The Software Encyclopedia 1996

(2 Vols)

A Guide for Personal, Professional and Business Users

This edition of
SOFTWARE ENCYCLOPEDIA 1996
was prepared by the R.R. Bowker Bibliographic Group
in collaboration with the Publication Systems Department

Martin Brooks, Senior Vice President-Business Manager/Publisher of Bowker Bibliographic Products
Leigh C. Yuster-Freeman, Vice President, Production - Bibliographies

Editorial
Beverley Lamar, Senior Managing Editor
Doret Dixon, Senior Editor
Dorothy Perry-Gilchrist, Associate Editor
Eleanor M. Schubauer, Assistant Editor

Subject Guide
Judy Salk, Executive Editor
Elsa Meyers, Senior Editor
Angela Barrett, Senior Associate Editor
Mark D. MacDonald and Joseph V. Tondi, Assistant Editors

Production
Doreen Gravesande, Production Director
Myriam Nunez, Managing Editor
Barbara Holton and Frank McDermott, Senior Editors
Megan Roxberry, Senior Associate Editor
Monalisa Massiah, Associate Editor
Clarice D. Isaacs, Assistant Editor

Publishers Authority Database
&
International Standard Book Number Agency
Doreen Gravesande, Production Director
Don Riseborough, Senior Managing Editor
Lynn Sahner and William D. McCahery, Senior Editors
Brenda Joseph, Pasquale Martirano, Margot Weidt, and Janet Weiss, Assistant Editors

Data Collection & Processing Group
Bonnie Walton, Manager
Cheryl Patrick and Rhonda McKendrick, Coordinators
Judy Harrison, Assistant Coordinator
Leslie Fisher, Sandy Minter, and Karen Santana, Editors

Computer Operations Group
Nick Wikowski, Director, Network/Computer Operations
Michael A. DeLuca, Production Control Manager
Jack Murphy, Production Coordinator

The Software Encyclopedia 1996

A Guide for Personal, Professional
and Business Users

Volume 1
Title Index ♦ Publisher/Title Index

R.R. BOWKER
A Reed Reference Publishing Company
New Providence, New Jersey

Published by R.R. Bowker
A Reed Reference Publishing Company
121 Chanlon Road, New Providence, NJ 07974

Andrew W. Meyer, Chief Operating Officer
Peter E. Simon, Executive Vice President, Business Development and Database Publishing
Gwyn Williams, Executive Vice President, Finance and Operations
Stanley Walker, Senior Vice President, Corporate Marketing
Edward J. Roycroft, Senior Vice President, Sales

Copyright © 1996 by Reed Elsevier Inc.
All rights reserved

No part of this publication may be reproduced or transmitted in any form or by any means, stored in any information storage and retrieval system, without prior written permission of R.R. Bowker, 121 Chanlon Rd., New Providence, New Jersey 07974, USA.

International Standard Book Numbers
Set: 0-8352-3735-4
Volume 1: 0-8352-3733-8
Volume 2: 0-8352-3734-6

Printed and bound in the United States of America.

No payment is either solicited or accepted for inclusion of entries in this publication. R.R. Bowker has used its best efforts in collecting and preparing material for inclusion in this publication, but does not warrant that the information herein is complete or accurate, and does not assume, and hereby disclaims any liability to any person for the loss or damage caused by errors or omissions in **The Software Encyclopedia 1996,** whether such errors or omissions result from negligence, accident or any other cause.

ISBN 0-8352-3735-4

Contents

Preface vii

How To Use The Software Encyclopedia viii

ISBN (International Standard Book Number) x

VOLUME 1

Title Index 1

Publisher/Title Index 1111

VOLUME 2

Guide To Systems xi

Guide To Applications xii

System Compatibility/Applications Index 1247

Preface

The Software Encyclopedia provides comprehensive and detailed information on microcomputer software. This 11th edition contains 50,000 software titles from 3,000 publishers, including 16,671 unique titles. All software is classified under one or more of the 580 subject headings or applications which are grouped under 38 major headings.

The editorial development and updating process of **The Software Encyclopedia** is an extensive effort. The information collected from software publishers is analyzed and styled for inclusion.

Information for **The Software Encyclopedia** is obtained primarily from the publishers. Secondary sources such as catalogs and brochures are also used in lieu of data from the publisher. Each title entry contains title, sub-title, version number, publication date, compatible hardware, operating system requirements, memory required, price, a description of the type of customer support available, package extras (i.e. manuals, etc.), and author if it differs from the publisher, when provided. ISBN (International Standard Book Number) or publisher order numbers are also supplied. Additionally, each record contains a brief annotation, as well as the publisher.

The Software Encyclopedia is simply organized. Volume 1 contains the Title Index, an alphabetical listing by title of all software, and the Publisher/Title Index, an alphabetical listing of all publishers with full address and telephone, as well as a listing of their titles. Volume 2 contains the System Compatibility/Applications Index which provides software organized by system, subject/application heading, and titles.

Two guides help the user find specific application needs: the Guide to Systems is a simple alphabetical listing of systems included in **The Software Encyclopedia** with a starting page number for each; the second Guide to Applications is provided in two parts: the first lists the Major Headings, and the Major Headings with the Applications under each heading. The second part lists specific applications and where each will be found under the major heading(s).

Every effort was made by publishers to submit their material with consideration for its accuracy throughout the life of **The Software Encyclopedia**. But given the immense amount of change and volatility in the microcomputer field, changes in price, availability, version, and other information have occurred and will continue to do so. The editorial staff is continuously updating the database so that the latest information can be reflected in future publications, as well as in the online version of the database available through Knight-Ridder Information, Inc's DIALOG Service (File 278—Microcomputer Software Guide Online). Most prices shown are list prices, but actual purchase prices will vary due to the wide availability and discount pricing of software through its many distribution channels.

The Software Encyclopedia database will soon undergo a major systems upgrade. As a result, all software titles will require an ISBN for each version. We urge all publishers of software to assign ISBN, if you are not doing so already. Please contact the ISBN Agency, R.R. Bowker, New Providence, NJ, USA, 908-665-6770, for an ISBN Prefix Application form and information. There is a service fee for the assignment of an ISBN Prefix.

The editors have used their best efforts to list software products and their publishers accurately; however, there are sure to be errors or omissions. We would appreciate receiving the correct information.

The Software Encyclopedia was carefully designed to meet the needs of its users, and be an easy to use reference tool. As standards develop for the cataloging and description of microcomputer software, Bowker editors will continue to play a key role in providing the information that will be needed, in whatever formats are appropriate. We strongly encourage you to contact us with suggestions and comments for future editions, as well as comments on this 11th edition. **The Software Encyclopedia** is your information tool, and your feedback is essential.

We trust that you will find this source of information on software valuable, accurate, well-organized and easy to use.

Leigh C. Yuster-Freeman
Vice President
Production-Bibliographies

How To Use The Software Encyclopedia 1996

The software product information in the Software Encyclopedia is accessible through the use of five provided indexes:

- ◆ TITLE INDEX
- ◆ PUBLISHER/TITLE INDEX
- ◆ GUIDE TO SYSTEMS
- ◆ GUIDE TO APPLICATIONS
- ◆ SYSTEM COMPATIBILITY/APPLICATIONS INDEX

These indexes were designed to allow the reader to access listings of software packages by title (if the reader is looking for a specific program) or by system/application (if the reader is looking for a type of program for a specific computer). The indexes are arranged as follows:

1. Title Index

Software products are arranged alphabetically in Volume 1. Entries include the following information (when available) on each product:

Title; sub-title; series; version; author(s); release date; compatible hardware; program language; operating system(s) required; memory required; general requirements; items included; customer support; system-specific price, ISBN, order number, and related information; annotation; publisher.

Ordering information for all publishers is given in the Publisher/Title Index.

TITLE INDEX SAMPLE ENTRY

❶ Snake Accounting: **❷** General Ledger.   **❸** Accounting for Small Business Series.

❹ Version: 7.1.   **❺** Chris King & Staff.   **❻** July 1995.   **❼** Items Included: Spiral-Bound Manual.   **❽** Customer Support: 90 Days toll-free tech support; each additional year $150.00.

❾ MS-DOS 2.1 or higher (384k).   **❿** IBM PC, PC XT, PC AT, & compatibles; BASIC.

⓫ 3.5" disk   **⓬** $700.00   **⓭** (ISBN 1-667431-07-0,   **⓮** Order no.: 102757)

⓯ Nonstandard peripherals required: Sound Blaster.   **⓰** Addl. software required: Microsoft Windows '95.

⓱ Optimal Configuration: Super VGA with 512K,   **⓲** Networks Supported: Lantastic.

⓳ Handles up to 9998 Accounts in the User Defined Chart of Accounts. Maintains a Financial History of the Past Twelve Months. Transactions Can Be Posted to Prior or Future Months.   **⓴** Snake Software Corp.

KEY

- **❶** Title
- **❷** Sub-Title
- **❸** Series Title
- **❹** Version
- **❺** Author(s)
- **❻** Release Date
- **❼** Also Included in the Package
- **❽** Customer Support
- **❾** Operating System; Minimum Memory Required
- **❿** Compatible Hardware; Language
- **⓫** Format
- **⓬** Price
- **⓭** ISBN
- **⓮** Order Number
- **⓯** Peripherals Required
- **⓰** Additional Software Required
- **⓱** Optimal Configuration
- **⓲** Networks Supported
- **⓳** Annotation
- **⓴** Company Name

2. Publisher/Title Index

This section lists the 3,000 software publishers whose products appear in this publication. Entries include Publisher name, ISBN prefix, address, telephone number, toll-free number, fax number, and distributor information. In addition, all products a company has listed in the Title Index appear below that company's listing.

PUBLISHER/TITLE INDEX SAMPLE ENTRY

❶ ASCP Pr., Div. of American Society of Clinical Pathologists. **❷** (0-89189).
❸ 2100 W. Harrison St., Chicago, IL 60612. **❹** Tel. 312-738-1336;
❺ Toll-free: 800-621-4142. **❻** FAX: 312-738-1619. **❼** Dist. by: PubCats, Inc.,
❽ 772 Norwich Lane, Knoxville, TN 37086 **❾** Tel. 615-776-8970; **❿** Toll-free: 800-999-7773; **⓫** FAX: 615-776-8971 **⓬** Titles: Banko (Order). Bleedo. Casequiz. ConverSion: A Program for Medical SI Unit Conversion. D. Tree. Emergency Transfusion. Intellipath. Reporter.
*The ISBN is being widely used by software publishers as a unique identifier for their products and is a standard part of the bibliographic description. The ISBN system is administered at R.R. Bowker.

KEY
❶ Publisher Name
❷ ISBN Prefix*
❸ Address
❹ Telephone Number
❺ Toll-Free Number
❻ Fax Number
❼ Distributor Name
❽ Distributor Address
❾ Distributor Telephone Number
❿ Distributor Toll-Free Number
⓫ Distributor FAX Number
⓬ Product Title(s)

---

3. Guide to Systems

The 15 major system headings under which the programs are grouped in Volume 2 are listed alphabetically, with the starting page given for each heading. Once placed under these headings the programs are further subdivided by application.

4. Guide to Applications

The applications are listed in three ways, so that the reader can easily determine where a broad or specific application would be listed. First, the 38 major headings are given; second, the specific applications found under each major heading are shown; and third; each specific application is given and is referred back to the major heading(s) where it can be found.

Within the contents of the book, programs are listed under broad heading-specific application.

5. System Compatibility/Applications Index

Software products are arranged first by system compatibility, then by specific application, and then alphabetically. In order to keep this index at a manageable length, while also eliminating cross-references for multiple-system and multiple-application programs, it was necessary to abridge the entries. However, we have tried to include enough information so that the user can easily locate the product in the Title Index if more information is desired. Entries include the following information when available:

Title, sub-title, volume number, number of disks/CD-ROMs, version, annotation, publisher name.

Ordering information for all publishers is listed in the Publisher/Title Index.

SYSTEM COMPATIBILITY/APPLICATIONS INDEX SAMPLE ENTRY

❶ APPLE MACINTOSH **❷** ACCOUNTING-PAYROLL **❸** Aatrix Payroll.
❹ Version 4.1. **❺** Designed to Manage Paychecks for Both Salaried & Hourly Employees. Handles All Check Printing: Calculates, Accumulates, & Deducts Taxes; Prints Reports Summarizing Gross Pay & Withholding at All levels by End-of-Payroll, Date, Months, Quarter, & Year; & Provides Password Protection. **❻** Aatrix Software.

KEY
❶ Operating System Heading (each new heading begins on a new page)
❷ Application Heading
❸ Title
❹ Version
❺ Annotation
❻ Publisher Name

ISBN SYSTEM

The International Standard Book Number (ISBN) System was developed to address the need for a unique identification number for publisher's products, including books and non-print materials such as computer software & CD-ROMs. The ISBN, accompanying the product from production through distribution to sale, contributes considerably to the simplification of ordering, stock control, accounting, royalty payments, etc. In addition, the ISBN system is used to identify the publisher, producer, or manufacturer with the address, all communication numbers & ordering information. The bibliographic databases of R.R. Bowker are using ISBNs as the standard identifier for electronic data transmission from publishers. Soon all R.R. Bowker databases will require that product information include an ISBN for each format. It is for these reasons that the Database Publishing Group of R.R. Bowker and the ISBN Agency would like to express their appreciation to all software abd CD-ROM producers who currently assign ISBN numbers to their products.

For additional information related to the ISBN System, please contact Don Riseborough, Senior Managing Editor, of the Publishers Authority Database & ISBN Agency, c/o R.R. Bowker.

Guide To Systems

APPLE II FAMILY & COMPATIBLES 1247
   (Includes Apple IIgs)

APPLE MACINTOSH 1333

ATARI 8-BIT MICROS 1505
   (Includes Atari 400, 600, 800, 1200, XLs, XEs)

ATARI ST 1519

COMMODORE 8-BIT MICROS 1531
   (Includes Commodore PET, 64, 128)

COMMODORE AMIGA 1567

CP/M, MP/M ENVIRONMENTS 1585

DIGITAL EQUIPMENT CORP. MICROS 1619

HEWLETT-PACKARD MICROS 1657

IBM PC FAMILY & MS-DOS COMPATIBLES 1679
   (Among those included are: AT&T 6300 PC; Compaq;
   IBM PS/2 series; Tandy 1000, 3000, etc.)

OS/2 2317

RADIO SHACK TRS-80 FAMILY 2357

TEXAS INSTRUMENTS HOME COMPUTERS 2381
   (Includes TI-99/4, 99/4A)

UNIX & UNIX-LIKE ENVIRONMENTS 2389

XEROX MICROS 2453

Guide To Applications

Once applications software are grouped by compatibility they are classified under one or more of 38 major subject headings; and within these headings by specific applications. The applications software are presented alphabetically by heading/application, and within the heading/application by title. The following three indexes will help the reader locate any general or specific application he or she is looking to find. The first index gives the 38 major subject headings; the second gives the headings together with the specific applications that are listed under them; and the third lists the specific applications and shows the major subject headings they are found under. Note that the third index also incorporates applications which are not specifically listed, but which can be found under other application listings.

Major Subject Headings

ACCOUNTING
AGRICULTURE & RANCHING
BANKING
BUSINESS MANAGEMENT
CONSTRUCTION
DATABASE MANAGEMENT
DESKTOP PUBLISHING
ENGINEERING & SCIENCE
FINANCIAL ANALYSIS
FOOD & LODGING SERVICES
GAMES & ENTERTAINMENT
GENERAL SERVICES
GOVERNMENT
GRAPHICS
HOBBIES
HOMEMAKING & NUTRITION
INSURANCE
INTEGRATED SOFTWARE
INVENTORY, PURCHASING & INVOICING
LEGAL
LIBRARY SERVICES
MANUFACTURING
MARKETING & SALES
MEDIA
MEDICAL
MUSIC & SOUND
COMPUTING
PERSONAL FINANCE & BUDGETING
PERSONAL RECORDKEEPING
PROGRAMMING TOOLS
PUBLIC SERVICES
REAL ESTATE
RELIGION
SPORTS & RECREATION
SPREADSHEETS
TELECOMMUNICATIONS
TRANSPORTATION & TRAVEL
WORD PROCESSING

Major Subject Headings With The Applications Under Them

Accounting
Accounts Payable
Accounts Receivable
Auditing
Bookkeeping
Certified Public Accounting
Checkbook Accounting
Client Accounting
Client Billing
Fixed Asset Accounting
General Ledger
Integrated Software
Job Cost Accounting
Lease Accounting
Miscellaneous
Payroll
Point of Sale
Professional Time Accounting
Self Study
Tax Preparation

Agriculture And Ranching
Accounting
Business Management
Crop Farming
Dairy Farming
Feed Mills
Financial Analysis
Forestries
General
Invoicing
Livestock—Feed Blending

Livestock—General
Livestock—Poultry
Machinery Management
Spreadsheets

Banking
Accounting
Asset Management
Bond Calculations
Business Management
Cash Flow Analysis
Check Processing
Credit Management
Financial Analysis
General
Loan Accounting
Loan Amortization Schedules
Loans—General
Mortgage Loans
Savings and Loan
Spreadsheets
Teller Systems

Business Management
Administration
Appointment Management
Calendars
Client Information
Critical Path Scheduling
Decision Support
Employee Productivity
Employee Scheduling
Integrated Office Administration
Mailroom Management
Management Modeling
Miscellaneous
Office Management
Operations Research
Personal Productivity
Personnel Management
Portfolio Management
Problem-Solving
Project Management
Property Management
Protection and Security
Report Writer
Resource Management
Scheduling
Telephone Dialer
Training

Construction
Accounting
Business Management
Contractor Industry
Estimating
Financial Analysis
General
Heating
Home Building
Job Cost Accounting
Production Control and Scheduling

Project Management
Spreadsheets
Surveying

Database Management
Accessing and Indexing Techniques
Data Collection
Data Entry
Database Management Systems
Filing
ISAM Routines
Miscellaneous
Report Generator
Text Retrieval
Tutorials

Desktop publishing
Clip-Art Libraries
Font Libraries
Graphics Processing
Miscellaneous Utilities
Page Layout
Presentations
Scanner Systems
Text Processing
Tutorials

Engineering And Science
Aerospace
Architecture
Artificial Intelligence
Astronomy
Building Design
Business Management
CAD-CAM
Chemical Engineering
Circuit Board Analysis
Civil Engineering
Computer Science and Software Development
Curve Fitting
Data Entry
Database Management
Digitizer Graphics
Drafting
Electrical Engineering
Electronics
Energy Management
Expert Systems
Financial Analysis
General
Geometry
Graphics
Harmanic Motion
Hydraulics
Industrial Engineering
Integrated Software
Laboratory Aids
Landscaping
Linear Programming
Mapping
Math Routines
Mathematics

Mechanical Engineering
Mining
Physics
Programming Tools
Project Management
Projectile Motion
Science for Industry
Spreadsheets
Statistics
Surveying
Word Processing

Financial Analysis
Asset Management
Bond Calculations
Cash Flow Analysis
Commodity Stock Trading
Credit Management
Depreciation Schedules
Disbursement Planning and Control
Economic Analysis
Estimating
Expense Account Analysis
Forecasting
General
Investments
Liability Management
Loan Analysis
Pension Management
Profit Analysis
Statistics
Stock Market
Tax Planning and Preparation

Food And Lodging Services
Accounting
Business Management
Camp Management
General
Hotel-Resort Management
Meat Cutting Industry
Restaurant Management

Games And Entertainment
Adventure
Arcade
Card and Casino
Chess
Educational
General
Puzzle
Simulation
Strategy
Trivia
Word

General Services
Appliance Dealer
Auction Systems
Auto Dealerships
Beauty Salons
Cemetery Management

Distribution
Employment Agencies
Exterminators
Florists
Foundry
Funeral Homes
Gas Station Management and Auto Repair
Interior Decorating
Jewelry Stores
Liquor Stores
Miscellaneous
Oil and Gas
Plumbing
Printer
Rental Companies
Retail Industry Control
Textiles and Clothing

Government
Census
General
Municipal and Local
Political Campaigns
Taxation

Graphics
Animation
Business
CAD-CAM
Development
Drawing and Painting
General
Program Editor
Utilities

Hobbies
Astrology
Astronomy
Automotive
Biorhythms
Coin Collecting
Crafts
Erotica
Fortune Telling
Gambling Aids
Gardening
Genealogy
Ham and Amateur Radio
Language Instruction
Meteorology
Miscellaneous
Morse Code
Music
Numerology
Occult
Ornithology
Pets
Photography
Religious Studies
Speed Reading
Stamp Collecting
Wine

Homemaking And Nutrition
Basic Living Skills
Calorie Counter
Consumer Education
Diets
Fitness
General
Health and Hygiene
Home Safety
Inventory
Meal Planning
Recipes
Shopping Aids
Store Coupon Management

Insurance
Accounting
Auto Insurance
Business Management
Client Accounting and Billing
Database Management
Financial Analysis
General
Home Insurance
Independent Agents and Brokers
Integrated Software
Life and Health Insurance
Pension Management
Property and Liability Insurance
Property Management
Prospect Tracking

Integrated Software
Business
General Purpose
Tutorials

Inventory, Purchasing And Invoicing
Barcode Programs
Customer Lists
Distribution
General
Inventory Control
Invoice Generators
Invoice Preparation
Job Cost Accounting
Mail Order Accounting
Order Entry
Order Scheduling And Shipping
Purchasing—Ordering
Retail Industry Control
Warehouse Management

Legal
Accounting
Asset Management
Bailbonding
Calendar System
Claims and Litigation
Client Accounting and Billing
Collection Agencies
Court Decision Research
Database Management
Dictionaries
Docket Scheduling
Escrow Accounts
Estate Planning
Expert Systems
File Management
Financial Analysis
Forms Generators
General
Government
Incorporation
Information Retrieval
Integrated Software
Leases
Liability Management
Office Management
Pension Management
Portfolio Management
Professional Time and Billing
Property Management
Real Estate Analysis
Spreadsheets
Tax Form Printer
Tax Planning and Preparation—Corporations
Tax Planning and Preparation—Individuals
Wills
Word Processing

Library Services
Acquisitions
Audio—Visual
Cataloging
Circulation
General
Information Retrieval
Integrated Software
Interlibrary Loan
On-Line
Periodicals
Reference and Information
Serials

Manufacturing
Accounting
Barcode Programs
Bill of Materials
Business Management
Database Management
Equipment Maintenance
Expert Systems
Factory Management
Financial Analysis
General
Integrated Software
Inventory Control
Invoicing
Job Cost Accounting
Measure and Control
Order Inventory Management
Order Scheduling and Shipping

Process Control
Production Control and Scheduling
Purchasing
Sales
Shop Floor Control
Spreadsheets
Statistical Data Systems
Warehouse Management

Marketing And Sales
Cash Register
General
Mailing Lists
Ordering
Prospect Tracking
Sales Accounting
Sales Analysis
Sales Management
Trend Analysis

Media
Ad Agency Management
Books
Broadcasting Management
Cable TV
Circulation and Subscription Management
General
Motion Pictures
Multi-Media Presentations
Newspapers
Periodicals
Publishing Data

Medical
Accounting
Ambulance Dispatching
Anesthesiology
Billing Systems for Multiple Physicians
Cardiology
Chiropractic
Clinic Administration
Database Management
Dental—General
Dental Office Management
Dictionaries
Education
Expert Systems
Financial Analysis
Fitness
General
Graphics
Hospital Management
Insurance Claims and Forms
Integrated Software
Laboratory
Nursing
Nursing Home Management
Obstetrics—Gynecology
Office Management
Ophthalmology—Optometry
Orthodontics
Pathology

Patient Accounting and Billing
Patient Data Management
Pediatrics
Pharmacy Management
Prescription Forms
Psychiatry-Psychology
Radiology
Treatment and Diagnosis
Veterinary Medicine
Word Processing

Music And Sound
Audio Spectrum Analysis
General
Instruction
Music Synthesizer
Speech Synthesizer
Voice Pattern Recognition

Personal Computing
Desk Accounting
Disk-File Librarian
Disk-File Utilities
DOS Shells
File-Data Compression
Keyboard Enhancements
Memory Management
Operating Systems
Printer Utilities
Security
Systems Utilities
Tutorials
Virus Detection and Protection

Personal Finance And Budgeting
Budget Aids
Calculator
Cash Management
Checkbook Accounting
Consumer Education
General
Insurance
Investments
Loan and Mortgage Analysis
Personal Accounting
Retirement Planning
Stock Charting
Tax Planning and Preparation

Personal Recordkeeping
Address Book
Calendar
Diary
Dictionaries and Encyclopedias
General
Home Inventory
Personal Database Management
Resume Writer
Telephone Utilities

Programming Tools
Cross-Development Tools

Development Tools
Language Tutorials
Languages
Program Libraries
Program Translators
Text-Screen Editors
Utilities

Public Services
Clubs and Community Affairs
Fire Houses
General
Law Enforcement
Museum Systems
Non-Profit Organizations
Utilities

Real Estate
Accounting
Brokerage Management
Building Management
Condominium Management
Database Management
Depreciation Schedules
Financial Analysis
General
Investment Financial Analysis
Loan Analysis and Schedules
Property Assessment
Property Management
Prospect Tracking
Real Estate Analysis
Real Estate Listing
Real Estate Settlement Statement
Taxation
Tenant Billing

Religion
Bible
Church Management
Donations
General
Non-Profit Organizations

Sports And Recreation
Baseball Scouting-Recordkeeping
Bowling League Secretary
Football Scouting-Recordkeeping
General
Golf

Spreadsheets
Add-Ons
General
Tutorials

Telecommunications
Bulletin Board
Electronic Mail
Facsimile Transmission
File Transmission
Information Retrieval
Multi-Purpose
Networking
Terminal Emulators

Transportation and Travel
Air Traffic Control
Aviation
Flight Simulator
General
Travel Agency
Travel Guides
Trucking

Word Processing
Add-Ons
Forms Generators
General
Indexing
Mail Merge Utilities
Mailing Labels
Outliners
Printer Utilities
Proofreading Systems
Spelling Checkers and Dictionaries
Thesaurus
Tutorials
Writing Aids

SPECIFIC APPLICATION	WILL BE FOUND UNDER THE FOLLOWING MAJOR HEADING(S)
A	
Accessing and Indexing Techniques	Database Management
Accounting (for specific industries)	Agriculture and Ranching; Banking; Construction; Food and Lodging Services; Insurance; Legal; Manufacturing; Medical; Real Estate
Accounts Payable	Accounting
Accounts Receivable	Accounting
Acquisitions	Library Services
Ad Agency Management	Media
Ada	Programming Tools (under Languages)
Ada Tutorials	Programming Tools (under Language Tutorials)
Add-Ons	Spreadsheets; Word Processing
Address Book	Personal Recordkeeping
Administration	Business Management
Adventure (games)	Games and Entertainment
Advertising Agency Management	General Services (under Ad Agency Management)
Aerospace	Engineering and Science
Air Traffic Control	Transportation and Travel
Amateur Radio	Hobbies (under Ham and Amateur Radio)
Ambulance Dispatching	Medical
Amortization Schedules	Banking (under Loan Amortization Schedules)
Anesthesiology	Medical
Animation	Graphics
Apple Tutorials	Personal Computing (under Tutorials)
Appliance Dealer	General Services
Appointment Management	Business Management
Arcade (games)	Games and Entertainment
Architecture	Engineering and Science
Artificial Intelligence	Engineering and Science
Assembler	Programming Tools (under Development Tools)
Assembly	Programming Tools (under Languages)
Assembly Tutorials	Programming Tools (under Language Tutorials)
Asset Management	Banking; Financial Analysis; Legal
Astrology	Hobbies
Astronomy	Engineering and Science; Hobbies
Atari Tutorials	Personal Computing (under Tutorials)
Auction Systems	General Services
Audio Spectrum Analysis	Music and Sound
Audio—Visual	Library Services
Auditing	Accounting
Auto Dealerships	General Services
Auto Insurance	Insurance
Automotive (consumer)	Hobbies
Aviation	Transportation and Travel
B	
Bailbonding	Legal
Barcode Programs	Inventory; Purchasing and Invoicing; Manufacturing
Baseball Scouting-Recordkeeping	Sports and Recreation
BASIC	Programming Tools (under Languages)
Basic Living Skills	Homemaking and Nutrition
BASIC Tutorials	Programming Tools (under Language Tutorials)
Beauty Salons	General Services

SPECIFIC APPLICATION	WILL BE FOUND UNDER THE FOLLOWING MAJOR HEADING(S)
Bible	Religion
Bill of Materials	Manufacturing
Billing Systems for Multiple Physicians	Medical
Biorhythms	Hobbies
Bond Calculations	Banking; Financial Analysis
Bookkeeping	Accounting
Books	Media
Bowling League Secretary	Sports and Recreation
Broadcasting Management	Media
Brokerage Management	Real Estate
Budget Aids	Personal Finance and Budgeting
Buffers	Programming Tools (under Utilities)
Building Design	Engineering and Science
Building Management	Real Estate
Bulletin Board	Telecommunications
Business Graphics	Graphics (under Business)
Business Management	(for specific industries) Agriculture and Ranching; Banking; Construction; Engineering and Science; Food and Lodging Services; Insurance; Manufacturing

C

SPECIFIC APPLICATION	WILL BE FOUND UNDER THE FOLLOWING MAJOR HEADING(S)
C	Programming Tools (under Languages)
C Tutorials	Programming Tools (under Language Tutorials)
Cable TV	Media
CAD-CAM	Engineering and Science; Graphics
Calculator	Personal Finance and Budgeting
Calendar	Personal Recordkeeping
Calendar System	Legal
Calendars	Business Management
Calorie Counter	Homemaking and Nutrition
Camp Management	Food and Lodging Service
Card and Casino (games)	Games and Entertainment see also Hobbies (under Gambling Aids)
Cardiology	Medical
Cash Flow Analysis	Banking; Financial Analysis
Cash Management	Personal Finance and Budgeting
Cash Register	Marketing and Sales
Casino (games)	Games and Recreation (under Card and Casino) see also Hobbies (Gambling Aids)
Cataloging	Library Services
Cemetery Management	General Services
Census	Government
Certified Public Accounting	Accounting
Check Processing	Banking
Checkbook Accounting	Accounting; Personal Finance and Budgeting
Chemical Engineering	Engineering and Science
Chess	Games and Entertainment
Chiropractic	Medical
Church Management	Religion
Circuit Board Analysis	Engineering and Science
Circulation	Library
Circulation and Subscription Management	Media
Civil Engineering	Engineering and Science
Claims and Litigation	Legal
Client Accounting	Accounting
Client Accounting and Billing (for specific industries)	Insurance; Legal
Client Billing	Accounting

SPECIFIC APPLICATION	WILL BE FOUND UNDER THE FOLLOWING MAJOR HEADING(S)
Client Information	Business Management
Clinic Administration	Medical
Clip-Art Libraries	Desktop Publishing
Clubs and Community Affairs	Public Services
COBOL	Programming Tools (under Languages)
COBOL Tutorials	Programming Tools (under Language Tutorials)
Coin Collecting	Hobbies
Collection Agencies	Legal
Commodity Stock Trading	Financial Analysis
Commodore Tutorials	Personal Computing (under Tutorials)
Compiler	Programming Tools (under Development Tools)
Compress Data	Personal Computing (under File-Data Compression)
Computer-Aided Design/Computer-Aided Manufacturing	Engineering and Science (under CAD-CAM); Graphics (under CAD-CAM)
Computer Language	Programming Tools (under Languages)
Computer Literacy (general)	Personal Computing (under Tutorials); Programming Tools (under Language Tutorials)
Computer Programming (general)	Programming Tools (under Language Tutorials and under Languages)
Computer Science and Software Development	Engineering and Science
Condominium Management	Real Estate
Consumer Education	Homemaking and Nutrition; Personal Finance and Budgeting
Contractor Industry	Construction
Conversion Aids	Personal Computing (under Disk-File Utilities)
Coupon Management	Homemaking and Nutrition (under Store Coupon Management)
Court Decision Research	Legal
CPA	Accounting (under Certified Public Accounting)
CP/M	Personal Computing (under Operating Systems)
Crafts	Hobbies
Credit Management	Banking; Financial Analysis
Critical Path Scheduling	Business Management
Crop Farming	Agriculture and Ranching
Cross Assembler	Programming Tools (under Cross-Development Tools)
Cross Compiler	Programming Tools (under Cross-Development Tools)
Cross-Development Tools	Programming Tools
Curve Fitting	Engineering and Science
Customer Lists	Inventory, Purchasing and Invoicing

D

Dairy Farming	Agriculture and Ranching
Data Collection	Database Management
Data Compression	Personal Computing (under File-Data Compression)
Data Entry	Database Management; Engineering and Science
Database Management (for specific industries)	Engineering and Science; Insurance; Legal; Manufacturing; Medical; Real Estate
Database Management Systems (general)	Database Management
Database Tutorials	Database Management (under Tutorials)
Debugger	Programming Tools (under Development Tools)
Decision Support	Business Management
Dental—General	Medical
Dental Office Management	Medical
Depreciation Schedules	Financial Analysis; Real Estate
Desk Accessories	Personal Computing
Development Tools	Programming Tools
Diagnosis	Medical (under Treatment and Diagnosis)
Diary	Personal Recordkeeping

SPECIFIC APPLICATION	WILL BE FOUND UNDER THE FOLLOWING MAJOR HEADING(S)
Dictionaries (for general word processing)	Word Processing (under Spelling Checkers and Dictionaries)
Dictionaries (for specific topics)	Legal; Medical
Dictionaries and Encyclopedias (general topics)	Personal Recordkeeping
Diets	Homemaking and Nutrition
Digitizer Graphics	Engineering and Science
Disassembler	Programming Tools (under Utilities)
Disbursement Planning and Control	Financial Analysis
Disk Backup	Personal Computing (under Disk-File Utilities)
Disk Conversion	Personal Computing (under Disk-File Utilities)
Disk Diagnostic	Personal Computing (under Disk-File Utilities)
Disk-File Librarian	Personal Computing
Disk-File Utilities	Personal Computing
Disk Organization	Personal Computing (under Disk-File Utilities)
Disk Recovery	Personal Computing (under Disk-File Utilities)
Distribution	General Services; Inventory, Purchasing and Invoicing
Docket Scheduling	Legal
Documentation Aids	Programming Tools (under Development Tools)
Donations	Religion
DOS	Personal Computing (under Operating Systems)
DOS Shells	Personal Computing
Drafting	Engineering and Science
Drawing and Painting	Graphics
Driver Utilities	Personal Computing (under Disk-File Utilities or under Printer Utilities)

E

Easywriter Tutorials	Word Processing (under Tutorials)
Economic Analysis	Financial Analysis
Educational (games)	Games and Entertainment
Electrical Engineering	Engineering and Science
Electronic Mail	Telecommunications
Electronics	Engineering and Science
Employee Productivity	Business Management
Employee Scheduling	Business Management
Employment Agencies	General Services
Encyclopedias	Personal Recordkeeping (under Dictionaries and Encyclopedias)
Energy Management	Engineering and Science
Equipment Maintenance	Manufacturing
Erotica	Hobbies
Escrow Accounts	Legal
Estate Planning	Legal
Estimating	Construction; Financial Analysis
Expense Account Analysis	Financial Analysis
Expert Systems	Engineering and Science; Legal; Manufacturing; Medical
Exterminators	General Services

F

Facsimile Transmission	Telecommunications
Factory Management	Manufacturing
Feed Blending	Agriculture and Ranching (under Livestock—Feed Blending)
Feed Mills	Agriculture and Ranching
File Backup	Personal Computing (under Disk-File Utilities)
File Conversion	Personal Computing (under Disk-File Utilities)
File-Data Compression	Personal Computing
File Librarian	Personal Computing (under Disk-File Librarian)

SPECIFIC APPLICATION	WILL BE FOUND UNDER THE FOLLOWING MAJOR HEADING(S)
File Management	Legal
File Recovery	Personal Computing (under Disk-File Utilities)
File Transmission	Telecommunications
File Utilities	Personal Computing (under Disk-File Utilities)
Filing	Database Management
Financial Analysis (for specific industries)	Agriculture and Ranching; Banking; Construction; Engineering and Science; Insurance; Legal; Manufacturing; Medical; Real Estate
Fire Houses	Public Services
Fitness (consumer)	Homemaking and Nutrition
Fitness (professional)	Medical
Fixed Asset Accounting	Accounting
Flight Simulator	Transportation and Travel
Florists	General Services
Font Libraries	Desktop Publishing
Football Scouting-Recordkeeping	Sports and Recreation
Forecasting	Financial Analysis
Forestries	Agriculture and Ranching
Forms Generators	Legal; Word Processing
FORTH	Programming Tools (under Languages)
FORTH Tutorials	Programming Tools (under Language Tutorials)
FORTRAN	Programming Tools (under Languages)
FORTRAN Tutorials	Programming Tools (under Language Tutorials)
Fortune Telling	Hobbies
Foundry	General Services
Framework Tutorials	Integrated Software (under Tutorials)
Funeral Homes	General Services

G

Gambling Aids	Hobbies see also Games (under Card and Casino)
Gardening	Hobbies
Gas Station Management and Auto Repair	General Services
Genealogy	Hobbies
General Ledger	Accounting
Geometry (professional)	Engineering and Science
Golf	Sports and Recreation
Graphics (for specific topics)	Engineering and Science; Medical
Graphics Libraries	Programming Tools (under Program Libraries
Graphics Processing	Desktop Publishing
Gynecology	Medical (under Obstetrics-Gynecology)

H

Ham and Amateur Radio	Hobbies
Harmonic Motion	Engineering and Science
Health and Hygiene	Homemaking and Nutrition
Health Insurance	Insurance (under Life and Health Insurance)
Heating	Construction
Home Building	Construction
Home Insurance	Insurance
Home Inventory	Personal Recordkeeping
Home Safety	Homemaking and Nutrition
Hospital Management	Medical
Hotel-Resort Management	Food and Lodging Services
Hydraulics	Engineering and Science
Hygiene	Homemaking and Nutrition (under Health and Hygiene)

I

IBM Tutorials	Personal Computing (under Tutorials)

SOFTWARE ENCYCLOPEDIA 1996 — GUIDE TO APPLICATIONS

SPECIFIC APPLICATION	WILL BE FOUND UNDER THE FOLLOWING MAJOR HEADING(S)
Incorporation	Legal
Independent Agents and Brokers	Real Estate
Indexing	Word Processing
Industrial Engineering	Engineering and Science
Information Retrieval	Legal; Library Services; Telecommunications
Insurance (for individual planning)	Personal Finance and Budgeting
Insurance Claims and Forms	Medical
Integrated Office Administration	Business Management
Integrated Software (for specific industries)	Accounting; Engineering and Science; Insurance; Legal; Library Services; Manufacturing; Medical
Integrated Software Tutorials	Integrated Software (under Tutorials)
Interior Decorating	General Services
Interlibrary Loan	Library Services
Inventory	Homemaking and Nutrition
Inventory Control	Inventory; Purchasing and Invoicing; Manufacturing
Investment Financial Analysis	Real Estate
Investments	Financial Analysis; Personal Finance and Budgeting
Invoice Generators	Inventory; Purchasing and Invoicing
Invoice Preparation	Inventory; Purchasing and Invoicing
Invoicing	Agriculture and Ranching; Manufacturing
I/O Library	Programming Tools (under Program Libraries)
ISAM Routines	Database Management

J

Jewelry Stores	General Services
Job Cost Accounting	Accounting; Construction; Inventory; Purchasing and Invoicing; Manufacturing

K

Keyboard Enhancements	Personal Computing

L

Laboratory	Medical
Laboratory Aids	Engineering and Science
Landscaping	Engineering and Science
Language Instruction (foreign)	Hobbies
Language Tutorials (computer)	Programming Tools
Languages (computer)	Programming Tools
Law Enforcement	Public Services
Lease Accounting	Accounting
Leases	Legal
Liability Insurance	Insurance (under Property and Liability Insurance)
Liability Management	Financial Analysis; Legal
Life and Health Insurance (professional)	Insurance
Linear Programming	Engineering and Science
Linkers	Programming Tools (under Languages)
Liquor Stores	General Services
LISP	Programming Tools (under Languages)
LISP Tutorials	Programming Tools (under Language Tutorials)
Litigation	Legal (under Claims and Litigations)
Livestock—Feed Blending	Agriculture and Ranching
Livestock—General	Agriculture and Ranching
Livestock—Poultry	Agriculture and Ranching
Living Skills	Homemaking and Nutrition (under Basic Living Skills)
Loan Accounting	Banking
Loan Amortization Schedules	Banking
Loan Analysis	Financial Analysis
Loan Analysis and Schedules	Real Estate
Loan and Mortgage Analysis (consumer)	Personal Finance and Budgeting

SPECIFIC APPLICATION	WILL BE FOUND UNDER THE FOLLOWING MAJOR HEADING(S)
Loans—General	Banking
Local Government	Government (under Municipal and Local)
LOGO	Programming Tools (under Languages)
LOGO Tutorials	Programming Tools (under Language Tutorials)
Lotus 1-2-3 Tutorials	Spreadsheets (under Tutorials)

M

Machinery Management	Agriculture and Ranching
Mail Merge Utilities	Word Processing
Mail Order Accounting	Inventory; Purchasing and Invoicing
Mailing Labels	Word Processing
Mailing Lists	Marketing and Sales see also Business Management (under Mailroom Management)
Mailroom Management	Business Management
Management Modeling	Business Management
Mapping	Engineering and Science
Math Libraries	Programming Tools (under Program Libraries)
Math Routines	Engineering and Science
Mathematics	Engineering and Science
Meal Planning	Homemaking and Nutrition
Measure and Control	Manufacturing
Meat Cutting Industry	Food and Lodging Services
Mechanical Engineering	Engineering and Science
Memory Management	Personal Computing
Menu Generators	Programming Tools (under Development Tools)
Meteorology	Hobbies
Mining	Engineering and Science
Modula-2	Programming Tools (under Languages)
Modula-2 Tutorials	Programming Tools (under Language Tutorials)
Morse Code	Hobbies
Mortgage Loans	Banking
Motion Pictures	Media
MS-DOS	Personal Computing (under Operating Systems)
Multi-Media Presentations	Media
MultiMate Tutorials	Word Processing (under Tutorials)
Multiplan Tutorials	Spreadsheets (under Tutorials)
Municipal and Local (government)	Government
Museum Systems	Public Services
Music	Hobbies
Music Synthesizer	Music and Sound

N

Networking	Telecommunications
Newspapers	Media
Non-Profit Organizations	Public Services; Religion
Numerology	Hobbies
Nursing	Medical
Nursing Home Management	Medical

O

Obstetrics—Gynecology	Medical
Occult	Hobbies
Office Management	Business Management; Legal; Manufacturing
Oil and Gas	General Services see also Engineering and Science (under Mining)
On-Line (access)	Library Services
Operating System Tutorials	Personal Computing (under Tutorials)
Operating Systems	Personal Computing
Operations Research	Business Management

SPECIFIC APPLICATION	WILL BE FOUND UNDER THE FOLLOWING MAJOR HEADING(S)
Ophthalmology—Optometry	Medical
Order Entry	Inventory; Purchasing and Invoicing
Order Inventory Management	Manufacturing
Order Scheduling and Shipping	Inventory; Purchasing and Invoicing; Manufacturing

Ordering	Marketing and Sales
	  see also Inventory; Purchasing and Invoicing
	  (under Purchasing-Ordering)

Ornithology	Hobbies
Orthodontics	Medical
Outliners	Word Processing

P

Page Layout	Desktop Publishing
Pascal	Programming Tools (under Languages)
Pascal Tutorials	Programming Tools (under Language Tutorials)
Pathology	Medical
Patient Accounting and Billing	Medical
Patient Data Management	Medical
Payroll	Accounting
PC-DOS	Personal Computing (under Operating Systems)
Pediatrics	Medical
Pension Management	Financial Analysis; Insurance; Legal
Periodicals	Library Services; Media
Personal Accounting	Personal Finance and Budgeting
Personal Database Management	Personal Recordkeeping
Personal Productivity	Business Management
Personnel Management	Business Management
Pets	Hobbies
Pharmacy Management	Medical
Photography	Hobbies
Physics (professional)	Engineering and Science
PILOT	Programming Tools (under Languages)
PILOT Tutorials	Programming Tools (under Language Tutorials)
Plumbing	General Services
Point of Sale	Accounting
Political Campaigns	Government
Portfolio Management	Business Management; Legal
Poultry	Agriculture and Ranching (under Livestock—Poultry)
Prescription Forms	Medical
Presentations	Desktop Publishing
Printer	General Services
Printer Utilities	Personal Computing; Word Processing
Problem-Solving	Business Management
Process Control	Manufacturing
Production Control and Scheduling	Construction; Manufacturing
Professional Time and Billing	Accounting
Professional Time Accounting	Legal
Profit Analysis	Financial Analysis
Program Editor	Graphics
Program Generators	Programming Tools (under Development Tools)
Program Libraries	Programming Tools
Program Translators	Programming Tools
Programming Languages	Programming Tools (under Languages)
Programming Tools (for a specific subject)	Engineering and Science
Programming Utilities	Programming Tools (under Utilities)
Project Management	Business Management; Construction; Engineering and Science
Projectile Motion	Engineering and Science
Proofreading Systems	Word Processing

SPECIFIC APPLICATION	WILL BE FOUND UNDER THE FOLLOWING MAJOR HEADING(S)
Property and Liability Insurance	Insurance
Property Assessment	Real Estate
Property Management	Business Management; Insurance; Inventory, Purchasing and Invoicing; Legal
Prospect Tracking	Insurance; Marketing and Sales; Real Estate
Protection and Security	Business Management
Psychiatry-Psychology (professional)	Medical
Public Utilities	Public Services (under Utilities)
Publishing Data	Media
Purchasing	Manufacturing
Purchasing—Ordering	Inventory, Purchasing and Invoicing
Puzzle(s)	Games and Entertainment

R

Radiology	Medical
Ranching	Agriculture and Ranching (under many specific applications)
Real Estate Analysis	Legal; Real Estate
Real Estate Listing	Real Estate
Real Estate Settlement Statement	Real Estate
Recipes	Homemaking and Nutrition
Reference and Information	Library Services
Religious Studies	Hobbies
Rental Companies	General Services
Report Generator	Database Management
Report Writer	Business Management
Resource Management	Food and Lodging Services (under Hotel-Resort Management)
Resource Management	Business Management
Restaurant Management	Food and Lodging Services
Resume Writer	Personal Recordkeeping
Retail Industry Control	General Services; Inventory, Purchasing and Invoicing
Retirement Planning	Personal Finance and Budgeting

S

Sales	Manufacturing
Sales Accounting	Marketing and Sales
Sales Analysis	Marketing and Sales
Sales Management	Marketing and Sales
Savings and Loan	Banking
Scanner Systems	Desktop Publishing
Scheduling	Business Management
Science (professional)	Engineering and Science (under many specific applications)
Science for Industry	Engineering and Science
Screen Editor	Programming Tools (under Text-Screen Editor)
Security	Personal Computing
Serials	Library Services
Shop Floor Control	Manufacturing
Shopping Aids	Homemaking and Nutrition
Simulation (games)	Games and Entertainment
Softball Scouting-Recordkeeping	Sports and Recreation (under Baseball Scouting-Recordkeeping)
Software Tutorials (general)	see specific applications under major headings: Database Management; Integrated Software; Spreadsheets; Word Processing
Speech Synthesizer	Music and Sound
Speed Reading	Hobbies
Spelling Checkers and Dictionaries	Word Processing

SOFTWARE ENCYCLOPEDIA 1996 — GUIDE TO APPLICATIONS

SPECIFIC APPLICATION	WILL BE FOUND UNDER THE FOLLOWING MAJOR HEADING(S)
Spreadsheets (for specific industries)	Agriculture and Ranching; Banking; Construction; Engineering and Science; Legal; Manufacturing
Stamp Collecting	Hobbies
Statistical Data Systems	Manufacturing
Statistics (professional)	Engineering and Science
Stock Charting	Personal Finance and Budgeting
Stock Market	Financial Analysis
Store Coupon Management	Homemaking and Nutrition
Strategy (games)	Games and Entertainment
Subscription Management	Library Services (under Circulation and Subscription Management)
Supercalc Tutorials	Spreadsheets (under Tutorials)
Surveying	Construction; Engineering and Science
Symphony Tutorials	Integrated Software (under Tutorials)
Systems Utilities	Personal Computing

T

Tax Form Printer	Legal
Tax Planning and Preparation (consumer)	Personal Finance and Budgeting
Tax Planning and Preparation—Corporations	Legal
Tax Planning and Preparation—Individuals	Legal
Tax Planning and Preparation (professional)	Financial Analysis
Tax Preparation	Accounting
Taxation	Government; Real Estate
Telephone Dialer	Business Management
Telephone Utilities	Personal Recordkeeping
Teller Systems	Banking
Tenant Billing	Real Estate
Terminal Emulators	Telecommunications
Texas Instruments Tutorials	Personal Computing (under Tutorials)
Text Processing	Desktop Processing
Text Retrieval	Database Management
Text-Screen Editors	Programming Tools
Textiles and Clothing	General Services
Thesaurus	Word Processing
Training (for business)	Business Management
Travel Agency	Transportation and Travel
Travel Guides	Transportation and Travel
Treatment and Diagnosis	Medical
Trend Analysis	Marketing and Sales
Trivia	Games and Entertainment
TRS and Tandy Tutorials	Personal Computing (under Tutorials)
Trucking	Transportation and Travel
Tutorials (computer or operating system)	Personal Computing
Tutorials (database)	Database Management; Integrated Software; Spreadsheets; Wordprocessing
Tutorials (integrated software)	Integrated Software
Tutorials (programming languages)	Programming Tools (under Language Tutorials)
Tutorials (spreadsheets)	Spreadsheets
Tutorials (word processing)	Word Processing

U

UNIX	Personal Computing (under Operating Systems)
Utilities (graphics)	Graphics
Utilities (personal computing)	Personal Computing (under Disk-File Utilities)
Utilities (programming)	Programming Tools
Utilities (public)	Public Services

V

Veterinary Medicine	Medical

SPECIFIC APPLICATION	WILL BE FOUND UNDER THE FOLLOWING MAJOR HEADING(S)
Virus Detection and Protection	Personal Computing
Visicalc Tutorials	Spreadsheets (under Tutorials)
Voice Pattern Recognition	Music and Sound

W

Warehouse Management	Inventory, Purchasing and Invoicing; Manufacturing
Wills	Legal
Wine	Hobbies
Word (games)	Games and Entertainment
Word Processing (for specific industries)	Engineering and Science; Legal; Medical
Word Processing Tutorials	Word Processing (under Tutorials)
WordPerfect Tutorials	Word Processing (under Tutorials)
WordStar Tutorials	Word Processing (under Tutorials)
Writing Aids	Word Processing

X

XENIX	Personal Computing (under Operating Systems)

Title Index

A-C-C-E-S-S: Microcomputer Network System.
Compatible Hardware: Apple II+, IIe, IIgs.
Operating System(s) Required: Apple DOS 3.3.
Language(s): Assembly. *Memory Required:* 48k.
General Requirements: Modem, clock card, 2 disk drives. *Items Included:* user manual.
disk $250.00.
175.00 ea. add'l. system.
BBS & Network System. Features Full 80-Column Messages. Provides Automatic Announcements at Log-On, Help Function, Automatic Forward & Retrieval, Electronic Mail, Automatic Form Fill Out, Automatic Log File, Automatic Message Numbering, Automatic Log-Off, Information File, Automatic Answer & Disconnect, & Automatic Baud Rate Settings. Also Provides User Selectable Modes, Security Passwords, Variable Message Length, Autolog, Subject Searching, etc.
Information Intelligence, Inc.

A-Cross. *Version:* 2.50. *Compatible Hardware:* IBM PC XT, PC AT, PS/2 & compatibles.
Operating System(s) Required:
PC-DOS/MS-DOS 2.15 or higher. *Memory Required:* 512k. *General Requirements:* Hard disk; monochrome, color, EGA & VGA monitors supported. *Items Included:* Manual, diskettes, tutorial. *Customer Support:* First 90 days free, $60.00/hr. thereafter.
disk $995.00.
Run-Time version $99.00.
Cross-Tabulation Program for the Analysis of Survey Research Questionnaire & Market Research Data. Handles up to 16.8 Million Respondents with up to 9,999 Variables per Respondent. Features T-Tests & Chi-Squares. Accepts ASCII, Column Binary, & DBASE Files. Outputs Directly to Laser Printers, ASCII Files, & Lotus .Wks Files.
Analytical Computer Service, Inc.

A-Maze-Ing. *Compatible Hardware:* TI-99/4A with PLATO interpreter solid state cartridge.
contact publisher for price (Order no.: PHM 3030).
Variety of Mazes from Simple to Complex - You're the Mouse Attempting to Capture Cheese While Avoiding Clever Cats.
Texas Instruments, Personal Productivit.

A Plus Electronic Flashcards. *Version:* 1.1. Mar. 1995. *Items Included:* Runtime Helix Engine, full instruction in program. *Customer Support:* Free phone support.
Windows. Macintosh (2Mb). CD-ROM disk $39.95.
A New Learning Utility Which Helps Students Quickly Learn Any Subject at the Computer & Improve Grades. Type the Questions & Answers Once, Then Review Material by Taking the Quiz. A Great Gift for Students As They Move from Subject to Subject, Grade to Grade, Kindergarten Through College.
Breakthrough Productions.

A>Recipes. May 1986. *Compatible Hardware:* Apple II, II+, IIe, IIc; Commodore 64, 128; IBM PC. *Operating System(s) Required:* MS-DOS 1.1, 2.0, 2.1. *Memory Required:* Apple 48k, Commodore 64k, IBM 128k. *Customer Support:* Free.
disk $15.00 ea.
East Hampton Industries, Inc.
  Natural Food Recipes from Rodale Press.
    IBM. (Order no.: 527I).
    Apple. (Order no.: 527A).
    Commodore. (Order no.: 527C).
    Recipes Contain No Salt & Very Little Fats & Cholesterol. User Can Change Serving Sizes, & Print Out the Recipes & a Shopping List.
  Recipes for Parents & Kids.
    IBM. (Order no.: 528I).
    Apple. (Order no.: 528A).
    Commodore. (Order no.: 528C).
    Collection of Recipes to Help Parents & Kids Cook Together. Designed to Teach Techniques of Healthy Cooking to Children. User Can Also Change Serving Sizes, & Print Out Recipes & a Shopping List.

A-Talk. Marco Tatta. Nov. 1990. *Items Included:* Runtime Windows. *Customer Support:* Free phone support.
Windows 3.0 (512k). Amiga. 3.5" disk $99.95.
Supports Tectronix Terminals.
Oxxi, Inc.

A-Talk for Windows. *Version:* 1.6. Sep. 1993. *Items Included:* Bound manual. *Customer Support:* 213-669-1497.
PC-DOS/MS-DOS & Microsoft Windows 3.1. IBM PC & compatibles (2M). disk $79.95 (ISBN 1-884992-00-5).
Microsoft Office Compatible Telecommunications Program with VT220 Tertronix 4014, MS-MAIL, CC:MAIL & Network DDE Support. Version for Microsoft Windows 3.1, Windows for Workgroups.
Felsina Software.

A-Talk for Windows. Feb. 1994. *Items Included:* 220 page manual. *Customer Support:* 90-day free support by phone, fax, mail & networks (Compuserve, Internet).
Microsoft Windows, Windows for Workgroups. Any PC compatible w/386/486 processor (2Mb). disk $49.95 (ISBN 1-884992-00-5).
Optimal configuration: Hayes compatible modem, MS-MAIL, CC:Mail. *Networks supported:* Novell, Windows for Work Groups.
Microsoft Windows NT. 386/486, MIPS, ALPHA (8Mb). disk $99.95. *Optimal configuration:* Hayes compatible modem, MS-MAIL, CC:Mail. *Networks supported:* LAN Manager/Windows NT.
A Comprehensive Telecommunications Package for the Windows NT, Windows 3.1 & Windows for Workgroups Operating Systems. A-Talk Supports Microsoft Mail, CC:Mail, Lotus Notes, Network DDE, Drag & Drop, Tektronix 4014 Emulation & Speech.
Felsina Software, Inc.

A-Talk for Windows NT. *Version:* 1.6. Sep. 1993. *Items Included:* Bound manual. *Customer Support:* 213-669-1497.
Windows NT. IBM PC & compatibles (8Mb), MIPS & Power PC (16Mb). disk $159.95 (ISBN 1-884992-00-5). *Nonstandard peripherals required:* Serial ports, LAN adapter (for LAN Manager & Telnet). *Optimal configuration:* 12Mb RAM. *Networks supported:* LAN Manager (Microsoft).
A Version of A-Talk for the High-Performance Microsoft Windows NT Operating System - Supports LAN Manager, Telnet & Other LANs.
Felsina Software.

A-Talk III. *Version:* 1.3. *Compatible Hardware:* Commodore Amiga.
3.5" disk $99.95.
Includes Tektronics Emulation.
Oxxi, Inc.

A*Video: Professional Font System. *Items Included:* 3 manuals, utilities.
Commodore Amiga 500, 1000, 2000, 3000. 3.5" disk $249.95. *Addl. software required:* Video Character Generator.
Variety of Video Fonts in 3 Formats.
CLASSIC CONCEPTS Futureware.

A-Z Form Templates for Excel. Jun. 1990. *Customer Support:* Phone support, 90 days unlimited warranty.
Macintosh. 3.5" disk $49.95. *Addl. software required:* Microsoft excel 2.2 or higher.
A Collection Calculating Input Automated Business & Personal Form Templates for Excel. Each Form is Ready for Input & Calculates the Input Data. Developing a User Defined Bookkeeping System or Individual Data Records is Achieved by Linking the Forms & Data to User Specifications Using Excel. Includes Templates for Accounts Receivable, Business Mileage, Travel Expense, Mileage Log, Equipment Maintenance, Spread Sheets, Invoices, Purchase Orders, Job Estimates, Job Costs, Pricing Sheet, Material Cost, Time Keeping, Time Cards, Tax Records, Statements, Sales Records, Check Book Register, Personal & Popular Record Keeping Categories.
Freemyers Design.

AA Computer Systems Accounts Payable. (Charterhouse Restaurant Programs Ser.). Jan. 1979. *Compatible Hardware:* IBM PC & compatibles, PC XT, PC AT, 80386-based machines; TRS-80 Model II, Model III, Model 4, Model 12, Model 16. *Operating System(s) Required:* MS-DOS, TRSDOS. *Language(s):* BASIC, C. *Memory Required:* 420k. *General Requirements:* Hard disk, printer.
disk $700.00.
Vendor Invoice Processing with Automatic Expense Distribution to General Ledger & Automatic Recording of Inventory & Unit Cost Changes to Inventory & Cost Control Cash or Accrual Accounting Check Processing.
Advanced Analytical/CharterHouse.

AA Computer Systems Club Accounts Receivable with Billing. (Charter House Restaurant Programs Ser.). Jan. 1979. *Compatible Hardware:* IBM PC & compatibles, PC XT, PC AT, 80386-based machines; TRS-80 Model II, Model III, Model 4, Model 12, Model 16. *Operating System(s) Required:* MS-DOS, TRSDOS. *Language(s):* BASIC, C. *Memory Required:* 420k. *General Requirements:* Hard disk, printer.
disk $1000.00 (ISBN 0-922121-09-5, Order no.: AP917).
One-Time Entry System with Optional Links to General Ledger, Order Entry, Inventory, & Manufacturing Bill of Materials.
Advanced Analytical/CharterHouse.

AA Computer Systems General Ledger. (Charter House Restaurant Programs Ser.). Jan. 1979. *Compatible Hardware:* IBM PC & compatibles, PC XT, PC AT, 80386-based machines. *Operating System(s) Required:* MS-DOS, networks. *Language(s):* BASIC, C. *Memory Required:* 420k. *General Requirements:* Hard disk, printer.
disk $1000.00 (ISBN 0-922121-08-7, Order no.: GL916).
Custom Chart of Accounts. Generates Balance Sheet, Income Statement, Financial Schedules, Working Trial Balance & Journal Transaction. Departmental Reporting, Budgeting & G/L Yearly History.
Advanced Analytical/CharterHouse.

AAIS Full Control Prolog. *Version:* 3.0. *General Requirements:* Hard disk drive, 2Mb memory partition. *Items Included:* Two volumes of manual, two diskettes, software. *Customer Support:* Via telephone/Applelink.
Macintosh Plus or higher (4Mb). 3.5" disk $598.00.
Powerful Extended Edinburgh Prolog Program Development System. Features Include Object-Oriented Commands for Creating Windows, Menus, Buttons, Controls, etc. with No Need for Understanding ROM Traps; & Foreign Code Resources; Extensive Debugging Commands; Dynamic Assertions/Retractions; Real Strings; Indexed Rules; & DCG Rules. Sample Programs Include the Source Defining the User Interface for Our Development Environment Which Is Built on Top of Our Object-Oriented Kernel. A Run-Time System for the Distribution of Applications Is Available Seperately. Educational & Site License Pricing are Available.
Advanced A.I. Systems.

AAPlanner for Windows. *Version:* 4.11. May 1995. *Compatible Hardware:* IBM PC, PC XT, AT, PS/2 or compatible. *Memory Required:* 8000k. *General Requirements:* Hard disk. *Items Included:* User's manual in 3-ring binder & cloth covered slipcase. *Customer Support:* 90-day telephone technical support included in purchase price; extended technical support with toll-free number is $150 per year.
IBM. $1495.00.
Calculates Eight Factor-Availability Analyses & Utilization Analyses & Prepares Goals Reports Used in an Affirmative Action Plan. Accesses External Workforce Data from Census Occupation Diskettes. Combines & Weights Data for Different Geographic Areas to Create Custom Recruiting Areas. Receives Internal Workforce Files Imported from Mainframe or Microcomputer. Offers Choice of Methods for Calculating Underutilization Including the 80% Rule, the Any Difference Rule, the Standard Deviation Test, & Exact Binomial Test. All Worksheets Can Be Printed for Inclusion in Final AAP. Does Not Require Programming Skills. Includes Three User-Selected Census Diskettes. Companion Program to Work Force/Job Group Analyst & Adverse Impact Monitor.
PRI Assocs., Inc.

Aatrix Payroll. *Version:* 7.0. *Compatible Hardware:* Macintosh Plus or above. *Memory Required:* 2000k. *General Requirements:* Hard disk. *Items Included:* Tax tables for federal & all 50 states. *Customer Support:* 30 days free, then $10.00 per month (includes tax tables).
3.5" disk $199.00.
Designed to Manage Paychecks for Both Salaried & Hourly Employees. Handles All Check Printing; Calculates, Accumulates, & Deducts Taxes; Prints Reports Summarizing Gross Pay & Withholding at All Levels by End-of-Payroll, Date, Month, Quarter, & Year; & Provides Password Protection.
Aatrix Software.

AB-RK (Soft Alphabet). 1987.
MS-DOS. IBM PC, PC XT, PC AT & compatibles. disk $30.00 (ISBN 0-938245-53-8).
Nonstandard peripherals required: Epson or compatible 9-pin dot matrix printer.
Soft English/Hebrew/Pointing Font for Downloading to Epson Compatible Dot Matrix Printers. Includes Utilities for Downloading & Protecting Printer from Reset.
Inverted-A, Inc.

Abacus Law Plus. *Version:* 10.0. Brian Hays. *Items Included:* User guide, Getting Started guide. *Customer Support:* Free 3 months telephone support (toll free), Annual maintenance contract available, 3-month moneyback guarantee.
MS/PC-DOS 3.0 or higher. IBM compatibles with a hard disk. $399.00 Singleuser, $599.00 Multiuser (1-5 users), $99.00 ea. (California FastTrack Rules, Civil Procedure Timelines, General Practice Templates). *Optimal configuration:* Supports B&W or color, mouse (if available), laser & dot matrix printers, hard disk needed. *Networks supported:* All Netbios compatible: Novell, Lantastic, etc.
Database Program Combines Calendaring/ Docketing, Case Management & Conflicts Checking into One Package. Features Include Docketing (Including Automatic Calculation of Court Required Dates); Information on Clients; Expert Witness Lists, etc. Over 16 Pages of Notes Can Be Kept on Each Matter & Client.
Abacus Data Systems, Inc.

ABASIC Utility Pak, No. 1. Dennis Allen. *Compatible Hardware:* TRS-80 Model I, Model III, Model 4, Tandy 2000. *Operating System(s) Required:* PC-DOS, MS-DOS, CP/M. *Memory Required:* 64k.
disk $29.95 ea.
CP/M. (Order no.: DCABU1).
Tandy 2000. (Order no.: D2ABU1).
Model 4. (Order no.: D4ABU1).
Model I & Model III. (Order no.: D8ABU1).
MS-DOS. (Order no.: DMABU1).
Includes HELP, LVAR (Lists Program Variables to Screen, Printer and/or Disk), CREF (Cross Reference Program Variables), XVAR (Translates Variables Between Different Forms of BASIC), & XLATE (a General Purpose Translator) to Assist User with Converting from 1 Dialect of BASIC to Another. Utilities May Be Used with Any File.
The Alternate Source.

ABASIC Utility Pak, No. 2. Dennis Allen. *Compatible Hardware:* TRS-80 Model I, Model III, Model 4, Tandy 2000. *Operating System(s) Required:* MS-DOS, PC-DOS, CP/M. (source code included). *Memory Required:* 64k.
disk $29.95 ea., incl. manual.
CP/M. (Order no.: DCABU2).
Model 4. (Order no.: D4ABU2).
MS-DOS. (Order no.: DMABU2).
Includes File Editors for Both Balanced TREE Index (BTREE) & Random Access LABEL Date Files.
The Alternate Source.

ABC Caterpillar. *Compatible Hardware:* Commodore 64/128. *General Requirements:* Joystick.
disk $21.00 (Order no.: 46755).
Children Control a Bright Green Caterpillar to Help Learn the Alphabet & Spelling. There Are Five Separate Games, Teaching the Alphabet, the First Letter of a Number of Objects, a Simple Three & Four Letter Spelling Game, & a Sketch Pad.
Avalon Hill Game Co., The Microcomputer Games Div.

ABC Flowcharter. *Version:* 2.0.
MS-DOS 3.1 or higher, Windows 3.1. IBM 386 & compatibles (2Mb). 3.5" disk $495.00 (Order no.: AB3L20ENG). *Addl. software required:* Windows 3.1. *Networks supported:* Windows 3.1 compatible.
Provides All the Capabilities Needed for Creating Diagrams, Developing Quality Management Programs, Designing PC & Mainframe Networks, Defining Requirements, Designing Office Layouts, & Documenting Auditing Procedures. Designed for Quick & Easy Flowcharting in Windows.
Micrografx, Inc.

ABC's Monday Night Football.
MS-DOS. IBM PC & compatibles (512K). contact publisher for price. *Addl. software required:* CGA, EGA required.
Commodore 64/128. contact publisher for price. *Nonstandard peripherals required:* 1 disk drive, color monitor or Joystick.
Commodore Amiga 500/1000/2000. Commodore Amgia 500/1000/2000 (512K). contact publisher for price.
ABC's Monday Night Football Gives You Football Action Like You've Never Seen Before! This is the Only Game That Takes You from the

TITLE INDEX

Bright Lights of the Announcers Booth to the Gut Wrenching Action on Th Field. You Are the Quarterback- Check Off Your Receivers & Find the Open Man. You'll Feel the Hits, Hear the Grunts, & Experience Football As Only the Best Players Can.
Data East U.S.A., Inc.

ABC's of Americans with Disabilities Act. *Items Included:* Full manual. No other products required. *Customer Support:* Free telephone support - no time limit, 30 day warranty.
MS-DOS 3.2 or higher. IBM & compatibles (512k). disk $89.95. *Optimal configuration:* IBM, MS-DOS 2.0 or higher, 512k RAM, & hard disk (will use 2.3Mb of disk space).
Provides a Quick & Efficient Way to Learn the Parts of the Law Which Affect You. Includes the Complete Text of ADA, As Well As a Summary, Fact Sheet, Q & A, Telephone Numbers for Contacting Agencies, & So On. Also Functions As a Tool for Searching the Text for Material Which May Specifically Affect You. Searches Are Not Just Limited to Multiple Keywords, but Also May Include Phrases.
Dynacomp, Inc.

ABC's of Americans with Disabilities Act. 1992. *Items Included:* Detailed manuals included with all Dynacomp products. *Customer Support:* Free telephone support to original customer - no time limit; 30 day limited warranty.
MS-DOS 3.2 or higher. IBM PC & compatibles (512k). $89.95 (Add $5.00 for 3 1/2" format; 5 1/4" format standard). *Optimal configuration:* IBM, MS-DOS 2.0 or higher, 512k RAM, & a hard disk (will use 2.3Mb of disk space).
ADAABC Provides a Quick & Efficient Way to Learn the Parts of the Law Which Affect You. Includes the Complete Text of ADA, As Well As a Summary, Fact Sheet, Q & A, Telephone Numbers for Contacting Agencies, & So On. Also Functions As a Tool for Searching the Text for Material Which May Specifically Affect You. Searches Are Not Just Limited to Multiple Keywords, but Also May Include Phrases.
Dynacomp, Inc.

ABE. *Compatible Hardware:* TRS-80 Model I. *Operating System(s) Required:* TRSDOS 2.3 or NEWDOS 80. *Memory Required:* 32-48k.
disk $19.95 (Order no.: 5026RD).
Accelerates Writing & Editing of BASIC Programs. Provides Formatted Screen, Line Copy Ability, & Assignable Keys.
Instant Software, Inc.

ABECAS Assets. *Version:* 3.3. *Operating System(s) Required:* MS-DOS. *Customer Support:* On site training unlimited support services for first 90 days & through subscription thereafter.
contact publisher for price.
Depreciation Management System That Tracks Historical, Current & Replacement Costs for Each Asset & Calculates Depreciation As Required.
Argos Software.

Abel's Island. Intentional Education Staff & William Steig. Apr. 1996. *Items Included:* Program manual. *Customer Support:* Free techncial support,.
- School ver.. System 7.1 or higher. Macintosh (4Mb). 3.5" disk contact publisher for price (ISBN 1-57204-381-4). *Nonstandard peripherals required:* 256 color monitor, hard drive, printer.
- Lab pack. System 7.1 or higher. Macintosh (4Mb). 3.5" disk contact publisher for price (ISBN 1-57204-357-1). *Nonstandard peripherals required:* 256 color monitor, hard drive, printer.
- Site license. System 7.1 or higher. Macintosh (4Mb). 3.5" disk contact publisher for price (ISBN 1-57204-382-2). *Nonstandard peripherals required:* 256 color monitor, hard drive, printer.
- School ver.. Windows 3.1 or higher. IBM/Tandy & 100% compatibles (4Mb). disk contact publisher for price (ISBN 1-57204-358-X). *Nonstandard peripherals required:* VGA or SVGA 640 x 480 resolution (256), mouse, hard drive, sound device.
- Lab pack. Windows 3.1 or higher. IBM/Tandy & 100% compatibles (4Mb). disk contact publisher for price (ISBN 1-57204-383-0). *Nonstandard peripherals required:* VGA or SVGA 640 x 480 resolution (256), mouse, hard drive, sound device.
- Site license. Windows 3.1 or higher. IBM/Tandy & 100% compatibles (4mb). disk contact publisher for price (ISBN 1-57204-359-8). *Nonstandard peripherals required:* VGA or SVGA 640 x 480 resolution (256), mouse, hard drive, sound device.

This companion for young adult literature is ideal for students who don't know how to start that book report, or give that needed summary. Gentle prompts throughout the guide section of the program include Warm-up Connections, Thinking about Plot, Quoting & Noting, Keeping a Journal, If I Were ———' Responding to Questions, Using Quotations, Taking a Personal View, Write to Others, & Write a Sequel.
Lawrence Productions, Inc.

ABFAB Assembly Disk. *Compatible Hardware:* Atari. *Language(s):* BASIC & Assembly.
disk $24.95 (ISBN 0-936200-30-8).
Contains the Assembly Language Programs from Atari BASIC in Both Source Code & Object File Format. Includes Sort Routines, MiniDOS & Other Functions.
Blue Cat.

ABFAB Demo Applications Disk. *Compatible Hardware:* Atari. *Operating System(s) Required:* DOS. *Language(s):* BASIC.
disk $24.95 (ISBN 0-936200-32-4).
Provides 11 Applications Programs & 14 Demonstration Programs, Including Many Utilities. Converts Machine Language Routines to BASIC Data Statements. Also Tests the Disk Drive & Analyzes DOS Files.
Blue Cat.

ABFAB Library Disks. *Compatible Hardware:* Atari. *Language(s):* BASIC.
disk $24.95 (ISBN 0-936200-31-6).
Provides BASIC & Machine Language Subroutines. Includes Sound Effects, String Manipulations & Video Formatters.
Blue Cat.

ABM. Silas Warner. Feb. 1981. *Compatible Hardware:* Apple II, IIe, II+. *Operating System(s) Required:* Apple DOS 3.2, 3.3. *Language(s):* Assembly. *Memory Required:* 48k.
disk $7.98 (ISBN 0-87190-001-7).
The Player Controls the Launch & Trajectory of Anti-Ballistic Missiles Defending the East Coast from Nuclear Attack. Enemy Attack Intensifies As the Game Goes On. The Player Must Be on Constant Alert for the MIRV Missile Which Splits into Multiple Warheads.
Muse Software.

Abrams Battle Tank. Dynamix. Mar. 1989. *Items Included:* Manual or ref card. *Customer Support:* Customer hint hotline (415) 572-9560.
PC/MS-DOS (512k). IBM. disk $14.95. *Optimal configuration:* Graphics: CGA, EGA, Tandy, Hercules.
Command One of the World's Most Powerful Battletanks, the Abrams M1A1. Advanced Weapon Intelligence, Tank Maneuverability, Modern Weaponry, 4 Different Battle Perspectives, 15 Types of Allied & Soviet Vehicles to I.D. or Destroy.
Electronic Arts.

ABRAXAS. *Compatible Hardware:* IBM PC & compatibles. *Memory Required:* 640k. *General Requirements:* Hard disk (40Mb). *Customer Support:* Toll free - No charge.
$695.00.
$995.00 network version.
ABRAXAS Is a First-Time Marriage of Management & Accounting. You Create the Documents That You Would Normally Generate on Paper: Sales Orders, Invoices, Packing Slips, Timecards, Checks & Deposit Slips. ABRAXAS Does the Accounting - Automatically & Instantly. Inventory, Clients, Vendors, Commission, Cash & Every Other Related File Are Updated Each Time a Document Is Entered or Edited. You Know Where You Stand Every Minute of Every Day.
ApTech, Inc.

ABS Accounts Payable.
disk $1995.00. *Networks supported:* Novell.
manual $35.00.
Fully Featured Accounts Payable System Processes Vendors, Vouchers, Checks, Cash Management. Works Independently or Integrates with Other ABS Accounting Programs.
Applied Business Software, Inc.

ABS Accounts Receivable.
$1995.00. *Networks supported:* Novell.
manual $35.00.
Supports up to 32,000 Customers with Both Itemized & Balance Forward Billing. Interest & Late Charges, Recurring Charges, Even "Dunning Letters" Generated Automatically. Integrates with Other ABS Accounting Programs, or Stands Alone.
Applied Business Software, Inc.

ABS General Ledger.
$1995.00. *Networks supported:* Novell.
manual $35.00.
Supports up to 9999 General Ledger Accounts. Maintains Departmentalized Records for Separation of Profit Centers. Automatically Does Month-End & Year-End Closing Entries. Maintains 24 Months of Data On-Line. Integrates with Other ABS Accounting Programs, or Stands Alone. Produces "Year at a Glance" Financials Detailing 12 Months in Columnar Format.
Applied Business Software, Inc.

ABS-IMS (Information Management System). $1295.00.
Database System That Allows User to Create, Define & Maintain Files by Means of a Menu-Driven Program. Receives Data from Other ABS Programs, Allowing for Complex Searches of All Data Files & Creation of Custom Reports.
Applied Business Software, Inc.

ABS/Inventory. *Operating System(s) Required:* PC-DOS, MS-DOS, UNIX, XENIX, VMS, AIX, ULTRIX.
$995.00. *Networks supported:* Novell.
A Fully Featured Inventory System That Lets User Keep Track of All Inventory Items & Transactions That Affect Inventory Count. Produces a Full Range of Inventory Reports That Tell Inventory Value, When to Re-Order Items, & All Transactions That Affected the Items. Works Independently or Integrates with Other ABS Accounting Packages.
Applied Business Software, Inc.

ABS Order Entry. *Operating System(s) Required:* PC-DOS, MS-DOS, UNIX, XENIX, VMS, AIX, ULTRIX.

ABS PAYROLL

$995.00. *Networks supported:* Novell.
Lets User Create, Update, & Issue Invoices. It Also Prints Packing Lists & Shipping Labels. ABS/OE is Designed to Work with ABS Accounts Receivables, So All Invoices Created Automatically Update the Receivable Files.
Applied Business Software, Inc.

ABS Payroll.
disk $1995.00.
manual $35.00.
Supports up to 10,000 Employees with 5 Miscellaneous Earning/Deductions & Withholding of Both State & Federal Tax per Employee. Processes Weekly, Biweekly, Semi-Monthly & Monthly Pay Intervals. Allows for up to 9 Departments for Cost Analysis. Produces Numerous Reports Such As 941 Federal Quarterly Report, DE-3 State Quarterly Report, W-2's, 1099s, etc.
Applied Business Software, Inc.

Absoft F77 SDK for Power Macintosh. *Version:* 4.2. Jan. 1996. *Items Included:* Complete documentation, linker, debugger, graphics libraries, subroutine libraries, MRWE application framework. *Customer Support:* 90 day warranty, free telephone support, internet support.
MacOS System 7.1.2 or higher. PowerPC 601 (16Mb). 3.5" disk $699.00 (Order no.: FPP3MAC1).
Complete Native Power Macintosh FORTRAN 77 Development Kit. Two Code Generators: 68K & PowerPC. Native Linker, Debugger, Graphics Libraries, MRWE Application Framework. VAX/VMS Compatible, CodeWarrior 7.0 & Later Link Compatible.
Absoft Corp.

Absoft F77 SDK for Power Macintosh. *Version:* 4.1.1. Aug. 1995. *Items Included:* Complete documentation, linker, debugger, graphics libraries, subroutine libraries, MRWE application framework. *Customer Support:* 90 day warranty, free telephone support, internet support.
Windows 95/Windows NT. 486DX (8Mb), VGA. disk $699.00 (Order no.: F863WIN1).
Complete Native Power Macintosh FORTRAN 77 Development Kit. Two Code Generators: 68K & PowerPC. Native Linker, Debugger, Graphics Libraries, MRWE Application Framework. VAX/VMS Compatible, CodeWarrior 7.0 & Later Link Compatible.
Absoft Corp.

Absoft Fortran 90 for Power Macintosh. *Version:* 2.0. May 1996. *Items Included:* Complete documentation. *Customer Support:* 90 day warranty, free telephone support, internet support.
MacOS System 7.1.2 or higher. PowerPC 601 (16Mb). disk $899.00.
ANSI Standard Fortran 90 Compiler. Linker, Debugger, Graphics Libraries, Subroutine Libraries, MRWE Application Framework. Link Compatible with Absoft F77 for Power Mac. Two Code Generators: 68K & Power PC. CodeWarrior 7.0 & Later Link Compatible.
Absoft Corp.

Absoft FORTRAN 77 for 386/486. *Version:* 3.1. Feb. 1991. *Items Included:* Complete documentation. *Customer Support:* Free unlimited telephone support, maintenance agreement available.
SCO Unix. 386/387 or 486DX (4Mb). $995.00 (Order no.: F865UV32).
SCO-ODT. 386/387 or 486DX (4Mb). $995.00 (Order no.: F865ODT2).
Intel SVR4. 386/387 or 486DX (4Mb). $995.00 (Order no.: F865VR42).
VAX/VMS Compatible, Full 32 Bit FORTRAN 77 Compiler for 386/486 Unix Systems. Fully Validated ANSI X3.9-1978/ISO 1539-1980 Compiler Which Supports all Dod MIL-STD 1753 Extensions & Is Fully FIPS 69-1, iBCS & POSIX Compliant. Includes Structure & Pointer.
Absoft Corp.

Absoft FORTRAN 77. *Version:* 3.2. Feb. 1993. *Items Included:* Complete documentation. *Customer Support:* Free unlimited telephone support, maintenance agreement available.
Windows NT. Intel 486 or Pentium processors (4Mb). disk $995.00. *Addl. software required:* Windows NT SDK.
Windows NT. Intel 386/387, Intel 486DX, Pentium processor (4Mb). disk $750.00.
ANSI Standard FORTRAN Compiler with All MIL-STD 1753 Extensions. VAX/VMS, IBM/VS, Sun/Cray, Fortran 90 Extensions, All VAX Intrinsic Functions.
Absoft Corp.

Absoft FORTRAN 77. *Items Included:* Software, manuals. *Customer Support:* 1 full year of support is included with each product purchased. Support includes hotline phone support, technical mailings, & free upgrades.
PDOS. Motorola 680 x 0 based systems. disk $2800.00. *Networks supported:* Ethernet, map.
ANSI FORTRAN 77 Compiler Written in 68000 Assembler. It Is Especially well Suited for Scientific, Industrial, Engineering, & Other Real-Team Applications As It Has No Limitation on Code Size. It Is Designed to Facilitate Running Mainframe Programs on the More Cost Efficient Micros on Which PDOS Is Implemented. Generated Code Is Both Position Independent & Re-Entrant. FORTRAN 77 Compilation Is Also Supported Through an Optional Compilation Switch.
Eyring Corp.

Absolut: Business & Inventory Management Software. Mar. 1984. *Compatible Hardware:* AT&T, DEC VAX, IBM RISC 6000, HP, NCR, Sequent, any 486. *Operating System(s) Required:* AIX, SCO, UNIX. *Language(s):* C & Unify R.D.B.M.S. *Memory Required:* 4000k. *General Requirements:* Hard disk, printer, modem.
$50,000.00 and up.
Complete Order Entry/Inventory Management Package Which Includes Prospect Tracking, Quotation Generating, & Activation into Order, Serialized & Multi-Site Inventory, AR, AP, & GL, Customer & Supplier Billing, Point of Sale Interface, Concurrent Customer File & Order Entry Functions, Credit Card Charge & Billing & Stock Alias Functions. Suitable for Distributors, Wholesalers, Importers, Retailers, Mail-Order & Phone Order Houses, & Manufacturers Distributing Durable & Nondurable Merchandise & Apparel.
Absolut Software, Inc.

Absolute Coordinate Dimensioning Plus. Rick McElhinney. Feb. 1987. *Compatible Hardware:* Apple Macintosh II; IBM PC. *Memory Required:* 640k. *General Requirements:* Hard disk, AutoCAD program.
disk $275.00.
For Users in the Tool & Die Industry with Needs in Absolute Coordinate Dimensioning. Gives Drawing Capabilities for the Dimensioning of Dies & Sheet Metalwork. Includes All of the Features of ACD Plus Inside Dimensioning, Variable Extension Lines & Locations, & Variable Unit Formats.
Vector Systems, Inc.

ABtab. *Version:* 4.2. Mar. 1989. *Items Included:* 250 page comprehensive manual; complete tutorial; sample data set. *Customer Support:* Support plus package included with purchase. Includes 1 year telephone technical support, free upgrades. Subsequent years: $200.00. 30 day money back guarantee; training available on site.
PC-DOS/MS-DOS 2.0 or higher. IBM PC, PS/2, AT & compatibles (512k). CD-ROM disk single use license: $995.00; site license: $1995.00 (ISBN 0-917955-01-3). *Nonstandard peripherals required:* 10Mb hard disk, printer.
Survey Information Management System (SIMS) For Market & Survey Researchers. Turns Survey Data into Meaningful Reports & Analyses - Cost Effective Alternative to On-Line Services & Data Vendors. Low "Learning Curve"; Menu Orientation; Compatible with Many Data File Formats. Documentation Included.
Bruce Bell & Assocs., Inc.

ABT's Time Line Interface: Interface to Project Workbench System.
PC/MS-DOS (512k). IBM PC & compatibles. contact publisher for price. *Addl. software required:* Project workbench system.
Enables Users to Quickly & Easily Convert Project Files Created with Time Line to a Format That Can Be Imported into Project Workbench. Free of Charge to Registered Project Workbench Users.
ABT Corp.

AC: Access Control. Nov. 1985. *Compatible Hardware:* IBM PC. *Operating System(s) Required:* MS-DOS. *Memory Required:* 640kk. *General Requirements:* Hard disk.
contact publisher for price.
Controls Access to Buildings, Computer Rooms, Computer Networks, Computer Usage, Elevators, & Environmental Controls by Means of an Electronic Card Issued to Personnel. A Total History of Card Usage May Be Retrieved from the System. Alarm Points May Also Be Monitored.
KMS Systems, Inc.

AC Circuit Analysis. *Compatible Hardware:* HP 85, 86/87, 216/220, 226/236 with BASIC 2.0. *Memory Required:* 100k.
HP 85. data cartridge, 3-1/2" or 5-1/4" disk $95.00 ea. (Order no.: 82810A).
HP 86/87. 3-1/2" or 5-1/4" disk $95.00 ea. (Order no.: 82840A).
HP 216/220. 3-1/2" or 5-1/4" disk $500.00 ea. (Order no.: 98825A).
HP 226/236. 5 1/4" disk $500.00 ea.
Helps Users Model Their Circuits & Examine Their AC Performance. Determines Steady-State Behavior of Electrical Networks Including Resistors, Capacitors, Inductors, Voltage-Controlled & Independent Current Sources. The HP 85/86/87 Versions Are a Subset of the Series 200 Package.
Hewlett-Packard Co.

AC Circuit Analysis Library. *Compatible Hardware:* TI 99/4A.
contact publisher for price (Order no.: PHD 5044).
Two Programs Which Assist In Determining the Performance of Circuits in Handling Alternating Currents.
Texas Instruments, Personal Productivit.

Academy of Reading. *Version:* 1.03. Ron Trites & Christina Fiedorowicz. Nov. 1995. *Items Included:* CD-ROM, teacher manual. *Customer Support:* Free on-site training, manuals, & 1-800 number.
DOS, Windows 3.1. 386XS-33, 486 recommended (8Mb). CD-ROM disk Contact publisher for price (ISBN 1-883919-14-2). *Optimal configuration:* SVGA (640x480-256 colors), 80Mb.
A Comprehensive Software Program That Will Help Both Children & Adults Realize Their Full Potential. The Program Contains a Wide Variety

TITLE INDEX

of Assessment Tools & Several Training Programs That Will Help Develop the Skills That Are Necessary for Successful Reading. These Include Phonetic Training, Word Blending, Comprehension.
Autoskill New York, Inc.

ACAP-Active Circuit Analysis Spice Circuit Simulation. *Items Included:* Full manual. No other products required. *Customer Support:* Free telephone support - no time limit, 30 day warranty.
MS-DOS 3.2 or higher. IBM & compatibles (512k). disk $39.95.
Active & Passive Circuit Analysis Program. It Can Be Used to Solve the Node Voltages of a Network. Circuit Elements Which Can Be Analyzed by ACAP are Resistors, Capacitors, Inductors, Voltage Sources, Current Sources, & a Voltage-Controlled Current Source.
Dynacomp, Inc.

ACCELL-IDS. *Version:* 2.0. *Compatible Hardware:* IBM PC & compatibles. *Items Included:* Software, Manuals, release notes.
Price varies.
UNIX-Based Application Development Product Designed to Maximize Developer Productivity Through a Tightly Integrated Combination of Fourth Generation Technologies. ACCELL IDS Includes a Complete 4GL, Visual Application Generator, Powerful Relational Database Management System & Cooperative Processing Option. ACCELL IDS Features Full Internationalization, Enhanced Formatting & Continue & Break Statements.
Unify Corp.

ACCELL/SQL. *Version:* 1.3. 1990. *Items Included:* Complete set of manuals, release notes, technical tips & hardware notes.
Any major UNIX OS System V.3 & V.4. Any Standard UNIX Platform. $1770 and up. *Optimal configuration:* 8-12Mb RAM. *Networks supported:* TCP/IP, NFS & PC Networks.
Open Systems, UNIX-Based Application Development Technology. Font-End Tool with an Integrated 4GL & Generator That Cut Development Time by up to 80 Percent. Graphical User Interfaces (Motif, OPENLOOK & Microsoft Windows) Are Available - with No Additional Programming. Utilizes Different Platforms, OSs, RDBMSs & GUIs.
Unify Corp.

ACCENT GraphicVUE: Visual Project Management. Aug. 1992. *Customer Support:* Telephone, FAX, E-Mail, On-Site - 30 days warranty.
UNIX. Sun, IBM, I&P, Silicon Graphics. $1450.00 per network sent. *Networks supported:* TCP/IP.
Offers "Mainframe-Class" Project Management Benefits to Network, Workstation & Visual Computing Environments. Build Plans Graphically with Motif/X-Windows; Manage Shared Resources Across Multiple Projects; Plan for Contingencies with "What-If" Analysis; Compare Estimates with Actual Performance; Promote Better Staff Communication; Focus on Quality/ Customer Satisfaction.
National Information Systems, Inc.

Accent R. *Version:* 11.22. 1980. *Compatible Hardware:* DEC VAX, MicroVax, Macintosh II. *Operating System(s) Required:* VMS, A/UX. *Language(s):* C.
$3,300.00-$108,400.00 depending on CPU.
Multi-User Applications Developed with ACCENT R, Meet the Demands of Users While Reducing Development Costs, Time, & Maintenance. ACCENT R's 4th Generation Language Replaces 3rd GLs, & Provides a 10:1 Reduction of Code. Features Include a Structured Programming Language, Debugging Tools, Error & Syntax Checking, & SQL.
National Information Systems, Inc.

ACCENT RDM: User Application Developer. *Version:* 4.4B. Aug. 1992. *Customer Support:* Telephone, FAX, E-Mail, On-Site - 30 days warranty.
UNIX, DOS, VMS. VAX. $895.00 for DOS. *Networks supported:* DECNET.
Development Tool for End-Users. Enables User to Create Detailed Reports with Automatic Selections. Users Can Quickly Paint Data Entry Forms & Include Such Features As Multi-File Access, Pre-Defined Input Options & Scrolling Windows. Applications Are Completely Portable Between Different Operating Systems Without Modification.
National Information Systems, Inc.

ACCENTR Fourth Generation Language: SQL-Based 462. *Version:* 11.41. Aug. 1992. *Customer Support:* Telephone, FAX, E-Mail, On-Site - 30 days warranty.
VMS. VAX. $2995.00. *Optimal configuration:* VMS. *Networks supported:* DECNET.
SQL-Based Applications Development Environment Which Includes a Fourth Generation Language, a Relational Database Management System & CASE Tools for Building Applications. It Generates Optimized, Compiled Code That Can Handle High-Volume Production Processing with RMS, Rdb/VMS, Sybase, Oracle & Ingres Databases.
National Information Systems, Inc.

ACCESS Accounts Payable. *Version:* 4.0. Jan. 1987. *Compatible Hardware:* IBM PC & compatible. *Language(s):* Compiled BASIC. *Memory Required:* 512k. *Items Included:* Disks, manuals, & demo data. *Customer Support:* Yes. disk $200.00.
Integrated Accounts Payable Package Features Company Master File & Check-Writing Function. Can Be Customized.
Software Design, Inc.

ACCESS Accounts Receivable. *Version:* 4.0. 1987. *Compatible Hardware:* IBM PC & compatible. *Language(s):* Compiled BASIC. *Memory Required:* 512k. *Items Included:* Disks, manuals, & demo data. *Customer Support:* Yes. disk $200.00.
Integrated Accounts Receivable Package Handles Cash Flow, Sales & Profit Analysis.
Software Design, Inc.

ACCESS General Ledger. *Version:* 4.0. 1987. *Compatible Hardware:* IBM PC & compatible. *Language(s):* Compiled BASIC. *Memory Required:* 512k. *Items Included:* Disks, manuals, & demo data. *Customer Support:* Yes. disk $200.00.
Integrated Ledger Package Handles General Journal, Cash Receipts & Cash Disbursements.
Software Design, Inc.

ACCESS Order Entry-Inventory. *Version:* 4.0. 1988. *Compatible Hardware:* IBM PC & compatible. *Language(s):* Compiled BASIC. *Memory Required:* 512k. *Items Included:* Disks, manuals, & demo data. *Customer Support:* Yes. disk $200.00.
Integrated Package Features Inventory File Which Can Be Adjusted As Invoices Are Written.
Software Design, Inc.

ACCESS Payroll. *Version:* 3.5. 1987. *Compatible Hardware:* IBM PC & compatible. *Language(s):* Compiled BASIC. *Memory Required:* 512k. *Items Included:* Disks, manuals, & demo data. *Customer Support:* Yes. disk $200.00.
Integrated Payroll Package Features Master Record for Each Employee with Constant & Variable Data. Provides Employee, Company & Governmental Reporting Information.
Software Design, Inc.

THE ACCOUNTANT

Access-64. *Compatible Hardware:* Commodore Amiga.
contact publisher for price.
Transfers C-64/C-128 Files to Amiga. Includes Software & an Adapter Plug That Fits into Amiga's Serial Port. Transparent.
Progressive Peripherals & Software, Inc.

ACCI Project Management Accounting System. *Version:* 9.0. Jul. 1992. *Compatible Hardware:* IBM PC, PC AT, PC XT, PS/2. *Operating System(s) Required:* MS-DOS 3.3 & higher. *Language(s):* Microsoft QuickBASIC. *Memory Required:* 384k. *General Requirements:* 132-column printer. *Customer Support:* $295 per year.
PC-DOS single user. $6200.00.
Novell Network. $11,000.00.
manual $150.00.
Emulates the AIA or ACEC Standardized Accounting for Architect's/Engineer's Structure. Accepts Time Sheet & Expense Data, & Updates All Project Files As Well As All Related Accounting Files Such As Payroll, Accounts Payable, Accounts Receivable & General Ledger.
ACCI Business Systems, Inc.

Accident/Incident Control. *Items Included:* Manuals, training exercises, quick refefence guide.
IBM PC, XT, AT, & compatibles. contact publisher for price.
Management Reporting from Any Angle.
Beechwood Software.

Account. *Version:* 2.2. Jul. 1982. *Compatible Hardware:* Altos, IBC, Onyx. *Operating System(s) Required:* Oasis. *Language(s):* BASIC & C. *Memory Required:* 64k.
contact publisher for price.
Interactive General Ledger/Accounts Receivable/ Accounts Payable Accounting Packages.
Business Design Software.

Account Sales Receivables. *Version:* 3.50. Dallas T. DeFee. Aug. 1985. *Compatible Hardware:* IBM PC & compatibles, PC XT, PC AT. *Memory Required:* 256k. *General Requirements:* Printer; Lotus 1-2-3 or Symphony.
disk $249.90.
Receivables & Order Processing System That Maintains Transaction History & Journals, Prepares Invoices & Statements, Mailing Labels, & Sales Reports, Calculates Sales Tax & Commissions, Updates & Graphs Receivables. Integrates with +ACCOUNT GENERAL LEDGER.
Computer Software Consultants, Inc.

The Accountant. *Version:* 2.0. *Compatible Hardware:* Commodore Amiga 500; 2000; 1000. *Items Included:* 2 disks: day-to-day activities; KFS (monthly & weekly) activities; data disk; indexed documentation. *Customer Support:* Customizing services; upgrade club indexed documentation $24.95, lifetime w/newsletters for tax info; upgrades for $9.95/disk; customer service phone line 813-584-2355 10am-4pm, Mon.-Fri..
3.5" disk $299.50.
Includes Accounts Receivable/Payable, General Ledger, Payroll, Inventory; Cash Register, Invoice Writer & 2 Other Point-of-Sale Options.
KFS Software, Inc.

The Accountant. *Compatible Hardware:* Apple II, II+, IIe, IIc.
contact publisher for price.
Enter Any Number of Transactions into a Single System. Over 4000 Can Be Stored on One Side of a Disk. Features On-Screen Help. Can Retrieve, Print or Remove Any Transaction (or Selected Group of Transactions). Printed Reports Display the Entire System Including All Monthly Totals.
Schmidt Enterprises.

ACCOUNTANT

Accountant, Inc. *Version:* 3.0. *Customer Support:* 30 days from first call to Tech Support line. Macintosh Plus or higher (1Mb). 3.5" disk $595.00.
This Complete Business Accounting Package Includes General Ledger, Accounts Receivable, Accounts Payable, Payroll, Inventory Control, Job Costing, Project Management & Time Billing. The General Ledger Tracks All Account Balances & Transactions; Payroll Calculates Income & Deduction, As Well As Prints Checks & Generates Tax Reports; Accounts Receivable Ledger Tracks Sales & Income; Accounts Payable Ledger Records & Tracks Purchases & Payments; Inventory Tracks Both Goods & Services; Job Costing Uses a Form Similar to Invoicing, That Can Be Printed & Presented to a Client; & Project Management Tracks Income & Expenses That Are Associated with a Project. Other Features Include: Customer & Vendor Mailing Labels; Form Printing; Detailed Audit Trails Which Are Generated Automatically. Information & Reports Can Be Exported to Spreadsheets, Databases, & Word Processing Files.
Softsync, Inc.

Accountant's Pac I. *Version:* 4.5. 1994. *Items Included:* Complete operating manual. *Customer Support:* Unlimited telephone support.
MS-DOS. IBM PC or compatible (256k). $50.00.
Optimal configuration: IBM PC or compatible, 256k RAM, printer. *Networks supported:* Novel, Unex.
Collection of Frequently Used Programs for Practical Day-to-Day Use for Accoutants, Businessmen, Bankers, & Investors. Contains Seven Loan Analysis Programs, Financial Statement Ratio Analysis, Mortgage Amortization Tables, Rule of 78's Interest, Apportionment by Ratios, Compute IRS Form 6252 (Installment Sale), & a Complete Client List Organizer.
Omni Software Systems, Inc. (Indiana).

Accountant's Pac II. *Version:* 4.5. 1994. *Items Included:* Complete operating manual. *Customer Support:* Unlimited telephone support.
MS-DOS. IBM PC or compatible (256k). $50.00.
Optimal configuration: IBM PC or compatible, 256k RAM, printer. *Networks supported:* Novel, Unex.
Includes Seven Investment Analysis Programs, a Complete Checkwriting System, Bank Reconciliation & an Individual Mailing Label Generating Program. These Programs Will Allow User to Make Calculations & Decisions Quickly & Accurately Without the Use of a Pencil, Calculator or Just Plain Guesswork.
Omni Software Systems, Inc. (Indiana).

Accountant's Practice Management. *Version:* 1.07. *Operating System(s) Required:* UNIX, XENIX, DOS. *Memory Required:* 48k.
disk $1900.00.
Client Time & Billing System for General Use by a Professional. User Can Create a Customized System. Generates Reports Organized by Client, by Professional or by Task Classification. Handles up to 90 Different Hourly Rates.
Dataverse Corp.

Accountant's Stock System. *Version:* 4.0. 1994. *Items Included:* Complete operating manual. *Customer Support:* Unlimited telephone support. MS-DOS. IBM PC or compatible (256k). $125.00. *Optimal configuration:* IBM PC or compatible, 256k RAM, printer. *Networks supported:* Novel, Unex.
Designed for the Professional Accountant Who Does Work for Various Clients Who Have Several Stock Transactions During the Year. The System Collects All of the Information That Is Essential for the Accountant to Have for Year End Tax Reporting Including Purchase Date, Total Cost, Dividends Received, Sale Date & Gains or Losses on Each Stock. Computation of Long Term or Short Term Gains or Losses Is Automatic. Attachments for Schedule B & Schedule D, IRS Form 1040 Are Prepared at Year End. Eliminates the Need to Input Repetitive Information Year After Year. Several Clients May Be Kept on a Single Disk for Easy Access to Several Client Files.
Omni Software Systems, Inc. (Indiana).

Accountant's 1040. 1980. *Compatible Hardware:* IBM PC & compatibles, PC XT, PC AT, PS/2. *Operating System(s) Required:* MS-DOS. *Language(s):* CBASIC. *Memory Required:* 128k.
disk $995.00.
Designed for the Income Tax Accountant or the Individual Taxpayer. Enables the User to Produce 1040 Form Returns for Business or Individuals. Also Compiles & Formats Data for Selected State Returns.
KIS Computer Corp.

Accountant's Trial Balance (ATB). *Version:* 3.0. Jul. 1991. *Items Included:* 1 wiro-bound manual. *Customer Support:* Free for the first 3 months; $195 annual fee after that.
DOS 3.1 or higher. 100% IBM compatible PC (490k). disk $423.75 nonmember; $381.37 AICPA member. *Optimal configuration:* 100% IBM compatible PC, DOS 3.1 or higher, 640k RAM, printer capable of printing condensed or compressed. *Networks supported:* Novell, 3COM, LANtastic.
Trial Balance Package Designed for Accountants by Accountants. Lets User Define up to 64 Source Journals, 16 User Definable Schedules & Compute 34 Preprogrammed Financial Ratios. You Can Keep Your Books on 4 Bases of Accounting: Accrual, Federal Tax, State Tax & Other. Lets User Print: Trial Balance, General Ledger Listing, Adjusting Journal Entries, Source Journals, 5-Year Comparative Reports & More.
American Institute of Certified Public Accountants.

Accounting & Finance Abbreviations & Acronyms. *Version:* 7.4. (Books-on-Disk Ser.). Mark W. Greenia. Jan. 1996. *Items Included:* On-Screen "Help" file. *Customer Support:* Free tech support 90 days.
DOS. IBM & compatibles. 3.5" disk $15.00 (ISBN 0-944601-39-1).
Complete Reference Guide to over 10,000 Abbreviations & Acronyms Used in Accounting, Finance, Real Estate, Banking Securities Trading, Business & Investments & Computing. This Is a Complete Textbook on Diskette. A Comprehensive Resource Guide with Automated Text Search Features Built In.
Lexikon Services.

Accounting Applications for the Microcomputer, 4 disks. S. S. Hamilton. 1983. *Compatible Hardware:* Apple II with Applesoft, II+; TRS-80 Model III. *Operating System(s) Required:* Apple DOS 3.3, TRSDOS 1.3. *Memory Required:* 32k. *General Requirements:* 2 disk drives.
Apple. disk $180.00 (ISBN 0-07-025739-6). TRS-80. disk $180.00 (ISBN 0-07-025738-8). Practice Set. $7.95 (ISBN 0-07-049197-6). wkbk. $9.68 (ISBN 0-07-025736-1).
Prepare for Jobs in Accounting & Bookkeeping by Assuming the Role of Accounting Clerk in a Retail Business.
Gregg/McGraw-Hill.

Accounting Database-Word Processor-Programmer Interface. *Operating System(s) Required:* MS-PC/DOS. *Language(s):* Compiled MS-COBOL. *Memory Required:* 256k. *Customer Support:* Support agreements available or on a per-call basis.
contact publisher for price.
Provides Access to the Master & Detail Data Base Files from MBA's General Accounting Applications to the Data Base Management Systems, Word Processors, & Programming Languages. Separate Modules Are Available for General Ledger, Accounts Receivable, Accounts Payable, Payroll, & Inventory. Information Entered into One System Automatically Transfers into All Other Applicable Systems. File Manager Eliminates the Use of Sorting Routines. The Full-Screen Data Entry & Review System Lets the User View Full Pages of Information on One Screen. Validation & Editing of Information Is Done On-Line. Financial Statements & Reports Can Be Generated at Any Time. Source Code Available.
MBA Business Accounting Software.

Accounting 4 Construction. *Version:* 1.2. *Compatible Hardware:* Apple Macintosh 512KE. *General Requirements:* ImageWriter. Hard disk recommended.
3.5" disk $2000.00.
Integrated Construction Accounting System.
Software Constructors, Inc.

Accounting-Job Costing. Richard T. Scott. Feb. 1980. *Compatible Hardware:* IBM PC XT, PC AT, PS/2 & compatibles. *Operating System(s) Required:* MS-DOS. *Language(s):* BASIC. *Memory Required:* 128k. *General Requirements:* 10Mb hard disk, printer.
disk $1868.00 (ISBN 0-923933-21-2).
video tape demo avail.
source code avail.
Integrated System Covers Accounts Payable/Receivable, General Ledger & Job Costing Functions. Calculates Current Earned Profit, over or under Bill, Cash Requirements & Pertinent Information by Job.
Esccomate.

Accounting Package. James O. Godloin & Glenn Butler. Mar. 1983. *Operating System(s) Required:* CP/M, CP/M-86, MS-DOS, PC-DOS. *Language(s):* DBASE II (source code included). *Memory Required:* 64k.
disk $129.00.
Masters Software Co.

Accounting Plus. *Version:* 8.1. Apr. 1990. *Compatible Hardware:* IBM PC, PC XT, PC AT, & compatibles, PS/2. *Operating System(s) Required:* PC-DOS/MS-DOS, OS/2, UNIX, XENIX; Alloy, Novell & other LAN. *Language(s):* C. *Memory Required:* 640k. *General Requirements:* 132-column printer.
contact publisher for price.
source code at additional cost avail.
Addresses the Needs of Four Vertical Market Areas: the Retail Industry Service Businesses, the Wholesale Industry, & the Medical Market As a Complementary Package to the Medical Manager. Offers Integrated Modules Designed to Meet These Needs for Each of the Four Industries. Conforms to Standard Accounting Principles & Safeguards Against Simple Accounting Mistakes While Providing a Complete Audit Trail. Supplies Comprehensive Reports Which Enable Managers to Make Well-Informed Business Decisions.
Systems Plus, Inc.

Accounting Trial Balance Worksheets. Jul. 1987. *Compatible Hardware:* IBM PC & compatibles. *Memory Required:* 256k. *General Requirements:* Lotus 1-2-3 release 1A.
$35.00.
Computes & Checks the Accuracy of Trial-Balance Input. Helps Set Up a New Year's Trial-Balance Worksheet.
Triad Computers.

TITLE INDEX

ACCOUNTS PAYABLE & ACCOUNTS PAYABLE-M

Accounting Tutorial. Allen. *Compatible Hardware:* TRS-80 Model III, Model 4; Apple II+, IIe, IIc; IBM PC. *Memory Required:* Apple & TRS-80 Model III, Model 4 48k; IBM PC DOS 1.1 64k; PC DOS 2.0, 2.1 128k.
TRS-80 Model III & Model 4. disk $59.50 (ISBN 0-538-02792-4, Order no.: B796-3).
Apple. disk $59.50 (ISBN 0-538-02192-6, Order no.: B797-3).
IBM. disk $59.50 (ISBN 0-538-02793-2, Order no.: B798-1).
txt. wkbk. $3.10 (ISBN 0-538-02790-8, Order no.: B79).
tchr's. manual avail. (Order no.: B79M).
Provides Exercises & Drills That Reinforce Basic Accounting Concepts.
South-Western Publishing Co.

The Accounting XPert. *Version:* 6.0. Jun. 1992. *Items Included:* Reference library, On-Line tutorial. *Customer Support:* Service contracts.
DOS 5.0 or higher, UNIX, CTOS, Windows/NT. IBM 486 & compatibles (4Mb) (Sun, HP, DEC). $4995.00 & up.
Integrated Multi-Company General Business Software. Includes Accounts Receivable & Payable, Sales Order Processing, PO, Inventory, Payroll, Sales Analysis, General Ledger, Bank Reconciliation, Reference Library & the Tutorial. Network Option Available, Language: MAGIC 46L, Internet Options Including Order Processing, Managing Third Party Solutions.
Micronetics, Inc.

AccountMate Professional. *Version:* 4.0. *Compatible Hardware:* IBM PC & compatibles, PC XT, PC AT; AT&T PC. *Operating System(s) Required:* PC-DOS/MS-DOS 2.0 or higher. *Language(s):* XBASE (source code included). *Memory Required:* dBASE II & III version 256k, dBASE III Clipper compiled version 640k. *General Requirements:* Hard disk for integrated version.
General Ledger. $295.00 single user, $595.00 multi-user.
Sales Order Inventory. $295.00 single user, $595.00 multi-user.
Purchase Order Inventory. $295.00 single user, $595.00 multi-user.
Accounts Receivable Inventory. $295.00 single user, $595.00 multi-user.
Accounts Payable. $295.00 single user, $595.00 multi-user.
Payroll/State Tax Program. $295.00 single user, $595.00 multi-user.
Time & Billing. $295.00 single user, $595.00 multi-user.
Fund Accounting. $295.00 single user, $595.00 multi-user.
Manufacturing Inventory Control. $795.00 single user, $995.00 multi-user.
Modular PC Accounting Software System Written in XBASE. All Modules Can Be Integrated to Form a Comprehensive Accounting System or Stand Alone. Programs Available Include: General Ledger, Accounts Receivable, Accounts Payable, Payroll, Sales Order, Purchase Order & Inventory Control. In Addition, There Are Job Cost, Manufacturer's Inventory, Fund Accounting, Executive Summary, Bank Reconciliation, & Contact Manager Modules Available. Working Demos Are Available for $25.00.
SourceMate Information Systems, Inc.

Accounts Payable. *Version:* 14.0. (Accounting Software Ser.). Sep. 1993. *Compatible Hardware:* IBM PC & compatibles. *Operating System(s) Required:* MS-DOS, PC-DOS 3.x & up. *Language(s):* MegaBASIC. *Memory Required:* 640k. *General Requirements:* Hard disk, wide carriage printer. *Customer Support:* (203) 790-9756.
disk $295.00, Network Option ,300.00 more. manual $50.00.
Allows Partial Payment, Automatic Payment & Selected Payment of Invoices. Auto Posting of Purchases, Receipts from Vendor. Automatic Tie-In to General Ledger, Detailed Aging, Extensive Audit Trial, Allows Entry of Terms & Discount Days/Percentage, Automatic Check Printing, Checkbook Balancing, Posts Handwritten Checks, Maintenance of Vendor/Address Records, Produces Supporting Statements. Choose Balance Forward or Archiving of Zero Balance.
Applications Systems Group (CT), Inc.

Accounts Payable. *Version:* 5.8. May 1993. *Language(s):* DIBOL & C, COBOL. *General Requirements:* Depends on specific configuration. *Customer Support:* Full service, update service; by quotation.
VMS, Open VMS. DEC VAX Series, DEC Alpha AXP. disk $2500.00-$15,000.00.
source code by quotation.
Includes: User-Designed Checks, Manual or Automatic Check Posting, Multiple Discount Dates, Selective Invoice Payments, Unapplied Payments & Recurring A/P. Automatic Check Reconciliation & Check Voiding. Major Reports Include: Aged Accounts Payable, Invoice/Payments Analysis, Cash Requirements.
Compu-Share, Inc.

Accounts Payable. (Service Management Ser.). 1996.
DOS,Unix. IBM PC. disk contact publisher for price.
FastTraks "Accounts Payable" module will help control disbursements by tracking all vendor invoices.
Core Software, Inc.

Accounts Payable. *Version:* 2.5.4. 1988. *Language(s):* C. *Memory Required:* 640k. *General Requirements:* Hard disk, 132-column printer. *Items Included:* Disks & manuals. *Customer Support:* Through VARs, support contracts available.
MS-DOS, PC-DOS, Concurrent DOS, Unix, Xenix. All IBM-compatible systems. single user $795.00. *Networks supported:* Novell & Microsoft.
multi-user, Unix, Xenix, multi-site discounts $995.00.
demo disk & manual $20.00.
Automated, Open-Order Accounts Payable System. Custom Report Writer Available.
INMASS/MRP.

Accounts Payable. *Version:* 450.3. 1979. *Compatible Hardware:* IBM PC & compatibles. *Operating System(s) Required:* MS-DOS, PC-DOS. *Language(s):* QuickBASIC. *Memory Required:* 512k. *General Requirements:* Hard disk. *Items Included:* System diskettes, users guide, training tutorial. *Customer Support:* Telephone; annual contracts available.
disk $395.00 to $495.00.
A Full Open Voucher Payables System with Check Writing Capabilities. The System Projects Cash Requirements for Any Three Week Period Plus Future. User May Selectively Pay Full or Partial Vouchers by Vendor Number, Voucher Number, or Pay All Vouchers Due. Automatically Applies Early Payment Discounts. Summarizes Vouchers by Vendor & Prints Consolidated Checks. Checks May Be Distributed to Multiple Ledger Accounts. Primary Reports Include Vendor Master List, Open Voucher Report, Paid Voucher Report, Voucher Register, & Check Register. The Number of Vendors & Transactions Are Limited Only By Capacity of Hard Disk. Accounts Payables Interfaces with IMS General Ledger & May be Run Single User or Multi-User on Many Networks.
International Micro Systems, Inc.

Accounts Payable. Nov. 1988. *Operating System(s) Required:* PC-DOS/MS-DOS. *Memory Required:* 384k. *Customer Support:* 60 days free phone support.
disk $149.00.
Produces Vendor Checks, Labels, Rolodex Cards, Check Register, Purchase Orders, Outstanding Bill Reports, Cash Requirements, etc. Designed for Small to Medium Sized Businesses.
MiccaSoft, Inc.

Accounts Payable. *Version:* 3.3. (Integrated Manufacturing & Financial System Ser.). *Compatible Hardware:* VAX, IBM PC. *Operating System(s) Required:* MS-DOS, Novell, VAX/VMS, UNIX. *Language(s):* DIBOL.
MS-DOS. 750.00 single-user.
DEC, VAX. $1500.00 multi-user.
Provides Manufacturer with Material Costs & Price Variances. Compares Vendor Invoices to Receivings; Handles Debit & Credit Memos; Pays Accordingly & Passes Material Outside Service & Other Costs to GENERAL LEDGER by General Ledger Account Number. Reports Include Cash Requirements, Vendor Checks & Register, Aged Trial Balance, General Ledger Distribution, Vendor Analysis; & 1099 Forms.
Primetrack.

Accounts Payable. *Version:* 6.0. Nov. 1990. *Items Included:* User guide, technical reference manual. *Customer Support:* Training included with purchase. Hot-line & remote diagnostic service included with maintenance.
VAX/VMS (2Mb). Digital VAX. $27,000 up.
An Interactive AP System Which Provides Effective Payables & Cash Management. It Provides Immediate Validation & Updates of Multi-Currency Payables Information &, When Used with RossPO, It Allows for Automated Invoice/Purchase Order/Receipt/Matching. The System is Completely Integrated with RossGL for Distribution & Reconciliation Purposes.
Ross Systs CA.

Accounts Payable (a part of ABECAS). *Version:* 3.3. Jan. 1989. *Customer Support:* On-site training, unlimited support services for first 90 days & through subscription service thereafter.
PC/MS-DOS 3.x. IBM PC & compatibles.
Contact publisher for price. *Nonstandard peripherals required:* Hard disk (30Mb or higher); 132 column printer.
Provides Complete Control over User's Trade Payables. Allows Invoices/Credits to Be Entered When Received (Along with Supplies & Merchandise Inventory) & Managed Until Paid. Optional Pre-Defined Distribution Codes Simplify Entry. Selection of Items to Pay May Be Manual or Automatic. Checks May Be Printed or Manually Written. Check Register May Be Maintained for As Long As Needed & Reconciled Checks May Be Entered. Prints Mailing Labels. Maintains Summary & Detailed Transaction History by Vendor. Numerous Reports Available Including Vendor Query, Aging, Cash Requirements, Transaction Recap & More. 1099's Can Be Printed for Vendors, As Appropriate. Multi-User Version Available for Novell, NTNX, 10-Net, Unix/Xenix, Turbo DOS & Others. Unique Features Include Ability of Each Module to Distribute Transactions to the Cost Accounting Accounts & Specialized Modules Designed Around Needs of Specific Industries.
Argos Software.

Accounts Payable & Accounts Payable-M. 1992. *Customer Support:* 30 days' free support, 1 yr. maintenance $250.00.
PC-DOS/MS-DOS, networks such as Novell & LANtastic. PC or PC-compatibles (640k). disk $495.00. *Networks supported:* Novell,

ACCOUNTS PAYABLE GOLD

LANtastic, networks supporting DOS 3.1 record-locking calls.
Integrates to CheckWrite or May Be Used Standalone. Payables Can Be Prioritized As to Importance. Lists of Payables Can Be Produced by Calendar Days or by Vendor. Monthly Calendars of All Payables & Memory-Resident Vendor Lists. If Integrated, Payables Are Checked off & Sent to CheckWrite When Checks Are Printed. Available for Networked Systems.
Micro Craft, Inc.

Accounts Payable Gold. *Version:* 1.9. Oct. 1988. *Customer Support:* 120 days free, 15% of purchase price per year.
OS/2, Windows 3.1 or higher. IBM 386 & 100% compatible. Contact vendor for price. *Nonstandard peripherals required:* VGA monitor.
Tracks Vendor Payables & Prints Checks Based on User-Defined Criteria. Prints 1099's by Company, Produces Invoice Register & Check Register for Multiple Owners/Properties. Check Reconciliation Feature Clears Checks, Prints Check Reconciliation Report.
Timberline Software Corp.

Accounts Payable: Module 3. *Version:* 7.11. Jul. 1991. *Items Included:* Perfect bound manual. *Customer Support:* 90 day toll-free technical phone support, each additional year $150.00.
MS-DOS 3.1 or higher. IBM PS/2, PC, PC XT, PC AT & compatibles (384k). disk $295.00. *Addl. software required:* System manager. *Networks supported:* PC-LAN, 3COM, Novell, LANtastic.
Allows the User to Enter Vendor Invoices & Keep Track of Discount & Payment Terms. By Generating Cash Flow & Discount Analysis Reports, the User Can Evaluate Cash Situations & Determine the Best Payment Schedule. The System Enables the User to Choose Either Manual or Automatic Payment of Invoices.
Manzanita Software Systems.

Accounts Payable-Purchase Order. *Version:* 4.6. 1995. *Operating System(s) Required:* MS-DOS, XENIX. *Language(s):* Compiled BASIC. *Memory Required:* 256k. *General Requirements:* Hard drive, printer, monitor. *Items Included:* Manual, demo, disk. *Customer Support:* Free phone support for 90-days; $25.00 per call after. disk $200.00 ea.
(ISBN 0-918185-11-4).
(ISBN 0-918185-12-2).
3.5" or 5.25" disk $200.00 (ISBN 0-918185-13-0).
Invoiced Linked, Interactive System. Purchase Order Capability with Posting to Accounts Payable & Applicable General Ledger Accounts. Features Aging Ledger & Check Calculation & Printing.
Taranto & Assocs., Inc.

Accounts Payable-Purchase Order-Vendor Programs. *Operating System(s) Required:* DOS, UNIX, XENIX. *Language(s):* Sculptor 4GL. *Memory Required:* 640k.
contact publisher for price.
3 Programs Allowing for Total Control & Tracking of Transactions. Vendor Program Assigns Vendor Number & Prints Vendor List & Directory. Purchase Program Automatically Prints Purchase Orders after Entering & Updating. Accounts Payable Posts Purchase Orders or Posts Payables Directly.
Universal Data Research, Inc.

Accounts Payable: Series 900 to 2000.
Compatible Hardware: IBM System/36, System/36 PC; AS/400.
contact publisher for price.
Payables Are Recorded on an Accrual Basis & Checks Can Be Printed As Required. Payables & Cash Requirements Reports & Vendor Statistics for Amounts Paid & Discounts Taken Are Available. Fully Integrated with the General Ledger & the Client Disbursement Accounting.
Manac-Prentice Hall Software, Inc.

Accounts Payable System. *Version:* 8. Feb. 1987. *Compatible Hardware:* IBM PC & compatibles. *Operating System(s) Required:* PC-DOS Ver. 3.1 or higher. *Memory Required:* 384k. *General Requirements:* Hard disk, printer. *Items Included:* Binder with documentation. *Customer Support:* Maintenance fee $108/yr. entitles user to phone support, quarterly newsletters & enhancements released during the year.
disk $500.00.
demo disk $35.00.
System Designed to Automate Payables. Keeps Track of Vendor Discounts, Recurring Payables. Accumulates Dollars for Form 1099. Allows Computer Check Writing from 9 Checking Accounts, or Checks May Be Manually Drafted. When Integrated with STI's GLS, Users Can Post Unpaid Invoices & Run Modified Accrual Statements. Then, User Can Unpost Unpaid Invoices & Be on Cash Basis Again. Integrates with TABS III, TABS III-M & GLS.
Software Technology, Inc.

Accounts Payable System Jr. *Version:* 8. *Items Included:* Binder with documentation. *Customer Support:* 1 yr. maintenance $65, entitles user to phone support, newsletter & enhancements released during the year for their computer.
PC-DOS/MS-DOS Ver. 3.1 or higher. IBM PC & compatibles (384k). disk $250.00. *Nonstandard peripherals required:* Hard drive. *Networks supported:* Novell, IBM PC Network & compatibles.
Designed to Integrate with STI's Jr Versions of TABS III & General Ledger System. Users Can Print Manual or Computer Checks from up to 9 Separate Checking Accounts. Allows Partial or Full Payment. Jr Version Provides All of the Features of STI's Regular Systems.
Software Technology, Inc.

Accounts Payable System-M. *Version:* 8. Feb. 1987. *Compatible Hardware:* IBM PC & compatibles. *Operating System(s) Required:* DOS Ver. 3.1 or higher; Novell Netware, IBM PC Network, or other NETBIOS compatible network. *Memory Required:* 384k. *General Requirements:* Hard disk, printer. *Items Included:* Binder with documentation. *Customer Support:* Maintenance fee $144/yr. entitles user to phone support, quarterly newsletters & enhancements released during the year.
disk $700.00.
demo disk $35.00.
Multi-User Version of STI's APS Allowing up to 30 Terminals to Enter or Retrieve APS Information, Print Checks, & Post to General Ledger System-M & TABS III-M.
Software Technology, Inc.

Accounts Receivable. (Service Management Ser.). 1996.
DOS, Unix. IBM PC. disk contact publisher for price.
The FasTrak A/R package updates & utilizes the same data files as other FasTrak modules, providing real time information on the account status of your customer base. Some features are; Open item invoices & credit memos, User definable aging periods, Accurate & up-tp-date Accounts Receivable aging reports, Payment screen allows overpayment of invoice, Automatic computation of finance charges based on date entered by operator, etc.
Core Software, Inc.

SOFTWARE ENCYCLOPEDIA 1996

Accounts Receivable. *Version:* 2.5.4. 1989. *Language(s):* C. *Memory Required:* 640k. *General Requirements:* Hard disk & 132-column printer. *Items Included:* Disks & manuals. *Customer Support:* Free.
Altos, Compupro, Compaq, Fujitsu, Heath-Zenith, HP, Tandy. All IBM-compatible syste,s. single-user $795.00.
muti-user, Unix, Xenix, multi-site discounts $995.00.
demo disk & manual $20.00.
Features Daily Account Aging & Provides Current Aged Trial Balance & Detailed Customer Inquiry Functions.
INMASS/MRP.

Accounts Receivable. *Version:* 4.5. 1995. *Compatible Hardware:* IBM PC & compatibles, PC XT, PC AT, 386, 486, Pentium, PS/2. *Operating System(s) Required:* PC-DOS/MS-DOS 3.X, 4X, 5X, 6X, Windows 3.1, Windows 95. *Language(s):* C, Assembler. *Memory Required:* 640k. *General Requirements:* Stand-alone or 2Mb Network file server. *Customer Support:* 90 days warranty, onsite training, telephone support.
$995.00.
Keeps Track of Customers & Associated Financial Information, Prints Monthly Statements & Delinquency Notices & Provides Sales Analysis Information. Can Optionally Interface to Billing, Sales Analysis & General Ledger Systems. Optionally Handles Multi-Company Processing.
LIBRA Corp.

Accounts Receivable. *Version:* 6.50. 1978. *Compatible Hardware:* IBM PC & compatibles, PC XT, PC AT, PS/2. *Operating System(s) Required:* MS-DOS, PC-DOS. *Language(s):* Fortran. *Memory Required:* 640k. *Items Included:* Manual. *Customer Support:* 1 hour per package purchased.
$495.00.
Produces Invoices, Credit Memos, Customer Statements, Aging & Cash Receipt Listings, In-Depth Sales Analysis, Customer Lists, & Labels. Allows Either Open Item or Balance Forward Accounting Methods, & Automatically Creates the Sales & Cash Receipt Journals for Direct Posting to General Ledger.
MCC Software (Midwest Computer Ctr. Co.).

Accounts Receivable. *Version:* 3.3. (Integrated Manufacturing & Financial System Ser.). *Compatible Hardware:* IBM PC, VAX. *Operating System(s) Required:* MS-DOS, Novell, VAX/VMS, UNIX. *Language(s):* DIBOL.
MS-DOS. 750.00 single-user.
DEC PDP-11/VAX. $1500.00 multi-user.
Handles Sales, Cash, & Debit/Credit Memos. Produces Statements & Passes Revenue to GENERAL LEDGER System by Account Number & Product Group. Features Automatic Calculation of Multi-State Sales Taxes, Salesmen Commissions, Customer/State/Salesmen Sales Analysis, Reporting by Division or Cost Center, Alphabetic Customer Sort Keys, & Payment Due Date Calculations.
Primetrack.

Accounts Receivable. *Items Included:* User guide, technical reference manual. *Customer Support:* Training included with purchase. Hot-line & remote diagnostic service included with maintenance.
VAX/VMS (2Mb). Digital VAX. $26,000.00 up.
A Sophisticated Credit & Cash Management System That Provides Users with the Resources Needed to Effectively Manage Revenue Stream & Maintain Accurate Invoice Tracking. Assures Maximum Efficiency in Every Phase of AR Management from Automatic Invoice Loading & Cash Posting Through Real Time Customer Balance Inquiry & Transaction Analysis.
Ross Systems, Inc.

TITLE INDEX

Accounts Receivable (a part of ABECAS).
Version: 3.1. Jan. 1989. Customer Support: On site training unlimited support services for first 90 days & through subscription thereafter.
PC/MS-DOS 3.x. IBM PC & compatibles. Contact publisher for price. Nonstandard peripherals required: Hard disk (30Mb or higher); 132 column printer.
Provides Complete Control over Customer Collections & Credit Sales. Interfaces to All Billing/Invoicing Modules & Is Directly Updated from These Modules. Invoices May Be Printed or Entered After-the-Fact with or Without Cash Receipts. Pre-Defined Distribution Codes Simplify Entry. Finance Charges Can Be Automatically Computed. Unpaid Balances Are Maintained As Open Items. Cash Automatically Computed. Cash Receipts May Be Applied Automatically or by Transaction. Credits May Be Automatically Applied to Matching Invoices. Prints Detailed, Projected & Summary Aging Reports, Statements, Overdue Notices, Mailing Labels, Customer Lists & More. Special Program Also Allows Quick Review of Customer's Open Items & History. Maintains Summary & Detailed History by Customer & Provides Summary Sales Analysis. Multi-User Version Available for Novell, NTNX, 10-Net, Unix/Xenix, Turbo DOS & Others. Unique Features Include Ability of Each Module to Distribute Transactions to the Cost Accounting Account.
Argos Software.

Accounts Receivable Balance Forward. Version: 4.6. 1995. Operating System(s) Required: MS-DOS, XENIX. Language(s): Compiled BASIC. Memory Required: 256k. General Requirements: Hard drive, printer. Items Included: Free phone support for 90-days; $25.00 per call after.
disk $200.00 ea.
(ISBN 0-918185-54-8).
(ISBN 0-918185-55-6).
3.5" or 5.25" disk $200.00 (ISBN 0-918185-56-4).
Features Full Recurring Transaction Facility, Aged Statements, Mailing & Shipping Label Program & Cash or Accrual Basics. Linked to General Ledger System. Not Invoice Oriented.
Taranto & Assocs., Inc.

Accounts Receivable Collections: Series 900 to 2000. Compatible Hardware: IBM System/36, System/36 PC, AS/400.
contact publisher for price.
Assists in Reducing Bad Debts. Client Reminder Statements Are Available on Demand & Interest Can Be Charged to All or Selected Clients.
Manac-Prentice Hall Software, Inc.

Accounts Receivable-Invoicing-Sales Analysis.
Version: 4.92. 1995. Operating System(s) Required: MS-DOS, XENIX. Language(s): Compiled BASIC. Memory Required: 256k. General Requirements: Hard drive, printer. Items Included: Manual, disk, demo. Customer Support: Free phone support for 90-days; $25.00 per call after.
disk $200.00 ea.
(ISBN 0-918185-06-8).
(ISBN 0-918185-07-6).
3.5" or 5.25" disk $200.00 (ISBN 0-918185-08-4).
Interactive, Invoice-Oriented System. Includes Sales Analysis with Commission Reporting, Mailing & Shipping Label Program, Posting to General Ledger Accounts.
Taranto & Assocs., Inc.

Accounts Receivable: Module 4. Version: 7.11. Jul. 1991. Items Included: Perfect bound manual. Customer Support: 90 days toll-free technical phone support, each additional year $150.00.
MS-DOS 3.1 or higher. IBM PS/2, PC, PC XT, PC AT & compatibles (384k). $295.00. Addl. software required: Systems manager. Networks supported: PC-LAN, 3COM, Novell, LANtastic.
Records All Accounts Receivable Activity, Including Sales Receipts, Finance Charges, Payments & Debit/Credit Adjustments. Data Such As Customer Activity, Collection Requirements, Credit History, & Sales Performance Can Be Retrieved & Reviewed by the User. Can Maintain Information for an Unlimited Number of Customers.
Manzanita Software Systems.

Accounts Receivable Package.
MS-DOS, Unix, Xenix (512k). IBM PC, PC XT, PC AT, & compatible mini/micros. contact publisher for price.
Includes One-Step Invoice Generation, Special Insurance Rate Change Billings, Invoicing & Analysis for Special Events, e.g. Luncheons, Cash Receipts or Direct Payments.
Universal Data Research, Inc.

Accounts Receivable Program. Version: 14.0. (Accounting Software Ser.). Sep. 1993. Compatible Hardware: IBM PC & compatibles. Operating System(s) Required: MS-DOS, PC-DOS 3.x & up. Language(s): MegaBASIC. Memory Required: 640k. General Requirements: Hard disk, wide carriage printer. Customer Support: (203) 790-9756.
disk $295.00, Network Option ,300.00 more. manual $50.00.
Features Entry & Maintenance of Customer Invoices, Provides Records of Credits, Debits, etc. Provides: Aging, Statements (All or Selected), Entry & Maintenance of Customer Name/Address Info, Allows Automatic Posting of Invoices, Automatic Payment, Selected or Partial Payment. Detailed Audit Trail, General Ledger Tie-In. Choose Balance Forward or Archive Zero Balances. Checkbook Balancing, Cash Receipt Journal. Calculates Late Charges (Several Methods Available).
Applications Systems Group (CT), Inc.

ACCPAC Plus Accounting. 1982. Compatible Hardware: IBM PC, PS/2 & compatibles. General Requirements: Hard disk, double-sided diskette drive, monitor. Customer Support: Available.
$795.00 per module.
Windowing System Manager $195.00; ScanPAC $595.00; Sales Analysis $495.00; LanPak $395.00; DynaView $249.00.
A Modular, Multi-User Accounting System for Medium-Sized Businesses & Divisions of Large Corporations. It Offers Customizable Options, Reports, & Forms. Generates on DOS, LAN, & OS/2. Modules Include: GL, AR, AP, Order Entry, Inventory Control, Purchase Order, Job Cost, Payroll, Retail Invoicing, Sales Analysis, ScanPAC, Windowing System Manager, LanPak, & DynaView.
Computer Assocs. International, Inc.

ACCPAC Plus Accounting Accounts Payable.
1983. Compatible Hardware: IBM PC, PS/2 & compatibles. Operating System(s) Required: DOS, OS/2. Language(s): C. Memory Required: 640k. Customer Support: Available.
$795.00.
Prints Checks, Current & Historical Vendor Status & Statistics. Takes Discounts, Defers Payments & Makes Partial Payments. Controls Maximum Payment Amount. Supports Unlimited Bank Accounts. Built-In Multicurrency Capabilities Support Revaluation of Open Transactions & Handling of Cash Transactions in Currencies Other Than Source.
Computer Assocs. International, Inc.

ACCPAC PLUS ACCOUNTING LANPAK

ACCPAC Plus Accounting Accounts Receivable. 1983. Compatible Hardware: IBM PC, PS/2 & compatibles. Operating System(s) Required: DOS, OS/2. Language(s): C. Memory Required: 640k. Customer Support: Available.
$795.00.
Includes Customer Statements, Collection Letters & Mailing Labels. Produces Aging & Printed Reports. Calculates Finance Charges with User-Defined Periods & Interest Rates. Posts Recurring Charges. Built-In Multi-Currency Capabilities Support Revaluation of Open Transactions & Handling of Cash Transactions in Currencies Other Than Source.
Computer Assocs. International, Inc.

ACCPAC Plus Accounting DynaView. 1991. Customer Support: Available.
DOS, OS/2. IBM PC, PS/2 & compatibles (640k). disk $249.00. Networks supported: Novell, LANManager, Banyan & others.
Information Management Tool That Enables Users to Dynamically Link Accounting Data to CA-SuperCalc or Lotus 1-2-3. Simultaneously Accesses Accounting Transactions & Master File Information, Establishes Hoi Links with ACCPAC Plus Accounting Data, Reads Information in Detail or Summary Form, Uses Statistical Functions to Display Minimum & Formats Columns & Cells Automatically According to Data Size & Type. Includes Data API & DLLs.
Computer Assocs. International, Inc.

ACCPAC Plus Accounting General Ledger & Financial Reporter. 1979. Compatible Hardware: IBM PC, PS/2 & compatibles. Operating System(s) Required: DOS, OS/2. Language(s): C. Memory Required: 640k. Customer Support: Available.
$795.00.
Maintains up to 26 Months of Previous Balances by Account. Provides User-Nominated Chart of Accounts with Unlimited Distributions & Redistributions. Compares Closing of Income & Expense Accounts to Retained Earnings at Fiscal Year End. Carries Budget Controls by Month. Generates Reports from GL Financial Data. Multicurrency Capabilities Allow Entry & Posting of Transactions in International Currencies.
Computer Assocs. International, Inc.

ACCPAC Plus Accounting Inventory Control & Analysis. 1982. Compatible Hardware: IBM PC, PS/2 & compatibles. Operating System(s) Required: DOS, OS/2. Language(s): C. Memory Required: 640k. Customer Support: Available.
$795.00 (ISBN 0-87210-006-5).
Prepares Perpetual IC Records, IC Status Analyses, Out-of-Stock Reports, Current Inventory Valuations & Gross Margin Analyses. User-Tailored IC Item Numbers with up to 16 Characters. Allows up to 999 IC Classifications or Departments. Offers User-Selectable Components in IC Record. Tracks Unlimited Number of Items for More Than 64,000 Locations.
Computer Assocs. International, Inc.

ACCPAC Plus Accounting Job Costing. 1985. Customer Support: Available.
DOS, OS/2. IBM PC, PS/2 & compatibles (512k). disk $795.00.
Monitors & Controls Job or Project Costs. Measures Profitability. Reports Journals/Listings, Job Status & Cost Analysis. Generates AIA Billing Worksheet & Sets up Cost Tracking Jobs That Requires No Estimates. Integrates with Other ACCPAC Plus Programs.
Computer Assocs. International, Inc.

ACCPAC Plus Accounting LanPak. 1985. Customer Support: Available.
DOS, OS/2. IBM PC, PS/2 & compatibles (640k). disk $395.00. Addl. software required:

ACCPAC Plus Windowing System Manager. *Networks supported:* Novell, PC LAN, LAN Manager, Banyan, LANtastic.
Provides Interface Between Novell, MS LAN Manager, IBM PC-LAN, Banyan & LANtastic & ACCPAC Plus Integrated Accounting Applications.
Computer Assocs. Imnternational, Inc.

ACCPAC Plus Accounting Order Entry. 1983. *Compatible Hardware:* IBM PC, PS/2 & compatibles. *Operating System(s) Required:* DOS, OS/2. *Language(s):* C. *Memory Required:* 640k. *Customer Support:* Available.
$795.00.
Generates Order Confirmations. Calculates Prices to 5 Discount & Tax Categories. Tax Tables Allow Multiple Locations & Special Taxes. Prints Picking Slips, Invoices, Credit Notes, Reports & Multiple Ship-To Addresses. Reclassifies & Confirms Future, Recurring, On-Hold, Active & Back Orders. Handles Multicurrency Accounting.
Computer Assocs. International, Inc.

ACCPAC Plus Accounting Purchase Orders. 1992. *Customer Support:* Available.
DOS, OS/2. IBM PC, PS/2 & compatibles. disk $795.00.
Module of ACCPAC Plus Accounting System. Integrated with AP, IC, OE, & GL Modules. Produces Customized Requisitions & Purchase Orders. Tracking Capabilities by Item Number, Vendor, Receipt, & Expected Arrival Date.
Computer Assocs. International, Inc.

ACCPAC Plus Accounting Retail Invoicing. 1985. *Compatible Hardware:* IBM PC, PS/2 & compatibles. *Operating System(s) Required:* DOS, OS/2. *Language(s):* C. *Memory Required:* 512k. *Customer Support:* Available.
$795.00.
Handles Invoices, Credit Notes, Layaways & Quotations for Medium/Large Ticket Inventory Items. Allows Payment by Cash, Credit Cards & on Account. Tracks Commissions by Inventory Category or Salesperson. User-Customized Formats for Invoices, Credit Notes & Quotations. Works with Cash Drawers & Light Pens.
Computer Assocs. International, Inc.

ACCPAC Plus Accounting Sales Analysis. 1987. *Customer Support:* Available.
DOS, OS/2. IBM PC, PS/2 & compatibles (512k). disk $495.00. *Addl. software required:* ACCPAC Plus Windowing System Manager. *Networks supported:* Novell, Banyan & others.
Provides Management Reports Using Data from Order Entry, Accounts Receivable, & Retail Invoicing. Helps Managers Plan, Forecast, & Track Sales; Gauge Sales Performance; & Determine Key Market Segments. Up to 99 Different Reports Let User Summarize, Subtotal, & Compare the Information in the Order Specified to Help Make Better-Informed Sales & Marketing Decisions. Helps Make More Accurate Forecasts by Comparing Budgeted Sales to Actual Sales.
Computer Assocs. International, Inc.

ACCPAC Plus Accounting ScanPAC. 1993. *Customer Support:* Support Agreement Available.
DOS, OS/2. IBM PC, PS/2 & compatibles (640k). disk $595.00.
Barcode Scanning Solution Integrated with ACCPAC Plus Accounting Inventory Control & Order Entry. Includes a Symbol Technology Model 1720 Hand Held Scanner. Define Multiple Bar Codes for Each Inventory Item, Supports Multiple Symbologies.
Computer Assocs. International, Inc.

ACCPAC Plus Accounting U. S. Payroll. 1982. *Compatible Hardware:* IBM PC, PS/2 & compatibles. *Operating System(s) Required:* DOS, OS/2. *Language(s):* C. *Memory Required:* 640k. *Items Included:* Canadian version available. *Customer Support:* Available.
$795.00.
Handles Payroll Calculations, Record Keeping, Payment & Reporting, Cafeteria & 401K Plans, Wage Garnishments, Commissions, Bonuses, Tips, Shift Differentials, Overtime & Piece-Rate Pay. Calculates & Records up to 94 Deductions, Payrolls. Imports & Exports Time Cards.
Computer Assocs. International, Inc.

ACCPAC Plus Accounting Windowing System Manager. 1986. *Compatible Hardware:* IBM PC, PS/2 & compatibles. *Operating System(s) Required:* DOS, OS/2. *Language(s):* C. *Memory Required:* 640k. *Customer Support:* Available.
$195.00.
Proprietary Windowing System for ACCPAC Plus Modules. Controls Operation of All Programs & Provides Collective Features Such As Hotkey Application Switching, Macros, Intelligent Database Searching, Interactive Pop-Up Calculator & Networking Capabilities on Most Popular LANs. Will Operate in DOS Box under OS/2.
Computer Assocs. International, Inc.

AccSys for Paradox. *Version:* 5.00. *Customer Support:* Yes.
PC-DOS/MS-DOS, OS/2, Dos Extenders, Windows. IBM PC & compatibles. $495.00. *Networks supported:* Novell, IBM PC LAN, 300M, MS-Network.
$1195.00 with source.
Provides Set of Library Functions for Interface Between Microsoft C (All Memory Models), Turbo C, Zortech C, QuickBasic, & Visual Basic for Paradox Database Files (with All Index Files). Ability to Create, Add, Delete, Modify & Update Database Files. Allows Different Index & Record Access Methods. Network Ready.
Copia International, Ltd.

AccSys for xBASE. *Version:* 2.92. *Items Included:* Fully descriptive manual. *Customer Support:* 60 day guarantee.
MS-DOS, PC-DOS, OS/2, Windows, DOS extenders. IBM PC & compatibles (256k). $495.00. *Networks supported:* Novell, 3COM, IBM PC LAN, MS-Network.
$1195.00 with source.
Enables Programmers to Create/Revise All xBASE, dBASE III & IV Files. Interface Provides Full Support & Control over DBF Files, MDX & NDX Index Files & DBT Memo Files. Also Handles DBF, NDX & DBT Files of dBASE III Plus. Network Ready. Clipper & FoxPro Support.
Copia International, Ltd.

ACCT-M2. *Version:* 2.0. 1980. *Compatible Hardware:* TRS-80 Model II, Model 16. *Operating System(s) Required:* TRSDOS. *Language(s):* BASIC (source code included). *Memory Required:* 32k.
disk $149.00.
manual $12.00.
Calculates Sales Tax, Shipping Costs, & Credit Checking, Aging Analysis, Invoices, etc.
Micro Architect, Inc.

ACCT-III. *Version:* 2.0. 1986. *Compatible Hardware:* TRS-80 Model I, Model III, Model 4. *Operating System(s) Required:* TRSDOS. *Language(s):* BASIC. *Memory Required:* 48k.
disk $99.00.
manual $10.00.
Manages Client Accounts & Accounts Receivables.
Micro Architect, Inc.

Accudraw Computer-Aided Design System. *Items Included:* Full manual. No other products required. *Customer Support:* Free telephone support - no time limit, 30 day warranty.
MS-DOS 3.2 or higher. Apple II series. disk $99.95.
Complete Computer Aided Design System for Floor Plan, Landscape, or Electronics Designers. Unlike Other Apple II Drawing or Paint Programs, ACCUDRAW Creates Accurate-to-Scale Drawings up to 6 by 8 Feet in Size on Any Dot-Matrix Printer. In Addition, It Uses an Icon Menu for Selecting All Drawing Tools & Is Controlled Just Like a Typical Paint Program.
Dynacomp, Inc.

AccuFarm-MGR. *Version:* 4.11a. Jun. 1995. *Items Included:* Manual, Report Booklet. *Customer Support:* Quarterly maintenance fee $165-$440. Phone support, On-site training also available.
PC-DOS/MS-DOS; Xenix (8Mb). $2900.00-$8300.00. *Networks supported:* Novell.
Double-Entry GL System for Professional Farm Managers. Includes Multi-Client Accounting System with Customized Reporting Capabilities. Includes Automatic Interest Allocation & Automatic Fee Transactions.
AccuTech Systems Corp.

Accufarm Plan. Sep. 1985. *Compatible Hardware:* IBM PC & compatibles. *Operating System(s) Required:* MS-DOS, PC-DOS. *Memory Required:* 256k.
$2500.00.
Modeling, Budgeting, & Credit Analysis Tool for Agricultural Lenders in Preparation for Agricultural Loan Decisions. The Ag Loan Officer Can Create or Project a Cash Flow & Other Financial Aspects of a Farm Operation. Create "What If" Plans, Complete Schedules, & Generate Reports in CFS Format.
Ontario Systems Corp.

Accuplus Integrated Distribution Logistics System. *Version:* 1.8.4. Sep. 1993. *Compatible Hardware:* HP 9000, Vectra RS/20; RS 6000 IBM PS/2 Model 80/95; Texas Instruments. *Operating System(s) Required:* Xenix, Unix, AIX. *Memory Required:* 1000k. *General Requirements:* 70Mb on hard disk. *Items Included:* 900 plus page 2 volume manual & system managers manual. *Customer Support:* 24 hrs/7 days a week.
contact publisher for price.
Handles Inventory, Stock Location, Sales Analysis, Billing, Accounts Receivable, Pallet Exchange, Cartage, & Labor Management. Additional Subsystems. Accu-4GL, Pool/Freight, Freight Consolidation, Distributor Broker, WINS, & RF/Point of Transaction, Enhance the System to Meet the Warehouseman's Expanded Data Processing Needs. Updated Quarterly.
LDS, Inc.

AccuRec Time Recording-Wage Totalling System. Oct. 1989. *Compatible Hardware:* Apple II+, IIe, IIc, IIgs; IBM PC & compatibles. *Operating System(s) Required:* Apple DOS. *Language(s):* Applesoft BASIC, IBM BASIC (source code included). *Memory Required:* 48k. *Items Included:* Manual & software. *Customer Support:* In-house, call 707-546-6781.
disk $329.00.
Records & Totals Timecard Hours & Calculates Wage Totals for Standard, Premium & Overtime Hours. Simultaneously Handles Pay-Class Variations Weekly, Bimonthly, Every 2 Weeks, & Monthly. Supports up to 150 Employees Including Overtime Schedules of Daily/Weekly for 3 Different Shifts. Total Company Payroll & Total of All Employee Hours Are Tallied at End of Pay Period. Federal, State & 10 Other Deductions Can Be Calculated to Produce Net Payroll.
Individualized Operand (IO).

TITLE INDEX

AccuTrust. *Version:* 4.11. Jun. 1995. *Items Included:* Manual, Report Booklet. *Customer Support:* Quarterly maintenance fee $165-$440. Phone support, On-site training also available. PC-DOS/MS-DOS; Xenix (8Mb). $2900.00-$7900.00. *Networks supported:* Novell.
Performs Budgeting, Modeling & Credit Analysis. Converts Production Information into Financial Information. Calculates What-If Plans. Budgets at Detail Levels Including Field or Lot Level. Reports Balance Sheets, Projected Cash Flow, Break-Even by Enterprise & Proforma Financial Statements.
AccuTech Systems Corp.

AccuWeather.
IBM. disk $24.95.
MAC. 3.5" disk $24.95.
Now, You Can Log on to the World's Largest On-Line Weather Service - AccuWeather...the Weather Service Used by Network TV Stations, Radio Forecasters & Major U.S. Newspapers. The Accu-Weather Forecaster Provides a Customized Account Name & Password.
Software Toolworks.

ACE. *Version:* 2.0. 1989. *Items Included:* Getting started manual, primer, system guide, security booklet, installation guide. *Customer Support:* Through Dealer.
MS-DOS. IBM & compatibles (640K). disk $4995.00 - $9995.00. *Nonstandard peripherals required:* Dallas Key. *Networks supported:* Novell.
Digitizer-Based Assembly Estimating Program That Speeds Take-Offs, Calculates Estimates & Produces Bills of Material by Job Phase. It Features Graphic Display to the Screen of the Blueprint Taken Off, Digitizer Keypad for Easy Entry, Assemblies That Can Be Changed at the Time of Take-Off, Pricing That Can Vary by Job (without Changing the Price for Other Jobs) & Bid Analysis Including up to 20 Extras or Change Orders & Integration to Software Shop's Job Cost Accounting.
Software Shop Systems, Inc.

Ace File Try & Buy. Ace Software Corporation Staff. *Items Included:* The package includes 3.5" diskettes, a mini-manual & a Try & Buy Brochure. Windows 3.X. IBM compatible with 286, 386 or 486 processor (2Mb). disk $49.99 (ISBN 1-57548-009-3). *Addl. software required:* Phone dialer requires Hayes compatible modem.
It Is a Powerful Sophisticated Fully Featured Database Management Program. It Allows Users to Store & Manage Customer Lists, Orders, Employee Records & Appointments.
IBM Software Manufacturing Solutions (ISMS).

Acecalc. *Version:* 2.173. 1983. *Compatible Hardware:* Franklin Ace 1000, 2000 Series & 500. *Operating System(s) Required:* Apple DOS 3.3. *Language(s):* Assembly. *Memory Required:* 64k.
disk $39.95 (ISBN 0-917963-05-9).
Spreadsheet. Same As MagiCalc but Modified for FRANKLIN Owners.
Artsci, Inc.

Aces, Eagles & Birdies: Picture Perfect Golf; Tom Kite-Shotmaking; Best Places to Play. Lyriq Intl. et al. Feb. 1996. *Items Included:* Set-up instruction sheet. *Customer Support:* Telephone number (503) 639-6863 8AM-7PM PST M-F. 386 or higher, DOS 3.1 or higher (Picture Perfect); 486-33 MHz, Windows 3.1, DOS 5.0 (Tim Kite-Shotmaking); 486 SX/25, Windows 3.1 (Best Places). 486/25 (4Mb, 5Mb HD) (Picture Perfect); 486/25 (4Mb, 2Mb HD) (Tom Kite); 486/25 (4Mb, 7Mb HD) (Best Places). CD-ROM disk $34.95 (ISBN 1-887783-53-9, Order no.: 5300-8005). *Addl. software required:* CD-ROM drive, IBM PC or compatible, DOS 3.1, SVGA, soundblaster (Picture Perfect); mouse, SVGA, soundcard (Tom Kite); double speed CD-ROM drive, SVGA (Best Places).
Computerized Golfing, Instructional Golf Tips for Game Improvement, Rated Golf Courses.
Entertainment Technology.

Acewriter II. *Version:* 2.06. 1983. *Compatible Hardware:* Franklin Ace 1000, 2000 Series & 500. *Operating System(s) Required:* Apple DOS 3.3. *Language(s):* Assembly. *Memory Required:* 48k.
disk $39.95 (ISBN 0-917963-04-0).
Word Processor. Same As MAGICWINDOW but Modified for Franklin Owners.
Artsci, Inc.

Achievement Motivation Profile (AMP). *Version:* 1.010. Jotham Friedland et al. Apr. 1996. *Customer Support:* Free unlimited phone support.
Windows 3.X, Windows 95. 286 (4Mb). disk $185.00 (Order no.: W-1093). *Nonstandard peripherals required:* Printer.
This Convenient Self-Report Inventory Is an Ideal Way to Evaluate Underachieving or Unmotivated Students, Ages 14 & Up. It Gives You a Complete Picture of the Personal Factors That Affect an Individual's Academic Performance & Provides Specific Recommendations for Improvement.
Western Psychological Services.

ACHWorks. Oct. 1988. *Compatible Hardware:* IBM PC & 100% compatibles. *Operating System(s) Required:* MS-DOS. *Memory Required:* 640k. *General Requirements:* 2400 baud modem. *Customer Support:* Telephone support, regulatory compliance, product enhancements, newsletters.
disk $2000.00.
Bank Customers Can Make Preauthorized Banking Transactions (Withdrawals or Deposits) or Consolidate Deposits from Several Locations. The Bank's Customer Enters Transaction Information into a PC & Then They Electronically Transmit the Information to the Bank via Modem. Banks Reduce Their Costs Because It Is Less Expensive to Process ACH Items Than Checks & Deposit Tickets (CCD, CCD, Plus, PPD).
Learned-Mahn.

ACI. Aug. 1986. *Compatible Hardware:* DEC VAX/VMS, PDP/RSX. *Language(s):* FORTRAN. *General Requirements:* AutoCAD 2.0 or higher, Intergraph 8.0 or higher.
$3500.00-$4500.00.
Provides Two-Way Conversion Between AUTOCAD 2.0 Drawing Interchange Files & Intergraph Design Files. Graphics Files Created on Either System Can Be Converted for Use on the Other System. The Translation Process Is Controlled by a Specification File Which Allows the User to Define the Translation Parameters.
Decision Graphics, Inc. (Alabama).

The Acid-Base Diagnostician. Martin Goldberg. May 1993. *Items Included:* User manual & HyperCard. *Customer Support:* Free, unlimited technical support via our toll-free number (1-800-945-4551).
Macintosh. Macintosh with a hard drive (2Mb). 3.5" disk $150.00 (ISBN 1-57349-059-8). *Addl. software required:* System 6.0.7 or higher. *Networks supported:* All LANs.
A HyperCard-Based Learning Tool Which Uses Text, Sound, Animation & Sophisticated Analytical Techniques to Illustrate the Principles of Acid-Base Metabolism. Includes a Computerized Version of the Acid-Base Map, a Diagnostic Module for Interactive Learning, & a Casebook of Data on 10 Hypothetical Patients for Use with the Diagnostic Module.
Keyboard Publishing, Inc.

ACNAP: AC Network Analysis Program. *Version:* 3.25. Jan. 1985. *Compatible Hardware:* AT&T 6300; DEC Rainbow, DEC VT 180; HP-125; IBM PC, PC jr, PC XT, PC AT & compatibles; Tandy 1000, 1200, 2000; TI Professional; Xerox 820, 820-II, 860. *Operating System(s) Required:* PC-DOS/MS-DOS. *Language(s):* Compiled BASIC. *Items Included:* disk & manual. *Customer Support:* free technical support to registered owners.
MS-DOS (256k). disk $195.00.
IBM PC's & compatibles. 3.5" disk $349.95.
Stand-Alone, General Purpose Electronic Circuit Analysis Program Which Analyzes Passive & Active Circuits Consisting of Resistors, Capacitors, Inductors, Trasistors, Operational Amplifiers, FET's, etc. Commands Are Menu-Driven & Interactive. Calculates the Response of a Typical 5-Node Circuit in 0.4 Seconds. Features: Built-In Editor, Automatic Impedance Calculations, Monte-Carlo Analysis, Sensitivity Analysis, etc.
BV Engineering.

ACNAP3. *Compatible Hardware:* Apple Macintosh. *Items Included:* disk & manual. *Customer Support:* free phone support to registered owners.
3.5" disk $350.00.
Easy-to-Use General Purpose Linear Circuit Analysis Program Which Analyzes Passive & Active Circuits Consisting of Resistors, Capacitors, Inductors, Transistors, Operational Amplifiers, FET's, Transformers, etc. Circuits Can Be Stored to Disk for Editing & Analysis. Machine Code Is Optimized for Speed. Performs Magnitude, Phase & Delay Calculations. Can Compute Input & Output Impedances at Any Node over Frequency Range. Will Compute Component Sensitivities, & Uses Tolerance to Perform Monte Carlo Analysis & Calculate Worst Case Outputs. Results Can Be Graphed to Screen, Imagewriter or Laserwriter.
BV Engineering.

Acquisition Manager. *Version:* 3.11. Apr. 1993. *Items Included:* Manual. *Customer Support:* Free phone support.
MS-DOS or Windows. IBM PC & compatibles (640k). disk $695.00.
Manages Book Selection, Placement of Orders, Recording of Receipts, Returns & Cancellations, Tracking of Overdue Items, Fund Control. Produces Newsletter Describing Recent Acquisitions.
Professional Software.

Acquisitions Manager. *Version:* 3.0a. Jun. 1993. *Compatible Hardware:* IBM PC, PC XT, AT, PS/2 & compatibles; Apple IIc, IIe, IIgs. *Memory Required:* 640k. *General Requirements:* Hard disk, printer. *Items Included:* Disks, complete illustrated instructions binder. *Customer Support:* Technical 8:30-4pm M-F telephone no charge.
disk $169.00 (IBM) (Order no.: ACQ).
disk $99.00 (Apple).
Network version $459.00.
$239.00 Windows version.
$439.00 Windows Network version.
Simple Program for Ordering Books or Other Materials. Prints Out Orders, Maintains Items in Memory. Features Built-In Spreadsheet to Keep Track of Budgets. Package Includes Starter Pack of Non-Carbon Acquisition Forms.
p.r.n. medical software.

Across Five Aprils. Intentional Education Staff & Irene Hunt. Apr. 1996. *Items Included:* Program manual. *Customer Support:* Free technical support, 90 day warranty.
School ver.. System 7.1 or higher. Macintosh (4Mb). 3.5" disk contact publisher for price (ISBN 1-57204-249-4). *Nonstandard peripherals required:* 256 color monitor, hard

drive, printer.
Lab pack. System 7.1 or higher. Macintosh (4Mb). 3.5" disk contact publisher for price (ISBN 1-57204-250-8). *Nonstandard peripherals required:* 256 color monitor, hard drive, printer.
Site license. System 7.1 or higher. Macintosh (4Mb). 3.5" disk contact publisher for price (ISBN 1-57204-275-3). *Nonstandard peripherals required:* 256 color monitor, hard drive, printer.
School ver.. Windows 3.1 or higher. IBM/Tandy & 100% compatibles (4Mb). disk contact publisher for price (ISBN 1-57204-251-6). *Nonstandard peripherals required:* VGA or SVGA 640 x 480 resolution (256), mouse, hard drive, sound device.
Lab pack. Windows 3.1 or higher. IBM/Tandy & 100% compatibles (4Mb). disk contact publisher for price (ISBN 1-57204-276-1). *Nonstandard peripherals required:* VGA or SVGA 640 x 480 resolution (256), mouse, hard drive, sound device.
Site license. Windows 3.1 or higher. IBM/Tandy & 100% compatibles (4Mb). disk contact publisher for price (ISBN 1-57204-252-4). *Nonstandard peripherals required:* VGA or SVGA 640 x 480 resolution (256), mouse, hard drive, sound device.
This companion for young adult literature is ideal for students who don't know how to start that book report, or give that needed summary. Gentle prompts throughout the guide section of the program include Warm-up Connections, Thinking about Plot, Quoting & Noting, Keeping a Journal, If I Were ———' Responding to questions, Using Quotations, Taking a Personal View, Write to Others, & Write a Sequel.
Lawrence Productions, Inc.

ACS. *Compatible Hardware:* IBM PC & compatibles. *Operating System(s) Required:* MS-DOS. *Language(s):* Fortran. *General Requirements:* AutoCAD 2.0 or higher, Intergraph 8.0 or higher.
$1500.00.
Provides Two-Way Conversion Between AUTOCAD 2.0 Drawing Interchange Files & INTERGRAPH ISIF Files. Graphics Files on Either System Can Be Converted for Use on the Other System. The Translation Process Is Controlled by a Specification File Which Allows the User to Define the Translation Parameters.
Decision Graphics, Inc. (Alabama).

ACS-Query. *Version:* 4.1. *Items Included:* Manual included. *Customer Support:* 30 hours free support with training; otherwise 8 hours free support. $60.00 per hour thereafter. On-site training - $480.00 per day plus expenses.
MS-DOS & novell network. IBM PC & compatibles (640K). $5000.00 & up. *Addl. software required:* Word Processor. *Networks supported:* All.
PC-Based Interviewing Software for Marketing Research, Telemarketing & Political Polling. Lets User Create Questionnaire, Conduct Interviews, List & Sort Open-Ended Responses, Run Marginals (Frequency Counts), One-by-One Cross Tabs, Disposition Reports, Productivity Reports. Full Sampling & Call Management Capabilities & Quota Control.
Analytical Computer Service, Inc.

ACS Time Series. *Compatible Hardware:* IBM PC, PC XT, PC AT & compatibles. (source code included).
disk $495.00.
Complete Time Series Analysis Package Which Contains Very High Speed FFT's, Filter Generations, Convolutions, Transfer Function Calculations, Cepstrum, Curve Fitting Algorithms, Coherence Calculations, & Other Associated Routines.
Alpha Computer Service.

ACSL-PC: Advanced Continuous Simulation Language-PC. *Version:* 10. Jan. 1985. *Compatible Hardware:* IBM PC with Microsoft FORTRAN or Microway NDP FORTRAN. *Operating System(s) Required:* PC-DOS/MS-DOS. *Memory Required:* 512k. *Items Included:* Diskettes, documentation, installation instructions, security key. *Customer Support:* Telephone hotline support; updates at nominal fees.
disk $2300.00 to $3950.00 (Order no.: 6011).
Tool for the Scientist or Engineer Who Models & Analyzes Continuous Systems Described by Time-Dependent, Non-Linear Differential Equations or Transfer Functions. Enables the User to Interact with Models & Fully Explore Dynamic Behavior. ACSL Is Also Available on Convex, Cray, VAX, HP, Silicon Graphics, IBM, & SUN Workstations & Mainframes.
Mitchell & Gauthier Assocs., Inc.

Act! *Version:* 2.1. *Compatible Hardware:* IBM PC & compatibles. *Operating System(s) Required:* PC-DOS/MS-DOS 3.1 or higher. *Memory Required:* 640k. *General Requirements:* Hard disk. *Customer Support:* Available to registered users, no charge.
disk $395.00.
Database Program Customized for Contact Management. Includes a Calculator, a Calendar, & a Phone Dialer.
Contact Software International, Inc.

ACT: Activated Sludge. The Water Doctor. *Compatible Hardware:* IBM PC. *Operating System(s) Required:* DOS. (source code included). *Memory Required:* 256k. *General Requirements:* Printer, Lotus 1-2-3.
disk $250.00.
LOTUS 1-2-3 Template Which Performs Design Calculations for Activated Sludge System Design. Uses Major Sizing & Performance Criteria in US Units & Also Considers Four Common Process Modifications Including Extended Aeration. Because It Is Spreadsheet Based, It Lets Users Vary Input Data to See the Effect on Plant Design. This Ability to Study Numerous Combinations of Design Criteria Enables Design Optimization in Addition to Providing Data for Flow Modeling & Permits. Report Is Macro (Automatically) Driven. Help Screens Are Available for Many of the Parameters.
Techdata.

ACT! for Windows. Jun. 1992. *Items Included:* 3.5" & 5.25" disks; user's guide, reference manual, & Getting Started Guide. *Customer Support:* Free to registered users.
Windows 3.X. IBM compatible 286, 386 or 486 (2Mb). disk $495.00. *Nonstandard peripherals required:* Hard disk, mouse recommended. *Addl. software required:* Microsoft Windows 3.X.
Contact Manager. Incorporates Industry Standard dBASE File Format Contact Database, with Comprehensive Scheduling & Calendar Management Functions, Tightly Coupled with a Word Processor & Communication Tools.
Contact Software International, Inc.

ACT! Network. *Version:* 2.1. Apr. 1991. *Customer Support:* Free unlimited support for registered users; 30 day warranty on product.
DOS 3.1 or higher. IBM PC compatibles (640k). Server plus 1-$595.00; 5-user-$1295.00. *Networks supported:* Any DOS based network.
Now Available for Single-User or Network Environments, Is a Powerful yet Easy to Use Program That Provides Functions Needed to Organize the Day-to-Day Activities of Business People.
Contact Software International, Inc.

Act 1 Plus. *Version:* 8.2. *Compatible Hardware:* IBM PC & compatibles. *Operating System(s) Required:* MS-DOS/PC-DOS 2.0 or higher. *Items Included:* G/L; A/P; A/R; O/E; Inv; Check Reconciliation; Payroll; Purchase Order; Lynx (ASCII) file converter. *Customer Support:* Toll free per hour: $75.00; $195.00 6 mos.; $295.00 12 mos..
disk $199.50.
Contains Nine Modules.
Cougar Mountain Software, Inc.

Act 4 Plus. *Version:* 8.2. *Compatible Hardware:* 80386-based PCs, SCO Xenix, Unix System V or compatible. *Items Included:* G/L; A/R; A/P; O/E; Check Reconciliation; P/R; P/O; Invoice Inventory; Lynx. *Customer Support:* Toll free per hour: $75.00; $195.00 6 mos.; $295.00 12 mos..
$1995.00.
Separates. $599.50.
Contains Nine Modules.
Cougar Mountain Software, Inc.

ACTFIL: Active Filter Design/Realization. *Version:* 2. Jul. 1985. *Compatible Hardware:* Apple Macintosh; AT&T 6300; DEC VT 180; HP-125; IBM PC, PC XT, PC AT & compatibles; Tandy 1000, 1200, 2000; TI Professional; Xerox 820, 820-II, 860. *Operating System(s) Required:* Apple DOS, PC-DOS/MS-DOS. *Language(s):* Compiled BASIC. *Memory Required:* IBM 256k, Apple 512k.
disk $150.00.
Active Filter Design & Synthesis Program. Low Pass, Band Pass, High Pass & Band Reject Filters May Be Designed Using This Menu-Driven System. Computes the Number of Stages, Transfer Function Coefficients, Magnitude, Phase & Time Delay Characteristics for the above Filter Types for Infinite Gain Multiple Feedback & Voltage Controlled Voltage Source Implementations. Either Chebychev or Butterworth Response May Be Selected. Files Are Fully Compatible with BVE's Signal Processing Program (SPP) to Perform Transient Analysis & PCPLOT & PLOTPRO Graphics Programs.
BV Engineering.

Action! *Version:* Mac 1.0, IBM 3.0. *Items Included:* Manuals. *Customer Support:* Registered users get first 90 days free phone support, fax & online support. Call Macromedia for information about Priority Access support.
DOS 3.3 or higher, Windows 3.1 or higher. 386/25 MHz IBM & compatibles (4Mb RAM). disk $199.00. *Nonstandard peripherals required:* 16-color VGA graphics card & monitor. *Optimal configuration:* 486/33 MHz recommended, 8Mb recommended, hard disk, 3.5" high density disk drive.
6.07 or higher. Macintosh (4Mb). 3.5" disk $199.00. *Optimal configuration:* Mac II or higher, 8Mb RAM, 7.0 system.
Enables Business Computer Users to Create Dazzling Multimedia Presentations in Minutes. Users Assemble Presentations Quickly in the Outliner, Then Use the Automated Text Motion Feature, Transitions, Pauses & Fades to Create a Multimedia Presentation. Create Your Outline, Select One of 300 Pre-Designed Templates, & Presto! - a Multimedia Presentation That People Will Remember.
Macromedia, Inc.

Action & Bumping Games. *Compatible Hardware:* Apple II, II+, IIe; Franklin Ace. *Operating System(s) Required:* Apple DOS 3.3. *Language(s):* BASIC. *Memory Required:* Apple 32k, Franklin 48k.
disk $24.95.
Six Games: Cycle Jump, Mine Rover, Road Machine, Obstacle Course, Hustle & Bumper

Blocks. Jump Over Vehicles in Cycle Jump. Cross a Mine Field with Mobile Mines in Mine Rover. Drive Twisting Mountain Roads at High Speeds in Road Machine-8 Skill Levels. Run a Path of Hurdles, Tires, Ladders & Penalty Areas in Obstacle Course. Race to Reach Disappearing Blocks in Hustle. Bumper Blocks Involves Evading & Colliding with Blocks-5 Skill Levels.
Compuware.

Action Art. (Art Ser.). 1984. *Compatible Hardware:* IBM PC & compatibles, PCjr, PC XT, PC AT. *Operating System(s) Required:* PC-DOS/MS-DOS 2.0 or higher. *Language(s):* C. *Memory Required:* 128k. *General Requirements:* CGA card.
disk $49.95 (ISBN 0-922928-17-7, Order no.: 1020).
Will Enable Users to Draw Detailed Diagrams with Various Color & Shading Combinations. Images Can Be Temporarily Stored in a Buffer or Permanently Stored on a Disk. Helps Children Develop an Appreciation of Spatial Relationships, Eye-Hand Coordination, Keyboard Skills, & Directional Concepts.
GemStar Partnership.

Action Games. *Compatible Hardware:* Apple II, II+, IIe; Franklin Ace. *Operating System(s) Required:* Apple DOS 3.3. *Language(s):* BASIC. *Memory Required:* 16k.
disk $24.95.
Three-Game Package. Jump over Vehicles in Cycle Jump. Cross a Field of Moving Mines in Mine Rover. Drive at High Speeds Over Twisting Mountain Roads in Road Machine. Eight Skill Levels.
Compuware.

Action Games. *Compatible Hardware:* HP 86/87. *Memory Required:* 64k.
3-1/2" or 5-1/4" disk $39.00 ea. (Order no.: 92248DA).
Includes Six Arcade-Style Video Games: CRISS-CROSS, a Galactic Shooting Gallery; DODGE BALL Like the Schoolyard Game; RACE, Drive a Formula I Car; MOUSER, You Are a Mouse Trapped Inside a Three-Dimensional Maze; SPOOLS, Jump from Spool to Spool; HEEBIE-GEEBIES, Trap Them by Leaving a Trail.
Hewlett-Packard Co.

Action Pack, No. 1. *Items Included:* CD Manual. Win '95. IBM. Contact publisher for price (ISBN 0-87321-000-X, Order no.: CDD-3107).
Activision, Inc.

Action Pack, No. 1. *Items Included:* Installation guide.
Cotact publisher for price (ISBN 0-87321-145-6, Order no.: CDD-3290-000-43).
Activision, Inc.

Action Pack, No. 2. *Items Included:* CD Manual. Win '95. IBM. Contact publisher for price (ISBN 0-87321-001-8, Order no.: CDD-3108).
Activision, Inc.

Action Pack, No. 2. *Items Included:* Installation guide.
Contact publisher for price (ISBN 0-87321-146-4, Order no.: CDD-3300-000-U3).
Activision, Inc.

ActionTracker. *Version:* 4.0. *Compatible Hardware:* IBM PC & compatibles. *Operating System(s) Required:* PC-DOS/MS-DOS 2.0 or higher. *Memory Required:* 384k. *General Requirements:* Hard disk.
disk $1498.00.
Project Management Application Capable of Integrating the Activities of Each Member of a Network Allowing All Members to Know Who Is Responsible for What & When. Includes PROJECT QUERY LANGUAGE (PQL), a Relational Report Writer.
Information Research Corp.

ACTIVE: Active Filter Design. *Version:* 2.08t. R & L Software. 1994. *Compatible Hardware:* 8086 family of computers IBM XT/AT & compatibles. *Operating System(s) Required:* MS-DOS or PC-DOS. *Language(s):* Basic. *Memory Required:* 512k. *General Requirements:* Parallel printer port. *Items Included:* 5.25" DS/DD, (3.5" diskette available on special order.) User's manual. Code plug. *Customer Support:* 30 day unlimited warranty.
disk $245.00 (ISBN 0-927449-77-3, Order no.: A2PM).
A Specialized, Design Specific, Software Package for the Computer-Aided Synthesis & Analysis of Active & Switched Capacitive Filters. Easy-to-Use, Interactive Dialogue-Based Menus Makes It Possible to Reach an Optimal Filter Design Within Minutes. Filters May Be Defined As a Butterworth, Chebyshev, Bessel, Real Pole, Gaussian, Linear Phase or Elliptic Filter Operating As an LPF, HPF, BPF, All Pass or Notch Filter. As Part of the Definition Process, the Filter to Be Synthesized May Be Defined by Its Polynomial Transfer Function, by Its Poles & Zeros, or by Attenuation Requirements. Conversely, for a Filter That Has Already Been Built, Based on 45 Different Circuit Network Topologies Populated with Specified Component Values, Will Detail the Filters' Performance. In the Latter Case, the Product Is Already Built, & Now Is Being Evaluated.
Tatum Labs, Inc.

Active Circuit Analysis Program (ACAP). *Compatible Hardware:* Apple II with Applesoft; CP/M based machines with MBASICS; IBM PC. *Language(s):* BASIC (source code included). *Memory Required:* 48k-128k. *Items Included:* Manual. *Customer Support:* Free hot line, 30 day warranty.
disk $39.95, incl. manual.
Solve for the Node Voltages of a Network.
Dynacomp, Inc.

The Active Eye. *Version:* 1.2. Michael Mills & William Schiff. 1989. *Items Included:* 150 page guidebook. *Customer Support:* Free technical support, 90 days limited warranty.
Macintosh Plus or higher (2.5Mb). single user copy $99.00 (Order no.: S-030-4).
Nonstandard peripherals required: 20Mb hard disk. *Addl. software required:* Hypercard.
site license-multiple users $750.00 (ISBN 1-56321-033-9, Order no.: S-033-9).
A Graphically Advanced Hypercard Software Stack Designed as a Teaching Tool in the Area of Visual Perception. Presents More Than 50 Well-Crafted Animations, Experiments, & Tutorials Covering a Range of Visual Phenomena.
Lawrence Erlbaum Assocs. Software & Alternate Media, Inc.

Active Investor. *Customer Support:* 800-929-8117 (customer service).
MS-DOS. IBM/PS2. disk $99.99 (ISBN 0-87007-556-X).
Determines the Most Effective Use of User Investment Dollars. Calculate Internal Rate of Return, Future Value, Necessary Investments & Payback Period for an Investment with Varying Yearly Investments & Withdrawals.
SourceView Software International.

Activision Action Pack 2600: 7 Pack, Vol. 2. *Items Included:* Installation Guide. Atari. Contact publisher for price (ISBN 0-87321-004-2, Order no.: CDD-3058S).
Activision, Inc.

Activision Action Pack 2600: 7 Pack, Vol. 2. *Items Included:* Installation Guide. Atari. Contact publisher for price (ISBN 0-87321-005-0, Order no.: MS2-3058S).
Activision, Inc.

Activity Log System: Instructional Enterprises. *Items Included:* Manual & 3 1/2" disk. *Customer Support:* 800-966-3382, Fax: 612-781-7753 <g>.
IBM PC & compatibles. disk $59.95.
Accountability System for the IBM. May Use the Standard Categories Provided, or User Can Create New Ones. Uses a Windows-Type Pull down Menu System. Keep Track of the Amount of Time You Spend in Different Functions with a Variety of Counselee Categories. Data Compiled & Analyzed with Ease & Stored in Safety.
Educational Media Corp.

ACTOMP - AutoCAD to Mass Properties. NASA Goddard Space Flight Center. Apr. 1989. *Items Included:* Source code. *Customer Support:* Limited telephone support from COSMIC.
PC-DOS (5k). IBM PC series. $150.00 Program; $12.00 documentation (Order no.: GSC-13228). *Addl. software required:* AutoCAD.
System Was Developed to Facilitate Quick Mass Properties Calculations of Structures Having Many Simple Elements in a Complex Configuration Such as Trusses or Metal Sheet Containers. Calculating the Mass Properties of Structures of This Type Can Be a Tedious & Repetitive Process, but ACTOMP Helps Automate the Calculations. The Structure Can Be Modelled in AutoCAD or a Compatible CAD System in a Matter of Minutes Using the 3-Dimensional Elements. This Model Provides the Geometric Data Necessary to Make a Mass Properties Calculation of the Structure. It Reads the Geometric Data of a Drawing from the Drawing Interchange File (DXF) Used in AutoCAD. The Geometric Entities Recognized Include POINTs, 3DLINEs, & 3DFACEs. ACTOMP Requests Mass, Linear Density, or Area Density of the Elements for Each Layer, Sums the Elements & Calculates the Total Mass, Center of Mass (CM) & the Mass Moments of Inertia (MOI).
COSMIC.

ACT1 Plus Series. *Version:* 8.2. Aug. 1982. *Compatible Hardware:* IBM PC & compatibles with hard disk. *Operating System(s) Required:* PC-DOS/MS-DOS 2.1 or higher. *Memory Required:* 640k.
disk $199.50, all nine modules.
Accounting System Consisting of General Ledger, Accounts Payable, Accounts Receivable, Payroll, Inventory & Order Entry. Check Reconciliation; Purchase Order & Lynx. Each Module Can Be Used Alone or Integrated with Other Modules. System Is a Single User Series with Capabilities of Handling 250 Companies, with Ledger Consolidation. Upgradable to ACT2 Plus Network Version. Multiple Departments with P & L on Each Department. Complete Audit Trail. Report Generator Included. Up to 15 Alphanumerics in Account Numbers. Financial Reports. User-Defined Checks, Statements, & Invoices. Two Help Messages on Each Screen. Two Passwords in Each Module. Four Methods of Inventory.
Cougar Mountain Software, Inc.

ACTOR. *Version:* 4.0. May 1991. *Compatible Hardware:* IBM PC XT, PC AT & compatibles, PS/2. (source code included). *Memory Required:* 1000k. *General Requirements:* Mouse, graphics card, Windows 3.0.
disk $895.00.
Object-Oriented Programming Environment Which Runs Under MICROSOFT WINDOWS. Produces Stand-Alone Windows Applications. Includes Substantial Library of Code. Not Copy Protected. Educational Pricing is Available.
The Whitewater Group.

ACT2 Plus Series. Version: 8.2. Aug. 1982. Compatible Hardware: IBM PC & compatibles. Operating System(s) Required: PC-DOS/MS-DOS 3.1 compatible with the following networks - PC NetWork, StarLAN, NOVELL NetWare, Microsoft NetWorks, PCNet II, NetWork OS, LANtastic; Grapevine; PC MOS; Concurrent DOS. Language(s): C, Assembly. Memory Required: 640k. General Requirements: Hard disk. Items Included: G/L; A/R; A/P; INV; P/R; Check Recon; P/O; Lynx. Customer Support: Toll free per hour: $75.00; $195.00 6 mos.; $295.00 12 mos.. all nine modules $999.50.
Fully Integrated, Multiuser Accounting Package. Permits As Many Users on One CPU as the Hardware & the Operating System Allow, Featuring True Record & File Locking with Complete Integrity. Can Be Used As a Single-User System. Functions Include General Ledger, Accounts Receivable, Sales Invoicing, Billing, Inventory, Accounts Payable, Payroll. Check Reconciliation; Purchase Order & Lynx (ASCII File Converter). Date Sensitive User-Defined Fiscal Calendar; User-Defined Financial Reports; User Can Categorize Accounts Receivable; Vendors, Payroll, & Inventory by User-Defined Type; User Can Design Checks, Invoices, Statements, & W2's; User-Defined Chart of Accounts, Account Numbers, & Stock Numbers up to 15 Alphanumerics.
Cougar Mountain Software, Inc.

Acuview.
Contact publisher for price.
Graphics Package That Is Integrated with ACUCOBOL-85. Allows Users to Draw Variations of Five Categories of Business Charts, Including Bar Charts, Pie Charts, Line Charts, Tables of Data, & Word Charts.
Acucobol, Inc.

ACX: Air Cooled Heat Exchanger Design & Rating Program. Heat Transfer Consultants. Items Included: Manual.
MS-DOS. IBM & compatibles (640K). $3000.00.
Designs & Rates Air Cooled Heat Exchangers.
Techdata.

Ad/Art/Plus: Architectural Graphics. Version: 2. Compatible Hardware: Apple Macintosh. General Requirements: ImageWriter, LaserWriter, MacDraw, Adobe Illustrator.
3.5" disk $49.95.
Contains Object-Oriented Architectural Graphic Drawings & Symbols Created in MacDraw Format. Contains Landscape Design Graphics & a Selection of Designs for Creating User-Defined Architectural & Landscape Graphic Drawings & Shapes. Includes Shading & Line Widths Which Can Be Modified. Features a Selection of Trees, Bushes, Foliage, Rocks, Building Blocks, Windows, Architectural Symbols, Plumbing, Electrical, Fixtures & Basic Three-Dimensional Graphics for Constructing Three-Dimensional Drawings. Available in PICT or Adobe Illustrator Format.
Freemyers Design.

Ad/Art/Plus: Borders, Vol. 2. Version: 1. Compatible Hardware: Apple Macintosh. General Requirements: ImageWriter, LaserWriter, MacDraw.
3.5" disk $49.95.
Contains Complete Border Sizes & a Selection of Designs for Customizing User-Defined Border Sizes. Border Sizes Can Be Changed & Textures Can Be Added with a Paint Program to Provide Unlimited Varieties & Combinations. Available in PictureBase or MacPaint Format.
Freemyers Design.

Ad/Art/Plus: Cartoon Designer. Compatible Hardware: Apple Macintosh.
3.5" disk $49.95.
Contains Complete Selection of Cartoon Expressions & Features for Designing & Constructing User-Defined Characters. Includes Libraries of Cartoon Characters for Immediate Use. Drawing Sizes, Line Width & Shading Can Be Modified. Available in MacDraw or Adobe Illustrator Format.
Freemyers Design.

Ad/Art/Plus: Forms. Jun. 1990. Customer Support: Phone support, 90 days unlimited warranty.
Macintosh (1Mb). 3.5" disk $49.95. Addl. software required: Page layout, or MACDRAW or PICT FORMAT Application.
Collection of Popular Business Forms. Statements, Invoices, Credit Memo, Cash Receipt, Purchase Orders, Pricing Sheet, Price Quotation, Accounts Receivable. Time Cards, Time Records, Job Estimates, Job Costs, Fax Transmission, Service Call, Message Reply, Phone Call Message.
Freemyers Design.

Ad/Art/Plus: LaserArt-Borders. Version: 1. Compatible Hardware: Apple Macintosh.
3.5" disk $49.95.
Contains Object-Oriented Border Designs & Rules Created in MacDraw Format. Provides Complete Border Sizes, As Well As a Selection of Designs for Customizing User Defined Border Sizes. Border Sizes & Line Widths Can Be Modified.
Freemyers Design.

ADA Compliance Kit. Items Included: Full manual. No other products required. Customer Support: Free telephone support - no time limit. 30 day warranty.
MS-DOS 3.2 or higher. IBM & compatibles (512k). disk $139.95.
Includes the ADAABC Software Package along with Worksheets & Tools to Assist in Compliance Checking. Tools Include an Angle Finder to Ascertain the Correct Angle of Ramps, Scale to Determine If Doors Are Within the Proper Push/Pull Force Restrictions, & a Tape Measure. Also, Purchasers of the Compliance Kit Are Eligible for Free Telephone Consultation with Dr. R.L. Lessne, Director of the ADA Compliance Specialists Network.
Dynacomp, Inc.

Ada Programming, 2 discs. Customer Support: All of our products are unconditionally guaranteed.
DOS, Unix, OS/2. CD-ROM disk $39.95 (Order no.: ADA). Nonstandard peripherals required: CD-ROM drive.
1000 MB of Ada Source Code, Programs & Documentation.
Walnut Creek CDRom.

ADAABC-ADA Compliance Program: The ABC's of the Americans with Disabilities Act. Version: 1.3. MC2 Engineering Software. Jul. 1992. Items Included: Manual; program is also available with ADA compliance kit of instruments. Customer Support: Technical assistance hotline, 1-yr. warranty.
PC-DOS/MS-DOS. IBM & compatibles (512k), monochrome or color, any printer. disk $99.00; $149.00 full compliance kit. Networks supported: Any - on individual user basis.
An Indexing & Reference Program Containing the Full Text of the Americans with Disabilities Act, Its Regulations, Summaries, Outlines, Comments & Questions & Answers. All These Documents Can Be Instantly Accessed by Paragraph & Section, & Any Subject Can Be Searched for Throughout All Documents In Just Moments. References May Be Printed. Architectural Specifications Given for Compliance with ADA. A "Must" for All Business & Industrial Managers, Architects, Employment Managers, & Engineers to Assist Them in Compliance with ADA.
ADA Compliance Specialists.

ADAABC-ADA Compliance Program: The ABC's of the Americans with Disabilities Act. Version: 1.3. MC2 Engineering Software. Jul. 1992. Items Included: Manual; Program is also available with ADA compliance kit of instruments. Customer Support: Technical assistance hotline, 1-yr. warranty.
PC-DOS/MS-DOS. IBM & compatibles, monochrome or color, any printer (512k). $99.00 ($149.00 for full compliance kit). Networks supported: Any - on individual user basis.
An Indexing & Reference Program Containing the Full Text of the Americans with Disabilities Act, Its Regulations, Summaries, Outlines, Comments & Questions & Answers. All These Documents Can Be Instantly Accessed by Paragraph & Section, & Any Subject Can Be Searched for Throughout All Documents In Just Moments. References May Be Printed. Architectural Specifications Given for Compliance with ADA. A "Must" for All Business & Industrial Managers, Architects, Employment Managers, Engineers, ADA Compliance Specialists.

Adabas. Version: 1.5. Compatible Hardware: DEC VAX/VMS.
$10,000.00-$80,000.00.
Database-Management System Includes a File Information Utility, a Monitor Utility, an Algorithm Enhancement & Improved Security Features.
Software AG.

AdaFlow. Version: 1.07. Items Included: Ada-oriented design & Ada development tool. Customer Support: Telephone.
Macintosh Plus or higher. 3.5" disk $1495.00.
Ada-Oriented Design Tool.
ICONIX Software Engineering, Inc.

The Adam Osborne Software Collection, 4 disks. Compatible Hardware: Apple II with Applesoft; Atari 400, 800 with Atari BASIC; Canon AS-100; Commodore PET; Cromemco; Heath-Zenith Z-100; IBM PC; NEC PC 8000; North Star; Osborne; TRS-80 Model I, Model III, Model 4 with level II BASIC; CP/M based machines with BASIC. Language(s): BASIC (source code included). Memory Required: 48k. Items Included: Manual. Customer Support: Free hot line, 30 day warranty.
Disk set. $39.95.
Set. 8" disk $49.95.
disk $9.95 ea.
8" disk $12.45 ea.
Contains Math Problems, Basic Statistical Problems & Common Financial Programs.
Dynacomp, Inc.
  Some Common Basic Math Programs, Disk A. Contains: Greatest Common Divisor, Area of Integers, Parts of a Triangle, Coordinate Plot, Linear Interpolation, & Other Programs.
  Some Common Basic Math Programs, Disk B. Contains: Simpson's Rule, Trapezoidal Rule, Derivatives, Roots of Equations, Linear Programming, & Other Programs.
  Some Common Basic Statistical Programs. Contains: Mann-Whitney U-Test, Geometric Mean Derivation, Chi-Square Test, Linear Regression, System Reliability, & Other Programs.
  Some Common Financial Programs. Contains: Tax Depreciation, Map Check, Future Value of Investment, Salvage Value, Mortgage Amortization Table, & Other Programs.

TITLE INDEX

Adaptive Filters: Filter Design & Analysis.
Items Included: Bound manual. *Customer Support:* Free hotline - no time limit; 30 day limited warranty; updates are $5/disk plus S&H. MS-DOS 3.0 or higher. IBM & compatibles (640k). disk $379.95. *Nonstandard peripherals required:* Hard disk (or a 1.2Mb floppy); math coprocessor & mouse are supported, but not necessary. Requires CGA, MCGA, EGA, VGA, Hercules, IBM 8514, AT&T 440, PC 3270 or compatible graphics capability.
Includes Both the Least Mean Squares (LMS) & Fast Least Squares (FLS) Algorithms. Filters May Be Implemented in Fixed-Point or Floating-Point Arithmetic. The Resulting Filter Designs May Be Tested with Both Real-World & Simulated Data.
Dynacomp, Inc.

AdaptSNA. *Version:* 4.3. *Compatible Hardware:* IBM PC & compatibles.
$585.00 3270 is $245.00 & LUO.
APPC $285.00.
RJE $785.00.
Family of PC-to-Host Communications Products Enhanced to Support IBM's Device-Independent System Application Architecture. Each Package Is Now Link-Independent, Allowing the Same Software Package to Be Used Over Any Physical Link.
Network Software Assocs. (NSA), Inc.

AdaptSNA APPCplus 3270. May 1989. *Compatible Hardware:* IBM PC & compatibles, PS/2. *Memory Required:* 190k.
Allows Concurrent 3270 & IBM Logical Unit 6.2 Sessions Via PC-to-Host Linkup. Runs in a Systems Network Environment, lets Users Toggle Between the Two Modes Without Terminating Either Session; Users Can Perform a 3270 Inquiry to Locate Information in a Host Data Base, Toggle to APPC for a File Transfer, & Toggle Back to 3270 Without Having to Log Off the Host Computer. Can Be Used with Several Linkups: Remote Synchronous Data Link Control Connection with an SDLC Board & Synchronous Modem; Coax Adapter Board; Asynchronous Link Through Users PC's COM Port; a LAN-to-Host Link with NSA's AdaptSNA LAN GAteway; Directly to the Host Via IBM's Token Ring Interface Card; an SDLC Link with an Integrated SDLC/Modem Board; or a Modem with AutoSync Capabilities.
Network Software Assocs. (NSA), Inc.

AdaptSNA LU6.2/APPC. *Version:* 4.3. Sep. 1986. *Compatible Hardware:* IBM PC, PC XT, PC AT, & compatibles, PS/2. *Operating System(s) Required:* PC-DOS 2.0 or higher. *Memory Required:* 256k. *General Requirements:* Hard disk, modem, SDLC Card.
disk $285.00.
Implements Logical Unit 6.2 (LU6.2), Physical Unit Type 2.1 (PU2.1) Protocol on IBM PCs, XTs, ATs, & Compatibles. The Software Product Provides Both Advanced Program-to-Program Communications & a User-Friendly Tool-Kit (AdaptSNA LU6.2 ASSIST) Which Provides an Application Sub-System & a Comprehensive Set of Learning, Simulation & Implement Tools. Both Mapped & BASIC Conversation Verbs Are Supported. Using AdaptSNA LU6.2, PCs Can Be Configured to Communicate with Mainframes, Minicomputers & Other PCs on a True Peer-to-Peer Basis. PCs Can Communicate Without the Need for Host Resources to Manage the Interaction.
Network Software Assocs. (NSA), Inc.

AdaptSNA 3270. Jan. 1984. *Compatible Hardware:* IBM PC & compatibles, PC XT, PC AT, PS/2, lap-tops. *Operating System(s) Required:* PC-DOS 2.0 or higher. *Language(s):* C. *Memory Required:* 256k.

disk $245.00.
Interactive SNA Micro-to-Mainframe Emulator Using the IBM 3270 Protocol.
Network Software Assocs. (NSA), Inc.

ADControl. *Version:* 2.0. *Items Included:* Diskette, user manual. *Customer Support:* Free telephone technical support.
Apple Macintosh (1Mb). 3.5" disk $379.00.
Enables a Macintosh to Monitor & Control Its External Environment. This Software Reads, Records, & Plots Data Obtained from Sensors That Respond to Environmental Changes (Temperature, Pressure, Humidity, Energy Usage, etc.). Can Automatically Issue Commands to Control External Devices (Appliances, Machinery, or Electronic Equipment) via IF...THEN...Rules. No Knowledge of a Programming Language Is Required. Operates in Background So the Macintosh May Be Used for Other Tasks While Monitoring Continues. Weather Measurements, Environmental Monitoring, Energy Management, Home Control, Product Testing, Small-Scale Process Control, Agriculture, & Industrial Research Labs Are Areas Where ADControl Is Appropriate.
Remote Measurement Systems, Inc.

ADDITOR (Arithmetic Editor). 1989.
MS-DOS (256k). IBM PC, PC XT, PC AT & compatibles. disk $30.00 (ISBN 0-938245-55-4). *Addl. software required:* BRIEF by Underware, Inc.
Provides for Arithmetic Operations Within BRIEF Editor. Arrange Numbers in Text at User Convenience. Product Will Perform Arithmetic On Selected Numbers & Insert Result in Text Where Placement Is Desired. Features Automatic Addition of Columns & Rows.
Inverted-A, Inc.

Address Book. Ed Zaron. Mar. 1981. *Compatible Hardware:* Apple II, II+, IIe, IIc. *Operating System(s) Required:* Apple DOS 3.2, 3.3. *Language(s):* Applesoft BASIC. *Memory Required:* 48k.
disk $24.98 (ISBN 0-87190-002-5).
Stores 700 Names & Addresses, Prints Envelopes & Mailing Labels; Can Sort by Name, Address, Zip & Assorted Categories. Labels Can Be Printed from 1-6 Across.
Muse Software.

Address File Generator. *Compatible Hardware:* Apple II, II+. *Language(s):* Applesoft II. *Memory Required:* 48k. *General Requirements:* Printer.
disk $29.95 (Order no.: 10028).
Allows User to Create Any Number of Four Types of Address Files: Holiday, Birthday, Home, & Commercial. Contains Menu of Seven Commands Used to Create, Add, Edit, Display, Search, Sort, & Reorganize Files. Up to Three Fields May Be Used for Sort Criteria.
Powersoft, Inc.

Address Pro. 1984. *Compatible Hardware:* Apple II. *Operating System(s) Required:* Apple DOS 3.3. *Language(s):* BASIC. *Memory Required:* 48k.
disk $16.95.
Allows User to Make & Store an Address List of up to 300 Addresses per File. Prints Address Lists or Labels in Single or Double Row.
Interkom.

Addresser. *Version:* 4.0. Harry Briley. 1991-92. *Compatible Hardware:* Commodore 64, 128; IBM PC & compatibles. *Operating System(s) Required:* CBM DOS; DOS 2.1 or higher. *Language(s):* Compiled BASIC, Compiled .EXE for IBM. *Memory Required:* C64 64k, IBM 512k. *General Requirements:* Printer, color monitor.
disk $25.00 (Order no.: D115F C-64; D0621

IBM).
Mailing Labels & Directory. Up to 300 (C64) 450 (IBM) Names per File, Four Lines with Phone, 8 User-Defined Flags. Merges Smaller Files Together. Able to Load from LeagueBowl Data to Speed up Creation of Address List. Uses C64 Mode in C128.
Briley Software.

Adjustments Scoresheets. *Compatible Hardware:* Altos Series 5-15D, Series 5-5D, 580-XX, ACS8000-XX; DEC Rainbow 100 with 2 disk drives, Rainbow 100+ with 10MB hard disk; IBM PC with 2 disk drives, PC XT, & compatibles; Kaypro II/IV with 2 disk drives, Kaypro 10; Xerox 820 with 2 disk drives; ZILOG MCZ-250. *Operating System(s) Required:* CP/M, MP/M, CP/M-86/80, PC-DOS, MS-DOS.
contact publisher for price (Order no.: AJE).
Monitors the Status of Proposed & Recorded Adjustments Continuously Throughout the Audit. Enhances the Timeliness & Quality of Discussions with Clients Concerning Adjustments. When the Client Decides to Record One or More of the Adjustments, Data Can Be Moved from the "Proposed Adjustments" Section to the "Recorded Adjustments" Section of the Scoresheet, & the Relative Significance of Proposed Adjustments Are Automatically Recalculated.
Coopers & Lybrand.

Adman. *Version:* 3.5. Jul. 1994. *Items Included:* Complete documentation in 2 three-ring binders, newsletters, technical bulletins & a test company that can be used for experimentation, training & initial setup. *Customer Support:* Telephone support at $150/hr. billed in quarter hours, Train classes - 3 day session for $695, On-Site consulting $750 per day, Total Maintenance Package price varies by the size of the system & number of users.
DOS. IBM PC & compatibles (640k). $700.00 to $16,995.00, varies by modules & workstations. *Optimal configuration:* 486-33 with 4Mb RAM & 100Mb hard drive. *Networks supported:* Novell Netware, Lantastic.
Contains 13 Integrated Modules Including: Time & Production Billing, Media Billing, Accounts Payable, Accounts Receivable, General Ledger, Time History, Profit Reporting, Job Trafficking, Media Ordering, Job Estimating, Checkbook Manager, Cash Planning & Time Importing. Modules Are Specifically Designed to Meet the Need of the Advertising Industry.
Marketing Resources Plus.

The Adman System, 13 modules. *Version:* 3.5. Jul. 1994. *Compatible Hardware:* IBM PC AT & compatibles. *Operating System(s) Required:* Lantastic, Novell Netware, PC-DOS/MS-DOS. *Language(s):* Compiled BASIC. *Memory Required:* 640k. *General Requirements:* 40 Mb hard disk, 132-column printer. *Customer Support:* 30 days free telephone support.
1 module single user $700.00.
13 module single user $6995.00.
7 module network $4695.00.
13 module network $16,095.00.
videotape demo $25.00.
manuals $150.00.
Consists of Thirteen Integrated Modules That Perform the Basic Accounting, Billing & Reporting Functions Required by Small to Medium-Sized Advertising Agencies & Related Businesses.
Marketing Resources Plus.

Adobe Illustrator Collector's Edition. *Compatible Hardware:* Apple Macintosh, Macintosh Plus. *General Requirements:* PostScript Printer.
3.5" disk $125.00.
Package of Hundreds of Pre-Built Adobe Illustrator Basic Graphic Shapes. The Collection

of Art Is Designed for Ease of Use & Can Be Edited & Manipulated by a User. Features Numerous Basic Graphic Shapes That Illustrators Frequently Use. Package Contains 100 Borders & More Than 300 Dingbats. There Is a Medium Weight Serif & San Serif Typeface That Can Be Edited & Modified by an Artist to Create Logotypes. All Images Can Be Used with Other Adobe Illustrator & Adobe Illustrator 88 Files.
Adobe Systems, Inc.

Adobe Illustrator: Windows Version. *Items Included:* Video demonstration tape for learning basic & advanced features.
DOS: Version 3.1 or higher, Windows 3.0 or higher. IBM PC or compatible. disk $495.00.
Professional-Quality Graphics Tool Featuring Freehand Sketching Tools, Automatic Tracing & Text Manipulation.
Adobe Systems, Inc.

Adobe Illustrator: with Adobe Type Manager. *Version:* 3.2.
Macintosh Plus, SE, or higher (1Mb). 3.5" disk $595.00. *Nonstandard peripherals required:* Scanner, PostScript printer.
Designed to Produce High Quality Illustrations. Uses Lines & Curves Instead of Dots to Form an Image. Allows Users to Enter the Scanned Image of a Photograph, Logotype, Blueprint, Sketch, or Other Picture, & Modify & Incorporate That Image into Individual Artwork & Graphics. Keeps Every Image in Small "Art Files", & Allows Users to Recall, Refine, Combine, & Change Images. Works with Most Popular Page Layout Systems. A Significant New Function Is the Text Tool Which Allows User to Enter & Manipulate Text Directly on the Page without Working Through a Dialog Box. With the Text Tool, User Can Mix Typefaces, Sizes, Styles, & Colors in a Text Block. Place Text on a Curve, Rotate, Skew & Scale Text or Wrap Text Around Graphics. Program Includes ADOBE TYPE MANAGER Which Gives User WYSIWYG Capability, Including Smooth Screen Fonts & Better ImageWriter Output. System 7 Compatible.
Adobe Systems, Inc.

Adobe Streamline. *Version:* 2.0. *General Requirements:* Adobe Illustrator 88.
Macintosh Plus or higher. 3.5" disk $195.00.
Line Art Conversion.
Adobe Systems, Inc.

Adobe Type Manager. *Version:* 2.0. *Items Included:* 13 LaserWriter outline fonts including Helvetica, Times, Courier & Symbol.
System 6.0 or higher (1Mb). Mac Plus, SE, SE/30, II, IIx, IIcs. disk $99.00.
Enables Existing Applications to Display & Print Adobe Outline Fonts in Any Point Size Without Any Jagged Edges. Supports All Fonts in the Adobe Type Library.
Adobe Systems, Inc.

Adobe Type Reunion.
System 6.02 or higher. Macintosh family of computers (1Mb). 3.5" disk $99.00.
Alphabetizes All Your Different Post Script Language Fonts by Family Name with Handy Little Submenus for Different Styles & Weights.
Adobe Systems, Inc.

Adobe Type Set Packages. *Items Included:* 32 Page How-To booklet.
PC-DOS or MS-DOS version 3.1 or higher; Microsoft Windows 3.0 or OS/2 software. IBM PC or compatible (1Mb). $149.00.
System 6.02 or higher. Macintosh family of computers (1Mb). $149.00.
Four Type Packages: Letters, memos & Faxes; Overheads & Slides; Invitations & Awards; Spreadsheets & Graphs. These packages Give You a Simple, Cost-Effective Way to Create Professional Looking Business Communications.
Adobe Systems, Inc.

Adobe TypeAlign.
System Software 6.02 or higher. Macintosh family of computers (1Mb). 3.5" disk $99.00.
DOS: 3.0 or higher; Microsoft Windows 3.0 or higher. IBM PC or compatible (1Mb). disk $99.00.
Exclusively for ATM Owners: Rotate, Wrap, Skew & Kern Type Then Add Special Effects Like Outlines & See It on Screen.
Adobe Systems, Inc.

Adobe Typeface Library. *Compatible Hardware:* Apple Macintosh. *Memory Required:* 512k. *General Requirements:* LaserWriter.
$95.00 to $370.00.
Adobe Fonts Are Downloadable Typefaces for All PostScript Devices. Includes Over 1000 Typefaces.
Adobe Systems, Inc.

AdPack Classified Management System. *Items Included:* Documentation. *Customer Support:* On-site training & support, 90-day warranty, toll-free number, maintenance.
MS-DOS, Windows (512k). PC & compatibles. contact publisher for price. *Nonstandard peripherals required:* HP Laser Printer. *Addl. software required:* PageMaker, Work Station Basic. *Optimal configuration:* 286 clone, 80Mb or higher.
Automates Classified Advertising for Shoppers, Newspapers & Other Periodicals. Performs Word Count, Calculates Billing Information, Tracks Cash Received, Creates Customer Records & Stores Advertisement for Publication. Selects Ads to Publish, Sorts & Typesets Them & Generates Strips of Typeset Ready & Paste Ready Ads. Prints a Variety of Reports.
Hansco Information Technologies, Inc.

ADS Accounts Payable. *Version:* 9.0. Jul. 1990. *Operating System(s) Required:* MS-DOS 3.2 & higher. *Language(s):* MBASIC. *Memory Required:* 640k. *General Requirements:* Hard disk. *Items Included:* Manual, training exercises, free support. *Customer Support:* 3 months free.
disk $195.00.
Provides a Means of Managing Cash Requirements on Either a Cash Basis, Accrual Basis or Combination of the Two. Reports Will Selectively Reflect Invoices Backward to Show Oldest Items or Forward to Show Future Cash Needs. Features Open Item Worksheet Which Becomes a Turnaround Document & Valid Account Number Verification of General Ledger Distribution.
ADS Software, Inc.

ADS Accounts Payable. ADS Software, Inc. *Compatible Hardware:* TI Professional with printer, 2 disk drives. *Operating System(s) Required:* MS-DOS. *Memory Required:* 128k. $485.00.
Cash Management System-Cash Basis, Accrual Basis or Combination of the Two.
Texas Instruments, Personal Productivit.

ADS Accounts Receivable. ADS Software, Inc. *Compatible Hardware:* TI Professional with printer, 2 disk drives. *Operating System(s) Required:* MS-DOS. *Memory Required:* 128k. $485.00.
Provides High Volume Debit/Credit Posting, Sales Analysis, Sales Tax & Miscellaneous Charges Breakout.
Texas Instruments, Personal Productivit.

ADS Club Accounting. *Version:* 10.0. *Items Included:* All manuals spiral-bound, 500 statements. *Customer Support:* 90 days unlimited support, 30 days money back guarantee.
MS-DOS 3.1 or higher, Windows. 286 or higher (1Mb). $999.00 ($200.00 for multi-user).
Designed for Clubs Whose Primary Income Is from Membership Dues, Miscellaneous Charges & Auxiliary Services. Provides for Automatic Dues Billing, Unlimited Number of Recurring Charges, Minimum Tracking, Assessments & Finance Charges. Automatic Charges Can Be Viewed, Listed & Modified Before Posting. A One Step Process Prints Statements, Trial Balance & Then Performs All Updates. The Package Has Easy Error Correction, Lookup Windows & User Definable Reports & Mailing Labels. Package Comes with Payroll, Accounts Payable & General Ledger.
ADS Software, Inc.

ADS General Ledger. *Version:* 9.0. Jul. 1990. *Operating System(s) Required:* MS-DOS 3.2 & higher. *Language(s):* Microsoft BASIC. *Memory Required:* 640k. *General Requirements:* Hard disk. *Items Included:* Manual, training exercises, support. *Customer Support:* 3 months free.
disk $195.00.
Made up of Two Parts: General Ledger Posting & Related Reports & Financial Statements. Incorporates 100% Latitude in Account Numbering & Report Formatting. Allows for Departmental Profit Analysis & Consolidation, Multiple Companies, Budget, & Last Year Comparison.
ADS Software, Inc.

ADS General Ledger. ADS Software, Inc. *Compatible Hardware:* TI Professional with printer & 2 disk drives. *Operating System(s) Required:* MS-DOS. *Memory Required:* 128k. $485.00.
Features General Ledger Posting & Related Reports & Financial Statements.
Texas Instruments, Personal Productivit.

ADS Light Accounting for Retail Florist. *Version:* Light. Jul. 1991. *Items Included:* Manuals, training exercises, support. *Customer Support:* Free - 3 months.
MS-DOS 3.2 & higher. Hard drive (640k). disk $399.00.
Designed for Small Florist with Less Than 1,500 Customers to Be Held in Accounts Receivable. Package Includes Accounts Receivable, General Ledger, Accounts Payable & Payroll. Accounts Receivable Provides Sales Analysis & Wire Service Reconciliation, along with the Ability to Run Statements, Invoices & Past Due Notices.
ADS Software, Inc.

ADS-MGMStation-Architecture. *Version:* 1.1. *Compatible Hardware:* Apple Macintosh. *Memory Required:* 512k. *Customer Support:* Free phone support.
3.5" disk $195.00.
Library of Architectural Symbols--to ANSI Standards. Symbols in Plan Form As Well As Elevation. Arranged in 31 Distinct Libraries That Are Instantly Accessible. Floor Plans Drawn in Minutes with Pull Down Menus. Snap in Doors & Windows with the Mouse. Pull Entire Bathrooms & Kitchens from the Library. Includes: Stairs, Doors, Windows, Furniture, Kitchen, Laundry, Plumbing, Electrical, Landscape, Foundations, Materials, Fireplaces, Bathrooms, Kitchens, Handicapped Public Bathrooms, Steel, Welding, & Graphic Symbols.
Compu-Arch.

ADS-MGMStation-Electronics. *Version:* 1.1. *Customer Support:* Free phone support.
Macintosh (512k or higher). disk $195.00.
Comprehensive Compilation of Electronic, Electro-Mechanical & Electrical Symbols Developed Specifically to Allow Creation of Complex Electronic Schematics & Drawings. There Are More Than 15 Libraries Covering All the Primary ANSI Symbols. They Are Accessible by Mouse to

Any Position on a Drawing. Used in Conjunction with MGMStation CAD Package, Program Transforms Macintosh into CAE Capture Work Station. Fully Compatible with Variety of Plotters & Laser Printers.
Compu-Arch.

ADS-MGMStation-Interiors. Version: 1.1. Compatible Hardware: Apple Macintosh. Memory Required: 512k. Customer Support: Free phone support.
3.5" disk $195.00.
Library of Interior Design Symbols. The Same Familiar Symbols Found in Standard Drawing Templates. Symbols in Plan Form As Well As Elevation. Draw a Floor Plan or Room Layout with Pull Down Menus. Snap in Furniture or Cabinetry or Pull Down Entire Rooms. Includes: Bathroom, Brick Patterns, Office Furniture, Equipment, Children's Furniture, Lighting, Outdoor Furniture, Wood Patterns, Tables, Landscape, Parking Layouts, Bedroom, Chairs, Cabinets, Kitchens, Living Room, Tile Patterns, Games, Store Fixtures, Swimming Pools & Spas.
Compu-Arch.

ADS-MGMStation-Mechanical. Version: 1.1. Customer Support: Free phone support. Macintosh (512k or higher). disk $195.00.
Integrated Compilation of Mechanical Symbols Stored in Libraries Developed Specifically for Mechanical Engineers, Plumbing Contractors, Specialists in HVAC Systems & Other Design Professionals. Allows Creation of Complex Schematics & Drawings. There Are More Than 20 Libraries, All Conforming to MIL STD & Architectural Standards. Used in Conjunction with MGMStation CAD Package, ADS Library Transforms Macintosh into Schematic Design Workstation. Symbols Used Are Precise Representations of the Most Commonly Utilized Mechanical Templates.
Compu-Arch.

ADS Payroll. Version: 9.0. Jul. 1990. Operating System(s) Required: MS-DOS 3.2 & higher. Language(s): Microsoft BASIC. Memory Required: 640k. General Requirements: Hard disk. Items Included: Manual, training exercises, support. Customer Support: 3 months free.
disk $195.00.
Payroll Journal Which Can Be Run Optionally by Department. Allows Multi-State Payroll Tax Calculation with up to Six Automatic Deductions per Pay Period. Provides for Operator Override of All Withholding Calculations & Allows Handling of Early Pay Offs. May Be Integrated with General Ledger to Provide Reports. 4011k Cafeteria Plan Available.
ADS Software, Inc.

ADS Payroll. ADS Software, Inc. Operating System(s) Required: MS-DOS. Memory Required: 128k.
$485.00.
Texas Instruments, Personal Productivit.

Adult Airway Management: Principles & Techniques. Raphael Ortega & Harold Arkoff. Dec. 1994. Customer Support: Toll-free technical support - no charge. In U.S. 9AM - 5PM EST 800-343-0064; in U.K. 44(0)81-995-8242.
Microsoft Windows 3.1. 386 IBM-Compatible PC (8Mb). CD-ROM disk $175.00, Individual, ,495.00 Institutional (ISBN 1-57276-015-X, Order no.: SE-015-001). Nonstandard peripherals required: CD-ROM drive (MPC Standard) 640x480 display with 256 colors, MPC Standard Soundboard & Speakers.
System 7.0 or higher. Apple Macintosh (8Mb). CD-ROM disk $175.00, Individual, ,495.00 Institutional. Nonstandard peripherals required: CD-ROM drive.

This Program Describes the Use & Indications of the Airway Control Adjuncts, the Risk & Benefits of the Airway Control Adjuncts, & the Complications of Airway Management. Through the Full Use of Multimedia, This Program Illustrates the Anatomy & Physiology of the Human Airway & Explains the Various Procedures & Techniques Used in Airway Management.
SilverPlatter Education.

Adult Parole Management. Version: 2.2. (Criminal Justice Ser.). Palladium Software Corp. Aug. 1992. Compatible Hardware: IBM, Digital Alpha. Operating System(s) Required: Windows 95 & NT. Language(s): Level 5, Clarion, Illustra DBM. Memory Required: 4000k.
contact publisher for price.
Provides for the Management of Paroles. Personal & Parole Agency Data Pertinent to Current Control of Parole Is Maintained Including All Reporting Requirements & Dates. Specifically Designed for Correction Adminstration. Consists of 4 Application Modules.
Ellington Duval, Inc.

Advance Booking. Version: 5.1. 1994. Items Included: Manual. Customer Support: One year of CSAP is provided at N/C; 30 day no risk guarantee.
MS-DOS. IBM & compatibles (640k). 5.25" disk $895.00 (ISBN 0-927875-36-5, Order no.: 1800). Addl. software required: Winnebago CIRC. Optimal configuration: Same as Winn CIRC. Networks supported: Netbios or IPX compatible.
3.5" disk $895.00 (ISBN 0-927875-35-7, Order no.: 1800).
An Optional Add-On Program That Interfaces with Winnebago CIRC. This Program Books Library/Media Center Materials in Advance: Gives Patrons Access to the Materials Needed, When They Are Needed. Advance Booking Also Assists in Managing & Tracking the Library's Bookings & Prints a Variety of Reports & Notices.
Winnebago Software Co.

Advance Booking. 1994. Items Included: Manual. Customer Support: 1 year free customer support agreement including 800 support & our 2 hour call-back guarantee.
MS-DOS. IBM PC & compatibles (640k). disk $895.00.
Allows You to Reserve Materials (Books, AV Equipment, Films, Rooms, Athletic Facilities, etc.) Days, Weeks, Even Months in Advance. Interfaces with Winnebago CIRC. Can Print Advance Booking Reports.
Winnebago Software Co.

Advance Booking. Apr. 1994. Items Included: Included in the IBM CIRC/CAT manual 428 pg. 3 ring binder. Customer Support: Guaranteed 2 hr call-back; 1st year of support included with program purchase; toll-free 1-800 number; modem support; program updates & manual revisions; replacement program disks if necessary; subscription to the WUG Letter, 30 day money back guarantee.
MS-DOS. IBM or compatible PC-Based computer, DOS 3.0 or higher (640k). 3.5" disk $895.00 (ISBN 0-927875-35-7, Order no.: 1800). Nonstandard peripherals required: Epson or compatible printer with tractor feed, barwand, or keyboard. 2Mb hard drive space. Optimal configuration: 486 or higher processor, MS-DOS 5.0 or higher, 1Mb RAM, 2Mb hard disk space for every 1,000 MARC records in database. Networks supported: Winnebago LAN, Novell, ICLAS, & LANtastic.
5.25" disk $895.00 (ISBN 0-927875-36-5, Order no.: 1810).
Integrates with Winnebago CIRC & CIRC/CAT.

You Can Book Items via Modem or a Remote Workstation. You Can Book Items a Year or More in Advance. Other Features Include Various Reports, Fine Capabilities, Log of Booking Activity, Set Destination, & Patron & Material Set-Up.
Winnebago Software Company.

Advanced Accounting. Version: 4.03. Sep. 1993. Items Included: Sample data, tutorial, full manual (3-ring binder). Customer Support: Free installation support (via phone) first 30 days; FAX & Bulletin Board: free, with response within 1-3 days; Phone support: 1 year, unlimited calls, 1-5pm M-F $150/year; Training is available from 3rd party.
DOS 3.3 or higher. PC compatibles/clones (2Mb). disk $399.00. Addl. software required: Recommend an expanded memory manager. Optimal configuration: Intel 486 or clone, DOS 5.0, 4Mb RAM, 386 MAX memory manager, Novell 3.12 network (for multiuser). Networks supported: Any NetBIOS compatible network; recommend Novell or LANtastic.
Includes 7 Fully Integrated Modules: G/L, A/R, A/P, Sales Order, Purchase Order, Inventory, Payroll. Add-On's for Job Costing, Bill of Materials, & Point of Sale Available. Real-Time Transaction Posting. Multiuser Ready. Supports Profit Centers, Departmentalization, Automatic Backorders, Partial Shipments, Recurring Billing, Multiple Inventory Locations, Complex Price & Discount Structures. Source Code Is Available.
Business Tools Software.

Advanced Air Traffic Controller. Compatible Hardware: Apple II, II+, IIe; Franklin Ace. Operating System(s) Required: Apple DOS 3.3. Language(s): Machine, BASIC. Memory Required: 32k.
disk $21.95.
By Ordering When to Turn, Hold or Change Altitude, Control 26 Prop Planes & Jets Landing, Taking Off & Flying in a Given Airspace. Keep Track of Altitude, Heading & Fuel Levels. New Challenges Come with Five Different Radar Maps & 84 Skill Levels.
Compuware.

Advanced Aircraft Analysis (AAA). Version: 1.6. Apr. 1995. Items Included: 3-ring bound AAA Users Manual. Customer Support: 90 days included with purchase, yearly support - $995.00.
Domain OS 10.3, 10.4. Apollo Workstation DN Series (8Mb). disk $4995.00 (ISBN 1-884885-12-8, Order no.: AAA-APB). Optimal configuration: 8Mb RAM, 10Mb hard disk.
Sun OS 4.1x, Solaris 2.x, Open Windows. Sun SPARCStation (8Mb). disk $4995.00 (ISBN 1-884885-13-6, Order no.: AAA-SUN). Optimal configuration: 8Mb RAM, 10Mb hard disk.
IRIX 4.x, Motif Window Manager. Silicon Graphics (8Mb). disk $4995.00 (ISBN 1-884885-16-0, Order no.: AAA-SGI). Optimal configuration: 8Mb RAM, 10Mb hard disk.
AIX 3.x, AIX Windows. IBM RISC System/6000 (8Mb). disk $4995.00 (ISBN 1-884885-14-4, Order no.: AAA-IBM). Optimal configuration: 8Mb RAM, 10Mb hard disk.
HP-UX 8.x, HP VUE. Hewlett Packard 9000 Series 700 (8Mb). disk $4995.00 (ISBN 1-884885-15-2, Order no.: AAA-HP7). Optimal configuration: 8Mb RAM, 10Mb hard disk.
Provides a Powerful Framework to Support the Interactive & Nonunique Process of Aircraft Preliminary Design. The AAA Program Allows Design Engineers to Rapidly Evolve a Preliminary Aircraft Configuration from Early Weight Sizing Through Open-Loop & Closed-Loop Dynamic Stability & Sensitivity Analysis, While Working Within Civil & Military Regulations & Cost Constraints. Operates in Either British or Metric Units. The Design Methodology Used in the

Development of the AAA Program Is Based on Airplane Design, Parts I-VIII, & Airplane Flight Dynamics, Parts I-II, by Dr. Jan Roskam. DARcorporation.

Advanced BASIC Faster & Better. *Compatible Hardware:* TRS-80. *Operating System(s) Required:* TRSDOS. *Language(s):* Microsoft BASIC.
disk $19.95, incl. bk. (Order no.: BABFB).
disk $19.95 (Order no.: DMABFB).
The Alternate Source.

Advanced Basic Meta-Analysis. *Version:* 1.10. Brian Mullen. 1993. *Customer Support:* Free technical support, 90 day limited warranty.
MS-DOS. IBM & compatibles (640k). disk $99.95 (ISBN 1-56321-132-7).
3.5" disk $99.95 (ISBN 1-56321-133-5).
text, 184 pages $29.95 (ISBN 0-8058-0502-8).
An Integrated & Comprehensive Combination of Meta-Analytic Tools for the Statistical Integration of Independent Study Results.
Lawrence Erlbaum Assocs. Software & Alternate Media, Inc.

Advanced Blackjack. Paul Dayton & Lois Slade. Jul. 1983. *Compatible Hardware:* Apple II, II+, IIe, IIc. *Operating System(s) Required:* Apple DOS 3.2, 3.3. *Language(s):* BASIC. *Memory Required:* 48k.
disk $19.98, incl. bklt. & reference card (ISBN 0-87190-001-7).
Teaches the Zen Counting Method for Strategic Blackjack. Improves All Skills of Blackjack Playing; Ex: Betting, Odds, Drawing Cards, etc.
Muse Software.

Advanced Concepts Accounts Payable. (source code included).
Online History Inquiry. $285.00.
Two Digit Pay to Vendor Name & Address. $175.00.
Post Line Item Detail to General Ledger Journal. $175.00.
Provides History Information for Vendor Transactions.
Advanced Concepts, Inc.

Advanced Concepts Payroll.
Print Other Pay Types 2, 3, & 4 Separately on Check Stub. $125.00.
Print up to 3 Different Wage Categories of Hours Worked, Earnings, & Department on Check Stub. $125.00.
Hours Worked History. $175.00.
Payroll Check History. $175.00.
Union Reporting. $345.00.
Union Deduction. $175.00.
Advanced Concepts, Inc.

Advanced DB Master Level IV. *Version:* 4.2. 1990. *Compatible Hardware:* IBM PC & compatibles. *Memory Required:* 512k. *Items Included:* Program diskettes, 600 Pg. manual, sample files. *Customer Support:* 30-day money back guarantee, upgrade maintenance program, on-site training/application development available.
MS-DOS/PC-DOS, 2.1 & Higher. IBM PC/XT/AT & compatibles. $695.00 single user; $1195.00 3 user; $1695.00 8 user; $2595.00 16 user; $4595.00 32 user; $6995.00 64 user. *Nonstandard peripherals required:* Hard disk or two floppy drives. *Networks supported:* Novell, Lantastic, Grapevine, Starlan, Most Others. Call for Complete List.
Full Relational Support (up to 30 Files Open Simultaneously with Automatic Read/Update), Programming Language, User-Definable Menus, & User-Definable Windows. Packed Records Save 50 to 70% over Fixed Length Records (i.e. dBASE, Paradox). Update File Structure at Will, Records/Formats Automatically Updated.
Macon Systems, Inc.

Advanced Disk Editor (ADE). *Compatible Hardware:* Apple II, II+, IIe. *Operating System(s) Required:* DOS. *Language(s):* Machine. *Memory Required:* 48k.
disk $39.95.
Permits Menu-Aided Manipulation of Disk Data on a Byte-by-Byte Level. Designed for Advanced Programmers.
Dynacomp, Inc.

Advanced Drafting Tools 1. Dec. 1992. *Items Included:* Manual, diskettes. *Customer Support:* Free with registration.
Macintosh. Macintosh Plus or higher (2Mb). 3.5" disk $79.00. *Addl. software required:* PowerDraw or PowerCADD.
Set of Externals for PowerDraw Version 4.0. Externals Contain Specialized Menu & Tool Items That Add Features to PowerDraw. Tools Included are a Trim/Extend Tool, Faired Curve Spline Tool, Spline Polygon, Projection Line, & Insulation Tool. Some of the Added Menu Commands Are Cut Curve with Line, Convert to Bezier, Divide, Duplication, Rotate & Mirror by Line. The Insulation Tool is a Special Interactive Tool That Allows You to Draw the Standard Architectural Symbol for Insulation. Many of the Tools Were Developed to Produce Aircraft Engineering Drawings & Exploded Isometric Assembly Illustrations. PowerDraw Users Will Find These Tools a Must for Enhanced Productivity.
Engineered Software.

Advanced Drafting Tools 2. Dec. 1992. *Items Included:* Manual, diskettes. *Customer Support:* Free with registration.
Macintosh. Macintosh Plus or higher (2Mb). 3.5" disk $79.00. *Addl. software required:* PowerDraw or PowerCADD.
Set of Externals for PowerDraw Version 4.0. Externals Contain Specialized Menu & Tool Items That Add Features to PowerDraw. Thirteen Baseline Tools Emulate the Manual Drafting Machine, Only Easier, to Allow You to Work at Odd Angles. Another Set of Tools Allows You to Copy & Paste with One Click or Copy the Attributes of One Object to Another. Twelve Specialized Isometric Tools Allow You to Draw Various Objects in an Isometric Plane. There Is Also a Balloon Text Tool. Some of the Added Menu Commands Are Blend & Join. The LaserPrint External Is Provided to Aid in PostScript Printing. This Specialized Tool Provides a Multitude of Capabilities Such As Printing Just Selected Objects or Print What Is Contained on the Windows, or Print a D Size Drawing on an 8 1/2 Size Sheet. PowerDraw Users Will Find These Tools, Especially LaserPrint, a Must for Enhanced Productivity.
Engineered Software.

Advanced Ear Training - Tutorial & Testing Programs. Jun. 1986. *Compatible Hardware:* Apple II, II+, IIe. *Memory Required:* 48k. *General Requirements:* DAC board with headphones or speakers.
disk testing $150.00.
disk tutorial $200.00.
Designed for 2nd-Year Ear Training Students. Covers All of the Materials in the Text "Advanced Ear Training" (Benward). The Software Is Designed for Student Use As a Supplement to Classroom Instruction. The Testing Programs Present Musical Selections to Test the Student on Material Covered in the Book & on the Tutorial Programs to Accompany the Book. They Contain a Total Score Record for the Individual Student. The Programs Require the Student to Identify Notes & Chords Played by the Computer.
Wm. C. Brown Pubs.

Advanced HyperCard Skills. *Compatible Hardware:* Apple Macintosh Plus. *Customer Support:* Hot line support.
3.5" disk $900.00.
Instructor-Led Course Training Materials.
Logical Operations.

Advanced Intelligent Network: An Overview. Dec. 1994. *Items Included:* User manual. *Customer Support:* Free technical support & a 30-day warranty (1-800-521-CORE).
MS-DOS. IBM & compatibles (512k). 3.5" disk $199.00 (ISBN 1-57305-007-5). *Nonstandard peripherals required:* High-density 3.5" disk drive; VGA color monitor. *Addl. software required:* MS-DOS version 3.3 or higher. *Optimal configuration:* IBM (512k), MS-DOS version 3.3 or higher, VGA color monitor, keyboard, Microsoft compatible mouse (optional).
Provides a High Level Technical View of the Switching System & Intelligent Service Node Functions Necessary for Providing Advanced Intelligent Network Customer Services. Because the AIN Provides the Telephone Subscriber with a Service "Customization" Interface, the Service Creation Model Is Discussed. The AIN-O CBT Also Provides the Basis for a More Advanced Study of the "Bits & Bytes" of AIN Functions. Training Will Take Approximately 2 Hours.
Bellcore.

Advanced Job Shop System. *Version:* 3.08. DBA Software Staff & Mike Hart. Jun. 1992. *Items Included:* Documentation. *Customer Support:* Available additional cost of $75/hour at time of purchase, as required. On-site training available at $75/hr. as well.
MS-DOS. IBM & compatibles (1Mb). $199.00 Single-User; $999.00 Multi-User; $249.00 Accounting Interface. *Networks supported:* Novell, Lantastic, M-S NT, M-S Lan Manager.
Software That Inferaces with Lake Avenue's Accounting Modules for a Complete Accounting Application. Interface Module Allows for Data Linking Between Lake's Inventory, Sales Order, Customer, Vendor & Employee Files to Download into This DBA Manufacturing Specific Software, Including: Manufacturing Inventory, Purchase Orders, Bills of Material, Light Work Orders, Routing's, Advanced Work Orders, Job Costing, Estimating, Scheduling, Features & Options, Data Collections, Lot Control & Serial Control. It Is Designed for Companies with Annual Sales of 1-10 Million, (10-200 Employees).
Lake Avenue Software.

Advanced Logo: A Language for Learning. Michael Friendly. 1988. *Customer Support:* Free technical support; 90 days limited warranty.
MS-DOS. IBM or compatibles (640k). disk $29.95 (ISBN 1-56321-149-1). *Addl. software required:* LOGO.
MAC. disk $29.95 (ISBN 1-56321-055-X). *Addl. software required:* LOGO.
cloth text, 676p. $99.95 (ISBN 0-8058-0933-3).
pap. text $45.00 (ISBN 0-8058-0074-3).
LOGO Procedures Disk to Accompany Text "Advanced Logo: A Language for Learning".
Lawrence Erlbaum Assocs. Software & Alternate Media, Inc.

Advanced Machine Design. Simha & Hsu. 1988. *Items Included:* Spiral manual contains theory, sample runs. *Customer Support:* Free phone, on-site seminars.
MS-DOS. IBM (512k). disk $140.00. *Addl. software required:* FORTRAN, hard graphics.
A Collection of Programs for the Design of Machine Elements Including Spur Gears, Stepped Shafts, 2, 3, 4 & 5 Position Synthesis of a 4 Bar Mechanism, Cayley's Construction to Find Link Lengths According to Theorem of Roberts-

TITLE INDEX

Chebychev, Kinematic & Kinetic Analysis of a 4 Bar Mechanism, 3 Position Synthesis of a Slider Crank, Path Cognate of a Slider Crank, Design of a 4 Bar Function Generator with 3 Point Accuracy Using Freudenstein's Method.
Kern International, Inc.

Advanced Manufacturing System. *Version:* 3.08. DBA Software Staff & Mike Hart. Jun. 1992. *Items Included:* Documentation. *Customer Support:* Available seperately at $75/hour purchased with software, as required. On-site available at same hourly rate.
 MS-DOS. IBM & compatibles (1Mb). $199.00 Single-User; $999.00 Multi-User; $249.00 Accounting Interface. *Networks supported:* Novell, Lantastic, M-S NT, M-S Lan Manager.
Software That Inferaces with Lake Avenue's Accounting Modules for a Complete Accounting Application. Interface Module Allows for Data Linking Between Lake's Inventory, Sales Order, Customer, Vendor & Employee Files to Download into This DBA Manufacturing Specific Add on Which Includes: Inventory Management, Purchase Orders, Bills of Material, Light Work Orders, Routing's, Advanced Work Orders, Job Costing, Estimating, Scheduling, Features & Options, Data Collections, Lot Control & Serial Control. It Is Designed for Companies with Annual Sales of 1-10 Million, (10-200 Employees).
Lake Avenue Software.

Advanced Math Graphics. 1992. *Items Included:* Detailed manuals are included with all DYNACOMP products. *Customer Support:* Free telephone support to original customer - no time limit; 30 day limited warranty.
 MS-DOS 3.2 or higher. IBM PC & compatibles, Apple (512k). $39.95 (Add $5.00 for 3 1/2" format; 5 1/4" format standard).
AMG Is a Menu-Driven Collection of Seven Programs Which Graphically (HI-RES) Demonstrate Many of the Functions & Concepts Encountered in Advance High-School & Beginning College Mathematics. Subject Areas Covered Are: Polynomial Functions, Rational Polynomials, Trigonometric Functions, Polar Plotting, Conic Sections (2D), Conic Sections (3D), Fourier Series.
Dynacomp, Inc.

Advanced Netware: Network Operating System. *Version:* 2.0a. Jun. 1986. *Compatible Hardware:* IBM PC & compatibles, PC AT, PC XT with hard disk. *Operating System(s) Required:* PC-DOS/MS-DOS 2.0, 2.1, 3.0, 3.1, 3.2. *Memory Required:* 512k.
 disk $1595.00 (Order no.: 883-XX-XXX).
Local Area Network (LAN) Operating System Software, Which Runs on 27 Different LAN Hardware Configurations. Up to 50 Workstations Can Be Connected to each File Server & Multiple File Servers Are Supported.
Novell, Inc.

Advanced Netware-286 Network Operating System. Oct. 1985. *Compatible Hardware:* IBM PC & compatibles, PC AT, PC XT with hard disk. *Operating System(s) Required:* PC-DOS/MS-DOS 2.0, 2.1, 3.0, 3.1. *Memory Required:* 512k.
 $1,695.00-$2,190.00.
Local Area Network (LAN) Operating System Software, Which Supports 27 Different LAN Hardware Configurations. Each File Server Can Support up to 100 Workstations. Multiple File Servers Are Supported.
Novell, Inc.

Advanced Professional Services Monitor. *Compatible Hardware:* TRS-80 Model I Level I, Model II, Model III, Model 4, Model 12, Model 16. *Operating System(s) Required:* TRSDOS, CP/M. *Language(s):* BASIC. *Memory Required:* 64k.
 disk $350.00.
Provides Support for Professional Consultants; e.g. Attorneys, Salespersons, Productivity Analysts. Input Includes Employee Data, Changes in Business Categories & Other Variables. Trends Are Plotted over Time, over Money Billed & over Revenue per Unit of Time. Also Features User-Selected Variables & Prompted Data Entry.
Advance Computer Concepts, Inc.

Advanced Programming ROM. *Compatible Hardware:* HP 85, 86/87.
 HP 85. ROM cartridge $195.00 (Order no.: 00085-15005).
 HP 86/87. (Order no.: 00087-15005).
Extends Control over Data Programs & Series 80 System Operations with the Functions, Statements, & Commands Provided.
Hewlett-Packard Co.

Advanced Programming Techniques for Your ATARI Including Graphics & Voice Programs. Linda M. Schreiber. 1983. *Compatible Hardware:* Atari 400, 800. *Operating System(s) Required:* Apple DOS. *Memory Required:* 16k.
 disk $39.95, incl. bk. (ISBN 0-8306-5021-0, Order no.: 5021C).
Shows How to Get the Most Out of Micro's Sound & Graphics Capabilities.
TAB Bks.

Advanced Revelation. *Version:* 3.0. *Compatible Hardware:* Intel-based PC using 286 or higher microprocessor. *Operating System(s) Required:* MS-DOS 3.1 or higher, OS/2. *Memory Required:* RAM 640k. *General Requirements:* Hard disk (7 Mb free disk space); one 5.25" (1.2 Mb) or 3.5" (1.44 Mb) disk drive. *Items Included:* Workstation manuals. *Customer Support:* First 3 months free; $400 per year thereafter.
 disk $1195.00.
A Complete Application Development Environment for PCs & LANs. Includes an Advanced Set of Development Tools Coupled with a Relational Database Management System. Features Include: Rapid Application Generator, Active Data Dictionary, ANSI SQL-Compatible Development & Programming Tools, & Intelligent Gateway Technology That Seamlessly & Simultaneously Accesses Diverse Data Formats (i.e., DBZ, dBASE, SQL Server ORACLE, NetWare SQL, Lotus 1-2-3).
Revelation Technologies, Inc.

Advanced Revelation: Runtime. Oct. 1987. Intel-based PC using 286 or higher microprocessor. disk $200.00 (ISBN 0-923387-04-8). Nonstandard peripherals required: 2Mb hard disk.
Creates an Execute-Only Version of Your Advanced Revelation Application for Cost-Effective Delivery to Users.
Revelation Technologies, Inc.

Advanced Scientific Analysis & Graphics. *Items Included:* Full manual. No other products required. *Customer Support:* Free telephone support - no time limit. 30 day warranty.
 MS-DOS 3.2 or higher. IBM & compatibles (512k). disk $129.95.
Contains 50 Interesting Programs Written in BASIC Which Can Be Run by Themselves, or Incorporated As Modules in Custom Programs. Here Are a Few of the 50 Topics Covered: GRID Draws Linear & Log Grids for Plotting; SHAD Plots a 2-D Array As a 3-D Surface; 2DFFT Displays Fourier Transform of an Array As a 3-D Map; COMPLEX Generates Bode Plots.
Dynacomp, Inc.

Advanced Scientific Analysis & Graphics. 1992. *Items Included:* Detailed manuals are included with all DYNACOMP products. *Customer Support:* Free telephone support to original customer - no time limit; 30 day limited warranty.
 MS-DOS 3.2 or higher. IBM PC & compatibles (512k). $129.95 incl. book (Add $5.00 for 3 1/2" format; 5 1/4" format standard). *Optimal configuration:* IBM, 128k, graphics adapter (color for some programs).
Contains 50 Interesting Programs Written in BASIC Which Can Be Run by Themselves, or Incorporated As Modules in Custom Programs. Topics Covered: GRID, SHAD, 3DMAP, FFT, 2DFFT, AUTO, RADTR, FACET, COMPLEX & Much More! If You Are at All Interested in Science or Engineering, This Collection Is for You.
Dynacomp, Inc.

Advanced String Library. *Compatible Hardware:* Apple Macintosh, IBM PC. *Memory Required:* 1000k. *General Requirements:* True BASIC. 3.5" disk $79.95.
Programming Tools Package.
True BASIC, Inc.

Advanced SystemPac. DBI Software Products. *Compatible Hardware:* TI Professional with printer. *Operating System(s) Required:* MS-DOS, CP/M-86. *Memory Required:* 64k.
 $695.00.
Data Base Management System, File Handler, File Manager, Form Generator & a BASIC Code Generator.
Texas Instruments, Personal Productivit.

Advanced Training for dBase 4. *Version:* 2. Jacqueline Jonas. 1989. *Items Included:* Quick Reference Guide, audio tapes, practice disk. *Customer Support:* 30 day-right of return; Editorial support for course content/exercises.
 DOS. IBM & compatibles. disk $175.00 (ISBN 0-917792-66-1, Order no.: 306). *Addl. software required:* dBase IV.
Self-paced training for advanced techniques in using dBase IV to query & get reports from databases.
OneOnOne Computer Training.

Advanced Training for Lotus 1-2-3 for Windows: Graphs & Charts. Charles R. Wolf. 1991. *Items Included:* Data disk, quick reference guide. *Customer Support:* Call with questions about taking the course or course exercises.
 Windows. IBM. disk $95.00 (ISBN 1-56562-010-0).
Self-Studio, Audio-Based Course for Lotus 1-2-3 for Windows Teaches Advanced Charting & Spreadsheet Publishing.
OneOnOne Computer Training.

Advanced Training for Lotus 1-2-3 for Windows: Macros. B. Alan August. 1991. *Items Included:* Data disk, quick reference guide. *Customer Support:* Call with questions about taking the course or course exercises.
 Windows. IBM. disk $95.00 (ISBN 1-56562-008-9).
Self-Studio, Audio-Based Course for Lotus 1-2-3 for Windows Teaches Advanced Macro Creation & Editing Techniques; Loop Macros & Autoexecute Macros, Much More.
OneOnOne Computer Training.

Advanced Training for Lotus 1-2-3 Rel. 1 for Windows: Functions & Analysis. Charles R. Wolf. 1991. *Items Included:* Data disk, quick reference guide. *Customer Support:* Call with questions about taking the course or course exercises.
 Windows. IBM. disk $95.00 (ISBN 1-56562-009-7).

Self-Studio, Audio-Based Course for Lotus 1-2-3 for Windows Teaches Advanced Techniques for Creating Formulas & Using Functions & Solving Common Business Problems.
OneOnOne Computer Training.

Advanced Training for Lotus 1-2-3 Rel. 5 for Windows. Version: 5. Charles R. Wolf. 1995. *Items Included:* Data disk, quick reference guide. *Customer Support:* Call with questions about taking the course or course exercises.
Windows. IBM. disk $175.00 (ISBN 1-56562-062-3).
Self-Studio, Audio-Based Course for Lotus 1-2-3 Teaches Creating, Saving, Editing, Printing Spreadsheets; Includes Creating Formulas, Using Functions, Creating Simple Graphs & Macros.
OneOnOne Computer Training.

Advanced Training for Microsoft Excel for Windows 95. Version: 7. B. Alan August. 1996. *Items Included:* Data disk, quick reference guide. *Customer Support:* Call with questions about taking the course or course exercises.
Windows. IBM. disk $175.00 (ISBN 1-56562-073-9).
Self-Studio, Audio-Based Course for Excel for Windows 95 Teaches Advanced Techniques for Editing Formulas, Using/Applying Functions, Creating & Editing Macros, Using Modules, Advanced Types of Graphs & More.
OneOnOne Computer Training.

Advanced Training for Microsoft Excel for Windows. Version: 5. B. Alan August. 1995. *Items Included:* Data disk, quick reference guide. *Customer Support:* Call with questions about taking the course or course exercises.
Windows. IBM. disk $175.00 (ISBN 1-56562-063-1).
Self-Studio, Audio-Based Course for Excel for Windows Teaches Advanced Techniques with Formulas, Functions, Graphing & Macros.
OneOnOne Computer Training.

Advanced Training for Microsoft Word for Windows. Version: 6.0. Linda K. Schwartz. 1995. *Items Included:* Data disk, quick reference guide. *Customer Support:* Call with questions about taking the course or the course exercises.
Windows. IBM. disk $175.00 (ISBN 1-56562-066-6).
Self-Studio, Audio-Based Course for WinWord 6, Teaches Advanced Merges, Macros, Styles & Style Sheets, Importing Files & Graphics.
OneOnOne Computer Training.

Advanced Training for Paradox: Managing Data. Version: 4.0. Jacqueline Jonas. 1992. *Items Included:* Quick Reference Guide, audio tapes, practice disk. *Customer Support:* 30 day-right of return; Editorial support for course content/exercises.
DOS. IBM & compatibles. disk $95.00 (ISBN 1-56562-024-0, Order no.: 312). *Addl. software required:* Paradox.
Advanced database techniques for queries, reports, & data analysis.
OneOnOne Computer Training.

Advanced Training for Paradox: Personal Programmer. Version: 4.0. Jacqueline Jonas. 1992. *Items Included:* Quick Reference Guide, audio tapes, practice disk. *Customer Support:* 30 day-right of return; Editorial support for course content/exercises.
DOS. IBM & compatibles. disk $95.00 (ISBN 1-56562-023-2, Order no.: 314). *Addl. software required:* Paradox.
Self-paced training for using the Personal Programmer of Paradox to create, edit & run scripts; includes debugging & other advanced techniques.
OneOnOne Computer Training.

Advanced Training for Quattro Pro: Graphs & Charts. Version: 2 & 3. B. Alan August. 1992. *Items Included:* Quick Reference Guide, audio tapes, practice disk. *Customer Support:* 30 day-right of return; Editorial support for course content/exercises.
DOS. IBM & compatibles. disk $95.00 (ISBN 0-917792-91-2, Order no.: 248). *Addl. software required:* Quattro Pro.
Self-paced training for advanced techniques for graphing & charting (creating, editing, printing) with Quattro Pro through version 4.
OneOnOne Computer Training.

Advanced Training for Quattro Pro: Macros. Version: 2 & 3. B. Alan August. 1991. *Items Included:* Quick Reference Guide, audio tapes, practice disk. *Customer Support:* 30 day-right of return; Editorial support for course content/exercises.
DOS. IBM & compatibles. disk $95.00 (ISBN 0-917792-89-0, Order no.: 246). *Addl. software required:* Quattro Pro.
Advanced techniques for macros with Quattro Pro 2 & 3.
OneOnOne Computer Training.

Advanced Training for Quattro Pro (Versions 2 & 3): Formulas & Functions. Version: 2 & 3. B. Alan August. 1991. *Items Included:* Quick Reference Guide, audio tapes, practice disk. *Customer Support:* 30 day-right of return; Editorial support for course content/exercises.
DOS. IBM & compatibles. disk $95.00 (ISBN 0-917792-90-4, Order no.: 244). *Addl. software required:* Quattro Pro.
Self-paced training for advanced techniques with formulas & functions of Quattro Pro versions 2 & 3.
OneOnOne Computer Training.

Advanced Training for WordPerfect. Version: 5.X. Sally Hargrave. 1990. *Items Included:* Quick Reference Guide, audio tapes, practice disk. *Customer Support:* 30 day-right of return; Editorial support for course content/exercises.
DOS. IBM & compatibles. disk $175.00 (ISBN 0-917792-68-8, Order no.: 430). *Addl. software required:* WordPerfect 5.1.
Self-paced training in advanced macro & merge techniques for WordPerfect 5.1.
OneOnOne Computer Training.

Advanced Trianing for WordPerfect for Windows. Version: 6.1. Kimi Nance & Sally Hargrave. 1995. *Items Included:* Data disk, quick reference guide. *Customer Support:* Call with questions about taking the course or course exercises.
Windows. IBM. disk $175.00 (ISBN 1-56562-065-8).
Self-Studio, Audio-Based Course for WordPerfect 6.1 for Windows Teaches Advanced Merges, Macros & Styles.
OneOnOne Computer Training.

AdvanceLink. *Compatible Hardware:* HP 150 Touchscreen, IBM PC. *Operating System(s) Required:* PC-DOS/MS-DOS 2.0 or higher. *Memory Required:* 256k. *General Requirements:* Touch screen for IBM.
HP. 3.5" disk $295.00 (Order no.: 45431A).
IBM. disk $295.00 (Order no.: 45431E).
Transfers Data Files Between the Personal Computer & the HP 3000 System, IBM PCs, Touchscreens, Public Data Bases, etc. The CREATE REMOTE Capability Allows Applications That Run on Remote Hosts to Be Installed into RAM.
Hewlett-Packard Co.

ADVANTAGE C++. AT&T. *Compatible Hardware:* IBM PC & compatibles, AT&T. *Operating System(s) Required:* PC-DOS, MS-DOS, UNIX, XENIX. *Memory Required:* 512k. *General Requirements:* Compatible C compiler.
contact publisher for price.
PC Implementation of AT&T's Object-Oriented Language, Including Full Support for MICROSOFT WINDOWS. Fully Compatible with All Existing C Source Code, Libraries, & Tools & Supports Object-Oriented Programming. Provides Features That Include Stronger Type Checking, Data Abstraction, Inheritance, Operator Overloading, a Broad Selection of Language Constructs, etc. Other Improvements over Traditional C Include Symbolic Constants, Inline Substitution of Functions, Default Function Argument, Free Storage Management Operations, & a Reference Type. Full C++ Source Level Debugging Is Provided for CodeView & PIX. Supports Virtual Models.
Lifeboat Assocs.

ADVANTAGE Disassembler. *Compatible Hardware:* IBM PC & compatibles. *Operating System(s) Required:* CP/M-86, PC-DOS/MS-DOS 2.0 or higher. *Memory Required:* 256k.
contact publisher for price.
Memory-Resident Program That Gives Programmers the Ability to Disassemble Executable Source Files (.EXE & .COM Files) to Produce Documented Assembly Language Source Code. The Programmer Can Add Additional Comments, Make Changes to Code, Define Labels for Subroutines, Data Areas or I/O Port Addresses, Check Conflicts in Memory, or Add More Code. The File Can Then Be Reassembled Including Those Modifications Made During Disassembly. Will Display the Contents of Memory in Hex/ASCII Format, Helping Users Decide Which Areas to Mark As Data in the Control Table As Part of the Disassembly Process. Allows Users to Suspend Disassembly at Any Point, Save the Intermediate Results, & Later Resume the Disassembly Process. Supports the 8087/80287 Math Coprocessors. Includes Two Tutorials Providing Example Disassembly of .EXE & .COM Files.
Lifeboat Assocs.

ADVANTAGE Graphics. *Compatible Hardware:* IBM PC, PC XT, PC AT. *Operating System(s) Required:* PC-DOS 2.0 or higher. *Memory Required:* 192k.
contact publisher for price.
Graphics Development Toolkit for C-Based Graphics Applications. Provides an Expanded Set of Graphics Drawing Functions, Device Independence over a Broad Range of Graphics Peripherals, & an Open Development Environment That Allows Full Access to All Levels of the Graphics System. Through a Series of External Data Structure Interfaces, Its Open Hardware Architecture Allows Developers to Define Support for New Custom Graphics Peripherals Not Directly Provided or to Implement Special Device-Independent Graphics Algorithms. Supports Multi-Window Desktop Applications, Treating Each Window As a Logically Separate & Independent Display. Package Includes ADVANTAGE PLOT, a Support Pack Which Adds Pen Plotter Output Capabilities to the Application. Includes Support for Both Direct Plotter Output & Spooled Plotter Operations.
Lifeboat Assocs.

ADVANTAGE Link. *Compatible Hardware:* IBM PC, PC XT, PC AT. *Operating System(s) Required:* PC-DOS/MS-DOS 2.0 or higher. *Memory Required:* 256k.
contact publisher for price.
Linker That Will Generate Symbol Tables for the CodeView Debugger Included in the

MICROSOFT C & FORTRAN Compilers. Takes Full Advantage of Expanded Memory (EMS). Will Operate with Any Language Which Delivers Object Modules in the INTEL Relocatable File Format for the 8086/8088 Chip Family & Libraries in the INTEL or MICROSOFT Library Indexing Format. The Program Is a Two Pass Linkage Editor Which Combines All Object User Specifies, Finds & Extracts Routines Called by Other Modules, Assigns Variables & Routines (Symbols) to Memory Areas & Addresses, Supplies All Routines with the Addresses, Supplies All Routines with the Addresses of the Symbols They Have Mentioned External to Themselves, Re-Orders Link Script Files into Optimal Sequences for Finding All References, Has No "Ancestor Worship." Overlays Can Call Other Overlays Without Restrictions. Provides 54 Commands.
Lifeboat Assocs.

ADVANTAGE Make. *Compatible Hardware:* IBM PC & compatibles. *Operating System(s) Required:* PC-DOS/MS-DOS 2.0 or higher. *Memory Required:* 128k.
contact publisher for price.
MS-DOS Version of the UNIX MAKE Utility. Useful for Software Projects Being Developed by Several Programmers. Keeps Track of File Dependencies & Automates the Output Generation Process Ensuring That Only Those Modules Which Have Been Changed or Are Dependent upon Change Are Updated, Thus Eliminating Re-Assembling of Modules Which Have Not Been Modified. Support Batch Files, Multiple Targets in a Single Definition, Intrinsic Surrounds & Full Pathname Definitions. Also Supports UNIX MAKE Scripts, Self-Referencing Macros, & Includes Files to Process Multiple Files. A Debugging Option Is Also Provided.
Lifeboat Assocs.

ADVANTAGE 386 C. *Compatible Hardware:* 8086/286/386-based system to develop, 80386-based system to run. *Memory Required:* 512k. *General Requirements:* Hard disk.
contact publisher for price.
Extended Version of the C Language Designed to Take Advantage of the 80386 Chip As Well As to Allow Programmers to Develop PC Software Products That Will Run on 386 PC's. Includes an ANSI Subset for Portable Applications. Provides Code Generation with Optimizations: Automatic Allocation of Variables to Registers, Cross-Jumping, Common Subexpressing, & Dead Code Elimination. Produces a Listing of Source Input with Generated Code Interleaved with Mnemonics, Addresses, & Hexadecimal Encoding of Instructions. Supports Embedded Applications & Symbolic Debuggers. Compatible with PHAR LAP's Products for 386 Applications Development under 386/DOS Extender.
Lifeboat Assocs.

ADVANTAGE 386 Pascal. *Compatible Hardware:* 8086/286/386-based system to develop, 80386-based system to run. *Memory Required:* 512k. *General Requirements:* Hard disk.
contact publisher for price.
Extended Version of PASCAL Allowing Users to Develop 386 Protected Mode Applications in This High Level Language. Designed for Professional Programmers, It Compiles Large Systems of Modules & Squeezes Programs into Small (Embedded) Spaces. Includes an ANSI Subset for Portable Applications. Produces ROMable Code for Embedded Applications. Supports Five Memory Models: Small, Compact, Medium, Big, & Large. Features User Error Reporting & Recovery. The Enhanced PASCAL Type-Protection (with Optional Override) Allows for Easier Bug Detection.
Lifeboat Assocs.

ADVANTAGE Version Control Management System (VCMS). *Compatible Hardware:* IBM PC, PC XT, PC AT. *Operating System(s) Required:* MS-DOS 2.0 or higher. *Memory Required:* 512k. *General Requirements:* Hard disk; ANSI X3.64(VT-100), VT-52 or H19 compatible.
contact publisher for price.
Set of Programs Designed to Increase Productivity by Eliminating Redundant Tasks Associated with Software Development. Will Maintain a Complete Revision History for Each Module in a Project, Provide Text Compression to Reduce Storage, Maintain Automatic Audit Trail Records & Reports, Support Revision Branching, Networking, Wild Card, & Exception Cases. Includes a High Level MAKE Utility Which Will Automatically Reconstruct Any Version of a Product Using a Single Command. Also Included Is a Full Screen, Menu-Driven Shell Which Hides the Details of Running the Tools & Speeds Development.
Lifeboat Assocs.

AdvanTax: 1040 Tax Preparation System. *Version:* 11.0. Feb. 1989. *Compatible Hardware:* IBM PC & compatible, THEOS compatible. *Operating System(s) Required:* MS-DOS, THEOS, UNIX. *Language(s):* THEOS BASIC, UX-BASIC. *Customer Support:* On-line.
1st year $1000.00.
Federal & State Tax Preparation Package Designed for Accountant or Tax Professional for Use in Personal Interview. Entry Screens Are IRS Form Oriented. IRS Approved Computer Generated Return. Proformas.
Comcepts Systems.

Adventure. *Compatible Hardware:* HP 150 Touchscreen, HP 110 Portable; HP Series 200 Personal Technical Computers 216/220 with BASIC 2.0 or 3.0, HP 217/237 with BASIC 3.0.
HP 150. 3.5" disk $39.95 (Order no.: 92443D). HP 216/220, 217/237. (Order no.: 92244GA).
Offers More Than 100 Rooms to Explore, 15 Treasures to Collect, & Many Objects to Locate & Use During Your Journey Through the Cave. Be Prepared to Encounter Many Dangers As You Venture into the Fascinating World of the Colossal Cave.
Hewlett-Packard Co.

Adventure Game. *Compatible Hardware:* TRS-80.
contact publisher for price.
Instant Software, Inc.

Adventure International Series. *Compatible Hardware:* TI 99/4A.
disk, cartridge, or cassette - contact publisher for price.
With the Adventure Cartridge & One of the 11 Cassette- or Disk-Based Games, You Can Experience Many Different Adventures.
Texas Instruments, Personal Productivit.

The Adventure System. *Compatible Hardware:* TRS-80 Model I, Model III. *Language(s):* Machine Language. *Memory Required:* 48k.
disk or tape with manual $39.95.
Permits User to Create Individualized Adventure Games.
The Alternate Source.

Adventure: The Original by Crowther & Woods. *Compatible Hardware:* Apple Macintosh; 9000 Series, 200, 300, 520, 9845. *Language(s):* BASIC.
HP. disk $29.95.
Macintosh. $29.95.
You Are Somewhere in Colossal Cave, Where Magic Is Said to Work. Some Who Have Entered Are Rumored to Have Never Been Seen Again. Enter & Explore, Find Treasure, Outsmart Trolls, & Experience Adventure.
James Assocs.

Adventureland. *Compatible Hardware:* TI-99/4A. disk or cassette - contact publisher for price. *Adventure Game.*
Texas Instruments, Personal Productivit.

Adventures. Jun. 1993. *Items Included:* User Guide. *Customer Support:* 30 day warranty.
Windows. IBM & compatibles (4Mb). disk $14.95 (ISBN 1-885638-02-7).
From Sailing off the Coast of Maine to Eco-Tours of the Amazon to Cooking Schools in Italy, Adventures Has It All. Filled with Full-Color Photographs, Video, Audio & Text, Adventures Offers Descriptions of More Than a Thousand Tours, Treks, Schools, Cultural Programs Throughout the World. Search by Type of Activity, Location, Time of Year, Choose specific Activities, & View In-Depth Tour Information with the Click of the Mouse.
Deep River Publishing, Inc.

Adventures in Musicland. George F. Litterst et al. 1995. *Items Included:* Manual. *Customer Support:* ECS offers technical support to registered users. Call (217) 359-7099. Other than the telephone call - technical support is no charge.
6.0.5 or higher, 256 color monitor. Macintosh (1Mb). $49.95 MSRP/$250.00 Network (Order no.: MAC-1358). *Nonstandard peripherals required:* 8Mb free hard disk drive space.
Windows 3.1 (4Mb). $49.95 MSRP/$250.00 Network (Order no.: W-1358). *Nonstandard peripherals required:* 8Mb hard disk drive space, VGA (SVGA recommended), sound card.
Set of Music Games Features Characters from Lewis Carroll's Alice in Wonderland. Players Learn Through Pictures, Sounds & Animation Which Help Develop Understanding of Musical Tones, Composers, & Musical Symbols. Games Include MusicMatch, Melody Mixup, Picture Perfect, & Sound Concentration.
Electronic Courseware Systems, Inc.

The Adventures of Batman & Robin: Interactive MovieBook. *Version:* 1.5. Nov. 1995. *Items Included:* Manual, registration card, promotional flyers. *Customer Support:* Phone technical support - toll call.
Windows 3.1 or higher. 386/33 or higher (8Mb). CD-ROM disk $29.95 (ISBN 1-57303-026-0). *Nonstandard peripherals required:* Sound card, CD-ROM drive. *Optimal configuration:* 486/33 with 8Mb RAM, Win 3.1 or higher 2X CD-ROM drive, SVGA monitor.
An Exclusively Licensed Computer Adventure/Activity Book for Children. There Are Three Complete Stories, Each with Interactive Animations, Movies, Sounds, Educational Word Activities, Puzzles & Dictionary Definitions, Plus an Optional Narrator That Reads Text Aloud As It Activates Multimedia Events. Other Activities Include Treasure Hunts, Mazes & Memory Games.
Sound Source Interactive.

The Adventures of Huckleberry Finn. *Version:* 1.5. Feb. 1995. *Items Included:* BookWorm Student Reader (diskette). *Customer Support:* 30 day MBG. Technical support (toll call) - no charge.
System 7.0 or higher. Macintosh (5Mb). CD-ROM disk $29.95 (ISBN 1-57316-024-5, Order no.: 16159). *Nonstandard peripherals required:* CD-ROM drive, 12" color monitor. *Optimal configuration:* 13" color monitor recommended.
Windows 3.1 or higher. IBM compatible (MPC) 386 DX (4Mb). CD-ROM disk $29.95. *Nonstandard peripherals required:* Standard multimedia compatible CD-ROM. *Optimal*

configuration: 8Mb RAM recommended, 256 color monitor recommended.
Since 1884, Mark Twain's Classic American Novel Has Fascinated Generations of Readers Young & Old. Incorporating All of the Features Available in the BookWorm Student Library, This Edition, Rendered Directly from the Author's Original Manuscript, Includes the Original Illustrations As Well As Easy-to-Use Annotations That Explain All of the Colloquial Language in the Text. Features Complete Sound Allowing the User to Listen to All or Part of Each Work.
Communication & Information Technologies, Inc. (CIT).

The Adventures of Notationman: A Computerized Introduction to Labanotation. Georgette Gorchoff. Oct. 1992.
System 7. Macintosh II or higher. 3.5" disk $50.00 (ISBN 1-878084-05-4).
Teaches the Method of Recording Bodily Movement (as in a Dance) by Means of Direction & Other Symbols That Can Be Aligned with Musical Accompaniment.
Danscores.

The Adventures of Ricky Racoon: Lost in the Woods. Jan. 1996. *Items Included:* School version contains CD & teacher's resource guide. Consumer version contains CD & parent's guide. *Customer Support:* 1-800-824-5179 product information; 1-800-543-0453 technical support.
Windows 3.1 or higher. 486 SX 25MHz (4Mb). CD-ROM disk $49.95 (ISBN 0-538-66550-5). *Nonstandard peripherals required:* Double speed CD-ROM, 256 color driver, sound blaster of 100% compatible sound card.
Macintosh, Power Mac compatible. 68030 (5Mb). CD-ROM disk $49.95 (ISBN 0-538-64291-2). *Nonstandard peripherals required:* Double speed CD-ROM.
A CD-ROM Based Multimedia Program Aimed at Children Ages 6 to 10. Using High Quality, Engaging, & Entertaining Software, the Young Learner Is Challenged to Read & Write at an Accelerated Pace & Be Thoroughly Entertained. Includes Language Arts & Science Activities.
South-Western Publishing Co.

The Adventures of Tom Sawyer. Version: 1.5. Feb. 1995. *Items Included:* BookWorm Student Reader (diskette). *Customer Support:* 30 day MBG. Technical support (toll call) - no charge.
System 7.0 or higher. Macintosh (5Mb). CD-ROM disk $29.95 (ISBN 1-57316-025-3, Order no.: 16160). *Nonstandard peripherals required:* CD-ROM drive, 12" color monitor. *Optimal configuration:* 13" color monitor recommended.
Windows 3.1 or higher. IBM compatible (MPC) 386 DX (4Mb). CD-ROM disk $29.95. *Nonstandard peripherals required:* Standard multimedia compatible CD-ROM. *Optimal configuration:* 8Mb RAM recommended, 256 color monitor recommended.
Out of Boyhood Memories Growing up on the Mississippi, Mark Twain Has Created a Cast of Characters That Continue to Entertain Children of All Ages. This Edition Includes Complete, Unabridged Text & In-Dept Critical Commentaries Extracted from Articles Written by Leading Authorities on Mark Twain & His Work. Features Complete Sound Allowing the User to Listen to All or Part of Each Work.
Communication & Information Technologies, Inc. (CIT).

Adverse Impact Monitor. Version: 8.16. May 1992. *Items Included:* Step-by-step user's manual in 3-ring binder & cloth covered slipcase. *Customer Support:* Telephone technical support for 90 days included in purchase price; extended technical support with toll free number cost $150.00 for 12 months.
MS/PC-DOS 2.1 or higher. IBM PC, PS/2 & compatible (512k). disk $400.00.
Performs Adverse Impact Calculations Required in Affirmative Action Plans. Calculates Impact Ratios for Hires, Promotions, Transfers, Terminations, & User-Defined Transactions. Processes Summary Employee Activity Information That Can Be Imported from Mainframe or Microcomputer or Entered Manually. Performs Adverse Impact Analyses by Race, Gender, & Age Using the Same Methodology Accepted by the OFCCP. Sorts Data by Job Group, Department, Job Title, & Date for Report Flexibility. Does Not Require Any Special Computer Training.
PRI Assocs., Inc.

Advertiser & Agency Red Books Plus.
MS-DOS. IBM or compatibles. CD-ROM disk $1195.00 for 1 year (Order no.: RB110). CD-ROM disk $3406.00 for 3 years.
Details on 33,000 corporate advertisers, including sales volume, budgets, media usage, & more. Names & titles of more than 197,000 corporate & agency personnel in management, creative, & media positions. Records on 12,000 domestic & international advertising agencies & branch officers. Descirptions & cross-references to the 62,000 products & services handled by entrants. Automatically retrieve full agency profiles from the advertiser record.
R. R. Bowker.

Advertising Edge. May 1989. *Items Included:* User manual & software tutorials. *Customer Support:* 30 day money back guarantee, free phone support, on line tutorials & help in software.
DOS or O/S2 (256k). IBM PC, XT, AT, PS/2 or compatibles. $109.00 (US & Canada), $149.00 (International). *Nonstandard peripherals required:* CGA, EGA, VGA, or Hercules graphics board. *Addl. software required:* Lotus 1-2-3 release 2. 2.01, 2.2, or 3. *Optimal configuration:* IBM PCAT, DOS 2.1 or higher, 640k RAM, EGA board, 1-2-3 release 2 or higher. *Networks supported:* All that are supported by Lotus 1-2-3.
Provides Expert Criteria for Quickly Developing the Framework for a Successful Ad, & a Success Rating System for Evaluating (Approving or Disapproving) Proposed Advertising Programs, Ensures a Well Targeted Ad for the Intended Audience. Provides a Consistent Advertising Evaluation System & Ensures the Effectivity of Advertising Expenditures.
Successware.

The Advertizer. May 1984. *Compatible Hardware:* IBM PC, PC XT, PC AT. *Memory Required:* 64k.
disk $39.00.
Menu Driven Software Turns the PC into a Text Slide Projector. Provides Two Size Letter Fonts. Runs Continuously.
Sylvia Products.

AEasy. Version: 4.5. Aug. 1987. *Items Included:* Comprehensive manual, sample tutorial, tutorial data files. *Customer Support:* 90 days free telephone support & program updates after purchase. Unlimited, toll free, telephone support & updates for 1 year $400-$1300. Maintenance for 1 year $250-$690. Training classes available nationally or at Timberline Corporate. Timberline National certified consultant network. Timberline consultants are also available.
MS-DOS. IBM PC XT, PC AT, PS/2, & 100% compatibles (640k). single-user starting at $1390.00; multi-user starting at $1990.00. *Nonstandard peripherals required:* 1 diskette drive, 1 hard drive, printer. *Networks supported:* Local area networks including Novell Advanced NetWare, IBM LAN Server & Microsoft LAN Manager.
Financial Management Software Designed for the Small to Medium Sized Architect & Engineering Firm. AEasy Reduces the Time It Takes User to Manage Projects & Analyze Performance. Major Benefits Include: Simple Setup, Ease of Use, No Employee Limits, Security Integration, Pop-Up Windows, "On-the-Fly" Setup of Project/Phases & Vendors During Entry, & Flexible Invoicing Producing Accurate Accounts Receivable Statements to Help Ensure a Steady Cash Flow. Also a Fully Integrated Accounting Package.
Timberline Software Corp.

AEasy Plus. Version: 4.5. Aug. 1991. *Items Included:* Full documentation, sample tutorial, & sample tutorial datafiles. *Customer Support:* 90 days free support.
DOS 3.1 or higher. IBM PC XT, AT, PS/2 & 100% compatibles. disk $2390.00 first station. *Nonstandard peripherals required:* Hard disk required.
Gives User Timely Information to Assist in Making Business Decisions on a Firm's Project & Financial Position. Major Benefits Include: Simple Set-Up, Ease of Use, 11 Flexible Billing Types, Comprehensive Reporting, Historical Detail Stored Indefinitely, Departmentalization, Ability to Void an Invoice & Reinstate Work in Process at Any Time. Also a Fully Integrated Accounting Package.
Timberline Software Corp.

Aegis Animagic. Version: 1.1. Gary Bonham. Jul. 1990. *Customer Support:* Unlimited toll support.
Amiga DOS. Amiga (512). 3.5" disk $99.95.
Creates Over 200,000 Effects with Animations & Images.
Oxxi, Inc.

Aegis Audiomaster III. Peter Norman. Sep. 1990. *Items Included:* Co-player software, oscilliscope software. *Customer Support:* Free phone support.
Amiga DOS (512k). 3.5" disk $99.95.
Sound Editor. Samples Sounds in up to 56k SPS. Wide Range of Special Effects, Including Flange & Echo.
Oxxi, Inc.

Aegis Express Paint. Steve Vermilian. Jan. 1989. *Customer Support:* Free phone support.
Amiga (512k). 3.5" disk $139.98.
Full-Featured Paint Program for Amiga. Includes Postscript Support.
Oxxi, Inc.

AEGIS: Guardian of the Fleet. Mar. 1994. *Customer Support:* Free phone-in assistance with game-playing & technical questions.
MS-DOS 5.0. IBM PC compatible 386SX, 386DX, 486 (570k). CD-ROM disk $89.95. *Nonstandard peripherals required:* Supports 256 color VGA or VESA-compatible SVGA video cards. *Optimal configuration:* 640k RAM, 2Mb, EMS, SoundBlaster, 1Mb SVGA Video Card.
CD-ROM Based Modern Naval Warfare Simulation, Spanning 1982-2002 Naval Career As Captain of an Aegis Class Cruiser. Actual Video Footage of Weapons Systems, Ships & Aircraft, Political & Diplomatic Challenges As Well As Highly Realistic Combat Situations.

Aegis Oran 2000. Bill Volk. Aug. 1980. *Customer Support:* Free phone support.
Amiga DOS (512k). 3.5" disk $279.95.
Full-Featured Amiga CAD. Program Includes Auto-Dimension, & Full Plotter Support.
Oxxi, Inc.

TITLE INDEX

Aegis Showcase FX. Tony Kubis. Feb. 1989. *Customer Support:* Free phone support.
Finder (2Mb). MAC II. disk $395.00.
Videotitler for Macintosh.
Oxxi, Inc.

Aegis Sonix. *Version:* 2.0. Mark Riley. Jan. 1988. *Customer Support:* Free phone.
Amiga (512k). 3.5" disk $29.98.
Allows User to Score Songs & Play them Back with Extreme Clarity. Includes Built-In Synthesizor to Create Personal Notes.
Oxxi, Inc.

Aegis Videoscape 3D. *Version:* 2.02. Alan Hastings. Sep. 1988. *Items Included:* Pro/Motion motion system. *Customer Support:* Free phone support.
Amiga (512k). 3.5" disk $199.95.
Fast 3-D Animation Program.
Oxxi, Inc.

Aegis Videotitler 3D. Gary Bonham. Sep. 1990. *Customer Support:* Free phone support.
Amiga (1Mb). 3.5" disk $159.95.
Creates Text with Over 100 Styles, Then Animates Them.
Oxxi, Inc.

Aeris for Windows, Aeris for MS-DOS. *Version:* 2.0. Scott Kelley. Sep. 1993. *Items Included:* Free bonus Aeris ScriptPak, which includes example date & time scripts that calculate new dates & times (handles holidays & weekends), 96 page, printed bound end-users manual. *Customer Support:* 90 days free support; optional support available thereafter.
MS-DOS. IBM PC & compatibles (640k). disk $45.95, Quantity discounts, site licenses available (Order no.: (509) 468-1434).
Optimal configuration: MS-DOS 3.0 or higher, 286 or higher, 640k memory, hard disk.
Networks supported: All NetBIOS Networks compatible.
Microsoft Windows. IBM PC & compatibles (2Mb). disk $45.95, Quantity discounts, site licenses available (Order no.: 509-468-1434). *Nonstandard peripherals required:* EGA monitor or higher. *Optimal configuration:* Windows 3.1 or higher, 386 or higher, 2Mb memory, hard disk, EGA monitor or higher. *Networks supported:* All NetBIOS Networks compatible.
Delivers Automated File Processing. Customizable Pull-Down Menus, Dialogs, Pick Lists. Built-In Scripts Handle Reformatting, Pattern Matching, Paste, Replace, View, & Search of File Contents, Columns, Records, Fields. Multiple Key Sorts, Cuts, Merges. Filter, Convert Files. Complex Searching. Change Line Terminators. Calculates Dates, Times. International Formats. Network Capable. Dynamic Language.
BlueRithm Software.

The Aerobics Master. *Version:* 10.8. Roger W. Bodo. 1983. *Compatible Hardware:* Apple II, II+, IIc, IIe, & compatibles; Franklin Ace. *Operating System(s) Required:* Apple DOS 3.3, ProDOS. *Language(s):* BASIC (source code included). *Memory Required:* 48k. *Items Included:* Operation instructions booklet. *Customer Support:* By phone, evenings.
Apple. disk $19.95.
Records & Computes Value of Daily Aerobic Exercise. Accumulates & Computes Data Averages & Shows Exercise Progress in List or Chart Form.
Bodo, Bodo & Co., Inc.

Aesop's Fables. Feb. 1995. *Items Included:* CD-ROM booklet. *Customer Support:* Free technical support via phone as of release date.
MPC/Windows. 386.25 or higher IBM compatible (4Mb). CD-ROM disk $29.95 (ISBN 1-885784-12-0, Order no.: 1172). *Optimal configuration:* MPC CD-ROM player, S-VGA graphics card (640x480x256 colors) with compatible monitor, MPC compliant sound card, mouse, Windows 3.1.
Discover the Morals of Aesop's Fables As They Are Brought to Life Through Multimedia Interaction. The Wise & Witty Tales Aesop Wrote More Than 2500 Years Ago Are Modernized by Colorful Illustrations, Dictionary-Linked Hot Spots & Narrates Whose Voices Invite Children to Read Along. The Morals Are Ageless.
Technology Dynamics Corp.

AffiniFile. *Version:* 1.1. *Compatible Hardware:* Apple Macintosh. *Memory Required:* 512k.
3.5" disk $79.95.
Office-Management Utility Providing Quick Access to Notes & Graphs.
Affinity Microsystems, Ltd.

Afikoman Adventure. *Compatible Hardware:* Apple II+, IIe, IIc. *Language(s):* BASIC, Assembly. *Memory Required:* 48k.
disk $14.95.
Game in Which Player Must Attempt to Find the Afikoman, an Elusive Fragment of Matzoh Eaten at the Conclusion of the Seder Meal. Exploration of New Worlds.
Davka Corp.

A4. *Version:* 3.1. *Customer Support:* 30 days included, customization available.
Macintosh SE/30 or higher (2Mb). disk $3595.00. *Nonstandard peripherals required:* Hard disk drive (20Mb).
fully functional demo $30.00.
Accounting, Sales Lead Tracking & Business Communications Program.
Softek Design, Inc.

AfroRoman. *Version:* 5.1. Nov. 1993. *Items Included:* User manual, Keyboard Layout Chart, Keycap Sticker Sheet. *Customer Support:* Free telephone support, defective disks replaced.
Macintosh. Macintosh (1Mb). 3.5" disk $99.95. *Addl. software required:* Any Word Processor. *Optimal configuration:* 4Mb RAM & a hard drive.
(Roman Script) Times-Style African Languages Font. Includes Afrikaans, Akan, Akuapim, Asante, Brong, Hausa, Santi, Swahili, Twi, Zulu (Bantu), Zulu-Kafir, & Many More (Including American Indian & European Languages). Over 130 Languages in One Font! ATM-Compatible, Type-1 & TrueType Plain, Bold, Italic, & Bold-Italic Fonts. Features 41 Overstrike Accents with Automatic, Non-Deleting Backspacing. Also Includes EuroScript System for Ease in Typing.
Linguist's Software, Inc.

AfroRoman for Windows. *Version:* 2.0. Mar. 1994. *Items Included:* User manual, Keyboard Layout Chart, Keycap Sticker Sheet, & ANSI Chart. *Customer Support:* Free telephone support, defective disks replaced.
Windows. IBM & compatibles (4Mb). disk $99.95. *Addl. software required:* Microsoft Windows or ATM. *Optimal configuration:* 4Mb RAM & 386.
(Roman Script) African Lanuages Font, As Well As American Indian & European Languages - over 130 Languages in One Font! Contains Professional-Quality, Hinted, Plain, Bold, Bold-Italic, & Italic Styles. Type 1 Works with ATM & Windows; Also Works with Word 6 for DOS, WordPerfect 6.06 for DOS, OS/2 & AutoCAD r.13. WordPerfect for Windows Users Must Upgrade to WordPerfect 6.0a or Newer. A NeXT Version Is Available. Features 41 Overstrike Accents & Diacritical Mark Keys Each Having Automatic, Non-Deleting Backspacing for Typing over Any Letter or Symbol & in Any Combination. Provides Four Characters per Key in Windows.
Linguist's Software, Inc.

AFS Asset-Based Lending. 1988. *Items Included:* Documentation for AFS Systems consists of several 3-ring binders: (1) System Documentation (general system narrative), & (2) Technical Documentation (program flow charts, run procedures, user manual, installation aids). *Customer Support:* AFS Systems are sold with a specified number of on-site support days. AFS recommends use of these days: (1) for implementing & running the AFS test system & representative test data from the client, (2) orientation for system users & technical support staff.
DOS, DOS/VSE, MVS/*, CICS. IBM System/370 architecture. contact publisher for price.
Monitors Loans Requiring Collateral Attention, Such As Accounts Receivable & Inventory Loans. Provides Bulk Assignment Processing for Invoices in Small Dollar Amounts or Not Requiring Detail Review. Accounting for Ineligibles, Deferral of Collection or Cash Collateral Processing, Sales, Average Receivables, Loan Yields & Histories. Confirmation Processing Provides a Means of Auditing.
Automated Financial Systems, Inc.

AFS Combined Deposit System. Jun. 1983. *Items Included:* Documentation for AFS Systems consists of several 3-ring binders: (1) System Documentation (general system narrative), & (2) Technical Documentation (program flow charts, run procedures, user manual, installation aids). *Customer Support:* AFS Systems are sold with a specified number of on-site support days. AFS recommends use of these days: (1) For implementing & running the AFS test system & represnative test data from the client, (2) Orientation for system users & technical support staff.
DOS, DOS/VSE, MVS/*, CICS. IBM 370, 43XX, 303X, 308X, 309X. contact publisher for price.
Provides Data Processing Support for Interest-Bearing & Non-Interest-Bearing Accounts, Including Checking, NOW, Savings, Clubs, Time Open & IRA Deposits. Combines Descriptive Statements, & Account Analysis Pricing/Statements. CIF Interface for Name/Address, Relationship Pricing, Combined Statement & Funds Management Provided. Complete On-Line Entry & Inquiry.
Automated Financial Systems, Inc.

AFS Commercial Lending (Level III, II PLUS). *Items Included:* Documentation for AFS Systems consists of several 3-ring binders: (1) System Documentation (general system narrative), & (2) Technical Documentation (program flow charts, run procedures, user manual, installation aids). *Customer Support:* AFS Systems are sold with a specified number of on-site support days. AFS recommends use of these days: (1) for implementing & running the AFS test system & representative test data from the client, (2) orientation for system users & technical support staff.
DOS, DOS/VSE, MVS/*, CICS. IBM 370, 43XX, 303X, 308X, 309X. contact publisher for price.
Allows Financial Institutions to Design, Implement, & Administer Wide Variety of Commercial Lending Products. They Provide Multiple Accruals, Optional Fees, Base Rate Interest Structures, Tiered Rates, Principal Recapture, On-Line Inquiries, Full On-Line Data entry & Validations, Obligations, & Effective Data Processing. Extensive Reporting Capabilities.
Automated Financial Systems, Inc.

AFS COMPUTER-BASED TRAINING

AFS Computer-Based Training. *Items Included:* Documentation for AFS Systems consists of several 3-ring binders: (1) System Documentation (general system narrative), & (2) Technical Documentation (program flow charts, run procedures, user manual, installation aids). *Customer Support:* AFS Systems are sold with specified number of on-site days. AFS recommends use of these days: (1) for implementing & running the AFS test system & representative test data from the client, (2) orientation for system users & technical support staff. DOS, DOS/VSE, MVS/*, CICS. IBM 370, 43XX, 303X, 309X. contact publisher for price.
An Award-Winning Program That Provids AFS Level III & II PLUS Loan System Users with Programmed Training on Any Terminal in Their System. Users Can Learn on Their Schedule, at Their Own Pace. Incorporates Real-Life Examples & Gives Encouragement with Praise for Correct Answers. Enables Managers to Monitor Progress.
Automated Financial Systems, Inc.

AFS Consumer Lending (Level III, II PLUS). *Items Included:* Documentation for AFS Systems consists of several 3-ring binders: (1) System Documentation (general system narrative), & (2) Technical Documentation (program flow charts, run procedures, user manual, installation aids). *Customer Support:* AFS Systems are sold with a specified number of On-Site support days. AFS recommends use of these days: (1) for implementing & running the AFS test system & representative test data from the client, (2) orientation for system users & technical support staff. DOS, DOS/VSE, MVS/*, CICS. IBM 370, 43XX, 303X, 308X, 309X. contact publisher for price.
These Systems Enable Financial Institutions to Be More Creative in Developing Lending Products. They Process Dealer Loans, Coupons (& Billing) & Insurance. High Volume Capability. Provide Various Calculations for Interest & Fees. Offer On-Line Inquiry, Reporting & Analysis for Memo Accruals, Personal Lines of Credit, Combined Liability Total.
Automated Financial Systems, Inc.

AFS Customer Information File. 1982. *Items Included:* Documentation for AFS Systems consists of several 3-ring binders: (1) System Documentation (general system narrative), & (2) Technical Documentation (program flow charts, run procedures, user manual, installation. *Customer Support:* AFS Systems are sold with a specified number of on-site support days. AFS recommends use of these days: (1) for implementing & running the AFS test system & representative test data from the client, (2) orientation for system users & technical support staff. DOS, DOS/VSE, MVS/*, CICS, IMS/DB. IBM 370, 43XX, 303X, 308X, 327X, 4700. contact publisher for price.
A Complete, Interactive System That Links Each Customer's Assets, Liabilities, & Services into One File. Supports Cross Selling of Services & Provides Base for Customer Asset/Liability Management, Selective Marketing & Personalized Services Other Corporate & Retail Customers & Services.
Automated Financial Systems, Inc.

AFS Dealer Floor Plan. 1989. *Items Included:* Documentation for AFS Systems consists of several 3-ring binders: (1) System Documentation (general system narrative), & (2) Technical Documentation (program flow charts, run procedures, user manual, installation aids). *Customer Support:* AFS Systems are sold with a specified number of on-site support days. AFS recommends use of these days: (1) for implementing & running the AFS test system & representative test data from the client, (2) orientation for system users & technical support staff. DOS, DOS/VSE, MVS/*, CICS. IBM 370, 43XX, 303X, 308X, 309X. contact publisher for price.
An Extension to the AFS Level III & II PLUS Collateral Feature. Tracks the Dealer's Entire Relationship from Commercial Loans to Installment Loans. Provides Comprehensive Unit Tracking & Streamlined Unit Booking, Pricing Flexibility Through Tiered Rates, & the Ability to Maintain Multiple Accruals Simultaneously, & Detailed Billing Statements.
Automated Financial Systems, Inc.

AFS Executive Line of Credit. *Items Included:* Documentation for AFS Systems consists of several 3-ring binders: (1) System Documentation (general system narrative), & (2) Technical Documentation (program flow charts, run procedures, user manual, installation aids). *Customer Support:* AFS Systems are sold with a specified number of om-site support days. AFS recommends use of these days: (1) for implementing & running the AFS test system & representative test data from the client, (2) orientation for system users & technical support staff. DOS, DOS/VSE, MVS/*, CICS. IBM 370, 43XX, 303X, 308X, 309X. contact publisher for price.
Allows Financial Institutions to Price Credit Lines Competitively & Profitably Using Multi-Accruals, Such As Tiered Rates & Variable Rates Tied to Any Number of Base Rate Indices. Automates Credit Line Booking, Collateral Monitoring, Insurance Processing, Billing, & Late Notices. Extensive Reporting Capabilities in Accordance with FASB 91 & Regulation.
Automated Financial Systems, Inc.

AFS Interest Reporting System. 1982. *Items Included:* Documentation for AFS Systems consists of several 3-ring binders: (1) System Documentation (general system narrative), & (2) Technical Documentation (program flow charts, run procedures, user manual, installation. *Customer Support:* AFS Systems are sold with a specified number of on-site support days. AFS recommends use of these days: (1) for implementing & running the AFS test system & representative test data from the client, (2) orientation for system users & technical support staff. DOS, DOS/VSE, MVS/*, CICS. IBM 370, 43XX, 303X, 308X, 309X. contact publisher for price.
Provides Complete Regulatory Reports, Including W9 Support, Backup Witholding, Year-End Reporting, & Remittance Provisions. Supports Application Processing Systems Generating Customr Earnings Such As CDs, IRAs, & NOWs, on an Account or Customer Level. Eliminates Need to Change Every Application Separately Each Time Tax Laws Change or IRS Issues New Guidelines.
Automated Financial Systems, Inc.

AFS Level III Mortgage Lending System. *Items Included:* Documentation for AFS Systems consists of several 3-ring binders: (1) System Documentation (general system narrative), & (2) Technical Documentation (program flow charts, run procedures, user manual, installation aids). *Customer Support:* AFS Systems are sold with a specified number of on-site support days. AFS recommends use of these days: (1) for implementing & running the AFS test system & representative test data from the client, (2) orientation for system users & technical support staff. DOS, DOS/VSE, MVS/*, CICS. IBM 370, 43XX, 303X, 308X, 309X. contact publisher for price.
Provides Financial Institutions with the Ability to Efficiently Process Regular & Participated Loans, Variable Due & Billing Dates, Escrow Analysis & Interest, Audit Reporting, Activity, Multiple Prepayments, New Loans & Foreclosures. Applies Late Charges. Handles Daily Maintenance. Generates Reports & Transaction Journals Through Parameter.
Automated Financial Systems, Inc.

AFS On-Line Collection System. 1985. *Items Included:* Documentation for AFS Systems consists of several 3-ring binders: (1) System Documentation (general system narrative), & (2) Technical Documentation (program flow charts, run procedures, user manual, installation aids). *Customer Support:* AFS System are sold with a specified number of on-site support days. AFS recommends use of these days: (1) for implementing & running the AFS test system & representative test data from the client, (2) orientation for system users & technical support staff. DOS, DOS/VSE, MVS/*, CICS. IBM 370, 43XX, 303X, 308X, 309X. contact publisher for price.
Monitors & Manages Collection Activities of Past-Due Accounts in a Multibank, Multiapplication Environment. Emphasis Is Placed on Supervisor Control Through On-Line Inquiry & Data Entry. Schedules Assignments. Provides Access to Contact Activity, Account Status & Payment History. Generates User-Designed Letters. Displays Past Due Accounts for Borrower on One Screen. Tracks Promises at Multiple Levels & Keeps Statistics on Those That Are Kept or Broken.
Automated Financial Systems, Inc.

AFS Product Definition. *Items Included:* Documentation for AFS Systems consists of several 3-ring binders: (1) System Documentation (general system narrative), & (2) Technical Documentation (program, flow charts, run procedures, user manual, installation aids). *Customer Support:* AFS systems are sold with a specified number of on-site support days. AFS recommends use of these days: (1) for implementing & running the AFS test system & representative test data from the client, (2) orientation for system users & technical support staff. DOS, DOS/VSE, MVS/*, CICS. IBM 370, 43XX, 303X, 308X, 309X. contact publisher for price.
Automates Loan Origination by Providing a Format for Loan Products. Users Enter Information Unique to the New Loan, e.g., Amount, Maturity, Customer Name, & Address. The System Makes the Related Entries & Performs Calculations Based on Predefined Parameters. Works with AFS Level III & II PLUS.
Automated Financial Systems, Inc.

AFS Task Management System. *Items Included:* Documentation for TMS consists of installation information, technical information, & user information. *Customer Support:* AFS Systems are sold with a specified number of on-site support days. AFS recommends use of these days: (1) for implementing & running the AFS test system & representative test data from the client, (2) orientation for system users & trechnical support staff. OS/2, WIN NT, APPC. PS/2 3865X & compatibles. contact publisher for price.
A Workflow Monitor System That Allows Centralized Control of Job Processes in a Decentralized Environment. Financial Institutions

TITLE INDEX

Can Schedule Work, Prioritize Job Tasks & Ensure Data Control, All Within Defined Time Parameters. Whenever Possible the System Simplifies the User's Task by Defaulting Information Through Access to Other Systems. After Approval Is Granted, Application Data Is Dynamically Uploaded from the Intelligent Workstation to Mainframe Systems.
Automated Financial Systems, Inc.

After Dark. Version: 2.0. Items Included: Software & documentation. Customer Support: 510-540-5535, 8am-5pm PST, M-F.
Macintosh 512KE or higher. 3.5" disk $49.95.
A Comprehensive Screen Saver for Business & Personal Environments. Select from over 30 Displays, & SOUND! Users Can See & Hear Thunder & Lightning, Screen Munching Worms, & Exploding Stars. Displays Include Flying Toasters, Fish!, Logo, Messages & MultiModule. SystemIQ Provides an Intelligent System Monitoring Package That Maximizes System Efficiency While Running After Dark. Programmers Can Write Their Own Screen Savers. After Dark Enables Users to Put the Screen to Sleep in Auto or Manual Password-Protected Mode.
Berkeley Systems, Inc.

After Dark: For Windows. Version: 2.0. Feb. 1992. Items Included: Dual media, documentation. Customer Support: 510-540-5535, available 8am-5pm PST weekdays.
Windows 3.0 or higher. IBM AT, XT, 286, 386, 486 & clones (1Mb). $49.95. Networks supported: All.
Save Your Screen with over 40 Incredible Displays - 2.0 Features 5 Brand New Displays, Digital Sound, True Color VGA & Super VGA Graphics, WallZapper (Turns an After Dark Display into Wallpaper), Network Password Support, New Fish, MultiModule & Password Protection for Windows & DOS! Also Includes DOS Blanking to Black & System IQ Activity Monitor.
Berkeley Systems, Inc.

After-the-Fact Payroll. Version: 9.9. 1995. Compatible Hardware: IBM PC & compatibles. Operating System(s) Required: MS-DOS 2.1. Language(s): C (source code included). Memory Required: 128k. General Requirements: 2 disk drives or hard disk.
disk $250.00.
manual $25.00.
Collection of Programs & Subroutines for Use by Professional Accountant to Record Payroll Information Taken from Client's Records. All Programs Are Self-Prompting. Prints Several Reports, Including W-2 Forms, Schedule of Wages for Quarterly Unemployment Reporting, Employee Lists, & Employee Payroll Records. Includes Program to Print Labels for Each Employee for Use on Payroll Records or Time Cards. Payroll Records for Several Different Clients Can Be Kept on One Disk.
Omni Software Systems, Inc. (Indiana).

After the Fire: American Literature in the Age of Expansion, 1865-1914. Version: 1.5. Feb. 1995. Items Included: BookWorm Student Reader (diskette). Customer Support: 30 day MBG. Technical support (toll call) - no charge.
System 7.0 or higher. Macintosh (5Mb). CD-ROM disk $29.95 (ISBN 1-57316-018-0, Order no.: 16153). Nonstandard peripherals required: CD-ROM drive, 12" color monitor. Optimal configuration: 13" color monitor recommended.
Windows 3.1 or higher. IBM compatible (MPC) 386 DX (4Mb). CD-ROM disk $29.95. Nonstandard peripherals required: Standard multimedia compatible CD-ROM. Optimal configuration: 8Mb RAM recommended, 256 color monitor recommended.
This Anthology Brings Together Some of the Most Brilliant Works of a Crucial Period in American History: the Post-Civil War Expansion That Forged a Modern Nation. Contains Works of Mark Twain, Henry James, Emily Dickinson, Frederick Douglass & Others.
Communication & Information Technologies, Inc. (CIT).

AFTOFF. Compatible Hardware: IBM PC. (source code included).
disk $89.00.
Text Utility That Adapts TEX Files on IBM PC & Compatibles to Access ADOBE Fonts on the LaserWriter. Can Be Also Used on Mainframe Computers.
Western Wares.

AG COUNT Extra. 1991. General Requirements: Two floppy disk drives or one floppy disk & hard disk drive. Items Included: manual, accounting handbook, worksheets. Customer Support: no charge.
Macintosh; Apple IIgs; IBM PC & compatibles (all 512k or higher). $395.00.
Farm Accounting Program. Every Check & Deposit Is Saved Automatically; Add Titles Anytime During the Year. Program Includes Tax Worksheet, Financial Statements, & Enterprise Analysis. Free Demo Disks Available. Free Crop Production Software Included.
AG PLUS Consulting.

AG Finance. Version: Blue Ribbon Plus. Compatible Hardware: IBM & compatibles. Operating System(s) Required: DOS. Language(s): Turbo Pascal. Memory Required: 640k. General Requirements: 1 drive & hard disk.
disk $395.00.
Accounting System That Helps with Check Writing, Check Registers, Account Summaries, & Accounting on a Cash Basis. Prints Checks & Records Financial Information at the Same Time. Handles Multiple Bank Accounts. Uses Numeric Codes & Identifies up to 1,000 Separate Enterprises. Ratio Analysis.
Countryside Data, Inc.

Ag. Marketing & Commodity Futures. 1982. Compatible Hardware: Apple II, IIe, IIc. Memory Required: 32k. General Requirements: Printer.
disk $50.00 (Order no.: FM004 D-A).
Series of Programs That Allow User to Evaluate the Different Marketing Alternatives of Hedging, Forward Contracts, Cash & Speculating Cash Price Required to Meet the Best Alternative.
Micro Learningware.

AG Payroll. Version: Blue Ribbon Plus. Operating System(s) Required: DOS. Language(s): Turbo Pascal.
disk $295.00.
Payroll Program to Meet the Needs of Agricultural Employees. Provides Check Writing Capabilities, Generates Labor Reports, State & Federal Forms (W-2, W-3, 940, 941, etc.). Also Included Are Different Methods of Payment, Piece Rate, Hourly, Salary & 8 Different Payroll Deductions.
Countryside Data, Inc.

AG Planner. Version: Blue Ribbon Plus. Compatible Hardware: Apple III. Operating System(s) Required: MS-DOS. Language(s): Compiled Pascal. Memory Required: 640k.
disk # part of AG Finance cost.
Designed to Be Used with the AG Finance Accounting System to Control Cash Flow & Income by Using Either User-Input Data or Generated Data. Generates a Profit/Cost Report & a Cash Flow Report for the Coming Production Year. User Can Alter Any or All of the Revenue, Cost, & Cash Flow Items to Perform Break-Even Analysis & to Evaluate Cash Flow Issues. 5 Year Enterprise Analysis.
Countryside Data, Inc.

AGA Orifice Flow Element Calculations. Items Included: Full manual. No other products required. Customer Support: Free telephone support - no time limit. 30 day warranty.
MS-DOS 3.2 or higher. IBM & compatibles (512k). disk $289.95.
Additional Module for INSTRUCALC. American Gas Association Updated Their Standards for Sizing Flow Elements. Now There Are Two Standards: This One (AGA) & the ISO Standard. The Orifice Sizing Calculations in INSTRUCALC Are Based on the ISO Standards. With These New Calculations Installed in INSTRUCALC, You Can Choose Either ISO or AGA Standards When Sizing Your Flow Elements.
Dynacomp, Inc.

AgAccounts. Compatible Hardware: Apple Macintosh Plus.
3.5" disk $395.00.
Accounting System for Farmers & Ranchers.
Komstock Co.

AgCHEK Accounting. Version: 5.0. Operating System(s) Required: MS-DOS. Items Included: Manual. Customer Support: 3 Different technical support plans.
$595.00-$1385.00.
Three Modules Allow User to Tailor Farm Accounting. General Ledger ($595) Provides Double-Entry Accounting & Financial Record Keeping. Crop Management Module ($395) Provides Crop Enterprise Analysis & Record Keeping. Livestock Management Module ($395) Provides Record Keeping & Analysis.
Red Wing Business Systems, Inc.

AgChek IV: Crop & Livestock Modules & Pesticide. Version: 5.0. Red Wing Business System Inc. Items Included: Spiral bound manual. Customer Support: Available.
MS-DOS 2.0 or higher. IBM compatible (640k). contact publisher for price. Addl. software required: AgChek IV Accounting. Optimal configuration: Hard disk & an 80 column printer recommended.
Allows User to Manage Crop & Livestock Production. Enables User to Allocate Income & Expenses to a Crop, Pesticides or Livestock Enterprise Analyzing Profitability. Also Keeps Track of Input, Inventory, Budgets & Histories. Records Kept on a Production Cycle Basis As Well As a Calendar Year Basis.
Farmer's Software Assn.

AgChek IV: General Ledger. Version: 5.0. Red Wing Business Systems Inc. Items Included: 1 applications & use manual, spiral bound. Customer Support: Available.
MS-DOS 2.0 or higher. IBM compatible computer (640k). contact publisher for price. Optimal configuration: Hard disk preferred, 80 column printer.
A Farm & Ranch Financial Management System That Is a Double Entry, Cash & Accrual Accounting Systems. It's Features Include Enterprise Analysis, Cash Flow & Budgeting. Allows User to Keep Track of Checks, Deposits, Expenses, Income Aids in Tax Preparation.
Farmer's Software Assn.

AgData Accounts Payable. Version: 1994. Dan Boeger. Jun. 1994. Items Included: User manual. Customer Support: One year free software support; renewable yearly at 13% of program

cost. Unconditional 45-day full refund guarantee.
MS-DOS 3.1 Plus. IBM & compatibles (640k).
  disk $595.00. *Addl. software required:* AgData General Ledger. *Optimal configuration:* 486/33 computer with 1Mb RAM, 60Mb hard drive.
  Networks supported: Novell.
Enter Payables for Payment Later. Payables Are Listed by Due Date Alone, or by Vendor Account, Sorted & Subtotaled by Due Date. Payables Are Grouped or Marked Individually into Ready or Hold Status. Use Either Cash or Accrual Basis Bookkeeping. Reverses Accrual Bookkeeping for Cash Basis Reporting.
AgData.

AgData Accounts Payable (Cash Basis). *Version:* 1994. Dan Boeger. *Items Included:* User manual. *Customer Support:* One year free software support; renewable yearly at 13% of program cost. Unconditional 45-day full refund guarantee.
MS-DOS 3.1 Plus. IBM & compatibles (640k).
  disk $395.00. *Addl. software required:* AgData General Ledger. *Optimal configuration:* 486/33 computer with 1Mb RAM, 60Mb hard drive.
  Networks supported: Novell.
Computer Checkwriting for Cash Basis Clients.
AgData.

AgData Accounts Receivable. *Version:* 1994. Dan Boeger. Jun. 1994. *Items Included:* User manual. *Customer Support:* One year free software support; renewable yearly at 13% of program cost. Unconditional 45-day full refund guarantee.
MS-DOS 3.1 Plus. IBM & compatibles (640k).
  disk $895.00. *Addl. software required:* AgData General Ledger. *Optimal configuration:* 486/33 computer with 1Mb RAM, 60Mb hard drive.
  Networks supported: Novell.
Program Prints Invoices, Statements, Customer Billing Histories, & Mailing Labels. Formats May Be Customized. Histories List All Transactions or Just Those Remaining Unpaid. Features Include Automatic Payment Resolution, Partial Payments, Selective Interest Charges, & Reprinting of Lost Invoices. Reverses Accrual Bookkeeping for Cash Basis Reporting, & Carries Forward Outstanding Payables.
AgData.

AgData Blue Skies Cost Accounting. *Version:* 1995. Dan Boeger. Jan. 1995. *Items Included:* User manual. *Customer Support:* One year free software support; renewable yearly at 13% of program cost. Unconditional 45-day full refund guarantee.
DOS 5.0 w/Windows 3.1. 386/33 IBM compatible w/mouse (4Mb). Contact publisher for price. *Addl. software required:* Windows 3.1. *Optimal configuration:* 486/66 computer with 8Mb RAM.
Supplements General Ledger to Provide Production Cost Analysis, & Evaluation Reports for Each Enterprise Cost Center. Enterprise Codes Are User-Definable. Specific P&L Statements Are Generated for Each Enterprise, Crop Years May Overlap & Carry Forward Through Calendar or Fiscal Accounting Years. Labor Costs Integrated Automatically If Payroll Module Installed.
AgData.

AgData Blue Skies General Ledger. *Version:* 1995. Dan Boeger. Jan. 1995. *Items Included:* User manual. *Customer Support:* One year free software support; renewable yearly at 13% of program cost. Unconditional 45-day full refund guarantee.
DOS 5.0 w/Windows 3.1. 386/33 IBM compatible w/mouse (4Mb). Contact publisher for price. *Addl. software required:* Windows 3.1. *Optimal configuration:* 486/66 computer with 8Mb RAM.

Provides Automated double-Entry Accounting. Generates Transaction Registers & Detail Reports, Plus Reports for Cash Flow Management, Budgeting, & Tax Preparation. No Monthly Closings, Correct Errors at Any Time & Data Is Saved Automatically. Computerized Check Printing Available. Integrates with AgData Accounting Series for a Complete Accounting System.
AgData.

AgData Blue Skies Payroll. *Version:* 1995. Dan Boeger. Jan. 1995. *Items Included:* User manual. *Customer Support:* One year free software support; renewable yearly at 13% of program cost. Unconditional 45-day full refund guarantee.
DOS 5.0 w/Windows 3.1. 386/33 IBM compatible w/mouse (4Mb). Contact publisher for price. *Addl. software required:* Windows 3.1. *Optimal configuration:* 486/66 computer with 8Mb RAM.
Prints Paycheck Details; Quarterly & Annual State & Federal Payroll Reports. Integrates with the Optional General Ledger & Cost Accounting Modules. Prints W2 & Immigration Reports. Offers Magnetic Media Reporting & High-Speed Timecard Scanning to Larger Employers. Labor Contractor's Payroll Available. Calculates All Withholdings & Prints Payroll Checks Using Multiple Piecework & Hourly Rate Combinations. Timecards May Be Entered Daily or All-at-One-Time. Piecework Gross Is Compared to Minimum Wage.
AgData.

AgData Check Reconciliation. *Version:* 1994. Dan Boeger. *Items Included:* User manual. *Customer Support:* One year free software support; renewable yearly at 13% of program cost. Unconditional 45-day full refund guarantee.
MS-DOS 3.1 Plus. IBM & compatibles (640k).
  disk $395.00. *Addl. software required:* AgData General Ledger. *Optimal configuration:* 486/33 computer with 1Mb RAM, 60Mb hard drive.
  Networks supported: Novell.
Works with the Check & Deposit Details Found in the AgData General Ledger Program. This Program Lets You Quickly & Easily Mark the Outstanding Entries & Print a Report That Reconciles Your Books to Your Bank Statement.
AgData.

AgData Cost Accounting 1. *Version:* 1994. Dan Boeger. Jun. 1994. *Items Included:* User manual. *Customer Support:* One year free software support; renewable yearly at 13% of program cost. Unconditional 45-day full refund guarantee.
MS-DOS 3.1 Plus. IBM & compatibles (640k).
  disk $395.00. *Addl. software required:* AgData General Ledger. *Optimal configuration:* 486/33 computer with 1Mb RAM, 60Mb hard drive.
  Networks supported: Novell.
Supplements General Ledger to Provide Production Cost Analysis, & Evaluation Reports for Each Enterprise Cost Center. Enterprise Codes Are User-Definable. Specific P&L Statements Are Generated for Each Enterprise, Crop Years May Overlap & Carry Forward Through Calendar or Fiscal Accounting Years. Labor Costs Integrated Automatically If Payroll Module Installed.
AgData.

AgData Cost Accounting 2. *Version:* 1994. Dan Boeger. Jun. 1994. *Items Included:* User manual. *Customer Support:* One year free software support; renewable yearly at 13% of program cost. Unconditional 45-day full refund guarantee.
MS-DOS 3.1 Plus. IBM & compatibles (640k).
  disk $595.00. *Addl. software required:* AgData General Ledger. *Optimal configuration:* 486/33 computer with 1Mb RAM, 60Mb hard drive.
  Networks supported: Novell.
Cost Accounting Level 1 Plus Operation (E.G.

Harvest) Costs & Equipment Costing. Supplements General Ledger to Provide Production Cost Analysis, & Evaluation Reports for Each Enterprise Cost Center. Enterprise Codes Are User-Definable. Specific P&L Statements Are Generated for Each Enterprise, Crop Years May Overlap & Carry Forward Through Calendar or Fiscal Accounting Years. Labor Costs Integrated Automatically If Payroll Module Installed.
AgData.

AgData Database Import-Export Utility. *Version:* 1994. Dan Boeger. *Items Included:* User manual. *Customer Support:* One year free software support; renewable yearly at 13% of program cost. Unconditional 45-day full refund guarantee.
MS-DOS 3.1 Plus. IBM & compatibles (640k).
  disk $395.00. *Optimal configuration:* 486/33 computer with 1Mb RAM, 60Mb hard drive.
  Networks supported: Novell.
Exports Selected General Ledger or Payroll Timecard Data to Spreadsheet, Database, Graphics, or Other Custom Programs in Standard ASCII Format, or Uses ASCII Data Generated from Another Program for Automated Import into AgData.
AgData.

AgData Enterprise Power Budgeting. *Version:* 1994. Dan Boeger. Jun. 1994. *Items Included:* User manual. *Customer Support:* One year free software support; renewable yearly at 13% of program cost. Unconditional 45-day full refund guarantee.
MS-DOS 3.1 Plus. IBM & compatibles (640k).
  disk $395.00. *Addl. software required:* AgData Cost Accounting, AgData General Ledger. *Optimal configuration:* 486/33 computer with 1Mb RAM, 60Mb hard drive. *Networks supported:* Novell.
Creates a New Full-Year Budget for Each Cost Accounting Enterprise Cost Center, Using the Grower's Actual Enterprise Income & Expense Records. Changes in Acreage or Percentage Are Factored Automatically. Monthly Enterprise Budget-to-Actual Reports Generate Variances & Remaining Balances. Totals Enterprise Budgets to Create the Overall Bank Budget.
AgData.

AgData Farm Labor Contractor's Payroll. *Version:* 1994. Dan Boeger. *Items Included:* User manual. *Customer Support:* One year free software support; renewable yearly at 13% of program cost. Unconditional 45-day full refund guarantee.
MS-DOS 3.1 Plus. IBM & compatibles (640k).
  disk $595.00. *Addl. software required:* AgData Payroll. *Optimal configuration:* 486/33 computer with 1Mb RAM, 60Mb hard drive.
  Networks supported: Novell.
The Report Lists Both Worker Pay & Deductions. Federal Law Requires Farm Labor Contractors to Give Reports to Their Farm Customers That Identify Farm Workers, Demonstrate They Have Been Paid Properly, & Show That Accurate Deductions Have Been Withheld. Program Is an Add-On to Payroll Reports & the Payroll Checkwriting Programs.
AgData.

AgData General Ledger. *Version:* 1994. Dan Boeger. 1994. *Operating System(s) Required:* MS-DOS. *Memory Required:* 640k. *Items Included:* User manual. *Customer Support:* One year free software support, renewable yearly at 13% of program cost. Unconditional 45-day full refund guarantee.
disk $895.00 (ISBN 0-922020-14-0).
Provides Automated Double-Entry Accounting. Generates Transaction Registers & Detail Reports, Plus Reports for Cash Flow

TITLE INDEX

Management, Budgeting, & Tax Preparation. No Monthly Closings, Correct Errors at Any Time & Data Is Saved Automatically. Computerized Check Printing Available. Integrates with AgData Accounting Series for a Complete Accounting System.
AgData.

AgData Inventory. *Version:* 1994. Dan Boeger. *Items Included:* User manual. *Customer Support:* One year free software support; renewable yearly at 13% of program cost. Unconditional 45-day full refund guarantee.
MS-DOS 3.1 Plus. IBM & compatibles (640k). disk $395.00. *Optimal configuration:* 486/33 computer with 1Mb RAM, 60Mb hard drive. *Networks supported:* Novell.
Tracks Quantitites & Rates for Bulk Inventories Either Grown or Purchased.
AgData.

AgData Land Leveling. *Version:* 1994. Dan Boeger. 1994. *Operating System(s) Required:* MS-DOS. *Memory Required:* 640k. *Items Included:* User manual. *Customer Support:* One year free software support, renewable yearly at 13% of program cost. Unconditional 45-day full refund guarantee.
disk $995.00 (ISBN 0-922020-36-1).
Designs Cut-&-Fill Maps & Engineers a 'Best Fit' Analysis. Prints Cut-&-Fill Tables or Color Countour Maps. Adjusts Automatically for Laser Transit Slant Angles.
AgData.

AgData Magnetic Media Reporting. *Version:* 1994. Dan Boeger. *Items Included:* User manual. *Customer Support:* One year free software support; renewable yearly at 13% of program cost. Unconditional 45-day full refund guarantee.
MS-DOS 3.1 Plus. IBM & compatibles (640k). disk $395.00. *Addl. software required:* AgData Payroll. *Optimal configuration:* 486/33 computer with 1Mb RAM, 60Mb hard drive. *Networks supported:* Novell.
If You Have 250 or More Employees, You Must Submit Payroll Reports on Floppy Disk (Magnetic Media) Instead of Paper to Avoid a Penalty of $50/Employee. This Report Allows These Larger Growers to Comply with Magnetic Media Reporting Requirements.
AgData.

AgData Payroll Checkwriting. *Version:* 1994. Dan Boeger. Jun. 1994. *Items Included:* User manual. *Customer Support:* One year free software support; renewable yearly at 13% of program cost. Unconditional 45-day full refund guarantee.
MS-DOS 3.1 Plus. IBM & compatibles (640k). disk $395.00. *Addl. software required:* AgData Payroll. *Optimal configuration:* 486/33 computer with 1Mb RAM, 60Mb hard drive. *Networks supported:* Novell.
Calculates All Withholdings & Prints Payroll Checks Using Multiple Piecework & Hourly Rate Combinations. Timecards May Be Entered Daily or All-at-One-Time. Piecework Gross Is Compared to Minimum Wage.
AgData.

AgData Payroll Reports. *Version:* 1994. Dan Boeger. 1994. *Operating System(s) Required:* MS-DOS. *Memory Required:* 640k. *General Requirements:* Hard drive, printer. *Items Included:* User manual. *Customer Support:* One year free software support, renewable yearly at 13% of program cost. Unconditional 45-day full refund guarantee.
CP/M-80. disk $895.00 (ISBN 0-922020-04-3).
Prints Paycheck Details; Quarterly & Annual State & Federal Payroll Reports. Integrates with the Optional General Ledger & Cost Accounting Modules. Prints W2 & Immigration Reports. Offers Magnetic Media Reporting & High-Speed Timecard Scanning to Larger Employers. Labor Contractor's Payroll Available.
AgData.

AgData Small Farm Series. *Version:* 1994. Dan Boeger. *Items Included:* User manual. *Customer Support:* One year free software support; renewable yearly at 13% of program cost. Unconditional 45-day full refund guarantee.
MS-DOS 3.1 Plus. IBM & compatibles (640k). disk $1495.00. *Optimal configuration:* 486/33 computer with 1Mb RAM, 60Mb hard drive. *Networks supported:* Novell.
If You Write Fewer Than 300 Checks per Year & Do Not Use Cost Accounting, This Program Will Provide Payroll with Checkwriting, General Ledger with Cash Basis Checkwriting, & Cost Accounting for the Small Farmer.
AgData.

The Age of Choice: Commentaries on Public & International Affairs. Harlan Cleveland. 1990.
DOS. Any type of IBM (64k). $14.95 (ISBN 1-56178-013-8).
MAC. Any type of Macintosh (64k). $14.95 (ISBN 1-56178-030-8).
Collection of Commentaries on Current Events, 1987-1990 by Former Ambassador to NATO.
Connected Editions, Inc.

Agency Accounting. *Customer Support:* Free on-site training, monthly maintenance/support - $350.00 per month.
MS-DOS. MICRO Based (640k). $10,000.00 software license.
This System Is Designed for the Managing General Agent or Surplus Lines Broker & Provides for Policy Maintenance, Premium Accounting, General Ledger Reporting, Premium Statistical, & Business Directory.
Insurance Technology Consultants.

"Agency" Advertising Management System. *Version:* 4.20. Jun. 1992. *Compatible Hardware:* Data General. *Operating System(s) Required:* DG/UX. *Language(s):* Interactive COBOL. *Memory Required:* 16,000k. *General Requirements:* Hard disk 520Mb.
2-port $5995.00.
$7995.00 4-port.
$11,995.00 11-port.
$15,995.00 23-port.
$19,995.00 35-port.
Includes Time/Media Billing, Accounts Receivable, Accounts Payable, Purchase Order, General Ledger, Payroll, Estimating, Traffic & Scheduling, Media Scheduling & Buying, Budgeting, Agency Business Analyses & Security. Optional Modules Include: Word Processing, Spreadsheet, Report Writer, Electronic Mail, Calendaring, Telephone Messaging, PC & MAC Terminal Emulation, Networking & Communications. Prices Include Installation, Training, & 1 Year Support/Enhancements.
Admark Systems, Inc.

Agency Information Management System. *Compatible Hardware:* IBM PC & compatibles. *Operating System(s) Required:* DOS, XENIX, UNIX, Novell, Alloy. *Memory Required:* 640k. *Items Included:* Vendor site training. *Customer Support:* Toll-free telephone.
$2795.00 single user, $3895.00 multi-user.
Designed to Automate Accounting, Claims, Suspense, Marketing, Management, & Policy Retrieval Systems of Insurance Industry Agencies. Produces ACORD Forms & Can Be Integrated with Word Processing Software.
Insurance Rating Systems, Inc.

AGREEMENTOR

The Agency Manager. Nov. 1983. *Compatible Hardware:* IBM PC AT, PS/2, & compatibles. *Operating System(s) Required:* MS-DOS, PC-DOS. *Language(s):* C. *Memory Required:* 256k.
$5750.00 & up.
Integrated Insurance Agency Management Package Handles Accounting, Customer/Policy Database, over 100 Different Marketing Reports, over 100 Different Sales Presentation Aids, Word Processing, Telecommunications Capabilities, Utilities & ACORD Forms. Contains the Optional Ability to Link, via Telecommunications, to Insurance Data Networks Including the Insurance Value Added Network Systems (IVANS). Also Includes Personal & Commercial Lines Rating & Custom Forms.
Applied Systems.

AGENCYMASTER: Insurance Agency Accounting. *Version:* 6.0. Aug. 1993. *Items Included:* Instruction manuals. *Customer Support:* First 90 days free, annually 15% of purchase price. Training customer site $800.00 per day plus expenses - training vendor office $500.00 per day.
MS-DOS, AIX, UNIX, VMS. Intel 486, IBM RS6000, DEC VAX (2Mb), ALPHA. disk $5800.00 (1-5 user) plus Progress. *Addl. software required:* Progress runtime. *Optimal configuration:* 486-50mhz 16Mb Ram, 1.44 Mb diskette, 525Mb QIC tape, 1.0 GB hard disk, 8 port MUX & printer. *Networks supported:* Lantastic, Novell, Powerfusion.
MS-DOS, AIX, Novell, UNIX, VMS. 486-50mhz (4Mb). disk $5800.00 (1-5 user) plus Progress. *Addl. software required:* Progress runtime & report writer. *Optimal configuration:* 486-50mhz 16Mb RAM, 1.44 Mb diskette, 5.25Mb Qic tape, 1.0 GB hard disk, 8 port MUX & printer. *Networks supported:* Lantastic, Novell, Powerfusion.
Comprehensive Agency Accounting Including: Policy Data, Storage & Retrieval, Invoicing, Accounts Receivables, Payable & Company Account Current Reconciliation, Expiration Controls, Premium & Commission Statistics, General Ledger & Financial Statements, Multi-Company with Profit Center Controls.
Automation Resources Corp.

Agenda Master. *Customer Support:* 800-929-8117 (customer service).
MS-DOS. IBM/PS2. disk $199.99 (ISBN 0-87007-379-6).
Commodore 128; CP/M. disk $399.99 (ISBN 0-87007-725-2).
Complete Corporate Office Appointment Scheduling Software for Unlimited Numbers of Professionals; Variable Time Periods Are Supported. Once an Individual Is Logged into the System, He or She May Check the Graphical Representation of Scheduled & Non-Scheduled Hours for Blocks of Days & for Large or Small Blocks of Time Until a Convenient Time Is Found. By Pressing One Key an Appointment Screen Appears, Where the Name & Phone Number of the Appointment Holder Is Keyed in, Followed by a Personal Free Form Notepad for Appointment Information. Previous Appointments May Be Archived for Legal Reasons, or Removed from the System.
SourceView Software International.

AgentBase. *Compatible Hardware:* Apple Macintosh 512KE. *General Requirements:* Hard disk drive, ImageWriter.
3.5" disk $1500.00.
Insurance Agency Marketing Office Management.
Business Systems Group/Merry Maid, Inc.

AgreeMentor. *Version:* 2.2. Apr. 1991. *Compatible Hardware:* IBM PC & compatibles; Macintosh. *Items Included:* Manual & software

diskette. *Customer Support:* Free installation & technical support; limited warranty call JIAN 415-941-9191.
$99.00. *Addl. software required:* PC's: word processor compatible with MS Word, PCWrite, Q&A, PFS First Choice, WordPerfect, WordStar, & most others. Macintosh's: word processor, MacWrite 5.0 or Microsoft Word 3.01 compatible.
Pre-Written, Fill-in-the-Blank Business Agreements on Diskette, Written in Everyday Language to Be Understood by Non-Lawyers. Can Be Edited to Suit the Specific Purposes. Agreements Include: Independent Sales Representative, Non-Disclosure, Lehman Formula Partnership, Power of Attorney, & Purchase Agreement.
JIAN Tools for Sales.

Agri-Quiz: Conduct of Meetings. *Version:* 4.1. 1992. *Items Included:* Diskettes & instruction manual. *Customer Support:* Free telephone customer support. (414) 629-5577.
 ProDOS. Apple IIe (enhanced), IIc, or IIgs (128k). disk $39.95 (ISBN 1-56719-002-2, Order no.: ACM-A5 (5.25") OR ACM-A3 (3.5")).
 MS-DOS. IBM & compatible (128k). disk $39.95 (ISBN 1-56719-003-0, Order no.: ACM-I5 (5.25") OR ACM-I3 (3.5")).
Procedure of Conducting Meetings, Duties & Responsibilities of Officers, & Basic Parliamentary Procedure for Beginning Members Are Covered.
Midwest Agribusiness Services, Inc.

Agri-Quiz: FFA Instruction. *Version:* 4.1. 1992. *Items Included:* Diskettes & instruction manual. *Customer Support:* Free telephone customer support.
 ProDOS. Apple IIe (enhanced), IIc, IIgs (128k). disk $39.95 (ISBN 1-56719-004-9, Order no.: AFI-A5 (5.25") OR AFI-A3 (3.5")).
 MS-DOS. IBM & compatible. disk $39.95 (ISBN 1-56719-005-7, Order no.: AFI-I5 (5.25") OR AFI-I3 (3.5")).
This Program Covers All Phases of the FFA Organization. INSTRUCTOR FEATURES: 1) Print Customized Tests with Questions Selected by Number, Topic, or Randomly by the Computer. 2) Mix Question Types & Print Individual Headings for Each Set on the Same Test. 3) Print Student Answer Sheets & an Answer Key Overlay. STUDENT FEATURES: 1) Review or Actually Take a Test Using the Computer. 2) Receive Immediate Reinforcement after Answering. 3) Review Question Answered Incorrectly. 4) Send Quiz Results to Printer or Disk.
Midwest Agribusiness Services, Inc.

Agri-Quiz: Floriculture. *Version:* 4.0. 1989. *Items Included:* Diskettes & instruction manual. *Customer Support:* Free customer telephone support. (414) 629-5577.
 ProDOS. Apple IIe (enhanced), IIc, IIgs (128k). disk $39.95 (ISBN 0-940135-88-4, Order no.: AFL-A5 (5.25") OR AFL-A3 (3.5")).
 MS-DOS. IBM & compatibles (128k). disk $39.95 (ISBN 0-940135-89-2, Order no.: AFL-I5 (5.25") OR AFL-I3 (3.5")).
Disk Can Be Used to Review, Make Up Work, or for Contest Preparation. Many FFA Teams Have Used This Program to Prepare for Competition.
Midwest Agribusiness Services, Inc.

Agri-Quiz: Greenhouse I. *Version:* 4.0. 1989. *Items Included:* Diskettes & instruction manual. *Customer Support:* Free telephone customer support. (414) 629-5577.
 ProDOS. Apple IIe (enhanced), IIc, IIgs (128k). disk $39.95 (ISBN 0-940135-90-6, Order no.: AG1-A5 (5.25") OR AG1-A3 (3.5")).
 MS-DOS. IBM & compatibles ((128k). disk $39.95 (ISBN 0-940135-91-4, Order no.: AG1-I5 (5.25") OR AG1-I3 (3.5")).
Topics Include the Greenhouse Industry, Plant-Growing Structures, Environmental Growth Factors, Fertilizers, Growing Media, Scientific Names, Plant Physiology, & Plant Nutrition.
Midwest Agribusiness Services, Inc.

Agri-Quiz: Greenhouse II. *Version:* 4.0. 1989. *Items Included:* Diskettes & instruction manual. *Customer Support:* Free telephone customer support. (414) 629-5577.
 ProDOS. Apple IIe (enhanced), IIc, or IIgs (128k). disk $39.95 (ISBN 0-940135-92-2, Order no.: AG2-A5 (5.25") OR AG2-A3 (3.5")).
 MS-DOS. IBM & compatibles (128k). disk $39.95 (ISBN 0-940135-93-0, Order no.: AG2-I5 (5.25") OR AG2-I3 (3.5")).
Program Contains Questions on Watering Techniques, Asexual Propagation, Container-Grown Crops, Handling & Marketing, & cut Flower Crops.
Midwest Agribusiness Services, Inc.

Agri-Quiz: Horticulture I. *Version:* 4.0. 1989. *Items Included:* Diskettes & instruction manual. *Customer Support:* Free telephone customer support. (414) 629-5577.
 ProDOS. Apple IIe (enhanced), IIc, or IIgs (128k). disk $39.95 (ISBN 0-940135-94-9, Order no.: AH1-A5 (5.25") OR AH1-A3 (3.5")).
 MS-DOS. IBM & compatibles (128k). disk $39.95 (ISBN 0-940135-95-7, Order no.: AH1-I5 (5.25") OR AH1-I3 (3.5")).
Questions Include Pesticide Safety, Lawn Care, Plant Growth & Development, Growth Media, Using Small Gas Engine Equipment & Employment.
Midwest Agribusiness Services, Inc.

Agri-Quiz: Horticulture II. *Version:* 4.0. 1989. *Items Included:* Diskettes & instruction manual. *Customer Support:* Free telephone customer support. (414) 629-5577.
 ProDOS. Apple IIe (enhanced), IIc, IIgs (128k). disk $39.95 (ISBN 0-940135-96-5, Order no.: AH2-A5 (5.25") OR AH2-A3 (3.5")).
 MS-DOS. IBM & compatibles (128k). (ISBN 0-940135-97-3, Order no.: AH2-I5 (5.25") OR AH2-I3 (3.5")).
Topics Encompass Plant Identification, Careers in the Horticulture Industry, Plant Handling, Diseases & Pesticides, & Business Management.
Midwest Agribusiness Services, Inc.

Agri-Quiz: Nursery - Landscape. *Version:* 4.0. 1989. *Items Included:* Diskettes & instruction manual. *Customer Support:* Free telephone customer support.
 ProDOS. Apple IIe (enhanced), IIc, IIgs (128k). disk $39.95 (ISBN 0-940135-98-1, Order no.: ANL-A5 (5.25") OR ANL-A3 (3.5")).
 MS-DOS. IBM & compatible (128k). disk $39.95 (ISBN 0-940135-99-X, Order no.: ANL-I5 (5.25") OR ANL-I3 (3.5")).
Program Can Be Used for Review, Contest Preparation, or Individual Study. Widely Used by FFA Teams in Preparing for Contests.
Midwest Agribusiness Services, Inc.

Agri-Quiz: Parliamentary Procedure II. *Version:* 4.1. 1992. *Items Included:* Diskettes & instruction manual. *Customer Support:* Free telephone customer support (414) 629-5577.
 ProDOS. Apple IIe (enhanced), IIc or IIgs (128k). disk $39.95 (ISBN 1-56719-006-5, Order no.: AP2-A5 (5.25") OR AP2-A3 (3.5")).
 MS-DOS. IBM & compatible (128k). disk $39.95 (ISBN 1-56719-007-3, Order no.: AP2-I5 (5.25") OR AP2-I3 (3.5")).
Midwest Agribusiness Services, Inc.

Agri-Quiz: Small Engine. *Version:* 4.0. 1989. *Items Included:* Diskettes & instruction manual. *Customer Support:* Free telephone customer support.
 ProDOS. Apple IIe (enhanced), IIc, IIgs (128k). disk $39.95 (ISBN 1-56719-000-6, Order no.: ASE-A5 (5.25") OR ASE-A3 (3.5")).
 MS-DOS. IBM or compatible (128k). disk $39.95 (ISBN 1-56719-001-4, Order no.: ASE-I5 (5.25") OR ASE-I3 (3.5")).
Topics Include Principles, Construction, Fuel, Carburetion, & Governing, Ignition Systems & Starters.
Midwest Agribusiness Services, Inc.

AI Learning Lab. *Version:* 3.1. Apr. 1990. *Items Included:* 200 page manual. *Customer Support:* Phone tech support.
 MS-DOS, PC-DOS. IBM PC. disk $299.95. *Optimal configuration:* 640k, VGA or EGA, hard drive.
Useful in Corporate Training Sessions to Quickly Bring Programmers Managers up to Speed with Latest Hands on Experience with Artificial Intelligence Software.
Thinking Software, Inc.

AI Logo. 1992. *Items Included:* Detailed manuals are included with all DYNACOMP products. *Customer Support:* Free telephone support to original customer - no time limit; 30 day limited warranty.
 MS-DOS 3.2 or higher. IBM PC & compatibles (512k). $59.95 (Add $5.00 for 3 1/2" format; 5 1/4" format standard). *Optimal configuration:* IBM, 128k RAM & color graphics card. Printer is supported.
An Easy-to-Use, Powerful, & Interactive Educational Programming Language. It Is Command Compatible with Apple Logo. Procedures (Programs) Are Created by Combining Previously Defined Commands & Procedures. Using This "Building Block" Approach, There Is Virtually No Limit to the Complexity of These Procedures. Includes a Spiral-Bound 240-Page Reference Manual.
Dynacomp, Inc.

AIDS: CHOICES. Sep. 1991. *Items Included:* Users manual. *Customer Support:* 90 day limited warranty.
 IBM MS-DOS. IBM PC & compatibles - for 5.25" disk & 3.5" disk (280k). $59.95 (3.5 & 5.25)-Lab Pack of 10-$195.00 (Note: replaces ISBN 0-929857-00-3) $59.95 (3.5)-Lab Pack of 10-$245.00 (Order no.: 1032). *Optimal configuration:* EGA graphics card for 3.5" disk.
A Graphic Interactive Computer Program Discussing All Facets of AIDS in a Straight-Forward, Serious Manner. Sections Include: 1. What Is AIDS?; 2. How Long Do People Live with HIV Infections?; 3. How Do People Get AIDS?; 4. How Can I Prevent Catching AIDS?; 5. What Can I Do If Someone I Know Gets AIDS? Includes Interaction Reviews of Material & Records of How Well the User Understands the Program & AIDS Materials.
GemStar Partnership.

AIDS Information Game. *Compatible Hardware:* Commodore Amiga.
 3.5" disk $29.95.
Designed for Ages High School Through Adult.
Micro-Ed.

AIDS "Trivia" Update for Nineties: The AIDS Prevention & Education Game. Thomas J. Rundquist. Nov. 1994. *Items Included:* HIV/AIDS Surveillance Report from US Dept. of Health, Flash Card Version, Health Education & Prevention Information. *Customer Support:* Fax support 1-616-796-7539, Phone support 10-5 EST 616-796-7539.

DOS 6.0, Windows 3.0 or higher. PC IBM & compatibles (2Mb). disk $39.95 (ISBN 1-884239-02-1). *Optimal configuration:* PC IBM compatible (2Mb), DOS 6.0, Windows 3.0. Networks supported: All.
A Quiz about AIDS Educaton & Prevention. 36 Questions with Multiple Choice Answers on Computer. Running Totals. Is Based on Surgeon General's Report for 1987 & Has Been Sold since 1987 As a Hard Copy Version Thru Several Health Catalogs for Many Years. Can Be Used in 3 Different Offices at the Same Address per Purchase. Thomas J. Rundquist Has a Masters in Counseling & Has Counseled for over 20 Years Substance Abusers.
Nova Media, Inc.

AIDS Trivia Update for Nineties Updated: PC IBM Windows Version. Thomas J. Rundquist. Aug. 1994. *Items Included:* Flash Card Version & 20 page report (HIV/AIDS Surveillance Report) by U.S. Public Health Service. *Customer Support:* Questions answered by phone or FAX. 9:30-5PM EST.
MS-DOS 6.0, Windows 3.1. IBM & compatibles 3 1/2 disk (2Mb). disk $39.95 (ISBN 1-884239-02-1). *Optimal configuration:* MS-DOS 6.0, Windows 3.1. Networks supported: Usual.
Update in the Surgeon General's Report on HIV/AIDS As of 1994, As Compares to 1987! Surgeon General Report. Questions & Answers Include Latest Copy of HIV/AIDS Surveillance Report by U.S. Public Health Service.
Nova Media, Inc.

AIDSaide. *Customer Support:* Toll free telephone support.
DOS 3.1 or higher. IBM PC & compatibles. disk $595.00.
This Solution is a Personal Tumor Registry for Medical Facilities That are Responsible for the Care & Followup of HIV+ Patients & Their Contacts & is Built along Similar Precepts to the Above Registries. Demographic Data is Managed, Followed by the Input of Clinical Data that Includes the Results of Tuberculin Skin Tests, Chest Xrays, EIA, Western Blot, Antigen Testing as Well as T-Cell Levels & Ratios, Therapy, Social-Support Interventions, Referrals, Risk Factors, Current Status & Return Date. Another Set of Data is Collected for Contacts. When Installed in a Multiple Clinic Environment, Each Local Database Can be Sent on Floppy Diskettes to the Central Facility for Master Inspection. The Solution was Designed with the Consultation of a Team of Public Health Specialists.
SRC Systems, Inc.

AIDSLINE CD-ROM Database. Jul. 1992.
MS Windows 3.1 or higher. IBM & compatibles (4Mb). CD-ROM disk $245.00-$395.00; Networks $795.00 & up. *Nonstandard peripherals required:* Magnetic or CD-ROM, using ISO 9660. *Optimal configuration:* IBM & compatibles, 80386 or higher, 4Mb RAM, 20Mb hard disk, mouse, MS Windows 3.1 or higher.
System 6.0.7 or higher. Apple Macintosh (3Mb). CD-ROM disk $245.00-$395.00; Networks $795.00 & up. *Optimal configuration:* Apple Macintosh Plus or higher, 3Mb RAM, System 6.0.7 or higher.
AIDSLINE Is an Electronic Reference Database to the Published Literature on AIDS Research & Treatment. Contains Bibliographic References Published by the U.S. National Library of Medicine since 1980, Covering the Biomedical, Epidemiologic, Social & Behavioral Sciences Literature on AIDS. The Database Contents, Including more than 60,000 References & Abstracts, Are Distributed on CD-ROM (Compact Disc, Read-Only Memory) Optical Disc. Knowledge Finder Search-&-Retrieval Software Makes Searching of the AIDSLINE Database Easy, Effective & Fast. After the User Types a Phrase or Sentence Describing the Information Needed, It selects the References in the Database That Appear to Best Match the Request, & Presents Them in Order of likely relevance. The AIDSLINE Database Covers Materials Published since 1980.
Aries Systems Corp.

AIM for Utility Companies: Utility Company Processing for Digital Equipment Corporation Systems. Version: 2. 1985. *Compatible Hardware:* DEC, VAX. *Operating System(s) Required:* VMS. *Language(s):* DIBOL (source code included).
contact publisher for price.
Features Meter Reading Sheets, Route Sorting & Statistical & Financial Reporting for Residential, Commercial, & Industrial Customers.
Philip Lieberman & Assocs., Inc.

AIM Problem Solver. Version: 1.1.1. 1990. *Items Included:* Manual, tutorials. *Customer Support:* 30 day money back guarantee, maintenance.
DOS. IBM PC or compatibles (640k). disk $1495.00. *Optimal configuration:* Hard drive, math coprocessor.
Macintosh. 3.5" disk $1495.00.
Advanced Machine Learning That Automatically Models Relationships in a Database of Numerical Data. Using Abductive Reasoning Technology. Given a Database of Operational, Simulated, Historical, or Expert-Generated Examples, the Product Synthesizes Abductive Networks & Encodes Them into Computer Subroutines That Can Be Readily Incorporated into Application Software. An Abductive Network Is a Feed-Forward Layered Network of Functional Nodes. Unlike Other Neural Network Techniques, Network Connectivity, Node Types, & Coefficient Values Are All Determined Automatically.
AbTech Corp.

AIM Resource Accounting. Version: 2.0. 1989. *Items Included:* Users manual. *Customer Support:* Annual update service $270.00-$1980.00 (telephone support, updates) price dependant upon class of computer, on-site training $900.00 per day plus expenses & preparation, 60 day warranty on defective merchandise.
UNIX (300k). $1350.00-$9000.00 dependant on class. *Addl. software required:* Standard UNIX accounting software.
Monitors UNIX Resource Usage by Users, Groups of Users & Projects. Allocated System Resource Charges to Distinctive User Groups, & Generates Charge Statements. Provides Various Levels of Usage Reports on Information Such As User, Resource, & Time Period.
AIM Technology, Inc.

AIM Suite III Multiuser Benchmark. Version: 3.1. 1986. *Items Included:* Users manual. *Customer Support:* On-site training $900.00 per day plus expenses & preparations, annual update service (telephone support, product updates) $2950.00.
UNIX (128k). $8900.00. *Addl. software required:* C-Compiler.
A Software Tool for Measuring & Comparing System Performances of Multi-User, Multiprocessor UNIX Systems. Suite III Uses 31 Functional Tests to Evaluate Multiuser & Multiprocess System Performance under User-Defined Application Mixes. Provides Graphic Reports Showing Multiuser Response Time & User Throughout. Measures the Effects of Commonly Used System Resources.
AIM Technology, Inc.

Air Defense. *Compatible Hardware:* TRS-80 Model I, Model III, Model 4 with Level II BASIC. *Language(s):* Language. *Memory Required:* 16k.
disk $18.95.
cassette $14.95.
Arcade Game.
Dynacomp, Inc.

Air Flight Simulation. *Compatible Hardware:* TRS-80.
contact publisher for price.
Instant Software, Inc.

Air Pre-Heat. Version: 2. Information Resource Consultants. Jan. 1988. *Compatible Hardware:* IBM PC. *Language(s):* BASIC. *Memory Required:* 128k.
disk $100.00 ea.
IBM PC. (Order no.: 05-251).
Predicts Fuel Savings on Fired Heaters & Specifies the Air Pre-Heater Performance. Program Allows Specification of System Leakage & Temperature Drops for Precise Efficiency & Economical Analysis. Program Features Flue Gas Generator, Bridgewall & Flue Gas Temperature Properties for Both Natural Draft & Air Pre-Heat Conditions. Program Calculates Radiant/Convection Duty Shift for Natural Draft & Air Pre-Heat Conditions & Back Checks Both Conditions Against Total Heater Absorbed Duty for Proper Closure.
Information Resource Consultants.

Air Systems. Jul. 1994. *Items Included:* User Manual on disk. *Customer Support:* 90 Days.
DOS 3.1 or higher. 286 or higher. disk $499.95 (ISBN 0-933735-02-2). Networks supported: All that Clarion Supports.
A Program for Tracking Service & Customer Information.
Tin Man Software.

Airball. Micro Deal. Jul. 1987. *Compatible Hardware:* Atari ST. *Memory Required:* 512k.
3.5" disk $39.95 (ISBN 0-923213-77-5, Order no.: AT-AIR).
Guide the Airball Through a Maze of 3-D Graphic Rooms in Search of the Spell Book.
MichTron, Inc.

Airball Construction Set. Microdeal. Nov. 1987. *Compatible Hardware:* Atari ST. *Memory Required:* 512k.
3.5" disk $24.95.
User Can Construct Airball Game Rooms Without Learning Programming.
MichTron, Inc.

Airborne Ranger. 1988. *Compatible Hardware:* Commodore 64/28, IBM PC. *Customer Support:* Free customer service, (410) 771-1151, Ext. 350.
Commodore. disk $19.95.
IBM. 3.5" or 5.25" disk $19.95.
A Fast Paced Action Simulation Where You Experience the Danger & Excitement of Infiltration & Combat. Includes a Variety of Missions, Extensive Graphics, Realistic Action & Modern Weapons.
MicroProse Software.

AIRCON Pneumatic Conveying System Analysis. *Items Included:* Bound manual. *Customer Support:* Free hotline - no time limit; 30 day limited warranty; updates are $5/disk plus S&H.
MS-DOS 2.0 or higher. IBM & compatibles (512k). disk $149.95. *Nonstandard peripherals required:* Printer supported (Epson, IBM, Toshiba, NEC, & HP).
Analyzes Bulk Material (Positive Pressure, Dilute Phase) Pneumatic Conveying Systems. For a Given Set of Design Conditions, AIRCON Calculates Responses Such As Total Pressure Drop; Material Ratio; Pickup Velocity; Heat Transfer Between Air & Product; & More.
Dynacomp, Inc.

Airflow. *Items Included:* Bound manual, demo diskette. *Customer Support:* Free hotline - no time limit; 30 day limited warranty; updates are $5/disk plus S&H.
MS-DOS 2.0 or higher. IBM & compatibles (128k). disk $119.95. *Nonstandard peripherals required:* Printer supported, but not necessary.
Helps HVAC Engineers Select Duct & Fan Sizes. It Calculates Direct Velocity & Pressure As Well As Brake Horsepower Requirements under Standard & Nonstandard Conditions. Analyzes Square, Rectangular, & Round Ducts.
Dynacomp, Inc.

Airheart. Dan Gorlin Productions. Sep. 1986. *Compatible Hardware:* Apple IIe, IIc, IIgs. *Memory Required:* 128k. *General Requirements:* Joystick or mouse, Apple Graphics Tablet, or KoalaPad.
disk $34.95 (Order no.: APDSK-27).
You'll Have to Find the Sleeping Prince Flying over the Ocean in an Amazingly Quick, Jet Powered Sled That Can Maneuver on a Dime. You'll Fight Wave After Wave of Robot Defenses. Spirit Guardians Will Present You with Specific Tasks You Must Accomplish in Order to Fight the Final Battle. Features 16-Color Double Hi-Resolution Graphics & 3-D Animation.
Broderbund Software, Inc.

Airline 500: A Buyer's Guide. Interavia Magazine Staff & Charles Miller. Feb. 1995. *Items Included:* Self running. *Customer Support:* 90 day unlimited warranty.
Macintosh. CD-ROM disk Contact publisher for price.
Pyramid Media Group.

Airline 500. 1995.
Windows (4Mb). CD-ROM disk $200.00. *Nonstandard peripherals required:* CD-ROM drive. *Addl. software required:* Pyramid Software.
Each Year INTERAVIA, an Aerospace Industry Monthly, Surveys All Airlines Carrying Half a Million Passengers or More a Year. This Product is a Buyers Guide Based on the INTERAVIA Survey & Packaged in a Convenient, Comprehensive CD-ROM Format That Includes More Than Three Hundred Airlines. Classifies the World's Major International & Regional Airlines by Region & by Type. Each Entry Includes Traffic Statistics & Information on the Airline's Principle Routes, the Composition of its Fleet, Its Senior Executives, & More. Other Features Include Text Search & a Glossary of Abbreviations & Acronyms.
Howell Pr., Inc.

Airmail Pilot. *Compatible Hardware:* TRS-80. contact publisher for price.
Instant Software, Inc.

AISCBEAM. 1984. *Compatible Hardware:* IBM PC. *Operating System(s) Required:* MS-DOS. *Language(s):* BASIC. *Memory Required:* 128k. $395.00.
Solution Provides Reactions, Shears, Moments, Deflection & Angles of Rotation at Beam Ends, Date for Plotting Curves for Shear, Moment & Deflection is Provided. Superpositioning of Two or More Beam Loading Conditions Is Possible. Over 50 Cases Included, Covering Almost All Possible Types of Loading.
Technical Research Services, Inc.

AKSATINT - Satellite Interference Analysis & Simulation Using Personal Computers. NASA Jet Propulsion Laboratory. Aug. 1988. *Items Included:* Source code. *Customer Support:* Limited telephone support from COSMIC.
PC-DOS. IBM PC series. $200.00 Program; $16.00 documentation (Order no.: NPO-17500).
Macintosh.
COSMIC.

AL-Qadin: The Genie's Curse (Jewel Case CD). Nov. 1995. *Customer Support:* 30 day limited warranty.
DOS 5.0 or higher. 386/33 (4Mb). CD-ROM disk $9.95 (ISBN 0-917059-46-8, Order no.: 062671). *Optimal configuration:* 486, 16Mb hard drive space, VGA.
This Single Character Fantasy Role-Playing Game Is an Arabian Nights Tale of High Magic & Dark Deeds. An Advanced Dungeons & Dragons Fantasy Role-Playing Game.
Strategic Simulations, Inc.

ALA Lab System. *Version:* 1.5. Luan Nguyen et al. Sep. 1992. *Items Included:* Teacher's manual, student manual, authors' guide, updates, headphones & PC audio card. *Customer Support:* 10% mandatory software maintenance. Includes phone service, replacement disks, & all software updates.
DOS 3.1 or higher. IBM or compatible (640k). $2000.00. *Networks supported:* Novell, Netware, LANtastic, ArcNet.
Computer Assisted Language Learning for IBM & Apple II - IBM Product. Includes Digitized Audio, Authoring/Editing - Preprogrammed Lessons & Exercises.
Regents/ALA Co.

Alaska Gunlog. Marvin J. Andresen & Ronald W. Gatterdam. Oct. 1989. *Items Included:* User manual. *Customer Support:* 30 day unlimited warranty. 1 yr. maintenance $200.00.
MS-DOS 2.0 or higher. $79.95.
Microcomputer Program for Recording & Retrieving Firearm Acquisitions & Dispositions. Program Satisfies BATF Requirements. Queries Can Be Made by Book Number (Range), by Acquisition or by Sales Date (Range), by Buyer or by Seller, by Manufacturer, Type, Model, Caliber, Action, &/or Serial Number. Reports Are Summary or All Details, & Can Be for Sold, Unsold, or All.
AK-D Software.

Albert J. Lowry Real Estate Investment & Management. Jun. 1987. *Compatible Hardware:* Apple II+, IIe, IIc, IIgs; IBM PC, PC XT, PC AT. *Operating System(s) Required:* PC-DOS 2.0 or higher for IBM PC, PC XT; PC-DOS 3.0 or higher for IBM PC AT. *Memory Required:* Apple 64k, IBM 256k. *General Requirements:* Apple: 1 or 2 floppy disk drives, & a Videx UltraTerm, Videx VideoTerm or Apple 80-column display card and monitor; IBM: 2 double-sided floppy disk drives or 1 double-sided floppy disk drive & 1 fixed disk drive.
contact publisher for price.
Will Help Users Target Best Buys, Recognize Properties That Will Increase in Value, Minimize Down Payment & Develop Cost Effective Management Strategies.
Brady Computer Bks.

Alcor Pascal. *Compatible Hardware:* Apple II; Kaypro; Osborne 1; TRS-80 Model I, Model III, Model 4, Model 12, Model 16. *Operating System(s) Required:* CP/M, TRSDOS. *Memory Required:* 48k.
disk $199.00.
Compiled Language. When Using This Program It Is Necessary to Have the Program Translated into an Object Format.
Alcor Systems.

Alcor Pascal & Advanced Development Package. *Compatible Hardware:* TRS-80 Model I, Model III. *Operating System(s) Required:* CP/M, NEW-DOS-80, L-DOS, TRSDOS. *Memory Required:* 48k.
contact publisher for price.
Alcor Systems.

Aldus Dictionary for Macintosh. Jul. 1993. *Customer Support:* For customer service, product registration, upgrades, technical support, & CustomerFirst service plans, customers may call Aldus Customer Services at (206) 628-2320.
Macintosh. Contact publisher for price (ISBN 1-56026-189-7).
Aldus Corp.

Aldus Dictionary for Windows. Jun. 1993. *Customer Support:* For customer service, product registration, upgrades, technical support, & CustomerFirst service plans, customers may call Aldus Customer Services at (206) 628-2320.
Windows. Contact publisher for price (ISBN 1-56026-188-9).
Aldus Corp.

Aldus Digital Darkroom. *Version:* 2.0. *Compatible Hardware:* Apple Macintosh Plus, SE or II. *Memory Required:* 1000k. *General Requirements:* Hard disk recommended; Mac II or SE/30 & grayscale or color video card, monitor required for grayscale viewing. *Customer Support:* Free technical support.
3.5" disk $395.00.
Offers an Image-Processing Program for the Macintosh That Functions As a Computerized Darkroom to Enhance & Compose Scanned Images, Such As Photos. The Program Includes "Intelligent" Tools for Automatic Image Manipulation, As Well As Tools for Detailed Retouching, to Give Users Complete Control Over Their Work. Features Include Auto Trace, Automatic Tracing of Gray-Scale & Other Bit-Mapped Images to Convert Them into Object-Oriented Graphics. The Selection Tools, Such As the "Magic Wand" for Automatically Choosing Areas Based on Gray Values, Allow Selection of Precise Areas for Image Enhancement. Selections Can Be Blended with or Pasted into Existing Images. Selected Areas of an Image Can Be Rotated, Scaled, Flipped or Distorted. For Detailed Retouching, There Are Brushes & Filters That Blur, Sharpen, Remove Noise or Create Special Effects.
Aldus Corp. (Consumer Division).

Aldus Gallery Effects: Classic Art, Volume 1. *Version:* 1.5. Aug. 1991. *Items Included:* User manual. *Customer Support:* Free technical support.
System 6.0.5 or higher, Finder 6.1 or higher. Macintosh SE/30, Classic II, or LC (2Mb). 3.5" disk $199.00. *Nonstandard peripherals required:* 32-bit QuickDraw 1.2 compatible with System 7.0; Color monitor & color card for SE/30 or II; hard drive. *Optimal configuration:* Macintosh II series, Quadra 700 or 900, 5Mb of RAM, hard drive.
Windows 3.0 or higher. 286 based DOS compatible computer (2Mb). Contact publisher for price. *Nonstandard peripherals required:* 20 Mb hard disk, Windows compatible graphics display card, mouse. *Optimal configuration:* 386 or 486 based DOS compatible computer, 4Mb of RAM, 80Mb hard disk, 16 or 24 bit graphics card.
Graphics Software Package That Gives Graphic Designers the Power to Transform Any Bitmapped Image, Including Color & Gray-Scale Scans, into Sophisticated Art. Package Includes Plug-In Filters That Provide Access to the Effects Directly from Within Many Industry-Leading Graphics Programs; a Stand-Alone Application & Desk Accessory Are Also Provided for Additional Flexibility. Volume 1, Classic Art, Provides Sixteen Master Effects with Thousands of Variations. Easy-to-Use Dialog Box Has Adjustable Settings Controls & Preview Capability. User Can Save up to 25 Customized Settings by Name with Each Filter. Effects Can Be Applied to Unique Selection Areas or to the

Entire Image. Effects Can Be Overlapped. Animator Format Available for Applying Effects to PICS Animation. Support for 8-Bit & 24-Bit Color.
Aldus Corp.

Aldus IntelliDraw. *Version:* 1.0. Jun. 1992. *Items Included:* Reference manual, user's guide, 90 minute training video. *Customer Support:* Free technical support.
- Windows 3.0 or higher. 286-based DOS compatible computer (4Mb). disk $299.00. *Nonstandard peripherals required:* Hard disk, EGA card, mouse. *Addl. software required:* Adobe Type Manager 2.0.
- System 6.0.5 or higher. Macintosh Plus, SE, Classic, Portable, or Powerbook 100, (2Mb). 3.5" disk $299.00. *Nonstandard peripherals required:* Hard disk. *Addl. software required:* Adobe Type Manager 2.0.

Cross Platform Drawing Program. Smart Tools Link Graphics in Drawings So They Respond to Changes Automatically. Create Visual "What-If" Scenarios with "Flip Books" & Intelligent Clip Art & Templates That Have Pre-Defined Relationships Built-In to Save Time. Link Objects to Maintain Specific Relationships Such As Size, Alignment, Distance, & Angle. Use the Symmetrigon & Connectigon Tools To Produce Symetric Shapes & Connect New Shapes to Existing Objects. Autoalignment, Shape Blending, Arrows & Dashes, Text Handling Capabilities, Unlimited Layers, Color Gradients, Object Animation, Slide Show Mode, Standard Draw Tools, & More. Shares Files Between Macintosh & Windows Versions.
Aldus Corp.

Aldus PageMaker for Macintosh. *Version:* 5.0. Apr. 1993. *Customer Support:* For customer service, product registration, upgrades, technical support, & CustomerFirst service plans, customers may call Aldus Customer Services at (206) 628-2320.
- System 7, also runs under System 6.0.7 with Finder 6.1.7 or higher. Apple Macintosh LC series or Classic II, Sytem 6.0.7 (4Mb). $716.00 license pack; $5728.00 10-user package. *Optimal configuration:* Any Apple Macintosh II series, Quadra, or SE/30 computer, System 7.0 or higher, 5-8Mb RAM, & an 80Mb hard drive.

Design & Redesign Quickly, Freely, Precisely - You Can Control the Entire Creative Process, from Idea Generation to Color Separation, Without Ever Leaving PageMaker. Create Documents of Any Length & Complexity - Even Customize PageMaker to Suit Your Unique Design & Publishing Needs. Import Text & Graphics Files with a Single Keystroke & Easily Share Publications with Colleagues - You Can Collaborate Creatively, Spending Less Time Struggling with File Formats & More Time Designing. Lay Out Your Publications Quickly & Easily with a Smooth, Simple Interface That Doesn't Get in the Way of Your Creative Process & Natural Work Style.
Aldus Corp.

Aldus PageMaker for Windows. *Version:* 5.0. Apr. 1993. *Customer Support:* For customer service, product registration, upgrades, technical support, & CustomerFirst service plans, customers may call Aldus Customer Services at (206) 628-2320.
- Microsoft Windows 3.1 or higher & Windows 3.1-compatible hardware. 386-based DOS-compatible computer (4Mb). $716.00 license pack; $5728.00 10-user package. *Optimal configuration:* 486- or 386-based DOS-compatible computer, 4Mb RAM, 80Mb hard drive, high-resolution graphics adaptor card (such as a Super VGA or XGA), & a mouse.

Import Virtually Any Text or Graphics File with a Single Keystroke & Easily Share Publications with Colleagues - You Can Collaborate Creatively, Free from the Hassles of Incompatible Hardware & Software. Create Any Kind of Document - Long or Short, Black-&-White or Color, Simple or Complex - Plus Increase Your Productivity & Efficiency by Customizing PageMaker to Suit Your Specific Publishing Needs. Freely Explore, Then Refine & Perfect Your Designs - You Can Control the Entire Creative Process, from Generating Concepts to Finalizing Prepress Preparations, Without Ever Leaving PageMaker. Lay Out Your Publications Quickly & Easily with a Smooth, Simple Interface That Doesn't Get in the Way of Your Creative Process & Natural Work Style.
Aldus Corp.

Aldus Personal Press. *Version:* 2.0. *Items Included:* Workbook for text & graphic storage, post-it note facility, navigator, word processor with Hyphenation, thesaurus, search & replace & spelling checker. *Customer Support:* Free technical support.
- Mac Plus (1Mb); Mac II or higher (2Mb) for color. disk $199.00.

Page-Layout Software That Automatically Assembles Text & Graphics. AutoCreate Feature Assembles Text & Graphics Through Intelligent Templates That Guide User Through Basic Design Choices & Build a Document. Interactive Previews Provide Constant Feedback & Automate Routine Tasks. Includes a Full-Featured Word Processor That Provides for Editing & Creation of Text Directly within the Application with Spelling Checker & Thesaurus. Also Includes the Link Navigator, which Visually Locates & Moves Through Components of a Story; the Workbook Which Acts As a Scrapbook Attached to each Document; Posted-Notes to Electronically Document Work; & On-Line Help with Inactive Menu Items. On-Screen Free Rotation of Text & Graphics, Text Wrap Around Graphics & Other Text, Support for Spot Color Seperation Are Included.
Aldus Corp. (Consumer Division).

Aldus Supercard. *Version:* 1.6. May 1989. *Customer Support:* Full manual, language guide, program disk & samples disk.
- Macintosh Plus, SE, Mac II or x. 3.5" disk $299.00. *Nonstandard peripherals required:* 2Mb recommended, required for color viewing.

User Can Create Custom Macintosh Applications That Work Like Commercial Software. HyperCard Compatible. Features Menus, Multiple Windows, Draw & High-Resolution Printing Using SuperTalk.
Aldus Corp. (Consumer Division).

Aldus SuperPaint. *Version:* 3.5. *Customer Support:* Free technical support.
- Macintosh Plus or higher. 3.5" disk $149.95.

Combines Painting, Drawing & Image Enhancement Capabilities in One Graphics Program. Access 1-Bit through 32-Bit Documents without 24-Bit Card. Interface Includes Pop-Ups, Tear-Away Menus, & Hot Keys to Easily Access Tools & Palettes. Tools & Features Work Together Intuitively - No Restriction to Use Particular Tools for Particular Effects. Custom & Provided Textures & Gradients Can Easily Add Dramatic Effects to Projects. SuperBits (Bitmap Graphics in Draw Layer) Can Be Edited at any Resolution. Scan Images Directly in, & Use Image-Enhancement Tools for Basic Editing. Draw & Paint Layer Plug-In Tools & Support for Aldus Gallery Effects. RGB, HSB, & CMYK Color Models. Exports as TIFF or EPS. Imports Color, Black & White, & Grayscale TIFF, PICT, PICT2, EPS, Startup Screen, & MacPaint Files.
Aldus Corp. (Consumer Division).

Aldus TechNotes for Aldus FreeHand for the Macintosh. *Version:* 3.1. Oct. 1992. *Customer Support:* For customer service, product registration, upgrades, technical support, & CustomerFirst service plans, customers may call Aldus Customer Services at (206) 628-2320. Macintosh. Contact publisher for price (ISBN 1-56026-183-8).
Aldus Corp.

ALE. *Version:* 1.5. *Compatible Hardware:* TRS-80 Model I, Model III. *Operating System(s) Required:* TRSDOS, L-DOS, NEW-DOS-80, DOSPLUS. *Language(s):* Z80 Assembly.
disk $49.95, incl. documentation, hot-line support & reference manual.
documentation $20.00.
Disk-Based Assembly Language Editor & Assembler for TRS-80 Systems.
The Alternate Source.

Alexandria. *Version:* 3.7. Feb. 1995. *Items Included:* Perfect bound 320 page manuals, network sharing software for Multi User versions, training tutorial. *Customer Support:* 24 Hour Support Hotline, Unlimited FAX/AppleLink Support, Software Updates, Version Upgrades, COMPanion Newsletters, User Group Sponsorship, & Area Training Seminars. The first year of support is included with purchase. Annual support renewal is $399.00.
- MAC O/S. Macintosh SE or higher (1Mb). 3.5" disk $1195.00-$4395.00. *Optimal configuration:* LC475 or Power Macintosh. *Networks supported:* All Macintosh compatible networks, including AppleTalk, EtherNet, Local Talk & Novell.

Offers Fully Integrated Macintosh Library Automation. Modules Include Circulation, Reports, Budgets, Orders, Subscriptions, & a Powerful Catalog with Advanced Searching Capabilities, Including Boolean Logic & a Phonetic 'Sounding-Like'. Full MARC compatible, & Is the Only Macintosh Product to Integrate Directly with Brodart's PRECISION ONE.
COMPanion Corp.

ALFA: Automated Law Firm Accounting System, Level II. 1981. *Compatible Hardware:* IBM PC & compatibles. *Operating System(s) Required:* PC-DOS, MS-DOS. *Memory Required:* 512k. *General Requirements:* Hard disk, printer, RM COBOL Systems Package.
disk $990.00-$2690.00.
GL & AP System. Prepares Law Firm's Financial Statements Including Income Statements, Balance Sheets, Trial Balance Worksheets, GL, & Statements of Partner's Capital. Includes Report Writer for User-Defined Report Formats. Integrated with BARRISTER's BILLING & TIME ACCOUNTING (B&TA) System.
Barrister Information Systems Corp.

Alfred's Adult Piano Theory: Level 1. *Version:* 3.1. Sandy Feldstein. Aug. 1989. *Memory Required:* 48k. *Items Included:* Manual. *Customer Support:* 90-day warranty, phone support.
- Apple, Commodore. disk $49.95 (ISBN 0-88284-465-2, Order no.: 3104).
- Atari. disk $49.95 (ISBN 0-88284-466-0, Order no.: 3105).
- IBM PC & compatibles. 3.5" disk $49.95 (ISBN 0-88284-463-6, Order no.: 3106).
- IBM PC & compatibles. disk $49.95 (ISBN 0-88284-464-4, Order no.: 3107).
- Macintosh. disk $59.95 (ISBN 0-88284-467-9, Order no.: 3116).
- Yamaha CI. disk $49.95 (ISBN 0-88284-468-7, Order no.: 3115).
- Apple 3.5. disk $49.95 (ISBN 0-88284-476-8, Order no.: 3950).

Correlates with Alfred's Adult Piano Course Book 1. A Game Approach for Piano Education Reinforcement, MIDI Compatible.
Alfred Publishing Co., Inc.

Alfred's Basic Band Computer Tutor. Sandy Feldstein & John O'Reilly. *Compatible Hardware:* Apple II series, Commodore 64/128. *Memory Required:* 48k. *Customer Support:* Available.
disk $29.95 (ISBN 0-88284-374-5, Order no.: 2525).
Teaches How to Play Band Instruments. Includes Tuning, Rhythm Exercises, Duets That Can Be Played with the Computer, On-Screen Conductor, & Theory Games for Flute, Oboe, Clarinet, Bass Clarinet, Alto/Tenor/Baritone Sax, Cornet/Trumpet, French Horn, Baritone (B.C. & T.C.), Eb Horn, Trombone, Bassoon, Tuba & Mallet Percussion.
Alfred Publishing Co., Inc.

Alfred's Basic Piano Theory: Levels 3-5. *Version:* 3.1. Sandy Feldstein. *Compatible Hardware:* Apple II series, Atari XL/XE, Commodore 64/128, IBM PC & compatibles, Macintosh, Yamaha C1. *Memory Required:* 48k. *Customer Support:* Available.
IBM. 3.5" disk $49.95 (ISBN 0-88284-389-3, Order no.: 3146).
IBM. disk $49.95 (ISBN 0-88284-390-7, Order no.: 3147).
Apple, Commodore. disk $49.95 (ISBN 0-88284-391-5, Order no.: 3148).
Atari. 3.5" disk $49.95 (ISBN 0-88284-392-3, Order no.: 3513).
Macintosh. 3.5" disk $59.95 (ISBN 0-88284-393-1, Order no.: 3119).
Yamaha C1. ROM cartridge $49.95 (ISBN 0-88284-394-X, Order no.: 3120).
Apple 3.5. disk $49.95 (ISBN 0-88284-478-4, Order no.: 3949).
Correlates With Alfred's "Basic Piano Library" Books 3, 4 & 5. A Game Approach for Piano Education Reinforcement. MIDI Compatible.
Alfred Publishing Co., Inc.

Alge-Blaster 3.
Windows. IBM & compatibles. CD-ROM disk $59.95 (Order no.: R1233). *Nonstandard peripherals required:* CD-ROM drive.
Guide Yourself Through an Entire Year's Algebra Course Using This Program As an Interactive Tutor. Four Separate Activities Use Enhanced Graphics & Animation to Help Teach about Integers, Monomials, Polynomials, Factoring, Algebraic Fractions, Radical Expressions, Quadratic Equations, Graphing & Word Problems.
Library Video Co.

Algebra: Equation-Solving Skills. (Micro Learn Tutorial Ser.).
MAC. IBM (128k), Macintosh (2 Mb), Apple II Series, (48k), Commodore 64. 5.25" disk, $39.95 (Lab pack/5 $99.00), 3.5" disk, $44.95 (Lab pack/5 $115.00). Apple, IBM or Macintosh network, $249.00 (ISBN 1-57265-057-5).
IBM. (ISBN 0-939153-51-3).
APP. disk (ISBN 0-939153-99-8).
Tutorial Covers the Skills & Concepts Needed to Solve Equations & Word Problems. Topics Include Properties, Order of Operations, Simplifying Expressions, Substituting, Evaluating Expressions, Equations, Inequalities & Word Problems. Tutorial & test mode. Tutorial mode gives explanations for each answer choice.
Word Assocs., Inc.

Algebra I, Vol. 1: Sets & Notation. 1995. *Items Included:* Full manual. *Customer Support:* Free telephone support - 90 days, 30-day warranty.
MS-DOS 3.2 or higher. 286 (584k). disk $44.95. *Nonstandard peripherals required:* CGA/EGA/VGA.
Essential Concepts That Form the Basis for Many Disciplines Including Computers.
Dynacomp, Inc.

Algebra I, Vol. 2: Number Systems. 1995. *Items Included:* Full manual. *Customer Support:* Free telephone support - 90 days, 30-day warranty.
MS-DOS 3.2 or higher. 286 (584k). disk $44.95. *Nonstandard peripherals required:* CGA/EGA/VGA.
Learn All about the Number Line, Integers, Fractions, Prime Factors, Rational Numbers & More.
Dynacomp, Inc.

Algebra III, Vol. 1: Polynomials. 1995. *Items Included:* Full manual. *Customer Support:* Free telephone support - 90 days, 30-day warranty.
MS-DOS 3.2 or higher. 286 (584k). disk $44.95. *Nonstandard peripherals required:* CGA/EGA/VGA.
Learn about Coefficients, Roots, Quadratics & More.
Dynacomp, Inc.

Algebra II, Vol. 1: Equations & Formulas. 1995. *Items Included:* Full manual. *Customer Support:* Free telephone support - 90 days, 30-day warranty.
MS-DOS 3.2 or higher. 286 (584k). disk $44.95. *Nonstandard peripherals required:* CGA/EGA/VGA.
Learn Word Statements, Polynomials, Powers, Solving Linear Equations, Inequalities, & More.
Dynacomp, Inc.

Algebra II, Vol. 2: Linear Relations. 1995. *Items Included:* Full manual. *Customer Support:* Free telephone support - 90 days, 30-day warranty.
MS-DOS 3.2 or higher. 286 (584k). disk $44.95. *Nonstandard peripherals required:* CGA/EGA/VGA.
Learn How to Solve Linear Equations, Use Graphs, Determinants, Functions & More.
Dynacomp, Inc.

Algebra 1. Jan. 1994. *Items Included:* Program on CD-ROM, CD Booklet, & Registration Card. *Customer Support:* Free unlimited support via telephone.
Windows 3.1 or higher running under DOS 5.0 or higher. 386 SX (4Mb RAM; 500k low Dos Mem; 6Mb free disk space). CD-ROM disk $49.00 (ISBN 1-57268-022-9, Order no.: 53102). *Nonstandard peripherals required:* Sound card (either: Sound Blaster - 8, 16, PRO; Media Vision ProAudio Spectrum; or Microsoft Sound System); MPC Compatible CD-ROM drive; VGA monitor; & microphone. *Optimal configuration:* 25MHz 386 SX.
High School Math for Windows. These Programs Offer Interactive Instruction for High-School-Aged Students. These CD-ROMs Contain Interactive Lessons Which Parallel the Pre-Algebra Concepts Taught in Eighth & Ninth Grades. Algebra 1 Reinforces Major Algebraic Concepts Your Child Must Master in School. Individual CD-ROMs for Geometry, Algebra 2, & Trigonometry Complement Programs for Grades Nine Through Twelve.
Conter Software.

Algebra 1. Jan. 1994. *Items Included:* Program on CD-ROM, CD Booklet, & Registration Card. *Customer Support:* Free unlimited customer support via telephone.
Windows 3.1 or higher running under DOS 5.0 or higher. 386 SX (4Mb RAM; 500k low Dos Mem; 6Mb free disk space). CD-ROM disk $249.00 (ISBN 1-57268-056-3, Order no.: 13101). *Nonstandard peripherals required:* Sound card (either: Sound Blaster - 8, 16, PRO; Media Vision ProAudio Spectrum; or Microsoft Sound System); MPC compatible CD-ROM drive; VGA monitor; & microphone. *Optimal configuration:* 25 MHz 386 SX.

High School Math for Windows: These Programs Offer Interactive Instruction for High-School-Aged Students. These CD-ROMs Contain Interactive Lessons Which Parallel the Pre-Algebra Concepts Taught in Eighth & Ninth Grades. Algebra 1 Reinforces Major Algebraic Concepts Your Child Must Master in School. Individual CD-ROMs for Geometry, Algebra 2, & Trigonometry Complement Programs for Grades Nine Through Twelve.
Conter Software.

Algebra 2. Jan. 1994. *Items Included:* Program on CD-ROM, CD Booklet, & Registration Card. *Customer Support:* Free unlimited support via telephone.
Windows 3.1 or higher running under DOS 5.0 or higher. 386 SX (4Mb RAM; 500k low Dos Mem; 6Mb free disk space). CD-ROM disk $49.00 (ISBN 1-57268-024-5, Order no.: 53104). *Nonstandard peripherals required:* Sound card (either: Sound Blaster - 8, 16, PRO; Media Vision ProAudio Spectrum; or Microsoft Sound System); MPC Compatible CD-ROM drive; VGA monitor; & microphone. *Optimal configuration:* 25MHz 386 SX.
High School Math for Windows. These Programs Offer Interactive Instruction for High-School-Aged Students. These CD-ROMs Contain Interactive Lessons Which Parallel the Pre-Algebra Concepts Taught in Eighth & Ninth Grades. Algebra 1 Reinforces Major Algebraic Concepts Your Child Must Master in School. Individual CD-ROMs for Geometry, Algebra 2, & Trigonometry Complement Programs for Grades Nine Through Twelve.
Conter Software.

Algebra 2. Jan. 1994. *Items Included:* Program on CD-ROM, CD Booklet, & Registration Card. *Customer Support:* Free unlimited customer support via telephone.
Windows 3.1 or higher running under DOS 5.0 or higher. 386 SX (4Mb RAM; 500k low Dos Mem; 6Mb free disk space). CD-ROM disk $249.00 (ISBN 1-57268-058-X, Order no.: 13103). *Nonstandard peripherals required:* Sound card (either: Sound Blaster - 8, 16, PRO; Media Vision ProAudio Spectrum; or Microsoft Sound System); MPC compatible CD-ROM drive; VGA monitor; & microphone. *Optimal configuration:* 25 MHz 386 SX.
High School Math for Windows: These Programs Offer Interactive Instruction for High-School-Aged Students. These CD-ROMs Contain Interactive Lessons Which Parallel the Pre-Algebra Concepts Taught in Eighth & Ninth Grades. Algebra 1 Reinforces Major Algebraic Concepts Your Child Must Master in School. Individual CD-ROMs for Geometry, Algebra 2, & Trigonometry Complement Programs for Grades Nine Through Twelve.
Conter Software.

Algorithms in SNOBOL4. James F. Gimpel. Nov. 1986. *Compatible Hardware:* Apple Macintosh, IBM PC & compatibles. *Operating System(s) Required:* MS-DOS for IBM, Mac/OS, OS/2. *Language(s):* SNOBOL4 (source code included). *Memory Required:* 128k. *General Requirements:* SNOBOL4 or SPITBOL compiler or interpreter. *Items Included:* Diskette & book. *Customer Support:* Free.
$45.00 ea., incl. 500-page textbk.
IBM. (ISBN 0-939793-02-4, Order no.: ALGDOS).
Macintosh. (ISBN 0-939793-04-0, Order no.: ALGMAC).
SNOBOL4 Functions for Solving Commonly Encountered Programming Problems. The 140 Files Cover: Conversions, String & Array Manipulations, List Processing, Document Formatting, Pattern Construction, Sorting,

Permutations, Games, Simulations, Assemblers, Compilers, & Macro Processors. All Functions Are Provided in Ready-to-Use, "Plug-In" Form. The Textbook Deals with SNOBOL Software Engineering Techniques.
Catspaw, Inc.

Alice. Feb. 1995. *Items Included:* Warranty/registration card, game manual. *Customer Support:* Technical Support Number: 1-800-734-9466, 90 days limited warranty.
Windows 3.1; Macintosh System 7 or higher. IBM i80486SX or higher, 33MHz i80486DX recommended (8Mb); Macintosh 16MHz 68030 or higher, 25 MHz 68LC040 or higher (8Mb). CD-ROM disk $79.99 (ISBN 1-888158-04-2). *Nonstandard peripherals required:* Double-speed CD-ROM drive. *Addl. software required:* MS-DOS 5.0 or higher.
This Interactive Museum Is Set in a Brilliantly Wild Background Where Special Paintings Literally Jump & Move with a Touch of a Mouse. Reminiscent of a Maze, the Secret Passages & Rooms Draw You into Viewing the Pictures Without Even Knowing It. Cryptic Cards Assist You on Your Journey.
Synergy Interactive Corp.

Alien Arcade. Astro Cavey & Cosmil Callahan. Sep. 1995. *Customer Support:* Telephone support - free (except phone charge).
Windows 3.1. IBM & compatibles (386 DX-20) (4Mb). CD-ROM disk $12.99 (ISBN 1-57594-001-9). *Nonstandard peripherals required:* 2x CD-ROM player, Sound Card, VGA monitor. *Optimal configuration:* 486 SX-33.
6 Non-Violent Arcade Games from the Depths of Outer Space.
Kidsoft, Inc.

Alien Arcade. Sep. 1995. *Customer Support:* Telephone support - free (except phone charge).
Windows 3.1. IBM & compatibles (386 DX-20) (4Mb). CD-ROM disk $12.99 (ISBN 1-57594-040-X). *Nonstandard peripherals required:* 2x CD-ROM player, Sound Card, VGA monitor. *Optimal configuration:* 486 SX-33.
6 Non-Violent Arcade Games from the Depths of Outer Space. Blister Pack Jewel Case.
Kidsoft, Inc.

Alien Attack Force. *Compatible Hardware:* TRS-80.
contact publisher for price.
Instant Software, Inc.

Alien Fires 2199 A.D. *Compatible Hardware:* Commodore Amiga.
contact publisher for price.
Futuristic Science Fiction Role Playing Game Where You Assume the Role of a Time Lord on a Quest to Find the Insane Genius, Samuel Kurtz & Destroy His Time Machine Which Threatens the Stability of the Time Continuum. The Time Elders Deposit You on the Surface of the Mining Colony of Galaxy's End Where You Must Negotiate the Maze of Corridors Filled with Exotic Aliens, Who Can Provide Clues to Kurtz's Whereabouts or Engage You in Combat. Prior to Each Game You Create Your Own Custom Time Lord, Determining His Strengths in Seven Different Skills Including Fighting, Quickness, & Diplomacy. Features Professionally Composed & Digitized Rock Sound Track, 3D Color Graphics, Speech Synthesis, etc.
Paragon Software Corp. (Pennsylvania).

Alien Logic. Cendus Software Staff. Sep. 1995. *Items Included:* CD in jewel case. *Customer Support:* 30 Day Limited Warranty.
DOS 5.0 or higher. PC CD (4Mb). CD-ROM disk $9.95 (ISBN 0-917059-33-6, Order no.: 062561). *Optimal configuration:* 486 DX/66.
Fantasy Role Playing Game Based on the Acclaimed SkyRealms of Jorune Game System.
Strategic Simulations Inc.

Alien Mind. May 1988. *Compatible Hardware:* Apple IIgs. *Memory Required:* 512k. *General Requirements:* RGB monitor. Supersonic stereo card recommended.
3.5" disk $54.95.
Space Arcade Adventure Game That Challenges Users to Neutralize Adversaries & Regain Control of a Research Space Station.
PBI Software, Inc.

Aliens. *Compatible Hardware:* TRS-80 Model I, III.
disk $24.95.
If the Player Can Escape Annihilation by Blasting the Bombs from the Sky, He or She Will Face Landing Crafts Piloted by Suicidal Warriors.
Blue Cat.

AlisaMail. *Version:* 4.3. Apr. 1993. *Items Included:* All documentation & software media. *Customer Support:* Annual support contracts available.
VAX 3100 or higher. VT, Mac, PC. Entry level - $10,000.00/100 users. *Nonstandard peripherals required:* Ethernet board for PC server. *Addl. software required:* VMS 5.4 or higher.
An Electronic Mail Integration System Which Provides Exchange of E-Mail Messages & Binary File Attachment for Users of the Following E-mail Systems; Microsoft Mail/Mac, QuickMail, CC:Mail, Da Vinci Mail, Microsoft Mail/PC, WordPerfect Office, VMS Mail & All-in-1.
Alisa Systems, Inc.

Alkaatib International. *Version:* 2.0. Sep. 1993. *Items Included:* Arabic & English manual; 50 plus Arabic TrueType fonts, 1 English font; Arabic Keycap stickers, template. *Customer Support:* 30 days unlimited warranty; customer support is free via telephone.
IBM PC or 386 (1Mb). disk $595.00. *Addl. software required:* Windows 3.1 or higher.
Fully Windows 3.1 compatible. It Offers Both Ease of Use & Desktop Publishing. Fonts & Support for Nearly Any Printer Supported by Microsoft Windows Offers the Power to Create Arabic & Multilingual Documents. Includes Features Like Arabic/English Spell Checking, Graphics Integration (TIF, NMF, PCX) & More.
Eastern Language Systems.

All-in-One V2. *Version:* 2.02. Apr. 1994. *Items Included:* 110 page manual. *Customer Support:* 60 day limited warranty, unlimited telephone support.
Any 386, 486 or higher. disk $795.00. *Nonstandard peripherals required:* hard disk. *Addl. software required:* MS-DOS. *Optimal configuration:* Any 386, 486 or higher.
Horse Race Handicapping Software.
Cynthia Publishing Co.

All Stars. *Compatible Hardware:* TRS-80.
contact publisher for price.
Instant Software, Inc.

Ali-Tech Project Simulator. *Customer Support:* Free, brief phone consultation; on-site consultation available.
MS-DOS. IBM PC & compatibles (256K). disk $49.00. *Addl. software required:* Lotus 1-2-3 2.0, 2.1.
"Monte-Carlo" Simulation of Project Performance That Indicates the Minimum, Maximun, Average & Probability Distribution of Time Durations That a Project is Likely to Require. It is an Essential Risk-Evaluation Tool for All Projects, but it is Especially Valuable for R&D Efforts. Supplementary Calculations Help Define the Likely Duration of Experimental Work & Alternate Strategies to Reduce Uncertainty.
All-Tech Project Management Services.

All-Time Favorite Dances: Macintosh CD-ROM. Oct. 1995. *Items Included:* Instruction & information booklet in CD-ROM jewel case. *Customer Support:* Telephone technical support. No charge.
Mac OS 7.x. Macintosh 68040 recommended. Recommended for Power PC (8Mb-16Mb). CD-ROM disk $39.95 (ISBN 0-9649190-0-1, Order no.: TIG ICN 50101). *Addl. software required:* Apple Quicktime 2.0 (Included). *Optimal configuration:* Mac 68040 66 MHz Mac OS 7.5 8Mb RAM, 16-bit color (Thousands), Double-speed CD-ROM drive, optimized for Performa 575. *Networks supported:* Any Macintosh work station network.
Features High Quality Quicktime Movies of Eleven Dances, a Library Section Presenting the History of the Songs & Dances, & Costume Sections Where the User Can Dress Girls & Boys in Regional Costumes. Interactive Navigational Features Include Switching Between English & Spanish Anywhere in the Program.
Advance Multimedia.

All Track Applicant Tracking System. *Items Included:* Bound manual. *Customer Support:* Free hotline - no time limit; 30 day limited warranty; updates are $5/disk plus S&H.
MS-DOS 3.1 or higher. IBM & compatibles (512k). $899.95-$1399.95. *Nonstandard peripherals required:* Hard disk, works with monochrome or CGA/EGA/VGA; supports Epson (or compatible) & laser printers; modem (for autodialing) must be internal or external Hayes (or compatible).
demo disks & guide $19.95.
Applicant Tracking System Geared to Users Having Large Relational Databases & Needing Detailed Record-Keeping. It Is Well-Suited to Personnel Departments, Recruiting & Search Firms, & Temporary Job Placement Agencies. Locate Candidates According to Specified Requirements, & Automatically Pull up the Candidate's Records, Contacts, & Other Data. Autodialing & Networking.
Dynacomp, Inc.

Allegro CL. *Version:* 4.3. *Items Included:* Installation guide & release notes plus two books: Common LISP: the Language 2nd Ed. & Allegro CL User's Guide. *Customer Support:* Included 1st yr., renewable thereafter.
UNIX & UNIX-like operating systems (8Mb plus 80Mb hard disk) HPUX, IRIX, Solaris. Contact vendor for price.
Complete Implementation of the Common LISP Standard, Including CLOS (Common Lisp Object System). Includes an Interpreter & Compiler, Debugging Facilities & a LISP Runtime Library. Enhancements Include the Foreign Function Interface, Multiprocessing Facilities, Generation Scavenging Garbage Collection, & Allegro Presto, an Automated Runtime Delivery Solution.
Franz, Inc.

Allegro CL for Windows: Object Oriented Development Systems. *Version:* 3.0. Sep. 1995. *Items Included:* Three volume set documentation, communication package for Franx Forum BBS. *Customer Support:* 60 days support free; additional support packages available.
Microsoft Windows 3.1, Windows 95 & Windows NT. 386, 486 or Pentium based PC (4Mb). disk $595.00.
Object Oriented Development Environment for Windows. Features CLOS, the Common Lisp Object System. Common Lisp Is a Programming Language with Incremental Compilation, Automatic Memory Management, Complete Debugging Facilities & Free Delivery.
Franz, Inc.

ALLEGRO COMPOSER

Allegro Composer. Version: 2.0. Items Included: Installation guide & release notes, plus Allegro Composer Users Guide. Customer Support: First year's support, maintenance, & updates included. Support package renewable for 25% of initial price per year.
Unix (12Mb). Contact vendor for price. Addl. software required: Allegro CL, X.11 windows. Optimal configuration: 12Mb or more; 120Mb hard disk.
An Interactive Window-Based Program Development Environment Designed to Improve Common LISP Programmer Productivity. Features Include Class & Process Browsers, Windowized Debugger, Graphical Profilers, Inspector, & Cross Referencer.
Franz, Inc.

Allergy Case Studies. William Doley. Feb. 1995. Customer Support: Toll-free technical support - no charge. 9AM - 5PM EST 800-343-0064.
System 7.0 or higher. Apple Macintosh (8Mb). CD-ROM disk $175.00, Individual, ,495.00 Institutional (ISBN 1-57276-016-8, Order no.: SE-016-001). Nonstandard peripherals required: CD-ROM drive.
Microsoft Windows, Version 3.1. 386 IBM-Compatible PC (8Mb). CD-ROM disk $175.00, Individual, ,495.00 Institutional. Nonstandard peripherals required: MPC Standard CD-ROM player, 640x480 display w/256 colors, MPC Standard Soundboard & Speakers.
This CD-ROM Reviews the Etiology, Pathogenesis, Diagnosis, & Management of Commonly Encountered Clinical Problems in Allergy-Immunology. The Three Case Types Are Rhinosinusitis, Obstructed Lung Disease, & Skin Disease. The Case Scenarios Are Illustrative of Situations in Which Primary Care Physicians & Subspecialists Can Collaborate in Patient Care.
SilverPlatter Education.

Alley Cat. SynSoft. Compatible Hardware: IBM PC, PC XT, PCjr, Portable PC. Memory Required: 128k. General Requirements: IBM Color Display or color TV.
disk $24.95 (Order no.: 6276621).
Freddy the Cat Is Madly in Love with Felicia & Will Do Almost Anything to "Cat-ch" up to Her. To Reach His Sweetheart, He Must Avoid Catastrophic Events. If He Is Caught He Loses a Life. If He Succeeds, He Can Reach Felicia, Receive a Kiss, Earn Bonus Points & an Extra Life.
Personally Developed Software, Inc.

Alley Stats. Items Included: Bound manual. Customer Support: Free hotline - no time limit; 30 day limited warranty; updates are $5/disk plus S&H.
Apple (48k). disk $49.95. Nonstandard peripherals required: One disk drive (two optional) & a serial printer interface.
Reports Include: A Complete Weekly Summary Sheet with All Standings, High Games & Sets, Averages, & All Other Necessary Data; a Complete Individual or Team Sheet; a Weekly Run of the Current Scores; a Sorted Average Sheet; a Final Average Sheet; a Most-Improved Bowlers List.
Dynacomp, Inc.

Alliance Plus. Version: 1.00. Jan. 1990. Items Included: Quarterly CD-ROM data discs, operating software in 3.5" & 5.25" format, documentation, & one year of toll-free 800 telephone support. Alliance Plus subscription renewals are available after the first year & must be purchased to continue receiving updated operating software & documentation, quarterly CD-ROM data discs, & toll free support. Customer Support: Support services include 90 days unlimited warranty. Free phone support. One year subscription renewal at $450.00.
IBM PC-MS/DOS. MS/DOS compatible (640k). CD-ROM disk $950.00 single site license (Order no.: BM099). Nonstandard peripherals required: Hard disk. Addl. software required: Circulation Plus or Catalog Plus. Optimal configuration: MS-DOS compatible, 640k RAM, one floppy disk drive, one 150 9660 format compatible CD-ROM player with card & cable (external), one hard disk drive. Networks supported: Novell.
A Specialized CD-ROM Data Disc Based on the Library of Congress Marc Database. Contains More Than 400,000 Book, Audio-Visual, & Serial Records - Many of Which Have Been Enhanced with: Reading Level; Interest Level; Review Source, Annotations; & LC, LC Children's, & Sears Subject Headings. New & Enhanced Records Are Being Added on an Average of 15,000 Each Quarter. This Product Is a Tool for Library Cataloging, Shelflist Data Entry, & Curriculum-Collection Development. The Perfect Retrospective Conversion Tool, Given Its Ability to Directly Interface with Both Circulation Plus Version 7 & All Versions of Circulation-Catalog Plus.
Follett Software Co.

Allied General Power Mac. Halestorm. Dec. 1995. Items Included: 96 page perfect bound manual. Customer Support: 30 day limited warranty.
Mac System 7 or higher. Mac 20MHz or Power Mac (8Mb). CD-ROM disk $59.95 (ISBN 0-917059-16-6, Order no.: 012291). Nonstandard peripherals required: Requires 13" 256 color monitor, CD-ROM 1X drive. Optimal configuration: System 7.5, 3mb free hard drive space, 2X CD-ROM drive.
World War II Strategy Game. Play 3 Campaign Games As an American, British or Soviet General Against the German Army or Choose from over 35 Scenarios That Let You Play As Either the Allied or Axis Side.
Strategic Simulations, Inc.

Allied General Win 95. Halestorm. Dec. 1995. Items Included: 64 page perfect bound manual. Customer Support: 30 day limited warranty.
Windows 3.1 or Windows 95. 486/66 CD2X (8Mb). CD-ROM disk $69.95 (ISBN 0-917059-13-1, Order no.: 052291). Optimal configuration: Pentium & 12Mb RAM.
Choose to Be an American, British or Russian General & Battle the German Army. The Three Complete Campaigns Include: the Desert, Western Front & Eastern Front.
Strategic Simulations, Inc.

Allie's Activity Kit. (Allie's Activity Ser.).
MS-DOS 5.0 or higher, Windows 3.1 or higher. 386 processor (4Mb). CD-ROM disk $59.95 (Order no.: R1251). Nonstandard peripherals required: CD-ROM drive. Optimal configuration: 386 processor operating at 16Mhz or higher, 30Mb hard drive, mouse, VGA graphic adapter & VGA color monitor (SVGA recommended), 4Mb RAM, external speakers or headphones (with sound card) that are Sound Blaster compatible.
Special Learning Activities Include Association Skills, Number Recognition, Puzzle Solving, Memory Skills, Build Your Own Town, Plant a Garden & Much More.
Library Video Co.

Allie's Activity Series.
MS-DOS 5.0 or higher, Windows 3.1 or higher. 386 processor or higher (4Mb). CD-ROM disk $119.90, Set (Order no.: R0908). Nonstandard peripherals required: CD-ROM drive. Optimal configuration: 386 processor operating at 16Mhz or higher, 30Mb hard drive, mouse, VGA graphic adapter & VGA color monitor (SVGA recommended), 4Mb RAM, external speakers or headphones (with sound card) that are Sound Blaster compatible.
Specifically Designed to Teach Youngsters about the World They Live in, This Program Encourages Children to Explore, Interact & Create. Designed by Experts from Both the Montessori & Public School Systems. 2 Volume Set.
Library Video Co.

Allie's Playhouse. (Allie's Activity Ser.).
MS-DOS 5.0 or higher, Windows 3.1 or higher. 386 processor or higher (4Mb). CD-ROM disk $59.95 (Order no.: R1250). Nonstandard peripherals required: CD-ROM drive. Optimal configuration: 386 processor operating at 16Mhz or higher, 30Mb hard drive, mouse, VGA graphic adapter & VGA color monitor (SVGA recommended), 4Mb RAM, external speakers or headphones (with sound card) that are Sound Blaster compatible.
Macintosh (4Mb). (Order no.: R1250A). Nonstandard peripherals required: 14" color monitor or larger, CD-ROM drive.
Special Learning Activities Include Counting, Telling Time, Alphabet, Spelling, Geography, Animals, Music & More.
Library Video Co.

Allotype Typographics. Compatible Hardware: Apple Macintosh. Memory Required: 512k. General Requirements: LaserWriter.
$40.00 to $160.00.
Downloadable LaserWriter Fonts.
Allotype Typographics.

AllPage.
Macintosh Plus or higher. 3.5" disk $649.00.
Hebrew/English Page-Layout Program.
Davka Corp.

AllScript. Compatible Hardware: Macintosh Plus or higher. Memory Required: 2000k.
3.5" disk $350.00.
Hebrew-English Word Processor.
Davka Corp.

Allways. Version: 1.2. Oct. 1988. Compatible Hardware: IBM PC, PC XT, PC AT & compatibles, PS/2. Operating System(s) Required: PC-DOS/MS-DOS 2.0 or higher. Memory Required: 128k. General Requirements: CGA, EGA, VGA, or Hercules display adapter, most standard printer, PostScript printers, Lotus 1-2-3 R 2.0/2.01 & Symphony R 1.1/1.2/2.0.
disk $195.00.
unconditional 30-day, money-back guarantee when purchased through Funk Software.
Produces Presentation Quality Reports from Lotus 1-2-3 Worksheets. User Can Highlight Data with Background Shading, Borders, Boxes, Lines, Grids, & Single or Double Underlining, & Apply Different Type Styles, Weights, & Sizes to Individual Cells or to Entire Ranges. Program Includes Five Fonts: Courier, Times, Times Italic, Triumvirate (Similar to Helvetica), & Triumvirate Italic. Can Embed As Many 1-2-3 Graphics in Printed Worksheet As Printer Can Resolve on the Page. Automatically Scales Graphs to Fit the Range.
Funk Software.

Almanac of WWII. Customer Support: Free, unlimited.
System 6 Mac. 030 Mac, 256 colors (4Mb). CD-ROM disk $24.95. Nonstandard peripherals required: Sound card, CD-ROM drive. Networks supported: Yes.
Windows 3.1 PC. 486 PC (4Mb). Nonstandard peripherals required: Any Windows supported sound card, CD-ROM drive.
An Extensive Resource of Information about World War II: Its People, Events, & Machinery.

TITLE INDEX

This Interactive CD-ROM Is Organized into Eight Separate Categories Including Battles, Dates, Documents, Leaders, Miscellaneous, Speeches, Statistics, & Weapons. Read the Complete Texts of the Japanese Surrender, Learn about the Feared German Stuka Dive-Bomber, View Information about General Patton & His Exploits, or View Images That Remind Us of the Horrors of War. Contains a Myriad of Text & Pictures for Both the Casual Reader & the Hardened War Buff.
BeachWare.

ALODS. Version: 1.0. 1982. Compatible Hardware: IBM PC & compatibles. Operating System(s) Required: MS-DOS. Language(s): BASIC. Memory Required: 128k.
$395.00.
Solves for Allowable Loads Which May Be Applied to a Nozzle under Internal Pressure in Spherical Shells. The External Loads and/or Pressure May Be Limited by Either Shell Stress or Nozzle Wall Stress & Is So Indicated on the Output.
Technical Research Services, Inc.

ALOSWARE HD. Version: 2.1. Aug. 1987. Compatible Hardware: IBM PC & compatibles, PC XT. Operating System(s) Required: PC-DOS/MS-DOS 3.0 or higher. Memory Required: 640k. General Requirements: Hard disk, serial port.
contact publisher for price.
Allows Documents to Be Quickly Retrieved from a File of Thousands of Images on Rollfilm.
ALOS Micrographics Corp.

ALPAL & Big ALPAL. Compatible Hardware: Apple Macintosh.
ALPAL $21.50.
Big ALPAL $21.50.
Linear Programming by Graphical, Algebraic & Simplex.
Kinko's.

Alpha-Draw. Compatible Hardware: TRS-80 Color Computer. Language(s): BASIC. Memory Required: 32k.
cassette $8.95.
A Subroutine Designed to Allow User to Draw All Upper Case, Lower Case, & Special Keyboard Characters on Graphics Screen at the Coordinates User Specifies. The Size, Color, & Orientation of the Characters Can Be Changed by a Simple DRAW Statement in User's Program. The Subroutine Is Fast Because It Does Not Use Any DATA or READ Statements or Array Storage. Uses Five Variables & Very Little Character Manipulation. Developed to Allow User to Change or Expand the Character Set & Delete Unnecessary Characters to Conserve Program Storage. Includes a Sample Program to Demonstrate Subroutine Use. Also Includes Instructions for a True Line Numbered Tape Merge of BASIC Program Files (Similar to Disk MERGE) to Add This Subroutine to User's BASIC Programs.
Custom Software Engineering, Inc.

Alpha Paint. Sep. 1994. Items Included: Manual, tutorials, keyboard template, registration card. Customer Support: Free tech support. 24 hr. tech Fax line.
Amiga (12Mb). disk $699.96 (Order no.: 510-638-0800). Nonstandard peripherals required: Video Toaster, 030 or 040 accel. Addl. software required: Toaster 2.0 or higher.
Elevates Painting Quality & Performance on the Video Toaster to Unprecedented New Heights with 36-Bits of Painting Power! Breaks New Ground with Full-Screen Realtime 24-Bit Painting & Exclusive 12-Bit Alpha Channel Support for Anti-Aliasing, Blending & Compositing. Advanced Set of Image Enhancement, Painting & Drawing Tools. Sophisticated Text Tool with Full Support for Toaster, Chroma & PostScript Fonts. Pressure Sensitive Drawing Tablet Support. Compatible with Video Toaster 2.0, 3.0, 3.1 & Toaster 4000. The All-in-One Professional Paint Solution.
InnoVision Technology.

Alpha Plot. Bert Kersey & Jack Cassidy. Sep. 1984. Compatible Hardware: Apple II, II+, IIe, IIc, IIgs. Operating System(s) Required: Apple DOS 3.3. Language(s): Applesoft BASIC. Memory Required: 48k.
disk $39.50.
Allows the User to Manipulate High Resolution Images. Enables User to Draw Pictures on Screen from Keyboard & Then Combine, Compare & Copy Them. Besides These Functions the User Can Label & Title the Images That Have Been Created.
Beagle Brothers.

Alpha Window. Compatible Hardware: TRS-80 Model I, Model III, Model 4. Operating System(s) Required: TRSDOS.
disk $10.00 ea.
Model I. (Order no.: D1AW).
Model III. (Order no.: D3AW).
Model 4. (Order no.: D4AW).
In-Memory Data File Manager for Maintaining Small Lists Sorted on Any Single Key.
The Alternate Source.

Alphabet Blocks. (The/Talking Tutor Ser.). Windows. IBM & compatibles. CD-ROM disk $44.95 (Order no.: R1027). Nonstandard peripherals required: CD-ROM drive. Optimal configuration: 386 processor or higher, MS-DOS 3.1 or higher, 20Mb hard drive, 640k RAM, external speakers or headphones (with sound card) that are Sound Blaster compatible, VGA graphics & adapter, VGA color monitor.
Macintosh (4Mb). (Order no.: R1027A).
Nonstandard peripherals required: 14" color monitor or larger, CD-ROM drive.
This Outstanding Series Uses Puzzles, Exciting Stories, Color-Animation & Music to Teach the Basics (Ages 3-6).
Library Video Co.

Alphabetic Keyboarding. Version: 3. 1994. Memory Required: Apple IIgs 256k, IBM/Tandy 128-512k, Macintosh-Apple IIe & IIc 54k. Customer Support: 1-800-354-9706.
Apple II series; IIgs. 5.25" disk Contact publisher for price (ISBN 0-538-61180-4, Order no.: Z367-3C).
Apple II series; IIgs. 3.5" disk Contact publisher for price (ISBN 0-538-62084-6, Order no.: Z368-1C).
DOS. 5.25" disk Contact publisher for price (ISBN 0-538-61181-2, Order no.: Z368-8C).
DOS. 3.5" disk Contact publisher for price (ISBN 0-538-61182-0).
MAC. 3.5" disk Contact publisher for price (ISBN 0-538-62046-3).
3 Combination Diskettes (1 Disk Only for PS/2 Version) Which Contain 12 Lessons Helping Students Master Letter Keys & Most Frequently Used Punctuation Keys. Can be Used with any Keyboarding Program.
South-Western Publishing Co.

AlphaBonk Farm. Dec. 1994. Items Included: Poster, Rhyme Book. Customer Support: 30 day unlimited warranty, free telephone technical support, Internet technical support.
Macintosh System 6.0.7; DOS, Windows 3.1. Macintosh 68040/25MHz (4Mb); IBM & compatibles, 80386/33MHz (8Mb). CD-ROM disk $34.95 (ISBN 1-886503-00-1).
Nonstandard peripherals required:
Double-speed CD-ROM drive.
Provides over 90 Engaging Activities for Kids 4 & up in a Colorful & Lively Farm. With Pioneering Interactive Programming, AlphaBonk Results in 35 Hours of Inventive Play & Development of Language, Problem-Solving, & Decision-Making Skills.
Headbone Interactive, Inc.

Alphacat. Compatible Hardware: Apple II with Applesoft. Operating System(s) Required: Apple DOS 3.2, 3.3. Language(s): Machine. Memory Required: 48k.
disk $14.95.
Organizes Directories on Diskettes. Sorts & Organizes Alphabetically by Name or Type, or Arranges According to File Size. The Disk Directory Is Rewritten with the Organization Chosen by the User.
Dynacomp, Inc.

AlphaLEDGER: Complete Business Accounting System. Version: 94.1. Mar. 1978. Compatible Hardware: Alpha Micro, UNIX, DOS, Novell. Operating System(s) Required: AMOS, UNIX, DOS, Novell. Language(s): BASIC. Memory Required: 200k. General Requirements: Hard disk. Items Included: Documentation, free training 1/2 day per module. Customer Support: 30 days free 800 hot line support - after which support contract available.
$1500.00-$25,000.00 disk, VCR, streamer (based on number of users).
Fully Integrated Accounting Software - Accounts Payable, Accounts Receivable, Check Reconciliation, Fixed Assets, General Ledger, Order Entry/Inventory Control, Payroll, Purchase Order, Report Writer, Screen Writer, File Manager, System Manager, User Manager. Other modules available - Manufacturers & Contractors Job Costing, Dealer Support, Property Management, Prospect Tracking, Serial Number Tracking, EDI.
Christensen Computer Company, Inc.

The Alpine Encounter. Compatible Hardware: Apple II, II+, IIe; Atari 800, 1200; Commodore 64; IBM PC, PC XT.
contact publisher for price.
Ibidinc.

Alpine Legal Management: Time Billing. Version: 6.1. Jan. 1994. Items Included: User manual; System Manager Manual; 30 or 90 day unlimited warranty including telephone support, updates (free). Customer Support: On-site consultation at $600.00 per day plus expenses; Custom programming; Annual or monthly support at $2800.00 or $250.00 per month; Alpine Helpline/Alpine Immediate Helpline, User Conferences.
VMS, MS-DOS, UNIX. DEC VAX, IBM & compatibles (2Mb), Altos. $995.00-$15,000.00. Networks supported: NetBIOS compatible.
High Quality, Proven Software to Handle Full Billing, Accounting, & Management-Reporting Needs of the Small to Medium Law Firm. All Modules Are Integrated for Higher Efficiency. Specific Features Include Unlimited Narrative, Word-Processing Type Editing, Receipt & Realization Reporting, & 70 User-Defined Statement Formats. The Software Accommodates the Specific Needs of Various Types of Legal Practices. ABA Approved.
Alpine Datasystems.

Alpine Project Time Management for Architects & Engineers: Time-Billing. Version: 6.1. Jan. 1994. Items Included: User manual; System Manager Manual; 30 or 90 day unlimited warranty including telephone support, updates (free). Customer Support: On-site consultation at $600.00 per day plus expenses; Custom programming; Annual or monthly support at

$2800.00 or $250.00 per month; Alpine Helpline/Alpine Immediate Helpline, Regional Seminars, User Conferences.
VMS, MS-DOS, UNIX. DEC VAX (1Mb), IBM & compatibles (2Mb), Altos. $995.00-$15,000.00. *Networks supported:* NetBIOS compatible.
Maintains Records for Each Employee, Client, Project & Project Type, Phase & Task Within a Project, Staff, & Departmental Assignment & Activity. Records & Posts Each Time, Expense, & Accounts Receivable Transaction by Client & Project. Adjusts Work-in-Progress & Billing Amounts; Prints Detailed or Summarized Statements in Several User-Selected Formats; & Ages Accounts Receivable, Unbilled Time & Expense Transactions, & Prints Aging Reports. Integrates with the Vendor's Accounts Payable, Report Generator, General Ledger, & Several Other Supporting Applications.
Alpine Datasystems.

Alpiner. *Compatible Hardware:* TI 99/4A with PLATO interpreter solid state cartridge.
ROM cartridge write for info. (Order no.: PHM 3056).
Mountain Climbing Game for 1 or 2 Players.
Texas Instruments, Personal Productivit.

ALS Prolog. *Version:* 1.2. *Compatible Hardware:* Apple Macintosh-PowerMac 68000 Mac; 386 DOS SCO UNIX; Windows; Sun, HP, AIX, NeXT, SGI, Linux. *Memory Required:* 4Mk. *General Requirements:* Hard disk recommended. *Items Included:* Documentation & binder. *Customer Support:* 1 year free updates.
$800.00.
Features Incremental Interactive Compiler for Edinburgh Prolog. Provides Complete Garbage Collection & Tail Recursion. Standard Debugger, Assert, Clause, etc. Operate on Compiled Code. Other Features Include: C Interface, Real Strings, Screen Control, Interrupt Handling, DCGs. Virtual Memory.
Applied Logic Systems, Inc.

alt. J. Weaver, Jr. May 1986. *Compatible Hardware:* Atari ST. *Operating System(s) Required:* TOS. *Memory Required:* 512k.
3.5" disk $29.95 (ISBN 0-923213-17-1, Order no.: AT-ALT).
Utility Converts Strings of Text or Commands into One Keystroke. Can Be Installed As a GEM Desktop Accessory. All 36 ALT Key Combinations Can Be Replaced by Strings up to 60 Characters Each. Can Be Made to Automatically Load the Setup When the Desktop Is Initialized.
MichTron, Inc.

Altar Boy Scheduler. *Version:* 1.2. Jan. 1989. *Compatible Hardware:* IBM PC & compatibles. *Operating System(s) Required:* PC-DOS/MS-DOS. *Memory Required:* 128k. *General Requirements:* Printer.
contact publisher for price.
Creates a Schedule of Altar Boys for Church Services.
Specialized Software.

Alternate BASIC. Dennis Allen. 1985. *Compatible Hardware:* TRS-80 Model I, Model III, Model 4, Tandy 2000. *Operating System(s) Required:* CP/M, MS-DOS, PC-DOS. *Memory Required:* 64k.
disk $59.95 ea.
Model I & Model 2. (Order no.: D8TAB).
Model 4. (Order no.: D4TAB).
MS-DOS. (Order no.: DMTAB).
Tandy 2000. (Order no.: D2TAB).
CP/M. (Order no.: DCTAB).
The Alternate Source.

Alternate Inventory. *Version:* 8A. Sep. 1993. *Compatible Hardware:* PC-DOS, XENIX, UNIX; IBM, DG. *Language(s):* R/M COBOL 85. *Memory Required:* Single user 500k, multi-user 1000k. *General Requirements:* Integrated Accounting. *Customer Support:* Included with the support for the Integrated Accounting.
Single-User. disk $200.00.
Multiuser. $400.00 up.
Can Be Added to Integrated Accounting So User Can Sell an Inventory Item in As Many Different Units - Such As Box, Carton, Gross, Bottle, Case. Suits the Needs of Many Types of Business-Stationery Stores, Lumberyards, Liquor & Beverage Stores, & Many Others. Keeps Prices Straight, Speeds Order-Taking & Check-Out, & Eliminates Manual Calculations & Pricing Errors.
Trac Line Software, Inc.

Alternate Pricing. 1996.
DOS, Unix. IBM PC. disk contact publisher for price.
Features Quantity Break Pricing up to 8 levels for each unit of measure. Up to 10 units of measure allowed per stock number. A price record can apply to a specific stock #, an entire category, or an entire revenue account number (product group).
Core Software, Inc.

Alternate Reality: The City. Paradise Programming. Nov. 1985. *Compatible Hardware:* Apple II, Macintosh; Atari XL/XE, ST; Commodore 64/128, Amiga; IBM PC. *Memory Required:* Atari XL/XE 48k; Apple II, Commodore 64k; Amiga, Atari ST, IBM PC, Macintosh 512k.
disk $29.95 ea.
Atari XL/XE. (ISBN 0-88717-122-2, Order no.: 1445WDO).
Commodore 64/128. (ISBN 0-88717-123-0, Order no.: 1445CDO).
Apple. (ISBN 0-88717-121-4, Order no.: 1445ADO).
$39.95 ea.
Atari ST. (Order no.: 1445WSO).
Apple Macintosh. (Order no.: 1445MDO).
Amiga. (Order no.: 1445AMO).
IBM. (Order no.: 1445IDO).
Role-Playing Game in Which You Choose a Character, Give Him Virtues Such As Courage & Intelligence, & Arm Him So That He Will Be Prepared to Face the Danger & Obstacles He Will Encounter in the Game.
IntelliCreations, Inc.

Alternate Reality: The Dungeon. May 1987. *Compatible Hardware:* Apple II series, Macintosh; Atari XL/XE, ST; Commodore 64/128, Amiga; IBM PC. *Memory Required:* Apple II, Atari XL/XE, Commodore 64k; Amiga, Atari ST, IBM, Macintosh 512k.
disk $29.95 ea.
Apple II. (ISBN 0-88717-165-6, Order no.: 1455ADO).
Atari XL/XE. (ISBN 0-88717-163-X, Order no.: 1455WDO).
Commodore 64/128. (ISBN 0-88717-164-8, Order no.: 1455CDO).
$39.95 ea.
Amiga. (Order no.: 1445AMO).
Atari ST. (Order no.: 1445WSO).
IBM. (Order no.: 1445IDO).
Second in the Alternate Reality Series. The Dungeon Lies Beneath the City. It Is a World Shrouded in Mystery, Where Turning a Corner Can Bring You Face-to-Face with Apparitions from Your Worst Nightmares. As in the City, Things Are Not Always What They Appear to Be. Meet Such Beings As Acrinimiril the Wizard, the Kings of the Trolls & Goblins, the Fearsome Dragon Lawrencio, & Many Other Mysterious Creatures. Join a Guild, Learn the Secrets of the Wizards & Acquire Great Wealth & Treasure.

There Are 4 Levels, Each Taking You Further into the Depths & Closer to Solving the Mystery of Alternate Reality.
IntelliCreations, Inc.

Alternative Sentencing: Criminal Justice Application System. *Version:* 3.0. Palladium Software Corporation. Oct. 1992. *Items Included:* Full documentation manual & a Quick Start manual. *Customer Support:* On-Line Electronic Bulletin Board Service - $200.00 Annual fee Technical support - 90 day unlimited warranty, On-site training & consulting services.
MS-DOS, Windows 95 & NT Server. IBM, Alpha, HP. disk $7000.00 (Order no.: CJ-A100). *Networks supported:* Novell, Banyan, any Peer to Peer, NT.
Provides Application Systems to Administer All Aspects of Alternative Programs to Incarceration: Administration, - Receiving, Processing, Release; Scheduling, - All Activities; Profile, - History Employment, Education, Criminal, Contacts & Associates; Operations, - Administration, Financial, Human Resource, & Analysis; Work & Time, - Industry, Education, Training, Counseling; Control, - Security, Custody & Scheduling (Employees); & Productivity, Productive Work, Time & Infraction Management Designed to Integrate & Expedite the Administration & Review of Offender Performance. This Application Systems Provides a Full Cost Analysis, Audit Trails, & a Quality of Time Served Measure.
Ellington Duval, Inc.

Altos Accountant Level III, 14 modules. *Version:* 3.X. Mar. 1986. *Compatible Hardware:* Altos 486, 586, 886, 986, 1086, 2086. *Operating System(s) Required:* XENIX. *Language(s):* BBX Business BASIC (source code included). *Memory Required:* 512k.
Set. $595.00-$995.00.
Integrated Series of Accounting Applications Which Can Be Run Standalone. Features On-Line Access to Altos Office Manager Productivity Tools.
Altos Computer Systems.

Altos Executive Financial Planner. *Compatible Hardware:* Altos. *Operating System(s) Required:* XENIX. *Language(s):* C.
disk $295.00.
8" disk $295.00.
Altos Computer Systems.

Altos Executive Word Processor. *Compatible Hardware:* Altos. *Operating System(s) Required:* XENIX.
disk $295.00.
Altos Computer Systems.

Alvin. *Compatible Hardware:* Atari 400, 800. *Language(s):* Atari BASIC (source code included). *Memory Required:* 16k.
disk $21.95.
cassette $17.95.
Ground/Space Attack Arcade Game.
Dynacomp, Inc.

Alvin, 2 disks. *Version:* 1.01. *Compatible Hardware:* IBM PC & compatibles. *Operating System(s) Required:* PC-DOS/MS-DOS. *Memory Required:* 256k. *General Requirements:* Hard disk recommended. *Items Included:* 32 pg. Thinking Software catalog.
5.25" or 3.5" disks $59.95.
Natural Language Query System Which Answers Most Questions about DOS.
Thinking Software, Inc.

AM Professional. *Version:* 3.0.
OS/2 1.1 or 1.2. 3.5" disk $7400.00.
Runtime module $250.00.
Application Managers for OS/2. Development

TITLE INDEX

Tools That Help User Integrate the Communications, Database, & Graphical Capabilities of This Operating System.
Intelligent Environments.

Amalgamated Pharmomatic Mark II. Version: 2.0. Nov. 1988. *Compatible Hardware:* IBM PC & compatibles. *Operating System(s) Required:* PC-DOS/MS-DOS 3.2. *Language(s):* Clarion. *Memory Required:* 640k. *General Requirements:* 20Mb Hard disk.
disk $2500.00, incl. PCS Recap Program.
Program for the Management of a Pharmacy. Using Files Based on Drugs & Current Prices, Patient Information & Physicians Who Write Prescriptions, System Can Print Labels, Provide Hard Copy of Transaction & Total Prescription Price. Will Provide Customer Profile to Include Purchase of New Prescriptions, Provide Log of Sales by Vendor for Welfare Patients & Allow Month-to-Date & Year-to-Date Accounts of Units Dispensed. Utility Programs Are Available. Compatible with MediSpan Price Update Diskettes & Drug Interaction Crosschecks.
Dusek Pharmacy.

Amanda Stories.
Windows. IBM & compatibles. CD-ROM disk $39.95 (Order no.: R1001). *Nonstandard peripherals required:* CD-ROM drive.
Macintosh (4Mb). (Order no.: 1001). *Nonstandard peripherals required:* 14" color monitor or larger, CD-ROM drive.
Ten Children's Adventures by Amanda Goodenough with Hundreds of Sound Effects, Charming Illustrations, & Lessons about Love, Friendship & Loyalty.
Library Video Co.

Amanda Stories, Vol. 1. *Compatible Hardware:* Apple Macintosh Plus. *General Requirements:* HyperCard.
3.5" disk $19.95.
Children's Stories Combine the Art of Storyteller with the Interactive Potential of HyperCard: Volume 1 Contains Four Stories That Enable Children to Lead the Main Character, Indigo the Cat, Through Many Adventures.
The Voyager Co.

Amanda Stories, Vol. 2. *Compatible Hardware:* Apple Macintosh Plus. *General Requirements:* Hypercard.
3.5" disk $19.95.
Children's Stories Combine the Art of the Storyteller with the Interactive Potential of HyperCard: Volume 2 Includes Two More Similar Interactive Stories.
The Voyager Co.

Amas. MicroDeal. Jan. 1989.
Amiga (512k). disk $169.95.
Full-Featured 8-Bit Stereo Audio Digitizer, Complete with Full MIDI Interface Built into a Hardware Unit That Complements User's Amiga.
Michtron, Inc.

AMAS: Agency Management Automation System. Oct. 1988. *Compatible Hardware:* IBM PC, PC XT, PC AT; HP 150. *Memory Required:* 256k. *General Requirements:* 2 disk drives, hard disk, printer.
disk $1950.00.
IBM PC AT. (Order no.: IB-AT-A).
IBM PC XT. (Order no.: IB-XT-A).
HP 150. (Order no.: HP-150-A).
Fully Integrated In-House Computer-Based Insurance Agency Management Automation System. AMAS Is Available in Several Different Configurations. Starter System Provides the Following Functions: Invoice & Credit Memo Production & Maintenance (On-Line Information Retrieval), Statement Production, & Expiration Reports. Enhancement Modules Include: Accounts Payable Reports, Accounts Receivable Reports with Age Breakdown, Line of Business Reports, Account Current Reports, Earned Premium Reports, Policy Register, Sales Journal, Statement History, Surplus Lines Report, & On-Line Loss Information by Invoice. Word Processing, Mailing List Management, Graphics, Spreadsheets, & Communications Options Are Available.
Howard W. Myers & Assocs.

Amazing Animations. *Customer Support:* All of our products are unconditionally guaranteed.
DOS, Windows, Mac. CD-ROM disk $19.95 (Order no.: AMAZANIM). *Nonstandard peripherals required:* CD-ROM drive.
2000 Files of the Latest CAD Rendered Animations. All Royalty Free.
Walnut Creek CDRom.

Amazing Art Adventure. Mar. 1994. *Items Included:* Kids Club Magazine.
DOS 3.1 or higher. IBM 386 minimum & compatibles (4Mb). SRP $59.95 (ISBN 1-57187-001-6, Order no.: AA3L10ENG). *Nonstandard peripherals required:* VGA video. *Addl. software required:* Windows 3.1. *Optimal configuration:* 12Mb minimum disk requirement, 10Mb hard disk space, Windows 3.1, mouse or pointing device.
Crayola Amazing Art Adventure Is the First & Only Creativity Program Specially Designed for the Early Creativity Needs of Children Ages 3-6. The Product Is Loaded with 12 Different Art Activities & Packed with Exciting Animations & Sounds Which Provide Endless Opportunity for Creative Exploration & Fun.
Micrografx, Inc.

Amazon: Guardians of Eden. Version: DOS. *Items Included:* Manual. *Customer Support:* 90 days unlimited warranty, hint line 1-800-793-8324.
286/12mhz CPU. IBM PC & compatibles (640k). disk $69.95. *Nonstandard peripherals required:* Hard disk drive, VGA display, mouse. *Optimal configuration:* 386/20mhz CPU or higher, hard disk drive, 640k RAM (540k available) Super VGA display, mouse, sound card.
Captures the Fun of Drive-In Movies of the '50's with Full Motion Video. Action-Packed Parody with Turns & Twists Throughout the Adventure. Brief Synopsis Goes Like This: You Are Jason Roberts, Living Somewhere in the United States. Your Brother Is Working with a Scientific Expediton Deep in the Amazon. You Must Fend off TEN FOOT Ants & Find the Emeralds Stolen by Cortez! And That's Only for Openers.
Access Software, Inc.

Amazonia. Jun. 1994. *Items Included:* NSTA Content Core, Teacher's Guide Level III, installation guide, laser disk, Pioneer MCI drivers (Windows).
Windows. IBM PC & compatibles (4Mb). CD-ROM disk Contact publisher for price (ISBN 1-57026-012-5). *Nonstandard peripherals required:* Sound blaster, laser disk player Pioneer 2200, 2400, 4200. *Addl. software required:* Pioneer MCI driver (included).
Macintosh. IBM PC & compatibles (4Mb). CD-ROM disk Contact publisher for price (ISBN 1-57026-007-9). *Nonstandard peripherals required:* Pioneer laser disk player.
An Interactive CD-ROM & Laserdisk Product That Explores the Biodiversity of the Amazon Rainforest.
Computer Curriculum Corp.

Amazonia, Level 1. Jun. 1994. *Items Included:* Teachers guide Level 1 with bar codes.
disk laser disk Contact publisher for price (ISBN 1-57026-009-5). *Nonstandard peripherals required:* Pioneer laser disk player 2200, 2400, 4200.
Contains 30 Minutes of Video of the Amazon Rainforest. Interviews with Smithsonian Scientists & Screen Slots of the CD-ROM Product.
Computer Curriculum Corp.

Amazonia Macintosh Installation Guide. 1994.
disk (ISBN 1-57026-005-2).
Computer Curriculum Corporation.

Amazonia Teacher's Guide, Level I. Susan Espinosa. *Items Included:* Teachers guide.
Laser disk. disk contact publisher for price (ISBN 1-57026-001-X).
Teachers guide with Bar codes for the Amazonia Level I laser disk. A study of the rain forest Biome.
Computer Curriculum Corp.

Amazonia Teachers Guide: Level III. Computer Curriculum Staff & Susan Espinosa. 1994.
disk (ISBN 1-57026-000-1).
Multimedia Users Guide teacher lessons for the CD-ROM software, Amazonia, an indepth exploration of the Rainforest Biome.
Computer Curriculum Corporation.

Amazonia Windows Installation Guide. Computer Curriculum Corporation. 1994.
disk (ISBN 1-57026-006-0).
Soft Installation Guide.
Computer Curriculum Corporation.

Ambassador English-Japanese for the Macintosh. Jun. 1992. *Items Included:* 2 manuals (one English, one Japanese). *Customer Support:* Free telephone support for registered customers.
Macintosh KanjiTalk 6.0.5 or higher or System 7.1 & Japanese Language Kit. Macintosh Plus or higher (2Mb). 3.5" disk $295.00 (ISBN 1-882465-00-8). *Optimal configuration:* Macintosh Plus or higher & 4Mb RAM, KanjiTalk 6.0.7 or System 7.1 & Japanese Language Kit.
Program Allows the User to Compose Business Correspondence Using Flexible Pre-Translated Bilingual Templates/Letters. The Product May Also Be Used to Automate the Production of Routine Business Correspondence in One Language.
Language Engineering Corp.

Ambassador French-Japanese for the Macintosh. Sep. 1992. *Items Included:* 2 manuals (one English, one Japanese). *Customer Support:* Free telephone support for registered customers.
Macintosh KanjiTalk 6.0.5 or higher or System 7.1 & Japanese Language Kit. Macintosh Plus or higher (2Mb). 3.5" disk $295.00 (ISBN 1-882465-01-6). *Optimal configuration:* Macintosh Plus or higher & 4Mb RAM, KanjiTalk 6.0.7 or System 7.1 & Japanese Language Kit.
Program Allows the User to Compose Business Correspondence Using Flexible Pre-Translated Bilingual Templates/Letters. The Product May Also Be Used to Automate the Production of Routine Business Correspondence in One Language.
Language Engineering Corp.

Ambrose's Chronology of History. Jul. 1994. *Items Included:* 1 spiral-bound manual, 1 brochure - Getting Started Quickly. *Customer Support:* 30 day limited warranty, 1-800 for questions.
MS-DOS. IBM PCs & ATs & compatibles (640k). disk $29.95 (ISBN 0-9639502-2-3). *Optimal configuration:* Color monitor, 640k RAM.
Software History Research/Reference Tool for

AMBULANCE

IBM PCs & Compatibles. Runs under DOS. Provides Information about the World's Major Events from 4300 B.C. to 1900. Designed for Students & Professionals As Well As History Buffs. Selected Reading Lists Available for All History Entries.
Historical Enterprises.

Ambulance. *Compatible Hardware:* Commodore PET. *Language(s):* BASIC (source code included). *Memory Required:* 16k.
disk $18.95.
cassette $14.95.
Real-Time Game.
Dynacomp, Inc.

AME: Access Managed Environment. *Version:* 2.1. 1992. *Items Included:* Manual, reg. card. *Customer Support:* Free phone support.
6.02 & higher. Macintosh (1Mb). 3.5" disk $159.00 single; $599.00 5 site pack; $999.00 10 site pack (Order no.: M201; M205; M210).
Complete Security Solution for the Macintosh with Virus Protection. Provides Everything from Simple, Limited Hard Drive Access to a Completely Secure Government or Corporated Environment.
Casady & Greene, Inc.

Amegas. *Compatible Hardware:* Commodore Amiga. *Customer Support:* Backup disk available.
3.5" disk $14.95.
Breakout-Style Arcade Game with 40 Levels.
Digitek Software.

America Adventure. Sep. 1995. *Customer Support:* Telephone support - free (except phone charge).
Windows 3.1. IBM & compatibles (386 DX-20) (4Mb). CD-ROM disk $12.99 (ISBN 1-57594-029-9). *Nonstandard peripherals required:* 2x CD-ROM player, Sound Card, VGA monitor. *Optimal configuration:* 486 SX-33.
Tour the Country from Sea to Sea to Learn Its Geography & History.
Kidsoft, Inc.

America Adventure. Sep. 1995. *Customer Support:* Telephone support - free (except phone charge).
Windows 3.1. IBM & compatibles (386 DX-20) (4Mb). CD-ROM disk $12.99 (ISBN 1-57594-068-X). *Nonstandard peripherals required:* 2x CD-ROM player, Sound Card, VGA monitor. *Optimal configuration:* 486 SX-33.
Tour the Country from Sea to Sea to Learn Its Geography & History. Blister Pack Jewel Case.
Kidsoft, Inc.

America Adventure.
Windows, MS-DOS 3.1 or higher. IBM & compatibles, 386 or higher (640k). CD-ROM disk $49.95 (Order no.: R1114). *Nonstandard peripherals required:* CD-ROM drive. *Optimal configuration:* 386 processor or higher, MS-DOS 3.1 or higher, 20Mb hard drive, 640k RAM, 1.44Mb floppy disk drive, external speakers or headphones (with sound card) that are Sound Blaster compatible, VGA graphics & adapter, VGA color monitor.
Journey from the Past to the Present, Tour the Country from Sea to Sea, & Discover the People & Places of America. This Interactive Program Reinforces Learning about American History, Popular Culture & Native Americans. (Ages 6 & Up).
Library Video Co.

America Cooks American: Cookbook-on-Disk.
Dec. 1985. *Compatible Hardware:* Apple II+, IIe, IIc, Macintosh; Atari ST; Commodore 64, 128; IBM PC, PCjr. *Operating System(s) Required:* MS-DOS, PC-DOS 1.1, Apple DOS 3.3. *Memory Required:* Apple 48k, IBM 128k.
disk $14.95 ea.
Apple. (ISBN 0-935745-39-4, Order no.: AK11).
Commodore. (ISBN 0-935745-51-3, Order no.: CK11).
IBM. (ISBN 0-935745-27-0, Order no.: MK11).
21 Top Restaurant Chefs Reveal Secret Recipes & Wine Suggestions.
Concept Development Assocs., Inc.

America Cooks Chinese: Cookbook-on-Disk.
Sep. 1985. *Compatible Hardware:* Apple II series, Macintosh; Atari ST; Commodore 64, 128; IBM PC, PCjr. *Operating System(s) Required:* PC-DOS/MS-DOS 1.1, Apple DOS 3.3. *Memory Required:* 48k-128k.
disk $14.95 ea.
Commodore. (ISBN 0-935745-49-1, Order no.: CK9).
IBM. (ISBN 0-935745-25-4, Order no.: MK9).
Provides More Than 160 Recipes from Chefs of over 21 of the Best Chinese Restaurants in America, Including Imperial Palace, in San Francisco, Mr. Chow's, in New York, & Christine Lie's, in Miami. Each Features a Full Course with Easy-to-Follow Instructions.
Concept Development Assocs., Inc.

America Cooks French: Cookbook-on-Disk.
Dec. 1985. *Compatible Hardware:* Apple II+, IIe, IIc, Macintosh, Commodore 64, 128; Atari ST; IBM PC & compatibles. *Operating System(s) Required:* MS-DOS, PC-DOS 1.1, Apple DOS 3.3. *Memory Required:* Apple 48k, IBM 128k.
disk $14.95 ea.
Apple. (ISBN 0-935745-40-8, Order no.: AK12).
Commodore. (ISBN 0-935745-52-1, Order no.: CK12).
IBM. (ISBN 0-935745-28-9, Order no.: MK12).
Chefs of over 21 of the Best French Restaurants in America Share More Than 160 Recipes with Easy-to-Follow Instructions for Preparation. Restaurants Featured Include Le Bagetelle, in Washington D.C., L'Etoile, in San Francisco, & Cafe Plaza, in Boston.
Concept Development Assocs., Inc.

America Cooks Italian: Cookbook-on-Disk.
Dec. 1985. *Compatible Hardware:* Apple II series, Macintosh; Atari ST; Commodore 64, 128; IBM PC, PCjr. *Operating System(s) Required:* MS-DOS, PC-DOS 1.1, Apple DOS 3.3. *Memory Required:* 64-128k.
disk $14.95 ea.
Commodore. (ISBN 0-935745-38-6, Order no.: CK10).
IBM. (ISBN 0-935745-26-2, Order no.: MK10).
Chefs from over 21 of the Best Italian Restaurants in America Share Cooking Secrets in More Than 160 Recipes from Restaurants Like Lello, in New York, & Al Bistro, in Seattle.
Concept Development Assocs., Inc.

America Cooks Mexican: Cookbook-on-Disk.
Dec. 1985. *Compatible Hardware:* Apple II+, IIe, IIc; Commodore 64, 128; IBM PCjr. *Operating System(s) Required:* PC-DOS/MS-DOS 1.1, Apple DOS 3.3. *Memory Required:* Apple 48k, IBM 128k. *General Requirements:* Micro Kitchen Companion program.
disk $14.95 ea.
Apple. (ISBN 0-935745-41-6, Order no.: AK13).
Commodore. (ISBN 0-935745-53-X, Order no.: CK13).
IBM. (ISBN 0-935745-29-7, Order no.: MK13).
Recipes & Wine Suggestions from 21 Top Mexican Chefs.
Concept Development Assocs., Inc.

America Remembered: Views You Can Use.
Jun. 1993. *Items Included:* 1 8-page booklet.
Macintosh System 6.07 or higher. 13" Monitor Macintosh (5Mb). CD-ROM disk $19.95 (ISBN 1-883596-00-9). *Optimal configuration:* 8Mb RAM, 24-bit color, 13" color monitor.
CD-ROM for the Macintosh with 500 Pict Images of Old America Scanned at 72 DPI & 300 DPI for Desktop Publishers to Print Copyright Free.

American College of Allergy & Immunology.
Customer Support: Toll-free technical support - no charge. In U.S. - 9AM-5PM EST 800-343-0064; In U.K. - 44(0)81-995-8242.
Microsoft Windows, Version 3.1. 386 IBM-Compatible PC (4Mb). CD-ROM disk 150.00 ACAI members; $225.00 Non-members; $595.00 Institutions (ISBN 1-57276-005-2, Order no.: SE-005-999). *Nonstandard peripherals required:* MPC Standard CD-Rom player 640 x 480 display with 256 colors, MPC standard soundboard, speakers.
System 7.0 or higher. Apple Macintosh. CD-ROM disk $150.00 ACAI members; $225.00 Non-members; $595.00 Institutions (Order no.: SE-005-999). *Nonstandard peripherals required:* CD-ROM drive.
This Collection of Four CD-ROM's Features Narration, Text, & Slide Images Captured from Twenty-Four Hours of Plenary Sessions at the ACAI's 1993 Annual Meeting in Atlanta. Volume 1 - Asthma, Volume 2 - Rhinitis, Volume 3 - Clinical Immunolgoy, Volume 4 - Allergy & Immunology.
SilverPlatter Education.

American College of Allergy & Immunology.
Feb. 1994. *Customer Support:* Toll-free technical support - no charge. In U.S. 9AM - 5PM EST 800-343-0064; in U.K. 44(0)81-995-8242.
System 7.0 or higher. Apple Macintosh (4Mb). CD-ROM disk $150.00, ACAI members, ,225.00 Non-members, ,595.00 Institutions (ISBN 1-57276-005-2, Order no.: SE-005-999). *Nonstandard peripherals required:* CD-ROM drive.
Microsoft Windows, Version 3.1. 386 IBM-Compatible PC (4Mb). CD-ROM disk $150.00, ACAI members, ,225.00 Non-members, ,595.00 Institutions. *Nonstandard peripherals required:* MPC Standard CD-ROM players, 640x480 display with 256 colors, MPC Standard Soundboard, Speakers.
This Collection of Four CD-ROMs Features Narration, Text, & Slide Images Captured from Twenty-Four Hours of Plenary Sessions at the ACAI's 1993 Annual Meeting in Atlanta. Volume 1 - Asthma, Volume 2 - Rhinitis, Volume 3 - Clinical Immunology, Volume 4 - Allergy & Immunology.
SilverPlatter Education.

American Family Physician on CD-ROM: DOS-MAC. Feb. 1994. *Items Included:* Registration Card. *Customer Support:* Creative Multimedia Corporation warrants the CD-ROM disc & diskettes to be free from defects in materials & workmanship under normal use & service for a period of 90 days from date of purchase. Creative Multimedia Corporation offers Technical Support to customers as needed.
MS-DOS 3.1 or higher. IBM PC & compatibles with VGA monitor (350k). CD-ROM disk $295.00 Suggested Retail Price (ISBN 1-880428-31-8, Order no.: 10529). *Optimal configuration:* Super VGA with 512k video memory capable of 640x480x256 colors. Networks supported: All.
System Software 6.0.5 or higher. Macintosh Plus, SE, Classic, SE/30, LC & any Model II (2Mb). CD-ROM disk $295.00 Suggested Retail Price. *Optimal configuration:* Color display requires 8-bit color, 32-bit QuickDraw & color monitor. Networks supported: All.
AFP Provides Continuing Medical Education for Family Physicians & Other Physicians Involved in

TITLE INDEX

Primary Care. Each Issue of AFP Contains Original Scientific Articles with Emphasis on Diagnostic & Therapeutic Techniques, As Well As Abstract from Major Medical Journals & Reports on Recent Developments in Medicine. All Articles Are Written by Physicians & Are Peer-Reviewed Before Publications. AFP Is Edited by a Family Physician Jay Siwek, MD, Department of Community & Family Medicine, Georgetown University School of Medicine.
Creative Multimedia Corp.

The American Heritage Dictionary. *Customer Support:* Free technical support for the life of product; 30 day money back guarantee; free BBS service.
  Microsoft Windows 3.0 or higher. IBM or 100% compatible (1Mb) with 3Mb free disk space. disk $99.00.
  MS-DOS 2.1 or higher. IBM or 100% compatible (43k) with 3Mb free disk space. Contact publisher for price. *Nonstandard peripherals required:* Hard disk.
  Macintosh System 6.0.2 or higher. Any Macintosh (1Mb) with 3Mb free disk space. Contact publisher for price.
The Dictionary Has 116,000 Words with Full Definitions, Spelling, Parts of Speech, Proper Usage. We Use Roget's II Electronic Thesaurus with More Than Half a Million Synonyms. Wordhunter Feature Lets User Find Words with Only a Vague Definition or Related Concept. The Wildcard Feature Allows User to Find Words Without Knowing All the Letters. Anagram Feature Allows Finding Other Words Hidden in the One Keyed.
WordStar International, Inc.

American History Atlas for Windows. Parsons Technology. Dec. 1993.
  3.5" disk Contact publisher for price (ISBN 1-57264-042-1).
Parsons Technology.

American History: Becoming a World Power, 1865-1912. (Micro Learn Tutorial Ser.). *Items Included:* Teacher-student materials. *Customer Support:* Free telephone support.
  MAC. IBM (128k), Macintosh (2 Mb), Apple II series, (48k), Commodore 64. $39.95 (Lab pack/5 $99.00). 3.5" disk, $44.95 (Lab Pack/5 115.00) Apple or Macintosh 249.00 (ISBN 1-57265-054-0).
  IBM. (ISBN 1-57265-001-X).
  APP. (ISBN 0-939153-97-1).
Tutorial Covers Reconstruction, Industry, Frontier, Reformers, U.S. As World Power. Topics Include Radical Republicans, Post-Civil War Amendments, Jim Crow Laws, Growth of Trusts, Labor Organizations, the West, Immigration & Growth of Cities, Populists, Progressives, Foreign Policy. Tutorial mode gives explanations for each answer choice, correct & incorrect.
Word Assocs., Inc.

American History: Decades Game 1, 2 & 3. Jun. 1983. *Items Included:* Teacher's guide. *Customer Support:* 90-day limited warranty.
  Apple-DOS 3.3. Apple II Family (48k). disk $39.00, each.
  Commodore 64/128 (64k). disk $39.00, each.
Historical Dating Game That's More Than Just a Collection of Trivia. Players Get an Outline of History, Learn When Major U. S. Cultural, Political, Eocnomic & Technological Events Took Place. Includes 15 Different Games on 3 Disks. For Ages 14 & up.
BrainBank/Generation Ahead of Maryland.

The American Investor: The Official Simulation of the American Stock Exchange. *Operating System(s) Required:* MS-DOS. *Customer Support:* (800) 572-2272, 90-day money back guarantee, $7.50 for replacement disks after 90-days..
  disk $149.95.
Simulation That Uses Historical Stock Market Data to Teach Investment Techniques.
Compton's NewMedia, Inc.

American Journey 1896-1945. Nov. 1994. *Customer Support:* Phone support.
  Windows. 486 (PC) or higher (4Mb). CD-ROM disk $59.95 (ISBN 0-9637731-1-9). *Optimal configuration:* IBM/compatible PC, 486 or higher processor, 4Mb RAM, hard drive, CD-ROM drive, audio board, mouse, VGA 256 colors, Windows 3.1 or higher.
Combines Vintage Photographs (over 1,300, All Printable); Original Audio (over 20 Hours of Radio Broadcasts, Speeches & Narration); Maps; Charts; Text; & Video (Including Japanese Footage of the Attack on Pearl Harbor, the Explosion of the Hindenburg, & World War I Footage) to Explore American History from the Klondike Gold Rush to the End of World War II.
Ibis Communications, Inc.

American Standard Version Add-On Module. Jun. 1988. *Customer Support:* No fee is charged for our customer support: 30 day money back return guarantee; lifetime warrenty on defective disk replacement; free telephone technical support.
  PC or MS-DOS 2.0 or higher. IBM PC/XT/AT or compatible. $5.00 upon return of the PC Study Bible's registration card (a $49.95 value). *Addl. software required:* PC STUDY BIBLE. *Optimal configuration:* Hard disk with 1.5Mb hard disk space for each Bible version.
The Text of the American Standard Version. Add-On Bible Version to Be Used with BIBLESOFT'S PC STUDY BIBLE.
Biblesoft.

Americans in Space. Jun. 1993. *Items Included:* Manual. *Customer Support:* Free telephone technical support.
  DOS & Microsoft Windows 3.1. 12 Mhz 80386SX (2Mb). CD-ROM disk Contact publisher for price (ISBN 1-884014-15-1). *Nonstandard peripherals required:* MPC-compatible CD-ROM drive (680Mb); SVGA display; audio board; mouse, 486DX processor. *Addl. software required:* Microsoft CD-ROM extensions v.2.2. *Optimal configuration:* 4Mb RAM; double-speed CD-ROM drive.
  Macintosh System 6.05. Color Macintosh (256 colors) (3.5Mb free RAM). CD-ROM disk Contact publisher for price (ISBN 1-884014-27-5). *Nonstandard peripherals required:* CD-ROM drive. *Optimal configuration:* Double speed CD-ROM; 13" color monitor; 8Mb RAM; fast processor.
CD-ROM Based Software Product Covering All American Space Missions with People on Board. Starting with Early Rocket Experiments, & Covering the Shuttle Program & Space Station Freedom, Americans in Space Mixes Audio, Video & Full Color Photographs.
Multicom Publishing, Inc.

America's Cup. 1995.
  Windows or Macintosh. CD-ROM disk $49.95 (ISBN 1-882949-94-3, Order no.: 10025101ED).
Navigate Through the Prestigious 144-Year History of Sport's Longest Standing International Competition on the First America's Cup Interactive CD-ROM. Containing Historical Data since 1851 along with Hundreds of Pictures & Paintings That Help Bring the Past to Life. Meet the Skippers & the Crews, Tour the Boats, Witness the Controversies & Relive the Drama of the 1995 America's Cup Races Climaxing with the Final Showdown Between Team New Zealand & Dennis Conner.
Paragon Media.

THE AMIGA COMPANION SERIES

Ami. *Version:* 1.2. *Compatible Hardware:* 80286/80386-based PCs. *Operating System(s) Required:* Microsoft Windows 386, Microsoft Windows 286, Microsoft Windows 3.0. *Customer Support:* Unlimited toll number, Compserve. $199.00.
Word-Processing Package Specifically Designed for the WINDOWS Environment. Features WYSIWIG Screen Display, Keyboard or Mouse Commands, 130,000-Word Spelling Checker, Mail Merge, Footnotes, Search & Replace, Headers & Footers, Undo Function & Context Sensitive Help. Formatting Can Be Done After Text Is Entered. Includes 25 Style Sheets.
Samna Corp.

Ami Professional. *Version:* 1.2. Oct. 1989. *Compatible Hardware:* IBM PC AT & compatibles, PS/2. *Operating System(s) Required:* Microsoft Windows. *Memory Required:* 640k. *Customer Support:* Unlimited free toll. $495.00, incl. runtime version.
Includes Macro Capabilities, a Built-In Drawing Program, & Support for the Dynamic Data Exchange Protocol. Using DDE, Changes in a Spreadsheet Automatically Update a Graph in the Word Processing Program. Adds Features that Support the Needs of Businesses: Merge, Complex Header & Footer, Indexing, & Table Capabilities. Tables, a Worksheet-Oriented Function, Lets Users Format Tabular Data from Spreadsheets & Include It with Text. Users Can Define a Block of Text, Graphics, or a Table & Anchor It to the Main Body of Text. Frames Are Automatically Repositioned Within a Document as Users Edit the Text. Users Can Annotate Documents with Hideable Notes, & the Program Supports Strikethrough, Allowing Users to Keep a Record of All Edit Changes Made on a Document. Other Added Features Include Undelete, a Thesaurus, Two Open Documents at Once, & the Ability to Import PIC (Lotus Graphics) & XLC (Excel) Graphics Files.
Samna Corp.

Ami...Alignment System. May 1989. *Items Included:* Manual describing alignment procedure & containing diagrams of various Amiga-compatible disk drives. *Customer Support:* Free telephone at 215-683-5699.
  Amiga DOS (512k). 3.5" disk $49.95.
Utility to Check 3.5" Disk Drive Alignment, Speed & Read/Write Performance.
Free Spirit Software, Inc.

Amiga BASIC Companion. *Compatible Hardware:* Commodore Amiga.
  3.5" disk $34.95.
Disk Based Manual.
Omega Star Software.

The Amiga Coloring Book: Borders. *Compatible Hardware:* Commodore Amiga.
  3.5" disk $34.95.
Over Fifty Borders.
The Dragon Group, Inc.

The Amiga Coloring Book: Sampler. *Compatible Hardware:* Commodore Amiga.
  3.5" disk $34.95.
Assorted IFF Clip Art.
The Dragon Group, Inc.

The Amiga Coloring Book: The World. *Compatible Hardware:* Commodore Amiga.
  3.5" disk $34.95.
Maps from Around The Globe.
The Dragon Group, Inc.

The Amiga Companion Series. *Compatible Hardware:* Commodore Amiga.
  3.5" disk $29.95.
Intuition-Based Interactive Help System.
Omega Star Software.

Amiga FFT C Package. *Compatible Hardware:* Commodore Amiga.
3.5" disk $152.00.
Fast Fourier Transform Routines.
ACDA Corp.

Amiga Graphics Starter Kit. Bill Volk et al. Aug. 1990. *Items Included:* Arazok's Tomb-game. *Customer Support:* Unlimited free tech support.
Amiga (512k). 3.5" disk $99.95.
Includes Paint, Animation, Draw, Clip Art & a Free Game.
Oxxi, Inc.

Amiga Programmer's Library. *Compatible Hardware:* Commodore Amiga.
$200.00.
Contains 10 Utilities, Four of Which Allow for File Transfer Both to & from the Amiga of Either Binary or Text Files.
Tardis Software.

Amiga View. *Compatible Hardware:* Commodore Amiga.
3.5" disk $79.95.
Intuition & Graphics Object Libraries.
ACDA Corp.

Amiga 184-A Light Pen & Driver. Oct. 1988.
Amiga 500, 1000, 2000, & (A2000). 3.5" disk $129.95.
A Transparent Light Pen Drive Coupled with a Two-Touch Switch Light Pen, Can Be Installed & Used in Conjuction with a Two-Button Mouse, Giving Amiga Owners Complete Data Entry Control with the Current Most Popular Amiga Software Programs. Works in Interlace, Non-Interlace & Overscan.
Inkwell Systems.

Amine Process Simulator Absorption & Stripping. *Items Included:* Full manual. No other products required. *Customer Support:* Free telephone support - no time limit. 30 day warranty.
MS-DOS 3.2 or higher. IBM & compatibles (512k). disk $589.95.
demo disk $5.00.
AMINE Models Processes for Absorption & Stripping of H2S & CO2 in Any Type of Gas Stream. It Is Particularly Accurate for H2S Absorption Near Atmospheric Pressure, a Task Much More Expensive Amine Simulators Can Not Do. Also, the Stripping Algorithms in the Program Will Converge in Most of the Really Difficult Cases.
Dynacomp, Inc.

Aminet. *Customer Support:* All of our products are unconditionally guaranteed.
Amiga. CD-ROM disk $29.95 (Order no.: AMINET). *Nonstandard peripherals required:* CD-ROM drive.
600 MB of Amiga Sounds, Images & Software.
Walnut Creek CDRom.

AMORT-ZIT. *Version:* 1.2. Peter C. Vonderhorst. Mar. 1981. *Compatible Hardware:* IBM PC, PC XT, PC AT; TRS-80 Model II, Model IV. *Operating System(s) Required:* TRSDOS, PC-DOS, MS-DOS. *Language(s):* Compiled BASIC. *Memory Required:* 48k. *General Requirements:* Printer.
disk $97.50.
Calculates & Prints Standard Amortization Table. Accumulates & Totals Interest (Annual or Fiscal Year) to Printout Formats. Fully Default Oriented (Monthly, Bimonthly, Biweekly, Quarterly, Semi Annual, Annual) Fixed Principal Payment Routine Discovers Any Missing Variable.
Computx.

Amort-I. Nov. 1983. *Compatible Hardware:* IBM PC; TRS-80 Model I, Model II, Model III, Model 4, Model 12, Model 16. *Operating System(s) Required:* CP/M, PC-DOS. *Memory Required:* 48k. *General Requirements:* Printer.
TRS-80 Model II, 12, 16. disk $25.00.
CP/M. 8" disk $25.00.
TRS-80 Model I, III, 4. disk $20.00.
IBM. write for info.
Takes Any 3 of 4 Loan Parameters & Calculates the 4th. Prints Amortization Schedules for Clients. Also Calculates Payments & Revises Schedule for Selling "On Time".
Documan Software.

Amortization-Plus. *Version:* 7.2. Jun. 1995. *Compatible Hardware:* IBM PC. *Operating System(s) Required:* PC-DOS 2.1. *Language(s):* C (source code included). *Memory Required:* 128k.
disk $40.00.
manual $95.00.
Computes & Prints Loan Amortization Schedule Using Principal Amount, Annual Interest Rate, Term of Loan, & Monthly Payment, Determining Fourth Variable If Necessary. Computation Methods Used Are Regular Mortgage with Constant Interest Amount per Unit Borrowed. Schedule Printout Can Be Displayed or Printed with Lender, Borrower, Terms, Payment Number, Due Date, Date Received, Principal Payment, Interest Payment, & Remaining Principal Balance with Annual Totals.
Omni Software Systems, Inc. (Indiana).

Amortizer. *Compatible Hardware:* TRS-80 Model I, Model III.
write for info.
Realsoft, Inc. (Florida).

Amortizer Plus: Professionals Count on It. *Version:* 3.01. 1991. *Items Included:* 1 Spiral bound manual, 1 set diskettes, warranty, software license agreement. *Customer Support:* Free Telephone Support on 214-713-6370; FAX Support on 214-713-6308.
MS-DOS 3.1 or higher; Windows 3.0 or higher. IBM or compatible (640k). disk $99.95.
Easy to Use Yet Powerful Loan Amortization Tool. User can Calculate Almost Any Kind of Loan, Including Multi-Phase & Variable Rates. Menu-Driven, Providing a Simple, Intuitive User Interface. User Enters any Three of Four Variables, Original Amount, Interest Rate, Number of Periods, and Payment Amount Automatically Calculates the Fourth! Override Feature can be Used to Enter all Four of the Variables. User Can Print the Amortization Schedule or Change the Variables and Perform "What-If" Scenarios. Accommodates Variable Phase Loans such as Adjustable Rate, Graduated Payment, Negative Amortization, Interest Only and Multiple Balloons. Interest Compounding Periods Include Annual, Semi-annual, Quarterly, Monthly, Bi-weekly, Weekly, and Exact Day. Accommodates Rule of 78's, Fixed Principal and Principal Only Loans, Payments in Advance, (leases) and More. Prints Detailed or Summary Amortization Schedules. Windows Version Includes Payment History Feature.
Good Software Corp.

Amos Fortune Free Man. Intentional Education Staff & Elizabeth Yates. Apr. 1996. *Items Included:* Program manual. *Customer Support:* Free technical support, 90 day warranty.
School ver.. Mac System 7.1 or higher. Macintosh (4Mb). 3.5" disk contact publisher for price (ISBN 1-57204-396-2). *Nonstandard peripherals required:* 256 color monitor, hard drive, printer.
Lab pack. Mac System 7.1 or higher. Macintosh (4Mb). 3.5" disk contact publisher for price (ISBN 1-57204-372-5). *Nonstandard peripherals required:* 256 color monitor, hard drive, printer.
Site license. Mac System 7.1 or higher. Macintosh (4Mb). 3.5" disk contact publisher for price (ISBN 1-57204-397-0). *Nonstandard peripherals required:* 256 color monitor, hard drive, printer.
School ver.. Windows 3.1 or higher. IBM/Tandy & 100% compatibles (4Mb). disk contact publisher for price (ISBN 1-57204-373-3). *Nonstandard peripherals required:* VGA or SVGA 640 x 480 resolution, 256 monitor, mouse, sound device.
Lab pack. Windows 3.1 or higher. IBM/Tandy & 100% compatibles (4Mb). disk contact publisher for price (ISBN 1-57204-398-9). *Nonstandard peripherals required:* VGA or SVGA 640 x 480 resolution, 256 monitor, mouse, sound device.
Site license. Windows 3.1 or higher. IBM/Tandy & 100% compatibles (4Mb). disk contact publisher for price (ISBN 1-57204-374-1). *Nonstandard peripherals required:* VGA or SVGA 640 x 480 resolution, 256 monitor, mouse, sound device.
This companion for young adult literature is ideal for students who don't know how to start that book report, or give that needed summary. Gentle prompts throughout the guide section of the program include Warm-up Connections, Thinking about Plot, Quoting & Noting, Keeping a Journal, If I Were ———,' Responding to Questions, Using Quotations, Taking a Personal View, Write to Others, & Write a Sequel.
Lawrence Productions, Inc.

AmPack. *Compatible Hardware:* Apple Macintosh. *Memory Required:* 128k or 512k.
AmPack 128k. 3.5" disk $75.00.
AmPack 256k. 3.5" disk $99.00.
Amortization Package Designed for Professionals.
Softflair, Inc.

Amusement Trivia! John Girard. Jan. 1995. *Customer Support:* Telephone support, 30 day money back guarantee.
DOS 3.1 or higher. IBM PC & compatibles (512). Contact publisher for price (ISBN 1-886770-01-8). *Nonstandard peripherals required:* VGA. *Optimal configuration:* Sound Blaster & mouse recommended.
Four Trivia Games for PC Compatibles. Uses VGA Graphics & SoundBlaster Cards. Includes Four Additional Strategy Games for a Total of 8 Games on Each CD-ROM. All Games Run from the CD.
Neon Publishing.

Anaheim Bid. *Items Included:* Disks, manual. *Customer Support:* 60 day telephone support.
IBM PC, XT, AT, PS/2 or compatibles (640k). disk $495.00. *Nonstandard peripherals required:* Hard disk, 640 RAM.
Software Package Used for Pricing Bids, Proposals & Quotations. System Predicts Competitive Bid Outcomes & Recommends a Winning Price & Sales Strategies. A Pricing Model Calculates the Highest Profit Possible, at the Best Chances of Beating the Competition. Designed for Manufactures, Construction Contractors, Service Firms, Resellers & Government Suppliers.
Anaheim Technologies, Inc.

Analog. *Compatible Hardware:* IBM PC compatibles; 120 (or more) column printer. *Language(s):* Machine.
disk $49.95.
Simulates the Operation of an Analog Computer. Used for Continuous System Simulation Work.
Dynacomp, Inc.

TITLE INDEX

Analysis of Continuous Beams. *Items Included:* Full manual. No other products required. *Customer Support:* Free telephone support - no time limit. 30 day warranty.
MS-DOS 3.2 or higher. IBM & compatibles (512k). disk $49.95.
Program for Analyzing Determinate & Indeterminate Beam Structures. Calculates Joint Displacements & Rotations, Member End Shear Forces, Bending Moments, & Section Top & Bottom Stresses. Loading May Be Defined by Concentrated Loads & Moments, & Member-Uniform & Linearly Distributed Loads. Also Capable of Analyzing Support Settlement.
Dynacomp, Inc.

Analysis of Continuous Beams. 1992. *Items Included:* Detailed manuals are included with all DYNACOMP products. *Customer Support:* Free telephone support to original customer - no time limit; 30 day limited warranty.
MS-DOS 3.2 or higher. IBM PC & compatibles (512k). $49.95 (Add $5.00 for 3 1/2" format; 5 1/4" format standard).
ACB Is a Program for Analyzing Determinate & Indeterminate Beam Structures. It Calculates Joint Displacements & Rotations, Member End Shear Forces, Bending Moments, & Section Top & Bottom Stresses. Loading May Be Defined by Concentrated Loads & Moments, & Member-Uniform & Linearly Distributed Loads. Also Capable of Analyzing Support Settlement. Includes a 35-Page Manual.
Dynacomp, Inc.

Analysis of Continuous Beams II with Graphics. 1992. *Items Included:* Detailed manuals are included with all DYNACOMP products. *Customer Support:* Free telephone support to original customer - no time limit; 30 day limited warranty.
MS-DOS 3.2 or higher. IBM PC & compatibles (512k). $89.95 (Add $5.00 for 3 1/2" format; 5 1/4" format standard). *Optimal configuration:* IBM, 256k RAM, MS-DOS 2.0 or higher & CGA, EGA, VGA, or Hercules Graphics or Equivalent.
ACB II Treats Multiple-Span Beam Structures with up to 200 Nodes & 199 Members. It Calculates Joint Displacements & Rotations, Member End Shear Forces, Bending Moments, Section Top & Bottom Stresses, & Restraint Reactions. Displays the Beam Model During the Development Process with Note, Member, Property, Material, & Restraint Numbering Options.
Dynacomp, Inc.

Analysis of Continuous Beams 2 with Graphics. *Items Included:* Full manual. No other products required. *Customer Support:* Free telephone support - no time limit. 30 day warranty.
MS-DOS 3.2 or higher. IBM & compatibles (512k). disk $89.95.
Treats Multiple-Span Beam Structures with up to 200 Nodes & 199 Members. Calculates Joint Displacements & Rotations, Member End Shear Forces, Bending Moments, Section Top & Bottom Stresses, & Restraint Reactions. You May Obtain the above Results at up to 20 Intervals Within Any Member Span. ACB II Accepts Gravity Loading, Concentrated Loads & Moments, & Member Uniform & Tapered Loads. Results May Be Sent to the Screen or to a Printer.
Dynacomp, Inc.

Analysis of Large Deflection Frames with Graphics. *Items Included:* Full manual. No other products required. *Customer Support:* Free telephone support - no time limit. 30 day warranty.
MS-DOS 3.2 or higher. IBM & compatibles (512k). disk $169.95.
Used for Analyzing Beam-Columns & Two-Dimensional Frame Structures with up to 50 Nodes & 75 Members. Results Include the Secondary Effects of Deflected Shape under Load. Interactive Analysis Method Is Used with the Frame-Stiffness Matrix Changing As the Geometry Changes with Each Iteration. The Iteration Diverges If the Structure Is Unstable for the Given Loading. LDF Calculates Node Displacements & Rotations, Member End Axial & Shear Forces, Bending Moments, Section Top & Bottom Combined Axial & Bending Stresses, & Restraint Reactions.
Dynacomp, Inc.

Analysis of Large Deflection Frames with Graphics. 1992. *Items Included:* Detailed manuals are included with all DYNACOMP products. *Customer Support:* Free telephone support to original customer - no time limit; 30 day limited warranty.
MS-DOS 3.2 or higher. IBM PC & compatibles (512k). $169.95 (Add $5.00 for 3 1/2" format; 5 1/4" format standard). *Optimal configuration:* IBM, 256k RAM, MS-DOS 2.0 or higher & a CGA, EGA, VGA, or Hercules Graphics card or equivalent.
LDF Is Used for Analyzing Beam-Columns & Two-Dimensional Frame Structures with up to 50 Nodes & 75 Members. Results Include the Secondary Effects of Deflected Shape under Load. Displays the Frame Model During the Development Process with Node, Member, Property, Material, & Restraint Numbering Options. A Node & Member Generation Option Is Included to Simplify the Model-Development Process.
Dynacomp, Inc.

Analysis of Plane Frames. *Items Included:* Full manual. No other products required. *Customer Support:* Free telephone support - no time limit. 30 day warranty.
MS-DOS 3.2 or higher. IBM & compatibles (512k). disk $69.95.
Designed to Analyze Determinate & Indeterminate Plane Frame Structures. Calculates Horizontal, Vertical, & Rotational Displacements at the Joints, As Well As Axial Forces, Shear Forces, Bending Moments, & Section Top & Bottom Stresses at the Member Ends. Loading May Be Defined As Concentrated Loads or Moments and/or Member-Uniform or Linearly Distributed Loads in Either the Horizontal or Vertical Directions. Fully Capable of Analyzing a Support Settlement Case.
Dynacomp, Inc.

Analysis of Plane Frames. 1992. *Items Included:* Detailed manuals are included with all DYNACOMP products. *Customer Support:* Free telephone support to original customer - no time limit; 30 day limited warranty.
MS-DOS 3.2 or higher. IBM PC & compatibles (512k). $69.95 (Add $5.00 for 3 1/2" format; 5 1/4" format standard).
APF Is Designed to Analyze Determinate & Indeterminate Plane Frame Structure. APF Calculates Horizontal, Vertical, & Rotational Displacements at the Joints, As Well As Axial Forces, Shear Forces, Bending Moments, & Section Top & Bottom Stresses at the Member Ends. Loading May Be Defined As Concentrated Loads or Moments and/or Member-Uniform or Linearly Distributed Loads in Either the Horizontal or Vertical Directions.
Dynacomp, Inc.

Analysis of Plane Frames II with Graphics. *Items Included:* Bound manual. *Customer Support:* Free hotline - no time limit; 30 day limited warranty; updates are $5/disk plus S&H.
MS-DOS 2.0 or higher. IBM & compatibles (256k). disk $149.95. *Nonstandard peripherals required:* CGA, EGA, VGA, or Hercules graphics card (or equivalent).
Used for Analyzing Two-Dimensional Frame Structures with up to 150 Nodes & 200 Members. It Will Calculate Joint Displacements & Rotations, Member End Axial Forces, Shear Forces, Bending Moments, Section Top & Bottom Combined Axial & Bending Stresses, & Restraint Reactions. Displays the Frame Model During the Development Process with Node, Member, Property, Material, & Restraint Numbering Options.
Dynacomp, Inc.

Analysis of Plane Frames 2 with Graphics. *Items Included:* Full manual. No other products required. *Customer Support:* Free telephone support - no time limit. 30 day warranty.
MS-DOS 3.2 or higher. IBM & compatibles (512k). disk $149.95.
Used for Analyzing Two-Dimensional Frame Structures with up to 150 Nodes & 200 Members. Will Calculate Joint Displacements & Rotations, Member End Axial Forces, Shear Forces, Bending Moments, Section Top & Bottom Combined Axial & Bending Stresses, & Restraint Reactions. You May Obtain the Member Results at up to 20 Intervals Within Any Member Span. Accepts Gravity Loading, Concentrated Loads & Moments, & Member Uniform & Tapered Loads.
Dynacomp, Inc.

Analysis of Plane Grids. *Items Included:* Full manual. No other products required. *Customer Support:* Free telephone support - no time limit. 30 day warranty.
MS-DOS 3.2 or higher. IBM & compatibles (512k). disk $69.95.
Used for Analyzing Plane Grid Structures. Calculated Out-of-Plane Displacements & X & Y Axis Rotations at the Joints, As Well As Shear Forces, Torsion Moments, Bending Moments, & Section Top & Bottom Stresses at the Member Ends. Loading May Be Defined As Concentrated Loads or Moments and/or Member-Uniform or Linearly Distributed Loads. Also Capable of Analyzing a Support Settlement Case.
Dynacomp, Inc.

Analysis of Plane Grids. 1992. *Items Included:* Detailed manuals are included with all DYNACOMP products. *Customer Support:* Free telephone support to original customer - no time limit; 30 day limited warranty.
MS-DOS 3.2 or higher. IBM PC & compatibles (512k). $69.95 (Add $5.00 for 3 1/2" format; 5 1/4" format standard).
APG Is the Third Member of the Series & Is Used for Analyzing Plane Grid Structures. Calculates Out-of-Plane Displacements & X & Y Axis Rotations at the Joints, As Well As Shear Forces, Torsion Moments, Bending Moments, & Section Top & Bottom Stresses at the Member Ends. Loading May Be Defined As Concentrated Loads or Moments and/or Member-Uniform or Linearly Distributed Loads.
Dynacomp, Inc.

Analysis of Plane Grids II with Graphics. *Items Included:* Bound manual. *Customer Support:* Free hotline - no time limit; 30 day limited warranty; updates are $5/disk plus S&H.
MS-DOS 2.0 or higher. IBM & compatibles (256k). disk $129.95. *Nonstandard peripherals required:* CGA, EGA, VGA, or Hercules Graphics (or equivalent).
Analyzes Two-Dimensional Grid Structures with up to 150 Nodes & 200 Members. It Calculates Joint Displacements & Rotations, Member End Shear Forces, Torsion Moments, Bending Moments, Section Top & Bottom Bending Stresses, & Restraint Reactions.
Dynacomp, Inc.

Analysis of Plane Grids 2 with Graphics. *Items Included:* Full manual. No other products required. *Customer Support:* Free telephone support - no time limit. 30 day warranty.
MS-DOS 3.2 or higher. IBM & compatibles (512k). disk $129.95.
Analyzes Two-Dimensional Grid Structures with up to 150 Nodes & 200 Members. Calculates Joint Displacements & Rotations, Member End Shear Forces, Torsion Moments, Bending Moments, Section Top & Bottom Bending Stresses, & Restraint Reactions. You May Obtain the above Results at up to 20 Intervals Within Any Member Span. Accepts Gravity Loading, Concentrated Loads & Moments, & Member Uniform & Tapered Loads. Results May Be Set to the Screen or to a Printer.
Dynacomp, Inc.

Analysis of Plane Trusses. *Items Included:* Full manual. No other products required. *Customer Support:* Free telephone support - no time limit. 30 day warranty.
MS-DOS 3.2 or higher. IBM & compatibles (512k). disk $69.95.
Specifically Suited to Analyzing Determinate & Indeterminate Plane Truss Structures. Calculates Horizontal & Vertical Displacements at the Joints, & Axial Forces & Stresses in the Members. Loading Is Defined As Concentrated Joint Loads in Either the Horizontal or Vertical Direction. Also Capable of Analyzing a Support Settlement Case.
Dynacomp, Inc.

Analysis of Plane Trusses. 1992. *Items Included:* Detailed manuals are included with all DYNACOMP products. *Customer Support:* Free telephone support to original customer - no time limit; 30 day limited warranty.
MS-DOS 3.2 or higher. IBM PC & compatibles (512k). $69.95 (Add $5.00 for 3 1/2" format; 5 1/4" format standard).
Similar to APF, but Is Specifically Suited to Analyzing Determinate & Indeterminate Plane Truss Structures. Calculates Horizontal & Vertical Displacements at the Joints, & Axial Forces & Stresses in the Members. Loading Is Defined As Concentrated Joint Loads in Either the Horizontal or Vertical Direction. APT Is Also Capable of Analyzing a Support Settlement Case.
Dynacomp, Inc.

Analysis of Plane Trusses II with Graphics.
Items Included: Bound manual. *Customer Support:* Free hotline - no time limit; 30 day limited warranty; updates are $5/disk plus S&H.
MS-DOS 2.0 or higher. IBM & compatibles (256k). disk $129.95. Nonstandard peripherals required: CGA, EGA, VGA, or Hercules Graphics card (or equivalent).
Used for Analyzing Two-Dimensional Truss Structures with up to 250 Nodes & 500 Members. It Will Calculate Node Displacements, Member Axial Forces & Stresses, & Restraint Reactions.
Dynacomp, Inc.

Analysis of Plane Trusses 2 with Graphics. *Items Included:* Full manual. No other products required. *Customer Support:* Free telephone support - no time limit. 30 day warranty.
MS-DOS 3.2 or higher. IBM & compatibles (512k). disk $129.95.
Used for Analyzing Two-Dimensional Truss Structures with up to 250 Nodes & 500 Members. Will Calculate Node Displacements, Member Axial Forces & Stresses, & Restraint Reactions. Accepts Gravity Loading & Concentrated Loads in Horizontal & Vertical Directions. Results May Be Sent to the Screen or Printer.
Dynacomp, Inc.

Analysis of Three-Dimensional Frames. *Items Included:* Bound manual. *Customer Support:* Free hotline - no time limit; 30 day limited warranty; updates are $5/disk plus S&H.
MS-DOS. IBM & compatibles, CP/M, TRS-80 (256k). disk $99.95.
Designed to Analyze Three-Dimensional Frame Structures. It Calculates Displacements & Rotations in Three Directions at Each Joint & Axial Forces, Shear Forces, & Bending Moments in Two Directions, As Well As Torsional Moments & Combined Stresses at Each Member End. Stress Output Is Optional for Each Member & You May Have up to Four Locations on a Member Cross-Section with Combined Axial & Bending Stresses in Two Directions.
Dynacomp, Inc.

Analysis of Three Dimensional Frames. *Items Included:* Full manual. No other products required. *Customer Support:* Free telephone support - no time limit. 30 day warranty.
MS-DOS 3.2 or higher. IBM & compatibles (512k). disk $99.95.
Designed to Analyze Three-Diemensional Frame Structures. Calculates Displacement & Rotations in Three Directions at Each Joint & Axial Forces, Shear Forces, & Bending Moments in Two Directions, As Well As Torsional Moments & Combined Stresses at Each Member End. Stress Output Is Optional for Each Member & You May Have up to Four Locations on a Member Cross-Section with Combined Axial & Bending Stresses in Two Directions.
Dynacomp, Inc.

Analysis of Three-Dimensional Trusses. *Items Included:* Bound manual. *Customer Support:* Free hotline - no time limit; 30 day limited warranty; updates are $5/disk plus S&H.
MS-DOS. IBM & compatibles (256k). disk $119.95.
Designed to Analyze Three-Dimensional Truss Structures. It Calculates Displacements in Three Directions at Each Joint & Axial Forces & Stresses in Each Member. It Treats Concentrated Joint Loads in Directions x, y, & z in Accordance with the Defined Coordinate System. A Support Settlement Load Case May Also Be Analyzed with This Program.
Dynacomp, Inc.

Analysis of Three Dimensional Trusses. *Items Included:* Full manual. No other products required. *Customer Support:* Free telephone support - no time limit. 30 day warranty.
MS-DOS 3.2 or higher. IBM & compatibles (512k). disk $119.95.
Designed to Analyze Three-Dimensional Truss Structures. Calculates Displacement in Three Directions at Each Joint & Axial Forces & Stresses in Each Member. Treats Concentrated Joint Loads in Directions X, Y, & Z in Accordance with the Defined Coordinate System. Support Settlement Load Case May Also Be Analyzed with This Program.
Dynacomp, Inc.

Analysis of Variance (ANOVA). *Compatible Hardware:* IBM; Apple. *Operating System(s) Required:* MS-DOS. (source code included). *Memory Required:* 48k-128k.
disk $39.95.
Contains 4 Programs. One-Way ANOVA Produces the Treatment Screen of Square, Mean Square, & F Ration along with the Error Mean Square. Two-Way ANOVA Performs an Analysis of Either Fixed or Random Factors with Equal Numbers of Replicates per Cell. N-Way (for N up to 5 Factors) Accepts up to 4 Levels per Factor. YATES Analysis Computes the Mean Square & Half Effect for Two-Level Factorial & Fractional Factorial Experiments.
Dynacomp, Inc.

@nalyst. *Compatible Hardware:* IBM PC & compatibles. *Memory Required:* each library (at most) 32k. *General Requirements:* Lotus 2.0 or higher.
IBM PC & compatibles (32k each utility). Financial & Stats @nalyst $195.00. *Addl. software required:* Lotus 1-2-3 2.0 & 2.1. other three libraries $495.00 ea. all five libraries $1495.00.
Five @ Function Libraries That Perform Financial & Investment Calculations Directly on Spreadsheet, Providing Total of 135 New Functions. Financial @nalyst Has Functions for Generalized Cash Flow, Amortized Loans/Annuities, Date Calculations Using Actual or 30/360 Calendar Conventions, Business Day Calculations, Quote Conversion & General Mathematics. Bond @nalyst Has Functions for Bonds, Bills & CDs with Calculations for Yield to Maturity, Price & Accrued Interest. Options @nalyst Provides Options Valuation & Sensitivity Analysis Using modified Black-Scholes & Binomial Pricing Models. Mbs @nalyst Functions for Mortgage-Backed Securities, Calculating Yield, Price, Duration, etc. Stats @nalyst Is a Library of Probability & Statistics Functions.
Tech Hackers, Inc.

Analyst. *Version:* 2.1. *Compatible Hardware:* Apple Macintosh II. *Memory Required:* 5000k. *General Requirements:* ParcPlace Systems Smalltalk-80 DE.
3.5" disk $1095.00.
Integrated Set of Application Packages That Provides Information Analysis Capabilities for Engineers.
Xerox Corp.

Analyst/Designer Toolkit. *Compatible Hardware:* IBM PC & compatibles, PC XT, PC AT.
disk $1995.00.
Automates Structural Analysis & Design Techniques & Increases Productivity. Supports Techniques Such As Entity-Relationship Diagrams, Data-Flow Diagrams, Structure Charts & State-Transition Diagrams for Both Business & Real-Time Applications Development.
Prentice Hall (Yourdon).

The Analyz-r. *Version:* Fall, 1994. Sep. 1985. *Compatible Hardware:* 486 PCs (DOS). *Operating System(s) Required:* DOS 6.0 or higher, Windows. *Language(s):* Clipper. *Memory Required:* 540k. *General Requirements:* 15Mb hard disk, 132 column printer, multi- or single-user. *Items Included:* Documentation, annual updates. *Customer Support:* Users manuals, conference, workshop, telephone support, training.
disk $1500.00 single user; $2500.00 multi-user.
Competitive Pricing Tool, Calculate After-Tax Yields on Your Lease Portfolio.
LeaseTek, Inc.

ANALYZER+. *Version:* 7.1. Oct. 1987. *Items Included:* Complete 3-ring binder manual with room for updates, help screens behind all input stages. *Customer Support:* On-site training, unlimited telephone support & all new enhancements throughout the year.
MS-DOS 5.0 (2Mb). IBM AT/XT, PS/2 & compatibles, IBM System 36, 38 & AS400MS. single-user $3000.00; Local Area Network $4500.00; Wide Area Network $10,500.00. Nonstandard peripherals required: Dot matrix printer, 132-column-wide carriage. *Addl. software required:* LOANLEDGER+ Networks supported: Novell, 3-Com, IBM PC NET.
Adds Tax & Insurance Accounting to the LOANLEDGER+ Environment. Can Do Escrow Analysis At Any Time During the Year. On-Screen Look-Up of Impounds/Escrows. Up to 10

TITLE INDEX

Unique Fields per Customer. Reports by Category Description or by Payee Number. Impound Balance Reports & Agings. Check Writing Automatically Updates the Payee/Vendor Files.
Dynamic Interface Systems Corp.

Anatomy & Anesthesia of the Mandibular Nerve. Arto Demirjian. *Customer Support:* Toll-free technical support - no charge. In U.S. - 9AM-5PM EST 800-343-0064. In U.K. - 44(0) 81-995-8242.
Microsoft Windows, Version 3.X. 386 IBM-compatible PC (3Mb). CD-ROM disk $249.00 Individual; $599.00 Institutional (ISBN 1-57276-010-9, Order no.: SE-010-001). *Nonstandard peripherals required:* MPC Standard CD-ROM drive, SVGA (640 x 480) 256 colors, MPC standard soundboard & speakers.
System 6.0.7 or higher. Apple Macintosh (3Mb). CD-ROM disk $249.00 Individual; $599.00 Institutional (Order no.: SE-010-001). *Nonstandard peripherals required:* CD-ROM drive.
This Instructional Disk Provides High Level Clinical Education That Crosses Many Specialties. The Content Is Divided into the Following Chapters: Osteology, Dissection, Clinic, Quiz. The Quiz Provides Self-Assessment in Dissection & Osteology.
SilverPlatter Education.

Anatomy & Anesthesia of the Mandibular Nerve. Arto Demirjian. Jan. 1994. *Customer Support:* Toll-free technical support - no charge. In U.S. 9AM - 5PM EST 800-343-0064; in U.K. 44(0)81-995-8242.
System 6.0.7 or higher. Apple Macintosh (3Mb). CD-ROM disk $249.00, Individual, ,599.00 Institutional (ISBN 1-57276-010-9, Order no.: SE-010-001). *Nonstandard peripherals required:* CD-ROM drive.
Microsoft Windows, Version 3.X. 386 IBM-Compatible PC (3Mb). CD-ROM disk $249.00, Individual, ,599.00 Institutional. *Nonstandard peripherals required:* MPC Standard CD-ROM drive, SVGA (640x480) 256 colors, MPC Standard Soundboard & Speakers.
This Instructional Disk Provides High Level Clinical Education That Crosses Many Specialties. The Content Is Divided into the Following Chapters: Osteology, Dissection, Clinic, Quiz. The Quiz Provides Self-Assessment in Dissection & Osteology.
SilverPlatter Education.

Anatool. Version: 3.1. *Compatible Hardware:* Apple Macintosh. *Memory Required:* 512k. *General Requirements:* Hard disk; ImageWriter or LaserWriter.
3.5" disk $925.00.
Structured Systems Analysis & CASE Tool.
Advanced Logical Software.

The Ancient Art of War. Dave Murry & Barry Murry. 1984-1985. *Compatible Hardware:* Apple Macintosh; IBM PC & compatibles, PCjr; Tandy. *Operating System(s) Required:* PC-DOS 2.0 or higher. *Memory Required:* 128k. *General Requirements:* CGA card for IBM.
IBM. disk $44.95 (ISBN 0-922614-67-9, Order no.: 10410).
Macintosh. 3.5" disk $44.95 (ISBN 0-922614-66-0, Order no.: 10455).
Players Test Their Skills in Armed Combat Against Eight of the Great Commanders in Myth & History, Including the Goddess Athena, Julius Ceasar, Genghis Khan & Geronimo. Plan the Campaign, Choose Troops, Lead the March, Direct the Battle, & Even Zoom in to Engage Close-Up, in Animated Conflict. Game Generator Lets User Create Games. Strategy Guide on the Wisdom of Sun Tzu & Other Military Strategists Is Included. Battles Are in Real Time. Includes a Strategy Guide That Tells User the Enemy's Greatest Strengths & Weaknesses. A Game Generator Allows Users to Create Their Own Campaigns.
Broderbund Software, Inc.

The Ancient Art of War at Sea. *Compatible Hardware:* Apple IIe, IIc, IIgs, Macintosh; IBM PC & true compatibles; Tandy. *Operating System(s) Required:* PC-DOS/MS-DOS 2.0 or higher. *Memory Required:* Apple II 128k, IBM 256k, Macintosh 512k. *General Requirements:* EGA, CGA, or Hercules monochrome card.
disk $44.95.
IBM. (Order no.: IBMFDK-401).
Macintosh. (Order no.: 11555).
You'll Be Planning Your Strategy Against One of Five of the Most Brilliant Naval Commanders, Including the Bloodthirsty Pirate Blackbeard, the "Yankee Pirate" John Paul Jones, & the Legendary Admiral Lord Nelson. Your Mission: to Sink His Ships Before He Sinks Yours. You Can Zoom in to Take Command of Individual Ships, & Lead the Boarding Parties As You Engage in Hand-to-Hand Combat on Enemy "Territory". Choose from 11 Classic Campaigns, or Use the GAME GENERATOR to Create Your Own. Includes Illustrated Guide to the Enemies' Known Strategies & Tactics. Features Real-Time Action & Three Levels of Zoom Down to the Deck of an Individual Ship.
Broderbund Software, Inc.

Ancient Art of War in the Skies. Dave Murry et al. Oct. 1992. *Items Included:* Manual, technical supplement, poster. *Customer Support:* Free customer service, 1-410-771-1151.
80286/80386/80486; hard disk required 10MHz. IBM PC & compatibles (640k). disk $59.95. *Nonstandard peripherals required:* VGA-256 Color. *Optimal configuration:* 545k memory DOS 3.0 or higher; Joystick, mouse, keyboard; supports Roland, Adlib, Sound Blaster (Sound Blaster required for digital sound F/X).
The Only Strategic Air-Based War Game on World War I Which Is Based on the Tactics of the Ancient Warlord Sun Tzu. With an Emphasis on Playability Rather Than Historical Accuracy, the Game Combines the Traditional Elements Found in Strategy War Games with a Fast-Paced Action Oriented Arcade Style That Provides Players Many Satisfying Hours of Computer Entertainment.
MicroProse Software.

Ancient Egyptian Art: The Brooklyn Museum: Jewel Case. Robb Lazarus et al. Jun. 1994. *Items Included:* Instructional manual, upgrade card (if available). *Customer Support:* Call-in, 1-800, fax back & on-line support are available at no charge for the lifetime of the disk.
Macintosh with 68030 processor or higher (8Mb). CD-ROM disk $49.95 (ISBN 1-886664-35-8). *Nonstandard peripherals required:* Double speed CD-ROM drive, 24-bit graphics card strongly recommended.
Windows 3.1 or higher (8Mb). CD-ROM disk $49.95 (ISBN 1-886664-36-6). *Nonstandard peripherals required:* 24-bit graphics card strongly recommended.
Digital Collections, Inc.

Ancient Egyptian Art: The Brooklyn Museum. Version: 6.94. Robb Lazarus et al. *Items Included:* Instruction manual, upgrade card (if available). *Customer Support:* Call-in, 1-800, fax back & on-line support are available at no charge for the lifetime of the disk.
Macintosh with 68030 processor or higher. Macintosh, double speed CD-ROM drive (8Mb). CD-ROM disk Contact publisher for price. *Nonstandard peripherals required:* 24-bit graphics card strongly recommended.
Windows 3.1 or higher. Windows System 3.1 or higher (8Mb). Contact publisher for price. *Nonstandard peripherals required:* 24-bit graphics card strongly recommended.
Explore the Brooklyn Museum's Famed Collection of Ancient Egyptian Art. The Collection, Which Spans over Four Millennia, Contains a 195 Full Color Images Enhanced by Multiple Views & Details. This CD-ROM Is an Ideal Way to Learn about This Intriguing Culture's Art.
Digital Collections, Inc.

... and now Miguel. Intentional Education Staff & Joseph Srumgold. *Items Included:* Program manual. *Customer Support:* Free technical support, 90 day warranty.
School ver.. System 7.1 or higher. Macintosh (4Mb). 3.5" disk contact publisher for price (ISBN 1-57204-286-9). *Nonstandard peripherals required:* 256 color monitor, hard drive, printer.
Lab pack. System 7.1 or higher. Macintosh (4Mb). 3.5" disk contact publisher for price (ISBN 1-57204-262-1). *Nonstandard peripherals required:* 256 color monitor, hard drive, printer.
Site license. System 7.1 or higher. Macintosh 4Mb). 3.5" disk contact publisher for price (ISBN 1-57204-287-7). *Nonstandard peripherals required:* 256 color monitor, hard drive, printer.
School ver.. Windows 3.1 or higher. IBM/Tandy & 100% compatibles (4Mb). disk contact publisher for price (ISBN 1-57204-263-X). *Nonstandard peripherals required:* VGA or SVGA 640 x 480 resolution (256), mouse, hard drive, sound device.
Lab Pack. Windows 3.1 or higher. IBM/Tandy & 100% compabitles (4Mb). disk contact publisher for price (ISBN 1-57204-288-5). *Nonstandard peripherals required:* VGA or SVGA 640 x 480 resolution (256), mouse, hard drive, sound device.
Site license. Windows 3.1 or higher. IBM/Tandy & 100% compabitles (4Mb). disk contact publisher for price (ISBN 1-57204-264-8). *Nonstandard peripherals required:* VGA or SVGA 640 x 480 resolution (256), mouse, hard drive, sound device.
This companion for young adult literature is ideal for student's who don't know how to start that book report, or give that needed summary. Gentle prompts throughout the guide section of the program include Warm-up Connections, Thinking about Plot, Quoting & Noting, Keeping a Journal, If I were ———' Responding to Questions, Using Quotations, Taking a Personal View, Write to Others, & Write a Sequel.
Lawrence Productions, Inc.

Anderson's Bankruptcy Filing System. Version: 2.1. John Mancini. Dec. 1993. *Items Included:* 80 page user's guide. *Customer Support:* Unlimited toll-free telephone support - no charge.
MS-DOS Version 2.1 or higher. IBM PC & compatibles (490k). Single User $495.95; Network $995.95 (3 Users); Add'l Workstations $99.95; Single User/Chapter 7 Only Version $295.95. *Optimal configuration:* Computer with 386 processor or higher. *Networks supported:* Most networks including, but not limited to Novell, Lantastic & Banyan.
Completes All Forms Necessary to Commence Filing of Chapter 7, 11, 12 or 13 Bankruptcy. Performs All Math Calculations, Alphabetizes Creditor Lists, Automatically Completes Summary of Schedules & Assembles Creditor Address Matrix.
Anderson Publishing Co.

Anderson's Ohio EPA on CD-ROM. *Items Included:* Complete documentation & quick reference card. *Customer Support:* Monthly newsletter keeps subscribers apprised of all developments in Ohio environmental law, toll-free technical support, 1 year's free upkeep service (quarterly updates), 30-day money-back guarantee.
Windows 3.1 or higher. 386 or higher (4Mb). CD-ROM disk $750.00 single user; $1050.00 2 simultaneous users; $200.00 each additional user. *Nonstandard peripherals required:* CD-ROM reader.
Related Ohio Revised Code Statutes. Ohio Administrative Code Regulations Relating to the Ohio EPA & to the Ohio Fire Marshal's Oversight of Underground Storage Tanks. Ohio EPA Policies. Annotations of Federal, State, & Environmental Board of Review Decisions. Ohio Attorney General Opinions. Cross-References to Related Statutory & Regulatory Provisions.
Anderson Publishing Co.

Anderson's Ohio Law on Disc. *Version:* Folio Views for Windows 3.1, DOS 2.5. Nov. 1994. *Items Included:* Documentation; Template; Three CD-ROM discs; Runtime version of Folio Views 3.1 (Windows); 2.5 (DOS). *Customer Support:* Toll-free telephone support, no charge; Free on-site training, no charge; 30 day money-back guarantee; Up to 2 1/2 hours of continuing legal education on site, no charge.
DOS 3.3 or higher. 386, 486 or 586 (Pentium) (1Mb). CD-ROM disk Single User $1500.00; Network $160.00 for 2 users, each additional concurrent user $300.00; prices subject to change without notice. *Nonstandard peripherals required:* CD-ROM Double Spin (Minimum). *Optimal configuration:* IBM or compatible 286 computer (higher recommended) & monitor (color recommended) 1Mb RAM; hard disk (requires only 1/2 Mb for installation); CD-ROM drive. *Networks supported:* Novell, Banyan Vines, Lantastic & many other networks.
Contents of Discs Include Page's Ohio Revised Code, Annotated; Approved Ohio Administrative Code with Appendix Material; Ohio Official Reports from 1821 to Date; Unreported Ohio Appellate Decisions from 1973; Ohio Administrative Code; Ohio Attorney General Opinions from 1977. Uses Folio Search Engine & Hypertext Link Capabilities. Find Pertinent Cases or Statutes & Follow Links to the Full Text of Referenced Material.
Anderson Publishing Co.

Andrew Tobias' Managing Your Money. *Version:* 9.0. Oct. 1992. *Compatible Hardware:* Tandy 1000, 1200 HD & 3000; IBM, PS/2 or compatible; Toshiba 3100, 1100. *Operating System(s) Required:* MS-DOS 3.0 or higher. *Memory Required:* 256k. *Items Included:* Documentation. *Customer Support:* Technical support, (203) 255-7562.
disk $79.95.
Complete, Integrated Home & Small Business Financial Management Package. Features Include a Portfolio Management Section, Including: A Link to Dow Jones News Retrieval to Update Securities Prices & Track Indexes As Well As a Utility to Download On-Line Trades with PC Financial Network Through Prodigy or Fidelity Brokerage Services Through Fidelity On-Line Express, a Budget & Checkbook Section Which Handles Numerous Accounts & Tracks Income & Expenses, a Tax Estimator, an Insurance Analyzer & an Analyzer for Major Financial Decisions, Such As Mortgage Refinancing & Rent/Lease/Buy. Users Can Also Print Checks. Not Copy Protected. The IBM Version Contains CheckFree, an Electronic Bill Payment System.
MECA Software, Inc.

Andrew Tobias' TaxCut. Oct. 1992. *Compatible Hardware:* IBM PC & compatibles, PS/2. *Memory Required:* 640k.
3.5" or 5.25" disk $79.95.
The Program's "Expert System" Allows User to Prepare a Professional Quality Tax Return Without the Help of an Accountant. Automatically Calculates & Prints Form 1040 Tax Returns & Other IRS Approved Forms & Schedules. Also Gathers Information via an Interview Format Conducted in Layman's Terms.
MECA Software, Inc.

Android Attack. *Compatible Hardware:* TRS-80 Color Computer. *Memory Required:* 32k.
contact publisher for price.
Spectral Assocs.

Andy Finds a Turtle. Nan Holcomb & Jane Steelman. Oct. 1993. *Items Included:* Directions on use of the program, registration card. *Customer Support:* 90 days limited warranty, replacement disks for fee of $10.00 & proof of purchase.
6.07. MAC LC (2Mb). 3.5" disk $29.95 (ISBN 0-944727-25-5). *Optimal configuration:* MAC LC, System 7.1, 4Mb RAM.
Turtle Books, Known As Super Stories on Disks, Allow Children with Developmental Disabilities to Click on a Button on the Screen or Use a Switch to Hear the Story Read Word by Word or Sentence by Sentence As the Text Is Highlighted in Color of Choice.
Jason & Nordic Pubs.

Andy Opens Wide. Nan Holcomb & Jane Steelman. Oct. 1993. *Items Included:* Directions on use of the program, registration card. *Customer Support:* 90 days limited warranty, replacement disks for fee of $10.00 & proof of purchase.
6.07. MAC LC (2Mb). 3.5" disk $29.95 (ISBN 0-944727-23-9). *Optimal configuration:* MAC LC, System 7.1, 4Mb RAM.
Story about Andy Who Has Problems with Voluntary Motor Control. User Can Click on a Button on the Screen or Use a Switch to Hear the Story Read Word by Word or Sentence by Sentence As the Text Is Highlighted in Color of Choice.
Jason & Nordic Pubs.

ANESafe. *Version:* 2.1. Sep. 1983. *Compatible Hardware:* IBM PC. *Operating System(s) Required:* PC-DOS. *Language(s):* Quicksilver. *Memory Required:* 640k. *Customer Support:* Toll free telephone support.
$595.00.
Interviews Patients Coming to Hospital or Surgicenter Admission Prior to General Anesthesia. Fifty Risk Factors Screened & Translated As Described under SYMPTOMATIX. Both English-to-English & Spanish-to-English Formats Are Included. Processing Time Is Less Than Seven Minutes for Production of a Finished Typed Report for the Anesthesiologist.
SRC Systems, Inc.

Anespec. 1984. *Operating System(s) Required:* Theos 286V. *Memory Required:* 640k. *General Requirements:* Hard disk, printer.
disk $2495.00.
Menu Driven Accounts Receivable & Billing System Designed Especially for Medical Specialties. Features Custom Third Party Billing, Practice Analysis, Collection Letters & a Comprehensive Age Analysis.
Medispec Management Services, Inc.

Anesthesia Practice Management System. Professional Software Associates, Inc. *Compatible Hardware:* TI Professional. *Operating System(s) Required:* UCSD p-System. *Memory Required:* 128k. *General Requirements:* Winchester second drive, printer.
$3495.00.
Generates Reports, Statements, & Insurance Forms, & Recalls & Maintains Detail As Desired. Allows On-Screen Calculations.
Texas Instruments, Personal Productivit.

Angling for Words in Bits & Bytes - Advance Level. Barbara Whitwell & Martha Keiser. Jul. 1991. *Items Included:* Manual & binder.
Apple II system disk. Apple II Plus, e, c, GS. disk $30.00 (ISBN 0-87879-937-0).
Provides Drill & Practice Exercises Which Help Students to Learn All Sound Concepts Including All Six Syllables & Multi-Syllabic Words.
Academic Therapy Pubns., Inc.

Angling for Words in Bits & Bytes - Intermediate Level. Barbara Whitwell & Martha Keiser. Jul. 1991. *Items Included:* Manual & binder.
Apple II system disk. Apple II Plus, e, c, GS. disk $30.00 (ISBN 0-87879-936-2).
Provides Drill & Practice Exercises Which Help Students to Learn Vowel-Consonant-E Words, Vowel-R Controlled Words, Some Vowel Teams & Some Multi-Syllabic Words.
Academic Therapy Pubns., Inc.

Angling for Words in Bits & Bytes-Beginner's Program. Barbara Whitwell. Jan. 1991. *Items Included:* Manual & binder.
Apple DOS 3.3. Apple II Plus, e, c, GS. $30.00 (ISBN 0-87879-918-4, Order no.: 918-4).
Provides Drill & Practice Exercises with Short Vowel Words. There are 15 Sequential Lessons, with 7 Different Activities per Lesson. Students Can Work Independently Once Introduced to the Specific Lesson.
Academic Therapy Pubns., Inc.

Animal Data Disks. *Items Included:* User's Guide. *Customer Support:* Free technical support.
PC-DOS/MS-DOS. IBM PC & compatibles. disk $50.00 ea. (2 free disks with each MIXIT program). *Addl. software required:* Any MIXIT Program. *Optimal configuration:* Same as for MIXIT Program used. *Networks supported:* Novell.
Data Disks Containing Ingredient & Nutrient Information to Formulate Nutritionally Balanced, Least Cost Rations for All Commercial Animals Are Available for MIXIT-2 & MIXIT-2 Plus Users. Currently Offered Are Data for: Beef & Dairy, Swine & Poultry, Horses, Turkeys, Sheep, Goats, Catfish & Tilapia, Shrimp, Trout & Salmon, Petfood, Zoo Animals, Mink & Fox, Game Bird & Waterfowl, Fertilizer, Ice Cream & Sausage. Many Disks Are Available in Spanish.
Agricultural Software Consultants, Inc.

The Animal Tales Electronic Books.
Macintosh. CD-ROM disk $49.95 (Order no.: AT1000).
Windows. CD-ROM disk $49.95.
These Stories Have Been Favorites of Parents, Teachers, & Guidance Counselors for Years & Are Now Available on CD-ROM. Each Story Is Designed to Enrich the Emotional Development of Young Children. Topics Covered Include Self-Acceptance, Respect, Overcoming Fear, & Many Other Hard to Teach Moral Values. The Wonderful Voices & Illustrations Really Bring These Stories to Life & Children Want to Read Them over & over Again. Each Package Includes Two Stories. DOS/Windows Versions Are Available.
Milliken Publishing Co.

Animals & Nature. (Studio Ser.). *Items Included:* Visual index, user's guide. *Customer Support:* Free & unlimited technical support to registered

TITLE INDEX

users; 60 day money-back guarantee.
Macintosh. Macintosh (Minimum required for program with which you want to use ClickArt). 3.5" disk $99.95. *Nonstandard peripherals required:* PostScript compatible printer. *Addl. software required:* Any desktop publishing, word processing or works application that accepts EPS files.
Windows V.3.0 or higher. IBM PC & compatibles (Minimum needed for application with which you will use ClickArt). 3.5" disk $99.95. *Addl. software required:* Any desktop publishing, word processing or works program that accepts CGM or WMF files.
MS-DOS V.3.3 or higher. IBM PC & compatibles (Minimum needed for application with which you will use ClickArt). 3.5" disk $99.95. *Addl. software required:* Any desktop publishing, word processing or works program that accepts WMF or CGM files.
Over 150 Images! Highest-Quality Full-Color Images Available; Ready-to-Use, or Changed in Appropriate Drawing Program; Designed in Full-Color (CMYK); Ready for Color Separations & Commercial Printing; Produced to Print in Detailed Greyscale on Black & White Printers.
T/Maker Co., Inc.

Animate. Jul. 1986. *Compatible Hardware:* Apple IIe, IIc, IIgs. *Operating System(s) Required:* ProDOS. *Memory Required:* 128k. *General Requirements:* Mouse, joystick, KoalaPad, or Apple Graphics Tablet.
disk $69.95 (Order no.: APDSK-35).
backup disk $10.00.
Create Drawings & Bring Them to Life in Double Hi-Res Movies & Cartoons. Create Scenes Pixel-by-Pixel, or Use Pre-Drawn Characters & Backgrounds. Allows Control of up to 16 Characters in a Single Scene. Includes Pull-Down Menus, Preview, & Edit. Offers Pre-Drawn Objects & Integrated Sound.
Broderbund Software, Inc.

Animate 3-D. *Compatible Hardware:* Commodore Amiga.
contact publisher for price.
Animation Program Which Allows Users to Control Details of Object Rotation, Camera Movements, Timing, & Action Through a Graphical Interface or a Script Language. Individual Objects Can Be Linked to Orchestrate Complex Hierarchical Movements That Simulate Live Action. The Final Production Can Be Stored As a Compressed Animation File Playable from RAM or Recorded on Videotape. Additional Output Options Include Single Frame VCR Control or Image Rendering to a Frame Buffer Card. Animations Can Incorporate Either Solid Modeling or Ray Tracing.
Byte by Byte.

Animation. *Compatible Hardware:* TRS-80 Model I Level II. *Operating System(s) Required:* TRSDOS. *Language(s):* Assembly. *Memory Required:* 16k.
cassette $39.95.
Extends the BASIC Programming Language to Provide 3 Dimensional Animation Capabilities. Contains High-Level Priorities to Allow Instant Scale, Rotation, Clip & Hidden Line Adjustments & Quality Definition.
Algorithmic Assocs.

Animation. Jul. 1988. *Compatible Hardware:* IBM PC & compatibles. *Operating System(s) Required:* MS-DOS. *Memory Required:* 640k. *Items Included:* Manual & software.
disk $1495.00 (ISBN 0-937197-02-5).
Educational Institutions. $250.00.
Animation Automatically Generates Graphics for Micro Saint Module.
Micro Analysis & Design, Inc.

Animation Games & Sound for the Apple IIe. *Compatible Hardware:* Apple II+, IIe. *Memory Required:* 48k.
disk $33.95, incl. bk.
Allows Beginners to Explore the Graphics Capabilities of the Computer While Learning to Create Monsters, Spacecrafts, & Other Objects. When the User Becomes Adept at Creating Graphics, Sound Can Be Added Making the Image Move, Turn, Fire & Attack.
Prentice Hall.

Animation Station: Computer Design Pad & Graphics Program. Jun. 1984. *Compatible Hardware:* Apple II, II+, IIe, IIc; Commodore 64, 128.
Apple. disk $84.95 (Order no.: GTA).
Commodore. disk $79.95 (Order no.: GTC).
Selection of Printer Dump Routines & Built-In Character Sets.
Suncom Technologies.

The Animator. *Compatible Hardware:* Commodore 64. *Memory Required:* 64k.
disk $29.95.
Dynacomp, Inc.

Animator. *Compatible Hardware:* IBM RT PC. *Operating System(s) Required:* UNIX. *Language(s):* COBOL.
$1200.00.
Tool for Migrating Applications from One Environment to Another. It Allows the Developer to Spot Problems That Occur. Execution Can Be Suspended at Any Time, Query or Change Data Items, Set Conditional or Unconditional Breakpoints, Alter the Flow of Control, View the User Screen, or Compile & Execute Additional COBOL Statements On-Line.
Micro Focus, Inc. (California).

AnnaBios. John O. Foster. *Items Included:* 3-ring binder with 3.5" diskette. *Customer Support:* By telephone or fax, normally no charge, 30 day money back gurantee.
IBM & compatibles (640k). disk disk $995.00 plus $4.00 royalty per production unit (ISBN 0-929392-30-2). *Nonstandard peripherals required:* Hard disk, prom programmer. *Addl. software required:* Microsoft C & MASM 6.0.
Allows User to Create & Customize an XT or AT BIOS. It Includes a Diskette That Contains a Completed BIOS, the Source Code for the BIOS, & All the Utilities the User Needs to Form a New BIOS Out of the BIOS Files. Also Includes a Setup Programme & a Monitor/Debugger Called SysVue. SysVue Is Particularly Useful for Those Developing Diskless Systems.
Annabooks.

Annal of Internal Medicine, 1992-1994. Jun. 1994. *Items Included:* Registration Card. *Customer Support:* Creative Multimedia Corporation warrants the CD-ROM disc & diskettes to be free from defects in materials & workmanship under normal use & service for a period of 90 days from date of purchase. Creative Multimedia Corporation offers Technical Support to customers as needed.
System Software 6.0.5 or higher. Macintosh Plus or higher (1Mb). CD-ROM disk SRP $195.00 (ISBN 1-880428-39-3, Order no.: 10613-001). *Optimal configuration:* Color display requires 8-bit color, 32 bit QuickDraw & color monitor.
MS-DOS 3.1 or higher. IBM-PC & compatibles (512k). CD-ROM disk SRP $195.00 (Order no.: 10613-001). *Optimal configuration:* For graphics display, Super VGA card w/512k memory & VESA extensions recommended, standard VGA supported.
Microsoft Windows 3.1. 386/33 or higher (4Mb). CD-ROM disk SRP $195.00 (Order no.: 10613-001). *Optimal configuration:* Super VGA card w/512k memory, standard VGA supported.
Three Years of the Leading Journal in Internal Medicine Exploring Topics Pertinent to General Internal Medicine & Related Subspecialties Such As Cardiology, Gastroenterology, Hematology, & Infectious Disease.
Creative Multimedia Corp.

Annatommy.
Windows. IBM & compatibles. CD-ROM disk $49.95 (Order no.: R1219). *Nonstandard peripherals required:* CD-ROM drive.
This Wild & Adventurous Journey Through the Human Body Educates As Users Control Anna & Tommy's Miniature Spaceship Through the Body's systems & Organs (Ages 8 & Up).
Library Video Co.

AnnaTommy: An Adventure into the Human Body. Mayo Clinic Staff. Sep. 1994. *Customer Support:* Free 800 Number Technical Support.
Windows. PC with 486SX 33MHz or higher (8Mb). disk $29.95 (ISBN 1-884899-08-0). *Addl. software required:* This program will install video for Windows 1.1 if not already installed. *Optimal configuration:* 486SX 33MHz or higher PC, 8MB RAM, double-speed CD-ROM drive, VGA Plus 640x480 monitor displaying 256 colors, Windows 3.1, stereo headphones or speakers, hard disk space, joystick or gamepad recommended, 16-bit sound card.
Join Copilots Anna & Tommy in Their Miniaturized Spaceship on a Wild Journey of Exploration & Adventure Through the Human Body. Twenty-Eight Challenging, Multi-Level, Arcade-Style Games Entertain & Reinforce Learning As Kids Work Their Way Through the Body, Exploring 10 Separate Body Systems. AnnaTommy Teaches the Fundamentals of Anatomy, Biology & Logic.
IVI Publishing, Inc.

Anno's Learning Games.
MS-DOS 5.0 or higher, Windows 3.1 or higher. 386 processor or higher (4Mb). CD-ROM disk $44.95 (Order no.: R1244A). *Nonstandard peripherals required:* CD-ROM drive. *Optimal configuration:* 386 processor operating at 16Mhz or higher, MS-DOS 5.0 or higher, Windows 3.1 or higher, 30Mb hard drive, mouse, VGA graphic adapter & VGA color monitor (SVGA recommended), 4Mb RAM, external speakers or headphones (with sound card) that are Sound Blaster compatible.
Macintosh (4Mb). (Order no.: R1244B). *Nonstandard peripherals required:* 14" color monitor or larger, CD-ROM drive.
Based on the Book "Anno's Math Games," Kids Open Doors to Higher Learning Through These Delightful Games Where They Find Lots of Fun New Ideas about Numbers, Counting, Shapes, Sets & Many Other Elements of Math & Logic (Ages 6-10).
Library Video Co.

Annual Horse Chronicles, 1996. Sep. 1995.
CD-ROM disk Contact publisher for price (ISBN 0-9647699-0-5).
Orion Publishing, LLC.

Annual Reviews Index on Diskette for DOS.
$45.00 single copy; $120.00 one year subscription (4 quarterly additions).
Bibliographic Database for Searching Every Annual Review Published since 1986.
Annual Reviews, Inc.

Annuity Table. *Compatible Hardware:* Commodore 64, IBM PC, TI 99/4A Home Computer. *Language(s):* Extended BASIC.
disk $14.95 (Order no.: 200XD).
IBM, Commodore. contact publisher for price.
River City Software, Inc.

ANOVA PACKAGE. R. C. Gray. Nov. 1990. *Items Included:* Saddle stitched manual. *Customer Support:* Free telephone support (no collect calls).
MS-DOS 2.1 or higher. IBM & compatibles (520k). disk $79.95 (ISBN 1-880762-00-5, Order no.: ANOVA 11-90-1.1).
Analysis of Variance Package. 1-5 Factors, Latin Square, Split Plot, Split-Split Plot, Balanced Lattice. Means, SD, SE & F Test.
Computers A Z, Inc.

Anova 2. *Items Included:* Full manual. No other products required. *Customer Support:* Free telephone support - no time limit. 30 day warranty.
MS-DOS 3.2 or higher. IBM & compatibles (512k). disk $139.95.
Accepts: 1 to 5 Factors, 2 to 36 Levels per Factor, Randomize Block Design, Repeated-Measures Designs, Equal or Unequal N (Unweighted Means Analysis), Randomized Designs with up to 10,000 Data Points, Mixed Designs with up to 1,200 Observations per Group, & Completely Repeated Measures Designs with up to 1,200 Data Points. Performs: Analysis of Variance, Analysis of Covariance with a Single Covariate, Latin Square Analysis, Data Disk-File Creation, Data Review/Edit, Data Transformations (Such As Arcsin, Power, Log in, etc.), & Data-File Joining. Calculates: Anova Tables, SS Between Regression, SS Within Regression, F Values, P Values, & Within-Group Correlation. Produces: Complete Summary Table with F-Test & P-Values on CRT or Printer; Mean, Standard Deviation, & Sum-of-Square for Each Cell on CRT or Printer, & High-Resolution Plots & Bar Graphs on CRT to Disk Files.
Dynacomp, Inc.

ANSI BASIC Software Interpreter. *Compatible Hardware:* Z-80 based microcomputer systems. contact publisher for price.
ANSI BASIC Interpreter.
Thomson Semi Conductors-Mostek Corp.

ANSI-66 Fortran Compiler. *Items Included:* Full manual. No other products required. *Customer Support:* Free telephone support - no time limit, 30 day warranty.
MS-DOS 3.2 or higher. IBM & compatibles (512k). disk $149.95.
Easy-to-Use, Two-Pass Compiler Which Conforms to the ANSI-66 Standards. Features Include: Standard: Full ANSI 66 Standard with Extensions. Code Generation: Object Files or Intermediate Code Files (Saves Disk Space). External Routines May Be Called. Data Types: Byte, Integer, Real Double Precision, Complex, Logical, Character, & Varying Length Strings. Operations: All Standard Operations, Plus String Comparisons, Assignments, & XOR. Debug Support: Subscript Checking, Good Runtime Messages.
Dynacomp, Inc.

ANSYS. *Version:* 5.0. *Compatible Hardware:* IBM & compatibles, Apollo, Convex, Hewlett Packard, Honeywell, VAX, Sun SG. *Items Included:* Documentation (reference & training manuals). *Customer Support:* Seminars, telephone hotline support, international conference highlighting applications, ANSYS support distributors located throughout the world to provide support, training & licensing.
contact publisher for price.
Finite-Element Analysis Programs for Engineers. Provides a Complete Engineering Environment -- Preprocessing, Solid Modeling, Analysis, Postprocessing, Graphics, Magnetics & Design Optimization. The Program Features 2 or 3-Dimensional, Static or Dynamic, Linear or Nonlinear Structural Analysis; 2 or 3-Dimensional, Steady-State or Transient, Linear or Nonlinear Thermal Analysis; Coupled Field Analysis (Fluid-Structural, Piezoelectric, Electro-Magnetic, Magneto-Structural, Thermal-Structural, Thermal-Electric, & Thermal-Fluid Flow); Graphics Based User Interface with Mouse-Driven Menu System & Comprehensive On-Line Help; Extensive Graphics Capabilities Including Color, Hidden Line Removal, Section, Contour, Variable-Versus-Path Display, & X-Y Graphs.
Swanson Analysis Systems, Inc.

ANSYS-PC/Linear: Finite Element Analysis. *Version:* 5.0. *Customer Support:* Seminars, telephone hotline support, International conference highlighting applications, ANSYS support distributors located throughout the world to provide support, training & licensing.
IBM PS/2 (Model 70 & above); COMPAQ DESKPRD 386; H-P VECTRA 486; NEC PowerMate 386; or 100% compatible. contact publisher for price. *Nonstandard peripherals required:* Hard disk drive; 68020/68030 processor; 68881/68882 math floating point coprocessor.
Handles Wide Range of Analysis Types Including Static, Modal, Dynamic Response & Random Vibration in One, Two & Three Dimensions. Analyses Are Performed on Models Built with the Library That Contains Shell, Solid, Beam, Pipe, Gap & Other Elements. Interactive Preprocessor, Included with Program, Contains Comprehensive Routines for Model Building in Two & Three Dimensions. Once Models Are Built, Analysts Can Specify Boundary Conditions of Acceleration, Force, Nodal Displacement, Pressure Load & Thermal Load. Post-Processing Can Be Done Via Graphic Displays or with Tabular Listings for Both Static & Dynamic Analyses. Solution Output Can Be Sorted & Selected with Database Language. Onscreen Help Menu Available.
Swanson Analysis Systems, Inc.

The Antagonists. Hal Renko & Sam Edwards. *Compatible Hardware:* Apple, Commodore, IBM. contact publisher for price.
Apple. (ISBN 0-201-16490-6).
Commodore. (ISBN 0-201-16491-4).
IBM. (ISBN 0-201-16492-2).
Over 100 Illustrations, Maps, & Other Information Hidden Throughout the Book, Provide the Keys to Escaping the Antagonist & Surviving.
Addison-Wesley Publishing Co., Inc.

Anti-Aircraft. Duane Bristow. *Compatible Hardware:* TRS-80 Model I, Model III. *Operating System(s) Required:* TRSDOS. *Language(s):* BASIC. *Memory Required:* 4k.
cassette $9.95.
disk $9.95.
Aim Your Gun & Shoot Enemy Aircraft.
Duane Bristow Computers, Inc.

The Anti-Virus Kit. Mar. 1989. *Customer Support:* Hotline 617-783-7118.
MAC-OS (512k). Macintosh 512KE, MacPlus SE, Macintosh II or higher. disk $79.95.
Easy-to-Use Product for Detecting & Preventing Viral Infections on Macintosh Computers. Consists of Three Utilities: VirusGuard, Inoculator & Same/Diff. Protects Against Infection by Viruses, Damage Caused by Malicious Programs, Directories Being Corrupted or Destroyed & Damage to Documents. Includes Advice in Manual on How to Cope with Virus Threat.
1st Aid Software.

AntivirusPlus. Oct. 1990.
IBM PC & compatibles. disk $100.00 (ISBN 1-879013-03-7).
3.5" disk $100.00 (ISBN 1-879013-04-5).
Computer Virus Detection & Elimination. Computer Immunization Against Viruses.
T.C.P. Techmar Computer Products, Inc.

ANVIL-5000. *Version:* 2.2. *Compatible Hardware:* 386-486 PCs, major UNIX workstations, most major workstations, superminis, mainframes. *Customer Support:* Telephone hot line, training classes.
depends on software configuration.
3-D CAD/CAM Program with Wireframe, Surface & Solids Modeling; Drafting; Finite-Element Mesh; N/C.
Manufacturing & Consulting Services, Inc.

Any P. I. A. Software: Social Security Software. Jun. 1995.
3.5" disk $55.00 (ISBN 1-57402-306-3).
disk $55.00 (ISBN 1-57402-305-5).
Athena Information Management, Inc.

Anyone for Cards? Jun. 1995. *Items Included:* Manual, company catalog. *Customer Support:* Technical support line - customer pays for call.
Windows 3.1 or higher. IBM 386/33 PC or compatible, 486 highly recommended. CD-ROM disk $34.00 (ISBN 1-57519-011-7). *Addl. software required:* CD-ROM player & software. *Optimal configuration:* SVGA, VGA-mouse required, Windows compatible sound card.
Mac System 6.5 or higher. Macintosh (4Mb RAM 1Mb hard drive space for optional install). CD-ROM disk $34.00.
Twelve All-Time Favorite Card Games - Gin Rummy, Pinochle, Cribbage, Hearts, Spades, Whist, Euchre, Crazy 8's, 31, 99, George, Oh Hell. Choice of 18 Partners or Opponents. Eight Unique Cardback Designs. Twelve Realistic Tabletop Patterns.
IntraCorp/Capstone.

AnyText II: Full Proximity Boolean Search Engine & Index Generator. *Version:* 4.1. Jul. 1991. *Items Included:* User's manual, AnyText & HyperCard diskettes. *Customer Support:* Telephone support, defective disks replaced free.
System 6.0.7 or higher. Macintosh (2Mb) or higher with a hard drive (2Mb). 3.5" disk $99.95. *Addl. software required:* WorldScript I.
HyperCard Based Program That Allows You to Create Concordances & Do Fast Word Searches on Ordinary Text Files in English, Greek, Russian, Hebrew, Aramaic, & Several Other Semitic & Cyrillic Languages. Can Be Used with Any Text-Only File. Provides: Two Indexed Word Lists for Fast Proximity Word Searches; Boolean AND & OR Functions for Operations Between the Two Indexed Word Lists; Boolean NOT for Inverting the Result of a Search; Lookup by Verse Reference; Wild Card String Searches Through the Indexed Word Lists for Finding Imbedded Strings - Great for Finding Base Forms & Root Words in Latin, Greek, & Hebrew; Search by Grammatical Form Using the Grammatically-Tagged BHS, NT, or LXX; Option of Having Two Files of Different Languages Open for Searching; Concordances with the Key Words in Context Aligned in the Center of the Screen; Area for Collecting & Taking Notes.
Linguist's Software, Inc.

Anytime Windows: PRO AT3. *Version:* 3.0. Apr. 1995. *Items Included:* User's guide, 3 1/2-diskettes. *Customer Support:* Free 800-331-3313.
IBM & compatibles. Contact publisher for price (ISBN 0-918617-04-9).
The Best Value in a Full-Featured Personal Organizer with the Widest Variety of Great-Looking Calendars...Includes Scheduling, To-Do List, Address Book & Hot Features Such As Drag-n-Drop, Envelope Printing, AutoDial, Autoschedule, & Quick Planner Views by Week, Month & Year.
Individual Software.

TITLE INDEX

AOM: Altos Office Manager Suite. 1985. *Operating System(s) Required:* XENIX. *Memory Required:* 512k.
Altos 486, 586, & 986. disk $995.00.
Altos 886, 1086, & 2086. disk $1650.00.
Provides Solutions for the Needs of Today's Office. Consists of 7 Interactive Productivity Applications That Fulfill the Office Automation Needs of Small & Medium-Sized Businesses. Includes Word Processing, Business Graphics, Communications, Electronic Spreadsheet, Calendar Manager, & Electronic Mail.
Altos Computer Systems.

AP*Plus (Accounts Payable). *Version:* 6.33. Apr. 1989. *Compatible Hardware:* IBM PC & compatibles. *Operating System(s) Required:* PC-DOS/MS-DOS 3.1. *Memory Required:* 640k. *Items Included:* Complete documentation manual & Quickstart Users Guide. *Customer Support:* 6 months toll free telephone support & updates. 90 days unlimited warranty; annual support & update fee $150.00.
$795.00.
Includes: Aging Reports, Cash Requirements, Check Register & Discounts.
UniLink.

Apartment Mortgage Analysis. *Customer Support:* 800-929-8117 (customer service).
MS-DOS. Apple II. disk $49.99 (ISBN 0-87007-825-9).
Helps Users Analyze Whether or Not an Apartment Complex Is a Good Buy.
SourceView Software International.

APBA Baseball/Baseball Wizard. *Version:* 2.0. Nov. 1991.
MS-DOS 3.1 or higher (256k). IBM & compatibles. Contact publisher for price (ISBN 0-941847-28-4, Order no.: PW1ZI).
Nonstandard peripherals required: Hard disk. *Addl. software required:* at least one season data disk.
Creates Players & Projects Ratings from Actual Baseball Statistics. Add Players to APBA Data Disks. Imports Statistics from Duerk's Encyclopedia. Includes Innovator.
Miller Assocs.

APBA Baseball Classic Deluxe. *Version:* 2.0. *Customer Support:* Telephone support (4.5 hrs. weekdays).
DOS 3.1 or higher, hard drive; 640k RAM; high density 3.5" disk drive. IBM (640k). Contact publisher for price.
An Upgrade to APBA Baseball Classic That Combines APBA Baseball Classic Version 2.0 with MicroManager & All the Most Recent Versions of the Most Popular APBA Baseball Programs - StatMaster, Draft, Old Timers Vol. 1, General Manager, New Main Menu Organizer.
Miller Assocs.

APBA Baseball Classic: Master Edition.
Version: 1.5. *Memory Required:* 640k.
MS-DOS 2.1 or higher. IBM PC & compatibles. Contact publisher for price.
Professional Baseball Simulation. Allows You to Manage Your Team in a Realistic Baseball Situation. You Make the Dynamic Decisions. Includes All Defensive & Offensive Options, Replays, Quick Play, & Boxscores. Also Includes the Most Recent Years Data & Programs to Draft Teams & Organizations of Your Own.
Miller Assocs.

APBA Baseball for Windows Ballparks Disks.
IBM. Contact publisher for price. *Addl. software required:* APBA Baseball for Windows.
Images of the Following Ballparks for Use with APBA Baseball for Windows, Each Sold Separately: Baltimore, Boston, California, Chicago, Cincinnati, Cleveland, Colorado, Florida, Houston, Kansas, Los Angeles, Milwaukee, Minnesota, Montreal, NY Queens, Oakland, Philadelphia, Pittsburgh, San Diego, Shibe, St. Louis, Texas, Toronto.
Miller Assocs.

APBA Baseball General Manager. *Version:* 1.5. *Items Included:* Instructions, Communications package.
MS-DOS 3.1 or higher (640k). IBM & compatibles. Contact publisher for price. *Nonstandard peripherals required:* Hard disk, printer, Modem (1200 or 2400). *Optimal configuration:* hard disk, one or two floppies, 640k. *Networks supported:* Computer Sports Network (Houston).
Contact publisher for price.
On-line Baseball League Manager. Hooks into Computer Sports Network of Houston. Compete Nationally Against Other APBA Fans. Electronic Mail & Communications Functions Built in. Manages Franchises, Drafts, Trades, Full-season Schedule, Playoffs, & Championships. Rule Book Sold Separately.
Miller Assocs.

APBA Baseball/Old Timers, Vol. 1. 1990.
MS-DOS. IBM PC & compatibles (640k). disk $19.95. *Addl. software required:* APBA Baseball Classic.
3.5" disk $19.95.
Baseball Data. 20 Teams & Special Ratings; Every Decade.
Miller Assocs.

APBA Baseball/Old Timers, Vol. 2. Jul. 1987. *Compatible Hardware:* IBM PC & Compatibles. *Operating System(s) Required:* MS-DOS. *Memory Required:* 540k. *General Requirements:* APBA Baseball Classic.
disk $19.95.
3.5" disk $19.95.
Baseball Data - 20 Teams & Special Ratings - from All Decades, Including Pittsburgh '09, New York '11, Boston '14, Chicago '29, Cincinnati '40, Brooklyn '47, Philadelphia '50, San Francisco '62, St. Louis '67, Houston '80, Philadelphia '11, Cleveland '20, St. Louis '22, New York '37, Chicago '59, Minnesota '65, Detroit '68, Boston '75, Kansas City '80, & Milwaukee '82. For Use with APBA MAJOR LEAGUE PLAYERS BASEBALL (for DOS & Windows).
Miller Assocs.

APBA Baseball/Old Timers, Vol. 3. 1990.
MS-DOS. IBM PC & compatibles (640k). disk $19.95. *Addl. software required:* APBA Baseball Classic.
3.5" disk $19.95.
Baseball Data. 20 Teams & Special Ratings; Every Decade.
Miller Assocs.

APBA Baseball/Old Timers, Vol. 4. 1990.
MS-DOS compatible (640k). disk $19.95. *Addl. software required:* APBA Baseball Classic.
3.5" disk $19.95.
Baseball Data. 20 Teams & Special Ratings; Every Decade.
Miller Assocs.

APBA Baseball/Original Franchise All-Stars.
MS-DOS (640k). IBM & compatibles. Contact publisher for price. *Addl. software required:* APBA Major League Players Baseball.
Contact publisher for price.
The Best Players in Their Best Years for Each of the 16 Original Professional Franchises.
Miller Assocs.

APBA Baseball StatMaster. *Version:* 2.2. Danny Landers. Nov. 1991. *Compatible Hardware:* IBM PC & compatibles. *Operating System(s) Required:* MS-DOS 3.1 or higher, hard disk. *Memory Required:* 640k. *General Requirements:* APBA Baseball game, either computer or board game, & appropriate season data disk.
Contact publisher for price.
Contact publisher for price.
Allows Player to Compile & Evaluate Modern Statistics from Games Played on APBA BASEBALL (Board Game) or APBA MAJOR LEAGUE PLAYERS BASEBALL. Updates Games & on the Leader Boards, Select How Many Leaders You Want, 58 Leader Boards, P-File Flexibility.
Miller Assocs.

APBA Major League Players Baseball.
Compatible Hardware: IBM PC, PCjr, PC XT; Apple IIe, IIc. *Operating System(s) Required:* MS-DOS 2.0, 2.1, 3.0; Apple DOS 3.3. *Memory Required:* 128k. *General Requirements:* For IBM: color monitor & CGA card, or monochrome monitor & monochrome graphics adapter.
disk $59.95.
Simulation of the Board Game, APBA Baseball. Includes Statistics of All Players on the 26 Major League Teams in 1984, 1985, & Historic Games. You Play the Part of Manager, Responsible for All Decisions Made on the Field.
Random Hse., Inc.

APBA Presents Baseball for Windows.
Customer Support: Telephone support (5 hrs. 4 wkdays 6 hrs. wknd).
Microsoft Windows 3.1 or 100% compatible; 20Mhz, 386 or higher processor (3Mb RAM). IBM (3Mb). Contact publisher for price. *Nonstandard peripherals required:* 12Mb free hard disk space, VGA/SVGA printer & mouse recommended.
Strategy Game That Profits from Windows Power. You Can Act As Manager, Scout, Pitching Coach & Commissioner, Drafting the Players, Setting Lineup & Rotations. Play Against Two Expert Computer Managers, a Friend or Relax in Spectator Mode. Includes Four Programs APBA Baseball, StatMaster, League Manager & Advance Draft.
Miller Assocs.

Aphasia I: Noun Associations. Fred Weiner. Jun. 1985. *Compatible Hardware:* Apple II+, IIe, IIc, IIgs; IBM PC, PCjr, PC XT. *Memory Required:* 48k. *General Requirements:* Printer.
Apple. disk $99.50 (ISBN 0-942763-05-X).
IBM. disk $99.50 (ISBN 0-942763-06-8).
User Must Match Words with Correct Association by Pressing the Space Bar to Move Word to Appropriate Place on the Screen.
Parrot Software.

Aphasia II: Opposites & Similarities. Fred Weiner. Jun. 1985. *Compatible Hardware:* Apple II+, IIe, IIc; IBM PC, PCjr, PC XT. *Memory Required:* 48k.
Apple. disk $99.50 (ISBN 0-942763-07-6).
IBM. disk $99.50 (ISBN 0-942763-08-4).
User Must Match Word with Correct Opposite or Similarity by Pressing the Space Bar to Move the Word to the Appropriate Place on the Screen.
Parrot Software.

Aphasia III: Categories. Fred Weiner. Jun. 1985. *Compatible Hardware:* Apple II+, IIe, IIc, IIgs; IBM PC, PCjr, PC XT. *Memory Required:* 48k.
Apple. disk $99.50 (ISBN 0-942763-09-2).
IBM. disk $99.50 (ISBN 0-942763-10-6).
User Is Presented with a Category & Then Words Are Displayed. User Must Press Space Bar for Every Word Within the Category.
Parrot Software.

Aphasia IV: Reading Comprehension. Fred Weiner. Sep. 1985. *Compatible Hardware:* Apple II Plus, IIe, IIc, IIgs; IBM PC. *Memory Required:* 48k.
disk $99.50 (ISBN 0-942763-11-4).
Literal & Inferential Questions Are Asked about a Story. User's Incorrect Responses Trigger a Teaching Strategy to Help Improve Reading Comprehension.
Parrot Software.

API C Library. *Compatible Hardware:* IBM PC & compatibles.
disk $199.95.
Provides C Language Interfaces for the Entire Set of API Functions, etc.
Quarterdeck Office Systems.

API Reference. *Compatible Hardware:* IBM PC & compatibles.
disk $59.95.
Provides Information on How to Write Assembly Language Programs & Defines the DESQview API.
Quarterdeck Office Systems.

APITANK. *Compatible Hardware:* IBM PC & compatibles. *Operating System(s) Required:* MS-DOS. *Language(s):* BASIC. *Memory Required:* 128k.
$165.00.
Provides the Calculations for API Tank Design Which Includes the Required Thickness of Shell, Cone Roof, Dome Roof, & Supported Cone Roof. Sizes Rafters & Provides Center Column Loading for Supported Roof.
Technical Research Services, Inc.

APL*Plus III for Windows. *Version:* 1.2. Apr. 1994. *Items Included:* 2 manuals, 3 disks (3.5" only). *Customer Support:* 90 days free telephone support. $99 support plan lasting 12 months.
Windows 3.1. IBM 803865X or higher (4Mb). disk $995.00. *Optimal configuration:* 80486 or Pentium processor, 8-16Mb of RAM. *Networks supported:* All major.
Windows NT. IBM 80386 or higher (8Mb). disk $995.00. *Optimal configuration:* 80486 or Pentium Processor, 32Mb of RAM. *Networks supported:* All major.
*A 32-Bit Application Development System for the Windows Environment. Win32 Based, APL*PLUS III Runs under Windows 3.1, WFW 3.11 & Windows NT & Is a Perfect Tool for Both Prototyping & the Development of Enterprise Wide Production Systems.*
Manugistics, Inc.

APL*Plus-PC. *Version:* 11. Jan. 1993. *Compatible Hardware:* IBM PC. *Operating System(s) Required:* MS-DOS. *Memory Required:* 512k. *Customer Support:* 90 days free.
disk $195.00 (ISBN 0-926683-02-0, Order no.: P109).
Extended APL Language Featuring: Full-Screen Editing, a Built-In Terminal Emulator, Communications, Graphics Primitives, & Report Formatting; Plus Concise Notation for Programs Like Sorting, Matrix Inversions, String Searching, etc.
Manugistics, Inc.

APL*Plus-PC Financial & Statistical Library. Oct. 1983. *Operating System(s) Required:* PC-DOS. *Memory Required:* 256k.
disk $275.00 (ISBN 0-926683-03-9, Order no.: P096).
Collection of More Than 200 APL Programs That Is Specially Prepared to Work with STSC's APL Plus/PC System. Allows User to Perform Financial Calculations, Manipulate & Forecast Time Series, Compute Statistical Measures & Generate Probability Distribution. Combination of the Library & the APL Plus/PC System Provides an Environment That Includes a Full-Screen Editor, Graphics, Communications, File Management, Report Formatting, 8087 Co-Processor Support & a Library of Financial, Forecasting, & Statistical Routines.
Manugistics, Inc.

APL*Plus-PC TOOLS, Vol. 1, 3 disks. Sep. 1984. *Operating System(s) Required:* PC-DOS 2.0. *Memory Required:* 256k. *General Requirements:* 2 disk drives.
disk $295.00 (ISBN 0-926683-04-7, Order no.: P118).
Programming Tools Consist of Implementations of Commonly-Required Algorithms, Integrated Application Building Blocks, Interfaces to Popular Microcomputer Hardware & Software, Utilities to Maintain Software Configurations.
Manugistics, Inc.

APL*Plus for UNIX. *Version:* 5. Jun. 1993. *Compatible Hardware:* IBM RS6000, SUN SPARC, SUN4, DEC System, DEC Stations, HP 9000. *Operating System(s) Required:* UNIX. *Memory Required:* 1024k. *Customer Support:* 90 days free.
AT&T-3B2. disk $2500.00 (ISBN 0-926683-05-5, Order no.: P113).
HP. ROM cartridge $3495.00 (ISBN 0-926683-05-5, Order no.: P113).
Provides Full Compatibility with STSC's Other APL Plus Systems. Features Include the Partial Compilation of APL Functions the First Time They Are Executed, Full-Screen Features for Display & Editing, & a Shared-File System for Data Management.
Manugistics, Inc.

APL*Plus II for DOS. *Version:* 5.2. *Customer Support:* 90 days free.
An 80386-based system under MS-DOS. $895.00.
Complete 32-Bit Implementation of APL in Extended Environment. Highly Compatible with IBM APL2. Includes Interfaces to Lotus, DBASE, Paradox & Compiled C & Fortran Routines.
Manugistics, Inc.

Apollo. *Compatible Hardware:* Apple II, II+, IIe, IIc; IBM PC & compatibles, PC XT.
disk $125.00, incl. manual.
Database Management Program That Stores Mailing Lists, Invoices, & Cookbooks, etc. Retrieve, Print, Remove, or Transfer Any File (or Selected Group of Files). Files Can Be Sorted Alphabetically by Any Field, Either in Ascending or Descending Order.
Schmidt Enterprises.

Apollo 13: A Week to Remember. Jun. 1995. *Items Included:* CD-ROM in Jewel Case only. No other materials. *Customer Support:* Customer support is free. By phone 314/231-5001 or by E-mail 74754.303-compuserve.com.
Windows 3.1 or Windows 95; Macintosh System 7. Mac; IBM & compatibles (8Mb PC; 5Mb Mac). CD-ROM disk $39.95 Box (ISBN 0-9647565-0-1). *Nonstandard peripherals required:* 2x CD-ROM drive, monitor capable of 256 colors, sound card. *Optimal configuration:* 8Mb RAM, thousands of colors, Quad speed DE-ROM player.
CD-ROM disk $39.95 Jewel Case (ISBN 0-9647565-1-X).
CD-ROM disk $69.95 Educational Package (ISBN 0-9647565-2-8).
This CD-ROM Tells the Story of the Apollo 13 Space Flight Through a Combination of Still Images, Narration, an Original Soundtrack, Newspaper Notices & Interviews with the Astronauts & Five of the Controllmen Who Worked the Flight.
Odyssey Interactive.

APPC-PLUS. *Operating System(s) Required:* UNIX or UNIX-like environments. *Memory Required:* 1000k.
contact publisher for price.
Provides Services for Program-to-Program Communications over Peer-to-Peer or Micro-to-Mainframe Connections. Enables Information Exchange & Access to Applications Without Regard to the Location of the Application in the Network, or to the Specific Operating Environment. Services Strictly Adhere to SNA LU 6.2/PU 2.1 Architectures. Features Include Support for Concurrent & Parallel Sessions, Primary & Secondary Logical Units, Basic & Mapped Conversations, Control Operator Functions. Includes Standard Rabbit Product Features Such As Profitable System Configuration, Highly Portable Code, Fully Integratable with Other Rabbit Components.
Rabbit Software Corp.

Appgen. *Compatible Hardware:* Apple II, II+, IIe. *Operating System(s) Required:* Apple Pascal. *Language(s):* Pascal. *Memory Required:* 48k. *General Requirements:* 2 disk drives, printer, MSI Handheld Computer.
contact publisher for price.
Automatic Program Generator Includes Standard Data Key Handling, Standard Data Edits, Multiple Accumulators, Memory Management, High Speed Search, Record Chaining, Wand Scanning Codes & Supports 1-Way Communication.
MSI Data Corp.

Apple Alarm. *Version:* 2.0. E. Neiburger. 1980. *Compatible Hardware:* Apple II, II+, IIe; Basis 6502; Franklin Ace. *Operating System(s) Required:* Apple DOS 3.3. *Language(s):* BASIC (source code included). *Memory Required:* 48k. *General Requirements:* Printer, paddles.
Apple. disk $20.00 (ISBN 0-914555-01-4).
Attach On-Off Sensor to Paddle Buttons to Turn Computer into a Sentry; Keeping Track of Fire, Smoke, Intrusion, Motion, Moisture, etc. The Program Is Not Copy Protected.
Andent, Inc.

Apple Assembly Language. Douglas W. Maurer. 1984. *Compatible Hardware:* Apple II+, IIe. *Operating System(s) Required:* Apple DOS 3.3. *Language(s):* Assembly. *Memory Required:* 64k. *General Requirements:* Lisa Assembler for Apple II.
disk $20.00 (ISBN 0-914894-85-4).
txbk $23.95 (ISBN 0-914894-82-X).
Tutorial on Apple Assembly Language.
W. H. Freeman & Co. (Computer Science Press).

Apple Clinic. *Compatible Hardware:* Apple II+. *Operating System(s) Required:* DOS 3.2. *Language(s):* Applesoft BASIC. *Memory Required:* 32k.
disk $29.95 (Order no.: 268AD).
Programming Aids Package. DISK DOC Aids in Documenting & Maintenance of Apple DOS 3.2 & Compares Line-by-Line Differences Between Two Versions of the Same Program. APDOC Assists Applesoft II Programmers.
Instant Software, Inc.

Apple Graphics Made Easy. *Version:* 3. Sharon G. Chumley. 1994. *Items Included:* Apple data disk & 1 reproducible book, 100pp. *Customer Support:* Unlimited toll-use telephone support, 30 day approval policy, money back guarantee.
Apple II Series (64k). disk $63.95 (ISBN 0-8251-2476-X, Order no.: 0-2476X).
Step-by-Step Lessons to Teach Programming Skills in AppleSoft BASIC. Worksheets Plus Demo Programs Illustrate Concepts. Work with GR, HLIN, PLOT, COLOR, POKE & CALL Statements, Subroutines & Loops.
J. Weston Walch Pub.

TITLE INDEX

Apple Mechanic Type Face. Bert Kersey. Sep. 1984. *Compatible Hardware:* Apple II, II+, IIe, IIc, IIgs. *Operating System(s) Required:* Apple DOS 3.3. *Language(s):* Applesoft BASIC. *Memory Required:* 48k.
disk $20.00.
The User Can Obtain 26 Additional High Resolution Fonts That Are Compatible with Apple Mechanics Xtyper & Hiwriter Programs. The Font Comes in Both Large & Small Sizes & Can Be Positioned Anywhere on the Screen. Virtually All Are 96 Character Fonts & Several Are Equipped with Unique Graphic Characters. A Beagle Menu Is Included.
Beagle Brothers.

Apple Panic. *Compatible Hardware:* TRS-80.
disk $24.95 (ISBN 0-915149-14-1).
cassette $19.95 (ISBN 0-915149-09-5).
Crazed Apples Chase the Player over Many Ladder-Connected Brick Levels.
Blue Cat.

Apple Pascal: A Self-Study Guide for the Apple II Plus, IIe, & IIc. 1985. *Compatible Hardware:* Apple II+, IIe, IIc. *Operating System(s) Required:* UCSD. *Memory Required:* 64k.
disk $20.00 (ISBN 0-88175-095-6).
Contains Material from Text: APPLE PASCAL; A SELF-STUDY GUIDE FOR THE APPLE II PLUS, IIe, & IIc.
W. H. Freeman & Co. (Computer Science Press).

The Apple Pie Series. Version: 2.0. 1990. *Items Included:* Storage folder, user guide/teacher manual, 1 disk. *Customer Support:* Free telephone support.
Apple 2 - DOS 3.3 or Pro DOS. Apple II (128k). $249.95 (Order no.: AP8-A). *Optimal configuration:* Computer with printer.
MS-DOS. IBM or 100% compatible (256k). $289.95 (Order no.: AP8-I). *Optimal configuration:* Computer with printer.
A Complete Nutrition Education Curriculum Featuring Seven Stand-Alone Titles. Users Learn about Nutrition Through Diet Analysis, Simulations, Tutorials, & Games. Topics Include: Diet Content, Weight Control, Healthy Snacks, Sugar, Fat, Cholesterol, Sodium, & Much More. The Seven Units Can Be Purchased Separately. Will Be Available for Macintosh in 1992.
DDA Software.

Apple II Computer Graphics. *Compatible Hardware:* Apple II+.
disk $19.95.
Offers Explanation of Apple II & IIe Graphics Techniques, Including Placing Dots on the Screen to Artificial Color Generation, Animation, & Byte-Move Techniques.
Brady Computer Bks.

Apple II Security. 1981. *Compatible Hardware:* Apple II Series. *Operating System(s) Required:* Apple DOS 3.3. *Language(s):* Applesoft (source code included). *Memory Required:* 48k.
disk $49.95.
Set of Programs Which Enables User to Secure Disks Against Listing & Modifications. Optionally, Disk Can Be Protected Against Copying with Normal Copy Programs by Leaving Track Uninitialized. Enables User to Relocate VTOC to Track User Chooses, Remove DOS from Data Disks & Arrange Disks with Same Security As Program Disk, & Allow or Disallow Any Other Command Except RUN, CATALOG, or LOAD. Also Permits User to Rename Certain DOS Commands, Such As LOAD, BLOAD, SAVE, BSAVE, INIT, CATALOG, BRUN, EXEC, RENAME, & MON. User Can Rename Disk Volume Header When Cataloging. Includes Modified Copy Program Which Allows Copying of Secured Disks When Track Is Left Blank. Machine Language Program Is Loaded When Booting & Will Not Permit User to LIST, PRINT, PEEK, or POKE from Immediate Execution Mode.
Professional Computerware.

Apple II/6502 Assembly Language Tutor. Richard Haskell. 1983. *Compatible Hardware:* Apple II, II+, IIe. *Operating System(s) Required:* Apple DOS. *Language(s):* Assembly.
disk $34.95 (ISBN 0-13-039230-8).
Tutorial-Monitor Program Using Unique Program TUTOR.
Prentice Hall (Spectrum).

Apple Utility Pak. Oct. 1985. *Compatible Hardware:* Apple II series. *Operating System(s) Required:* Apple DOS 3.30. *General Requirements:* Apple Fontrix software.
disk $30.00.
Designed to Aid FONTRIX (Apple) in Graphics Creation. Lines Can Be Plotted, & Geometric Shapes May Be Drawn by Giving X,Y Coordinates. Frame Styles May Be Selected from a Menu of Choices.
Data Transforms, Inc.

Apple '21'. 1980. *Compatible Hardware:* Apple II, II+, IIe, IIc, IIgs; Franklin Ace; Laser 128. *Operating System(s) Required:* Apple DOS 3.3. *Language(s):* BASIC. *Memory Required:* 48k.
disk $8.95
illustration files on disk avail.
Play Casino Blackjack at Home. Players May Join or Leave at Any Time Without Affecting the Game.
Artsci, Inc.

The Apple's Core: An Introduction to Applesoft Computer Programming.
Apple DOS 3.3. Apple II, II+, IIe, IIc. disk $49.95.
An Introduction to Applesoft Computer Programming for the Beginner: (Disk 1) 14 Teaching Modules; (Disk 2) Learning Tutorials.
The Professor Corp.

The Apple's Core, Pt. II: The Seed. 1983. *Compatible Hardware:* Apple II, II+, IIe, IIc; Franklin Ace. *Operating System(s) Required:* Apple DOS 3.3. *Language(s):* BASIC, Machine. *Memory Required:* 48k. *Customer Support:* Lifetime warranty on all disks. Help at (305) 977-0686.
Disk Set. $59.95, incl. manual (ISBN 0-87284-027-1).
Teaches Advanced Methods of Using & Programming the Apple II Series. Areas Covered: Low-Resolution Graphics, High-Resolution Graphics, How to Use Tab Commands, Do Complex Editing, Improve the Visual Impact of Screen Displays, Incorporate Paddles & Sound into Programs, Generate & Use Random Numbers, Work with Data on Disks, Implement the Built-In Math Functions for Formulas Such As Sine, Cosine & Tangent.
The Professor Corp.

The Apple's Core, Pt. III: Advanced BASIC. 1984. *Compatible Hardware:* Apple II, II+, IIe, IIc; Franklin Ace. *Operating System(s) Required:* Apple DOS 3.3. *Language(s):* BASIC, Machine. *Memory Required:* 48k. *Customer Support:* Help at (305) 977-0686.
Disk set. $69.95, incl. manual (ISBN 0-87284-028-X).
Designed to Teach Users Advanced Ways to Use & Program the Apple. A Variety of Topics Are Discussed Including Complex Editing, Low & High Resolution Graphics, Working with Data Lists, etc. There Are 2 Disks Included: One Is a Program Disk with 13 Teaching Modules; the Other Is a Tutorial Disk Containing over 70 Programs Using the Easytype Error Proof Entry System.
The Professor Corp.

APPLICATION BROWSER

Applesoft BASIC Toolbox. Larry G. Wintermeyer. Mar. 1985. *Compatible Hardware:* Apple II, II+, IIe, III. *Memory Required:* 48k.
disk $29.95, incl. bk. & reference card (ISBN 0-201-14779-3).
Provides Lessons in Advanced Programming Technique. Disk Contains over 100 Ready-to-Run Programs That Illustrate How to Design BASIC Programs. Package Emphasizes Commands & Programming Techniques Needed to Organize, Store, & Retrieve Information on Disks.
Addison-Wesley Publishing Co., Inc.

Applestat: Regression-Correlation Programs on the Apple II, IIe. Peter Rob. Jan. 1984. *Compatible Hardware:* Apple II, IIe; Franklin Ace. *Operating System(s) Required:* Apple DOS 3.3. *Language(s):* Applesoft BASIC (source code included). *Memory Required:* 48k.
disk $49.95, incl. bk. & audio cassette (ISBN 0-13-038951-X).
Designed for Beginning Apple Users Who Work with Statistics. Contains Regression/Correlation Programs for Linear Bivariate, Multivariate, Non-Linear Problems, Statistical Significance Tests, & Other Functions.
Prentice Hall.

AppleWorks in Your Classroom: A Student Introduction. David E. Chesebrough. 1991. *Items Included:* Student activity text; data disk; reproducible book, 152pp.; teacher resource disk. *Customer Support:* Unlimited toll-free telephone support, 30 day approval policy, money back guarantee.
Apple II Series (64k). disk $99.95 (ISBN 0-8251-1826-3, Order no.: 0-18263).
$10.95 student bk.; 10 or more copies $9.95 ea. (ISBN 0-8251-1519-1, Order no.: 0-15192).
Users Will Master the AppleWorks Program by Learning Its Overall Structure & Concepts in the Workbook. The Disk Contains Files for Users to Manipulate About the Program's Word Processor, Spreadsheet & & Database.
J. Weston Walch Pub.

Appleworks Management Templates, 3 disks. William Choat. 1986. *Compatible Hardware:* Apple IIe, IIc. *Memory Required:* 128k. *General Requirements:* 2 disks drives, Appleworks program. *Items Included:* 3 disks & 2 bks.
disk $39.95 set (ISBN 1-55603-040-1).
Offers an Alterable Framework Around Which to Build Filing Systems to Manage Equipment, Office & Classroom Supplies, & Other Audio Devices.
Electronic Courseware Systems, Inc.

AppleWriter Enhancer. *Items Included:* Manual. *Customer Support:* 800-929-8117 (customer service).
MS-DOS. Apple II. disk $79.99 (ISBN 0-87007-410-5).
An Enhancement Utility That Increases the Capability of the AppleWriter Text Editing System. Existing A/W Files Will Work Fine with AppleWriter Enhancer. Added Features Include: Backspace, Word/Character Underscore, Overstrike, Text-Embedded Printer Control & Format commands, 12 Added Characters Such as Curly & Square Brackets, Tilde, & Backslash. It Makes It Possible to Drive a Serial Printer Through the Game I/O Port or with an Apple COM Card. AppleWriter Is an Obsolete Apple Corp. Software Product & Is Required to Use the Enhancer.
SourceView Software International.

Application Browser. *Customer Support:* Technical support, maintenance & updates, education, consulting services on a fee basis. Any DOS-capable PC, 286 & higher. 286 (580k). disk $3995.00.

PC-Based Tool That Analyzes Existing COBOL Programs & Graphically Represents the Program Design, Structure, Control Flow, & Logic to Provide Immediate Understanding of Source Code. Can Be Used to Assist with Documentation, Maintenance, Functional Enhancements, Technology Changes, Architecture Changes, & Migration to New Platforms.
Visible Systems Corp.

Application Tool Kit Diskette to Accompany "Understanding the TI PC: A Programming Digest". J. B. Dawson. Jun. 1985. *Compatible Hardware:* TI Professional with 2 disk drives. *Operating System(s) Required:* MS-DOS 2.11 or higher. *Language(s):* BASIC, MS-DOS, Macro Assembly (source code included). *Memory Required:* 128k.
disk $15.00 (ISBN 0-9615084-1-8, Order no.: TIPCD100).
Includes 53 Files of Source Code, Ready-to-Use Assemble Object Code, BLOADable Code, & Ready-to-Run Programs to Accompany the Book UNDERSTANDING THE TI PC: A PROGRAMMING DIGEST.
J. B. Dawson.

Applications of Logs & Exponentials for the Nuclear Industry, 4 lessons. General Physics Corp. 1985. *Compatible Hardware:* IBM PC with 2 disk drives, McGraw-Hill Interactive Authoring System, & color graphics adapter. *Operating System(s) Required:* PC-DOS 2.0 or higher. *Memory Required:* 128k.
Set. $300.00 (ISBN 0-87683-700-3).
disk $75.00 ea.
Designed As an Alternative to GP Courseware Modular Programs. Allows Users to Build Their Own Programs from the More Than 300 Lessons Available. Each Lesson Is on a Single Diskette. A Separate Delivery Diskette, Which Works with All the Lesson Diskettes, Is Required to Make the Lesson Operational. Each 20- to 30-Minute Lesson Begins with the Learning Objectives for the Lesson. There Are Typically 1 or 2 Learning Objectives for Each Lesson. Lessons Are Interactive, Allowing for Practice & Review. Provides a Posttest at the End of Each Lesson to Assess the Student's Understanding of the Material, & a Report on the Student's Performance Is Produced.
GP Publishing, Inc.
  pH of Solutions.
    (ISBN 0-87683-551-5).
  Radiation Shielding.
    (ISBN 0-87683-552-3).
  Radioactive Decay.
    (ISBN 0-87683-550-7).
  Reactor Period & Startup Rate.
    (ISBN 0-87683-553-1).

Applied Environmetrics: Hydrological Tables. T. Beer. 1991. *Items Included:* Manual, Shareware program for graphing.
MS-DOS 2.1 or higher. IBM PC & compatibles (256k). software pkg. $222.00 (ISBN 1-56252-228-0).
Combine Traditional Scientific Tables with Flexibility of Computer Program. Contains Following Tables: Catchment Hydrology; Open water Evaporation; Sediment Transport; Drought Indices; Soil Moisture Properties; Beaufort Scale; Special Funcitons; Longitudinal Dispersion; Physical Properties of Water; Open Channel Flow; Radiation Through a Cloudy Atmosphere; Forest Fire Tables; Extreme Value Statistics; SI, Metric, US Units Conversion; Dissolved Gases in Fresh Water.
Computational Mechanics, Inc.

Applied Environmetrics: Meteorological Tables. T. Beer. 1990. *Items Included:* Manual, Shareware program for graphing.
MS-DOS 2.1 & higher. IBM PC & compatibles (256k). software pkg. $222.00 (ISBN 1-56252-229-9).
Combines Traditional Scientific Table with Advantages in Flexibility of a Computer Program. Contains Following Tables: Hygrometry, Psychrometry, Vertical Wind Profile, Reference Atmosphere, Gaussian Plumes, Beaufort Scale, Vertical Properties of the Atmosphere, Physical Properties of Air, Meteorological Temperatures, Radiation Incident on Slopes, Grassland Fire Tables, Saturation Vapour Pressure, Transport Properties of Air.
Computational Mechanics, Inc.

Applied Environmetrics: Oceanographic Tables. T. Beer. 1989. *Items Included:* Manual, Shareware program for graphing.
MS-DOS 2.1 & higher. IBM PC & compatibles (256k). software pkg. $222.00 (ISBN 1-56252-230-2).
Combines Traditional Scientific Table Format with Flexibility of Computer Program. Contains Tidal Prediction Tables; Dynamic Oceanography; Geodetic Tables; Ekman Spiral; Wind Wave & Ideal Wave Properties; Beaufort Scale, Wind Speed Conversions; Saturation Vapor Pressure, Latent Heats, Physical Properties of Seawater; Transport Properites of Seawater; Blackbody Radiation; Normal & X2 Distribution; Weibull Distribution; Sediment Deposition; Dissolved Gases in Seawater.
Computational Mechanics, Inc.

Applied Environmetrics: Set of 3 Tables & Dust Emissions Software. T. Beer. 1991. *Items Included:* Applied Environmetrics: Hydrological Tables, Meteorological Tables, Oceanographic Tables; manual; Share program for graphing; Dustcon program.
MS-DOS 2.1 or higher. IBM PC & compatibles (256k). software pkg. $667.00 (ISBN 1-56252-231-0).
Combines Traditional Scientific Format with Convenience & Flexibility of Computer Program.
Computational Mechanics, Inc.

Applied Information Payroll Package. *Version:* 7.0. Applied Information Management Sciences, Inc. 1989. *Compatible Hardware:* '286, '386, '486, Pentium. *Operating System(s) Required:* MS-DOS, Unix, Xenix. *Language(s):* RM/COBOL. *Memory Required:* 640k. *General Requirements:* Hard disk; RM/COBOL Runtime. *Customer Support:* Telephone, modem; support & maintenance retainer required.
$1495.00.
Comprehensive Payroll system with Personal Information; 401k & "Cafeteria" Features; Supports E.I.C.
AIMS, Inc.

Applied Multivariate Statistics for the Social Sciences. James P. Stevens. *Customer Support:* Free technical support, 90-day limited warranty.
DOS. Contact publisher for price (ISBN 1-56321-107-6).
A Useful Statistical Program That Covers a Wide Range of Applied Multivariate Statistics.
Lawrence Erlbaum Assocs. Software & Alternate Media, Inc.

Appointment Calendar. *Compatible Hardware:* Commodore 64, IBM PC, TI 99/4A Home Computer. *Language(s):* Extended BASIC.
disk $12.95 (Order no.: 101XD).
IBM, Commodore. contact publisher for price.
River City Software, Inc.

Appointment Calendar: Word for the Day. Parsons Technology. Aug. 1993.
3.5" disk Contact publisher for price (ISBN 1-57264-000-6).
Parsons Technology.

Appointments. *Version:* 3.0. G. Lyle. 1980. *Compatible Hardware:* Apple II, IIc, IIe; Franklin Ace; Basis 6502. *Operating System(s) Required:* Apple DOS 3.3. *Language(s):* BASIC (source code included). *Memory Required:* 48k.
Apple. disk $75.00 (ISBN 0-914555-02-2).
Manages an Appointment Book. Allows Search by Name, Comments, Scrolling, etc.
Andent, Inc.

Appraisal Management System. *Version:* 3.0. Raymond C. Whisnant. Sep. 1983. *Compatible Hardware:* IBM PC, PC XT, PC AT, PS/2. *Operating System(s) Required:* PC-DOS/MS-DOS 3.0. *Language(s):* PASCAL. *Memory Required:* 540k.
disk $695.00 (ISBN 0-926911-01-5, Order no.: PC 093).
Used by Professional Jewelry Appraisers to Construct Professionally Worded Appraisals. Has the Ability to Calculate by Formula the Approximate Weight of a Set Stone. Simpplifies the Writing, Storage, Retrieval, Modification & Printing of Appraisal. Demo Available on Request.
Sound Decisions.

Apprentice: Definitive Collection of Source Code & Utilities for Mac Programmers. *Customer Support:* Available for support questions between 9:AM to 4:PM. Also available on E-Mail Celestin-pt.olympus.nej.
System 7 or higher. Macintosh computers (4Mb). CD-ROM disk $35.00 (ISBN 1-886545-50-2, Order no.: 07009). *Nonstandard peripherals required:* CD-ROM drive. *Addl. software required:* Development system.
Apprentice Contains over 450 Megabytes of Mac Source Code & Programmer Utilities. Most of the Code Is in C, C Plus Plus, Pascal. You'll Find Computer Working Examples of Full-Blown Applications, Games, Control Panels, Extensions, Utilities & Much, Much, More.
Celestin Co.

APPS. *Version:* 2.0. 1981. *Compatible Hardware:* IBM PC AT. *Operating System(s) Required:* PC-DOS. *Language(s):* FORTRAN. *Memory Required:* 512k.
$10,000.00 software & support.
Digitizer or Coordinate Measuring Machine-Based System for Programming NC/CNC Machine Tools Primarily Developed to Handle Nondimensioned Shapes Using Contour & Point-to-Point Input. Provides for Conventional Keyboard Entry of Part Coordinates. Full Range of Plot/Display, Editing & Hardcopy Support Are Included.
Alden Computer Systems Corp.

APR Check & Dealer Reserve. *Compatible Hardware:* Sharp ZL-6100 System, ZL-6500 System. *Language(s):* Sharp Microcode.
$400.00.
Checks the APR by Either the Actuarial or U.S. Rule Methods Using Either an Actual Calendar or "Federal Calendar" to Count Days to the 1st Payment. Find APR to Either 2 or 3 Decimal Places & the Equivalent Add-On Rate. 5 Different Methods of Computing the Dealer Reserve Are Included & the Reserve Can Be Paid on Any Amount.
P-ROM Software, Inc.

APR Loan Analysis. 1979. *Compatible Hardware:* Apple; IBM PC & compatible; TRS-80. *Operating System(s) Required:* Apple DOS 2.2, MS-DOS. *Language(s):* BASIC. *Memory Required:* 48k.
disk $75.00.
Calculates True Annual Percentage Rate for Amortized Loans or Interest Only Loans. Handles Balloon Payments.
Realty Software.

TITLE INDEX

APS (Accounts Payable System). Version: 8. Feb. 1987. Compatible Hardware: IBM PC & compatibles. Operating System(s) Required: DOS Ver. 3.1 or higher. Memory Required: 384k. General Requirements: Hard disk. Items Included: Binder with documentation. Customer Support: Maintenance fee $108/yr entitles user to phone support & enhancements released during the year.
disk $500.00.
annual maintenance fee (optional) $108.00.
demo disk $35.00.
System Designed to Automate Payables; Keeps Track of Vendor Discounts, Recurring Payables, Accumulates Dollars for Form 1099, Allows Computer Check Writing from Nine Checking Accounts, or Checks May Be Manually Drafted. Unposted Checks Can Be Automatically Transferred to STI's GLS to Allow Users to Run Modified Accrual Statements. Users Can Elect to Unpost Unpaid Invoices & Maintain Their Financials on a Cash Basis. Integrates with TABS III, TABS III-M & GLS.
Software Technology, Inc.

APS: Agents Processing Systems. Version: 2.5. Items Included: SW support, manuals, training, updates, enhancements, & user group membership. Customer Support: Full training for executives, managers, & operators. We can customize our package. Maintenance fee 14.5% software. Hot line with 800 number. Full customer support unit.
Novell 386, 2.0 or higher; MS-DOS 3.1 or higher. Any IBM-AT compatible 286, 386 or 486 based computer with 2Mb memory (640k) RAM workstation. $33,000.00-$75,000.00. Addl. software required: Dataflex version run time 2.3B for multiuser MS-DOS is required to execute the software. Carbon Copy Plus 5.0 (included in purchase). Networks supported: Novell.
A Menu-Driven Policy Processing & Accounting System that Addresses Management & Operational Needs for the General Agent. Provides a Function for Every Type of Money Transaction. All Money Transactions Become Part of an Automated Invoice Which Interfaces with Insurance Accounting. Most Management & Accounting Reports are Generated, Including a Reconciliation Process for Payable Companies. Software Can be Modulized for the Smaller Installation.
Agents Processing Systems, Inc.

APS Premium Finance System. Version: 2.3. Memory Required: 640k RAM & 2000k. Items Included: Operations manual; training, user group & support. Customer Support: Full training. System may be customized to your own approved forms. Technical assistance center with a hot line. Maintenance fee 14.5% of software. MS-DOS 3.1 or higher. IBM AT compatible 286, 386 or 486 based computer. $15,000.00 with general ledger. Addl. software required: Dataflex run time 2.3B for multiuser, MS-DOS. Carbon Copy Plus 4.0 or higher (included in purchase). Optimal configuration: 386 with 2Mb memory as network file server. 100Mb hard disk. Networks supported: Novell 286 V2.0A or higher, modem 2400 bauds & higher.
Provides Management Reports, Multi-Policy Loan Financing, Automatic Loan Processing Including Interest Calculation, Automatic Intents, Cancels, Reinstates & Check Issuance for Insureds, Companies or Agents. Integrated System Including Interface to APS GL. Provides Option for Coupon Books or Monthly Bills. Full Loan History for End of Year Reporting & Inquiries.
Agents Processing Systems, Inc.

APSS Plus: Aristo Parcel Shipping System. Version: 12.50. Compatible Hardware: IBM PC, PC XT, PC AT, PS/2, & compatibles. Memory Required: 640k. General Requirements: 1 to 3 Printers. Fixed Disk.
APSS. $995.00 & up.
Automates Shipping Process with UPS, USPS, Fed Ex, Airborne, DHL, RPS, LTLs & Other Carriers. Eliminates Hand Writing of Pickup Records, C.O.D. Tags, & Shipping Labels; Saves Customer Database & Shipping History. Automatically Calculates Zones & Charges. Handles All UPS Zones & Services. Prints, Manifests, C.O.D. Tags, Shipping Labels, Optional Audit Label, & an Unlimited Number of Management Reports. Report Generator Creates Customized Reports & Forms. Data Files Are Compatible with dBASE III; Not Copy Protected.
Aristo Computers, Inc.

APT-ZAP. Andy Tuken & APT Software. Feb. 1987. Compatible Hardware: Apple II, II+, IIe, IIc, IIgs. Operating System(s) Required: ProDOS. Memory Required: 64k.
disk $25.00 (ISBN 0-926567-06-3, Order no.: APT-ZAP).
ProDos, Menu-Driven Disk Zap Program Supports Both Block & File Operations.
Rettke Resources.

AQM: Automated Quality Measurement. Version: 1.1. Aug. 1992. Items Included: Disks, manual.
DOS. PC 386 (640k). disk $15,000.00.
Nonstandard peripherals required: VGA. Optimal configuration: 386, VGA, laser, large hard disk. Networks supported: Novell.
System That Tracks Department & Corporate Quality Indicators Such As Customer Satisfaction, Accuracy, Timeliness, Profitability, Growth, & Reports These Results at Any Desired Organizational Level.
Robert E. Nolan Co., Inc.

AR*Plus (Accounts Receivable). Version: 6.37. May 1991. Compatible Hardware: IBM PC & compatibles. Operating System(s) Required: PC-DOS/MS-DOS 3.1. Memory Required: 640k. Items Included: Complete documentation manual; Quick Start Users Guide. Customer Support: 6 months toll free telephone support & updates; 90 day unlimited warranty; annual maintenance (support & updates) $150.00.
$795.00.
Includes: Aging Reports, Sales Analysis, Open Item or Balance Forward, & Invoicing or Statements or Both.
UniLink.

ARAM - Automated Reliability-Availability-Maintainability. Version: 2.0. NASA Langley Research Center. Dec. 1988. Items Included: Source code. Customer Support: Limited telephone support from COSMIC.
PC-DOS (512k). IBM PC series. $400.00 Program; $23.00 documentation (Order no.: LAR-13997). Nonstandard peripherals required: 132 column printer.
One of the Tools Designed to Assess Candidate Space Station Data Management System Architectures. It Evaluates the Reliability, Availability, & Maintainability Characteristics of the System Concepts. Uses the Data Representing the System Architecture Redundancy Characteristics (Redundancy Diagram), the System Maintainability Characteristics, & the Hardware Component Reliability Parameters. Reliability is the Probability That a Function Performs Without Interruptions Within a Given Time Interval. For Any Unit, the Time Between Failures is Assumed to Have an Exponential Probability Distribution Defined by Its Mean Time Between Failures. Maintainability is the Probability That a Function is Restored Within a Given Time Interval. Parameters Include Repair Service Priority, Mean Time to Repair, & Availability of Spares. Maintainability Includes Global Parameters Such as Spare Parts Replenishment Period & Number of Repairmen.
COSMIC.

Arborist. Version: 2.0. Apr. 1986. Compatible Hardware: Texas Instruments; IBM PC & compatibles. Memory Required: 512k.
disk $595.00.
Decision Tree Program Designed for Examining Complex Decisions & Incorporating Uncertain Data into Spreadsheet Analysis. Allows a Decision-Maker to Structure & Represent a Problem Graphically & to Identify the Best Course of Action. Employs the Decision Analysis Technique of Representing Problems in a Tree Structure, with Decision Branches Leading to Different Outcomes or to Subsequent Alternatives.
Texas Instruments, Personal Productivit.

ARC-Monitor Plus. Operating System(s) Required: PC-DOS/MS-DOS 3.1 or higher. Memory Required: 256k. General Requirements: ARCnet card.
$75.00.
Designed for Networks Using the ARCnet Cabling & Access Protocol Scheme, It Enables Experienced Network Managers & Installers to Determine Where the Problems Lie or How Much of the Network Is Used.
Westcon, Inc.

Arcade Champ Kit. Compatible Hardware: Atari XL/XE.
ROM cartridge $24.95 (Order no.: KX7102).
Atari Corp.

Arcade Game Construction Kit. May 1988. Compatible Hardware: Commodore 64, 128. Memory Required: 64k. General Requirements: Joystick.
disk $29.95 (Order no.: 12630).
Creates Maze & Arcade "Shoot 'em Up" Style Games. Complete with Sound, Music, & Full Color Animation. Does Not Require Programming.
Broderbund Software, Inc.

Arcade Poker. Feb. 1986. Compatible Hardware: IBM PC, PC XT, PC AT. Language(s): Compiled BASIC. Memory Required: 128k. General Requirements: Both color & B&W in same program.
disk $25.00.
Resembles the Video Game Played in Arcades, Bars, & Nevada or New Jersey Casinos. Two Different Games Are Provided.
Robert L. Nicolai.

Archetype Designer. Version: 3.0. Operating System(s) Required: Windows 3.0. Customer Support: 30 days free support.
IBM PC 386 & compatibles (4Mb). disk $745.00.
Runs under Microsoft Windows. Designed for Advertising & Page Layout for Graphic Arts Professional. Features Include TIFF Compatibility for Importing Scanned Graphics, Automated Irregular Runarounds, Five User-Definable Tracking Levels, & Multi-Language Hyphenation in 17 Languages.
Archetype, Inc.

Archetype Designer. Version: 3.0B. 1991. Items Included: 1 spiral bound manual; a tutorial (manual & disk); free CD ROM offer. Customer Support: 30 days free phone support.
MS-DOS & Windows 3.0. IBM PC or compatibles 80386 or 80486 (2Mb). disk $745.00. Addl. software required: Windows

3.0. *Networks supported:* Novell, 3COM.
Microsoft Windows Based Page Make-Up Program for the Creation & Production of Design Intensive Documents (i.e. Flyers, Forms, Ads, Catalogs, Free Sheets, Magazines, etc.). Designer Addresses the Flexible Needs of the Artist/Designer While Providing the Tools Necessary in a Production Environment. It Allows the User to Quickly Create Complex Color Page Layouts Combining Sophisticated Typography & Graphics. Pages Can Be Output to Any Postscript Color Proofing Devices & High Resolution ImageSetters. Designer Provides 24 Bit Color & Outline Type Display, Rotation of All Objects, Free Text, Precession Typography & Placement.
Archetype, Inc.

Archetype InterSep. 1991. *Items Included:* 2 spiral-bound manuals.
MS-DOS & Windows. IBM PC or compatible 80386 or 80486 (4Mb). $9950.00/10 users. *Addl. software required:* Novell 3.10 or later, Windows 3.0. *Networks supported:* Novell 3.1x.
Multifinder 6.1.5 or higher, System 6.0.5 or higher, 32 bit QuickDraw 1.2. Macintosh (2Mb). $9950.00/10 users. *Nonstandard peripherals required:* 32 Bit QuickDraw 1.2. *Networks supported:* Novell 3.1x.
Novell-Compatible Desktop Publishing Workgroup Accelerator. Dramatically Increases Productivity by Reducing the Time to Search for Images, to Place Them into Any of the Popular Macintosh or Windows DTP Packages, & to Print Completed Pages to PostScript Output Devices. Off-Loads Image Processing & PostScript Integration Tasks to a Central High-Speed Picture Database Freeing up Client Workstations & Reducing Network Traffic.
Archetype, Inc.

Archibald's Guide to the Mysteries of Ancient Egypt. Sep. 1994. *Customer Support:* Free technical support - Call/Fax/Mail, Phone: 305-567-9996, Fax: 305-569-1350.
Windows 3.1. 386SX or higher (4Mb). CD-ROM disk $39.95. *Nonstandard peripherals required:* CD-ROM drive, Sound Blaster or 100% compatible, mouse, Super VGA graphics.
Macintosh System 7 or higher. Macintosh. *Nonstandard peripherals required:* Mouse, color monitor, CD-ROM drive.
Archibald Takes Kids Around the World in This Fun & Educational Geography Lesson. Prompted by Questions & Clues, Kids Lead Archibald to the Four Corners of the Earth. Kids Hear & See Facts & Landmarks about Countries, Oceans & States in the U.S. Then Play an "Around-the-World" Expedition Game.
SWFTE International, Ltd.

Archibald's Guide to the Mysteries of Ancient Egypt. Jun. 1994. *Customer Support:* Free technical support - Call/Fax/Mail, Phone: 305-567-9996, Fax: 305-569-1350.
Windows 3.1 (4Mb). CD-ROM disk $39.95. *Nonstandard peripherals required:* CD-ROM drive. *Optimal configuration:* Sound Blaster or 100% compatible, Super VGA or higher, Microsoft mouse or compatible.
Macintosh System 7 or higher (4Mb). CD-ROM disk $39.95. *Nonstandard peripherals required:* CD-ROM drive. *Optimal configuration:* Mouse, Macintosh color monitor.
Archibald, the Son of a British Explorer, Takes Kids on an Animated Adventure to the Pharaohs. Kids Learn about Hieroglyphics, How Mummies Were Made, & Watch the Myth of Osiris Come to Life on the Computer Screen.
SWFTE International, Ltd.

Archimedes Apprentice. *Compatible Hardware:* TRS-80.
contact publisher for price.
Instant Software, Inc.

Architectural/Engineering Master Accounting System Plus (AEMAS Plus). *Version:* 1.40. 1993. *Compatible Hardware:* IBM PC & compatibles, 386, 486, RT, RISC/6000; Sun Microsystems. *Operating System(s) Required:* MS-DOS, UNIX, XENIX, AIX, NOVELL, LANTASTIC. *Language(s):* COBOL (source code included). *Memory Required:* 4000k. *Items Included:* Full documentation. *Customer Support:* Various support & training options available.
disk contact publisher for price.
An Integrated Accounting/Project Management Software System Designed Specifically for Architects & Engineers. Includes Full Complement of Accounting Modules. Job Costing Allows Instant Review of Budgets, Billings, Costs, Cash Flow & Profitability. Advanced Automated Invoicing Simplifies the Invoicing Process While Increasing the Clarity of Information.
Data-Basics, Inc.

Archive. *Version:* I. Bill Hall. Apr. 1984. *Compatible Hardware:* IBM PC & compatibles. *Operating System(s) Required:* PC-DOS, MS-DOS. *Language(s):* C. *Memory Required:* 64k. *General Requirements:* Printer optional.
disk $39.95.
Allows (Binary As Well As Text) Files to Be Saved in One File with a Significant Savings in Disk Space. Also Allows User to Create an Archive File Whose Contents Can Be Listed, Updated, Appended, Extracted, or Deleted. Allows Immediate Access. Date, Time & Comments May Be Added.
Generic Computer Products, Inc. (GCPI).

Archive-Link. *Version:* 4.5. *Compatible Hardware:* IBM PC. *Customer Support:* Free product support.
$395.00.
Provides Word Processing Document Conversion Between Wang 5-1/4" Archive Format & the Following IBM PC Wang Word Processing Formats: WordPerfect, OfficeWriter, Multimate, MicrosoftWord, DisplayWrite, PFS: ProfessionalWrite, Word Star & ASCII.
M/H Group.

Archivebowl. *Version:* D4. Ron Gunn. 1994. *Compatible Hardware:* Commodore 64, 128; IBM PC & compatibles. *Operating System(s) Required:* DOS 2.1 or higher; CBM DOS. *Language(s):* BASIC for C64, Compilied .EXE for IBM. *Memory Required:* C64 64k, IBM 512k. *General Requirements:* Color monitor, printer.
disk $25.00 ea. *Addl. software required:* Leaguebowl.
Archivebowl-(IBM). (Order no.: D058I).
Archivebowl-(C-64). (Order no.: D021F).
End of Season Summary of Teams & Individuals. Handles 2, 3, & 4 Game Series Data Disks. Requires LEAGUEBOWL Data Disks.
Briley Software.

ArchiveCommand. 1992.
VMS 5.x. VAX. Contact publisher for price.
Film Archive & Retrieval System That Allows VAX/VMS Sites to Store Information on Inexpensive Offline Media. Package Provides a System for Moving Dated Information to Alternate Storage Media by Combining Options for User Driven Archiving & Management-Controlled Automatic Archiving. All Archiving Is Tracked Through a Card Catalog System. Indexing Capabilities Allow Users to Search for Archived Data Based on Combinations of 52 Different Fields, Including Archive History, User Notes & Owner Information.
Raxco, Inc.

Area Moment of Inertia. Dec. 1983. *Compatible Hardware:* Apple II; HP Series 85; IBM PC. *Operating System(s) Required:* PC-DOS, Apple DOS 3.3. *Language(s):* BASIC (source code included). *Memory Required:* HP 32k, Apple 48k, IBM 128k. *Customer Support:* Telephone.
$125.00.
Determines Area Moment of Inertia & Neutral Axis Location of Built-Up Sections Composed of up to 25 Rectangular & Special Sub-Sections.
PEAS (Practical Engineering Applications Software).

Arena. *Version:* 2.00. Jan. 1985. *Compatible Hardware:* IBM PC with printer. *Operating System(s) Required:* MS-DOS. *Memory Required:* 256k.
contact publisher for price.
Sports & Entertainment Facility Management System for Season Ticket Subscribers.
Programmers & Analysts, Ltd.

ARGUS. *Version:* 3.1. May 1985. *Compatible Hardware:* IBM PC XT with printer. *Operating System(s) Required:* PC-DOS, MS-DOS. *Language(s):* Clipper, dBASE III Plus. *Memory Required:* 512k.
disk or cassette $4500.00 ea.
PDP-11/RSX-11M or M+. (ISBN 0-922866-25-2).
PDP-11/RSTS. (ISBN 0-922866-26-0).
PDP-11/RT11 or TSX+. (ISBN 0-922866-27-9).
VAX/VMS. cassette $4500.00 (ISBN 0-922866-28-7).
IBM. disk $4500.00 (ISBN 0-922866-29-5).
Provides Facilities Maintenance Personnel with a Tool for Planning, Analysis, & Historical Tracking. Designed for Use in Manufacturing Plants, HVAC Systems, Offices, & Other Areas Where Groups of Equipment Require Programmed Maintenance. Helps Reduce Equipment Downtime, Breakdown Repair & Replacement Cost While Increasing Facility Operation Reliability, Equipment Life, & Effectiveness of Maintenance Department Personnel.
Centaurus Systems, Inc.

Argus Perceptual Mapper. *Items Included:* Bound manual. *Customer Support:* Free hotline - no time limit; 30 day limited warranty; updates are $5/disk plus S&H.
MS-DOS. IBM & compatibles (256k). disk $99.95.
A Multidimensional Scaling (MDS) & Hierarchial Clustering Package for Discovering Hidden Structure in Data Tables. Data Can Be Entered Either As Distances (Dissimilarities) Between Pairs of Objects, or As Profiles of Objects on a Set of Attributes. ARGUS Transforms This Data into a Two-Dimensional Graph That Shows the Objects As Labeled Points & the Attributes As Labeled Vectors. A Tree Diagram Showing How the Objects Cluster Together on the Basis of Profile Similarity, Is Also Displayed.
Dynacomp, Inc.

ARGUS: Perceptual Mapper. *Version:* 1.22. Mar. 1993. *Items Included:* On-line DOCS/Manual, Hi-Res graphics, spreadsheet, multidimensional scaling, hierarchical clustering, quick clustering. *Customer Support:* Free to get started, after that, $2.00/minute minimum 10 minutes.
MS-DOS 3.1 or higher. PC, XT, AT, PS2 or compatibles (385k). $40.00 3.5" or 5.25" disk or (2) 360k disks, $40.00 hard copy manual (Order no.: AD001). *Optimal configuration:* 640k RAM, math co-processor, laser or ink jet printer, color monitor (VGA, EGA, CGA, HGA), hard disk.
MS Windows 3.0 or higher. PS2 or compatibles (386 or 486) (2Mb). $40.00 3.5" or 5.25" disk or (2) 360k disks, $40.00 hard copy manual

TITLE INDEX

(Order no.: AW001). *Addl. software required:* MS-DOS & Windows 3.X. *Optimal configuration:* 486, 33Mb, VGA, hard disk, laser or ink jet printer.
Accepts Data in Table Format (OBJECTS As Rows, ATTRIBUTES As Columns) & Transforms This Data into a Visually Attractive Perceptual Map. Map Enables User to See Relationships Between OBJECTS & VARIABLES As Well As CLUSTERS of OBJECTS Based on Profile Similarity. Most Common Use Is As "Pattern Recognition" Tool in Exploratory Data Analysis.
Spring Systems, Inc.

ARIC: Allocation Resource Identification & Costing. *Version:* 2.0. M. James Bahr. 1988. *Items Included:* 2 data entry manuals, Scantron manual, Reports Generation manual. *Customer Support:* Free on-site training, 90 day warranty, annual maintenance fee, 12% of purchase price (24 hour "hotline"), 90 day free maintenance with purchase.
SCO XEXIX. Compaq (4Mb). $40,000.00-$100,000.00 depending on size of the institute. *Addl. software required:* Accell Database ROMS.
A Nursing Database Management System Used for Staffing, Budgeting, & for Costing Nursing Care by Patient. Uses Sophisticated Techniques Such As Simulation & Regression for Budgeting & Forecasting Purposes. It Has Self-Correcting Features Which Allow the User to Keep the System up to Date.
James Bahr Assocs., Ltd.

Aristo Parcel Shipping System.
IBM PC & compatibles. Contact publisher for price.
Automates the Outbound Shipping Process for Carriers Such As: UPS, Mail Manifesting, RPS, FedEx, Airborne, LTL's, & Most Local Carriers. The System Is Menu-Driven & Requires no Programming Knowledge to Customize the System to Meet Your Application. APSS Allows Modification of Label & Form Formats to Include Carrier Related Bar Codes & Bar-Coding of Shipment Information. An In-Put Device Can Be Incorporated to Read Shipping Data from a Bar Code, Thus Reducing the Keystrokes Required to Process a Shipment. Can Provide Seamless Integration with Your Host Application with Our ScreenLink Option.
Aristo Computers, Inc.

Aristo Receiving Management System.
MS-DOS 5.0 or higher. IBM & compatibles, 386 or higher (2Mb). Contact publisher for price.
Tracks Incoming Time Sensitive Items, Then Automates Internal Delivery. Functions As a Stand-Alone System or Networked Solution. Reduces Receiving Time by Capturing Data with Hand-Held Scanners. Facilitates the Internal Delivery Process by Producing Barcoded Internal Delivery Labels. A Hand-Held Data Collection Device Can Be Incorporated to Read the Bar Code of the Item Being Delivered & That of the Receiver, Which Closes the Loop on the Entire Process. Menu-Driven & Requires No Programming Knowledge to Customize the System to Meet Your Unique Application. Easy to Install, Easy to Upgrade & Maintain, & Integrates with Your Current Shipping System, or Aristo Parcel Shipping System (APSS).
Aristo Computers, Inc.

Arithmetic Skills Assessment Test. Howard Behrns. 1994. *Items Included:* Diskette & teachers guide & binder. *Customer Support:* Toll free customer service Hot Line 1-800-645-3739 (9a.m. - 5p.m. Eastern Time) software guaranteed for two years.
Mac 6.0 Plus. Macintosh (4Mb). 3.5" disk $89.00 (Order no.: DK20004).
This Comprehensive Test Provides a Complete Profile of Each Student's Strengths & Weaknesses-Indicating Which of the 119 Skills Were Passed, Missed, Skipped, or Failed.
Educational Activities Inc.

Arity Combination Pack. *Version:* 6.1. 1992. *Compatible Hardware:* IBM PC & compatibles, PC XT, PC AT. *Operating System(s) Required:* PC-DOS/MS-DOS, OS/2. *Memory Required:* 640k. *General Requirements:* Hard disk. *Items Included:* 4 manuals. *Customer Support:* 30 days free w/purchase - $250.00/year.
$1295.00.
Includes: Arity/Prolog Compiler & Interpreter, the Arity/Expert Systems Development Package, Arity/SQL Development Package, Arity/Windows Toolkit.
Arity Corp.

Arity/Expert System Development Package. *Version:* 1.61. 1992. *Compatible Hardware:* IBM PC & compatibles, PC XT, PC AT. *Operating System(s) Required:* PC-DOS/MS-DOS, OS/2. *Memory Required:* 640k. *General Requirements:* Hard disk. *Items Included:* 1 manual.
disk $295.00.
Designed to Speed the Construction of Expert Systems & Knowledge Intensive Programs. Provides Two Ways of Representing Knowledge, a Taxonomy of Frames & a Rule Based System. Provides the Ability to Optimize Backward Chaining & Interface to Other Languages. Features a Two-Directional Interface, Two Gigabyte Capacity of Virtual Memory When Accessing Arity/Prolog Database, Four Megabytes of Memory Allocated for Storage of up to 20,000 Rules, & a Built-In Explanation & Questioning Facility for Quick Generation of User Interfaces.
Arity Corp.

Arity OS/2 Integrated Prolog. *Version:* 6.1. 1992. *Items Included:* 1 perfect-bound manual. *Customer Support:* 1 yr. maintenance $250.00.
OS/2. $1000.00.
Full Prolog Compiler for OS/2 Including Object-Oriented Programming Extensions & Presentation Manager Support.
Arity Corp.

Arity/Prolog Compiler & Interpreter. *Version:* 6.1. 1992. *Compatible Hardware:* IBM PC & compatibles, PC XT, PC AT. *Operating System(s) Required:* PC-DOS/MS-DOS, OS/2. *Memory Required:* 640k. *General Requirements:* Hard disk. *Items Included:* 1 manual.
disk $650.00.
Designed to Provide the Speed & Power Required for Developing Applications. Provides Floating-Point Arithmetic, String Support for Text Handling, Text Screen Manipulation, Interface to Other Programming Languages, & Shell to MS-DOS, & Definite Clause Grammar Support. Offers a Virtual Database That Supports Two Gigabytes of Memory & Both Hashed & B-Tree Indexing, a Fully Automated Development Environment (Including a Source Level Debugger), Support of All Microsoft Languages, Assembly Language, & Lattice C, & Speed of Execution Comparable to Compiled PROLOG Running on Mainframe & Specialized Hardware.
Arity Corp.

Arity/Prolog Interpreter. *Version:* 6.1. 1992. *Compatible Hardware:* IBM PC & compatibles, PC XT, PC AT. *Operating System(s) Required:* PC-DOS/MS-DOS, OS/2. *Memory Required:* 640k. *General Requirements:* Hard disk. *Items Included:* 1 manual.
disk $295.00.
Designed to Provide the Speed & Power Required for Developing Applications. Provides Floating-Point Arithmetic, String Support for Text Handling, Text Screen Manipulation, Interface to Other Programming Languages, & Shell to MS-DOS, & Definite Clause Grammar Support. Offers a Virtual Database That Supports Two Gigabytes of Memory, & Both Hashed & B-Tree Indexing, a Fully Automated Development Environment (Including a Source Level Debugger), Support for All Microsoft Languages, Assembly Language, & Lattice C, & Speed of Execution Comparable to Compiled PROLOG Running on Mainframes & Specialized Hardware. Includes All the Features of ARITY/PROLOG Without the Production Capability.
Arity Corp.

Arity/Prolog32 Compiler & Interpreter. Aug. 1992. *Customer Support:* Six months of technical support with purchase of Prolog32. $250 per year after.
OS/2 V2.0. IBM PC or compatible, PC XT, PC AT. $2450.00. *Addl. software required:* OS/2 V2.0. *Optimal configuration:* 650k hard drive running OS/2 V2.0.
Includes the Following Features & Enhancements over Arity/Prolog for the 16-Bit Environment: 32-Bit Internal Processing Removes the 64k Limit on Stacks. Code No Longer Needs to Be Broken into 64k Segments (Far Prolog Has Been Eliminated). Speed Increment of 2 to 5 Times Faster Implementation (Depending on the Sophistication of the Program) Than Arity/Prolog 16-Bit. Code Is No Longer Compiled Through the Database, Allowing Easier Recompilation for Third Party Development. Databases & Applications Are Now Independent, Therefore One Application Can Easily Access Information in a Database That Was Modified in Another Application. Code Is Upward Source Compatible with the 16-Bit Version of Arity/Prolog.
Arity Corp.

Arity SQL Development Package. *Version:* 1.61. 1992. *Compatible Hardware:* IBM PC & compatibles, PC XT, PC AT. *Operating System(s) Required:* PC-DOS/MS-DOS, OS/2. *Memory Required:* 640k. *General Requirements:* Hard disk & either Arity/Prolog Compiler or Arity/Prolog Interpreter. *Items Included:* 2 manuals.
disk $295.00.
Complete Implementation of the SQL (Structural Query Language) Database Lanaguage Which, When Used in Conjunction with ARITY/PROLOG, Helps User to Build Intelligent Database Applications.
Arity Corp.

Arity/Windows Toolkit. 1991. *Customer Support:* 1 year technical support $250.00.
MS-DOS. IBM PC or compatible, PC XT, PC AT (650k). disk $350.00. *Addl. software required:* Arity/Prolog Compiler & Interpreter, Microsoft SDK. *Optimal configuration:* IBM PC or compatible, 650k hard disk.
OS/2. IBM PC or compatible, PC XT, PC AT (650k). disk $350.00. *Addl. software required:* Arity/Prolog Compiler & Interpreter, Microsoft SDK. *Optimal configuration:* IBM PC or compatible, 650k hard disk.
Write Applications for Microsoft Windows Version 3.0, Taking Full Advantage of All of the Microsoft Windows Version 3.0 System Features. User Can Build Applications That Run in Either Protected Mode or 386 Enhanced Mode. Access Any of the Dynamically Linked Libraries Provided by Microsoft As Well As Other Vendors. Gives All of the Advantages of Programming in Prolog with the Benefits of Microsoft Windows Version 3.0. Full Integration Is Done Through the Embedded C Feature of Arity/Prolog. The Arity/Windows Toolkit Is a Set of Runtime Libraries That Provide Support for the Memory Management Function Calling Microsoft Windows Version 3.0. Works in Conjunction with the Arity/Prolog Compiler & Interpreter.
Arity Corp.

Arizona High Tech Directory, 1996: ACT for Windows Electronic Database Edition.
Version: 2.0. Sep. 1995. *Items Included:* Spiral bound printed copy of the Arizona High Tech Directory. *Customer Support:* 90 day unlimited warranty & support.
Windows 3.X. 386 or higher. disk $149.00 (ISBN 1-885797-09-5, Order no.: KE 004). *Addl. software required:* ACT 2.0 for Windows.
ACT for Windows Edition Is Available for Use with ACT for Windows in the Windows 3.X Environment. Up to 15 Key Individuals & Titles Are Placed in the ACT USER Fields.
Keiland Corp.

Arizona High Tech Directory, 1996: Electronic Database Edition. *Items Included:* Spiral bound printed copy of the Arizona High Tech Directory. *Customer Support:* 90 day unlimited warranty & support.
MS-DOS/PC-DOS & Windows 3.1. 80286 or higher (2Mb). disk $149.00 (Order no.: KE002). *Addl. software required:* dBASE, spreadsheet or word processor. *Optimal configuration:* 80286 or higher, 2Mb RAM, 20Mb HD.
Macintosh Systems 6 or 7. Macintosh (2Mb). 3.5" disk $149.00 (ISBN 1-885797-08-7, Order no.: KE003). *Addl. software required:* dBASE, spreadsheet, or word processor. *Optimal configuration:* Mac Plus or higher, 2Mb RAM, 20Mb HD.
Available in PC Compatible & Macintosh Formats Including: dBase, Spreadsheet, & ASCII Test. May Be Used Directly with Such Programs As Microsoft Word, Word Perfect, EXCEL, Lotus 1-2-3, & Numerous dBase Applications. Contains Basic Company Information, Names & Titles of Key Personnel. Also Categorized by Activities of Firm.
Keiland Corp.

Armageddon. *Customer Support:* 800-929-8117 (customer service).
MS-DOS. Apple II. disk $29.99 (ISBN 0-87007-060-6).
A Machine Language Arcade Game. Amass Enough Points in Air Battles & Dogfights to Move up to Increasingly More Complex Levels from World War I Planes to Space Fights. There are Seven Levels of Difficulty.
SourceView Software International.

Armor Premier Accounting Software. *Version:* 3.20. Oct. 1992. *Compatible Hardware:* Altos, AT&T, COMPAQ, Epson, IBM, Leading Edge, NEC, Radio Shack, Sun, Texas Instruments, Zenith. *Operating System(s) Required:* MS-DOS, Concurrent DOS, SCO Unix, SCO Xenix, Altos Unix, Altos Xenis, Sun System 3, Sparc. *Language(s):* C. *Memory Required:* 512k. *General Requirements:* Hard disk. *Customer Support:* $125.00/module for six months.
contact publisher for price.
Integrated Business & Accounting System of 18 Modules Offering Flexible Features for Better Management Control.
Armor Systems, Inc.

Around the World. *Version:* 2.0. (Dr. T's Sing-A-Long Ser.). Jan. 1994. *Customer Support:* Free, unlimited.
Windows 3.1 or higher. IBM 386 or higher (4Mb). disk $24.95 (ISBN 1-884899-25-0).
Dr. T's Music Software, Inc.

Arrhythmias: Case Studies in Management.
Edward P. Hoffer & G. Octo Barnett. Nov. 1985. *Compatible Hardware:* IBM PC/XT/AT/PS/2 or true compatible. *Operating System(s) Required:* MS-DOS 2.0 or higher. *Memory Required:* 128k.
IBM. disk $98.50 (ISBN 0-683-16805-3).
Assists in Making Diagnostic & Management Decisions in Order to Save the Simulated Patients As They Experience a Variety of Cardiac Arrhythmias.
Williams & Wilkins.

ARS-A Reporting System. *Compatible Hardware:* Motorola MC68000 based 16-bit microcomputers.
contact publisher for price.
The Computer Co.

Art & Science of Decision Making. *Compatible Hardware:* IBM PC & compatibles, PC XT. *Operating System(s) Required:* PC-DOS 2.0 or higher.
disk $95.00.
Introduction to the Basic Ideas of Quantitative Decision Making. General Decision Problem Is Formulated & Criteria for Decision Making Are Developed.
Softext Publishing Corp.

Art Companion, Vol. I. *Compatible Hardware:* Commodore Amiga.
3.5" disk $29.95.
200 Medium-Res IFF for Use in Desktop Publishing.
MicroSearch.

Art Companion, Vol. II, III, IV. *Compatible Hardware:* Commodore Amiga.
3.5" disk $29.95.
200 Hi-Res IFF Graphics per Package.
MicroSearch.

The Art Department. *Version:* 1.0.3. Jun. 1989.
Amiga DOS 1.3 or higher. Commodore Amiga - All models (3Mb). $90.00.
Entry Level Image Processing System Providing a Wide Range of Input Formats, Processing Tools & Rendering Methods. Perfect for the Casual User of Products Which Produce or Use Color Imagery.
Elastic Reality, Inc.

Art Department Professional. *Version:* 1.0.3.
Amiga DOS 1.3 or higher. Commodore Amiga - all models (3Mb). $240.00.
Professionally Oriented Image Processing System Offering Total Input, Processing & Output Flexibility with Full Programmability via ARexx. A Large Number of Image Formats Are Supported for Both Reading & Writing Including Many Non-Amiga Formats, Optional Modules Allow Control over Input & Output Devices Such As Scanners & Film Recorders.
Elastic Reality, Inc.

ART EPS: Borders 1. *Version:* 1. Jan. 1989. *Items Included:* Pictorial index. *Customer Support:* Phone support & warranty.
Macintosh (512k). 3.5" disk $49.95. *Addl. software required:* PostScript or compatible.
Collection of 17 PostScript Border Designs Created in Adobe Illustrator 88 That Produce High Resolution Printing on Laser Printers. Useful for Creating Advertisements, Newsletters, Card Designs, Letterheads for Desktop Publishing, Business, School or Personal Use. Star, Pinstripe, Geometric, Flourishes, Bullet & Diamond Included. Collection Contains Completely Assembled Borders. Border Sizes Can Be Stretched or Reduced to Specification in Page Layout Program.
Freemyers Design.

Art EPS: Cartoon Characters. Jan. 1990. *Items Included:* Pictorial index. *Customer Support:* Phone support, 90 day unlimited warranty.
Macintosh (1Mb), or IBM & compatibles. 3.5" disk $49.95. *Addl. software required:* Page layout or postscript compatible application.
A Variety of PostScript Format Cartoon Characters: Sports, Recreation, Business.
Freemyers Design.

Art EPS: Cartoon Critters. Jan. 1990. *Items Included:* Pictorial index. *Customer Support:* Phone Support, 90 days unlimited warranty.
Macintosh (1Mb), or IBM & compatibles. 3.5" disk $49.95. *Addl. software required:* Page Layout, PostScript compatible application.
Variety of PostScript Format Cartoon Critters. (Chipmunk, Beaver, Bull, Bird, Deer, Peacock, Crab, Donkey, Elephant, Giraffe, Bee, Bear, Lion, Mouse, Duck, Turtle, Penguin, Rabbit, Seal, Dog, Cat, Chicken, Turkey, Woodpecker, & Racoon).
Freemyers Design.

ART EPS: Designs 1. *Version:* 1. Jan. 1989. *Items Included:* Pictorial Index. *Customer Support:* Phone Support & warranty.
Macintosh (512k). disk $49.95. *Addl. software required:* Post Script or compatible.
A Collection of 44 PostScript Decorative & Geometric Designs Created in Adobe Illustrator 88 That Produce High Resolution Printing on Laser Printers. Useful for Enhancing Advertisements, Newsletters, Card Designs Page Background, Logos or Creating Border Designs. Works with Applications That Accept POSTSCRIPT Format Files.
Freemyers Design.

ART EPS: Designs 2. *Version:* 1. Jan. 1989. *Items Included:* Pictorial Index. *Customer Support:* Phone support & warranty.
Macintosh (512k). $49.95. *Addl. software required:* PostScript or compatible.
A Collection of 40 PostScript Decorative & Geometric Designs Created in Adobe Illustrator 88 That Produce High Resolution Printing on Laser Printers. Useful for Enhancing Advertisements, Newsletters, & More. Works with Applications That Accept POSTSCRIPT Format Files.
Freemyers Design.

ART EPS: Holiday (Christmas). *Version:* 1. Jan. 1989. *Items Included:* Pictorial Index. *Customer Support:* Phone support & warranty.
Macintosh (512k), or IBM & compatibles. $49.95. *Addl. software required:* PostScript or compatible.
An 800k Disk with a Collection of Christmas Subjects in Adobe Illustrator 88 That Produce High Resolution Printing on Laser Printers. The Designs are Useful for Creating Advertisements, Newsletters, or Card Designs, for Desktop Publishing, Business, School, or Personal Use. Graphics Included are Christmas Candle with Holly Leaf, Christmas Bell with Ribbon, Christmas Star, Santa & More. Size of Graphics Can Be Stretched or Reduced to Your Specifications in User's Page Layout Program. Available in PostScript Format.
Freemyers Design.

Art EPS: Industry 1. Jan. 1990. *Items Included:* Pictorial Index. *Customer Support:* Phone support, 90 days unlimited warranty.
Macintosh (1Mb). 3.5" disk $49.95. *Addl. software required:* Page layout, postscript compatible application.
Includes a Variety of Business, Industrial, & Construction Equipment Images.
Freemyers Design.

ART EPS: Patterns 1. *Version:* 1. Jan. 1989. *Items Included:* Pictorial Index. *Customer Support:* Phone support & warranty.
Macintosh (512k). $49.95. *Addl. software required:* Adobe Illustrator 88.
A Collection of PostScript Design Patterns to Be Used with Adobe Illustrator 88. Ready to Use with Pattern Fill Feature. Can Be Copied & Pasted into an Open Document & Be Used to Paint Paths & Fill Areas. Useful in Creating Textures in Drawings, Illustrations, & Graphic

TITLE INDEX

Designs or As Page Background Designs. All Designs Can Be Edited, Skewed, Rotated, & Scaled Using the Pattern Editing Feature in Adobe Illustrator 88. Patterns Included Are a Variety of Cross Hatch, Abstract, Geometric, & Decorative Designs.
Freemyers Design.

Art EPS: Restaurant & Foods. Jan. 1990. *Items Included:* Pictorial index. *Customer Support:* Phone support, 90 days unlimited warranty.
Macintosh (1Mb). 3.5" disk $49.95. *Addl. software required:* Page layout, postscript compatible application.
Collection of PostScript Clip Art of Restaurant & Food Subjects, Illustrations & Objects. (Hamburger, Bread, Glass, Beer Mug, Fish, Turkey, Waiter, Champaign Bottle, Glass, Cheese, Muffin, Coffee Cup, Mushroom, Lobster,) & More.
Freemyers Design.

ART EPS: Symbols 1. *Version:* 1. Jan. 1989. *Items Included:* Pictorial index. *Customer Support:* Phone support & warranty.
Macintosh (512k). 3.5" disk $49.95. *Addl. software required:* PostScript or compatible.
Collection Contains Symbols for Airport, Arrows, Baggage, Bar/Drink, Bicycle, Bus, Car, Computer (Mac), Dollar Sign, Female, Male, Fire Extinguisher, Handicap, Heart, Key, Light Bulb, Man, Woman, Mask (Theater, Happy & Sad), Music (Treble Clef), No Smoking, Smoking, Phone, Poison (Skull/Cross Bones), Attorney (Scale of Justice), Sleep/Rest, Stars, Sun/Sad, Sun/Happy, Taxi, Turkey & Trumpet. Symbols & Sizes Can Be Stretched or Reduced to Specification in Page Layout Program or Edited in Draw Program.
Freemyers Design.

ART EPS: Symbols 2. *Version:* 1. Jan. 1989. *Items Included:* Pictorial Index. *Customer Support:* Phone support & warranty.
Macintosh (512k). $49.95. *Addl. software required:* PostScript or compatible.
A Collection of 42 PostScript International Sign Symbol Designs Created in Adobe Illustrator 88 That Produce High Resolution Printing on Laser Printers. Useful for Desktop Publishing, Business, School, or Personal Use. Collection Includes Artist Brush, Baseball, Hand, Question Mark, Flower, Fire Extinguisher, & More. Symbols Can Be Stretched or Reduced in Page Layout Program or Edited in Draw Program that Accepts Encapsulated PostScript. Available in PostScript Format.
Freemyers Design.

Art EPS: Trees. Jan. 1990. *Items Included:* Pictorial index. *Customer Support:* Phone support, 90 days unlimited warranty.
Macintosh (1Mb). 3.5" disk $49.95. *Addl. software required:* Page layout, postscript compatible application.
Illustrated Hardwood & Evergreen Trees & Bushes.
Freemyers Design.

Art Gallery I & II. *Compatible Hardware:* IBM PC & compatibles. *General Requirements:* PrintMaster Plus program. *Items Included:* 1 users manual. *Customer Support:* 510-748-6938.
$39.95 ea.
Supplementary Files Which Provide Additional Graphics for PrintMaster PLUS.
Unison World.

The Art of Negotiating. *Version:* 2.1. Roy A. Nierenberg & Jonathan Llewellyn. 1988. *Compatible Hardware:* Hard disk or 2 disk drives. *Operating System(s) Required:* PC-DOS/MS-DOS 2.0 or higher. *Language(s):* Pascal. *Memory Required:* 256k. *Items Included:* Manual, Book "The Complete Negotiator". *Customer Support:* telephone hotline.
3.5" disk $97.50 (ISBN 0-928615-02-2, Order no.: 133).
Trains People to Negotiate Better As They Prepare for Their Own Negotiations. The Program Asks Questions & Makes Suggestions Which Stimulate the User's Awareness of Both Sides' Viewpoints. Helps the User Develop Useful Plans of Action, Including a Strategic Agenda.
Experience in Software, Inc.

The Art of Negotiating. *Version:* 1.1. *Compatible Hardware:* IBM PC & compatibles. *Operating System(s) Required:* PC-DOS/MS-DOS. *Memory Required:* 256k. *General Requirements:* Hard disk. *Items Included:* 32 pg. Thinking Software catalog.
5.25" or 3.5" disk $195.00.
Prepares Users to Negotiate a Deal or Agreement.
Thinking Software, Inc.

The Art of Negotiating 2. *Items Included:* Bound manual. *Customer Support:* Free hotline - no time limit; 30 day limited warranty; updates are $5/disk plus S&H.
MS-DOS. IBM & compatibles (256k). $179.95-$279.95.
System Is Based on the Highly Successful Methods of Gerard I. Nierenberg, Author of Fundamentals of Negotiating & Negotiation Manual, Both of Which Are Included with the Program. Also Included Are the Disks, a User's Guide, & a One-Hour Video Tape.
Dynacomp, Inc.

Art Parts, 2 vols. *Compatible Hardware:* Apple IIgs. *Operating System(s) Required:* ProDOS 16. *Memory Required:* 768k. *General Requirements:* DeluxePaint II (Electronic Arts).
3.5" disk $29.95, ea. vol.
Each Volume (Disk) Provides Clip-Art for DELUXEPAINT II.
Electronic Arts.

Art Studio. Mar. 1994. *Items Included:* Kids Club Magazine.
DOS 3.1 or higher. IBM 386 minimum & compatibles (4Mb). SRP $59.95 (ISBN 1-57187-000-8, Order no.: AS3L10ENG). *Nonstandard peripherals required:* VGA video. *Addl. software required:* Windows 3.1. *Optimal configuration:* 12Mb minimum disk requirement, 10Mb hard disk space, Windows 3.1, mouse or pointing device.
Creativity Program Designed by Kids for Kids Ages 6-12. The Program Is Loaded with 16 Different Games, Crafts & Creative Activities Designed to Provide Challenge & Fun. The Program Is Packed with Exciting Animations & Sounds Which Provide Endless Opportunity for Creative Exploration & Fun.
Micrografx, Inc.

Artagenix: Planes of Fame. *Compatible Hardware:* Apple Macintosh.
3.5" disk $39.50.
Clip Art Designed for User's Favorite Paint Program Modern American Military Aircraft.
Devonian International Software Co.

Artapart Collectors Edition. Apr. 1995. *Items Included:* Special bonus offer & chance to win free software. *Customer Support:* Phone 201-845-3357, Fax 201-845-4638, Compuserv 76605.1506, Genie C. Niehoff, American Online C. Niehoff, Internet 76605.1506 Compuserv.COM, Fido Netmail Andy Schmidt 1:2604/511.
Windows version 3.1 or higher. IBM PC or compatible (2Mb). disk $39.95 (ISBN 1-885936-04-4). *Optimal configuration:* IBM or compatible, 4Mb RAM, 386 or higher, VGA high resolution with 256 colors & sound card. *Networks supported:* Windows NT & Windows for WorkGroups.
Take Great Artwork & Create a Jigsaw Puzzle with Real Interlocking Pieces. You Decide on the Size & Number. Do You Feel Like Finishing a Quick One with 20 Pieces or Take the Challenge of 2000? Don't Worry If You Don't Finish It. You Can Always Save a Game & Come Back to It Later.
Argos Gameware.

ArtClips. *Version:* 2.0. *Items Included:* Disks, manual & addendums. *Customer Support:* Free unlimited phone technical support, FAX & modem service. America Online, CompuServe, Applelink.
Macintosh System 6.0.5 & higher. Mac Plus & higher (1Mb RAM). 3.5" disk $149.00. *Addl. software required:* EPS compatible S/W. Adobe 88 for editing image.
A Collection of EPS Clip Art & Symbols for Use with Desktop Publishing Applications. This Volume Contains: Graphics & Symbols, Olympic Symbols, Hand Tools, People, Cars, Boats, Business Images, Computers, Office Furniture, Maps, People, Office Equipment, Supplies, & More.
Olduvai Corp.

ArtDisk 7 "Christian Images". Dec. 1989. *Items Included:* Printed catalog of artwork on the disks. *Customer Support:* Unlimited customer support. All customers receive quarterly newsletter free.
Apple DOS 6.0 or higher. Macintosh Plus or higher (1Mb). 3.5" disk $79.00. *Addl. software required:* Page layout, Adobe Illustrator.
Contains over Fifty Images in the Christian Motif. All Drawings Are Saved As Encapsulated Postscript for the Macintosh.
D.V. Franks.

ArtDisks 1, 2, 3, & 4. *Compatible Hardware:* Apple Macintosh. *General Requirements:* MacPaint.
3.5" disk $39.95.
Clip Art.
D.V. Franks.

Artemis ProjectView. *Version:* 3.1. *Items Included:* 1 set of documentation, Runtime Version of SQLBASE & QUEST. *Customer Support:* 1 year free; 20% of purchase price thereafter includes toll free support. Training available for a fee.
MS-DOS 3.X, 8Mb RAM, MS-Windows 3.X. IBM & compatibles. disk $7795.00 S/U PC. *Addl. software required:* MS-Windows, SQLBASE (included). *Optimal configuration:* Client/Server - VAX or UNIX server with PC Windows as clients. *Networks supported:* Banyan Vines, Novell.
Formerly Artemis Prestige. Incorporates Planning; Activity, & Resource Scheduling; Progress Tracking; & Cost Management Across an Entire Orgnaization.
CSC; Artemis Products & Services.

Artemis Schedule Publisher. *Version:* 4.2. Advanced Management Solutions Inc. Aug. 1994. *Items Included:* 2 manuals. *Customer Support:* 90 day warranty; hotline; newsletter.
Windows 3.0 or higher. IBM or compatible with 386 or higher processor (1Mb); All UNIX using X-Windows. disk $1995.00. *Addl. software required:* Drawing Package recommended, not required; PC or MS-DOS 3.1 or higher; windows 3.0 or higher. *Optimal configuration:* IBM or compatible with 386 processor, hard disk with 1.5 Mb of disk space, color monitor with graphics card, mouse.
Macintosh System 6.0 or higher. Macintosh Plus, SE or Macintosh II. disk $2000.00. *Addl.*

software required: Drawing Package recommended, not required PC or MS-DOS 3.1 or higher. *Optimal configuration:* IBM or compatible with 386 processor, hard disk with 1.5 Mb of disk space, color monitor with graphics card, mouse.
Macintosh. Mac Plus, Mac SE, or Mac II (1Mb). 3.5" disk $1995.00. *Addl. software required:* System software 6.0 or higher (compatible with System 7.0). *Optimal configuration:* MAC II, hard disk with 1.5Mb of disk space, color monitor with graphics card.
A Unique Graphical Planning & Scheduling Tool Providing Advanced Project Management Functions Without Sacrificing Ease of Use or Performance. A Distinctive Feature of the System Is It's Real-Time Processing of Schedule, Cost, & Resource Information to Provide Instant Answers to Support Rapid Decisions.
CSC; Artemis Products & Services.

Artemis 7000. *Version:* 7.5. Jun. 1994. *Items Included:* 6 manuals, samples/tutorial database. *Customer Support:* Hot line, maintenance, new releases, 90 day warranty.
VMS, Unix, DOS, Vax. IBM 386 based PCs; Unix & Vax. disk $6000.00.
A 4GL Project Modeling System That Consists of a Powerful Relational Database, Flexible Report Writer with Full Graphics Capability & Menu & Command Driven Modes of Operation. Provides Total Information Management Through the Integration of Planning & Scheduling Functions with the Database, Graphics, & Report Writer Features.
CSC; Artemis Products & Services.

Arterial Blood Gases. Edward P. Hoffer & G. Octo Barnett. Oct. 1985. *Compatible Hardware:* Apple II with 2 disk drives; IBM PC, PCjr with 80 column display, PC XT, PC AT. *Operating System(s) Required:* MS-DOS 2.0 or higher. *Memory Required:* Apple 64k, IBM 128k.
Apple. disk $85.00 (ISBN 0-683-16806-1).
IBM. disk $85.00 (ISBN 0-683-16807-X).
Teaches a 4-Step Approach to Interpretation of ABG Data & Shows How to Calculate the Alveolar-Arterial Gradient. Students Face a Series of Realistic Patient Cases Where They Analyze Blood Gas Results.
Williams & Wilkins.

ArtFonts. *Version:* 2.1. *Items Included:* Disks, manual & addendums. *Customer Support:* Free unlimited phone technical support, FAX & modem service. America Online, CompuServe, Applelink.
Macintosh System 6.0.5 & higher. Mac Plus & higher (1Mb RAM). 3.5" disk $149.00.
Collection of 21 High Quality PostScript Typefaces. This Is a Four Disk Set Which Also Includes a TypeFace Use & Selection Guide As Well As a PictureKeys Font. Type 1 & TrueType Formats Are Included.
Olduvai Corp.

Arthur's Birthday. (Living Book Ser.). Marc Brown.
MS-DOS 5.0 or higher, Windows 3.1 or higher. 386 processor or higher (4Mb). CD-ROM disk $49.95 (Order no.: R1187). *Nonstandard peripherals required:* CD-ROM drive. *Optimal configuration:* 386 processor operating at 16MHz or higher, MS-DOS 5.0 or higher, Windows 3.1 or higher, 30Mb hard drive, mouse, VGA graphic adapter & VGA color monitor (SVGA recommended), 4Mb RAM, external speakers or headphones (with sound card) that are Sound Blaster compatible.
Macintosh (4Mb). (Order no.: R1187).
Nonstandard peripherals required: 14" color monitor or larger, CD-ROM drive.
Highly Interactive Animated Stories for Children That Have Hundreds of Beautiful Animations & Have Received Countless Awards. In English & Spanish.
Library Video Co.

Arthur's Teacher Trouble. (Living Book Ser.). Marc Brown.
MS-DOS 5.0 or higher, Windows 3.1 or higher. 386 processor or higher (4Mb). CD-ROM disk $49.95 (Order no.: R1043). *Nonstandard peripherals required:* CD-ROM drive. *Optimal configuration:* 386 processor operating at 16MHz or higher, MS-DOS 5.0 or higher, Windows 3.1 or higher, 30Mb hard drive, mouse, VGA graphic adapter & VGA color monitor (SVGA recommended), 4Mb RAM, external speakers or headphones (with sound card) that are Sound Blaster compatible.
Macintosh (4Mb). (Order no.: R1043).
Nonstandard peripherals required: 14" color monitor or larger, CD-ROM drive.
$35.00 Jewel case only (Order no.: R1043J).
Highly Interactive Animated Stories for Children That Have Hundreds of Beautiful Animations & Have Received Countless Awards. In English & Spanish (Ages 6-10).
Library Video Co.

Artic Business Vision: Interactive Screen/ Keyboard Processor. *Version:* 3.1. 1992. *Compatible Hardware:* IBM PC & compatibles, PC XT, PC AT, PS/2; other 80286 or 80386-based micros, NEC Multispeed & Toshiba laptops. *Operating System(s) Required:* PC-DOS, MS-DOS. *Memory Required:* 100k. *General Requirements:* 2 disk drives, 215, 225, 245, 315, Crystal or Artic TransPort, speech synthesizer. *Customer Support:* Phone.
$895.00-$1295.00 bundle with synthesizer. upgrade from ARTIC VISION $100.00.
Contains All the Functions of ARTIC VISION Plus Some New Modes to Tracking Reverse Video Cells Used by Spreadsheet Programs. Also Included Is a 10 Memory Talking Calculator. Will Work with LOTUS 1-2-3 & VP-PLANNER.
Artic Technologies.

Artist Designer II. *Compatible Hardware:* Apple II+, IIe with game paddles. *Memory Required:* 64k.
contact publisher for price.
Drawing System Designed for Artists Which Allows the User to Produce Irregular Shapes, Curves, & Shading with Random Dots & Textures. Includes 6 Colors & Mixtures by Alternating the Basic Colors in Stripes, Zigzags, or Dots. Can Re-Perform Stored Designs by Redrawing Them Step-by-Step. Students, Artists, & Teachers Have the Opportunity to Observe the Drawing Process. Allows the User to Save Screens to Preserve Particular Images. Can Do a Story Board of a Performance, & Step Through the Scenes Like a Series of Slides. A Series of Drawing Procedures, Storage & Retrieval Procedures, & Interactive & Editing Procedures Are the Main Components of the System.
CAPS Software.

Artistry & Borders. (Studio Ser.). *Items Included:* Visual index, user's guide. *Customer Support:* Free & unlimited technical support to registered users; 60 day money-back guarantee.
Macintosh. Macintosh (Minimum required for program with which you want to use ClickArt). 3.5" disk $99.95. *Nonstandard peripherals required:* PostScript compatible printer. *Addl. software required:* Any desktop publishing, word processing or works application that accepts EPS files.
Windows V.3.0 or higher. IBM PC & compatibles (Minimum needed for application with which you will use ClickArt). 3.5" disk $99.95. *Addl. software required:* Any desktop publishing, word processing or works program that accepts CGM or WMF files.
MS-DOS V.3.3 or higher. IBM PC & compatibles (Minimum needed for application with which you will use ClickArt). 3.5" disk $99.95. *Addl.*

software required: Any desktop publishing, word processing or works program that accepts WMF or CGM files.
Over 375 Images! Highest-Quality Full-Color Images Available; Ready-to-Use, or Changed in Appropriate Drawing Program; Designed in Full-Color (CMYK); Ready for Color Separations & Commercial Printing; Produced to Print in Detailed Greyscale on Black & White Printers.
T/Maker Co., Inc.

The Artistry of Henry James. *Version:* 1.5. Feb. 1995. *Items Included:* BookWorm Student Reader (diskette). *Customer Support:* 30 day MBG. Technical support (toll call) - no charge.
System 7.0 or higher. Macintosh (5Mb). CD-ROM disk $29.95 (ISBN 1-57316-027-X, Order no.: 16162). *Nonstandard peripherals required:* CD-ROM drive, 12" color monitor. *Optimal configuration:* 13" color monitor recommended.
Windows 3.1 or higher. IBM compatible (MPC) 386 DX (4Mb). CD-ROM disk $29.95. *Nonstandard peripherals required:* Standard multimedia compatible CD-ROM. *Optimal configuration:* 8Mb RAM recommended, 256 color monitor recommended.
Henry James Was One of America's Greatest Literary Masters. This Collection Shows Him at His Best, in Fiction & Criticism, Probing Deep into the Human Condition, Exploring Themes of Perception, the Supernatural, & the Problems of the Creative Personality.
Communication & Information Technologies, Inc. (CIT).

ArtPack. Jul. 1988. *Compatible Hardware:* IBM PC & compatibles. *Operating System(s) Required:* PC-DOS/MS-DOS. *Memory Required:* 256k. *General Requirements:* CGA, EGA or VGA card.
disk $29.95.
Generates 10 Types of Computer Art, Including Fractals, Moirre Patterns, Roses from Polar Equations, Serendipitous Circles, Spirographs, One & Two Dimensional "Life" Patterns, Wallpaper Art, Sierpinski Curves & Picture Generation from Names or Text.
Zephyr Services.

Arts & Letters Apprentice. *Version:* 1.2. Feb. 1993. *Items Included:* Users guide & clipart book. *Customer Support:* Free telephone support for all registered users.
IBM 286, 386, 486/compatibles with DOS 5.0 or higher, Windows 3.0 or 3.1 & a pointing device (4Mb). disk $169.00 (Order no.: 44065). *Optimal configuration:* 386 w/at least 30Mb, Win 3.1, mouse. *Networks supported:* Novell, etc. any windows supported network.
Graphics, Drawing & DTP Program for Homes or Small Businesses. Apprentice Comes with 4,000 Art Forms & Clip-Art Symbols, & 90 Scalable, Editable Typefaces. Includes Data-Driven Charting, Predefined Colors, Lines, & Fill Styles, Automatic Kerning, Typeface Preview, Vector, Raster & Gradient Fills. Also Included Are Easy-to-Use Special Effects Such As Warp/Perspective, Text along a Path & Interactive Size/Slant/Rotate Features. Compatible with Many Desktop Publishing & Word Processing Programs. Runs under Windows V 3.0 or 3.1.
Computer Support Corp.

Arts & Letters Editor. *Version:* 3.12. Jun. 1992. *Compatible Hardware:* IBM PC AT, PS/2 & compatibles. *General Requirements:* Microsoft Windows 3.1; Windows-supported drawing device. *Items Included:* User's guide, tutorials, clip art handbook. *Customer Support:* Free telephone support for all registered users.
$695.00.
Optional libraries. $99.00 to $129.00.

TITLE INDEX

Lets User Create Professional-Quality Graphics in Minutes. More Than 8,000 Clip-Art Images, 90 Versatile Typefaces, Data-Driven Charting & an Activity Manager. Offers Such Highly Advanced Features As Warp/Perspective, Hole Cutting, Shape & Color Interpolation, Bezier Curve Drawing/Editing, & Automatic 4-Color Separation.
Computer Support Corp.

Arts & Letters Jurassic ART. Apr. 1993. *Items Included:* Scenerio users guide, Jurassic ART users guide, & Age of Dinosaurs book. *Customer Support:* Free telephone support for all registered users.
MS-DOS 5.0 or higher, Windows 3.0 or 3.1. 286/386/486 & compatibles (4Mb). disk $59.95 (Order no.: 59269). *Networks supported:* Novell & any other Windows supported network.
Consists of Arts & Letters Scenerio Bundled with The Age of Dinosaurs. The Age of Dinosaurs Can Be Installed for Use with Any Arts & Letters Product. The Collection Contains Dozens of Dinosaurs, Including the Greatest Carnivore of All Time - Tyrannosaurus Rex. A Special Typeface, Dinosauria, Was Created Just for This Collection. Prehistoric Plants & Trees Add Authenticity to the Sample Compositions. A Handy Reference Guide Contains a General Discussion of the Life & Times of Dinosaurs, Interesting Facts about Dinosaurs, a List of Museums That Display Dinosaur Artifacts & a Bibliography for Further Reading.
Computer Support Corp.

Arts & Letters Picture Wizard. *Version:* 1.1. Feb. 1993. *Items Included:* Users guide. *Customer Support:* Free telephone support for all registered users.
MS-DOS 5.0 or higher, Windows 3.0 or 3.1. 286/386/486 & compatibles (4Mb). disk $89.95 (Order no.: 44165). *Networks supported:* Novell & any other Windows supported network.
Drawing & Graphics Program for All Newcomers to Computer Graphics. Features Concise & Easy-to-Understand Instructions & Comes with 1,500 Clip Art Images & 15 Scalable Typefaces. Comes Complete with Line & Curve Drawing Tools, Automatic Charting, Vector & Raster Fills, & an Activity Manager. A Clip Art Manager Catalogs Images in a Variety of Subjects Including Airplanes, Animals, Sports, World Maps, & More.
Computer Support Corp.

Arts & Letters Scenerio. Jan. 1993. *Items Included:* Users guide. *Customer Support:* Free telephone support for all registered users.
MS-DOS 5.0 or higher, Windows 3.0 or 3.1. 286/386/486 & compatibles (4Mb). disk $39.95 (Order no.: 59266). *Networks supported:* Novell & any other Windows supported network.
Perfect Gift for Friends & Family Who Are Just Getting Started with Computer Graphics. Fully-Functional Drawing Program That Features Many of the Capabilities of Other Arts & Letters Products, Scenerio Includes over 300 Award-Winning Clip-Art Images, 8 Outline Typefaces, Vector & Raster Fills, Support for ATM & Adobe Typefaces, & Instant Art. Instant Art Is a Composition System Using Modular Art Backgrounds That Can Be Broken Apart & Used in Combination with Other Scenery & Props to Create Finished Artwork in Minutes.
Computer Support Corp.

Arts Info 1.0. *Version:* 1.0. Peter Duran. Aug. 1991. *Items Included:* 1 spiral bound manual. *Customer Support:* Toll free number 800-343-0095.
DOS 3.2 or higher. 286-386 (512k). disk $395.00.
This Database Application Is Designed to Meet Specific Needs of Low Vision & Blind Entrepreneurs, Administrators, & Teachers. It, in Particular, Permits Information to Be Displayed in Two Ways: in a Form Most Convenient for Voice & Large Print Access & in a Manner Best Suited for Standard Visual Presentation.
Arts Computer Products, Inc.

Artwork. *Version:* 2.56. Bill Ferster & Oov Jacobson. 1981. *Compatible Hardware:* IBM PC, PC XT, PC AT & compatibles. *Operating System(s) Required:* PC-DOS/MS-DOS. *Language(s):* C. *Memory Required:* 512k. *General Requirements:* Graphics card.
Targa 16. included in StudioWorks System.
VISTA. included in StudioWorks VISTA System.
ACL (Artwork Control Language). included in StudioWorks System.
SHOOT (Matrix 4000 Line QCR/PCR Driver). included in StudioWorks System.
A2PLP (NAPLPS Driver). included in StudioWorks System.
Fonts. $300.00 ea.
29 Fonts Pak $3900.00.
Interactive Graphics-Design Program. Using an Input Tablet, the Designer Can Draw, Modify, Edit & Store 20-30 Graphic Elements. Gives the Designer the Power & Flexibility of a Mainframe System. Used in Conjunction with Other StudioWorks Modules.
West End Film, Inc.

As Times Go: Concise Encyclopedia, Our Century in Depth (Sci-Tech). Software Toolworks Staff. Sep. 1995. *Items Included:* Set up instruction sheet, registration card. *Customer Support:* Customer support helpline 503 639-6863.
DOS. IBM PC (1Mb). CD-ROM disk $34.95 Our Century in Depth (ISBN 1-887783-09-1, Order no.: 5400-8002). *Optimal configuration:* IBM PC 486, DOS 5.0, IBM RAM w/580k free memory, Vera VBE 1.2, Super VGA graphics card & color monitor, Sound Blaster or Pro Audio Spect. or 100% sound card, HD w/2Mb avail., CD-ROM, CD-ROM extension, mouse.
Win 3.1. IBM PC 386 or higher (8Mb). CD-ROM disk $34.95 Concise Encyclopedia (Order no.: 5400-8002). *Optimal configuration:* IBM PC 386 or higher, Win 3.1, 8Mb RAM, VGA or SVGA, double speed CD-ROM, mouse, soundcard.
Great Reference Source of World Events, (Biblical, Sports, Science, Technology, Etc).
Entertainment Technology.

ASCII Express: Mouse Talk. *Version:* 1.5. Mark Robbins & Bill Blue. Nov. 1986. *Compatible Hardware:* Apple IIe, IIc, IIgs. *Operating System(s) Required:* Apple DOS, ProDOS. *Language(s):* Assembly. *Memory Required:* 128k. *General Requirements:* Printer, modem, color monitor.
contact publisher for price.
Communications Program for Electronic Mail, File Transfer & Terminal Emulators.
United Software Industries.

ASCII Printer Sharing Switches. *Compatible Hardware:* Apple II+, IIe, III, Lisa, Macintosh; IBM PC, PC XT, PCjr. *Operating System(s) Required:* CP/M-80, CP/M-86, CP/M-68000, MP/M-80, MP/M-86, MP/M-68000, UNIX, XENIX, UCSD p-System. *Language(s):* ASCII (source code included). *Memory Required:* 1k.
contact publisher for price.
Communications Program. Handles Electronic Mail & Terminal Emulators.
Advanced Systems Concepts, Inc.

ASCII PRO. *Version:* 4.24. Nov. 1984. *Compatible Hardware:* IBM PC, PCjr, PC XT, PC AT. *Operating System(s) Required:* MS-DOS. *Language(s):* Assembly. *Memory Required:* 128k. *General Requirements:* Modem, color monitor.
contact publisher for price.
Communication Program for Electronic Mail, File Transfer & Terminal Emulators.
United Software Industries.

ASCOM 86. Lifeboat Associates. *Compatible Hardware:* TI Professional with asynchronous communications board. *Operating System(s) Required:* MS-DOS, CP/M-86, Concurrent CP/M-86. *Memory Required:* 64k.
$175.00.
Asynchronous Communication Facility to Interact with Remote Time-Sharing Services or Local Computers to Transfer Data Files & Programs.
Texas Instruments, Personal Productivit.

ASCOM IV. *Version:* 1.42. *Operating System(s) Required:* MS-DOS, PC-DOS. *Language(s):* Assembly. *Memory Required:* 64k. *Customer Support:* (516) 462-6961.
disk $195.00, incl documentation.
documentation $45.00.
Asynchronous Communication Package Features Interactive & Menu-Driven Batch Operations. Batch Command Facilities May Be Used to Simulate a Network Environment.
DMA, Inc.

ASET: Advanced Staff Evaluation Techniques. *Compatible Hardware:* IBM PC. *Operating System(s) Required:* DOS. *Language(s):* COBOL. *Memory Required:* 512k. *Items Included:* One year maintenance, site license. *Customer Support:* Telephone support.
$18,000.00.
Used to Report the Progress of a Work Measurement Program & to Plan Future Work Distributions at a Unit Level.
Robert E. Nolan Co., Inc.

ASH PLUS Automated Social History. Joseph Waldron. 1990. *Items Included:* Ring-binder manual. *Customer Support:* Toll-free phone support available.
MS-DOS 3.1 or higher. IBM PC, XT, AT, PS/2 (640k). disk $345.00.
Produces Narrative Social History Report Covering Most Important Areas of Subject's Social & Personal Functioning. Covers 13 Areas: Religion, Family, Education, Sex, Military, Employment, Crime, Alcohol/Drug Abuse, Marriage, Parents, Personality Traits, Items, Risk Analysis & Summary.
Anderson Publishing Co.

askSam. *Version:* 5.1. Mar. 1992. *Compatible Hardware:* IBM PC, PC XT, PC AT & compatibles. *Operating System(s) Required:* PC-DOS 2.0 or higher. *Language(s):* C. *Memory Required:* 384k. *Customer Support:* unlimited free support.
disk $395.00.
Free Form, Text-Oriented DBMS That Allows Storage & Access to Data Without Knowing in Advance How It Will Be Used. Data Can Be Stored in Fields or Free-Form Style, Can Handle 1600 Characters per Field, Unlimited Characters per Record, Unlimited Fields per Record, & Unlimited Records per File. Supports Boolean Searches. Route Output to Screen, Printer, or Disk; & Update Records with a Full Screen Text Editor. Update Records with Batch Operations, Design Templates, Exchange ASCII Files with Other Systems. Perform Math Operations, & Use Word Processing Features. Retrieve on Any Combination of Anything Found in the Records - Even a Single Character. Developer's & Newtork Versions Available.
askSam Systems.

ASKSAM for Windows. Version: V.1.0. May 1993. Items Included: Reference guide & tutorial. Customer Support: Unlimited free support (phone 904-584-6590).
Windows V.3.1 & DOS 3.1. IBM or 100% compatibles with min. 386 processor (4Mb). disk $395.00. Optimal configuration: 4Mb RAM, 2Mb disk space.
Freeform Database. Structured Data, Straight Text or a Combination of the Two May Be Quickly Stored, Searched, Organized, Reported on & Updated. Include Images, Sounds, Video & Other Graphical Information in Documents via OLE Links.
AskSam Systems.

AskSam Network Version. Version: 5.1. Mar. 1992. Items Included: Reference manual, user manual, getting started manual, index manual. Customer Support: Free telephone technical support. Training available in our office or on site. We offer application development in house or on site.
PC-DOS/MS-DOS. IBM PC & compatibles (384k). $1095.00 5 users; $1995.00 10 users; $2800.00 15 users. Optimal configuration: 640k RAM, hard disk. Networks supported: All NetBIOS compatible, Novell.
An Information Manager Combining Database, Word Processing, & Text Retrieval Functions. This Combination of Functions Make AskSam Unique. Requires No Structure. User Can Search Thru Entire Information for a Word or Phrase, Like a Text Retrieval Package. If the Data Has Some Structure, AskSam Is Like a Database Program & Can Output Fields, Sort Data, Perform Arithmetic & Create Reports. Can Help User Manage Nearly Any Type of Information, Including Names & Addresses, E-Mail, Research, Legal Texts, Notes, Letters & Regular Structured Information.
askSam Systems.

ASM Utility. Compatible Hardware: IBM PC & compatibles; Tandy 2000; Kaypro II, 4; Apple II (Z80), Osborne, Morrow, other CP/M based systems. Operating System(s) Required: PC-DOS/MS-DOS 2.0 or higher, CP/M-80 2.2 or higher.
disk $10.00.
Allows Users to Link Object Files Created by Microsoft's MASM or M80 Assemblers. Numerous Assembly Language Functions Are Included As Examples.
MIX Software.

ASM-68000. Compatible Hardware: DEC PDP-11, VAX.
contact publisher for price.
Permits Assembly Language Programming on the MK-68000 Microprocessor.
Thomson Semi Conductors-Mostek Corp.

ASP. Version: 1.2. Compatible Hardware: Apple Macintosh Plus. Memory Required: 2000k. General Requirements: ParcPlace Systems Smalltalk-80.
3.5" disk $495.00.
Analytic Spreadsheet Package for Engineers.
Xerox Corp.

ASP: The Integrity Shell. Version: 3.1. Jun. 1990. Items Included: Tech support manual. Customer Support: Free 30 day warranty & customer support; 1 year maintenance & upgrades & customer support, $250.
PC-DOS 2.1 or higher. IBM PC & compatibles; PS/2 (256K). disk $250.00. Optimal configuration: Hard disk.
UNIX. AT&T 3B2. contact publisher for price.
Integrity Package & Computer Virus Defense. Includes Completely Automatic Detection & Eradication & Many Other Features.
ASP.

Assem-Zsim. Compatible Hardware: TRS-80.
contact publisher for price.
Instant Software, Inc.

Assemble to Order: Through Sales Order Entry. 1996. Customer Support: Free telephone & BBS technical support.
MS/PC DOS; Concurrent DOS, Xenix, Unix. IBM PC/XT/AT & compatibles; IBM PS/2 (512k). disk $495.00. Networks supported: Novell, Lantastic, Banyan VINES; all NETBIOS compatible.
The assemble to Order module impacts users of INMASS/MRP's Ball of Materials & Inventory Control. Assemble to Order (ATO) allows the user to issue a single level Work Order for an Assembly or Finished good with a Bill of Material. ATO provides more information to the order processors. This information appears in various windows on the Order Entry screen.
INMASS/MRP.

Assembler. Greg Susong. Oct. 1984. Compatible Hardware: Radio Shack Model 100, NEC PC-8201A, Tandy 200. Memory Required: 3k.
Radio Shack. cassette $32.95 (ISBN 0-932095-00-3).
NEC PC. cassette $32.95 (ISBN 0-932095-01-1).
Custom Software Engineering, Inc.

Assembler Editor. Compatible Hardware: Atari XL/XE. Operating System(s) Required: AOS.
ROM cartridge $24.95 (Order no.: CXL4003).
Has Both Editor & Assembler in Memory at the Same Time. All Lines Are Assigned a Line Number. A Full Screen Editing Feature Allows for Editing Individual Lines. Capable of Saving Object Code to Disk, Tape, or Memory. Also Contains a Debugger.
Atari Corp.

Assembler Plus Tools. Compatible Hardware: IBM PC, Apple. Operating System(s) Required: CP/M, CP/M-86, UCSD p-System.
disk $200.00.
Consists of Assemblers & a Set of Software Development Tools Designed for Professional Programmers. Tools Consist of Linkers, Librarians, Cross-Reference Utilities, & Symbolic Instruction Debuggers.
Digital Research, Inc.

Assembler ROM. Compatible Hardware: HP 85, 86/87. General Requirements: HP 82928A, 82929A.
HP 85. ROM cartridge $295.00 (Order no.: 00085-15007).
HP 86/87. (Order no.: 00087-15007).
Allows User to Write Customized Assembly Language Programs That Can Be Executed from Series 80 User Memory to Be Burned into EPROM's.
Hewlett-Packard Co.

Assembly Lines, Vol. I. Compatible Hardware: Apple II series, IIgs. Language(s): Assembly (source code included).
disk $15.95 (ISBN 0-927796-24-4).
bk. $19.95 (ISBN 0-927796-99-6).
Provides 50 Source Listings & Assembled Object Files from "Assembly Lines: The Book".
Roger Wagner Publishing, Inc.

Assembly Lines, Vol. II. Compatible Hardware: Apple II series. Operating System(s) Required: ProDOS 8. Memory Required: 64k.
book $19.95 (ISBN 0-927796-34-1, Order no.: 920).
disk $15.95 (ISBN 0-927796-35-X, Order no.: 920D).
Book Leaves off & Details Calling Machine Language Routines from Applesoft Programs, Passing Variables Between Applesoft & Machine Language, Coverage of HI-Resolution Graphic Routines. Also Includes New Material on Double Hi-Res Graphics & 80-Column Screen Access Routines. Appendices Include a Listing of Useful Internal Entry Points in the Applesoft ROMs.
Roger Wagner Publishing, Inc.

Asset, 4 modules. Software Products International. Compatible Hardware: IBM PC; Sage II, IV.
Set. $1290.00.
manual $100.00.
disk $390.00 ea.
Integrated Accounting Package Available As Individual Program or As a Package. Includes Accounts Payable, Accounts Receivable, General Ledger, Inventory Control.
Datamed Research, Inc.

Asset Allocation Tools, 3 disks. William Sharpe. Compatible Hardware: IBM PC, PC XT, PC AT. Memory Required: 640k. General Requirements: Hard disk, Lotus 1-2-3.
$2500.00 (ISBN 0-89426-957-7).
Lotus 1-2-3 Based System That Uses a Set of Programs, Over 150 Proxy Data Bases, & Lotus 1-2-3 Templates to Optimize Returns on Asset Portfolios.
Boyd & Fraser Publishing Co.

Asset Depreciation. Version: 5.1.1. Oct. 1991. Compatible Hardware: IBM PC & compatibles. Operating System(s) Required: MS-DOS, PC-DOS. Language(s): Compiled BASIC. Memory Required: 640k. General Requirements: hard disk. Customer Support: 3 different technical support plans available.
disk $495.00.
Accommodates All Current Depreciation Methods Including New ACRS (the 1986 Tax Reform Act), Straight Line, Sum of the Year's Digits, 150%, 200% Declining Balance, ACRS/Alternate ACRS & MACRS. Prints Tax Information to Help Complete Form 4562 (Depreciation Ledger). Integrates with Red Wing General Ledger. Posts Asset Activity As It Occurs, & Posts Depreciation Expense At Month End or Year End. Produces Complete Asset Listing by Group or profit center, 5 Year Depreciation Spread, & Gains/Losses from Sale of Assets. Maintains Both Book & Market Value Assets.
Red Wing Business Systems, Inc.

ASSET/PACK: Fixed Asset Manager. Version: 95.1. Jesse Tarshis. Jun. 1986. Compatible Hardware: IBM PC, PC XT, PC AT, & compatibles. Operating System(s) Required: PC-DOS/MS-DOS, Novell. Language(s): Compiled Microsoft Professional BASIC. Memory Required: 512k. General Requirements: Hard disk. Items Included: Software, documentation. Customer Support: Toll free technical support, updates via modem & disks.
IBM. disk $395.00 (Order no.: ASSET-MSDOS).
demo disk $25.00.
Records, Tracks & Depreciates Assets for Book, Federal, State & AMT. All Depreciation Methods & Conventions. Full Screen Editor. Multiple Divisions, Locations or Departments Within a Company. Depreciate by Month. Automatic Depreciation User's Choice of Method & Life. Calculates Recapture.
Alpine Data, Inc.

ASSIA Plus: Applied Social Science Abstracts. Items Included: Quarterly Updated.
MS-DOS. IBM or compatibles. disk $1895.00 1 year (Order no.: DAS110).
Explore practical & theoretical issues with all the social sciences - from the nursing health sciences to the fields of economics, communications, social studies, & more.
Bowker-Saur.

Assistant Coach: Basketball. *Items Included:* Manual.
Apple II (48k). $39.95, Lab pack/5 $99.00 (ISBN 0-939153-37-8). *Optimal configuration:* Apple II, 48k, 1 drive.
Basketball Statistics Scoring Program That Calculates Complete Statistics for Any Coach - Jr. High Through NBA. Calculates Summaries of Games & Performances by Individual Players & by Teams, by Game & by Season. Each Individual Is Given a Computer-Rating by Game & Season. Even Sorts by Computer Ratings, Points or Nine Other Selected Criteria. So Easy-to-Use That Students Can Operate Without the Coach's Assistance.
Word Assocs., Inc.

The Assistant Controller: Order Entry/Invoicing. *Version:* 7.2. 1985. *Compatible Hardware:* IBM PC & compatibles, Apple Macintosh, Unix. *Language(s):* DBASE III Plus, dBASE IV. *Memory Required:* 512k. *General Requirements:* Hard disk. *Items Included:* 3-ring binder with 5.25" or 3.5" program disks. *Customer Support:* Phone support available at $75/hour.
disk $195.00 Single user; $395.00 Multi user. Source code (free to dealer). per module $200.00.
Monitors Sales Information & Generates Invoices. Can be Interfaced to the Accounts Receivable & Inventory Systems.
Lake Avenue Software.

The Assistant Controller Series. *Version:* 7.2. 1982. *Compatible Hardware:* Apple Macintosh, IBM PC, UNIX. *Operating System(s) Required:* PC-DOS, MS-DOS, UNIX. *Language(s):* DBASE III PLUS, dBASE IV. *Memory Required:* 384k. *General Requirements:* Hard disk. *Items Included:* 3-ring binder with 5.25" or 3.5" program disks. *Customer Support:* Telephone support & on-site training available at $75/hour.
disk $195.00 ea. single user.
$395.00 ea. Multi-user Enhanced version.
source code per Module (Free to dealer) $200.00 ea.
source code avail.
dBASE III/IV Compatible Accounting System Consisting of Separate Modules That Can Be Used Alone or Integrated to Form a Larger System. Key Features in All Systems Include: Password Protection, Complete Audit Trail, Accrual & Cash Basis Accounting, up to 1,000 Departments/Cost Centers & Amounts up to $99,999,999.00, DATA DOCTOR, a Program to Reconstruct Damaged Files, & Automatic Back-Up of Data Files.
Lake Avenue Software.
Accounts Payable.
Enables User to Keep Track of Cash Disbursements & to Project Cash Requirements. Reports Include: Review of Individual General Ledger Account Activity, Distribution, Payee, Check Register, Cash Requirements, Aged Payables, & Vendor Analysis. Prints Checks or Allows for Manual Check Input.
Accounts Receivable.
Provides Up-to-the-Minute Reports on Accounts Receivable Balances. These Include: Accounts Receivable Aging, Cash Receipts Register, Distribution/Sales, Review of Individual General Ledger Account Activity, Customer Statements & Invoicing Capability.
Financial Reporting.
Offers Certain Enhanced Features Not Provided in the GENERAL LEDGER System. Balance Sheet & Income Statement Can Be Saved in a "Text File" That a Word Processor Can Access. Allows for Spreadsheet Journal Entries for Financial Statement Presentation. Non-Consecutive Departments Can Be Consolidated; Budgets; Comparative Analysis of Current & Prior Months & Year to Date, Provides for "Both" Cash & Accrual Financial Statements.
General Ledger.
Offers Double-Entry Bookkeeping, Complete Audit Trail. Error-Checking; Reports Include: Distribution, Trial Balance/Chart of Accounts Listing, Payee Register, Check Distribution, Check Register, Cash Receipts Register, 1099 Recipient, Review of Individual Account Groups, Balance Sheet/Income Statement, Working Trial Balance Spreadsheet. Interfaces with Computax, Time Slips, LACERT & Others.
Inventory.
Raw Materials & Finished Goods Inventory Levels Are Monitored Using LIFO, FIFO or Moving (Weighted) Average Costing Methods, EOQ Calculation, Cross Reference Vendor & User Numbers, Consignment Inventory Control, Tracking by Warehouse, Lot/Bin & Project Number & Purchase Order Tracking. Unlimited Bill of Materials Levels.
Job Costing.
Monitors Labor, Material & Sub-Contractor Costs Against Budget by Project/Job Number. Allocation of Overhead from General Ledger. Accrual or Cash Basis Reports.
Payroll.
Handles Payroll Calculations, Prints Payroll Checks and/or Stubs & Generates Information Necessary for Federal & State Payroll Tax Reporting. Prints 941 Federal Quarterly's & Some State Forms. Summarizes Time Charges for JOB COSTING or PROFESSIONAL TIME & INVOICING. Reports Include: Employee Status File; Employee History; Payroll by Pay Period; Monthly, Quarterly & Annual Payroll; Summary for Preparation of State Forms & Federal 940 & 941; Time Charge Summary; Union Report; Certified Payroll; Multi-State & Multi-Company Capability; Works with Electronic Time Keeping Systems; Multi-Level Bill-of-Materials Feature. Works with Magnetic Media Reporting Programs for Filing with Federal & State.
Professional Time & Invoicing.
Captures Time & Expense Charges to Create a Letter-Quality Invoice. Reports Include: Staff Utilization, Quick Review, Time & Expense Charges, Client Activity, Staff History.

The Assistant: Integrated Library Automation Software. *Version:* 4.0. Apr. 1989. *Items Included:* Software & documentation. *Customer Support:* $380.00 - $440.00 per module, unlimited telephone support & software upgrades.
DOS 3.1 or higher (640k). IBM PC/AT, PS/2 & compatibles. single-user per module $2300.00, multi-user per module $2800.00. *Nonstandard peripherals required:* 10Mb Hard Disk.
Networks supported: Novell, 3COM, Banyon, AT&T Starlan, Lantastic.
Designed for Libraries Seeking Software That Will Run on a Single PC or in a Networked PC (LAN) Environment. Product Line Offers Cataloging, Online Public Access Catalog (OPAC), Circulation, Serials Control, & Acquisitions. Modules May Be Purchased & Used Singly or in any Combination. Provides the Following Features: A Fully Integrated Library System Designed for Small to Medium-Sized Libraries of all Types (Corporate, Academic, Legal, School, Public, Medical, Special); Menu Driven Modules That Make Extensive Use of Windowing; Interface to Other Systems & Utilities for Importing MARC Records; Multiple Levels of System Security.
Inlex, Inc.

Association Accounter: Accounting for Associations. *Version:* 2.2. Stephen R. Krause. Oct. 1988. *Items Included:* Instruction manual & runtime disks. *Customer Support:* 1 year unlimited warranty. On-site installation & training is available for fee.
DOS 3.1 & higher, Novell Netware for multi-user. IBM PC/AT & compatibles (640k). disk $1995.00 single user, $2995.00 LAN (Order no.: ASSO-2.2). *Optimal configuration:* IBM AT or compatible 640k RAM, 40Mb hard disk drive (minimum), 133-column dot matrix printer or laser printer. *Networks supported:* Novell.
Programs Provide Accounting, Invoicing, & a Series of Collection Letters for Association Dues & Maintenance Fees for Members/Owners. Keeps a Full Five Year History of All Payments & Fees. Tracks Violations of By-Laws & Followup Rules. Especially Valuable for Homeowner Associations Where Violations Need to Be Tracked. Provides Payment Registers, Aging Accounts Receivable Reports, Lists by Owners, Streets, etc. & Provides Mailing Labels for Association/Group Newsletters & Announcements.
Tele Vend, Inc.

Asteroids. *Compatible Hardware:* Atari XL/XE. ROM cartridge $6.95 (Order no.: CXL4013).
Atari Corp.

Astro-Aid Plus. Jul. 1983. *Compatible Hardware:* IBM PC, PC XT. *Operating System(s) Required:* PC-DOS, MS-DOS. *Memory Required:* 256k.
disk $49.95.
Collection of 44 Astronomical Functions Selectable by Menu. Includes Coordinate Conversions, Nutation, Telescope Design, & Kepler's/Newton's Laws.
Zephyr Services.

Astro Blast. *Compatible Hardware:* TRS-80 Color Computer, TDP-100. *Memory Required:* 16k.
cassette $24.95.
Protect Earth from Wave after Wave of Alien Invaders.
Mark Data Products.

Astro Edit I: Astrological Report Editor. Michael Bullock. Oct. 1986. *Compatible Hardware:* IBM PC & compatibles. *Memory Required:* 256k. *General Requirements:* 2 disk drives. *Items Included:* Manual. *Customer Support:* Free phone support.
disk $50.00 (ISBN 0-87199-063-6).
Allows Users to Rewrite Text of the Following Astrological Report Programs: Astro-Scope Report, Sex-O-Scope Report, Contact Astro-Report, Composite Astro-Report, Progressed Astro-Report, Monthly Astro-Report, Daily Astro-Report.
Astrolabe, Inc.

Astro Edit II: Astrological Report Editor. Michael Bullock & Michel Roch. May 1989. *Items Included:* Manual. *Customer Support:* Free phone support.
IBM PC & compatibles (256k). disk $50.00 (ISBN 0-87199-098-9). *Nonstandard peripherals required:* Hard disk.
Allows Users to Rewrite Text of the Following Astrological Report Programs: Advanced Natal Report, Astro-Scope Report, Sex-O-Scope Report, Contact Astro-Report, Composite Astro-Report, Progressed Astro-Report, Monthly Astro-Report, Daily Astro Report.
Astrolabe, Inc.

Astro-Grover. Children's Television Workshop. *Compatible Hardware:* Apple II; Atari XL, XE; Commodore 64, IBM PC & compatibles.
disk $9.95.
Numbers Game Which Develops Addition & Subtraction Skills.
Hi Tech Expressions, Inc.

Astro Logical Chart Package: M-30. 1979. *Compatible Hardware:* Apple II; Commodore 64. *Language(s):* Compiled BASIC. *Memory Required:* 32k. *General Requirements:* Printer.
Apple II. disk $50.00 (ISBN 0-925182-28-1, Order no.: M-30).
Commodore 64. disk $50.00 (ISBN 0-925182-29-X, Order no.: M-30).
Professional Horoscope Calculator & Chart File. Produces Accurate Natal Charts for Anywhere on the Globe in the 20th Century. Includes a Built-in Screen Dump to Printer.
Matrix Software.

Astro-Scope Report. Steve Blake & Robert Hand. 1981. *Compatible Hardware:* Apple II with Applesoft, Apple II+, IIe, IIc, Macintosh; CP/M-based machines; IBM PC & MS-DOS compatibles. *Operating System(s) Required:* Apple DOS, CP/M-80, PC-DOS, MS-DOS, MacFinder. *Language(s):* BASIC. *Memory Required:* Apple & CP/M 48k, PC-DOS 256, MS-DOS 128k or 256k, Macintosh 512k, Commodore 64k. *General Requirements:* 2 disk drives, printer. *Items Included:* Manual. *Customer Support:* Free phone support.
disk $150.00 ea.
CP/M (Kaypro 2). (ISBN 0-913637-38-6, Order no.: 514).
IBM PC. (ISBN 0-913637-39-4).
MS-DOS. (ISBN 0-913637-61-0).
Apple. (ISBN 0-913637-37-8).
Macintosh. (ISBN 0-87199-041-5).
Computes & Prints Natal Horoscope & 1800-Word Interpretation. Includes Batch Loader & License to Sell Printed Output. Spanish, French, German & Other Foreign-Language Versions Are Available for $200.
Astrolabe, Inc.

Astro-Scope: Screen Version. (Ancient Arts Ser.). Steve Blake. 1980. *Compatible Hardware:* Apple II with Applesoft, Apple II+, IIe, IIc, IIgs, III, Macintosh; Commodore 64; CP/M-based machines; IBM PC & MS-DOS compatibles. *Operating System(s) Required:* Apple DOS, Commodore DOS, CP/M-80, MacFinder, MS-DOS, PC-DOS. *Language(s):* BASIC. *Memory Required:* Apple & TRS-80 32k, Commodore & CP/M 64K, IBM & MS-DOS 128k, Macintosh 512k. *General Requirements:* 2 disk drives for Macintosh; 5-1/4" disk drive for Apple IIgs. *Items Included:* Manual. *Customer Support:* Free phone support.
disk $39.95 ea., incl. manual.
Apple. (ISBN 0-913637-33-5).
Commodore. (ISBN 0-87199-014-8).
CP/M (Kaypro 2). (ISBN 0-87199-012-1).
IBM & MS-DOS. (ISBN 0-87199-011-3).
Macintosh. (ISBN 0-87199-047-4).
Computes Natal Horoscope & Interprets It in 1500 Words or More. The Text Delineates All Planets by Aspect & House, & All but Jupiter Through Pluto by Sign.
Astrolabe, Inc.

Astro Star I. Doug Kellogg. Jul. 1981. *Items Included:* Manual. *Customer Support:* Free phone support.
CP/M-80. CP/M compatibles & Commodore 128 (64kb). disk $150.00 (ISBN 0-913637-22-X).
Nonstandard peripherals required: Printer.
A Fast, One-Disk Astrological Calculation Program That Lets User View All Types of Charts on the Screen & Make Printouts at Will. Includes Natal, Progressed, Solar- and Lunar-Return Charts, Composite Charts & Synastry, in Two Zodiacs & over 10 House Systems. Lists, Natal Aspects & Midpoints, & Lists Transmitting Aspects at Regular Intervals. Includes "Uranian" Planets & Helio, Right Ascension & Altitude/Azimuth Positions As Well As the More Usual Calculations.
Astrolabe, Inc.

Astro Talk: M-11. 1983. *Compatible Hardware:* Apple II+, IIe, IIc; Commodore 64, PET; IBM PC, PCjr. *Language(s):* Compiled BASIC. *Memory Required:* PET 32k, Apple 48k, Commodore 64k, IBM 128k.
disk $39.95 ea., incl. user's guide.
Commodore 64. (ISBN 0-925182-00-1).
IBM. (ISBN 0-925182-01-X).
Apple. (ISBN 0-925182-02-8).
Home Use Version of the Professional Horoscope Interpreter #M90. Takes an In-Depth Look at You, Your Friends & Family, & Answers Questions So You Can Learn Astrology at Your Own Pace.
Matrix Software.

The AstroAnalyst. *Version:* 1.01. Bill Meridian & Robert Hand. Feb. 1989. *Operating System(s) Required:* PC-DOS/MS-DOS. *Memory Required:* 640k. *General Requirements:* Hard disk; 8087 co-processor; EGA, Hercules, VGA or CGA; Epson or IBM compatible dot matrix printer, Hewlett-Packard compatible laser or inkjet printer. *Items Included:* Manual. *Customer Support:* Phone support.
disk $1250.00 (ISBN 0-87199-080-6).
3.5" disk $1250.00 (ISBN 0-87199-081-4).
Extends Conventional Technical Market Analysis with Indicators Derived from Planetary Cycles & Other Astronomical Events. Draws Price Charts with Trendlines, Moving Averages, Oscillators, Stochastics, Fibonacci Retracements, Gann Lines, etc., & Allows You to Access Instant Planetary Positions for Any Point in a Price Graph. Also Has a Planetary Diagram in Which You Can Watch the Prices Change as Planets Move. Also Computes Timing of a Large Variety of Astronomical Cycles, & Enables User to Examine any Price Data Series for the Presence of Astronomical & Other Cycles, Either Single or Combined. Includes Dow Jones Industrial Database & Provision for Importing Price Data from Standard Sources Such as CompuTrac & CSI.
Astrolabe, Inc.

Astrobase Plus. Feb. 1984. *Compatible Hardware:* IBM PC, PC XT. *Operating System(s) Required:* PC-DOS, MS-DOS. *Memory Required:* 256k.
disk $59.95.
Database System for Astronomical Objects. Includes 2000 Galaxies, Stars, Nebulae, etc. User May Add More.
Zephyr Services.

Astrocalc Plus. *Version:* 2.5. Sep. 1982. *Compatible Hardware:* IBM PC, PC XT. *Operating System(s) Required:* PC-DOS, MS-DOS. *Memory Required:* 256k.
disk $59.95, incl. user's guide.
Provides Fundamental Astronomical Data for Sun, Moon & All Planets, Given Any Time, Date & Location.
Zephyr Services.

AstroDay: Personal Version. Josh Prokop & Bruce Scofield. Mar. 1996. *Customer Support:* Free phone support.
MS-DOS. 8088 (640k). $50.00 per year (ISBN 0-87199-137-3). *Nonstandard peripherals required:* High-density floppy drive, Hercules Mono.
Shows User's Personal Astrological Transits Each Day When Computer Is Booted Up. Detailed Text by Bruce Scofield Includes Aspects by the Transiting Moon As Well As the Other Planets. Disk Includes Forecasts for One Year; Please Supply Date, Time & Place of Birth, & Date You Want the Forecasts to Start On.
Astrolabe, Inc.

AstroDay with Global Transits. Josh Prokop & Bruce Scofield. Mar. 1996. *Customer Support:* Free phone support.
MS-DOS. 8088 (640k). $70.00 per year (ISBN 0-87199-138-1). *Nonstandard peripherals required:* High-density floppy drive, Hercules Mono.
Besides Everything That Is in AstroDay: The Personal Version, This Includes the Aspects Between the Transiting Planets Themselves. This Gives the User a Daily Report on Astrological Conditions for the World in Addition to a Personal Daily Astrological Forecast.
Astrolabe, Inc.

Astrolabe Font 1. Gary Christen. Sep. 1993. *Items Included:* Manual. *Customer Support:* Free phone support.
PC-DOS/MS-DOS, Windows. IBM PC & MS-DOS & compatibles. disk $50.00 (ISBN 0-87199-125-X). *Addl. software required:* Any word-processing, desktop publishing or graphics program that uses TrueType or Type 1 fonts.
Optimal configuration: High-resolution printer.
Scalable Font with Astrological Characters, Including All Zodiacal Signs; Planetary Symbols with Additional European & Old-Style Glyphs; Chiron & Asteroids; Uranian & Other Hypothetical Planets; Aspect Symbols; Numerals & Degree, Minute & Second Marks; Subscripts; Moon-Phase & Eclipse Symbols; Arrows, Stars & More. Disk Includes Complete TrueType & Type 1 Versions of the Same Font.
Astrolabe, Inc.

The Astrologer's Companion: An Astrological Clock Program. Robert S. Hand. May 1987. *Compatible Hardware:* IBM PC & compatibles. *Memory Required:* 256k, recommended 512 or 640k. *General Requirements:* Hard disk. *Items Included:* Manual. *Customer Support:* Free phone support.
disk $75.00 (ISBN 0-87199-066-0).
Memory-Resident Astrological Clock Program, Providing an Instant Pop-Up Astrological Chart for the Present Time & Place, or Any Other Moment. Includes Horoscope Wheel; Aspectarian; Midpoint List; Moon Calendar, Planetary Hours, Complete Speculum of Planetary Position, & Heliocentric Sidereal, & Multi-House Options. Works in DOS 5 or Higher with Programs That Do Not Do Screen Graphics, & Is Also Accessible in Windows. New Version Can Place Any Nova-Compatible Birth Chart Next to the Current Chart on the Screen.
Astrolabe, Inc.

Astrological Chart Service: M65A. 1982. *Compatible Hardware:* Apple II+, IIe, IIc; Commodore 64, PET; IBM PC, PCjr; TRS-80. *Language(s):* BASIC, Assembly. *Memory Required:* PET 32k; Apple & TRS-80 48k; Commodore 64k; IBM 256k. *General Requirements:* 2 disk drives, printer.
disk $300.00 ea. (Order no.: M65A).
(ISBN 0-925182-03-6).
IBM. (ISBN 0-925182-04-4).
Apple. (ISBN 0-925182-05-2).
Complete Chart Service for the Professional Astrologer. Performs Complex Techniques Such As Transits, Progressions & Returns, & Will Batch Processes up to 40 Charts Unattended. File System Stores Client Information for Later Use. Many Customizing Modules Are Available, Including Ones for Hi-Res Graphics & Astrological Research.
Matrix Software.

Astrological Horoscope Interpreter. 1982. *Compatible Hardware:* Apple II+, IIe, IIc; Commodore 64, PET; IBM PC; TRS-80. *Language(s):* BASIC. *Memory Required:* PET 32k, Apple & TRS-80 48k, Commodore 64 64k, IBM

TITLE INDEX

256k. *General Requirements:* 2 disk drives, printer.
disk $300.00 ea. (Order no.: M90).
Commodore 64. (ISBN 0-925182-06-0).
IBM. (ISBN 0-925182-07-9).
Apple. (ISBN 0-925182-08-7).
Writes Multipage Horoscope Interpretations for Resale. 12-Page Reports Include Cover Sheet, Instructions & Planet Listings. 10 Chapters Cover Love Life, Career, & More. Designed to Expand Astrologer's Client Base to Include Those Not Yet Ready for Personal Interviews.
Matrix Software.

Astrological Professional PC Computer Shareware Pack: Software for Personalized Astrological Charts & Accessories Programs.
Jan. 1996. *Items Included:* Instruction booklet.
DOS & Windows. PC (640k). disk $19.90 (ISBN 1-56087-131-8). *Optimal configuration:* Min. 286, DOS or Windows, 2k RAM.
The Ideal Computer Program for Medium, Advanced & Professional Astrologers. Creates Serious, Complex & Extensive Personalized Charts, Takes into Consideration Time & Location. Plus a Program of Famous People Born on Any Date, & a Professional Program for Appointment Tracking, & File & Contact.
Top of the Mountain Publishing.

Astrological Transit Reporter: M91. 1982.
Compatible Hardware: Apple II+; Commodore 64, PET; TRS-80; IBM PC. *Language(s):* BASIC.
Memory Required: Apple & Commodore 32k, IBM 256k. *General Requirements:* 2 disk drives, printer.
disk $5000.00.
Apple. (ISBN 0-925182-11-7).
Commodore 64. (ISBN 0-925182-09-5).
IBM. (ISBN 0-925182-10-9).
For the Professional Astrologer: Compares Transitting Planets with Natal Planets for Your Customer & Provides Day-by-Day Interpretations for That Individual.
Matrix Software.

Astrology. *Compatible Hardware:* Apple II; TRS-80 Model I, Model III. *Memory Required:* 16-28k.
Apple II. disk $19.95 (Order no.: 0242AD).
TRS-80. cassette $14.95 (Order no.: 0241R).
Supplies Calculations & Planetary Placement Data Necessary for a Trained Astrologer to Interpret.
Instant Software, Inc.

Astrology Gift Pack. 1995. *Items Included:*
Operating manual. *Customer Support:* Free telephone technical support 1-800-850-7272.
DOS 3.1, Windows 3.1; Macintosh. 33Mhz 80486DX, VGA video/display at 256 colors (4Mb); Macintosh, System 6.07, 68030 processor or higher (4Mb). CD-ROM disk Contact publisher for price (ISBN 1-884014-65-8). *Nonstandard peripherals required:* CD-ROM drive. *Optimal configuration:* 8Mb, Dual speed CD-ROM.
Multicom Publishing, Inc.

Astrology Source. *Items Included:* Manual, registration card, flier describing all our titles, occasional promotional offers. *Customer Support:* Free telephone technical support.
DOS & Microsoft Windows 3.1. 12 MHz 80386SX. CD-ROM disk Contact publisher for price (ISBN 1-884014-16-X). *Nonstandard peripherals required:* MPC compatible. CD-ROM drive (680Mb) SVGA display, audio board, mouse, 486 DX processor. *Addl. software required:* Microsoft CD-ROM Extensions v.2.2.
Macintosh System 6.05. Color Macintosh (256 colors) (3.5Mb). CD-ROM disk Contact publisher for price (ISBN 1-884014-28-3).

Optimal configuration: Single speed CD-ROM, 13" color monitor, 8 Mb RAM.
Create Natal Charts & Daily Horoscopes. Evaluate Your Compatability with Others. Learn the Fundamentals of Astrology with Illustrations & Information on the Houses, Planets, & Sun, Moon & Ascendant Signs.
Multicom Publishing, Inc.

Astrology Source. 1995. *Items Included:*
Operating manual. *Customer Support:* Free telephone technical support 1-800-850-7272.
DOS 3.1, Windows 3.1; Macintosh. 33Mhz 80486DX, VGA video/display at 256 colors (4Mb); Macintosh, System 6.07, 68030 processor or higher (4Mb). CD-ROM disk $59.95 (ISBN 1-884014-62-3). *Nonstandard peripherals required:* CD-ROM drive. *Optimal configuration:* 8Mb, Dual speed CD-ROM.
An Interactive Astrological Guide with Background Information Daily Horoscopes That Can Be Personally Tailored for the User & a Compatibility Feature with Historical & Famous Figures. Bundled with Book.
Multicom Publishing, Inc.

Astronomy. *Version:* 3.0. *Compatible Hardware:* Apple Macintosh. *Memory Required:* 512k.
3.5" disk $19.95.
Astronomical Plots.
E & M Software Co.

Astronomy Data Bytes. Richard Tolman. Jan. 1985. *Compatible Hardware:* Apple II+, IIe. *Operating System(s) Required:* Apple DOS 3.3. *Language(s):* Apple-BASIC. *Memory Required:* 48k.
disk $59.95 (ISBN 0-8331-0188-9, Order no.: 188).
Reference of Up-to-Date Facts in Astronomy. Data Bank Consists of Information Regarding Asteroids, Celestial Phenomena, Comets, Discoveries, Events, Instruments, Meteors, Moon, Planets, Stars & the Sun.
Hubbard Scientific.

Astronomy: Planet Orbits 1500-2400 AD.
1985. *Compatible Hardware:* IBM PC, Tandy 1000. *Operating System(s) Required:* PC-DOS, MS-DOS. *Language(s):* BASIC (source code included). *Memory Required:* 16k.
disk $20.00, incl. documentation.
Designed to Find Heliocentric, Geocentric & Altazimuth Coordinates of the 9 Planets on Any Date Between 1500-2400 AD. Julian Calendar Day & Position of Halley's Comet Can Also Be Found. Plot of Positions for IBM PC, XT, AT.
Don Carrera.

Astroquest. *Items Included:* Bound manual. *Customer Support:* Free hotline - no time limit; 30 day limited warranty; updates are $5/disk plus S&H.
MS-DOS 2.0 or higher. IBM & compatibles (128k). disk $29.95. *Nonstandard peripherals required:* Graphics capability.
Desktop Astrologer. User Can Choose a Personality (Natal) Reading Based on the Time of Birth, or Use the Daily Horoscope to Determine How Planetary Alignment Will Affect You Today. You Can Chart Your Future Three Different Ways: with the Placidus System, the Equal House System, or the Koch System.
Dynacomp, Inc.

AstroTutor. Jul. 1988. *Compatible Hardware:* IBM PC & compatibles. *Operating System(s) Required:* PC-DOS/MS-DOS. *Memory Required:* 256k. *General Requirements:* CGA card or EGA/VGA with CGA emulation.
disk $29.95.
Explains the Solar System & Planets, Galaxies, Stars & Their Evolution & The Methods & History of Astronomy. Uses Graphics & Animation to Illustrate Key Ideas.
Zephyr Services.

ASYNC PROFESSIONAL FOR WINDOWS

Async COMPAC. 1983. *Compatible Hardware:* CP/M-86 based micros; IBM PC, PC XT, PC AT. *Operating System(s) Required:* PC-DOS. *Language(s):* BASIC. *Memory Required:* 64k.
disk 300 baud $40.00.
disk 1200 baud $60.00.
disk 9600 baud $195.00.
Allows Asynchronous Communication Through an IBM RS-232 Interface or Via a Frontier Technologies Advanced Communications Board.
Frontier Technologies Corp.

ASYNC Professional. *Version:* Pascal 2.0, C 2.1. Dec. 1995. *Items Included:* Manual, online help system. *Customer Support:* 60 day money-back guarantee, free technical support, CompuServe Technical support, free electronic maintenance updates.
MS-DOS 2.0. IBM PC or compatible (256k). disk $199.00 Pascal; $249.00 C Plus Plus. *Nonstandard peripherals required:* At least one com port. *Addl. software required:* Turbo Pascal 5.5, 6.0, 7.0, Borland C Plus Plus 3.1 or higher, Microsoft C/C Plus Plus 7.0 or higher.
Library of Asynchronous Communications Functions for Pascal & C Plus Plus Programmers Working in the DOS Environment. Features Include Object-Oriented & Procedural Programming Interfaces, Buffered I/O up to 115k Baud, Buffered UART Support, File Transfer Protocols Including ZMODEM & Kermit, FAX Send & Receive, Built-In Tracing & Debugging, Terminal Emulation & Modem Control. Supports DOS Protected Mode. Full Source Code Included. No Royalties.
TurboPower Software.

Async Professional for Delphi. Dec. 1995. *Items Included:* Manual, online help, example programs. *Customer Support:* Free technical support, 60 day money-back guarantee, free electronic maintenance updates, E-mail technical support.
Windows 3.1 or higher. 386 IBM PC (4Mb). disk $179.00. *Nonstandard peripherals required:* Comport. *Addl. software required:* Borland Delphi 1.0.
A Collection of Native VCL Components for Serial Communications under Windows. It Has an Event-Driven Architecture Tuned for Performance & Efficiency That Supports Full Background Operation. Delphi Events for Serial Data Are Generated under Conditions That You Define. Includes Integrated Serial Debugging Tools. Supports XMODEM, YMODEM, ZMODEM, Kermit, CompuServe B Plus, & ASCII File Transfers. Also Includes a Terminal Component with Scrollback, ANSI Emulation, & File Capture. Plus a Modem Database with over 100 Entries, an Event-Driven Dialing Engine, Modem Status Lights Component, & a Collection of Dialogs for Modem Database Editing & Phone Number Management. Full Source Code Included.
TurboPower Software.

Async Professional for Windows. Aug. 1995. *Items Included:* Manual, online help, example programs. *Customer Support:* Free technical support, 60 day money-back guarantee, free electronic maintenance updates, E-mail technical support.
Windows 3.1 or higher. 386 IBM PC (4Mb). disk $199.00. *Nonstandard peripherals required:* Comport. *Addl. software required:* Borland Pascal 7.0, Turbo Pascal for Windows 1.5, Borland C Plus Plus 4.0 or higher, Microsoft Visual C Plus Plus 1.0 or higher.
A Powerful Object-Oriented Serial Communications Library Tightly Integrated with OWL for Pascal & C Plus Plus & MFC for C Plus Plus. It Has an Event-Driven Architecture Tuned for Performance & Efficiency That Supports Full Background Operation. Includes Integrated Serial

Debugging Tools. Supports XMODEM, YMODEM, ZMODEM, Kermit, CompuServe B Plus, & ASCII File Transfers. Also Includes a Terminal Window with Scrollback, ANSI Emulation, & File Capture. Plus a Modem Database with over 100 Entries, an Event-Driven Dialing Engine, & a Collection of Dialogs for Modem Database Editing & Phone Number Management. Full Source Code Included.
TurboPower Software.

ASYST, 4 modules. Version: 4.0. May 1992. Compatible Hardware: IBM PC & compatibles, PC XT, PC AT. Operating System(s) Required: PC-DOS 3.0 or higher. Memory Required: 384k of LIM 4.0 expanded memory, 640k. General Requirements: 5Mb hard disk, high density floppy disk drive, compatible graphics card (IBM EGA, CGA or 100% compatible). Items Included: Master disk, help system disk, sample applications backup master, tutorial manual, reference manual, & index. Customer Support: Free newsletter & 90 days of software support at no charge.
4 module set. $2295.00 (ISBN 0-924729-14-7).
4 Separate, but Fully Integrated, Software Tools Designed for Scientific & Engineering Applications. Offers a Complete Set of High Level Commands for Sophisticated Analysis & Graphics, Analog-to-Digital, Digital-to-Analog Acquisition, & RS-232 & GPIB/IEEE-488 Intrument Interfacing. Provides Hundreds of Built-In Commands Such As FFT, INTEGRATE.DATA, MATRIX.INV & LOCAL.MAXIMA. Utilizes PC's 8087 Coprocessor. All Intermediate Calculations Taken to the 80-Bit Precision Level.
Keithley Asyst.
  Module 1. Systems-Graphics-Statistics.
  Modules 1 & 2 Establish ASYST Environment. Module 1 Provides Data Representation & Storage Capability; Supplies Arithmetic, Trigonometric, Hyperbolic & Other Mathematical & Statistical Functions; Also Provides Direct Graphics Output to Screen & Plotter. Includes Array Manipulation, Control of Vectors & Matrices, Automatic Plotting, Bar & Pie Charts, Error Bars, Color & High Resolution Graph, File Manipulation, Programming Control Structures, Gamma, Besse & Error Functions, RS-232 Support & Built-In Text Editor.
  Module 2. Analysis.
  Modules 1 & 2 Establish ASYST Environment. Module 2 Reduces & Analyzes Data, & Includes Selection of Analytical Functions Such As Eigenvalues, Eigenvectors & Polynomials. Among the Automatic Functions Provided Are Least Squares Approximation, Curve Fitting, Convolutions, Integration, Differentiation, Smoothing Fourier Transform, Axonometric & Contour Plots, R2 (Cross-Correlator Non-Linear Regression), ANOVA, & F-Tests.
  Module 3. Acquisition.
  Interfaces ASYST & Personal Computer to Laboratory Instruments. Standard Commands Such As "A/D.IN" Are Used to Control Communication Between ANSYST & Standard Interface Boards. Supports High-Speed A/D & D/A Conversions, Digital I/O, Timing, Triggering & DMA.
  Module 4. GPIB-IEEE-488.
  Supports Interface Between ASYST & the GPIB BUS. Features Include Complete Support for IEEE-488 Protocol, Parallel & Serial Polling, Synchronous & Asynchronous Operation, DMA, Buffering of Data & Device-Dependent Commands, Real-Time Synchronization.

ASYSTANT. Version: 1.1. Compatible Hardware: IBM PC, PC XT, PC AT, & compatibles. Operating System(s) Required: MS-DOS 2.0 or higher. Memory Required: 512k, recommended 640k. General Requirements: Hard disk; 8087/80287/80387 math co-processor; CGA, EGA, VGA, Hercules, or AT&T monochrome graphics card. Customer Support: Free newsletter, assistance available.
$495.00 (ISBN 0-924729-20-1).
Stand Alone, Integrated Software Package for Scientific Data Analysis, Statistics, & Graphics. Provides the Following Features: Menu-Driven; Performs Sophisticated Operations Such As ANOVA, FFT, & Curve Fitting; Calculations Are Executed Immediately; Function Keys Can Be Programmed for Repeated Operations. Can Be Used for: Classroom Instruction, Scientific Computing, Desktop Analysis, Presentation Graphics, Signal Processing, Data Modeling, etc.
Keithley Asyst.

ASYSTANT - Student Version. Version: 1.1. Sep. 1989. Items Included: Student manual. Customer Support: Extended support (usable only by licensee) $145.00/yr.
MS-DOS 2.0 or higher (640k). IBM PC, PC XT, PC AT & compatibles, PS/2, 386-based computer in real mode. disk $44.95 (ISBN 0-924729-01-5). Nonstandard peripherals required: Math coprocessor - Intel 8087, 80287, 80387.
Allows User to Design Sophisticated Analysis Routines (Including Array & Matrix Operations, Statistics, Polynomials, Differential Equations & Curvefits) Quickly & Easily. Program Menus Also Offer Powerful Waveform Processing, Signal Processing & Plotting Options for Instant Data Display.
Keithley Asyst.

ASYSTANT GPIB, 5 disks. Version: 1.01. Compatible Hardware: IBM PC, PC XT, PC AT, & compatibles. Operating System(s) Required: MS-DOS 2.0 or higher. Memory Required: 512k, recommended 640k. General Requirements: Hard disk; 25-pin standard printer port; 8087/80287/80387 math co-processor; CGA, EGA, Hercules, or AT&T monochrome graphics card.
contact publisher for price (ISBN 0-924729-21-X).
Stand-Alone, Menu-Driven Package Which Gives All the Analysis & Graphics Capabilities of ASYSTANT Coupled with IEEE-488 Interface Support. Menu-Driven & Programmable.
Keithley Asyst.

AT&T Multimedia Designer for Windows. Version: 1.5. Dec. 1995. Items Included: Installation CD-ROM, user guide, quick reference guide, tutorial (for Windows 3.1/95 versions only), 250 Truetype fonts, font manual, high quality photo/texture CD-ROM, sample scenes (for Windows 3.1/95 versions only), over 50 presentation templates (for Windows 3.1/95 versions only). Customer Support: Toll free customer support for first 90 days; free customer support after 90 days - will cost phone charges.
Windows 3.1/95. 386 (8Mb). $495.00 MSRP - $295.00 Intro. Nonstandard peripherals required: Math co-processor, 24-bit graphics card, mouse or digitizing pad, high color monitor. Addl. software required: Microsoft Windows 3.1 or higher in enhanced mode. Windows 95 or Windows NT.
A Full-Color 32-Bit Imaging Solution with Easy-to-Use Tools That Meet the Needs of Both Design Professional & Non-Artists. The Object-Oriented Architecture Seamlessly Pulls Text, Graphics & Images Together to Create Illustrations for Multimedia, Presentation, Layout, Print & Photographic Applications.
AT&T Multimedia Software Solutions.

AT&T Multimedia Designer for Windows. Feb. 1995. Items Included: Installation CD-ROM, user guide, quick reference guide, tutorial (for Windows 3.1/95 versions only), 250 Truetype fonts, font manual, high quality photo/texture CD-ROM, sample scenes (for Windows 3.1/95 versions only), over 50 presentation templates (for Windows 3.1/95 versions only). Customer Support: Toll free customer support for first 90 days; free customer support after 90 days - will cost phone charges.
Windows NT. 386 (16Mb). $595.00 MSRP - $395.00 Intro. Nonstandard peripherals required: Math co-processor, Windows NT compatible mouse, digitized pad, high color display card-24-bit, high color monitor. Addl. software required: Microsoft Windows NT.
A Full-Color 32-Bit Imaging Solution with Easy-to-Use Tools That Meet the Needs of Both Design Professional & Non-Artists. The Object-Oriented Architecture Seamlessly Pulls Text, Graphics & Images Together to Create Illustrations for Multimedia, Presentation, Layout, Print & Photographic Applications.
AT&T Multimedia Software Solutions.

@Base. Dec. 1987. Compatible Hardware: IBM PC & compatibles. Memory Required: 76k, plus for each open database file 8k.
$195.00.
optional indexing & linking module for dBase III $89.95.
Creates a Disk-Based Relational Database That Is Compatible with dBase III & dBase III Plus, Requiring No File Conversion. Accesses Multiple Data Files Concurrently, & Includes Multilevel Data Sorting, & a Multifield Search & Replace Capability. Allows As Many As 254 Characters per Field, 128 Fields per Record, & an Unlimited Number of Records per File. Not Copy Protected.
Personics Corp.

At Dream's End: A Kingdom in the Balance. (The/Destiny Chronicles Ser.). William R. Stanek. Feb. 1995.
PC-DOS/MS-DOS, Novell DOS 3.1 or higher. IBM PC, XT, AT, PS/2 or 100% compatibles (640k). disk $9.50 (ISBN 1-57545-002-X). Optimal configuration: IBM PC, XT, AT, PS/2 or 100% compatibles, VGA/SVGA or compatible graphics card & monitor, 640k minimum RAM, hard disk, PC-DOS/MS-DOS or Novell DOS 3.1 or higher. Will also run on Windows system.
PC-DOS/MS-DOS, Novell DOS 3.1 or higher. IBM PC, XT, AT, PS/2 or 100% compatibles (640k). disk $9.50 (ISBN 1-57545-003-8). Optimal configuration: IBM PC, XT, AT, PS/2 or 100% compatibles, VGA/SVGA or compatible graphics card & monitor, 640k minimum RAM, hard disk, PC-DOS/MS-DOS or Novell DOS 3.1 or higher. Will also run on Windows system.
Interactive Fiction on Floppy Disk.
Virtual Pr., The.

At Ease. Version: 1.04. 1988. Customer Support: Available for 90 day limited warranty.
write for info.
A Powerful Tool for Simplifying the Creation of Reports, Budgets, Plans, Forecasts & Other Basic Spreadsheet Tasks, Thereby Greatly Increasing the Productivity of Lotus Users. Contains Functions for Generating Any Series of Dates, Subtotals, Grandtotals, Centering Headings, Summing up Dates & Many Other Functions to Create Worksheets.
Spreadsheet Solutions Corp.

At Fixed Income. Version: 1.08 for DOS. 1988. Customer Support: Available for 90 day limited warranty.
write for info.
A Library or over 50 New FUNCTIONS for 1-2-3, 20/20, & Wingz. Uses the Standards Set by

TITLE INDEX

the Securities Industry Association & Includes -Functions Which Represent Standard Calculations for the Fixed Income Securities Industry. In a Lotus Worksheet, User Can Construct an Infinite Assortment of Models Including: Yield Curve Analysis, Interest Rate Swaps, Plus Many Others.
Spreadsheet Solutions Corp.

At Home Household Organizer Try & Buy. Ace Software Corporation Staff. *Items Included:* The package includes a 3.5" diskette, a mini-manual & a Try & Buy Brochure.
DOS, Microsoft Windows 3.1 or higher running DOS 3.3 or higher. IBM PC & compatibles, 286, 386, or 486 PC (2Mb). disk $29.99 (ISBN 1-57548-008-5). *Nonstandard peripherals required:* VGA or SVGA video card supported by Windows 3.3.
A Home Office Product That Allows Users Quick Access to Office Records.
IBM Software Manufacturing Solutions (ISMS).

At Home Personal Post Office Try & Buy. Ace Software Corporation Staff. *Items Included:* The package includes 3.5" diskettes, a mini-manual & a Try & Buy Brochure.
Microsoft Windows 3.1 or higher running DOS 3.3 or higher. IBM PC AT or compatible 386 or 486 PC (4Mb). disk $29.99 (ISBN 1-57548-007-7).
This Product Would Allow Users to Print Envelopes & Labels Within Minutes.
IBM Software Manufacturing Solutions (ISMS).

@Liberty. *Version:* 2.01. *Operating System(s) Required:* PC-DOS/MS-DOS 2.0 or higher. *Customer Support:* 9:00 AM to 5:30 PM EST (603) 644-5555.
$295.00, incl. license for unlimited run-time. upgrade $35.00 to current @Liberty users.
New Version of the Spreadsheet Compiler, Includes a Context-Sensitive Help Facility, 230-Column Printer Support, Improved Performance in Displaying Data & Executing @Sum & VLookup Functions.
SoftLogic Solutions.

At Play for Windows. Jan. 1994. *Items Included:* Manual, diskette, response card. *Customer Support:* Call 303-673-9046, No charges for support, 90 day limited warranty, support via phone, modem, fax.
MS-DOS 3.3, MS-Windows 3.1, MS-Windows 95. Intel 486, IBM compatible PC (2Mb). disk $21.95 (ISBN 1-884791-04-2, Order no.: 01-2103-0100). *Optimal configuration:* 486-processor, MPC-compatible sound card, mouse, color VGA.
Entertainment Software for Microsoft Windows Incorporating Flipover, Highscore, Whirlwind, At Play for Windows with an Educational Twist.
Technological Computer Innovations Corp.

@RISK. *Compatible Hardware:* IBM PC & compatibles, Macintosh. *General Requirements:* Hercules, CGA, EGA, or VGA card. *Items Included:* Documentation. *Customer Support:* 90 days free tech support (maintenance contract avail.).
3.5" or 5.25" disk $395.00.
Lotus 1-2-3/Microsoft Excel Add-In Designed for Situations Where There Is Uncertainty in the Values Entered in a Spreadsheet. Lets Users Enter a Range of Values & Then Uses Probability Distribution & Simulation Techniques to Evaluate the Situation. Each Simulation Calculates Hundreds or Thousands of What-If Scenarios, & Then the Program Shows the Probability of Each Outcome Occurring. Output Is Displayed Graphically in Various Formats Including Histograms, Cumulative Curves, Summaries over Range of Cells, or Overlays. Graphic Output Is in Standard 1-2-3/Excel Format.
Palisade Corp.

@ Risk. *Items Included:* Program disk, reference manual. *Customer Support:* 3 months technical support.
MS-DOS. IBM PC/XT/AT or PS/2 & compatibles, (512k). disk $395.00 (Order no.: PAL 1001). *Nonstandard peripherals required:* Hard disk recommended. *Addl. software required:* Lotus 1-2-3 version 2.X. *Optimal configuration:* 80286 microprocessor or higher, MS-DOS 3.0 or higher. *Networks supported:* Most PC based servers.
MS-DOS. 80386 microprocessor or higher (2Mb). disk $395.00 (Order no.: PAL 1002). *Addl. software required:* Lotus 3.1 or higher DOS based software. *Optimal configuration:* 80486, MS-DOS 5.0 or higher, 4Mb RAM.
Microsoft Windows 3.0 or higher. 286 or higher (2Mb). disk $395.00 (Order no.: PAL 1005). *Addl. software required:* Microsoft Excel 3.0 or higher. *Optimal configuration:* 486, Microsoft Windows 3.1, Microsoft 4.0.
Macintosh. 68030 16MHz or higher (2Mb). 3.5" disk $395.00 (Order no.: PAL 1004). *Nonstandard peripherals required:* Math coprocessor highly recommended. *Addl. software required:* Microsoft Excel 3.0 or higher.
Uses Monte Carlo Simulation to Analyze Uncertainty. Probability Distributions Are Added to Cells in the Worksheet Using 30 New Probability Distribution Built-In Functions, Including Normal, Lognormal, Beta, Uniform & Triangular. Simulations Are Controlled from an Excel/Lotus-Style Menu That Lets Users Choose Monte Carlo or Latin Hypercube Sampling, Select Output Ranges & Start Simulating. Results Are Displayed Graphically & Detailed Statistics Reports Are Generated. Probability Distribution Built-In Functions Can Be Used Anywhere in a Worksheet, Either Alone in a Cell or As Part of Other Expressions, & Their Parameters Can Be References to Other Cells. Dependencies Can Be Specified. Seed or Random Number Generator Can Be Specified. High-Resolutions Graphics Enhance Manipulation or Output Results. Simulations Can Be Paused & Restarted.
Palisade Corp.

@RISK for Project. *Items Included:* Program diskettes, reference manual. *Customer Support:* 3 months technical support.
Microsoft Windows 3.1. IBM 286 or compatible with hard disk (3Mb). Contact publisher for price (Order no.: PAL 1007). *Addl. software required:* Microsoft & Excel 4.0 or higher, Microsoft Project version 3.0 or higher. *Optimal configuration:* 486, Microsoft Windows 3.1, 4Mb, mouse.
Links Directly to Microsoft Project to Add Risk Analysis Capabilities. After a Simulation Is Run, @RISK Displays All Results in Excel, Providing All the Necessary Tools for Reviewing & Editing Reports & Charts. Allows You to Define Uncertain Cell Values in Project As Probability Functions Using Excel-Style Functions. Distribution Functions Can Be Added to Many Tasks & Resources Throughout Your Project & Can Include Arguments That Are Dates, Durations, Dollar Amounts, etc.
Palisade Corp.

AT-RTX. *Version:* 3.0. Apr. 1985. *Compatible Hardware:* IBM PC AT with hard disk. *Operating System(s) Required:* IRMX86. *Language(s):* PL/M86, C86, Pascal 86, FORTRAN 86. *Memory Required:* 512k.
disk $1495.00.
Implementation of Intel's IRMX86 Operating System Configured to IBM AT Device Driver Specifications. Supports up to 15Mbytes RAM Disk Storage & IBM's Enhanced Graphics Adapter. Performs Real-Time Events Based on Priority Task Scheduling.
Real-Time Computer Science Corp.

ATARI 2600 ACTION PACK

At the Movies: The Complete Resource on over 10,000 Movies. Jun. 1994. *Items Included:* Registration card, instruction sheet. *Customer Support:* 900 support number $2.00 per minute; limited 60 day warranty.
DOS. IBM PC & compatibles (512k). disk $9.95 (ISBN 1-57269-004-6, Order no.: 3202 42115). *Addl. software required:* DOS 3.0 or higher. *Optimal configuration:* Single floppy drive. Will run on hard disk drive.
The Consummate Guide to the Movies of Yesterday & Today. Identify Your Viewing Desires - & the Movies That Fit the Criteria Show up on the Screen.
Memorex Products, Inc., Memorex Software Division.

ATAC: Advanced Tactical Air Command. Aug. 1992. *Items Included:* Manual. *Customer Support:* Free customer support, 1-410-771-1151, Ext. 350.
80286, 16MHz, hard disk required, DOS 5.0 required, VGA/EGA, Joystick, Adlib/Roland, Sound Blaster sound cards. (1Mb). disk $49.95 (ISBN 1-55884-188-1). *Optimal configuration:* 386, 16MHz, hard disk, DOS 5.0, VGA, Joystick, Adlib/Roland, Sound Blaster sound cards.
Provides a Unique Gaming Experience That Combines the Excitement of a State-of-the-Art Flight Simulation with the Challenge of a Top Notch Strategy Game. Lead a Squadron of F-22s or Pilot an Apache Helicopter. Command a Force of 250 Undercover Agents As You Root-Out Cocaine Processing Labs in the Mountains of Colombia.
MicroProse Software.

Atari Action Pack, No. 1. *Items Included:* Installation Guide.
MAC. Contact publisher for price (ISBN 0-87321-010-7, Order no.: MAC-3057).
Activision, Inc.

Atari Action Pack, No. 1. *Items Included:* Installation Guide.
MAC. Contact publisher for price (ISBN 0-87321-009-3, Order no.: CDM-3057).
Activision, Inc.

Atari Electric Pencil. *Compatible Hardware:* Atari.
cassette $79.95 (ISBN 0-936200-39-1).
Word Processing System Which Adds Support for Most Character & Dot Matrix Printers with Parallel or Serial Interfaces. Provides a Comprehensive Search & Replace Function.
Blue Cat.

Atari ST Graphics & Sound Programming. Henry Simpson. Nov. 1986. *Compatible Hardware:* Atari ST. *Memory Required:* 512k.
disk $34.95, incl. bk. (ISBN 0-8306-5231-0, Order no.: 5231C).
Offers the Potentials of the 68000 Microprocessor, Icon Data Management, Animation, & 250 Colors. Creates Graphics & Sound Concepts. Complete with Descriptions, Program Listings, & Summaries of Each Program's Results. Also Provides the Know-How Users Need to Begin Writing Their Own Original Programs for Almost Any Application.
TAB Bks.

Atari Utilities. *Compatible Hardware:* Atari 400, 800. *Language(s):* Atari BASIC (source code included). *Memory Required:* 24k.
disk $5.00.
Renumber Program & Disk RPM Test Program.
Dynacomp, Inc.

Atari 2600 Action Pack. *Items Included:* Installation Guide.
Atari. Contact publisher for price (ISBN 0-87321-007-7, Order no.: CDD-3057).
Activision, Inc.

ATARI 2600 ACTION PACK

Atari 2600 Action Pack. *Items Included:* Installation Guide.
Atari. Contact publisher for price (ISBN 0-87321-006-9, Order no.: MS2-3057).
Activision, Inc.

Atari 2600 Action Pack, No. 1. *Items Included:* Installation Guide.
Atari PC. Contact publisher for price (ISBN 0-87321-011-5, Order no.: CDD-3057-NFR).
Activision, Inc.

Atari 2600 Action Pack, No. 2. *Items Included:* Installation Guide.
Atari PC. Contact publisher for price (ISBN 0-87321-015-8, Order no.: MS2-3058).
Activision, Inc.

Atari 2600 Action Pack, No. 2. *Items Included:* Installation Guide.
Atari PC. Contact publisher for price (ISBN 0-87321-014-X, Order no.: CDD-3058).
Activision, Inc.

Atari 2600 Action Pack, No. 2. *Items Included:* Installation Guide.
MAC. Contact publisher for price (ISBN 0-87321-013-1, Order no.: MAC-3058).
Activision, Inc.

Atari 2600 Action Pack, No. 2. *Items Included:* Installation Guide.
MAC. Contact publisher for price (ISBN 0-87321-012-3, Order no.: CDM-3058).
Activision, Inc.

Atari 2600 Action Pack, No. 3. *Items Included:* Installation Guide.
Atari PC. Contact publisher for price (ISBN 0-87321-019-0, Order no.: MS2-3099).
Activision, Inc.

Atari 2600 Action Pack, No. 3. *Items Included:* Installation Guide.
Atari PC. Contact publisher for price (ISBN 0-87321-018-2, Order no.: CDD-3099).
Activision, Inc.

Atari 2600 Action Pack, No. 3. *Items Included:* Installation Guide.
MAC. Contact publisher for price (ISBN 0-87321-017-4, Order no.: MAC-3099).
Activision, Inc.

Atari 2600 Action Pack, No. 3. *Items Included:* Installation Guide.
MAC. Contact publisher for price (ISBN 0-87321-016-6, Order no.: CDM-3099).
Activision, Inc.

Atari 2600 Action Pack, No. 21. *Items Included:* Installation Guide.
Atari PC. Contact publisher for price (ISBN 0-87321-020-4, Order no.: CDD-3121).
Activision, Inc.

Atari 2600 Action Pack, No. 22. *Items Included:* Installation Guide.
Atari PC. Contact publisher for price (ISBN 0-87321-021-2, Order no.: CDD-3122).
Activision, Inc.

Atari 2600 Action Pack: 7 Pack. *Items Included:* Installation Guide.
Atari. Contact publisher for price (ISBN 0-87321-008-5, Order no.: CDD-3057S).
Activision, Inc.

AtariWriter Plus. *Compatible Hardware:* Atari XL/XE. *Operating System(s) Required:* AOS. *Memory Required:* 48k.
disk $49.95 (Order no.: AX2034).
Word Processing Package. Files Can Be Saved to Disk or Tape & Sent to Any Atari Printer. Includes a Print Review Option for Setting Margins & for Changing Files.
Atari Corp.

ATB Consolidations. *Version:* 1.2. Jul. 1991. *Items Included:* 1 wiro-bound manual. *Customer Support:* Free for the first 3 months; $195 annual fee after that.
DOS 3.1 or higher. 100% IBM compatible PC (490k). disk $156.00 nonmember; $140.40 AICPA member. *Addl. software required:* Accountant's Trial Balance, Version 3.0. *Optimal configuration:* 100% IBM compatible PC, DOS 3.1 or higher, 640k RAM, printer capable of printing condensed or compressed. *Networks supported:* Novell, 3COM, LANtastic.
Allows User to Consolidate Trial Balances Produced by the AICPA's Accountant's Trial Balance & Financial Statements Produced with ATB Financial Statements. Links & Combines Accounts of Related Groups into One Consolidated Company. Makes It Easy to Handle Related Corporate Groups or Nonprofit Institutions.
American Institute of Certified Public Accountants.

ATB Conversion. *Version:* 1.4. May 1993. *Items Included:* 1 wiro-bound manual. *Customer Support:* Free for the first 3 months; $195 annual fee after that.
DOS 3.1 or higher. 100% IBM compatible PC (490k). disk $280.00 nonmember; $252.00 AICPA member. *Addl. software required:* Accountant's Trial Balance, Version 3.0. *Optimal configuration:* 100% IBM compatible PC, DOS 3.1 or higher, 640k RAM, printer capable of printing condensed or compressed. *Networks supported:* Novell, 3COM, LANtastic.
Automatically Imports a Company's Data from General Ledger & Workpaper Packages Directly to the AICPA's Accountant's Trial Balance (ATB) & from ATB to Certain Tax Packages. User Can Import Data Directly from: ACCPAC BPI, ACCPAC Plus, ACE, Business Works, Champion, CYMA, FAST!, FAST-CPA, Great Plains, Macola, MAS90, One-Write Plus, Open Systems, Platinum, Real World, Solomon, Timberline Medallion, ASCII, Lotus or dBASE. User Can Export to the Following Tax Packages: CCH Computax Lacerte (GL Bridge), CLR/FastTax, A-Plus Tax, AMI Tax Machine or Digitax Business Returns, Ron Callis Tax & Generic Tax Text File.
American Institute of Certified Public Accountants.

ATB Financial Statements. *Version:* 1.2. Jul. 1991. *Items Included:* 1 wiro-bound manual. *Customer Support:* Free for the first 3 months; $195 annual fee after that.
DOS 3.1 or higher. 100% IBM compatible PC (490k). disk $156.00 nonmember; $140.40 AICPA member. *Addl. software required:* Accountant's Trial Balance, Version 3.0. *Optimal configuration:* 100% IBM compatible PC, DOS 3.1 or higher, 640k RAM, printer capable of printing condensed or compressed. *Networks supported:* Novell, 3COM, LANtastic.
Gives User the Added Flexibility of Creating Financial Statements with the AICPA's Accountant's Trial Balance. Report Writing Feature Acts Like a Combination Word Processor/Spreadsheet. With ATB Financial Statements, Simply Create Your Trial Balance, Select the Report You Want, Customized to Suit Your Needs. Create Balance Sheets, Income Statements, Cash Flow Statements, Notes to Financial Statements, Supplemental Schedules, Additional Statements & More.
American Institute of Certified Public Accountants.

SOFTWARE ENCYCLOPEDIA 1996

ATB Write-Up. Sep. 1992. *Items Included:* 2 wiro-bound manuals. *Customer Support:* 3 months of free support.
DOS 3.1 or higher. IBM compatible 286 or higher (530k). disk $1100.00 nonmember; $990.00 AICPA member. *Optimal configuration:* 100% IBM compatible 386 PC, DOS 3.1 or higher, 640k RAM, printer capable of printing condensed or compressed. *Networks supported:* Novell, 3COM, LANtastic.
Features Powerful Options That Make Analyzing Information & Generating Reports & Financial Statements a Matter of a Few Keystrokes. Allows 13 Periods per Year for Any Given Company. This Gives User the Flexibility to Generate Annual, Semi-Annual, Quarterly or Monthly Reports. Allows User to Set up As Many Departments As Needed. Produces a 16-Column Financial Statement. Has After-the-Fact Payroll & W-2/1099 Support.
American Institute of Certified Public Accountants.

ATC: Advanced Teller Controls. *Compatible Hardware:* IBM PC. *Operating System(s) Required:* PC-DOS. *Language(s):* Compiled BASIC. *Memory Required:* 512k. *Customer Support:* Telephone support.
$10,000.00.
Simulates a Working Environment Involving the Queuing of Customers or Tasks in Order to Aid in the Determination of the Most Effective Staffing Solutions.
Robert E. Nolan Co., Inc.

Athena II. *Compatible Hardware:* Atari 1040 ST or 520 ST upgraded to 1Mb. *General Requirements:* 1 double-sided or 2 single-sided disk drives.
contact publisher for price.
Full-Color, Two Dimensional CAD Program. Features Include: Autodimensioning; B-Splines - 256 Layers (16 Colors); Circles (Radius, Diameter, & Three Point); Lines - Horizontal, Vertical, Parallel, Perpendicular, Tangental, Line at an Angle, Line Between Lines, Rectangles, Line Tangent to Two Circles, etc.; Transformation - Move, Copy, Rotate, Scale, Mirror, Trim (Adjust Any Line or Circle So That It Will Exactly Intersect with Any Given Line or Circle); Parts - Creating Parts from an Existing Drawing & Save Them, Load Parts from Libraries & Place Them Anywhere on Any Drawing; Isometrics - Semi-Automatically Transform Existing Drawings into an Isometric View; Full Zooming Capabilities.
Iliad Software, Inc.

The Athlete's Dairy. *Version:* Macintosh 3.0, Windows 3.0, DOS 2.2. Steven Patt. Jun. 1990. *Items Included:* Manual. *Customer Support:* Free by phone, fax & e-mail.
Macintosh Plus or higher, Windows 3.1, Windows 95, DOS. 3.5" disk $59.95 (Version 3.0).
IBM PC & compatibles. disk $39.95 (Versions 2.2).
$59.95 (Windows Version 3.0).
Special-Purpose Database Enabling Users to Keep a Log of Athletic Activity in up to Eight Different Sports. Calculates Pace, Totals, Averages by Week or Month. Tracks Equipment Use. Selects by Multiple Criteria. Graphs Time, Distance, Pace or Any Other User-Defined Value. Displays Personal Records.
Stevens Creek Software.

ATI Training Modules. American Training International. *Operating System(s) Required:* MS-DOS. *Memory Required:* 64k.
$75.00.
Interactive Software Training Program.
Texas Instruments, Personal Productivit.

TITLE INDEX

ATI Workshop Course: Lotus 1-2-3, Module 2 (Advanced).
$1495.00.
$239.40 set of 12 additional student guides. instruction training & workshop customization available at extra cost.
Includes Instructor's Kit, Seven Student Training Guides, Master Exercise Disk, & Toll-Free Instructor Support Line.
American Training International, Inc.

ATI Workshop Course: Lotus 1-2-3, Module 1 (Introductory).
$1495.00.
additional set of 12 student guides $239.40. instructor training & workshop customization available at extra cost.
Includes Instructor's Kit, Seven Student Training Guides, Master Exercise Disk, ATI Software Sampler Disk, & Toll-Free Instructor Support Line.
American Training International, Inc.

ATLAS*GIS. Version: 2.1. 1993. *Items Included:* Manuals, disks, installation guide. *Customer Support:* Unlimited free telephone support; extended service available - call for prices.
DOS 3.0 or higher. IBM PC XT, PC AT, PS/2 & compatibles (640k). disk $2595.00. *Networks supported:* LAN.
First Full-Featured Desktop Geographical Information System (GIS) to Combine the Most Important Features Found on Mainframe Computers with Base-of-Use & Affordability of Desktop Mapping Software.
Strategic Mapping, Inc.

Atlas MapMaker: For Windows. Version: 1.0. Sep. 1991. *Items Included:* Documentation, starter kit of boundary & data files, tutorial. *Customer Support:* Free unlimited telephone support with return of registration card. Custom application work available - call for more information.
Windows 3.0. IBM PC compatible (2Mb). disk $395.00. *Nonstandard peripherals required:* Graphics monitor. *Addl. software required:* Windows 3.0. *Networks supported:* All supported by Windows 3.0.
Data Driven Map Presentation Program. Built-In Data Spreadsheet & Graphics Display Tools Enable the User to Create a Wide Variety of Map Graphics.
Strategic Mapping, Inc.

Atlas of Clinical Rheumatology. Version: 2. David Nashel. *Customer Support:* Toll-free technical support - no charge. In U.S. - 9AM-5PM EST 800-343-0064. In U.K. - 44(0)81-995-8242.
Microsoft Windows 3.1. 386 IBM - Compatible PC (4Mb). CD-ROM disk $175.00 Individual, $495.00 Institutional (ISBN 1-57276-002-8, Order no.: SE-002-002). *Nonstandard peripherals required:* CD-ROM drive (MPC Standard) 640 x 480 display with 256 colors, MIC standard sound board, speakers.
Provides training in the Identification of Disease-Associated Images in Rheumatology. Provides Color Images & Commentary on the Following Conditions: Osteoarthritis/DJD, Rheumatoid Arthritis, Crystal-Induced Disease, Serongative Arthritis, Connective Tissue Diseases, Infectious Arthritis, Miscellaneous Conditions.
SilverPlatter Education.

Atlas of Clinical Rheumatology. Version: 2.0. David Nashel. Mar. 1993. *Customer Support:* Toll-free technical support - no charge. In U.S. 9AM - 5PM EST 800-343-0064; in U.K. 44(0) 81-995-8242.
Microsoft Windows 3.1. 386 IBM-Compatible PC (4Mb). CD-ROM disk $175.00, Individual, ,495.00 Institutional (ISBN 1-57276-002-8, Order no.: SE-002-002). *Nonstandard peripherals required:* CD-ROM drive (MPC Standard) 640x480 display with 256 colors, MPC Standard Soundboard, Speakers.
Provides Training in the Identification of Disease-Associated Images in Rheumatology. Provides Color Images & Commentary on the Following Conditions: Osteoarthritis/DJD, Rheumatoid Arthritis, Crystal-Induced Disease, Serongative Arthritis, Connective Tissue Diseases, Infectious Arthritis, Miscellaneous Conditions.
SilverPlatter Education.

Atlas of Myocardial Perfusion Imaging. Edited by Frans J. Wackers & Daniel S. Berman. Sep. 1993. *Items Included:* Software supplied on CD-ROM disc, User's Manual, & videodisc.
Macintosh. Macintosh II or Quadra with minimum of 13 inch 256-color display (8Mb). CD-ROM disk $499.00 (ISBN 1-884012-01-9, Order no.: 93-001). *Nonstandard peripherals required:* CD-ROM drive to load software. *Optimal configuration:* Macintosh IIci, fx, LC, or Quadra with 13 inch or larger color monitor, 8Mb RAM, with CD-ROM drive. *Networks supported:* AppleShare.
Provides Radiologists & Cardiologists with an Encyclopedic Collection of over 120 Cases in SPECT & Planar Perfusion Imaging of the Heart. Topics Also Include Patient Positioning, Image Quality Control, & Illustrations of the Gross Anatomy of the Heart As Seen by Nuclear Imaging.
Yale Univ., Schl. of Medicine, Ctr. for Advanced Instructional Media.

Atlas Pro: For DOS. Version: 2.1. 1993. *Items Included:* Documentation, starter kit of boundary & data files, tutorial. *Customer Support:* Free unlimited telephone support with return of registration card. Custom Application work available - call for more information.
DOS 3.0 or higher. IBM PC compatible (2Mb). disk $795.00. *Nonstandard peripherals required:* EGA graphics card & monitor, mouse. *Optimal configuration:* 80286 or higher CPU, VGA graphics, 40Mb hard disk. *Networks supported:* LAN compatible.
Geographic Data Analysis & Presentation Software Program. Built-In Geographic Database Manager & Extensive Map Creator & Layout Tools for Performing Analysis & Designing a Wide Variety of Presentation Maps.
Strategic Mapping, Inc.

Atlas Pro: For Macintosh. Version: 1.5. 1993. *Items Included:* Documentation, starter kit of boundary and data files, tutorial. *Customer Support:* Free unlimited telephone support with return of registration card. Custom application work avaliable - call for more information.
System 6.05 or higher, Apple Macintosh. Apple Macintosh (1Mb for 6.05 or higher 2Mb for System 7.0). 3.5" disk $795.00. *Networks supported:* Apple.
Program for Managing, Presenting & Publishing Geographic Information. Completely System 7.0 "Savvy". Combines Data Management & Analysis Capabilities with Sophisticated Presentation Mapping.
Strategic Mapping, Inc.

ATLIS/PC. Jun. 1987. *Compatible Hardware:* IBM PC XT, PC AT. *Operating System(s) Required:* MS-DOS 3.2. *Memory Required:* 640k. *General Requirements:* Hard disk.
$4995.00.
Complete Microbased Litigation Support System. The Software Combines a Custom On-Line Inputting System & a Search & Retrieval Package Which Provides Full Text & Abstracted Data Searching & Reporting. Volume Discounts Apply.
Atlis Systems, Inc.

ATP: CODE FREE TYPESETTING

ATM: A Technical Overview. Sep. 1994. *Items Included:* User manual. *Customer Support:* Free technical support & a 30-day warranty (1-800-521-CORE).
MS-DOS. IBM & compatibles (512k). 3.5" disk $199.00 (ISBN 1-57305-005-9). *Nonstandard peripherals required:* High-density 3.5" disk drive; VGA color monitor. *Addl. software required:* MS-DOS version 3.3 or higher. *Optimal configuration:* IBM (512k), MS-DOS version 3.3 or higher, VGA color monitor, keyboard, Microsoft compatible mouse (optional).
A Computer-Based Training Program (CBT) Course That Describes How ATM Meets the Challenges of the Increasing Demands of Information Processing. This Training Package Explains the Evolution of the Information Processing Environment, the Basics of Cell Relay Technology & How ATM Uses That Technology, & the Capabilities of ATM Compared to Alternatives.
Bellcore.

ATM, F-R, SMDS: An Applications Overview. Dec. 1994. *Items Included:* User manual. *Customer Support:* Free technical support & a 30-day warranty (1-800-521-CORE).
MS-DOS. IBM & compatibles (512k). 3.5" disk $199.00 (ISBN 1-57305-008-3). *Nonstandard peripherals required:* High-density 3.5" disk drive; VGA color monitor. *Addl. software required:* MS-DOS version 3.3 or higher. *Optimal configuration:* IBM (512k), MS-DOS version 3.3 or higher, VGA color monitor, keyboard, Microsoft compatible mouse (optional).
This Course Begins with an Overview of the Capabilities & Characteristics of the Underlying Technologies & Services of ATM, Frame Relay, & SMDS. Then, Generic Advantages of These Networks Versus Traditional Networks Are Examined. Specific Horizontal Applications Are Explained, Beginning with the Support for LAN Internetowrking & the Support of Traditional "Legacy" Networks. This Is Followed by a Discussion of Emerging Imaging, Voice, & Video Applications. Finally, Information Is Presented Concerning the Availability of Products & Services.
Bellcore.

ATM Local Area Networks: An Overview. Dec. 1994. *Items Included:* User manual. *Customer Support:* Free technical support & a 30-day warranty (1-800-521-CORE).
MS-DOS. IBM & compatibles (512k). 3.5" disk $199.00 (ISBN 1-57305-015-6). *Nonstandard peripherals required:* High-density 3.5" disk drive; VGA color monitor. *Addl. software required:* MS-DOS version 3.3 or higher. *Optimal configuration:* IBM (512k), MS-DOS version 3.3 or higher, VGA color monitor, keyboard, Microsoft compatible mouse (optional).
This Course Begins with an Explanation of How ATM LANs Work with a Description of Their Components & Characteristics. Then, the Benefits of Utilizing ATM LANs Are Explored. Next, ATM LANs Are Compared with Other LAN Technologies & Possibilities for Interworking with These Other Technologies Are Explained. Finally, Similarities & Differences with ATM WANs Are Discussed.
Bellcore.

atp: Code Free Typesetting. Ron Laroche & Debborah Knotts. Nov. 1985. *Compatible Hardware:* IBM PC & compatibles.
disk $550.00.
Process for Preparing Manuscript for Typesetting on Normal Word Processing or PC Equipment Without the Insertion of Visible Typesetting

ATS Maintenance Management Systems.
Codes. Discs Containing Clean Copy, but Prepared Using "atp" Conventions, Are Then Sent to George Lithograph for Typesetting or the Copy Is Telecommunicated. Proofs Are Returned Overnight for Revision, or Telecommunicated Back Immediately on a Laser Printer.
George Lithograph, Graphics Div.

ATS Maintenance Management Systems. Version: 7.4. Feb. 1988. *Compatible Hardware:* IBM PC & compatibles. *Operating System(s) Required:* MS-DOS. *Language(s):* BASIC & C. *Memory Required:* 256k. *General Requirements:* Hard disk, printer, modem. Color monitor recommended. Add'l. RAM needed for network systems. Backup system required.
$9500.00.
Full Turnkey Maintenance Management System. Featuring P.M. & Open Order Scheduling, Labor Forecasting, Machine History, Comprehensive Reporting, Browse, Help Features & Look-Up Windows. Modules Such As Machine Breakdowns, Manpower Resources, Trend Analysis, Material/Labor Update, Machine Parts, Data Export & Spare Parts Inventory System Available Separately.
Auto Tell Services, Inc.

ATS SPI System: Spare Parts Inventory Control. Version: 5.3. Nov. 1988. *Compatible Hardware:* IBM PC & compatibles. *Operating System(s) Required:* MS-DOS. *Language(s):* BASIC & C. *Memory Required:* 256k. *General Requirements:* Hard disk, printer, modem. Color monitor recommended. Add'l. RAM needed for network systems. Backup system required.
$9500.00.
Full Turnkey Spare Parts Inventory System. Featuring Inventory Control, Multi Storeroom Capability, Comprehensive Reporting, Browse, Help Features & Look up Windows. Modules Such As Material/Labor Update, Purchasing, Physical Inventory, Machine Parts & Our Maintenance Management System Available Separately.
Auto Tell Services, Inc.

The Attack. *Compatible Hardware:* TI 99/4A.
contact publisher for price (Order no.: PHM 3031).
Maneuver Your Ships to Avoid the Aliens & Fire Missiles to Destroy the Enemy.
Texas Instruments, Personal Productivit.

Attendance. *Compatible Hardware:* IBM PC; TRS-80 Model II, Model III, Model 4, Model 12, Model 16; Tandy 2000.
contact publisher for price.
Maintains Attendance Record for up to 160 Functions. Gives Church Functions in Chronological or Attendance Order, Gives Grand Totals & Percentage Attendance, & Attendance Record by Individual, Using Church Donations Data Base.
Custom Data (New Mexico).

Attitude for Success. Crisp Publications. Nov. 1995. *Items Included:* Manual, registration card, one CD-ROM disk, product catalog, product brochure, America Online user card. *Customer Support:* Free technical support allows users to call support technicians anytime between 8:00am to 5:00pm Pacific Standard Time Monday through Friday.
Windows 3.1, Windows 95 or higher. 486 33MHz PC or higher (8Mb). CD-ROM disk $49.95 (ISBN 1-888226-03-X). *Nonstandard peripherals required:* Double speed CD-ROM drive, SVGA, mouse, 8 bit sound card. *Optimal configuration:* 486 33MHz PC or higher, double speed CD-ROM drive, SVGA, mouse, 16Mb RAM, 16 bit sound card.
A CD-ROM Based Software Product That Provides Life-Changing Attitude Adjustment Techniques & Tips for Self-Improvement.
Midisoft Corp.

Attitude Scales. 1986. *Compatible Hardware:* IBM PC & compatibles. *Operating System(s) Required:* PC-DOS/MS-DOS. *Memory Required:* 128k. *General Requirements:* Joystick recommended but not required. *Items Included:* Disk, instructions.
disk $19.95 (ISBN 0-926152-57-2).
Designed to Record Scaled Responses to Questions or Statements As Commonly Used in Marketing or Opinion Survey Research.
Persimmon Software.

Attorney's Trust Accounting: ATAS. Version: TAS 3.0.1. 1983. *Compatible Hardware:* IBM PC & compatibles. *Operating System(s) Required:* PC-DOS. *Language(s):* MicroFocus COBOL. *Memory Required:* 512k. *General Requirements:* Hard disk, 80-column printer or laser. *Items Included:* Disks, manuals, 90 days of support. *Customer Support:* Direct from Morningstar.
$295.00 single-user; $395.00 multi-user.
demo disk $50.00.
Provides the Legal Firm with Audit Trails of Client Trust Accounts. Designed for Firms Dealing with Real Estate Closings, Collections Work or Bankruptcies, As Well As General Practice. Prints Checks, Ledgers, & Bank Reconciliations, Integrates to General Ledger & Time Accounting & Billing.
Morningstar Technology Corp.

ATV2: Real Estate Valuation Software. 1983. *Compatible Hardware:* IBM PC & compatibles. *Memory Required:* 512k. *General Requirements:* Hard disk, printer.
contact publisher for price.
Valusoft, Inc.

A2B: AutoCAD to BMP Interface System. Version: 11.0. Apr. 1986. *Compatible Hardware:* IBM PC. *Operating System(s) Required:* MS-DOS. *Language(s):* C-BASIC. *Memory Required:* 128k. *General Requirements:* Hard disk, printer. *Customer Support:* 1 year free telephone support.
disk $295.00.
Uitlizes AutoCAD's Attribute Definition & Extract Features to Generate Bills of Material (Single-Level or Indented, Costed or Uncosted) Directly from the User's AutoCAD Drawing Files. A2B Will Also Automatically Add a Bill of Materials to the BMP Data Base, Saving Much Data Entry Time. In Addition, the Simplicity of A2B's Interface File Makes It Compatible with a Wide Variety of Other Micro-Based CAD Systems.
Alliance Manufacturing Software.

The AUCTIONEER. Version: 1.4. 1995. *Items Included:* Manual. *Customer Support:* 90-days free phone support, $25.00 per call after.
MS-DOS. IBM PC & compatibles (2Mb). disk $99.00.
Simplifies the Process of Running a Live or Silent Auction While Allowing You Total Control of All Functions of the Auction for Non-Profit Organizations. Provides Printed Receipts & Reduces the Time Required to Pay for & Collect Items. Maintains Record of Each Item Available for Sale Including Description, Donor, Value & Minimum Bid; a Record of Each Bidder's Name & Address; a Record of Each Bidder's Purchases, the Price Paid for Each Item, & Their Actual Cash Payment. Prints: Bill for Bidder W/Without Payment Indication; of Bidder's & Their Purchases; of Sales by Item & Includes Price Paid, Includes Unsold Items. User May Create a Text File of Items Which Can Be Input into a Word Processing or Spread Sheet Program.
Taranto & Assocs., Inc.

AuData Business Turbine PC Package. Version: 1.1. *Items Included:* Operater's manual. *Customer Support:* Phone-in assistance available; on-site training available.
MS-DOS. IBM compatible (640k). write for info. *Optimal configuration:* 286 or higher; DOS 3.3; 640k RAM; 80Mb hard drive.
Displays the Name & Address of Every Operator of Business Jets & Turboprops Worldwide. Additional Data Includes the Aircraft Make, Model & Serial Number, the Date of Purchase, Year of Manufacture & a Field for Operator-Entered Comments.
Aviation Data Service, Inc.

Audio Mirror for SoundBlaster. G. David Peters. *Customer Support:* 90 day warranty against defective software.
IBM 386/468 (2Mb). disk $79.95 (Order no.: I-1441). *Nonstandard peripherals required:* Hard drive, SoundBlaster (or compatible) sound card, VGA or SVGA monitor, microphone.
Allows You to Practice Singing & Matching Pitches Using the Latest in Technology. Audio Mirror "Listens" to Notes in Real-Time & Determines Not Only the Note Being Sung, but How Sharp or Flat the Note Is in Cents. The User Can Set the Sensitivity of the Program to Compensate for Various MIC Level Inputs & Impedances, Plus Record Keeping Is Included So Progress Can Be Tracked & Performance Evaluated.
Electronic Courseware Systems, Inc.

Manager Series Audio/Visual Handler Module: Manager Series Library Automation System. Version: 4.0. 1992. *Compatible Hardware:* IBM PC & compatibles. *General Requirements:* One floppy & one hard disk, printer. *Items Included:* Floppy disk, tutorial manual. *Customer Support:* Turn-key vendor: hardware, peripherals, hardware/software support contracts, toll-free phone & Internet access to product support, installations, training, user groups, technical newsletter.
IBM. 3.5" or 5.25" disk, Business/Professional $2450.00; School discount, multiple purchase discounts & GSA pricing available (ISBN 0-929795-05-9). *Networks supported:* Novell, Banyan, 3COM, IBM, LANtastic, PathWorks, Windows NT, NetWare.
Integrated, Menu-Driven System That Ties Together Six Major Media Center Functions. These Include Rental Film Control, Vendor File Control, Booking File Control, Facilities Management, Media Cataloging, & Inventory File Control. Other Features Include a Booking Calendar, Thorough Searching Tools, Equipment, Label Printing & a Variety of Reports, Including Vendor Utilization, Media Activity, User Activities & Order Summary.
Data Trek, Inc.

Audiomedia 2. *Items Included:* 1 spiral bound manual, Sound Designer II software, NuBus card. *Customer Support:* Free telephone technical support.
Macintosh II, IIx, IIcx, IIci, IIfx; Quadra. 3.5" disk $1295.00.
Allows User to Record CD Quality Sound for Audio Production & Multimedia Presentations. Plays Directly from User's Hard Disk - a CD Quality Soundtrack Uses Only 50k of RAM & Loads Instantly, Allowing the Majority of Computer's RAM to Be Dedicated to Visuals.
Digidesign, Inc.

AUDIT. Version: 2.0. Jan. 1988. *Compatible Hardware:* IBM PC, PC XT, PC AT & compatibles. *Memory Required:* 256k.
3.5" or 5.25" disk $395.00.
Elite Software Development, Inc.

AUDIT: Background User Session Monitoring. Version: 4.0A. 1990. *Compatible Hardware:* DEC Micro VAX & VAX. *Operating System(s)*

Required: VMS, MICROVMS 4.6 or higher. *Language(s):* Basic. *Memory Required:* 3k per on-line user plus 100k. *Items Included:* 1 year maintenance, quarterly newsletter. *Customer Support:* 30 days free.
$1242.00-$17,714.00 quantity & cluster discounts; site licensing.
Records Terminal I/O Activity & Analyzes User Session/Operator Logs. It's Useful for Pinpointing & Correcting Troublesome Application Errors. It Can Monitor Specific User Accounts, Such As Operator Accounts & Those with Privileged Access to the System. Uses Less Than 3 Percent of the CPU Resource, Even When Monitoring All Terminals. It Provides Necessary Raw Data for Security Analysis & Evidence.
Raxco, Inc.

Audit Program Generator. *Version:* 2.02. Dec. 1989. *Items Included:* 1 wiro-bound manual. *Customer Support:* Free for the first 3 months; $95 annual fee after that.
 DOS 3.1 or higher. 100% IBM compatible PC (490k). disk $295.00 nonmember; $265.50 AICPA member. *Optimal configuration:* 100% IBM compatible PC, DOS 3.1 or higher, 640k RAM, printer capable of printing condensed or compressed.
Word Processing Program That Allows User to Create or Edit Checklists. APG Automatically Renumbers Existing Steps When You Delete or Add a Step. APG Keeps Track of Sign-Off Columns So User Can Concentrate on Editing & Not Worry about Line Wrapping. Comes With an Audit Program Ready to Be Tailored to Your Clients Needs.
American Institute of Certified Public Accountants.

AUDIT: Residential Energy Analysis. *Items Included:* Manual. *Customer Support:* Free toll free telephone support.
 IBM PC & compatibles (256k). disk $395.00.
Calculates Annual Heating & Cooling Costs for Residential & Light Commercial Buildings. Follows Exact ACCA Manual J Calculation Procedures. Virtually Any Type of Cooling & Heating System Can Be Simulated by AUDIT Including Standard DX, Evaporative, Air Source Heat Pumps, Water Source Heat Pumps, & All Types of Fossil Fueled Furnaces & Boilers.
Elite Software Development, Inc.

AuditCube. Robert C. Coffey. Jun. 1987. *Operating System(s) Required:* MS-DOS, PC-DOS. *Memory Required:* 640k. *General Requirements:* Hard disk, printer.
disk $2000.00.
Microcomputer Auditing System That Turns the Computer into an Electronic Audit Binder.
Blackman, Kallick, Bartelstein, Certified Public Accountants/Consulting.

Aura CAD/CAM. *Version:* 2.52 II. *Compatible Hardware:* Apple Macintosh. *Memory Required:* 1000k. *Items Included:* 2 days on-site training, 4 days off-site training. *Customer Support:* Technical phone support.
CAD only black & white, $999.00.
CAD only color, $1399.00.
CAD/CAM with one module $7000.00.
Additional modules $1000.00.
CAD Program for Architecture Featuring Symbols Library, Macro Facilities, Text Editor, On-Line Help & Area Calculation. Links Provided to Spreadsheet Data via Macro Language. Imports & Exports IGES & .DXF File Formats. Technical Phone Support Available.
aura CAD-CAM, Inc.

Aural Skills Trainer. Vincent Oddo. *Customer Support:* 90 day warranty against defective software.
 System 6.0.4 - 7.1. Macintosh (1Mb). 3.5" disk $99.95 (Order no.: MAC-1101). *Optimal configuration:* Apple external MIDI interface - MIDI compatible keyboard.
 DOS 3.3 or higher. IBM (640k). disk $99.95 (Order no.: I-1101). *Nonstandard peripherals required:* CGA display minimum.
 DOS 3.3. Apple II (48k). disk $99.95 (Order no.: A-1101).
Designed to Improve a Music Student's Ability to Perceive & Identify Intervals, Basic Chords, & Seventh Chords. These Programs Keep Student Records Including Diagnostic Information, Progress Reports, & Completion Scores.
Electronic Courseware Systems, Inc.

Author's Aid. *Customer Support:* 800-929-8117 (customer service).
 MS-DOS. IBM/PS2. disk $99.99 (ISBN 0-87007-291-9).
This Program Stores Information about Where to Locate Research Material, One That Converts Sizes of Illustrations, One That Converts Typed Copy to Printed Copy & One That Simplifies the Task of Writing Captions for Illustrations.
SourceView Software International.

Author's Guide to Journals in the Behavioral Sciences. Alvin Wang. 1989. *Customer Support:* 90 days limited warranty.
 MS-DOS. IBM or compatibles (640k). disk $49.95 (ISBN 1-56321-054-1).
3.5" disk $49.95 (ISBN 1-56321-053-3).
$24.95 paper text (ISBN 0-8058-0313-0).
This Computerized Reference Guide Provides the Most Current & Readily Accessible Information about Editorial Policies for Periodicals of Interest to Psychologists & Other Behavioral Scientists.
Lawrence Erlbaum Assocs. Software & Alternate Media, Inc.

Authorware. *Version:* 2.0. *Items Included:* Manuals. *Customer Support:* Registered owners get first 90 days free phone support, fax & online support. Call Macromedia for information about Priority Access support.
 System 7.X. Macintosh (4-8Mb RAM). 3.5" disk $4995.00. *Optimal configuration:* Mac II w/ 2Mb RAM (w/System 6.0.7) 4Mb RAM (w/ System 7.X).
 Windows 3.0 or higher, 1 DOS 3.3 or higher. IBM & compatibles (4-8Mb). disk $4995.00. *Optimal configuration:* 20 MHz 386 w/4Mb RAM, 16-color VGA, 40Mb hard disk & a mouse. 33 plus MHz w/8Mb RAM recommended.
Authorware's Built-In Interactivity, Data-Measurement Functions, & Media-Integration Controls Bring the Power of Multimedia to Educators, Corporate Trainers, & Developers. Authorware's Iconic Authoring Makes Complex Applications Easy to Develop. Its Extensive Variables & Functions Provide the Basis for Collecting, Storing & Analyzing Data; Built-In Computer Managed Instruction (CMI) Variables Make It Easy to Manage Performance & Data.
Macromedia, Inc.

Auto-AOC: Automated Advanced Office Controls. *Version:* 2.1. *Compatible Hardware:* IBM PC. *Operating System(s) Required:* DOS. *Language(s):* COBOL. *Memory Required:* 128k. *Customer Support:* Telephone support.
$10,000.00.
Used to Establish Work Measurement Standards for Office Clerical or Technical Activities.
Robert E. Nolan Co., Inc.

Auto-Exec: Accounts Receivable. Cyber Enterprises. *Compatible Hardware:* TRS-80 Model I, Model III, Model 4. *General Requirements:* 2 or 4 disk drives, single- or double-density, with 35, 40, 77 or 80 tracks.
disk $149.95.
Handles 200 to 1400 Customers & 1150 to 8300 Transactions Between Cycles. May Be Run with or Without AUTO-EXEC GENERAL LEDGER.
Blue Cat.

Auto-Exec: General Ledger. Cyber Enterprises. *Compatible Hardware:* TRS-80 Model I, Model III, Model 4. *General Requirements:* 2 or 4 disk drives.
disk $149.95.
Accommodates 200 to 300 General Ledger Accounts & 2 Journals with 600 to 1800 Entries Between Cycles. Can Be Run with or Without AUTO-EXEC ACCOUNTS RECEIVABLE.
Blue Cat.

AUTO-GRAPH. *Compatible Hardware:* TRS-80 Model I, Model III.
contact publisher for price.
Modtec, Software Div.

Auto Insurance. Duane Bristow. *Compatible Hardware:* TRS-80 Model I, Model III. *Operating System(s) Required:* TRSDOS. *Language(s):* BASIC. *General Requirements:* Line printer.
disk $195.95.
Rating Program for Independent Insurance Agents. Custom Designs Auto Insurance for Clients with up to 4 Vehicles.
Duane Bristow Computers, Inc.

Auto-Intelligence. *Customer Support:* Free on-line tech support.
 IBM PC & compatibles. 3.5" or 5.25" disk $490.00. *Nonstandard peripherals required:* Hard disk (20Mb); CGA or EGA.
Automates Learning Task by Interactively Interviewing a Human Expert & Generates Rules in a Variety of Formats. Interview Process Helps Expert Clarify His Own Knowledge.
IntelligenceWare, Inc.

Auto Journal System: Cash Flow Analyzer. Oct. 1986. *Compatible Hardware:* IBM PC. *Operating System(s) Required:* PC-DOS 3.1. *Memory Required:* 256k. *General Requirements:* Printer.
contact publisher for price.
Online Interactive Account System Designed for Journalizing Transactions of Multiple Bank Accounts & Analyzing Actual Cash Flow. Online Functions for Maintaining the Database of Bank Account Journals Include: Adding, Changing & Deleting Accounts, Receipts & Disbursements. Features Password Protection, Automatic Error Detection, & Correction Capabilities. Cash Flow Analysis Includes the Account Balance for Each Transaction with: Average Daily Balance, Average Daily Receipts, Average Daily Disbursement, & the Average Receipt & Disbursement.
Automatronics.

Auto-Laws-Automatic Legal, Administrative Word Processing System. *Compatible Hardware:* IBM PC, PC XT. *Operating System(s) Required:* MS-DOS. *Language(s):* BASIC. *Memory Required:* 256k. *General Requirements:* 2 disk drives, hard disk, printer. *Customer Support:* Mon-Fri EST 9:00AM-5:00PM, Modem support & on-site.
contact publisher for price.
demo $50.00.
Allows Data to Be Processed by Client, Lawyer & Activity. Features Time & Billing Which Allows Input of Time Sheets, Produces Bills, Produces a Billable Report, Reports Attorney's Expenses, Shows Profitability & Documents Caseloads. The Calendar Management/Docket Control Does Automatic Scheduling, Groups Dates & Appearances & Avoids Data Conflicts. The Diary Uses an Internal Clock to Alert the Attorney to Future Deadlines & Provides Check-Off Lists. The

Word Processor Handles All Aspects of Text Management, Utilizing the Database for Stored Information. Full Financials Are Provided.
M&C Systems, Inc.

Auto Mac. *Version:* 1.2. PC Consulting. 1984. *Compatible Hardware:* IBM PC. *Operating System(s) Required:* PC-DOS 1.0 or higher. *Memory Required:* 192k. *General Requirements:* 2 disk drives, Lotus 1-2-3.
disk $49.95.
Create LOTUS 1-2-3 Keyboard Macros. Keystroke Sequences Can Be Saved As You Run 1-2-3 & Then Later Be Output As Macros Automatically. Also Provides a "Quick Write" Mode to Speed up the Manual Writing of Keyboard Macros by Automatically Converting Special Keys to Its Proper LOTUS Macro Format.
DataSource Publishing Co.

Auto-Nutritionist IV. *Version:* 4.0. Jun. 1995. *Items Included:* User's manual. *Customer Support:* Included with purchase.
Windows 3.1 or Windows for Workgroups 3.11. 386 (4Mb). disk $495.00. *Addl. software required:* DOS 5.0 with Windows 3.1 or WG 3.11.
Assists in Menu Creation Based on Diet Requirements & Restrictions. Automatically Generate Menus for One or More Days, Allowing the Software to Choose Foods from the Database of 500 Plus Specially Coded Foods & Recipes or Design Menus Manually.
First DataBank.

Auto-Nutritionist IV. *Version:* 4.1. Jun. 1996. *Items Included:* User's manual. *Customer Support:* Included with purchase.
Windows 3.1 or Windows for Workgroups 3.11 or Windows 95. 386 (4Mb). disk $495.00. *Addl. software required:* DOS 5.0 with Windows 3.1 or WG 3.11.
Assists in Menu Creation Based on Diet Requirements & Restrictions. Automatically Generate Menus for One or More Days, Allowing the Software to Choose Foods from the Database of 500 Plus Specially Coded Foods & Recipes or Design Menus Manually.
First DataBank.

Auto Proofing System: Cash Flow Analyzer.
Oct. 1986. *Compatible Hardware:* IBM PC. *Operating System(s) Required:* PC-DOS 3.1. *Memory Required:* 256k.
contact publisher for price.
Online Interactive Accounting System Designed for Consolidating & Proofing Multiple Bank Account Statements & Analyzing Actual Cash Flow. Online Functions for Maintaining the Database of Statements & Transactions Include: Adding, Changing & Deleting Statements, Receipts & Disbursements. Features Password Protection, Extensive Error Detection & Correction Capabilities. Cash Flow Analysis Includes: Account Balance for Each Transaction with Average Daily Balance, Average Daily Receipts, Average Daily Disbursements, & the Average Receipt & Disbursement.
Automatronics.

AutoBASE. Nov. 1985. *Compatible Hardware:* IBM PC & compatibles. *Memory Required:* 512k. *General Requirements:* AutoCAD & dBASE III.
disk $295.00.
Complete Menu-Driven Program Allowing Users to Extract & Manage Drawing Information Using dBASE under Menu Control. Creates a Direct AutoCAD to dBASE Link, Enhances dBASE by Making It Easier to Use. Allows Users to Create Their Own Attribute Definitions, Updating AutoCAD & Automatically Building dBASE Files.
Sensible Designs.

Autobox. *Version:* 3.0. Mar. 1993. *Compatible Hardware:* IBM PC & compatibles. *Operating System(s) Required:* MS-DOS, PC-DOS. *Language(s):* FORTRAN IV. *Memory Required:* 550k. *General Requirements:* 2 disk drives.
disk $395.00 (ISBN 0-928400-03-4).
Short-Term Forecasting Tool Which Can Be Used to Build Models Either Automatically or Not, & Automatically Build Box-Jenkins Models. Includes Automatic Univariate, Transfer Function & Intervention Modeling. Common Applications Include Forecasting Sales, Interest Rates, Cash Flow, Inventory Levels, Economic Indicators & Utility Demand.
Automatic Forecasting Systems, Inc.

AutoCAD. *Version:* 10. 1982. *Compatible Hardware:* Apple Macintosh II; IBM PC, PS/2 & compatibles; DEC VAX Station 2000, GPX; Apollo Domain Series; Sun Microsystems-2, -3, 386i; Compaq 386. *Operating System(s) Required:* PC-DOS/MS-DOS 3.0 or higher; Sun OS; DEC VMS; Apollo Aegis; Mac OS. *Language(s):* C. *Memory Required:* 640k. *General Requirements:* Hard disk. IBM requires graphics card & 8087/80287 coprocessor. *Items Included:* Reference manual, tutorial, digitizer template. *Customer Support:* Authorized dealer.
$3000.00, incl. user's manual, reference guide, programmer's reference to AutoLISP, & audio tape tutorial.
French, German, Italian, Kanji, Spanish, Swedish, & Russian editions avail.
IBM PC. (ISBN 0-922414-59-9).
IBM PS/2. (ISBN 0-922414-61-0).
Design & Drafting Software for Desktop Computers & Workstations. Useful in Environments Such As Architecture, Engineering, Facilities Management, Manufacturing, & Surveying. Three of Its Main Features Are: Open Architecture; an Integrated High-Level Programming Language, AutoLISP; & the Autodesk Device Interface (ADI) Used to Configure AutoCAD to Operate with a Wide Variety of Peripherals. Not Copy Protected.
Autodesk, Inc.

AutoCAD-86. Autodesk, Inc. *Compatible Hardware:* TI Professional. *Operating System(s) Required:* CP/M-86, MS-DOS, MS-DOS 2.1. *Memory Required:* 256k.
TI version. $1000.00.
2-Dimensional Computer Aided Drafting & Design System.
Texas Instruments, Personal Productivit.

AutoCAD Reference Guide Disk: 2nd Edition.
Aug. 1990.
IBM PC & compatibles. disk $14.95 (ISBN 0-934035-84-9).
Companion Support Disk for the Book, AutoCAD Reference Guide Updated/Revised for Release II. Contains Commands Featured in the Book.
New Riders Publishing.

AUTOCAST. *Version:* 3.0. 1990. *Compatible Hardware:* IBM PC & compatibles. *Operating System(s) Required:* MS-DOS. *Language(s):* Compiled BASIC. *Memory Required:* 100k. *General Requirements:* Printer. *Items Included:* Disk & documentation. *Customer Support:* Phone inquiry.
$395.00.
Automated Character Count & Book Length Adjustment for Modern Typesetting Options.
Autospec, Inc.

AUTOCAST II- Expert Forecasting. *Version:* 1.6. E. S. Gardner, Jr. Jul. 1991. *Items Included:* 160-page manual with examples & technical documentation. *Customer Support:* 90 days unlimited warranty, free telephone support, consulting/training on-site available, customized programming.
MS-DOS 2.0 or higher (512k). IBM PC & compatibles. $349.00, batch ,1900.00. *Optimal configuration:* Hard disk, math coprocessor, color graphics card, IBM/EPSON/HP Laserjet printer.
Expert Forecasting System That Automatically Identifies Correct Combination of Trend & Seasonal Cycle in Historical Data, Makes Projections, Identifies & Corrects Extreme Observations & Simulates Forecast Accuracy. Reads from Lotus 1-2-3 & Symphony Worksheets. Includes On-Screen Editor for Data Entry & Correction. Provides Modeling with User Options, Graphical & Laser Printer Output Capabilities. Optional Large Volume Batch Version Available.
Delphus, Inc.

AUTOCAST II/BATCH: Volume Forecasting. *Version:* 1.01. E. S. Gardner, Jr. Jul. 1991. *Items Included:* 10 page user's manual with tutorials example. *Customer Support:* 1 year unlimited warranty, free telephone support 8 AM-6 PM EST, customized programming services, training services on forecasting.
MS-DOS 2.0 & higher. IBM PC & compatibles (640k). disk $1900.00. *Optimal configuration:* IBM PC/AT/386/486 & compatibles, 640k, hard disk, graphics cards (EGA/VGA), math coprocessor (optional).
AUTOCAST II/BATCH Is an Expert Forecasting System for Large Volume Users. Using Expert System Logic, the System Identifies the Best Statistical Model from a Selection of Nine Alternative Specification for Each Item Forecasted. The Program Reads LOTUS 1-2-3 Worksheets & a Wide Variety of ASCII Formats. Features of the System Include (1) Interactive AUTOCAST II Version Is Fully Integrated, (2) Program Can Run from Menu Operation or With Command Line Option. Module for Modeling With Inventory Management Options Is Also Available.
Delphus, Inc.

AutoCIVIL. *Version:* 7.0. May 1995. *Compatible Hardware:* IBM PC & compatibles. *Operating System(s) Required:* PC-DOS/MS-DOS, Windows. *Memory Required:* 4000k. *General Requirements:* AutoCAD release 12/386 or higher for DOS, Windows. *Items Included:* Manual, 120-day free maintenance. *Customer Support:* 1 year maintenance for $200.
$995.00 for all 10 modules.
Design & Drafting Program, Runs Interactively Inside AutoCAD. Features Interactive Graphics, Pull down Menus & Icons. MODULES Include AutoCollect, AutoSurvey, & AutoContour, AutoDTM, AutoRoads, AutoTemplate, AutoStorm, AutoSewer, & AutoWater.
Research Engineers.

AutoClerk. *Version:* 2.0B. *Compatible Hardware:* IBM PC & compatibles. *Operating System(s) Required:* SBOS, CBOS, MBOS, BOS/LAN. *Language(s):* BOS COBOL. *Memory Required:* 256k.
Single-User computer. disk $450.00.
Multi-User computer. disk $900.00, incl. documentation.
Single-User computer.
Multi-User computer. training/day $150.00.
manual $20.00.
Program Builder Enables Commercial Programs/Reports to Be Developed.
BOS National, Inc.

Autodesk Multimedia Explorer. 1991. *Items Included:* Reference manual, tutorial. *Customer Support:* 800 number provided.
MS-DOS 3.1 or higher. IBM & compatibles (80286 or higher recommended). disk $199.00

(ISBN 0-922414-94-7).
Combines Three Comprehensive Tools to Get Started with Multimedia: AUTODESK ANIMATOR for Producing Animations at VGA Resolution; ANIMATION CLIPS (on CD-ROM), a Library of Still Images & Animation Clip Art; AUTODESK ANIMATION PLAYER for WINDOWS to Arrange Animation & Graphics into a Final Presentation. Sound Can Be Added with MULTIMEDIA EXTENSIONS to WINDOWS.
Autodesk, Inc.

AutoDialog. *Compatible Hardware:* Apple Macintosh. *Memory Required:* 512k.
3.5" disk $79.00.
Dialog-Manager Interface.
Jam Technologies.

Autodraw. *Version:* 6.03. Sep. 1990. *Customer Support:* 1 year warranty.
MS-DOS. IBM PC (640k). disk $500.00.
  Optimal configuration: 386, 486 with 4Mb RAM. *Networks supported:* Novell.
Architectural Libraries & Autocad Enhancement Tools. (GUI) for Autocad.
AI Systems, Inc.

Autofinance. *Version:* 2200/2201. Jun. 1986. *Compatible Hardware:* Sharp ZL-6500 System. *Language(s):* Sharp Microcode.
$700.00.
Computes Monthly Installment Loans with Odd Days, Downpayments, Trade-Ins, Sales Tax, Credit-Life & Disability Insurance, "After Sales". 4 Roll-Backs Are Provided. Includes Routines That Compute Comparison Fuel Cost, Interest Earned on Cash-Conversion & Dealer Reserve by 6 Different Methods.
P-ROM Software, Inc.

AUTOFLOW. *Version:* 2.0. 1989.
PC/MS-DOS (384k). IBM PC & compatibles. $29.95.
Automatically Generates a Flow Diagram from BASICA Programs. Reads BASICA/GWBASIC Program & Creates Two Optional Structured & Indented Versions - One with Flow Lines to Delimit Conditional Logic & Active Loops; One for Import by QUICKBASIC. In Addition it Produces Line Number, Variable & String Literal Cross-Reference Reports.
Educational Micro Systems, Inc.

Autoform Print Utility. Jan. 1986. *Compatible Hardware:* IBM PC. *Operating System(s) Required:* PC-DOS 3.1. *Memory Required:* 256k.
contact publisher for price.
Programmer Aid Used for Obtaining a Formatted Listing of Program Files. Options Include: Variable Line Numbering & Incrementation, Page-Length Formatting, Tab Replacement with Spaces, Footing Printed on Each Page, Automatic Printing of Processed File, & Display of Statistics for Each File Processed.
Automatronics.

Autogen. *Compatible Hardware:* MSI/85 or MSI/88 HandHeld Computer. *Operating System(s) Required:* TOS. *Language(s):* ADL. *Memory Required:* 8k.
contact publisher for price.
Terminal Program Generator. Includes: Standard Data Key Handling, Standard Data Edits, Multiple Accumulators, Program Source, High Speed Search, Record Chaining, Wand Scanning Codes & Supports 1-Way Communication.
MSI Data Corp.

Automan. Jun. 1995. *Items Included:* User Manual on disk. *Customer Support:* 90 Days.
  DOS 3.1 or higher. 286 or higher. disk $499.95 (ISBN 0-933735-01-4). *Networks supported:* All that Clarion Supports.
A Program for Tracking Auto Service & Expenses.
Tin Man Software.

Automated Cognitive Rehabilitation Laboratory: ACRe Lab. Robert Geeslin & Richard Bost. Sep. 1993. *Items Included:* Home-based laboratory consists of a 386 & VGA (with sound & voice command, alternative input devices optional). Clinical laboratory adds hard disk storage as required. Modem. Access to software library. Complete manualization. Full graphical, clinical reports. *Customer Support:* Full day of training at the College (please contact for CME credit). On-line access to the ACRe Lab Administration Host, telephone support, patient referrals may occasionally be accepted. Contact OSU-COM Dept. of Psychiatry & Behavioral Science for costs, other details.
Supplied. Both satelight & home-based units are supplied. Contact Dr. Bost or Dr. Geeslin to discuss your patients' needs. *Optimal configuration:* Must use supplied hardware/software.
System for Automating Many of the Cognitive Rehabilitation Exercises That Have Heretofore Been Handled Only in Face-to-Face Therapy with Resulting Improvement in Costs, Convenience, Compliance, & Accuracy of Both Administration & Scoring. Both Hardware & Software Are Supplied, & Both Are Tailored for the Patient's Needs. A "Lending Library" of Configurable Software Is Available for All Levels of Recovery from Awareness to Problem-Solving. Typically, the Patient Works at Home Twice a Day for 6 Days a Week & Sees the Therapist Once, a Big Improvement over Non-Automated Therapy. Progress Is Reported Automatically & Graphical, Comparative Reports Are Generated for the Clinician. Developed by a Neuropsychologist for Use with His Own Patients Because Other Offerings Were Not Complete or Did Not Offer a Depth of Practice in Some Areas.
Oklahoma State University College of Osteopathic Medicine.

Automated Document Tracking System. Aug. 1994. *Items Included:* Documentation manuals. *Customer Support:* Modem support 9:00AM to 5:00PM EST Monday-Friday - $85.00/hr. or part thereof. On-site support available at same rate within 50 miles otherwise expenses charged for support person.
MS-DOS. IBM PC & compatibles (1Mb). Contact publisher for price. *Addl. software required:* Bridge.Net Data Collection Management software. *Optimal configuration:* 386/486 PC, MS-DOS, 1Mb RAM minimum, Bridge.Net scanners & barcode reading equipment. *Networks supported:* Novell Netware.
Provides the Ability to Record & Track Flow of Documents from Central Filing Dept. to Each Individual's Desk & Back to Central Filing. Each Movement Date & Time Stamped & Stations ID Number. Who It Was Sent to & Where It Was Sent. Ability to Locate Document by Number from Any Terminal. Comprehensive Management Reports; Volume of Files in Flow; Number of Files at a Particular Station; an Individual File's Elapsed Time on a Desk; Noting When a File Skipped an Assigned Movement; Historical Analysis.
M&C Systems, Inc.

Automated Infection Control II. Robert Chalice. 1989. *Compatible Hardware:* IBM PC & compatibles. *Operating System(s) Required:* MS-DOS, PC-DOS. *Language(s):* PASCAL (source code included). *Memory Required:* 640k. *Items Included:* Tutorial manual & program diskettes. *Customer Support:* Hotline.
disk $1595.00.
Reports Numbers of Hospital Infections by Causative Organism, by Site, by Service, & by Physician. Automatically Produces 5 Reports & 5 Graphs Required by Infection Control Personnel. Features Menus & On-Screen Forms.
MIPS, Inc.

Automated Nurse Staffing. Robert Chalice. 1985. *Compatible Hardware:* IBM PC & compatibles, PC XT, PC AT. *Operating System(s) Required:* PC-DOS/MS-DOS 2.0 or higher. *Language(s):* Compiled BASIC. *Memory Required:* 192k. *Items Included:* Tutorial manual, program diskettes, installation. *Customer Support:* Hotline.
Automated Nurse Staffing. disk $6800.00.
Add-On Graphics Module. disk $1495.00.
Add-On Extended Management Reporting Module. disk $1495.00.
Staffs Each Hospital Nursing Unit Based upon Patient Census or Acuity. Monitors Nursing Staff Utilization Through Daily & Cumulative Management Reports. Numerous Graphs Plainly Show Trends. Requires 2 Hours Training & No Additional Staff to Operate. Can Save up to 10% of the Nursing Budget Annually Through More Objective Staffing.
MIPS, Inc.

Automated Social History, Automated Social History II. Joseph Waldron. 1984-1986. *Compatible Hardware:* Apple IIe; IBM PC; TRS-80 Model I, Model II, Model III, Model 4, Model 12, Model 16. *Operating System(s) Required:* MS-DOS, CP/M. *Memory Required:* 64-120k.
disk $395.00 ea.
ASH. (ISBN 0-87084-050-9).
ASH II. (ISBN 0-87084-337-0).
Produces Narrative Social History Reports Covering Most Important Areas of Subject's Social & Personal Functioning. Covers Thirteen Areas: Religious, Family, Education, Sexual, Military, Employment, Criminal, Alcohol/Drug Abuse, Marital, Parental, Personality, Interests & Medical Histories. ASH II Is an Enhanced Version.
Anderson Publishing Co.

Automatic Filer. *Compatible Hardware:* TI 99/4A. *Operating System(s) Required:* DX-10. *Language(s):* Extended BASIC. *Memory Required:* 48k.
disk or cassette $37.95.
Database Management Program Which Allows Files Containing up to 200 Records & 11 Categories. Performs Multiple Searches Through the Database & Files Can Be Sub-Divided or Combined, Searched for a Keyword or Searched Based on Relational Criteria. Files Can Be Stored on Disk or Cassette, Routed to a Printer or Displayed on the Screen. Categories Can Be Added/Deleted from a File, & the Contents of Any Category Can Be Sorted.
Eastbench Software Products.

Automatic Graphing of Functions. *Compatible Hardware:* TRS-80 Model I Level II, Model III. *Operating System(s) Required:* TRSDOS. *Memory Required:* 16k.
disk $24.95.
Puts the Graphs of Formulas Like $y=f(x)$ or $y=y+f(x)$ on the Screen Display. The X & Y Axes Are Positioned Automatically & the Y Axis Range Can Be Controlled Manually & Automatically.
Modtec, Software Div.

Automax. J. B. Rose. Mar. 1987. *Compatible Hardware:* Data General. *Operating System(s) Required:* RDOS/ICOBOL.
disk $250.00.
Establishes Set-Up for Running RDOS/ICOBOL Reorganization. Creates a Command File Dialogue.
Infodex, Inc.

Automobile Rating & Policy Issuance.
Customer Support: Free on-site training, monthly maintenance/support - $400.00 per month.
MS-DOS. MICRO Based (640k). $12,500.00 software license.
This System Is Designed to Provide Rating & Policy Issuance for Private Passenger & Commercial Auto Business. The System Interfaces with ITC's Accounting System to Provide a Fully Comprehensive Package for the Complete Management of the Automobile Business.
Insurance Technology Consultants.

Automotive Diagnosis. *Compatible Hardware:* Apple II, II+. *Language(s):* Integer BASIC. *Memory Required:* 16k.
disk $19.95 (Order no.: 10035).
Assists User in Diagnosing Most Automobile Problems. Narrows down Problem to Small Number of Highly Probable Causes after User Responds to Some General Questions. Program Does Not Describe Repair Procedures.
Powersoft, Inc.

Automotive Information Management System: AIMS. *Version:* 5.0. 1984. *Compatible Hardware:* IBM PC & compatibles, PC XT, PC AT, PS/2. *Operating System(s) Required:* MS-DOS, PC-DOS. *Language(s):* FORTRAN. *Memory Required:* 640k. *Items Included:* Manual. *Customer Support:* 1 hour per package purchased.
$1875.00.
disk accounts receivable is optional $525.00.
Includes General Ledger, Financial Analysis, Accounts Payable, & Payroll. Allows for Multiple Stores and/or Corporations.
MCC Software (Midwest Computer Ctr. Co.).

AutoPLOT 1. *Version:* 2.23. Richard Morris. Mar. 1990. *Items Included:* Manual. *Customer Support:* Full-time technical support for registered users; 30 day money back, no risk guarantee.
PC, MS-DOS 3.0 or higher. IBM, PS/2, Microchannel or compatibles (18k). disk $99.95.
Invisible Memory Resident Program Designed to Plot AutoCAD Plot Files in the Background While Your Computer is Free to Continue Drawing in the Foreground. Can Hyperspool, Plot Any File Size, Cancel Plot Jobs At Any Time & Only Take 18k of RAM.
Software Machine, Inc.

AutoPLOT 2. *Version:* 2.90. Richard Morris. Mar. 1990. *Items Included:* A manual for installation & use of the software. *Customer Support:* Full-time tech support for registered users, 30 day money back guarantee.
PC, MS-DOS 3.0 or higher. IBM PC & compatibles & PS/2 computers (30k). disk $179.95 (Order no.: AP II). *Networks supported:* Novell, 10net, & any network with a designated plot station.
Allows User to Be in AutoCAD, Wordperfect, dBASE, Lotus 1-2-3, VersaCAD, & Other Programs While Plotter/Printer Is Plotting in the Background, Uninterrupted. The System Will Save up to 94% Waiting Time.
Software Machine, Inc.

AutoPLOT 3. *Version:* 1.30. Richard Morris. Mar. 1991. *Items Included:* Manual & Extensive on-line context sensitive help. *Customer Support:* Full-time technical support for registered users; 30 day money back; no risk guarantee.
PC, MS-DOS 3.0 or higher. IBM, PS/2, Microchannel & compatibles (20k). $249.95 single user, $349.95 Network. *Optimal configuration:* IBM or compatible, DOS 3.0 or higher. *Networks supported:* Novell, 10 net & any network with a designated plot station.
Extensive Plot/Print Management Software Capable of Plotting/Printing in the Background to up to 8 Printers or Plotters Simultaneously. Contains: Automatic Queuing, Hyperspooling, Standard Graphics Pop up & Extensive On-Line Help. Saving 95 Percent of Plotting Time Allows the User Much More Drawing Time.
Software Machine, Inc.

AutoProject. *Version:* 2.0. Jan. 1995. *Items Included:* Manual, 120-day free maintenance. *Customer Support:* 1 yr. maintenance for $200.
MS-DOS, Windows (8Mb). disk $995.00. *Addl. software required:* AutoCAD Release 12 or 13.
The World's First Comprehensive Project Management Software That Works Entirely Within AutoCAD. Equipped with a Powerful, Open Relational Database & Uses State-of-the-Art Algorithms to Solve the Network for Time, Resource, & Cost. Allows for Multiple Calendars, Hammock & Activity Split, Multiple Resource Leveling, Resource Constrained Time Scheduling, Crashing & Time-Cost Trade-Off, Earned Value Analysis, Resource Overload Diagram, Cost-Performance S-Curves, & More.
Research Engineers.

AutoSave II. *Version:* 2.01.
Macintosh 512KE or higher. 3.5" disk $49.95.
An INIT That Automatically Saves Work in Progress Using a Preset Time Interval. Works with All Major Applications in UniFinder or MultiFinder, System 7 Compatible.
Magic Software, Inc.

AUTOSEND. *Version:* 2.0. Aug. 1990. *Items Included:* 1 spiral-bound manual; at least 1 voice digitizer. *Customer Support:* On-site training option of $350.00 per day; 1 yr. maintenance $400.00; Annual support retainer of at least $900.00.
DOS. UNIX. 286, 386, or 486-based (640k). $4800.00 & up. *Nonstandard peripherals required:* 1 voice digitizer supplied with each system. *Addl. software required:* RM/COBOL Runtime. *Optimal configuration:* DOS - 640k RAM, 60Mb disk, 300 cps printer, 1 serial port.
SCO XENIX, SCO UNIX. 386, 486-based (4Mb), Pentium (8Mb). $4800.00 & up. *Nonstandard peripherals required:* Number of voice digitizers scaled to customer's needs. *Addl. software required:* RM/COBOL Runtime. *Optimal configuration:* 286 or 486, Pentium with 8Mb RAM, 125Mb hard disk, 500 cps printer, multiple serial ports.
System That Automates the EPA's Formula for Daily Inventory Reconciliation of UST Inventories. To Send in Tank Measurements & Fuel Sales Figures AUTOSEND Only Requires a Touch-Tone Phone at Retail or Commercial Accounts. The AUTOSEND Software, Running on a PC in the Distributor's Office, Performs Inventory Reconciliations & Produces Prioritized Fuel Dispatch Reports.
AIMS, Inc.

AutoShade. *Version:* 2. *Compatible Hardware:* DOS 386, 486 & compatibles. *Operating System(s) Required:* PC-DOS/MS-DOS 3.3 or higher, PharLap DOS Extender, AutoCAD R10 or R11. *Memory Required:* 4000k. *General Requirements:* 1.2Mb floppy disk or 3.5" floppy disk drive, 20Mb hard disk; math co-processor; Monochrome Hercules Graphics Card, CGA, EGA, Orchid TurboPGA, Professional Graphics Controller, or Autodesk Device Interface; mouse, table, or joystick; AutoCAD program R10 or R11.
disk $500.00.
Enables Users to Create Perspective, Reflections, & Full-Color Hard-Copy Output of Drawings Created Using the Three-Dimensional Capabilities of AUTOCAD. Uses the Color Elements of AUTOCAD As a Basis for Color in the Finished Output & Also Supports the Monochrome & Color Implementations of POSTSCRIPT. Users Can Generate a 256 Color-Output File or a Continuous-Output File with a Floating-Point Representation of up to 16 Million Colors.
Autodesk, Inc.

AutoSim: A Process Control Software Lab. Len Klochek. *Items Included:* 3-ring bound user's manual & companion text.
MS-DOS. IBM PC & compatible (256k). disk $250.00 (ISBN 1-55617-266-4, Order no.: A266-4). *Nonstandard peripherals required:* CGA, EGA, or VGA graphics.
Allows User to Interact with a Simulated Industrial Process with a Real-Time Control System. Teaches Operating & Tuning Concepts & Techniques.
Instrument Society of America (ISA).

AutoSim: The Marketing Laboratory. *Version:* 2.04. Stuart James et al. Jan. 1996. *Items Included:* Manual & floppy disk with administrator's guide available. *Customer Support:* Free weekday support.
DOS. 386 (2Mb). $25.00 MBA, $95.00 Consult (ISBN 1-885837-00-3).
Windows. 386 (2Mb). $25.00 MBA, $95.00 Consult (ISBN 1-885837-01-1).
Macintosh. $25.00 MBA, $95.00 Consult (ISBN 1-885837-02-X).
Compete Against Japanese & U.S. Automakers in the Small-Car Segment. Conduct Market Reserach, Formulate Strategies & Production Runs, & Much More.
Interpretive Software, Inc.

AUTOSIR. Apr. 1994. *Items Included:* User documentation. *Customer Support:* Support Included with Purchase; support by voice phone & modem.
DOS. IBM PC & coamptibles, 486/DX4 (640k). $5000.00 & up.
UNIX. 486/DX4 (8Mb). $5000.00 & up.
Networks supported: No.
An In-House S.I.R. System. A Combination of AUTOSEND (Produced by AIMS, Inc.) & Simmons SIRVEY's S.I.R. Software. It Provides the Marketer with the Means to Gather Tank Inventory Data, Correct Errors in the Data, & Process the Data with the Embedded SIR Software.
AIMS, Inc.

Autoskill Component Reading Subskill Program. Ron Trites & Christina Fiedorowicz. *Items Included:* Software discs, teacher manual, video training tape. *Customer Support:* Includes free on-site teacher training & support & 1-800 number.
System 6.0 or 7.0. Macintosh Classic II, SE30; LC; LC11, Powerbook Family (2Mb). 3.5" disk $2395.00 (ISBN 1-883919-01-0). *Optimal configuration:* Macintosh 40Mb hard drive, 4Mb memory.
System 6X 20Mb hard drive. Macintosh (2Mb). Contact publisher for price.
IBM DOS platform. Contact publisher for price.
Research Based, Computer Assisted Oriented Learning Resource Aimed at Promoting the Acquisition of Skills Needed for the Mastery of Reading. This Is a Skills Based Program.
Autoskill New York, Inc.

Autoskill Mathematics Program. Ron Trites & Christina Fiedorowicz. *Items Included:* Software discs, teacher manual, video training tape. *Customer Support:* Includes free on-site teacher training & support & 1-800 number.
System 6.0 or 7.0. Macintosh Classic II, SE30; LC; LC11, Powerbook Family (2Mb). 3.5" disk $2395.00 (ISBN 1-883919-00-2). *Optimal*

TITLE INDEX

configuration: Macintosh 40Mb hard drive, 4Mb memory.
System 6X 20Mb hard drive. Macintosh (2Mb). Contact publisher for price.
IBM DOS. Contact publisher for price.
Computerized, Curriculum Based Learning Resource Aimed at Promoting the Acquisition of Skills Necessary for the Mastery of Mathematics.
Autoskill New York, Inc.

Autosort-86M. *Version:* 1.30A. Jan. 1991. *Items Included:* Spiral-bound manual, disk with program. *Customer Support:* Technical Support by Phone (813-961-7566) or Fax (813-963-6180) No charge.
PC-DOS/MS-DOS 2.1 or higher, Windows. IBM or compatible (128k). disk $150.00. *Addl. software required:* Programming Languages: C, Basic, Pascal, Fortran, Cobol.
OS/2 1.1 or higher. IBM or compatible (2Mb). 3.5" disk $150.00. *Addl. software required:* Programming Languages: Basic, C, Fortran, Pascal Lattice C. *Networks supported:* LAN-Manager & all Net-Bios compatible.
SORT/MERGER/SELECT Utility Written in Assembly, Designed for Very Large Files with Fixed-Length Fields with Fixed Length Records for Fast Sorting & High Transfer Rate. May Be Used Memory Resident of Linked Directly with Application Program. May Be Used with MS-DOS Compatible Networks. File Size Limited Only by DOS/Disk Space. Record Sizes in Excess of 5,000 Bytes Permitted. Path Names Supported.
Computer Control Systems, Inc.

AUTOSPEC. *Version:* 3.0. 1990. *Compatible Hardware:* IBM PC & compatibles. *Operating System(s) Required:* PC-DOS, MS-DOS. *Language(s):* Compiled BASIC. *Memory Required:* 150k. *General Requirements:* Printer. *Items Included:* Disk & documentation. *Customer Support:* Phone inquiry.
$475.00.
Automatic Typographic Specification Program for Books & Booklets Which Follows the Needs of the User: Any Trimmed Size, Typeface, Number of Columns, etc.
Autospec, Inc.

AutoTrace DOS. *Version:* 1.1. Jun. 1991. *Items Included:* 1 Complete Documentation Manual, Software on either 3.5" or 5.25". *Customer Support:* Free Technical support; 30 day money back guarantee.
MS-DOS. PC XT, AT or compatibles (640k). disk $119.00 (Order no.: ATD). *Addl. software required:* CAD Software package. *Optimal configuration:* 386 or faster, MS-DOS, 640K RAM, VGA Card, Mouse, Turbo CAD or Generic CADD.
Loads Non-CAD Drawings into CAD Based Systems. Interactive Menu Driven Program That Converts Bit-Mapped Graphic Images (.PCX) into Vector Based Images. After Conversion, the New File Can Be Imported Directly into a CAD Package That Supports the Industry Standard .DXF Tile Format. Also Produces Files in HPGL, Turbo C, & Turbo Pascal Formats.
Blue Mountain Software.

AutoWriter. *Version:* 2.01. *Compatible Hardware:* IBM PC & compatibles. *Operating System(s) Required:* PC-DOS/MS-DOS. *Memory Required:* 256k. *General Requirements:* Hard disk recommended. *Items Included:* 32 pg. Thinking Software catalog.
3.5" or 5.25" disk $59.95.
Includes an Automated Paragraph Generator That Searches & Selects Sentences from Any Text File & Writes up to 40 Pages on Any Topic. Has a Built-In Word Processor (Others Can Be Used), 20-Minute Tutorial, & Online Help. Also Included Is the WORDFREQ Program for Counting the Word Frequency in Any Text File.
Thinking Software, Inc.

Auxal 2: A PC Program for Auxological Analysis of Longitudinal Measurements of Human Stature. R. Darrell Bock et al. 1994. *Customer Support:* Free technical support, 90-day limited warranty.
DOS extender. disk $550.00 (ISBN 1-56321-181-5).
Extender. disk $450.00 (ISBN 1-56321-180-7).
demo disk Contact publisher for price (ISBN 1-56321-183-1).
This Program Provides Accurate Fitting or Same Thing of Growth Curves for Height, Velocity, & Acceleration & Displays the Height & Velocity Curves in Publication Quality Graphic Output Applied Multivariate Statistics.
Lawrence Erlbaum Assocs. Software & Alternate Media, Inc.

AVAGIO Publishing System. *Version:* 2.0. Jun. 1991. *Items Included:* 1 users manual; 1 "A Practical Guide to Adding Pizazz to Your Documents". *Customer Support:* 800 Number for registered owners.
MS/PC DOS 3.3 or higher. IBM & compatibles (640k). disk $149.95. *Nonstandard peripherals required:* Hard disk, mouse.
Full-Featured Desktop Publishing Program. Features Include Color Printing, 360 Degree Text Rotation, Text Fitted to Curves, Scanner Image Manipulation, Fully Scalable Fonts & Graphics, & Incredible Print Quality.
Unison World.

Avalon CIIM. *Version:* 8.5. May 1993. *Items Included:* Documentation, CASEmod's. *Customer Support:* 24 hr. phone support, on-site training, modifications.
Unix. All Unix based, IBM RS6000, HP9000, DEC, Data General, Sun, Unisys, NCK (16Mb). Contact publisher for price. *Addl. software required:* Oracle or Sybase RDBMS. *Networks supported:* TCP/IP.
Avalon Software.

Avalon Publisher. *Version:* 2.0. *Compatible Hardware:* Sun 3 & 4, SPARC stations, HP 9000/300, 400, 700 & 800, DEC station, IBM RS/6000, 386/486 PC's. *General Requirements:* 18Mb of disk space, 8Mb of main memory, X11 windowing system. *Items Included:* Color text & graphics; automatic multi-level table of contents; keyboard accelerators; point sizes from 1-1000; mail merge; clip art library. *Customer Support:* Documentation, phone, FAX.
$995.00.
additional concurrent license $995.00 ea.
Desktop Publishing System Which Provides Pagination, Graphics, Page/Document Layout & Word Processing under a Mac-Like Environment.
Elan Computer Group, Inc.

Avant Cards. *Version:* 2.3. Harvey E. Hahn. *Compatible Hardware:* IBM PC, PS/2 & compatibles. *Operating System(s) Required:* MS-DOS 2.10 or higher. *Memory Required:* 256k. *General Requirements:* Two floppy disk drive or hard disk & printer. IBM version: asynchronous communications adapter w/serial printer. *Items Included:* Documentation. *Customer Support:* Yes.
disk $250.00.
Creates & Prints Catalog Cards, Either in Single Sets, or Multiple Sets. Labels Can Be Produced in Single Sets or Multiple Sets. For School, Academic, Special & Public Libraries.
Avant Software Enterprises.

AVANTI. 1974. *Compatible Hardware:* IBM System 34. *Operating System(s) Required:* CP/M. *Language(s):* RPG II (source code included). *Memory Required:* 30k.
8" disk $5000.00.
Integrated Accounting System.
Advanced Data Systems, Inc.

AvCase 2 8051 Family Package. *Version:* 2.11. *Customer Support:* Free technical support, 30 day unconditional guarantee.
MS-DOS. PC or compatible, 386 or higher. disk $1795.00 (Order no.: AVCASE 51).
Integrated Set of Tools for the 8051 Family Embedded-Systems Software Development. Includes a C Compiler, Macro Assembler, Simulator with Source Level Debugging, On-Line Reference Guide, Integrated Editor, & MAKE Utility.
Avocet Systems, Inc.

AvCase 68000 Family C Package. *Version:* 3.23. 1991. *Items Included:* C Compiler, Macro Assembler, C-Source Level Simulator, Remote Monitor Debugger. *Customer Support:* One year free technical support; 30 day unconditional money back guarantee.
MS-DOS. PC (640k). disk $1895.00. *Networks supported:* Any DOS based network.
Integrated Set of Tools for the 68000 Family. Includes an Optimizing ANSI-Standard C Compiler, Macro Assembler, C-Source Level Simulator Debugger, Remote Monitor Debugger, On-Line Reference Guide, Editor & Project MAKE Utility.
Avocet Systems, Inc.

Aviation Department Management System III ADMS III. 1982. *Compatible Hardware:* IBM PC, PC XT, PC AT, PS/2. *Operating System(s) Required:* MS-DOS 3.0 or higher. *Language(s):* C Plus Plus. *Memory Required:* 512k. *General Requirements:* Hard disk, printer, modem. Carbon copy, remote or other similar packages for remote operations.
Set. annual subscription fee $179.00 to $3995.00.
$310.00 expanded airport & navigation databases.
free unlimited (800) telephone support.
$55.00 manual.
Comprised of 4 Modules, Each Module Will Stand-Alone, However, if Another Module Is Present on the System They Will Exchange Information As Necessary.
Aviation Analysis, Inc.
 Budget.
  Provides a Standard Aviation Budget, Using Account Codes & Names Supplied by User. Prints a Monthly Budget vs. Actual Reports. Breaks out Cost By Fixed & Variable Expense Reports.
 Scheduling.
  Assembles a 16 Leg Itinerary, Computing Time Enroutes, Using Standard Wind Factors. Computes Arrival, Departure, or Ground Time As Requested by the Operator & Always Considers Time Zone Changes.
 Maintenance-Inventory.
  Maintains the Aircraft & Inventory Parts Information. Provides Maintenance Due Lists, Status Reports. May Be Used with Any Type of Aircraft. Customers Track Maintenance on the Ground Support Equipment.
 Record Keeping.
  Collects & Assimilates the Flight Data into the Following Reports: Manpower Usage, Aircraft Monthly Usage, Aircraft Annual Usage, FLT Dept, Pilot Flight Logs, I.R.S Information (Taxable Benefits) & Aircraft Usage By Accounts.

AVLIB. *Compatible Hardware:* CP/M-80 or CP/M-86 systems, IBM PC & compatibles, Prime, mini or mainframes with standard FORTRAN-77. *Language(s):* FORTRAN.
contact publisher for price.
Designed to Manage the Inventory in an Audio-Visual Library. Handles Items on Hand, Inventory, Items Checked Out to Subscribers & Items Put on Hold or Reserved for Specific Subscribers.

AVMACZ80: Z80

Maintains Information on Stock Number, Title, Sub-Title, Type Item, Subject Class, Classification Code, Rack Shelf, Restriction Code, Title Authority Code, Issue Code, Volume Copy, Birth Date of Item, Last Date Issued, Due Date, Request Form, Condition Code, Distribution Status, Times Issued, Reservations, Command Codes, Hold Status, & Reserve Status. Provides for Entering New Titles & Looking up Items by Stock Number, Old Number, & by Title.
Management Systems, Inc.

AVMACZ80: Z80, Z180, HD64180 Macro Assembler. *Version:* 2.24. *Compatible Hardware:* PC & compatibles. *Operating System(s) Required:* MS-DOS. *Language(s):* Assembly. *Memory Required:* 256k. *Customer Support:* One-year free technical support - 30 day unconditional money-back guarantee.
disk $395.00, incl. documentation.
write for info.
Advanced Macro-Assembler Package for the Z80 Family of Microprocessors. The Macro Assembler Accepts Z80 Assembly Language As Input & Produces Relocatable Object Modules. The Linker Then Combines These Modules to Produce an Absolute Object File in Intel, Motorola, or Tektronix HEX Format, Suitable for Downloading to an EPROM Programmer, Debugger, or Emulator. Package Includes: AVMACZ8 Assembler, AVLINK Linker, AVREF Cross-Reference Generator, AVLIB Librarian, & Utility Programs.
Avocet Systems, Inc.

AVMAC05: 6805 Family Macro Assembler. *Version:* 2.23. *Compatible Hardware:* PC & compatibles. *Operating System(s) Required:* MS-DOS. *Language(s):* Assembly. *Memory Required:* 256k. *Customer Support:* One-year free technical support - 30 day unconditional money-back guarantee.
MS-DOS, PC-DOS. disk $395.00, incl. documentation.
write for info.
Advanced Macro-Assembler Package for the 6805/6305 Family of Microprocessors. The Macro Assembler Accepts 6805 Assembly Language As Input & Produces Relocatable Object Modules. The Linker Then Combines These Modules to Produce an Absolute Object File in Intel, Motorola, or Tektronix HEX Format, Suitable for Downloading to an EPROM Programmer, Debugger, or Emulator. Package Contains: AVMAC05 Assembler, AVLINK Linker, AVREF Cross-Reference Generator, AVLIB Librarian, & Utility Programs.
Avocet Systems, Inc.

AVMAC09: 6809 Macro Assembler. *Version:* 2.23. *Compatible Hardware:* PC & compatibles. *Operating System(s) Required:* MS-DOS. *Language(s):* Assembly. *Memory Required:* 256k. *Customer Support:* One-year free technical support - 30 day unconditional money-back guarantee.
MS-DOS, PC-DOS. disk $395.00, incl. documentation.
write for info.
Advanced Macro-Assembler Package for the 6809 Family of Microprocessors. The Macro Assembler Accepts 6809 Assembly Language As Input & Produces Relocatable Object Modules. The Linker Then Combines These Modules to Produce an Absolute Object File in Intel, Motorola, or Tektronix HEX Format, Suitable for Downloading to an EPROM Programmer, Debugger, or Emulator. Package Contains: AVMAC09 Assembler, AVLINK Linker, AVREF Cross-Reference Generator, AVLIB Librarian, & Utility Programs.
Avocet Systems, Inc.

AVMAC11: 6811 Macro Assembler. *Version:* 2.27. *Compatible Hardware:* PC & compatibles. *Operating System(s) Required:* MS-DOS. *Language(s):* Assembly. *Memory Required:* 256k. *Customer Support:* One-year free technical support - 30 day unconditional money-back guarantee.
MS-DOS, PC-DOS. disk $395.00, incl. documentation.
write for info.
Advanced Macro Assembler Package for the 68HC11 Family of Microprocessors. The Macro Assembler Accepts 68HC11 Assembly Language As Input & Produces Relocatable Object Modules. The Linker Then Combines These Modules to Produce an Absolute Object File in Intel, Motorola, or Tektronix HEX Format, Suitable for Downloading to an EPROM Programmer, Debugger, or Emulator. Package Contains: AVMAC6811 Assembler, AVLINK Linker, AVREF Cross-Reference Generator, AVLIB Librarian, & Various Utility Programs.
Avocet Systems, Inc.

AVMAC18: 1802 Macro Assembler. *Version:* 2.20. *Compatible Hardware:* PC & compatibles. *Operating System(s) Required:* MS-DOS. *Language(s):* Assembly. *Memory Required:* 256k. *Customer Support:* One-year free technical support - 30 day unconditional money-back guarantee.
MS-DOS, PC-DOS. disk $395.00, incl. documentation.
write for info.
Advanced Macro-Assembler Package for the 1802/1805/1806 Family of Microprocessors. The Macro Assembler Accepts 1802 Assembly Language As Input & Produces Relocatable Object Modules. The Linker Then Combines These Modules to Produce an Absolute Object File in Intel, Motorola, or Tektronix HEX Format, Suitable for Downloading to an EPROM Programmer, Debugger, or Emulator. Package Contains: AVMAC18 Assembler, AVLINK Linker, AVREF Cross-Reference Generator, AVLIB Librarian, & Utility Programs.
Avocet Systems, Inc.

AVMAC48: 8048 Macro Assembler. *Version:* 2.20. *Compatible Hardware:* PC & compatibles. *Operating System(s) Required:* MS-DOS. *Language(s):* Assembly. *Memory Required:* 256k. *Customer Support:* One-year free technical support - 30 day unconditional money-back guarantee.
MS-DOS, PC-DOS. disk $395.00, incl. documentation.
write for info.
Advanced Macro-Assembler Package for the 8048/8041 Family of Microprocessors. The Macro Assembler Accepts 8048 Assembly Language As Input & Produces Relocatable Object Modules. The Linker Then Combines These Modules to Produce an Absolute Object File in Intel, Motorola, or Tektronix HEX Format, Suitable for Downloading to an EPROM Programmer, Debugger, or Emulator. Package Contains: AVMAC48 Assembler, AVLINK Linker, AVREF Cross-Reference Generator, AVLIB Librarian, & Utility Programs.
Avocet Systems, Inc.

AVMAC65: 6500-6502 Macro Assembler. *Version:* 2.21. *Compatible Hardware:* PC & compatibles. *Operating System(s) Required:* MS-DOS. *Language(s):* Assembly. *Memory Required:* 256k. *Customer Support:* One-year free technical support - 30 day unconditional money-back guarantee.
MS-DOS, PC-DOS. disk $395.00, incl. documentation.
write for info.
Advanced Macro-Assembler Package for the 6500/6502/65C02/6511 Family of Micro Processors. The Macro Assembler Accepts 6502/6500 Assembly Language As Input & Produces Relocatable Object Modules. The Linker Then Combines These Modules to Produce an Absolute Object File in Intel, Motorola, or Tektronix HEX Format, Suitable for Downloading to an EPROM Programmer, Debugger, or Emulator. Package Contains: AVMAC65 Assembler, AVLINK Linker, AVREF Cross-Reference Generator, AVLIB Librarian, & Utility Programs.
Avocet Systems, Inc.

AVMAC68: 6800-6301-6303-6801 Macro Assembler. *Version:* 2.27. *Compatible Hardware:* PC & compatibles. *Operating System(s) Required:* MS-DOS. *Language(s):* Assembly. *Memory Required:* 256k. *Customer Support:* One-year free technical support - 30 day unconditional money-back guarantee.
MS-DOS, PC-DOS. disk $395.00, incl. documentation.
write for info.
Advanced Macro-Assembler Package for the 6801/6301 Family of Microprocessors. The Macro Assembler Accepts 6801 Assembly Language As Input & Produces Relocatable Object Modules. The Linker Then Combines These Modules to Produce an Absolute Object File in Intel, Motorola, or Tektronix HEX Format, Suitable for Downloading to an EPROM Programmer, Debugger, or Emulator. Package Contains: AVMAC68 Assembler, AVLINK Linker, AVREF Cross-Reference Generator, AVLIB Librarian, & Utility Programs.
Avocet Systems, Inc.

AVMAC85: 8085 Macro Assembler. *Version:* 2.21. *Hardware:* PC & compatibles. *Operating System(s) Required:* MS-DOS. *Language(s):* Assembly. *Memory Required:* 256k. *Customer Support:* One-year free technical support - 30 day unconditional money-back guarantee.
MS-DOS, PC-DOS. disk $395.00, incl. documentation.
Advanced Macro-Assembler Package for the 8085 Family of Microprocessors. The Macro Assembler Accepts 8085 Assembly Language As Input & Produces Relocatable Object Modules. The Linker Then Combines These Modules to Produce an Absolute Object File in Intel, Motorola, or Tektronix HEX Format, Suitable for Downloading to an EPROM Programmer, Debugger, or Emulator. Package Contains: AVMAC85 Assembler, AVLINK Linker, AVREF Cross-Reference Generator, AVLIB Librarian, Utility Programs.
Avocet Systems, Inc.

AVMAC04: 6804 Macro Assembler. *Version:* 2.20. *Compatible Hardware:* PC & compatibles. *Operating System(s) Required:* MS-DOS. *Language(s):* Assembly. *Memory Required:* 256k. *Customer Support:* One-year free technical support - 30 day unconditional money-back guarantee.
MS-DOS. disk $395.00, incl. documentation.
write for info.
Advanced Macro-Assembler Package for the Motorola 6804 Family of Microprocessors. The Macro Assembler Will Accept 6804 Assembly Language As Input & Produce Relocatable Object Modules. The Linker Then Combines These Modules to Produce an Absolute Object File in Intel, Motorola, or Tektronix HEX Format, Suitable to Downloading to an EPROM Programmer, Debugger, or Emulator. The Package Consists of: AVMAC04 Assembler, AVLINK Linker, AVREF Cross-Reference Generator, AVLIB Librarian, & Various Utility Programs.
Avocet Systems, Inc.

TITLE INDEX

Avocet C Compiler Series. *Customer Support:* One-year free technical support, 30 day unconditional guarantee.
MS-DOS. PC or compatible (256k). disk $695.00 (Order no.: AVXCXX).
Translate C Language Programs to Produce Optimized Code. Integrates AVMAC Assembler Code with C Code. Performs Type Checking & Issues Warnings about Constructs That May Represent Programming Errors. Target Families Available Are 6801, 68HC11, Z80/64180/Z180.
Avocet Systems, Inc.

AVScripter. *Version:* 4.1. *Items Included:* Disk, documentation, command card, free updates for six months. *Customer Support:* phone or correspondence.
MS-DOS. IBM & compatibles. disk $40.00. *Nonstandard peripherals required:* Printer. *Addl. software required:* word processor capable of ASCII file output.
Program for Formatting Two Column TV & Audio-Visual Scripts. Includes the Following Features: Two Column Output to Printer, Screens or Editable Disk File; Variable-Width Video & Audio Columns; Output Prompter-Narrator Scripts from the Audio Column to Printer, Screen, or Disk File (for Computer Prompting Systems); Automatic Scene Numbers & Page Numbers; Automatic Page Breaks with "CONTINUED's"; Title Lines Automatically Centered; Headers; Switch to Page-Width Text in Middle of Script; Printer Commands Sent to Any Printer; Selective Page Printing Multiple Copies; Scene Lists Sorted by Location etc. "A Very Worthwhile Product" - VIDEOGRAPHY. "Value Rating! Excellent" - VIDEOMAKER.
Tom Schroeppel.

AVSIM65. *Version:* 1.60. *Operating System(s) Required:* MS-DOS. *Memory Required:* 256k. *Customer Support:* One-year free technical support - 30 day unconditional money-back guarantee.
disk $595.00.
Programming Development Tool, Full-Screen Software Simulator/Debugger for the 6502 Family. Simulates 6502 Series Chips, Including RAM/ROM Boundaries & On-Chip Peripherals, Interrupts, & I/O Handled in a Flexible Way. Features Advanced Debugging with Breakpoint Facilities & an UNDO Key Which Single Steps in Reverse Through Recently Issued Instructions.
Avocet Systems, Inc.

AVSIMZ80: Z80 Simulator/Debugger. *Version:* 1.60. *Compatible Hardware:* PC & compatibles. *Operating System(s) Required:* MS-DOS. *Language(s):* Assembly. *Memory Required:* 256k. *Customer Support:* One-year free technical support - 30 day unconditional money-back guarantee.
MS-DOS. disk $595.00, incl. documentation. write for info.
Full-Screen Software Simulator/Debugger for the Z80 Microprocessor Family. Simulates Z80-Series Chips, Including RAM/ROM Boundaries & On-Chip Peripherals. Interrupts & I/O Are Handled in a Flexible Way. Advanced Debugging Features Include a Breakpoint Facility & a UNDO Key Which Single-Steps in Reverse Through Recently-Executed Instructions.
Avocet Systems, Inc.

AVSIM05: 6805 Simulator/Debugger. *Version:* 1.60. *Compatible Hardware:* PC & compatibles. *Operating System(s) Required:* MS-DOS. *Language(s):* Assembly. *Memory Required:* 256k. *Customer Support:* One-year free technical support - 30 day unconditional money-back guarantee.
PC-DOS, MS-DOS. disk $595.00, incl. documentation.
write for info.
Full-Screen Software Simulator/Debugger for the 6805/6305 Microprocessor Family. Will Simulate 6805-Series Chips, Including RAM/ROM Boundaries & On-Chip Peripherals. Interrupts & I/O Are Handled in a Flexible Way. Advanced Debugging Features Include a Breakpoint Facility & an UNDO Key Which Single-Steps in Reverse Through Recently-Executed Instructions.
Avocet Systems, Inc.

AVSIM09: 6809 Simulator/Debugger. *Version:* 1.60. *Compatible Hardware:* PC & compatibles. *Operating System(s) Required:* MS-DOS. *Language(s):* Assembly. *Memory Required:* 256k. *Customer Support:* One-year free technical support - 30 day unconditional money-back guarantee.
MS-DOS. disk $595.00, incl. documentation. write for info.
Full-Screen Software Simulator-Debugger for the 6809 Microprocessor Family. Simulates the 6809-Series Chips, Including RAM/ROM Boundaries & On-Chip Peripherals. Interrupts & I/O Are Handled in a Flexible Way. Advanced Debugging Features Include a Breakpoint Facility & an UNDO Key Which Single-Steps in Reverse Through Recently-Executed Instructions.
Avocet Systems, Inc.

AVSIM48: 8048 Simulator/Debugger. *Version:* 1.60. *Compatible Hardware:* PC & compatibles. *Operating System(s) Required:* MS-DOS. *Language(s):* Assembly. *Memory Required:* 256k. *Customer Support:* One-year free technical support - 30 day unconditional money-back guarantee.
MS-DOS. disk $595.00, incl. documentation. write for info.
Full-Screen Software Simulator-Debugger for the 8048 Microprocessor Family. Simulates 8048-Series Chips, Including RAM/ROM Boundaries & On-Chip Peripherals. Interrupts & I/O Are Handled in a Flexible Way. Advanced Debugging Features Include a Breakpoint Facility & a UNDO Key Which Single-Steps in Reverse Through Recently-Executed Instructions.
Avocet Systems, Inc.

AVSIM51: 8051 Simulator/Debugger. *Version:* 1.60. *Compatible Hardware:* PC & compatibles. *Operating System(s) Required:* MS-DOS. *Language(s):* Assembly. *Memory Required:* 256k. *Customer Support:* One-year free technical support - 30 day unconditional money-back guarantee.
MS-DOS. disk $595.00, incl. documentation. write for info.
Full-Screen Software Simulator-Debugger for the 8051/8052 Microprocessor Family. Simulates the 8051-Series Chips, Including RAM/ROM Boundaries & On-Chip Peripherals. Interrupts & I/O Are Handled in a Flexible Way. Advanced Debugging Features Include a Breakpoint Facility & a UNDO Key Which Single-Steps in Reverse Through Recently-Executed Instructions.
Avocet Systems, Inc.

AVSIM68: 6801 Simulator/Debugger. *Version:* 1.60. *Compatible Hardware:* PC & compatibles. *Operating System(s) Required:* MS-DOS. *Language(s):* Assembly. *Memory Required:* 256k. *Customer Support:* One-year free technical support - 30 day unconditional money-back guarantee.
MS-DOS. disk $595.00, incl. documentation. write for info.
Full-Screen Software Simulator-Debugger for the 6801/6301 Microprocessor Family. Simulates 6801-Series Chips, Including RAM/ROM Boundaries & On-Chip Peripherals. Interrupts & I/O Are Handled in a Flexible Way. Advanced Debugging Features Include a Breakpoint Facility & a UNDO Key Which Single-Steps in Reverse Through Recently-Executed Instructions.
Avocet Systems, Inc.

AVSIM85: 8085 Simulator/Debugger. *Version:* 1.60. *Compatible Hardware:* PC & compatibles. *Operating System(s) Required:* MS-DOS. *Language(s):* Assembly. *Memory Required:* 256k. *Customer Support:* One-year free technical support - 30 day unconditional money-back guarantee.
MS-DOS. disk $595.00, incl. documentation. write for info.
Full-Screen Software Simulator/Debugger for the 8085 Microprocessor Family. Simulates 8085-Series Chips, Including RAM/ROM Boundaries & On-Chip Peripherals. Interrupts & I/O Are Handled in a Flexible Way. Advanced Debugging Features Include a Breakpoint Facility & a UNDO Feature Which Single-Steps in Reverse Through Recently-Executed Instructions.
Avocet Systems, Inc.

The Awakening. *Version:* 1.5. Feb. 1995. *Items Included:* BookWorm Student Reader (diskette). *Customer Support:* 30 day MBG. Technical support (toll call) - no charge.
System 7.0 or higher. Macintosh (5Mb). CD-ROM disk $29.95 (ISBN 1-57316-030-X, Order no.: 16165). *Nonstandard peripherals required:* CD-ROM drive, 12" color monitor. *Optimal configuration:* 13" color monitor recommended.
Windows 3.1 or higher. IBM compatible (MPC) 386 DX (4Mb). CD-ROM disk $29.95. *Nonstandard peripherals required:* Standard multimedia compatible CD-ROM. *Optimal configuration:* 8Mb RAM recommended, 256 color monitor recommended.
Kate Chopin's Novel of One Woman's Difficult Liberation Met a Hostile Reception When First Published, but Is Now Regarded As a Masterpiece of American Literature. This Edition Provides Extensive Background on the Novel's Historical & Biographical Context, & Profuse Illustrations of Its Setting, Old New Orleans. Features Complete Sound Allowing the User to Listen to All or Part of Each Work.
Communication & Information Technologies, Inc. (CIT).

Award Maker Plus (Apple Version). *Version:* 44011. Greg Miller. Jan. 1987. *Compatible Hardware:* Apple II+, IIe, IIc, IIgs. *Operating System(s) Required:* ProDOS. *Language(s):* Assembly. *Memory Required:* 128k.
disk $59.95.
backup $12.50.
update $17.50.
Enables Users to Create Awards, Certificates, Licenses, Coupons, or Other Documents of Their Own Design. The Program Will Print Hundreds of Predesigned Award Styles, Allowing Users to Choose a Text Style, Enter a Message, Select the Border Style & Color, & in Some Styles Enter Their Own Hi-Res Picture. Features Color or Black & White Borders, Gold Embossed Press-On Seals, & Class Name File Capability. Hard Disk Version Available. Supports Most Printers & Interfaces.
Baudville.

Award Maker Plus (IBM).
MS-DOS. IBM PC & compatibles (256k). disk $49.95 (Order no.: 23745). *Nonstandard peripherals required:* DOT Matrix Printer. *Networks supported:* Novell or compatible Network version required.
Allows the User to Create & Print Quality Awards, Certificates, Licenses, Coupons or Other Documents. The Program Includes Hundreds of Award Styles, Allowing the User to Enter New Text Select Border Styles. Also Allows User to Compile & Print Awards from Name Lists of up to One Hundred People.
Baudville.

Award Maker Plus (Macintosh Version).
Version: 23727. *Compatible Hardware:* Apple Macintosh.
3.5" disk $49.95.
Software Tool That Lets a User Create & Print Professional Quality Awards, Certificates, Licenses, Coupons or Other Documents. The Program Will Print Hundreds of Predesigned Award Styles, Allowing a User to Enter Text, Select the Border Style &, in Some Styles, Enter a User's Own Picture. The Program Comes with Hundreds of Different Awards & Certificates to Pick from for Sports, School, Home & Business; Several Styles of Borders; Sample Awards; Gold Embossed Press on Seals; a Special Price on Pin-Feed Parchment Paper, & the Ability to Create Name Files & Print Out Awards for an Entire Class or Group.
Baudville.

AwardWare. *Compatible Hardware:* Apple II+, IIe, IIc; Atari 400/800, 800XL, 1200XL, 130XE; Commodore 64, 128; IBM PC, PCjr, PC XT, PC AT. *Memory Required:* Apple 64k, IBM 256k. *General Requirements:* Color Graphics Adapter for IBM. Supports the following printers & interfaces: Writer, Scribe, Star, Gemini, Okidata 92/93, Epson, Citizen, Star, Tandy DMP 130, Panasonic 1090/1091, IBM (except ProPrinter); super serial card, standard serial, Apple IIc standard parallel, & Apple II parallel.
disk $14.95.
Allows Users to Design & Print Customized Certificates, Awards, Announcements, Stationery, Memos, Checks, Coupons, & Tickets. Users May Choose the Create-an-Award-Disk Option Which Allows Them to Design an Award, Copy It on a Disk, & Send the Disk to a Friend. When the Addressee Loads the Disk, the Award Appears on the Screen in a Flashing Marquee. The Award Can Then Be Printed.
Hi Tech Expressions, Inc.

Aware. *Version:* 2.2. *General Requirements:* Hard disk drive.
Macintosh Plus or higher. $795.00 General Ledger only; $1,495.00; G/L, A/L, A/P.
General Ledger, Accounts Receivable, Accounts Payable.
Database International, Inc.

AXCENT on Accounting: Accounts Payable.
Version: 1.83. Jun. 1989. *Compatible Hardware:* IBM PC & compatibles. *Operating System(s) Required:* PC-DOS/MS-DOS 2.1 or higher. *Language(s):* Pascal. *Memory Required:* 256k. *General Requirements:* 2 disk drives or hard disk.
disk $495.00 (ISBN 0-938929-01-1).
Features Include: User Defined Fields; Retain Invoices/All Periods & Search Duplicate Invoices; Import/Export Data; Passwords; Prepay Invoices; Installment Payments; One-Time Vouchers; Automatic Numbering; Aged Cash Requirement Reports; Pre-Disk Register; User-Defined Checks; User-Defined Aging Periods; Check Reconciliation; User-Defined Reports; Vendor Analysis; Monthly Activity Summary; Vendor Aged Balance; Pop-Up Windows for Vendors, Invoices, GL Accounts, Terms Codes, Screen Formats, & Clients.
Axcent Software, Inc.

AXCENT on Accounting: Client Write-Up.
Version: 2.91. Aug. 1991. *Compatible Hardware:* IBM PC & compatibles. *Operating System(s) Required:* PC-DOS/MS-DOS 2.1 or higher. *Language(s):* BASIC, Pascal. *Memory Required:* 256k. *General Requirements:* 2 disk drives or hard disk. *Items Included:* Client Ledger, Financial Report Writer, Post-Facto Payroll, User's manual. *Customer Support:* Free telephone support for 60 days & free training classes for 6 months.
disk $1585.00 (ISBN 0-938929-00-3).
Designed for Professional Accountants with Flexible, Easy-to-Use Features & Very Powerful Capabilities. Features Include: Design Account Codes up to 24 A/N Characters, Function Keys, Streamline Entry, User-Defined Screens, Help Facility, Fund Accounting, File Import/Export, Cash Management, Automatic Unattended Printing, Client Time Reporting, 3 Level Password Security, Built-In Word Processor & Spreadsheet, No Sorting, Automatic Data File Repair, Automatic Backup, & up to 28 Accounting Periods Online.
Axcent Software, Inc.

AXIOM: Scientific Computation System. Robert Sutor & Richard Jenks. Nov. 1991. *Items Included:* Software, installation instructions, hardbound user's guide, complete on line documentation. *Customer Support:* Annual maintenance $190-$250.
UNIX. IBM RX/6000; SUN/SPARC (32Mb). disk $1200.00. *Optimal configuration:* 32Mb RAM, 200Mb swapspace.
Powerful Computer Algebra & Visualization System for Mathematical Analysis & Graphics. Object Oriented Construction, Easily Extensible via Internal Compiler. Includes Intuitive Graphical User Interface & Complete On-Line User's Guide Implemented in Hypertext. Used to Solve Problems Symbolically, Numerically & Visually.
Numerical Algorithms Group, Inc.

Axys. *Version:* 2.0. Feb. 1996. *Items Included:* Full documentation. *Customer Support:* 800 number customer support w/maintenance fee; regional training; annual user conferences.
Windows 95, Windows NT Workstation, Windows 3.1 in enhanced mode. IBM Pentium 100MHz (8Mb). $15,000.00 & up. *Nonstandard peripherals required:* 80486 DX66MHz. *Addl. software required:* Excel for Windows 5.0.
A Windows-Based Portfolio Management System. Investment Professionals Rely on Axys to Integrate Portfolio Management, Trading Support, Client Reporting & Performance Measurement. Features Include 200 Standard Reports Plus a Report Writer for Customizing Reports, Automated Linking to Microsoft Excel, & Available Interfaces to Data Providers, Brokerage & Clearing Firms.
Advent Software, Inc.

Azimuth. *Version:* 2.5. Jan. 1992. *Items Included:* Spiral bound manuals, data disks. *Customer Support:* Free technical support Mon-Fri 9:00-5:30 EST; 30-day money back guarantee.
MAC-DOS (1Mb). Macintosh Plus, LC, SI, SE, IIx & higher. 3.5" disk $395.00. *Optimal configuration:* 2Mb.
World Mapping Program on MAC - NOT Clip Art! Allows User to Draw Dramatic Global Views of All Countries in the World & All the United States. This Is Done Quickly & Easily with Perfect Accuracy from Any Distance & at Any Angle. Combines Power of Full-Featured 2D Drafting System with Ease of Macintosh Interface. High-Accuracy Coordinate System Allows User to Draw Maps with Perfectly Meshed Country Borders. Add Text at Any Scale. Easily Create Drop Shadows by Duping Object & Filling with Black, 9 Map Projections.
Graphsoft, Inc.

Aztec Astro-Report. *Version:* 2.0. Bruce Scofield & Barry Orr. Dec. 1990. *Items Included:* Manual. *Customer Support:* Free phone support.
MS-DOS, PC-DOS. IBM PC & MS-DOS compatibles (256k). disk $195.00 (ISBN 0-87199-104-7). *Nonstandard peripherals required:* Hard disk or two 360k floppy drives.
Applies the Astrology of Ancient Mexico & Central America to Modern Situations. Printouts Can Include a 4- to 5-Page Character Interpretation Based on One of the 20 Aztec Day-Signs Combined with the Day Number in a 13-Day Cycle & the Phase of Venus. Two Additional Pages Can Answer a Question Using One of Several Aztec Systems of Divination, & Two More Pages Provide an Introduction to Aztec Astrology. The Program Is Easy to Use & Requires Only the Date of Birth. Researchers Can Use the Program to Convert Modern Dates Into Dates in the Aztec Sacred Calendar & Mayan Long Count Calendar.
Astrolabe, Inc.

Aztec Astrology. *Version:* 1.x. Bruce Scofield & Barry Orr. Dec. 1990. *Items Included:* Manual. *Customer Support:* Free phone support.
MS-DOS, PC-DOS. IBM PC & MS-DOS compatibles (256kb). disk $39.95 (ISBN 0-87199-106-3). *Nonstandard peripherals required:* Hard disk or two 360k floppy drives.
Accepts Input of a Day, Month & Year of Birth, Converts This to the Aztec Sacred Calendar, & Displays an Interpretation of the Aztec Day-Sign & 13-Day Cycle on the Computer Screen. User Can Also Have a Question Answered Using Aztec Systems of Divination.
Astrolabe, Inc.

Aztec C. *Version:* 4.1. *Compatible Hardware:* IBM PC & compatibles. *Memory Required:* 512k.
Aztec C $125.00.
Aztec C plus SDB $189.00.
Aztec MPW C $189.00.
Aztec SDB $125.00.
Aztec C UniTools $125.00.
Aztec C Library Source $250.00.
Source-Code Debugger Integrated with Compiler, Overlay, Assembler & Linker. Compatible with Manx C86 Language. Supports 8086, 8087 & 80186 Instruction Sets, Multiple Monitors & 43-Line Code. Features Full Screen Interface; Code & Data Windows Displays; & Instruction Execution, Memory Change & Expression Breakpoint Types. Also Includes Single Step at Assembly & Source Level & Script Capabilities.
Manx Software Systems.

Aztec C86. *Compatible Hardware:* IBM PC & compatibles. *Memory Required:* 256k.
$75.00 to $499.00.
C Compiler Featuring Assembler Access, Integrated Linker, MAKE, Integrated Editor, Compiler Subdirectories, Integral Assembly Language, Screen/Cursor Control, DOS Service Functions & Low Level Keyboard Input. Compilation Is an Added-Step Process. Supports Math Coprocessor & Technical Hot Line.
Manx Software Systems.

Aztec C65. *Compatible Hardware:* Apple II; Commodore 64, 128. *Operating System(s) Required:* CP/M, Apple DOS 3.3, ProDOS.
Aztec C65-c ProDOS & DOS 3.3. disk $299.00.
Aztec C65-d Apple DOS 3.3. disk $199.00.
Aztec C65-r Apple Prime system. disk $75.00.
Aztec C65-a Apprentice C. disk $19.00.
System Includes a Full Optimized C Compiler, 6502 Assembler, Linkage Editor, UNIX Library, Screen & Graphics Libraries, Shell, etc. Apprentice, Personal, & Developer Versions Are Available for Commodore 64 & 128 Machines.
Manx Software Systems.

Aztec C68k/Am-p Professional System 3.6.
Version: 3.6. *Compatible Hardware:* Commodore Amiga.
3.5" disk $199.00.
Library Source. $300.00.
C Development System Featuring: Optimized C with Selectable 68020 & 68881 Support; 680x0 Macro Assembler with 68881 Support; Linker/Librarian with Overlays, Scatter, Load, & Segmentation; Symbolic Debugger; Supports

TITLE INDEX

Amiga Object Format; UNIX, Amiga, & General Purpose Run Time Routines; Runs under CLI & Supports All the Workbench Functions; Creates CLI & Workbench Applications; Supports Both 1.1 & 1.2 Amiga DOS; 600 Pages of Documentation & Example Programs.
Manx Software Systems.

Aztec ROM Systems: 6502/65C02, 8080/Z80, 8086/80x86, 680x0. *Compatible Hardware:* Apple Macintosh, IBM PC.
Initial host plus target. $750.00.
Additional targets. $500.00.
ROM support package. $500.00.
ROM Code Development System.
Manx Software Systems.

B-Coder: For DOS or For Windows. *Version:* DOS 3.0, Windows 2.0. 1993. *Items Included:* Complete manual 80 pages. *Customer Support:* Complete, unlimited FREE phone support for all registered users.
DOS. 8088 XT or AT min. (60k). $99.00-$199.00 (Order no.: BC30 OR BC30PDF). Networks supported: All.
Windows. 386, or 486, Pentium or Power PC (256k but Windows needs 4Mb min.). $199.00-$359.00 (Order no.: BC20WP). *Addl. software required:* Any Windows program. *Optimal configuration:* 386 PC & 8Mb RAM & any printer supported by DOS.
Install B-Coder & Start Generating High Quality Bar Codes Today! Easy to Use with WYSIWYG Display & Intuitive Pull down Menus. Quickly Produce Professional Quality, Fully Scalable, Bar Codes for All Types of applications - Product Labels, Document Tracking, Packing Slips, etc.
T.A.L. Enterprises.

B-Tree Filer. *Version:* Pascal 5.5, C 3.5. Aug. 1995. *Items Included:* Manual, online help. *Customer Support:* Free technical support, 60 day money-back guarantee, free electronic maintenance updates, Compuserve technical support.
MS-DOS 3.0 or higher (360k). IBM PC, AT, PS/2, compatibles. $199.00 (Pascal), $249.00 (C). *Addl. software required:* Turbo Pascal 6.0, 7.0 or Turbo Pascal for Windows, Borland C Plus Plus 3.1 or higher, Microsoft C/C Plus Plus 7.0 or higher, Borland Delphi 1.0. *Optimal configuration:* Hard disk, 640k RAM. *Networks supported:* Novell, 3Com, MS-NET, PC LAN, VINES, all NetBIOS compatibles.
A Toolbox of Routines to Make Writing Multi-User Database Applications Easy & Reliable in Delphi, Turbo Pascal & C Plus Plus. Applications Can Run in Single User Mode, or on Novell, MS-NET, 3Com, & Many Other Networks. Offers B-Tree Indexing Techniques with Dynamic Page Caching & Balancing for Optimized Performance, up to 2 Billion Records & 100 Indexes per File. Supports Fixed & Variable Length Records, & Also Includes a Failsafe Mode to Guarantee High Reliability of Transaction-Oriented Databases. Supplies Utilities for Browsing Databases, Rebuilding Corrupted Indexes & Sorting. Includes Network-Specific Units for Message Passing, Printer Control, & File Management on Novell, NetBIOS, & SHARE Compatible Networks.
TurboPower Software.

B-Tree HELPER. *Version:* 2.0. Sep. 1989. *Customer Support:* Telephone or mail for registered users.
Macintosh (512k). disk $75.00. *Addl. software required:* C or Pascal compiler, or HyperCard & ResEdit.
A Set of Code Resources & XFCNs to Insert, Find & Delete Records from a B-Tree File. Multiple Trees May Exist in a File. Keys May Be Nonunique. Records Are Independent of Keys. Pascal Source Code Available for $200.00 Additional.
Magreeable Software, Inc.

B-1 Nuclear Bomber. *Compatible Hardware:* Apple II+, IIe; Atari 800/XL/XE; Commodore 64, PET; IBM PC & compatibles; Tandy 1000; TI 99/4A. *Operating System(s) Required:* MS-DOS. *Language(s):* BASIC. *Memory Required:* 16-48k.
Apple, Atari, IBM, TI. disk $21.00.
Apple, Atari, Commodore, IBM. cassette $16.00.
Object of Game Is to Fly B-1 Nuclear Bomber Through Stiff Russian Defenses to Target City, Bomb It, & Return Home Safely. Computer Controls Soviet MIG Fighters & Surface-to-Air Missiles. Player Must Rely on Self-Defense Missiles & Electronic Counter Measures.
Avalon Hill Game Co., The Microcomputer Games Div.

Babble Terror. *Compatible Hardware:* TRS-80. disk $24.95 (ISBN 0-915149-16-8).
cassette $19.95 (ISBN 0-915149-11-7).
Babbles Are Roaming the Maze-Like Complex Everywhere, but the Player Can See Only a Few Yards Ahead.
Blue Cat.

Babe: Interactive MovieBook. *Version:* 1.5. Nov. 1995. *Items Included:* Manual, registration card, promotional flyers. *Customer Support:* Phone technical support - toll call.
Windows 3.1 or higher. 386/33 or higher (4Mb). CD-ROM disk $29.95 (ISBN 1-57303-028-7). *Nonstandard peripherals required:* Sound card, CD-ROM drive. *Optimal configuration:* 486/33 with 8Mb RAM, Win 3.1 or higher, 2X CD-ROM drive, SVGA monitor.
Exclusively Licensed Computer Story/Activity Books for Children. Taken from the Movie Version, the Story Appears on the Computer in Book Form Which the Child Can Read or Have Read to Them in a Boy's or Girl's Voice. Pictures Are Included Which, by Clicking the Mouse, Become Short Clips from the Actual Movie. Many Learning Activities Included.
Sound Source Interactive.

Baby/4XX. *Version:* 1.5. Jun. 1994. *Items Included:* Perfect bound manuals. *Customer Support:* First 30 days free. Free Bulletin Board service (714) 835-BABY. $750.00 per year for personal technical support.
OS/2 Release 1.2 or higher. 386 Based PS/2 PS's or 100% compatibles (8Mb). disk $3500.00 Development System, $750.00 Runtime Support System. *Nonstandard peripherals required:* For multi-users I/O cards. *Optimal configuration:* Minimum 4 to 5 Mb RAM, Minimum 60Mb disk. *Networks supported:* IBM PC NET, Novell NetWare.
Full-Featured Software System Designed to Emulate the AS/400 Environment on Personal Computers. Provides Users with the Power of the AS/400 & Cost Savings of the PC Systems. By Off-Loading RPG-400 Applications Development to a Low Cost PC Environment, AS/400 Users Can Dramatically Improve Productivity & Midrange Systems Performance.
California Software Products, Inc.

Baby/36 for Windows. *Version:* 6.3. Mar. 1985. *Items Included:* Documentation. *Customer Support:* Technical support via fax, Bulletin Board system or CompuServe. First 30 days telephone support free.
Windows 3.1, Windows 95. 286 or higher (4Mb). $3500.00 development system; from $350.00/user for system services.
A Comprehensive Software Package That Allows Users to Migrate System/36 RPGII Applications to PCs & PC Networks Running Windows & Windows 95. Includes a Graphical Processor Which Automatically Creates Windows Forms in Place of Previous Text Based RPG Screens Without Any Recoding. Converted Windows Can Be Further Enhanced Using a Point & Click

BACKAID SOFTWARE

Graphical Editor. The Development Tool-Set & System Support of the System/36 (RPGC, SFGR, SEU, SDA, DSU, OGL, DRU etc.) Are Replicated on the PC to Allow On-Going Maintenance of Migrated Applications. Also Runs under DOS with a Text Only Display.
California Software Products, Inc.

Babylon 5: Limited Edition CD-ROM Entertainment Utility. *Version:* 1.5. Nov. 1995. *Items Included:* Manual, registration card, promotional flyers. *Customer Support:* Phone technical support - toll call.
Windows 3.1 or higher. 386/33 or higher (8Mb). CD-ROM disk $29.95 (ISBN 1-57303-025-2). *Nonstandard peripherals required:* Sound card, CD-ROM drive. *Optimal configuration:* 486/33 with 8Mb RAM, Win 3.1 or higher, 2X CD-ROM drive, SVGA monitor.
Multimedia Entertainment Utility Featuring Licensed Audio & Videoclips from the Hit TV Series, Babylon 5. Includes Wallpaper Images & Custom Babylon 5 Screensaver, & Personal Desktop Which Allows the User to "Attach" Audioclips to Various Windows Events. Requires Win 3.1 or Later. Win 95 Compatible.
Sound Source Interactive.

Baccarat. *Compatible Hardware:* Atari 400, 800. *Language(s):* Atari BASIC. *Memory Required:* 24k.
disk $22.95, incl. documentation.
cassette $18.95, incl. documentation.
Casino Game.
Dynacomp, Inc.

Back-It for Windows. *Version:* 2.0. Aug. 1994. *Items Included:* Manual. *Customer Support:* 30-day money-back guarantee. Technical support representatives available for phone calls from 8am to 5pm Mountain Standard Time.
Microsoft Windows 3.1. IBM PC, XT, AT, PS/2 & compatibles (2Mb). disk $79.00.
Provides Automatic, Multi-Volume, Background Backups in an Easy-to-Use Windows Environment with Data Compression Rates up to 75%, Support for Scores of Tapes, & Advanced Error Correction/Prevention.
GTM Software.

Back-It 4. *Version:* 1.4. Apr. 1993. *Operating System(s) Required:* PC-DOS/MS-DOS 2.0 or higher. *Memory Required:* 384k. *General Requirements:* Hard disk or any mass storage device. *Items Included:* Manual. *Customer Support:* 30-day money-back guarantee, technical support (toll).
disk $79.00.
Hard Disk Backup Software. Allows Backup by Directory, Filename (Specifically Include or Exclude Files by Name), Range of Dates or a File's "Modified" Status. Writes to DOS Compatible Diskettes. Requires No Preparation to Backup since Diskettes Are Formatted (Only If Needed) During Backup. Bad Sectors Are Locked Out. Backup from/to Any DOS Device. Network Version Available. Mouse Compatible. Offers Support for Many Tape Drives. Windows Version Available.
GTM Software.

Backaid Software. Mar. 1987. *Items Included:* Instruction guide. *Customer Support:* 90-day limited warranty.
Apple-DOS 3.3. Apple II Family (48k). disk $99.00 (ISBN 0-917277-73-2).
PC-DOS/MS-DOS 2.0 or higher. IBM & compatibles (128k). disk $99.00 (ISBN 0-917277-65-1).
Illustrates & Explains the Nature of the Most Common Types of Back Pain, Introduces Chronic Back Pain Sufferers to Remedial Practices, & Helps Them to Identify & Track the Factors That

75

Contribute to Their Discomfort. Program Offers a Combination of Awareness, Self-Help, Education & Individually Recommended Exercises.
BrainBank/Generation Ahead of Maryland.

Backflow Records. *Items Included:* Bound manual. *Customer Support:* Free hotline - no time limit; 30 day limited warranty; updates are $5/disk plus S&H.
MS-DOS 2.0 or higher. IBM & compatibles (384k). full system $695.00. *Nonstandard peripherals required:* Hard disk recommended, but not necessary. Supports both monochrome & color displays, as well as an 80-column (or wider) printer.
demo diskette $10.00.
Database System for Maintaining Cross-Connection Control Records, Providing Reports, & Preparing Customer Mailings for Scheduling Backflow Preventer Tests.
Dynacomp, Inc.

Backgammon. *Version:* 2.0. *Compatible Hardware:* Apple II with Applesoft; Atari 400, 800 with Atari BASIC; Canon AS-100; Commodore PET; CP/M based machines with MBASIC; Cromemco; Heath Zenith Z-100; IBM PC; NEC PC-8000; North Star; TRS-80 Model I, Model III, Model 4 with Level II BASIC. *Language(s):* BASIC (source code included). *Memory Required:* 16k, Atari 24k, IBM 128k.
disk $19.95.
8" disk $26.45.
cassette $19.95.
Test Skills & Improve Game.
Dynacomp, Inc.

Backgammon. John E. Hoel. *Compatible Hardware:* IBM PC, PCjr with BASIC cartridge, PC XT, PC AT, Portable PC, 3270 PC. *General Requirements:* IBM Color Display.
disk $19.95 (Order no.: 6276502).
Computer Screen Becomes an Animated Game Board. Users Can Play Against the Computer or a Friend, Choose from Beginner or Advanced Skill Levels, Select Screen Colors, Change the Computer Playing Style by Altering Its Back Game & Running Game, etc.
Personally Developed Software, Inc.

BackGrounder II Task Switching System for CP/M. *Operating System(s) Required:* CP/M 2.2. *Memory Required:* 64k.
3.5", 5.25" or 8" disk $74.95.
Allows User to Switch to Another Program from Withing Running Program. User Can Cut & Paste Between Programs. Also Includes Key Redefinition, Print-Spooler, Calculator Bi-Directional File Viewing, & Help Menu.
Elliam Assocs.

Badge-Scan System. Greg M. Taylor. 1994. *Items Included:* Users guide, wand scanner, wedge reader, interface converter. *Customer Support:* 90 day free support; $150.00 year renewable.
MS-DOS, Windows. IBM PC & compatibles (512k). disk $3295.00 (Order no.: BADGE-SCAN). *Nonstandard peripherals required:* Included with system. *Addl. software required:* ED-U-Keep II. *Optimal configuration:* VGA monitor, 486 computer, 80Mb hard drive & Laptop for remote capture. *Networks supported:* Novell.
System Reads Employee Badges (Mag Strip or Bar Code) for Attendance Taking at Class Site. Includes Scanning Hardware & Software. Also Prints Bar Codes.
The Edukeep Co.

BadgeMaker. 1992. *Items Included:* Manual, tutorial, sample paper products. *Customer Support:* Free technical support via telephone.
MS-DOS. IBM PC, XT, AT or compatible (640k). disk $129.00 (ISBN 0-930393-69-4, Order no.: 46715). *Optimal configuration:* IBM AT or compatible with 1Mb, Hewlett Packard or compatible inkjet or laser printer.
Macintosh 6.0 or higher. Macintosh (1Mb). 3.5" disk $129.00 (ISBN 0-930393-71-6, Order no.: 46217). *Optimal configuration:* Macintosh with 1Mb of RAM, any Macintosh compatible with laser or inkjet printer.
Will Produce Badges or Labels of Any Size. The User Can Modify Pre-Designed Templates, or Create Their Own. PICT or PCX Graphics Can Be Imported & Scaled. A Database Feature Will Allow Importing of an ASCII File to the Database That Can Contain 10 Mergable Fields onto the Badge.
Baudville.

Baffles II. John Ridge. 1986. *Compatible Hardware:* IBM PC, PCjr, PC XT. *Operating System(s) Required:* PC-DOS 2.10-3.10. *Language(s):* BASIC, Assembly. *Memory Required:* 128k.
disk $60.00, incl. user's notes & backup (Order no.: BIO600I).
Interactive Game Designed to Challenge a Player's Deductive Skills. To Be Successful at Playing the Game, Students Must Use Some Form of Scientific Inquiry, That Is, They Must Formulate & Test Hypotheses While Keeping Accurate Records of Their Results & Conclusions.
CONDUIT.

Bailey's Book House.
Windows. IBM & compatibles. CD-ROM disk $49.95 (Order no.: R1313). *Nonstandard peripherals required:* CD-ROM drive. *Optimal configuration:* 386 processor operating at 16Mhz or higher, MS-DOS 5.0 or higher, Windows 3.1 or higher, 30Mb hard drive, mouse, VGA graphic adapter & VGA color monitor (SVGA recommended), 4Mb RAM, external speakers or headphones (with sound card) that are Sound Blaster compatible.
Macintosh (4Mb). (Order no.: R1313). *Nonstandard peripherals required:* 14" color monitor or larger, CD-ROM drive.
Designed by Early-Learning Experts, This Enchanting Environment Encourages Children to Develop Early Reading Skills. Children Are Invited to Explore the Sounds & Meanings of Letters, Words, Rhymes & Stories.
Library Video Co.

Bake 'n Taste. 1986-1991. *Items Included:* Disk(s), user's guide, warranty card. *Customer Support:* 90 day unlimited warranty; 800 toll free number, 800-221-7911, 8:00 a.m.-5:00 p.m. Arizona time; Updates $10.
Macintosh System 6 or higher. Macintosh (1Mb monochrome, 2Mb color). 3.5" disk $69.99 (ISBN 1-55772-268-4, Order no.: 0602). *Optimal configuration:* 2Mb color monitor, Macintosh LC. *Networks supported:* Digicard.
MS-DOS. IBM, Tandy, MS-DOS compatible (128k). disk $49.99 (ISBN 0-918017-11-4, Order no.: 0601). *Nonstandard peripherals required:* VGA or CGA card. *Optimal configuration:* 128k, color monitor, VGA card. *Networks supported:* Velan, Novell, Digicard.
DOS. Apple II, Apple IIe, Apple IIGS, Apple II Plus (48k). disk $49.99 (ISBN 0-918017-10-6, Order no.: 0600). *Optimal configuration:* Apple II, printer, color monitor, 48k. *Networks supported:* Digicard.
Award Winning Bake & Taste Reinforces Following Directions, Measuring & Introduction to Fractions. This Realistic Game Encourages Players to Read for Detail & Comprehension. They Measure, Mix, Set Oven Time & Temperature, & Bake. The Taste Team Decides How "Yummy" the Desserts Are. Ages 8 to Adult.
Mindplay.

BakerForms Accounting Applications.
Macintosh (512k or higher). $49.95 each package. *Nonstandard peripherals required:* Hard disk drive; pin-feed computer forms. *Addl. software required:* Microsoft Works 1.0 or higher, ImageWriter.
all four Packages $169.00.
Accounts Receivable, Accounts Payable, Payroll & Purchasing Packages.
Baker Graphics.

Balance of the Planet. Apr. 1990. *Items Included:* 136 page manual. *Customer Support:* Free telephone support, 90 day warranty.
System 3.2 or higher (1Mb). Apple Macintosh. 3.5" disk $49.95 (ISBN 0-9625733-0-2). *Nonstandard peripherals required:* Hard disk drive.
MS-DOS. IBM or compatible (512k). 5.25" disk $49.95 (ISBN 0-9625733-2-9); 3.5" disk $49.95 (ISBN 0-9625733-1-0). *Nonstandard peripherals required:* Hard disk drive.
An Environmental Policy Simulation Game Using a "Hypertext" Format with 150 Screens of Information.
Chris Crawford Games.

Balancing Act. 1994. *Items Included:* Book & software (teacher's manual). *Customer Support:* Technical support available - no charge; free upgrading.
System 7.0 or higher. Mac LC or higher (1Mb). $79.95 school; $129.95 5-user; $179.95 10-user; $379.95 30-user (ISBN 1-57116-006-X).
Computers & Mathematical Models Make a Powerful Learning Combination. Balancing Act Combines Devices Which Are Used to Represent Equality & Inequality to Create a Unique Computer-Based Learning Environment Where Students Explore Operations Involving Whole Numbers, Integers, Fractions, & Decimals. Select the Learning Environment from the Tool Menu, Set the Options for the Proper Difficulty Level & Instantly Your Macintosh Computer Becomes a Power Tool for Investigating Fundamental Math Concepts. Students Will Find Working with Balancing Act to Be a Delightful Experience. Tutorials Lead Students to an Understanding of Important Mathematical Concepts. Terms & Phrases Used in the Program Are Explained Through the On-Line Glossary. Teachers Will Find the Reproducible Black Line Masters a Valuable Classroom Resource. Activities Help to Integrate Math & Science, Two Curriculum Areas Where the Study of Equality & Inequality Are Essential.
Ventura Educational Systems.

Baler Spreadsheet Compiler. *Version:* 6.0. 1992. *Compatible Hardware:* IBM PC, PC XT, PC AT, PS/2; 80X87-based systems. *Operating System(s) Required:* PC-DOS/MS-DOS 3.3 or higher. *Language(s):* Assembler, C. *Memory Required:* 640k. *General Requirements:* Hard disk. *Items Included:* Royalty free license. *Customer Support:* Free, unlimited. 60 day money back guarantee.
$499.00.
Free Demo Disk.
Turns Lotus 1-2-3 Spreadsheets into Secure, .EXE Files That Run Directly from DOS. Formulas Become Invisible & Unchangeable. Macros & Calculations Run Faster. Create Pull-Down or Pop-Up Menus, or Custom F1-Key Help. Print Spreadsheet - Publishing Output.
Baler Software Corp.

Baler XE. *Version:* 2.0. *Customer Support:* Free, unlimited. 60 day money back guarantee.
$799.00.
A Superset of Baler 6.0. Allows User to Call C Routines from Macros & Functions in Compiled Spreadsheets. Over 150 "Hooks" Are Provided into the Spreadsheet Engine. Other Features

TITLE INDEX

Include the Ability to Print Graphs Directly from the Compiled Worksheet, dBASE-Like Input Validation & a Macro-Debugger.
Baler Software Corp.

Ball Turret Gunner. *Compatible Hardware:* TRS-80.
write for info.
Instant Software, Inc.

Balloon Stack. Jan. 1991. *Items Included:* 30 specialty balloons. *Customer Support:* 30 day unlimited warranty; 800 number phone support; no shipping charges.
Macintosh Classic, Plus or higher. 3.5" disk $35.00. *Addl. software required:* Hypercard 1.0 or higher.
Hypercard Program Illustrating How to Make over 30 Different Balloon Figures. Each Figure Is Fully Illustrated & Cross Referenced.
BugByte, Inc.

Ballyhoo. Jeff O'Neill. Jan. 1986. *Compatible Hardware:* Atari XL/XE, ST; Apple II, II+, IIe, IIc, Macintosh; Commodore 64, 128, Amiga; IBM PC, PCjr, PC XT, PC AT. *Memory Required:* 48k. disk $39.95.
You Find Yourself in a Mysterious Crime-Ridden Underworld Where a Kidnapping Has Taken Place. Your Mission Is to Solve the Crime.
Activision, Inc.

B&TA: Billing & Time Accounting System. 1981. *Compatible Hardware:* IBM PC & compatibles. *Operating System(s) Required:* PC-DOS, MS-DOS. *Memory Required:* 512k. *General Requirements:* Hard disk, printer.
disk $990.00-$3550.00.
Handles Attorney Timekeeping, Disbursements, Billing, Trust Accounting, & Financial Reporting. Produces Aged AR, Aged WIP, & Realization Cash/Receipt Allocation. Includes Report Writer for User-Defined Reports & Inquiries; Extensive Password Security Protection, & Audit Trails. Integrated with BARRISTER's LAW FIRM ACCOUNTING Package (ALFA). Network Version Available.
Barrister Information Systems Corp.

Bank Accounts Payable. *Version:* 6.03. *Items Included:* 8 1/2" X 11" hard-cover manual. *Customer Support:* 90-day free telephone support; optional annual maintenance, $300; On-site training & other services available; 30-day limited guarantee.
MS-DOS 3.3x or higher. IBM PC/XT, AT, PS/2 & compatibles (640K). disk single user $995.00. *Networks supported:* Novell, 3-COM, Token Ring, etc.
A Complete Accounts Payable System. Use Existing Checkforms. Unlimited G/L Distribution. Standard Distributions May Be Defined. Supports Cash & Accrual Basis Accounting.
Weston & Muir.

Bank*Count*Calc. Nov. 1986. *Items Included:* Instruction manual. *Customer Support:* Telephone support, Instruction, modem support.
PC-DOS (128k). IBM PC, PC XT, PC AT & compatibles. 3.5" or 5.25" disk $675.00. *Addl. software required:* Microsoft Quick Basic Compiler.
Stand-Alone Dedicated Turnkey Savings Account Application Program for Micros. Menu-Driven, Keyed to Date-of-Entry for Variable Applications, (Regular Deposit Account - CD's - IRA's - Quarterly Compound Xmas Clubs - etc.). Provides Simple Customer Profile with Expanded Fields.
Computx.

Bank-On-It. *Items Included:* Modem & communicatons software. *Customer Support:* Telephone support, regulatory compliance, product enhancements, newsletters. Windows & DOS-based systems. 486. Contact publisher for price.
PC-Based System That Enables Banks to Deliver Electronic Cash Management Services to Business Customers. This System Eliminates Time-Consuming Tasks & Improves Efficiency for Both Banks & Their Customers. Banks Choose the Modules They Need: Balance & Statement Reporting - Customers Access Account Information at Their PCs; Reconcile - Customers Automate Account Reconciliation at Their PCs; Transact - Customers Originate ACH Transactions at Their PCs; Wire - Customers & Bank Departments Initiate Wire Transfers at Their PCs. Extensive Security Features, Communications Software, & Electronic Mail Capability Are Included with Each System.
Learned-Mahn.

Bank Reconciliation. *Version:* 7.2. 1989. *Items Included:* Documentation, 3.5" or 5.25" program diskettes. *Customer Support:* 1 hour telephone support included, additional support on a fee basis, on-site training $75 hr.
PC-DOS, MS-DOS (384k). IBM PC. disk $125.00. *Optimal configuration:* Hard disk. *Networks supported:* Novell, LANTASTIC, MS Windows.
DOS (512k). disk $125.00. *Nonstandard peripherals required:* Hard disk.
Interfaces with General Ledger, Accounts Receivable, Accounts Payable & Payroll to Automatically Perform Bank Reconciliation & Print Reports.
Lake Avenue Software.

Bank Street Filer. Bank Street College of Education & Franklin E. Smith. *Compatible Hardware:* Apple IIe, IIc, IIgs; Commodore 64, 128. *Memory Required:* Commodore 64k, Apple 64-128k.
Apple IIe, IIc with 128k. disk $69.95 (Order no.: 30251).
Commodore 64/128. disk $29.95 (Order no.: 84130).
Data Management & Filing System for Small Business, Schools & the Home. Uses Simple English Sentences to Select & Sort Data, Includes "Browse" Function, "Comment" Fields & On-Screen Field Positioning.
Broderbund Software, Inc.

Bank Street Writer. Bank Street College of Education et al. *Compatible Hardware:* Apple II+, IIe, IIc, IIgs; Atari 400, 800, XL, XE series; Commodore 64, 128; IBM PC, & compatibles, PCjr; Tandy. *Operating System(s) Required:* AOS, Apple DOS 3.3, CBM DOS, MS-DOS. *Language(s):* Pascal. *Memory Required:* Atari & Commodore 48k; Apple 64k; IBM & Tandy 128k.
Apple II+, IIe with 64k. disk $69.95 (Order no.: APDSK-80).
Apple IIe, IIc with 128k. disk $69.95 (Order no.: APDSK-800).
Atari. disk $49.95 (Order no.: ATDSK-81).
Commodore. disk $49.95 (Order no.: COMDSK-82).
IBM & Tandy. disk $79.95 (Order no.: IBMDSK-83).
Word Processing Program Which Does Not Contain Codes That Need to Be Memorized but Which Uses Plain English, On-Screen Prompts & Menu to Guide User. Features Include Print Format Routines in Memory; Automatic Word Wrap; Centering; Indexing & Page Numbering; Universal Search & Replace; Password Protection; Document Chaining; Page Headers; Upper & Lower Case; Add, Move, Insert or Delete Single Words, Lines or Entire Blocks of Text; Indent; Utility Programs & Back-Up Disk. Apple IIe & IIc Have Mouse Option.
Broderbund Software, Inc.

BAR CODE FACTORY

Banko (Order). Byron A. Myhre & Henry M. Taylor. Mar. 1987. *Compatible Hardware:* IBM PC & compatibles, PCjr, PC XT, PC AT. *Operating System(s) Required:* MS-DOS 2.XX. *Language(s):* BASIC. *Memory Required:* 128k. disk $47.00, incl. documentation (ISBN 0-89189-248-6, Order no.: 68-9-007-20).
Tests the User's Knowledge of Blood Type Compatibilities & Blood Bank Management Skills.
ASCP Pr.

Bankreporter I. *Compatible Hardware:* IBM PC. *Operating System(s) Required:* MS-DOS, PC-DOS. *Memory Required:* 512k. *General Requirements:* 132-column printer.
contact publisher for price.
Asset/Liability Management System When Coupled with GAPMANAGER I. Accepts Forecasted Balances & Rates Then Produces Detailed Reports.
Distributed Planning System Corp.

The Banner Machine. *Version:* 4.0. Jan. 1989. *Compatible Hardware:* IBM PC & compatibles. *Operating System(s) Required:* MS-DOS. *Language(s):* Compiled BASIC. *Memory Required:* 256k. *General Requirements:* Epson MX printerwith Graftrax, Epson LX, FX, RX. *Items Included:* Manual, disk. *Customer Support:* Free call 703-491-6502.
$59.95.
Creates Signs, Banners, Posters, & Announcements. User Can Make Signs up to 14 Inches Tall by Any Length. Eight Sizes of Letters Are Available from 3/4" to 6 1/2" High. Ten Fonts (Letter Styles), 26 Graphic Symbols, 20 Textured Background Shades & 30 Different Border Styles Are Included.
Cardinal Software (Virginia).

Banner Magic. 1982. *Compatible Hardware:* Apple II series. *Language(s):* Compiled Applesoft BASIC. *Memory Required:* 48k. *Customer Support:* 1 backup disk.
disk $39.95.
Allows User to Create Banners on the Printer for Picnics, Parties, Special Celebrations, or Sporting Events. Uses Seven Inch Letters on Large Banners. Lab packs Available.
American Eagle Software, Inc.

Banner Printer. 1981. *Compatible Hardware:* Commodore 16, Plus 4, 64, 128, VIC-20; TRS-80 Model I, Model III, Tandy 16B, 6000. *Language(s):* BASIC & MBASIC. *Memory Required:* 16k.
disk $14.95.
cassette $9.95.
listing $3.95.
Prints Letters & Characters in Banner Style on Printer.
Raymond L. Reynolds.

BannerMania.
Macintosh. 3.5" disk $35.00.
Lets User Produce Banners, Posters, Bumperstickers, & All Kinds of Messages with Incredible Special Effects Like Stretch Type, Distort Shapes, Shadows, Perspective, 3D, & More. Can Form Banners, into Arches, Ribbons, Pennants, & 24 Others Shapes. Choose from 19 Fonts, 40 Ready-to-Use Designs, 68 Colors for Color Printers, & 13 Shades with Four Patterns on Monochrome Printers. Regardless of Printer, User Gets Smooth, High-Quality Output, Easy Resizing, & Preview Any Time Before Printing.
Broderbund Software, Inc.

Bar Code Factory. 1988. *Items Included:* Software & documentation. *Customer Support:* Free telephone support.
Apple Macintosh Plus, SE. 3.5" disk $179.95.
Bar Code Printing Software. Creates Sequential List of Codes. Creates Duplicate Codes from Bar Code Reader Scans.
Computext.

BAR CODE GENERATOR & READER SOFTWARE

Bar Code Generator & Reader Software.
Version: 3.2. *Compatible Hardware:* IBM PC & compatibles. *Operating System(s) Required:* MS-DOS/PC-DOS. *Language(s):* Compiled BASIC. *Memory Required:* 128k. *General Requirements:* Printer, bar code reader; subsystem requires bar code wand.
disk $295.00.
Menu-Driven, Interactive Program Designed to Print Bar Code Symbols for Various Products. Allows the Following Bar Code Symbologies: Alpha-Numeric Code 39, Numeric Interleaved Two or Five, Numeric Code Two or Five, Numeric Codabar, Numeric UPC Version A. Features Included Are Auto Increment/Decrement of Numeric Fields, User-Specified Bar Codes Heights & Label Sizes, Interpretation Line Printed in OCR-A Font.
Dataflow Technologies, Inc.

Bar Code Labeler. *Version:* 1.2. 1992. *Compatible Hardware:* Apple Macintosh. *Language(s):* Pascal. *Memory Required:* 512k. *General Requirements:* Supports LaserWriter or ImageWriter printers. *Customer Support:* Free telephone support.
3.5" disk $89.00 (Order no.: TWS-005).
Allows Users to Design Custom Labels, All Macintosh Font & Type Styles Can Be Used to Print Mailing, Bar Code, & Other Types of Labels. Uses Information from Any Program That Saves Information in a Text Format, Such As MS EXCEL, FILEMAKER, & MSWORD. Prints on Label Stock Using Either the LaserWriter or ImageWriter Printers.
Videx, Inc.

Bar Code Labeler 2. Jan. 1994. *Items Included:* Complete manual supporting both entry & technical users. *Customer Support:* Free telephone support.
System 7. Macintosh (2Mb). 3.5" disk $149.00 (Order no.: BLS-001). *Optimal configuration:* Any Macintosh with 2Mb or higher.
Full-Featured Bar Code Printing Software Program That Lets You Create, Print & Edit Bar Codes with Ease. All Popular Bar Code Symbologies Are Supported: Code 3of9, 1 2of5, Code 128, Code 93, WPC (A&R), EAN, & Codabar. You Can Create Labels by Keying Data in or Merging Data from a File. Detailed Graphics Can Be Used from Other Programs & Bar Codes from Bar Code Labeler II Can Be Pasted into Other Application Software.
Videx, Inc.

Bar Code Printer. *Items Included:* Bound manual. *Customer Support:* Free hotline - no time limit; 30 day limited warranty; updates are $5/disk plus S&H.
MS-DOS 2.0 or higher. IBM & compatibles (128k). disk $39.95. *Nonstandard peripherals required:* Dot matrix printer (IBM, Epson, Okidata, or compatible).
Prints the Widely Used Code 39 & Interleaved 2-of-5 Bar Codes. The Bar Codes Have a Resolution of 120 x 70 Dots per Inch, & Meet the Standard Tolerances to Assure High Readability. Adjusts to Any Label Size or Position. Data Can Be Entered Directly from the Keyboard or from a Data File (e.g., Text Files, Lotus 1-2-3 & Symphony Print Files, or dBASE II & dBASE III Plus Database Files). Human-Readable Characters Can Be Printed Below the Bar Code & the Bar Code Can Be Printed Anywhere on the Page.
Dynacomp, Inc.

Bar Code Pro. *Version:* 3.0. Feb. 1996. *Items Included:* Disk, manual with registration cards. *Customer Support:* Telephone support - Eastern Standard Time Mon-Fri 9:00am - 5:00pm (718) 369-2944.
System 6.0 or newer. (System 7.0 compatible. Macintosh Plus or higher (1Mb). $195.00 for all 18 codes (ISBN 1-880773-00-7). *Nonstandard peripherals required:* Printer.
Desk Accessory That Generates EPS or PICT Graphics for Code 39, Code 25, ITF (Interweave 2 of 5), ITF-14, Codabar, Code 128, UPC(A), UPC(E), EAN-8, EAN-13, ISSN, ISBN, POSTNET/FIM. Can Be Used with Any Popular Desktop Publishing Software Application; Pantone Colors Now Available.
Synex.

Bar Code Pro Filemaster. Feb. 1996. *Items Included:* Manual, 188 pages.
System 7.0 or higher. Macintosh (2Mb). Contact publisher for price.
A Single Solution for All Inventory, Tracking, & Labeling Needs. Allows User to Customize Database, Add Bar Code, Graphics, Video Images, Text or Numbers & Print Any Sort of Bar Coded Label Imaginable. The Perfect Solution for Inventory Control, Warehouse Management, Libraries, Filing, Personnel Files, Job Tracking, Name Badges, Mail Lists, Tags, & Collections. Enables User to Create Databases with Text, Numbers & Graphics. Choose from Any of the 100 Plus Preformatted Templates or Create Your Own Labels with Photos, Bar Code, Text or Graphics. Merge the Database Information with Your Own Custom Label Designs & Print to Any Macintosh Compatible Printer. Perfect for Tracking & Printing Bar Coded Labels. Powerful Features Allow You to Batch Print, Sort, & Color, Serialize, & Adjust Bar Width to Get Perfect Bar Code Every Time.
Synex.

Bar Code Pro Reader: User's Guide. Allen Lubow. Jul. 1995. *Items Included:* Bar code Pro Reader Cable, Manual. *Customer Support:* 30 day money back guarantee. Tech support 718-369-2944 M-F 9:00AM-5:00PM EST.
System 6.7 (System 7 Rec). Mac Plus or higher (1Mb). disk $199.00 (ISBN 1-880773-20-1).
A Durable, Compact, & Light-Weight Bar Code Reader Which Plugs Directly into the ADB Port of Your Computer or Keyboard. Requires No Additional Software or Power Supply. Data Is Sent to Your Computer Just Like Keyboard Entry. It Reads All Major Symbologies.
Synex.

Bar Coding. *Memory Required:* 512k. *Customer Support:* Free.
MS-DOS. IBM/PC/XT/AT & compatibles, IBM PS/2 (512k). single-user or Network (without barcode hardware) $595.00. *Nonstandard peripherals required:* Hard disk, 132 column printer.
The Bar Code System of INMASS II, MC Software's Integrated Manufacturing Software Package, Includes a Program for Printing Bar Codes, a "Wedge" Type Bar Code Reader, a Descriptive Manual with Templates & a Short Card That Fits into Any IBM PC or Compatible Machine. MC Software Eliminates the Problem of Finding Compatible Manufacturing Software & Bar Code Hardware. The Flexibility of This System Allows the User to Lay Out His Own Reports, Mixing Bar Coded Information with Normal Text Information. The User Decides what Information Is to Be Bar Coded & How It Is to Be Presented.
INMASS/MRP.

Bar-Min-Ski: Consumer Product. *Version:* 2.0. Webster Lewin et al. Jul. 1995. *Items Included:* Small booklet. *Customer Support:* Users may call us directly for support.
MAC; IBM. MAC Power PC (8Mb); IBM 386SX or higher, 640X480 color display 256 colors (8Mb). CD-ROM disk $39.95 (ISBN 0-9647676-0-0). *Addl. software required:* Quicktime 1.61 or higher; Microsoft Windows 3.1 MS-DOS 5.0.
Features the Work of Noted Los Angeles Artist Bill Barminski, Who Takes Aim at America's Consumer Based Society Through His Paintings, Music & Interactive Art. This Award-Winning Program Contains over 160 Paintings, the Artist's Original Comics, Video Interviews, Plus "SUB-VERT" the Game Where You Are a Crazed Ad Person.
De-Lux'O Consumer Productions.

Barbarian. *Customer Support:* 90 day warranty.
MS-DOS 2.1 or higher (384K). disk $14.99. *Nonstandard peripherals required:* Requires CGA, EGA, Tandy, Hercules, MCGA or VGA Graphics.
Commodore 64 (64K). *Nonstandard peripherals required:* Joystick required.
disk $14.99.
In the Best Tradition of the Most Popular Arcade Games, Now Comes Hegor the Barbarian. Battle Powerful Warriors & Horrific Monsters. Use Your Wits to Defeat Cunning Traps & Ingenious Machines Protecting the Path to Necron's Lair.
Virgin Games.

The Bard's Tale, 2 disks. *Compatible Hardware:* Apple II, II+, IIe, IIc; Commodore 64, 128, Amiga. *Language(s):* Machine. *Memory Required:* 64k.
Apple. $14.95.
Commodore. $14.95.
Features 4 Classes of Magic Users, Including Wizard & Sorcerer, & 85 Magic Spells. There Are 128 Monsters (Many Animated), Full-Color 16-Level Scrolling Dungeons, & a 3-D City. Can Be Played with Characters from WIZARDRY or ULTIMA III.
Electronic Arts.

The Bard's Tale II: The Destiny Knight. Michael Cranford & Interplay Productions. *Compatible Hardware:* Apple II, II+, IIe, IIc, IIgs; Commodore 64, 128, Amiga.
Commodore. disk $14.95.
Apple II. disk $14.95.
Amiga. 3.5" disk $19.95.
Adventure into 6 Cities, 25 Dungeons, & an Entire Wilderness. Discover Clues & Monsters. You Can Bring Your Entire Party from the BARD'S TALE & Mold Your Characters into Powerful Warriors, Bards, & Magicians, or Start with New Characters. Features the Ability to Summon a Monster to Become a Permanent Part of the Party; New Combat Strategies Such As Long-Range Weapons & Head-to-Head Combat; New Places Like the Casino & Bank. Apple Version Uses Characters from WIZARDRY, ULTIMA II, & ULTIMA III.
Electronic Arts.

BARE BONES Accounting. Aug. 1993. *Items Included:* 113 page bound manual with screen illustrations. *Customer Support:* 1 year free training & support by telephone.
PC-DOS 2.1 or higher, MS-DOS 2.1 or higher. IBM PC & compatibles (640k). disk $55.00. Networks supported: Inquire with author.
Bookkeeping for Multiple Funds & Projects Operated Jointly from Same Bank Accounts. Reports for All Combined or Each Separately. Designate One Account to Be Increased or Decreased & the Program Determines Whether the Other Chosen Account Is Increased or Decreased. Automatic Allocation of Interest According to Daily Average Balances.
J W Funsten Publisher.

BarGen. *Version:* 3.22. Mar. 1982. *Compatible Hardware:* IBM PC, PC XT, PC AT, PCjr & compatibles; Xerox 820; Kaypro; North Star;

Osborne; Morrow; Superbrain. *Operating System(s) Required:* CP/M, MS-DOS, PC-DOS. *Language(s):* CB-86. *Memory Required:* 64k. *General Requirements:* IBM or Epson Graphics compatible printer (MX, FX, RX, LQ or EX). *Customer Support:* Tech phone support.
disk $345.00.
Bar Code Label Generating System for Microcomputers. Allows User to Create Bar Code on Any Size Gummed Labels (As Well As on Plain Paper & Special Stock) for Their Products, Customer Names, Payroll Numbers, & Other Data, Which Can Then Be Read in with Bar Code Reader. Utilizes Code-39, & Prints at Either 3.5 or 6 Characters per Inch Using All Letters in Alphabet, All Numbers, & Space. Program Generates Varying Sizes of Bar Code. User Can Change All Default Values to Vary Height & Width of Bars, Label Size, & Add up to 25 Lines of Text above & under Bar Code. Also Generates OCR Font to Meet U.S. Government Requirement for Incoming Products. Accepts Data Entry from Keyboard or Standard Data File.
KDA Systems.

Barney O'Blarney's Magic Spells. 1992. *Items Included:* Detailed manuals are included with all DYNACOMP products. *Customer Support:* Free telephone support to original customer - no time limit; 30 day limited warranty.
MS-DOS 3.2 or higher. IBM PC & compatibles (512k). $29.95 (Add $5.00 for 3 1/2" format; 5 1/4" format standard).
Will Improve Your Child's Spelling & Math Reasoning Ability. Barney O'Blarney Will Lead Your Child on a Chase Through the Forest in Search of the Famous Pot of Gold. Barney Gives Clues about the Location of the Pot of Gold in Reward for Correctly Spelling His Words. A Special Reward Awaits the Child Who Learns All 500 Spelling Words. The Word List Supplied Covers Grades 1 Through 7, but You Can Easily Add Your Own Words.
Dynacomp, Inc.

Barnstorming Microstation 3-D. 1996. *Customer Support:* ECS offers technical support to registered users. Call (217) 359-7099. Other than the telephone call - technical support is no charge.
Windows 3.1. IBM. disk $199.95, MSRP (Order no.: I-1480). *Addl. software required:* Microstation.
Macintosh. 3.5" disk $199.95, MSRP. *Addl. software required:* Microstation.
This Program Is an Interactive "Hypermedia" Tutorial Designed to Completely Cover the Concepts of MicroStation's 3-D Capabilities. Compatible with DOS & Windows.
Electronic Courseware Systems, Inc.

BARON: The Real Estate Simulation. Blue Chip Software, Inc. *Compatible Hardware:* HP 150 Touchscreen, IBM PC.
3.5" disk $59.95 (Order no.: 92243KA).
Economic Simulation Based on a Complex Historical Model of the Real Estate Market. You Start with $35,000 & Have 60 Simulated Months to Parlay It into a Fortune by Buying, Selling, & Developing Different Kinds of Properties in Five U.S. States.
Hewlett-Packard Co.

BaronData Personal CAT: Computer Aided Transcription System, 13 disks. May 1986. *Compatible Hardware:* IBM PC, PC XT, PC AT. *Operating System(s) Required:* PC-DOS 3.1. *Memory Required:* 640k.
IBM PC AT set. $8995.00 (Order no.: 120-2000).
IBM PC XT set. $8995.00 (Order no.: 920-2001).
Personal CAT set. $5000.00 (Order no.: 920-2005).
Allows Court Reporters & Other Steno Machine Users to Produce Transcripts of Court Proceedings, Depositions or Hearings.
Stanograph Corp.

The Barrister Financial Management System. *Operating System(s) Required:* MBOS, MBIX. *Memory Required:* 1024k.
contact publisher for price.
Automated System for Timekeeping, Billing, & Financial Reporting That Will Track the Firm's Financial Data. Provides Several Reports to Help Users Assess Their Financial Condition & Manage Their Firm More Effectively. Some of the Programs Available Through the FINANCIAL MANAGEMENT SYSTEM Include: Time & Disbursement Accounting, General Ledger Accounting, Accounts Payable, Client Trust Accounting, Checkwriter, & Supercomp Financial Modeling.
Barrister Information Systems Corp.

Barrister/Messager Electronic Mail. 1987. *Compatible Hardware:* IBM PC & compatibles, minicomputers. *Operating System(s) Required:* PC-DOS, MS-DOS, MBOS, MBIX.
contact publisher for price.
Multi-User Messaging System Designed to Simplify Intra- & Inter-Office Communications in Law Firms. Messages Can Be Sent to Any User of the System, or Any Groups of Users. Messages Are Automatically Time & Date Stamped & May Be Tagged 'Urgent' by the Sender. Telephone Messaging Also Allows for Phone Message Relay to Mail Users. Also Features Security Safeguards & Message Management Capabilities.
Barrister Information Systems Corp.

Barrister/Publisher Document Finishing System. 1987. *Compatible Hardware:* IBM PC & compatibles. *Operating System(s) Required:* MS-DOS. *Memory Required:* 2048k. *General Requirements:* Hard disk, printer. Modem optional.
contact publisher for price.
Provides Text & Graphics Output at Near-Typeset Quality. The Workstation Is Based on a BARRISTER 80286/80386 PC with 40-80Mb Hard disk. Can Be Networked with a Minicomputer or Microcomputer System.
Barrister Information Systems Corp.

The Barrister Relational Database Management System. *Operating System(s) Required:* MBOS, MBIX. *Language(s):* C. *Memory Required:* 1024k.
$7,900.00-$13,900.00.
Information Storage & Retrieval System That Can Be Applied to Most Information Needs of a Law Office. May Be Used to Automate a Variety of Functions Including: Litigation Support Document Management, Calendar/Docket Control, Conflict of Interest Checking, Attorney Work Product Retrieval, Case Management/Case Status Tracking, File Room Management, Library Card Indexing. Features Include Menus & Prompts; Menu Bypass; SQL-Standard English Command Language; Cursor-Based Interactive Data Entry, Edit & Delete; Global Edit & Delete; Batch or Interactive Data Entry; Form Windowing.
Barrister Information Systems Corp.

The Barrister Word Processing System. *Version:* 4.5. Nov. 1988. *Compatible Hardware:* IBM PC, PC XT, PC AT & compatibles. *Operating System(s) Required:* MS-DOS, MBOS. *Memory Required:* 640k.
contact publisher for price.
Simplifies Professional Document Production by Automating Complex Functions Such As Footnoting, Paragraph & Page Numbering, & Outlining. The System Combines Editing Features with Formatting Features & Creates Tables of Contents & Authorities Automatically. Other Features Include Spell Checking with a Coaching Option, Keystroke Memory, Enhanced Background Functions, & List File Merge That Allows Users to Combine a Single Document with Many Sets of Available Data, Such As the Same Letter Sent to Many Addresses.
Barrister Information Systems Corp.

Barry the Bear: Explore the Polar World with Your New Friend Barry. *Items Included:* Pamphlet of instructions. *Customer Support:* Tech support, 60 day money-back guarantee.
Windows; Macintosh. IBM compatible 386SX or higher (4Mb); Mac LC or higher (2.5Mb). CD-ROM disk $39.95 (ISBN 0-924677-05-8). *Nonstandard peripherals required:* Audio board, mouse, CD-ROM drive. *Addl. software required:* Video card 640x480 with 256 colors; Quicktime 2.0.
Explore the Polar World with Barry the Bear. Six Activities & Games Are Introduced by "Nalaag," the Young Eskimo Boy, As You Learn about Polar Bears in Greenland.
IMSI (International Microcomputer Software, Inc.).

Bartender's Friend. 1981. *Compatible Hardware:* Commodore 64, 128. *Language(s):* BASIC (source code included). *Memory Required:* 40k.
disk $14.95.
cassette $9.95.
Contains Liquor Recipes & Terms.
Raymond L. Reynolds.

BAS. *Compatible Hardware:* Cromemco Systems. *Operating System(s) Required:* UNIX. *Memory Required:* 1024k.
$1995.00.
BASIC Language System.
Cromemco, Inc.

BAS-C: BASIC to C Converter, 14 disks. *Version:* 5.7. Jun. 1992. *Operating System(s) Required:* PC-DOS, MS-DOS, XENIX, UNIX. (source code included). *Memory Required:* 640k. *General Requirements:* 2 disk drives.
$495.00 to $875.00.
Converts BASIC Source Programs into C Source Programs Which Can Be Compiled Directly by Any C Compiler. Also Transforms "Spaghetti-Code" to Structured Statements Such As Switch, While, Do-While, If-Then-Else. Gotoless Conversion.

BAS-C 286: BASIC to C Translator. *Version:* 5.7. Joe Smith. Jun. 1992. *Items Included:* 3 spiral-bound manual, 14 diskettes. *Customer Support:* BBS 214-625-6905.
MS-DOS. IBM PC (640k). disk $1189.00. *Addl. software required:* C compiler. *Optimal configuration:* 640k hard disk.
Converts BASICA/QUICK BASIC into C Source Programs Which Can Be Compiled Directly by Any C Compiler. Also Restructures Any Spaghetti Code into Indented Top-Down Modules. Gotoless Conversion.

BAS-C386 XENIX: Basic to C Translator. *Version:* 5.3. Joe Smith. Jun. 1990. *Items Included:* 3 spiral-bound manual. 14 diskettes. *Customer Support:* BBS 214-625-6905.
XENIX 386. IBM PC (1Mb). disk $1129.00. *Addl. software required:* XENIX 386 Development System. *Optimal configuration:* 1MB memory, 20Mb hard disk.
Converts BASICA/QUICK BASIC into C Source Programs Which Can Be Compiled Directly by XENIX C Compiler. Also Restructures Any Spaghetti Code into Indented Top-Down Modules. Gotoless Conversion.

BAS-PAS: BASIC to Pascal Converter. *Version:* 2.5. Ken Hasimoto. Feb. 1986. *Operating System(s) Required:* PC-DOS/MS-DOS 2.1 or higher. (source code included). *Memory Required:* 192k.
disk $199.00.
Menu-Driven Software That Converts BASIC to Pascal. Transforms "Spagetti" Code into Structured Code Such As IF-THEN-(ELSE), REPEAT-UNTIL, WHILE-END, & CASE Statement Automatically. Separates Complex, Overlapped BASIC into Many Pascal Procedures in the Top-Down Fashion.
Gotoless Conversion.

Baseball Book Statistics. *Compatible Hardware:* TRS-80 Model III. *Operating System(s) Required:* TRSDOS. *Memory Required:* 32k.
cassette $29.95.
Helps User Maintain a Cumulative Total of Baseball Players' Performance Records. Scorebook Entries Include Bats, Runs Batted in, & Hits & Errors. Averages & Season Histories Can Be Produced for Single Players or Entire Teams.
Educational Data Systems, Inc.

The Baseball Database. *Compatible Hardware:* Apple IIgs, IIe, IIc; Commodore 64/128.
Apple. disk $49.95.
Commodore. disk $39.95.
Baseball Database. Keep Track of Your Team's Baseball Stats.
Jacobsen Software Designs.

Baseball League Statistics. *Version:* 1.1. May 1985. *Compatible Hardware:* IBM PC, PCjr, PC XT, PC AT, PS/2. *Operating System(s) Required:* PC-DOS 2.1 or higher. *Language(s):* Compiled BASIC. *Memory Required:* 256k. *Items Included:* Disk, User Guide. *Customer Support:* 800 number phone support.
$39.95.
Allows Team Manager to Maintain All Statistics on Individual Team Members. Batting, Pitching, & Fielding Statistics Can Be Maintained for Single Team or Entire Leagues. Full Game-by-Game History Records Are Also Maintained. Several Reporting Options Allow Reporting on Individual Players or Entire Teams.
Mighty Byte Computer, Inc.

Baseball Power. *Customer Support:* 800-929-8117 (customer service).
MS-DOS. IBM/PS2. disk $49.99 (ISBN 0-87007-853-4).
One Can Make All of the Managers Decisions in Major League Baseball. Great for Boning up on the Strategy of Major League Baseball.
SourceView Software International.

Baseball Records. Merle W. Wagner. 1983. *Compatible Hardware:* Apple II+, IIe, IIc. *Operating System(s) Required:* Apple DOS 3.3. *Language(s):* BASIC. *Memory Required:* 48k. *General Requirements:* Printer.
disk $49.95, incl. manual (ISBN 0-922900-43-4, Order no.: CFS-830).
additional manual $19.95.
back-up disk $9.95.
Baseball Statistics Program That Can Be Used by Several Teams. Entry Includes: Identification Code, Player, Opponent, Innings Pitched, Earned Runs, Games, Wins/Losses, Hits Given up, Runs, Strikeouts, Shutouts, Saves, Chances, Errors, Putouts, Assists, At Bats, Hits, Base on Balls, Doubles, Triples, Home Runs, Steals, Runs Batted In, & Average. Reports Can Be on an Individual or Several Players.
Cherrygarth, Inc.

The Baseball Statbook. 1984. *Compatible Hardware:* IBM PC. *Operating System(s) Required:* PC-DOS. *Memory Required:* 256k.
disk $69.00.
Maintains Game, Year-to-Date, & Historical (Lifetime) Baseball/Softball Statistics.
RJL Systems.

Baseball the Series: Pitching Clinic. Nov. 1995. *Customer Support:* 60 Day Limited Warranty.
Windows. PC Compatible (4mg). CD-ROM disk $49.95 (ISBN 1-887209-26-3). *Addl. software required:* Windows 3.1. *Optimal configuration:* 80486/33 mhz PC with MPC compatible sound card, mouse, speakers, color VGA, 8 bit VGA adapter (256 colors), 4 MB Ram (8 MB or greater preferred) DC-ROM Drive, 6 MB or greater free disk space, MSDOS 5.0 or later & Windows 3.1.
Personal Interactive Training Camp on CD-ROM Teaching the Fundamentals of Proper Pitching Mechanics. The Major Aspects of Pitching Are Covered, Including Arm Preparation, Proper Warm-Up, Pitching Mechanics, Covering First Base, Pitching Tips, Etc. Images, Photos, Videos, Graphics, & Animation Enhance the Actual Detailed Audio Lessons As They Are Presented.
Spirit of St. Louis Software Co.

BASIC. *Items Included:* Software, manuals. *Customer Support:* 1 full year of support is included with each product purchased. Support includes hotline phone support, technical mailings, & free upgrades.
PDOS. Motorola 680 x 0 based systems. disk $900.00 (Order no.: 3520). *Networks supported:* Ethernet, MAP.
Combines Compiler Performance with the Convenience of an Interpreter in a Unique Approach to Program Development. While Most Microcomputer Interpreters Are Slow, PDOS BASIC Executes As Fast As Many Threaded Code Compilers. PDOS BASIC Commands Are Parsed into Executable Tokens During Program Entry & Not at Execution Time. As a Result, Program Lines Do Not Require Passing Every Time They Execute.
Eyring Corp.

Basic Accounting Course. *Version:* 2.0. Mar. 1994. *Items Included:* Workbooks & computer graded testing. *Customer Support:* Consultation by mail, certificate upon satisfactory completion.
MS-DOS. IBM & compatibles (256k). $360.00 (installment plan available). *Optimal configuration:* Printer needed.
Teaches All Phases of Small Business Accounting Procedures. Comprehensive Workbook Included. Computer Tested & Graded at End of Each Lesson with Hard Copy of Test Results. Quick Backup to Previous Screens for Review Purposes. Graphics to Aid in Visualizing Concepts.
D W N.

Basic Aircraft Performance. S. A. Powers. 1984. *Compatible Hardware:* IBM PC, Macintosh. *Operating System(s) Required:* Macintosh, PC-DOS 2.0. *Language(s):* BASIC (source code included). *Memory Required:* 64k.
disk $180.00 ea. incl. manual & documentation.
IBM Kit. (Order no.: 810-IK).
Macintosh Kit. (Order no.: 810-AK).
A System of 8 Interacting Programs Which Can Be Used to Estimate the Performance of Aircraft, Both on Prescribed Missions & in Maneuvering Flight at Prescribed Conditions. Drag Prediction Program, a Thrust/Fuel Input & Evaluation Program, & a Simple Method of Describing Complex Missions Are Included. User Is Taken from a Three-View Drawing of an Aircraft with a Table of Thrust/Fuel Flow Data for the Engine to a Completed Performance Envelope & a Mission Performance Description.
Kern International, Inc.

Basic Builder II. *Version:* 4.5. Feb. 1990. *Compatible Hardware:* IBM PC, AT & compatibles, 286,386. *Operating System(s) Required:* PC-DOS, MS-DOS. *Memory Required:* 640k. *General Requirements:* Printer.
contact publisher for price.
Designed for the Small Volume Builder & a Single-User System. Includes 4 Integrated Modules: Job Cost, Accounts Payable, Accounts Receivable & General Ledger. Optional Modules Include Payroll, Basic Bid (Estimating), Billing Inventory.
Construction Data Control, Inc. (CDCI).

Basic Business Finance. *Compatible Hardware:* IBM PC & compatibles, PC XT. *Operating System(s) Required:* PC-DOS 2.0 or higher.
disk $95.00.
Introduces the PC User to the Basic Ideas of Business Finance, Assets, Liabilities, Shareholders Equity, the Balance Sheet, Cash Flow, Income & Corporate Profitability. Allows User to Develop the Appropriate Business Forms.
Softext Publishing Corp.

Basic Business Forecasting. *Compatible Hardware:* IBM PC & compatibles, PC XT. *Operating System(s) Required:* PC-DOS 2.0 or higher. *Memory Required:* 192k.
disk $95.00.
All the Basic, Easy to Use Methods of Statistical Forecasting Including Data Smoothing, Moving Averages, Exponential Smoothing, Extrapolation, Curve Fitting & Seasonal Analysis.
Softext Publishing Corp.

Basic Business Graphics. *Compatible Hardware:* IBM PC & compatibles, PC XT. *Operating System(s) Required:* PC-DOS 2.0 or higher.
disk $95.00.
Covers the Use of All the Basic Types of Business Presentation Graphics. Allows the User to Plot All the Basic Types of Graphs, Scatter Plots & Various Combinations of These Graphs.
Softext Publishing Corp.

BASIC Cross Reference Facility. Robert L. Nicolai. Apr. 1983. *Compatible Hardware:* IBM PC & compatibles. *Operating System(s) Required:* MS-DOS. *Language(s):* BASIC, Compiled BASIC (source code included). *Memory Required:* 64k. *General Requirements:* Printer.
disk $25.00 (ISBN 0-925825-00-X).
Finds All Literal Variables in Any BASIC Program, Alphabetizes Them & Prints Them along with a Line Number Cross Reference.
Robert L. Nicolai.

BASIC Development System: BDS. *Version:* 3.1. Dec. 1982. *Compatible Hardware:* Compaq; IBM PC, PC XT, PC AT. *Operating System(s) Required:* PC-DOS, MS-DOS. *Language(s):* Assembly. *Memory Required:* 128k.
PC-DOS. disk $125.00 (ISBN 0-926944-00-2).
MS-DOS. disk $125.00 (ISBN 0-926944-01-0).
Integrated Set of BASIC Language Programming Tools Co-Resident with the Interpreter So That All Functions Are Immediately Available Within the Basic Environment.
BetaTool Systems.

Basic Diet Analysis. 1993. *Items Included:* Disks, instruction binder with all of program's screens & all print outs. *Customer Support:* Technical, M-F 8:30 - 4 pm, Telephone, no charge.
DOS 3.1 or higher. IBM & compatibles (640k).
disk $259.00 (Order no.: DIET). *Optimal configuration:* DOS, hard drive, color monitor, printer.
$269.00 DOS version.
$289.00 Windows version.
$499.00 Network version (either).
User Can Enter Menus in Cycles. Dozens of

TITLE INDEX

Foods Already Installed. Dietary Breakdowns of Installed Foods by Calories, Fat, Protein, Cholesterol. Patient Records Retained in Database. Print Reports by Meal, Day, Week. Eliminates Constant "Figuring Out". Repeat Menus, Edit, or Change Completely. Customize Menus for Your Hospital. Saves Hundreds of Hours Weekly. Edit or Delete Records Instantly. Print Paper Copies As Required by Law. Easy to Learn, Easy to Use.
p.r.n. medical software.

Basic Dispersion Models, 3 diskettes. *Items Included:* Bound manual. *Customer Support:* Free hotline - no time limit; 30 day limited warranty; updates are $5/disk plus S&H.
MS-DOS. IBM & compatibles (256k). $149.95. *Nonstandard peripherals required:* One disk drive; printer supported, but optional.
Apple (64k). $149.95.
Predicts: the Location & Amount of Maximum Ground Level Concentration from a Single Point Source (for Example, an Incinerator Stack) for Various Conditions of Wind Speed & Atmospheric Stability; the Amount of Ground Level Pollution from a Single Point Source at Varying Distances from the Source; the Amount of Ground Level Pollution from Multiple Point Sources at Arbitrary Locations on an x-y Grid.
Dynacomp, Inc.

BASIC EMG #1. *Compatible Hardware:* Commodore 64, 128. *General Requirements:* Standard or Biofeedback EMG sensors.
disk $19.95 (Order no.: DISC64-03-003).
Used to Facilitate Muscle Control & Coordination. Contains Simple BASIC Programs - PONG, PETIT PRIX, SLALOM, & BOMB SQUAD.
Bodylog.

BASIC Fun for the Commodore 64 Beginner. Arthur T. Denzau & Kent L. Forrest. Jun. 1984. *Compatible Hardware:* Commodore 64, Executive 64. *Language(s):* BASIC 20. *Memory Required:* 64k. *General Requirements:* Commodore 1541, 2031, or 4010 disk drive.
disk $19.95, incl. bk. (ISBN 0-13-061441-6).
Programs Use Sprite Graphics, Music Synthesizer & Special Features of the 64.
Prentice Hall.

Basic Gas & Liquid Flow Calculator. *Items Included:* Full manual. No other products required. *Customer Support:* Free telephone support - no time limit, 30 day warranty.
MS-DOS 3.2 or higher. IBM & compatibles (512k). disk $69.95.
Provides 11 Basic Flow Calculations for Liquids & Gases, Including: Fanning's Friction Factor; Frictional Pressure Drop; Flow Rate Versus Pressure Difference; Pressure Drop for Non-Isothermal Flow; Z-Factor; & Six More. Handles Both U.S. & Metric Units. Menu-Driven, with Clear Prompts for Every Input.
Dynacomp, Inc.

Basic Gas & Liquid Flow Calculator. 1992. *Items Included:* Detailed manuals included with all Dynacomp products. *Customer Support:* Free telephone support to original customer - no time limit; 30 day limited warranty.
MS-DOS 3.2 or higher. IBM PC & compatibles (512k). $69.95 (Add $5.00 for 3 1/2" format; 5 1/4" format standard). *Optimal configuration:* IBM, MS-DOS 2.0 or higher, 640k RAM.
Provides 11 Basic Flow Calculations for Liquids & Gases, Including: Fanning's Friction Factor; Frictional Pressure Drop; Flow Rate Versus Pressure Difference; Pressure Drop for Non-Isothermal Flow; Z-Factor; & Six More. Both U.S. & Metric Units.
Dynacomp, Inc.

Basic Gramarcy: The Word Game. Oct. 1986. *Compatible Hardware:* IBM PC, PC XT, PC AT. *Operating System(s) Required:* PC-DOS 2.0 or higher. *Language(s):* Compiled Basic. *Memory Required:* 128k. *General Requirements:* Double-sided disk drive, printer, RAM disk recommended.
disk $15.00.
Computerized Educational Word Game for One Player That Emulates the Word Game Found in the Daily Newspapers.
Robert L. Nicolai.

Basic Lung Volume Calculation. *Compatible Hardware:* Apple II, II+, IIe, IIc; IBM PC, PC XT, PC AT.
$200.00, incl. back-up disk (Order no.: PIP 86100).
Presents Definitions of Common Lung Volumes with Abbreviations.
Educational Software Concepts, Inc.

Basic Math Competency Skill Building. Michael P. Conlon. 1994. *Items Included:* Diskette, teachers guide & binders. *Customer Support:* Toll free customer service Hot Line 1-800-645-3739 (9a.m. - 5p.m. Eastern Time) software guaranteed for two years.
Mac 6.0 Plus. Macintosh (4Mb). 3.5" disk $369.00 (Order no.: DKCOMP3).
These Programs Teach Math Skills, Frequently Checking for Understanding & Emphasize Step-by-Step Problem Solving, Ensuring That Students Do Not Bypass Any Steps in the Process.
Educational Activities Inc.

Basic Photography, 2 diskettes. *Items Included:* Bound manual. *Customer Support:* Free hotline - no time limit; 30 day limited warranty; updates are $5/disk plus S&H.
Apple II. $19.95. *Nonstandard peripherals required:* One disk drive; color monitor helpful, but not required.
Part I Begins by Exploring the Parts That Are Common to Most Cameras: the Iris, Shutter, Lens, Viewfinder, & Film Holder. The Instructional Units Compare Reflex & Non-Reflex Viewing Systems, Show the Differences Between Wide-Angle & Telephoto Lenses, & Illustrate the Effects of Various Iris & Shutter Settings. Part II Concentrates on the Basic Characteristics of Film. After Showing Film Formats That Are Commonly Used, the Tutorial Illustrates the Meaning of the ISO (ASA/DIN) Numbers That Indicate a Film's Sensitivity to Light. The Unit About Black-&-White Film Explains How Black-&-White Negatives & Prints Are Produced. The Color-Film Unit Discusses Color Film, Color Prints, & Color Slides (Transparencies).
Dynacomp, Inc.

Basic Photography. 1992. *Items Included:* Detailed manuals are included with all DYNACOMP products. *Customer Support:* Free telephone support to original customer - no time limit; 30 day limited warranty.
MS-DOS 3.2 or higher. Apple II. $19.95 (Add $5.00 for 3 1/2" format; 5 1/4" format standard). *Optimal configuration:* Apple II with 1 disk drive, Color monitor is helpful, but not required.
Designed to Help the Person Who Would Like to Develop an Interest in Photography, but Is Overwhelmed by the Complexity of the Equipment & Technical Language. Part I Begins by Exploring the Parts That Are Common to Most Cameras: the Iris, Shutter, Lens, Viewfinder, & Film Holder. Part II Concentrates on the Basic Characteristics of Film. After Showing Film Formats That Are Commonly Used, the Tutorial Illustrates the Meaning of the ISO (ASA/DIN) Numbers That Indicates a Film's Sensitivity to Light.
Dynacomp, Inc.

BASIC PROGRAMMER'S LIBRARY

Basic Piano Theory Level 1A, 1B & 2. Sandy Feldstein. 1986. *Compatible Hardware:* Atari, Apple II, Commodore 64, IBM PC & compatibles, Macintosh, Yamaha C1. *Language(s):* BASIC, machine. *Memory Required:* 48k. *General Requirements:* CGA card & color monitor for IBM.
IBM. 3.5" disk $49.95 (ISBN 0-88284-395-8, Order no.: 3149).
IBM. disk $49.95 (ISBN 0-88284-396-6, Order no.: 2107).
Apple, Commodore. 3.5" disk $49.95 (ISBN 0-88284-397-4, Order no.: 2102).
Atari. 3.5" disk $49.95 (ISBN 0-88284-398-2, Order no.: 3512).
Macintosh. 3.5" disk $59.95 (ISBN 0-88284-399-0, Order no.: 3117).
Yamaha C1. disk $49.95 (ISBN 0-88284-450-4, Order no.: 3118).
Apple 3.5. disk $49.95 (ISBN 0-88284-477-6, Order no.: 3948).
Correlates with Alfred's "Basic Piano Library" Books 1A, 1B, & 2. A Game Approach for Piano Education Reinforcement. MIDI Compatible.
Alfred Publishing Co., Inc.

Basic Primer. 1992. *Items Included:* Detailed manuals are included with all DYNACOMP products. *Customer Support:* Free telephone support to original customer - no time limit; 30 day limited warranty.
MS-DOS 3.2 or higher. IBM PC & compatibles (512k). $19.95 (Add $5.00 for 3 1/2" format; 5 1/4" format standard). *Optimal configuration:* IBM, 128k RAM & BASIC or GWBASIC or equivalent.
An Electronic Book with Pages, a Table of Contents, & an Index. This Is a Special Book, However, Because BASIC PRIMER Takes Advantage of Screen Animation & Color to Teach Programming Concepts Like Loops, Variables, & Program Control. It Checks Your Responses & Allows Easy Access to the BASIC Interpreter So That You Can Practice Each New Concept. An Attractive Package for the Computer Novice.
Dynacomp, Inc.

Basic Program Mender. Jan. 1986. *Compatible Hardware:* IBM PC, PC XT, PC AT. *Operating System(s) Required:* PC-DOS/MS-DOS 1.1 or higher. *Language(s):* Compiled BASIC. *Memory Required:* 64k.
disk $20.00.
Allows User to Read & Print Parts of Files, Providing a Means of Reconstructing a Lost File Save in Tokenized Basic.
Robert L. Nicolai.

BASIC Program Printer. Jan. 1985. *Compatible Hardware:* IBM PC, PC XT, PC AT. *Operating System(s) Required:* PC-DOS/ MS-DOS 1.1 or higher. *Language(s):* Compiled BASIC. *Memory Required:* 64k. *General Requirements:* Printer.
disk $25.00.
Reads Any ASCII or Tokenized BASIC Program File Whether or Not That File Is Saved with the P Option (Protected) & Outputs As Desired.
Robert L. Nicolai.

BASIC Programmer's Library. *Compatible Hardware:* HP 150 Touchscreen.
3.5" disk $110.00 (Order no.: 45310A).
Collection of Subroutines, Variable Definitions & Functions That Make the HP Touchscreen's Features Accessible by Calling up a Subroutine. Users Can Access Screen Control Functions, Keyboard Control, Control of the User-Defined Function Keys, Line & Math Character Sets, BIOS Routines via AGIOS Calls, Datacomm & Plotter Devices.
Hewlett-Packard Co.

BASIC Programming Assistant. *Compatible Hardware:* TRS-80 Model I. *Memory Required:* 16-48k.
cassette $19.95 (Order no.: 0203R).
Helps in Writing & Debugging Programs.
Instant Software, Inc.

Basic Property Management. *Version:* 3.3. *Items Included:* Disks, manual, sample data. *Customer Support:* 90 days of free telephone support.
IBM PC, XT, AT, PS/2 & compatibles (512k).
disk $495.00.
Menu Driven with the Following Program Capacities: 100 Properties, 400 Tenants, 250 Vendors, 100 Recurring Expenses, & 100 Accounts. Features Include Automatic Check Writer, Tenant Billing, Report Writing & More.
Yardi Systems.

BASIC RAM Database. Jan. 1985. *Compatible Hardware:* Apple II+, IIe, IIc. *Operating System(s) Required:* Apple DOS. *Language(s):* Applesoft BASIC (source code included). *Memory Required:* 48k.
disk $9.95 (ISBN 0-918547-01-6).
illustration files on disk avail.
Database System That Operates Entirely in Random Access Memory.
AV Systems, Inc.

BASIC-S. *Version:* 3.0. *Compatible Hardware:* TRS-80 Model I Level II, Model III. *Operating System(s) Required:* TRSDOS. *Memory Required:* 48k.
disk $89.95.
Subset Compiler That Puts the Z80 Language into BASIC to Help a Program to Run Faster. Recognizes Only Part of the BASIC Language System. Designed to Be Used in Advanced Commercial Program Development, Which Requires That the Final Program Be Efficient & Tamper-Proof. Syntax Must Be Used When Writing a Program. Incorporates Subtle Differences from Regular BASIC.
Powersoft, Inc.

BASIC Scientific Subroutines, Vol. 1.
Compatible Hardware: Apple II, Atari, Commodore PET, CP/M Machines, CBM; IBM, Osborne; NEC PC 8000; North Star; Superbrain; TRS-80. *Operating System(s) Required:* CP/M. *Language(s):* BASIC. *Memory Required:* 48k-128k.
disk $31.95-$69.95.
Provides Users with Scientific Subroutines Designed to Facilitate the Application of Microcomputers to Scientific Tasks. Includes Alphanumeric Data Plotting, Complex Variables, Vector & Matrix Operations, Random Number Generators & Series Approximations.
Dynacomp, Inc.

BASIC Scientific Subroutines, Vol. 2, 8 collections. *Compatible Hardware:* Apple II with Applesoft; Atari 400, 800 with Atari BASIC; Canon AS-100; Commodore PET; CP/M based machines with MBASIC; Cromemco; Heath Zenith Z-100; IBM PC; NEC PC 8000; North Star; TRS-80 Model I, Model III, Model 4 with Level II BASIC. *Language(s):* BASIC (source code included). *Memory Required:* 48k-128k.
Set. $31.95-$119.95.
8" disk set $144.95.
Cassette set. $99.95.
disk $18.95 ea.
8" disk $21.45 ea.
cassette $14.95 ea.
Dynacomp, Inc.
 No. 1. Least Square Approximation.
 Includes: First-Order Least Squares, Second-Order Least Squares, Nth-Order Least Squares, Multi-Dimensional Least Squares, etc.
 No. 2. Series Approximation Techniques.
 Includes: Taylor Series & Horner's Rule, Asymptotic Series, Bessel Function, Gamma Function, Economization, Polynomial Reversion & Inversion, etc.
 No. 3. Functional Approximations by Iteration & Recursion.
 Includes: Roots of Iteration, Tangent Iteration, Arcsine by Recursion, Bessel Functions by Recursion, etc.
 No. 4. CORDIC Approximation Techniques & Alternatives.
 Includes: Trigonometric Functions, Inverse Trigonometric Functions, Exponential Functions, Inverse Hyperbolic Trigonometric Functions, etc.
 No. 5. Table Interpolation, Differentiation & Integration.
 Includes: Lagrange Interpolation, Semi-Spline Interpolation, Calculating Derivatives from Tables, etc.
 No. 6. Finding the Real Roots of Functions.
 Includes: Interval Searches, Successive Substitution, Newton's Method, Aitken Acceleration, etc.
 No. 7. Finding the Complex Roots of Functions.
 Includes: Interval Search, Mueller's Method in One Dimension, Quadratic Formula, Lin's Method, Bairstow's Method, etc.
 No. 8. Optimization by Steepest Descent.
 Includes: Steepest Descent with Functional Derivatives & Steepest Descent with Approximate Derivatives.

BASIC Scientific Subroutines, Vol. 3, Chapter II. *Compatible Hardware:* Apple II with Applesoft; Macintosh; Canon AS-100; Commodore PET; CP/M based machines with MBASIC; Cromemco; Heath Zenith Z-100; IBM PC; NEC PC-8000; North Star; Commodore PET; TRS-80 Model I, Model III, Model 4 with Level II BASIC. *Language(s):* BASIC (source code included). *Memory Required:* 48k, IBM 128k, Macintosh 512k.
disk $29.95.
8" disk $27.45.
Provides Scientific Subroutines in BASIC. Programs Are Loaded in 1 Step & Called According to Menu Selection.
Dynacomp, Inc.

Basic Scientific Subroutines, Vol. 3, Chapter 1: Basic Probability Distributions. 1992. *Items Included:* Detailed manuals are included with all DYNACOMP products. *Customer Support:* Free telephone support to original customer - no time limit; 30 day limited warranty.
MS-DOS 3.2 or higher. IBM PC & compatibles (512k). $29.95 incl. manual (Add $5.00 for 3 1/2" format; 5 1/4" format standard).
This Chapter Includes an Introduction to Volume III, As Well As a Coordinated Set of Routines for Accurately Calculating Probability Density, Cumulative, & Inverse-Cumulative (for Hypothesis Testing) Distribution Functions. The Functions Covered Are: Normal; Student's T; Chi-Square; Poisson; & Snedecor F. Each Routine Is Fully Demonstrated. Includes a Perfect-Bound 210-Page Manual.
Dynacomp, Inc.

BASIC-68k. *Compatible Hardware:* TRS-80 Model II, Model 12, Model 16 Enhanced; Tandy 6000. *Operating System(s) Required:* CP/M. *Memory Required:* 128k.
$25.00, incl. manual.
Dialect of the BASIC Language Implemented As a Compiler/Interpreter. File Handling Capabilities Include Sequential, Random & ISAM (Indexed Sequential) Support. XCALL Statement Allows Use of Subroutines Written in C Language. Screen Handling Functions Are Provided for Most Hardware Systems.
TriSoft.

Basic Statistical Subroutines, Vol. 1.
Compatible Hardware: Apple II with Applesoft; CP/M based machines with MBASIC; IBM PC. *Language(s):* BASIC (source code included). *Memory Required:* 48k-128k.
disk $69.95, incl. instruction bk.
Collection of Non-Parametric Statistics Routines Keyed to the Text "Non-Parametric Statistics for the Behavioral Sciences" by Sidney Siegal. Subjects Covered Include: Binomial Test, Chi Square One Sample, Kolmogorov-Smirnov One Sample, McNemar Test, Wilcoxon Matched Pairs Signed Ranks Test, Walsh Test, & Randomization Test for Matched Pairs.
Dynacomp, Inc.

Basic Statistics & Data Manipulation.
Compatible Hardware: HP 85, 86/87.
HP 85. data cartridge, 3-1/2" or 5-1/4" disk $95.00 ea. (Order no.: 82805A).
HP 86/87. 3-1/2" or 5-1/4" disk $95.00 ea. (Order no. 82835A).
Provides Common Database for Other Hewlett-Packard Statistics Software Pacs (Excludes GENERAL STATISTICS). Routines for Data Entry, Editing, Output, Sorting, & Transformation Are Included. Computes Many Basic Statistics.
Hewlett-Packard Co.

BASIC Subroutines. Alan G. Porter & Martin G. Rezmer. *Compatible Hardware:* Apple II, II+, IIe; IBM PC. *Memory Required:* 32k.
Apple. disk $29.95, incl. bk. (ISBN 0-201-05692-5).
IBM. disk $29.95, incl. bk. (ISBN 0-201-05662-3).
bk. $12.95 (ISBN 0-201-05663-1).
Provides Specific Techniques for Solving the Most Common Programming Problems.
Addison-Wesley Publishing Co., Inc.

BASIC Tutor Kit. *Compatible Hardware:* Atari XL/XE. *Memory Required:* 16k.
cassette $19.95 (Order no.: KX7099).
Atari Corp.

BASIC Windows. *Version:* 2.0. Jan. 1985. *Compatible Hardware:* IBM PC, PC XT, PC AT, PS/2 & compatibles. *Operating System(s) Required:* PC-DOS/MS-DOS 2.X or 3.X. *Language(s):* Assembler 8086 (source code included). *Memory Required:* 64k. *General Requirements:* Microsoft Quick BASIC or C, or Borland Turbo Pascal 4 (specify language).
disk $69.00.
source code $250.00.
Language Enhancements to Provide WINDOW Functions for the Programmer. Create Windows, Write to Windows (with Automatic Word Wrap), GET Input (From a User) in a Window, Scroll Windows up or Down or Clear, Change Colors or Reverse Windows, Restore Windows or TOSS It. Many Other Features Using a CALL Statement. Works with IBM or Microsoft BASIC & C Compilers (Also Borland Turbo Pascal 4).
Hawkeye Grafix.

Basics of Servomechanisms & Operational Amplifiers. *Compatible Hardware:* TRS-80 Model I, Model III.
contact publisher for price.
OMNI Systems Co.

BASIS Desktop. *Version:* 3.1. 1995. *Customer Support:* Telephone support, training, seminars, documentation, applications development, performance tuning, custom programming, installation.
DEC, OSF/1; DEC VAX, Alpha AXP/VMS, OpenVMS, Ultrix, IBM mainframe, RS6000 MVS/TSO, AIX, Unisys; SunSparcstation/ SunOS, Solaris, HP9000 Series 800/HP-UX; Silicon Graphics ITRIX: UnixWare. Intel 386 PC

TITLE INDEX

or higher (4Mb). $5000.00 plus. *Addl. software required:* Supported network transport. *Networks supported:* Windows Sockets 1.1 compatible, Novell LAN Workplace, Sun PC-NFS, DEC PAT Works, FTP PC/TCP.
Fully Customizable Client/Server Windows Application for Tracking, Updating & Safeguarding All Kinds of Documents at Personal, Workgroup & Enterprise Levels. Designed for Organizations with an Urgent Need for Reliable, Ready Access to Business-Critical Information, BASIS Desktop Offers Advanced Content-Based Retrieval, Intelligent Search Assistance, Mixed Object Management, & Intelligent Printing, As Well As Controls Document Versioning, Routing, & Approval Processes. Delivered As a Starter Application with an Underlying Visual Basic Toolkit, It Can Be Adapted to Accommodate Specific Business Requirements & System Configurations. It Easily Integrates with Windows Applications & Toolkits & Is Portable Across Multiple Server Platforms.
Information Dimensions, Inc.

BASIS SGMLserver. 1993. *Customer Support:* Maintenance fee 15% of list price per yr.; phone support.
AT&T UNIX System V; DEC VAX/VMS; Digital UNIX, Sun/SunOS, Solaris; HP/HP-UX; IBM/AID (2Mb). $5000.00-$31,000.00.
Nonstandard peripherals required: Disk space 13Mb.
Object-Oriented Programming Interface for Building Applications That Manipulate, Store, Search, Retrieve & Update SGML Documents. Recognizes SGML Components & Hierarchical Relationship Between Them. Parses & Validates Every Document That Enters Database. Integrates with Other SGML Tools.
Information Dimension.

BASIS WEBserver. 1994. *Customer Support:* Maintenance fee 15% of list price per yr.; phone support.
DEC VAX, Alpha AXPlums, Open VMS, ULTRIX, Digital UNIX, IBM mainframe, RS/6000, MVS/TSO, VM/CMS, AIX; Unisys; Sun SPARCstation/SunOS, Solaris, HP9000 series 800, HP-UX; Silicon Graphics/IRIX, UNIXware. $5000.00-$25,000.00.
Extends Industry-Accepted WEBservers & Browsers to More Intelligently Store, Manage, Navigate, & Retrieve Document Repositories & Other Information Collections. Supports Text, Word-Processing, & HTML Documents Without Conversion. Document Links Can Be Managed Using Database Queries.
Information Dimension.

BASISplus. *Version:* L1G.2. 1995. *Compatible Hardware:* CDC's Cyber Series; DEC's ALPHA & VAX Series; IBM 43xx, 3xxx, & 370 Series, 9370 Series, RS6000; Sun SPARC, HP 9000; Intel PCs; SGI Indigo; Unisys. *Operating System(s) Required:* AIX, MVS, VM/CMS, NCS/VE, IRIX, HP-UX, OSF/1, SunOS/Solaris 2, Ultrix, UnixWare, VMS/OpenVMS. *Language(s):* C, Assembler, FORTRAN, Uniface. *Memory Required:* 16000k. *Items Included:* Full documentation, training. *Customer Support:* Telephone support, training seminars, documentation, applications development, performance, tuning, custom programming installation.
Contact publisher for price.
Relational Database Management System for Documents, Consisting of Database Manager & 14 Modules, that Possesses Capabilities for Advanced Retrieval, Manipulation, & Storage of Textual Image, Graphic, & Numeric Data. System Offers a Range of Desktop & Server User Interfaces, Supports Compound Document Architecture, Features Advanced Content-Based Retrieval with Intelligent Search Assistance, Interchange, & Markup, & Uses a Fully Relational DBMS & Client/Server Architecture.
Information Dimensions, Inc.

Basketball. *Compatible Hardware:* Atari XL/XE. ROM cartridge $6.95 (Order no.: CXL4004).
Atari Corp.

Basketball Challenge. *Version:* 1.01. Dec. 1987. *Compatible Hardware:* IBM PC, PC XT, PC AT & true compatibles.
3.5" disk $39.95.
Real Time, Five-on-Five College Basketball Simulation Game. Select from 20 Teams, Add Your Own Coaching Ability, & See How Many Victories You Can Chalk up in Your Win Column.
XOR Corp.

Basketball Coach's Assistant. *Items Included:* Bound manual. *Customer Support:* Free hotline - no time limit; 30 day limited warranty; updates are $5/disk plus S&H.
MS-DOS 2.0 or higher. IBM & compatibles (256k). disk $39.95. *Nonstandard peripherals required:* Printer supported, but not required.
Will Record Game Statistics for the Following Categories: Points; Total Rebounds; Assists; Field Goals Made/Attempted; Free Throws Made/Attempted; Three Point Field Goals Made/Attempted; Steals; Turnovers; Fouls; Blocked Shots; Minutes; & Fast Break Points. Game Totals Can Be for Individual Players on Either Team, As Well As for Teams As a Whole. Rosters Can Be Maintained for up to 20 Players on the Two Playing Teams for Each Game Played. Can Handle up to 100 Games. Can Review & Print Reports on: Individual Players for Any Game; Final Game Totals; Up-to-Date Averages for Any Player on Your Team; Team Averages; & More.
Dynacomp, Inc.

Basketball League Statistics. Aug. 1988. *Items Included:* 10 page user guide. *Customer Support:* 90 day free telephone support via 800 number.
MS-DOS 2.1 or higher. IBM PC & compatibles (256k). disk $39.95.
Program Maintains & Updates the Full Complement of Player Offensive & Defensive Statistics for Each Team Member. Full Player Game by Game Records Are Also Maintained, Allowing for a Variety of Reports on Both Team & Individual Statistics.
Mighty Byte Computer, Inc.

The Basketball Statbook. 1985. *Compatible Hardware:* IBM PC & compatibles. *Operating System(s) Required:* PC-DOS, MS-DOS. *Memory Required:* 256k.
disk $59.00.
Maintains/Prints Game, Year-to-Date, & Historical Statistics; Provides Team/League Leaders & Team Standings.
RJL Systems.

Basketbal! Statistician. *Compatible Hardware:* TI Home Computer.
contact publisher for price.
Helps Basketball Statisticians Keep Statistics for Individual Players.
Texas Instruments, Personal Productivit.

BasketMath. *Version:* 1.1. Robert Cummings. Apr. 1993. *Items Included:* 1 - 10 page manual. *Customer Support:* Voice-Mail Technical support for "Registered Users".
PRODOS. AppleIe, AppleIIc, AppleIIGS (64k). disk $69.00 (ISBN 0-9623926-3-4, Order no.: BMA3.5). *Optimal configuration:* Color monitor, Imagewriter or compatible printer, 3.5" disk drive.
PRODOS. AppleIe, AppleIIc, AppleIIGS (64k). disk $69.00 (ISBN 0-9623926-6-9, Order no.: BMA5). *Optimal configuration:* Color monitor, Imagewriter or compatible printer, 5.25" disk drive.
A Mathematics Drill & Practice Software in a Basketball Game Format. Fashioned after the New York State Mathematics Regents Competency Test, BasketMath's Diagnositc Capability Tests 40 Different Mathematics Areas & Provides Results of Possible Areas Needing Remediation or Review. The Game Format Makes This Software Entertaining As Well As Educational.
Science Academy Software.

BasketMath: For IBM Computers. *Version:* 1.1. Robert Cummings. Dec. 1993. *Items Included:* 1 - 10 page manual. *Customer Support:* Voice-Mail Technical support for "Registered Users".
MS-DOS. IBM PS/2, IBM PCs EGA/VGA (640k). disk $69.00 (ISBN 0-9623926-5-0, Order no.: BMI). *Optimal configuration:* Color monitor, hard disk, printer, 3.5" disk drive format.
A Mathematics Drill & Practice Software in a Basketball Game Format. Fashioned after the New York State Mathematics Regents Competency Test, BasketMath's Diagnositc Capability Tests 40 Different Mathematics Areas & Provides Results of Possible Areas Needing Remediation or Review. The Game Format Makes This Software Entertaining As Well As Educational.
Science Academy Software.

BASTOC. *Version:* 2.2. Mar. 1986. *Compatible Hardware:* AT&T; DEC; IBM PC, PC XT; NCR; TRS-80 Model 16. *Operating System(s) Required:* UNIX, Idris, PC-DOS, XENIX, MS-DOS. *Language(s):* C (source code included). *Memory Required:* 256k. *General Requirements:* 2 disk drives.
disk single-user $495.00.
1 to 8 users $695.00.
manual $25.00.
Translates BASIC Programs into C Source Code. Useful for Migrating BASIC Programs from BASIC Oriented Environments to Newer Systems Supporting UNIX or MS-DOS with a C Compiler. Supports Microsoft DISK BASIC Without the Extension Added for Each Host Operating System. Also, IBM's BASICA, Digital Research CBASIC. Under Control of an Option, the Program Will Perform a Limited Amount of Code Restructuring, Attempting to Form C Functions from BASIC Subroutines. Performs Optimization on Source Code.
JMI Software Consultants, Inc.

BAS34 Conversion Utility. Dennis Allen. *Compatible Hardware:* TRS-80 Model I, Model III, Model 4, Tandy 2000. *Operating System(s) Required:* CP/M, MS-DOS, PC-DOS. *Memory Required:* 64k.
disk $49.95 ea.
CP/M. (Order no.: DCB34).
MS-DOS. (Order no.: DMB34).
Tandy 2000. (Order no.: D2B34).
Model 4. (Order no.: D4B34).
Model I & Model III. (Order no.: D8B34).
Enables User to Use BASIC Code from TRS-80 Models I & III on the Model 4, & the Code from These 3 Machines on the Tandy 2000 & Sanyo 550, 555. Inserts Necessary Spaces, Assists User with Converting Between 64 x 16 & 80 X 24 Screens & Points to Lines Where Possible Misinterpretations Can Be Made.
The Alternate Source.

BAS43. *Compatible Hardware:* TRS-80 Model I, Model III, Model 4. *Operating System(s) Required:* CP/M, MS-DOS, PC-DOS. *Memory*

Required: 64k.
disk $49.95 ea.
CP/M. (Order no.: DCB43).
MS-DOS. (Order no.: DMB43).
Model 4. (Order no.: D4B43).
Mode I & Model III. (Order no.: D8B43).
Performs the Opposite of BAS34. Long Variable Names Are Converted to 2 Characters, & Other Appropriate Changes Are Made.
The Alternate Source.

Batch Distillation. *Items Included:* Full manual. No other products required. *Customer Support:* Free telephone support - no time limit, 30 day warranty.
MS-DOS 3.2 or higher. IBM & compatibles (512k). disk $989.95. *Addl. software required:* Steady State Continuous Distillation plus Dynamic & Continuous Distillation.
Models Batch Distillation Columns by Solving the Necessary Differential Equations Derived from the Column & Control Loop Dynamics. Uses U.S. SI, & Metric Units. Includes a Complete & Detailed Manual Which Describes All Procedures.
Dynacomp, Inc.

Batchwork Quilt: The Menu Control Program. *Version:* 2.1C. Sep. 1992. *Items Included:* Loading instructions. Order form for other products; Manual is on the disk. *Customer Support:* 7 day money back warranty. Short phone questions answered free. Questions longer than 12 minutes at $2.00 per minute.
DOS 4.01 or higher. IBM or compatible with hard drive; package requires 2Mb (128k). disk $99.95 (ISBN 0-916161-06-4, Order no.: S06). *Addl. software required:* DOS, Menu finds & loads over 250 application programs. *Optimal configuration:* 640k 30Mb Disk or more. *Networks supported:* Any supporting DOS Logical Drives.
A DOS Based Menu Program Using Simple 1 to 3 Letter Commands to Execute All DOS Commands & Load over 250 Commercial Software Packages. Based on Batch Files It Requires No RAM Overhead & Leaves the User at DOS. Over 350 Help Screens Are Also Provided.
Computer Training Corp.

Bati-Texte: French Storyboard. Wida Software. Sep. 1987. *Compatible Hardware:* Apple II. *Operating System(s) Required:* Apple DOS 3.3. *Memory Required:* 48k. *Customer Support:* 800-654-8715 for technical assistance.
site license disk $139.95 (ISBN 0-940503-34-4).
Research Design Assocs., Inc.

Battery Watch Pro for DOS & Windows: Release IV. *Version:* 4.0. *Compatible Hardware:* IBM PC & compatibles. *Memory Required:* 6 to 14k. *Customer Support:* (206) 483-8088. $49.95.
For Laptops. Pop up Fuel Gauge Shows How Much Longer Computer's Battery Will Last. Tune-Up Feature Watches User's Usage Pattern & Will Assign a New Battery Capacity Estimate Based on How Battery Has Performed over Past Cycles. A Deep Discharge Feature Trains User's Battery to Remember Its Original Charge Capacity for Longer Battery Life.
Traveling Software, Inc.

Battle Isle 2220: Shadow of the Emperor. Feb. 1996. *Items Included:* 75 page manual.
Win 95, Win 3.11 (NT). 486/33 local Bus (8Mb). CD-ROM disk $49.95 (ISBN 1-888533-00-5, Order no.: 96001). *Nonstandard peripherals required:* 2X CD-ROM, Soundblaster, 34Mb of hard drive space. *Optimal configuration:* Pentium, Win 95, 4X CD-ROM drive, Soundblaster. *Networks supported:* Novell, Windows.

The Third Part of the Classic Battle Isle Series. With Texture Mapped 3-D Battles, Network Play, Win 95 Compatibility, & over an Hour of Full Motion Video, Your Strategical & Logistical Abilities Will Be Put to the Ultimate Test in a Bid to Secure Total Victory.
Blue Byte Software, Inc.

Battledroidz. *Compatible Hardware:* Commodore 64/128. *Memory Required:* 64k. *General Requirements:* Joystick optional.
disk $24.95 (ISBN 0-88717-210-5, Order no.: 16051-43499).
In the Abandoned Mining Caverns of a Far Away Planet, the Remote-Controlled Mine Droids Are Now Used for Sport. The Mine Grids Are Interconnnected Hexagons, Each of Which is a War Zone. User Selects a Hexagon & Sends the Battle Droid into Combat with the Resident Aliens & Collects Four Energy Pods Before Escaping. Complete a Row of Hexagons & the Player Has Won the Game. Features Include 3-D Scrolling Action, Thirty-Seven Different Landscapes to Explore, Selection of Three Different Battle Droids, View Level Map Option & Bonus Levels.
IntelliCreations, Inc.

Battlefield!!! *Compatible Hardware:* Apple II with Applesoft; Atari 400, 800 with Atari BASIC; Canon AS-100; Commodore PET; CP/M based machines with MBASIC; Cromemco; Heath Zenith Z-100; IBM PC; NEC PC-8000; North Star; TRS-80 Model I, Model III, Model 4 with Level II BASIC. *Language(s):* BASIC (source code included). *Memory Required:* 48k-128k.
disk $19.95.
8" disk $26.45.
Provides 8 Games of Tactical War Simulation.
Dynacomp, Inc.

Battlefield Warriors: Jetfighter II, Operation Combat, Project X. Velocity Development Corp. Staff et al. Aug. 1995. *Items Included:* Set up instruction sheet. *Customer Support:* (503) 639-6863.
DOS 2.1 or higher. IBM PC & compatibles. $14.95 Jetfighter II (ISBN 1-887783-03-2, Order no.: 5300-4003). *Optimal configuration:* IBM PC 386 or higher, 640k RAM, DOS 2.1 or higher, VGA, EGA or CGA. Supports (but does not require) AdLib, Soundblaster, Analog joystick or mouse.
DOS 5.0. IBM PC & compatibles. $14.95 Operation Combat (Order no.: 5300-4003). *Optimal configuration:* IBM PC 386 or higher, DOS 5.0 or higher, VGA. Supports AdLib, Soundblaster & compatibles.
DOS 3.0. IBM PC & compatibles. $14.95 Project X (Order no.: 5300-4003). *Optimal configuration:* IBM PC 386 or higher, DOS 3.0 or higher, VGA, 2Mb RAM, keyboard or joystick, AdLib, Soundblaster or Gravis compatible board, PC speakers.
A Game Compilation of Battle Games. The Game Player Plays Against Enemy Aircraft, Ground Forces & Interplanetary Enemies.
Entertainment Technology.

Battlefield Warriors: JetFighter II, Operation Combat, Project X. Velocity Development Corp. et al. Jan. 1996. *Items Included:* Set-up instruction sheet. *Customer Support:* 310-403-0043.
Jet Fighter: DOS 2.1 or higher; Operation Combat: DOS 5.0; Project X: DOS 3.0 or higher. IBM PC or compatibles. disk $14.95 (ISBN 1-887783-21-0, Order no.: 5200-3003). *Optimal configuration:* IBM PC 386 or higher: Jet Fighter: 640k RAM, DOS 2.1 or higher, VGA/EGA/CGA. Supports but does not require Adlib, Soundblaster, Analog, joystick or mouse; Operation Combat: DOS 5.0 or higher, VGA. Supports Adlib, soundblaster &
compatibles; Project X: DOS 3.0 or higher, VGA, 2Mb RAM, keyboard or joystick, Adlib, Soundblaster or Gravis PC speakers.
A Game Compilation of Jetfighter II, Operation Combat & Project X Which Are Battle Games. The Game Player Plays Against Enemy Aircraft, Ground Forces & Inter-Planetary Enemies.
Entertainment Technology.

Battleground. *Compatible Hardware:* TRS-80. contact publisher for price.
Instant Software, Inc.

Battleground: Ardennes: Battle of the Bulge. Sep. 1995. *Items Included:* Players guide. *Customer Support:* Tech support - 410-821-7282. CompuServe - Go Gamepubc or Email 75162, 2132. Internet - 75162.2132-Compuserve.com. 90 day warranty.
Windows 3.1 - CD-ROM - SVGA Graphics. IBM PC & 100% compatibles, 2x CD-ROM, SVGA (4Mb). CD-ROM disk Contact publisher for price (ISBN 1-57519-050-8). *Optimal configuration:* 486DX66 - 8Mb RAM - 4x CD-ROM, Accelerated Windows, Graphics card. *Networks supported:* Modem to Modem.
Historical Strategy Game of World War II. Small Unit Tactics Based on the Most Famous American Land Battle Called "The Battle of the Bulge." Fast & Furious Action, Multimedia Enhanced, Easy to Play, Difficult to Master.
TalonSoft, Inc.

Battles of Napoleon, 2 disks. David Landrey & Chuck Kroegel. 1988. *Compatible Hardware:* Apple II series; Commodore 64/128; IBM PC/ compatibles. *Memory Required:* Apple & Commodore 64k, IBM 256k. *General Requirements:* IBM version supports CGA & EGA cards. *Items Included:* Rulebook. *Customer Support:* 14 day money back guarantee/30 day exchange policy; tech support line: (408) 737-6850 (11:00 - 5:00 PST); customer service: (408) 737-6800 (9:00-5:00 PST).
disk $49.95.
Allows You to Simulate Practically Any Napoleonic Engagement on a Detailed, Tactical Level by Giving You All the Tools to Create Any Battle of That Historic Era. Use the Computer to Generate Random Maps, Then Modify Them as You Choose. Or Start From Scratch by Building Your Own Maps, Square-by-Square (Each Representing 100 Yards). Your Terrain Options Include Five Levels of Elevation, Woods, Roads, Fields, Swamps, Water, Towns and Redoubts. Create Your Own Armies or Adjust the Armies Provided to Suit Your Exact Specifications: Number of Men, Type of Units, Weapons & Nationality. Rate Your Units for Melee Strength, Leadership & Morale.
Strategic Simulations, Inc.

Battletech. *Items Included:* Installation Guide. IBM PC. Contact publisher for price (ISBN 0-87321-079-4, Order no.: CDD-3017).
Activision, Inc.

Battletech. *Items Included:* Installation Guide. IBM PC. Contact publisher for price (ISBN 0-87321-078-6, Order no.: MSD-3017).
Activision, Inc.

BCS League Finance Manager. Jack Phelps. *Compatible Hardware:* IBM PC & compatibles. *Operating System(s) Required:* DOS 2.1 or higher. *Memory Required:* 256k. *General Requirements:* 2 disk drives, printer.
disk $100.00 (Order no.: D925I).
Weekly Dues, Paid-Out Funds (up to 7 User-Defined Categories). Reports Include: Weekly Worksheets, Team & League Transactions, & Financial Summary.
Briley Software.

TITLE INDEX

BEACON: The Multimedia Guidance Resource. Dec. 1992. *Items Included:* User's Guide, headphones, video, poster, teaching units. *Customer Support:* "800" number for free customer technical support Monday through Friday, 9:00AM-5:30PM EST & Saturday 9:00AM-5:00PM EST.
MS-DOS 3.1 or higher. IBM or compatible 286 or higher, VGA monitor, hard disk (640k). CD-ROM disk $695.00 (ISBN 1-56574-005-X). *Nonstandard peripherals required:* CD-ROM drive with headphone minijack. *Addl. software required:* MS-DOS CD-ROM extension (MSCDEX) Version 2.1 or higher. *Optimal configuration:* IBD 386 or 486 4Mb RAM, MSCDEX Ver. 2.21, expanded memory.
Comprehensive CD-ROM Information System for the Development of Educational & Career Plans. Combining Powerful Search Software, a User-Friendly Interface & Expert Advice, BEACON Helps Students Make Smart Educational & Career Choices. Information Includes: 3,400 Undergraduate Colleges; 1,100 Graduate Schools; 900 Career Paths; 2,150 Grants, Scholarships, Fellowships & Loan Programs.

Beagle Bag. Bert Kersey. *Compatible Hardware:* Apple II, II+, IIe, IIc, IIgs. *Operating System(s) Required:* Apple DOS 3.3. *Language(s):* Applesoft BASIC. *Memory Required:* 48k.
disk $29.50.
Consists of 12 Games with Instructions & Copyable Disk. User Can Change Programs or List Them to Learn by Seeing How They Work.
Beagle Brothers.

Beagle BASIC. Mark Simonsen. Jun. 1985. *Compatible Hardware:* Apple II, II+, IIe, IIc, IIgs. *Operating System(s) Required:* Apple DOS 3.3. *Language(s):* Machine, BASIC. *Memory Required:* 64k.
disk $34.95.
AppleSoft Enhancement Utility. AppleSoft Is Moved into RAM Where Users Can Customize & Enhance It. Users May Rename AppleSoft Commands & Error Messages. Will Add New Commands to AppleSoft: ELSE, TONE, PAGE, & HSCRN. It Also Lets GOTO & GOSUB a Variable. No Memory Is Lost Because These New Commands & Features Replace Unused Cassette Commands.
Beagle Brothers.

Beagle Compiler. Alan Bird. *Compatible Hardware:* Apple II, II+, IIe, IIc, IIgs. *Operating System(s) Required:* ProDOS. *Memory Required:* 64k.
disk $74.95.
AppleSoft Speed-Up Utility. Programs Can Be Compiled from Any Standard ProDOS Disk, Including Floppies, Hard Disks, & UniDisk 3.5's. Programs Can Be Saved in Compiled Format. Not Copy-Protected.
Beagle Brothers.

Beagle Graphics. Mark Simonsen. Mar. 1985. *Compatible Hardware:* Apple IIe, IIc. *Operating System(s) Required:* Apple DOS 3.3, ProDOS. *Language(s):* Machine. *Memory Required:* 128k. *General Requirements:* Mouse, graphics tablet, KoalaPad, joystick, paddles, or keyboard. $59.95.
"Double-Res" Drawing Package. Users Can Select from Sixteen Hi-Res Colors or a 560x192-Pixel Screen (Twice the Resolution of Standard Hi-Res Graphics). Users Can Draw or "Paint" Directly on the Double "Hi-Res" Screen. Hi-Res Icons (Pencil, Scissors, etc.) Make Drawing & Editing Easy. Data May Be Compressed to Save Disk Space. Existing Standard Hi-Res Programs Can Be Converted So They Work in Double Hi-Res & Normal Hi-Res Pictures Can Be Converted to Double Hi-Res. Double Lo-Res Graphics Are Supported. Users Can "Fill" Double Hi-Res Shapes in 16 Solid Colors, or Choose from over 200 Color Mixes for a Wide Range of Effects.
Beagle Brothers.

Beagle Screens. Fred Crone & Sara Crone. *Compatible Hardware:* Apple IIe, IIc, IIgs. *Operating System(s) Required:* ProDOS. *Memory Required:* 128k.
disk $34.95.
Full-Screen Captionable Clip Art. Includes 40 Captionable Full-Screen Pictures on Disk. Each Picture Has a Blank Area Where Users Can Add Their Own Message. 20 of the Pictures are Automatically Animated. Printer Dump Software Not Included.
Beagle Brothers.

Beam Analysis. Jun. 1983. *Compatible Hardware:* Apple II+, IIe; HP-85; IBM PC. *Operating System(s) Required:* PC-DOS, Apple DOS 3.3. *Language(s):* BASIC (source code included). *Memory Required:* HP 32k, Apple 48k, IBM 128k. *Customer Support:* Telephone.
$125.00.
Determines Deflection, Bending Stresses, Shear Stresses, Moments & Reactions for Determinate & Indeterminate Simple Beams Subject to Point Loads, Distributed Loads & Moments. Graphics Included.
PEAS (Practical Engineering Applications Software).

Beam Analysis with Selection. Jun. 1983. *Compatible Hardware:* Apple II+, IIe; HP-85; IBM PC. *Operating System(s) Required:* PC-DOS, Apple DOS 3.3. *Language(s):* BASIC (source code included). *Memory Required:* HP 32k, Apple 48k, IBM 128k. *Customer Support:* Telephone.
$200.00.
Provides the Same Features As BEAM ANALYSIS, with the Addition of Automatic, Standard AISC Wide Flange Selection Based on User Allowable Bending Stress. For the IBM Version, the BEAM ANALYSIS with Selection Program Has Been Enhanced to Include 30 Point Loads for the General Modules. In Addition, the Selection Tables Now Include the Following: W, M, HP, & S Shapes, C & MC (Channels), L (Angles), Pipes, & Structural Tubing.
PEAS (Practical Engineering Applications Software).

Beam Analyzer. 1989. *Items Included:* Spiral manual contains theory, sample runs. *Customer Support:* Free phone, on-site seminars.
MS-DOS. IBM (128k). disk $120.00.
Analyzes Continuous Beams with Constant or Variable Cross Section & Intermediate Supports. Up to 10 Concentrated & 5 Distributed Loads. End Conditions May Be Any Combination of Clamped, Simply Supported or Free. Up to 10 Intermediate Supports. Output Displays Shear & Moment Diagrams, Slope & Deflection with Numerical Values.
Kern International, Inc.

Beam-Column Analysis & Second Order Frame Analysis. *Items Included:* Bound manual. *Customer Support:* Free hotline - no time limit; 30 day limited warranty; updates are $5/disk plus S&H.
MS-DOS. IBM & compatibles, TRS-80, CP/M (256k). disk $89.95 ea.
User-Interactive Programs for Solving Multiple-Span Beams & Columns & Plane-Frame Structures in the Elastic Range, & Include the Secondary Effects of Deflected Shape under Load.
Dynacomp, Inc.

Beam-Column Analysis: Second Order Frame Analysis. 1995. *Items Included:* Full manual. *Customer Support:* Free telephone support - 90 days, 30-day warranty.
MS-DOS 3.2 or higher. 286 (584k). disk $89.95. *Nonstandard peripherals required:* CGA/EGA/VGA.
User-Interactive Programs for Solving Multiple-Span Beams & Columns & Plane-Frame Structures in the Elastic Range, & Include the Secondary Effects of Deflected Shape under Load.
Dynacomp, Inc.

Beam Deflection. *Compatible Hardware:* Apple II with Applesoft; IBM PC. (source code included). *Memory Required:* 48k-128k.
disk $39.95.
Series of Structural Analysis Programs; Allows Development of Data Files & Performs Calculations for Problems.
Dynacomp, Inc.

Beam Deflection 2. *Items Included:* Full manual. No other products required. *Customer Support:* Free telephone support - no time limit, 30 day warranty.
MS-DOS 3.2 or higher. IBM & compatibles (512k). disk $49.95.
Upgraded & Enhanced Version of Beam Deflection. Includes All of the Same Features As Beam Deflection, & Has the Additional Capability of Being Able to Include up to 5 Torsional Springs along the Beam Length.
Dynacomp, Inc.

Beam Sections. B. J. Korites. 1983. *Compatible Hardware:* Apple, IBM PC. *Operating System(s) Required:* PC-DOS 2.0 or higher. *Language(s):* BASIC (source code included). *Memory Required:* 64k.
disk $120.00 ea.
IBM Kit. (Order no.: 603-IK).
Apple Kit. (Order no.: 603-AK).
Calculates Properties of Homogeneous & Composite Beam Cross Sections. Sections Can Have Any Shape & May Contain Holes, Inclusions of Different Materials & Reinforcing Rods.
Kern International, Inc.

Beams & Columns. Version: 5.3. N. Alterman. Jan. 1986. *Compatible Hardware:* IBM PC & compatibles. *Memory Required:* 4000k. *General Requirements:* AutoCAD Software (Autodesk, Inc.), hard disk, digitizer, plotter. *Items Included:* 1 day free training. *Customer Support:* Unlimited telephone.
Contact publisher for price.
Aids Fabricators & Detailers in Creating Shop Fabrication Drawings. Composed of Screen & Tablet Menus. Parameter Compositions of Beams, Columns & All Other Structural Elements. Creates Bill of Material & Shop Cutting Lists.
Computer Detailing Corp.

Beams One-Two-Three, 2 diskettes. *Items Included:* Bound manual. *Customer Support:* Free hotline - no time limit; 30 day limited warranty; updates are $5/disk plus S&H.
MS-DOS. IBM & compatibles (256k). $99.95. *Nonstandard peripherals required:* IBM graphics card; 80-column (or wider) printer supported, but not necessary. To get printed beam diagrams, printer capable of hi-res screen dumps is needed.
Designed to Be Used to Design, Analyze, & Study the Reactions of Many Types of Beam-Loading Configurations. It Uses Analytical Solutions & the Principle of Superposition (Finite Elements, etc., Are Not Employed) to Very Quickly & Accurately Determine the Reactions (& Deflections, etc.) under 60 Commonly Used Beam-Loading Configurations. Three Types of

Beams May Be Examined: Simply Supported, Cantilevered, & Fixed Ended. The Cases Covered Include 29 Statically Supported & 31 Statically Indeterminate. Calculate & Display (or Print) All Values of the Shear, Moment, Deflection, Bending Stress, & Shearing Stress in Three Ways: for Design, All Maximum Values Are Calculated; for Analysis, All Values at Any Location May Be Calculated; for Study, All Values at Equally Spaced Points May Be Calculated.
Dynacomp, Inc.

The Bean Machine. *Compatible Hardware:* Atari 400, 800 with Atari BASIC, APX. *Memory Required:* cassette 24, disk 32k. *General Requirements:* Joystick.
Atari APX. disk $24.95.
Atari 400, 800. disk $21.95.
Atari 400, 800. cassette $17.95.
Maneuver 33 Beans along Troughs, Elevators, Conveyor Belts, etc.
Dynacomp, Inc.

Beanstalk. (Creative Pastimes Ser.). Mike Orkin & Ed Bogas. *Compatible Hardware:* Atari, Commodore 64, IBM PCjr.
Atari. disk $29.95 (ISBN 0-8359-0441-5).
Commodore 64. disk $39.95 (ISBN 0-8359-0442-3).
IBM PCjr. disk $34.95 (ISBN 0-8359-0443-1).
Animated Strategy Game, Requiring a Sharp Memory & Skillful Decision Making. To Win, Jack Has to Compete on Five Levels, Outwitting Beanstalk Creatures & Overcoming Difficult Situations As He Goes.
Prentice Hall.

Bear Essentials. 1992. *Items Included:* Manual. *Customer Support:* Free telephone support, defective disks replaced free.
Macintosh System 6.0.7 or higher. Macintosh (1Mb). 3.5" disk $19.95. *Addl. software required:* Hypercard.
Educational Program for Children. Contains Four Hypercard Stacks for Learning to Count by Ones, Twos, Fives, & Tens. Uses Teddy Bears to Teach Number Concepts.
Master Software.

A Bear Family Adventure. Sep. 1995. *Customer Support:* Telephone support - free (except phone charge).
Windows 3.1. IBM & compatibles (386 DX-20) (4Mb). CD-ROM disk $12.99 (ISBN 1-57594-000-0). *Nonstandard peripherals required:* 2x CD-ROM player, Sound Card, VGA monitor. *Optimal configuration:* 486 SX-33.
Your Child Joins the Bear Family on an Enchanting Journey Thru the Park - Exploring & Learning.
Kidsoft, Inc.

A Bear Family Adventure. Sep. 1995. *Customer Support:* Telephone support - free (except phone charge).
Windows 3.1. IBM & compatibles (386 DX-20) (4Mb). CD-ROM disk $12.99 (ISBN 1-57594-039-6). *Nonstandard peripherals required:* 2x CD-ROM player, Sound Card, VGA monitor. *Optimal configuration:* 486 SX-33.
Your Child Joins the Bear Family on an Enchanting Journey Thru the Park - Exploring & Learning. Blister Pack Jewel Case.
Kidsoft, Inc.

Bearings. *Compatible Hardware:* IBM PC, PC XT. *Memory Required:* 256k. *General Requirements:* 80-column printer.
disk $24.95.
Helps Radio Amateurs Get Precise Bearings on Distant Locations Using Azimuth System.
Zephyr Services.

BearWare. *Compatible Hardware:* Apple Macintosh. *General Requirements:* Paint program or page makeup program.
Twenty bears per disk. 3.5" disk $12.00 ea.
Entire package of 12 disks. 3.5" disk $99.99.
Catalog. $1.00.
Clip Art of 180 Teddy Bears Which Are Elaborately Costumed & Suitable for Many Holidays.
Collector Software.

Beast War. Jan. 1984. *Compatible Hardware:* Apple II, II+, IIe, IIc. *Memory Required:* 48k. disk $25.00 (Order no.: 48952).
The People of Alaxis Have Come up with a Novel Way to Resolve Conflict. On a Circular Board, Holographic Creatures Maneuver & Attack, Draining Energy from Each Other & Being Revived in the Center of the Vortex. There Are Four Levels of Play. For up to Four Players.
Avalon Hill Game Co., The Microcomputer Games Div.

Beastly Funnies: ClickArt Cartoons. *Customer Support:* Free & unlimited technical support to registered users; 60 day money-back guarantee.
Macintosh. Macintosh, System 6.0.7 or higher (1Mb). 3.5" disk $49.95. *Addl. software required:* Any word-processing, desktop publishing or works program that accepts graphics.
Windows MS-DOS. IBM PC & compatibles. 3.5" disk $49.95. *Addl. software required:* Any word processing, desktop publishing or works program that accepts graphics.
Over 100 Images! Black & White Cartoons; Ready-to-Use, or Changed in Appropriate Drawing Program; Contains 12 Bonus Images Pre-Colored for Use in Presentations; Includes the ClickArt Trade Secret - Images Traded to Every Popular Graphics Format, Guaranteed to Work with All Popular Applications.
T/Maker Co., Inc.

Beasy: Acoustic Design. *Version:* 6.0. 1996. *Items Included:* Complete user guide (3000 pages). *Customer Support:* Hot-line telephone support, bug files, software updates included with purchase price for 1st 90 days. Available on an annual-fee basis following this period. Training & consulting services available.
UNIX. Contact publisher for price. *Addl. software required:* PHIGS graphics run-time library.
DOS. 386 (8Mb). Contact publisher for price. *Nonstandard peripherals required:* Math coprocessor for 386 systems, mouse, VGA.
Typical Applications Include Computing Sound Levels in the Passenger Compartments of Automobiles & Aircraft, Structural Acoustic Scattering & Radiation & Many Other Noise Control Problems. A Powerful Feature Is Its Ability to Compute the Sensitivity of the Acoustic Solution to the Structural Velocity etc. Diagnostic Features Compute the Contribution of Individual Parts of the Structure to the Sound Perceived at a Specific Point, Providing the Information Designers Need. Can Be Applied to Three Dimensional Structures & Systems.
Computational Mechanics, Ltd.

Beasy: Corrosion & CP. *Version:* 6.0. 1996. *Items Included:* Complete user guide (3000 pages). *Customer Support:* Hot-line telephone support, bug files, software updates included with purchase price for 1st 90 days. Available on an annual-fee basis following this period. Training & consulting services available.
UNIX. Contact publisher for price. *Addl. software required:* PHIGS graphics run-time library.
DOS. 386 (8Mb). Contact publisher for price. *Nonstandard peripherals required:* Math coprocessor for 386 systems, mouse, VGA.
Given the Basic Geometry & the Polarisation Characteristics of the Materials the System Can Produce Detailed Predictions of Potential & Current Density on All the Surfaces. It Can Be Used to Optimise the Design of CP Systems & Evaluate Their Performance & Life Expectancy. Can Also Be Used to Simulate Other Electro-Chemical Processes.
Computational Mechanics, Ltd.

Beasy: Fatigue & Crack Growth. *Version:* 6.0. 1996. *Items Included:* Complete user guide (3000 pages). *Customer Support:* Hot-line telephone support, bug files, software updates included with purchase price for 1st 90 days. Available on an annual-fee basis following this period. Training & consulting services available.
UNIX. Contact publisher for price. *Addl. software required:* PHIGS graphics run-time library.
DOS. 386 (8Mb). Contact publisher for price. *Nonstandard peripherals required:* Math coprocessor for 386 systems, mouse, VGA.
Analysis Assumes a Piece-Wise Linear Discretisation of the Unknown Crack Path. The Dual Boundary Element Method Is Applied to Carry Out a Stress Analysis of the Cracked Structure & the J-Integral Is the Technique Used for the Evaluation of the Stress Intensity Factory.
Computational Mechanics, Ltd.

BEASY-Mechanical Design: Boundary Element Analysis System. *Version:* 6.0. 1996. *Items Included:* Complete user guide, 3000p. *Customer Support:* Hot-line telephone support, bug fixes, software updates incl. with purchase for 1st 90 days. Available on an annual fee basis following this period. Training & consulting services.
Unix. Sun, HP, SGI, IBM RS/6000, Cray. Contact publisher for price. *Addl. software required:* PHIGS graphics run-time libraries.
MS-DOS. 386, 486, or Pentium PC IBM-compatible (8Mb). Contact publisher for price. *Nonstandard peripherals required:* Math coprocessor (80387) for 386 platforms, mouse, VGA. *Optimal configuration:* Pentium, DOS, 16Mb Plus RAM, mouse, VGA.
BEASY-Mechanical Design is a comprehensive environmental design analysis of engineering components & structures including all the capabilities of BEASY-Stress, BEASY-Thermal & BEASY-Code.
Computational Mechanics, Inc.

Beat Design & Analysis System. 1988. *Memory Required:* 512k.
PC-DOS/MS-DOS. disk $495.00.
Used by Police Departments to Evaluate Alternative Assignments of Patrol Areas to Response Units. Maintains a Data Base of Additive Beat Level Characteristics Such as Population, Area, Calls for Service. Calculates Beat Workloads. Prescribes Modifications to Beat Plan to Balance One of These Characteristics.
Computing Power Applied.

BeckerTools 4: Windows Disk & File Management Utilities. *Version:* 4.0. Jan. 1993. *Items Included:* 1 saddle-stitched manual, registration card. *Customer Support:* 60 day money back guarantee - free technical support.
Windows. IBM PC & compatibles (2Mb). disk $129.95 (ISBN 1-55755-170-7, Order no.: S170). *Optimal configuration:* 2Mb RAM, 286 or higher. *Networks supported:* Novell.
Collection of Powerful & Essential Programs for Every Windows User. Includes Many Useful Features & Utilities: the Shell, Launcher, Disk Utilities, File Finder, Group Service, File Compactor/Extractor, Disk Info, Disk Optimizer, Icon Editor; BTBackup, Print Service, Recover, Undelete, Disk Librarian, File Viewer, HexEditor, Disk Editor, Text Editor, & Blackout (a Screen Saver).
Abacus.

TITLE INDEX

Bed & Breakfasts & Country Inns. Dec. 1991. *Items Included:* Operating instructions. *Customer Support:* Bulletin board support will be available. Macintosh (1Mb). 3.5" disk $50.00 (ISBN 1-879196-00-X).
This Supercard-Based Stack (Supercard Not Needed to Run Database) Lists Bed & Breakfasts & Country Inns in the U.S., Canada, Virgin Islands. Thousands of Inexpensive Places to Stay. Also Includes Points of Interest, Reservation Organizations, Complete Descriptions.
Hollow Earth Publishing.

Beechwood Accounts Payable Package. contact publisher for price.
Handles Regular Accounts Payable Functions & Provides Managerial Cost Control Features.
Beechwood Software.

Beechwood General Ledger Package. contact publisher for price.
Handles All General Ledger Functions & Financial Reporting.
Beechwood Software.

Beechwood Payroll Package. contact publisher for price.
Prints Out Summaries for Detailed Cost Analysis & Reporting.
Beechwood Software.

Beef Cattle Management. Agri-Management Services, Inc. *Compatible Hardware:* TI Professional. *Operating System(s) Required:* MS-DOS. *Memory Required:* 64k. *General Requirements:* Printer.
$995.00.
Permits Recall of Information in Many Forms: Cow's Lifetime History, Cows Sorted by Production, Cows Due to Wean, etc. Bull & Inseminator Summaries.
Texas Instruments, Personal Productivit.

Beef Herd & Herd Health Management. *Compatible Hardware:* IBM PC, PC XT & compatibles.
$500.00.
Farm Management Systems of Mississippi, Inc.

Beef Herd History. Merle W. Wagner. 1983. *Compatible Hardware:* Apple II Plus, IIe, IIc; IBM. *Operating System(s) Required:* Apple DOS 3.3, MS-DOS 2.2. *Language(s):* BASIC. *Memory Required:* 48k, 640k.
disk $49.95 (ISBN 0-922900-26-4, Order no.: CFH-390).
add'l. manual $19.95.
back-up disk $9.95.
Breeding & Health History for the Life of the Cow. 40 Cows per Data Disk.
Cherrygarth, Inc.

Beef Herd Management: Decision Aid. Merle W. Wagner. 1982. *Compatible Hardware:* Apple II Plus, IIe, IIc; IBM. *Operating System(s) Required:* Apple DOS 3.3, MS-DOS 2.0. *Language(s):* BASIC. *Memory Required:* 48k, 640k.
disk $29.95 (ISBN 0-922900-15-9, Order no.: CFD-334).
Budget Analysis for a Cow-Calf Operation. Twenty-Nine Data Entries. Ten Calculations.
Cherrygarth, Inc.

Beef History Information, 2 disks. *Compatible Hardware:* Apple II Plus, IIe, IIc; IBM. Set. $49.95.
Individual History of Each Cow, for a Period of up to 10 Years, Can Be Maintained, Including Information on the Cow & the Calf. One Record Is Reserved for Each Year with Calculations Such As the 205 Day Adjusted Weight. The Record of Any Cow or Cows, Year or Years, Can Be Produced at Any Time.
Cherrygarth, Inc.

Beef Manager. *Version:* 2. Jan. 1991. *Items Included:* Direction manual in 3 ring binder. *Customer Support:* 30 minutes free; Pay-per-call at $1.95/minute.
3.1 or higher. IBM XT, AT, 386 & PS/2 models (640k). disk $395.00.
Gives You the Tools to Track Your Most Productive Cows Bulls, & Calves, So You Can Select the Fastest Gaining Heifers or the Offspring of the Most Consistently Productive Cows to Hold Back into the Herd. You Can Make Your Cow-Calf Herd More Productive. You Can See At a Glance an Animal's History & Compare Each Animal's Performance to the Others.
Harvest Computer Systems, Inc.

Beef Production Records. Merle W. Wagner. 1981. *Compatible Hardware:* Apple II Plus, IIe, IIc; IBM. *Operating System(s) Required:* Apple DOS 3.3, MS-DOS 2.0. *Language(s):* BASIC. *Memory Required:* 48k, 640k. *General Requirements:* Printer.
disk $49.95, incl. manual (ISBN 0-922900-03-5, Order no.: CF9-333).
Income/Expense Information for a Complete Beef Operation. Four Hundred Cows per Disk. Breeding & History Available for Each Cow.
Cherrygarth, Inc.

BEEFPRO (Windows & DOS). *Version:* 2.0. 1993. *Items Included:* User's Guide. *Customer Support:* Free technical support.
PC-DOS/MS-DOS. IBM PC & compatibles (384k). disk $195.00. *Optimal configuration:* IBM PC compatible computer with MS-DOS, minimum 384k RAM, 80-column printer. *Networks supported:* Novell.
MS Windows 3.0 or higher. IBM PC & compatibles (384k). disk $195.00. *Optimal configuration:* IBM PC compatible computer with MS-DOS, minimum 384k RAM, 80-column printer. *Networks supported:* Novell.
Projects the Profitability & Calculates the Breakeven Prices for Feeding Out & Finishing Beef Cattle in Feedlots. Suggests Most Profitable Feeding Schedule Using up to Five Pens & Produces Reports That Include Buy/Sell Prices, Feeding Costs, Daily Intake/Gain, & More. With Windows, Menus, Mouse Support, Context Sensitive Help. Also Available in Spanish.
Agricultural Software Consultants, Inc.

BeefUp. *Version:* 4.0. 1990. *Compatible Hardware:* IBM PC, PC XT. *Operating System(s) Required:* CP/M, CP/M-86, MP/M, MP/M-86, PC-DOS, MS-DOS. *Language(s):* CB-80, CB-86. *Memory Required:* 48k. *General Requirements:* 2 disk drives or hard disk. *Items Included:* manual. *Customer Support:* Unlimited telephone support.
disk $100.00.
demo disk $10.00.
manual $25.00.
Cow/Calf Herd Management Performance Data System Designed for Commercial Beef Producers & Purebred Breeders. Program Flags Herd Management Jobs That Need Tending to, Including Calving Due-Dates, Pregnancy Checks, Open Cows to Breed, etc. Provides 12 Different Types of Updated Reports.
St. Benedict's Farm.

Beer. *Customer Support:* All of our products are unconditionally guaranteed.
Windows. CD-ROM disk $39.95 (Order no.: BEER). *Nonstandard peripherals required:* CD-ROM drive.
Complete Reference & Tutorial on Brewing Beer at Home.
Walnut Creek CDRom.

Begat. *Version:* 1.1. Jun. 1990. *Items Included:* Manual. *Customer Support:* 30 day money-back guarantee, free tech support (you pay only for the call), On-Line help, interactive tutorial.
6.0.5 or higher (7.0 compatible). MAC Plus or higher (1Mb). Contact vendor for price. *Nonstandard peripherals required:* 800k drive. *Addl. software required:* HyperCard 1.0 or higher. *Optimal configuration:* 6.0.7, MAC Plus, 1Mb RAM.
Takes the Ho-Hum Out of Bible Genealogies. It Is a In-Depth Family Tree of Practically Everyone in the Old Testament in an Easy to Access, Visually Based HyperCard Stack. Use the Find Command to Find Any Name in Seconds. Is Very Easy to Use: Just Point & Click on Any Character to See Detailed Biographical Information & Scripture References. You Can Even Add Notes from Your Own Studies. See a Family Tree of the Twelve Sons of Israel. Trace the Line of Jesus All the Way from Adam to Mary & Joseph.
Beacon Technology, Inc.

Beginner's Adventures, 5 games. *Compatible Hardware:* TRS-80 Model I, Model III, Model 4 with Level II BASIC. (source code included). disk $13.95 ea.
Mini-Adventures for First Time Adventure Players. Includes KING REX III'S TOMB, MEDUSA'S REVENGE, MISSILE SUBMARINE WARFARE, MONASTERY OF GWYDION, & PITS OF HEMLOCK.
Dynacomp, Inc.

Beginners Charts: M-309 Printing Package 1. 1982. *Compatible Hardware:* Commodore 64 with printer. *Memory Required:* 64k.
disk $100.00 (ISBN 0-925182-39-7).
Chart with Planets & Signs Spelled Out.
Matrix Software.

Beginning Reading. (The/Talking Tutor Ser.). Windows. IBM & compatibles. CD-ROM disk $44.95 (Order no.: R1025). *Nonstandard peripherals required:* CD-ROM drive. *Optimal configuration:* 386 processor or higher, MS-DOS 3.1 or higher, 20Mb hard drive, 640k RAM, external speakers or headphones (with sound card) that are Sound Blaster compatible, VGA graphics & adapter, VGA color monitor. Macintosh (4Mb). (Order no.: R1025A). *Nonstandard peripherals required:* 14" color monitor or larger, CD-ROM drive.
This Outstanding Series Uses Puzzles, Exciting Stories, Color-Animation & Music to Teach the Basics (Ages 4-7).
Library Video Co.

Beginning Tarot PC. Jan. 1996. *Items Included:* Instruction handbook.
DOS & Windows. PC (640k). disk $19.90 (ISBN 1-56087-132-6). *Optimal configuration:* Min. 286, DOS or Windows, 2k RAM.
Learn from Two Easy-to-Use Beginning Tarot Card Training Programs. Three Dynamic Shareware Programs. Bonus Program to Test Your Psychic Abilities...& Your Friends Too.
Top of the Mountain Publishing.

Beginning Word. *Version:* 5.1. Dec. 1992. *Items Included:* 90-minute audio cassette with instructions, practice disk with lesson files & examples, Quick Reference Card, Extra Practice Card. *Customer Support:* Free technical support 800-832-2499, 100% satisfaction guarantee.
Macintosh Plus, SE or II. 3.5" disk $39.95 (ISBN 0-944124-10-0). *Optimal configuration:* Microsoft Word 5.1, Mactinosh Plus, SE or II, 2 disk drives, or 1 disk drive plus a hard disk, printer, mouse & cassette tape recorder.
Personal Training for Microsoft Word 5.1. Learn to Enter & Edit Information, Use the Spelling Checker, Set Margins & Tabs, & Use Styles to Format Text.
Personal Training Systems.

Bell Object Relations & Reality Testing Inventory. Version: 2.010. Morris D. Bell. Customer Support: Free unlimited phone support with a toll free number.
Windows 3.X, Windows 95. IBM or 100% compatible. disk $250.00 (Order no.: W-1074). Optimal configuration: Hard disk with 1Mb free disk space, printer.
This New Self-Report Inventory Gives Clinicians a Quick, Convenient, & Reliable Way to Evaluate Adults with Character Disorders & Psychoses. Identifies Clients with Borderline Personality Disorder, Tells You Whether They Are Likely to Benefit from Therapy, & Offers Helpful Treatment Guidelines.
Western Psychological Services.

BEM Starter Pack for Acoustics. R. Adey et al. Jul. 1994. Items Included: Book: Boundary Element Methods in Acoustics; Self-Study Guide; BEASY acoustics code for the PC.
MS-DOS 3.0 or higher. IBM PC & compatibles (386 or higher) (8Mb). software pkg. $384.00 (ISBN 1-56252-261-2). Nonstandard peripherals required: Math co-processor.
Contains Special PC Version of the Advanced Commercial Boundary Elements Program, BEASY. The Code Has Full Capabilities & Allows up to 80 Three-Dimensional Elements. A Self-Study Guide Includes Tutorial Sessions Covering Several Applications.
Computational Mechanics, Inc.

BEM Starter Pack for Fracture Mechanics & Crack Growth. R. Adey et al. Jul. 1994. Items Included: Book: Numerical Fracture Mechanics; Self-study guide; general theoretical guide; BEASY-Crack Growth code for the PC.
MS-DOS 3.0 or higher. IBM PC & compatibles (386 or higher) (8Mb). software pkg. $384.00 (ISBN 1-56252-262-0). Nonstandard peripherals required: Math co-processor.
Contains Special PC Version of Advanced Commercial Boundary Elements Code, BEASY. The Code Is Fully Functional, Including Crack Propagation, & Allows up to 30 Two-Dimensional Elements to Define the Original Geometry. There Is No Restriction on Additional Elements Generated During Crack Propagation. The Self-Teaching Guide Includes Several Tutorial Sessions Where Representative Examples Are Run.
Computational Mechanics, Inc.

BEM Starter Pack for Stress Analysis. R. Adey et al. May 1994. Items Included: Book: Boundary Elements for Engineers: Theory & Applications; Self-Teaching Guide to BEASY-Stress Analysis code for the PC; BEASY-Stress code for the PC.
MS-DOS 3.0 or higher. IBM PC & compatibles (386 or higher) (8Mb). software pkg. $384.00 (ISBN 1-56252-260-4). Nonstandard peripherals required: Math co-processor.
Contains Special PC Version of the Advanced Boundary Elements Program, BEASY. The Code Has Fuel Capabilities & Allows up to 30 Two-Dimensional & 80 Three-Dimensional Elements. Self-Teaching Guide Includes Tutorial Sessions That Involve Solving Representative Examples.
Computational Mechanics, Inc.

BENCHMARK. Version: 3.0. Jun. 1993. Items Included: User manual, practice database. Customer Support: phone consultation; periodic updates.
PC-DOS 3.1 & higher (512k). IBM PC XT, AT & compatibles. disk $395.00 (ISBN 0-924945-07-9, Order no.: 7). Addl. software required: PC-File:DB version 1.1. Optimal configuration: Hard disk, printer.
Database Management Package for Tracking Book Repairs in Libraries. Prints Job Tickets, Statistics, Reports, & Graphs. Uses the Shareware Package PC-File:DB.
Logic Assocs.

Benchmark Modula-2. Compatible Hardware: Commodore Amiga.
3.5" disk $199.95.
Interactive Modula-2 Development System.
Avant-Garde Software.

Benchmark Survey System. Version: 7.0. Compatible Hardware: IBM & compatibles. General Requirements: Hard disk. Customer Support: Included for 90 days.
Options: Benchmark/Autocad Interface-$195.00; Benchmark Advanced Graphics Options-$195.00; BenchPlot II-printer plotting-$195.00; Benchmark Astro/Bench-Astronomic Observation-$195.00.
Professional Survey System $795.00.
Land Surveying & Subdivision Design Program.
Computersmith, Inc.

Benchmarking with Dr. H. James Harrington. H. James Harrington. Aug. 1993. Items Included: 1 manual. Customer Support: 90 days unlimited warranty.
Windows 3.1 or higher. 386 or higher (2Mb). Contact publisher for price. Optimal configuration: 386 SX 25Mhz, Windows 3.1 2Mb.
One of the Best Ways to Improve Organization Is to Implement a Benchmarking Program. Takes the Complex Benchmarking Process & Breaks It down into Simple, Step-by-Step Activities, Greatly Reducing the Time & Expense Related to Benchmarking. Provides User with Specific Guidelines to Help Start & Maintain a Benchmarking Program.
LearnerFirst.

BeneQuick. Jun. 1993. Items Included: Software documentation/owner manual & Arthur Andersen & Co. booklets. Customer Support: Customer service is provided to all customers free of charge for 30 days after the purchase date. After that time, maintenance may be purchased at $95 per year.
IBM DOS. IBM compatible (640k). disk $249.00 Stand Alone DOS Version (ISBN 0-943293-02-). Optimal configuration: Mouse. Networks supported: Novell, Lantastic & Banyon.
Microsoft Windows. IBM compatible (2Mb). disk $249.00 Stand Alone Windows Version (ISBN 0-943293-03-0). Addl. software required: Windows. Optimal configuration: Mouse. Networks supported: Novell, Lantastic & Banyon.
Charitable Trust Planning Software Which Calculates the Charitable Deduction & Other Information for Charitable Lead & Charitable Remainder Unitrusts & Annuity Trusts. Also Calculates for Pooled Funds & Charitable Gift Annuities. Calculates for up to 5 Lives, Includes a Pop-Up Calculator & Text Explanations.
ViewPlan, Inc.

Benoit. Compatible Hardware: Apple Macintosh. Memory Required: 512k.
3.5" disk $30.00.
Fractal Generator in Desk Accessory Form, Featuring Sound Capability, 3-D Graphics & Color Support.
Comlink.

Best Access. Feb. 1990. Items Included: Text Search (Fuzzy) & Relational Database (Open). Customer Support: 90 day free phone support maintenance contract.
SUN O/S 4.1 (8Mb), Solaris 2.3, Novell 3.1. Client: M/S Windows; MAC; SUN(Motif). Server: SUN SPARC, Novell NLM. $500.00-$1500.00 per user. Optimal configuration: Clients: 8Mb RAM, SVGA monitor; Server: 32Mb RAM, 1 GB disk. Networks supported: PC-NFS, Novell 3.1, TCP-IP.
Work Management System Designed for All Commercial & Government. Client-Server Workgroups: SUN & Novell Servers, M/S Windows, MAC, & SUN Desktop Client. Word, Frame & WordPerfect Document Processors. Litigation & Work Product. Documents Are Accessible As Full Text, Images, or in the Document Catalog. Integrated Applications Include Viewers, Spreadsheets, Secure Work Area Management, Document Version Control.
Liticom, Ltd.

Best Aps. Customer Support: All of our products are unconditionally guaranteed.
DOS. CD-ROM disk $49.95 (Order no.: BEST AP). Nonstandard peripherals required: CD-ROM drive.
A Collection of the Best Applications of Business & Home Shareware.
Walnut Creek CDRom.

Best Bid. May 1988. Customer Support: Free for six months included in purchase price $100.00 annually thereafter.
PC-DOS/MS-DOS 2.0 or higher. IBM PC XT, AT, PS/2 & compatibles. 3.5" or 5.25" disk $499.95. Addl. software required: Lotus 1-2-3 256k; Symphony 448.
Menu-Driven Bond Bidding, Analysis & Reporting System. Figures Net Interest Cost (NIC). True Interest Cost (TIC), Average Life Years & at the User's Choice TRUERATE%, Math Corp's Own Index of the True Rate of return. The System Can Figure Serial Bonds, Term Bonds & Zero Coupon Bonds. All Data entry Is Automatically Produced. Pricipal or Interest Installments Can Occur Annually, Semi-Annually, Quarterly or Monthly. Also Offers an Excellent Reporting System for Analysis, Final Proposals, etc. All Calculations Are Performed Using Standa rd SIA (Security Industry Association) Conventions.
Math Corp.

Best Case Bankruptcy Filing System. Version: 2.1. Dec. 1993. Items Included: User's Guide, Client Interview Worksheets. Customer Support: Unlimited toll-free telephone support, 60-day money back guarantee.
MS-DOS 2.1 or higher. IBM PC & compatibles (490k). Single-user $495.95; Network version $995.95; Single-user/Chapter 7 only $295.95. Optimal configuration: PC compatible with 386 processor or higher. Networks supported: Novell, Lantastic, Banyan, most others.
Produces All Forms Necessary for Filing Chapter 7, 11, 12, & 13 Bankruptcy Petitions. Client Files Are Permanently Saved in the Database So That Changes or Additions May Be Made at Anytime. Time-Consuming Tasks Such As Alphabetizing Lists of Creditors, Totaling Schedules, Counting Continuation Sheets, & Assembling the Creditor Address Matrix Are Performed by the Computer. Completed Forms Emerge from the Printer with a Crisp, Professional Appearance.
Best Case Solutions, Inc.

Best Choice 3 Decision Making. Items Included: Full manual. No other products required. Customer Support: Free telephone support - no time limit, 30 day warranty.
MS-DOS 3.2 or higher. IBM & compatibles (512k). disk $89.95.
Helps User Solve Problems & Make Better Decisions. It Does This by Organizing, Simplifying, & Quantifying the Decision-Making Process. Then a Proprietary Optimization Algorithm Is Used to Score the Choices in Descending Order.
Dynacomp, Inc.

Best ESP: Electronic Statement Preparation. Compatible Hardware: IBM PC & compatibles, PS/2. Memory Required: 640k. General Requirements: DOS 3.0 or higher; Lotus 1-2-3

TITLE INDEX

Release 2.01 or higher; hard disk with 10 meg available; HP LaserJet laser printer recommended. *Customer Support:* Toll free technical product support available. contact publisher for price.
Assists the Insurance Company with Compilation of Accounting Information for Mandatory Financial Filings. User Can Generate Electronic Filings & Also Print the Forms Approved by the National Association of Insurance Commissioners & State Insurance Departments for Annual & Quarterly Filings.
A. M. Best Co.

Best Fantasy 1996. (Best Fantasy Ser.). Edited by William R. Stanek. Jun. 1996.
PC-DOS/MS-DOS, Novell DOS 3.1 or higher. IBM PC, XT, AT, PS/2 or 100% compatibles (640k). disk $9.95 (ISBN 1-57545-008-9).
Optimal configuration: IBM PC, XT, AT, PS/2 or 100% compatibles, VGA/SVGA or compatible graphics card & monitor, 640k minimum RAM, hard disk, PC-DOS/MS-DOS or Novell DOS 3.1 or higher. Will also run on Windows system.
PC-DOS/MS-DOS, Novell DOS 3.1 or higher. IBM PC, XT, AT, PS/2 or 100% compatibles (640k). disk $9.95 (ISBN 1-57545-009-7).
Optimal configuration: IBM PC, XT, AT, PS/2 or 100% compatibles, CGA/VGA or compatible graphics card & monitor, 640k minimum RAM, hard disk, PC-DOS/MS-DOS or Novell DOS 3.1 or higher. Will also run on Windows system.
Interactive Fiction on Floppy Disk.
Virtual Pr., The.

The Best Food & Wine, Vol. 1: MPC - Stand-Alone. *Items Included:* Operating manual, catalog, registration card. *Customer Support:* Free technical support 206-622-5530.
DOS 3.1, Windows 3.1, Windows 95. 486SX 25MHz or higher (8Mb RAM). CD-ROM disk Contact publisher for price (ISBN 1-884014-70-4). *Addl. software required:* Double speed CD-ROM drive.
An Interactive Experience in Gourmet Cooking Presented on a CD-ROM Disc for PC & MAC. Contains Recipes from the Best of Food & Wind & Gourmet Cooking Video Featuring Chefs from the Aspen Classic. There Are Wine Suggestions from Wine Authority Ronn Wiegand & an On-Line Connection to the Experts at Best of Food & Wine.
Multicom Publishing, Inc.

Best Friend. William W. Smith. Sep. 1985. *Compatible Hardware:* IBM PC, PC XT, PC AT, & compatibles. *Operating System(s) Required:* MS-DOS. *Memory Required:* 128k. *General Requirements:* 2 disk drives.
3-1/2", 5-1/4" or 8" disk $84.95.
Provides Six Functions: File Services (Copy, Delete, Rename, View, Sort, & Spool Files), Disk Services (Format, Copy & Compare Disks), Input/Output Options (Set Serial Port Parameters & Specify a Printer to Any Port), Printer Output Redirection (Capture the Printer Output from Any Program into a Disk File), Typewriter (Emulates Full Featured Electronic Typewriter), & a Full Featured Scientific/Business Calculator (Includes over 50 Math & Business Functions). Each Function of BEST FRIEND Is Menu Driven So That No DOS Commands Are Needed.
Elite Software Development, Inc.

Best Mystery 1996. (Best Mystery Ser.). Edited by William R. Stanek. Jun. 1996.
PC-DOS/MS-DOS, Novell DOS 3.1 or higher. IBM PC, XT, AT, PS/2 or 100% compatibles (640k). disk $9.95 (ISBN 1-57545-010-0).
Optimal configuration: IBM PC, XT, AT, PS/2 or 100% compatibles, VGA/SVGA or compatible graphics card & monitor, 640k minimum RAM, hard disk, PC-DOS/MS-DOS or Novell DOS 3.1 or higher. Will also run on Windows system.
PC-DOS/MS-DOS, Novell DOS 3.1 or higher. IBM PC, XT, AT, PS/2 or 100% compatibles (640k). disk $9.95 (ISBN 1-57545-011-9).
Optimal configuration: IBM PC, XT, AT, PS/2 or 100% compatibles, CGA/VGA or compatible graphics card & monitor, 640k minimum RAM, hard disk, PC-DOS/MS-DOS or Novell DOS 3.1 or higher. Will also run on Windows system.
Interactive Fiction on Floppy Disk.
Virtual Pr., The.

Best of Breed: The American Kennel Club's Multimedia Guide to Dogs. Nov. 1995. *Customer Support:* 800 number (free), online support forums.
Windows 486SX, 25MHz; Macintosh. IBM & compatibles (8Mb); Performa 550 (33MHz 68030) (8Mb). CD-ROM disk $49.95 (ISBN 1-57595-004-9). *Nonstandard peripherals required:* Double-speed CD-ROM drive, Super VGA color card-256 color display, "SoundBlaster" compatible sound card; Double-speed CD-ROM drive.
The World's Most Authoritative & Comprehensive Resource on Dogs. Includes Hundreds of Pictures, over an Hour of Training Video, & Text from Twenty Howell Book House Titles Including the Bestselling "The Complete Dog".
Macmillan Digital U. S. A.

The Best of Food & Wine, Vol. 1. Oct. 1995. *Items Included:* Operating manual, catalog, registration card. *Customer Support:* Free technical support 206-622-5530.
Macintosh. 68030 processor System 7.1 or higher (8Mb RAM). CD-ROM disk Contact publisher for price (ISBN 1-884014-71-2). *Addl. software required:* Double speed CD-ROM drive, keyboard, 13" monitor, Quicktime 1.61 or higher mouse.
Prepare Yourself for an Enchanting, Interactive Gourmet Cooking Experience, Featuring over 100 Video Clips, Audio Instruction, & Masterful Dinner Planning Assistance with The Best of Food & Wine.
Multicom Publishing, Inc.

The Best of Food & Wine, Vol. 1: Mac-MPC Book Bundle. Oct. 1995. *Items Included:* Operating manual, catalog, registration card. *Customer Support:* Free technical support 206-622-5530.
DOS 3.1, Windows 3.1, Windows 95; Macintosh. 486SX 25MHz or higher (8Mb RAM); 68030 processor System 7.1 or higher (8Mb RAM). CD-ROM disk Contact publisher for price (ISBN 1-884014-72-0). *Addl. software required:* Double speed CD-ROM drive.
A Gourmet Cookbook on CD-ROM with over 200 Recipes from the Chefs at the Famous Aspen Classic. Learn to Cook Gourmet & Even about Which Wines to Serve with Your Meal. The Best of Food & Wine Will Be Bundled with a Gourmet Cookbook.
Multicom Publishing, Inc.

The Best of Multimedia. 1995. *Items Included:* Operating manual. *Customer Support:* Free telephone technical support 1-800-850-7272.
DOS 3.1, Windows 3.1; Macintosh. 33Mhz 80486DX (4Mb); Macintosh, System 6.07, 68030 processor or higher (4Mb). CD-ROM disk $5.95 (ISBN 1-884014-56-9). *Nonstandard peripherals required:* CD-ROM drive.
A Unique Way to Sample the Wide Range of Multicom Products Through Interactive Browsing.
Multicom Publishing, Inc.

The Best of Multimedia: CD-ROM Sampler. May 1995. *Items Included:* Manual on how to use the CD-ROM. *Customer Support:* Free telephone technical support 1 800 850-7272. Support available Mon - Fri 7:30am - 7:30pm, Sat. 9-5:00pm, Sun 10:00-4:00pm.
DOS 3.1 (or higher) & Microsoft Windows. 33 MHz 80486DX or higher (4Mb) (8Mb recommended). CD-ROM disk Contact publisher for price (ISBN 1-884014-56-9). *Nonstandard peripherals required:* MPC compatible CD-ROM drive, VGA video/display at 256 colors. *Addl. software required:* Microsoft CD-ROM extensions 2.2 or higher Soundblaster, compatible audio board. *Optimal configuration:* Double speed CD-ROM drive.
Contains (Almost) Full Functioning Examples of Multicom's Fine Line of Titles. This Title Includes Samplers of American in Space, Journey to the Planet, Wines of the World, National Parks of America, Better Homes & Gardens Complete Guide to Gardening, Better Homes & Gardens Cool Crafts, Better Homes & Gardens Healthy Cooking CD-ROM Cookbook, Warren Miller's Ski World, Astrology Source, Legends of Oz & Dandy Dinosaurs.
Multicom Publishing, Inc.

The Best of Muse. Ed Zaron & Silas Warner. Mar. 1981. *Compatible Hardware:* Apple II, II+, IIe. *Operating System(s) Required:* Apple DOS 3.2, 3.3. *Language(s):* Assembly. *Memory Required:* 32k.
disk $7.98 (ISBN 0-87190-003-3).
Provides Muse's Most Popular Cassette Games on One Disk. Includes TANK WAR, ESCAPE, MUSIC BOX, MAZE GAME, & SIDE SHOWS.
Muse Software.

Best of Wok Talk. *Items Included:* Bound manual. *Customer Support:* Free hotline - no time limit; 30 day limited warranty; updates are $5/disk plus S&H.
MS-DOS. IBM & compatibles (256k). disk $29.95.
Over 100 Recipes from All Regions of China. Select Recipes by Ingredients, Type of Cuisine, or Key Words. Automatically Scales Ingredient Quantities to Fit Amounts on Hand or Portions Needed. Package Includes a 22-Page Chinese Cooking Primer.
Dynacomp, Inc.

Best Sci-Fi 1996. (Best Sci-Fi Ser.). Edited by William R. Stanek. Jun. 1996.
PC-DOS/MS-DOS, Novell DOS 3.1 or higher. IBM PC, XT, AT, PS/2 or 100% compatibles (640k). disk $9.95 (ISBN 1-57545-012-7).
Optimal configuration: IBM PC, XT, AT, PS/2 or 100% compatibles, VGA/SVGA or compatible graphics card & monitor, 640k minimum RAM, hard disk, PC-DOS/MS-DOS or Novell DOS 3.1 or higher. Will also run on Windows system.
PC-DOS/MS-DOS, Novell DOS 3.1 or higher. IBM PC, XT, AT, PS/2 or 100% compatibles (640k). disk $9.95 (ISBN 1-57545-013-5).
Optimal configuration: IBM PC, XT, AT, PS/2 or 100% compatibles, CGA/VGA or compatible graphics card & monitor, 640k minimum RAM, hard disk, PC-DOS/MS-DOS or Novell DOS 3.1 or higher. Will also run on Windows system.
Interactive Fiction on Floppy Disk.
Virtual Pr., The.

BestBet. Bob Nadler. May 1988. *Operating System(s) Required:* PC-DOS/MS-DOS. *Memory Required:* 4.1 or 4.2 versions 256k, 5.0 or 5.1 version 512k. *General Requirements:* WordPerfect 4.1, 4.2, 5.0 or 5.1. *Items Included:* User's Manual. *Customer Support:* Yes.
disk $24.95 (ISBN 0-933596-39-1).

3.5" disk $29.95 (ISBN 0-933596-40-5).
Compact Collection of Two-Key Macros That Make WordPerfect 5.1, 5.0, 4.2, or 4.1 Faster, Easier to Use & Learn. Macros Add New Functions, Features & Editing Tools While They Cut Numbers of Keystrokes & Menu Responses. Macros Included Enable Users to Make Full-Line Cuts or Left-of-Cursor Cuts with the Cursor Anywhere on the Line, Transpose Words or Letters, Make Case Changes, Add Initial Caps, Restore Cuts, Address Envelopes, Make Quick Cursor Moves, Send a Printer "Go", or Directly Embed Epson Printer Codes.
F/22 Pr.

BestChoice 3. *Version:* 3.0. Nov. 1989. *Items Included:* 116 page, perfect bound manual, 2 disk 3.5" & 5.25" media. *Customer Support:* 90 day unlimited warranty; 24 hour Fax 213-821-8122; 24 hour BBS 619-228-3159 Voice Tech 213-453-7937, 8:30am-5:00pm.
PC/MS-DOS 2.0 or higher. IBM PC, PC/XT, PC/AT, PC/Jr, PS/2 & compatibles (256k). disk $99.00.
Decision System Assists You or Your Team in Any Problem Requiring Alternative Analysis. Useful for Determining Program Design Specifications, Personnel Review, Hiring & Firing, Any Purchase (Equipment, Property, Stocks). Logical Process, Simple to Learn & Easy to Use.
Sterling Castle.

BestChoice3: Decision Making. 1992. *Items Included:* Detailed manuals included with all Dynacomp products. *Customer Support:* Free telephone support to original customer - no time limit; 30 day limited warranty.
MS-DOS 3.2 or higher. IBM PC & compatibles (512k). $89.95 (Add $5.00 for 3 1/2" format; 5 1/4" format standard). *Optimal configuration:* IBM, MS-DOS 2.0 or higher, 256k RAM.
Helps You Solve Problems & Make Better Decisions. Your Problem Models May Have up to 255 Choices, with up to 56 Criteria, Each Weighted. There May Be up to 54 Decision Makers Involved (for a Consensus), & You May Identify the "Experts" & Weigh Their Choices More Highly. Case-Study Examples Are Included on Disk & in the 120-Page Manual. They Include Marketing Campaigns, Settlement Considerations, Purchasing, Sports, Finance, Personal Review, Risk Management, Nurse Scheduling, etc.
Dynacomp, Inc.

BestFit. *Version:* 1.01. *Items Included:* Program diskette, reference manual. *Customer Support:* 3 months technical support.
Microsoft Windows 3.0 or higher. 286 or higher microprocessor (1Mb). Contact publisher for price. *Addl. software required:* Microsoft Windows 3.0 or higher. *Optimal configuration:* Microsoft Windows 3.1, 1Mb RAM, a mouse compatible with Windows. *Networks supported:* Most server based PC networks.
BestFit Finds the Distribution That Best Fits Your Input Data. Just Read in Your Data, Click Start & BestFit Automatically Runs a Thorough Analysis. The Fit Is Optimized Using the Levenberg-Marquardt Method with 18 Distribution Types. The Goodness-of-Fit Is Measured for the Optimized Function, Chi-Square, Anderson-Darling & Kolmogorov-Smirnov Tests Are Performed. All Functions Are Compared & the Lowest Goodness-of-Fit Value Is Considered the Best Fit. Graphs & Statistics Are Generated for Further Examination of the Results.
Palisade Corp.

BET-A-BIT. *Version:* 3.0. Oct. 1991. *Compatible Hardware:* IBM PC & compatibles. *Operating System(s) Required:* MS-DOS. *Language(s):* BASIC. *Memory Required:* 256k. *Items Included:* 5.25" or 3.5" disk & manual. *Customer Support:* Customer support available.
disk $29.95 (ISBN 0-918741-17-3).
Comparative Rating System for Picking Possible Winning Race Horses. Uses Past Performance Data of Competing Race Horses, Jockey & Trainer Ratings & Other Pertinent Factors. Prints Results for Use at Track.
D W N.

Better Homes & Gardens Complete Guide to American Cooking. Sep. 1994. *Items Included:* Manual, registration card, flier describing all our titles, occasional promotional offers. *Customer Support:* Free telephone technical support.
DOS & Microsoft Windows 3.1. 12 MHz 80386SX. CD-ROM disk Contact publisher for price (ISBN 1-884014-14-3). *Nonstandard peripherals required:* MPC compatible. CD-ROM drive (680Mb) SVGA display, audio board, mouse, 486 DX processor. *Addl. software required:* Microsoft CD-ROM Extensions v.2.2.
Macintosh System 6.05. Color Macintosh (256 colors) (3.5Mb). CD-ROM disk Contact publisher for price (ISBN 1-884014-26-7). *Optimal configuration:* Single speed CD-ROM, 13" color monitor, 8 Mb RAM.
Savor over 500 Recipes with Thousands of Full Color Photographs Showing Recipes from Beginning to End. You Can Add Your Own Recipes to the Database, Keeping Them Organized & Handy. Search for Recipes by Ingredients, Preparation Time, & Nutritional Information Using the Innovative "What's for Dinner" Feature.
Multicom Publishing, Inc.

Better Homes & Gardens Complete Guide to Gardening. Jun. 1994. *Items Included:* Manual, registration card, flier describing all our titles, occasional promotional offers. *Customer Support:* Free telephone technical support.
DOS & Microsoft Windows 3.1. 12 MHz 80386SX. CD-ROM disk Contact publisher for price (ISBN 1-884014-17-8). *Nonstandard peripherals required:* MPC compatible. CD-ROM drive (680Mb) SVGA display, audio board, mouse, 486 DX processor. *Addl. software required:* Microsoft CD-ROM Extensions v.2.2.
Macintosh System 6.05. Color Macintosh (256 colors) (3.5Mb). CD-ROM disk Contact publisher for price (ISBN 1-884014-29-1). *Optimal configuration:* Single speed CD-ROM, 13" color monitor, 8 Mb RAM.
Complete Information Regarding Plant Size, Color, Growing Season, Maintenance, Disease Prevention & More. Contains Video Demonstrations Showing Gardening Techniques. Regional & Seasonal Guides Allow You to Pick the Right Plants for Your Yard.
Multicom Publishing, Inc.

Better Homes & Gardens Cool Crafts. 1994. IBM. CD-ROM disk $22.75.
Meredith Bks.

Better Homes & Gardens Cool Crafts: Incredible Activities for Kids. Sep. 1994. *Items Included:* Manual, registration card, flier describing all our titles, occasional promotional offers. *Customer Support:* Free telephone technical support.
DOS & Microsoft Windows 3.1. 12 MHz 80386SX. CD-ROM disk Contact publisher for price (ISBN 1-884014-13-5). *Nonstandard peripherals required:* MPC compatible. CD-ROM drive (680Mb) SVGA display, audio board, mouse, 486 DX processor. *Addl. software required:* Microsoft CD-ROM Extensions v.2.2.
Macintosh System 6.05. Color Macintosh (256 colors) (3.5Mb). CD-ROM disk Contact publisher for price (ISBN 1-884014-25-9). *Optimal configuration:* Single speed CD-ROM, 13" color monitor, 8 Mb RAM.
A Title with Innovative Crafts, Coloring & Activity Pages, All Encouraging Children to Use Their Imagination. Kids Find Projects with the "What Can I Make?" Feature Using Supplies They Have Available. For Parents There Is a "Grownups Corner", a Special Section Outlining Safety Tips & Helpful Advice.
Multicom Publishing, Inc.

Better Homes & Gardens Health Cooking CD Cookbook. Jun. 1993. *Items Included:* Manual. *Customer Support:* Free telephone technical support.
DOS & Microsoft Windows 3.1. 12 Mhz 80386SX (2Mb). CD-ROM disk Contact publisher for price (ISBN 1-884014-18-6). *Nonstandard peripherals required:* MPC-compatible CD-ROM drive (680Mb); SVGA display; audio board; mouse, 486DX processor. *Addl. software required:* Microsoft CD-ROM extensions v.2.2. *Optimal configuration:* 4Mb RAM; double-speed CD-ROM drive.
Macintosh System 6.05. Color Macintosh (256 colors) (3.5Mb free RAM). CD-ROM disk contact publisher for price (ISBN 1-884014-30-5). *Nonstandard peripherals required:* CD-ROM drive. *Optimal configuration:* Double speed CD-ROM; 13" color monitor; 8Mb RAM; fast processor.
Interactive CD-ROM Cookbook Based on New Dieter's Cook Book (ISBN 0-696-01974-4). *Features over 400 Recipes & Suggests Menu Items Based upon Nutritional Value; Sodium, Fat, or Cholesterol Restrictions; or Available Ingredients. Title Features Narration, Music, Video, Color Photographs, & Illustrated Techniques.*
Multicom Publishing, Inc.

Better Homes & Gardens Planning Your Home. Oct. 1995. *Items Included:* Operating manual, catalog, registration card. *Customer Support:* Free technical support 206-622-5530.
DOS 3.1, Windows 3.1, Windows 95. 486SX 25MHz or higher (8Mb RAM). CD-ROM disk Contact publisher for price (ISBN 1-884014-73-9). *Addl. software required:* Double speed CD-ROM drive, mouse, keyboard, MPC compliant audio.
Macintosh. 68030 processor System 7.1 or higher (8Mb RAM). CD-ROM disk Contact publisher for price (ISBN 1-884014-74-7). *Addl. software required:* Double speed CD-ROM drive, keyboard, 13" monitor, Quicktime 1.61 or higher mouse.
Planning Your Home Is a Title Designed to Assist a Potential Homeowner Through All the Steps in Planning & Building a Dream Home. Take Advantage of 3-D Technology to Allow You to "Walk" Through Different Home Styles. There Are Approximately 600 2-Dimensional Floor Plans for You to Browse Through.
Multicom Publishing, Inc.

Better Working Desktop. 1987. *Compatible Hardware:* IBM PC & true compatibles. *Operating System(s) Required:* MS-DOS 2.1 or higher. *General Requirements:* Hayes compatible modem. Hard disk supported. *Customer Support:* (617)494-1220, 494-1221.
disk $29.95.
Desktop Organizer. Includes: MEMO PAD Supporting Preset Memo Formats; WORLD CLOCK Capable of Showing the Time in 16 Cities Around the World; CALENDAR That Will Keep Track of User's Schedule; ADDRESS BOOK with Autodial Feature; TO-DO LIST; & UTILITIES Option Providing an On-Screen Menu That

TITLE INDEX

Allows Users to Format & Copy Disks, & Erase, Rename, & View Files Without Leaving the Program. Can Be RAM-Resident in a 512k Computer.
Spinnaker Software Corp.

BetterWorking Eight-in-One. *Version:* 2.0. *Compatible Hardware:* IBM PC & true compatibles. *Operating System(s) Required:* PC-DOS 2.1 or higher. *Memory Required:* 512k. *General Requirements:* Graphics card for graphics output. Hard disk supported, mouse optional. *Customer Support:* (617) 494-1220, (617) 494-1221.
disk $59.95.
Integrated Productivity Package. The Eight Applications Included Are: DESKTOP ORGANIZER - Keeps Track of Appointments, Issues Reminders of Birthdays & Anniversaries, Maintains a "To-Do" List, & Includes an Address Book; OUTLINER; WORDPROCESSOR; 100,000 Word SPELLING CORRECTOR; SPREADSHEET with 1-2-3 File Import & Export Capability; DATA BASE Which Can Read & Write DBASE III Compatible Files; GRAPH - Creates Bar Charts, Point & Line Graphs, & Pie Charts; & COMMUNICATIONS - Takes Advantage of the Features of HAYES Compatible Modems.
Spinnaker Software Corp.

The BetterWorking One Person Office. *Customer Support:* (617) 494-1221/1220. IBM PC (512k). disk $69.95.
Program Tracks Expenses, Invoices Clients & Provides Contact Database. Includes More Than 60 Pre-Defined Expense Categories. User Can Organize Expenses by Category, Date or Project. Once Names, Addresses & Notes Are Entered, Program Tracks Each Contact & Issues Reminders for Follow-Up Calls. Can Also Use Database to Print Mailing Labels, Mail Merge for Customized Letters & Sort Reports by Location or Code. Reports Include Invoices by Job, Date, Outstanding Balances, Sales Tax Due & More.
Spinnaker Software Corp.

BetterWorking: The Resume Kit. *Version:* 1.32. Jun. 1988. *Customer Support:* Unlimited free support: (617) 494-1220, (617) 494-1221. PC-DOS/MS-DOS 2.0 or higher (384k). disk $39.95.
Macintosh (512k). disk $59.95.
Takes User Through a Step-by-Step Process to Organize the Important Information Needed in a Resume. Fill in On-Screen Forms with Experience, Skills, Interests, Education. Then Select from Nine Resume Types for Style: Quick & Easy, General, Standard, Business, Engineering, Student, Computer, Professional, Academic. Includes Automatic Formatting (Chronological, Curriculum Vitae, Target Skill, or Accomplishment), On-Screen Template, 10,000 Word Spell Checker, On-Screen Calendar System, Interview Tips, & Job Hunting Guide.
Spinnaker Software Corp.

BetterWorking Word Processor. 1987. *Compatible Hardware:* Apple IIe, IIc; IBM PC & true compatibles. *Memory Required:* Apple IIe & IIc 128k, IBM 256k. *General Requirements:* CGA for graphics output. Supports hard disk. *Customer Support:* (617) 494-1220, (617) 494-1221.
disk $29.95.
WYSIWYG Word Processor. Includes an Outliner & a 100,000 Word Spelling Corrector That Suggests Spelling Alternatives. Supports over 240 Printers. Features On-Line Context-Sensitive Help & Pull-Down Menus. Print Features Supported Include Underlining, Boldface, Italics, Double-Width, Enhanced, & Compressed. Page Layout Capabilities Include Headers, Footers, Centering, Automatic Table of Contents, & Automatic Page Numbering. Other Layout Features Include Text Justification, Line Spacing, Tabs, Margins, & Upper & Lower Case Option. Allows Mailmerge for Personalized Mass Mailings.
Spinnaker Software Corp.

BetterWorking Word Publisher. *Version:* 5.0. May 1989. *Customer Support:* Unlimited free support: (617) 494-1220, (617) 494-1221. PC-DOS 2.1 or higher, DOS 3.3 or higher required for 3.5" disks. $59.95.
Has 22 Word Processing Features. Comes Complete with Fully Integrated Outliner. Features a Wide Variety of Fonts, Type Styles, & Sizes; On-Screen Prompts, Dropdown Menus, Context Sensitive Help, 4 Standard Columns of Text, WYSIWYG Preview Mode. More Than One Document Can Be Edited at a Time. Includes 100,000 Word Spelling Corrector & Thesaurus. Supports over 250 Printers, Can Import TIFF & PCC.
Spinnaker Software Corp.

Betting Analyst. *Version:* 1.01. Dick Mitchell. *Items Included:* Complete manual. *Customer Support:* 60 days limited money back guarantee; telephone support-handicapping & technical. MS-DOS. IBM & compatible (512K). disk $249.00.
Record-Keeping & Analysis Program for Thoroughbred Handicappers. The Handicappper Writes His Bets Down on the Track Program. After the Day's Races, It Takes about 15 Minutes to Input the Day's Bets into the Betting Analyst. The Program Has Available up to 35 Separate Reports on the Betting Records Input into It. It Will Report on Win Percentage, Average Mutual, Profit/Loss, Return on Investment, Suggested Bankroll Bet Percentage, etc. It Breaks down its Analysis into Many Different Subcategories Such As Sprints, Routes, Dirt & Turf. It Will Track All Types of Bets-Win, Place, Show or Exotics.
Cynthia Publishing Co.

Betty Crocker's Fortieth Anniversary Cookbook. *Items Included:* Full manual. No other products required. *Customer Support:* Free telephone support - no time limit, 30 day warranty.
MS-DOS 3.2 or higher. IBM & compatibles (512K). disk $34.95.
Similar to the MICROWAVE COOKBOOK, Except That 1000 Microwave, Grilling, Broiling, & Stove-Top Recipes Are Included, but There Is No Nutritional Information. Requirements & Options Are the Same.
Dynacomp, Inc.

Betty Crocker's Microwave Cookbook. *Items Included:* Full manual. No other products required. *Customer Support:* Free telephone support - no time limit, 30 day warranty.
MS-DOS 3.2 or higher. IBM & compatibles (512K). disk $29.95. *Optimal configuration:* IBM, MS Windows 3.1 or higher, 2Mb RAM, color graphics capability. Printer, mouse, & sound card are supported, but optional.
Everything You Want - & Need - to Plan Delicious Microwave Meals on Your Computer Is Right Here at Your Fingertips. Features Include: 600 Quality-Tested Recipes. Complete Nutrition Information for Every Recipe, Including Calories, Protein, Carbohydrates, Fat, Cholesterol, Sodium, & The Top 8 U.S. RDA Percentages per Serving. High Quality Color Displays Showing Creative Presentations. On-Line Help, with Guidelines on Microwave Techniques, Safety & Equipment. Includes Micro-Kitchen Light, a Simple-to-Use, Abridged Version of Micro-Kitchen Companion. Colorful Pull-Down Menus.
Dynacomp, Inc.

BEYOND THE WALL OF STARS: MPC JEWEL

Betty Crocker's Old-Fashioned Cookbook. *Items Included:* Full manual. No other products required. *Customer Support:* Free telephone support - no time limit, 30 day warranty. MS-DOS 3.2 or higher. IBM & compatibles (512k). disk $24.95.
Similar to the 40th ANNIVERSARY COOKBOOK (Including Requirements & Options), Except That It Has 250 Classic, Heritage Recipes Which Recapture the Tantalizing Flavors of a Bygone Era.
Dynacomp, Inc.

Beverly Hills Models. *Items Included:* Instruction inserts. *Customer Support:* Free phone tech support. One year exchange warranty. Macintosh; Windows; 3DO & CD1. Any Macintosh with QuickDraw Software (4Mb); IBM PC AT or compatible 80386 or 80486 (4Mb); 3DO player/photo CD player (4Mb). CD-ROM disk $24.95 (Order no.: 00011). *Nonstandard peripherals required:* Color monitor & Photo CD compatible CD-ROM drive; VGA display or higher, Photo CD compatible CD-ROM drive; Television with monitor.
Still Shot Photo CD Involving Five Girls. Arranged in a Book to Flip Through & Pick Who You Would Like to View. Blow up Picks to Larger Size on Screen.
MacDaddy Entertainment.

BEX. *Version:* 3.1. Dec. 1987. *Compatible Hardware:* Apple II series, IIgs. *Memory Required:* 128k. *Items Included:* Print, braille, audio documentation. *Customer Support:* Unlimited telephone support.
disk $450.00.
Designed for Use with Visual Impairments. Braille Translation, Braille Input/Output Options & Voice Output to Speech Synthesizers. Large Print Screen & Output Options.
Raised Dot Computing, Inc.

Beyond Basic BASIC. (Private Tutor Ser.). Randolph W. Cabell. *Compatible Hardware:* IBM PC, PCjr, PC XT, PC AT, Portable PC. *Memory Required:* 128k. *General Requirements:* Double-sided disk drive, IBM Display; also requires IBM Private Tutor 1.10, 2.00, or IBM Private Tutor Presenter 1.10 program. disk $19.95 (Order no.: 6276532).
Covers Subroutines & Addresses Other Topics Such As Input/Error Handling, String Functions, Uppercase & Lowercase Conversion, Printer Control, Use of Color & Music, Use of the Function Keys, & Menu Design.
Personally Developed Software, Inc.

Beyond Castle Wolfenstein. Eric Ace et al. May 1984. *Compatible Hardware:* Apple II+, IIe, IIc; Atari 400, 800, 1200XL; Commodore 64; IBM PC, PCjr. *Operating System(s) Required:* Apple DOS 3.2, 3.3, MS-DOS 1.1, 2.0, 2.1. *Language(s):* Assembly. *Memory Required:* Apple 48k, Commodore 64k.
disk $13.98 ea., incl. instr. bklt.
Apple. (ISBN 0-87190-031-9).
Commodore. (ISBN 0-87190-032-7).
Sequel to CASTLE WOLFENSTEIN.
Muse Software.

Beyond the Wall of Stars: MPC Jewel Case. R. A. Montgomery. *Items Included:* Registration card. *Customer Support:* Creative Multimedia Corporation warrants the CD-ROM disc & diskettes to be free from defects in materials & workmanship under normal use & service for a period of 90 days from date of purchase. Creative Multimedia Corporation offers Technical Support to customers as needed.
CD-ROM drive with MS-CDEX 2.0 or higher, Microsoft Windows 2.0 with Multimedia

Extensions or Windows 3.1. 386SX PC or higher, hard drive required (2Mb). CD-ROM disk $49.99 (ISBN 1-880428-12-1, Order no.: 10195). *Optimal configuration:* SuperVGA with 512k+ Video Memory capable of 640x480x256 colors with Windows Driver supported. Sound Card with Windows drivers (sound is not required to use this product.). *Networks supported:* All.
The Planet Celadon Is in Trouble & Needs Help. In This Story, You Will Become Part of the Expedition Team Which Will Try to Reach Tara, a Recently Settled Planet Far Beyond the Wall of Stars. Along the Way, You'll Get to Affect the Outcome of the Story by Making a Series of Critical Decisions about Direction, Strategy, Tactics & Teamwork. You'll Solve Puzzles & Use Other Problem-Solving Techniques.
Creative Multimedia Corp.

Beyond the Wall of Stars: MPC-MAC Jewel Case. R. A. Montgomery. *Items Included:* Registration Card. *Customer Support:* Creative Multimedia Corporation warrants the CD-ROM disc & diskettes to be free from defects in materials & workmanship under normal use & service for a period of 90 days from date of purchase. Creative Multimedia Corporation offers Technical Support to customers as needed.
CD-ROM drive with MS-CDEX 2.0 or higher, Microsoft Windows 2.0 with Multimedia Extensions or Windows 3.1. 386SX PC or higher, hard drive required (2Mb). CD-ROM disk $49.00 Suggested Retail Price (ISBN 1-880428-29-6). *Optimal configuration:* Super VGA with 512k or higher, Video Memory capable of 640x480x256 colors with windows driver supported. Sound Card with Windows Drives (Sound is not required to use this product). *Networks supported:* All.
System Software 6.0.7 or higher. Macintosh Plus or higher (2.5Mb). CD-ROM disk $49.00 Suggested Retail Price. *Optimal configuration:* 8-bit color & color monitor. *Networks supported:* All.
The Planet Celadon Is in Trouble & Needs Help. In This Story, You Will Become Part of the Expedition Team Which Will Try to Reach Tara, a Recently Settled Planet Far Beyond The Wall of Stars. Along the Way, You'll Get to Affect the Outcome of the Story by Making a Series of Critical Decisions about Direction, Strategy, Tactics & Teamwork. You'll Solve Puzzles & Use Other Problem-Solving Techniques.
Creative Multimedia Corp.

Beyond the Wall of Stars: MPC-MAC Retail Box. R. A. Montgomery. *Items Included:* Registration Card. *Customer Support:* Creative Multimedia Corporation warrants the CD-ROM disc & diskettes to be free from defects in materials & workmanship under normal use & service for a period of 90 days from date of purchase. Creative Multimedia Corporation offers Technical Support to customers as needed.
CD-ROM drive with MS-CDEX 2.0 or higher, Microsoft Windows 2.0 with Multimedia Extensions or Windows 3.1. 386SX PC or higher, hard drive required (2Mb). CD-ROM disk $49.00 Suggested Retail Price (ISBN 1-880428-30-X). *Optimal configuration:* Super VGA with 512k or higher, Video Memory capable of 640x480x256 colors with windows driver supported. Sound Card with Windows Drives (Sound is not required to use this product). *Networks supported:* All.
System Software 6.0.7 or higher. Macintosh Plus or higher (2.5Mb). CD-ROM disk $49.00 Suggested Retail Price. *Optimal configuration:* 8-bit color & color monitor. *Networks supported:* All.
The Planet Celadon Is in Trouble & Needs Help. In This Story, You Will Become Part of the

Expedition Team Which Will Try to Reach Tara, a Recently Settled Planet Far Beyond The Wall of Stars. Along the Way, You'll Get to Affect the Outcome of the Story by Making a Series of Critical Decisions about Direction, Strategy, Tactics & Teamwork. You'll Solve Puzzles & Use Other Problem-Solving Techniques.
Creative Multimedia Corp.

Beyond Zork. *Compatible Hardware:* Apple II, II+, IIe, IIc, Macintosh; Atari ST; Commodore 128, Amiga; IBM PC & true compatibles. $49.95.
Takes You to the Troubled Kingdom of Quendor, Across the Sea from the Great Underground Empire. In Quendor, the Wizards Have Mysteriously Disappeared, & Vicious Monsters Haunt the Streets & Wastelands. Fate Has Directed That You, a Lowly Peasant, Must Unravel the Meaning Behind These Ominous Events. Luckily, You Have an Arsenal of New Weapons & Abilities at Your Disposal. You Start by Designing Your Own Character. You Can Execute Frequently-Used Commands with a Single Keystroke by Pressing a Function Key. There Is Also an On-Screen Map to Chart Your Progress.
Activision, Inc.

BFBDEM. Lewis Rosenfelder. *Compatible Hardware:* TRS-80 Model I, Model III. *Language(s):* BASIC.
disk $19.95 (ISBN 0-936200-16-2).
Includes 32 Demonstrations of BASIC Overlays, Video Handlers, Sorts, & Other Functions.
Blue Cat.

BFBLIB. Lewis Rosenfelder. *Compatible Hardware:* TRS-80 Model I, Model III.
disk $19.95 (ISBN 0-936200-15-4).
Contains the Following: 121 Functions, Subroutines & User Routines; Search, Merge, Compare & Program Listing Routines; Array Handlers, BASIC Overlays & Video Drivers.
Blue Cat.

BHI Plus: British Humanities Index. 1996. *Items Included:* Quarterly Updated.
MS-DOS. IBM or compatibles. CD-ROM disk 1300.00 1 year (Order no.: DBH110).
"BHI Plus" delivers an astonishing range of information about the arts, economics, history, philosophy, Politics, & society.
Bowker-Saur.

Bi-Wheel Printer: M-311 Printing Package 3. 1982. *Compatible Hardware:* Commodore 64, IBM PC. *Memory Required:* 64k. *General Requirements:* Printer.
Commodore. disk $150.00 (ISBN 0-925182-41-9).
IBM. disk $100.00 (ISBN 0-925182-42-7).
Prints 2 Charts on the Same Wheel for Purposes of Comparison.
Matrix Software.

BIAS. *Version:* 4.0. 1983. *Compatible Hardware:* IBM PC & compatibles, PC XT, PC AT. *Operating System(s) Required:* PC-DOS, MS-DOS, OS/2, UNIX V, LANs. *Language(s):* C. *Memory Required:* 512-640k. *General Requirements:* Printer.
$686.00-$1986.00.
Integrated Accounting System Comprised of Several Separate Modules Such As General Ledger, Accounts Payable, Accounts Receivable, etc. User Selects Modes According to His Company's Specific Requirements.
Bristol Information Systems.

Bible/Master: Cross References & Marginal Notes. *Version:* 3.0. Lockman Foundation. Jun. 1993. *Items Included:* Manual. *Customer Support:* 30-day money-back guarantee, free

technical support.
PC-DOS/MS-DOS v. 2.1 or higher. IBM PC, PC/XT, PC/AT, PS/2 series or 100% compatibles (640k). 5.25" disk $39.95 (ISBN 1-885217-23-4, Order no.: CB502-IBM). *Addl. software required:* NAS Computer Bible v 2.0 or higher. *Optimal configuration:* 640k RAM hard disk, 1.6Mb space on hard disk.
IBM PC, PC/XT, PC/AT, PS/2 series or 100% compatibles (640k). 3.5" disk $39.95 (ISBN 1-885217-22-6, Order no.: CB502-IBM).
Standard Set of Crossreferences in the New American Standard Bible, Plus All Marginal Notes, Alternate Renderings & Literal Translations.
Foundations Pubns., Inc.

Bible/Master: King James Version Computer Bible. *Version:* 3.0. Lockman Foundation. Jun. 1993. *Items Included:* Manual. *Customer Support:* 30-day money-back guarantee, free technical support.
PC-DOS/MS-DOS v 2.1 or higher. IBM PC, PC/XT, PC/AT, PS/2 series or 100% compatibles (640k). $59.95 as basic set; $39.95 as add-on (Order no.: CB521-IBM; CB522-IBM (ADD-ON)). *Optimal configuration:* 512k RAM, 2.7Mb space on hard disk, monochrome or color monitor.
Macintosh 6.0 or higher. Macintosh (1Mb). $59.95 as basic set; $39.95 as add-on (Order no.: MAC521; MAC522 (ADD-ON)). *Optimal configuration:* 1Mb on hard disk.
King James Version Bible on Floppy Disk for IBM & Macintosh. Bible Search Program, Text Editor, Wild Card Search, Three Windows, Note Pad. Modules Can Be Added.
Foundations Pubns., Inc.

Bible/Master: La Biblia de las Americas. *Version:* 3.0. Lockman Foundation. Jun. 1993. *Items Included:* Manual. *Customer Support:* 30-day money-back guarantee, free technical support.
MS-DOS. IBM & compatibles (512k). 5.25" disk $59.95 basic set (ISBN 1-885217-17-X, Order no.: CB601-IBM).
IBM & compatibles (512k). 3.5" disk $59.95 basic set (ISBN 1-885217-16-1, Order no.: CB601-IBM).
IBM & compatibles (512k). 5.25" disk $39.95 add-on module (ISBN 1-885217-19-6, Order no.: CB607-IBM).
IBM & compatibles (512k). 3.5" disk $39.95 add-on module (ISBN 1-885217-18-8, Order no.: CB607-IBM).
Spanish NASB on 5.25" & 3.5" Disks for IBM & Compatible. Bible Search Program, Text Editor, Wild Card Search, Three Windows, Note Pad & More. Modules Can Be Added.
Foundations Pubns., Inc.

Bible/Master: NAS Computer Bible. *Version:* 3.0. Lockman Foundation. Jun. 1993. *Items Included:* 36 page manual. *Customer Support:* 30-day money-back guarantee, free technical support.
MS-DOS. IBM & compatibles (512k). $59.95 basic; $39.95 as add-on module (Order no.: CB501-IBM; CB507-IBM (ADD-ON)).
Macintosh 6.0 or higher. Macintosh (1Mb). $59.95 basic; $39.95 as add-on module (Order no.: MAC501; MAC507 (ADD-ON)). *Optimal configuration:* 1Mb on hard disk.
New American Standard Bible on Floppy Disk (3.5" or 5.25") for IBM & Compatible & Macintosh. Bible Search Program, Text Editor, Wild Card Search, Three Windows, Note Pad. Modules Can Be Added.
Foundations Pubns., Inc.

TITLE INDEX

Bible/Master: NAS Hebrew-Greek Transliterated Dictionary. Version: 3.0. Lockman Foundation. Jun. 1993. Items Included: Manual. Customer Support: 30-day money-back guarantee, free technical support.
MS-DOS. IBM PC, PC/XT, PC/AT, PS/2 series or 100% compatibles (640k). 5.25" disk $39.95 (ISBN 1-885217-21-8, Order no.: CB505-IBM). Addl. software required: NAS Computer Bible v 2.0 or higher. Optimal configuration: 640k RAM hard disk.
IBM PC, PC/XT, PC/AT, PS/2 series or 100% compatibles (640k). 3.5" disk $39.95 (ISBN 1-885217-20-X, Order no.: CB505-IBM).
System 6 or higher. Macintosh (1Mb). 3.5" disk $39.95 (ISBN 1-885217-34-X, Order no.: MAC505). Addl. software required: NAS Computer Bible v 2.0 or higher. Optimal configuration: 1Mb hard disk.
Hebrew, Aramaic & Greek Dictionary of the Bible with Strong's Numbering, Accessible in Four Formats.
Foundations Pubns., Inc.

Bible/Master: New International Version. Version: 3.0. Lockman Foundation. Jun. 1993. Items Included: Manual. Customer Support: 30-day money-back guarantee, free technical support.
PC-DOS/MS-DOS v 2.1 or higher. IBM PC, PC/XT, PC/AT, PS/2 series or 100% compatibles (640k). $69.95 as basic set; $49.95 as add-on (Order no.: CB591-IBM; CB592-IBM (ADD-ON)). Optimal configuration: 512k RAM, 2.8Mb on hard disk, monochrome or color monitor.
Macintosh 6.0 or higher. Macintosh (1Mb). $69.95 as basic set; $49.95 as add-on (Order no.: MAC591; MAC592). Optimal configuration: 1Mb on hard disk.
New International Version Bible on Floppy Disk for IBM & Compatible & Macintosh. Bible Search Program, Text Editor, Wild Card Search, Three Windows, Note Pad. Modules Can Be Added.
Foundations Pubns., Inc.

Bible/Master: New Revised Standard Version. Version: 3.0. Jun. 1993. Items Included: Manual. Customer Support: 30-day money-back guarantee, free technical support.
MS-DOS. IBM & compatibles (512k). 5.25" disk $59.95 (ISBN 1-885217-09-9, Order no.: CB561-IBM).
IBM & compatibles (512k). 3.5" disk $59.95 (ISBN 1-885217-08-0, Order no.: CB561-IBM).
IBM & compatibles (512k). 5.25" disk $39.95 add-on module (ISBN 1-885217-11-0, Order no.: CB562-IBM).
3.5" disk $39.95 add-on module (ISBN 1-885217-10-2, Order no.: CB562-IBM).
New RSV Bible on Floppy Disk for IBM or Compatible. Bible Search Program, Text Editor, Wild Card Search, Three Windows, Note Pad. Modules Can Be Added.
Foundations Pubns., Inc.

Bible/Master: Topical Studies. Version: 3.0. Lockman Foundation. Jun. 1993. Items Included: Manual. Customer Support: 30-day money-back guarantee, free technical support.
PC-DOS/MS-DOS v. 2.1 or higher. IBM PC, PC/XT, PC/AT, PS/2 series or 100% compatibles (640k). 5.25" disk $39.95 (ISBN 1-885217-25-0, Order no.: CB506-IBM). Addl. software required: NAS Computer Bible v 2.0 or higher. Optimal configuration: 640k RAM hard disk, 2.3Mb on hard disk.
IBM PC, PC/XT, PC/AT, PS/2 series or 100% compatibles (640k). 3.5" disk $39.95 (ISBN 1-885217-24-2, Order no.: CB506-IBM).
Macintosh 6.0 or higher. Macintosh (1Mb). Contact publisher for price (Order no.: MAC506).
Data Base of 20,000 Topics, Sub-Topics, & Sub-Sub-Topics Accessing Bible Verses.
Foundations Pubns., Inc.

Bible/Master: Treasury of Scripture Knowledge. Version: 3.0. Lockman Foundation. Items Included: Manual. Customer Support: 30-day money-back guarantee, free technical support.
PC-DOS/MS-DOS v. 2.1 or higher. IBM PC, PC/XT, PC/AT, PS/2 series or 100% compatibles (640k). 5.25" disk $39.95 (ISBN 1-885217-27-7, Order no.: CB509-IBM). Addl. software required: Basic BIBLE/MASTER Computer Bible, any Bible Version, software v. 2.0 or higher. Optimal configuration: 640k RAM, 1Mb on hard disk, monochrome or color monitor.
IBM PC, PC/XT, PC/AT, PS/2 series or 100% compatibles (640k). 3.5" disk $39.95 (ISBN 1-885217-26-9, Order no.: CB509-IBM).
Data Base of Cross References of Bible Verses Based on the Book: TREASURY OF SCRIPTURE KNOWLEDGE.
Foundations Pubns., Inc.

Bible - RSV, NRSV, KJV, RVR (Spanish Bible), RLB (German), NVSR (French), or Vulgate for Windows. Version: NRSV 1.3, RVR 1.1. Items Included: User's manual. Customer Support: Free telephone support; defective disks replaced free.
IBM & compatibles (4Mb). disk $59.95.
Entire Text of the Bible in Any One of the Following Versions: Revised Standard Version (RSV), New Revised Standard Version (NRSV), King James Version (KJV), Reina Valera Spanish Bible (RVR), Revised Luther Bible-1985 (RLB), Nouvelle Version Segond Revisee-1978 (NVSR), or Latin Vulgate. Each Includes the New Testament, Old Testament, & Apocrypha.
Linguist's Software, Inc.

Bible Builder. Nov. 1992. Items Included: NIV Bible, Manual. Customer Support: 90-day warranty - customer support 8:30-5:30 PST (415) 368-3200.
DOS 2.1 or higher. IBM PC & compatibles, VGA/EGA (640k). disk $49.95 (ISBN 0-00-102820-0, Order no.: 80105HD/T). Optimal configuration: Hard disk, mouse, Sound Blaster, Ad-Lib compatible sound card, 3.5 diskettes (720k), 5.25 diskettes (1.2Mb).
Bring the Bible to Life on Home Computers! Fun & Easy to Play Educational Game. Suitable for Ages 7 - Adult. Six Levels of Difficulty. 50 Plus Animated Color Bible Scenes. 700 Plus Bible References. View Maps of the Holy Lands. Hear 33 Actual Hymns. Suitable for All Denominations. Free NIV Bible Included - (Also Supports KJV, RSV & The Living Bible).
Epyx, Inc.

Bible Builder Software. Nov. 1992. Items Included: NIV Bible, manual, 3-3.5 diskettes, 2-5.25 diskettes. Customer Support: 90 day warranty, customer service available 8:30-5:30 PST (415) 368-3200.
DOS 2.1 or higher. IBM PC & compatibles, VGA/EGA (640k). disk $49.95 (ISBN 0-00-102820-0, Order no.: 80105HD/T). Optimal configuration: Hard disk, mouse, Sound Blaster, Ad-Lib compatible sound card, 3.5 diskettes (720k), 5.25 diskettes (1.2Mb).
Bring the Bible to Life on Home Computers! Fun & Easy to Play Educational Game. Suitable for Ages 7 - Adult. Six Levels of Difficulty. 50 Plus Animated Color Bible Scenes. 700 Plus Bible References. View Maps of the Holy Lands. Hear 33 Actual Hymns. Suitable for All Denominations. Free NIV Bible Included (Also Supports KJV, RSV & The Living Bible).
Everbright Software.

Bible Illustrator for DOS. Parsons Technology. Jul. 1990.
3.5" disk Contact publisher for price (ISBN 1-57264-001-4).
Parsons Technology.

Bible Illustrator for Windows. Parsons Technology. Jun. 1994.
3.5" disk Contact publisher for price (ISBN 1-57264-002-2).
Parsons Technology.

The Bible on Disk. Items Included: Bound manual. Customer Support: Free hotline - no time limit; 30 day limited warranty; updates are $5/disk plus S&H.
MS-DOS. IBM & compatibles, CP/M (256k). disk $39.95.
Apple. disk $39.95.
King James Version of the Bible on Disk.
Dynacomp, Inc.

Bible: RSV, NIV, KJV, Vulgate, NRSV, RLB, or RVR (Spanish Bible), (German), NVSR (French). Version: KJV 4.0, NIV 3.3, RSV 3.2, NRSV 1.4, Vulgate 3.0. Jun. 1989. Items Included: User's manual. Customer Support: Telephone support, defective disks replaced free.
Macintosh (1Mb). 3.5" disk $59.95.
Entire Text of the Bible in Any One of the Following Versions: Revised Standard Version (RSV), New Revised Standard Version (NRSV), New International Version (NIV), King James Version (KJV), Reina Valera Spanish Version (RVR), Revised Luther Bible-1985 (RLB), Nouvelle Version Segond Revisee-1978 (NVSR), or Latin Vulgate. Each Includes the New Testament, Old Testament, & (Except NIV) Apocrypha.
Linguist's Software, Inc.

BibleMaster for Macintosh: Bible Bundle, No. 2. Feb. 1996.
Macintosh. disk $69.95 (ISBN 1-885217-65-X, Order no.: MAC402).
Treasury of Scripture Knowledge, NASB - 200.5, NASB update - 220.5, Topical Studies - 220.2, NASB Strong's Hebrew/Greek Transliterated Dictionaries - 220.3, KJV - 220, Spanish NASB - 220.5, NASB Cross References, NASB Updated Cross References.
Foundation Pubns., Inc.

BibleMaster for Windows: Bible Bundle, No. 2. Feb. 1996.
Windows. disk $69.95 (ISBN 1-885217-64-1, Order no.: WIN402).
Treasury of Scripture Knowledge, NASB - 200.5, NASB update - 220.5, Topical Studies - 220.2, NASB Strong's Hebrew/Greek Transliterated Dictionaries - 220.3, KJV - 220, Spanish NASB - 220.5, NASB Cross References, NASB Updated Cross References.
Foundation Pubns., Inc.

BibleMaster on CD-ROM. (NASB BibleMaster Reference Library: Vol. 1). Edited by Lockman Foundation Staff. Nov. 1995.
IBM. CD-ROM disk $49.95 (ISBN 1-885217-63-3, Order no.: CD401).
Treasury of Scripture Knowledge, NASB, NASB Update, Topical Studies, NASB Strong's Hebrew/Greek Transliterated Dictionaries, KJV, LBLA (Spanish NASB), NASB Cross References, NASB Updated Cross References.
Foundation Pubns., Inc.

Biblesoft's Greek-Hebrew Word Study Series. Aug. 1991. Customer Support: No fee is charged for our customer support: 30 day money back return guarantee; lifetime warranty on defective disk replacement; free telephone technical support.
PC or MS-DOS 2.0 or higher. IBM PC/XT/AT or compatible. 3.5" or 5.25" disk $129.95. Addl. software required: PC Study Bible & King James Version of Bible. Optimal configuration: 6Mb on the hard drive is required for the Greek-Hebrew Word Study Series.
Add-On Module for PC STUDY BIBLE. It Is a

Powerful Combination of Strong's Greek-Hebrew Dictionary, Englishman's Greek-Hebrew Concordance, Vine's Expository Dictionary of New Testament Words, & Nelson's Expository Dictionary of the Old Testament. It Makes Original Language Research Easy to Everyone Who Uses a Computer.
Biblesoft.

Biblical Hebrew Grammar. Version: 3.0. Oct. 1988. Items Included: Hebrew keyboard layout chart, user's manual (which includes Hebrew verb charts). Customer Support: Telephone support, defective disks replaced free.
Macintosh (1Mb). 3.5" disk $49.95. Addl. software required: MacHebrew or LaserHebrew plus Microsoft Word.
Fifty Hebrew Grammar Lectures, Typically with Grammar, Word Lists, Exercises & Vocabulary Tests in Microsoft Word Formatting. Includes Verb Parsing Charts, Subject Index, Hebrew-English & English-Hebrew Glossaries, Vocabularies, Word Lists, Translation Materials & Cross References to Lambdin's Grammar.
Linguist's Software, Inc.

Biblio-Link II Packages. Mar. 1992. Customer Support: Free phone service Mon-Fri 9-5, 30 day money-back guarantee, free newsletter.
PC-DOS/MS-DOS, Windows 3.1 or higher. IBM PC or compatible (256k). CD-ROM disk Contact publisher for price. Addl. software required: Pro-Cite for IBM, DOS 2.0 256k RAM minimum, DOS 3.0 320k RAM, hard disk or two DS disk drives.
Companion Program to ProCite Bibliographic Reference Management Software. Biblio-Links Transfer Records Retrieved from On-Line Services, Automated Library Systems, CD-ROM Services, & Diskette Data Products Directly into a ProCite Database. The Automatic Parsing Feature Separates Information & Places Each Item in the Appropriate ProCite Field. Available for the DOS Operating System. Online Package Works with BRS, DIALOG, MEDLARS, SilverPlatter, & STN. Library Package Works with USMARC, NOTIS, OCLC, WILSONDISC, MUMS, SCORPIO, DOBIS, & DROLS.
Personal Bibliographic Software, Inc.

Biblio-Link II. Version: 1.1. Jul. 1993. Items Included: Disk, manual. Customer Support: Free phone support Mon-Friday 9-5, 30 day money-back guarantee, free newsletter.
6.0.2 or higher. Macintosh (1Mb). CD-ROM disk Contact publisher for price. Nonstandard peripherals required: Hard disk recommended. Addl. software required: Pro-Cite Version 2.1 or higher.
System 6.02. IBM PC & compatibles (2Mb). CD-ROM disk Contact publisher for price.
Companion Program to ProCite Bibliographic Reference Management Software. Transfers Records Retrieved from On-Line Services, Automated Library Systems, CD-ROM Services, & Diskette Data Products Directly into a ProCite Database. The Automatic Parsing Feature Separates Source Field Information & Places Each Item in the Appropriate ProCite Field. User Is Able to Print Log File to Review How Information Was Transferred.
Personal Bibliographic Software, Inc.

Bibliography Builder. Version: 1.2. Dec. 1991. Items Included: Manual. Customer Support: Free telephone support, defective disks replaced free.
Macintosh System 6.0.7 or higher. Macintosh (1Mb). $49.95 Word Version; $49.95 Hypercard Version; $79.95 Dual Version. Addl. software required: Hypercard or Microsoft Word.
Formats Raw Data into Bibliography, Reference or Footnote Lists with the Appropriate Order, Italicization & Punctuation. Covers More Than 30 of the Most Common Formats from the Fifth Edition of Turabian's "A Manual for Writers." Microsoft Word Version Allows Users to Enter & Format Bibliographies & Then Export the Data to Other Word Processors & Database Programs.
Master Software.

Bibliography of Published Studies Using the Child Behavior Checklist & Related Materials, 1995. Version: 8.0. Jill S. Brown & Thomas M. Achenbach. Jul. 1995. Customer Support: Free telephone support for unlimited time.
MS-DOS. IBM-PC & compatibles (512k). $45.00 (ISBN 0-938565-38-9). Optimal configuration: IBM-PC compatible with 512k.
Lists 1500 Published References for Studies That Have Used the Child Behavior Checklist & Its Related Assessment Materials. Studies Are Keyed According to 200 Topics. Users Can Display & Print References Individually or by Topic or Author.
Univ. of Vermont, Dept. of Psychiatry.

BiComM-3270. Dynamic Microprocessor Assoc. Feb. 1984. Compatible Hardware: Data General One; HP 150 Touchscreen I & II; IBM PC AT, PC XT; Toshiba T3100 & T1100 Plus; Visual Commuter. Operating System(s) Required: MS-DOS, VENIX. Memory Required: 64k.
disk $895.00 ea., incl. controller.
PC XT/MS-DOS 3270i.
PC AT/MS-DOS 3270a.
PC XT/Venix V3270i.
PC AT/Venix V3270a.
disk $495.00 ea.
DG/One 3270g.
HP 150 Touchscreen 3270p.
Visual Commuter.
Allows Most MS-DOS or PC-DOS Microcomputers to Emulate the Functions of an IBM 3270 Display System. Applications Include Single Transaction Processing, On-Line Inquiries, As Well As Large-Scale Database Access, & Data Entry in a Time-Sharing Environment.
Packaged Solutions, Inc.

BiComM-3700. Version: 5.0. Wilmot Systems, Inc. Feb. 1984. Compatible Hardware: Data General One; HP 150 Touchscreen I & II; IBM PC AT, PC XT; Toshiba T3100 & T1100 Plus, Visual Commuter. Operating System(s) Required: MS-DOS, VENIX. Memory Required: 64k.
disk $895.00 ea., incl. controller.
PC XT/MS-DOS 3700i.
PC AT/MS-DOS 3700a.
PC XT/Venix 3700i.
PC AT/Venix 3700a.
DG/One 3700g. disk $495.00 ea.
HP 150 Touchscreen 3700p.
Visual Commuter 3700v.
Allows an MS-DOS Microcomputer to Emulate the IBM 2780/3780/2770/3741 Series of Remote Job Entry Stations. Utilizes the BISYNC Point-to-Point Communications Protocol to Communicate at up to 19.2k baud with a Mainframe or Other Computer.
Packaged Solutions, Inc.

Bicycle Baccarat. Sep. 1995. Items Included: Installation instructions, registration card. Customer Support: Phone support by calling 302-234-1750, no charge. Fax support by faxing to 302-234-1760, no charge. E-Mail support at Compuserve ID 76004,3520 or MCI Mail/560-7116, no charge.
DOS; Windows 3.1 or higher. 286 or higher. disk $17.75 (ISBN 1-887468-45-5). Optimal configuration: PC-DOS/MS-DOS 3.1 or higher, EGA, VGA, 8514/t or higher resolution monitor, mouse, hard disk recommended.
Brings the Action & Excitement of the High-Stakes European Casino Game to Your Computer. Learn the Basics, & Soon You'll Be Playing Like the European Royalty That Made This Game a Popular Casino Attraction.
SWFTE International, Ltd.

Bicycle Baccarat. Sep. 1995. Items Included: Installation instructions, registration cards. Customer Support: Telephone 302-234-1750, Fax 302-234-1760, E-Mail, CompuServe 76004, 3520, E-mail, MCI mail 560-7116 - no charge.
DOS. 286 or higher. 3.5" disk $17.75 (ISBN 1-887468-45-5). Optimal configuration: PC-DOS/MS-DOS 3.1 or higher, EGA, VGA, 8514t or higher resolution monitor, mouse, hard disk recommended.
Windows. 286 or higher. Optimal configuration: PC-DOS/MS-DOS 3.1 or higher, EGA, VGA, 8514/t or higher resolution monitor, mouse, hard disk recommended, Windows 3.1 or higher.
Brings the Action & Excitement of the High-Stakes European Casino Game to Your Computer. Learn the Basics, & Soon You'll Be Playing Like the European Royalty That Made This Game a Popular Casino Attraction.
Swfte International, Ltd.

Bicycle Casino. Aug. 1995. Items Included: Installation instructions, registration card. Customer Support: Phone support by calling 302-234-1750, no charge. Fax support by faxing to 302-234-1760, no charge. E-Mail support at Compuserve ID 76004,3520 or MCI Mail/560-7116, no charge.
Windows. 286 or higher. CD-ROM disk $49.95 (ISBN 1-887468-43-9). Optimal configuration: Microsoft Windows 3.1 or higher, PC-DOS/MS-DOS 3.1 or higher, Windows compatible mouse, hard disk, double-speed CD-ROM drive, EGA, VGA or higher resolution monitor.
A Collection of Baccarat, Blackjack, Poker & Roulette. Includes a Bonus "Book of Tells" Program That Teaches How to Read the Nonverbal Cues Given off by Poker Players.
SWFTE International, Ltd.

Bicycle Casino. Aug. 1995. Items Included: Installation instructions, registration cards. Customer Support: Telephone 302-234-1750, Fax 302-234-1760, E-Mail, CompuServe 76004, 3520, E-mail, MCI mail 560-7116 - no charge.
Windows. 286 or higher. CD-ROM disk $49.95 (ISBN 1-887468-43-9). Optimal configuration: Microsoft Windows 3.1 or higher, PC-DOS/MS-DOS 3.1 or higher, Windows compatible mouse, hard disk, double-speed CD-ROM drive, EGA, VGA or higher resolution monitor.
A Collection of Baccarat, Blackjack, Poker & Roulette. Includes a Bonus "Book of Tells" Program That Teaches How to Read the Nonverbal Cues Given off by Poker Players.
Swfte International, Ltd.

Bicycle Classics. Aug. 1995. Items Included: Installation instructions, registration card. Customer Support: Phone support by calling 302-234-1750, no charge. Fax support by faxing to 302-234-1760, no charge. E-Mail support at Compuserve ID 76004,3520 or MCI Mail/560-7116, no charge.
Windows. 286 or higher. CD-ROM disk $49.95 (ISBN 1-887468-44-7). Optimal configuration: Microsoft Windows 3.1 or higher, PC-DOS/MS-DOS 3.1 or higher, Windows compatible mouse, hard disk, double-speed CD-ROM drive, EGA, VGA or higher resolution monitor.
A Collection of Bridge, Cribbage, Gin & Solitaire. Includes a Bonus Interactive Betting Guide to Help Hone Bridge Skills.
SWFTE International, Ltd.

TITLE INDEX

Bicycle Classics. Aug. 1995. *Items Included:* Installation instructions, registration cards. *Customer Support:* Telephone 302-234-1750, Fax 302-234-1760, E-Mail, CompuServe 76004, 3520, E-mail, MCI mail 560-7116 - no charge.
Windows. 286 or higher. CD-ROM disk $49.95 (ISBN 1-887468-44-7). *Optimal configuration:* Microsoft Windows 3.1 or higher, PC-DOS/MS-DOS 3.1 or higher, Windows compatible mouse, hard disk, double-speed CD-ROM drive, EGA, VGA or higher resolution monitor.
A Collection of Bridge, Cribbage, Gin & Solitaire. Includes a Bonus Interactive Betting Guide to Help Hone Bridge Skills.
Swfte International, Ltd.

Bicycle Gin. Sep. 1995. *Items Included:* Installation instructions, registration card. *Customer Support:* Phone support by calling 302-234-1750, no charge. Fax support by faxing to 302-234-1760, no charge. E-Mail support at Compuserve ID 76004,3520 or MCI Mail/560-7116, no charge.
DOS; Windows 3.1 or higher. 286 or higher. disk $17.75 (ISBN 1-887468-46-3). *Optimal configuration:* PC-DOS/MS-DOS 3.1 or higher, EGA, VGA, 8514/t or higher resolution monitor, mouse, hard disk recommended.
Puts You Head-to-Head Against an Expert Opponent in the High-Stakes Game Made Popular by the Glitz & Glamour of Hollywood. It Tallies the Score & Gives Bonus Points Automatically.
SWFTE International, Ltd.

Bicycle Gin. Sep. 1995. *Items Included:* Installation instructions, registration cards. *Customer Support:* Telephone 302-234-1750, Fax 302-234-1760, E-Mail, CompuServe 76004, 3520, E-mail, MCI mail 560-7116 - no charge.
DOS. 286 or higher. 3.5" disk $17.75 (ISBN 1-887468-46-3). *Optimal configuration:* PC-DOS/MS-DOS 3.1 or higher, EGA, VGA, 8514t or higher resolution monitor, mouse, hard disk recommended.
Windows. 286 or higher. *Optimal configuration:* PC-DOS/MS-DOS 3.1 or higher, EGA, VGA, 8514/t or higher resolution monitor, mouse, hard disk recommended, Windows 3.1 or higher.
Puts You Head-to-Head Against an Expert Opponent in the High-Stakes Game Made Popular by the Glitz & Glamour of Hollywood. It Tallies the Score & Gives Bonus Points Automatically.
Swfte International, Ltd.

Bicycle Limited Edition - CD-ROM. Dec. 1993. *Customer Support:* Free technical support - Call/Fax/Mail, Phone: 305-567-9996, Fax: 305-569-1350.
Windows 3.1 (2Mb). CD-ROM disk $49.95. *Nonstandard peripherals required:* EGA, VGA or higher graphics, CD-ROM drive. *Optimal configuration:* Mouse required.
Includes Variations of Favorite Card Games, Solitaire, Poker, Cribbage & Bridge.
SWFTE International, Ltd.

Bicycle Master. Version: 1.2. Mar. 1992. *Items Included:* 32 page manual. *Customer Support:* Free telephone support, customer satisfaction guarantee.
MS-DOS 3.21 or higher. IBM compatible (512k). disk $29.95. *Optimal configuration:* Need 2 drives; hard disk recommended but not required. Need CGA, EGA, or VGA monitor.
Display, Analyze & Plot Data Recorded in Riding/Training & Racing Diaries. Also Record Bicycle Identification & Maintenance Data, Display Training, Riding, & Safety Checklists, Print On-Bike Gearing Chart, Perform US-Metric Conversions, Calculate Spoke Size, Establish Weight-Reducing Riding Program, Provide Reference Source Lists, Display Tour de France Resutls 1903-1993, Display Long-Ride Training Program, & Much More for the Bicycle Enthusiast. Uses Sophisticated, Easy-to-Use Pull-Down Menus. Print to Dot-Matrix or Laser Jet Printers.
Bridget Software Co.

Bid Lite. Jul. 1992. *Items Included:* Documentation manual, startup instructions. *Customer Support:* 30-day free telephone. Always: phone $25/15-minutes.
DOS. IBM PC & compatibles (640k). disk $495.00. *Optimal configuration:* IBM PC-compatible, 640k RAM, hard disk, color or monochrome monitor.
Basic Estimating & Job-Cost for Smaller Companies or First-Time Computer Users. Derived from SSD's Full-Featured Construction Management Software, It Can Be Upgraded with No Loss or Re-Entry of Data. Includes Bid Sheet, Job Status Report, Variance Report, Job Cost Reports, & More.
SSD (Small System Design), Inc.

Bid Magic. Aug. 1993. *Items Included:* 1 manual. *Customer Support:* Free phone support, free newsletter.
Macintosh. Macintosh (1Mb). 3.5" disk $295.00. *Optimal configuration:* Mac Plus or higher, hard disk.
Windows. IBM AT or PS/2 compatibles. *Optimal configuration:* IBM or clone, hard disk.
Quick Rough Estimating for Residential & Light Commercial Construction. Also Produces Finished Bids. Links to MACNAIL.
Turtle Creek Software.

The Bid Team. *Items Included:* 2 manuals-user guide, reference guide; installation. *Customer Support:* Training classes-(hands on) $595-3 days; telephone support-$425/year, (90 days free); maintenance plan-$450/year.
MS-DOS. PS/2, 286 & 386 & compatibles (512k). contact publisher for price. *Optimal configuration:* 286-640k, 40 Mb hard disk, 132 column printer. *Networks supported:* Novell.
Interactive System Designed to Meet the Needs of Both the Advanced & the Basic Estimator. Simplifies the Estimating Process Due to its Unique Design & Through the Use of Procedures. By Providing a Comprehensive Set of Functions, Such as Four Methods of Take-Off (Procedures, Assemblies/Work packages, Material Selections, Lump Sums), Full Audit Trail, Plus Automatic Adjustment of Regional Variables Such As Labor Productivity & Material Cost; the Needs of Both the Commercial & Residential Industries are Met.
Construction Data Control, Inc. (CDCI).

Bidsheet. Version: 2.1. Feb. 1990. *Items Included:* 5.25" or 3.5" diskette, manual. *Customer Support:* Free. 30 day money back guarantee.
IBM PC & 100% compatibles (512k). disk $49.00. *Addl. software required:* Lotus 1-2-3 (any version). *Optimal configuration:* IBM PC or compatible, 640k memory, hard disk or 2 floppy disk drives. *Networks supported:* Any network that supports Lotus 1-2-3.
Helps Construction Industry Estimators to Create Bids Quickly & Easily by Entering Parts Quantities Needed for Job, Labor & Parts Overhead Percentage & Rental Permit Costs. Enables Rapid Creation of Bids & Painless Changes for "What-If" Variations for Overhead & Profit to Create More Competitive Bids.
PC Software Solutions.

Big Anthony's Mixed-Up Magic.
MS-DOS 5.0 or higher, Windows 3.1 or higher. 386 processor or higher (4Mb). CD-ROM disk $49.95 (Order no.: R1007). *Nonstandard peripherals required:* CD-ROM drive. *Optimal configuration:* 386 processor operating at 16Mhz or higher, MS-DOS 5.0 or higher, Windows 3.1 or higher, 30Mb hard drive, mouse, VGA graphic adapter & VGA color monitor (SVGA recommended), 4Mb RAM, external speakers or headphones (with sound card) that are Sound Blaster compatible.
Macintosh (4Mb). (Order no.: R1007A). *Nonstandard peripherals required:* 14" color monitor or larger, CD-ROM drive.
Children Can Read Tomie dePaola's Book, "Strega Nona Meets Her Match" or Explore Strega Nona's Wonderful World of Calabria Through the Help of This Delightful Program. Includes Games, Adventures, Activities, Sing-a-Long Songs, Music & More.
Library Video Co.

The Big Apple. Adrian Vance. Nov. 1984. *Compatible Hardware:* Apple II. *Operating System(s) Required:* Apple DOS. *Language(s):* Applesoft BASIC (source code included). *Memory Required:* 48k.
disk $19.95, incl. bk. (ISBN 0-918547-06-7).
"Textbook of Apple Compressed Data Systems" Revealing New Formation Technology Designed to Make Major Data Compressions in Order That As Many As 30,000 Records May Be Made on One Apple Disk. Several Systems Have Already Been Used for Recording Such Databases As the "Apple Tree" & "TAPIT".
AV Systems, Inc.

Big Bird's Special Delivery. *Compatible Hardware:* Atari XL, XE; Commodore 64; IBM PC & compatibles.
disk $9.95.
Matching Game Which Develops Object Recognition.
Hi Tech Expressions, Inc.

Big Brother. Version: 2.0. Open Door Software Division. Oct. 1993. *Items Included:* Spiral manual, video (when available). *Customer Support:* 30 day free customer support; 900 line $2.00/min.; 1 yr. maintenance $400/mo. Includes: toll free line & fax back priority service.
DOS. IBM compatible 386, 25Mhz, 5Mb free space on hard disk, VGA monitor, 3.5" floppy, keyboard, mouse, (1Mb). disk $395.00 # Network version $1395.00 (ISBN 1-56756-059-8, Order no.: OD9001). *Addl. software required:* Operating system. *Optimal configuration:* IBM or compatible 486, 66Mhz, 5Mb free space on hard disk, 4Mb RAM-3Mb expanded usable, VGA monitor, 3.5" high density floppy, keyboard, mouse, tape backup, & uninterruptable power supply. *Networks supported:* Novell Netware Lite.
Windows. IBM compatible 386, 25Mhz, 5Mb free space on hard disk, VGA monitor, 3.5" floppy, keyboard, mouse (1Mb). disk $395.00 (ISBN 1-56756-063-6, Order no.: OD905W). *Addl. software required:* Windows 3.1 or higher. *Optimal configuration:* IBM or compatible 486, 66Mhz, 5Mb free space on hard disk, 4Mb RAM-3Mb expanded usable, VGA monitor, 3.5" high density floppy, keyboard, mouse, tape backup, & uninterruptable power supply. *Networks supported:* Novell Netware Lite.
MAC. 3.5" disk $395.00 (ISBN 1-56756-059-8, Order no.: OD920M). *Addl. software required:* System 7.
Complete Business Operating System Integrating Everything Most Businesses Need into One Accessible Package. Has Separate Modules for Each Business Need, Including Sales Automation, Administration, Contact Management, Personnel Services, Word Processing, Finance/Accounting, Inventory, E-Mail, Reports, List Management, Services Management, Project Management,

Scheduling & Knowledge Bases That Contain Information on Everyday Needs Such As Direct Mail, Copyrighting, Employment Contracts & Hundreds of Other Topics. Add to the Knowledge Bases to Build Your Own Online Procedure Manual for Your Employees. Standalone & Novel Network Ready.
Advantage International.

The Big Bug Alphabet Book.
MS-DOS 5.0 or higher, Windows 3.1 or higher. 386 processor or higher (4Mb). CD-ROM disk $39.95 (Order no.: R1235). *Nonstandard peripherals required:* CD-ROM drive. *Optimal configuration:* 386 processor operating at 16Mhz or higher, MS-DOS 5.0 or higher, Windows 3.1 or higher, 30Mb hard drive, mouse, VGA graphic adapter & VGA color monitor (SVGA recommended), 4Mb RAM, external speakers or headphones (with sound card) that are Sound Blaster compatible.
Macintosh (4Mb). (Order no.: R1235A). *Nonstandard peripherals required:* 14" color monitor or larger, CD-ROM drive.
Children Learn to Identify Both Upper & Lower Case Letters by Hearing & Participating in This Animated Story. Matching, Hidden-Letter Search & Hide-&-Seek Games Help Children in Word & Letter Recognition (Ages 3-7).
Library Video Co.

The Big Bug Alphabet Book.
Windows. CD-ROM disk $39.95 (Order no.: BBC1001).
Macintosh. CD-ROM disk $39.95.
This CD-ROM Book Contains Excitement Galore! Buzzy (a Whimsical Character in the Story) Is Ready to Take Your Child to the Big Bug Alphabet Circus, Where Together They Will Discover Entertaining & Unusual Bugs, Plus Hidden Facts about Each Letter of the Alphabet. With Just a Click of the Mouse, Your Child Can Explore the Fun & Surprises That Await As Each Page Unfolds. The Alphabet Rap & Hidden-Letter Search Are Just a Few of the Many Activities That the Big Bugs Have in Store. Enchanting Artwork & Animations, Plus a High-Quality Sound Track with Multiple Voices & Sound Effects Make Learning the Alphabet More Fun Than Ever Before. Also Included Is the Original Paperback Book Written by Authors Patricia & Frederick McKissack, Winners of the Coretta Scott King & Caldecott Honor Awards. Available in Both DOS/Windows & Macintosh Versions.
Milliken Publishing Co.

Big Foot: Arcade Plus Series. *Compatible Hardware:* TI 99/4A with Milton Bradley's MBX System.
contact publisher for price (Order no.: PHM3151).
Try to Dodge Boulders & Eagles to Climb High & Capture Big Foot. 6 Mountains. Pick up Supplies & Gold for Bonus Points. Speech Synthesis & Voice Recognition.
Texas Instruments, Personal Productivit.

Big U. Randy Brandt. Apr. 1986. *Compatible Hardware:* Apple II, II+, IIe, IIc, IIgs. *Operating System(s) Required:* ProDOS. *Memory Required:* Apple II+ 64k, some programs require 128k. *General Requirements:* 80-column hardware.
disk $34.95.
Set of ProDOS Utilities. Includes FileMover, CRT Writer, RAM-Load, etc. Lets Users Add 18 Commands Such As COPY, XLIST, ANYCAT, MON & NONMON, SHOW, & SEE.
Beagle Brothers.

BigEars. *General Requirements:* Macintosh.
3.5" disk $129.00.
Music Courseware.
MacMIDI Distributing.

BigPrint. 1987. *Operating System(s) Required:* MS-DOS/PC-DOS 2.0 or higher. *Memory Required:* 384k. *General Requirements:* Toshiba, Citizen, Epson LQ or compatible printer. IBM PC & compatibles. disk $49.95.
M.A.P. Systems, Inc.

BigThesaurus. *Version:* 2. *Compatible Hardware:* Apple Macintosh. *Memory Required:* 2000k.
3.5" disk $99.95.
Electronic Thesaurus.
Deneba Software.

Bikini Open, Vol. 1. Jun. 1994. *Items Included:* License agreement & registration card. *Customer Support:* 1-900-420-5005, $3.00 per minute.
Windows 3.1 or System 7. IBM & compatibles & Macintosh (2.0Mb). CD-ROM disk $39.00 MSRP (ISBN 0-9634008-3-5). *Nonstandard peripherals required:* CD ROM drive. *Optimal configuration:* 386, 20MHz, 4Mb RAM, VGA monitor with 256 colors.
One Hundred Photo CD Images with Corel Utilities for Image Conversion & Screensavers for Windows & Macintosh.
Cascom International, Inc.

Bikini Open, Vol. 2. Jun. 1994. *Items Included:* License agreement & registration card. *Customer Support:* 1-900-420-5005, $3.00 per minute.
Windows 3.1 or System 7. IBM & compatibles & Macintosh (2.0Mb). CD-ROM disk $39.00 MSRP (ISBN 0-9634008-4-3). *Nonstandard peripherals required:* CD ROM drive. *Optimal configuration:* 386, 20MHz, 4Mb RAM, VGA monitor with 256 colors.
One Hundred Photo CD Images with Corel Utilities for Image Conversion & Screensavers for Windows & Macintosh.
Cascom International, Inc.

Bilinear Transform Tutorial. (Electrical Engineering Tutorial Ser.: No. 5). *Compatible Hardware:* Apple, IBM. *Operating System(s) Required:* Apple DOS 3.2, 3.3; MS-DOS. *Language(s):* Applesoft/Machine (source code included). *Memory Required:* 48k-128k.
disk $39.95.
Deals with the Bilinear Transform & How It Can Be Used to Derive Filters from Analog RLC Filters.
Dynacomp, Inc.

Bill-It. *Version:* 4.42. Nov. 1989. *Customer Support:* First 90 days free, $79.00 annually thereafter.
Macintosh Plus or higher (1Mb). disk $99.00 (ISBN 1-879815-02-8, Order no.: B12). *Nonstandard peripherals required:* External hard disk drive (800k); printer.
Sales, Bids, Billing, Invoicing, Inventory, Packing Slips, Automatic Recurring Billing, Accounts Receivable, Customer Files, Mail Merge Files, & Mailing Labels.
Shopkeeper Software International, Inc.

Bill James All Time All-Stars.
IBM. Contact publisher for price. *Addl. software required:* Bill James Electronic Baseball Encyclopedia.
Compare Players of Today to the Best of the Past. Complete Career Records of 472 of the Greatest Players of All-Time from All Decades since 1876, Players Who Set More Than 80% of the Top-20 Records of All Time.
Miller Assocs.

Bill James Electronic Baseball Encyclopedia.
Customer Support: Telephone support (4.5 hrs. weekdays).
EGA or VGA, hard drive, 640k RAM, & DOS 3.1 or higher. IBM. Contact publisher for price.
Unified Edition of the Complete Career Record
for Every Major League Player Who Appeared since 1989 along with a Powerful Stat Analyzer for Fans to Study Baseball Player Careers.
Miller Assocs.

Bill of Material Processor: BOMP. *Version:* 1.50. 1978. *Compatible Hardware:* IBM PC XT & compatibles, PC AT, PS/2. *Operating System(s) Required:* MS-DOS, PC-DOS. *Language(s):* FORTRAN. *Memory Required:* 320k. *General Requirements:* Hard disk. *Items Included:* Manual. *Customer Support:* 1 hour per package purchased.
$395.00.
3.5" disk write for info.
Provides Users with the Ability to Input & Maintain Standard Lists of Materials Used to Generate Inventory Orders. Inventory Stock Requirements Can Automatically Be Generated. Requires That MCC's INVENTORY MANAGEMENT Be Installed & in Use Before Processing Can Begin. Includes a Materials Requirements Planning Report Which Provides Quantity & Cost of Each Part, Cost to Order, BOM Using the Part, & Total Cost to Build.
MCC Software (Midwest Computer Ctr. Co.).

Bill of Material Record. Al Brudlie & Lee Todnem. 1985. *Compatible Hardware:* Apple II series. *Operating System(s) Required:* 64. *Memory Required:* 64k. *General Requirements:* Printer, VisiCalc spreadsheet, Appleworks Spreadsheet. *Items Included:* Disk, documentation.
disk $21.50 (ISBN 1-55797-109-9, Order no.: AP2-AG309).
Works in Conjunction with the VISICALC or APPLEWORKS Spreadsheet to Record the Bill of Material Used in a Building or Project. Will Calculate the Cost & Give a Printout for Easy Analysis. Serves As a Checklist of Nearly All Materials Needed to Construct a Building.
Hobar Pubns.

Bill of Materials. *Version:* 14.0. (Accounting Software Ser.). Aug. 1993. *Compatible Hardware:* IBM & compatibles. *Operating System(s) Required:* MS-DOS, PC-DOS. *Language(s):* MegaBASIC. *Memory Required:* 640k. *General Requirements:* Hard disk, wide carriage printer. *Customer Support:* (203) 790-9756.
disk $295.00, Network Option ,300.00 more.
manual $50.00.
Requires the Inventory Program. Ability to Cost B.O.M., Calculates Quantity to Build Based on On-Hand & On-Order Quantity, Pulls from Inventory As B.O.M. Is Built. Automatic Update of Inventory with Sales, Orders, Returns, Receipts. Reports Include Physical Inventory Forms, Cost vs. Price Analysis & Many Other Reports.
Applications Systems Group (CT), Inc.

Bill of Materials. *Version:* 4.0. Dec. 1993. *Items Included:* Sample data, full manual. *Customer Support:* Free installation support (via phone) first 30 days; FAX & Bulletin Board: free, with response within 1-3 days; Phone support: 1 year, unlimited calls, 1-5pm M-F $150/year; Training is available from 3rd party.
DOS 3.3 or higher. PC compatibles/clones (2Mb). disk $249.00 (Order no.: BOM 4.0). *Addl. software required:* Recommend an expanded memory manager; must have Advanced Accounting 4.03. *Optimal configuration:* Intel 486 or clone, DOS 5.0, 4Mb RAM, 386 MAX memory manager, Novell 3.12 network (for multiuser). *Networks supported:* Any NetBIOS compatible network; recommend Novell or LANtastic.
Add-On to Advanced Accounting 4.03 That Manages Inventory Assembled from Components

TITLE INDEX

or Subassemblies into Finished Products. Easy Specification & Editing of Bills of Material. Up to 9 Levels of Assemblies. Create To-Build Orders & Instructions. Record the Building or Un-Building of Products. Include Both Labor & Materials in Product. Source Code Is Available.
Business Tools Software.

Bill of Materials. Compatible Hardware: Apple II+, IIe, III; IBM PC. Operating System(s) Required: CP/M, PC-DOS. Language(s): BASIC (source code included). Memory Required: 48k.
disk $148.50.
Designed for Small Manufacturers. Handles Inventory Control, Materials Required Planning & Explodes User's Bill of Materials. Sets up & Maintains a Stock File Containing Descriptive Information for Each Item, a Scheduling File Containing Production Schedule Date, & a Bill of Materials File That Defines Product Structures. Inventory Information Is Updated by Entry of Issue & Receive Transactions &/or by Processing of Inventory Net-Out after the Bill of Materials Program Is Run. General Ledger Programs (MAXILEDGER or MICROLEDGER) Automatically Post a Journal File. Reports Include: Standard Stock Status Showing Inventory Valuation at Cost, Discounted Retail or Retail, Material Requirement Planning, Maximum/Minimum, ABC Analysis, & Bill of Materials Explosion.
Compumax, Inc.

Bill of Materials. Version: 2.5.4. 1989. Language(s): C. Memory Required: 640k. General Requirements: Hard disk, 132-column printer. Items Included: Disks & manuals. Customer Support: Free.
MS-DOS, PC-DOS, Concurrent DOS, Unix, Xenix. All IBM compatibles. single user $995.00. Networks supported: Novell & Microsoft. multi-user $1295.00.
demo disk with manual $25.00.
Creates & Lists Multiple Level Bills of Materials.
INMASS/MRP.

Bill of Materials. Customer Support: Free telephone & BBS technical support.
DOS, Concurrent DOS, Xenix, Unix. IBM PC/XT/AT & compatibles, IBM PS/2 (512k). single-user $995.00. Nonstandard peripherals required: Novell, Lantastic, Banyan VINES; all NETBIOS compatibles.
milti-user or Network $1295.00.
"Bill of Materials" may contain up to 100 assembly levels & any number of items within each level. BOM's may be copied from a single "master" & then modified as necessary (global parts replacement capability may be used). Requirements reports & job issues may be exploded to a single level or down to raw materials level. Features cost update. Raw materials are transferred from available to allocated inventory when a job is issued. When the job is completed raw materials are removed from inventory & the number of finished items available is updated. Labor, process & burden may be included in a BOM with the materials. The assembly cost can be calculated with or without non-material costs. Bills can be printed as costed or non-costed manufacturing bills & can be printed in indented or single-level format with their components in order by part number or a user-assigned sequence number.
INMASS/MRP.

Bill of Materials. May 1983. Compatible Hardware: IBM PC, PC XT, PC AT. Operating System(s) Required: PC-DOS. Language(s): COBOL. Memory Required: 192k. General Requirements: 2 disk drives.
disk $1750.00 to $3050.00.
Defines the Relationship Between Various Parts & Assemblies Required to Produce the Product. Supports 20 Levels of Bills of Materials. The Reports Include the Bill of Material, Where Used & Summarized. The Engineering Change Module Controls the Starting & Stopping of a Bill of Material or Router. The Secondary Description Module Appends Descriptive Text to the Primary Description.
Twin Oaks, Inc.

Bill of Materials (a Part of ABECAS). Version: 3.3. Customer Support: On site training unlimited support services for first 90 days & through subscription thereafter.
PC/MS-DOS. IBM PC & compatibles. Contact publisher for price. Nonstandard peripherals required: Hard disk (30Mb or higher); 132 column printer.
Assembly or Sub-Assembly Inventory Items May Be Exploded into Component Detail Through Bill of Material. This May be Used to Relieve Component Inventory Items when Parent Item Is Received into Inventory. Various Analysis Reports Available, Such As Usage Reports. Requires Inventory Management Module. Multi-User Version Avaiable for Novell, NTNX, 10-Net, Unix/Xenix, Turbo-DOS.
Argos Software.

Bill of Materials Plus (BMP): Engineering Documentation Control System. Version: 11.0. C. R. Smolin. Nov. 1983. Compatible Hardware: IBM PC & compatibles. Operating System(s) Required: MS-DOS. Language(s): C-BASIC. Memory Required: 128k. General Requirements: Hard disk. Customer Support: 1 year free telephone support.
disk $1295.00.
Complete Bill-of-Materials Processor & Engineering Documentation Control System Designed to Run on Microcomputers. Supports Multiple Databases of up to 32,000 Parts per Database & Includes Extensive Costing & Cost Roll-Up Features. Reports Which Have Comprehensive Sort & Data Selection Capabilities Include Part Master, Single Level, Indented & Summary Bills-of-Materials, "Where Used", & Manufacturer's Cross Reference.
Alliance Manufacturing Software.

Bill of Materials Processor. Version: 5.8. May 1993. Items Included: User's Guides & other documentation all included. Customer Support: 90 days free customer service, full service and update maintenance available. Call for pricing.
Digital VAX/VMS, Open VMS. Digital VAX Platform, DEC Alpha AXP. $3500.00-$15,000.00.
Designed for the Manufacturer or Wholesale Distributor to "Assemble Kits" (Process Work Oders). Processing May Include Finish Work, Assembly, Or Required Sub-Processing Steps. "Pack & Ship" Work Orders Can Be Processed with More Sophisticated Work Order Assembly. Work Orders Can Be Stored for Kit Assembly or Custom Work Orders. Components of Kits Can Include Inventories Products, Labor, Special-Order Products. Texts Can Be Inserted on Any Work Order for Processing & Assembly Instructions. Integrated with the OE Order Entry, IC Inventory Management, & AR Accounts Receivable. Automatic Component Substituting Procedures Fill Work Orders Allowing Kits to Be Finished. New Inventory Receipts Automatically Fill Backordered Components. Component Commitments Are Taken into Account for Recommended Purchasing Calculations.
Compu-Share, Inc.

Bill of Materials-Routing. Version: 3.3. (Integrated Manufacturing & Financial System Ser.). Compatible Hardware: Micro/VAX, UNIBUS/VAX; IBM PC. Operating System(s)

BILLING CLERK WITH ACCOUNTS

Required: MS-DOS, Novell, VAX/VMS, UNIX. Language(s): DIBOL.
MS-DOS. single-user $750.00.
DEC PDP-11/VAX. $1500.00 multi-user.
Handles Multi-Level Structure of Materials & Routing Specifications. Includes a Drawing Number, Engineering Change Number & Date, Economic Order Quantity, & Unit Cost. BILL OF MATERIALS EXPLOSION Shows All Levels of a Bill, along with Routings. REQUIREMENTS REPORT Calculates Quantity & Cost of Parts Needed to Build an Item.
Primetrack.

Bill-85. Version: 6.1. Oct. 1984. Compatible Hardware: IBM. Operating System(s) Required: MS-DOS. Language(s): COBOL. Memory Required: 640k. General Requirements: Hard disk.
disk $5000.00 (ISBN 0-926987-00-3).
Loan Management & Billing System Designed to Amortize Loans, Print Bills, Receive Payments, Credits & Charges for Loans, Interfaces to General Ledger, Btrieve Compatible.
Software Creations.

Billboard. Duane Bristow. Compatible Hardware: TRS-80. Operating System(s) Required: TRSDOS. Language(s): BASIC.
cassette $19.95.
Allows Merchants to Use TRS-80 Video Screen As Moving Billboard Advertising Daily Specials or Conveying Other Messages.
Duane Bristow Computers, Inc.

Billing. Version: 4.5. 1979. Compatible Hardware: IBM PC & compatibles, PC XT, PC AT, 386, 486, Pentium, PS/2. Operating System(s) Required: PC-DOS/MS-DOS 3.X, 4X, 5X, 6X, Windows 3.1, Windows 95. Language(s): BASIC. Memory Required: 640k. General Requirements: Stand-alone or 2Mb Network file server. Customer Support: 90 day warranty, onsite training, telephone support.
$200.00.
Uses Several Pricing Methods Including Simple, Customer Class, Quantity Discount & Contract Billing. Features Various Discounting Methods, Commissions Optionally Computed Based on Sales or Profit, Computer Sales or Excise Sales or Excise Taxes, Entry of Prepaid Amounts, Supports 2 Standard Invoice Formats, Handles Pre-Billing & Post Billing, Allows Creation of Fixed Invoices on a Recurrent Cycle, & Optionally Interfaces to LIBRA Accounts Receivable, Inventory Control, General Ledger/Client Write-Up, Sales Analysis, & Job Costing.
LIBRA Corp.

Billing Clerk with Accounts Receivable. Version: 2.01. Jul. 1992. Items Included: 150 page wire bound manual. Customer Support: Free installation help via phone, Free fax support, 900 number at $2.00 per minute with no minimum.
MS-DOS 3.0 or higher with hard disk. Any 8088, 86, 286, 386 or 486 MS-DOS compatible (640k). disk $179.00 (Order no.: 1-800-880-0887/FAX 512-629-4341). Optimal configuration: 640k RAM, hard disk, printer. Networks supported: Most. Not multi user, but network compatible.
Ability to Do Recurring Billing, Invoicing, Statements, Aging, Past Due Notices, Late Charges, Multi-Tax Rate, Discount, Multi-Tier Pricing, Save-Recall Invoices, Labels, Rolodex Cards, Product & Service Code Can Be Created. Prints on Standard Forms or Blank Paper. Sales Tracking-Inventory Module Available. Custom Modifications Available. Designed Specifically to Be Extremely Easy to Operate. Self Installs in Less Than Two Minutes. Typical Customers up & Running in Less Than One Hour.
Dilloware, Inc.

97

BillMaster. *Operating System(s) Required:* CP/M, MP/M.
$395.00.
Practical Solutions, Inc.

BILOG. *Version:* 3.04. Robert J. Mislevy & R. Darrell Bock. 1993. *Items Included:* Manual. *Customer Support:* Free technical support, 90 day limited warranty.
MS-DOS. IBM & compatibles. disk $285.00 (ISBN 1-56321-064-9)
3.5" disk $285.00 (ISBN 1-56321-065-7).
3.5" disk $345.00, BILOG 3.07 386 DOS Extender Version (ISBN 1-56321-111-4).
170p. manual $35.00 (ISBN 1-56321-123-8).
Implements Modern Item Response Theoretic (IRT) Methods of Item Analysis & Test Scoring in a Fast, User-Oriented Computer Program. Designed for a Wide Range of IRT Applications to Practical Testing Problems with Long or Short Tests, Multiple Subtests, & Multiple Test Forms.
Lawrence Erlbaum Assocs., Software & Alternate Media, Inc.

BIMAIN. *Version:* 2. Michele Zinowskil et al. 1993. *Items Included:* Manual. *Customer Support:* Free technical support, 90 day limited warranty.
MS-DOS. IBM & compatibles. disk $385.00 386 DOS Extender (ISBN 1-56321-128-9).
101p. manual $35.00 (ISBN 1-56321-122-X).
Special Form of the BILOG Program Designed to Detect & Estimate Item Parameter Drift (DRIFT) & Differential Item Functioning (DIF). Extremely Versatile, BIMAIN Is Essentially a Multiple-Group BILOG.
Lawrence Erlbaum Assocs., Software & Alternate Media, Inc.

Binary Phase Equilibria Curve Fitting. *Items Included:* Bound manual. *Customer Support:* Free hotline - no time limit; 30 day limited warranty; updates are $5/disk plus S&H.
MS-DOS. IBM & compatibles (256k). disk $99.95. *Nonstandard peripherals required:* Requires CGA (or equivalent) graphics capability; printer supported.
Apple II series (64k). disk $99.95.
Fits Empirical Curves to Sparse Binary Vapor-Liquid Equilibrium Data at Constant Moderate Pressure in Order to Permit Interpolation or Extrapolation. The Empirical Models Available for the Calculation of the Activity Coefficient Are the Margules, Van Laar, & Wilson Functions. Vapor Pressure Options Include the Wagner & Antoine Equations, or Raw Vapor Pressure Data. Means Are Provided for Easy Recalculation Based on Different Data Points & Different Models. Graphic Displays Allow Comparison Between the Fitted Model & Data.
Dynacomp, Inc.

Bio-Data. *Compatible Hardware:* IBM PC, PC XT. *Memory Required:* 256k.
disk $19.95.
Birthdate Data Includes Biorhythm Chart, Julian Day, the Number of Days Since the Birth, & the Day of the Week of the Birth. Calculates the Celestial Longitude of the Sun & the Astrological Sign.
Zephyr Services.

Bioinformation on the World Wide Web: An Annotated Directory of Molecular Biology Tools. *Version:* 2.0. Cynthia S. Smagula. Apr. 1996. *Items Included:* Acrobat Reader 2.1 Software, Web Link Plug-In Extension information on obtaining Netscape Navigator Browser, Readme File explaining organization & use of PPF files. *Customer Support:* Biota Web Site will supply information on changed URLS, E-Mail support, Book format available: ISBN 0-9649044-9-7.
Macintosh System 7.0 or higher. Macintosh with 68020 processor or higher (4Mb). 3.5" disk $29.95 (ISBN 0-9649044-8-9, Order no.: BIOINFO.PDF V2.0). *Nonstandard peripherals required:* 14.4k modem or higher. *Addl. software required:* Mac TCP 2.04, SLID or PPP dial up account, Netscape Navigator (V1.1 or higher, 1 for Macintosh). *Optimal configuration:* Power PC, System 7.5, 8Mb RAM, Mac TCP 2.0.6, PPP dial-up connection, Netscape Navigator V1.1 for Power Macintosh.
3.5" disk $49.95, incl. book (ISBN 0-9649044-9-7).
Microsoft Windows 3.1 in 386 enhanced mode. 386, 486 PC (4Mb). *Nonstandard peripherals required:* 14.4k modem. *Addl. software required:* Winsock TCP/IP stack, Netscape Navigator for Windows (latest version). *Optimal configuration:* 486 with 8Mb RAM, SVGA monitor, 28.8k modem, Winsock TCP/IP stack, Netscape Navigator for Windows (latest).
An Annotated Guide to Online Resources Providing Access to the Global Megadatabases & Their Associated Analytic Tools. Over 450 Sites Are Classified by Function, Forming an Integrated Tool Kit. Each of the 10 Adobe Acrobat Files Are Accessible via a Hyperlinked Table of Contents & Index.
Biota Publications.

BioInformation on the World Wide Web: Annotated Directory of Molecular Biology Tools. *Version:* 3.0. Cynthia S. Smagula. Mar. 1996. *Items Included:* Text version. *Customer Support:* Biota Publications Web Site will make available updates.
Apple System 7.0 or higher. Macintosh with 68020 processor or higher (5Mb). CD-ROM disk $29.95 (ISBN 0-9649044-7-0). *Nonstandard peripherals required:* 14.4k modem, CD-ROM drive. *Addl. software required:* Mac TCP 2.0.4, SLIP or PPP dial up (Internet connection), Netscape Navigatotr V1.1 for Macintosh. *Optimal configuration:* Power PC System 7.5, 8Mb RAM, Mac TCP 2.0.6, PPP dial up connection, 28.8k modem, Netscape Navigator V1.1 for Power Macintosh.
Microsoft Windows 3.1. 386 or 486 based PC (8Mb). *Nonstandard peripherals required:* 14.4k modem, CD-ROM drive. *Addl. software required:* Winsock TCP/IP stack, Netscape Navigator for Windows (latest). *Optimal configuration:* 486-based PC with 8Mb RAM, SVGA monitor, 28.8k modem, Winsock TCP/IP stack, Netscape Navigator for Windows (latest).
Contains All the Material Contained in the Software Version (Netscape Navigator Formatted Chapters with Hypertext TOCS & Indexes) Plus the Full-Length Text with the Complete TOC & a Comprehensive Index Viewable with "Viewer" Software (Included). Site Documentation Archives Will Also Be Included.
Biota Pubns.

BioInformation on the World Wide Web: Annotated Directory of Molecular Biology Tools. *Version:* 2.0. Cynthia S. Smagula. Dec. 1995. *Items Included:* Text version. *Customer Support:* Biota Publications Web Site will make available updates.
Apple System 7.0 or higher. Macintosh with 68020 processor or higher (4Mb). disk $29.99 (ISBN 0-9649044-8-9). *Nonstandard peripherals required:* 14.4k modem. *Addl. software required:* Mac TCP 2.0.4, SLIP or PPP dial up (Internet connection), Netscape Navigaotr V1.1 for Macintosh. *Optimal configuration:* Power PC System 7.5, 8Mb RAM, Mac TCP 2.0.6, PPP dial up connection, 28.8k modem, Netscape Navigator V1.1 for Power Macintosh.
Microsoft Windows 3.1 in 386 enhanced mode. 386 or 486 based PC (4Mb). *Nonstandard peripherals required:* 14.4k modem. *Addl. software required:* Winsock TCP/IP stack, Netscape Navigator for Windows (latest). *Optimal configuration:* 486-based PC with 8Mb RAM, SVGA monitor, 28.8k modem, Winsock TCP/IP stack. Netscape Navigator for Windows (latest).
Formatted So That Individual Chapters May Be Opened in the Netscape Web Browser & Used As a "Jump-Pad", Directly Linking Described Sites to the Actual Web Sites. Each Chapter Includes a Hypertext TOC & Index, Giving a Comprehensive Over-View & Facilitating Rapid Searching.
Biota Pubns.

Biological Age. Arto Demirjian. *Customer Support:* Toll-free technical support - no charge. In U.S. - 9AM-5PM EST 800-343-0064. In U.K. - 44(0)81-995-8242.
System 6.0.7 or higher. Apple Macintosh (3Mb). CD-ROM disk $249.00 Individual; $599.00 Institutional (ISBN 1-57276-007-9, Order no.: SE-007-001). *Nonstandard peripherals required:* CD-ROM drive.
This CD-ROM Presents the Subject of Child Growth & Development. The Content Includes Several Thousand Dental, Hand/Wrist & Maxillo-Facial X-Rays, along with Charts, Diagrams, & Accompanying Text.
SilverPlatter Education.

Biological Age. Arto Demirjian. Jan. 1994. *Customer Support:* Toll-free technical support - no charge. In U.S. 9AM - 5PM EST 800-343-0064; in U.K. 44(0)81-995-8242.
System 6.0.7 or higher. Apple Macintosh (3Mb). CD-ROM disk $249.00, Individual, ,599.00 Institutional (ISBN 1-57276-007-9, Order no.: SE-007-001). *Nonstandard peripherals required:* CD-ROM drive.
This CD-ROM Presents the Subject of Child Growth & Development. The Content Includes Several Thousand Dental, Hand/Wrist & Maxillo-Facial X-Rays, along with Charts, Diagrams, & Accompanying Text.
SilverPlatter Education.

Biology, Vol. 1: Respiration. 1995. *Items Included:* Full manual. *Customer Support:* Free telephone support - 90 days, 30-day warranty.
MS-DOS 3.2 or higher. 286 (584k). disk $44.95. *Nonstandard peripherals required:* CGA/EGA/VGA.
Learn the Mechanism & Anatomy of Respiration. Conduct "Virtual" Dissections, & Much More.
Dynacomp, Inc.

Biology, Vol. 2: Digestion & Nutrition. 1995. *Items Included:* Full manual. *Customer Support:* Free telephone support - 90 days, 30-day warranty.
MS-DOS 3.2 or higher. 286 (584k). disk $44.95. *Nonstandard peripherals required:* CGA/EGA/VGA.
Learn the Complete Functioning of the Digestive System, Effects of Nutrition, Exercise, & Sleep, etc.
Dynacomp, Inc.

Biology, Vol. 3: Reproduction & Development. 1995. *Items Included:* Full manual. *Customer Support:* Free telephone support - 90 days, 30-day warranty.
MS-DOS 3.2 or higher. 286 (584k). disk $44.95. *Nonstandard peripherals required:* CGA/EGA/VGA.
A Clear Animated Treatment of the Human Reproductive System & Physical Development.
Dynacomp, Inc.

TITLE INDEX

BISINESS CONSTRUCTION ACCOUNTING

Biology, Vol. 4: Circulation & the Heart. 1995. *Items Included:* Full manual. *Customer Support:* Free telephone support - 90 days, 30-day warranty.
MS-DOS 3.2 or higher. 286 (584k). disk $44.95. *Nonstandard peripherals required:* CGA/EGA/VGA.
A Fantastic Voyage into the Blood Stream Including Arteries, Veins, Capillaries, Lymph Glands, & More.
Dynacomp, Inc.

Biometrics. *Version:* 10.0. (Professional Ser.). 1989. *Compatible Hardware:* Apple Macintosh, IBM PC & compatibles. *Memory Required:* 512k. *Items Included:* Disks, book, program instructions. *Customer Support:* Telephone.
disk $145.00 (ISBN 0-920387-26-8).
Intended to Serve the Needs of People Engaged in the Biological & Life Sciences. Covers the Materials in the Well-Known Reference Biometry by R.R. Sokal & F. James Rohlf with a Few Exceptions & Considerable Additions. For Descriptive Statistics Various EDA Techniques Are Adapted Including, Stem-&-Leaf Displays, Boxplots, Coded Tables; Standard Techniques Such As Histograms, Simple Data Entry & T-Test Analysis Are Also Provided. Statistical Distributions & Statistical Inference Are Covered in Detail As Is Hypothesis Testing (Parametric & Non-Parametric). A Set of Programs for the Analysis of Variance of Experiments Is Included; Factorials with Replications, Unbalanced Factorials, Nested Designs, Repeated Measures. Includes the Duncan Multiple Range Test, etc.
Lionheart Pr., Inc.

Bionutritional Blood Analysis. *Operating System(s) Required:* MS-DOS, PC-DOS, CP/M, Concurrent DOS, Novell. *Memory Required:* 256k. *General Requirements:* Hard disk.
disk $495.00.
After the Results of a Standard Blood Analysis Is Entered, the Program Will Produce a Report Outlining the Function, Meaning, & Importance of Each Result. Suitable As a Patient Education Tool.
ProGroup.

Biorhythm. *Compatible Hardware:* TRS-80 Model I, Model III.
contact publisher for price.
Modtec, Software Div.

Biorhythm Graph & Interpreter. 1983. *Compatible Hardware:* Apple II+, IIe, IIc; Commodore 64, PET; IBM PC with 2 disk drives. *Language(s):* BASIC. *Memory Required:* PET 32k, Apple 48k, Commdore 64k, IBM 256k. *General Requirements:* Printer.
disk $300.00 ea. (Order no.: M92).
Commodore 64. (ISBN 0-925182-14-1).
IBM. (ISBN 0-925182-15-X).
Apple. (ISBN 0-925182-16-8).
Biorhythm Report Writer Complete with Monthly Biographs, Key-Day Charts, & Event Interpretations.
Matrix Software.

Biorhythm Master. *Customer Support:* 800-929-8117 (customer service).
MS-DOS. IBM/PS2. disk $49.99 (ISBN 0-87007-795-3).
Computes & Prints Out Person's Biorhythms for a Given Period of Time.
SourceView Software International.

BioScan OPTIMAS. *Version:* 3.0. Sep. 1991. *Operating System(s) Required:* MS-DOS, windows 3.0. *Memory Required:* 640k. *General Requirements:* Frame grabber board, video source, optional additional monitor. *Items Included:* Software, manuals. *Customer Support:* Free technical support/training classes.
disk $3995.00.
Image Processing, Measurement & Analysis Application Running Under Windows 3.0 for IBM PC AT, PS/2 & Compatibles. Permits Scientists & Technicians to Gather Measurements from Images, Communicate Results to Other Programs & Automate Procedures. Images Are Saved in TIFF Format & Can Be Printed Directly from Laserprinters or Placed in Desktop Publishing Programs. A Comprehensive Macro Programming Environment Also Permits Users to Automate Work Procedures, Link to Custom Algorithms, Create Custom User Interfaces in Windows, & Interact with Other Word Processing Graphics & Animation Packages Through DDE & DLL Links.
BioScan, Inc.

BioScan SnapShot+. *Version:* 3.0. Sep. 1991. *Items Included:* 1 installation guide, 1 user guide, BioScan OPTIMAS tour, software. *Customer Support:* 1 year free technical support.
MS-DOS, Microsoft Windows. PS/2, AT, 386 (& 486), PC compatible (640k, 2Mb recommended). disk $295.00. *Nonstandard peripherals required:* Frame grabber board. *Addl. software required:* Microsoft Windows. *Optimal configuration:* 386 PC, MS Windows, 640k, choice of over 25 frame grabber boards (2Mb).
Entry-Level Image Processing Software, Allows Users to Capture, Enhance & Manage Digital Images. Saves Images in Industry-Standard TIFF Format for Placing Images into Word Processing or Publishing Software for Publication. Supports over 25 Frame Grabbers or Can Run Without Frame Grabber Using 256 Color VGA Card. Extension Modules Available for Scientific Image Analysis.
BioScan, Inc.

Biquad Filter Design Tutorial. *Items Included:* Bound manual. *Customer Support:* Free hotline - no time limit; 30 day limited warranty; updates are $5/disk plus S&H.
MS-DOS. IBM & compatibles (256k). disk $29.95.
Apple. disk $29.95.
Allows the Determination of the Poles & Zeroes Required to Produce Various Filters Including: Analog Anti-Aliasing; Digital Low Pass, High Pass, & Band Stop. Design Butterworth & Chebyshev Low Pass/High Pass (up to 8 Poles) & Band Pass (up to 4 Poles) Digital Filters, & Graphically Observe Both the Analog & Digital Responses. To Use, You Must Be Familiar with the Bilinear Transform (an Earlier Tutorial in This Series).
Dynacomp, Inc.

Bird Brain: The Birding Database for Macintosh. *Version:* 3.0. Dec. 1995. *Items Included:* 2 manuals, software on 2 disks. *Customer Support:* 30-day unlimited warranty, free telephone technical support, detailed manuals included with software.
Mac Plus, Mac II, Power Mac recommended. Macintosh Plus or higher, Mac II recommended (2Mb). 3.5" disk $79.95 (ISBN 0-934077-09-6). *Optimal configuration:* Mac Plus, Mac II recommended, hard disk.
Lets Birder Easily Record Birding Observations. Program Automatically Creates Life Lists, Year Lists, State-, Nation-, County-, & Place-Life Lists, State-&-Province Checklists & Target Lists. All Data Can Be Exported. Simple Data Entry: Pick Birds' Names from Pop-Up Menus. Reference Database Includes All 1972 Birds of North & Central America, Mexico, & Hawaii. Upgrade to World List Available for $20.
Ideaform Inc.

Bird Classification. *Compatible Hardware:* Apple II.
contact publisher for price.
American Avicultural Art & Science.

The Birdhouse Cathedral. William Dubie. 1990.
DOS. Any type IBM (64k). $4.95 (ISBN 1-56178-000-6).
MAC. Any type Macintosh (64k). $4.95 (ISBN 1-56178-017-0).
Poetry-Collection of Poems.
Connected Editions, Inc.

Business Accounts Payable System. *Version:* 4.0. 1974. *Compatible Hardware:* IBM PC & compatibles, PC XT, PC AT. *Operating System(s) Required:* MS-DOS, PC-DOS, OS/2, UNIX V, LANs. *Language(s):* C. *Memory Required:* 512k. *General Requirements:* Printer.
disk $686.00.
Online, Real Time, Interactive System. User Has Option to Pay Invoices by Date or Vendor, Except When Held, or to Pay Only As Released. Other Features Include: Multi-Company, Multi-File, Multi-User with Password Security; Vendor Statistics; Batch & Voucher Controls; & Help Screens.
Bristol Information Systems.

Business Accounts Receivable System (AR). *Version:* 4.0. 1975. *Compatible Hardware:* IBM PC & compatibles, PC XT, PC AT. *Operating System(s) Required:* MS-DOS, PC-DOS, OS/2, UNIX V, LANs. *Language(s):* C. *Memory Required:* 512k. *General Requirements:* Printer.
disk $686.00.
Open-Item System Designed to Accept Data, Based upon Specific Invoice Inquiry. Offers Multi-File/MultiUser/Multi-Company Capacity with Password Security.
Bristol Information Systems.

Business Balance Forward Accounts Receivable (BFAR). *Version:* 3.0. 1979. *Compatible Hardware:* IBM PC & compatibles, PC XT, PC AT. *Operating System(s) Required:* MS-DOS, PC-DOS, OS/2, UNIX V, LANs. *Language(s):* C. *Memory Required:* 512k. *General Requirements:* Printer.
disk $686.00.
Provides Control over Accounting & Supervision of Accounts Receivable, Billing, Inventory Control, & Sales Analysis. Built upon a Customer File, Transaction File & Combined Sales/Cash Receipts File. Provides Customer Credit Controls & Complete Audit Trails & Can Maintain a Retail Product File. Features Password Security, Multi-File/Multi-Company/Multi-User Capacity, Unlimited File Size, 12 Reports with Multiple Options, Rolodex Cards & Mailing Labels.
Bristol Information Systems.

Business Check Reconciliation System. 1981. *Compatible Hardware:* IBM PC & compatibles, PC XT, PC AT. *Operating System(s) Required:* PC-DOS, MS-DOS, OS/2, UNIX V, LANs. *Language(s):* C. *Memory Required:* 512k. *General Requirements:* Printer.
disk $386.00.
Designed to Provide User with a Way of Maintaining & Providing a List of Outstanding Checks. Check Numbers Can Be Manually Input. Also Accepts Data from Almost Any Other Packaged or Custom Check Writing System. Allows Returned Checks to Be Input in Block Mode.
Bristol Information Systems.

Business Construction Accounting System. 1976. *Compatible Hardware:* IBM PC & compatibles, PC XT, PC AT. *Operating System(s) Required:* MS-DOS, PC-DOS, OS/2, UNIX V, LANs. *Memory Required:* 512k. *General*

BISINESS EQUIPMENT MANAGEMENT

Requirements: Printer.
disk $3986.00.
Integrated Accounting & Cost Control System Designed Specifically for the Construction Industry. Also Designed to Handle Prime & Sub-Contractors of Varying Sizes in All Phases of Construction. Includes Job Cost, Payroll, Accounts Payable & General Ledger.
Bristol Information Systems.

Bisiness Equipment Management. *Version:* 4.0. 1982. *Compatible Hardware:* IBM PC & compatibles, PC XT, PC AT. *Operating System(s) Required:* PC-DOS, MS-DOS, OS/2, UNIX V, LANs. *Memory Required:* 512k. *General Requirements:* Printer.
disk $986.00.
Provides Accounting for Business Equipments Such As: Trucks, Tractors, Printing Presses, etc. Provides for Control over Assets from Depreciation Calculations to Analysis of Costs & Revenue. It Is a Subsystem of the Business Fixed Assets System, Specifically Designed for Owners of Numerous Pieces of Equipment. In Addition to Depreciation Accounting & Tax & Insurance Analysis That Are Standard in the Fixed Assets System, It Provides Control over Expense Revenue, & Billing Data for Each Piece of Equipment Owned.
Bristol Information Systems.

Bisiness Fixed Asset System. *Version:* 4.0. 1975. *Compatible Hardware:* IBM PC & compatibles, PC XT, PC AT. *Operating System(s) Required:* MS-DOS, PC-DOS, OS/2, UNIX V, LANs. *Memory Required:* 512k. *General Requirements:* Printer.
disk $686.00.
Provides a System of Depreciation Accounting, along with Report Printing Capabilities That Can Be Utilized at Every Level. Allows Modification to Meet Company's Specific Needs. Simplifies the Handling of Fixed Asset Accounting. Nine Methods of Depreciation Calculation Are Provided.
Bristol Information Systems.

Bisiness General Ledger System. *Version:* 4.0. 1972. *Compatible Hardware:* IBM PC & compatibles, PC XT, PC AT. *Operating System(s) Required:* MS-DOS, PC-DOS, OS/2, UNIX V, LANs. *Memory Required:* 512k. *General Requirements:* Printer.
disk $686.00.
Designed to Produce All Required General Accounting Reports. When Used in Conjunction with Other Business Systems, the Appropriate Amounts Are Automatically Posted from Accounts Payable, Accounts Receivable, Payroll & Other Accounting Systems. A User-Defined Financial Report Generator & Budgeting Are Included.
Bristol Information Systems.

Bisiness Inventory Control System. *Version:* 4.0. 1972. *Compatible Hardware:* IBM PC & compatibles, PC XT, PC AT. *Operating System(s) Required:* MS-DOS, PC-DOS, OS/2, UNIX V, LANs. *Memory Required:* 512k. *General Requirements:* Printer.
disk $686.00.
Accepts Interactive Keyboard Input for Orders, Receipts, Usage, Physical Inventory, Sales, Transfers, Adjustments, Returns & Damages As Well As for Adding, Deleting & Changing Item Information. Reports Supply the Information That Management Needs for Proper Maintenance of Inventory.
Bristol Information Systems.

Bisiness Order Entry Billing System. *Version:* 3.0. 1984. *Compatible Hardware:* IBM PC & compatibles, PC XT, PC AT. *Operating System(s) Required:* MS-DOS, PC-DOS, OS/2, UNIX V, LANs. *Memory Required:* 512k.
disk $686.00.
Provides the Entire Order Process from Order Entry, Inventory, & Automatic Backlog Control, Through Automatic Posting to Accounts Receivable. Features Provided Include: Multi-Company Processing; File & Users with Password Security; Menus & Help Screens; Credit Checking; Accounts Receivable Customer File; Tax Rates & Codes for Control of Sales Tax Calculations.
Bristol Information Systems.

Bisiness Payroll System. 1972. *Compatible Hardware:* IBM PC & compatibles, PC XT, PC AT. *Operating System(s) Required:* MS-DOS, PC-DOS, OS/2, UNIX V, LANs. *Memory Required:* 512k. *General Requirements:* Printer.
disk $886.00.
Handles over 30 Different Payroll Formulas for Gross Pay Including Hourly, Overtime, Double Time, Salary, Multi-Rate, Commissions, No Check, No Pay, Salary with Commission & Shift Premiums. All Federal & All 50 State Taxes Are Supported Including City, County, &/or School Taxes, for Any Period, Plus 12 Deductions with 16 Deduction Formulas Including Percent & Hourly. Optional Modules: Labor Distribution, General Ledger Interface, & Check Reconciliation.
Bristol Information Systems.

Bisiness Property Management System. *Version:* 4.0. 1979. *Compatible Hardware:* IBM PC & compatibles, PC XT, PC AT. *Operating System(s) Required:* MS-DOS, PC-DOS, OS/2, UNIX V, LANs. *Memory Required:* 512k. *General Requirements:* Printer.
disk $1586.00.
Designed to Give the User Control over All Aspects of the Accounting & Supervision Needed to Maintain a Profitable Real Estate Project. The Main Master File Contains Data about Each Unit & Also the Lease, Occupants, Billing Cost, & Maintenance. Also Provides Additional Fields in Which Special Information Can Be Stored.
Bristol Information Systems.

Bisiness Purchase Order System. *Version:* 4.0. 1981. *Compatible Hardware:* IBM PC & compatibles, PC XT, PC AT. *Operating System(s) Required:* MS-DOS, PC-DOS, OS/2UNIX V, LANs. *Language(s):* C. *Memory Required:* 512k. *General Requirements:* Printer.
disk $686.00.
Designed to Provide Each User with a Method of Maintaining & Controlling Purchasing. Some Features Are: Multi-Department/Division Capabilities, Blanket Order/Partial Order Fulfillment, Cash Requirements Analysis, Automatic Updating of Inventory, Purchasing History, Audit Trail & Multi-Level Security.
Bristol Information Systems.

Bismarck-The North Sea Chase. *Compatible Hardware:* Apple II; Atari; Commodore 64/128. *Memory Required:* 64k. *General Requirements:* Joystick Optional.
Apple. disk $29.95 (ISBN 0-88717-179-6, Order no.: 15753-43499).
Atari. disk $29.95 (ISBN 0-88717-229-6, Order no.: 15758-43499).
Commodore. disk $29.95 (ISBN 0-88717-178-8, Order no.: 15751-43499).
Multi-Level Game with Torpedo Attacks, Armament Controls & Bridge Controls, Radar Search, Weather Forecasting, Reconnaissance & Map Screens, etc.
IntelliCreations, Inc.

BisPlan Master. *Customer Support:* 800-929-8117 (customer service).
MS-DOS. IBM/PS2. disk $199.99 (ISBN 0-87007-558-6).
A Dedicated Program Which Is Designed to Churn Out a Variety of Business Plans, Including the Financial Reporting Sections. It Includes a Considerable Store of Boiler Plates That Can Be Adapted Readily by Any Fledgling Concern. The User Is Led Through Screen Prompts to Enter Data Concerning His Business Plans. User Can Enter Estimates of a Business Proposal That Is Being Considered & Produce Projections of Potential Earnings. Helps the User Access Financing Requirements. Loan Payoff Rate, Length of Time Before Return of Investment & Profit Potential. Estimates Can Be Projected up to Five Years & Dumped from Screen to Line Printer. This Is a Standalone Program Not Dependent on Having a Spreadsheet.
SourceView Software International.

BitCom. *Version:* 3.5. *Compatible Hardware:* IBM PC & compatibles. *Operating System(s) Required:* PC-DOS/MS-DOS 2.0 or higher. *Memory Required:* 256k.
disk $69.00.
Automates Communication Tasks. Supports the Hayes Command Set, As Well As Transmission Rates of 110 to 19,200 Bits per Second. Has Built-In Buffers & Xon/Xoff Flow Control. Allows User to Change Protocols Before Sending or Receiving a File. Supports Include Xmodem with Check-Sum, Xmodem-CRC, Relaxed Xmodem, Xmodem 1K, Ymodem Batch & Kermit.
BIT Software, Inc.

BITS & PIECES. *Compatible Hardware:* Commodore 64.
disk $14.95, incl. instr's. manual.
A Multiple Software Utility Program.
Applied Technologies, Inc.

BiWeibullSMITH. Robert Abernethy & Wes Fulton. Jul. 1994. *Customer Support:* 30 day limited warranty.
MS-DOS. IBM (512k). disk $320.00 (Order no.: S106). *Optimal configuration:* 5Mb storage on hard disk required.
Program Will Solve Two Weibull Fit Lines from One Set of Data. Covers Both Infant Mortality Data at the Beginning of Component Life & Wearout Data at End of Component Life. Also Simulates the Entire Range of Product Life with a Curve on a Weibull Graph, Usually Known As a Bathtub Curve.
Gulf Publishing Co.

BiWeibullSMITH: Dual Weibull Analysis. 1995. *Items Included:* Full manual. *Customer Support:* Free telephone support - 90 days, 30-day warranty.
MS-DOS 3.2 or higher. 286 (584k). disk $319.95. *Nonstandard peripherals required:* CGA/EGA/VGA.
Fits Dual Weibull Curves Represented by One Set of Data. Based on the Technique Developed by Alan Townsend for Use in Warranty Models, This Procedure Can Cover Both Infant Mortality Data at the Beginning of Component Life & Wearout Data at the End of Component Life. It Can Simulate the Entire Range of Product Life with a Plot on a Weibull Graph, Usually Known As the Bathtub Curve.
Dynacomp, Inc.

BizPlanBuilder. *Version:* 4.1. *Items Included:* Software disk (360k 5.25" & 720k 3.5" diskette, or single 800k 3.5" for Macintosh) has pre-formatted text & financial spreadsheets. Manual includes a reference guide of key business terms & concepts, sample finished business plan, & hard copy of the disk's contents. *Customer Support:* Provided by JIAN at (415) 941-9191.
IBM PC & compatibles (512K), Macintosh. $129.00. *Nonstandard peripherals required:* Hard disk recommended. *Addl. software*

required: PC's: word processor compatible with MS Word, PCWrite, Q&A, PFS First Choice, WordPerfect, WordStar & most others. PC's: spreadsheets, Lotus 1-2-3 compatible including Lotus, QuattroPro, Excel, MS Works & others. Macintosh: word processors, MacWrite 5.0 or MS Word 3.01 compatible. Macintosh: spreadsheets, SYCK compatible including Excel, MS Works & others.
Working Business Plan Template with Descriptive & Analytic Text Files, Enhanced by Financial Spreadsheets. It Is Sales & Marketing Oriented & Covers a Wide Variety of Topics from Product/Service Description to Marketing Strategy & Analysis to Basic Financials. Manual Includes a Reference Guide to Key Business Terms & Concepts, Sample Finished Business Plan, & Hard Copy of the Disk's Contents. Designed to Allow the Businessperson to Edit & Customize a Pre-Formatted Business Plan Rather Than Write One from Scratch.
JIAN Tools for Sales.

Black Beauty: Interactive Moviebook. *Version*: 1.5. Nov. 1994. *Items Included*: Manual, registration card, sound list. *Customer Support*: Phone technical support.
Windows 3.1. 386 DX 25MHz or higher (4Mb). CD-ROM disk $19.95 (ISBN 1-57303-010-4). *Nonstandard peripherals required*: Sound card. *Optimal configuration*: 486 or higher with 8Mb RAM, Windows 3.1 or later, 15Mb free hard drive space available, sound card, 256 color monitor.
Interactive MovieBooks Are Exclusively Licensed Computer Storybooks for Children. Taken from the Movie Version, the Story Appears on the Computer Screen in Book Form Which the Child Can Read on, or by Clicking the Mouse, Can Have Read to Them in a Boy's or Girl's Voice. Pictures Are Included Which, by Clicking the Mouse, Turn into Short Clips from the Actual Movie.
Sound Source Interactive.

Black Hawk. *Compatible Hardware*: Atari XL/XE. disk $15.00.
Fly from Your Aircraft Carrier Across Hostile Enemy Territory, Land at the Embassy to Rescue the Hostages, Then Fly Back to the Carrier. Beware of Surface to Air Missiles & Enemy Aircraft. Features 3-D Scrolling Arcade Style Graphics, Multiple Difficulty Levels, Color or Black & White Display Options.
Orion Software (Texas).

The Black Hole. *Compatible Hardware*: TRS-80. disk $24.95 (ISBN 0-915149-13-3). cassette $19.95 (ISBN 0-915149-08-7).
Player Must Survive the Perils of the Black Hole in Seeking to Find & Destroy the Dorfian Leader.
Blue Cat.

Black Hole. *Compatible Hardware*: Apple II with Applesoft. *Operating System(s) Required*: Apple DOS 3.2, 3.3. *Memory Required*: 16k. disk $19.95.
cassette $15.95.
Space Arcade Game.
Dynacomp, Inc.

Black Jack Tutorial. *Compatible Hardware*: Apple II. *Language(s)*: Integer BASIC. *Memory Required*: 16k.
disk $14.95 (Order no.: 10036).
Designed to Teach User to Play Winning Game by Eliminating Poor Play.
Powersoft, Inc.

The Blackacre Conveyancer. Steven R. Kursh. *Items Included*: 3 manuals. *Customer Support*: Technical support available.
DOS 3.1 or higher. IBM PC & compatibles (640k). Contact publisher for price. *Addl.*

software required: WordPerfect V5.1. *Networks supported*: Novell 3.11.
Comprehensive & Flexible System Designed Specifically for Real Property Attorney's & Their Staffs. Provides a Complete Single-Entry System for Producing All Documents, Tracking Activities, Generating Reports, & Doing All Calculations. Customized System Designed Specifically for Your Needs & Statutory Requirements.
Shepard's/McGraw-Hill, Inc.

Blackacre's Foreclosure System. Steven R. Kursh. *Items Included*: 3 manuals. *Customer Support*: Technical support available.
DOS 3.1 or higher. IBM PC & compatibles (640k). Contact publisher for price. *Addl. software required*: WordPerfect V5.1. *Networks supported*: Novell 3.11.
Customized Comprehensive & Flexible System for Managing Residential & Commercial Loan Workouts & Foreclosures. Provides a Complete Single-Entry System for Producing Summary Management Reports for Clients, Tracking All Activities by State & Local Calendars, Responsible Person, or Key Events, & Producing All Documents.
Shepard's/McGraw-Hill, Inc.

Blackacre's RESPA. *Version*: 7.0. Steven R. Kursh. Aug. 1993. *Items Included*: 1 manual. *Customer Support*: Toll free phone support.
DOS 3.1 or higher. IBM PC & compatibles (640k). Contact publisher for price. *Networks supported*: Novell 3.11.
Handles Real Estate Closing by Producing HUD-1 Form, HUD Addendum, FHA HUD Addendum, Plus Buyer's & Seller's Statement & Fixed Rate Loan Amortization Schedules. Expand Your RESPA Software with the Following Additional Modules: Network Module, Checkwriting Module, IRS Form 1099 Module, & WordPerfect Link Module.
Shepard's/McGraw-Hill, Inc.

Blackjack. *Compatible Hardware*: Atari XL/XE. cassette $6.95 (Order no.: CX4105).
Atari Corp.

Blackjack. Wayne Hammond. *Compatible Hardware*: IBM PC, PCjr, PC XT, Portable PC with IBM Color Display. *Operating System(s) Required*: DOS 1.10, 2.00, 2.10, 3.00, 3.10. *Memory Required*: IBM PCjr 256k, all others 128k.
disk $19.95 (Order no.: 6276503).
User Can Compete with As Many As Six Players at a Time, & Also Select Terms or Options for Each Game. Review Card Counts in Simple or Intermediate Formats. Check the Strategy Screen for Game Conditions, & Learn Several Variations of Rules.
Personally Developed Software, Inc.

Blackjack Academy. *Compatible Hardware*: Apple II, II+, IIe, IIc, IIgs; Atari ST; Commodore 64/128; Amiga; IBM PC.
$24.95.
A Professional Primer to Beat the Odds. Learn 2nd Play BlackJack.
Microillusions, Inc.

Blackjack Analyzer: Rules & Strategy Simulation. 1992. *Items Included*: Detailed manuals included with all Dynacomp products. *Customer Support*: Free telephone support to original customer - no time limit; 30 day limited warranty.
MS-DOS 3.2 or higher. IBM PC & compatibles (512k). $39.95 (Add $5.00 for 3 1/2" format; 5 1/4" format standard). *Optimal configuration*: IBM, MS-DOS 2.0 or higher, 128k RAM. Can be run in either monochrome or color modes.

Has Three Main Functions. First, It Is a Game. Second, It Will Generate a Table of Basic Strategy under Almost Any Set of Rules. Third, It Runs High Speed Simulations. The Card Display Is Attractive & Easy to Read. For Any Set of Rules You Wish, You May Build a Strategy Table. Has Received Rave Reviews.
Dynacomp, Inc.

Blackjack & Poker. *Compatible Hardware*: TI 99/4A.
contact publisher for price (Order no.: PHM3033).
Computer-Simulated Card Games Allow Betting with a Bankroll. Up to 4 Players.
Texas Instruments, Personal Productivit.

Blackjack Coach. *Compatible Hardware*: Apple II with Applesoft; CP/M based machines with MBASIC; IBM PC. (source code included). *Memory Required*: disk 48k-128k.
disk $29.95.
Helps the User to Learn & Practice Blackjack Skills.
Dynacomp, Inc.

BlackJack Master. *Version*: 2.1. *Items Included*: Program disk & manual.
DOS 2.1 or higher. IBM PC & compatibles (256k). disk $49.95.
Three Modes: Play, Practice, Simulate. Play Mode Permits All Popular Casino Rules; Practice Mode Enables User to Rehearse a Variety of Playing Situations; & Simulate Mode Which Is the Program's Main Features, Enables User to Test Playing Strategies at 80,000 Hands per Hour.
Elite Software.

Blackjack Trainer. *Version*: 2.0. Mar. 1992. *Items Included*: Manual. *Customer Support*: Limited phone support.
Macintosh System 6.0 or System 7. Macintosh (1024k). $75.00 plus shipping (ISBN 1-886070-00-8, Order no.: 9202). *Optimal configuration*: Color monitor supported but not required.
Microsoft Windows. PC compatible (2048k). $75.00 plus shipping (ISBN 1-886070-02-4, Order no.: 9304). *Optimal configuration*: Color monitor (not required), Sound Board (not required).
Teaches the Professional Play of Blackjack. Basic Strategy & Balance or Unbalanced Counts. High Speed Simulation Capability. Extensive Counting & Strategy Drills.
ConJelCo.

Blackjack Tutor. *Compatible Hardware*: Commodore 64, 128; IBM PC & compatibles. *Operating System(s) Required*: CBM DOS, DOS 2.1 or higher. *Language(s)*: Compiled BASIC, Compiled .EXE for IBM. *Memory Required*: Commodore 64k, IBM 256k. *General Requirements*: Color monitor.
Commodore. disk $35.00 ea. (Order no.: D210F).
IBM. disk $35.00 (Order no.: D210I).
Users Learn to Hit, Stand, Double, & Split. Features Full Card Graphics with 150 Practice Scenarios. Assumes the Use of Two Decks, i.e., NO Card-Counting Scheme. Teaches & Tests Strategy Skills.
Briley Software.

Blackjack Tutor. *Customer Support*: 800-929-8117 (customer service).
MS-DOS. IBM/PS2. disk $79.99 (ISBN 0-87007-485-7).
Teaches Proper Blackjack Strategy According to Five Worldwide Rules: Las Vegas, Reno, London, Bahamas & Hong Kong. Users Learn by Doing, with Gentle Reminders of Ways to Increase the Odds at Crucial Points. User Can Choose from Three Methods -- Point Count, Theoretical and None.
SourceView Software International.

Black's Law Dictionary. 1983. *Compatible Hardware:* Apple II, II+, IIc, IIe, IIgs. *Operating System(s) Required:* Apple DOS 3.3, ProDOS. *Memory Required:* 48k-64k. *General Requirements:* Sensible Speller Program.
disk $39.95 (ISBN 0-926776-02-9).
Combines 20,000 Words for the Legal Profession with 15,000 Words from the Random House Dictionary on a Single Disk. This Reference Work on Legal Terminology May Be Used Alone or in Conjunction with Other Random House Dictionary Disks Used by the Sensible Speller Program.
Sensible Software, Inc.

Black's Law Dictionary Legal Word Speller. Reference Software International Staff. May 1989. *Items Included:* License, installation card, disks. *Customer Support:* Free support at these toll numbers: DOS (801) 228-9918, Windows (801) 228-9919.
DOS. IBM PC & compatibles (100k). $89.00 SRP. *Addl. software required:* WordPerfect 5.0 or 5.1 only! Compatibility with WP 6.0. *Optimal configuration:* Hard disk recommended. *Networks supported:* Network ready.
Windows. IBM PC & compatibles (100k). Contact publisher for price. *Addl. software required:* WordPerfect 5.1 or 5.2 for Windows. *Networks supported:* Network ready.
A Definitive Legal Spelling Reference for WordPerfect Users. The Product Allows 16,000 Legal Terms & Phrases of American & English Jurisprudence to Be Merged into WordPerfect's Main Spelling Dictionary to Ensure Accurate Legal Spelling in All WordPerfect Documents.
WordPerfect Corp.

The Blackwell Data Collection. *Version:* 1.x. Arthur Blackwell et al. Aug. 1990. *Items Included:* Manual. *Customer Support:* Free phone support.
MS-DOS. IBM PC & compatible (512k). disk $50.00.
MacFinder. Apple Macintosh (1Mb). 3.5" disk $50.00.
Contains over 500 Meticulously Sourced Celebrity Horoscopes, from the Emperor Augustus to the First Test-Tube Baby, Pre-Calculated & Ready to Display On-Screen or Printed Out. Also Contains Dates of Life Events for Studying Forecasting Techniques. Database Can Be Edited & Added to by the User.
Astrolabe, Inc.

BLAST: Blocked ASynchronous Transmission. Communications Research Group. 1980. *Compatible Hardware:* AT&T, Data General, DEC, HP, IBM, Prime, Sperry, Wang. *Operating System(s) Required:* CP/M, UNIX, VMS, RDOS, AOS, AOSVS. *Memory Required:* 256k.
IBM. disk $250.00 (ISBN 0-917721-00-4, Order no.: PCBLAST).
CP/M. disk $250.00 (ISBN 0-917721-05-5, Order no.: CPBLAST).
DEC VAX. cassette $895.00 (ISBN 0-917721-04-7, Order no.: VBLAST).
$495.00-$1295.00 ea.
Data General. (ISBN 0-917721-01-2, Order no.: DGBLAST).
UNIX. (ISBN 0-917721-06-3, Order no.: UBLAST).
Communications Family of Products That Is Used As a Multi-Vendor Data Communications Program. Features Error-Free Communications Compatibility among Most Computers As Well As for Networks & Services. Also Allows Both Sites of a Computer to Send & Receive at the Same Time. Both Channels Are Used on Asynchronous Full Duplex Modems. ACK/NAK Does Not Use Both Channels, but Must Stop & Wait for ACK (Acknowledgement) Following Each Data Block. The Program's SDLC-Like Protocol Sends Data in Both Directions Simultaneously, Re-Transmitting Only the Erroneous Blocks.
U.S. Robotics, Inc.

BLAST Professional. 1991. *Items Included:* User's guide; reference manual; quick reference card. *Customer Support:* Unlimited customer support; 30 day money back guarantee.
MS-DOS. PC compatibles. $295.00 single user; $695.00 multi-user. *Optimal configuration:* 286 or higher. *Networks supported:* Works with all popular LANs.
Initially Designed for the Demanding Needs of Data Center Managers; Now Available on over 30 Different Operating Systems. Handles File Transfer, Terminal Emulation & Remote Control. Protects Data from Line Noise for 100 Percent Error-Free Throughout. Works with All Popular LANs.
U.S. Robotics, Inc.

BLAST II: Blocked ASynchronous Transmission. *Compatible Hardware:* IBM (VM/CMS & MVS/TSO), AMDAHL; DEC (VAX/VMS; PDP/RSX, RT-11, TSX+); Prime (Primos); HP 3000 (MPE) 1000 (RTE), 9000 (UNIX); Data General (all OS); Wang VS; AT&T 3B1, 3B2, 3B5, 3B15, 3B20, PC6300; Harris VOS; NCR Tower; Apple (DOS, CP/M); Macintosh; Burroughs-BTOS; Convergent Technologies-CTOS; IBM PC & compatibles, PC XT, PC AT (MS-DOS); CP/M; UNIX (System V & Berkeley 4.2). *Memory Required:* 256k.
Micros. disk $250.00.
Minis. $495.00-$895.00.
Mainframes. $2495.00 up.
Provides Data Transfer Among PC's, Minis, & Mainframes Under Any of 30 Different Operating Systems. Data Is Converted Between Systems Automatically. Includes VT 100 Emulation, Lotus-Style Menus, On-Line Help Screens, Automated Dialing, Text Editor for Messages & Scripts for Repetitive Menus, Unattended Operations, Special Routines, Polling Remote Sites, etc.
U.S. Robotics, Inc.

Blasto. *Compatible Hardware:* TI 99/4A.
contact publisher for price (Order no.: PHM3032).
1 or 2 Player Tank. Challenge to Destroy a Field of Mines While Avoiding Your Opponent's Fire.
Texas Instruments, Personal Productivit.

Bleedo. Byron A. Myhre & Henry M. Taylor. Dec. 1986. *Compatible Hardware:* IBM PC & compatibles, PC XT, PC AT. *Operating System(s) Required:* MS-DOS 2.XX. *Language(s):* BASIC (source code included). *Memory Required:* 128k.
disk $47.00, incl. documentation (ISBN 0-89189-246-X, Order no.: 68-9-006-20).
Educational Game Intended to Sharpen or Refresh the User's Transfusion Skills. The Imaginary Patient Is Initialized as to Weight, Sex, & Clinical Conditions, & Deficiencies of Various Hematologic Factors. The Computer Simulates a Patient's Changing Blood Analysis As the User Bleeds & Transfuses Platelets, Plasma, Albumin, etc. Bleeding Continues Until a Selected Total Volume Has Been Passed. The Final Condition of the Patient Is Then Displayed.
ASCP Pr.

Blender Magazine. *Version:* 1.1. Nov. 1994. *Items Included:* Quicktime 2.0; Quicktime 1.1 for Windows; Shareware, Fonts. *Customer Support:* Technical support line.
MAC System 7; PC WIndows 3.1; 640x480 256 color monitor. Macintosh; Windows - cross platorm disc (4Mb). CD-ROM disk $19.95 (ISBN 1-886009-00-7). *Nonstandard peripherals required:* CD-ROM drive (double speed). *Addl. software required:* Quicktime; Quicktime for Windows (supplied). *Optimal configuration:* MAC: Quadra; 8Mb free. WINDOWS: 486; 8Mb.
An Interactive Guide to Current Pop-Culture, Incorporating Music & Video to Complement the Written Text. Blender Is a MAC/PC Hybrid CD-ROM Disk, with Original Content, Operating As a Periodical.
Dennis Publishing.

Blender Magazine. *Version:* 1.2. Feb. 1995. *Items Included:* Quicktime 2.0; Quicktime 1.1 for Windows; Shareware, Fonts. *Customer Support:* Technical support line.
MAC System 7; PC Windows 3.1; 640x480 256 color monitor. Macintosh; Windows - cross platform disc (4Mb). CD-ROM disk $19.95 (ISBN 1-886009-01-5). *Nonstandard peripherals required:* CD-ROM drive (double speed). *Addl. software required:* Quicktime; Quicktime for Windows (supplied). *Optimal configuration:* MAC: Quadra or higher, System 7.1, 8Mb RAM, double speed CD-ROM. WINDOWS: 486 66MHz, Windows 3.1, 8Mb RAM, double speed CD-ROM.
An Interactive Guide to Current Pop-Culture, Incorporating Music & Video to Complement the Written Text. Blender Is a MAC/PC Hybrid CD-ROM Disk, with Original Content, Operating As a Periodical.
Dennis Publishing.

BLKPLOT, BLKMAP: BLOCKPLOT, BLOCKMAP. *Version:* 2.4. Nov. 1985. *Compatible Hardware:* IBM PC, PC AT, PC XT & compatibles. *Operating System(s) Required:* MS-DOS, PC-DOS. *Language(s):* FORTRAN. *Memory Required:* 512k. *General Requirements:* Printer, plotter.
disk $1250.00 ea.
Used to Produce Plotter & Printer Maps of Blocks & Their Corresponding Values. Generates Maps of Gridded Blocks at Any Specified Scale. Up to 10 Values or Variables May Be Displayed Inside the Blocks, with Format Options Left to the User's Requirements.
Geostat Systems International, Inc. (GSII).

Block & Tackle: Fantasy Football, Tom Landry Football, Pro Football Scorecard. Fantasy Sports Properties Staff et al. Aug. 1995. *Items Included:* Set up instruction sheet. *Customer Support:* (503) 639-6863.
DOS. IBM PC. $14.95 Fantasy Sports (ISBN 1-887783-07-5, Order no.: 5300-4006). *Optimal configuration:* DOS 5.0, EGA, VGA or SVGA, 640k RAM.
DOS. IBM PC. $14.95 Tom Landry Football (Order no.: 5300-4006). *Optimal configuration:* IBM PC 386 or higher, DOS 5.0 or higher, 640k RAM, VGA, mouse.
DOS. IBM PC. $14.95 Pro Football Scorecard (Order no.: 5300-4006). *Optimal configuration:* IBM PC 286 or higher, DOS 3.3 or higher, 640k RAM, EGA.
A Compilation of Football Statistical Programs & an Actual Game Program Where the Player Calls the Plays in a Computer Simulated Football Game.
Entertainment Technology.

Block & Tackle: Fantasy Football, Tom Landry Football, Pro Football Scorecard. Fantasy Sports Properties et al. Jan. 1996. *Items Included:* Set-up instruction sheet. *Customer Support:* 310-403-0043.
DOS. IBM PC. disk $14.95 (ISBN 1-887783-24-5, Order no.: 5200-3006). *Optimal configuration:* Fantasy Sports: DOS 5.0, EGA/VGA/SVGA, 640k RAM; Tom Landry Football: IBM PC 386 or higher, DOS 5.0 or higher, 640k RAM, VGA, mouse; Pro Football: IBM PC 286 or higher, DOS 3.3 or higher, 640k RAM, EGA.
A Compilation of Football Statistical Programs & an Actual Game Where the Player Calls the Plays in a Computer Simulated Football Game.
Entertainment Technology.

TITLE INDEX

Block It. John M. Eddins & Cheryl Presley. 1986. *Customer Support:* ECS offers technical support to registered users. Call (217) 359-7099. Other than the telephone call - technical support is no charge.
Apple DOS 3.3. Apple. disk $39.95 (Order no.: A-1140).
DOS 3.3 or higher. IBM. $39.95 single station/ $200.00 network (Order no.: I-1140).
An Educational Computer Game for Mathematics Students Learning Place Value. Graphic Representation of Counting Blocks Are Displayed to Reinforce the Concept of Place Value in the Base-Ten Numbers. Use of Manipulative Tools in Mathematics Is Reinforced. Student Scores Are Retained.
Electronic Courseware Systems, Inc.

Blood Bank Archives.
dBASE III+ IBM PC & compatibles. Contact publisher for price.
An Archival Storage System for Essential Transfusion Information. It Replaces the Typical Manual Card File, Enabling More Accurate & Complete Information Such As Patient Demographics, ABO/Rh, Antibody Screen, Direct Coombs, Number & Identification of Units Transfused, Antibody Identifications, & Transfusion Reactions. Inquiries to the Database Are Easily Made for Patients Who Are Either Active, Inactive, or Purged (Moved to a Floppy Disk for Long-Term Retrievals). Other Reports Allow Retrievals & Tracking Not Otherwise Possible in a Manual System. The System Runs Either As a Stand-Alone System, or Can Be Interfaced with an LCI Laboratory Information System for Efficient Transfer of Pertinent Data. Easy to Use, the Blood Bank Archives Provides an Organized Method to Deal with This Critical Information Function.
LCI.

Blood Bank Systems. *Customer Support:* Software warranty; 24 hours, days a week; 800 number; hardware/software staging; training & seminars; documentation; system personalization; consulting services.
DSM, OpenVMS, DOS, AIX, MSM, OSF/1, HP-UX. DEC, IBM & HP platforms (2Mb). contact publisher for price.
ANTRIM Corp.

Blood Bank Systems. *Customer Support:* Software warranty; 24 hours, days a week; 800 number; hardware/software staging; training & seminars; documentation; system personalization; consulting services.
DEC VAX, Alpha AXP, DECStation & PC platforms using OpenVMS, DMS, OSF/1 or DOS; IBM RISC System 6000 under AIX, Micronetic MUMPS, or DOS; HP9000 under HP-UX. DEC, IBM & HP platforms (2Mb). contact publisher for price.
Meets the Needs of Both the Medical Laboratory & Blood Centers. Donor Management Application Addresses: 1) Donor Processing, Including Registration, Donor Screening & Blood Collection, & Management Reporting, 2) Blood Processing, Including Clearinghouse Login, Worklists, Components Processing, Results Processing, Label & Release to Inventory, & Management Reporting, & 3) Inventory, Including Updates, Manipulation of Components, Shipping, & Management Reporting. Transfusion Services Application Addresses: 1) Clearinghouse Login, Including Worklist Processing, Results Processing, Label & Release to Inventory, & Management Reporting, 2) Crossmatch, Including Transfusion Request Verification, Patient Results Processing, Manipulation of Components, Reserving Blood, Updating Inventory, & Management Reporting, & 3) Inventory, Including Shipping Products & Management Reporting.
ANTRIM Corp.

Blood Gas Consultant 2.0. (Consultant Ser.). *Compatible Hardware:* IBM PC, PC XT, PC AT. *Operating System(s) Required:* PC-DOS, MS-DOS 2.0 or higher. *Language(s):* Compiled BASIC. *Memory Required:* 256k.
disk $50.00.
manual $15.00.
Acid-Base Program Designed to Interpret Arterial Blood Gas Data & Generate Reports. Also Calculates Acute Disorders Overlying Chronic Acid-Base Disturbances.
Rapha Group Software, Inc.

Blood Review. Michael P. Hansen. Jan. 1985. *Compatible Hardware:* Apple. *Operating System(s) Required:* Apple DOS 3.3. *Memory Required:* 64k.
contact publisher for price (ISBN 0-931261-00-7).
Assists Students in Reviewing Important Concepts about the Four Major Components of the Blood: Plasma, Red Blood Cells, White Blood Cells, & Platelets.
Concord Regional Vocational Ctr.

Blown Away: Twisted Villain, Twisted Logic, Twisted Games. Imagination Pilots & MGM-UA Staff. Oct. 1994. *Customer Support:* Free 800 Number Technical Support.
Windows. PC with 486SX 33MHz or higher (8Mb). disk $19.95 (ISBN 1-884899-32-3). Optimal configuration: 486SX 33MHz or higher IBM-compatible full Multimedia PC Level 2 system, 8Mb RAM & 5Mb free hard disk space, double-speed CD-ROM drive with minimum 300 KB/sec transfer rate, VGA plus 640x480 monitor displaying 256 colors, MS-DOS 5.0 or higher, Windows 3.1, MS-DOS CD-ROM Extensions, stereo headphones or speakers, mouse or compatible positioning device, 16 bit Microsoft Windows compatible Sound Card.
In This Adventure Game Sequel to the Successful Movie of the Same Name, the Player Assumes the Role of Jimmy Dove, a Boston Bomb Squad Expert, Who Must Match Wits with an Ingenious Villain Names Justus. In a Race Against Time, the Player Uses Knowledge & Intellect, As Opposed to Violence, to Overcome Various Challenges, Obstacles & Other Clever Puzzles to Rescue Hostages & Save His Daughter.
IVI Publishing, Inc.

BLOX Graphics Builder. Andrew J. Rubel. Feb. 1983. *Compatible Hardware:* DEC VAX; 68000-based systems; 80186, 80286, 80386-based systems. *Operating System(s) Required:* VAX/VMS, VAX/UNIX, other 68000/UNIX. *Language(s):* FORTRAN. *Memory Required:* 10000k. *General Requirements:* FORTRAN compiler, 20Mb on hard disk.
Masscomp, Sun, MicroVAX & other 68000's. contact publisher for price.
VAX/VMS & VAX/UNIX systems. contact publisher for price.
User Interface Management System Creates Graphic Application Programs Interactively. User Interfaces Can Be Designed, Prototyped & Tested Without Writing Any Code.
Rubel Software.

Blue for System Flowcharts. Version: 20. *Compatible Hardware:* Apple Macintosh. *General Requirements:* ImageWriter or LaserWriter.
3.5" disk $1875.00.
CASE Tool.
Advanced Logical Software.

Blue Lodge Program Package. John M. Taylor. *Compatible Hardware:* IBM PC & compatibles. *Operating System(s) Required:* MS-DOS 2.11 or higher. *Language(s):* Compiled BASIC. *Memory Required:* 256k. *General Requirements:* Line printer.
disk $89.00 (ISBN 0-939321-02-5, Order no.: BLPP-M).
Programs Assist a Masonic Lodge Secretary Perform His Duties Such As Posting Dues, Furnishing Name & Address Rosters, Making Mailing Labels for Due Notices, Preparing Merge Files for Form Letters, & Most of All, Aspects of Grand Lodge Reporting That May Be Required in Each State.
Fraternal Software.

Blue Max 2001. Bob Polin. *Compatible Hardware:* Atari 400, 800, XL, XE Series; Commodore 64. *General Requirements:* Joystick.
Atari & Commodore versions on flip sides of same disk. $29.95 (Order no.: A/CDSK-6090).
As a Direct Descendant of Max Chatsworth You Are Called upon to Fight the FURXX Empire Which Has Captured Earthbase Gamma IV. Your Mission Is to Breach Their Defenses, Destroy the Hoverfields with Gravonic Penetrators, & Smash the Symbol on Which the FURXX Empire Is Built.
Broderbund Software, Inc.

Blue Pencil. *Compatible Hardware:* TRS-80.
disk $89.95 (ISBN 0-936200-14-6).
Proofreads a Document for Spelling & Typographical Errors. Words That Are Not Found Are Identified & Displayed on the Screen. Either ELECTRIC PENCIL or RED PENCIL Can Be Used to Correct Mistakes.
Blue Cat.

Blue/60: Data Modeling.
Macintosh (512k or higher). disk $1875.00. *Addl. software required:* ImageWriter or LaserWriter.
Development & Maintenance Tool for System Designers, Database Administrators & Others Involved in Optimizing Data Processing. Used to Create & Maintain Data Models. Features Include Ability to Enter Detailed Information About Entities & Attributes, & to Make the Link to Layout of a Physical Database. User Can Draw Data Model (Bachman) Diagrams & Define the Relationships Between All Objects in the Data Dictionary. Program Can Perform Normalization to Third Normal Form Following Boyce-Codd Method, & Automatically Generate New Entities. Also Helps User with Access Path Analysis & Optimizing Response Times & Disk Space.
Advanced Logical Software.

Blue Star. 1985. *Compatible Hardware:* IBM PC & compatibles. *Memory Required:* 256k. *General Requirements:* 2 disk drives, printer.
disk $300.00 (ISBN 0-925182-13-3, Order no.: M-67).
Astrological System: Home Chart Service, Chart Filing System, & Transits & Progressions.
Matrix Software.

Blue Star 64. 1985. *Compatible Hardware:* Commodore 64 with printer. *Memory Required:* 64k.
disk $100.00 (ISBN 0-925182-12-5, Order no.: B5-64).
Professional Chart Service Program.
Matrix Software.

Blue Star Time Change Atlas. 1985. *Compatible Hardware:* IBM with 2 disk drives & printer. *Memory Required:* 256k.
disk $50.00 (ISBN 0-925182-30-3).
Provides Longitude, Latitude & Time Changes for 1200 Cities World-Wide.
Matrix Software.

BlueFish. *Compatible Hardware:* IBM PC & compatibles. *Operating System(s) Required:* PC-DOS. *Language(s):* Assembly, C. *Memory Required:* 256k.

single-user site license $750.00.
publishing license $3500.00.
Evaluation Kit $100.00.
BlueFish CD-ROM. 50 fully searchable full-text CD-ROMs from user's own ASCII files $9800.00.
Full Text Data Base Management for the PC. Offers English-Language Syntax for All Commands & Operations; Boolean & Range Searches by Sentence, Paragraph, or Document; Full-Screen Display with Forward & Backward Scrolling Through the Entire Database; Pattern-Matching "Wild Card" Searches; Building Speeds over 4Mb per Hour on a Standard IBM PC AT; Indexes up to 1 Million Words; Automatically Masks All Words Occurring over 32,000 Times in a Single Database. Builds Databases Larger Than 32Mb with Additional Software. Works with Floppies, Hard Disks, or CD-ROM's. Search & Retrieval Only Module Is Available for Redistribution.
Lotus Development Corp.

Blueprint. *Version:* 5. Aug. 1994. *Items Included:* 300-page manual in binder, 2 template disks. *Customer Support:* Free technical support Mon-Fri 9-5:30 EST, 30-day money back guarantee.
MAC-DOS (1Mb). Macintosh, LC, SI, Plus, SE, II, IIx, IIcx & higher, Native Power Macintosh. 3.5" disk $295.00. *Optimal configuration:* 2Mb.
Professional 2D CAD Package. Offers High Precision, Speed, Ease of Use & Reliability at an Affodable Price. Features: Layers, Double Lines, Dashed Lines, Fillets, Hatching, Mirroring, Editable Fill Patterns, Cubic & Bezier Splines, Multiple Keyboard, Palette & Menu Options for Drawing Many Features, Auto-Dimensioning, & Array Duplication - along with More Advanced Features Such As Built-In DXF Translator, Auto-Wall Tool, Tolerancing, Encapsulated PostScript, Hierarchical Symbol Library, Test That Rotates by Degrees, Minutes & Seconds, Nine Decimal Place Precision & Object-by-Object Color.
Graphsoft, Inc.

Blueprint of a LAN. Craig Chaiken. Sep. 1989.
MS-DOS. IBM PC & compatibles. disk $23.95 (ISBN 1-55851-052-4).
MS-DOS. IBM PC & compatibles. disk $38.95, incl. book (ISBN 1-55851-066-4).
Provides Hands-On Introduction to Microcomputer Networks & Affords an Opportunity to Use a Network, View the Code That Makes It Run, & Customize the Code. Includes Introduction to LAN Theories, Discussions on Building & Installing LAN Communication Cables & Configuring & Troubleshooting Network Hardware & Software. Complete Intel 8086 Source Code & Object Files Included.
M & T Bks.

BMDP Statistical Software. *Compatible Hardware:* IBM PC XT, PC AT, or compatible hard disk systems (including mainframes & minis). contact publisher for price.
Users Can Choose Any Combination of Programs That Suit Their Needs. Routines Available Include: Frequencies & Percents, Chi Square, Scatterplots & Histograms, Analysis of Variance & Covariance, Planned & Post Hoc Comparisons, Stepwise Logic Regression, Nonlinear Regression, Factor Analysis, Repeated Measures ANOVA, Canonical Correlation, Spectral Analysis, Time Series, etc.
BMDP Statistical Software.

BNA Corporate Foreign Tax Credit Planner. *Version:* 93.1. Peter Whitehead. Jun. 1993. *Items Included:* Manual inside 3-ring binder. *Customer Support:* Initial price: Single-user $1995, Network $2495. Renewal price: Single-user $995, Network $1250 per year. Includes all updates & toll-free telephone support.
MS-DOS. IBM PC & compatibles (400k). disk $1995.00 single user, $2495.00 network, 45-day approval evaluation avail. *Nonstandard peripherals required:* Hard disk. *Networks supported:* Novell.
Powerful New Software Program That Helps U.S. Multinational Corporations Optimize Their Use of the Foreign Tax Credit (FTC) & Evaluate Numerous "What If" Foreign Tax Credit Scenarios. Utilizing the Full Capability of the BNA Corporate Tax Spreadsheet, the BNA Corporate Foreign Tax Credit Planner Offers Practitioners the Ability to Calculate the Allowable FTC for up to 12 Categories (Baskets) of Foreign Income with Emphasis on Applicable Section 904 Limitations.
BNA Software.

BNA Corporate Tax Spreadsheet. *Version:* 93.1. *Compatible Hardware:* IBM PC, PS/2, AT & compatibles. *Operating System(s) Required:* PC-DOS/MS-DOS 2.0, 3.2. *Memory Required:* 500k. *General Requirements:* Hard disk. *Items Included:* Full program, users' manual. *Customer Support:* Toll-free hotline: 1-800-424-2938.
Single-user version, $995.00; network version, $1495.00. Free working model available.
Calculates Federal & State Taxes for Domestic C Type, Personal Service, or Closely-Held Corporations & Automatically Handles the Carryback & Carryover of NOLs, Credits, Capital Losses, Contributions, & More. Analyzes up to 12 Years at Once; Displays up to Three Multi-Year Scenarios on Screen at Once; Complete Set of Reports.
BNA Software.

BNA Estate Tax Spreadsheet. *Version:* 94.2. May 1985. *Compatible Hardware:* IBM PC PS/2, XT, AT & compatibles. *Operating System(s) Required:* DOS 2.0, 3.2. *Memory Required:* 520k free RAM - program will run with one case on as little as 490k. *Items Included:* Full program, users' manual. *Customer Support:* Toll-free hotline: 1-800-424-2938.
Single-user version, $1295.00; network version, $1945.00. Free working model available.
Computes Federal Estate & State Death Taxes for All 50 States & the District of Columbia & Handles Many Sophisticated Computations Including Interrelated Residue Calculations for Marital & Charitable Deductions, GST, Section 6166 Interrelated Interest Calculations, Gift Tax Computations Including GRITS, GRATS, GRUTS & More. Simultaneously Calculates Three Family Estate Plans or Six Plans for a Single Decedent; Comprehensive Reports Include an Estate Tax Summary & Liquidity Analysis. Tested & Approved by the American Bar Association.
BNA Software.

BNA Fixed Asset Management System. *Version:* 94.2. *Items Included:* Full program, user's manual. *Customer Support:* Toll-free hotline: 1-800-424-2938.
IBM PC, PS/2, XT, AT or compatibles (500k). Single-user version, $995.00; network version, $1495.00. Free working model available. *Nonstandard peripherals required:* Hard disk drive.
Six Depreciation Books Available Including Book, Federal, State, AMT, ACE, & Earnings & Profits; All Caclutated Automatically. Program Supports 32 Depreciation Methods, Handles up to 20,000 Assets for Each Company, & Provides a Complete Set of Tax & Asset Management Reports. Handles Numerous Automatic Calculations Including Section 179 Expense & Application of Company Limit, & Determination & Enforcement of the Mid-Quarter Convention.
BNA Software.

The BNA Income Tax Spreadsheet with Fifty State Planner. *Version:* 94.2. Sep. 1983. *Compatible Hardware:* IBM PC, PS/2, XT, AT or compatibles. *Memory Required:* 500k. *General Requirements:* Hard disk required; printer recommended. *Items Included:* Full program, users' manual. *Customer Support:* Toll-free hotline: 1-800-424-2938.
Single-user version, $890.00; network version, $1,335.00. Federal only: single-user version, $495.00; network version, $750.00. Free working model available.
Recognized As the Industry's Leading Tax Planner, This Program Calculates Federal & State Income Taxes for Individuals from 1987 on, Provides Projections for 10 Years and/or Cases, Handles Input from K-1s & 1099s with a Complete Audit Trail, & with the Fifty State Planner, Handles Taxes for All 50 States, the District of Columbia, & New York City. Automatically Handles Complete Tax Limitations & Phase-Outs & Provides over 60 Reports.
BNA Software.

BNA Real Estate Investment Spreadsheet. *Version:* 90.1. Apr. 1985. *Compatible Hardware:* IBM PC, PS/2, XT, AT & compatibles. *Operating System(s) Required:* DOS 2.0 256k, DOS 3.2. *Memory Required:* 500k. *General Requirements:* Hard disk, printer recommended. *Items Included:* Full program, users' manual. *Customer Support:* Toll-free hotline: 1-800-424-2938.
Single-user version, $395.00; network version, $595.00. Free working model available.
Computes Yearly Cash Flows & Rates of Return for up to a 40-Year Period & Handles Many Tedious Calculations Such As Depreciation, Loan Amortization, Taxes & Rates of Return. Complete Set of Reports Includes Income Statement, Balance Sheet, & Statement of Cash Flows.
BNA Software.

Bo Jackson Baseball.
MS-DOS. IBM PC XT/AT & compatibles (512K). contact publisher for price. *Nonstandard peripherals required:* 16 color, VGA 5.25" or 3.5" disk drive. *Addl. software required:* CGA, EGA.
Kickstart 1.2 or higher. Commodore Amiga 500/1000/2000 (512K). contact publisher for price. *Nonstandard peripherals required:* 1 disk drive, color monitor required.
What's More Exciting Than Professional Baseball? Bo Jackson Baseball Captures the Energy & Drive of Pro Baseball's Hottest Star. Learn & Compete with Bo in Big League Play. Practice Batting Techniques with the All Star Himself. Then Battle the Big League Pitchers in Intense One on One Competitions That Really Test Your Skills.
Data East U.S.A., Inc.

Boa. *Compatible Hardware:* Apple II. *Operating System(s) Required:* Apple DOS 3.2, 3.3. *Language(s):* Applesoft, Machine. *Memory Required:* 48k. *General Requirements:* Paddle or joystick recommended.
disk $29.95.
Maze-Chase Game.
Dynacomp, Inc.

Boardroom Graphics. *Version:* 4.0. Mark Haley & Marjorie Haley. *Compatible Hardware:* IBM PC XT. *Memory Required:* 384k.
disk $150.00.
Presentation-Graphics Package for On-Screen Slide Shows with Sound Capability & Optional Run-Time Version. Graphics & Chart-Making Features Include Zoom & Undo Commands; Bar, Line, Pie, Text, Organization, Scatter, 3-D & Flow Charts; X/Y Plots, Trend Lines with Linear or Curvilinear Trends; Multiple Charts On One Screen; & Free Positioning of Charts on Screen. Color Schemes Are Included with 8 User-

TITLE INDEX

Selectable Colors. Four Typefaces & 4 Font Sizes Are Available. Output Options Include HP Laserjet, Dot-Matrix Printer, Film Recorder Plotter & Color Ink-Jet Printer. Imports ASCII, WKS, DIF & SLK File Formats. Also Includes On-Screen Help & Scientific Plotting.
Analytical Software, Inc.

Body Chemistry 3: Point of Seduction. May 1995. *Customer Support:* Dedicated voice mail phone number; will respond back to consumer.
Windows 3.1 or higher; Macintosh. IBM or 100% compatible 486SX 25MHz (4Mb); 68030/68040 Color Mac System 7.1 or higher (4Mb). CD-ROM disk $19.99 (ISBN 1-57339-012-7, Order no.: ROMI2931NH). *Nonstandard peripherals required:* 2X CD-ROM drive.
Andrew Stevens & Morgan Fairchild Star in This Erotic Thriller about a Hollywood Writer Who Thinks the Story of His Best Friends Death May Be His Ticket to Fame & Fortune.
Image Entertainment.

Body Park. Sep. 1994. *Customer Support:* Free unlimited customer support.
Windows. 386 or higher (4Mb). CD-ROM disk $49.95 (ISBN 1-886031-00-2, Order no.: 10001). *Nonstandard peripherals required:* Sound Board, CD-ROM drive. *Optimal configuration:* 486 33MHz, 8Mb RAM.
Macintosh. Macintosh (4Mb). CD-ROM disk $49.95 (ISBN 1-886031-01-0, Order no.: 10102). *Nonstandard peripherals required:* CD-ROM drive, color monitor. *Addl. software required:* System 6.0.7 or higher.
An Interactive Adventure Where Kids Learn about Anatomy, Nutrition, Health & Safety Through Games, Songs & Cartoon Characters.
Virtual Entertainment, Inc.

Body Shots - Business. Oct. 1993. *Items Included:* Manual & user guide, reference card, hints & tips for use. *Customer Support:* 90 day warranty, unlimited internal use of Bodyshot Images, unlimited commercial use of images with free registration, restrictions apply to repackaging or resale of images.
Macintosh System 6 or System 7. MAC II or higher (4Mb). CD-ROM disk $295.00 (ISBN 1-883481-02-3). *Nonstandard peripherals required:* CD-ROM drive. *Addl. software required:* High end DTP, Image Editor or Presentation, Paint, Draw Software or any application that imports TIFF Files. *Networks supported:* Network license available.
PC-DOS & Windows. 386 or higher (4Mb). disk $295.00 (ISBN 1-883481-03-1). *Nonstandard peripherals required:* CD-ROM drive. *Addl. software required:* High end DTP, Image Editor or Presentation, Paint, Draw Software or any application that imports TIFF files. *Networks supported:* Network license available.
Offers Designers & Desktop Publishers a Photographic Stock Collection of Very High Resolution Images of People in an Extensive Variety of Activities. Images Are Shot by Top Photographers Using Professional Models, Make-Up Artists, & Stylists. Titles in the Series Feature Professional & Business Activities; Sports, Health & Keep-Fit Poses; & Romantic Situations. Additional Lifestyle Titles Are Being Developed. Individual Images Can Be Assembled to Compose a Scene of Your Choice. Each CD-ROM Offers a Specific Title Theme for Unlimited Commercial Use in Advertising, Publishing & Multimedia. Each Image Is Stored in 24-Bit Color TIFF & Is Typically 2200 X 1000 Pixels or Greater. First Title in the Series.
Digital Wisdom, Inc.

The Body System: Complete Personal Fitness Program. Berthold Brecht. Jan. 1993. *Items Included:* Complete manual & 3.5" or 5.25" disk. *Customer Support:* 90 days warranty, free phone support.
DOS 3.0. IBM PC or 100% compatibles (640k). disk $49.95.
Builds Perfectly Balanced Workout Routines That You Can Take to the Gym with You. These Customized Routines Are Based on Your Personal Statistics, Goals & Progress. Included Is Animation of All Exercises, Complete Anatomical Figures That Identify Ideal Exercises & Graphs to Display Progress. Many, Many Other Features.
Vision Technologies.

Bodylink. *Compatible Hardware:* Commodore 64, 128.
$99.95, incl. demo program (Order no.: BDLC64-03-001).
Dual Channel Microprocessor Driven Body Signal Monitor for Collecting EMG, GSR, EEG, EKG, Temperature, Heart Rate, Blood Pressure, Breath, Sounds, Optics, & Posture.
Bodylog.

Bodyscope. *Compatible Hardware:* Commodore 64, 128.
ROM cartridge $69.95 (Order no.: SOFC64-07-012).
Used with Any Sensor, Cartridge Is Multi-Purpose & Can Be Used to: (a) Monitor & Display up to Four Channels of Body Signals, (b) Immediately Display Moving Graphs of Three Signals Simultaneously, (c) Save Data on Disk & Printer, (d) Customize the Graphs with the Threshold, Adapt, & Zoom Options to: Create Personalized Games, Conduct Small Experiments, or Design Self-Help Coaching Protocols for Sports Skills, Muscle Rehabilitation, Stress Reduction, & Body Signal Control, (e) Write BASIC Programs That Control the BODYLINK's Data Collection & Signal Manipulation, or (f) Load & Store Programs or Data on a Disk or on a MICROMEM Cartridge.
Bodylog.

Bond Analysis. *Compatible Hardware:* Atari 800. *Operating System(s) Required:* AOS. *Language(s):* Atari BASIC. *Memory Required:* 24k.
disk $9.95 (Order no.: CX8106).
Gives the User the Current Yield & the Total Yield of a Bond Held to Maturity. Accrued Interest for a Specific Bond When Given the Annual Coupon Payment Is Displayed for the User, As Is the Redemption Price At Maturity, Time to Maturity, & Requested Rate of Return. A Tool for Investors on a Fixed Income.
Atari Corp.

Bond Computation. *Compatible Hardware:* Commodore 64, IBM PC, TI 99/4A.
Language(s): Extended BASIC.
TI. disk $14.95 (Order no.: 201XD).
IBM, Commodore. contact publisher for price.
River City Software, Inc.

Bond Portfolio Manager. Version: 92.6. Lawrence R. Rosen. *Items Included:* Complete on-disk documentation & Reports. *Customer Support:* Free telephone consultation.
MS-DOS. PCs, PS/2 (128k). disk $89.00. *Addl. software required:* Spreadsheet, including Lotus 1-2-3.
Macintosh (128k). 3.5" disk $89.00. *Addl. software required:* Excel, Microsoft Works or Claris Works.
PRODOS or DOS 3.3. Apple II Series (64k). disk $89.00. *Addl. software required:* Appleworks.
Bond Portfolio Analysis Features Include: (A) Calculates Market Value of Each Bond & the Entire Portfolio, Priced to Lesser Value of Call or Maturity; (B) Month & Day Each Interest Payment Is Due (So That As Interest Is Received or Coupons Clipped They Can Merely Be Checked off on the List for That Month of Receivables Expected & So That Interest Receipts Can Be Balanced by Month Throughout the Year); (C) Call Dates & Put Dates in Chronological Order; (D) Unrealized Gain or Loss for Each Bond Ranked in Order of Magnitude from Largest Loss to Largest Gain. Calculations Are Made Using Taxable Basis Adjusted for Amortization. Calculates Duration & Convexity for Each Bond & the Entire Portfolio.
Larry Rosen Co.

Bond Smart. 1985. *Compatible Hardware:* IBM Micros & compatibles. *Operating System(s) Required:* PC-DOS/MS-DOS. *Language(s):* C. *Memory Required:* 640k. *General Requirements:* 70Mb hard disk. *Items Included:* Operator's manual, conversion manual, auditors manual. *Customer Support:* Onsite training, telephone support, annual maintenance; first year free, $950.00 next year.
monthly lease, initial customization $900.00.
Networks supported: Banyan, Novell, etc.
Bond Accounting & Decision Making Package That Consists of Five Modules: Bond Swap, Bond Accounting, Bond Portfolio Management, Bond Calculator & Mortgage Calculator. Features Include: Cash & Accrual Accounting, Amortization & Accretion, Automatic Pricing, Tax & Book Profits, Institutional & Personal Swaps, Single & Multi Bond Swaps, GAAP & Tax Swaps, Duration & Immunization, Realized Yields, Optional Spread Analysis & "What-If" Capability. Handles Variable Rate Bond, Paydown Bond, GL Accounting, Multiportfolios & Choices of Amortization Accretion. Over 100 Standard Reports, Plus a Report Writer. Module Available for Dollar & Reverse Repos.
Wall Street Consulting Group.

Bond Value. 1982. *Compatible Hardware:* MS-DOS & IBM & compatibles. *Operating System(s) Required:* MS-DOS. *Language(s):* Microsoft BASIC & BASICA.
disk $65.00 (Order no.: 263).
Calculates Present Value of Available Bonds to the Analyst or Potential Bond Investor.
Resource Software International, Inc.

Bonds & Interest Rates Software. Version: 2.0. Albert Bookbinder. Aug. 1993. *Compatible Hardware:* IBM PC. *Operating System(s) Required:* PC-DOS/MS-DOS. *Language(s):* BASIC. *Memory Required:* 64k. *Items Included:* Handbook. *Customer Support:* Telephone support.
disk $144.00 (ISBN 0-916106-08-X).
Includes 16 Interactive Programs on Bonds & Interest Rates; Evaluates Price, Return, & Risk on Fixed Income Investments. Programs Included Are: Moving Average, Exponential Moving Average, Exponential Smoothing for Forecasting, Multiple Correlation, Value of Treasury Bill, Yield on 91-Day Treasury Bill, Yield on 6-Month Treasury Bill, Yield on One-Year Treasury Bill, Compound Interest, Yield on Notes & Bonds, High-Coupon Bond Yield Tables, Monthly Mortgage Payments, Present Value of Annuity, Present Value of Future Lump Sum, Rate of Return on Investment, & Bond Yield after Taxes.
Programmed Pr.

BondScholar. Version: 7.1. *Compatible Hardware:* IBM PC & compatibles, PC XT, PC AT. *Operating System(s) Required:* MS-DOS. *Memory Required:* 358k. *General Requirements:* Epson, IBM, or similar printer. *Items Included:* Basic system-additional modules $500.00 ea. *Customer Support:* Telephone with maintenance contract. $1995.00.

Computes Prices, Cashflow Yields, Yields to Average Life, After Tax Yields, Compound Rates of Returns, Durations on Almost Any Type of Fixed Income Security (Bonds, Mortgages, Preferred Stocks, Treasuries, CATS, TIGRS, etc.). Additional Modules Provide Other Analytical Functions; Prepayment Models for MBS, Swaps, CPR/Yield Sensitivity, Reinvestment Rate/Yield (Total Return) Sensitivity etc.
Investek, Inc.

Book & Tax Depreciation. Version: 2.02. *Compatible Hardware:* Altos Series 5-15D, Series 5-5D, 580-XX, ACS8000-XX; Burroughs B20-3 with 2 disk drives; DEC Rainbow 100 with 2 disk drives, Rainbow 100+ with 10Mb hard disk; IBM PC with 2 disk drives, PC XT, PC AT, IBM compatibles; Kaypro 11/IV with 2 disk drives, Kaypro 10; Xerox 820 with 2 disk drives; ZILOG MCZ-250. *Operating System(s) Required:* CP/M, MP/M, CP/M-86/80, PC-DOS, MS-DOS.
License fee unit. $750.00 (Order no.: BOOK AND TAX).
License fee site. $1125.00.
Maintenance unit. $250.00.
Maintenance site. $370.00.
Designed to Store Asset Information & Compute Annual Depreciation for Both Financial Statement Preparation & Tax Return Preparation (Form 4562). Computes Depreciation under ACRS (Accelerated Cost Recovery System), ADR (Class Life Asset Depreciation Range) & Other (Pre-1971 Assets Guidelines, Post-1970 Facts & Circumstances). Interfaces with PRE-AUDIT.
Coopers & Lybrand.

Bookdex. Theodore Hines. 1982. *Compatible Hardware:* IBM PC & Compatibles. *Operating System(s) Required:* MS-DOS. *Language(s):* BASIC. *Memory Required:* 64k.
disk $450.00.
Capital Systems Group, Inc.

Bookends Extended. Jonathan D. Ashwell. May 1985. *Compatible Hardware:* Apple IIe, IIc, IIgs. *Operating System(s) Required:* ProDOS. *Memory Required:* 128k. *General Requirements:* 80 column display.
3-1/2" & 5-1/4" disk included $149.95.
Database Program That Helps Users Enter & Print Out Information about Magazines, Books & Journals into an "Electronic" Card Catalog. Allows Data to Be Printed in Fully Customized Bibliographic & Footnote Formats. Creates Alphabetical List of Authors or Keywords. Output Can Go to Screen, Printer or Text File.
Sensible Software, Inc.

Bookends Extended-SP: School Pak, 10 5-1/4" or 3-1/2" disks. Jonathan Ashwell. 1987. *Compatible Hardware:* Apple IIe, IIc, IIgs. *Operating System(s) Required:* ProDOS. *Memory Required:* 128k. *General Requirements:* 80-column display.
$449.85.
Database Program That Helps Users Enter & Print out Information about Magazines, Books & Journals into an "Electronic" Card Catalog. Allows Data to Be Printed in Fully Customized Bibliographic & Footnote Formats. Creates Alphabetical List of Authors or Keywords.
Sensible Software, Inc.

Bookends II. May 1991.
Macintosh Classic, Plus, SE, LC, SE/30, SI, II, IIci, IIcx, IIx, IIfx (1Mb). 3.5" disk $124.95 (ISBN 0-926776-27-4).
Specialized Database for Keeping Track of Magazine Articles, Journals, & Books. Enter References, Find Information & Generate Reports or Bibliographies. Product is a Hypercard Stack That Runs in Conjunction with Hypercard (Version 2) Which Is Supplied with the Program. Stores Titles, Author, Journal, Volume, Page Number, Location, Key Words, & Abstract, up to 30,000 Characters per Field. Imports from Dialog, BRS Medline, Tab Delimited Text Files, & Other Bookends.
Sensible Software, Inc.

Bookends PC. Aug. 1987. *Compatible Hardware:* IBM PC, PC XT, PC AT & compatibles. *Memory Required:* 256k.
disk $149.95 (ISBN 0-926776-08-8).
Expanded Database Program That Helps Users Enter & Print out Information about Magazines, Scientific Journals, Newspapers, & Books in an "Electronic" Card Catalog. Allows Data to Be Printed in Fully Customized Bibliographic & Footnote Formats. Uses up to 640k of Memory for References. Able to Search by Any Combination of Categories.
Sensible Software, Inc.

Bookie Buster I Football Analysis. 1986. *Compatible Hardware:* Apple I, II; Commodore 64/128; IBM PC & compatibles. *Memory Required:* IBM 256k, Apple 64k, Commodore 64k.
3.5" or 5.25" disk $99.95.
Long-Term Trend Analysis Including a Complete Data Base of All NFL Games from 1978. There Are Twenty-One Separate Analyses Used to Project the Spread Winner. For Professional Football Only.
Professor Jones Professional Handicapping Systems.

Bookie Buster II Football Analysis. 1986. *Compatible Hardware:* Commodore 64/128, IBM PC & compatibles. *Memory Required:* Commodore 64, IBM 256k.
3.5" or 5.25" disk $179.95.
Contains More Analysis Systems Than the BOOKIE BUSTER I. Performs Sixty-One Separate Analysis & Allows the User to Select the Number of Years to Be Analyzed in the Regression Analysis Before Predicting a Winner.
Professor Jones Professional Handicapping Systems.

Bookkeep. *Compatible Hardware:* IBM. (source code included). *Memory Required:* 128k.
disk $69.95.
General Ledger & Financial Statement Preparation Program Designed for Small Business Use.
Dynacomp, Inc.

The Bookkeeper. Irvine Center Software. *Operating System(s) Required:* MS-DOS. (source code included).
disk $99.00.
Includes Accounts Receivable & Accounts Payable Ledgers, Income Statement, Balance Sheet, IRS Depreciation Schedules, & Loan Amortization Schedules. Finished Statements Can Be Printed in Standard Accounting Format.
ILAR Systems, Inc.

Bookmobile Software. 1992. *Items Included:* Manual. *Customer Support:* One year of customer support is included in purchase price of software. The program is at no charge when a CIRC/CAT is purchased for the main library & one for the bookmobile.
MS-DOS. IBM AT, PS/2 & compatibles (640k).
5.25" disk N/C if purchase a CIRC/CAT for main library & Bookmobile (ISBN 0-927875-29-2, Order no.: 1910). *Optimal configuration:* 386/486 processor, 2Mb RAM, hard disk drive access speed of less than 20ms, DOS 5.0 or higher. *Networks supported:* Any NetBIOS Network.
MS-DOS. IBM AT, PS/2 & compatibles (640k).
3.5" disk N/C if purchase a CIRC/CAT for main library & Bookmobile (ISBN 0-927875-32-2, Order no.: 1910). *Optimal configuration:* 386/486 processor, 2Mb RAM, hard disk drive access speed of less than 20ms, DOS 5.0 or higher. *Networks supported:* Any NetBIOS Network.
Lets You Merge the Circulation & Catalog Data from Your Bookmobile's CIRC/CAT Program into the CIRC/CAT at Your Main Library. Patrons Benefit from Full On-Line Catalog & Circulation Features. Program Also Lets User Print Separate Bookmobile Reports.
Winnebago Software Co.

Books In Print Plus. 1995. *Items Included:* Monthly Updates. *Customer Support:* Information & Assistance Hotline; Electronic Bulletin Board.
DOS 3.1 or higher; Windows 3.1 or later. IBM 386 or higher. CD-ROM disk $1095.00 for 1 year (Order no.: BP110). *Nonstandard peripherals required:* CD-ROM Player running under MS-DOS Extensions 2.0 or later.
System 6.02 or later. Macintosh Plus, Classic, SE, IIci, IIsi, Quadra Series, Powerbook or equivalent (1Mb). CD-ROM disk $3121.00 for 3 years. *Nonstandard peripherals required:* Apple CD SC, Toshiba, or other compatible CD-ROM reader.
Features All Genres & Forms of Material among the 1.5 Million Citations Included. Includes 45,000 Publishers & Their Addresses, over 72,000 LC Subject Headings, & over 7,000 Sears & LC Subject Headings for Children.
R. R. Bowker.

Books In Print Plus: With Book Reviews. 1995. *Items Included:* Monthly Updates. *Customer Support:* CD-ROM hotline support line & electronic bulletin board.
DOS 3.1 or higher or Windows 3.1. IBM 286 or higher (535k) for DOS; IBM 386 or higher ((4Mb) for Windows. CD-ROM disk $1595 for 1 year (Order no.: RV110). *Nonstandard peripherals required:* Hard disk (minimum 10 Mb free space); CD-ROM player running under MS-DOS extensions 2.0 or later.
System 6.02 or higher. Macintosh Plus, Classic, SE, IIci, IIsi, Quadra Series, Powerbook, or equivalent (1Mb). CD-ROM disk $4546 for 3 years. *Nonstandard peripherals required:* Apple CD SC, Toshiba, or other compatible CD-ROM reader & Macintosh CD-Setup system disk or appropriate drivers.
Complete with the Unabridged BOOKS IN PRINT Database, This Value-Added CD-ROM Features over 225,000 Full Text Reviews from 12 of the Most Esteemed Book Reviewing Media: Publisher's Weekly, Library Journal, School Library Journal, Choice, ALA Booklist, Kirkus Reviews, the Bookstore Journal, Reference and Research Book News, Sci-Tech Book News, University Press Book News, BIOSIS, & VOYA.
R.R. Bowker.

Books In Print with Book Reviews Plus. 1996. *Customer Support:* Call 1-800-323-3288 for availability of VOYA reviews.
IBM version. MS-DOS. CD-ROM disk for 1 year $1595.00 (Order no.: RV 110).
IBM version. CD-ROM disk for 3 years $4546.00 (Order no.: RV 110).
Macintosh version. CD-ROM disk for 1 year $1595.00 (Order no.: RVM 110).
Macintosh version. CD-ROM disk for 3 years $4546.00.
Complete with the Unabridged BOOKS IN PRINT Database, This Value-Added CD-ROM features over 225,000 full text reviews from Library Journal, Publisher's Weekly, School Library Journal, Choice, Booklist, Reference & Research Book News, Sci-Tech Book News, University Press Book News, Kirkus, BIOSIS, Bookstore Journal, VOYA, & more to come - all on the same CD-ROM.
R. R. Bowker.

TITLE INDEX

Books Out Of Print Plus. 1995. *Items Included:* Quarterly Updates. *Customer Support:* Information & Assistance Hotline; Electronic Bulletin Board.
DOS 3.1 or higher. IBM 286 or higher (535k). CD-ROM disk $195.00 for 1 year.
Nonstandard peripherals required: Hard disk (minimum 10 MB free space); CD-ROM player running under MS-DOS extensions 2.0 or later.
CD-ROM disk $585.00 for 3 years.
Every Year, Thousands of Titles Are Declared Out-of-Print or Out-of-Stock Indefinitely. This CD-ROM Archive Allows User to Identify, Evaluate, & Verify the Status of Some 680,000 Titles Which Have Lapsed into O/P Status from 1979 to the Present. A Valuable Support Tool for Used Book Dealers, Reference Librarians, & Interlibrary Loan.
R.R. Bowker.

Books Out Of Print Plus: With Book Reviews. 1995. *Items Included:* Quarterly Updates. *Customer Support:* Information & Assistance Hotline, Electronic Bulletin Board.
DOS 3.1 or higher. IBM 286 or higher (535k). CD-ROM disk $395.00 for one year (Order no.: OP110). *Nonstandard peripherals required:* Hard disk (10 Mb of free space); CD-ROM player running under MS-DOS extensions 2.0 or later.
CD-ROM disk $1126.00 for three years.
Each Year, Thousands of Titles Are Declared Out-of-Print or Out-of-Stock Indefinitely. This CD-ROM Archive, Newly Enhanced with Full Text Reviews from 12 Key Reviewing Media, Allows User to Identify, Evaluate, & Verify the Status of Some 680,000 Titles Which Have Lapsed into O/P Status from 1979 to the Present.
R. R. Bowker.

Boring Logs. Dec. 1988. *Compatible Hardware:* IBM PC & compatibles. *Operating System(s) Required:* PC-DOS/MS-DOS. *Memory Required:* 640k. *General Requirements:* IBM or AT compatible monitor, graphics printer (Epson; HP Laser Jet II; HP 7475 Plotter).
3.5" or 5.25" disk $400.00.
Designed for Input of Boring Data. Flexibility in Design of Final Page & File Management for Retrieval & Editing.
Rambow Enterprises.

Borland C++. *Version:* 2.0. Mar. 1991. PC/MS-DOS 3.0 or higher. IBM & compatibles (640k). disk $495.00 (ISBN 0-87524-226-X). *Nonstandard peripherals required:* Hard disk, Microsoft Windows 3.0.
Complete C & C++ Programming Environment for DOS & Windows. Compiler & Tools with Everything Needed to Develop & Debug Microsoft Windows 3 & DOS Applications.
Borland International, Inc.

Borlog. *Version:* 2.1. Nov. 1988. *Compatible Hardware:* IBM PC & compatibles. *Operating System(s) Required:* PC-DOS/MS-DOS. *Memory Required:* 128k. *General Requirements:* Dot matrix or laser printer.
contact publisher for price.
Creates a Log Based on Laboratory Tests Results & Field Observations of Borings of Variable Depth. Test Results Including: Natural Moisture, Strain, Unconfined Shear Stress, RQD, Loss on Ignition, Unit Dry Weight, Blow Count. Provides Graphic Representation of Material Encountered, Sampling Method Indicated.
Specialized Software.

BOS/Accounts Payable. *Version:* 6.1. *Compatible Hardware:* IBM PC & compatibles. *Operating System(s) Required:* SBOS, CBOS, MBOS, BOS/LAN, DOS, NOVELL, UNIX, VMS. *Language(s):* BOS COBOL. *Memory Required:* 256k. *General Requirements:* Hard disk.
Single-User. with documentation $600.00.
Multi-User. $1200.00.
manual $16.00.
15% of list annually.
Menu-Driven Program That Validates Data on Entry & Integrates with the General Ledger & AutoClerk for Special Reports. Maintains Vendor Accounts, Prints Checks, & Provides a Variety of Management Reports Such As Disbursement Journals, Job Cost Analysis, Purchase Details, & Trial Balances. Vendors Can Be Given Priorities Used for Selection During Automatic Payment Runs.
BOS National, Inc.

BOS/Accounts Receivable. *Version:* 3.0B. *Compatible Hardware:* IBM PC & compatibles. *Operating System(s) Required:* BOS/5, MBOS/5, BOS/LAN, DOS, NOVELL, UNIX, VMS. *Language(s):* BOS COBOL. *Memory Required:* 256k.
Single-User. disk $600.00.
Multi-User. $1200.00.
15% of list annually.
manual $16.00.
Allows User to Enter Invoice & Credit Details, Make Adjustments, Allocate Payments to Invoices, Choose Balance Forward or Open-Item Accounting Method, Select an Accounting Period, Maintain Customer Statistics, Calculate Finance Charges, Generate Management Reports & Inquire on Account Status. Integrates With BOS/General Ledger. Compatible with AUTOCLERK. When Used Together, Customized Reports & Programs Can Be Created to Meet User Specifications.
BOS National, Inc.

BOS COBOL. *Compatible Hardware:* IBM PC, PC XT, PC AT,386. *Operating System(s) Required:* SBOS, CBOS, MBOS, BOS/LAN, NOVELL, DOS, VMS, UNIX, OS/2. *Language(s):* BOS COBOL. *Memory Required:* 45k. *General Requirements:* 2 disk drives. *Customer Support:* 15% for annual maintenance.
contact publisher for price.
single user with documentation $450.00.
multi-user with documentation $900.00.
manual $30.00.
COBOL Language Containing All Standard ANSI COBOL Verbs, with Structured Programming & Overlay Management Features. Data Management Facilities Include File & Record Locking, Spooling, & Logical Physical Unit Assignments. Overlay Management Capability & Sort Facilities Are Standard Features. Arithmetic Is 18 Decimal Digits.
BOS National, Inc.

BOS/COBOL Symbolic Debug: Delopment Pack. *Version:* 6.1. Oct. 1988. *Compatible Hardware:* IBM PC & compatibles. *Memory Required:* 256k. *General Requirements:* BOS operating system.
$1500.00 to $6000.00.
Complete Development Environment for Multi-User COBOL Applications Source-Code & Symbolic Debugger Integrated with Compiler, Linker, Cross-Referencer, Editor & Other Utilities. Operates on Intermediate Instruction Codes. Supports Multiple Monitors, 43-Line Mode & 50-Line Mode. Full Screen & Command Line Interface & Code & Data Windows Display. Supports BOS National & BOS/COBOL Overlays. Features Source, Jump & Breakpoint Stepping, Resident/Non-Resident Mode, Script Capabilities & Multiple Windows at a Single Screen.
BOS National, Inc.

BOS/Finder. *Compatible Hardware:* IBM PC & compatibles. *Operating System(s) Required:* SBOS, CBOS, MBOS, BOS/LAN, DOS, NOVELL, UNIX, VMS. *Language(s):* MICROCOBOL. *Memory Required:* 256k.
Single-User computer. disk $450.00, incl. documentation.
15% of list annually.
Multi-User computer. Training/Day service $135.00.
manual $16.00.
$900.00, incl. documentation.
Stores, Controls, & Maintains Business Facts & Figures. Information Retrieval & Storage Software, Uses Data Base Techniques.
BOS National, Inc.

BOS/General Ledger. *Version:* 6.0. *Compatible Hardware:* IBM PC & compatibles. *Operating System(s) Required:* SBOS, CBOS, MBOS, BOS/LAN, DOS, NOVELL, UNIX, VMS. *Language(s):* MICROCOBOL. *Memory Required:* 256k.
Multi-User. disk $1200.00, incl. documentation.
Single-User. with documentation $600.00.
15% of list annually.
manual $16.00.
Menu-Driven Package That Can Be Used Alone or Integrated with the Accounts Receivable & Accounts Payable System. Journal Entries, Accruals, & Prepayments Can Be Input Directly & the General Ledger Accepts Automatic Expenditure Input via the Accounts Payable System. The Format of the Balance Sheet, Profit & Loss Statement, Income Statement, & Other Operating Reports Can Be Produced to the Users' Specifications. Two Periods Can Be Held Open At Once to Simplify End-of-Period Accounting. End of Year Procedures Allow the New Budget to Be Created & Old Balances to Be Transferred Automatically. Budgets Can Be Established & Comparison Reports Can Be Produced.
BOS National, Inc.

BOS/Inventory Control. *Version:* 3.0B. *Compatible Hardware:* IBM PC & compatibles. *Operating System(s) Required:* SBOS, CBOS, MBOS, BOS/LAN, DOS, NOVELL, UNIX, VMS. *Language(s):* BOS COBOL. *Memory Required:* 256k.
Multi-User. disk with documentation $1200.00.
Single-User. with documentation $600.00.
15% of list annually.
manual $16.00.
Interactive, Menu-Driven Package That Can Be Used Alone or Integrated with the Accounts Receivable & Invoicing Programs. Controls Stock Movements & Produces a Variety of Management & Stock Analysis Reports Including Inventory Status, Stock on Order, Reorder Point, & Cost Analysis. When Used with Invoicing, All Invoices & Credit Memos Can Generate Appropriate Entries for the System Automatically.
BOS National, Inc.

BOS/Invoicing. *Version:* 3.0B. *Compatible Hardware:* IBM PC & compatibles. *Operating System(s) Required:* SBOS, CBOS, MBOS, BOS/LAN, DOS, NOVELL, UNIX, VMS. *Language(s):* BOS COBOL. *Memory Required:* 256k.
Multi-User. disk with documentation $1200.00.
Single-User. with documentation $600.00.
15% of list annually.
manual $16.00.
Invoicing & Sales Analysis System for Use in Conjunction with BOS Accounts Receivable & Inventory Control.
BOS National, Inc.

BOS/LAN. Version: 6.1. Compatible Hardware: IBM PC & compatibles, DEC PDP-11, VAX. Operating System(s) Required: BOS, NOVELL, DOS. Language(s): BOS COBOL & Assembler. Memory Required: 256k.
contact publisher for price.
manual $10.00.
Networking Capabilities Provide Full File Sharing & Record Protection.
BOS National, Inc.

BOS Office Products Package. Version: 6.0. Compatible Hardware: IBM PC XT, PS/2. Memory Required: 256k. General Requirements: 10Mb hard disk.
$1350.00 per single user.
$2700.00 multi-users.
Integrated Package Featuring Word Processing, Database, Spreadsheet, Graphics, Communications, Spelling Checker & BOS Operating System. Includes Context Switching, 65,000 Database Tables Linked in One Query, Mail/Merge Database Link, 60 by 9999 Spreadsheet Matrix Size & On-Screen Help. Edits 65,000 Files Simultaneously. Pastes & Links Spreadsheet Sections & Graphics into Word-Processing Files. Imports & Exports ASCII & DIF File Formats. Also Available in Separate Modules.
BOS National, Inc.

BOS/Planner. Version: 6.0A. Compatible Hardware: DEC PDP-11, IBM PC & compatibles, PC XT, PC AT; 386. Operating System(s) Required: SBOS, CBOS, MBOS, BOS/LAN. Language(s): BOS COBOL. Memory Required: 256k.
single-user disk $450.00.
multi-user disk $900.00.
Financial Planning & Modeling System. Provides Budgeting, Cash Flow Forecasting & "What If" Calculations. Plan Size Is Not Restricted by Memory Size of the Computer. Handles up to 10,000 Lines & up to 60 Columns. Compatible with AUTOCLERK.
BOS National, Inc.

BOS/WRITER. Version: 6.0. Compatible Hardware: IBM PC & compatibles. Operating System(s) Required: SBOS, CBOS, MBOS, BOS/LAN. Language(s): BOS COBOL. Memory Required: 256k.
Single-user computer. disk $450.00, incl. documentation.
Multi-user computer. disk $900.00, incl. documentation.
Single-user Computer. 15% of list annually.
Multi-user computer. Training/Day service $135.00.
manual $10.00.
Full Screen Word Processing System with Mailing List, Filing, & Print Spooling Capabilities. Spell-Checker Also Integrated.
BOS National, Inc.

Boss 1-2-3. Version: 1.1. Oct. 1983. Operating System(s) Required: PC-DOS, MS-DOS. Language(s): Compiled BASIC. Memory Required: 128k. General Requirements: Lotus 1-2-3.
disk $195.00.
Allows Actual Financial Data from the BOSS to Be Transferred into LOTUS 1-2-3.
Mesa Software.

BOTTOM$LINE+, 3 disks. Version: 7.1. 1986. Compatible Hardware: IBM PC & compatibles, PC XT, PC AT. Operating System(s) Required: PC-DOS/MS-DOS 5.0 Plus. Language(s): Compiled BASIC, Assembly. Memory Required: 2000k.
Set. $1995.00.
Micro-Based Environment for Full Loan Servicing. Standard System Offers Mortgages, Simple-Interest, Rule-of-78. Computes Interest & Late Charges. Calculates & Displays Payoffs.
Dynamic Interface Systems Corp.

Bottomline Capitalist. Version: 2.0. Oct. 1985. Operating System(s) Required: MS-DOS. (source code included). Memory Required: 128k. General Requirements: Printer.
disk $125.00.
Business Management Game Where Up to Four Teams Can Play. Teaches Financial Management, Marketing, Planning, Human Resource Management & Even Lets You Build a Management Team.
ILAR Systems, Inc.

Bottomline GRAF. Oct. 1985. Operating System(s) Required: MS-DOS. Language(s): DBASE II. Memory Required: 256k. General Requirements: Plotter, dot addressable printer or screen camera.
disk $99.00.
Graphics Program Designed for Businesses. Example Problems Are Documented, Menu-Driven & Interactively Run. Has Screen Plot, Dot Addressble Printer & Plotter Capability.
ILAR Systems, Inc.

Boulder Dash. (Series A).
All Apple IIs. disk $5.00. Optimal configuration: Apple II, joystick.
Commodore 64. disk $5.00. Optimal configuration: Commodore 64, joystick.
It Isn't Easy to Find Butterflies in an Underground Cave, Let Alone Transform Them into Precious Stones. But with Your Help, Rockford Can Do It. The Real Problem Is - How Do You Get Him Out of There Alive? As Boulders Crash down All Around Him, Rockford Digs Frantically Through 16 Magical Caves & 5 Levels of Difficulty. If He Collects the Required Number of Diamonds, the Hidden Escape Tunnel Will Be Revealed. But He Needs Skillful Guidance to Drop Boulders Through an Enchanted Wall, Block the Amoeba, Turn Butterflies into Gems. If You Think You Can Do It, You've Got Rocks in Your Head.
Word Assocs., Inc.

Bounce. Compatible Hardware: IBM PC. Memory Required: 64k.
disk $29.95.
Combines Pool, Hockey, & Soccer into an Action Game. The User Can Curve the Ball During Active Play. Play One-on-One with Two or Four Players.
Prentice Hall.

Boundary Element Starter Packs. R. Adey et al. Jul. 1994. Items Included: Special PC versions of boundary elements code (BEASY) for acoustics, stress analysis, & fracture mechanics & crack growth; Self-teaching guides for each code; 3 books giving theoretical background.
MS-DOS 3.0 or higher. IBM PC & compatibles (386 or higher) (8Mb). software pkg. $995.00 (ISBN 1-56252-263-9). Nonstandard peripherals required: Math co-processor.
Contains Special PC Versions of the Advanced Commercial Boundary Elements Code, BEASY, for Stress Analysis, Acoustics, & Fracture Mechanics & Crack Growth. The Codes Are Fully Functional, but with Limits on the Elements Allowed. Self-Teaching Guides Include Tutorial Sessions Involving the Solution of Representative Examples.
Computational Mechanics, Inc.

Bounded Linear Program: RAMLP. W. Candler. Oct. 1985. Compatible Hardware: IBM PC & compatibles. Language(s): Machine. Memory Required: 128k. General Requirements: Printer.
disk $139.00.
Uses a Matrix Generator to Generate Problems up to 100 Real Consonants & 130 Real Activities, or 130 by 100, & Bounds on Real Activities. Solves Resulting Bounded Linear Program, with Full Reports.
Miniware, Inc.

Bowen Digital Bibliography of Works on Intelligence, Security, & Covert Activities. Sep. 1991. Items Included: Manual describing search techniques & history of Bowen. Customer Support: Unlimited telephone assistance.
MS-DOS. IBM & compatibles (512k). disk $400.00 (ISBN 1-878292-02-1). Nonstandard peripherals required: Minimum 7Mb Hard disk space available.
Digital Bibliography Provides Access to More Than 8000 Intelligence Books. Using Text Database Engine (Runtime Version Supplied with Database), Searchers Can Access Thousands of Key Words. Half of the Entries Contain Full Descriptive Outlines or Summaries of the Books Followed by Hundreds of Important Names & References Mentioned in the Text, Often Not Always in the Index of the Book Itself. Database Handles Complicated Boolean Searches, & Full Help Manual Is Online & Available at All Times.
National Intelligence Book Center.

Bowker/Whitaker Global Books In Print Plus. 1995. Items Included: Monthly Updates. Customer Support: Toll free CD-ROM hotline assistance; monthly updates to database; electronic bulletin board.
DOS 3.1 or later. IBM 286 or higher (535k). CD-ROM disk $1995.00 for 1 year (Order no.: BG110). Nonstandard peripherals required: Hard disk with minimum 10 Mb free space; CD-ROM player running under MS-DOS extensions 2.0 or later.
CD-ROM disk $5686.00 for 3 years.
Features 1.2 Million U.S. Bindings from BOOKS IN PRINT, 500,000 U.K. Bindings from Whitaker's BOOKBANK, 220,000 Bindings from INTERNATIONAL BOOKS IN PRINT & 57,000 Bindings from AUSTRALIAN & NEW ZEALAND BOOKS IN PRINT. In Addition, 32,000 Canadian Titles, Produced in Cooperation with CANADIAN TELEBOOK Will Be Added This Year.
R. R. Bowker.

Bowler. Compatible Hardware: Commodore 64, 128.
$39.95.
File Tracking & Maintenance System for a League Secretary. Up to 100 Bowlers & 20 Teams Can Be Kept on One Disk for up to 50 Games. Maintains Individual String Scores & Every Combination of Report(s) are Generated. Some Examples Are: Team Standing, Player History, Player Standing & Weekly Update.
Raymond L. Reynolds.

Bowler's Database. Compatible Hardware: Atari 400, 800. Language(s): Atari BASIC (source code included). Memory Required: cassette 32k, disk 48k.
disk $16.95.
cassette $12.95.
Keeps Track of Bowling Scores.
Dynacomp, Inc.

Bowler's Diary. Version: 1.0. Apr. 1991. Items Included: Program disc, manual. Customer Support: Free, unlimited.
PC-DOS, MS-DOS version 2.X or greater. IBM PC & compatibles (256k). disk $19.95.
Easy-to-Use Statistics Package for Individual Bowlers. Tracks Progress, High Scratch/Handicap Game/Series. Sets Goals for Increasing Average. Can Be Used for up to 5 Leagues Plus Open Bowling.
CDE Software.

TITLE INDEX

Bowling League Record System 2, 2 diskettes.
Items Included: Bound manual. *Customer Support:* Free hotline - no time limit; 30 day limited warranty; updates are $5/disk plus S&H. PC-DOS/MS-DOS 2.1 or higher. IBM PC, PC/XT, PC/AT, PS/2 & compatibles (256k). $99.95. *Nonstandard peripherals required:* Two floppy drives (either 5.25" or 3.5") or one floppy & one hard disk; monochrome, color, or EGA monitor.
IBM PC, PC/XT, PC/AT, PS/2 & compatibles (384k). expanded version $124.95.
Nonstandard peripherals required: Any printer which can be programmed to print underline, normal, double-wide, & condensed fonts is supported (e.g., Epson, etc.).
Set of Programs Designed to Facilitate Accurate Record Keeping of All Team & Individual Bowling Scores Following the Guidelines of the American Bowling Congress (ABC) & the Women's International Bowling Congress (WIBC). The System Provides the Following Features: Female, Male, & Mixed Leagues Bowling, Either Scratch or Handicap Scoring, Are Supported; Weekly Scoring Input Is Keyed off the League Bowling Schedule & Team Lineup; Automatic Archiving & Update of Team & Individual Records; Separate Handicap Base, Percentage, & Maximum Handicap for Female & Male Members; Team & Individual High Series over High Game Score Is Supported & More.
Dynacomp, Inc.

Bowling League Secretary. *Version:* 4.0. Aug. 1991. *Compatible Hardware:* IBM PC & compatibles. *Operating System(s) Required:* PC-DOS/MS-DOS version 2.x & higher. *Language(s):* PL/1, Assembly. *Memory Required:* 256k. *General Requirements:* 2 floppy disk drives, 1 3-1/2" drive, or hard disk. *Items Included:* Program disk, manual, sample files, sample forms. *Customer Support:* Free, unlimited. disk $74.95.
Easy to Use Package Designed to Manage the Results of Bowling Leagues. Maintains Team Standings, Totals, Bowler Averages, Handicaps, & Standings for up to 40 Teams, 12 Bowlers per Team & 44 Weeks. Also Records High Games & Series (Both Scratch & Handicap) for the League, Teams, & Bowlers for Awards & Bowlers Recognition.
CDE Software.

Bowling League Secretary. *Compatible Hardware:* TRS-80 Model I, Model III. *Memory Required:* 48k.
disk $49.95 (Order no.: 0095RD).
Records Individual Handicaps & Stores up to 250 Bowlers & 40 Teams.
Instant Software, Inc.

Bowling League Secretary. *Version:* 4.57. Feb. 1980. *Compatible Hardware:* Apple II, II+, IIe, IIc; IBM PC, PC/XT, PC AT; MS-DOS based computers. *Operating System(s) Required:* Apple DOS 3.3, PC-DOS 2.1 or higher. *Memory Required:* IBM 256k, Apple 48k. *Items Included:* 15 page user guide. *Customer Support:* 800 phone number.
Apple. disk $44.95.
IBM PC. disk $44.95.
MS-DOS compatibles. disk $44.95.
Full Function Statistics Manager for All Sizes of Bowling Leagues. Maintains Statistics on Teams & Individuals in Regular & Mixed Leagues. Standard ABC Reports May Be Output to Computer Screen or Attached Printer. Report Module Allows Users to Customize Their Own Reports from Several Formats.
Mighty Byte Computer, Inc.

Bowling League Statistics System. *Compatible Hardware:* TRS-80 Model I, Model III. *Memory Required:* 16k.
cassette $24.95 (Order no.: 0056R).
Enter Weekly Scores & Program Provides a Complete List of Bowler, Team & League Stats. Variety of Scoring Options.
Instant Software, Inc.

Bowling Secretary. *Customer Support:* 800-929-8117 (customer service).
MS-DOS. Apple II. disk $39.99 (ISBN 0-87007-409-1).
IBM PC, PS/2. disk $99.99 (ISBN 0-87007-652-3).
Maintains Bowling Averages, Team Standing & Assignments & Has Built-in Word Processor for Personalized Letters to League Members. The Same as Bowling League Secretary but with Significant Improvements in the Interface & Capacity.
SourceView Software International.

BOX-B. *Version:* 2.1. Sridhar Seshdari & Stanley N. Deming. 1989. *Items Included:* Manual, 3.5" diskette. *Customer Support:* Free telephone support to registered users.
MS-DOS. IBM PC/XT/AC & compatibles (384k). disk $295.00 (ISBN 0-932651-21-6). *Optimal configuration:* Suggested 512k.
Program for Using Box-Behnken Designs to Investigate 3-Factor & 4-Factor Surfaces. These 3-Level Designs Detect/Describe Curvature Effects 2-Level Designs Cannot. Prints Worksheets & Analyzes Results.
Statistical Programs.

BOXCALC 1000. *Version:* 1.06. Robert Cotton. Feb. 1987. *Compatible Hardware:* IBM PC XT, PC AT. *Operating System(s) Required:* PC-DOS 2.0 or higher. *Memory Required:* 256k.
disk $139.00.
Calculation Program That Allows Combination of Figures with Text. Instead of Using Pre-Determined Rows & Columns, Users Can Type Text & Place Calculation "Boxes" Anywhere on the Screen. Accepts up to 1000 Calculation Boxes per File; Boxes Can Be Relocated on Screen under Cursor Control; a File Can Contain up to 1000 Pages; Boxes Can Be Calculated Sequentially, or in Any Specified Order; Full Replication Feature Allows for Fast Creation of Box Formulas; Any Page or Combination of Pages Can Be Printed; Accepts Data from Other BOXCALC Files & ASCII Files. Full Featured Word Processing. Not Copy Protected.
Cotton Software, Inc.

Boxes: Champion Edition. *Version:* 4.0. Feb. 1995. *Items Included:* Game comes on one 3 1/2" High Density diskette. *Customer Support:* 90 days unlimited warranty on materials. Technical support phone for registered users. America Online Account (DTGames   aol.com).
Windows 3.1. 386 or higher (IBM & compatibles) (4Mb). disk $20.00 (ISBN 1-885708-10-6). *Nonstandard peripherals required:* Sound Blaster, or compatible, sound card - optional, but recommended. *Addl. software required:* None - All drivers supplied & automatically installed by setup program. *Optimal configuration:* 486/33 MHz or higher; Windows 3.1; 4Mb RAM; Sound Blaster, or compatible, sound card; 5Mb free hard drive space.
Innovative Mind-Challenging Windows Arcade Game. Stack Falling Colored Boxes to Solve All 150 Levels. Instead of Succumbing to Its Speed (since You May Not Have the Reflexes of an Android), You Need to Think Your Way Through This Game. BOXES Will Challenge Neural Transmitters More Than Punish Carpel Tunnels.
DynoTech Software.

BPI GENERAL ACCOUNTING

Boxx. *Version:* 3.0. Mar. 1993. *Compatible Hardware:* IBM PC & compatibles. *Operating System(s) Required:* MS-DOS, PC-DOS. *Language(s):* FORTRAN IV. *Memory Required:* 550k. *General Requirements:* 2 disk drives.
disk $195.00 (ISBN 0-928400-02-6).
Delivers Non-Automatic Univariate, Transfer Function & Intervention Modeling Capabilities. User Answers Prompts with Clearly Stated Defaults. Stores Models for Recall. Educationally-Oriented.
Automatic Forecasting Systems, Inc.

BPI Accounts Payable. BPI Systems, Inc. *Compatible Hardware:* HP 150 Touchscreen. 3.5" disk $425.00 (Order no.: 45457A).
Computerizes Vendor Control, Check Writing, & Cash Requirements Management. User Can Select the Method of Accounting, Maintain Detailed Vendor Files, Edit Invoices, Select Check Disbursements, Write Checks Automatically, & Maintain Multiple Bank Accounts. Aging & Cash Requirements Reports Along with Check Registers, Voucher Registers, Ledger, & Journals Can Be Printed. Can Be Used As a Stand Alone Product or Merged with BPI General Accounting, BPI Inventory Control, & BPI Job Cost.
Hewlett-Packard Co.

BPI Accounts Payable. BPI Systems, Inc. *Compatible Hardware:* TI Professional with Winchester second drive. *Operating System(s) Required:* MS-DOS. *Language(s):* MBASIC. *Memory Required:* 128k.
$395.00 (Order no.: TI P/N 2311447-0001).
Enables Small Business to Take Advantage of Computerized Accounting Techniques by Providing Cash Management Tools Like Vendor Control & Check Writing.
Texas Instruments, Personal Productivit.

BPI Accounts Receivable. BPI Systems, Inc. *Compatible Hardware:* HP 150 Touchscreen. 3.5" disk $425.00 (Order no.: 45456A).
Allows User to Set up Accounts Receivable Ledger Based on Either the Balance Forward or the Open Item Method of Maintaining Accounts. Supports Four Kinds of Customer Accounts Including Nonrevolving & Revolving Accounts, Those with Fixed, Required Payments, & Customer Accounts with Repetitive Charges. Users Can Set up Two Levels of Finance Charges, & Determine the Number of Days in a Billing Period & the Month That Marks the End of the Fiscal Year. Prints Customer Statements, Past Due Notices, Mailing Labels, Current Period Journal Activity, & Both Customer & General Ledgers. Detailed Analyses of Customer Accounts Can Be Printed. Can Be Set up As a Stand Alone System, or Can Be Designed to Merge with BPI General Accounting.
Hewlett-Packard Co.

BPI Accounts Receivable. BPI Systems, Inc. *Compatible Hardware:* TI Professional with printer, color monitor, Winchester second drive. *Operating System(s) Required:* MS-DOS. *Language(s):* MBASIC. *Memory Required:* 128k.
$395.00 (Order no.: TI P/N 2311446-0001).
Allows Statement Preparation, Aging Reports & Credit Analysis.
Texas Instruments, Personal Productivit.

BPI General Accounting. BPI Systems, Inc. *Compatible Hardware:* HP 150 Touchscreen. 3.5" disk $425.00 (Order no.: 45455A).
Users Can Automatically Record a Single Transaction As a Double Entry to Designated Control Accounts, Merge the System with Other Books with a Single Entry for Each Account, or Use It Independently As a Stand-Alone System. Prints up to 10 Profit-&-Loss Sub-Statements for Various Branches or Departments, Plus a

Consolidated Profit-&-Loss Statement. Trial Balance, Profit-&-Loss Statements, & Balance Sheet May Be Printed at Any Time During the Month. Up to 2000 Accounts Are Available to Be Divided Among General Ledger, A/R, A/P, Payroll, & Cash Disbursements.
Hewlett-Packard Co.

BPI Inventory Control. BPI Systems, Inc. *Compatible Hardware:* HP 150 Touchscreen.
3.5" disk $425.00 (Order no.: 45460A).
Allows Users to Choose One of Three Accounting Methods: FIFO, LIFO, or Average. User Can Establish up to 10 Departments or 10 Branch Locations, Produce a Single or Consolidated Income & Expense Statement, or Multiple Statements for Various Departments, Can Create Back Orders Automatically; Track Low Balance Inventory Items, & List the Inventory Items 12 Different Ways. Prints Purchase Orders, Sales Invoices, Journal Activity, Price Labels, Packing List, & End-of-Period Reports. Can Be Used As a Stand Alone System, or Merged with BPI Accounts Receivable, Accounts Payable, or General Accounting.
Hewlett-Packard Co.

BPI Job Cost. BPI Systems, Inc. *Compatible Hardware:* HP 150 Touchscreen.
3.5" disk $425.00 (Order no.: 45461A).
Allows Users to Report Job Income Either by Completed Job or by Percentage of Completion. Users Can Put Together & Print a Job Estimate Either by Entering Job Codes, Work Codes, & Combinations of Quantities, Rates, & Dollar Amounts. Can Also Compare Actual & Estimated Costs & Quantities on a Percentage of Completion Basis. Produces Reports Such As Job Status, Job Profit & Loss, Job Cost General Ledger & Journal, & Monthly Cost Summary Reports. Can Be Used As a Stand Alone System or Merged with BPI Accounts Payable & General Accounting.
Hewlett-Packard Co.

BPI Payroll. BPI Systems, Inc. *Compatible Hardware:* HP 150 Touchscreen.
3.5" disk $425.00 (Order no.: 45461A).
Provides for Automatic Payroll Processing, Check Printing, & Transfer of Data to the Operational BPI General Ledger. Using Standard Double-Entry Accounting, It Will Calculate All Taxes & Deductions, Track Vacation Days & Pay, Sick Days & Pay, Tips, Advances, & Reimbursements. Also Allows for an Employer-Sponsored IRA. Employees May Be Salaried, Hourly, or Commissioned & Can Live in Different States, or Even Be on Different Pay Cycles. Also Handles up to 100 Employees.
Hewlett-Packard Co.

BPI Payroll. BPI Systems, Inc. *Operating System(s) Required:* MS-DOS. *Language(s):* MSBASIC. *Memory Required:* 128k.
$395.00 (Order no.: TI P/N 2311449-0001).
Texas Instruments, Personal Productivit.

BPI Personal Accounting System. BPI Systems, Inc. *Compatible Hardware:* HP 150 Touchscreen.
3.5" disk $195.00.
Users Can Set up Their Own Set of Accounts Within Five Categories: Assets, Liabilities, Net Worth, Income & Expenses. Calculates the Balance of Each Account & Prints Reports Describing User's Financial Status. Printed Reports from the System Can Include: a List of Checks Written & Deposits Made for Each of 10 Checking Accounts, a List of Outstanding Checks & Deposits in Transit; a General Journal; an Amortization Schedule; & Two Different Statements of Net Worth. Also Does Profit & Loss Statements, Lists of Accounts, & Lists of Payees & Payers.
Hewlett-Packard Co.

BPS-II (Batch Processing). *Version:* 9.0. 1983. *Compatible Hardware:* IBM & compatibles. *Operating System(s) Required:* MS-DOS, PC-DOS 2.0 or higher. *Language(s):* CB-86. *Memory Required:* 512k. *General Requirements:* Hard disk, 132-column printer.
$95.00.
Batch Processor That Allows PMS-II, RMS-II & MMS-II Reports to Be Run Unattended. Subsystem to PMS-II.
North America MICA, Inc.

The Braille Editor (Edgar). *Version:* 2.7. Joseph E. Sullivan & Peter J. Sullivan. Feb. 1991. *Items Included:* Disks & print manuals. *Customer Support:* Free unlimited support by telephone, 1 year access to updates & support by Bulletin Board.
PC-DOS, MS-DOS. PC, AT, XT & compatible (512k). single-user license $295.00 (Order no.: 18-C6).
Allows Blind or Sighted Transcribers to Compose & Edit Braille in What-You-See-Is-What-You-Get Fashion by Means of ASCII Characters or a Graphical Representation of the 6 Dot Cells on the Screen. The System Is Compatible with VGA, CGA, EGA, & Hercules Graphics. For Those Users Who Are Learning Braille, the System Is Capable of Translating English to Grade II Braille & Vice Versa.
Duxbury Systems, Inc.

Brain Booster: Reasoning by Visual Analogy. Thomas M. Kemnitz.
IBM PC. disk $29.99 (Order no.: 1278).
disk $39.99, incl. backup disk (Order no.: 1278B).
Apple II. 3.5" disk $29.99 (Order no.: 1081).
3.5" disk $39.99, incl. backup disk (Order no.: 1081B).
Presents Nine Geometric Shapes in a Grid of Three Across & Three Down. The Player Must Determine Which Shape Does Not Belong. Designed for Very Young Children, This Program Proved Extremely Popular with Gifted High School Students. The Program Has Four Speeds & Presents 52 Screens. Speed & Complexity Give Depth So It Appeals to All from Young Children to Adults. Reasoning by Visual Analogy Is Used for Many I.Q. Tests. It Can Be Taught & Practiced. This Software Does Both. Tests Have Shown That Exercises Such As Those Provided by This Software Can Significantly Increase an Individual's Score on I.Q. Tests.
Trillium Pr.

Brain Browser. Floyd E. Bloom et al. Dec. 1989. *Items Included:* Casebound concealed wire-o manual. *Customer Support:* User support provided by electronic mail on CompuServ & Genie.
Apple Hypercard 1.2.1 or higher (1Mb). Macintosh. disk $299.00 (ISBN 0-12-107250-9). *Optimal configuration:* System 4.1 or higher, Finder 5.5 or higher, 2Mb RAM, hard disk, printer. *Networks supported:* All Apple.
HyperCard-Based Program Designed to Assist Neuroscience Students & Researchers Organize, Analyze & Report Neuroanatomical & Neurochemical Data. Includes Computerized Rat Brain Atlas, Bibliographic & Neurochemical Databases, & Comprehensive Import-Export Facilities.
Academic Pr., Inc.

Brain Browser. *Version:* 1.0 for Windows. Floyd E. Bloom et al. Dec. 1993. *Items Included:* Casebound concealed wire-o manual. *Customer Support:* User support provided by electronic mail on CompuServ.
Microsoft Windows 3.1. IBM PC with Intel 80386 or 80486 (2Mb). disk $99.00 (ISBN 0-12-107240-1). *Nonstandard peripherals required:* Must have 8Mb available space on hard disk drive; Microsoft Windows VGA; Mouse. *Optimal configuration:* 4 Mb RAM recommended, 1.44Mb 3.5 disk drive.
Hypertext-Based Program Using Spinnaker PLUS Runtime Engine. Designed to Assist Neuroscience Students & Researchers Organize, Analyze, & Report Neuroanatomical & Neurochemical Data. Includes Computerized Rat Brain Atlas, Bibliographic & Neurochemical Databases, & Comprehensive Import-Export Facilities.
Academic Pr., Inc.

Brain Damage. *Customer Support:* 800-929-8117 (customer service).
MS-DOS. IBM/PS2. disk $29.99 (ISBN 0-87007-851-8).
Users Sprint a Way Through the Various Levels of Mazes, Gathering Gold, Killing Monsters & Amassing an Ever Larger Score, Going from Level of Difficulty to Ever Higher Levels. For Those Times When Users Want to Damage the Brain.
SourceView Software International.

Brain Quest CD - Grades 1-2. Nov. 1995. *Items Included:* Installation instructions, registration cards. *Customer Support:* Telephone 302-234-1750, Fax 302-234-1760, E-Mail, CompuServe 76004,3520, E-mail, MCI mail 560-7116 - no charge.
Windows 3.1. 386 or higher (4Mb). CD-ROM disk $29.95 (ISBN 1-887468-03-X). *Nonstandard peripherals required:* Double-speed CD-ROM drive, color VGA or higher, mouse, sound card (optional). *Optimal configuration:* 486 processor, 8Mb RAM.
Macintosh. System 7 or higher (4Mb, 2.5Mb of free RAM). *Nonstandard peripherals required:* Double-speed CD-ROM drive, 13 inch color monitor or higher.
Based on the Best-Selling Q&A Card Decks & Software of the Same Name (Brain Quest). It Features In-Depth Answers Highlighted with Video Footage, Sound Effects, Graphics & Animation. Challenges Kids with over 1750 Questions.
Swfte International, Ltd.

Brain Quest CD - Grades 2-3. Nov. 1995. *Items Included:* Installation instructions, registration cards. *Customer Support:* Telephone 302-234-1750, Fax 302-234-1760, E-Mail, CompuServe 76004,3520, E-mail, MCI mail 560-7116 - no charge.
Windows 3.1. 386 or higher (4Mb). CD-ROM disk $29.95 (ISBN 1-887468-04-8). *Nonstandard peripherals required:* Double-speed CD-ROM drive, color VGA or higher, mouse, sound card (optional). *Optimal configuration:* 486 processor, 8Mb RAM.
Macintosh. System 7 or higher (4Mb, 2.5Mb of free RAM). *Nonstandard peripherals required:* Double-speed CD-ROM drive, 13 inch color monitor or higher.
Based on the Best-Selling Q&A Card Decks & Software of the Same Name (Brain Quest). It Features In-Depth Answers Highlighted with Video Footage, Sound Effects, Graphics & Animation. Challenges Kids with over 2000 Questions.
Swfte International, Ltd.

Brain Quest CD - Grades 3-4. Nov. 1995. *Items Included:* Installation instructions, registration cards. *Customer Support:* Telephone 302-234-1750, Fax 302-234-1760, E-Mail, CompuServe 76004,3520, E-mail, MCI mail 560-7116 - no charge.
Windows 3.1. 386 or higher (4Mb). CD-ROM disk $29.95 (ISBN 1-887468-05-6). *Nonstandard peripherals required:*

TITLE INDEX

Double-speed CD-ROM drive, color VGA or higher, mouse, sound card (optional). *Optimal configuration:* 486 processor, 8Mb RAM. Macintosh. System 7 or higher (4Mb, 2.5Mb of free RAM). *Nonstandard peripherals required:* Double-speed CD-ROM drive, 13 inch color monitor or higher.
Based on the Best-Selling Q&A Card Decks & Software of the Same Name (Brain Quest). It Features In-Depth Answers Highlighted with Video Footage, Sound Effects, Graphics & Animation. Challenges Kids with over 2200 Questions.
Swfte International, Ltd.

Brain Quest CD - Grades 4-5. Nov. 1995. *Items Included:* Installation instructions, registration cards. *Customer Support:* Telephone 302-234-1750, Fax 302-234-1760, E-Mail, CompuServe 76004,3520, E-mail, MCI mail 560-7116 - no charge.
Windows 3.1. 386 or higher (4Mb). CD-ROM disk $29.95 (ISBN 1-887468-06-4). *Nonstandard peripherals required:* Double-speed CD-ROM drive, color VGA or higher, mouse, sound card (optional). *Optimal configuration:* 486 processor, 8Mb RAM. Macintosh. System 7 or higher (4Mb, 2.5Mb of free RAM). *Nonstandard peripherals required:* Double-speed CD-ROM drive, 13 inch color monitor or higher.
Based on the Best-Selling Q&A Card Decks & Software of the Same Name (Brain Quest). It Features In-Depth Answers Highlighted with Video Footage, Sound Effects, Graphics & Animation. Challenges Kids with over 2400 Questions.
Swfte International, Ltd.

Brain Quest CD - Grades 5-6. Nov. 1995. *Items Included:* Installation instructions, registration cards. *Customer Support:* Telephone 302-234-1750, Fax 302-234-1760, E-Mail, CompuServe 76004,3520, E-mail, MCI mail 560-7116 - no charge.
Windows 3.1. 386 or higher (4Mb). CD-ROM disk $29.95 (ISBN 1-887468-07-2). *Nonstandard peripherals required:* Double-speed CD-ROM drive, color VGA or higher, mouse, sound card (optional). *Optimal configuration:* 486 processor, 8Mb RAM. Macintosh. System 7 or higher (4Mb, 2.5Mb of free RAM). *Nonstandard peripherals required:* Double-speed CD-ROM drive, 13 inch color monitor or higher.
Based on the Best-Selling Q&A Card Decks & Software of the Same Name (Brain Quest). It Features In-Depth Answers Highlighted with Video Footage, Sound Effects, Graphics & Animation. Challenges Kids with over 2400 Questions.
Swfte International, Ltd.

Brain Quest CD - Grades 6-7. Nov. 1995. *Items Included:* Installation instructions, registration cards. *Customer Support:* Telephone 302-234-1750, Fax 302-234-1760, E-Mail, CompuServe 76004,3520, E-mail, MCI mail 560-7116 - no charge.
Windows 3.1. 386 or higher (4Mb). CD-ROM disk $29.95 (ISBN 1-887468-08-0). *Nonstandard peripherals required:* Double-speed CD-ROM drive, color VGA or higher, mouse, sound card (optional). *Optimal configuration:* 486 processor, 8Mb RAM. Macintosh. System 7 or higher (4Mb, 2.5Mb of free RAM). *Nonstandard peripherals required:* Double-speed CD-ROM drive, 13 inch color monitor or higher.
Based on the Best-Selling Q&A Card Decks & Software of the Same Name (Brain Quest). It Features In-Depth Answers Highlighted with Video Footage, Sound Effects, Graphics & Animation. Challenges Kids with over 2400 Questions.
Swfte International, Ltd.

Brain Quest CD - Preschool & Kindergarten. Nov. 1995. *Items Included:* Installation instructions, registration cards. *Customer Support:* Telephone 302-234-1750, Fax 302-234-1760, E-Mail, CompuServe 76004,3520, E-Mail, MCI mail 560-7116 - no charge.
Windows 3.1. 386 or higher (4Mb). CD-ROM disk $29.95 (ISBN 1-887468-22-6). *Nonstandard peripherals required:* Double-speed CD-ROM drive, color VGA or higher, mouse. *Optimal configuration:* Sound card.
Macintosh. System 7 or higher (4Mb). *Nonstandard peripherals required:* Double-speed CD-ROM drive, 13 inch color monitor or higher, mouse.
Features over 300 Narrated & Colorful, Illustrated Questions & Answers, Fun Animations & Catchy Music. Children Are Encouraged & Rewarded Each Step of the Way As They Build Language, Reading & Math Skills.
Swfte International, Ltd.

Brain Quest CD: Grades 1-2. Nov. 1995. *Items Included:* Installation instructions, registration card. *Customer Support:* Phone support by calling 302-234-1750, no charge. Fax support by faxing to 302-234-1760, no charge. E-Mail support at Compuserve ID 76004,3520 or MCI Mail/560-7116, no charge.
Windows 3.1; Macintosh. 386 or higher (4Mb); Macintosh running system 7 or higher (4Mb). CD-ROM disk $29.95. *Nonstandard peripherals required:* Double-Speed CD-ROM drive.
Based on the Best-Selling Q&A Card Decks & Software of the Same Name (Brain Quest), It Features In-Depth Answers Highlighted with Video Footage, Sound Effects, Graphics & Animation. Challenges Kids with over 1750 Questions.
SWFTE International, Ltd.

Brain Quest CD: Grades 1-2. Nov. 1995. *Items Included:* Installation instructions, registration card. *Customer Support:* Phone support by calling 302-234-1750, no charge. Fax support by faxing to 302-234-1760, no charge. E-Mail support at Compuserve ID 76004,3520 or MCI Mail/560-7116, no charge.
Windows 3.1; Macintosh. Windows, 386 or higher (4Mb); Macintosh, System 7 or higher (4Mb). CD-ROM disk $29.95 (ISBN 1-887468-60-9). *Nonstandard peripherals required:* Double-speed CD-ROM drive.
Features In-Depth Answers Highlighted with Video Footage, Sound Effects, Graphics & Animation. Challenges Kids with over 1750 Questions. Mac/Win on CD-ROM in One Package - Jewelcase.
SWFTE International, Ltd.

Brain Quest CD: Grades 2-3. Nov. 1995. *Items Included:* Installation instructions, registration card. *Customer Support:* Phone support by calling 302-234-1750, no charge. Fax support by faxing to 302-234-1760, no charge. E-Mail support at Compuserve ID 76004,3520 or MCI Mail/560-7116, no charge.
Windows 3.1; Macintosh. 386 or higher (4Mb); Macintosh running system 7 or higher (4Mb). CD-ROM disk $29.95 (ISBN 1-887468-04-8). *Nonstandard peripherals required:* Double-Speed CD-ROM drive.
Based on the Best-Selling Q&A Card Decks & Software of the Same Name (Brain Quest), It Features In-Depth Answers Highlighted with Video Footage, Sound Effects, Graphics & Animation. Challenges Kids with over 2000 Questions.
SWFTE International, Ltd.

Brain Quest CD: Grades 2-3. Nov. 1995. *Items Included:* Installation instructions, registration card. *Customer Support:* Phone support by calling 302-234-1750, no charge. Fax support by faxing to 302-234-1760, no charge. E-Mail support at Compuserve ID 76004,3520 or MCI Mail 560-7116, no charge.
Windows 3.1; Macintosh. Windows, 386 or higher (4Mb); Macintosh, System 7 or higher (4Mb). CD-ROM disk $29.95 (ISBN 1-887468-61-7). *Nonstandard peripherals required:* Double-speed CD-ROM drive.
Features In-Depth Answers Highlighted with Video Footage, Sound Effects, Graphics & Animation. Challenges Kids with over 2000 Questions. Mac/Win on CD-ROM in One Package - Jewelcase.
SWFTE International, Ltd.

Brain Quest CD: Grades 3-4. Nov. 1995. *Items Included:* Installation instructions, registration card. *Customer Support:* Phone support by calling 302-234-1750, no charge. Fax support by faxing to 302-234-1760, no charge. E-Mail support at Compuserve 76004,3520 or MCI Mail/560-7116, no charge.
Windows 3.1; Macintosh. 386 or higher (4Mb); Macintosh running system 7 or higher (4Mb). CD-ROM disk $29.95 (ISBN 1-887468-05-6). *Nonstandard peripherals required:* Double-speed CD-ROM drive.
Based on the Best-Selling Q&A Card Decks & Software of the Same Name (Brain Quest), It Features In-Depth Answers Highlighted with Video Footage, Sound Effects, Graphics & Animation. Challenges Kids with over 2200 Questions.
SWFTE International, Ltd.

Brain Quest CD: Grades 3-4. Nov. 1995. *Items Included:* Installation instructions, registration card. *Customer Support:* Phone support by calling 302-234-1750, no charge. Fax support by faxing to 302-234-1760, no charge. E-Mail support at Compuserve 76004,3520 or MCI Mail/560-7116, no charge.
Windows 3.1; Macintosh. Windows, 386 or higher (4Mb); Macintosh, System 7 or higher (4Mb). CD-ROM disk $29.95 (ISBN 1-887468-62-5). *Nonstandard peripherals required:* Double-speed CD-ROM drive.
Features In-Depth Answers Highlighted with Video Footage, Sound Effects, Graphics & Animation. Challenges Kids with over 2200 Questions. Mac/Win on CD-ROM in One Package - Jewelcase.
SWFTE International, Ltd.

Brain Quest CD: Grades 4-5. Nov. 1995. *Items Included:* Installation instructions, registration card. *Customer Support:* Phone support by calling 302-234-1750, no charge. Fax support by faxing to 302-234-1760, no charge. E-Mail support at Compuserve 76004,3520 or MCI Mail/560-7116, no charge.
Windows 3.1; Macintosh. 386 or higher (4Mb); Macintosh running system 7 or higher (4Mb). CD-ROM disk $29.95 (ISBN 1-887468-06-4). *Nonstandard peripherals required:* Double-Speed CD-ROM drive.
Based on the Best-Selling Q&A Card Decks & Software of the Same Name (Brain Quest), It Features In-Depth Answers Highlighted with Video Footage, Sound Effects, Graphics & Animation. Challenges Kids with over 2400 Questions.
SWFTE International, Ltd.

Brain Quest CD: Grades 4-5. Nov. 1995. *Items Included:* Installation instructions, registration card. *Customer Support:* Phone support by calling 302-234-1750, no charge. Fax support by faxing to 302-234-1760, no charge. E-Mail

support at Compuserve ID 76004,3520 or MCI Mail/560-7116, no charge.
Windows 3.1; Macintosh. Windows, 386 or higher (4Mb); Macintosh, System 7 or higher (4Mb). CD-ROM disk $29.95 (ISBN 1-887468-63-3). *Nonstandard peripherals required:* Double-speed CD-ROM drive.
Features In-Depth Answers Highlighted with Video Footage, Sound Effects, Graphics & Animation. Challenges Kids with over 2200 Questions. Mac/Win on CD-ROM in One Package - Jewelcase.
SWFTE International, Ltd.

Brain Quest CD: Grades 5-6. Nov. 1995. *Items Included:* Installation instructions, registration card. *Customer Support:* Phone support by calling 302-234-1750, no charge. Fax support by faxing to 302-234-1760, no charge. E-Mail support at Compuserve ID 76004,3520 or MCI Mail/560-7116, no charge.
Windows 3.1; Macintosh. 386 or higher (4Mb); Macintosh running system 7 or higher (4Mb). CD-ROM disk $29.95 (ISBN 1-887468-07-2). *Nonstandard peripherals required:* Double-Speed CD-ROM drive.
Based on the Best-Selling Q&A Card Decks & Software of the Same Name (Brain Quest), It Features In-Depth Answers Highlighted with Video Footage, Sound Effects, Graphics & Animation. Challenges Kids with over 2400 Questions.
SWFTE International, Ltd.

Brain Quest CD: Grades 5-6. Nov. 1995. *Items Included:* Installation instructions, registration card. *Customer Support:* Phone support by calling 302-234-1750, no charge. Fax support by faxing to 302-234-1760, no charge. E-Mail support at Compuserve ID 76004,3520 or MCI Mail/560-7116, no charge.
Windows 3.1; Macintosh. Windows, 386 or higher (4Mb); Macintosh, System 7 or higher (4Mb). CD-ROM disk $29.95 (ISBN 1-887468-64-1). *Nonstandard peripherals required:* Double-speed CD-ROM drive.
Features In-Depth Answers Highlighted with Video Footage, Sound Effects, Graphics & Animation. Challenges Kids with over 2400 Questions. Mac/Win on CD-ROM in One Package - Jewelcase.
SWFTE International, Ltd.

Brain Quest CD: Grades 6-7. Nov. 1995. *Items Included:* Installation instructions, registration card. *Customer Support:* Phone support by calling 302-234-1750, no charge. Fax support by faxing to 302-234-1760, no charge. E-Mail support at Compuserve ID 76004,3520 or MCI Mail/560-7116, no charge.
Windows 3.1; Macintosh. 386 or higher (4Mb); Macintosh running system 7 or higher (4Mb). CD-ROM disk $29.95 (ISBN 1-887468-08-0). *Nonstandard peripherals required:* Double-Speed CD-ROM drive.
Based on the Best-Selling Q&A Card Decks & Software of the Same Name (Brain Quest), It Features In-Depth Answers Highlighted with Video Footage, Sound Effects, Graphics & Animation. Challenges Kids with over 2400 Questions.
SWFTE International, Ltd.

Brain Quest CD: Grades 6-7. Nov. 1995. *Items Included:* Installation instructions, registration card. *Customer Support:* Phone support by calling 302-234-1750, no charge. Fax support by faxing to 302-234-1760, no charge. E-Mail support at Compuserve ID 76004,3520 or MCI Mail/560-7116, no charge.
Windows 3.1; Macintosh. Windows, 386 or higher (4Mb); Macintosh, System 7 or higher (4Mb). CD-ROM disk $29.95 (ISBN 1-887468-65-X). *Nonstandard peripherals required:* Double-speed CD-ROM drive.
Features In-Depth Answers Highlighted with Video Footage, Sound Effects, Graphics & Animation. Challenges Kids with over 2400 Questions. Mac/Win on CD-ROM in One Package - Jewelcase.
SWFTE International, Ltd.

Brain Quest CD: Preschool & Kindergarten. Nov. 1995. *Items Included:* Installation instructions, registration card. *Customer Support:* Phone support by calling 302-234-1750, no charge. Fax support by faxing to 302-234-1760, no charge. E-Mail support at Compuserve ID 76004,3520 or MCI Mail/560-7116, no charge.
Windows 3.1 or higher; Macintosh. Windows, 386 or higher (4Mb); Macintosh, System 7 or higher (4Mb). CD-ROM disk $29.95 (ISBN 1-887468-22-6). *Nonstandard peripherals required:* Double-speed CD-ROM drive.
Features over 300 Narrated & Colorful Illustrated Questions & Answers, Fun Animations & Catchy Music. Children Are Encouraged & Rewarded Each Step of the Way As They Build Language, Reading & Math Skills. Packaged in a Box.
SWFTE International, Ltd.

Brain Quest CD: Preschool & Kindergarten. Nov. 1995. *Items Included:* Installation instructions, registration card. *Customer Support:* Phone support by calling 302-234-1750, no charge. Fax support by faxing to 302-234-1760, no charge. E-Mail support at Compuserve ID 76004,3520 or MCI Mail/560-7116, no charge.
Windows 3.1 or higher; Macintosh. Windows, 386 or higher (4Mb); Macintosh, System 7 or higher (4Mb). CD-ROM disk $29.95 (ISBN 1-887468-23-4). *Nonstandard peripherals required:* Double-speed CD-ROM drive.
Features over 300 Narrated & Colorful Illustrated Questions & Answer, Fun Animations & Catchy Music. Children Are Encouraged & Rewarded Each Step of the Way As They Build Language, Reading & Math Skills. Packaged in a Jewel Case.
SWFTE International, Ltd.

Brain Quest: Grade 1. Nov. 1994. *Items Included:* Installation instructions, registration card. *Customer Support:* Phone support by calling 302-234-1750, no charge. Fax support by faxing to 302-234-1760, no charge. E-Mail support at Compuserve ID 76004,3520 or MCI Mail/560-7116, no charge.
DOS 3.1 or higher; Windows 3.1 or higher; Macintosh. DOS, 286 (2Mb); Windows, 386 (2Mb); Macintosh, System 7 or higher (4Mb). disk $9.95 (ISBN 1-887468-15-3).
Interactive Software on 3.5" Disk. Children Test Their Knowledge of History, English, Geography, Math, Science & More, Answering over 750 Questions.
SWFTE International, Ltd.

Brain Quest: Grade 1. Nov. 1994. *Items Included:* Installation instructions, registration card. *Customer Support:* Phone support by calling 302-234-1750, no charge. Fax support by faxing to 302-234-1760, no charge. E-Mail support at Compuserve ID 76004,3520 or MCI Mail/560-7116, no charge.
DOS 3.1 or higher; Windows 3.1 or higher. DOS, 286 (2Mb); Windows, 386 (2Mb). disk $9.95 (ISBN 1-887468-25-0). *Addl. software required:* Color VGA or higher graphics adapter, Microsoft mouse or compatible pointing device, Windows compatible sound card. *Optimal configuration:* 486 processor, speakers.
Macintosh. System 7 or higher (4Mb). 3.5" disk $9.95 (ISBN 1-887468-32-3). *Nonstandard peripherals required:* Hard disk, 3 1/2" high density drive, 13" monitor or higher, Macintosh mouse, 2.5 Mb free.
Interactive Software on 3.5" Disk. Children Test Their Knowledge of History, English, Geography, Math, Science & More, Answering over 750 Questions.
SWFTE International, Ltd.

Brain Quest: Grade 2. Nov. 1994. *Items Included:* Installation instructions, registration card. *Customer Support:* Phone support by calling 302-234-1750, no charge. Fax support by faxing to 302-234-1760, no charge. E-Mail support at Compuserve ID 76004,3520 or MCI Mail/560-7116, no charge.
DOS 3.1 or higher; Windows 3.1 or higher; Macintosh. DOS, 286 (2Mb); Windows, 386 (2Mb); Macintosh, System 7 or higher (4Mb). disk $9.95 (ISBN 1-887468-16-1).
Macintosh. System 7 or higher (4Mb). 3.5" disk $9.95. *Nonstandard peripherals required:* Hard disk, 3 1/2" high density drive, 13" monitor or higher, Macintosh mouse, 2.5Mb free.
Interactive Software on 3.5" Disk. Children Test Their Knowledge of History, English, Geography, Math, Science & More, Answering over 1000 Questions.
SWFTE International, Ltd.

Brain Quest: Grade 2. Nov. 1994. *Items Included:* Installation instructions, registration card. *Customer Support:* Phone support by calling 302-234-1750, no charge. Fax support by faxing to 302-234-1760, no charge. E-Mail support at Compuserve ID 76004,3520 or MCI Mail/560-7116, no charge.
DOS 3.1 or higher; Windows 3.1 or higher. DOS, 286 (2Mb); Windows, 386 (2Mb). disk $9.95 (ISBN 1-887468-26-9). *Addl. software required:* Color VGA or higher graphics adapter, Microsoft mouse or compatible pointing device, Windows compatible sound card. *Optimal configuration:* 486 processor, speakers.
Macintosh. System 7 or higher (4Mb). 3.5" disk $9.95 (ISBN 1-887468-33-1). *Nonstandard peripherals required:* Hard disk, 3 1/2" high density drive, 13" monitor or higher, Macintosh mouse, 2.5 Mb free.
Interactive Software on 3.5" Disk. Children Test Their Knowledge of History, English, Geography, Math, Science & More, Answering over 1000 Questions.
SWFTE International, Ltd.

Brain Quest: Grade 3. Sep. 1994. *Items Included:* Installation instructions, registration card. *Customer Support:* Phone support by calling 302-234-1750, no charge. Fax support by faxing to 302-234-1760, no charge. E-Mail support at Compuserve ID 76004,3520 or MCI Mail/560-7116, no charge.
DOS 3.1 or higher; Windows 3.1 or higher; Macintosh. DOS, 286 (2Mb); Windows, 386 (2Mb); Macintosh, System 7 or higher (4Mb). disk $9.95 (ISBN 1-887468-17-X).
Interactive Software on 3.5" Disk. Children Test Their Knowledge of History, English, Geography, Math, Science & More, Answering over 1000 Questions.
SWFTE International, Ltd.

Brain Quest: Grade 3. Sep. 1994. *Items Included:* Installation instructions, registration card. *Customer Support:* Phone support by calling 302-234-1750, no charge. Fax support by faxing to 302-234-1760, no charge. E-Mail support at Compuserve ID 76004,3520 or MCI Mail/560-7116, no charge.
DOS 3.1 or higher; Windows 3.1 or higher. DOS, 286 (2Mb); Windows, 386 (2Mb). disk $9.95 (ISBN 1-887468-27-7). *Addl. software required:* Color VGA or higher graphics

TITLE INDEX

adapter, Microsoft mouse or compatible pointing device, Windows compatible sound card. *Optimal configuration:* 486 processor, speakers.
Macintosh. System 7 or higher (4Mb). 3.5" disk $9.95 (ISBN 1-887468-34-X). *Nonstandard peripherals required:* Hard disk, 3 1/2" high density drive, 13" monitor or higher, Macintosh mouse, 2.5 Mb free.
Interactive Software on 3.5" Disk. Children Test Their Knowledge of History, English, Geography, Math, Science & More, Answering over 1000 Questions.
SWFTE International, Ltd.

Brain Quest: Grade 4. Aug. 1994. *Items Included:* Installation instructions, registration card. *Customer Support:* Phone support by calling 302-234-1750, no charge. Fax support by faxing to 302-234-1760, no charge. E-Mail support at Compuserve ID 76004,3520 or MCI Mail/560-7116, no charge.
DOS 3.1 or higher; Windows 3.1 or higher; Macintosh. DOS, 286 (2Mb); Windows, 386 (2Mb); Macintosh, System 7 or higher (4Mb). disk $9.95 (ISBN 1-887468-18-8).
Interactive Software on 3.5" Disk. Children Test Their Knowledge of History, English, Geography, Math, Science & More, Answering over 1200 Questions.
SWFTE International, Ltd.

Brain Quest: Grade 4. Aug. 1994. *Items Included:* Installation instructions, registration card. *Customer Support:* Phone support by calling 302-234-1750, no charge. Fax support by faxing to 302-234-1760, no charge. E-Mail support at Compuserve ID 76004,3520 or MCI Mail/560-7116, no charge.
DOS 3.1 or higher; Windows 3.1 or higher. DOS, 286 (2Mb); Windows, 386 (2Mb). disk $9.95 (ISBN 1-887468-28-5). *Addl. software required:* Color VGA or higher graphics adapter, Microsoft mouse or compatible pointing device, Windows compatible sound card. *Optimal configuration:* 486 processor, speakers.
Macintosh. System 7 or higher (4Mb). 3.5" disk $9.95 (ISBN 1-887468-35-8). *Nonstandard peripherals required:* Hard disk, 3 1/2" high density drive, 13" monitor or higher, Macintosh mouse, 2.5 Mb free.
Interactive Software on 3.5" Disk. Children Test Their Knowledge of History, English, Geography, Math, Science & More, Answering over 1200 Questions.
SWFTE International, Ltd.

Brain Quest: Grade 5. Aug. 1994. *Items Included:* Installation instructions, registration card. *Customer Support:* Phone support by calling 302-234-1750, no charge. Fax support by faxing to 302-234-1760, no charge. E-Mail support at Compuserve ID 76004,3520 or MCI Mail/560-7116, no charge.
DOS 3.1 or higher; Windows 3.1 or higher; Macintosh. DOS, 286 (2Mb); Windows, 386 (2Mb); Macintosh, System 7 or higher (4Mb). disk $9.95 (ISBN 1-887468-19-6).
Interactive Software on 3.5" Disk. Children Test Their Knowledge of History, English, Geography, Math, Science & More, Answering over 1200 Questions.
SWFTE International, Ltd.

Brain Quest: Grade 5. Aug. 1994. *Items Included:* Installation instructions, registration card. *Customer Support:* Phone support by calling 302-234-1750, no charge. Fax support by faxing to 302-234-1760, no charge. E-Mail support at Compuserve ID 76004,3520 or MCI Mail/560-7116, no charge.
DOS 3.1 or higher; Windows 3.1 or higher. DOS, 286 (2Mb); Windows, 386 (2Mb). disk $9.95 (ISBN 1-887468-29-3). *Addl. software required:* Color VGA or higher graphics adapter, Microsoft mouse or compatible pointing device, Windows compatible sound card. *Optimal configuration:* 486 processor, speakers.
Macintosh. System 7 or higher (4Mb). 3.5" disk $9.95 (ISBN 1-887468-36-6). *Nonstandard peripherals required:* Hard disk, 3 1/2" high density drive, 13" monitor or higher, Macintosh mouse, 2.5 Mb free.
Interactive Software on 3.5" Disk. Children Test Their Knowledge of History, English, Geography, Math, Science & More, Answering over 1200 Questions.
SWFTE International, Ltd.

Brain Quest: Grade 6. Aug. 1994. *Items Included:* Installation instructions, registration card. *Customer Support:* Phone support by calling 302-234-1750, no charge. Fax support by faxing to 302-234-1760, no charge. E-Mail support at Compuserve ID 76004,3520 or MCI Mail/560-7116, no charge.
DOS 3.1 or higher; Windows 3.1 or higher; Macintosh. DOS, 286 (2Mb); Windows, 386 (2Mb); Macintosh, System 7 or higher (4Mb). disk $9.95 (ISBN 1-887468-20-X).
Interactive Software on 3.5" Disk. Children Test Their Knowledge of History, English, Geography, Math, Science & More, Answering over 1200 Questions.
SWFTE International, Ltd.

Brain Quest: Grade 6. Sep. 1994. *Items Included:* Installation instructions, registration card. *Customer Support:* Phone support by calling 302-234-1750, no charge. Fax support by faxing to 302-234-1760, no charge. E-Mail support at Compuserve ID 76004,3520 or MCI Mail/560-7116, no charge.
DOS 3.1 or higher; Windows 3.1 or higher. DOS, 286 (2Mb); Windows, 386 (2Mb). disk $9.95 (ISBN 1-887468-30-7). *Addl. software required:* Color VGA or higher graphics adapter, Microsoft mouse or compatible pointing device, Windows compatible sound card. *Optimal configuration:* 486 processor, speakers.
Macintosh. System 7 or higher (4Mb). 3.5" disk $9.95 (ISBN 1-887468-37-4). *Nonstandard peripherals required:* Hard disk, 3 1/2" high density drive, 13" monitor or higher, Macintosh mouse, 2.5 Mb free.
Interactive Software on 3.5" Disk. Children Test Their Knowledge of History, English, Geography, Math, Science & More, Answering over 1200 Questions.
SWFTE International, Ltd.

Brain Quest: Grade 7. Aug. 1994. *Items Included:* Installation instructions, registration card. *Customer Support:* Phone support by calling 302-234-1750, no charge. Fax support by faxing to 302-234-1760, no charge. E-Mail support at Compuserve ID 76004,3520 or MCI Mail/560-7116, no charge.
DOS 3.1 or higher; Windows 3.1 or higher; Macintosh. DOS, 286 (2Mb); Windows, 386 (2Mb); Macintosh, System 7 or higher (4Mb). disk $9.95 (ISBN 1-887468-21-8).
Interactive Software on 3.5" Disk. Children Test Their Knowledge of History, English, Geography, Math, Science & More, Answering over 1200 Questions.
SWFTE International, Ltd.

Brain Quest: Grade 7. Aug. 1994. *Items Included:* Installation instructions, registration card. *Customer Support:* Phone support by calling 302-234-1750, no charge. Fax support by faxing to 302-234-1760, no charge. E-Mail

BRAIN QUEST: GRADES 6-7

support at Compuserve ID 76004,3520 or MCI Mail/560-7116, no charge.
DOS 3.1 or higher; Windows 3.1 or higher. DOS, 286 (2Mb); Windows, 386 (2Mb). disk $9.95 (ISBN 1-887468-31-5). *Addl. software required:* Color VGA or higher graphics adapter, Microsoft mouse or compatible pointing device, Windows compatible sound card. *Optimal configuration:* 486 processor, speakers.
Macintosh. System 7 or higher (4Mb). 3.5" disk $9.95 (ISBN 1-887468-38-2). *Nonstandard peripherals required:* Hard disk, 3 1/2" high density drive, 13" monitor or higher, Macintosh mouse, 2.5 Mb free.
Interactive Software on 3.5" Disk. Children Test Their Knowledge of History, English, Geography, Math, Science & More, Answering over 1200 Questions.
SWFTE International, Ltd.

Brain Quest: Grades 1-2. Sep. 1995. *Items Included:* J. *Customer Support:* Phone support by calling 302-234-1750, no charge. Fax support by faxing to 302-234-1760, no charge. E-Mail support at Compuserve ID 76004,3520 or MCI Mail/560-7116, no charge.
DOS 3.1 or higher; Windows 3.1 or higher; Macintosh. DOS, 286 (2Mb); Windows, 386 (2Mb); Macintosh, System 7 or higher (4Mb). disk $19.95 (ISBN 1-887468-66-8).
Interactive Software on 3.5" Disk. Children Test Their Knowledge of History, English, Geography, Math, Science & More, Answering over 1750 Questions. DOS/WIN/MAC Versions in One Package.
SWFTE International, Ltd.

Brain Quest: Grades 3-4. Sep. 1995. *Items Included:* Installation instructions, registration card. *Customer Support:* Phone support by calling 302-234-1750, no charge. Fax support by faxing to 302-234-1760, no charge. E-Mail support at Compuserve ID 76004,3520 or MCI Mail/560-7116, no charge.
DOS 3.1 or higher; Windows 3.1 or higher; Macintosh. DOS, 286 (2Mb); Windows, 386 (2Mb); Macintosh, System 7 or higher (4Mb). disk $19.95 (ISBN 1-887468-67-6).
Interactive Software on 3.5" Disk. Children Test Their Knowledge of History, English, Geography, Math, Science & More, Answering over 2200 Questions. DOS/WIN/MAC Versions in One Package.
SWFTE International, Ltd.

Brain Quest: Grades 4-5. Sep. 1995. *Items Included:* Installation instructions, registration card. *Customer Support:* Phone support by calling 302-234-1750, no charge. Fax support by faxing to 302-234-1760, no charge. E-Mail support at Compuserve ID 76004,3520 or MCI Mail/560-7116, no charge.
DOS 3.1 or higher; Windows 3.1 or higher; Macintosh. DOS, 286 (2Mb); Windows, 386 (2Mb); Macintosh, System 7 or higher (4Mb). disk $19.95 (ISBN 1-887468-68-4).
Interactive Software on 3.5" Disk. Children Test Their Knowledge of History, English, Geography, Math, Science & More, Answering over 2200 Questions. DOS/WIN/MAC Versions in One Package.
SWFTE International, Ltd.

Brain Quest: Grades 6-7. Sep. 1995. *Items Included:* Installation instructions, registration card. *Customer Support:* Phone support by calling 302-234-1750, no charge. Fax support by faxing to 302-234-1760, no charge. E-Mail support at Compuserve ID 76004,3520 or MCI Mail/560-7116, no charge.
DOS 3.1 or higher; Windows 3.1 or higher; Macintosh. DOS, 286 (2Mb); Windows, 386

(2Mb); Macintosh, System 7 or higher (4Mb). disk $19.95 (ISBN 1-887468-69-2).
Interactive Software on 3.5" Disk. Children Test Their Knowledge of History, English, Geography, Math, Science & More, Answering over 2200 Questions. DOS/WIN/MAC Versions in One Package.
SWFTE International, Ltd.

Brain Quest Interactive Software. Aug. 1994. *Customer Support:* Free technical support - Call/Fax/Mail, Phone: 305-567-9996, Fax: 305-569-1350.
Windows 3.1 or higher (2Mb). disk $14.95. *Nonstandard peripherals required:* 3 1/2 floppy disk drive, VGA or higher graphics. *Optimal configuration:* VGA recommended, Microsoft mouse, Windows-compatible sound card & speakers.
DOS 3.1 or higher (640k). disk $29.95.
Macintosh System 7 or higher. Macintosh (4Mb, 2.5Mb RAM free). *Optimal configuration:* Macintosh, hard disk, 3 1/2" high density drive, 13" monitor or higher, Macintosh mouse required, color monitor recommended.
The Best-Selling Kids Educational Card Game Comes to the Home Computer. Each Brain Quest Game Complements School Curriculum & Provides a Fun Way for Kids to Learn & Have Fun, Too. Grades 1 (One) Through 7 Are Available.
SWFTE International, Ltd.

BrainStormer. Sep. 1983. *Compatible Hardware:* IBM PC & compatibles. *Operating System(s) Required:* MS-DOS. *Language(s):* MBASIC. *Memory Required:* 56k. *General Requirements:* 2 disk drives.
disk $75.00, incl. manual.
disk multi-user $100.00.
Problem Solving Tool Enabling Flexible Thinking, Discovering New Products, Identifying New Markets & Exploring Personal or Organizational Problems.
Soft Path Systems.

Branch - HQ Integrated System. *Version:* 1.2. 1987. *Compatible Hardware:* IBM PC. *Operating System(s) Required:* MS-DOS, UNIX. *Language(s):* Informix. *Memory Required:* 640k. contact publisher for price.
Data Transport Systems.

Branch Marketing. Nov. 1992. *Items Included:* Contact vendor. *Customer Support:* Contact vendor.
MS-DOS. 386 (4Mb). Contact publisher for price. *Addl. software required:* AtlasPro from Strategic Mapping. *Networks supported:* Lantastic, Novell Netware.
The System Maintains Demographic & Geographic Information on a Companies Offices & Other Offices Such As State Agencies That Impact the Company Offices. This Information Can Be Used to Perform Searches, Sorts & Logical Selections Between Offices. Reports & Geographic Displays Can Be Generated As a Result of the Operations Performed Against the Various Data Bases. Has Tie in with AtlasPro GIS Package from Strategic Mapping, Inc., for the Display of Marketing Plan Maps. Various Graphics & Reports Can Be Produced for Managing a Marketing Program.
Management Systems, Inc.

Branch Store Retailing. *Version:* 8A. Sep. 1993. *Operating System(s) Required:* PC-DOS/MS-DOS, UNIX, XENIX. *Language(s):* COBOL 85. *Memory Required:* Multi-user 3Mb or higher, Single user 1000k. *General Requirements:* Trac Line's Integrated Accounting, Retailing, & Distributing software. *Customer Support:* Included with the supported for the Integrated Accounting.
UNIX & XENIX. disk $1800.00.
MS-DOS. disk $1000.00.
Full Point of Sale Recording System for Small Chains. Operates Computer Terminals & Electronic Cash Drawers As Cash Registers, Running As Many "Registers" As the Hardware System Permits. This Module Gathers Information to Be Fed into the Main Accounting System - INTEGRATED ACCOUNTING & Master POINT-OF-SALE Software Running at the Chain's Main Location. Handles Cash, Check, Charge, Gift Certificate, Coupons, or Layaways. Uses Bar Code Readers.
Trac Line Software, Inc.

BRANCHBANKER. *Version:* 11.3. *Compatible Hardware:* IBM PS/2 & compatibles. *Operating System(s) Required:* PC-DOS 5.0 or higher. *Language(s):* C. *Memory Required:* 256k. *Items Included:* Manuals. *Customer Support:* Training & maintenance available, hot line, electronic bulletin board & annual users' conference.
Enterprise license contact publisher for price.
The BRANCHBANKER Software Solution Is Designed to Turn the PC into a Powerful Tool for Selling, Cross-Selling, & Delivering the Retail Products & Services of a Financial Institution. BB Guides Bank Personnel in Presenting a Spectrum of Products & Services to Current & Prospective Customers. It Handles "What-If" Calculations, Cross-Sell Recommendations, Host Communications, Graphic Presentations, Document Preparation, Laser Generated Forms, Account Opening, & Much More.
Ampersand Corp.

BRANCHTELLER. *Version:* 4.1. May 1989. *Items Included:* Manual. *Customer Support:* Training & maintenance available, hot line, electronic bulletin board & annual users' conference.
PC-DOS 5.0 or higher (256k). IBM PS/2 compatible. Enterprise license contact publisher for price.
A Full-Function Teller Automation Software Solution. The Program Is Designed As a Complementary System to BRANCHBANKER, Fully Integrating Teller, Platform, Administrative, & Back Office Functions Within a Local Area Network Universal Workstation Environment. There Is an On-Line Host Link Facility Within the System Which Allows for Real Time Posting of Transactions. BT Has the Capability for Picture & Signature Verification As Well As the Ability to Process a Wide Variety of Teller Functions.
Ampersand Corp.

Brass. *General Requirements:* ImageWriter, LaserWriter or other PostScript-compatible printer.
Macintosh Plus or higher (1Mb). 3.5" disk $195.00.
Music Notation.
Shaherazam.

Brass Instrument Tutor. Will Gaddy & Dan Harding. *Items Included:* Controller module. *Customer Support:* 90 day warranty against defective software.
DOS 3.3 or higher. IBM (640k). disk $179.95 (Order no.: I-1418). *Nonstandard peripherals required:* Minimum CGA.
Designed to Teach Students Fingerings for Trumpet, Horn, Euphonium, & Tuba. Scale Patterns & Random Drills Are Included. The Controller Module Reinforces Actual Valve Interaction.
Electronic Courseware Systems, Inc.

Breach. *Version:* 1.0 - 1.1. Aug. 1987. *Compatible Hardware:* Apple Macintosh, Atari ST, IBM PC, Commodore Amiga. *Memory Required:* 512k.
disk $39.95 ea.
Macintosh. (ISBN 0-932549-09-8, Order no.: BR-MA-1).
Atari. (ISBN 0-932549-08-X, Order no.: BR-AT-1).
IBM. (ISBN 0-932549-10-1, Order no.: BR-MS-1).
Amiga. (ISBN 0-932549-11-X, Order no.: BR-AM-1).
Strategy/Role-Playing Game Set in the 23rd Century.
Omnitrend Software, Inc.

Breakers. Bob Smith et al. *Compatible Hardware:* Apple II+, IIe, IIc, IIgs; Atari ST; Commodore 64, 128; IBM PC & compatibles, PCjr; Tandy. *Memory Required:* Apple 48k, Commodore 64k, IBM & Tandy 128k; Atari ST 512k.
Apple. disk $44.95 (Order no.: APDSK-1913).
Atari ST. 3.5" disk $44.95 (Order no.: ATDSK-2059).
Commodore. disk $39.95 (Order no.: COMDSK-3203).
IBM & Tandy. disk $44.95 (Order no.: IBMDSK-4210).
The Breakers Are the Slimiest, Most Evil Creatures Ever to Crawl Across the Landscape of Planet Borg. The Natives, the Mystical Laus, Have Been Overcome by These Desperate Misfits, & It's up to You to Save Them If You Can. You'll Move Through an Ever Changing Web of Plots & Subplots, As You Communicate in English with a Group of Sleazy Desperados Who Have Definite Minds of Their Own. It Will Take All Your Sophisticated Intellect & Moral Superiority to Outwit the Breakers - & That May Not Be Enough.
Broderbund Software, Inc.

Breakeven Analysis. 1982. *Compatible Hardware:* IBM PC compatibles & MS-DOS based machines. *Operating System(s) Required:* MS-DOS. *Language(s):* Microsoft BASIC & BASICA.
disk $45.00 (Order no.: 267).
Calculates Breakeven Points for Profit.
Resource Software International, Inc.

BREAKPOINT: For Shopping Center Management. *Version:* 3.4. Oct. 1991. *Items Included:* Advanced Commercial Escalations (ACE). *Customer Support:* Toll-free telephone support, local on-site or classroom training, consultation, & on-line help. Users can join one of many nationwide SOFTA user groups. Annual updates & enhancement subscription available.
MS-DOS 3.1 or higher. IBM & compatibles 386 & higher. disk $3495.00.
Software Package for Performance Analysis & Management of Retail Property from The SOFTA Group. Forecasts & Analyzes Performance on Space & Tenants, Automates Retail Billing & Collection, & Handles the Details of Lease Administration.
The SOFTA Group, Inc.

Breakthrough Backgrounds. *Items Included:* Browser/installer/copier front end software. *Customer Support:* 90 day warranty, free call back technical support.
Windows 3.1. IBM 386 (4Mb). CD-ROM disk $9.95. *Nonstandard peripherals required:* CD-ROM drive. *Optimal configuration:* 486, 8Mb RAM.
BeachWare.

Breaktrust Accounting System. *Compatible Hardware:* IBM PC & compatibles. *Memory Required:* 256k. *General Requirements:* Printer. $7900.00.
Menu-Driven System Generates Customer Statements, Investment & Management Review Reports, & Regulatory & Audit Reports. Accutrust

Enables the Trust Department to Streamline Their Banking Operations Through Use of Cash Sweeps, Interest/Dividend Automatic Generation, Tickler Transactions & Automatic Pricing of Assets.
Ontario Systems Corp.

Breakup. *Compatible Hardware:* Commodore PET with Commodore BASIC. *Memory Required:* 16k.
disk $16.95.
cassette $12.95.
Dynacomp, Inc.

Breeze. *Customer Support:* 800-929-8117 (customer service).
MS-DOS. IBM/PS2. disk $199.99 (ISBN 0-87007-855-0).
Set up Screens, Database Structures, Allows Full Control of Applications, & Produces Ideal Source Code Ready for Compiling Without Error. Speeds up the Development Process Manyfold.
SourceView Software International.

IRS Interest. *Version:* 4.10. Feb. 1991. *Compatible Hardware:* IBM & compatibles. *Memory Required:* 448k. *Items Included:* User manual & 12 months of maintenance coverage. *Customer Support:* 1-800-367-1040, Annual maintenance contract: $71.00.
3.5" or 5.25" disk $179.00.
Handles IRS Interest & Penalties & State Interest Calcs from 1954 to 1999. Includes 120% Tax Motivated Transactions & Refund Rates. Stores Interest Rates for Future Quarters. Penalty Coverage Includes Failure to File, Failure to Pay, Negligence, Fraud, Substantial Overstatement, Valuation Over/Understatement. Penalty Relationships Automatically Handled.
CCH ACCESS Software.

Bridge Baron. *Items Included:* Full manual. No other products required. *Customer Support:* Free telephone support - no time limit, 30 day warranty.
MS-DOS 3.2 or higher. Apple II series; IBM & compatibles (512k). disk $29.95.
C-64. disk $34.95.
Macintosh; Atari ST. 3.5" disk $45.95.
Features Include: Standard American Bidding with 5-Card Major Opening Bids. Strong or Weak 2-Bids. Takeout, Penalty, & Balancing Doubles. Blackwood, Gerber, & Stayman Conventions. Replay Any Deal, Switching Sides If You Wish. When You Are Not Sure of What to Play, Just Ask the Bridge Baron for Its Recommended Play. Rubber Bridge Scoring Option. Two-Person Mode, in Which You & Your Favorite Partner Play Against the Computer. Input Your Own Deals. Save Computer Deals or Your Own Deals to Disk.
Dynacomp, Inc.

Bridge Baron II. *Compatible Hardware:* Apple II+, IIe, IIc, IIgs, Macintosh; IBM PC & compatibles.
disk $49.95.
Winner of First Computer Bridge Tournament. Provides over a Billion Deals & Allows User to Input Personal Deals. User May Bid, Play, or Bid & Play Deals. Also Bid & Play South Hand While the Computer Bids & Plays the Other Hands. Two-User Option Allows User to Play with Another User As a Partner or One of User's Opponents.
Great Game Products.

Bridge Bidding I. *Compatible Hardware:* TI Home Computer.
contact publisher for price (Order no.: PHD5026).
cassette write for info. (Order no.: PHT6026).
Teaches the Art of Expert Bidding to the Bridge Player. For Intermediate & Advanced Players.
Texas Instruments, Personal Productivit.

Bridge Bidding II. Robert Hammen & Robert Wolff. *Compatible Hardware:* TI Home Computer.
contact publisher for price (Order no.: PHD5039).
cassette write for info. (Order no.: PHT6039).
Helps You Practice Slam Bidding.
Texas Instruments, Personal Productivit.

Bridge Bidding III. *Compatible Hardware:* TI Home Computer.
disk write for info. (Order no.: PHD5041).
contact publisher for price (Order no.: PHT6041).
Tex Inst Prsnltive Bidding.
Texas Instruments, Personal Productivit.

Bridge Champ I. *Compatible Hardware:* IBM PC.
disk $26.95.
After User Plays a Hand, Computer Evaluates User's Move. Features 200 Play Hands.
Barclay Bridge Supplies, Inc.

Bridge-It. Jul. 1985. *Compatible Hardware:* IBM PC. *Operating System(s) Required:* MS-DOS. (source code included). *Memory Required:* 256k. *General Requirements:* 2 disk drives or hard disk. *Items Included:* 1 spiral bound manual, 5 1/4" IBM diskette. *Customer Support:* 800 number, no charge.
disk $125.00.
Processes Complete Displays That Have Been "Downloaded" from WLN's On-Line System So They Can Be Used by a Database Program Running on the PC. Opens the Way for WLN Participants to Move Useful Data from WLN onto Their PC Where It Can Be Employed for a Wide Variety of Purposes.
WLN.

Bridge-It 3.5. *Version:* 2.08. Mar. 1989.
MS-DOS, PC-DOS (256k). disk $49.00.
Device Driver to Support 3.5" 1.44 Mb Diskette Drives on Older IBM A/T's & compatibles. Provides Simplified DOS Operations.
Microbridge Computers.

Bridge Manager Program. Aug. 1989. *Items Included:* User guide. *Customer Support:* Phone support 6 AM to 5 PM Pacific time; 90-day limited warranty.
IBM Token-Passing Ring. IBM PC, PC AT, PS/2, or compatible that will accept a token-ring adapter. 3.5" or 5.25" disk $495.00. *Nonstandard peripherals required:* IBM or Andrew source routing bridge required, token-ring adapter card required for PC. *Addl. software required:* IBM Lan support program or Novell Netware.
Manages & Configures Token-Ring Bridge Network from Any Designated Workstation.
Andrew Corp.

Bridge Master. *Compatible Hardware:* Apple II with Applesoft; Macintosh; IBM PC. *Memory Required:* MS-DOS 128k.
disk $29.95.
Dynacomp, Inc.

Bridge Master 2. *Items Included:* Bound manual. *Customer Support:* Free hotline - no time limit; 30 day limited warranty; updates are $5/disk plus S&H.
MS-DOS. IBM & compatibles (128k). disk $34.95. *Nonstandard peripherals required:* One disk drive.
Apple (48k). disk $34.95.
The Usual Customer Evaluation of BRIDGE MASTER Is "Excellent". So What Could We Do to Improve an Already Great Product? Well, We Did Find a Few Things: We Improved the Bidding. More Than 90% of the Time the Right Contract Will Be Bid (If You Hold up Your End); We Improved the Playing. Better Finesses & Trumping, Too.
Dynacomp, Inc.

Bridge Parlor. *Items Included:* Bound manual. *Customer Support:* Free hotline - no time limit; 30 day limited warranty; updates are $5/disk plus S&H.
MS-DOS. IBM & compatibles (256k); not available for PS/2 Model 80. disk $69.95. *Nonstandard peripherals required:* Printer supported, but not necessary.
General Bridge Package for Any Player, Beginning or Advanced. Features: Deals That Can Be Biased for Distribution & High Cards; One to Three Humans Can Play; Four- or Five-Card Majors, Weak or Strong Two Bids; Optional Signals: Ace/King, Upside down, Count, Fourth Best; Match Point Replay; Graphics; Bid/Play with All Cards up; Cancel, Claim, Concede, Hints, Take-Back; Bid Review While Playing; Printed Records of Bid/Play & More.
Dynacomp, Inc.

Bridge Partner Alice. *Items Included:* Bound manual. *Customer Support:* Free hotline - no time limit; 30 day limited warranty; updates are $5/disk plus S&H.
MS-DOS 2.0 or higher. IBM & compatibles (128k). disk $49.95.
Bidding Method Operates in Two Modes: Practice & Learning. Comes Already Programmed to Bid Standard American Five Card Major. In the Learning Mode, All the Hands Are Turned Up. ALICE Will Bid for Each of the Three Other Players. Each Time She Bids You Can Either Accept Her Bid or You Can Tell Her What a Better Bid Might Be. She Will Evaluate What You Told Her & Store That Information. Uses Standard Opening Leads (e.g., King from Touching Ace-King, Fourth from the "Longest & Strongest," etc.). She Will Take Finesses, Lead to Promote Tricks, etc.
Dynacomp, Inc.

Bridge Scorer. *Compatible Hardware:* Osborne with MBASIC. *Operating System(s) Required:* CP/M, MS-DOS. (source code included). *Memory Required:* 48k-128k.
disk $29.95.
Provides Scoring.
Dynacomp, Inc.

Bridge to Terabithia. Intentional Education Staff & Katherine Peterson. *Items Included:* Program manual. *Customer Support:* Free technical support, 90 day warranty.
School ver.. Mac System 7.1 or higher. Macintosh (4Mb). 3.5" disk contact publisher for price (ISBN 1-57204-341-5). *Nonstandard peripherals required:* 256 color monitor, hard drive, printer.
Lab pack. Mac System 7.1 or higher. Macintosh (4Mb). 3.5" disk contact publisher for price (ISBN 1-57204-317-2). *Nonstandard peripherals required:* 256 color monitor, hard drive, printer.
Site license. Mac System 7.1 or higher. Macintosh (4Mb). 3.5" disk contact publisher for price (ISBN 1-57204-342-3). *Nonstandard peripherals required:* 256 color monitor, hard drive, printer.
School ver.. Windows 3.1 or higher. IBM/Tandy & 100% compatibles (4Mb). disk contact publisher for price (ISBN 1-57204-318-0). *Nonstandard peripherals required:* VGA or SVGA 640x480 resolution (256), mouse, hard drive, sound device.
Lab pack. Windows 3.1 or higher. IBM/Tandy & 100% compatibles (4Mb). disk contact publisher for price (ISBN 1-57204-343-1). *Nonstandard peripherals required:* VGA or SVGA 640x480 resolution (256), mouse hard drive, sound device.
Site license. Windows 3.1 or higher. IBM/Tandy & 100% compatibles (4Mb). disk contact publisher for price (ISBN 1-57204-319-9).

Bridge 5.0

Nonstandard peripherals required: VGA or SVGA 640x480 resolution (256), mouse, hard drive, sound device.
This companion for young adult literature is ideal for students who don't know how to start that book report, or give that needed summary. Gentle prompts throughout the guide section of the program include Warm-up Connections, Thinking about Plot, Quoting & Noting, Keeping a Journal, If I Were ———' Responding to Questions, Using Quotations, Taking a Personal View, Write to Others, & Write a Sequel.
Lawrence Productions, Inc.

Bridge 5.0. Artworx. *Compatible Hardware:* Apple II series, Macintosh; Commodore 64; IBM PC.
disk $34.95.
Random Deal Bridge Program.
Barclay Bridge Supplies, Inc.

BridgeMaster Championship Edition. Great Game Products, Inc. Staff. May 1995. *Items Included:* Manual - 8 1/2" x 5 1/2", Intracorp Catalog, Next Move Series Cross-Seller, Warranty Card. *Customer Support:* 90 day limited warranty, free phone support Monday thru Friday 9:00AM to 6:00PM.
  Windows 3.1 or higher. 386/33 PC or compatibles with 1Mb hard drive free (4Mb). CD-ROM disk Contact publisher for price (ISBN 1-57519-005-2). *Nonstandard peripherals required:* CD-ROM player, mouse required. *Addl. software required:* CD-ROM driver software. *Optimal configuration:* SVGA - 256 color recommended. *Networks supported:* Novell 3.1.1 & above, Lantastick.
  Mac 68k or Power Mac, System 7.0 or higher.
  Mac 68k or Power Mac, System 7.0 or higher (4Mb). CD-ROM disk Contact publisher for price. *Nonstandard peripherals required:* CD-ROM player, mouse required. *Addl. software required:* CD-ROM driver software.
Offers a Winning Combination of Intelligent Game Play & a Wealth of Features on a Single, Multi-Format IBM & MAC CD-ROM. Master the Art of Playing Bridge with the Perfect Partner & Personal Tutor. It's the All New Champion of Bridge Programs.
IntraCorp/Capstone.

BridgeMaster: Championship Edition. Great Game Products Staff. Jun. 1995. *Items Included:* Manual. *Customer Support:* 90 day limited warranty, free phone support 9AM-6PM Monday thru Friday.
  Windows. 386/33 PC or compatible (4Mb). CD-ROM disk Contact publisher for price (ISBN 1-57519-008-7, Order no.: 081159975876). *Nonstandard peripherals required:* CD-ROM drive. *Addl. software required:* CD-ROM software.
Offers a Winning Combination of Intelligent Game Play & a Wealth of Features on Windows CD-ROM. With Network & Modem Play, Helpful Computer Hints & an Easy-to-Use Interface Bridgemaster Is the Perfect Partner & Personal Tutor.
IntraCorp/Capstone.

BridgeMaster Championship Edition. *Items Included:* manual. *Customer Support:* 90 day limited warranty. Free telephone support, 9-am to 6-pm monday thru friday.
  Mac System 7.1 or higher. Mac 68k or Power Mac. CD-ROM disk contact publisher for price. *Nonstandard peripherals required:* CD-ROM drive.
IntraCorp/Capstone.

BriefCASE: The Collegiate Systems Development Tool. 1990.
  IBM PC. contact publisher for price (ISBN 0-538-80304-5, Order no.: DH83A8).
  IBM PS/2. contact publisher for price (ISBN 0-538-80693-1, Order no.: DH83A8H88).
  Lab Manual & Diskette Package for Use as a Supplement in Systems Analysis & Design Courses. Contains an Integrated Set of CASE Tools for Developing Software Documentation (Including: Word Processor, Data Dictionary Template Files, Report/Form Design Program, Screen Design Program; Graphics Design Program.) Available Spring 1989.
South-Western Publishing Co.

Brimstone. James Paul et al. *Compatible Hardware:* Apple II+, IIe, IIc, Macintosh; Atari 400, 800, XL, XE Series, 520 ST; Commodore 64; IBM PC & compatibles, PC XT, PCjr. *General Requirements:* 2 disk drives for Atari 400, 800, XL, & XE series.
disk $44.95 ea.
  Apple II+, IIe & IIc. (Order no.: APDSK-1209).
  Atari 520 ST. (Order no.: ATDSK-2290).
  IBM. (Order no.: IBMDSK-4209).
  Macintosh. 3.5" disk $49.95 (Order no.: MACDSK-5209).
  Commodore. disk $39.95 (Order no.: COMDSK-3209).
  Atari 400, 800, XL & XE Series. disk $39.95 (Order no.: ATDSK-2209).
Electronic Novel Featuring a Parser with an over 1200-Word Vocabulary & a Continuously Changing Real-Time Universe. Sir Gawain, a Knight of the Round Table, Has Been Given His Most Difficult Quest - to Escape from the Underworld of Ultro with the Five Mystical Words, or Be Trapped for Eternity.
Broderbund Software, Inc.

Bristow Accounts Receivable. Duane Bristow. *Compatible Hardware:* TRS-80 Model III. *Operating System(s) Required:* TRSDOS. *Language(s):* BASIC. *Memory Required:* 48k. *General Requirements:* 2 disk drives.
disk $195.95.
Keeps up to 4000 Transactions per Month for up to 4500 Customers Including Date, Description, Units, Cost & Tax for Each Transaction. Also Prints Bills with Customized Messages.
Duane Bristow Computers, Inc.

Bristow Accounts Receivable II. *Compatible Hardware:* TRS-80 Model III, Model 4. *Memory Required:* 48k. *General Requirements:* 2 disk drives.
$295.00.
Keeps up to 2000 Transactions per Month for up to 800 Customers. Includes Account Aging 30, 60, 90 Days & up to 1600 Time Accounts. Time Accounts Keep Monthly Payment, Remaining Balance, Amount Payments in Arrears & % Monthly Carrying Charge for Overdue Payments: Date, Description & Amount for Each Transaction.
Duane Bristow Computers, Inc.

British Foreign Direct Investment in the United States 1974-1994. May 1995. *Items Included:* Spiral bound manual. *Customer Support:* Unlimited telephone support.
  MS-DOS 6.0/Windows 3.1 or higher. PC Clone 486 or higher (4Mb). disk $125.00 (ISBN 1-878974-11-4). *Addl. software required:* Database Versions are available for MS Access 2.0, Excel, Lotus, Paradox, Foxpro, and dBASE. *Optimal configuration:* PC clone with MS-DOS 6.0/Windows 3.1 or higher. Must have MS Access 2.0, or Excel, or Lotus or Paradox or FoxPro or dBASE.
Database of All British Foreign Investment Transactions in the United States 1974-1994.
Jeffries & Associates, Inc.

Broadband: An Overview. Oct. 1994. *Items Included:* User manual. *Customer Support:* Free technical support & a 30-day warranty (1-800-521-CORE).
  MS-DOS. IBM & compatibles (512k). 3.5" disk $199.00 (ISBN 1-57305-009-1). *Nonstandard peripherals required:* High-density 3.5" disk drive; VGA color monitor. *Addl. software required:* MS-DOS version 3.3 or higher. *Optimal configuration:* IBM (512k), MS-DOS version 3.3 or higher, VGA color monitor, keyboard, Microsoft compatible mouse (optional).
A Computer-Based Training Course That Describes Elements/Functions of Broadband Systems, Advantages of Broadband Packet Networking, Current & Emerging Technologies That Utilize Broadband Packet Networking, & the Future of These Networks & Technologies. It Is a Stand-Alone Course but Is Also a Helpful Prerequisite for More Advanced Training Related to Broadband Packet Networking.
Bellcore.

Broadcast Titler 2. Version: 2.0. *Compatible Hardware:* Commodore Amiga. *Customer Support:* Free telephone support with registration.
3.5" disk $389.95.
Broadcast Quality Character Generator for the Amiga. Features 16 Anti-Aliased Fonts, High Performance Transition Effects, a Menu & Mouse Driven Interface, Graphics Import Capabilities, & Hardware Genlock Control. New Super High Res Upgrade Addresses 35-Nanosecond Resolution of 1472 x 480.
InnoVision Technology.

Broadcast Titler 2: Font Enhancer.
  AmigaDOS Workbench 1.3 or higher. Commodore Amiga (1.5Mb). disk $169.95. *Addl. software required:* Broadcast Titler 2.
Converts Any Single-Color Amiga Font into Broadcast Titler 2's Anti-Aliased Format. The Resulting Font Has Improved Kerning & Is Free of Jagged Edges. Fonts Can Also Be Accurately Resized to Smaller Sizes While Preserving Original Detail.
InnoVision Technology.

Broadcast Titler 2: Font Pack 1.
  AmigaDOS Workbench 1.3 or higher. Commodore Amiga (2Mb). disk $169.95. *Addl. software required:* Broadcast Titler 2.
Includes 10 Anti-Aliased Typestyles in Six Sizes Each for Use with the Broadcast Titler 2 Character Generator. Each Font Includes Special Symbols & International Characters. A Jumbo-Size Amiga Font in Each Style Is Also Included for Use with Other Graphics Software.
InnoVision Technology.

Broadcast Wan-Lan Simulation Toolbox: ADA Broadcast Wan-Lan Simulation. Jan. 1996. *Items Included:* Sample input & output files & users manuals on disk. *Customer Support:* Assistance in formulative inputs & understanding outputs, price free or variable.
  MS-DOS. IBM PC (8Mb). disk $6000.00 (Order no.: 841). *Nonstandard peripherals required:* Math coprocessor. *Addl. software required:* FORTRAN Compiler & Linker. *Optimal configuration:* Source code can be compiled & linked for execution on any Machine with a FORTRAN compiler & linker.
ADA Source Code Version of Product 840 Which Performs Discrete Event Simulations of Wide Area Broadcast Networks & Bus-Based Local Area Networks. Other Source Code Versions Are Available in BASIC(842), "C"(843), PASCAL(844), MODULA-2(845), FORTRAN(846), & COBOL(847). Each of the Seven Versions Is Available Individually or

Collectively at a Significantly Reduced Price. The 840 Series Is Intended to Facilitate the Development of Simulation Models in the Language of the User's Choice & to Support Courses in Simulation Model Development & Comparative Programming Languages.
Cane Systems.

Broadcast Wan-Lan Simulation Toolbox: BASIC Broadcast Wan-Lan Simulation. Jan. 1996. *Items Included:* Sample input & output files & users manuals on disk. *Customer Support:* Assistance in formulative inputs & understanding outputs, price free or variable.
MS-DOS. IBM PC (8Mb). disk $6000.00 (Order no.: 842). *Nonstandard peripherals required:* Math coprocessor. *Addl. software required:* FORTRAN Compiler & Linker. *Optimal configuration:* Source code can be compiled & linked for execution on any Machine with a FORTRAN compiler & linker.
BASIC Source Code Version of Product 840 Which Performs Discrete Event Simulations of Wide Area Broadcast Networks & Bus-Based Local Area Networks. Other Source Code Versions Are Available in ADA(841), "C"(843), PASCAL(844), MODULA-2(845), FORTRAN(846), & COBOL(847). Each of the Seven Versions Is Available Individually or Collectively at a Significantly Reduced Price. The 840 Series Is Intended to Facilitate the Development of Simulation Models in the Language of the User's Choice & to Support Courses in Simulation Model Development & Comparative Programming Languages.
Cane Systems.

Broadcast Wan-Lan Simulation Toolbox: "C" Broadcast Wan-Lan Simulation. Jan. 1996. *Items Included:* Sample input & output files & users manuals on disk. *Customer Support:* Assistance in formulative inputs & understanding outputs, price free or variable.
MS-DOS. IBM PC (8Mb). disk $6000.00 (Order no.: 843). *Nonstandard peripherals required:* Math coprocessor. *Addl. software required:* FORTRAN Compiler & Linker. *Optimal configuration:* Source code can be compiled & linked for execution on any Machine with a FORTRAN compiler & linker.
"C" Source Code Version of Product 840 Which Performs Discrete Event Simulations of Wide Area Broadcast Networks & Bus-Based Local Area Networks. Other Source Code Versions Are Available in ADA(841), BASIC(843), PASCAL(844), MODULA-2(845), FORTRAN(846), & COBOL(847). Each of the Seven Versions Is Available Individually or Collectively at a Significantly Reduced Price. The 840 Series Is Intended to Facilitate the Development of Simulation Models in the Language of the User's Choice & to Support Courses in Simulation Model Development & Comparative Programming Languages.
Cane Systems.

Broadcast Wan-Lan Simulation Toolbox: COBOL Broadcast Wan-Lan Simulation. Jan. 1996. *Items Included:* Sample input & output files & users manuals on disk. *Customer Support:* Assistance in formulative inputs & understanding outputs, price free or variable.
MS-DOS. IBM PC (8Mb). disk $6000.00 (Order no.: 847). *Nonstandard peripherals required:* Math coprocessor. *Addl. software required:* FORTRAN Compiler & Linker. *Optimal configuration:* Source code can be compiled & linked for execution on any Machine with a FORTRAN compiler & linker.
COBOL Source Code Version of Product 840 Which Performs Discrete Event Simulations of Wide Area Broadcast Networks & Bus-Based Local Area Networks. Other Source Code Versions Are Available in ADA(841), BASIC(843), "C"(843), PASCAL(844), MODULA-2(845), & FORTRAN(846). Each of the Seven Versions Is Available Individually or Collectively at a Significantly Reduced Price. The 840 Series Is Intended to Facilitate the Development of Simulation Models in the Language of the User's Choice & to Support Courses in Simulation Model Development & Comparative Programming Languages.
Cane Systems.

Broadcast Wan-Lan Simulation Toolbox: FORTRAN Broadcast Wan-Lan Simulation. Jan. 1996. *Items Included:* Sample input & output files & users manuals on disk. *Customer Support:* Assistance in formulative inputs & understanding outputs, price free or variable.
MS-DOS. IBM PC (8Mb). disk $6000.00 (Order no.: 846). *Nonstandard peripherals required:* Math coprocessor. *Addl. software required:* FORTRAN Compiler & Linker. *Optimal configuration:* Source code can be compiled & linked for execution on any Machine with a FORTRAN compiler & linker.
FORTRAN Source Code Version of Product 840 Which Performs Discrete Event Simulations of Wide Area Broadcast Networks & Bus-Based Local Area Networks. Other Source Code Versions Are Available in ADA(841), BASIC(843), "C"(843), PASCAL(844), MODULA-2(845), & COBOL(847). Each of the Seven Versions Is Available Individually or Collectively at a Significantly Reduced Price. The 840 Series Is Intended to Facilitate the Development of Simulation Models in the Language of the User's Choice & to Support Courses in Simulation Model Development & Comparative Programming Languages.
Cane Systems.

Broadcast Wan-Lan Simulation Toolbox: MODULA-2 Broadcast Wan-Lan Simulation. Jan. 1996. *Items Included:* Sample input & output files & users manuals on disk. *Customer Support:* Assistance in formulative inputs & understanding outputs, price free or variable.
MS-DOS. IBM PC (8Mb). disk $6000.00 (Order no.: 845). *Nonstandard peripherals required:* Math coprocessor. *Addl. software required:* FORTRAN Compiler & Linker. *Optimal configuration:* Source code can be compiled & linked for execution on any Machine with a FORTRAN compiler & linker.
MODULA-2 Source Code Version of Product 840 Which Performs Discrete Event Simulations of Wide Area Broadcast Networks & Bus-Based Local Area Networks. Other Source Code Versions Are Available in ADA(841), BASIC(843), "C"(843), PASCAL(844), FORTRAN(846), & COBOL(847). Each of the Seven Versions Is Available Individually or Collectively at a Significantly Reduced Price. The 840 Series Is Intended to Facilitate the Development of Simulation Models in the Language of the User's Choice & to Support Courses in Simulation Model Development & Comparative Programming Languages.
Cane Systems.

Broadcast Wan-Lan Simulation Toolbox: PASCAL Broadcast Wan-Lan Simulation. Jan. 1996. *Items Included:* Sample input & output files & users manuals on disk. *Customer Support:* Assistance in formulative inputs & understanding outputs, price free or variable.
MS-DOS. IBM PC (8Mb). disk $6000.00 (Order no.: 844). *Nonstandard peripherals required:* Math coprocessor. *Addl. software required:* FORTRAN Compiler & Linker. *Optimal configuration:* Source code can be compiled & linked for execution on any Machine with a FORTRAN compiler & linker.
PASCAL Source Code Version of Product 840 Which Performs Discrete Event Simulations of Wide Area Broadcast Networks & Bus-Based Local Area Networks. Other Source Code Versions Are Available in ADA(841), BASIC(843), PASCAL(844), MODULA-2(845), FORTRAN(846), & COBOL(847). Each of the Seven Versions Is Available Individually or Collectively at a Significantly Reduced Price. The 840 Series Is Intended to Facilitate the Development of Simulation Models in the Language of the User's Choice & to Support Courses in Simulation Model Development & Comparative Programming Languages.
Cane Systems.

Brock Disk Librarian for Macintosh. *Version:* V-AI. Nov. 1985. *Compatible Hardware:* Apple Macintosh, Macintosh XL. *Memory Required:* 128k. *General Requirements:* Hard disk.
3.5" disk $29.95.
Organizes Diskettes or Files on a Hard Disk. Stores All Information in One Location. Searches for a Specific File, Prints Reports Listing the Diskette Library in User-Specified Order or Prints User-Defined Diskette Labels.
Brock Software Products, Inc.

Brock Keystroke Data Base. *Version:* AI. Feb. 1985. *Compatible Hardware:* Apple III, Macintosh, Lisa. *Memory Required:* 128k. *General Requirements:* 2 disk drives.
$199.00.
Includes All the Functions of BROCK KEYSTROKE FILER, Plus Cross-Reference Capability & Batch Update (Allows User to Perform Any Record-by-Record Function to an Entire File or to Selected Records of a File).
Brock Software Products, Inc.

Brock Keystroke Data Base Advanced-Encrypted. *Version:* MAC+. Feb. 1985. *Compatible Hardware:* Apple Macintosh. *Memory Required:* 128k. *General Requirements:* 2 disk drives.
3.5" disk $149.00.
Includes All the Functions of BROCK KEYSTROKE DATA BASE, Plus Password Protection, Data Encryption & Merging to Other Applications.
Brock Software Products, Inc.

Brock Keystroke Filer. *Version:* AI. Feb. 1985. *Compatible Hardware:* Apple Macintosh. *Memory Required:* 128k. *General Requirements:* 2 disk drives.
3.5" disk $49.95.
Database Manager Which Allows Free-Form Input Forms, Field Formatting, Defaults, Form Letter Merge, etc. The 128k Installation Supports 2 Billion Records per File, 50 Fields per Record, 2048 Characters per Field, 4 Rapid Search Fields, 49 Computed Fields, 68 Characters in a Formula, & 10 Computed Columns in a Report.
Brock Software Products, Inc.

Brock Keystroke: Relational Data Base & Report Generator. *Version:* AI. *Compatible Hardware:* Apple III, Lisa, Macintosh. *Memory Required:* 128k.
Apple III Set. $150.00.
Macintosh. 3.5" disk $99.00.
Lisa. 8" disk $200.00.
Relational Database & Report Generator $199.00.
Relational Database & Report Generator Advanced Encrypted $147.00.
Disk Librarian $29.95.
Free Form Integrated Relational Data Base, Supports MacWrite Form Letter Merge, SILK, PFS, & DIF Formats, & Wide ImageWriter Printer. Accepts up to 2 Billion Records per File, with a Maximum of 50 Fields per Record with 128k RAM & 255 Fields with 512k. Up to 2 Files Can Be Opened at Once.
Brock Software Products, Inc.

Broderbund Accounts Receivable. *Compatible Hardware:* Apple II, II+, IIe. *Operating System(s) Required:* Apple DOS 3.3. *Memory Required:* 64k. *General Requirements:* 2 disk drives.
disk $395.00.
Accounts Receivable Program for the Apple II Family.
Broderbund Software, Inc.

Broderbund General Ledger with Payables. *Compatible Hardware:* Apple II, II+, IIe. *Operating System(s) Required:* Apple DOS 3.3. *Language(s):* Pascal. *Memory Required:* 64k. *General Requirements:* 2 disk drives.
disk $495.00.
Integrated Accounting Package Capable of Modular Expansion to Include Accounts Receivable, Payroll, Budget & Other Systems. Designed for Use by General Businesses or Small Bookkeeping & Accounting Service Firms. Features Include: 2,000 GL Accounts Including 256 Divisions or Subaccounts, a Three-Level Account Numbering System (9999.255.255), a Maximum Dollar Amount $9,999,999,999.00, & a Built-In Report Writer.
Broderbund Software, Inc.

Broderbund Payroll. *Compatible Hardware:* Apple II, II+, IIe. *Operating System(s) Required:* Apple DOS 3.3. *Language(s):* Pascal, Assembly. *Memory Required:* 48k. *General Requirements:* 2 disk drives.
disk $395.00.
Handles up to 300 Employees, 15 Divisions, Stores or States. Includes 5 Standard Deductions & 30 Additional Deductions of User's Choice; Tax Computations for All States & Most Local Governments. Yearly Updates Available.
Broderbund Software, Inc.

Broiler Management. *Compatible Hardware:* IBM PC, PC XT & compatibles.
$500.00.
Farm Management Systems of Mississippi, Inc.

Broiler Production: Decision Aid. Merle W. Wagner. 1982. *Compatible Hardware:* Apple II Plus, IIe, IIc; IBM. *Operating System(s) Required:* Apple DOS 3.3, MS-DOS 2.0. *Language(s):* BASIC. *Memory Required:* 48k, 640k. *General Requirements:* Printer.
disk $29.95 (ISBN 0-922900-22-1, Order no.: CFD-668).
Designed for Any Poultry Feeding Operation. Fifteen Data Entries; Ten Calculations.
Cherrygarth, Inc.

Brooklyn Bridge. *Version:* 3.0. Guy Gordon. *Items Included:* 1 manual, 1 parallel cable, 1 serial cable. *Customer Support:* Free, toll call. PC/MS-DOS 2.1 or higher. IBM & compatibles (256k). disk $139.95.
File Transfer Package for IBM Compatibles. It Is Valuable as a Stand-Alone DOS Interface.
Fifth Generation Systems, Inc.

Brother John. *Version:* 4.6. Aug. 1989. *Compatible Hardware:* IBM PC & compatibles. *Operating System(s) Required:* XENIX, PC-DOS/MS-DOS. *Language(s):* C. *Memory Required:* 256k.
PC-DOS/MS-DOS. $995.00-$2,495.00.
PC-XENIX. $2,495.00-$3,995.00.
Designed for Churches & Synagogues. Integrates All Data Is Within a True Data Base. Includes Membership Census, Contribution Accounting, Ministry Scheduling, Standard Reports Such As Family Directory, Church Statistics, etc., As Well As Labels, Envelopes, Tuition/Pledge Accounting & Billing Statements, Contribution Statements, & Fund Accounting. A Report Generator (SQL Type Query Language) Allows Demand-Specific Data Pathing & Data Extraction for Presentation on Screen, Printer or Data File.
CompuData, Inc. (Pennsylvania).

Browse. *Version:* 2.00. Gordon Waite. Jan. 1988. *Compatible Hardware:* IBM PC. *Operating System(s) Required:* MS-DOS. *Memory Required:* 256k. *Customer Support:* Free telephone support.
disk $24.99 (ISBN 0-934777-03-9).
Lets User Look at Any ASCII Text File. Simple Key Strokes Allow Viewing of Files Page by Page or Left to Right & Back Again. The "HOME" Key Lets User Jump to the Top of the File, & the "END" Key Jumps to the Bottom. Texts Which Are More Than 80 Characters Wide Can Be Displayed.
Pico Publishing.

Browstext. Robert J. Quickle. Jul. 1986. *Compatible Hardware:* IBM PC, PCjr, PC XT, PC AT, Portable PC, 3270 PC. *Operating System(s) Required:* PC-DOS 2.00, 2.10, 3.00, 3.10. *Memory Required:* 128k.
disk $49.95 (Order no.: 6276635).
File Manager, Hex Editor, Sector Editor, & Text Editor in One Package. Program Displays a Directory Listing of User's Files, Then User Selects a File to Browse or Edit. The Directory Listing Can Be Also Used to Copy, Rename, or Print Files. Function Keys Can Be Set by User As Desired. Includes a Help Facility Providing Specific Information about Any Command.
Personally Developed Software, Inc.

BRS/Search. *Version:* 6.0. 1991. *Language(s):* Assembly, C. *Customer Support:* 90 days warranty, 800-number telephone support, annual maintenance - 15% of license.
MS-DOS, MVS/CICS, Novell, Unix, VMS. contact publisher for price. *Networks supported:* Novell, LAN Manager, DECNet.
Offers Instant Access to Any Document, Using Boolean Logic, Positional Operators, & Wild Card Searching. Hypertext Links Allow Integrated Retrieval of Text, Images, & Graphics. With the Fully Integrated Thesaurus, Users Can Expand Searching to Related Idaes. A Report Writer & Applications Integration Toolkit Are Available.
Ovid Technologies.

Bruce Lee. Ron Fortier. Apr. 1984. *Compatible Hardware:* Apple II; Atari 400, 800, 1200; Commodore 64, 128; IBM PC, PCjr. *Memory Required:* Atari 48k, Apple & Commodore 64k.
Atari, Commodore. disk $19.95 (ISBN 0-88717-119-2).
Apple. disk $19.95 (ISBN 0-88717-007-2).
IBM. disk $24.95 (ISBN 0-88717-008-0).
Martial Arts Game with Bruce Lee Mixing It up with the World's Meanest Opponents, Fighting off One Challenge after Another. Warrior, Teacher, & Street Fighter, Bruce Lee Is a Match for the Most Powerful Imaginations. His Body Is His Weapon & Now He's Ready to Join Forces with You.
IntelliCreations, Inc.

Brushwork. *Version:* 3.10. Nov. 1988. *Compatible Hardware:* IBM PC, PC XT, PC AT & compatibles. *Operating System(s) Required:* PC-DOS/MS-DOS. *Language(s):* C. *Memory Required:* 512k. *General Requirements:* Graphics card.
Targa 16. included in StudioWorks System.
VISTA. included in StudioWorks Vista System.
Graphics Design Product Designed to Work in Conjunction with ARTWORK & Other StudioWorks Modules. Provides the Power Required to Perform Graphics Manipulation in Raster (or Bit-Map) Mode. "Painting", Using a Tablet & Pen, the Designer Can Draw, Airbursh, Cut & Paste, & Store Screen Images. Also Supports the Definition & Storing of Brush Patterns.
West End Film, Inc.

BSDnet. *Items Included:* Software, manuals. *Customer Support:* One full year of support is included with each product purchased. Support includes hotline phone support, technical mailings, & free upgrades.
PDOS. Motorola 680 x 0 based systems, PC, Sun & HP Hosts. $700.00-$6000.00.
Provides Ethernet & TCP/IP Support for PDOS. System Supports FTP for File Transfer, TELNET for Remote Login, & a Socket Interface Allowing Applications to Transfer Data Directly to Application on Other PDOS or Non-PDOS Systems. Runs on CPUs with an On-Board Ethernet Controller or with an Intelligent Ethernet Controller on a Separate Card. In the Latter Case, the Structure of the EMOD Allows the Most Time-Consuming Tasks to Run on the Ethernet Card, Freeing the CPU for the Real-Time Work. Features: TELNET R Login Support, ITP File Transfer Support, TCP/IP Supported Via Berkeley Socket Interface.
Eyring Corp.

BSO/Assembler Microprocessor Relocating Assemblers. 1976. *Compatible Hardware:* DEC VAX, Sun 3, Sun 4, HP/Apollo, IBM PC DECstation, IBM Risc. *Operating System(s) Required:* UNIX, VMS, ULTRIX, DOS, Sun OS, HP/UX, OS/2, AIX. *Language(s):* Assembly. *Memory Required:* 1000k. *Items Included:* Software & documentation. *Customer Support:* 90 days warranty included in product purchase, 1 year maintenance contract available.
starting at $600.00. Write for info.
90 days free maintenance & support avail. training & customizing avail.
A Family of Cross Assemblers Specifically Designed to Produce Code for Real-Time Embedded Microprocessors. The Cross Assemblers Are Full Macro Assemblers That Are Compatible with the Manufacturer's Assembly Language. The Product Is Used by Software & Hardware Engineers to Produce Relocatable Object Code for Microprocessors That Are Embedded in the Product They Are Designing & Manufacturing. Assemblers Are Available for a Number of Different Microprocessors.
BSO/Tasking.

BSO/C: BSO C Compiler. *Version:* 2.1. 1984. *Items Included:* Software & Documentation. *Customer Support:* 90 days warranty included in price; 1 year maintenance contracts available starting at $240.00.
VMS, DOS, OS2, UNIX, ULTRIX, SUNOS, DOMAIN HPUX, AIX. DECVAX, PC, DECStation, SUN 3 & 4, HP/Apollo, IBM Risc. Starting at $900.00. *Networks supported:* Novell, Ethernet.
A Family of ANSI C Cross Compilers for Use by Software & Hardware Engineers to Produce Code for Microprocessors That Are Embedded in a Product.
BSO/Tasking.

BSO/Debug: Microprocessor Symbolic Debuggers. 1977. *Compatible Hardware:* DEC VAX. *Operating System(s) Required:* VMS. *Language(s):* Assembly. *Memory Required:* 2000k. *Items Included:* Software & documentation. *Customer Support:* 90 days warranty included in product purchase, 1 year maintenance contract available.
starting at $2000.00. Write for info.
90 days free maintenace & support avail. training & customizing avail.
A Symbolic Simulator Debugger Used, by Software & Hardware Engineers, for Simulating Different Microprocessors, So That Object Code for the Microprocessor Can Be Run & Debugged Without Microprocessor Hardware.
BSO/Tasking.

TITLE INDEX

BSO/Pascal Compiler. 1979. *Compatible Hardware:* DEC VAX. *Operating System(s) Required:* VMS. *Language(s):* Pascal. *Memory Required:* 2000k. *Items Included:* Software & documentation. *Customer Support:* 90 days warranty included in product purchase, 1 year maintenance contract available.
starting at $2100.00. Write for info.
90 days free maintenance & support avail. training & customizing avail.
A Family of Cross Compilers Specifically Designed to produce Code for Real-Time Embedded Microprocessors. Compilers Produce Highly Optimized, ROMable Reentrant Code for a Number of Different Microprocessors. For Use by Software & Hardware Engineers.
BSO/Tasking.

BSO/PLM Compiler. 1984. *Compatible Hardware:* DEC VAX, IBM PC, Sun 3, Sun 4, HP/Apollo, DECstation, IBM Risc. *Operating System(s) Required:* VMS, UNIX, ULTRIX, Sun OS, OS/2, DOS, AIX. *Memory Required:* 2000k. *Customer Support:* 90 days warranty included in product purchase, 1 year maintenance contract available.
starting at $1495.00. Write for info.
90 days free maintenance & support avail. training & support avail.
A PL/M Cross Compiler Specifically Designed to Produce Code for Real-Time Embedded 8051 Applictions. Produces Highly Optimized, ROMable Reentrant Code for the 8051 Family. For Use by Software & Hardware Engineers.
BSO/Tasking.

Btrieve. *Version:* 5.0. Dec. 1988. *Compatible Hardware:* IBM PC, PC XT, PC AT, PS/2. *Operating System(s) Required:* PC-DOS/MS-DOS 2.X, 3.X, 4.X, Xenix, OS/2. *Language(s):* C, BASIC, PASCAL, COBOL, etc.. *Memory Required:* 64k.
Single user. disk $245.00.
PC-DOS 3.1/MS-DOS networks, IBM PC networks, Multitasking DOS, Xenix. disk $595.00.
Applications Development in BASIC, Pascal, COBOL, C, FORTRAN, & APL. BTRIEVE Is a Key-Indexed Record Management System Which Can Be Used with Any Programming Language for High-Performance File I/O. Subroutine Calls Retrieve, Store, & Update Records in BTRIEVE Files. No Run-Time License Fees Are Required. BTRIEVE Is Implemented As a Value-Added Process for NetWare.
Novell, Inc.

Btrieve. SoftCraft, Inc. *Compatible Hardware:* TI Professional. *Operating System(s) Required:* MS-DOS. *Memory Required:* 128k. *General Requirements:* Winchester hard disk, printer.
$145.00.
Provides Application Developers Both Random & Sequential Keyed Access to Data Base from Problems Written in BASIC, Pascal, COBOL & C.
Texas Instruments, Personal Productivit.

B20 Asynchronous Terminal Emulator. *Compatible Hardware:* B-20 series, B-22. *Operating System(s) Required:* BTOS. *Language(s):* PL/M. *Memory Required:* 256k.
disk $500.00.
Designed to Emulate an Asynchronous Character-Oriented ASCII Terminal. Received Data May Be Displayed on Screen or Stored in a File for Later Review or Printing. Receives & Transmits ASCII or Binary Data at Speeds up to 192k & Allows Entire Files to Be Transferred from Work Station to Another Computer. Supports Both ASCII & Binary File Transfer Protocols in Blocked & Character Stream Modes.
Burroughs Corp.

B20 BASIC Interpreter. *Compatible Hardware:* B-20 series, B-22. *Operating System(s) Required:* BTOS. *Language(s):* Pascal. *Memory Required:* 256k.
disk $750.00.
Provides an Interactive Programming Environment for Business & Scientific Applications. Features Include Built-In Editor & Debugger, Command Set, Screen I/O, & Disk I/O. Allows up to 40-Character Variable Names, Multiple Variable Types & Arrays of up to 255 Dimensions. CALL Statements Allow Access to All B20 Operating System Services, Form Facility & ISAM.
Burroughs Corp.

B20 COBOL Compiler. *Compatible Hardware:* B-20 series, B-22. *Operating System(s) Required:* BTOS. *Language(s):* Pascal. *Memory Required:* 256k.
disk $750.00.
Allows COBOL Programs Which Reside in Disk Files to Be Compiled into a Compact Intermediate Code Which Is Then Executed by the B20 COBOL Run-Time System. Permits Full Access via Calls to All System Facilities: Data Management Facilities ISAM, & Forms, Which Displays Forms, Prompts User for Input, Accepts Data into Fields, & Supplies Data to Programs.
Burroughs Corp.

B20 Customizer Package. *Compatible Hardware:* B-20 series, B-22. *Operating System(s) Required:* BTOS. *Language(s):* BASIC. *Memory Required:* 256k.
disk $895.00.
Set of Structured Software Components Designed to Speed & Simplify Development of Application Programs. Includes Operating System, Utilities, Optional Languages, Program Development Tools, Data Management Facilities & All Generators Needed to Produce a Custom Application Software Package. Also Provides Multi-Partition & Batch Manager Facilities, Support for Standard Communication Protocols, etc.
Burroughs Corp.

B20 Forms Facility. *Compatible Hardware:* B-20 series, B-22. *Operating System(s) Required:* BTOS. *Language(s):* PL/M Assembly. *Memory Required:* 256k.
disk $990.00.
Allows Application-Defined Collection of Graphical Rulings & Text Captions to Be Displayed on B20 Screen. Consists of Two Major Parts: Interactive Forms Editor for Designing & Testing Forms, & Run Time Modules Which May Be Linked with Application Programs to Display Forms & Accept User-Supplied Data. Allows Interactive Design & Test of Business Graphics, Forms, Protected & Unprotected Text, etc.
Burroughs Corp.

B20 FORTRAN Compiler. *Compatible Hardware:* B-20 series, B-22. *Operating System(s) Required:* BTOS. *Language(s):* Pascal. *General Requirements:* Printer.
disk $750.00.
Implementation of the Subset Level of ANSI FORTRAN 77. Features Include Double Precision Floating Point, Multiple Named Commons with up to 64K Bytes Each, & FORTRAN 66 Compatibility Switch. The Compiled Object Code Modules May Be Linked with Other Language Programs & All B20 Modular Software Building Blocks.
Burroughs Corp.

B20 Pascal Compiler. *Compatible Hardware:* B-20 series, B-22. *Operating System(s) Required:* BTOS. *Language(s):* Pascal. *Memory Required:* 256k.
disk $750.00.
Conforms to Current Draft of ISO Proposed Standard. Contains Major Extensions, Making It Adequate for Both Application Programming & Development, As Well As System Implementation. Includes Generation of Efficient Object Code, Independent Compilation Support with Cross-Module Type Checking & Extensions Such As New Constants, New Data Types, Additional String Manipulation Functions, etc.
Burroughs Corp.

B20 Poll-Select Data Communications Protocol. *Compatible Hardware:* B-20 series, B-22. *Operating System(s) Required:* BTOS. *Language(s):* PL/M. *Memory Required:* 256k.
disk $500.00.
Allows a B20 to Be Interfaced to Burroughs Host Computer System. Operates in Both Stand-Alone & Cluster Environments. When Implemented on Master Workstation of a Cluster, Allows Each Station in Cluster to Communicate with the Burroughs Host. Allows User to Establish a Station Address, Read from the Host, Write to the Host & Interrogate Line or Buffer Status.
Burroughs Corp.

B20 3270 Emulator. *Language(s):* PL/M.
contact publisher for price.
Designed to Support Data Flow Control for 3270's, Which Is a Subset of Architected DFC Functions, & 3270 Command Processing Functions Necessary for SLU Type 213 Support. In Addition to DFC Processing, Program Supports 3270 Command & Data Stream Processing. A Screen-Oriented Interface, to Be Provided, Eliminates the Need for the Application Programmer to Be Aware of Underlying SNA Protocols.
Burroughs Corp.

B20 3270 SNA Emulator. *Compatible Hardware:* B-20 series. *Operating System(s) Required:* BTOS. *Language(s):* PL/M. *Memory Required:* 256k. *General Requirements:* Printer.
disk $995.00.
Enables the B20 Workstation to Emulate IBM 3270 Devices, Utilizing Binary Synchronous Communications Protocol. Consists of Two Segments: a Communications Package, Which Handles Data Link Interface to the Remote Mainframe; & the Screen Handler, Which Provides Necessary Formatting to Display Data on the Screen. Supports 80 or 132 Columns & up to 31 Line Displays.
Burroughs Corp.

B22 Font Designer. *Compatible Hardware:* B-22. *Operating System(s) Required:* BTOS. *Language(s):* PL/M Assembly. *Memory Required:* 256k.
disk $500.00.
Designed to Allow User to Create, Modify & Display Any Number of Characters. Allows User to Alter the Standard Character Set to Create Multiple Custom Character Sets by Loading Sets from Disk to RAM.
Burroughs Corp.

B20 X.25 Communications Manager. *Compatible Hardware:* B-20 series, B-22. *Operating System(s) Required:* BTOS. *Language(s):* PL/M. *Memory Required:* 256k.
disk $500.00.
Supports Three Levels of Access to Public Packet Switching Networks: Packet, Bytestream & Terminal Emulation. Enables User to Send & Receive Complete Packets of Data & Allows Development of Interfaces to other Computers. Bytestream Allows Sending of Data to other Systems via X.25 Network & Device Independent I/O via B20 Sequential Access Method. Terminal Lets User Appear As a Terminal to a Computer on Any X.25 Network.
Burroughs Corp.

Buck Actval. *Items Included:* User manual & telephone hotline number. Training is available. *Customer Support:* Continually enhanced to meet regulatory & accounting requirements.
IBM,MVS, XA. contact publisher for price.
Parameterized Actuarial Valuation System. Can Be Used for Valuation of Pension, Retiree Life & Retired Medical Plans, Projections of Cash Flows, Cost Studies of Plan Changes, Determination of Liabilities in Event of Plan Termination, Mergers or Spinoff.
Buck Consultants, Inc.

Buck BENCAL/PC. 1988. *Items Included:* Purchase of the system includes a user manual & on-line help. *Customer Support:* Continually maintained to reflect plan provisions & changes in Social Security laws, if applicable; Plan specific updates charged on an individual basis.
PC & MS-DOS (640k). Contact publisher for price.
Performs All Types of Defined Benefit Calculations/Options. Determines Service, Annual Compensation from Rates, Variety of Average Final Compensations. Social Security Benefit/Tax Exclusion Functions Part of the System Determinations. Output Includes Letters, Worksheets, Trustee Reports, Flat Files for Various Uses (e.g., SSA & Valuation Reporting). Files Hold Data/Results.
Buck Consultants, Inc.

Buck IDP (Interactive Data Program). 1970. *Items Included:* User manual. *Customer Support:* Staff training, hotline number available.
IBM/MVS/XA. Contact publisher for price.
An Interactive Program Used to Manage Valuation, Record-Keeping & Research Data. Allows the User to View & Update Data, Add New Data, Perform Data Distributions, Extract Information, Compare Data Files, Perform Calculations on Data & Store Data.
Buck Consultants, Inc.

Buck Recordkeeping Plus. 1987. *Items Included:* User manual. *Customer Support:* Continually maintained to accommodate federal regulations; fees charged on an individual basis. Training available.
IBM, MVS, XA. contact publisher for price.
Comprehensive Defined Contribution Plan Administration & Loans System. Includes Employee Data, Employee Election, Contributions, Transfers, Loans, Distributions, & Account Balance Details. Customized Batch Interfaces to Any Payroll & Valuation System. Reports Include Payroll Reconciliation, Loan Repayment & Transaction Summary. May Be Integrated with Defined Benefit & Human Resources Databases.
Buck Consultants, Inc.

Buck Social Security. 1988. *Customer Support:* Continually maintained to reflect current Social Security law.
PC-MS/DOS. disk $500.00, plus ,100.00 annual maintenance fee.
Both PC & Mainframe Versions Calculate & Project Social Security Benefits. Compensation History May Be Projected, Pre-Set with Maximums (or Zero) or Entered Directly. Can Perform Old-Age, Death, & Disability Calculations. All Input Data & Calculation Results Included in Printed Report. Online Help.
Buck Consultants, Inc.

Buck Tax Exclusion/PC. 1988. *Items Included:* Purchase of the system includes a user manual & on-line help. *Customer Support:* Continually maintained to stay current with relevant legislation.
disk $1200.00.
Determines Taxable & Non-Taxable Portions of Pension Payments Under Internal Revenue Code Section 72. Support Wide Range of Annuity Variations. Money Amounts Can Be Erased to Reflect Various Payment Schedules. On-Line Help. Printed Output.
Buck Consultants, Inc.

Budapest Gambit: Electronic Chessbook. Edited by A. C. Van der Tak. Sep. 1993. *Items Included:* Book & disk with 500 or more games (over 200 annotated). *Customer Support:* Telephone support by appointment.
MS-DOS 2.0 or higher (512k). 3.5" disk $25.00, incl. softcover text (ISBN 0-917237-01-3).
Atari ST (520k). Atari. disk $25.00.
Nonstandard peripherals required: Monochrome monitor DS/DD drive.
Authoritative Introduction to & Analysis of an Important Chess Opening.
Chess Combination, Inc.

Budget Analysis. Version: 3.2. Aug. 1986. *Items Included:* Comprehensive manual, sample tutorial, tutorial data files. *Customer Support:* 90 days free telephone support & program updates after purchase. Unlimited, toll free, telephone support & updates for 1 year $400. Maintenance for 1 year $200. Training classes available nationally or at Timberline Corporate. Timberline National certified consultant network. Timberline consultants also available.
MS-DOS. IBM PC XT, PC AT, PS/2, & 100% compatibles (512k). single user $730.00; multi-user $1030.00. *Nonstandard peripherals required:* 1 diskette drive, 1 hard drive, printer. *Networks supported:* Local area networks including Novell Advanced NetWare, IBM LAN Server & Microsoft LAN Manager.
Helps User to Develop Accurate Cost Estimates & Monitor the Fine Details of Project's Performance. It Helps User to Predict the Potential Profitability of a Project Based on Actual or Average Billing Rates & Budgeted Costs, Including Overhead Multipliers. Lets User Create Detailed Budgets by Hours, Fees or Costs. User Can Budget for Individual Staff Members, Staff Types (Job Titles), Labor or Expense Items. Can Use Average Staff Rates to Develop Feasibility Budgets or Cost Estimates. Project Management Reports Provide Detailed Budget Information for Your Analysis.
Timberline Software Corp.

The Budget Express. *Items Included:* manual, tutorial. *Customer Support:* 30 day, money-back guarantee.
IBM PC/XT, AT, PS/2 or compatibles. disk $149.00. *Addl. software required:* IBM PC version of Lotus 1-2-3 Release 2.0, 2.01, or 2.2.
Features Include Spreadsheet Outlining, Spreadsheet Construction & Modification, Configurable Columns & Fiscal Periods, Consolidation of Dissimilar Spreadsheets & Goal Tracking.
Symantec Corp.

Budget Model Analyzer. *Compatible Hardware:* Atari 400, 800. *Language(s):* Atari BASIC. *Memory Required:* cassette 32k, disk 40k.
disk $23.95.
cassette $19.95.
Financial Planning Tool Designed to Provide a Clear Picture of Overall Cash Flow Situation.
Dynacomp, Inc.

Budget Solutions. Version: 1.10. Feb. 1988. *Memory Required:* recommended 320k.
$99.95.
Defines Budget in a Form Window & Then Displays a Hierarchical Tree Containing Variables & Intermediate Accounts. The User Defines the New Budget Value, Which the Program Allocates Proportionally to All Variables, Sets Limits for Values or Cells with Formulas, & Imposes Limits As Absolutes or Percentage Values in Relation to the Current Variable Value or to the New Budget Value.
Enfin Software Corp.

Budget System. Version: 1.02. *Compatible Hardware:* IBM PC Compatible 286, 386, 486. *Operating System(s) Required:* 3.1 or higher. *Memory Required:* 640k. *General Requirements:* 1 floppy, 10 MB HardDisk Space. *Customer Support:* 90 day Free Telephone Support.
Single User. $450.00 (ISBN 0-925961-03-5, Order no.: BUS).
Multi-User. $950.00 (ISBN 0-925961-31-0, Order no.: BUM).
A Budgetary System Integrated with Full Featured Purchase Order System.
Organic Computing.

Budgetary Accounting-General Ledger. *Compatible Hardware:* AT&T 3B2; IBM PC & compatibles, PC XT, PC AT, System 36 PC. *Operating System(s) Required:* PC-DOS, UNIX. *Language(s):* BASIC (source code included). *Memory Required:* 512k. *General Requirements:* Wide-carriage printer.
contact publisher for price.
Double Entry Accounting-Single Activity Entry Resulting in True Double Entry Bookkeeping.
Diversified Computing.

Budgetary Control System: BUCS. Version: 95.0. 1978. *Operating System(s) Required:* XENIX, UNIX, L.A.N, MS-DOS. *Language(s):* COBOL. *General Requirements:* 132-column printer, hard disk, COBOL Runtime. *Items Included:* Users' Guide. *Customer Support:* Yes; phone & modem - contact vendor for features.
contact publisher for price.
Fully Integrated Fund Accounting System with G/L, A/P, Receipts, Encumbrances, Accounts Receivable, Budget Planning, Combining Reports, Fixed Assets. Check Reconciliation for Governmental & Non-Profit Organizations. Functions As a Modified Accrual or Cash System Where Each Account Has 24 Periods of Posting History. Appropriation & Vendor Limits Are Automatically Checked & Offers a 29 Position Free Form Account Number.
Donald R. Frey & Co., Inc.

Budgetary Planning-Financial Modeling. *Compatible Hardware:* AT&T 3B2; IBM PC & compatibles, PC XT, PC AT, PC 36. *Operating System(s) Required:* MS-DOS, PC-DOS, UNIX. *Language(s):* BASIC (source code included). *Memory Required:* 512k. *General Requirements:* Wide carriage printer.
contact publisher for price.
Application Based on LOTUS 1-2-3 & SYMPHONY. Compares Multiple Years of Budget Information, & If Changes Need to Be Made, Automatically Recalculates Sub-Totals & Totals.
Diversified Computing.

Buffer-Master. *Compatible Hardware:* IBM PC, PCjr, PC XT, PC AT, PC compatibles.
disk $29.95.
Keyboard Buffer Extender from 15 to 2000 Key Type Ahead.
Software Matters.

Bug Adventure. Sep. 1995. *Customer Support:* Telephone support - free (except phone charge). Windows 3.1. IBM & compatibles (386 DX-20) (4Mb). CD-ROM disk $12.99 (ISBN 1-57594-005-1). *Nonstandard peripherals required:* 2x CD-ROM player, Sound Card, VGA monitor. *Optimal configuration:* 486 SX-33.
Exciting, Inviting Interactive Journey into the Creepy, Crawly World of Insects.
Kidsoft, Inc.

TITLE INDEX

Bug Adventure. Sep. 1995. *Customer Support:* Telephone support - free (except phone charge). Windows 3.1. IBM & compatibles (386 DX-20) (4Mb). CD-ROM disk $12.99 (ISBN 1-57594-044-2). *Nonstandard peripherals required:* 2x CD-ROM player, Sound Card, VGA monitor. *Optimal configuration:* 486 SX-33.
Exciting, Inviting Interactive Journey into the Creepy, Crawly World of Insects. Blister Pack Jewel Case.
Kidsoft, Inc.

Bug Adventure (3-D).
Windows. IBM & compatibles. CD-ROM disk $49.95 (Order no.: R1180). *Nonstandard peripherals required:* CD-ROM drive. *Optimal configuration:* 386 processor operating at 16Mhz or higher, MS-DOS 5.0 or higher, Windows 3.1 or higher, 30Mb hard drive, mouse, VGA graphic adapter & VGA color monitor (SVGA recommended), 4Mb RAM, external speakers or headphones (with sound card) that are Sound Blaster compatible.
Take a Journey to the Creepy, Crawly World of Insects. Narrated Text Allows Non-Readers & Early Readers to Learn All about Their Favorite Bugs. Contains a Detailed, Cross-Referenced Exploratory Environment, & Features a 3-D Bug Basement for Viewing Favorite Bugs (Ages 3-10).
Library Video Co.

Builder. Jul. 1993. *Items Included:* 3-ring bound manual, paid versions of software, 2 free programs. *Customer Support:* Phone support, upgrade notification.
MS-DOS v3.3. IBM PC & compatibles (400k). disk $99.00. *Addl. software required:* Clipper Compiler, Summer '87 or higher. *Optimal configuration:* IBM compatible running DOS 5.0 2Mb RAM.
Clipper Program Source Code Generator & Function Library. Creates Drop down Menuing Applications. Features Automatic File Maintenance Creation & Report Source Code Generator. Create Four Types of Text Windows: File Maintenance, Picklist, Menu, Dialog. Extensive & Powerful Function Library. Shareware ASP.
Aeolus Software.

BUILDER PLUS. *Version:* 7.1. Jul. 1991. *Items Included:* Full 3 ring binder manual with room for updates. Help screens behind all input stages. *Customer Support:* on site-training; maintenance service gives unlimited telephone support & all new enhancements throughout the year. Maintenance agreement available at 15% of total system.
MS-DOS 5.0 plus (2Mb). Hard disk required, AT/XT, PS/2 & compatibles; IBM System 36, 38 & AS400MS- $3000.00 single-user; $4500.00 local area network; $10,500.00 wide area network. *Addl. software required:* Dot matrix printer, 132 column wide carriage, LOANLEDGER plus, FLEX-RATE plus, OPEN$LINE plus. *Networks supported:* Novelle, 3-Com, IBM-PC NET.
Gives LOANLEDGER Plus the Ability to Track the Progress of Construction Loans Utilizing Cost Breakdown Schedules. Easy, up to the Minute Loan Analysis for Both Payments & Funding. Requires OPEN$LINE Plus & FLEX-RATE Plus. Cost Breakdown & Construction Summary & Other Reports Provide Necessary Information on a Loan's Progress. Some of the Information Given Includes Amount Budgeted, Amount Paid, % Paid % Complete, Projected Overrun, Funds Received, Funds Disbursed Balance, & LIP Available.
Dynamic Interface Systems Corp.

Builder's Apprentice. *Version:* 2.9. Jun. 1989. *Items Included:* Manual. *Customer Support:* Free phone support; on-site training for a fee.
Macintosh (1Mb). 3.5" disk $1400.00 (Order no.: M30). *Networks supported:* AppleTalk, EtherTalk.
Comprehensive General or Sub-Contracting System for the Small to Medium-Sized Contractor. Includes Fully Integrated Estimating, Job Casting, General Ledger, Receivables, Payables, & Payroll. Can Be Customized to Suit Special Requirements.
Exceiver Corp.

Building Cost Analysis. 1982. *Compatible Hardware:* MS-DOS based machines. *Language(s):* Microsoft BASIC & BASICA. disk $85.00 (Order no.: 255).
Designed for Real Estate Investors As a Tool in Analyzing the Intended Investment.
Resource Software International, Inc.

Building Heat Gain & Heat Loss. W. C. Dries. 1980. *Compatible Hardware:* IBM PC. *Operating System(s) Required:* PC-DOS. *Language(s):* FORTRAN. *Memory Required:* 128k. *General Requirements:* Printer.
disk $250.00 (ISBN 0-9606344-3-6).
Calculates Instantaneous Heat Gain & Loss for All Types of Buildings.
Blitz Publishing Co.

Building Heating Energy Use Estimator. W. C. Dries. 1980. *Compatible Hardware:* IBM PC. *Operating System(s) Required:* PC-DOS. *Language(s):* FORTRAN. *Memory Required:* 128k. *General Requirements:* Printer.
disk $100.00 (ISBN 0-9606344-5-2).
Estimates Monthly & Annual Energy Used to Heat a Building.
Blitz Publishing Co.

Building Local Area Networks. Patrick H. Corrigan & Aisling Guy. Jun. 1989. *Operating System(s) Required:* MS-DOS.
book & disk $39.95 (ISBN 1-55851-010-9). book only $24.95 (ISBN 1-55851-025-7).
Discusses the Specifics of Building & Maintaining PC LANs, Including Hardware Configurations, Software Development, Cabling, Selection Criteria, Installation, & On-Going Management. Gives Particular Emphasis to Novell's Netware, Version 2.1. Additional Topics Covered Include the OS/2 LAN Manager, Tops, Banyan, VINES, Internetworking, Host Computer Gateways, & Multisystem Networks That Link PCs, Apples, & Mainframes.
M & T Bks.

Building Productivity. 1984. *Compatible Hardware:* Apple II; IBM PC & compatibles. *Operating System(s) Required:* PC-DOS 2.0. *Memory Required:* Apple-64k, IBM-128k.
Apple. disk with supervisor's hdbk. $89.00 ea. (Order no.: PAD6-018).
IBM. (Order no.: PAD8-018).
Self-Training Program for Supervisors to Learn Applied Techniques to Increase Productivity.
Bureau of Business Practice.

Bulk Mailer. *Version:* 3.25. Joe Marinello & Chris LeCroy. May 1985. *Compatible Hardware:* IBM PC; Apple II, IIe, Macintosh. *Operating System(s) Required:* MS-DOS. *Memory Required:* Macintosh 512k. *Items Included:* Manual, disk. *Customer Support:* Free phone support.
IBM version. $125.00.
Hard disk version (IBM - 57,000 names, Macintosh - 90,000 names). $350.00.
Macintosh. 3.5" disk $149.00.
manual $15.00.
Features: 57,000 Name Capacity (IBM) 90,000 (Macintosh), Eliminates Duplications & Displays Any "Close Calls", Finds Fastest Possible Zip Sort/Label Printout, Special CODE Feature to Sort Any Entry, etc.
Satori Software.

Bulk Mailing Master. *Customer Support:* 800-929-8117 (customer service).
MS-DOS. IBM/PS2. disk $199.99 (ISBN 0-87007-819-4).
Bulk Mailing System Which Includes File Maintenance & Printing of Labels for Large Bulk Mailings. Allows the User To Create/Name Multiple Files with Full Screen Editing. Similar Information May Be Carried over from Previous Records While Adding or Unused Fields May Be Skipped. Utilities Include: Automatic Insert/Update of Carrier Route Numbers Using the Postal Service's CRIS (Carrier Route Information System) Update Tapes on Diskette. Merge Two Files Together. Eliminate Duplicates from a File Keying on Company Name, Person's Name, Address etc. Create Mail Merge Files That Are Compatible with Most Word Processors. Menu-Driven, & Complete Documentation Is Included.
SourceView Software International.

BulkMail. P. L. Mariam. Apr. 1987. *Operating System(s) Required:* PC-DOS/MS-DOS 2.0 or higher. *Memory Required:* 640k. *General Requirements:* 2 disk drives or hard disk.
disk $49.95 (ISBN 0-935509-08-9, Order no.: 6000.01).
Will Sort Users Mailing List & Print Mailing Labels in Exact Bulk Mail Sorting Order. Bundling & Bagging Instructions Are Contained in Mailing Labels. The Program Comes with Its Own Data Base & Is Compatible with dBASE III+ Files. Program Offers 6 Other Sorting Configurations Which the User Can Print on a Hard Copy Report or Print-Out Mailing Labels. Manual Contains Complete Overview of Bulk Mail Postal Requirements.
FlowSoft, Inc.

Bulletin Board Construction Set. *Customer Support:* 800-929-8117 (customer service).
MS-DOS. Apple II. disk $99.99 (ISBN 0-87007-023-1).
IBM PC, PS/2. disk $99.99 (ISBN 0-87007-565-9).
A Totally Configurable Machine Language Bulletin Board System. Supports 2400 Baud. Needs the Original 6502 Chip, Will Not Work with the Enhanced 6502 Chip or the GS. User is Allowed to Completely Create His or Her Own Menu Structure, Allocate Areas for 5 Uploading & Downloading Programs, & Monitor Online Transaction with Users.
SourceView Software International.

Bulletins & Newsletters: ClickArt Cartoons. *Customer Support:* Free & unlimited technical support to registered users; 60 day money-back guarantee.
Macintosh. Macintosh, System 6.0.7 or higher (1Mb). 3.5" disk $49.95. *Addl. software required:* Any word-processing, desktop publishing or works program that accepts graphics.
Windows MS-DOS. IBM PC & compatibles. 3.5" disk $49.95. *Addl. software required:* Any word processing, desktop publishing or works program that accepts graphics.
Over 100 Images! Black & White Cartoons; Ready-to-Use, or Changed in Appropriate Drawing Program; Contains 12 Bonus Images Pre-Colored for Use in Presentations; Includes the ClickArt Trade Secret - Images Traded to Every Popular Graphics Format, Guaranteed to Work with All Popular Applications.
T/Maker Co., Inc.

BURCOM: DEC - Unisys Communication System. *Version:* 4.0. Aug. 1980. *Compatible Hardware:* VAX, Alpha AXP, Intel. *Operating System(s) Required:* Micro-RSX, Micro VMS, UNIX, MS Windows. *General Requirements:* Hardware interface.
Contact publisher for price.
Allows DEC & UNIX Computers to Communicate with Unisys Computers. DEC Terminals Can Be Used to Emulate Unisys Terminals. Also Provides Print Routing & File Transfer.
Applied Information Systems, Inc.

Bureaucracy. Douglas Adams. Mar. 1987. *Compatible Hardware:* Apple II, II+, IIe, IIc, Macintosh; Atari ST; Commodore 128, Amiga; IBM PC & compatibles. *Memory Required:* 128k.
Apple II, Macintosh, Amiga, IBM. disk $39.95. Commodore. $34.95.
Everyone, at One Time or Another, Feels Bound in an Endless Swathe of Red Tape. In BUREAUCRACY, Adams Draws on His Own Battles with Beadledom to Create a Comic Misadventure. The Goal of the Story Is to Get Your Bank to Acknowledge Your Change-of-Address Form. While Trying to Complete This Seemingly Easy Task, You Become Entangled in a Series of Bureaucratic Mishaps That Take You from the Feeding Trough of a Greedy Llama to the Lofty Branches of a Tree Deep in the Zalagasan Jungle.
Activision, Inc.

Burrelle's Media Directory 1994. Dec. 1993. *Items Included:* 12-page instruction manual for Electronic Data Files. Loose-leaf instruction binder for CD-ROM. *Customer Support:* No fees, customer service through Burrelle's for electronic data files. No fees, technical service through Silver Platter for CD-ROM.
DOS. IBM & compatibles (4Mb). disk $500.00 (ISBN 1-885601-07-7). *Addl. software required:* Database management system. *Optimal configuration:* 60Mb hard drive.
DOS. IBM & compatibles (4Mb). CD-ROM disk $795.00 (ISBN 1-885601-06-9). *Optimal configuration:* CD-ROM player. *Networks supported:* Novell, Banyan.
A Database of Broadcast & Print Media Organizations in the United States & Some Media Organizations in Canada.
Burrelle's Information Services.

Burrelle's Media Directory 1995. Dec. 1994. *Items Included:* 12-page instruction manual for Electronic Data Files. Loose-leaf instruction binder for CD-ROM. *Customer Support:* No fees, customer service through Burrelle's for electronic data files. No fees, technical service through Silver Platter for CD-ROM.
DOS. IBM & compatibles (4Mb). disk $500.00 (ISBN 1-885601-19-0). *Addl. software required:* 100Mb hard drive. *Optimal configuration:* Database management system.
MAC. IBM & compatibles (4Mb). 3.5" disk $500.00 (ISBN 1-885601-20-4). *Addl. software required:* Database management system. *Optimal configuration:* 100Mb hard drive.
DOS. IBM & compatibles (4Mb). CD-ROM disk $795.00 (ISBN 1-885601-18-2). *Optimal configuration:* CD-ROM player. *Networks supported:* Novell, Banyan.
A Database of Broadcast & Print Media Organizations in the United States, Canada, & Mexico.
Burrelle's Information Services.

Burrelle's Media Directory 1996. Dec. 1995. *Items Included:* 12-page instruction manual for electronic data files. Loose-leaf instruction binder for CD-ROM. *Customer Support:* No fees, customer service through Burrelle's for electronic data files. No fees, technical service through Silver Platter for CD-ROM.
DOS. IBM & compatibles (4Mb). disk $500.00 (ISBN 1-885601-34-4). *Addl. software required:* Database management software. *Optimal configuration:* 100Mb hard drive.
MAC. Apple (4Mb). 3.5" disk $500.00 (ISBN 1-885601-35-2). *Addl. software required:* Database management software. *Optimal configuration:* 100Mb hard drive.
DOS. IBM & compatibles (4Mb). CD-ROM disk $795.00 (ISBN 1-885601-36-0). *Optimal configuration:* CD-ROM player. *Networks supported:* Novell, Banyan.
Provides ASCII Comma Delimited Data Files of Broadcast & Print Media Organizations in the United States, Canada, & Mexico.
Burrelle's Information Services.

BusBASIC. *Items Included:* Detailed Manual. *Customer Support:* 800-929-8117 (customer service).
MS-DOS. Apple II. disk $49.99 (ISBN 0-87007-071-1).
An Interpreted & Compiled BASIC with Extensions for More Efficient Programming of Business Applications. Compacts to a Tight Code Which Is Usually Contained Within a 48Kb Memory Space. Source Programs May Be Run in an Interpreted or Compiled Version for Ease of Development. For Programmers, & Provides Several Built-In Development Tools. There Is No Distribution Fee for Including a Runtime Version with Applications Programs.
SourceView Software International.

Business Address & Information System. *Compatible Hardware:* TRS-80 Model III, Model 4. *Operating System(s) Required:* TRSDOS. *Language(s):* BASIC. *Memory Required:* 48k. *General Requirements:* Printer.
disk $24.95.
Information on Company Name, Address, Phone Number & Comments Can Be Stored, Edited or Changed When Needed. Can Search By Name or By One or Two Key Phrases. Capable of Printing Whole Entries or Mailing Labels if User Has the Proper Equipment.
Compuware.

Business Agreements. *Compatible Hardware:* IBM, Sanyo.
disk $49.95.
Provides 50 Standard Legal Forms.
MichTron, Inc.

Business Aids Library - Cash Management. *Compatible Hardware:* TI Home Computer. *Language(s):* BASIC.
contact publisher for price (Order no.: PHD5029).
Provides a Method of Forecasting the Amount of Cash Available to Company.
Texas Instruments, Personal Productivit.

Business Aids Library - Financial Management. *Compatible Hardware:* TI Home Computer. *Language(s):* BASIC.
contact publisher for price (Order no.: PHD5022).
Helps Project How Much Money Is Needed to Sustain a Business & How Much Capital Costs Will Be.
Texas Instruments, Personal Productivit.

Business Aids Library - Inventory Management. *Compatible Hardware:* TI Home Computer.
contact publisher for price (Order no.: PHD5024).
Allows for Inventory Update & Movement Tracking.
Texas Instruments, Personal Productivit.

Business Aids Library - Invoice Management. *Compatible Hardware:* TI Home Computer.
contact publisher for price (Order no.: PHD5027).
Keeps Current Customer Information in One System. Includes 7 Programs. Used with PERSONAL RECORD KEEPING or STATISTICS.
Texas Instruments, Personal Productivit.

Business Aids Library - Lease-Purchase Divisions. *Compatible Hardware:* TI Home Computer.
contact publisher for price (Order no.: PHD5038).
cassette write for info. (Order no.: PHT6038).
With the Capital Investment Analysis Model User Can Determine Whether an Investment in Any Capital Project Will Be Economically Beneficial.
Texas Instruments, Personal Productivit.

Business Analysis. *Compatible Hardware:* TRS-80 Model I, Model II, Model III. *Memory Required:* 32k.
disk $99.95 (Order no.: 0152RD).
cassette $75.00 (Order no.: 0140R).
Examines & Forecasts Any Type of Monthly, Quarterly, or Annual Data.
Instant Software, Inc.

Business Analyst. 1981. *Compatible Hardware:* Apple II with printer. *Memory Required:* 48k.
disk $55.00.
Designed for Analyzing the Expenses of a Small Company, by Comparing Historical to Projected Data. Calculates Effects of Changes in Income, Labor Costs, Material Costs, Overhead & G&A Expense on Company Operations. Printouts of Complete Expense Plans Are Available & Burden Rate Percentages Are Computed for Cost Accounting & Bidding Purposes.
Navic Software.

Business Architect: For the Business You Imagine. Sep. 1992. *Items Included:* Bound user manual. *Customer Support:* Free telephone support; 90 day warranty on disks; 30 day money back guarantee.
MS-DOS 3.0 or higher. IBM PC AT, PS12, Compaq or other 100% compatible (530k). disk $149.00. *Optimal configuration:* 386 computer, current release of MS-DOS, 600k memory, 2Mb hard drive space, HP laser jet or compatible laser printer.
Provides a Comprehensive Step-by-Step Approach to Business Planning. User Is Guided Through Three Key Planning Phases: Assessing Your Opportunity, Building a Business Plan, & Implementing That Plan. Features Like Expert Help, Notepads, Spreadsheets, Matrices, Milestone Planner, Action Planner, Calculator, & Loan Calculator Ensure a High Quality Printed Plan.
Enterprising Solutions, Inc.

Business Art. (Studio Ser.). *Items Included:* Visual index, user's guide. *Customer Support:* Free & unlimited technical support to registered users; 60 day money-back guarantee.
Macintosh. Macintosh (Minimum required for program with which you want to use ClickArt). 3.5" disk $99.95. *Nonstandard peripherals required:* PostScript compatible printer. *Addl. software required:* Any desktop publishing, word processing or works application that accepts EPS files.
Windows V.3.0 or higher. IBM PC & compatibles (Minimum needed for application with which you will use ClickArt). 3.5" disk $99.95. *Addl. software required:* Any desktop publishing, word processing or works program that accepts CGM or WMF files.
MS-DOS V.3.3 or higher. IBM PC & compatibles (Minimum needed for application with which

you will use ClickArt). 3.5" disk $99.95. *Addl. software required:* Any desktop publishing, word processing or works program that accepts WMF or CGM files.
Over 200 Images! Highest-Quality Full-Color Images Available; Ready-to-Use, or Changed in Appropriate Drawing Program; Designed in Full-Color (CMYK); Ready for Color Separations & Commercial Printing; Produced to Print in Detailed Greyscale on Black & White Printers.
T/Maker Co., Inc.

Business BASIC Compiler. *Compatible Hardware:* MS-DOS based machines. *Memory Required:* 32k. *General Requirements:* 2 disk drives.
disk $295.00.
Facilitates the Development of Business Applications Software in Microsoft BASIC.
Microsoft Pr.

Business Board System. *Version:* 1.2. Jul. 1986. *Compatible Hardware:* IBM PC, PC XT, PC AT, PS/2 & compatibles. *Operating System(s) Required:* DOS 2.X, 3.X. *Language(s):* BASIC & Assembler (source code included). *Memory Required:* 256k. *General Requirements:* Modem.
disk $349.00 (ISBN 0-924354-12-7, Order no.: HG12).
disk $149.00 (ISBN 0-924354-11-9, Order no.: HG11).
disk $99.00 (ISBN 0-924354-10-0, Order no.: HG10).
Provides a 24-Hour Information Center. No Programming Is Required to Configure to Meet Individual Business Needs. Users Can Provide Business Info and/or Take Product Orders & Inquiries. Data Entry Forms Can Be Designed by Users to Meet Their Needs.
Hawkeye Grafix.

Business Card Maker: Small Office Home Office. Mike Chapin. May 1995. *Items Included:* 8 1/2 x 5 1/2 manual, warranty card, sample paper pack & paper catalog, 3 8 1/2 x 11 "layout" sheets. *Customer Support:* 90 day limited warranty, free phone support Monday thru Friday 9:00AM to 6:00PM, 305-373-3700.
Windows 3.1 or higher. 386 or higher with 2Mb hard drive free (4Mb). CD-ROM disk $49.95 (ISBN 1-57519-002-8, Order no.: 976613). *Nonstandard peripherals required:* CD-ROM player. *Addl. software required:* CD-ROM driver software. *Optimal configuration:* 386 or higher, Win 3.1 or higher, CD player & software, 4Mb RAM, 2Mb hard drive, VGA or higher resolution.
Includes Everything a User Needs to Instantly Design Professional, Quality Business Cards, Post Cards, Labels & More! With 1000 High Quality Color Clipart Images & Designer Paper Samples - Plus, a Point-&-Click Windows Interface.
IntraCorp/Capstone.

Business Case for Implementing Broadband Networks. Dec. 1994. *Items Included:* User manual. *Customer Support:* Free technical support & a 30-day warranty (1-800-521-CORE).
MS-DOS. IBM & compatibles (512k). 3.5" disk $199.00 (ISBN 1-57305-010-5). *Nonstandard peripherals required:* High-density 3.5" disk drive; VGA color monitor. *Addl. software required:* MS-DOS version 3.3 or higher. *Optimal configuration:* IBM (512k), MS-DOS version 3.3 or higher, VGA color monitor, keyboard, Microsoft compatible mouse (optional).
This CBT Product Addresses Both the Pricing Issues That Customers Must Deal with in Making a Decision to Use or Not to Use a Broadband Service Like Frame Relay, ATM, or SMDS & the Parameters That Typically Are Included in the Pricing Structure. It Also Includes Example Pricing of Analyses for Specific Case Studies Involving a Network Using Frame Relay vs. More Traditional Services. Finally, the Student Has the Opportunity to Apply the Same Tools to Generate a Network of Their Own Design.
Bellcore.

Business Communication for the Microcomputer. 1989.
IBM PC. contact publisher for price (ISBN 0-538-70163-3, Order no.: WC44A8).
IBM PS/2. contact publisher for price (ISBN 0-538-70194-3, Order no.: WC44AH88).
Text & Software Package Covering the Essentials of Good Business Writing & Microcomputer Document Formatting.
South-Western Publishing Co.

Business Cycle Analysis. *Compatible Hardware:* Apple II+.
disk $59.95.
Allows User to Do Product Planning, Analyze Various Business Climates & Cycles, Analyze Stocks, Company Trends, & Growth Rates, & Store Graphs on Cycles & Trends That Aid in Decision-Making.
Instant Software, Inc.

Business Graphics. *Compatible Hardware:* B-20 series, B-22. *Operating System(s) Required:* BTOS. *Language(s):* PL/M. *Memory Required:* 256k.
disk $750.00.
Business Graphics Package Which May Be Used to Graphically Display & Print Data Used in Release 2.0 or Higher MULTIPLAN. Allows Cut & Paste Graphics for Presentation Material, Interactive Manipulation of Charts & Graphs with Merge, Scale, Interactive Changes in Shading & Label Font Styles, etc.
Burroughs Corp.

Business Graphics Toolkit. *Compatible Hardware:* Macintosh, IBM PC. *General Requirements:* True BASIC 2.0 or higher. 3.5" disk $79.95.
Produces Business Charts from Data. Selects the Scale, Chooses Good Looking Numbers for the Axes & Draws the Chart. The Business Graphics Toolkit Works in All the True BASIC Graphics Modes. The Program Features Bar Charts, Histograms, Line Charts, Area Charts, Scatter Plots, Comparison Tables, I-Beam & High-Low-Close Charts. Multiple Data Sets May Be Plotted on a Graph & Overlaid Graphs Are Available. In Addition, 13 Point Styles, Four Line Styles & Full Color Support Are Provided.
True BASIC, Inc.

Business GuardDog. *Version:* 2.0. Feb. 1992. *Compatible Hardware:* Macintosh; IBM PC & compatibles. *Items Included:* Manual & diskette(s) (one 360k 5.25" & one 720k 3.5" for the PC, one 800k 3.5" for the Mac). *Customer Support:* Provided by JIAN   415-941-5191.
disk $159.00. *Addl. software required:* PC's: word processor compatible with MS Word, PCWrite, Q&A, PFS First Choice, WordPerfect, WordStar & most others. Macintosh: word processor, MacWrite 5.0 or MS Word 3.01 compatible.
Over 60 Policies & Procedures to Uncover & Prevent Business Losses & Abuses - from Employee Carelessness to Criminal Intent. Formatted in Popular Wordprocessing Files for Editing & Customization.
JIAN Tools for Sales.

Business Horizon: Small Business Accounting. *Version:* 6. *Items Included:* direction manual. *Customer Support:* 30 minutes free; Pay-per-call at $1.95/minute.
MS-DOS 3.1 or higher. IBM & compatibles (640k). disk $725.00. *Networks supported:* Novell, Lantastic.
Double Entry Accounting Deigned for Non-Farm Businesses with Expanded Accounts Receivable Needs. Password Protection Included. Reports Include. Daily Journal Report, Receivables Statements, Aged Receivables, Aged Payables, & Financial Analysis. Checks May Be Written Individually or in a Batch. Vendors Names & Addresses Automatically Looked up. Flexible Enterprise Tagging Allows You to Mark Entries for Special Reports.
Harvest Computer Systems, Inc.

Business Illustrations: ClickArt. *Items Included:* Visual index, user's guide. *Customer Support:* Free & unlimited technical support to registered users; 60 day money-back guarantee.
Macintosh. Macintosh, System 6.0.7 or higher (1Mb). 3.5" disk $49.95. *Addl. software required:* Any word-processing, desktop publishing or works program that accepts graphics.
Windows MS-DOS. IBM PC & compatibles. 3.5" disk $49.95. *Addl. software required:* Any word processing, desktop publishing or works program that accepts graphics.
Over 275 Images! Full-Color Images; Ready-to-Use, or Changed in Appropriate Drawing Program; Designed in Full-Color (CMYK); Produced to Print in Detailed Greyscale on Black & White Printers; Includes the ClickArt Trade Secret - Images Traded to Every Popular Graphics Format, Guaranteed to Work with All Popular Applications.
T/Maker Co., Inc.

Business in a Box. *Version:* 3.5. *Compatible Hardware:* IBM PC XT. *Memory Required:* 640k. *General Requirements:* 20Mb hard disk.
disk $995.00.
Integrated Package Featuring Word-Processing, Database & Communications Modules. Includes Mail/Merge Database Link, On-Screen Help & Built-In Language & Single Custom Application in the Database. Imports ASCII File Formats; Exports ASCII, DIF, SYLK & SDF File Formats.
EKD Computer Sales & Supplies Corp.

Business Insight. *Version:* 4.0. Dec. 1994. *Items Included:* Tutorial disk. *Customer Support:* Unlimited free technical support at (512) 251-7541.
MS/PC-DOS, Windows; 3.1 or higher. IBM PC, XT, AT or compatibles (640k). disk $495.00. *Nonstandard peripherals required:* Hard disk required. *Networks supported:* LAN.
Expert Systems Designed to Help User Accurately Measure the Potential Risks & Rewards of Business Ideas. The Expert System Is Programmed to Make Observations on Target Markets, Promotion Strategy, Sales Methods, Inventory Management, & More. It Also Includes a Sophisticated Spreadsheet Manager (Compatible with Lotus 1-2-3).
Business Resource Software.

Business Law, Comprehensive Volume. 1987.
IBM/Tandy. contact publisher for price (ISBN 0-538-51061-7, Order no.: Q30062).
Microcomputer Study Guide for Use With Business Law, Comprehensive Volume (L68) or with Standard Volume (L69).
South-Western Publishing Co.

Business Learning System. Oct. 1986. *Items Included:* Provided with each simulation is a manual describing the various simulation decisions & a facilitators guide that explains simulation set-up & terminology. *Customer Support:* Included in all Licensing Agreements is a service contract that entitles Licensees to a Train-the-Trainer program & an 800 support phone number.

PC/MS-DOS 2.0 & higher. IBM PC/XT/AT & compatibles (256k). disk $475.00. *Nonstandard peripherals required:* 2 disk drives &/or a hard disk.
Comprehensive MBA Level Business Simulation in the Areas of Marketing, Finance, Operations & Strategic Planning.
Strategic Management Group, Inc.

Business Letter Base. *Compatible Hardware:* Apple Macintosh Plus. *Memory Required:* 1000k. *General Requirements:* 2 800k floppy disk drives or hard disk, HyperCard. *Customer Support:* Free.
3.5" disk $99.95.
Expandable Letter Database with Writing Guide.
Milum Corp.

Business Letters for Publishers. *Version:* 1.1. Jan. 1988. *Compatible Hardware:* Apple Macintosh, IBM PC & compatibles. *Operating System(s) Required:* PC-DOS/MS-DOS, Apple DOS, Windows. *Memory Required:* 640k. *Items Included:* Manual. *Customer Support:* Yes.
3.5" disk $29.95 (ISBN 0-915516-47-0).
Collection of 75 Letters Drafted for Publishers. Includes Promotion, Marketing, Collections, Letters to Printer, etc.
Para Publishing.

Business Letters Go! *Version:* 2.0. *Compatible Hardware:* Apple Macintosh. *Memory Required:* 512k. *General Requirements:* 800k disk drive; Double Helix. *Customer Support:* Free.
3.5" disk $49.95.
Business Letter Templates & Letter Writing Guide.
Milum Corp.

Business Management, Pt. V: Econometrics.
Operating System(s) Required: CP/M. *Memory Required:* 56k.
disk $310.00.
Application Software System for Performing & Analyzing Two & Three-Stage Least Squares Estimates of Parameters in "Simultaneous Equation" Econometric Models As Well As "Interdependent" Econometric Models.
Century Software Systems.

Business Management System. *Version:* 5.2. Jan. 1987. *Compatible Hardware:* IBM PC, PC AT, PC XT, PC XT 286, P/S 2. *Operating System(s) Required:* PC-DOS. *Language(s):* Compiled BASIC. *Memory Required:* 512k. *Customer Support:* First year support is free. contact publisher for price.
Construction Management Program. Basic Modules Are Job Cost, Payables & Receivables, General Ledger. Payroll & Estimating (Integrated) Available As Option, Report Writer.
Enterprise Computer Systems, Inc.

Business Management System. Fisher Business Systems, Inc. *Compatible Hardware:* TI Professional. *Operating System(s) Required:* MS-DOS. *Memory Required:* 128k. *General Requirements:* Printer.
$1800.00.
Functions Include Accounts Payable, Accounts Receivable, Payroll & General Ledger. Other Applications May Be Integrated Later.
Texas Instruments, Personal Productivit.

Business Manager. *Compatible Hardware:* IBM PC & compatibles. *Memory Required:* 512k. *General Requirements:* Hard disk.
$295.00 per module.
Financial/Accounting Software. Posts Recurring Transactions, Automatic Posting from Other Modules, Report Format User Definable, Reports Comparative Statements, Links with External Software Programs, Password Access, Audit Trail, Error Recovery, Source Code Available Dbase Compatible, Reject Erroneous Account Numbers & On-Line Help.
Custom Software Consulting Services, Inc.

Business Mastery Supplemental Software.
May 1995. *Items Included:* Instruction booklet. *Customer Support:* Free telephone support.
MS-DOS, DOS/Windows, OS/2, Macintosh. X86. Single-User $24.95, Multi-User (up to 5) $59.95, Schools-Associatons $129.95 (ISBN 0-9621265-6-X). *Addl. software required:* Any word processor that can import text files. *Optimal configuration:* 1Mb disk space.
A Text-Based Computer Disk Offering Quick & Easy Access to Exercises, Forms & Business Plan Outline from the Book Business Mastery; More Than 150 Letters, Announcements, Forms & Checklists; & a Completed Massage Practice Business Plan.
Sohnen-Moe Assocs.

Business Mathematics for Colleges. 1988. IBM/Tandy. contact publisher for price (ISBN 0-538-51065-X, Order no.: Q30066).
Text-Workbook & Microcomputer Study Guide Covering Basic Business Math. Exercises Give Students Experience Using the Microcomputer to Solve Practical Math Problems. Software Features Help Screens & a Pop-Up Calculator.
South-Western Publishing Co.

Business Pack: Business Program Collection, 2 diskettes. *Items Included:* Bound manual. *Customer Support:* Free hotline - no time limit; 30 day limited warranty; updates are $5/disk plus S&H.
MS-DOS. IBM & compatibles (256k). $99.95.
Collection of 100 Ready-to-Run Programs for Various Business Calculations Such as Bond Value, Depletion Analysis etc.
Dynacomp, Inc.

Business Plan Package. Jan. 1989. *Compatible Hardware:* IBM PC & compatibles. *Operating System(s) Required:* PC-DOS. *Memory Required:* 512k. *General Requirements:* Hard disk.
disk $89.95 (ISBN 1-55571-056-5).
Includes the Self-Help Manual "Develop Your Business Plan" & Companion Software Combining Word Processing & Spreadsheet Functions. Enables the User to Make Projections for Balance Sheets, Income Planning, Market Penetration, Market Size, Sales Planning, & Sales Ratios. Assists the User in Calculating Results.
Oasis Pr.

Business Plan Pro. Tim Berry. Nov. 1994. *Items Included:* Manual. *Customer Support:* Free technical support (toll call) for 1 year via phone, fax, email.
Windows 3.1 or higher, including Windows 95 (4Mb). disk $149.95. *Nonstandard peripherals required:* 5Mb hard disk space.
A Complete, Versatile Package That Shows You What a Business Plan Is, Walks You Through the Preparation Process, & Produces the Finished Product Practically & Efficiently. It Gives You All the Tools That You Need to Create a Surprisingly Polished Business Plan Without Going Through Extensive Training.
Palo Alto Software.

Business Plan Toolkit. *Version:* 6.0. Tim Berry. Feb. 1996. *Items Included:* Manual. *Customer Support:* Free technical support (toll call) for 1 year via phone, fax, email.
Macintosh with at least 2Mb hard disk (2Mb). 3.5" disk $149.95. *Addl. software required:* Excel 4.0 or higher (Excel 5.0 recommended) & Word 5.1 or higher; or Microsoft Works 3.0 or higher, or Claris Works 2.1 or higher.
An All-in-One Package That Covers Everything from Financial Analysis to Market Forecasting. Includes a Robust Set of Spreadsheet Templates As Well As an Ingenious Text Editor for Writing a Business Plan. The Manual Gives Clear, Commonsense Advice on Business Plan Preparation, Including Tips on What to Leave Out of the Plan. It's a Top Choice for Start-Up Entrepreneurs.
Palo Alto Software.

Business Planner. *Version:* 3.0. *Compatible Hardware:* IBM PC & compatibles, PS/2. *Memory Required:* 115k. *General Requirements:* Lotus 1-2-3 release 2/2.01, or Symphony. disk $295.00.
Contains Goal-Seeking, Budgeting, Scenario-Analysis, Risk-Analysis, Forecasting, & Linear-Optimization Add-In Programs. Each Program Is Self-Contained & Any One Can Be Used for Decision Analysis Without Having to Alter Worksheet.
Enfin Software Corp.

Business Planning Master. *Customer Support:* 800-929-8117 (customer service).
MS-DOS. Apple II. disk $49.99.
Provides the Tools for Making a Variety of Business Decisions. Included are: Future Value of an Investment, Future Value of Annuity, Future Value of Savings, Withdrawals from Investment, Loan Price, Minimum Investment for Income, Loan Payment Schedules, Income from Investment, Nominal, Effective & Earned Interest Tables, Annual Depreciation, Mortgage Amortization, Loan Repayment, Salvage Value, Depreciated Investment, Discounted Commercial Paper, Final Loan Payment & Remaining Loan Balance.
SourceView Software International.

Business Planning Model for Forecasts & Projections. Jun. 1987. *Compatible Hardware:* IBM PC & compatibles. *Memory Required:* 348k. *General Requirements:* Lotus 1-2-3 Release 2. *Customer Support:* Free telephone Support. $195.00.
Model Helps Analyze & Present Prospective Financial Information & Serves As a Guide to American Institute of Certified Public Accountants Guidelines & Standards. User May Set Monthly, Quarterly, or Yearly Periods Within a 12-Period Time Horizon. Immediately Calculates Input Changes & Allows Screen Scrolling to Review Additions. Determines Break-Even Point & Helps Set Goals & Manage Surplus or Deficit Financing. Produces Graphs.
Accounting Professionals Software, Inc.

Business Pro-Pak. *Customer Support:* 800-929-8117 (customer service).
MS-DOS. IBM/PS2. disk $99.99 (ISBN 0-87007-293-5).
Converts All Types of Weights & Measures, Maintains an Appointment Calendar, Converts Any Amount of U.S. Currency to Any Other Currency & Vice Versa, Analyzes Advertising Costs & Keeps an Accurate Record of Research Material. Features a Perpetual Calendar, Name & address List, & Prints Labels.
SourceView Software International.

Business Problem Solving Using the IBM PC & PC XT. *Compatible Hardware:* IBM PC.
disk $35.00.
Includes Dozens of Programs Designed for Use by Business People in Problem Solving & Decision Making. Describes Select Commercial Software & Offers Guidance in Writing Programs & in Revising or Customizing the Programs Listed in the Text.
Prentice Hall.

Business Simulator. 1986. *Items Included:* Provided with each simulation is a manual describing the various simulation decisions & a facilitators guide that explains simulation set-up & terminology. *Customer Support:* Included in all Licensing Agreements is a service contract that entitles licensees to a Train-the-Trainer program &

an 800 support phone number.
PC/MS-DOS 2.0 & higher. IBM PC/XT/AT (256k). 3.5" or 5.25" disk $69.95.
Nonstandard peripherals required: 2 disk drives &/or a hard disk.
Mac & compatibles.
Competitive Business Simulation to Build Skills in Production, Marketing & Financial Planning to Win Big in Business.
Strategic Management Group, Inc.

Business Simulator Collegiate Edition w Business Week Articles. 1988. *General Requirements:* 2 floppy disk drives or 1 floppy disk drive & 1 hard drive. Colorgraphics card & color monitor necessary for analysis mode only.
IBM PC. contact publisher for price (ISBN 0-538-80088-7, Order no.: GC71AC).
Package Contains: System Disk, Tutorial Disk, & User's Guide. Focuses on Decision-Making Skills at 3 Levels of a Business Environment (Start-up; Growth; Independence). Allows for Individual or 2-Person Sessions. It Includes Relevant Business Week Articles. Software Contains Help Screens, On-Line Tutorial, & "Pro-Forma Planner" Analysis/Consulting Modes.
South-Western Publishing Co.

Business Statistics. *Version:* 10.0. (Professional Ser.). 1989. *Compatible Hardware:* Apple Macintosh, IBM PC & compatibles. *Memory Required:* 512k. *Items Included:* Disks, book, program instructions. *Customer Support:* Telephone.
disk $145.00 (ISBN 0-920387-10-1).
Statistical Tools Likely to Be of Use in a Business Setting. The Coverage Is Similar to That of EXPERIMENTAL STATISTICS but Less Emphasis Is Placed on the Variety of Design of Experiments & Analysis of Variance; Instead Concentration Is Made on Those Types of Experiments Which Are Most Applicable in a Business Ambiance (2k Factorials, Fractional Factorials, Blocked Factorials). Sampling Procedures Are Given Special Attention, & Sections on Quality Control & System Reliability Are Included. A Section on Forecasting Techniques Is Provided with Examples of Time-Series.
Lionheart Pr., Inc.

Business Ties. *Version:* 1.01. Jan. 1994. *Items Included:* Complete documentation, extensive on-line Help. *Customer Support:* 90-day evaluation period, 30-day money-back guarantee, unlimited toll-free support for 12 months, product updates for 12 months.
DOS. IBM PC & compatibles (512k). $395.00 per module. *Addl. software required:* SystemManager. *Optimal configuration:* IBM PC or compatible, MS-DOS 3.1 or higher, 512k RAM, Business Ties System Manager. *Networks supported:* Novell, LANtastic, PC-LAN & most DOS networks.
Suite of Integrated Accounting Products Including General Ledger, Accounts Receivable, Accounts Payable, Inventory Control, Order Entry, Payroll, & Job Cost. The Unique Integration That Connects Business Ties Data to Other Prentice Hall Applications Is the Characteristic That Separates Business Ties from Any Other Suite of Accounting Products. By Retrieving Their Clients' Transactions & End-of-Year Balances from Business Ties, Accountants Can Use Their Prentice Hall Packages for Client Write-Up Work, Workpaper & Trial Balance Engagements, Business Tax Returns, & W-2s & 1099s. All Business Ties Modules Feature Fast & Easy Setup, Single & Multiple Users, & Complete File Locking.
Prentice Hall Professional Software.

Business Tools. Fern Benson & Paul Benson. *Compatible Hardware:* Atari ST.
3.5" disk $49.95.
Includes 215 Attorney-Prepared Business Documents: 77 Business Forms, 33 Contracts, & 105 Letters. The Forms, Contracts, & Letters Are Saved As Word Processing Templates & Can Be Used & Customized with Any Word Processor. Includes 8 Business Appendices with Information Like Weights & Measures, Abbreviations, & Telephone Area Codes.
MichTron, Inc.

Business Utility I. *Compatible Hardware:* Apple II+. *Memory Required:* 32k.
disk $49.95.
Deals with the Areas of Real Estate, Banking, Securities, Leasing, Investment Analysis, & Statistics. Allows Rapid Access to Ten Frequently Occurring Business Decisions in Areas Which Require Speed & Accurate Analysis of Data. The Subroutines Presented in the Program Include Linear Regression-Exponential Curve Fit, Accumulated Interest/Remaining Balance, Wrap-Around Mortgage, Discounted Cash Flow Analysis/Net Present Value, Interest at Maturity-Securities, Discounted Securities Analysis, Internal Rate of Return, Direct Reduction Loans-Sinking Fund, Depreciation Schedules & Amortization Schedules.
Powersoft, Inc.

Business Utility II. *Compatible Hardware:* Apple II+. *Memory Required:* 32k.
contact publisher for price.
Applicable to Real Estate, Banking, Investments, Securities, & Insurance Analysis Requirements. Subroutines Presented in the Program Include Calendar Functions, Best Curve Fit Analysis, Constant Payment to Principal Loan, Advanced Payments to Loan, Add-On Date Installment Loan, Savings-Compounding Period Different from Payment Period, Interest Rebate-Rule 78, Simple Interest, Interest Conversions & Let's Make a Deal.
Powersoft, Inc.

Business Utility Master. *Customer Support:* 800-929-8117 (customer service).
MS-DOS. IBM/PS2. disk $79.99 (ISBN 0-87007-857-7).
A Collection of Math, Statistics & Financial Calculation Programs Similar to What Is Available on Specialized Handheld Calculators. Designed for the Quick Decision Where There Are Few Known Data Points.
SourceView Software International.

Business Valuation. Feb. 1985. *Compatible Hardware:* IBM PC & compatibles. *Operating System(s) Required:* PC-DOS, MS-DOS. (source code included). *General Requirements:* Lotus 1-2-3. *Customer Support:* Free telephone Support.
disk $195.00.
Estimates the Value of Businesses. Templates Are Provided for Both Regular & Professional Corporations. Several Common Methods of Valuation Including Discounted Future Earnings Method Are Provided. Low, Medium, & High Valuation Alternatives for Each Method Can Be Displayed Simultaneously. Input of Balance Sheet & Income Statement Information Follows Format of the Corporate Income Tax Return.
Accounting Professionals Software, Inc.

Business Valuation Template. Jan. 1990. *Customer Support:* Telephone customer support, documentation with sample problems.
MS-DOS. IBM PC & compatibles (640k). disk $195.00 (Order no.: 956). *Nonstandard peripherals required:* Printer, hard disk. *Addl. software required:* Lotus 1-2-3.
Macintosh (512k). 3.5" disk $195.00 (Order no.: 956). *Nonstandard peripherals required:* Printer, hard disk. *Addl. software required:* Excel.
Produces Results for the Eight Most Common Business Valuation Methods - Low, Medium, & High, As Follows: Capitalization of Earnings, Discounted Future Earnings, Discounted Cash Flow, Dividend Paying Capacity, Excess Earnings - Return on Net Assets, Excess Earnings - Return on Net Sales, Adjusted Net Assets, & Price-Earnings Ratio (Multiple of Earnings). Includes 41 Pre-Defined Graphs & 51 Statement Ratios, All of Which Are Produced Automatically. A Total of 15 Professional Reports are Generated. Each Report Prints on a Separate Page. Program Is Menu - Driven & Interactive with Graphics & Works with Lotus 1-2-3 Or As a Stand-Alone Version.
ILAR Systems, Inc.

Business Week's Business Advantage. Jun. 1987. *Items Included:* Provided with each simulation is a manual describing the various simulation decisions & a facilitators guide that explains simulation set-up & terminology. *Customer Support:* Included in all Licensing Agreements is a service contract that entitles licensees to a Train-the-Trainer program & an 800 support phone number.
PC/MS-DOS 2.0 & higher. IBM PC/XT/AT (384k). 3.5" or 5.25" disk $69.95.
Nonstandard peripherals required: 2 disk drives &/or a hard disk.
Mac & compatibles.
Interactive Business Simulation Designed to Develop Your Business Skills in All Aspects; Comes Complete with an "Expert Insight" Feature for Evaluating Decisions; Also Has a Library of 14 Specific Industry Case Scenarios.
Strategic Management Group, Inc.

BusinessWorks Bundle (Apple). *Version:* 5.1. Sep. 1986. *Compatible Hardware:* Apple IIe with 80-column display, IIc, IIgs. *Operating System(s) Required:* ProDOS. *Language(s):* Assembly, BASIC. *Memory Required:* 128k. *General Requirements:* 2 3.5" drives or ProDOS compatible hard disk or 1 3.5" drive & 1Mb available memory. *Items Included:* System Manager, General Ledger, Accounts Payable, Accounts Receivable, Inventory Control; manuals included. *Customer Support:* 90 days toll-free support; $150 for each additional yr. of phone support.
$495.00.
Full-Featured Accounting System Which Provides Numerous Reports, Including Summary "Flash" Reports, Help Messages, & Windows. Can Be Used with AppleWorks. Up to 50 Companies Can Be Installed on a Hard Disk, or User Can Keep Track of an Unlimited Number of Companies on Floppy Disks.
Manzanita Software Systems.
  Module 1. System Manager (with Labels Plus). *Version:* 5.1 (Apple).
  3.5" disk $95.00.
  Handles Password Security, Company Information, Payment Terms, & Various Utilities. Allows the Use of Payroll Modules Separately or Combined into One Complete Accounting Package. Includes LABELS PLUS, a Mailing Labels Program That Allows User to Produce Lists & Labels for Any Names Entered, As Well As for Employees, Customers, or Vendors Entered in the Other Modules.
  Module 2. General Ledger. *Version:* 5.1 (Apple).
  not sold separately, included in the bundle.
  Handles up to 1000 Accounts in the User-Defined Chart of Accounts. Maintains a Financial History of the Previous 13 Months. Transactions Can Be Posted to Prior or Future Months. Entries Are Posted As Soon As They Are Entered. Various Reports Are Available in Several Different Formats.

BUSINESSWORKS INVENTORY CONTROL:

Module 4. Accounts Receivable. *Version:* 5.1 (Apple).
not sold separately, included in the bundle. *Maintains Complete Information on Customers, Including Total Sales & Payments, Credit History, Payment Terms, & Credit Limit. Handles Debit & Credit Memos, Open Credits, Three Levels of Sales Tax, Discounts, Finance Charges, Recurring Invoices, Open Item Statements, & Balance Forward Statements. Sales Can Be Posted to up to 16 Different General Ledger Accounts, & Can Be Tracked by Sales Representative. Generates Various Reports.*
Module 3. Accounts Payable. *Version:* 5.1 (Apple).
not sold separately, included in the bundle. *Automatically Performs Cash Management Tasks Such As Determining Whom to Pay & When to Pay, Taking Advantage of All Available Discounts. User Can Produce Checks for Either the Full Invoice Amount or a Partial Payment. Supports Check Voiding & Reconciliation. Maintains Complete Vendor & Invoice Information, Including Payment Terms, Year-to-Date Purchases & Payments, & Current Balances Owed. Produces Various Reports.*
Module 4. Inventory Control. *Version:* 5.1 (Apple).
not sold separately, included in the bundle. *For Each Part Entered, the System Tracks Month-to-Date & Year-to-Date Receipts, Issues & Adjustments, Order Points, & Minimum Order Quantities. Prints Purchase Orders & Retains the Information until All Ordered Items Have Been Received. Supports Global Price Changes. Produces Summary or Detailed Reports.*
Module 6. Payroll. *Version:* 5.1 (Apple). 3.5" disk $195.00.
Automatically Produces Checks with Detailed Stubs for Weekly, Biweekly, Monthly, or Semimonthly Pay Periods. Also Produces Government Reports Such As 940 & 941 & W-2 Forms. System Can Prepare Payroll for Hourly, Salaried, Commissioned & Piece Rate Employees, & Can Handle up to 25 Extra Deductions (Ten per Employee). Maintains 200 Job Codes & Allows User to Record Handwritten Payroll Checks. Requires System Manager If Not Integrated with the Businessworks Bundle.

BusinessWorks Inventory Control: Module 6. *Version:* 7.11. Jul. 1991. *Items Included:* Perfect bound manual. *Customer Support:* 90 days toll-free technical phone support, each additional year $150.00.
MS-DOS 3.1 or higher. IBM PS/2, PC, PC XT, PC AT & compatibles (384k). disk $295.00. *Addl. software required:* System manager. *Networks supported:* PC-LAN, 3COM, Novell, LANtastic.
Maintains Complete Information for Each Inventory Part, Including On-Hand & On-Order Quantities, Vendors, Substitute Items, Components & Transaction History. Automatically Makes Global Price Changes, Prints Purchase Orders & Retains Information Until All Ordered Items Have Been Received. Allows One of Four Costing Methods: Standard, Average, LIFO or FIFO.
Manzanita Software Systems.

BusinessWorks PC Bundle. *Version:* 7.11. Jeff Gold. Jul. 1991. *Items Included:* Perfect-bound manuals. *Customer Support:* 90 days toll-free technical phone support; each additional year costs $150.
MS-DOS 3.1 or higher (384k). disk $795.00, bundle includes System Manager, General Ledger, Accounts Receivable & Accounts Payable. *Nonstandard peripherals required:* Hard disk. *Networks supported:* PC-LAN, 3COM, Novell, Lantastic.
Full-Featured Accounting System Which Provides Numerous Reports, Including Summary "Flash" Reports, Help Messages, & Windows. Up to 100 Companies Can Be Installed. All Modules Are Fully Integrated to Allow for Automatic Posting to the General Ledger.
Manzanita Software Systems.

Busipack. 1989. *Items Included:* Manual & sourcecode in BASIC.
MS-DOS 2.X -4.X. IBM PC/XT/AT; PS/2 (512K). disk $12.95 (Order no.: 521). *Addl. software required:* Basica/GWbasic.
This Integrated Package Combines Invoice Writing, Inventory Control, & Mailing List. The Inventory Control & the Mailing List Can Be Used as Standalone Programs. The Inventory Control Allows User to Enter Reorder Level. The Value of All Products on Stock Can Be Calculated by Resale Prices & Wholesale Prices. The Mailing Lists Allows User to Search, to Print Labels & Lists. When Writing Invoices, the Addresses Are Retrieved from the Mailing List & the Description & Prices for the Items Are Retrieved from the Inventory Control. The Inventory File is Updated Automatically Everytime an Item is Sold.
Elcomp Publishing, Inc.

Busytown. (Richard Scarry Ser.). Feb. 1995.
MS-DOS 3.1 or higher. 386 processor or higher (640k RAM). CD-ROM disk $49.95 (Order no.: R1159). *Nonstandard peripherals required:* CD-ROM drive. *Optimal configuration:* 386 processor or higher, MS-DOS 3.1 or higher, 20Mb hard drive, external speakers or headphones (with sound card) that are Sound Blaster compatible, VGA graphics & adapter, VGA color monitor.
Macintosh (4Mb). (Order no.: R1159A). *Nonstandard peripherals required:* 14" color monitor or larger, CD-ROM drive.
This Delightful Educational Adventure Challenges Creativity & Helps Children Develop Language & Social Skills, Exercise Creative Thinking, Build Memory, & Practice Problem Solving Through Games, Songs, Counting, Real Life Situations & More (Ages 3 & Up).
Library Video Co.

buttonFile. *Version:* 1.0. May 1993. *Items Included:* 1 bound manual. *Customer Support:* 800-809-0027: $15/call or 900-555-8800: $2/min.
Windows. IBM PC, XT, AT, PS/2 or compatible (1Mb). disk $69.96; Network LAN version $199.95. *Addl. software required:* Microsoft Windows 3.0 or higher. *Optimal configuration:* IBM compatible machine with 1Mb free RAM, VGA monitor, Microsoft Windows & a mouse. *Networks supported:* Microsoft LAN Manager, Novell Netware, Artisoft LANtastic, Banyan Vines.
Personal Database Manager for the Windows Operating System. No Other Program Lets User Perform the Essential Database Tasks As Quickly & Easily: Manage Mailing Lists, Team Rosters, Phone Directories, Inventory Lists, Catalogs or Even Recipe Collections. Auto-Dial Any Phone Number & Create a List of Frequently-Used Speed-Dial Numbers. Design & Print Mailing Labels, Envelopes, Rolodex & 3x5 Cards, & a Myriad of Reports. Does All This Better Than a Rolodex & with More Ease Than Full-Blown Database Managers.
Outlook Software.

Buy Low-Sell High. *Compatible Hardware:* TRS-80 Model I, Model III, Model 4 with Level II BASIC. (source code included). *Memory Required:* 32k.
disk $19.95.
Stock Market & Investment Simulation.
Dynacomp, Inc.

Buysel. *Compatible Hardware:* IBM PC. (source code included).
disk $99.95.
Dynacomp, Inc.

Byte 'N Bass. *Version:* 2.1. Braston DeGaruio. Sep. 1995. *Customer Support:* Free telephone support or via Compuserve.
DOS 3.X, Windows 3.X. 386 (640k). disk $99.95. *Nonstandard peripherals required:* Mouse recommended.
Relational Database That Includes a Fishing Diary, Lake Database, & Lure Database. Includes Graphic Analysis of Daily & Seasonal Fishing Patterns, Computer Assisted Lure Selection, over 400 Pages of On-Line Information on Bass Fishing, Color Graphics on Knots & Rigging, GPS Support, Personal Tournament Stats, & More.
Rapha Group Software, Inc.

Bytes of Fright. *Compatible Hardware:* Apple Macintosh.
contact publisher for price.
A.A.H. Computer Graphics Productions.

C. *Items Included:* Software, manual. *Customer Support:* One full year of support is included with each product purchased. Support includes hotline phone support, technical mailings, & free upgrade.
PDOS. Motorola 680 x 0 based systems. disk $1400.00 (Order no.: 3550). *Networks supported:* Ethernet, MAP.
The PDOS C Compiler Is Written in C & is a Full C Language Implementation As Defined by Kernighan & Ritchie in The C Programming Language. System Supports the Draft-Proposed American National Standards Institute (ANSI) C Standard. Programs Are Easily Moved to or from Other Systems Running C. PDOS C Programs Can Use the Full 32 Bit Address Space of the 680 x 0 CPU. Floating Point Aritthmetic Is Supported in Software Using the Motorola Fast Floating Point or the IEEE Floating Point Format. PDOS 68020/68030 C Support Floating Point Using the Motorola Floating Point Co-Processor.
Eyring Corp.

C. A. Cutter's Three-Figure Author Table. Richard Cutter. 1969.
IBM & compatibles. CD-ROM disk $17.00 (ISBN 0-87287-209-2). *Nonstandard peripherals required:* CD-ROM drive.
Library Resource.
Libraries Unlimited, Inc.

C. A. Cutter's Two-Figure Author Table. Richard Cutter. 1969.
IBM & compatibles. CD-ROM disk $11.00 (ISBN 0-87287-208-4). *Nonstandard peripherals required:* CD-ROM drive.
Library Resource.
Libraries Unlimited, Inc.

C.A.R.-FREE. *Version:* 2.0. Open Door Software Division. Oct. 1993. *Items Included:* Spiral manual, video (when available). *Customer Support:* 30 day free customer support; 900 line $2.00/min.; 1 yr. maintenance $400/mo. Includes: toll free line & fax back priority service.
DOS. IBM compatible 386, 25Mhz, 5Mb free space on hard disk, VGA monitor, 3.5" floppy, keyboard, mouse (1Mb). disk $495.00 (ISBN 1-56756-055-5, Order no.: OD8001). *Addl. software required:* Operating system. *Optimal configuration:* IBM or compatible 486, 66Mhz, 5Mb free space on hard disk, 4Mb RAM-3Mb expanded usable, VGA monitor, 3.5" high density floppy, keyboard, mouse, tape backup, & uninterruptable power supply. *Networks supported:* Novell Netware Lite.
Windows. IBM compatible 386, 25Mhz, 5Mb free space on hard disk, VGA monitor, 3.5"

TITLE INDEX

floppy, keyboard, mouse (1Mb). disk $495.00 (ISBN 1-56756-068-7, Order no.: OD805W). *Addl. software required:* Windows 3.1 or higher. *Optimal configuration:* IBM or compatible 486, 66Mhz, 5Mb free space on hard disk, 4Mb RAM-3Mb expanded usable, VGA monitor, 3.5" high density floppy, keyboard, mouse, tape backup, & uninterruptable power supply. *Networks supported:* Novell Netware Lite.
MAC. 3.5" disk $495.00 (ISBN 1-56756-056-3, Order no.: OD820M). *Addl. software required:* System 7.
Corporate Car Rental Rate Comparison Software Application Designed for Purchasing Agents of Mid to Large Companies That Rent Cars Regionally, Nationally, or Internationally. Saves Time & Money by Giving Purchasing Agents the Advantage of Having a Highly Sophisticated Program to Compare Up-to-Date Costs & Savings of Each of the Car Rental Company Alternatives. Compare Apples to Apples by Having This Software to Give Accurate Comparisons of the per Rental Rates, Costs per Rental per Car Type per City per Region per Year, Include or Exclude CDW, All with Graphical Output. It Would Take an Expert at LOTUS or EXCEL 6 Months to Build an Analysis As Sophisticated As This Software.
Advantage International.

C. A. S. Classroom Administration System.
Apple II (48k). $99.00, Lab pack/5 $250.00. *Optimal configuration:* Apple II, 48k, 1 or 2 drives.
Teacher's Management Program Offers Complete Integration in a Single Program. Prepare a Data Bank of Multiple-Choice, Matching, Fill-In or Essay Questions. Produce Word-Processed Tests with These or Other Questions. Choose Test Questions Individually, in Groups, by Searching. Maintain an Electronic Gradebook for up to 800 Students. Connect to Card Reader/Scanner to Enter Grades Automatically into the Gradebook. Generate a Great Variety of Individual Grade Reports & Class Comparisons. You Can Curve Tests, Do Item Analyses, Histograms, Keep Question Histories, Mark Standardized Tests (Criterion & Norm-Referencing), Produce Virtually Any Statistic.
Word Assocs., Inc.

C. Breeze. Paul Beskeen. Nov. 1988. *Compatible Hardware:* Atari ST. *Memory Required:* 512k.
3.5" disk $49.95.
Features Customizable Menu & Keyboard Commands. On-Screen Help Facilities. Advanced Commands for Editing C Source Code.
MichTron, Inc.

C Chest & Other C Treasures from Dr. Dobb's Journal. Edited by Allen Holub. *Operating System(s) Required:* MS-DOS.
book & disk $39.95 (ISBN 0-934375-49-6).
book only $24.95 (ISBN 0-934375-40-2).
Anthology Containing the "C Chest" Columns from Dr. Dobb's Journal of Software Tools along with the Philosophical & Practical Discussions They Inspired, & Other Articles by C Experts. All Subroutines & Programs Are Written in C & Are Available on Disk with Source Code.
M & T Bks.

C-COMP. Version: 2.1. 1988. *Operating System(s) Required:* PC-DOS/MS-DOS 2.1 or higher. *Memory Required:* 256k. *Items Included:* Manual, 3.5" diskette. *Customer Support:* Free telephone support to registered users.
disk $295.00 (ISBN 0-932651-17-8).
Pair of Experimental Design Computer Programs for Investigating 2 or 3 Factor Response Surfaces in R&D Processes by Central-Composite Designs.
Statistical Programs.

C-D-Calc. Version: 1.1. Peter C. Vonderhorst. 1982. *Compatible Hardware:* IBM PC, PC XT, PC AT & compatibles; TRS-80 Model II, Model IV. *Language(s):* Compiled BASIC. *Memory Required:* 48k. *General Requirements:* 132-column printer.
disk $525.00.
Calculates Monthly Interest Costs to Bank for Any Length C-D. Prints Notices of Due Date, 1099's, Monthly Reports Projecting Entire Year's Interest Rate, List of Accounts for Payment, etc.
Computx.

C EXECUTIVE. Version: 2.3A. 1990. *Compatible Hardware:* DEC; IBM PC; Intel; Motorola; any system with a standard C compiler. *Language(s):* C, Assembly. *Memory Required:* 5-10k.
Binary. $575.00, incl. documentation.
Source. $5075.00, incl. documentation.
Real-Time, Multi-Tasking, ROMable Monitor for C Programs Especially Suited for High-Volume, Low-Cost Board Products for Instrumentation Control, Data Acquisition, & Other Real-Time Applications, Military Avionics, Robotics/Vision Systems, Cardiac Monitors, Intelligent Terminals, Laser Printer, Controllers, etc. Also, Optional File System.
JMI Software Consultants, Inc.

The C-Food Smorgasboard. *Compatible Hardware:* IBM PC, Victor 9000. *Operating System(s) Required:* MS-DOS, CP/M-86, PC-DOS, SB-86. *Memory Required:* 64k.
disk $150.00.
Collection of C Routines That Can Be Added to Standard Latice C Library or Used to Form a New Library. Included Are Routines for the Following: Decimal or Floating Decimal Arithmetic up to 16 Significant Digits; Low-Level Input/Output on CRT Keyboard Printer & Asynchronous Port; IBM PC or Victor 9000 BOIS Interface for Managing a Screen As If It Were a Normal CRT. Also Supports Fundamental Graphics.
Lifeboat Assocs.

C-Graphics. B. J. Korites & M. Novack. May 1984. *Compatible Hardware:* IBM PC. *Operating System(s) Required:* PC-DOS. *Language(s):* BASIC, C (source code included). *Memory Required:* 64k.
IBM PC. disk $75.00, incl. manual (ISBN 0-940254-51-4, Order no.: 206-ID).
Tutorial That Shows User How to Create Machine Language Graphics Routines Using C Language. Contains a Library of Machine Language Routines.
Kern International, Inc.

The C. H. A. O. S. Continuum: MAC Jewel Case. Sep. 1993. *Items Included:* Registration card. *Customer Support:* Creative Multimedia Corporation warrants the CD-ROM disc & diskettes to be free from defects in materials & workmanship under normal use & service for a period of 90 days from date of purchase. Creative Multimedia Corporation offers Technical Support to customers as needed.
System Software 7.0 or higher. Macintosh II or higher; hard drive with 1Mb of free space, 13" or larger color monitor w/8-bit display required (2.5Mb). CD-ROM disk $79.99 (ISBN 1-880428-15-6, Order no.: 10412). *Addl. software required:* CD-ROM extensions. *Optimal configuration:* CD-ROM drive with 150k/second transfer rate, 380ms or less access rate recommended. *Networks supported:* All.
In the Year 2577, Titan Colony Is Being Held Captive by the Sentient Supercomputer, C.H.A.O.S. Trapped in a Parallel Continuum by the Computer, the Colonists & the Scientists Who Created the Supercomputer Are Seeking Help - from You! The C.H.A.O.S. Continuum Is a Dramatic New Development in CD-ROM Entertainment, Incorporating Movie-Style Special Effects, Detailed Story Line & a Comprehensive Educational Database.
Creative Multimedia Corp.

The C. H. A. O. S. Continuum: MPC Jewel Case. Sep. 1993. *Items Included:* Registration card. *Customer Support:* Creative Multimedia Corporation warrants the CD-ROM disc & diskettes to be free from defects in materials & workmanship under normal use & service for a period of 90 days from date of purchase. Creative Multimedia Corporation offers Technical Support to customers as needed.
Microsoft Windows 3.1, MS-CDEX 2.2 or higher. 386/33 or higher; hard drive with 1Mb free disk space (4Mb). CD-ROM disk $79.99 (ISBN 1-880428-16-4, Order no.: 10373). *Nonstandard peripherals required:* Sound Card with Window Driver. *Optimal configuration:* SuperVGA resolution with 256 colors. Double-speed CD-ROM drive is recommended. *Networks supported:* All.
In the Year 2577, Titan Colony Is Being Held Captive by the Sentient Supercomputer, C.H.A.O.S. Trapped in a Parallel Continuum by the Computer, the Colonists & the Scientists Who Created the Supercomputer Are Seeking Help - from You! The C.H.A.O.S. Continuum Is a Dramatic New Development in CD-ROM Entertainment, Incorporating Movie-Style Special Effects, Detailed Story Line & a Comprehensive Educational Database.
Creative Multimedia Corp.

The C. H. A. O. S. Continuum: MPC Retail Box. Sep. 1993. *Items Included:* Registration card. *Customer Support:* Creative Multimedia Corporation warrants the CD-ROM disc & diskettes to be free from defects in materials & workmanship under normal use & service for a period of 90 days from date of purchase. Creative Multimedia Corporation offers Technical Support to customers as needed.
Microsoft Windows 3.1, MS-CDEX 2.2 or higher. 386/33 or higher; hard drive with 1Mb free disk space (4Mb). CD-ROM disk $79.99 (ISBN 1-880428-17-2, Order no.: 10427). *Nonstandard peripherals required:* Sound Card with Windows Drivers. *Optimal configuration:* SuperVGA resolution with 256 colors. Double-speed CD-ROM drive is recommended. *Networks supported:* All.
In the Year 2577, Titan Colony Is Being Held Captive by the Sentient Supercomputer, C.H.A.O.S. Trapped in a Parallel Continuum by the Computer, the Colonists & the Scientists Who Created the Supercomputer Are Seeking Help - from You! The C.H.A.O.S. Continuum Is a Dramatic New Development in CD-ROM Entertainment, Incorporating Movie-Style Special Effects, Detailed Story Line & a Comprehensive Educational Database.
Creative Multimedia Corp.

C-ISAM. Version: 2.10. Feb. 1985. *Compatible Hardware:* IBM PC, PC XT, PC AT, PC compatibles; DEC; AT&T. *Operating System(s) Required:* UNIX, XENIX, MS-DOS, PC-DOS. *Language(s):* C. *Memory Required:* 24k.
contact publisher for price.
Library of C-Language Functions for Creating & Manipulating Indexed File Systems. Features B-Tree Based Access Method That Allows Programmers to Create, Manipulate, & Retrieve Data Using Indexed Files. Designed for Software Applications That Require an Indexed Sequential Access Method Without the Additional Capabilities Provided by a Database Management System.
Relational Database Systems, Inc.

C LANGUAGE

C Language. *Compatible Hardware:* Apple II; Kaypro; Osborne 1; TRS-80 Model I, Model II, Model III, Model 4, Model 12, Model 16. *Operating System(s) Required:* CP/M, TRSDOS & compatibles. *Language(s):* C. *Memory Required:* TRS-80 Model I & Model III 48k; Model 4, Model 12; CP/M 52k.
$139.00.
General Purpose Programming Language Which Provides the Structure & Portability of a High Level Language While Retaining the Low Level Characteristics of an Assembly Language. Allows Bit Level Manipulation of Data While Providing Control Structures, Data Typing, & Other Functions.
Alcor Systems.

C-Language Cross Compilers: A-554. 1989. *Operating System(s) Required:* PC-DOS, MS-DOS. *Memory Required:* 512k. *General Requirements:* 2 disk drives. *Customer Support:* Telephone support & customer/product service.
8 bits & 16 bits $895.00.
American Automation.

"C" Language Library for Benchmark Modula-2. *Items Included:* 200 pages of documentation with tutorial & many examples. *Customer Support:* Free telephone & mail technical support.
Amiga DOS (512k). $99.95. *Addl. software required:* Benchmark Modula-2.
A Library of Routines Similiar to That Provided with "C" Compilers. Allows Standard "C" Functions to Be Used in Programs Written in Benchmark Modula-2.
Avant-Garde Software.

C Language Scientific Subroutine Library Version 2.0. *Version:* 2.0. *Compatible Hardware:* IBM PC & compatibles. *Language(s):* Microsoft C, Lattice C (source code included). *Memory Required:* 256k. *Customer Support:* 212-850-6194/6788.
disk $739.00, incl. documentation (ISBN 0-471-61233-2).
Consists of More Than 100 Pretested & Precompiled Mathematical & Statistical Subroutines, Supplied on Disk As a Linkable Library & As a Source Code. The Subroutines Cover Formulas for: General Statistics, Probability, Analysis of Variance, Regressions, Matrices, Interpolations, Fourier Analysis, Cross Tabulations, Differential Equations, Roots of Bioquadratic Equations, Function Evaluations, Systems of Equations, Solution of Equations, Time Series Analysis, etc.
John Wiley & Sons, Inc.

C-Light. *Version:* 1.6. Jan. 1989. *Items Included:* Spiral bound manual, 3D object editor, Stereoscopic 3D viewer.
Amiga DOS (512k). $24.95. *Optimal configuration:* Amiga running Amiga DOS with 512k or more of RAM & an external floppy drive or hard disk.
A 3D Graphics & Animation Program for All Amiga Computers. It Features an Easy-to-use Real-time Wireframe Editor for Creating Scenes Using Spheres, Cubes & Cylinders as Building Blocks Which Can Be Stretched, Squashed & Rotated. A Ray Tracer Then Renders Smoothly Shaded Surfaces, Mirrored Surfaces & True Shadows. Support Is Included for Haitex X-Specs 3D Stereoscopic Viewing Glasses.
Peterson Enterprises.

C Math Functions. *Compatible Hardware:* IBM PC. *Operating System(s) Required:* PC-DOS 2.0. *Language(s):* C, BASIC (source code included). *Memory Required:* 64k.
disk $45.00, incl. manual (Order no.: 210-IK).
Self-Teaching Guide That Shows User How to Write C Functions to Generate Math Functions Such As SIN(x), COS(x), ATAN(x), & LOG(x).
Kern International, Inc.

C.O.T.S/BOSS. Jan. 1991. *Customer Support:* On-site training, hotline.
Windows NT. PS/2, IBM PC & compatibles (16Mb). $60,000.00-$200,000.00 license. *Networks supported:* NetWare, Vines, LAN Manager, Pathworks.
UNIX (AIX), SUN(SPARC). RS/6000 (16Mb). $60,000.00-$200,000.00 license.
Comprehensive Risk Management & Treasury Operations System for Off-Balance Sheet Transactions, with Specialized Functions for: Deposits, FRA's Caps/Floors/Collars, Swaps & Swaptions; FX & FX Options, with Theoretical Valuation & Sensitivity Analysis; Physical Commodities, with Location-Based Pricing; Energy Products, with P/1 for Cargo Hedge Positions; Futures Brokerage, with Client & Clearingbroker Margins; Portfolio Management, with Multicurrency Profit/Loss.
Software Options, Inc.

C Optimizing Compiler. *Version:* 5.1. *Compatible Hardware:* IBM PC & compatibles. *Memory Required:* 448k. *General Requirements:* Hard disk.
disk $450.00.
C Compiler Featuring Assembler Access, Integrated Linker, MAKE, Source Debugger, Compiler Wildcards & Subdirectories, Screen/Cursor Control, DOS Service Functions & Low Level Keyboard Input. Compilation Is an Added-Step Process. Supports Math Coprocessor & Technical Hot Line & Is MASM & LINK-Compatible.
Microsoft Pr.

C Plus Plus/Views. *Version:* 3.0.1. *Items Included:* Complete documentation set, including C Plus Plus/Views Class Catalog, C Plus Plus/Views User's Guide, C Plus Plus/Views Release Notes & C Plus Plus/Views Constructor User's Guide. *Customer Support:* 30-day warranty; additional support options available.
MS Windows, MS Windows NT. Intel 286/386/486. disk $749.00-$999.00.
OS/2 PM. Intel 386/486. disk $999.00 up.
OSF/Motif. Sun SPARC, HP 9000, RISC/6000. disk $1999.00 up.
A Leading Object-Oriented Application Framework for Developing Multi-Platform, Native GUI Programs Using C Plus Plus. Includes a Library of over 100 C Plus Plus Classes for Developing Your Entire GUI Application. It Also Includes C Plus Plus/Views Constructor, a Unique Visual Development Tool That Unites an Interface Builder with a Class Browser.
Liant Software Corp.

C Programmer's Toolbox. *Version:* 3.0. Aug. 1992. *Items Included:* 400 plus page manual. *Customer Support:* 30 day unconditional money back guarantee; nominal update.
DOS 3.2 or higher. IBM PC, XT, AT, PS/2 & compatibles (123k). Professional Edition $395.00; 386 Edition $225.00; all 3 vols. $300.00; any 2 vols. $225.00; 1 vol. $125.00; site license avail. (Order no.: PCPE; 386; V123; V12; V1).
Apple Macintosh (2Mb). 3.5" disk $295.00 (site license avail.).
Sun 3, Sun 4 & SparcStation. disk $495.00 (site license avail.).
Contains 38 Plus Tools That Enhance Entire C & C Plus Plus Development Environment & Process. There Are Tools That: Determine & Graph How a Program Is Organized; How/Where Variables Are Used (XREF); Cleanup Source Code (Pretty Printer); Find Unintended Programming Mistakes (Lint); Find Performance Bottlenecks (Monitor); Archive Files/Directories/Disks & More. The Tools Work with Microsoft C/C Plus Plus, MPW C/C Plus Plus, Borland C Plus Plus, ANSI C.
MMCAD Systems.

C Programming for MIDI. Jim Conger. *Operating System(s) Required:* MS-DOS. *General Requirements:* Microsoft C or Turbo C.
book & disk $37.95 (ISBN 0-934375-90-9).
book only $22.95 (ISBN 0-934375-86-0).
Provides an Introduction to C Programming Fundamentals As They Relate to MIDI. Shows How to Write Customized Programs to Create the Desired Sound Effects. All Programs Are Available on Disk with Full Source Code.
M & T Bks.

C. S. M. S. *Compatible Hardware:* Apple II. contact publisher for price.
NSP, Inc.

C-scape. *Version:* 4.0. *Items Included:* Complete documentation set, including Function Reference Manual, Look&Feel Manual, OWL Function Reference Manual, Quick Reference Card, & Release Notes. *Customer Support:* 30-day warranty; additional support options available.
MS-DOS. Intel 286/386/486. disk $499.00.
VMS. disk $2999.00 up.
UNIX, AIX, HP-UX, Sys V ATT, Sun. Intel, HP, RISC/6000, Sun. disk $1999.00.
The C-scape Interface Management System Is a Professional-Strength Library of C Functions for Designing Portable, Character-Based User Interfaces. Includes the Look & Feel Screen Designer - an Interactive Design Tool That Generates K & R C or ANSI C Code.
Liant Software Corp.

C-scape. *Version:* 3.0. Jun. 1986. *Compatible Hardware:* IBM PC & compatibles; Unix, VMS Workstations; OS/2. *Language(s):* C (source code included). *Memory Required:* 256k.
disk $399.00.
complete package including source avail. for Borland, Lattice, Microsoft, & other leading compilers $399.00.
Screen & Keyboard Interface Management for C Programmers. Enables Users to Create Pop-Up Windows, Pull-Down Menus, Data Entry Screens, Text Screens, Editing, Fully Definable Keystrokes, & Complete Validation. Supports Graphics: Includes LOOK & FEEL, a WYSIWYG Screen Designer Which Lets Users Design the Screen into Readable C Code. Features Automatic Horizontal & Vertical Scrolling, Line Draw, & Erase. Includes Context-Sensitive Help.
Oakland Group, Inc.

C Scientific Libraries: CSL. May 1986. *Compatible Hardware:* IBM PC & compatibles; Z-100. *Operating System(s) Required:* PC-DOS, MS-DOS.
Complete set of over 300 functions. $245.00, incl. manual & examples.
without manual $200.00.
manual $55.00.
demo disk $5.00.
CSL annotated index of functions $2.50.
C Compiler. $298.00.
Eigenware Technologies.
  Advanced Matrix Computations. $55.00.
    Over 80 Functions & 163 Manual Pages.
  Complex Variables & Polynomials. $35.00.
    Over 25 Functions & 53 Manual Pages.
  Differential Equations, Quadrature & Derivatives. $49.00.
    Over 30 Functions & 63 Manual Pages.
  Graphics, Utilities, Finance & Calendar. $49.00.
    Over 60 Functions & 123 Manual Pages.
  Nonlinear Equations, Optimization & Interpolation. $39.00.
    Over 25 Functions & 23 Manual Pages.

TITLE INDEX

Special Math Functions.
$49.00.
*Over 50 Functions & 103 Manual Pages.
Statistics, Probability & Time Series.*
$49.00.
Over 50 Functions & 103 Manual Pages.

The C Shroud. *Version:* 1.0. Feb. 1990. *Items Included:* reference manual. *Customer Support:* 30 day money back guarantee, free telephone tech support.
All that support C. All that Support C. $1298.00 for binary license.
Any Supporting C. Any Supporting C (640k). $1298.00 & up depending on hardware, Software MS-DOS diskettes, is distributed in "shrouded source" form. *Addl. software required:* K&R or ANSI C Compiler.
A C Source Code Protection Utility for Use by Anyone Who Wants to Distribute an Application in C Source Form & Still Safeguard the Source Code He Has Written. It Will Accept Your Nicely Structured C Source Code & Produce an Obscure Version That Is Very Difficult to Understand But Can Be Easily Translated by a C Compiler.
Gimpel Software.

C-64 15 Pack. *Items Included:* Installation guide. Windows 95. IBM. Contact publisher for price (ISBN 0-87321-112-X, Order no.: CDD-3126).
Activision, Inc.

C-Star. 1985. *Compatible Hardware:* Commodore 64/128. *Language(s):* BASIC. *Memory Required:* 64k. *General Requirements:* Commodore 1541 or MSD SD2 disk drive. *Items Included:* Manual. *Customer Support:* Free phone support.
disk $65.00 (ISBN 0-87199-040-7).
Computes, Stores on Disk & Prints Natal, Progressed, & Solar & Lunar-Return Horoscopes.
Astrolabe, Inc.

C Subroutines. 1983. *Operating System(s) Required:* MS-DOS. *Memory Required:* 64k.
contact publisher for price.
Allows User to Develop Programs Specific to Their Applications While Using FRONTIER Graphic Controllers.
Frontier Technologies Corp.

C3D. *Version:* 2.0. 1988. *Compatible Hardware:* IBM PC, PC XT, PC AT, PS/2. *Operating System(s) Required:* MS-DOS 2.00 or higher. *Language(s):* QcuikBASIC. *Memory Required:* 640k. *General Requirements:* Plotter; EGA or VGA card.
$349.00.
3-D Drafting Package. True Perspective, Orthographic or Axonometric Projection of Any Object Entered by Coordinates. Disk Storage of Coordinate File for Plotting Different Views.
AeroHydro, Inc.

C Thru ROM. *Version:* 1.3. *Compatible Hardware:* IBM PC & compatibles. *Operating System(s) Required:* MS-DOS. *Memory Required:* 285k.
disk $495.00.
Stand-Alone Source-Code Debugger. Reads Microsoft .EXE File Format & Intel Absolute OMF Format. Compatible with MS C 5.0/5.1 & MASM 5.0/5.1 Languages. Supports 8086, 80186, 8087 & 80187 Instruction Sets & Remote Debugging. Includes Full Screen & Command Line Interface; Code, Data, Register Value & Expressions Windows Display; & Fixed & Conditional Breakpoint Types. Also Features Assembly Single Step, Assembly Program Stepping, Source Single Step, Source Program Stepping, Script Capabilities, Resident/Non-Resident Mode, ROMable Startup Code, ROMable Library & Locater.
Datalight.

c-tree Plus File Handler. *Version:* 6.5A. *Compatible Hardware:* Apple Macintosh; DOS; OS/2; UNIX; QNX 4.X; Coherent; XENIX; RISC platforms; DEC Alpha; supports most commercial grade C compilers. *Items Included:* Choice of up to 26 Developer's Servers, perfectbound Programmer's Reference Guide & Function Reference Guide. *Customer Support:* 3 months free technical support; maintenance plan thereafter.
3.5" disk starts at $895.00.
Royalty Free. Provides Fast, Highly Portable BPlus Tree Functions for Multikey ISAM File Management. Low Level Functions Provide Individual Control over Data/Index Files. ISAM Functions Operation on Data Files & Indexes Simultaneously. Compile C Source Code for Single-User or Multi-User Network Applications. Ported to over 90 CPU/OS Environments. ANSI Standard C Source Included.
FairCom Corp.

C2D: Spatial Autocorrelation in 2 Dimensions. *Version:* 1.2. Geoffrey M. Jacquez. Oct. 1990. *Items Included:* User's manual. *Customer Support:* 60 day warranty. Free technical support by phone.
DOS 2.0 or higher. IBM & compatible (512k). disk $100.00. *Nonstandard peripherals required:* Hard disk suggested. *Addl. software required:* EGA/VGA. *Optimal configuration:* IBM 386, DOS 2+, 640k RAM, VGA, Math coprocessor, hard disk.
site license $300.00.
Program for Spatial Autocorrelation Statistics in Two Dimensions. It Calculates Directional Correlograms Which Express Geographic Variation in a Data Set As Spatial Autocorrelation in Different Compass Directions & Distances. Spatial Autocorrelation Coefficient Includes Both Moran's I & Gary's C.
Exeter Software.

C-User Group. *Customer Support:* All of our products are unconditionally guaranteed.
DOS, Unix. CD-ROM disk $49.95 (Order no.: CUG). *Nonstandard peripherals required:* CD-ROM drive.
Entire C User's Group Collection. Vol. 100-411.
Walnut Creek CDRom.

C-Vision for C/C Plus Plus. *Version:* 4.0. Mar. 1992. *Items Included:* User manual. *Customer Support:* 30 day money-back guarantee. Fax, phone & mail technical support included.
MS-DOS or OS/2. PC compatible (640k). disk $239.00. *Optimal configuration:* Intel 80386 or higher recommended. *Networks supported:* All.
OS/2 (640k). disk $239.00. *Networks supported:* All.
Set of Tools to Help Analyze, Understand & Maintain C & C Plus Plus Programs. Includes Four Main Components: an Intelligent Source Code Lister, a Cross-Referencer, a Function Call Diagrammer & a Reformatter. Supports K&R & ANSI C & ANSI/ISO C Plus Plus & Uses DOS Extender Technology to Handle Huge Applications When Run on a 386 or Higher. The Lister Will Print Outlined Listings of Your Code. The Cross-Referencer Provides Highly Detailed Symbol Descriptions Including Symbol Usage (Assigned, Declared, Address Used) & Type Information. The Tree Diagrammer Is Customizable to Show Different Views of Your Code (to Flow Downwards or Upwards) & Trees Can be Pruned in Many Different Ways. The Reformatter Supports Independent Control of Curly-Braces, Labels, Preprocessor Statements, Case/Default Statements & More & Also Includes a Comment Reformatter.
Gimpel Software.

CA-ACCPAC/2000 ACCOUNTS RECEIVABLE

The C Workshop. *Version:* 2.0. Sep. 1992. *Items Included:* 368-page book. *Customer Support:* Free by mail & phone.
MS-DOS (320k). IBM PC-XT-AT-PS/2 & compatible. $89.00 single user license (ISBN 0-917419-13-8).
An Interactive Software & Book Package Which Teaches the C Programming Language. It Gives Feedback on Over 100 Program Exercises Completed with the Built-in Editor & C Compiler. The User May Also Write His Own Programs up to a Limit of 65 KB. On-Line Help & a Coordinated Textbook Are Included.
Wordcraft.

C-Zar. *Version:* 2.4. *Compatible Hardware:* Commodore Amiga. *Memory Required:* 512k. *General Requirements:* MIDI interface; Casio CZ-101 or CZ-1000 keyboard. *Items Included:* 86-page manual with binder. *Customer Support:* Phone.
3.5" disk $99.00.
Music Editor & Librarian for the Casio CZ-101 & CZ-1000 Keyboards. Provides Over 200 Instruments & Sound Effects. Users Can Tune the Keyboard's Six Eight-Step Envelopes; Pitch, Tone, & Loudness Envelopes Are Color-Coded & Drawn in Eight Colors in a 1024- by 200-Pixel Area. More Than One Envelope Can Be Displayed at Once. Provides a Time Display Logarithmically. The Mouse Can Drag Segments of an Envelope Around the Screen. Also Enables Users to Record Sequences & Automatically Play Them Back, & Maintain a Library With Up to 6000 Sounds. Other Features Include Line Copying & Detuning, Key Transpose, Key Follow, Pitch Bend, Vibrato, Modulation, Portamento, & Waveform Selection. Eight Programmable Tone Mixes Are Provided in Every Bank of Sounds.
Diemer Development.

CA ACCESS Library. 1986. *Customer Support:* Available.
DOS, OS/2. IBM, PS/2 & compatibles (512k). disk $1695.00. *Networks supported:* Novell, LAN Manager, Banyan, & others.
Allows Developers to Develop Products & Provide Custom Programming Services That Extend Capabilities fo CA's ACCPAC Plus Accounting Line. Provides Increased Database Capacity, Enhanced Sequential File SORT & MERGE Utilities & Extended Application Programming Interface. Includes International & Multi-Currency Support & Improved Low Level Screen I/O Support & Print Control.
Computer Assocs. International, Inc.

CA-Accpac/2000 Accounts Payable. *Customer Support:* Available.
Windows. Contact publisher for price.
Integrates with Bank & Tax Services to Provide Comprehensive Management of Company's Payables. Vendors Can Be Assigned to Groups, Vendor Statistics Can Be Kept by Fiscal or Calendar Periods. Invoices Can Be Distributed Manually or Automatically Using Distribution Sets.
Computer Assocs. International, Inc.

CA-Accpac/2000 Accounts Receivable. *Customer Support:* Available.
Windows. Contact publisher for price.
Integrates with Bank & Tax Services to Provide Comprehensive Management of Company's Receivables. Customers Can Be Assigned to Groups & National Accounts. Customer & Sales Statistics Kept by Fiscal or Calendar Periods. Invoices Can Be Printed Using Items Set up in Item Price List.
Computer Associates International, Inc.

CA-Accpac/2000 General Ledger. *Customer Support:* Available.
Windows. Contact publisher for price.
Features Multicompany & Multicurrency Support. Allows for 45 Character GL Account Numbers. Up to 99 Years of History & Budget Data. Financial Reporter Provides Spreadsheet & Graphics Functionality.
Computer Associates International, Inc.

CA-Accpac/2000 Lanpak. *Customer Support:* Available.
Windows. Contact publisher for price.
Lanpak for Novell Netware Allows Users to Access Licensed CA-Accpac/2000 Applications from Any Workstation of the Network.
Computer Associates International, Inc.

CA-Accpac/2000 System Manager. *Customer Support:* Available.
Windows. Contact publisher for price.
Financial Management System Featuring Multicompany & Multicurrency Support. System Manager Is Foundation of System, Providing Centralized System Services, Security Administration, Data Management & Macro Language Capability.
Computer Associates International, Inc.

CA-Accpac/2000 U. S. Payroll. *Customer Support:* Available.
Windows. Contact publisher for price.
Comprehensive Payroll Processing & Reporting System. Supports Nine Pay Frequencies, Multiple Work States, Multiple Years of History, & Unlimited Earnings, Deductions, Benefits, Accruals, Advances, & Expense Reimbursements. Features Cost Center Posting to Allow Detailed Tracking of Payroll Expenses & Liabilities.
Computer Associates International, Inc.

CA-ACCPAC/2000. 1994. *Customer Support:* Support Agreement Available.
Windows. IBM PC, PS/2 & compatibles (8Mb). Contact publisher for price. *Networks supported:* Novell NetWare.
Windows-Based Financial Management System Designed for Medium to Large Sized Businesses. Features Comprehensive Multi-Company & Multicurrency Support; Graphic Report Designer; Macro Language; Customizable to Organize Accounting Tasks by Business Processes; Query by Example for Searches on Key Fields; Shares User, Security, & Currency Information & Data Common to All Applications.
Computer Assocs. International, Inc.

CA-ACF2/PC PC Only Option. *Customer Support:* Available.
PC-DOS/MS-DOS. Contact publisher for price.
Enforces Individual Accountability & Prevention of Unauthorized Use Through User Sign-On. Protects Directories, Files & Programs. Controls System Prompt Use & Restricts DOS Commands. Enables User to Create Customized User Menus. Logs Selected Computer Activity in Security Reports. Includes MS-Windows Application for Security Administration.
Computer Associates International, Inc.

CA-ACF2. 1978. *Customer Support:* Support Agreement Available.
MVS, VSE, VM. IBM S/370-390. Contact publisher for price.
Provides Access Control to Protect Your Computer Data from Accidental or Deliberate Destruction, Modification, Disclosure and/or Misuse. Allows You to Control Who Uses Your Computer Resources, & Provides You with All the Facts to Monitor Your Security Policy Effectively. Attempts to Access Unauthorized Resources Are Automatically Denied & Logged. Any Authorized Use of Sensitive Resources May Also Be Logged for Subsequent Review. Logging, Reporting & Online Monitoring Capabilities Give You or Other Authorized Personnel a Range of Opportunities to Analyze & Evaluate Computer Access Activities & Trends. Optional VSE/ESA Feature Further Exploits VSE/ESA, Providing VSE/ESA Data Space Support, the Ability to Monitor Activity in Both Static & Dynamic Partitions, & the Extension of IUCV to Dynamic Partitions to Allow Communication among Systems Operating As Guests under VM.
Computer Assocs. International, Inc.

CA-ACF2/DB2. 1991. *Customer Support:* Support Agreement Available.
MVS. IBM S/370-390. Contact publisher for price.
Enables Security Administrator to Protect DB2 Databases, Table Spaces, Tables, Views, Plans, Elements & Management Functions & Utilities Using CA-ACF2 Administrative Tools. Provides Comprehensive Auditing & Reporting Facilities. Eliminates DB2 Cascade Effect. Controls Security for Multiple DB2 Subsystems from Single Point.
Computer Assocs. International, Inc.

CA-ACF2/PC. 1991. *Customer Support:* Support Agreement Available.
Windows, DOS. IBM PC & compatibles (512k). Contact publisher for price.
Provides Centralized Mainframe Control & Validation of PC Sign-Ons & PC to Mainframe Connections. Allows Single Point Registration of Multi-Platform Users. Provides Single-Sign on Capabilities. Security for PC Resources Includes Files, Directories & Commands. Offers Standardized, Automatic Maintenance & Auditing from CA-ACF2 MVS Security Program.
Computer Assocs. International, Inc.

CA-ACF2/Secman for VAX. 1989. *Items Included:* Documentation included. *Customer Support:* Available.
MVS, VAX/VMS. IBM System 370/390 Architecture; Digital VAX (500k). Contact vendor for price. *Addl. software required:* CA-ACF2 MVS; Digital VAX/VMS; DECnet SNA gateway with 3270 Data Streaming, Interlink connection, or a protocol converter with VT100 emulation.
Provides Integrated Security Administration for Sites with Mixed IBM MVS & DEC VAX/VMS Network Environments. Allows MVS Security Administrators to Protect All Networked Users & Resources Using Concepts & Standard Facilities of CA-ACF2 Environments & Enhances Native VAX/VMS Security.
Computer Assocs. International, Inc.

CA-ACF2/Viewpoint. 1991. *Customer Support:* Support Agreement Available.
MVS. IBM S/370-390 (1Mb). Contact publisher for price.
Windowing User Interface Option to CA-ACF2 Based on IBM's SAA/CUA Standards. Integrates Across CA Systems Management Solutions to Enable Multi-Product Communication. SQL-Based Query Facility Allows for Complex Searches. Object-Oriented Database Capabilities Add Flexibility to Administration of Security Records.
Computer Assocs. International, Inc.

CA-ADS. 1981. *Customer Support:* Support Agreement Available.
MVS, VSE, VM. IBM S/370-390 (5Mb). Contact publisher for price.
Environment for Development of On-Line Transaction-Based Production Systems. Incorporates 4GL Forms Generator, System-Assisted Prototyping & Dictionary Integration. Shares Backup/Recovery Capabilities & Query & Reporting Facilities of CA-IDMS/DB.
Computer Assocs. International, Inc.

CA-ADS/PC. 1985. *Memory Required:* 4000k. *Customer Support:* Available.
PC-MS/DOS. IBM PC AT, PS/2 or compatibles. contact publisher for price.
A Complete Application Design, Development & Processing Environment for the PC That Is Compatible with Mainframe CA-ADS. Adds Fourth-Generation Screen Painting, Programming & Prototyping Tools to the Dictionary-Driven Database Management Capabilities of CA-IDMS/PC. CA-ADS/PC Runs in a Single-User Environment, or in the Multi-User, Client-Server Environment of CA-IDMS/PC Lanpack.
Computer Assocs. International, Inc.

CA-APCDDS. 1990. *Customer Support:* Support Agreement Available.
MVS. IBM S/370-390 (4Mb). Contact publisher for price.
Automates Report & File Balancing. Eliminates Production Delays & Reruns. Integrates with CA-7, CA-Scheduler, CA-Opera & CA-Netman.
Computer Assocs. International, Inc.

CA-APCDOC. 1988. *Customer Support:* Support Agreement Available.
MVS. IBM S/370-390 (1Mb). Contact publisher for price.
On-Line Data Center Documentation System for Storage & Retrieval of Information Necessary to Data Center Operations. Produces Cross-Reference Information, Tape Pull Lists & Generates Job Network Flowcharts from Production Scheduling Databases.
Computer Assocs. International, Inc.

CA-Archiver. 1982. *Items Included:* Documentation included. *Customer Support:* Available.
VAX/VMS. Digital VAX (512k). Contact vendor for price.
Disk to Tape and/or Optical Disk Archive & Retrieval. Reduces User Disk Storage. Stores Critical or Seldom Accessed Files on Magnetic Tape or Optical Disk. Maintains an Online Directory of Files Archived to Each User, Provided for Automated Disk Management & Data Retrieval Functions. Intelligently Sorts Tape Mount Requests to Eliminate Multiple Mount Requests for the Same Tape.
Computer Assocs. International, Inc.

CA-ASM/Archive. 1990. *Customer Support:* Support Agreement Available.
VSE. IBM S/370-390. Contact publisher for price.
Rule-Based Tool That Automates Management of DASD Backup, Archive & Restore Processing. Includes Batch, On-Line & Realtime Components, Automatic & On-Demand Processing, Incremental Backup & Inactive Dataset Archive. Provides Automatic Restore on Access, Customized Dataset Grouping, Automatic Dataset Activity Tracking, Access Method & Device Independence.
Computer Assocs. International, Inc.

CA-ASM/Workstation. 1991. *Operating System(s) Required:* PC-DOS. *Customer Support:* Available.
IBM AT & compatibles. Contact Vendor.
Automated Media Management Tracking System. Includes Automated Search & Management of Tapes, Real-Time Tape Retrieval, Loading & Filing, Tape Movement & Verification Control, Tape Inventory System, Automated Update, Statistical Data for Tape Operations Analysis, Off-Site Tape Movement & Pulls Verification, Control over On-Site Scratch Pools, Vault Management & Clean Processing & On-Line Update of Tape Status.
Computer Assocs. International, Inc.

TITLE INDEX

CA-ASM2. 1974. *Customer Support:* Support Agreement Available.
MVS. IBM S/370-390 (512k). Contact publisher for price.
Manages Disk Space on Any System-Supported Disk or Mass Storage Direct Access Device. Manipulates & Reorganizes Data & Data Sets & Provides Automatic or Explicit Backup & Archival of Data to Tape. Supports IBM Storage Management Subsystems, Implementation of Integrated Product Catalog & VSAM Sphere Processing.
Computer Assocs. International, Inc.

CA-Blockmaster. 1985. *Customer Support:* Support Agreement Available.
MVS. IBM S/370-390. Contact publisher for price.
Performance Optimizer Which Blocks Sequential Datasets to Reduce I/O Activity, CPU Usage & DASD Space Requirements. Selects Datasets for Reblocking Using User-Defined Control Parameters Including Dataset Name, VOLSER, Volume Type & Job Name.
Computer Assocs. International, Inc.

CA-BPI Accounting II. 1986. *Customer Support:* Available.
IBM DOS. IBM PC, XT, AT, PS/2, COMPAQ or compatibles (512k). $229.00.
Supports Departmental & Divisional Reporting. Includes GL, AR, AP, OE, Payroll, IC & LanPak. Provides Automatic Generation & Customization of Financial Reports. Handles Dollar Amounts up to 99 Billion. Provides Bank Reconciliation. Multiple Sales Tax Authorities & Tax Groups Can Be Modified for Accurate Tax Calculation & Reporting. 1099 Reporting Provided in AP. LAN Compatible up to 40 Workstations.
Computer Assocs. International, Inc.

CA-CAS/AD Manufacturing & Logistics Management System for Aerospace & Defense. 1985. *Customer Support:* Support Agreement Available.
HP-UX; MVS, VSE, VM; BS2000; MSP/AE; VOS-3. HP9000; IBM S370/390; Siemens; Fujitsu; Hitachi. Contact publisher for price.
Complies with DoD Standards for Material Management & Accounting System. Modules Include BOM, Cost Control, Forecasting Management, OE, IC, MPS, MRP, Shop Floor Control, Purchasing, AP, AR, GL & Fixed Assets.
Computer Assocs. International, Inc.

CA-CAS:AP. *Customer Support:* Available.
HP-UX, MVS, VSE, VM, BS2000, MSP/AE, VOS-3. Contact publisher for price.
Provides Vendor Information, Name Search Facility & Statistics. Payment Selection, Duplicate Invoice Checking, Customized Check Formats & Check Reconciliation. Matches PO, Receivables, Inspection & Invoice Information. Handles Cash Requirements, Projections, Employee & Expense Processing. Integrated with CA-CAS:Purchasing & CA-CAS:General Ledger Applications.
Computer Associates International, Inc.

CA-CAS:AR. *Customer Support:* Available.
HP-UX, MVS, VSE, VM, BS2000, MSP/AE, VOS-3. Contact publisher for price.
On-Line Credit & Collection Options, Customer Payment & Aging Analysis, Aged Trial Balances & Audit Trails. Customer Correspondence, Note Pad & Dunning Letters. Performs Autocash, Lock Box & Direct Cash Application. Integrates with CA-CAS:Order Entry & CA-CAS:General Ledger Applications.
Computer Associates International, Inc.

CA-CAS:BOM. *Customer Support:* Available.
HP-UX, MVS, VSE, VM, BS2000, MSP/AE, VOS-3. Contact publisher for price.
Central Resource of Information about Each Part & Product. Includes Definition & Maintenance of Part Master & Product-Structure Data, On-Line Material Catalog, Multiple Product-Structure Views, Part Master Browsing by Part Number or Description, On-Line & Hard Copy Reporting & On-Line History of All Changes.
Computer Associates International, Inc.

CA-CAS:COE. *Customer Support:* Available.
HP-UX, MVS, VSE, VM, BS2000, MSP/AE, VOS-3. Contact publisher for price.
Maintains Detailed Customer Profiles, Supports Flexible Pricing Schemes, Increases Available-to-Promise Accuracy & Includes Customer Credit Checking. Allocates Inventory, Schedules Shipments & Generates Pick Lists, Invoices, Acknowledgments & Backorders.
Computer Associates International, Inc.

CA-CAS:COST. *Customer Support:* Available.
HP-UX, MVS, VSE, VM, BS2000, MSP/AE, VOS-3. Contact publisher for price.
Values Shop Floor Activity, Purchasing & Inventory Activity/Levels Using Standard & Actual Costing Techniques. Maintains Standard Costs, Collects Actual Costs, Provides Cost Comparisons, Calculates Variances, Values Inventory & Handles Fixed, Variable & Material Overhead.
Computer Associates International, Inc.

CA-CAS:Data Collection. *Customer Support:* Available.
MVS, VSE, VM. Contact publisher for price.
Automates Data Collection Through Real-Time Processing. Provides Integrated Error-Free Information on Status of Production Reporting, Purchase Receipts, Inventory Accuracy & Customer Shipments. Full Integration with CA-CAS.
Computer Associates International, Inc.

CA-CAS:FA. *Customer Support:* Available.
HP-UX, MVS, VSE, VM, BS2000, MSP/AE, VOS-3. Contact publisher for price.
Multi-Functional Program for Controlling Fixed Assets, Calculating Depreciation in Accordance with GAAP & Latest Federal Tax Laws & Controlling Leased Property Maintenance Construction-in-Progress & Other Requirements of Fixed Asset Accounting. Integrates with CA-CAS:General Ledger & CA-CAS:Accounts Payable.
Computer Associates International, Inc.

CA-CAS:GL. *Customer Support:* Available.
HP-UX, MVS, VSE, VM, BS2000, MSP/AE, VOS-3. Contact publisher for price.
Realtime Financial Reporting, Analysis & Control. Flexible Account/Reporting Structures, Multi-Company/Multi-Fiscal Year Capabilities, Budgeting, Account Creation, Allocations, Variance Calculations, Consolidations with Eliminations.
Computer Associates International, Inc.

CA-CAS:INV. *Customer Support:* Available.
HP-UX, MVS, VSE, VM, BS2000, MSP/AE, VOS-3. Contact publisher for price.
Tracks Location, Quantity & Movement of Inventory Across Multiple Bins, Stockrooms & Plants for Control over Raw Materials, Parts, Assemblies & Finished Goods. Provides ABC Classification, Automatic Cycle Count Notification & Lot & Serial Number Traceability. Maintains Statistics to Measure Inventory Accuracy & Manage Production Schedules, Rework Processing, Subcontract Requirements & Transfer Orders.
Computer Associates International, Inc.

CA-CAS Logistics & Financial Management System. 1982. *Customer Support:* Support Agreement Available.
HP-UX; MVS, VSE, VM; BS2000; MSP/AE; VOS-3. HP9000; IBM S370/390; Siemens; Fujitsu; Hitachi. Contact publisher for price.
Integrated Applications Set Including GL, AR, AP & Fixed Assets. Provides On-Line Accessibility to Date for Financial Management. Standalone or Integrates with CA-CAS Manufacturing Management System.
Computer Assocs. International, Inc.

CA-CAS Manufacturing & Logistics Management System. 1981. *Customer Support:* Support Agreement Available.
HP-UX; MVS, VSE, VM; BS2000; MSP/AE; VOS-3. HP9000; IBM S370/390; Siemens; Fujitsu; Hitachi. Contact publisher for price.
Addresses Make-to-Order, Make-to-Stock Manufacturers' Requirements by Supporting Production Scheduling & Inventory Management Policies to Optimize Overall Productivity. Modules Include BOM, Cost Control, Forecasting Management, Customer OE, Distribution Requirements Planning, IC, Master Production Scheduling, MRP, Shop Floor Control & Purchasing. Incorporates JIT Characteristics & Includes I/O Control & Backflushing Capabilities. Includes E-Mail & Enhanced Security Control. Integrated with CA-CAS Logistics & Financial Management Applications.
Computer Assocs. International, Inc.

CA-CAS:MPS. *Customer Support:* Available.
HP-UX, MVS, VSE, VM, BS2000, MSP/AE, VOS-3. Contact publisher for price.
Production & Rough-Cut Capacity Planning. Defines Product Families & Uses Forecasts & Planning Information at Family or End-Item Level to Improve Master Scheduling. Includes Final Assembly Scheduling, Multi-Plant Processing, Two-Level Master Scheduling & Planner's Workbench to Prioritize Exception Conditions & Allow Planners to Reschedule Receipts.
Computer Associates International, Inc.

CA-CAS:MRP. *Customer Support:* Available.
HP-UX, MVS, VSE, VM, BS2000, MSP/AE, VOS-3. Contact publisher for price.
Keeps Inventory Low Without Creating Shortages or Jeopardizing Sales. Supports Multi-Plant Processing, Automatic PO Generation, Unlimited Horizons & Multi-Level Pegging. Incorporates Multiple Lead-Time Elements, Scrap/Yield Percentages & Safety Stock Usage into Replenishment Planning.
Computer Associates International, Inc.

CA-CAS:PUR. *Customer Support:* Available.
HP-UX, MVS, VSE, VM, BS2000, MSP/AE, VOS-3. Contact publisher for price.
Handles Procurement Process with Vendor Profiles, Dock-to-Stock Tracking & Requisition Traceability. Supports Single- & Multi-Level Approvals, Blanket, Master & Service Orders & Receipt & Inspection Capabilities.
Computer Associates International, Inc.

CA-CAS:SFC. *Customer Support:* Available.
HP-UX, MVS, VSE, VM, BS2000, MSP/AE, VOS-3. Contact publisher for price.
Schedules & Tracks Production Line Routings & Work Center Activities Material Tracking. Maintains Work Center & Routing Information & Calculates Current & Future Capacity Loan Requirements.
Computer Associates International, Inc.

CA-CICSORT. 1988. *Customer Support:* Support Agreement Available.
MVS, VSE. IBM S/370-390. Contact publisher for price.

CA-CLASSIC/OPEN: FLEXCOMP

Native Sorting Facility for CICS Applications. Extends CICS to Permit Use of COBOL Sort Feature Without Performance Degradation. Includes Standard VS COBOL & COBOL II Verb & PL/1 & Assembler Language Support. Provides Off-Load of Sort Data to Secondary Address Space.
Computer Assocs. International, Inc.

CA-Classic/Open: FlexComp. 1980. *Items Included:* Documentation included. *Customer Support:* Available.
UNIX, SCO UNIX, AIX, HP-UX, SVR4, AVIION, DG-UX, VS. IBM RS/6000, NCR/3000, HP/9000, SCO, HP-9000, DG, Wang. Contact vendor for price.
Flexible Compensation Administration. Sets Cost Ceilings on Total Benefits Package While Allowing Employees to Tailor Benefits to Meet Individual Needs. Prepares/Edits Enrollment Forms. Processes Claims. Reports on Confirmations, Account Status & History. Performs 401(k) Discrimination Tests.
Computer Assocs. International, Inc.

CA-Classic/Open: Payroll. 1978. *Items Included:* Documentation included. *Customer Support:* Available.
UNIX, SCO UNIX, AIX, HP-UX, SVR4, AVIION, DGUX, VS. IBM RS/6000, NCR/3000, HP/9000, SCO, DG, Wang. Contact vendor for price.
Includes Time & Attendance Reporting, Labor Cost Analysis, Payroll Reporting & Several Check Options Including Direct Deposit. Provides Earnings & Deducitons Calculations, User-Defined Data Elements, Data Entry Customization & History Retention. Supports Tax Calculations & Reporting Requirements for U. S. & Canada.
Computer Assocs. International, Inc.

CA-Classic/Open. 1978. *Items Included:* Documentation included. *Customer Support:* Available.
UNIX, AIX, HP-UX, SVR4, SCO UNIX, AVIION, DG-UX, VS. IBM RS/6000, NCR/3000, HP/9000, SCO UNIX, DG Wang. Contact vendor for price.
Fully Integrated Human Resource Enterprise Solution. Includes Payroll, Personnel/Benefits & Flex Comp Modules Which Operate Standalone or Integrated. Includes Customizable Data Screens & Calculations.
Computer Assocs. International, Inc.

CA-Classic/Open: Personnel/Benefits. 1978. *Items Included:* Documentation included. *Customer Support:* Available.
UNIX, SCO UNIX, AIX, HP-UX, SVR4, AVIION, DG-UX, VS. IBM RS/6000, SCO, HP9000, NCR3000, DG, Wang. Contact vendor for price.
Includes Government Compliance Reporting for EEOC, OSHA, AAP, Applicant Tracking with Recruitment Cost Tracking, Skills Inventory, Wage & Salary Administration & Benefit Administration. Uses Personnel Tickler File for Employee Anniversary Tracking, Service Awards & Probation Periods. Includes COBRA Processing & History. Provides User-Defined Fields.
Computer Assocs. International, Inc.

CA-Clipper. 1984. *Items Included:* Documentation included. *Customer Support:* Available.
PC-DOS/MS-DOS. IBM PC & compatibles. disk $795.00.
Application Development System. Includes User-Extensible Command & Function Sets, Pre-Processor, Replaceable Database Drivers, Linker, Debugger, Virtual Memory Management, Run-Time Error Handling & Compiler. Supports Concurrent Use of Multiple Database Drivers for Access to Alternate Data Formats & Client-Server Technologies. French, German, Spanish, Portuguese, Japanese, Polish, Russian & English Versions Available.
Computer Assocs. International, Inc.

CA-Clipper/Compiler Kit for dBASE IV. 1991. *Items Included:* Documentation included. *Customer Support:* Available.
PC-DOS/MS-DOS. IBM PC & compatibles. disk $395.00.
Creates Stand-Alone, Executable Files from dBASE IV Programs. Produces .EXE Files That Can Be Freely Distributed Across Local Area Networks Without Royalty or Runtime Software Requirements. Includes Preprocessor, Custom Header File, User-Defined Function Library & dBASE IV Replaceable Database Driver Components. Includes CA-Clipper.
Computer Assocs. International, Inc.

CA-Clipper/ExoSpace. 1993. *Customer Support:* Support Agreement Available.
DOS. IBM PC & compatibles (1.5Mb). Contact publisher for price.
DOS Extender for CA-Clipper Which Runs Applications in Protected Mode to Make More Memory Directly Available. Allows Users to Link & Run CA-Clipper Applications While Shelled Out from Another CA-Clipper Application or Editor. Includes Protected Mode Linker Which Automatically Overlays Code & Data.
Computer Assocs. International, Inc.

CA-Clipper Tools. 1988. *Items Included:* Documentation included. *Customer Support:* Available.
PC-DOS/MS-DOS. IBM PC & compatibles. disk $695.00.
Extension Library for CA-Clipper Application Development System. Includes over 700 Functions Including Multiple Window Customization, Ability to Work with 2 Separate Screens, Multiple Output Effects & Disk Utilities. Provides 2 Reference Utilities for Locating Appropriate Functions, File Backup, Serial Interfacing, Functions for Novell Networks & Printer Management Within Networks, Mathematical & Trigonometric Function & Character String Manipulation.
Computer Assocs. International, Inc.

CA-Consol. 1972. *Customer Support:* Support Agreement Available.
MVS, VSE, VM. IBM S/370-390. Contact publisher for price.
Supports Financial Consolidation & Management Reporting in Medium to Large Organizations. Handles Thousands of Accounts & Reporting Units. Can Rollup by 14 Consolidation Criteria Simultaneously with No Practical Hierarchical Limits. Includes Intercompany Eliminations, Foreign Currency Capability, Integration with GL, Ad Hoc Reporting & Exception Analysis.
Computer Assocs. International, Inc.

CA-Consol/PC. 1987. *Items Included:* Documentation included. *Customer Support:* Available.
PC-DOS/MS-DOS. IBM AT, PS/2 & compatibles (640k). Contact vendor for price.
PC-Based Version of CA's Mainframe Financial Consolidation & Management Reporting System. Includes Intercompany Elimination, User-Designed Adjusting Entries, Foreign Currency Translation & Statement & Ad Hoc Reporting. Uploads/Downloads Mainframe Data. Exchanges Data with Spreadsheet, Financial Planning & Other PC Programs.
Computer Assocs. International, Inc.

CA-Consol/WS. 1993. *Customer Support:* Support Agreement Available.
Windows. IBM PC & compatibles (4Mb). Contact publisher for price.
Windows-Based, Graphical, Icon-Driven Financial Consolidation & Management Reporting System. Includes Intercompany Elimination, User-Designed Adjusting Entries, Foreign Currency Translation & WYSIWYG Reporting. Exchanges Data with Spreadsheets, Financial Planning & Other PC Programs.
Computer Assocs. International, Inc.

CA-Convertor. 1973. *Customer Support:* Support Agreement Available.
MVS, VSE. IBM S/370-390. Contact publisher for price.
DOS-to-MVS & VSE-to-MVS Conversion. Performs Program & File Inventory, Program Source Conversion, Generation of Job Control & Documentation. Compares Results of Conversion vs. Pre-Conversion. Supports Installation Standards & Non-IBM System Software Products. Converts DOS/VS COBOL to OS/VS COBOL or VS/COBOL II.
Computer Assocs. International, Inc.

CA-Corporate Tie. 1986. *Items Included:* Documentation included. *Customer Support:* Available.
PC-DOS, VSE, MVS. Contact vendor for price.
Mainframe to Micro Network Communications System. Performs High-Speed File Transfer with Interactive Menus & PC-Based Command Language. Contains Facility Which Allows Exchange of Data Between Micro Network & Mainframe During Periods of Low Network Activity or While PC Is Unattended. Includes Screen-Driven Virtual Disk System Which Transparently Extends Storage Available to Microcomputers.
Computer Assocs. International, Inc.

CA-Cricket Draw III. 1986. *Memory Required:* 2000k. *Customer Support:* Available.
Macintosh Plus, SE, SE/30, Classic, LC, Portable, or Macintosh II Series. $129.00.
Object-Oriented Drawing Package. Includes Intuitive User Interface, Bezier Tools, Color Capabilities & PostScript Generation.
Computer Assocs. International, Inc.

CA-Cricket Graph III. 1985. *Compatible Hardware:* Macintosh Plus, SE, Classic, SE/30, Portable, LC or Macintosh II Series. *Memory Required:* 1000k. *Customer Support:* Available. $129.00.
Charting Application for Scientists, Engineers, & Business Professionals. Creates High-Quality Graphs & Charts for Reports, Presentations, or Data Analysis. Graph Types Include Scatter, Line, Stacked Bar, Pie, Column, Text, Area, Stacked, Double Y Axes, Bar, Polar, Quality Control, & Overlay Combinations & Provides Various Fonts, Sizes, & Styles.
Computer Assocs. International, Inc.

CA-Culprit. 1969. *Customer Support:* Support Agreement Available.
MVS, VSE, VM, BS2000, MSP, VOS-3. IBM S/370-390; Siemens, Hitachi, Fujitsu FACOM. Contact publisher for price.
Creates Reports Based on Data Stored in CA-IDMS/DB & Other Databases & VSAM Files. Creates & Updates Data Tables That Reside in CA-IDMS/DB or CA-ICMS.
Computer Assocs. International, Inc.

CA-DADS/Plus. 1988. *Customer Support:* Support Agreement Available.
MVS. IBM S/370-390. Contact publisher for price.
CICS Resource Management Tool. Maximizes CICS Availability. Controls CICS Data Sets, Programs, Load Libraries & Tables & Streamlines Operations in CICS & Batch. Dynamic Allocation

of Files, Databases, Transient Data Queues & Load Libraries. FCT/DCT Table Management. Program/Module Management.
Computer Assocs. International, Inc.

CA-DASDCheck. 1982. *Customer Support:* Support Agreement Available.
MVS. IBM S/370-390 (256k). Contact publisher for price.
Recovers DASD Data That Has Become Unreadable Due to Permanent Input/Output Error. Recovers Data from Critical Datasets Such As VTOCs, VSAM & JES Checkpoint Datasets. Reads SYS1.LOGREC File & Reports Errors Utilizing SAS Interface.
Computer Assocs. International, Inc.

CA-Datacom/PC Runtime. 1991. *Customer Support:* Available.
PC-DOS/MS-DOS. IBM PC AT, PS/2 or compatible (2Mb). Contact publisher for price. *Networks supported:* NetBIOS.
Complete, Standalone, Database Management & Application Execution System. Also for Use in Conjunction with CA-Datacom/PC Runtime Server in Multi-User LAN-Based Client/Server Environment. Compatible with the CA-Datacom Product Line on the Mainframe & UNIX & Is Intended for Use As a CA-Datacom Workstation for the Execution of Downsized Applications. Includes ODBC Support.
Computer Assocs., International, Inc.

CA-Datacom/PC Runtime Server. 1992. *Customer Support:* Available.
PC-DOS/MS-DOS. LAN that may include IBM AT, PS/2 or compatibles with any standard network topology that supports a NetBIOS-compatible interface running on PC or MS-DOS; 386 or higher recommended (2Mb). Contact publisher for price. *Networks supported:* NetBIOS.
LAN-Based Database Management System for the PC Environment. Designed to Run with CA-Datacom/PC Runtime Clients, It Provides a Multi-User Environment with a Shared Dictionary & Database on a Central Database Server. Compatible with the CA-Datacom Product Line on the Mainframe & UNIX. Includes Interactive SQL Facilities, Data & Dictionary Transport Facilities & Various Support Utilities. ODBC Support Is Provided.
Computer Assocs., International, Inc.

CA-Datacom/STAR. 1981. *Customer Support:* Support Agreement Available.
MVS, VSE. IBM S/370-390 (250k). Contact publisher for price.
Distributed DBMS Product That Distributes Data & Programs Without Impacting Applications. Supports Local Autonomy or Centralized Control of Environment. Handles Integrity, Security, Restart & Recovery Capabilities of CA-Datacom/DB Throughout Distributed Environment. Provides Partitioning, Replication & Multi-Site Updating with 2-Phase Commit Protocol.
Computer Assocs. International, Inc.

CA-Datacom/STAR PC. 1991. *Customer Support:* Available.
PC-DOS or MS-DOS. IBM PC AT, PS/2 & compatibles. Contact Vendor.
Provides Transparent Data Distribution Services for Single- or Multi-User, LAN-Based CA-Datacom/PC. Supports Call-Level or SQL Access to Data on Local CA-Datacom/PC and/or Remote CA-Datacom/DB System, Including Update with 2-Phase Commit Protocol. Exchanges Transaction & Control Data with CA-Datacom/Star.
Computer Assocs. International, Inc.

CA-Datacom/UNIX. 1993. *Items Included:* Documentation included. *Customer Support:* Available.
HP-UX, AIX, DG AVIION, DG-UX. IBM RS/6000/AIX, HP 9000, DG AVIION. Contact vendor for price.
DBMS Compatible with CA-Datacom/DB & CA-Datacom/PC. Includes Integrated Dictionary & Precompiler for SQL Embedded in COBOL or C. Supports CA-Datacom Call-Level Access & CA-Ideal/UNIX. Includes Facility to Transport Data & Definitions Between Platforms. Client/Server Access Available from Both UNIX Workstations & PCs.
Computer Assocs. International, Inc.

CA-Datacom/CICS Services. 1982. *Customer Support:* Support Agreement Available.
MVS, VSE. IBM S/370-390. Contact publisher for price.
Provides Application Programs Designed to Run under CICS with Access to CA-Datacom/DB. Includes Functions Which Allow User to Control On-Line System Resources & Display Status Information On-Line.
Computer Assocs. International, Inc.

CA-Datacom/DB. 1974. *Customer Support:* Support Agreement Available.
MVS, VSE, VM, HP-UX, AIX, DG-UX. IBM S/370-390; HP9000, DG, RS/6000 (2Mb). Contact publisher for price.
ROBMS Which Stores Data in Tables. Provides Relational Index System, Query System, Accounting Facilities, Data Access & Security. Provides Program Development, Maintenance & Information Center Support. Includes Data Dictionary for Definition, Design, Reporting, Auditing & Control UNIX Version Supports Call-Level & SQL Access for COBOL, C & CA-Ideal/UNIX. Includes Facility to Transfer Data Between Platforms. ODBC-Compliant Server & GUI PC Tools.
Computer Assocs. International, Inc.

CA-Datacom/DL1 Transparency. 1985. *Customer Support:* Support Agreement Available.
MVS, VSE. IBM S/370-390 (100k). Contact publisher for price.
Database Migration Tool That Converts DL/1 & IMS/DB Files to CA-Datacom/DB Databases. Redesigns Database & Loads Data into New Database. Existing DL/1 Programs Operate Against CA-Datacom/DB Without Changes to Program Logic, Recompile or Relink.
Computer Assocs. International, Inc.

CA-Datacom Fast Restore. 1994. *Customer Support:* Support Agreement Available.
MVS, VSE. IBM S/370-390. Contact publisher for price.
Provides Ultra-Fast Recovery from Database or Hardware Failures for CA-Datacom/DB. Expedites Database Recovery Process. Optimizes Recovery Information. Eliminates Duplicate Updates. Fully Multi-Threaded. Operates in Parallel with Ongoing DBMS Activity.
Computer Assocs. International, Inc.

CA-Datacom/IMSDC Services. 1987. *Customer Support:* Support Agreement Available.
MVS. IBM S/370-390. Contact publisher for price.
Provides Applications Executing in IMS/DC Environment with Access to CA-Datacom/DB Database Management System. Programs Can Execute in MPP or BMP Regions. Programs Can Use IMS DL/I, SQL or Record-at-Time to Access CA-Datacom.
Computer Assocs. International, Inc.

CA-Datacom/PC. 1989. *Customer Support:* Available.
PC-MS/DOS. IBM PC AT, PS/2 & compatibles (2Mb). contact publisher for price.
DBMS Compatible with Mainframe CA-Datacom/DB & CA-Datacom/UNIX. Includes DataDictionary & DataQuery Components & PreCompiler for Embedded SQL in COBOL. Supports CA-Datacom Call-Level Access & CA-Ideal/PC. Includes Graphical Data Dictionary Facility & ODBC Support. Run-Time Versions Available for Server & Workstations.
Computer Assocs. International, Inc.

CA-Datacom/PC Lanpack. 1991. *Items Included:* Documentation included. *Customer Support:* Available.
PC-DOS/MS-DOS. IBM AT, XT, PS/2 & compatibles (2Mb); 386-based machine recommended for use as Database Server. Contact vendor for price.
LAN-Based DBMS & Application Development System with Client/Server Architecture. Compatible with Mainframe & UNIX CA-Datacom Product Line. Provides Shared, Integrated Dictionary & Database on Centralized Database Server for Development & Downsizing of CA-Datacom Applications. Includes Interactive & Embedded SQL Facilities, Data & Data Definition Transport Facilities, ODBC Support & CA-Ideal/PC, CA-MetaCOBOL Plus/PC & CA-Realia COBOL Application Development Environments.
Computer Assocs. International, Inc.

CA-Datacom Presspack. 1992. *Customer Support:* Support Agreement Available.
MVS. IBM S/370-390. Contact publisher for price.
Data Compression Program. Uses Enhanced Huffman Encoding Technique to Compress Data. Integrates with CA-Datacom/DB & Includes Compression Estimation Report Utility.
Computer Assocs. International, Inc.

CA-Datacom Resource Analyzer. 1994. *Customer Support:* Support Agreement Available.
MVS. IBM S/370-390. Contact publisher for price.
Analyzes Database Table Definitions & Program Usage to Identify Possible Problem Areas. Recommends Changes to Enhance Performance & Reduce Resource Usage. Operates Online in Real Time. Utilizes Actual Operational Data. Completely Menu-Driven.
Computer Assocs. International, Inc.

CA-Datacom Server. 1993. *Customer Support:* Available.
Windows; MVS. IBM PC & compatibles; IBM S/370-390. Contact publisher for price.
Provides Access to CA-Datacom Mainframe Databases from Client PC Applications Executing under Microsoft Windows & Utilizing Microsoft ODBC API. Windows Required on Client.
Computer Assocs., International, Inc.

CA-Datacom/SQL Option. 1989. *Customer Support:* Support Agreement Available.
MVS, VSE, VM. IBM S/370-390. Contact publisher for price.
Provides Access & Manipulation of Data via Industry-Standard SQL. Supports ANSI, FIPS & CA-Extended SQL. Integrity Management Facilities Provide Referential, Domain, Entity & Data Type Integrity Restraints. SQL Can Be Used to Manipulate Tables Even If Tables Were Not Created Using SQL.
Computer Assocs. International, Inc.

CA-Datacom/Total Transparency. 1987. *Customer Support:* Support Agreement Available.
MVS, VSE. IBM S/370-390. Contact publisher for price.

Migrates Applications from Cincom's Total to CA-Datacom/DB Environment. Restructures Data. Includes Database Designer, Data Transfer & Application Transparency Facilities. Existing Total Programs Operate Against CA-Datacom/DB Without Changes to Program Logic, Recompile or Relink.
Computer Assocs. International, Inc.

CA-Datacom/Transparency for DB2. 1993. *Customer Support:* Support Agreement Available.
MVS. IBM S/370-390. Contact publisher for price.
Allows DB2 Applications to Run Against CA-Datacom/DB Without Program Modification. Includes Catalog Conversion Utility, Data Conversion Utility, DBRM Conversion Utility & DB2 Request Interceptor.
Computer Assocs. International, Inc.

CA-Datacom/VSAM Transparency. 1984. *Customer Support:* Support Agreement Available.
MVS, VSE. IBM S/370-390 (100k). Contact publisher for price.
Migration Tool for Converting VSAM Applications to CA-Datacom/DB Environment. Supports Access from Both Environments to Permit Phased Migration. Allows Existing Applications to Operate in CA-Datacom/DB Environment Without Modifications or Relink.
Computer Assocs. International, Inc.

CA-Datacom VSE/ESA Option. 1991. *Customer Support:* Support Agreement Available.
VSE/ESA. IBM S/370-390. Contact publisher for price.
Provides Exploitation of VSE/ESA's Enhanced Processing Capacity.
Computer Assocs. International, Inc.

CA-Datamacs/II. 1985. *Customer Support:* Support Agreement Available.
MVS, VSE. IBM S/370-390 (500k). Contact publisher for price.
Creates Test Data Files from Scratch and/or Existing Production Files. Masks Confidential Data Fields. Resides in Data Division of COBOL Program in Comment Fashion for Regression Testing. Optional Interfaces to Dump/Modify/Populate IMS, CA-IDMS & CA-Datacom Databases. ISPF Interface Builds CA-Datamacs/II Control Statements & JCL.
Computer Assocs. International, Inc.

CA-Dataquery. 1976. *Customer Support:* Support Agreement Available.
MVS, VSE, VM. IBM S/370-390 (500k). Contact publisher for price.
Ad Hoc Query, Data Management & Reporting System. Includes Novice, Intermediate & Expert Modes of Operation. Provides Multi-Language Facilities, Procedural Operations, Model Queries & Interactive SQL Support. Integrates with CA-Datacom/DB & Other CA Products.
Computer Assocs. International, Inc.

CA-Dataquery for VAX. 1988. *Items Included:* Documentation included. *Customer Support:* Available.
VAX/VMS. Digital VAX. Contact vendor for price.
Ad Hoc Query, Data Management & Reporting System. Supports Data Exchange Between VAX & Mainframe. Provides SQL Interface, Ad Hoc Query Facility, Data Download/Upload, Data Export/Import for Exchanging Data Between VAX Spreadsheet & Application Software, Report Writer & Unattended/Repetitive Task Support.
Computer Assocs. International, Inc.

CA-Dataquery/PC. 1984. *Items Included:* Documentation included. *Customer Support:* Available.
PC-DOS/MS-DOS. IBM XT, AT, PS/2 & compatibles (395k). Contact vendor for price.
Ad Hoc Query, Data Mangement & Reporting System. Supports Data Exchange Between PC & Mainframe, SQL Interface & Data Import/Export. Includes Novice, Intermediate & Expert Operation Modes.
Computer Assocs. International, Inc.

CA-DataVantage. 1982. *Customer Support:* Support Agreement Available.
MVS, VSE. IBM S/370-390 (128k). Contact publisher for price.
Simplifies Development, Testing & Maintenance of DL/1 Applications. Creates Subsets of Production Databases & Maintains Logical Relationships. Lists, Replaces, Deletes or Inserts Segments with On-Line or Batch Commands. Compares Before & after Images of Database & Lists Differences.
Computer Assocs. International, Inc.

CA-Director. 1986. *Customer Support:* Support Agreement Available.
VM. IBM S/370-390 (2Mb). Contact publisher for price.
Simplified VM Directory Maintenance with Business-Oriented Departmental/Division Organization. Provides Decentralized Administration with Synchronization Between Remote VM Systems. Supports Single-Point Registration. Interfaces to CA-Top Secret & CA-ACF2. DRCT Line Commands Enable CA-Director to Follow Group Authority Restrictions & Controls.
Computer Assocs. International, Inc.

CA-Dispatch. 1984. *Customer Support:* Support Agreement Available.
MVS. IBM S/370-390 (3.5Mb). Contact publisher for price.
Manages Report Distribution. Report Archiving Eliminates Lost Report Job Reruns. Control of Sysout Parameters On-Line Replaces Change Control for JCL. Output Grouped by Destination Rather Than Job. On-Line Viewing Can Replace Hard Copy. Provides On-Line Tracking of Reports & Security Interface. PC Component Available.
Computer Assocs. International, Inc.

CA-Dispatch/Notepad. 1991. *Customer Support:* Support Agreement Available.
MVS. IBM S/370-390 (2Mb). Contact publisher for price.
Provides Centralized, Integrated Recording & Viewing of User Notes Made During CA-Dispatch Operations. Provides TSO/ISPF Interface, Help Facility & External Security Integration.
Computer Assocs. International, Inc.

CA-Dispatch/PC. 1991. *Customer Support:* Available.
Windows. IBM PC or compatibles. Contact Vendor.
Extends User Accessibility & Functionality of Mainframe-Generated Reports to PC Workstaiton or LAN. Requests Reports from Local Hard Disk, LAN Server or Mainframe. Allows Concurrent Viewing of Multiple Reports. Provides 3270 Emulation & Prints Reports on Local PC Printer, LAN Printer or Any Printer Connected to JES. Windows Required for Report Viewing & Manipulation.
Computer Assocs. International, Inc.

CA-Dispatch/Viewpoint. 1991. *Customer Support:* Support Agreement Available.
MVS. IBM S/370-390 (2Mb). Contact publisher for price.
Object-Oriented Windowing Interface for CA-Dispatch Report Distribution System. Utilizes IBM's SAA Common User Access Standard. Includes Report Management & On-Line Viewing.
Computer Assocs. International, Inc.

CA-Disspla. 1970. *Compatible Hardware:* DEC VAX/VMS, OpenVMS AXP, ULTRIX; HP9000 Series 300, 400, 700, 800, Apollo Domain/IX, HP-UX, Aegis, Alliant/Concentrix; Convex; CDC/NOS/VE; Cray; DG AVIION/AOS/VS; IBM Mainframe MVS, VM/CMS, RS/6000/AIX; Prime/Primos; SGI/IRIX; Unisys OS1100; PC-MS/DOS; Solaris, OSF/1, DecAlpha, SUN, MIPS Co UNIX (RISC). *Items Included:* Documentation included. *Customer Support:* Available.
Contact vendor for price.
Visualization Library for Use When Developing Graphics in Distributed Environment. Graphics Types Include Maps, Charts, Graphs, Contours, Surfaces, 2D or 3D Designs & Set of 2D & 3D Graphics Primitives with Attributes. Supports Raster Imaging & 3D Scene & Object Rendering. Provides Math Utilities & Algorithms. Supports CGM, PostScript, 400 Graphics Devices & X-Windows.
Computer Assocs. International, Inc.

CA-Disspla COBOL. 1989. *Customer Support:* Support Agreement Available.
MVS. IBM S/370-390 (1.3Mb). Contact publisher for price.
Tool for COBOL Application Development Programmers for Incorporating Presentation-Quality Graphics into Any COBOL Application. Includes Line, Pie, Bar, Area, High-Low, Scatter, Print/Image Graphics, Multiple Charts per Page, Customized Graphics. Uses Modular COBOL Record Source, Programs & Statements.
Computer Assocs. International, Inc.

CA-Driver. 1979. *Customer Support:* Support Agreement Available.
VSE. IBM S/370-390. Contact publisher for price.
Job Control Management System for Control of Storage, Maintenance & Manipulation of JCL. Enhances JCL by Conditional Procedure Expansion, Variable Parameter Substitution & Arrays, Procedure Nesting & Branching, Conditional Execution & Job Submission, Password Protection for Library & Procedures & Global Maintenance Functions.
Computer Assocs. International, Inc.

CA-DUO. 1970. *Customer Support:* Support Agreement Available.
MVS. IBM S/370-390 (4Mb). Contact publisher for price.
VSE to MVS Conversion Aid. Allows VSE Programs to Execute under MVS Without Source Change. All MVS Facilities Available to VSE Batch Program. Supports Most Database Systems, DBOMP, VSE Compilers & Utilities, Power Segmentation & COMREG/SYSCOM Access.
Computer Assocs. International, Inc.

CA-Dynam/B. 1983. *Customer Support:* Support Agreement Available.
VM. IBM S/370-390 (4Mb). Contact publisher for price.
Backs up CMS Files, Minidisks or Full Volumes on Regularly Scheduled Basis or When Requested. Provides Disaster Recovery to Ensure Data Integrity & User-Controlled File Archival System to Offload CMS Files. Supports the Shared File System (SFS) for Backup, Restore, Archive & Recall. Able to Run Unattended Backups & Schedule IPLable DDR Backups.
Computer Assocs. International, Inc.

TITLE INDEX

CA-Dynam/D. 1977. *Customer Support:* Support Agreement Available.
VSE. IBM S/370-390. Contact publisher for price.
Management Facility for DASD Resources & Datasets. Provides Dynamic Allocation & Automatic Secondary Allocation of DASD File Space. Supports DASD Pool Management & Automatically Controls Dataset Usage & Retention. Uses CA-Dynam Catalog for Seamless File Management Without Frequent Program & JCL Changes. Provides Automatic Volume Recognition, Audit Trail, Standard & Custom Reporting, On-Line Catalog Query & Update.
Computer Assocs. International, Inc.

CA-Dynam/FastVTOC. 1991. *Customer Support:* Support Agreement Available.
VSE. IBM S/370-390. Contact publisher for price.
Indexing Facility for DASD Volume Table of Contents Access. Builds & Automatically Maintains Indexed VTOC. Addresses Performance Issues That Occur Primarily During Open & Close Processing. Utilizes Storage above 16 MB Line for Site Running VSE/ESA Release 1.3. Compatible with Most Disk Management Software.
Computer Assocs. International, Inc.

CA-Dynam/FI. 1979. *Customer Support:* Support Agreement Available.
VSE. IBM S/370-390. Contact publisher for price.
File Independence Facility for Tape, Disk & Unit-Record Devices. Redefines Device Characteristics, Such As Device Type, Record Format, Record & Block Size, to Transparently Adapt Applications to Device Differences Without Program Modifications or JCL Changes. Provides Automatic Block File Optimization, Disk/Tape Switching, File Concatenation & Unit Record Device Simulation.
Computer Assocs. International, Inc.

CA-Dynam/T VM. 1983. *Customer Support:* Support Agreement Available.
VM. IBM S/370-390 (4Mb). Contact publisher for price.
Comprehensive Tape/Vault Management System for VM User. Automates Dataset Usage, Controls Access & Secures Data from Accidental Destruction or Loss. Includes Audit Trail & Disaster Recovery Capabilities, Volume Recognition, Catalog Control & Dataset Retention. Includes Interfaces to STK 4400 & Memorex's LMS.
Computer Assocs. International, Inc.

CA-Dynam/T VSE. 1977. *Customer Support:* Support Agreement Available.
VSE. IBM S/370-390. Contact publisher for price.
Tape Management System Providing Automatic Control of Tape Dataset Usage & Retention. Provides Control at Dataset & Volume Levels, Automatic Attach/Detach & Standard IBM Tape Label Support for Unlabeled Tape Files. Includes Vault Location Control, CA-Dynam Catalog for File Management Without Program & JCL Changes, On-Line Catalog Query & Update, On-Line Option Definition, VSAM History File & Audit Trail.
Computer Assocs. International, Inc.

CA-Dynam/TLMS. 1972. *Customer Support:* Support Agreement Available.
MVS. IBM S/370-390 (64k). Contact publisher for price.
Tape Library Management & Dataset Protection. Facility for Offsite Vault Movement & Scratch Pool Management. On-Line Interface to MVS Production Scheduling, DASD Management Products & CMS/VSE Tape Management Software.
Computer Assocs. International, Inc.

CA-Dynam/TLMS/Copycat. 1992. *Customer Support:* Support Agreement Available.
MVS. IBM S/370-390. Contact publisher for price.
Provides Tape Media Conversions, Media Consolidation/Stacking & Media Replacement Operations. Assists in Disaster Recovery by Facilitating Tape Backup & Electronic Vaulting. Allows User to Cop Data Sets or Volumes to Other Tapes Without Requiring Cataloging of Backup Version. Protects Data from Old or Faulty Media.
Computer Assocs. International, Inc.

CA-Dynam/TLMS/Viewpoint. 1992. *Customer Support:* Support Agreement Available.
MVS. IBM S/370-390. Contact publisher for price.
Provides Windowing User Interface to CA-Dynam/TLMS Based on IBM's SAA/CUA Standard. Includes Self-Refreshing Tape Device Display, Device Support, Boolean Selection Logic, On-Line Documentation & Volume Set.
Computer Assocs. International, Inc.

CA-Earl. 1972. *Customer Support:* Support Agreement Available.
MVS, VSE, VM. IBM S/370-390 (260k). Contact publisher for price.
Produces Reports Using High Level Language Supporting IMS, VSAM, Sequential Files, CA-Datacom, CA-IDMS, DB2, SQL/DS, & Other Data Sources. Performs Data Analysis, Production of Multiple Reports & File Maintenance.
Computer Assocs. International, Inc.

CA-EasyProclib. 1978. *Customer Support:* Support Agreement Available.
MVS. IBM S/370-390 (2Mb). Contact publisher for price.
Allows User to Create, Maintain & Execute JCL from Private Procedure Libraries. Reduces JES Failure Probability Due to System Proclib Problems. Handles Change Control Procedures.
Computer Assocs. International, Inc.

CA-Easytrieve/IQ. 1987. *Customer Support:* Support Agreement Available.
MVS, VSE, VM. IBM S/370-390 (256k). Contact publisher for price.
Provides Mainframe Information Query & Report Writing Capabilities for End Users. Allows User to Create Comprehensive Reports, Download Relational & Non-Relational Information to Workstation & Produces Graphics. Enables Immediate Access to Data with No Programming.
Computer Assocs. International, Inc.

CA-Easytrieve/Online. 1991. *Customer Support:* Support Agreement Available.
MVS, VSE, VM. IBM S/370-390 (2Mb). Contact publisher for price.
Extends Batch Language Capabilities of CA-Easytrieve for CICS, TSO & CMS. Tool for Interactively Creating, Testing & Implementing Reports & Applications & Enterprise-Wide Data Retrieval & Information Management. Kanji Version Available.
Computer Assocs. International, Inc.

CA-Easytrieve Plus. 1973. *Customer Support:* Support Agreement Available.
MVS, VSE, VM, BS2000. IBM S/370-390; Siemens (256k). Contact publisher for price.
Information Retrieval & Data Maintenance/Management Tool. Includes English-Like Programming Language for Producing Reports & Applications for IBM Mainframe & PC. Provides Sequential and/or Random Access to Data Located in Various DBMSs. Separate Options Available for Query Access to Several Popular Mainframe Databases, Including Total, Supra, Oracle, IMS, DL/1, DB2, SQL/DS, CA-IDMS & CA-Datacom.
Computer Assocs. International, Inc.

CA-Easytrieve/Toolkit. 1986. *Customer Support:* Support Agreement Available.
MVS, VSE, VM. IBM S/370-390. Contact publisher for price.
Provides Utilities Which Allow User to Optimize Capabilities of CA-Easytrieve Plus. Includes Date & Time Routines for Executing Conversions/Computations, File Comparison Routines to Validate Accuracy, & Test Generation Routines to Create Numeric, Alphabetic or Alphanumeric Data in Random, Sequenced or Constant Format.
Computer Assocs. International, Inc.

CA-Easytrieve/Workstation. 1992. *Items Included:* Documentation included. *Customer Support:* Available.
PC-DOS/MS-DOS. IBM PC & compatibles (256k). Contact vendor for price. *Networks supported:* Novell, Banyan, Token Ring, 3COM.
Uses Same Syntax As Mainframe CA-Easytrieve Products. Allows Manipulation of Multiple File Types Including CA-Datacom/PC, CA-IDMS/PC, Lotus, CA-SuperCalc, dBase, BTRIEVE, EBCDIC & ASCII Record Formats. Allows Unlimited Number of Files to Be Used to Generate Reports or Graphs.
Computer Assocs. International, Inc.

CA-EDP Auditor. 1971. *Customer Support:* Support Agreement Available.
MVS, VSE, VM, BS2000, MSP, VOS-3. IBM S/370-390; Siemens; Fujitsu; Hitachi. Contact publisher for price.
Library of CA-CULPRIT Routines for Audit Community. Routines Provide Algorithms & Reports for Confirmations, Statistical Sampling, Statistical Sample Analysis & Summary/Graphical Analysis.
Computer Assocs. International, Inc.

CA-11. 1973. *Customer Support:* Support Agreement Available.
MVS. IBM S/370-390 (256k). Contact publisher for price.
Rerun Handling & Tracking System. Executes Reruns with No JCL Changes. Eliminates NOT CATLGD 2 Situations. Job Status Information & Automatic Adjustment of OS Catalog Entries. Pinpoints & Reports Causes of Reruns.
Computer Assocs. International, Inc.

CA-11/Disaster Recovery Planning. 1991. *Customer Support:* Support Agreement Available.
MVS. IBM S/370-390 (2Mb). Contact publisher for price.
Component of CA-11 That Allows Users to Develop, Maintain & Test Comprehensive, Company-Wide Disaster Recovery Plans in Centralized Mainframe Environment. Provides Preformatted Templates & Allows Users to Customize or Create Templates Through On-Line Screens.
Computer Assocs. International, Inc.

CA-11/Notepad. 1991. *Customer Support:* Support Agreement Available.
MVS. IBM S/370-390 (1Mb). Contact publisher for price.
Provides Centralized, Integrated Recording & Viewing of User Notes Made During CA-11 Operations. Provides TSO/ISPF Interface, External Security Integration & On-Line Screen Print.
Computer Assocs. International, Inc.

CA-11/Reports+. 1991. *Customer Support:* Support Agreement Available.
MVS. IBM S/370-390 (4Mb). Contact publisher for price.
Provides Presentation-Quality Graphic Reporting Capabilities. Assists Production Control Managers, Data Center Executives, Operations Analysts & End-Users in Analyzing All Facets of Data Center Rerun Activity.
Computer Assocs. International, Inc.

CA-11/Viewpoint. 1991. *Customer Support:* Support Agreement Available.
MVS. IBM S/370-390 (1Mb). Contact publisher for price.
Brings Windowing to MVS Mainframe Environment & Provides Integrated, Centralized Interface to CA-11 & Other CA Solutions Which Utilize Viewpoint Option. Follows IBM's SAA/CUA Standards. Features Include Single Screen Control, Movable Windows, Pull-Down Menus, Choice Lists & Auto-Refresh Capabilities.
Computer Assocs. International, Inc.

CA-eMail+. 1982. *Customer Support:* Support Agreement Available.
MVS, VSE, VM. IBM S/370-390 (800k). Contact publisher for price.
Provides Full E-Mail Capabilities Including Message Creation, Automated Message Management, Calendaring & Scheduling, Resource Coordination, Electronic Forms, Multiple BBSs, Fax & Telex, Voice Interface, Mail Security & On-Line Help. Facilities Include X.400 Gateway Option, PC Connectivity Option with CA-eMail Plus Companion, Standard Exits & Interfaces to Other Software.
Computer Assocs. International, Inc.

CA-eMail+ Companion. 1993. *Items Included:* Documentation included. *Customer Support:* Available.
PC-DOS/MS-DOS. IBM PC & compatibles (340k). Contact vendor for price. *Addl. software required:* CA-eMail Plus.
Works with CA-eMail Plus to Allow E-Mail Processing Capabilities on PC Connected to Mainframe or in Disconnected Mode. Allows User to Create Messages, Replies & Other E-Mail Related Activities on PC Via Built-In or Common Word Processor & Route into CA-eMail Plus Network. Performs File Transfer, Word Processing Document Conversion & Printing.
Computer Assocs. International, Inc.

CA-eMail+ X.400 Option. 1993. *Items Included:* Documentation included. *Customer Support:* Available.
OS/2. IBM PS/2 (6Mb). Contact vendor for price. *Nonstandard peripherals required:* Eicon X.25 card. *Addl. software required:* CA-eMail Plus.
E-Mail Gateway Between CA-eMail Plus & Other X.400 Standard E-Mail Systems. Provides Full Support for Converting to/from X.400 Originator/Recipient Names, Message Security, References & Other Standard X.400 Capabilities.
Computer Assocs. International, Inc.

CA-ESP/Upgrade. 1989. *Customer Support:* Support Agreement Available.
OS/400. IBM AS/400. Contact publisher for price.
Automates Process of Integrating Custom Programming Modifications with Vendor's Latest Release of Application Software. Includes Relate Audit & Management Component, Compare Component Which Compares 2 Separate Source File Members or Groups of Members & Merge Component Which Compares 2 Independent Sets of Changes to Original Files.
Computer Assocs. International, Inc.

CA-Estimacs. 1982. *Memory Required:* 640k. *Customer Support:* Available.
MS-DOS. IBM PC & compatibles. contact publisher for price.
Knowledge-Based System for Business Application Estimating Verified on Approximatley 13,000 Projects. Supports MIS Management Decision Process with Financial Data, Risk Analysis & Grouping of Estimated Projects into Portfolios for Horizon Planning. For Budget Preparation, Staffing & Auditing Reviews.
Computer Assocs. International, Inc.

CA-ETC. 1974. *Customer Support:* Support Agreement Available.
MVS, VSE. IBM S/370-390 (250k). Contact publisher for price.
Text Composition System for Large Volume Documents. Split-Screen to Simultaneously View Final Form & Raw Form of Document. Macro Language to Facilitate Special Formatting Needs. Interfaces to Data Files for Mail/Merge Applications. Interfaces to CA-eMail Plus for Electronic Document Distribution. Supports Multiple Fonts for Non-Impact, All Points Addressable Page Printers.
Computer Assocs. International, Inc.

CA-Examine. 1986. *Customer Support:* Support Agreement Available.
MVS. IBM S/370-390 (4Mb). Contact publisher for price.
Reviews, Verifies & Analyzes MVS & Associated System Software Integrity & Control Mechanisms. Reports Status of System Options & Parameters, Tables, Libraries, Files & Application Programs. Identifies Inconsistencies, Potential Exposures & Unauthorized Modifications. Includes Interactive On-Line Displays. Natural Language Interface. Uses Expert System Techniques to Analyze MVS Software Installation/Options & Detect Potential Errors/Threats.
Computer Assocs. International, Inc.

CA-Examine/PC. 1992. *Customer Support:* Available.
DOS. IBM PC, XT, AT, PS/2, COMPAQ or compatible (2Mb). Contact publisher for price.
Auditing Tool Providing a Computer-Aided Method for Identification of Organization's PC Hardware & Software Inventory. Electronically Identifies & Collects PC Hardware & Software Information Through Scanning Process.
Computer Assocs., International, Inc.

CA-Eztest/CICS. 1982. *Customer Support:* Support Agreement Available.
MVS, VSE. IBM S/370-390 (40k). Contact publisher for price.
Debugging for CICS Environment. Captures & Repairs Storage Violations & Other Common Abends. Allows Actual COBOL, COBOL II, COBOL/370, PL/1 & Assembler Statement Display, Conditional & Unconditional Pauses & Instruction Stepping. Displays & Updates Files & Storage to Authorized Users.
Computer Assocs. International, Inc.

CA-FastDASD. 1980. *Customer Support:* Support Agreement Available.
MVS, VM. IBM S/370-390 (256k). Contact publisher for price.
Performance Measurement, Tuning & Analysis System for Improving DASD & Cache Performance. Provides Online Monitor Displaying DASD I/O Service Time Metrics. Recommends Optimum Data Set Placement Based on Information Collected about Seek Activity. Aids in String Balancing & Cache Control Unit Analysis. Produces Reports & Control Statements for Input to Volume Reorganization by CA-ASM2, FDR, Compaktor, DF/DSS, DDR & Cross-Volume by CA-ASM2. Provides System Managed Storage (SMS) Reporting.
Computer Assocs. International, Inc.

CA51 Cross Assembler for 8051 Microcontrollers. *Version:* 1.5. John G. MacDougal. Jun. 1991. *Items Included:* Distribution diskette (5.25" only) containing: CA51.EXE program, README.DOC instruction booklet, TEST51.ASM sample source file; installation instructions. *Customer Support:* Free technical support by phone.
MS-DOS version 2.0 or higher. IBM PC compatible (256k). $150.00 postage pre-paid to continental U. S. (ISBN 0-9628535-1-8, Order no.: CA51). *Nonstandard peripherals required:* Prom programmer. *Addl. software required:* Text editor or word processor for preparing source code files.
Processes a Source Code File & Generates an Object Code File & an Assembly Listing. Knowledge of the 8051 Family of Embedded Controllers Is Required the Standard (Intel) Mnemonics Is Required.
Oak Manor Pr.

CA-Filesave/RCS. 1986. *Customer Support:* Support Agreement Available.
MVS. IBM S/370-390 (512k). Contact publisher for price.
Automated Forward/Backward Recovery of VSAM or BDAM Datasets. Generates Recovery JCL. Simulates Recovery Process. Manages, Copies, Reblocks & Analyzes CICS & Batch Journals. Creates Journals from Batch Programs. Merges Multiple CICS/Filesave Journals. Summarizes/Lists Journal Contents.
Computer Assocs. International, Inc.

CA-FPXpert. 1992. *Items Included:* Documentation included. *Customer Support:* Available.
PC-DOS. IBM PC & compatibles (640k). Contact vendor for price. *Networks supported:* Novell.
Automates Calculation of IFPUG Function Point Measure & Repository for FP Measure Applications. Provides Guidance on Methods.
Computer Assocs. International, Inc.

CA-Gener/OL. 1982. *Customer Support:* Support Agreement Available.
MVS, VSE. IBM S/370-390 (500k). Contact publisher for price.
4GL Development Tool. Includes Interactive Screen Development, Incremental Compilation, Variety of System Utilities, On-Line Debugging Capabilities & Access to Large Number of Common Database Management Systems.
Computer Assocs. International, Inc.

CA-Graphics Connection. 1988. *Compatible Hardware:* IBM VM/CMS; MVS; & Digital VAX/VMS operating systems (1Mb). *Items Included:* Documentation included. *Customer Support:* Available.
Contact vendor for price.
Links Graphics-Producing Applications to Any Graphics Output Device. Imports, Translates & Manipulates Graphics Formats Including HPGL, CGM, ADMGDF, PICT, DDIF & DISSOP. Supports 400 Graphics Devices. Provides Device-Independent Output Formats, Including CGM & PostScript. Allows for Integration of Existing Graphics Applications with Text & Graphics Systems. Includes Pull-Down Menus & Batch Capabilities.
Computer Assocs. International, Inc.

CA-HRISMA. 1993. *Customer Support:* Available.
IBM MVS, RS6000/AIX, HP-9000/HP UX. IBM S/370-390, RS6000; HP9000. Contact publisher for price.
Integrated, Multi-Company, Multi-Platform Client/Server Human Resource Management Software Solution. Provides Payroll, Personnel & Benefits Administration. GUI Provides Navigation & User Customization with Imaging Interface. Features Flexible End-User Access Tools with Visual Information Access for Reporting & Modeling.
Computer Assocs., International, Inc.

CA-Ideal. 1982. *Customer Support:* Support Agreement Available.
MVS, VSE, VM, AIX, HP-UX. IBM S/370-390, RS6000; HP-9000. Contact publisher for price.
Application Development System for Program Creation/Maintenance. Provides Development of Batch & On-Line Applications. Dictionary Facility

Controls Applicaiton Development Process. Integrates with CA-Datacom/DB & DB2 Supporting Tables, Views, Dataviews & Sequential & VSAM Files. Includes Screen Painter, Report Generator, Debugger & Structured Procedural Language. Applications Compatible Across Mainframe, PC, & UNIX Platforms.
Computer Assocs. International, Inc.

CA-Ideal DB2 Option. 1988. *Customer Support:* Support Agreement Available.
MVS. IBM S/370-390 (2Mb). Contact publisher for price.
On-Line Workstation for Development of Both Batch & On-Line Applications. Includes Screen Painter, Nonprocedural Report Generator, Structured Procedural Language, Symbolic Debugger, Dictionary Facility, Version & Status Control, DB2 Catalog Integration, Dynamic/Static SQL, DB2 Plan Definition Fill-Ins & Batch Generate Facility.
Computer Assocs. International, Inc.

CA-Ideal/PC. 1991. *Customer Support:* Available.
PC-DOS. IBM PC AT, PS/2 & compatibles (2Mb). contact publisher for price.
Application Development Tool Compatible with Mainframe CA-Ideal. Provides High-Level Procedural Language with SQL Support & Non-Procedural Report & Panel Definition. Supports COBOL & CICS COBOL Subprograms. Supports Editing, Compilation, Execution & Dictionary Reporting. Provides Transport Facility to Transfer Applications to & from Mainframe CA-Ideal Supporting Downsizing Applications or Offloading Ideal Development to PC.
Computer Assocs. International, Inc.

CA-IDMS/PC Runtime. 1985. *Customer Support:* Available.
PC-DOS/MS-DOS. IBM PS/2, AT or compatible PCs (640k). Contact publisher for price.
Execution-Only Dictionary-Driven DBMS. Includes Facilities for Query & Update, Dictionary & User-Database Integrity Verification, Reporting & Other Supporting Features. Can Be Accessed & Updated with SQL. CA-ADS/PC, COBOL-Batch, COBOL-DC, COBOL-CICS, DMLO & C. Allows Clients to Run CA-IDMS/PC Applications on Single-User Workstation or PC LAN.
Computer Assocs. International, Inc.

CA-IDMS/PC Runtime Server. 1985. *Customer Support:* Available.
PC-DOS/MS-DOS. IBM PS/2, AT & compatibles. Contact publisher for price.
Networks supported: NetBIOS.
Execution-Only Dictionary-Driven DBMS. Includes Query/Update Database Integrity Verification, Reporting, Database Recovery, Multiple Database Support & Concurrent Usage. Language Support Includes SQL, CA-ADS/PC, COBOL-Batch, COBOL-DC, COBOL-CICS, DMLO & C. Allows Execution of CA-IDMS Applications in Multi-User LAN Environment.
Computer Assocs. International, Inc.

CA-IDMS/UNIX. 1992. *Items Included:* Documentation included. *Customer Support:* Available.
HP-UX. HP 9000. Contact vendor for price.
Navigational DML, DML Online, ADS/A, ADS/O, COBOL-DB/DC & Relational Access Through ANSI Standard SQL & ODBC. Includes Security Management, Database Administration, Distributed Processing, Database Tuning & Integrates Data Dictionary Support. Client Requires PC-MS/DOS.
Computer Assocs. International, Inc.

CA-IDMS/ADS Alive. 1989. *Customer Support:* Support Agreement Available.
MVS, VSE, VM, BS2000, MSP/AE. IBM S/370-390; Siemens; Fujitsu. Contact publisher for price.
Source Level Testing & Debugging Utility for CA-ADS Dialogs. Provides Understanding of Internal Data Representations or Structure of CA-ADS Run-Time Control Blocks.
Computer Assocs. International, Inc.

CA-IDMS/ADS Trace. 1985. *Customer Support:* Support Agreement Available.
MVS, VSE, VM, BS2000, MSP/AE. IBM S/370-390; Siemens; Fujitsu. Contact publisher for price.
On-Line Facility Which Allows ADS Developer to Specify Locations in ADS Dialog Process & Debug ADS Dialog in Same Way As COBOL Batch Trace Facility.
Computer Assocs. International, Inc.

CA-IDMS/APPC. 1989. *Customer Support:* Support Agreement Available.
MVS, VSE, VM, BS2000, MSP/AE, VOS-3. IBM S/370-390; Siemens; Fujitsu; Hitachi (2Mb). Contact publisher for price.
Provides Communications Facilities for Cooperative Processing under CA-IDMS/DC & CA-IDMS/UCF. Allows User to Exchange Messages & Data on Mainframe or Across Platforms & Exchange Messages & Data Between CA-ADS Dialogs Running on Mainframe & Other CA-ADS Dialogs on Mainframe, PC or LAN or Other Application Programs Which Conform to IBM LU 6.2 Protocols Running on Other Platforms.
Computer Assocs. International, Inc.

CA-IDMS/CMS Option. 1983. *Customer Support:* Support Agreement Available.
VM/CMS. IBM S/370-390 (4Mb). Contact publisher for price.
Allows CA-IDMS/DB Central Version to Operate in CMS & Use VMCF Facility to Make Communications Possible from One Virtual Machine to Another in VM.
Computer Assocs. International, Inc.

CA-IDMS/Database Extractor. 1988. *Customer Support:* Support Agreement Available.
MVS, VSE, VM, BS2000, MSP/AE. IBM S/370-390; Siemens; Fujitsu. Contact publisher for price.
On-Line Utility Used to Specify & Generate Test CA-IDMS Databases. User Specifies Selection Criteria, Sets up JCL & Database Extractor Extracts Records from Existing Database & Stores in Test Database.
Computer Assocs. International, Inc.

CA-IDMS/DB. 1973. *Customer Support:* Support Agreement Available.
MVS, VSE, VM, BS2000, MSP/AE, VOS-3. IBM S/370-390; Siemens; Fujitsu; Hitachi (256k). Contact publisher for price.
General Purpose DBMS. Provides All Necessary Functions for Data Definition, Manipulation & Control. Includes Tuning Facilities & Open System Architecture. Supports Navigational & Relational Processing Through SQL. ODBC-Compliant Server & GUI PC Tools. ODBC-Compliant Server & GUI PC Tools.
Computer Assocs. International, Inc.

CA-IDMS/DB Analyzer. 1982. *Customer Support:* Support Agreement Available.
MVS, VSE, VM, BS2000, MSP/AE. IBM S/370-390; Siemens; Fujitsu. Contact publisher for price.
Performs Physical Analysis of Databases & Produces Variety of Reports That Describe Database's Physical Organization. Information Contained in Reports Can Be Used to Plan Database Reorganization & Expansion. Reports Focus on 4 CA-IDMS Database Structure Types Including Area, Record, Set & Index.
Computer Assocs. International, Inc.

CA-IDMS/DB Audit. 1982. *Customer Support:* Support Agreement Available.
MVS, VSE, VM, BS2000, MSP/AE. IBM S/370-390; Siemens; Fujitsu (500k). Contact publisher for price.
Batch Utility Used to Examine Physical Integrity of Database & Correct Any Errors. Shows Error Corrections in Simulate Mode Before Correcting Them.
Computer Assocs. International, Inc.

CA-IDMS/DB Reorg. 1982. *Customer Support:* Support Agreement Available.
MVS, VSE, VM, BS2000, MSP/AE. IBM S/370-390; Siemens; Fujitsu. Contact publisher for price.
Batch Utility That Physically Reorganizes Selected Areas of Database Without Unloading & Reloading Entire Database.
Computer Assocs. International, Inc.

CA-IDMS/DBOMP Transparency. 1981. *Customer Support:* Support Agreement Available.
MVS, VSE. IBM S/370-390 (800k). Contact publisher for price.
Facilitates Conversion from DBOMP or CFMS to CA-IDMS/DB Environment. Permits DBOMP Applications to Execute in CA-IDMS/DB Environment. Includes Integrated SQL Support for Relational Processing.
Computer Assocs. International, Inc.

CA-IDMS/DC. 1978. *Customer Support:* Support Agreement Available.
MVS, VSE, VM; BS2000; MSP/AE; VOS-3. IBM S370/390; Siemens; Fujitsu; Hitachi (600k). Contact publisher for price.
Teleprocessing Monitor for Accessing/Updating CA-IDMS/DB Databases. Screen Painting, Editing, Data Validation, Statistics & Support for CA-ADS, PL/1, COBOL, RPG or Assembly. Supports BTAM, VTAM & TCAM. Integrates with CA-IDMS/DB in Single or Multiple Address Space Architecture.
Computer Assocs. International, Inc.

CA-IDMS/DC Sort. 1985. *Customer Support:* Support Agreement Available.
MVS, VSE, VM; BS2000; MSP/AE. IBM S370/390; Siemens; Fujitsu. Contact publisher for price.
On-Line Sort Tool for CA-IDMS/DC Environment. Invokes Multiple Sorts with Different Sort Sequences During On-Line Programming. Supports End-User Ad Hoc Reporting Requirements.
Computer Assocs. International, Inc.

CA-IDMS/DDS. 1980. *Customer Support:* Support Agreement Available.
MVS, VSE, VM; BS2000; MSP/AE; VOS-3. IBM S370/390; Siemens; Fujitsu; Hitachi (2Mb). Contact publisher for price.
Maintains CA-IDMS/DB Databases at Each Network Location & Makes Data Available on Demand Basis to Applications at Other Locations. Application Needs No Knowledge of Location of Data. Handles Network Management, Transaction & Routing Functions & Automatic Recovery.
Computer Assocs. International, Inc.

CA-IDMS/Dictionary Migrator. 1984. *Customer Support:* Support Agreement Available.
MVS, VSE, VM; BS2000; MSP/AE. IBM S370/390; Siemens; Fujitsu. Contact publisher for price.

Migrates Systems or Components from One CA-IDMS Dictionary to Another. Reports, Tracks & Validates Each Migration. Identifies Discrepancies. Documents Migration Activities.
Computer Assocs. International, Inc.

CA-IDMS/Dictionary Module Editor. 1984. *Customer Support:* Support Agreement Available.
MVS, VSE, VM, BS2000, MSP/AE. IBM S/370-390, Siemens, Fujitsu. Contact publisher for price.
On-Line Editor for Creating, Editing & Deleting Dictionary Modules. Keeps Track of User IDs & Dates of Last Update.
Computer Assocs. International, Inc.

CA-IDMS/DLI Transparency. 1982. *Customer Support:* Support Agreement Available.
MVS, VSE. IBM S/370-390 (800k). Contact publisher for price.
Automated Migration Tool for Transition of DL/I & IMS/DB Applications to CA-IDMS/DB Environment. Permits DL/I Applications to Operate with CA-IDMS/DB Without Requiring Coding Changes in Application Programs. Provides Access to Database Technology & Productivity Tools in CA-IDMS Environment Including Fully Integrating SQL Support for Relational Processing.
Computer Assocs. International, Inc.

CA-IDMS/DML Online. 1982. *Customer Support:* Support Agreement Available.
MVS, VSE, VM, BS2000, MSP/AE. IBM S/370-390, Siemens, Fujitsu. Contact publisher for price.
Interactive Utility for Immediate Access & Update of Database Records. Executes CA-IDMS/DML Commands Interactively with Full Functionality & Error Reporting.
Computer Assocs. International, Inc.

CA-IDMS/Enforcer. 1984. *Customer Support:* Support Agreement Available.
MVS, VSE, VM, BS2000, MSP/AE. IBM S/370-390, Siemens, Fujitsu. Contact publisher for price.
On-Line, Menu-Driven Database Utility for Defining & Enforcing Naming Standards for Attempts to Add Entities to IDMS Dictionary.
Computer Assocs. International, Inc.

CA-IDMS/Journal Analyzer. 1980. *Customer Support:* Support Agreement Available.
MVS, VSE, VM, BS2000, MSP/AE. IBM S/370-390, Siemens, Fujitsu. Contact publisher for price.
Audits Statistics in CA-IDMS/DC Archive Journal & Produces Detailed Time-Based Reports on Overall Run-Unit Activity, Database & Program Activity.
Computer Assocs. International, Inc.

CA-IDMS/Log Analyzer. 1982. *Customer Support:* Support Agreement Available.
MVS, VSE, VM, BS2000, MSP/AE. IBM S/370-390, Siemens, Fujitsu. Contact publisher for price.
Produces Reports on Database & System Performance from Information in CA-IDMS/DB Log File. Reports Reflect Activity at Task Level by User, Transaction, Terminal or Account Number Which Can Be Used for Charge Back or Billing Purposes.
Computer Assocs. International, Inc.

CA-IDMS/Masterkey. 1987. *Customer Support:* Support Agreement Available.
MVS, VSE, VM, BS2000, MSP/AE. IBM S/370-390, Siemens, Fujitsu. Contact publisher for price.
On-Line Facility That Enables DBA to Control How Terminal Looks & Feels to User. Includes Ability to Design Menus & Assign Tasks to Each of 24 PF Keys & 2 PA Keys.
Computer Assocs. International, Inc.

CA-IDMS/PC. *Customer Support:* Available.
PC-MS/DOS. IBM PC AT, PS/2 or compatibles (640k). contact publisher for price.
Dictionary-Driven DBMS. Compatible with CA-IDMS/DB. Includes PC-Based Utilities, Facilities for Import/Export, Query & Update, Reporting & Other Supporting Features. Can Be Accessed & Updated with CA-ADS/PC, COBOL-Batch, COBOL DC, COBOL-CICS, DMLO & C Language. Run-Time & LAN Versions Available.
Computer Assocs. International, Inc.

CA-IDMS/PC Lanpack. 1985. *Items Included:* Documentation included. *Customer Support:* Available.
PC-DOS/MS-DOS. IBM AT, PS/2 & compatibles (640k). Contact vendor for price.
Multi-User, Dictionary-Driven Database Server for PC LANs. Includes Shared Multi-User Environment for Data Dictionary & User Database Access, Development/Execution Compatibility with CA-IDMS/DB & CA-ADS, DBMS, Language Support for CA-ADS/PC, COBOL, COBOL-DC, COBOL-CICS, SQL, C & DMLO, Dicitonary Reports, Migration Facilities, User Database Utilities, Batch Generation & Windowing Facilities.
Computer Assocs. International, Inc.

CA-IDMS Performance Monitor. 1986. *Customer Support:* Support Agreement Available.
MVS, VSE, VM, BS2000, MSP/AE, VOS3. IBM S/370-390, Siemens, Fujitsu, Hitachi (2Mb). Contact publisher for price.
On-Line Monitor for CA-IDMS/DB & CA-IDMS/DC Activity. Analyzes, Controls & Refines CA-IDMS/DB Run-Time Environment. Includes Facilities for Performance Monitoring & Tuning. Provides Data for Chargeback & Billing Purposes, Resource Analysis & System Capacity Planning.
Computer Assocs. International, Inc.

CA-IDMS Presspack. 1987. *Customer Support:* Support Agreement Available.
MVS, VSE, VM, BS2000, MSP/AE, VOS3. IBM S/370-390, Siemens, Fujitsu, Hitachi (2Mb). Contact publisher for price.
Data Compression & Decompression Utility for CA-IDMS/DB. Determines Compress Rate Based on Sampling of Actual Data.
Computer Assocs. International, Inc.

CA-IDMS/SASO. 1985. *Customer Support:* Support Agreement Available.
MVS, VSE, VM, BS2000, MSP/AE. IBM S/370-390, Siemens, Fujitsu. Contact publisher for price.
Enables Access to & Maintenance of Documents Such As CA-IDMS/SP&G That Reside on Database. Features Multiple Database Environment under Single Central Version When Documentation Is Housed on CA-IDMS/DB Database. Access & Maintain Documentation Using On-Line & Batch Features of CA-IDMS/SASO. Documents Organized by Chapter, Subject & Topic.
Computer Assocs. International, Inc.

CA-IDMS/Schema Mapper. 1982. *Customer Support:* Support Agreement Available.
MVS, VSE, VM, BS2000, MSP/AE. IBM S/370-390, Siemens, Fujitsu. Contact publisher for price.
Batch Utility That Produces Automatic or Manual Database Structure Diagrams from Schema & Subschema Information.
Computer Assocs. International, Inc.

CA-IDMS Server. 1992. *Customer Support:* Available.
Windows; MVS; UNIX. IBM PC & compatibles; IBM S/370-390, AT&T UNIX System V. Contact publisher for price.
Client/Server Connectivity Tool Consisting of Set of Microsoft Windows & Mainframe/UNIX Programs That Support Access to Data Stored in Databases from Windows Applications. Provides ODBC Support Drivers Which Enables Open Access to Databases by CA Software & Other Third-Party Tools/Applications That Adhere to ODBC Interface Protocol. Windows Required on Client.
Computer Assocs., International, Inc.

CA-IDMS SQL Option. 1990. *Customer Support:* Support Agreement Available.
MVS, VSE, VM, BS2000, MSP/AE, VOS-3. IBM S/370-390; Siemens; Fujitsu; Hitachi (1Mb). Contact publisher for price.
Provides SQL to CA-IDMS Databases, Both SQL & Non-SQL Defined. Allows Client/Server Access to Existing Information in CA-IDMS Databases. Conforms to ANSI, FIPS & CA-Extensions. Supports Microsoft ODBC API.
Computer Assocs. International, Inc.

CA-IDMS/Task Analyzer. 1985. *Customer Support:* Support Agreement Available.
MVS, VSE, VM, BS2000, MSP/AE. IBM S/370-390, Siemens, Fujitsu. Contact publisher for price.
CA-IDMS/DC Task Reporting Utility. Uses Multiple CA-IDMS/DC Exits to Gather Statistics. CA-ADS Dialogs, Tasks & Integrated Indexes. Writes Statistics into CA-IDMS Log or SMF File. Produces Reports Including Billing, Program, CA-ADS, Abend, Program Loads, Integrated Index & Ranking Reports. CA-IDMS.
Computer Assocs. International, Inc.

CA-IDMS/Total Transparency. 1981. *Customer Support:* Support Agreement Available.
MVS, VSE. IBM S/370-390 (1Mb). Contact publisher for price.
Allows Applications Written for TOTAL to Access CA-IDMS/DB Without Modification. Includes Run-Time Interface That Allows Existing Batch & CICS Application Programs to Access & Update CA-IDMS/DB Database.
Computer Assocs. International, Inc.

CA-IDMS/UCF. 1980. *Customer Support:* Support Agreement Available.
MVS, VSE, VM, BS2000, MSP/AE, VOS-3. IBM S/370-390, Siemens, Fujitsu, Hitachi (600k). Contact publisher for price.
TP Monitor-to-CA-IDMS/DB Bridge. Enables CA-IDMS/DB On-Line Application Development & Execution under CICS, TSO & VM/CMS. Handles Terminal & File I/O Operations, Dispatches Concurrent Processing Activities & Validates User Requests for Services.
Computer Assocs. International, Inc.

CA-IDMS/VSAM Transparency. 1982. *Customer Support:* Support Agreement Available.
MVS, VSE. IBM S/370-390 (800k). Contact publisher for price.
Program Interface Enabling Application Programs Written for VSAM to Execute in CA-IDMS/DB Environment. Assists Users in Migrating from VSAM to CA-IDMS/DB Environment.
Computer Assocs. International, Inc.

CA-IDMS VSE/ESA Option. 1992. *Customer Support:* Support Agreement Available.
VSE/ESA. IBM 370-390 (2Mb). Contact publisher for price.
Allows Exploitation of IBM's VSE/ESA Enhanced Processing Capacity. Reduces I/O Operations Through Implementation of Data Spaces.
Computer Assocs. International, Inc.

CA-Infopoint. *Customer Support:* Available.
MVS, VSE. Contact publisher for price.
Integrated Applications Software for Financial

TITLE INDEX

Industry. Over 25 Packages Provide Deposits, Transaction Processing, Customer, Loans, Collections, Recovery & Financial Management Applications.
Computer Associates International, Inc.

CA-Infopoint Account Analysis. *Customer Support:* Available.
MVS, VSE. Contact publisher for price.
Provides for Account Analysis, Service Charge Processing & Statement Modeling. Analyzes Commercial/Retail Customers at Individual Account, Relationship or Cross-Bank Level. Supports Loan Compensating Balances, AR Billing, Posting, Tracking for Service Charges, Full On-Line Statement for Account Officers, Printed Customer TMA Standard Statement & EDI Transmission Statements & Analysis Reports.
Computer Associates International, Inc.

CA-Infopoint Accounts Payable System.
Customer Support: Available.
MVS, VSE. Contact publisher for price.
Provides Check Writing & Reconciliation, PO Control, Employee Expense, Use Tax, 1099 Accounting, Vendor Analysis, Reporting, Recurring Payments, 3-Way Matching of Receiver, Invoice & PO Data, Optimum Pay Data Calculations, Reporting, Duplicate Invoice Tracking & Simulation of Disbursements. Handles On-Line Entry & Inquiry.
Computer Associates International, Inc.

CA-Infopoint Automated Clearing House.
Customer Support: Available.
MVS, VSE. Contact publisher for price.
NACHA Compliant ACH System Providing On-Line Scheduling of Incoming & Outgoing Files, Concurrent Batch & On-Line Processing, Interbank & Intrabank Transfers, On-Line Origination, Risk Analysis Management, Service Charging, Corporate Reporting & Automated Settlement.
Computer Associates International, Inc.

CA-Infopoint Cashtran. *Customer Support:* Available.
MVS, VSE. Contact publisher for price.
Facilitates Reporting of 4789 Large Cash Transactions to IRS or Magnetic Tape. Includes Multi-Institution Processing, Exemption & Suspect Tracking, Geographic Targeting, Monetary Logging of Bank Instruments, On-Line Help & Customer & Capture System Interface. Certified by IRS.
Computer Associates International, Inc.

CA-Infopoint Collection Management.
Customer Support: Available.
MVS, VSE, OS/400. Contact publisher for price.
Provides Total Portfolio Control by Processing Accounts Established. Allows Tailoring of Each Account. Performs Tracking, Provides Facts & Figures On-Line & Through Various Standard & Requested Reports, Supports Collectors in Handling Large Volumes of Accounts & Automatically Generates Hundreds of Personalized Collection Letters.
Computer Associates International, Inc.

CA-Infopoint Combined Interest Reporting.
Customer Support: Available.
MVS, VSE. Contact publisher for price.
Provides Combined Customer Account Year-End Statements by Tax ID Number. Supports IRS Forms, Tax ID Certification & B Notice Processing. Scans by Tax ID Number. Handles Internal Report Processing & Retains Taxpayer ID File Maintenance History.
Computer Associates International, Inc.

CA-Infopoint Combined Statement. *Customer Support:* Available.
MVS, VSE. Contact publisher for price.
Reports Detail & Summary Information for Any Group of Related Accounts on Single Statement. Includes Selective Marketing Messages, On-Line Set up for Combining Accounts, Enclosure Processing, Optional Individual Statements, Unrestricted Accounts Combined Including Detail for Multiple DDA Accounts, Bulk Filing Support, Bar Coding for Enclosures & Relational Copies Provided.
Computer Associates International, Inc.

CA-Infopoint De-Dupe. *Customer Support:* Available.
MVS, VSE. Contact publisher for price.
Analyzes Customer Information in Search of Duplicates. Identifies, Automatically Combines Duplicate Customer Records, Analyzes/Reports Suspected Duplicate Customers for On-Line Presentation/Resolution. Resolves Suspected Duplicates Who Are Actually Different Customers. Provides Options to Analyze Segments of Database or Entire Database on Initial & Ongoing Basis.
Computer Associates International, Inc.

CA-Infopoint Deposits. *Customer Support:* Available.
MVS, VSE. Contact publisher for price.
Handles Various Account Types Including DDA, NOW, Money Market, Club, Golden, Home Equity Lines, Statement & Passbook Savings, Commercial Servicing & Relationship Management, Commercial & Retail Cash Management, NSF, Overdraft, & Funds Transfer Processing, Tax Withholding, Stops, Cautions & Holds & Customizable Reporting Capabilities.
Computer Associates International, Inc.

CA-Infopoint Desktop Budgeting. *Customer Support:* Available.
MVS, VSE. Contact publisher for price.
Client/Server Enhancement to CA-Infopoint Financial Control System. Performs Complete Budgeting Process on PC. Includes All FCS Budget Functionality Using Spreadsheet Approach. Prints Reports. Mainframe Programs Perform Host Security, Upload/Download Functions. Provides Ability to Import/Export Files on PC. Client Requires Windows.
Computer Associates International, Inc.

CA-Infopoint Exception Administrator.
Customer Support: Available.
MVS, VSE. Contact publisher for price.
Tracks Current Status of Bank Exceptions, NSF, OD, RDI & Service Charges. Prepares Automated Cash Letters. Provides for Comments & Referrals. Presents Items Posted for Selective Rehandling. Monitors Officer Actions, Automatic Stop, Hit & Suspect Recognition. Initiates Printing of Notices. Provides User Transaction Input from Multiple Applications.
Computer Associates International, Inc.

CA-Infopoint Financial Control System.
Customer Support: Available.
MVS, VSE. Contact publisher for price.
Makes Month-End Adjustments Posting & Shows Impact On-Line. Handles Budget Adjustments, Report Format Modification, Subsystem Interfacing Data Conversion, Consolidation of Like Entries, Multiple Entry Generation, High Volume Reversal, What-If Viewing, On-Line & Real-Time Functionality, Suspense Posting, Account Reconciliation, Multiple Cost Allocation Methods, Multiple Close-Outs, up to 9 Working Budgets, Multiple Annualization Techniques & Standard Reports.
Computer Associates International, Inc.

CA-Infopoint Household Marketing. *Customer Support:* Available.
MVS, VSE. Contact publisher for price.

CA-INFOPOINT RELATIONSHIP CIF

Turns Customer Information into Household Profiles of Customers, Accounts, Balances & Demographics. Prepares Product Mix, Product Penetration & Household Patterns to Assist Marketing & Client Support Representatives in Identifying Households with Greatest Propensity to Acquire New Product.
Computer Associates International, Inc.

CA-Infopoint Integrated Commercial Loans.
Customer Support: Available.
MVS, VSE. Contact publisher for price.
Provides Account, Commitment, Note, Participation, History & Collateral Processing. Provides Transaction Processing, Backdating & Reversals. Offers Automated Stop Accrual, Late Fee & Century Overflow, Charge-Off & Recovery Processing, GL Interface, over 100 Reports, On-Line, Real-Time Maintenance & Loan Consolidation Reporting in Conjunction with Other CA Loan Products & Selective On-Line History.
Computer Associates International, Inc.

CA-Infopoint Integrated Installment Loans.
Customer Support: Available.
MVS, VSE. Contact publisher for price.
Multi-Institution, Multi-Branch Processing. Includes Dealer, Insurance & Student Loan Accounting, Backdating & Reversal Processing, Accrual, Rebate & Fixed, Variable, Split & Tiered Rate Processing Options, GL Interface, Charge-Off Processing with Recovery Options & Revolving Line of Credit. Provides On-Line, Real-Time Maintenance & Loan Consolidation Reporting in Conjunction with Other CA Loan Products.
Computer Associates International, Inc.

CA-Infopoint Multisort. *Customer Support:* Available.
MVS, VSE. Contact publisher for price.
Provides Multi-Bank Processing, Cycle Sorting/ Exception Outsort, Fine Sorting/Exception Outsort, Statement Account Sorting, Directed Statement Sorting, Return Item Sorting, Nested Group Sorting, Zip Code Sorting, Item Level Sequence Checking & Restart, Signature Verification Pull & On-Line Research Facility for Vaulted Items.
Computer Associates International, Inc.

CA-Infopoint Profitability. *Customer Support:* Available.
MVS, VSE. Contact publisher for price.
Provides Multiple Entity Processing, Customer Relationship Pricing, Loan Relationships/Analysis, Account Grouping, Service Charge Routines, Officer Performance/Incentive, Tiered/Ranged Pricing, On-Line History Statement & Cross-Bank Customer Analysis. Handles Statement Customization, Receivables Processing, Effective Date of Service Price Changes, Loan Compensating Balances Protection, Customer Product Profitability & Reporting. NCCMA Compliant.
Computer Associates International, Inc.

CA-Infopoint Recovery Management. *Customer Support:* Available.
MVS, VSE. Contact publisher for price.
Provides Accounting & Collection Management Features for Recovery Department. Tracks Infinite Number of Variables, Communicates with Existing Corporate Information Systems & Databases, Provides Updated Information to Credit Bureaus, Checks Verification Services & Coupon Book Suppliers & Interacts with On-Line Collection System. Provides for Complete Agency Tracking.
Computer Associates International, Inc.

CA-Infopoint Relationship CIF. *Customer Support:* Available.
MVS, VSE. Contact publisher for price.

Provides On-Line Access to Customer Profiles Containing Name, Address & Demographic Data at Both Relationship & Account Levels. Features Sociographic Information, Operational/Marketing/Management Reporting, On-Line Documentation, Breakaway Maintenance, Comment Information, Account Instructions, Selection Capabilities & Database Flexibility.
Computer Associates International, Inc.

CA-Infopoint Relationship Pricing. *Customer Support:* Available.
MVS, VSE. Contact publisher for price.
Allows Bank to Price Services Based on Customer's Total Relationship Rather Than on Individual Account Balance. Maintains Record of Customer's Related Accounts, Balance & Control Parameters. Tracks Individual Account Minimum Balances, As Well As Customer's Combined Balance for Entire Relationship of Accounts. Determines If Balance Criteria Is Sufficient to Waive Service Charges.
Computer Associates International, Inc.

CA-Infopoint Scrub. *Customer Support:* Available.
MVS, VSE. Contact publisher for price.
Converts Names & Addresses, Customer & Account Demographic Data, & Account Relationships to Create Initial Customer Information File. Analyzes/Standardizes Format for Names/Addresses. Can Be Used to Add RCIF As Mergers/Acquisitions Occur. Determines/Assigns Customer Gender & Account Relationships. Includes Exception Reporting, Audit Trail & Multiple Customer Support.
Computer Associates International, Inc.

CA-Infopoint Super MICR. *Customer Support:* Available.
MVS, VSE. Contact publisher for price.
On-Line, Real-Time Item Processing Solution Providing MICR & Non-MICR Capture, On-Line Reject Reentry & Reconciliation, On-Line Cash Management, Release Extract, Sort Pattern Creation, Cash Letter Production, Float Analysis & Management Reporting. Supports 389x/XP Devices, LU6.2 Communications for 3891/XP Machines & 3880/XP in Native Mode.
Computer Associates International, Inc.

CA-Infopoint Teller/Transaction Gateway.
Customer Support: Available.
MVS, VSE. Contact publisher for price.
On-Line Link Between Terminal & Permanent Customer Files. Features On-Line Processing, Control Through Access Authorization, Complete Daily Transaction, Passbook Processing, Regulation CC Compliance, End-of-Day Balancing, Reporting, Transaction History & Calculations. Provides Batch Update to On-Line Availability.
Computer Associates International, Inc.

CA-Infopoint Time Investment. *Customer Support:* Available.
MVS, VSE. Contact publisher for price.
Processes CDs, IRAs, Original Issue Discount, Savings, Time Deposit Open Accounts, Money Market Certificates & User-Defined Products. Handles Multiple Instrument/Single Customer Tracking, Reporting & Statements, Transaction & Cycle Service Charging, On-Line Payment/Premature Withdrawal Forecasting/Posting, Advanced Interest, Maturity, Notice & Check Processing, Tax Withholding Support, Descriptive & Combined Statement Processing, Transaction Backdating with Automatic Reaccrual & Adjustments & Regional Pricing.
Computer Associates International, Inc.

CA-InterTest. 1977. *Customer Support:* Support Agreement Available.
MVS, VSE. IBM S/370-390. Contact publisher for price.
Interactive Testing & Debugging Tool for CICS Applications Written in COBOL, COBOL II, COBOL/370, Assembler & PL/1. Allows Programmers to Work Directly from Source Listing. Prevents All Storage Violations, Program Check/Abends & CICS Abends in Command Level Programs.
Computer Assocs. International, Inc.

CA-InterTest/Batch. 1984. *Customer Support:* Support Agreement Available.
MVS. IBM S/370-390. Contact publisher for price.
Interactive Tool for Debugging & Testing Batch, IMS/DC, COBOL, COBOL II & COBOL/370 Programs Through TSO or CA-Roscoe Interface. Provides Symbolic Debugging Directly from On-Line Source Listing to Resolve Errors in Single Session. Automatically Converts Batch JCL into CLIST or ALIB Statements.
Computer Assocs. International, Inc.

CA-ISS/Three. 1984. *Customer Support:* Support Agreement Available.
MVS, DOS. IBM S/370-390, IBM PC & compatibles. Contact publisher for price.
Computer System Capacity Management Tool. Assists in Analyzing & Eliminating Capacity Bottlenecks Through Modeling Capabilities, Advanced Expert Systems Logic, & Knowledge Base.
Computer Assocs. International, Inc.

CA-JARS. 1973. *Customer Support:* Support Agreement Available.
MVS, VSE, VM. IBM S/370-390. Contact publisher for price.
Performance Management System with Comprehensive Reporting Facilities. You Can Effectively Report on, & Account for, Resource Utilization, Manage Your Data Center's Performance & Analyze Current Activity with a Reporting System That Provides Accurate & Easy-to-Understand Reports. Produces Standard, As Well As User-Customized, Reports from a Broad Spectrum of Reporting Environments to Provide an Outstanding Source of Performance Information. Provides the Necessary Data Collection, Reporting & Archival Facilities to Ensure That Critical Data Is Available for Informed Decision Making. System Accounting Information Is Collected & Then Stored on the CA-JARS Common Historical Database for Future Reference. You Can Manage Your Data Center's Performance: Control Data Center Costs; Improve Operations Management; & Anticipate Future Data Center Requirements.
Computer Assocs. International, Inc.

CA-JARS/CICS. 1976. *Customer Support:* Support Agreement Available.
MVS, VSE. IBM S/370-390 (40k). Contact publisher for price.
CICS Performance Reporting & Tuning Facility. Provides Data Collection, Real-Time Reporting, On-Line Graph Reports, On-Line Tutor to Assist with CICS Tuning, Batch Graph Reports & Interface with CA-JARS for Additional Tabular Reporting & Chargeback.
Computer Assocs. International, Inc.

CA-JARS/DSA. 1984. *Customer Support:* Support Agreement Available.
MVS. IBM S/370-390 (2Mb). Contact publisher for price.
DASD Accounting Option. Provides Performance & DASD Utilization Statistics & Chargebacks Based on DASD Space Occupancy. Billing & Chargeback Interface to CA-JARS MVS & CA-PMA/ChargeBack. Collects Disk Space Usage Statistics Through DADSM Exit Including System Management Storage (SMS) Statistics.
Computer Assocs. International, Inc.

CA-JARS IDMS. 1985. *Customer Support:* Support Agreement Available.
MVS, VSE. IBM S/370-390 (1Mb). Contact publisher for price.
Provides Management Tools for Analyzing CA-IDMS/DB Activity. Measures CA-IDMS/DB User Productivity & Environment, Evaluates CA-IDMS/DB Application Software & Provides Equitable Customer Billing & Cost Distribution.
Computer Assocs. International, Inc.

CA-JARS/IMS. 1980. *Customer Support:* Support Agreement Available.
MVS. IBM S/370-390 (2Mb). Contact publisher for price.
Reports Application Performance & Resource Utilization, Application Database Activity, Transaction Change Exception, Line, Terminal & Network Reliability & Management Goals. Projects Future Service Requirements & Work Load with Graphs Depicting Availability, Response Time, Transaction Volume & CPU Utilization.
Computer Assocs. International, Inc.

CA-JARS/Interface for VAX. 1989. *Items Included:* Documentation included. *Customer Support:* Available.
MVS; VAX/VMS. IBM System 370/390 Architecture; Digital VAX (4Mb). Contact vendor for price.
Optional Component of CA-JARS MVS Providing Performance Measurement & Chargeback Capabilities for VAX/VMS OS. Combines VAX/VMS Data with MVS, CICS, VSE or VM Data for Multi-System Reporting & Billing.
Computer Assocs. International, Inc.

CA-JARS/Reports+. 1991. *Customer Support:* Support Agreement Available.
MVS. IBM S/370-390 (2.3Mb). Contact publisher for price.
Provides Customizable CA-JARS Reports Using Advanced APA Print & Graphical Charting Facilities. Includes Flexible Charting to Allow User-Defined Data Ranges, Timeframes & Titles for Customized Reports, Set of Pre-Coded Graphic Reports Including Pie, Bar, Area, Curve, High-Low & Stacked Bar & Modifiable Reports to Meet Specific Requirements.
Computer Assocs. International, Inc.

CA-JARS/SMF. 1981. *Customer Support:* Support Agreement Available.
MVS. IBM S/370-390 (256k). Contact publisher for price.
Provides Automated Control & Handling of SMF (System Management Facility) Data. Manages the Automatic Selection & Dumping of SMF, Validates SMF Records, Maintains Index of SMF Data & Selectively Processes SMF Records on User-Defined Extraction Criteria.
Computer Assocs. International, Inc.

CA-JCLCheck. 1980. *Customer Support:* Support Agreement Available.
MVS. IBM S/370-390 (256k). Contact publisher for price.
Validates JCL Stream Before Submitted for Execution. Enables Programmer or Production Control Analyst to Eliminate JCL Errors in Batch Mode or On-Line to Assure Job Runs to Completion.
Computer Assocs. International, Inc.

CA-JobWatch. 1991. *Customer Support:* Support Agreement Available.
VM. IBM S/370-390 (2Mb). Contact publisher

TITLE INDEX

for price.
Batch Execution Environment for Production & General Batch Work. Includes Operations Interface, CMS Extensions, Job Accounting/Chargeback & Security Interfaces. Supports User Inquiry of Job Status & Monitoring Capabilities via Full-Screen Panels or Commands.
Computer Assocs. International, Inc.

CA-KBM. 1994. *Customer Support:* Support Agreement Available.
OS/400. AS/400. Contact publisher for price. *Developed for Manufacturers Who Need to Respond to Customer Request for Varying Product Characteristics Including Colors & Sizes. Features Manufacturing Database Generator Which Creates Complete Manufacturing Product Database in Form of Item Records Including Definition & Planner Data, Pricing Formulas & Multi-Level BOM.*
Computer Assocs. International, Inc.

CA-KBM Accounts Payable. 1985. *Customer Support:* Support Agreement Available.
OS/400. AS/400. Contact publisher for price. *Maintains Strict Control over Invoice Processing. On-Line Inquiry Permits Viewing of Account Activity & Reports May Be Created on Request. Supports Multiple Currencies; Transactions May Be Entered in Any User-Defined Currency. Function Keys are Provided on All Screens to Display Transactions in Functional or Foreign Currency.*
Computer Assocs. International, Inc.

CA-KBM Accounts Receivable. 1985. *Customer Support:* Support Agreement Available.
OS/400. AS/400. Contact publisher for price. *Works in Concert with Sales Order Management to Control Order Processing, Enforce Credit Policies, Identify Potential Credit Problems, & Improve Timely Payment from Clients.*
Computer Assocs. International, Inc.

CA-KBM Bar Code. 1994. *Customer Support:* Support Agreement Available.
OS/400. AS/400. Contact publisher for price. *Modular, Closed-Loop MRP II System. Designed for Use in Repetitive, Discrete & Process Manufacturing Environments That Use Bar Code Data Collection. Provides Shop Floor Data Collection for Labor & Inventory, Time/Attendance Reporting & Client/Server Connection of AS/400. RF Bar Code Interface Available.*
Computer Assocs. International, Inc.

CA-KBM Business Planning. 1981. *Customer Support:* Support Agreement Available.
OS/400. AS/400. Contact publisher for price. *Translates High Level "Non-Unit" Production Goals & Forecasts, Such As Dollar Sales or Dollar Production Goals Specified by Top Management & Marketing, into a Detailed Unit Production Plan at the Master Production Schedule (MPS) Level. Uses Production Plan & Customer Forecast As Input; the Production Plan Forms Top Management's Primary Input to MPS.*
Computer Assocs. International, Inc.

CA-KBM Cash Management. 1985. *Customer Support:* Support Agreement Available.
OS/400. AS/400. Contact publisher for price. *Provides Centralized Control of Bank Transactions Including All Cash Receipts, Cash Disbursements, & General Ledger Journal Entries. Provides Manual & Automatic Check Printing. Also Records Cash Receipts Processed in Accounts Receivable. All General Ledger Journal Entries to Cash Control Accounts Are Passed to Cash Management.*
Computer Assocs. International, Inc.

CA-KBM Detail Capacity Planning. 1981. *Customer Support:* Support Agreement Available.
OS/400. AS/400. Contact publisher for price. *Audits Production Plan from MRP & Is Final Check of Scheduling Integrity Prior to Commencement of Value Added Manufacturing. Performs Detailed Analysis of Load Versus Capacity Available for Each Work Center & Machine Group in the Manufacturing Facility.*
Computer Assocs. International, Inc.

CA-KBM EDI. 1994. *Customer Support:* Support Agreement Available.
OS/400. AS/400. Contact publisher for price. *Supports Electronic Transfer of Outgoing POs & Incoming Sales Orders Between CA-KBM Users & Their Trading Partners, Regardless of Trading Partners' Application or Hardware Platform. Prepares Data for Electronic Transfer from CA-KBM: Manufacturing Module to Vendor & Receives Orders from Customers into CA-KBM: Sales Order Management.*
Computer Assocs. International, Inc.

CA-KBM Financial Statements. 1985. *Customer Support:* Support Agreement Available.
OS/400. AS/400. Contact publisher for price. *Allows Creation of Custom Financial Reports. Report Writing Tool Allows Formatting of Reports Based on General Ledger Account Balances and/or Budget Values for Any Organization, from Single Department to Multi-Company Consolidation. No Formal End-of-Period Processing Is Required to Run a Particular Report or Statement; Reports Can Be Created & Printed at Any Time.*
Computer Assocs. International, Inc.

CA-KBM Financials. 1994. *Customer Support:* Support Agreement Available.
OS/400. AS/400. Contact publisher for price. *Management Tool for Planning & Controlling Manufacturing Environment. Includes GL, AP, AR, Fixed Assets, Cash Management, Financial Statements & Ratio Analysis Modules. Includes Open-Coded Database & Variable List Report Writer. Performs Key-Edit-Posting to Transfer Transactions from Manufacturing to Accounting, Validates Entry & Posts to GL & Applications Ledgers Daily. Payroll Interface Available.*
Computer Assocs. International, Inc.

CA-KBM General Ledger. 1985. *Customer Support:* Support Agreement Available.
OS/400. AS/400. Contact publisher for price. *Provides Complete Financial Control over a Manufacturing Business. Designed for Maximum Flexibility, While Ensuring Data Integrity Through Strict System Controls. Supports Posting from All Financial Applications, Including Accounts Payable, Accounts Receivable, Cash Management, & Fixed Assets. Allows Warehouse, Shipping, Inventory, & Shop Floor Activities to Be Posted Directly to General Ledger - on the Same Day They Occur in the Plant.*
Computer Assocs. International, Inc.

CA-KBM Inventory Management. 1981. *Customer Support:* Support Agreement Available.
OS/400. AS/400. Contact publisher for price. *Maintains Inventory Balances by Location or by Location/Lot on All Levels of Purchased, Assembled, or Manufactured Parts in an On-Line, Real-Time Environment. Records Inventory Movements Through On-Line Inventory Transaction Processor. Updates Inventory Transactions On-Line, Real-Time.*
Computer Assocs. International, Inc.

CA-KBM Manufacturing. 1994. *Customer Support:* Support Agreement Available.
OS/400. AS/400. Contact publisher for price. *Integrated Customer-Responsive Manufacturing Management Package Including Integrated Financial System. Uses Relational Database Capabilities & Expanded Communications of IBM AS/400. Multi-MFG Planning, Bar Code, Sales Order Management & Process Modules Available. Supports Large & Small Manufacturing Companies.*
Computer Assocs. International, Inc.

CA-KBM Master Production Schedule. 1981. *Customer Support:* Support Agreement Available.
OS/400. AS/400. Contact publisher for price. *Determines What Products Will Be Produced, & in What Quantities. Is the Basis for All Scheduling of Production & Procurement Activities. Intercepts the Demand (Forecast & Actual Customer Orders) & Allows MPS to Satisfy That Demand with Planned Orders & Scheduled Receipts Based on Production Plan Targeted Inventory Balances, Plant Capacity, & Material Availability.*
Computer Assocs. International, Inc.

CA-KBM Material Requirements Planning. 1981. *Customer Support:* Support Agreement Available.
OS/400. AS/400. Contact publisher for price. *Determines Procurement & Manufacturing Schedules Required to Meet Business Plan. Calculates What to Buy & Manufacture, How Much, & When. Provides the Output That Drives the Detail Capacity Planning Module to Generate Complete Information on the Capacity Loading That a Given Production Schedule Will Place on Each Work Center in Facility.*
Computer Assocs. International, Inc.

CA-KBM Multi-Manufacturing Planning. 1994. *Customer Support:* Support Agreement Available.
OS/400. AS/400. Contact publisher for price. *Provides Formalized Method of Communication Between Multiple, Autonomous Operating Units of Demand Planning & Product Transportation & Serves As Building Block of JIT Manufacturing. Incorporates Unit of Measure Conversion Function, Distribution Losses & Alternate Codes to Facilitate Passing of Requirements to Multiple Suppliers.*
Computer Assocs. International, Inc.

CA-KBM Process. 1994. *Customer Support:* Support Agreement Available.
OS/400. AS/400. Contact publisher for price. *Integrated MRP II Process Package. Uses Relational Database Capabilities of IBM AS/400. Provides Lot Control, By-Product/Co-Product Scheduling, Decimalization & Potency Functions.*
Computer Assocs. International, Inc.

CA-KBM Product Structure. 1981. *Customer Support:* Support Agreement Available.
OS/400. AS/400. Contact publisher for price. *Creates & Maintains Product Structure Records Used to Describe Product. Maintains Bills of Material in Single Level Parent-Component Relationships. Provides Full Use of from/to Effective Dates on Product Structure Records. Provides Alternate Bills of Material & User-Defined Bills of Material Sequencing.*
Computer Assocs. International, Inc.

CA-KBM Purchase Order Management. 1981. *Customer Support:* Support Agreement Available.
OS/400. AS/400. Contact publisher for price. *Controls Purchase Orders from Release to Fulfillment of Last Receipt. Maintains Up-to-Date Accurate Information on Scheduled Receipts of Material from Outside the Company. Tracks Incoming Material from Receipt into Plant Through Incoming Inspection Operations until Material Is Actually Transferred into on Hand Inventory. Maintains Vendor History Information.*
Computer Assocs. International, Inc.

CA-KBM Rough Cut Capacity Planning. 1981. *Customer Support:* Support Agreement Available. OS/400. AS/400. Contact publisher for price. Compares Critical Capacity Load Points with Requirements of MPS or Production Plan. Investigates Feasibility of MPS from Standpoint of User-Specified Critical Capacity Areas Which Are Distinct from Actual Shop Floor Work Centers.
Computer Assocs. International, Inc.

CA-KBM Sales Order Management. 1994. *Customer Support:* Support Agreement Available. OS/400. AS/400. Contact publisher for price. Allows User to Enter, Cancel, Promise, Configure, Discount, Invoice & Handle All Facets of Order Processing for Make-to-Stock & Make-to-Order Environments. Provides Interactive Entry of New Orders & Shipments Made Against Existing Orders & Incorporates Sales Tax, Multinational Currencies, Sales Commission, Discounting & Invoicing Information.
Computer Assocs. International, Inc.

CA-KBM Shop Floor Control. 1981. *Customer Support:* Support Agreement Available. OS/400. AS/400. Contact publisher for price. Determines Priorities & Manages Activities on the Shop Floor. Provides Information Needed to Execute Established Production Plan. "Daily Dispatch" Contains a List, by Work Center, or All Work Orders to Be Worked on, Arranged in Operation Due Date Sequence, & a List of All Work Orders That Are One Operation Away from the Work Center.
Computer Assocs. International, Inc.

CA-KBM Standard Product Cost. 1981. *Customer Support:* Support Agreement Available. OS/400. AS/400. Contact publisher for price. Contains the Tools Needed to Track & Maintain the Cost Involved in Manufacturing Products. Provides Accurate & Up-to-Date Information on the Value of WIP Inventory.
Computer Assocs. International, Inc.

CA-KBM Windows. 1991. *Customer Support:* Support Agreement Available. Windows. IBM PC & compatibles. Contact publisher for price. Integrated Closed Loop MRP II Package Including Integrated Financial System. Allows Users to Run up to 32 Sizeable CA-KBM Windows Simultaneously for Viewing or to Cut-&-Paste Data. Utilizes DDE to Link Current Data from AS/400 Applications to Windows Applications. Distribution Resource Planning, Bar Code, Sales Order Management & Process Modules Available. Supports Large & Small Manufacturing Companies.
Computer Assocs. International, Inc.

CA-KBM Work Order Management. 1981. *Customer Support:* Support Agreement Available. OS/400. AS/400. Contact publisher for price. Links MRP & Execution Phases of CA-KBM System. Creates Repository of Information Pertaining to Open & Completed Work Orders, Providing Pertinent Work Order Data for Use by MRP, MPS, Shop Floor Control, Detail Capacity Planning & Standard Product Cost Modules. Allows JIT Work Orderless Transactions.
Computer Assocs. International, Inc.

CA-Librarian. 1969. *Customer Support:* Support Agreement Available. MVS, VSE, VM. IBM S/370-390 (180k). Contact publisher for price. Provides General Purpose Source Library Management Services. Change Control Facility (CCF) Complements Source Code Management Services by Providing Comprehensive Methodology for Managing Application Development Life Cycle.
Computer Assocs. International, Inc.

CA-Librarian/JCL Validation. 1991. *Customer Support:* Support Agreement Available. MVS. IBM S/370-390 (180k). Contact publisher for price. Automatic Syntax Checking of MVS JCL under ELIPS (Extended Librarian Interactive Productivity, Dialog-Based Interface Between TSO/ISPF/PDF & CA-Librarian) for CA-Librarian. Provides Comprehensive JCL Syntax Checking & Validation from Within ELIPS Environment. Locates & Reports JCL Problems Which Could Cause Execution Time Failures. Generates Diagnostic Messages into Monitor Display Using JCK Command While Editing CA-Librarian Master File.
Computer Assocs. International, Inc.

CA-Link. 1985. *Compatible Hardware:* IBM PC & compatibles; IBM S/370-390. *Operating System(s) Required:* IBM MVS, VM, VSE, PC-MS/DOS, OS/2. *Customer Support:* Available. contact vendor.
contact vendor.
PC-to-Host Communications System. Provides 3270 or Async Terminal Emulation with Built-In Intelligent File Transfer Facility. Includes Foundation for CA90S-Common Communications Interface & CAICCI Service Which Enables CA Products to Operate in Multiplatform Distributed Environment.
Computer Assocs. International, Inc.

CA-Look. 1979. *Customer Support:* Support Agreement Available. VSE. IBM S/370-390. Contact publisher for price. Real-Time Performance Management System. Provides On-Line Diagnosis, Long-Term Measurement & Threshold Monitoring for VSE & Host VM Systems. Includes CICS, CA-Datacom/DB & Overall System Monitoring. Produces Tabular Summaries, Histograms & Point Plots. Provides System Programmer Productivity Tools to Eliminate IPLs.
Computer Assocs. International, Inc.

CA-MANMAN/X:Distribution & Inventory Location Management. *Customer Support:* Available. AIX, SunOS, Solaris, HP-UX, OSF/1. Contact publisher for price. Provides Distribution Planning & Location Management Capabilities & Visibility of Inventory Status. Maintains Optional Inventory Levels Across Distribution Locations, Full Lot Traceability, Assignment of Storage Locations & Selection Release. Lets Users Create Hierarchy of Distribution Facilities That Operate As Supply Chain with Demand Created Automatically When Any Distribution Location Falls Below Target Levels.
Computer Associates International, Inc.

CA-MANMAN/X:Sales & Purchasing Management. *Customer Support:* Available. AIX, SunOS, Solaris, HP-UX, OSF/1. Contact publisher for price. Provides Order Management & Purchase Activities Analysis Capabilities. Provides Real-Time Control over Profitability, Featuring Blocking Controls over Orders Whose Margin Is Below or Above Allowable Percentage. Provides Visibility of Problem Accounts or Orders & Allows Range of Options for Handling Business in These Accounts.
Computer Associates International, Inc.

CA-MANMAN/X. 1992. *Customer Support:* Support Agreement Available. HP-UX, OSF/1, Solaris, AIX, SCO. HP9000, DEC Alpha, SUN, IBM RS/6000. Contact publisher for price. Manufacturing Business Management System. Consists of Modules That Automate Manufacturing Process, Including Planning, Costing, Engineering Control, Project Control, Inventory, Shop Floor Control, Sales Management, Purchasing, Finance, Customer Service & Maintenance. Supports Concurrent Operation in Multiple Languages Including French, German & English. Supports CA-Ingres, ORACLE, Informix, ISAM Databases, & X-Windows.
Computer Assocs. International, Inc.

CA-MANMAN/X Accounts Payable. 1992. *Customer Support:* Support Agreement Available. HP-UX, OSF/1, Solaris, AIX, SCO. HP9000, DEC Alpha, SUN, RS6000. Contact publisher for price. Manages Open Entries, Generates Payment Advice, Supports Electronic Funds Transfer, Supports Debit Memos, Provides 1099 Reporting, Matches Invoices, POs, Receipts. Integrated with CA-MANMAN/X GL & CA-MANMAN/X Purchasing Control.
Computer Assocs. International, Inc.

CA-MANMAN/X Accounts Receivable. 1992. *Customer Support:* Support Agreement Available. HP-UX, OSF/1, Solaris, AIX, SCO. HP9000, DEC Alpha, SUN, IBM RS6000. Contact publisher for price. Liquidity Forecast Shows Projected Cash Flow, Credit Management, Debit Credit Memos, Open Entries, Electronic Funds Transfer, Accounts Reminders, Customer Payment & Aging Analysis, Integrated with CA-MANMAN/X GL & CA-MANMAN/X Sales Order Processing.
Computer Assocs. International, Inc.

CA-MANMAN/X Capacity Requirements Planning. 1992. *Customer Support:* Support Agreement Available. HP-UX, OSF/1, Solaris, AIX, SCO. HP9000, DEC Alpha, SUN, RS6000. Contact publisher for price. Integrated with CA-MANMAN/X Manufacturing Planning & Execution, Calculates Work Center Capacity Using Number of Resources, Scheduled Work Period, & Work Center Calendar, Integrates Graphical Capacity Analysis Tool with Planning Board, Provides Visibility of Project Cash Flow Based on Current MRP.
Computer Assocs. International, Inc.

CA-MANMAN/X Cost Center Administration. 1992. *Customer Support:* Support Agreement Available. HP-UX, OSF/1, Solaris, AIX, SCO. HP9000, DEC Alpha, SUN, IBM/RS6000. Contact publisher for price. Cost Center Administration System to Manage & Organize Cost Categories So That All Transactions May Be Processed Automatically into Cost Centers. Offers Flexibility in Allocating Financial Data over Multiple Cost Centers. Default Cost Center Distributions Can Be Defined for Each Ledger Account.
Computer Assocs. International, Inc.

CA-MANMAN/X Distribution Requirements Planning. 1992. *Customer Support:* Support Agreement Available. HP-UX, OSF/1, Solaris, AIX, SCO. HP9000, DEC Alpha, SUN, IBM RS/6000. Contact publisher for price. Maintain Optimal Inventory Levels Across All Distribution Locations. Material Requisitions Provide a Mechanism for Transfers Between Warehouses. Accommodates a Flexible Network of Distribution Sites, Allowing Users to Define Network Structure & Multiple Sources of Supply. Segregate Distribution Inventory from Produciton Inventory to Assure Proper Levels of Inventory for All Requirements.
Computer Assocs. International, Inc.

TITLE INDEX

CA-MANMAN/X Drawing Control. 1992.
Customer Support: Support Agreement Available.
HP-UX, OSF/1, Solaris, AIX, SCO. HP9000, DEC Alpha, SUN, IBM RS/6000. Contact publisher for price.
Provides the Capability to Manage Engineering Drawings, Maintain Engineering Bills of Material, & Maintains Relationships Between Drawings & Items and/or EBOMs. Provides a Link with CAD Software. Maintain Drawings by Category & Size. EBOMs Can Be Defined by Drawing, by Version, or by Product Number. Display & Reporting Including Where-Used, Structure Printing, & Summary Bill with Order Quantities, & Sorting by Dimensions.
Computer Assocs. International, Inc.

CA-MANMAN/X Electronic Data Interchange. 1992. *Customer Support:* Support Agreement Available.
HP-UX, OSF/1, Solaris, AIX, SCO. HP9000, DEC Alpha, SUN, RS/6000. Contact publisher for price.
Electronic Data Interchange Support for CA-MANMAN/X. Supports Inbound Sales Orders, Outbound Invoices, Outbound Purchase Orders, & Outbound Order Acknowledgments. Supports Industry-Standard Message Formats Including ANSI X.12, EDIFACT, ODETTE, & UAC-TRANSCOM.
Computer Assocs. International, Inc.

CA-MANMAN/X Financial Management System. 1992. *Customer Support:* Support Agreement Available.
HP-UX, OSF/1, Solaris, AIX, SCO. HP9000, DEC Alpha, SUN, RS6000. Contact publisher for price.
Integrated Application Set Including GL, AR, AP, FINANCIAL REPORTING, COST CENTER ADMINISTRATION & FIXED ASSET REGISTRATION. Interactive Accessibility to Data for Financial Management. These Modules Can Be Used in a Fully Integrated Manufacturing or Distribution Environment or As a Standalone Suite of Applications.
Computer Assocs. International, Inc.

CA-MANMAN/X Financial Statements. 1992. *Customer Support:* Support Agreement Available.
HP-UX, OSF/1, Solaris, AIX, SCO. HP9000, DEC Alpha, SUN, IBM RS/6000. Contact publisher for price.
Provides Control over the Format & Content of Financial Reports. Users Define Detail & Summary Levels for Reporting, Including Columns Showing Actuals, Budgets, Comparisons, & Ratios. Define up to 99 Ratios Based on Statement Accounts.
Computer Assocs. International, Inc.

CA-MANMAN/X Fixed Asset Registration. 1992. *Customer Support:* Support Agreement Available.
HP-UX, OSF/1, Solaris, AIX, SCO. HP9000, DEC Alpha, SUN, IBM RS/6000. Contact publisher for price.
Supports Asset Management & Recording Activities. Assets Are Maintained by Location & the System Maintains Straight-Line Depreciation Tables for Asset Groups. Maintains Three Types of Depreciation per Asset: Book, Tax, & Simulation.
Computer Assocs. International, Inc.

CA-MANMAN/X General Ledger. 1992. *Customer Support:* Support Agreement Available.
HP-UX, OSF/1, Solaris, AIX, SCO. HP9000, DEC Alpha, SUN, RS6000. Contact publisher for price.
Maintains All Accounting Transactions by Account for Multiple Companies, Departments, Projects. Manages Foreign Currency Transactions, Chart of Accounts, Links to External GL's, User Defined Fiscal Calendar, 14 Financial Periods per Fiscal Year, Executes Inter-Company Transactions.
Computer Assocs. International, Inc.

CA-MANMAN/X Hours Accounting. 1992.
Customer Support: Support Agreement Available.
HP-UX, OSF/1, Solaris, AIX, SCO. HP9000, DEC Alpha, SUN, RS6000. Contact publisher for price.
Integrated with CA-MANMAN/X Manufacturing Planning & Execution, Maintains Standard Work Hours Information Including Schedule Breaks, Tracks Both Production Order Direct Labor & Non-Direct Labor, Maintains Overtime Hours Budgets & Automatically Calculates Overtime.
Computer Assocs. International, Inc.

CA-MANMAN/X Inventory Location Control. 1992. *Customer Support:* Support Agreement Available.
HP-UX, OSF/1, Solaris, AIX, SCO. HP9000, DEC Alpha, SUN, IBM RS/6000. Contact publisher for price.
Maintains Inventory by Warehouse, Physical Inventory & Cycle Counting, & Inventory Location Control.
Computer Assocs. International, Inc.

CA-MANMAN/X Lot Control. 1992. *Customer Support:* Support Agreement Available.
HP-UX, OSF/1, Solaris, AIX, SCO. HP9000, DEC Alpha, SUN, IBM RS/6000. Contact publisher for price.
Provides Full Traceability for Lots & Serial Numbers. Functions Meet ISP-9001 Certification Standards. Lot Control Is Specified by Item & Users Can Define the Types of Information That Need to Be Collected for Each Item. Provides Full Lot Genealogy Beginning with the Origin, at Purchasing, of Component Materials.
Computer Assocs. International, Inc.

CA-MANMAN/X Manufacturing Planning & Execution. 1992. *Customer Support:* Support Agreement Available.
HP-UX, OSF/1, Solaris, AIX, SCO. HP9000, DEC Alpha, SUN, RS6000. Contact publisher for price.
Modules Consist of Business Planning, Master Production Scheduling (MPS), Material Requirements Planning (MRP), Capacity Requirements Planning (CRP), Production Planning, Production Control, Hours Accounting, Drawing Control, & Product Classification. The System Calculates Projected Revenue, Gross Profit, Quantities, & Cost for Each Product Family.
Computer Assocs. International, Inc.

CA-MANMAN/X Master Production Scheduling. 1992. *Customer Support:* Support Agreement Available.
HP-UX, OSF/1, Solaris, AIX, SCO. HP9000, DEC Alpha, SUN, IBM RS/6000. Contact publisher for price.
Provides Extensive Simulation Capabilities; Supports Master Scheduling for Make-to-Order, Make-to-Stock, Assemble-to-Order, & Engineer-to-Order Operations. Define Multiple Levels of Product Families. Drive the Master Schedule from Statistical Forecast or Actual Demand. Production & POs Can Be Firmed & Released Automatically.
Computer Assocs. International, Inc.

CA-MANMAN/X Material Requirements Planning. 1992. *Customer Support:* Support Agreement Available.
HP-UX, OSF/1, Solaris, AIX, SCO. HP9000, DEC Alpha, SUN, IBM RS6000. Contact publisher for price.
Integrated with CA-MANMAN/X Manufacturing Planning & Execution, Supports Net Change & Regenerative MRP, Uses Smoothing Factors to Control Unnecessary Rescheduling, Allows Selective & Simulated MRP, Provides Graphical Analysis.
Computer Assocs. International, Inc.

CA-MANMAN/X Product Classification. 1992.
Customer Support: Support Agreement Available.
HP-UX, OSF/1, Solaris, AIX, SCO. HP9000, DEC Alpha, SUN, IBM RS/6000. Contact publisher for price.
Allows for Classification of Items by Their Characteristics & Use Those Characteristics As Search Criteria. Create a Customized Classification & Coding System Specific to Product Characteristics & Structure. User-Defined Questions & Answers Facilitate Item Searches. Classify Products Based on Logical Features.
Computer Assocs. International, Inc.

CA-MANMAN/X Product Configurator. 1992.
Customer Support: Support Agreement Available.
HP-UX, OSF/1, Solaris, AIX, SCO. HP9000, DEC Alpha, SUN, RS6000. Contact publisher for price.
Rules-Based System Allowing Users to Create a Customized Product with Minimum Effort. Structure Product Options & Generate Custom BOMs & Routings with Unique Costs & Pricing.
Computer Assocs. International, Inc.

CA-MANMAN/X Production Control. 1992.
Customer Support: Support Agreement Available.
HP-UX, OSF/1, Solaris, AIX, SCO. HP9000, DEC Alpha, SUN, RS/6000. Contact publisher for price.
Manages Each Phase of the Production Cycle; Fully Integrated with CA-MANMAN/X Planning Modules Providing a Closed Loop from Planning Through Execution. Includes: Production Master Data Maintenance, Production Planning, Shop Floor Control, Hours Accounting, & Product Costing.
Computer Assocs. International, Inc.

CA-MANMAN/X Production Master Data. 1992. *Customer Support:* Support Agreement Available.
HP-UX, OSF/1, Solaris, AIX, SCO. HP9000, DEC Alpha, SUN, RS/6000. Contact publisher for price.
Control Production Activities Using Both Shop Orders and/or Production Schedules. Identify Items & Sub-Assemblies As Phantom Parts on Either the Item Master of a BOM, Maintains BOMs for All Production Parts. Includes BOM Maintenance & Reporting. Define Main & Sub-Work Centers. Maintains Capacity Data & a Company Wide Timetable for Scheduling.
Computer Assocs. International, Inc.

CA-MANMAN/X Production Planning. 1992.
Customer Support: Support Agreement Available.
HP-UX, OSF/1, Solaris, AIX, SCO. HP9000, DEC Alpha, SUN, RS/6000. Contact publisher for price.
Translates MPS & MRP into Detailed Plan of Action. Supports Forward & Backward Scheduling for Standard & Customized Manufactured Parts. Schedule Any Part for Production Using a Produciton Order. Includes Repetitive/JIT Scheduling. Planning Board Provides a Gantt Chart for Each Order Detailing Current Operations & Recorded Completions Against Those Operations.
Computer Assocs. International, Inc.

CA-MANMAN/X Project Budgeting. 1992.
Customer Support: Support Agreement Available.
HP-UX, OSF/1, Solaris, AIX, SCO. HP9000, DEC Alpha, SUN, RS6000. Contact publisher for price.
Creates Project Bids to Integrate with CA-MANMAN/X. Bids Can Be Converted to Projects & Used to Create Sales Quotations & Sales Orders.
Computer Assocs. International, Inc.

CA-MANMAN/X PROJECT CONTROL

CA-MANMAN/X Project Control. 1992.
Customer Support: Support Agreement Available.
HP-UX, OSF/1, Solaris, AIX, SCO. HP9000, DEC Alpha, SUN, IBM/RS6000. Contact publisher for price.
Provides the Detailed Planning & Control Needed for Integrated Online Management. Includes Customized BOMs & Routings, Detailed Project Budgeting & Cost Tracking, Planning for Project Material & Capacity Requirements, & Simulations of Project Impact on Manufacturing Capacity.
Computer Assocs. International, Inc.

CA-MANMAN/X Project Management. 1992.
Customer Support: Support Agreement Available.
HP-UX, OSF/1, Solaris, AIX, SCO. HP9000, DEC Alpha, SUN, RS6000. Contact publisher for price.
Configure Final Products to Customer Specifications & in the Process Generates Customized BOMs & Routing Sheets, Make and/or Buy Customized Products, Designs, Develops & Carries Out Job & Projects. Integrated with CA-MANMAN/X Manufacturing Planning.
Computer Assocs. International, Inc.

CA-MANMAN/X Project Network Planning. 1992. *Customer Support:* Support Agreement Available.
HP-UX, OSF/1, Solaris, AIX, SCO. HP9000, DEC Alpha, SUN, IBM/RS6000. Contact publisher for price.
Allows Users to Schedule Project Activities Using a PERT-Style Network Technique with Graphical Reporting to Help Determine the Critical Path & Identify Capacity Bottlenecks. Also Allows Users to Schedule & Re-Schedule Tasks & Activities That Are Linked to Project Production Orders.
Computer Assocs. International, Inc.

CA-MANMAN/X Purchase Quotations. 1992.
Customer Support: Support Agreement Available.
HP-UX, OSF/1, Solaris, AIX, SCO. HP9000, DEC Alpha, SUN, IBM RS/6000. Contact publisher for price.
Maintains Detailed Information about Supplier Price & Delivery Quotations. Users Can Analyze & Compare Pricing & Discount Structures by Supplier & Maintain Historical File of Prior Quotations. Records Data Requested, Required Delivery, & Required Return Date.
Computer Assocs. International, Inc.

CA-MANMAN/X Purchasing Statistics. 1992.
Customer Support: Support Agreement Available.
HP-UX, OSF/1, Solaris, AIX, SCO. HP9000, DEC Alpha, SUN, IBM RS/6000. Contact publisher for price.
Tracks Purchasing Statistics & Supplier Performance. Provides User-Defined Selection & Analysis of Purchasing Statistics & Budget Information.
Computer Assocs. International, Inc.

CA-MANMAN/X Return Material Administration. 1992. *Customer Support:* Support Agreement Available.
HP-UX, OSF/1, Solaris, AIX, SCO. HP9000, DEC Alpha, SUN, IBM RS/6000. Contact publisher for price.
Tracks Information on Returned Materials Including Items Repaired, Returned, Scrapped, or Inventoried for Future Disposition. Supports Return for Restock, Repair & Restock, Repair & Return, Failure Analysis, & Replacement Types of Material Return.
Computer Assocs. International, Inc.

CA-MANMAN/X Sales & Marketing Information. 1992. *Customer Support:* Support Agreement Available.
HP-UX, OSF/1, Solaris, AIX, SCO. HP9000, DEC Alpha, SUN, IBM RS/6000. Contact publisher for price.
Maintains & Provides Sales Statistics for CA-MANMAN/X. Graphical Reports Provide Trend Information for Analysis. Maintains Order History for All Transactions. Monitors & Reports Prospecting Activities.
Computer Assocs. International, Inc.

CA-MANMAN/X Sales & Purchase Control. 1992. *Customer Support:* Support Agreement Available.
HP-UX, OSF/1, Solaris, AIX, SCO. HP9000, DEC Alpha, SUN, IBM RS/6000. Contact publisher for price.
Includes Purchase Quotations, Sales Quotations, Purchase Contracts, Sales Contracts, Purchase Order Management, Sales Order Management, Sales Statistics, & Sales & Marketing Information. Integrated with Manufacturing Planning.
Computer Assocs. International, Inc.

CA-MANMAN/X Sales Contracts. 1992.
Customer Support: Support Agreement Available.
HP-UX, OSF/1, Solaris, AIX, SCO. HP9000, DEC Alpha, SUN, IBM RS/6000. Contact publisher for price.
Maintains Sales Contracts for a Time Period and/or Specified Quantities by Item or Groups of Items. Tracks Contract Start & End Dates, Supplier & Delivery Data, Quantity Ordered & Quantity Received to Date, Min/Max Quantities, Price & Discounts, & Delivery Schedule.
Computer Assocs. International, Inc.

CA-MANMAN/X Sales Quotations. 1992.
Customer Support: Support Agreement Available.
HP-UX, OSF/1, Solaris, AIX, SCO. HP9000, DEC Alpha, SUN, IBM RS/6000. Contact publisher for price.
Allows Users to Create Quotations for Standard, New, & Configured Items & Convert the Quotation to a Sales Order upon Customer Acceptance. Customer & Prospect Information Can Be Created with the Quotation Entry. Optionally Include Quotations in Forecasting & Planning. Provides Detailed Win/Loss Information for Analysis. Quotations Can Be Printed in Foreign Languages & Priced Accordingly.
Computer Assocs. International, Inc.

CA-MANMAN/X Sales Statistics. 1992.
Customer Support: Support Agreement Available.
HP-UX, OSF/1, Solaris, AIX, SCO. HP9000, DEC Alpha, SUN, RS/6000. Contact publisher for price.
Manages Sales Activity. Provides Reports in Graphical & Custom Formats. Shows Deliveries by Period As Well As Sales above & below Defined Margins.
Computer Assocs. International, Inc.

CA-MANMAN/X Service Management. 1992.
Customer Support: Support Agreement Available.
HP-UX, OSF/1, Solaris, AIX, SCO. HP9000, DEC Alpha, SUN, RS6000. Contact publisher for price.
Provides Management & Control of All Service, Maintenance Activities, & Return Material Processing. Includes Functionality for Managing Service Calls, Service Contracts, Customer Site & Equipment Information, & Return Material Processing. Automatic Dispatching & Invoicing.
Computer Assocs. International, Inc.

CA-MANMAN/X Service Order Processing. 1992. *Customer Support:* Support Agreement Available.
HP-UX, OSF/1, Solaris, AIX, SCO. HP9000, DEC Alpha, SUN, IBM RS/6000. Contact publisher for price.
Service Order Processing System Manages All Repair & Maintenance Activities at Customer Sites & User Facilities. Tracks Service Activities, Manages the Activities of Customer Service Engineers, Creates RMAs Automatically for Service-Exchangeable Items.
Computer Assocs. International, Inc.

CA-Manufacturing Workbench. *Customer Support:* Available.
Windows. Contact publisher for price.
Provides Access to Manufacturing & Financial Data. Includes Queries, Reports & Worksheets Which Provide Up-to-the-Minute Data on Customers, Order, Inventory, Financials & Other Aspects of Business Operations. Features Ad Hoc Query & Reporting Capability.
Computer Assocs. International, Inc.

CA-Masterpiece/2000 Accounts Payable.
Customer Support: Available.
MVS, VSE, OS/400, AIX, VAX, OpenVMS, OSF/1, HP-UX, DYNIX/ptx, System V, ICL/UNIX, DG-UX, Solaris, Windows, SCO/ODT. Contact publisher for price.
Module of CA-Masterpiece/2000 Series. Tracks Due Dates & Discount Terms. Determines Pay Dates & Cash Requirements. Provides Check Register. Allows Manual Check Processing. Includes Check Reconciliation, Discount Availability, 1099 Reports, PO Integration, International Language & Tax Support & Currency Conversion.
Computer Associates International, Inc.

CA-Masterpiece/2000 Accounts Receivable.
Customer Support: Available.
MVS, VSE, OS/400, AIX, VAX, OpenVMS, OSF/1, HP-UX DYNX/ptx, System V, ICL/UNIX, DG-UX, Solaris, Windows, SCO/ODT. Contact publisher for price.
Module of CA-Masterpiece/2000 Series. Multi-Corporate, Multi-Division Support. Provides Customer billing, Tracks Credit Limits & Assesses Finance Charges on Specified Customer Billing, Tracks Credit Limits & Assesses Finance Charges on Specified Customers. Real-Time Posting to CA-Masterpiece/2000 GL. Includes Multiple Bill-To Locations for Each Ship-To Location. Provides Lock-Box Receipts Processing & User-Directed Cash Application Techniques.
Computer Associates International, Inc.

CA-Masterpiece/2000 Fixed Assets. *Customer Support:* Available.
MVS, VSE, OS/400, AIX, VAX, OpenVMS, OSF/1, HP-UX DYNX/ptx, System V, ICL/UNIX, DG-UX, Solaris, Windows, SCO/ODT. Contact publisher for price.
Module of CA-Masterpiece/2000 Series. Multi-Corporate, Multi-Division Support. Tracks Assets by Responsibility Center & Depreciates with Unlimited Books. Calculates Depreciation Monthly & Posts to CA-Masterpiece/2000 GL Selectively or En Masse. Conforms to FASB Guidelines. Includes Standard & Custom Reporting.
Computer Associates International, Inc.

CA-Masterpiece/2000 Fund Accounting.
Customer Support: Available.
MVS, VSE, OS/400, AIX, VAX, OpenVMS, OSF/1, HP-UX DYNX/ptx, System V, ICL/UNIX, DG-UX, Solaris, Windows, SCO/ODT. Contact publisher for price.
Module of CA-Masterpiece/2000 Series. Consists of GL, AP, Purchasing & IC. Monitors & Controls Spending in Non-Profit Environment. Includes Links to Ad Hoc query & Reporting, Host-to-PC Linking, Host & PC Spreadsheet Interface, Graphics Production Systems & Business Decision Support Facilities.
Computer Associates International, Inc.

TITLE INDEX

CA-Masterpiece/2000 General Ledger.
Customer Support: Available.
MVS, VSE, OS/400, AIX, VAX, OpenVMS, OSF/1, HP-UX DYNX/ptx, System V, ICL/UNIX, DG-UX, Solaris, Windows, SCO/ODT. Contact publisher for price.
Module of CA-Masterpiece/2000 Series. Capabilities for Multi-Company & Multi-Division Processing Include Multiple Currency & Management Support, Budgeting, Accruals & Reversals, Recurring Journal Entries & Allocations. Supports 12/13-Period Accounting. Provides Standard & Custom Reports. Relationship Structure Provides On-Line Access to All Summary-Level Data.
Computer Associates International, Inc.

CA-Masterpiece/2000 Inventory Control.
Customer Support: Available.
MVS, VSE, OS/400, AIX, VAX, OpenVMS, OSF/1, HP-UX, DYNIX/ptx, System V, ICL/UNIX, DG-UX, Solaris, Windows, SCO/ODT. Contact publisher for price.
Module of CA-Masterpiece/2000 Series. Designed to Match IC Levels to Customer Demand. Tracks On-Hand, Allocated, Ordered, Back-Ordered, in Transit & Available IC. Records Re-Order Point, Maximum, Minimum & EQQ. Audits Material Movement by Activity Type, Date & Part Number. Supports Stock Requests, Multiple Currencies, VAT Taxing, International Data Format & Foreign Language Screen Sets. Integrates with CA-Masterpiece/2000 Purchasing & General Ledger.
Computer Associates International, Inc.

CA-Masterpiece/2000 Job Cost. *Customer Support:* Available.
MVS, VSE, OS/400, AIX, VAX, OpenVMS, OSF/1, HP-UX, DYNIX/ptx, System V, ICL/UNIX, DG-UX, Solaris, Windows, SCO/ODT. Contact publisher for price.
Module of CA-Masterpiece/2000 Series. Provides Integrated Financial & Cost Accounting System for Government & Project-Oriented Commercial Firms. Receives Transaction Information from Other CA-Masterpiece/2000 Applications & Tracks, Updates & Reports All Expenditures Applied to Given Project from Inception to Completion.
Computer Associates International, Inc.

CA-Masterpiece/2000 Labor Distribution.
Customer Support: Available.
MVS, VSE, OS/400, AIX, VAX, OpenVMS, OSF/1, HP-UX, DYNIX/ptx, System V, ICL/UNIX, DG-UX, Solaris, Windows, SCO/ODT. Contact publisher for price.
Module of CA-Masterpiece/2000 Series. Timesheet Driven System. Controls & Reports Labor Costs for Government Contractors & Commercial Firms. Tracks & Reports Timesheet Items Including Project, Labor Grade & Pay Code & Posts Detailed Labor Cost Information to CA-Masterpiece/2000 GL & Job Cost.
Computer Associates International, Inc.

CA-Masterpiece/2000 Order Processing.
Customer Support: Available.
MVS, VSE, OS/400, AIX, VAX, OpenVMS, OSF/1, HP-UX, DYNIX/ptx, System V, ICL/UNIX, DG-UX, Solaris, Windows, SCO/ODT. Contact publisher for price.
Module of CA-Masterpiece/2000 Series. Processes & Monitors Orders from Entry Point Through Invoicing. Includes Auto Updating of Inventory Levels, Multiple Warehouse File Maintenance & Reporting, Invoice Printing, customer Credit Management, Order Confirmation, Picking List & Sales Analysis Report Writer.
Computer Associates International, Inc.

CA-Masterpiece/2000 Purchasing. *Customer Support:* Available.
MVS, VSE, OS/400, AIX, VAX, OpenVMS, OSF/1, HP-UX, Solaris, DYNIX/ptx, System V, ICL/UNIX, DG-UX, Windows, SCO/ODT. Contact publisher for price.
Module of CA-Masterpiece/2000 Series. Real-Time Purchasing/Receiving/Requisition Management & Analysis. POs Include Multiple Line Items & Delivery Dates. Monitors Order Status or Anticipated Receipt of Parts with Respect to POs & Late Shipments Tracked by Vendor. Integrates with CA-Masterpiece/2000 AP, IC & GL Applications.
Computer Associates International, Inc.

CA-Masterpiece/2000 Workbench. 1994.
Customer Support: Support Agreement Available.
Windows. IBM PC & compatibles. Contact publisher for price.
Desktop, GUI-Based Client/Server Extension to CA-Masterpiece/2000. Provides Ad Hoc Inquiry, Reporting, Decision Support & Analysis of Financial Data at Desktop. Dynamically Links to Server SQL Database on All Platforms, Including MF, UNIX, VAX & AS/400.
Computer Assocs. International, Inc.

CA-Masterpiece/2000. 1976. *Compatible Hardware:* IBM System 370/390 MVS, VSE; AS/400-OS/400; DEC VAX-VMS; UNISYS 1100 series, 2200-1100 OS; Data General Eclipse MV series-AOS/VS, HP9000 HP/UX, Sequent DYNIX/ptx, AT&T GIS, UNIX MP RAS, ICL/UNIX, DG AVIION/DG-UX, Sun Solaris.
Items Included: Documentation included.
Customer Support: Available.
Contact vendor for price.
Includes Integrated General Ledger, Accounts Payable, Accounts Receivable, Fixed Assets, Purchasing, Inventory Control, Job Cost, Labor Distribution, Order Processing, & Fund Accounting Modules.
Computer Assocs. International, Inc.

CA-Mazdamon. 1983. *Customer Support:* Support Agreement Available.
MVS. IBM S/370-390 (2Mb). Contact publisher for price.
Network Performance Monitoring System. Collects Performance Data for Every Component on Entire VTAM Network. Reports Data Through Use of Real-Time & History Reporting Facilities. Interfaces with CA-ISS/Three for Network & Host Capacity Planning.
Computer Assocs. International, Inc.

CA-MetaCOBOL+. 1989. *Customer Support:* Support Agreement Available.
MVS, VSE. IBM S/370-390 (2Mb). Contact publisher for price.
High-Level Application Development & Maintenance Workstation for Batch & CICS COBOL Users. Augments Editor Functions under TSO/ISPF, CA-Roscoe or CA-Vollie. Creates Program Shells, Generates Prevalidated Code, Submits Jobs & Allows On-Line Browsing of Output. Includes COBOL Language Extensions for Database Access, Structured Programming & CICS Programming. Provides Panel Painter for Creating BMS Maps.
Computer Assocs. International, Inc.

CA-MetaCOBOL+/PC. 1992. *Customer Support:* Available.
PC-DOS/MS-DOS. IBM AT, PS/2 & compatibles. Contact vendor for price.
Develops COBOL Applications & Downsizes COBOL & CA-MetaCOBOL Plus Applications. Includes COBOL Extensions for On-Line Applications, CA-Datacom Access, Structured Programming, QA Standards Enforcement & Formatting. Includes CA-Realia PC COBOL Compiler. Transfers Programs Between PC & Mainframe.
Computer Assocs. International, Inc.

CA-Metrics. 1992. *Items Included:* Documentation included. *Customer Support:* Available.
PC-DOS/MS-DOS. IBM PC & compatibles (640k). Contact vendor for price.
Measurement & Tracking System for IS Organizations. Allows User to Collect, Analyze & Present Key Measures for Success Including Quality, Productivity & Customer Satisfaction. Provides Metrics Repository, Toolbox of Analysis Tools, Decision Support for IS Management & TQM/S Defect Tracking System.
Computer Assocs. International, Inc.

CA-Migrate/COBOL. 1988. *Customer Support:* Support Agreement Available.
MVS, VSE. IBM S/370-390 (1.5Mb). Contact publisher for price.
Converts IBM OS/VS COBOL, DOS/VS COBOL & Older COBOL Dialects into IBM VS COBOL II or COBOL/370. Converts Macro-Level DL/1 Programs & CICS/VS to Command-Level. Provides Analysis, Manipulation & Transformation Capabilities for Existing Programs. Allows Enforcement of Standards & Formatting. Provides Extensive Reporting Facilities.
Computer Assocs. International, Inc.

CA-Mindover. 1987. *Customer Support:* Support Agreement Available.
MVS. IBM S/370-390 (512k). Contact publisher for price.
Expert System for MVS Performance Management. Collects & Analyzes Data, Reports Findings & Conclusions & Offers Recommendations to Solve Performance Problems.
Computer Assocs. International, Inc.

CA-Netman. 1981. *Customer Support:* Support Agreement Available.
MVS, VSE, VM. IBM S/370-390 (1Mb). Contact publisher for price.
Integrated On-Line Database for Managing Data Centers & Communications Networks. Relates Problems, Changes, Network Configurations, Inventory, Contracts, Invoices, Budgets, User Chargeback, Order Tracking & Vendor Management Applications. Inventory/Configuration Manager, Financial Manager, Problem Tracking & Change Manager Modules. Interfaces with CA-ACF2, CA-Top Secret, CA-Scheduler, CA-Dynam/TLMS & CA-Opera.
Computer Assocs. International, Inc.

CA-Netman/Workbench. *Customer Support:* Available.
Windows. Contact publisher for price.
Integrated Client/Server Business Solution to Manage CA-Netman MVS Environment from a PC Workstation.
Computer Associates International, Inc.

CA-Netman/Bar Code. 1993. *Customer Support:* Support Agreement Available.
DOS. IBM PC & compatibles (640k). Contact publisher for price.
Collects Hardware Inventory Data. Provides Communication Utility to Upload Gathered Data from Owner Information, Tag Number/Logical Name, Serial Number, Manufacturer & Product Code to PC. Provides Utilities to Update CA-Netman MVS & CA-Netman/PC.
Computer Assocs. International, Inc.

CA-Netman/DB. 1991. *Customer Support:* Support Agreement Available.
MVS. IBM S/370-390 (750k). Contact publisher for price.
Relational Option for Data Centers Using CA-Netman. Reduces Data Storage, Provides Database Logging & Recovery, Uses Same Database from CICS & TSO & Moves Data Center Toward 24 Hour Environment.
Computer Assocs. International, Inc.

CA-Netman for VAX. 1988. *Items Included:* Documentation included. *Customer Support:* Available.
VAX/VMS. Digital VAX (2Mb). Contact vendor for price.
Provides Management with Reports & Information Required to Track & Manage All Hardware & Software Inventory. Integrates Problem Help Desk to Assist Computing Center Staff in Managing End-User Problems, Requests & Support Needs.
Computer Assocs. International, Inc.

CA-Netman/OLCF. 1985. *Customer Support:* Support Agreement Available.
MVS. IBM S/370-390 (1Mb). Contact publisher for price.
On-Line Customization Facility for CA-Netman. Data Dictionary Tracks Netman System & User-Defined Fields. Allows User to Write Reports, Paint Screens or Add User Fields to Database.
Computer Assocs. International, Inc.

CA-Netman/PC. 1986. *Customer Support:* Available.
PC-DOS. IBM PC or compatible micro computers. Contact Vendor. *Networks supported:* IBM PC Network Program, Novell, Banyan, 3Com, NetBIOS (Operating over a LAN requires a dedicated AT-class machine to act as a "database engine".).
Integrated Software Tool for Automating Mangaement & Support of End User Computing Resources. Includes Inventory Tracking, System Configuration Management, Network Management, Warranty Maintenance Management, Purchasing & Receiving, End User Support & Problem Tracking. Provides 225 Reports, Report Writer, Import/Export Facilities, Customization Utility, Automatic Database Recovery & Record Locking.
Computer Assocs. International, Inc.

CA-Netman/Reports+. 1991. *Customer Support:* Support Agreement Available.
MVS. IBM S/370-390. Contact publisher for price.
Codebok Containing Customizable CA-Netman Reports Using Advanced APA Print & Graphical Charting Facilities. Includes Graphical Representation of CA-Netman Problem Management Information & Flexible Charts Allowing User-Defined Date Ranges. Provides Charts-by-Problem Category, Allows for Multiple Chart Definitions & Provides On-Line Help.
Computer Assocs. International, Inc.

CA-9/R+. 1976. *Customer Support:* Support Agreement Available.
MVS. IBM S/370-390 (512k). Contact publisher for price.
Tracks/Analyzes Temporary & Permanent Failures for Tapes/Drives, DASD, CPUs, Core, Channels, TD & Unit Devices. Pinpoints Sources of Device Degradation. Compares Device Degradation/Failure Characteristics to National Standards.
Computer Assocs. International, Inc.

CA-OLQ. 1977. *Customer Support:* Support Agreement Available.
MVS, VSE, VM, BS2000, MSP, VOS-3. IBM S/370-390; Siemens, Fujitsu, Hitachi. Contact publisher for price.
Retrieves Information from CA-IDMS/DB Databases or Sequential Files for Creating Reports, Performing Ad Hoc Queries or Creating Extracts of Production Data for Downloading to PC Through CA-ICMS.
Computer Assocs. International, Inc.

CA-1. 1971. *Customer Support:* Support Agreement Available.
MVS. IBM S/370-390 (64k). Contact publisher for price.
Tape Library Management. Protects Against Accidental Deletion of Any Type of Tape Dataset, Streamlines Tape Handling & Provides Information on All Tape Usage. On-Line ISPF Inquiry & Update. Offsite Vaulting Facilities & Subpooling Capabilities. Interfaces with Production Scheduling, DASD & Automated Restart Products.
Computer Assocs. International, Inc.

CA-1/Copycat. 1991. *Customer Support:* Support Agreement Available.
MVS. IBM S/370-390. Contact publisher for price.
Tape Management Utility. Provides Tape Copy, Media Replacement & Consolidation Functions. Facilitates Reel-to-Cartridge Conversions, Consolidation of Small Files on Multiple Tapes to Single Tape. Supports Electronic Ejecting of Volumes Controlled by Robotic System. Provides Duplication Allowing for Replacement of Old/Faulty Tapes. Electronically Vaults Tapes to Off-Site Location & Provides Backup Facility.
Computer Assocs. International, Inc.

CA-1/Viewpoint. 1991. *Customer Support:* Support Agreement Available.
MVS. IBM S/370-390. Contact publisher for price.
Windowing User Interface Option to CA-1 Based on IBM's SAA/CUA Standards. Provides Continuous Monitoring, Single-Screen Operation, Errorless Commands & Data Center Integration Capabilities.
Computer Assocs. International, Inc.

CA-OpenIngres. *Customer Support:* Available.
SunSPARC Solaris, SunOS; HP 9000/HP-UX; AT&T GIS SVR4; IBM RS/6000/AIX; Bull DPX/20, Bull OS; DEC VAX/VMS, VAXSEVMS, Alpha OpenVMS, DEC UNIX; ICL DRS6000 NX, V7 L7; SCO UNIX, OpenServer; Pyramid system V; MIServer; Sequent DYNIX/ptx; Novell Netware, DG AViiON DG-UX, Intel-based DG-UX, Intel x86 UNIXware. Contact publisher for price.
Provides Foundation to Support Mission-Critical Production Applications, Such As Multithreaded, Multi-CPU Architecture for OLTP, Data Management for OLCP, Scalability, Distributed Processing Services, Enterprise Systems Management & Real-World Data. Provides Name Server Load Balancing, Spatial Objects Library, Client/Server Data Access. Includes Query & Reporting Tools, Data, Object & Knowledge Management.
Computer Associates International, Inc.

CA-OpenIngres/Desktop. *Customer Support:* Available.
Windows. Contact publisher for price.
A Complete DBMS for the Windows 3.1 & Windows 95 Desktop Environment, with Replication Technology to Automatically Synchronize Changes Between the Desktop Database & the CA-OpenIngres Server Database As Well As Other CA-OpenIngres/Desktop Users.
Computer Associates International, Inc.

CA-OpenIngres/DTP. *Customer Support:* Available.
AIX, HP-UX. Contact publisher for price.
Set of Libraries & Programming Extensions to Enable X/Open DTP-Compliant Applications to Be Developed & Deployed Against CA-OpenIngres/Server. Used to Integrate Database with Transaction Processing Monitors Such As IBM CICS/6000, Transarc Encina & Novell Tuxedo.
Computer Associates International, Inc.

CA-OpenIngres/Enhanced Security. *Customer Support:* Available.
VAX, SEVMS, Sun 4, Trusted Solaris. Contact publisher for price.
Secure RDBMS. Allows Government Agencies & Commercial Organizations to Store & Protect Data with Diverse Security Classifications in One Database. Implements Discretionary Access Controls for Users & Groups, Mandatory Access Controls, Configurable Security Auditing, Protection Against Object Reuse & Least Privilege.
Computer Associates International, Inc.

CA-OpenIngres/Enterprise Access. *Customer Support:* Available.
DEC Alpha AXP, VAX, DECstation, DECsystem/OSF/1, VMS, ULTRIX; HP 3000, 9000/MPE/iX, HP-UX; SCO UNIX; Sun-4, SPARCstation/SunOS, Solaris; UnixWare; IBM RS/6000/AIX; DG AViiON/DG/UX. Contact publisher for price.
Provides Full, Transparent READ/WRITE Access to Existing Data in Relational & Non-Relational Systems. Provides Common, Portable, Open Interface Across Variety of Operating Environments While Maintaining Access to Existing Data. Protects Existing Investments & Provides Access to Information.
Computer Associates International, Inc.

CA-OpenIngres/Net. *Customer Support:* Available.
DEC Alpha AXP, VAX/OpenVMS, VMS; HP 9000 series 700, 800/HP-UX; Sun SPARCsystem/SunOS, Solaris, Trusted Solaris; IBM RS/6000/AIX. Contact publisher for price.
Allows Distributed Access to CA-OpenIngres Databases Connected in Computer Networks, Including Different Operating Environments. Accesses CA-OpenIngres Information from Remote Computers While Running CA-OpenIngres Tools/Applications Locally.
Computer Associates International, Inc.

CA-OpenIngres/Object Management Extension & Spatial Object Library. *Customer Support:* Available.
SUN SPARCsystem/SunOS, Solaris, Trusted Solaris; IBM RS/6000/AIX; HP 9000 series 700, 800/HP-UX; DEC Alpha AXP, VAX/OpenVMS, VMS. Contact publisher for price.
Provides Object Management Capabilities to Relational Database Model by Allowing CA-OpenIngres/Server to Understand & Manipulate New Types of Data. Features Application Development, Spatial Data Relationships Handled Like Traditional Characters & Numbers, User-Defined Data Types, Operators & Functions, Programmable As SQL Statements.
Computer Associates International, Inc.

CA-OpenIngres/Server. *Customer Support:* Available.
Sun SPARCsystem/SunOS, Solaris, Trusted Solaris; IBM RS/6000/AIX; HP 9000 series 700, 800/HP-UX; DEC Alpha AXP, VAX/OpenVMS, VMS. Contact publisher for price.
Multithreaded, Multiclient/Multiserver RDBMS Supporting OLTP & Decision Support Systems. Includes Query & Report Writing Facilities, Character-Based Application Programming, Data, Knowledge, Object Management & Security.
Computer Associates International, Inc.

CA-OpenIngres/Star. *Customer Support:* Available.
DEC Alpha AXP, VAX/OpenVMS, VMS; HP 9000 series 700, 800/HP-UX; Sun SPARCsystem/SunOS, Solaris, Trusted Solaris; IBM RS/6000/AIX. Contact publisher for price.
Distributed Database Manager That Provides Ability to Access & Update Data As Single

TITLE INDEX

Database Without Regard to Format or Location. Provides Global View of Enterprise-Wide Data, Facilities for Intelligent Distributed Database Management, Centralized Administration of Distributed Systems, & Transparent 2-Phase Commit for Distributed Data Integrity.
Computer Associates International, Inc.

CA-OpenIngres Replicator. *Customer Support:* Available.
SunSPARC Solaris, SunOS; HP9000/HP-UX; AT&T GIS SVR4; IBM RS/6000/AIX, OS/2; Bull DPX/20; DEC VAX/VMS, VAX SEVMS, Alpha OpenVMS, DecVAX; ICL DRS 6000; SCO Unix; Pyramid System V MIServer; Sequent DYNIX/ptx; DG Aviion/DG-UX; DG Intel-based DG-UX; Intel x86 Unixware. Contact publisher for price.
Enables Users to Maintain Copies of Designated Data in One or More Databases. Supports Maintenance of Information Warehouses That Provide Data to Users by Writing Information Throughout Organization in Peer-to-Peer Relationship.
Computer Associates International, Inc.

CA-OpenRoad. *Customer Support:* Available.
SunSPARC Solaris, SunOS; HP 9000/HP-UX; AT&T GIS SVR4; IBM RS/6000/AIX; ICL DRS6000 NX V7 L7; SCO UNIX; Pyramid System V, Sequent DYNIX/ptx; Data General AViion DG-UX; 386/486 UNIX; MS Windows 3.1; MS Windows NT; UNIXware. Contact publisher for price.
Graphical, Object-Oriented Application Development Environment. Provides Driver Technology, Frame & Field Templates & Styles, Edit Multiple Applications, On-Line Help, Integration with 3rd Party Databases, Editable Table-Field Menus, Developer-Controlled Color, System & User Classes, Local Procedures, Debugger & Preprocessor.
Computer Associates International, Inc.

CA-Opera. 1987. *Customer Support:* Support Agreement Available.
MVS, VM, VSE. IBM S/370 & 390. Contact publisher for price.
Facilitates Unattended Computer Operations & Day-to-Day Processing. Provides Console Message Routing, Message Suppression & Automates Response. Message Selection Is by Message Number, Job Name, Accounting Codes, CPU ID, Time, Day, Message Text Scan, Generic Messages, Frequency of Occurrence & Message ID Pattern Matching.
Computer Assocs. International, Inc.

CA-Opera/PC. 1990. *Customer Support:* Available.
MS-DOS. IBM PC or compatibles. contact publisher for price.
Console Management Tool. Facilitates Unattended Computer Operation & Daily Processing. Includes Pager Notification, Remote & Automatic IML/IPL of Target Mainframe System, Remote System Console Operation, Scripting & Playback of Console Activities, Monitoring of & Reaction to Console Events & Remote File Backup.
Computer Assocs. International, Inc.

CA-Optimizer. 1970. *Customer Support:* Support Agreement Available.
MVS, VSE, VM. IBM S/370-390 (256k). Contact publisher for price.
Includes Optimizer, Detector & Analyzer Components. Reduces Object Module Size/Runtime. Identifies Unexecutable Code. Provides Enhanced Source Listings. Replaces Hex Dumps with Intelligent Abend Information & Captures Multiple Abends in One Pass. Tests Verify Programs & Identifies Potentially Inefficient Source Code.
Computer Assocs. International, Inc.

CA-Optimizer/II. 1986. *Customer Support:* Support Agreement Available.
MVS, VSE. IBM S/370-390 (160k). Contact publisher for price.
Provides Optimizer, Detector, Analyzer & On-Line COBOL II Help Facility. Replaces Hex Dumps with Abend Information. Identifies Inefficient & Unexecutable Code. Extended Detector Provides Reports for Production Abends Without Source Change, JCL Changes & Execution Time Overhead. Extended Optimization Support for CICS.
Computer Assocs. International, Inc.

CA-Pan/LCM. 1989. *Items Included:* Documentation included. *Customer Support:* Available.
MS-DOS, OS/2 LAN, HP-UX, SCO UNIX, AIX, SunOS. IBM PC, OS/2 & compatibles, HP9000, SCO, RS/6000, Sun Solaris (250k). Contact vendor for price.
Provides Workstation Application Development Tools That Support All Phases of Development Life Cycle. Includes Version Mangaer Which Tracks All Activity Within Workstation Development Projects & Indicates Who, What, When & Why Changes Were Made. Advanced Make Facility Allows for Building & Generation of Applications to Simplify Development & Maintenance. Compatible with All Batch Mode Driven Compilers, Linkers, Editors & Components.
Computer Assocs. International, Inc.

CA-Pan/LCM Configuration Manager. 1993. *Customer Support:* Support Agreement Available.
MVS, VSE. IBM S/370-390 (1Mb). Contact publisher for price.
Configuration Management System That Determines Dependencies Between Application Components. Automates Process of Recompiling, Reassembling & Relinking Application Software Systems. Assures All Modules Affected by Change Are Recompiled or Reassembled & Relinked. Provides Impact Analysis Information.
Computer Assocs. International, Inc.

CA-Pan/Merge. 1990. *Customer Support:* Support Agreement Available.
MVS. IBM S/370-390 (1Mb). Contact publisher for price.
Allows User to Combine Separate Sets of Program Changes into One Program. Identifies All Change Overlays & Marks All Conflicts. Provides Option to Resolve Conflicts On-Line Immediately Following Merge. Provides Detailed Summary Reports.
Computer Assocs. International, Inc.

CA-PanAPT. 1988. *Customer Support:* Support Agreement Available.
MVS. IBM S/370-390 (2mb). Contact publisher for price.
Automates Program Turnover Process Required to Identify, Approve & Move Applications into Production Libraries. Manages Migration of Application Entities. Provides History of Promotion Process.
Computer Assocs. International, Inc.

CA-PanAPT DB2 Option. 1989. *Customer Support:* Support Agreement Available.
MVS. IBM S/370-390. Contact publisher for price.
Automates DB2 Production Turnover Process. Validates DB2 Moves. Allows Grouping of DB2 Entities Including Plans & Packages with Other Entities in Move Request & Shows Plan/DBRM Associations.
Computer Assocs. International, Inc.

CA-PanAPT JCLCheck Option. 1994. *Customer Support:* Support Agreement Available.
MVS. IBM S/370-390. Contact publisher for price.
Verification Procedure for CA-PanAPT, CA's Turnover Product. Verifies MVS JCL at Setup Time, As Verification Procedure, As Well As Prior to Moving JCL into Production.
Computer Assocs. International, Inc.

CA-PanAudit Plus. 1979. *Customer Support:* Support Agreement Available.
MVS, VSE. IBM S/370-390 (256k). Contact publisher for price.
File Interrogation & Audit Solution Based on CA-Easytrieve PLUS Information Retrieval & Data Management System. Routines Include Statistical Sampling, Integrity Testing, Data & Time Conversions & Calculations, Numeric Calculations, File Distribution Analysis Comparison, Test Data Generation & SMF Analysis.
Computer Assocs. International, Inc.

CA-PanAudit Plus CPS. 1990. *Items Included:* Documentation included. *Customer Support:* Available.
MVS, VSE; PC-DOS/MS-DOS. IBM System 370/390 Architecture; IBM PC & compatibles. Contact vendor for price.
Computer-Based Auditing System Integrating Mainframe & PC Versions of CA-PanAudit Plus into Single Solution for Auditors of All Technical Skill Levels. Allows Auditors to Build Requests on PC & Execute Them Directly Against Mainframe & PC Data.
Computer Assocs. International, Inc.

CA-PanAudit Plus PC. 1990. *Items Included:* Documentation included. *Customer Support:* Available.
PC-DOS/MS-DOS. IBM PC & compatibles (400k). Contact vendor for price.
Audit System Which Enables User to Execute All Functions of Mainframe CA-PanAudit Plus on PC. Features Fill-in-Blanks Access to Information for Use By EDP Auditors with No Formal Data Processing Knowledge. Contains CA-Easytrieve Plus Information Retrieval & Data Management System. Includes Statistical Sampling, Distribution Analysis, Integrity Testing, Date & Time Conversion & Calculations, Numeric Calculations, File Comparison & Test Data Generation. Includes LAN Support.
Computer Assocs. International, Inc.

CA-Panexec. 1977. *Customer Support:* Support Agreement Available.
MVS. IBM S/370-390 (1Mb). Contact publisher for price.
Library Management System for Object & Executable Programs & Listings. Safeguards Integrity of Executable Programs. Protects Production Status Executable from Modification. Accumulates Statistics Including Frequency of Use. Provides Multilevel Access Code System & Security Exit. Includes Management Reports & ISPF Interface.
Computer Assocs. International, Inc.

CA-Panvalet. 1969. *Customer Support:* Support Agreement Available.
MVS, VSE. IBM S/370-390 (384k). Contact publisher for price.
Source Program Library Management, Security & Access Control System. Provides Program Status Directory Listing. Produces Library Activity Record. Prevents Data Loss Due to Disaster, Theft & Unauthorized Modification. Controls Program Deletion. Maintains Current Backup. Identifies Inactive Members. DASD Error Detection.
Computer Assocs. International, Inc.

CA-PFF. 1989. *Customer Support:* Support Agreement Available.
MVS. IBM S/370-390 (4Mb). Contact publisher

for price.
Allows User to Store & Maintain IBM's PDS Libraries. Includes Execution of Commands in On-Line or Batch Mode to Merge, Copy, Print, Backup, Restore & Delete PDS Members. Allows Storage of Multiple Members of Same Name on Protection File.
Computer Assocs. International, Inc.

CA-Planmacs. 1984. *Memory Required: 640k. Customer Support: Available.*
MS-DOS. IBM PC & compatibles. contact publisher for price.
Builds Detailed Phase, Task & Activity Definitions for Project Management Packages. Allows Project Manager to Graphically Edit Project Plan at Any Level & Adjust Relationsihps Between Individual Phases, Tasks & Activities. Entire Phases Can Be Added, Deleted, Lengthened or Shortened for Specific Project Before Detail Activities Are Generated.
Computer Assocs. International, Inc.

CA-Plot Optimizer. 1989. *Customer Support: Support Agreement Available.*
MVS, VM. IBM S/370-390 (1Mb). Contact publisher for price.
Improves Print Speeds of Laser Printers. Increases Graphics Output Capabilities Without Impacting Other Resources. Includes Optimized Laser Printer Drivers, Graphics Software Interfaces & IBM Text Interfaces. FORTRAN 77 Runtime for Execution.
Computer Assocs. International, Inc.

CA-PMA/ChargeBack. 1990. *Customer Support: Support Agreement Available.*
MVS. IBM S/370-390 (4Mb). Contact publisher for price.
Provides Comprehensive Cost Management Through Assignment of Costs for IS Resource Units. Distributes Costs to Proper Clients. Enables Users to Input Resource Accounting, Chargeback & Cost Data from CA-JARS, CA-Netman, CA-JARS Interfaces & User-Defined Data. Accomplishes Chargeback Configuration & Implementation Through IBM SAA/CUA Compliant On-Line Screens Which Provide Look & Feel of PC. Includes On-Line Rate & Budget Definition, Forecasting, Rate Determination & On-Line Query Capabilities.
Computer Assocs. International, Inc.

CA-PMA/ChargeBack for VAX. 1991. *Items Included: Documentation included. Customer Support: Available.*
VAX/VMS. Digital VAX. Contact vendor for price.
Provides Comprehensive Cost Management Through Assignment of Costs for IS Resource Units. Distributes Costs to Proper Clients. Enables Users to Input ACCOUNTING.DAT, QUOTA. DAT & User-Defined Data. Accomplishes Chargeback Configuration & Definition, Forecasting, Rate Determination & On-Line Query Capabilities.
Computer Assocs. International, Inc.

CA-PMA/Look. 1991. *Customer Support: Support Agreement Available.*
MVS. IBM S/370-390 (352k). Contact publisher for price.
Real-Time System Performance Management System. Provides Color Graphics for Immediate System Status. Includes Real-Time Monitoring of MVS, CICS, DASD, TSO, CA-Datacom/DB & CA-Roscoe. Includes Interactive Threshold & Exception Monitoring to Produce Early Warning Alerts & Status Messages. Provides User-Defined Summary Reports, Histograms & Point Plots for Long-Term Trend Analysis. Provides System Programmer Productivity Tools.
Computer Assocs. International, Inc.

CA-Power/Bench. 1992. *Customer Support: Available.*
Windows. IBM PC, PS/2 & compatibles (2Mb). Contact publisher for price.
System Which Assists in Implementation Process & Serves As Training Tool. Includes Graphical Presentation, Flow Charts of Processes, Detailed Project Plans & Narrative System Descriptions. Customizable.
Computer Assocs., International, Inc.

CA-PRMS:Accounts Payable. *Customer Support: Available.*
OS/400. Contact publisher for price.
Provides Control & Management of Cash Through Invoice Entry & Payments Processes, Cash Requirement Reporting & Vendor Analysis. Includes Multiple Banks, Recurring Payables, Void Check Processing, Variance Reporting, Check Reconciliation, Bank Drafts, Standard Distribution & VAT. Analyzes POs & Issues & Pays in Foreign Currency.
Computer Assocs. International, Inc.

CA-PRMS:Accounts Receivable. *Customer Support: Available.*
OS/400. Contact publisher for price.
Provides Accurate Customer Account Control Through Cash Posting & Statement Processing, On-Line Customer Inquiry into Current & Historical Data & Receivables Reporting. Includes Terms Codes & Dunning Notices.
Computer Assocs. International, Inc.

CA-PRMS:Capacity Requirements Planning. *Customer Support: Available.*
OS/400. Contact publisher for price.
Balances Material Plan Created by MRP Against Work Center or Production Line Capacities at Individual Work Center or Department Levels. Includes Work Center Profiles, Planning Horizons, Production Line Capacity, Work Center Capacity, Demand Pegging & What-If Planning. Includes Rough Cut Capacity Planning Capabilities.
Computer Assocs. International, Inc.

CA-PRMS:CIM Series. *Customer Support: Available.*
OS/400, DOS, OS/2. Contact publisher for price.
Open Architecture System Which Connects CA-PRMS to Plant Floor & Engineering Applications. Utilizes Standard API. Includes Links to, OnSchedule for Finite Scheduling, POMS Process Operations Management Component & PRMS Scan for Links to Bar Code Data Collection Devices.
Computer Assocs. International, Inc.

CA-PRMS:Distribution Requirements Planning. *Customer Support: Available.*
OS/400. Contact publisher for price.
Provides Method for Scheduling All Resources Necessary to Obtain, Handle, Move & Store Material Throughout Company's Network of Plants & Warehouses. Includes Forecasting & Generation of Requirements for Warehousing Network, DRP Simulation, Time Fences, Requirements Pegging, Bucketless Data Processing, Exception Message Filters & Suggested Warehouse Replenishment.
Computer Associates International, Inc.

CA-PRMS Distribution Solution. 1985. *Customer Support: Support Agreement Available.*
OS/400. AS/400. Contact publisher for price.
Package for Repetitive, Discrete, Process & Coexistent Manufacturers. Includes Support for AP, AR, Distribution Requirements Planning, Forecasting & Inventory Control. Supports Order Entry & Billing, Purchasing & Receiving & Replenishment. Integrated with CA-PRMS Manufacturing & Financial Solutions. Interfaces with CA-Warehouse Boss.
Computer Assocs. International, Inc.

CA-PRMS Enterprise Solution. 1982. *Customer Support: Support Agreement Available.*
OS/400. IBM AS/400 (8Mb). Contact publisher for price.
Closed-Loop Manufacturing System. Integrated Manufacturing, Distribution & Financial Applications. Handles Discrete, Repetitive, Process or Coexistent Environments. Defines Needs, Analyzes Resource Availability & Cost, & Schedules Purchasing & Production. MRP II, Master Production Scheduling, Product Structure & Standard Costing, Shop Floor Control, Capacity Requirements Planning, Rough Cut Capacity Planning, & Distribution Requirements Planning.
Computer Assocs. International, Inc.

CA-PRMS Financial Solution. 1985. *Customer Support: Support Agreement Available.*
OS/400. AS/400. Contact publisher for price.
Package for Repetitive, Discrete, Process & Coexistent Manufacturers. Includes Support for AP, AR, Fixed Assets, Complete Forecasting, GL, Human Resources, Payroll, & Purchasing & Receiving. Integrated with CA-PRMS Manufacturing & Distribution Solutions & CA-Warehouse Boss.
Computer Assocs. International, Inc.

CA-PRMS:Fixed Assets. *Customer Support: Available.*
OS/400. Contact publisher for price.
Provides Information Necessary to Compute & Project Book & Tax Depreciation, Monitor Asset Locations, Track Disposals with Gain/Loss Reporting & Satisfy Governmental Reporting Requirements. Include Multiple Company Processing, 12 or 13 User-Defined Accounting Periods & 11 Different Depreciation Methods.
Computer Assocs. International, Inc.

CA-PRMS:Forecasting Workbench. *Customer Support: Available.*
OS/400. Contact publisher for price.
Provides Planning Tool for Future Demand for Each Product. Utilizes Forecast to Manage Inventory Levels to Meet Required Product Demand. Simulation Capability Answers What-If Questions. Includes Multiple Forecasting Techniques, Group-Level Forecasts, Single-Item Forecasts, Seasonality & Trends & Performances Reporting.
Computer Assocs. International, Inc.

CA-PRMS:General Ledger. *Customer Support: Available.*
OS/400. Contact publisher for price.
Accounting & Reporting Application Combining GL Accounting, Financial Reporting & Budget Reporting for One or More Companies. Includes Customizable Report Formats, Budget Comparisons, Prior Period Adjustments, 12/13 Account Periods, Recurring Journal Entries, Budgets, Consolidations & Integration with Other CA-PRMS Applications.
Computer Assocs. International, Inc.

CA-PRMS:Human Resources. *Customer Support: Available.*
OS/400. Contact publisher for price.
Shares Database with Payroll Application, Tracking & Reporting Employee & Position Information Including Applicants, Job Openings, Attendance, Benefits & Grievances. Provides Employee Database, Position Control & Reporting, Management Reporting & Education & Training History.
Computer Assocs. International, Inc.

CA-PRMS:Inventory Control. *Customer Support: Available.*
OS/400. Contact publisher for price.
Helps Maintain Accurate Inventory Levels.

TITLE INDEX

Handles OLTP, User-Specified Inventory Tracking, On-Line Transaction History, Multiple Products per Lot, Multiple Warehouses, Random Locations, Backflushing, Performance Routing & User Interfaces to CA-Warehouse Boss.
Computer Assocs. International, Inc.

CA-PRMS Manufacturing Solution. 1985.
Customer Support: Support Agreement Available.
OS/400. AS/400. Contact publisher for price.
Subset of CA-PRMS Integrated Manufacturing System. Designed for Repetitive, Discrete, Process & Coexistent Manufacturers. Supports Computer Integrated Manufacturing, Capacity Requirements Planning, Distribution Requirements Planning, Demand Forecasting, Inventory Control, Master Production Scheduling, Material Requirements Planning, Product Costing, BOM, Replenishment Orders, Shop Floor Control, Rough Cut Capacity Planning & Complete Shop Data.
Computer Assocs. International, Inc.

CA-PRMS:Master Production Scheduling.
Customer Support: Available.
OS/400. Contact publisher for price.
Balances Demand & Supply on Corporate or Plant Level, Merging Forecasts & Customer Orders for Products or Product Families. Nets Against On-Hand Inventory & Existing Production Schedules, Resulting in End-Item Manufacturing Schedule. Includes Multilevel MPS, Interplant Demand, Time Fences, Planning Bills, Demand Source Rules & Actions Messages.
Computer Assocs. International, Inc.

CA-PRMS:Material Requirements Planning.
Customer Support: Available.
OS/400. Contact publisher for price.
Ensures Creation of Time-Phased Planned Manufacturing or POs to Meet Dependent & Independent Demands. Includes JIT Support, Interplant Demand, Dynamic Lot Sizing, By-Product Planning, Full or Net Change, MRP Regeneration, Order Action Exception Messages, Planning Factors & Automatic Rescheduling. Creates Planned Orders to Satisfy Requirements.
Computer Assocs. International, Inc.

CA-PRMS:Order Desk. *Customer Support:* Available.
Windows. Contact publisher for price.
PC-Based, Customer OE Module Designed for Use with CA-PRMS. Uses Pull-Down Menus & Help Facility to Provide User with All Necessary Information.
Computer Assocs. International, Inc.

CA-PRMS:Order Entry & Billing. *Customer Support:* Available.
OS/400. Contact publisher for price.
Sales OE/Billing System. Allows for Entry, Confirmation, Shipment & Billing of Customer Orders. Includes EDI Customer Order Processing, Full-Screen Entry, Order Quotations, User-Specified Order Types, Allocation Control, Supersede & Substitute Capabilities, Contract Pricing, Matrix Pricing, Kit Processing, Available-to-Promise, Credit Memo Processing, Trade Allowances & Order Entyr Product Configuration. Includes Client/Server GUI for OE & Customer Maintenance. Client Runs on Windows.
Computer Assocs. International, Inc.

CA-PRMS:Order Entry Configurator. *Customer Support:* Available.
OS/400. Contact publisher for price.
Module Enables User to Configure New Products with Unique Product Numbers, Manual & Automatic Selection Options & Component Parts. Product Master Information & Optional Text Are Created On-Line upon Acceptance. Creates BOM & Routing Information in Batch If Requested by User. Identifies Product to CA-PRMS for Inventory, Allocation, Orders, Planning, Shipping & Forecasting. Provides Full Costing Capabilities.
Computer Assocs. International, Inc.

CA-PRMS:Payroll. *Customer Support:* Available.
OS/400. Contact publisher for price.
Provides Complete System Which Satisfies Payroll Requirements & Meets Governmental & External Reporting Needs. Includes Tax Table Maintenance, Cafeteria Plan, Lead Man Earnings, Check Reconciliation, Voluntary Deductions, Direct Deposit, 401(k) Support, Salaried & Hourly Payrolls & Special Payrolls.
Computer Assocs. International, Inc.

CA-PRMS:Product Costing. *Customer Support:* Available.
OS/400. Contact publisher for price.
Collects Information from Other CA-PRMS Applications to Calculate, Track & Revise Cost Information. Costs for Any Product or Component at Each Level of Product Structure Are Accessible Separately & Used to Compute Total Costs. Includes Standard Costing, Actual Costing, Landed Cost Calculations, Product & Warehouse Costs & Selected Cost Roll-Ups.
Computer Assocs. International, Inc.

CA-PRMS:Product Structure. *Customer Support:* Available.
OS/400. Contact publisher for price.
Enables Maintenance, Modification & Inquiry into Structuring of Components for BOM. Serves As Central Repository for All Assembly & Component Relationships on System. Includes Explosion Capability Which Details Assembly's Entire Component Structure. Simulation Function Helps Determine Assembly & Component Structures Before Going Live. Includes ECN Control, Phantom Bills & Single & Multilevel Backflush.
Computer Assocs. International, Inc.

CA-PRMS:Purchasing & Receiving. *Customer Support:* Available.
OS/400. Contact publisher for price.
Creates & Records Requisitions, Quotes & POs & Tracks Received Goods Through Purchasing Cycle. Includes Quotation Subsystem & Pricing, Calendar Days Leadtime, Performance Reporting, On-Line Requisition Processing, On-Line Action from MRP, Time-Phased Order Point Processing, Outside Operations Support, Lot Control & Traceability, AP Invoice Matching, Blanket POs & Releases, EDI Interface & Interfaces to CA-Warehouse Boos, Client/Server PO Entry & Vendor Maintenance. Client Runs on Windows.
Computer Assocs. International, Inc.

CA-PRMS:Quality Control. *Customer Support:* Available.
OS/400. Contact publisher for price.
Enables Manufacturers to Document Procedures & Standards. Provides Support in Meeting Documentation Requirements of ISO 9000 Standard of Quality Set by European & Other Foreign Countries. Also Conforms with Domestic Requirements of U.S. Food & Drug Administration. Establishes Test Criteria, Triggers Test Scheduling, Saves & Compares Test Results to Requirements.
Computer Assocs. International, Inc.

CA-PRMS:Replenishment Orders. *Customer Support:* Available.
OS/400. Contact publisher for price.
Includes All Activities Involved in Control & Movement of Inventory from One Warehouse to Another. Includes Regular & Backorder Processing, Intra- & Inter-Plant Transfer, in Transit Reconciliation, Lot & Location Handling, Multiple Shipments per Order, Performance Reporting & Order Text.
Computer Assocs. International, Inc.

CA-PROAUDIT

CA-PRMS Sales Analysis Workbench. 1993.
Customer Support: Support Agreement Available.
Windows. IBM PC & compatibles (4Mb). Contact publisher for price.
PC-Based Windows Application Integrated with CA-PRMS: Enterprise Solution That Provides Data in Client/Server Environment As Aspect of Client Focused Manufacturing. E/S Brings Access to Sales Performance Indicators Throughout Sales Administration. GUI Uses Point & Click Assistance for All Levels of Management.
Computer Assocs. International, Inc.

CA-PRMS:Sales Analysis Workbench. *Customer Support:* Available.
Windows. Contact publisher for price.
PC-Based Windows Application Integrated with CA-PRMS:Enterprise Solution That Provides Data in Client/Server Environment As Aspect of Client Focused Manufacturing. EIS Brings Access to Sales Performance Indicators Throughout Sales Administration. GUI Uses Point-&-Click Assistance for All Levels of Management.
Computer Assocs. International, Inc.

CA-PRMS: SCAN for Windows. 1993. *Customer Support:* Support Agreement Available.
Windows. IBM PC & compatibles. Contact publisher for price.
Bar Code Data Collection for CA-PRMS. Provides Interface Modules for Each Logical Data Collection Entry Point in CA-PRMS. System Control Module Allows System Tailoring, Default & Polling Control, Data Flow Control & Output Flow Control. Data Collection Accomplished from Receiving Dock Through to Manufacturing and/or Distribution Facility to Shipping Dock.
Computer Assocs. International, Inc.

CA-PRMS: Shop Floor Control. *Customer Support:* Available.
OS/400. Contact publisher for price.
Provides Dispatch Management, I/O Control & Material Control for Job Shops & Rate-Based Management, Scheduling, Backflushing, Routing, Work Centers, Production Lines, Employees, Crews & Generational Standards to Model Plant Floor. Includes Production Scheduling Workbench, By-Product Reporting, Shop Packet, WIP Tracking, Skid Ticket Processing & Employee/Crew Reporting. Supports Definition of Alternate Production Methods, Engineering Change Control & Use of Rate Codes & Copy Functions for Routing Maintenance. Supports Orderless Shop-Floor Management.
Computer Associates International, Inc.

CA-PRMSVision. 1993. *Customer Support:* Support Agreement Available.
Windows. IBM PC & compatibles (4Mb). Contact publisher for price.
Executive Information System Which Provides Access to Key Performance Indicators from Manufacturing, Distribution & Financial Areas of Business. Includes Graphical Presentation, Class A MRP II Key Indicators, Multi-Dimensional Spreadsheet, Information Retrieval & Reporting. Allows User to Drill-Down into Data.
Computer Assocs. International, Inc.

CA-ProAudit. 1989. *Customer Support:* Support Agreement Available.
MVS. IBM S/370-390 (2Mb). Contact publisher for price.
Custom Audit Trail Facility for DB2. Provides Auditors & Database & Security Administrators Access to DB2 Data. Reports on Changes in DB2 Data, Eliminating Need to Maintain Application Audit Trails. Provides Audit Information on DB2 Plans Including Details about Object Dependencies, Plan Parameters & Associated SQL. Tracks Unauthorized Access, Utility Runs & Changes to Object Definitions. Allows Creation of Custom Reports to Complement Standard Report Formats.
Computer Assocs. International, Inc.

CA-ProBuild. 1987. *Customer Support:* Support Agreement Available.
MVS. IBM S/370-390. Contact publisher for price.
Interface That Provides Access to DB2 from TSO CLIST or REXX Exec. Provides DB2 User with Ability to Build Prototype Applications & Develop CLIST Tools for DB2. Embeds SQL Directly into CLIST Eliminating Need to Code & Debug COBOL or PL/1. Includes Library of Sample Tools, Including Source Code.
Computer Assocs. International, Inc.

CA-ProEdit. 1987. *Customer Support:* Support Agreement Available.
MVS. IBM S/370-390 (2Mb). Contact publisher for price.
Builds DB2 Test Environment Incorporating Referential & Entity Integrity, Manipulates Data in DB2 Tables & Tests SQL Code. Includes Panel-Driven Create Table/Index, Load/Unload, ISPF-Like Table Edit, Logical Table Compare, Embedded SQL Testing & SPUFI Emulator.
Computer Assocs. International, Inc.

CA-ProOptimize. 1988. *Customer Support:* Support Agreement Available.
MVS. IBM S/370-390 (2Mb). Contact publisher for price.
Provides Automated Recommendations for Efficient DB2 Application Tuning. Analyzes DB2 Access Path Selection & Application Plans. Identifies Inefficient SQL Statements, Recommends Coding Improvements & DB2 Physical Design Changes & Shows How DB2 Data Is Being Accessed & Why DB2 Chose That Specific Access Path.
Computer Assocs. International, Inc.

CA-ProSecure. 1987. *Customer Support:* Support Agreement Available.
MVS. IBM S/370-390 (2Mb). Contact publisher for price.
Manages DB2 Security. Groups DB2 Users, Objects & Access Privileges Together. Generates SQL Grant & Revoke Statements from Menu-Driven ISPF-Like Interface, Analyzes Consequences of Drop & Restores Authorizations on Dropped Objects As Required. Reports on DB2 Security Authorizations & Activity. Executes in Batch or On-Line Mode.
Computer Assocs. International, Inc.

CA-Quickserv. *Customer Support:* Available.
MVS, VSE. Contact publisher for price.
Provides Real-Time, Interactive Client/Server Access to Legacy Data Including VSAM, IMS, DL/I or Total. Provides Utilities to Migrate Legacy Data to Relational Storage Structure.
Computer Associates International, Inc.

CA-Ramis. 1977. *Customer Support:* Support Agreement Available.
MVS, VSE, VM. IBM S/370-390 (4Mb). Contact publisher for price.
4GL. Provides Reporting, Data Retrieval & Application Development. Reports & Applications Can Be Created & Executed on Either IBM Mainframe, UNIX, or Programmable Workstation. Includes Facilities for Report Writing, Graphics, Data Management, Statistics & Micro-Mainframe Communications & Database Management. Provides Compiled Application Development Language & Screen Painter.
Computer Assocs. International, Inc.

CA-Raps. 1982. *Customer Support:* Support Agreement Available.
MVS, VSE. IBM S/370-390. Contact publisher for price.
A Print Management System Designed to Provide the Data Center with Immediate, Online Control over the Remote Printing & Distribution of Reports.
Computer Assocs. International, Inc.

CA-Realia CICS. 1986. *Compatible Hardware:* IBM PC, PC XT, PC AT, 3270 PC. *Operating System(s) Required:* PC-DOS/MS-DOS, OS/2. *Language(s):* COBOL. *Memory Required:* 640k. *Customer Support:* Available.
Contact vendor for price.
CICS Applications Development on PC, for Execution on Mainframe or PC. Converts CICS Command-Level COBOL Programs to Form That Can Be Compiled by CA-Realia COBOL. BMS Macro Processor Produces Tables & COBOL Copy Members Required for Mapped Screen Use. Includes Map Editor.
Computer Assocs. International, Inc.

CA-Realia COBOL. 1984. *Compatible Hardware:* IBM PC & compatibles, PC AT, PC XT, 3270 PC. *Operating System(s) Required:* PC-DOS/MS-DOS, OS/2. *Language(s):* COBOL. *Memory Required:* 290k. *Customer Support:* Available.
Contact vendor for price.
High-Speed Compiler Compatible with IBM VS COBOL. Supports VS COBOL II & ANSI-85 Capabilities. Error-Checking, Program Editor & Interactive Symbolic Debugging. DOS, Windows, OS/2, C, HLLAPI, Assembler & Machine-Level Interfaces.
Computer Assocs. International, Inc.

CA-Realia DL/I. 1988. *Items Included:* Documentation included. *Customer Support:* Available.
PC-DOS/MS-DOS, OS/2. IBM PC & compatibles (512k). Contact vendor for price.
Allows Mainframe COBOL Programs Issuing IMS/DB or DL/I Database Calls to Run Unchanged in Single or Multi-User Mode. Includes Database Access, Query, Real-Time Trace/Debug Utilities & Full Database Unload, Reload & Rebuild Functions.
Computer Assocs. International, Inc.

CA-Realia/MS. 1989. *Items Included:* Documentation included. *Customer Support:* Available.
PC-DOS/MS-DOS, OS/2. IBM PC & compatibles (384k). Contact vendor for price.
Provides Compatible PC Environment for Users of Mainframe IMS Programs. Creates New Programs or Downloads Existing Mainframe Programs, Without Conversion for Development or Maintenance. Tests & Debugs Programs.
Computer Assocs. International, Inc.

CA-Realia JCL. 1993. *Customer Support:* Support Agreement Available.
DOS, OS/2. IBM PC & compatibles (1.1Mb). Contact publisher for price.
Runs Mainframe JCL Streams on PC. Downsizes Applications from Mainframe for Execution on PC with Little or No Modification. Builds, Tests & Runs Applications on PC with Option of Migrating Back to Mainframe. Trains Programmers in MVS JCL on PC, Avoiding High Mainframe Resource Expenses.
Computer Assocs. International, Inc.

CA-Realia ScreenIO. 1988. *Items Included:* Documentation included. *Customer Support:* Available.
PC-DOS/MS-DOS. IBM PC & compatibles (384k). Contact vendor for price.
Screen Manager Used to Develop, Maintain & Display Screens for Programs Compiled under CA-Realia COBOL. Includes Panel Editor Facilities Which Establish Screen Defaults, Create Windows, Draw Boxes & Specify Field-Level Definitions & Tabbing Order. Provides Subroutines to Simplify Programming & Accommodate Processing Options.
Computer Assocs. International, Inc.

CA-Realia II Workbench for MVS Batch. *Customer Support:* Available.
MVS, OS/2. Contact publisher for price.
Allows MVS Batch COBOL Programs to Be Analyzed & Debugged under a GUI CA-Realia II Workbench Windows Interface. Detects & Prevents Abends. Automates Uploading & Downloading of Source Members Between Host PDS, CA-Librarian & CA-Panvalet Libraries & PC Files.
Computer Associates International, Inc.

CA-Realia II Workbench for MVS CICS. *Customer Support:* Available.
MVS CICS, Windows, OS/2. Contact publisher for price.
Allows Mainframe MVS CICS COBOL Programs to Be Analyzed & Debugged under a GUI CA-Realia II Workbench Windows Interface. Detects & Prevents Abends. Automates Uploading & Downloading of Source Members Between Host PDS, CA-Librarian & CA-Panvalet Libraries & PC Files.
Computer Associates International, Inc.

CA-Realia II Workbench for VSE CICS. *Customer Support:* Available.
MVS CICS, Windows, OS/2. Contact publisher for price.
Allows Mainframe VSE CICS COBOL Programs to Be Analyzed & Debugged under the GUI CA-Realia II Workbench Windows Interface. Detects & Prevents Abends. Automates Uploading & Downloading of Source Members Between CA-Vollie, CA-Librarian, CA-Panvalet & VSE Libraries & PC Files.
Computer Associates International, Inc.

CA-Realia II Workbench. 1993. *Customer Support:* Available.
Windows, OS/2. IBM PC & compatibles. Contact publisher for price.
Complete Development System Provides Mainframe-Compatible COBOL Development on PC. GUI Shell Simplifies Development, Maintenance, Analysis & Testing of COBOL Programs. Includes COBOL Compiler, Integrated Editor & Life Cycle Management Tool.
Computer Assocs., International, Inc.

CA-Realia 370. 1990. *Items Included:* Documentation included. *Customer Support:* Available.
PC-DOS/MS-DOS, OS/2. IBM PC & compatibles (384k). Contact vendor for price.
Debugger for S/370 Compatible Assembler Programs & Subroutines. Emulates Assembler under DOS/VSE or MVS with Full Mainframe XA Instruction Set. Supports IBM Assembler H, In-Line & Library Macros, Copy Libraries, Supervisor Calls, Abend Processing, Source Listings Containing Generated Code Listing, CSect Map, Cross-References of Symbols/Literals & EBCDIC. Includes Single/Multi-Speed, Quiet Mode Tracing, Program Scrolling, Quick Searching for Label, Modification of Memory/PSW/Registers & Multiple Breakpoints/Watchpoints.
Computer Assocs. International, Inc.

CA-Realizer. 1991. *Items Included:* Documentation included. *Customer Support:* Available.
Windows; OS/2. IBM PC & compatibles. disk $99.00.
Combines Structures Superset of BASIC, Extended to Access Windows or OS/2 Object Resources with Programmable Application Tools, Such As Charts, Spreadsheets, Forms, Animation & Command Scheduler. Includes Integrated Debugger, Visual Form Designer, Report Generator, Support for DDE, DLL & Serial Communication.
Computer Assocs. International, Inc.

TITLE INDEX

CA-Roscoe. 1969. *Customer Support:* Support Agreement Available.
MVS. IBM S/370-390 (3.5Mb). Contact publisher for price.
On-Line Development System. Provides Complete Development Environment with Multiple Active Workspaces for Data Entry & Manipulation, Programming Facility, Job Processing Facility, Printing Services & Library System. Features Extended Time-Sharing Option for Execution of Site-Written or Purchased Applications.
Computer Assocs. International, Inc.

CA-RSVP. 1992. *Customer Support:* Support Agreement Available.
MVS. IBM S/370-390. Contact publisher for price.
Storage Reporting Facility That Produces Reports Based upon Multiple Sources, Including VTOCs, System Catalogs, SMS Constructs & CDS. Provides over 20 Standard Reports. Can Serve As Pre-Processor to Drive Other Systems. Allows User to Define Installation Storage Criteria & Subsequent Management Actions. Includes DASD Billing System.
Computer Assocs. International, Inc.

CA-Scheduler. 1971. *Customer Support:* Support Agreement Available.
MVS, VSE, VM. IBM S/370 & 390. Contact publisher for price.
Automates the Entire Production Workload. As a Scheduling & Workload Management System, It Provides the Means to Define & Monitor the Work Load in an Online Environment, Enforcing Predecessor Conditions & Enabling Automatic Recovery. Simulation & Forecasting Allow a Data Center to Depict Production Service Levels in the Future, Including the Impact of Future Changes in the Environment.
Computer Assocs. International, Inc.

CA-Scheduler/Notepad. 1993. *Customer Support:* Support Agreement Available.
MVS. IBM S/370-390 (2Mb). Contact publisher for price.
Provides Centralized, Integrated Recording & Viewing of User Notes Made During CA-Scheduler Operations. Provides TSO/ISPF Interface, Help Facility & External Security Integration.
Computer Assocs. International, Inc.

CA-Scheduler/Report Balancing. 1993. *Customer Support:* Support Agreement Available.
MVS. IBM S/370-390 (4Mb). Contact publisher for price.
Performs Automatic Balancing & Verification of Report Data for CA-Scheduler Managed Jobs. Includes On-Line TSO/ISPF Menus, Rule Simulation Facility & Security Integration.
Computer Assocs. International, Inc.

CA-Scheduler/Reports+. 1993. *Customer Support:* Support Agreement Available.
MVS. IBM S/370-390 (4Mb). Contact publisher for price.
Reporting Option That Provides Presentation Quality Graphic Reporting Capabilities. Assists Production Control Managers, Data Center Executives, Scheduling Personnel & End Users in Analyzing Facets of Production Workload Performance & Management. Performs Trend Analysis & Helps Pinpoint Problem Areas.
Computer Assocs. International, Inc.

CA-Scheduler/Smart Console. 1993. *Customer Support:* Support Agreement Available.
MVS. IBM S/370-390 (4Mb). Contact publisher for price.
Automates CA-Scheduler-Related Console & CICS Functions for Operations Personnel. Provides Automatic Responses & Routing of CA-Scheduler Commands Based on CA-Scheduler. CICS or Console Activity Across Multiple MVS Systems.
Computer Assocs. International, Inc.

CA-Scheduler/Viewpoint. 1991. *Customer Support:* Support Agreement Available.
MVS. IBM S/370-390 (2Mb). Contact publisher for price.
Windowing User Interface Option to CA-Scheduler Based on IBM's SAA/CUA Standards. Enables Users to Control & Organize Dynamic, Fluid or Complex Batch Workloads.
Computer Assocs. International, Inc.

CA-7. 1977. *Customer Support:* Support Agreement Available.
MVS. IBM S/370-390 (2Mb). Contact publisher for price.
Schedules, Balances Workload & Tracks Data Center Production. Provides Reporting & Productivity Aids. Includes Separate Batch Planning Facility. Supports TSO/ISPF. Integrates with CA-11, CA-Dispatch, CA-JCLCheck, CA-Opera, CA-APCDDS, CA-Netman, CA-ACF2 & CA-Top Secret. Includes CA-Earl for Customized Reporting.
Computer Assocs. International, Inc.

CA-7 for AS/400. 1985. *Customer Support:* Support Agreement Available.
MVS. IBM S/370-390 (2Mb). Contact publisher for price.
Automates Job Scheduling & Provides Forecast & Demand Scheduling. Provides Dependency Feature, Allowing Priorities & Relationships to Be Established among Jobs. Includes 8 Inquiry & Report Programs to Display or Print Information Contained Within System. Provides Recovery, Security & Calendaring Features.
Computer Assocs. International, Inc.

CA-7/Notepad. 1991. *Customer Support:* Support Agreement Available.
MVS. IBM S/370-390 (1Mb). Contact publisher for price.
Provides Centralized, Integrated Recording & Viewing of User Notes Made During CA-7 Operations. Provides TSO/ISPF Interface, Help Facility & External Security Integration.
Computer Assocs. International, Inc.

CA-7/Report Balancing. 1991. *Customer Support:* Support Agreement Available.
MVS. IBM S/370-390 (4Mb). Contact publisher for price.
Automatic Balancing & Verification of Report Data for CA-7 Managed Jobs. Includes On-Line TSO/ISPF Menus, Rule Simulation Facility & Security Integration.
Computer Assocs. International, Inc.

CA-7/Reports+. 1991. *Customer Support:* Support Agreement Available.
MVS. IBM S/370-390 (4Mb). Contact publisher for price.
Provides Presentation-Quality Graphic Reporting Capabilities. Assists Production Control Managers, Data Center Executives, Scheduling Personnel & End-Users in Analyzing All Facets of Production Workload Performance & Management.
Computer Assocs. International, Inc.

CA-7/Smart Console. 1991. *Customer Support:* Support Agreement Available.
MVS. IBM S/370-390 (4Mb). Contact publisher for price.
Automates CA-7-Related Console & CICS Functions for Operations Personnel. Provides Automatic Responses & Routing of CA-7 Commands Based on CA-7, CICS or Console Activity Across Multiple MVS Systems.
Computer Assocs. International, Inc.

CA-7/Viewpoint. 1991. *Customer Support:* Support Agreement Available.
MVS. IBM S/370-390 (1Mb). Contact publisher for price.
Brings Windowing to MVS Mainframe Environment & Provides Integrated, Centralized Interface to CA-7 & Other CA Solutions Which Utilize Viewpoint Option. Follows IBM's SAA/CUA Standards. Features Include Single Screen Control, Movable Windows, Pull-Down Menus, Choice Lists & Auto-Refresh Capabilities.
Computer Assocs. International, Inc.

CA-ShareOption/5. 1990. *Customer Support:* Support Agreement Available.
MVS. IBM S/370-390 (8Mb). Contact publisher for price.
Allows Sharing of VSAM Sets Without Changes to Applications. Provides Continuous Availability of VSAM Data. Reads/Updates Datasets from Batch During On-Line Processing Windows. Forward/Backward Recovery Facilities Enlarge Batch Window by Eliminating Need for Daily Full-File Backups.
Computer Assocs. International, Inc.

CA-Sort. 1971. *Customer Support:* Support Agreement Available.
MVS, VSE, VM. IBM S/370 & 390. Contact publisher for price.
Full IBM Sort Capability. Include/Omit Record Selection, Multi-Sort Facility & In-Core Sort Capability. Supports 31-Bit Addressing. VSE Version Has Direct Interface with CA-Dynam Family of Products. Includes CA-Dart. MVS Version Interfaces to CA-Examine & CA-Blockmaster.
Computer Assocs. International, Inc.

CA-Spoolman. 1988. *Customer Support:* Support Agreement Available.
VM. IBM S/370 & 390. Contact publisher for price.
Spool Management Facility. Provides Realtime Monitoring & Viewing Capabilities of VM Spool Activity. Allows Multiple, Authorized Users to View Operator Console Log in Realtime & with Search Capabilities Including Ability to Scroll Backward/Forward Through Operator Console Log. Provides Security Interfaces to CA-ACF2 & CA-Top Secret.
Computer Assocs. International, Inc.

CA-SRAM. 1971. *Customer Support:* Support Agreement Available.
MVS. IBM S/370-390. Contact publisher for price.
Sort Re-Entrant Access Method Allows Multiple Sorts to Be Processed Concurrently. Permits Multiple Sort Calls from Single Application Program. Supports 31-Bit Addressing.
Computer Assocs. International, Inc.

CA-Stabilize/CICS. 1986. *Customer Support:* Support Agreement Available.
MVS, VSE. IBM S/370-390. Contact publisher for price.
Repairs Problems Including Corruption of CICS Management Modules or Control Blocks, Storage Violations, Loops & Abends. Provides On-Line or Batch Diagnostics for Each Error Detected.
Computer Assocs. International, Inc.

CA-SuperProject. *Compatible Hardware:* Any 286, 386 or 486 PC capable of running Microsoft Windows 3.0 or higher; SUN Solaris. *Operating System(s) Required:* PC-DOS/MS-DOS, Microsoft Windows; OS/2; SUN Solaris UNIX. *Memory Required:* 6000k. *Customer Support:* Available.
Contact publisher for price. *Networks supported:* Novell, 3COM, IBM Token Ring, Banyan. *Project Management & Presentation Tools.*

Includes Customizable Gantt, Cost/Resource, PERT & WBS Charts. Interactive GUI with Pull-Down Menus, Mouse Support & Hi-Res Graphics. WYSIWYG Reporting & Presentation Output. Supports Multiple Document Interface Allowing Multiple Views of Same Project or Different Projects Simultaneously. Includes Tool Bar with Icons, DDE, DLL, Macro Language, User-Defined Fields & Formulas.
Computer Assocs. International, Inc.

CA-SuperProject for DOS. 1983. *Compatible Hardware:* IBM PC, XT, AT, PS/2 & compatibles. *Operating System(s) Required:* MS-DOS. *Memory Required:* 640k. *Customer Support:* Available.
$649.00. *Networks supported:* Novell, 3COM, IBM Token Ring, Banyan.
Set of Project Management & Presentation Tools. Features Include Interactive Project Creation in PERT, Gantt & WBS Views, Pull-Down Menus, Assist Mode for Pro-Active Context-Sensitive Help & On-Line Tutorial. Provides User-Defined WYSIWYG Graphics, Preview to Screen, Multiple Outlines, Effort, Elapsed, Workday & Span Driven Tasks, Input & Tracking of Actuals.
Computer Assocs. International, Inc.

CA-SuperProject for VAX. 1992. *Items Included:* Documentation included. *Customer Support:* Available.
VAX/VMS. Digital VAX (2Mb). Contact vendor for price. *Networks supported:* Pathworks.
Project Management System Includes Graphics with Gantt, PERT/WBS & Cost-Resource Charts, Planning/Tracking Tools with Multiple Outlines & Input/Tracking of Actuals & Resource Management Functionality Including Cross-Project Resource Leveling. Allows Project Files to Be Moved from PC to VAX & Vice-Versa.
Computer Assocs. International, Inc.

CA-SymDump. 1988. *Customer Support:* Support Agreement Available.
MVS. IBM S/370-390. Contact publisher for price.
On-Line Facility Which Allows Users to Analyze CICS Transaction Dumps Symbolically & Use CA-InterTest to Resolve Problems. Presents Dumps Symbolically in Source Statement Format. Generates Automatic Breakpoint Display at Source Statement Which Triggered Abend.
Computer Assocs. International, Inc.

CA-System/Manager. 1978. *Customer Support:* Support Agreement Available.
VSE. IBM S/370-390. Contact publisher for price.
Integrated Disk & Tape Management System. Provides MVS-Like JCL Commands to Manage Tape & DASD Resources. Includes Catalog Management & Maintenance, Secondary Allocation, Pool Management & Dynamic Allocation. VSE/ESA Functionality Includes Dynamic Partition Execution & Data Space Exploitation.
Computer Assocs. International, Inc.

CA-Teleview. 1984. *Customer Support:* Support Agreement Available.
MVS. IBM S/370-390 (1.5Mb). Contact publisher for price.
VTAM Multi-Session Management Solution. Includes Concurrent Session Management of Large Numbers of Terminals & Applications, Optional Distributed Extension for Single Image Operation of Distributed Environment, Customizable Panels, Data Compression, Session Windowing & Real-Time Viewing of User's Screens from Monitoring Terminals.
Computer Assocs. International, Inc.

CA-Tellagraf. 1975. *Compatible Hardware:* DG AOS/VS, DEC VAX/VMS, HP9000-HP/UX, IBM MVS, VM/CMS, PC-DOS, SUN3-OS-3 SUN4OS-4, Sparc, Sparc II. *Items Included:* Documentation included. *Customer Support:* Available.
Contact vendor for price.
Graphics Software System with Multiple User-Interfaces. Provides Device & Industry-Standard Output Support Including CGM & PostScript. Includes Tables, Stock Market, Error, Management & Comparison Charts in 2D, 3D & Thematic Mapping. Axes Types Includes Linear, Log, Monthly, Boxed Date & Labeled Types. Provides SQL Access to Data in CA-DB, CA-Datacom & IBM DB2. Provides Rdb Access on Digital Platform.
Computer Assocs. International, Inc.

CA-Telon. 1981. *Customer Support:* Support Agreement Available.
MVS. IBM S/370-390. Contact publisher for price.
Supports Design, Prototyping, Rule-Based Generation & Testing for Development & Maintenance of MVS, CICS, IMS/DC, AS/400, UNIX, MS/DOS, OS/2 & VSE On-Line & Batch Target Applications on Mainframe or Workstation. Generates COBOL, COBOL II or PL/1 Code. Supports Data Access for IMS/DB, CA-IDMS, CA-Datacom, VSAM, Sequential & Variety of RDBMS.
Computer Assocs. International, Inc.

CA-Telon AS/400 Target Option. 1989. *Customer Support:* Support Agreement Available.
MVS, OS/2, DOS. IBM S/370-390; IBM PC & compatibles. Contact publisher for price.
Supports Development & Maintenance of On-Line & Batch COBOL/400 Applications for OS/400 Environment. Supports Design, Prototyping, Rule-Based Generation & Testing on Mainframe or Workstation.
Computer Assocs. International, Inc.

CA-Telon PWS. 1989. *Items Included:* Documentation included. *Customer Support:* Available.
MS-DOS, OS/2. IBM PC & compatibles (8Mb). Contact vendor for price.
Allows User to Design, Prototype, Generate & Test On-Line & Batch Programs for Development/Maintenance on Workstation for MVS, CICS, IMS/DC, AS/400, UNIX, VSE, PC-MS/DOS & OS/2 Target Applications. Generates COBOL, COBOL II & PL/1 Code. Supports Data Access for IMS/DC, CA-IDMS, CA-Datacom, VSAM & Variety of RDBMs. Includes Testing & Debugging Capabilities.
Computer Assocs. International, Inc.

CA-Telon UNIX Target Option. 1994. *Customer Support:* Available.
DOS, OS/2; MVS. IBM PC, PS/2 & compatibles; IBM S370-390. Contact publisher for price.
Supports Development & Maintenance of On-Line & Batch COBOL Applications for UNIX Target Environments. Supports Design, Prototyping, Rule-Based Generation & Testing on Mainframe or Workstation.
Computer Assocs., International, Inc.

CA-Telon VSE Target Option. 1994. *Customer Support:* Support Agreement Available.
MVS, OS/2, DOS. IBM S/370-390; IBM PC & compatibles. Contact publisher for price.
Provides the Ability to Generate COBOL & PL/1 Application Programs That Can Execute in a VSE Environment. Applications Can Be Designed, Prototpyed, Generated & Tested Using CA-Telon. The Application Can Then Be Transmitted to the VSE Environment for Execution.
Computer Assocs. International, Inc.

CA-Top Secret. 1981. *Customer Support:* Support Agreement Available.
MVS, VSE, VM. IBM S/370-390. Contact publisher for price.
Provides Access Control to Protect Your Computer Data from Accidental or Deliberate Destruction, Modification, Disclosure and/or Misuse. Allows You to Control Who Uses Your Computer Resources, & Provides You with All the Facts to Monitor Your Security Policy Effectively. Attempts to Access Unauthorized Resources Are Automatically Denied & Logged. Any Authorized Use of Sensitive Resources May Also Be Logged for Subsequent Review. Logging, Reporting & Online Monitoring Capabilities Give You or Other Authorized Personnel a Range of Opportunitites to Analyze & Evaluate Computer Access Activities & Trends. An Optional VSE/ESA Feature Further Exploits VSE/ESA, Providing VSE/ESA Data Space Support, the Ability to Monitor Activity in Both Static & Dynamic Partitions, & Support for Transaction Routing Between CICS Regions Active in Static or Dynamic Partitions, Regardless of Address Space.
Computer Assocs. International, Inc.

CA-Top Secret/PC-PC Only Option. *Customer Support:* Available.
PC-DOS/MS-DOS. Contact publisher for price.
Enforces Individual Accountability & Prevention of Unauthorized Use Through User Sign-On. Protects Directories, Files & Programs. Controls System Prompt User & Restricts DOS Commands. Enables User to Create Customized User Menus. Logs Selected Computer Activity in Security Reports. Includes MS-Windows Application for Security Administration.
Computer Associates International, Inc.

CA-Top Secret/DB2. 1991. *Customer Support:* Support Agreement Available.
MVS. IBM S/370-390 (46k). Contact publisher for price.
Protects DB2 Databases, Table Spaces, Tables, Views, Plans, Packages, Collections, Elements & Management Functions & Utilities Using CA-Top Secret Structures & Administrative & Reporting Tools. Provides Auditing Facilities. Enables Separation of DBA & Security Functions. Centralizes Security for Multiple DB2 Subsystems. Eliminates DB2 Revoke Cascade Effect. Supports DB2 Distributed Data Facility. Includes DB2 Catalog to CA-Top Secret Security Migration Tools & Automated Synchronization Facility.
Computer Assocs. International, Inc.

CA-Top Secret/PC. 1993. *Customer Support:* Available.
MS-DOS, PC-DOS. IBM AT, XT, PS/2 or compatibles (256k). Contact Vendor. *Addl. software required:* CA-Top Secret MVS. Optimal configuration: 10Mb hard disk, one 360k or 720k diskette drive.
Provides Centralized Mainframe Control & Validation of PC Sign-Ons & PC to Mainframe Connection. Allows Single Point Registration & True Single-Sign on of Multi-Platform Users. Provides Security for PC Resources Including Files, Directories, Programs, Commands & DOS Prompts. Offers Standardized, Automated Installation, & Maintenance & Audit from CA-Top Secret MVS Product.
Computer Assocs. International, Inc.

CA-Top Secret/Secman for VAX. 1989. *Items Included:* Documentation included. *Customer Support:* Available.
MVS, Digital VAX/VMS. IBM System 370/390 Architecture; Digital VAX (500k). Contact vendor for price. *Addl. software required:* CA-TOP SECRET MVS; Digital VAX/VMS; DECnet SNA gateway with 3270 Data Streaming, Interlink connection, or a protocol

converter with VT100 emulation.
Provides Integrated Security Administration for Sites in Mixed IBM MVS & DEC VAX/VMS Network. Enables Use of Single-User ID Throughout System. Allows Security Administrator to Use Standard CA-Top Secret MVS Facilities to Define User Sign-On & Resource Access Controls for VAX/VMS Network. Consolidates Auditing of Both Environments & Enhances Native VAX/VMS Security.
Computer Assocs. International, Inc.

CA-Top Secret/Viewpoint. 1993. *Customer Support:* Support Agreement Available.
MVS. IBM S/370-390 (4Mb). Contact publisher for price.
Windowed User Interface Option to CA-Top Secret Based on IBM's SAA/CUA Standards. Provides Multi-Windowed View under a Single Screen. Enables Simplified Navigation to CA-Top Secret Information & Direct On-Screen Modification of ACID & Resource Definitions & System Options. Incorporates On-Line Documentation & Integrated Security.
Computer Assocs. International, Inc.

CA-Transit. 1977. *Customer Support:* Support Agreement Available.
MVS, VSE. IBM S/370-390 (1.5Mb). Contact publisher for price.
Non-IBM-to-IBM Conversion Aid. Handles Preconversion Analysis & Reporting, Program & Copybook Translation, Program & Data Translation, JCL Generation & Management Reporting. Coordinated Program/Data Translation, Status/Cross-Reference Reporting, Customization & Program/JCL Standardization.
Computer Assocs. International, Inc.

CA-Traps. 1986. *Customer Support:* Available.
PC-DOS. IBM PC, XT, AT, PS/2 & compatibles (300k). Contact Vendor. *Networks supported:* Novell, 3Com, Token-Ring, All NETBIOS LANs are supported for storage or execution.
Automates Software Testing & Provides Early Detection of Defects. Compares Responses from Both System & Application Programs, Prototype Applications, Views Mismatches in Data, Cursor Positioning & Color, Measures End-to-End Response Times, Changes Test Scripts & Automatically Play Back Test Cases. Includes Security Functions & Management Reporting Facility Documents.
Computer Assocs. International, Inc.

CA-Ucandu. 1972. *Customer Support:* Support Agreement Available.
MVS. IBM S/370-390 (48k). Contact publisher for price.
Utility for Selective Copying, Dumping or Listing of Datasets, Generation of Test Datasets, Backup & Restore of Datasets, Reorganization and/or Backup of ISAM Files & Random Record Selection. Provides Editing, Field Modification & Tallying.
Computer Assocs. International, Inc.

CA-UFO. 1976. *Customer Support:* Support Agreement Available.
MVS, VSE, VM. IBM S/370-390. Contact publisher for price.
4GL for Developing On-Line Applications. Provides Active Dictionary & Screen Painting Facility. Creates Models of Applications & Test Datasets Before Code Is Written. Integrates Nonprocedural & Procedural Development Approaches. Includes Field Level Validation Capability & On-Line Debugger.
Computer Assocs. International, Inc.

CA-Unicenter. 1992. *Items Included:* Documentation included. *Customer Support:* Maintenance & training available.
HP-UX, OS/2, Windows NT Solaris, AIX, DYNIX/ptx, SVR4, Guardian, DG-UX, UNIX, Netware, OS/400. Hewlett-Packard model 9000, Series 800, SunSPARC, IBM RS/6000, Sequent Symmetry, AT&T GIS, DG AVIION, Pyramid MisServer, Siemens (32Mb). Contact vendor for price.
Integrated Systems Management Solution for Client/Server Environments Which Provides File Backup & Archive, Tape Management, Problem Management, User & Resource Security, Resource Accounting & Chargeback, Performance Monitoring, Workload Scheduling, Report Management, Event Management & Spool Controls.
Computer Assocs. International, Inc.

CA-Unicenter/Agent Factory. *Customer Support:* Available.
HP-UX, AIX, SCO/ODT, DYNIX/ptx, Solaris, SunOS. Contact publisher for price.
Development Environment for Building Extensible Agents for Distributed Enterprise Management. Enables Users to Develop CA-Unicenter Agents for the Remote Monitoring & Control of IT Resources Enterprise-Wide.
Computer Associates International, Inc.

CA-Unicenter/AHD Advanced Help Desk. *Customer Support:* Available.
Server: HP-UX, Solaris, AIX; Client: Windows NT, Windows, OS/2 WARP. Contact publisher for price.
Automates Help Desk Service Tasks to Reduce Service Response Time, Ensure the Availability of Enterprise-Wide Resources, & Optimize Responses to User Requests.
Computer Associates International, Inc.

CA-Unicenter/DB Alert. *Customer Support:* Available.
SunOS, Solaris, AIX, HP-UX. Contact publisher for price.
Implementation of CA-Unicenter/Systems Alert, Allows Users to Monitor Databases & Database Applications. Provides View of Status & Condition of Database Resources & Database-Based Applications Throughout Network. Identifies Changes in Status That Threaten Service Levels & Notifies Operator. Lets Users Access Remote Database Systems, Gather Information & Take Pre-Defined Actions for Problem Resolution.
Computer Associates International, Inc.

CA-Unicenter/OSM Open Storage Manager. *Customer Support:* Available.
HP-UX, Solaris, AIX. Contact publisher for price.
Employs Advanced Hierarchical Storage Management Methods to Increase Disk Storage Capacity.
Computer Associates International, Inc.

CA-Unicenter/Software Delivery. *Customer Support:* Available.
SunOS, Solaris, AIX, HP-UX. Contact publisher for price.
Application for Management & Distribution of Software & Data from a Central Point Across a Network of Multi-Vendor Systems. Automates Delivery, Installation, Activation & Removal of Software Packages. Includes Versioning, Which Allows Distribution of Only Changes Between Releases.
Computer Associates International, Inc.

CA-Unicenter/Systems Alert. *Customer Support:* Available.
SunOS, Solaris, AIX, HP-UX. Contact publisher for price.
Distributed Client/Server Application Based on Manager/Agent Architecture. Provides Central Monitoring & Control of IT Services in Multi-Vendor Networked Systems. Monitors Applications, File Systems, OS, Queries, & Devices. Executes Pre-Defined Actions to Resolve Problems, Either Automated or Interactive.
Computer Associates International, Inc.

CA-Unicenter/TNG. *Customer Support:* Available.
WindowsNT, OS/2, UNIX, OS/400, DOS. Contact publisher for price.
Integrated Object-Oriented Systems Management Solution for Client/Server Environments Which Provides File Backup & Archive, Tape Management, Problem Management, User & Resource Security, Resource Accounting & Chargeback, Performance Monitoring, Workload Scheduling, Report Management, Event Management & Spool Controls.
Computer Associates International, Inc.

CA-Unicenter for VMS. 1993. *Customer Support:* Available.
VAX/VMS. Digital. Contact publisher for price.
Provides Full Data Center Automation Functionality Encompassing the Areas of Automated Production Control, Automated Storage Management, Data Center Administration, & Performance Management & Accounting.
Computer Assocs., International, Inc.

CA-Unicenter/II. 1985. *Customer Support:* Support Agreement Available.
MVS, VSE, VM; VAX/VMS. IBM S/370-390; Digital. Contact publisher for price.
Data Center Automation & Management. Includes CA Production Control, Performance Measurement & Accounting, Security Control & Auditing, Storage & Resource Management & MVS & VSE Data Center Administration Mainframe Software. VAX/VMS Version Provides System Managers with Full Data Center Automation Functionality in Areas of Automated Production Control, Automated Storage Management, Data Center Administration & Performance Management & Accounting.
Computer Assocs. International, Inc.

CA-Unicenter SSO Single Sign-On. *Customer Support:* Available.
Windows (client); HP-UX, AIX, Solaris (server). Contact publisher for price.
Allows Single Sign-On Access for Microsoft Windows Users to UNIX, Windows, & Mainframe-Based Network Applications. Single Network Sign-On Provided via CA-Unicenter Security Server. Application Access via Dynamic Icon Container. CA-ACF2 & CA-Top Secret Token Management, IBM Pass Tickets & Other Ticketing Schemes Supported. Policy Auditing & Automatic Violation Notification Provided.
Computer Associates International, Inc.

CA-Unicenter/STAR. 1994. *Customer Support:* Support Agreement Available.
OS/2. IBM PC & compatibles (16Mb). Contact publisher for price.
Integrated Systems Management Client Application for Administering CA-Unicenter Servers Throughout Heterogeneous, Distributed Environment. Provides Common GUI to Shield Administrators from Complexities of Underlying Platforms. Enables Distributed Management, While Enforcing Consistent Image of Management Policies.
Computer Assocs. International, Inc.

CA-Verify. 1985. *Customer Support:* Support Agreement Available.
MVS, VSE. IBM S/370-390 (30k). Contact publisher for price.

CA-VERIFY/EEO

Automated CICS Quality Assurance Testing Tool Which Performs Unit, Regression, Stress, Concurrency, Migration & System Testing. Logs Screen Outputs & Inputs into Test Cases. Allows Use in Batch & On-Line Mode.
Computer Assocs. International, Inc.

CA-Verify/EEO. 1990. *Customer Support:* Support Agreement Available.
MVS. IBM S/370-390. Contact publisher for price.
Automates Unites, Regression, Stress, Concurrency, Migration & System Testing for All MVS On-Line Applications. Streamlines Testing of New Modified Applications by Logging Screen Inputs & Outputs into Test Cases.
Computer Assocs. International, Inc.

CA-VISA: VAX Integrated System Administration. 1991. *Items Included:* Documentation included. *Customer Support:* Available.
Digital VAX/VMS. Digital VAX (8Mb). Contact vendor for price.
VAX Integrated System Administration. Supports User Account Management, Process Management, Identifier Management, Disk Quota Management & Queue Management. Provides Interface That Streamlines System Management for Novice & Expert System Managers.
Computer Assocs. International, Inc.

CA-Visual Express. 1994. *Customer Support:* Support Agreement Available.
Windows. IBM PC & compatibles (4Mb). Contact publisher for price.
Client/Server Access, Query & Reporting with Intuitive & Scalable Interface Accommodating Wide Range of User Skills & Query Complexities. Transparent Support for ODBC, Optional Data Servers & Personal Database Provide Users with Enterprise-Wide Information Access to Relational & Non-Relational Sources.
Computer Assocs. International, Inc.

CA-Visual Express/Easytrieve Server. 1993. *Customer Support:* Support Agreement Available.
MVS, Windows. IBM S/370-390; IBM PC & compatibles (2Mb). Contact publisher for price.
Enables CA-Easytrieve Users to Access Data on Multiple Platforms & Feed Results to CA-Visual Express or Any Other Windows Application. Supports Microsoft ODBC Standards for Distributed Processing & Provides Access to Non-Relational Data Sources, Such As VSAM & IMS. Includes GUI Client/Server Access, Reporting & Decision Support.
Computer Assocs. International, Inc.

CA-Visual Express/Host Server. 1993. *Customer Support:* Support Agreement Available.
MVS, Windows. IBM S/370-390; IBM PC & compatibles (2Mb). Contact publisher for price.
Enables Windows End-Users to Access All Critical Corporate Data on Multiple Platforms & Feed Results Directly into CA-Visual Express or Any Other Windows Application. Open DataBase Connectivity (ODBC) Is Provided via Servers for Both CA-IDMS & CA-Datacom. Includes Programming Language for Access to Non-Relational Data Sources, Such As VSAM, IMS & Sequential Files.
Computer Assocs. International, Inc.

CA-Visual Objects. *Customer Support:* Available.
Windows. Contact publisher for price.
Xbase Based Fully Object-Oriented Language. Native Code Compiler Integrated with GUI Development Environment for Windows Application Development. Replaceable Database Drivers for Network/Stand-Alone Applications. ODBC Drivers for Client/Server Applications. Visual Editing Tools for Forms, Menus, Icons, Reports, Databases (DBF/SQL) & Fields.
Computer Associates International, Inc.

CA-Visual Objects Lite. *Customer Support:* Available.
Windows. Contact publisher for price.
Xbase Based Fully Object-Oriented Language. Geared Towards Object-Oriented Xbase Windows Application Development for Network/Standalone Applications. Native Code Compiler Integrated with GUI Development Environment for Windows Application Development. Does Not Include the Enterprise Database Access Components of CA-Visual Objects: CA-RET, ODBC Drivers, & the Class Libraries That Accompany Them. Upgradeable to CA-Visual Objects.
Computer Associates International, Inc.

CA-Visual Objects SDK. *Customer Support:* Available.
Windows. Contact publisher for price.
Enables Developers to Create Integrated Add-On Tools Such As Source Editors, Business Graphics & Multimedia Editors to Enhance Functionality of CA-Visual Development Environment & Provide Access to New Database Formats. Includes APIs for IDE, RDD, Item, & Error Subsystems.
Computer Associates International, Inc.

CA-Visual Realia. 1994. *Customer Support:* Support Agreement Available.
Windows. IBM PC & compatibles (8Mb). Contact publisher for price.
Integrated Toolset for Developing GUI Client/Server COBOL Application. Uses COBOL for Business Logic & GUI Windows Tools for User Interface. Forms Editor Simplifies Creation of Standard Windows Elements. Provides Access to Local & Host Databases. Includes over 20 ODBC Database Drivers.
Computer Assocs. International, Inc.

CA-Visual Telon. *Customer Support:* Available.
Windows. Contact publisher for price.
Tool for Developing Enterprise-Level Distributed Applications. Provides GUI Applications for End-Users & Provides Developers with Choice of Architectures for Distributing Applications for End-Users & Provides Developers with Choice of Architectures for Distributing Applications in Client/Server Environments. Integrated Visual Development Environment Gives Developers Set of Tools Similar to That Used for Rapid Application Generation.
Computer Associates International, Inc.

CA-Vivid. 1990. *Items Included:* Documentation included. *Customer Support:* Available.
VAX/VMS. Contact vendor for price.
Creates Business Graphs/Charts for Reports, Analysis & Presentations. Supports More Than 30 Types of Graphs/Charts. Hold up to 16 Data Series per Graph & up to 10,000 Data Points per Data Series. Accommodates Headlines, Bulleted Lists & Tables. Generates X-Y Plots, Scatter Diagrams & Free Form Drawings. Incorporates into Slide Show Presentations.
Computer Assocs. International, Inc.

CA-Vman. 1987. *Customer Support:* Support Agreement Available.
MVS. IBM S/370-390 (4Mb). Contact publisher for price.
MVS/VTAM Network & Session Manager. Allows Single or Multi-Session Mode Selection by Terminal or User. Provides Single-Entry Point to VTAM, Menu Selection of Network Applications & Security Interfaces. Enables Single-Point Sign-On Capabilities Through Cross-System VMAN Communication. Generates VTAM & NCP Parameters.
Computer Assocs. International, Inc.

CA-VMLib. 1980. *Customer Support:* Support Agreement Available.
VM. IBM S/370-390 (2Mb). Contact publisher for price.
Library Management & Change Control System for CMS. Provides Centralized File Management of & Tracks Changes to Files Accessed by Multiple Users. Manages Development Process from Initial Coding Through Testing, Validation & Production.
Computer Assocs. International, Inc.

CA-Vollie. 1977. *Customer Support:* Support Agreement Available.
VSE. IBM S/370-390. Contact publisher for price.
On-Line Program Development/Production System for Native VSE & VSE Guests under VM. Allows User to Create, Maintain & Submit Jobs, Display Queues & Act As Alternate System Console. Includes Multiple Window Display, Full-Screen Editor, XEDIT Line Editing Commands, Direct Access to VM, On-Line Access to VSE Libraries/Sublibraries & Self-Reorganizing, Maintenance-Free Library System.
Computer Assocs. International, Inc.

CA-Vterm. 1981. *Customer Support:* Support Agreement Available.
VM. IBM S/370-390 (4Mb). Contact publisher for price.
Virtual Terminal Support for IBM VM/CMS. Allows 16 Simultaneous Sessions from One Terminal. Includes Conversational Procedural Language, Data Compression, Color & VSE/VTAM Support. Duplex Facility Allows 2 Users to Work on Same Session. Provides On-Line Screens to Alter Environment & Options & Includes Screen SEND/PRINT Facility.
Computer Assocs. International, Inc.

CA-Warehouse Boss. 1989. *Customer Support:* Support Agreement Available.
OS/400. AS/400 (8Mb). Contact publisher for price.
Warehouse Management System. Controls All Warehouse Operations, Including Receiving, Putaway, Order Management, Picking & Shipping. Supports Activity-Based Random Locating, System Directed RF Picking & Putaway, Automatic Replenishment, Lot Tracking, Bar Code Reading Equipment, ANSI X12.10 EDI Ship Notice/Manifest.
Computer Assocs. International, Inc.

CA-1 for VAX. 1991. *Items Included:* Documentation included. *Customer Support:* Available.
VAX/VMS. Digital VAX (2Mb). Contact vendor for price.
Tape Management System Providing Protection Against Inadvertent Destruction of Tape Files. Provides Management Controls & Comprehensive Reporting. Features Scratch Pools, Tape Retention & Protection, TMSTIQ Interface, Audit Trail, Relational Database Support, Automated Device Selection, Optical Support, VMS BACKUP Command Support & Image & File Level Disk Backup & Restore.
Computer Assocs. International, Inc.

CA-7 for VAX. 1991. *Items Included:* Documentation included. *Customer Support:* Available.
VAX/VMS. Digital VAX (2Mb). Contact vendor for price.
Automates Scheduling by Addressing Accurate & Complete Work Load Definition, Work Load Processing Management, Performance Tracking & Reporting & Work Load Planning. Workloads May Be Scheduled Based on Calendar and/or System Events. Provides Automatic Job Selection, Facilities for Simulation & Forecasting, Advanced DCL Functionality & On-Line Inquiry/Update Capabilities.
Computer Assocs. International, Inc.

TITLE INDEX

Cabri: The Interactive Geometry Notebook.
Yves Baulac et al. 1992. *Items Included:* One 3 1/2" disk & a paperback "Guide to Cabri". *Customer Support:* Unlimited technical support to registered users.
  MS-DOS 3.1 or higher. IBM or compatibles (640k). disk $50.00 (ISBN 0-534-17586-4, Order no.: 800-354-9706). *Nonstandard peripherals required:* Mouse is recommended but not required; compatible with most graphics cards, prints on all types of matrix printers, HP Laserjet, & standard HPGL plotters. *Optimal configuration:* Mouse is recommended but not required.
  Site license avail. $400.00 (ISBN 0-534-17587-2).
  Macintosh. Macintosh 4.0 or higher (500k). 3.5" disk $97.25 (ISBN 0-534-17058-7, Order no.: 800-354-9706).
  Site license avail. $300.00 (ISBN 0-534-17059-5).
  Allows Users to Construct Precise Figures from Basic Geometric Components, Control the Graphical Look of Geometric Elements with the Click of a Mouse, Save & Reuse Macros for Creating Complex Geometric Constructions, & Manipulate Geometric Figures & Watch All Related Parts & Measure Quantities Update Continuously.
Brooks/Cole Publishing Co.

CAche. *Version:* 3.0. *Customer Support:* Toll free telephone support.
  DOS 3.1 or higher. IBM PC & compatibles. disk $595.00.
  This Solution is a Personal Tumor Registry That Closely Resembles Traumatix in Principle. It Uses 690 Different ICD-9-CM Diagnostic Codes in Storage, Including Benign, In-situ & Hematological Neoplasia. T, N, M & Staging Date are Recorded. Then the Appropriate Morphology Code is Picked from 674. Tumor Grading Follows. Next, Therapy Goals & Treatments are Recorded. Finally, Patient Response is Registered -- Based on Karnofsky's Performance Classification.
SRC Systems, Inc.

Cache86 for DOS. *Version:* 4.13g. Oct. 1991. *Language(s):* Assembly. *Items Included:* Manual & diskette. *Customer Support:* Telephone support, 9-5 M-F CST; 30 day moneyback guarantee.
  PC-DOS/MS-DOS (64K). IBM & compatibles. $49.95. *Optimal configuration:* PC-DOS 2.1 or higher.
  Fastest, Safest, Most Memory Efficient Disk Cache Program. Increase Productivity - Cache86 Speeds up Data Transfer. Write Back & Write Through Are Available at the User's Option. In Expanded Memory, a 4Mb Cache Can Use As Little As 1k of Conventional Memory. Includes Benchmark Program to Measure System Performance & Memory Map Utility.
The Aldridge Co.

Cache86 for Windows & DOS. *Version:* 6.0. Feb. 1994. *Items Included:* 1 manual, diskette. *Customer Support:* Telephone technical support 9-5 Central Time M-F, 30 day money back guarantee.
  PC-DOS/MS-DOS 2.0 or higher. IBM & compatibles (64k). disk $89.95. *Optimal configuration:* IBM compatible 486, MS DOS 6.0, 16Mb RAM, memory manager.
  Windows, PC-DOS/MS-DOS 4.0 w/Windows 3.1 or higher. IBM & compatibles (4Mb). disk $89.95. *Addl. software required:* Memory manager. *Optimal configuration:* Pentium w/ Windows, DOS 6.0, 32Mb RAM, memory manager (QEMM, 386 Max, Himen-Sys).
  The Windows Accelerator Controllable On-the-Fly. The Smallest, Fastest Disk Cache Program Speeds up Your System & Graphically Displays Statistics Including Real Time Gauges of System Performance Improvement. Reconfigure, Disable, Re-Enable & Flush the Cache from Within Windows.
The Aldridge Co.

Cactus League Baseball. *Compatible Hardware:* Atari 400, 800. *Language(s):* Atari BASIC. *Memory Required:* 40k. *General Requirements:* 2 joysticks.
  disk $19.95.
  2-Player Baseball.
Dynacomp, Inc.

The CAD - CAM Starter Kit. Edited by Patrick D. Halloran. Nov. 1994. *Items Included:* 2 manuals, 2 diskettes.
  DOS 3.3. 80286 w/coprocessor, EGA, 7Mb HD, HD Floppy (2Mb). disk $100.00 (ISBN 1-887777-02-4). *Nonstandard peripherals required:* Mouse. *Optimal configuration:* 486, 4Mb RAM, DOS 6.X, VGA, 15"-17" monitor, laser printer.
  An Inexpensive Means to Explore CAD/CAM (Computer Aided Design/Computer Aided Manufacturing). It Is a Functional, Educational Oriented System Designed to Introduce & Teach CAD/CAM, the Principles & Processes Involved, & Answers the Questions; What Is CAD/CAM & How Does It Work.
Datacut, Inc.

CAD-Access. *Version:* 3.2. *Compatible Hardware:* IBM PC & compatibles; Unix - Hewlett Packard, Apollo & Sun. *Items Included:* IGES & Direct Read modules. *Customer Support:* Yes.
  $2500.00 & up.
  Mechanical Drafting & Design Program Allowing Access to All Major CAD Systems for Non-Designers, Management & Engineers Including View, Mark-Up, Plus & Professional Tools.
Xysys, Inc.

CAD for Linear & Planar Antenna Arrays of Various Radiating Elements. Aleksander Nesic & Miodrag Mikavica. Oct. 1991. *Items Included:* 200 page user's manual.
  IBM PC compatible. disk $300.00 (ISBN 0-89006-567-5, Order no.: C1U567).
  This Practical Software Program Allows for the Fast & Accurate Design & Analysis of Linear & Two Dimensional Planar Arrays. It Delivers Comprehensive Coverage of Linear & Planar Antenna Arrays, Including a Variety of Element Types, Excitations, Ground Interference & Random Error Effects.
Artech Hse., Inc.

CAD-1+. *Version:* 1.1. 1982. *Compatible Hardware:* Apple II, IIe, IIgs. *Language(s):* Assembler. *Memory Required:* 128k. *Items Included:* Software, manual, interface module. *Customer Support:* 800 number technical support.
  disk $695.00.
  Design & Drafting System. Includes Rubber Banding, Angle Locks, Grids, & Mirroring.
Robo Systems International, Inc.

CADKEY, 7 disks. *Version:* 7.0. 1994. *Compatible Hardware:* IBM PC, 386 & 486 & compatibles. *Operating System(s) Required:* MS-DOS 3.3 or higher, UNIX. *Language(s):* C. *Memory Required:* 8000k. *General Requirements:* Hard disk. Graphics card & 8087/80287 coprocessor recommended. *Customer Support:* 30 day free.
  disk $495.00, incl. user reference manual, customization guide, & hardware setup bklt.
  Integrated 2-D & True 3-D Computer-Aided Design & Drafting System for the Personal Computer. There Are Currently over 90,000 Installed CADKEY Systems Worldwide in Applications Such As Mechanical Engineering, Tooling, Drafting & Other Manufacturing & Design Areas in the Naval, Aerospace & Automotive Industries. Features Include: True Three-Dimensional Geometric Modeling, Compliance with ANSI & ISO Drafting Standards, Precision Accuracy, & a Three-Dimensional Programming Language (CADL) Which Provides Virtually Unlimited Links to Applications Programs Including Numerical Control, Finite Element Analysis, Desktop Publishing, Mesh Generation, Multiple Viewports, Construction Planes, Tolerance & Clearance Checking, etc.
Cadkey, Inc.

CADKEY Advanced Modeler. *Version:* 7.0. 1994. *Items Included:* Manual. *Customer Support:* 30 day free technical support.
  IBM. MS-DOS 3.3 or higher. IBM PC, 386, 486 & compatibles. disk $1250.00 (Order no.: D025-3500). *Addl. software required:* Cadkey 7.
  DOS 3.3 & higher. PCs. *Addl. software required:* Cadkey 7.
  Powerful Easy-to-Use Solids Modeling Tool. Features Include Calculation of Mass Properties, Boolean Operations, Smooth Shading & More. Engineers & Designers Can Now Create Solids Models from Wireframe Designs, Verify Design Integrity, Analyze Input Geometry Errors & Output Solids Models In CADL Format, Which Is Compatible with over 200 Third Party Programs Including FEA, Numerical Control, Sheet Metal Foldout & More.
Cadkey, Inc.

CADlab. *Compatible Hardware:* Apple IIe; IBM PC, PC XT, PC AT. *Memory Required:* IBM PC 360k; PC XT & AT 640k.
  disk $1000.00 to $1500.00 copy protected.
  Designed As a Teaching Tool. Trains Students in the Use of Any CAD System. Networkable on Cascade Speedlink.
Cascade Graphics Systems.

CADleaf Plus. *Version:* 3.0. Jul. 1992. *Compatible Hardware:* Sun; SPARC; HP workstations; IBM-RS-6000 & DEC. *Customer Support:* 90 days unlimited warranty.
  Contact publisher. *Addl. software required:* Motif/X-Windows.
  Software Product for Converting, Viewing, & Redlining CAD Files into Several Desktop Publishing Formats. Lets User Monitor the Translation Process as It Occurs. Also Lets User Convert Any CAD or Drawing Program That Exports IGES, HPGL, CalComp960, AutoCAD, or CGM Format into CGM, EPSI, Sun Raster, CCI TT GP4, TIFF Interleaf, or Framemaker Format.
Carberry Technology, Inc.

CADMAX 3D. *Compatible Hardware:* IBM PC & compatibles. *Customer Support:* Yes.
  disk $3950.00.
  Includes 2-D, 3-D & Wire-Frame Features.
Vector Automation, Inc.

CADMAX TrueSurf. *Version:* 4.0. *Compatible Hardware:* 80386-based computers. *Customer Support:* Yes.
  disk $4750.00.
  Mechanical Design Package Including 2-D & 3-D Capabilities.
Vector Automation, Inc.

CADMover. *Version:* 3.4. *Compatible Hardware:* Apple Macintosh Plus or higher. *Items Included:* Program & user manual. *Customer Support:* (703) 532-0213.
  3.5" disk $495.00.
  Vector Graphics Translation Utility. Creates Connectivity Between Mainframes, Workstations,

PC's & the Macintosh. Translation Options
Include Multiple Layers & Levels, Multiple
Drawings Within a File. Scaling Between Most
Formats. Unit Measurement Conversion (Metric
to English Standard etc.). Unlimited File Size with
Use of a Hard Disk & Full Color. System 7.0
Compatible.
Kandu Software Corp.

CADPAK. *Items Included:* Bound manual.
Customer Support: Free hotline - no time limit; 30
day limited warranty; updates are $5/disk plus
S&H.
MS-DOS. IBM & compatibles (256k). disk
$119.95. *Nonstandard peripherals required:*
Color-graphics card or digitizer & a graphic
printer or plotter are recommended.
Computer (CADD) Program for First-Pass or
Conceptual Design & Drafting Creates 2-D
Drawings.
Dynacomp, Inc.

CADPAK-64 Enhanced. *Version:* 2.0. Roy
Wainwright. 1984. *Compatible Hardware:*
Commodore 64. *Memory Required:* 64k.
disk $39.95 (ISBN 0-916439-18-6, Order no.:
770).
Graphics Design & Drawing Package. User Can
Create Detailed Designs with Dimensioning,
Scaling, Text, Rotating, etc. Can Be Used with or
Without a Lightpen.
Abacus.

CadPLUS 3D. *Version:* 12.13. Nov. 1995. *Items
Included:* Manual, 120-day free maintenance.
Customer Support: 1 yr. maintenance for $200.
MS-DOS, Windows/NT (16Mb). disk $795.00.
Addl. software required: AutoCAD Release 12
or 13.
A Comprehensive Architectural Drafting,
Detailing, & Scheduling Software Inside
AutoCAD. It Offers Seamless Integration among
All A/E Disciplines Such As Architectural, Facility
Management, Structural, Civil, Mechanical,
Electrical, Fire Protection, etc. Also Incorporates
an Extensive Library of Pre-Drawn Details. Its
Universal Scheduler Offers Complete Take-Off
Reports for Any Items in the Drawing.
Research Engineers.

**CADRA Design Drafting Mechanical Design
Software.** *Version:* 9.2. Jul. 1994. *Items
Included:* Manuals included: a two volume users
guide & a installation & systems manager guide.
Customer Support: 90 day warranty on software,
maintenance available at 1%/month of software
list price, variety of training available either on-
site or at an Adra Training Center. All customers
with a maintenance contract receive hot line
support & software updates.
ULTRIX 4.1 & 4.2, SUN O/S, SUN Solaris, HP-
UX, SGI/IRIX, AIX, DEC ALPHA NT, DEC
ALPHA OSF, Windows 3.1, Windows NT.
DECstation 3100 & 5000; SUN Workstations;
Silicon Graphics Workstation; HP 700 Series;
IBM RS6000; DEC ALPHA; IBM Compatible
PCs. $5995.00 (CADRA-III). *Optimal
configuration:* Any of the above, 16Mb,
300Mb disk, mouse, 19" color monitor.
Networks supported: NFS, TCP/IP, Novell.
MS-DOS 3.3 & higher, Windows 3.1, Windows
NT. IBM compatible, 386 & 486 (8Mb).
$3995.00 (CADRA Design Drafting for
Personal Computers). *Nonstandard peripherals
required:* VGA or SVGA graphics. *Optimal
configuration:* 486, MS-DOS 6.0, 8Mb, mouse,
SVGA Graphics, 19" color monitor, hard disk
drive. *Networks supported:* TCP/IP, Novell,
PathWorks.
Specifically for Design & Drafting Professionals &
Features Advanced Graphics Techniques to
Maximize Performance for the Creation of
Production Engineering Drawings. Has Several
Options Which Extend Its Flexibility in the Design-
Drafting Area. This Includes: CADRA-Raster,
CADRA-3D, Autogeometry Programming
Language, ADT, IGES, DWG, DXF Data
Exchange & Plotting Capabilities Software
Supports the UNIX DOS & Windows Operating
Systems & Runs on a Variety of High-
Performance Workstations & 386 & 486 Based
Personal Computers.
Adra Systems, Inc.

**CADRA-NC: Numerical Control Graphics
Programming Language.** *Version:* 9.2. May
1994. *Items Included:* Manuals included: User's
Guide, Installation guide. *Customer Support:* 90
day warranty on software, maintenance available
at 1%/month of software list price, variety of
training available either on-site or at Adra
Training Center. All customers with a maintenance
contract receive hot line support & software
updates.
ULTRIX 4.1 & 4.2, SUN O/S, SUN Solaris, HP-
UX, SGI/IRIX, AIX, DEC ALPHA NT, DEC
ALPHA OSF, Windows 3.1, Windows NT.
DECstation 3100 & 5000; SUN Workstations;
Silicon Graphics Workstation; HP 700 Series;
IBM RS6000; DEC ALPHA; IBM Compatible
PCs. Contact publisher for price. *Optimal
configuration:* Any of the above, 16Mb,
300Mb disk, mouse, 19" color monitor.
Networks supported: TCP/IP, NFS, Novell.
A Full Function 2 1/1 to 5 Axis Interactive
Numerical Control Programming System & Post
Processor Generator. Provides Programming
Capabilities for 2 or 2 1/2 Axis Machine Tools,
Including Milling Machines, Wire EDMs, &
Lathes. Includes Interactive Error Checking,
Extensive Geometry Definitions & Complete
Collision Checking for Geometry & Motion.
Supports Full 3-Axis Machining on Any Complex
Surface & 5-Axis Module Gives Full Control of
the Tool Axis & Allows Positioning of Tools
Perpendicular or at a Specified Angle to Any
Complex Surface. Adra's Postprocessors take
CADRA-NC & Other Cutter Location (CL) Files &
Generate Machine Control Date for Your
Controller & Machine Combination. The User
May Also Develop Their Own Post- Processor
with CADRA-NC'S Menu-Driven, Interactive
Custom Postprocessor Generator.
Adra Systems, Inc.

**CADRA-View: View Only Software for
Engineer Drawing.** *Version:* 9.2. May 1994.
Items Included: Manuals included. Users guide &
a installation guide. *Customer Support:* 90 day
warranty on software, maintenance available at
1%/month of software list price, varity of
training available eihter on-site or at an Adra
Training Center. All customers with a maintenance
contract receive hot-line support & software
updates.
ULTRIX 4.1 & 4.2, SUN O/S, SUN Solaris, HP-
UX, SGI/IRIX, AIX, DEC ALPHA NT, DEC
ALPHA OSF, Windows 3.1, Windows NT.
DECstation 3100& 5000; SUN Workstations;
Silicon Graphics Workstation; HP 700 Series;
IBM RS6000; DEC ALPHA; IBM compatible
PCs. Contact publisher for price. *Optimal
configuration:* Any of the Above, 16Mb,
300Mb disks, mouse, 19" color monitor.
Networks supported: TCP/IP, NFS.
MS-DOS 3.3 & higher; DOS/Windows 3.
1;Windows NT. IBM compatible, 386 & 486
(8Mb). $795.00. *Nonstandard peripherals
required:* EGA or VGA graphics. *Optimal
configuration:* 486, MS-DOS 6.0, 8Mb, mouse,
SVGA Graphics, 19" color monitor, hard disk
drive. *Networks supported:* TCP/IP, Novell,
PathWorks.
Product Allows Sharing of Engineering Drwaings
within a Manufacturing Company, Providing
View-only & Red-lining Abilities to Supprot
Concurrent Engineering Environments. Product is
Intended for the Display of Drawings in
Engineering, Manufacturing & Finance
Departments for the Purpose of Checking
Engineering Drawings.
Adra Systems, Inc.

CADVANCE. *Version:* 5.0. *Compatible Hardware:*
IBM PC & compatibles. *Memory Required:*
4000k. *General Requirements:* Hard disk.
Customer Support: 90 day free support.
disk $1995.00.
CADVANCE for Windows Is a Full-Featured 2D/
3D Design & Drafting Package Designed
Specifically for the Microsoft Windows
Environment. It Completely Integrates CAD
Drawings & Database Information with Other
Applications Using Standard Windows Tools,
Including Dynamic Data Exchange (DDE), Object
Linking & Embedding (OLE) & the Clipboard &
Supports Simultaneous Displays of Multiple Views
& Multiple Drawings. A Built-In Raster Display
Capability Allows Fast, Easy Display of Scanned
Blueprints & Redline Drawings, Plus Import/
Export of Photos, Logos & Other Images. Besides
Including a Built-In DXF Translator, CADVANCE
Also Directly Reads & Writes AutoCAD .DWG
Files. Also Features Built-In Capabilities for
Architectural/Engineering & Facilities
Management Applications, Such As Two-Line
Walls, Automatic Insertion of Doors & Windows,
Automatic Insertion Clean-Up, & Building Grids.
Offers Complete Support for Networks. Includes
a Standard Embedded BASIC Language for
Macro Programming.
ISICAD, Inc.

**CADvent Integrated System: Computer-Aided
Drafting-Design System.** Sep. 1991. *Items
Included:* 3 ring binder with documentation,
various utilities. *Customer Support:* Free training
& telephone support; service contracts available
for hardware and/or software; free updates for
the first year; if a service contract is maintained,
all updates are included free of charge.
DOS 3.3. IBM PC compatible 80286/80386
(8Mb). Contact Vendor. *Nonstandard
peripherals required:* EGA, VGA or P8514A
monitor & board, math coprocessor, hard disk,
mouse (printer & plotter recommended).
Integrated Architectural/Sheet Metal/Piping CAD
with Downloading Capabilities to Manufacturing/
Estimating Systems; AutoCad (DXF)/IGES File
Export/Import; High Speed 3D Multiple Views
(Ortho, Iso, Rotational); Manufacturer's
Catalogs; Dynamic Editing; Automatic Features:
Detailing, True Dynamic/Static Collision
Checking, Joint & Connector Make-Up
Allowances, Spooling with Dimensioning, Report
Generation, Piece & Spool Numbering/Tagging,
Labor Tracking.
East Coast Sheet Metal Fabricating Corp.

**CADvent Piping System: Computer-Aided
Drafting-Design System.** Sep. 1991. *Items
Included:* 3 ring binder with documentation,
various utilities. *Customer Support:* Free training
& telephone support; service contracts available
for hardware and/or software; free updates for
the first year; if a service contract is maintained,
all updates are included free of charge.
DOS 3.3. IBM PC compatible 80286/80386
(8Mb). Contact Vendor. *Nonstandard
peripherals required:* EGA, VGA or P8514A
monitor & board, math coprocessor, hard disk,
mouse (printer & plotter recommended).
Includes: High Speed Operation; 3-D Multiple
Views; Dynamic Editing; Direct Downloading to
Manufacturing/Estimating Systems; AutoCad
(DXF)/IGES File Export/Import; Manufacturer's
Catalogs; Graphics-Oriented/Icon-Based
Interface; Automatic Features: Detailing, True
Dimensional Dynamic/Static Collision Checking,

TITLE INDEX

Joint Make-Up Allowances, Spooling with Dimensioning, Report Generation, Piece & Spool Numbering/Tagging, Labor Tracking.
East Coast Sheet Metal Fabricating Corp.

CADvent Sheet Metal System: Computer-Aided Drafting-Design System. Sep. 1991. *Items Included:* 3 ring binder with documentation, various utilities. *Customer Support:* Free training & telephone support; service contracts available for hardware and/or software; free updates for the first year; if a service contract is maintained, all updates are included free of charge.
DOS 3.3. IBM PC compatible 80286/80386 (8Mb). Contact Vendor. *Nonstandard peripherals required:* EGA, VGA or P8514A monitor & board, math coprocessor, hard disk, mouse (printer & plotter recommended).
Includes: Specification-Driven High Speed Operation; d-D Multiple Views; Dynamic Editing; Direct Downloading to Manufacturing/Estimating Systems; AutoCad (DXF)/IGES File Export/Import; Rectangular/Round Fitting Libraries; Graphics-Oriented/Icon-Based Interface; Automatic Features: Duct Routing/Detailing, True Dimensional Dynamic/Static Collision Checking, Connector Make-Up Allowances, Duct Dimensioning, Piece Numbering/Tagging, Acoustic Lining, Report Generation, Labor Tracking.
East Coast Sheet Metal Fabricating Corp.

CAI Integration Toolset. 1987. *Customer Support:* In addition to the development of products, CAI also provides full after-sales service in training, installation, skills transfer, & ongoing support. Annual maintenance - 18% of license fee; 15% per year on 3 year contract.
UNIX. HP-UX on the HP9000; AIX on the IBM RS6000; DG-UX on DG Aviion; DEC Ultrix on DEC RISC platforms; Unix 5.4 on the Unisys U6000; Unix 5.4 on the NCR3000; Unix 5.4 on the AT&T StarServer; Solaris on SUN Sparc; Interactive on Intel platforms. Per workstation charge based on configuration - Quantity discounts available for larger installations.
Series of Products That Provide for Inter-Application Data Synchronization, Seamless Information Access, the Enhancing of Existing End User Views of Information, the Creation of New End-User Views, & an Object-Oriented Development Environment for Easy Programming & Reusability of Code.
Century Analysis, Inc.

Cal LottoMaster. *Compatible Hardware:* Commodore 64; IBM PC, PS/2. *Customer Support:* 800-929-8117 (customer service).
MS-DOS. disk $39.99 (ISBN 0-87007-559-4).
Increases User's Chances of Winning California Lotto by Drawing Truly Random Numbers.
SourceView Software International.

Calc Merge. DBI Software Products. *Operating System(s) Required:* MS-DOS, CP/M-86. *Memory Required:* 64k.
$150.00.
Interfaces Any DBI File with MULTIPLAN, VISICALC, LOTUS 1-2-3 or Similar Spreadsheet Programs.
Texas Instruments, Personal Productivit.

Calc-Pad. *Compatible Hardware:* IBM PC, PCjr, PC XT, PC AT, PC compatibles.
disk $29.95.
RAM Resident Calculator. Operates in Hex, Octal, Binary, & Decimal. Works in Any Graphic Mode. Supports Unlimited Parentheses Nesting.
Software Matters.

Calc Result. May 1985. *Compatible Hardware:* IBM PC & compatibles, Victor 9000. *Operating System(s) Required:* MS-DOS. *Memory Required:* 128k. *General Requirements:* 2 disk drives, printer.
disk $45.00.
demo disk $5.00.
3-Dimensional, 32-Page Spreadsheet with 64 Columns & 256 Rows. Designed to Handle Financial, Mathematical & Statistical Functions. Produces Bar Charts & Pie Charts with up to 12 Segments. Built-In Text Editor Allows User to Enter & Edit Text Across Cells for Titles, Memos, Reports, etc. Comes with 9 Languages: Danish, Dutch, Finnish, French, German, Italian, Norwegian, Spanish, & Swedish.
ScanAm Enterprises, Inc.

Calc Result Advanced. *Compatible Hardware:* Commodore 64, CBM 8000 series. *Operating System(s) Required:* CBM DOS. *Memory Required:* 64k.
Commodore 64. disk $15.00.
CBM 8000 Series. disk $35.00.
Full-Featured, 3-Dimensional Spreadsheet Program Offers Users Many Features of VISICALC. Features Split Screen & Window Capabilities That Allow Different Files to Be Displayed at One Time. Files up to 32 Pages in Length Can Be Accommodated & an On-Line Help Menu Contains Frequently Used Commands.
ScanAm Enterprises, Inc.

Calc Result Easy. *Compatible Hardware:* Commodore 64. *Operating System(s) Required:* CBM DOS. *Memory Required:* 64k.
disk $15.00.
Combines Full-Function Editing with a Spreadsheet of 63x254 Cells for the Commodore 64. Information Can Be Presented in Graphic Form on the Screen or Formatted for Printing. IF-THEN-ELSE & AND, OR, & NOT-ELSE Commands Manipulate Data in Each Cell of the Spreadsheet for Unlimited What-If Capability. This Software Also Offers Replicate, Copy & Move Operations to Transfer Data.
ScanAm Enterprises, Inc.

CalComp ColorMaster Presenter.
Macintosh, IBM PC. disk $2995.00.
Uses Thermal Transfer to Produce Fast, High-Resolution Hard Copy for CAD/CAM, Graphic Arts & Presentation Graphics Applications. Images at Speed of Approximately One Minute per Color Page; Plots in Seven Solid Colors & Resolves at 200 DPI. Features Built-In Rasterizer. Other Features Include: Image Rotation Mode to Produce Graphics in Either Portrait (Vertical) or Landscape (Horizontal) Format; Produces Both Color & Black & white Graphics & Text on ANSI-Size or ISO-Size A4 Cut-Sheet Paper or Overhead Transparency Film.
CalComp, Inc.

The Calcgram Stock Options System. *Items Included:* Bound manual. *Customer Support:* Free hotline - no time limit; 30 day limited warranty; updates are $5/disk plus S&H.
MS-DOS. IBM & compatibles (256k). disk $99.95.
manual only $19.95.
Analytic Power for Full Control of Risk & Profit in Option Investments. The First Program in the Software Package Computes Normal (Theoretical) Values, Differences from Actual Prices, & Implied Volatilities for the Options on a Stock. This Is What You Need for Picking Candidates for Your Spreads. The Main Program, Options Hedging, Lets User Examine the Prospects of Spreads & Combinations. You Can Determine the Best Ratios among the Options, & Find the Probability As Well As the Magnitude of Future Profit. Gain Curves Are Presented Both in Graphic & Tabular Form, & for Any Selected Future Date. Round-Trip Commission & Margin Requirements Are Calculated, & Net Profit Tables Are Printed.
Dynacomp, Inc.

CALENDAR

Calculated Beauty: A Journey Through Mandelbrot Space. James N. Perdue. Sep. 1993. *Items Included:* N/A. Documentation available on disc. *Customer Support:* 90-day warranty on defective disc. Telephone support to distributors & retailers - no charge.
7.0 or higher. Macintosh (4Mb). CD-ROM disk $44.00 Retail (ISBN 1-885237-00-6, Order no.: RMDP 101-001). Optimal configuration: MAC II or higher, Floating Point Unit (FPU), 5Mb or more RAM, 300k or faster CD-ROM, 20MHz or faster CPU, QuickTime INIT.
A Unique Interactive CD-ROM with over 6,000 Sq. Ft. of MOSAICs of Fascinating Color Images & Sounds Created by the Mandelbrot Fractal Equation. The MandelDisplay Program Permits Browsing & Customizing the Mosaics for Posters, Presentations, Educational Studies, & Computer Art. Shareware, QuickTime Movies, & Art Gallery Included.
Rocky Mountain Digital Peeks.

Calculator Construction Set. Version: 2.09.6. *Compatible Hardware:* Apple Macintosh 512KE. *Customer Support:* Free to registered users.
3.5" disk $99.95.
Application That Creates Calculators (Saved As Applications or Desk Accessories).
Dubl-Click Software.

Calculator HP-UX. *Compatible Hardware:* HP Series 200 HP-UX Models 217, 220, 236, the Integral PC.
Single-user. 3.5" disk $75.00 (Order no.: 45413G).
Linus tape $200.00.
Multi-user. 3.5" disk $150.00 (Order no.: 45413H).
Linus tape $275.00.
Functions Provided Include: Mathematical & Scientific Calculations, Trigonometric Calculations & Coordinate Conversions, Statistical & Trend Analysis, & Business & Financial Solutions.
Hewlett-Packard Co.

Calendar. Duane Bristow. *Compatible Hardware:* TRS-80 Model I, Model III. *Operating System(s) Required:* TRSDOS. *Language(s):* BASIC.
cassette $9.95.
Prints Calendar Page for Any Month from 99 B.C. to 9999 A.D. & Calculates Number of Days Between Dates.
Duane Bristow Computers, Inc.

The Calendar. *Compatible Hardware:* HP 150 Touchscreen, HP 110 Portable.
3.5" disk $49.95 (Order no.: 35151D).
Turns the Personal Computer into an Appointment Calendar. Lets the User Move Between Daily, Monthly & Yearly Calendar Screens. Provides Scans for Available Times; Enter, Change or Delete Appointments; Maintain Notes for Each Appointment, Print Copies of Any Calendar; or Write Reminder Notes Throughout the Day.
Hewlett-Packard Co.

Calendar.
contact publisher for price.
Prints a Complete Calendar for Any Modern Year Specified. Holidays Are Marked.
James Assocs.

Calendar. J. Weaver, Jr. Apr. 1986. *Compatible Hardware:* Atari ST, IBM PC with GEM or DOS, Sanyo MBC 55X. *Operating System(s) Required:* TOS, MS-DOS. *Memory Required:* 512k.
disk $29.95 ea.
Atari. 3.5" disk $29.95 (ISBN 0-923213-15-5, Order no.: AT-CAL).
Sanyo, MS-DOS. disk $24.95 (ISBN 0-923213-18-X, Order no.: SA-CAL).
IBM. disk $24.95.

Appointment & Reminder System Permanently Available As a DESKTOP Accessory from Within Any Application. Users Can Display or Print Calendars of Any Selected Year and Month. Messages for Any Date & Time, up to 2099, Can Be Saved to Disk with the Possibility of Attaching Alarms to Any or All Reminder Messages to Notify User of Special Events As They Occur. Alarms or Hourly Chimes Appear Automatically on the DESKTOP During GEM Programs, Even When CALENDAR Itself Is Not on the Screen.
MichTron, Inc.

Calendar Creater Plus Try & Buy. Softkey International, Inc. Staff. *Items Included:* The package includes a 3.5" diskette, a mini-manual & a Try & Buy Brochure.
Windows 3.1 or higher or MS-DOS 5.0 or higher. IBM PC & compatibles, 386 or higher (4Mb). disk $44.99 (ISBN 1-57548-002-6). *Nonstandard peripherals required:* Microsoft or compatible mouse.
Product Allows Users to Create Calendars. Once Calendars Are Created, Users Can Schedule Meetings, Trips, Vacation, etc.
IBM Software Manufacturing Solutions (ISMS)

Calendar Creator. *Compatible Hardware:* IBM PC, PCjr, PC XT, PC AT; Compaq Portable, Plus, DeskPro. *Operating System(s) Required:* PC-DOS 2.0, Compaq DOS. *General Requirements:* Any of the following graphics printers: IBM Graphics, Epson MX 80/100 (with Graftrax), RX 80/100, FX 80/100, LQ 1500; Okidata 84, 92, 93, 182, 192, 193; C. Itoh Prowriter; IDS 460, 560, Prism; NEC 8023; Toshiba P351.
disk $39.95 (Order no.: 1030).
Works with Multiple Event Files That Let User Enter Both Unique & Recurring Events. Allows Entry of Irregular Dates (e.g. the Third Thursday of Each Month). Custom Calendars Can Be Printed by Selecting Event Files to Include. Events Files Can Be Updated at Any Time, After Which a New Calendar Can Be Printed. Users Can Choose Between Three Calendar Types: One Week, One Month, or One Year per Page; or Print the Event Files Alone, Apart from the Calendar. Output Can Be on Either Standard or Wide Paper.
Channelmark Corp.

Calendar/Docket System. *Version:* 1.5. 1988. *Items Included:* Complete manual. *Customer Support:* 90-day unlimited warranty, software update & service agreement after warranty $55/yr.
MS-DOS 2.1 or higher (384k). IBM PC & compatibles. standalone $395.00, network $495.00. *Nonstandard peripherals required:* Dual floppy drive. *Optimal configuration:* Hard disk. *Networks supported:* Novell Netware, Net Blas.
Designed Exclusively for Law Firms. Attacks Number One Cause of Malpractice: Inadequate Calendaring. Reminds User of Appointment, Court Appearance or Statute of Limitations Prior to Its Due Date.
Data Law.

Calendar Magic. 1987. *Compatible Hardware:* Apple II series, IIgs; Laser 128. *Operating System(s) Required:* Apple DOS. *Memory Required:* 64k. *General Requirements:* Prints in color with Imagewriter II.
disk $29.95.
Custom Calendars (Weekly, Monthly, Yearly or Events Calendar). Customize Special Events, Add or Remove Events at Anytime. New Calendars Printed Until the Year 1999. Will Keep Track of 150 Calendar Events each Year. Menu Driven: A) Add Events, E) Edit Events, D) Delete Events, S) Same Events, N) Next Page of Events, P) Previous Page of Events & M) Main Menu.
Artsci, Inc.

The Calendar Program. *Compatible Hardware:* TI 99/4A. *Operating System(s) Required:* DX-10. *Language(s):* BASIC. *Memory Required:* 48k. cassette $14.95.
Displays a Calendar Showing the Correct Days of the Week for Any Year after 4712 B.C.
Eastbench Software Products.

CalendarMaker. *Version:* 4.0. Donald Brown. *Compatible Hardware:* Mac Plus or higher. *Memory Required:* 2000k. *Items Included:* CM disk, manual. *Customer Support:* Free support. 3.5" disk $59.95.
Custom Calendar Generator That Imports from Appointment Diary, More, SideKick, BatteryPack, Text Files & Other CalendarMaker Files So That Individual Calendars Can Be Combined into a Master Calendar. Setup of Preferences for Page Style, Text Style, Monthly Pictures, Printing Colors & Monthly Icons Is Built into the Menus.
CE Software, Inc.

CalendarMaker for Windows. *Version:* 3.0.1. Steven W Stoner. *Memory Required:* 640k. *Items Included:* Disk, User manual. *Customer Support:* Free to registered users.
MS-DOS 3.1 or higher. disk $49.00.
Creates Calendars Incorporating Holidays & Periodic Events. Includes Date Accents & Floating Notes for Individual Text.
CE Software, Inc.

Calfex & Calfex G-T. *Items Included:* Bound manual. *Customer Support:* Free hotline - no time limit; 30 day limited warranty; updates are $5/disk plus S&H.
MS-DOS. IBM & compatibles (128k). disk $99.95.
Apple (48k). disk $149.95.
General-Purpose Menu-Driven Equation Processor for Engineering & Scientific Analysis. Features: Graphs & Tables; Maxima & Minima, Can Be Found Automatically; Simultaneous Equations, up to 10; Numerical Integration; Array or Simple Variables, up to 120 Inputs & 120 Outputs.
Dynacomp, Inc.

California Challenge: The Collection. *Customer Support:* 90 days limited warranty, customer support phone: (408) 296-8400, hrs: M-F 8-5pm. Also Bulletin Board (408) 296-8800.
PC-DOS 2.1 or higher; CGA, HERC 384k; EGA, TGA (Tandy) 512k. $49.95 (Order no.: CGPC/P3).
PC only $14.95.
Apple IIgs/ProDOS 16 (512k). Contact publisher for price.
3.5" disk $21.95.
Scenery Add on Disk to "The Duel".
Accolade, Inc.

California Corporation Formation Package & Minute Book. Kevin W. Finck. May 1986. *Compatible Hardware:* IBM PC & compatibles. *Operating System(s) Required:* PC-DOS 2.0 or higher. *Memory Required:* 256k.
disk $39.95, incl. manual (ISBN 1-55571-006-9).
WORDSTAR-Compatible Word Processing Program Is Provided on the Disk, Together with the Text Files from the Book, Which Include All the Letters, Bylaws, Articles of Incorporation & Other Forms Incorporated in the Book.
Oasis Pr.

California Corporation Software: (Text Files). *Items Included:* 3-ring binder edition of "California Corporation Formation Package & Minute Book" by Kevin W. Finck. *Customer Support:* Free technical support over phone; limited warranty.
DOS. IBM & compatibles. disk $69.95 (ISBN 1-55571-317-3, Order no.: CACPBASC31). *Addl. software required:* Word processor.
Macintosh. Macintosh. 3.5" disk $69.95 (ISBN 1-55571-318-1, Order no.: CPPWBAXC3M). *Addl. software required:* Word processor.
ASCII Text File Forms for Generating By-Laws, Minutes & the Many Other Forms Required for Starting Regular Federal 'C' Corporations (H Corp. under California State Law). Covers Subchapter S Corporations. The Software Does Not Replace the Book, but Instead Complements It with Forms, Minutes & By-Laws That Can Be Edited.
Oasis Pr., The.

California Games. *Compatible Hardware:* Apple II; Commodore 64/128, Amiga; IBM PC. contact publisher for price.
Features Events Such As BMX Bike Races, Skating, Surfing, & Skateboarding.
Epyx, Inc.

California Games II. *Version:* 1.2. Jun. 1991. *Customer Support:* 90 day warranty, customer service available 8:30-5:30 PCT.
DOS 3.3 or higher. IBM-PC (512k). Call manufacture for price (Order no.: 19405D). *Nonstandard peripherals required:* Color or Hercules monochrome monitor. *Optimal configuration:* Joystick compatible.
Features Five Events: Body Boarding, Skate-Boarding, Hang Gliding, Jet-Surfing, Snow-Boarding.
Epyx, Inc.

California Incorporator. *Version:* 1.2. Anthony Mancuso & Legisoft. *Compatible Hardware:* IBM PC, XT, AT, PS/2 & compatibles. *Operating System(s) Required:* PC-DOS/MS-DOS 2.0 or higher. *Memory Required:* 256k. *Items Included:* PC: both 3.5" & 5.25" disks & a 336 page manual. *Customer Support:* Free technical support Monday-Friday, 9-5 PST; unlimited money back guarantee.
3.5" disk & 5.25" disk included $129.00 (ISBN 0-87337-027-7).
Provides Legal Documentation for Businesses Wishing to Incorporate in CA.
Nolo Pr.

The California Nonprofit Corporation Handbook. Anthony Mancuso. *Customer Support:* Free technical support Monday-Friday, 9-5 PST; unlimited money back guarantee.
PC-DOS/MS-DOS 2.0 or higher. IBM PC & compatibles. 69.96 5.25" & 3.5" disks, incl. book (ISBN 0-87337-095-3).
Macintosh. 3.5" disk $69.95, incl. book (ISBN 0-87337-212-3).
(ISBN 0-87337-097-X).
The Standard Work on How to Form a Nonprofit Corporation in California Includes Forms for the Articles, Bylaws & Minutes, As Well As Regular & Special Director & Member Minute Forms.
Nolo Pr.

California Travel. *Items Included:* CD-ROM booklet. *Customer Support:* Free technical support via phone as of release date.
MPC/Windows. 386 or higher (4Mb). CD-ROM disk $29.95 (ISBN 1-885784-63-5, Order no.: 1316). *Optimal configuration:* MPC CD-ROM player, S-VGA graphics card (640x480x256 colors) with compatible monitor, MPC compliant sound card, mouse, Windows 3.1 or higher, Windows 95 compatible.
System 7.0 or higher. Macintosh (4Mb). CD-ROM disk $29.95 (ISBN 1-885784-55-4, Order no.: 1552). *Optimal configuration:* CD-ROM drive, color monitor, mouse.
Experience California with Renowned Travel Writer Lee Foster, Winner of the Coveted Lowell Thomas Award. This Personal Tour of the Golden State Features Video Clips & over 1000 Full-Color Photos of Exciting California Vacation

TITLE INDEX

Sights; Recommendations for Restaurants, Museums, Shopping, & More; & Maps with Easy-to-Print Directions.
Technology Dynamics Corp.

California Travel: Jewel. *Items Included:* CD-ROM booklet. *Customer Support:* Free technical support via phone as of release date.
MPC/Windows. 386 or higher (4Mb). CD-ROM disk $29.95 (ISBN 1-885784-08-2, Order no.: 1319). *Optimal configuration:* MPC CD-ROM player, S-VGA graphics card (640x480x256 colors) with compatible monitor, MPC compliant sound card, mouse, Windows 3.1 or higher, Windows 95 compatible.
System 7.0 or higher. Macintosh (4Mb). *Optimal configuration:* CD-ROM drive, color monitor, mouse.
Experience California with Renowned Travel Writer Lee Foster, Winner of the Coveted Lowell Thomas Award. This Personal Tour of the Golden State Features Video Clips & over 1000 Full-Color Photos of Exciting California Vacation Sights; Recommendations for Restaurants, Museums, Shopping, & More; & Maps with Easy-to-Print Directions.
Technology Dynamics Corp.

California Verbal Learning Test (CVLT) Research Edition. Dean C. Delis et al. Jul. 1987. *Compatible Hardware:* Apple II, II+, IIe; IBM PC, PC XT, PC AT. *Memory Required:* Apple 64k, IBM 320k. *General Requirements:* 2 disk drives or hard disk, Epson or compatible graphics capable dot matrix parallel printer. IBM version also supported by HP Laserjet. *Items Included:* Software user's guide, keyboard overlay. *Customer Support:* 210-228-0752, 1 for Menu, 6 for Support.
disk $192.00 (Order no.: 8030-470).
Apple. (Order no.: 8030-660).
IBM. (Order no.: 8030-652 (5.25"); 8030-454 (3.5")).
Assesses Verbal Learning & Memory Deficits in the Elderly & the Neurologically Impaired. Suited for Tailoring Individualized Cognitive Rehabilitation Programs & for Assessing the Effectiveness of These Interventions. Measures Aspects of How Learning Occurs or Fails to Occur, in Addition to Measuring the Amount of Verbal Material Learned.
Harcourt Brace Jovanovich, Inc. (Psychological Corp.).

California Wills & Trusts: CAPS Practice System Series. Robert A. Mills. Sep. 1991. *Items Included:* Current version of CAPS/User, which is a document assembly software platform needed to run this application. A systems manual that includes explanation of the substance of the product, a Basic Tutorial, & an Advanced Tutorial. Transmittal sheets to inform operator of attorney's decisions about documents. *Customer Support:* Free hotline support through an 800 number.
MS-DOS or PC-DOS version 3.0 or higher. IBM XT, AT or PS/2 or compatible with hard disk (450k). disk $475.00 (Order no.: 894 & 993).
Addl. software required: Word processing program recommended. *Optimal configuration:* IBM PC & compatible, or PS/2, with 80286 microprocessor or higher with at least 5Mb of free disk space.
Enables User to Assemble Simple & Complex, Complete, Legally Accurate Wills, Inter Vivos Trusts, & Durable Powers of Attorney Based on the User's Answers to Questions. On-Line Help Screens Include Legal Guidance & Cross-References to Other Matthew Bender Publications. Integrates with User's Word-Processor.
Matthew Bender & Co., Inc.

Caligari. *Version:* 2.0. *Items Included:* Tutorial video tape, manual, diskette & warranty card. *Customer Support:* Hot line to Octree offices for phone support.
Amiga DOS (1Mb). $249.00 Consumer Version, $2000.00 - $3500.00 Professional Version. *Nonstandard peripherals required:* Targa board for Broadcast Renderer. *Optimal configuration:* 2-8Mb.
Conceptual 3D Modeler Using Intuitive Real Time Response, Allowing the User to Perform the Initial Conceptual Stage of the Project Directly on the Screen. At the Heart of the System Is a Unique Real Time Interface That Requires Only Minutes of Training Time in Order for a User to Become Highly Productive.
Octree Software.

Calixto Island. *Compatible Hardware:* TRS-80 Color Computer, TDP-100.
contact publisher for price.
Mark Data Products.

Call Option Writing. *Compatible Hardware:* Commodore 64, IBM PC, TI 99/4A Home Computer. *Language(s):* Extended BASIC.
TI. disk $14.95 (Order no.: 202XD).
IBM, Commodore. contact publisher for price.
River City Software, Inc.

Call Reporter I. Jun. 1984. *Memory Required:* 384k. *General Requirements:* Hard disk.
contact publisher for price.
Provides Means for Preparing the FFIEC Quarterly Call Report. Versions 002, 031, 032, 033 & 034 Are Available.
Distributed Planning System Corp.

Caller ID Developer Toolkits: Single Line & Multi-Line. *Version:* 1.01. Jan. 1991. *Items Included:* ANI-232 Caller ID Computer Adaptor; ANI-232 Interface specifications & Incoming Call Line Identification Message Format; royalty-free Device Driver; Application examples in C, Pascal, BASIC, & Fox Pro; Emulation program & RS-232 Interface cable. *Customer Support:* Free customer support for one year, free software upgrades within one year from date of purchase, limited one year warranty for ANI-232.
MS-DOS 3.0 or higher, Windows, OS/2, UNIX, Macintosh. IBM compatibles with one available serial port (512k). single line $495.00; multi-line $595.00. Networks supported: LAN.
Allows a PC to Emulate the Data & Control Signals of an ANI-232 under Various Line Conditions. Program Emulates Ringing, Calling Number, Calling Name, & On-Hook/Off-Hook. It Can Also Be Used to Create Error Conditions Such As an Incorrect or Missing Check Sum. An Essential Building Block for Developing Single Line & Multi-Line, Computer-Based Caller ID Applications.
Rochelle Communications, Inc.

Caller ID+ Plus, Single Line & Multi-Line. *Version:* 1.04. Apr. 1991. *Items Included:* ANI-232 Caller ID Computer Adaptor, telephone cord, "T" adaptor, limited warranty card, User's manual. *Customer Support:* Free customer support for 90 days, free software upgrades within one year from date of purchase, 30-day money back guarantee, limited one year warranty for ANI-232.
MS-DOS 2.1 or higher. IBM PC, XT, AT, PS/2 & compatibles (384k). disk $199.00 single line (ISBN 0-9629249-0-3). *Nonstandard peripherals required:* Requires that user subscribe to the caller ID telephone service (not available in all states). Requires a serial RS-232 port (COM1 or COM2 on all PC's, also COM3/3 on PS/2 models 50 & above), one to four incoming telephone lines.
disk $495.00 multi-line.

Integrated Caller Identification System. Designed to Work with the New Telephone Service Known As Caller ID (or Call Display in Canada). Identifies the Calling Number & Brings up a Database of Information on the Caller Before the Call Is Answered. Potential Users: Accountants, Medical Professionals, Construction Industry, Lawyers, Salespersons, Home Users, Publishers, Hospitality, Real Estate.
Rochelle Communications, Inc.

Callme. *Version:* 3.5. *Customer Support:* 90 days free support - then $150.00 per year. 24 hour bulletin board system.
Multiuser DOS & REAL/32. $275.00.
Nonstandard peripherals required: Multiport board required for more than two remote users.
Remote Console Supervisor. Allows Remote Users Complete Access To a Concurrent DOS Installation. Security Options Include Log In, Drive, Directory & Program Access Classes. Includes Complete Bulletin Board System & File Transfer Utilities.
Logan Industries, Inc.

Calorix Savant. *Version:* 3.1. Aug. 1985. *Compatible Hardware:* IBM PC. *Operating System(s) Required:* PC-DOS. *Language(s):* Quicksilver. *Memory Required:* 640k. *Customer Support:* Toll free telephone support.
$195.00.
Conduct a 24-Hour Diet Recall from Any Patient. Ideal Body Weight Is Computed. Foods Are Entered by Name & Quantity (Household Units). Effects of Work & Exercise Are Then Addressed Showing What Was Done, How Long & Its Benefits to Projected Weight.
SRC Systems, Inc.

CALOUT PLUS: Computer-to-Computer Communications. *Version:* 1.7. 1991. *Compatible Hardware:* MicroVAX, VAX. *Operating System(s) Required:* VMS, MICROVMS. *Language(s):* Basic, Macro. *Memory Required:* 220k. *Items Included:* 1 year maintenance, quarterly newsletter. *Customer Support:* 6:00 a.m.-6:00 p.m. MST. depending on CPU included in ClydeSupport (formerly ProSupport).
A Communications Program That Lets Support Personnel Dial into Remote Sites & Transfer Trouble-Shooting Information & Repaired Software. It Also Lets a User Access Remote Systems, Transfer All Types of Files & Even Automate Communications Procedures.
Raxco, Inc.

Calx. *Version:* 2.0. Cliff Joyce. Jan. 1996. *Items Included:* 1 manual, 2 diskettes (1 Macintosh, 1 Windows), 1 brochure. *Customer Support:* Free telephone support.
Newton operating system. Newton. floppy disk $49.95 (ISBN 1-884447-00-7, Order no.: M2741LL/A). *Nonstandard peripherals required:* For floppy version - Newton Connection Kit & RAM card.
Collection of 16+ Calculators Designed for the Newton. Included Are Lifestyle Calculators (Sales Tax/Tip, Dates, etc.), Professional Calculators (Architecture, Film Editing, etc.) & Standard Calculators (Math/Science, Statistics, etc.).
Dubl-Click Software.

Calx. *Version:* 2.0.
disk $49.95, upgrade for ,29.95.
While Still Compatible with the Newton 1.0 Platform, Calx 2.0 Is Optimized for Newton 2.0 - Resulting in Significantly Faster Performance. A Collection of Many Calculators, Now Separately Installable. Whether It's Figuring the Tip in a Restaurant, Paying the Babysitter, an Equation in Calculus Class, or the number of Tablespoons in a Cup. Calx takes the Hassel Out of Numbers.

Professionals Will Appreciate Calx 2.0's Powerful Set of Scientific, Statistical, & Industry-Specific Calculators, Including Solutions for Film Editors, Architects, & Computer Programmers.
Dubl-Click Software.

CAM Design Software. 1985. *Compatible Hardware:* IBM PC. *Operating System(s) Required:* PC-DOS 2.0. *Language(s):* BASIC (source code included). *Memory Required:* 64k. disk $110.00 incl. manual.
Designed As a Teaching Aid in CAM Design. Graphically Shows CAM Rotation with the Motion of a CAM Follower.
Kern International, Inc.

Cam Master: Kinematic Cam Design. *Items Included:* Bound manual. *Customer Support:* Free hotline - no time limit; 30 day limited warranty; updates are $5/disk plus S&H.
MS-DOS 2.0 or higher. IBM & compatibles (512k). disk $199.95. *Nonstandard peripherals required:* CGA (or equivalent) graphics capability; printer supported, but not required.
Accurate Design & Analysis of Roller-Follower Cams. The User May Choose from a Menu of Several Types of Motion to Be Applied over Segments of the Cam's Rotation to Form the Complete Description. The Software Computes & Graphically (or in Table Format) Displays the Pitch Curve (Choice of Polar or Cartesian Coordinates) & Follower Displacement, Velocity, & Acceleration. Also Provided Are Displays of the Radius of Curvature (Which May Limit Roller Diameter), Roller Force, & Pressure Angle.
Dynacomp, Inc.

Cam Master: Kinematic Cam Design. 1992. *Items Included:* Detailed manuals included with all Dynacomp products. *Customer Support:* Free telephone support to original customer - no time limit; 30 day limited warranty.
MS-DOS 3.2 or higher. IBM PC & compatibles (512k). $199.95 (Add $5.00 for 3 1/2" format; 5 1/4" format standard). *Optimal configuration:* IBM, MS-DOS 2.0 or higher, 512k RAM, CGA or equivalent graphics capability. A printer is supported, but not required.
Simplifies the Accurate Design & Analysis of Roller-Follower & Slider-Follower Cams. It Is Applicable to Rotating As Well as Linear Cams (up to 360 Defined Points). The User May Choose from a Menu of Several Types of Motion to Be Applied over Portions (up to 16) of the Cam's Rotation to Form the Complete Description.
Dynacomp, Inc.

Camp Planning System. *Version:* 4.02. Daniel Sykora. Jul. 1989. *Items Included:* Users manual, sample data files.
MS-DOS (512k). IBM compatible. disk $995.00. *Optimal configuration:* IBM compatible, MS-DOS 2.0 or higher.
Camper, Group, Staff & Activity Scheduler Based on User Defined Criteria. Issues Daily: Camper, Bunk, Division, Staff, & Fair & Rainy Weather Schedules as Well as Various Management Reports. Also Divides & Sorts Campers into Groups. Projects How Many Times Each Group Will Be Assigned Each Activity & How Often Staff & Facilities Will Be Used. User Defined Scheduling Criteria Can Then Be Modified to Obtain Desired Results. Enables Dynamic Error-Free Programming.
Specialized Software.

Campaign Manager III. *Version:* 3.0. Jan. 1996. *Compatible Hardware:* IBM PC & compatibles, Macintosh, Windows 95. *Operating System(s) Required:* PC-DOS/MS-DOS or Windows. *Language(s):* Machine/FoxPro. *Memory Required:* 4000k. *General Requirements:* 10Mb disk space. *Items Included:* Media documentation. *Customer Support:* Included 24 hours toll free. $995.00.
Features Candidate's Schedule Fundraising Analysis, Campaign Budget, Polling Analysis, Media Buy Analysis, Targeting Report, Research Data Bases, Treasurer's Report, Word Processing & File Card.
Aristotle Industries.

Camping One. *Version:* 4. Sep. 1994. *Items Included:* User manual. Interactive tutorial. *Customer Support:* Installation support toll-free. 1 yr. telephone support $100.
MS-DOS Version 5.0 or higher. IBM PC (1Mb). $795.00 Single-user; $1795.00 Multi-user. *Optimal configuration:* 2Mb RAM, hard drive. *Networks supported:* All.
Assigns Campsites. Reports Revenue, etc. Add Your Own Reports. User-Defined Attributes Allow Customization. Displays Sites & Reservation Data in a Spreadsheet-Like Format for User Manipulation. Version Is Based on Borland International's Paradox Database.
Paracomp, Inc.

Camping II. *Version:* 3. Sep. 1992. *Compatible Hardware:* IBM PC. *Operating System(s) Required:* PC-DOS 3.0 or higher. *Memory Required:* 512k. *General Requirements:* Hard disk, printer; color monitor recommended. *Items Included:* Interactive tutorial. User manual. *Customer Support:* 30 days, updates & telephone support included. Additional support available. disk $595.00 Single User, $1595.00 Multi-User.
Assigns Campsites Based on Availability & Site Features. Allows Flexible Charging & Customization for Individual Campgrounds. Displays Sites & Reservation Data in a Spreadsheet-Like Form for User Manipulation. Reports Available Include Invoices & Receipts, Occupancy, Check-In, & Many More. Content-Sensitive Help.
Paracomp, Inc.

CAN-FAX. *Compatible Hardware:* IBM PC & compatibles. *Memory Required:* 512k. *Items Included:* disks, manuals, cabling interface. *Customer Support:* No charge for support. $195.00 & up.
Enables Computer to Communicate with Canon Fax Phone 25, 26, 210, 222, 225, 245, T301, 350, T701, 705, 750, 730, L770, L920 & Others. Fax Machines Are Connected to the PC via the RS232C Port. Option to Scan into DXF File Format for AutoCAD. Also, Works with PIC, PCX, TIFF, & ASCII.
LA Business Systems, Inc.

Canadian Foreign Direct Investment in the United States 1974-1994. May 1995. *Items Included:* Spiral bound manual. *Customer Support:* Unlimited telephone support.
MS-DOS 6.0/Windows 3.1 or higher. PC Clone 486 or higher (4Mb). disk $125.00 (ISBN 1-878914-10-6). *Addl. software required:* Database Versions are available for MS Access 2.0, Excel, Lotus, Paradox, Foxpro, & dBASE. *Optimal configuration:* PC clone with MS-DOS 6.0/Windows 3.1 or higher. Must have MS Access 2.0, or Excel, or Lotus or Paradox or Foxpro or dBASE.
Database of All Canadian Foreign Direct Investment Transactions in the United States 1974-1994.
Jeffries & Associates, Inc.

CANCERLIT CD-ROM Database. Apr. 1989. MS Windows 3.1 or higher. IBM & compatibles (4Mb). CD-ROM disk $695.00-$2790.00; Networks $2395.00 & up. *Nonstandard peripherals required:* Magnetic or CD-ROM, using ISO 9660. *Optimal configuration:* IBM & compatibles, 80386 or higher, 4Mb RAM, 20Mb hard disk, mouse, MS Windows 3.1 or higher.
System 6.0.7 or higher. Apple Macintosh (3Mb). CD-ROM disk $695.00-$2790.00; Networks $2395.00 & up. *Optimal configuration:* Apple Macintosh Plus or higher, 3Mb RAM, System 6. 0.7 or higher.
CANCERLIT Is an Electronic Reference Database to the Published Cancer Literature. Database Contents, Selected from Some 3,000 Biomedical Journals, from Papers Presented at Meetings, & from Books, Reports & Doctoral Theses, Are Distributed on CD-ROM (Compact Disc, Read-Only Memory) Optical Disc. Knowledge Finder Search-&-Retrieval Software Makes Searching of the CANCERLIT Database Easy, Effective & Fast. After the User Types a Phrase or Sentence Describing the Information Needed, It selects the References in the Database That Appear to Best Match the Request, & Presents Them in Order of likely relevance. The CANCERLIT Database Covers the Most Recent Five Years.
Aries Systems Corp.

Cancerlit Knowledge Finder. *Version:* 1.5. Jun. 1989. *Customer Support:* Documentation, telephone support, software upgrades.
Macintosh; Windows. MAC Plus & higher; PC/Windows 80386 & higher. CD-ROM disk $695.00-$2395.00 (International higher). *Nonstandard peripherals required:* Compatible CD-ROM player. *Networks supported:* Appleshare, Tops, Novell.
Produced by the National Cancer Institute, in Conjunction with the National Library of Medicine. The Database Is a Comprehensive Collection of Citations & Abstracts of Published Cancer Literature. Database Contents Are Selected from Some 3,000 Biomedical Journals, from Papers Presented at Meetings, & from Books, Reports & Doctoral Theses. The Database Includes Material Indexed During the Current & Four Prior Years (CD-ROM Discs Created During 1989 Cover Back Through 1985). English & Non-English Article References Are Pre-Selected into Separate Databases to Facilitate Searching of English Language References.
Aries Systems Corp.

Canis Dog Owner's Database. *Items Included:* Bound manual. *Customer Support:* Free hotline - no time limit; 30 day limited warranty; updates are $5/disk plus S&H.
MS-DOS 2.0 or higher. IBM & compatibles (256k). disk $39.95. *Nonstandard peripherals required:* VGA (or compatible) graphics capability is required if illustrations are desired; mouse is supported.
Canine Database for Present or Prospective Dog Owners. It Covers the Most Popular Breeds. Included Are VGA Color Illustrations (Optional) & Historical Data, As Well As Information on Specific Nutritional Needs, Diseases, Health, & Temperament. Enter Your Personal Requirements, & CANIS Will Provide a Selection of Dogs Which Best Fit Your Life Style. Do Your Own Health Exams Following the Guidelines Given & Maintain a Complete Medical History for Your Dog. Prepare Printed Guardian Instructions for Emergencies or Travel. Print Birth Certificates for Litters.
Dynacomp, Inc.

Canopy Color Program: Computerized Color Pattern Selection. *Version:* 1.1. Gary Peek. Jan. 1993. *Items Included:* Fabric samples, manual. *Customer Support:* Unlimited warranty, free telephone support.
MS-DOS. IBM (640k). disk $14.95 (ISBN 0-915516-83-7, Order no.: CANCOLOR). *Optimal configuration:* EGA or VGA color

monitor.
Parachute Canopy Color Combinations May Be Viewed & Compared on the Screen. This Program Replaces Paper & Color Pencils.
Para Publishing.

Canopy Formation Planner: Computerized CRW Formation Planner. *Version:* 1.1. Gary Peek. 1995. *Items Included:* Instruction sheet. *Customer Support:* Free telephone support.
MS-DOS. 386 (640k). disk $19.95 (ISBN 1-56860-016-X). *Nonstandard peripherals required:* VGA.
Now You Can Plan Canopy Formation Skydives & Save Them to Disk for Later Recall. There Are up to 24 Skydivers, Eight Different Colors & 16 Different Rotational Positions. Slots Can Be Added or Deleted Either in the Middle of the Lineup or at the End. Grid Lines for Precise Alignment of the Slots Are Available.
Para Publishing.

Canostat Statistical Process Control. *Items Included:* Bound manual. *Customer Support:* Free hotline - no time limit; 30 day limited warranty; updates are $5/disk plus S&H.
MS-DOS 2.0 or higher. IBM & compatibles (256k). disk $169.95.
Spreadsheet-Based Statistical Quality Control System. Full-Screen Spreadsheet Editing, Storage, Retrieval; X-Bar & R Control Charts; X & Moving Range Control Charts; Histograms; Printed Charts (Dot Matrix Graphics Not Needed); Titles & Labels; File Splicing for Historical Analysis; Spreadsheet Cells Can Be Initialized with Common Digits & More.
Dynacomp, Inc.

Canterbury Tales. *Version:* 1.5. Feb. 1995. *Items Included:* BookWorm Student Reader (diskette). *Customer Support:* 30 day MBG. Technical support (toll call) - no charge.
System 7.0 or higher. Macintosh (5Mb). CD-ROM disk $29.95 (ISBN 1-57316-029-6, Order no.: 16114). *Nonstandard peripherals required:* CD-ROM drive, 12" color monitor. *Optimal configuration:* 13" color monitor recommended.
Windows 3.1 or higher. IBM compatible (MPC) 386 DX (4Mb). CD-ROM disk $29.95. *Nonstandard peripherals required:* Standard multimedia compatible CD-ROM. *Optimal configuration:* 8Mb RAM recommended, 256 color monitor recommended.
The BookWorm Edition of the Canterbury Tales, Edited by the Renowned Chaucerian Authority Dr. John Fisher, Provides the Modern Student with the First Electronic Edition of These Ancient Classics, Marking a New Chapter in the English Literary Tradition That Chaucer's Work Began. Full of Illustrations, Recordings, & Works of Art from the Author's Time Period.
Communication & Information Technologies, Inc. (CIT).

Cantus, the Music Improviser. Created by Michael Riesman.
contact publisher for price.
Plays Computer-Generated Music Continually, Without Repeating Itself. Instead of Typing in Notes, the User Enters Choices for Tempo, Harmony, Rhythm, Counterpoint, Voice Range, & Tone Color Which Become the Basis from Which the Program Creates, in Real-Time, Its 3-Voice Improvisations. Each Set of User Choices Becomes a "Patch", Which Can Be Saved to Disk & Recalled & Played at Will. The Program Comes Supplied with over 65 Such Patches, Representing a Broad Range of Musical Styles. Produces a Graphic Real-Time Display of the Notes Being Played. Includes a Glossary of Musical & Technical Terms.
Algo-Rhythm Software.

Canvas. *Version:* 3.5. 1993. *Items Included:* 2 manuals & 5 disks.
Apple System 6.02 or higher. Mac Plus, SE, SE30, II, IIx, IIcx, IIci, or Portable, Quadra, Centris, LC family, Classic family (1Mb). 3.5" disk $399.00.
Precision Drawing & Graphics Product . For Paint & Draw. Supports Bezier Curve, Unlimited Layers, 16.7 Million Colors & PostScript Greyscales in 1% Increments. Built-In Translators for Multi-Platform Formats Like CGM, IGES, & DXF. Conversion of PostScript Type 1 Fonts to Customizable Bezier Outlines. Technical Drawing Features Include Custom Dynamic Hatching, Custom Parallel Lines & Curves, Custom Dashed Lines, Curves & Borders. Automatic Dimension Lines, Area & Perimeter Calculations, & a Smart Mouse Drawing Aide.
Deneba Software.

Canvas: Windows Version. 1993. *Items Included:* User guide & reference manual. *Customer Support:* 30-day money back guarantee, technical support line available free.
Windows 3.X or higher. IBM Compatible 286 or higher (2Mb). disk $399.00 (Order no.: 3055965644). *Optimal configuration:* 486 compatible, Windows 3.1, 4Mb RAM, 24-bit video card.
Precision Drawing Tool for Professionals. Only Windows Graphics Program That Integrates Precision Drawing & Bitmap Editing. Ideally Suited for Such Diverse Applications As Technical Illustrations, Graphics Design, Business Graphics, Desktop Presentations, Desktop Publishing, Engineering, & Architecture. Boasts a Wealth of Technical Illustration Features, Excellent Text Handling, & Rich CMYK & PANTONE Colors. Based on Deneba's Modular, Extensible Open Architecture Technology. Features Full Support for Windows 3.1 Technology Including Multiple Document Interface, Object Linking & File Embedding. Shares the Same File Format & Interface with the Popular Canvas 3 for Macintosh.
Deneba Software.

CAP Accountant. Feb. 1996. *Items Included:* Printed manual. *Customer Support:* 60 days free support with purchase. Support after that via 800 toll free numbers is $399 per year.
DOS. 486 (1Mb). Contact publisher for price (ISBN 0-917081-06-4). *Nonstandard peripherals required:* Mono/EGA/VGA. *Networks supported:* Novell Netware 3.X, 4.X, Lantastic.
A Simple DOS Based Accounting System That Can Be Run on a Cash or Accrual Basis. It Will Generate Real Time Financial & Accounting Reports. Can Be Used with the SellWise or CAP Cash'nCarry to Create a Fully Integrated POS & Accounting Solution. In Addition to Doing Regular General Ledger Accounting Functions It Will Also Keep Track of Your Checkbook Balance & Allow Easy Bank Reconciliation.
CAP Automation.

CAP BackOffice. Feb. 1996. *Items Included:* Printed manual. *Customer Support:* 60 days free support with purchase. Support after that via 800 toll free numbers is $399 per year.
Windows. 486 (1Mb). Contact publisher for price (ISBN 0-917081-35-8). *Nonstandard peripherals required:* VGA. *Networks supported:* Novell Netware 3.X, 4.X, Lantastic.
Provides Managers with Real-Time Graphical Information & Allows Powerful Data Analysis by Linking to Microsoft Excel & Lotus 1-2-3. A Combination of Three Components: 1) Reports Allow You to View & Print Data Related to Sales, Customers, & Inventory. 2) Ability to Display Graphs. 3) Excel Link Is the Answer for All Business Owners Who Want to Go Beyond the Predefined Report.
CAP Automation.

CAP Cash 'n Carry. *Version:* 96.1. Sep. 1994. *Items Included:* Demo disk, training book. *Customer Support:* 30 days free. FAX free. Toll free after 30 days for $299/year (includes $150 update).
DOS. IBM & compatibles (640k). disk $995.00 (ISBN 0-917081-32-3). *Nonstandard peripherals required:* Cash drawer, receipt printer. *Optimal configuration:* Bar code scanner. *Networks supported:* Novell, LANtastic.
Capture Front Counter Sales Data Quickly & Report All Information in the Back Office, 'Live.' The Color, Legend Keys Make It Easy to Learn & To Use. Enter Items for Sale with Bar Code Scanner or Key Pad. Do Ordering, Receiving, Vendors, Inventory & Sales Reports. Add More Sales Stations & Stores. Low Cost DOS Equipment. Novell & LANtastic. Links to Popular Accounting Programs Like BusinessWorks.
CAP Automation.

CAP Head Quarters. Feb. 1996. *Items Included:* Printed manual. *Customer Support:* 60 days free support with purchase. Support after that via 800 toll free numbers is $399 per year.
Windows NT or Windows 95 with Microsoft Plus. 486 (4Mb). Contact publisher for price (ISBN 0-917081-36-6). *Nonstandard peripherals required:* VGA. *Networks supported:* Novell Netware 3.X, 4.X, Lantastic.
Allows, from One Location, Control of Inventory at One or More Locations Which Are Using Either CAP SellWise of CAP Cash'nCarry. Will View Inventory, Edit Inventory, Consolidate Ordering, Remote Receiving & Replenishment, & Stock Transfers & Balancing. The Answer for Managing Inventory for More Than One Location Easily.
CAP Automation.

CAP POS. *Version:* 96.1. (Inventory Management Ser.). 1995. *Compatible Hardware:* IBM PC & compatibles. *Operating System(s) Required:* PC-DOS/MS-DOS. *Language(s):* CB-86, Btrieve File Manager. *Memory Required:* 640k. *Items Included:* Manual on disk. *Customer Support:* $199.00 per year.
$295.00-$495.00 (ISBN 0-917081-30-7).
Tracks a User's Parts Inventory, Prints Sales Invoices, Lists the Inventory, Orders & Receives Items, Prints Labels & Price Tags, & Gets Reports on Sales & Stock. When User Enters the Quantity & Stock/Locator Number, the Computer Prints a Sales Ticket & Manages the Inventory Simultaneously. User Can Continue to Order Parts in the Usual Way, or If Desired, the Program Performs This Function Automatically. Reports Include Backorders, Review Today's Sales, Sales Summary, Turnover, under or Overstock, Vendor Parts Lists, Parts with Zero Sales, & Parts Status. Also Keeps Track of Customers If Needed.
CAP Automation.

Capacity Planning. *Version:* 1.3. Apr. 1992. *Compatible Hardware:* UNIX compatibles. *Operating System(s) Required:* AIX, Opus, UNIX, XENIX. *Language(s):* C. *Memory Required:* 1000k.
contact publisher for price.
Tool for Creating & Maintaining a Picture of Planned Capacity & Load for Each Work Center.
Solid State Software, Inc. (Missouri).

Capgain. *Compatible Hardware:* IBM PC, PC XT, PCjr, & compatibles; TRS-80. *Operating System(s) Required:* MS-DOS. *Language(s):* BASIC. *Memory Required:* 32k. *General Requirements:* 2 disk drives, 132-column printer.
contact publisher for price.
Tracks Investor's Capital Gains & Losses Periodically Throughout Tax Year. By Setting up

Random Access Data File Which Records Each Sale of Capital Asset During Year, Program Calculates Gain or Loss Which Are Long & Short Term, & Separately Totals All Gains & Losses to Date for Year. Holds & Carries Forward Long & Short Term Losses from Previous Years & Factors These into Indicated Gains & Losses for Taxable Year. Each Sale Can Be Reviewed at Random on Monitor Display. Periodic Printouts, & Particularly Report for December 31 of Any Year (or Any Given Fiscal Year End), Provide Listing of Information Needed for Preparing Capital Gains & Losses Schedule for Income Tax Purposes.
R & M Assocs.

Capital Cashflow Templates. *Version:* Professional Series. Nov. 1991.
MS-DOS. IBM or compatible (256k). disk $29.95. *Addl. software required:* Lotus compatible spreadsheet.
Selection of Cashflow & Income Flow Templates to Aid in Business Planning. Also Includes Disbursements & Receipts Templates. Ideal for the Accountant. Customization Available.
Capital Enterprises.

Capital Financial Templates. (Professional Ser.). Nov. 1991. *Compatible Hardware:* IBM PC & compatibles. *Memory Required:* Recommended 384k.
$59.95.
Helps Perform Loan & Yield Calculations. Provides Detailed Monthly Mortgage Loan-Amortization Schedules for As Many As 30 Years. Includes Rule of 78's. Customization Available.
Capital Enterprises.

Capital Investment Analysis. *Customer Support:* 800-929-8117 (customer service).
MS-DOS. Apple II. disk $79.99 (ISBN 0-87007-540-3).
Analyze Capital Investments as a Return on Investment, Net Present Value, or Internal Rate of Return. Method Uses Annual Cash Flows as Input.
SourceView Software International.

Captain Blood. *Compatible Hardware:* Atari ST; Commodore 64/128, Amiga; IBM PC & compatibles; Macintosh; Apple IIgs.
Atari ST & Amiga. 3.5" disk $49.95.
Commodore 64/128. disk $24.94.
IBM. $39.95.
Apple IIgs. disk $44.95.
Macintosh. 3.5" disk $49.95.
Science Fiction Adventure Game. Find 5 Clones Before They Destroy You. Includes Spectacular Graphics, Icon Language, Trips Through Hyperspace.
Software Toolworks.

Captain Goodnight & the Islands of Fear.
Michael Wise. *Compatible Hardware:* Apple II+, IIe, IIc. *Memory Required:* 64k.
disk $34.95 (Order no.: APDSK-37).
Players Battle Against the Clock in This Feature-Length Arcade Adventure, Fighting Their Way by Land, Sea, & Air Towards Dr. Maybe's Hideout on Doom Island.
Broderbund Software, Inc.

Captivate. *Version:* 4.5. Mar. 1995. *Compatible Hardware:* Apple Macintosh. *Memory Required:* 512k. *Items Included:* Manual. *Customer Support:* Free Tech support for registered users.
3.5" disk $89.95.
Saves Any Portion of a Macintosh Screen to the Clipboard or Scrapbook; Saves in PICT, TIFF or MacPaint Formats. Converts Graphics to Many Standard Graphics Formats. Stores & Organizes Graphics, Text, Sounds, & QuickTime Movies. Power Mac Native.
Mainstay.

The Car Disk. Oct. 1985. *Compatible Hardware:* Apple II, II+, IIe, IIc. (source code included). *Memory Required:* 48k.
disk $9.95.
Includes "The Road Navigator" to Help in Trip Planning. Determines the Amount of Time & Fuel Needed to Complete a Particular Trip. Computes the Time of Departure to Meet a Specific Arrival Time or the Time of Arrival When Given Time of Departure. Also Includes Trip Recording & Mileage Computing Routines As Well As a Trip Cost System in Order to Decide Whether to Drive or Fly & Has a Program for Computing the Ideal Time to Trade or Sell a Particular Car.
AV Systems, Inc.

Car Sales & Rental Software. 1987. *Compatible Hardware:* IBM PC, PC XT, PC AT & compatibles. *Memory Required:* 640k. *General Requirements:* 20Mb hard disk, printer.
disk $499.00 (Order no.: LSC-2029).
Capable of Keeping Track of Customer Information & Checks Expiration Date of Credit Cards. Keeps Track of Late Charges. Features Daily Sales Report & Summary of Transactions by Individual Sales Clerk. Keeps Track of Car Inventory During Invoice Generation, Reservations & Returns. Inventory Can Be Traced by Car Code, License Number, Customer Code or Invoice Number. Security Deposits Received & Returned Are Reported.
Lizcon Computer Systems.

CARBONCopy. *Version:* 3.3. 1986. *Items Included:* Manuals (system, reference, installation), 1 year maintenance, quarterly newsletter. *Customer Support:* 6am-6pm, MST.
MicroVMS & VMS 4.6 & higher. MicroVAX & VAX (100k). Included in ClydeSupport (formerly ProSupport).
A Trouble-Shooting Tool. Unobtrusively Records All the Activity at a Terminal So Support Personnel Can Determine Exactly Where & When Software Problems Occur. As a Documentation Tool, It Easily Creates User Examples for Virtually Any Program.
Raxco, Inc.

Card & Label Manager (CALM). *Version:* 4.0. Aug. 1989. *Items Included:* Manual, sample data files. *Customer Support:* 30-day preview without obligation, phone support.
Macintosh. $169.00 (ISBN 0-918161-00-2, Order no.: C40M).
MS-DOS/PC-DOS. IBM PC, PS/2, & compatibles (256k). $169.00 (ISBN 0-918161-00-2, Order no.: C40A).
Apple Pro DOS. Apple IIc, IIe, IIgs, (64k). $169.00 (Order no.: C40A).
Produces Library Catalog Cards &/or Card & Pocket Labels & Spine Labels. Data Saved in Disk File & Fully Editable.
Speak Softly, Inc.

Card-Cat. 1987. *Compatible Hardware:* Apple II series. *Memory Required:* 48k. *Customer Support:* 800 no., Guaranteed to load & run 1 year.
disk $59.95 (ISBN 0-917729-41-2, Order no.: AP833).
Program Allows User to Input, Edit & Print the Required Catalog Cards & Spine Labels Needed for Library Use. Includes a Program Diskette & a Data Disk Which Will Hold up to 160 Different Titles. Program Diskette Can Be Used to Create As Many Additional Data Disks As Are Required.
Compu-Tations, Inc.

Card/Fax. *Items Included:* Database of 28,000 Topps baseball cards, user's guide. *Customer Support:* Free tech. support.
Apple Macintosh (512k). 3.5" disk $95.00.
Apple II with ProDOS (128k). disk $95.00.
IBM (384k). disk $95.00.
Sports Card Collection Inventory & Evaluation.
Compu-Quote.

Card Shop. *Compatible Hardware:* Apple Macintosh.
3.5" disk $39.95.
Contains an Assortment of 45 Greeting Cards That Can Be Used As Is or Customized with a User's Own Personal Message. The Cards Cover a Variety of Occasions, Including Birthdays, Christmas, Party Invitations, Bar Mitzvahs, Thanksgiving, Baby Announcements, Friendship, Sympathy, Get Well, Thank You, Anniversary, Valentine, Congratulations, Halloween, Easter etc.
Artsci, Inc.

Card Shop: Greeting Cards for the Mac. Sep. 1986. *Compatible Hardware:* Apple Macintosh, Macintosh Plus. *General Requirements:* Printer.
3.5" disk $39.95 (ISBN 0-917963-20-2).
48 Original Cards for Birthdays, Party Invitations, Romance, "Thank You", etc. Can Be Customized. Samples of Colored Paper & Envelopes Are Included.
Artsci, Inc.

Cardiac Muscle Mechanics. *Compatible Hardware:* IBM PC & compatibles. *Memory Required:* 256k.
disk $125.00 (Order no.: COM 4202B).
Simulates the Mechanical Behavior of an Isolated Strip of Heart Muscle to Represent the Function of the Heart As a Whole. Simplifies Anatomical Teaching Techniques. A Series of 17 Pictures Can Be Called up to Further Illustrate the Principle Points of the Simulation.
COMPress.

Cardio-Pulmonary Exercise Testing. 1985. *Compatible Hardware:* Apple II+, IIe, IIc; IBM PC & compatibles. *Operating System(s) Required:* Apple DOS 3.3, MS-DOS. *Language(s):* BASIC. *Memory Required:* Apple 48k, IBM 512k.
disk $200.00 (Order no.: PIP-81301).
Identifies the Ventilatory & Cardiac Responses to Exercise That Typifies the Normal, Sedentary, Cardiac, & Pulmonary Limited Patients. The Learner Will Use This Information to Determine Appropriate Exercise Prescriptions for These Patient Groups.
Educational Software Concepts, Inc.

Cardio Pulmonary Master. *Customer Support:* 800-929-8117 (customer service).
MS-DOS. Apple II. disk $69.99 (ISBN 0-87007-533-0).
Allows Simulation of 20 Hemodynamic Parameters Including BSA, CI, SU, SI, TVR, PVR, LVMWI, RVMWI, Saturation, Consumption, PO-2 & Shunt for Educational Purposes.
SourceView Software International.

Cardionet. 1982. *Compatible Hardware:* IBM PS/2 based LAN Nestar, token ring network. *Operating System(s) Required:* MS-DOS, PC-DOS. *Language(s):* Compiled BASIC. *Memory Required:* 640k. *General Requirements:* Nestar Network.
contact publisher for price.
Create a Local Area Network Administrative System with the Cath Lab Support System, Echocardiography Support System, CCU Support System, Pacemaker Followup System & a Stress Test Analysis System.
Trinity Computing Systems, Inc.

CardLine CD-ROM Database for Cardiology. Mar. 1991.
MS Windows 3.1 or higher. IBM & compatibles (4Mb). CD-ROM disk $325.00-$995.00; Networks $1895.00 & up. *Nonstandard peripherals required:* Magnetic or CD-ROM, using ISO 9660. *Optimal configuration:* IBM & compatibles, 80386 or higher, 4Mb RAM, 20Mb hard disk, mouse, MS Windows 3.1 or

TITLE INDEX

higher.
System 6.0.7 or higher. Apple Macintosh (3Mb). CD-ROM disk $325.00-$995.00; Networks $1895.00 & up λ03249645. *Optimal configuration:* Apple Macintosh Plus or higher, 3Mb RAM, System 6.0.7 or higher.
CardLine Is an Electronic Reference Database to the Cardiology Journal Literature. Cardiology-Specific Excerpts (Including Abstracts) from the National Library of Medicine's MEDLINE Database Are Distributed on CD-ROM (Compact Disc, Read-Only Memory) Optical Disc. Knowledge Finder Search-&-Retrieval Software Makes Searching of the CardLine Database Easy, Effective & Fast. After the User Types a Phrase or Sentence Describing the Information Needed, It selects the References in the Database That Appear to Best Match the Request, & Presents Them in Order of Likely Relevance. The CardLine Archive CD-ROM Contains More Than 385,000 References to Articles Published in 185 Cardiology-Related Journals over the Most Recent 10 Full Years.
Aries Systems Corp.

Cards. J. Weaver, Jr. May 1986. *Compatible Hardware:* Atari ST. *Operating System(s) Required:* TOS. *Memory Required:* 512k.
Atari ST. 3.5" disk $39.95 (ISBN 0-923213-02-3, Order no.: AT-CAR).
Includes: Blackjack, Cribbage, Klondike, Poker Squares, & Solitaire.
MichTron, Inc.

Care-DM. *Version:* 5.0. 1990. *Compatible Hardware:* VAX, Micro VAX. *Operating System(s) Required:* VMS, VAX-11 BASIC, Micro VMS. *Language(s):* BASIC Plus 2, VAX-11 BASIC. *Memory Required:* 1000k.
$4750.00.
Healthcare Office Automation System Designed to Be Used Interactively in the Practice As a Tool to Capture, Control, Process & Analyze Patient Service Information. Emphasis Is Placed on Accounts Receivable Management.
Care Information Systems, Inc.

Care Plan. G. B. Cook. Jun. 1985. *Compatible Hardware:* IBM PC. *Language(s):* Quicksilver. *Memory Required:* 640k. *Customer Support:* Toll free telephone support.
disk $995.00 (Order no.: 285-03).
Designed for Both Institutional & Community Nursing to Develop, Store & Utilize Customized Care Plans.
SRC Systems, Inc.

Care Plans. *Items Included:* Manuals, training exercises, quick reference guide.
IBM PC, XT, AT & compatibles; PS/2. contact publisher for price.
Patient Care Plans & Management of Objectives, Time Tables, & Approaches.
Beechwood Software.

Career Compass. *Version:* 5.10. *Items Included:* User's guide.
DOS. IBM & compatibles. disk $95.00 (ISBN 1-56191-318-9, Order no.: 3099). *Optimal configuration:* Computer, software, printer.
R.R. 3. Apple II. disk $95.00 (ISBN 1-56191-349-9, Order no.: 3098). *Optimal configuration:* Computer, software, printer.
Covers General Career Clusters, Major Work Groups & Specific Occupations Based on Student's Responses to 70 Work Activity Questions. Program Printout Covers: 1) Career Interest Profile Describing Student's Interest, 2) Interest Area Descriptions Providing Additional Information for the Top Three Interest Clusters.
Meridian Education Corporation.

Carets & Cursors. *Version:* 1.3. 1991. *Items Included:* Disk & Instruction. *Customer Support:* 8-5 MST.
MS Windows. IBM compatible (20k). disk $49.00. *Addl. software required:* MS Windows 3.0.
A MS-Windows Utility for Controlling the Edit Caret & Mouse Cursor in Application & System Windows. Provides a Large Selection of Shapes, Sizes, & Colors. Changing the Window Coloring Will Often Make the Caret & Cursor Difficult to See. Changing the Text Font Will Often Make the Carrot Seem Inappropriate. Common Caret & Cursor Colors Makes Them Difficult to Distinguish. Provides a Quick Solution to Better Colors Shapes. Caret Blinking Can Also Be Disabled.
Instant Replay Corp.

Carina BBS, 2 disks. Jun. 1986. *Compatible Hardware:* Atari 800, XL/XE. *Language(s):* BASIC, Machine. *General Requirements:* Modem.
disk $55.00.
Hayes compatibility handler for the MPP modem $10.00.
Hayes compatiblity handler for the 1030/XM301 $15.00.
Modular Design for a BBS Set-Up Allowing Customization for Individual Needs. Features Upload/Download Capability, a Message Board, & Sysop/User Chat Mode. Compatible with Most Modems.
Carina Software Systems.

Carnasaur. Mar. 1995. *Customer Support:* Dedicated voice mail phone number; will respond back to consumer.
Windows 3.1 or higher; Macintosh. IBM or 100% compatible 486SX 25MHz (4Mb); 68030/68040 Color Mac System 7.1 or higher (4Mb). CD-ROM disk $19.99 (ISBN 1-57339-000-3, Order no.: ROMI2930NH).
Nonstandard peripherals required: 2X CD-ROM drive.
A Deranged Geneticist Brings Dinosaurs Back to Life from Chicken Eggs.
Image Entertainment.

Carol's Big Helper: Interest on Deposits. Richard Olin. Jan. 1985. *Operating System(s) Required:* CP/M, MS-DOS. *Memory Required:* 64k.
disk $100.00 (ISBN 0-931815-04-5, Order no.: CBH-C). MS-DOS. disk $100.00 (ISBN 0-931815-05-3, Order no.: CBH-M).
Savings Account Type Program That Calculates Interest on Deposits for Unlimited Number of Accounts. Fixed or Floating Interest Rates. Prints 1099 Forms at Year End. Designed for Use in Consumer Finance Company or Credit Union.
Commercial Investment Assocs.

Carrier Strike: Jewel Case CD. Nov. 1995. *Customer Support:* 30 day limited warranty.
DOS 5.0 or higher. 386 CD-ROM with hard drive (2Mb). CD-ROM disk $9.95 (ISBN 0-917059-39-5, Order no.: 062601).
All the Great Carrier Battles of the South Pacific, Linked up in One Big Campaign. WWII Wargame.
Strategic Simulations, Inc.

CARS: Computer Assisted Repair System. *Version:* 6.27. Oct. 1988. *Compatible Hardware:* IBM PC & compatibles. *Memory Required:* 640k. disk $1495.00 single user; $2495.00 multi-user.
Creates Work Orders for Technicians, Invoices; Provides Service History. Reminds Operator & Customer When Vehicle is Due for Service (Individual & Fleet). Computers Shop Gross P & L, Technician Pay. Tracks Inventory Usage & Prints Inventory Vendor Orders Based upon Reorder Points.
Miramar, Ltd.

CASE MASTER III

Cars Wars. *Compatible Hardware:* TI 99/4A with PLATO interpreter solid state cartridge.
contact publisher for price (Order no.: PHM 3054).
Pit Your Speed & Skill Against the Computer's As You Try to Get Your Car Around the Track Without Getting Crashed off the Field. Various Levels of Difficulty.
Texas Instruments, Personal Productivit.

Cartooners. Dec. 1988. *Items Included:* Manual or ref card. *Customer Support:* Customer hint hotline (415) 572-9560.
Apple IIgs (1Mb). disk $24.95 (Order no.: 3045).
IBM. disk $49.95.
Wide Variety of Animated Graphics, Vibrant Scenery, & Lively Music, Combined with an Easy-to-Use Interface. A Computer Movie Studio for Kids of All Ages.
Electronic Arts.

Cascade I. Jan. 1984. *Compatible Hardware:* Apple, IBM PC. *Operating System(s) Required:* Apple DOS, MS-DOS. *Language(s):* UCSD Pascal. *Memory Required:* 64k.
Apple. $895.00.
IBM PC. $995.00.
Computer Aided Drafting & Design Package. Includes: Crosshatch, Arcs, Circles, Automatic Dimensioning, Rotate, Scale, Mirror & Groups.
Cascade Graphics Systems.

CasCode Component Application Guide, 1966-1993. May 1993.
disk $49.95 (ISBN 0-8019-8518-8).
Professional Mechanics.
Chilton Bk. Co.

CASDIS. *Compatible Hardware:* Atari 400, 800, 1200XL. *Language(s):* BASIC.
$24.95 (ISBN 0-936200-18-9).
Machine Language Utility That Transfers Most "Boot" Tapes & Cassette Data Files to Disk.
Blue Cat.

CASDUP. *Version:* 2.0. *Compatible Hardware:* Atari. *Language(s):* BASIC.
cassette $24.95 (ISBN 0-936200-17-0).
Copies Most "Boot" Tapes & Cassette Data Files. Includes a File Copier & a Sector Copier.
Blue Cat.

Case & File Management (Mailings & Records Management): Series 900 to 2000. *Compatible Hardware:* IBM System/36, System/36 PC; AS/400.
contact publisher for price.
Helps to Administer & Locate Client Files. Produces Client Directory, File Labels & Bring-Forward Dates. When Closed, the Archives Number & Date to Destroy Are Noted.
Manac-Prentice Hall Software, Inc.

Case Load. *Compatible Hardware:* TI Professional Computer. *Operating System(s) Required:* MS-DOS. *Language(s):* DBASE II. *Memory Required:* 128k. *General Requirements:* 2 disk drives.
disk $700.00.
Track Accounts Receivable from Blue Cross & Others. Handles Case Loads & Provides Summaries. Designed for Use by Professionals Such As Visiting Nurses, Therapists, etc.
Computer/Business Services.

Case Master III. *Version:* 2. May 1989. *Items Included:* Binder with documentation. *Customer Support:* 1 yr. maintenance, $175.00, provides phone support, quarterly newsletters & any enhancements released for their computer during the year at no charge.
PC-DOS/MS-DOS Ver. 3.3 or higher. IBM &

compatibles (512k). disk $995.00. *Nonstandard peripherals required:* Hard disk. *Optimal configuration:* 640k RAM. *Networks supported:* Novell, IBM PC networks, 3COM Plus network.
Provides a Convenient Method of Tracking Client & Case Information. This Information Is Then Used to Automatically Prepare Documents & Management/Status Reports. Tracks the Time Spent on Each Case & Includes a Calendar Tickler, Automatic Docket Entry System, Document Tracking & Location System, Conflict of Interest & Statute of Limitations Checking, Document Assembly Allows If/Then/Else Conditional Logic & More. Integrates with TABS III. For CASEMASTER III for Windows Users Hot Docs Document Assembly Engine.
Software Technology, Inc.

Case Master III-M. *Version:* 2. *Items Included:* Binder with documentation. *Customer Support:* 1 yr. maintenance, $250-$2,500, provides phone support, quarterly newsletters & all enhancements released during the year on their computer at no charge.
DOS Ver. 3.1 or higher. IBM & compatibles (512k). contact publisher for price.
Nonstandard peripherals required: Hard disk. *Optimal configuration:* 640k RAM. *Networks supported:* Novell, IBM PC networks, PC network.
Multi-User Version of CM-III When Used with a Network. It Provides Client Tracking & Case Information for Automatic Preparation of Documents & Management/Status Reports. A Calendar Tickler, Automatic Docket Entry System, Document Tracking & Location System, Conflict of Interest & Statute of Limitations Checking & More. Integrates with TABS III-M. Case Master III Is Licensed Based on the Number of Active Users Not on the Number of Timekeepers. Case Master III-M for Windows Uses Hot Docs Document Assembly Engine.
Software Technology, Inc.

Case Master III. *Version:* 2.2. 1989. *Items Included:* Bound manual, tutorial, runtime of Hot Docs. *Customer Support:* Maintenance includes free phone support from STI, user newsletter, free updates released during the maintenance period & retention of value if user needs to.
DOS Version 3.3. or higher. Math Co-processor recommended (512k). $995.00-$15,000.00.
Addl. software required: Hot Docs optional, TABS III optional. *Networks supported:* Novell, IBM PC Network & compatibles.
Provides a Convenient Method of Tracking All Client & Case Information. Includes Calendar/Docket, Conflict of Interest, Statute of Limitations, Value Billing. Document Assembler Automatically Merges & Assembles Client & Case Data into Documents Templates Created with Hot Docs, Information Entered During the Assembly Process Is Written Back into Case Master III Files.
Software Technology, Inc.

Case Mix Library. *Compatible Hardware:* DEC Micro Vax II; IBM PC, IBM 4300 & compatibles. *Operating System(s) Required:* VM/CMS, DOS-VSE.
contact publisher for price.
Offers Managers of Both Hospitals & Multi-Hospital Groups a Wide Range of Decision Support Applications to Aid in Effective Management under the Prospective Payment System. Financial Applications Include Case Mix Budgeting & Profitability Analysis. Clinical Applications Allows Physician Practice Pattern Evaluation, Examination of Exceptional or Problem Physicians, Patient Groups, Departments, & Complete Length of Stay Analysis.
HBO & Co., Inc.

Case Studies in Gastroenterology: GastroMaster. Ingram M. Roberts & William M. Steinberg. Dec. 1994. *Customer Support:* Toll-free technical support - no charge. In U.S. 9AM - 5PM EST 800-343-0064.
Microsoft Windows, Version 3.1. 386 IBM-Compatible PC (8Mb). CD-ROM disk $175.00, Individual, ,495.00 Institutional (ISBN 1-57276-017-6, Order no.: SE-017-001). *Nonstandard peripherals required:* CD-ROM drive (MPC Standard) 640x480 display with 256 colors, MPC Standard Soundboard & Speakers.
Provides Exposure of Gastroenterological Scenarios So That Physicians Can Review Their Interpretive Abilities. Physicians Will Gain a Better Understanding of Gastroenterology Through Reading X-Rays, CT Scans, & Pathology Material Such As Biopsies. The Program Is Organized Around 30 Case Scenarios Based on Real Patient Material.
SilverPlatter Education.

CaseFlow Management System. *Compatible Hardware:* Apple Macintosh SE or II. *General Requirements:* ImageWriter II or LaserWriter, hard disk drive recommended, multiuser version requires AppleShare & Ethernet.
single user $2950.00.
Track's a Court's Civil Cases from Filing Through Disposition.
Diamante Software.

CaseLode (FKA PROMIS). 1982. *Compatible Hardware:* Alpha Micro, IBM PC & compatibles. *Memory Required:* 100k. *General Requirements:* Hard disk, printer, modem.
Alpha Micro. VCR tape $4,250.00-$10,500.00. IBM. $4250.00.
Total Law Office Management System of Word Processing, Time & Billing Accounting, Trust (Escrow) Funds Accounting, Management Reporting, Docket & Conflicts of Interest Control, Litigation Support, & Telephone & Photocopy Chargeback Systems. ABA Approved. Both Single & Multi-User.
Alpha Microsystems.

Casequiz. Byron A. Myhre & Henry M. Taylor. Apr. 1987. *Compatible Hardware:* IBM PC & compatibles, PC XT, PC AT. *Operating System(s) Required:* MS-DOS 2.XX. *Language(s):* BASIC (source code included). *Memory Required:* 128k.
disk $45.00, incl. documentation (ISBN 0-89189-244-3, Order no.: 68-9-005-20).
Educational Assessment Tool for All Blood-Banking Personnel. The User Selects the Proper Tests for Ten Simulated Patients with Varying Blood Related Symptoms. Questions Are Asked Concerning Each Patient, with Four Possible Answers Given for Each. The User Diagnoses the Problem by Employing Test Results; Scores Are Derived by How Many Tries the User Needs to Diagnose the Correct Condition.
ASCP Pr.

Cash & Credit. *Version:* 4.1. Stephen R. Krause. Nov. 1983. *Compatible Hardware:* IBM PC & compatibles. *Operating System(s) Required:* MS-DOS, PC-DOS. *Language(s):* DBASE III Plus, DBASE IV & Foxbase, Foxpro. *Memory Required:* 640k. *General Requirements:* 20Mb hard disk. *Customer Support:* 6 months free telephone support.
5-1/4" or 3.5" disk $1900.00.
Accounts Receivable System & Inventory Control for a Small Shop Owner. Handles Cash & Credit Customer & Provides a History File of All Transactions.
Tele Vend, Inc.

Cash Controller. 1982. *Compatible Hardware:* Apple II, Commodore 64, IBM PC. *Memory Required:* 64k. *General Requirements:* Printer.
disk $39.00.
Helps the Small Businessman to Apply Available Funds, by Combining Both Age of Invoice & Dollar Amount in Pay Decision. Accommodates up to 300 Invoices at a Time, with Routines for Totaling, Finding, Deleting, Correcting, Updating, & Listing the Entire Database. Printouts Sorted by Age & Amount; Complete List & Combine Payout List Are Selectable from Main Menu. Program Does Not Print Checks.
Navic Software.

Cash Flow Analysis. *Customer Support:* 800-929-8117 (customer service).
MS-DOS. Apple II. disk $49.99 (ISBN 0-87007-832-1).
Provides a Process for Analyzing Existing & Projected Cash Flow in Terms of Adequacy & Various Principles of Good Business.
SourceView Software International.

Cash-Flow Forecaster Plus. *Version:* 1.1. Sep. 1987. *Compatible Hardware:* IBM PC & compatibles. *Memory Required:* Lotus Release 1A 256k, Release 2 320k. *General Requirements:* Lotus 1-2-3 Release 1A or 2. *Items Included:* Manual, startup procedure, software. *Customer Support:* Telephone.
$99.95.
optional Consolidation Module $30.00.
both $129.95.
Projects Income-Statement Results, Financial Ratios, Monthly Sales, Costs, Income, Balance-Sheet Changes, & Cash-Flow Results for a One-Year Period. Prints Monthly & Quarterly Income Statements, Balance Sheets (Includes Accounts-Receivable & Accounts-Payable Aging Formulas), Cash-Flow Forecasts, & Financial Ratios Reports. Graphs Trends, Ratios, Sales, Cost of Goods Sold, Operating Expenses, & Net Income. Supports Normal & Condensed Printing on 80- & 132-Column & Laser Printers. Optional CONSOLIDATION MODULE Consolidates Worksheets Across Multiple Years & Separate Departments, Divisions or Companies.
Bryley Systems, Inc.

Cash Flow Management with Lotus 1-2-3. W. M. Greenfield & Dennis P. Curtin. *Compatible Hardware:* IBM PC & compatibles. *Memory Required:* 128-192k.
disk $38.95, incl. bk. (Order no.: 12013-9).
Prentice Hall.

Cash Flow Management with Symphony. W. M. Greenfield & Dennis P. Curtin. *Compatible Hardware:* IBM PC & compatibles. *Memory Required:* 320k.
disk $38.95, incl. bk. (Order no.: 12015-4).
Lets User Devise a Cash Budget, Project Inflows & Outflows, Monitor Accounts Receivable, Calculate Trade Discounts & Realize the Most Economic Ordering Quantity.
Prentice Hall.

Cash Flow Plan. Duane Bristow. *Compatible Hardware:* TRS-80 Model I, Model III. *Operating System(s) Required:* TRSDOS. *Language(s):* BASIC.
disk $44.95.
cassette $29.95.
Allows User to Label up to 100 Categories of Income & Expense Items & Enter the Amount of Income & Expense in Each Category for Each Month of the Year.
Duane Bristow Computers, Inc.

Cash Flow Planner. Jun. 1987. *Compatible Hardware:* IBM PC & compatibles. *Memory Required:* 348k. *General Requirements:* Lotus 1-2-3. *Customer Support:* Free telephone Support.
$95.00.
Tracks Historical or Projected Cash Flows for 12

TITLE INDEX

Periods. Helps Schedule Dividend Payments, Purchase of Assets, Sale of Investments, & Borrowing & Marketing Efforts. Analyzes Alternate Business Strategies. Includes a Sample File & Instructs in Using the Model in Different Business Situations.
Accounting Professionals Software, Inc.

Cash Flow Pro. Dec. 1985. *Compatible Hardware:* Apple Macintosh with printer. *Memory Required:* 128k.
disk $49.95.
Loan Computation/Analysis Program That Amortizes with up to 4 Rates of Interest or Amortization, 2 Types of Balloons, C.C.P., etc.
Realsoft, Inc. (Florida).

Cash Ledger. *Version:* 2.1. *Compatible Hardware:* Apple Macintosh. *Memory Required:* 512k. *Items Included:* Diskette & manual. *Customer Support:* 60 days free support, starting with the first call. $79/year extended support plan.
3.5" disk $99.00.
An Entry-Level Accounting System for Those Who Don't Need Inventory, Payables, or Receivables. All Transactions Handled Through the 3 Journals (General, Receipts, & Disbursements). Prints Checks & Bank Reconciliation Report along with Several Other Useful Reports.
CheckMark Software, Inc.

Cash Management for Holding Companies (CMS). Alan Chwick & Joel Katzman. Jun. 1990. *Items Included:* All documentation, Novell LAN server, communications server (for 5 in-bound & 1 out-bound), all software & customization. *Customer Support:* Maintenance & support: $5000.00/month; 90 day unlimited warranty.
Novell LAN server included in package. $100,000.00 complete with hardware & customization (ISBN 0-928407-05-5, Order no.: CMS-V100).
The CMS System Is a Complete Funds Control System for Holding Companies. It Is Designed to Acquire Bank & Ledger Information (Automatically & Manually) & Produce All Needed Reports. Multiple Receipt & Disbursement Banks Are Supported. Customization Required at Each Installation (Included in Price). Wire Transfer Is Not Part of System for Security Reasons.
The Complete Machine.

Cash Reconcilement & Statement Proofing System: Cash Flow Analyzer. Oct. 1986. *Compatible Hardware:* IBM PC. *Operating System(s) Required:* PC-DOS 3.1. *Memory Required:* 256k.
contact publisher for price.
Online Interactive Accounting System with Password Protection Designed for Consolidating, Proofing, & Reconciling. Comprised of Three Operationally Independent Sub-Systems: Journal, Statement Proofing, & Cash Reconcilement. Cash Flow Analysis Is Provided for the Journal & Statement Proofing Sub-Systems. The Following Averages Are Provided for Each Journal Bank Account & Proofed Statement: Average Daily Balance, Average Daily Receipts, Average Daily Disbursement, & the Average Receipt & Disbursement. Cash Reconcilement Listings Include Non-Reconciled or Reconciled Transactions & Provide Reconciled & Non-Reconciled Totals & Final Adjusted Balances.
Automatronics.

Ca$hCollector. *Version:* 2.0c. Jul. 1990. *Items Included:* Manual & diskette. *Customer Support:* Free installation & technical support: limited warranty, call JIAN 415-941-9191.
MS-DOS. IBM PC & compatibles (512K). disk $199.00. *Nonstandard peripherals required:* Hard drive with min 2Mb free.
Generates a Variety of Collection Notices - from Nice & Polite to Threatening - Necessary to Collect Debts. If User Needs to Threaten Legal Action, Ca$hCollector Produces Appropriate Local Court Documentation. The Process Extends All the Way Through Garnishment of Wages or Attachment of Property.
JAIN Tools for Sales.

Ca$hFlow. *Compatible Hardware:* IBM PC, PC XT, PC AT & compatibles, PS/2. *Operating System(s) Required:* PC-DOS/MS-DOS 2.10 or higher. *Memory Required:* 320k. *General Requirements:* Hard disk. *Customer Support:* 60 days toll-free.
disk $695.00, 10 timekeepers/400 matters. $295.00, 5 timekeepers/200 matters.
Complete Accounts Receivable, Time Management, Billing, & Report Production Package for Small Law Firms or Other Small Firms That Bill on a Time & Expenses Basis. Enables Users to Store up to 10 Timekeepers, 10 Case Types, 74 Service Codes, & 400 Individual Matters/Cases. In Addition to 3 Standard Billing Types & 6 Standard Statement Formats, Users Can Customize Statements for an Individual Client, a Timekeeper's Cases, or the Firm As a Whole. Will Print Complete Audit Trials of All Entries, Changes, & Deletions. Users Can Enter Write-Offs, Write-Ups & Adjustments, Calculate Discounts & Sales Tax. Sorting & Printing Procedures Enable Users to Select Which Cases to Include in Almost All Reports.
CompuLaw, Ltd.

Cashman. Bill Dunlevy & Harry Lafnear. 1985. *Compatible Hardware:* Sanyo MBC 555, TRS-80 Color Computer. *Memory Required:* 128k. *General Requirements:* Joystick recommended.
Sanyo. disk $34.95 (ISBN 0-923213-27-9, Order no.: SA-CAS).
Arcade Game with over 40 Screens in Which User Searches for Gold.
MichTron, Inc.

CASHMAX: Investment Management System. 1974. *Compatible Hardware:* IBM PC, PC XT, PC AT & compatibles; Prime. *Operating System(s) Required:* PC-DOS/MS-DOS, PRIMOS. *Language(s):* C, ANSI FORTRAN 77. *Memory Required:* 512k.
contact publisher for price.
Designed for Corporate Cash Treasury Management. Provides On-Demand Investment Accounting & Management Reports; Rate of Return Calculations for Individual Securities, Market Sectors & Security Types Within the Portfolio; Daily Market Pricing, Evaluation of Investment Buy, Sell, & Borrowing Strategies; Yield Spread & Bond Swap Analysis Using User-Defined Trading Considerations; & Management of Revolving Credit Lines, Commercial Paper, & Other Debt Instruments. Modules Include Portfolio Management Reporting, Performance Measurement & Analysis, Cash Flow Forecasting & Tracking, Cash Management Strategy, Investment & Reporting.
Wismer Assocs., Inc.

CashPlan. Ben Ettelson. May 1986. *Compatible Hardware:* IBM PC & compatibles. *Operating System(s) Required:* PC-DOS 2.0 or higher. *Memory Required:* 256k.
disk $39.95 (ISBN 0-916378-90-X).
Helps Estimate Cash Needs, Living Expenses, Pro Forma Income Statement & Balance Sheet for Start-Up Business. Works with the Publishing Services, Inc. Series of STARTING & OPERATING A BUSINESS IN... Books; Disk Can Be Equally Useful Working Alone.
Oasis Pr.

CASINO LITE SEVEN CARD STUD

CashTrax Point of Sale. Jan. 1996. *Customer Support:* Free reseller support, user support on a fee basis.
DOS 5.0 or higher. 386 CPU or higher (2Mb). disk $1100.00. *Nonstandard peripherals required:* Modem (for on-line authorizations). *Addl. software required:* RealWorld Version 6.5/6.6 or 7. *Networks supported:* Novell 3.11 or higher.
The Ultimate Point-of-Sale Solution, CashTrax Is an Easy-to-Use Front-End System That Is 100% Compatible with RealWorld Accounting & Business Software & Provides Easy Data Consolidation for Analysis & Quick Operational Performance Feedback.
RealWorld Corp.

CashWise Retail Systems. *Version:* 2.1. 1986. *Compatible Hardware:* IBM PC & compatibles, PC XT, PC AT. *Operating System(s) Required:* PC-DOS, MS-DOS. *Language(s):* PL/I. *Memory Required:* 256k. *General Requirements:* Hard disk.
contact publisher for price.
Series of Data Base, Point-of-Sale, Processing, & Communications Modules for Single & Multiple Retail Store Management. Daily & Periodic Reports Control Inventory, Analyze Sales, & Monitor Price Accuracy & Personnel Productivity. Operations Modules Automate Inventory Ordering, Receiving & Distribution, Perform Point-of-Sale Functions, & Link to a Variety of Point-of-Sale Terminals.
Technovation Corp.

Casino Craps. *Compatible Hardware:* Atari 400, 800; IBM. *Language(s):* Atari BASIC. *Memory Required:* 48k-128k.
disk $23.95.
cassette $19.95.
Teaches Users the Game of Craps.
Dynacomp, Inc.

Casino Games. *Version:* 2.1.0. May 1987. *Compatible Hardware:* Apple II series. *Memory Required:* 64k.
3.5" disk $9.95 (ISBN 1-55616-025-9).
Casino Simulations.
DAR Systems International.

Casino Lite Omaha Hold'Em. Wayne Russell. Aug. 1993. *Items Included:* Disk, manual, registration card. *Customer Support:* Free technical support, free sales support, guaranteed satisfaction or full refund.
MS-DOS 3.1 or higher. IBM & compatibles (640k) 1Mb hard disk. disk $14.99 (ISBN 1-882586-03-4). *Nonstandard peripherals required:* Mouse, supports all sound cards. *Optimal configuration:* Sound Card.
Played in the Casinos of Las Vegas. This Game Includes On-Line Strategy Tips from One of the Experts Bob Ciaffone. You Play a Realistic Game of Poker with Strong Players, Loose Players & Maniacs. It Tracks Total Wins & Losses for up to 6 Players.

Casino Lite Seven Card Stud. Wayne Russell. Aug. 1993. *Items Included:* Disk, manual, registration card. *Customer Support:* Free technical support, free sales support, guaranteed satisfaction or full refund.
MS-DOS 3.1 or higher. IBM & compatibles (640k) 1Mb hard disk. disk $14.99 (ISBN 1-882586-01-8). *Nonstandard peripherals required:* Mouse, supports all sound cards. *Optimal configuration:* Sound Card.
One of the Most Popular Forms of Poker. Very Realistic Poker Play Includes Strong Players, Loose Players & Maniacs. On-Line Help with Strategy Tips from David Sklansky & Mason Malmuth. Tracking of Total Wins & Losses for up to 6 Players.

Casino Lite Texas Hold'Em. Wayne Russell. Aug. 1993. *Items Included:* Disk, manual, registration card. *Customer Support:* Free technical support, free sales support, guaranteed satisfaction or full refund.
MS-DOS 3.1 or higher. IBM & compatibles (640k) 1Mb hard disk. disk $14.99 (ISBN 1-882586-02-6). *Nonstandard peripherals required:* Mouse, supports all sound cards. *Optimal configuration:* Sound Card.
The Game Played in the World Series of Poker. On-Line Help Includes Strategy Tips from Experts David Skalansky & Mason Malmuth. Play a Realistic Poker Game Against Strong Players, Loose Players & Maniacs. The Game Tracks Total Wins & Losses for up to 6 Players.

Casino Pack One.
Microsoft Windows 3.0 or higher. IBM & compatibles (1Mb). disk $49.95. *Optimal configuration:* 80286-486PC's & PS/2s, & PC's with 80386 add-in boards; Microsoft Windows 3.0 or higher; 1Mb of RAM, & a hard drive; VGA monitor & VGA Graphics Card; Windows compatible mouse or other pointing device.
Here Are All Your Las Vegas Favorites - Poker, Roulette, Black Jack & Keno. Hours of Fun for Everyone - Novice to Shark. And Your Life-Savings Are Safe.
Software Toolworks.

Casino Poker. Mar. 1986. *Compatible Hardware:* IBM PC, PC XT, PC AT. *Language(s):* Compiled BASIC. *Memory Required:* 128k. *General Requirements:* Both color & B&W in same program.
disk $30.00.
Plays the Game of Draw Poker Against up to Six Players & Simulates Play as If the Opposing Players Chosen Were Real.
Robert L. Nicolai.

Cassandra: Medical Office Manager. Jul. 1991. *Items Included:* Manual & various utility files. *Customer Support:* Four hours free start-up support (on-line on-screen). Telephone & on-line on-screen support $105/hr thereafter.
Macintosh. Macintosh IIfx or IIci (4Mb). $3500.00. *Nonstandard peripherals required:* 9600 baud modem compatible with Timbuktu/Remote. *Addl. software required:* Double Helix with client/server software: Timbuktu/Remote. *Optimal configuration:* Standalone: Mac IIfx with LaserWriter & ImageWriter. Network: IIfx for server & IIci for each client, networked printers. *Networks supported:* Appletalk.
A Medical Office Management System Based on the Peg Board with Which Nearly Every Physician Is Familiar. Developed in an Operational Setting over a Two-Year Period. Easy-to-Use Yet Comprehensive Accounts Receivable & Medical Records Application.
Preceptor Systems, Inc.

Cassette Scope. *Compatible Hardware:* TRS-80 Model I. *Memory Required:* 16-48k.
cassette $14.95 (Order no.: 0192R).
Locates Lost Files & Files Names. Finds & Loads Addresses & Entry Points, Then Reads & Displays All Addresses in Hexidecimal.
Instant Software, Inc.

Castle Wolfenstein. Silas Warner. *Compatible Hardware:* Apple II+, IIe, IIc; Atari 400, 800, 1200XL; Commodore 64; IBM PC, PCjr. *Language(s):* Assembly. *Memory Required:* Atari 32k, Apple 48k, Commodore 64k.
disk $11.98 ea.
Apple. (ISBN 0-87190-010-6).
Atari. (ISBN 0-87190-017-3).
Commodore. (ISBN 0-87190-025-4).
Arcade-Adventure Game in Which Player Is a GI Attempting to Escape Nazi Interrogation & Torture.
Muse Software.

The Castles of Doctor Creep. Ed Hobbs. *Compatible Hardware:* Commodore 64 with 1 joystick.
disk $29.95 (Order no.: COMDSK-254).
Thirteen Castles Containing over 200 Rooms Await Your Inspection. Confront Force Fields, Electrostatic Generators, Death Rays, Wandering Mummies, & Other Dangers. Can Be Played by Two Players.
Broderbund Software, Inc.

The Cat Ate My Gymsuit. Intentional Education Staff & Paula Danziger. Apr. 1996. *Items Included:* Program manual. *Customer Support:* Free technical support, 90 day warranty.
School ver.. System 7.1 or higher. Macintosh (4Mb). 3.5" disk contact publisher for price (ISBN 1-57204-228-1). *Nonstandard peripherals required:* 256 color monitor, hard drive, printer.
Lab pack. System 7.1 or higher. Macintosh (4Mb). 3.5" disk contact publisher for price (ISBN 1-57204-204-4). *Nonstandard peripherals required:* 256 color monitor, hard drive, printer.
Site license. System 7.1 or higher. Macintosh (4Mb). 3.5" disk contact publisher for price (ISBN 1-57204-229-X). *Nonstandard peripherals required:* 256 color monitor, hard drive, printer.
School ver.. Windows 3.1 or higher. IBM/Tandy & 100% compatibles (4Mb). disk contact publisher for price (ISBN 1-57204-205-2). *Nonstandard peripherals required:* VGA or SVGA 640 x 480 resolution (256), mouse, hard drive, sound device.
Lab pack. Windows 3.1 or higher. IBM/Tandy & 100% compatibles (4Mb). disk contact publisher for price (ISBN 1-57204-230-3). *Nonstandard peripherals required:* VGA or SVGA 640 x 480 resolution (256), mouse, hard drive, sound device.
Site license. Windows 3.1 or higher. IBM/Tancy & 100% compatibles (4Mb). disk contact publisher for price (ISBN 1-57204-206-0). *Nonstandard peripherals required:* VGA or SVGA 640 x 480 resolution (256), mouse, hard drive, sound device.
This companion for young adult literature is ideal for students who don't know how to start that book report, or give that needed summary. Gentle prompts throughout the guide section of the program include Warm-up Connections, Thinking about Plot, Quoting & Noting, Keeping a Journal, If I Were———' Responding to Questions, Using Quotations, Taking a Personal View, Write to Others, & Write a Sequel.
Lawrence Productions, Inc.

CAT (Computer-Aided-Teaching). *Items Included:* Bound manual. *Customer Support:* Free hotline - no time limit; 30 day limited warranty; updates are $5/disk plus S&H.
MS-DOS 2.0 or higher. IBM & compatibles (128k). disk $39.95. *Nonstandard peripherals required:* Color graphics card; printer supported but optional. *Addl. software required:* BASICA (or GWBASIC).
TRS-80 (48k). disk $39.95.
Package Consists of Two Programs, CATGEN & CAT. CATGEN Is Used to Create Lesson, Test & Lesson Plan Files. CAT Is Used to Run the Lessons & Tests Created by the Teacher. It Can Be Used in Business & Industry for Training.
Dynacomp, Inc.

C.A.T. III.
Macintosh. Contact publisher for price.
Maintains a Rolodex of Name Cards, Call Logs, Appointments, & To-Do's. Automates Follow-Up Letters & Can Be Customized To Automate Company Forms. Use It To Print Follow-Up Correspondence, Labels, Mail Merges, Phone Books, & Custom Reports.
Chang Laboratories, Inc.

Cat Reader OCR Software for Hand-Held Scanners. *Version:* 1.54. Dec. 1988. *Items Included:* Manual with quick start-up sheets in binder/slipcase. *Customer Support:* Free on-site training, free telephone technical support.
MS-DOS 3.1, 3.2, 3.3 (640k). IBM PC XT, PC AT & 100% compatible. $295.00. *Nonstandard peripherals required:* Hand-held scanner, Hercules, CGA, EGA, or VGA display graphics adapter.
Fully Trainable, Accurate, Affordable Optical Character Recognition Software for Hand Scanners (Logitech, Complete PC, Niscan, Geniscan, DFI Handy Scanner, Mitsubishi, & More). Handles up to 10 Degree Skew, Pulls Separate Columnar Scans into One Complete Page of Text, Reads Monospaced, Proportional, & Typeset Characters, Automatically Eliminates Graphics, Has Built-In Font Dictionaries.
Computer Aided Technology, Inc.

CAT200.
IBM PC PS/2 & compatibles (including laptops). $395.00; 222 Digital Oscilloscope, $2450.00. *Nonstandard peripherals required:* Hard disk drive; EGA or VGA graphics card; serial port.
Used to Control 222 Digital Handheld Oscilloscope Through Standard RS-232C Serial Link. Reproduces Oscilloscope Front Panel on Computer screen, Allowing User to Acquire, Analyze, Reduce & Store Data. User Can Point & Click Mouse to Activate 222 Controls. Can Also Store Commonly-Used Setups for Nearly Hands-Free Use in the Field. Package Can Display up to Six Different Waveforms. Features Built-In Support for Hayes-Compatible Modems. Computer Can Be Linked to Remotely-Located 222 Scope. Uses Delta Cursors to Measure Voltage, Time & Frquency of Acquired Signals. Also Outputs Waveforms to Hardcopy Using Any Standard Printer.
Tektronix, Inc.

Catacombs. *Customer Support:* 800-929-8117 (customer service).
MS-DOS. IBM/PS2. disk $29.99 (ISBN 0-87007-852-6).
Another Variation of the Favorites. Requires CGA or EGA.
SourceView Software International.

CataList. *Version:* 5.01. Alan Stewart. Nov. 1982. *Compatible Hardware:* IBM PC, PC XT, PC AT & compatibles. *Operating System(s) Required:* PC-DOS/MS-DOS, OS/2. *Language(s):* Compiled BASIC A. *Memory Required:* 256k.
Single User. disk $250.00.
Network version. disk $795.00.
Menu-Driven, Mini-Database, List Processor, File Manager & Mailing List Handler for International & USA Mailings.
Automation Consultants, International.

Catalist: File Manager Support for Your Word Processor. *Version:* 2.9. Automation Consultants Intl. Oct. 1983. *Compatible Hardware:* IBM PC, PC XT; Compaq. *Operating System(s) Required:* MS-DOS, PC-DOS 1.1, 2.0 or 2.1. *Language(s):* CBASIC. *Memory Required:* 128k.
disk $250.00 (Order no.: 100).
Mini Data Base Manager & Mailing List Handler Able to Prepare Compatible Interface Diskettes That Can Be Merged with Form Letters Created by Most Word Processors. User Can Delete or Select Items by Name, Partial Name, Nine-Digit Zip Code, Record Number. The XT Version Can Handle up to 32,000 Items.
Stone & Assocs.

Catalog Card & Label Maker. *Version:* 6. Wehner. 1989. *Items Included:* 3-ring binder, manual.
DOS. IBM, Tandy, & compatibles (512k). disk

TITLE INDEX

$199.00 (ISBN 0-943646-13-8). *Optimal configuration:* Hard disk, printer. *Networks supported:* None supported. However, may be networked at one site only.
Creates Catalog Cards & Labels Individually or in Batch Mode. All Entries Are Saved on a Data Disk Which May Be Accessed Through a Database Program. Easy to Follow Instructions. Good for Entry Level Users & Catalog Card Production Facilities (Not AACR2).
K-12 Micromedia Publishing, Inc.

Catalog Card & Label Writer. *Items Included:* Bound manual. *Customer Support:* Free hotline - no time limit; 30 day limited warranty; updates are $5/disk plus S&H.
MS-DOS. IBM & compatibles (256k). disk $189.95. *Nonstandard peripherals required:* 80-column printer; single disk drive. Requires continuous-form cards & labels; lower-case adapter required for the Apple II Plus.
Apple. disk $189.95.
Macintosh. 3.5" disk $189.95.
Formats & Prints Catalog Cards & Book Pockets & Spine Labels, As Many Copies As Needed. Provides Individual Flexibility in Card Format While Not Sacrificing Ease of Entering Information. User Can Do Hanging Indentations, Long Subject Entries &, If More Information Than Will Fit on One Card, It Will Do a Second Card. Author or Title Main Entry Is Provided For.
Dynacomp, Inc.

Catalog Card & Label Writer: V6Pro. *Compatible Hardware:* Apple IIc, enhanced IIe, IIgs. *Memory Required:* 128k. *General Requirements:* Printer. *Customer Support:* Telephone.
disk $199.00 (ISBN 0-943646-13-8, Order no.: 8258).
Store Information to Disk; Patch Print; Print Accession Lists, Save to AppleWorks, Easy to Follow Instructions.
K-12 MicroMedia Publishing, Inc.

Catalog Card/Labels Program. *Version:* 3.2. *Compatible Hardware:* Apple II series; IBM PC & compatible; TRS-80, Model 4; Tandy 1000. *Memory Required:* TRS-80 48k, Apple 64k, IBM 256k. *General Requirements:* Two disk drives, tractor-feed printer, continuous pin-fed catalog cards, hard disk (IBM only). *Items Included:* Manual, disks. *Customer Support:* free updates. disk $250.00 (ISBN 0-918811-04-X).
Designed for Libraries. Enables Users to Maintain Book Lists with Inventory, Subject List, & New Book Categories. Can Produce Full Sets of Catalog Cards & Individual Cards. Can also Delete Entries, Sort Fiction Alphabetically by Author, & Sort Numerically by Call Numbers. Supports Dewey, Library of Congress, or Local Cataloging Procedures. Users can Designate Books as Reference, Paperback, or Professional, & Perform Subject Searches by Keyword or Groups of Call Numbers.
G-N-G Software.

Catalog Card Maker IV. *Version:* 2.1. Nels Aakre. 1986. *Compatible Hardware:* Apple IIe, IIc, IIgs. *Memory Required:* 128k. *General Requirements:* Printer. *Customer Support:* Manual.
disk $179.00 (ISBN 0-927875-08-X, Order no.: 451).
Formats & Prints Catalog Cards & Also Spine, Book & Pocket Label Sets. Allows Users to View the Card in Card Format on the Screen During Data Entry. Easy Editing Features Have Been Added.
Winnebago Software Co.

CATALOG-MASTER. *Version:* I. David Powers. Apr. 1983. *Compatible Hardware:* IBM PC & compatibles. *Operating System(s) Required:* MS-DOS, PC-DOS. *Language(s):* Compiled BASIC. *Memory Required:* 128k. *General Requirements:* 2 disk drives.
disk $39.95.
Disk Cataloging Program That Provides for Selection Criteria & File Descriptions for Master Directories (Sorted by Filename). Menu-Driven. Output to Terminal, Printer or Disk File.
Generic Computer Products, Inc. (GCPI).

Catalog Plus. *Version:* 7.71. 1989. *Customer Support:* Toll-free support included for the first year, with continuing support available as a renewal option. 90 days support service. Maintenance fee $150.00 after first year.
MS-DOS Plus 3Mb extended. MS-DOS compatibles (640k). disk $1295.00 (Order no.: B92750D). *Nonstandard peripherals required:* Hard disk, Workstations. *Addl. software required:* Circulation Plus. *Networks supported:* Novell.
On-Line Public Access Catalog. Integrates with Circulation Plus. Allows User to Add, Change or Delete Information Stored in Bibliographic Records via Word Processing Functions at Certain Prescribed Terminals. Provides Searchable Fields, Including Title, Author, Call Number, LCCN/ISBN Series & Subject. Includes Key Word Searching & Supports Boolean Terms in Key Word Search Field.
Follett Software Co.

Cataloger. Robert H. Geeslin. 1986. *Operating System(s) Required:* MS-DOS, PC-DOS. *Memory Required:* 640k. *General Requirements:* hard disk, printer. *Items Included:* Software, instructions for use. *Customer Support:* Custom modification available.
disk $695.00.
Full-Screen Editor to Enter Descriptions of Products, Breeding of Livestock, Video-Cassettes, etc. Prints & Sorts Catalog.
Robert H. Geeslin (Educational Programming).

Catch a Hamantash. *Compatible Hardware:* Apple II+, IIe, IIc. *Language(s):* BASIC, Machine. *Memory Required:* 48k.
disk $14.95.
Object of the Game Is to Grab the Falling Hamantashen Before They Splatter on the Ground.
Davka Corp.

Catch Weight 2001: CW2001. *Version:* 3.0. *Customer Support:* As required, training, interfaces to host.
DOS. PC LAN (8Mb). varies $30,000.00-$75,000.00. *Nonstandard peripherals required:* Optional radio terminals (LXE, Norand, TELXON). *Addl. software required:* PROGRESS RDBMS (Runtime). RADIOS (Proprietary Data Index Software). *Optimal configuration:* IBM PC 486 Plus w/LAN. *Networks supported:* Novell (NetBIOS).
CW2001 Captures the Weight of Cartons of Meat Against a Purchase Order & Ships the Meat with Weight & Price Extended Against Invoices to the Customer.
Data Index, Inc.

CatchWord. *Version:* 1.2. Aug. 1991. *Items Included:* Manual. *Customer Support:* 7 days a week customer support (telephone), CompuServe, Logitech BBS, FAXBack.
DOS 3.0 or higher. IBM PC, XT, AT, PS/2 & compatibles (640k). disk $249.00.
Omnifont OCR Package That Supports Logitech's ScanMan Family of Hand-Held Scanners. Features Include Full-Page Scan Option with Automatic Merging, Multiple Languages,

CAULDRON

Scanning Direction Options (L to R, R to L, Vertical). Stores Text in All Popular Word Processing Formats As Well As ASCII.
Logitech, Inc.

CatchWord Pro: OCR Software for Windows. Aug. 1992. *Items Included:* 1 manual (CatchWord Pro software); 1 manual (scanner, when bundled). *Customer Support:* Tech support hotline (7-days-a-week); Logitech BBS; FaxBack; CompuServe.
Windows 3.0 or higher. IBM AT or compatible with 286 processor or higher (4Mb). disk SRP $299.00. *Nonstandard peripherals required:* Scanner, mouse. *Optimal configuration:* IBM AT or compatible with 286 processor or higher (4Mb); Windows 3.0 or higher; scanner, mouse; 3Mb free disk space.
A Windows-Based OCR Package That Meets Special Requirements of Hand-Held Scanners While Working with Flatbed Models As Well. OmniFont Capability Permits Capture of a Wide Range of Fonts & Point Sizes with No Software Training Required. Features Button Bar Icons, 11-Language Capability, Automatic Stitching, Multiple Modes, Multiple Document Interface, Background Recognition. Reads Slightly Skewed Text & Offers a "Deskew" Feature for Extremely Skewed Text. Includes Text Filters for Exporting Text to All Popular Word Processing, DTP, & Spreadsheet Applications.
Logitech, Inc.

The Cath Lab Support System. 1981. *Compatible Hardware:* IBM PC AT, PC XT, PS/2 Model 30. *Operating System(s) Required:* MS-DOS. *Language(s):* C. *Memory Required:* 640k.
contact publisher for price.
Designed to Provide Reports for Both the Numeric Calculations, As Well As Graphic & Textual Recap of the Procedure Being Analyzed. Additionally, the Reports Are Archived & Can Subsequently Be Queried So That Retrospective Data Can Be Obtained.
Trinity Computing Systems, Inc.

Catskills. *Version:* 2.0.
IBM PC or compatibles with Windows. disk $39.95 (Order no.: 1488).
Macintosh Plus or higher. 3.5" disk $39.95 (Order no.: M488).
An Adaptation of a Classic Face That Presents English Letters in a Hebrew Style. Available in TrueType & Type 1 Formats.
Davka Corp.

Cattle Ration Analysis. Merle W. Wagner. 1983. *Compatible Hardware:* Apple II Plus, IIe, IIc; IBM. *Operating System(s) Required:* Apple DOS 3.3, MS-DOS 2.0. *Language(s):* BASIC. *Memory Required:* 48k, 640k. *General Requirements:* Printer.
disk $49.95 (ISBN 0-922900-31-0, Order no.: CFR-180).
Designed for Any Cattle Operation, Beef or Dairy. Provides Twenty-Six Nutrient Entries for Each Feed.
Cherrygarth, Inc.

Cauldron. Palace Software. *Compatible Hardware:* Commodore 64, 128. *Memory Required:* 64k. *General Requirements:* Joystick.
disk $29.95 (Order no.: COMDSK-269).
Two Arcade Games in One. In the First Game, You Are a Witch Whose Golden Broom Has Been Stolen by the Pumpking. In the Second Game, You Play a Pumpkin Warrior, Out to Destroy the Evil Witch Queen. In Both Games, the Only Way to Defeat Your Opponent Is to Brew a Magic Spell in the Seething Cauldron. You'll Need Special Ingredients to Do It. Features 64 Locations in CAULDRON I & 128 Locations in CAULDRON II.
Broderbund Software, Inc.

CAV-ASL: Computerized Animated Vocabulary of ASL. 1987. *Compatible Hardware:* Apple II series, Apple IIgs, Macintosh; IBM PC & compatibles. *Memory Required:* Apple II 48k, Macintosh 512k, IBM 256k. *General Requirements:* 2 disks drive, CGA card for IBM.
Apple II series Talking. disk $995.00.
Apple II series Silent. disk $695.00.
Apple IIgs Talking. disk $995.00.
Apple IIgs Silent. disk $695.00.
Macintosh Talking. 3.5" disk $995.00.
Macintosh Silent. 3.5" disk $695.00.
IBM. $695.00.
Provides Children with an Interest in Secret Languages to Learn ASL Sign Language. Vocabulary Consists of 160 Words Which Are Translated into the Equivalent ASL Signs. Signs Are Displayed with or Without Captions. Motions of Signs Can Be Slowed, Frozen or Repeated to Make Learning Easier.
E&IS SignWare.

Caveman Ugh-Lympics. Greg Johnson & Dynamix. Oct. 1988. *Items Included:* Manual or ref card. *Customer Support:* Customer hint hotline (415) 572-9560.
Commodore, IBM. $14.95. *Optimal configuration:* Joystick, graphics: IBM - EGA, CGA, Hercules, Tandy 1.6 color.
All-Time Great Neanderthal Athletes Compete for Medals in Events That Started it All: Ugh-Lympics . . . When Competition Was Rugged . . . When Brute Strength Was Worth More Than a Commercial-Appealing Smile . . . When Clubbing Earned Medals. Six Wild Events.
Electronic Arts.

Cavern Cobra. May 1988. *Compatible Hardware:* Apple IIgs. *Operating System(s) Required:* ProDOS. *Memory Required:* 768k.
3.5" disk $49.95.
Action Arcade Game Involving a Mission to Destroy the World's Most Dangerous Terrorist.
PBI Software, Inc.

The Caverns of Freitag. David Shapiro. *Compatible Hardware:* Apple II+, IIe, IIc. *Operating System(s) Required:* Apple DOS 3.2, 3.3. *Language(s):* BASIC. *Memory Required:* 48k.
disk $9.98 (ISBN 0-87190-014-9).
Player Is a Thechu Warrior out to Free the Enchanted Isles from the Reign of Terror Imposed by the Dragon Freitag. Weapons Are a Sword, Shield, & Bow with 12 Arrows. The Magic Spell Can Help Fight the Way Through Monsters until the Ultimate Terror Is Met.
Muse Software.

The Cay. Intentional Education Staff & Theodore Taylor. Apr. 1996. *Items Included:* Program manual. *Customer Support:* Free technical support, 90 day warranty.
School ver.. System 7.1 or higher. Macintosh (4Mb). 3.5" disk contact publisher for price (ISBN 1-57204-384-9). *Nonstandard peripherals required:* 256 color monitor, hard drive, printer.
Lab pack. System 7.1 or higher. Macintosh (4Mb). 3.5" disk contact publisher for price (ISBN 1-57204-360-1). *Nonstandard peripherals required:* 256 color monitor, hard drive, printer.
Site license. System 7.1 or higher. Macintosh (4Mb). 3.5" disk contact publisher for price (ISBN 1-57204-385-7). *Nonstandard peripherals required:* 256 color monitor, hard drive, printer.
School ver.. Windows 3.1 or higher. IBM/Tandy & 100% compatibles (4Mb). disk contact publisher for price (ISBN 1-57204-361-X). *Nonstandard peripherals required:* VGA or SVGA 640 x 480 resolution (256), mouse, hard drive, sound device.
Lab Pack. Windows 3.1 or higher. IBM/Tandy & 100% compatibles (4Mb). disk contact publisher for price (ISBN 1-57204-386-5). *Nonstandard peripherals required:* VGA or SVGA 640 x 480 resolution (256), mouse, hard drive, sound device.
Site license. Windows 3.1 or higher. IBM/Tandy & 100% compatibles (4Mb). disk contact publisher for price (ISBN 1-57204-362-8). *Nonstandard peripherals required:* VGA or SVGA 640 x 480 resolution (256), mouse, hard drive, sound device.
This companion for young adult literature is ideal for students who don't know how to start that book report, or give that needed summary. Gentle prompts throughout the guide section of the program include Warm-up Connections, Thinking about Plot, Quoting Noting, Keeping a Journal, If I Were ———' Responding to Questions, Using Quotations, Taking a Personal View, Write to others, & Write a Sequel.
Lawrence Productions, Inc.

CB Tree. *Compatible Hardware:* Commodore Amiga.
3.5" disk $159.00.
C Programming Tool.
Peacock Systems, Inc.

CBASIC. *Compatible Hardware:* IBM PC, Apple II. *Operating System(s) Required:* CP/M, MP/M II, CP/NET, CP/NOS. *Memory Required:* 48k.
IBM PC, 8086 CPU. disk $200.00.
Format 3740, 8-bit. 8" disk $150.00.
Apple II, 8-bit. disk $150.00.
Format 3740, 8086. 8" disk $325.00.
IBM Display Writer, 8086. $325.00.
Commercial Dialect of the BASIC Language Implemented As a Compiler/Interpreter. Designed Specifically to Develop Business Applications. A Source Code File, Created by a Text Editor or Word Processor, Is Compiled by CBASIC into an Intermediate File Composed of Pseudo-Code (P-Code) Instructions. During Execution, the CBASIC Run-Time Monitor Interprets Each P-Code Instruction & Performs the Operation. This Process Allows the Program to Use Less Random Access Memory Space. Maintains Real Numbers in a Binary Coded Decimal Floating Point Format, Retaining 14 Significant Digits. Decimal Arithmetic Assures That Fractional Parts of Dollar Amounts Will Be Exact & That Ledgers Will Be Balanced.
Digital Research, Inc.

CBASIC Compiler. *Compatible Hardware:* Apple II, IBM PC.
Apple. disk $500.00.
IBM. 8" disk $500.00.
Code Compiler Designed Specifically for Commercial Applications. Allows Separate Modules to Be Written, Tested & Then Combined to Create a Complete Program. Includes a Linkage Editor & Librarian. The Linkage Editor Combines Output Generated by the Compiler with Required Routines from the Run-Time Library to Create a Composite Program. Also Produces Overlay Modules for Use with CBASIC Compiler's Chain Statement. The Librarian Combines Many Relocatable Modules into an Indexed Library for Rapid Access by the Linkage Editor.
Digital Research, Inc.

CB80 Language Utilities. William H. Zaggle. Oct. 1983. *Compatible Hardware:* Apple II; DEC Rainbow, DEC VT180; Hewlett-Packard; IBM PC; Kaypro; Morrow; North Star; Osborne; SuperBrain; TRS-80 Model I, Model III; Vector Graphics, Victor; Zenith. *Operating System(s) Required:* CP/M, CP/M-86, MS-DOS, PC-DOS. *Language(s):* CB80. *Memory Required:* CP/M 64k, MS-DOS 128k. *General Requirements:* 2 disk drives, printer.
disk $149.00.
8" disk $149.00.
3.5" disk $149.00.
demo disk $38.00.
Provides the Applications Programmer with Tools for Creating "Friendly" Programs.
Elite Software Development, Inc.

CBook. 1979. *Compatible Hardware:* IBM PC; TRS-80 Model I, Model II, Model III, Model 4, Model 12, Model 16. *Operating System(s) Required:* TRSDOS, PC-DOS. *Language(s):* Basic. *Memory Required:* 48-64k.
TRS-80 Model, III, 4. disk $159.95.
IBM PC. disk $159.95.
TRS-80 Model I, Model II, Model 4. 8" disk $159.95.
Single-Entry Bookkeeping System That Prepares Profit & Loss Statements from Data Entries. User Can Prepare or Update a Set of Profit & Loss Figures Directly On-Screen & Print the Statement. Program Then Records Each Profit & Loss under the Month & Year for Which It Applies. When the User Has Recorded Two or More of Such Monthly (or Other Period) Statements, the Program Automatically Totals Them, Line for Line, & Produces a Year-to-Date Profit & Loss That Gives the History of the Business up to That Point. Reads the Figures, Converts Them to the Format Required by the IRS Schedule C, Profit/Loss from Business or Profession & Prints Out That Schedule in IRS Approved Format, Ready for Filing with the Client's Tax Return.
Contract Services Assocs.

CBT Analyst. *Version:* 3.0. May 1988. *Compatible Hardware:* IBM PC & compatibles. *Operating System(s) Required:* PC-DOS 2.1 or higher. *Language(s):* Pascal. *Memory Required:* 256k.
3.5" or 5.25" $39.95.
Expert System That Helps Training. Enables Computer Managers to Make Effective Decisions about Computer-Based Training.
Park Row Software.

CBT Development Stacks. *Version:* 1.1. *Compatible Hardware:* Apple Macintosh Plus. *General Requirements:* External disk drive; HyperCard.
3.5" disk $135.00.
Routines, Tools, Templates, Demonstrations.
First Reference, Inc.

CBTree. *Compatible Hardware:* Apple Macintosh, Commodore Amiga, UNIX- or XENIX-based systems.
disk $99.00.
Assists Users With Programming in C by Providing a B+ Tree Record Indexing System. Users Can Allocate, Deallocate, & Re-Allocate Fixed-Length Data Records, Examine the Index With Debugging Tools, & Use Multiple Index Keys or Concatenated Keys. Also Includes Record-Locking & 6000 Lines of C Source Code. Operations Provided Include Absolute Positioning, Exact Matching, Lexical Relations (>, <, <=, >=), Relative Positioning, & Partial Matching. Users Can Add, Update, & Delete Keys With or Without Records. Data & Indexes are Stored in Separate Files.
Peacock Systems, Inc.

cc:Mail LAN Package. *Operating System(s) Required:* PC-DOS/MS-DOS 3.1 or higher. *Memory Required:* 320k.
disk $595.00.
E-Mail Service Includes a Point & Shoot Menu System with a Main Menu & Submenus for Message Reading, Storage & Creation. Users Can Also Establish Private Listings & Then Share the List with Others. Full-Screen Text Editor Helps

the User Create Messages & the Program Makes It Easier to Find the Name of the Mailbox User Wants to Send the Message To. Other Features Include Snapshot Utility That Allows the User to Capture Graphic Images.
CC:Mail.

CC-RIDER Professional: The C-CH Programmer's Companion. *Version:* 5.0. Rick Hollinbeck. Mar. 1994. *Items Included:* API Library, manual, BBS access. *Customer Support:* BBS, phone, email.
MS-DOS, Windows, Windows NT or OS/2. IBM & compatibles. disk $279.00 (Order no.: CCRPROF). *Networks supported:* All.
A Complete Source Code Analysis, Browsing & Documentation Tool for Large & Small C/C Plus Plus Projects. Version 5 Includes Graphic Reports of All Tree Charts, along with Automated Windows Help File Generation. All Current Compilers Are Supported, Including Templates & Exception Handling.
Western Wares.

CC-RIDER: The C & C Plus Plus Programmers Companion. *Version:* 5.0. Mar. 1994. *Operating System(s) Required:* PC-DOS/MS-DOS/Windows/OS/2. *Memory Required:* 320k. *Items Included:* CC-RIDER Professional for DOS, OS/2 & Windows. disk $279.00.
Includes a Sophisticated C Symbol Analyzer, Together with a Unique & Powerful POP-UP SYMBOL CROSS REFERENCER. CC-RIDER Gives You Instant Access to All the MACRO, TYPEDEF, SCALAR, STRUCTURE, UNION, & ENUM DEFINITIONS Throughout Your C Applications & from Within Your Own Editor & Only a Hot Key Away.
Western Wares.

CCC. *Compatible Hardware:* Cromemco Systems. *Operating System(s) Required:* UNIX. *Language(s):* C. *Memory Required:* 20000k. $1995.00.
C Compiler.
Cromemco, Inc.

CCRS Horoscope Program 92: by Mark Pottenger. *Version:* 92. Dec. 1988. *Compatible Hardware:* Apple Macintosh, Commodore Amiga, IBM PC & compatibles. *Operating System(s) Required:* Apple DOS, PC-DOS/MS-DOS. *Memory Required:* Macintosh & Amiga 1Mb, MS-DOS 512k. *General Requirements:* Hard disk, Dot-matrix printer or HP LaserJet. *Items Included:* Manual. *Customer Support:* Free phone support.
IBM. disk $225.00 (ISBN 0-87199-121-7).
Apple Macintosh XL, Plus or SE. 3.5" disk $225.00 (ISBN 0-87199-122-5).
Commodore Amiga. 3.5" disk $225.00 (ISBN 0-87199-123-3).
IBM. 3.5" disk $225.00 (ISBN 0-87199-121-7).
Research-Oriented Astrological Calculation Program. Computes Natal, Progressed, Directed, Composite, Synastry, Harmonic & Solar/Lunar Return Horoscopes; Lists Fixed-Star & Asteroid Positions; Includes Astro-Clock with Rectification & Electional Assist Features; Includes Atlas of 100 City Longitudes/Latitudes with Room for up to 500 Locations in Each City File & Also Accesses the More Complete ACS PC Atlas; New High-Accuracy Ephemeris Spans 12,000 Years & Has "Big Five" Asteroids from A.D. 1487-2101; Prints Custom Ephemerides & Tables of Houses; Lists Dynamic Transit & Progressed "Hits"; Tallies Common Factors in Large Groups or Charts, or Selects Charts with One or More Common Factors; Does Charts from Viewpoint of Any Planet in Solar System, Synodic & Metonic Sun-Moon Angles; Station Position Printouts, Uranian Planets, Geodetic Midheavens, etc.

Draws Intriguing Mandala-Like Diagrams Derived from Motions of Any Pair of Planets or Asteroids.
Astrolabe, Inc.

CCS - SS7. Apr. 1993. *Items Included:* User manual. *Customer Support:* Free technical support & a 30-day warranty (1-800-521-CORE).
MS-DOS. IBM & compatibles (512k). 3.5" disk $495.00 (ISBN 1-57305-000-8). *Nonstandard peripherals required:* High-density 3.5" disk drive; VGA color monitor. *Addl. software required:* MS-DOS version 3.3 or higher. *Optimal configuration:* IBM (512k), MS-DOS version 3.3 or higher, VGA color monitor, keyboard, Microsoft compatible mouse (optional).
Advances in Common Channel Signaling Have Revolutionized Telecommunications. By Using Common Channel Signaling You Can: Increase the Volume of Signaling Information Sent over the Network, Use Trunks to Carry Voice & Data More Efficiently, Reduce Call Setup Time, Detect Fraud More Easily, & Implement New Services Faster & More Efficiently. This Computer-Based Training Package Explores How the CCS/SS7 Network Operates & the Benefits It Offers.
Bellcore.

CD-Cabin Pro: For Windows with Link'n Logging. *Version:* 1.42. Jan. 1996. *Items Included:* User guides, runtime version of Video for Windows, 2 diskettes. *Customer Support:* Technical support 9-5 CST M-F, 30 day money back guarantee.
Windows 3.X, Windows 95 or Win/OS/2. 386 (4Mb). disk $199.95 (Order no.: OW1435). *Nonstandard peripherals required:* VGA, PC speaker. *Optimal configuration:* Pentium 133 with 120Mb RAM, PC1 Video with 4Mb, CD-ROM drive, Zip or Jazzdrive, sound system & hires video card.
Multimedia Suite Includes 14 Separate Applications Accessible from a Single User Interface: Image Viewer/Editor, File Manager, Text Editor, Thumbnail Creator/Viewer, Multimedia Slide Show Presenter, Audio CD Player, Text Search Engine, HMM Indexer with Automatic Multimedia Librarying, MIDI, WAV, & VFW Play, Format Converter, Image Acquisition/Conversion, & Screen Capture.
The Aldridge Co.

CD-Cabin: With Link'n'Logging for Windows. *Version:* 1.1. Abelbeck Software. 1988. *Items Included:* 1 manual, 1 diskette. *Customer Support:* Free to registered end-users 610-779-0522, fax 610-370-0548, Internet tech syynergy.com.
MS-DOS 3.1 with MS Windows 3.1. 80386SX (2Mb). CD-ROM disk $99.95. *Nonstandard peripherals required:* CD-ROM drive. *Addl. software required:* MSCDEX or equivalent. *Optimal configuration:* Pentium with MS-DOS 6.22, 32Mb RAM, Windows 3.1, Cache86 for Windows, triple-speed CD-ROM or higher.
Windows 3.1, NT, 95, WFWG 3.11. 80386 or higher (6Mb). (Order no.: SYNWIN333). *Optimal configuration:* 80386 or higher, 6Mb RAM, 5Mb hard drive space, Windows compatible mouse.
Provides Virtually Instant Access to CD-ROM Information. Automatically Reads & Remembers All of Your CD-ROM Data. Allows You to (Search, Find, Sort, View, Copy, Execute, Retrieve) All (Files, Programs, Data, Pictures, Sounds) Across Multiple CD-ROM Discs. Enables User to Group, Categorize, & Index Entire CD-ROM Collections.
The Aldridge Co.

CD Companion Series: Igor Stravinsky, The Rite of Spring. *Customer Support:* M-F 9 AM-5 PM Pacific Time (213) 451-1383.
Macintosh Plus, SE, II or Portable (1 Mb). CD-ROM disk $99.95. *Nonstandard peripherals required:* Macintosh-compatible CD-ROM drive, hard disk, speakers or headphones. *Addl. software required:* Hypercard 2.0 or higher.
Contains Six Interrelated Parts: A Pocket Guide, Provides a One-Screen Orientation to the Entire Work; Stravinsky's World is an Engrossing Discussion of Stravinsky's Life & Times; Rite Listening, an Informative Introduction to Listening to Music; Dancing the Rite, Explores the Actual (& Now Rarely-Experienced) Ballet Production of The Rite of Spring; A Close Reading Delivers Continuous Real-Time Commentary Across the Entire Work. The Rite Game is a Question & Answer Game That Tests the Users' Comprehension of Stravinsky Using Audio-Based Questions.
The Voyager Co.

CD Companion Series: Ludwig Van Beethoven, Symphony No. 9. *General Requirements:* CD-ROM drive; HyperCard. *Items Included:* 1 audio CD, 2 800k floppy disks, user's guide. *Customer Support:* M-F 9 AM-5 PM Pacific Time (213) 451-1383.
Macintosh Plus, SE, II or Portable (1 Mb). CD-ROM disk $99.95. *Nonstandard peripherals required:* Macintosh-compatible CD-ROM Drive, hard disk, speakers or headphones. *Addl. software required:* Hypercard 1.2.2 or higher.
Music Exploration. Consists of a Five-Part Interactive HyperCard Program Combined with a Commercially Available Compact Disc Recording of the Vienna Philharmonic Orchestra, Which Includes: Pocket Guide, a Single-Screen Schematical Overview of the entire Symphony; Beethoven's World, Examines Maestro's Life & Times; Art of Listening Uses Examples from Ninth Symphony; Close Reading, Contains Detailed Real-Time Commentary on Every Passage of the Work; Ninth Game Is a Listener-Proficiency Q & A Game.
The Voyager Co.

CD Connection. *Version:* 3.0. *Items Included:* 1-5 1/4" software disk, 1 Installation manual in slipcase & binder. *Customer Support:* 30 day money back guarantee, 60 day warranty, free telephone tech support.
MS-DOS. IBM Compatible 286, 386 or 486 (640k). 10 user-$695.00; 100 user-$1395.00; 255 user-$1995.00. *Nonstandard peripherals required:* Extended memory, 1.2Mb floppy drive, CD-ROM host adapter, monochrome video adapter; monitor, CD-ROM drive. *Optimal configuration:* 2MB. *Networks supported:* Novell Netware (286/386/1PX/NetBIOs), Network-OS, 3COM, Banyan, IBM PC LAN, PCSA, MS-Net, Open NET, most other NetBIOs LANs.
Allows CD-ROM Users to Access Multiple CD-ROM Drives Simultaneously Over a Local Area Network. With CD Connection, a CD-Rom Disc is As Accessible As a Regular Disk Drive to All Networked Stations. Because the Software is Installed on Top of an Existing LAN, Using CD Connection Doesn't Mean Replacing User's Present Network.
CBIS, Inc.

CD Game Pack. *Customer Support:* Technical support is available at 818-885-1078, 9AM-5PM PST.
IBM CD-ROM. CD-ROM disk $59.25. *Optimal configuration:* CR-ROM Drive & software driver; IBM PC, XT, AT, PS/2 & compatibles; CGA, EGA, VGA; MS-DOS CD-ROM Extensions, Version 2.0 or higher; 512k; keyboard, joystick or mouse.

Over $180 Worth of Thrills: Life & Death, Bruce Lee Lives, Beyond the Black Hole, The Chessmaster 2000 & Gin King/Cribbage King. Software Toolworks.

CD Game Pack Two.
IBM CD-ROM (640k). CD-ROM disk $79.95. *Optimal configuration:* 640k RAM, CD-ROM drive & software driver; MSCDEX version 2.1 or higher; MS-DOS version 3.3 or higher; CGA, EGA, or VGA, (Puzzle Gallery requires EGA or VGA).
Ten of Your Favorite Disk-Based Games, Now on One CD! Includes: The Chessmaster 2100, The Software Toolworks Robot Tank, Beyond the Black Hole, Life & Death, Gin King/Cribbage King, Checkers, Loopz, Puzzle Gallery, Bruce Lee Lives, & Backgammon.
Software Toolworks.

CD Helpdesk Series: Novell Products. Deni Connor & Ronald Nutter. Nov. 1995. *Items Included:* Instructions; licenses; third party software demos. *Customer Support:* Free technical support, 30 day limited warranty, site licenses available.
Windows 3.1 or higher; DOS. IBM & compatibles (4Mb). CD-ROM disk $39.95 (ISBN 1-886801-12-6). *Nonstandard peripherals required:* CD-ROM drive. *Optimal configuration:* 486 or higher; 8Mb RAM.
Contains Practical, Hands-On Questions & Answers about Using the Best Selling Novell Products. Hyperlinking Allows You to Use a Keyword Search to Select a Topic, Find an Answer, & Download Appropriate Third Party Software to Help Resolve Problems.
Charles River Media.

CD-ROM Selector: A Directory of CD-ROMs for DOS & Windows. Roger Cox & Kathy Cox. Mar. 1994. *Items Included:* Access Software for both MS-DOS & Windows is included. *Customer Support:* 30 day money-back guarantee. 90 day free customer phone support.
MS-DOS. IBM PC & compatibles (640k). CD-ROM disk $39.95 for standalone; $59.95 for network license (ISBN 1-885023-00-6, Order no.: CDRS-PC). *Nonstandard peripherals required:* CD-ROM drive, VGA graphics with color monitor. *Optimal configuration:* PC compatible with 2Mb RAM, CD-ROM drive, Windows 3.1, SVGA graphics, color monitor, Windows-compatible sound card, printer. *Networks supported:* Works wiht most networks.
A Directory of DOS & Windows CD-ROM Titles. Over 1600 CD-ROMs Are Listed with Title Name, System Requirements, Description, Price, & Full Publisher Contact Information. 70 Subject Categories Permit Easy Browsing. Included Are 235 Actual CD-ROM Screen Shot Samples. Delivered on a CD-ROM That Is Both Windows & MS-DOS Compatible.
Save the Planet Software.

CD TimeSketch. Douglas Short. *Items Included:* 1 small 3-ring binder. *Customer Support:* 90 day warranty against defective software.
Windows 3.1. IBM 386 or 486 (2Mb). disk $99.95 (Order no.: W-1420). *Nonstandard peripherals required:* VGA or SVGA monitor, 1 hard disk drive, 1 floppy disk drive, CD ROM.
This Program Has Been Designed to Facilitate Listening & Aurally Analyzing CD Music under CDROM & Computer Control. Program Can Be Used to Create Unique "Teacher-Developed" Listening Lessons with Any Audio CD. The Annotated Listening Format Can Be Applied to a Number of Classes & Activities, Plus the Music Performance Curriculum. A Glossary of Terms Includes Dynamics, Temp Markings, Stylistic Expression Markings, Music Symbols, & Standard Musical Terms.
Electronic Courseware Systems, Inc.

CDexecutive. *Customer Support:* 90 day warranty, installation, hotline support, hardware maintenance, software maintenance.
Windows NT 3.5 or higher. 486/DX2 (16Mb). CD-ROM disk Contact publisher for price. *Nonstandard peripherals required:* SCSI interface. *Networks supported:* NetBEUI, IPX/SPX, TCP/IP, DECnet.
Software Provides a Total CD-ROM Management Solution for Windows NT Environments. Features Include CDcatalog, CDlaunch, CDstatus & CDmeter Which Facilitate the Usage. Logicraft Has Networking Solutions for the DOS, Windows, Windows NT, Windows 95 & Macintosh Markets.
Logicraft.

CDIBOL. *Operating System(s) Required:* UNIX. *Language(s):* C, Machines.
contact publisher for price.
Compiles & Executes Programs Written in CTS-500 DIBOL, Version 4D & Provides a Calling Interface to Subroutines Written in the C Programming Language. Designed for Business Applications.
BBN Software Products Corp.

CDS-M (Critical Date Systems-M). *Version:* 8. Feb. 1979. *Compatible Hardware:* IBM PC & compatibles, IBM PS/2. *General Requirements:* Hard disk. *Items Included:* Binder with documentation. *Customer Support:* 1 yr. maintenance, $84.00, entitles user to phone support, quarterly newsletters & enhancements made available for their computer during the year at no charge.
DOS Ver. 3.1 or higher; Novell Netware or IBM PC Network software (470k). disk $400.00.
maintenance fee (optional) $84.00.
demo disk $35.00.
True Multi-User Version of CDS, Allowing up to 200 Terminals to Enter or Retrieve Appointments & Critical Date Information. Displays Calendar on Screen, Showing Number of Entries Which Were Designated As Critical. Includes a Scheduler Which Locates Available Time Slots & Checks for Conflicts. More Than One Employee Can Be Scheduled at One Time with Comparisons for Conflicts. Schedule Appointments after Locating Available Time for up to 99 Timekeepers. CDS-M Will Display Any Conflict & State If the Conflict Is "Critical" or Not. Print Reports for 1 Timekeeper or the Firm, One Client or All, & for a Given Date or Range of Dates. An Even Planner Allows "Plus/Minus" Days from a Given Date for Automatic Scheduling. Integrates with TABS III-M.
Software Technology, Inc.

Cecil Textbook of Medicine CD-ROM. Claude Bennett & Fred Plum. Edited by Lisette Bralow. Jul. 1996.
CD-ROM disk Contact publisher for price (ISBN 0-7216-6417-2).
Saunders W. B. Co.

C86. *Compatible Hardware:* IBM PC & compatibles. *Memory Required:* 192k.
disk $1295.00.
C Compiler Featuring Assembler Access, Source Debugger & Compiler Subdirectories. Compilation Is an Added-Step Process. Supports Math Coprocessor. Technical Hot Line Available for Registered Users.
Real-Time Computer Science Corp.

C86 C Compiler for QNX. *Version:* 3.4. Aug. 1988. *Operating System(s) Required:* QNX 2. 15D. *Memory Required:* 640k. *Items Included:* Symbolic debugger, libraries, quick make, linker. *Customer Support:* Telephone technical support 10am-5pm (EST) Monday through Friday.
3.5" or 5.25" disk $595.00 per single node.
Brings High-Quality Code Generation, ANSI Compatibility, & Multiple Memory Models to the QNX Operating System. On Intel X86 Machines, Programs Have Access to up to 16Mb of Memory. This Means Large-Scale Applications Can Be Developed (or Ported from Other Operating Systems) with Greater Ease. The C86for/QNX Run-Time Library Contains ANSI-Standard As Well As Many QNX-Specific Functions. Specific QNX Functions Are Included for Terminal Independence, Video Access, File System Access, & Inter-Process Communication. Includes a Source Level Debugger (SID) That Features C Program Debugging at the C Source Level. Symbolic Information Is Available in a Multi-Window Debugging Environment.
Computer Innovations, Inc.

Celeste I: Natal Horoscope Calculation Program. *Version:* 1.x. Linda Sherrill. Jul. 1991. *Items Included:* Manual. *Customer Support:* Free phone support.
MacFinder, MultiFinder. Macintosh (1Mb). 3.5" disk $75.00 (ISBN 0-87199-111-X). *Nonstandard peripherals required:* Hard disk & a dot-matrix, laser or inkjet printer.
Calculates Natal Horoscopes & Displays Them on the Screen or Prints Them Out in a Wide Choice of Wheel Styles (At Printer's Highest Resolution If User Desires). Includes Charts in the Tropical or Any Sidereal Zodiac, in Geocentric or Heliocentric Coordinates, & Any of 39 House Systems. Chart Wheel & Aspectarian Pages Can Be Converted to PICT or PNTG Files for Use in Desktop Publishing.
Astrolabe, Inc.

Celestial BASIC. *Compatible Hardware:* Apple, Commodore 64, IBM. *Language(s):* BASIC (source code included). *Memory Required:* 48k-128k.
contact publisher for price.
Dynacomp, Inc.

Celestial Body Angular Distance. *Compatible Hardware:* TI 99/4A with Extended BASIC module. *Operating System(s) Required:* DX-10. *Memory Required:* 48k.
cassette $16.95.
Calculates Angular Distance in Degrees Between Any 2 Celestial Bodies.
Eastbench Software Products.

CELLULA. *Version:* 1.04. *Items Included:* Diskette & manual. *Customer Support:* Telephone inquiries.
MAC-DOS (1Mb). Macintosh, all models. disk $49.95.
Simulate Dynamic Behavior of 1-Dimensional Cellular Automaton, Using Additive, Boolean or Monte-Carlo Rules (Color Mac II).
Atlantic Software.

Cement Pyro Processing. *Version:* 2. 1988. *Compatible Hardware:* IBM PC. *Operating System(s) Required:* PC-DOS 3.0. *Language(s):* BASIC. *Memory Required:* 128k.
disk $100.00 ea.
IBM PC. (ISBN 0-931821-21-5, Order no.: 07-101).
IBM PS/2. (ISBN 1-55804-980-0).
Based on an Input of Charge Composition, (% wt SiO2, % wt AL2O3, % wt FE2O3, % CaO, % wt free CaO) Program Determines A/F Ratio, L-2550%, (C(2)S)x/Cx Ratio, Burn Index, Burning Zone Temperature. Allows New Trial Charge Mixes Holding A/F, Fe(2)O(3), Al(2)O(3) or L-2550 Constant. For Each Option, S28 Value As Group A, B & C Trial Cements for Comparison with Trial Mix S28 Value, Is Determined.
Information Resource Consultants.

TITLE INDEX

Cemetery Accounting. 1980. *Compatible Hardware:* IBM & compatibles. *Language(s):* BASIC. *Memory Required:* 128k. *General Requirements:* Printer.
contact publisher for price.
Each Sales Entry Creates Historical Data to Maintain Burial, Lot Owner & Memorial Records; Address File to Lot Owners for Billing & Direct Mail; Sales Analysis Data by Customer, Salesman, & Product; & Accounts Receivable Data for Billing & Commission.
Zeltner Assocs., Inc.

Census Data System '90. *Version:* 1.5. 1992-94. *Items Included:* Manuals. *Customer Support:* 90 days telephone support is free.
MS-DOS 3.0. IBM PC & compatibles (512k). CD-ROM disk Modular $150.00 to $395.00. *Nonstandard peripherals required:* VGA or EGA graphics, CD-ROM. *Optimal configuration:* 640k RAM, CD-ROM drive, EGA or VGA graphics, minimum 40Mb hard disk. *Networks supported:* Novell Netware.
Specialized Data Extraction Tools Which Work with the 1990 Census Data That Is Available on CD-ROM Disks. Much More Flexible & Easier to Use Than the Census "GO" Software That Is Provided on the Disks. Allows Instant Verification of the Data. Data Files Can Be Used by Mapping Systems, Spreadsheets, & Database Programs.
Sammamish Data Systems, Inc.

Centerpiece. *Version:* 3.2. *Compatible Hardware:* IBM PC, PC XT, PC AT, PS/2 or compatibles. *Operating System(s) Required:* PC-DOS 2.0. *Memory Required:* 640k. *Items Included:* 310 page manual. *Customer Support:* After the first year, $150.00 per year, includes upgrades & unlimited toll-free technical support.
disk $895.00.
$25.00-60 day trial copy.
Professional Portfolio Management & Performance Measurement System (Time Weighted Rate of Return, BAI Recommended Method). Produces 45 Clear, Comprehensive Reports. The System Provides Outstanding Performance & Analytical Measures, Detailed Tax Lot Accounting, & Superior Decision Support Tools. Comprehensive Billing Module Included. Call (800) 528-9595 for a Brochure or a Sixty Day Trial Copy.
Performance Technologies, Inc.

Centipede. *Compatible Hardware:* Atari XL/XE. ROM cartridge $19.95 (Order no.: CXL4020).
Atari Corp.

Central Offender Processing System: Criminal Justice Application System. *Version:* 2.0. Palladium Software Corp. Aug. 1992. *Operating System(s) Required:* IBM/DB2, MS-DOS, Windows 95 & NT. *Language(s):* Objectview, Level 5. *Memory Required:* 4000k.
disk $7000.00 ea.
MS-DOS Windows. (ISBN 0-931755-82-4, Order no.: CJ 410/3).
Windows NT. (ISBN 0-931755-83-2, Order no.: CJ 410/4).
Windows 95. (ISBN 0-931755-84-0, Order no.: CJ 410/5).
Manages All Aspects of Offender Processing, Arrest Processing, Detention & Release; Contains Property Management, Pre-Arrainment, Notification System; Fully Integrated with Other CJAS Modules.
Ellington Duval, Inc.

Central Point Anti-Virus. *Version:* 2.0. Jun. 1993. *Items Included:* Documentation, registration card, 3.5" or 5.25" diskettes. *Customer Support:* Toll-call telephone technical support; BBS, 60-day warranty; 24-hour virus hotline, Faxback virus signature service.
MS-DOS 3.3 or higher. IBM PC, XT, AT, PS/2, 286 or 100% compatibles (512k). disk $129.95.
Combines Virus Detection, Removal & Prevention with an Innovative Virus Protection Service Plan Designed to Address New Viruses As They Are Discovered. Protects Against Virus Infection in DOS, Windows & Networked Environments. The Main Application Scans & Cleans on Command. An Optional Memory-Resident Program Works in the Background Detecting & Removing Virus Infections. Central Point Anti-Virus Recognizes over 2000 Known Viruses & Can Detect Unknown Viruses. The Program's Immunization Feature Makes Files Self-Protecting, Protects Against Stealth Viruses & Virus Created by the Mutation Engine. Includes a Unique Expert System to Provide the Highest Left of Generic Detection Available.
Central Point Software, Inc.

Central Point Anti-Virus for Macintosh. *Version:* 2. Oct. 1992. *Items Included:* Documentation, registration card, 3.5" diskettes. *Customer Support:* Toll-call telephone technical support; BBS; 60-day warranty; 24-hour virus hotline, Faxback virus signature service.
Macintosh System 7 compatible System 6.0.5 & Finder 6.0 or higher. Macintosh Plus or higher (2Mb). 3.5" disk $69.95.
Identical to the Powerful Anti-Virus Program Found in Central Point's MACTOOLS. Detects & Eradicates All Known Macintosh Viruses.
Central Point Software, Inc.

Central Point Anti-Virus for NetWare. *Version:* 1.1. Apr. 1993. *Items Included:* Documentation, registration card, Server edition as well as workstation programs, DOS, Windows & Macintosh. *Customer Support:* Toll-call telephone technical support; BBS; 60-day warranty; 24-hour virus hotline, Faxback virus signature service.
DOS Version 3.3 or higher. IBM PS/2, PC, XT, AT & most DOS-based computers with 512k RAM (4Mb). disk $1199.00. *Networks supported:* Novell NetWare Version 3.11.
An Anti-Virus Solution That Provides Centralized Virus Management for Clients & Servers on Novell NetWare 3.11 Networks. Program Provides Three Simultaneous Lines of Defense: at the Desktop, to Prevent Virus Entry into the System; at the Server, to Prevent Virus Entry into the Local Area Network; & Between Servers to Prevent Virus Propagation Throughout the Enterprise.
Central Point Software, Inc.

Central Point Anti-Virus for Windows. Mar. 1992. *Items Included:* Documentation, registration card, 3.5" or 5.25" diskettes. *Customer Support:* Toll-call telephone technical support; BBS; 60-day warranty; 24-hour virus hotline, Faxback virus signature service.
Microsoft Windows 3.0 or higher. IBM AT or higher, or 100% compatibles (2Mb). disk $129.95.
Detects & Removes More Than 1,500 Known Viruses, As Well As Unknown & Stealth Viruses, & Is Optimized for Windows 3.1.
Central Point Software, Inc.

Central Point Backup for DOS. *Version:* 8.0. *Items Included:* Documentaion; Registration card; 3.5" or 5.25" diskettes. *Customer Support:* Toll-call telephone technical support; BBS; 60 day warranty.
IBM PC, XT, AT, PS/2 or 100% compatibles. disk $129.95.
The Same Backup Program Found in PC Tools, with Central Point Backup You Can Back up to Floppy, Networks or Bernoulli Drives, As Well As Virtually Any QIC-40/80 Tape Drive. And If You Have Large Storage Needs, SCSI Tape Drives Are Also Supported. Other Features Include High-Speed Data Compression, Data Encryption, File Viewers & Expanded Virus Protection.
Central Point Software, Inc.

Central Point Backup for Windows. *Version:* 2.0. *Items Included:* Documentation; registration card; 3 1/2" or 5 1/4" diskettes. *Customer Support:* BBS; 60-day warranty.
Windows. Contact publisher for price.
Offers the Same Hard Disk Backup Speed, Reliability & Ease-of-Use As the Backup Function Found in PC TOOLS for WINDOWS. User Can Backup Data to Floppy, Network, & Bernouli Drives, As Well As Virtually All QIC-40/80 Tape Drives. And If You Have Large Storage Needs, SCSI Tape Drives Are Also Supported. Other Features Include High-Speed Data Compression, Data Encryption, File Viewers & Expanded Virus Protection.
Central Point Software, Inc.

Centrifugal Compressor Design & Rating. *Items Included:* Full manual. No other products required. *Customer Support:* Free telephone support - no time limit, 30 day warranty.
MS-DOS 3.2 or higher. IBM & compatibles (512k). disk $289.95.
demo disk $5.00.
Includes a Database of 30 Component Gases, & the User May Add More. It Is Based on Theories of Elliot & Ingersoll-Rand & Will: Design a Compressor & Analyze Multi-Stage Compressors with up to Four Stages of Compression. It Can Determine the Proper Number of Stages for a Desired Service Based on the Maximum Gas Temperature. Analyze the Performance of an Existing Compressor by Calculating New Operating Conditions Based on the Design Conditions, Compressor Curve, & the Actual Process Conditions. The Flow Versus Discharge Performance Curve Is Displayed. Calculate the Thermodynamic Properties of a Gas Mixture, Including Molecular Weight, Critical Temperature, Critical Pressure, Specific Heat Ratio, & Gas Constant. Test Compressor Performance.
Dynacomp, Inc.

Centrifugal Pump Selection & Rating. *Items Included:* Full manual. No other products required. *Customer Support:* Free telephone support - no time limit, 30 day warranty.
MS-DOS 3.2 or higher. IBM & compatibles (512k). disk $389.95.
Either Provides Commercially Available Pump Designs to Best Suit Given Operating Conditions & Requirements, or Revises Existing Pump Curve Data for New Pumping Conditions. It Also Calculates Approximate Impeller Design, As Well As Viscosity Correction Factors Based on the Hydraulic Institute Charts. In Addition, It Covers Suction Specific Speed, Efficiency, Nozzle Rating, Shaft Size, Minimum Continuous Flow, & Affinity Laws.
Dynacomp, Inc.

Centrifugal Pump Selection & Rating. 1995. *Items Included:* Full manual. *Customer Support:* Free telephone support - 90 days, 30-day warranty.
MS-DOS 3.2 or higher. 286 (584k). disk $389.95. *Nonstandard peripherals required:* CGA/EGA/VGA.
Either Provides Commercially Available Pump Designs to Best Suit Given Operating Conditions & Requirements, or Revises Existing Pump Curve Data for New Pumping Conditions. It Also Calculates Approximate Impeller Design, As Well As Viscosity Correction Factors Based on the Hydraulic Institute Charts. In Addition, It Covers Suction Specific Speed, Efficiency, Nozzle Rating, Shaft Size, Minimum Continuous Flow, & Affinity Laws.
Dynacomp, Inc.

CERTIFICATE MASTER-AWARD CERTIFICATE

Certificate Master-Award Certificate Creation.
Items Included: Full manual. No other products required. *Customer Support:* Free telephone support - no time limit, 30 day warranty.
MS-DOS 3.2 or higher. IBM & compatibles (512k). disk $39.95. *Optimal configuration:* IBM, MS-DOS 2.1 or higher, 256k RAM, CGA/EGA/VGA or compatible graphics capability & dot matrix printer.
Apple. disk $39.95. *Optimal configuration:* Apple, 64k RAM, dot matrix printer.
Macintosh. 3.5" disk $39.95. *Optimal configuration:* Macintosh, 512k, Plus, SE or II, ImageWriter, LaserWriter, or compatible printer.
Easy-to-Use Package That Enables You to Create Attractive, Personalized Awards. It Provides More Than 200 Professionally-Designed, Partially-Completed Certificates. To Make a Certificate, All You Have to Do Is Select the Template You Want, Choose a Border & Type Style, & Fill in the Blanks with the Recipient's Name & Achievement. As a Finishing Touch, You Can Add One of the 36 Seals & Stickers That Come with Certificate Master.
Dynacomp, Inc.

Certificates & Awards Designer. W. Andrew Bear. 1986. *Compatible Hardware:* Apple IIe. *Operating System(s) Required:* Apple DOS 3.3. *Memory Required:* 48k. *General Requirements:* Grappler Series interface card, dot matrix printer. *Items Included:* Disk, documentation.
disk $43.50 (ISBN 1-55797-180-3, Order no.: AP2-AG515).
Will Help Create Certificates & Awards. Written with the Non-Graphic Designer in Mind. Predesigned Certificates & Awards Are Stored on the Disk. Users Enter the Basic Information & Make Selections from the Different Menus.
Hobar Pubns.

Certified Dental Assistant. *Compatible Hardware:* TRS-80 Model III.
contact publisher for price.
Nappo Computer Service.

CertiFLEX. Computer Program Associates. *Compatible Hardware:* TI Professional. *Operating System(s) Required:* MS-DOS. *Memory Required:* 128k. *General Requirements:* 2 disk drives, printer.
$549.00.
Hard Disk System Supported, Fast Retrieval & Update of Data Items, Flexible Stock Numbers. Interfaces with Accounts Receivable. Suggested Order Report Shows Quantities Needed Based on Minimum On-Hand Amount. Keeps Track of Sales & Cost of Sale by Item.
Texas Instruments, Personal Productivit.

CertiFLEX Accounts Payable with Check Writing. Computer Program Associates. *Compatible Hardware:* TI Professional. *Operating System(s) Required:* MS-DOS. *Memory Required:* 128k. *General Requirements:* 2 disk drives, printer.
$549.00.
Generates Entire Check Run. Cut a Check, Post Transaction to General Ledger, Update Vendor's Account, Enter Invoice for Payment at Later Date.
Texas Instruments, Personal Productivit.

CertiFLEX Accounts Receivable with Billing. Computer Program Associates. *Compatible Hardware:* TI Professional. *Operating System(s) Required:* MS-DOS. *Memory Required:* 128k. *General Requirements:* 2 disk drives, printer.
$549.00.
Lists Accounts Receivable & Past Due Accounts. Generates Statements.
Texas Instruments, Personal Productivit.

Certiflex Dimension Accounting Software. *Version:* 6.20. 1994. *Items Included:* Full documentation. *Customer Support:* On-site training available by contract, technical support available at $120.00/60 minutes, 1 yr. maintenance $90.00/module.
MS-DOS. IBM PC & compatibles (640k). $695.00 module. *Optimal configuration:* 80386 or higher w/1Mb RAM & hard disk sufficient to handle volume of data. Program req. approx. 3Mb/module. *Networks supported:* Novell Advanced NetWare.
General Business & Professional Accounting System May Be Operated Stand-Alone by Functional Requirement or Interactively. Employs Unique Concept of Integrating Business Accounting & Reporting with the Professional Accountant & Tax Compilation & Reporting. System Features Include Word-Processor Type Edit, Controlled User Access & Security, Unlimited Printer Support, User Definable Custom Menus, Multi-Indices (Name and/or Number) for Ease of Data Access, & On-Line Context Sensitive Help.
The Versatile Group, Inc.

CertiFLEX Fixed Assets-Depreciation. Computer Program Associates. *Compatible Hardware:* TI Professional. *Operating System(s) Required:* MS-DOS. *Memory Required:* 128k. *General Requirements:* 2 disk drives, printer.
$549.00.
Calculates Book & Tax Depreciation - Monthly, Quarterly or Annually. Investment Tax Credit & Recapture Fully Supported, Along with Gain or Loss on Disposition of Assets. Complies with Latest in Tax & Accounting Methods, Including ACRS.
Texas Instruments, Personal Productivit.

CertiFLEX General Ledger. Computer Program Associates. *Compatible Hardware:* TI Professional. *Operating System(s) Required:* MS-DOS. *Memory Required:* 128k. *General Requirements:* 2 disk drives, printer.
$549.00.
Provides General Ledger Functions, from Entry of Transactions Reports.
Texas Instruments, Personal Productivit.

CertiFLEX Payroll with Check Writing. Computer Program Associates. *Compatible Hardware:* TI Professional. *Operating System(s) Required:* MS-DOS. *Memory Required:* 128k. *General Requirements:* 2 disk drives, printer.
$549.00.
Calculates Gross Wages, FICA, Withholding & Net Pay. Prints Paychecks, Journal Entry on Paycheck, W-2's & Special Earnings & Deductions.
Texas Instruments, Personal Productivit.

CFO Advisor.
Windows. IBM PC & compatibles. disk $995.00.
*Gives Immediate Solutions to Business Problems. Direct Input or Interfaces with Most High-End General Ledger Systems, e.g., AECPAE Plus, Plus DDE with Excel; Graphics, etc.
Financial Feasibilities.*

CG-Survey for AutoCAD. *Version:* 12.07. Jul. 1994. *Items Included:* Complete documentation, tutorial, diskettes, & hardware lock. *Customer Support:* 90 days free technical support & updates at time of purchase. Annual fee thereafter is $400/first workstation & $80/each additional workstation.
MS-DOS, Windows NT. 486 or higher (8Mb). disk $1495.00. *Addl. software required:* AutoCAD release 12.C2 or higher. *Optimal configuration:* 486, 8Mb RAM, Super VGA monitor, 2 serial ports, 1 parallel port, 200 or higher Mb hard drive, laser printer or pen plotter. *Networks supported:* Novell, Lantastic, Windows for Workgroups.
ADS Application Running Inside AutoCAD. Features Include Complete COGO, Contouring, Earthwork Volume Computations, Manual or Electronic Data Entry, & Liberal Import/Export Capability. Includes an Interactive COGO/CAD Systems for Surveyors by Surveyors. Mature Product with 16 Years of Refinement in the Marketplace.
C&G Software Systems, Inc.

CG-Survey for DOS. *Version:* 4.40. Sep. 1994. *Items Included:* Complete documentation, tutorial, diskettes, & hardware lock. *Customer Support:* 90 days free technical support & updates at time of purchase. Annual fee thereafter is $400/first workstation & $80/each additional workstation.
MS-DOS. 386, 486 or higher (4Mb). disk $1295.00. *Optimal configuration:* 486, 8Mb RAM, Super VGA monitor, 2 serial ports, 1 parallel port, 200 or higher Mb hard drive, laser printer or pen plotter. *Networks supported:* Novell, Lantastic, Windows for Workgroups.
Complete Field-to-Finish Surveying Computational/CAD Package. Includes Manual or Electronic Data Entry/Adjustment/Balance, Complete COGO, Contouring, Earthwork Volume Computations, Liberal Import/Export Capability, Legal Description Generator, & User Macro Generation. Features an Interactive COGO/CAD System for Surveyors by Surveyors. Mature Product with 16 Years of Refinement in the Marketplace.
C&G Software Systems, Inc.

CG-Survey for MicroStation. *Version:* 4.08. Apr. 1994. *Items Included:* Complete documentation, tutorial, diskettes, & hardware lock. *Customer Support:* Varies with product supply source.
MS-DOS, UNIX, Windows NT. 486 or higher (16Mb). disk $1995.00. *Addl. software required:* Intergraph MicroStation 4.0 or higher. *Optimal configuration:* 486, 16Mb RAM, Super VGA monitor, 2 serial ports, 1 parallel port, 200Mb or higher hard drive, laser printer or pen plotter. *Networks supported:* Novell, Lantastic, Windows for Workgroups.
MDL Application for MicroStation Versions 4.0 or Greater. Features an Interactive COGO/CAD System by Surveyors for Surveyors, Manual or Electronic Data Entry/Adjustment/Balance, Liberal Import/Export Capability, Note Reduction/Adjustment. Available with 16 Years of Experience & Refinement in the Surveying Software Industry.
C&G Software Systems, Inc.

CGCAL. 1982. *Compatible Hardware:* IBM PC & compatibles. *Operating System(s) Required:* MS-DOS. *Language(s):* BASIC. *Memory Required:* 128k.
$150.00.
Used to Calculate the Center of Gravity of the Vessel or Heat Exchanger.
Technical Research Services, Inc.

Chaco: Canyon of Mystery. Dan Yankosky et al. Jan. 1995. *Items Included:* Captions Identifying Each Image.
MAC OS. Mac II, Centris, Performa, Quadra, Power PC (4Mb). CD-ROM disk $29.99 (ISBN 0-9643689-0-0). *Nonstandard peripherals required:* Photo CD compatible CD-ROM drive. *Addl. software required:* Quicktime, Photo CD Extension, optional: photo manipulation software (ie Adobe Photoshop). *Optimal configuration:* Mac Quadra 8 Plus Mb RAM, Photo CD compatible CD-ROM drive, 24-Bit Video, Quicktime, Adobe Photoshop.
Windows 3.1. PC Compatible (4Mb). CD-ROM disk $29.99. *Nonstandard peripherals required:*

Photo CD compatible CD-ROM drive. *Addl. software required:* Photo manipulation or viewing software (ie Corel Photopaint). *Optimal configuration:* PC compatible 8 Plus Mb RAM, 24-Bit Video, Photo CD compatible CD-ROM drive, Corel Photo CD Lab.
CD-1 or Photo CD. CD-ROM disk $29.99.
Nonstandard peripherals required: Television plus CD-1 player or Photo CD player.
This Photo CD Contains 100 Full-Color, High-Resolution, Professional Photos from North America's Most Intriguing Prehistoric Site, Chaco Canyon, New Mexico. The Images Include All Major Anasazi Towns, Houses, & Kivas As Well As Petroglyphs, Pictographs, Some Flora & Fauna, & the Famous Sun Dagger Celestial Calendar.
Confluence Creations.

Chadwick & the Sneaky Egg Thief. Jul. 1994. *Items Included:* Registration card, manual. *Customer Support:* Free customer support for registered users via 1-800 Number.
DOS 3.1 or higher. IBM & compatibles, 386 CPU or higher (2Mb). $49.95 MSRP (ISBN 0-9642108-0-0, Order no.: CT-001-DF).
Nonstandard peripherals required: Sound Blaster or compatible sound card required for sound. Printer required for printing. *Optimal configuration:* IBM or compatible 386 DX, 4Mb RAM, DOS 3.1, Sound Blaster sound card & printer.
An Interactive Coloring Book Adventure for Children Ages 3 to 8. Available on Floppy Disks for IBM PC & Compatibles This Adventure Comes to Life As Children Color & Animate the 20 Page Storybook Featuring Chadwick, a Young Dinosaur, & His Companions.
KnowWare.

Chadwick & the Sneaky Egg Thief. Jul. 1994. *Items Included:* Registration card, manual. *Customer Support:* Free customer support for registered users via 1-800 number.
DOS 3.1 or higher. IBM & compatibles 386 CPU or higher (2Mb). disk $49.95 (ISBN 0-9642108-0-0, Order no.: C1-V10-PF).
Nonstandard peripherals required: Sound Blaster or compatible required for sound. Printer required for printing. *Optimal configuration:* IBM or compatible 386DX, 4Mb RAM, DOS 3.1, Sound Blaster compatible sound card & color printer.
DOS 3.1 or higher. IBM & compatibles 386 CPU or higher (2Mb). disk $49.95 (ISBN 0-9642108-1-9, Order no.: C1-VID-PC).
Nonstandard peripherals required: CD-ROM drive, Sound Blaster or compatible for sound. Printer required for printing. *Optimal configuration:* IBM or compatible 386DX, 4Mb RAM, DOS 3.1, Sound Blaster compatible sound card & color printer.
An Interactive Coloring Book Adventure for Children Ages 3 to 8. Available on Floppy Disks for IBM PC & Compatibles. This Adventure Comes to Life As Children Color & Animate the 20 Page Storybook Featuring Chadwick, a Young Dinosaur, & His Companions.
KnowWare.

Chain Reference. *Version:* 6.1. Kent Ochel & Bert Brown. Oct. 1989. *Items Included:* Tutorial disk; 3-ring binder with manual. *Customer Support:* Unlimited free technical support at (512) 251-7541.
Any DOS or any Windows. IBM PC; XT; AT or compatibles (512k). disk $49.95.
Any Macintosh. 3.5" disk $49.95.
Provides the User with over 55000 Chains That Associate a Specific Word in the Bible Verse with a List of Other Verses to Which Additions or Deletions May Be Made. VERSE SEARCH Is Required.
Bible Research Systems.

Chain 4. 1985. *Compatible Hardware:* Apple II, II+, IIe, IIc. *Memory Required:* 48k.
disk $24.95 (ISBN 0-87492-017-5, Order no.: INT 6014A).
Game of Strategy & Tactics for 1 or 2 Players.
Intellectual Software.

Chains & Belts. *Version:* Disk, documentation. Dennis Brunsvold. 1984. *Compatible Hardware:* Apple II series. *Operating System(s) Required:* Apple DOS 3.3. *Memory Required:* 48k. *General Requirements:* Printer.
disk $49.50 (ISBN 1-55797-221-4, Order no.: AP2-IE704).
Aids the User in Selecting Chains & Belts Based on Specifications of Sprockets & Pulleys, Ratios, Length of Chain, Type of Pulley, Speeds, Torque & Contact Angles. Terms Are Defined, Equations for Calculations Are Shown & All Output Data & Design Specifications Can Be Printed.
Hobar Pubns.

Challenge of the Five Realms: Spellbound in the World of Nhagardia. Sep. 1992. *Items Included:* Manual, technical supplement, poster. *Customer Support:* Free contact support, 1-410-771-1151.
80286 minimum-hard disk required 16MHz. IBM PC & compatibles (640k). disk $59.95.
Nonstandard peripherals required: VGA/MCGA-256 Color. *Optimal configuration:* DOS 2.11 or higher; mouse recommended; Joystick, keyboard; Roland, Adlib, Sound Blaster.
The Only Fantasy Role Playing Game Based on the Works of Award Winning Game Designer Marc Miller. Players Will Find the Game to Have More of an Imaginary "Colorful Fantasy-Feel" Rather Than the "Dismal Environment" Approach Which Is the Benchmark of Most RPG's.
MicroProse Software.

Chameleon. *Version:* 3.0. *Compatible Hardware:* Apple Macintosh. *Customer Support:* Unlimited telephone support.
3.5" disk $49.95.
Weights & Measures Conversion.
Spectrum Computing, Inc.

Chameleon Laboratory Information Management System. *Customer Support:* 24 hour/day, 7 day/week customer support; 90 day warranty; yearly maintenance fee approx. 15% of software purchase price.
DOS, Novell, Windows. IBM PCs & compatibles. Contact publisher for price. *Networks supported:* Novell.
Features Capabilities Vital to the Laboratory Manager Who Must Continuously Improve Communications & Quality with Fewer Staff & Lower Budgets. Communications Between Multi-Site Facilities Is Easily User Customized to Track Specimens, Change Performing Locations, & Route Reports. Quality Is Supported with Real-Time Turnaround Alerts & Result Correlation. Fewer Staff Are Aided by More Efficient Data Entry Using Picklists, Logic, Barcodes, Lightpens, & Touch Screens & by Immediate Access to Procedure Manuals, Doctor Phone Numbers, & Mail Messages. Uses PC Workstations on a Novell Network. It Provides You Capability to Develop & Maintain Your Own Databases, Screens, Reports, & Logic Which in Turn Allows You to Gain the Full Benefits of the New Features.
LCI.

Chameleon Laboratory Information System. *Customer Support:* 24 hours/day, 7 days/week. DOS/Novell/Windows. IBM PCs & clones (8Mb). Contact publisher for price. *Networks supported:* Novell Netware.
Based on New OMNIS Technology. OMNIS Incorporates Microcomputer Workstations on a Novell Network Platform Utilizing Object-Oriented Technology. This Approach Supports New User Design Options for Specifying Data Records, Ad Hoc Data Browsers, & Creating Screens with Intelligent Screen Control. Efficiency Is Also Enhanced with Use of Barcoding, Mouse, Touchscreen & Light Pen Technology. Initial Release Will Consist of the Microbiology Module; Full Functionality Will Be Available with Subsequent Product Releases.
LCI.

Chameleon Remote. *Compatible Hardware:* IBM PC XT, PC AT & compatibles. *Memory Required:* 512k.
disk $3995.00.
Lets Typesetting Facilities Transmit Plain Paper Proofs Via Modem to Customers Who Have Laser Printers. Can Also Send Out Proofs While Still Producing Output On-Site.
Applied Publishing.

Champion Accounting Software. *General Requirements:* 8Mb free disk space.
IBM & compatibles, 386 or higher. contact publisher for price.
Package Includes General Ledger Receivable, Accounts Payable, Payroll, Inventory, Job Costing, Cost Estimating & ReportWriter.
Champion Business Systems, Inc.

Champion Accounts Payable. *Version:* 9409. Sep. 1994. *Compatible Hardware:* IBM PC & compatibles. *Operating System(s) Required:* MS-DOS. *Language(s):* Clipper. *Memory Required:* 640k. *General Requirements:* Printer.
disk $595.00 multi-user.
Maintains the Vendor List, Accounts Payable Journal, Vendor Ledgers, Purchase Order Register, Accounts Payable Aging Report. Provides a Prepayment Edit List, & Prints Vendor Checks.
Champion Business Systems, Inc.

Champion Accounts Receivable. *Version:* 9409. Sep. 1994. *Compatible Hardware:* IBM PC & compatibles. *Operating System(s) Required:* MS-DOS. *Language(s):* Clipper. *Memory Required:* 640k. *General Requirements:* Printer.
MS-DOS. disk $595.00.
MS-DOS, multi-users. disk $595.00 module.
Accounts Receivable Program That Provides Both Point-of-Sale Invoicing & Invoicing from Sales Orders, Sales Analysis Reports, Accounts Receivable Aging & Billing Statements, Open Orders, Open Invoices & More.
Champion Business Systems, Inc.

Champion Business Accounting System Bookkeeper. *Version:* 9409. Sep. 1994. *Compatible Hardware:* IBM PC & compatibles. *Operating System(s) Required:* MS-DOS. *Language(s):* Clipper (source code included). *Memory Required:* 640k. *General Requirements:* Hard disk recommended.
disk $195.00.
Includes 6 Modules to Be Used As an Integrated Accounting System, Written in Clipper. General Ledger, Accounts Receivable, Accounts Payable, Payroll, Reportwriter.
Champion Business Systems, Inc.

Champion Controller - Integrated Accounting Software: Business Accounting. *Version:* 9409. *Compatible Hardware:* IBM PC & compatibles. *Operating System(s) Required:* MS-DOS. *Language(s):* Clipper. *Memory Required:* 640k. *General Requirements:* Printer; hard disk recommended.
disk $1295.00.
Integrated Accounting Program with Six Modules Include: General Ledger & Financial Statements,

Champion General Ledger: Business
Accounts Payable (with Purchase Order); Inventory; Payroll; & Accounts Receivable (with Order Entry & Point-of-Sale Functions) & Report-Writer.
Champion Business Systems, Inc.

Champion General Ledger: Business Accounting. *Version:* 9409. Sep. 1994. *Compatible Hardware:* IBM PC & compatibles. *Operating System(s) Required:* PC-DOS, MS-DOS, CP/M-80, CP/M-86. *Language(s):* Clipper (source code included). *Memory Required:* 640k. *General Requirements:* Printer; hard disk recommended.
Single user. disk (PC-DOS) $395.00.
Multi-user. disk $595.00.
Automatically Updates the Cash Receipts Journal, Cash Disbursements Journal, General Ledger, & Financial Statements. Maintains the Cash Disbursements Journal, Detailed & General Ledger Transactions, General Ledger Activity by Code, Trial Balance Work-Sheet, Financial Statement, Schedules to Financial Statements, etc.
Champion Business Systems, Inc.

Champion Inventory. *Version:* 9409. Sep. 1994. *Compatible Hardware:* IBM PC & compatibles. *Operating System(s) Required:* PC-DOS/MS-DOS. *Language(s):* Clipper. *Memory Required:* 640k. *General Requirements:* Printer; hard disk recommended.
Contact publisher for price.
Multi-user. disk $595.00 MS-DOS.
Maintains the Inventory Master List, History, Planning Report, Adjustments Journal, Reorder Report, etc. Product Assembly & Bill of Materials Included.
Champion Business Systems, Inc.

Champion Payroll. *Version:* 9409. Sep. 1994. *Compatible Hardware:* IBM PC & compatibles. *Operating System(s) Required:* MS-DOS, MS-DOS, CP/M-86, CP/M-80. *Language(s):* Clipper (source code included). *Memory Required:* 640k. *General Requirements:* Printer; hard disk recommended.
Multi-user. disk 595.00 MS-DOS.
Multi-user. disk MS-DOS $495.00.
Produces Payroll for All Fifty States. Maintains the Payroll Journal, Employee Information & History Report, & Worksheets for Federal Unemployment (Form 940) Federal Withholding & F.I.C.A. (Form 941), & State Unemployment Reports. Produces a Prepayment Edit List Before the Payroll Checks Are Printed. Also, Provides a Company Payroll Summary Total Report for Each Payroll & Prints W-2's at the End of the Year, etc.
Champion Business Systems, Inc.

Champion Report Writer. *Version:* 9409. Champion Business Systems, Inc. Jan. 1985. *Compatible Hardware:* IBM PC & compatible. *Operating System(s) Required:* PC-DOS, MS-DOS, CP/M-80, CP/M-86. *Language(s):* DBASE III Plus. *Memory Required:* 640k. *General Requirements:* Printer; hard disk recommended.
disk $249.00.
Custom Report Generator & Spreadsheet Interface Program Designed Specifically to Increase the Power & Versatility of CHAMPION Integrated Business Accounting Software.
Champion Business Systems, Inc.

Champions of Krynn. S.S.I. Special Projects Team. *Customer Support:* Technical support line: (408) 737-6850 (11am-5pm, PST); 14 day money back guarantee/30 day exchange policy.
IBM PC & compatible (512k, Tandy (640k). $49.95 (2 SKUs, one for 3.5" disk & one for 5.25"). *Nonstandard peripherals required:* Requires a color monitor & a graphics adaptor (i.e., CGA, EGA, Tandy 16-color) if playing on floppies, requires 2 disk drives.
Commodore 64/128 (64k). disk $39.95.
Workbench. Amiga (512k). 3.5" disk $49.95.
Apple II (128k). disk $49.95. *Nonstandard peripherals required:* 80 column explanation card (to expand to 128k).
Guide a Party of Characters Through a Web of Combat & Intrigue. Uncover & Then Thwart a Plot to Establish the Dark Queen Takhisis As Krynn's Undisputed Ruler. Player Characters Include Kenders & Knights of Solamnia As well As Most of the Races & Classes Found in POOL OF RADIANCE & CURSE OF THE AZURE BONDS. Meet & Work with the Characters from the DRAGONLANCE Novels -- Tanis, Tasselhoff, & Caramon -- As They Struggle to Overcome the Forces of Evil. New Features Include Moons with Phases That Affect a Mage's Power & Gods That Grant Special Abilities to Their Clerics.
Strategic Simulations, Inc.

Championship Baseball. *Compatible Hardware:* Commodore Amiga.
3.5" disk $39.95.
Baseball Simulation.
Activision, Inc.

Championship Baseball: Arcade Plus Series. *Compatible Hardware:* TI 99/4A with Milton Bradley's MBX System.
contact publisher for price (Order no.: PHM3148).
Baseball Diamond Action with a Computer Umpire to Call out the Plays & Pitches. Make up Team Names for the Scoreboard. Realistic Player Movements & Ballpark Music. Speech Synthesis & Voice Recognition.
Texas Instruments, Personal Productivit.

Championship Basketball. *Compatible Hardware:* Commodore Amiga.
3.5" disk $44.95.
Two on Two Basketball Game.
Activision, Inc.

Championship Blackjack. *Compatible Hardware:* IBM PC. *Operating System(s) Required:* MS-DOS. *Memory Required:* 192k.
disk $34.95.
Provides a Realistic Table Layout, Complete Rules, Player Statistics, & Two Playing Strategies. Supplies Computer Players & Allows up to Six Players.
PC Software.

Championship Golf. *Compatible Hardware:* Commodore Amiga.
3.5" disk $39.95.
Golf Simulation.
Activision, Inc.

Championship Lode Runner. Doug Smith. *Compatible Hardware:* Apple II+, IIe, IIc; Atari 400, 800, XL, XE Series; Commodore 64; IBM PC, PC XT, PCjr. *General Requirements:* CGA card for IBM.
disk $34.95 ea.
Apple. (ISBN 0-922614-73-3, Order no.: 10150).
Commodore. (ISBN 0-922614-96-2, Order no.: 10130).
IBM. (ISBN 0-922614-91-1, Order no.: 10110).
Atari. disk $29.95 (Order no.: ATDSK-137).
hint bk. $9.95 (Order no.: SUP-300).
50 All-New Levels for Lode Runner Experts with Special Screen Titles for Each Completed Level. The Hint Book Provides Step-by-Step Hints for Solving Every Level & Diagrams of Every Screen.
Broderbund Software, Inc.

CHAMPIPE: Piping Materials Inventory & Control. *Version:* 2.5. WJJ Computer Systems. Sep. 1988. *Compatible Hardware:* IBM PC, PC XT, PC AT & compatibles. *Operating System(s) Required:* PC-DOS/MS-DOS 3.1. *Language(s):* COBOL. *Memory Required:* 512k. *General Requirements:* 10Mb on hard disk. *Customer Support:* 30 day money-back guarantee.
3.5" or 5.25" disk $1995.00, incl. 75-page manual (Order no.: 181).
Replicates the Manual Procedures of Piping Material Control That Most Engineering Firms in the USA, Canada, & the UK Use. Isometric Drawings, Bills of Material, Requisitions, Purchase Orders, Receiving Vouchers, & Shipping Orders Are Parts of the Program & Its Products. It Is a Tool Designed for Consulting Engineering Firms in Particular. Can Do the Control Job Whenever Piping Is to Be Designed, Procured, & Installed. Tracks Piping Materials Through All Stages of Engineering, Procurement & Construction, Covering Any Number of Projects Concurrently.
Gulf Publishing Co.

Change & Configuration Control (CCC) Enterprise Wide Life-Cycle Management. *Customer Support:* Training courses, periodic updates & enhancements, hotline, customization, consultation.
PC, XT, AT & compatibles, IBM 370, 30xx, 43xx, RS16000, 9370; Digital VAX, MicroVAXstation; Honeywell Bull; Data General MV AViiON; Sun Microsystems; Gould; Harris Night Hawk, HCX & MCX; Hewlett-Packard 9000 Series 300, 400, 700, & 800 models. Contact publisher for price.
Provides Change Control, Configuration Management & Life-Cycle Management for All Activities in the Software Life Cycle, Independently of Platform, Life-Cycle Phases & Methodologies.
Softool Corp.

The Chaos Continuum: MAC Retail Box. Sep. 1993. *Items Included:* Registration Card. *Customer Support:* Creative Multimedia Corporation warrants the CD-ROM disc & diskettes to be free from defects in materials & workmanship under normal use & service for a period of 90 days from date of purchase. Creative Multimedia Corporation offers Technical Support to customers as needed.
System Software 7.0 or higher. Macintosh II or higher; hard drive w/1Mb of free space; 13" or larger color monitor 2/8-bit display required (2.5Mb). CD-ROM disk $79.99 (ISBN 1-880428-27-X, Order no.: 10520). *Addl. software required:* CD-ROM extensions required. *Optimal configuration:* A CD-ROM drive with 150k/second transfer rate, 380ms or less access rate recommended. *Networks supported:* All.
In the Year 2577, Titan Colony Is Being Held Captive by the Sentient Supercomputer, C.H.A.O.S. Trapped in a Parallel Continuum by the Computer, the Colonists & the Scientists Who Created the Supercomputer Are Seeking Help - from You! The C.H.A.O.S. Continuum Is a Dramatic New Development in CD-ROM Entertainment, Incorporating Movie-Style Special Effects, Detailed Story Line & a Comprehensive Educational Database.
Creative Multimedia Corp.

Chaos Data Analyzer. *Items Included:* Full manual. No other products required. *Customer Support:* Free telephone support - no time limit, 30 day warranty.
MS-DOS 3.2 or higher. IBM & compatibles (512k). disk $99.95.
Research Tool Consisting of 14 Programs for Detecting Hidden Determinism in Seemingly Random Data. Calcuations Such As the

TITLE INDEX

Probability Distribution, Power Spectrum, Lyapunov Exponent, & Various Measures of the Fractal Dimension Enable You to Determine Properties of the Equations Governing the Observed Behavior. Data May Be Displayed in Phase-Space Plots, Time Records, Return Maps, & Poincare Movies.
Dynacomp, Inc.

Chaos Data Analyzer. 1995. *Items Included:* Full manual. *Customer Support:* Free telephone support - 90 days, 30-day warranty.
MS-DOS 3.2 or higher. 286 (584k). disk $99.95. *Nonstandard peripherals required:* CGA/EGA/VGA.
A Research Tool Consisting of 14 Programs for Detecting Hidden Determinism in Seemingly Random Data. Calculations Such As the Probability Distribution, Power Spectrum, Lyapunov Exponent, & Various Measures of the Fractal Dimension Enable You to Determine Properties of the Equations Governing the Observed Behavior. Data May Be Displayed in Phase-Space Plots, Time Records, Return Maps, & Poincare Movies.
Dynacomp, Inc.

Chaos Demonstrations. 1995. *Items Included:* Full manual. *Customer Support:* Free telephone support - 90 days, 30-day warranty.
MS-DOS 3.2 or higher. 286 (584k). disk $69.95. *Nonstandard peripherals required:* CGA/EGA/VGA.
A Collection of 22 Colorful Demonstrations, Many of Which Can Be Viewed in 3-D, Illustrating Chaos in Physical & Biological Systems. It Encourages an Appreciation & Understanding of the Complexity & Beauty of Chaotic Systems. The Demonstrations May Be Used by an Instructor in the Classroom, As a Tutorial by Individual Students, or As an Exhibit Using the Museum-Mode Setting. Some of the Animations Included Are the Driven Pendulum, Duffing Oscillator, Random & Deterministic Fractals, & Magnetic Quadrupole.
Dynacomp, Inc.

Chaos Path: The Hands of over Earth. (The/Destiny Chronicles Ser.). William R. Stanek. Jun. 1996.
PC-DOS/MS-DOS, Novell DOS 3.1 or higher. IBM PC, XT, AT, PS/2 or 100% compatibles (640k). disk $11.95 (ISBN 1-57545-006-2). *Optimal configuration:* IBM PC, XT, AT, PS/2 or 100% compatibles, VGA/SVGA or compatible graphics card & monitor, 640k minimum RAM, hard disk, PC-DOS/MS-DOS or Novell DOS 3.1 or higher. Will also run on Windows system.
PC-DOS/MS-DOS, Novell DOS 3.1 or higher. IBM PC, XT, AT, PS/2 or 100% compatibles (640k). disk $11.95 (ISBN 1-57545-007-0). *Optimal configuration:* IBM PC, XT, AT, PS/2 or 100% compatibles, CGA/VGA or compatible graphics card & monitor, 640k minimum RAM, hard disk, PC-DOS/MS-DOS or Novell DOS 3.1 or higher. Will also run on Windows system.
Interactive Fiction on Floppy Disk.
Virtual Pr., The.

Chaos Simulations. 1995. *Items Included:* Full manual. *Customer Support:* Free telephone support - 90 days, 30-day warranty.
MS-DOS 3.2 or higher. 286 (584k). disk $69.95. *Nonstandard peripherals required:* CGA/EGA/VGA.
Includes Fifteen Simulations of Nonlinear Systems. It Is a Highly Sophisticated Learning Aid for Graduate & Advanced Undergraduate Students. The Simulations Show Chaos in Phenomena of Ascending Order of Mathematical Difficulty, from the Simple Algebraic Equation That Defines the Logistic Model for Population Fluctuation Through Differential Equations.
Dynacomp, Inc.

Chaotic Mapper: Linear - 2D Iterative Maps. 1995. *Items Included:* Full manual. *Customer Support:* Free telephone support - 90 days, 30-day warranty.
MS-DOS 3.2 or higher. 286 (584k). disk $69.95. *Nonstandard peripherals required:* CGA/EGA/VGA.
An Exploratory Tool That Enables You to Examine 22 Linear & Two-Dimensional Iterative Maps of Chaotic Systems & Three-Dimensional Differential Equations. Its Elaborate Plotting Capabilities Let Your Create Bifurcation Cascades & Fractal Basin Boundaries.
Dynacomp, Inc.

The Character Factory. *Version:* 2.1. David Hecker. Dec. 1986. *Compatible Hardware:* Apple II+ (with lower-case adapter), IIe, IIc, IIgs. *Operating System(s) Required:* ProDOS. *Language(s):* BASIC, Assembly. *Memory Required:* 64k. *General Requirements:* Printer that allows downloaded characters. *Items Included:* Some math & foreign language characters. *Customer Support:* 11-5 Mon-Fri EST 904-576-9415 or on-line through AppleLink, America Online, GEnie & CompuServe.
disk $24.95 (ISBN 0-931277-09-4).
Lets Users of APPLEWORKS, APPLEWRITER, & Other Programs Print Characters Not Pictured on the Keyboard. User Can Print Characters for Mathematics, Foreign Languages, Science, & Other Subject Areas. Hundreds of Characters Are Supplied. Additional Characters, Typefaces, & Graphic Designs May Be Added.
Seven Hills Software Corp.

Charitable Financial Planner. *Version:* 4.02. Sep. 1991. *Compatible Hardware:* IBM & compatibles. *Operating System(s) Required:* PC-DOS/MS-DOS 2.0 or higher. *Memory Required:* 512k. *Items Included:* User manual & 12 months of maintenance coverage.
3.5 or 5.25" disk $249.00.
Coverage Includes Charitable Remainder Unitrusts & Annuity Trusts, Charitable Lead Unitrusts & Annuity Trusts, Gift Annuities (Immediate & Deferred), Pooled Income Funds, & Charitable Remainders in Personal Residence or Farm. Term of Year, One- & Two-Life Calcs.
CCH ACCESS Software.

Charlotte's Web. Intentional Education Staff & E. B. White. Apr. 1996. *Items Included:* Program manual. *Customer Support:* Free technical support, 90 day warranty.
School ver.. System 7.1 or higher. Macintosh (4Mb). 3.5" disk contact publisher for price (ISBN 1-57204-390-3). *Nonstandard peripherals required:* 256 color monitor, hard drive, printer.
Lab pack. System 7.1 or higher. Macintosh (4Mb). 3.5" disk contact publisher for price (ISBN 1-57204-366-0). *Nonstandard peripherals required:* 256 color monitor, hard drive, printer.
Site license. System 7.1 or higher. Macintosh (4Mb). 3.5" disk contact publisher for price (ISBN 1-57204-391-1). *Nonstandard peripherals required:* 256 color monitor, hard drive, printer.
School ver.. Windows 3.1 or higher. IBM/Tandy & 100% compatibles (4Mb). disk contact publisher for price (ISBN 1-57204-367-9). *Nonstandard peripherals required:* VGA or SVGA 640 x 480 resolution (256), mouse, hard drive, sound device.
Lab pack. Windows 3.1 or higher. IBM/Tandy & 100% compatibles (4Mb). disk contact publisher for price (ISBN 1-57204-392-X). *Nonstandard peripherals required:* VGA or SVGA 640 x 480 resolution (256), mouse, hard drive, sound device.
Site license. Windows 3.1 or higher. IBM/Tandy

CHART 'N GRAPH TOOLBOX

& 100% compatibles (4Mb). disk contact publisher for price (ISBN 1-57204-368-7). *Nonstandard peripherals required:* VGA opr SVGA 640 x 480 resolution (256), mouse, hard drive, sound device.
This companion for young adult literature is ideal for students who don't know how to start that book report, or give that needed summary. Gentle prompts throughout the guide sections of the program include Warm-up Connections, Thinking about Plot, Quoting & Noting, Keeping a Journal, If I were ———' Responding to Questions, Using Quotations, Taking a Personal View, Write to Others, & Write a Sequel.
Lawrence Productions, Inc.

Charlton Heston Voyage Through the Bible: A Voyage of Discovery on CD-ROM. Oct. 1995. *Customer Support:* Free 800 number.
Windows; Macintosh. CD-ROM disk Contact publisher for price. *Nonstandard peripherals required:* CD-ROM drive.
A Spellbinding Adventure Through the World of the Bible in Which Charlton Heston Relates Some of Its Most Powerful Stories. Travel Back in Time to Jerusalem in Jesus' Day, & Walk Through the Second Temple. Motion Video - 3-D Animation, Art Works. Interactive Tours Through 3-D Models. Music from Great Composers.
Jones Interactive Systems, Inc.

CHARM. Jan. 1985. *Compatible Hardware:* IBM PC & compatibles, PC XT, PC AT. *Operating System(s) Required:* PC-DOS. *Memory Required:* 512k. *General Requirements:* Dot matrix line printer, graphics card, hard disk.
disk $9500.00.
Calculates the Probable Dispersion Pattern of a Toxic Gas Cloud Caused by Accidental Release of Hazardous Chemical Compounds. Can Function in Planning or Emergency Response Modes. Predictions Are Based on Physical Properties of a Chemical Compound, Nature of the Release, & Prevailing Meteorological Conditions. Displays a Map Showing the Toxic Cloud's Dispersion & Concentration & Information on Health Hazards Emergency Procedures. Users Can Customize the Maps to Include Local Features & Define Concentration Scales & Altitudinal Parameters.
Radian Corp.

Chart Eas-Alyzer. *Compatible Hardware:* Apple II with 2 disk drives. *Memory Required:* 48k.
disk $395.00.
Provides Charts That May Be Displayed on the Video Monitor & Printed on Most Dot Matrix Printers. There Is No Limit to the Number of Stocks That Can Be Followed. Features Include: Line Charts, Bar Charts, On-Balance Volume, Moving Averages (up to 200 Days or Weeks), Relative Strength, Momentum, Speed Resistant Lines & Trend Lines. Provides Automatic Updating form Remote Computing Corp. (Which Has Historical Information Available for Most Stocks & over 200 Market Indicators Going Back to 1970).
Wall Street Graphics, Inc.

Chart 'N Graph Toolbox. *Version:* 8.9. *Compatible Hardware:* Apple II, II+, IIe, IIc, IIgs. *Operating System(s) Required:* Apple DOS 3.3, ProDos 8. *Language(s):* Assembly, BASIC. *Memory Required:* 128k.
disk $39.95 (ISBN 0-927796-20-1).
Collection of Hi-Res & Double Hi-Res Plotting Commands Designed to Help Users Create Their Own Chart Graphics. Integrated Commands Include Automatic Scaling & Axes Generation, Area Fill, Move, Plot, Draw, Window Frame, Clipping Window, Window Clear, Window Reverse, Tic Marks, Grid Pattern, Zoom/Unzoom, & Vertical & Horizontal Labels. Includes Easy Chart, a Free Chart Drawing Program.
Roger Wagner Publishing, Inc.

Chart Printer: Printing Package 3. *Compatible Hardware:* Commodore 64, PET; IBM PC. *General Requirements:* Printer.
disk $100.00.
Allows the User to Print Any Two Charts in a Bi-Wheel Format.
Matrix Software.

CharterHouse Accounting Systems. *Compatible Hardware:* IBM PC & compatibles. *Memory Required:* 384k. *General Requirements:* Hard disk.
$99.95 to $1700.00 per module.
Financial/Accounting Package. Posts Recurring Transactions, Automatic Posting from Other Modules, Report Format User Definable, Reports Comparative Statements, Wild Card, Links with Other Software Programs, Password Access, Audit Trail, Error Recovery, Reject Erroneous Account Numbers, On-Line Help & Source Code Available.
CharterHouse Software Corp.

CharterHouse Accounts Payable. 1979. *Compatible Hardware:* IBM PC & compatibles, PC XT, PC AT. *Language(s):* GW-BASIC, BASICA, C, Compiled BASIC. *Memory Required:* 256k.
one-time fee $700.00.
lease $50.00, per mo.
maintenance $220.00, per yr.
Designed for Restaurants. Single & Multi-User, Multi-Company. Unlimited Vendor Files, History, & Transactions. Prints Checks, Aged AP Reports, Cash Requirements & Discounts Taken. Stands Alone or Integrates with Other CharterHouse Modules.
Advanced Analytical/CharterHouse.

CharterHouse Accounts Payable System: A-P. Sep. 1985. *Compatible Hardware:* IBM PC, PC XT, PC AT & compatibles. *Operating System(s) Required:* MS-DOS 2.0 or higher. *Language(s):* MS-BASIC.
disk $700.00 (Order no.: CSCAP001).
source code avail.
Allows Processing of Vendor Invoices with Automatic Expense Distribution to General Ledger, Job Costing & Purchase Order Systems. Features Include: Cash or Accrual Methods of Accounting, Aged A/P Trial Balance, Cash Requirements Reports (Variable Periods), Processing of Hand-Written Checks, Automatic Vouchering, Recurring Invoices, Flexible Payment Selection (Vendor, Due-Date, Hold), Partial Payments, Automatic Cash Discounts Computation, Voucher Register, G/L Distribution Summary &/or Detail, Check Writing, Check Register (Session & Monthly), Vendor & Expense Accounts Listings, & 1099 Forms for Selected Vendors.
CharterHouse Software Corp.

CharterHouse Accounts Receivable, Billing & Inventory Control System: A-R. Sep. 1985. *Compatible Hardware:* IBM PC & compatibles, PC XT, PC AT. *Operating System(s) Required:* MS-DOS 2.0 or higher. *Language(s):* MS-BASIC. *Memory Required:* 384k.
disk $1700.00 (Order no.: CSCAR002).
source code avail.
Prints Invoices, Reduces Inventory, Posts to Customer Ledger & Accumulates Sales Analysis & Purchase History. Features Include: Open Item with Details of Charges & Payments or Balance Forward A/R, On-Line Invoicing with Default Discounts, Ship-To File, Credit Checks, Sales Tax Computation, Credit Memos, Sales Journal, Cash Receipts Processing with On-Screen Look-Up of Open Items, On-Line Customer Profile, Summary &/or Detail A/R Aging, Monthly Statements with Optional Finance Charges, Revenue Analysis & Detail Distribution, Sales Analysis (Salesman, Territory, State), & Sales Commissions. Prints Inventory Status & Exception Reports, Physical Inventory Worksheets, Item Labels, Price Lists, Inventory Valuations Using LIFO, FIFO (Unlimited Layers), or Average Cost, Suggested Purchase Orders & Inventory Projections. Integrates with CharterHouse O/E, Manufacturing, Job Costing, P/O & G/L Systems.
CharterHouse Software Corp.

CharterHouse Accounts Receivable with Billing & Inventory. 1979. *Compatible Hardware:* IBM PC & compatibles, PC XT, PC AT. *Language(s):* GW-BASIC, BASICA, C, Compiled BASIC. *Memory Required:* 420k.
one-time fee $1700.00.
lease $80.00, per mo.
maintenance $220.00, per yr.
Designed for Restaurants. Single & Multi-User, Multi-Company. Includes Customer Profiles, Inventory, Salesman & Territory Reports. Unlimited Customer Files. Unlimited Inventory. Stands Alone or Integrates with Other Modules.
Advanced Analytical/CharterHouse.

CharterHouse Accounts Receivable with Billing. 1979. *Compatible Hardware:* IBM PC & compatibles, PC XT, PC AT. *Language(s):* GW-BASIC, BASICA, C, Compiled BASIC. *Memory Required:* 256k.
one-time fee $1000.00.
lease $50.00, per mo.
maintenance $220.00, per yr.
Designed for Restaurants. Single & Multi-User, Multi-Company. Includes Invoicing, Customer Profiles, Salesman & Territory Reports. Unlimited Customer Files, On-Line Help. Stands Alone or Integrates with Other Modules.
Advanced Analytical/CharterHouse.

CharterHouse Fixed Assets. 1979. *Compatible Hardware:* IBM PC & compatibles, PC XT, PC AT. *Language(s):* GW-BASIC, BASICA, C, Compiled BASIC. *Memory Required:* 256k.
$99.00, one-time fee.
lease $50.00, per mo.
maintenance $220.00, per yr.
Designed for Restaurants. Calculates Depreciation by All Accepted Methods. Depreciation History Reports for Each Asset. GL Posting Options for Federal Taxes, States, & Internal Use. Stands Alone or Integrates with GL.
Advanced Analytical/CharterHouse.

CharterHouse Fixed Assets System. 1986. *Compatible Hardware:* IBM PC & compatibles, PC XT, PC AT. *Operating System(s) Required:* MS-DOS 2.0 or higher. *Memory Required:* 384k. *General Requirements:* Hard disk.
disk $99.95.
source code avail.
Continuously Updated since 1979, the Software Provides for up to 34 Depreciation Methods & Current Requirements for Luxury Auto Cap. Designed for Use with Multiple Companies, the Software Can Process an Unlimited Number of Clients. The Program Even Automatically Determines Whether the Mid-Quarter Convention Applies & Adjusts Year-to-Date Depreciation in the Fiscal Year's Last Quarter. For Each Asset, the Depreciation Method, Life, Salvage, Type, Location, & Serial Number Can Be Set up Differently for Book, Federal, State, & Two Other Types of Side-by-Side Reporting - Including Alternative Minimum Tax.
CharterHouse Software Corp.

CharterHouse General Ledger. 1979. *Compatible Hardware:* IBM PC & compatibles, PC XT, PC AT. *Language(s):* GW-BASIC, BASICA, C, Compiled BASIC. *Memory Required:* 420k.
one-time fee $1000.00.
lease $50.00, per mo.
maintenance $220.00, per yr.
Designed for Restaurants. Single & Multi-User, Multi-Company. Consolidated, Divisional & Departmental Reports. Unlimited Chart of Accounts & Transactions. Two Years Detail. No Closing. Stands Alone or Integrates with Other Modules.
Advanced Analytical/CharterHouse.

CharterHouse General Ledger System: G-L. *Version:* 1.1. Sep. 1985. *Compatible Hardware:* IBM PC, PC XT, PC AT with 2 double-sided disk drives or hard disk. *Operating System(s) Required:* MS-DOS 2.0 or higher. *Language(s):* MS-BASIC. *Memory Required:* 256k.
disk $1000.00 (Order no.: CSCGL001).
source code avail.
Allows User-Controlled Formatting of Financial Statements or Using "Simplified Set-Up" of the Supplied Standard Charts of Accounts. Features Include: Flexible Account Numbers (8-Digit; 4-Major, Last 4 Define Division & Department), User-Defined Journals (up to 89; Recurring, Reversing), User-Defined Periods (13 or 12 Calendar), Interim Year-End Close, Immediate Financial Reports for Any Period in the "Two-Open" Years, Flexible Financial Statements Against Same Period of Prior Year or Against Budget, Separate Schedules, Automatic Inventory Adjustment (Based on Predetermined Gross Profit Percentage), Automatic State & Federal Tax Accrual Entries (Based on User-Estimated Tax Rates), Divisional & Departmental Reporting & Consolidation.
CharterHouse Software Corp.

CharterHouse Manufacturing Inventory/Bill of Materials. 1979. *Compatible Hardware:* IBM PC & compatibles, PC XT, PC AT. *Language(s):* GW-BASIC, BASICA, C, Compiled BASIC. *Memory Required:* 420k.
one-time fee $1700.00.
lease $80.00, per mo.
maintenance $220.00, per yr.
Designed for Restaurants. Single & Multi-User, Multi-Company. Schedules Finished Goods by Allocating Raw Material Components & Sub-Assemblies. Receives Inventory. Works in Conjunction with CharterHouse ACCOUNTS RECEIVABLE WITH BILLING.
Advanced Analytical/CharterHouse.

CharterHouse Manufacturing Inventory Control System. *Version:* 2.0. Sep. 1985. *Compatible Hardware:* IBM PC, PC XT, PC AT & compatibles. *Operating System(s) Required:* MS-DOS 2.0 or higher. *Language(s):* MS-BASIC. *Memory Required:* 384k.
disk $1000.00 (Order no.: CSCMF001).
source code avail.
Offers Integrated Control of Finished Goods, Subassemblies & Component Inventories & Allows Costing Using a Multi-Level, Indented Bill-of-Material Processor. Features Include: Inventory File Maintenance (20 Alphanumeric Part Key), Bill-of-Material File Maintenance, Product Cost Reporting, Production Activity Entry, Bill-of-Material Explosion & Update, Status of Commitment of Finished Goods &/or Component Inventories, Suggested Component Pruchase Order Reports, Pick-Lists & Where Used Reports. Prints Physical Inventory Worksheets, Item Labels, Price Lists, Component Inventory Valuations Using LIFO, FIFO (Unlimited Layers), or Average Cost. Integrates with CharterHouse O/E, A/R with Billing, P/O & G/L Systems.
CharterHouse Software Corp.

CharterHouse Order Entry. 1979. *Compatible Hardware:* IBM PC & compatibles, PC XT, PC AT. *Language(s):* GW-BASIC, BASICA, C, Compiled BASIC. *Memory Required:* 320k.

one-time fee $700.00.
lease $50.00, per mo.
maintenance fee $220.00.
Designed for Restaurants. Single & Multi-User, Multi-Company. Creates & Maintains Orders & Backorders. Works in Conjunction with CharterHouse ACCOUNTS RECEIVABLE WITH BILLING & INVENTORY & with CharterHouse MANUFACTURING BILL OF MATERIALS.
Advanced Analytical/CharterHouse.

CharterHouse Order Entry System: Order Entry. *Version:* 1.1. Sep. 1985. *Compatible Hardware:* IBM PC & compatibles, PC AT, PC XT. *Operating System(s) Required:* MS-DOS 2.0 or higher. *Language(s):* MS-BASIC. *Memory Required:* 384k.
disk $700.00 (Order no.: CSCOE001).
Prints Customer Workorders (Pick-Lists) & Shipping Labels, Commits Finished Goods Ordered, Updates Customer Orders & Backorders. Features Include: Open & Backorder Reports by Customer &/or Inventory Item, Order Profile by Customer or Item (On-Screen or Print), Selective Partial Billing on Previously Entered Orders with Automatic Backorders & Order Corrections. Integrates with CharterHouse A/R with Billing & Manufacturing Systems.
CharterHouse Software Corp.

CharterHouse Payroll. 1979. *Compatible Hardware:* IBM PC & compatibles, PC XT, PC AT. *Language(s):* GW-BASIC, BASICA, C, Compiled BASIC. *Memory Required:* 420k.
one-time fee $700.00.
lease $50.00, per mo.
maintenance fee $220.00, per mo.
Designed for Restaurants. Single & Multi-User, Multi-Company. Provides Union Reporting Features. Prints Checks, W-2, 941 & 940 Deposits. Prints State-Specific Reports. Will Operate As Stand Alone or Integrates with CharterHouse GENERAL LEDGER. For All 50 States & Canada.
Advanced Analytical/CharterHouse.

CharterHouse Payroll System. Jan. 1987. *Compatible Hardware:* IBM PC & compatibles, PC XT, PC AT. *Operating System(s) Required:* MS-DOS 2.0 or higher. *Language(s):* MS-BASIC. *Memory Required:* 256k. *General Requirements:* Hard disk.
disk $99.95.
source code avail.
Payroll, Continuously Updated since 1979, Provides for Full-Function Payroll, After-the-Fact Entry & Laser Printing of Yearly (W2) & Quarterly (941, DE3) Forms. Designed for Use with Multiple Companies, the Software Can Process an Unlimited Number of Clients. System Functions Include Automatic Computation of Withholdings (Federal, State, Local, FICA, SDI), Accumulation of: Group Totals for Workman's Compensation, 401K Data, Tips Reported, & 125 Deductions, FICA & Federal/State Withholding Deposit Check Computation & Printing, Quarterly (941, DE3DP, DE3B) & Yearly (W2) Tax Reports.
CharterHouse Software Corp.

CharterHouse Purchase Order System. Mar. 1986. *Compatible Hardware:* IBM PC & compatibles, PC XT, PC AT. *Operating System(s) Required:* MS-DOS 2.0 or higher. *Language(s):* MS-BASIC (source code included). *Memory Required:* 384k. *General Requirements:* Hard disk.
disk $700.00.
source code avail.
Offers Integrated Control of Goods & Services Being Ordered with Automatic Preparation of Accounts Payable Vouchers & Posting of Received Items to Inventory. Features Include: Purchase Order Form Printing (Identifying the Items Being Ordered by User or Vendor ID, the Time & Mode of Delivery, & the Expected/Negotiated Cost, On-Line Purchase Order Profile (by Vendor or Item), Open Purchase Order Reports (by Vendor, Buyer, or PO), Incoming Item Analysis Report in Date Requested Sequence (by Vendor, Buyer, or User's Item ID), Vendor Item Cross Reference Listing (20 Alphanumeric Item ID). Ties in with CharterHouse A/P & Inventory Systems.
CharterHouse Software Corp.

ChartEx. *Version:* 3.0. Nov. 1991. *Items Included:* Tutorial book, reference manual. *Customer Support:* 90 days free support, yearly support contract $879.00.
MS-DOS 5.0. IBM PC compatible, 486 (4Mb). $2995.00 & up. *Optimal configuration:* IBM PC compatible, 486 or higher, 4Mb or higher. *Networks supported:* Novell, LANtastic, most NetBIOS.
Problem Oriented Medical Record Program That Links a Patient's Medical History, Problem List, & Progress Notes Together. A Patient's Medical History Is Used to Generate a List of Problems for the Patient. Every Progress Note Written for a Patient Is Associated with Problems on the Problem List. The Problem List Provides a Reference Point & Anchor for the Patient's Medical Record.
Pacific Medsoft, Inc.

Chartics: Business-Science Graphic System. Jun. 1985. *Compatible Hardware:* Apple II. *Memory Required:* 64k.
disk $250.00, incl. manual (ISBN 0-922238-00-6).
Produces 8 Types of Charts & Read/Write DIF. FILE Database File on Disk for Business & Science Applications. Enables User to Calculate & Plot up to 280 Data Cells in a Single Operation Which May Be Generated from a Spreadsheet Program or Transmitted with Modem.
American Avicultural Art & Science.

Charting Gallery. *Compatible Hardware:* HP 150 Touchscreen.
3.5" disk $265.00 (Order no.: 45513A).
Transforms Numerical Data into Line, Pie & Bar Charts, & Scattergrams. Information Can Be Transferred from Existing Spreadsheets, or Entered Manually. The Charts Can Be Enhanced, or Merged into EXECUTIVE MEMOMAKER Documents.
Hewlett-Packard Co.

Charts for Agricultural Commodities (Price Charting). 1982. *Compatible Hardware:* Apple II, IIe, IIc. *Memory Required:* 48k.
disk $50.00 (Order no.: FM006 D-A).
Allows User to Store & Chart Agricultural Commodities on a Daily Basis. Enter High, Low & Closing Volumes.
Micro Learningware.

Charts Unlimited. *Version:* 2.0. Stan Webber. May 1983. *Compatible Hardware:* IBM PC XT, PC AT, & compatibles. *Operating System(s) Required:* MS-DOS, PC-DOS 2.0 or higher. *Language(s):* Assembler. *Memory Required:* 512k. *General Requirements:* Printer.
IBM. $49.95.
Graphic/Text Processor That Can Be Used to Draw Almost Any Type of Charts Including: Flow Charts, Floor Plans, Office Layouts, Organiation Charts, Forms, PERT Charts, Business Charts, Block/Wire/Circuit Diagrams. User Can Rearrange, Enlarge, Or Overlay Charts. Offer 256 Column by 1000 Row Drawing Area. Mixes Three Kinds of Text with 36 Predefined Objects & 36 Special Symbols. Replicates, Enlarges, Shrinks, Or Rearranges Objects.
Graphware, Inc.

Chartwheels II. *Version:* 1.X. *Items Included:* Manual. *Customer Support:* Free phone support.
MS-DOS 3.x (512k). disk $125.00 (ISBN 0-87199-086-5). *Nonstandard peripherals required:* Hercules, EGA or VGA graphics card; two 360k floppy drives or one hard drive; 8087-type math processor recommended; IBM- or Epson-compatible printer, or Hewlett Packard compatible laser printer.
3.5" disk $125.00 (ISBN 0-87199-093-8).
Produces Readable Round Horoscope Wheels on Screen or Printer. Allows Two Charts on a Wheel. Features Rectification Assist, Dial Charts, Solar Arcs, Progressions & Directions, Asteroids & Uranian Planets, Astroclock & Synastry. Works with Nova Chart Files or Alone.
Astrolabe, Inc.

CHARTWORK. *Version:* 3.10. Nov. 1988. *Compatible Hardware:* IBM PC, PC XT, PC AT & compatibles, 80386-based PCs. *Language(s):* C. *Memory Required:* 512k. *General Requirements:* Graphics card.
contact publisher for price (Order no.: TARGA 16).
Business Graphics Program for Creating Business & Word Charts for High-Resolution Slide or Hard Copy Output.
West End Film, Inc.

El Cheapo Mail Program. *Compatible Hardware:* IBM PC; TRS-80 Model I Level I, Model III, Model 4, Color Computer, Tandy 1000. *Operating System(s) Required:* TRSDOS. *Language(s):* BASIC. *Memory Required:* 16k.
cassette $19.95.
Designed for Administrative Office Use for Those Who Want to Produce Personalized Mailings to Parents, Alumni, Fraternities, Clubs, etc. Prepares Letters, Envelopes, Labels, & Offers Other Features. Personalization Is Permitted for 1-4 Lines.
Viking, Inc.

The Cheapware Tax Record. Aug. 1984. *Compatible Hardware:* IBM PC, PC jr, PC XT & compatibles. *Operating System(s) Required:* PC-DOS/MS-DOS 3.X. *Language(s):* Compiled BASIC. *Memory Required:* 64k. *General Requirements:* Printer, CGA card, medium resolution color monitor & RAM card recommended.
disk $40.00 (ISBN 0-925825-08-5).
Collect Income & Expense Records in Eight Classes & 32 Types for Any Calendar Year in One Displayable File.
Robert L. Nicolai.

Cheats, Hacks, & Hints. *Customer Support:* Free, unlimited.
System 6 Mac. 030 Mac, 256 colors (4Mb). CD-ROM disk $19.95. *Nonstandard peripherals required:* Sound card, CD-ROM drive.
Windows 3.1 PC. 486 PC (4Mb). *Nonstandard peripherals required:* Any Windows supported sound card, CD-ROM drive.
This Disc Is Crammed with Hundreds of Maps, Walk-Throughs, Cheating Utilities, FAQs (Frequently Asked Questions), Extra Game Levels, Clues, Game Editors, Secret Keyboard Codes, & Patches for Your Favorite Games. A Must-Have for Any Serious Computer Gamer.
BeachWare.

Check Exec. *Version:* 2.0. May 1983. *Operating System(s) Required:* CP/M-86, PC-DOS, MS-DOS. *Language(s):* CB-86. *Memory Required:* 128k.
$249.95.
Checkbook System That Includes Computerized Error Checking, Balance Keeping, Monthly Payment Tracking, Deposit Totalling, etc.
Data Source One, Inc.

Check Ledger. *Compatible Hardware:* IBM PC & compatibles. *Memory Required:* 512k.
disk $100.00.
Single-Entry Bookkeeping System Serves the Accounting Needs of the Small to Medium-Sized Business, a Department Within a Large Organization, or Personal Use. Reports Include Detail Ledger, Year-to-Date Ledger, Outstanding Checks, Check Register, Summary Ledger, Issued Checks, Adjustments & Deposits. The Flexible Chart of Accounts Offers up to 99 Subaccounts or Departments. Accounts Payable & Payroll Can Post Directly to Check Ledger.
Computerware.

Check*Mate. *Version:* 1.1. Aug. 1989. *Operating System(s) Required:* PC-DOS/MS-DOS 3.1 or higher. *Memory Required:* 640k. *General Requirements:* Microsoft C or QuickC (5.0 or higher). *Items Included:* Users guide; reference manual; quick reference guide. *Customer Support:* Upgrades; full telephone support.
first copy annual license $5750.00.
contact publisher for multi-copy purchase rate.
PC-Based Capture/Replay Tool for Automation of PC, Minicomputer, or Mainframe-Based Application Software Testing. Testers "Capture" Their Keystrokes & Screens, Generating Scripts As They Step Through a Test Manually. "Replayed" Scripts Emulate the Tester & Check the Responses. Includes Facilities to Develop & Debug Scripts, Run Suites of Tests, & Document Testing Activity.
Pilot Research Assocs.

Check Services Model PLUS CSM PLUS. Oct. 1993. *Items Included:* Documentation. *Customer Support:* Training included, annual maintenance, limited warranty.
OS/2 or Windows. IBM 386 or higher & compatibles (4Mb-OS/2) (2Mb-Windows). Contact publisher for price. *Addl. software required:* Database Manager for OS/2, Access for Windows. *Optimal configuration:* 486DX 33mhz machine, OS/2, 8Mb RAM, printer, Database Manager.
Check Product Management & Clearing Analysis Tool with Routines to Identify Availability & Pricing Structures & Compute the Lowest Clearing Cost Alternatives.
Automated Financial Systems, Inc.

Check Write & Check Write-M. *Version:* 7.1. 1992. *Compatible Hardware:* IBM PC & compatibles. *Operating System(s) Required:* PC-DOS/MS-DOS; Networks such as Novell, Lantastic. *Customer Support:* 30 days' free support, 1 yr. maintenance $250.00.
$495.00.
Legal Checkwriting/Cash Disbursements Program. Produces Computer Checks & Cash Disbursements Posting Registers of All Checks Written for Each of User's Checking Accounts. All Checks Are Kept Track of for up to 15 Regular & Trust Checking Accounts. Additional Reports Include Vendor Reports on All Companies & Persons to Whom Checks Are Written on a Regular or Frequent Basis, Vendor Inquiries Listing Every Check Written to a Vendor for the Year to Date, Alphabetized Vendor Lists, & Audit Reports of Deletions & Changes. Can Be Used Standalone or Integrated to VERDICT, to GENERAL LEDGER FOR PROFESSIONALS, or to Both. Check Write-M is available for networked systems.
Micro Craft, Inc.

Check Writer. *Items Included:* Bound manual. *Customer Support:* Free hotline - no time limit; 30 day limited warranty; updates are $5/disk plus S&H.
MS-DOS 2.0 or higher. IBM & compatibles (128k). disk $39.95.
Prints Home or Small-Business Checks on Your Own Blanks, Keeps Track of Each Transaction, Reconciles Your Bank Statement, Monitors Budget Deviation, & Summarizes Income Tax Deductible Expenditures. Checks Can Be Printed by Budget Number, Check Number, Payee, or Checks That Have Not Cleared the Bank. A List of Budgeted Amounts to Date Versus Expenditures Can Be Printed at Any Time.
Dynacomp, Inc.

Check Writer. *Compatible Hardware:* Apple II+. disk $29.95.
Allows the User to Print Checks & Vouchers from Text Files Created by Super Checkbook III. Checks Can Also Have Addresses Printed for Window Envelopes & Are Compatible with the NEBS Brand.
Powersoft, Inc.

Checkbook Manager. *Compatible Hardware:* TI 99/4A with Pascal Language card. *Operating System(s) Required:* DX-10. *Language(s):* UCSD Pascal. *Memory Required:* 16k.
disk or cassette $14.95.
Maintains User's Checkbook. Up to 50 Categories Including Food, Transportation & Mortgage Payment. Current Balance for Each Category & the Total Are Maintained. Program Updates Disk File When Transactions Are Entered.
Eastbench Software Products.

Checkbook Manager. *Compatible Hardware:* TI Home Computer.
contact publisher for price (Order no.: PHD 5021).
Maintains Bank Records.
Texas Instruments, Personal Productivity Products.

The Checkbook Solution. Sep. 1989. *Items Included:* Accountant receives Accountant's utilities manual's checkbook manual with His/Her master license. *Customer Support:* 2 hrs included on Master License to accountant. All support is to the accountant only. Additional support is billed at $48/hr broken into 10 minutes.
DOS 3.XX or higher. IBM & compatibles (512K).
master license $995.00. *Nonstandard peripherals required:* Hard disk required for client. *Addl. software required:* Accountant needs Write-Up Solution II.
checkbook basic $125.00.
calculating payroll $225.00.
A Checkwriting Package Which Offers Total Integration Between the Accountant & His/Her Client. The Client Enters Unpaid Invoices, Prints Checks & Distributes to G/L Accounts. He Also Records Cash Receipts Thereby Maintaining an Accurate Cash Balance. Other Information Such as the Chart of Accounts, Vendor & Employee Information is Transferred Initially from the Accountant, Then the Monthly Activity is Transferred Back to the Accountant's G/L at Month-End via Disk or Modem, Thereby Saving Redundant Data Entry of Transactions by Accountant. An Additional Payroll Module is Also Available.
Creative Solutions, Inc. (Michigan).

Checkers 3.0. *Compatible Hardware:* Commodore 64. *Language(s):* Machine. *Memory Required:* 32k.
disk $20.95.
cassette $16.95.
Offers 10 Levels of Play.
Dynacomp, Inc.

Checking Account Manager. *Version:* 2.5. Randolph Constan. Jan. 1990. *Items Included:* 14 page tutorial & reference guide.
Atari XL/XE (48k). $12.95 documentation on disk; $14.95 printed manual. *Optimal configuration:* 64k RAM for extended features.
Fast & Instinctive Database Package Specifically Designed for Checking Account Management. Full Search & List Capabilities with Bargraph Analysis for Spotting Trends. The Key Features of a Business Quality Database, in a User Friendly Program That Is Easily Mastered in One Evening.
Elfin Magic.

Checking Account Package.
contact publisher for price.
Has Automatic Procedures for Reconciling Checkbook & Bank Statement & Recording All Transactions.
Beechwood Software.

CheckMark MultiLedger. *Version:* 4.0. *Items Included:* Diskette & manual. *Customer Support:* 60 days free support, starting with the first call. $79/year extended support plan.
Apple Macintosh (1Mb). 3.5" disk $199.00.
A Complete Integrated Accounting System for Small & Medium-Sized Businesses. Combines General Ledger, Accounts Payable, Accounts Receivable, & Inventory Tracking into a Single Program. Prints Checks, Invoices, & Statements As Well As a Number of Management & Financial Reports. Multi-User Capabilities Are Built-In for up to 10 Users.
CheckMark Software, Inc.

Checkmate II. 1986. *Compatible Hardware:* IBM PC & compatibles. *Operating System(s) Required:* PC-DOS/MS-DOS. *Language(s):* BASIC. *Memory Required:* 512k. *General Requirements:* Hard disk, printer. *Customer Support:* 1 year telephone support; maintenance contract available.
disk $3300.00 (Order no.: 49031).
EBSCO Download Records. disk $300.00 (Order no.: 50032).
demo disk & manual $45.00 (Order no.: 59012).
10% discount to CLASS members avail.
Completely Redesigned Version of CHECKMATE I. New Features Include Faster & More Powerful Keyboard Searching, Truncated Word Searching, Cursor-Controlled Check-In, & More Sophisticated Management Reports. Also Includes Many of the Standard Serials Functions Such As Check-In, Claiming, Routing, Fund Accounting, Subscription Alert & Tracking. In Addition, EBSCO Subscription Service Customers Can Have Their Bibliographic Records Downloaded into CHECKMATE II, Thus Bypassing the Need to Manually Input Bibliographic Data.
CLASS (Cooperative Library Agency for Systems & Services).

!Checkout. *Version:* 2.0. Sep. 1990. *Customer Support:* On Line - Unlimited trianing, report modification, some screen modification. $695.00-annual fee. Telephone - Unlimited telephone access to customer support staff. $495.00-annual fee.
DOS/Windows. IBM PC & compatibles (640k-up to 16Mb). disk $1750.00. *Optimal configuration:* 386 Class or higher. *Networks supported:* Novell, Banyan.
Automates the Check In/Out of Tools, Equipment, Files & Other Shared Resource Items Utilizing Bar Code Technology. Complete System Includes Everything Needed Except PC & Report Printer. Training & Customization Available.
ASAP Systems.

Checks & Balances. *Version:* 4.18 (IBM) 4.1 (CP/M). Apr. 1991. *Compatible Hardware:* CP/M-based machines, IBM PC & compatibles. *Operating System(s) Required:* CP/M, PC-DOS, MS-DOS. *Language(s):* Assembly. *Memory Required:* CP/M 64k; PC-DOS/MS-DOS 256k. *General Requirements:* 2 floppy disk drives, 1 3-1/2" drive, or hard disk. *Customer Support:* Free, unlimited.

TITLE INDEX

disk $74.95, incl. bk.
Financial Package for Home or Small Business. Provides Balance Sheets, Budget Reports, & Profit/Loss Reports. Prints Labels, Cards, & Address Envelopes from the Address File. Keeps Logs of Mileage & Travel for Tax Records. Keeps a Full Year at a Time (Calendar or Fiscal). Single-Entry System. Prints Checks. Supports LaserJet Printers.
CDE Software.

CheckTrack PLUS. *Version:* 4.0. Dec. 1992. *Items Included:* Documentation. *Customer Support:* 90 day limited warranty, annual maintenance - business hours, 12% of license fee, extended hours of support available, training included.
DOS 5.0. Industry standard, 80386 equipped or higher (4Mb). $125,000.00 one site. *Optimal configuration:* IBM compatible 80386/80486, DOS, 4Mb. *Networks supported:* Novell Netware, LAN Manager, Banyan, DLink, Lantastic.
Work Flow Control System with the Capability to Track, Report & Model Each Step of Check Processing. System Actively Monitors Workflow & Enables the User to Adjust Resources to Meet the Demands of Conventional & Image Check Processing Environment. Interfaces to Other Applications, Such As Branch Teller & Check Processing Systems Are Key Components.
Automated Financial Systems, Inc.

Checkup Rx. *Version:* 1.2.
Macintosh 512KE or higher. 3.5" disk $49.95.
Analyzes Macintosh Disks for Viral Infections.
OITC, Inc.

The Checkwriter. *Version:* 4.7. Sep. 1995. *Compatible Hardware:* IBM PC with 2 disk drives. *Operating System(s) Required:* DOS 2.1. *Language(s):* C (source code included). *Memory Required:* 128k.
disk $125.00.
Automates User's Check Writing & Procedures & Prepares Checks on the Printer Without the Use of an Accounts Payable System. A Separate Stand-Alone Bank Reconciliation Program Provided Will Prepare a Report for the User & Client.
Omni Software Systems, Inc. (Indiana).

Checkwriter+: The Electronic Pegboard. Feb. 1985. *Compatible Hardware:* Symphony. *Memory Required:* 512k.
$285.00.
Records & Prints Checks Using Symphony Database. Each Check Amount May Be Distributed to an Unlimited Number of Accounts. Reports Include a Check Register & a Monthly Recap, Summarized & Totaled by Account Number.
Computools, Inc.

Checkwriter Pro. *Version:* 5.0. *Items Included:* Comes with program & manual. *Customer Support:* Free support.
Macintosh system 6.05 or higher (64k). Mac Plus, or above. $79.00. *Optimal configuration:* Plus with system 6.0.5 with hard disk.
Prints on Checks Right From Your Personal Checkbook! Tear Out a Check & Begin. Any Checkform, Even Laser Forms can be Used. Offers Budgeting, Graphing, an Address Database With Envelope/Label Printing, Tax Summaries, Cash Projections, income vs. Expense Reports, Importing/Exporting, MacInTax Link, & Converts Quicken Files. Small Businesses, Use the Direct Link With Aatrix Payroll for a Complete Accounting Solution.
Aatrix Software.

Chef's Accountant. *Items Included:* Bound manual. *Customer Support:* Free hotline - no time limit; 30 day limited warranty; updates are $5/disk plus S&H.
MS-DOS 2.0 or higher. IBM & compatibles (512k). $34.95-$54.95. *Nonstandard peripherals required:* Two disk drives or a hard disk.
Home Food Manager. Plan Nutritious Meals & Save Money by Gaining Control of Your Food Dollars. Recipe Manager; Grocery Manager; Communications; Chef's Handbook; Additional Features - Full-Color Menus with Light-Bar Selection; On-Line Context-Sensitive Help; Pop-Up Calculator; Full-Featured Text Editor; DOS Window; User-Definable Drive/Directory Setup.
Dynacomp, Inc.

CHEKBOOK. *Compatible Hardware:* TRS-80 Model I, Model III. *Operating System(s) Required:* NEW-DOS-80, L-DOS & DOSPlus. *Memory Required:* 48k.
disk $49.95, incl. documentation.
Keeps Track of & Verifies Personal Checkbook Transactions.
The Alternate Source.

Chemcalc Multiphase & General Fluid Flow. *Items Included:* Full manual. No other products required. *Customer Support:* Free telephone support - no time limit, 30 day warranty.
MS-DOS 3.2 or higher. IBM & compatibles (512k). disk $399.95.
Contains Four Programs for Pipeline & Process Engineering: (1) Multiphase Flow, (2) Economic Pipe Diameter, (3) General Fluid Flow, & (4) Compressible Flow Calculations. Programs Will Handle Any Degree of Inclination along the Pipe. Each Program Is Completely Documented with Numerous Example Cases. Programs Operate in Both Metric & U.S. Units.
Dynacomp, Inc.

Chemcalc 2: Gas & Liquid Flow Calculation. C. S. Fang. Jan. 1985. *Compatible Hardware:* IBM PC, PC XT, PC AT & compatibles. *Operating System(s) Required:* PC-DOS/MS-DOS 2.0. *Language(s):* Compiled BASIC. *Memory Required:* 64k. *Customer Support:* 30 day money-back guarantee.
3.5" or 5.25" disk $49.00, incl. 110-page manual (ISBN 0-87201-086-4).
Offers Programs for Calculating the Following: Fanning's Friction Factor, Frictional Pressure Drop, Total Pressure Drop, Power Requirements for Liquid Flow, Flow Rate Vs. Pressure Difference, Pressure Drop for Non-Isothermal Flow, Minimum Diameter, System Head Calculations, Gas Compression, Z-Factor, & Pressure Drop of Real Gas. Operates in SI & U.S. Units.
Gulf Publishing Co.

Chemcalc 3: Heat Transfer Calculations. C. S. Fang. Jan. 1985. *Compatible Hardware:* IBM PC, PC XT, PC AT & compatibles. *Operating System(s) Required:* PC-DOS/MS-DOS 3.0. *Language(s):* Compiled BASIC. *Memory Required:* 64k. *Customer Support:* 30 day money-back guarantee.
3.5" or 5.25 disk $49.00, incl. 82-page manual (ISBN 0-87201-087-2).
System Offers Calculating Heat Transfer Coefficients (Natural Convection, Forced Convection, Forced Convection in Annulus, Jacketed-Wall & Coils, & Condensation), Heat Transfer in Boiling, Combined Boiling & Radiant Heat Transfer, Rate of Simple Convection, & Rate of Convective Heat Transfer. Operates in SI & U.S. Units.
Gulf Publishing Co.

CHEMCALC 7: CHEMICAL COMPOUND

Chemcalc 4: Multiphase Flow & General Fluid Calculations. *Version:* 2.0. Mahesh Talwar. May 1985. *Compatible Hardware:* IBM PC, PC XT, PC AT & compatibles. *Operating System(s) Required:* PC-DOS/MS-DOS 3.0. *Language(s):* Compiled BASIC. *Memory Required:* 64k. *Customer Support:* 30 day money-back guarantee.
3.5" or 5.25" disk $395.00, incl. 198-page manual (ISBN 0-87201-088-0).
System Comprises Four Programs for Pipeline & Process Engineering: Multi-Phase Flow, Economic Pipe Diameter, General Fluidflow Calculations, & Compressible Flow Calculations. Will Handle Any Degree of Inclination Along the Pipe. It Is Exhaustive, Using the Redlich-Kwong Equation of State & NGPA K-Values for Calculating Thermodynamic & Physical Properties & Flashing along the Pipe. Also Calculates Steam/Condensate Two-Phase Flow. Optimum Pipe Sizes for Gas & Liquid Flow in General, As Well As for Compressor & Pump Piping Circuits, May Be Calculated Using the Economic Parameters Diameter Program. Twenty Different Economic Parameters Are Used. Each Program Is Completely Documented with Numerous Example Cases. Operates in SI & U.S. Units.
Gulf Publishing Co.

Chemcalc 5: Heat Exchanger Network Optimization. Jim C. Otar. Jan. 1985. *Compatible Hardware:* IBM PC & compatibles, PC AT, PC XT. *Operating System(s) Required:* MS-DOS 2.0. *Language(s):* BASIC. *Memory Required:* 128k. *Customer Support:* 30 day money-back guarantee.
disk $295.00 ea., incl. manual (ISBN 0-87201-089-9).
Analyzes & Optimizes Several Heat Exchanger Network Configurations. Allows Engineer to Define Variables. Accepts Imperial or Metric Units. Utilizes an Algorithm Based in Minimum Utility Consumption & Operates Within User-Defined Constraints. Also Contains a Powerful, Four-Level Stream Compatibility Facility Allowing Manipulation of Non-Matching Streams.
Gulf Publishing Co.

Chemcalc 6: Heat Exchanger Design (Shell-&-Tube). *Version:* 2.06. Mahesh Bhatia, Chemsoft, Inc. Jan. 1988. *Compatible Hardware:* IBM PC, PC XT, PC AT & compatibles. *Operating System(s) Required:* PC-DOS/MS-DOS 3.1. *Language(s):* Compiled BASIC. *Memory Required:* 256k. *General Requirements:* 2Mb hard disk space. *Customer Support:* 30 day money-back guarantee.
3.5" or 5.25" disk $995.00, incl. 128-page manual (ISBN 0-87201-090-2).
Totally Integrated Heat Exchanger Design Package. Covers 15 Different Types of Exchangers. Designs Are Based on the Latest Research, Methods, & Algorithms, & Conform with Industry, TEMA & ASME Standards. Handles Thermal & Mechanical Design, & Both Rating & Design Modes Are Included Together with Cost & Weight Estimates. Operates in Imperial & Metric Units. Designs Are Optimized with up to 15 Intermediate Possibilities Explores for Each Case. Offers Complete Flexibility for Using Your Own Data & Simple, Quick Change Options to Examine "What If" Conditions. All Designs Are Thoroughly Tested Against Actual Performance Criteria.
Gulf Publishing Co.

Chemcalc 7: Chemical Compound Databank. *Version:* 2.0. Mahesh Bhatia, Chemsoft, Inc. Jan. 1990. *Compatible Hardware:* IBM PC, PC XT, PC AT & compatibles. *Operating System(s) Required:* PC-DOS/MS-DOS 3.1. *Language(s):* Compiled BASIC. *Memory Required:* 128k. *General Requirements:* 1Mb hard disk space.

Customer Support: 30 day money-back guarantee.
3.5" or 5.25" disk $595.00, incl. 58-page manual (ISBN 0-87201-093-7).

Unit Can Be Used to Estimate Properties at Virtually Any Temperature or Pressure Within a Specified Range. Operates in Metric or Imperial Units. Will Be Useful to Engineers Performing Calculation for Heat Exchanger or Distillation Unit Design, Heat & Material Balance Calculations, Drying, Flash Tank, Incinerator or Effluent Calculations, & Other Common Process & Mechanical Design Calculations. Has Library of 400 Compounds. Allows Users to Add 100 Compounds of Their Own.
Gulf Publishing Co.

Chemcalc 8: Centrifugal Pump Selection & Rating. *Version:* 1.4. Gordon S. Buck. Jan. 1986. *Compatible Hardware:* IBM PC, PC XT, PC AT & compatibles. *Operating System(s) Required:* PC-DOS/MS-DOS 3.0. *Language(s):* Compiled BASIC. *Memory Required:* 240k. *General Requirements:* Graphics card (color or monochrome) optional. *Customer Support:* 30 day money-back guarantee.
3.5" or 5.25" disk $395.00, incl. 44-page manual (ISBN 0-87201-112-7).

Assists Users in Selecting a New Pump or Re-rating an Existing One. Produces Commercially Available Pump Designs to Best Suit Given Operating Conditions & Requirements, or Revises Existing Pump Curve Data for New Pumping Conditions. Calculates Approximate Impeller Design, & the Viscosity Correction Section Calculates Correction Factors Based on the Hydraulic Institute Charts. In Addition, It Covers Suction Specific Speed, Efficiency, Nozzle Ration, Shaft Size, Munimum Continuous Flow, & Affinity Laws.
Gulf Publishing Co.

Chemcalc 10: Heat & Mass Transfer Equilibrium Calculations. Mahesh Bhatia, Chemsoft, Inc. Jan. 1987. *Compatible Hardware:* IBM PC, PC XT, PC AT & compatibles. *Operating System(s) Required:* PC-DOS/MS-DOS 3.1. *Language(s):* Compiled BASIC. *Memory Required:* 192k. *General Requirements:* 2 disk drives. *Customer Support:* 30 day money-back guarantee.
3.5" or 5.25" disk $295.00, incl. 114-page manual (ISBN 0-87201-081-3).

System Covers Many Types of Chemical Engineering Heat & Mass Transfer Equilibrium Equations, Including Process Design Calculations & Simulations. It Is Integrated with an Extensive Databank of Chemical Properties of 400 Compounds. On-Line Help Is Available at Every Stage. Error-Checking Capabilities Save Time. Checks Entries for Validity, Practicality, & Consistency, & Guides Users on How to Correct Entries. Contains Full-Screen Editing Capabilities. Capabilities Include: Distillation Simulation, Calculations for Flash & Drying Stages, Dew-Point & Bubble-Point Temperatures & Pressures, Phase Envelopes, Condenser & Vaporizer Heat-Exchanger Designs.
Gulf Publishing Co.

Chemcalc 11: Amine Process Simulator. *Version:* 2. Douglas L. Erwin. Nov. 1992. *Compatible Hardware:* IBM PC, PC XT, PC AT & compatibles. *Operating System(s) Required:* PC-DOS/MS-DOS 3.0. *Language(s):* BASIC. *Memory Required:* 640k. *Customer Support:* 30 day money-back guarantee.
3.5" or 5.25" disk $595.00, incl. 48-page manual (ISBN 0-87201-080-5).

Models the Absorption & Stripping of H26 & CO2 in Any Type of Gas Stream. For Hydrocarbon Gases, the Program Will Also Determine Hydrocarbons Absorbed & Stripped. System will Determine Required Amine Circulation, Pressure-Temperature Conditions, Number of Theoretical Trays, Slippage of Absorber Gas Remainder, & Stripping Limitations. All of the Commonly Used Amines Are Included (MDEA, DGA, MEA & DEA). True Equilibrium with Chemical Reaction Is Produced Using the Kent-Eisenberg Model.
Gulf Publishing Co.

Chemcalc 12: Flare Network Analysis. *Version:* 1.01. Mahesh Talwar. Jan. 1988. *Compatible Hardware:* IBM PC, PC XT, PC AT & compatibles. *Operating System(s) Required:* PC-DOS/MS-DOS 2.1. *Language(s):* Compiled BASIC. *Memory Required:* 256k. *Customer Support:* 30 day money-back guarantee.
3.5" or 5.25" disk $295.00, incl. 80-page manual (ISBN 0-87201-077-5).

Will Satisfy the Needs of Engineers Who Need to Design Safe & Economical Flare Network Systems Using Accepted Approaches Such As Fault-Tree Analysis & Failure Mode Expectancy Analysis (FMEA). Can Model Complex Networks. Calculates Pressure Drop, Velocity & Diameter for Each Pipe in the Network, Optimum Pipe Sizes, & Pressure & Velocity Profiles. Operates in U.S. & SI Units.
Gulf Publishing Co.

Chemcalc 14: Boiler Efficiency Analysis. Bruce A. Barna. Jan. 1988. *Compatible Hardware:* IBM PC, PC XT, PC AT & compatibles. *Operating System(s) Required:* PC-DOS/MS-DOS 2.0. *Language(s):* BASIC. *Memory Required:* 128k. *Customer Support:* 30 day money-back guarantee.
3.5" or 5.25" disk $395.00 (ISBN 0-87201-940-3).

Calculates Both the ASME Thermal Efficiency & Overall Efficiency of Boilers (Taking into Account Losses Due to Blowdown, Feed Water Stream Heating, etc.). User Inputs the Proper Operating & Environmental Data & the Program Calculates the Necessary Thermodynamic Properties & Performs the Efficiency Analysis According to Same Power Test Code Heat Loss Method. This Version Is Suitable for Both Process & Utility Boilers.
Gulf Publishing Co.

Chemcalc 15: Centrifugal Compressor Design & Rating. Alistair A. Tees. Jan. 1990. *Compatible Hardware:* IBM PC, PC XT, PC AT & compatibles. *Operating System(s) Required:* PC-DOS/MS-DOS 2.1. *Language(s):* PowerBASIC/ASS. *Memory Required:* 256k. *Customer Support:* 30 day money-back guarantee.
3.5" or 5.25" disk $295.00 (ISBN 0-87201-605-6).

Users Rate & Design Centrifugal Compressors. Based on the Theories of Ingersoll-Rand the Program Will Design a Compressor & Analyze a Multi-Stage Compressor with up to Four Stages of Compression. Will Also Determine the Proper Number of Stages for a Desired Service Based on a Maximum Gas Temperature, Analyze the Performance of an Existing Compressor. Will Test Compressor Performance & Calculate the Thermodynamic Properties of a Gas Mixture, Specific Heat Ratio, & Gas Content. Also Includes a Database of 30 Component Gases.
Gulf Publishing Co.

Chemcalc 16: Liquid-Liquid Extraction. Douglas L. Erwin. 1991. *Compatible Hardware:* IBM PC, PC XT, PC AT & compatibles. *Operating System(s) Required:* PC-DOS/MS-DOS 3.0. *Language(s):* Compiled BASIC. *Memory Required:* 240k. *Customer Support:* 30 day money-back guarantee.
$595.00.

Determines Material Balance, Number of Theoretical Stages, & Stage Efficiency in Extraction Operations. Provides Up-to-Date Analysis of Liquid-Liquid Equilbria Behavior Using Proven Data. The Following Processes Are a Few of the Typical Liquid-Liquid Extraction Cases That Can Be Run: Solvent Dewaxing (Lube Oils Using MEK-Toluene); Propane (Butane) Decarbonizing (FCCU Feed); Amine/Water Solvent with Stripping; Gasoline Sweetening Using Amine (DEA, MDEA, MEA, DGA, etc.); Ethylene Pit Caustic Wash for CO2 Removal; Aromatics Recovery Using Liquid Di-, Tri- & Tetra-Ethylene Glycol; Caustic Removal of Mercaptans & Hydrogen Sulfide from Varied Hydorcarbon Streams, Fuels & Lube Oils; Crude Oil Dewaxing Using Selected Solvents. Will Display Stage-by-Stage Analysis & Terminal Analysis Along with a Stage Efficiency Prediction for an Actual Stage & Will Give Users the Number of Actual Stage Contact required for One Theoretical Stage.
Gulf Publishing Co.

Chemcalc 17: EPA Storage Tank Emissions Analysis. *Customer Support:* 30 day money-back guarantee.
MS-DOS 3.0 or higher (256k). IBM PC, PC XT, PC AT, PS/2 & compatibles. 3.5" or 5.25" disk $495.00 (Order no.: 213). *Nonstandard peripherals required:* Epson FX compatible printer.

Program Saves Time & Effort. User Can Estimate Liquid Tank Emissions per Recommended EPA Standards with Simple Screens & Choices. Program Uses Consistent & Simple User Interface to Query User About Specific Tank Design & Liquid Stored. Then Program Retrieves Appropriate Factors from Database & Performs Calcuations Needed to Estimate the Organic Liquid Tank Emissions According to EPA Published Procedures. Supports All Tank Configurations in EPA Procedures & Other Pertinent Considerations, Including: Welded & Riveted Tanks, Any Tank Diameter & Height in Feet, Any Tank Capacity in Barrels, Shell Condition, etc.
Gulf Publishing Co.

Chemical Compounds Databank. *Items Included:* Full manual. No other products required. *Customer Support:* Free telephone support - no time limit, 30 day warranty.
MS-DOS 3.2 or higher. IBM & compatibles (512k). disk $579.95.

Allows User to Estimate Properties at Virtually Any Temperature or Pressure Within a Specified Range. Has One of the Largest Physical Properties Databanks Available (Covering 500 Compounds), & User May Add up to 100 More. Included Are EPA & OSHA Toxicity Data, DOT Notations, As Well As a Directory of Manufacturers (Including Addresses) for Each Compound.
Dynacomp, Inc.

Chemical Engineering 1: Chemical & Process Engineering. *Items Included:* Bound manual. *Customer Support:* Free hotline - no time limit; 30 day limited warranty; updates are $5/disk plus S&H.
MS-DOS 2.0 or higher. IBM & compatibles (128k). disk $399.95. *Nonstandard peripherals required:* For graphics plots, a CGA (or equivalent) is required. *Addl. software required:* Microsoft BASIC (e.g., BASIC, BASICA, GWBASIC, etc.).
manual only $49.95.

Set of Chemical Engineering Software Covering Heat Exchangers, Fuel Cells, Thermodynamic Properties, Autothermal Reformers, & Fluid Flow. The Software Comes in Module Form, & Includes the Source Code on Disk. The Associated 500-Page Manual Describes the Operation of Each

Module, As Well As the Program Code (in BASIC), So That You May Modify the Code and/or Include It in Your Own Programs (Not for Re-Sale, Though!). The Modules Include: Heat Exchanger Analysis; Fuel Cell Analysis; Pressure Drop Distribution Analysis; Fluid Analysis; Reactor Analysis; Thermodynamic Analysis.
Dynacomp, Inc.

Chemical Laser Labels. *Version:* 2.0. Feb. 1996. *Items Included:* Labels Unlimited software, instruction manual, starter pack of yellow label stock & vinyl overlays. *Customer Support:* 30 day return guarantee, free telephone support.
Microsoft Windows 3.1 or higher. 386 (4Mb). disk $199.00. *Addl. software required:* Labels Unlimited software (included with package).
Template Software Which Prints, via Laser Printers, Container Labels for Workplace Chemicals. Includes Prewritten Labels with Hazard Pictograms for 100 Chemicals in Two Sizes, 8.5 by 11 Inches & 4.25 by 5.5 Inches. Includes Prewritten Labels with Hazard Pictograms for 900 Chemicals in a 4 by 2 inch Label Size. User Can Add New Materials & Edit Existing Labels.
Genium Publishing Corp.

Chemical Manufacturing Control System. Oct. 1979. *Compatible Hardware:* IBM PC XT, PC AT, & compatibles. *Operating System(s) Required:* PC-DOS/MS-DOS, UNIX, XENIX. *Language(s):* BASIC & Assembler (source code included). *Memory Required:* 512k. *General Requirements:* Hard disk. *Items Included:* Disks, manual. *Customer Support:* 90 days free, then 15% of the current price per year. On-site installation & training available at $700.00 per day.
$4495.00 - $12,990.00. *Networks supported:* Novell, 3COM, Lantastic.
sample disk avail.
Inventory, Formulations Blending, Bill of Materials (BOM) Control & Materials Requirements Planning System (MRP) Featuring Multi-Level Traceability by Lot. Purchase Orders & Numerous Reports Are Generated. User-Defined Fields Provide Flexibility for Diverse Chemical Manufacturing Firms. Customization Available. Assists in Complying with the FDA Good Manufacturing Practices, EPA, & Other Governmental Record-Keeping Requirements. Inventory Records Are Kept at Both the Item & the Lot Level. Handles Real-World Situations Such as Variances Between Planned & Actual Consumption. Calculates Costs Based on Lot Costs, Standard Costs, Average Costs, FIFO or LIFO. Optional Order Processing Module Provides for Sales Order Entry, Generation of Pick Lists & Packing Lists, Sales Analysis, Invoices, & Back-Order Lists. Handles Various Discount & Price Structures. Interfaces to Accounting Packages.
Stolzberg Research, Inc.

Chemical Week Buyers' Guide, 1996. Chemical Week Associates. Nov. 1995. *Customer Support:* 30 day return guarantee, free telephone support.
Microsoft Windows 3.1 or higher. 386 (4Mb). CD-ROM disk $129.00. *Nonstandard peripherals required:* CD-ROM drive.
Macintosh System 7.0 or higher. Macintosh 68030 (8Mb). CD-ROM disk $129.00. *Nonstandard peripherals required:* CD-ROM drive.
Provides Names, Mailing Addresses & Telephone Numbers of over 6,000 Chemical Suppliers & the 20,000 Chemicals & 5000 Tradename Products Available from Them. Also Includes Directories for Chemical Packaging Suppliers, Hazardous Waste & Environmental Services, Chemical Transportation Services, & Chemical Consultants.
Genium Publishing Corp.

ChemIntosh. *Version:* 2.1.1. Mar. 1993. *Compatible Hardware:* Apple Macintosh. *Memory Required:* 1000k. *General Requirements:* Hard disk. *Customer Support:* Unlimited telephone support, free newsletter. Free demo available.
3.5" disk $499.00.
Drawing Program Designed to Create Publication Quality Graphics for Chemical Reports & Papers. Compatible with Other Macintosh Drawing Applications & Word Processors. Features Include Album & Template Tools, an Integrated Scrapbook, & an Online Tutorial That Guides You As You Work. Other Features Include Drawing Tools for Rings & Bonds, an Acyclic Chain Tool That Draws in Any Direction, Bezier Curves & Arrows, Lewis Dots, Circled Charges, Multiple Undo Commands, Restored Editing When Pasting Back from Other Applications, One-Electron Arrows, Orbitals, Rulers, Align & Space Commands, a Reduced View Option, Ovals & Arcs, & the Ability to Use Any Font, Style or Size of Text for Captions & Labels.
SoftShell International, Ltd.

Chemistry Facts. Duane Tutaj & Melvin Sedlacek. *Customer Support:* 90 day warranty against defective software.
Apple II (48k). disk $49.95 (Order no.: A-1163).
DOS 3.3 or higher. IBM (640k). disk $49.95 (Order no.: I-1163).
Introduces the Periodic Table of Elements. The Element Names Section Asks the Student to Correctly Spell or Abbreviate the Names of the Randomly Presented Elements. The Tutorial Section Describes How to Read Information Contained in the Table. The Periodic Table Quiz Tests the Student on How Well He Can Locate Information from the Periodic Table. The Student Is Asked to Identify the Atomic Mass, Atomic Number, Number of Protons & Electrons, etc. Hall of Fame, Student Evaluation, & Record-Keeping Are Also Included in This Program.
Electronic Courseware Systems, Inc.

Chemistry Laboratory Simulations Parts I & II COM 4030B. Robert D. Allendoerfer. 1986. *Compatible Hardware:* IBM PC & compatibles. *Operating System(s) Required:* MS-DOS 2.1-3.1. *Memory Required:* 256k. *General Requirements:* CGA card.
Part I & II sold alone at $75.00 each. Pkg price $135.00 (ISBN 0-88720-326-4, Order no.: COM4030B).
Designed to Illustrate the Principles of Qualitative Analysis Through a Lab Simulation & to Teach the Analysis of Kinetic Data Through the Simulation of Reaction Rate Response to Variations in Temperature & Concentration.
COMPress.

Chemistry, Vol. 1: The Atom. 1995. *Items Included:* Full manual. *Customer Support:* Free telephone support - 90 days, 30-day warranty.
MS-DOS 3.2 or higher. 286 (584k). disk $44.95. *Nonstandard peripherals required:* CGA/EGA/VGA.
An Historical Review of Atomic Theories to Modern Times. Includes Dalton's Model, Rutherford's Experiment, Sub Levels, & More.
Dynacomp, Inc.

Chemistry, Vol. 2: The Periodic Table. 1995. *Items Included:* Full manual. *Customer Support:* Free telephone support - 90 days, 30-day warranty.
MS-DOS 3.2 or higher. 286 (584k). disk $44.95. *Nonstandard peripherals required:* CGA/EGA/VGA.
Learn the Periodic Table Using Memory Aids & Animation, Making It Easy to Understand.
Dynacomp, Inc.

Chempat: A Program to Assist Hazard Evaluation & Management. 1996. *Items Included:* Diskette, user's guide.
DOS. IBM. disk $195.00 (ISBN 0-8169-0701-3).
American Institute of Chemical Engineers.

ChemStock: Database Management for Chemical Inventory. *Version:* 1.0.1. Matt Neilson. Jun. 1991. *Items Included:* One spiral-bound manual. *Customer Support:* Free customer support, 800 number.
System 4.1 or higher. Macintosh (1Mb). disk List $199.00; Academic $149.00 (ISBN 0-8412-1926-5).
IBM clone w/MS Windows. disk List $299.00; Academic $249.00 (ISBN 0-8412-2841-8).
Tracks Chemical Inventory. Quickly Checks Quantities, Locations, Suppliers, etc. Using Simple Standard Macintosh Application Features. Can Search & Sort by Chemical Name or Formula, Quickly Reducing a Structural Formula to Its Molecular Formula for Searching. Alphabetizes from a Chemist's Point of View, Giving Numbers Secondary Priority, Ignoring Certain Characters, Ordering the Entries the Way a Chemist Would. MS Windows Version Also Includes Item-Level Tracking up to 6 User-Defined Fields, & Enhanced Reporting Capability.
American Chemical Society.

ChemWindow. *Version:* 2.1.1. Jun. 1993. *Customer Support:* Unlimited telephone support, free newsletter. Free demo both 3 1/2" & 5 1/4".
MS-DOS (2Mb RAM). IBM compatible 286 or faster. disk $499.00. *Nonstandard peripherals required:* Graphics adapter, hard disk, mouse, Microsoft Windows 3.0 & Adobe type manager or Windows 3.1.
Drawing Program Designed to Create Publication Quality Graphics for Chemical Reports & Papers. Compatible with Many Other Drawing Applications & Word Processors. Features Include Album & Template Tools, an Integrated Scrapbook, & an Online Tutorial That Guides You As You Work. Other Features Include Drawing Tools for Rings & Bonds, an Acyclic Chain Tool That Draws in Any Direction, Bezier Curves & Arrows, Lewis Dots, Circled Charges, Multiple Undo Commands, Restored Editing When Pasting Back from Other Applications, One-Electron Arrows, Orbitals, Rulers, Align & Space Commands, a Reduced View Option, Ovals & Arcs, & the Ability to Use Any Font, Style or Size of Text for Captions & Labels.
SoftShell International, Ltd.

ChemWindow Classic. *Version:* 1.36. Aug. 1991. *Items Included:* 1 manual, Runtime version of Windows. *Customer Support:* Unlimited telephone support, free newsletter. Free demo both size 3 1/2" & 5 1/4".
MS-DOS. IBM compatible - 80286 or faster recommended (512k). disk $199.00. *Nonstandard peripherals required:* Graphics card supported by Microsoft Windows, Hard disk, mouse. *Addl. software required:* A limited runtime version of Windows 2.11 can be provided by SoftShell.
Has 30 Drawing & Text Tools Specifically Designed for Creating Chemistry Graphics. There are Tools for Drawing Rings, Bonds, Arrows, Labels, & Captions. User Can Also Make Curved Arrows, Benzene Rings, Circles, Ovals, & More. When Writing Captions & Labels, User can use any Available Font at Sizes 8 to 36 Point. Can Be Integrated into Presentation Materials & Word Processing Documents Including Microsoft Windows Applications & WordPerfect. Also Features Undo Facility & Ability to Scale Objects.
SoftShell International, Ltd.

Chess. Adrian Vance. Oct. 1985. *Compatible Hardware:* Apple II. *Operating System(s) Required:* Apple DOS. (source code included). *Memory Required:* 48k.
disk $9.95 (ISBN 0-918547-41-5).
Computerized Version of the Classic Game. An Artificial Intelligence System. For Beginning or Expert Players.
AV Systems, Inc.

Chess Master. *Compatible Hardware:* IBM. *Memory Required:* 128k.
disk $19.95.
Provides 5 Playing Levels.
Dynacomp, Inc.

The Chessmaster 3000.
Multimedia PC or equivalent. CD-ROM disk $79.95. *Optimal configuration:* DOS 3.1 or higher; CD-ROM drive; Microsoft Windows 3.0 or higher; Microsoft Multimedia Extensions 1.0 or higher; MPC-compatible sound card; VGA color graphics card; Microsoft-compatible mouse recommended, 4Mb memory.
DOS. CD-ROM disk $49.95.
Windows. CD-ROM disk $59.95.
Meet the Most Intelligent Computer Chess Game Available - on CD-ROM! Offers Teaching & Hint Modes to Help All Levels of Players Master the Game. Choose from a Library of Computer Opponents or Create a New Personality. During a Game, Open up to Eight Informative Chess Windows, Such As Thinking, Best Line, & Captured Pieces. New Features Include Audio Help, On-the-Fly Audio Advice, Game Sounds, Fantasy Chess Set, & Voice Annotation. In Addition, the MPC Version Now Includes Grand Master Anatoly Karpov Talking about His Best Games.
Software Toolworks.

CHESSNET for Windows. *Version:* 2.0. Jun. 1991. *Items Included:* 5.25" & 3.5" disks; manual; registration card. *Customer Support:* Free technical support; free sales support.
Windows 3.0 or higher. IBM; Tandy or compatible (512k). $49.95 (ISBN 0-9624419-2-9). *Networks supported:* Novell, NetBios.
Allows Users to Play Against the Computer at Various Skill Levels. Also Lets User Play Against Others via Modem or Networked Computers. The 1990 World Chess Championship Games are Included on Disk. Replay Any Game & Analyze Variations. Save Game to Disk & Resume Later. Real Time Clocks & Algebraic or Coordinate Notations Are Available.
Masque Publishing.

The Chief Software. *Version:* 3.7. *Operating System(s) Required:* PC-DOS/MS-DOS, OS/2. *Memory Required:* 640k. *General Requirements:* Hard disk.
$1200.00 to $20,000.00 for various modules.
Complete Modular Maintenance Management System. 24 Modules Presently Available. Standard Stock Versions or Full Custom Systems Are Available. Stock & Custom Bar Code Applications Are Also Available.
Maintenance Automation Corp.

Child Care, 3 disks. 1985. *Compatible Hardware:* Apple, IBM PC & compatibles. *Operating System(s) Required:* Apple DOS, MS-DOS. *Memory Required:* 48k.
disk $195.00 (Order no.: PMCCIA).
Deals with the Following Child Care Subjects: Physical Development/Social & Emotional Growth/Intellectual Development, Children's Behavior/Discipline of Children, Goals & Objectives/The Importance of Play.
Aquarius Instructional.

Child of the Owl. Intentional Education Staff & Laurence Yep. Apr. 1996. *Items Included:* Program manual. *Customer Support:* Free technical support, 90 day warranty.
School ver.. Mac System 7.1 or higher. Macintosh (4Mb). 3.5" disk contact publisher for price (ISBN 1-57204-399-7). *Nonstandard peripherals required:* 256 color monitor, hard drive, printer.
Lab pack. Mac System 7.1 or higher. Macintosh (4Mb). 3.5" disk contact publisher for price (ISBN 1-57204-400-4). *Nonstandard peripherals required:* 256 color monitor, hard drive, printer.
Site license. Mac System 7.1 or higher. Macintosh (4Mb). 3.5" disk contact publisher for price (ISBN 1-57204-425-X). *Nonstandard peripherals required:* 256 color monitor, hard drive, printer.
School ver.. Windows 3.1 or higher. IBM/Tandy & 100% compatibles (4Mb). disk contact publisher for price (ISBN 1-57204-401-2). *Nonstandard peripherals required:* VGA or SVGA 640 x 480 resolution, 256 monitor, mouse, sound device.
Lab pack. Windows 3.1 or higher. IBM/Tandy & 100% compatibles (4Mb). disk contact publisher for price (ISBN 1-57204-426-8). *Nonstandard peripherals required:* VGA or SVGA 640 x 480 resolution, 256 monitor, mouse, sound device.
Site license. Windows 3.1 or higher. IBM/Tandy & 100% compatibles, (4Mb). disk contact publisher for price (ISBN 1-57204-402-0). *Nonstandard peripherals required:* VGA or SVGA 640 x 480 resolution, 256 monitor, mouse, sound device.
This companion for young adult literature is ideal for students who don't know how to start that book report, or give that needed summary. Gentle prompts thoughout the guide sections of the program include Warm-up Connections, Thinking about Plot, Quoting & Noting, Keeping a Journal, If I Were ———' Responding to Questions, Using Quotations, Taking a Personal View, Write to Others, & Write a Sequel.
Lawrence Productions, Inc.

Children's Carrousel. 1992. *Items Included:* Detailed manuals are included with all DYNACOMP products. *Customer Support:* Free telephone support to original customer - no time limit; 30 day limited warranty.
MS-DOS 3.2 or higher. IBM PC & compatibles, Apple, Atari, Commodore 64 (512k). $19.95 (Add $5.00 for 3 1/2" format; 5 1/4" format standard).
Composed of Nine Menu-Selected Games Which Have Great Color & Sound (Include the Carrousel & Alphabet Songs). The Games Include Matching Shapes, Counting, Letter Recognition & More. It Has Been "Field Tested" with Many Children.
Dynacomp, Inc.

Children's Reference Plus. 1995. *Customer Support:* Information and Assistance Hotline; Electronic Bulletin Board.
DOS 3.1 or later. IBM 286 & or higher & compatibles (535k). CD-ROM disk $595.00 for 1 year. *Nonstandard peripherals required:* Hard disk (10 Mb free space).
CD-ROM disk $1696.00 for 3 years.
Integrates over 50 Bibliographies, Full-Text Critical Guides, & Professional Resources for Children & Young Adult Specialists on a Single CD-ROM. Citations on all Juvenile & YA Titles from: CHILDREN'S BOOKS IN PRINT, SUBJECT GUIDE TO CHILDREN'S BOOKS IN PRINT, EL-HI BOOKS IN PRINT & More. Full Text Critical Book Reviews from: PUBLISHERS WEEKLY, LIBRARY JOURNAL, and Five Other Prestigious Reviewing Media. Full-Text of Selective & Annotated Bibliographies, Including BOWKER'S BEST BOOKS Series. Full-Text of Activity Books & Professional Resources Including SCHOOL LIBRARIAN'S SOURCEBOOK, PRIMARYPLOTS, INTRODUCING BOOKPLOTS 3, JUNIORPLOTS 3, & SENIORPLOTS.
R.R. Bowker.

Child's Play One. 1992. *Items Included:* Detailed manuals are included with all DYNACOMP products. *Customer Support:* Free telephone support to original customer - no time limit; 30 day limited warranty.
MS-DOS 3.2 or higher. Apple (48k). $19.95 (Add $5.00 for 3 1/2" format; 5 1/4" format standard). *Optimal configuration:* Apple, 48k RAM & game paddle.
Contains Four Programs: SHAPES PRIMER - Helps Teach Young Children How to Identify Shapes That Are Smaller Than, Larger Than, & Different from Other Shapes. NUMBERS PRIMER - Three Activities to Help Children Learn to Count to Ten. ANT MAZE - Helps Teach Directions & Simple Keyboard Use. DRAWING FUN - A "Just for Fun" Activity That Turns the Screen into a Magic Slate. Has Great Graphics & Sound.
Dynacomp, Inc.

Chinese Checkers. *Items Included:* Bound manual. *Customer Support:* Free hotline - no time limit; 30 day limited warranty; updates are $5/disk plus S&H.
MS-DOS 2.0 or higher. IBM & compatibles (128k). disk $19.95. *Nonstandard peripherals required:* CGA (or equivalent) graphics capability.
Played on the Standard Six-Pointed-Starboard Using Graphics. You Move Your Marble, & Everyone Else Quickly Responds. The Challenge Is to Not Come in Last.
Dynacomp, Inc.

Chinese Clip Art. *General Requirements:* HyperCard 2.0 v2 or higher.
Macintosh Plus or higher. 3.5" disk $30.00.
Chinese Images.
Heizer Software.

ChipChat: Communications Software for OS/2. *Version:* 1.3 (16-Bit), 2.0 (32-Bit). 1989. *Operating System(s) Required:* OS/2 1.3 or higher. *Language(s):* C & ASSEMBLER. *Memory Required:* 512k. *General Requirements:* Modem. *Customer Support:* telephone support for 90 days, BBS support & updates for 90 days. $299.00.
Performs Communications Tasks, File Transfers, Terminal Emulations, Electronic Mail, Using OS/2 Presentation Manager. Designed Specifically for OS/2, ChipChat Takes Advantage of the Advanced Features of OS/2, Such As Dynamic Data Exchange & Dynamic Link Libraries. Supports Xmodem, Ymodem, Zmodem, Kermit File Transfer Protocols. Emulates DEC VT-100, VT-220, VT-320, IBM-3101 Terminals, ANSI, & TTY Terminals. ChipChat 2.0 Is a 32-Bit Version of ChipChat Designed Especially for OS/2 2.0. Both ChipChat 1.3 (16-Bit) & ChipChat 2.0 (32-Bit) Are Available.
ChipChat-Cawthon Software.

Chips Challenge. Aug. 1991. *Customer Support:* 90 day warranty, customer service available 8:30-5:30 PCT.
DOS 3.3 or higher. IBM PC (512k). Contact publisher for price (Order no.: 12305D). *Nonstandard peripherals required:* Graphics card. *Optimal configuration:* Joystick compatible, CGA, EGA, VGA, Hercules monochrome compatible.
Commodore 64/128. Contact publisher for price (Order no.: 12307D). *Optimal configuration:* Joystick compatible.

TITLE INDEX

Amiga. Contact publisher for price (Order no.: 12309D). *Optimal configuration:* Joystick compatible.
One Hundred Forty-Four of Timed Puzzle Solving Challenge.
Epyx, Inc.

ChiroMac. *Version:* 3.9. Mar. 1993. *Compatible Hardware:* All Macintosh. *Language(s):* Assembler, C & Pascal - combination. *Memory Required:* Minimum of 4000k. *General Requirements:* Minimum of a 40Mb hard disk, LaserWriter printer. *Items Included:* Software, all user manuals. *Customer Support:* 90 days free initial support; 1 year Technical Support Enhancement Contract, $795.00 - single user; $995.00 - network user. Toll Free: 800-627-7344, Fax: 402-466-9044.
single user $1995.00.
network $3495.00.
Office Management System Designed for a Chiropractic Office.
HealthCare Communications.

Chiropractic. CYMA Corp. *Compatible Hardware:* TI Professional. *Operating System(s) Required:* CP/M-86, MS-DOS. *Memory Required:* 64k. *General Requirements:* Printer.
$1695.00 (Order no.: SY P/N T039-145).
Provides Patient Billing, Third Party Billing, Practice Analysis & Patient Analysis. Generates Insurance Forms. Analyzes All Activity of Practice.
Texas Instruments, Personal Productivit.

Chiropractic Data System. *Version:* 2.8. Mark Waldo. Sep. 1985. *Compatible Hardware:* Apple IIe; IBM PC, PC XT, PC AT & compatibles. *Operating System(s) Required:* PRODOS, MS-DOS. *Language(s):* Applesoft, C (source code included). *Memory Required:* 128k. *General Requirements:* Hard disk.
Apple. disk $3450.00, incl. training (Order no.: CDSA).
IBM. disk $4850.00, incl. training (Order no.: CSDI).
Keeps Track of Patient Billing Information & Prints Out Daily Reports; Insurance Forms; Patient Statement; 30, 60, 90-Day Notices; New Patient Letters; Referral Letters; Automatic Timed Letters; Birthday Notices; Re-Xray Notices; Dated Messages; Practice Statistics Graphs; Practice Analysis, etc.
Professional Computerware.

Chiropractic Practice Management System. Professional Software Associates, Inc. *Compatible Hardware:* TI Professional. *Operating System(s) Required:* UCSD p-System. *Memory Required:* 128k. *General Requirements:* Winchester hard disk, printer.
$2995.00.
Generates Various Reports, Statements, & Insurance Forms. Recalls & Maintains Detail as Desired. Capable of Custom Diagnostic Codes.
Texas Instruments, Personal Productivit.

Chirp Invaders. *Compatible Hardware:* Commodore PET with Commodore BASIC. *Memory Required:* 16k.
disk $18.95.
Dynacomp, Inc.

Chisholm Trail. *Compatible Hardware:* TI 99/4A with PLATO interpreter solid state cartridge.
contact publisher for price (Order no.: PHM 3110).
User Moves a Steer Through the Maze on the Screen in Order to Kill Four Brand Monsters & a Wrangler.
Texas Instruments, Personal Productivit.

The Chocolate War. Intentional Education Staff & Robert Cormier. Apr. 1996.
School ver.. System 7.1 or higher. Macintosh (4Mb). 3.5" disk contact publisher for price (ISBN 1-57204-195-1). *Nonstandard peripherals required:* 256 color monitor, hard drive, printer.
Lab pack. System 7.1 or higher. Macintosh (4Mb). 3.5" disk contact publisher for price (ISBN 1-57204-196-X). *Nonstandard peripherals required:* 256 color monitor, hard drive, printer.
Site license. System 7.1 or higher. Macintosh (4Mb). 3.5" disk contact publisher for price (ISBN 1-57204-197-8). *Nonstandard peripherals required:* 256 color monitor, hard drive.
School ver.. Windows 3.1 or higher. IBM/Tandy & 100% compatibles (4Mb). disk contact publisher for price (ISBN 1-57204-198-6). *Nonstandard peripherals required:* VGA or SVGA 640 x 480 resolution (256), hard drive, sound device, mouse.
Lab pack. Windows 3.1 or higher. IBM/Tandy & 100% compatibles (4Mb). disk contact publisher for price (ISBN 1-57204-199-4). *Nonstandard peripherals required:* VGA or SVGA 640 x 480 resolution (256), hard drive, sound device, mouse.
Site license. Windows 3.1 or higher. Macintosh (4Mb). disk contact publisher for price (ISBN 1-57204-200-1). *Nonstandard peripherals required:* VGA or SVGA 640 x 480 resolution (256), hard drive, sound device, mouse.
This companion for young adult literature is ideal for students who don't know how to start that book report, or give that needed summary. Gentle prompts throughout the guide section of the program include warm-up connections, Thinking about Plot, Quoting & Noting, Keeping a Journal, If I Were———' Responding to Questions, Using Quotations, Taking a Personal View, Write to Others, & Write a Sequel.
Lawrence Productions, Inc.

Choice! Jul. 1984. *Operating System(s) Required:* MS-DOS, VAX/VMS, MPE V, any DOS, NETWORK, A1X, UNIX, XENIX, AOS/VS, VMS, or other system. *Language(s):* COBOL. *Memory Required:* 256k.
contact publisher for price.
Allows User's Programs Written in Data General's Interactive COBOL to Directly Run on Almost Any Popular Machine from the IBM PC to the Largest Mainframe. All Programs & Data Files Stay Data General Compatible & Are Easily up & down Loaded as Desired. There Is No Source Code Modification & No Data File Restructuring.
Wild Hare Computer Systems, Inc.

Cholesterol Education Group.
Mac II or higher (5Mb, 4Mb without sound); Mac Plus, SE (black & white). for medical schools & other health care facilities free. *Nonstandard peripherals required:* Hard disk drive; 8-bit color card. *Addl. software required:* HyperCard 1.22 or higher (for black & white).
Interactive Program for Physicians, Medical Students, Pharmacologists, Nurses & Other Professionals Who Want to Learn More About Preventive Management of Blood Cholesterol Levels. Provides Data from Clinical Studies Examining Link Between High Blood Cholesterol Levels & Coronary Heart Disease. Full-Color Graphics Describe Atherosclerosis & 9.5 Minute Animation Discusses Lipids, Lipoproteins & Lipid Transport. Interactive Exercises Include Patient Case Studies. Tutorial Covers Basic Food Education. Includes Glossary, Bibliography, General Diet & Fat Intake Information, & Drug therapy Data.
American Heart Assn., Inc.

CHRISTIAN ILLUSTRATIONS: CLICKART

Chompelo. *Compatible Hardware:* Atari 400, 800. *Language(s):* Atari BASIC (source code included). *Memory Required:* 16k.
disk $18.95.
Dynacomp, Inc.

Choplifter. Don Gorlin. *Compatible Hardware:* Apple II+, IIe, IIc; Atari 400, 800, XL, XE Series; Commodore 64. *Memory Required:* 48k. *General Requirements:* Joystick.
disk $34.95 ea.
Apple. (Order no.: APDSK-20).
Atari. (Order no.: ATDSK-120).
Commodore. (Order no.: COMDSK-245).
Player Must Fight off Air Mines, Enemy Jet Fighters, Tank Fire & Air-to-Ground Missiles. The Object Is to Rescue Hostages Held Behind the Enemy Line & Bring Them Home Alive.
Broderbund Software, Inc.

Christa's Science Adventure, No. 1: The Manuscript. Sep. 1992. *Items Included:* Complete documentation.
MS-DOS or Windows. IBM PS/2 & compatibles (1Mb). Contact publisher for price. *Optimal configuration:* Hard disk required, mouse suggested. *Networks supported:* Novell.
Helps Students Learn Basic Scientific Facts in an Enjoyable, Interactive, Highly Motivational, Adventure Game Format. Students Play the Role of Christa, a Contemporary Ninth Grader Who Must Use Her Knowledge of Physical Science, Life Science & Earth Science to Collect Chapters of Her Father's Manuscript. Christa Moves with the Touch of an Arrow Key or a Click of the Mouse. She Interacts with the Program When the User Enters Commands Such As "Look at the Mine" or "Wire the Circuit." Over Fifty Screens of 256 Color Graphics, Animated Characters, & Verbal Interactions All Help "Christa's Science Adventure - The Manuscript" Set a New Standard for Enjoyable Educational Software. Although Based upon the Scientific Ideas Taught in Grades 7 Through 9, the Program Is Engaging for Students & Adults in a Broad Range of Ages.
Basics & Beyond, Inc.

Christian Books In Print Plus. *Items Included:* Monthly Updates.
MS-DOS, Apple DOS. IBM, Macintosh Compatible. CD-ROM disk $995 for 1 year.
CD-ROM disk $2836 for 3 years.
Reflecting the combined resources of the Christian Booksellers Association, Evangelical Christian Publishers Association, Gospel Music Association & R. R. Bowker, this unique, industry-wide CD-ROM provides bibliographic information for ordering all Christian books, bibles, gifts, & music. Through the value-added X-Net network, the system is electronically linked to the original suppliers, enabling merchants to process orders electronically, receive confirmation of orders, & secure advance shipping notice to track arrival dates.
R. R. Bowker.

Christian Illustrations: Bookstore Edition. (ClickArt Ser.).
WIN/DOS. disk $39.95 (ISBN 0-918183-01-4).
Macintosh. 3.5" disk $39.95 (ISBN 0-918183-00-6).
Christian Illustrations.
T/Maker Co., Inc.

Christian Illustrations: ClickArt. *Items Included:* Visual index, user's guide. *Customer Support:* Free & unlimited technical support to registered users; 60 day money-back guarantee.
Macintosh. Macintosh, System 6.0.7 or higher (1Mb). 3.5" disk $49.95. *Addl. software required:* Any word-processing, desktop publishing or works program that accepts graphics.

CHRISTIAN IMAGES

Windows MS-DOS. IBM PC & compatibles. 3.5" disk $49.95. *Addl. software required:* Any word processing, desktop publishing or works program that accepts graphics.
Over 200 Images! Full-Color Images; Ready-to-Use, or Changed in Appropriate Drawing Program; Designed in Full-Color (CMYK); Produced to Print in Detailed Greyscale on Black & White Printers; Includes the ClickArt Trade Secret - Images Traded to Every Popular Graphics Format, Guaranteed to Work with All Popular Applications.
T/Maker Co., Inc.

Christian Images. Parsons Technology. Jul. 1993. 3.5" disk Contact publisher for price (ISBN 1-57264-003-0).
Parsons Technology.

Christian Images Bundle. Parsons Technology. Jul. 1993.
3.5" disk Contact publisher for price (ISBN 1-57264-004-9).
Parsons Technology.

Christian Products Video. Parsons Technology. Jun. 1994.
3.5" disk Contact publisher for price (ISBN 1-57264-047-2).
Parsons Technology.

A Christmas Carol. Feb. 1995. *Items Included:* CD-ROM booklet. *Customer Support:* Free technical support via phone as of release date. MPC/Windows. 386.25 or higher IBM compatible (4Mb). CD-ROM disk $29.95 (ISBN 1-885784-16-3, Order no.: 1196). *Optimal configuration:* MPC CD-ROM player, S-VGA graphics card (640x480x256 colors) with compatible monitor, MPC compliant sound card, mouse, Windows 3.1.
This Holiday Classic by Charles Dickens Is Brought to Life Through the Multimedia Use of Sir Arthur Rackham's Distinct Illustrations. Transport Yourself to the World of Bob Cratchit & His Cruel Boss Ebenezer Scrooge. Discover the True Spirit of Christmas As Scrooge Rediscovers His Humanity. Interact with One of the Most Famous & Popular Works of English Literature.
Technology Dynamics Corp.

Christmas Mail. 1983. *Compatible Hardware:* Apple II with printer. *Memory Required:* 48k. disk $24.00, incl. labels.
Stores up to 250 Names, Alphabetizes & Prints Address Labels with Greeting Message. Also Prints Return Address Labels. 500 Labels Included.
Navic Software.

ChromaTools. *Version:* 2.3. *Compatible Hardware:* IBM PC.
disk $249.00.
Converts TGA, PCX, GIF, TIF, & VST Images to TGA, PCX, GIF, TIF, VST & Color/Black & White PostScript. Supports All Screen Modes Including Super VGA, VGA, EGA, CGA & Hercules. Includes Multiple Color Reduction Algorithms, Multiple Dithering Patterns, Sizing, Cropping & Rescaling Algorithms. Featuring Controls Such As the Spot Meter & Optimized Palette Reduction. Also Converts Between Color Depths Supporting 1, 2, 4, 8, 15, 24, or 32 Bit Color Images. Supporting Resolutions up to 1024x768 by 256 Colors. Offers Support for Most Super VGA Cards Including Tseng, Paradise, Video 7, ATI, Genoa, STB, Orchid & Others. Also Included Is a Screen Grabber for Capturing Screen Images. Works with or Without a TARGA Board Installed. Menu Driven or Batch Mode Operation.
Videotex Systems, Inc.

Chronological Bible. *Version:* 6.1. Kent Ochel & Bert Brown. Oct. 1989. *Items Included:* TutoriL DISK: 3-ring binder with manual. *Customer Support:* Unlimited free technical support at (512) 251-7541.
Any DOS or Windows. IBM PC; XT; AT & compatibles (512k). disk $49.95.
Any Macintosh. 3.5" disk $49.95.
Presentation of the Bible in Chronology Sequence. A Chronological Bar Chart of the Bible Is Displayed & the User May Select Any Point in Time to Begin Studying. The Time Sequenced Outline of the Bible Shows Each Event Keyed to the Scripture Text. VERSE SEARCH Is required.
Bible Research Systems.

Chubby Checker. *Version:* 3.1. Oct. 1983. *Compatible Hardware:* IBM PC. *Operating System(s) Required:* PC-DOS. *Language(s):* Quicksilver. *Memory Required:* 640k.
disk $95.00.
Food & Total Calorie Program with a Code-Free Data Base of 640 Foods & 44 Work & Sports Activities.
Health & Habitation, Inc.

Chuck Yeager's Advanced Flight Trainer. *Compatible Hardware:* IBM PC.
disk $14.95.
Simulates the Characteristcs of 14 Different Planes, from Those of the World War I Era Through the Present. User Must Learn the Basics of Flying, Which Are Taught in the Manual.
Electronic Arts.

Church Administration/Accounting. *Version:* 6.0. Jean Vandenbroucke. May 1984. *Compatible Hardware:* IBM PC & compatibles. *Operating System(s) Required:* PC-DOS, MS-DOS. *Memory Required:* 256k. *General Requirements:* Hard disk.
contact publisher for price.
Mailing List, Interests & Skills, Attendance, Membership, Contributions Accounting with Pledges & Receipt, Disbursements & Payables, General Ledger Fund Accounting, Budget, Interface to Word Processor.
Church Software.

Church Business Manager Plus. *Compatible Hardware:* Apple Macintosh 512KE. *Memory Required:* 512k. *General Requirements:* External disk drive or hard disk.
Church Business Manager Plus (includes Omnis 3 Plus). 3.5" disk $799.00.
Church Business Manager (includes Omnis 3 Plus). 3.5" disk $599.00.
Church Member Management.
CP Software.

Church Contribution Record System. *Version:* 4.3. 1995. *Items Included:* Complete operating manual. *Customer Support:* Unlimited telephone support.
MS-DOS. IBM PC or compatible (256k). $125.00. *Optimal configuration:* IBM PC or compatible, 256k RAM, printer. *Networks supported:* Novel, Unex.
Contribution Record Keeping System That Keeps Track of Individual's Gifts & Contributions to Any Number of Funds & Provides a Quarterly Statement to Contributors. Designed for the First Time User. Entirely Menu Driven & Is Easy to Use & Install. All Reports Are Printed on Standard Letter Size Paper. All Modules Are Menu-Driven with On-Screen Information Available Throughout to Guide Operators in Their Tasks. Annual & Quarterly Statements Are Prepared Automatically & an Analysis of the Congregation's Giving May Be Produced. Will Accommodate up to 1000 Members. These Statements May Be Used for Income Tax Purposes.
Omni Software Systems, Inc. (Indiana).

SOFTWARE ENCYCLOPEDIA 1996

Church Data Master Plus. *Version:* 3.0.2. *Compatible Hardware:* Apple Macintosh. *Memory Required:* 1000k. *General Requirements:* Hard disk. *Items Included:* 230 pg. manual. *Customer Support:* Yes.
3.5" disk $795.00.
Demo. 3.5" disk $10.00.
Allows Large or Small Local Congregations to Maintain Membership, Financial, Pastoral Records.
Suran Systems, Inc.

Church Denominations. *Compatible Hardware:* TRS-80 Model I, Model II, Model III.
contact publisher for price.
Custom Data (New Mexico).

Church Directory & Financial Records System. *Version:* 1.0. *Compatible Hardware:* TRS-80 Model II. *Operating System(s) Required:* TRSDOS 2.0. (source code included). *Memory Required:* 64k.
disk $5.00, (Public Domain).
source code (Public Domain) $5.00.
Keeps Track of Church Members & Financial Status of Church.
Computer Guidance & Support.

Church Donations. *Compatible Hardware:* IBM PC; TRS-80 Model II, Model III, Model 4, Model 12, Model 16, Tandy 2000. *Memory Required:* 48k. *General Requirements:* 2 disk drives.
disk $190.00.
Allows Entry of Congregation Member Information. Produces Quarterly Reports with Totals by Individual or Category, & Lists Mailing Labels for the Complete Congregation or for Selected Members.
Custom Data (New Mexico).

Church Financial Accounting. ADS Software, Inc. *Compatible Hardware:* TI Professional; with printer, 2 disk drives. *Operating System(s) Required:* MS-DOS. *Memory Required:* 128k. $895.00.
Membership/Contribution System. Flags Members Falling Short of Pledge, Retains Unpaid Prior Year Pledge. Maintains Membership Type/Activity Tables. Budgeted Financial Reporting.
Texas Instruments, Personal Productivit.

Church Ledger. *Compatible Hardware:* IBM PC; TRS-80 Model II, Model III, Model 4, Model 16, Tandy 2000.
contact publisher for price.
General Ledger Interface with the Church Donations Program for Producing Chart of Accounts, Trail Balance Sheet, Statement of Income/Expenses, Check Register, Checkbook Reconciliation, Budget Report, & Session Transaction Journal.
Custom Data (New Mexico).

Church Management System. *Version:* 450.2. 1982. *Compatible Hardware:* IBM PC & compatibles. *Operating System(s) Required:* PC-DOS, MS-DOS. *Language(s):* QuickBASIC. *Memory Required:* 512k. *General Requirements:* Hard disk. *Items Included:* System diskettes, users guide, training tutorial. *Customer Support:* Telephone; annual contracts available.
disk $695.00 to $995.00.
Tracks Congregation Member's Names & Addresses, Family Units, Occupations, Skills, Anniversaries, & Committee Assignments. Prepares Numerous Reports & On-Line Inquiries from This Data Base. System Monitors Pledges & Contributions & Prints Contribution Summary for Members' Tax Records. Mailing Lists & Label Facilities Are Included. Other Modules Include: A Fund Accounting Ledger System with Budgeting, Encumbrancing, & Church Financial Reports, Accounts Payable with Cash Requirements

TITLE INDEX

Projection & Check Writing, Scheduling Module for Scheduling Personnel, Rooms, & Equipment, & an Attendance Module for Worship Services, Sunday School, & Meetings. Optional Interface with IMS Payroll System.
International Micro Systems, Inc.

Church Membership-Contribution. Version: 2.0. May 1982. Compatible Hardware: Intel 80286, 80386, 80486, etc.. Operating System(s) Required: MS-DOS, Novell, THEOS, UNIX, Win 95, Win/NT. Language(s): BASIC. Memory Required: 44k.
disk $1595.00.
Provides a System for Maintaining Records on Church Memberships & Contributions. Interfaces Word Processing & Produces Directory Listings & Contribution Statements.
COMPASS.

Church Stewardship Program. Compatible Hardware: Apple Macintosh. Memory Required: 512k.
Single user with Omnis 3 Plus Runtime. 3.5" disk $395.00.
Multiuser (requires Multiuser Omnis 3 Plus). 3.5" disk $495.00.
Keeps Track of Various Member Information.
H&D Leasing.

ChurchMaster. Version: 7.03. Jun. 1983. Compatible Hardware: IBM PC, PC AT, PC XT, PS/2. Operating System(s) Required: PC-DOS. Language(s): Compiled BASIC. Memory Required: 512k. Items Included: Reference manual, tutorial manual, procedures manual. Customer Support: Phone/modem support included first year, nominal fee thereafter. disk $800.00 (ISBN 0-924068-04-3, Order no.: CH5).
Multi-User Church Management System Featuring Word Processing (Personalized Letters, Envelopes, & Labels), Accounting (Fund Accounting & Budgeting), & Membership Management (Pledges, Contribution, Attendance, Personal, Membership/Leadership, & Interest Information).
Fogle Computing Corp.

Churchstar. Church Computer Systems of America. Compatible Hardware: TI Professional. Operating System(s) Required: MS-DOS. Memory Required: 64k. General Requirements: Winchester hard disk, printer.
$695.00.
Church Congregation Accounting. Keeps Track of All Members, Contributions & Activities. Can Also Be Used by Other Clubs & Groups.
Texas Instruments, Personal Productivit.

Churchware. Charnette Trimble. Memory Required: 256k.
contact publisher for price.
Maintains Church Member Mailing Lists, Donations, Church Assets, etc.
Compu-Nette, Inc.

CHVAC: Commercial HVAC Loads Calculation. Items Included: Manual. Customer Support: Free toll free telephone support.
IBM PC & compatibles (256k). disk $295.00.
Commercial HVAC Load Calculation Program That Is Based on the Exact CLTD Procedures Described in the 1989 ASHRAE Handbook of Fundamentals. Calculates Peak Heating & Cooling Loads As Well As CFM Air Quantity Requirements with Complete Psychrometrics.
Elite Software Development, Inc.

CIA EMS Management Software. Version: 11.0. Aug. 1991. Memory Required: 640k. General Requirements: 10Mb IBM; 90Mb UNIX, XENIX, 90Mb Novell, LANtastic. Items Included: Software, training, manuals. Customer Support: Free 90 days, $695.00 per year single-user, $1295.00 multi-user, optional.
IBM. disk $1500.00.
UNIX; XENIX; Novell; LANtastic. disk $3995.00.
Designed to Accommodate All Types of Billing & Accounts Receivable Needs. Private, Hospital, Medicare, Medicaid & Various Other Insurance & Electronics Claims Processing. Captures & Reports Trip Statistics. Perform Vehicle Maintenance & Dispatching Functions, Even Electronic Reconciliation Is Available & Trip Sheet Programs.
Computer Investment Advice, Inc.

CIA Interstate Fuel & Mileage Software. May 1988. Operating System(s) Required: PC-DOS/MS-DOS, Unix, Xenix. Memory Required: 256k. General Requirements: PC-DOS/MS-DOS 10Mb hard disk, UNIX/XENIX 90Mb hard disk.
$1500.00.
Designed to Help the User Calculate State Taxes. Includes Reports That Show Individual Driver Mileage & Fuel Consumption & State's Reports to Assist the User at Tax Time. Also Captures Data About Drivers, Which States They Are Permitted in, & Information About Their Trucks.
Computer Investment Advice, Inc.

CIA Relational Data Base System. Compatible Hardware: IBM PC, LANtastic, Novell, UNIX. Language(s): Compiled BASIC. Items Included: Software, manuals. Customer Support: Free 90 days.
A. disk $295.00.
B. disk $595.00.
C. disk $995.00.
Menu-Driven & Machine Independent Program. Version A Is an End User Version with 3 Report Generators Included. Version B Adds the Ability for End Users to Define New Files. Version C Has Screen Generation & Interface to Basic Language.
Computer Investment Advice, Inc.

CIA Vehicle Maintenance Software. Version: 4.0. Jan. 1987. Operating System(s) Required: PC-DOS/MS-DOS, Unix, Xenix. Memory Required: 640k. General Requirements: IBM 10Mb; UNIX, XENIX 20Mb, Novell, LANtastic.
contact publisher for price.
Management System Designed to Show User Cost of Keeping a Vehicle on the Road & Saves User Money by Reminding User of Scheduled Maintenance. Also Designed to Report Fuel Consumption, Average Miles per Gallon & Cost per Mile for Each Vehicle.
Computer Investment Advice, Inc.

CICA, 2 discs. Customer Support: All of our products are unconditionally guaranteed.
Windows. CD-ROM disk $29.95 (Order no.: CICA). Nonstandard peripherals required: CD-ROM drive.
1050 MB of Windows Programs with Multilingual Interface.
Walnut Creek CDRom.

CICS/pc. Version: 2.1. Jul. 1990.
PC/MS-DOS. IBM compatibles (512k). disk $795.00 (Order no.: 805-003).
Simulator for Use in Computer Programming.
PLE, Inc.

Cimarron. Version: 4.2.1. Items Included: Manual, DOS. Customer Support: 24-hour unlimited software support included for first 12 months. $490.00 per year after first 12 months. 2 days training at one of 6 training centers - $500.00.
MS-DOS or IBM PC-DOS 3.2 or higher. IBM or compatible (640k). disk full software $3995.00.
Nonstandard peripherals required: 20Mb fixed disk, 1 floppy drive; C.A.T. shorthand writer. disk edit software $1995.00.
Computer-Assisted-Transcription Software for Court/Convention Reporters Translates into English Text Stenographic Notes of Court, Convention, Deposition Verbatim Proceedings. Notes Are Written on a Computerized C.A.T. Shorthand Machine to a 3.5" Floppy Disk, Then Translated by Matching Steno Notes to Personalized English Dictionary Via the C.A.T. Software for Editing/Printing Via Built-In Word Processor.
Stenograph Corp.

Cinema Master. Customer Support: 800-929-8117 (customer service).
MS-DOS. IBM/PS2. disk $199.99 (ISBN 0-87007-290-0).
Used for the Budgeting of Any Type of Motion Picture Production from TV Commercials to Feature Motion Pictures or Mini Series. Ideal for Creative People Who Want the Grounding of the Business End to Production Budgeting. Allows Budgeted & Actual Cost Figures to Be Entered in for over 50 Functional Categories & Has Several Hundred Budget Line Items Normally Found Related to Minor & Major Productions.
SourceView Software International.

CineWrite. Version: 2.14. Compatible Hardware: Apple Macintosh Plus. General Requirements: Hard disk or external disk drive; ImageWriter or LaserWriter.
3.5" disk $495.00.
Word Processing System Linking 3 Phases of Film, Television, Video & Advertising Production: Writing, Storyboarding & Presenting.
Max 3, Inc.

Circuit Database II. Compatible Hardware: Atari XL/XE. Language(s): Atari BASIC. Memory Required: 48k.
disk $12.95.
Electronic Circuit Design Software Allowing Design & Editing of Electronic Circuits, & Storage of up to 60 Complete, Labeled Programs on One Disk Side. Includes a Text-to-HiRes Converter Which Produces Vertical Printouts on Any Dot-Matrix Printer with a Vertical Printhead.
Elfin Magic.

Circulation-Catalog Plus Multiuser. Version: Novell-Compatible 7.8XN. 1991. Customer Support: toll-free support included for the first year, with continuing support available as a renewal option.
DOS 3.3 or higher. MS-DOS compatible, hard disk drive. disk $3190.00 (Order no.: MJM94955A). Nonstandard peripherals required: One high-density 3.5" or 5.25" floppy disk drive, color or Monochrome display, 80-column printer. Addl. software required: Netware 386, SFT Netware, Advanced Netware, ELS Netware Level I, ELS Netware Level II, Netware 2.2 & Netware 3.11. Optimal configuration: All Workstations must have 470k free RAM after booting up & logging onto the Network.
A Circulation Management System & On-Line Public Access Catalog Which Is Fully Integrated & Marc Based. With Circulation Plus & Catalog Plus Combined You Have A Compete Automated Circulation Management System along with All the Benefits of an On-Line Catalog. Circulation-Catalog Plus, Which Features File Card-Style Menus, Currently Manages a Maximum of 65,000 Full Marc Records & Accommodates up to 15,000 Patrons or Higher, Depending on the Number of Records in the System. Circulation-Catalog Plus Novell-Compatible Version Can Be Installed Under ICLAS.
Follett Software Co.

Circulation Manager. *Version:* 3.19. Jan. 1992. *Compatible Hardware:* IBM PC & compatibles, PC XT, PC AT. *Operating System(s) Required:* MS-DOS or Windows. *Memory Required:* 640k. disk $695.00.
Produces Overdue Notices, Reserve Item Notices, & Notices to People Who Are Leaving the Institution & Who Have Items Out on Loan. Keeps Circulation Statistics by Patron-Type & Item-Type. Can Be Used Stand-Alone or Integrated with "Online Catalog" Via Barcode Linkage.
Professional Software.

Circulation Plus (Apple). *Version:* Apple. 1983. *Customer Support:* Toll-free support included for the first year, with continuing support available as a renewal option. One year support services. Maintenance fee $125.00 after first year.
ProDOS. Apple ProDOS (128k). $895.00 (Order no.: B92547A). *Nonstandard peripherals required:* Apple IIe, IIgs, 80-column display, minimum 10Mb hard disk drive & one 3.5" or 5.25" floppy disk drive, printer. *Optimal configuration:* hard disk, printer, barcode scanner; one floppy disk drive.
A Complete Library Management System Which Utilizes Barcode Labels & a Barcode Scanner for Fast & Accurate Circulations, in Addition to, over Dues, Statistical Reports, Complete Inventory, etc. The Quick, Menu-Driven System Operates Using a Hard Disk Drive. The Apple Version of Circulation Plus Features File-card- Style Menus & Comes in Three Version Sizes - 15,000, 30,000 & 65,000 Items - to Better Accommodate the Needs of Your Library.
Follett Software Co.

Circulation Plus (MS-DOS). *Version:* MS-DOS. 1983. *Customer Support:* Toll-free support included for the first year, with continuing support available as a renewal option. One year support services. Maintenance fee $125.00 after first year.
DOS 3.3. MS-DOS compatibles (640k). disk $895.00 (Order no.: B92550A). *Nonstandard peripherals required:* MS-DOS compatibles, 80286, 640k RAM, 20Mb hard disk drive (depending on size of collection & number of patrons). *Optimal configuration:* Call Follett's Sales Department for hard disk drive specifications, One 3.5" or 5.25" floppy disk drive, color or monochrome display, 80 column printer. *Networks supported:* Novell.
A Complete Marc Library Management System Utilizing Barcode Labels & a Barcode Scanner for Fast & Accurate Circulations, in Addition to Overdues Statistical Reports, Complete Inventory, etc. The Quick, Menu-Driven System Operates Using a Hard Disk Drive the MS-DOS Version Features File-Card Style Menus & Manages a Maximum of 65,000 Full Marc Records, or If You Choose, the Program Will Permit a Brief Record Format Allowing Management of up to 200,000 Brief Records. The Program Accommodates up to 15,000 Patrons; However, the Number Could Be Higher Depending on the Number of Records in the System.
Follett Software Co.

Circus Maximus. *Compatible Hardware:* IBM PC & compatibles, Tandy 1000. *General Requirements:* CGA card for IBM. disk $25.00 (Order no.: 46554).
Travel Back in Time to the Days of Chariot Racing in the Roman Colosseum. In This Simultaneous Movement Game, Players Design Their Own Chariot's Weight, Speed, Horse Endurance, Armament, & Driver's Skills. Each Turn, Enter Your Movement Orders, Then Sit Back & Watch the Animated Action from the Overhead View. The Campaign Game Allows Players to Bet on the Outcome of Each Race. For up to 12 Players.
Avalon Hill Game Co., The Microcomputer Games Div.

CIS COBOL. *Operating System(s) Required:* CP/M, MP/M, CP/M-86. *Language(s):* COBOL. *Memory Required:* 64k. disk $850.00.
Permits the Implementation of Standard ANSI'74 COBOL. Comes with a COBOL Source Code Generator, Forms 2, Which Will Allow the User to Create a Fully Operational Program. Can Generate Standard Code & Expand on It & Perform Interactive Debugging, Screen Creation, & Dynamic Loading of Modules.
Micro Focus, Inc. (California).

CIS COBOL. Digital Research. *Compatible Hardware:* TI Professional. *Operating System(s) Required:* CP/M-86, Concurrent CP/M-86. *Memory Required:* 64k.
$850.00 (Order no.: SS P/N DRT-006).
Compact, Interactive & Standard Implementation of COBOL. GSA Certified.
Texas Instruments, Personal Productivit.

CIS COBOL with FORMS-2 for Apple. *Operating System(s) Required:* DOS 3.2. *Memory Required:* 48k. disk $950.00.
Generates Standard COBOL Code & Offers All the Power of ANSI COBOL File Handling.
Micro Focus, Inc. (California).

CiteRite II. *Version:* 4.0. *Compatible Hardware:* IBM PC & compatibles. *Operating System(s) Required:* PC-DOS/MS-DOS 2.0 or higher. *Memory Required:* 270k. *Customer Support:* Extended support & upgrade program.
disk $180.00.
Based on the Rules in the Harvard Law Review's "Bluebook". Automatically Locates & Checks Cites. When an Error Is Found, an Error Message Is Displayed. Cross Referenced to the Rules of the "Bluebook". Compatible with Most Major Word Processing Programs.
Jurisoft.

Citi Desk. *Compatible Hardware:* Commodore Amiga.
3.5" disk $149.95, incl. manual.
Desktop Publishing Program Supporting PostScript & LaserJet+ Printers. Features Automatic Kerning & Leading, Embedded Commands Options, Unlimited Font Changes in the Text, Flow Text Around Graphics, & Any Number of Fonts on a Line. All Types of Printers Are Supported. Prints IFF Pictures. Prints Color Pictures in Gray Scales. Text & Graphics Editors Are Included. Not Copy Protected.
MicroSearch.

City Desk. *Version:* 2.0. *Compatible Hardware:* Commodore Amiga.
3.5" disk $199.95.
Page-Layout with PostScript Support.
MicroSearch.

CLAN. *Compatible Hardware:* TRS-80 Model III, Model 4. *Memory Required:* 64k.
disk $10.00 (Order no.: D8CLAN).
For Maintaining a Genealogical Data Base for User's Family Tree. Reports Include an INDEX of Persons, INDIVIDUAL DATA SHEETS on Persons, ANCESTOR CHARTS to 5 Generations, & DESCENDANT LISTS to 7 Generations. Will Handle up to 5 Marriages per Person, & 18 Children per Marriage.
The Alternate Source.

Clarion. *Version:* 1.1. *Compatible Hardware:* IBM PC AT or compatibles. *Memory Required:* 320k. *General Requirements:* Hard disk.
disk $395.00.
upgrade from version 1 $100.00.
Enables Users to Write, Compile, Run, & Debug Applications Without the Need of Writing the Code. Users Will Design the Screen Using the SCREENER Utility, & Then CLARION Will Write the Souce Code & Compile It Automatically. Likewise, REPORTER Can Be Used to Create Reports. CLARION HELPER Will Allow Users to Design Pop-Up, Context-Sensitive Help Screens. Provides Declarations, Procedures, & Functions to Process Dates, Strings, Screens, Reports, Indexed Files, DOS Files, & Memory Tables. The FILER Utility Will Enable the User to Create a New File by Just Naming the Source Module & the Statement Label of a File Structure Within It; Will Also Automatically Rebuild Existing Files to Match a Changed File Structure. This Version Includes 15 Major Enhancements, Including a "Converter" Utility Which Allows the Import/ Export of DIF, dBASE II, dBASE III, & BASIC Files.
Barrington Systems, Inc.

Clarion Personal Developer. *Version:* 2.0. Sep. 1989. *Items Included:* 8 programs are included in the package, & may be modified to meet user's specific needs. *Customer Support:* Free 90-day technical support includes unlimited telephone assistance & bulletin board access, & a subscription to our quarterly newsletter.
DOS 2.0 or higher. IBM PC, XT, AT, PS/2 & compatibles (512k). disk $79.00.
Designed for the Non-Programmer Who Wants to Write Programs. It Offers Two Development Methods: Quick Start Automatically Generates an Application Board on a File Layout. The Custom Method Enables User to Design Complex Programs.
Clarion Software.

Clarion Professional Developer. *Version:* 3.0. Apr. 1990. *Customer Support:* Free 90-day product technical support includes unlimited telephone assistance & bulletin board access & subscription to our quarterly newsletter, "The Clarion Developer".
DOS 2.0 or higher operating system. IBM PC, XT, AT, PS/2 & compatibles (512k). disk $995.00. *Nonstandard peripherals required:* 1 double-sided disk drive & hard disk (approximately 4.5Mb free). *Networks supported:* All leading networks are supported, including Novell, 3COM, IBM PC Net & Token Ring.
Upgrade from version 2.0 $150.00.
Provides a Complete Environment for Developing PC Applications. It Comes with 14 Utility Programs Which Include: Database Functions; Network Support, a Modem, Comprehensive Language; Application Generator; Debugger; Editor; Converter; & an Ad-Hoc Report & Query Generator.
Clarion Software.

Clarion Report Writer. Apr. 1990. *Customer Support:* Free 90-day technical support includes unlimited telephone assistance & bulletin board access, & a subscription to our quarterly newsletter.
IBM DOS 2.0 or higher. IBM PC, XT AT, PS/2 & compatibles (512k). disk $199.00. *Optimal configuration:* IBM PC, XT, AT, PS/2 & compatibles, IBM DOS 2.0 or higher, 512k memory, 1 double-sided diskette drive & 1 hard disk (approx. 1Mb free). *Networks supported:* All leading networks are supported.
Enables Developers & End-Users to Produce Personalized Custom Queries & Reports from Existing Databases. This Menu-Driven Program Allows Users to Design Reports on a Screen Called a Worksheet. Users Can Create New Databases from Calrion, dBase, DiF, Or ASII files. User Can Create New Files, Use Report Filters & Run-Time Values, As Well As Calculate Totals.
Clarion Software.

TITLE INDEX

Claris Emailer. 1995.
System 7.0 or later. Any Macintosh with a 68020 processor (4Mb recommended). 3.5" disk $69.00. *Nonstandard peripherals required:* 3 mb available hard drive space.
Claris Emailer software is the flexible way to manage all kinds of email. Whether a user subscribes to the Internet, America Online, Compuserve, eWorld or RadioMail, Claris Emailer gives users the power to send, recieve, reply, forward, & store all their email messages & files quickly & easily.
Claris Corporation.

Claris Organizer for Macintosh. 1995.
System 7.0 or higher. Macintosh Plus or higher. 3.5" disk $99.00. *Nonstandard peripherals required:* Hard drive with minimum 1 MB disk space; 2Mb full installation with sample files & on-line help.
Claris Organizer is the award-winning all-in-one, intelligent personal information manager (PIM) for the Macintosh that seemlessly integrates calendar, contacts, tasks, & notes in one easy-to-use, compact application.
Claris Corporation.

ClarisDraw for Macintosh. 1996.
2Mb of memory required for System 6.0.7 or later; 4 mb for System 7.x. Apple Macintosh Plus, SE, Centris, Classic, LC, SE, Performa, PowerBook, II, or Quadra families. 3.5" disk $399.00.
Designed with the needs of the generalist graphics user in mind, ClarisDraw incorporates 75 new features compared to its predecessor, MacDow Pro. These new features integrate revolutionary graphics intelligence with versatile tools, including full color painting, advanced text handling & presentation effect, to master virtually any graphics job.
Claris Corporation.

ClarisDraw for Windows. 1996.
Windows 3.X or higher. IBM & compatible personal computers, 386 or higher (8Mb). 3.5" disk $129.00. *Nonstandard peripherals required:* Hard disk drive with 15Mb. 3.5" disk $99.00.
Designed for the graphics "generalist," ClarisDraw for Windows integrated revolutionary intelligence, painting & image editing effects, advanced text handling, presentation features, & comprehensive drawing tools to master virtually any business graphics task.
Claris Corporation.

ClarisImpact for Windows, Macintosh & Power Macintosh. Version: 2.0. 1996.
Windows 3.1 or later. IBM 386; Apple Macintosh 680X0-based or Power Macintosh families. 3.5" disk $129.00. *Nonstandard peripherals required:* Hard disk drive (17Mb); Windows 3.1 or later (4Mb); System 6.0.7 or later (2Mb); System 7 (4Mb) Power Macintosh (8Mb).
ClarisImpact is the only cross platform business diagramming application for creating & editing organizational, flow, & data charts, network diagrams, project time line & calenders. It offers both speed or creation & high quality delivery, including back & white or color printing onscreen presentation. Version 2.0 adds significant enhancements & features.
Claris Corporation.

ClarisWorks. Version: 4.0.
System 7.0 or higher. Macintosh computer with 68020. 3.5" disk $129.00. *Nonstandard peripherals required:* Requires a hard disk & 4 mb RAM.
PC with any 386 or higher processor. 3.5" disk $49.00. *Nonstandard peripherals required:* Requires a hard disk drive & 8 mb RAM; VGA or better video.
Windows 95.
With full-featured word-processing, spreadsheet, database, graphics, & presentation capabilities, ClarisWorks 4.0 customers can create everything they need from memos to presentations, customer lists to mailing labels, letters to college term papers, flyers to invitations, home budgets to balance sheets, & family newsletters to business reports.
Claris Corporation.

ClarisWorks in Your Classroom: A Student Introduction. Version: 3.0. Keith Humphrey & Robert Delio. 1996. *Items Included:* 1 reproducible teacher book, 95 pp., 1 student activity text, 195 pp. Additional copies of activity text available for $13.95; 10 or more copies, each $12.95. *Customer Support:* Call 1-800-341-6094 for free technical assistance, 30 day approval policy, money back guarantee.
Macintosh. 3.5" disk $79.95 (ISBN 0-8251-2777-7, Order no.: 0-27777). *Addl. software required:* ClarisWorks.
Windows. IBM & compatibles. disk $79.95 (ISBN 0-8251-2779-3, Order no.: 0-27793). *Addl. software required:* ClarisWorks.
Students Learn the Program's Word Processing, Database, Spreadsheet, & Drawing Modules, & How to Integrate One Type of Information with Another. The Data Disk Provides the Files That Students Manipulate According to Directions in the Activity Text.
J. Weston Walch Pub.

Clark Howard's Consumer Survival Kit. Clark Howard & Mark Meltzer. 1993. *Items Included:* CD-ROM only. *Customer Support:* Free replacement if defective due to manufacturing.
Windows. 80386 SX (486 recommended) (2Mb). CD-ROM disk $39.95. *Nonstandard peripherals required:* Windows compatible sound card with speakers; CD-ROM drive, SVGA video card. *Addl. software required:* Microsoft Windows 3.1 or higher. *Optimal configuration:* 80486, 2Mb RAM, SVGA video card/2 button mouse.
Lively, Informative CD-ROM Will Help You Make Safer, Smarter Purchases. Whether Buying a Car, Selling Your House, Arranging a Vacation on a Budget, or Reinvesting a 401(K) Payout, This May Be the Only Guide You Need. Easy to Use, Hundreds of Money Saving Tips.
Mescon Multimedia.

Clash of Steel: Jewel Case. Nov. 1995.
Customer Support: 30 day limited warranty.
DOS 5.0 or higher. 386 CD-ROM with hard drive (2Mb). CD-ROM disk $9.95 (ISBN 0-917059-40-9, Order no.: 062611). *Optimal configuration:* 386, hard drive, CD-ROM, 256 color VGA.
World War II Strategic Wargame. The Campaign Game Covers the Entire European Theater in 60-80 Hours of Play. Several Levels of Difficulty for All Wargames - Beginner, Intermediate & Advanced.
Strategic Simulations, Inc.

Class Record. 1992. *Items Included:* Detailed manuals are included with all DYNACOMP products. *Customer Support:* Free telephone support to original customer - no time limit; 30 day limited warranty.
MS-DOS 3.2 or higher. IBM PC & compatibles (512k). $49.95 (Add $5.00 for 3 1/2" format; 5 1/4" format standard).
Can Meet the Requirements of Teachers at Every Level, from Elementary Through University. Features: Speed. Written in Turbo PASCAL & Is Compiled for Quick Execution. Automatically Sorts & Displays the Names of Students Together with Optional ID Numbers & Credit/No Credit (or Pass/Fail) Status. Can Record up to 10 Assignments & 8 Quizzes. Choice of Grading Systems. Print Out All Records for Each Student. All Bookkeeping, Scaling, etc., Is Done Automatically. Posting Marks. New Subject. New Marking Period. Password Option.
Dynacomp, Inc.

Class Scheduling System. 1992. *Items Included:* Detailed manuals are included with all DYNACOMP products. *Customer Support:* Free telephone support to original customer - no time limit; 30 day limited warranty.
MS-DOS 3.2 or higher. Apple. $469.95 (Add $5.00 for 3 1/2" format; 5 1/4" format standard).
Handles: up to Nine Periods per day; up to Ten Requests per Student; up to 1,200 Students/400 per Grade. Allows: Multiple Section Courses, No Limits; Balanced Section Enrollment; 1 or 2 Alternate Selections per Course; You to Set Maximum Class Size; You to Track Students & Prioritize Courses; Multiple Period Courses, up to Three Periods Long. Prints: Alphabetized Class Rosters; Student Schedules; Student ID Number & Grade on All Forms; on Virtually Any Printer.
Dynacomp, Inc.

Class Struggle. *Compatible Hardware:* Apple II+, IIe, IIc.
contact publisher for price.
Begin As a Worker, a Capitalist, a Student, Businessman, or Professional & Join the Marxist Struggle for Power. Includes Avalon Hill's CLASS STRUGGLE Boardgame.
Avalon Hill Game Co., The Microcomputer Games Div.

Classes of Nouns. Apr. 1983. *Items Included:* Teacher's guide. *Customer Support:* 90-day limited warranty.
Apple-DOS 3.3. Apple II Family (48k). disk $59.00 (ISBN 0-917277-51-1).
Commodore 64/128 (64k). disk $59.00 (ISBN 0-917277-62-7).
Five Computer Programs Teach User the Difference Between Common, Proper & Special Classes of Nouns. Also Covers That Tricky Area of Capitalizaiton. Complete with Review Test. Ages 13 & Up.
BrainBank/Generation Ahead of Maryland.

Classic BASIC Games. *Compatible Hardware:* HP 9000 Series 200, 300 with graphics.
Language(s): BASIC (source code included). disk $29.95.
Collection of Games That Includes BLACKJACK, HANGMAN, GOMOKU, BITE, MAZE, SPACEWAR, QUADGT & More.
James Assocs.

Classic Collection: Adventure - Fantasy. Sep. 1993. *Customer Support:* Free technical support 810-477-1205.
MS-DOS 3.1 or higher. IBM 386 or higher, or compatibles (640k). CD-ROM disk $29.95 (ISBN 1-57037-003-6). *Optimal configuration:* CD-ROM drive, 4Mb free hard disk space, VGA card & monitor, mouse (recommended); joystick (optional); Sound Board (optional).
Featured Software Packages Are: "Zak McKracken & The Alien Mindbenders" by LucasArts Entertainment Co. Hilarious One-Liners in This Easy-to-Use Classic. "The Savage Empire" by Origin Systems - Interact with Dozens of Characters in the Most Advanced Ultima Role-Playing System Ever Created. "Bill & Ted's Excellent Adventure" by Capstone - Four Levels of Difficulty Require Most Excellent Playing to Ensure You Are Triumphant in Your "Homework." Party on Dudes! "Maniac Mansion" by LucasArts Entertainment - Get Ready for the Funniest Adventure of Your Life.
SelectWare Technologies, Inc.

Classic Collection: Greatest Air Battles. Aug. 1993. *Customer Support:* Free technical support 810-477-1205.
MS-DOS 3.1 or higher. IBM 386 or higher, or compatible (640k). CD-ROM disk $29.95 (ISBN 1-57037-004-4). *Optimal configuration:* CD-ROM drive, 4Mb free hard disk space, VGA card & monitor, Mouse (recommended); Joystick (optional); Sound board (optional). *The Featured Software Packages Are:* "Knights of the Sky" by MicroProse - Challenge Germany's Most Celebrated Pilots to Determine Who Is WWI's Ace of Aces. "F-14 Tomcat" by Activision - Put Your Talents to the Test Against 15 Elite Pilots to Become the Top Gun. "JetFighter I" by Velocity - Fly over 30 Sweat-Drenching Missions. "F-19 Stealth Fighter" by MicroProse - With Dazzling Graphics & Authentic Real-World Scenarios, F-19 Creates Action-Packed Excitement That Keeps You Coming Back for More.
SelectWare Technologies, Inc.

The Classic Collection Plus: 4 Disc Set Jewel Case. *Items Included:* Registration card. *Customer Support:* Creative Multimedia Corporation warrants the CD-ROM disc & diskettes to be free from defects in materials & workmanship under normal use & service for a period of 90 days from date of purchase. Creative Multimedia Corporation offers Technical Support to customers as needed.
MS-DOS version 3.1 or higher. IBM PC & compatibles with VGA monitor (640k). CD-ROM disk $129.99 4 disc set (ISBN 1-880428-13-X, Order no.: 10193). *Optimal configuration:* SuperVGA monitor with 512k Video Memory capable of 640x480x256 colors with VESA extensions recommended. *Networks supported:* All LAN.
System Software 6.0.5 or higher. Macintosh Plus or higher (2Mb). $129.99 4 disc set (Order no.: 10193). *Optimal configuration:* Color requires 8-bit color display, 32-bit QuickDraw & Color Monitor. *Networks supported:* All.
Contains the Works of the Greatest Playwright of All Times, SHAKESPEARE, & the Classic Stories of Detection by SHERLOCK HOLMES & Dr. Watson. Also Included, the Rare & Complete 1840 Edition of "Quadrupeds of North America" in MULTIMEDIA AUDUBON'S MAMMALS, & Audubon's Complete 1840 First Edition Plates in the Disc of MULTIMEDIA AUDUBON'S BIRDS.
Creative Multimedia Corp.

Classic Science Fiction. *Compatible Hardware:* Apple Macintosh.
contact publisher for price.
A.A.H. Computer Graphics Productions.

Classic Season Disks.
IBM. Contact publisher for price. *Addl. software required:* APBA Baseball & Baseball for Windows.
Baseball Data Disk from the Following Seasons, Each Sold Separately: 1889, 1913, 1919, 1920, 1920, 1924, 1927, 1929, 1930, 1931, 1934, 1935, 1938, 1939, 1940, 1941, 1946, 1947, 1948, 1950, 1951, 1953, 1955, 1956, 1957, 1958, 1959, 1960, 1961, 1962, 1963, 1964, 1965, 1966, 1967, 1969, 1970, 1971, 1972, 1975, 1977, 1978, 1980, 1982, 1983, 1984, 1985, 1986, 1987, 1988, 1989, 1990, 1991, 1992, 1993.
Miller Assocs.

Classical Compact Disc Guide. *Compatible Hardware:* Apple Macintosh Plus. *General Requirements:* Printer optional.
3.5" disk $29.95.
hard disk version $39.95.
demo disk $10.00.
Lists & Reviews Classical Compact Discs.
Somerville Assocs.

Classified! II. *Compatible Hardware:* Apple Macintosh. *Memory Required:* 512k. *General Requirements:* Microsoft Word, any draw or paint program.
3.5" disk $295.00.
Classified Ad Management System for Medium-Size Newspapers. Contains All the Usual Classified Ad Headings, & User Is Shown How to Create Additional Headings. When a Classified Ad Is Submitted, A User Goes to the Proper Heading & Types in the Ad, Complete with Expiration Code. A User Then Opens the Billing Files & Enters the Billing Information. The Complete Galley of Classified Ads & a Current Classified Billing Can Be Printed Out Anytime. The Invoice Formats Are Included on Disk. User Can Also Search & Delete All Expired Ads. The Search System Makes it Simple to Locate & Post Each Account As Payment Comes In. Also Included Is a Provision for Integrating All Small (One or Two Inch) Display Ads into the Same System.
Nick Murray.

ClearingHouse. *Version:* 1.0. Bob Nadler. Apr. 1985. *Compatible Hardware:* Apple II+, IIc, IIe, IIgs; Atari 400, 800, 600XL, 800XL, 1200XL, 1400XL, 1450XLD, 65XE, 130XE; Commodore 64/128; IBM PC XT,AT & compatibles, PCjr. *Operating System(s) Required:* Atari DOS 2.0, 2.5 or 3.0 Apple DOS 3.3, PC-DOS/MS-DOS 2.1 or higher. *Language(s):* Compiled TurboBASIC on PC-DOS/MS-DOS systems. *Memory Required:* 48k; PC-DOS/MS-DOS machines 128k. *Items Included:* User's Manual. *Customer Support:* Yes.
disk $49.95 ea., incl. manual.
Commodore. (ISBN 0-933596-22-7, Order no.: CH-C).
IBM. (ISBN 0-933596-24-3, Order no.: CH-I).
Apple. (ISBN 0-933596-25-1, Order no.: CH-A).
Atari. (ISBN 0-933596-26-X, Order no.: CH-AT).
Identifies Over 95% of All Bad Checks & Warns Users Not to Cash Them. Visual & Audible Warnings Are Provided When a Problem Is Detected with a Check. Complete Report on Each Check Is Available on Screen or Printer.
F/22 Pr.

ClearView.
IBM PC or higher (512k). disk $79.00. *Nonstandard peripherals required:* Hard disk drive. *Addl. software required:* Microsoft Windows 2.0 or higher.
Improves Graphics & Functionality of Windows Desktop. User Can Customize Placement, Size & Arrangement of Windows. Features Automatic Program Loading & Desktop Customization for Layout Selection. Windows & Non-Windows Applications Can Be Accessed from Same Menu. List Feature Automates Window Movement.
Wang Laboratories, Inc.

Clef Notes. G. David Peters. *Customer Support:* 90 day warranty against defective software.
DOS 3.3. Apple II (48k). disk $39.95 (Order no.: A-1105).
DOS 3.3 or higher. IBM (640k). disk $39.95 (Order no.: I-1105).
System 6.0.7 - System 7.1. Macintosh (1Mb). 3.5" disk $59.95 (Order no.: MAC-1105).
Designed to Improve the Speed with Which a Student Can Identify Music Notes As They Are Placed on the Staff, Using Treble, Alto, Tenor & Bass Clefs. Correct Answers Are Selected on a Graphics Display, Using a Movable Cursor. Ten Notes Must Be Identified Consecutively to Complete a Session. Scores Are Stored in a Hall of Fame at the End of Each Session.
Electronic Courseware Systems, Inc.

CLEO 3780Plus. Richard Newberry. 1983. *Compatible Hardware:* Altos; Arete; AT&T 3B2, 3B5, DEC RISC; DEC VAX; DG AViiON; HP9000; IBM PC & compatibles; IBM RS/6000; NCR System 3000; Sun SPARC. *Operating System(s) Required:* AIX, DG-UX, HP-US, PC-DOS/MS-DOS, SunOS, UNIX, Ultrix, VMS, XENIX. *Language(s):* C. *Memory Required:* 128k. *Items Included:* Software. *Customer Support:* Toll-free phone support.
$995.00-$9995.00, depending on platform. manual $50.00.
Allows a Microcomputer to Emulate a 2780/3780 RJE Station. Features Include: Forms Control, Auto Dial/Auto Answer, Scripting Command Language, Applications Program Interface (API), Attended & Unattended Operation, & Are Available Under MS-DOS, UNIX, XENIX, AIX, 386/ix VENIX & Others. There Are Several Hardware Options to Meet Your Needs. Boards with a Built-In Coprocessor, Off-Load Communications Processing from the CPU, freeing It for Applications Processing. Our Unique SYNCoable Allows Synchronous Communications Activity Through Standard Asynchronous Ports. Modem Boards Allows User to Combine 2780/3780 Terminal Emulation Software with a High-Speed Modem on One Board. When Application Demands an External Modem, Synchronous Cards Can Provide a Complete, Cost-Effective Solution.
CLEO Communications.

Clerk of the Works: Accounting Software for Architects & Engineers. *Version:* 2.0. Nov. 1989. *Items Included:* 150 page manual. *Customer Support:* 1 Month free telephone, $1 per minute or $695 per year.
System 6.0 or higher. MAC Classic. 3.5" disk $2495.00.
High End Integrated Accounting Package Written Especially for Architects & Engineers. It Conforms to AIA Accounting Practices; is a One Imput System That Distributes the Information to Projects & General Ledger at the Time of Input; Budget & Tracks Projects by Phase & Tasks; Allows Different Billing Rates for the Same Person on the Same Project; Bills Time & Reimbursables, Fixed Fee, % Construction, Payables to Project & Phase & General Ledger Accounts from the Vendor Invoice Entry Screen; Has Nine Levels of Password Protection; Number of Records Limited Only by Disk Space; Custom Reports. Product's Five Modules Include: Time & Expenses; Billing & AR; General Ledger; Payables; & Payroll.
Samsara, Ltd.

Clever & Smart. *Customer Support:* Back up disks available.
Amiga (512k). 3.5" disk $14.95.
Atari (512k). 3.5" disk $14.95.
Join the Fun in This Action Strategy Game With Clever & Smart, the Bumbling Detectives, As They Accomplish Their Lifetime Mission of Recovering the Kidnapped Dr. Bacterius.
DigiTek Software.

ClickArt EPS Symbols & Industry, Vol. 1. Oct. 1990. *Items Included:* EPS Symbols & Industry manual, ClickArt catalog. *Customer Support:* Free & unlimited to registered users - via phone, FAX, & online service.
Macintosh. 3.5" disk $129.95. *Nonstandard peripherals required:* PostScript compatible printer. *Addl. software required:* Application that reads EPS files.
MS-DOS or Windows. IBM PC & compatibles. disk $129.95. *Nonstandard peripherals required:* PostScript compatible printer. *Addl. software required:* Application that reads EPS files.
Collection of More Than 260 High-Quality

TITLE INDEX

PostScript Images Created by Professional Artists for Use in Brochures, Newsletters, Reports, Charts, Signs, & Other Published Documents. Image Categories Include General Business & International Symbols, Military Armaments & Ranks, Medical Symbols & Equipment, Science & Engineering Symbols & Equipment, & Much More.
T/Maker Co., Inc.

ClickChange. *Version:* 2.5.2. Cliff Joyce. Nov. 1995. *Customer Support:* Free phone support to registered users.
Macintosh 6.04 or newer. Mac plus or higher (1 meg). $89.95 (Order no.: 94627-00027).
Optimal configuration: Mac plus or higher.
Allows Users to Customize Their Macintosh. Windows & Buttons May Be Replaced by Many Interesting Alternatives. Over 100 Animated Color Cursors & a Cursor Editor Are Included. Dubl-Arrowed Custom Scrollbars, Custom color Sets, & the Ability to Use a Variety of Sounds for System Events Round Out the Features.
Dubl-Click Software.

Clicktracks.
Macintosh 512KE higher. 3.5" disk $349.00.
Professional Film & Video Timing Software.
Passport Designs, Inc. (California).

Client Accounting. CYMA Corp. *Compatible Hardware:* TI Professional. *Operating System(s) Required:* CP/M, MS-DOS. *Memory Required:* 64k. *General Requirements:* Printer.
$1695.00 (Order no.: SY P/N T039-105).
Texas Instruments, Personal Productivit.

Client Accounting System. *Compatible Hardware:* IBM PC & compatibles. *Operating System(s) Required:* MS-DOS, Xenix. *Language(s):* COBOL. *Memory Required:* 640k.
disk $595.00.
Designed for the Accounting Professional. Capable of Doing Batch Processing, & Multi-Client &/or Multicompany Processing. A Complete Variety of Reports Needed by an Accountant Is Included. Supports up to 999 User-Defined Account Numbers per Client, 99 Departments, Sub-Accounts, Prior Period Adjustments, User-Defined Exhibits, & Unlimited Subtotals & User-Formatted Financial Statements.
Rowlette Enterprises, Inc.

Client & Lawyer Financial: Series 500 & 600. *Compatible Hardware:* IBM PC, PS/2.
contact publisher for price.
Processes Client Descriptive & Financial Data, Including Time Worked, Disbursements, Trust Activity, Billings & Accounts Receivable. Data Can Be Edited & Printed According to Formats Predefined by the Law Firm. Produces Reminder Statements & Interest Charges to All or Selected Clients.
Manac-Prentice Hall Software, Inc.

Client Asset Management System (dbCAMS+). *Version:* 3.32. Jun. 1992. *Operating System(s) Required:* PC-DOS/MS-DOS. *Memory Required:* 640k. *General Requirements:* 20Mb hard disk. *Items Included:* Teaching tapes, manual. *Customer Support:* Users Support Group.
disk $725.00.
demo disk $25.00.
Complete Client Management System That Provides Client Tracking, Asset Allocation, Portfolio Management, & Financial Statements. Features a TODO Suspense System, a Phone Management System, a Mailmerge Facility, & a Variety of Reports. dbCAMS + Interfaces with Several Financial Planning Packages & Broker Dealers. Pricing Service, Downloading Client Billing & Time Management Are Also Available.
Financial Computer Support, Inc.

Client Data System (CDS). *Version:* 2.8. Morgan P. Underwood, III. Jul. 1992. *Operating System(s) Required:* MS-DOS, PC-DOS. *Language(s):* C. *Memory Required:* 512k. *General Requirements:* Hard disk, printer. *Items Included:* 4 diskettes, users manual. *Customer Support:* Via regular phone lines $245.00/annually.
disk $675.00.
Designed to Assist in the Management of Client Investments. Tracks All Types of Investments, from Stocks & Mutual Funds to Variable Annuities, Insurance & Limited Partnerships. The Program's Sorting Feature Provides the Ability to Find Groups of Clients. Provides a Variety of Client Statements. Statements May Be Output to the Screen, Printer or Spreadsheet Readable Formats. Also Very Strong Activity Management & Office Automation Features.
E-Z Data, Inc.

Client Database. *Version:* 2.0. *Compatible Hardware:* IBM PC & compatibles, PS/2. *Memory Required:* 512k. *General Requirements:* Lotus 1-2-3 release 2/2.01. *Items Included:* Users' manual. *Customer Support:* Phone support, unlimited.
$25.00.
Allows User to Record Standard Items for up to 2,000 Clients. Entries Include Name, Phone Number, Company, Address, Profession, & Remarks. Database Entries Can Be Found by Entering a Shortened Character String That Ensures a Unique Match. Prints Mailing Labels from the Database.
Compusense.

Client Dental Billing System. *Compatible Hardware:* Apple II, II+, IIe with 80-column text card; IBM PC. *Memory Required:* Apple II, II+ 48k; Apple IIe 64k; IBM PC 320k. *General Requirements:* 2 to 4 disk drives, 132-column printer; SmarTerm for Apple.
Apple II. disk $1595.95 (Order no.: D-099).
Apple II, II+. disk $1595.95 (Order no.: D-111).
IBM. disk $1595.95 (Order no.: D-121).
demo disk $100.00.
source code avail.
Designed for Accounting Firms & Billing Services to Use in Handling Private Patient Billing & Claim Form Preparation for Dentist's Clients. Allows for the Development of Separate Databases for Each Client Office.
CMA Micro Computer.

Client-Entry Program for the CBCL - 4-18, YSR, & TRF. Thomas M. Achenbach. Mar. 1996. *Items Included:* Detailed manual. *Customer Support:* Free telephone support with no time limit.
MS-DOS 3.1 or higher. IBM & compatibles 386 with color monitor (2Mb). disk $175.00 (ISBN 0-938565-39-7).
Enables Users to Have Clients Directly Keyboard Their Own Data for Scoring by CBCL/4-18, YSR, TRF, or Cross-Informant Program.
University of Vermont, Dept. of Psychiatry.

Client Files, Conflict & Dates: Series 500 & 600. *Compatible Hardware:* IBM PC & PS/2.
contact publisher for price.
Classifies & Retrieves Client & Matter Descriptive Data, Records Archives Numbers & Advises of Bring-Forward Dates.
Manac-Prentice Hall Software, Inc.

Client Financial Management: Series 900 to 2000. *Compatible Hardware:* IBM System/36, System/36 PC; AS/400.
contact publisher for price.
Enables Lawyers to Keep Track of Work Performed & Disbursements Made for Clients, to Bill on a Timely Basis, to Monitor Accounts Receivable & to Control Client Trust Funds.
Manac-Prentice Hall Software, Inc.

THE CLIENT MEDICAL BILLING SYSTEM

Client Information Management System: CIMS. *Version:* 2.0. Jan. 1989. *Compatible Hardware:* IBM PC & compatibles. *Operating System(s) Required:* MS-DOS/PC-DOS. *Memory Required:* 640k. *General Requirements:* Hard disk. *Customer Support:* $200/yr.
disk $595.00 (ISBN 0-941433-02-1, Order no.: 10020).
Designed to Allow for Fast Very Flexible Input/Output of Client Information & Reporting by Individuals with Limited Computer Experience. Automatically Maintains Accurate Accounting of Unduplicated Participants. Tracks Services by Client, Date or Type & Provides Cross Reference Capability for a Wide Range of Variables. Designed for use by Meals on Wheels Programs & Provider of Service under the Older Americans Act.
Texas Software.

Client List. 1982. *Compatible Hardware:* Apple II, Commodore 64, IBM PC. *Operating System(s) Required:* PC-DOS, Apple DOS 3.3. *Memory Required:* 64k. *General Requirements:* Printer.
disk $35.00.
Sorts & Prints Alphabetized Lists with Optional Categories. Records Name, Address, Affiliation & Phone Number, & Prints Labels up to 3-Across Arranged by Zip Code.
Navic Software.

Client List II. *Compatible Hardware:* Apple II, Commodore 64, IBM PC. *Memory Required:* 48-64k.
$35.00.
Sorts & Prints Alphabetized Lists with Optional Categories. Records Name, Address, Affiliation & Phone Number & Prints Labels up to 3-Across Arranged by Zip Code. Accommodates up to 250 Names. Features: Membership Records for Churches, Clubs or Organizations, Realtors Listing Directories, Patient Records for Doctors & Dentists, Client Records for Lawyers & Accountants, & Marketing Sales Leads.
Navic Software.

The Client Management System. *Version:* 5.5. *Compatible Hardware:* IBM PC XT, PC AT & compatibles, PS/2. *Operating System(s) Required:* PC-DOS 2.1 or higher. *Language(s):* Pascal. *Memory Required:* PC-DOS 2.1 256k, PC-DOS 3.0 or higher 320k. *General Requirements:* 2 disk drives or hard disk. *Customer Support:* 60 days toll-free.
disk $1295.00.
Designed to Handle the Billing Problems of Small to Medium-Sized Law Firms. The System Performs the Following Functions: Time, Expense, & Payment Recording; Billing; Accounts Receivable; Trust Accounting; Retainer Accounting; Work-in-Process Management; Management Reports Production; & Historical (Archival) Data Management.
CompuLaw, Ltd.

The Client Medical Billing System. *Compatible Hardware:* Apple II, II+, IIe; IBM PC. *General Requirements:* 2 to 4 disk drives, printer.
disk $1595.95 ea. (Order no.: D-098).
Apple II, II+.
IBM PC. (Order no.: D-120).
preview manual $50.00.
source code avail.
demo disk $100.00.
Designed for Accountants & Billing Services to Use in Handling the Patient Billing & Claim Form Preparation for Their Physician Clients. Allows for Development of Separate Databases for Each Physician Client Containing Patient Data for the Daily Input & Reporting of Billing Activity, for the Preparation of Private Patient Statements & for Preparation of the Universal AMA Claim Form.
CMA Micro Computer.

Client Record-Bill Preparation. *Compatible Hardware:* Apple. *Language(s):* Applesoft. *Memory Required:* 32k.
disk $49.95 (Order no.: 0284AD).
Create Files about Each Client Including Charges for Time, Materials, & Expenses. Print Invoices.
Instant Software, Inc.

Client-Sales Master. *Items Included:* Bound manual. *Customer Support:* Free hotline - no time limit; 30 day limited warranty; updates are $5/disk plus S&H.
MS-DOS 2.0 or higher. IBM & compatibles (128k). disk $89.95. *Nonstandard peripherals required:* Printer.
Track Your Clients & Prospective Clients. Easily Maintain Client/Customer List. Print Mailing Labels (One to Four Across). Compiled Programs for Super-Fast Performance. Assign As Many As 40 Different Classes or Types to Each Address or Person That You Have Defined. Unlimited Number of Files or Addresses (Limited Only by Available Disk Space) & More.
Dynacomp, Inc.

Client Statements: Series 900 to 2000. *Compatible Hardware:* IBM System/36, System/36 PC; AS/400.
contact publisher for price.
Produces Client Statements for Billing Purposes.
Manac-Prentice Hall Software, Inc.

Client Write-Up. *Version:* 3.3. *Operating System(s) Required:* PC-DOS, MS-DOS. *Language(s):* BASIC. *Memory Required:* 256k. *Customer Support:* $250 annually. 45 days unlimited warranty.
disk $695.00.
Allows User to Design Any Financial Statement or Compilation Report Free-Form on the Video Screen. Current or Year-to-Date GL Can Be Produced at Any Time.
E. F. Haskell & Assocs.

Client Write-Up General Ledger Accounting Module. *Compatible Hardware:* DECmate II, DECmate III, PDP 11-53, VAX. *Operating System(s) Required:* COS-310, MICRO-RSX. *Language(s):* DIBOL-83. *Customer Support:* One month.
$1875.00, incl. user's guide (Order no.: 85-1).
Combines the Features of a Financial Statement Presentation with Purchase Transaction Recording, to Serve the Special Needs of Companies That Need to Present Financial Statements & Keep a History of Transactions.
Corporate Consulting Co.

Client Write-Up System. Fisher Business Systems, Inc. *Operating System(s) Required:* MS-DOS. *Memory Required:* 64k.
$1695.00 (Order no.: SY P/N TO39-105).
Texas Instruments, Personal Productivit.

Client Write-Up System: PASS, Vol. 1. Plenary Systems, Inc. *Compatible Hardware:* TI Professional; with printer, 2 disk drives. *Operating System(s) Required:* MS-DOS, RM/COBOL Run Time. *Memory Required:* 128k.
$1995.00.
Professional Financial Reporting Package. Features General Ledger, Report Generator, After the Fact Payroll Reporting, Electronic Spreadsheet & Asset Management System.
Texas Instruments, Personal Productivit.

ClienTrak. *Version:* 3.5. Oct. 1985. *Compatible Hardware:* Altos; General Automation; IBM PC AT. *Operating System(s) Required:* PICK, Revelation, PC-DOS, MS-DOS. *Language(s):* BASIC. *Memory Required:* 640k.
contact publisher for price.
Sales Management Tool That Provides Targeted Prospecting, Reduces Paperwork, Improves Sales Productivity, Provides Client Service, etc.
Intelligent Technology Group.

Clients & Profits for Advertising Agencies. *Version:* 5.0. *Compatible Hardware:* Apple Macintosh Plus. *General Requirements:* Hard disk; ImageWriter or LaserWriter. *Customer Support:* Free.
$3895.00 single user.
$4995.00 multi-user.
Advertising Agency Management Package.
Working Computer.

CLIM: Common Lisp Interface Manager. *Version:* 2.1. Jan. 1996. *Items Included:* Manual. *Customer Support:* First year's support, maintenance, updates included. Support package renewable thereafter.
UNIX. Sun/SPARC, IBM RS/6000, HP9000, DEC Alpha, SGI, most Unix workstations. Contact publisher for price.
Portable, High-Level User Interface Manager for Creating Graphical, Windowized User Interfaces for Lisp-Based Applications. Compatible with CLIM on Symbolics' Lisp Machines.
Franz, Inc.

CLImate. *Compatible Hardware:* Commodore Amiga.
3.5" disk $39.95.
File Management Utility. Enables Users to Use the Mouse to Bypass the Keyboard for Most Operations. Supports up to 3 External Disk Drives, 2 Hard Drives, & RAM Disks. Users Can Copy, Delete, Move Files & Directories, View IFF Pictures, & Print Files with Control of Print Format.
Progressive Peripherals & Software, Inc.

Climatedata Hourly-Precipitation. *Version:* 3.0. Jan. 1993. *Items Included:* Bound Documentation, License. *Customer Support:* Unlimited telephonic support. On-Site by contract.
DOS. IBM-PC or compatible 20 mg Hard Drive (512k). CD-ROM disk $995.00, Subscribe ,495.00 year one, ,250.00 future years (ISBN 1-884632-05-X). *Nonstandard peripherals required:* CD-ROM Drive. *Addl. software required:* MS Extention 2.0 Plus or substitute.
Optimal configuration: 640k RAM, 20mg Hard Drive Math Coprocessor.
TD-3240 Precipitation Records Compiled by the National Climatic Data Center. Access to Observations from Nearly 5000 Stations Nationwide via Our Proprietary Data Retrieval Software. Three Discs Cover the Entire United States.
Hydrosphere Data Products, Inc.

Climatedata Monthly Summary GIS. May 1994. *Items Included:* Bound Documentation, License. *Customer Support:* Unlimited telephonic support. On-Site by contract.
Designed for use with ESRI software. System configuration for software use varies: DOS, Windows, UNIX. CD-ROM disk $995.00 (ISBN 1-884632-00-9). *Addl. software required:* ArcView, ArcInfo, PC ArcInfo, ArcCAD.
Summary Statistical Analyses on over 57,000 Meteorological Observations from over 17,000 Measurement Stations Nationwide. NCDC TD-3200 Data is the Basis for Statistical Summaries. Native ArcInfo, ArcData, & ArcCAD Data Sets. We Are an ESRI Authorized ArcData Publisher.
Hydrosphere Data Products, Inc.

Climatedata Quarter-Hourly Precipitation. Jan. 1993. *Items Included:* Bound Documentation, License. *Customer Support:* Unlimited telephonic support. On-Site by contract.
DOS. IBM-PC or compatible 20 mg Hard Drive (512k). CD-ROM disk $995.00, Subscribe ,495.00 year one, ,250.00 future years (ISBN 1-884632-04-1). *Nonstandard peripherals required:* CD-ROM Drive. *Addl. software required:* MS Extention 2.0 Plus or substitute.
Optimal configuration: 640k RAM, 20mg Hard Drive Math Coprocessor.
TD-3260 Precipitation Records Compiled by the National Climatic Data Center. Access to Observations from Nearly 2,500 Stations Nationwide via Our Proprietary Data Retrieval Software. One Disc Covers Entire United States.
Hydrosphere Data Products, Inc.

Climatedata Summary of the Day. *Version:* 4.0. Jan. 1993. *Items Included:* Bound Documentation, License. *Customer Support:* Unlimited telephonic support. On-Site by contract.
DOS. IBM-PC or compatible 20 mg Hard Drive (512k). CD-ROM disk $995.00, Subscribe ,495.00 year one, ,250.00 future years (ISBN 1-884632-03-3). *Nonstandard peripherals required:* CD-ROM Drive. *Addl. software required:* MS Extention 2.0 Plus or substitute.
Optimal configuration: 640k RAM, 20mg Hard Drive Math Coprocessor.
TD-3200 Climatological Data Compiled by the National Climatic Data Center. Access to Observations from Nearly 25,000 Stations in All Fifty States via Our Proprietary Data Retrieval Software. Includes Precalculations of Frequently Used Statistics.
Hydrosphere Data Products, Inc.

Clinic Management System (CMS). *Version:* 4.01. 1987. *Items Included:* User manual. *Customer Support:* 90 days unlimited support after installation & training, ongoing support & maintenance $375/yr.
PC-DOS 3.30 (384k). PC AT & compatibles.
single user $2500.00, Novell $3500.00 (ISBN 0-928246-13-2, Order no.: CMS-SU).
Nonstandard peripherals required: Hard disk. *Addl. software required:* "PC Anywhere" for remote support. *Optimal configuration:* AT 286; EGA monitor; 640k RAM. *Networks supported:* Novell.
Totally Automated, Replaces One-Write System in Use in Most Clinics Today. Unlike Manual System, Also Captures Significant Management Data & Produces Many Reports Not Available Without an Automated System.
HEL Custom Software, Inc.

Clinical Cost Accounting. *Compatible Hardware:* DEC Micro Vax II; IBM PC, IBM 4300 & compatibles. *Operating System(s) Required:* VM, MVS, VSE, Micro VMS.
contact publisher for price.
Provides the Capability to Analyze & Allocate Costs from the General Ledger, Cost Center Level, to the Individual Patient to Reflect the Actual Cost of Treating Each Patient.
HBO & Co., Inc.

Clinical Pharmacology. Alexander Shephard. Mar. 1989.
IBM PC. $99.95.
MS-DOS 2.1 (192k). IBM PC, PC XT, PC AT.
Explains Pharmacokinetic Process by Showing the Following Stages of an Antibiotic: Absorption, Distribution, Drug Action, Metabolism, & Elimination. Also Discusses Management of Drug Therapy.
Cardinal Health Systems, Inc.

CLINICALL. *Version:* 2.1. Jun. 1991. *Customer Support:* Toll free telephone support.
MS-DOS 3.1. IBM PC. disk $495.00.
Personal Medical Encyclopedia That Arrives Filled with Topical Information That Can Be Used Immediately & Also Can Be Enlarged Effortlessly over a Physician's Lifetime of Practice.
SRC Systems, Inc.

TITLE INDEX

Clip Animation Sampler. *Compatible Hardware:* Apple Macintosh. *General Requirements:* 800k disk drive, VideoWorks II or VideoWorks Professional.
3.5" disk $59.95.
Animated Clip Sequences for Use with VideoWorks II & VideoWorks Professional Animation Programs. Three Categories Are Included: Business & Industry, Sales & Marketing & Borders & Symbols.
Desktop Video Productions.

Clip*Video*Art "Animation Effects". *Version:* 1. *Compatible Hardware:* Apple Macintosh 512KE. *General Requirements:* Hard disk or external disk drive, VideoWorks II.
3.5" disk $59.95.
Collection of Short Animated Clips for Enhancing Animated Presentations. Includes Special Effect Animated Graphic Symbols & Shapes That Move, Spin, Explode, Highlight, Fade & Race Across the Screen. Clips Can Be Combined to Create User-Defined Effects.
Freemyers Design.

Clip*Video*Art "Presentation Animation". *Version:* 1. *Compatible Hardware:* Apple Macintosh 512KE. *General Requirements:* Hard disk or external disk drive, VideoWorks II.
3.5" disk $59.95.
Collection of Short Animations for Enhancing Animated Presentations. Includes Animated Special Effects, Pie Charts, Bar Charts, Borders, Marquees, Graphic Arts Aids, Arrows, Symbols & Selected Clip Art.
Freemyers Design.

Clipart Cornucopia. *Customer Support:* All of our products are unconditionally guaranteed.
DOS, Windows. CD-ROM disk $39.95 (Order no.: CLIPART). *Nonstandard peripherals required:* CD-ROM drive.
5050 Clip Art Images in 95 Categories. PCX & WPG Formats.
Walnut Creek CDRom.

CLIPS. *Version:* 6.0. NASA Johnson Space Center. 1993. *Compatible Hardware:* Apple Macintosh, DEC VAX, IBM PC & compatibles, UNIX. *Operating System(s) Required:* PC-DOS, MS-DOS, VMS, Unix. *Language(s):* C (source code included). *Memory Required:* 256k. *General Requirements:* Hard disk; ANSI C compiler.
disk $350.00 (Order no.: MSC 21208).
Forward Chaining Rule-Based Language for Developing Expert Systems. Contains an Inference Engine & a Language Syntax. Based on the Rete Algorithm Which Enables Efficient Pattern Matching. Program's Syntax Allows the Inclusion of Externally Defined Functions & Outside Functions Which Are Written in a Language Other Than CLIPS. Can Be Embedded in a Program Such That the Expert System Is Available As a Simple Subroutine Call.
COSMIC.

Clips for QuickTime. *Customer Support:* All of our products are unconditionally guaranteed.
Windows, Mac. CD-ROM disk $19.95 (Order no.: CLIPS). *Nonstandard peripherals required:* CD-ROM drive.
224 Full Color Movie Clips with Sound in QuickTime Format.
Walnut Creek CDRom.

CliqAccessories. *Compatible Hardware:* AT&T; DEC; DG; ENCORE; Hewlett-Packard; IBM PC RT, IBM RS6000; Motorola; NCR; Pyramid; UNISYS; XENIX, MS-DOS. *Language(s):* C. *Items Included:* 1 set of user manuals. *Customer Support:* Telephone/on site support; training classes; maintenance releases.
contact publisher for price.
Integrated Office Automation Package Comprised of 5 Software Modules Including CliqDate, Calendar-Scheduler; CliqMail, Electronic Mail; CliqCall, Phone Directory; CliqMath Full Function Calculator & CliqNote, Notepad-Index Program.
Quadratron Systems, Inc.

CliqCalc. *Operating System(s) Required:* UNIX, XENIX, MS-DOS. *Language(s):* C. *Customer Support:* Telephone/on site support; training classes; maintenance releases.
contact publisher for price.
Easy-to-Use Spreadsheet for Collecting, Manipulating & Analyzing Data. CliqCalc's Complete Lotus 1-2-3 Work-Alike Interface Will Cut Learning Curve to Almost Zero, Further Flexibility Is Provided with 100% Compatible Between CliqCalc & 1-2-3 Release 2 Files. Features Include 8192 Rows by 256 Columns; to 16 Simultaneously Updated Windows; Insert & Delete Rows, Columns or Windows; Sort Rows or Columns; & On-Line Context Sensitive Help Information.
Quadratron Systems, Inc.

CliqDCA. Feb. 1990. *Compatible Hardware:* AT&T; DEC; Hewlett-Packard; IBM PC & compatibles; MOTOROLA; NCR; UNISYS, UNISYS, IBM RS/6000, IBM RT, Encore, DG, Pyramid. *Customer Support:* Telephone/on site support; training classes; maintenance releases.
contact publisher for price.
Allows Two-Way Interchange of the IBM DCA RFT/FFT Formats & CliqWord Word-Processor Document Files. Runs Interactively or As a Background Task & Is Designed to Work with DIA Communications Programs & Services.
Quadratron Systems, Inc.

CliqPage. Feb. 1990. *Operating System(s) Required:* Unix, Xenix, MS-DOS. *General Requirements:* Postscript printer. *Customer Support:* Telephone/on site support; training classes; maintenance releases.
contact publisher for price.
Tool for Producing Typeset Output from Quadratron's CliqWord Word-Processor. Includes a Wide Range of Font Types, Styles & Sizes That Allow the User to Create Professional Looking Documents. Operates Transparently & Interactively with CliqWord. All Typographic Elements of Page Production Are Controlled Including Typeface, Point Size, Leader, Control, & Kerning. Features Page Layout, Header & Footer Layout & Content, Footnoting & Multicolumn Presentation. Adds Line & Box Drawing As Well As Shading & Patterning, Plus Integration of Graphics.
Quadratron Systems, Inc.

CliqWord. *Compatible Hardware:* AT&T; DEC; DG; Encore; Hewlett-Packard; IBM PC & compatibles, PC RT, IBM RS6000; Motorola; NCR; Pyramid; Sun; UNISYS. *Operating System(s) Required:* UNIX, XENIX, MS-DOS. *Language(s):* C. *Customer Support:* Telephone/on site support; training classes; maintenance releases.
contact publisher for price.
Word Processor. Features Include: Records Processing for Mass Mailings; Spelling Correct or with an 80,000 Word Dictionary Plus Optional Legal & Medical Dictionaries; Thesaurus; Capability to Edit Multiple Files Simultaneously Using Windows; Ability to Copy/Move Text Between Documents, Automatic Hyphenation/ Pagination; Footnoting; Multi-Column Capability, & Global Search/Replace Capability. Special Character Attributes Are Available, Including Bold, Underline, & Overstrike.
Quadratron Systems, Inc.

CLOSE-UP: REMOTE

Clock Shop. *Version:* 2.1. Aug. 1993. *Items Included:* Manual & 1 disk.
System 6.0.7 or higher. Macintosh Plus or higher (1Mb). 3.5" disk $57.95 (ISBN 0-940081-66-0).
Windows 3.1. 386SX or higher. 3.5" disk $57.95 (ISBN 0-940081-73-3). *Nonstandard peripherals required:* Mouse, SVGA, sound card.
Macintosh & Windows. CD-ROM disk $57.95 (ISBN 1-57374-013-6).
Teaches Children to Read & Write Digital & Analog Time with Eight Lesson Options. Begin by Learning to Set Time by Hours. More Challenging Problems Ask for Answers in Half-Hour, Quarter-Hour, Ten Minute, Five Minute, & One Minute Intervals. Correct Answers Are Rewarded with Time for the Clock Shop Game.
Nordic Software, Inc.

Clone. *Version:* 3.0A. James W. Moody. May 1990. *Items Included:* Manual, if not OEM version. *Customer Support:* Free phone, other support by agreement.
DOS386 (15k). 8088 thru 80486 (128k, Clone 15k). $49.95 (ISBN 0-924626-04-6). *Optimal configuration:* 386 4Mb RAM DOS 386.
Multitasking Executive That Allows DOS386 to Run Several Windows Using the Command, (CLONE/128/128/128). (640k SYS) This Gives the System Four Windows. The Main Process or Task Has 256k, the Other Windows 128k Each. These Windows Can Be Any Size That Fits the Applications & Memory Size.
Intelligent Machines.

The Clone Machine. *Compatible Hardware:* Commodore VIC-20. *General Requirements:* Joystick.
contact publisher for price.
Micro-W Distributing, Inc.

Close. Stuart Adler. 1983. *Compatible Hardware:* IBM PC & compatibles. *Operating System(s) Required:* MS-DOS. *Language(s):* DBASE III & IV, FOXPlus. *Memory Required:* 384k. *Items Included:* Manual. *Customer Support:* Telephone support at $75.00 per quarter. Three hours maximum.
disk $150.00. *Networks supported:* Novell.
source code option $450.00.
Client & Policy Database System Primarily for Insurance Agents. Prints Various Client & Policy Reports. Compatible with WordStar & Can Create Mailmerge Files.
Adler Computer Technology.

Close-Up/LAN Pro. *Version:* 6.1. May 1995. *Items Included:* Hard copy manual is included within the package. *Customer Support:* Technical support services are unlimited for registered users.
PC-DOS/MS-DOS 3.3 or higher. IBM PC, XT, AT, PS/2 (Host 47k, Remote 375k). 2-user $399.00; 5-user $499.00; 20-user $999.00. *Networks supported:* Novell (IPX).
The Quick & Easy Way to Remotely Control PCs on Your Network. Hold Workgroups, Conferences & Classrooms by Sharing Screens & Keyboards with Multiple PC over Your LAN or WAN. Product Features Include Support of Both Windows & DOS, Self Installations, File Transfers, Modem Version for Dial-In/Dial-Out Capabilities.
Norton-Lambert Corp.

Close-Up: Remote. *Version:* 6.0. May 1994. *Items Included:* Spiral bound user manual, either 5.25" or 3.5" disk. *Customer Support:* Technical support services unlimited for registered users, 90 day warranty for disks. Phone No. 805-964-6767.
DOS 2.0 or higher, DOS 5.0, Windows 3.0 or

CLOSE-UP REMOTE COMMUNICATIONS: HOST

higher. IBM PC, AT, XT, PS/2 & 100% compatibles (153k to 244k). Close-Up Support/ACS - $245.00 retail. *Nonstandard peripherals required:* Over 670 modems supported. *Optimal configuration:* 2 computers, 2 modems. *Networks supported:* All popular networks - NetBIOS or IPX protocol.
Remote Communications.
Norton-Lambert Corp.

Close-Up Remote Communications: Host & Remote. *Version:* 6.0. May 1994. *Items Included:* User manual, either 5.25" or 3.5" disk. *Customer Support:* Technical support services unlimited for registered users, 90 day warranty for disks. Phone No. 805-964-6767.
DOS 2.0 or higher, DOS 5.0, Windows 3.0 or higher. IBM PC, AT, XT, PS/2 & 100% compatibles, (34k-81k). Close-Up Host/Remote - $199.00 retail (Order no.: 420). *Nonstandard peripherals required:* Over 670 modems supported. *Optimal configuration:* 2 computers, 2 modems. *Networks supported:* All popular networks - NetBIOS or IPX protocol.
New Close-Up 6.0 Delivers Faster Windows Performance, Faster File Transfer, a New Look & Feel, & a Long List of Exciting Features Such As the Ability to Remotely Print in Windows & Virus Checking Security.
Norton-Lambert Corp.

Close-Up Remote Communications: Host & Remote. *Version:* 6.0. May 1994. *Items Included:* User manual, either 5.25" or 3.5" disk. *Customer Support:* Technical support services unlimited for registered users, 90 day warranty for disks. Phone No. 805-964-6767.
DOS 2.0 or higher, DOS 6.0, Windows 3.0 or higher. IBM PC, AT, XT, PS/2 & 100% compatibles (153k to 244k). disk $199.00, incl. Host & Remote sides. *Nonstandard peripherals required:* Over 670 modems supported. *Optimal configuration:* 2 computers, 2 modems. *Networks supported:* All popular networks - NetBIOS or IPX protocol.
First Modem Remote Control Software for Both Windows & DOS. Lets You View & Operate PCs Miles Away by Modem. Run Office PCs from Home or On-the-Road via Laptop. Give Instant Windows Support to Customers at Any Location, Without Leaving Your Office. Remotely Run Multiple Windows & DOS Applications in Different Windows on Your Own Screen. Access Networks. Fastest Remote Screens & File Transfers. Hi-Speed VGA/EGA/CGA Graphics. Remote Mouse Control. Includes Both Sides, Host & Remote.
Norton-Lambert Corp.

Clothing Retail Management System. *Version:* 1.0. L. Williams. 1983. *Compatible Hardware:* Cromemco, IBM PC, Kaypro, Eagle, Zenith, Epson. *Operating System(s) Required:* CROMIX, MS-DOS, CP/M-86, MP/M, CP/M 2.2, C DOS. *Language(s):* BASIC. *Memory Required:* 48k. disk $995.00.
Tightens Inventory Control by Recognizing Fast Selling Items for Prompt Reorder, by Recognizing Slow Sellers for Timely Markdowns & Adjustments of Reorders, by Zeroing in on Proper Size Structuring, by Reducing Accounting & Clerical Costs & by Increasing the Overall Productivity of the Business.
Microtec Information Systems.

CLR Anova. *Compatible Hardware:* Apple Macintosh. *Memory Required:* 512k.
3.5" disk $75.00.
Statistical Analysis.
Clear Lake Research.

CLR HyperArrays. *Version:* 2.0.
Macintosh Plus or higher. 3.5" disk $100.00.
XCMDs & XFCNs for Working Efficiently with Numeric Arrays.
Clear Lake Research.

CLR StatCalc. *Compatible Hardware:* Apple Macintosh Plus. *Memory Required:* 1000k. *General Requirements:* HyperCard.
3.5" disk $35.00.
One-year site license for educational institutions. $150.00.
Solves Small Statistical Problems.
Clear Lake Research.

CLS Law Office Management System. *Version:* 5.4. Apr. 1986. *Compatible Hardware:* AT&T; Compaq; IBM; SCO Xenix, Unix; SUN. *Operating System(s) Required:* AIX, Novell, PC-DOS, SUN O/S, Unix, Xenix. *Language(s):* C, COBOL, Informix. *Memory Required:* 640k. *General Requirements:* Printer, modem, terminal, tape drive. *Items Included:* CLS' Time Accounting & Management System, CLS' Administrative Systems, CLS' Business Support Systems, CLS' Professional Support Systems. *Customer Support:* Telephone hotline, on-line help, training, newsletters, annual client symposium.
contact publisher for price.
Designed for Law Firms, System Includes Business Applications (Time & Disbursement Accounting, Billing, General Ledger, Accounts Payable, Trust Accounting, Accounts Receivable), Professional Applications (Case Management, Conflict of Interest, Docket/Calendar Control, Document Indexing) Administrative Applications (List Manager, Export Interface, Import Interface), & Word Processing Applications.
Computer Law Systems, Inc.

The Club Controller: Health & Country Club Management System. Jun. 1984. *Compatible Hardware:* AIX (RS600), IBM PC & compatibles, XENIX, UNIX. *Memory Required:* 512k. *General Requirements:* 2 disk drives or hard disk, printer, modem.
contact publisher for price.
Dataverse Corp.

Club-Pak. *Version:* 2.0. Robert P. King. 1983. *Operating System(s) Required:* PC-DOS, TurboDOS, CP/M-86, MP/M-86. *Language(s):* CB-80, CB-86. *Memory Required:* 64k.
contact publisher for price.
Billing & Accounting System for Clubs & Organizations.
Crownsoft Applications.

CLUB-PLAN-CALC. *Version:* 1.1. Peter C. Vonderhorst. Jun. 1982. *Compatible Hardware:* IBM PC & compatibles, PC XT, PC AT; TRS-80. *Operating System(s) Required:* TRSDOS, PC-DOS, MS-DOS. *Language(s):* Compiled BASIC. *Memory Required:* 64k. *General Requirements:* Printer.
disk $350.00.
Christmas or Vacation Club Plans for Banks' or Retail Merchants' Merchandising Club Plans. Can Be Programmed to Print Checks or List of Accounts.
Computx.

Club Receivables/Membership. *Version:* 1.95. *Compatible Hardware:* PS/2, 386, 486, Pentium & RISC, & compatibles. *Operating System(s) Required:* MS/DOS, UNIX, XENIX, Windows, NT. *Language(s):* Visual BASIC. *Memory Required:* 4000k. *General Requirements:* Hard disk. *Customer Support:* Toll free hotline.
Contact publisher for price.
A Club-Exclusive, Integrated Club Management System. Maintains Extensive Membership Profiles, Member Billing, Accounts Receivable, Accounts Payable, Payroll, General Ledger, Golf Handicapping & Tournaments. Also Interfaces with the Most Popular Point-of-Sale Cash Registers for Automatic Posting of Daily Charges. Tracks Membership by Classification & Activity. Maintains Minimums Spent, Year-to-Date Spending Amounts, Family History, Lockers, Etcetera. Automatic Posting of Dues, F & B Minimums, Handicap Charges, Assessments, Late Charges, Hole-in-One Club. Interfaces with COSMOS' Proshop Management System.
Cosmos International, Inc.

Cluster Analysis. *Version:* 10.0. *Compatible Hardware:* Apple Macintosh, IBM PC & compatibles. *Items Included:* Disks, book, program instructions. *Customer Support:* Telephone.
disk $145.00 (ISBN 0-920387-76-4).
Include Procedures Based on Arbitrary Clustering Criteria, Sum-of-Squares of Distance Criteria, HMEANS & KMEANS, Criteria Involving Invariants, WMEANS, the Multiple-Location Allocation Problem, the Sum of Absolute Distance Criterion, Divisive & Agglomerative Procedures, & Some Miscellaneous Procedures Such As the Bond Energy Criterion Technique. Appropriate Programs Provide Results for the Plotting of Dendograms; a Dendogram Plotting Program Is Also Provided.
Lionheart Pr., Inc.

ClydeSENTRY. *Version:* 1.8. 1991. *Operating System(s) Required:* VMS & MicroVMS 4.6 & higher. *Language(s):* Basic. *Items Included:* Manuals, 1 year maintenance, quarterly newsletter. *Customer Support:* 6am-6pm, MST. MicroVAX, VAX (200k + 3k per on-line user). $2269.00-$30,371.00.
Provides Effective Protection of Data Against Internal or External Theft, Tampering or User Error. Includes: AUDIT, a Terminal/System Monitoring Module That Creates Terminal I/O Logs & Summary Reports of Security-Sensitive Activities; CONTRL, Allows User to Observe in Real Time What's Happening at Any Terminal & Intervene If Necessary; KBlock-Lets Users Lock Keyboards & Clear Screens with a Single Keystroke; DIALBACK, Protects Dial-in Lines from UnAuthorized Access; LOCK, Builds Menus to Restrict Access to Security-Sensitive Functions; RTMON, Allows Both CONTRL & AUDIT to Monitor DECnet RT Devices; FRAMER, Converts Log Files to Printable Formats.
Raxco, Inc.

ClydeSupport. *Version:* 1.7. 1991. *Items Included:* Manuals (system, reference & installation), 1 year maintenance, quarterly maintenance. *Customer Support:* 6am-6pm, MST.
MicroVMS, VMS 4.6 & higher. MicroVAX, VAX (220k). $798.00-$8869.00 depending on CPU.
Enables In-House Support Personnel to Create a Centralized Help Desk Providing Efficient Computer Support. This Package Allows Users to Interact with Users On-Line; Increase User Productivity Through Multiple Terminal Sessions; Provides Debugging Tools; System & Performance Monitoring; Replaying Recorded User Sessions; Support Dial-Up Sites. Includes: CNTRL, a Support Tool to Let an Expert Tutor Users in Any Application; WINDOW, Which Creates Multiple Sessions from a Single VT Terminal; CARBONCopy, Records All the Activity at a Terminal So Support Personnel Can Determine Exactly Where & When Software Problems Occur; CALOUT-Plus, Lets a User Access Remote Systems, Transfer All Types of Files, & Automate Communications Procedures.
Raxco, Inc.

CMA Dental for the Macintosh. *Compatible Hardware:* Apple Macintosh. *General Requirements:* Hard disk.
3.5" disk $1995.00.
Dental Office Management Program.
CMA Micro Computer.

CMA Medical for the Macintosh. *Compatible Hardware:* Apple Macintosh. *General Requirements:* Hard disk.
3.5" disk $1995.00.
Medical Office Management Program.
CMA Micro Computer.

CMINER. *Version:* 1.2. May 1985. *Compatible Hardware:* IBM PC, PC XT, PC AT & compatibles. *Operating System(s) Required:* MS-DOS, PC-DOS. *Language(s):* FORTRAN. *Memory Required:* 512k. *General Requirements:* Printer.
disk $2500.00 (Order no.: CMINER).
Static Cone Miner Program That Simplifies the Development of a Production Schedule for an Open Pit Mine. Uses a 3-D Block Model of an Ore Deposit That Has Had Pit Limits Imposed by a Pit Optimization Program. Computes the Reserves Within the Defined Cone & Updates the Topographic Model.
Geostat Systems International, Inc. (GSII).

Cmodem Telecommunications Program.
Operating System(s) Required: OS-9, UNIX, XENIX, SKDOS. (source code included). *Memory Required:* 64k.
disk $50.00.
disk with source $100.00.
Allows Communication with Most Systems Over Telecommunications Facilities. Supports Dumb-Terminal Mode, Upload & Download in Non-Protocol Mode, & Christensen Protocol.
Computer Systems Consultants.

CMOS.COM: CMOS Save - Restore - Compare.
Version: 1.11. Scott Hoopes. Aug. 1995. *Items Included:* Information file. *Customer Support:* Free upgrades for 1 year.
DOS 4.0 or higher. IBM PC & compatibles (200k). disk $5.00 (Order no.: CMOS1.11). *Networks supported:* Any (operation not dependent on network).
Saves CMOS Data & Restores It in the Event of a CMOS Battery Failure. Data Can Be Compared Regularly to Warn User of a Failing Battery. Even Saves/Restores Extended CMOS Data. Creates NO DATA Files. Fast, "Goof-Proof" Design Makes Restoring CMOS Data a Breeze.
S & J Software.

CMS/Advantage. *Version:* 3.703. May 1994. *Items Included:* Complete documentation including Installation, Tutorial, & Operations manuals. *Customer Support:* Free technical support for customers using current version, or two previous versions. Training available at Hertzler Systems Goshen, IN facilities, $300/day; or at customer's plant, $1000/day plus expenses. BBS offers 24-hour support/information.
Windows 3.1. IBM compatible PCs (4Mb). disk $1295.00 (Order no.: QWIN-000 (STAND-ALONE); QWIN-500 (NETWORK)). *Networks supported:* All PC networks.
Advanced Quality Management Software Package Offering Variable & Short Run SPC. Runs in Windows, but Allows Data Entry to Be Done in DOS As Well. This System Is Ideal for Local Area Network (LAN) Users Wishing to Share Quality Data on Processes Plantwide. Features Include: Real-Time Charting & Analysis; Non-Normal Distribution; Monitor the Network Screens; Pareto of Events (Out-of-Control Alarms, Change of Shift/Tool/Operator, etc.).
Hertzler Systems Inc.

CMT Personal Movie Database, 2 disks. *Compatible Hardware:* IBM PC, PC XT, PC AT. *Operating System(s) Required:* PC-DOS, MS-DOS. *Memory Required:* 256k. *General Requirements:* 2 disk drives or hard disk.
contact publisher for price.
The First Disk Contains the Program & the Second Disk Contains over 2000 Movies with Ratings. The Program Allows the User to Add, Modify, & Delete Movies with Fast Search & Find Capabilities. These Features Are Used for Selecting Movie Title, Category, Actor, Year, MPAA Rating, or Star (*) Ratings. The Program Also Allows a Look-Up for Taking Notes or Reviews for a Particular Movie (16k/Movie). Movie Lists Can Be Printed. The Data Base Does Not Contain Any X-Rated Material. Not Copy Protected.
Consolidated Micro Technology.

CNC. Walter Wheeler. 1985. *Compatible Hardware:* Gimex, IBM PC & compatibles. *Operating System(s) Required:* MS-DOS or PC-DOS, OS9. *Memory Required:* 64k. *General Requirements:* 2 disk drives. *Items Included:* Manual. *Customer Support:* Yes.
disk $795.00.
Job Estimating & Actual Cost Program for Computer Control of Manufacturing Operations. Allows Storage & Retrieval of Estimates by Customer & Part Number. Shows Bid Price per Piece to Be Delivered & Percentage Profit on the Job.
Trend Computer Systems.

CO-Graphics. *Compatible Hardware:* IBM PC, PC XT, PC AT, IBM 3270 PC, Portable PC. *Operating System(s) Required:* DOS 2.0, 2.1, 3.0. *Memory Required:* 256k. *General Requirements:* 2 360k disk drives or hard disk.
contact publisher for price.
Provides Micro Focus COBOL Programmers with Graphics Capabilities Previously Available Through Special Graphics Packages. By Means of This COBOL Interface, Applications Programmers Can Create Business Graphics on Microcomputers Directly from the Same COBOL Programs That Collect, Process, & Manage Business Data. Designed to Be Used with Micro Focus PROFESSIONAL COBOL or Micro Focus LEVEL II COBOL Version 2.6.
Micro Focus, Inc. (California).

CO-Math. *Compatible Hardware:* IBM PC & compatibles, PC XT, PC AT, 3270 PC. *Operating System(s) Required:* PC-DOS/MS-DOS 2.0, 2.1, 3.0. *Language(s):* COBOL. *Memory Required:* 256k. *General Requirements:* Micro Focus LEVEL II COBOL (v. 2.6 or later), Professional COBOL, VS COBOL Workbench, VS COBOL Packages.
disk $200.00.
Library of Math Functions Provides Application Developers with Extended Math Functions That Are Not Available in the Standard COBOL Language, Enabling Users to Perform Numerical Analysis of COBOL Data Records from Micro Focus COBOL without Requiring a Math-Oriented Language, Such As FORTRAN. Its Routines Provide Such Mathematic Operations As Logarithmic Scaling of Data, Exponentiation, Power, Square Root, Natural Log, Log(10), Sine, Cosine, Arcsine, & Arctangent XY.
Micro Focus, Inc. (California).

Coach's Corner. *Compatible Hardware:* Apple II with Applesoft. *Operating System(s) Required:* Apple DOS 3.2, 3.3. (source code included). *Memory Required:* 48k.
disk $29.95.
Offers 10 Levels of Play. Coach Rather Than Play Football.
Dynacomp, Inc.

COB-XS. *Compatible Hardware:* Cromemco Systems. *Operating System(s) Required:* UNIX. *Language(s):* COBOL. *Memory Required:* 2000k. $995.00.
COBOL Compiler, GSA High Level.
Cromemco, Inc.

COBOL. Microsoft, Inc. *Compatible Hardware:* HP 150 Touchscreen.
3.5" disk $750.00 (Order no.: 45448A).
Provides Part of a Complete Development Environment on the Touchscreen for Users Whose Applications Are Written in COBOL, & Would Prefer to Further Develop Their Applications in the Same Language & Methodology. The System Features a 2-Pass Compiler & Four Levels of Overlays, & Complies with the ANSI X3.23-1974 Standard at the Low Intermediate Level for All the Level-1 & Some Level-2 ANSI-74 Standard Features.
Hewlett-Packard Co.

COBOL. *Compatible Hardware:* IBM PC & compatibles. *Operating System(s) Required:* MS-DOS. *Memory Required:* 384k.
disk $900.00.
Includes 4 Utilities: Menu Handler, Cross-Reference Utility, Mouse-Input Module & an Interactive Symbolic Debugger.
Microsoft Pr.

COBOL Developer's Toolkit. *Compatible Hardware:* IBM RT PC. *Operating System(s) Required:* UNIX.
Set. $3750.00.
Includes 4 of MICRO FOCUS's Products: Compact Level II COBOL/ET, ANIMATOR, FORMS-2, & Upgrade III. Products Can Be Purchased Separately.
Micro Focus, Inc. (California).

COBOL-Plus. *Version:* 5.0. *Compatible Hardware:* DEC Professional 350. *Operating System(s) Required:* RT-11, TSX-Plus, RT-11XM. *Memory Required:* 32k.
contact publisher for price.
Features Extended Memory Support, Compatibility with Popular COBOL Syntax Extensions, & Compatibility with the Latest Version of RT-II Operating System.
S & H Computer Systems, Inc.

COBOL Source Analyst. *Version:* 2.0. Sep. 1993. *Items Included:* Manual, disk. *Customer Support:* Free telephone technical support, 30-day money-back guarantee.
PC-DOS/MS-DOS, OS/2; compatible w/ Windows 3.1. IBM PC & compatibles, 386 Plus (2Mb). $99.00 per license. *Addl. software required:* Editor of choice. *Optimal configuration:* Min. RAM required - 2Mb, disk storage required - 3Mb, IBM PC or compatible, DOS 3.1 Plus, 386 Plus or OS/2 (2.1 Plus).
CSA Offers a Fully Interactive & Intuitive Analysis Environment on the PC. Ideal for Use with COBOL Source Code Downloaded from a Mainframe. Features Outlining, Formatting, Colorization & Instant Syntax Check, All Without Compiling or Batch Steps. Compatible with All Popular COBOL Environments & Standards.
Command Technology Corp.

COBOL Source Analyst for SPF-PC. *Version:* 2.0. Mar. 1994. *Items Included:* Manual, disk. *Customer Support:* Free telephone technical support, 30-day money-back guarantee.
PC-DOS/MS-DOS, OS/2; compatible w/ Windows 3.1. IBM PC & compatibles, 386 Plus (2Mb). $99.00 per license. *Addl. software required:* SPF/PC V 3.0. *Optimal configuration:* Min. RAM required - 2Mb, disk storage required - 3Mb, IBM PC or compatible, DOS 3.1 Plus, 386 Plus or OS/2 (2.1 Plus).

CSA for SPF/PC Offers a Fully Interactive & Intuitive Analysis Environment from Within SPF/PC V. 3.0 Plus. Ideal for Use with COBOL Souce Code Downloaded from a Mainframe. Features Outlining, Formatting, Colorization & Instant Syntax Check, All Without Compiling. Compatible with All Popular COBOL Environments & Standards.
Command Technology Corp.

COBRA. Version: 1.2. Jul. 1991. Items Included: Full documentation for COBRA & documentation for custom report writer (WRL, Welcom Report Language), comes in 2 binders. Customer Support: Free telephone support 8 AM - 5 PM CST, maintenance free for first year, renewable for a fee each year; training & consulting available.
MS-DOS (640k). IBM PC, XT, AT or 100% compatible. $5000.00 single user PC version. Addl. software required: Foxbase Plus. Networks supported: 3Com, IBM token ring, Banyan, Novell.
Designed to Comply with Government Standards. It Is Compliant with C/SCSC Guidelines & Its Standard Reports Include DOD/DOE CPR & CSSR Reports, the NASA 533. All Screens & Reports Are User-Definable & COBRA Includes WRL (Welcom Report Language) to Assist the Customization.
Welcom Software Technology.

CoCoPro. Version: 1.1. Compatible Hardware: Apple Macintosh. Memory Required: 512k. Items Included: 1 disk, Project Cost-Estimating Program. Customer Support: Telephone.
3.5" disk $1495.00.
Software Costing Estimation Tool.
ICONIX Software Engineering, Inc.

CoCounsel III. Nov. 1988. Compatible Hardware: IBM PC, PC XT, PC AT & compatibles. Operating System(s) Required: PC-DOS, MS-DOS; Novell, 3Com or other compatible networks. Customer Support: 60 days toll-free.
$1495.00-$4995.00.
Full-Text Litigation Support System with a Database Document Management Option. The Program Gives Litigating Attorneys the Ability to Identify, Extract, Organize & Summarize the Pertinent Data Faster Than It Would Take If Conventional Methods Were Employed. Features Advanced Keyword Searching Capabilities Including the Unlimited Use of Wildcard, Boolean & Proximity Searches. To Summarize Documents, the User May Enter Annotations and/or Issue Codes Throughout the Document at Relevant Locations. When the Document Is Reviewed Later, the Annotations Will Appear in a Window on the Page Where They Were Entered, Allowing the User to View Both the Text of the Document & the Notes Concurrently; Hypertext-Like Cross-Referencing from One Document to Another Are Also Allowed. Database Includes Data Validation, One-to-Many Fields & a Report Writer.
CompuLaw, Ltd.

CODA. John Aitchison. Oct. 1986. Compatible Hardware: IBM.
$220.00 (ISBN 0-412-28950-4, Order no.: 1044).
Microcomputer Package for the Statistical Analysis of Compositional Data.
Routledge, Chapman & Hall, Inc.

CODECHECK. Version: 6.0. Compatible Hardware: Apple Macintosh; IBM PC & compatibles, PS/2; UNIX. Operating System(s) Required: MS-DOS 3.4 or higher; OS/2 Standard or Extended edition; System 6.0 or higher with Finder or MultiFinder. Memory Required: DOS 512k, Macintosh 1Mb, OS/2 2000k. Customer Support: Free for first year.
DOS or MAC, $495.00; OS/2 NT, $995.00; UNIX, $1995.00 single seat server license.
Designed to Target Code for Portability Between DOS, OS/2, UNIX, VMS, & the Macintosh Environments. Analyzes Source Code for Portability, Maintainability, & Style, Without Requiring the Programmer to Own More than One Operating-System Based Machine. The Expert System Allows Users to Modify Its Rules, Allowing Them to Tailor It for Just One Platform That Users Want to Port to, or to Conform to Corporate or Individual Standards. Users Can also Alter the Program to Work in a Foreign Language.
Abraxas Software, Inc.

Codegen: DSP Filter Code Generator. Items Included: Bound manual. Customer Support: Free hotline - no time limit; 30 day limited warranty; updates are $5/disk plus S&H.
MS-DOS 3.0 or higher. IBM & compatibles (640k). disk $89.95. Nonstandard peripherals required: Math coprocessor & mouse are supported, but not necessary. Requires CGA, MCGA, EGA, VGA, Hercules, IBM 8514, AT&T 440, PC 3270 or compatible graphics capability.
Digital Signal Processing Filter Source Code Generator Applicable to All DSP Microprocessors. Contains a Macro-Preprocessor & Template. Create Code Output for Different Applications, Different DSP Microprocessor Boards, & Even Different DSP Microprocessors.
Dynacomp, Inc.

CodeProbe Debugger for RPG. Aug. 1993. Items Included: User manual (1 book). Customer Support: Bulletin Board Support; 30-day free technical support - subsequent support is available through a 900 number. FAX number available also.
MS-DOS 5.0 or higher, 350k disk storage (2Mb). disk $350.00. Addl. software required: Lattice RPG II Development System 4.02 or higher.
Interactive Source-Level Debugger for Lattice RPG on the PC, Allowing User to Closely Examine the Behavior of a Program Written in the RPG Language. Complete Set of Controls Lets User Track Program Logic & Observe Data Values As the Program Executes. Provides RPG Programmers with the Same Debugging Power Found in Other PC Languages, Such as C & Pascal. With CPR, User Can Quickly Single-Step Through RPG Programs; Step over or into Sub-Routines; Set Breakpoints & Watch Breakpoints; Examine & Change Variable Values or Array Elements; View & Manipulate Indicators; List Field Types; Establish Watch Lists for Continuously Monitoring Variables or Array Elements; View Code in RPG or Assembly Format; & Easily Stop & Restart Program Execution.
Lattice, Inc.

CodeView. Version: 2.2. Mar. 1988. Compatible Hardware: IBM PC, PC XT, PC AT & compatibles, PS/2, 80386. Memory Required: 200k, in windows 150k.
$150.00 MASM 5.1.
$450.00 C & FORTRAN 4.1.
$300.00 Pascal 4.0.
$295.00 BASIC.
Stand-Alone Source-Code & Symbolic Debugger. Reads Microsoft .OBJ File Formats. Compatible Languages Are MS FORTRAN, COBOL, C 4.0 & Higher, QuickBASIC 4.0, QuickBASIC 6.0 & Higher & Pascal 4.0 & Higher. Supports 8088, 8080, 80186, 80286, 80386, 8087 & 80287 Instruction Sets, Multiple Monitors, 43-Line Mode, 50-Line Mode & Microsoft Overlay Linker 3.36 or Higher. Features Full Screen & Command Line Interfaces; Code, Data & Register Values Windows Displays; & Watchpoint & Truepoint Breakpoint Types. Also Includes Continuous Execution, Source Single Step, Step over Function Call, Assembly Instruction Trace, Script Capabilities, 80386 Debug Register Support, On-Line Help, Debugs Threads & Dynalinks under OS/2 & Supports All Math Types.
Microsoft Pr.

CodeWatch. Version: 5.2 UNIX V.3 & V.4, 386/486. Sep. 1988. Compatible Hardware: 80386/80486, Sparc. Operating System(s) Required: Unix. Memory Required: 1000k. incl. with compilers.
Window-Based Interactive Source-Level Debugger That Comes with Liant's Compilers. Works on Actual Liant Source Code Without Using an Interpreted Intermediate Language. Programmers Interact in the Conventions & Symbols of the Source Language Not the Machine Language. The Window Interface Displays the User's Source Program & Program Output Simultaneously While Allowing the User to Enter Commands. The Graphical-Based Interface Uses All the Capabilities of the Powerful Motif User Interface & X-Windows.
Liant Software Corp.

CodeWriter. Dynatech Microsoftware, Inc. Compatible Hardware: TI Professional; with printer, monitor, 2 disk drives. Operating System(s) Required: MS-DOS. Memory Required: 64k.
$249.00.
Program Design System for Non-Programmers.
Texas Instruments, Personal Productivit.

Cognitive Disorders I: Category Naming & Completion. Fred Weiner. Jan. 1987. Compatible Hardware: Apple II+, IIe, IIc, IIgs; IBM PC. Memory Required: 48k.
disk $99.50 (ISBN 0-942763-02-5).
User Will First Determine Category of a Short List of Words & Then Add a Word to the List.
Parrot Software.

The Cognitive Rehabilitation Series: Categorization, Sequencing, Association, Memory, Authoring Program, 5 disks. Version: 8-15-86. Jan. 1984. Compatible Hardware: Apple II+, IIe, IIc; IBM PC, PCjr. Operating System(s) Required: Apple DOS 3.3, MS-DOS. Language(s): BASIC. Memory Required: Apple 48k, IBM 128k.
Set. $595.00, incl. documentation & library storage binder.
Designed to Address the Variety of Organizational Deficits Which Typically Result from Traumatic Brain Injury & Other Neurological Impairments.
Hartley Courseware, Inc.

Cognitive Retraining with Print Shop Pictures, 1 3-1/2" or 2 5-1/4" disks. Fred Weiner. Apr. 1987. Compatible Hardware: Apple IIe, IIc, IIgs; IBM PC. Memory Required: 48k.
$99.50 (ISBN 0-942763-01-7).
Allows Users to Create Multiple Choice Lessons in Which They Choose Between Three Descriptions of a Print Shop Picture or Two Print Shop Pictures.
Parrot Software.

COGO PC Plus: Coordinate Geometry Program. Version: 3.10. Mar. 1993. Compatible Hardware: IBM PC, PC XT, PC AT & true compatibles. Operating System(s) Required: MS-DOS, PC-DOS. Language(s): Fortran. Memory Required: 640k. General Requirements: Hard disk, printer. Items Included: Manual, 120-day free maintenance. Customer Support: 1 year maintenance for $200.
$795.00.

Design Program for Surveying & Mapping. Coordinate Geometry System That Is Capable of Processing Field Data & Producing Final Maps. Solves Geometric Problems in Mapping, Highway & Roadway Design, Subdivision Design, Parcel & Tract Maps & Utility Alignments. Both Batch & Interactive Processing Capabilities Are Available. Interfaces to Most Popular Micro-Based CAD Programs.
Research Engineers.

CogoMaster II. *Compatible Hardware:* Apple Macintosh 512k, SE, Mac II. *General Requirements:* Hard disk or 800k disc.
3.5" disk $75.00.
Surveying Program.
Guenzi Surveys.

CogoMate. *Version:* 2.8. Jamie E. Sletten et al. May 1989. *Items Included:* Manual with tutorial. *Customer Support:* 120 days free phone support; 90 day moneyback guarantee.
MS-DOS 2.1 or higher (640k); Windows 3.0 or higher. IBM PC & compatibles. disk $249.00, incl. manual (ISBN 0-932071-07-4).
Nonstandard peripherals required: 1 floppy & 1 hard drive. *Addl. software required:* AutoCAD Release 9 or higher; or AutoCAD for Windows.
A Coordinate Data File Interface Program to AutoCAD Releases 9 or Higher. Provides a Menu-Driven Drawing Assistant Which Uses Coordinate Data to Construct Drawings. Supports Many Third Party COGO Data File Formats.
Simplicity Systems, Inc.

Coin Collection & Inventory Valuation System. *Compatible Hardware:* TRS-80 Model I, Model II, Model III. *Language(s):* BASIC (source code included). *Memory Required:* TRS-80 Model I, III 32k, TRS-80 Model II 64k.
TRS-80 Model I. disk $39.95.
TRS-80 Model II. disk $49.95.
TRS-80 Model III. disk $44.95.
Maintains a Direct Access File of Coins in a Coin Collection (or Business Inventory). Includes Full Updating Capabilities.
Computer Guidance & Support.

Coin Collector. E. Neiburger. 1982. *Compatible Hardware:* Apple II, II+, IIe, IIc; Basis 6502; Franklin Ace; IBM PC, PC XT, PC AT & compatibles. *Operating System(s) Required:* Apple DOS 3.3, PC DOS 3.1. *Language(s):* BASIC (source code included). *Memory Required:* Apple 48k, IBM 256k. *General Requirements:* Printer.
disk $49.00 (ISBN 0-914555-03-0).
6 Collection Information Programs for Numismatists. Includes: Foreign Coin List, Domestic Coin List, Meetings List, Sources List, Data Base & File Transfer.
Andent, Inc.

Coin Critters. *Version:* 2.1. Aug. 1993. *Items Included:* Manual & 1 disk.
System 6.0.7 or higher. Macintosh Plus or higher (1Mb). 3.5" disk $57.95 (ISBN 0-940081-67-9).
Windows 3.1. 386 or higher. 3.5" disk $57.95 (ISBN 0-940081-74-1). *Nonstandard peripherals required:* Mouse, SVGA, sound card.
Macintosh & Windows. CD-ROM disk $57.95 (ISBN 1-57374-014-4).
Helps Children Discover What Coins Are All About. Begins by Teaching Children to Identify Heads & Tails of U.S. Coins. Lesson Objectives Include Recognizing the Face Value of Coins, Purchasing, & Counting Back Change. Children Will Love the Color, Sound, & Animation As They Enrich Their Understanding of Money.
Nordic Software, Inc.

Coindata & Stampdata. *Items Included:* Bound manual. *Customer Support:* Free hotline - no time limit; 30 day limited warranty; updates are $5/disk plus S&H.
MS-DOS. IBM & compatibles (256k). $69.95 set; $39.95 ea.
High-Speed Compiled BASIC (Source Included) Programs Which Use Random-Access Files to Compactly Store & Quickly Retrieve Stamp & Coin Collection Information.
Dynacomp, Inc.

COINS. *Items Included:* Bound manual. *Customer Support:* Free hotline - no time limit; 30 day limited warranty; updates are $25/disk plus S&H.
MS-DOS. IBM & compatibles (256k). disk $49.95. *Nonstandard peripherals required:* Two drives & an 80-column (or wider) printer.
Apple. disk $49.95.
Short for COmputerized Inventory of Numismatic Stock. It Is Written by Marvin C. Mallon, a Noted Columnist for Coin World Magazine. Enables the Serious Numismatist to Catalog an Entire Collection & Obtain Several Reports That Serve for Personal Investment Information. The Principal Feature Is Its Built-In Standard Coin File. Sixteen-Hundred Common U.S. Coin Descriptions, along with the Latest Market Value for Most Grades, Are Included. The Data File Includes: All Small Cents since 1856; All Nickel Five-Cent Pieces since 1883; All Dimes since 1892; All Quarters since 1892; All Half-Dollars since 1839; All Dollars since 1878.
Dynacomp, Inc.

Coins/Plus. M. Mallon. 1983. *Language(s):* DBaseII Plus. *General Requirements:* Printer. *Items Included:* Database with prices of U.S. coins, user's guide. *Customer Support:* Free tech. support.
ProDOS (128k). Apple IIgs, II+, IIe. $95.00 (ISBN 0-923027-03-3).
PC-DOS (384k). $95.00 (ISBN 0-923027-00-9).
MS-DOS (384k). $95.00 (ISBN 0-923027-01-7).
TRS-80 (384k). $95.00 (ISBN 0-923027-02-5).
Enables the Coin Collector to Catalog an Entire Collection & Obtain Various Reports That Serve for Personal Investment Information. Data File with the Latest Prices for 2300 U.S. Coins Across Most Grades Is Included, with Annual Updates Available.
Compu-Quote.

Colbert's Medico. Roman Colbert Ph. D. Aug. 1991. *Items Included:* A printed book of 322 pages; audio cassette, 5.25 or 3.5 disks, instruction sheets. *Customer Support:* Ninety days warranty limited to the material on the magnetic disk(s) only & does not apply to the overall software program supplied "as is".
DOS 3,3 or higher. IBM or compatible (512k). 1 program $495.00 not network supported for several programs or network support, write for information (ISBN 0-9630253-0-9). *Optimal configuration:* IBM or compatible, DOS 3.3 or higher. *Networks supported:* Two versions; 1) Not Network supported, 2) Network support for single user at a time.
Designed As a Reference Tool to Enable to Communicate Immediately with the Spanish-Speaking Patients. Rather Than Provide Just Medical Terms & Definitions. Bridges the Communication Gap by Promoting Free Flowing Conversational Interviews... Thus Leading to Better Understanding. English- Spanish & Spanish-English Dictionaries Are Included.
Colbert's Medico.

La Coleccion. *Customer Support:* All of our products are unconditionally guaranteed.
DOS, Windows, UNIX. CD-ROM disk $39.95 (Order no.: LA COLECCION). *Nonstandard peripherals required:* CD-ROM drive.
5,000 DOS, Windows, & OS/2 Programs in English & Spanish.
Walnut Creek CDRom.

Collage Complete. *Version:* 1.1. Jun. 1993. *Items Included:* 2 manuals. *Customer Support:* No charge business hours support via normal toll line.
DOS, Windows. IBM compatible PC running MS Windows V3.1 or higher (4Mb). disk $199.00. *Optimal configuration:* 4 Mb or higher (386 Enhanced Mode is recommended). *Networks supported:* All major.
One-Product Solution for High Quality Screen Capture & Image Management in Windows & DOS. Capture Windows Screen to File, Clipboard, or Printer. Easily Print, Scan, Convert, Crop, Annotate, Size, Flip, Rotate, Invert, & Combine Images. Build Thumbnail Catalogs for Image Browsing & Batch Operations. See Why Many Major Publishing Houses Standardize on Collage.
Inner Media, Inc.

Collage PM. *Version:* 1.01. Feb. 1990. *Items Included:* User's manual. *Customer Support:* No charge business hours support via normal toll line.
OS/2 version 1.2 or higher. IBM AT or compatible. $199.00. *Optimal configuration:* 4Mb or higher. *Networks supported:* All major.
Screen Capture, Image Handling, & Format Conversion Program for the OS/2 PM Environment. Supports PCX, TIFF, BMP, Metafile & Clipboard Formats in Color, B/W, Dithered Grayscale, & TRUE Gray. Provides Image Cropping, Printing, & Ability to Easily Locate/View Images.
Inner Media, Inc.

Collect-a-Debt. *Version:* 2.1. Aug. 1994. *Items Included:* Manual, Reg. card, 1 5 1/4" disk, 1 3 1/2" disk. *Customer Support:* Tech. support 801-565-8753.
DOS, Windows 3.1, Windows 95. IBM PC & compatibles (512k RAM). disk $99.00 (Order no.: CD10SB).
Software Program That Will Automate the Entire Debt-Collections Process. Designed Primarily for the Small- or Home-Office, Collect-a-Debt Will Automatically Generate Collection Letters for Those Customers Whose Accounts Are Overdue. Includes Automated Debtor Tracking, Payment History, Automated Tickler System, Rapid Debtor Search, & Much More. Now You Can Collect the Money They Owe You, Automatically.
GTM Software.

Collectibles Manager. 1996.
100% on screen prompts; 100% menu driven. disk $99.00.
Collectibles Manager is the perfect program to catalog & manage all your collectibles; expensive or inexpensive, large or small, antique or modern, sensible or silly. Easy to install & learn, efficient, affordable, & effective.
RIGHT ON PROGRAMS.

Collection Ledger Accounting System. *Version:* 2.1. 1986. *Items Included:* Complete manual & installation insstructions. *Customer Support:* 90-day unlimited warranty, yearly software update & service agreement $120.
MS/PC-DOS 2.1 & up (384k). IBM PC, PC XT, PC AT & compatibles. disk $695.00. *Nonstandard peripherals required:* Dual floppy drive. *Optimal configuration:* PC AT, matrix printer.
Software That Allows Law Firm, Collection Agency or Collections Department to Account for Collections Made. In Addition, Software Also Interfaces with Most Widely-Used Word Processing Programs to Automatically Produce Standard Collection Letters.
Data Law.

Collection Management System: ColMan System. Version: 7.1. Aug. 1991. Items Included: Step-by-Step instruction manual. Customer Support: Free support by phone, FAX, correspondence, or modem. On-site training and/or installation, $229.00 per day plus expenses. MS/PC DOS 3.0 or higher. PC, 286, 386, 486; Tandy 3000 or higher (640k). disk $995.00 (Order no.: 1201). Nonstandard peripherals required: Interface to Touch-Tone requires our voice digitization board. Programs without Touch-Tone interface do not require nonstandard peripherals, boards. Optimal configuration: 386SX computer with a fast hard disk & our telephone interface board. Networks supported: Novell.
Check-Out of Materials, Check-In, Quickly & Easily from Labels Printed by the System. Prints "Who Has What," Where to Find It, & Numerous Other Reports. Customized for Each Application.
Robert H. Geeslin (Educational Programming).

Collection-Master: Legal Collection-Master. Version: 4.0. May 1992. Compatible Hardware: IBM PC AT & compatibles. Operating System(s) Required: PC-DOS/MS-DOS, UNIX, XENIX; Netware, Netbios networks. Language(s): BASIC & C (source code included). Memory Required: 420k. General Requirements: Wide carriage printer, hard disk. Customer Support: Toll free 9AM-8PM ET, free for first year.
From $8900.00.
Integrated Word Processing & Data Base Management System for Law Offices Specializing in Collections, Collection Agencies & Credit & Collection Departments.
Commercial Legal Software, Inc.

Collection One: Collections for Dental & Medical Offices. 1995. Items Included: Full manual. Customer Support: Free telephone support - 90 days, 30-day warranty.
MS-DOS 3.2 or higher. 286 (584k). $29.95-$289.95. Nonstandard peripherals required: CGA/EGA/VGA.
An Add-On Module for Use with the DENTAL ONE & MEDICAL ONE Office Management Systems. Along with Many Other Features, It Will: Print a Summary Master Aging Report That Gives a Short, Two-Page Report Listing Your Total Receivables by Aging Category. Selectively Print, in Various Sequences, Your Receivables Reports by Aging Category & More.
Dynacomp, Inc.

Collection Resource System. Version: 3.02. Compatible Hardware: IBM PC, PC AT; NCR Tower; Tandy 6000; UNISYS (Sperry) 5000. Operating System(s) Required: XENIX, UNIX System V. Memory Required: 1024k. General Requirements: Hard disk, printer. Items Included: Turnkey systems.
contact publisher for price.
Designed to Automate All Phases of the Collection Process of Past Due Accounts, & to Be Used by Collection Agencies & by the In-House Collection Departments of Larger Corporations.
CR Software, Inc.

Collections Manager. Version: 1.1. Jun. 1986. Compatible Hardware: IBM PC & 100% compatibles. Operating System(s) Required: MS-DOS. Language(s): C. Memory Required: 640k. General Requirements: Hard disk drive. Customer Support: Unlimited telephone support, regulatory compliance, product enhancement, newsletters.
$3000.00-$15,000.00 plus options.
PC-Based System Designed to Process Domestic Collection Letters in a Bank. Examples of Domestic Collections Would Be Coupons, Bonds, Drafts, & NSF Checks. Benefits of the System Are Reduced Labor Requirements, Lowered Forms Cost, More Consistent Follow-Up & a Way to Track & Identify Waived Fees.
Learned-Mahn.

Collections Plus. Version: 2.5. Apr. 1994. Items Included: Booklet "Increasing Cash from Delinquent Accounts", Paid in full stamp, manual, 1 3 1/2" diskette, reg. cards. Customer Support: Tech. support 801-565-8753.
IBM PC (512k). disk $399.95 (Order no.: CP10S3). Networks supported: Yes.
Software Program That Will Automate the Entire Debt-Collections Process. With Collections Plus You Can Import Debtor Data Directly from Existing Accounting Systems & Immediately Begin Printing Standard or Custom Collections Letters. Includes Automated Debtor Tracking, Payment History, Automated Tickler System, Rapid Debtor Search, & Much More. Use Collections Plus with Your Own Word Processor, or Use the Text Editor Included.
GTM Software.

Collector Connector: Data Collector Communications for Your PC. Version: 2.01. Shirl A. Vonasek. May 1991. Items Included: Manual. Customer Support: 120 days free phone support; 1 yr unlimited (on all Simplicity Software), $249.00; 90 day moneyback guarantee.
PC-DOS/MS-DOS 3.0 or higher. IBM PC, XT, AT, PS/2 & compatibles (512k). disk $199.00, incl. manual (ISBN 0-932071-10-4). Optimal configuration: 1 hard drive, 640k RAM, mouse.
A Low-Cost PC to Data Collector Communications Program. Provides Quick, Convenient Data Transfer to & from Portable Data Collectors Through Your Computer's Serial Port. Formats Down-Loaded Data Directly for use with Simplicity's SURVEY 4.0 Coordinate Geometry Program As Well As Several Third-Party COGO Programs. Easy-to-Use, Menu-Driven Format.
Simplicity Systems, Inc.

COLLECTOR PLUS. Version: 7.1. Jul. 1991. Items Included: Full 3 ring binder manual with room for updates. Help screens behind all input stages. Customer Support: on site-training; maintenance service gives unlimited telephone support & all New enhancements throughout the year. Maintenance agreement available at 15% of total system.
MS-DOS 5.0 plus (2Mb). Hard disk required, IBM AT/XT, PS/2 & compatibles; System 36, 38 & AS400MS- $3500.00 single-user; $6900.00 local area network; $16,500.00 wide area network. Addl. software required: LOANLEDGER plus, Dot matrix printer, 132 column wide carriage. Networks supported: Novelle, 3-Com, IBM-PC NET.
Gives LOANLEDGER Plus the Ability to Simplify & Expedite Loan Collections. Auto-Dialer Feature Improves Productivity. Tickler Reports Monitor the Number of Calls & Length & Result of Calls, etc. Unlimited Notepad Captures Comments, Promises & Legal Notes. Additional Bank of 40 User Defined Letters. On Line Inquiry Showing Complete Payment History, User Defined Fields, Last Promise to Pay & Last Letter Sent, Queing.
Dynamic Interface Systems Corp.

Collector's Bookcase. May 1989. Items Included: 2.0.
IBM PC & compatibles (512k). disk $29.95.
Macintosh (512k). 3.5" disk $29.95.
Personal Library Software.
Future Visions Software.

Collector's Paradise. Compatible Hardware: IBM. (source code included). Memory Required: 128k. disk $29.95.
3 Collectors Inventory Programs: Coin Collection, Stamp Collection, Rare Collectibles.
Dynacomp, Inc.

College Accounting - Practice Sets. 1986. Memory Required: 64k; 256k. General Requirements: 80-column card is required to run these on Apple IIe.
Apple II Series; IIgs, Pt. 1. contact publisher for price (ISBN 0-538-51031-5, Order no.: Q30032).
PC-DOS/MS-DOS, Pt. 1. contact publisher for price (ISBN 0-538-51032-3, Order no.: Q30033).
Apple II Series; IIgs, Pt. 2. contact publisher for price (ISBN 0-538-51033-1, Order no.: Q30034).
PC-DOS/MS-DOS, Pt. 2. contact publisher for price (ISBN 0-538-51034-X, Order no.: Q30035).
Apple II Series; IIgs, Pt. 3. contact publisher for price (ISBN 0-538-51035-8, Order no.: Q30036).
PC-DOS/MS-DOS, Pt. 3. contact publisher for price (ISBN 0-538-51036-6, Order no.: Q30037).
Apple II Series; IIgs, Pt. 4. contact publisher for price (ISBN 0-538-51037-4, Order no.: Q30038).
PC-DOS/MS-DOS, Pt. 4. contact publisher for price (ISBN 0-538-51038-2, Order no.: Q30039).
Pt. 1 - Creative Designs: Automated Accounting for the Microcomputer; Pt. 2 - Bi-Lo Appliances: Automated Accounting for the Microcomputer; Pt. 3 - Two-Wheelers: Automated Accounting for the Microcomputer; Pt. 4 - Liberty Electronics In a Computerized Job Order Simulation.
South-Western Publishing Co.

College & Retirement Planning. Version: 3.0. Eugene J. Aubert & Matt Stephens. Aug. 1991. Items Included: 5.25" disk or 3.5" disk plus 21 page manual on disk. Customer Support: Provided on limited basis over telephone.
PC DOS 2.0 or higher. IBM PC, XT, AT or compatible (256k). disk $10.00 (ISBN 0-929416-04-X). Addl. software required: Lotus 1-2-3 or compatible. Optimal configuration: 1 floppy drive & 1 hard drive.
Five Programs, Three Examples Plus Manual. Runs with LOTUS 1-2-3, Includes One to Assist with College Financial Planning - Looking at College As a Financial Investment, College Costs & Financial Aide, & Predicting College Costs & Savings Required. Three Alternative Programs to Assist with Retirement Planning - Estimating Retirement Budget & Income & Savings Required for a Satisfying Retirement Lifestyle.
Advanced Financial Planning Group, Inc.

College Cost Explorer Fund Finder, 1993. Version: MS-DOS. Nov. 1993. Items Included: User manual. Customer Support: (212) 529-1840.
MS-DOS. MS-DOS/IBM compatibles (512k). disk $495.00 (ISBN 0-87447-462-0, Order no.: 004620). Optimal configuration: 512k RAM PC-DOS 2.1 or higher; MS-DOS 3.2 or higher required; hard drive required. Networks supported: Network & site.
Users Can Locate Public & Private Scholarships, Fellowships, & Loans for Undergraduate & Graduate Study on the Basis of Such Individual Characteristics As Academic & Career Interests, Ethnic & Minority Background, Military Service, & More. The Program Provides Customized Lists from a Data Base of Thousands of Private Sources of Scholarships & Loans; Current Costs & Financial Aid at 2,800 Two- & Four-Year Institutions; Interactive Electronic Worksheets for Dependent & Independent Students to Calculate Expected Family Contribution; & More. Also: Loan Calculator for the Repayment of Government & Other Loans; Data Entry Screens for Adding Scholarships of Local Interest; Bulletin Board Screen for Posting Notices on Financial Aid Workshops, Application Deadlines, etc.
The College Board.

TITLE INDEX

College Explorer Plus, 1993. *Version:* MS-DOS. Oct. 1993. *Items Included:* User manual. *Customer Support:* Hotline (212) 529-1840.
MS-DOS. MS-DOS/IBM compatibles (256k). disk $295.00 (ISBN 0-87447-496-5, Order no.: 004965). *Optimal configuration:* 256k RAM PC DOS 2.1 or higher; MS-DOS 3.2 or higher required; hard drive required. *Networks supported:* Network & site.
This Unique, Comprehensive Search Program Provides Current Facts on 2,800 Undergraduate Colleges; 1,200 Graduate & Professional Schools; & 10 Professional Degree Programs Including Law, Medicine, & Dentistry. The Undergraduate Data Base of Two- & Four-Year Colleges May Be Searched Using over 800 Options, Including CLEP Policies & 580 Majors, Get Facts on 1,200 Accredited Graduate & Professional Degree Programs, & Find Requirements & Special Services for Foreign Students at Each Institution.
The College Board.

College Explorer: 1994. 1993. *Items Included:* User's manual worksheets. *Customer Support:* Hotline (212) 529-1840.
Apple II family (128k). disk $125.00 ea.
5.25" & 3.5" disk (ISBN 0-87447-464-7, Order no.: 004647).
3.5" disk
MS-DOS 2.1 or higher (256k). disk $125.00 ea.
5.25" & 3.5" disk (ISBN 0-87447-463-9, Order no.: 004639).
3.5" disk
Lets Students Search Through 2,800 Two- & Four-Year Colleges to Find the Ones Best for Them. The Program Has Complete, Onscreen Information about Any College in the Data Base. Special Features Include the Ability to Sort Customized College Lists & It Tells Why a Specific College Is Not Included in the Search Results.
The College Board.

College Funding. *Version:* 1.0. Floyd Henderson. Mar. 1985. *Compatible Hardware:* Atari 400, 800, 1200, 800XL; Commodore 64; IBM PC, PC AT & compatibles. *Language(s):* BASIC (source code included). *Memory Required:* 48k.
disk $29.95 ea.
Commodore. (ISBN 0-917263-07-3).
(ISBN 0-917263-06-5).
Atari. (ISBN 0-917263-08-1).
Calculates College Funding Requirements for All Children in the Family. Calculates Yearly Savings or Lump Sum Required to Fund All College Expenses.
Advanced Financial Planning.

College League Option Module. *Items Included:* Manual, catalog, update card. *Customer Support:* Always free over the phone, disks replaced free for first 30 days, disks replaced for $10.00 after 30 days.
MS-DOS. IBM PC & Compatibles (512k). $14.95.
Commodore 64, 128. $14.95.
Commodore Amiga 500, 1000, 2000 (512k). $14.95.
Lead One of the Top 64 College Teams in the Nation Through the Annual Championship Tournaments. Comes Complete with Actual Players & Stats. One or Two People Can Play.
SportTime Computer Software.

The College Majors Search System. *Version:* 1993. Dec. 1993. *Customer Support:* Free telephone support.
PC-DOS/MS-DOS 2.0 or higher. IBM PC & compatibles (640K). disk $250.00.
Nonstandard peripherals required: hard drive.
Enables High School Seniors to Match Their Academic & Career Interests with Distinctive College Departments Throughout the Country. The Datafile Covers Statistical Information for Some 900 Colleges with Descriptions of More Than 8000 Distinctive Major Departments. It Allows Students to Choose Colleges Based on Their Strengths in Specific Majors.
Custom Databanks, Inc.

College Money Finder Program: Financial Aid Software. *Version:* 4.0. Sep. 1994. *Items Included:* Software users guide, College Money Finder Student's Guide. *Customer Support:* Free phone support to subscribers.
PC-DOS. IBM & compatibles with hard drive (12Mb min). Initial subscriber-HS & Undergrad Database $300.00 yr. for min. 2 updates per year (ISBN 1-884002-02-1). *Optimal configuration:* 2.0 DOS or higher; 256k RAM min. *Networks supported:* Compatible with all multi-user systems.
PC-DOS. IBM & compatibles with hard drive (12Mb min). Initial subscriber-HS & Undergrad & Grad Databases $375.00 yr. for min. 2 updates per year (ISBN 1-884002-03-X). *Optimal configuration:* 2.0 DOS or higher; 256k RAM min. *Networks supported:* Compatible with all multi-user systems.
PC-DOS. IBM & compatibles with hard drive (12Mb min). Initial subscriber-Undergratuate & Graduate Databases $375.00 yr. for min. 2 updates per year (ISBN 1-884002-04-8). *Optimal configuration:* 2.0 DOS or higher; 256k RAM min. *Networks supported:* Compatible with all multi-user systems.
PC-DOS. IBM & compatibles with hard drive (12Mb min). Initial subscriber-Undergrad Database $300.00 yr. for min. 2 updates per year (ISBN 1-884002-00-5). *Optimal configuration:* 2.0 DOS or higher; 256k RAM min. *Networks supported:* Compatible with all multi-user systems.
PC-DOS. IBM & compatibles with hard drive (12Mb min). Initial subscriber-Graduate Database $300.00 yr. for min. 2 updates per year (ISBN 1-884002-01-3). *Optimal configuration:* 2.0 DOS or higher; 256k RAM min. *Networks supported:* Compatible with all multi-user systems.
Self-Contained Software Allows Students to Get On-the-Spot Financial Aid Reports. Student Can Enter Personal Information Directly into Computer, or Use a Written Form Which is Batch-Entered by 1 Person. Students Can Also Scan the Databases & Select Any Listing to Print. User Subscribes to HS, Undergrad, Graduate Databases with Updates from 2 Times to 9 Times per Year.

College Money Finder Program: Financial Aid Software. *Version:* 4.0. Sep. 1994. *Items Included:* Software users guide, College Money Finder Student's Guide. *Customer Support:* Free phone support to subscribers.
Macintosh. Macintosh with hard drive (12Mb min). Initial subscriber-HS & Undergraduate Databases $300.00 yr. for min. 2 updates per year (ISBN 1-884002-05-6). *Optimal configuration:* 1Mb RAM, System 4.2 or higher, Finder 6.0. *Networks supported:* Compatible with all multi-user systems.
Macintosh. Macintosh with hard drive (12Mb min). Initial subscriber-HS & Undergrad & Graduate Databases $375.00 yr. for min. 2 updates per year (ISBN 1-884002-06-4). *Optimal configuration:* 1Mb RAM, System 4.2 or higher, Finder 6.0. *Networks supported:* Compatible with all multi-user systems.
Macintosh. Macintosh with hard drive (12Mb min). Initial subscriber-Undergrad & Graduate Databases $375.00 yr. for min. 2 updates per year (ISBN 1-884002-07-2). *Optimal configuration:* 1Mb RAM, System 4.2 or higher, Finder 6.0. *Networks supported:* Compatible with all multi-user systems.
Macintosh. Macintosh with hard drive (12Mb min). Initial subscriber-Undergrad Databases $300.00 yr. for min. 2 updates per year (ISBN 1-884002-08-0). *Optimal configuration:* 1Mb RAM, System 4.2 or higher, Finder 6.0. *Networks supported:* Compatible with all multi-user systems.
Macintosh. Macintosh with hard drive (12Mb min). Initial subscriber-Graduate Databases $300.00 yr. for min. 2 updates per year (ISBN 1-884002-09-9). *Optimal configuration:* 1Mb RAM, System 4.2 or higher, Finder 6.0. *Networks supported:* Compatible with all multi-user systems.
Self-Contained Software Allows Students to Get On-the-Spot Financial Aid Reports. Student Can Enter Personal Information Directly into Computer, or Use a Written Form Which is Batch-Entered by 1 Person. Students Can Also Scan the Databases & Select Any Listing to Print. User Subscribes to HS, Undergrad, Graduate Databases with Updates from 2 Times to 9 Times per Year.

College Money Finder Program: Financial Aid Software. *Items Included:* Profile forms, master codes, 32 page user manual. *Customer Support:* Unlimited with annual subscription.
Contact publisher for price.
Financial Aid Finders.

College Planner. Apr. 1990. *Items Included:* User's manual. *Customer Support:* (212) 529-1840.
Apple II. disk $35.00 ea.
5.25" & 3.5" disk (ISBN 0-87447-368-3, Order no.: 003683).
3.5" disk (ISBN 0-87447-368-3, Order no.: 003683).
MS-DOS 2.1 or higher. IBM PC, XT, AT, PS/2 & compatibles (256k). disk $35.00 ea.
5.25" & 3.5" disk (ISBN 0-87447-370-5, Order no.: 003705).
3.5" disk (ISBN 0-87447-370-5, Order no.: 003705).
Helps High School Students Manage College Admissions Tasks Independently. Its Electronic Calendar Allows Users to Plan an Overall Schedule Including Dates for Personal & School Events, As Well As Dates Directly Related to College Admissions. Students Can Create a Personalized Data Base of College Information & Print Out Letters Requesting Application Materials &/or College Interviews.
The College Board.

College Season Disk 1990. *Items Included:* Manual, catalog, update card. *Customer Support:* Always free over the phone, disks replaced free for first 30 days, disks replaced for $10.00 after 30 days.
Amiga 500, 1000, 2000 (512k). $14.95.
Data Disk with Actual Players & Stats from the 1990 College Basketball Season. The College League Module Is Required to Play.
SportTime Computer Software.

Collier's Topform: Bankruptcy Filing Program. *Version:* 3.0. Arthur L. Moller (Editorial Consultant). 1991. *Items Included:* User's manual includes instructions on operating the program & a tutorial; attorney's manual includes form illustrations & discussion of substance; transmittal sheets collect client information. *Customer Support:* Free hotline support through an 800 number.
MS-DOS or PC-DOS version 2.0 or higher. IBM XT, AT, or PS/2 (512k) or compatible with hard disk. disk $825.00 (Order no.: 885).
This Menu-Driven Document Assembly Program Enables the User to Draft the Forms Necessary to File a Voluntary Bankruptcy Case under Chapters

7, 11, 12, & 13. *The Program Maintains a Database for Each Client, Makes Necessary Mathematical Calculations, & Includes an On-Line Help Feature.*
Matthew Bender & Co., Inc.

Collins Electronic English Dictionary & Thesaurus. Reference Software International Staff. 1992. *Items Included:* License, User's Guide, disks. *Customer Support:* Customer support available at these numbers: DOS (801) 228-9918, Windows (801) 228-9919.
DOS. IBM PC (640k). Contact publisher for price. *Optimal configuration:* 9.2Mb of hard disk space required for full installation.
Windows. IBM PC (640k). Contact publisher for price. *Optimal configuration:* 9.2Mb of hard disk space required for full installation.
A Word Processor Add-On That Lets Users Search & Query for 190,000 Definitions & over 275,000 Synonyms & Antonyms. Collins Electronic Is Based on the 1991 Collins English Dictionary & the 1984 Collins Thesaurus.
WordPerfect Corp.

Color Convert. Kendall J. Redburn. Mar. 1990. *Customer Support:* 90 day unlimited warranty, toll free support.
Macintosh OS. Macintosh II, IIci, IIcx, IIfx (1Mb). 3.5" disk $55.00. *Optimal configuration:* Macintosh II, 8 bit color video, 2Mb memory, Imagewriter II.
Converts Color Images on a Macintosh II into a Format That Will Then Print on Image Writer II Printer. Has Multiple Dithering Methods, Special Effects & Mirror Imaging for Iron on Transfers.
BugByte, Inc.

Color Digital Photos, Vols. 1-7.
Windows or Macintosh. CD-ROM disk $199.95 (ISBN 1-882949-67-6, Order no.: 10044108ND).
Each Volume Contains 200 Quality Photographs from Award Winning Stock Photo Libraries for Your Unlimited Royaltyfree Use in Any Commercial or Non-Commercial Application. Perfect for Creating Reports, Presentations, Newsletters, Packaging, Advertising, Software Developing, & Much More!
Paragon Media.

Color Digital Photos, Vol. 1: Premier.
Windows or Macintosh. CD-ROM disk $34.95 (ISBN 1-882949-68-4, Order no.: 10044101ND).
Contains 200 Quality Photographs from Award Winning Stock Photo Libraries for Your Unlimited Royaltyfree Use in Any Commercial or Non-Commercial Application. Perfect for Creating Reports, Presentations, Newsletters, Packaging, Advertising, Software Developing, & Much More!
Paragon Media.

Color Digital Photos, Vol. 2: Space.
Windows or Macintosh. CD-ROM disk $34.95 (ISBN 1-882949-69-2, Order no.: 10044102ND).
Contains 200 Quality Photographs from Award Winning Stock Photo Libraries for Your Unlimited Royaltyfree Use in Any Commercial or Non-Commercial Application. Perfect for Creating Reports, Presentations, Newsletters, Packaging, Advertising, Software Developing, & Much More!
Paragon Media.

Color Digital Photos, Vol. 3: Floral.
Windows or Macintosh. CD-ROM disk $34.95 (ISBN 1-882949-70-6, Order no.: 10044103ND).
Contains 200 Quality Photographs from Award Winning Stock Photo Libraries for Your Unlimited Royaltyfree Use in Any Commercial or Non-Commercial Application. Perfect for Creating Reports, Presentations, Newsletters, Packaging, Advertising, Software Developing, & Much More!
Paragon Media.

Color Digital Photos, Vol. 4: Planes.
Windows or Macintosh. CD-ROM disk $34.95 (ISBN 1-882949-71-4, Order no.: 10044104ND).
Contains 200 Quality Photographs from Award Winning Stock Photo Libraries for Your Unlimited Royaltyfree Use in Any Commercial or Non-Commercial Application. Perfect for Creating Reports, Presentations, Newsletters, Packaging, Advertising, Software Developing, & Much More!
Paragon Media.

Color Digital Photos, Vol. 5: Paramount.
Windows or Macintosh. CD-ROM disk $34.95 (ISBN 1-882949-72-2, Order no.: 10044105ND).
Contains 200 Quality Photographs from Award Winning Stock Photo Libraries for Your Unlimited Royaltyfree Use in Any Commercial or Non-Commercial Application. Perfect for Creating Reports, Presentations, Newsletters, Packaging, Advertising, Software Developing, & Much More!
Paragon Media.

Color Digital Photos, Vol. 6: Glamour.
Windows or Macintosh. CD-ROM disk $34.95 (ISBN 1-882949-73-0, Order no.: 10044106ND).
Contains 200 Quality Photographs from Award Winning Stock Photo Libraries for Your Unlimited Royaltyfree Use in Any Commercial or Non-Commercial Application. Perfect for Creating Reports, Presentations, Newsletters, Packaging, Advertising, Software Developing, & Much More!
Paragon Media.

Color Digital Photos, Vol. 7: Underwater.
Windows or Macintosh. CD-ROM disk $34.95 (ISBN 1-882949-74-9, Order no.: 10044107ND).
Contains 200 Quality Photographs from Award Winning Stock Photo Libraries for Your Unlimited Royaltyfree Use in Any Commercial or Non-Commercial Application. Perfect for Creating Reports, Presentations, Newsletters, Packaging, Advertising, Software Developing, & Much More!
Paragon Media.

Color It! *Version:* 2.0. *Items Included:* Manual. *Customer Support:* Unlimited technical support; 60 day moneyback guarantee.
MAC. Macintosh (2Mb). 3.5" disk $149.95. *Addl. software required:* System 6.05 or higher, 32-bit QuickDraw. *Optimal configuration:* MAC Classic II, SE/30, LC, Si or II family, hard drive, mouse.
Powerful Easy-to-Learn Color Paint & Image Editing Program. Use Color It! to Create Dynamic Images from Scratch or Enhance Existing Clip Art. Supports Pressure Sensitive Tablets & Adobe Photoshop or Digital Darkroom Plug-Ins & Filters. Has Built-In Virtual Memory for Working with Multiple or Large Filters.
Timeworks, Inc.

Color Presentation Magic Simplified Graphics Generation. *Items Included:* Full manual. No other products required. *Customer Support:* Free telephone support - no time limit, 30 day warranty.
MS-DOS 3.2 or higher. IBM & compatibles (512k). disk $39.95. *Optimal configuration:* 386/25 or higher, MS-DOS 5.0 or higher or Windows 3.1 or higher, 4Mb RAM, 3-1/2" disk drive, mouse, & VGA w/256 video card.
Enables User to Create Professional Looking Presentations Without Special Graphics Training & Technical Expertise - All from Your Everday Office PC. If You Can Change the Channel on Your TV, You Can Pull up Color Backgrounds That Create Compelling-Looking presentations on Paper or Transparencies. Sensible Features & Straightforward Control Console Enable User to Create & Print Bar (2-D & 3-D), Line, Pie (Single/Double/Exploded), & Bullet Charts; Tables; Free-Form Text (with a Spelling Checker); Four-on-a-Page Handouts; & More. And All Within Minutes of Installation.
Dynacomp, Inc.

Color Spectral Doppler Ultrasound of the Carotid Arteries & Peripheral Vessels: An Interactive Compendium. Stephen Baker. Oct. 1994.
Mac/Windows PC (5Mb). disk $250.00 (ISBN 1-56815-040-7). *Optimal configuration:* PC Windows 3.1.
Mosby Multi-Media.

Colorado Corporation Formation Package & Minute Book. Collon C. Kennedy, III et al. May 1986. *Compatible Hardware:* IBM PC & compatibles. *Operating System(s) Required:* PC-DOS 2.0 or higher. *Memory Required:* 256k. disk $39.95, incl. manual (ISBN 1-55571-007-7).
WORDSTAR-Compatible Word Processing Program Is Provided on the Disk, Together with the Text Files from the Book, Which Include All the Letters, Bylaws, Articles of Incorporation & Other Forms Incorporated in the Book.
Oasis Pr.

ColorBIZ Biorhythm. 1982. *Compatible Hardware:* IBM PC. *Operating System(s) Required:* MS-DOS, PC-DOS. *Language(s):* BASIC. *Memory Required:* 48k.
disk $59.97.
Exploits the Natural Body Cycle in Personal, Social, or Business Situations. Used by Fortune 500 Companies to Help Prevent Accidents. Features: Congemahty Comparisons, Display, Graphic Printout, Storage, Retrieval of Names & Birthdates.
RetailFORCE, Inc.

ColorBIZ Gambler. 1982. *Compatible Hardware:* IBM PC. *Operating System(s) Required:* MS-DOS, PC-DOS. *Language(s):* BASIC. *Memory Required:* 48k.
disk $59.95.
Casino Game Package with "Vegas Rules" Includes Blackjack, Beno, Baccarat.
RetailFORCE, Inc.

ColorBIZ Inventory. *Compatible Hardware:* IBM PC & compatibles. *Operating System(s) Required:* PC-DOS. *Language(s):* BASIC. *Memory Required:* 64k. *General Requirements:* 132-column printer.
$498.00.
Interactive Database & Report Generator Suitable for Multistore. Provides Dual Item #, Location Codes, etc. Record Capacity Is Limited Only by Disk Space. Transactions Includes: Sales, Returns, Orders Receipts, Cancel Order, Scrap Loss, & Physical Count.
RetailFORCE, Inc.

ColorBIZ Loan. 1982. *Compatible Hardware:* IBM PC. *Operating System(s) Required:* MS-DOS, PC-DOS. *Language(s):* BASIC. *Memory Required:* 48k.
disk $59.97.
Analyzes Numerous Financing Alternatives for Loan Situations. Calculates Any Loan Value, Stores Loans, Prints or Displays Monthly or Yearly Amortization Schedules.
RetailFORCE, Inc.

ColorCourse/Imagesetting. ColorExpert. Oct. 1995.
IBM. CD-ROM disk $49.95 (ISBN 1-56609-186-1).
Peachpit Pr.

TITLE INDEX

ColoRIX-VGA Paint. *Version:* 1.38. *Compatible Hardware:* IBM PC & compatibles. *Memory Required:* 384k. *General Requirements:* Hard disk recommended. *Items Included:* Manual, flow chart, demo. *Customer Support:* 90-day unlimited warranty, extended support $50/yr.
disk $199.00.
Presentation-Graphics Package for On-Screen Slide Shows with Animation, Dissolves, Wipes & Color Sweeps. Graphics Features Include Object Rotation, Image Enlargement & Reduction & Zoom & Undo Commands. Provides 256 User-Selectable Colors from a Palette of 256,000, Color Schemes, 34 Typefaces & 34 Font Sizes. Outputs to HP LaserJet, Dot-Matrix Printer, Film Recorder, Color Ink-Jet Printer & Thermal Printer. Features File Compression & Imports PCX, IMG, TARGA ,ASCII, Taff, Word Perfect File Formats & Gif.
RIX Softworks, Inc.

Colorizer. *Version:* 1.1. *Compatible Hardware:* Apple Macintosh II. *Memory Required:* RAM 2Mb, video RAM 512k. *General Requirements:* Color monitor recommended. *Customer Support:* Illustrated manual, limited warranty, sample documents, & technical support. Tel: 619-721-7000.
3.5" disk $49.95, incl. manual.
Object-Oriented Drawing Program Which Lets Users Manipulate the Objects in Color. Objects Can Be Drawn, Grouped, or Ungrouped. Users Can Also Select Foreground & Background Color. Enables Users to Add Colors to Otherwise Black & White Applications. Several Pre-Set Color Palettes Are Available, or Users Can Create Their Own Palettes. Color Screens Can Be Captured to a File or Dumped to an ImageWriter II Printer.
Palomar Software, Inc.

Column Buckling. Sep. 1983. *Compatible Hardware:* Apple II+, IIe; HP-85; IBM PC. *Operating System(s) Required:* PC-DOS, Apple DOS 3.3. *Language(s):* BASIC (source code included). *Memory Required:* HP 32k, Apple 48k, IBM 128k. *Customer Support:* Telephone.
$125.00.
Utilizes the AISC Method for Determining the Acceptability of Columns Subject to Axial Loads, Off-Center Loads & End Moments. Output Includes Allowable & Critical Loads, As Well As Applicable AISC Determinants.
PEAS (Practical Engineering Applications Software).

Column: Multicomponent Separation Processes. Bob Nealon. Jan. 1990. *Customer Support:* 30-day money back guarantee, MES available.
MS-DOS. IBM (640k). disk $995.00 (Order no.: S031). *Nonstandard peripherals required:* Math coprocessor. *Optimal configuration:* 3Mb hard disk space required.
Simulates the Separation of Feeds up to 50 Components in Columns of up tp 100 Stages. User Can Choose from Nine VLE Methods & Program Will Select the Most Appropriate Algorithm. Also Contains a Databank of More Than 1,300 Components; User Can Add up to 1,000 More.
Gulf Publishing Co.

COLUMNS. Mar. 1986. *Operating System(s) Required:* CP/M 2.2, CP/M Plus. *Memory Required:* 40k.
disk $35.00 (ISBN 0-924945-05-2, Order no.: 005).
"Cut & Paste" Software for Text. Allows Manipulating Columns of Text As Easily As Word Processors Manipulate Paragraphs of Text. Can Automatically Convert a Single Column of Text into Multi-Column Pages, with Appropriate Margins & Column Spacing. Supports Proportional Printing & Proportional Justification. Accepts Standard ASCII Text As Input, Generates Standard ASCII Text As Output. Output Can Be Sent to the Console, to the Printer, or to a Disk File.
Logic Assocs.

COM-CAP Class. *Compatible Hardware:* Sharp Pocket Series; IBM PC & compatibles. *Language(s):* BASIC (source code included). *Memory Required:* 3k.
disk or cassette $19.95.
Horseracing Program.
COM-CAP.

COM-CAP Pace. Apr. 1986. *Compatible Hardware:* IBM PC. *Language(s):* BASIC (source code included).
disk or cassette $99.99.
Horseracing Program.
COM-CAP.

COM-CAP Racing Records. Apr. 1986. *Compatible Hardware:* IBM PC. *Language(s):* BASIC (source code included).
disk $99.99.
Horseracing Database Program.
COM-CAP.

Com/ment. *Version:* 5.29. *General Requirements:* UNIX operating system, All UNIX Platforms, SCO. *Items Included:* Complete ready to use Bulletin Board, EMail. *Customer Support:* Available.
Macintosh II, ITEL, R86000, HP, DEC, MIPS, Motorola, SCO. $895.00 - $4995.00.
Communications Management Program, Bulletin Board, Electronic Mail, W/Internet Connection. User Configurable.
Sans Souci Consulting.

COMAL. Jun. 1984. *Compatible Hardware:* Commodore 64, PET. *Language(s):* BASIC, Pascal. *Memory Required:* 16k.
disk $19.95.
Disk for Teaching of COMAL Language for Home or School.
COMAL Users Group, USA, Ltd.

COMAL Starter Kit, 5 disks. *Compatible Hardware:* Commodore 64.
$29.95, incl. 2 books: "COMAL from A to Z" & "Graphics Primer", 5 newsletters: "COMAL Today".
COMAL Language Package. Includes: 1541 Fast Loader, Disk Backup, File Copier, Full C64 COMAL .14, & More Than 100 Other Programs.
COMAL Users Group, USA, Ltd.

COMAL Super Chip. *Compatible Hardware:* Commodore 64, 128.
ROM cartridge $29.95.
Upgrade to COMAL 2.0 (the 16k Chip Plugs into Empty Socket of COMAL 2.0 Cartridge). Features C128 Support, C64 Auto Boot System, 1541 Fast Loader, & over 100 Added Commands.
COMAL Users Group, USA, Ltd.

COMAL 2.0. *Compatible Hardware:* Commodore 64.
ROM cartridge $74.95.
64k Language Cartridge with Empty Socket.
COMAL Users Group, USA, Ltd.

COMBO. *Version:* 1.03. *Compatible Hardware:* Altos Series 5-15D, Series 5-5D, 580-XX, ACS8000-XX; Burroughs B20-3 with 2 disk drives; DEC Rainbow 100 with 2 disk drives, Rainbow 100+ with 10Mb hard disk; IBM PC with 2 disk drives, PC XT, PC AT, & compatibles; Kaypro 11/IV with 2 disk drives, Kaypro 10; Xerox 820 with 2 disk drives; Zilog MCZ-250. *Operating System(s) Required:* CP/M, MP/M, MS-DOS, CP/M-86/80, PC-DOS.
License fee unit. $600.00 (Order no.: COMBO).
License fee site. $900.00.
Maintenance unit. $120.00.
Maintenace site. $180.00.
Series of Programs Designed to Automate Some of the Common, Labor-Intensive Review Procedures Associated with Consolidations. Accommodates Any Type of Financial & Hierarchical Group Structure. User Can Post the Consolidating Journal Entries, Produce Consolidation Worksheets (in Horizontal & Vertical Format) & Produce the Consolidated Financial Statements.
Coopers & Lybrand.

COMCALC: Communications Design Spreadsheet. Charles H. Gould. Apr. 1986. *Compatible Hardware:* AT&T 6300; HP-125; IBM PC, PC jr, PC XT, PC AT, & compatibles; Tandy 1000, 100, 2000; TI Professional; Xerox 820, 820-II, 860. *Operating System(s) Required:* MS-DOS, PC-DOS. *Memory Required:* 256k.
disk $95.00.
Design Tool for the Radio Communications System Designer or User. Components of the System Such As Transmitter Power, Frequency, Transmission Path Attenuation, Receiver Noise Figure, etc. Are Entered & Performance Characteristics Are Displayed. Displays a Communications "Budget" Which Tells the Designer How Much Signal Energy Margin the User Has.
BV Engineering.

ComedyWriter. Vincent J. Constantino. Jul. 1995. *Items Included:* 68 page manual, sample files. *Customer Support:* 90 days replacement warranty, 30 day money-back guarantee, 90 days free technical support.
Windows 3.1 or higher. disk $109.95 (ISBN 0-9648239-0-X).
ComedyWriter Is a Windows-Based Program for Creating Humorous Scenes, Characters, Situations, Dialogue, & Expressions. It Includes a Database of References from Popular Culture & History.
Ideascapes.

Comfort Call. Jun. 1994. *Items Included:* User manuals; phone interface board; latest version of SERVICE CALL Maintenance Management software. *Customer Support:* Free telephone support; training seminars - included in purchase price; rapid implementation services - fees vary with service provided.
DOS. IBM or compatible 386/486 4Mb RAM (640k). $14,000.00 & up. *Optimal configuration:* 486 PC with 8Mb RAM, latest DOS. *Networks supported:* Novell, NetBios, Banyan Vines.
Links the Telephone in Each Hotel Guest Room with the Engineering Department's Work Order System, SERVICE CALL MAINTENANCE MANAGEMENT. Housekeeper's Submit Maintenance Requests in Seconds Without Writing or Speaking. Each Request Is Made via Touch-Tone Phone, & Work Orders Are Generated & Printed Automatically in the Engineering Department.
OmniComp, Inc.

Comic-Pro. *Version:* 1.5. John Arocho. Jan. 1991. *Items Included:* Hard cover 3-ring binder.
PC-DOS/MS-DOS. IBM PC & compatibles (512k). disk $30.00 (Order no.: CP15). *Optimal configuration:* Mouse compatible (optional), printer (optional).
demo disk $5.00.
Extensive Comic Management System. Easy to

Use. Mouse Compatible. Title Collection Reports, Missing Issue Reports & Checklists. Fast Data Entry. Unlimited Capability; Stores 100,000's of Comics.
Visionary Technology.

COMIS. Version: 3.0. Jun. 1978. Compatible Hardware: IBM PC & compatibles. Operating System(s) Required: Novell, PC-DOS, UNIX, Windows NT. (source code included). Memory Required: 4000k.
disk $5000.00.
Medical Information System.
Southern Software Systems, Inc.

Comm Desk. Compatible Hardware: IBM PC, PC XT, PC AT & compatibles.
contact publisher for price.
MCI International.

Command. Compatible Hardware: Apple Macintosh.
3.5" disk $149.95.
Enables Users of MICROSOFT WORKS to Create Macros Similar to Those Possible with EXCEL.
Lundeen & Assocs.

Command Post. Version: 7.0. Jun. 1990. Items Included: Manual & disk. Customer Support: (206) 937-9335.
MS-DOS 3.x or 4.x; MS-Windows. IBM PC, XT, AT, & compatibles (30k). disk $49.95.
MS Windows Menuing Application That Allows Windows Users Complete Control Over Windows Environment & the Initiation of Other Applications Via the Creation of Drop Down Menus. Menu Items Can Be Added to Start Applications, Change Directories, & Load Files. Double Directory Windows & a Tree Structured Directory Listing Allowing File Moves & Copies Between Disks & Directories. Features Include Window Arrangement, Time/Date Display, File Viewing Utility, Display Blanking & Menu Customization.
Wilson WindowWare.

Command Stream Processor. Compatible Hardware: TRS-80 Color Computer. Language(s): Machine. Memory Required: 16k.
cassette $19.95.
Designed to Run Other Programs. Allows User to Prepackage a Stream of Direct System Commands As Well As INPUT & LINE INPUT to BASIC Programs, Resulting in a Totally Automated Stream of Activity. Advanced Features Allow Intermixing Actual Keyboard Input with User's Routine & Provide for Subroutines. User Has the Options of Displaying Command Lines Used or Hiding Them. Intended for Users Who Have a Good Understanding of Their Computer & the Flow of Activity Required for Its Total Operation.
Custom Software Engineering, Inc.

Commander FDC. Items Included: Reference manual, "What's New", keyboard template, service bulletin, installation guide. Customer Support: Optional training & maintenance package. Training available through headquarters or locally. Unlimited help line (8-8 EST) with maintenance agreement.
DOS 3.1 or higher. IBM PS/2 series. Contact publisher for price. Networks supported: Novell, Banyan, IBM, PathWorks.
Consolidation & Reporting for Multi-Location Organizations. Graphic User Interface LAN- or PC-Based System to Solve Problems of International Currency Translations, Intercompany Eliminations, Account Reclassifications, Financial Restatements & Changing Reporting Needs. Automatically Creates Forms for Reporting Financial Results; Transmits to Reporting Units; Enables Local Editing & Data Validation. Ad-Hoc Query & Analysis. Menu Driven. Lotus Interface. Integrated Multidimensional Modeling for Product Profitability Analysis & Budgeting.
Comshare, Inc.

Commander Software for Managerial Applications. Version: 3.0. Compatible Hardware: DEC VAX, MicroVAX; IBM PC AT, PS/2 series, 30XX series, 43XX series, 9370 series; Macintosh; MS-DOS-based hardware. Operating System(s) Required: Macintosh OS System 6.7, MS-DOS, MVS, OS/2, VM, VMS, Windows. Memory Required: 640k. Customer Support: Training available through headquarters or locally. Unlimited help line with maintenance agreement.
IBM. disk $60,000.00-$225,000.00.
DEC. disk $54,000.00-$186,000.00.
Managerial Applications Software for Managers & Executives. Facilitates Effective Analysis, Planning, & Control Through Applications for Enterprise Budgeting, Statutory/Management Reporting, Profit Management, Executive Support Systems, & Quality Initiative Reporting. Includes Commandless Electronic Briefing Book, Exception Reporting, News & Competitive Information Tracking, E-Mail, & Reminder. Dynamic Data Acquisition from DBMS. Complete Application Management Tools for Distributed Environments & Builder Tools. Supports Macintosh, IBM OS/2 & DOS with Consistent Executive Interface.
Comshare, Inc.

Commander Ultra Terminal-64. Compatible Hardware: Commodore 64. General Requirements: Modem.
contact publisher for price (Order no.: C-1700). Self-Contained Modem Program Which Provides the Ability to Download, Dump to Printer, etc.
Creative Equipment.

Commercial Aircraft: History & Specifications. 1995.
Macintosh (2Mb); System 7.1 requires 4Mb.
3.5" disk $29.95 (ISBN 0-944188-01-X).
Interactive Software Which is Perfect Companion for Flight Simulator Users. Dependable & Comprehensive Source on Every Passenger & Cargo Aircraft. More than One Hundred Models Are Featured, from TurboProps Operated by Today's Commuter Airlines to Retired Jet & Propeller Aircraft & Classic Transports Such as the Constellation, the Comet, & the DC-3. Each Entry Includes Detailed Specifications & Information on the Craft's design, Evolution, & Varients. Includes a Glossary of More Than 600 Aerospace Terms, Names, Abbreviations, & Acronyms with Direct Link to Every Image & Data Entry.
Howell Pr., Inc.

Commercial Aircraft: History & Specifications. Version: 1.5. A. Gesar & D. Quast. Jan. 1995. Items Included: Instructions for installation & use included on inside cover. Customer Support: Very simple/self supporting, if malfunction - we will replace. 90 days unlimited warranty.
6.08 or higher. Macintosh (2Mb). 3.5" disk $29.95 (ISBN 0-944188-01-X).
Pyramid Media Group.

Commercial Building Energy Consumption. 1995. Items Included: Full manual. Customer Support: Free telephone support - 90 days, 30-day warranty.
MS-DOS 3.2 or higher. 286 (584k). disk $949.95. Nonstandard peripherals required: CGA/EGA/VGA.
Utilizes the Latest ASHRAE Bin Energy Estimation Methods & Calculation Procedures with Many Additional Enhancements. It Has Convenient Entry Screens, with Input Error Checking & Easy-to-Read Prompts. A Complete Run Can Be Made on a Minimal 386-33 Computer in Less Than 20 Seconds.
Dynacomp, Inc.

Commercial Cooling & Heating. Items Included: Bound manual. Customer Support: Free hotline - no time limit; 30 day limited warranty; updates are $5/disk plus S&H.
MS-DOS. IBM & compatibles (256k). $99.95-$899.95.
demo disk $5.00.
Uses the Latest ASHRAE Methods to Calculate Cooling & Heating Loads in Commercial Buildings. It Develops Required Air Quantities for Each Zone & Air System, Calculates Air Handling Equipment Specifications, & Runs a Series of Load Check Figures. Set up to Handle Large Multi-Story Buildings but Is Also Sufficiently Convenient to Be Applied to Small Buildings (& Even Residences). Printed Reports Include Full Details of Inputs, As Well As Independently Calculated Zone, System, & Building Loads & Air-Handling System Specifications.
Dynacomp, Inc.

Commercial Cooling & Heating Load - CL4M. Version: 1965. 1979. Compatible Hardware: IBM PC & compatibles. Operating System(s) Required: MS-DOS, PC-DOS. Language(s): Compiled & Assembly Language. Memory Required: 256k. Customer Support: Technical hotline, "Lifetime" support at no charge.
$450.00-$995.00.
Commercial Cooling/Heating Loads - CL4M Uses Latest ASHRAE Methods to Calculate Cooling/Heating Loads, Air Requirements & Coil Specifications for Large Commercial Buildings & Residences. Capacity 255 Zones/Air Systems. Separately Calculates Zones, Air Systems & Building Design Loads, Displays Detail for Verification, Optimization. Runs Series of Load Check Figures. Handles Shading Projections, Return Air Plenums, Five Exposures Per Zone, Multiple Wall, Window & Shading Types for Each Exposure, Ventilation, Infiltration Air. Any Location, Latitute, Altitude Corrected. Permits Building Rotation, Reversal. Fully Compiled, Powerful, Prompted, Interactive. Fast (1/4 sec. per Zone-Hour), Flexible. English Units Only.
MC2 Engineering Software.

Commercial Cooling & Heating Load Program: CHVAC. Version: 4.0. William W. Smith. May 1988. Compatible Hardware: IBM PC & compatibles. Operating System(s) Required: CP/M, CP/M-86, MS-DOS, PC-DOS. Language(s): CB-80. Memory Required: 256k. General Requirements: 2 disk drives, printer.
$595.00.
8" disk $595.00.
3.5" disk $595.00.
demo disk $38.00.
Calculates Heating & Cooling Loads on Commercial Buildings Having As Many As 1000 Zones & 100 Air Handler Systems. Computes Zone Loads, Outside Air Loads, Tonnage Requirements, CFM Air Requirements, Chilled Water Flow Rates, & All Necessary Psychrometrics Data. Provides Glass Exterior Shading, Internal Operating Load Profiles, Automatic Building Rotation, Positive & Negative Pressure Allowances, Reheat & Subcooling Considerations, Minimum Supply CFM Settings, Seasonal Infiltration & Ventilation Requirements, Automatic Disk Storage of All Project Data.
Elite Software Development, Inc.

Commercial Credit Matrix: For Lotus 1-2-3 & Symphony. Version: 2.1. James E. Kristy. Jan. 1993. Compatible Hardware: IBM PC & compatibles, PC XT AT. Memory Required: 256k. General Requirements: Lotus 1-2-3 or Symphony.

TITLE INDEX

Items Included: 48 page booklet: Analyzing Financial Statements: Quick & Clean. *Customer Support:* Phone support: (714) 523-0357.
Lotus 1-2-3. disk $89.00, incl. bklt. (ISBN 0-932355-13-7, Order no.: 248).
A Unique Template That Sifts the Information in a Company's Financial Reports & Grades the Company's Strength on a Numeric Scale. The Package Includes an Example to Help Novices.
Books On Business.

Commercial Finance Lending System.
Operating System(s) Required: UNIX, CP/M. contact publisher for price.
Mnemotech Financial Systems, Inc.

Commercial-Industrial Real Estate Applications. *Version:* 3.0. 1991. *Compatible Hardware:* Apple Macintosh; IBM PC & compatibles. *Memory Required:* IBM 640k, Macintosh 4000k. *General Requirements:* Speadsheet program, printer, IBM Lotus 1-2-3 or MS-Excel; MAC: MS-Excel. *Items Included:* Complete users manual. *Customer Support:* Unlimited, Free phone support.
disk $150.00.
Project Development Tool Which Allows the Use of a Spreadsheet Program to Help Plan & Develop Complex Commercial or Industrial Real Estate Projects.
RealData, Inc.

Commerical Printing Guide for Aldus FreeHand. *Version:* 4.0. Nov. 1993. *Customer Support:* For customer service, product registration, upgrades, technical support, & CustomerFirst service plans, customers may call Aldus Customer Services at (206) 628-2320.
Macintosh. Contact publisher for price (ISBN 1-56026-251-6).
Aldus Corp.

Commission Comparisons. *Version:* 1.2. Jules Brenner. Jul. 1991. *Operating System(s) Required:* MS-DOS. *Language(s):* QUICKBASIC. *Memory Required:* 30k. *Items Included:* Manual. *Customer Support:* Telephone or mail.
disk $39.95 (ISBN 0-930437-30-6).
Designed to Show the Market Trader How 14 Selected Discount Brokerages & One Full-Service Brokerage Compare in Commission Costs for Any Particular Transaction. User Enters Number of Shares & Price per Share; Program Will Then Calculate Each Brokerage Commission & Sort Them Accordingly. Includes Vital Statistics on Each Brokage.
NewTEK Industries.

Commission Comparisons for Windows. Sep. 1994. *Items Included:* Comb-bound manual. *Customer Support:* Free phone support.
DOS 2.1 or higher. PC (256k). disk $39.95 (ISBN 0-930437-33-0). *Addl. software required:* Windows 3.1. *Optimal configuration:* 800 x 600 x 64 colors, video standard.
Brokerage Database Designed to Show the Market Trader How Selected Discount Brokerages & One Full-Service Brokerage Compare in Commission Costs for Any Particular Transaction in Stocks, Options or Bonds. User Enters Number of Shares, Contracts or Bonds, & Price; Program Will Then Calculate Each Brokerage Commission & Sort Them Accordingly. Trader Can Readily See How They Compare; Exact Differences; How the Comparison Changes According to the Transaction; How a Particular Trade Can Be Designed for Minimum Commission. At the Press of a Number Key, Vital Statistics Concerning the Brokerage of Choice Is Displayed on the Screen, Including Toll Free Numbers, Nationwide Offices & Special Trading Requirements If Applicable. Users May Request Brokerages to Be Added for Nominal Fee.

Updated As Brokerage Rates Are Changed. Number of Brokerages Varies, Generally Between 15 & 17.
NewTEK Industries.

Commodities & Futures Package. *Version:* 2.0. Albert Bookbinder. Aug. 1993. *Compatible Hardware:* IBM PC. *Operating System(s) Required:* PC-DOS/MS-DOS. *Language(s):* BASIC (source code included). *Memory Required:* 64k. *Items Included:* Handbook. *Customer Support:* Telephone support.
disk $144.00 (ISBN 0-916106-10-1).
Forecasts & Evaluates Price, Risk & Return on Commodity Futures.
Programmed Pr.

Commodity Merchandising. *Customer Support:* Free on site training; first 6 months support free; yearly support is 13% of cost of software; modem & phone support; classroom training & "user group" meetings.
IBM PC & compatibles (4mb). Contact publisher for price. *Networks supported:* Novell primarily.
Accounting Software to Track Contract Purchases & Sales from Start to Finish. System Tracks Discounts/Premiums, Sales, Advances, Brokers Commissions, Trucking Freight, Shipping Schedules, As Well As Rail, Barge, & Vessel Transport Areas. System Also Integrates to All Other Grossman Accounting Packages for a Complete Solution.
Grossman & Assocs., Inc.

Commodore Logo. *Items Included:* Complete manual, quick reference card. *Customer Support:* Terrapin Times newsletter (free); 90 day limited warranty; free courteous telephone support.
Commodore 64, 128 (64K). $49.95; 5-pack $99.95; 10-pack $149.95; 20-pack $199.95 (Order no.: LGXC5). *Optimal configuration:* C-64 & C-128 with color monitor.
Used to Introduce Computer Skills in Educational & Home Settings. Excellent for Problem-Solving, Mathematics & Geometry, & Computer Programming. This Powerful yet Easy to Use Programming Language Includes Turtle Graphics, yet is a Complete Language- A Subset of LISP Developed at MIT. User Defined Commands Extend Language. Available in Lab Packs & Site Licenses.
Terrapin, Inc.

Commodore 64 Assembly Language Diskette.
W. D. Maurer. 1986. *Compatible Hardware:* Commodore 64. *Memory Required:* 64k.
disk $20.00 (ISBN 0-88175-041-7).
Contains Material from Text "Commodore 64 Assembly Language: A Course of Study Based on the DEVELOP-64 Assembler/Editor/Debugger".
W. H. Freeman & Co. (Computer Science Press).

Commodore 64 Tutorial, Vol. 1. *Compatible Hardware:* Commodore 64. *Operating System(s) Required:* CBM DOS. *Language(s):* BASIC.
disk $24.95.
Introduction to the Commodore 64 Computer Keyboard & Programming in BASIC. Consists of Two Major Topics: Introduction to the Keyboard (Which Describes the Operation & Function of Each Key on the Commodore 64 Keyboard), & Introduction to BASIC Which Explains the Fundamentals of the BASIC Programming Language & Method of Data Storage.
Dynacomp, Inc.

Commodore 64 Tutorial, Vol. 2. *Compatible Hardware:* Commodore 64. *Operating System(s) Required:* CBM DOS. *Language(s):* BASIC.
disk $24.95.
Introduction to Sound & Graphics of the Commodore 64 Computer. Requires Only

Minimal Knowledge of BASIC. Consists of Two Major Topics: Fundamentals of Sound (Explores the Sound Synthesis Process & the Built-In Features of the Commodore 64 Sound Interface Device); & Fundamentals or Graphics (Explores the Nature & Function of Sprite & Character Graphics).
Dynacomp, Inc.

Commodore 64/128 Graphics & Sound Programming. Stan Krute. 1983. *Compatible Hardware:* Commodore 64, 128. *Operating System(s) Required:* CBM, CP/M. *Language(s):* BASIC. *Memory Required:* 64k.
disk $29.95, incl. bk. (ISBN 0-8306-5179-9, Order no.: 5179C).
Includes over 50 Examples, 300 Illustrations, Charts & Codes.
TAB Bks.

Common Stock Decision Aide. Apr. 1990. *Items Included:* Detailed instruction manual. *Customer Support:* Free telephone support.
IBM & compatibles (240K). disk $49.00. *Addl. software required:* Lotus 1-2-3 V. 2+
Provides Unique Characteristics of a Common Stock with Little Effort from Readily Available Data. Calculates After-Tax (0%-15%-28%) Compounded Returns from Each of Up to 12 Past Years to the Present, Total Returns Each Year Including Dividend Credits, Earnings Growth Rates, Dividend Yields, Price/Earnings Ratio Ranges, Projected Current-Year High & Low Price/Share, & Compounded Returns on One's Own Investment. Compare with DJIA & S&P 500.
V. A. Denslow & Assocs.

GiftMaker: (Entry Level System). *Version:* 3.2. Aug. 1994. *Items Included:* Complete operations guide (manuals); Quarterly newsletter. *Customer Support:* 60 day money back guarantee; Annual support agreement-provides unlimited telephone support & free upgrades. Cost-$195 per year.
All Macintosh & PC with Windows 3.1. $975.00 single user; $1675.00 multi-user (2-5 users): Additional users over 5, $700.00 per 5 users. *Addl. software required:* Word Processing. *Networks supported:* TOPs, Appleshare, Netware, System 7 FileSharing. All major networks.
IBM PC or compatibles, 386 or 486 required (4Mb). $975.00 single user; $1675.00 multi-user (2-5 users); additional users over 5, $700.00 ea. *Addl. software required:* Word Processing. *Networks supported:* Netware, Lantastic. All major networks.
Mail List, Membership & Fund-Raising Management Program Designed for Small to Medium Sized Non-Profits or a Non-Profit Just Beginning a Development Program. It Enables an Organization to Perform Personalized Mailings, Manage On-Going Membership Campaigns, Tracks All Fund-Raising Campaigns & Generate Reports for Analysis Purposes.
Campagne Assocs., Ltd.

CommTax Telecommunication Tax Compliance System. *Items Included:* National Telecommunications Tax Directory; Documentation; State & Local Tax Matrices. *Customer Support:* First year support included; renewal year support is based on original purchase price.
IBM PC & compatibles (1Mb). contact publisher for price.
Provides Telecommunications Utilities with a Call Processing Taxation System. Tells the Billing System What to Tax, When to Tax It, & How Much to Tax. Interfaces Directly with the Utlity's Call Rating & Billing System. Includes a Data File for Every Taxing State & Locality in the U.S., & a Calculation Module.
Vertex, Inc.

COMMUNICATE

Communicate! Crisp Publications. Oct. 1995. *Items Included:* Manual, registration card, one CD-ROM disk, product catalog, skills product brochure, America Online user card. *Customer Support:* Free technical support allows users to call support technicians anytime between 8:00am to 5:00pm Pacific Standard Time Monday through Friday.
Windows 3.1, Windows 95 or higher. 486 33MHz PC or higher (8Mb, 16 recommended). CD-ROM disk $49.95 (ISBN 1-888226-02-1). *Nonstandard peripherals required:* Double speed CD-ROM drive, SVGA graphics, 8 bit sound card. *Optimal configuration:* 486 33MHz PC or higher, Windows 3.1 or higher, double speed CD-ROM drive, SVGA graphics card (256 colors 640x480), 16Mb RAM, 16 bit sound card.
A CD-ROM Based Software Product That Provides Proven Techniques for Improving Communication Skills in Writings, Presenting & Interacting with Others in Meetings.
Midisoft Corp.

Communicating Safety Awareness. Dec. 1983. *Compatible Hardware:* Apple IIe, IBM PC. *Memory Required:* 64k. *Items Included:* Supervisor's Book of Safety Meetings.
disk $89.00 ea.
IBM. (Order no.: CSD4).
Apple. (Order no.: CAD5).
Interactive Training Program for Industrial Supervisors That Uses a Step-by-Step Method to Teach Safety Improvement Skills. Training Manual Included.
Bureau of Business Practice.

Communications Central. *Compatible Hardware:* TRS-80. *Operating System(s) Required:* CP/M, TRSDOS. *Memory Required:* 48k.
5-1/4" or 8" disk $175.00.
Includes File Transfer, Programmable Function Keys, On-Line Help & DEC VT-100 Terminal Emulation.
IMPACC Assocs., Inc.

Communications Library. 1988. *Items Included:* PRIVATE-TALK (ready-to-use communications package), 100-page manual. *Customer Support:* By phone Mon-Fri 8:30 AM-5:30 PM CST.
MS-DOS. IBM PC, PC XT, PC AT & compatibles, PS/2. disk $99.00 (Order no.: 108411).
Saves Many Programming & Debugging Hours by Providing Both Low- & High-Level Commands. Adds Full-Featured Communications Capabilities to New or Existing Programs. These Features Include Error Detection Routines, Auto Encryption & Decryption Facilities & Batch Processing Support. User Can Integrate Communications & Thus Provide Customers with Remote Diagnostics, Automatic Updates & On-Site Processing.
Glenco Engineering, Inc.

Communications Library. Version: 1.0. *Items Included:* User manual.
MS-DOS 2.1 or higher; OS/2 1.0 or higher. IBM PC & 100% compatibles. disk $250.00.
Gives User a Comprehensive Set of High- & Low-Level Functions for Managing Asynchronous Communications Programs.
Lattice, Inc.

Communications Support Toolkit. *Compatible Hardware:* Apple Macintosh, IBM PC. *Memory Required:* 1000k.
3.5" disk $79.95.
Desktop-Communications Program.
True BASIC, Inc.

The Communicator. *Compatible Hardware:* TRS-80 Model I. *Memory Required:* 16-48k.
cassette $14.95 (Order no.: 0126R).
Provides Economical Communication Between Host & Remote Terminals.
Instant Software, Inc.

CommUnity: DECnet for Non-DEC Systems. *Items Included:* User manual, release notes. contact publisher for price.
Networks supported: DECnet.
UNIX BSD 4.3, System V or Proprietary operating system. PC, mini, minisuper, work station. Version 5.0 (04/1989) Call for Info. *Nonstandard peripherals required:* Ethernet controller. *Addl. software required:* DECnet Phase IV. *Networks supported:* DECnet.
Offers DECnet Capabilities for UNIX, MS-DOS, Macintosh, & Proprietary Operating Systems. Includes Such Standard DECnet Functions as Virtual Terminal, File Server with Compatibility with DEC's VAX/VMS Services for MS-DOS, File Access Listener (FAL), Task-to-Task Communication, & Network Management. No Additional Software or Hardware is Required to Communicate with DECnet Systems.
Technology Concepts, Inc.

Community Exploration. Jan. 1994. *Items Included:* Program on CD-ROM, CD Booklet, & Registration Card. *Customer Support:* Free unlimited customer support via telephone.
Macintosh System 7.0 or higher. Macintosh LC or higher (4Mb). CD-ROM disk $59.00 (ISBN 1-57268-085-7, Order no.: 20702). *Nonstandard peripherals required:* 12 inch monitor or larger; CD-ROM drive. *Optimal configuration:* 5Mb RAM.
Windows 3.1 or higher running under DOS 5.0 or higher. 386 SX (6Mb RAM; 500k low Dos Mem; 6Mb free disk space). CD-ROM disk $59.00 (Order no.: 20702). *Nonstandard peripherals required:* Sound card (either: Sound Blaster - 8, 16, PRO; Media Vision ProAudio Spectrum; or Microsoft Sound System; MPC compatible CD- ROM drive; VGA monitor; & microphone. *Optimal configuration:* 25 MHz 386 SX.
This Interactive, Language-Building Program Allows You to Explore 52 Places & See How the People of Cornerstone Work & Live. You Can Take Trips to the Airport, Supermarket, Library, Museum, Bank, Bus Station & More! Over 500 Word Labels Identify the People, Places, Animals & Objects.
Conter Software.

Community Exploration. Jan. 1994. *Items Included:* Program on CD-ROM, CD Booklet, & Registration Card. *Customer Support:* Free unlimited customer support via telephone.
Windows 3.1 or higher running under DOS 5.0 or higher. 386 SX (6Mb RAM; 500k low Dos Mem; 6Mb free disk space). CD-ROM disk $59.00 (ISBN 1-57268-086-5, Order no.: 21702). *Nonstandard peripherals required:* Sound card (either: Sound Blaster - 8, 16, PRO; Media Vision ProAudio Spectrum; or Microsoft Sound System; MPC compatible CD-ROM drive; VGA monitor; & microphone. *Optimal configuration:* 25 MHz 386 SX.
This Interactive, Language-Building Program Allows You to Explore 52 Places & See How the People of Cornerstone Work & Live. You Can Take Trips to the Airport, Supermarket, Library, Museum, Bank, Bus Station & More! Over 500 Word Labels Identify the People, Places, Animals & Objects.
Conter Software.

Community Exploration. Jan. 1994. *Items Included:* Program on CD-ROM, CD Booklet, & Registration Card. *Customer Support:* Free unlimited customer support via telephone.
Macintosh System 7.0 or higher. Macintosh LC or higher (4Mb). CD-ROM disk $59.00 (ISBN 1-57268-087-3, Order no.: 22702). *Nonstandard peripherals required:* 12 inch monitor or larger; CD-ROM drive. *Optimal configuration:* 5Mb RAM.

SOFTWARE ENCYCLOPEDIA 1996

This Interactive, Language-Building Program Allows You to Explore 52 Places & See How the People of Cornerstone Work & Live. You Can Take Trips to the Airport, Supermarket, Library, Museum, Bank, Bus Station & More! Over 500 Word Labels Identify the People, Places, Animals & Objects.
Conter Software.

CommWorks. Version: 1.4. Jan. 1986. *Compatible Hardware:* Apple IIe, IIc, IIgs. *Operating System(s) Required:* ProDOS. *Memory Required:* 128k.
$95.00.
Telecommunications Software Package That Has an AppleWorks-Type Interface with On-Line Help. For Easier Use, the Program Incorporates 4 Features: CommWorks Communications Files, Which Allow Users to Define & Save Often-Used Communications Parameters & Commands for Terminal Sessions; an Automatic Log-On Facility, Which Lets Users Define a Set of Macros That They Can Instruct Program to Execute by Using a Single Keystroke; CommWorks Macros, Which Allow Users to Define up to 18 Separate Sets of Macros & Keep Them in a Library; & CommWorks Text Editors, with Which Users Can Create or Modify Their ProDOS Documents.
PBI Software, Inc.

COMMX. Version: A.05. 1978. *Compatible Hardware:* Apple with CP/M; Data General; IBM PC, PC XT, PC AT, PS/2 & compatibles; Kaypro; Sanyo; TRS-80 with CP/M; most CP/M 80 based machines.. *Operating System(s) Required:* CP/M-80, PC-DOS, MS-DOS. *Language(s):* Assembly. *Memory Required:* 48k. *General Requirements:* Serial port with external modem or internal modem.
COMMX. disk $119.00.
COMMX/PC. $99.00.
Menu Driven Terminal Emulator & File Transfer Program for Access & Data Transfer with Timeshare Services for all Mainframe & Mini-Computers. Supports XMODEM, Kermit & Commx Protocol File Transfer (Also ASCII XON/XOFF). Emulates VT100, VT102, VT52, IBM 3101-1X, HP2624, Adds Regent, WYSE 50, Televideo 950. Macros for Unattended Operations Such As Electronic Mail & Auto-Dial-Log-On.
Hawkeye Grafix.

COMMX-M. Version: 1.3. 1982. *Compatible Hardware:* DEC VAX, DEC 10/20; HP 3000; IBM 308X; Prime. *Operating System(s) Required:* VMS, TOPS-10, MVS/TSO, Primos. *Language(s):* FORTRAN (source code included). *Memory Required:* 64k.
disk $1500.00.
Allows a Micro Running COMMX to Transfer Binary & Text Files Using CRC 16 Error Correcting Protocol with a Mainframe/Mini Running the FORTRAN Compatible COMMX.
Hawkeye Grafix.

Comp Computing Standard MUMPS (CCSM). Version: 5.04. Mar. 1985. *Compatible Hardware:* IBM PC & compatibles. *Operating System(s) Required:* PC-DOS, MS-DOS. *Memory Required:* 128k. *Customer Support:* (409) 883-8537 for technical support.
Multi-user 386 version, 256k. $795.00.
Single-user, multi-tasking. $159.95.
Single-user, single-tasking. $89.95.
MUMPS Programming Language.
MGlobal International, Inc.

COMPAC Z. *Compatible Hardware:* IBM PC, PC XT. *Operating System(s) Required:* PC-DOS. *Language(s):* C. *Memory Required:* 64k.
disk $695.00.
Provides: Asynchronous Communication Through

TITLE INDEX

Any RS-232C Interface & Bisync, HDLC/SDLC & X.25 Protocols on Frontier Technologies AdCom 2 Controllers. Provides Uploading & Downloading ASCII Files, Defining Function Keys & Programmable Baud Rates.
Frontier Technologies Corp.

Compact Level II COBOL/ET. *Compatible Hardware:* IBM RT PC. *Operating System(s) Required:* UNIX.
$2000.00.
ANSI 74 COBOL Compiler. Produces Code Which, with a Run Time Library, Can Be Used in the RT PC Multi-User Environment. The Compiler Generates Intermediate Code from Source Programs Created Using a Standard UNIX Editor. Support Is Provided for Very Large Programs, All Four COBOL File Formats, & Calls to Programs Written in C.
Micro Focus, Inc. (California).

Companies International IBM CD ROM Plus PK. (Companies Internaitonal IBM CD ROM Plus Ser.). Edited by K. Forster. Dec. 1995.
IBM. CD-ROM disk $4995.00, incl. hard cover bk. (ISBN 0-7876-0600-6, Order no.: 109696).
CD-ROM disk $4995.00 (ISBN 0-7876-0601-4, Order no.: 109697).
Companies Active in Domestic & International Trade.
Gale Research, Inc.

Companies International IBM Manual Plus. (Companies International IBM CD ROM Plus Ser.). Edited by K. Forster. Dec. 1995.
IBM. CD-ROM disk Contact publisher for price (ISBN 0-7876-0602-2, Order no.: 109698).
Companies Active in Domestic & International Trade.
Gale Research, Inc.

Companies International IBM Plus Help. (Companies International IBM CD ROM Plus Ser.). Edited by K. Forster. Dec. 1995.
IBM. CD-ROM disk Contact publisher for price (ISBN 0-7876-0604-9, Order no.: 109700).
Companies Active in Domestic & International Trade.
Gale Research, Inc.

Companies International IBM 96, Pt. 1.
(Ward's World Business IBM Network CD Ser.). Edited by K. Forster. Dec. 1995.
IBM. CD-ROM disk $2945.00 (ISBN 0-8103-5128-5, Order no.: 101840).
Companies Active in Domestic & International Trade.
Gale Research, Inc.

Companions of Xanth. Michael Lindner. Oct. 1993. *Items Included:* Disks, game manual, warranty card, product catalog, "Demons Don't Dream," by Piers Anthony. *Customer Support:* Toll free technical assistance (1-800-658-8891). Computer operated pre-recorded hintline (1-900-933-CLUE). Hint book $9.95 plus s/h.
DOS 5.0 or higher. IBM & compatibles (640k). disk $59.95 (ISBN 1-880520-23-0, Order no.: CX). *Nonstandard peripherals required:* Microsoft compatible mouse, Sound Blaster compatible sound card. *Optimal configuration:* 386/33 with 640k RAM, Sound Blaster compatible audio card & Microsoft compatible mouse.
An Adventure Game Where You Explore the Magical World of Xanth & Become a Player in a Game Where the Stakes Are the Existence of Magic Itself.
Legend Entertainment.

Companions of Xanth. Michael Lindner. May 1994. *Items Included:* CD-Disk, Game Manual, warranty card, product catalog, "Demons Don't Dream," by Piers Anthony. *Customer Support:* Toll free technical assistance (1-800-658-8891). Computer operated pre-recorded hintline (1-900-933-CLUE). Hint book $9.95 plus s/h.
DOS 5.0 or higher. IBM & compatibles (640k). CD-ROM disk $59.95 (ISBN 1-880520-24-9, Order no.: CXCD). *Nonstandard peripherals required:* CD-ROM, Microsoft compatible mouse, Sound Blaster compatible sound card. *Optimal configuration:* 386/33 with 640k RAM, Sound Blaster compatible audio card, Double Speed CD-ROM. Microsoft compatible mouse.
An Adventure Game Where You Explore the Magical World of Xanth & Become a Player in a Game Where the Stakes Are the Existence of Magic Itself.
Legend Entertainment.

Company & Business: ClickArt Cartoons.
Customer Support: Free & unlimited technical support to registered users; 60 day money-back guarantee.
Macintosh. Macintosh, System 6.0.7 or higher (1Mb). 3.5" disk $49.95. *Addl. software required:* Any word-processing, desktop publishing or works program that accepts graphics.
Windows MS-DOS. IBM PC & compatibles. 3.5" disk $49.95. *Addl. software required:* Any word processing, desktop publishing or works program that accepts graphics.
Over 100 Images! Black & White Cartoons; Ready-to-Use, or Changed in Appropriate Drawing Program; Contains 12 Bonus Images Pre-Loaded for Use in Presentations; Includes the ClickArt Trade Secret - Images Traded to Every Popular Graphics Format, Guaranteed to Work with All Popular Applications.
T/Maker Co., Inc.

A Company Policy & Personnel Workbook. Ardella Ramey & Ronald Mrozek. May 1986. *Compatible Hardware:* IBM PC & compatibles. *Operating System(s) Required:* PC-DOS 2.0 or higher. *Memory Required:* 256k.
disk $39.95, incl. manual (ISBN 1-55571-005-0).
WORDSTAR-Compatible Word Processing Program Is Provided on Disk, Together with the Text Files from the Book for Each of the over 40 Business Policies & Alternates.
Oasis Pr.

Company Policy Manual Package. Jan. 1989. *Compatible Hardware:* Apple Macintosh, IBM PC & compatibles. *Memory Required:* Macintosh 1Mb, IBM 256k. *General Requirements:* Word processing software.
IBM. disk $89.95 (ISBN 1-55571-055-7).
Macintosh. 3.5" disk $79.95.
Provides a Way to Develop Company Policies. Package Includes a Step-by-Step Manual "A Company Policy & Personnel Workbook" & Companion Text Files That Give over 50 Model Policies. The Policies Are Ready for Use As Is, or They Can Be Modified to Suit User's Specific Company.
Oasis Pr.

Company Policy Manual (Standalone). Ardella Ramey & Ronald A. Mrozek. *Items Included:* Available with companion workbook. *Customer Support:* 15 day unlimited warranty - telephone technical.
DOS 2.1 or higher. IBM PC, XT, AT, PS2 & compatibles (512K). (software only) $69.95; (software & workbook) $99.95. *Addl. software required:* Hard disk & floppy drive or a dual floppy disk drive or a high density disk drive.
Macintosh (512K). (software only) $69.95; (software & workbook) $99.95.
Way to Develop Company's Policies in a Fast & Affordable Manner Without Months of Expensive Research, Development, & Legal Clarification or

COMPARATIVE MARKET ANALYSIS

Weeks of Keying in Information. The Software is a Complete Policy Development Program That Provides More Than 50 Model Policies - Each Ready to Be Printed or Customized to Meet a Particular Company's Needs. Some of the Many Different Areas Covered Are: Company Description; Employment Policies; Compensation; Employee Benefits; Employee Expenses; Miscellaneous Employee Legal Issues, Miscellaneous Policies.
Oasis Pr.

Company Policy: (Standalone). Nov. 1993. *Items Included:* Combination package contains 3-ring binder edition of "A Company Policy & Personnel Workbook" by Ardella Ramey & Carl R.J. Sniffen ISBN 1-55571-315-7. *Customer Support:* Free technical support over phone; limited warranty.
DOS 3.2 or higher. IBM & compatibles (356k). disk $99.95 (ISBN 1-55571-316-5, Order no.: CPPWSS/A31). *Nonstandard peripherals required:* Hard disk with 2Mb free space. *Optimal configuration:* Mouse supported, printer beneficial.
DOS 3.2 or higher. IBM & compatibles (356k). disk $125.95, incl. bk. (ISBN 1-55571-315-7, Order no.: CPPWBS/A31). *Nonstandard peripherals required:* Hard disk with 2Mb free space. *Optimal configuration:* Mouse supported, printer beneficial.
Create Your Companies Policies with Ease Using COMPANY POLICY Software. Contains 65 Model Policies You Can Use Verbatim or Customize to Fit Your Company's Particular Needs. Includes Information on New Federal Laws Such As the Americans with Disabilities Act & the Civil Rights Act.
Oasis Pr., The.

Comparative Lease Analysis. 1992. *Items Included:* User manual. *Customer Support:* Unlimited free telephone support.
Windows 3.1 or Windows 95. IBM & compatibles (4Mb). disk $295.00. *Nonstandard peripherals required:* Printer. *Addl. software required:* Lotus 1-2-3 2.01 or higher, MS-Excel 4.0 or higher. *Optimal configuration:* 4Mb RAM.
System 6 or 7 (MAC). MAC 030 or higher (4Mb). 3.5" disk $295.00. *Nonstandard peripherals required:* Printer. *Addl. software required:* MS-Excel Ver. 4.0 or higher. *Optimal configuration:* 8Mb.
Compare up to Six Different Real Estate Leases with Varying Provisions for CPI's, Pass-Throughs, Build-Outs, & Other Considerations. See How the Leases Really Stack up Economically. Play "What If?" with Leases As You Negotiate the Terms That Suit You Best. Includes Detailed & Summary Reports.
RealData, Inc.

Comparative Market Analysis. David Hunter. 1985. *Compatible Hardware:* IBM PC. *Operating System(s) Required:* PC-DOS 3.3 or higher. *Language(s):* QuickBasic. *Memory Required:* 640k.
NEC APC III. disk $49.95 (ISBN 0-942132-35-1, Order no.: N-1152).
IBM. disk $49.95 (ISBN 0-942132-37-8, Order no.: I-1152).
Designed to Give Real Estate Personnel & Homeowners a Precise Method for Determining the Comparative Market Value of Any Home. As Many As Thirteen Individual Home Features Can Be Defined, Such As Location, Type of Structure, Square Footage, Lot Size, Number of Baths, & Type of Financing Available. Once the Features of the Subject Property & Comparable Properties Have Been Identified, the Program Generates & Displays a Detailed Analysis & the Computed Market Value of the Subject Property.
Electronic Courseware Systems, Inc.

Compare-A-Loan. *Version:* 1.1. Jan. 1990. *Compatible Hardware:* IBM PC, PC XT, PC AT & compatibles. *Operating System(s) Required:* MS-DOS, OS/2. *Memory Required:* 360k. *Items Included:* 90 page manual & loan textbook. *Customer Support:* Call in 30 days, no charge.
disk $95.00.
Investment Analysis Tool That Constructs, Analyzes, Prints Schedules, & Compares Any Types of Loans. One Page Summary or Detailed Results Can Be Stored for Other Programs.
AA Software Development.

CompareRite: The Instant Redliner. *Version:* 4.1. *Compatible Hardware:* IBM PC & compatibles, Wang VS. *Operating System(s) Required:* PC-DOS/MS-DOS 2.0 or higher. *Memory Required:* 399k. *General Requirements:* 2 disk drives, printer.
disk $160.00.
Compares & Redlines Two Drafts of a Document, Highlights the Differences Between Them, & Generates a Comparison Draft. Allows User to Define How They Wish to See the Changes, Additions, Deletions or Moved Text in Any Number of Ways. Compatible with All Major Word-Processing Programs.
Jurisoft.

Comparison. *Items Included:* Instruction included on disk. *Customer Support:* 90 days unlimited warranty.
MS-DOS, Windows 3.1. IBM XT, AT or compatibles (512K). disk $34.95 plus $3.50 S&H. *Addl. software required:* Lotus 1-2-3 Version 4.0 or higher. *Optimal configuration:* IBM AT, 640k RAM.
Compares Terms of Various Mortgages. Includes Options for 15 to 30 Year Term, Fixed Interest, Variable Interest, etc.
Compiled Systems.

Compass Accounts Payable. *Version:* 3.0. Oct. 1982. *Compatible Hardware:* Intel 80286, 80386, 80486, etc.. *Operating System(s) Required:* MS-DOS, Novell, THEOS, UNIX, Win 95, Win/NT. *Language(s):* BASIC. *Memory Required:* 44k.
disk $1995.00.
Provides Multi-Company, Multi-Division, Departmentalized Payables, As Well As Check-Writing for Multiple Banks. Accounts Payable Interfaces with the Compass General Ledger Package.
COMPASS.

Compass Accounts Receivable. *Version:* 2.5. Aug. 1983. *Compatible Hardware:* Intel 80286, 80386, 80486, etc.. *Operating System(s) Required:* MS-DOS, Novell, THEOS, UNIX, Win 95, Win/NT. *Language(s):* BASIC. *Memory Required:* 44k.
disk $1995.00.
Provides Records of Invoices, Credit Memos, & Partial Payments. Offers Full Reporting Capability & Flexible Statements. Interfaces with the Compass General Ledger Package.
COMPASS.

Compass Fixed Assets. *Version:* 1.5. Jun. 1985. *Compatible Hardware:* Intel 80286, 80386, 80486, etc.. *Operating System(s) Required:* MS-DOS, Novell, THEOS, UNIX, Win 95, Win/NT. *Memory Required:* 44k.
disk $1995.00.
Provides Multiple Depreciation & Amortization Schedules. All Accepted Depreciation Methods Are Supported Including Accelerated Cost Recovery, Sum of the Years Digits, & Straight Line. Provides Multiple Depreciation Schedule by Fixed Asset, Supports All Accepted Depreciation Methods, Handles Assets Purchased or Sold During Fiscal Year, & Reports on Tax Requirements.
COMPASS.

Compass General Ledger. *Version:* 2.0. Oct. 1982. *Compatible Hardware:* Intel 80286, 80386, 80486, etc.. *Operating System(s) Required:* MS-DOS, Novell, THEOS, UNIX, Win 95, Win/NT. *Language(s):* BASIC. *Memory Required:* 44k.
disk $1995.00.
Multi-Company, Multi-Division, Departmentalized Ledger Package. Permits Manual Check-Entry & Check Writing, & Provides a User-Oriented Report Generator.
COMPASS.

Compass Job Cost & Estimating. *Version:* 1.5. Jan. 1987. *Compatible Hardware:* Intel 80286, 80386, 80486, etc.. *Operating System(s) Required:* MS-DOS, Novell, THEOS, UNIX, Win 95, Win/NT. *Language(s):* BASIC.
disk $4500.00.
Incorporates Standard & Nonstandard Operations. These Standard Operations Can Be Used As Templates for New Job Estimating. Bill of Materials Can Be Automatically Pulled & Exploded. Raw Material Requirements, Machine & Operating Hours, Overhead Rate, & Number of Persons Required Are Stored by Operation. Reports Include the Detailed Job Estimate, the Job Ticket, the Open Jobs List, the Job Cost Summary, & the Monthly Production Analysis Report.
COMPASS.

Compass Job Queue. *Version:* 5.5. May 1982. *Compatible Hardware:* Intel 80286, 80386, 80486, etc.. *Operating System(s) Required:* MS-DOS, Novell, THEOS, UNIX, Win 95, Win/NT. *Language(s):* BASIC.
disk $340.00.
free with purchase of 2 other Compass applications.
Provides Greater Productivity by Scheduling & Processing Jobs. Operator Time Is Saved Because Terminals Are Not Tied up While Reports Are Running. During Peak Reporting Periods Such As the End of the Month, Program Processes All Report Requests Without Manual Intervention. Additional Features Include the Following: Frees Terminals for Data Entry & Inquiry; Multiple Jobs Can Be Scheduled at One Time; Automatic Restart of "Active" Jobs; Multiple Job Queues Processing at the Same Time; Job Queue Management Commands.
COMPASS.

Compass Material Requirements Planning (MRP). Oct. 1988. *Compatible Hardware:* Intel 80286, 80386, 80486, etc.. *Operating System(s) Required:* MS-DOS, Novell, THEOS, UNIX, Win 95, Win/NT.
disk $2500.00.
Permits the User to Enter a Master Production Schedule. Calculates the Material Requirements Based on the Demand Required to Meet This Master Schedule. This Material Requirement Is Compared with the Quantity on Hand in Inventory & All Shortages Are Identified. Net & Expanded Material Requirements Reports Are Available. Features Include: 13 Periods of History on Requirements, on Hand Balance, Planned Order Receipts, Planned Order Quantities, & Current On-Order Quantities; Shopping History by Customer &/or Product; Interfaces with Inventory & Purchase Order Modules.
COMPASS.

Competitive Review. May 1993. *Items Included:* 150 page manual, Step-by-Step tutorial, data entry worksheet, automatic report writer, graphs. *Customer Support:* 60 days free.
MS-DOS. IBM PC compatible. disk $149.00.
A Financial Analysis Program That Calculates Key Ratios & Percentages, Thus, Allowing You to Review the Operating Performance of Your Target Company. You Can Then Work with What- If Scenarios, in Order to Determine What Changes You Should Be Making in Your Operating Procedures.
ValuSource.

Compile 1-to-C. *Compatible Hardware:* IBM PC & compatibles, PS/2. *Memory Required:* 200k. *General Requirements:* Lotus 1-2-3, Symphony, Excel, Quattro, SuperCalc, Surpass or VP-Planner.
disk $299.00.
Allows User to Prevent Menu Options from Appearing on a Compiled Spreadsheet While Keeping the Menu Commands Active Within Macros. Formula-Protection Feature Allows Others to Use the Compiled Spreadsheet but Not to See or Alter the Formulas. For Speedier Recalculation, Math Coprocessor Can Be Accessed from the Compiled Spreadsheet.
Resource Analysis International Corp.

Compiled BASIC. Microsoft, Inc. *Compatible Hardware:* HP 150 Touchscreen, HP 110 Portable.
3.5" disk $395.00 (Order no.: 45446D).
Optimizing Compiler Designed to Complement HP's Series 100/BASIC. Users Can Develop & Debug BASIC Programs Using the Series 100/ BASIC Interpreter, Then Streamline Program Execution Using Compiled BASIC. The Package Allows Users to Create Programs That, in Most Cases, Execute Faster Than the Same Interpreted Programs, Require Less Memory & Provide Source-Code Security.
Hewlett-Packard Co.

CompileIt! *Version:* 2.6.1. *General Requirements:* 1Mb RAM (2Mb RAM recommended), hard disk, any System compatible with HyperCard (recommend version 6.05 or higher). Supports all versions of HyperCard & SuperCard. Macintosh Plus or higher. 3.5" disk $149.00 (Order no.: 30-0612).
A Complete Development System for the Creation of Compiled Code Resources Such As HyperCard External Commands & Functions (SCMDs & XFCNs). In Addition to HyperCard SCMDs, CompileIt! Directly Supports the Creation of Many Other Common Code Resource Types Such As LDEFs, WDEFs, CDEFs & Others. Can Be Used to Create Virtually Any Type of Code Resource Found on the Macintosh. Externals (SCMDs & XFCNs) Expand the Capabilities of Products Like HyperCard & SuperCard. Supports the Macintosh ROM Toolbox, System 7.0, the Extended SCMD Interface, SuperCard Language & Callback Extensions, User-Defined Symbols, & Much More. Can Increase the Speed of Routines Written in HyperTalk & Protect Sensitive Code from Prying Eyes.
Heizer Software.

Compiling Roots & Branches. *Compatible Hardware:* TRS-80 Model II, Model 12, Model 16. *Operating System(s) Required:* TRSDOS. *Language(s):* BASIC-80. *Memory Required:* 64k.
disk $250.00.
Genealogy System That Aids the User in Recording Names, Dates, & Places. Enables the User to Create Indices to Names & Dates, Pedigree & Descendant Charts, & Add to Family Books.
Armstrong Genealogical Systems.

The Compleat Alfredo: Animated Adventures, 2 vols. 1987. *Compatible Hardware:* Apple II series. *Memory Required:* 48k.
3.5" disk $12.95.
Features Alfredo the Animated Hero of Misadventures.
Softdisk, Inc.

TITLE INDEX

The Complete Audubon: DOS-MAC Retail Box.
Items Included: Registration card. *Customer Support:* Creative Multimedia Corporation warrants the CD-ROM disc & diskettes to be free from defects in materials & workmanship under normal use & service for a period of 90 days from date of purchase. Creative Multimedia Corporation offers Technical Support to customers as needed.
MS-DOS 3.1 or higher. IBM PC & compatibles with VGA Monitor (640k). CD-ROM disk $79.99 2 disk set (ISBN 1-880428-02-4, Order no.: 10269). *Optimal configuration:* SuperVGA with 512k+ video memory. *Networks supported:* All LAN.
System Software 6.0.5 or higher. Macintosh Plus or higher (2Mb). $79.99 2 disk set (Order no.: 10269). *Nonstandard peripherals required:* Images display on all systems. *Optimal configuration:* Color image display requires 8-bit color, 32-bit QuickDraw & Color monitor. *Networks supported:* All.
John James Audubon, Best Known for His Famous Prints of Birds, Also Produced Equally Brilliant Prints of North American Mammals. This Two-Disc Set Includes the Complete 1840 First Edition "Octavo" Set of Books. All of the Color Plates & Text, As Well As the CD-Quality Audio Recordings of Bird Calls & Mammals Make This a True Collector's Edition.
Creative Multimedia Corp.

Complete Bond Analyzer. *Version:* 90.01.
Compatible Hardware: Apple Macintosh, Apple II Series, IBM PC's & PS/2.
3.5" or 5.25" disk $89.00.
Financial Program Featuring Bond Yield Calculation & Accrued Interest, Spot Rates & Duration.
Larry Rosen Co.

Complete Catalog of Forty-Fives. Charlie Holz. May 1993. *Items Included:* Disk (high density only), manual, newsletter. *Customer Support:* 1 year free support, 30 day unlimited warranty.
DOS Version 3.2 or higher. IBM & compatibles (400k). disk $19.95 per volume (17 volumes). *Optimal configuration:* 100Mb of hard disk space, EGA/VGA/SVGA color video.
A Computer Based Catalog of Nearly Every 45 That Has Been Released from 1947 until the Present. Includes Software for Reading, Sorting, Cross Referencing the Catalog. Discographics for Any Artist Can Be Created Instantly.
PSG-HomeCraft Software.

Complete Catalog of 45s. Aug. 1994. *Items Included:* Free software for accessing the catalog. *Customer Support:* One year free support via phone, mail, fax & BBS.
DOS 3.3 or higher. Any IBM compatible with 100Mb of free hard disk space (440k). disk $199.95. *Optimal configuration:* 640k RAM & 100Mb of free hard disk space.
A Computer-Based Catalog with Information about Every 45rpm Record Released since 45s Were Invented in 1949.
PSG-HomeCraft Software.

Complete Church Management Applications.
Compatible Hardware: IBM PC; Apple II+, IIe.
disk $1495.00.
Helps to Minimize Recordkeeping for Writing Checks, Recording Contributions, & Analyzing Membership Participation.
Scott, Foresman & Co.

The Complete Dickens. Charles Dickens. Mar. 1994. *Items Included:* CD ROM disc, The Complete Dickens User's Guide, Registration Card, License Agreement. *Customer Support:* 1) 30 days to return product 2) Software will perform substantially in accordance w/ accompanying written materials for 90 days from receipt date 3) Media containing software will be free from defects for 1 year from date of receipt 4) Technical support for all products.
DOS 3.30 or higher. 80386SX or higher processor (running at 16Mhz) 4-bit VGA graphics adapter w/color VGA monitor (2Mb). CD-ROM disk $39.95. *Nonstandard peripherals required:* MPC compatible CD-ROM drive, MPC-compatible audio board, headphones or speakers, Microsoft compatible mouse. *Addl. software required:* Microsoft Windows operating system 3.1 or higher (enhanced mode). *Networks supported:* Network version available through Bureau Development, Inc.
The Merry Old England of Dickens Comes Alive with This Complete Multimedia Collection of His Works. Get All the Novels & Hard-to-Find Short Stories & Essays. You Also Get Respected Literary Criticism & Authoritative Dickens Biography, & Hundreds of Color Illustrations & Voice Overs! Designed for Use by Students, Teachers, Adults, & Librarians, the Complete Dickens Is a Complete & Authoritative Addition to Your Home Reference Collection.
Bureau Development, Inc.

The Complete Edgar Cayce Readings. Jan. 1993. *Items Included:* Operator's manual, 94 pages. *Customer Support:* In-house customer service/data processing dept.
PC-DOS/MS-DOS. IBM & compatibles (640k). disk $500.00 (ISBN 0-87604-297-3). *Nonstandard peripherals required:* Non-standard hard drive.
The Complete 14,000 Discourses Given by Edgar Cayce on Subjects: Holistic Health, Parapsychology, Comparative Religions, Ancient History, Death & Rebirth, Meditation & Earth Changes, & Others.
A.R.E. Pr.

Complete House. Dec. 1992. *Items Included:* User Guide. *Customer Support:* 30 day warranty.
Windows. IBM & compatibles (4Mb). disk $14.95 (ISBN 1-885638-01-9).
A Multimedia Exploration of American Residential Architecture, Ideal for People Who May Be Building, Remodeling or Just Interest in House Design. Hundreds of Photos, Plans, Drawings & Audio Segments Explain & Illustrate the Major Points of House Design. Also Includes CAD/FP Floor Planner, a Powerful Easy-to-Use Software Tool That Lets You Create Customized Floor Plans.
Deep River Publishing, Inc.

Complete League Series. *Version:* 1.03. Jerry A. Ostler. 1984. *Compatible Hardware:* IBM PC, XT, AT, PS/2. *Operating System(s) Required:* MS-DOS. *Language(s):* C, Pascal, Force. *Memory Required:* 640k. *General Requirements:* 2 disk drives, printer, hard disk recommended.
disk $125.00 ea.
Provides League Statistics, Tournament Assignments, Team Statistics, Administrative (Assignment to Leagues, Assignments to Playing Fields, Time Assignments & Unassigned Team Members), Utilities, Telecommunications & Bulletin Boards. Covers Baseball, Basketball, Football, Hockey, Soccer or Softball.
Score Book Software.

Complete Multimedia Bible.
Macintosh. CD-ROM disk $49.95. *Nonstandard peripherals required:* CD-ROM drive.
Offers an Intensive Examination of the King James Bible with Special Features That Provide a Comprehensive Historical Work. Users May Easily Navigate Through the Bible Stories & Parables, Guidance & Inspiration, Maps & Multimedia.
Compton's NewMedia, Inc.

COMPLETE TEAM SERIES

Complete Oil Marketers Perpetual Accounting System (COMPAS). *Version:* 7.0. Applied Information Management Systems, Inc. 1976. *Compatible Hardware:* '286, '286, '486, Pentium. *Operating System(s) Required:* PC-DOS/MS-DOS, UNIX, XENIX. *Language(s):* RM/COBOL. *Memory Required:* 640k. *General Requirements:* Hard disk, RM/COBOL Runtime. *Customer Support:* Telephone, modem; support & maintenance retainer required.
IBM. $10,000.00, plus $1000.00 for each additional user.
Interactive Accounting & Tax Reporting Systems for Wholesale Petroleum Marketers.
AIMS, Inc.

Complete Personal Accounting (CPA).
Compatible Hardware: Heath-Zenith.
contact publisher for price.
Reichert Digital Systems.

Complete Property Manager-II. *Version:* 1.51. Apr. 1991. *Items Included:* Complete manual, tutorial & program disks (2). *Customer Support:* Free toll-free voice support "800" number.
MS-DOS (256k). IBM compatible. disk $795.00 (ISBN 0-929770-10-2). *Optimal configuration:* MS-DOS, 256k memory, 2 floppy disks or hard disk, printer.
Complete Integrated Accounting (General Ledger, Accounts Receivable, Accounts Payable) Plus Four Databases (Properties, Tenants, Vendors, Past Tenants). Designed for the Property Manager Who is Not Computer Literate, It Writes Checks, Prints Bills & Pays Disbursements. Ages Receivables, DVNS Late-Pays, Meets Guidelines for the Tax Revision Act. Handles Residential & Commercial Properties. Maintains a Balanced Set of Books Automatically. Data Can Be Exported to Any Other Program.
!Solutions! Publishing Co.

Complete Real Estate Investor. *Version:* 2.04. Apr. 1991. *Items Included:* Complete manual, tutorial & program disk. *Customer Support:* Free toll-free voice support "800" number.
MS-DOS (256k). IBM compatible. disk $595.00 (ISBN 0-929770-00-5). *Optimal configuration:* MS-DOS, 256k memory, 2 floppy drives or hard disk, printer.
Helps Investor Quickly Analyze Property, Play "What If" Games & Print Reports Needed for Profitable Decisions. Prints Analysis for Owner, Negotiating Sheet for Buyer, Cash-Flow Proforma Statements for Banker. Also Analyzes Wraparound Mortgages, Shared-Equity Participation Using Bonds as Collateral, Appreciation, Depreciation, Amortization Tables, Compares Mortgage Payments, Qualifies Conventional Loans, Produces Year- by-Year Analyses & the Real Cost of Ownership Analysis. Does Internal Rate of Return, Depreciation, Future Value, & More.
!Solutions! Publishing Co.

Complete Team Series. Jerry A. Ostler. 1984. *Compatible Hardware:* IBM PC, XT, AT, PS/2. *Operating System(s) Required:* MS-DOS. *Language(s):* C, Pascal, Force. *Memory Required:* 640k. *General Requirements:* 2 disk drives, printer, hard disk recommended.
disk $125.00 ea.
Provides Team Statistics, Practice Sessions, Scouting Statistics, Scouting Tutor, Individual Training, League Statistics, Scoring Tutor, Team Administration, Utilities & Telecommunications. Covers Baseball, Basketball, Football, Hockey, Soccer, or Softball.
Score Book Software.

The Complete Works: Shakespeare & Sherlock Holmes. *Items Included:* Registration card. *Customer Support:* Creative Multimedia Corporation warrants the CD-ROM disc & diskettes to be free from defects in materials & workmanship under normal use & service for a period of 90 days from date of purchase. Creative Multimedia Corporation offers Technical Support to customers as needed.
MS-DOS 3.1 or higher. IBM PC & compatibles with VGA Monitor (640k). CD-ROM disk $49.99 2 disk set (ISBN 1-880428-05-9, Order no.: 10268). *Optimal configuration:* SuperVGA with 512k, video memory. *Networks supported:* All LAN.
System Software 6.0.5 or higher. Macintosh Plus or higher (2Mb). $49.99 2 disk set (Order no.: 10268). *Nonstandard peripherals required:* Images display on all systems. *Optimal configuration:* Color image display requires 8-bit color, 32-bit QuickDraw & Color monitor. *Networks supported:* All.
Two Disc-Set Contains the Complete Unabridged & Total Works of the Greatest Playwright of All Times, Shakespeare, & the Classic Stories of Detection by the World's Greatest Consulting Detective Sherlock Homes & Dr. Watson.
Creative Multimedia Corp.

Completely Randomized Designs: One-Way Analysis of Variance. Bruce E. Trumbo. 1984. *Compatible Hardware:* Apple II+, IIe, IIc. *Operating System(s) Required:* Apple DOS 3.3. *Memory Required:* 48k.
disk $50.00 (ISBN 0-933694-33-4, Order no.: COM 3103A).
Covers the Topics: Computing ANOVA Tables from Data, Conclusions, Multiple Comparing & Simulations Exploring the Power of the F-Test.
COMPress.

Complex Mathematics. *Compatible Hardware:* TI 99/4A. *Operating System(s) Required:* DX-10. *Language(s):* Console BASIC. *Memory Required:* 16k.
disk or cassette $17.00.
Menu-Driven Program Adds, Subtracts & Divides Complex Numbers. Complex Polynomials Can Be Evaluated & Trigonometric Functions Including COSH, SINH & TANH Can Be Calculated.
Eastbench Software Products.

Complex Matrix Master. *Items Included:* Bound manual. *Customer Support:* Free hotline - no time limit; 30 day limited warranty; updates are $5/ disk plus S&H.
MS-DOS. IBM & compatibles, TRS-80 (256k). disk $39.95 single precision; $49.95 double precision.
Apple. disk $39.95 single precision.
For Complex (Real Plus Imaginary) Matrices. The Real & Imaginary Parts of the Matrix A'(I,J) Are Encoded into the BASIC Matrix As Follows: Re A'(I,J) Equals A(1,2 J) - Im A'(I,J) Equals A(1,2 J Plus I).
Dynacomp, Inc.

Complex Variable Boundary Elements. T. V. Hromadka. 1987. *Compatible Hardware:* IBM PC & compatibles. *Operating System(s) Required:* MS-DOS 3.0 or higher. *Language(s):* FORTRAN 77. *Memory Required:* 256k. *Items Included:* Disk, manual, binder. *Customer Support:* Limited warranty.
software pkg. $395.00 (ISBN 0-931215-15-3).
Provides a Mathematical Modeling Technique for Approximating Boundary Value Problems of the LaPlace Equation in Two Dimensions. Can Be Used to Solve Potential Problems Involving Steady State Flow, Soil Water Flow, Electrostatics, Stress-Strain Torsion Effects, etc., Numerically.
Computational Mechanics, Inc.

Components Accounts Payable. *Version:* 1.0. Chris LeCroy & David Johnson. Aug. 1989. *Items Included:* Manual, disk. *Customer Support:* Free phone support, due to ease of programs use, qualified installers, authorized dealers.
Macintosh Plus or higher (1Mb). $595.00.
Tracks Detailed Info Regarding Vendors & Purchases. P.O.'s Can Be Designed in Any Format. It Also Projects Due Dates for Invoices & Prints Checks. Custom Reporting Using a DTP Environment, & Easily Posts to the General Ledger.
Satori Software.

Components Accounts Receivable with Invoicing. Chris LeCroy & David Johnson. Aug. 1989. *Items Included:* Manual, disk. *Customer Support:* Free phone support, due to ease of programs use, qualified installers, authorized dealers.
Macintosh Plus or higher (1Mb). $595.00.
Allows Users to Creatively Design Their Own Invoices, Has Unlimited Ship-to-Addresses, Tracks Sales History, Commissions, Receipts, Etc., Detailed Reporting at Every Level, Customizable Entry Windows, Tracks Open Item or Balance Forward. Users Can Use & Modify On-Line Help.
Satori Software.

Components General Ledger. Chris LeCroy & David Johnson. *Compatible Hardware:* Apple Macintosh. *Memory Required:* 1000k. *General Requirements:* Hard disk. *Items Included:* manual, disk. *Customer Support:* Free phone support, qualified installers, authorized dealers.
3.5" disk $595.00.
An Object-Oriented, Customizable Accounting Package.
Satori Software.

COMPOS. *Version:* 3.31. Mar. 1986. *Compatible Hardware:* IBM PC, PC XT, PC AT & compatibles. *Operating System(s) Required:* MS-DOS, PC-DOS. *Language(s):* FORTRAN. *Memory Required:* 320k. *General Requirements:* Printer.
disk $1500.00 (Order no.: COMPOS).
Composites Irregular Drill Hole Data in 3 Modes: by a Constant Length Starting at the Collar, by a Constant Bench Height or by Seam Name or Rock Code.
Geostat Systems International, Inc. (GSII).

Composite & Relationship Charts: M-17. *Compatible Hardware:* Commodore 64, PET, VIC-20.
disk $30.00.
cassette $30.00.
Displays Natal Charts for Both Individuals & Their Composite/Relationship Simultaneously.
Matrix Software.

Composite & Relationship Charts: M-34. *Compatible Hardware:* Apple II+; Commodore 64, PET; TRS-80.
disk $50.00.
Commodore 64, PET; TRS-80. cassette $50.00.
Performs 2 Synastry Techniques: Composite & Relationship Charts.
Matrix Software.

Composite Astro-Report. Lynne Cochran & Robert S. Hand. 1983. *Compatible Hardware:* Apple II with Applesoft, Apple II+, IIc, IIe, III; Macintosh, CP/M-based machines with 2 148-200k disk drives or 1 300k disk drive; IBM PC compatibles. *Operating System(s) Required:* Apple DOS, CP/M-80, MacFinder, MS-DOS, PC-DOS. *Language(s):* BASIC. *Memory Required:* Apple & TRS-80 48k, CP/M 64k, PC-DOS 256k, MS-DOS 128k or 256k, Macintosh 512k. *General Requirements:* Printer, Dot-Matrix or Hewlett Packard Laser. *Items Included:* Manual. *Customer Support:* Free phone support.
disk $195.00 ea.
IBM PC. (ISBN 0-913637-50-5).
MS-DOS. (ISBN 0-913637-64-5).
CP/M (Kaypro 2). (ISBN 0-913637-49-1).
Apple. (ISBN 0-87199-027-X).
Macintosh. (ISBN 0-87199-051-2).
Produces a 10-12 Page Report Analyzing a Romantic Relationship from the Composite Horoscope of Two People. Includes License to Sell Printed Output. Also Available in Spanish in IBM Compatible Version for $250.
Astrolabe, Inc.

Composite Image. *Compatible Hardware:* Unix Sun, HP-UX, Aegis; HP Apollo; DEC ULTRIX. *Items Included:* Documentation. *Customer Support:* Maintenance plan, training; 800 number.
contact publisher for price.
Composite Image is an Interactive Raster Editing Option Used with Series 5000 Graphics Software. User Can Revise Existing, Scanned, or digital Raster Images & Add Vector Entitles to Create a "Composite File". In the Composite File, User Can Edit Raster data, Vector Data or Both Simultaneously without Raster Conversion.
Auto-Trol Technology Corp.

Comprehensive Index to ASM CD-ROM. 1994. Windows 3.1. IBM or compatible. CD-ROM disk $153.00 (Order no.: 6508B).
ASM International.

Comprehensive Integrated Payroll System: CHIPS. *Version:* 95.0. 1986. *Operating System(s) Required:* XENIX, UNIX, L.A.N, MS-DOS. *Language(s):* COBOL. *General Requirements:* 132-column printer, hard disk, COBOL Runtime. *Items Included:* Yes; phone & modem - contact vendor for features. *Customer Support:* Yes; phone & modem.
contact publisher for price.
On-Line Interactive Payroll System Which Can Be Integrated with BUCS. Offers the User the Ability to Define & Maintain the Tables Necessary to Compute All Federal, State & Local Taxes As Well As Numerous Other Pays & Deductions. The System Handles Various Fixed Pay Categories & up to Twelve Fixed Deductions. Additional Deductions & Earnings Can Be Set for Each Employee.
Donald R. Frey & Co., Inc.

Comprehensive Utility Billing & Control System: CUBIC. *Version:* 94.0. 1981. *Operating System(s) Required:* XENIX, UNIX, L.A.N., MS-DOS. *Language(s):* COBOL. *General Requirements:* 132-column printer, hard disk, COBOL Runtime. *Items Included:* Users' Guide. *Customer Support:* Yes; phone & modem - contact vendor for features.
Contact publisher for price.
Designed to Meet the Needs of Utility Service Operations. Offers the Ability to Process Metered Service Such As Water, Sewer, Gas & Electric, As Well As Unmetered Services Such As Sanitary Pickup, Street Lights, Sprinklers & Other Services. Statistical Reporting Is Available to Track Services by Billings, Penalties, Payments & Volumes, etc. Inquiry Capabilities Are Available by Account, Customer Name, Service Address & Billing Address for Information on Customer/ Owner Data & Billing, Payment & Usage Data by Service. Supports a Multi-User Option. Integrated with the BUCS System for Speed & Control.
Donald R. Frey & Co., Inc.

CompreMED. *Compatible Hardware:* 486, Pentium, IBM RISC. *Operating System(s) Required:* SuperDOS, SCO UNIX & AIX. *Memory Required:* 1000k. *General Requirements:*

TITLE INDEX

Hard disk with tape cartridge for back-up, printer, modem.
contact publisher for price.
Designed to Enhance the Efficiency of a Medical Practice. The Basic Package Consists of Patient Demographic Information, Billing, Accounts Receivable Management, Practice Analysis, Practice Marketing, & Electronic Mail. Optional Modules Include Electronic Claims Transmission, Clinical Information, Report Generator, Appointment Scheduling, Surgery Scheduling, A/R Open Item Method, Patient Budgeting, Accounts Payable, Payroll, General Ledger, & Word Processing, Electronic Posting of Payment, Refund Check Generation, Managed Care & Innoculation Tracking.
Ranac Computer Corp.

COMPRESS. *Version:* 5.32. *Items Included:* Manual - 3 ring box binder. *Customer Support:* $600/year updates & technical support, 1st year free.
DOS. 386 or higher (2Mb). disk $4000.00.
Designs ASME Pressure Vessels, Including Heads, Shells, Transitions, Flanges, Nozzles, Reinforcing Pad, Skirts, Legs, & Saddles. It Considers Internal & External Pressure, Wind & Earthquake & Calculates Minimum Thickness, MAP & MAWP for All Vessel Components, & with Corrosion Rate Data Determines Replacement Date.
Techdata.

Compression Utility Pack. *Compatible Hardware:* TRS-80.
cassette $19.95 (Order no.: 0246R).
Compacts BASIC Programs into a Smaller Amount of Memory.
Instant Software, Inc.

Compton's Concise Encyclopedia. Sep. 1995. *Customer Support:* Telephone support - free (except phone charge).
Windows 3.1. IBM & compatibles (386 DX-20) (4Mb). CD-ROM disk $12.99 (ISBN 1-57594-031-0). *Nonstandard peripherals required:* 2x CD-ROM player, Sound Card, VGA monitor. *Optimal configuration:* 486 SX-33.
Entire 15 Volumes of Compton's Encyclopedia Plus Multimedia Pictures, Animation, Sounds & Video.
Kidsoft, Inc.

Compton's Concise Encyclopedia. Sep. 1995. *Customer Support:* Telephone support - free (except phone charge).
Windows 3.1. IBM & compatibles (386 DX-20) (4Mb). CD-ROM disk $12.99 (ISBN 1-57594-070-1). *Nonstandard peripherals required:* 2x CD-ROM player, Sound Card, VGA monitor. *Optimal configuration:* 486 SX-33.
Entire 15 Volumes of Compton's Encyclopedia Plus Multimedia Pictures, Animation, Sounds & Video. Blister Pack Jewel Case.
Kidsoft, Inc.

Compu/Chart. *Version:* 1.3. Jun. 1994. *Compatible Hardware:* IBM PC & compatibles. *Operating System(s) Required:* PC-DOS/MS-DOS 2.1 to 6.2. *Language(s):* QUICKBASIC. *Memory Required:* 640k. *General Requirements:* 1200 Baud Modem, EGA/VGA card, hard disk. *Items Included:* User manual. *Customer Support:* Phone or mail.
3.5" or 5.25" disk $239.95 (ISBN 0-930437-28-4).
Automatic Data Retrieval & Technical Analysis Employing 16-Color, High-Resolution Graphics for an Optimal Display of Charts & Indicators on Screen As Well As for Printer Output. Capabilities Include the Intra-Day Monitor with Dynamic Bar, Moving up & down Volume Ratio, Back Scanner, Flagged Report During Retrieval Updates, Last Trade Chart Market & Status Report & Others. Includes 5 Unique Chart Screens Including Comparison Charting: Web Page: Http:11www.loop.com/nvariagate/ntpge.htm.
NewTEK Industries.

Compu-Chart EGA: Technical-Graphic Market Analyzer. *Items Included:* Bound manual. *Customer Support:* Free hotline - no time limit; 30 day limited warranty; updates are $5/disk plus S&H.
MS-DOS 3.2 or higher. IBM & compatibles (640k). disk $299.95. *Nonstandard peripherals required:* High density floppy or hard drive. For downloading by telephone, a Hayes (or compatible) or Racal Vadic modem is necessary.
Tool for Performing Technical Market Analysis Based on Graphical Representations. It Is Applicable to Both Short Term & Long Term Trading, & Can Be Used by Novices & Veterans Alike. Data Is Quickly & Painlessly Downloaded by Modem (from the Hale System/Track Service). Historical Market Files Can Hold up to 7 Months (Daily) to 33 Months (Weekly) of Data on Any of the Stocks, Indices, or Funds Which You Care to Follow.
Dynacomp, Inc.

The Compu-Counter Accounts Payable: Business Accounting Software. *Version:* 4.0.5. Dec. 1993. *Compatible Hardware:* IBM PC & compatibles. *Operating System(s) Required:* PC-DOS/MS-DOS 3.3 or higher. *Language(s):* Microsoft PDS. *Memory Required:* 256k. *General Requirements:* Hard disk. *Customer Support:* 12 months free telephone support.
IBM. 3.5" or 5.25" disk $95.00 (ISBN 0-923945-10-5).
Designed to Keep Track of Current & Aged Accounts Payable. Maintains Complete Record for Each Vendor, Suggests Vendors to Pay Based upon Due Date or Discount Date or Within Certain Cash Requirements, & Automatically Prints Checks & a Check Register. Integrates with the General Ledger.
Excalibur Systems, Inc.

The Compu-Counter Accounts Receivable: Business Accounting Software. *Version:* 4.0.5. Dec. 1991. *Compatible Hardware:* IBM PC & compatibles. *Operating System(s) Required:* PC-DOS/MS-DOS 3.3 or higher. *Language(s):* Microsoft PDS. *Memory Required:* IBM 256k. *General Requirements:* Hard disk. *Customer Support:* 12 months free telephone support.
IBM. 3.5" or 5.25" disk $95.00 (ISBN 0-923945-08-3).
Invoicing & Monthly Statement Generating System. Keeps Track of Current & Aged Accounts Receivable. Maintains a Customer Master File & Transaction File. Master File Contains Detailed Customer Information & Transaction File Contains Information Regarding Each Posted Invoice & Payment. Integrates with General Ledger.
Excalibur Systems, Inc.

The Compu-Counter General Ledger: Business Accounting Software. *Version:* 6.1.3-91. Jul. 1992. *Compatible Hardware:* IBM PC & compatibles. *Operating System(s) Required:* PC-DOS/MS-DOS 3.3 or higher. *Language(s):* Microsoft PDS. *Memory Required:* 256k. *General Requirements:* Hard disk. *Customer Support:* 12 months free telephone support.
IBM. 3.5" or 5.25" disk $95.00 (ISBN 0-923945-14-8).
Designed to Record & Balance Financial Transactions, Provide Accurate & Timely Financial Statements, & Provide Comparative Financial Data for Previous Year. Departmentalized Income Statements for up to 90 Departments Can Be Generated & Chart of Accounts Can Be User Defined.
Excalibur Systems, Inc.

The Compu-Counter Payroll: Business Accounting Software, Payroll. *Version:* 4.0.5. Jul. 1992. *Compatible Hardware:* IBM PC & compatibles. *Operating System(s) Required:* PC-DOS/MS-DOS 3.3 or higher. *Language(s):* Microsoft PDS. *Memory Required:* 256k. *General Requirements:* Hard disk. *Customer Support:* 12 months free telephone support.
IBM. 3.5" or 5.25" disk $95.00 (ISBN 0-923945-12-1).
Prepares Periodic Payroll for Hourly, Salaried & Commissioned Employees & Accumulates Information Necessary to Prepare Monthly, Quarterly, & Annual Tax Reports. User-Definable Tables for Federal, State, & Local Withholdings & FICA Are Provided. Automatically Produces Payroll Checks & W2s & Integrates with the General Ledger.
Excalibur Systems, Inc.

Compu-Crete. *Items Included:* Software & documentation. *Customer Support:* Optional on-site training & support, 90-day warranty, toll-free #, maintenance.
MS-DOS (512k). PC & compatibles. contact publisher for price. *Addl. software required:* Work Station Basic operating system. *Optimal configuration:* 286 clone, 100Mb operating system.
Specialized Billing, Accounts Receivable & Analysis System with Interface to Truck Scale & Batch Plants. System Is Designed for Bulk Materials Dealers Such As Sand & Gravel or Ready-Mix Concrete.
Hansco Information Technologies, Inc.

Compu-Cutter: Paper Cutting Calculator. *Version:* 4.0.4, Compu-Cutter. Mar. 1991. *Compatible Hardware:* IBM PC & compatibles. *Operating System(s) Required:* PC-DOS/MS-DOS 3.3 or higher. *Memory Required:* 128k. *General Requirements:* Hard disk; graphics board optional for graphic display. *Customer Support:* 12 months free telephone support.
3.5" or 5.25" disk $95.00.
Calculates Number Out & Percent Yield from Parent Sheets.
Excalibur Systems, Inc.

Compu-Opoly. *Compatible Hardware:* TRS-80 Model I, Model III, Model 4 with Level II BASIC. *Memory Required:* disk 32k.
disk $23.95.
Rules of the Game Are Similar to Parker Brothers' Monopoly.
Dynacomp, Inc.

The Compu-Printer Customer History Module. *Version:* 4.0.5. Jul. 1992. *Compatible Hardware:* IBM PC & compatibles. *Operating System(s) Required:* PC-DOS/MS-DOS 3.3 or higher. *Language(s):* Microsoft PDS. *Memory Required:* 512k. *General Requirements:* Minimum 10Mb hard disk & Level III of COMPU-PRINTER Print Shop Management Software. *Customer Support:* 12 months free telephone support.
3.5" or 5.25" disk $195.00.
Stores Customer Order/Invoice Details for Later Recall & Analysis. Displays & Prints Reports by Customer, Invoice, Date Ranges, etc. Disk Files Are in ASCII Format, Enabling Access by User's Word Processor, Data-Base System or Other Programs for All Types of Analysis.
Excalibur Systems, Inc.

The Compu-Printer: Paper Inventory. *Version:* 4.0.5. Mar. 1991. *Customer Support:* 12 months free telephone support.
MS-PC DOS 3.3 or higher. IBM-PC compatible (512k). disk $195.00.
An Inventory System for Print Shop Paper Stock. Integrates with Order Entry & Paper Pricing Files

to Automatically Deduct Disbursements. Produces Status, Activity, Re-Order & Physical Inventory Reports. Displays Description, Code Price, on Hand, Minimum & Re-Order Quantities, Total Value. Also Available As a Stand-Alone Module.
Excalibur Systems, Inc.

The Compu-Printer: Print Shop Estimating-Quoting, Level II. *Version:* 4.0.5. Jul. 1992. *Compatible Hardware:* IBM PC & compatibles. *Operating System(s) Required:* PC-DOS/MS-DOS 3.3 or higher. *Language(s):* Microsoft. *Memory Required:* 512k. *General Requirements:* Hard disk. *Customer Support:* 12 months free telephone support.
IBM. 3.5" or 5.25" disk $195.00 (ISBN 0-923945-02-4).
Designed for Medium to Small Sized Commercial & Quick Printers. User-Defined Data Base, Interacting with a Set of Copyrighted Formulas, Produces Customized Printing Price Lists & Complete Quotations.
Excalibur Systems, Inc.

The Compu-Printer: Print Shop Management System, Level III. *Version:* 4.0.5. Jul. 1992. *Compatible Hardware:* IBM PC & compatibles. *Operating System(s) Required:* MS-DOS/PC-DOS 3.3 or higher. *Language(s):* Microsoft PDS. *Memory Required:* 512k. *General Requirements:* Hard disk. *Customer Support:* 12 months free telephone support.
IBM. disk $485.00 (ISBN 0-923945-00-8).
Designed for Medium to Small Sized Commercial & Quick Printers. A User-Defined Data Base, Interacting with a Set of Copyrighted Formulas, Produces Customized Price Lists, Quotations, Workorders, Invoices, Customer Statements, Accounts Receivable Aging, Sales Analysis, & Numerous Other Reports. Integrates with Accounts Payable, Payroll, & General Ledger Modules.
Excalibur Systems, Inc.

Compu-Share General Ledger. *Version:* 5.8. May 1993. *Language(s):* DIBOL & C, COBOL. *General Requirements:* Depends on specific configuaration. *Customer Support:* Full service, update service; by quotation.
VMS, Open VMS. DEC VAX Series, DEC Alpha AXP. disk $2500.00-$15,000.00.
Includes: User Defined Charts of Accounts Scheme, Account Number Format, Date Format, Automatic Recurring Postings, Automatic Allocations & Accounting Periods, etc. Almost Any Style of Financial Statement Can Be Designed.
Compu-Share, Inc.

Compu-Share Receivables Management RE/CS. *Version:* 5.8. May 1993. *Compatible Hardware:* VMS, Open VMS. *Operating System(s) Required:* VMS. *Language(s):* DIBOL, C, COBOL. *Customer Support:* Full service, update service; by quotation.
disk $2500.00-$15,000.00.
Features: User Designed Statements & Invoices, Numeric or Alpha Customer Codes, Discount Capabilities, Finance Charge Computation, Credit Limit Checking, Recurring A/R, up Applied Payments, etc. Reports Available on a Customer, Salesperson, Sales Type & Customer Class on a Date-Range Basis.
Compu-Share, Inc.

Compu-Soft's Pro-Performance Management Series: Service Performance. *Version:* 2.0. Christine Schad & Michael Schad. Jun. 1994. *Items Included:* 1 3-ring bound manual. *Customer Support:* 90 day limited warranty; yearly support contract w/product updates, $145.00.
MS-DOS 3.3. IBM compatible 8088 w/1Mb HD space (640k). disk $795.00, incl. manual.

Nonstandard peripherals required: Any color monitor, printer. *Optimal configuration:* 386 SX16, DOS 3.3 or higher, 640k RAM, 1Mb HD space, any color monitor.
A System That Allows Your Employee's to Know Exactly What Is Expected of Them, Keeping Them Informed of Their Progress & If Desired, Rewarding Them for Their Efforts. The Program Includes Detailed Manager Reports on a Monthly Basis.
Compu-Soft.

Compu-U-Temp: Temperature Data Acquisition. Feb. 1986. *Compatible Hardware:* Commodore 64, 128. *Memory Required:* 48k.
Version 2.0 8 channel. disk $139.95, incl. 2 Sensors.
Version 3.0 16 channel. disk $189.95, incl. 4 Sensors.
add'l. Sensors $7.50 ea.
Inexpensive Temperature Monitor & Data Logger. Data Storage to & from Disk, Temperature Monitoring From 15 Degrees Fahrenheit to 180 Degrees Fahrenheit.
Applied Technologies, Inc.

Compuchurch Plus Combo Pak. *Version:* 2.89. 1984. *Compatible Hardware:* IBM PC & compatibles. *Operating System(s) Required:* MS-DOS. *Language(s):* Assembly, Compiled BASIC, C. *Memory Required:* 512k. *General Requirements:* Hard disk. *Items Included:* Word processor interface. *Customer Support:* 1st 6 months included, nominal fee thereafter.
disk $275.00, incl. manual.
Integrated Version of COMPUCHURCH GIFTS, COMPUCHURCH SHEPHERD; Church Ledger for Church Administration.
MTS, Inc.

CompuCite. *Compatible Hardware:* IBM PC, PC XT, PC AT & compatibles, PS/2. *Operating System(s) Required:* PC-DOS/MS-DOS 2.10 or higher. *Memory Required:* 320k. *Customer Support:* 60 days toll-free.
$129.00.
Scans Legal Documents & Automatically Locates the Citations Without the Need to Mark the Beginning & End of Citation & Checks the Form of the Citation with "A Uniform System of Citation - 14th Edition (the Blue Book)". A Copy of the "Blue Book" Is Included in the Package. Reads Most Leading Word Processor Files Directly; Also Includes a USER DEFINED Format Which Allows Users to Customize the System to Work with Additional Word Processors. Includes a 'Pop-Up' Table Which Allows Users to Set the Order of Jurisdictional Searching. As Errors Are Located, 13 Types of Diagnostics Are Produced: Alternate Reporter, Court Designation, Case Name, Capitalization & Punctuation, Date, Introductory Signal, Page, Prior & Subsequent History, Parallel Reporter, Paranthetical, Parsing, & Volume.
CompuLaw, Ltd.

Compuledger: Single-Entry General Ledger. *Items Included:* Bound manual. *Customer Support:* Free hotline - no time limit; 30 day limited warranty; updates are $5/disk plus S&H.
MS-DOS. IBM & compatibles (128k). disk $49.95. *Nonstandard peripherals required:* 132-column printer.
Single-Entry Accounting System Designed for Small Businesses (Less Than 25 Employees). A Combination of up to 99 Accounts/Subaccounts Are Allowed. User Can Incrementally Step Through Checks. Transaction Descriptions Can Be up to 20 Characters Long. When You Enter Account Codes, the Account Description (up to 35 Characters) Is Displayed. Data May Be Stored in up to 50 Named Files (e.g., by Month). Reports Can Be Prepared Using Totals

by Category/Subcategory; Chronological Sorting; & Other Selection Techniques. All Reports May Be Saved on Disk in ASCII Format for Passing to Other Programs, Such As a Word Processor.
Dynacomp, Inc.

Compulize: Accounts Payable. *Version:* 5.0. Jan. 1991. *Items Included:* 3 ring binder user manual. *Customer Support:* $93.00 yearly support contract, toll free number, & software maintenance & updates.
MS-DOS 3.3 or higher. IBM & compatible (640k). Contact publisher for price. *Optimal configuration:* 368, MS-DOS 4.01, 1Mb RAM, VGA color. *Networks supported:* LANtastic, Novell.
Accounting Tool for Fertilizer Dealers. Handles Both Product & General Payables. Tracks Vender Activity. Applies Freight- Trucking & Rebate Checks to Product Cost. Check Writing & Check Register. Matches Bill of Lading with Invoices. Updates General Ledger.
Hutch Computer Industries, Inc.

Compulize: Accounts Receivable. *Customer Support:* Annual toll-free software maintenance, includes updates & annual training, $93.00.
MS-DOS 3.3 or higher. IBM compatibles (640k). disk $935.00. *Optimal configuration:* 386 MS-DOS 4.01, 1Mb RAM, VGA color letter quality 80 column printer. *Networks supported:* Lantastic, Novell.
This Program Automatically Posts Invoices to Customers's Accounts, Produces End-to-End Statement, Adds Finance Charges, Creates Aged Trial Balance, Prints Invoice Listing, & Allows User to Look up Customer's Balance & Detail at Time. Interfaces with Compulize Invoices & Prepay.
Hutch Computer Industries, Inc.

Compulize: Cash Crop Breakeven. *Customer Support:* Annual toll-free software maintenance, includes updates & annual training, $69.00.
MS-DOS 3.3 or higher. IBM compatibles (640k). disk $250.00. *Optimal configuration:* 386 MS-DOS 4.01, 1Mb RAM, VGA color letter quality, 80 column printer. *Networks supported:* Lantastic, Novell.
Leads Farmer Through the Cost of Raising Any Crop Calculating Breakeven Price & Profitability of the Crop. Also Calculates Buying & Rental Breakeven Prices on Land Based on the Cost of Raising a Crop. Interfaces with Compulize Soil Recommendation Program.
Hutch Computer Industries, Inc.

Compulize: Data Base Reports. *Customer Support:* Annual toll-free software maintenance, includes updates & annual training, $105.00.
MS-DOS 3.3 or higher. IBM compatible. disk $1050.00. *Optimal configuration:* MS-DOS 4.01, 1Mb RAM, VGA color letter quality 80 column printer. *Networks supported:* Lantastic, Novell.
Allows User to Operate Reports on Any Information from Any Compulize Programs. Allows User to Find Who Bought What, When, Where, & How Much. Provides Restricted Use Pesticide Reports, Tonnage Tax Reports, & a Variety of Reports on Customers, Sales, Purchases, & Product.
Hutch Computer Industries, Inc.

Compulize: Formulation. *Customer Support:* Annual toll-free software maintenance, includes upgrades & annual training, $150.00.
MS-DOS 3.3 or higher. IBM compatible (640k). disk $1525.00. *Optimal configuration:* 386 MS-DOS 4.01, 1Mb RAM, VGA color letter quality, 80 column printer. *Networks supported:* Lantastic, Novell.
Prescription Blend Fertilizer to a Soil Test

Recommendation or Blend Grade Creating a Batch Sheet/Delivery Ticket. Determines Pounds or Gallons Per Acre, Weight Per Gallon or Cubic Foot, & Final Analysis. Calculates Cost Per Acre, Ton & Batch. Interface with Compulize Invoicing & Inventory Control & Compulize Soil Test Recommendation.
Hutch Computer Industries, Inc.

Compulize: Invoicing & Inventory Central.
Customer Support: Annual toll-free software maintenance, includes updates & annual training, $235.00.
MS-DOS 3.3 or higher. IBM compatibles (640k). disk $2350.00. *Optimal configuration:* 386 MS-DOS 4.01, 1Mb RAM, VGA color letter quality 80 column printer. *Networks supported:* Lantastic, Novell.
Creates an Invoice & Controls Inventories on up to 26 Product Categories of Over 25,000 Items. This Point-of-Sale Program Provides Immediate & Perpetual Inventory. Eliminates the Need for a Cash Register. Interfaces with Compulize Formulation, Accounts Receivable Prepay, Data Base Reports, General Ledger, & Accounts Payable.
Hutch Computer Industries, Inc.

Compulize: Lab Telecommunications. *Customer Support:* Annual toll-free software maintenance, includes updates & annual training, $60.00.
MS-DOS 3.3 or higher. IBM compatibles (640k). disk $129.00. *Optimal configuration:* 386 MS-DOS 4.01, 1Mb RAM, VGA color, letter quality 80 column printer. *Networks supported:* Lantastic, Novell.
Hook up Via MODEM to Major Soil Test Labs to Telecommunicate Soil Test Results Directly to the Field History Program. Saves Time & Costly Mistakes.
Hutch Computer Industries, Inc.

Compulize: Prepay. *Customer Support:* Annual toll-free software maintenance, includes updates & annual training, $79.00.
MS-DOS 3.3 or higher. IBM & compatibles (640k). disk $795.00. *Networks supported:* Lantastic, Novell.
Allows User to Enter the Amount of Product, Price, & Price Level When a Customer Prepays Products. Program Will Then Use This Information at the Time of Invoicing. Allows Prepay of Product, Category of Product, or a General Prepay for All Customer Purchases. Interfaces with Compulize Invoicing & Accounts Receivable.
Hutch Computer Industries, Inc.

Compulize: Soil-Field History. *Customer Support:* Annual toll-free software maintenance, includes updates & annual training, $93.00.
MS-DOS 3.3 or higher. IBM compatibles (640k). disk $935.00. *Optimal configuration:* 386 MS-DOS 4.01, 1Mb RAM, VGA color, letter quality, 80 column printer. *Networks supported:* Lantastic, Novell.
Stores Five Soil Test Reports on Each Field, with Unlimited Number of Fields. Stores recommendations. Graphic Displays of Soil Test Nutrient Levels, Compare Graphically Nutrients from Last Five Tests, to Compare Fertility. Allows up to 15 Scouting Notes Per Field. Interfaces with Compulize Soil Test Recommendation & Lab Telecommunications.
Hutch Computer Industries, Inc.

Compulize: Soil Test Recommendation.
Customer Support: Annual toll-free software maintenance, includes updates & annual training, $235.00.
MS-DOS 3.3 or higher. IBM compatible (640k). disk $2350.00. *Optimal configuration:* 386 MS-DOS 4.01, 1Mb RAM, VGA color letter quality 80 column printer. *Networks supported:* Lantastic, Novell.
Sales Tool for Fertilizer Dealer to Make Soil Recommendations, & Price Them Using a Program Approach. Cost of Fertilizer Per Acre, Bushel, & Per Field Included. Allows Different Yield Goals, up to 100 User Defined Crops & User Tuned Recommendations. Interfaces with Compulize Soil History, Compulize Formation & Cash Crop Breakeven.
Hutch Computer Industries, Inc.

Compumedic. *Version:* 1.40. 1981. *Compatible Hardware:* IBM PC & compatibles, 286, 386, 486. *Operating System(s) Required:* PC-DOS, MS-DOS. *Language(s):* Compiled BASIC. *Memory Required:* Windows 8000 Mb, DOS 640k. *Items Included:* On-site installation, training, support, two updates, General Ledger. *Customer Support:* $720/yr. after first 6 months. disk $1995.00.
Complete Medical Management Program Including Electronic Billing Through EMC.
Data Strategies, Inc.

Compusec Portfolio Manager. *Items Included:* Bound manual. *Customer Support:* Free hotline - no time limit; 30 day limited warranty; updates are $5/disk plus S&H.
Apple (84k). disk $99.95. *Nonstandard peripherals required:* Printer supported, but not required; can be used with or without a modem.
Ranks Each Stock in Any Portfolio, Showing Which Stocks Should Be Reduced or Eliminated, & Which Should Be Increased. Calculates for Any Stock, the Compound Growth Rate Between the Earnings-per-Share for an Earlier Time Period & the Earnings-per-Share for a Later Time Period. Calculates the Payback Period (Years to Earn Back the Market Price), Based on the Calculated Growth Rate or Your Own Estimated Growth Rate. Shows Daily Volume & More.
Dynacomp, Inc.

CompuServe Navigator. *General Requirements:* Double-sided 800K disk drive; hard disk drive; System 4.1 or later, Hayes-compatible modem. Macintosh 512KE or higher. 3.5" disk $99.95.
Automated Access Software.
CompuServe, Inc.

Compusketch. *General Requirements:* Hard disk drive; ImageWriter, LaserWriter (Windows compatible) or 9 pin dot matrix. *Items Included:* Disk, manuals, paint program - MS Window for DOS version. *Customer Support:* 800-722-3729 (8-5 PST).
MS-DOS (640k). Macintosh SE or higher. 3.5" disk $4500.00.
Composite Sketch Software for Law Enforcement Agencies.
Visatex Corp.

CompuSystems Payroll System. *Version:* 2.1. Nov. 1984. *Compatible Hardware:* IBM PC, PC XT, Displaywriter. *Operating System(s) Required:* MS-DOS 2.0. *Language(s):* BASIC. *Memory Required:* 128k. *General Requirements:* 2 disk drives, printer.
IBM PC, PC XT. disk $500.00 (ISBN 0-923067-15-9, Order no.: PC-PRSA).
Displaywriter. cassette $495.00 (ISBN 0-923067-14-0, Order no.: DW-PRSA).
Displaywriter. 8" disk $812.50, incl. source code (ISBN 0-923067-13-2, Order no.: DW-PR).
Displaywriter. 8" demo disk $50.00 (ISBN 0-923067-16-7, Order no.: DW-PR-DEMO).
Maintains Records for Employees; Prints Checks, Check Register, Monthly Reports, Quarterly Reports, Annual Reports, W-2 Forms, 1099 Forms etc. Hard Disk Version Is Available.
CompuSystems, Inc.

Compute Pursuit. 1984. *Compatible Hardware:* Apple II, Commodore 64, IBM PC. *Memory Required:* 64k.
disk $34.00.
Spinning Wheel with 20 Categories of Trivia Information Stops at Random. Words & Phrases Are Indicated by Groups of Arrows on Screen. Player Chooses While Scoring Clock Ticks Down. If He Fails to Guess the Word or Phrase in Time He Is "Bankrupt" & Must Spin Again for a New Category. Otherwise He Completes 5 Turns to Get the Cumulative High Score.
Navic Software.

Computer Acquire. Sep. 1991. *Items Included:* Rulebook. *Customer Support:* 60 days warranty; free replacement of defective software; replacement after 60 days-$12.00.
MS-DOS. IBM PC (256k). disk $25.00 (Order no.: 49354).
Players Create Chains of Hotels & Expand Them Through Mergers & Acquisitions. Buy Stock in Any Active Chain & Even Overtake Those Begun by Your Opponents. The Player Controlling the Largest Chain at the End of the Game Is Declared the Hotel Tycoon of the World.
Avalon Hill Game Co., The Microcomputer Games Div.

Computer Aid Payroll: PayMaster for Hotels, Restaurants & Multi Location Businesses.
Version: 7.0. Jul. 1983. *Compatible Hardware:* IBM PS/2 & compatibles. *Operating System(s) Required:* MS-DOS, Novell Netware 3.11 or 4. *Language(s):* Compiled MBASIC & Assembler. *Memory Required:* 2000k. *General Requirements:* Floppy disk drives, printer, hard disk.
Version 1. disk $4000.00.
Version 2. disk $2500.00.
Version 3. disk $1000.00.
demo disk $55.00.
Contains Tip Allocation for Large Food & Beverage Establishments Using Gross Receipts or Hours. Includes 3 Versions: Screen Data & Corrections, Batch Processing of Entire Payroll, & Department Summaries. The Computation of All Taxes Required by Federal, State & Local Payroll Laws Includes: Federal Income Tax Withholding, 52 Different State Taxes, City & County Taxes, FICA, FUTA, & SUTA, Federal Wage-Hour Law, Disability Insurance, Advance Earned Income Credit, Tip Credit, Vacation Pay, Sick, Banquet Wages, Banquet Tips, Commissions, Uniform & Meals Allowance. The Program Contains Error Checking & Corrections, & Prints Totals On-Screen Before Processing Payroll.
Computer Aid Corp.

Computer-Aided Construction Take-Off & Estimating System: CACTES. 1976. *Compatible Hardware:* All IBM compatible PCs; all Novel networks; any UNIX-based PC. *Operating System(s) Required:* Standard OS for hardware selected. *Language(s):* BASIC (source code included). *Memory Required:* 640k. *General Requirements:* Hard disk.
Single-User. $7895.00.
System to Take-Off, Calculate & Report Quantities, Costs & Hours for All Cost Items of a Construction Project. User-Designed Reports, Multiple Look-Up Methods, Supports Digitizers; Transfer Data from/to Other Systems (Spreadsheets, Job-Cost, Scheduling, Pricing Systems, CAD); User Designed Cost Codes, Questions, Formulas, Indexes, etc.
E. F. Paynter & Assocs., Inc.

Computer-Aided Design for Inductors & Transformers. *Version:* III. KG Magnetics, Inc. Jun. 1990. *Items Included:* Operating manual & design examples. *Customer Support:* Full telephone support by KG Magnetics personal. Apple Macintosh & IBM. contact publisher for

price.
DOS 2.1 & higher. IBM PC, XT, AT & compatibles (128k). contact publisher for price. *Magnetics Design Program That Allows Engineers to Quickly Evaluate Transformer & Inductor Designs, Given Their Basic Electrical Parameters. Comes with a Basic Data Base of Magnetic Core Information.*
E.J. Bloom Assocs., Inc.

Computer Aided Design System, 4 diskettes.
Items Included: Bound manual. *Customer Support:* Free hotline - no time limit; 30 day limited warranty; updates are $5/disk plus S&H.
DOS 3.3 & ProDOS. Apple (48k or 64k). $139.95.
Complete Computer-Aided Design System for the Apple. It Includes an Extensive Drawing System (CADDRAW), Utility for Creating New Symbols (CADDRAW SYMBOL MAKER/EDITOR), & a Printer Dump (by Beagle Bros.).
Dynacomp, Inc.

Computer Aided Drafting. *Items Included:* Bound manual. *Customer Support:* Free hotline - no time limit; 30 day limited warranty; updates are $5/disk plus S&H.
MS-DOS. IBM & compatibles, TRS-80 (256k). disk $79.95.
Apple. disk $79.95.
Now Students Can Learn about Computer Aided Drafting Without the Expense of a CAD System! This Menu-Driven Package Includes "Career Opportunities in CAD", "Is CAD for You", "An Introduction to CAD Basics", "CAD Hardware", & "Applications of CAD Principles". This Software Tutorial Is Ideal for Introducing the Subject of Computer Aided Design, or Is a Perfect Supplement for Any Class That Already Uses an Actual CAD System. Each Lesson Is Followed by a Computer-Generated Quiz. Student Scores Are Automatically Recorded & May Be Printed.
Dynacomp, Inc.

Computer Applications for Introduction to Business. Ronald S. Burke. 1988. *Items Included:* Data disk, instructor's manual. *Customer Support:* Software Service Center: 1-800-437-3715 (New York residents call 212-512-6665 collect) 9AM-4PM EST.
PC-DOS. IBM PC & compatibles. site license fee $150.00.
Consists of Four Applications Requiring Students to Use Spreadsheets & Databases in Making Operational & Strategic Decisions for a Hypothetical but Realistic Business. May Be Used with Any Introduction to Business Program. Each Application Focuses on a Key Functional Area of Business Management - Production, Marketing, Human Resources & Finance. Computer Tools Used Are Spreadsheet & Database Programs Drawn from McGraw-Hill Integrated Software.
Gregg/McGraw-Hill.

Computer Applications in Retail Management & Entrepreneurship for the Apple II Series.
Ruth A. Keyes. *Compatible Hardware:* Apple II, II+, IIe.
disk $75.00 (ISBN 0-13-163775-4).
Prentice Hall.

Computer Applications in Retail Management & Entrepreneurship for the IBM PC. Ruth A. Keyes. *Compatible Hardware:* IBM PC.
disk $75.00 (ISBN 0-13-163445-3).
Prentice Hall.

Computer Assisted Charting: Nurse Charting.
Jan. 1986. *Compatible Hardware:* IBM PC, PS/2 & compatibles. *Operating System(s) Required:* MS-DOS. *Language(s):* BASIC, C. *Memory Required:* 256k. *Items Included:* Extensive documentation on-line, pop-up windows & printed manual. *Customer Support:* 800-line available to licensed users on software maintenance plan. contact publisher for price.
Collects Patient Care & Billing Data from Terminal and/or Pocket-Sized Bar Code Wand. Prints Patient Care Plans, Charts, & Billing Summaries. Source Code Available for the Report Generation Modules.
New Century Products.

Computer-Assisted Investment: Handbook.
Albert Bookbinder. 1983. *Compatible Hardware:* Apple, Macintosh; Commodore; DEC; IBM PC; Kaypro; Sanyo; Tandy; TRS-80. *Operating System(s) Required:* Apple DOS, CBM, CP/M, Macintosh, MS-DOS, TRSDOS. *Language(s):* BASIC (source code included). *Memory Required:* 64k. *Customer Support:* Telephone support.
disk containing all 50 programs Ready-to-Run $119.95.
Forecasts & Evaluates Price, Risk, & Return on Exchange of Foreign Currencies in International Trade or Investment. Includes 11 Interactive Programs for Foreign Currency Exchange.
Programmed Pr.

Computer Assisted Loss Management System (CALMS): Intelligent Query.
IBM. Contact publisher for price (ISBN 0-88061-111-1).
International Loss Control Institute, Inc.

Computer Assisted Loss Management System (CALMS): Task Analysis Module.
IBM. Contact publisher for price (ISBN 0-88061-110-3).
International Loss Control Institute, Inc.

Computer Bidding. *Version:* 2.0.
Macintosh 512K or higher. 3.5" disk $695.00.
AICP TV Commercial Bidding.
Max 3, Inc.

Computer Casino: The Most Realistic Gaming Experience Ever. Jun. 1994. *Items Included:* Registration card, instruction sheet. *Customer Support:* 900 support number $2.00 per minute; limited 60 day warranty.
DOS. IBM & compatibles (512k). disk $9.95 (ISBN 1-57269-005-4, Order no.: 3202 42125). *Addl. software required:* DOS 2.1 or higher. *Optimal configuration:* Mouse is optional.
Memorex Computer Casino Gives You the Authentic Draw Poker Casino Without Venturing Farther Than Your PC.
Memorex Products, Inc., Memorex Software Division.

Computer Chef. *Items Included:* Bound manual. *Customer Support:* Free hotline - no time limit; 30 day limited warranty; updates are $5/disk plus S&H.
MS-DOS. IBM & compatibles (256k). disk $29.95.
Home Data Base That Makes Page Flipping & Portion Figuring a Thing of the Past. Tell It the Ingredients on Hand, & COMPUTER CHEF Will Quickly Suggest Recipes Using Them. Saves You Money By Finding Recipes for This Week's Supermarket Bargains. Automatically Scales the Recipe to Fit Your Individual Needs. Prints Recipes On Your Printer. Contains over 70 Kitchen-Tested Recipes from Salad to Desert, Plus Make Even More Use of All These Capabilities by Entering Your Own Recipes Too.
Dynacomp, Inc.

Computer Concepts. 1989. *Items Included:* 3 ring binder with program disk(s), teacher's guide & reproducible student worksheets. *Customer Support:* (805) 473-7383.
Macintosh (1Mb). $59.95 single, $109.95 5-user, $159.95 10-user, $359.95 30-user (SL/Ntwk) (ISBN 0-917623-81-9). *Networks supported:* All.
IBM/Tandy (512k). $59.95 single, $109.95 5-user, $159.95 10-user, $359.95 30-user (SL/Ntwk) (ISBN 0-917623-82-7). *Networks supported:* All.
Apple II (128k). $59.95 single, $109.95 5-user, $159.95 10-user, $359.95 30-user (SL/Ntwk) (ISBN 0-917623-10-X). *Networks supported:* All.
Provides an Excellent Overview of Computer Fundamentals & the Topics Covered Have Become an Essential Part of the Curriculum for an Information Age. The Easy-to-Use Menues & Game-Like Format Make the Program Fun for Students Who Are New to Computers. Provides a Survey of Important Topics in Computer Literacy. Uses a Game-Like Format to Teach Terms & Key Concepts Relevant to: Computer History, How a Computer System Works, BASIC Statements, Understanding Computers, Flowcharts, Computer Uses, Computer Components, & Peripherals.
Ventura Educational Systems.

Computer Crossword. *Compatible Hardware:* IBM PC.
contact publisher for price.
Swiftware Corp.

Computer Diplomacy. Calhammer & Sutherland. Apr. 1984. *Compatible Hardware:* Commodore 128, IBM PC. *Operating System(s) Required:* PC-DOS 2.0. *Language(s):* Assembly. *Memory Required:* Commodore 128k, IBM 256k. *General Requirements:* CGA card for IBM.
Commodore. disk $35.00.
IBM. disk $50.00.
Spread User's Influence & Control over Other Territories, with Diverse Methods, from Diplomacy & Political Strategies, to Back-Stabbing & Psychological Intimidation.
Avalon Hill Game Co., The Microcomputer Games Div.

Computer Generated Chemistry Exams & Homework Assignments. 1995. *Items Included:* Full manual. *Customer Support:* Free telephone support - 90 days, 30-day warranty.
MS-DOS 3.2 or higher. 286 (584k). $29.95 ea.; $395.00 complete set. *Nonstandard peripherals required:* CGA/EGA/VGA.
Completely Menu-Driven. All Needed Instructions Are Clearly Displayed on the Screen. Each of the 16 Packages Consists of Three Modules That Permit the Creation, Generation, & Grading of the Unique Problem Sets Given Each Student. Unit A Introductory Concepts; Unit B Compounds & Bonding; Unit C Chemical Reactions; Unit D The Mole; Unit E Gravimetric Stoichiometry; Unit F Behavior of Gases; Unit G Solutions; Midterm Review of Units A-G; Unit H Chemical Bonding; Unit I Organic Chemistry; Unit J Energy; Unit K/L Kinetics & Equilibrium; Unit M Electrochemistry; Unit N Acids & Bases; Unit O/P Nuclear & Industrial Chemistry; Final Review of Units A-P.
Dynacomp, Inc.

The Computer Geoboard: Visualized Geometry. Mary Luckas. 1994. *Items Included:* Disk comes with software guide. *Customer Support:* Returnable if not satisfied. Call 1-800-341-6094 for technical support. 30-day preview available.
MS-DOS. IBM & compatibles (128k). disk $49.95 (ISBN 0-8251-2606-1, Order no.: 0-26061).
Apple. Apple IIE (128k). disk $49.95 (ISBN 0-8251-2348-8, Order no.: 0-23488).
Students Use the Computer Geoboard to Construct & Visualize Geometric Figures of

Various Types. The Program Describes the Construction, Then Offers Hints for Incorrectly Answered Questions. Teachers May Keep Records of Students' Performances on the Disk.
J. Weston Walch Pub.

Computer Glossary of Abbreviations: SuperGlossary. Version: 7.1. Mark Greenia. Dec. 1995. *Items Included:* Includes printed instructions, install program & help screens. *Customer Support:* Free 90-day Tech Support via Internet E-mail to Lexikon2-aol.com.
MS-DOS. IBM PC & compatibles 80286 (1Mb), VGA color. 3.5" disk $15.00 (ISBN 0-944601-66-9, Order no.: SGL).
A Full Glossary of over 11,000 Abbreviations, Acronyms & Symbols Used in the Fields of Computers, Information Systems, Law, Criminal Justice, Business, Medicine, Photography, Security, Accounting, Budgeting, & Much More. Fast Search Utility Lets You Search for Any Abbreviation or Term in Seconds. A Unique Quick Reference Guide. Includes Install Program & Help Screen. Very Easy to Use.
Lexikon Services.

Computer Industry Forecasts: The Source for Business Information on Computers, Peripherals, & Software. Jan. 1985. *Compatible Hardware:* IBM PC & compatibles with 2 disk drives or hard disk. *Memory Required:* 256k. *General Requirements:* Lotus 1-2-3 or compatible.
disk $295.00 (ISBN 0-936677-01-5).
Quarterly Subscription Service Delivering the Latest Business Information: Sales & Shipment Forecasts, Market Share, Installed Base on Computers, Related Equipment, & Software in a Form Useful for Planning & Analysis. Data from the Major Computer & Business Publications is Abstracted into Tables. Delivered on a Lotus 1-2-3 Formatted Data Disk, Lotus Graphics May Be Used to Make Pie Charts of Market Share, X-Y Plots of Forecasts. Information Can Be Combined with Letters, Reports & Presentations. Print Version Available.
Data Analysis Group.

Computer Innovations C++. Version: AT&T v. 2.1. 1990. *Items Included:* Full documentation included. Also included, Teach Yourself C++ *Customer Support:* Technical telephone/BBS support at no charge.
QNX v.2.15D. Microcomputer 80286/386/486 (1Mb). $595.00. *Addl. software required:* C86 C Compiler v.3.4.
Combines the Standard AT&T Version 2.1 C+ Language with a Developmental Environment Familar to QNX Developers Using Computer Innovations C86 C Compiler. The Package Includes: AT&T Version 2.1 C++ Translator, Integrated CC Compiler/Linker/Debugger Driver, SID++ C++ Debugger, Standard C+ Class Libraries, & Needed Utilities. The C+ Language Definition Supported is Standard, & Portable to Other Environments, Including CI's C+ for UNIX. Documentation to Help Developers Learn & Use C+ Is Included.
Computer Innovations, Inc.

Computer Literacy. H. I. Mathis. 1987. *Compatible Hardware:* Apple II+, IIe; IBM PC. *Operating System(s) Required:* Apple DOS, MS-DOS. *Language(s):* BASIC. *Memory Required:* Apple 48k.
disk $29.95 (ISBN 0-917729-78-1, Order no.: CC111).
Interactive Quiz Program for Teaching Computer Literacy.
Compu-Tations, Inc.

Computer Models of Epidemiology. 1992. *Items Included:* Manual with theory & sample runs, program listings in BASIC. *Customer Support:* Free phone, on-site seminars.
MS-DOS. IBM (128k). disk $130.00.
Macintosh. Macintosh. 3.5" disk $130.00.
2 Programs That Model Transmission of Disease in a Population. (1) SIR - Models a System in Which Susceptibles Become Infectives & Are Removed from the Population by Immunity, Isolation or Death. (2) SIRS - An Extension of SIR, Models a System in Which Some Removed Lose Their Immunity & Return to Become Infected Again. Programs Plot Number of Infectives vs. Time Alongside a Phase Diagram of Infectives vs. Susceptibles.
Kern International, Inc.

Computer Models of Pattern Formation in Biology. 1992. *Items Included:* Manual with theory & sample runs, program listings in BASIC. *Customer Support:* Free phone, on-site seminars.
MS-DOS. IBM (128k). disk $130.00.
Macintosh. Macintosh. 3.5" disk $130.00.
3 Programs That Demonstrate Principles of Pattern Formation in Biology. (1) Stripes - Shows How Stripes Are Formed on Animal Coats As A Result of Reaction-Diffusion (Turing) Mechanism. (2) Spots - Same As Stripes but Shows How Spots Are Formed. (3) Spread - Shows How a Colony of Microorganisms Spreads Through Diffusion into Surrounding Area Combined with Exponential Growth of the Population.
Kern International, Inc.

Computer Models of Population Dynamics. 1991. *Items Included:* Manual with theory & sample runs, program listings in BASIC. *Customer Support:* Free phone, on-site seminars.
MS-DOS. IBM (128k). disk $130.00.
Macintosh. Macintosh. 3.5" disk $130.00.
14 Programs That Simulate Various Processes in Population Biology Including: Growth Processes, Growth with Age & Site Dependence, the Cobweb Method, Growth of the Baleen Whale Population, Density Dependent Growth, Interacting Populations That Follow the Nicholson-Bailey Model, Parasitoid-Host Populations, Phase Planes, Continuous & Discrete Growth Models, Predator-Prey System Modelled by the Lotka-Volterra Equations, Populations in Competition.
Kern International, Inc.

Computer Models of the Chemostat. 1992. *Items Included:* Manual with theory & sample runs, program listings in BASIC. *Customer Support:* Free phone, on-site seminars.
MS-DOS. IBM (128k). disk $130.00.
Macintosh. Macintosh. 3.5" disk $130.00.
2 Programs That Simulate Operation of a Chemostat (Bioreactor). TRSTAT - Plots Transient Response for Given Startup Conditions, Specifically the Bacteria Concentration & Critical Nutrient Concentration vs. Time. SSSTAT - Plots Steady State Response of Bacteria & Critical Nutrient Concentrations vs. Dilution Rate.
Kern International, Inc.

Computer Models of the Environment. 1991. *Items Included:* Manual with review of theory, sample runs. *Customer Support:* Free phone, on-site seminars.
MS-DOS. IBM (128k). disk $130.00.
Macintosh. Macintosh. 3.5" disk $130.00.
16 Programs That Solve Environmental Problems Including Water Quality, Sag Curves in Rivers & Streams, Water Table Contours, Plumes of Contaminants in Ground Water, Stack Plumes of Gaseous Contaminants, Global Warming Due to Atmospheric Pollutants, Oil Slick Spreading, Risk Analysis.
Kern International, Inc.

Computer Programs for Cognitive Rehabilitation. Version: 2.0. Rosamond Gianutsos & Carol Klitzner. *Compatible Hardware:* Apple II, IBM PC. *Operating System(s) Required:* Apple DOS 3.3; PC-DOS 2.1 & higher. (source code included). *Memory Required:* 64k. *Customer Support:* Telephone. $250.00, incl. manuals & documentation.
8 Programs & Handbook Identify & Treat Cognitive Defects in Strokes & Brain Injuries. Memory & Perception Tasks Are Included. Other Volumes in This Series Are Available.
Life Science Assocs.

Computer Resource Guide, Third Edition: Principles of Accounting. Version: 3.0. John W. Wanlass. Nov. 1989. *Compatible Hardware:* IBM PC, PS/2. *Memory Required:* 256k. *General Requirements:* 1 or 2 disk drives, printer. *Customer Support:* 619-699-6227; will accept collect calls, prefer calls from instructors, not students.
disk $19.95, incl. student manual (ISBN 0-15-512758-6, Order no.: 05-12758).
Complete System for Working Beginning Financial Accounting Problems. Includes General Ledger System & Electronic Spreadsheet Templates.
Harcourt Brace Jovanovich, Inc. (College Div.).

Computer Slots: Realistic Casino Slots Action. Oct. 1994. *Items Included:* Registration card, instruction sheet. *Customer Support:* 900 support number $2.00 per minute; limited 60 day warranty.
Windows. IBM PC & compatibles (4Mb). disk $9.95 (ISBN 1-57269-012-7, Order no.: 3202 42155). *Addl. software required:* Windows 3.1 or higher. *Optimal configuration:* VGA or higher monitor, hard disk required (1Mb disk space available), sound card optional.
Experience True Las Vegas-Style Casino Fun with the Absolutely Addictive Play of Memorex Computer Slots.
Memorex Products, Inc., Memorex Software Division.

Computer Starfinder. Larry Ciupik & Jim Seevers. Jan. 1985. *Compatible Hardware:* Apple II+, IIe. *Operating System(s) Required:* Apple DOS 3.3. *Language(s):* Applesoft BASIC. *Memory Required:* 48k.
disk $39.95 (ISBN 0-8331-0187-0, Order no.: 187).
Graphic Demonstration of Constellation, Star & Planet Positions According to Year, Month, Day, Hour & Minute for the Years 1900 to 2100 A.D.
Hubbard Scientific.

Computer Stocks & Bonds. *Compatible Hardware:* Apple II+, IIe; Atari 800/XL/XE; Commodore 64/128; IBM PC. *Operating System(s) Required:* MS-DOS. *Memory Required:* 48k.
Apple, Commodore, IBM. disk $25.00.
Apple, Commodore. cassette write for info.
Game That Allows Players to Select General Strategy & Invest in Stocks That Fit Their Game Plan. Players May Gamble, "Play It Safe", or Do Both. Through Game Transactions, Person Who Makes Most Money Is Winner.
Avalon Hill Game Co., The Microcomputer Games Div.

Computer Third Reich. Sep. 1991. *Items Included:* Rulebook, map. *Customer Support:* 60 days warranty; free replacement for defective software; after 60 days-$12.00.
IBM PC or compatibles (256k). disk $34.95 (Order no.: 45954).
Macintosh. 3.5" disk $34.95 (Order no.: 45956).
Amiga. disk $34.95 (Order no.: 45957).
A Grand Strategic Simulation of the European Theater in WW2. The Player Takes the Role of

the Axis or Allied Powers, & Concentrating on the Many Strategic Decisions Facing Them If They Hope to Attain Victory.
Avalon Hill Game Co., The Microcomputer Games Div.

Computer Upgrades & Repair. Edited by Joseph Desposito.
disk $24.80, incl. 160p. text (ISBN 0-929321-17-0).
Repairing Your IBM Computer & Performing Upgrades.
WEKA Publishing, Inc.

Computerized Classic Accounting. *General Requirements:* 20 MB hard disk drive. Macintosh Plus or higher. $99.00 General Ledger; $300.00 Accounts Receivable, Accounts Payable & Inventory Control; $300.00 Job Costing; $695.00 Client Write-Up.
Accounting for Excel Users.
Absolute Solutions, Inc.

Computerized Classic Bookkeeping. *General Requirements:* 20Mb hard disk drive; ImageWriter or LaserWriter.
Macintosh Plus or higher. 3.5" disk $1295.00.
Complete Accounting/Spreadsheet Program.
Absolute Solutions, Inc.

Computerized Daily Book. *Version:* 6.0. K. Lugo. Jan. 1996. *Compatible Hardware:* IBM PC, PS/2 & compatibles. *Operating System(s) Required:* MS-DOS 6.0 or higher. *Language(s):* C-BASIC, C, C Plus Plus. *Memory Required:* 2000k. *General Requirements:* Hard disk 40Mb. *Customer Support:* On site training, 1st year support via Modem.
disk $3370.00 ea.
IBM PS/2. (ISBN 0-934537-07-0).
PC compatibles. (ISBN 0-934537-08-9).
Integrated Set of 7 Programs (Daily Book, Sales & Receivables, Purchases & Payables, Inventory, Commissions, Vehicle History, & Follow-Up) & Financials. Written in C. Used for C-Stores, Car Wash, Gas Only, & Repair Service Stations.
Service Station Computer Systems, Inc.

The Computerized D.O.T. *Version:* 2.0. Aug. 1992. *Items Included:* Manual. *Customer Support:* Unlimited 800 support line (free); 30 day unlimited warranty.
DOS 3.1 & higher. IBM XT & higher (640k). 3.5" or 5.25" disk $239.00. *Nonstandard peripherals required:* 7Mb hard disk. *Networks supported:* Novell, Lantastic.
DOS 3.1 & higher. Macintosh (1Mb). 3.5" disk $239.00. *Nonstandard peripherals required:* 7Mb hard disk. *Addl. software required:* Hypercard 1.2.5 & higher.
Provides Rapid Access to All Definitions in the Dictionary of Occupational Titles. Offers 4 Ways to Search for Occupations - by Key Word, Interest Area, Industry, & DOT Classification System.
Wintergreen Software.

The Computerized D.O.T. Plus. *Version:* 2.0. Marilyn E. Maze & Patricia Waldren. Aug. 1992. *Items Included:* Manual. *Customer Support:* Unlimited 800 support line (free), 80 day unlimited warranty.
DOS 3.1. IBM XT (640K). 3.5" or 5.25" disk $399.00. *Nonstandard peripherals required:* 7Mb hard disk. *Networks supported:* Novell, Lantastic.
DOS 3.1 or higher. Macintosh (1Mb). 3.5" disk $399.00. *Nonstandard peripherals required:* 7Mb hard disk. *Addl. software required:* Hypercard 1.2.5 & higher.
Includes All the Features of the Computerized DOT, Plus Lists the Worker Traits for Each Occupation & Offers to Print or Save Descriptions on the Disk.
Wintergreen Software.

Computerized Farm Records "Farmware".
1989. *Compatible Hardware:* Apple II Plus, IIe, IIc; IBM PC, PCjr & compatibles. *Memory Required:* Apple 48k, IBM 64k. *General Requirements:* 2 disk drives, printer.
Apple II+, IIe, IIc. disk $199.00 (Order no.: FM001 D-A).
IBM PC, PCjr. disk $249.00 (Order no.: FM001 D-PC).
Provides the Farming Business with Management Information & Eliminates the Processes Associated with Manual Record Keeping.
Micro Learningware.

Computerized Inventory Procedures. Allen. 1986. *Compatible Hardware:* Apple II+, IIe, IIc; IBM PC, PCjr; TRS-80 Model III, Model 4, Tandy 1000. *Operating System(s) Required:* Apple DOS; PC-DOS 1.1, 2.0, 2.1, 3.0; TRSDOS. *Language(s):* BASIC. *Memory Required:* Apple & TRS-80 48k, IBM 128k, Tandy 256k.
TRS-80 (Individual). disk $42.50 (ISBN 0-538-19041-8, Order no.: S046-3).
TRS-80 (Driver). disk $62.50 (ISBN 0-538-19042-6, Order no.: S046-30).
Apple (Individual). disk $42.50 (ISBN 0-538-19043-4, Order no.: S0473).
Apple (Driver). disk $62.50 (Order no.: S047-30).
IBM, Tandy (Individual). disk $42.50 (Order no.: S048-1).
IBM, Tandy (Driver). disk $62.50 (Order no.: S048-10).
txbk. $8.50 (Order no.: S04).
South-Western Publishing Co.

Computerized Operations Planning & Engineering (COPE). *Version:* 4.5. Jun. 1985. *Compatible Hardware:* IBM PC, Texas Instruments. *Operating System(s) Required:* PC-DOS/MS-DOS 1.1 or higher. *Language(s):* BASIC. *Memory Required:* 128k. *General Requirements:* Hard disk, plotter.
disk $395.00.
All Purpose Financial Planning & Modeling Program That Is a Spreadsheet & Decision Support System. Features Statistical Analysis Functions Such as Goal Seeking, Regression Analysis, Trend Analysis, & Learning Curve Operations. Can Integrate with over 2000 Software Programs Without Modification.
Antech, Inc.

Computerized Practice Management System: CPMS. Kelon Corp. *Compatible Hardware:* TI Professional. *Operating System(s) Required:* MS-DOS. *Memory Required:* 128k. *General Requirements:* Printer.
$5000.00 (Order no.: CPMS/PC).
Accounts Receivable, Statement Preparation, Claim Preparation Using Patient Name or Account Number. Reports Based on Physician, Diagnoses, Procedures, Payment Type, Insurer Category, Classification & Place of Service.
Texas Instruments, Personal Productivit.

Computerized Stock Market Analysis.
1983-1986. *Compatible Hardware:* Apple II+, IIe; IBM PC. *Language(s):* BASIC (source code included). *Memory Required:* 64k. *General Requirements:* Printer.
contact publisher for price.
Contains 11 Techniques Using Any of 4 Applicable Data Bases at the Pressing of Menu Selected Key. Over 22 Reports Can Be Generated, Present & Future Stock Trends.
Dalex Pubns.

Computerized Telephone Directory. *Compatible Hardware:* TI 99/4A. *Operating System(s) Required:* DX-10. *Language(s):* Extended BASIC. *Memory Required:* 48k.
disk $24.95.
Menu-Driven Telephone Information Storage & Retrieval System Which Stores Phone Numbers, Addresses & Notes of Conversations on Disk. Automatically Dials a Selected Number If User Has a Touch Tone Dialing System.
Eastbench Software Products.

Computerized Test Bank to Accompany INTERNATIONAL MARKETING, 3rd Edition. Michael R. Czinkota & Ilkka A. Ronkainen. Mar. 1993.
IBM. instr's. software 5.25" $13.50 (ISBN 0-03-097042-3).
Dryden Pr.

Computerized Test Bank to Accompany CONTEMPORARY BUSINESS, 7th Edition. Louis E. Boone & David L. Kurtz. Mar. 1993.
Apple. instr's. software $13.50 (ISBN 0-03-074696-5).
Dryden Pr.

Computerized Test Bank to Accompany CONTEMPORARY BUSINESS, 7th Edition. Louise E. Boone & David L. Kurtz. Feb. 1993.
IBM. instr's. software $13.50 (ISBN 0-03-097598-0).
instr's. software $13.50 (ISBN 0-03-092837-0).
Dryden Pr.

Computerized Test Bank to Accompany CONSUMER BEHAVIOR, 7th Edition. James F. Engel et al. Feb. 1993.
IBM. disk $16.00 (ISBN 0-03-097047-4).
MAC. 3.5" disk $13.50 (ISBN 0-03-097048-2).
Dryden Pr.

Computerized Test Bank to Accompany CONCEPTS OF TAXATION, 1993 Edition. Ray M. Sommerfeld et al. Feb. 1993.
IBM. instr's. software 3.5" $13.50 (ISBN 0-03-097630-8).
Macintosh. instr's. software $13.50 (ISBN 0-03-097632-4).
Dryden Pr.

Computerized Test Bank to Accompany FINANCIAL ACCOUNTING, 2nd Edition. Richard F. Kochanek et al. Feb. 1993.
IBM. instr's. software 5.25" $10.00 (ISBN 0-15-500357-7).
instr's. software 3.5" $13.50 (ISBN 0-15-500356-9).
Dryden Pr.

Computerized Test Bank to Accompany FINANCIAL INSTITUTIONS, MARKETS, & MONEY, 5th Edition. David S. Kidwell et al. Mar. 1993.
IBM. instr's. software $13.50 (ISBN 0-03-092958-X).
Dryden Pr.

Computerized Test Bank to Accompany MONEY, BANKING, & FINANCIAL MARKETS, 2nd Edition. Meir Kohn. Mar. 1993.
IBM. instr's. software $13.50 (ISBN 0-03-097103-9).
Dryden Pr.

Computerized Test Bank to Accompany PROMOTION MANAGEMENT & MARKETING COMMUNICATIONS, 3rd Edition. Terence A. Shimp. Feb. 1993.
Macintosh. instr's. software $13.50 (ISBN 0-03-097912-9).
Dryden Pr.

Computerized Test Bank to Accompany PROFESSIONAL SELLING. Mary A. Oberhaus et al. Mar. 1993.
IBM. instr's. software $16.00 (ISBN 0-03-097023-7).
Dryden Pr.

TITLE INDEX

Computerized Test Bank to Accompany STRATEGIC MANAGEMENT: TEXT & CASES, 5th Edition. James M. Higgins & Julian W. Vincze. Mar. 1993.
IBM. instr's. software $13.50 (ISBN 0-03-054758-X).
MAC. instr's. software $13.50 (ISBN 0-03-097208-6).
Dryden Pr.

Computers in Business. 1992. *Operating System(s) Required:* PC-DOS/MS-DOS. *Memory Required:* 640k. *General Requirements:* dBASE IV or dBASE II Plus, Lotus 1-2-3, WordPerfect, DOS.
3.5" or 5.25" disk $29.95 (ISBN 0-935987-24-X).
Self Study Guide Provides a Survey Course Designed to Acquaint Students with Popular PC Applications. Students are Taught the Basics of DOS, Lotus 1-2-3, dBASE & WordPerfect. Step-by-Step Instructions Are Provided in the Student Guide Which Utilize the Data Files Provided. Basic Computer Terminology is Also Covered.
Edutrends, Inc.

Computerware Accounts Payable. *Compatible Hardware:* IBM PC & compatibles. *Operating System(s) Required:* MS-DOS. *Memory Required:* 512k. *General Requirements:* Hard disk, printer.
disk $195.00.
Helps Manage & Track Cash Liabilities by Collecting Vendor & Invoice Information & by Reporting the Business Cash Commitments & Payment History. On-Screen Inquiry, Timely Payment Information, & Annual Purchase Summaries Keeps User Aware of Current Credit Information. Features a Variety of Reports, Including Vendor Master, Accounts Past Due, Vendor Labels, Adjustments & Payments, Aged Vendor, Invoice Summary, Payment Forecast. Autoposting to General Ledger or Check Ledger Is Available.
Computerware.

Computerware Accounts Receivable.
Compatible Hardware: IBM PC & compatibles. *Operating System(s) Required:* MS-DOS. *Memory Required:* 512k. *General Requirements:* Hard disk, printer.
disk $195.00.
Shows Which Accounts Are Past Due, Forecasts Monies Receivable for Cash Flow Planning & Prints Statements Automatically. System Records Customer Information & Tracks Invoices Input from the Point-of-Sale or Manufacturer's Inventory Systems or Entered Directly. Reports Include Account Master, Accounts Past Due, Customer Labels, Adjustments & Payments, Accounts Aged, Account Summary, Payment Forecast & Statements.
Computerware.

Computerware General Ledger. *Compatible Hardware:* IBM PC & compatibles. *Operating System(s) Required:* MS-DOS. *Memory Required:* 512k. *General Requirements:* Hard disk, printer.
disk $195.00.
Double-Entry System Features Audit Trails, Closing Procedures, & Full Reporting. Reports Include Income Statements, Trial Balance Sheets, Transaction Registers of Journal Entries & Balance Sheets Can Be Printed for Current Month, Prior Month or Year to Date. Also Includes a User-Defined Chart-of-Accounts Which Can Accommodate up to 3 or 4 Digit Account Codes & Offers Up to 99 Subaccounts or Departments. Accounts Payable & Payroll Can Post Directly to General Ledger.
Computerware.

Computeware Payroll. *Compatible Hardware:* IBM PC & compatibles. *Operating System(s) Required:* MS-DOS. *Memory Required:* 512k. *General Requirements:* Hard disk, printer.
disk $195.00.
Accommodates All Pay Types & Periods: Hourly, Salary, Weekly, Biweekly, Monthly & Semimonthly. Includes Federal & State Tax Reporting, Quarterly Tax Statements, W-2s, Paychecks, Pay-Stubs & Labor Cost Accounting. Also Features Four User-Specified Deductions, Automatic Accrual of Vacation Time, General Ledger or Check Ledger Interactivity, 401(k) Wage, User Changeable Rate Tables & Password Protection.
Computerware.

Computhello. *Compatible Hardware:* Atari 400, 800. *Language(s):* Atari BASIC. *Memory Required:* disk 32k. *General Requirements:* Joystick.
disk $23.95.
Dynacomp, Inc.

Computing Without Mathematics: BASIC, Pascal, Applications. Jeffrey Marcus & Marvin Marcus. 1986. *Compatible Hardware:* Apple II, II+, IIe, IIc. *Memory Required:* 64k. *General Requirements:* 2 disk drives, USCD Apple Pascal.
double-sided disk $20.00 (ISBN 0-88175-106-5).
disk $32.95, incl. txt. bk. (ISBN 0-88175-110-3).
Contains Material from Text "Computing Without Mathematics: BASIC & Pascal Applications".
W. H. Freeman & Co. (Computer Science Press).

COMPUTRAC-PC. *Items Included:* Manual. *Customer Support:* 1 year maintenance; $300 prorated first year. Includes phone support & newsletter.
MS-DOS 3.0 or higher. IBM PC or compatible (640k). disk contact publisher for price. *Optimal configuration:* PC or compatible, 640k, math coprocessor, MS-DOS 3.3, hard disk.
Macintosh SE or higher (1Mb). 3.5" disk $695.00. *Optimal configuration:* Macintosh SE 3.0, System 6.0.5, Finder 6.1.5, hard disk.
A Technical Anaylsis Software Utilizing Historical Data for Stocks, Commodities, Futures, Options & Mutual Funds. It is Fully Automated Including the Ability to Test & Optimize the User's Trading Strategy. Users May Add Their Own Formulas. Semi-Annual Updates.
CompuTrac, A Telerate Co.

Comsen Energy Distribution System. 1982. *Compatible Hardware:* IBM PC, PC XT, PC AT, PS/2 & compatibles. *Operating System(s) Required:* MS-DOS. *Language(s):* RPG (source code included). *Memory Required:* 1000k. *General Requirements:* Printer.
disk $1,000.00-$15,000.00 (ISBN 0-923302-01-8).
Management Information System. Allows an Energy Company to Operate from Ticket Generation to Financials.
Comsen Services, Inc.

Comsen Trucking System. 1982. *Compatible Hardware:* IBM PC, PC XT, PC AT, PS/2 & compatibles. *Operating System(s) Required:* MS-DOS. *Language(s):* RPG (source code included). *Memory Required:* 1000k. *General Requirements:* Printer.
disk $1,000.00-$15,000.00 (ISBN 0-923302-00-X).
Management Information System for the Operations & Financial Reporting of a Truckload Carrier.
Comsen Services, Inc.

ComServe. *Compatible Hardware:* Apple Macintosh.
$195.00 per server.
Provides Telecommunications Services to AppleTalk Network Users. Eliminates the Need for a Modem at Each Computer. Provides Network-Wide Access to Modems, Mainframes, & Minis. Eliminates Dedicated Hardware. Runs Transparently in the Background. AppleShare Compatible.
Infosphere.

Comtronic Contract Collector. *Version:* 3.7. Jeffrey A. Dantzler. Dec. 1995. *Compatible Hardware:* IBM PC compatibles & networks. *Operating System(s) Required:* MS-DOS, PC-DOS. *Language(s):* Revelation. *Memory Required:* 640k. *General Requirements:* Hard disk drive, 132-column printer or laser printer. *Items Included:* Complete documentation, Revelation run time. *Customer Support:* 120 days free, single-user $315/yr, network system $445/yr.
single user $1595.00, five user network $2995.00.
demonstration system & manual $40.00.
Manage Any Type of Installment Payment Loan, Note or Contract for Yourself or Third Parties.
Comtronic Systems, Inc.

Comtronic Debtmaster: Debt Collection System. *Version:* 4.0. Dec. 1995. *Compatible Hardware:* IBM PC & compatibles, networks. *Operating System(s) Required:* MS-DOS. *Language(s):* Advanced Revelation. *Memory Required:* 640k. *General Requirements:* Hard disk, printer. *Items Included:* Complete documentation, Revelation run time. *Customer Support:* 120 days free, single-user $365/yr, network system $650/yr, $995 for 20-users & larger.
Single-user. $2495.00.
Five-user network. $4995.00.
demonstration system & manual $40.00.
Collections of Third Party Delinquent Debts.
Comtronic Systems, Inc.

Comtronic Property Manager for Windows. *Version:* 2.2. *Compatible Hardware:* IBM PC & compatibles, networks. *Memory Required:* 4000k. *General Requirements:* 40Mb hard disk & printer. *Items Included:* Documentation, FoxPro Runtime. *Customer Support:* 120 days free, single-user $315/yr, network system $425/yr.
single copy $1595.00.
five-user network version $2995.00.
demonstration system & user manual $40.00.
Complete Management of Residential, Commercial & Retail Properties.
Comtronic Systems, Inc.

Conan. Eric Robinson & Eric Parker. Nov. 1984. *Compatible Hardware:* Apple II; Atari XL/XE; Commodore 64, 128. *Memory Required:* Apple & Atari - standard; Commodore 64k.
Commodore. disk $14.95 (ISBN 0-88717-095-1, Order no.: 1420CDO).
Atari. disk $14.95 (ISBN 0-88717-096-X, Order no.: 1420WDO).
Apple. disk $14.95 (ISBN 0-88717-097-8, Order no.: 1490ADO).
The Mighty Conan of Films, Novels & Comics Comes to the Home Computer Screen. Your Goal Is to Find & Destroy the Villainous Volta Who Resides Deep Within an Ancient Castle Inhabited by Frightful Creatures. Battle Your Way Through 7 Levels in This Game Filled with Graphics & Adventure.
IntelliCreations, Inc.

ConCensus. *Version:* 2.0. Sep. 1990. *Compatible Hardware:* Apple Macintosh. *Memory Required:* 1000k. *General Requirements:* Hard disk. *Items Included:* Operating manual. *Customer Support:* 90 days phone support.
3.5" disk $695.00 (ISBN 0-940169-00-2, Order no.: 101).

CONCENTRATION

Contributions & Census System for Church Management. Provides Automation of Church Membership & Contribution Records.
Liturgical Pubns., Inc.

Concentration. Adrian Vance. Oct. 1985. *Compatible Hardware:* Apple II. *Operating System(s) Required:* Apple DOS. *Memory Required:* 48k.
disk $9.95 (ISBN 0-918547-39-3).
illustration files on the disk avail.
Computerized Version of the Classic Card Game. Features Graphics. Not Copy Protected.
AV Systems, Inc.

Concentrator Solar Cell Modelling. *Compatible Hardware:* HP 9000 Series 200, 300, 520, MSDOS. *Language(s):* BASIC (source code included).
Circular Active Area Planar Silicon & Gas Cell with Radial Grid Lines $1975.00.
Rectangular Active Area Planar Silicon Cell with Linear Grid Lines $1975.00.
Square Active Area Silicon Cell with Linear Grid Lines Ending on Diagonals $2575.00.
Takes a Short Circuit Current Flux Density File & Uses It to Calculate a Cell I-V Curve.
James Assocs.

Concept Booster. Bob Olivier & Helen Olivier. Apple II (64k). 3.5" disk $29.99 (Order no.: 1383).
3.5" disk $39.99, incl. backup disk (Order no.: 1383B).
Designed to Help Children Develop Some of the Essential Concepts & Relationships That Young Children Have to Learn. Screens Present Relationships Such As, "The Red Circle Is Bigger Than the Blue Square," with Appropriate Graphics & Words. Younger Children Need Assistance, but Quickly Develop the Ability to Recognize the Screens & Then to Read the Letters. Each Key Gives the Child a Different Screen. An Automatic Display Will Change the Screens If the Child Does Not Want to Push Keys. Excellent for Giving Young Children That Special Boost in Development.
Trillium Pr.

Concepts in Electromyography. 1988. *Compatible Hardware:* Apple II, II+, IIe, IIc, IIgs. *Memory Required:* 64k.
$49.95.
Basic Electrical Concepts, Skeletal Muscle Physiology, & the Detection, Amplification, & Processing of EMG Signals Are Stressed.
Biosource Software.

Concepts in Thermography. 1988. *Compatible Hardware:* Apple II, II+, IIe, IIc, IIgs. *Memory Required:* 64k.
$49.95.
Basic DC Concepts, Peripheral Vascular Physiology, Detection of Peripheral Temperature, & the Amplification & Processing of DC Signals Are Presented.
Biosource Software.

Conceptual Process Cost Estimator Labor, Materials, & Subcontracts. *Items Included:* Full manual. No other products required. *Customer Support:* Free telephone support - no time limit, 30 day warranty.
MS-DOS 3.2 or higher. IBM & compatibles (512k). disk $689.95. *Optimal configuration:* IBM, MS-DOS 3.1 or higher, 640k RAM, & 132-column (or wider) printer.
Uses Widely Accepted Data from Page's Conceptual Cost Estimating Manual to Produce a Six-Page Comprehensive Conceptual Estimate of Total Cost (Labor, Materials, & Subcontracts). This Gives Engineers, Contractors, & Managers a Fast & Incredibly Inexpensive Way to Evaluate the Economic Feasibility of Refinery & Chemical/Petrochemical Plant Construction Projects.
Dynacomp, Inc.

ConcertWare+. *Version:* 4. Aug. 1987. *Compatible Hardware:* Apple Macintosh 512k, Macintosh Plus, Macintosh SE, Macintosh II. *Memory Required:* 512k.
3.5" disk $69.95.
Integrated Package That Includes the Music Writer, the IntrumentMaker Application, & the Music Player. Full-Length Musical Pieces May Be Entered Using the Mouse; Then Edited, Played & Printed. Allows Users to Experiment with Music & Learn about Music Theory, Composition, & the Physics of Sound. Reads CONCERTWARE & MUSICWORKS Files. Original Instrumental Sounds May Be Designed with the InstrumentMaker. For Beginners As Well As Amateur & Accomplished Musicians.
Great Wave Software.

ConcertWare+MIDI. *Version:* 5. Aug. 1987. *Compatible Hardware:* Apple Macintosh 512k, Macintosh Plus, Macintosh SE, Macintosh II. *Memory Required:* 512k.
3.5" disk $69.95.
Includes All Features of CONCERTWARE+. Provides Full Support for Most MIDI Functions. With the Use of a MIDI Adapter, the Program Allows the Macintosh to Control Any MIDI Compatible Electronic Keyboard, Synthesizer, or Drum Machine. Can Play Back Any CONCERTWARE+ File Through a Synthesizer. MIDI Playback Allows up to 8 Tracks Simultaneously with Unlimited Program (Instrument Sound) Changes.
Great Wave Software.

ConcertWare+Music, Vol. 1: Instrumental Favorites. Boyd Edwards & Nadine Edwards. 1985. *Compatible Hardware:* Apple Macintosh. *Memory Required:* 128k. *General Requirements:* Printer, ConcertWare & software.
3.5" disk $15.00.
Contains a Variety of Musical Selections Including Classical, Ragtime, & an Original Work.
Great Wave Software.

ConcertWare+Music, Vol. 2: Die Kunst der Fuge. Twelve Tone Productions. Aug. 1985. *Compatible Hardware:* Apple Macintosh. *General Requirements:* Printer, ConcertWare & software.
3.5" disk $15.00.
Contains the Entire Work "The Art of Fugue" by Johann Sebastian Bach.
Great Wave Software.

ConcertWare+Music, Vol. 3: Christmas Favorites. Robert Gardner & Debbie Gardner. Oct. 1985. *Compatible Hardware:* Apple Macintosh. *Memory Required:* 128k. *General Requirements:* Printer, ConcertWare software.
3.5" disk $15.00.
Contains a Wide Selection & Variety of Holiday Favorites As Well As a Large Selection of Music from Handel's Messiah.
Great Wave Software.

ConcertWare+Music, Vol. 4: Early Music. Richard Rae. Oct. 1985. *Compatible Hardware:* Apple Macintosh. *Memory Required:* 128k. *General Requirements:* Printer, ConcertWare software.
3.5" disk $15.00.
Contains Renaissance Selections & 29 Original Baroque Instruments.
Great Wave Software.

ConcertWare+Music, Vol. 5: Classical Selections. Michael Benson. Mar. 1985. *Compatible Hardware:* Apple Macintosh. *Memory Required:* 128k. *General Requirements:* Printer, ConcertWare software.
3.5" disk $15.00.
Contains Classical Selections, Including Vivaldi's "The Four Seasons", Which Plays for Almost 40 Minutes.
Great Wave Software.

ConcertWare+Music, Vol. 6: Popular Music 1900-1930. Aug. 1987. *Compatible Hardware:* Apple Macintosh. *Memory Required:* 128k.
3.5" disk $15.00.
Contains a Selection of Broadway & Other Musical Favorites from 1900-1930.
Great Wave Software.

ConcertWare+Music, Vol. 7: Jazz with a French Twist. Lionel Lumbroso & Richard Rae. Aug. 1988. *Compatible Hardware:* Apple Macintosh. *Memory Required:* 512k. *General Requirements:* ConcertWare+ or ConcertWare+MIDI.
3.5" disk $15.00.
Original Jazz Music Written for ConcertWare+
Great Wave Software.

Concord: A Study Package. *Items Included:* 3-ring hard-back user manual, diskette binder, slipcase. *Customer Support:* Free hot-line support, free Concord news letter - "Spectrum".
Macintosh System 6.0. Mac Plus or higher (1Mb). 3.5" disk $550.00. *Nonstandard peripherals required:* Hard disk required (13Mb).
DOS 2.0 or higher. IBM XT & compatibles (512k). disk $550.00. *Nonstandard peripherals required:* Hard disk required - Data base (5 - 10 Mb).
Book Study/Reference Program for: The Bible (KJV); the Published Writings of Mary Baker Eddy; the Christian Science Hymnal. Provides: Complete Text of These Books; Comprehensive Querying, Concordances, & Cross-Referencing; Reference Management; Note Taking; Print/Copy Features; Four-Part Harmony Hymn Player for Internal Speaker or MIDI Interface.
The Christian Science Publishing Society.

Concord Management System: CS1000, CS2000. *Compatible Hardware:* IBM & compatibles; IBM AS/400. *Operating System(s) Required:* Unix; MS-DOS; OS/400. *Memory Required:* OS/400 2Mb, Unix 1Mb, MS-DOS 512k. *General Requirements:* Concord Applications; Accounts Rec, Accounts Payable, 6L, Payroll, Job Cost, Contract Status, Equipment, AIA Bill., T&M Bill., Inventory, Purchase Orders. *Items Included:* Professional documentation, on-line Help, Lotus Download. *Customer Support:* Class room education, on-site consulting, phone support, fees vary.
contact publisher for price.
Provides a Complete Turn-Key Computer/Software Solution for Single User & Multi-User Systems. System Works Specifically in Construction in Providing a Complete Computer System with Local Training & Support.
Concord Management Systems, Inc.

Concordance. *Version:* 5.21. *Compatible Hardware:* IBM PC & compatibles, PS/2. *Memory Required:* 512k. *General Requirements:* Hard disk. *Items Included:* 400 page manual, 3-ring binder & slipcase. *Customer Support:* Free via phone.
$495.00-$3000.00.
Full-Text Database That Can Edit & Retrieve Formatted & Unformatted Data. Accepts Virtually Any Source, Including Existing Text & Database Files, Optical Scanners & Keyboard Entry. Program Also Searches & Retrieves Records According to the Words & Phrases They Contain. Records Are Displayed with Key Words Highlighted. User Can View, Reference & Build upon Previous Queries to Refine & Tailor Search Results. All Features Are Accessible Through Menus or Function Key Shortcuts. Supports Boolean, Context, Proximity, & Relational Searching. Programming Language Available.
Dataflight Software.

TITLE INDEX

Concrete. *Items Included:* Full documentation - 3 ring binder.
MS-DOS 3.0 or higher. IBM PC XT, AT or compatible (640k). $495.00. *Optimal configuration:* Hard drive, Epson Dot Matrix printer, color monitor/graphics card. Networks supported: BASIC source code not available.
Designed to Assist in the Design & Analysis of Reinforced Concrete Projects. It Includes the Standard Handbooks As Well As Sections on: Column Design & Analysis, Flexure Design & Analysis & Soil-Structure Design & Analysis. The Handbook Tables Are Used for Reinforcement, Beam Sizing, Beam Strength, Shear Strengths, Rectangular Columns, & Circular Columns. Flexure of Joists, Continuous Beams & Stirrups & Ties are Considered. The Soil- Structures Section Is an Excellent Analysis Tool for Isolated Footings & Retaining Wall Problems.
Engineering Software Co.

Concrete Beam Design - ST16M. *Version:* 04/1988. 1982. *Compatible Hardware:* IBM PC & compatibles. *Operating System(s) Required:* MS-DOS, PC-DOS. *Language(s):* Compiled & assembly language. *Memory Required:* 256k. *Customer Support:* Technical hotline, "Lifetime" support at no charge.
$395.00.
Concrete Beam Design - ST16M Uses the ACI 1983 Ultimate Strength Method to Design Concrete Beams. Outputs Area of Reinforcing Steel, Design Live & Dead Shear & Moment Loads, Inflection Points, Recommended Number, Size & Spacing of Top & Bottom Steel, & Stirrup Spacing. Prompting, Interactive. Fully Compiled. SI Metric or English Units.
MC2 Engineering Software.

Concrete Column Design - ST18M. *Version:* 07/1988. 1982. *Compatible Hardware:* IBM PC & compatibles. *Operating System(s) Required:* MS-DOS, PC-DOS. *Language(s):* Compiled & Assembly language. *Memory Required:* 448k. *Customer Support:* Technical hotline, "Lifetime" support at no charge.
$295.00.
Concrete Column Design - ST18M (New Update) Automatically Designs or Checks Near-Optimum Reinforced Concrete Round, Square & Rectangular Tied Columns, Using the Ultimate Strength Interaction Diagram Methods of the 1984 CRSI Handbook. Calculates Six Key Points & Graphically Displays & Prints the Interaction Diagram. Checks Slenderness Both Directions & Moment Magnification, Braced Columns. Latest Windowed Pop-up Screens, Defaults Error Checking Super-Convenient Entries for Column Stack Design.
MC2 Engineering Software.

Concrete Mix Designs. *Version:* 4. Nov. 1980. *Compatible Hardware:* TRS-80 Model II, Model 12, Model 16; Tandy 6000. *Operating System(s) Required:* TRSDOS. *Language(s):* BASIC (source code included). *Memory Required:* 64k.
contact publisher for price.
Prints Out Batch Weights for Concrete Ready Mix Plants.
Palmer & Palmer.

Concrete Retaining Wall Analysis. 1995. *Items Included:* Full manual. *Customer Support:* Free telephone support - 90 days, 30-day warranty.
MS-DOS 3.2 or higher. 286 (584k). disk $99.95. Nonstandard peripherals required: CGA/EGA/VGA.
RWALL Is an Interactive, Easy to Use Analysis Package for Cantilevered Retaining Walls. Inputs Include Trial Wall Dimensions, Surcharge, Active & Passive Pressures, Dead & Live Loads with Eccentricity, Friction Coefficient, Rebar Cover & Area. Outputs Include Base Soil Pressures, Moments (Resisting & Overturning), Safety Factors (Sliding & Overturning), Area of Steel Required, Section Moment of Inertia (Effective, Gross, & Cracked), & Deflection at the Top of the Wall (Instantaneous & Long-Term).
Dynacomp, Inc.

Concrete Shear Wall & Column Design. *Items Included:* Full manual. No other products required. *Customer Support:* Free telephone support - no time limit, 30 day warranty.
MS-DOS 3.2 or higher. IBM & compatibles (512k). disk $269.95.
demo disk $5.00.
Interactively Designs Variably-Shaped Concrete Shear Walls & Columns, According to Chapter 10 of ACI 318-77, by Calculating the Interaction Curve for the Wall or Column. Determines the Ultimate Load & Moment Capacities at Various Positions of the Neutral Axis of the Wall & Column Configuration, & Interactively Reduces the Neutral Axis until the Ultimate Load Is Zero. The Ultimate Moment Using Phi Equals 0.90 Is Defined at Pu Equals 0.
Dynacomp, Inc.

Concrete Spread Footing Design. 1995. *Items Included:* Full manual. *Customer Support:* Free telephone support - 90 days, 30-day warranty.
MS-DOS 3.2 or higher. 286 (584k). disk $99.95. Nonstandard peripherals required: CGA/EGA/VGA.
SPREAD Designs Concentrically Loaded Rectangular Footings. Inputs Include Material Strengths, Dead & Live Loads, Column Size, & Footing Dimensions. Outputs Include Required Footing Area, Required Effective Reinforcement Depth, Moment Capacity (X & Y Direction), & Required Reinforcement (X & Y Direction).
Dynacomp, Inc.

Concurrent DOS 386. *Version:* 2.0. *Compatible Hardware:* IBM 386-based machines & compatibles. *Operating System(s) Required:* PC-DOS 3.3. *General Requirements:* Hard disk, terminals which support PC emulation. 640k needed for single PC, 1Mb additional memory needed for each three additional users.
contact publisher for price.
Operating System Designed for Multiuser & Multitasking, Being Able to Handle up to 255 Tasks Simultaneously. This Version Enables Users of Workstations & Terminals to Run Two Programs at a Time. Works with TSR (Terminate & Stay Resident) Applications.
Digital Research, Inc.

Condex United States Stamps (1902-1921).
May 1990. *Items Included:* Diskettes, instruction book.
PC-DOS/MS-DOS. IBM & compatibles (540k). disk $29.95 (ISBN 0-945541-03-1, Order no.: 031).
Allows a Collector of U.S. Stamps to Readily Integrate the Data for Any One, or More, of the Following Factors: Scott Catalog Numbers & Identification; Design Type (from Scott); Year of Issue; Type of Perforation; Color Variations of the Stamp; Scene, Portrait or Theme Depicted; Type of Watermark; Type of Printing (Engraved, Offset); Size of Design (mm); Type & Variation of Paper; Horizontal & Vertical Separation of Designs, & More.
CSY Publishing, Inc.

Condo Manager. *Version:* 5.0. David Coleman. Jul. 1982. *Compatible Hardware:* IBM PC & compatibles. *Operating System(s) Required:* MS-DOS. *Language(s):* Compiled BASIC. *Memory Required:* 512k. *Customer Support:* Telephone support.
disk $995.00.
Property Management System, Customized for Community Associations, Combined with a Simplified General Ledger. Emphasis of the Design Is on Member Payments & Charges & the Generation of Various Accounting Reports. In Addition, There Is Provision for Passing Data to Electronic Spreadsheet & Word Processor Programs.
Coleman Business Systems.

Condominium Control System: Reservations Only, Front Desk, General Ledger, Accounts Payable & Owner Billing & Receivables, Group-Company Billing, Guest History, Enhanced Report Writer. *Version:* 8.00. 1981. *Compatible Hardware:* IBM PC, PC XT, PC AT or compatibles. *Operating System(s) Required:* MS-DOS 2.0. *Language(s):* Compiled Basic. *Memory Required:* 640k. *General Requirements:* Hard drive, printer.
Complete System. $3000.00-$11,000.00 single-user.
Complete System. $6000.00-$16,000.00 multi-user.
evaluation kit $95.00.
single-user $2000.00 ea.
General Ledger & Accounts Payable. single-user $1000.00.
General Ledger & Accounts Payable. multi-user $2000.00.
Property Management/Reservation/Billing System. Features Include: On-Line Reservations, Priority Scheduling of Units, Deposit Tracking, Reservation History Sorted by Owner, & Maid Scheduling Using Check Out Report. Prints Monthly Owner Statements, Mailing Lists, & Reservation Confirmations. Includes On-Line Help Facility. Integrated Accounting Systems Available Include: Accounts Receivable, Accounts Payable, & General Ledger.
Resort Data Processing, Inc.

Condor Jr. *Version:* 2.11.11. Dec. 1984. *Compatible Hardware:* IBM PC & compatibles. *Operating System(s) Required:* MS-DOS. *Memory Required:* 128k.
disk $99.00.
File Management System. As Needs Grow Can Be Upgraded to CONDOR 3.
Condor Computer Corp.

Condor 1. Condor Computer Corp. *Compatible Hardware:* HP 150 Touchscreen.
3.5" disk $300.00 (Order no.: 45415A).
Condor 1 to 3 Upgrade Kit. 3.5" disk $500.00 (Order no.: 45417A).
Includes HELP Menus Allowing the Use of Databases for Daily Applications with Minimal Training. Databases Can Be Created by Typing a Form on the Screen. Data Can Be Entered, Updated, & Listed Using the Same Form. Sorts Data, Computes Simple Statistics, & Produces Simple Row & Column Reports. Can Be Upgraded to Condor 3.
Hewlett-Packard Co.

Condor 3. *Version:* 2.20. Nov 1987. *Compatible Hardware:* DEC Rainbow, Professional; HP 125, 150 Touchscreen; IBM PC & compatibles, PC XT, PC AT, PS/2 ; Tandy 2000. *Operating System(s) Required:* CP/M, CP/M-86, MS-DOS, PC-DOS. *Language(s):* Assembly. *Memory Required:* CP/M 64k; MS-DOS or PC-DOS 128k (minimum), recommended 256k.
5.25" or 3.5" disk $495.00.
tutorial $59.95.
Combines a File Manager with a Database Management System for Non-Programmers. Program Is Menu-Driven, & Features Plain English Commands & Extensive On-Line Help. Supports up to 65,000 Records per File with up to 127 Fields per Record.
Condor Computer Corp.

Condor 3. Condor Computer Corp. *Compatible Hardware:* HP 150 Touchscreen. 3.5" disk $700.00 (Order no.: 45416A). *Provides All the Capabilities of CONDOR 1 Plus Relational Database Functions, Allowing User to Retrieve, Sort, & Print Information from Databases. Commands That Allow User to Join, Project, Post, & Combine Multiple Files Are Included. The Report Generator Allows the Creation of Customized Reports in a Wide Variety of Formats. Also Provided Is an Indexing Feature.*
Hewlett-Packard Co.

The ConEstCo Contractor: AI/I. *Version:* 3. Ken Lipton. 1990. *Compatible Hardware:* MS-DOS based machines. *Operating System(s) Required:* PC-DOS, MS-DOS. *Language(s):* CBASIC. *Memory Required:* 256k.
disk $699.00.
Business/Accounting Data Manipulation System Allowing User to Build (or Have CONESTCO Customize) Multitiered Data Modules. Create Integrated Programs That Do Estimating, Cost Accounting & Accounting, Financial Planning, Loan Payment & Other Similar Functions.
Construction Estimating Co. (ConEstCo).

CONEXUS: MIST Plus Communications NEXUS. *Version:* 1.3. Johnson & Lenz. Apr. 1984. *Compatible Hardware:* IBM PC, PC XT, PC AT, PS/2. *Operating System(s) Required:* PC-DOS 2.0 or higher. (source code included). *Memory Required:* 256k. *Items Included:* MISTplus, resources, online documentation. *Customer Support:* Unlimited.
$50.00 incl. MIST (ISBN 0-918659-00-0).
Integrated Conferencing, Electronic Mail & Bulletin Board System Designed for Easy System Management & a Professional Environment Allows Private & Topic Specific Communication Between up to 900 Members Who Can Access the System Using Any Kind of TTY Device.
OMM Corp.

Confined Space Entry Tracking. *Version:* 1.2. 1992. *Items Included:* One year of free telephone technical support, an operations manual in a 3-ring binder, the Runtime Version of Revelations. *Customer Support:* After the first year of free telephone technical support, additional technical support can be purchased if needed.
MS-DOS. IBM PC & compatibles (320k). disk $499.00. *Networks supported:* Novell, IBM PC-NET, Banyan Vines, LAN Manager for MS-DOS, & most other DOS compatible networks. Pathworks or Digital Equipment Corp.'s VMS. VAX (320k). Contact publisher for price. *Networks supported:* DECNET.
UNIX, SUNOS. SPARC Station. Contact publisher for price.
The Program Helps to Identify, Classify, Inventory, & Track Confined Spaces. It Prompts You with a Series of Questions to Aid in Classifying the Space. The Program Generates an "Equipment Requirements Form", a "Pre-Entry Checklist", & the "Confined Space Permit". Also Warns You When Permits Are Not Closed.
Pro-Am Software.

Conflict. *Customer Support:* 90 day warranty. MS-DOS 2.1 or higher. IBM (384K). disk $14.99. *Nonstandard peripherals required:* CGA, EGA, Tandy or VGA Graphics required. *You've Just Been Sworn into Office As the Leader of Israel. Your Mission: To Force the Collapse of All Neighboring Governments. Should You Maintain Good Relations Diplomatically While Covertly Supporting Anti-Government Activity? Or Should You Remain Neutral & Allow the SuperPowers to Turn Their High-Tech Military Gadgetry Agaist Each Other.*
Virgin Games.

Conflict Catcher II. *Version:* 2.1. Aug. 1993. *Customer Support:* Free phone support.
7.0 or higher. Macintosh. 3.5" disk $79.95.
Utility That Solves Startup File Problems - Crashes, Freezes, Printing Problems & More - Puts User in Control of Startup Software - Saves Memory & Time.
Casady & Greene, Inc.

Conflict in Jerusalem: Jesus' Last Days.
Windows 3.1 or higher. 386 or higher IBM PC & compatibles (4Mb). 3.5" disk $49.95 (Order no.: SW938-4G). *Optimal configuration:* 386 or higher IBM PC-compatible, Windows 3.1 or higher, 4Mb RAM, approximately 10Mb of hard disk space, & mouse.
A Bible Adventure Game from Colonnade Technologies, a Subsidiary of Logos Research Systems. Centers on the Critical Passover Week Leading up to & Including the Crucifixion & Resurrection of Jesus Christ. Players Are Cast onto Ancient Streets Where They Assume Various Disguises While Solving Puzzles & Advancing Through the Unfolding Events. Although the Game Uses Some Fictional Representative Characters, the Events Are Biblically Accurate & Players Will Learn History & Geography As Well As Confronting the Essential Truths of the Gospel Message. Suitable for Ten Years Old & Up.
Gospel Films Inc.

Conflict of Interest. Mar. 1994. *Items Included:* Disks, manual & installation procedures. *Customer Support:* 90 days of telephone support & product updates included in purchase; agreement available thereafter for 20% of purchase price annually.
MS-DOS/Networks. Any Net Bios Compatible (526k). $195.00 Single-User; $295.00 Multi-User. *Optimal configuration:* PC, 640k, DOS 5.0 or higher, printer. *Networks supported:* Novell, Lantastic, etc.
Product Allows Firm to Enter All Parties to a Case & Then to Search for Potential Conflicts When Taking on New Cases. Search Criteria Is Not Case Sensitive. Interfaces with Our Time & Billing System. May Also Run Stand Alone.
Morningstar Technology Corp.

Conflict of Interest: Series 900 to 2000. *Compatible Hardware:* IBM System/36, System/36PC; AS/400.
contact publisher for price.
Records & Searches the Names & Relationships of Clients & Related Parties to Avoid Conflict of Interest.
Manac-Prentice Hall Software, Inc.

Conflix-A. *Version:* 2.1. *Compatible Hardware:* IBM PC. *Operating System(s) Required:* PC-DOS. *Language(s):* Quicksilver. *Memory Required:* 640k. *Customer Support:* Toll free telephone support.
$195.00.
Accomplishes Direct Patient Retrieval of Essential Baseline Data in Screening Persons for Alcoholism Using Mayo Clinic Criteria. Patients Appreciate & Benefit from the Privacy & Give the Physician an Opening Wedge in Resolving These Prevalent Serious Problems. Both English & Spanish Interviews.
SRC Systems, Inc.

Congressional Masterfile 1. 1995.
MS-DOS. IBM or compatibles. CD-ROM disk
A Comprehensive archive perserving 200 years of congressional information, this database emcompasses 400,000 records on historical congressional publications from 1789 to 1969.
Congressional Information Service.

Congressional Masterfile 2. 1995.
MS-DOS. IBM or compatibles. disk (Order no.: C2C110).
The CD-ROM edition of the award-winning CIS/Index to Publications of the United States Congress allows users to pinpoint information contained in all congressional reports, documents, published hearings, & committee prints since 1970. A current index is issued with quarterly updates; retrospective discs are also available.
Congressional Information Service.

Congressional Portraits: Desktop Publishers' Collection. Jul. 1995. *Customer Support:* 90 days unlimited warranty.
Windows 3.1 or higher. IBM compatible PC with 80Mb hard drive & SVGA monitor (4Mb). disk $39.90 (ISBN 0-9647419-0-3). *Optimal configuration:* IBM compatible PC with 8 to 16Mb RAM & 80Mb hard drive; CD player & Windows 3.1 or higher operating system & an SVGA monitor capable of displaying 24 bit colors.
Individual Black & White Portraits of All Members of the 104th Congress Available for Unlimited Use. Files Organized in a Catalog That Uses Keyword Search. Color Images Supplied of Some Members. Free Use of B&W. Additional Fees Must Be Paid to Use Color Files.
Amphora Media.

Connect for Success: Connect with Others & Influence Them. Feb. 1994. *Customer Support:* Toll-free telephone number for technical support. 90 days warranty for defects in materials & workmanship.
Macintosh System 7.0. Macintosh with 68040 processor (5Mb). CD-ROM disk $49.95 (ISBN 1-886806-02-0). *Nonstandard peripherals required:* Double speed CD-ROM drive. *Addl. software required:* QuickTime (included on CD-ROM disc).
Microsoft Windows 3.1. PC compatibles; 486/33 MHz (runs slow on 386/25MHz) (8Mb). CD-ROM disk $49.95. *Nonstandard peripherals required:* 256 color display card (640x480); double speed CD-ROM drive. *Addl. software required:* QuickTime for Windows (included on CD-ROM disc).
Uses Simple Communication Tools to Help Build Stronger Relationships & Gain Cooperation with Others. You Are Immersed in a Role & Through Highly Interactive Video Experiences Are Asked to Respond & React, & Determine What Action to Take Next. The Situations Are Fun & Realistic.
Wilson Learning Corp.

Connect for Success Plus Repacking Your Bags: Two CD-ROMs to Improve Your Family Life. Nov. 1995. *Items Included:* Two CD-ROMs in package: Connect for Success & Repacking Your Bags, Repacking Your Bags Journal. *Customer Support:* Toll-free telephone number for technical support, 90 days warranty for defects in materials & workmanship.
Macintosh System 7.0. Macintosh with 68040 processor (5Mb). CD-ROM disk $49.95 (ISBN 1-886806-12-8). *Addl. software required:* QuickTime (included on CD-ROM disc).
Microsoft Windows 3.1. PC compatibles; 486/33MHz (runs slow on 386/25MHz) (8Mb). *Nonstandard peripherals required:* 256 color display card (640x480); double speed CD-ROM drive. *Addl. software required:* QuickTime for Windows (included on CD-ROM disc).
Connect for Success Helps You Improve Communication & Gain Cooperation. Repacking Your Bags Helps You Get Your Life under Control. Each Program Invites You to a World of Learning Where You Are a Player in Several Unfolding Stories That Help You to Understand & Practice Important New Relationship & Life Skills. You Are Immersed in Different Roles & Through

Highly Interactive Video Experiences, Are Asked to Respond, React, & Determine What Action to Take Next. The Situations Are Fun & Realistic. You Can Explore Different Approaches & Learn by Doing Without Risk.
Wilson Learning Corp.

Connect Four. *Compatible Hardware:* TI 99/4A.
contact publisher for price (Order no.: PHM3038).
Vertical Strategy Game. Players Must Get 4 Markers in a Row - Down, Across or Diagonally to Win.
Texas Instruments, Personal Productivit.

Connex Professional Correspondence Manager. *Compatible Hardware:* IBM PC & compatibles. *Memory Required:* 640k. *General Requirements:* Hard disk, modem.
$495.00.
Send Documents from Personal Computer Via the Post Office, Telex, Telegram, Electronic Mail or Other Services. Features Mail List Management & a Business Contact Database.
Productivity Performance, Inc.

CONPLOT Contour Plotter. *Items Included:* Bound manual. *Customer Support:* Free hotline - no time limit; 30 day limited warranty; updates are $5/disk plus S&H.
MS-DOS 2.0 or higher. IBM & compatibles (128k). disk $89.95. Nonstandard peripherals required: Color graphics card. *Addl. software required:* BASICA (or GWBASIC).
General-Purpose Contour Plotter Which Allows Engineers, Scientists, Surveyors, Mathematicians, or Anyone with (X, Y, Z) Data or Functions, to Easily Create Clear & Intelligible Contour Plots. Accepts User Input in Several Forms: Multi-Line Functions Written in BASIC; ASCII Numeric Data Files (e.g., from a Word Processor or Spreadsheet); Previously Saved Contour Plots.
Dynacomp, Inc.

Conplot Contour Plotter. 1995. *Items Included:* Full manual. *Customer Support:* Free telephone support - 90 days, 30-day warranty.
MS-DOS 3.2 or higher. 286 (584k). disk $89.95. Nonstandard peripherals required: CGA/EGA/VGA.
A General-Purpose Contour Plotter Which Allows Engineers, Scientists, Surveyors, Mathematicians, or Anyone with (X, Y, Z) Data or Functions, to Easily Create Clear & Intelligible Contour Plots. Accepts User Input in Several Forms: 1. Multi-Line Functions; 2. XYZ Data Entered from the Keyboard; 3. ASCII Numerical Data Files (e.g., from a Word Processor or Spreadsheet); 4. Previously Saved Contour Plots.
Dynacomp, Inc.

Conquering the Commodore 64 Kingdom: 25 Original Games in Dazzling Sight & Sound.
Bill L. Behrendt. May 1984. *Compatible Hardware:* Commodore 64 & Portable 64. *Operating System(s) Required:* CBM DOS. *Language(s):* BASIC (source code included). *Memory Required:* 64k.
disk $29.95 (ISBN 0-13-167925-2, Order no.: 16792-4).
bk. $14.95 (ISBN 0-13-167917-1, Order no.: 16791-6).
Book Provides Original Arcade Games (Adventure, Space, Strategy). Also Included Are 3 Trilogies.
Prentice Hall.

Conquering the PCjr Kingdom: 25 Original Games in Dazzling Sight & Sound. Bill L. Behrendt. Sep. 1984. *Compatible Hardware:* IBM PCjr. *Operating System(s) Required:* PC-DOS 2.1. *Language(s):* Cartridge BASIC (source code included). *Memory Required:* 64k.
disk $29.95 (ISBN 0-13-167909-0, Order no.: 16790-8).
bk. $14.95 (ISBN 0-13-167891-4, Order no.: 16789-0).
Space, Adventure, Arcade-Type & Strategy Games.
Prentice Hall.

CONSOLX. *Version:* 5. 1980. *Compatible Hardware:* IBM PC & compatibles; CP/M based machines. *Operating System(s) Required:* CP/M-80, MS-DOS, PC-DOS. *Language(s):* Assembly (source code included). *Memory Required:* 48k. *General Requirements:* Hayes compatible modem.
disk $99.00.
Provides Remote Control Access to a System for Applications Such As Electronic Mail, Bulletin Board Systems & Use of an Office System from Home. Password, Auto Run Applications, Batch Execution at Logoff & Many Other Options.
Hawkeye Grafix.

Constant-Payment-to-Principal Loan. *Compatible Hardware:* Sharp ZL-6100 System, ZL-6500 System. *Language(s):* Sharp Microcode.
$400.00.
Finds the Range of Payments, Finance Charge & APR for This Type of Loan Where an Equal Amount of Principle Plus Accrued Interest Is Paid Each Period. Origination Fee Can Be Charged & an Actual or Mixed Calendar System Can Be Used.
P-ROM Software, Inc.

Constellation III For Macintosh. *General Requirements:* Ominet network hardware.
Macintosh 512K or higher. 3.5" disk $495.00.
Network Management. Allows File Transfers, Disk Sharing & Printer Sharing at Speeds of 1Mbps; Supports MFS & HFS File Structures & Conversions of MFS Volumes to HFS. With Add-On Accessories, Allows Macs, PCs & Apple II Computers to Communicate & Transfer Across Same Network.
Corvus Systems, Inc.

Constituent Service. *Version:* 3.0. *Compatible Hardware:* IBM PC & compatibles, DEC, Macintosh, Windows 95. *Memory Required:* 4000k. *Items Included:* Media, documentation. *Customer Support:* Included 24 hours/day toll free.
contact publisher for price.
source code can be purchased separately.
Allows Each Legislative Staff Member to Operate Independently on Separate PC's on Functions Like Polling, Case Work, & Scheduling. Gives PC's Access to a Hard Disk Database Containing the Case Histories of Every Potential Voter.
Aristotle Industries.

Construction. CYMA Corp. *Compatible Hardware:* TI Professional. *Operating System(s) Required:* CP/M, MS-DOS. *Memory Required:* 64k. *General Requirements:* Printer.
$2795.00 (Order no.: SY P/N T039-095).
4 Program Construction Management Programs: General Ledger, Accounts Payable, Payroll & Accounts Receivable.
Texas Instruments, Personal Productivit.

Construction Accounting. *Version:* 5.5. *Items Included:* Disks, manuals, sample data. *Customer Support:* 90 days of free telephone support.
DOS 2.1 or higher. IBM PC/XT, AT, PS/2 & compatibles (640k). disk $795.00. Nonstandard peripherals required: Hard disk.
Menu Driven, NAHB Approved Accounting Program Designed for the Construction Trade.
Yardi Systems.

Construction Accounting Systems. *Compatible Hardware:* Apple II, II+. *Operating System(s) Required:* Apple DOS 3.3. *Language(s):* Applesoft BASIC. *Memory Required:* 48k. *General Requirements:* 2 disk drives, printer.
disk $2495.95 (Order no.: D-044).
documentation $50.00.
demo disk $100.00.
source code avail.
Designed for the Contractor or Sub-Contractor. Includes a General Ledger System, a Job Cost & Project Management System, a Complete Payroll System Including Record Keeping of Workers Compensation Data & a Document Process for Proposals & Bids. Provides a Trial Balance Report, a Monthly Balance Sheet, a Monthly Income Statement & Detailed Job Cost Reports.
CMA Micro Computer.

Construction Cash Flow Master. *Customer Support:* 800-929-8117 (customer service).
MS-DOS. disk $199.99 (ISBN 0-87007-365-6).
This Program Computes Points & Interest Reserves on all Loans, Produces Monthly Cash Flow Charts, Computes Monthly Interest on Loans Based on Either a Flat or Floating Interest Rate, Load Payback Amounts Based on When Properties Are Sold, Tracks All Loans & Expenses for up to 8 Years, Including as Many as Nine Construction Phase Loans Which Can Be Increased or Decreased with a Key Stroke, Create "What If" Scenarios & Know in Advance the Cash Flow Adjustments That Various Changes in Interest Rates Would Cause, Keep Track of Marketing Costs, Buyers' Loan Points, Taxes, Sales Model Costs, Land Loan & Land Development Loans, & Minimum Bank Payback Percentages.
SourceView Software International.

Construction Contractor Management. *Version:* 3.0. *Compatible Hardware:* Apple Macintosh. *Memory Required:* 1000k. *Customer Support:* Free phone support.
3.5" disk $1200.00.
with integrated accounting $2780.00.
Management System for General Contractors.
Exceiver Corp.

Construction Cost Control System CCS/PMS. 1984. *Compatible Hardware:* IBM & compatibles. *Operating System(s) Required:* PC-DOS/MS-DOS, OS/2, UNIX. *Memory Required:* 512k. *General Requirements:* Hard disk, printer.
disk $995.00 (ISBN 0-927558-04-1, Order no.: 301).
Provides On-Line Construction Project Tracking & Cost Control by CSI Codes. Features Immediate Update & Reporting Capabilities. Produces Project Cost Control Report. Data Can Be Accessed by Standard Database & Report Generators. Also Provides Dynamic Tracking of Proposals, Quotes, Change Orders, Contract vs. Actual, etc. Onsite Setup & Training Available.
Timon, Inc.

Construction Cost-Profit. 1978. *Compatible Hardware:* Apple II; IBM PC & compatibles. *Operating System(s) Required:* MS-DOS, Apple DOS. *Language(s):* BASIC. *Memory Required:* 48k.
disk $75.00.
Designed for Builders & Investors in Building Projects. Allows an Analysis of the Potential Profits. Legal Fees, Interest Rates, Construction Costs, Demolition, Land Draw, & Financing Are Considered in Calculating the Total Funds Necessary for Project Completion.
Realty Software.

CONSTRUCTION ESTIMATING

Construction Estimating. *Version:* 1.1-3.1, 3.4. Mar. 1982. *Compatible Hardware:* IBM PC, PCjr, PC XT, PC AT. *Operating System(s) Required:* MS-DOS. *Language(s):* Compiled MBASIC. *Memory Required:* 384k.
disk $300.00.
demo disk $50.00.
Menu Driven Program Based on the CSI Indexing System of 16 Divisions Such As by MEANS Cost Guide. Allows Estimator to Input Each Item, Quantity, Labor, & Unit Costs from Take-Off Sheets. Computer Places Items in Order, Extends Figures, Summarizes by Division & Category & Adds User's Mark-Up Percentages. Reports Include Detailed Breakdown of All Costs As Well As a Proposal for Clients Which Combines Overhead & Profit Amounts with Cost Items.
Rambow Enterprises.

Construction Estimator. Mesa Research, Inc. May 1984. *Compatible Hardware:* Apple II, IIe, III, Macintosh; IBM PC.
disk $69.95 ea.
Macintosh Multiplan Edition. (ISBN 0-8359-0957-3).
IBM Multiplan Edition. (ISBN 0-8359-0953-0).
IBM Lotus 1-2-3 Edition. (ISBN 0-8359-0945-X).
IBM VisiCalc Edition. (ISBN 0-8359-0947-6).
Apple II & IIe VisiCalc Edition. (ISBN 0-8359-0946-8).
Apple III VisiCalc Edition. (ISBN 0-8359-0947-6).
IBM PC SuperCalc Edition. (ISBN 0-8359-0948-4).
Computer Tool for Precise Estimation, Calculation, & Comparison of the Costs Involved in Any & All Real Estate or Construction Projects. Estimates Construction Costs, Property Values, Individual Component Costs. Compares Material & Lumber Suppliers & Cost Differences, Actual Costs & Estimated Costs. Calculates Cost Differences Between Suppliers, Percent of Monies Expended, Completion Percentages, Savings Realized by Item, etc.
Prentice Hall.

Construction Job Cost Estimating. Apr. 1982. *Compatible Hardware:* Apple II, II+, IIe; Atari 400, 800; Columbia; Compaq; Commodore CBM 8096; Franklin Ace; Fujitsu; HP 150 Touchscreen; IBM PC, PC jr, PC XT; LNW 80; Sharp PC 5000; Sperry; Tandy 2000; TI Professional; TRS-80 Model I, Model II, Model III, Model 4, Model 12, Model 16. *Operating System(s) Required:* CP/M, CP/M-86, MS-DOS, PC-DOS. (source code included). *Memory Required:* 48k. *General Requirements:* General Requirements- Visicalc, Supercalc, Multiplan or Lotus 1-2-3.
disk $59.95.
Consists of Spreadsheet Templates Specifically Designed for Architects & Contractors. Factors in Contingencies, Overhead, & Profit Margin to Estimate Residential Construction Costs. Spreadsheet Forecasting Functions Are Retained. Includes "What-If" Features.
Software Models.

Construction Management. Jun. 1984. *Operating System(s) Required:* PC-DOS, Windows. *Memory Required:* 640k.
disk $4200.00.
Integrated Accounting System for General & Sub-Contractors.
Hansco Information Technologies, Inc.

Construction Management Software Plus. *Version:* 5.0. Jan. 1991. *Items Included:* Pre-installation guide, installation guide, documentation. *Customer Support:* Support contract entitles you to 1 year of free telephone support, use of bulletin board (computerized information exchange), menu changes, periodic updates, & company name additions; price of service contract depends on software purchased; training, installation, & on-site work also available.
PC-DOS (640k). IBM PC, PC XT, PC AT, PS/2. disk $1495.00-$9995.00. *Nonstandard peripherals required:* 40Mb hard disk. *Optimal configuration:* Language - BASIC. *Networks supported:* Novell.
Full-Featured & Easy-to-Use System Designed for the Contractor, Homebuilder, & Remodeler. In One Integrated & Comprehensible Format, the Program Provides Effective Cost Control, Accurate Estimates, Accurate Financial Reports & Flexible Payroll. Other Capabilities Include Purchase Orders, Invoices, Direct Checkwriting, & Billing. Easy to Use Windows Allow for Error Free Account & File Entering.
SSD (Small System Design), Inc.

The Construction Manager. *Version:* 2.0. 1989. *Items Included:* Getting started manual, primer, system guide, security booklet & installation guide. *Customer Support:* Through Dealer.
MS-DOS. IBM & compatibles (640K). $5995.00 - $9995.00. *Nonstandard peripherals required:* Dallas Key or I/O Board. *Networks supported:* Novell.
Integrated Job Cost Accounting System Designed for Medium-Large Builders & Contractors. Its Sophisticated Networking Can Connect an Unlimited Number of IBM PC's (or Compatibles) to Meet Growth Needs. It's Colorful Screens Make the Learning Curve Short. It Performs Advanced Construction Functions Like Separate Accounting for up to 99 Companies with Consolidated Financial Statements, Projection of Cost to Complete for Each Job, Phase & Cost Code, Subcontractor Control of Billings, Payments & Retention, 401 (K) Payroll Plans, & More. Six Integrated Modules, Payroll, Accounts Payable/Receivables & Inventory.
Software Shop Systems, Inc.

Construction Master. *Customer Support:* 800-929-8117 (customer service).
MS-DOS. IBM PC, PS/2. disk $199.99 (ISBN 0-87007-501-2).
Commodore 128, CP/M. disk $299.99 (ISBN 0-87007-502-0).
Does Construction Estimating & Project Control. Cost Codes Reference Pre-Loaded Values under the Uniform System Adopted by the American Institute of Architects, Associated General Contractors of America & The Construction Specifications Institute, Inc.
SourceView Software International.

Construction Master Accounting System Plus (CMAS Plus). *Version:* 1.40. 1993. *Compatible Hardware:* IBM PC & compatibles, 386, 486, RT, RISC/6000; Sun Microsystems. *Operating System(s) Required:* MS-DOS, XENIX, UNIX, AIX, NOVELLL, LANTASTIC. *Language(s):* COBOL (source code included). *Memory Required:* 4000k. *Items Included:* Full documentation. *Customer Support:* Various support & training options available.
contact publisher for price.
An Integrated Job Costing, Service, & Accounting Software System Designed Specifically for Plumbing, HVAC, Mechanical & Electrical Contractors. Includes Full Complement of Accounting Modules. Job Costing Allows Instant Review of Budgets, Billings, Costs, Cash Flow & Profitability. Service Dispatch & Billing Streamline & Simplify Those Procedures.
Data-Basics, Inc.

Construction Software. *Version:* 7.0. *Compatible Hardware:* IBM PC & compatibles, IBM PS12, system 136, AS/400. *Operating System(s) Required:* DOS, Networking; Novell, or OS/400. *Language(s):* RPG (source code included). *Memory Required:* 51k. *Items Included:* Complete operator instructions available on-line. *Customer Support:* Onsite training, software support program available.
contact publisher for price.
Tracks All Facets of Construction Costing, AIA Billing, & Construction Loan Draws. Each of the Standard Applications: Payroll, Accounts Payable, Sub Contract Control, Accounts Receivable, Inventory & General Ledger Interface with Job Cost. Also Includes: Residential Sales Analysis & Budgeting, Property Management, & Fixed Assets.
Pac Corp.

Consulair MacC Jr. *Compatible Hardware:* Apple Macintosh. *Memory Required:* 512k.
3.5" disk $79.95.
C Development System.
Consulair Corp.

Consulair MacC/MacC Toolkit. *Version:* 6.0. *Compatible Hardware:* Apple Macintosh. *Memory Required:* 512k. *Customer Support:* Free telephone support.
3.5" disk $425.00.
C Compiler & Development Tools Program.
Consulair Corp.

Consulair MacC 68020/68881. *Version:* 6.0. *Compatible Hardware:* Apple Macintosh II. *General Requirements:* 68020/68881 board. *Customer Support:* Free telephone support.
3.5" disk $600.00.
upgrade $200.00.
C Compiler for Macintosh II & Other 020 Upgrades.
Consulair Corp.

Consulair 68000 Development System. *Version:* 2.1. Bill Duvall. Oct. 1984. *Compatible Hardware:* Apple Macintosh. *Memory Required:* 512k.
3.5" disk $79.95.
Collection of Software Tools for Developing Assembly Language Programs on the Macintosh. Includes a Multiple-Window Editor with UNDO Which Allows the User to Edit Several Files Simultaneously with Standard Macintosh Text-Editing Features. The Motorola 68000 Assembler Has a Macro Facility, Which Reduces Coding Time. The Linker/Librarian Supports Libraries & Modular Programming. A Motorola 68000 Manual Is Included with the Package. Site Licenses & University Discounts Are Available.
Consulair Corp.

Consulair 68020/68881 C Compiler. *Version:* 6.0. Oct. 1987. *Compatible Hardware:* Apple Macintosh. (source code included). *General Requirements:* 68020/6881 hardware board. *Customer Support:* Free telephone support.
3.5" disk $600.00.
$200.00, ASD upgrade.
Version of the Consulair MacC Development System Tailored to Take Full Advantage of the Macintosh II or Any Other Machine with 68020/68881 Processors. The Compiler Includes a Complete Built-In 68020/68881 Assembler & Emits Code Which Takes Advantage of the Expanded 68020/68881 Instruction Set. Floating Point Operations Are Compiled Directly to 68881 Instructions, & Intermediate Values Are Kept in the Internal 68881 Registers, Resulting in Fast Floating Point Execution Times. The Package Includes the Conslair MacC/MacC Toolkit Development System, or Is Available As an Upgrade to Existing Customers.
Consulair Corp.

Consulair 68020/030 Assembler. Bill Duvall. *Items Included:* User's manual, spiral bound manual, 3 diskettes. *Customer Support:* Free telephone support.

Macintosh. contact publisher for price. *Optimal configuration:* Macintosh with 68020 or 68030 board.
Allows Users to Take Full Advantage of the Extended Addressing Modes & Instructions Sets of the 68202 & 68030 Processors, the 68881 & the 68882 Math Coprocessor, & the 68851 Memory Management Unit. The 68020/030 Assembler Is Fully Compatible with the CDS at Both the Source File & Binary File Levels, & Files May Be Used Interchangeably Between the Two.
Consulair Corp.

Consultant. *Compatible Hardware:* IBM PC, PCjr, PC XT. *Operating System(s) Required:* MS-DOS, PC-DOS 1.1. *Memory Required:* 128k. *General Requirements:* Color monitor, printer.
$95.00.
demo package $30.00, incl. documentation.
Proposes a Proper Computer Hardware & Software Configuration. Performed Using Government Accepted Cost-Benefit Analysis Methods.
Antech, Inc.

Contact Astro-Report. Joan Negus & Robert S. Hand. 1983. *Compatible Hardware:* Apple II with Applesoft, Apple II+, IIe, IIc, III, Macintosh, CP/M based machines with 2 150-280k disk drives, or 1 284k disk drive; IBM PC. *Operating System(s) Required:* Apple DOS, CP/M-80, MacFinder, MS-DOS, PC-DOS. *Language(s):* BASIC. *Memory Required:* Apple 48k, CP/M 64k, IBM 256k, MS-DOS 128k or 256k, Macintosh 512k. *General Requirements:* Printer, Dot-Matrix or Hewlett Packard Laser. *Items Included:* Manual. *Customer Support:* Free phone support.
disk $195.00 ea.
IBM PC & MS-DOS. (ISBN 0-913637-48-3).
CP/M. (Kaypro 2). (ISBN 0-913637-47-5).
Apple. (ISBN 0-87199-029-6).
Macintosh. (ISBN 0-87199-052-0).
Computes & Compares Horoscopes of Two People for Romantic Compatibility, Producing a 25-Page Report. Includes License to Sell Printed Output. IBM-Compatible Version Is Also Available in Spanish for $250.
Astrolabe, Inc.

Contact Management (a Part of ABECAS). *Version:* 3.3. Jan. 1989. *Customer Support:* On site training unlimited support services for first 90 days & through subscription thereafter.
PC/MS-DOS 3.x. Contact publisher for price.
Nonstandard peripherals required: Hard disk (30Mb or higher); 132-column printer.
Networks supported: Novell, NTNX, 10-Net, UNIX/XENIX, Turbo DOS.
Master Records Can Be Entered at Various Levels of Detail with Any Amount of Contact Data. Multiple Interest Window-Accessible Data Is Available. Master Record Data Can Be Time & Date Stamped, Maintained & Analyzed. Program Also Prints Lists & Labels in Varying Sequences, & Interfaces with ABECAS Accounts Receivalble.
Argos Software.

Contacts & Facts. Steve Schwartz & David Linke. Dec. 1987.
MS-DOS (640k). disk $49.95 (Order no.: CF5).
Nonstandard peripherals required: 1 hard disk or 2 floppies.
3.5" disk $49.95 (Order no.: CF3).
An Electronic Address File. Affords a Way to Record Names, Addresses & Notes About People or Subjects. Can Be Searched by First Name, Last Name, Organization Name, ID Code, City or State.
Domain, Inc., Information Managers Div.

Contemporary Authors CD-ROM DOS-MAC 96 Manual. (Contemporary Authors CD-ROM Ser.). Edited by Brandon Trenz. Nov. 1995.
IBM; Mac. CD-ROM disk Contact publisher for price (ISBN 0-7876-0267-1, Order no.: 10919).
Gale Research, Inc.

Contemporary Authors CD-ROM DOS-MAC 96 CD 1. (Contemporary Authors CD-ROM Ser.). Edited by Brandon Trenz. Nov. 1995.
IBM; Mac. CD-ROM disk Contact publisher for price (ISBN 0-7876-0268-X, Order no.: 109200).
Gale Research, Inc.

Contemporary Authors CD-ROM DOS-MAC 96 Spine. (Contemporary Authors CD-ROM Ser.). Edited by Brandon Trenz. Nov. 1995.
IBM; Mac. CD-ROM disk Contact publisher for price (ISBN 0-7876-0270-1, Order no.: 109202).
Gale Research, Inc.

Contemporary Authors CD-ROM DOS-MAC 96 Package. (Contemporary Authors CD-ROM Ser.). Edited by Brandon Trenz. Nov. 1995.
IBM; Mac. CD-ROM disk Contact publisher for price (ISBN 0-7876-0272-8, Order no.: 109204).
Gale Research, Inc.

Contemporary Authors 96 Mac Help Card. (Contemporary Authors CD-ROM Ser.). Nov. 1995.
IBM; Mac. CD-ROM disk Contact publisher for price (ISBN 0-7876-0277-9, Order no.: 109210).
Gale Research, Inc.

Contest Tabulator & Scorecard Program I, 3 disks. Gary Sande. 1984. *Compatible Hardware:* Apple II, II+, IIe, IIc; IBM PC & compatibles. *Operating System(s) Required:* Apple DOS 3.3, MS-DOS 2.0 or higher. *Language(s):* BASIC. *Memory Required:* Apple 48k, IBM 64k.
3.5" or 5.25" disks $49.50 (ISBN 1-55797-016-5, Order no.: AP2-AG55).
3.5" or 5.25" disks $69.50 (ISBN 1-55797-017-3, Order no.: IBM-AG55).
Designed to Tabulate, Score, & Print out the Results of All Types of Contests, Including Skill-Type & Judging Contests. The User Adds Contestant Names & Numbers, Team Names, Scores, & Official Placings, & the Program Will Print out the Complete Team Scores by Individuals & Rankings of Teams & Individuals. Designed to Save Time & Add Accuracy to Contest Results. Accepts Data for Teams with 3 to 4 Team Members.
Hobar Pubns.

Contest Tabulator & Scorecard Program II, 3 disks. Gary Sande. *Compatible Hardware:* Apple II, II+, IIe, IIc; IBM PC & compatibles. *Operating System(s) Required:* Apple DOS 3.3, MS-DOS 2.0 or higher. *Language(s):* BASIC. *Memory Required:* 48k. *General Requirements:* 2 disk drives; printer.
3.5" or 5.25" disks $49.50 (ISBN 1-55797-018-1, Order no.: AP2-AG56).
3.5" or 5.25" disks $69.50 (ISBN 1-55797-019-X, Order no.: IBM-AG56).
Designed to Tabulate, Score, & Print out the Results of All Types of Contests, Including Skill- & Judging-Type Contests. The User Can Add Contestant Names & Numbers, Team Names, Scores, & Official Placings, & the Program Will Print out the Complete Team Scores by Individuals & Rankings of Teams & Individuals. Supports Teams of Three to Five Members.
Hobar Pubns.

Context MBA. Context Management Systems, Inc. *Compatible Hardware:* HP 150 Touchscreen, HP Series 200 Models 216/220, 236, 217/237 Personal Technical Computers. *Memory Required:* 512k.
HP 150. 3.5" disk $495.00 (Order no.: 45481A).
HP 216/220, 236, 217/237. 3.5" disk $795.00 (Order no.: 45481B).
HP 236, 217/237. 5-1/4" disk $795.00.
Helps Managers Generate Reports Analyzing Current Sales Data, Predict & Describe Current Budget Requirements Based on Current Year Expenses, Create a Model to Compare Planned Inventory with the Actual Inventory on Hand & Then Report the Findings, & Write Executive Memos & Reports. The Package Includes Spreadsheet, Graphics, Word Processing, Database Management, & Telecommunications. All These Functions Work with the Same Information - Once the Information Is Entered All Parts of the Program Have Access to It. The Windowing Feature Allows More Than One Function at a Time to Appear on the Screen, So Data Can Be Analyzed in Several Different Ways.
Hewlett-Packard Co.

Continuous Beam Analysis. *Version:* Beam86. 1989. *Compatible Hardware:* IBM PC & compatibles. *Operating System(s) Required:* PC-DOS/MS-DOS. *Language(s):* QBASIC. *Customer Support:* Telephone assistance.
disk $47.00, incl. user guide.
disk $127.00, incl. source code.
Data May Be Input from a Previously Created File or May Be Input As the Program Requests It. Up to 20 Spans May Be Analyzed with up to 40 Concentrated Loads & a Uniform Load on Each Span. Prismatic or Variable Cross-Sections May Be Specified & the Beam Ends May Be Fixed, Free or Cantilevered. Output Consists of End Shears & End Moments. User Has the Option of Echoing the Input Data to the Printer for Complete Problem Description.
Systek, Inc. (Mississippi).

Continuous Concrete Beam Design. 1995. *Items Included:* Full manual. *Customer Support:* Free telephone support - 90 days, 30-day warranty.
MS-DOS 3.2 or higher. 286 (584k). disk $99.95. *Nonstandard peripherals required:* CGA/EGA/VGA.
Assists in the Design & Selection of Reinforcing Steel for Continuous Concrete Beams in Braced Frames. It Handles Rectangular or T-Beams. Moments Are Computed for Dead Loads, Live Loads on All Spans, & Live Loads on Odd Spans & Even Spans.
Dynacomp, Inc.

Continuous Probability Distributions. Bruce E. Trumbo. 1985. *Compatible Hardware:* Apple II+, IIe, IIc. *Operating System(s) Required:* Apple DOS 3.3. *Language(s):* BASIC. *Memory Required:* 48k.
disk $50.00 (ISBN 0-933694-35-0, Order no.: COM 3108A).
Graphics Sequences Are Used to Demonstrate How to Compute Areas under Normal Curves from Tabled Values, Simulated Samples from the Standard Normal Distributions Are Plotted As Histograms. Complete Interactive Control of Precision Plots for Normal, T, Chi-Square, F, Gamma & Density Curves.
COMPress.

Continuous Span. Sep. 1983. *Compatible Hardware:* Apple II+, IIe; HP-85; IBM PC. *Operating System(s) Required:* PC-DOS, Apple DOS 3.3. *Language(s):* BASIC (source code included). *Memory Required:* HP 32k, Apple 48k, IBM 128k. *Customer Support:* Telephone.

$125.00.
Analyzes up to 8 Spans Using the "Theory of Three Moments", Calculates Moments, Reactions, Shears, & Deflections for All Spans.
PEAS (Practical Engineering Applications Software).

Contour. *Version:* 2.0. Thomas Dougherty. *Customer Support:* Free technical support, 90-day limited warranty.
Mac. 3.5" disk $89.95, incl. pamphlet (ISBN 1-56321-108-4).
A Hypercard Environment for Teaching about Subjective Contour & Related Visual Illusions As Well As about Subjective Contours As a Microcosm of Issues in Visual Perception.
Lawrence Erlbaum Assocs. Software & Alternate Media, Inc.

Contour PLOT. Oct. 1985. *Compatible Hardware:* IBM PC. *Operating System(s) Required:* PC-DOS. *Language(s):* BASIC. *Memory Required:* 512k.
disk $249.00.
Generates Contour Plots from Regularly or Irregularly Spaced Data.
Tesseract Enterprises, Ltd.

CONTOUR Plus: Contour Plotting Program.
Version: 2.03. Feb. 1991. *Compatible Hardware:* AT&T PC 6300; Compaq; IBM PC, PC XT. *Operating System(s) Required:* PC-DOS/MS-DOS. *Language(s):* FORTRAN, C. *Memory Required:* 640k. *Items Included:* Manual, 120-day free maintenance. *Customer Support:* 1 year maintenance for $200.
$595.00 (ISBN 0-922920-03-6, Order no.: PR0031).
Menu Driven Program. Allows User to Enter Random X, Y, Z Data & Create a Contour Map. Data May Be Entered Manually, Read from COGO-PC PLUS or from a User File. CONTOUR PLUS Allows for the Delineation of Creeks & Structures. The Meshing Feature Allows User to Create a 3-Dimensionally Rotated Model of the Contour Feature. Final Contour Map May Be Plotted on over 25 Pen Plotters or an Epson Printer to Scale. Interfaces to Most Popular Micro-Based CAD Programs.
Research Engineers.

Contract Collection Manager. *Version:* 2.0. Apr. 1984. *Compatible Hardware:* IBM PC & 100% compatibles. *Operating System(s) Required:* MS-DOS. *Language(s):* C. *Memory Required:* 640k. *Customer Support:* Unlimited telephone suport, regulatory compliance, product enhancement, newsletters.
$30000.00-$12,500.00 plus options.
PC-Based System Which Processes Third-Party Payments & Disbursements, Such As Escrows, Land Contracts, Installment Collections, Note Collections, Mortgage Notes or Rental Payments.
Learned-Mahn.

Contract Express. *Customer Support:* Unlimited telephone support, regulatory compliance, product enhancements, newsletters.
Windows. 486 (8Mb). Contact publisher for price. *Addl. software required:* Windows. *Networks supported:* Novell.
A Windows-Based, PC Software System Which Automates the Collection & Disbursement Service for Third-Party Contracts. The Contracts May Be Called Escrows, Land Contracts, Installment Collections, Mortgage Notes, Note Collections or Agreement of Sale. Other Applications Include Installment Purchase or Student Loans. Available in Single or Multi-User Versions. Features: ACH Credits & Debits Are Available; Interest Reporting with Magnetic Tape Production; Sales Tax Accounting; Automated Amortization & Assumption Accounting; Provides 1098 & 1099 Reporting; Automatic Assumptions & Wrap-Arounds; Extensive Security Features; Provides Accounting by Branches.
Learned-Mahn.

Contract Management. 1992. *Customer Support:* Free telephone & BBS technical support, documentation, training from local dealers &/or vendor's CFPIM, C.P.M., CIRM, CQA trainers. Customization available from vendor.
MS/PC DOS; Concurrent DOS, Xenix, Unix. IBM PC/XT/AT & compatibles; IBM PS/2 (512k). single or multi user $795.00. *Networks supported:* Novell, Lantastic, Banyan VINES; all NETBIOS compatible.
A date-sensitive pricing tool designed to handle special marketing & sales program pricing as well as high-volume, contract-price customers. This module overrides internal Order Entry & Inventory Control pricing schedules & automatically injects resident contract prices (by product by customer) into all Sales Orders for each designated customer or range of customers. Allows the use of start-dates & end-dates for each contract pricing schedule (by customer & product) & automatically re-sets price to pre-contract levels when each customer contract expires.
INMASS/MRP.

Contract Manager. *Compatible Hardware:* IBM PC, PC XT, PC AT. *Operating System(s) Required:* PC-DOS. *Memory Required:* 256k. *General Requirements:* Hard disk.
disk $5475.00.
Designed for the Construction Contractor. Includes Accounts Payable, Accounts Receivable, General Ledger, Job Costing & Payroll.
Business Computer Consultants/Merrill Street Software.

Contract Processing. (Service Management Ser.). 1996.
DOS, Unix. IBM PC. disk contact publisher for price.
Features Multiple coverage types per contract with appropriate charges for each type. 9,999 items per contract. Supports multiple addresses & response times on an individual contract with appropriate charges for each.
Core Software, Inc.

Contractor Cost Accounting System.
Compatible Hardware: DECmate II, DECmate III, PDP 11-23, MicroVAX. *Operating System(s) Required:* COS-310, MICRO-RSX.
$10,000.00, incl. user's guide (Order no.: 85-3).
Combines Job Cost Reporting for Management with an Accounting System to Serve the Special Needs of Construction Companies & Contractors. Reporting System Compares Actual Cost with Bid Estimate by Dividing Jobs into Distinct Activities & Activities into Multiple Lines According to the Organization of the Bid Sheet. Accounting System Records Labor, Billing, & Purchase Transactions, & Prints Payroll & Vendor Checks. Month-End Accounting Figures Collect to the General Ledger & Report on Financial Statements & Supporting Schedules. Special Features Include Separate Reporting for Smaller Time & Material Jobs, Subcontract Activity, & Change Orders, & Billing Using the Standard AIA Contractor Billing Report Format.
Corporate Consulting Co.

Contractor Management Program. *Compatible Hardware:* TRS-80 Model I, Model III, Model 4 with Level II BASIC; IBM PC. *Language(s):* BASIC (source code included). *Memory Required:* 48k-128k. *General Requirements:* Printer.
disk $99.95.
Designed to Assist General Contractors & Related Businesses in the Processes of Estimating, Planning, Scheduling & Controlling in the Contracting Business.
Dynacomp, Inc.

Contractor Management Program. *Items Included:* Full manual. No other products required. *Customer Support:* Free telephone support - no time limit, 30 day warranty.
MS-DOS 3.2 or higher. IBM & compatibles (512k). disk $99.95.
Management Tool Designed to Assist General Contractors & Related Businesses in the Processes of Estimating, Planning, Scheduling, & Controlling of the Contracting Business. Program Has a Large Menu of Functions Which Provide the User with Cost, Scheduling, & Resource Utilization Information in a Wide Variety of Formats.
Dynacomp, Inc.

Contractor Microcomputer Software. Bradbury & Co. *Compatible Hardware:* TI Professional. *Operating System(s) Required:* CP/M, MS-DOS. *Memory Required:* 64k. *General Requirements:* Winchester hard disk, printer.
$695.00.
4 Program Series; PAYMENT, MATERIAL, SHOPDRAW & DRASPEC. Process Payment Requests, Control Materials & Subcontractors & Expedite Material Deliveries.
Texas Instruments, Personal Productivit.

Contractor Three Lite. *Version:* 11.0.18L. Jan. 1996. *Items Included:* Operator's manual. Getting Started Guide, Startup Chart of Accounts & Job Cost Code Dictionary. *Customer Support:* Remote site, telephone hotline.
MS-DOS, Windows. 286, 386, 486, Pentium (640k). disk $1655.00. *Optimal configuration:* 386, MS-DOS 5.0 or higher, 640k RAM.
Fully Integrated Job Cost/Accounting Software System for Smaller Contractors/Subcontractors. System Includes Job Cost, General Ledger, Accounts Payable, Accounts Receivable, & Payroll. Also Includes One Year of Product Support & Free Enhancements.
A-Systems Corp.

Contractor III Plus. *Version:* 11.0.18P. Jan. 1996. *Compatible Hardware:* 286 or higher. *Operating System(s) Required:* PC-DOS/MS-DOS, Novell. *Language(s):* QuickBASIC & C. *Memory Required:* 640k. *Items Included:* Customer data, manuals, 1 year support & installation. *Customer Support:* Remote Site, Telephone Hotline.
PC-DOS/MS-DOS. $6435.00, incl. manual, training & support plus data conversion. *Networks supported:* Novell.
Fully Integrated Job/Cost Accounting System for the Construction Industry. 18 Open Fiscal Periods. Integrated Modules Include General Ledger, Job Cost, Payroll & Accounts Payable, Optional Integrated Modules Include Accounts Receivable, Equipment Costing, Purchase Orders, Multi-User Capability, Estimating. Includes 1 Year Support & Free Upgrade.
A-Systems Corp.

Contractor III Standard. *Version:* 11.0.18S. Jan. 1996. *Compatible Hardware:* 80286, 80386, 80486, Pentium. *Operating System(s) Required:* PC-DOS/MS-DOS, Novell. *Language(s):* QuickBASIC & C. *Memory Required:* 640k. *Items Included:* Customer data, manuals, 1 year support. *Customer Support:* Remote Site, Telephone Hot Line.
MS-DOS, Windows. disk $4195.00, incl. manual & training data conversion. *Networks supported:* Novell.
Modular Software Oriented to Contracting Industry. Integrates General Ledger, A/P, Payroll, & Job Costing. General Ledger & A/R Covers 18 Open Fiscal Periods. Optional Modules Include Equipment Costs, Purchase Orders, Multi-User, & Estimating. Includes 1 Year Support & Free Upgrades.
A-Systems Corp.

TITLE INDEX

Contractor's Dream. Version: 4.25. Dan Heilman & Joe Applegate. Jan. 1991. *Items Included:* Educational Manual; tutorial tape. *Customer Support:* 30 day unlimited warrantee; free telephone support; 800 number.
MS-DOS 3.0 or higher. IBM compatible with hard disk (640k). disk $275.00. *Optimal configuration:* 286 or faster; 20Mb or higher hard disk, 640k, EGA or higher.
A Complete Estimating & Cutting List Program for Small to Medium Sized Contractor's. Includes a Complete Data Base of Construction Materials. Estimates All Phases of Residential Construction, Including Walls, Floors, Roofs, Trim, Paint, Patio's, etc. Prepares Bid Sheets for Contractor, Client, & Lumber Yard. Includes Pop-up Full Featured Calculator.
Workhorses, Inc.

Contraption Zack. Nov. 1992.
MS-DOS version 3.3 or higher. IBM PC-AT or compatible (640k). 3.5" or 5.25" disk $39.95. *Optimal configuration:* IBM PC-AT or compatible (286 required, 386 recommended); 640k of RAM; 16MHz or faster, hard disk required; VGA Graphics Card required (256-color graphics throughout); joystick supported; Ad Lib, Sound Blaster, & Roland supported.
A Madcap Strategy Game in a Bizarre Universe of Overblown Machines. Find Lost Tools to Make Repairs, Solve Puzzles along the Way, & Singlehandedly Get Gadgetco Inc. up & Running - with Surprising Results.
Software Toolworks.

CONTRL: Security Monitoring. Version: 3.2. 1990. *Compatible Hardware:* MicroVAX & VAX. *Operating System(s) Required:* VMS, MICROVMS 4.6 or higher. *Language(s):* Basic. *Memory Required:* 220k. *Items Included:* Manuals, 1 year maintenance, quarterly newsletter. *Customer Support:* 6:00 a.m.-6:00 p.m. MST.
disk $614.00-$6822.00.
Lets an Authorized User Observe What Another User is Doing on the System & Interact in Real Time. Lets Security Personnel Monitor Suspicious Activities & Gather Evidence. Any Terminal on the System May Be Monitored. It Includes Many Configurations & Built-in Safeguards. Includes: INSTRUCTOR, a Training Tool for Demonstrating Software on Multiple Terminals Simultaneously; ATTEND, Lets Users Participate & Communicate with Their Tutor; FRAMER, Converts Screen-Oriented Logs into a Printable Format; RTMON, Allows Both CONTRL to Monitor DECnet RT Devices.
Raxco, Inc.

CONTRN. 1982. *Compatible Hardware:* IBM PC & compatibles. *Operating System(s) Required:* MS-DOS. *Language(s):* BASIC. *Memory Required:* 128k.
$115.00.
Calculates the Stresses in Cylinder-Cone Transitions for Half Apex Angles of up to 60 Degrees.
Technical Research Services, Inc.

Control-Net. W. J. Moody. May 1987. *Compatible Hardware:* IBM PC & compatibles. *Operating System(s) Required:* PC-DOS, MS-DOS. (source code included). *Memory Required:* 256k.
disk $495.00.
Software & Hardware Package to Monitor Analog & Digital Sensors in Buildings. There Is a Record of Events Kept in a Data Base. Responses to & Monitoring of These Events Can Be by Remote Telephone Access. Various Sensors Can Be Used, Such As Temperature, Refrigerator Status, Intrusion Monitors, & Other Parameters. According to Customer Needs, These Parameters Can Be Modified by the Customer. Control-Net Is Multi-Tasking & Concurrent, under PC-DOS.
Intelligent Machines.

Control Panel. Nov. 1988. *Customer Support:* Free telephone support (505) 345-7701.
IBM PC, XT, AT or compatibles MicroChannel (384k). contact publisher for price. *Networks supported:* NetBIOS, Novell.
Utility & Menu Shell (Non-Memory Resident) Providing Fast, One-Touch Access To Any Software Application in a Consistant, Easy-to-Use Interface. Incorporates 5 Major Functions: Menu Services, DOS Services, Disk Services, Desktop Services & Communication Services.
Promark, Ltd.

Control Plus. Version: 4.2. *Compatible Hardware:* IBM PC & compatibles. *Memory Required:* 128k.
disk $695.00.
Free-Form, Command & Menu-Driven Database-Management System Featuring Help Screen, On-Disk Tutorial, Automatic Indexing & Split Files. Offers a Maximum of 512 Fields per Record, 78 Characters per Field, Over 1 Million Records per File, 2048 Characters per Record, 1 Index per File, 1 Active Index & up to 16 Records Sorted. Allows User to Revise Field Descriptions at Will.
Phase 1 Systems.

CONTROL/EXCEL or CONTROL for Lotus 1-2-3. 1978. *Items Included:* 3 three-ringed manuals (1 user, 2 reference). *Customer Support:* Toll free number 1 year unlimited technical support, 1 yr. extended telephone support, national on-site training available.
PC-DOS 3.3, Windows, Database Servers (Oracle, Sybase, & DB2). 386/486. $500.00 & $4000.00 Modules Bundled with Support, Network package $17,500.00. *Optimal configuration:* 8Mb RAM. *Networks supported:* Novell, Windows NT Server, TCP/IP or IPX/SPX Protocols, LAN Manager, DEC Pathworks.
A Multi-Dimensional Financial Server & OLAP (On-Line Analytical Processor) That Works with Spreadsheet Front-Ends (EXCEL & Lotus 1-2-3). Capable of Producing Hundreds of Trillions of Potential Combinations for Analysis, CONTROL Allows Information Processing from an RDBMS Financial Database Providing Endusers the Tools for Budgeting, Forecasting, & Variance Reporting with Multi-Dimensional Data Needing to Be Consolidated or Drilled On.
KCI Computing, Inc.

Control Valve Sizing Fluid Control Analysis. *Items Included:* Full manual. No other products required. *Customer Support:* Free telephone support - no time limit, 30 day warranty.
MS-DOS 3.2 or higher. IBM & compatibles (512k). disk $199.95. *Optimal configuration:* IBM, MS-DOS 2.0 or higher, 256k RAM. Printer is supported.
Employs the Power of the Computer to Save Time in Iteratively Sizing Control Valves. At Each Stage in the Process, CVS Does Everything Possible to Simplify Data Input. ISA S75.01-1985 Methodology Is Followed, with Traceable Nomenclature & Equations. Calculated Results Are Automatically Checked Against This Standard to Ensure Accuracy. Both English & Metric Units Are Supported.
Dynacomp, Inc.

Control Valve Sizing: Fluid Control Analysis. 1992. *Items Included:* Detailed manuals included with all Dynacomp products. *Customer Support:* Free telephone support to original customer - no time limit; 30 day limited warranty.
MS-DOS 3.2 or higher. IBM PC & compatibles (512k). $199.95 (Add $5.00 for 3 1/2" format; 5 1/4" format standard). *Optimal configuration:* IBM, MS-DOS 2.0 or higher, 256k RAM. A printer is supported.
Employs the Power of the Computer to Save Time in Iteratively Sizing Control Valves. At Each Stage in the Process, CVS Does Everything Possible to Simplify Data Input. The ISA S75.01-1985 Methodology Is Followed, with Traceable Nomenclature & Equations. Calculated Results Are Automatically Checked Against This Standard to Ensure Accuracy. Both English & Metric Units Are Supported. Comes with an Excellent 120-Page Reference Manual.
Dynacomp, Inc.

Conv III to PC: Convert Model I-III BASIC to PC. Version: 2.0. 1985. *Compatible Hardware:* IBM PC & compatibles; TRS-80 Model I, Model III. *Memory Required:* 256k. *General Requirements:* 2 disk drives.
disk $139.95 (Order no.: CONV3TOPC).
Transfers TRS-80 Model I/III Files & BASIC Programs to PC Readable Diskettes & Automatically Performs 95% or More of the Syntax Changes Necessary to Run TRS-80 BASIC Programs on an IBM PC/XT/AT or Compatible.
Educational Micro Systems, Inc.

Conv 4 to PC: Convert Model 4 BASIC to PC. 1985. *Compatible Hardware:* IBM PC & compatibles; TRS-80 Model 4. *General Requirements:* 2 disk drives.
disk $139.95.
Transfers TRS-80 Model 4 Files & BASIC Programs to PC Readable Disks, & Automatically Performs 95% or More of the Syntax Changes Necessary to Run TRS-80 Model 4 BASIC Programs on an IBM PC/XT/AT or Compatible.
Educational Micro Systems, Inc.

Convective Heat Transfer. *Items Included:* Bound manual. *Customer Support:* Free hotline - no time limit; 30 day limited warranty; updates are $5/disk plus S&H.
MS-DOS. IBM & compatibles (128k). disk $119.95.
Apple (64k). disk $119.95.
Offers Programs for Calculating Heat Transfer Coefficients (Natural Convection, Forced Convection, Forced Convection in Annulus, Jacketed-Wall & Coils, & Condensation), Heat Transfer in Boiling, Combined Boiling & Radiant Heat Transfer, Rate of Simple Convection, & Rate of Convective Heat Transfer.
Dynacomp, Inc.

ConverSIon: A Program for Medical SI Unit Conversion. H. P. Lehmann et al. Mar. 1987. *Compatible Hardware:* Apple IIe, IIc; IBM PC & compatibles. *Operating System(s) Required:* PC-DOS/MS-DOS 3.1, ProDOS. *Language(s):* Applesoft BASIC, BASICA. *Memory Required:* 256k. *General Requirements:* Extended 80-column card for Apple IIe.
IBM & compatibles. disk $47.00, incl. documentation (ISBN 0-89189-250-8, Order no.: 68-9-022-20).
Apple IIe, IIc. disk $47.00, incl. documentation (ISBN 0-89189-249-4, Order no.: 68-9-023-33).
Can Convert Conventional Units of Measure to SI Units for More than 500 Laboratory Analytes. User Enters the First Three Letters for the Desired Analyte & the Test Results in Conventional Units & the Program Converts the Values to SI Units. It Can Also Convert SI Units to Conventional Units.
ASCP Pr.

Conversion Master. *Customer Support:* 800-929-8117 (customer service).
MS-DOS. Apple II. disk $59.99 (ISBN 0-87007-316-8).
Converts Over 1000 Common & Not so Common Unit Measures for Scientific & Mathematical Purposes.
SourceView Software International.

Conversion Plus. *Version:* 3.5. Dec. 1995. *Customer Support:* Free technical support line (203-268-0030) 9AM to 6PM Eastern. Windows 95, NT & 3.1. 386 or hgiher, VGA monitor (4Mb). disk $149.00.
Includes All the Capabilities of MacOpen Plus File Translation. Use Macintosh Disks, Removable Media & CD-ROMs in Your PC & Convert Files. the Included Macintosh Disk Mounting Utility Reads, Writes, & Formats High Density Mac Disks & Removable Media on Your PC. Also Includes Thousands of Convcersion Combinations for Popular Macintosh, DOS & Windows Word Processing, Spreadsheet, Database, & Graphics Programs. All Converted Documents Retain Original Formatting & Are Fully Usable. Supports Long File Names.
DataViz, Inc.

Convert. *Compatible Hardware:* Apple Macintosh. 3.5" disk $15.00.
Metric to Imperial Conversion Calculator.
Jam Technologies.

ConvertaCalc. *Version:* 1.55. L. A. Chapman. Sep. 1984. *Compatible Hardware:* DEC Rainbow; IBM PC & compatibles, PC XT, PC AT, PS/2; TI Professional; Wang PC. *Operating System(s) Required:* PC-DOS, MS-DOS. *Language(s):* Compiled BASIC. *Memory Required:* 192k. *Customer Support:* Yes.
disk $245.00.
Takes Models Developed under One Spreadsheet Program & Converts Them to Another. Can Be Used with Lotus 1-2-3, Symphony, MultiPlan, SuperCalc, VisiCalc, DIF, & Comma Separated Variables Files. Any Function That Is Not Available in the New Output Format Becomes a Label & the Program Gives the User a Detailed Report on Any Cells Which Need to Be Modified.
Micro Decision Systems (Pennsylvania).

The Convertible Bond Analyst. *Compatible Hardware:* Epson MX-80; IBM PC (5.25" disk only). *Operating System(s) Required:* PC-DOS/MS-DOS. *Language(s):* BASIC. *Memory Required:* 64k.
disk $99.95, incl. manual.
Evaluates Convertible Bonds Giving User All Ratios & Undervaluation Factor.
Analytical Service Assocs.

Converticalc. *Compatible Hardware:* Apple II. *Memory Required:* 64k.
contact publisher for price.
RPH Assocs.

Convoy 1942. Adrian Vance. Oct. 1985. *Compatible Hardware:* Apple II. *Operating System(s) Required:* Apple DOS. (source code included). *Memory Required:* 48k.
disk $9.95 (ISBN 0-918547-40-7).
illustration files on the disk avail.
Simulation of World War II Convoy from New York to Murmansk, Russia. Not Copy Protected.
AV Systems, Inc.

Cooking & Baking, 13 disks. 1985. *Compatible Hardware:* Apple II, IIc, IIe; IBM PC & compatibles. *Operating System(s) Required:* Apple DOS, MS-DOS. *Memory Required:* 48k.
Complete Cooking & Baking Unit. $775.00 (Order no.: PMCBCA).
Topics Include Food Service Responsibilities, First Aid/Safety, Meats, Recipe Conversion, Baking Ingredients, & Cooking & Baking Measurement.
Aquarius Instructional.
  Baking Ingredients, 2 disks. 1985. *Memory Required:* 48k.
    $140.00 (Order no.: APPLE PMCB5A, IBM BMCB51).
    Topics Included Are: Part I, Ingredients; Part II, Ingredients.
  Cooking & Baking Measurement, 5 disks. 1985. *Memory Required:* 48k.
    $295.00 (Order no.: APPLE PMCB6A, IBM BMCB61).
    Covers the Following Subjects: Baker's Scale, Ounce Measurement, Pound Measurement, Volume Measurement, & Coverting Equivalent Measurements.
  First Aid/Safety, 2 disks. 1985. *Memory Required:* 48k.
    $140.00 (Order no.: APPLE PMCB2A, IBM BMCB21).
    Covers First Aid/Review of First Aid, Safety.
  Food Service Responsibilities, 3 disks. 1985. *Memory Required:* 48k.
    $195.00 (Order no.: APPLE PMCB1A, IBM-BMCB11).
    Covers Sanitation/Food Poisoning, Hygiene, Receiving & Storing Food Supplies.
  Meats, 2 disks. 1985. *Memory Required:* 48k.
    $140.00 (Order no.: APPLE PMCB3A, IBM BMCB31).
    Covers Beef & Pork.
  Recipe Conversion. 1985. *Memory Required:* 48k.
    disk $80.00 (Order no.: APPLE PMCB4A, IBM BMCB41).
    Includes Recipe Conversion, Pts. I & II.

Cooking for Today: Chicken. Oct. 1995. *Items Included:* Operating manual, catalog, registration card. *Customer Support:* Free technical support 206-622-5530.
DOS 3.1, Windows 3.1, Windows 95. 486SX 25MHz or higher (8Mb RAM). Contact publisher for price (ISBN 1-884014-77-1). *Addl. software required:* Double speed CD-ROM drive, mouse, keyboard, MPC compliant audio.
Macintosh. 68030 processor System 7.1 or higher (8Mb RAM). Contact publisher for price (ISBN 1-884014-78-X). *Addl. software required:* Double speed CD-ROM drive, keyboard, 13" monitor, Quicktime 1.61 or higher mouse.
A Compilation of 50-60 Recipes Containing Chicken from The Better Homes & Gardens Cooking for Today - Chicken Cookbook. The User Can Search for Recipes on the CD Based on Available Ingredients.
Multicom Publishing, Inc.

Cooking for Today: Chicken (Hybrid Book Bundle). Oct. 1995. *Items Included:* Operating manual, catalog, registration card. *Customer Support:* Free technical support 206-622-5530.
DOS 3.1, Windows 3.1, Windows 95; Macintosh. CD-ROM disk Contact publisher for price (ISBN 1-884014-79-8). *Addl. software required:* Double speed CD-ROM drive.
Contains 50-60 Recipes on a Particular Topic. This CD Will Focus on Chicken Recipes & Will Be Bundled with the Better Homes & Gardens Cooking for Today Series, Chicken. The User Will Be Able to Search for Recipes Based on Available Ingredients.
Multicom Publishing, Inc.

Cooking for Today: Pasta. Oct. 1995. *Items Included:* Operating manual, catalog, registration card. *Customer Support:* Free technical support 206-622-5530.
DOS 3.1, Windows 3.1, (8Mb RAM). 486SX 25MHz or higher (8Mb RAM). CD-ROM disk Contact publisher for price (ISBN 1-884014-80-1). *Addl. software required:* Double speed CD-ROM drive, mouse, keyboard, MPC compliant audio.
Macintosh. 68030 processor System 7.1 or higher (8Mb RAM). CD-ROM disk Contact publisher for price (ISBN 1-884014-81-X). *Addl. software required:* Double speed CD-ROM drive, keyboard, 13" monitor, Quicktime 1.61 or higher mouse.
A CD-ROM Containing Recipes for Pasta from the Better Homes & Gardens Cooking for Today Series, Pasta Edition. The CD Will Contain 50-60 Recipes. The User Will Be Able to Search for Recipes Based on Available Ingredients.
Multicom Publishing, Inc.

Cooking for Today: Pasta (Hybrid Book Bundle). Oct. 1995. *Items Included:* Operating manual, catalog, registration card. *Customer Support:* Free technical support 206-622-5530.
DOS 3.1, Windows 3.1, Windows 95; Macintosh. 486SX 25MHz or higher (8Mb RAM); 68030 processor System 7.1 or higher (8Mb RAM). CD-ROM disk Contact publisher for price (ISBN 1-884014-82-8). *Addl. software required:* Double speed CD-ROM drive.
A Series of 50-60 Recipes from the Better Homes & Gardens Cookbook of the Same Name. Each Recipe Has a Photo, Ingredients, Directions, etc. There Is a Search Feature That Allows the User to Look for Recipes Based on Available Ingredients. The CD Will Come Bundled with the Better Homes & Gardens Cooking for Today Cookbook.
Multicom Publishing, Inc.

Cooking for Today: Stir Fry. Oct. 1995. *Items Included:* Operating manual, catalog, registration card. *Customer Support:* Free technical support 206-622-5530.
DOS 3.1, Windows 3.1, Windows 95. 486SX 25MHz or higher (8Mb RAM). CD-ROM disk Contact publisher for price (ISBN 1-884014-86-0). *Addl. software required:* Double speed CD-ROM drive, mouse, keyboard, MPC compliant audio.
Macintosh. 68030 processor System 7.1 or higher (8Mb RAM). CD-ROM disk Contact publisher for price (ISBN 1-884014-87-9). *Addl. software required:* Double speed CD-ROM drive, keyboard, 13" monitor, Quicktime 1.61 or higher mouse.
Will Contain 50-60 Recipes on Stir Fry Based on the Better Homes & Gardens Cookbook of the Same Name.
Multicom Publishing, Inc.

Cooking for Today: Stir Fry (Hybrid Book Bundle). Oct. 1995. *Items Included:* Operating manual, catalog, registration card. *Customer Support:* Free technical support 206-622-5530.
DOS 3.1, Windows 3.1, Windows 95; Macintosh. 486SX 25MHz or higher (8Mb RAM); 68030 processor System 7.1 or higher (8Mb RAM). CD-ROM disk Contact publisher for price (ISBN 1-884014-88-7). *Addl. software required:* Double speed CD-ROM drive.
Will Contain 50-60 Recipes on Stir Fry Based on the Better Homes & Gardens Cookbook of the Same Name.
Multicom Publishing, Inc.

Cooking for Today: Vegetarian. Oct. 1995. *Items Included:* Operating manual, catalog, registration card. *Customer Support:* Free technical support 206-622-5530.
DOS 3.1, Windows 3.1, Windows 95. 486SX 25MHz or higher (8Mb RAM). CD-ROM disk Contact publisher for price (ISBN 1-884014-83-6). *Addl. software required:* Double speed CD-ROM drive, mouse, keyboard, MPC compliant audio.
Macintosh. 68030 processor System 7.1 or higher (8Mb RAM). CD-ROM disk Contact publisher for price (ISBN 1-884014-84-4). *Addl. software required:* Double speed CD-ROM drive, keyboard, 13" monitor, Quicktime 1.61 or higher mouse.
A CD-ROM That Will Contain 50-60 Recipes

TITLE INDEX

from the Better Homes & Gardens Cookbook of the Same Name. The CD Will Allow the User to Search for Recipes Based on Available Ingredients.
Multicom Publishing, Inc.

Cooking for Today: Vegetarian (Hybrid Book Bundle). Oct. 1995. *Items Included:* Operating manual, catalog, registration card. *Customer Support:* Free technical support 206-622-5530.
DOS 3.1, Windows 3.1, (8Mb RAM); Macintosh. 486SX 25MHz or higher (8Mb RAM); 68030 processor System 7.1 or higher (8Mb RAM). CD-ROM disk Contact publisher for price (ISBN 1-884014-85-2). *Addl. software required:* Double speed CD-ROM drive.
A CD-ROM That Will Contain 50-60 Recipes from the Better Homes & Gardens Cookbook of the Same Name. The CD Will Allow the User to Search for Recipes Based on Available Ingredients.
Multicom Publishing, Inc.

CookSoft. Nov. 1994. *Items Included:* User's manual. *Customer Support:* 90 days limited warranty; technical support line.
Windows 3.1. IBM & compatibles (4Mb). disk $49.90 (ISBN 0-9643229-4-3, Order no.: CSW-100). *Optimal configuration:* IBM or compatible running Windows 3.1 or higher version; 4Mb RAM; 3 1/2" HD drive; 11Mb hard disk space; mouse; printer.
Picture Cookbook & Recipe Organizer with 202 Ethnic & American Recipes, Each with Color Photograph on Screen; Ability to Add User's Recipes. Recipes Are Resizable. Shopping List Organized by Store Location. Menu & Daily Planning Capabilities. Nutritional Information Provided for All Recipes, Menus & Daily Plans. Printing Capabilities. Friendly; Enjoyable.
Zangsoft, Inc.

Coopers & Lybrand Effective Analytical Review System: CLEAR. *Compatible Hardware:* ALTOS Series 5-15D, Series 5-5D, 580-XX, ACS8000-XX; IBM PC & compatibles, PC XT, PC AT with 2 disk drives; Kaypro 11/IV with 2 disk drives, Kaypro 10; Xerox 820 with 2 disk drives; Zilog MCZ-250. *Operating System(s) Required:* CP/M, MP/M, PC-DOS, MS-DOS.
contact publisher for price.
Designed for the Auditor or Consultant Who Is Evaluating the Performance of a Client Business. Can Be Used As a Tool for Assessing Sales, Production, & Financing of an Enterprise. Consists of a Series of Programs Designed to Increase Audit Efficiency by Automating Some of the Common, Labor-Intensive Procedures Associated with Financial Statement Analysis.
Coopers & Lybrand.

Coordinate Geometry. *Version:* Cogo89. 1989. *Compatible Hardware:* IBM PC & compatibles. *Operating System(s) Required:* PC-DOS/MS-DOS. *Language(s):* QBASIC. *Customer Support:* Telephone assistance.
disk $47.00, incl. user guide.
disk $127.00, incl. source code.
Includes 41 Commands for Locating Points, Calculating Areas, Distances, Azimuths or Bearings, Traverse Adjustment & Description of Streets. Data May Be Stored on Disk. Inputs Is Free-Format. Help Screens Available.
Systek, Inc. (Mississippi).

The Coordinated Financial Planning System: The CFP System. *Version:* 2.20. Jan. 1992. *Operating System(s) Required:* PC-DOS. *Memory Required:* 640k.
disk $1000.00 (ISBN 0-939119-01-3, Order no.: CFP).
Designed for the Financial Planning Industry.

Helps the Planner Analyze Important Aspects of a Financial Plan, from Investment, Tax, Cash Flow, Disability, & Retirement Planning, to Estate & Insurance Needs. Program Is Menu-Driven, with Help System. Provides "What-If" Capability - Different Versions of a Client's Plan Can Be Manipulated, Compared, & Then Summarized to Find the Best Combination of Recommendations.
The CPU Corp.

Copy-Tape. *Compatible Hardware:* TRS-80 Model I, Model III.
contact publisher for price.
Modtec, Software Div.

Copyfitting. Daniel Malenke & Andrew Bear. 1984. *Compatible Hardware:* Apple II series. *Operating System(s) Required:* Apple DOS 3.3. *Memory Required:* 48k. *General Requirements:* Printer.
disk $34.50 (ISBN 1-55797-206-0, Order no.: AP2-IE654).
Will Help Determine How Much Space a Manuscript Will Take When Set in Type. Set up to Work with 45 of the Most Commonly Used Type Faces Including: Bodoni, Century, English Times, Futura, Helios, Souvenir, Universe & Others. Output Provides Total Number of Characters, Number of Typeset Lines for a Specific Style, Size & Column Width & Copy Depth in Picas Converted to Inches.
Hobar Pubns.

The Copyist D.T.P. *Compatible Hardware:* Commodore Amiga, Atari ST, IBM PC.
3.5" disk $399.99.
Comes with Adobe Sonata Fonts; Prints 100 Pages & Transcribes to & from Popular Sequences.
Dr. T's Music Software, Inc.

The Copyist Professional DPT with QuickScore Deluxe. *Compatible Hardware:* Atari ST: Commodore Amiga 500, 1000, 2000; IBM PC. *General Requirements:* Epson FX, LX; HP InkJet, LaserJet supported.
3.5" disk $79.95, incl. 1.3 workbench.
Lets Users Transcript from KCS Format, Standard MIDI Files, or SMUS. Can also EXport SCores to SEquencer Programs & Enter & Edit Them on a PC Using a Mouse & a Set of Mnemonic Keystrokes. Users Can Place Notes, Text, Sybols, & Lines Anywhere on the Page. Comes with a Set of Symbols that Include Treble, Bass, Alto, Tenor, Soprano, & Percussion Clefs, Guitar Chord Grids, & 16-Stave Capability. Can Slant Beams or Print Them Horizontally & Can Generate Smooth Slurs, Ties, & Dynamics. There Is 4-Point Adjustment of Slur Curvature, Direction, & Height. Users Can also Creat & Transpose Indiviual Parts Directly from Score.
Dr T's Music Software, Inc.

Copyrights, Trademarks & Patents. *Version:* 2.5. *Compatible Hardware:* Apple Macintosh, Macintosh Plus. *General Requirements:* HyperCard. *Customer Support:* Free.
3.5" disk $49.95.
"How-To" Guide for Users Interested in the Actual Government Regulations Concerning Copyrights, Trademarks & Patents.
Milum Corp.

The Corbel Connection: Online. *Version:* 5.21. Jul. 1992. *Compatible Hardware:* IBM PC, PC XT, PC AT & compatibles, PS/2. *Operating System(s) Required:* PC-DOS 3.3 or higher. *Memory Required:* 640k. *General Requirements:* Hard disk, laser printer, MNP5 modem which implements standard Hayes "AT" command set. *Customer Support:* One year free support: pension hot-line to technical staff, updates on recent or anticipated legislative changes.

CORE CURRICULUM IN PRIMARY CARE:

disk $2500.00.
Generates Pension Plans, Profit Sharing Plans, Flexible Benefit Plans, Wills, Trusts, Estate Planning & Corporate Documents, Group Insurance Documents & Specifications for Architecture & Engineering.
Corbel & Co.

Core Curriculum in Primary Care: Asthma & Allergy Section. Michael Rees. Jun. 1995. *Customer Support:* Toll-free technical support - no charge. In U.S. 9AM - 5PM EST 800-343-0064.
System 7.0 or higher. Apple Macintosh (8Mb). CD-ROM disk $49.00, Single Copy, ,349.00 Full Set (ISBN 1-57276-992-0, Order no.: SE-018-001). *Nonstandard peripherals required:* CD-ROM drive.
Microsoft Windows, Version 3.1. 386 IBM-Compatible PC (8Mb). CD-ROM disk $49.00, Single Copy, ,349.00 Full Set. *Nonstandard peripherals required:* MPC Standard CD-ROM player, 640x480 display w/256 colors, MPC Standard Soundboard & Speakers.
This CD-ROM Delivers a Series of Outstanding Lectures in Adult Primary Care Medicine. These Lectures Are Given by Top Specialists from Harvard, Tufts, & Boston University to a Live Audience of Primary Care Providers. This Lecture Series Has Been Captured in Digital Media & Reconstructed in an Interactive, Multimedia Format. There Will Be a Total of Nine Discs Available Individually, or As a Set.
SilverPlatter Education.

Core Curriculum in Primary Care: Gastroenterology Section. Michael Rees. Dec. 1994. *Customer Support:* Toll-free technical support - no charge. In U.S. 9AM - 5PM EST 800-343-0064.
System 7.0 or higher. Apple Macintosh (8Mb). CD-ROM disk $49.00, Single Copy, ,349.00 Full Set (ISBN 1-57276-018-4, Order no.: SE-018-001). *Nonstandard peripherals required:* CD-ROM drive.
Microsoft Windows, Version 3.1. 386 IBM-Compatible PC (8Mb). CD-ROM disk $49.00, Single Copy, ,349.00 Full Set. *Nonstandard peripherals required:* MPC Standard CD-ROM player, 640x480 display w/256 colors, MPC Standard Soundboard & Speakers.
This CD-ROM Delivers a Series of Outstanding Lectures in Adult Primary Care Medicine. These Lectures Are Given by Top Specialists from Harvard, Tufts, & Boston University to a Live Audience of Primary Care Providers. This Lecture Series Has Been Captured in Digital Media & Reconstructed in an Interactive, Multimedia Format. There Will Be a Total of Nine Discs Available Individually, or As a Set.
SilverPlatter Education.

Core Curriculum in Primary Care: Metabolic Diseases Section. Michael Rees. May 1995. *Customer Support:* Toll-free technical support - no charge. In U.S. 9AM - 5PM EST 800-343-0064.
System 7.0 or higher. Apple Macintosh (8Mb). CD-ROM disk $49.00, Single Copy, ,349.00 Full Set (ISBN 1-57276-993-9, Order no.: SE-018-001). *Nonstandard peripherals required:* CD-ROM drive.
Microsoft Windows, Version 3.1. 386 IBM-Compatible PC (8Mb). CD-ROM disk $49.00, Single Copy, ,349.00 Full Set. *Nonstandard peripherals required:* MPC Standard CD-ROM player, 640x480 display w/256 colors, MPC Standard Soundboard & Speakers.
This CD-ROM Delivers a Series of Outstanding Lectures in Adult Primary Care Medicine. These Lectures Are Given by Top Specialists from Harvard, Tufts, & Boston University to a Live Audience of Primary Care Providers. This Lecture

Series Has Been Captured in Digital Media & Reconstructed in an Interactive, Multimedia Format. There Will Be a Total of Nine Discs Available Individually, or As a Set.
SilverPlatter Education.

Core Curriculum in Primary Care: Nephrology Section. Michael Rees. Mar. 1995. *Customer Support:* Toll-free technical support - no charge. In U.S. 9AM - 5PM EST 800-343-0064.
  System 7.0 or higher. Apple Macintosh (8Mb). CD-ROM disk $49.00, Single Copy, ,349.00 Full Set (ISBN 1-57276-996-3, Order no.: SE-018-001). *Nonstandard peripherals required:* CD-ROM drive.
  Microsoft Windows, Version 3.1. 386 IBM-Compatible PC (8Mb). CD-ROM disk $49.00, Single Copy, ,349.00 Full Set. *Nonstandard peripherals required:* MPC Standard CD-ROM player, 640x480 display w/256 colors, MPC Standard Soundboard & Speakers.
This CD-ROM Delivers a Series of Outstanding Lectures in Adult Primary Care Medicine. These Lectures Are Given by Top Specialists from Harvard, Tufts, & Boston University to a Live Audience of Primary Care Providers. This Lecture Series Has Been Captured in Digital Media & Reconstructed in an Interactive, Multimedia Format. There Will Be a Total of Nine Discs Available Individually, or As a Set.
SilverPlatter Education.

Core Curriculum in Primary Care: Office Surgery & Urology Section. Michael Rees. Jan. 1995. *Customer Support:* Toll-free technical support - no charge. In U.S. 9AM - 5PM EST 800-343-0064.
  System 7.0 or higher. Apple Macintosh (8Mb). CD-ROM disk $49.00, Single Copy, ,349.00 Full Set (ISBN 1-57276-997-1, Order no.: SE-018-001). *Nonstandard peripherals required:* CD-ROM drive.
  Microsoft Windows, Version 3.1. 386 IBM-Compatible PC (8Mb). CD-ROM disk $49.00, Single Copy, ,349.00 Full Set. *Nonstandard peripherals required:* MPC Standard CD-ROM player, 640x480 display w/256 colors, MPC Standard Soundboard & Speakers.
This CD-ROM Delivers a Series of Outstanding Lectures in Adult Primary Care Medicine. These Lectures Are Given by Top Specialists from Harvard, Tufts, & Boston University to a Live Audience of Primary Care Providers. This Lecture Series Has Been Captured in Digital Media & Reconstructed in an Interactive, Multimedia Format. There Will Be a Total of Nine Discs Available Individually, or As a Set.
SilverPlatter Education.

Core Curriculum in Primary Care: Ophthalmology & Neurology Section. Michael Rees. Apr. 1995. *Customer Support:* Toll-free technical support - no charge. In U.S. 9AM - 5PM EST 800-343-0064.
  System 7.0 or higher. Apple Macintosh (8Mb). CD-ROM disk $49.00, Single Copy, ,349.00 Full Set (ISBN 1-57276-994-7, Order no.: SE-018-001). *Nonstandard peripherals required:* CD-ROM drive.
  Microsoft Windows, Version 3.1. 386 IBM-Compatible PC (8Mb). CD-ROM disk $49.00, Single Copy, ,349.00 Full Set. *Nonstandard peripherals required:* MPC Standard CD-ROM player, 640x480 display w/256 colors, MPC Standard Soundboard & Speakers.
This CD-ROM Delivers a Series of Outstanding Lectures in Adult Primary Care Medicine. These Lectures Are Given by Top Specialists from Harvard, Tufts, & Boston University to a Live Audience of Primary Care Providers. This Lecture Series Has Been Captured in Digital Media & Reconstructed in an Interactive, Multimedia Format. There Will Be a Total of Nine Discs Available Individually, or As a Set.
SilverPlatter Education.

Core Curriculum in Primary Care: Preventive Medicine Section. Michael Rees. Apr. 1995. *Customer Support:* Toll-free technical support - no charge. In U.S. 9AM - 5PM EST 800-343-0064.
  System 7.0 or higher. Apple Macintosh (8Mb). CD-ROM disk $49.00, Single Copy, ,349.00 Full Set (ISBN 1-57276-995-5, Order no.: SE-018-001). *Nonstandard peripherals required:* CD-ROM drive.
  Microsoft Windows, Version 3.1. 386 IBM-Compatible PC (8Mb). CD-ROM disk $49.00, Single Copy, ,349.00 Full Set. *Nonstandard peripherals required:* MPC Standard CD-ROM player, 640x480 display w/256 colors, MPC Standard Soundboard & Speakers.
This CD-ROM Delivers a Series of Outstanding Lectures in Adult Primary Care Medicine. These Lectures Are Given by Top Specialists from Harvard, Tufts, & Boston University to a Live Audience of Primary Care Providers. This Lecture Series Has Been Captured in Digital Media & Reconstructed in an Interactive, Multimedia Format. There Will Be a Total of Nine Discs Available Individually, or As a Set.
SilverPlatter Education.

Core Curriculum in Primary Care: Psychiatry & Pain Management Section. Michael Rees. Dec. 1994. *Customer Support:* Toll-free technical support - no charge. In U.S. 9AM - 5PM EST 800-343-0064.
  System 7.0 or higher. Apple Macintosh (8Mb). CD-ROM disk $49.00, Single Copy, ,349.00 Full Set (ISBN 1-57276-999-8, Order no.: SE-018-001). *Nonstandard peripherals required:* CD-ROM drive.
  Microsoft Windows, Version 3.1. 386 IBM-Compatible PC (8Mb). CD-ROM disk $49.00, Single Copy, ,349.00 Full Set. *Nonstandard peripherals required:* MPC Standard CD-ROM player, 640x480 display w/256 colors, MPC Standard Soundboard & Speakers.
This CD-ROM Delivers a Series of Outstanding Lectures in Adult Primary Care Medicine. These Lectures Are Given by Top Specialists from Harvard, Tufts, & Boston University to a Live Audience of Primary Care Providers. This Lecture Series Has Been Captured in Digital Media & Reconstructed in an Interactive, Multimedia Format. There Will Be a Total of Nine Discs Available Individually or As a Set.
SilverPlatter Education.

Core Curriculum in Primary Care: Pulmonary Medicine & ENT Section. Michael Rees. Jan. 1995. *Customer Support:* Toll-free technical support - no charge. In U.S. 9AM - 5PM EST 800-343-0064.
  System 7.0 or higher. Apple Macintosh (8Mb). CD-ROM disk $49.00, Single Copy, ,349.00 Full Set (ISBN 1-57276-998-X, Order no.: SE-018-001). *Nonstandard peripherals required:* CD-ROM drive.
  Microsoft Windows, Version 3.1. 386 IBM-Compatible PC (8Mb). CD-ROM disk $49.00, Single Copy, ,349.00 Full Set. *Nonstandard peripherals required:* MPC Standard CD-ROM player, 640x480 display w/256 colors, MPC Standard Soundboard & Speakers.
This CD-ROM Delivers a Series of Outstanding Lectures in Adult Primary Care Medicine. These Lectures Are Given by Top Specialists from Harvard, Tufts, & Boston University to a Live Audience of Primary Care Providers. This Lecture Series Has Been Captured in Digital Media & Reconstructed in an Interactive, Multimedia Format. There Will Be a Total of Nine Discs Available Individually, or As a Set.
SilverPlatter Education.

Core-Reading & Vocabulary Development. Priscilla Hamilton & Barbara Hombs. *Items Included:* CD-ROM binder & documentation. *Customer Support:* Toll free customer service Hot Line 1-800-645-3739 (9a.m. - 5p.m. Eastern Time) software guaranteed for two years.
  System 6.07 or higher (2Mb); System 7.0 or higher (4Mb). Macintosh. CD-ROM disk $675.00 (Order no.: CDRCORE). *Nonstandard peripherals required:* CD-ROM drive.
Core Provides Extensively Guided Drill & Practice in the Core Vocabularies Used by So Many Major Reading Textbooks. The Program Begins with 36 Basic Words & Progresses to More Than 200. A Management System Keeps Track of Each Student's Performance & Reenters That Students at the Appropriate Activity Based on Previous Attempts.
Educational Activities Inc.

Cornerman. *Version:* Atari 2.1. J. Weaver, Jr. *Compatible Hardware:* Atari ST, IBM PC, Sanyo MBC 55x. *Operating System(s) Required:* MS-DOS, TOS. *Memory Required:* 512k. *General Requirements:* GEM for IBM.
  Atari. 3.5" disk $49.95 (ISBN 0-923213-14-7, Order no.: AT-COE).
  Sanyo, MS-DOS. 5-1/4" disk $49.95 (ISBN 0-923213-21-X, Order no.: SA-COR).
  IBM. 5-1/4" disk $49.95.
9-Function Utility Installed As a DESKTOP Accessory. Utilities Included Are: ASCII TABLE - Shows the ST's Symbols with Their Decimal & Hex Values; CALCULATOR - 16 Digit, Works in Decimal, Binary, Octal, & Hex with Floating Point, 3 Memory Registers, Standard Math, Square Root, Percents, & Pi Functions; CLOCK - Real Time in Analog or Digital; SECURITY; NOTE PAD - Accepts 7-Line Memos with Search, Save, & Delete Capabilities; PHONE BOOK/DIALER; PHONE LOG - Records the Date, Time, & Duration of User's Calls; DOS WINDOW; 15 SQUARE PUZZLE; SET-UP UTILITY - Users Can Customize the Format & Formation of CORNERMAN's Windows.
MichTron, Inc.

Cornerstone. Jan. 1985. *Compatible Hardware:* IBM PC, PC XT, PC AT, PC compatibles; Tandy 1000, 2000, 1200HD. *Memory Required:* 256k.
  disk $495.00.
Free-Form Relational Data Base System Supporting up to 250,000 Records per File with up to 160 Fields per Record. Up to 120 Files Can Be Opened at One Time. Includes Help Facilities & Interactive Reporting. Search & Sort Can Be Performed for Any Field. Permits Records Within Records. Also Supports Variable Length Fields, & Allows Any Field Can Be Multivalued.
Activision, Inc.

Cornucopia: A Source Book of Edible Plants. Stephen Facciola. Aug. 1994. *Items Included:* Manual.
  DOS 3.0/Windows 3.0. IBM PC (640k & 4Mb). disk $70.00 (ISBN 0-9628087-1-7). *Optimal configuration:* 386 or higher processor, 8Mb RAM, VGA or higher graphics card, 13Mb hard disk space.
Complete Reference & Source Book of Edible Plants of the World. 3,000 Species & 7,000 Varieties Are Included. More Than 1300 Catalog Sources for Seeds, Plants & Food Products Are Listed. Selected for Choice Outstanding Academic Books List. Electronic Edition Uses 25,000 Hypertext Links to Cross-Reference Information.
Kampong Pubns.

CORP 84. *Compatible Hardware:* IBM PC, Tandy 2000, Kaypro. *Operating System(s) Required:* TRSDOS, PC-DOS, MS-DOS. *Language(s):* BASIC. *Memory Required:* 64k.

disk $500.00.
Prepares Federal Tax Forms 1120 & 1120S & Their Most Important Schedules. Forms Are Printed on Continuous Forms & Lined Paper & Are Based on Model Approved by the IRS.
Computer Technical Services of New Jersey.

Corporate Affiliations Plus. *Customer Support:* Quarterly Updates.
MS-DOS. IBM or compatibles. CD-ROM disk 1995.00 for 1 year (Order no.: CA110).
CD-ROM disk 5686.00 for 3 years.
Profiles of 15,000 parent companies in the U. S. & abroad. Records on 97,000 subsidiaries, divisions, affiliates, manufacturing plants, & joint ventures. Names & titles of 286,000 top executives, financial officers, board of directors, purchasing agents, & other key personnel. Outside service firms such as auditors, legal firms, insurance carriers, bankers, pension managers, & transfer agents for the companies listed. Descriptions & current financials of each business, including; sales, revenue, net income/earnings, net worth, general assets & liabilities, pension assets, & fiscal year-ends.
R R Bowker.

Corporate Car Rental Sales Force Automator.
Version: 2.0. Open Door Software Divison. Oct. 1993. *Items Included:* Spiral manual, video (when available). *Customer Support:* 30 day free customer support; 900 line $2.00/min.; 1 yr. maintenance $400/mo. Includes: toll free line & fax back priority service.
DOS. IBM compatible 386, 25Mhz, 5Mb free space on hard disk, VGA monitor, 3.5" floppy, keyboard, mouse (1Mb). disk $2995.00 (ISBN 1-56756-051-2, Order no.: OD7001). *Addl. software required:* Operating system. *Optimal configuration:* IBM or compatible 486, 66Mhz, 5Mb free space on hard disk, 4Mb RAM-3Mb expanded usable, VGA monitor, 3.5" high density floppy, keyboard, mouse, tape backup, & uninterruptable power supply. *Networks supported:* Novell Netware Lite.
Windows. IBM compatible 386, 25Mhz, 5Mb free space on hard disk, VGA monitor, 3.5" floppy, keyboard, mouse (1Mb). disk $2995.00 (ISBN 1-56756-067-9, Order no.: OD705W). *Addl. software required:* Windows 3.1 or higher. *Optimal configuration:* IBM or compatible 486, 66Mhz, 5Mb free space on hard disk, 4Mb RAM-3Mb expanded usable, VGA monitor, 3.5" high density floppy, keyboard, mouse, tape backup, & uninterruptable power supply. *Networks supported:* Novell Netware Lite.
MAC. 3.5" disk $2995.00 (ISBN 1-56756-052-0, Order no.: OD720M). *Addl. software required:* System 7.
Sophisticated Corporate Rate Comparison Software Application Used As a Sales Tool by Car Rental Companies to Illustrate the Benefits of Renting from Their Company. Assists Sales Representatives by Comparing the Rates & Benefits of Their Company with the Competition. Comprehensive Analysis Features Comparisons of the Basic per Rental Rate, Cities That the Account Services, Mileage, Rental Regions, Types of Cars Rented, & Competition Selection with Graphical Displays. Can Print a Rental Contract from Within the Program, & Supports over 100 Printers Including Postscript.
Advantage International.

Corporate MBA. *Version:* 1.2. *Compatible Hardware:* IBM PC & compatibles, Hewlett-Packard 9000. *Memory Required:* 384k. *Customer Support:* Hot line.
disk $695.00.
Integrated Software Package Featuring Word-Processing, Spreadsheet, Database, Graphics & Communications Modules. Includes Context Switching, Mail/Merge Database Link, Built-In Language in All Modules, 95 by 999 Spreadsheet Matrix Size & Context-Sensitive On-Screen Help. Pastes & Links Spreadsheet Sections & Graphics into Word-Processing Files. Imports & Exports ASCII, dBASE II & III, SYLK & DIF File Formats.
Lemain, Inc.

Corporate Quarterly Estimated Tax Payments.
Compatible Hardware: Altos Series 5-15D, Series 5-5D, 580-XX, ACS8000-XX; DEC Rainbow 100 with 2 disk drives, Rainbow 100+ with 10Mb hard disk; IBM PC with 2 disk drives, PC XT, IBM compatibles; Kaypro 11/IV with 2 disk drives, Kaypro 10; Xerox 820 with 2 disk drives; ZILOG MCZ-250. *Operating System(s) Required:* CP/M, MP/M, CP/M-86, PC-DOS, MS-DOS.
disk write for info. (Order no.: QTRLYTAX).
Calculates the Corporate Quarterly Estimated Tax Payments under All Three Exceptions for the Underpayment of Estimated Taxes. Produces a Schedule Showing the Annual Total Estimated Payments, a Quarterly Breakdown of Estimated Payments, Including Any Reduction in Quarterly Payments for Refunds That Are to Be Credited, or Previous Payments on Earlier Estimates. Also Provides a Schedule Showing the Computation of Tax Liability under Each of These Exceptions.
Coopers & Lybrand.

The Corporate Real Estate Management System. *Version:* 4.0. Oct. 1993. *Items Included:* User manual; 30 day warranty period; 30 day technical support. *Customer Support:* Annual maintenance agreement. Included: unlimited telephone and/or modem support. Free new version, updates, documentation, input on future enhancements, plus special offers on new products (15% of license fee).
MS-DOS. IBM & compatibles (386sx) (1Mb). $995.00-$9995.00 (based on number of properties/leases). *Optimal configuration:* 486 or higher, 2Mb of RAM or higher, 100Mb HD, Color VGA monitor, laser printer. *Networks supported:* Lantastic, Novell.
A Comprehensive, PC Based Database System Especially Designed to Assist Real Estate Managers in Managing Information Regarding Leased and/or Owned Property. The System Allows You to Catalog, Retrieve, & Process Information on Any or All Properties in the System. A Complete Reporting System Is Available.
Classic Real Estate Systems, L.L.C.

Corporate Tax Planner. Apr. 1985. *Compatible Hardware:* IBM PC & compatibles, PC XT, PC AT. *Operating System(s) Required:* MS-DOS. *Customer Support:* Free telephone Support.
disk $150.00.
Allows User to See the Results of Various Tax Alternatives As Quickly As User Inputs Assumptions. Following the Layout of Federal Form 1120, It Allows User to Play "What If" Games or Check Manually Prepared Returns for Corporate Clients. Calculates the Charitable Contribution Limit, Net Long & Short Term Capital Gain & the Regular Tax, Alternative Tax & Minimum Tax.
Accounting Professionals Software, Inc.

Corporate Telephone Directory. *Items Included:* Bound manual. *Customer Support:* Free hotline - no time limit; 30 day limited warranty; updates are $5/disk plus S&H.
MS-DOS 2.1 or higher. IBM & compatibles (256k). disk $99.95. *Nonstandard peripherals required:* 80-character-wide (or wider) printer; 2 drives; color or monochrome monitor.
System for Generating Company Telephone Directories. The White Pages Contain the Names, Department Numbers (or Mail Stops), & Telephone Numbers of All Company Employees. The Yellow Pages Contain Similar Information for Company Departments. Output Can Go Directly to a Printer or to ASCII Disk Files for Use by Your Typesetter.
Dynacomp, Inc.

Corporate Vision: The Super Spreadsheet.
Version: 1.0d. Jun. 1993. *Items Included:* Manuals. *Customer Support:* 1 year free on-line tech support.
Windows 3.1 or higher. IBM PC & compatibles (4Mb). disk $690.00. *Networks supported:* LAN.
An Intuitive & Immediately Usable Multidimensional Point-&-Click Program That Helps You Visually Analyze Facts, Graphically See Your Corporate Data. Corporate Vision, Which Runs on Windows, Implements a Hypermedia Graphic User Interface to Provide Instantaneous Graphic Access to the Vital Information Needed to Monitor & Control a Business.
IntelligenceWare, Inc.

Corporate Voice. *Items Included:* Book-"Writing to Please Your Boss" GPOSTYLE V.1.2, Manual, Dual Media (Note: GPOSTYLE Shipped upon registration). *Customer Support:* Unlimited telephone/FAX support.
IBM PC, PC XT, PC AT, PS/2, 386 (256k). contact publisher for price (ISBN 1-878322-01-X). *Networks supported:* Network Version Available, Contact Publisher (NETBIOS compatible LAN-DOS 3.0 & higher.
Sophisticated Program Shows Writers How to Customize Writing to Fit Audience & Subject Material. Allows Writers to Replicate Writing Style of Anyone. Read WordPerfect, WordStar, Microsoftword, & ASCII File Formats.
Scandinavian PC Systems, Inc.

Corpse Killer. *Items Included:* Instruction manual. *Customer Support:* Free Telephone support.
DOS/Windows 95. IBM & compatibles (8Mb). Contact publisher for price. *Nonstandard peripherals required:* CD-ROM drive.
Saturn. Sega Saturn. Contact publisher for price.
Digital Pictures, Inc.

Correct Behavior: The Japanese Way, 2 disks.
(Baedeker Travelware Ser.). 1984. *Compatible Hardware:* Apple II, II+, IIe, IIc. *Memory Required:* 48k. *Items Included:* Operations manual.
English set. $49.95 (ISBN 0-88729-356-5).
Teaches Japanese Culture & Customs by Placing User into Situations He May Encounter on a Visit.
Langenscheidt Pubs., Inc.

Correct Grammar. Mar. 1992. *Customer Support:* Free technical support for the life of product; 30 day money back guarantee; free BBS service.
Microsoft Windows 3.0 or higher. IBM 286 or higher processor (1Mb). disk $99.00. *Networks supported:* Network compatible.
MS-DOS 2.1 or higher. IBM (512k). disk $99.00. *Nonstandard peripherals required:* 1 floppy & hard disk. *Networks supported:* Network compatible.
Macintosh (1Mb). 3.5" disk $99.00. *Nonstandard peripherals required:* 1 floppy drive & hard disk. *Networks supported:* Network compatible.
Corrects Errors in Grammar, Style, Usage, Punctuation & Spelling. Checks Your Work a Sentence at a Time. When It Finds an Error, Suggests How to Fix It & Explains the Grammar Rule Involved. User Can Customize Correct Grammar to Fit Personal Style. Modify or Write Your Own Rules or Choose One of the Nine Default Styles. Checks Readability.
WordStar International, Inc.

Correct Letters. *Customer Support:* Free technical support for the life of product; 30 day money back guarantee.
Microsoft Windows 3.0 or higher. IBM PC & compatibles (2Mb). disk $49.00. *Nonstandard peripherals required:* Hard disk; EGA or VGA graphics card; mouse or other pointing device.
MS-DOS 2.1 or higher. IBM PC & compatibles. disk $49.00.
Any Macintosh (1Mb). 3.5" disk $49.00. *Nonstandard peripherals required:* Hard disk & 1 floppy drive.
Has 250 Model Letters for Just about Every Occasion. All Letters Have Been Carefully Crafted by Noted Business Writers & Approved by the American Management Association.
WordStar International, Inc.

Correct Quotes. *Customer Support:* Free technical support for the life of product; 30 day money back guarantee.
MS Windows 3.0 or higher. IBM PC & compatibles (2Mb). disk $49.00. *Nonstandard peripherals required:* Hard disk; EGA or VGA graphics card; mouse or other pointing device.
MS-DOS 2.1 or higher. IBM PC & compatibles (56k). disk $49.00. *Nonstandard peripherals required:* Hard disk.
Macintosh Plus, SE, Classic, LC, SE/30, II, IIcx, IIx, IIsi, IIei, IIfx. 3.5" disk $49.00.
Has over 5,000 Quotations on 600 Topics. Quotes Are Arranged Alphabetically by Topic in a Convenient & Easy to Use Software Program. A Thorough Author List & Cross References Make It Even Easier to Find the Right Thought Every Time. User Can Even Search by Any Word with Instant Results.
WordStar International, Inc.

Correct Writing. *Customer Support:* Free technical support for the life of product; 30 day money back guarantee.
MS Windows 3.0 or higher. IBM PC & compatibles (2Mb). disk $49.00. *Nonstandard peripherals required:* Hard disk; EGA or VGA graphics card; mouse or other pointing device.
MS-DOS 2.1 or higher. IBM PC & compatibles (56k). disk $49.00. *Nonstandard peripherals required:* Hard disk.
Any Macintosh. 3.5" disk $49.00. *Nonstandard peripherals required:* Hard disk.
Puts an Encyclopedia of Writing Inside Your Computer. It Has All the Information You Need to Perfect Letters, Proposals, Reports You Write Every Day. Tells You Everything You Need to Know about Style, Punctuation & Better Writing Skills.
WordStar International, Inc.

Correctamente. *Version:* 2.0. *Compatible Hardware:* Apple Macintosh. *General Requirements:* External disk drive, Microsoft Word. *Items Included:* Diskette & manual in both English & Spanish. *Customer Support:* Complete telephone support, 90-day warranty.
3.5" disk $32.95 (Order no.: 48842-205).
demo disk $5.00.
Spanish Spelling Dictionary.
Medina Software, Inc.

Correction Administration - Health Services Administration: Criminal Justice Application System. *Version:* 3.0. Palladium Software Corp. Aug. 1992. *Operating System(s) Required:* MS-DOS, Windows 95 & NT. *Language(s):* Objectview, Level 5. *Memory Required:* 15000k.
$7000.00.
Alpha. (ISBN 0-931755-71-9, Order no.: CJ 250/2).
MS-DOS Windows. (ISBN 0-931755-72-7, Order no.: CJ 250/3).
Windows NT. (ISBN 0-931755-73-5, Order no.: CJ 250/4).
Windows 95. (ISBN 0-931755-74-3, Order no.: CJ 250/5).
(ISBN 0-931755-70-0, Order no.: CJ 250/1).
Manages Medical, Dental, Psychiatric & Pharmaceutical Operations with Patient Scheduling & Treatment Programs & a Perpetual Inventory for Supplies & Equipment.
Ellington Duval, Inc.

Correction Administration - Management Analysis: Criminal Justice Application System. *Version:* 3.0. Palladium Software Corp. Aug. 1992. *Operating System(s) Required:* MS-DOS, Windows 95 & NT. *Memory Required:* 15000k. *General Requirements:* IBM PC Pentium, DEC, Alpha, HP. *Customer Support:* Electronic BBS, telephone tech support.
$7000.00.
Windows 95. (ISBN 0-931755-46-8, Order no.: CJ 200/2).
MS-DOS, Windows. (ISBN 0-931755-47-6, Order no.: CJ 200/3).
NT Server. (ISBN 0-931755-49-2, Order no.: CJ 200/5).
Maintains Current & Historical Inmate Data, Creates Inmate Classification & Cell Assignment Exception Report. The Analysis Contributes an Operations Analytics Capability Unique to the Detention Facility. The Program Facilitates Critical Aspects of Security Planning, Efficient Resource Allocation, & Calculates the Quality of Time Served.
Ellington Duval, Inc.

Correction Administration - Offender Classification: Criminal Justice Application System. *Version:* 3.0. Palladium Software Corp. Aug. 1992. *Operating System(s) Required:* MS-DOS, Windows 95 & NT. *Language(s):* Objectview, Level 5. *Memory Required:* 15000k. *General Requirements:* IBM PC Pentium, DEC, Alpha. *Customer Support:* Electronic BBS, telephone tech support.
disk $7000.00.
MS-DOS Windows. (ISBN 0-931755-57-3, Order no.: CJ 220/3).
NT Server. (ISBN 0-931755-58-1, Order no.: CJ 220/4).
Windows 95. (ISBN 0-931755-59-X, Order no.: CJ 220/5).
Classifies Inmates, Assigns Them to Cells, Transfers & Tracks Them to Other Cells, Classifies All Housing Units & Prints Management & Analyses Reports.
Ellington Duval, Inc.

Correction Administration - Offender Finance: Criminal Justice Application System. *Version:* 3.0. Palladium Software Corp. Aug. 1992. *Operating System(s) Required:* MS-DOS, Windows, NT Server. *Memory Required:* 15000k.
disk $7000.00 ea.
MS-DOS, Windows. (ISBN 0-931755-92-1, Order no.: CJ 430/3).
NT Server. (ISBN 0-931755-93-X, Order no.: CJ 430/4).
Windows 95. (ISBN 0-931755-94-8, Order no.: CJ 430/5).
Manages the Collection & Allocation of Funds for Offenders.
Ellington Duval, Inc.

Correction Administration - Offender Profile: Criminal Justice Application System. *Version:* 3.0. Palladium Software Corp. Aug. 1992. *Operating System(s) Required:* MS-DOS, Windows, Windows 95, NT Server. *Language(s):* Objectview, Level 5. *Memory Required:* 15000k. *General Requirements:* IBM PC Pentium, DEC, Alpha. *Customer Support:* Electronic BBS, telephone tech support.
disk $7000.00.
NT Server. (ISBN 0-931755-61-1, Order no.: CJ 230/2).
MS-DOS Windows. (ISBN 0-931755-62-X, Order no.: CJ 230/3).
Windows 95. (ISBN 0-931755-64-6, Order no.: CJ 230/5).
Maintains In-Depth Personal Data Related to Inmate, Includes Family History, Employment, Education, Criminal Contacts & Associates, Any Gang Affiliations, Relationships & Position on Role, & Record of Correspondence & Visitors.
Ellington Duval, Inc.

Correction Administration - Offender Productivity Management: Criminal Justice Application System. *Version:* 3.0. Palladium Software Corp. Aug. 1992. *Operating System(s) Required:* MS-DOW, Windows, Windows 95, NT Server. *Language(s):* Objectview, Level 5. *Memory Required:* 15000k.
disk $7000.00 ea.
NT Server. (ISBN 0-931755-86-7, Order no.: CJ 420/2).
Windows 95. (ISBN 0-931755-87-5, Order no.: CJ 420/3).
Windows. (ISBN 0-931755-88-3, Order no.: CJ 420/4).
Digital Alpha. (ISBN 0-931755-89-1, Order no.: CJ 420/5).
Maintains Personal Data Relative to the Offender; Infraction, Disciplinary & Grievance History. Integrates Offender Productivity, Application, to Provide Automated Index of Quality of Time Served.
Ellington Duval, Inc.

Correction Administration - Offender Scheduling: Criminal Justice Application System. *Version:* 3.0. Palladium Software Corp. Aug. 1992. *Operating System(s) Required:* MS-DOS Windows, NT & Windows 95. *Language(s):* Level 5 & Illustra ODBMS. *Memory Required:* 15000k. *General Requirements:* IBM PC Pentium, DEC, Alpha. *Customer Support:* Electronic BBS, telephone tech support.
disk $7000.00 ea.
NT Server. (ISBN 0-931755-66-2, Order no.: CJ 240/2).
Windows 95. (ISBN 0-931755-67-0, Order no.: CJ 240/3).
Windows NT. (ISBN 0-931755-69-7, Order no.: CJ 240/5).
Provides for the Management & Control of Inmate's Activities, Including Court Appearances, Work, Education, Counseling, Medical, & Religious & Recreational Activities, & Work/Study Release Programs.
Ellington Duval, Inc.

Correction Administration - Operations Management: Criminal Justice Applications System, 8 modules. *Version:* 3.0. Palladium Software. Sep. 1992. *Operating System(s) Required:* MS-DOS, Windows, Windows 95, NT Server. *Language(s):* Level 5. *Memory Required:* 4000k.
disk $7000.00 ea.
NT Server. (ISBN 1-55505-056-5, Order no.: CJ350/2).
Windows 95. (ISBN 1-55505-057-3, Order no.: CJ350/3).
Windows 3.X. (ISBN 1-55505-058-1, Order no.: CJ350/4).
Provides Business Administration, Human Resource, Financial, Operations Management, Health Services, Food Service, Physical Plant, Logistics/Transportation/Warehousing, Administration Modules for Correction Administration.
Ellington Duval, Inc.

Correction Administration System Offender Administration: Criminal Justice Application System. Version: 3.0. Palladium Software Corp. Aug. 1992. Compatible Hardware: IBM, Alpha, HP. Operating System(s) Required: MS-DOS Windows, NT Server. Memory Required: 1400k. disk $7000.00 ea.
Windows 3.1. (ISBN 0-931755-51-4, Order no.: CJ 210/2).
Windows 95. (ISBN 0-931755-52-2, Order no.: CJ 210/3).
Windows NT. (ISBN 0-931755-53-0, Order no.: CJ 210/4).
Provides for Intake Including Receiving Assignments, Outstanding Wants & Warrants, Court Appearances, Responsible Agencies, Tracking & Remarks Relevant to Inmates Physical or Mental Conditions, etc.
Ellington Duval, Inc.

CORREL. Version: 1.0. Oct. 1985. Compatible Hardware: IBM PC, PC XT, PC AT & compatibles. Operating System(s) Required: MS-DOS, PC-DOS. Language(s): FORTRAN. Memory Required: 320k. General Requirements: Printer.
disk $700.00 (Order no.: CORREL).
Computes the Correlation Coefficient Between a Paired Data Set or Between Two Variables in the Same Data Set. The Correlation Coefficient Provides a Measure of the Degree of Confidence with Which the Analyst Can Predict the Value of One of a Pair Given the Other.
Geostat Systems International, Inc. (GSII).

Correlation. Items Included: Bound manual. Customer Support: Free hotline - no time limit; 30 day limited warranty; updates are $5/disk plus S&H.
MS-DOS. IBM & compatibles (256k). disk $39.95.
Apple. disk $39.95.
Engineering Tutorial Package Consists of a Manual Coordinated with Software. The Manual Presents the Theory & Describes How to Use the Software, & the Software Shows Visually the Principles Covered in the Manual. The Subject Areas Included Are: Autocorrelation, Power & Energy Spectra, Cross-Correlation, Cross-Spectral Density, Convolutions, & Matched Filters.
Dynacomp, Inc.

Correlation. 1992. Items Included: Detailed manuals are included with all DYNACOMP products. Customer Support: Free telephone support to original customer - no time limit; 30 day limited warranty.
MS-DOS 3.2 or higher. IBM PC & compatibles, Apple (512k). $39.95 (Add $5.00 for 3 1/2" format; 5 1/4" format standard).
Package Consists of a Manual Coordinated with Software. The Manual Presents the Theory & Describes How to Use the Software, & the Software Shows Visually the Principles Covered in the Manual. Subject Areas Included Are: Autocorrelation, Power & Energy Spectra, Cross-Correlation, Cross-Spectral Density, Convolutions, & Matched Filters. The Computer Examples Include Correlation (E.G., Burst Correlation, a Means for Radar Ranging) & Two-Dimensional Template Matching. High-Resolution Graphics Are Employed Wherever Possible to Make the Presentations Clear.
Dynacomp, Inc.

Correspondence Control System. Roberto Fuentes. Oct. 1990.
Contact publisher for price (ISBN 1-879185-00-8).
Software to Register, Control, & Follow up Correspondence & Other Matters Referred by an Executive for Action by Others in the Organization.
CompuConsultants.

Correspondence Control System: Control of In-House Referrals. Version: 2.1. Feb. 1990. Customer Support: 90 days maintenance - free; telephone support - free for 6 months.
MS-DOS 2.x or higher. PC XT; 286 or higher recommended (640k). disk $1600.00 (ISBN 1-879185-00-8, Order no.: MAIL 2.1). Addl. software required: SmartWare II (provided).
Software to Register, Control, & Follow-Up Correspondence & Other Matters Referred by an Executive to Be Handled by Others in the Organization.
CompuConsultants.

Corvus Omninet. Compatible Hardware: Apple II, Macintosh, IBM PC & compatibles.
disk $159.00 to $249.00.
Local Area Network for Personal Computers. Uses Twisted Pair Cable to Connect Microcomputers to Each Other & to Share Disk Systems & Printers. Connected to the Omninet Network by a Simple Tap Cable. Uses Bus Toplogy.
Corvus Systems, Inc.

Cosmetics Manufacturing Control System. Items Included: Manuals. Customer Support: 90 days included, then 15% per year of the current price..
MS-DOS, Xenix. IBM PC XT, AT, & compatible (512k). $4495.00 to $12,990.00. Networks supported: Novell, Lantastic, 3COM.
Inventory, Formulations Blending, Bill of Materials (BOM) Control & Materials Requirements Planning System (MRP) Featuring Multi-Level Traceability by Lot. Purchase Orders & Numerous Reports Are Generated. User-Defined Fields Provide Flexibility for Diverse Cosmetics Manufacturing Firms. Customization Available. Assists in Complying with the FDA Good Manufacturing Practices, EPA, & Other Governmental Record-Keeping Requirements. Inventory Records Are Kept at Both the Item & the Lot Level. Handles Real-World Situations Such As Variances between Planned & Actual Consumption. Calculates Costs Based on Lot Costs, Standard Costs, Average Costs, FIFO, or LIFO.
Stolzberg Research, Inc.

Cosmic Clones. Compatible Hardware: TRS-80 Color Computer, TDP-100.
contact publisher for price.
Mark Data Products.

Cosmic Patrol. Compatible Hardware: TRS-80.
contact publisher for price.
Instant Software, Inc.

Cosmic Relief. Compatible Hardware: Commodore 64/128, Amiga; Atari ST. Memory Required: Commodore 64k; Commodore Amiga, Atari ST 512k. General Requirements: Joystick or mouse optional.
Commodore Amiga. 3.5" disk $34.95 (ISBN 0-88717-223-7, Order no.: 165243499).
Commodore 64/128. disk $24.95 (ISBN 0-88717-224-5, Order no.: 1625143499).
Atari ST. 3.5" disk $34.95 (ISBN 0-88717-222-9).
Player Can Choose from One of Five Internationally Famous Adventurers, English, French, German, Japanese or American. The Quest is to Find Renegade. Player Must Survive Bizarre Creatures & Conditions Including Stone Snakes, Reptilian Birds & Acid Storms.
IntelliCreations, Inc.

Cosmos. Compatible Hardware: Atari 400, 800. Language(s): Atari BASIC. Memory Required: disk 32k. General Requirements: Joystick.
disk $16.95.
Collect Power Cells Scattered Throughout Maze-Like Playing Field.
Dynacomp, Inc.

COSMOS/M Designer II. Jan. 1996. Items Included: Manuals & installation notes. Customer Support: Same as all other products.
DOS, Windows NT, Windows 95, Unix. 486 or higher PC, Sun, HP & SGI EWS (24 or higher). CD-ROM disk $7000.00-$9500.00.
Provides a Comprehensive Design & Analysis System for Design Engineers by Integrating COSMOS/M & COSMOS/FFE with MicroStation Modeler. Engineers Can Design 2/Part, Apply Loads & Boundary Conditions, Analyze & View the Results in a Single Fully Integrated Software Suite. Will Also Work with All Other ACIS-Based CAD Designs, Including AutoCAD Designer & HP/PE Solid Designer.
Structural Research & Analysis Corp.

COSMOS/Works: Phase 1. Jan. 1996. Items Included: Manuals & installation notes. Customer Support: Same as all other products.
Windows 95, Windows NT. 486 or higher (32 or higher). disk $4995.00.
Provides an Integrated Analysis Solution for Users of SolidWorks 95. A Fully Integrated Version of COSMOS/WORKS Will Combine COSMOS/M & COSMOS/FFE Analysis Engines with the SolidWorks Parametric Solid Modeler to Provide Stress, Frequency, Buckling & Heat Transfer Analyses for Solid & Surface Models Directly in the SolidWorks User Interface.
Structural Research & Analysis Corp.

COSMOS/Works: Phase 2. May 1996. Items Included: Manuals & installation notes. Customer Support: Same as all other products.
Windows 95, Windows NT. 486 or higher (32 or higher). $4995.00; $3995.00 if purchased with SolidWorks 95.
Provides an Integrated Analysis Solution for Users of SolidWorks 95. A Fully Integrated Version of COSMOS/WORKS Will Combine COSMOS/M & COSMOS/FFE Analysis Engines with the SolidWorks Parametric Solid Modeler to Provide Stress, Frequency, Buckling & Heat Transfer Analyses for Solid & Surface Models Directly in the SolidWorks User Interface.
Structural Research & Analysis Corp.

COSMOS-M CAD Interface. Version: 1.71. Sep. 1994. Items Included: Manuals & installation notes. Customer Support: Maintenance available for 25% of list price (annual).
Windows NT, Windows 95, UNIX (specifics depend on EWS). HP9000/700 Series (16Mb), Sun, DEC, SGI, IBM, Pentium PC, Windows NT - disk, all others CD-ROM. $6500.00-$15,000.00. Addl. software required: Pro/ENGINEER, Pro/JR., Cadra, CADDS5, MicroStation Modeler, Unigraphics, SolidWorks 95.
Finite Element Analysis with a Variety of CAD Packages to Perform Mechanical Analyses in the Areas of Stress, Frequency, Buckling, Thermal, Nonlinear, Advanced Dynamics & Design Optimization.
Structural Research & Analysis Corp.

COSMOS-M Designer. Version: 2.0. Feb. 1994. Items Included: Manuals & installation notes. Customer Support: Maintenance available for 25% of list price (annual).
DOS 3.0 or higher. PC 386/486 & compatible (4Mb). $2500.00 for complete package. Addl. software required: AutoCAD version 12.1. Optimal configuration: Any 386/486 PC, mouse, 4Mb RAM or higher, 20Mb hard disk space, DOS 3.0 & higher.
Seamless Interface to AutoCAD Geometry, with AutoCAD Look & Feel, to Perform Mechanical Analysis on AutoCAD Designs in the Area of Stress, Frequency, Buckling & Thermal.
Structural Research & Analysis Corp.

COSMOS/M: Finite Element System. *Version:* 1.75. Aug. 1995. *Compatible Hardware:* Apple Macintosh II, Quadra; Apollo; Compaq; Digital; HP 9000; IBM PC & compatibles, IBM RS6000; SGI, Sun. *Operating System(s) Required:* MS-DOS 3.0 or higher for PCs; appropriate O/S for EWS. *Language(s):* C, Fortran. *Memory Required:* 32,000-64,000k. *General Requirements:* 40Mb hard disk, VGA card, math co-processor, mouse. *Items Included:* Manuals, 30 day tech support. *Customer Support:* Provided to maintenance subscribers.
Full Version. Dos or Windows 95 for PCs; appropriate O/S for EWS (Windows NT & UNIX). Call for details. *Optimal configuration:* 64Mb RAM.
Structural Version. Call for details.
Heat Transfer. Call for details.
Call for details.
Finite Element Program Which Consists of a Pre- & Post-Processor, Mesh & Model Generation, & Color Graphics. Performs Structural Static & Dynamic, Thermal, Fluid, Nonlinear, Fatigue, Electromagnetic & Design Optimization Analyses & Features COSMOS/M FFE (Fast Finite Element) for Solution Speeds up to 100 Times Faster Than Traditional Technologies & Gives Turnaround Speeds Comparable to That of Many Mainframe Computers. Interfaces with Many CAD Systems Including AUTOCAD & PRO/ ENGINEER.
Structural Research & Analysis Corp.

Cosmos II: Your Guide to the Celestial Sphere. Jun. 1994. *Items Included:* Registration card, instruction sheet. *Customer Support:* 900 support number $2.00 per minute; limited 60 day warranty.
DOS. IBM PC & compatibles (640k). disk $9.95 (ISBN 1-57269-003-8, Order no.: 3202 42105). *Addl. software required:* DOS 3.0 or higher. *Optimal configuration:* Dual floppy drive. Will run on hard disk drive.
Don't Just See the Skies with the Naked Eye. Instead, Explore Its Magic & Intrigue Like a Professional Astronomer with Cosmos II.
Memorex Products, Inc., Memorex Software Division.

COSORT. *Version:* DOS 4.4, Unix 2.5. 1980-86. *Operating System(s) Required:* UNIX, XENIX, MS-DOS. *Language(s):* Assembly & C. *Memory Required:* MS-DOS 52k, UNIX-XENIX 100k. *Items Included:* Software & documentation. *Customer Support:* Hotline; Fax; Email; first year for Unix users free, 15% thereafter.
MS-DOS. disk $200.00 (ISBN 0-917323-00-9, Order no.: COSORT (M)).
UNIX. disk $990.00 (ISBN 0-917323-01-7, Order no.: COSORT (U)).
XENIX. disk $490.00 (ISBN 0-917323-02-5, Order no.: COSORT (X)).
General Purpose High-Speed Sort/Merge Routine for Operations & Programming Use. Includes Stand-Alone Programs for Interactive & Batch Operations. Allows Any Number of Keys, Records & Data Types. Can Be Linked to All Languages, Facilities for Special Selection & Compares Using an I/O-Reducing Coroutine Interface.
Information Resources, Inc. (New York).

Cost Accounting. *Version:* 4.5. 1978. *Compatible Hardware:* IBM PC & compatibles, PC XT, PC AT, 386, 486, Pentium, PS/2. *Operating System(s) Required:* PC-DOS/MS-DOS 3.X, 4X, 5X, 6X, Windows 3.1, Windows 95. *Language(s):* BASIC, C, Assembler. *Memory Required:* 640k. *General Requirements:* Stand-alone or 2Mb Network file server. *Customer Support:* 90 day warranty, onsite training, telephone support.
$1295.00.
Automatically Receives Information from Payroll, Accounts Payable, Billing, Order Entry & Inventory Control. Provides Reports That Show Cost Breakdowns, Percentage Completed, Profit Projection, etc. Optional Feature Facilitates Billing Jobs with Different Methods. Optionally Handles Multi-Company Processing.
LIBRA Corp.

Cost Accounting. *Operating System(s) Required:* CP/M.
$2500.00.
Masters Software Co.

COST ACCOUNTING: Planning & Control - Practice Case. 1988. *Compatible Hardware:* IBM/Tandy.
Micro Job Order Cost Case - Practice Case & Template. write for info. (ISBN 0-538-51021-8, Order no.: Q30022).
Micro Process Cost Case - Practice Case & Template. write for info. (ISBN 0-538-51022-6, Order no.: Q30023).
Micro Standard Cost Case - Practice Case & Template. write for info. (ISBN 0-538-51023-4, Order no.: Q30024).
Micro Budgeting Case - Practice Case & Template. write for info. (ISBN 0-538-51024-2, Order no.: Q30025).
South-Western Publishing Co.

Cost Advantage. *Version:* 1.8.3. Aug. 1994. *Items Included:* Manual. *Customer Support:* Training, hotline, update support, maintenance, 90-day warranty.
SUN Solaris, Ultrix (8Mb), UNIX. SUN4/SPARC, IBM RS-6000, HP, Silicon Graphics. disk $5000.00 (Order no.: 384-022023).
Expert System allowing for the Capture of Expert Knowledge on Cost Estimation & Manufacturability Analysis. Generates Well-Documented, Auditable Cost Estimates for Complex Mechanical, Electronic & Assembly Designs Using Expert Knowledge Captured from Industry Standards & Merged with Company-Specific Parameters. Generates Costs More Quickly, More Accurately at Lower Cost Than Manual Methods. Allows Staff with Little Costing Experience to Generate Accurate Projections Using Expert Knowledge. Integrated with PTC-PRO/Engineers & SDRC-IDEAS & Cognition Mechanical Advantage.
Cognition Corp.

Cost/Benefits. Mar. 1986. *Compatible Hardware:* IBM PC & compatibles. *Operating System(s) Required:* PC-DOS 2.1 or higher. *Memory Required:* 256k.
5.25" or 3.5". disk $39.95.
Designed to Make Cost/Benefits Analysis Easier & Faster. Contains 10 Commonly Used Models.
Park Row Software.

Cost Center Reporting System. 1985. *Compatible Hardware:* DECmate, PDP 11-23. *Operating System(s) Required:* COS-310, MICRO-RSX. (source code included). *General Requirements:* Hard disk.
$4000.00.
Combines Project Cost Reporting for Management with a Transaction Entry System to Serve the Special Needs of Companies That Need Cost Analyses Without Detailed Accounting. Prints Detailed Labor & Purchase Distribution Reports & Shows Project & Task Activity on the Project Cost Reports. The P.C.R.'s Include Labor, Expense, & Line Item Budgets & Variances for Each Task, Transaction Entry Records Information for the Current Week, Month, Year-to-Date, & Project Life. Transaction Entry Records Labor & Purchase Transactions Using Purchase Order Management to Update the Reporting System Week, Period, & Project Life Data Files. Special Features Include Project Budgeting & User-Controlled Overhead Rate Applications.
Corporate Consulting Co.

Cost Development. May 1983. *Compatible Hardware:* IBM PC, PC XT, PC AT. *Operating System(s) Required:* PC-DOS. *Language(s):* COBOL. *Memory Required:* 192k. *General Requirements:* 2 disk drives.
disk $1660.00-$3085.00.
Develops Material, Labor, Burden & Outside Operation Costs for an Item. The Cost at That Level & All Lower Levels Are Supported. Cost Groups Include Standard & Current. Cost Types Include Elementary & Total. Reports Include a Stock Status, Bill of Material, & Cost Summary. The Cost Variance Module Provides Standard Job Cost & Variance Reporting for the Inventory, Purchasing, & Shop Floor Functions. General Ledger Data Is Provided for an Accounting System. Reports Are Produced for Material & Labor Variance, Word Order, & Purchase Order Cost Summaries & Inventory Accounting.
Twin Oaks, Inc.

Cost Estimating. *Compatible Hardware:* IBM PC. *Operating System(s) Required:* PC-DOS. *Language(s):* Microsoft BASIC (source code included). *Memory Required:* 64k. *General Requirements:* Lotus 1-2-3.
disk $100.00.
demo disk $20.00.
Calculates Estimated Construction Costs for Contractors, Engineers, & Architects. User Inputs Unit Costs of Labor & Materials, & Data Such As Total Unit Cost, Labor Cost, & Material Cost Is Output.
Caldwell Software.

Cost Management System. *Version:* 3.0. *General Requirements:* Hard disk drive.
Macintosh Plus or higher (2Mb). 3.5" disk $289.00.
Cost Management, Estimating, Job Costing.
Softouch Software, Inc.

Cost Manager Level I. *Version:* 3.1. *Customer Support:* On site training unlimited support services for first 90 days & through subscription thereafter.
MS-DOS, PC-DOS. Contact publisher for price. *Nonstandard peripherals required:* Hard disk (30Mb); 132-column printer. *Networks supported:* Novell, NTNX, 10-Net, Unix, Xenix, Turbo DOS (Multi-User version for all).
Transaction-Based Accounting System for Smaller Businesses. Supports up to 10 Departments. Allows Transactions to Be Broken Down by Type; Only Requirement Is That User Know Whether Transaction Increases or Decreases Balance.
Argos Software.

Cost Manager Level II. *Customer Support:* On site training unlimited support services for first 90 days & through subscription thereafter.
MS-DOS, PC-DOS. Contact publisher for price. *Nonstandard peripherals required:* Hard disk (30Mb); 132-column printer. *Networks supported:* Novell, NTNX, 10-Net, Unix, Xenix, Turbo DOS (Multi-User version for all).
Adds Cost Accounting to Cost Manager Level I. Supports up to 999 Jobs with Information Broken Down By Account & Activity for Each Job.
Argos Software.

COSTREP+. *Compatible Hardware:* Hewlett Packard Vectra; IBM PC & compatibles. *Memory Required:* 640k. *General Requirements:* Hard disk, printer.
contact publisher for price.
Produces HCFA Approved Cost Reports That Can Be Filed with All Intermediaries. Generates All Worksheets Including Supplementals for Titles V, XVIII & XIX in Exact Replica of HCFA Forms.
HBO & Co., Inc.

TITLE INDEX

COTA Examination Review Check. M. Teresa Mohler & Leonard Trujillo. Nov. 1995. IBM. disk $23.00 (ISBN 1-55642-262-8, Order no.: 32628).
Computer Program with Self-Check Study Questions for COTA Exam Review.
SLACK, Inc.

COTS/DEALER Options System. Oct. 1982. *Compatible Hardware:* IBM PC, PS/2. *Operating System(s) Required:* PC-DOS, MS-DOS. *Memory Required:* 640k. *General Requirements:* Hard disk, CGA card, printer. *Customer Support:* Hotline. $25,000.00-$80,000.00. *Networks supported:* Novell Netware.
A Comprehensive, Integrated & Modular Front Office, Treasury Operations/Backoffice & Risk Management System for Treasurers, Marketmakers & Hedgers. It Provides for Pricing & Revaluation of Interest Rate Swaps, Swaptions, Caps/Floors/Collars, Deposits/Loans, Banker's Acceptances, Fra's/Iro's & Futures/Options; Hedging of Exposures; Cashflow Management; Sensitivity Analysis, What-If Scenarios, Stress Testing, Value-at-Risk, Position & Loss Limits for Counterparties & Traders; Confirmations, Payments/Settlements, General Ledger Interface, Operations Control & Security.
Software Options, Inc.

Cotton Tales. Jan. 1990. *Items Included:* Disk(s), user's guide, poster, coloring book, warranty card, swap coupon. *Customer Support:* 90 day unlimited warranty; 800 toll free number, 800-221-7911, 8:00 a.m.-5:00 p.m. Arizona time; Updates $10.
Macintosh System 6 or higher. Macintosh (1Mb monochrome, 2Mb color). 3.5" disk $69.99 (ISBN 1-55712-024-X, Order no.: 4002). *Optimal configuration:* 2Mb color monitor, Macintosh LC. *Networks supported:* Digicard.
MS-DOS. IBM, Tandy, MS-DOS compatible (128k). disk $49.99 (ISBN 0-918017-94-7, Order no.: 4001). *Nonstandard peripherals required:* VGA or CGA card. *Optimal configuration:* 128k, color monitor, VGA card. *Networks supported:* Velan, Novell, Digicard.
DOS. Apple II, Apple IIe, Apple IIGS, Apple II Plus (48k). disk $49.99 (ISBN 0-918017-64-5, Order no.: 4000). *Optimal configuration:* Apple II, printer, color monitor, 48k. *Networks supported:* Digicard.
Award Winning Cotton Tales Helps Beginning Readers Express Themselves Creatively Through Words & Pictures. Cotton, the Bunny Cursor, Guides Children to Enter Pictures & Words by Using Publishing Tools Like Cut, Paste & Copy to Create Stories, Pictures or Letters to Grandma. 192 Graphic Library, 600 Word Dictionary, Picture to Text Translator. Ages 3 to 9.
Mindplay.

Counseling Data Base System: Instructional Enterprises. *Items Included:* Manual & 3 1/2" disk. *Customer Support:* 800-966-3382, Fax: 612-781-7753.
IBM PC & compatibles. disk $59.95.
Card File Formats Are Presented for Immediate Use. Simply Type Information for Card Files, Protect Files with a Password, & Retrieve, Print, & Edit Files at Ease. Students Can Obtain Information from the Files Without Being Able to Change or Tamper with the Files.
Educational Media Corp.

Countdown. (Visual Almanac Ser.).
Macintosh (4Mb). CD-ROM disk $29.95 (Order no.: R1107). *Nonstandard peripherals required:* 14" color monitor or larger, CD-ROM drive.
Build Intuition & Math Skills with This Innovative Program. Users Alter the Difficulty of Three Different Games to Apply New Approaches to Counting, Estimations & Other Match Concepts. Multilingual: Dutch, English, Spanish, French & Italian.
Library Video Co.

Counters. Gordon Waite. Jan. 1986. *Compatible Hardware:* IBM PC. *Operating System(s) Required:* MS-DOS. *Memory Required:* 128k. disk $9.95 (ISBN 0-934777-06-3).
Contains 2 Programs: TC - Counts the Number of Words & Lines in Any ASCII Test File; WORDFREQ - Reads Any ASCII Text File & Produces an Alphabetical List of the Individual Words Found in the File. Will Also Count the Number of Times the Word Was Found.
Pico Publishing.

Counting & Adding: Colorful Introduction to Numbers. Oct. 1994. *Items Included:* Registration card, instruction sheet. *Customer Support:* 900 support number $2.00 per minute; limited 60 day warranty.
Windows. IBM PC & compatibles (1Mb). disk $9.95 (ISBN 1-57269-009-7, Order no.: 3202 42175). *Addl. software required:* Windows 3.1 or higher. *Optimal configuration:* 286 or higher CPU, VGA or higher monitor, single 3.5" disk drive, any mouse.
Numbers Become a Magical Adventure in Counting & Adding. Music Games & Storytelling Teach the Essentials of Number Skills.
Memorex Products, Inc., Memorex Software Division.

Counting on Frank.
Windows. IBM & compatibles. CD-ROM disk $49.95 (Order no.: R1239). *Nonstandard peripherals required:* CD-ROM drive. *Optimal configuration:* 386 processor operating at 16Mhz or higher, MS-DOS 5.0 or higher, Windows 3.1 or higher, 30Mb hard drive, mouse, VGA graphic adapter & VGA color monitor (SVGA recommended), 4Mb RAM, external speakers or headphones (with sound card) that are Sound Blaster compatible.
Macintosh (4Mb). (Order no.: R1239A). *Nonstandard peripherals required:* 14" color monitor or larger, CD-ROM drive.
Based on the Book by Rod Clement, This Animated Program Presents Math Concepts in a Humorous, Imaginative Way. Children Learn about Word Problems, Estimations, Compound Equations, Multiplication, Fractions & More with Fran the Dog & His Math-Happy Owner.
Library Video Co.

County Outline Database. *Items Included:* Bound manual. *Customer Support:* Free hotline - no time limit; 30 day limited warranty; updates are $5/disk plus S&H.
MS-DOS. IBM & compatibles (256k). disk $95.00.
Includes County Outlines for All of the United States Except Alaska & Hawaii. This Database Can Be Used with MAPIT or Other Mapping Packages. The County Outlines Are Stored in 48 State Files As ASCII Text. Each County Outline Consists of a List of Coordinate Pairs Measured in Radians X 1,000. This Allows County Outlines from Two or More State Files to Be Combined. Also Included Is MTRANS, a Program for Scaling, Documenting, & Rotating Map Outlines.
Dynacomp, Inc.

Coupon Collector. 1982. *Compatible Hardware:* Apple II+, IIc, IIe; Franklin Ace; IBM PC, PC XT, PC AT. *Operating System(s) Required:* Apple DOS 3.3, MS-DOS 3.1. *Language(s):* BASIC (source code included). *Memory Required:* Apple 48k, IBM 256k.
disk $39.00.
Helps the Grocery-Retail Coupon Collector in Sorting, Indexing, Listing, & Trading. It Also Helps in Keeping Track of Expiration Date.
Andent, Inc.

Coupon Organizer. D. Stein & E. Neiburger. 1982. *Compatible Hardware:* Apple II, II+, IIe, IIc; Basis 6502; Franklin Ace; IBM PC, PC XT, PC AT & compatibles. *Operating System(s) Required:* Apple DOS 3.3, MS-DOS 3.1. *Language(s):* BASIC (source code included). *Memory Required:* Apple 48k, IBM 256k. *General Requirements:* Printer.
disk $39.00 (ISBN 0-914555-04-9).
Allows Cost Minded Shopper to Organize, Store, Sort & Select Thousands of Coupons. Handles: Qualifiers & Requirements, Coupon Trades, Double Coupon Days, Need Lists, Refund Tracking, Mail Coupons, Store Locations, Labels, Clearing Houses, Expiration Dates, Deadlines, etc.
Andent, Inc.

Coupon Padlock. Version: 4.58. 1983. *Operating System(s) Required:* PC-DOS, MS-DOS. *Memory Required:* 64k. *Customer Support:* Mon.-Fri. 8:30 AM-6:30 PM CST.
disk $149.99 (Order no.: 412108).
Coupon Disks Provide High Level Copy Protection with a Special Analog Magnetic Fingerprint. This Fingerprint - Placed on the Floppy with Equipment Designed & Used Exclusively at GLENCO - Contains a Unique Company Assigned ID No. & Sequentially Assigned S/Ns. The Serial Numbers Can Be Used to Set up a Tracking System, Version Control, or May Simply Be Displayed by the Program, In Addition, the Number of Times Program Can Run Is Preset. When the Last Coupon Is Used, the Fingerprint Is Wiped Out. The COUPON Copy Protection System Includes a COUPON Master Disk Along with the Appropriate Number of COUPON Preformatted or Duplicated Disks. The COUPON Master Disk Contains the Necessary Subroutines along with Example Programs in the Language Specified. An Option, Called HDCOPY, Frees the Need to Have a COUPON Key Disk in Drive A in Order for the Program to Run.
Glenco Engineering, Inc.

CouponOmizer. Feb. 1984. *Compatible Hardware:* IBM PC & compatibles. *Operating System(s) Required:* MS-DOS. *Language(s):* Assembler. *Memory Required:* 64k.
disk $29.95, incl. manual, & automatic installation.
Menus Provide Entry & Display of All Types of Discounts. Prepares Shopping List Highlighting Discount Opportunities. Tracks Rebate Requirements & Purges Expired Offers. User May Define Own Product Classification Categories. Verifies Computer Records Against Paper Records.
Natural Software Ltd.

Course Builder. Version: 4. Bill Appleton. Jan. 1991. *Items Included:* 340-page documentation, tutorials disk, guided tour disks, support & utilities disk, examples disks. *Customer Support:* Free telephone technical support, custom training classes - $500/day.
Apple operating system 6.05 or higher. Apple Macintosh (2Mb). 3.5" disk $1495.00, Academic & Site License pricing available. *Optimal configuration:* Macintosh IIci, Apple System 6.05, 5Mb RAM, 80Mb hard disk, 13" color monitor.
Visual Authoring Language to Create Interactive Training & Multimedia Applications. Built-In Features Make the Presentation of Information Easy & Powerful. Use Dialog Boxes, Mouse Clicks, & Simulated Controls to Receive & Interpret Input. Automatically Keeps Track of Performance & Allows the Course to Branch According to Past Answers.
TeleRobotics International, Inc.

COVERED OPTIONS

Covered Options. *Items Included:* Bound manual. *Customer Support:* Free hotline - no time limit; 30 day limited warranty; updates are $5/disk plus S&H.
MS-DOS. IBM & compatibles (128k). disk $99.95. *Nonstandard peripherals required:* 80-column printer for printouts; color graphics board desirable, but not necessary.
Designed for Managers & Conservative Investors with Portfolios Which Include Common Stocks & Convertible Bonds. It Introduces Techniques Which Will: Provide Increased Protection for Holdings; Significantly Increase Portfolio Yield. Gives Both Graphic & Tabular Representations of What Will Happen to the Gain As the Stock Price Changes, for Any Future Date. The Probability That the Stock Will Remain Within a Profitable Range Is Also Computed. Also Provided Is a Printed Report of the Gains or Losses in the Stock (Bond) & the Options, & the Present Annualized Option Yield.
Dynacomp, Inc.

Covert Action. Sid Meier. Oct. 1990. *Items Included:* Manual. *Customer Support:* Free customer service, (410) 771-1151, Ext. 350. IBM PC & compatibles (512k). 3.5" or 5.25" disk $59.95. *Nonstandard peripherals required:* Supports VGA/MCGA, EGA, CGA, Tandy 16-color.
Finally, An International Espionage Simulation That Portrays This Clandestine World the Way It Really Is. Espionage In the 1990s Thrives on High Technology; & In This Techno-Thriller, You'll Tap Phone Lines, Crack Complex Codes, & Defeat Computerized Defense Systems. Solve Masterplots That Involve Real World Animal Organizations.
MicroProse Software.

Cowboy Casino. *Version:* 2.0. *Items Included:* Brochure, manual, & product registration card. *Customer Support:* Unlimited free technical support via 1-800 line.
Macintosh System 6.0 or higher. Macintosh (4Mb). 3.5" disk $49.95 (ISBN 1-882284-73-9, Order no.: SCC-01-MAC). *Optimal configuration:* 8Mb available RAM.
Learn to Play Poker with Five Wisecracking Card Sharks in a Wild West Salon.
Intellimedia Sports.

CP/Emulator. *Version:* 2.7. 1984. *Compatible Hardware:* IBM PC, PC XT, PC AT, PC compatibles; Compaq, Leading Edge, Televideo. *Operating System(s) Required:* PC-DOS, MS-DOS, CNO. *Memory Required:* 128k.
disk $99.00.
Converts CPM 2.2 Programs to Run on MS/PC-DOS Machines. Contains a CPEmulator & a CP/M Conversion Utility That Allows Users to Read & Write Popular Disk Formats Such As Kaypro & Osborne. The Conversion Process Involves Two Steps: the Conversion Utility Will Copy the CP/M Program to a PC-DOS or MS-DOS Diskette. Then, the Bind Utility Will Attach the CPEmulator to the Program, Making It Ready to Run on a PC-DOS/MS-DOS Machine.
GTEK Development Hardware/Software.

CP-M. *Customer Support:* All of our products are unconditionally guaranteed.
CP/M. CD-ROM disk $39.95 (Order no.: CP/M). *Nonstandard peripherals required:* CD-ROM drive.
18,000 Files Including Programs, Docs, & More for the CP/M OS.
Walnut Creek CDRom.

CP/M Emulator. *Compatible Hardware:* Atari ST. contact publisher for price (Order no.: DS5023). Atari Corp.

CP/M Emulator for MS-DOS. *Items Included:* Bound manual. *Customer Support:* Free hotline - no time limit; 30 day limited warranty; updates are $5/disk plus S&H.
MS-DOS 2.0 or higher. IBM & compatibles (256k). disk $29.95.
Allows User to Run Osborne, Kaypro, etc., Software As Long As It Does Not Do Things Specific to Hardware (Like Look at the ROM, Monkey with the BIOS, etc.), or Depend on Specific Screen Cursor Controls. For Example, You Can Run CP/M MICROSOFT BASIC, CBASIC, EBASIC, MULTIPLAN, etc. on the IBM. That Means You Can Run BASIC Programs Which Were Written on CP/M Systems Directly on Your MS-DOS Machine, with Little or (Usually) No Modification.
Dynacomp, Inc.

CP/M Emulator Master. *Customer Support:* 800-929-8117 (customer service).
MS-DOS. IBM/PS2. disk $49.99 (ISBN 0-87007-824-0).
Users Can Execute All Their CP/M Software on the IBM Through the Use of This Software.
SourceView Software International.

CP/M-MS DOS Teaching Testing & Training Program. *Items Included:* Bound manual. *Customer Support:* Free hotline - no time limit; 30 day limited warranty; updates are $5/disk plus S&H.
MS-DOS. IBM & compatibles (256k). disk $49.95.
CP/M. disk $49.95.
The 3T Package Was Designed to Be a School in Itself, Simulating the Classroom Environment. There Are Text Lessons, Multiple-Choice Questions, & Coaching. Test Scores Are Used to Direct the Student Backwards or Forwards in the Lessons.
Dynacomp, Inc.

CP/M Plus. *Memory Required:* 10k.
disk $350.00.
Operating System for Z-80 & 8080 Based Microcomputers in Single-User Environments. Supports an Estimated 3,000 CP-M Based Application Programs Without the Necessity to Modify the Language. Lists File Directories, Transfers Files & Edits. File System Precludes the Need for Directory Searches by Utilizing a Hashing Technique to Access Directory Information. Utilities Allow Optional English Words.
Digital Research, Inc.

CP/M 2.2. *Memory Required:* 20k.
disk $150.00.
Includes Dynamic File Management, Fast Assembler, Debugger & a General Purpose Editor.
Digital Research, Inc.

CP/M-2.2mH. Pickles & Trout. Jul. 1983. *Compatible Hardware:* TRS-80 Model II, Model 12, Model 16, Tandy 6000. *Operating System(s) Required:* CP/M. *Memory Required:* 32k.
CP/M-2.2m. disk $25.00.
CP/M-2.2mH. disk $25.00.
TriSoft.

CP/M-68k. *Compatible Hardware:* TRS-80 Model II Enhanced Version, Model 16; Tandy 1000. *Language(s):* C. *Memory Required:* 96k.
disk $65.00, incl. 68000 Assembler & C-compiler. manual set $45.00.
Operating System That Adds Speed & Power of the 16/32-Bit MC68000 While Maintaining Compatibility with the Library of CP/M 2.2 Software. Runs in Conjunction with CP/M 2.2. Easy Context Switching Allows User to Quickly Go from CP/M-68K to CP/M 2.2 & Vice Versa. Z80 Processor Acts As an I/O Slave Freeing the 68000 from Mundane Tasks.
TriSoft.

SOFTWARE ENCYCLOPEDIA 1996

CP/M-80 Emulator for the IBM PC. *Items Included:* Bound manual. *Customer Support:* Free hotline - no time limit; 30 day limited warranty; updates are $5/disk plus S&H.
MS-DOS 1.0 or higher. IBM & compatibles (192k). disk $39.95.
Run CP/M-80 Software on Your IBM PC! Machine-Language 8080 Microprocessor Emulator Which Gives Your IBM PC an Effective CP/M Processor Speed of about One Megahertz. Its Only Limitations Are That It Cannot Handle Code Which Contains Z-80 Specific Instructions, Modifies the Operating System, or Accesses the Hardware Directly. Using the IBM Display Characteristics, ZP-EM Will Emulate Osborne, Kaypro (ADM-3), HZ-19, & DEC VT52 Screens.
Dynacomp, Inc.

CP/M-86 & CBASIC 86. Digital Research. *Compatible Hardware:* TI Professional. *Memory Required:* 128k. *General Requirements:* Winchester hard disk, printer.
$240.00 (Order no.: TI P/N 2232414-0001).
Operates with the 16-Bit Intel 8086-8088 Family of Microprocessors. Can Support Application Programs That Range from Simple to Complex.
Texas Instruments, Personal Productivit.

CPA Client Master. *Compatible Hardware:* IBM PC & compatibles. *Operating System(s) Required:* MS-DOS. *Language(s):* RBASE 4000. *Memory Required:* 270k.
contact publisher for price.
Set of Utilities Written for RBASE DBMS, the Product Manager's CPA Client Information. These Clients Can Be Corporations, Individuals, Partnerships, Proprietorships, & Non-Profit Organizations. Product Keeps Track of Company Names As Well As Individual Names; Social Security Numbers, Telephone Numbers, Federal Identification Numbers & State Identification Numbers, Estimated Payment Due Dates, Tax Return Due Dates, Extension Due Dates, Partner Data for Partnerships, Birth Dates & Other Important Dates. System Provides a Variety of Standard Reports for Client Information Such As Phone Books or Tax Return Due Date Reports. The System Is Menu Driven So That It Can Be Used by the Novice User but Can Also Be Driven Using RBASE Command Words for the More Experienced User.
Management Systems, Inc.

CPA: The Clan Practical Accountant. Robert Jahncke. Nov. 1989. *Items Included:* Four manuals (Beginner's Guide, Tutorial Guide, Reference Guide & Question & Answer Guide), wall chart, printer set-up card, stop sheet, warranty/registration card. *Customer Support:* Hotline, disk repair or replacement.
MS-DOS (256k). disk $39.95 (ISBN 0-926846-47-7, Order no.: 2162).
Fully Automated Accounting & Bookkeeping Package. Uses Widely Accepted Accounting Procedures & Terminology & Is Easily Adapted To Existing Accounting Systems. Tracks up To 128 Asset, Liability, Income & Expense Accounts Including Net Worth & up To 20 Bank Accounts. Provides Reconciliation of Any Bank Account at the Touch of a Button. Unique Features Include the Use of up To Eight Departments for a Small Business & User-Customized "Spreadsheet Style" Reports for 12 Full Months on a Single Page, Allowing "At a Glance" Trend Analysis Without the Use of Support Software.
Sir-Tech Software, Inc.

CPA Tickler Database. *Items Included:* 140 page illustrated manual. *Customer Support:* Phone support avail.: $35.00 per 20 minutes; 30-day money back guarantee.
IBM XT, PC AT, 386 & compatibles (640k). disk

TITLE INDEX

$259.00.
Based on Original CPA Tickler- the Widest Selling Spreadsheet Software for Due Date Monitoring & Tax Return Tracking. This Product Performs Significantly Faster Than the Original & Manages Much More Information. Incorporates a Tickler Database of Tax Returns, Events, & Due Dates, with Related Client Name & Address Database. 39 Different Reports Available, Including Due Date, Scheduling, Tax Return Status, Client Calendars & Listings, Personalized Letters, Mailing Labels, Index Cards & Rolodex Cards. User Can Print or View Either All or Selected Items. Inquiry Is Done Through Query by Example.
Front Row Systems.

CPAid Individual State Programs. *Version:* 1992. Andrew Rosenberg. 1982. *Compatible Hardware:* IBM PC & compatibles, PS/2. *Operating System(s) Required:* PC-DOS/MS-DOS 3.1 or higher. *Language(s):* Compiled BASIC. *Memory Required:* 640k. *General Requirements:* Hard disk.
$200.00-$360.00 single station.
$240.00-$435.00 small network.
$300.00-$540.00 large network.
$15.00 working models.
39 State Programs Available for Processing Tax Returns - Designed to Interface with the Master 1040: AL, AR, AZ, CA, CA Nonresident, CO, CT, DC, GA, IA, IL, IN, KS, KY, LA, MA, MD, ME, MI, MI Intangibles, MI Single Business, MN, MO, MT, NC, ND, NE, NJ, NM, NY, NYC Unincorporated Business, OH, OK, PA, SC, VA, WV, WI.
Best Information Services.

CPAid Individual Tax Planner. *Version:* 3.0. Andrew Rosenberg. 1981. *Compatible Hardware:* IBM PC & compatibles, PS/2. *Operating System(s) Required:* PC-DOS/MS-DOS 3.1 or higher. *Language(s):* Compiled BASIC. *Memory Required:* 640k. *General Requirements:* Hard disk.
disk $195.00, incl. manual.
working model $15.00.
Aids Tax Professionals in Making Tax Projections to Help Minimize Client Tax Liabilities. It Includes K-1 Detail Screens, Capital Gains Worksheet for "Kiddie Tax" Calculations, the Ability to Easily Handle Statutory Employee Reporting & Interfaces with All the State Tax Planning Programs (Available as an Option). Automatically Compares Married Filing Separate vs. Married Filing Joint Comparisions on the Same Screen. Four Different Scenarios May Be Compared in Each Tax Year & Up To Four Years Worth of Comparisions Can Be Made; Allowing for 16 Total Comparisions. Government Parameters Are User-Definable Which Allows Users To Make Tax Parameter Changes In-Between the Yearly Updates the Company Offers. Handles Computation of State Tax Liabilities. Allows Customized Entries for State Income, Deductions, Additions, Credits, Personal Exemption Amounts & Standard Deductions as State Laws Change.
Best Information Services.

CPAid Master Write-Up. *Version:* 2.0. 1991. *Compatible Hardware:* IBM PC & compatibles, PS/2. *Operating System(s) Required:* PC-DOS/MS-DOS 3.1 or higher. *Language(s):* Compiled BASIC. *Memory Required:* 640k. *General Requirements:* Hard disk.
$1395.00 single station. *Networks supported:* 3COM, Lantastic, Novell & compatibles.
$1695.00 small network.
$2195.00 large network.
$55.00 working model.
Best Information Services.

CPAid Master 1040. *Version:* 1992. Andrew Rosenberg. 1978. *Compatible Hardware:* IBM PC & compatibles, PS/2. *Operating System(s) Required:* PC-DOS/MS-DOS 3.1 or higher. *Language(s):* Compiled BASIC. *Memory Required:* 640k. *General Requirements:* Hard disk.
$795.00 single station. *Networks supported:* 3Com, Lantastic, Novell, & 100% compatibles.
$960.00 small network.
$1195.00 large network.
$15.00 working model.
Designed To Simplify the Preparation of Federal 1040 Tax Returns. Easy-To-Use Menus, On-Screen Forms View & Extensive On-Line Help. Batch or Interactive Data Entry. Prepares 78 Forms & Schedules. Automatically Chooses the Best Tax Calculation & Includes a Report Generator. Allows Users To Select & Access the Forms or Schedules In Order Desired (GOTO Menu). Return Is Automatically Recalculated as New Data Is Entered. New Security Option Allows for the Creation of Passwords for Confidential Access to Individual State Programs. Error Trapping for Tax Compliance. Ability to Calculate Keogh Limits, Vacation Home, SE Health Insurance, Interface Capabilities with Master Write-Up Schedule C, E, & F, Automatic Import of K-1 Data from Master 1120S & Master 1065, Multiples of Many Forms. Complete Diagnostic Report with Prior Year Comparison & Special Reports for Reviewers.
Best Information Services.

CPAid Master 1065. *Version:* 1992. Andrew Rosenberg. 1984. *Compatible Hardware:* IBM PC & compatibles, PS/2. *Operating System(s) Required:* PC-DOS/MS-DOS 3.1 or higher. *Language(s):* Compiled BASIC. *Memory Required:* 640k. *General Requirements:* Hard disk.
$760.00 single station. *Networks supported:* 3COM, Lantastic, Novel & compatibles.
$915.00 small network.
$1140.00 large network.
$15.00 working model.
39 State Programs Available for Processing Tax Returns - Designed to Interface with the Master 1040.
Best Information Services.

CPAid Master 1120. *Version:* 1992. Andrew Rosenberg. 1982. *Compatible Hardware:* IBM PC & compatibles, PS/2. *Operating System(s) Required:* PC-DOS/MS-DOS 3.1 or higher. *Language(s):* Compiled BASIC. *Memory Required:* Hard disk.
$760.00 single station. *Networks supported:* 3Com, Lantastic, Novell & compatibles.
$915.00 small network.
$1140.00 large network.
$15.00 working model.
Comprehensive Tax Program Designed for Preparing the 1120 Corporate Tax Return. Ability To Prepare 35 Forms & Schedules. 2 Year Diagnostic Report. Ability To Generate Override Reports of Calculated Fields. Recalculations Are Automatic as New Data Is Entered. Conversion Program Automatically Carries Forward Previous Year's Data. Automatic Conversion of Data To/From 1120 & 1120S. Automatically Chooses the Best Tax Calculation & Includes a Report Generator. New Security Option Allows For the Creation of Passwords For Confidential Access To Business State Programs. Interfaces with Business State Programs, Master Write-Up, & Master Fixed Asset. Import Data From Popular Accounting Packages Through the CPAid Tax Bridge Program.
Best Information Services.

CPR PROFESSIONAL: CUSTOMER PROFILE &

CPAid Master 1120S. *Version:* 1992. Andrew Rosenberg. 1987. *Operating System(s) Required:* PC-DOS/MS-DOS 3.1 or higher. *Memory Required:* 640k. *General Requirements:* Hard disk.
$760.00 single station. *Networks supported:* 3COM, Lantastic, Novell, & compatible.
$915.00 small network.
$1140.00 large network.
$15.00 working model.
Best Information Services.

CPaid Time & Billing Program. *Version:* 2.2. Andrew Rosenberg. 1986.
PC-DOS/MS-DOS 3.0 or higher. IBM PC, XT, AT, PS/2 & compatibles (640k). single station $195.00. *Nonstandard peripherals required:* Hard disk.
Designed for Professionals Who Bill at an Hourly Rate & Require an Efficient Method for Tracking Time & Expenses. Complies with the Client Billing Software Guidelines Established by the American Institute of Certified Public Accountants. Up to 5 Billing Rates Provided per Employee with Optional Override Capability. Create a List of Jobs That Are Chargeable & Non-Chargeable with a List of Expenses Incurred. Choose from 5 Different Standard Bills - Quick Bill - Created at a Moments Notice, Itemized Transaction Bill, Transaction Summary Bill, Monthly Retainer Bill, Billing Code Override Bill or Free Form Bill. Maintains Files for Staffs of One to 96 Members & Can Bill up to 3,000 Clients. Maintains Accounts Receivable Data Including the Ability to Generate Statements & Accounts Receivable Aging Reports at any Time.
Best Information Services.

CPNIX. *Customer Support:* 800-929-8117 (customer service).
MS-DOS. Commodore 128; CP/M. disk $99.99 (ISBN 0-87007-193-9).
Allows Communication Between CP/M "Local" Computers & UNIX "Host" Computers. Transfers Both ASCII Text Files & Binary Files. It Transfers Only the Desired File, Then Returns to Command Level. Permits the CP/M Computer to Use the More Powerful Resources of the UNIX Computer & to Act As an Intelligent Terminal with One Major Difference--It Can Also Write UNIX Files to a Local Disk, & Automatically Directs UNIX to Perform Activities Such as Editing, Listing & Removal of Files to Accomplish a Particular File Transfer. For All Transferred Files, It Compares the CP/M File Size Against the UNIX File Size. When Transferring Binary Files, Checksum Error Checking Every 16 Bytes Is Accomplished. To Allow Easy End-User Modifications, It Is Provided in a Source Code Form.
SourceView Software International.

CPplus. Taurus Software Corp. *Compatible Hardware:* TI Professional. *Operating System(s) Required:* MS-DOS. *Memory Required:* 64k.
$79.95.
Series of Programs That Interface to the MS-DOS & CP/M-86 Operating Systems.
Texas Instruments, Personal Productivit.

CPR Professional: Customer Profile & Retrieval. *Version:* 3.10. *Items Included:* 80 column display; 8 user definable tickler dates; auto dialing & 7 different formats for labels/rotary index cards reports & phone directories. *Customer Support:* 15 day unlimited warranty - telephone technical.
DOS 2.1 or higher. IBM PC & compatibles (640K). 3.5" or 5.25" disk $199.95. *Optimal configuration:* AT-286 or higher recommended.
Computer Program That Gives Instant Retrieval Capability for Accessing Detailed Information on Customers, Clients, Contacts, Vendors, or Employees. Built-in Sophistication Makes

CPRS: COAL PREPARATION RESPONSE

Handling of Complex Data Effortless. User Can Save Significant Amounts of Time; & Increase Revenues While Handling Business Activities & Communications. Has an Integrated Word Processor & Phone Dialer That Allows User User to Speed up & Automate Entire Maintenance Program While Reducing Errors.
Oasis Pr.

CPRS: Coal Preparation Response Surfaces. Sep. 1983. *Compatible Hardware:* IBM PC, PC XT, PC AT & compatibles. *Operating System(s) Required:* MS-DOS, PC-DOS. *Language(s):* FORTRAN. *Memory Required:* 512k. *General Requirements:* Printer, plotter.
disk $12,000.00 (Order no.: CPRS).
Shows in Three Dimensional Form the Washability Characteristics of Coal & the Performance of Plant Equipment. The Graphic Output Enables the Analyst to See Coal Size, Density & Content on a 3D Mesh Surface. Useful in Wash Plant Design & Operation.
Geostat Systems International, Inc. (GSII).

CPS/PC. Jan. 1985. *Compatible Hardware:* IBM PC & compatibles, PC XT, PC AT. *Operating System(s) Required:* PC-DOS. *Memory Required:* 512k. *General Requirements:* Graphics adapter, pen plotter, hard disk, 8087 co-processor.
disk $2495.00-$4995.00.
Menu- & Prompt-Driven Processing System That Generates Surface Models Based on X, Y, Z Data Points Derived from a Data-Base Application Program or Manual or Key Entry. Generates Two-Dimensional, Profile , & Three-Dimensional Displays; Performs Single & Multiple Surface Operations; & Calculates Surface Trends. Users Can Automate Maps with Text Blocks, Data Point Posting, & Polyline Data Such As Lease Boundaries. Options Include Fault Handling, Volumetrics, & Seismic Migrations.
Radian Corp.

CPT: Current Procedural Terminology. *Version:* 1993. Dec. 1992. *Compatible Hardware:* IBM PC, XT, AT or compatible. *Items Included:* Disk & CPT 1993, Book.
disk $175.00 (ISBN 0-89970-520-0, Order no.: OP-052493).
Medical Terminology.
American Medical Assn.

CPT 1996 Codes on Disk. Edited by American Medical Association. Dec. 1995.
disk $129.95 (ISBN 1-57066-047-6).
Disk & Softbound Version of Physicians' Current Procedural Terminology Which Is Used to Accurately Code Insurance Forms for Reimbursement.
Practice Management Information Corp.

CPYAT2PC. *Compatible Hardware:* IBM PC AT, Compaq Deskpro 286, Zenith Z-200, Kaypro 286i, AT&T 6300+, Tandy 3000, Sperry PC/IT, HP Vectra PC, Wang APC. *Operating System(s) Required:* PC-DOS, MS-DOS. *Customer Support:* 9-5 Mon-Fri Pacific time.
disk $49.00.
Allows Copying of IBM PC AT Files for Use On IBM PCs & Compatibles with No Modification of Existing Hardware or Software. A 360k Floppy Drive Is Not Required As the Program Resides on AT's Hard Disk & Can Copy Entire Subdirectories in One Step.
Microbridge Computers.

CQ-3270-BSC. *Version:* 3.4. Oct. 1994. *Items Included:* User's manual. *Customer Support:* Annual Software Maintenance Agreement, 20 percent of list price. Free telephone technical support available at current hourly rates.
MS-DOS. IBM PCs, PS/2's, Laptops, notebooks or compatibles. $495.00-$695.00 (Order no.: CQ-3270 BSC (DOS)). *Nonstandard peripherals required:* If using Hayes AutoSync or Motorola Sync-Up modem, no board required. Any other modem, synchronous adapter card required. *Optimal configuration:* IBM PC or compatible, Hayes AutoSync or Motorola Sync-Up modem.
BSC Single User Solution Provides Interactive PC-to-Mainframe Communications with Features Such As IBM's IND$FILE File Transfer, Multiple Host Sessions, Auto-Dialing, Auto-Answer, Automatic File Naming, User-Remappable Keyboards IBM's APIs, X.25 Support, MS-DOS, IBM's ADLC Support, DATAMODE-FULL, & Hotkey Function.
CQ Computer Communications.

CQ-3270-SNA. *Version:* 3.4. Oct. 1994. *Items Included:* User's manual. *Customer Support:* Annual Software Maintenance Agreement, 20 percent of list price. Free telephone technical support available at current hourly rates.
MS-DOS. IBM PCs, PS/2's, Laptops, notebooks or compatibles. $495.00-$695.00 (Order no.: CQ-3270-SNA (DOS)). *Nonstandard peripherals required:* If using Hayes AutoSync or Motorola Sync-Up modem, no board required. Any other modem, synchronous adapter card required. *Optimal configuration:* IBM PC or compatible, Hayes AutoSync or Motorola Sync-Up modem.
OS/2. IBM PCs, PS/2, laptops, notebooks, or compatibles. $695.00-$995.00 (Order no.: CQ-3270-SNA (OS/2)). *Nonstandard peripherals required:* If using Hayes AutoSync or Motorola Sync-Up modem, no board required. Any other modem, synchronous adapter card required. *Optimal configuration:* IBM PC or compatible, Hayes AutoSync or Motorola Sync-Up modem.
SNA Single User Solution Provides Interactive PC-to-Mainframe Communications with Features Such As IBM's IND$FILE File Transfer, Multiple Host Sessions, Auto-Dialing, Auto-Answer, Automatic File Naming, User-Remappable Keyboards IBM's APIs, X.25 Support, MS-DOS or IBM's OS/2, IBM's ADLC Support, DATAMODE-FULL, & Hotkey Function.
CQ Computer Communications.

CQ-3270-SNA LAN. *Version:* 3.4. Oct. 1994. *Items Included:* User's manual. *Customer Support:* Annual Software Maintenance Agreement, 20 percent of list price. Free telephone technical support available at current hourly rates.
MS-DOS. IBM PCs, PS/2's, Laptops, notebooks or compatibles (70k). $2395.00-$19,995.00 (Order no.: CQ-3270-SNA LAN (DOS)). *Nonstandard peripherals required:* If using Hayes AutoSync or Motorola Sync-Up modem, no board required. Any other modem, synchronous adapter card required. *Optimal configuration:* IBM PC or compatible, Hayes AutoSync or Motorola Sync-Up modem. *Networks supported:* Novell, NETBIOS.
OS/2. IBM PCs, PS/2, laptops, notebooks, or compatibles. $3995.00-$29,995.00 (Order no.: CQ-3270-SNA LAN (OS/2)). *Nonstandard peripherals required:* If using Hayes AutoSync or Motorola Sync-Up modem, no board required. Any other modem, synchronous adapter card required. *Optimal configuration:* IBM PC or compatible, Hayes AutoSync or Motorola Sync-Up modem. *Networks supported:* Novell, NETBIOS.
SNA Local Area Network (LAN) Solution Provides Interactive PC-to-Mainframe Communications with Features Such As IBM's IND$FILE File Transfer, Multiple Host Sessions, Auto-Dialing, Auto-Answer, Automatic File Naming, User-Remappable Keyboards IBM's APIs, X.25 Support, MS-DOS or IBM's OS/2 IBM's ADLC Support, DATAMODE=FULL, & Hotkey Function.
CQ Computer Communications.

CQ-3770. *Version:* 4.0. Dec. 1995. *Items Included:* User's manual. *Customer Support:* Annual Software Maintenance Agreement, 20 percent of list price. Free telephone technical support provided for installation, additional support available at current hourly rates.
MS-DOS. IBM PCs, PS/2's, Laptops, notebooks or compatibles (90k). $695.00-$995.00 (Order no.: CQ-3770). *Nonstandard peripherals required:* If using Hayes AutoSync or Motorola Sync-Up modem, no board required. Any other modem, synchronous adapter card required. *Optimal configuration:* IBM PC or compatible, Hayes AutoSync or Motorola Sync-Up modem.
SNA RJE Single User Solution, Ideal for Batch File Transfers. Features Include Auto-Dialing, Auto-Answer, Automatic File Naming, Full Multiple Logical Unit Support, Data Compaction & Compression, Unattended Operation, Automatic ASCII/EBCDIC Translation, APIs, Multiple Printer Support, X.25 Support, & Scripting.
CQ Computer Communications.

CQ-3770 LAN. *Version:* 4.0. Dec. 1995. *Items Included:* User's manual. *Customer Support:* Annual Software Maintenance Agreement, 20 percent of list price. Free telephone technical support provided for installation, additional support available at current hourly rates.
MS-DOS. IBM PCs, PS/2's, Laptops, notebooks or compatibles (70k). $4995.00-$22,295.00 (Order no.: CQ-3770-LAN). *Nonstandard peripherals required:* If using Hayes AutoSync or Motorola Sync-Up modem, no board required. Any other mode, synchronous adapter card required. *Optimal configuration:* IBM PC or compatible, Hayes AutoSync or Motorola Sync-Up modem. *Networks supported:* Novell, NETBIOS.
SNA RJE Local Area Network (LAN) Solution, Ideal for Batch File Transfers. Features Include Auto-Dialing, Auto-Answer, Automatic File Naming, Full Multiple Logical Unit Support, Data Compaction & Compression, Unattended Operation, Automatic ASCII/EBCDIC Translation, APIs, Multiple Printer Support, X.25 Support, & Scripting.
CQ Computer Communications.

CQ-3780. *Version:* 3.0. Nov. 1995. *Items Included:* User's manual. *Customer Support:* Annual Software Maintenance Agreement, 20 percent of list price. Free telephone technical support provided for installation, additional support available at current hourly rates.
MS-DOS. IBM PCs, PS/2's, Laptops, notebooks or compatibles (70k). $495.00-$695.00 (Order no.: CQ-3780). *Nonstandard peripherals required:* If using Hayes AutoSync or Motorola Sync-Up modem, no board required. Any other modem, synchronous adapter card required. *Optimal configuration:* IBM PC or compatible, Hayes AutoSync or Motorola Sync-Up modem.
BSC RJE Single User Solution, Ideal for Batch File Transfers. This 2780/3780 Emulation Feature Includes Auto-Dialing, Auto-Answer, Data Compression, Unattended Operation, Automatic File Naming, Automatic ASCII/EBCDIC Translation, APIs, & Scripting.
CQ Computer Communications.

CQ-5250. *Version:* 3.4. Oct. 1994. *Items Included:* User's manual. *Customer Support:* Annual Software Maintenance Agreement, 20 percent of list price. Free telephone technical support provided for installation, additional support available at current hourly rates.
MS-DOS. IBM PCs, PS/2's, Laptops, notebooks or compatibles (100k). $495.00-$695.00 (Order no.: CQ-5250 (DOS)). *Nonstandard peripherals required:* If using Hayes AutoSync or Motorola Sync-Up modem, no board

TITLE INDEX

required. Any other modem, synchronous adapter card required. *Optimal configuration:* IBM PC or compatible, Hayes AutoSync or Motorola Sync-Up modem.
OS/2. IBM PCs, PS/2, laptops, notebooks, or compatibles. $695.00-$995.00 (Order no.: CQ-5250 (OS/2)). *Nonstandard peripherals required:* If using Hayes AutoSync or Motorola Sync-Up modem, no board required. Any other modem, synchronous adapter card required. *Optimal configuration:* IBM PC or compatible, Hayes AutoSync or Motorola Sync-Up modem.
SNA Single User Solution Provides Interactive PC-to-System 3X or AS/400 Communications, with Features Such As Multiple Host Sessions, Auto-Dialing, Auto-Answer, Automatic File Naming, User Remappable Keyboards, X.25 Support, MS-DOS or IBM's OS/2, IBM's ADLC Support, & Hotkey Function.
CQ Computer Communications.

CQ-5250 LAN. *Version:* 3.4. Oct. 1994. *Items Included:* User's manual. *Customer Support:* Annual Software Maintenance Agreement, 20 percent of list price. Free telephone technical support provided for installation, additional support available at current hourly rates.
MS-DOS. IBM PCs, PS/2's, Laptops, notebooks or compatibles (70k). $2395.00-$19,995.00 (Order no.: CQ-5250 LAN (DOS)). *Nonstandard peripherals required:* If using Hayes AutoSync or Motorola Sync-Up modem, no board required. Any other modem, synchronous adapter card required. *Optimal configuration:* IBM PC or compatible, Hayes AutoSync or Motorola Sync-Up modem. *Networks supported:* Novell, NETBIOS.
OS/2. IBM PCs, PS/2, laptops, notebooks, or compatibles. $3995.00-$29,995.00 (Order no.: CQ-5250 LAN (OS/2)). *Nonstandard peripherals required:* If using Hayes AutoSync or Motorola Sync-Up modem, no board required. Any other modem, synchronous adapter card required. *Optimal configuration:* IBM PC or compatible, Hayes AutoSync or Motorola Sync-Up modem. *Networks supported:* Novell, NETBIOS.
SNA Local Area Network (LAN) Solution Provides Interactive PC-to-System 3X or AS/400 Communications with Features Such As Multiple Host Sessions, Auto-Dialing, Auto-Answer, Automatic File Naming, User-Remappable Keyboards, X.25 Support, MS-DOS or IBM's OS/2, IBM's ADLC Support & Hotkey Function.
CQ Computer Communications.

CQS-Linkware. 1985. *Compatible Hardware:* IBM PC & compatibles, PC XT, PC AT. *Memory Required:* 400k. *General Requirements:* TSO for MVS or CMS for VM.
contact publisher for price.
Audit, Data Retrieval & Micro-Mainframe Link Software. Extracts Data from an IBM Mainframe File (Including Multiple Types of Database Management Systems) As Reports, Data Extracts & Mainframe Files. Extracts Can Be Formatted for Input into Specific PC Software. Transfers Data Between Micro & Mainframe Computers. Features a Report Writer, Active Data Dictionary, & Micro-Mainframe Link Software. Operates in Batch Mode.
Carleton Corp.

Crack Growth Analysis in Anisotropic Materials. A. Portela & M. H. Aliabadi. Sep. 1994. *Customer Support:* Fax.
MS-DOS 3.0 or higher. IBM PC & compatibles (4Mb). disk $460.00 (ISBN 1-56252-270-1). *Addl. software required:* Crack Growth Analysis using Boundary Elements Basic Package. *Optimal configuration:* Laser printer.
Unix. Sun, IBM (4Mb). software pkg. $460.00.
VMS. VAX (4Mb). disk $995.00.

Module on Anisotropic Materials to Work with Basic Package Which Performs Crack Growth Analysis Using the Boundary Element Method.
Computational Mechanics, Inc.

Crack Growth Analysis in Stiffened Sheets. A. Portela & M. H. Aliabadi. Sep. 1994. *Customer Support:* Fax.
MS-DOS 3.0 or higher. IBM PC & compatibles (4Mb). software pkg. $460.00 (ISBN 1-56252-271-X). *Addl. software required:* Crack Growth Analysis Using Boundary Elements Basic Package. *Optimal configuration:* Laser printer.
Unix. Sun, IBM (4Mb). software pkg. $460.00.
VMS. VAX (4Mb). software pkg. $460.00.
Module on Stiffeners to Work with Basic Package Which Performs Crack Growth Analysis Using the Boundary Element Method.
Computational Mechanics, Inc.

Crack Growth Analysis Using Boundary Elements: Basic Package. A. Portela & M. H. Aliabadi. May 1992. *Items Included:* User manual; book: Dual Boundary Element Analysis of Crack Growth; example problems. *Customer Support:* Fax support.
MS-DOS 3.0 or higher. IBM PC & compatibles (4Mb). software pkg. $1035.45 (ISBN 1-56252-115-2). *Optimal configuration:* Laser printer.
Unix. Sun & IBM (4Mb). software pkg. $1035.45. *Optimal configuration:* Laser printer.
VMS. VAX (4Mb). software pkg. $1035.45. *Optimal configuration:* Laser printer.
This Software Uses the State-of-the-Art Boundary Element Method, Eliminating the Difficult & Time-Consuming Task of Remeshing. It Evaluates Stress Intensity Factors, for Which the BEM Is Renowned. It Uses the Established Criteria for Crack Propagation & Evaluates the Residual Strength As Well As Fatigue Life Calculation.
Computational Mechanics, Inc.

Crack Growth Analysis Using Boundary Elements: Three-Module Package. A. Portela & M. H. Aliabadi. Sep. 1994. *Items Included:* Crack Growth Analysis Using Boundary Elements: Anisotropy Module, Stiffener Module, Thermoelasticity Module. *Customer Support:* Fax.
MS-DOS 3.0 or higher. IBM PC & compatibles (4Mb). software pkg. $1074.00 (ISBN 1-56252-272-8). *Addl. software required:* Crack Growth Analysis Using Boundary Elements Basic Package. *Optimal configuration:* Laser printer.
Unix. Sun, IBM (4Mb). software pkg. $1074.00.
VMS. VAX (4Mb). software pkg. $1074.00.
Anisotropy, Stiffener & Thermoelasticity Modules to Go with Basic Package Which Performs Crack Growth Analysis Using the Boundary Element Method.
Computational Mechanics, Inc.

Cranston Manor Adventure. *Compatible Hardware:* IBM. *Memory Required:* 128k.
disk $19.95.
Fantasy Exploration Simulation in Which the Player Explores a Fantasy Land Using the Computer (an Android) As Eyes, Ears, Hands & Legs. Player Controls the Android by Sending It Two Word Sentences Consisting of a Verb & a Noun. The Objective Is to Find the Deserted Cranston Manor, Enter It, Collect the 16 Treasures & Leave.
Dynacomp, Inc.

Craps. *Version:* 2.1. 1981. *Compatible Hardware:* Apple, Franklin Ace, Laser 128. *Operating System(s) Required:* Apple DOS 3.3. *Language(s):* BASIC. *Memory Required:* 48k.
disk $8.95.
illustration files on disk avail.
Crap Table Game Simulation for One or Two Players.
Artsci, Inc.

CREATEABASE

Craps Academy. *Compatible Hardware:* Commodore Amiga.
3.5" disk $24.95.
Learn & Play Craps.
Microillusions, Inc.

Crash Barrier. *Version:* 1.1. Patrick Buckland. Oct. 1991. *Customer Support:* Free phone support.
Macintosh Plus or higher (2Mb). 3.5" disk $79.95.
Utility That Offers Alternatives to System Errors. Features: System Error Recovery & Prevention. Also Automatically Saves Data.
Casady & Greene, Inc.

Crazy Cars. *Compatible Hardware:* Commodore Amiga, IBM PC, Apple Macintosh, Atari ST, Commodore 64.
3.5" disk $39.95.
Drive Four Fast Cars on Six Race Courses.
Titus Software Corp.

Crazy Chase. *Compatible Hardware:* Atari 400, 800. *Language(s):* Atari BASIC. *Memory Required:* 24k.
disk $21.95.
cassette $17.95.
Arcade Game.
Dynacomp, Inc.

Create. *Compatible Hardware:* Apple Macintosh. *General Requirements:* Finder 4.1 or 5.3.
3.5" disk $8.00.
Pre-Writing Program Designed to Stimulate Ideas about the Direction a Document Should Take to Achieve Its Purpose.
Kinko's.

Create a Calendar. *Compatible Hardware:* Apple II & compatibles, Commodore 64/128, IBM PC & compatibles.
contact publisher for price.
Lets Users Design Daily, Weekly, Monthly, or Yearly Calendars. Includes Sets of Pictures, Graphics, & Fonts. Allows the Use of Pictures from the GRAPHICS SCRAPBOOKS, or PRINT SHOP Compatible Graphics Disks.
Epyx, Inc.

Create Your Dream Job: Four Key Questions to Design Your Life's Work. Feb. 1995. *Items Included:* Career Design Journal. *Customer Support:* Toll-free telephone number for technical support. 90 days warranty for defects in materials & workmanship.
Macintosh System 7.0. Macintosh with 68040 processor (5Mb). CD-ROM disk $69.95 (ISBN 1-886806-00-4). *Nonstandard peripherals required:* Double speed CD-ROM drive. *Addl. software required:* QuickTime (included on CD-ROM disc).
Microsoft Windows 3.1. PC compatibles; 486/33 MHz (runs slow on 386/25MHz) (8Mb). CD-ROM disk $69.95. *Nonstandard peripherals required:* 256 color display card (640x480); double speed CD-ROM drive. *Addl. software required:* QuickTime for Windows (included on CD-ROM disc).
Helps User Clarify Talents, Passions, Purpose, & Vision to Examine Options & Create a Vision & Plan for What You Want to Be. This Highly Interactive CD-ROM Program Includes Information, Exercises, Video, & Real-Life Examples to Help You Be Your Own Career Counselor.
Wilson Learning Corp.

CREATEABASE. *Version:* 7.0. NDX Corp. Sep. 1992. *Customer Support:* 800 number, free on-site training.
contact publisher for price.
General Purpose Text & Data Retrieval Product Which Provides High-Speed Search & Analysis of

Numeric & Coded Data Bases. Includes Modular Library, a Library of Function Calls to Allow Access to All CREATABASE Functions from Within a Company's Own Applications. Solution to Applications Requiring a Mixture of Text & Structured Data.
NDX Corp.

Creating a Memory of Casual Relationships: An Integration of Empirical & Explanation-Based Learning Methods. Michael J. Pazzani. 1990. *Customer Support:* 90 days limited warranty.
MS-DOS. IBM & compatibles (512K). disk $10.95, incl. manual (ISBN 1-56321-038-X). *Addl. software required:* LISP.
IBM & compatibles (512k). 3.5" disk $10.95, incl. manual (ISBN 1-56321-037-1). *Addl. software required:* LISP.
Macintosh Plus or higher (1Mb). 3.5" disk $10.95, incl. manual (ISBN 1-56321-039-8). *Addl. software required:* LISP.
cloth text, 360 pages $69.95 (ISBN 0-8058-0629-6).
paper text $29.95 (ISBN 0-8058-0789-6).
Artificial Intelligence Application.
Lawrence Erlbaum Assocs. Software & Alternate Media, Inc.

Creating User Pathways to Electronic Information: Synopsis of the 1991 Faxon Institute Annual Conference. Sep. 1991.
MS-DOS 2.0 or higher. IBM PC or compatible (126k). disk $50.00.
Captures the Exciting Dialog, Style, & Flow of Information Exchanged by Presenters & Participants Whose Conversations Went Beyond the Limitations Imposed by Traditional Conference Settings. This Electronic Publication Includes Summaries of the Presentations At the Assembled Conference, & the Exchanges & Related Ideas of Over 50 Electronic Conference Participants. Using the Hypertext Interface, Readers Can: Zero-In on the Sections of Most interest; Link to Related Material Throughout the Publication; Search for Any Word in the Text; Print Items of Particular Interest; Benefit from Participants' Networking; Review Reports on In-Progress Research & Suggested Related Readings.
Faxon Institute.

The Creator. *Version:* 5.0. Dec. 1988. *Items Included:* 130-page manual, applications disk. *Customer Support:* Free phone support, 30-day money-back guarantee.
PC-DOS 2.1. IBM PC or compatible (384k). disk $50.00. *Addl. software required:* Microsoft Quickbasic 4.0 or higher. *Optimal configuration:* IBM PC, DOS 3.1 or higher, Microsoft Quickbasic 4.0 or higher.
Generates & Reads Data Dictionaries & Entry Screens, & Writes Program & File Documentation. Includes a Report Program Generator with Import & Export Capabilities. The Creator Includes a Fast General-Purpose Sort, for Database Applications.
TNT Software.

The Creator. *Version:* 6.0. Jan. 1991. *Items Included:* 158 page manual. *Customer Support:* Free phone support, 30-day money-back guarantee.
MS-DOS 3.x or higher. IBM-PC, XT, AT, or 386 (640k). $99.00. *Addl. software required:* Quick BASIC 4.5 or BASIC PDS 7.0 or higher. *Optimal configuration:* MS-DOS 3.3, 640k RAM, 10 Mb hard disk space, BASIC PDS 7.1 (microsoft). *Networks supported:* All known.
MS-DOS 2.0. IBM compatible (512k). $99.00. *Addl. software required:* Quick BASIC 4.5 or Power BASIC 3.0. *Optimal configuration:* MS-DOS 2.0, two floppy drives, Quick BASIC 4.0, 512k RAM. *Networks supported:* All known.
Database Applications for Single or Multi-User Systems Which Allow Multi-Level Linked Files. Sophisticated Error Checking. Report Generation. Fast Sort Included. Also Includes Source Code for Library Routines, a Random File Editor, & Cross-Reference Program.
TNT Software.

Creator XCMD: (Developer's Version).
Compatible Hardware: Apple Macintosh, Macintosh Plus. *General Requirements:* HyperCard.
3.5" disk $5.00.
Allows Users to Create Stand-Alone Applications from Within HyperCard Stacks.
Comlink.

Credit Committee. *Version:* I.B.4. Jun. 1987. *Compatible Hardware:* IBM PC & compatibles. *Memory Required:* 512k. *General Requirements:* Lotus 1-2-3.
$395.00.
optional RMA Reporter module available for $100.00.
Compares, Analyzes, & Graphs 12 Periods of Financial Statements for Any Industry. Reports Include Changes from Prior Period, Reconciliations & Industry Comparisons (RMA or Other), Cash-Flow Analysis, & Financial Ratios (Liquidity, Efficiency, Capital Structure, Profitability, & Altman Z-Score). Nineteen Graphs Cover 64 Ratios & Balances. Macro-Driven Worksheet Application for 1-2-3.
C. M. Phelps & Co.

The Credit Rating Booster. *Compatible Hardware:* TRS-80 Model I, Model III, Model 4 with Level II BASIC. (source code included). *Memory Required:* 16k.
disk $29.95.
Designed to Give the Best Interest Rates on a Mortgage, Auto Loan or Any Other Type of Credit.
Dynacomp, Inc.

The Credit Rating Booster. 1995. *Items Included:* Full manual. *Customer Support:* Free telephone support - 90 days, 30-day warranty.
MS-DOS 3.2 or higher. 286 (584k). disk $19.95. *Nonstandard peripherals required:* CGA/EGA/VGA.
Designed & Written by a Data Processing Consultant to Major U.S. Banks. It Provides a Well Organized Printout, or Full Screen Displays of Your Up-to-Date Credit History in a Way That Is Designed to Suitably Impress a Loan Officer.
Dynacomp, Inc.

The Credit Reporter. 1986. *Compatible Hardware:* IBM PC series, COMPAQ. *Operating System(s) Required:* MS-DOS. *Language(s):* BASIC. *Memory Required:* 512k.
disk $395.00.
Contour Software, Inc.

Credit Union Management System.
contact publisher for price.
Illini Data Systems.

Creepy Crawlies.
MS-DOS 5.0 or higher, Windows 3.1 or higher. 386 processor or higher (4Mb). CD-ROM disk $39.00 (Order no.: R1121). *Nonstandard peripherals required:* CD-ROM drive. *Optimal configuration:* 386 processor operating at 16Mhz or higher, MS-DOS 5.0 or higher, Windows 3.1 or higher, 30Mb hard drive, mouse, VGA graphic adapter & VGA color monitor (SVGA recommended), 4Mb RAM, external speakers or headphones (with sound card) that are Sound Blaster compatible.
Macintosh (4Mb). (Order no.: R1121A).
Nonstandard peripherals required: 14" color monitor or larger, CD-ROM drive.
A Unique, Informative Reference Exploring 74 of the Most Creepy Critters Ever to Stalk the Earth. This Multimedia Guide Uses Full-Motion Video Clips, Full-Color Screen Images, & Text Description of Each Animal in Both English & French. For Students of All Ages.
Library Video Co.

Cribbage. *Compatible Hardware:* TRS-80 Model I, Model III, Model 4. *Memory Required:* 64k.
disk $19.95 (Order no.: D8CRI).
This Game Plays According to Hoyle. Offers a "Hint" Mode When in a Pinch - If You Are Not Winning.
The Alternate Source.

Cribbage. *Version:* 2.0. *Compatible Hardware:* IBM. *Memory Required:* 128k.
disk $29.95.
2-Handed Version of Classic Card Game.
Dynacomp, Inc.

The Cricket in Times Square. Intentional Education Staff & George Selden. Apr. 1996.
School ver.. Mac System 7.1 or higher. Macintosh (4Mb). 3.5" disk contact publisher for price (ISBN 1-57204-375-X). *Nonstandard peripherals required:* 256 color monitor, hard drive, printer.
Lab pack. Mac System 7.1 or higher. Macintosh (4Mb). 3.5" disk contact publisher for price (ISBN 1-57204-351-2). *Nonstandard peripherals required:* 256 color monitor, hard drive, printer 330 # 03.00 contact publisher for price.
Site license. Mac System 7.1 or higher. Macintosh (4Mb). (ISBN 1-57204-351-2). *Nonstandard peripherals required:* 256 color monitor, hard drive, printer.
School ver.. Windows 3.1 or higher. IBM/Tandy & 100% compatibles (4Mb). disk contact publisher for price (ISBN 1-57204-352-0). *Nonstandard peripherals required:* VGA or SVGA 640 x 480 resolution, 256 monitor, mouse, sound device.
Lab pack. Windows 3.1 or higher. IBM/Tandy & 100% compatibles (4Mb). disk contact publisher for price (ISBN 1-57204-377-6). *Nonstandard peripherals required:* VGA or SVGA 640 x 480 resolution, 256 monitor, mouse, sound device.
Site license. Windows 3.1 or higher. IBM/Tandy & 100% compatibles (4Mb). disk contact publisher for price (ISBN 1-57204-353-9). *Nonstandard peripherals required:* VGA or SVGA 640 x 480 resolution, 256 monitor, mouse, sound device.
This companion for young adult literature is ideal for students who don't know how to start that book report, or give that needed summary. Gentle prompts throughout the guide section of the program include Warm-up Connections, Thinking about Plot, Quoting & Noting, Keeping a Journal, If I were ---' Responding to Questions, Using Quotations, Taking a Personal View, Write to Others, & Write a Sequel.
Lawrence Productions, Inc.

The Criminal Justice System. *Version:* 4.0. Dec. 1989. *Items Included:* Application users manual-spiral bound. *Customer Support:* 1 year maintenance & telephone support; extensive training & hardware maintenance available; 1 year warranty.
DOS 3.x or Unix. IBM PC or compatible (640K), Unix compatible. contact publisher for price. *Networks supported:* Novell, Syntax TotalNet. UNIX, MS-DOS. HP, IBM, NCR, call publisher about others. contact publisher for price.
Provides Automated Record Keeping & Analysis for Major Functions of Public Safety Agencies

Including Police, Jails, Detectives, Animal Control, Courts, & Emergency Communications Centers. Includes the Following Modules: Records Manager (Police); Jailmanager; Courtmanager; Computer Aided Dispatch & Animal Manager.
OCS/Syntax.

Crisis Mountain. (Series A).
All Apple IIs. disk $5.00. *Optimal configuration:* Apple II, joystick.
You're in a Life or Death Race Against the Clock, with an Erupting Volcano & Hidden Bombs Waiting to Blow You Skyhigh! Nine Skill Levels on Two High-Res Screens Give You All the Action & Excitement You Can Handle, As You Try to Defuse Ticking Time Bombs Before They Turn the Western Hemisphere into a Smoldering Wasteland! You Have to Climb, Crawl & Leap Through the Treacherous Caverns...Avoid Tumbling Boulders, Falling Debris, Boiling Lava. And Watch Out for Bertram, the Radioactive Bat.
Word Assocs., Inc.

CRISP-R Real Estate Accounting. Version: 1.30. Oct. 1991. *Items Included:* 90 page user manual. *Customer Support:* One year of updates & telephone support.
$55.00.
Bookkeeping System for up to 100 or More Different Properties or Activities for One Year Using Just One Bank Account (or up to 3 Bank Accounts) for All Properties. Reports Are Made for All Properties Together or for Any One Property. It Is Appropriate for Property Management of Multiple Commercial, Investment, or Residential Properties.
James W. Funsten Pub.

CRISP Real Estate Accounting. Version: 3.30. 1990. *Items Included:* 80 page manual. *Customer Support:* One year of updates & one year of telephone support.
$55.00.
Bookkeeping System That Can Support 250 Individual Databases, Making It Appropriate for Property Management of Multiple Commercial or Investment Properties, or for Individual Accounting for Several Separate Projects or Professional Activities. It Is Designed to Keep the Accounting for Each Property or Activity Completely Separate from Any Other Property or Activity & to Maintain up to Three Separate Bank Accounts for Each.
James W. Funsten Pub.

Criterion CAE/CAD Schematic & PC-Board Design System. *Items Included:* Bound manual. *Customer Support:* Free hotline - no time limit; 30 day limited warranty; updates are $5/disk plus S&H.
MS-DOS. IBM PC/AT or higher (640k). full system $649.95. *Nonstandard peripherals required:* 80x87 math coprocessor; one 1.2Mb floppy & one hard disk; communications port & mouse; printer parallel port; EGA or better (640 x 350 or higher) graphics card with at least 256k RAM.
demo pkg. $10.00.
Completely Integrated Schematic & PCB Layout System. It Features Extensive Analog, Digital, RF, & SMD Support, Global Block Editing Commands, Easy-to-Use Definable Menus, & Can Handle Round Boards & Curved Traces. Up to 50 Design Layers May Be Treated.
Dynacomp, Inc.

Criterium. Version: 1.1. Feb. 1991. *Items Included:* three (3) bound manuals, one (1) Quick Reference Card, and one (1) Quick Tour Book. *Customer Support:* Customer dial-up support, long distance phone charges; customer on-site support, travel & expenses; free customer product training; free pre & post sale support;

unconditional 60 day money back guarantee; software updates available.
MS DOS 2.1 or later. IBM PC XT, AT, PS/2 or 100% compatable (512k). disk $495.00.
Desktop Decision Support Software. Combines Hard Data with Gut Instinct, Organizes & Analyzes Decision Components, Calculates the Best Decision Choice. Accepts Graphic, Numeric & Verbal Ratings. Provides Concise Executive Summaries & Supporting Data Reports in Order to Document & Present a Recommendation. Intuitive User-Interface. Seven Prebuilt Decision Models Included.
Sygenex, Inc.

Critical Care Nursing Simulations: Endocrine System. 1988. *Compatible Hardware:* IBM PC & compatibles. *Operating System(s) Required:* MS-DOS. *Memory Required:* 512k.
disk per module $725.00 (Order no.: CCN-3800).
5 Computerized Clinical Simulations for Critical Care Nursing Education/Module.
Educational Software Concepts, Inc.

The Critical Care Support System. 1982. *Compatible Hardware:* IBM PC AT, PC XT, PS/2 Model 30. *Operating System(s) Required:* MS-DOS. *Language(s):* C. *Memory Required:* 640k.
contact publisher for price.
Comprises a Group of Interactive Computer Programs Designed to Evaluate the Cardiovascular, Respiratory, Fluid Balance, Renal Status, & Nutritional Profiles of the Patient in Question. Uses Inputted Values Recorded in the Critical Care Environment, & Can Be Either Manually Entered or Automatically Acquired at the Source.
Trinity Computing Systems, Inc.

Critical Date System Jr. Version: 8. Feb. 1979. *Items Included:* Binder with documentation. *Customer Support:* 1 yr. maintenance $50 entitles user to phone support, quarterly newsletter & enhancements made available for their computer at no charge.
DOS Ver. 3.1 or higher. IBM PC & compatibles (470k). disk $200.00. *Nonstandard peripherals required:* Hard drive.
Schedule Multiple Activities from a Single Date Automatically for One Individual or 5 at One Time. Will Locate & Display/Print All Conflicts. Can Generate Reports for One Employee or the Firm for a Given Date, Client or Type of Activity. Integrates with TABS III Jr.
Software Technology, Inc.

Critical Date System JR-M. Version: 8. Feb. 1979. *Items Included:* Binder with documentation. *Customer Support:* 1 yr. maintenance $65 entitles user to phone support, quarterly newsletter & enhancements made available for their computer at no charge.
DOS Ver. 3.1 or higher. IBM PC & compatibles (470k). disk $300.00. *Nonstandard peripherals required:* Hard drive. *Networks supported:* Novell, IBM PC Networks & compatibles.
Multi-User Version of CDS Jr Allowing up to 10 Workstations to Enter & Retrieve Appointments & Critical Date Information. Allows the Scheduling of up to 5 Employees.
Software Technology, Inc.

Critical Mass: America's Race to Build the Atomic Bomb. 1996. *Items Included:* Manual, registration card. *Customer Support:* Phone technical & customer support Mon-Fri 9:00-5:00 PST. Email & Web-site support.
Microsoft Windows 3.1, Windows 95.
Multimedia PC with 486/33 or higher (8Mb). CD-ROM disk $45.00-$55.00 (ISBN 1-886802-02-5). *Nonstandard peripherals required:*

256-color Super VGA display, double-speed CD-ROM drive, 8-bit Windows-compatible sound card & speakers, mouse.
System 7.1. Macintosh 25MHz 68030 or higher (LCIII, IIVX, Centris, Quadra, performa, or higher) (8Mb, 12Mb for Power Mac). CD-ROM disk $45.00-$55.00 (ISBN 1-886802-03-3). *Nonstandard peripherals required:* Double-speed CD-ROM drive, 13" monitor or higher, 256 colors.
Discover the Extraordinary Science & People Behind a Pivotal Event in World History - the Building & Testing of the First Atomic Bomb. Critical Mass Is a Engrossing Multimedia CD-ROM Which Takes You Directly into the World of the Manhattan Project & the Renowned Scientists Responsible for One of the Most Provocative Scientific Achievements of Our Time.
Continuum Productions.

Critical Path Analysis. *Customer Support:* 800-929-8117 (customer service).
MS-DOS. Apple II. disk $49.99 (ISBN 0-87007-833-X).
Allows a Variable Maximum Number of Nodes & Paths Depending on Memory Size.
SourceView Software International.

Critical Path Method & Job Scheduling Program: CPMPERT. Version: 2.0. William W. Smith. Sep. 1987. *Compatible Hardware:* Apple II; DEC Rainbow, DEC VT180; Hewlett-Packard; IBM PC; Kaypro; Morrow; North Star; Osborne; Superbrain; TRS-80 Model I, Model III; Vector Graphics; Victor; Zenith. *Operating System(s) Required:* CP/M, CP/M-86, MS-DOS, PC-DOS. *Language(s):* CB-80. *Memory Required:* CP/M 64K, MS-DOS 256k. *General Requirements:* 2 disk drives, printer.
disk $249.00.
8" disk $249.00.
3.5" disk $249.00.
demo disk & documentation $38.00.
Job Scheduling Tool That Allows User to Evaluate the Status & Relative Importance of up to 700 Activities in a Project. Uses Both the Critical Path Method (CPM) & the Project Evaluation Review Technique (PERT). Reports Include: A Critical Path Report, an Activity Schedule Report, & Gantt Chart in Bar Graph Form. Features Include User Defined Hoildays, Printer Output Options, Special Weekday Modes, User Defined Calendar Files, & Automatic Disk Storage of All Project Data.
Elite Software Development, Inc.

Critical Path Project Management. *Items Included:* Bound manual. *Customer Support:* Free hotline - no time limit; 30 day limited warranty; updates are $5/disk plus S&H.
MS-DOS 2.0 or higher. IBM & compatibles (128k). full system $279.95. *Nonstandard peripherals required:* Two drives (or one drive & a hard disk); 80-column (or wider) printer.
demo disk $5.00.
Schedule Project Operations with Respect to Time Periods & Cost Constraints, Using Critical Path Method.
Dynacomp, Inc.

Critical Path Project Management - M2M. Version: 07/1991. 1979. *Operating System(s) Required:* MS-DOS, PC-DOS. *Language(s):* Compiled & Assembly Language. *Memory Required:* 448k. *Customer Support:* Technical hotline, "Lifetime" support at no charge.
disk $99.00.
Critical Path Project Management - M2M Uses CPM to Schedule Project Operations Against Time Periods & Cost Constraints. Capacity of 1400 Tasks (MS-DOS Version). Keeps Records of Actual Costs Versus to Budget by Materials, Overhead, & Labor. Variable Work Week, 40

Holidays. Calculates the Critical Path, Then Prints a Gantt Bar Chart, PERT Report, Cost Report & Activity List. Reports by Responsibility & for Overall Job. Tasks May Be Reorganized in Mid-Project for "What if . . ." Studies & Changes of Concept. Fully Compiled. Prompted, Interactive Inputs. Windowed Pop-Up Screens, Advanced User Interface, Automatic Installation.
MC2 Engineering Software.

Critical Path Scheduling. *Version:* 4.0. *Compatible Hardware:* Altos; AT&T; Compaq; IBM PC XT, PC AT, PC RT, 386, 486, RS6000. *Operating System(s) Required:* PC-DOS/MS-DOS, XENIX, UNIX V, Networks, AIX. *Language(s):* ACUCOBOL. *Memory Required:* 640k. *Customer Support:* Available with 800 number, regional & onsite training. contact publisher for price.
Enables Milestone Reporting, Holiday & Calendar Files, Track Total Float, Free Float, Resource Management, Time & Equipment Control & More.
Pro-Mation, Inc.

Critics Choice. Free Fall Associates, Microids Staff et al. Mar. 1995. *Items Included:* 1 perfect bound manual & 2 data cards. *Customer Support:* 30 day limited warranty.
DOS 5.0 or higher. IBM PC compatible with CD-ROM, Hard drive & Mouse (4Mb). CD-ROM disk $39.95 (ISBN 0-917059-22-0, Order no.: 062381). *Optimal configuration:* 386 required, 486 recommended.
Compilation Product Including Archon Ultra, Ultimate Domain, Dark Legions Serf City: Life Is Feudal, Chessmaster 3000.
Strategic Simulations, Inc.

CROMIX Plus. *Compatible Hardware:* Cromemco Systems. *Memory Required:* 1024k.
$1500.00.
Multi-User, Multi-Tasking UNIX-Like Operating System.
Cromemco, Inc.

Crop Duster. *Compatible Hardware:* Commodore 64, 128.
$29.95 (Order no.: SOFC64-05-004).
Used in Conjunction with COMET for Doing Isometric Exercises While Playing a Game.
Bodylog.

Crop Management System. *Compatible Hardware:* IBM PC, PC XT & compatibles.
$500.00.
Farm Management Systems of Mississippi, Inc.

Crop Production: Decision Aid. Merle W. Wagner. 1982. *Compatible Hardware:* Apple II Plus, IIe, IIc; IBM. *Operating System(s) Required:* Apple DOS 3.3, MS-DOS 2.0. *Language(s):* BASIC. *Memory Required:* 48k, 640k. *General Requirements:* Printer.
disk $29.95 (ISBN 0-922900-11-6, Order no.: CFD-112).
Designed for Budget Analysis of a Small Grains Operation. Accommodates up to 50 Students on an Individual Basis, 33 Data Entries, & 10 Calculations.
Cherrygarth, Inc.

Crop Production Records. Merle W. Wagner. 1981. *Compatible Hardware:* Apple II Plus, IIe, IIc; IBM. *Operating System(s) Required:* Apple DOS 3.3, MS-DOS 2.0. *Language(s):* BASIC. *Memory Required:* 48k, 640k. *General Requirements:* Printer.
disk $49.95, incl. manual (ISBN 0-922900-01-9, Order no.: CFR-111).
Income/Expense Information for Individual Fields. Useful for Any Small Grain. Four-Hundred Fields per Data Disk.
Cherrygarth, Inc.

Crop Weather Analyst. *Version:* 2.31. Jun. 1990. *Compatible Hardware:* IBM PC. *Operating System(s) Required:* PC-DOS/MS-DOS 2.1 to 3.3. *Language(s):* Machine. *Memory Required:* 512k. *Items Included:* disk, user's manual, & normal data. *Customer Support:* free telephone support.
disk $330.00.
Modular System of Weather & Crop Application Programs. In Order to Produce Estimates of Crop Development, Soil Moisture, & Crop Stress, the Integrated Software Utilizes Temperature, Precipitation, & Three More Optional Weather Variables. With Editing, Processing, & Report Functions Controlled by Menus, the Daily Weather Data Is Entered Via the Keyboard.
Climate Assessment Technology, Inc.

Crop Weather Analyst - Irrigator. Oct. 1985. *Operating System(s) Required:* PC-DOS 2.x-3.1, MS-DOS. *Memory Required:* 640k. *Items Included:* disks, user's manual, & normal weather data. *Customer Support:* free telephone support.
disk $560.00.
A Weather & Field Application Program for Crop Irrigation Scheduling & Other Management Functions Conducted by Professionals Handling Large Acreages. Provides Interactive Menu-Driven Operation, Including Fully Integrated Models of the Climate-Crop-Soil System. Outputs Include Daily Soil & Crop Moisture Estimates & Projections along with Graphical Displays of Most Quantities.
Climate Assessment Technology, Inc.

Crops Management. Agri-Management Services, Inc. *Compatible Hardware:* TI Professional. *Operating System(s) Required:* MS-DOS. *Memory Required:* 64k. *General Requirements:* Printer.
$495.00.
Provides 10-Year Record of Individual Field from Rainfall Through Lab Soil Analysis Recommendation. Also Includes Farm Equipment Program, Scheduling Routine & Payroll Accumulation Routine.
Texas Instruments, Personal Productivit.

Crops Records. *Compatible Hardware:* Apple II Plus, IIe; IBM. *Language(s):* BASIC. *Memory Required:* 48k, 640k.
disk $49.95.
back-up disk $9.95.
manual $19.95.
Generates Written Reports in Detailed Form for Each Individual Field, Individual Crop, or the Totals of All Fields Involved in the Farming Operation. All Expenses for Individual Fields Are Computed for Totals per Field Along with Most per Acre. Grain Sales Can Be Entered for Any Degree of Moisture & the Program Computes the Dried Grain in Pounds & Bushels. Income Is Computed for Totals per Individual Field & Income per Acre.
Cherrygarth, Inc.

Cross-Assemblers. *Compatible Hardware:* IBM PC, Motorola. *Operating System(s) Required:* OS-9, MS-DOS, UNIX, SKDOS. *Language(s):* Assembly (source code included). *Memory Required:* 64k.
disk $50.00 ea.
Set. $200.00.
Enables Program Development on 6809 or 68000 Computer System for 1802/5, 680X, 6502/3, 8080/5, 8048, 8051, Z-8, Z-80, 68000, 32000, 68HC11, 6301/3 Systems. Provides the Assembly Language & Listing Formats Which Are Standard on the Target Machine.
Computer Systems Consultants.

Cross Connect. *Version:* 4.0. Oct. 1990. *Compatible Hardware:* IBM PC & compatibles. *Operating System(s) Required:* PC-DOS/MS-DOS OS/2. *Memory Required:* 32k. *General Requirements:* Hard disk. *Items Included:* Cross Connect Outbound plus Cross Connect Inbound. *Customer Support:* Free.
Integrated dial in/out comm software. $495.00 1 modem version; $995.00 5 modem version; $1995.00 20 modem version.
All Features of Cross Connect Inbound & Outbound So You Can Dial in & Out of up to 20 Modems Located Anywhere on a LAN. TSR's Run in Background So No Dedicated Machine Required. Runs on All IPX & Netbios LANs. Compatible with All Modems.
Smith Micro Software, Inc.

Cross Connect Inbound. *Version:* 4.0. Aug. 1990. *Customer Support:* Free.
MS-DOS. IBM PC (30k). $295.00 1 modem version; $495.00 5 modem version; $995.00 20 modem version (ISBN 0-923426-58-2).
Remote Access to LAN Network Services. Dial in to up to 20 PCs Located Anywhere on a LAN to Remote Control Server Drives or Hard Drives. TSRs are 11k & Run in Background So No Need to Dedicate a PC for a Server. Password Protection. Upgrade to Dial Out.
Smith Micro Software, Inc.

Cross Connect Outbound. *Version:* 4.0. Jan. 1989. *Compatible Hardware:* IBM PC & compatibles. *Operating System(s) Required:* PC-DOS/MS-DOS, PS/2. *Memory Required:* 11k, recommended 512k. *General Requirements:* Hard disk. *Customer Support:* Free.
$295.00 1 modem version; $495.00 5 modem version; $995.00 20 modem version.
Allows Access to Any Modem (up to 20), Located on Any Networked PC, from Any Location on the Network, Without Affecting the User of the Terminal with the Installed Modem. Has Pop-Up Access Features, Allows File Transfers, & Offers Optional Security Access & Password Protection. X, Y Modem G, Z, ASCII File Transfer; Pull down Menus; Mouse Support; 38.4 BPS Support; Upgrade to Dial In.
Smith Micro Software, Inc.

Cross-Informant Program for the CBCL/4-18, YSR, & TRF. *Version:* 4.1. Thomas M. Achenbach. Jun. 1993. *Items Included:* Detailed manual. *Customer Support:* Free telephone support with no time limit.
MS-DOS. IBM-PC compatibles with hard disk (512k). disk $295.00 (ISBN 0-938565-31-1). *Optimal configuration:* IBM-PC compatible with 512k, hard disk, & printer capable of 132 character lines if user wishes to print profiles.
For Entering & Scoring the CBCL/4-18, Youth Self-Report, & Teacher's Report Form. Options Include Storing Scores for Analysis, Printing Profiles, & Comparing Scores from up to Five Forms. Computes Q Correlations Between Problem Item Scores & Between Syndrome Scale Scores for All Combinations of Informants. 1993 Version Computes Intraclass Correlations with Profile Types.
Univ. of Vermont, Dept. of Psychiatry.

Cross Reference Utility. *Compatible Hardware:* HP 150 Touchscreen.
3.5" disk $49.00 (Order no.: 92248BA).
Productivity Aid to Programmers Using Series 100/BASIC on the Touchscreen. Using a Standard BASIC File, User Can Generate a Complete Cross-Reference Listing Which Includes Variable Names, BASIC Function Names, & Math Operators, All Referenced by Line Number, & Resolved & Unresolved Line References. Output Can Be Directed to a Printer or a Disk File.
Hewlett-Packard Co.

Cross Reference Utility (CRF): A Programming Aid for the IBM PC. Sumar Corporation. Oct. 1983. *Compatible Hardware:* IBM PC. *Operating System(s) Required:* PC-DOS 1.1. *Language(s):* BASIC (source code included). *Memory Required:* 64k.
  disk $29.95, incl. bklt. (ISBN 0-13-194746-X).
  Provides Listing of Variables Within BASIC Program, Allowing User to Review, Analyze, & Modify Program. Also Helps Locate & Correct Typographical Errors, Identify Frequently Used Variables, & Change Variable Names When Necessary. Includes Booklet & Software Package.
  Prentice Hall.

Cross-Reference Words Database. 1996. *Items Included:* Manual. *Customer Support:* One year of the CSAP is provided at n/c; 30 day no risk guarantee.
  MS-DOS. IBM or compatibles (640k). disk $495.00 (ISBN 0-927875-69-1, Order no.: 1690). *Addl. software required:* Winnebago CIRC and/or CAT V 5.1 or higher. *Optimal configuration:* Same as Winnebago CIRC/CAT or Winnebago CAT, an additional 5Mb hard disk space needed. *Networks supported:* IPX or Netbios compatible.
  3.5" disk $495.00 (ISBN 0-927875-68-3, Order no.: 1690).
  Four Volumes of the Library of Congress U.S. Marc Subject Headings Which Combines Powerful Cross-Referencing & Indexing. The Files Load Easily & Automatically Merge with Your Local Collection. The Database Is a Virtual Thesaurus Online with over 50,000 Cross-Referenced Subject Headings.
  Winnebago Software Co.

CrossCode C for the 68000 Microprocessor Family. *Version:* 5.1. *Operating System(s) Required:* MS-DOS, UNIX, XENIX. *Customer Support:* One full year support, updates & hot line telephone support.
  $2000.00 & up.
  CrossCode C Generates ROMable Code for All Members of the Motorola 68000 Family, Including the 68302 & the Entire CPU32 Line of Microcontrollers. Compiler Output Code Is Split into Five Independent Memory Sections That Can Be Assigned into ROM or RAM As Needed. Sizes of Ints, Pointers, & Other Types Are User Selectable. ANSI Standard Language Features Are Provided. CrossCode C Comes with a Fully Featured Motorola Style Assembler, a Linker That Can Handle Very Large Loads, & a Downloader That Can Convert Any Load into Motorola S-Records & Other File Formats. A Librarian, Symbol Lister, & Other Utilities Are Also Provided. Works with the FreeForm Source-Level Debugger.
  Software Development Systems, Inc.

CrossConnect. *Version:* 4.7. *Items Included:* 1 spiral bound manual. *Customer Support:* 60 day free phone; BBS.
  DOS 3.0 or higher. IBM PC, AT, 386, 486 & compatibles (512k). disk $195.95-$695.95-$2495.95. *Nonstandard peripherals required:* Hayes AT or compatible modem. *Addl. software required:* Novell or NetBIOS Network. *Networks supported:* Novell or NetBIOS compatible.
  Powerful Modem Sharing & Remote Access Software Package for Novell & NetBIOS Networks. Users on the LAN Can Share Network Modems for Dial-Out Connections. Also Allows Remote Workstations to Dial into a Network Computer for Full LAN Communications. Provides Node-to-Node Remote Control on the Network - So You Can Share Resources & Run Diagnostics Interactively. Package Comes in a 1, 4 or 20 Modem Version.
  Smith Micro Software, Inc.

Crossdata. *Version:* 2.0. Award Software, Inc. Jan. 1984. *Compatible Hardware:* TI Professional. *Operating System(s) Required:* MS-DOS, CP/M. *Memory Required:* 64k. *General Requirements:* Winchester hard disk, printer.
  $99.00.
  Self-Contained Disk Format Conversion Program.
  Texas Instruments, Personal Productivit.

Crosstalk for Windows. *Version:* 2.0.1. Mar. 1993. *Items Included:* 2 manuals (CASL Programming Reference, User's Guide). *Customer Support:* Free telephone support (404-442-3210); free bulletin board system (BBS); CompuServe forum.
  Microsoft Windows 3.1. Systems capable of running Microsoft Windows 3.1 (400k). disk $195.00. *Addl. software required:* Microsoft Windows 3.1. *Optimal configuration:* Fast 386 or 486, serial port or modem equipped w/ 16550 VART.
  Crosstalk Communications.

Crosstalk Mark 4. *Version:* 2.1.1. *Compatible Hardware:* IBM PC & compatibles. *Operating System(s) Required:* PC-DOS/MS-DOS 2.1 or higher. *Memory Required:* 320k. *General Requirements:* 2 disk drives, modem.
  disk $295.00.
  Features CASL (Crosstalk Application Script Language) Which Enables Users to Completely Customize the Program by Creating Specialized Menu-Driven Communication Applications. Allows Accessing Mainframes & Minicomputers Through IRMA Interface & Exchanging Files Through a Data PBX. Up to 15 Communications Sessions Can Take Place Simultaneously in Windows or Individually in Full-Screen Format. Supports CROSSTALK, FAST, KERMIT, X.PC, XMODEM, & YMODEM, & CompuServe "B" File Transfer Protocols. All Function & Keypad Keys Are User-Programmable. Features Emulation for Most Terminals & Supports All Asynchronous, Full-Duplex Modems. The Programming Language Includes over 200 Commands, Statements & Functions, Floating Point Math, String & Numeric Operators, Full Control of Screen Windows & Colors.
  Crosstalk Communications.

Crosstalk XVI. *Version:* 3.8. 1990. *Compatible Hardware:* IBM PCs & 100% compatibles. *Operating System(s) Required:* PC-DOS 2.1 or higher, MS-DOS. *Language(s):* Assembly. *Memory Required:* 256k. *Customer Support:* Tech support via telephone, BBS, & CompuServe forum.
  disk $195.00, incl. manual.
  Data Communications Program That Enables Computer to Communicate with Variety of Other Brands & Models, with Remote Mainframes, & with Information Services Including the Source & CompuServe. Supports Speeds of up to 115,200 BPS & Allows Full Control of Stop Bits, Parity, Baud Rate, & Duplex. Supports Acoustic & Direct Connect Modems, & Auto-Answer & Auto-Dial Models. Additional Features Include: Capture to Printer, Disk, or Capture Buffer, Error Checking with Retransmission, Script File Facility Which Allows User Customization, & Terminal Emulation, Including IBM 3101, DEC VT-52 & VT-100/102, TI 940, & Televideo 920. Provides 40 User-Programmable Keys to Store Passwords & User ID Codes for Information Utilities or Mainframes.
  Crosstalk Communications.

Crosstalk XVI: Network Version. *Version:* 3.71. *Compatible Hardware:* IBM PC. *Operating System(s) Required:* PC-DOS 3.0 or higher; works under Windows, TopView, DeskView, & other windowing environments. *Memory Required:* 128k. *General Requirements:* IBM Asynchronous Communications Server software, modem. *Customer Support:* Tech support via telephone, BBS, & CompuServe.
  contact publisher for price.
  Shares Modems & Telephone Lines among Networked Computers, Eliminating the Need for Modems & Lines for Each Computer. Transfers Files among Networked Computers Without Routing Them Through the File Server. Functions Through Direct Commands or Menus with Help Screens. Allows Automated Communications Sessions for Novice Users with CROSSTALK Command Language. Provides Unattended Call-In Access & Password Protection in Answer Mode. Allows Data Capture to Disk, RAM, or Printer. Supports CROSSTALK & XMODEM File Transfer Protocols & Mainframe to PC File Transfer with KERMIT Error-Detection Protocol. Teminal Emulation Include Most Popular Types. Allows Access to Disk Directories & File Manipulation from Within the Program. Pre-Stored Codes & Passwords Can Be Sent with a Single Key. Size of Exchanged Files Is Limited Only by Available Disk Space. Provides over 70 Script Commands. Not Copy Protected.
  Crosstalk Communications.

CrossTarget. *Items Included:* "Discovering CrossTarget" trial manual (wirebound booklet). *Customer Support:* Maintenance & upgrades; software support by phone; on-site training & support (pricing varies regarding number of users & workstations, etc.).
  Macintosh OS, MS-DOS, UNIX, Ultrix, AIX. Macintosh, IBM PC, Sun, DECstation (2Mb). Averages $1500.00 per station. *Addl. software required:* Windows with MS-DOS. *Optimal configuration:* 8Mb of RAM. *Networks supported:* Banyan, Novell, AppleTalk, 3COM, Token Ring, etc.
  Data Analysis & Reporting Solution Gives Decisionmakers Fast, Direct Access to Large Volumes of Corporate Data with Point-&-Click Ease. It Runs on IBM PC, Macintosh, UNIX or Mixed Platforms in Standalone or Client/Server Modes.
  Dimensional Insight, Inc.

CrossView: CrossView Source Level Debugger. *Version:* 2.0. 1984. *Items Included:* Software & documentation. *Customer Support:* 90 day warranty included in price; 1 year maintenance contracts available starting at $330.00.
  VMS, DOS, OS2, UNIX, ULTRIOC, SUNOS, DOMAIN, HPUX, AIX. DECVAX, PC, DECStation, SUN 3 & 4, HP/Apollo, IBMRisc. start at $1650.00. *Networks supported:* Ethernet.
  A Family Source Level Debugger That Enable Users to Debug C & Assembly Language Applications for Embedded Microprocessors.
  BSO/Tasking.

Crossword Challenge. Wida Software. Sep. 1987. *Compatible Hardware:* Apple II. *Operating System(s) Required:* Apple DOS 3.3. *Memory Required:* 64k. *Items Included:* Disk, user manual. *Customer Support:* 800-654-8715, full lifetime guarantee.
  single site license disk $59.95 (ISBN 0-940503-38-7).
  site license disk $139.95.
  Crossword Generating Program.
  Research Design Assocs., Inc.

Crossword Creator. *Version:* 1.1. Jul. 1989. *Customer Support:* Free telephone support.
  AmigaDOS (512k). $49.95.
  Create Or Solve Crossword Puzzles. Pattern Matching 87,000 Dictionary. IFF Compatible.
  Polyglot Software.

Crossword Creator. *Compatible Hardware:* Commodore Amiga.
3.5" disk $49.95.
40,000+ Word Dictionary.
Polygon Software Corp.

Crossword Magic.
DOS. disk $49.95.
MAC. 3.5" disk $49.95.
Apple II. disk $49.95.
A Veritable Crossword Processor. Create, Play, Save & Print Crossword Puzzles Effortlessly. The Program Handles the Tedious Work, Including Creating the Puzzle Grid Automatically When You Enter a Word You Want in Your Puzzle. Make Puzzles to Entertain & Challenge. Build Them to Use As Study Aids, Greeting Cards or Invitations. Play Puzzles on the Computer or Print Them Out. Let Crossword Magic Work Its Spell on You.
Software Toolworks.

Crossword Master. Wida Software. Sep. 1987. *Compatible Hardware:* Apple II. *Operating System(s) Required:* Apple DOS 3.3. *Memory Required:* 64k. *Customer Support:* 800-654-8715, full lifetime guarantee.
single site license disk $59.95 (ISBN 0-940503-39-5).
site license disk $139.95.
Crossword Generating Program.
Research Design Assocs., Inc.

Crosswords. 1981. *Compatible Hardware:* Apple II+, IIe, IIc, IIgs; Franklin Ace. *Operating System(s) Required:* Apple DOS 3.3. *Language(s):* Assembly. *Memory Required:* 48k.
disk $8.95.
Work on the Existing High Resolution Crossword Puzzles, or Create Your Own.
Artsci, Inc.

Crosswords, Vol. I. Caribbean Software Staff. Aug. 1995. *Items Included:* Set up instruction sheet. *Customer Support:* (503) 639-6863.
DOS. IBM PC. disk $7.95 (ISBN 1-887783-01-6, Order no.: 4100-1001). *Optimal configuration:* IBM PC 286 or higher, DOS 3.3 or higher, EGA, VGA or SVGA, mouse.
A Crossword Puzzle Program for the Computer.
Entertainment Technology.

Crosswords Scrabble & Crossword Helper. *Items Included:* Bound manual. *Customer Support:* Free hotline - no time limit; 30 day limited warranty; updates are $5/disk plus S&H.
MS-DOS 2.0 or higher. IBM & compatibles (128k). disk $19.95. *Nonstandard peripherals required:* Two floppies (or one floppy & a hard disk); standard printers are supported.
Expandable Set of Menu-Driven Software Utilities Which Allow User to Manipulate Word Lists. For SCRABBLE, You May Specify the Letters You Have and/or Wish to Use on the Board, As Well As the Locations of Particular Letters (e.g., There Must Be an "E" in the Third Position & an "N" in the Fifth). CROSSWORDS Will Then Conditionally Search Its Database for All Allowable Words. For Crossword Puzzles, You May Specify the Length of the Word, & the Letters Already in Place (Which You Must Fit Around). CROSSWORDS Then Provides a List of Possible Words. Additional Utilities Include a Spelling Checker for ASCII Text Files & Several Entertaining Word Games (Including Hangman). A 35,000 Word Database Is Supplied (in ASCII). Utilities Are Provided for Adding to This List from the Keyboard, or for Merging in Other Word Files. Includes a Clear & Concise 21-Page Manual.
Dynacomp, Inc.

Crowley Manor. *Compatible Hardware:* NEC PC-6000.
ROM cartridge $34.95.
cassette $19.95.
Solve the Murder, Survive the Curse, & Battle the Occult to Win.
NEC Technologies.

Crozzzwords. Jan. 1991. *Items Included:* Disk(s), user's guide, poster, coloring book, warranty card, swap coupon. *Customer Support:* 90 day unlimited warranty; 800 toll free number, 800-221-7911, 8:00 a.m.-5:00 p.m. Arizona time; Updates $10.
Macintosh System 6 or higher. Macintosh (1Mb monochrome, 2Mb color). 3.5" disk $69.99 (ISBN 1-55772-269-2, Order no.: 6202). *Optimal configuration:* 2Mb color monitor, Macintosh LC. *Networks supported:* Digicard.
MS-DOS. IBM, Tandy, MS-DOS compatible (128k). disk $49.99 (ISBN 1-55772-062-2, Order no.: 6201). *Nonstandard peripherals required:* VGA or CGA card. *Optimal configuration:* 128k, color monitor, VGA card. *Networks supported:* Velan, Novell, Digicard.
DOS. Apple II, Apple IIe, Apple IIGS, Apple II Plus (48k). disk $49.99 (ISBN 0-918017-76-9, Order no.: 6200). *Optimal configuration:* Apple II, printer, color monitor, 48k. *Networks supported:* Digicard.
Puzzle Game for Playing & Creating Crossword Puzzles. Includes Work Ready-to-Play Puzzles on Various Subjects or Create Your Own Puzzles, Automatic & Manual Puzzle Creation, Variable Grid Size - Maximum Size 20x20. With CHALLENGE UPGRADE, Crozzzwords Can Fit the Needs of Individual Players. Ages 9 to Adult.
Mindplay.

CRT Emulator. Oct. 1983. *Compatible Hardware:* IBM PC with Kronos Timekeeper System. *Operating System(s) Required:* DOS 1.1, 2.0, 2.1. *Memory Required:* 64k.
contact publisher for price (Order no.: SD-04019-000).
Allows the Use of an IBM PC As a CRT Terminal. Conversion Gives User Interactive Communications with a KRONOS TIMEKEEPER System (Computerized Timeclock) & Therefore Allows Adding/Scheduling of Employees, Management Reporting, & Punch & Totals Editing.
Kronos, Inc.

Cruiser: Records Management for Law Enforcement. *Version:* 2.0. Jun. 1991. *Items Included:* Full documentation, written & on-line. *Customer Support:* On-site or class room training, 24 hour, 7-day support - Fees are related to number of users & size of installation.
MS-DOS. 286 or better compatible (640k). contact publisher for price (Order no.: CDOS, CNOV). *Addl. software required:* Informix Runtime, provided with Cruiser. *Networks supported:* Novell.
UNIX or derivitive. IBM RS/6000, ALTOS, AT&T, UNISYS, NCR, DEC, etc. (Order no.: CUNIX). *Addl. software required:* Informix Runtime, provided with Cruiser. *Optimal configuration:* IBM RS/6000, 16MB RAM, 400MB Disk, AIX operating system. *Networks supported:* TCP/IP.
Interactive Records Management & Reporting for Law Enforcement & Other Public Safety Agencies. Menu-Driven, Informix Based, Modular, & Simple-to-Use, Cruiser Is Well Suited to the Records Department & the Investigative Division. Comprehensive History is Maintained, with Criminal, Complainant, Arrest, Offense, Incident, Property, Vehicle & Officer Files. Complete UCR Reporting Functions.
Scorpion Systems, Inc.

Crumb Eater. *Compatible Hardware:* Apple II+, IIe, IIc. *Language(s):* BASIC. *Memory Required:* 48k.
disk $14.95.
Passover Is Coming & the Muncher Has to Eat All the Breadcrumbs. Player Must Be Fast or He Will Run into Trouble. If the Player Gobbles All the Crumbs in the Maze, There Are Still Lots More.
Davka Corp.

Crunch Interactive Statistical Package: Crunch, 5 disks. *Version:* 4.0. Jan. 1991. *Compatible Hardware:* IBM PC. *Operating System(s) Required:* DOS 2.1, 3.3. *Memory Required:* 500k. *General Requirements:* 1 disk drive and hard disk, printer. *Items Included:* Software & manual. *Customer Support:* Unlimited telephone support.
disk $247.50 (ISBN 0-923431-00-4).
Set of Statistical Procedures for the Analysis of Marketing, Survey, Social Science, & Medical Research. Included Is a Full Range of Utilities for the Management of Large Numerical Data Sets. Statistical Procedures Include: Multiple Regression (50 Variables); Nonlinear Regression (Users Enter Their Own Equations with up to 25 Variables); Analysis of Variance (10 Factors with Repeated Measures); Crosstabulation (Two Programs - Interactive & Batch); Nonparametric & Descriptive Statistics.
Crunch Software Corp.

CRYPT LIBRARY. *Version:* 1.15. *Customer Support:* By phone Mon-Fri 8:30 AM-5:30 PM CST.
MS-DOS. IBM PC, PC XT, PC AT & compatibles, PS/2. disk $99.00 (Order no.: 107111).
Features Subroutines to Encrypt Character Strings, Four Easy-to-Use Encryption Routines, Password Protection & Fast Algorithm to Convert Data Rapidly. Two Encryption Routines Feature Zero Exception. Crafted in Assembly Language for Maximum Speed & Minimum Size. Available for over 20 Languages/Compilers. Suited to Applications That Use Sensitive Information.
Glenco Engineering, Inc.

Crypt of Medea. A. Britto & A. Lamb. Dec. 1983. *Compatible Hardware:* Apple II, II+, IIe, IIc. *Language(s):* Machine. *Memory Required:* 48k. *Customer Support:* Hotline; disk repair or replacement.
disk $9.95 (ISBN 0-926846-12-4, Order no.: 114).
Adventure Game That Contains High-Resolution Graphics.
Sir-Tech Software, Inc.

Crypto-Mania. Russell P. Holsclaw et al. *Compatible Hardware:* IBM PC, PCjr, PC XT, PC AT, Portable PC with IBM Color Display, one double-sided disk drive, dot matrix printer (optional). *Operating System(s) Required:* DOS 1.10, 2.00, 2.10, 3.00, 3.10. *Memory Required:* 128k.
disk $19.95 (Order no.: 6276535).
As Time Ticks Away, the Player Must Race to Reveal the True Words Within the Cryptogram. The Challenge Is to Discover Which Letters Stand for the Real Letters of a Word. During the Game the Player Can Change All Like Letters Throughout the Cryptogram, Alter the Letter Selection, Request Hints, & Use the Screen Clock to Keep Track of Solving Time.
Personally Developed Software, Inc.

Crypto-Mania Puzzle Pac. Frank D. Dennison & Russell P. Holsclaw. *Compatible Hardware:* IBM PC, PCjr, PC XT, PC AT. *Operating System(s) Required:* DOS 1.10, 2.00, 2.10, 3.00, 3.10. *Memory Required:* 128k. *General Requirements:* 2 double-sided disk drives, Crypto-Mania

TITLE INDEX

program.
disk $14.95 (Order no.: 6276577).
Includes over 500 Cryptograms Featuring Famous Quotations, Historical Facts, & Movie Trivia.
Personally Developed Software, Inc.

CryptoMactic with EasyTrash & Incinerate: Integrated Desktop Encryption Shredding & Trash Management. Aug. 1993. *Items Included:* Manual. *Customer Support:* Free, unlimited technical support, 90 day warranty.
Macintosh 6.05 or higher. Mac Plus & higher (512k). 3.5" disk $99.00.
Hacker-Proof Security Built Directly into the Desktop. To Encrypt, Select an Icon, Press -1 & Enter a Codekey. Offers the Fastest, Most Rigorous Algorithms & Key Management Available. Create Self-Decrypting Files. Also Includes EasyTrash & Incinerate, Utilities Which Trash and/or Shred from the Desktop.
Kent Marsh Ltd.

Crystal Crazy. Patrick Buckland. 1993. *Items Included:* Instructions, reg. card. *Customer Support:* Free phone support.
6.02 & higher. Macintosh. 3.5" disk $49.95 (Order no.: M110).
Casady & Greene, Inc.

Crystal Fantasy. Jul. 1995. *Items Included:* Instruction inserts. *Customer Support:* Free phone tech support. One year exchange warranty.
Macintosh; Windows. Any Macintosh with QuickDraw Software (8Mb); IBM PC or compatible 80386 or 80486 (8Mb). CD-ROM disk $59.95. *Nonstandard peripherals required:* Mac System 6.0.5 or higher, color monitor & photo CD compatible CD-ROM drive; IBM VGA display or higher, Photo CD compatible CD-ROM drive.
Adult Interactive CD-ROM Game Involving 6 Girls to Choose from in Various Quicktime Videos, Talk with Me Segments (Q&A), & Still Shots. Various Print Functions Are Available.
MacDaddy Entertainment.

Crystal Paint. Oct. 1987. *Compatible Hardware:* Apple Macintosh 512k, Macintosh 512e, Macintosh Plus, Macintosh SE, Macintosh II. *Memory Required:* 512k.
3.5" disk $49.95.
Graphics Tool Which Allows Users to Draw Intricate & Precise Objects Using Any of More Than 30 Graphic Symmetries. These Drawings Can Then Be Printed or, Employing Copy & Paste Options, Used to Embellish Any Document. Provides Editing Capabilities Which Enable the User to Do Precision Detail Work by Editing One Trail at a Time or by Importing Other Graphics Files for Manipulation. Designed for Home Use, Education, & for Application in Desktop Publishing.
Great Wave Software.

Crystal Quest with Critter Editor. Patrick Burkland. 1987. *Items Included:* Instructions, reg. card. *Customer Support:* Free phone support.
6.02 & higher. Macintosh. 3.5" disk $31.95 (Order no.: M103).
A Fast Moving Macintosh Classic. Collect All the Crystals & Avoid All the Mines. 40 Different Waves. Change over 1,000 Parts of the Game with the Critter Editor.
Casady & Greene, Inc.

CrystalLaser Laser Typesetting. Jan. 1988. *Compatible Hardware:* Altos, ARIX, AT&T, IBM PC & compatibles, Intel, NCR, Toshiba, UNISYS. *Operating System(s) Required:* PC-DOS/MS-DOS 3.0 or higher, UNIX, XENIX. *Language(s):* C. *Memory Required:* each individual application 640k. *General Requirements:* Hard disk, HP Laserjet printer.
$445.00-$6,995.00 license fee.
Adds Laser Printer Typesetting Capabilities to the Crystal Document Management System (Crystal DMS). Generates the Typeset-Quality Output Specified in Crystal DMS Documents, Including Multiple Fonts, Font Families & Point Sizes, Plus Automatic Justification, Leading, Kerning, & Hyphenation. Typesetting Codes Definitions Are Specified in One Simple Menu of Crystal DMS.
Syntactics.

Crystals. *Compatible Hardware:* Atari 400, 800. *Language(s):* Atari BASIC (source code included). *Memory Required:* 16k.
disk $19.95.
Generates Color Patterns on Screen.
Dynacomp, Inc.

CrystalWriter Plus. *Version:* 4.0. Nov. 1985. *Compatible Hardware:* Altos, ARIX, AT&T, Convergent, DEC, Intel, NCR, Plexus, Pyramid, Sequent, Sun, UNISYS. *Operating System(s) Required:* UNIX, XENIX, DOS. *Language(s):* C. *Memory Required:* 512k-1000k.
$189.00-$6995.00 license fee.
Word Processor Designed for UNIX, XENIX & DOS Systems. Coordinates Standard Document Formats & Customizes Document Types, Defining Exactly How They Will Look. Function-Key Driven, Using Plain English Commands & On-Line Help. Features Include Automatic, On-Screen Formatting, Mail Merge, Spell Checker, Footnoting, Macros.
Syntactics.

CS-Interface. *Compatible Hardware:* Commodore Amiga.
contact publisher for price.
Use the Ricoh Color Scanner with the Amiga.
ACDA Corp.

CS-4: Residential Buy-Rent Software Package. Ted C. Jones. 1987. *Customer Support:* User-friendly format requires little support; free telephone consultation as needed.
MS-DOS. IBM PC compatible (256k). $20.00 (ISBN 1-56248-006-5). *Optimal configuration:* IBM PC compatible; minimum one floppy drive (3.50 or 5.25"); dot matrix printer.
Assists Prospective Homebuyers in Decision to Rent or Buy a Home. Considers Rental Rates & Other Rental Costs As Well As Associated Growth Rates, Changes in Property Values, Interest Rates & Terms of Proposed Mortgage, Growth Rates, Closing Costs & Resale Expenses. Contrasts Costs of Renting or Buying on Both a Pre- & Post-Tax Basis. Calculates Estimated Return on Homeowner's Investment Compared to Renting.
Texas A&M Univ., Real Estate Ctr.

CSC ChemDraw. *Version:* 3.0. *Compatible Hardware:* All current Apple Macintosh. *Items Included:* 1 spiral-bound manual. *Customer Support:* 6 mos. free updates/30 day money-back guarantee.
3.5" disk $595.00.
Industry Standard for Chemical Structure Drawing for Preparation of Scientific Presentation Materials. Includes Bond Tools, Ring Templates, Arrows, Orbitals, Text & Other Specialized Tools That Make It Easy to Draw Chemical Notations. Full Page Layout & PostScript Output. Support for EPS & PICT (Export Only) File Formats.
Cambridge Scientific Computing, Inc.

CSC ChemDraw Plus. *Version:* 3.0. *Compatible Hardware:* Apple Macintosh, UNIX. *Items Included:* 1 spiral bound manual. *Customer Support:* 6 mos. free updates/30 day money-back guarantee.
Macintosh OS. Macintosh Plus or higher (1Mb). 3.5" disk $795.00.
Industry Standard for Chemical Structure Drawing for Preparation of Scientific Presentation Materials. Features Include Bond Tools, Ring Templates, Arrows, Orbitals, Text & Other Drawing Tools, Full Page Layout, & PostScript Output. Includes Color Capability, User-Definable Templates & Support for EPS, PICT (Macintosh Export Only), MDL, MSI, SMD, & SMILES File Formats.
Cambridge Scientific Computing, Inc.

CSC Chem3D. *Version:* 3.0. *Compatible Hardware:* Apple Macintosh, Macintosh Plus. *Items Included:* 1 350-page spiral-bound manual. *Customer Support:* 6 mos. free updates/30 day money-back guarantee.
3.5" disk $495.00.
Molecular Modeling & Visualization Software for Analyzing Chemical Models. Translate CSC CHEMDRAW Structures into 3D. Display up to 6000 Atoms As Wire Frame, Ball & Stick or Space Filling (CPK) Models. Rotate Models, Create Real-Time Animation. Support for EPS, PICT, Alchemy, Brookhaven, Cambridge Crystal Data Bank, & Other Formats.
Cambridge Scientific Computing, Inc.

CSC Chem3D Plus. *Version:* 3.0. *General Requirements:* Color firmware required for color; 68020 & 68881 or 68030 & 68882 processors required for energy minimization & Molecular Dynamics. *Items Included:* 1 spiral-bound 350-page manual. *Customer Support:* 6 mos. free updates/30 day money-back guarantee.
Macintosh Plus or higher. 3.5" disk $995.00.
Molecular Modeling & Visualization Software for Analyzing Chemical Models. Translate CSC CHEMDRAW Structures into 3D. Display 6000 Atoms in Color As Wire Frame, Ball & Stick or Space Filling (CPK) Models. Rotate Models, Create Real-Time Animation. Energy Minimizations & Molecular Dynamics Computations. Supports CSC CHEM3D File Formats, SMD, MDL, MSI, & Others.
Cambridge Scientific Computing, Inc.

CSI Business System. Jan. 1983. *Compatible Hardware:* DEC PDP-11, RSX-11M. *Memory Required:* 64k. *General Requirements:* 2 disk drives, printer.
write for info.
User-Oriented System Which Can Be Used by a Small or Medium-Sized Business & Set up In-House. Includes Payroll, Accounts Payable, Accounts Receivable & General Ledger. Modules May Be Used Independently.
Creative Software.
  Accounts Payable.
  Accounts Receivable.
  General Ledger.
  Payroll.

CSL: C Scientific Programming Library. *Items Included:* Examples & functions reference manual. *Customer Support:* 30 days technical support; software maintenance service; annual free $200.00.
DOS. IBM PC, AT 386/486, UNIX, XENIX. $455.00. *Nonstandard peripherals required:* Hard disk. *Addl. software required:* Microsoft C Compiler.
UNIX or XENIX. AT 386/485 (4Mb). $455.00. *Addl. software required:* Microsoft C Compiler.
High Quality C Programming Library of over 600 Functions in Archived Libraries, Example Programs, & Optional Source Code. Just a Few of the Capabilities That CSL Can Provide Are Real & Complex Matrix Computations, Similarity Transformations, Inversions, & Decompositions. Linear Algebra & Eigensystem Analysis, Differential Equations, Multi-Dimensional Integrations, FFT & Kalman Filtering, Time Series, Statistics, & Optimization, Stepwise Regression, & Data Plotting.
Eigenware Technologies.

CSR TRAINER 4000. Version: 1.5. Jun. 1987. Compatible Hardware: IBM PC & compatibles, PC XT, PC AT, PS2. Operating System(s) Required: PC-DOS, MS-DOS. Memory Required: 256k.
$1820.00.
Allows Development & Presentation of CBT Courses on the IBM PC or Compatibles.
CSR Macmillan/McGraw-Hill.

CSS/3. Version: 3.1. 1988. Items Included: 2 loose-leaf & binder manuals, Quick Start manual, Addendum to the manual. Customer Support: Free technical support by phone, Fax, or mail; 14 day money back guarantee; service contract available.
MS-DOS (Version 3.1 or higher), DR DOS. PC/XT & compatibles with hard drive & 3 1/2" or 5 1/4" floppy drive (640k). Contact publisher for price (ISBN 1-884233-00-7). Optimal configuration: 386 SX/DX-25Mhz; MS-DOS 5.0 or higher; 640k RAM (expanded memory recommended); EGA or higher. Networks supported: Novell, Lantastic, Banyan Vines, & Others.
Powerful Statistical Analysis & Graphing System. Extensive Implementations of Statistical Tests with Hundreds of Graphs Integrated with All Analyses. Complete Statistical Database Management Includes Fast Spreadsheet Editor, Relational Joining of Files, Nested Sorting, Powerful Transformations, & Comprehensive Reporting Options. Intelligent Import of Many File Formats.
StatSoft, Inc.

CSS/3. Version: 3.1. May 1992. Customer Support: Technical support.
DOS/VSE. PC's AT & higher (640k). disk $595.00. Optimal configuration: DOS Version 5.0 or higher. Networks supported: All.
A Powerful Statistical Analysis & Graphing System. Extensive Implementations of Statistical Tests with Hundreds of Graphs Integrated with All Analyses. Complete Statistical Database Management Includes Fast Spreadsheet Editor, Relational Joining of Files, Nested Sorting, Powerful Transformations, & Comprehensive Reporting Options. Intelligent Import of Many File Formats.
StatSoft, Inc.

CSS:GRAPHICS. Version: 3.1. May 1992. Customer Support: Technical support.
DOS/VSE. PC's AT & higher (640k). disk $495.00. Optimal configuration: DOS Version 5.0 or higher. Networks supported: All.
A Comprehensive Graphics/Charting System with Data Management. Hundreds of Types of 2D & 3D Graphs, Including Interactive Onscreen Rotation. Features Onscreen Drawing, 19 Scalable Fonts, Overlaying of Multiple Graphs, & Other Customization Options. Supports Output Devices at Highest Resolution. Imports/Exports Data in 15 Formats.
StatSoft, Inc.

CSS: Graphics. Version: 3.1. 1988. Items Included: 1 loose-leaf & binder manual, Quick Start manual. Customer Support: Free technical support by phone, Fax, or mail; 14 day money back guarantee; service contract available.
MS-DOS (Version 3.1 or higher), DR DOS. PC/XT & compatibles with hard drive & 3 1/2" or 5 1/4" floppy drive (640k). Contact publisher for price (ISBN 1-884233-01-5). Optimal configuration: 386 SX/DX-25Mhz; MS-DOS 5.0 or higher; 640k RAM (expanded memory recommended); EGA or higher. Networks supported: Novell, Lantastic, Banyan Vines, & Others.
Comprehensive Graphics/Charting System with Data Management. Hundreds of Types of 2D & 3D Graphs, Including Interactive Onscreen Rotation. Features Onscreen Drawing, 19 Scalable Fonts, Overlaying of Multiple Graphs, & Other Customization Options. Supports Output Devices at Highest Resolution. Imports/Exports Data in 15 Formats.
StatSoft, Inc.

CT Spool. Version: 1.2. Compatible Hardware: Apple Macintosh. Items Included: User guide, templates. Customer Support: Hotline.
contact publisher for price.
Host to Local Printer Spooler via LAN.
Menlo Business Systems, Inc.

CTAccess. Version: 2.0. Sep. 1994. Items Included: User manual. Customer Support: Hotline Support.
Apple System 7.0 or higher. Macintosh or Power PC. Contact publisher for price. Nonstandard peripherals required: Ethernet card or gateway. Addl. software required: MacAM, TandemTalk.
Tandem Terminal Emulator Which Allows End User to Run Multiple Host Applications or Sessions Simultaneously. Works over LANs, WANs, ASYNCH, & AppleTalk Remote Access.
Menlo Business Systems, Inc.

CTAR. Version: 3.1. Compatible Hardware: IBM PC AT & compatible, Unix-based systems.
MS-DOS. disk $85.00.
All other versions. $75.00.
Backup Utility for MS-DOS, Unix, & Xenix that Features File-Compression Capabilities. Compresses Files by an Average of 40 to 60 Percent. Enables Users to Archive Entire File Systems Including Device Files, Links, Symbolic Links, Named Pipes, & Empty Directories. Users can Back Up only Files Added or Changed Since the Last Master Backup. Allows Large Tape Block Factors (up to 2048 on Motorola CPUs & up to 120 on Intel CPUs). Can Perform Unattended Backups Using Multiple Volumes & Multiple Drives, Perform Backups in the Background, & Backup Multiple Volumes While Checking Volume Number on Restore. Other Features Are File-Locking & Group-Tagging Capabilities.
Microlite Corp.

CTC Bridge: CTC Burroughs Micro to Mainframe Communication (Mac, Burroughs & Sperry connection). Version: IBM 4.0, Macintosh 3.0. Aug. 1984. Compatible Hardware: Apple Macintosh; IBM PC, PC XT, PC AT PS/2;. Operating System(s) Required: MS-DOS 2.1, PC-DOS 2.1, 3.1; IBM NetBios Gateway. Memory Required: 256k.
disk $395.00.
NETBIOS LAN version $895.00.
Supports the Standard Burroughs "Poll/Select" Communication Protocol. Micros May Be Attached Locally Using Burroughs TDI Direct Connect, or Remotely Via Asynchronous/Synchronous Leased or Switched Lines. Standard Speeds Vary from 300 to 19,200 bps.
Core Technology Corp.

CTI Plus: Current Technology Index. 1995. Items Included: Quarterly Updates.
MS-DOS. IBM or compatibles. disk $1400.00 1 year.
Use information technology to penetrate the fast-changing world of technology & its many applications - from civil engineering to radiochemistry to neural nets.
Bowker-Saur.

Ctrace Debugger. Compatible Hardware: IBM PC & compatibles. Operating System(s) Required: PC-DOS/MS-DOS 2.0 or higher. Memory Required: 256k.
disk $19.95.
C Source Debugger. The Animated Trace Will Show the Flow of Execution, Statement by Statement. Features Six Windows of Information: Source, Output, Variables, Watch, Memory, & Symbols. Features Pop-Up Menus & Single-Keystroke Commands.
MIX Software.

CTV-Plus. Apr. 1986. Compatible Hardware: IBM PC & compatibles. Memory Required: 256k.
contact publisher for price.
Full Function Multi Franchise Cable Billing System.
The Management.

CTXfer. May 1994. Items Included: User manual. Customer Support: Hotline Support.
Apple System 7.0 or higher, Tandem Guardian C30, D20 Plus. Macintosh (700k). Contact publisher for price. Addl. software required: Tandem Talk, AppleTalk, Remote Access.
High-Speed LAN File Transfer. Uses Client/Server Technology, with GUI for Point-&-Click Transfer.
Menlo Business Systems, Inc.

Cube & Tess. Version: 2.0. Items Included: Diskette & manual. Customer Support: Telephone inquiries.
Macintosh (1Mb). Macintosh, all models. 3.5" disk $34.95.
Two Challenging Puzzles Based on the Famous Six-colored Cube Game. 3-D Cube & 4-D Tesseract Version with Illustrated Manual Describing Group-Theory Concepts (Color Mac II).
Atlantic Software.

Cubik. Compatible Hardware: Apple II. Language(s): Integer BASIC. Memory Required: 32k.
disk $14.95 (Order no.: 10042).
High Resolution Graphics Game Which Provides Three-Dimensional Version of Tic-Tac-Toe Played on Four Planes, Each Plane Being Four Rows Wide. Object of Game Is to Place Four Tokens in Row or Diagonally along Any Three-Dimensional Plane. Can Be Played Against Computer or Another Person.
Powersoft, Inc.

CUBIT. Version: 4.0. Feb. 1986. Compatible Hardware: Compaq; IBM PC, PC XT, PC AT, PS/2 & compatibles. Operating System(s) Required: PC-DOS/MS-DOS 2.0 or higher. Memory Required: 228k. Customer Support: 9:00 AM to 5:30 PM EST - (603) 644-5555.
disk $49.95.
Compresses All Types of Files, Even 1-2-3 Files, by an Average of 70%. So with an Overstuffed 10 Megabyte Disk, User Can Free 7 Mb or more. Once Compressed, Transparently Makes Sure Your Files are Usable.
SoftLogic Solutions.

Cue. Memory Required: 128k.
disk $150.00.
Procedure-Based Communications Package for Straightforward Communications Between a PC & a Remote Computer System(s). Design Objectives Include Incorporating Knowledge of Remote System Protocols into a Standardized Framework That Can Be Taught & Transferred Across Several Sytems, & Adaptation to Varied Configurations of PC's & Remote System(s), with Working Knowledge of a Few Commands or Menus. Intermediate Users Can Modify Existing Procedure Files to Suit Specialized Needs. At the Expert or Programming Level, Sets of Procedures for New Remote System(s) Can Be Written.
Software Resources.

Culture: The Multi-Media Guide to Western Civilization. Version: 2.0. Walter W. Reinhold. Compatible Hardware: Macintosh; IBM PC & compatibles (System 3.5). Items Included: Disks.

computer software $249.00.
software & wkbk. set $294.00.
Set of Hypercard Stacks or HyperWriter Files Provides an Overview of More Than 3800 Years of Western Culture. Comprises 250 Graphics, 120 Signature Melodies, 32 Cultural Grids, 20,000 Internal HyperText Links & 5000 External Links to a Variety of Laserdiscs, Including the National Gallery of Art Laserdisc, & 131 Essays. 330-Page Complementary Workbook of Interdisciplinary Lessons & Worksheets Also Available.
Cultural Resources, Inc.

Culture: The Multi-Media Guide to Western Civilization. *Version:* 2.0. Walter W. Reinhold. 1992. *Items Included:* 10 floppy disks. *Customer Support:* Replacement of defective disks.
Macintosh. Macintosh (2.5Mb). 3.5" disk $249.00 (ISBN 0-9624372-3-9). *Addl. software required:* Hypercard. *Optimal configuration:* 12Mb hard drive space; 2.5Mb RAM. *Networks supported:* As in any Hypercard Product.
An Interdisciplinary, Contextual & Multimedia Guide to Western Civilization, Provides an Overview of More Than 3800 Years of Western Culture. The Program Includes More Than 250 Graphics, 120 Signature Melodies, 1000 Profiles of Famous People, 40 Historical Maps, 130 Essays on Topics Ranging from the Black Death to Impressionism, 4500 Cards & 25,000 Hypertext Links, Both Internal & to Such Sources As the National Gallery of Art Laserdisc. A Workbook Is Available.
Cultural Resources Inc.

Current Contents on Diskette (available in 7 editions). *Items Included:* User's guide; keyboard template (IBM); quick reference card (IBM); sample issue; starter supply of Request-A-Print card; *Customer Support:* Free customer support from ISI's U.S. & U.K. Offices; U.S. office can be reached via a toll-free number (800-336-4474); regional demonstration by User Education staff.
MS-DOS version 2.0 or higher. IBM PC, XT, AT & compatibles (512K). contact publisher for price.
Apple DOS 4.2 or higher. Macintosh Plus, II, SE. contact publisher for price. *Nonstandard peripherals required:* Hard disk & 800K floppy disk drive.
Provides the Tables of Contents Each Week from Current Books & the Latest Issues in the World's Leading Journals. Enables High-Speed Searching & Browsing. Custom Search Profiles Using Relevant Terms from the Searcher's Field Can Be Created. Search Results Can Be Exported in a Variety of Formats. Currently Available in 7 Editions: Life Sciences J-1200 (Covers 1,200 Journals); Life Sciences J-600 (Covers 600 Journals); Clinical Medicine (Covers 870 Journals); Agriculture, Biology & Environmental Sciences (Covers 900 Journals); Physical, Chemical & Earth Sciences (Covers 800 Journals); Engineering, Technology & Applied Sciences (Covers 810 Journals); Social & Behavioral Sciences (Covers 1,300 Journals).
Institute for Scientific Information.

Curse of the Azure Bonds. *Items Included:* Rulebook, adventurer's journal, code wheel. *Customer Support:* 14 day money back guarantee/30 day exchange policy; tech support line: (408) 737-6850 (11:00 - 5:00 PST); customer service (408) 737-6800 (9:00 - 5:00 PST).
Apple II (128k). 3 disks $49.95.
Commodore 64/128. 3 disks $39.95.
IBM PC & compatibles (512k). 4 disks $49.95.
Ambushed & Knocked Unconscious, You Awake with Five Azure-Blue Symbols Implanted Under the Skin of Your Right Arm. The Mystical Power of the Symbols Ensnares Your Will! Your Only Hope: Search the Forgotten Realm for Members of the Alliance Who Created the Bonds & Regain Control of Your Own Destiny. Only Then Can You Be Free of the Curse of the Azure Bonds.
Strategic Simulations, Inc.

Cursor & Keypad Editor: C.A.K.E. *Version:* I. *Compatible Hardware:* IBM PC & compatibles. *Operating System(s) Required:* PC-DOS, MS-DOS. *Language(s):* Assembly. *Memory Required:* 128k.
disk $49.95, incl. user's guide, installation guide & software registration form.
Full-Screen Text Editor That Allows User to Create & Change Text Files Using the Display Screen As a Window to the Particular File. Provides Text Formatting Features Such As Margin Setting, Combining or Dividing Lines, & TAB Control. Includes a Command Mode Which Allows Merging of Files, Saving All or Parts of Files, Deleting Files, & Listing Other Files While Running C.A.K.E.
Generic Computer Products, Inc. (GCPI).

CursorPower. *Version:* 1.4. Jun. 1993. *Items Included:* Manual, 3 1/2" disk. *Customer Support:* Free phone support.
Windows 3.X. IBM PC & compatibles. disk $49.95 (ISBN 0-9625126-2-1). *Addl. software required:* Windows 3.X. *Optimal configuration:* Mouse. *Networks supported:* All.
OS/2 2.1. IBM PC & compatibles. disk $49.95 site licenses avail. *Addl. software required:* OS/2 operating system. *Optimal configuration:* Mouse. *Networks supported:* All.
Changes System Cursors. Pointer, Wait, Resize & I-Beam Cursors. Use Pre-Defined or Draw Your Own. Modify Pre-Defined to Your Liking.
North Shore Systems, Inc.

CURVE. 1981-1985. *Compatible Hardware:* Atari 800, Commodore 64. *Language(s):* BASIC (source code included).
disk $200.00.
Graphics Tool Providing General-Purpose 2-Dimensional Hard Copy Graphics Capability. Used in Engineering, Scientific Research & Business Applications. All Output Is Directed to Any of Several Popular Plotters.
West Coast Consultants.

CURVE Appleplotter. 1982. *Compatible Hardware:* Apple II, II+, IIe. *Operating System(s) Required:* Apple DOS 3.3. *Language(s):* Applesoft BASIC (source code included). *Memory Required:* 48k.
disk $75.00, incl. manual.
Allows User to Plot Hardcopy of Any Graphic Generated with the APPLEPLOT Program. Supports Color Control of Graphics Components & Has Options for 3 Different Sizes.
West Coast Consultants.

Curve Copy. 1981. *Compatible Hardware:* Apple II+, II. *Operating System(s) Required:* Apple DOS 3.3. *Language(s):* Assembly, Applesoft BASIC (source code included).
disk $75.00.
Copies Contents of a High Resolution Display to Any HIPLOT DMP Plotter in 9 Sizes.
West Coast Consultants.

Curve Digitizer. Richard J. Knox. Jun. 1986. *Compatible Hardware:* IBM PC, PC XT, PC AT, & compatibles. *Memory Required:* 256k. *General Requirements:* EGA/CGA or Hercules mono-card, plotter and/or printer.
disk $149.00.
2-Dimensional Computer-Aided Design Package Hosting 80 Single-Key Graphics Commands. Accepts Input from Digitizers, Keyboard, Disk Files, Keypad-Control Drawings, & Plotters. The Plotter Input Mode Allows a User to Substitute the Device for Use As a "Discrete" Digitizer. Besides Featuring Most "Standard" CAD Graphics Commands, the Program Includes Smoothing, Shading, & Area Calculations of Complex Shapes. High-Resolution & Color Output Is Directible to Many Printers & Most Popular Plotters.
West Coast Consultants.

Curve-F: Polynomial Curve Fitting. *Version:* 2.00. Daniel V. Oaks Jr. 1988. *Compatible Hardware:* 8086 family of computers IBM PC/XT/AT & compatibles. *Operating System(s) Required:* MS-DOS or PC-DOS. *Language(s):* C. *Memory Required:* 256k. *Items Included:* 5.25" DS/DD, non-protected diskette (3.5" diskette available on special order). User's manual. *Customer Support:* 30 day unlimited warranty.
disk $120.00 (ISBN 0-927449-33-1, Order no.: IFPM).
Interactive Graphical Software Package Will Solve the Polynomial Coefficients to Fit Empirical Data Points, Allowing Simulation of a Complex Component, Circuit, Blackbox, etc. Using This Technique It May Be Possible to Simulate Analog Components That Would Otherwise Be Difficult If Not Impossible to Model. The Empirical Data Entry Can Be from External Files As a List of x & y Coordinates, from the Keyboard As x & y Coordinates, or As Points on a Graph. Subsequent Commands Graph the Data & Optimize the Equation That Approximates the Data. The Graphical Presentation Permits & Plots, Also Allows Adding Points & to See Their Effects in "Smoothing Out" the Computed Curve. The Program Permits up to 8000 Data Points & Computing up to a 19th Degree Polynomial.
Tatum Labs, Inc.

Curve-Fit. *Version:* 2.0. 1989. *Compatible Hardware:* Apple II+, IIe; Atari; IBM PC XT, PC AT & compatibles; TRS-80. *Language(s):* BASICA (source code included).
disk $99.00.
Hardcopy Graphics Program Which Can Be Used to Fit Data with up to 4 Types of Equations & Display All Results on High-Resolution Screen & to Most Popular Plotters & Printers.
West Coast Consultants.

Curve Fit Utility. *Items Included:* Bound manual. *Customer Support:* Free hotline - no time limit; 30 day limited warranty; updates are $5/disk plus S&H.
MS-DOS. IBM & compatibles (256k). disk $29.95.
Fits Curves to Data. It Provides Flexibility in Selecting Curve Types, Data Weighting Factors, & Data Input/Output Devices & Formats. Can Be Run Stand-Alone or Can Be Used in Conjunction with Other Software Such As Spread Sheets, Data Bases, Plotting Packages, or Other Scientific or Business Applications Software. Features: Data Input; Data Display & Edit; Curve Fitting; Curve Extrapolation; Curve Output; Graphing; Statistics.
Dynacomp, Inc.

Curve Fitter. *Compatible Hardware:* Apple II+, IIe; Franklin Ace. *Operating System(s) Required:* Apple DOS 3.3. *Language(s):* BASIC. *Memory Required:* 48k.
disk $34.95.
Uses Three Forms of Interpolation & Three Forms of Least Square to Make High Resolution Curves Out of Data. Interpolated Values Can Be Found Once a Curve Has Been Made. Data Can Be Entered from the Keyboard, Disk, or Analog Instruments. It Can Then Be Scaled, Changed to Log Form, or Offset by a Constant. Smoothing & Averaging Are among the Features Included. Data Can Be Saved on the Disk.
Compuware.

Curve Fitter. *Compatible Hardware:* TI 99/4A. *Operating System(s) Required:* DX-10. *Language(s):* Console BASIC. *Memory Required:* 16k.
disk or cassette $17.00.
2 Interactive Programs to Fit Smooth Curves to Experimental Data. 5 Curves Including Straight Line, Logarithmic & Polynomial Are Used for a Single Independent Variable. Multiple Linear Regression Is Used, with More Than One Independent Variable, to Derive Polynomial or Multiple Straight Line Fit.
Eastbench Software Products.

Curve Fitting & Data Manipulation. 1995. *Items Included:* Full manual. *Customer Support:* Free telephone support - 90 days, 30-day warranty.
MS-DOS 3.2 or higher. 286 (584k). disk $49.95. *Nonstandard peripherals required:* CGA/EGA/VGA.
Manipulates & Analyzes Two-Dimensional Data Sets & Presents the Results Efficiently Using a Menu-Driven Interface. It Fits Using a Simple Straight Line, a Simple Power Law, Linear Combinations of Legendre & Chebyshev Polynomials, & Nonlinear Combinations of Delayed, Gaussian, & Lorenzian Exponentials. It Also Smooths Data, Generates Derivatives & Integrals, Fits a Cubic Spline, or Calculates a Fast Fourier Transform of a Data Set. There Is a Lot of Power in This Tool.
Dynacomp, Inc.

Curve Fitting Software. Mar. 1992. *Items Included:* Spiral manual contains theory, sample runs. *Customer Support:* Free phone, on-site seminars.
MS-DOS. IBM (128k). disk $96.00.
Macintosh. Any Macintosh. 3.5" disk $96.00.
This Is a Book/Disk Package That Shows How to Write 2 & 3D Curve Fitting Software Using Splines, Lines, Functions & Regression. Includes Plotting Data Sets in 3 Dimensions, Editing & Filing Data Sets, Curve Fitting with A & B Splines, Function Fitting, Rotating Data Sets & Curves in 3 Dimensions.
Kern International, Inc.

Curve Perspective. 1987. *Compatible Hardware:* Apple II, II+, IIe, IIc; IBM PC, PC XT, PC AT. *Language(s):* Compiled BASIC. *Memory Required:* IBM 256k, Apple 48k.
Apple. disk $450.00.
IBM. disk $650.00.
Provides 3-D Graphics. Gives User Full Plotting Power for Arbitrary 3-D Objects. Allows User to Describe Complex Objects by Using As Many As 450 Interconnecting Lines Forming a Maximum of 50 Planes. Used by Drafters, Architects, Floor Planners, Designers, Machinists, Industrial Artists & Hobbyists.
West Coast Consultants.

Curve 3-D. 1984. *Compatible Hardware:* Apple II; Atari 800; Commodore PET; IBM PC; NEC PC-8001; North Star; TRS-80 Model I, Model III. *Operating System(s) Required:* MS-DOS. *Language(s):* BASIC (source code included). *Memory Required:* 256k.
disk $200.00.
Plots Surface Functions X, Y, Z, Data Arrays, Plot Space Curves, Rotate Through 360 Degrees; Scales Axes & Labeling. All Output Directed to Any of Several Popular Plotters.
West Coast Consultants.

Curve 3-D CRT. 1984. *Compatible Hardware:* Apple II+, IIe; IBM PC. *Language(s):* BASIC (source code included). *Memory Required:* 48-128k.
disk $250.00.
Plots Surface Functions X,Y,Z Data Arrays. Plots Space Curves, Rotates Through 360 Degrees; Scales Axes & Labeling. All Output Directed to High-Resolution Screen or to Any of Several Popular Plotters & Printers.
West Coast Consultants.

Curve II. 1981. *Compatible Hardware:* Apple II; Atari 800; CP/M based machines; Commodore PET; NEC PC-8001; TRS-80 Model I, Model III. *Language(s):* BASIC (source code included).
disk $275.00.
manual $25.00.
Graphics Tool for General-Purpose 2-Dimensional Hard Copy Graphics Capability. Used in Engineering, Scientific Research & Business Applications.
West Coast Consultants.

Curve II CRT. 1984. *Compatible Hardware:* Apple II+, IIe; IBM PC. *Language(s):* Applesoft BASIC, BASICA (source code included). *Memory Required:* IBM 128k, Apple 48k.
disk $250.00.
Graphics Tool for General-Purpose 2-Dimensional Hard Copy Graphics Capability. Used in Engineering, Scientific Research & Business Applications. A Preview of Each Chart May Be Directed to the High-Resolution Screen.
West Coast Consultants.

CurveFit: Curve Fitting Program. *Version:* 2.5. Dec. 1995. *Items Included:* User manual with sample problems. *Customer Support:* Free telephone support for 12-months.
PC-DOS/MS-DOS, Windows 3.1 & higher. Intel compatible machines, 386 or higher (4Mb). disk $149.00 (ISBN 0-932507-68-9). *Nonstandard peripherals required:* Color 640x480.
Fits Experimental Data to Various Polynomials, Splines, & Interpolating Functions. Handles up to 100 Data Points. Calculates Best-Fit Coefficients & Plots the Result on Screen or Printer. Calculates Y Value for Given X Value & Extrapolates Data. User-Definable Graph Titles for the X & Y Axis.
Systek.

Custom Auto-Pricing System: CAPS. *Version:* 1.2. Mar. 1994. *Items Included:* Full documentation manuals. *Customer Support:* 90 days free support, annual maintenance support at $995.00.
MS-DOS, UNIX. IBM PC & compatibles (4Mb). single user version $99.50. *Addl. software required:* Relational Database (Progress Runtime) license included. *Optimal configuration:* Standalone PC or LAN. *Networks supported:* Novell, LAN.
A Retail Store Headquarters, CAPS Accepts Item Cost Changes & Automatically Adjusts Retail UPC Prices to Reach Planned Gross Margins. Plans Sales, Downloads to Stores, Price-Markdown.
Data Index, Inc.

Custom Ledger. *Compatible Hardware:* IBM PC; TRS-80 Model II, Model III, Model 4, Model 12, Model 16.
contact publisher for price.
General Ledger Produces Chart of Accounts, Trial Balance, Transaction Journal, Balance Sheet, Statement of Income/Expenses, Check Register, Checkbook Reconciliation, Budget Report & Session Transaction Journal.
Custom Data (New Mexico).

Custom Payroll. *Version:* 8.25. Jan. 1985. *Compatible Hardware:* IBM PC, PC XT, PS/2 & compatibles. *Operating System(s) Required:* PC-DOS, MS-DOS Version 3.0 or higher. *Language(s):* Microsoft Professional BASIC Version 7.1 (source code included). *Memory Required:* 384k. *General Requirements:* hard disk with at least 2.5Mb free, plus at least one floppy disk drive, printer. *Items Included:* 310 plus pp manual, source code, compiled runtime system. *Customer Support:* 1 year free telephone support, 1 year limited warranty.
disk $695.00 (ISBN 0-917769-08-2).
Eight Categorized Pay Amounts (from 16 Categories), 12 User-Defined Regular Deductions Plus 5 Special Pay or Deduction Amounts with Tax Treatment Control. Automatic Federal, FICA, Medicare, State, Local, & Other Withholding Amounts for Any Pay Period from a Single Set of Easy-to-Maintain Annual Tax Tables, Preview, Modify & Recalculate. Previous-Period Check Reversal. Over 23 Reports Including Check, Paper & Diskette W-2's, & 1099-MISC's. Department, Company Totals, Job Cost. Handles Cash Advance/Payback, Vacations, Pension, Cafeteria Plans, Imputed Pay, Non-Cash, Tips, Earned Income Credit, Garnishment, Daily Payroll, Extra Payroll. Expandable.
Datasmith, Inc.

Custom/QC. *Version:* 3.96. Sep. 1983. *Compatible Hardware:* IBM PC, PC XT, PC AT, PS/2 & compatibles. *Operating System(s) Required:* PC-DOS/MS-DOS, UNIX, Windows. *Language(s):* C. *Memory Required:* 640k. *Customer Support:* 800, BBS, FAX, Optional Training.
PC-DOS, MS-DOS, UNIX. disk $495.00-$995.00 (ISBN 0-927236-01-X).
IBM, SUN. disk $495.00-$995.00 (ISBN 0-927236-02-8).
Menu-Driven Statistical Process Control Package. Accepts ASCII Formatted Data from Mainframes, Spreadsheets, Databases, Manual Entry, etc. Output Includes Configurable Graphics to Screen, Printer, or Plotter. Calculations & Charts: Mean, Median, Standard Deviation, Skewness, Kurtosis, Histogram, Run Test, CP, CPK, X-bar, R, Sigma, CuSum, P, NP, C, U, Min/Max, X, Moving R, Chi Square, T Square, Single & Multi Variable Analysis of Means, Multiple Regression, Trend Analysis, Process Evaluation, Process Capability, Auto Correlation, Sampling Plans, Curve Comparisons & Table Lookup.
Stochos, Inc.

Customer Histories: Order Entry-Accounts Receivable. *Customer Support:* Free telephone & BBS technical support.
MS/PC DOS, Concurrent DOS, Xenix, Unix. IBM PC/XT/AT & compatibles; IBM PS/2 (512k). single or multi-user $795.00. *Nonstandard peripherals required:* Novell, Lantastic, Banyan VINES; all NETBIOS compatible.
"Customer Histories" tracks all purchases made from all products by all customers. Additionally, OE/AR Customer Histories reports the payment & credit history of each customer over an extended period of time. All invoice & Sales Order activity may be viewed & analyzed, & a summary/analysis record may be prepared for each customer who has any purchase & or payment history information.
INMASS/MRP.

Customer Profile. *Compatible Hardware:* IBM. (source code included). *Memory Required:* 128k.
disk $59.95.
Provides a Way to Keep Track of Current & Prospective Customers According to Business Type, Services or Products Provided the Customer & Assigned Sales Representative or Territory.
Dynacomp, Inc.

Customer Profile II: Customer-Client Tracking. 1992. *Items Included:* Detailed manuals included with all Dynacomp products. *Customer Support:* Free telephone support to original customer - no time limit; 30 day limited warranty.
MS-DOS 3.2 or higher. IBM PC & compatibles

TITLE INDEX

(512k). $79.95 (Add $5.00 for 3 1/2" format; 5 1/4" format standard). *Optimal configuration:* IBM, 256k RAM, MS-DOS 2.0 or higher.
Provides an Easy Way to Keep Track of Current & Prospective Customers According to Business Type, Services or Products Provided to the Customer, & Assigned Sales Representative or Territory. Employs a Customer Data File & Three Tables. The Customer Data File Contains: Customer Name & Address, Customer Telephone Number, Sales Contact, Customer Status (Current or Prospective Customer), Business Type, Sales Code (User-Refined), Territory/Representative Assignment, Product/Service, Date of Most Recent Sale/Sales Call. The Three Tables Are: Business Type, Assignment, Products & Services.
Dynacomp, Inc.

Customer Profile System. Version: 1.50. 1991. *Items Included:* Manual. *Customer Support:* 1 hour phone support, annual support agreements ($150), hourly phone support ($1 per minute).
  MS-DOS version 2.10 or higher. PC & compatibles (640k). $795.00. *Nonstandard peripherals required:* Must have hard disk. *Addl. software required:* Optional MCC Accounts Receivable & Inventory Accounting. *Optimal configuration:* 386, MS-DOS 4.00, 640k, 80Mb hard disk, MCC Accounts Receivable & Inventory Accounting.
Maintains Complete Data & Chronological History of Customer or Prospect. Allows User to Search & Analyze Contact Data. Includes Options for Letter Writing, Labels, Order Entry & Invoicing, Inventory Lookup, Sales History, Aged Accounts Receivable Total, & Auto Dialing. Designed for Telemarketing, Prospecting & Sales Management.
MCC Software (Midwest Computer Ctr. Co.).

Customer Profile System. *General Requirements:* Host database with network link to Macintosh; Oracle for Macintosh; Hypercard 1.2.
  Macintosh (2Mb). contact publisher for price.
Detailed Analysis of Key Customer Accounts & Market Areas.
Softouch Software, Inc.

Customer Profile 2: Customer - Client Tracking. *Items Included:* Full manual. No other products required. *Customer Support:* Free telephone support - no time limit, 30 day warranty.
  MS-DOS 3.2 or higher. IBM & compatibles (512k). disk $79.95.
Provides an Easy Way to Keep Track of Current & Prospective Customers According to Business Type, Services or Products Provided to the Customer, & Assigned Sales Representative or Territory. Customer Data File Contains: Customer Name & Address, Customer Telephone Number, Sales Contact, Customer Status (Current or Prospective Customer), Business Type, Sales Code (User-Defined), Territory/Representative Assignment, Product/Service, Date of Most Recent Sale/Sales Call. The Three Tables Are Business Type, Assignment, Products & Service.
Dynacomp, Inc.

CustomGantt Plus. Version: 1.2. 1989. *Items Included:* 300-page user manual. *Customer Support:* Outside training available $750.00 per day plus expense.
  MS-DOS (256k). IBM PC PC XT, PC AT, PS/2 & compatibles. Version 1.2 $195.00. *Nonstandard peripherals required:* Dot matrix printer, laser printer or pen plotter required.
  SCOenix 286 & 386 (1Mb). $295.00-$395.00. *Nonstandard peripherals required:* Dot matrix printer, laser printer or pen plotter required. *Optimal configuration:* 2Mb RAM if running multiuser.
  Unix System V (1Mb). AT&T 3bx, Sun III, Motorola 8000, HP 9000/800. *Nonstandard peripherals required:* Dot matrix printer, laser printer or pen plotter required. *Optimal configuration:* 2Mb RAM or higher if running multiuser.
User Can Create Gantt Charts from Data Directly Entered into CustomGantt. Can Also Use Data Generated by Lotus 1-2-3, dBase II or III, Primavera Project Planner, Microsoft Project 4.0, Harvard Project Manager III or SuperProject Expert. User Can Display Pertinent Cost & Date Information, Can Show Detailed Project Time Line, or Summarize Project's Milestones.
SofTrak Systems.

Customizable Screen Symbol Library. Version: 10. Rick McElhinney. *Compatible Hardware:* Apple Macintosh II; IBM PC. (source code included). *General Requirements:* Hard disk, AutoCAD program.
  disk $195.00.
Consists of over 1000 Symbols in the Following Disciplines: Architecture, Electrical, Mechanical, Structural, Plumbing, Mapping, Process Control, Utilities, & Notes, Plus Room for Customizable Menus. Each Group of Symbols Is Contained on a Submenu & Is Found by Selecting the Correct Heading in Each Menu. The Software Creates Patterns for Other Symbols, Adding Functions for Differing Applications, or for Modification of the Existing Symbols. Restructuring & Changes of the Menus & Symbols, Locations, or Functions Is Possible.
Vector Systems, Inc.

Cut Planner 10, 20, 30. Version: 2.0. Sep. 1984. *Operating System(s) Required:* PC-DOS. *Language(s):* C. *Memory Required:* 1000k. *Customer Support:* Yes.
  386 or higher. disk $1500.00-$6000.00.
Automatically Creates & Displays Cutting Layouts. Determines How to Cut Small Rectangular Parts from Sheet Inventory for Glass, Metal, Wood Composites Panels & Plastic. Three Models Available to Fit All Types of Operations.
Pattern Systems International, Inc.

Cutter-Sanborn Tree-Figure Author Table. Richard Cutter. 1969.
  IBM & compatibles. CD-ROM disk $18.00 (ISBN 0-87287-210-6). *Nonstandard peripherals required:* CD-ROM drive.
Library Resource.
Libraries Unlimited, Inc.

Cutthroats. Michael Berlyn & Jerry Wolper. Sep. 1984. *Compatible Hardware:* Apple II, II+, IIe, IIc, Macintosh; Atari 400, 800, 1200, ST; Commodore 64, Amiga; IBM PC & compatibles; Kaypro. *Operating System(s) Required:* MS-DOS, CP/M.
  disk $39.95.
You're a Diver for Hire on an Isolated Island Populated by Disreputable Characters. When a Motley Band of Local Salts Gets Wind of a Shipwreck Laden with Sunken Treasures Somewhere in the Surrounding Waters, They Offer You a Piece of the Action in Exchange for Your Diving Skills & Knowledge. Now You Must Survive the Perils of the Deep (& the Even Greater Danger That Your Crew May Harbor a Cutthroat) If You Are to Recover the Treasure & Save Your Neck.
Activision, Inc.

Cutthroats. Infocom. *Compatible Hardware:* HP 150 Touchscreen, HP 110 Portable.
  3.5" disk $39.95 (Order no.: 92244AA).
Reader Becomes a Diver with an Untrustworthy Crew, & Tries to Recover Treasures from Shipwrecks.
Hewlett-Packard Co.

Lab Windows CVI. Sep. 1993. *Items Included:* Disks, manuals. *Customer Support:* Toll-free telephone support, paid on-site training, paid maintenance & support program.
  MS Windows 3.1. 386/33 PC with a 387 coprocessor (8Mb). disk $1995.00. *Optimal configuration:* 486/33 PC with Super VGA display. *Networks supported:* TCP/IP.
  Solaris 1.X or 2.X & MIT's X Windows System Version 11 Release 5. Sun SPARCstation (24Mb main memory, 32Mb disk swap space, 20Mb disk space). disk $3995.00. *Addl. software required:* LabWindows /CVI will run under Motif or Open Look. *Networks supported:* TCP/IP.
Used to Design Portable Instrumentation Applications with C That Run under Windows & Solaris. Includes a ANSI C Compiler, Linker, Debugger, Variable Trace Display, & Memory Checking Capabilities. Has Libraries for Designing User Interfaces; Acquiring, Analyzing, & Presenting Data; & Networking. DOS-Based LabWindows C Programs Can Run in LabWindows /CVI.
National Instruments Corp.

Cyberboogie with Sharon, Lois & Bram.
  MS-DOS 5.0 or higher, Windows 3.1 or higher. 386 processor or higher (8Mb). CD-ROM disk $49.95 (Order no.: R1308). *Nonstandard peripherals required:* CD-ROM drive. *Optimal configuration:* 386 processor operating at 16Mhz or higher, MS-DOS 5.0 or higher, Windows 3.1 or higher, 30Mb hard drive, mouse, VGA graphic adapter & VGA color monitor (SVGA recommended), 8Mb RAM, external speakers or headphones (with sound card) that are Sound Blaster compatible.
  Macintosh (8Mb). (Order no.: R1308A). *Nonstandard peripherals required:* 14" color monitor or larger, CD-ROM drive.
Featuring the Popular Songs of Sharon, Lois & Bram, Children Are Provided Hours of Creative Play As They Learn to Choreograph Musical Shows with Animated Characters or Just Relax, Sing & Dance along with Prerecorded Shows.
Library Video Co.

CyberBoogie with Sharon, Lois & Bram. Ehrlich Multimedia Staff. Oct. 1994.
  System 7.0.1. Mac II CX or higher (4Mb). CD-ROM disk $49.95 (ISBN 1-885551-03-7). *Nonstandard peripherals required:* CD-ROM (2x speed min). *Optimal configuration:* 8Mb RAM strongly recommended.
  Windows 3.1. Any MPC Level II (4Mb). CD-ROM disk $49.95 (ISBN 1-885551-02-9). *Optimal configuration:* 8Mb RAM strongly recommended.
CyberBoogie Is a Creative Play Program for Children Which Allows Them to Create Animated Shows to the Songs of Sharon, Lois & Bram. Animations Include 15 Scenes, 5 "Ani-Mates" & 20 Wacky Things for Kids to Choose From.
Times Mirror Multimedia.

Cyberchess. *Compatible Hardware:* Apple.
  disk $29.95.
Game Which Provides Immediate Penalty/Reward Feedback, & Features an Instruction Mode, 2 Modes of Timed Play for Tournament Drill, & 2 Modes of Speed Chess.
Blue Cat.

Cyberdesk. Version: 2.0. Jul. 1993. *Items Included:* Manual. *Customer Support:* 30 day money back guarantee, 60 days telephone support, 1 year online support. Contact CyberCorp, Inc., via e-mail cyber-netcom.com or phone 404-424-6240 or fax 404-424-8995.
  Windows 3.1. IBM & compatibles (1Mb). disk $99.00. *Optimal configuration:* 386 compatible with 4Mb RAM.

Gives Users a Windows Interface to the Internet. All a User Needs Is Cyberdesk & a Dial-Up UNIX Shell Account, SLIP, or PPP Account. Users Pick the Internet Service Provider They Like to Access the Net. Supports Internet Services Such As E-Mail, WWW, Newsgroups, FTP, Telnet, Gopher, Archie, Veronica, & IRC. Users Can Read & Respond to Messages Offline in Cyberdesk's Highly Graphical Windows Environment. Also Handles Accounts & Mailboxes on CompuServe, MCI Mail, CC:Mail, Microsoft Mail, Netware's MHS, & UNIX's Mail. Routinely Checks Each System for New Private E-Mail, & Public Messages in CompuServe's Forums & the Internet's Newsgroups. All the Messages from These Various Systems Appear in One Mailbox. Combines the Advantages of E-Mail, Off-Line Readers for Multiple Systems, Terminal Emulation & File Transfer into One Intuitive Environment.
CyberCorp, Inc.

Cyborg. Sentient Software. 1982. *Compatible Hardware:* Apple Macintosh. *Language(s):* FORTH.
3.5" disk $39.95 (Order no.: APDSK-51).
You Awaken in a Strange Environment & Discover You Have Been Turned into a Cyborg (Half Human, Half Machine). Your Two Halves Work Together to Discover Why You've Been Put Here & What You Must Do to Escape. You Will Travel Through 122 Locations & Try to Locate & Determine the Use of 28 Objects, Your Goal Not Being to Collect Treasure or Amass Points but to Complete Your Mission.
Broderbund Software, Inc.

Cyclones. Raven Soft Staff. Sep. 1995. *Items Included:* CD in jewel case. *Customer Support:* 30 Day Limited Warranty.
DOS 5.0 or higher. PC CD (4Mb). CD-ROM disk $9.95 (ISBN 0-917059-29-8, Order no.: 062521). *Optimal configuration:* 486/66.
Fantastic Fantasy Action Game.
Strategic Simulations Inc.

Cylinder & Shock Absorber Analysis. Apr. 1985. *Compatible Hardware:* Apple II+, IIe; IBM PC. *Operating System(s) Required:* PC-DOS, Apple DOS 3.3. *Language(s):* BASIC (source code included). *Memory Required:* Apple 48k, IBM 128k. *Customer Support:* Telephone.
$125.00.
Intended for Material Handling Applications. Contains 2 Sub-Programs Including Cylinder Analysis & Selection & Shock Absorber Analysis. Design Is Based on Criteria Such As Time, Acceleration, & Stopping Distance. Includes Graphics.
PEAS (Practical Engineering Applications Software).

CYMA Accounts Payable. CYMA Corp. *Compatible Hardware:* TI Professional with printer. *Operating System(s) Required:* CP/M-86, MS-DOS. *Memory Required:* 64k.
$1095.00.
Cash Management System. Cash Basis or Accrual Accounting Methods May Be Used.
Texas Instruments, Personal Productivit.

CYMA Accounts Receivable. CYMA Corp. *Compatible Hardware:* TI Professional with printer. *Operating System(s) Required:* CP/M, MS-DOS. *Memory Required:* 64k.
$1095.00 (Order no.: SY P/N TO39-035).
Provides up-to-the Minute Account Ledgers & Aging Detail on Receivables.
Texas Instruments, Personal Productivit.

CYMA Chiropractic Practice Management. Feb. 1985. *Compatible Hardware:* IBM PC & compatibles. *Operating System(s) Required:* PC-DOS/MS-DOS, TurboDOS, XENIX. *Language(s):* CYMA C-OPT. *Memory Required:* 256k.
DOS. disk $2295.00.
Xenix. disk $2495.00.
Provides for Patient Billing, Third Party Billing, Patient Recall, & Practice Analysis. Contains a Combination Open Item & Balance Forward System. Provides a Function for Printing Contract Accounts with Payment Book. Handles up to 26 Billing Codes & Includes Custom Printing Formatting. Also Includes Procedure Code Cross Referencing.
CYMA/McGraw Hill.

CYMA Client Accounting. Jan. 1981. *Compatible Hardware:* IBM PC & compatibles. *Operating System(s) Required:* PC-DOS/MS-DOS, TurboDOS, XENIX. *Language(s):* CYMA C-OPT. *Memory Required:* 128k.
DOS. disk $1195.00.
Xenix. disk $1295.00.
Features Job Costing with Budget Variance; Automatic Recurring, Reversing or Closing Entries; Update/Close into Specified Accounts; Roll Ending Balance into a Budget; Activity in Multiple Accounting Periods; Graphing of Accounts in Groups or Individually; File Lockouts, etc. Also Includes After-the-Fact Payroll.
CYMA/McGraw-Hill.

CYMA Dental Practice Management. Feb. 1985. *Compatible Hardware:* IBM PC & compatibles. *Operating System(s) Required:* PC-DOS/MS-DOS, TurboDOS, XENIX. *Language(s):* CYMA C-OPT. *Memory Required:* 128k.
DOS. disk $2295.00.
Xenix. disk $2495.00.
Gives Current Status on Patients & Accounts Receivable. It Provides an Open Item, Balance Forward System. The User May Create a Patients Account As a Contract Receivable, & the Program Will Print a Payment Book. This Software Has Patient Recall & Third Party Billing Capabilities. Dental Practice Can Be Used in Multiple Practices As Well. Includes Custom Report Formatting & Procedure Code Cross Referencing.
CYMA/McGraw Hill.

CYMA General Business System, 4 modules. *Version:* 2.3. Jan. 1980. *Compatible Hardware:* IBM PC & compatibles. *Operating System(s) Required:* PC-DOS/MS-DOS, TurboDOS, XENIX. *Language(s):* CYMA C-OPT. *Memory Required:* 128k.
DOS. $495.00-$595.00 per module.
Xenix. $595.00-$695.00 per module.
Offers the User an Automated Accounting System with Multi-User Capabilities. The Four Modules That Can Stand Alone or Integrate Are General Ledger, Accounts Payable, Accounts Receivable, & Payroll. Documentation Is Worded for Managers in Business Environments.
CYMA/McGraw Hill.

CYMA Job Control. *Version:* 2.3. Oct. 1985. *Compatible Hardware:* IBM PC & compatibles. *Operating System(s) Required:* PC-DOS/MS-DOS, TurboDOS, XENIX. *Language(s):* CYMA C-OPT. *Memory Required:* 128k.
DOS. disk $995.00.
Xenix. disk $1095.00.
Plots Information for Materials, Labor & Other Costs Based on Use Input. Also Tracks Man-Hours Worked, Wages Paid, & Invoices Rendered. Designed As a Manpower & Resource Management Aid.
CYMA/McGraw Hill.

CYMA Medical Practice Management. Feb. 1985. *Compatible Hardware:* IBM PC & compatibles. *Operating System(s) Required:* PC-DOS/MS-DOS, TurboDOS, XENIX. *Language(s):* CYMA C-OPT. *Memory Required:* 256k.
DOS. disk $2295.00.
Xenix. disk $2495.00.
Stores All Patient Transaction Information, Including All Necessary Treatments & Their Applicable Cost. Automates the Billing & Collection Procedure, Prints Insurance Forms. Sets up Patient Accounts under Different Formats: Open Item, Balance Forward or Contract Receivables. Custom Report Formatting. Includes Procedure Code Cross Referencing.
CYMA/McGraw-Hill.

CYMA Orthodontic Practice Management. *Version:* 3.0. Feb. 1985. *Compatible Hardware:* IBM PC & compatibles. *Operating System(s) Required:* PC-DOS/MS-DOS, TurboDOS, XENIX. *Language(s):* CYMA C-OPT. *Memory Required:* 256k.
DOS. disk $2295.00.
Xenix. disk $2495.00.
Allows the User to Add, Change, or Delete Patient Accounts, & to Post Entries to Patient Accounts. The Package Has Print Capabilities for Aging Reports of Patient Balances, Patient Statements or Insurance & Practice Analysis. Custom Report Formatting. Procedure Code Cross-Referencing.
CYMA/McGraw Hill.

CYMA Patient Billing. Jan. 1980. *Compatible Hardware:* IBM PC & compatibles. *Operating System(s) Required:* PC-DOS/MS-DOS, TurboDOS, XENIX. *Language(s):* CBASIC. *Memory Required:* 128k.
disk $995.00.
Provides Account Ledgers & Aging Details on Receivables. Produces Statements, Invoices, & Payment Coupon Books for Long-Term Payment Obligations. Audit Files Are Available.
CYMA/McGraw Hill.

CYMA Payroll. CYMA Corp. *Operating System(s) Required:* CP/M-86, MS-DOS. *Memory Required:* 64k. *General Requirements:* Printer.
$1095.00 (Order no.: SY P/N T039-045).
Texas Instruments, Personal Productivit.

CYMA Professional Accounting Series. 1986. *Compatible Hardware:* IBM PC & compatibles. *Operating System(s) Required:* PC-DOS, Xenix. *Memory Required:* 256k.
PC-DOS. $695.00-$995.00 per module.
Xenix. $895.00-$995.00 per module.
CYMA/McGraw-Hill.

Cypress for Dow Jones News-Retrieval. *Version:* 3.0. Sep. 1994. *Customer Support:* 1 year maintenance includes all upgrades - $100, unlimited phone support, 30-day money-back guarantee.
Windows 3.1, OS/2 2.1. IBM compatible 286 (4Mb). disk $179.00. *Nonstandard peripherals required:* Modem. *Addl. software required:* Windows 3.1. *Optimal configuration:* 386 running Windows w/8Mb RAM. *Networks supported:* All.
Macintosh, Windows. 68000 (2Mb). 3.5" disk $179.00. *Nonstandard peripherals required:* Modem. *Addl. software required:* System 6.0.3. *Optimal configuration:* 68030 w/8Mb RAM.
A Graphical Interface to Dow Jones News/Retrieval. Offers Push Buttons & Pull-Down Menus to Facilitate Gathering of Financial Data & News. Features Include Pull-Down Menus; User-Customizable Toolbar Buttons for Simplifying Common Queries; Buttons to Replace

Typed Commands & Menus; & a Capture Facility for Retrieving Information for Later Review & Formatting. Available Directly from Dow Jones.
Trax Softworks, Inc.

Cyrillic Alphabets, 2 disks. *Version:* 3.0. Jul. 1989. *Items Included:* Icon interface, utilities, font charts, 80-page manual with keymap guide. *Customer Support:* Phone support, free network support.
AmigaDOS (512k). Commodore Amiga 500, 1000, 2000, 3000. $59.95. *Addl. software required:* Applications software.
Variety of Workbench-Compatible Bitmap Cyrillic & English Fonts in 5 Languages Ranging from 8 to 120 Lines High. Works with Notepad & Popular Word Processing, & Paint Programs.
CLASSIC CONCEPTS Futureware.

Cyrillic II. *Version:* 8.1. Apr. 1992. *Items Included:* User's manual, keyboard layout charts, key caps sticker sheet. *Customer Support:* Telephone support, defective disks replaced free.
Macintosh (1Mb). 3.5" disk $149.95 ($249.95 for Cyrillic II Professional which includes all seven typefaces). *Nonstandard peripherals required:* Hard drive. *Addl. software required:* Any word processor.
Professional-Quality, Hinted, Scalable Bilingual Russian-English Fonts in Both TrueType & Type-1 Formats. These Fonts Are Available in Seven Typestyles, Each in Plain, Bold, Italic & Bold-Italic (Except Chan & Optina Are in Plain Only). Each Is Bilingual & Switches from English to Cyrillic Simply By Depressing the Caps Lock Key. Includes Five Optional Keyboard Layouts: Russian, AATSEEL Transliterated, Ukrainian, Serbian, & Bulgarian. Includes English & 17 Cyrillic Languages: Avar, Belarus, Bulgarian, Chechen, Evenki, Kabardian, Komi, Lak, Lezgin, Macedonian, Moksha, Moldavian, Mordvin, Russian, Serbian, Udmurt, & Ukrainian. Available in Times-Style, Helvetica-Style, Palatino-Style, Garamond-Style, Zapf Chancery-Style, Courier-Style, or Optina-Style.
Linguist's Software, Inc.

Cyrillic II for Windows. *Version:* 3.1. Jul. 1994. *Items Included:* User manual, Keyboard Layout Chart, Keycap Sticker Sheet, & ANSI Chart. *Customer Support:* Free telephone support, defective disks replaced.
Windows. IBM & compatibles (4Mb). $99.95; $249.95 for Cyrillic II Professional for Windows which includes all seven typefaces. *Addl. software required:* Microsoft Windows or ATM. *Optimal configuration:* 4Mb RAM & 386.
Professional-Quality, Hinted, Scalable Bilingual Russian-English Fonts in Both TrueType & Type 1 Formats: Cyrillic II, CyrliDos, & CyrliMac (Corresponding to Russian Windows, Russian DOS, & Russian Mac Font Arrangements) in Plain, Bold, Italic & Bold-Italic (Except Chan & Optina Are in Plain Only). These Three Formats Are Available in Seven Typestyles Each. For All Windows 3.1-Compatible Applications. Type 1 Works with ATM & Windows 3.X. Includes Five Optional Keyboard Layouts: Russian AATSEEL Transliterated, Ukrainian, Serbian, & Bulgarian. Includes English & 14 Cyrillic Languages: Avar, Belarus, Bulgarian, Chechen, Evenki, Kabardian, Lak, Lezgin, Macedonian, Moksha, Mordvin, Russian, Serbian, & Ukrainian. WordPerfect for Windows 6.0 Users Must Upgrade to 6.0a or Newer to Type Stress Marks.
Linguist's Software, Inc.

Cystic Fibrosis. *Version:* 2. 1988. *Compatible Hardware:* IBM PC & compatibles. *Operating System(s) Required:* MS-DOS. *Language(s):* BASIC. *Memory Required:* 512k.
disk $200.00 (Order no.: CCS-8112).
Deals with the Diagnosis & Treatment of a Cystic Fibrosis Patient. Chest Physiotherapy, Oxygen, Humidity & Aerosol Therapy Are Tested along with Home Care Procedures.
Educational Software Concepts, Inc.

D Code. *Version:* 1.1. Alan Bird. Aug. 1985. *Compatible Hardware:* Apple II, II+, IIe, IIc, IIgs. *Operating System(s) Required:* Apple DOS 3.3, ProDOS. *Language(s):* Machine, BASIC. *Memory Required:* DOS 3.3 48k, ProDOS 64k.
disk $39.95.
Program Compactor & Debugger. Will Reduce an AppleSoft Program to the Smallest Number of Program Lines Possible. The Total Bytes Saved Is Reported on the Screen. Lets Users Shorten Variable Names to One or Two Characters. REM Statements Are Removed (the "Remarked" Version Can Be Saved for Reference). Will Find Lines or Statements That Can't Possibly Be Executed & Let User Delete Them. Other Features Include: Program Comparer, the Ability to Uncover Program Errors Before Execution, Instant Syntax Checker, a TRACE Command, Break Point Control for Debugging Purposes, & the Ability to Find Occurrences of Any String or Variable in the Program.
Beagle Brothers.

D/Generation. Sep. 1991.
DOS. IBM PC & compatibles. disk $24.95. *Optimal configuration:* Full 256-color VGA, EGA, CGA.
Action Acdventure Meets Virtual Reality! Race Against Time to Search for Clues & Solve the Puzzles of the Strange Doings at the Genoq Corp. Headquarters & a Security System Run Amok. Incredible Graphics.
Software Toolworks.

D-Manager. *Items Included:* Bound manual included with software. *Customer Support:* Unlimited free technical support.
PC-DOS/MS-DOS Ver. 3.1 or higher. IBM PC/XT/AT, PS-2 (all models), & compatibles (640k). disk $295.00 (Order no.: DS-220). *Networks supported:* Ethernet.
A DOS-Based Network Management Program That Delivers a Host of Features for Monitoring & Evaluating the Performance of Different PCs on the Network & a Variety of Administrative Functions for Control.
D-Link Systems, Inc.

d-Marketcom. Aug. 1987. *Operating System(s) Required:* MS-DOS. *Memory Required:* 512k. *General Requirements:* Hard disk.
disk $299.00.
Maintains Mailing Lists & Phone Numbers, Types Letters, Memos, etc. Prints Labels & Envelopes. Uses Three Perpetually Sorted Index Files for Each Database. Ad Hoc Reports & Database Printouts, As Well As Scanning Are Included. Easy to Edit & Update Database.
ILAR Systems, Inc.

D-PLOT: For Amiga or IBM. Jan. 1990. *General Requirements:* BASIC.
Amiga, any series (256k). contact publisher for price (ISBN 0-9621208-6-3).
IBM PC (256k). contact publisher for price (ISBN 0-9621208-7-1).
Computer Programs for Data Organization, Analysis & Plot, 19 Analysis Operations, 9 Paper Types, Any Scale, 5 Plot Modes, 7 Label Modes, Screen, Sheet & Stripchart Plots. Math Function Plot Provided.
MiniLab Books.

D-Screen. *Compatible Hardware:* ASCII terminal capable of DCA, line DEL & INS, character DEL & INS, etc. *Operating System(s) Required:* CP/M. *Language(s):* CB80. *Memory Required:* 48k.
disk $100.00.
Programming Tool That May Be Used to Create Screen Images (Menus, etc.) That Are Stored in Screenfiles. Screenfile Entries May Then Be Retrieved by an Access Routine Within the User's Program & Displayed on an ASCII Terminal. The "Command" Mode Provides for Manipulation at the File Level (GET, SAVE, etc.) As Well As Providing a Way to Include Graphic Objects (Boxes, Lines) in the Screen Image. Graphic Support Includes Reverse Video, Highlight, Blink, & Alternate Character.
Design Software.

D The Data Language. *Operating System(s) Required:* PC-DOS/MS-DOS, Unix, XENIX 286, XENIX 386, Intel UNIX, Sco UNIX, Sys V, AIX PS/2s, DOS LANS, RISC 6000. *Customer Support:* 90 days free, then $200.00 per year. contact publisher for price.
Database Management System Provides On-Screen Help, Free-Form File Definition, Automatic Indexing, Split & Merge Files, Built-in Editor, Debugging Facilities, & Run-Time Version Available. Features Unlimited Fields Per Record; 4,096 Characters in Field; 4,088 Records Per File; Unlimited Characters in Record; Unlimited Indexes Per File; & Unlimited Active Files. Includes 103 Commands, Unlimited Functions, Full Screen of Lines Per Command File, & Unlimited Variables. Offers Comma-Delimited ASCII, DIF, DBF, SDF Data-Import/Export Capabilities. C & Assembler Are Languages Provided, Developer Transparent File & Record Locking (Multi-User Version).
Caltexsoftwareinc.

d-tree. *Version:* 3.5A. *Compatible Hardware:* Unix. *Items Included:* Perfectbound 2 vol. Programmer's Reference Guide, Function Reference Guide. *Customer Support:* 3 months free unlimited support; maintenance plan thereafter includes priority shipments of upgrades & free subscription to technical publication.
3.5" disk begins at $745.00.
Set of Application-Generation Modules Including a Data Dictionary. The Toolbox Allows Programmers to Design Their Own Development Environments by Providing Functions That Can Be Used to Create an Application Generator & Generate Structures to Use C-Tree & R-Tree. Features Include Faircom's Termcap for Screen & Keyboard Protability, Interface to C-Tree, Data Portability, File Reformatting, & General Utilities, Including a General Table Lookup Function, Screen F/O Functions & Date & Time Functions.
FairCom Corp.

D-View, SNMP Network Management Program. *Version:* 3.0. *Items Included:* Bound manual included with software. *Customer Support:* Unlimited free technical support.
MS-DOS 4.0 or higher, Windows 3.1 or higher. IBM PC & compatibles with 80386 processor (4Mb). disk $395.00 (Order no.: DS-200). *Nonstandard peripherals required:* For in band connection - D-Link Ethernet card. For out-of-band management, an asynchronous communication card. A modem is also needed for remote connection. *Networks supported:* Ethernet.
Network Management Package Delivers an Array of Features That Monitor, Evaluate, Improve & Plan Network Performance. It Implements the Simple Network Management Protocol (SNMP) Which Diagnoses & Controls the Network.
D-Link Systems, Inc.

DacEasy Accounting. *Version:* 4.3. *Compatible Hardware:* IBM PC & compatibles, PC XT, PC AT, hard disk. *Operating System(s) Required:* PC-DOS/MS-DOS 3.1 or higher. *Memory Required:* 640k. *General Requirements:*

(132-column printer) 80-column, 132 compressed mode.
disk $149.95.
Menu-Driven Accounting Package with Password Protection. File Capacity Is Limited Only by Disk Space. Modules Include General Ledger, Accounts Receivable, Accounts Payable, Cash Management Inventory, Product Assembly, Purchase Order, Billing, Budgeting Forecasting, Graphics & Report Generator.
DacEasy, Inc.

DacEasy Bonus Pack. *Version:* 4.3. *Compatible Hardware:* IBM PC & compatibles.
$199.95.
Includes: DACEASY ACCOUNTING 4.3 & DACEASY PAYROLL 4.3.
DacEasy, Inc.

DacEasy Instant Accounting. Jun. 1992. *Items Included:* 320 pg. manual (illustrated), 3 1/2" & 5 1/4" diskettes, also a conversion utility for users of our light checkbook accounting pkg. *Customer Support:* 60 days of free technical support from degreed accounting & computer professionals. Thereafter, $25 per year.
DOS 3.1 or higher (MS or PC DOS). IBM or compatible (512k). disk $49.95. *Nonstandard peripherals required:* Hard disk drive required; Mono; CGA, EGA, & VGA monitor; Mouse optional. *Optimal configuration:* Modems can be used for auto dialing to customers & vendors; also, Instant creates FAX format files for users with FAX boards & software; Mouse. Windows 3.0 or higher. IBM or compatible (1Mb with Windows). disk $49.95. *Nonstandard peripherals required:* Hard disk required; CGA, EGA, VGA monitor; Mouse. *Optimal configuration:* Modems can be used for customer/vendor dialing, FAX-format files can be created for use with FAX-modem boards. 2Mb of RAM is optimal in Windows version.
DOS & Windows Accounting System for Small Business. Intuitive & Easy-to-Read Screens Make Learning & Using It Simple. Use Either the DOS or Windows Version, or Both - They Are Both Included. This Is a Complete General Ledger Package.
DacEasy, Inc.

DacEasy Light. *Compatible Hardware:* IBM PC & compatibles. *Operating System(s) Required:* PC-DOS/MS-DOS 2.0 or higher. *Memory Required:* 256k. *General Requirements:* Printer.
disk $49.95.
Home or Office Accounting System.
DacEasy, Inc.

DacEasy Payroll. *Version:* 4.3. *Compatible Hardware:* IBM PC & compatibles, PC XT, PC AT (all require hard disk drives). *Operating System(s) Required:* PC-DOS/MS-DOS 3.1 or higher. *Memory Required:* 640k. *General Requirements:* (132-column printer) 80 column, 132 compressed mode.
disk $99.95.
Can Be Used As Stand-Alone, or Integrated with DAC EASY ACCOUNTING. Features Built-In Federal & State Tax Tables; Automatic Federal, City, & State Withholding Calculations; FICA & User-Defined Deductions; Continuous Form Checks & W2's; up to 99 Departments, with Earning & Deductions Codes per Department; Manages Hire Dates, Raises, Reviews, Terminations, Vacations, & Sick Time; Generates Complete Range of Management Reports; Supports Hourly or Salaried Employees, Four Different Payroll Periods, Tips, Piece-Rate, & After-the-Fact Payroll.
DacEasy, Inc.

DacEasy Payroll Self Paced. *Version:* 4.3. *Compatible Hardware:* IBM PC & compatibles. *Operating System(s) Required:* PC-DOS/MS-DOS 3.1 or higher. *Memory Required:* 640k.
disk $75.00.
Can Be Used by the Beginner or the Current User As a Stand-Alone Supplement to the User's Manual.
DacEasy, Inc.

DacEasy Point of Sale. Jan. 1992. *Items Included:* 1 manual. *Customer Support:* 2 per-call support options: "Credit Card Charge Line" $15.00 minimum charged to major credit card, $1.50/minute thereafter. "900" line telephone charge - no minimum charge, $1.50/minute thereafter. Annual contract fee of $50.00 for yearly unlimited support.
DOS 3.1 or higher (640k). IBM or compatibles or PC Based Point of Sale System. $149.95 single user; $299.95 network version. *Nonstandard peripherals required:* Hard disk drive. *Networks supported:* Network system available - runs on any NetBIOS compatible LAN.
Stand Alone Point of Sale System That Also Fully Integrates with DacEasy Accounting. Works with a Computer (IBM or Compatible) or Most Popular Cash Register Hardware to Ring up Sales, Scan & Print Bar Codes, Print Reports, Track Serial Numbers & More.
DacEasy, Inc.

DacEasy Self Paced. *Version:* 4.3. *Compatible Hardware:* IBM PC & compatibles. *Operating System(s) Required:* PC-DOS/MS-DOS 3.1 or higher. *Memory Required:* 640k. *Items Included:* Disk, manual, tape.
disk $75.00.
Can Be Used by the Beginner or the Current User As a Stand-Alone Supplement to the User's Manual.
DacEasy, Inc.

DADiSP: Data Analysis & Display. *Version:* 3.01. *Compatible Hardware:* Concurrent, DEC; IBM PC, IBM RS600 & compatibles, 32-bit workstations; Silicon Graphics, Sun, Vext. *Operating System(s) Required:* PC-DOS/MS-DOS 2.0 or higher. *Memory Required:* 640k. *General Requirements:* 2 disk drives or hard disk; CGA, EGA, VGA, or Hercules card. 80287 or 80387 math co-processor recommended. *Items Included:* Software media, documentation, registration card. *Customer Support:* 6 months free telephone support & product updates.
PC version $1795.00.
workstation version $4495.00.
Graphical, General Purpose Productivity Software for Scientists & Engineers. DADiSP Allows Users to Manipulate & Analyze Large Amounts of Data in Graphical or Tabular Format. Users Can Perform Various Complex Operations & View Results in Multiple Windows, up to 100 Windows in Each Worksheet. Includes Hundreds of Data Reduction, Mathematical, Statistical, Fourier Transform, Peak Analysis, & Graphical Tools. Users Also Can Define New Functions & Automate DADiSP Sessions. The Program Includes an Enhanced User Interface, an Extensive Set of Matrix Math & Statistical Functions, Powerful 3-D & 4-D Plotting Capabilities, & Presentation-Quality Output. Data Acquisition Support Is Also Available.
DSP Development Corp.

DAFRAC-The Diffraction Calculation Tool. *Compatible Hardware:* Apple Macintosh.
3.5" disk $20.00.
Tool for the Investigation of Wave Diffraction & Two-Dimensional Fourier Transforms.
Kinko's.

Dagar Home Health Care. *Version:* 2.00. 1988. *Operating System(s) Required:* PC-DOS/MS-DOS. *Memory Required:* 512k. *General Requirements:* 20Mb hard disk.
contact publisher for price.
For Person Providing In-Home Post-Hospital Medical Care. Provides Labels for Intravenous Solutions, Records Vital Signs in Graphic Form, Schedules Field Personnel Providing These Services & Handles the Insurance Billing to up to 4 Carrriers for Each Patient. Electronic Claim Submission Is Available.
Dagar-Software Development Corp.

Daily Astro-Report. Bruce Scofield & John Kahila. 1983. *Compatible Hardware:* Apple Macintosh with 2 disk drives; CP/M-based machines with 2 154-359k disk drives or 1 330k disk drive; IBM PC & MS-DOS compatibles with 2 double-sided disk drives. *Operating System(s) Required:* CP/M-80, MacFinder, MS-DOS, PC-DOS. *Language(s):* BASIC. *Memory Required:* CP/M 64k, PC-DOS, MS-DOS 128k or 256k, Macintosh 512k. *General Requirements:* 80-column printer, dot-matrix or laser. *Items Included:* Manual. *Customer Support:* Free phone support.
$195.00 ea.
CP/M (Kaypro 2). (ISBN 0-913637-51-3).
IBM PC & MS-DOS. (ISBN 0-913637-52-1).
Macintosh. (ISBN 0-87199-053-9).
Prints Multi-Page Forecasts Comparing Natal Horoscope with Current Transiting Planetary Positions. Includes License to Sell Printed Output. Also Available with Alternative "Keyword", "Relationship", or "Electional" Texts.
Astrolabe, Inc.

Daily Attendance Accounting System. *Version:* V8.01. 1982. *Items Included:* 1 full manual. *Customer Support:* 90 days unlimited warranty; unlimited technical support via telephone for $225/system per year.
MS-DOS. IBM or compatible (640k). disk $995.00. *Optimal configuration:* MS-DOS 6.2 or higher, 15Mb (including data) of space on a hard drive (to include all 5 systems). *Networks supported:* Novell, LANtastic, Windows NT.
Attendance Information Is Entered Using an Optical Scanner or Computer Keyboard. Within Minutes a Daily Attendance List of Absent, Tardy, Dismissed Students (Including Parent Information) Is Printed. Attendance Information Can Be Easily Updated, & a Variety of Reports May Be Printed.
Applied Educational Systems, Inc.

Daily Journal for Windows. Parsons Technology. Aug. 1993.
3.5" disk Contact publisher for price (ISBN 1-57264-043-X).
Parsons Technology.

Daily Manager: Accounts Payable. *Compatible Hardware:* IBM PC & compatibles. *Operating System(s) Required:* PC-DOS/MS-DOS, OS/2, UNIX. *Memory Required:* 640k. *General Requirements:* Hard disk, printer.
disk $995.00 (ISBN 0-927558-05-X, Order no.: 120).
Accounts Payable Option for DAILY MANAGER FINANCIAL ACCOUNTING SERIES. Includes Check Printing Option, On-Line Updating, Query. Allows Balance Forward or Open-Item Accounts. Handles Discounts & Optional Retainages. Data Format Allows the Use of Standard Database & Report Generator Packages. On Site Setup & Training Available.
Timon, Inc.

Daily Manager: Funds Development System. 1986. *Compatible Hardware:* IBM PC & compatibles. *Operating System(s) Required:*

PC-DOS/MS-DOS, OS/2, UNIX. *Memory Required:* 640k. *General Requirements:* Hard disk, printer.
disk $995.00 (ISBN 0-927558-03-3).
Provides Mailing List Management & Cross Referencing by Family, Employer, Church, School, etc. Handles Donations, Pledges, Funds, Promotions, Solicitations, etc., & Provides for Cross Referencing, Totaling, & Reporting Options. Data Can Be Accessed by Standard Database Packages & Report Generators. Onsite Setup & Training Available.
Timon, Inc.

Daily Manager: General Accounting System. 1982. *Operating System(s) Required:* PC-DOS/MS-DOS, OS/2, UNIX. *Memory Required:* 640k. *General Requirements:* Hard disk, printer.
disk $995.00 (ISBN 0-927558-01-7, Order no.: 101).
General Accounting Package Which Provides Reporting & Auditing Control, Multiple Organizations, & Consolidations. Allows Dynamic Posting to Multiple Fiscal Years, Includes Checking Account Controls with Bank Reconciliation. Follows AICPA Reporting Guidelines. Data Can Be Interfaced with Industry Standard Database Packages & Report Generators. Check Printing Option with Accounts Payable. (Includes OfficeMate Pop up Window for Help, Calculator, Financial Calculations, Notepad, Calendar & Datebook, Phone Book & Dialer, Project Scheduler, etc.) Onsite Setup & Training.
Timon, Inc.

Daily Manager: Horse Management. 1990. *Customer Support:* On site setup & training available. Phone support provided.
PC-DOS/MS-DOS, OS/2, Windows. IBM & compatibles (640k). disk $995.00 (ISBN 0-927558-14-9). *Networks supported:* Novell, Lantastic.
Provides Complete Management Control & Reporting for Horse Farm Business. Maintains Horse Health Records & Includes a Date Scheduler & Daily Reminder for Shots, Shoes, Teeth & Other Veterinarian Needs. Also Has Provision for General Dates (Shows, Special Events, Meetings, Birthdays). Historical Records Can be Maintained. Horse Show Option Can Track Horse Show Records & Results, Retain Rider/Handler Information & Print Class/Test Schedules, Results, etc.
Timon, Inc.

Daily Manager: Accounts Receivable with Optional Inventory/Billing. 1988. *Operating System(s) Required:* PC-DOS/MS-DOS, OS/2, Unix. *Memory Required:* 640k.
$1995.00 (ISBN 0-927558-07-6).
Includes Inventory, Invoicing, & Accounts Receivable Control & Reporting. Provides Replacement/Substitutes; Balance Forward & Open Item Accounts; Discounts; Optional Retainages. Has Scheduling/Reminder System That Can Be Tracked by Account or in General. Data Can Be Accessed by Standard Databases & Report Generators. Includes OfficeMate Pop-Up Window for Help, Calculator, Financial Calculations, Notepad, Calendar & Datebook, Phone Book, Etc.
Timon, Inc.

Daily Manager: Manufacturing Management Systems. 1988. *Operating System(s) Required:* PC-DOS/MS-DOS, OS/2, Unix. *Memory Required:* 640k.
$15,000.00 (ISBN 0-927558-08-4).
Includes Inventory Control, Production Cost/Price Control, Bill-of-Materials Management/Control, Routing, Job Scheduling, Invoicing & Receivables. Data Can Be Accessed by Standard Database & Report Generators.
Timon, Inc.

Daily Manager: Name & Address System. 1980. *Operating System(s) Required:* PC-DOS/MS-DOS, OS/2, UNIX. *Memory Required:* 512k. *General Requirements:* Hard disk, printer.
disk $295.00 (ISBN 0-927558-00-9).
Assists in Handling of Large & Small Mailing Databases. Includes: Add, Edit, Search, Pop-Up Notepad for Each Entry, Labels & List Features. USPS Bulk Rate Sorting Capabilities Data Can Also Be Interfaced with Industry Standard Database Packages & Report Generators.
Timon, Inc.

Daily Manager: Payroll System. 1983. *Compatible Hardware:* IBM & compatibles. *Operating System(s) Required:* PC-DOS/MS-DOS, OS/2, UNIX. *Memory Required:* 512k. *General Requirements:* Hard disk, printer.
disk $995.00 (ISBN 0-927558-02-5, Order no.: 140).
Offers the Following Options: Departmentalization of All Major Output (Checks, Reports, etc.); Full- & Part-Time, Bonuses, Tips, Multiple Rates, Changing Departments, Multiple Deductions. IRS W-2's (Hard Copy & Magnetic); Rates Can Be Hourly, Salary, or Daily; On-Line Updating & Control. Can Be Used by Any Site Organizations (Unlimited Number of Employees). New Features Include Job Accounting & Time/Attendance Tracking (Days or Hours: Sick, Absent, Personal, Vacations, etc.) with Carry over form Prior Years of Days/Hours Still Available & Related Reports. Also, Pop-Up Calculators, Notebook (Separate Notes for Each Employee.) On-Site Setup & Training Available, Annual Update Service Available.
Timon, Inc.

Daily Organizer. Stephen R. Nichols. *Compatible Hardware:* IBM PC, PCjr, PC XT, PC AT, Portable PC, 3270 PC. *Operating System(s) Required:* PC-DOS 2.00, 2.10, 3.00, 3.10. *Memory Required:* 128k. *General Requirements:* Double-sided disk drive; IBM Matrix Printer optional.
disk $19.95 (Order no.: 6276557).
Enables User to Store Information for Dates Spanning More Than Half a Century & Print a Pocket-Sized Listing of Their Reminders. Can Be Customized with Colors. Includes Online Help. Can Be Used with TOPVIEW.
Personally Developed Software, Inc.

Daily Reminder. A. Beyreuther. Jan. 1982. *Compatible Hardware:* IBM PC. *Operating System(s) Required:* MS-DOS. *Language(s):* Compiled BASIC. *Memory Required:* 64k.
disk $39.95.
Year-Round Computerized Notebook & Appointment Calendar for Home or Office. Up to 16 Separate Memos May Be Entered for Each Day of the Year - Birthdays, Holidays & Other Yearly Recurring Events Are Registered Permanently. A Monthly Calendar Highlights Important Days & Allows Instant Selection of Any Day for Reviewing Appointments, or to Enter New Ones. Also Available in Spanish (Mi Diario), French (Mon Journal) & German (Mein Tagebuch) Versions.
International Software.

Dairy Cattle Recordkeeping. *Compatible Hardware:* TRS-80 Model I, Model II, Model III. contact publisher for price.
GHQ, Ltd.

Dairy Cooperative Accounting. Version: 1.4. Anita M. Lenes. May 1985. *Compatible Hardware:* IBM PC, PC AT. *Operating System(s) Required:* PC-DOS 3.1, MS-DOS. *Language(s):* Compiled dBASE. *Memory Required:* 512k. *General Requirements:* Hard disk.
disk $6000.00 (ISBN 0-934075-01-8, Order no.: SS002).
Designed for the Administration of Dairy Farm Milk Collection of Cooperatives by Banks or Bulk Milk Buyers & Processors. Incorporates Data Collection, Correlation of Information Sorting, Accounting, & Technical Reporting.
Sunstar Systems.

Dairy Herd Management: Decision Aid. Merle W. Wagner. 1982. *Compatible Hardware:* Apple II Plus, IIe, IIc; IBM. *Memory Required:* 48k, 640k. *General Requirements:* Printer.
disk $29.95 (ISBN 0-922900-13-2, Order no.: CFD-223).
Budget Analysis for a Complete Dairy Operation. 32 Data Entries, 10 Calculations.
Cherrygarth, Inc.

Dairy Management. Agri-Management Services, Inc. *Compatible Hardware:* TI Professional. *Operating System(s) Required:* MS-DOS. *Memory Required:* 64k. *General Requirements:* Printer.
$995.00.
Financial & Ration Program Which Provides Information Recall in Various Forms, Including: Cow's Lifetime History, Order of Production, Due to Calf, Come in Heat, Pregnancy Check, Inseminator Summaries, & Vaccination History.
Texas Instruments, Personal Productivit.

Dairy Production Records. Merle W. Wagner. 1981. *Compatible Hardware:* Apple II Plus, IIe, IIc; IBM. *Memory Required:* 48k, 640k. *General Requirements:* Printer.
disk $49.95, incl. manual (ISBN 0-922900-02-7, Order no.: CFR-222).
Income/Expense Information for a Dairy Operation. 400 Cows per Data Disk. Breeding & History Available for Each Cow.
Cherrygarth, Inc.

Dairy Ration Evaluation. May 1984. *Compatible Hardware:* Altos; Compupro; Cromemco; DEC Rainbow; Digital Microsystems; Eagle II, Eagle III, Eagle 4, Eagle PC; Epson QX-10; Exo; HP 87, 125; IBM PC; IMS; Kaypro; Micromation; Molecular; Morrow; North Star; Osborne; TeleVideo; TRS-80 Model II, Model 12, Model 16; Xerox; Zenith. *Operating System(s) Required:* CP/M 2.2, MS-DOS. *Language(s):* FORTRAN. *Memory Required:* 48-215k.
$600.00.
demo package $30.00.
Loren Bennett.

Dairy Ration Formulation. May 1984. *Compatible Hardware:* Altos; Compupro; Cromemco; DEC Rainbow; Digital Microsystems; Eagle II, Eagle III, Eagle 4, Eagle PC; Epson QX-10; HP 87, 125; IBM PC; IMS; Kaypro; Micromation; Molecular; Morrow; North Star; Osborne; TeleVideo; TRS-80 Model II, Model 12, Model 16; Xerox; Zenith. *Operating System(s) Required:* CP/M 2.2 or MS-DOS. *Language(s):* FORTRAN. *Memory Required:* 48-215k.
$1000.00.
demo package $30.00.
Consists of 8 Programs: Profit Maximizing Ration, Least Cost Ration Milking & Dry, Least Cost Grower Ration, Feed Library with NRC Nutrient Analysis of 101 Ingredients, Dairy Ration Evaluation, Feed Library Editor, Load Sheet Calculator, Terminal Configuration.
Loren Bennett.

DAL Server for UNIX. *Items Included:* Documentation; product registration card included. *Customer Support:* Maintenance

available; customer support; warranty.
UNIX. Sun SPARC, H-P 9000 or IBM RS/6000. Up to 16 users $4000.00 (educational, quantity & special discounts avail.). *Addl. software required:* Used with a DAL-aware client application to access Ingres, Informix, Oracle or Sybase databases. *Networks supported:* TCP/IP, Async.
Access to UNIX Databases from Any Computer Running a DAL-Aware Client Application.
Pacer Software, Inc.

Dan Bricklin's Demo II. *Compatible Hardware:* IBM PC XT. *Memory Required:* 512k.
disk $245.00.
Presentation-Graphics Package for On-Screen Slide Shows with Animation, Wipes, Sound Capability & Run-Time Version. Supports Any Bit-Mapped Graphics Image. Chart-Making Features Include Bar, Line, Text & Organization Charts; Multiple Charts on One Screen; & Free Positioning of Charts, Labels & Titles on Screen. Provides 256 User-Selectable Colors, 1 Typeface & 1 Font Size. Outputs to PostScript Printer, HP LaserJet, Dot-Matrix Printer, Film Recorder, Plotter, Color Ink-Jet Printer & Thermal Printer. Imports PCX File Formats.
Peter Norton Computing, Inc.

Dance of the Planets. *Version:* 2.5s. *Items Included:* Comprehensive, award-winning manual. *Customer Support:* 1-800 number for technical & subject based support.
DOS or Windows. IBM & compatibles, 80286 CPU or higher (640k). Contact publisher for price. *Nonstandard peripherals required:* Co-processor recommended, hard drive required (2.3Mb).
Applying Planetary Theory & Gravitational Laws to Realistic Animated Graphics Dance Creates the Most Accurate & Comprehensive Solar System Simulator Ever. Includes All the Known Planets & Moons, over 5500 Asteroids, & 1400 Comets, & 10,500 Stars & DSO's. Select Any Site & Date, from 4680 BC to AD 10,000, to Observe Any Celestial Event on Earth or Go Off-World & Watch the Planets Dance from Space.
Applied Research Consultants.

Dandy Dinosaurs: A Max the Dragon CD-Storybook. *Items Included:* Manual, registration card, flier describing all our titles, occasional promotional offers. *Customer Support:* Free telephone technical support.
DOS & Microsoft Windows 3.1. 12 MHz 80386SX. CD-ROM disk Contact publisher for price (ISBN 1-884014-19-4). *Nonstandard peripherals required:* MPC compatible. CD-ROM drive (680Mb) SVGA display, audio board, mouse, 486 DX processor. *Addl. software required:* Microsoft CD-ROM Extensions v.2.2.
Macintosh System 6.05. Color Macintosh (256 colors) (3.5Mb). CD-ROM disk Contact publisher for price (ISBN 1-884014-31-3). *Optimal configuration:* Single speed CD-ROM, 13" color monitor, 8 Mb RAM.
This Storybook Adventure Offers Eleven Easy-to-Make Craft Projects, Games & an Interactive Narrated Story for Children Ages 3 to 9.
Multicom Publishing, Inc.

Dandy Dinosaurs: A Max the Dragon Interactive Storybook. Sep. 1993. *Items Included:* Manual. *Customer Support:* Free telephone technical support.
DOS & Windows 3.1. Tandy Sensation, Sensation II, MMPC Model 10 (2Mb). CD-ROM disk Contact publisher for price (ISBN 1-884014-19-4). *Nonstandard peripherals required:* MPC-compatible CD-ROM drive; SVGA 256 colors, sound card, mouse, 486SX processor 20Mhz or higher. *Addl. software required:* Microsoft CD-ROM extensions 2.2 or higher. *Optimal configuration:* 4Mb RAM; double-speed CD-ROM drive.
Mac. CD-ROM disk Contact publisher for price (ISBN 1-884014-31-3).
Interactive CD-ROM for Children Age 4 & Up. Contains Animated, Fully Narrated Max the Dragon Stories. Each Story Is Matched to Engaging Craft Projects Which Can Be Completed by the Child Using Inexpensive Materials Found Around the Home. The Craft Projects Have Been Tested by Childhood Education Experts to Be Interesting & Entertaining for This Age Group.
Multicom Publishing, Inc.

Danger in Orbit. *Compatible Hardware:* TRS-80. contact publisher for price.
Instant Software, Inc.

Dangerous Creatures.
Windows. IBM & compatibles. CD-ROM disk $59.95 (Order no.: R1309). *Nonstandard peripherals required:* CD-ROM drive. *Optimal configuration:* 386 processor operating at 16Mhz or higher, MS-DOS 5.0 or higher, Windows 3.1 or higher, 30Mb hard drive, mouse, VGA graphic adapter & VGA color monitor (SVGA recommended), 8Mb RAM, external speakers or headphones (with sound card) that are Sound Blaster compatible.
Macintosh (4Mb). (Order no.: R1309A). *Nonstandard peripherals required:* 14" color monitor or larger, CD-ROM drive.
Developed in Conjunction with the World Wildlife Fund, Get Close to More Than 250 of the Wildest Creatures on Earth Through Detailed Articles, Photographs & Narrated Videos. Explore by Geographic Regions, Habitats & Types of Animals, or Take One of Three Fully Narrated Tours.
Library Video Co.

Daniel the Dinosaur Teaches Concepts: Same & Different. Oct. 1993. *Customer Support:* 1 manual, 1 registration card, 1 license agreement/system requirements card, colored stickers to cover keys.
MS-DOS 3.3 or higher. IBM PC & compatibles (286) (1Mb). disk $34.99 SRP (ISBN 0-9638408-0-8, Order no.: 503 645-6760). *Optimal configuration:* Echo PC or Soundblaster optional. Touchwindow optional (TM Edmark Corp.).
Play & Learn Game for 2-4 Year Olds. A Talking, Dancing, Dinosaur Invites the Child to Choose Color, Shapes, or Objects; & "Same" or "Different" Drills. Daniel Responds to Each Effort. Volcanoes Explode, Dinosaur Eggs Hatch, & Music Plays to Celebrate Success.
Software Enterprise, Ltd.

DARAD IIe. *Version:* 4.0.3. Jan. 1988. *Compatible Hardware:* Apple II series. *Memory Required:* 128k. *General Requirements:* Extended 80-column card.
3.5" disk $49.95 (ISBN 1-55616-022-4).
File Manager Targeted at Home Users with Limited Database Needs.
DAR Systems International.

DARAD IIe Report Generator. *Version:* 1.0.1. Jan. 1988. *Compatible Hardware:* Apple II series. *Memory Required:* 128k. *General Requirements:* DARAD IIe.
3.5" disk $29.95 (ISBN 1-55616-051-8).
Custom Report Generator for DARAD IIe Users.
DAR Systems International.

Darby My Dalmatian. Apr. 1995. *Items Included:* Soft cover, stapled manual & registration card. *Customer Support:* Free customer service via our 800 number. Unlimited warranty on disk replacement.
System 7 or higher or Windows 3.1; 386 or higher. Any 256 color capable MAC or IBM Tandy & 100% compatibles (4Mb). CD-ROM disk $24.95 (ISBN 1-888046-56-2, Order no.: ISD1001H). *Nonstandard peripherals required:* 12" monitor or larger, mouse or Super VGA, Sound Card; 100% Sound Blaster compatibles.
An Interactive Storybook, Featuring Darby the Dalmatian As the Main Character. The Story Has 225 Animations, 20 Original Tunes & Sound Effects.
Image Smith, Inc.

Darius IV. *Compatible Hardware:* IBM PC. *Memory Required:* 64k.
disk $29.95.
Skill & Action Game That Challenges Common Sense & Reflexes. Players Must Avoid Air Mine Fields, Cannons, & Air Snakes Hoping to Discover the 15 Landing Sites on the Planet Darius IV. Treasure Is the Goal, & to Escape, the Final Achievement.
Prentice Hall.

Dark Castle. *Compatible Hardware:* Commodore Amiga.
3.5" disk $39.95.
Arcade Action Game.
360, Inc.

Dark Legions. Silicon Knights Staff. Sep. 1995. *Items Included:* CD in jewel case. *Customer Support:* 30 Day Limited Warranty.
DOS 5.0 or higher. PC CD (4Mb). CD-ROM disk $9.95 (ISBN 0-917059-32-8, Order no.: 062551). *Optimal configuration:* 486/33.
Fantasy, Strategy Action Game.
Strategic Simulations Inc.

Dark Lord. Kyle Freeman. *Compatible Hardware:* Apple II, II+, IIe, IIc, IIgs; Commodore 64.
disk $20.00.
The Evil Wizard Has Risen from His Grave & Enslaved the Realm. It's up to You to Storm the Castle & Overthrow This Dark Villain. Features: Over 80 Different Game Locations to Visit; High Speed Screen Drawing & Animation; Sound Effects & Original Music Score; Numerous Puzzles to Solve, Including Some with Real-Time Solutions; Built-In Beginner Demo.
Electronic Arts.

Dark Lord. *Compatible Hardware:* Apple II series; Commodore 64/128.
Apple. disk $19.95 (ISBN 0-88717-202-4, Order no.: 16003-43499).
Commodore. disk $19.95 (ISBN 0-88717-203-2, Order no.: 16001-43499).
Animated Graphic Adventure in Which User Becomes Heir to Grandfather's House & All It Contains, Including His Secret Journal Which Reveals Tale of Good & Evil. The Journal Tells of How He Became Involved in a Plot to Destroy the Evil Tyrant, Nequam, Whose Possession of a Magical Amulet Bestowed Great Power upon Him & Made Him Invulnerable to Attack. The Plot Succeeded; Nequam Was Killed & His Coffin Sealed Forever in Stone. Now the User Has the Opportunity to Relive His Grandfather's Adventure. The Game Has the Capability to Relocate Key Objects, Making It a Different Game Each Time It Is Played. Includes a Mini-Adventure for Beginners, a Self Running Demo, Animated Graphics & Original Music That Plays Throughout the Game.
IntelliCreations, Inc.

Dark Passages I: The Psychotron; Wrath of the Demon; Dark Seed. Merit S, W et al. Feb. 1996. *Items Included:* Set-up instruction sheet. *Customer Support:* Area code telephone number (503) 639-6863 8AM-7PM PST M-F.

TITLE INDEX

486SX 25MHz, Windows 3.1 (Psychotron); 486SX or higher, DOS 5.0 or higher (Wrath of the Demon); DOS 5.0 or higher (Dark Seed). IBM PC 486SX 25MHz (4Mb, 8Mb HD) (Psychotron); (505k) (Wrath). CD-ROM disk $14.95 (ISBN 1-887783-55-5, Order no.: 5300-4007). *Addl. software required:* MPC double speed CD-ROM drive, IBM PC, Windows compatible soundcard, SVGA (Psychotron); joystick or keyboard, Adlib or Roland sound card, CGA, EGA, VGA (Wrath of the Demon); Mouse, SVGA, CD-ROM drive (Dark Seed).
Entertainment Technology.

Dark Passages II: Crusaders of the Dark Savant; The C. H. A. O. S. Continuum; Demoniak. Sir-Tech S, W et al. Feb. 1996. *Items Included:* Set-up instruction sheet. *Customer Support:* Telephone number (503) 639-6863 8AM-7PM PST M-F.
486SX 25MHz, DOS 3.X or 5.0 (Crusaders); 486SX/25 MHz, Windows 3.1, HD 1Mb (CHAOS); 486SX/25 MHz DOS 2.1 or higher (Demoniak). IBM PC or compatible 486SX/25MHz or higher (557k-Crusaders, 8Mb-CHAOS, 640k-Demoniak). CD-ROM disk $14.95 (ISBN 1-887783-56-3, Order no.: 5300-4008). *Addl. software required:* Double-speed CD-ROM drive, 6.5Mb HD, AdLib, Roland or PC speakers, mouse or keyboard, VGA, EGA, soundblaster (Crusaders); double-speed CD-ROM drive, soundcard, VGA, SVGA (CHAOS); double-speed CD-ROM drive, VGA, VGA, EGA, Ad-Lib, or MT32, soundblaster (Demoniak).
Entertainment Technology.

Dark Sun II: Wake of the Ravage (Jewel Case CD). Nov. 1995. *Customer Support:* 30 day limited warranty.
DOS 5.0 or higher. 386 CD-ROM with hard drive (2Mb). CD-ROM disk $9.95 (ISBN 0-917059-45-X, Order no.: 062661).
Sequel to the Mega-Hit Shattered Lands. Fantasy Role Playing Game That Takes Place in the Scorching Dark Sun Game World.
Strategic Simulations, Inc.

Dark Sun: Shattered Lands (Jewel Case CD). Nov. 1995. *Customer Support:* 30 day limited warranty.
DOS 5.0 or higher. 386 CD-ROM with hard drive (2Mb). CD-ROM disk $9.95 (ISBN 0-917059-44-1, Order no.: 062661). *Optimal configuration:* 386, hard drive, CD-ROM, 256 color VGA.
An Advanced Dungeons & Dragon Fantasy Role Playing Game.
Strategic Simulations, Inc.

Darkhorn. Apr. 1987. *Compatible Hardware:* Apple II, II+, IIe, IIc, IIgs; Commodore 64/128. *Memory Required:* 64k. *General Requirements:* Joystick.
disk $30.00 (Order no.: 43794).
Strategy Game Featuring Simultaneous Movement & Combat. The Swift-Rising Storm Has Broken & There Is Civil War Among the Pretenders to the Throne of Darkhorn. In One Army, While a Group of Elves Is Attacking an Enemy's Castle, a Party of Dwarven Loyalists is Fortifying a Newly-Occupied Castle. And As a Third Group Marches Overland to Reinforce the Siege, a Fourth Is Busy Recruiting New Members to the Cause. For up to Four Players, with up to Three Computer Opponents.
Avalon Hill Game Co., The Microcomputer Games Div.

Darklands: Heroic Role-Playing Adventures in Medieval Europe. Aug. 1992. *Items Included:* Manual, map. *Customer Support:* Free customer service, 1-410-771-1151, Ext. 350.
80386 (80286 requires 12 Plus MHz & 606k free RAM) DOS 5.0, hard disk required. IBM 386 & 486 compatibles (1Mb). disk $69.95. *Nonstandard peripherals required:* VGA graphics. *Optimal configuration:* Mouse recommended; Sound Blaster & Roland sound cards supported.
The Industry's First Realistic Role-Playing Game, Draws on the Lore, Myths & Superstitions of Medieval Europe, Wearing a Detailed Tapestry of Gaming Innovation & State-of-the-Art Technology.
MicroProse Software.

Darkstar. *Version:* 2.0. Bob Nadler. Oct. 1990. *Compatible Hardware:* Apple II Plus, IIc, IIe, IIgs; Atari 400, 800, 600XL, 800XL, 1200XL, 1400XL, 1450XL, 65XE, 130XE; Commodore 64/128; IBM PC, XT, AT & compatibles, PCjr. *Memory Required:* Apple, Atari & Commodore 48k; IBM 128k. *Items Included:* User's manual. *Customer Support:* Yes.
disk $64.95 ea.
Apple. (ISBN 0-933596-28-6).
Atari. (ISBN 0-933596-29-4).
Commodore. (ISBN 0-933596-30-8).
IBM. (ISBN 0-933596-32-4).
Solves B&W & Color, Positive or Negative Printing Exposure Problems Involved with Print Size, Contrast, Paper Type, Lens Sharpness, Emulsion Batch, Density, Color Balance, Filtration, etc.
F/22 Pr.

Darkstar Plus (Combines Both Darkstar & Timestar). *Version:* 2.0. Oct. 1990. *Compatible Hardware:* Apple II+, IIc, IIe, IIgs; Atari 400, 800, 600XL, 800XL, 1200XL, 1400XL, 1450XLD, 65XE, 130XE; Commodore 64/128; IBM PC XT, AT & compatibles, PCjr. *Language(s):* Compiled Turbo Basic on PC-DOS/MS-DOS systems. *Memory Required:* 48k; PC-DOS/MS-DOS 128k. *Items Included:* Users Manual. *Customer Support:* Yes.
disk $89.95 ea.
Apple. (ISBN 0-933596-16-2).
Atari. (ISBN 0-933596-17-0).
Commodore. (ISBN 0-933596-18-9).
IBM. (ISBN 0-933596-20-0).
Provides All the Functions of DARKSTAR As Well As Those of TIMESTAR with Both Programs Available from the Main Menu.
F/22 Pr.

DARTS: Traffic & Billing System for Radio Broadcasters. *Version:* 7.13. *Items Included:* One Operator's manual, manager's guide & form examples. *Customer Support:* 90-days free support with system purchase. Beyond initial 90 days, system support & enhancements are available. On-site training is also available.
PC-DOS 3.3 - 6.2. IBM PC & compatibles. $4500.00-$12,000.00. *Optimal configuration:* 486 processor, VGA monitor, 40Mb, 640k. *Networks supported:* Novell, LANtastic.
Designed for Radio Broadcasters. Currently Serves over 1800 Users & 85 National Broadcast Groups. System Is Designed to Help Automate All Logging, Traffic, & Billing Aspects of a Broadcast Operation.
Datacount, Inc.

DAS Editor. *Version:* 3.0. *Compatible Hardware:* Apple IIe, IIc, IIgs. *Operating System(s) Required:* ProDOS. *Memory Required:* 64k.
disk $39.95.
Programming Tool Adds New Commands to the ProDOS/BASIC System Environment. Designed to Be Used When Entering, Editing, & Debugging Applesoft Programs. A Global FIND Command Allows the Programmer to Search & Replace Values Throughout the Program. The Editor Supports 2 Glossaries Which Allow the Addition of Applesoft Reserved Words & User-Defined Statements Using a Single Key Press with the Open & Closed Apple Keys. Package Includes the ProDOS System Utilities, FILER & CONVERT.
Nite Owl Productions.

DAS-Security. Jun. 1995. *Items Included:* User Manual on disk. *Customer Support:* 90 Days.
DOS 3.1 or higher. 286 or higher. disk $99.95 - $4999.95 (ISBN 0-933735-04-9). *Addl. software required:* Clarion Version 3 or higher. *Networks supported:* All that Clarion Supports.
A Security Add-On for Clarion Version 3 or Higher.
Tin Man Software.

DASTOOLS. Jun. 1994. *Items Included:* User manual. *Customer Support:* One year included.
DOS 3.1 or higher. 286 or higher. $49.95 incl. shipping within U.S. (ISBN 0-933735-00-6, Order no.: 11338). *Addl. software required:* CLARION Version 3 or higher. *Networks supported:* All that CLARION support.
A Set of Programming Add On's for CLARION Version 3 or Higher. Includes Routines for Date, Time, File, Directory, System, Video, Popup's, EMS, XMS, & Functions.
Tin Man Software.

The Data Acquisition Hardware Expert. *Items Included:* Bound manual. *Customer Support:* Free hotline - no time limit; 30 day limited warranty; updates are $5/disk plus S&H.
MS-DOS 2.0 or higher. IBM & compatibles (384k). disk $14.95.
Provides User with the Capability to Quickly Identify Analog I/O Hardware Meeting Desired Specifications. Eleven Manufacturers Are Included in the Software Database, Covering More Than 57 Different Hardware Configurations. Selection Criteria Include: A/D or D/A; Number of Channels Required; Maximum Throughput (KHz); Resolution (Number of Bits); Programmable Gain (A/D); Sampling Interval (A/D); Pre-Triggering (A/D); Streaming to Disk (A/D); Digital I/O Ports, Bus Type, Price.
Dynacomp, Inc.

Data Aid, 2 disks. *Compatible Hardware:* Atari 400, 800. *Language(s):* Atari BASIC. *Memory Required:* 48k.
Set. disk $29.95.
Stores, Organizes, Reorganizes & Retrieves Information of User's Choice.
Dynacomp, Inc.

Data Capture. *Version:* 5.0. *Compatible Hardware:* Apple II+. *Language(s):* Applesoft BASIC, Assembly. *Memory Required:* 48k. *General Requirements:* Modem or serial card.
disk $90.00.
Direct Update of DATA CAPTURE 4.0. Editor Is Included for Preparing Text to Send to Another Computer or for Editing Text Received from Another Computer.
Southeastern Software.

Data Capture IIe. *Compatible Hardware:* Apple IIe with modem or serial card. *Language(s):* BASIC, Assembly. *Memory Required:* 64k.
disk $90.00.
Features Character Oriented Line Editing for Rapid Editing of Text Files. User Can List, Edit, Print, Send, Delete a Disk File, & Scroll Forward & Backwards Through the Capture Buffer. Supports Auto Dial, Hangup, & Answer with Most Popular Modems, Load & Save Multiple Option Files, & Interrupt Support for 1200 Baud Operations. Modifications to the Program Are Possible.
Southeastern Software.

Data Capture III. *Compatible Hardware:* Apple III with modem or serial card. *Language(s):* Business BASIC, Assembly. *Memory Required:* 256k.
disk $90.00.
Uses All the Features of Data Capture IIe & the Ability to Capture Directly to the Disk for Profile Drive Owners.
Southeastern Software.

Data Capture PC. *Compatible Hardware:* IBM PC, PC XT. *Operating System(s) Required:* MS-DOS. *Language(s):* MBASIC, Assembly. *Memory Required:* 128k. *General Requirements:* Modem, asynchronous card, or internal modem.
disk $120.00.
Includes the Ability to Direct Incoming Data Directly to a Disk File Without Having to Set-Up File Handling Protocols with the Sending System.
Southeastern Software.

Data Comm. *Compatible Hardware:* B-20 series, B-22. *Operating System(s) Required:* BTOS. *Language(s):* PL/M. *Memory Required:* 256k.
disk $2500.00.
Communications Package for the Burroughs System. Incorporates the Asynchronous Terminal Emulator, the 2780 3780 RJE Terminal Emulator, the 3270 SNA Emulator, the Poll/Select, the X.25 Communications Manager & the MT 983 Emulator into a Single Communications System.
Burroughs Corp.

Data Communications. *Compatible Hardware:* HP 85 with 16k Memory Module (HP 82903A), Serial Interface (HP 82937A), Modem (HP 82950A); HP 86/87 with HP-IB Interface (HP 82937A), Advanced Programming ROM (00085-15005). *General Requirements:* ROM Drawer (HP 82936A), I/O ROM (HP 00085-15003).
data cartridge, 3-1/2" or 5-1/4" disk $200.00 ea.
(Order no.: 82821A).
Turns the Series 80 Computer into an Intelligent Remote Terminal That Can Communicate with Other Asynchronous Computers & Terminals. Transmission Rates Range from 50 to 9600 Baud. Data Can Be Up- or Downloaded. Allows User to Print Reports, Store & Retrieve Data, & Use Other Series 80 Peripherals While On-Line.
Hewlett-Packard Co.

Data Communications: Basics. *Version:* 2.0. 1990. *Operating System(s) Required:* MS-DOS/PC-DOS. *Memory Required:* 640k. *General Requirements:* Color monitor; CGA, EGA, or VGA graphics board, monochrome monitor with Hercules graphics.
3.5" or 5.25" disk $495.00 (ISBN 0-935987-32-0).
Computer Based Training Course Which Teaches Data Communications Basics. Topics Include Data Communications Terminology & Concepts, Components, Protocols, Network Types, Network Architectures, & Data Communications in Business Today. Animated Graphics Help Learning While Simulating Data Communications Concepts. Review Quizzes Evaluate Learning. Comprehensive Online Glossary, Electronic Bookmark.
Edutrends, Inc.

Data Communications: Equipment. *Version:* 2.0. 1990. *Operating System(s) Required:* PC-DOS/MS-DOS. *Memory Required:* 640k. *General Requirements:* Color monitor; CGA, EGA, or VGA graphics board, monochrome monitor with Hercules graphics.
3.5" or 5.25" disk $495.00 (ISBN 0-935987-34-7).
Interactive Computer Based Training Course Which Teaches User the Equipment Needed for Successful Data Transmission. Topics Covered Include Terminals & PCs, Modems, Data Service Unit/Channel Service Unit, Multiplexors, Concentrators, Front Ends, Gateways. Animated Graphics Simulate Data Communications Concepts. Review Quizzes Evaluate Learning. Comprehensive Online Glossary, Electronic Bookmark.
Edutrends, Inc.

Data Communications: Networks. *Version:* 2.0. 1990. *Operating System(s) Required:* PC-DOS/MS-DOS. *Memory Required:* 640k. *General Requirements:* Color monitor & CGA, EGA, or VGA graphics board, monochrome monitor with Hercules graphics.
3.5" or 5.25" disk $495.00 (ISBN 0-935987-33-9).
Interactive Computer Based Training Course Which Teaches Students About Networks. Topics Covered Include Review of Network Types, Switched Networks, Private Line Analog, Private Line Digital, Packet Switching, Satellite, Local Area Networks, & Private Transmission Systems. Use of Animated Graphics Helps Learning While Simulating Data Communications Concepts. Review Quizzes Evaluate Learning. Comprehensive Online Glossary, Electronic Bookmark.
Edutrends, Inc.

Data Converter. *Compatible Hardware:* TI 99/4A. *Operating System(s) Required:* DX-10. *Language(s):* Extended BASIC. *Memory Required:* 48k.
cassette $27.95.
Performs Numerical Operations on Files Created by AUTOMATIC FILER. Categories Can Be Numerically Converted to Another Form or Summed. Square Roots, Multiplication, Division, etc. May Be Performed on the Contents of 2 Categories. Character Strings Can Be Inserted into Records in Any Category. Modified Disk Files Can Be Deleted, Listed, or Saved.
Eastbench Software Products.

Data Desk. *Version:* 3.0. Paul Velleman. *Items Included:* Help file, sample datasets, demonstration diskettes, Handbook, Statistics Guide, Quickstart. *Customer Support:* Free for registered users.
Macintosh 512E & up (1 Mb). 3.5" disk $595.00.
Graphical Data Analysis & Statistics Program That Runs on Any Macintosh Computer with at Least 1MB of RAM. It Combines Traditional Statistics with the Power of Exploratory Data Analysis. Data Desk Employs a Finder-Like Interface & Built-In Expertise to Allow Users to Quickly & Easily Explore Their Data.
Data Description, Inc.

Data Disk to Accompany STEPPING THROUGH WORD 2.0 FOR WINDOWS. Electronic Learning Facilitators, Inc. Mar. 1993.
IBM. instr's. software 5.25" $13.50 (ISBN 0-03-097659-6).
instr's. software 3.5" $13.50 (ISBN 0-03-097658-8).
Dryden Pr.

Data Ease. Dec. 1991. *Items Included:* 3 perfect bound guides containing 3 reference guides, installation guide, database engine guide & tutorial. Also includes quick reference guide. *Customer Support:* Free 6 mos; subscription-based high priority phone support; Service Ease high priority support - $200 per year; advanced technical support program - a toll-free annual contract based program for developers of advanced LAN and/or client-saver apps for $2000-$3000 per year; on-site consulting services on contract basis; BBS.
DOS, OS/2, Windows. Minimal 80286, recommended 80386 (2Mb). single user, $795.00; SQL Connect, $495.00; Workstation 5 pak, $1995.00. *Addl. software required:* Server vendor network library which supports the specific network. *Optimal configuration:* 80386/80486 with 4Mb RAM. *Networks supported:* Named Pipes (Novell, LAN Manager compatible, Banyan Vines), TCP/IP (various), DECnet, AT&T Star group.
The Front-End Application Development System for SQL Database Engines in the Client/Server Environment. Provides Rapid Application Development Capabilities, Distributed Database Support, Transparent Access to Data, Easy Migration from File Server Environments & Application Scalability Across Platforms, Combined with the Performance, Integrity & Connectivity of SQL Database Engines. It Automatically Translates All DATAEASE Functions, Including 4GL Procedures, into SQL Optimized for the SQL Server. Includes Complete Two-Phase Commit Functionality, Server-Controlled Referential Integrity Options, a Form/SQL Table Synchronization Capability, & Trigger Integration Features. Provides a Single Install of Both DOS & OS/2 Versions.
DataEase International, Inc.

Data*Easy PC Accounts Payable. *Version:* 4.1. Jan. 1994. *Operating System(s) Required:* PC-DOS/MS-DOS. *Memory Required:* 256k. *General Requirements:* Printer, VGA monitor recommended; hard disk required.
disk $149.00.
demo disk $20.00.
*Can Be Used As a Stand-Alone System or Integrated with Other DATA*EASY Software. (1) Simplify Payables Accounting, (2) Print Payables Checks & (3) Print Distribution Registers. A Pay-Code Is Used to Indicate: (1) Pay Immediate, (2) Hold Payment, (3) Pay on Due-Date, (4) Pay If Within a Specified 1-9 Days of the Due-Date or (5) Pay If Within 2 Days of the Discount Date. After a Vendor-ID Has Been Entered, Its Last 15 Unpaid Invoices Are Displayed on the Screen. Each DIST File Record Can Hold up to 8 G/L# & Amount Sets. A Valid G/L# Is 1-7 Digits in Length. The Distribution Registers Can Be Listed by Invoice, by Vendor or (after Payment) by Check#. Manual Checks Are Entered Just Like To-Be-Paid Checks. A Complete Trial-Check Run Can Be Printed on Plain Paper Prior to Printing the Actual Checks. Provides for Input of 3 Discount Dates & Their Related Discount Amounts.*
Data Consulting.

Data*Easy PC Cash Register. *Version:* 4.1. *Operating System(s) Required:* PC-DOS/MS-DOS. *Memory Required:* 256k. *General Requirements:* Printer, VGA monitor recommended, hard disk required.
disk $249.00.
demo disk $25.00.
Processes Retail/Discount Sales, Prints Sales Receipts, Updates Inventory, Maintains a Customer Sales Receipts, Updates Inventory, Maintains a Customer Database, Tracks Employee Sales & Commissions, Logs Credit Card & Personal Check Usage, Prints Sales Analysis Reports, Accumulates Cash Register Totals, Provides for Automatic Customer Discounts & Writes Price Quotes. This Version Includes Global Price Markdowns by Vendor, Department or Class & Sales Analysis Reports by Department or Class.
Data Consulting.

Data*Easy PC Data Entry & Edit. *Version:* 3.9. Nov. 1994. *Operating System(s) Required:* PC-DOS/MS-DOS. *Memory Required:* 256k. *General Requirements:* Printer, VGA monitor recommended, hard disk required.
disk $149.00.

Data Files Are Easily Described by Using a Technique of Fill-in-the-Blanks. Data Entry Screens & Files Are Automatically Created. Data Entry Modes Are: Add, Change, Delete, Inquiry, Search, Verify, Field Duplicate & Field Backup. A Hash Total Is Accumulated in the Record-Add Mode. There Is Easy Field Duplication from the Prior Record. Output Is Standard ASCII Format with Several Ways to Handle Numerical Fields. There Is Chaining from One Screen Format to Another So That Different Layouts Can Be Entered in the Same File. Normal Limits Are: 16 Fields/Screen, 64 Characters/Field & 255 Characters/Record. However, These Limits Can Be Easily Circumvented.
Data Consulting.

Data*Easy PC Elementary A/R. Version: 3.9. Jan. 1994. Operating System(s) Required: PC-DOS/MS-DOS. Memory Required: 256k. General Requirements: Printer, VGA monitor recommended, hard disk required.
disk $69.00.
demo disk $15.00.
Accounts Receivable Program.
Data Consulting.

Data*Easy PC Inventory Control A, B & C. Version: 4.1. Jan. 1994. Operating System(s) Required: PC-DOS/MS-DOS. Memory Required: 256k. General Requirements: Printer, VGA monitor recommended, hard disk required.
disk $99.00-$149.00.
demo disk $20.00.
Can Be a Stand-Alone Module As Well As an Integrated Part of Other DATA*EASY Systems. There Are 20 Reports for Listing Inventory Data & Analysis. Bar Code Data Entry Is Built In & DCG Can Supply the Readers. The Calculated Value of the Inventory Is Based on Either Last Cost or Average Cost & Sale Price.
Data Consulting.

Data*Easy PC Names & Labels A. Version: 4.1. Nov. 1994. Operating System(s) Required: PC-DOS/MS-DOS. Memory Required: 256k. General Requirements: Printer, EGA monitor recommended, 10Mb hard disk.
disk $49.00-$129.00.
demo disk $15.00.
Interfaces with Other DATA*EASY Software. There Is Duplicate Record Detection/Display During Data Entry. There Is a Single-Key Duplication of the City-Zip from the Previous Record with Zip Override. It Can Store up to 8 Categories of User Defined Attributes. Attributes Can Be Used to Select Records for Lists, Labels, Counts or Deleting. Multiple Attributes Can Be Merged to Prevent Duplicate Mailing. New Records Can Be Automatically Assigned a Special Attribute in Order to Do One-Time Mailings. Attributes or Records Can Be Deleted Globally. 1-Up, 3-Up, Envelope & Packing Labels Are Supported. Up to 999 Copies of a Label May Be Printed. Records Can Be Sorted by any Fields or Attributes.
Data Consulting.

Data*Easy PC Mail Order System. Version: 4.1. Nov. 1994. Operating System(s) Required: PC-DOS/MS-DOS. General Requirements: Printer, EGA monitor recommended, 10Mb hard disk.
disk $249.00-$399.00.
demo disk $35.00.
Major Features Are: Sales Logging, Product Invoicing, Sales Analysis, Inventory Control & Analysis, Sales Tax Reporting, Customer Database & List/Label Printing. Consists of 4 Modules: Invoicing, Inventory, List Management & Sales Analysis.
Data Consulting.

Data*Easy PC Menu/Item Costing. Version: 3.9. Jan. 1994. Operating System(s) Required: PC-DOS/MS-DOS. Memory Required: 256k. General Requirements: Data*Easy PC inventory Control, printer, VGA monitor recommended, hard disk required.
disk $99.00.
demo disk $20.00.
Designed to Interface with Data*Easy PC Inventory Control, Which Provides the Basic Items Used in Costing. Allows Items to Be Purchased at the Usual Unit-of-Measure & Then Costed at a Use-Portion Using a Conversion Factor. Meals Can Consist of Both Previously Costed Entrees As Well As Individual Items. Entrees Are Made up of Only Items. Selling Price Can Be Set or Calculated Based on an Entered Multiplication Factor (Percent). Program Is Menu & Command Driven, Has Pop-Up Help & Uses Techniques to Prevent Errors.
Data Consulting.

Data*Easy PC Names & Labels B. Version: 4.1. Nov. 1994. Operating System(s) Required: PC-DOS/MS-DOS. Memory Required: 256k. General Requirements: Printer, VGA monitor recommended, hard disk required.
disk $99.00.
demo disk $20.00.
Includes Features of DATA*EASY PC Names & Labels A. Interfaces with Other DATA*EASY Software. There Is Duplicate Record Detection/Display During Data Entry. This Version Includes the Following: Records Can Be Imported from Either ASCII or DIF Files & Can Be Exported into Mail-Merge Word Processors. Price Tickets & Shelf Labels Can Be Printed.
Data Consulting.

Data*Easy PC Open Item A/R. Version: 4.1. Jan. 1994. Operating System(s) Required: PC-DOS/MS-DOS. Memory Required: 256k. General Requirements: Printer, VGA monitor recommended, hard disk required.
disk $149.00.
demo disk $20.00.
Open-Item Type of A/R for Receiving Money & Applying It to Invoices. All File Updates Are Done in Real-Time & a Transaction Log Is Maintained of All Additions or Modifications. Invoices, Whether Received from Other Systems or Created by This Module, Can Be Modified.
Data Consulting.

Data*Easy PC Product Invoicing. Version: 4.1. Jan. 1994. Operating System(s) Required: PC-DOS/MS-DOS. Memory Required: 256k. General Requirements: Printer, VGA monitor recommended, hard disk required.
disk $199.00.
demo disk $25.00.
(1) Generate Professional Invoices, (2) Maintain a Customer/Patient Database, (3) Provide Inventory Analysis & (4) Update Inventory Data. Invoices Can Be a Mix of Taxable & Non-Taxable Items or They Can Be Completely Tax Exempt. Terms & Payment Method Can Be Retrieved by a Single Keystroke or They Can Be Entered Manually. P/O#, Credit Card# & Tax Exempt# Can Be Printed on Invoices. Credit Card# Can Be Retrieved from Customer Records. Customer & Price Lookup Are Features. There Are 10 Plus Reports That Deal with Customer Invoice Activity. 1-99 Pages of Products or Services Can Be Billed on a Single Invoice with 1-9 Copies of Each Page (Plus 0-9 Packing Slips). New Features: (1) International Addressing, (2) Record Export & Import, (3) Estimate Writing, (4) 65,000 Records/File & More. For Details on Inventory See: PC INVENTORY CONTROL. Options: Multi-Part Item Invoicing, Back-Order Management, Sales & Commission Accounting, Rent-to-Rent Management.
Data Consulting.

Data*Easy PC Purchase Orders. Version: 4.1. Jan. 1994. Operating System(s) Required: PC-DOS/MS-DOS. Memory Required: 256k. General Requirements: Printer, VGA monitor recommended, hard disk required.
disk $199.00.
demo disk $25.00.
(1) Writes Purchase Orders, (2) Writes Price Quotation, (3) Logs Receipt & (4) Updates the Inventory. It Can Be Used with or Without the Built-In Inventory. Items Can Be Received by Individual Item or by Order#. Up to 99 Pages of Items Can Be Entered per Order. Automatic P/O# Incrementing, Job# Override & Quick Product Lookup Are among the Features. Terms & Ship-Via Test Can Be Retrieved by a Single Keystroke or They Can Be Entered Manually. There Are 10 Plus Reports That Deal with Vendor Purchase Activity Plus a Future Aging Report Based on Due-Date. The Name & Address File Holds Vendor Data & User Ship-To Data. This Permits Multiple Ship-To Locations. The Purchase Order Records Can Be Listed by Order#, Due-Date, Vendor or Job# Without Sorting. New Features: (1) International Addressing, (2) Record Export & Import, (3) Requests for Quote, (4) 65,000 Records/File & More. For Details on Inventory See: PC INVENTORY CONTROL B.
Data Consulting.

Data*Easy PC Tax Organizer. Version: 3.9. Jan. 1994. Operating System(s) Required: PC-DOS/MS-DOS. Memory Required: 256k. General Requirements: Printer, EGA monitor recommended, 10Mb hard disk.
disk $49.00.
Organize Payables & Expenses into User-Defined Categories. Whether Displayed, Listed or Printed, the Data Can Be Extracted on Date or Date Range Basis. This Permits Multiple Years of Data to Reside in the Same File.
Data Consulting.

Data*Easy PC Time Accounting. Version: 4.1. Jan. 1994. Operating System(s) Required: PC-DOS/MS-DOS. Memory Required: 256k. General Requirements: Printer, VGA monitor required, hard disk required.
disk $149.00-$199.00.
demo disk $25.00.
Allows the User to: Record Time & Materials Billing, Produce Professional Invoices, Report Sales Tax, Control Work in Process, Provide Billing Analysis, Track Employee Sales/Commissions/Time, & Billing Analysis, & Optionally, Service Accounts Receivable.
Data Consulting.

Data Entry Optimize, Store Front & Estimating. Compatible Hardware: IBM PC.
contact publisher for price.
DeMichele Systems, Inc.

Data Entry Workshop. Version: 2.0. Aug. 1995. Items Included: 2 Layflat manuals, online help. Customer Support: 60 day money-back guarantee, free technical support, CompuServe technical support, free electronic maintenance upgrades.
Windows 3.1 or higher. 286 or higher (2Mb).
disk $199.00. Addl. software included: Turbo Pascal for Windows 1.5, Borland Pascal 7.0, Borland C Plus Plus 3.1 or higher.
An Integrated System That Works with Borland's Resource Workshop & Object Windows Library to Make It Easy to Design & Use Sophisticated Data Entry Techniques in Microsoft Windows Programs. You Design Custom Controls Using Resource Workshop, Then Merge the Resources into Your Windows Programs Using Supplied Utilities. The Custom Controls Offer True Field-by-Field Validation of User Input, Picture Masks, Support for Calculated & Required Fields, &

Calculator-Style Numeric Entry. Also Provided Are Spin Controls, Meter Controls, Toolbars, Toolboxes, Large File Text Editors, Scrolling Table Controls, & File Browsers. Provides DLLs & Interfaces Callable from Pascal or C Plus Plus Programs. Includes Full Source Code, Windows Help File, Comprehensive Documentation, & Plenty of Examples. No Royalties.
TurboPower Software.

Data Grapher 200. *Compatible Hardware:* HP Series 200: Models 216/220, 217, 236 Personal Technical Computers. *Memory Required:* 512k.
disk $295.00.
One-Step Function Plotting Package. Specify the Function (Not the Points) & the Calculations & Plotting Are Done Automatically. Take Data from the Keyboard or a File. Other Functions Include Bar Charts (Clustered or Stacked, Positive or Negative), Pie Charts, & Histograms. Charts & Graphs Created with This Package Can Be Included in Documents Created by HP TECHWRITER Document Processor, As Well As in Diagrams Created with the HP ENGINEERING GRAPHICS System.
Hewlett-Packard Co.

Data Junction. *Version:* 4.2. Jan. 1993. *Items Included:* Diskettes & documentation. *Customer Support:* Phone support.
MS-DOS/PC-DOS 2.0 or higher (640); UNIX/XENIX. IBM PC, XT, AT, PS/2 & compatibles. Contact publisher for price. *Nonstandard peripherals required:* Hard disk.
Data Conversion Tool with "Hub & Spoke" Architecture That Allows User to Translate Native Data Files to & from Other File Formats. User Can Sort, Extract, Re-arrange, Edit, & Enter Records, Fields & Bytes into the Exact Output Format Required. Parameters Can Be Selected Interactively or Set Up for Automatic Batch Mode Operation. A Frontend Facility Is Also Provided to Capture Keyboard Data Entry.
Tools & Techniques, Inc.

Data Manager. *Compatible Hardware:* B-20 Series, B-22. *Operating System(s) Required:* BTOS. *Language(s):* Pascal. *Memory Required:* 256k.
disk $1200.00.
Facilitates Data File Creation, Entry, Maintenance, Update, Reporting & Inquiry. User Provides Specifications for Data Storage, Computations, Display & Print Formats, etc. Includes Consistent Function Key Assignment, Optional Batch Data Entry, Batch Update, Real Time Update, Field Editing & More.
Burroughs Corp.

Data Manager PC. *Version:* 3.1. *Items Included:* Manual. *Customer Support:* Unlimited technical support; 60 day moneyback guarantee.
DOS. IBM or compatibles (512k). disk $39.95.
Addl. software required: DOS 2.1 or higher. *Optimal configuration:* One or more disk drives or a hard drive.
Easy-to-Learn Information Storage & Retrieval System Ideal for Home, Small Business & School Use. Includes an Instant Help Index to Make the Novice Computer User Feel Comfortable, While Providing Enough Powerful Features for the Experienced User. Create Your Own Free-Form Address Lists, Customize Reports & Labels in Minutes - in Any Form You Like - from Simple Mailing Lists to Complex Inventory Records.
Timeworks, Inc.

Data Manger for Windows. Jan. 1993. *Items Included:* Manual. *Customer Support:* Unlimited technical support; 60 day moneyback guarantee.
Windows. IBM or compatibles (2Mb). disk $199.95. *Addl. software required:* DOS 3.1 or higher; MS Windows 3.0 or higher. *Optimal configuration:* DOS compatible computer; hard drive; any Windows-compatible video adapter card & monitor, mouse.
Graphical Database Publisher That Requires No Programming Experience. Combines Powerful Graphic Capabilities, Such As Importing Scanned, Videotaped or Clip Art Images, with a Built-In Report Designer. Also Includes User-Specific Security Features, a Built-In Query Language & Easy Data Linking.
Timeworks, Inc.

Data Merge. DBI Software Products. *Compatible Hardware:* TI Professional. *Operating System(s) Required:* MS-DOS, CP/M-86. *Memory Required:* 64k. *General Requirements:* Printer. $150.00.
Personalized Correspondence System.
Texas Instruments, Personal Productivit.

Data-O-Base Calendar. *Compatible Hardware:* TRS-80 Color Computer. *Language(s):* Extended Color BASIC. *Memory Required:* 32k.
Disk Date-O-Base Calendar. disk $19.95.
Tape Data-O-Base Calendar. $16.95.
General Calendar & Date Memo Pad. Permits up to Twelve 28-Character Memos per Day, & a Maximum of 300 Memos per Month. Key-Word Search of Memos Which Outputs to Screen or Printer.
Custom Software Engineering, Inc.

Data Pack & Disk Pack. *Compatible Hardware:* TDP-100; TRS-80 Color Computer.
contact publisher for price.
Cer-Comp.

Data Plot. Edward Zeidman. May 1981. *Compatible Hardware:* Apple II+, IIe. *Operating System(s) Required:* Apple DOS 3.2, 3.3. *Language(s):* Applesoft BASIC. *Memory Required:* 48k.
disk $19.98 (ISBN 0-87190-008-4).
Enables Users to Create & Include Bar Graphs, Line Graphs, Scatter Diagrams & Pie-Charts in Reports. Allows for Multiple Graphs & Stacked Bar Charts, & Figures the Standard Deviation & Mean of Entered Data.
Muse Software.

Data Plotter. *Items Included:* Bound manual. *Customer Support:* Free hotline - no time limit; 30 day limited warranty; updates are $5/disk plus S&H.
MS-DOS. IBM & compatibles (256k). disk $59.95.
Does Not Create Graphs on the Screen, but Rather on Your Printer. Unlimited Number of Labels Placed Anywhere on the Page. Uneven Spacing of Points (Either Axis). Unlimited Number of Functions on One Graph. Automatic Manual Scaling. Choice of Graph Size. Choice of Numbers, Words, or Both As Labels for X & Y Axis Divisions. 11 Different Symbols in Six Sizes for Line Graphs & Scatterplots. Distinctive Shadings for Pie Charts & Bar Graphs. Plots Data from an ASCII (Text) File. This Data Can Therefore Be Created by a Word Processor, dBASE II, SuperCalc, a Program You Have Written, etc. You Do Not Need to Program to Make DATA PLOTTER Graphs.
Dynacomp, Inc.

Data Plotting Software for Micros. B. J. Korites. 1982. *Compatible Hardware:* IBM PC. *Operating System(s) Required:* PC-DOS 2.0. *Language(s):* BASIC (source code included). *Memory Required:* 64k.
disk $50.00.
18 Complete Programs That Process & Display Data As Pie Charts, Bar Charts, & Stock Market Charts. Creates 3D Views of Surfaces & Performs Curve Fitting, Data Management, & Statistical Analyses. Package Also Includes 4 Database Management Systems That Create X, X-Y, X-Y-Z, & Stock Market Files & Store Them on Disks. Plotting Programs Read the Data Files & Carry Out Sorting & Statistical Analyses.
Kern International, Inc.

DATA+. Oct. 1990. *Items Included:* Software documentation/owners manual. *Customer Support:* Customer service is provided to all customers free of charge for 30 days after the purchase date. After that time, maintenance may be purchased at $150 per year.
IBM DOS. IBM compatible (640k). disk $119.00 Stand Alone Version (ISBN 0-943293-04-9). *Networks supported:* Novell, Lantastic & Banyon.
Designed for Entering Detailed Information Regarding Clients' Assets, on an Asset-by-Asset Basis. Asset Information Is Organized by Categories for Data Entry. Each Category Can Have up to 30 Assets with a Brief Description of the Asset, Indication of Asset Ownership, Value, Growth Rate & Whether or Not the Asset Is Liquid.
ViewPlan, Inc.

DATA Plus: For Windows. *Version:* 4.0. Oct. 1994. *Items Included:* Software Documentation/Owners Manual. *Customer Support:* Customer Service is provided to all customers free of charge for 30 days after the purchase date. After that time, maintenance may be purchased at $150 per year.
Microsoft Windows. IBM & compatibles (1Mb). $119.00 Stand Alone Version (ISBN 0-943293-09-X). *Addl. software required:* Windows version 3.0 or higher. *Optimal configuration:* Mouse. *Networks supported:* Novell, Lantastic & Banyon.
Allows for Detailed Gathering of Asset Information for Use in Estate Tax Planning.
ViewPlan, Inc.

Data Pro Accounting Series. *Compatible Hardware:* IBM PC & compatibles. *Memory Required:* 512k. *General Requirements:* Hard disk.
$695.00 per single user module.
$795.00 per network module.
Financial/Accounting Software. Posts Recurring Transactions, Automatic Posting from Other Modules, Report Format User Definable, Reports Comparative Statements, Ability to Jump Modules, Wild Card, Links with External Software Programs, Password Access, Encryption, Audit Trail, Error Recovery, Automatic Back-Up for Each Module, Log off Out-of-Balance & On-Line Help.
Data Pro Accounting Software, Inc.

Data Retrieval for Rehab. *Compatible Hardware:* Commodore 64, 128.
$199.95 (Order no.: DRRC64-03-001).
Works in Conjunction with the REHAB Program for Retrieval of Data Saved During a Therapy Session for Display of a Buffer or Frame on a Printer in Either Numeric or Graphic Formats. Also Allows On-Screen Viewing of Files for Analysis.
Bodylog.

Data Retrieval for Stress. *Compatible Hardware:* Commodore 64, 128.
$199.95 (Order no.: DRSC64-05-001).
Works in Conjunction with STRESS Program for Retrieval of Data Saved During Therapy Session for Display of a Buffer or Frame on a Printer or Graphic Formats. Also Allows On-Screen Viewing of Files for Analysis.
Bodylog.

TITLE INDEX

Data Retrieval System (DRS). *Compatible Hardware:* IBM PC. (source code included). *Memory Required:* 128k.
disk $29.95.
Dynacomp, Inc.

Data Smoother. *Compatible Hardware:* Apple II with Applesoft; IBM PC. *Memory Required:* 128k.
disk $39.95, incl. manual.
Provides User with a Means to Smooth Equally Spaced Data & Plot the Results Using Least Squares.
Dynacomp, Inc.

Data Smoother: Semi-Spline - Polynomial Data Smoothing. *Version:* 1.0 & 2.0. 1992. *Items Included:* Detailed manuals included with all Dynacomp products. *Customer Support:* Free telephone support to original customer - no time limit; 30 day limited warranty.
MS-DOS 3.2 or higher. IBM PC & compatibles (512k). $39.95-$49.95 (Add $5.00 for 3 1/2" format; 5 1/4" format standard). *Optimal configuration:* IBM, MS-DOS 2.0 or higher, 256k RAM. For high resolution graphics, CGA or equivalent graphics capability is required.
Provides a Fast & Easy Means to Smooth Equally-Spaced Data. Any Size Data Set May Be Processed (Within the RAM Limits of Your Computer). The Variation in Each Data Point Is Smoothed According to a Weighted Average of the Points Surrounding It. The Averaging Span Available Is 3 to 25 Points. The Order of the Local Smoothing Is Linear to Quintic Least-Squares (First to Fifth Degree Polynomial). Also Calculated Are the Smoothed First & Second Derivatives.
Dynacomp, Inc.

Data Team DDS: Dental Office Management. *Version:* 3.02. Mar. 1992. *Compatible Hardware:* IBM PC, PC XT, PC AT, PS/2, 286, 386, 486. *Operating System(s) Required:* MS-DOS 3.1 or higher. *Memory Required:* 512k. *Customer Support:* 60 days free.
disk $895.00.
$30.00 demo disk & documentation.
Complete Dental Office Management System Which Allows the Tracking & Managing of Patient Transactions & Insurance, Billing.
Data Team Corp.

A Database for Chemical & Environmental Compatibility of Plastics: POLCOM. *Items Included:* Bound product description & manual. *Customer Support:* Plastics Design Library technical support by phone, fax or mail. Registered users will receive announcements about updates.
MS-DOS. IBM & compatibles (640k). disk $549.00. (ISBN 1-884207-09-X, Order no.: 884207-6). *Optimal configuration:* Standard color monitor will enhance readability, minimum 9Mb hard drive space.
Reference Source Showing How Exposure Environments Influence the Physical Characteristics of Plastics. Data Include Resistance to: Thousands of Chemicals; Weathering & UV Exposure; Sterile Methods including Radiation, Ethelyene Oxide & Steam; Thermal Aging in Air & Water; Environmental Stress Cracking & More. Test Conditions Present Various Combinations of Exposure Times, Temperatures, Stress Levels, Concentrations & Test Details.
William Andrew, Inc.

Database 4. *Compatible Hardware:* Commodore Amiga.
3.5" disk $69.95.
Four Database Applications for Home Inventory.
MicroSearch.

Database Gateway. *Version:* 2.02. *Items Included:* Combination installation & reference guide. *Customer Support:* Introductory support plan includes 2 days on-site support, 1 year warranty, 6 months money-back guarantee. Fee Services: call for current fee schedule.
host software $60,000.00-$160,000.00; database gateway $4995.00 per OS/2 platform.
OS/2, AIX, & Windows NT Applications That Allow LAN-Based Front-End Applications to Directly Access DB2, SQL/DS, Teradata DBC/1012, SQL/400, VSM, ADABAS, IMS, & IDMS Data, Using the Microsoft SQL Server API. DOS, Windows, OS/2, UNIX & MAC Applications Which Support DB-Library or ODBC, Such As Paradox, Advanced Revelation, Forest & Trees, & Many Others Gain Transparent Access to Mainframe Data. A Transfer Facility Lets User Move Data Between SQL Server & the Mainframe, Enabling Use of the SQL Server for Transaction Processing or Decision Support. Runs on a TCP/IP LAN or a LAN Supporting Named Pipes, Such As Microsoft LAN Manager or Novell NetWare & Uses an APPC Mainframe Communications Facility Such As DCA/Microsoft Comm. Server.
Micro Decisionware, Inc.

Database Manager in MICROSOFT BASIC. Greg Greene. 1983. *Compatible Hardware:* TRS-80 Model III, Model 4. *Operating System(s) Required:* TRSDOS. *Memory Required:* 32k.
disk $45.50, incl. bk. (ISBN 0-8306-5033-4, Order no.: 5033C).
TAB Bks.

Database of Accounting Research-Search Software. *Version:* 2.0. 1992. *Items Included:* User manual. *Customer Support:* 90 day warranty, phone support for sales & technical questions.
MS-DOS 2.0 or higher (384k). $75.00 (ISBN 0-926606-00-X).
$150.00 site license.
Contains Information about Articles Published in 40 Accounting Journals over a 23 Year Period from January 1968 to December 1991. The Database Consists of 11 5.25" Diskettes, or 7 3.5" Diskettes. The Software Is Self Contained & Contains a Search Program to Search the Database & Extract Needed Records.
Pacific Research Pubns.

Database of Stress Intensity Factors. M. H. Aliabadi. Jan. 1996. *Items Included:* Manual. *Customer Support:* Fax.
MS-DOS 3.0 or higher. IBM PC & compatibles (4Mb). software pkg. $550.00 (ISBN 1-56252-220-5). *Addl. software required:* PCs: Windows 3.1.
Hundreds of Entries Covering All Main Fracture Mechanics Standard Specimens & Other Configurations. Each Entry Comprises Configuration Illustrations, Description, Table & Figure of Solutions, Accuracy, Definitions, Equations, References, etc.
Computational Mechanics, Inc.

Database Preparer. *Version:* 2.0. Dec. 1995. *Items Included:* Complete instructions included on disk. *Customer Support:* 90 days free support by phone or E-mail.
MS-DOS. IBM & compatibles (8Mb). disk $175.00. *Optimal configuration:* IBM compatible, MS-DOS Rel. 5.0 or higher, Windows 3.1, 8Mb RAM, printer (preferably laser or ink jet).
Produce Lotus 123 Databased Without Having the Knowledge of the Lotus Database Rules. Insures Accuracy of Data Through the Use of Help Lists Which Guarantees That Critical Data Is Always Spelled Correctly & Therefore, a Data

DATACOUNT MUSIC BOX: MUSIC MANAGEMENT

Extract Command Will Never Miss an Entry. All Entry & Extract Functions Are Handled by a Macro with Detailed Screen Prompts.
Compiled Systems.

Database/Supervisor. *Customer Support:* Free on-line technical support for all registered users.
IBM PC/AT/XT, PS/2 & compatibles. $490.00 3.5" or 5.25" disk. *Networks supported:* Supports database files in ASCII, Lotus, dBASE, Oracle, XDB, Interbase, Teradata, etc.
Data Quality & Data Integrity Control System. It Automatically Finds Errors & Atypical Patterns Within a Database & Uses Integrity Constraints to Prevent Errors. Both Statistics & Inference Are Used to Test Hypotheses & Enforce Integrity Contraints.
IntelligenceWare, Inc.

DataCAD. *Version:* 6.0. Oct. 1994. *Items Included:* Manuals, DataCAD tutorials available separately (videos) & on-line documentation. *Customer Support:* 30 day free technical support.
DOS 3.3 & higher. IBM 386 & 486 PCs & compatibles (640k). disk $149.95. *Optimal configuration:* 486 PC, 4Mb RAM or more, printer or plotter.
A 2D/3D Computer-Aided Design System Optimized for Architectural & Building Applications. You Can Design a Closet, House, or Complete Building with Features Like Framing, Automatic Clean-Up of Walls, Automatic Roof & Stair Modeling, Shading, Associative Dimensioning, Hidden-Line Removal, Automatic Insertion of Doors & Windows, & 1,650 Built in Symbols.
Cadkey, Inc.

DataCAD 128: 3-D Architectural Design & Drafting. *Items Included:* Bound manual. *Customer Support:* Free hotline - no time limit; 30 day limited warranty; updates are $5/disk plus S&H.
MS-DOS. IBM AT, PS/2 or compatible (640k). disk $349.00. *Nonstandard peripherals required:* Math coprocessor; hard disk (20Mb or larger recommended); mouse or digitizer; if using plotter, two serial ports are needed.
Computer-Aided Design Package for the Architect, Contractor, Home Designer, or Remodeler. It Efficiently Carries You from Initial Site Design Work & 30 Perspectives to Your Final Set of Working Drawings.
Dynacomp, Inc.

DataComm Software. *Compatible Hardware:* HP Series 200 HP-UX the Integral PC.
3.5" disk $195.00 (Order no.: 82815J).
Provides Data Communications Features Enabling User to: Operate the Computer As a Remote Terminal (Full-Duplex) of Another Computer System, Communicate Through Public Telephone Lines with Commercial Information Services, & Transfer Files Between PC's.
Hewlett-Packard Co.

Datacount Music Box: Music Management & Scheduling System. Jan. 1996. *Items Included:* One operator's manual. Conversion from any other Music Scheduler or Music Management System. *Customer Support:* 90 days free support with system purchase. Beyond initial 90 days, System support & enhancements are available. On-site training is also available.
MS-DOS 5.0-6.22. 80386-16MHz (2Mb). disk $1995.00. *Nonstandard peripherals required:* Not required but will use if available - CD-ROM & sound card, Monochrome. *Networks supported:* Novell, LANtastic.
A Comprehensive Music Management & Scheduling System for Commercial & Non-Commercial Radio Stations. System Allows Control of Dayparts, Time Periods, Tempo's &

253

Moods. System Also Protects by Artists, Groups, Duets, Songtypes, Themes, Locations & Packets. System Will Generate Necessary Files for CD & Digital Audio Automation Systems. Currently Serving over 100 Users.
Datacount, Inc.

DataDirect Developer's Toolkit. *Version:* 2.0. 1993. *Items Included:* Complete documentation: ODBC drivers, & sample applications built using Visual Basic, Toolbook, Actor, Excel. *Customer Support:* Free 30-day technical support with paid programs available; on-site & off-site training. Windows, OS/2, Solaris 2.02. IBM PC & compatibles (4Mb of RAM). $699.00 - Distribution License, call for information. *Networks supported:* All that support Windows. OS/2 PM 2.X & higher. IBM PC & compatibles (4Mb of RAM). $699.00 - Distribution License, call for information. *Networks supported:* All that support presentation manager.
Best Way to Develop ODBC-Compliant Applications. Includes a High Level Application Program Interface (the QELIB API) & ODBC-Compliant Drivers for over 30 Major Databases. Adds a Common Superset of Features for All Databases - DISTINCT, GROUP BY, HAVING, UNION, Subqueries, Cursor Scrolling, & More Are Added for Databases That Lack These Features. In Addition, Supports All Major Development Environments. Databases Supported Include: ALLBASE, Btrieve, Clipper, DB2, DB2/2, DB2/6000, dBASE, Excel, FoxBase, FoxPro, Gupta SQLBase, Image/SQL, Informix, Ingres, Microsoft SQL Server, Netware SQL, Oracle, Paradox Progress, SQL/400, SQL/DS, Sybase System 10, Sybase SQL Server 4, Teradata, Text Files, & XDB.
Intersolv.

DataDirect ODBC Pack. Oct. 1993. *Items Included:* On-line documentation. *Customer Support:* Free 30-day technical support with paid programs available, on-site & off-site training. Windows 3.0 or higher. IBM PC/AT, PS/2 & compatibles (1Mb). disk $499.00.
Comprehensive Suite of ODBC Drivers That Connect ODBC-Compliant Applications Across Multiple Platforms to All Major PC & SQL Databases. These Database Drivers Allow You to Seamlessly Access Important Corporate Data from the Familiar Desktop Applications You're Using Everyday. Drivers Provide a Consistent Level of ODBC Implementation. Every Driver Supports All the ODBC Core & Level 1 Functions As Well As Selected Level 2 Functions. This allows You to Interface with Each Database in Exactly the Same Way, Whether It's dBASE on Your PC or Oracle on the Server. Databases Supported Include ALLBASE, Btrieve, Clipper, DB2, DB2/2, DB2/6000, dBASE, Excel, FoxBase, FoxPro, Gupta SQLBase, Image/SQL, Informix, Ingres, Microsoft SQL Server, Netware SQL, Oracle, Paradox, Progress, SQL/400, SQL/DS, Sybase System 10, Sybase SQL Server 4, Teradata, Text Files & XDB.
Intersolv.

DataEase. *Version:* 4.5. *Compatible Hardware:* IBM PC & compatibles. *Items Included:* 3 perfect-bound manuals, 1 tutorial manual totalling 1000+ pages documentation. *Customer Support:* Six months of free, unlimited technical phone support to all registered users licensed in the U. S.; subscription-based high priority suppport. DOS 3.2 or higher. IBM PC & 100% compatibles (640k). disk 3-user LAN pack $795.00; 5-user LAN pack $1095.00.
Award-Winning Ease of Use & Speed of App-Development. Users Quickly Build Sophisticated Applications Using the Power & Control of DataEase's 4GL, the DataEase Language (DQL).
Version 4.2 Allows Applications to Address from 1 to 16Mb of Extended Memory on 286- & 386-Based PCs. The DataEase MultiForms Feature Provides Full Updating (Enter, Edit & View) of up to 32 Tables from a Single Form Without Programming. Special LAN Features Include: Automatic File & Record Locking, Automatic Screen Refresh, & User Conflict Messaging.
DataEase International, Inc.

DataEase Developer. *Version:* 4.2, 4.5. 1992. *Items Included:* Documentation, DataEase Runtime, unlimited free runtime copies. *Customer Support:* Six-month of free, unlimited technical phone support to registered users licensed in the U. S..
DOS 3.1 or higher. IBM, XT, AT, PS/2 & compatibles (640k). disk $795.00.
Automatically Generates Complete User & System Documentation. For DataEase Applications, & Outputs Data in Popular Desktop Publishing & Wordprocessing Formats. System Also Generates Encrypted, Serialized Distribution Copies of DataEase Applications.
DataEase International, Inc.

DataEdge. *Version:* 1.7F. *Compatible Hardware:* IBM PC & compatibles. *Items Included:* Disks, documentation manual, tutorial. *Customer Support:* Technical support line.
disk $395.00.
Free-Form, Menu-Driven Database-Management System Featuring Help Screen, On-Disk Tutorial, Automatic Indexing & Split/Merge Files. Offers a Maximum of 500 Fields per Record, 254 Characters per Field, 16,000 Characters per Record, 10 Indexes per File, 10 Active Indexes & up to 9 Records Sorted. (The Number of Records per File Is Limited by Hardware.) Allows User to Revise Field Descriptions at Will.
PCM, Inc.

DataEdge. *Version:* 1.7B. *Compatible Hardware:* IBM PC & compatibles, PS/2. *Operating System(s) Required:* DOS 3.1 or higher. *Memory Required:* 384k. *General Requirements:* Hard disk recommended.
$595.00 per 6 stations.
Networked, Relational Database Offering Menu-Driven Features Combined with a Fourth-Generation Programming Language Called PAL. Not Copy Protected.
PCM, Inc.

DataEze: For the Pharmacist. J. M. Moody. 1979. *Compatible Hardware:* IBM PC. *Operating System(s) Required:* MS-DOS, PC-DOS, Concurrent. (source code included). *Memory Required:* 256k.
disk $1195.00.
Features: Prescription Labels, Patient Profiles, Price Updates, Third Party Billing, Cost Control & Sig Codes in Traditional Latin Abbreviations.
Intelligent Machines.

Datafax. *Version:* 4.0. *Compatible Hardware:* IBM PC & compatibles. *Operating System(s) Required:* MS-DOS. *Memory Required:* 256k.
$99.00 intermediate version.
$299.00 business version.
Text Database-Management System with 28 Characters per Keyword per Field, 489,000 Characters per Record, 100 Fields per Record & 30,000 Records per File. Supports Boolean Searches, & Searches Can Be Restricted to a Specific Field or Other Qualifier. Other Features Include Ability to Build Own Data Files; Run in Background & in Memory-Resident Mode; & Import, Export & Append ASCII Files.
All Easy Software Corp.

DataFax. Link Systems, Inc. *Compatible Hardware:* HP 110 Portable.
$299.00 (Order no.: 45408C).
Unstructured Data Management System for the Organization of Non-Numeric Information. Unformatted Structure Allows Cross-Reference of Information in a Variety of Ways.
Hewlett-Packard Co.

DATAFAX: Filing Software. *Customer Support:* 90 days free phone support.
MS-DOS 2.0 or higher. IBM PC, AT, PS/2 & compatibles (256k). $99.00 Intermediate version; $299.00 Business version.
Create Files, Catalog, Store & Retrieve Information Using a PC. Compatible with Most Popular Word Processors.
All Easy Software Corp.

The DataFiler. *Version:* 1.11. Michael P. Agne. Jan. 1984. *Compatible Hardware:* IBM PC. *Operating System(s) Required:* MS-DOS. *Language(s):* BASIC. *Memory Required:* 256k.
disk $159.00.
List Manager Featuring Global Update or Deletion of Records. Select Records for Printing, Merging or Updating on up to 5 Criteria; Sort Resultant List up to 3 Levels Deep. Input Forms & up to 10 Report Functions May Be Created on Free Form Text Entry Program. Create Sublists, Master Lists & More.
MBS Software (Oregon).

DataFlash. *Compatible Hardware:* Apple Macintosh.
3.5" disk $995.00.
SCSI-Based Data Acquisition System.
CPSA.

DataFlex. *Version:* 3.X. *Items Included:* Complete documentation including: user's guide, encyclopedia, handbooks, reference guide, tutorial. *Customer Support:* CompuServe Forum. 90 day media warranty; maintenance service available, Tech support line, 800 line free sales support.
DOS 6.22 & higher, UNIX. IBM AT & compatibles (450k), various UNIX. disk $795.00 single user. *Networks supported:* Novell, IBM, AT&T.
disk $995.00 LAN.
Provides the Combined Functions of a Powerful 4GL, True Relational DBMS, Object-Oriented Programming, Application & Report Generators, Graphics & Powerful On-Line Transaction Processing Capabilities. A Comprehensive, Transportable Application Development Environment for 16 Bit, Single & Multi-User Systems.
Data Access Corp.

DataFund Systems. *Items Included:* Instruction manual. *Customer Support:* During 90-day warranty DataFund will provide up to 5 hours training for any 2 employees, & will take up to 15 calls (not to exceed 20 minutes each), excess calls will be billed at $25 per 20-minute call. Support Plan 1: 20 calls over one year, plus any product updates free. Support Plan 2, modem: initial fee $150, calls at $75 per hour. Support Plan 3: unlimited modem support for 1 year plus updates $750.
PC-DOS 3.x (640k). IBM PC AT & compatibles. disk $7500.00, single user (ISBN 0-9623482-0-1). *Nonstandard peripherals required:* Wide printer, condensed printing. *Networks supported:* IBM PC Network, IBM Token Ring Network, Local Area Networks, Novell Advanced Netware, UNIX & many others. network price available upon request.
Complete Financial Management Package for Fundraising. Handles Daily Cash Receipts, Deposit Slips, Checkbooks, Billing, Labels, History on

TITLE INDEX

Each Contributor, Reports on: Reservations, Guest Lists, Table Lists, Sales Lists, Ad Books, Raffles, Auctions, 6 Simultaneous Events, Tracking of Sponsor Credit, Contributions, Dues, Pledges, etc.
DataFund Systems, Inc.

DATAHANDLER. *Compatible Hardware:* IBM PC, PC XT, PC AT, PS/2; TRS-80 Model I, Model III, Model 4. *Operating System(s) Required:* MMSFORTH. *Language(s):* MMSFORTH (source code included). *Memory Required:* 32k.
disk $59.95, incl. 2 manuals.
PIMS manual $11.95, if ordered separately.
Application Program for MMSFORTH; Fast File Manager Suitable for Standard & Custom Applications. Can Run the Same Data Disk in All Supported Computers. Integrates with the MMSFORTH Applications FORTHWRITE, FORTHCOM, etc. Data Files Are Upward Compatible with DATAHANDLER-PLUS.
Miller Microcomputer Services.

DATAHANDLER-PLUS. *Version:* 1.2. 1987. *Compatible Hardware:* IBM PC, PC AT, PC AT, PS/2. *Language(s):* MMSFORTH. *Memory Required:* 128k.
disk $99.95, incl. manual.
Application Program for MMSFORTH Used As a Database Management System. Comes with Demonstration Program, Datafiles, & Documentation. Fast File Manager with Flexible Options Suitable for Standard & Custom Applications. Includes "Active-Window" Entry System, Table-Display Options for Data, Local & Global Function-Key Macros, Complex Search & Select Criteria on Multiple Fields & Various "Smart" Report Options, All with Named Presets for Ease of Use. Integrates with the MMSFORTH Applications FORTHWRITE, FORTHCOM, etc.
Miller Microcomputer Services.

DATALAW-PC. *Version:* 4.01. 1988. *Compatible Hardware:* IBM PC, PC AT, PC XT & compatibles, PS/2. *Operating System(s) Required:* MS-DOS 2.1 & up. *Language(s):* BASIC. *Memory Required:* 512k. *Customer Support:* 90-day unlimited warranty; yearly software update & service agreement priced/module.
$395.00-$3980.00.
manual $75.00.
Legal Management Program Featuring Time Keeping & Billing Management Reporting, General Ledger, Tickler Docket Calendar, & Report Generating.
Data Law.

DataLock. *Version:* 3.1. 1991. *Operating System(s) Required:* VMS, MicroVMS 4.6 & higher. *Language(s):* Basic. *Items Included:* Users manual, primer, release notes, software performance reports, 1 year maintenance, quarterly newsletter. *Customer Support:* 6am-6pm, MST.
770. $600.00-$7750.00.
Cross-Industry Product Providing Transparent Encryption for Existing Applications. Requires No Application Program Changes. Encrypts VMS Mail Messages. Used by Security Administrators, Data Security Managers, End Users.
Raxco, Inc.

Datamax. *Items Included:* Bound manual. *Customer Support:* Free hotline - no time limit; 30 day limited warranty; updates are $5/disk plus S&H.
MS-DOS 2.1 or higher. IBM & compatibles (512k). $29.95 to $59.95 ea. Regular Version; $39.95 to $69.95 ea. Math Coprocessor Version. Nonstandard peripherals required: CGA or EGA (or equivalent); printer supported.
$59.95 ea. Regular Version; $69.96 ea. Math Coprocessor Version.
Composed of Three Independent Packages, Each Aimed at a Different Class of Least Squares Regression. Each Package Contains Full Data Entry & Editing Capabilities, as Well as Graphic Output.
Dynacomp, Inc.

DataModeler. Apr. 1992. *Items Included:* Manual, lesson plan. *Customer Support:* 800 support, 800 BBS line, 30 day money back guarantee.
Mac OS. Macintosh (1Mb). 3.5" disk $39.00 (Order no.: 800-522-2286). *Optimal configuration:* MAC SE/30, 2.5Mb RAM, System 6.08 or higher. *Networks supported:* ATALK, Ethernet.
Provides Users a Variety of Options to Produce on Screen Forms to Enter, Edit, Display, & Print Many Types of Data. Features Unique Graphic Forms Capability While Displaying Various Types of Data Such As Text, Number, Date, Time, Phone, Sequence, Boolean, List, Document, Sound, Picture, & QuickTime Movies in User Defined Boxes. In Seconds It Will Recognize & Reflect on Screen Forms Created in Any Graphics Program or Printed Forms Digitized from a Scanner. Automatically Identifies Squares, Rectangles, & Lines As Boxes Where Users May Want to Insert Data. Users May Elect to Create, Size, & Position Boxes in the Interface As Well. Provides Convenient Entry & Display Filters along with Full Color Appearance Attributes. Options for 'Lock After', 'Mandatory', & 'Retain Last Entry' Are Included. Calculates Computed Fields & Displays Results on Screen. The Form & Data or Just the Data Can Be Printed at 300DPI.
1st Desk Systems, Inc.

DataPerfect. *Version:* 2.3. *Compatible Hardware:* IBM PC, PC XT, PC AT & compatibles, PS/2. *Operating System(s) Required:* PC-DOS 2.1 or higher; 3.0 required for network systems. *Memory Required:* 256k. *Items Included:* Workbook, reference manual, color coded template. *Customer Support:* Toll free customer support.
disk $495.00.
Simplifies Defining a Database Through a Menu-Definition Scheme. As Soon As a Database Structure Is Defined, Users Can View, Enter & Modify Data in the Same Files. Supports a Text Storage Capacity of up to 510 Million Bytes, with Data File Sizes of over 2 Billion Bytes & More Than 16 Million Records. Each Database Can Have up to 80 Panels, Each Panel Can Have up to 80 Fields, Each Field Can Have up to 32,000 Characters, Each Record Can Have up to 1.3 Million Characters. Supports Boolean Searches & Multiple Users. Also Features: Ability to Run in Memory-Resident Mode; Import & Append ASCII & WordPerfect Merge Text Files; Export ASCII, WordPerfect & WordPerfect Merge Text Files; & Lock at Field Level. Is a Relational Database Development & Management Program; Enables Users to Define Database Applications Without Programming. Is Network-Ready & Will Allow Concurrent Record & Report Access. Ships with a Wide Range of Pre-Designed Applications.
WordPerfect Corp.

Dataquick. *Compatible Hardware:* IBM PC & compatibles.
disk $495.00.
Menu-Driven Database-Management System Featuring Help Screen, Automatic Indexing & Split/Merge Files. Offers a Maximum of 100 Fields per Record, 2000 Characters per Field, Unlimited Records per File, 2000 Characters per Record, 1 Index per File, 1 Active Index & up to 10 Records Sorted. Allows User to Revise Field Descriptions at Will.
G&Z Systems, Inc.

Datasafe. *Version:* 1.3. 1984. *Compatible Hardware:* IBM PC, PC XT & compatibles, PC AT, PCjr, 3740. *Operating System(s) Required:* PC-DOS, MS-DOS, CP/M. *Language(s):* Assembly. *Memory Required:* 50k.
$99.00, incl. manual.
manual $20.00.
File Security System Which Protects the Confidentiality of Information Stored in Computer Files. Can Also Be Used to Protect Information Which Is to Be Transmitted over Telephone Lines or Local Networks, or Carried with a Portable Computer. Uses the Federal Data Encryption Standard (DES) Algorithm to Secure a File, Group of Files, or an Entire Disk. User Can Determine Whether a Particular File Has Been Tampered with or Altered, Either Accidentally or Deliberately.
Trigram Systems.

Datasmith Payroll. Sep. 1979. *Items Included:* Helpful 310 plus page user manual. *Customer Support:* One year limited warranty.
PC-DOS/MS-DOS 3.0 or higher, DR-DOS 6.0 or higher. IBM PC/XT/AT, PS/2 & compatibles (384k). 5.25" or 3.5" disk $695.00. *Optimal configuration:* At least 80 column capability at 10 cpi pitch required (132-column printer preferred) and/or HP Series II or Series III laser printer.
Optional Features/Pricing: Demonstration Package with Complete Manual ($35), Additional Tax Authorities ($60), Direct Deposit ($480), W2AUDIT ($99), Import/Export ($480), Automatic Federal/State Deposit Checks ($180), State/Federal Large Lien Handling ($180), Cost Center Allocation (Quoted to Spec.), Expanded Deduction Report ($120), Vacation, Sick Pay User-Defined Benefit Accrual ($480), Multiple Tax Homes/Year ($540). Hundreds of Other Options Available.
Datasmith, Inc.

Datasurf. *Items Included:* Bound manual. *Customer Support:* Free hotline - no time limit; 30 day limited warranty; updates are $5/disk plus S&H.
MS-DOS 2.0 or higher. IBM & compatibles (256k, 320k for optional printer support). disk $79.95.
Surface-Sketching Package. Using Data Tables, DATASURF Produces 3-D Graphic Images in Two Forms: As Continuous Two-Dimensional Surfaces, or As a Series of Sheets Shown in Three-Dimensional Perspective. Data May Be Read from ASCII Files Created by: Wordprocessors Such As WordStar, Multimate, etc. Spreadsheets Such As Lotus 1-2-3, Symphony, VisiCalc, etc. Programming Languages Such As Pascal, BASIC, FORTRAN, etc. Handles Tables of up to 32,000 Numbers. The Sheet Representation Is Drawn in True Perspective So That Individual Rows of Data May Be Examined Separately. Surfaces May Be Crosshatched. Axes May Be Included & Labelled & More.
Dynacomp, Inc.

Datasurf. 1992. *Items Included:* Detailed manuals are included with all DYNACOMP products. *Customer Support:* Free telephone support to original customer - no time limit; 30 day limited warranty.
MS-DOS 3.2 or higher. IBM PC & compatibles (512k). $79.95 incl. manual (Add $5.00 for 3 1/2" format; 5 1/4" format standard).
Produces 3-D Graphic Images in Two Forms: As Continuous Two-Dimensional Surfaces, or As a Series of Sheets Shown in Three-Dimensional Perspective. Data May Be Read from ASCII Files Created by: Wordprocessors Such As WordStar, Multimate, etc. Spreadsheets Such As Lotus 1-2-3, Symphony, VisiCalc, etc. Programming Languages Such As Pascal, BASIC, FORTRAN, etc. Handles Tables of up to 32,000 Numbers.

Surfaces May Be Crosshatched. Axes May Be Included & Labelled. Hidden Lines Are Removed Automatically but Can Be Restored If Desired. Full File Handling & Editing. A Bound 115-Page Manual Included.
Dynacomp, Inc.

DataTalker 3270.
contact publisher for price.
Offers Features to Increase the Productivity of Data Processing Networks, Users & Application Developers. Includes PC Cluster Support for 1 to 8 PCs Simultaneously; a Menu-Driven Interface; a Separate Communications Processor; an Application Program Interface (API); & Quickscreen, a Local Screen Storage & Retrieval Utility That Reduces Communications Line Traffic & Increases Responsiveness.
Winterhalter, Inc.

Datatree. Arizona Computer Systems Group, Inc. *Compatible Hardware:* TI Professional. *Operating System(s) Required:* UCSD p-System. *Memory Required:* 64k. *General Requirements:* Printer.
$249.00.
Generalized Program to Handle the Common Functions of Entering, Storing, Manipulating, Retrieving & Reporting Systems.
Texas Instruments, Personal Productivit.

Dataview: Data Management & Analysis Package. *Version:* 5.51. C. G. Renfro & Assoc. Oct. 1995. *Items Included:* Users manual, complete documentation, installation assistance, re-installation if accidentally destroyed. *Customer Support:* 1st year Alpha Plus support is free, subsequent years are optional & cost about 20% of the software price, includes telephone technical assistance, free updates with new releases, conferences, training & user seminars.
MS-DOS 3.0 or higher (640k); Windows 3.10; OS/2 2.1. IBM compatible XT & up. $650.00. *Nonstandard peripherals required:* Math coprocessor chip. *Networks supported:* Ethernet or Token Ring coaxil cable or twisted pair, Novell, 3 Com, IBM.
Executes Data Management Tasks: (Updates, Transformations, Difference, Growth & Index Calculations, Seasonal Adjustment, Frequency Conversions, Trend & Residual Calculations). Access Facilities Include Index & Keyword Search. Also Performs Statistical, Analysis & Time-Series Regression. Includes Reporting & Graphics.
Alphametrics Corp.

Dataview Plus: Market Forecasting Package. *Version:* 5.51. Oct. 1995. *Items Included:* Users manual, complete documentation, installation assistance, re-installation if accidentally destroyed. *Customer Support:* 1st year Alpha Plus support is free, subsequent years are optional & cost about 20% of the software price, includes telephone technical assistance, free updates with new releases, conferences, training & user seminars.
MS-DOS 3.0 or higher (640k); Windows 3.X; OS/2 2.X. IBM compatible XT & up. $750.00. *Nonstandard peripherals required:* Math coprocessor chip. *Networks supported:* Ethernet or Token Ring coaxil cable or twisted pair, Novell, 3 Com, IBM.
Supports quantification & Forecasting of Relationships Between Market Factors Using Time-Series Regression Techniques. Includes Data Management, Presentation Graphics, & Table Generation Facilities. Has Been Used in Executive Information Systems, Expert Systems Supporting Promotional Planning & Product Line Forecasting.
Alphametrics Corp.

DataVUE. *Compatible Hardware:* Alpha Micro. *Operating System(s) Required:* AMOS. *Memory Required:* 55k.

$1050.00-$3000.00 VCR tape.
Relational, High-Speed RAM-Based Database Which Sorts 1000 Records in Less Than 2 Seconds. Analyzes Sales, Inventory, Billing, Mailing Lists, etc. Databases Can Be Quickly Set Up. Views Information One Record at a Time or in Rows & Columns Like a Spreadsheet. Also Features Math Calculations, up to 20 Custom Print Reports, & Macros.
Provue Development Corp.

Datebook. *Compatible Hardware:* IBM. *Memory Required:* 128k.
disk $29.95, incl. manual.
Contains Perpetual Calendar.
Dynacomp, Inc.

DATEBOOK PRO. *Version:* 2.0. Apr. 1993. *Items Included:* User manual. *Customer Support:* Free technical support.
Macintosh 6.0.5 or higher. Macintosh Plus or higher (2Mb). $79.95 (DATEBOOK/TOUCHBASE PRO Bundle $149.95). *Nonstandard peripherals required:* Hard disk. *Addl. software required:* System 7.0 required for integration with TOUCHBASE PRO. *Optimal configuration:* Mac II family, color monitor, 2Mb RAM, System 7.0, hard disk. *Networks supported:* AppleTalk.
Combines Scheduling, To-Do Lists & Alarms into One Package to Keep You on Top of Your Appointments & Things to Do. User Can Print Wall Charts or Custom Schedules to Popular Day Timer, DayRunner & fILOFAX Formats. And DATEBOOK PRO Can Even Directly Communicate with Your TOUCHBASE PRO Contact Manager, Linking Your Meetings & To-Do Items with Their Associated Contacts.
Aldus Corp. (Consumer Division).

Datebook II. Organic Software, Inc. *Compatible Hardware:* HP 86/87 with CP/M System (HP 82900A).
3-1/2" or 5-1/4" disk $295.00 ea. (Order no.: 45581A).
Recommended for Doctors' Offices, Legal Firms, & Other Professional Offices. Appointments Can Be Scheduled, Cancelled, Modified, Moved, or Held Until They Can Be Rescheduled. Openings Can Be Searched by Time of Day, Day of Week, or Day of Year. Prints the Appointments for the Day, Displays All Scheduled Appointments for Any Person, or Schedules a Conference at a Convenient Time for All Attendees.
Hewlett-Packard Co.

Dates: Series 900 to 2000. *Compatible Hardware:* IBM System/36, System/36PC; AS/400.
contact publisher for price.
Records & Monitors Time-Dependent Deadlines.
Manac-Prentice Hall Software, Inc.

DAUDIT - Disk-Based Audit Trail System. *Version:* 11.0. Apr. 1986. *Compatible Hardware:* IBM PC & compatibles. *Operating System(s) Required:* MS-DOS. *Language(s):* C-BASIC. *Memory Required:* 128k. *General Requirements:* Hard disk, printer. *Customer Support:* 1 year free telephone support & upgrades.
free, with E-Z MRP.
Stores Standard Printer-Based Audit Trail Information of Inventory Transactions in a Disk File on Hard Disk & Allows for Flexible Report Generation Using Numerous Sort & Data Select Features. DAUDIT Is Ideal for Physical Inventory Transactions, Auditing Requirements, Lot or Serial Number Tracking, & Purchase Price Variance Reporting. Product included with E-Z MRP.
Alliance Manufacturing Software.

David Leadbetter's Greens: The Instructional 3D Golf Game. Sep. 1992. *Items Included:* Manual, technical supplement, maps. *Customer Support:* Free customer service, 1-410-771-1151, Ext. 350.
80386/80486; hard disk required (1Mb). disk $69.95. *Nonstandard peripherals required:* VGA or MCGA graphics. *Optimal configuration:* Supports mouse (recommended) & joystick; Roland, Adlib, Sound Blaster supported.
The First 3-D Golf Game Designed to Help Players Improve Their Golf Game While They Are Having Fun. The Player May Play Golf with up to Three Opponents or Against a Human Opponent via Modem in a Dozen Game Types.
MicroProse Software.

David's Midnight Magic. *Compatible Hardware:* Apple II+, IIe; Commodore 64. *General Requirements:* Paddles or joystick.
disk $34.95.
Hi-Res Pinball Game That Contains Dual Flipper Controls, Lower & Upper Playing Levels, Rollovers, Tilt Mechanism, Electromagnetic Deflectors, Multiple Ball Play, & Other Effects.
Broderbund Software, Inc.

Davka Bats.
IBM PC or compatibles with Windows. disk $39.95 (Order no.: 1489).
Macintosh Plus or higher. 3.5" disk $39.95 (Order no.: M489).
A Symbol Font That Contains 70 Judaic Symbols & Signs in PostScript on True Type Formats.
Davka Corp.

DavkaGraphics: Bitmaps. *Compatible Hardware:* Apple II; Macintosh; IBM.
3.5" disk $39.95.
Judaic Clip Art That Features a Wide Assortment of Graphics Suitable for Synagogue, School & Personal Use. Includes Pictures Appropriate for All Seasons & Occasions, Including Jewish Holidays & Israel Themes. Compatible for Use with FullPaint, MacPaint, The Print Shop & Other Macintosh Applications That Use Clip Art.
Davka Corp.

DavkaGraphics EPS: Jewish Holidays. *General Requirements:* Page-layout program, PostScript printer.
Macintosh Plus or higher. 3.5" disk $79.95.
EPS Clip Art.
Davka Corp.

DavkaGraphics EPS: Judaica.
Macintosh Plus or higher. 3.5" disk $79.95. *Nonstandard peripherals required:* PostScript printer. *Addl. software required:* Page Layout Program.
Collection of 66 PostScript Graphics Designed for Use with Synagogue Newsletters, Community Fliers & Announcements, Invitations, or Any Judaic-Oriented Publication. Includes Judaic Borders, Symbols, People, & Ritual Objects.
Davka Corp.

Dawn. *Compatible Hardware:* IBM PC. *General Requirements:* EGA graphics capability.
disk $39.95.
Screen Saver Program That Paints Landscapes on Your Monitor When Not in Use. Features Thousands of Variations & Dozens of Themes.
Iron Mountain Software.

Dax Plus with Voicedrive. SuperSoft, Inc. Apr. 1984. *Compatible Hardware:* TI Professional. *Operating System(s) Required:* MS-DOS. *Memory Required:* 128k. *General Requirements:* Winchester hard disk, Speech Command System, printer.
$495.00.

TITLE INDEX

DB-FABS-DABL

Management System Which Uses English Commands. List Data Files, Produce Reports, Sort Entries & Search for Specific Reports.
Texas Instruments, Personal Productivit.

Day-to-Day Calendar. Sep. 1994. *Items Included:* (1) User Manual, (1) Quick Reference Guide, (2) 3.5" HD disks. *Customer Support:* 30 day MBG - free tech support for reg. users: Direct 802-434-6300 9:00AM-5:00PM Monday-Friday EST. Fax 802-434-7000. CompuServe, America Online, AppleLink.
System 7.0 or higher. MAC w/hard disk & high density drive (4Mb). $79.95 SRP (Order no.: R53101).
The Easiest & Most Flexible Way to Make & Keep Track of Appointments, Meetings, To-Do's, Projects & Notes. It Is Intuitive & Easy to Use for Beginners, Yet Comprehensive Enough for a Business. Included Is Day-to-Day Assist, Which Offers Instance Access to Calendar Information from Within Any Macintosh Application for Fast & Easy Entry & Retrieval of Data, Without Opening the Calendar Application. It's Powerful & Varied Printing Abilities Make It the Perfect Partner to Any Personal Organizer for Accessibility to Calendar Information Anytime, Anywhere. Day-to-Day Calendar Works the Way You Work.
Portfolio Software, Inc.

Day-to-Day Complete Organizer. Sep. 1994. *Items Included:* (3) User Manuals, (2) Quick Ref. Guides, (2) 3.5" LD disks, (4) 3.5" HD disks, (1) Leather Organizer. *Customer Support:* 30 day MBG - free tech support for reg. users: Direct 802-434-6300 9:00AM-5:00PM Monday-Friday EST. Fax 802-434-7000. CompuServe - Go Macaven; America On-Line - "Portfolio" Forum; AppleLink - 3rd Parties Folder-Portfolio Software.
System 7.0 or higher. MAC w/hard disk drive (4Mb). $149.95 SRP (Order no.: R59101).
A Complete Set of Personal Information Tools for Organizing Your Home or Office. Includes Day-to-Day Calendar, Day-to-Day Contacts, & Day-to-Day Notepad. The Three Programs Are Tightly Integrated for Complete & Easy Organization of & Access to Your Personal Calendars, Contacts & Notes. Information Can Be Quickly & Easily Accessed & Entered Without Ever Launching the Individual Applications, Saving Time & Effort in Organizing & Managing Your Life...Day-to-Day.
Portfolio Software, Inc.

Day-to-Day Contacts. *Version:* MAC 3.5.2, WIN 3.0. 1994. *Items Included:* MAC: (2) 3.5" HD disks, (1) Quick Ref Guide, (1) User Manual. WIN: (1) 3.5" HD disk, (1) Quick Ref Guide, (1) User Manual. Both: AT&T 800 Directory, MCI 10 Free minutes calling card. ZipZapp Assist - which links all the day-to-day products seamlessly. *Customer Support:* 30 day MBG - free tech support for reg. users: Direct 802-434-6300 9:00AM-5:00PM Monday-Friday EST. Fax 802-434-7000. CompuServe, America Online, AppleLink.
MS Windows 3.1 or higher. 386 or higher IBM & compatibles (2Mb - 4 recommended). $79.95 SRP (Order no.: R61301).
6.0.4 or higher. Macintosh w/hard disk (2Mb). $79.95 SRP (Order no.: R51302).
Offers the Most Flexible Way to Organize & Manage the Names & Addresses of the Important People in Your Life, As Well As Keep Detailed Notes about Them. The Intuitive Interface Allows for Easy Set-Up & Fast Entry of Information. Powerful Database Features & Customizable Fields Allow Maximum Flexibility in Entering & Accessing Data. Also Included, Is Day-to-Day Assist, Which Gives You Instant Access to Your Contact Files from Within Any Macintosh Application for Fast & Easy Entry, Retrieval, & Editing of Data, All Without Opening the Day-to-Day Contacts Application. Powerful Printing Abilities Allow You to Print Your Address Book to a Personal Organizer or Any Other Format for Access to Your Contact Information Anytime, Anywhere. Day-to-Day Contacts Works the Way You Work.
Portfolio Software, Inc.

Day-to-Day Notepad. *Items Included:* MAC/WIN: (1) User Manual, (1) 3.5" LD disk. *Customer Support:* 30 day MBG - free tech support for reg. users: Direct 802-434-6300 9:00AM-5:00PM Monday-Friday EST. Fax 802-434-7000. CompuServe - Go Macaven; America On-Line - "Portfolio" Forum; AppleLink - 3rd Parties Folder-Portfolio Software.
MS Windows 3.1 or higher. IBM PC & compatibles 286 or higher (2Mb). $49.95 SRP (Order no.: R62102).
System 6.0.4 or higher. MAC w/hard disk (2Mb). $49.95 SRP (Order no.: R52102).
A Fast & Effective Way to Organize Notes, Create Outlines & Write Agendas. It's Simply Interface Allows for Fast & Easy Set-Up & Entry of Information. With Links to Both Day-to-Day Contacts & Day-to-Day Calendar, It Offers a Complete Solution for Organizing & Managing Notes Regarding Your Time, Schedule & the People You Need to Reach. Powerful Printing Abilities Allow You to Print Your Notes, Outlines & Agendas to a Personal Organizer & Other Formats So You Can Have This Information with You Anytime, Anywhere. Day-to-Day Notepad Works the Way You Work.
Portfolio Software, Inc.

DAY-2-DAY Pro. Ben Kirby. Sep. 1990. *Items Included:* Indexed manual. *Customer Support:* Update club with newsletters for $49.95 lifetime, allows for upgrades at $19.95 per disk. Customer support (813) 584-2355 open 10-4 weekdays. customizing available.
Amiga DOS or higher. Amiga (1Mb). retail $695.00; dealer/var: $395.00, Dist. $295.00. *Optimal configuration:* 3 Mb RAM with 68030 Processor & 100 Mb HD. (I.E. Amiga 3000). *Networks supported:* Ethernet, Arcnet.
Complete Point-of-Sale, Data Base System, with 4 Different P/O/S Interfaces. Perpetual Item Sales Tracking by Customer. Networkable on Amiga Based Ethernet or Arcnet. Tracks Backorders on A/R As Well As A/P. Many Database Functions. Limited by System Memory Only.
KFS Software, Inc.

DayFlo TRACKER. *Version:* 3.0. *Compatible Hardware:* IBM PC, PC XT, PC AT, PS/2 & compatibles. *Operating System(s) Required:* MS-DOS/PC-DOS. *Memory Required:* 448k. *General Requirements:* RAM disk or hard disk. *Items Included:* Documentation, support, demo disk, Smart Key. *Customer Support:* (714) 474-0229.
disk $249.00.
A Database/Information Manager Which Handles Both Text & Field Information. Word Processing Including Mailmerge Are Integral. Field Lengths Are Variable, 65,000 Records/Database With Full Reporting, Retrieving, Sorting & Tracking Capabilities. Included Is a Complete Application for the Management of Contacts & Correspondence.
DayFlo Software Corp.

Daylight. *Compatible Hardware:* TI 99/4A. *Operating System(s) Required:* DX-10. *Language(s):* BASIC. *Memory Required:* 48k. cassette $16.95.
Calculates Sunrise/Sunset & the Beginning/Ending of Nautical Twilight for Any Given Day.
Eastbench Software Products.

The Daylight Ephemeris Program. *Compatible Hardware:* TI 99/4A with Extended BASIC. *Operating System(s) Required:* DX-10. *Language(s):* Extended BASIC. *Memory Required:* 48k.
cassette $17.95.
Provides Several Variables Including Latitude & Longitude, Tabular Interval & Starting Date. Then Computes Several Times, Including Sunrise & Sunset, Nautical & Astronomical for Any Point on Earth.
Eastbench Software Products.

Daylite. *Version:* 2.0. Sep. 1984. *Compatible Hardware:* Apple Macintosh, IBM PC. *Operating System(s) Required:* MS-DOS, Apple OS. *Language(s):* Pascal. *Memory Required:* IBM 128k, Macintosh 512k. *General Requirements:* 2 disk drives.
contact publisher for price.
Computerized Daylighting Design & Analysis Tool Developed to Provide the Architect, Interior Designer, Electrical Engineer, Mechanical Engineer, & Lighting Designer with a Means of Designing an Efficient Natural Daylight Lighting System. Quantifies Effects of Natural Illumination & Calculates Glare & Contrast Values.
Solarsoft.

Daz-Zle Plus Try & Buy. Envelope Manager Software Staff. *Items Included:* The package includes a 3.5" diskette, a mini-manual & a Try & Buy Brochure.
Microsoft Windows 3.1 or higher. IBM PC. disk $34.99 (ISBN 1-57548-005-0). *Nonstandard peripherals required:* A Hayes compatible modem is required to use Dial-A-Zip. *Optimal configuration:* 1.5Mb of available disk space is required.
It Is a Product Designed for the Creation of Envelope Mailing.
IBM Software Manufacturing Solutions (ISMS).

Dazzle Draw. David Snider. *Compatible Hardware:* Apple IIe, IIc, IIgs. *Memory Required:* 128k. *General Requirements:* Mouse, Apple Graphics Tablet, KoalaPad, or joystick. Apple IIe requires extended 80-column card.
disk $59.95 (Order no.: APDSK-89).
Art Program That Provides User with a 16-Color Palette, Various Brushes, "Spray Paint" Option, & 30 Built-In Patterns. Utility Tools Let User Draw Geometric Shapes, Invert Images Vertically or Horizontally, Cut & Paste, Enlarge Sections. Text Feature Gives Different Type Styles & Sizes.
Broderbund Software, Inc.

DB CONVERT. Oct. 1993. *Items Included:* Contact vendor. *Customer Support:* Contact vendor.
MS-DOS 5.0 or higher. 386 (8Mb). Contact publisher for price. *Addl. software required:* Paradox 4.5 or higher. *Networks supported:* Novell Netware, Artisoft Lantastic.
Windows 3.1 or higher. 386/DX (8Mb). *Addl. software required:* Paradox 5.0 or higher. *Networks supported:* Novell Netware, Artisoft Lantastic, Windows for Workgroups.
Converts Paradox DB Files from 3.0 & 4.0 DOS to 4.0 DOS & 5.0 Windows. Converts DB Files from 4.0 Windows to 5.0 Windows. Transfers All Fields to New Tables. Transfers Memo Data to New Memo Tables.
Management Systems, Inc.

DB-FABS-DABL. *Version:* 3.0F. Feb. 1991. *Items Included:* 3-ring hard bound manual, disks with programs. *Customer Support:* Technical support by phone (813-961-7566) or Fax (813-963-6180).
PC/MS-DOS 2.1 or higher. IBM or compatible (256k). disk $195.00 (single user) $295.00 (Network).

DATA, SCREEN & REPORT Manager Consisting of Two Modes Modes of Operation: STAND-ALONE (for Non- Programmers) or RUNTIME (for Programmers). RUNTIME Allows Programmers to Handle File I/O, Indexing, Sorting, Screen Management/Report Generation by Calling DB-FABS from DABL or one of Many Higher Level Languages Supported. Millions of Records Permitted. 128 Fields Allowed. Automatically Maintains Indices on Multiple Keys. Easy to Use Tutorials. Net Bios Compatible Version Available for Network Use.
Computer Control Systems, Inc.

DB Master One. *Compatible Hardware:* Atari ST. 3.5" disk $49.95 (Order no.: DS5004).
Atari Corp.

db—QUERY. *Compatible Hardware:* IBM PC & compatibles; Unix, Xenix, VAX, MS Windows. *Operating System(s) Required:* MS-DOS, Unix, Xenix, VMS, OS/2, Windows. *Language(s):* C. $595.00 & up, depending upon configuration. SQL-Based Query System. Provides the Relational View of a db—VISTA Network Model Database. Includes Report Forms Source Code Available.
Raima Corp.

DB/write. *Version:* 2.1. Mar. 1989. *Customer Support:* 60 day free support, user manual; support contract available.
Mac Plus or higher (1Mb). disk $129.00.
An XCMD for HyperCard 2.0 That Adds Full Word Processing & Mail Merge Functionality. Also Compatible with 4th DIMENSION, & SuperCard.
Metropolis Software, Inc.

dBarcode: dBase Bar Code Printing. 1995. *Items Included:* Full manual. *Customer Support:* Free telephone support - 90 days, 30-day warranty.
MS-DOS 3.2 or higher. 286 (584k). disk $139.95. Nonstandard peripherals required: CGA/EGA/VGA.
Enables Any IBM PC-Compatible Computer to Print Bar Codes Using dBASE III Plus & dBASE IV. dBARCODE Supports the Following Printers: Any Dot Matrix Printer in the IBM Graphics Mode; Any 24-Pin Dot Matrix Printer in the Epson LQ1000 Mode; Hewlett Packard Laser Jet & Compatibles. Prints the Following Bar Codes: Code 39, Code 2 of 5, Interleaved 2 of 5, UPC Version A, EAN-13, & Code 93.
Dynacomp, Inc.

The dBASE Door. Tylog Systems, Inc. *Compatible Hardware:* TI Professional. *Operating System(s) Required:* MS-DOS, CP/M-86. *Language(s):* DBASE II. *Memory Required:* 64k. *General Requirements:* Printer.
$149.00.
Free Form dBASE II Report Generator. Allows 2 Databases to Appear on Report. 10 Accumulators Available for Totaling, Subtotaling, Averaging, Counting, etc.
Texas Instruments, Personal Productivit.

dBASE IV: Introduction Level 1, Introduction Level 2 & Advanced. *Version:* 1.1. May 1989. PC-DOS (640k). starter pack $900.00 (Order no.: 40-430-PK, 40-431-PK). Addl. software required: dBASE IV.
Instructor-Led Courseware. Starter Kit Includes Instructor's Guide & 12 Student Manuals with Practice Activities & Data Disks. Also, Instructor Guide Includes Overhead Transparencies & Two-Year Free Upgrade Service. Additional Student Manuals Available Separately for $28.00 each.
Logical Operations.

dBASE II. Ashton-Tate. *Compatible Hardware:* HP 86/87 with CP/M System (HP 82900A), HP 150 Touchscreen, HP 110 Portable.
HP 86/87. 3-1/2" or 5-1/4" disk $700.00 ea. (Order no.: 45583A).
HP 150, HP 110. 3.5" disk $500.00 (Order no.: 45468D).
Data Management Tool for Constructing & Manipulating Numeric & Character Information Files. A Special Feature Included Is the English-Style Program-Building Language. Users Can Sort, Edit, or Display a Database Directly from the Keyboard, or Write Menus & Programs to Support a Specific Application. Can Be Used for Such Applications As General Ledger, Journal of Accounts, Accounts Receivable, Accounts Payable, Sales Tax Records, Payroll, Check Management & Writing, Time Billing, Inventory Control, Job Costing, Tax Computation, & Document Cross-Referencing.
Hewlett-Packard Co.

dBASE II Programming: Making dBASE Work for Your Small Business. Albert Peabody & Richard Seabrook. May 1984.
disk $24.95 (ISBN 0-13-196130-6).
bk. $14.95 (ISBN 0-13-196148-9).
Shows How to Use dBASE II to Maximum Advantage in a Small Business. Goes into Software Development, Design, Coding, & Verification & Includes an Actual Order Entry/Inventory Tracking System.
Prentice Hall.

dBASE III PLUS, 8 disks. Dec. 1985. *Compatible Hardware:* IBM PC & true compatibles, PC XT, PC AT, 3270 PC. *Operating System(s) Required:* PC-DOS 2.0 to 3.0. (source code included). *Memory Required:* 256k. *General Requirements:* 2 360k floppy disk drives or 1 360k floppy disk drive & fixed hard disk; networking requires PC-DOS 3.1.
disk $695.00.
Upgrade from dBASE III. avail.
Improved Version of dBASE III. The ASSISTANT Provides Non-Programming Users with Easy-to-Use Pull-Down Menus for Creating, Using, & Modifying Multiple Databases. With The ADVANCED QUERY SYSTEM, Users Can Build Complex Queries by Selecting from the Pull-Down Menus. Sorting Is up to Two Times Faster, & Indexing Is up to Ten Times Faster Than dBASE III. Local Area Networking Capabilities Are Built In. For Developers There Is a New DATA CATALOG & More Than 50 New Commands & Functions. Also Included Are Improved Code Encryption & Linking, Debugging Aids, Assembly Language Calls, etc. Provides On-Screen Help, Structured File Definition, Split & Merge Files, & Built-In Editor. Features 128 Fields per Record, 254 Characters per Field, 1 Billion Records per File, 4,000 Characters per Record, 7 Indexes per File, & 7 Active Indexes. Includes 170 Commands, 74 Functions, Unlimited Lines per Command File, & 256 Variables.
Borland International, Inc.

dBASE III Plus in Business. Jul. 1987. *Compatible Hardware:* IBM PC & compatibles. *Memory Required:* 640k.
disk $29.95 (ISBN 0-935987-15-0).
Designed for Those Who Want to Use dBASE III Plus to Manage Information. Covers the Commands: Create Use, Append, Delete, Updating the Data Base, Reporting, Mailing Labels, Customized Data Entry Screens, History, Temporary Calculations, Advanced Query Mode, Querying the Database. Must Be Used in Conjunction with dBASE Plus Software.
Edutrends, Inc.

dBASE III PLUS LAN Pack. Jan. 1986. *Compatible Hardware:* IBM PC & true compatibles, PC XT, PC AT, PS/2. *Operating System(s) Required:* IBM Token-Ring Network, AT & T STARLAN NETWORK, 3COM 3Plus, Novell Advanced Netware, IBM PC Net, PC-DOS 3.1.
$995.00.
Allows up to Five Personal Computers to Share dBASE III Plus on a Network-Only Basis.
Borland International, Inc.

dBASE IV. *Version:* 1.1. *Compatible Hardware:* IBM PC & compatibles, Sun Workstations, VAX, Macintosh. *Operating System(s) Required:* PC-DOS/MS-DOS UNIX, VMS, Macintosh. *Memory Required:* 640k. *General Requirements:* Hard disk.
Standard Edition $795.00.
Developer's Edition $1295.00.
Database-Management System. Features up to 255 Fields per Record, up to 49 Indexes per Table, up to 99 Open Files with DOS 3.1, up to 1024 Characters per Field, up to 15,000 Memory Variables. Allows Multiple "Children" Files Related by Different Keys to a "Parent". The Language Has Been Enhanced with New Commands & Functions. Includes a Shell Program That Allows Non-Programmers to Develop Applications. Emulates SQL Using dBASE Data Tables.
Borland International, Inc.

dBASE IV for Everyone. *Operating System(s) Required:* PC-DOS/MS-DOS. *Memory Required:* 640k. *General Requirements:* dBASE IV software.
3.5" or 5.25" disk $29.95 (ISBN 0-935987-35-5). Optimal configuration: Hard disk drive.
Self-Study Guide Which Consists of a Student Guide with Step-by-Step Procedures, & a Data Disk. Topics Covered Include Getting Started, Creating & Updating Database, Creating Reports & Customized Data Entry, & Mailing Labels, Query by Example, Indexing. Must Be Used in Conjunction with dBASE IV Software.
Edutrends, Inc.

dBASE On-Line. *Version:* 2.0.
IBM PC (72k). disk $149.00.
Pop-Up Reference System for dBase Programmers. Powered by Norton Guides Reference Engine & Features Databases for dBase III Plus, dBase IV, FoxBase+, Clipper, Quicksilver & DBXL. Reference Topics Include Commands, Functions, Error Codes, DBF File Structure & Utility Programs. Clipper & Quicksilver Databases Also Include Data on Compiling, Linking, Debugging & C Interface Functions.
SofSolutions.

The dBASE Window. Tylog Systems, Inc. *Compatible Hardware:* TI Professional with printer. *Operating System(s) Required:* MS-DOS, CP/M-86. *Language(s):* DBASE II. *Memory Required:* 64k.
$249.00.
dBASE II Applications Generator. Allows Any Number of Databases in an Application. Each Database Can Have up to 5 Indexes.
Texas Instruments, Personal Productivit.

Db.Bas. *Items Included:* Detailed 100-page manual. *Customer Support:* 800-929-8117 (customer service).
MS-DOS. Commodore 128; CP/M. disk $99.99 (ISBN 0-87007-706-6).
CBASIC 2 Extendible Database System, Fully Operated with Menus.
SourceView Software International.

TITLE INDEX

dBC III Library. *Version:* 2.02. *Compatible Hardware:* IBM PC. *Operating System(s) Required:* MS-DOS 2.0 or higher, OS/2 1.0 or higher. *Items Included:* User manual. *Customer Support:* Bulletin Board support; 30-day free technical support - subsequent support is available through a 900 number. FAX number available also.
5.25" or 3.5" disk $250.00.
Program Stand-Alone dBASE Applications. The dBC IIIC Function Library Gives Users an Alternative to Programming in the dBASE Interpretive Language. With dBC III, Users Can Write C Programs That Create, Access, & Update Files That Are Compatible with Borland's dBASE III Database Management System. You Do Not Need dBASE in Order to Use the dBC III Library since dBC III Functions Give You a Complete Indexed Sequential Access Method (ISAM) Package by Itself.
Lattice, Inc.

DB86. Dec. 1988. *Compatible Hardware:* IBM PC, PC XT, PC AT & compatibles, PS/2. *Operating System(s) Required:* MS-DOS 3.0 or higher. *Memory Required:* 210k.
$750.00 includes Assembler/Linker package.
Stand-Alone Source-Code & Symbolic Debugger. Reads Intel OMF-86 Object Files. Compatible Languages Are Intel C-86, Pascal-86, FORTRAN-86, ASM-86 & PL/M-86. Supports 8086, 80286 Real Mode, 80386 Real Mode, 8088 & 80186/80188 Instruction Sets, Multiple Monitors, 43-Line Mode & Intel Link-86 Overlays. Features Full Screen & Command Line Interface; Code, Data, Stack Values & Register Values Windows Display; & Conditional on Data & Arbitrary Expressions Breakpoint Types. Also Includes Step by Assembly Instruction, Step by High-Level Language Line, Step over Calls, Step until Next Call or Next Return Is Executed, Script Capabilities, On-Line Help, Mixed Source/Assembly, 8087 Support, Callstack with All Stack Resident Variables, Walk Stack in Source Window & Browse to Any Arbitrary Point in Source Window.
Intel Corp.

DBLTS. *Compatible Hardware:* IBM PC & compatibles. *Operating System(s) Required:* MS-DOS. *Language(s):* BASIC. *Memory Required:* 128k.
$175.00.
Used to Perform the Calculations Outlined in ASME Publication 77-JPGC-NE-21. This Design Incorporates the Use of Two TubeSheets with a Space Between, Occupied by Tubes, To Replace a Single Conventional Tubesheet. This Design Is Used Where Mixing of Shell & Tube Side Streams Would Be Objectionable & At the Same Time It Utilizes the Strength of Tubes to Decrease Thickness of Tubesheets Required.
Technical Research Services, Inc.

dBMAN. *Version:* 3.0. *Compatible Hardware:* Commodore Amiga.
3.5" disk $350.00.
Features Relational On-Screen Report Generator.
VersaSoft.

dBMAN: Amiga Version. *Version:* 5.3. *Compatible Hardware:* Commodore Amiga. *Operating System(s) Required:* AmigaDOS. *Memory Required:* 512k.
3.5" disk $350.00.
Relational Database Manager Ported to Amiga from the IBM PC Version. Features File Compatibility with DBASE III & III Plus, Report Generator, & On-Line Help.
VersaSoft.

dBMAN: IBM Version. *Version:* 5.3. *Compatible Hardware:* IBM PC & compatibles. *Operating System(s) Required:* PC-DOS/MS-DOS 3.1. *Memory Required:* 256k.
Single-user interpreter. disk $350.00.
Run-time. disk $300.00.
Provides an Environment for Applications Development. Includes over 300 Commands & Functions. Features Include: dBASE III Plus Compatibility; Multi-User Record & File Locking for NOVELL & IBM PC LAN; Data Security, Password, Encryption, & Field Level Read/Write Protecion; Unlimited Number of Windows; Debugger; & User-Defined Routines for Validating Any Data. Runs on over 100 UNIX Platforms.
VersaSoft.

DBMAN 5. *Version:* 5.3. Dec. 1991. *Items Included:* Full documentation. *Customer Support:* 120 days free support.
UNIX (100 platforms), XENIX, ULTRIX, AIX, HP-UX, etc.; Sun OS (500k). $795.00-$8995.00.
Networks supported: Novell, 3COM, Banyan, PC Net, Promise LAN.
dBASE III Plus Compatible DBMS. With dBMAN, Most dBASE Applications Run with No Change on over 100 Platforms Including MS-DOS UNIX & Leading LANs. Includes Relational Report Generator. Application 4001 with over 300 Extensions of dBASE Language.
VersaSoft.

dBMann. *Compatible Hardware:* Atari ST.
3.5" disk $149.95 (Order no.: DS5034).
Atari Corp.

dbMed/Mac. *Version:* 3.0. *Compatible Hardware:* Apple Macintosh 512K. *General Requirements:* Hard disk or external disk drive. *Items Included:* User guide, 60 day free technical support contract, Foxrun. *Customer Support:* Toll-free hot line, on-site support, hardware maintenance, training.
3.5" disk $2995.00.
User Can Maximize Office Efficiency. Retrieves Patient Records Instantly. Reduces Administrative Demands with Automatic Ledger System. Provides Open Item Accounting for Easy Adjustments. Produces Itemized Statements to Simplify Billing. Includes House & CPT-ICDA Codes & Chart History. Maintains Complete History of All Transactions. Tracks Aged Accounts Receivable to Speed Collection Process. Automatically Generates Recall History & Appointment Reminders to Improve Recall Revenue. Generates Powerful Financial Reports for Performance Evaluation.
UNICOM.

DBMS/Copy. *Version:* 2.0. Nov. 1988. *Operating System(s) Required:* PC-DOS/MS-DOS. *Memory Required:* 384k. *Customer Support:* Toll free technical support; classes available.
$195.00.
Provides Direct Data Transfer Between Over 65 Packages Including Systems: SPSS, LOTUS SYMPHONY & 123, dBASE, PARADOX, REFLEX, ORACLE, R:BASE, CLIPPER, STATA, SAS, PRODOS, QUATTRO, SORITEC, DATAEASE, SMART, SCA, ABSTAT, BASS, AUTOBOX, BMDP, STAT PAC, GAUSS, PC-FILE, NCSS, STATA, GLIM, DATALEX, SYSTAT, MINITAB, ASCII Fixed Format, Free Format & Mail Merge. Transfers Are Done with No Intermediate Files. Dates, Missing Values, etc. Are All Handled Within the Limits of the More Restrictive of the Two Systems Involved in a Given Transfer Application. Features an Easy to Use Pop-up Menu User Interface.
Conceptual Software, Inc.

DBMS/Copy Lite. Jan. 1990. *Items Included:* Bound manual. *Customer Support:* Toll free technical support; Classes available.
MS-DOS. IBM PC or compatibles (384k). disk $89.00.
Menu-Driven File Transfer Utility That Converts Data Between 26 Spreadsheets, Databases, & ASCII Files on the IBM PC. Products Supported Include: Excel, Lotus, Quattro, Reflex, Paradox, Rbase & Many Others.
Conceptual Software, Inc.

DBMS/Copy plus. *Version:* 2.0. Jan. 1990. *Items Included:* Bound manual. *Customer Support:* Toll free technical support; classes available.
MS-DOS. IBM PC or compatible (350k). disk $295.00.
Offers Advanced Data Conversion for the Power User. Features Include a Programming Language That Allos the User to Select Variables, Filter Records, & Perform Computations During Conversion.
Conceptual Software, Inc.

DBMS Interface. *Compatible Hardware:* DEC MicroVAX II, VAX 8800.
MicroVAX II $1750.00.
VAX 8800 $8500.00.
Rental fees: $70 per month for MicroVAX II & $420 per month for VAX 8800.
Interface Between Focus 4GL & DEC's Codasyl VAX/DBMS.
Information Builders, Inc.

DBRx. *Operating System(s) Required:* CP/M, MS-DOS. *Language(s):* DBASE II, Assembly. *Memory Required:* 48k.
disk $150.00.
Employs Machine Language & dBASE II Code Functions to Increase dBASE II Capabilities. Allows User to Perform Sine, Cosine, Ln, Logarithm, Arc Tangent, Exponentiation, & Square Root Functions. Features Several String Functions, Including Removing Extra Blanks from the Left Side of a String or from Within a String.
Gryphon Microproducts.

dbSecure II. *Customer Support:* 800-929-8117 (customer service).
MS-DOS. Commodore 128; CP/M. disk $99.99 (ISBN 0-87007-186-6).
Compresses dBase II Files 30 to 50 Percent, Thereby Saving Disk Space for Large Complex Programs, While at the Same Time Encrypting dBase Command Files So They Can Be Run, but Not Examined or Modified. Nine Encryption Keys Are Used Rather Than by Any Known Utility. Handles Text/Endtext Properly. There Is no Royalty or Distribution Fee for Programs Using dbSecure II. Requires Dbase II to Run.
SourceView Software International.

DbsPay.
Macintosh (512K). 3.5" disk $395.00.
Payroll System.
Summit Systems, Inc.

dBXL. *Version:* 1.3R. *Compatible Hardware:* IBM PC & compatibles. *Memory Required:* 512k. *Customer Support:* 1 hour free technical support, extended support available; private & public bulletin board.
disk $249.00.
dBXL/LAN $599.00.
An Interpretiive Environment Adding Extended Language (XL) Features to the dBASE Language. Includes Wordtech R & R Relational Report Writer; Full dBASE Compatibility (Files & Syntax); dBXL INTRO Helps First Time Users; Unique Online HELP System Includes Two Levels of Context-Related Help; Memory Swapping; Advanced Memo Field Handling; Macro Creation; Records Have up to 512 Fields; &

Numerous Enhancements to dBASE Language Such as AUTOMEM Extensions to the REPLACE, USE & STORE Commands. Also Adds New Features: True Windowing; Multidimensional Arrays; User-Defined Functions; Graphing; VALID; & EMS Support.
WordTech Systems, Inc.

DCD Job Shop Control System. 1974. *Compatible Hardware:* AS/400, IBM PC, PS/2 & compatibles, IBM System/36/RS6000. *Operating System(s) Required:* PC-DOS/MS-DOS, AIX, OS/400, SSP. *Language(s):* RPG II. *Memory Required:* 1000k. *General Requirements:* hard disk, printer. *Customer Support:* Yes.
$4000.00 - $40,000.00.
Integrated Shop Floor Control System. Features Include: Job Costing, Job Scheduling, Shop Loading, Job Tracking, Efficiency Analysis, WIP, Estimating, Data Collection, Inventory/Purchasing, Bill of Materials, Financial Applications & Order Processing.
DCD Co.

DCI: Dry Cleaner Inventory. Dec. 1985. *Compatible Hardware:* IBM PC with printer. *Operating System(s) Required:* MS-DOS. *Memory Required:* 256k.
contact publisher for price.
Ticket Inventory System.
Programmers & Analysts, Ltd.

DCLUST. *Version:* 2.1. May 1984. *Compatible Hardware:* IBM PC, PC XT, PC AT & compatibles. *Operating System(s) Required:* PC-DOS, MS-DOS. *Language(s):* FORTRAN. *Memory Required:* 512k. *General Requirements:* Printer.
disk $700.00 (Order no.: DCLUST).
Utility Program That Declusters Data Irregularly Distributed in Space. Program Application Prevents the Histograms from Being Biased in Regions of High Drilling Density. To Decluster, DCLUST Either Takes the Averages of Samples in Cells of a 3-D Grid or Randomly Picks up One Sample in Each Cell.
Geostat Systems International, Inc. (GSII).

DCNAP: DC Network Analysis Program.
Version: 2. Jan. 1985. *Compatible Hardware:* AT&T 6300: DEC VT 180; HP-125; IBM PC, PC XT, PC AT, & compatibles; Tandy 1000, 1200, 2000; TI Professional; Xerox 820, 820-II, 860. *Operating System(s) Required:* PC-DOS/MS-DOS. *Language(s):* Compiled BASIC. *Memory Required:* 256k.
$150.95.
Stand-Alone, General Purpose DC Circuit Analysis Program Which Analyzes Passive & Active DC Circuits Consisting of Resistors, Voltage Sources, Independent Current Sources, Dependent Current Sources, Operational Amplifiers, Transistors, etc. All Commands Are Menu-Driven & the Program Is Interactive. Circuit Data Can Be Saved to Disk File for Use by ACNAP or for Later Editing &/or Analysis. Calculates All Node & Element Voltages, Branch Currents, & Component Power Dissipations of a Typical Five-Node Circuit in Less Than 5 Seconds. Features Built-In Editor, Sensitivity Analysis, Worst Case Voltages, & ACNAP Compatibility.
BV Engineering.

DCNAP2. *Compatible Hardware:* Apple Macintosh.
3.5" disk $200.00.
General Purpose Linear DC Circuit Analysis Program Which Works on Passive & Active DC Circuits Consisting of Resistors, Voltage Sources, Independent Current Sources, Operational Amplifiers, FET's, Transistors, etc. Machine Code is Optimized for Speed, Calculating All Node & Element Voltages, Branch Current & Component Power Dissipation of a Typical Five-Node Circuit in Less Than Three Seconds. Also Performs Sensitivity, Monte Carlo & Worst Case Analysis. In Addition, User May Iterate Value of a Component While Performing Node Voltage, Branch V I &W, or Node Impedance Calculations, Graphing the Result to the Screen, Imagewriter or Laserwriter. User May Access Supplied Component Libraries, Create Own Models, or Edit & Save Existing Models.
BV Engineering.

DDI*Amor: Loan Amortization. 1980. *Operating System(s) Required:* PC-DOS/MS-DOS, Xenix. *Memory Required:* 256k. *General Requirements:* Hard disk, printer. *Customer Support:* Annual support varies.
PC-DOS/MS-DOS. disk $75.00.
Xenix. disk $150.00.
Loan Schedules Generated with Due Date, Payment Number, Interest Amount, Loan Reduction, Loan Balance & Payments Remaining. Optional Yearly Totals. Schedules Can Be Printed Multiple Times. Variable-2- Line Schedule Description. Payment Amount or Number of Payments Optionally Calculated System Allowing User to Try Different Sets of Parameters Before Printing. Up to 999 Payments. Installment Period Variable. Interest Compounded per Defined Period. Optional Due Dates. Balloon Payments Can Be Defined by Payment Number or Payment Date.
DDI Inc.

DDI*Assets: Fixed Asset Accounting. 1982. *Operating System(s) Required:* PC-DOS/MS-DOS; XENIX, UNIX. *Memory Required:* 512k. *General Requirements:* Hard disk, printer. *Customer Support:* Annual support varies.
PC-DOS/MS-DOS. disk $600.00.
Xenix. disk $1000.00.
System for any Size Firm. Unlimited Number of Companies Can Be Set up, Each with up to 9999 Assets Which Can Be Categorized by Type, Location, & Vendor. Methods Include ACRS, MACRS, Tax Preference (AMT), ACE & all Standard Methods: Straight Line, Sum of Year Digits, Declining Balance with Optional Conversion to Straight Line, & Variable Percentages. Multiple Booking for Financial, Federal, & State Tax Reporting. Handles Reduced Basis ITC Calculations, Automatic Calculation of Gain or Loss & Tax Recapture upon Disposal & the Ability to Carry Foward on a Trade-In. Automatic Tie-In with DDI*Accounting, Southware Rev 2, 3, & 4 or Users Own Ledger System. Single & Multi-User Versions Available.
DDI, Inc.

DDI*LAW: Legal Time & Billing. *Version:* 4.0. 1986. *Operating System(s) Required:* PC-DOS/MS-DOS, UNIX, XENIX. *Memory Required:* 640k. *Customer Support:* Annual support available varies.
$995.00 & up.
Comprehensive System Adaptable to Any Size Firm, Giving Attorney Complete Control over Time & Expenses, Client Billing, Accounts Receivable & Financial Accounting. Designed to Be Easy to Install & Use & Allows for Unlimited Clients, Matters, Timekeepers & Transactions. Includes Flexible Billing Rates, over 280 Bill Formats, User-Defined Text & Many Other Features. Over 120 Built-In Management Reports Produced. Modules Include Trust Accounting, Conflict Checking, Fee Allocation, Budgeting, Court Dockets, Mailing Labels, General Ledger, Accounts Payable, Payroll, Remote Data Entry & Telephone/Copier Interfaces & Report Generator. Available in Single User, Multi-User & Small Office Versions.
DDI, Inc.

DDI-Mailbag: Mailing List/Labels. 1982. *Operating System(s) Required:* PC-DOS/MS-DOS; UNIX, XENIX. *Memory Required:* 640k. *General Requirements:* Hard disk, printer. *Customer Support:* Annual support available.
PC-DOS/MS-DOS. disk $350.00.
Xenix. disk $700.00.
Multi-User System for Printing Mailing Lists, Labels, Roladex Cards, & Index Cards. Record Includes: 4-Line N/A; Phone, Fax Number, 2 Contacts; Misc. Reference, & up to 8 User-Defined Codes Which Can Be Used to Select Records for Printing. Names Can Be Intermixed without Use of Sort Tags. User Can Select Specific Groups of Names for Printing & Can Print in Order by Name, Zip or Reference. Additional Selection by up to 12 Different Criteria or Combination of Criteria. Cards Include, Phone, Fax Number & Both Contacts. Multiple Sets Can Be Requested with User Defined Page, Label, & Card Sizes. Unlimited N/A Files That Can Be Merged &/or Seperated as Desired. System Has the Ability to Create ASCII File for Mail/Merge & DBase Applications.
DDI, Inc.

DDI*TIMETRAK: Professional Time & Billing Scheduling. *Operating System(s) Required:* PC-DOS/MS-DOS; UNIX, XENIX. *Memory Required:* 512k. *General Requirements:* Hard disk, printer.
PC-DOS/MS-DOS. $995.00 & up.
Xenix. disk $4895.00.
Designed for Accountants, Consultants & Other Professional Service Firms. Integrated & Modular System Which Provides Time & Expense Accounting, Client Billing, Accounts Receivable, Management Reporting, Job Monitoring, Staff Scheduling, Target Billing Goals, & Financial Accounting. Modules Include Trust Accounting, Fee Allocation, Scheduling, Mailing List Management, General Ledger, Accounts Payable, Payroll, Checkwriting & Remote Data Entry. Available in Single User, Multi-User & Entry Level Versions.
DDI, Inc.

DDX. *Version:* 7.7. 1985. *Compatible Hardware:* Altos 500, 1000, 2000, 1086, 2086; AT&T 362 & 6386, IBM PC, PC AT, & compatibles, PS/2, RT; H-P; WANG; WYSE; NEC ASTRA; TANDY Model 4000, 6000; Intel; NCR Tower, Tower XP; UNISYS 5000-20, 40, 55, 60, 80. *Operating System(s) Required:* PC-DOS/MS-DOS 3.1, UNIX version 7, UNIX System V, XENIX. *Language(s):* C. *Memory Required:* 2000k. *General Requirements:* 80Mb minimum disk storage, tractor feed printer with the ability to accept at least 2-part forms.
Calyx Corp.

   MDX: Financial Accounting Module.
   $3195.00.
   Maintains All Patient Data & Files. Enables Operator to Post Charges & Payments; Maintain Tables; Print Statements & Claim Forms; Generate a Variety of Reports, Including Recall Lists. Includes Audit Trail, Backup & Restoration Utilities, Data Conversions from Other Systems Available.

   DF.b: Budget Plans.
   Product is included in Financial Accounting Module.
   Establishes & Keeps Track of Payment Schedules of Individual Accounts. When a Payment Is Due, It Is Automatically Added to the Billing Statement. Budget Plans Can Be Updated If New Charges Are Incurred. Also Includes a Budget Plan Aging Analysis Report.

   DF.a: Route Slips.
   $695.00 Base price. Price varies with number of workstations.
   Stores Patient Scheduling Data; Creates Daily Route Slips & Day Sheets for Each Physician (but Is Not a Full Appointment Scheduling Package).

DF.b.c: Cycle Billing.
Included in Financial Accounting Module.
Allows Clinic to Specify Its Own Billing Cycle
& Ensures That Patients Are Always Billed on
the First Cycle after They Are Seen. Also
Offers Alphabetic Cycles.
DF.b.i: Insurance-First Billing.
Included in Financial Accounting Module.
Prevents a Patient from Receiving Billing
Statements until All Insurance Coverages Have
Been Exhausted.
DF.c.# Each Additional Claim Form.
$595.00 Base price. Price varies with number
of workstations.
Necessary If an Insurer Requires a Form Other
Than the Standard Form.
DF.d: Deposit Slip.
Included in Financial Accounting Module.
Facilitates Posting of Payments from
Explanation of Benefits or Other Bulk Checks;
Prepares Itemized Deposit Slips, Including
Cash Deposit & Credit Card Discounts.
DF.e: Electronic Claims.
$1695.00.
Submits Claim Data via Telephone Lines to a
Cooperating Insurance Carrier. Each Such
Format & Communication Is an Option.
DF.l: Letters.
$695.00.
Generates Letters with Operator-Specified
Variables; Incorporates Messages on Patient
Statements; Allows for Calculation of Interest
Charges on Patient Accounts.
DF.o: Offline Data Entry System (Batch).
$1295.00.
Enables Large Clinics to Perform Batch Data
Entry to Speed up the Process & to Minimize
System Loading.
DA: Appointment Scheduling Module.
$1195.00.
Maintains Appointment Calendars & Provides
Searches for Available Time. Also Includes All
Functions of "F.a".
DH: Clinical History Module.
$1895.00.
Offers Complete Freedom in Designing &
Maintaining Dental History Records. Allows
Searches Oriented by Time or by Problem.
Includes Several Forms of Summary Clinical
Record Printout, & the Ability to Find Patients
Based on the Contents of Those Records.
DR: Report Writer Module.
$2295.00.
Flexible Query Language Enables the
Operator to Specify Special Reports Based on
Any Data Stored in DDX. Also Allows the
System to Interface with Other Software
Packages (e.g. Graphics Packages,
Spreadsheets, etc.).
DE.d: Additional Data Base.
$1495.00.
Necessary If Two or More Separate Practices
with Separate Files Will Be Using the Same
Computer; Each Additional Practice Requires
an Additional Data Base.
DE.t: Each Additional Terminal.
Priced according to number of workstations.
Terminal License Fee Necessary for Each
Additional Concurrent Terminal.

The Deacon System. *Compatible Hardware:*
Apple II+, IIe. *Operating System(s) Required:*
Apple DOS 3.3. *Memory Required:* 48k. *General
Requirements:* 2 disk drives.
disk $450.00.
*Congregation Management System Which Stores
Data on Family & Individual Members. Prints
Labels, Listings, & Directories. Has the Capacity
for 1500 Individuals (about 500 Families) & 99
Church Activities or Interests.*
Scott, Foresman & Co.

**The Deacon System: Church Management
System.** 1986. *Operating System(s) Required:*
PC-DOS/MS-DOS, OS/2, UNIX. *Memory
Required:* 640k. *General Requirements:* Hard
disk, printer.
disk $1995.00 (ISBN 0-927558-06-8, Order no.:
501).
*Full Featured Financial, Accounting & Funds/
Development Software System. Onsite Setup &
Training Available.*
Timon, Inc.

Dead Sea Scrolls Revealed.
Windows. 486 DX33 (4Mb, 8Mb recommended).
CD-ROM disk $59.95 (Order no.: CD119-7C).
Optimal configuration: 486 DX33 with minimum
4Mb RAM (8Mb RAM recommended), 256
color display, CD-ROM drive, sound card, 5Mb
minimum hard drive space.
Macintosh LCIII (3Mb). *Optimal configuration:*
Macintosh LCIII with 3Mb RAM available to the
application & 8 bit color.
*A Unique Historical Documentary Style Program
Offering Footage of the Dead Sea Scrolls & the
Circumstances Surrounding Their Ancient Origins
& Recent Discovery. The CD Contains Historical
Overviews, Interviews with Dead Sea Scrolls
Scholars, Photos & Translations of the Scrolls
Themselves, with Commentary & 3D Depictions of
Khirber Qumran & Neighboring Caves. Its Full
Multi-Media Output with 70 Minutes of Videos,
One Hour of Interviews, & Hundreds of Photos,
Illustrations & Film Clips Make.*
Gospel Films Inc.

Deadline. Marc Blank. 1982. *Compatible
Hardware:* Amiga; Apple II Series, Macintosh;
Atari XL/XE, ST; Commodore 64; IBM.
Operating System(s) Required: MS-DOS, CP/M.
Memory Required: 32k.
disk $14.95.
*Puts the Case in Your Hands with a Dossier
Containing Lab Reports, Police Findings, & More.
To Track Down the Killer, You Will Sift Through
a Myriad of Clues & Motives. No Easy Feat, for
All Your Six Suspects Possess Minds of Their
Own - Coming & Going, Scheming &
Maneuvering Independently of Your Actions. And
Some of Them Are So Treacherous That, Should
You Make the Wrong Move, One May Do You
In.*
Activision, Inc.

Deadline. Infocom. *Compatible Hardware:* HP
150 Touchscreen, HP 110 Portable.
3.5" disk $49.95 (Order no.: 92243VA).
*Puts the Case in Your Hands with a Dossier
Containing Lab Reports, Police Findings, & More.
To Track Down the Killer, You Will Sift Through
a Myriad of Clues & Motives. No Easy Feat, for
All Your Six Suspects Possess Minds of Their
Own - Coming & Going, Scheming &
Maneuvering Independently of Your Actions. And
Some of Them Are So Treacherous That, Should
You Make the Wrong Move, One May Do You
In.*
Hewlett-Packard Co.

Dealerwerks. *Compatible Hardware:* Apple
Macintosh. *Memory Required:* 2000k. *General
Requirements:* 20Mb hard disk; ImageWriter II.
Complete set. 3.5" disk $1995.00.
Starting price for modules. 3.5" disk $95.00.
Showroom Management System for Retailers.
Dealership Systems.

The DEALMAKER: Automotive F&I. 1976.
Compatible Hardware: IBM PC & compatibles,
PS/2. *Operating System(s) Required:* MS-DOS,
PC-DOS. *Language(s):* Compiled BASIC.
Memory Required: DOS 3.1 or higher 512k,
otherwise 384k. *General Requirements:* Hard
disk. *Customer Support:* 90-day warranty then
service contracts suggested.
$795.00-$2,995.00 (ISBN 0-922627-00-2).
*System for Entering & Customizing Finance Deals
& Producing Paperwork Associated with the
Deal. Applicable to Automobile, Truck,
Motorcycle, Recreational Vehicle, Boat & Any
Other Consumer Financial Dealers. Allows
Complete Control of F&I Close; Calculates
Monthly Payment. "Rolls" Payment in Many
Ways & Allows "Odd Days", Does All Forms.
Includes F&I Analysis & the WORDS MAKER
Abreviation Processor.*
Bruzaud Assocs.

**The DEALMAKER: Automotive Leasing
Systems.** 1981. *Compatible Hardware:* IBM PC
& compatibles. *Operating System(s) Required:*
PC-DOS, MS-DOS. *Language(s):* Compiled
BASIC. *Memory Required:* 384k. *General
Requirements:* Hard disk. *Customer Support:*
90-day warranty, then service contract
suggested.
$795.00-$1495.00 (ISBN 0-922627-01-0).
*Many Leasing Systems Are Offered, Including
GMAC-DLP (& RLSP), Ford Red Carpet, Chrysler
Gold Key, GECAL, Money Factor, & Interest
Rate Plans. Designed to Help Develop a Lease
Which Satisfies Customer While Meeting Dealer's
Profit Requirements, & to Print Associated
Paperwork.*
Bruzaud Assocs.

The DEALMAKER: Data Conversion System.
Customer Support: 90-day warranty.
MS-DOS, PC-DOS (512k). PC & compatibles,
PS/2. contact publisher for price.
*Converts Data from the Dealmaker into Formats
Suitable for Importing into Lotus 1-2-3, dBASE
III, etc. Templets for Raw Data Provided.*
Bruzaud Assocs.

DealMaker III, Senior Analyst. *Version:* 4.0.
Compatible Hardware: IBM PC & compatibles,
PS/2. *Memory Required:* 640k. *Items Included:*
250 page manual, tutorial, data entry worksheet,
automatic report writer. *Customer Support:* 60
days free.
$495.00 includes Automatic Report Writer.
*Performs Detailed Business Valuations & Business
Transfer Analysis Using 15 Different Valuation
Methods. Allows User to Play with What-If
Scenarios in Structuring & Financing the Deal, So
User Can Find the Best Terms for the Situation.
Automatically produces a 20-50 Page Formal
Prospectus.*
ValuSource.

The DEALMAKER: Management Reports. 1988.
Operating System(s) Required:
PC-DOS/MS-DOS. *Memory Required:* 384k.
$595.00.
*Produces Management Reports from F & I Data.
User May Select by Range of Dates or Deals or
by Individual Deals. Many Reports Produced for
Both Accounting & Sales, or User Can Have "1-
2-3" Version.*
Bruzaud Assocs.

The DEALMAKER: Vehicle Inventory System.
1985. *Compatible Hardware:* IBM PC &
compatibles. *Operating System(s) Required:*
PC-DOS, MS-DOS. *Language(s):* Compiled
BASIC. *Memory Required:* 512k. *General
Requirements:* Hard disk. *Customer Support:*
90-day warranty, then service contract
suggested.
$495.00-$695.00 (ISBN 0-922627-02-9).
*Keeps Track of Current Inventory Such As On-
Hand, Incoming & On-Order (Preferenced)
Vehicles. Prints Analysis of Current Inventory
Including Reports by Year, Make, Model, etc., by
Date of Acquisition; Profitability Code, & Other
Criteria. Keeps Track of Used Vehicles. Users
May Define Their Own Reports.*
Bruzaud Assocs.

Dear Mr. Henshaw. Beverly Cleary. Apr. 1996. *Items Included:* Program manual. *Customer Support:* Free technical support, 90 day warranty.
  School ver.. System 7.1 or higher. Macintosh (4Mb). 3.5" disk contact publisher for price (ISBN 1-57204-183-8). *Nonstandard peripherals required:* 256 color monitor, hard drive, printer.
  Lab pack. System 7.1 or higher. Macintosh (4Mb). 3.5" disk contact publisher for price (ISBN 1-57204-184-6). *Nonstandard peripherals required:* 256 color monitor, hard drive, printer.
  Site license. System 7.1 or higher. Macintosh (4Mb). 3.5" disk contact publisher for price (ISBN 1-57204-185-4). *Nonstandard peripherals required:* 256 color monitor, hard drive, printer.
  School ver.. Windows 3.1 or higher (4Mb). IBM/Tandy & 100% compatibles (2Mb). disk contact publisher for price (ISBN 1-57204-186-2). *Nonstandard peripherals required:* VGA or SVGA 640 x 480 resolution (256), mouse, sound device, hard drive.
  Lab pack. Windows 3.1 or higher (4Mb). IBM/Tandy & 100% compatibles (2Mb). disk contact publisher for price (ISBN 1-57204-187-0). *Nonstandard peripherals required:* VGA or SVGA 640 x 780 resolution (256), mouse, sound device, hard drive.
  Site license. Windows 3.1 or higher. IBM/Tandy & 100% compatibles (4Mb). disk contact publisher for price (ISBN 1-57204-188-9). *Nonstandard peripherals required:* VGA or SVGA 640 x 480 resolution (256), mouse, sound device, hard drive.
  This companion for young adult literaure is ideal for students who don't know how to start that book report, or give that needed summary. Gentle prompts throughout the guide section of the program include Warm-up Connections, Thinking about Plot, Quoting & Noting, Keep a Journal, if I Were _____' Responding to Questions, Using Quotations, Taking a Personal View, Write to Others, & Write a Sequel.
  Lawrence Productions, Inc.

Death Gate. Glen Dahlgren. *Items Included:* CD disc, game manual, warranty card, short story by Margaret Weis & Tracey Hickman, product catalog. *Customer Support:* Toll free technical assistance (1-800-658-8891). Computer operated pre-recorded hint line (1-900-933-CLUE). Hint book $9.95 plus s/h.
  DOS 5.0 or higher. IBM PC 386/33 or higher (4Mb). CD-ROM disk $59.95 (ISBN 1-880520-17-6, Order no.: DE-CD). *Nonstandard peripherals required:* VESA compatible Super VGA, CD-ROM, Microsoft compatible mouse. *Optimal configuration:* 486/33 w/8Mb RAM, Sound Blaster compatible audio card, double-speed CD-ROM.
  A Fantasy Adventure Game Following the Main Character, Haplo, Through the Deathgate & into the Five Magical Realms As He Tries to Recover the Scattered Pieces of the World Seal That Were Broken upon the Sundering of the World Seal by the Sartan.
  Legend Entertainment.

Death in the Caribbean. (Micro Learn Learning Games Ser.).
  Apple II (48k). disk $35.00.
  Commodore 64. disk $35.00.
  Lab pack/5 $88.00.
  Strategy, Courage & High Adventure on a Lush, Lost Island in the Caribbean, Where Fabulous Treasure Is Hidden. Can You Descend the Cliff? Get Through Quicksand? Avoid the Man-Eating Ants? Conquer the Crocodile-Filled Swamp? Avoid These & Gain Riches. More Than 100 Different High-Res Color Screens, Plus a Printed Map, Guide You. Develops Critical Thinking, Inference, Visual Memory, Map-Reading & Language Skills. Gather & Use Facts; Learn Cause & Effect Relationships - All While Enjoying Yourself. Good for Small Groups or Individuals, Even Special Education.
  Word Assocs., Inc.

Death in the Caribbean. (Series C).
  All Apple IIs. $35.00; $15.00 if ordered with 40 or more games from series A. *Optimal configuration:* Apple II, keyboard.
  Commodore 64. $35.00; $15.00 if order with 5 or more games in series A. *Optimal configuration:* Commodore 64, keyboard.
  Strategy, Courage & High Adventure on a Lush, Lost Island in the Caribbean, Where Fabulous Treasure Is Hidden - & Unspeakable Terror Awaits You! More Than 100 Different High-Res Color Screens, Plus a Printed Map, Make It All Come Alive for You. Can You Descend the Cliff Without Falling to Your Death! Get Through the Quicksand! Avoid the Man-Eating Ants! Conquer the Crocodile-Filled Swamp! Escape These & Other Deadly Pitfalls, & You Will Have Untold Riches! Develops Critical Thinking, Inference, Visual Memory, Map-Reading & Language Skills. Gather & Use Facts; Learn Cause & Effect Relationships - All While Enjoying Yourself. Good for Small Groups or Individuals. Special Education Teachers Rave about This Game.
  Word Assocs., Inc.

Deathkeep 3DO. Lion Entertainment. Nov. 1995. *Items Included:* 48 page rulebook. *Customer Support:* 30 day limited warranty.
  3DO. CD-ROM disk $59.95 (ISBN 0-917059-15-8, Order no.: 032321).
  An AD&D Fantasy Role Playing Adventure Game in Full 3D. An Evil Necromancer Has Escaped from His Icy Prison & Is Quickly Converting the Land into His Evil Domain. You Must Work Your Way Through Multiple Dungeon Settings to Defeat Him.
  Strategic Simulations, Inc.

DEBT. *Version:* 1.01. *Compatible Hardware:* Altos Series 5-15D, Series 5-5D, 580-XX, ACS8000-XX; IBM PC with 2 disk drives, PC XT, & compatibles; Xerox 820 with 2 disk drives, Zilog MCZ-250. *Operating System(s) Required:* CP/M, MP/M, PC-DOS, MS-DOS.
  License fee unit. $195.00 (Order no.: DEBT).
  License fee site. $290.00.
  Maintenance unit. $40.00.
  Maintenance site. $60.00.
  Computes Amortization Using Five Most Common Methods of Debt Repayment: System-Calculated Combined Level Payment, Level Principal Payment, User-Defined Combined Level Payment, Draw-Down, Combined Level Balloon Payment. Output, Which Can Be Generated According to the Periodicity of Payments Serves As a Planning Tool. Also Generates a Consolidated Report for Debts Processed in a File.
  Coopers & Lybrand.

The Debt Analyzer. *Version:* 1.2. Michael D. Jones. Mar. 1993. *Items Included:* 1 manual. *Customer Support:* 90 day warranty, notification of major updates.
  MS-DOS. IBM PC, XT, AT & compatibles (512k). disk $20.00. *Optimal configuration:* 386 or higher, printer capable of condensed print - 15CPI or higher, hard drive.
  Designed to Help Reduce & Eliminate Debt. Debt Reduction Is Illustrated Through a Loan Payment Matrix or Through Loan Consolidation. Up to 20 Debts Can Be Processed at One Time. Use Minimum Payments, Current Payments or Accelerated Payments with Matrix. Debts Can Be Prioritized. Supports Multiple Clients.
  Insight Software Solutions.

Debug 2000. *Version:* 3.3. 1990. *Items Included:* Full documentation included. *Customer Support:* Technical telephone/BBS support at no charge.
  UNIX SVR3/SVR4, LynxOS. Microcomputer Intel 80386/486/Pentium. $595.00.
  Full-Screen, Multi-Window, Multi-File Source Level Debugger, for C, C+, FORTRAN, & Assembly Languages. Automatically Updated Windows Show You the Most Important Program Information, & Save Typing. Source-Code Environment. C+ Support Includes Automatic Name-Demangling & Class/Method Lists. Works with Popular Compilers. Easy to Learn & Use.
  Computer Innovations, Inc.

The Debugger VZ & MacNosy, 2 pts.
  Compatible Hardware: Apple Macintosh Plus, Macintosh SE, Macintosh II.
  3.5" disk write for info.
  Universal Version. 3.5" disk $350.00.
  High Level, Symbolic Debugger.
  Jasik Designs.

The DEC Rainbow 100: Use Applications & BASIC. Eric W. Kiebler. Edited by Paul Becker. Sep. 1984. *Compatible Hardware:* DEC Rainbow 100.
  disk $39.95, incl. bk. (ISBN 0-03-064181-0).
  Tutorial in BASIC Language Skills & the Fundamentals of Programming.
  Holt, Rinehart & Winston, Inc.

Decide for Sure: Add Certainty to Your Decision Making. Mar. 1994. *Customer Support:* Toll-free telephone number for technical support. 90 days warranty for defects in materials & workmanship.
  Macintosh System 7.0. Macintosh with 68040 processor (5Mb). CD-ROM disk $49.95 (ISBN 1-886806-07-1). *Nonstandard peripherals required:* Double speed CD-ROM drive. *Addl. software required:* QuickTime (included on CD-ROM disc).
  Microsoft Windows 3.1. PC compatibles; 486/33 MHz (runs slow on 386/25MHz) (8Mb). CD-ROM disk $49.95. *Nonstandard peripherals required:* 256 color display card (640x480); double speed CD-ROM drive. *Addl. software required:* QuickTime for Windows (included on CD-ROM disc).
  Helps You Evaluate Facts & Information to Make Sound Decisions. You Will Learn Proven Decision-Making Skills, Including the Need for Decisions, How to Generate Options, Reach a Decision, & Implement the Decision. This Highly Interactive CD-ROM Includes Video Exercisese & Simulations & a Self-Assessment Test.
  Wilson Learning Corp.

Decision Analysis. *Items Included:* Bound manual. *Customer Support:* Free hotline - no time limit; 30 day limited warranty; updates are $5/disk plus S&H.
  MS-DOS. IBM & compatibles (256k). disk $89.95.
  Will Help You Better Organize Your Choices & the Factors Involved, &, in Turn, Help You Make Better Decisions. Sees to It That You Define the Choices & Criteria Clearly, & Supply Ratings. Then It Analyzes Your Ratings to Show How Each Choice Compares with All the Others. The Analysis Is Presented in Three Tables of Paired Comparisons: Table of Advantages - How Much the Choices Outscore Each Other; Table of Disadvantages - How Much the Choices Are Outscored by Each Other; Table of Best Choices - Which Choices Are Superior to the Others. What You Do Is Simple. You Enter Your Choices, Criteria, & Levels of Confidence. There Are Several Options, Including the Weighting System, Confidence Levels, Date Printing, Saving, etc.
  Dynacomp, Inc.

TITLE INDEX

Decision Analysis by TreeAge. *Version:* 1.03. *Compatible Hardware:* Apple Macintosh. *Memory Required:* 512k. *Customer Support:* Free telephone support to registered users.
$495.00.
Allows Users to Implement the Techniques of Decision Analysis in an Intuitive Manner. Transforms Decision Analysis into a Visual Means of Organizing the Decision-Making Process.
TreeAge Software, Inc.

Decision Analysis for the Professional with Supertree. P. McNamee & J. Celona. Jun. 1987. *Compatible Hardware:* IBM PC, PC XT, PC AT; Macintosh. *Operating System(s) Required:* MS-DOS, PC-DOS. *Memory Required:* 512k. *General Requirements:* Hard disk.
IBM. $1500.00 ea.
Uses Decision Analysis Software Packages SUPERTREE & SENSITIVITY to Perform Routine Decision Analysis Calculations. Enables the Student to Experiment with Trees Linking Them with Such Modeling Packages As LOTUS 1-2-3 or EXCEL in Order to Obtain a Richer Understanding of the Material.
Boyd & Fraser Publishing Co.

Decision Analysis Techniques. *Version:* 10.0. (Professional Ser.). 1989. *Compatible Hardware:* Apple Macintosh, IBM PC & compatibles. *Memory Required:* 512k. *Items Included:* Disks, book, program instructions. *Customer Support:* Telephone.
disk $145.00 (ISBN 0-920387-16-0).
Decision Analysis Is a New Topic Which Is Gradually Working Its Way into Business, Jurisprudence, the Military, & Various Other Fields Where Decisions Must Be Reached in Terms of Incomplete & Sometimes Conflicting Information. The Book Covers the Major Reaches of Decision Theory; the Assistance & Mathematical Prog ramming, Decisions Under Uncertainty & Risk (Involving the Use of Utility Analysis & Bayesian Probability Theory), Decision Tables & Decision Trees, Group Decision Making, & the ELECTRE Technique Which Allows the Balancing of Concordance & Discordance in the Subjective or Objective Evaluation of People or Situations. Facilities for the Application of the Analytical Hierarchy Technique Are Provided. Although the Techniques Themselves Are Easy Enough to Use, the Ideas & Procedures Are Highly Sophisticated & Involve the "Next Level" of Statistical Assistance to Decision Making. A Specialized Book and Programs for Users Who Are Faced with Complex Decision Making Situations.
Lionheart Pr., Inc.

Decision Inventory Package. Hamid Noori & Frank Anatol. 1989.
DOS. IBM PC, XT, AT, or compatible (256k). disk $125.00 (ISBN 0-89806-101-6, Order no.: 153). *Addl. software required:* Lotus 1-2-3 2.0 or higher.
Software for Use with Lotus 1-2-3. Allows Inventory Decisions To Be Made by Calculating the Economic Order Quantity, Quantity Discounts, Inflation, Lead Time, & Finite Replenishment Rate. Includes MRP & Forecasting Functions.
Engineering & Management Pr.

Decision Pad. *Version:* 2.0. Dec. 1989. *Items Included:* User guide with tutorial & reference section, indexed; example decision models & self-running demo on disk. *Customer Support:* Free support hotline to registered owners, unlimited terms, 30 day unconditional guarantee.
MS-DOS 2.0 or higher. IBM PC/AT/PS2 or compatibles (348k). disk $395.00. *Optimal configuration:* Uses additional RAM up to 640K for worksheets. Hard disk, mouse, color displays optional.
Software System for Making Decisions Clear: Purchasing, Employee Hiring & Review, Real Estate, Financing, Closing Sales, Project Selection & Priorities. Products Unique Worksheet Metaphor, Modern User Interface, & Graphics Are Easy to Use. It's Also Easy to Understand, Crucial to Getting the Decision Implemented in an Organization.
Apian Software.

Decision Pad Lan Pack. *Version:* 2.0. Jan. 1990. *Items Included:* LAN Administrator's installation guide; complete user's guide documentation for each workstation server installation software. *Customer Support:* Free support hotline to registered owners, unlimited terms, 30 day unconditional guarantee.
MS-DOS 3.1 or higher (workstations can be diskless). IBM PC, AT, PS2 or compatibles (348K). five station pack $495.00. *Addl. software required:* Requires one copy of single-user DECISION PAD for installation on server. *Networks supported:* Novell, Banyan, MS Net, NETBOIS & other popular PC LANs.
Each LAN Pack Adds 5 Workstations to a DECISION PAD Installed on a Server. A Workgroup Can Share Decision Templates, Files & Printers. Multiple Evaluation Ballots Can Be Distributed & Collected Across the Network to Produce a 3D Model of Criteria, Alternatives & Evaluators.
Apian Software.

Decision Support I. *Version:* 1.2. Aug. 1987. *Items Included:* 600 pages of documentation, divided by modules. *Customer Support:* Free support.
PC-DOS (320k). IBM & compatibles. disk $695.00. *Addl. software required:* Lotus 1-2-3 version 2.0 or 2.1, or Symphony.
Contains Goal Solutions Plus (50 Goals/50 Variables), Optimal Solutions Plus (8000 Variables/Constraints), & Simulated Solutions Plus (18 Different Probability Distributions).
Enfin Software Corp.

DecisionMaker. Nov. 1994. *Items Included:* Manual. *Customer Support:* Free technical support (toll call) for 1 year via phone, fax, e-mail.
Windows 3.1 or higher, including Windows 95 (4Mb). disk $129.95. *Nonstandard peripherals required:* 2Mb hard disk space.
System 7.0 or higher. Mac Plus or higher (4Mb). 3.5" disk $129.95. *Nonstandard peripherals required:* 2Mb hard disk space.
Provides a Useful Way to Deal with - & Often Reduce - Uncertainty Which Can Also Reduce Your Risk. Employees Decision Tree Science - the Same Sophisticated Decision Analysis Method Taught in Leading Business Schools & Used in Large Corporations. Also Features Proprietary Business Analysis Charts to Quickly Visualize the Trade-Offs of a Decision. A Comprehensive Guidebook Full of Practical Examples Is Included to Step You Through the Decisionmaking Process.
Palo Alto Software.

Decisions: Computers & the Democratic Process. Donald B. Straus. 1990.
DOS. Any Type of IBM (64k). $9.95 (ISBN 1-56178-007-3).
MAC. Any Type of Macintosh (64k). $9.95 (ISBN 1-56178-024-3).
Nonfiction Monograph on the Ways That Computer Telecommunications May Revolutionize Our Democratic Form of Government.
Connected Editions, Inc.

DECK. *Version:* 1.03. Mats Myrbers et al. *Customer Support:* Free technical phone support.
Macintosh II, IIx, IIcx, IIci, IIfx. 3.5" disk $349.00.
Uses the Direct to Disk Recording Capabilities of SOUND TOOLS or AUDIOMEDIA to Turn the Macintosh into a CD-Quality Four Track Digital Recording Studio. Features Unlimited Track Bouncing & Sound on Sound Recording, Automated Mixdown, MIDI File Playback While Recording & Playing Audio, Digital Effect (with AUDIOMEDIA) & Optional 2:1 Data Compression.
Digidesign, Inc.

DeClass. *Compatible Hardware:* Apple Macintosh. *Memory Required:* 512k.
3.5" disk $225.00.
Data-Processing Support Tool for Classified Data.
OITC, Inc.

Deduct!: Payroll Processing. Mar. 1990. *Items Included:* Stitched Manual, order form for custom printed continuous form checks. *Customer Support:* Free telephone support, registered users are entitled to a 50% discount when ordering upgrades.
MS-DOS/PC-DOS 3.0 & higher. IBM PC, XT, AT, PS/2 & compatibles (384k). 3.5" or 5.25" disk $29.95. *Optimal configuration:* 8088 or higher, color monitor, 80 column printer, PC/MS-DOS 3.1 or higher, 384k RAM. *Networks supported:* Novell Netware, IBM PCLP, LANtastic.
Basic Payroll Program Intended for Small Business. Provides an Easy Method of Calculating Either Net from Gross or Gross from Net. Besides Printing Paychecks, Product Makes It Easy to Help Employees Who Want to Know How Their Check Would Be Affected If They Change Their Number of Deductions.
Marigold Computer Consultants.

Deep Space. 1995. *Items Included:* Full manual. *Customer Support:* Free telephone support - 90 days, 30-day warranty.
MS-DOS 3.2 or higher. 286 (584k). disk $29.95. *Nonstandard peripherals required:* CGA/EGA/VGA.
One of the Most Impressive Planet & Star Map Packages We Have Ever Seen. This Is a Powerful Evaluation Version Which Contains All the Features of the Full Version Except the 3-D Viewer Kit (for Stereographic Viewing), & Background Books. It Contains an 18,000-Star Atlas (down to 7.2 Magnitude).
Dynacomp, Inc.

Deep Space - Operation Copernicus. Paul Neurath & Ed Lerner. Nov. 1989. *Items Included:* Disk, manual, reference card, warranty/registration card. *Customer Support:* Hotline, disk repair or replacement.
MS-DOS (256k). Tandy 1000 SX, EX, TX, HX, SL, TL. disk $19.95 (ISBN 0-926846-49-3, Order no.: 2182). *Nonstandard peripherals required:* CGA card.
Innovative 3-D Animated Graphics Offer Speed & Detail in This Space Adventure. All Objects Follow Actual Laws of Motion Observed in Space, Realistic Spaceship Behavior & Navigation. Four Levels.
Sir-Tech Software, Inc.

Defender. *Compatible Hardware:* Atari XL/XE. ROM cartridge $19.95 (Order no.: CXL4025).
Atari Corp.

Deferred Charges. *Compatible Hardware:* Altos Series 5-15D, Series 5-5D, 580-XX, ACS8000-XX; IBM PC with 2 disk drives, PC XT & compatibles; Kaypro 11/IV with 2 disk drives, Kaypro 10; Xerox 820 with 2 disk drives; Zilog MCZ-250. *Operating System(s) Required:* CP/M, MP/M, PC-DOS, MS-DOS.
contact publisher for price (Order no.:

DCHARGES).
Worksheet Program Used to Calculate the Portion of a Prepaid Expense (Usually an Insurance Policy) to Be Allocated to a Prior Period, the Current Period, or Future Periods on a Simple Duration of Time Basis. In Addition, the Amount to Be Allocated to Future Periods Is Split Between Current & Long-Term. User Can Set up a File of Deferred Charges for Each Client, to Be Carried Forward from Year to Year. Policy Dates May Be Entered in the Form of a from/to Period or by Specifying a from Date & a Duration in Years, Months, or Days.
Coopers & Lybrand.

Definitive Wargame Collection. Strategic Simulations Staff et al. Jun. 1995. *Items Included:* Armor Attacks Novel by John F. Antal & data cards. *Customer Support:* 30 day limited warranty.
MS DOS 5.0 or higher. 386/33 or faster with hard drive, CD-ROM drive & Mouse (2Mb). CD-ROM disk $39.95 (ISBN 0-917059-03-4, Order no.: 062481). *Nonstandard peripherals required:* Uncompressed hard drive recommended. *Optimal configuration:* 386/33 or higher.
A Dozen World Class Wargames from 3 Different Top Publishers. Includes: Battles of Napoleon, Sword of Aragon, Tanks from Strategic Simulations Inc. Decisive Battles of the American Civil War Vol. I-III, Gold of the Americas, Panzer Battles, Reach for the Stars, & Warlords, from SSG. Conquest of Japan, D-Day, Global Domination, & When Two Worlds War, from Impressions.
Strategic Simulations, Inc.

Degree Day Handler. *Version:* 2.6. Raymond W. Merry. Mar. 1986. *Compatible Hardware:* IBM PC & compatibles. *Operating System(s) Required:* MS-DOS. *Language(s):* Compiled BASIC. *Memory Required:* 256k.
disk $100.00.
(ISBN 0-936561-14-9).
Stores & Prints Degree-Day Data by Day, by Month, & by Year. Will Also Print out Average, High, & Low Mean Temperatures in Any Period up to a Year, Change Degree Base, etc.
Rays Computers & Energy.

Delaware Corporation Formation Package & Minute Book. Wyman N. Bravard. May 1986. *Compatible Hardware:* IBM PC & compatibles. *Operating System(s) Required:* PC-DOS 2.0 or higher. *Memory Required:* 256k.
disk $39.95, incl. manual (ISBN 1-55571-008-5).
WORDSTAR-Compatible Word Processing Program Is Provided on the Disk, Together with the Text Files from the Book, Which Include All the Letters, Bylaws, Articles of Incorporation & Other Forms Incorporated in the Book.
Oasis Pr.

Delivery Control & Accounting System: A Software Package for Fuel Distributors.
Version: 4.4. Van Talmage. Nov. 1982. *Operating System(s) Required:* PC-DOS, MS-DOS. *Language(s):* QUICK BASIC. *Memory Required:* 512k. *General Requirements:* 20Mb hard disk.
$4500.00 (Order no.: DCAS).
Package for the Small to Medium-Sized Fuel Oil Dealer. DCAS Main Functions Include: Automatic Delivery Control, Ticket Printing, Accounts Posting, Daily and/or Monthly Billing, Management Report Generation, Individual Customer Inquiry. Customization Allows System to Be Altered to Fit the Individual Fuel Dealer's Methods of Operation. Installation & On-Site Training Are Included.
Briggs Mountain Co.

Dell Magazines Diabolical Digits. Perce Berloquin. Jun. 1995. *Items Included:* Multilingual on-line instruction. *Customer Support:* Technical support 215-625-8928.
PC CD-ROM. 486 or higher - Microsoft Windows 3.1 or higher. Contact publisher for price. *Nonstandard peripherals required:* MS-DOS 3.1 or higher, mouse, SVGA 256 or higher, speakers or headphones, sound card.
Macintosh LCII or higher, color monitor & CD-ROM drive. System 7 or higher (5Mb). Contact publisher for price.
The Concept Is Simple: No Two Numbers of Simular Value May Touch Each Other on a Grid. But When You Add 3-D Geometric or Twisting Shapes & Factors to Other Mathematics Variables & Spatial Relations That's When the Game Really Begins. With Thousands of Combinations & CD Quality Sound, Diabolical Digits Offers Endless Hours of Problem Solving Entertainment of All Ages.
Millennium Media Group, Inc.

DELTA: Docket Events & Legal Time Activities.
Compatible Hardware: IBM PC & compatibles. *Operating System(s) Required:* PC-DOS, MS-DOS. *Memory Required:* 512k. *General Requirements:* Hard disk, printer; B&TA (Barrister Billing & Time Accounting) program.
disk $950.00.
Tracks Docket Events in Date, Attorney, & Client Sequences. May Be Used for Simple Calendars As Well As Sophisticated Case Management Applications, Includes Report Writer for Custom Designed Reports, Personal Security Protection, & Integration with BARRISTER's TIME & BILLING (B&TA) System.
Barrister Information Systems Corp.

Deltek Government Contractor Accounting & Job Cost System. *Version:* 4.0. *Compatible Hardware:* IBM PC, PC LAN, DEC VAX. *Operating System(s) Required:* PC-DOS/MS-DOS, VMS, Novell Netware. *Language(s):* COBOL. *Memory Required:* 640k. *Items Included:* User manuals, additional supplements. *Customer Support:* Mon - Thur 9 -7; Fri 9 - 6 EST.
contact publisher for price.
Functions Are over 300 Separate Menu Commands & Hundreds of Standard Reports, Such As Job Costing & Billing, Payroll, Purchase Orders, Accounts Payable, General Ledger, & Budgeting & Forecasting. Improves Performance by Handling Jobs with Multiple Tasks, Calculates & Burdens Multiple Overhead Rates, Establishes Work Breakdown Structures, Handles Uncompensated Overtime & 401 Tracking, & Selects & Sorts Files to Produce Reports & Designated Formats. Integrated Inventory & Assembly Modules Are Available. The DELTEK Query Writer, a Flexible Tool, Allows the User to Generate On-Line Inquiry & Custom Reports Directly from DELTEK Data Files in Any of the Accounting, Job Cost, Materials or Purchasing Modules. Allegro, a Resource Management System, Is an Add-On Module Which Enables the User to Schedule Manpower & Other Resources & Also to Plan Individual Project Activity.
Deltek Systems, Inc.

Deltek Pro Pricing & Estimating System. *Items Included:* User manual; software diskettes; additional updates. *Customer Support:* 60-day money back guarantee; training classes provided to both east & west coast locations, $200.00 per day; customer support maintenance charge, includes first 3 months.
PC-DOS/MS-DOS. IBM PC or compatible, PC LAN (640k). contact publisher for price. *Nonstandard peripherals required:* Wide carriage printer, tape backup method, 15-20Mb disk system; power protection devices. *Addl.*

software required: Not a requirement, but system can be integrated with the DELTEK Government Contractor Accounting & Job Cost System. *Networks supported:* Novell Netware.
Provides Rapid Set Up for Each Proposal by Task, WBS & CLIN; Consistent Costing Methodology for Proposals & Supportive Cost Proposal Reports; Auditability, & "What-If" Analysis. Meets the FAR, DFAR, CAS & CRAG Regulations. Also Contains a QueryWriter Enabling Users to Create Custom Reports & Bar Graphs; Sales Tracking & Forecasting; Importing/Exporting Capabilities & User Security.
Deltek Systems, Inc.

Deluxe Music Construction Set. Geoff Brown. *Compatible Hardware:* Apple Macintosh, Commodore Amiga.
Amiga. 3.5" disk $99.95.
Macintosh. 3.5" disk $129.95.
Music Construction Tools Which Will Allow Users to Compose Music, Listen to Their Creation, & Print Sheet Music. Features: Complete MIDI Compatibility - Produces MIDI Output on 16 Channels; Complete Music Notation Tools: Triplets, Slurs, Beams, up to 8 Staffs with 2 Stacks per Staff, Multiple Time & Key Signatures in One Song, On-Screen Player Piano, Transposition. User Will Be Able to See & Hear Notes Before They Write Them; Control Dynamics, Volume, & Tempo; Choose from 16 Instruments & Play Styles. Sheet Music May Be Printed with Lyrics, Guitar Chords & Special Music Symbols.
Electronic Arts.

Deluxe Property Management. *Version:* 5.5. *General Requirements:* Hard disk. *Items Included:* Disks, manual, sample data. *Customer Support:* 90 days free telephone support.
IBM PC/XT, AT, PS/2 or compatibles (640k). disk $1195.00.
Designed for All Levels of Property Management. Includes a Complete General Ledger System, Integrated with a Comprehensive Property & Tenant Database. Handles Residential & Commercial Properties, Condominium Associations, Mini-Storage Units, Trailer Parks, Marina Slips, & Other Applications. Integrated General Ledger Includes Partnership Accounting, Accounts Payable & Complete Financial Reporting. Product Also Allows User to Schedule & Track Property & Unit Maintenance. A MultiUser Version of This Product is Available. An Expanded Capacity Version is Also Available.
Yardi Systems.

Deluxe Recorder.
Macintosh Plus or higher. 3.5" disk $149.95.
Home MIDI Recording Studio. Includes a 16-Track Real-Time MIDI Sequencer with Full Graphics Display & Editing Capabilities; Deluxe Recorder Provides Power of a Multitrack Tape Recorder As Well As Vital Controls For Recording & playing. Program Can Function Alone or in Conjunction with Other Music Software.
Electronic Arts.

Deluxe VisiCalc. Paladin Software Corp. *Compatible Hardware:* HP 150 Touchscreen. 3.5" disk $250.00 (Order no.: 45405A).
Enhanced Version of VisiCalc for Managers & Professionals. Features an Expanded Row Range of 500 Lines While Offering Consolidation, Command Files, & Block Replicating in Addition to Calendar, Business, & Statistics Functions.
Hewlett-Packard Co.

DeluxePaint II. *Compatible Hardware:* Apple IIgs, Commodore Amiga. *Operating System(s) Required:* ProDOS 16. *Memory Required:* 768k. *General Requirements:* Color monitor

TITLE INDEX

recommended.
Apple IIgs. disk $24.95.
Amiga. 3.5" disk $69.95.
Painting Program. Allows Users to View Their Work at Four Levels of Detail. Users Can Create Custom Gradient Color Ranges from a 4,096-Color Palette. Users Can Freeze an Image & Paint over It. Includes 3-D Perspective Tool & "Smoothing Tool" to Soften Jagged Edges & Color Transitions.
Electronic Arts.

DeluxePrint II (with Art Disk, Vol. 2).
Compatible Hardware: Commodore Amiga.
General Requirements: DeluxePrint program.
disk $79.95.
Additional Graphic Images to Be Used with DeluxePrint.
Electronic Arts.

DeluxeVideo 1.2. *Compatible Hardware:* Commodore Amiga.
3.5" disk $129.95.
Video Animation, Titling, & Music.
Electronic Arts.

DEMIN. John Migliavacca. Sep. 1984. *Compatible Hardware:* IBM PC. *Operating System(s) Required:* DOS. (source code included). *Memory Required:* 256k. *General Requirements:* Lotus 1-2-3.
disk $100.00 (ISBN 0-917405-01-3).
Design Program for Strong Acid/Strong Base Demineralizers. Sizes Vessel, Calculates Resin Volume & Regenerant Requirements, Finds Water per Service Run, Flow Rates Through Bed, Cost per 1000 Gallons of Products. Allows Two Level Acid Regeneration by HCl or H2SO4. Can Be Used to Check a Vendor's Offering or to Optimize a Design by Examining Alternates.
Techdata.

DEMO. *Compatible Hardware:* NEC PC-6000.
contact publisher for price.
Demo Program Showing the Bright, Clear, Highly Graphic & Colorful Screens You Can Design.
NEC Technologies.

Demo Program. *Compatible Hardware:* Commodore 64, 128.
included in BODYLINK $139.95 (Order no.: SOFC64-03-001).
A Series of Brief Programs Introducing the User to BODYLINK & Some of Its Applications.
Bodylog.

Demon Seed. Phil MacKenzie & Jeff Sorenson. 1985. *Compatible Hardware:* Sanyo MBC 555, TRS-80 Color Computer. *Language(s):* Machine. *Memory Required:* 128k. *General Requirements:* Joystick optional.
Sanyo. disk $34.95 (ISBN 0-923213-28-7, Order no.: SA-DEM).
Game in Which User Evades Deadly Bats & Demons in Order to Destroy the Mother Ship.
MichTron, Inc.

DENEB Construction Accounting & Estimating: Accounts Payable. Version: 6. Nov. 1984.
Compatible Hardware: Altos 586-3086, series 500, 1000, 2000; AT&T 6300, 7300, 3B1, 3B2, 6386 WGS, PC 3B; IBM PC, PC XT, PC AT, & compatibles, PS/2, RT PC, RS/6000; NCR PC4, PC6, PC8, Tower PC916; UNISYS 5000/7000; NEC ASTRA; IBC ENSIGN; PRIME EXL, SUN, DATA GENERAL AVIION. *Operating System(s) Required:* PC-DOS, UNIX, XENIX, AIX, MS-DOS, NETWORK DOS DG/UX OS/2. *Language(s):* ACUCOBOL-85. *Memory Required:* 640k. *General Requirements:* Hard disk, 132-column printer, COBOL runtime. *Items Included:* Manual. *Customer Support:* 90-day limited warranty; maintenance available.
disk $595.00-$1795.00.
source code at additional charge avail.
Permits On-Line Inquiry & Validation of Input with Distribution of Input by Job, GL Account, Inventory Item, Purchase Order. Payments May Be Made by Vendor Job or Paydate. Prints Checks, Check Register, & Detailed Reports for Audit Control. Handles Retainages & Maintains Vendor Masterfile. Interfaces to Other DENEB Applications: JOB COST, GENERAL LEDGER, INVENTORY, PURCHASE ORDER, BANK RECONCILIATION, & EQUIPMENT CONTROL. Splits Invoices for Partial Payment. Prints Waivers of Lien & Subcontractor Waivers of Lien. Handles Direct-Pay Use Tax & Vendor Sales Tax. Prints 1099s. Allows Use of Temporary Vendors. Posts to General Ledger or Bank Reconciliation of Another Company.
Deneb, Inc.

DENEB Construction Accounting & Estimating: Accounts Receivable. Version: 6. Feb. 1985.
Compatible Hardware: Altos 586-3080, series 500, 1000, 2000; AT&T 6300, 7300, 3B1, 3B2, 6386 WGS, PC 3B; IBM PC, PC XT, PC AT & compatibles, PS/2, RT PC, RS/6000; NCR PC4, PC6, PC8, Tower, PC916; UNISYS 5000/7000; NEC ASTRA; IBC ENSIGN; PRIME EXL, SUN, DATA GENERAL AVIION. *Operating System(s) Required:* PC-DOS, UNIX, XENIX, AIX, MS-DOS, NETWORK DOS DG/UX OS/2. *Language(s):* ACUCOBOL-85. *Memory Required:* 640k. *General Requirements:* Hard disk, 132-column printer, COBOL runtime. *Items Included:* Manual. *Customer Support:* 90-day limited warranty; maintenance available.
disk $595.00-$1795.00.
source code at additional charge avail.
Provides Control of Outstanding Invoices with an Open Item Accounts Receivable. Handles Retainages & Lump Sum Cash Receipts, As Well As Customer Aging & Customer History. Produces Variable Monthly Analysis Reports. Interfaces to DENEB's JOB COST, GENERAL LEDGER, BANK RECONCILIATION, ORDER ENTRY, ITEM BILLING & EQUIPMENT CONTROL. Provides Free-Form Invoicing, Point-of-Sale Invoicing.
Deneb, Inc.

DENEB Construction Accounting & Estimating: Bank Reconciliation. Version: 6. Oct. 1985.
Compatible Hardware: Altos 586-3086, series 500, 1000, 2000; AT&T 6300, 7300, 3B1, 3B2, 6386 WGS, PC 3B; IBM PC, PC XT, PC AT & compatibles, PS/2, RT PC, RS/6000; NCR PC4, PC6, PC8, Tower PC916; UNISYS 5000/7000; NEC ASTRA; IBC ENSIGN; PRIME EXL, SUN, DATA GENERAL AVIION. *Operating System(s) Required:* PC-DOS, UNIX, XENIX, AIX, MS-DOS, NETWORK DOS DG/UX OS/2. *Language(s):* ACUCOBOL-85. *Memory Required:* 640k. *General Requirements:* Hard disk, 132-column printer, COBOL runtime. *Items Included:* Manual. *Customer Support:* 90-day limited warranty; maintenance available.
included with general ledger module.
source code at additional charge avail.
Controls Bank Account Balances on up to 15 Accounts for Multiple Companies. Allows Direct Input of Deposits, Withdrawals, & Monitors Miscellaneous Transactions to Provide Up-to-Date Bank Account Balances. When Interfaced to Other DENEB Accounting Applications, Checks Are Automatically Posted from PAYROLL & ACCOUNTS PAYABLE, As Are Receipts from ACCOUNTS RECEIVABLE. Allows On-Screen Updates of Cleared Checks & Transactions. Provides On-Screen Inquiry of Current Bank Balances, On-Screen Inquiry or Printed Report of Transactions. Reconciles Statement to Actual Balance.
Deneb, Inc.

DENEB CONSTRUCTION ACCOUNTING &

DENEB Construction Accounting & Estimating: Contact Organizer & Mailing List. Version: 6. Jul. 1989. *Items Included:* Manual. *Customer Support:* 90-day limited warranty, maintenance available.
PC-DOS/MS-DOS, UNIX, XENIX, AIX, OS/2. 286, 386 & compatibles (640k). disk $595.00-$1795.00. *Addl. software required:* COBOL Runtime. *Optimal configuration:* Hard disk, 132-column printer.
Network DOS. 286, 386 & compatibles (640k). disk $595.00-$1795.00. *Addl. software required:* COBOL Runtime. *Networks supported:* Net Bios.
UNIX, XENIX, AIX, DG/UX. Altos, AT&T, Data General, IBC, IBM, NEC, SUN, Unisys 286/386/486 & compatibles. disk $595.00-$1795.00. *Addl. software required:* COBOL Runtime.
Tracks Contact with Current & Potential Customers & Produces Selective Mailings. Letters, Mailing Labels, Index Cards, & Reports Can Be Selected & Sorted with a Wide Variety of Options. Database Files May Be Loaded into or Unloaded from the Contact File.
Deneb, Inc.

DENEB Construction Accounting & Estimating: Estimating. Version: 6. Aug. 1985. *Compatible Hardware:* Altos 586-3086, series 500, 1000, 2000; AT&T 6300, 7300, 3B1, 3B2, 6386 WGS, PC 3B; IBM PC, PC XT, PC AT & compatibles, PS/2, RT PC, RS/6000; NCR PC4, PC6, PC8, Tower PC916; UNISYS 5000/7000; NEC ASTRA; IBC ENSIGN; PRIME EXL, SUN, DATA GENERAL AVIION. *Operating System(s) Required:* PC-DOS, XENIX, UNIX, AIX, MS-DOS, NETWORK DOS DG/UX. *Language(s):* ACUCOBOL-85. *Memory Required:* 640k. *General Requirements:* Hard disk, 132-column printer, COBOL runtime. *Items Included:* Manual. *Customer Support:* 90-day limited warranty; maintenance available.
disk $595.00-$1795.00.
source code at additional charge avail.
Multi-User Package with Control for Multiple Estimators & Multiple Companies. Costs Are Controlled by Labor, Material, & Four Additional Categories, Each with 10 Sub-Categories. Labor Rates, Fringes, Taxes, & Labor Overhead, Are Controlled at the Phase & Job Level. Other Overhead Is Controlled by Cost Category. Assemblies Are Built On-Screen with Database Lookup Function & Automatic Cost Update from Interfacing Inventory. Includes On-Screen Calculator Function & Full-Screen Cursor Movement. Transfers Estimate to Job Cost (When Interfaced) Once the Contract Is Awarded. Interfaces to ITEM BILLING. Load Prebuilt Industry-Specific Databases from a Variety of Pricing Services. Provides On-Line Takeoff, & Multiple Line-Item Takeoff from Database. Optional Security Feature Limits Access to Estimates.
Deneb, Inc.

DENEB Construction Accounting & Estimating: Equipment Control. Version: 6. Aug. 1986.
Operating System(s) Required: PC-DOS/MS-DOS, UNIX, Xenix, AIX, NETWORK DOS DG/UX. *Memory Required:* PC-DOS/MS-DOS 640k; UNIX, Xenix & AIX 1000k. *General Requirements:* Hard disk, 132-column printer, COBOL runtime. *Items Included:* Manual. *Customer Support:* 90-Day limited warranty; maintenance available.
disk $595.00-$1795.00.
3.5" disk $595.00-$1795.00.
Controls Profitability of Equipment Items. Handles Maintenance Through Meter Readings & Service Dates. Users Can Input Billing Three Different Ways. Generates Monthly Depreciation. Interfaces to DENEB JOB COST, PAYROLL, ACCOUNTS RECEIVABLE, INVENTORY CONTROL, PURCHASE ORDER, ACCOUNTS PAYABLE, & GENERAL LEDGER.
Deneb, Inc.

DENEB Construction Accounting & Estimating: General Ledger. Version: 6. May 1989. Compatible Hardware: Altos 586-3086, series 500, 1000, 2000; AT&T 6300, 7300, 3B1, 3B2, 6386 WGS, PC 3B; IBM PC, PC XT, PC AT, & compatibles, PS/2, RT PC, PS/6000; NCR PC4, PC6, PC8, Tower PC916; UNISYS 5000/7000; NEC ASTRA; IBC ENSIGN; PRIME EXL, SUN, DATA GENERAL AVIION. Operating System(s) Required: PC-DOS, XENIX, UNIX, AIX, MS-DOS, NETWORK DOS, DG/UX. Language(s): ACUCOBOL-85. Memory Required: 640k. General Requirements: Hard disk, 132-column printer, COBOL runtime. Items Included: Manual. Customer Support: 90-day limited warranty; maintenance available.
disk $595.00-$1795.00.
source code at additional charge avail.
Interfaces to DENEB'S PAYROLL, ACCOUNTS PAYABLE, & ACCOUNTS RECEIVABLE, Inventory Control & Equipment Control Systems. Provides Multiple Company Capacity, Multiple Profit Centers, Flexible Financial Statements, Budgets, & Year-End Procedure. Optional Password Protection.
Deneb, Inc.

DENEB Construction Accounting & Estimating: Item Billing. Version: 6. Jul. 1986. Operating System(s) Required: PC-DOS/MS-DOS, Unix, Xenix, AIX, NETWORK DOS DG/UX. Memory Required: 640k. General Requirements: Hard disk, 132-column printer, COBOL runtime. Items Included: Manual. Customer Support: 90-day limited warranty; maintenance available.
disk $595.00-$1795.00.
3.5" disk $595.00-$1795.00.
Produces Either a Progress Billing with Detail by Line Item or Detailed Billing Similar to the American Institute of Architects Format. Billings May Be in Quantity/Unit Price Format or Lump Sum/Percentage of Completion Format. Tracks Original Contract, Change Orders, Stored Materials, Retainages, & Other Functions. New Billings Can Be Created from DENEB Estimating. Also Interfaces to DENEB Job Cost & Accounts Receivable.
Deneb, Inc.

DENEB Construction Accounting & Estimating: Inventory Control. Version: 6. Jun. 1985. Items Included: Manual. Customer Support: 90-day limited warranty.
MS-DOS, PC-DOS. 286, 386 & compatibles (640k). disk $595.00. Addl. software required: COBOL Runtime. Optimal configuration: Hard disk, 132-column printer.
Network DOS. 286, 386 & compatibles (640k). disk $595.00-$1795.00. Addl. software required: COBOL Runtime. Optimal configuration: Hard disk, 132-column. Networks supported: Net Bios.
UNIX, XENIX, AIX, DG/UX. Altos, AT&T, Data General, IBC, IBM, NCR, NEC, SUN, Unisys 286/386/486 & compatibles. disk $595.00-$1795.00. Addl. software required: COBOL Runtime. Optimal configuration: Hard disk, 132-column printer.
Designed to Perform Functions Related to the Control of Inventory Items. It Provides Automatic Pricing & Costing of Material Sales with Flexible Inventory Costing Methods. It Provides Flexible Tax Coding for Sales Tax & Direct-Pay Use Tax.
Deneb, Inc.

DENEB Construction Accounting & Estimating: Job Cost. Version: 6. Oct. 1984. Compatible Hardware: Altos 486-2086, series 500, 1000, 2000; AT&T 6300, 7300, 3B1, 3B2, 6386 WGS, PC 3B; IBM PC, PC XT, PC AT, & compatibles, PS/2, RT PC, RS/6000; NCR PC4, PC6, PC8, Tower PC916; UNISYS 5000/7000; NEC ASTRA; IBC ENSIGN; PRIME EXL, SUN, DATA GENERAL AVIION. Operating System(s) Required: PC-DOS, XENIX, UNIX, AIX, MS-DOS, NETWORK DOS, DG/UX. Language(s): ACUCOBOL-85. Memory Required: 640k. General Requirements: Hard disk, 132-column printer, COBOL runtime. Items Included: Manual. Customer Support: 90-Day limited warranty; maintenance available.
disk $595.00-$1795.00.
source code at additional charge avail.
Brings Together the Contract, Estimate, Expenses, Billings & Purchases (Committed) from All Facets of the DENEB Construction Accounting & Estimating System into a Data Base for Reporting & Control. Reports Include: Job List, Unbilled Contract, Job Cost Analysis, Labor Analysis, Profit & Loss, Gross Profit, & Project Summary, & Job Cash Flow. Interfaces to DENEB's ESTIMATING, ACCOUNTS PAYABLE, ACCOUNTS RECEIVABLE, INVENTORY CONTROL, PAYROLL PURCHASE ORDER, EQUIPMENT CONTROL, & ITEM BILLING. Provides User-Defined Categories.
Deneb, Inc.

DENEB Construction Accounting & Estimating: Order Entry. Version: 6. Dec. 1985. Operating System(s) Required: PC-DOS/MS-DOS, UNIX, Xenix, AIX, NETWORK DOS, DG/UX. Memory Required: 640k. General Requirements: Hard disk, 132-column printer, COBOL runtime, DENEB accounts receivable module & Inventory Control Module. Items Included: Manual. Customer Support: 90-Day limited warranty; Maintenance Available.
disk $595.00-$1795.00.
3.5" disk $595.00-$1795.00.
Controls Open Orders, Backorders, & Committed Inventory. Handles Recurring Orders. Handles Contract Prices & Promotional Prices. Provides Various Pricing Options. Allows User-Defined Setup of Discounts, Invoice Numbers, Order Input Fields, & Other Functions.
Deneb, Inc.

DENEB Construction Accounting & Estimating: Office Tools. Version: 6. Apr. 1990. Items Included: Manual. Customer Support: 90-day limited warranty, maintenance available.
PC-DOS. 286, 386 & compatibles (640k). disk $595.00. Addl. software required: COBOL Runtime. Optimal configuration: Hard disk, 132-column printer.
Network DOS. 286, 386 & compatibles (640k). disk $595.00-$1795.00. Addl. software required: COBOL Runtime. Optimal configuration: Hard disk, 132-column printer. Networks supported: Net Bios.
UNIX, XENIX, AIX, DG/UX. Altos, AT&T, Data General, IBC, IBM, NCR, SUN, Unisys 286/386/486 & compatibles. disk $595.00-$1795.00. Addl. software required: COBOL Runtime. Optimal configuration: Hard disk, 132-column printer.
Provides an Appointment Calendar, a Personalized Phone Book, Reminder Notices, Notes, a Financial Calculator, & Utilities for the Entire DENEB System. The Program Is Packaged with the COBOL Runtime That Is Required to Run the DENEB System; the Price Listed Includes Both Office Tools & the Runtime.
Deneb, Inc.

DENEB Construction Accounting & Estimating: Payroll. Version: 6. Oct. 1984. Compatible Hardware: Altos 586-3086, series 500, 1000, 2000; AT&T 6300, 7300, 3B1, 3B2, 6386 WGS, PC 3B; IBM PC, PC XT, PC AT, & compatibles, PS/2, RT PC, RS/6000; NCR PC4, PC6, PC8, Tower PC916; UNISYS 5000/7000; NEC ASTRA; IBC ENSIGN; PRIME EXL, SUN, DATA GENERAL AVIION. Operating System(s) Required: PC-DOS, XENIX, UNIX, AIX, MS-DOS, NETWORK DOS, DG/UX. Language(s): ACUCOBOL-85. Memory Required: 640k. General Requirements: Hard disk, 132-column printer, COBOL runtime. Items Included: Manual. Customer Support: 90-Day limited warranty; maintenance available.
disk $595.00-$1795.00.
source code at additional charge avail.
Provides for Multiple Company Payrolls, with Multiple Pay Rates, Multiple State Taxes, Multiple Local Taxes, User Defined Deductions, & Variable Pay Frequencies. Prepares Government Documentation & Reports. Handles Union or Non-Union Shop. Maintains Employee Masterfile, Area Reports, & Timecard Input (by Employee or Job). Interfaces to DENEB's JOB COST, GENERAL LEDGER, BANK RECONCILIATION, & EQUIPMENT CONTROL. Supports 401(K) Plan.
Deneb, Inc.

DENEB Construction Accounting & Estimating: Purchase Order. Version: 6. May 1985. Compatible Hardware: Altos 586-3086, series 500, 1000, 2000; AT&T 6300, 7300, 3B1, 3B2, 6386 WGS, PC 3B; IBM PC, PC XT, PC AT & compatibles, PS/2, RT PC, RS/6000; NCR PC4, PC6, PC8, Tower PC916; UNISYS 5000/7000; NEC ASTRA; IBC ENSIGN; PRIME EXL, SUN, DATA GENERAL AVIION. Operating System(s) Required: PC-DOS, XENIX, UNIX, AIX, MS-DOS, NETWORK DOS, DG/UX. Language(s): ACUCOBOL-85. Memory Required: 640k. General Requirements: Hard disk, 132-column printer, COBOL runtime. Items Included: Manual. Customer Support: 90-day limited warranty; maintenance available.
disk $595.00-$1795.00.
source code at additional charge avail.
Provides Overall Control of Purchase Orders with Reports & Inquiry by Job, Purchase Order Supplier, Inventory Item, Customer, Requisition/Department or Buyer. Tracks Each Item of the Order by Type: Job, Customer Requisition/Department, or Stock. Interfacing Capabilities Allow Purchase Order Items to Be Applied to Committed Job Costs or Inventory on Order. Receipts May Be Entered in PurchaseOrders or Accounts Payable. Maintains Supplier Masterfile, New Orders, Change Orders, & Confirming Orders. Handles Direct-Pay Use Tax & Vendor Sales Tax. Information Consolidated from Accounts Payables to Provide Subcontract Reports, & Free-Form Purchase Orders.
Deneb, Inc.

DENEB Service Management. Version: 6. Sep. 1992. Items Included: Manual. Customer Support: 90-day limited warranty; maintenance available.
DOS. 286/386/486 compatibles (640k). disk $595.00. Addl. software required: DENEB Accounts Receivable, DENEB Inventory Control. COBOL Runtime. Networks supported: NetBIOS compatible.
UNIX/XENIX/AIX. Altos, AT&T, IBM, NCR, 6EC, Sun, Data General (1Mb plus 1Mb/User). disk $595.00-$1795.00. Addl. software required: DENEB Accounts Receivable, DENEB Inventory Control, COBOL Runtime.
Tracks the Status of Service Orders & Provides a Dispatching System. Service Orders in Process Update Committed Inventory, with Automatic Pricing & Costing of Materials Provided Through DENEB Inventory Control. Recurring Orders May Be Stored & Generated Automatically on Demand.
Deneb, Inc.

Deneba ArtWORKS. Jan. 1993. Items Included: Free clip art images on disk, user manual. Customer Support: 30-day money back guarantee, technical support line available free. Macintosh 6.0.5 or higher. Macintosh family w/

hard disk drive, except Macintosh 128 & 512/ KE (2Mb). 3.5" disk $149.95 (Order no.: 3055965644).
Fun, Flexible Graphics Package That Combines Advanced Drawing Power with a Full Set of 24-Bit Painting & Image Editing Features. Features Breakthrough Memory Handling & Support for Third-Party Plug-Ins Such As ADOBE PHOTOSHOP Filters & ALDUS GALLERY EFFECTS. Targeted As the Rapidly Growing Number of Home, Education & Small Business Macintosh Users. Both System 6 Compatible & System 7 Savvy. Supports Balloon Help, Publish, Subscribe, TrueType, Custom AppleEvents & Can Place, Play & Create QuickTime Movies.
Deneba Software.

Dennis Allen's ABASIC Combo. Dennis Allen. *Compatible Hardware:* TRS-80 Model I, Model III, Model 4. *Operating System(s) Required:* MS-DOS, TRSDOS, CP/M.
disk $19.95 ea.
Model I & Model III. (Order no.: D8ACOMBO).
Model 4. (Order no.: D4ACOMBO).
CP/M. (Order no.: DCACOMBO).
MS-DOS. (Order no.: DMACOMBO).
The Alternate Source.

DENPAC 80. 1990. *Compatible Hardware:* IBM PC & compatibles, PC XT, PC AT, PS/2. *Operating System(s) Required:* PC-DOS/MS-DOS 3.0 or higher. *Language(s):* Compiled Basic, Assembly. *Memory Required:* 640k. *General Requirements:* Hard disk. *Items Included:* Educational & technical support. *Customer Support:* Free updates, free phone support.
$2750.00.
Dental Practice Management Tool That Utilizes the ADA Standard Dental Procedure Code.
Denpac Systems, Inc.

Dental. CYMA Corp. *Compatible Hardware:* TI Professional. *Operating System(s) Required:* CP/M, MS-DOS. *Memory Required:* 64k. *General Requirements:* Printer.
$1695.00 (Order no.: S/N P/N T039-125).
Provides Patient Billing, 3rd Party Billing, Practice Analysis & Patient Recall. Generates Multiple Insurance Forms.
Texas Instruments, Personal Productivit.

Dental Account PAC. *Compatible Hardware:* Apple II & compatibles; IBM PC. *Memory Required:* 48k. *General Requirements:* 2 disk drives, 132-column printer.
disk $1595.95 (Order no.: D-123).
demo disk $100.00.
source code avail.
Integrated General Ledger, Payables & Payroll System for Small Practice.
CMA Micro Computer.

Dental Billing Accounts Receivables. *Version:* 1.5G & 1.9. 1979. *Compatible Hardware:* Apple II series, IBM PC & compatibles. *Operating System(s) Required:* Apple DOS 3.3, MS-DOS. *Language(s):* Applesoft BASIC (source code included). *Memory Required:* Apple 64k, IBM 256k. *General Requirements:* 10Mb on hard disk.
$1295.00.
Dental Management System Which Includes Recalls, Statements, Payroll, Inventory, & Payables.
Johnson Assocs. (Arizona).

Dental Development. Arto Demirjian. *Customer Support:* Toll-free technical support - no charge. In U.S. - 9AM-5PM EST 800-343-0064. In U.K. - 44(0)81-995-8242.
Microsoft Windows, Version 3.X. 386 IBM-compatible PC (3Mb). CD-ROM disk $249.00 Individual; $599.00 Institutional (ISBN 1-57276-009-5, Order no.: SE-009-001). *Nonstandard peripherals required:* MPC Standard CD-ROM drive, SVGA (640 x 480) 256 colors, MPC standard soundboard & speakers.
System 6.0.7 or higher. Apple Macintosh (3Mb). CD-ROM disk $249.00 Individual; $599.00 Institutional (Order no.: SE-009-001). *Nonstandard peripherals required:* CD-ROM drive.
Presents Dental Growth & Development. Includes 100 High-Resolution Images (X-Rays, Photographs, Diagrams) & over 800 Pages of Text. The Content of the CD-ROM Is Divided into Five Chapters; The Demirjian System, Training, Bibliography, Sample X-Rays, & Clinical Evaluation.
SilverPlatter Education.

Dental Development. Arto Demirjian. Jan. 1994. *Customer Support:* Toll-free technical support - no charge. In U.S. 9AM - 5PM EST 800-343-0064; in U.K. 44(0)81-995-8242.
System 6.0.7 or higher. Apple Macintosh (3Mb). CD-ROM disk $249.00, Individual, ,599.00 Institutional (ISBN 1-57276-009-5, Order no.: SE-009-001). *Nonstandard peripherals required:* CD-ROM drive.
Microsoft Windows, Version 3.X. 386 IBM-Compatible PC (3Mb). CD-ROM disk $249.00, Individual, ,599.00 Institutional. *Nonstandard peripherals required:* MPC Standard CD-ROM drive, SVGA (640x480) 256 colors, MPC Standard Soundboard & Speakers.
Presents Dental Growth & Development. Includes 100 High-Resolution Images (X-Rays, Photographs, Diagrams) & over 800 Pages of Text. The Content of This CD-ROM Is Divided into Five Chapters; the Demirjian System, Training, Bibliogrpahy, Sample X-Rays, & Clinical Evaluation.
SilverPlatter Education.

Dental Insurance Form Writer. J. McFarland. 1981. *Compatible Hardware:* Apple II, IIe, IIc; Franklin Ace; IBM PC, PC XT, PC AT. *Operating System(s) Required:* Apple DOS 3.3, MS-DOS 3.1. *Language(s):* BASIC (source code included). *Memory Required:* Apple 48k, IBM 256k.
disk $100.00 (ISBN 0-914555-06-5).
Prepares UNIVERSAL ADA INSURANCE FORMS. Master Form Can Be Prepared for Each Patient/Family & Saved for Later Use.
Andent, Inc.

Dental Laboratory System. *Operating System(s) Required:* UNIX, XENIX, DOS. *Language(s):* Sculptor 4GL. *Memory Required:* 640k.
contact publisher for price.
Collection of 5 Programs Designed to Work Interactively with the GENERAL LEDGER & INVENTORY Programs. Includes Order Entry, Job Scheduling, Accounts Receivable/Billing, Business Calendar, & Dentist/Job Code Tracking.
Universal Data Research, Inc.

Dental Master. *Customer Support:* 800-929-8117 (customer service).
MS-DOS. IBM/PS2. disk $299.99 (ISBN 0-87007-775-9).
Prints Insurance Company Forms. Maintains a Patient Database Which is Indexed by Both Chart Number & Name Code. Displays Main Menu & Loads the Desired Functional Program Based on the User's Selection.
SourceView Software International.

Dental-Medical Office Data. D. Stein & E. Neiburger. 1982. *Compatible Hardware:* Apple II, IIe, IIc; Basis 6502; Franklin Ace; IBM PC, PC XT, PC AT. *Operating System(s) Required:* Apple DOS 3.3, MS-DOS 3.1. *Language(s):* BASIC (source code included). *Memory Required:* Apple 48k, IBM 256k.
disk $50.00 (ISBN 0-914555-07-3).
Data Base Management System Which Includes: Appointments, Patient File, Dead Beat File, Phone List, Insurance Lists, Inventory, Checkbook, Investments, Employee Records, Subscription Index, Literature, Text Editor, Mail List, File Transfer & Data Base.
Andent, Inc.

Dental Office Management PC. *Compatible Hardware:* IBM PC & compatibles. *Memory Required:* 128k. *General Requirements:* 2 disk drives, printer.
disk $595.95 (Order no.: D-108).
demo disk $100.00.
source code avail.
Accounts Receivable System for Private Patient Billing, an Insurance Claims Management System for the Preparation & Collection of American Dental Association Standard Claims Preauthorizations, & a Special Appointment Management System with Patient Reminder Recall. Prepares Claim Forms, Bills Account Reviews, Attending Dentist's Statements, Monthly Age Accounts Receivable Reports, Daily Journals, & Practice Productivity Reports. Appointment System Automatically Prepares Recall Notices Based on the Schedule the Dentist Establishes for Each Individual Patient.
CMA Micro Computer.

Dental Office Management PCE. *Compatible Hardware:* IBM PC & compatibles. *Memory Required:* 128k. *General Requirements:* 2 disk drives, printer.
disk $795.95 (Order no.: D-115).
demo disk $100.00.
source code avail.
Handles the Following: Word Processing, Dental Records Management, Claim Form Preparation, Accounts Receivable, Appointment Management. Allows Users to Design a Free Form Data Base That Can Be Entered & Edited. Keeps Track of Patient Dental Histories, Chart Type Visit Records, & Continuous Transactions History. Makes Insurance Company Reports, & Records Transfer to Other Dentists.
CMA Micro Computer.

Dental Office Management PCH. *Compatible Hardware:* IBM PC, PC XT & compatibles. *Memory Required:* 128k. *General Requirements:* 2 disk drives, printer, hard disk.
disk $1595.95 (Order no.: D-109).
demo disk $100.00.
source code avail.
Office Management & Billing Program for up to 18,000 Patients.
CMA Micro Computer.

Dental Office Management PCHE. *Compatible Hardware:* IBM PC, PC XT & compatibles. *Memory Required:* 128k. *General Requirements:* 2 disk drives, printer, hard disk.
disk $1995.95 (Order no.: D-116).
demo disk $100.00.
source code avail.
Accounts Receivable System That Prepares Daily Reports for up to Ten Dentists, Private Patient Bills for up to 15,000 Patients per 5MB of Storage, an Aged Accounts Receivable Report, & the Universal American Dental Association Claim Forms. Generates Daily Appointment Logs, Recall Notices, Payment Receipts, & Time of Service Super Bills, etc.
CMA Micro Computer.

Dental Office Management System. *Version:* 450.3. 1982. *Compatible Hardware:* IBM PC & compatibles. *Operating System(s) Required:* MS-DOS, PC-DOS. *Language(s):* QuickBASIC. *Memory Required:* 512k. *General Requirements:* Hard disk. *Items Included:* System diskettes, users

guide, training tutorial. *Customer Support:* Telephone; annual contract available.
$1995.00 to $2495.00.
Designed for Sole Practitioners or Small Clinics with Several Dentists. Productivity Reports Are Prepared for Each Dentist & Consolidated Reports for Practice. System Uses ADA Codes to Itemize Patient Statements, Maintain Patient History, & Print Insurance Forms. Handles ADA Forms with Custom Forms Generator for Others. Accounts Receivable Module Uses Open Item & Balance Forward Methods. Prints Statements & Aged Trial Balance for Each Dentist. Uses Walk-Out Statements or Mail Statements & Open Times for Each Dentist. Schedules Up to Six Patients Per Time Slot. Appointment Times Variable from 5 to 30 Minutes. Comprehensive Patient Recall Features. Supports up to 50 Dentists. Interfaces with IMS General Ledger. Runs Single User or Multi-User on Many Networks.
International Micro Systems, Inc.

Dental Office Management System PC-Oral Surgeon. *Compatible Hardware:* IBM PC & compatibles. *Memory Required:* 128k. *General Requirements:* Printer, hard disk.
disk $3595.95.
demo disk $100.00.
source code avail.
Accounts Receivable System Designed for Private Patient Billing. Also an Insurance Claims Management System for Preparation & Collection of American Medical Association Standard Claims & Preauthorizations, & a Patient Reminder Recall. Prepares Claim Forms, Attending Dentist's Statements, Daily Journals, Account Reviews & Numerous Practice Productivity Reports. The Appointment System Can Automatically Prepare Recall Notices Based on the Schedule the Dentist Establishes for Each Patient.
CMA Micro Computer.

Dental Office Management I. *Compatible Hardware:* Apple II series. *Operating System(s) Required:* Apple DOS 3.3. *Memory Required:* 48k. *General Requirements:* 2 to 4 disk drives.
disk $595.95.
demo disk $100.00.
source code avail.
Cash Management, Appointment Scheduling, Private Patient Billing & Dental Insurance Claims Preparation System. A Professional Fee Schedule May Be Established & Third Party Pay or Accounts May Be Created. Automatically Locates Patients Who Need to Come in for Checkups. Makes Patient Appointment Reminders, Prints Daily Calendars, Enters Fees, Accepts Payments, & Prepares Claims.
CMA Micro Computer.

Dental Office Management II. *Compatible Hardware:* Apple II, II+, IIe.
disk $795.95.
demo disk $100.00.
source code avail.
Dental Office Administrative Package for Specialized Practitioners or Medium-Sized Group Practices. Includes Private Patient Accounts Receivable, Appointment Scheduling & Patient Recordkeeping, Insurance Company Claim Form Preparation, & Dental Treatment Records Management.
CMA Micro Computer.

Dental Office Solution. *Version:* 9.0. Oct. 1979. *Compatible Hardware:* CP/M, MS-DOS & PC-DOS based machines. *Operating System(s) Required:* MS-DOS, PC-DOS. *Language(s):* Compiled MBASIC. *Memory Required:* CP/M 64k, MS-DOS 256k. *General Requirements:* 10Mb hard disk, 80/132-column printer.
disk $2500.00.

Part of a Series of Computer Programs Designed to Perform the Routine Paperwork of a Dental Practice. Basic Functions Include: Telling Doctors What Was Done & Who Produced It, Keeping Records of Who Owes What, Permanent Record of Each Patient's Recall Time, Producing Insurance Claim Forms, Storing Detailed Data for an Itemized Statement, Sending Electronic Insurance Claims.
D.D.S., Inc.

Dental One: Dental Office Management System. *Items Included:* Full manual. No other products required. *Customer Support:* Free telephone support - no time limit, 30 day warranty.
MS-DOS 3.2 or higher. IBM & compatibles (512k). $29.95 introductory version (100 patient limit); $379.95 full version (99,999 patient limit); $649.95 full version with Networking. *Optimal configuration:* IBM, MS-DOS 3.3 or higher, 640k RAM, hard disk & any 80-column (or wider) dot matrix printer.
Low-Cost, User-Friendly Dental Office Management System Which Easily Adapts to Your Office Environment. It Not Only Offers Flexibility, but Also Large Capacity; It Can Handle an Entire Practice Having up to 100 Dentists. Up to 99,999 Accounts Can Be Set up under a Variety of Conditions, Such As Taxable/Nontaxable, Budget Plan, Discount, & Financing. There Can Be up to 100 Patients per Account. Each Account Can Be searched. No Special Forms Are Required. Includes 126-Page Bound Manual.
Dynacomp, Inc.

Dental One: Dental Office Management System. 1992. *Items Included:* Detailed manuals included with all Dynacomp products. *Customer Support:* Free telephone support to original customer - no time limit; 30 day limited warranty.
MS-DOS 3.2 or higher. IBM PC & compatibles (512k). $29.95 Introductory Version (100 patient limit); $379.95 Full Version (99,999 patient limit); $649.95 Full Version with Networking (Add $5.00 for 3 1/2" format; 5 1/4" format standard). *Optimal configuration:* IBM, MS-DOS 3.3 or higher, 640k RAM, a hard disk, & any 80-column or wider dot matrix printer.
Can Handle an Entire Practice Having up to 100 Dentists. Up to 99,999 Accounts Can Be Set up under a Variety of Conditions, Such As Taxable/Nontaxable, Budget Plan, Discount, & Financing. There Can Be up to 100 Patients per Account. Each Account Can Be Searched by the Patient's First or Last Name; Can Include an Assigned Dentist; Can Reference Two Insurance Carriers (& Have Assigned Billing); Can Be Assigned a Specific Charge Table (up to 100 Tables Possible); Can Have Unlimited Notes & History; & Can Be Scheduled for Multiple Recalls. Patient Profiles May Be Obtained at Any Time.
Dynacomp, Inc.

Dental Practice Management System. Professional Software Associates, Inc. *Compatible Hardware:* TI Professional. *Operating System(s) Required:* UCSD p-System. *Memory Required:* 128k.
$2495.00.
Generates Various Reports, Statements, Insurance Forms; Recalls & Maintains Detail As Desired. Uses Tooth Surface or Custom Codes.
Texas Instruments, Personal Productivit.

Dental-Rx: Dental Office Management System. *Version:* 4.1. May 1991. *Compatible Hardware:* IBM PS/2, 486, 586 & compatibles. *Operating System(s) Required:* PC-DOS 2.0 & higher. *Language(s):* MICRO FOCUS COBOL/2. *Memory Required:* 384k. *General Requirements:*

20Mb hard disk.
disk $4850.00 (Order no.: 321).
Dental Accounts Receivable Software Package Which Incorporates True Cycle Billing & Insurance Filing with Follow-Ups, Patient Recall with Birthdays, On-Demand Reports on Practice Statistics & Analysis, Aging, Labels, As Well As Automatic Daily-Monthly-Annual Audit. All Parts of the Program Are Explained & Prompted by the Screen.
Prose Software.

Dental WPC. *Compatible Hardware:* Wang. *Memory Required:* 192k. *General Requirements:* 2 disk drives, printer.
disk $595.95 (Order no.: D-117).
manual $50.00.
Office, Patient & Billing Management Designed to Take Full Advantage of the Wang Computer.
CMA Micro Computer.

Dental WPCH. *Compatible Hardware:* Wang. *Memory Required:* 256k. *General Requirements:* Printer.
disk $1595.95 (Order no.: D-119).
demo disk $100.00.
source code avail.
manual $50.00.
Offers Expandable Storage Capacity, Wang File Transfer Capabilities & Concurrent Applications Operations.
CMA Micro Computer.

Dental IIc. *Compatible Hardware:* Apple II with 132-column printer; Corvus hard disk with 10Mb. *Language(s):* Pascal. *Memory Required:* 64k. *General Requirements:* 10Mb Corvus hard disk, 132-column printer.
disk $1995.95 (Order no.: D-088).
demo disk $100.00.
source code avail.
Integrated Office Management System. Stores Files Directly on Hard Disk.
CMA Micro Computer.

Dental III. *Compatible Hardware:* Apple III. *Language(s):* BASIC (source code included). *Memory Required:* 128k. *General Requirements:* 2 to 4 disk drives, printer.
disk $595.95 (Order no.: D-089).
demo disk $100.00.
Features Cycle Billing & Unlimited Patient Base Size. Designed for Small Group or Medium-Sized Solo Practice.
CMA Micro Computer.

Dental III H. *Compatible Hardware:* Apple III with printer & hard disk. *Operating System(s) Required:* SOS. *Language(s):* BASIC (source code included). *Memory Required:* 256k.
disk $1595.95 (Order no.: D-090).
demo disk $100.00.
Designed for Large Group Practices or Practices with Large Patient Bases. Combines All the Features of the Floppy Based Version with Speed in Processing & "No Disk Swapping".
CMA Micro Computer.

DentaLab. *Compatible Hardware:* IBM PC.
contact publisher for price.
Turnkey System Developed for the Small to Medium Sized Dental Labs. Includes: Sales Reports; Accounts Receivable Statements, Orders Duel Lists, Invoices, Automatic Billing, Case Locations, Case Entry, Work Tickets. Allows User to Let a Lab Schedule a Case, Generate a Work Ticket, Add the Case to the Location File, Produce an Invoice, & Apply the Invoice to the Doctor's Statement. Each Invoice Contains the Case Number & the Patient's Name.
Dentcom, Inc.

TITLE INDEX

DentalChip. Version: 2.0. Michael S. Ettel. 1995. Compatible Hardware: IBM PC & compatibles. Operating System(s) Required: PC-DOS or Windows. Memory Required: 8000k. General Requirements: Hard disk, printer. Customer Support: Free 90 day support/dial-in remote access on line help.
Single user. disk $3450.00.
Multi-User Version. $4450.00.
Dental Office Management Program That Emphasizes the Marketing Aspect of the Dental Office & Allows User to Selectively Market to Various Types of Patients with Various Combinations of Attributes/Characteristics. Complete Billing & Recall Management & Scheduling. Direct Electronic Claims Capability Built in with Claim Status Inquiry.
Stanton Consulting & Software.

DentalMac. Version: 3.9.3. (MacHealth Ser.). Dec. 1995. Compatible Hardware: All Apple Macintosh. Language(s): Assembler, C & Pascal - combination. Memory Required: Minimum of 4000k. General Requirements: Minimum of 40Mb hard disk, Laser printer. Items Included: All software, standard insurance form files, fee files, all user manuals. Customer Support: 90 days free initial support; 1 year Technical Support/Enhancement Contract, $795.00 - single user; $995.00 - network user. Toll Free: 800-627-4344, Fax: 402-466-9044.
$1995.00 & up, single user.
Network $5495.00.
Management System Designed for the Dental Office.
HealthCare Communications.

DentalStack. Compatible Hardware: Apple Macintosh, Macintosh Plus. General Requirements: HyperCard 1.2.
3.5" disk $495.00.
Demo. 3.5" disk $75.00.
Replaces a Standard Chart for Chairside Use by a Dentist.
PBC Enterprises.

DentalWare. Version: 4.40. Aug. 1980. Compatible Hardware: IBM PC AT & compatibles, 286, 386, 486, 586. Operating System(s) Required: PC-DOS/MS-DOS. Language(s): Compiled BASIC. Memory Required: Windows 8000Mb, DOS 640kk. Items Included: On-site installation, training, support, two updates, General Ledger. Customer Support: $480/yr. after first yr..
disk $1995.00.
Consists of a Series of over 60 Integrated Programs for Veterinary Office Management. Complete Practice Management, Automatic Recall. System Enables Accurate Billing, Posting Payments & Charges, Computing Late Charges & Installment Records, Punctuality of Notices, Statements & Insurance Forms.
Data Strategies, Inc.

Dentist's Appointment Scheduler & Projects Organizer. Larry Friedman & Steven Friedman. May 1989. Items Included: Diskettes, manual, book/folder, 8 1/2"x 11' pages of each application & form. Customer Support: 30 day exchange or refund if package seals unopened.
MS-DOS (256k). IBM PC compatibles. $74.00 (ISBN 1-877766-00-3, Order no.: APPT-5). Addl. software required: Word Processor Program. Optimal configuration: Form generator software.
$74.00 (ISBN 1-877766-01-1, Order no.: APPT-3).
$34.00, manual only (ISBN 1-877766-03-8, Order no.: APPT-M).
Appt. Scheduling Forms, Telephone Technique, Appointment Sheets, Daily/Weekly/Monthly/Yearly Projects, Insurance & Fee Tables for Quick Form Fill-in, Insurance Tracking & Preauths & Abbrev., Employee Progress & Competancy Reviews, Solution Changing Records, Ordering Supplies List, Repair Log, Pregnancy & Medical Alert Forms, X-Ray Techniques, Staff Meeting Formats, Job Descriptions, Bookkeeper Checklist, Petty Cash Receipts. Not Copy-Protected.
On the Mark Computer Software Co.

Dentist's Checklist & Tray Setup System. Larry Friedman & Steven Friedman. Oct. 1988. Items Included: Diskettes, manual, book/folder, 8 1/2" x 11" pages of each application & form. Customer Support: 30 day exchange or refund if package seals unopened.
MS-DOS (256k). IBM PC & compatibles. disk $64.00 (ISBN 1-877766-69-0, Order no.: TRA8-5). Addl. software required: Word processor.
3.5" disk $64.00 (ISBN 1-877766-70-4, Order no.: TRA8-3).
manual $24.00 (ISBN 1-877766-71-2, Order no.: TRA8-M).
Dentist, Doctor, & Health Professional Computer Generated Forms. Instruments & Supplies for Each Procedure Are Listed. Training/Office Manual & Organizational Aid for New Staff. Step-by-Step Outlines for Each Office Procedure. Medical Emergency info. Tray Set-ups Color Coding, Instrument ID, Inventory & Bank Financing Info. Decrease Overstocking Problems. Well-organized & Fast-reading. Customize & Create New Forms Easily. Reorder Supplies & Instruments Quickly. Not Copy- Protected.
On the Mark Computer Software Co.

Dentist's Employee Record. Larry Friedman & Steven Friedman. May 1989. Items Included: Diskettes, manual, book/folder, 8 1/2" x 11" pages of each application & form. Customer Support: 30 day exchange or refund if package seals unopened.
MS-DOS (256k). IBM PC & compatibles. disk $94.00 (ISBN 1-877766-17-8, Order no.: EMPL-5). Addl. software required: Word Processor, Lotus 1-2-3 or compatible spreadsheet, PC-FILE+ or PC-FILE:dB or dBASE III. Optimal configuration: 512k Ram, Hard disk.
3.5" disk $94.00 (ISBN 1-877766-18-6, Order no.: EMPL-3).
$54.00, manual only (ISBN 1-877766-19-4, Order no.: EMPL-M).
BENEFITS: Hourly/Daily/Monthly/Yearly Wages, Benefits, Raises, Sick Pay, Vacation Pay, Bonus Plan, Wage Analyses, Salary Increases. INTERVIEWING/HIRING/FIRING: Ads, Phone Technique, Leads Data Base, Interview Applications, Math Test & Answers, Referral Form, Licenses & Degrees, Letter of Recommendation, References. DUTIES & PROGRESS REVIEWS: Employee & Doctor Data, Competency Evaluations, New & Leaving Employee Checklist, Jobs & Duties, Not Copy-Protected.
On the Mark Computer Software Co.

Dentist's Fee Schedule Analyzer. Larry Friedman & Steven Friedman. May 1989. Items Included: Diskettes, manual, book/folder, 8 1/2" x 11"pages of each application & form. Customer Support: 30 day exchange or refund if package seals unopened.
MS-DOS (256k). IBM PC & compatibles. disk $94.00 (ISBN 1-877766-20-8, Order no.: FEE-5). Addl. software required: Word Processor, Lotus 1-2-3 or compatible spreadsheet. Optimal configuration: Hard disk, 512k Ram, PC-FILE;dB or dBASE III.
3.5" disk $94.00 (ISBN 1-877766-21-6, Order no.: FEE-3).
$54.00, manual only (Order no.: FEE-M).
Over 545 Fees Ready for Your Evaluation Diagnostic, Preventive, Restorative, Endodontic, Periodontic, Fixed & Removable Prosthethics, Surgery, Orthodontics, General & Misc. Fees. Use the Power of Lotus 1-2-3 Spreadsheet for Analysis on 5 Parameters. Daily & Often Used Fee Lists, Appointment Time List, Insurance Maximum Fees, Medi-Caid & New Fees, Percentage Raise/Discount of Fees. Add New Fees as They Develop. Not Copy-Protected.
On the Mark Computer Software Co.

Dentist's Humorous Side. Larry Friedman & Steven Friedman. May 1989. Items Included: Diskettes, manual, book/folder, 8 1/2" x 11" pages of each application & form. Customer Support: 30 day exchange or refund if package seals unopened.
MS-DOS (256k). IBM compatible. disk $54.00 (ISBN 1-877766-23-2, Order no.: HUMR-5). Addl. software required: Word processor, form generator program. Optimal configuration: Graphics capability.
3.5" disk $54.00 (ISBN 1-877766-24-0, Order no.: HUMR-3).
$24.00, manual only (ISBN 1-877766-25-9, Order no.: HUMR-M).
Over 100 Cartoons, Drawings, Illustrations, Dental Humor, Hints, Tips, Traps & Suggestions for the Entire Staff Modify these 8 1/2" X 11" Forms & Insert These Humorous Pages in Your Own Office Manual. Make the Learning Process Fun & Reinforce Your Messages. See Good Ol' Doc; Nurse Kandi, Receptionist - Pam Perfect; Office Manager - Mrs. Tuff; Sandy Scale RDH, & a Variety of Patients & Everyday Experiences. Pictures are Printed on Each Enclosed Sheet. Not Copy-Protected.
On the Mark Computer Software Co.

Dentist's Insurance Organizer. Larry Friedman & Steven Friedman. May 1989. Items Included: Diskettes, manual, book/folder, 8 1/2"x 11" of each application & form. Customer Support: 30 day exchange or refund if package seals unopened.
MS-DOS (256k). IBM PC & compatibles. disk $94.00 (ISBN 1-877766-26-7, Order no.: INS-5). Addl. software required: Word processor, Lotus 1-2-3 or compatible spreadsheet; PC-FILE or PC-FILE:dB or dBASE III. Optimal configuration: 512k Ram, hard disk.
3.5" disk $94.00 (ISBN 1-877766-27-5, Order no.: INS-3).
$54.00, manual only (ISBN 1-877766-27-5, Order no.: INS-M).
INSURANCE BILLING: Insurance Staff Duties, Paperwork Simplifiers, Fee Schedules to Post, Appointment Time Scheduling List. INSURANCE COMPANY DATA: Details of Each Employer & Insurance Co. on Data Base. Percentages & Allowances of Each Employer's Group. Preauthorization Worksheets & Forms Enclosed. TRICKS OF THE INSURANCE INDUSTRY: Fee Adjustments, Waiting Periods, Limitation, Exclusions, Dept. of Insurance Can Aid You, See How You Can Win. Not Copy-Protected.
On the Mark Computer Software Co.

Dentist's Management System. Version: 2.0. Larry Friedman & Steven Friedman. May 1989. Items Included: Diskettes, manual, book/folder, 8 1/2" x 11" pages of each application & form. Customer Support: 30 day exchange or refund if package seals unopened.
MS-DOS (256k). IBM PC & compatibles. disk $74.00 (ISBN 1-877766-42-9, Order no.: MGMT-5). Addl. software required: Word processor, Lotus 1-2-3 or compatible spreadsheet program. Optimal configuration: Form generator program.
3.5" disk $74.00 (ISBN 1-877766-43-7, Order no.: MGMT-3).
$34.00, manual only (ISBN 1-877766-44-5,

Order no.: MGMT-M).
Dentist, Doctor & Health Professional Computer Generated Forms & Spreadsheets. Fee Analysis Templates, Customized Patient Literature, Production Projections, Appointment Scheduling Forms, Patient Recall Organizers. Insurance Benefit Analysis, Logs & Tracing. Collection Policy & Office Manual. Ordering Supplies & Solutions Changed Lists. Macros Simplify Use. Over 75 Forms for Doctor, Staff, Patients & Bookkeeper. Not Copy-Protected.
On the Mark Computer Software Co.

Dentist's Management System for the IBM. Larry Friedman & Steven Friedman. Apr. 1984. *Items Included:* Diskettes, manual, book/folder, 8 1/2" x 11" pages of each application & form. *Customer Support:* 30 day exchange or refund if package seals unopened.
MS-DOS (256k). IBM PC & compatibles. disk $74.00 (ISBN 1-877766-39-9, Order no.: MAN4-5). *Addl. software required:* Work processor, Lotus 1-2-3 or compatible program.
3.5" disk $74.00 (ISBN 1-877766-40-2, Order no.: MAN4-3).
$34.00, manual only (ISBN 1-877766-41-0, Order no.: MAN4-M).
Dentist, Doctor & Health Professional Computer Generated Forms & Spreadsheets. Fee Analysis Templates, Customized Patient Literature, Production Projections, Appointment Scheduling Forms, Patient Recall Organizers. Insurance Benefit Analysis, Logs & Tracing. Collection Policy & Office Manual. Ordering Supplies & Solutions Changed Lists. Macros Simplify Use. Over 75 Forms for Doctor, Staff, Patients & Bookkeeper. Not Copy-Protected.
On the Mark Computer Software Co.

Dentist's Patient Literature & Handouts. Larry Friedman & Steven Friedman. May 1989. *Items Included:* Diskettes, manual, book/folder, 8 1/2" x 11" pages of each application & form. *Customer Support:* 30 day exchange or refund if package seals unopened.
MS-DOS (256k). IBM compatible. $64.00 (ISBN 1-877766-36-4, Order no.: LIT-5). *Addl. software required:* Word processor. *Optimal configuration:* Form generatior program.
$64.00 (ISBN 1-877766-37-2, Order no.: LIT-3).
$34.00, manual only (ISBN 1-877766-38-0, Order no.: LIT-M).
FRONT OFFICE: Dental Insurance Reference Forms, Release & Assignment, Department of Insurance, Insurance Letters, Patient Estimate, Refund, School Note. BACK OFFICE: Medical Consult, Pregnancy Consent Form, Oral Hygiene Instructions, Post Operative Instructions for Oral & Periodontal Surgery. DOCTOR: Credit Application, 4 Billing Statements & Final Notice, Correspondence Coordinator Forms, Customize Your Own Forms. Not Copy-Protected.
On the Mark Computer Software Co.

Dentist's Recall System. Larry Friedman & Steven Friedman. May 1989. *Items Included:* Diskettes, manual, book/folder, 8 1/2" x 11" pages of each application & form. *Customer Support:* 30 day exchange or refund if package seals unopened.
MS-DOS (256k). IBM PC & compatibles. disk $84.00 (ISBN 1-877766-56-9, Order no.: RCL-5). *Addl. software required:* Word processor, PC-FILE+ or PC-FILE/dB or dBASE III. *Optimal configuration:* 512k Ram & hard disk.
3.5" disk $84.00 (ISBN 1-877766-57-7, Order no.: RCL-3).
$34.00, manual only (ISBN 1-877766-58-5, Order no.: RCL-M).
DATA BASE: The Easiest Program to Learn & Train the Staff, Search by Name, Last Prophy, or Balance Due/Date. Print Reports of Overdue,

Money Owed, New Patients, etc. *REPORTS & LETTERS: Monthly Recall & Billing Checklists, Mailing Labels, Mail Merge Letters, Statements Customized for Your Office! Preauths, Overdue, Perio Letters, & More. SPECIAL FEATURES: Weekly & Advertising Planner, Correspondence Coordinator, Monthly Duties, New Info Form. Not Copy-Protected.*
On the Mark Computer Software Co.

Dentist's Songs, Poetry, & Nursery Rhymes. Larry Friedman & Steven Friedman. May 1989. *Items Included:* Diskettes, manual, book/folder, 8 1/2" x 11" pages of each application & form. *Customer Support:* 30 day exchange or refund if package seals unopened.
MS-DOS (256k). IBM compatible. $34.00 (ISBN 1-877766-62-3, Order no.: SONG-5). *Addl. software required:* Word processor. *Optimal configuration:* Form generator program.
$34.00 (ISBN 1-877766-63-1, Order no.: SONG-3).
$18.00, manual only (ISBN 1-877766-65-8, Order no.: SONG-M).
SONGS & RHYMES: To Remember & Sing to Your Patients & Family, Cartoons, Drawings, Illustrations, Dental Humor for the Entire STAFF. Modify These 8 1/2" x 11" Poems & Songs & Put in Your Office Manual! Make Your Office Distinct, Different, & Memorable! Poetry to Lament the Woes of the Dental Profession. Enjoy These Gems While Taking a Bathroom Break. Include the Office Staff in the Fun & Creativity. Remember Your Patients & Everyday Experiences. Pictures Are Printed on Each Enclosed Sheet. Not Copy-Protected.
On the Mark Computer Software Co.

Dentist's Technique Manual. Larry Friedman & Steven Friedman. May 1989. *Items Included:* Diskettes, manual, book/folder, 8 1/2" x 11" pages of each application & form. *Customer Support:* 30 day exchange or refund if package seals unopened.
MS-DOS (256k). IBM compatible. $74.00 (ISBN 1-877766-66-6, Order no.: TECH-5). *Addl. software required:* Word processor.
$74.00 (ISBN 1-877766-67-4, Order no.: TECH-3).
$34.00, manual only (ISBN 1-877766-68-2, Order no.: TECH-M).
Back Office: Crown & Bridge, Ortho, Composite Bonding, Endo, Oral/Perio Surgery, Pedo, Color Coding, Medical Emergencies, Dentures. Step-By-Step Outlines: Assisting the Doctor, X-Ray taking, Analgesia/N20, Pregnancy, Anesthetics, New/Recall & Emergency Patients, Lab Cases. Quick Reference Guide: Sterilization, Impression Taking, Inventory of Equipment, & Humor! Speed Up the Training Process. Customize the Steps for Your Way of Doing Things. Avoid Problems by Having It in Writing! Not Copy-Protected.
On the Mark Computer Software Co.

Dentist's Tray Setup Checklist System. *Version:* 2.0. Larry Friedman & Steven Friedman. May 1989. *Items Included:* Diskettes, manual, book/folder, 8 1/2" x 11" pages of each application & form. *Customer Support:* 30 day exchange or refund if package seals unopened.
MS-DOS (256k). IBM compatible. $64.00 (ISBN 1-877766-72-0, Order no.: TRAY-5). *Addl. software required:* Word processor. *Optimal configuration:* Form generator program.
$64.00 (ISBN 1-877766-73-9, Order no.: TRAY-3).
$24.00, manual only (ISBN 1-877766-74-7, Order no.: TRAY-M).
Dentist, Doctor, & Health Professional Computer Generated Forms. Instruments & Supplies for Each Procedure Are Listed. Training/Office Manual & Organizational Aid for New Staff. Step-by-Step Outlines for Each Office Procedure.

Medical Emergency Info. Tray Set-ups Color Coding, Instrument ID. Inventory & Bank Financing Info. Decrease Overstocking Problems. Well-organized & Fast-reading. Customize & Create New Forms Easily. Reorder Supplies & Instruments Quickly. Not Copy-Protected.
On the Mark Computer Software Co.

Depreciate-II. 1983. *Compatible Hardware:* Apple II, IIe; IBM PC; TRS-80 Model I, Model II, Model III, Model 4, Model 12, Model 16. *Operating System(s) Required:* CP/M-80, PC-DOS. *Memory Required:* TRS-80 Model I, Model III 48k; TRS-80 Model II, Model 4, Model 12, Model 16, Apple 64k. *General Requirements:* Printer.
TRS-80 Model II, Model 12, Model 16. disk $50.00.
CP/M. disk $50.00.
disk $35.00 ea.
TRS-80 Model I, Model III, Model 4; IBM; Apple.
Maintains Lists of Depreciable Goods, Corresponding Costs, Dates, & Depreciation Rates. Items Are Automatically Updated Each Year. Also Prints Reports.
Documan Software.

Depreciation. *Version:* 92.04. Jul. 1993. *Items Included:* 1 wiro-bound manual. *Customer Support:* One year free support.
DOS 3.1 or higher. 100% IBM compatible PC (490k). disk $495.00 nonmember; $445.50 AICPA member. *Optimal configuration:* 100% IBM compatible PC, DOS 3.1 or higher, 640k RAM, printer capable of printing condensed or compressed. *Networks supported:* Novell, 3COM, LANtastic.
Network, unlimited version $695.00 nonmember; $625.50 AICPA member.
Calculates Depreciation for Six Separate Reporting Bases: Book, Federal, State, AMT, ACE & "Other." Depreciation Applies Various Methods to Any of These Reports & Prints Out Complete Worksheets Showing Changes in Various Property Accounts & the Necessary Journal Entries to Record Depreciation for the Year.
American Institute of Certified Public Accountants.

Depreciation-Amortization Estimator. *Compatible Hardware:* Altos Series 5-15D, Series 5-5D, 580-XX, ACS8000-XX; DEC Rainbow 100 with 2 disk drives, DEC Rainbow 100+ with 10MB hard disk; IBM PC with 2 disk drives, IBM PC XT, & compatibles; Kaypro 11/IV with 2 disk drives, Kaypro 10; Xerox 820 with 2 disk drives; Zilog MCZ-250. *Operating System(s) Required:* CP/M, MP/M, CP/M-86/80, PC-DOS, MS-DOS.
contact publisher for price (Order no.: DAEST).
Developed to Assist the Auditor in Performing Reasonableness Tests of Depreciation. Estimates Current-Year Depreciation (or Amortization) Expense Based on Prior-Year Relationships. Helps the Auditor Determine the Nature & Extent of Other Substance Tests of Depreciation.
Coopers & Lybrand.

Depreciation Calculator. *Version:* 2.30. Jul. 1992. *Compatible Hardware:* IBM & compatibles. *Operating System(s) Required:* PC-DOS/MS-DOS 2.0 or higher. *Memory Required:* 384k. *Items Included:* User manual & 12 months of maintenance coverage. *Customer Support:* 1-800-367-1040, Annual maintenance contract: $51.00.
3.5" or 5.25" disk $129.00.
Handles Virtually Every Depreciation Method. Includes HACRS, ACE, ACRS & Luxury Auto Limitations. Conventions Include Half-Year, Mid-Quarter, & Mid-Month. Provides Help Messages & Input Validations to Aid in Selecting Methods, Recovery Periods, & Adjustments to Basis.
CCH ACCESS Software.

Depreciation Comparison. 1982. *Compatible Hardware:* MS-DOS. *Language(s):* Microsoft BASIC.
disk $45.00 (Order no.: 259).
Compares 3 Standard Methods of Depreciating Fixed Assets for Any Investment Amount & Any Length of Asset Life.
Resource Software International, Inc.

Depreciation Log. *Version:* 5. *Compatible Hardware:* IBM PC & compatibles. *Operating System(s) Required:* MS-DOS. *Language(s):* Foxpro. *Memory Required:* 640k. *General Requirements:* Hard disk. *Items Included:* Program on disk & manual. *Customer Support:* Pay-per-call - $1.95/minute.
disk $295.00.
demo disk $45.00.
Maintains Control of Depreciation Decisions & Monitors Tax Status Months Ahead of Year-End to Provide Capital Spending & Depreciation Decisions. Prints Information on the Tax Form.
Harvest Computer Systems, Inc.

Depreciation Master. *Customer Support:* 800-929-8117 (customer service).
MS-DOS. Apple II. disk $49.99 (ISBN 0-87007-838-0).
Calculates Annual Depreciation Using Straight Line Sum-of-Years Digits, or Multiple Declining Balance with the Option of Switching to S.L. or S.Y.D. at Optimal. Calculates Interest Payments, Loans, Investment, Deposits & Amoritizations.
SourceView Software International.

Depreciation-Master II. *Version:* 8.0. David Powers. Mar. 1988. *Compatible Hardware:* IBM PC & compatibles. *Operating System(s) Required:* PC-DOS, MS-DOS. *Language(s):* Pascal. *Memory Required:* 384k. *General Requirements:* 2 disk drives, printer.
disk $249.00, incl. 3-ring binder, manual & software registration form.
$99.00 update from version 7.0.
manual $20.00.
Allows User to Create & Maintain Asset Inventory Records & Depreciation Schedules. Supports All IRS Depreciation Methods, Including Straight-Line, Sum-of-the-Digits, Declining Balance & ACRS. User Can Select from up to 7 Different Report Formats, Including Tax Form 4562.
Generic Computer Products, Inc. (GCPI).

Depreciation Schedule. *Version:* 2.0. Jim Hunt & CPA. Feb. 1989. *Compatible Hardware:* IBM PC. *Operating System(s) Required:* MS-DOS. *Memory Required:* 256k. *General Requirements:* Printer. *Items Included:* Manual. *Customer Support:* Customer support available.
IBM. disk $79.95 (ISBN 0-918741-46-7).
Calculates Monthly & Accumulated Depreciation under Any One of Five Accepted Methods. Allows Users to Categorize Each Item & Gives a Breakdown of the Overall Total by Those Categories. Features Add, Change & Delete Modes; Screen Inquiry; & Calculation of Gains &/or Losses.
D W N.

The Depreciation Solution II. *Version:* 1.1.2. 1989. *Compatible Hardware:* IBM PC XT & compatibles, PC AT, PS/2. *Operating System(s) Required:* PC-DOS/MS-DOS 3.X, 4.x. *Language(s):* C. *Memory Required:* 512k. *Customer Support:* 2 free hours in first year.
$695.00.
Network version $995.00. *Networks supported:* Novell, ELS I, ELS II, SFT; LANTASTIC Version 3.0.
Enables the Computerization of the Necessary Record Keeping Associated with the Acquisition, Depreciation & Disposition of an Organization's Fixed Assets.
Creative Solutions, Inc. (Michigan).

Derive, A Mathematical Assistant. *Version:* 3.0. Oct. 1994. *Items Included:* diskette & manual. *Customer Support:* Limited 90 day warranty, technical support by mail..
MS-DOS/PC-DOS, OS/2 (versions 2.1 or higher) (512k). IBM PC & compatibles. $125.00 suggested retail price, available through dealers. *Optimal configuration:* IBM PC compatibles with 512k RAM. Display adapter & appropriate monitor (MDA, CGA, EGA, MCGA, VGA or Hercules), For graphics printing: screen capture & print software compatible with MS/PC-DOS.
A Menu Driven Computer Algebra System for Personal Computers. Does Symbolic & Numerical Equation Solving, Exact & Approximate Arithmetic, Calculus, Trigonometry, Matrices & More. Supports 2D & 3D Expression Plotting. Supports Monochrome & Color Graphics Monitors. Contains a Full Range of Elementary Functions & a Number of Statistical & Financial Functions.
Soft Warehouse, Inc. (Hawaii).

Dermatology & Trichology, 5 disks. 1987. *Compatible Hardware:* Apple II, IIc, IIe; IBM PC & compatibles. *Operating System(s) Required:* Apple DOS, PC-DOS/MS-DOS. *Memory Required:* 48k.
Apple. disk $310.00 (ISBN 0-87354-274-6, Order no.: CSMT2A).
IBM. 3.5" or 5.25" disk $310.00 (Order no.: BMC7).
Program Contents: Skin & Scalp, Epidermis & Dermis, Massage Movements, Trichology/Hair Root, Nerves in the Skin, Sweat & Oil Glands, Structure of the Hair, Properties of the Hair.
Aquarius Instructional.

DES-PAC. *Version:* 3.0. Jan. 1985. *Compatible Hardware:* IBM PC, PC AT, PC XT, PS/2 & compatibles. *Operating System(s) Required:* PC-DOS/MS-DOS 2.X or 3.X. *Language(s):* MicroSoft C (source code included). *Memory Required:* 64k. *General Requirements:* Communications software & modem optional.
disk $249.00.
Allows Government-Approved Encryption of Data. Package Includes Data Compression & Telecommunications Formatting. Any File Can Be Compressed, Encrypted & Formatted for Transmission with Users' Own Comm Software. Users Can Store Sensitive Information on Any Information Service for a Later Pickup.
Hawkeye Grafix.

DeScribe Word Processor. *Version:* 3.0. *Customer Support:* 90 days free, optional extended support, optional corporate support.
Any OS/2 Network; Windows 3.0. Stand-alone/server $495.00; client, $350.00.
American dictionaries $149.95 ea.
Graphical Word Processor with Extensive Desktop Publishing Features.
DeScribe, Inc.

Descriptions Now! *Version:* 3.0. Apr. 1995. *Items Included:* User manual, online tutorial. *Customer Support:* Unlimited free phone support for registered users.
Windows 3.1 or higher. 386 or higher (4Mb). disk $79.00, Multi-user pricing avail. *Optimal configuration:* Windows 3.1 compatible graphics card & monitor, mouse, 8Mb space on hard disk, floppy disk drive. *Networks supported:* Most Local Area Networks.
MS-DOS 3.0 or higher. PC, XT, AT, PS/2 or compatible (640k). disk $79.00. *Optimal configuration:* Color or Monochrome monitor, 6Mb space on hard disk, mouse recommended.
A Knowledge-Based Interactive Software Program That Writes Customized Job Descriptions, Starting from a Library of over 2,800 Jobs. Based on User Input, KnowledgePoint's Intelli-Text Technology Writes Sections on Physical Demands, Qualifications, Supervisory Responsibilities & Work Environment. Creates Job Descriptions That Comply with the Americans with Disabilities Act (ADA).
KnowledgePoint.

Descriptions Write Now!: ADA-Ready Job Descriptions. *Items Included:* Full manual. No other products required. *Customer Support:* Free telephone support - no time limit, 30 day warranty.
MS-DOS 3.2 or higher. IBM & compatibles (512k). disk $149.95. *Optimal configuration:* IBM & compatibles, word processor which can read ASCII files.
Gives Managers & Business Owners the Benefit of Clear, Practical, & Complete Job Descriptions in Just Minutes. Covering More Than 1200 Job Titles, Program Gives You the Ability to Locate & Merge Text to Clearly Describe the Essential Duties for Any Job.
Dynacomp, Inc.

Desert War 1991. Oct. 1991. *Compatible Hardware:* Apple II, II+, IIe, IIc. (source code included). *Memory Required:* 48k.
disk $9.95 (ISBN 0-918547-19-9).
illustration files on disk avail.
Simulation of Conflict Between Ten Countries with Five on Each Side.
AV Systems, Inc.

Design. *General Requirements:* Systat. *Items Included:* Documentation. *Customer Support:* Free technical support.
Macintosh Plus or higher, IBM PC, 286 or higher & compatibles. 3.5" disk $110.00.
Provides Sample Size Estimation, Tables of Expected Mean Squares for Balanced Experiments & Randomization Plans.
Systat, Inc.

Design Advantage. *Version:* 3.5.14. Aug. 1994. *Compatible Hardware:* SUN Solaris 2.3, HP 9000/700, Silicon Graphics, IBM RS6000. *Items Included:* Manual. *Customer Support:* Hotline, maintenance, update, training, 90 day warranty.
$600.00 to $5000.00.
A Family of 2-D & 3-D Mechanical CAD Software for Drafting.
Cognition Corp.

Design Center - with Circuit File Entry: Direct Program Management. *Version:* 6.1. Jul. 1994. *Items Included:* Circuit Analysis Users Guide, Circuit Analysis Reference Manual, Installation Manual, Application Notes Manual. *Customer Support:* Customer Technical Support is free with purchase of software.
SUN OS 4.12, Solaris 2.1 or higher, Open Windows 3.0, HP-UX 9.01. HP9000/700 Network, SUN-4 SPARC Station or Solbourne (1Mb). $10,000.00-$11,900.00. *Nonstandard peripherals required:* λ.
Analog Only or Mixed Analog/Digital Circuit Simulation with PSpice, Including Analog Behavioral Modeling, Monte Carlo & Sensitivity Worst-Case Statistical Analysis, Fully Integrated Event-Driven Digital Simulation, Graphical Waveform Analysis Using Probe, Stimulus Generation, Device Characterization & Extensive Analog & Digital Model Libraries (over 9,000 Parts). Options Available Include: Device Equations - All Platforms & Filter Designer - IBM PC, DOS & Cadence Integration, Mentor Integration on Sun & HP Platforms.
MicroSim Corp.

Design Center - with Extended DOS Control Shell. *Version:* 6.1. Jul. 1994. *Items Included:* Circuit Analysis Users Guide, Circuit Analysis

THE DESIGN CENTER WITH PARAGON:

Reference Manual, Installation Manual, Application Notes Manual, Filter Synthesis Users Guide with purchase of Filter Designer option. *Customer Support:* Customer Technical Support is free with purchase of our software.
MS-DOS 5.0 or higher. IBM PC (640k, 2Mb extended memory for 16M). $1495.00-$5450.00. *Nonstandard peripherals required:* 80387 floating point coprocessor.
DOS Control Shell Front-End Environment Analog Only with PSpice Digital Only with PLogic, & Mixed Analog/Digital Circuit Simulation with PSpice A/D. Includes Analog Behavioral Modeling, Monte-Carlo & Sensitivity Worst Case Statistical Analyses, Fully Integrated Event-Driven Simulation, Graphical Waveform Analysis Using Probe, Stimulus Generation, Device Characterization, & Extensive Analog & Digital Model & Symbol Libraries (over 9,000 Parts). Options Available - Device Equations - Source Code for Semiconductor Devices, & Filter Designer - Active & Passive Filter Synthesis.
MicroSim Corp.

The Design Center with Paragon: Analog Performance Optimization. *Version:* 6.1. Jul. 1994. *Items Included:* Circuit Analysis Manual Set, Analog Performance Optimization User's Guide. *Customer Support:* Free technical support w/purchase of product.
MicroSoft Windows 3.1 or higher, MS-DOS 5.0 or higher. IBM-PC. disk $1900.00. *Nonstandard peripherals required:* 80387 floating-point coprocessor. *Addl. software required:* PSpice with Schematics, or PSpice AID with Schematics. *Networks supported:* Novell, IPX, or Net Bios protocol.
Sun OS 4.1.2 or higher or Solaris 2.3 or higher. Sun-4 SPARC Station, or Solbourne computer. disk $3900.00. *Addl. software required:* PSpice with Schematics or PSpice AID with Schematics. *Networks supported:* Sun Network.
Paragon - Analog Performance Optimization Implementing Both Unconstrained & Constrained Minimization & Least-Squares Algorithms. User Has Complete Control over Design Goals & Constraints. Design Parameter Values Are Adjusted until the Solution Is Found That Best Meets the Specified Goals Subject to the Constraints. Optimization of Designs with Nonlinear Goals and/or Constraints Is Supported.
MicroSim Corp.

Design Center with Schematic Capture: Schematic Capture Front-End. *Version:* 6.1. Jul. 1994. *Items Included:* Schematic Capture User's Guide, Circuit Analysis Users Guide, Circuit Analysis Reference Manual, Installation Manual, Application Notes Manual, Filter Synthesis User's Guide - with Filter Designer Option. *Customer Support:* Free Customer Technical Support with purchase.
Microsoft Windows 3.1 or higher. IBM PC 80386/80486 or compatible (640k). $4900.00-$8200.00; Stand-alone Schematics $950.00. *Nonstandard peripherals required:* 80387 floating point coprocessor.
Open Window 3.0, Sun OS 4.1.2 or higher, Solaris 2.3 or higher. Sun-4, SPARC Station, or Solbourne. $14,000.00-$15,900.00; Stand-alone Schematics $4000.00.
Contributes Significantly to Simplifying the Design Engineer's Job. Provides a Unified System for Drawing Circuits for Single or Multiple Page Drawings, Flat & Hierarchical Designs, Performing PSpice Simulations, & Graphically Analyzing Waveform Results, All Without Having to Leave the Circuit Drawing Environment. Features Include: Extensive Analog/Digital Symbol & Package Libraries, & Interface to External Layout Packages Such As PADs, PCAD, TangoPro, Protel, & CADSTAR. The Signal Integrity Analysis Option, Polaris Can Also Be Purchased with This Package. Other Options Include: Filter Designer, the Active & Passive Filter Synthesis Design Aid Supporting Both LC Active, Switched Capacitor, & LC Ladder Filters. Device Equations, Source Code for Semiconductor Devices, PLSyn - Programmable Logic Synthesis Tool & Paragon - the Analog Performance Optimization Tool.
MicroSim Corp.

Design/CPN: CPN Analysis Methods. *Version:* 2.0. *Items Included:* Binder manuals. *Customer Support:* Tutorials, customized support & consulting services.
Macintosh II or Quadra (8Mb); SUN Microsystems - SUN 3 & 4; HP 9000 Model 400. disk $24,000.00.
Highly Sophisticated, Graphically-Based Simulation Tool That Incorporates Colored Petri-Net Technology for Performance Evaluation & Validation Testing of Extremely Large, Complex Models Which Involve Concurrency. Design/CPN Produces a Wide Variety of Reports & Tests Which Assist in Analyzing & Optimizing a Redesigned Business Process.
Meta Software.

Design Dimensions. *Version:* 2.0.
Macintosh Plus or higher. contact publisher for price.
Three Dimensional Design, Analysis, Presentation & Surface Modeling. Provides a Flexible Set of Tools for Conceptual Design, Analysis, Modification & Presentation.
Visual Information, Inc.

Design-Ease Design of Experiments. *Items Included:* Full manual. No other products required. *Customer Support:* Free telephone support - no time limit, 30 day warranty.
MS-DOS 3.2 or higher. IBM & compatibles (512k). disk $379.95.
Enables User to Quickly & Easily Design & Analyze Factorial Experiments. It Provides a Full Range of Powerful Two-Level Factorial, Fractional Factorial (up to 15 Variables), & Plackett-Burman (up to 31 Variables) Designs. These Designs Will Quickly Identify Critical Variables & Directions for Improvement. They Are Particularly Well-Suited for the Early Stages of Product or Process Optimization.
Dynacomp, Inc.

Design-Ease: Design of Experiments. 1995. *Items Included:* Full manual. *Customer Support:* Free telephone support - 90 days, 30-day warranty.
MS-DOS 3.2 or higher. 286 (584k). disk $379.95. *Nonstandard peripherals required:* CGA/EGA/VGA.
Enables You to Quickly & Easily Design & Analyze Factorial Experiments. It Provides a Full Range of Powerful Two-Level Factorial, Fractional Factorial (up to 15 Variables), & Plackett-Burman (up to 31 Variables) Designs. These Designs will Quickly Identify Critical Variables & Directions for Improvement. They Are Particularly Well-Suited for the Early Stages of Product or Process Optimization.
Dynacomp, Inc.

Design Estimator. *Version:* Windows 6.0, DOS 4.2, Macintosh 6.0.
Windows 3.1 or higher. disk $69.95 (Order no.: 744734 60160 6). *Optimal configuration:* Windows 3.1 or higher, 4Mb RAM, 9-13Mb hard drive space.
DOS 3.0 or higher. disk $59.95 (Order no.: 744734 60130 9). *Optimal configuration:* DOS, 640k, DOS 3.0 or higher, mouse & hard drive recommended.
System 7. Macintosh (4Mb). 3.5" disk $99.95 (Order no.: 744734 60150 7). *Optimal configuration:* Macintosh, System 7, 4Mb RAM, 9Mb hard drive space.
This Is an Estimating, Bidding & Quoting System That Has Produced Accurate & Quick Results in over 240 Industries. Estimator Was Specifically Designed to Reduce the Amount of Time & Effort Spent Calculating Labor & Material Costs. Now You Can Draw Your Floorplans & Any Other Home Designs with Any of Abracadata's Design Your Own Home Programs, Then Estimate the Cost of Your Projects Before You Build Them. Your Drawings Are Estimated in Seconds Without Re-Typing & Your Budget Can Be Tracked by Such Programs As Quicken.
Abracadata, Ltd.

Design Expert Response Surface Methods & Design of Experiments for Mixtures. *Items Included:* Full manual. No other products required. *Customer Support:* Free telephone support - no time limit. 30 day warranty.
MS-DOS 3.2 or higher. IBM & compatibles (512k). disk $749.95. *Optimal configuration:* IBM, MS-DOS 3.1 or higher, 640k RAM (EMS OK), hard disk, & CGA/EGA/VGA or Hercules (or compatible) graphics capability. Supports dot matrix, laser & postscript printers. Mouse & math coprocessors are supported, but not required.
Sets up & Analyzes Response Surface & Mixture Designs. For Response Surface Designs You Can Choose Central Composite, Box-Behnken, or D-Optimal Designs. If You Do Formulation Works, Choose a Mixture Design: Simplex, Extreme Vertices, or D-Optimal.
Dynacomp, Inc.

Design/IDEF. *Version:* 2.5. *Compatible Hardware:* Apple Macintosh Plus, Mac II or Quadra; IBM AT & compatibles (Windows 3.0); SUN Microsystems; HP 9000 Model 400. *General Requirements:* ImageWriter or LaserWriter. *Customer Support:* Maintenance program, $600.00/year.
3.5" disk $3995.00.
IDEF Methodologies Modeling Tools Used in CIM Modeling & Planning for Engineering, & Business Process Redesign.
Meta Software.

Design/OA. *Version:* 3.0. Jun. 1986. *Compatible Hardware:* Apple Macintosh; IBM 386 PC PS/2 & compatibles; SUN Microsystems; HP 9000 Model 400. *Operating System(s) Required:* Macintosh, DOS/Windows 3.0; UNIX X Window System. *Language(s):* C (source code included). *Memory Required:* 2000k-3000k. *Items Included:* Binder manuals. *Customer Support:* Consulting Services.
disk $9000.00. *Nonstandard peripherals required:* Hard disk.
C Language Construction Kit for the Rapid Prototyping & Implementation of Diagram-Based Applications.
Meta Software.

Design to Print. *Compatible Hardware:* IBM PC & compatibles. *Memory Required:* 512k. *Customer Support:* (800) 572-2272.
disk $49.95.
Low-End Desktop Publishing Package. Enables Users to Place Clip Art & Text Anywhere on the Page or Design Their Own Clip Art.
Compton's NewMedia, Inc.

Design Your Own Home, Architecture. *Compatible Hardware:* Apple II series, IIgs, Macintosh; IBM, all PC's, PS/2, Windows (3.1 or higher). *Operating System(s) Required:* DOS 3.0 or higher. *Memory Required:* Apple 64k, IIgs 1Mb, Macintosh 2Mb, Windows 4Mb, IBM 640k. *General Requirements:* Graphics card, hard drive, mouse recommended. *Customer*

Support: No charge telephone tech support.
Apple II series. 3.5" & 5.25" disks $49.95 (ISBN 0-939377-12-8, Order no.: 1011-011).
IBM. dual disks $59.95.
Macintosh. 3.5" disk $99.95.
Apple IIgs. 3.5" disk $59.95 (ISBN 0-939377-22-5, Order no.: 1011-412).
Windows. 3.5" disk $59.95.
Draw Floorplans, Side-View Building Plans & Structural Details. Features Pull-Down Menus, Icons, Grid Snap Lines, Layering, Stud-Beam Repeater, Regular Polygons, Circles, Ellipses, Arcs, Horizontal & Vertical Text. Pre-Drawn Shapes That Can Be Rotated & Arranged at Will. Includes Standard Architectural Scales & Automatically Displays Distances, Areas, Diagonals & Angles in Decimal Feet, Feet & Inches or Metric. User Can Also Create Custom Objects.
Abracadata, Ltd.

Design Your Own Home: Architecture. *Version:* Windows 2.02, DOS 3.7, Macintosh 2.0.
Windows 3.1 or higher. disk $59.95 (Order no.: 744734 10160 1). *Optimal configuration:* Windows 3.1 or higher, 4Mb RAM, 5Mb hard drive space.
DOS 3.0 or higher. disk $59.95 (Order no.: 744734 10130 4). *Optimal configuration:* DOS, 640k, DOS 3.0 or higher, mouse & hard drive recommended.
Macintosh (1Mb). 3.5" disk $99.95 (Order no.: 744734 10150 2). *Optimal configuration:* Macintosh, 1Mb, hard drive recommended.
Apple II (64k). disk $49.95.
Apple IIGS (1Mb). disk $59.95.
With Architecture You Can Easily Draw Floor Plans, Side-View Building Plans & Structural Details. The Program Has a Unique Stud Repeater Tool Which Speeds Drawing & Aids in Lumber Estimates. An Overlay Feature Allows up to Nine Levels of Layering of Details Such As Electrical or Plumbing Schematics & Multiple Floors. Access to Dozens of Architectural Symbols Is Faster & Easier Than with Other Comparable Products.
Abracadata, Ltd.

Design Your Own Home: Architecture. 1992.
Items Included: Detailed manuals are included with all DYNACOMP products. *Customer Support:* Free telephone support to original customer - no time limit; 30 day limited warranty.
MS-DOS 3.2 or higher. IBM PC & compatibles (512k). $99.95 (Add $5.00 for 3 1/2" format; 5 1/4" format standard). *Optimal configuration:* IBM, 640k RAM, MS-DOS 2.1 or higher, CGA/EGA/Hercules or compatible graphics. Supports mouse & graphics printer.
Apple II series (64k); Apple IIgs (1Mb). $99.95 (Add $5.00 for 3 1/2" format; 5 1/4" format standard). *Optimal configuration:* Apple II series, 64k RAM; Apple IIgs, 1Mb RAM, supports paddles & joystick, mouse & graphics printer.
Macintosh (1Mb). $99.95 (Add $5.00 for 3 1/2" format; 5 1/4" format standard). *Optimal configuration:* Macintosh, 1Mb RAM, supports mouse & graphics printer.
Enables You to Draw Floor Plans, Side-View Elevation Plans, & Structural Details in a Fraction of the Time It Would Take to Draft Them by Hand. Plans Can Easily Be Rearranged, Adding Keynotes & Labels. Features Include: Dozens of Sample Plans Which Can Be Modified. Calculates Distances, Diagonals, Areas, Angles. Employs All Appropriate Architectural Scales, Plus You Can Specify Your Own. Icons for Box, Line, Circle, Ellipse, Arc, Regular Polygons, & Sketching. Grids & Snap Lines. Overlays for Adding Plans (E.G., Plumbing, Electrical). Plans Can Extend over 4 (2x2) Screens. Pull-Down Menus, Full Editing, & More.
Dynacomp, Inc.

Design Your Own Home, Interiors. *Compatible Hardware:* Windows 3.1 or higher, Apple II series, IIgs, Macintosh; IBM, all PC's, PS/2. *Memory Required:* Windows, Macintosh 2Mb, Apple II series, IIgs 1Mb, IBM 640k. *General Requirements:* Graphics card, hard drive, mouse recommended. *Customer Support:* No charge telephone tech support.
Apple II series. 49.95 dual disks (ISBN 0-939377-14-4, Order no.: 1021-011).
Apple IIgs. 3.5" disk $59.95.
IBM. disk dual disks $59.95.
Windows. 3.5" disk $59.95.
Create Room Plans, Arrange Furnishings & Color Schemes. Enables User to Keep Plans & Showcase of Furnishings True-to-Scale. Automatically Draws Side Views from Top View.
Abracadata, Ltd.

Design Your Own Home: Interiors. *Version:* Windows 2.1, DOS 1.9, Macintosh 2.0.
Windows 3.1 or higher. disk $59.95 (Order no.: 744734 10260 8). *Optimal configuration:* Windows 3.1 or higher, 2Mb RAM, 9Mb hard drive space.
DOS 3.0 or higher. disk $59.95 (Order no.: 744734 10230 1). *Optimal configuration:* DOS, 640k, DOS 3.0 or higher, mouse & hard drive recommended.
Macintosh (1Mb). 3.5" disk $99.95 (Order no.: 744734 10250 9). *Optimal configuration:* Macintosh, 1Mb, hard drive recommended.
Apple II (64k). disk $49.95.
Apple IIGS (1Mb). disk $59.95.
Interiors Makes It Easy to Plan the Decor of Your Home or Office. Use the Drawing Tools & Supplied Patterns to Bring Your Interiors to Life! Choose from Hundreds of Pre-Drawn Furniture Objects & Appliances to Create Rooms from the Top View, & the Program Can Automatically Show You What Your Rooms Will Look Like from All Four Sides. Side Views Are Rendered in 3-D Perspective with 2-D Speed.
Abracadata, Ltd.

Design Your Own Home: Interiors. 1992. *Items Included:* Detailed manuals are included with all DYNACOMP products. *Customer Support:* Free telephone support to original customer - no time limit; 30 day limited warranty.
MS-DOS 3.2 or higher. IBM PC & compatibles (512k). $99.95 (Add $5.00 for 3 1/2" format; 5 1/4" format standard). *Optimal configuration:* IBM, 640k RAM, MS-DOS 2.1 or higher, CGA/EGA/Hercules or compatible graphics. Supports mouse & graphics printer.
Apple II series (64k); Apple IIgs (1Mb). $99.95 (Add $5.00 for 3 1/2" format; 5 1/4" format standard). *Optimal configuration:* Apple II series, 64k RAM; Apple IIgs, 1Mb RAM & supports paddles & joystick, mouse & graphics printer.
Macintosh (1Mb). $99.95 (Add $5.00 for 3 1/2" format; 5 1/4" format standard). *Optimal configuration:* Macintosh, 1Mb RAM. Supports mouse & graphics printer.
You Can Use Interiors with Your Computer to Easily Draw Floor Plans in Seconds, Rearrange Furnishings, & Explore Color Schemes. Features Include: Hundreds of Pre-Drawn, to Scale Furniture Pieces. Keeps Plans & Furniture True to Scale Automatically. Arranges Furnishings in 8 Different Rotations. Automatically Transforms Top Views into Side Views, with Depth. Pull-Down Menus, On-Screen Measurements, Distance Finder. Line, Box, Circle Drawing Tools. Color-Fill, Horizontal & Vertical Text. Dozens of Sample Plans for You to View & Modify.
Dynacomp, Inc.

Design Your Own Home: Landscape. *Version:* Windows 2.0, DOS 1.9, Macintosh 2.0.
Windows 3.1 or higher. disk $59.95 (Order no.: 744734 10360 5). *Optimal configuration:* Windows 3.1 or higher, 4Mb RAM, 6Mb hard drive space.
DOS 3.0 or higher. disk $59.95 (Order no.: 744734 10330 8). *Optimal configuration:* DOS, 640k, DOS 3.0 or higher, mouse & hard drive recommended.
Macintosh (1Mb). 3.5" disk $99.95 (Order no.: 744734 10350 6). *Optimal configuration:* Macintosh, 1Mb, hard drive recommended.
Apple II (64k). disk $49.95.
Apple IIGS (1Mb). disk $59.95.
Landscape Gives Users Libraries of Pre-Drawn Trees & Shrubs, & a Variety of Drawing Tools & Patterns to Help Them Plan Their Perfect Landscape. Users Can Choose from the Hundreds of Plants Provided, or They Can Draw Their Own Trees, Shrubs, Flowers, or Landscaping Objects. This Program Allows Users to Automatically See Their Designs from Four Different Side-View Perspectives, & a Unique Aging Feature Lets Them View Their Landscape after Years of Growth. Also Prints Plans & Plant Shopping Lists.
Abracadata, Ltd.

Design Your Own Home: Landscape. 1992.
Items Included: Detailed manuals are included with all DYNACOMP products. *Customer Support:* Free telephone support to original customer - no time limit; 30 day limited warranty.
MS-DOS 3.2 or higher. IBM PC & compatibles (512k). $99.95 (Add $5.00 for 3 1/2" format; 5 1/4" format standard). *Optimal configuration:* IBM, 640k RAM, MS-DOS 2.1 or higher, CGA/EGA/Hercules or compatible graphics. Supports mouse & graphics printer.
Apple II series (64k); Apple IIgs (1Mb). $99.95 (Add $5.00 for 3 1/2" format; 5 1/4" format standard). *Optimal configuration:* Apple II series, 64k RAM; Apple IIgs, 1Mb RAM. Supports paddles, joystick, mouse & graphics printer.
Macintosh (1Mb). $99.95 (Add $5.00 for 3 1/2" format; 5 1/4" format standard). *Optimal configuration:* Macintosh, 1Mb RAM, supports mouse & graphics printer.
Addresses the Difficult Problem of Visualizing & Recording the Appearance of Landscaping Designs. Features Include: Dozens of Sample Plans Which Can Be Modified. Trees & Shrubs Can Be Scaled to See the Effects of Aging on the Landscaping Plan. Identify & Label Each Plant. Automatic Inventory List of Trees & Sizes. Dozens of Pre-Drawn Trees & Shrubs Included. Line, Box, Circle, & Arc Drawing Tools. Paint & Color-Fill. Horizontal & Vertical Text for Labeling. Create Your Own Trees & Shrubs!. Special South View Which Shows Entire Plan.
Dynacomp, Inc.

Design Your Own Home, Landscape: Landscape. *Compatible Hardware:* Windows 3.1 or higher, Apple II series, IIgs, Macintosh; IBM PC & compatibles. *Memory Required:* Windows 4Mb, Macintosh 2 Mb, Apple II series 64k, IIgs 1Mb, IBM 640k. *General Requirements:* Graphics card, mouse recommended. *Customer Support:* No charge telephone support.
Apple II series. $49.95 dual disks (ISBN 0-939377-13-6, Order no.: 1031-011).
Apple IIgs. 3.5" disk $59.95.
Macintosh. 3.5" disk $99.95.
IBM. dual disks $59.95.
Windows. 3.5" disk $59.95.
Create Complete Landscape Plans, Age Plants to Determine Correct Placement, & Prepare Shopping List for Nursery. Generates Automatic Side Views from Top View Drawing.
Abracadata, Ltd.

Design Your Own Railroad. 1990. *Items Included:* Manual. *Customer Support:* No charge telephone tech support.

DESIGN YOUR OWN RAILROAD

Diversidos. Apple II. $49.95 (ISBN 0-939377-39-X). *Optimal configuration:* Mouse recommended, printer optional.
MS-DOS. IBM PC & all compatibles (640k). dual disks $59.95 (ISBN 0-939377-42-X). *Optimal configuration:* Printer optional - color monitor recommended, CGA, EGA, VGA or Hercules video cards supported.
Macintosh (1Mb). 3.5" disk $79.95. *Optimal configuration:* Hard drive.
Precision To-Scale Model Railroading Layout Design Program. Runs Realistic Operation Simulation & Allows for Custom Design of Train Cars & Scenery.
Abracadata, Ltd.

Design Your Own Railroad. *Version:* DOS 1.35, Macintosh 1.12.
DOS 3.0 or higher. disk $59.95 (Order no.: 744734 50530 0). *Optimal configuration:* DOS, 640k, DOS 3.0 or higher, mouse & hard drive recommended.
Macintosh (1Mb). 3.5" disk $79.95 (Order no.: 744734 50550 8). *Optimal configuration:* Macintosh, 1Mb, hard drive recommended.
Apple II (64k). disk $49.95. *Optimal configuration:* Apple II, 64k, mouse, paddles, or joystick.
Allows Users to Design Precision Track Layouts to Scale, & Then Build & Operate Trains on That Railroad System! This Complete Railroad Design Program Allows You to Operate Switches, Specify Cargo & Destinations, Couple & Uncouple Cars, Control Train Direction & Speed, Crashes, Revenue Tracking & Switching Puzzles. Design Tools Include: Layout CAD Tools, Layout & Scenery Design Tools, Track-Laying Tools, Grids & Rulers, Car, Loco & Station Design Tools. Zoom in on Waybills of the Rolling Stock for a Large, Detailed, Full-Color View Complete with Associated Data, Running Sounds & Horn, & Dozens of Railroad Pictures in a Complete Manual.
Abracadata, Ltd.

Design Your Own Train. *Compatible Hardware:* Apple II series. *Memory Required:* 64k. *Items Included:* Manual. *Customer Support:* No charge telephone tech support.
3.5" disk $49.95, Apple (ISBN 0-939377-25-X, Order no.: 5160-012).
Allows Users to Design & Operate Their Own Train, Subway, Trolley, or Bus Layout. Offers: up to 26 Operational Switches; 4 Independently Controllable Trains; 99 Layout Speeds; Hundreds of Straight & Curved Track, with Crossings. Provides Top View of Systems Created. Build Custom Locomotives On-Screen. Features Pull-Down Menus & Icons. Operates with Keyboard, Mouse, Paddles, Pad, or Joystick.
Abracadata, Ltd.

Design Your Own Train: Train-Transit System Construction Set. 1992. *Items Included:* Detailed manuals are included with all DYNACOMP products. *Customer Support:* Free telephone support to original customer - no time limit; 30 day limited warranty.
MS-DOS 3.2 or higher. IBM PC & compatibles (512k). $54.95 (Add $5.00 for 3 1/2" format; 5 1/4" format standard). *Optimal configuration:* IBM, 512k, CGA or EGA or equivalent & supports Epson/IBM Prowriter or compatible printer. Supports mouse.
Apple II series (64k). $54.95 (Add $5.00 for 3 1/2" format; 5 1/4" format standard). *Optimal configuration:* Apple II series, 64k RAM. Supports mouse & paddles/Joystick.
Macintosh (512k). $54.95 (Add $5.00 for 3 1/2" format; 5 1/4" format standard). *Optimal configuration:* Macintosh, 512k RAM, supports mouse.
Lets You Enjoy Model Railroading Without the Expense & Space Requirements Usually Associated with That Hobby. You Create Your Trains, Truck Systems, & Scenery Using Icons, Pull-Down Menus, & Libraries of Pre-Drawn Shapes. You Can Even Design Your Own Locomotives. Operation Can Be Pre-Programmed, or You Can Run Your System Manually, Throwing Every Switch, Slowing for the Curves, etc. Features Include: 26 Operating Switches; 4 Independently Controllable Trains; 90 Layout Speeds; Operating Freight Stations; Library of 100 Plus Scene Shapes; Painting, Color-Fill, Text; & More.
Dynacomp, Inc.

DesignCAD (DOS): DesignCAD 2D for DOS. *Version:* 6.0. Robert Webster & Chao-Chyuan Shih. Nov. 1992. *Items Included:* 3 perfect-bound manuals, digitizer template, quick reference card. *Customer Support:* Unlimited free technical support via toll number; seminars (for fee).
DOS. IBM & compatibles (2Mb). disk $349.95 (Order no.: 714-2600-3 (3.5"); 714-2600-5 (5.25")). *Addl. software required:* DOS 5 or higher. *Optimal configuration:* Faster the computer, the faster it runs.
Computer-Aided Design (CAD) Drafting & Design Program with 500 Pre-Drawn Symbols. Extensive Editing Control; Automatic, Associative Dimensioning; Zooms; Macros; User-Definable, Graphical Command Icons; Digitizer Menu; Programming Language; Unlimited Views; Extensive Peripheral Support & File Exchange.
American Small Business Computers, Inc.

DesignCAD: The Expert Suite. *Version:* 2.0. Robert Webster et al. Apr. 1993. *Items Included:* 7 perfect-bound manuals, 2 digitizer templates, 2 quick reference cards, 1 spiral bound manual. *Customer Support:* Unlimited free technical support via toll number; seminars (for fee); videos; BBS support.
MS-DOS & MS-Windows. IBM & compatibles (2-4Mb). disk $995.00 (Order no.: 714-5000-3 (3.5"); 714-5000-5 (5.25")). *Optimal configuration:* Faster the computer, the faster it runs.
Four Graphics Programs Combined into One High End CAD Package. DESIGNCAD 2D: Two Dimensional CAD System. DESIGNCAD 3D: True 3D CAD Modeling Package. SCANPRO: Raster-to-Vector Conversion Software. DESIGNSYM: Professional Symbols Library with over 6,700 CAD Symbols.
American Small Business Computers, Inc.

DesignCAD Windows: DesignCAD 2D for Windows. *Version:* 7.0. Robert Webster et al. Sep. 1993. *Items Included:* 3 perfect-bound manuals, digitizer template, quick reference card. *Customer Support:* Unlimited free technical support via toll number; seminars (for fee).
MS-DOS. IBM & compatibles (4Mb). disk $349.95 (Order no.: 714-2W70-3 (3.5"); 714-2W70-5 (5.25")). *Addl. software required:* MS-Windows 3.1 or higher. *Optimal configuration:* Faster the computer, the faster it runs.
Computer-Aided Design (CAD) Drafting & Design Program with 500 Pre-Drawn Symbols. Uses Windows Fonts (Including True-Type & Adobe). Extensive Editing Control; Automatic, Associative Dimensioning; Zooms; Macros; User-Definable, Graphical Command Icons; Digitizer Menu; Programming Language; Unlimited Views; Extensive Peripheral Support & File Exchange; Genuine Windows Interface.
American Small Business Computers, Inc.

DesignCAD 2D/3D Macintosh. *Version:* 3.0. Steve Davis. Jul. 1991. *Items Included:* 500 symbols, manual. *Customer Support:* Free unlimited phone support.
System 7 or higher of MAC/OS. MAC Plus or higher (3Mb). 3.5" disk $299.95 (Order no.: 710-3000). *Optimal configuration:* MAC II or higher with 2Mb.
Two Dimensional/Three Dimensional CAD, 32-Bit Floating-Point Accuracy, Extensive Geometric Construction, Cubic Spline/Bi-Cubic Surface Geometry, Complete Dimension/Annotation. Shading, Real-Time Rotation, Parametric Surface Construction & Modification. Wireframe, Surface, & Solid Geometry Within Unified Database Representation. Transfers to/from DXF, IGES, HPGL, PICT - Plus DesignCAD MS-DOS Files.
American Small Business Computers, Inc.

DesignCAD 3D. *Version:* 4.0. *Items Included:* 3 manuals, quick reference card, digitizer template. *Customer Support:* Free, unlimited; videos; books; training for a fee.
IBM PC (2Mb) under MS-DOS with graphics card. $499.95 (Order no.: 714-3400-3 (3.5"); 714-3400-5 (5.25")).
First True Low-Cost 3D CAD in 1987, New Version 4.0 Adds Smooth Shading with Surface Texturing, Approaching Photorealism for under $500. A Strong Design & Modeling Foundation Uses 3D Solids with Boolean Operations, Key-Frame Animation, Dimensioning, Hidden Lines, Real-Time Positioning, & 4 Simultaneous Views - for Starters.
American Small Business Computers, Inc.

Designer. *Version:* 4.0. Jul. 1993.
MS-DOS 3.1 or higher. IBM 386 or higher (4Mb). disk $695.00 (Order no.: D52L40ENG). *Addl. software required:* Windows 3.1. *Optimal configuration:* 16Mb RAM, CD-ROM.
Easy, Precise, Powerful. Professionals' Choice for Graphics Illustrations, Offers Windows Users a Whole New Level of Accuracy in Technical Illustration & Graphic Design. Delivers Sophisticated Symbol Creation & Editing Features, Impressive Text Handling, Advanced Color Creation & Separation Capabilities & More.
Micrografx, Inc.

The Designer. *Version:* 1.8. Mar. 1993. *Items Included:* All manuals. *Customer Support:* Included.
PC-DOS/MS-DOS. IBM PC/AT/XT/386/486 or compatible (640k). disk $1495.00. *Nonstandard peripherals required:* Color graphics, hard disk. *Optimal configuration:* 486, high res graphics, 40Mb hard disk, 3-button mouse. *Networks supported:* Novell, most DOS-based.
CAE/CAD Integrated Software Package That Includes: Schematic Layout & Full Post Processing Capability.
Team Visionics Corp.

Designer Bath Plans. *Version:* 1.2. Michael E. Nelson. 1995. *Items Included:* Complete instructions & plan book of layouts (symbol files). *Customer Support:* 30 day warranty.
DOS Version AutoCAD Format. Any DOS computer w/AutoCAD. disk $49.95 (ISBN 1-886917-07-8). *Addl. software required:* AutoCAD.
Designer Bath Plans, Symbols Files with 100 Layouts to Choose. AutoCAD Format.
Nelson Michael E. & Assocs., Inc.

Designer Bath Plans. *Version:* 1.1. Michael E. Nelson. 1995. *Items Included:* Complete instructions & plan book of layouts (symbol files). *Customer Support:* 30 day warranty.
DOS Version AutoCAD Format. Any DOS computer w/AutoCAD. disk $49.95 (ISBN 1-886917-08-6). *Addl. software required:* AutoCAD.
Designer Bath Plans, Symbols Files with 75 Layouts to Choose. AutoCAD Format.
Nelson Michael E. & Assocs., Inc.

TITLE INDEX

Designer Bath Plans. *Version:* 1.1. Michael E. Nelson. 1995. *Items Included:* Complete instructions & plan book of layouts (symbol files). *Customer Support:* 30 day warranty.
DOS Version with CAD Program excepting DXF format. Any DOS computer w/CAD Program. disk $49.95 (ISBN 1-886917-11-6). *Addl. software required:* CAD Program excepting DXF format.
Designer Bath Plans, Symbols Files with 75 Layouts to Choose. DXF Format.
Nelson Michael E. & Assocs., Inc.

Designer Bath Plans. Michael E. Nelson. 1995. *Items Included:* Complete instructions & plan book of layouts (Symbols Files). *Customer Support:* 30 day warranty.
DOS Version with CAD Program Excepting DXF Format. Any DOS computer w/CAD Program. disk $49.95 (ISBN 1-886917-04-3). *Addl. software required:* CAD Program excepting DXF Format.
Symbols Files with 100 Layouts to Choose. DXF Format.
Nelson Michael E. & Assocs., Inc.

Designer Kitchen & Breakfast Plans. *Version:* 1.1. Michael E. Nelson. 1995. *Items Included:* Complete instructions & plan book of layouts (symbol files). *Customer Support:* 30 day warranty.
DOS Version AutoCAD Format. Any DOS computer w/AutoCAD. disk $49.95 (ISBN 1-886917-05-1). *Addl. software required:* AutoCAD.
Kitchen & Breakfast Room Plans, Symbols Files with 50 Layouts to Choose. AutoCAD Format.
Nelson Michael E. & Assocs., Inc.

Designer Kitchen & Breakfast Plans. *Version:* 1.1. Michael E. Nelson. 1995. *Items Included:* Complete instructions & plan book of layouts (symbol files). *Customer Support:* 30 day warranty.
DOS Version with CAD Program excepting DXF Format. Any DOS computer w/CAD Program. disk $49.95 (ISBN 1-886917-09-4). *Addl. software required:* CAD Program excepting DXF Format.
Kitchen & Breakfast Room Plans, Symbols Files with 50 Layouts to Choose. DXF Format.
Nelson Michael E. & Assocs., Inc.

Designer Kitchen & Breakfast Room Plans. *Version:* 1.2. Michael E. Nelson. 1995. *Items Included:* Complete instructions & plan book of layouts (symbol files). *Customer Support:* 30 day warranty.
DOS Version AutoCAD Format. Any DOS computer w/AutoCAD. disk $49.95 (ISBN 1-886917-06-X). *Addl. software required:* AutoCAD.
Kitchen & Breakfast Room Plans, Symbols Files with 66 Layouts to Choose. AutoCAD Format.
Nelson Michael E. & Assocs., Inc.

Designer Pop-up-Menu Software. *Version:* 4.20. 1983. *Compatible Hardware:* IBM PC & compatibles, PCjr, PC XT, PC AT. *Operating System(s) Required:* PC-DOS 2.0, 2.1, 3.0 or 3.1. *General Requirements:* Lotus 1-2-3, Personal Editor, VisiCalc, WordStar, Volkswriter, or MultiPlan.
$50.00.
Provides Mouse Interfaces for Most of the Major Applications Packages on the Market Today i.e.: Lotus 1-2-3, Symphony, Framework, Wordstar, dBASE II, III, Wordperfect, Time Line.
MSC Technologies, Inc.

Designer Series. *Compatible Hardware:* IBM PC. disk $100.00.
Printer Utility That Allows a Dot Matrix Printer to "Plot" High Resolution Charts & Graphs.
Matrix Software.

Designer's Club. Jan. 1989. *Items Included:* Image Quest electronic indexing system; Ideas & Images - a monthly creative supplement with layout suggestions & manipulation ideas; Printed pictorial index; Disk storage case; Binders for Ideas & Images & indexes. *Customer Support:* Free technical support via telephone to customers.
Macintosh (1Mb). CD-ROM disk Monthly subscription is $49.50 per month. *Addl. software required:* Page layout or draw program that accepts EPS files. *Optimal configuration:* Macintosh Plus or larger & a PostScript compatible printer device or phototypesetter.
IBM or compatibles (640k). CD-ROM disk Monthly subscription is $49.50 per month. *Addl. software required:* Page layout or draw program that accepts EPS files. *Optimal configuration:* IBM or compatible with 640k memory & a PostScript compatible printer device or phototypesetter.
EPS Illustrations Available on a Monthly Basis; Includes Disks with at Least 50 EPS Images in a Variety of Styles & Subjects. Issues are Electronically Indexed for Easy Organization, Identification & Retrieval of Graphics with Image QUEST. Images are in the Adobe Illustrator Format. Product Is Available in 3.5" Disk, 5.25" Disk or CD-ROM.
Dynamic Graphics, Inc.

DesignMaster. *Customer Support:* 800-929-8117 (customer service).
MS-DOS. IBM/PS2. disk $399.99 (ISBN 0-87007-287-0).
A Computer Assisted Drawing, Drafting & Systems Design Program That Supports a Myriad of Matrix Printers, Plotters & Laser Printers. There Are Special Templates for Business Presentation Graphics, Engineering Applications, Drawing Organizational Charts, Systems Design Charts Using Bubble Technology As Well As Conventional Electronic, & Systems Logic Design Methods. Fonts May Be Generated, & Miscellaneous Uses Such as Producing Disk Labels of Directory Contents or Large Banners Are Provided. Lotus Reports Also May Be Used As Input & Modified.
SourceView Software International.

Designs. Duane Bristow. *Compatible Hardware:* TRS-80 Model I, Model III. *Operating System(s) Required:* TRSDOS. *Language(s):* BASIC. cassette $19.95.
User Can Draw Design in One Corner of Video Screen & the Computer Will Create Pattern by Repeating This Design.
Duane Bristow Computers, Inc.

DesignSYM: Professional Symbols Library. *Version:* 2.0. Jun. 1991. *Items Included:* Manual, Flip-Top Disk Case. *Customer Support:* Free unlimited telephone support.
DOS 3.0 or higher. IBM & compatible (2Mb). disk $179.00 (Order no.: 716-0000-3 (3.5"); 716-0000-5 (5.25")). *Nonstandard peripherals required:* EGA or higher. *Addl. software required:* DesignCAD 2D or DesignCAD 3D or DesignCAD 2D/3D Macintosh. *Optimal configuration:* Math coprocessor. *Networks supported:* Novell Netware.
Macintosh. 3.5" disk $149.95 (Order no.: 711-0000).
Extensive Computer-Aided Design System of Over 6700 Pre-Drawn Symbols in Over 40 Separate Libraries. Compatible with DesignCAD 2D, DesignCAD 3D & DesignCAD Macintosh. Retrieve Symbols into Drawing at Any Location, Angle, Size & Quantity. Edit & Resave Symbols Under Same Name or Another & Have Two Symbols.
American Small Business Computers, Inc.

DESKMATE

Desk. *Version:* 3.03. *Compatible Hardware:* Macintosh. *Customer Support:* 60 day money back guarantee.
3.5" disk $399.95.
Integrated Software Program with Seven DAs That Can Handle Everything Users Need to Do with Mac. Includes Word Processing, Time Management, Spreadsheet & Charting, a Database, a Paint Program, a Draw & Page-Layout Module, & Telecommunications.
Zedcor, Inc.

The Desk Organizer. *Compatible Hardware:* IBM PC with 2 disk drives. *Memory Required:* 128k. contact publisher for price.
Files Information, Organizes & Retrieves It. Does Numerical Calculations, Runs Formulas, Constructs Mini-Models. Writes & Prints Memos, Letters, Meeting Reports. Manages Your Time & Work Flow. Retrieves Phone Numbers from User's Files & Makes Telephone Calls.
Warner Bks., Inc.

Desk Toppers. Dec. 1984. *Compatible Hardware:* Apple Macintosh. *Memory Required:* 128k. 3.5" disk $19.95.
Set of 5 Desk Accessories That Includes a Calendar/Appointment Book, Little Black Book, a Doodle Pad Where User Can Add a Sketch & Save Drawings from MacWrite, a Music Maker Which Plays Back Notes & Tunes, a Scrapbook Library Where Users Can Create & Access New Scrapbooks.
Harvard Assocs., Inc.

Desket Design Edition. *Version:* 4.0. *Compatible Hardware:* IBM PC & compatibles. *Memory Required:* 640k. *Items Included:* 8 fonts, ruling, reverse video, vertical justification, multi-column, pagination & WYSIWYG preview Postscript 8 laser master drivers. *Customer Support:* 10% of a software product purchase price per year.
$2495.00.
$1495.00 typesetter-driver option.
Desktop-Publishing Package Including Such Page-Formatting Features as Automatic Pagination, Automatic Numbering of Pages, Automatic Columning, Hyphenation, Justification, Kerning & Leading. Supports ASCII, WordPerfect & WordStar Word-Processing Programs; Dr. Halo, Lotus & PC Paintbrush Graphics Programs; EGA, CGA, Hercules, Genius & WYSE WY 700 Graphics Cards; & Typesetters, Laser & Dot-Matrix Printers. Compatible with COMPUGRAPHIC 8000 & 9000 Series Typesetters, Tegra/Varityper Image Setters & Any Canon Sx/Lx Engine Laser Printers.
GO Graphics, Inc.

DeskLink: Release II. *Version:* 2.21d. *Compatible Hardware:* IBM PC/XT/AT or PS/2 & compatibles. *Customer Support:* (206) 483-8088. disk $169.95, incl. universal cable & 25 feet of RJ-11 wire.
High-Speed Serial-Transfer Program Which Lets User Share Disk Drives & Printers Between IBM PCs & Compatibles (Including Laptops & Networked Computers). Transfer Speeds of up to 115,000 bps Reported. Pop-Up Menu Lists Auxilliary Devices. When User Wants to Access Another Computer's Printer or Disk, Talk Box Can Be Utilized.
Traveling Software, Inc.

DeskMate. *Version:* 3.5. 1990. *Compatible Hardware:* Tandy; IBM PC & compatibles. *Memory Required:* 360k. *Items Included:* Manuals.
3.5" & 5.25" disk $99.95 (Order no.: 25-1250).
Includes Spreadsheet, Word Processing, Filer, Address, Calendar & Telecom.
Radio Shack.

DeskPack Plus. *Compatible Hardware:* Commodore 64, 128. *Operating System(s) Required:* GEOS or GEOS 128.
disk $29.95.
Includes Four Applications: a Graphics Grabber for Importing Art from PRINT SHOP, NEWSROOM, & PRINT MASTER Graphics; a Calendar; an Icon Editor, & a Black Jack Dealer. Available in 80 Columns for Commodore 128.
Berkeley Softworks.

DeskPaint & DeskDraw. *Version:* 3.03. *Compatible Hardware:* Apple Macintosh. *Operating System(s) Required:* System 6.05 or higher. *Memory Required:* 512k.
3.5" disk $199.95.
A Complete Graphics Package That Provides Users with Paint, TIFF & Draw Editing in Two Desk Accessories. Loads, Edits & Saves Bitmap Graphics, Including TIFF, MacPaint & PICT Formats. A Feature Included is Auto Trace, a Facility for Tracing Bitmap Images to PICT Objects. Other Features Include: Air Brush, Charcoal, Duplicate Distort, One & Two Point Perspective, Cropping, Transparent Paint, Inverse Paint, Halftoning Effects, Printing of Posters & Billboards, Edit Patterns, Scale Selections from One Percent to 3,999 Percent, Paste Unscaled (Pastes Images Back at Their Original Size), Browse Features for Looking Through Folders of Clip Art or Scrapbooks & Free Rotating Bitmaps in 2 Degree Increments. Creates, Loads Edits & Saves Images Consisting of Graphics & Text Objects, Bitmaps (up to 4,000 DPI) & Rotate PostScript Text & Is Similar to MacDraw.
Zedcor, Inc.

DeskSet PS Edition. *Operating System(s) Required:* PC-DOS/MS-DOS 2.0 or higher. *Memory Required:* 512k. *General Requirements:* 2 disk drives.
disk $495.00.
Similar in Functionality to DeskSet Design Edition but Supports PostScript Printers, Including the LinoType PostScript Typesetter.
GO Graphics, Inc.

Desktop Accountant. *Customer Support:* 800-929-8117 (customer service).
MS-DOS. IBM/PS2. disk $399.99 (ISBN 0-87007-860-7).
An Integrated, Compiled Full Charge Accounting System with General Ledger, Payroll, Accounts Receivable, Accounts Payable, Order Entry, Sales Analysis, & Inventory Modules. Powerful & Easy to Use. A Complete Audit Trail Is Provided for All Changes.
SourceView Software International.

Desktop Architect. *Compatible Hardware:* Apple Macintosh 512k or higher. *General Requirements:* SuperPaint/MiniCAD 4.0+ *Items Included:* 3-ring binder, manual, SuperPaint Version 8-800 K diskettes, MiniCAD Version 4-800 K diskettes. *Customer Support:* 8-5:30 M-F.
8" & 3.5" disks $299.00.
Detailing System That Allows User to Assemble New Drawings from Pre-Drawn Components. Components Are Organized in Individual Documents Called Kit Parts, Which Include Wall Sections, Cross Sections, Plain View Details, Structural Steel Detailing, Door Details, Window Details, Interior Elevations, Door Elevations, Window Elevations & Roof Truss Diagrams.
Desktop Architect.

Desktop Bibliography. *Compatible Hardware:* IBM. *Memory Required:* 128k.
disk $29.95.
Designed to Allow Users to Construct a Bibliographic Reference System.
Dynacomp, Inc.

The Desktop Fractal Design System. *Version:* 2.0. Michael F. Barnsley. Aug. 1992. *Items Included:* 32 page manual entitled The Desktop Fractal Design Handbook. *Customer Support:* 90 day warranty that the magnetic diskette on which the program is recorded is free from defects in material & faulty workmanship under normal use.
PC-DOS 2.0 (640k). IBM or compatible PC. $29.95 (ISBN 0-12-079066-1). *Nonstandard peripherals required:* EGA. *Optimal configuration:* Hyundai 80286 or Everex 80386 computer, CGA & VGA compatible.
This Interactive System Introduces Deterministic & Randomly Generated Fractals. Among Its Features Are a Library of Complex Images, Each of Which Can Be Manipulated by the User, & a Gereralized Mandelbrot Set Which Can Be Examined at Various Levels of Magnification. It Also Allows Users to Design Entirely New Fractals.
Academic Pr., Inc.

The Desktop Fractal Design System: Macintosh Version. *Version:* 2.0. Michael Barnsley. Aug. 1992. *Items Included:* 48-page manual entitled "The Desktop Fractual Design Handbook". *Customer Support:* 90 day warranty that the magnetic diskette on which the program is recorded is free from defects in material & faulty workmanship under normal use.
MAC DOS 6.0 or higher. Macintosh Plus, SE, II (1Mb). 3.5" disk $29.95 (ISBN 0-12-079065-3). *Optimal configuration:* Macintosh IIci, Mac 6.0 OS (or higher), 1Mb RAM (no peripherals needed but color monitor preferable).
This Interactive System Introduces Deterministic & Randomly Generated Fractals. Among Its Features Are a Library of Complex Images, Each of Which Can Be Manipulated by the User, & a Generalized Mandelbrot Set Which Can Be Examined at Various Levels of Magnification. It Also Allows Users to Design Entirely New Fractals.
Academic Pr., Inc.

Desktop Publishing (PFS): First Publisher. Richard Bonen & Darla Babcock. 1991. *Items Included:* Diskette with practice exercises.
MS-DOS 2.0 or greater. IBM PC or compatible (640k). disk $29.50.
Training for Using a Low-Cost Desktop Publishing Program; Includes Basic Word Processing, Page & Format Design, Fonts, Art Files, Importing Text, Using Various Types of Printers.
Career Publishing, Inc.

Desktop Publishing with WordPerfect. *Version:* 5.1. Sally Hargrave. 1991. *Items Included:* Quick Reference Guide, audio tapes, practice disk. *Customer Support:* 30 day-right of return; Editorial support for course content/exercises.
DOS. IBM & compatibles. disk $175.00 (ISBN 0-917792-39-4, Order no.: 432). *Addl. software required:* WordPerfect 5.1.
Self-paced training in using WordPerfect to desktop publish a variety of documents.
OneOnOne Computer Training.

Desktop Time and Billing. *Customer Support:* 800-929-8117 (customer service).
MS-DOS. IBM/PS2. disk $99.99 (ISBN 0-87007-856-9).
A General Time & Billing Package for the Small Professional Office. Allows 4500 Time/Expense Entries per Mb of Hard Disk. More Productivity When Run in Conjunction with Desktop Accountant.
SourceView Software International.

Desktop Video Productions Clip Art. *Compatible Hardware:* Apple Macintosh. *Memory Required:* 512k. *General Requirements:* 400k disk drive, MacPaint or compatible.
3.5" disk $39.95.
Clip Art Collection Including Faces, Hands, Beatles, Portraits of Prince, Romantic Images, & Landscapes Categories.
Desktop Video Productions.

DeSmet C 8086/8088 Development Package(DeSmet DC88). *Version:* 3.1m. Mark DeSmet. Apr. 1983. *Compatible Hardware:* IBM PC & compatibles. *Operating System(s) Required:* PC-DOS, MS-DOS. *Language(s):* C. *Memory Required:* 192k. *Items Included:* Editor, Linker, Assembler, Debugger, Librarian.
3 disks $99.00, incl. symbolic debugger (Order no.: DC88).
Full K&R C Compiler, Assembler, Linker, Librarian, Execution Profiler, Overlays, & Full Screen Editor. Includes Complete STDIO Library with More Than 120 Functions.
C Ware.

DESQview: A Guide to Programming the DESQview Multitasking Environment. Stephen R. Davis. Mar. 1989. *Operating System(s) Required:* MS-DOS.
book & disk $39.95 (ISBN 1-55851-028-1). book only $24.95 (ISBN 1-55851-006-0).
Topics Discussed Include the Object-Oriented DESQview API (Application Program Interface) & Multitasking Concepts Necessary to Program the DESQview Environment. These Concepts Are Applied by Creating Example Programs That Control & Interact with DESQview's API. The Book Demonstrates Such Concepts As Windowing, Intertask Communication, Memory Management, Software Objects, & Subtask Control by Using API.
M & T Bks.

DESQview Companions 1: Calculator, Datebook, Link, Notepad. *Version:* 1.1. Nov. 1986. *Compatible Hardware:* IBM PC & compatibles. *Operating System(s) Required:* PC-DOS/MS-DOS 2.0 or higher. *Memory Required:* 200k. *General Requirements:* Hard disk, printer, modem; DESQview or TopView compatible integrator program. *Customer Support:* Includes DESQview Datebook, D. Notepad, D. Link, D. Calculator.
disk $99.95 (ISBN 0-926433-02-4).
Set of Four Programs: DATEBOOK (Calendar), NOTEPAD (Word Processor), CALCULATOR, & LINK (Communications). They Are Designed Specifically for Use with DESQview to Take Full Advantage of DESQview's Multi-Tasking, Windowing, & Data Transfer Capabilities.
Quarterdeck Office Systems.

DESQview: The Multi-Window Software Integrator. *Version:* 2.6. Gary W. Pope. Aug. 1988. *Compatible Hardware:* IBM PC & compatibles. *Operating System(s) Required:* MS-DOS, PC-DOS 2.0 or higher. *Memory Required:* EMS 4 expanded memory recommended, 640k. *General Requirements:* 2 disk drives or hard disk. *Customer Support:* 90 days from date of first call to technical support.
disk $99.95 (ISBN 0-926433-00-8).
Allows Users to Load More than One Program & Instantly Switch from One Program to Another. Provides Consistent User Interface to Programs (Menus, In-System Help, Mouse Selecting); Multi-Program Support So That As Many As 9 Programs Can Run Simultaneously & Transfer Data Between Programs; & Customization (Keystroke Macros, Menu Building) for Tailoring to Individual & Vertical Market Applications.
Quarterdeck Office Systems.

Desserts Cookbook. *Compatible Hardware:* Commodore Amiga.
3.5" disk $14.95.
Recipes.
Meggido Enterprises.

TITLE INDEX

Destination Japan: Multimedia Business & Education Reference. *Version:* 1.5. May 1995. *Items Included:* 1 manual, 1 registration card, 1 software license. *Customer Support:* 90 days unlimited warranty. Customer support numbers: Phone: 916-757-2323, Phone: 916-757-2992. Windows 3.1 or higher. PC compatible (8Mb). disk $69.00 (ISBN 0-9646582-0-8). *Optimal configuration:* PC-compatible computer, Windows 3.1 or higher, 8Mb RAM, 15Mb of disk space.
Developed for Windows PCs, Destination Japan Contains Hundreds of Articles, Including Profiles of over 600 Companies & Dozens of Industries; Explanations of Japan's Financial, Political, & Educational Systems; Overviews of the Japanese Language, Geography, & History; & Much More.
Digital Destinations.

Destiny: Business Info & Planning. *Version:* 1.06. Jul. 1993. *Items Included:* Spiral bound manual, 2 diskette. *Customer Support:* 90 days unlimited warranty.
Windows. IBM PC 386 or higher (2Mb). disk $129.00. *Optimal configuration:* 4Mb RAM w/ any system above 386 (meaning computer running on Intel 80386 processor). *Networks supported:* Novell.
Creates Business Models That Make Real Sense of Business. A Dynamic Business Modeling, Risk Analysis, Forecasting, Budgeting & Business Plan Writing Software. Can Easily Tie to Other Accounting & Project Management Programs. Immediately Useful to Businessmen, Fortune 500 Management Entrepreneurs & Financial Officers. No Other Tools Necessary.
International Business Software, Inc.

Detention Center Management: Correction Administration System. *Version:* 3.0. Palladium Software Corp. Aug. 1992. *Compatible Hardware:* IBM, VAX. *Operating System(s) Required:* MS-DOS Windows, NT Server. *Language(s):* Level 5. *Memory Required:* 4000k. *General Requirements:* IBM, VAX. *Items Included:* Documentation & quick start manuals.
  write for info. (ISBN 1-55505-025-5, Order no.: CJ550/1).
  Windows 3.X. (ISBN 1-55505-026-3, Order no.: CJ550/2).
  Windows 95. (ISBN 1-55505-027-1, Order no.: CJ550/3).
  Windows NT. (ISBN 1-55505-028-X, Order no.: CJ550/4).
Developed to Monitor & Administer Offender Administration: Receiving, Processing, Release, Offender Classification, Housing Assignments, Offender Scheduling, Transfers, Appearances, Activities, & an Offender Profile: Inmate History, Contacts & Associates, & Property Management.
Ellington Duval, Inc.

Determining Damages: Economic Loss in Personal Injury & Wrongful Death Cases. *Version:* 2.0. Evan Schouten & Ronald Schouten. May 1989. *Compatible Hardware:* IBM PC, PC XT, PC AT. *Operating System(s) Required:* PC-DOS/MS-DOS 2.0 or higher. *Memory Required:* 512k.
disk $500.00.
Provides the Attorney with an Immediate Analysis of the Present & Future Values of an Injured Party's Losses. Provides Income Information for 503 Different Occupations, Each of Which Is Broken into Six Separate Educational Levels & Five Different Age Levels, As Well As by Race & Sex of the Injured Party. The Program Bases Its Calculations & Default Values on Current Statistics from the Bureau of the Census of the Department of Labor. In Addition to Its Application in Personal Injury Cases, It Will Calculate Losses for Use in Wrongful Death Cases of Both Minors & Adults.
Shepard's/McGraw-Hill, Inc.

DETPROB: Probability of Detection Calculation. Jun. 1991. *Items Included:* Manual.
IBM PC & compatibles. disk $100.00 (ISBN 0-89006-561-6).
Tabulates the Probability of Detection of Various Types of Radar Targets for a Wide Variety of Conditions.
Artech Hse., Inc.

Deuce of a Time. Paul Levinson. 1990.
DOS. Any type IBM (64k). $8.95 (ISBN 1-56178-001-4).
MAC. Any type of Macintosh (64k). $8.95 (ISBN 1-56178-018-9).
Science Fiction Novel.
Connected Editions, Inc.

Deutsch Aktuell One. Ariane-Cathy Culot et al. *Items Included:* Software program guide. *Customer Support:* Customer support is available through our toll-free number 800-328-1452, ask for Technical Support. Free on-site training is also available through the same number.
MS-DOS. IBM & compatibles (256k). disk $350.00 (ISBN 0-8219-1234-8, Order no.: 95800H). *Nonstandard peripherals required:* CGA or better graphics adaptor. *Optimal configuration:* Color monitor & printer. *Networks supported:* Not designed for networks, but can be installed to a network.
MS-DOS. IBM & compatibles (256k). disk $350.00 (ISBN 0-8219-0698-4, Order no.: 95800G). *Nonstandard peripherals required:* CGA or better graphics adaptor. *Optimal configuration:* Color monitor & printer. *Networks supported:* Not designed for networks, but can be installed to a network.
Apple PRODOS. Apple IIe or higher (128k). disk $350.00 (ISBN 0-8219-0684-4, Order no.: 95800F). *Nonstandard peripherals required:* 80-column card for 64k Apple II's. *Optimal configuration:* Color monitor & printer. *Networks supported:* Not designed for networks, but can be installed to a network.
Designed to Review, Drill, & Apply the Vocabulary, Structures, & Cultural Information Presented in the Textbook in an Easy-to-Use Interactive Environment.
EMC Publishing.

Deutsch Aktuell Two. Ariane-Cathy Culot et al. *Items Included:* Software program guide. *Customer Support:* Customer support is available through our toll-free number 800-328-1452, ask for Technical Support. Free on-site training is also available through the same number.
MS-DOS. IBM & compatibles (256k). disk $350.00 (ISBN 0-8219-1235-6, Order no.: 95813H). *Nonstandard peripherals required:* CGA or better graphics adaptor. *Optimal configuration:* Color monitor & printer. *Networks supported:* Not designed for networks, but can be installed to a network.
MS-DOS. IBM & compatibles (256k). disk $350.00 (ISBN 0-8219-0826-X, Order no.: 95813G). *Nonstandard peripherals required:* CGA or better graphics adaptor. *Optimal configuration:* Color monitor & printer. *Networks supported:* Not designed for networks, but can be installed to a network.
Apple PRODOS. Apple IIe or higher (128k). disk $360.00 (ISBN 0-8219-0815-4, Order no.: 95813F). *Nonstandard peripherals required:* 80-column card for 64k Apple II's. *Optimal configuration:* Color monitor & printer. *Networks supported:* Not designed for networks, but can be installed to a network.
Designed to Review, Drill, & Apply the Vocabulary, Structures, & Cultural Information Presented in the Textbook in an Easy-to-Use Interactive Environment.
EMC Publishing.

DEVELOPMENTAL PROFILE II

Develop Your Business Plan. Richard L. Leza & Jose Placencia. *Items Included:* Available with 3 ring workbook or software only. *Customer Support:* 15 day unlimited warranty, telephone technical support.
PC-DOS/MS-DOS 2.0 or higher. IBM PC & compatibles (512K). 3.5" or 5.25" disk $69.95; with wkbk. $99.95. *Addl. software required:* Hard disk & single floppy drive or one high density floppy drive or a dual floppy drive system.
Macintosh. 3.5" disk $69.95; with wkbk. $99.95. *Addl. software required:* Excel.
For the Business Owners & Managers Who Want to Develop a Professionally Designed Business Plan as Quickly as Possible. The WorkBook Contains Thorough Step-by-Step Guidelines for Completing a Business Plan, While the Software Saves Time in Calculating the Financial Statements, Typing & Text Formatting. It Helps User Through Seven Major Areas of a Business Plan Such As: Company Analysis; Industry Analysis; Market Analysis; Competition Analysis; Strategic Planning; Management/Team Description & Executive Summary Statements.
Oasis Pr.

Developer Disk 1. *Compatible Hardware:* Apple IIe, IIc, IIgs. *Operating System(s) Required:* ProDOS.
disk $19.95.
Includes NORT (The Nite Owl Run Time Package) Which Adds New ProDOS Commands to the ProDOS/Basic. System Environment. NORT Includes a Quick Index (QI) Command Which Displays All Locked Files & Subdirectories Listed in a Directory; Can Be Used to Organize 3-1/2" & Hard Disk Directories Too. PACKER Packs Standard HIRES Pictures into BRUNable Binary Files. SETDATE Is a Relocatable Binary Program Which Sets the ProDOS Date Register for Proper Dating of Disk Files. Flip Side Contains the INTRODUCTION to ProDOS & APPLESOFT & Several Demonstration Manuals.
Nite Owl Productions.

Developer Disk 2. May 1986. *Compatible Hardware:* Apple II+, IIe, IIc, IIgs. *Operating System(s) Required:* ProDOS. *Memory Required:* 64k.
disk $39.95 (Order no.: D102).
Nite Owl Productions.

Developer's Kit.
OS/2. disk $495.00.
Programming Tools That Let User Write OS/2 Client- & Server-Based Applications. Also Includes OS/2 Requester, Which Allows OS/2 Workstations to Access NetWare Services. Supplies Connectivity Between OS/2 Workstations & File Servers Running NetWare 2.1 or Higher. Supports Standard OS/2 API's (Application Programming Interfaces). Once Network Application Has Been Developed, Users Have Complete Access to NetWare 2.1 & Higher & NetWare 386 Print, File & Communications Services. Applications Can Run on an Application Server That's Configured with Just OS/2 & the NetWare Requester. Includes: NetWare API Documentation for OS/1.1 & 1.2, NetWare Requester for OS/2 1.2, Pre-Release Version of NetWare Requester for OS/2 1.2. Also Includes Header & Import Libraries for the NetWare OS/2 API's.
Novell, Inc.

Developmental Profile II. *Version:* 1.100. Gerald Alpern et al. *Customer Support:* Free unlimited phone support.
IBM PC & 100% compatibles. 3.5" or 5.25" disk $195.00 (Order no.: W-1009 (5.25"); W-1024 (3.5")). *Optimal configuration:* DOS 3.0 or higher; DOS cannot be running in high memory,

printer.
Assesses Child's Development from Birth to 9 Years of Age, Generating Scale Scores in the Following Five Areas: Physical Age, Self-Help Age, Social Age, Academic Age, & Communication Age.
Western Psychological Services.

DEX-88 Spooler. *Compatible Hardware:* IBM PC. *Operating System(s) Required:* DOS.
disk $89.95 (ISBN 0-936200-47-2).
Prints Data from Memory or Disk While Running Another Program. Requires DEX/88.
Blue Cat.

DFBLOAD. Lewis Rosenfelder. *Compatible Hardware:* TRS-80 Model I, Model III. *Language(s):* BASIC.
disk $29.95 (ISBN 0-936200-26-X).
Includes 25 BASIC Demonstration Programs & a Library of Disk I/O Subroutines.
Blue Cat.

DFE-DFU: Data File Editor-Data File Utility. *Version:* 1.0. *Items Included:* 2 perfect-bound manuals. *Customer Support:* Bulletin Board support; 30-day free technical support - subsequent support is available through a 900 number; Fax number available also.
PC-DOS/MS-DOS version 3.1 or greater. IBM PC or 100% compatible (384k). disk $350.00. *Networks supported:* Any net BIOS compatible network.
DFU allows you to Create Data Files, Update Existing Files, & Produce Reports Based on the Data in Those Files. Can Be Used By Programmers & Non-Programmers Who Need a Simple Way to Manage Data Files. Compatible with IBM DFU Specifications & with the IBM ENTER, UPDATE, INQUIRY, & LIST Procedures. Can Be Used with Any dBASE Compatible Database. Comes with an Easy-to-Use Configuration Program That Lets Individual Users Select a System/36 or IBM PC Keyboard Layout, Control Screen Colors, & Set a Variety of Other Run-Time Options. Also Network Compatible, Lattice DEE Provides Easy-to-Use Editing Functions to Manually Update or Review Records in Raw Data Format. DFE Works with EBCDIC, ASCII & dBASE Files to Allow You to Quickly Open a Data File & Make Changes or Fixes to Data Records.
Lattice, Inc.

Dfile. *Compatible Hardware:* Atari, CP/M, North Star. *Language(s):* Machine. *Memory Required:* 48k.
contact publisher for price.
Dynacomp, Inc.

DFT: Direct File Transfer. Timothy Purves. Apr. 1986. *Compatible Hardware:* Atari ST. *Operating System(s) Required:* TOS. *General Requirements:* Modem or null modem cable.
3.5" disk $49.95 (ISBN 0-923213-13-9, Order no.: AT-DFT).
Performs File Transfers Between Atari ST & IBM Computers. All ASCII Data Files Can Be Converted to Atari-Readable Format. Does Not Transfer Programs.
MichTron, Inc.

DFWEDGE. *Version:* 1.2. Jan. 1990. *Items Included:* Manual. *Customer Support:* Telephone, bulletin board support - 24 hours.
DOS 2.0 & higher. IBM PC/XT/AT/386 (128k). disk $95.00.
Terminate & Stay Resident Program Which Receives Data via Any User Defined RS-232 Port (Comm Port) & Puts Data into the Keyboard Buffer. Used to Wedge Barcode Scanners Data into Keyboard Buffer But Can Be Used by Scales & Other RS-232 Devices.
Dataflow Technologies, Inc.

The DGI Cryptogram. Charles D. Blish. May 1987. *Compatible Hardware:* Apple II+, IIe, IIc; IBM PC & compatibles. *Operating System(s) Required:* Apple DOS 3.3, MS-DOS 2.1 or higher. *Memory Required:* Apple 64k, IBM 128k. *General Requirements:* Printer.
disk $24.95 ea.
Apple. (ISBN 0-932779-11-5, Order no.: CRYP.AP).
IBM. (ISBN 0-932779-12-3, Order no.: CRYP.IBM).
Creates Cryptograms Using Over 2500 Codes & Allows Users to Decode Them, Providing the Encryption Code Is Known. (Cryptograms Are Codes Which Replace One Letter with Another Letter).
Decision Graphics, Inc. (Colorado).

DGI LOTTO MGR. *Version:* 1.14. Aug. 1991. *Items Included:* Instructions.
MS-DOS 2.10 or higher. IBM PC, XT, AT & compatibles (256k). disk $24.95.
Macintosh (512k). 3.5" disk $24.95.
Provides Statistical Analysis of All Pick 6 Lottos. Finds Hot & Overdue Numbers. Stores up to 500 Past Drawings. Includes Data for All US Pick 6 Lottos. Includes Smart Pick Number Selection.
Decision Graphics, Inc. (Colorado).

DGI Organization Chart Manager. *Version:* 1.06. Sep. 1988. *Operating System(s) Required:* PC-DOS/MS-DOS 2.1 or higher. *Memory Required:* 256k.
3.5" or 5.25" disk $59.95 (ISBN 0-932779-13-1, Order no.: ORG.MGR).
Create & Manage Free-Form Organization Charts. Features a Cross Between a Graphics Spreadsheets & Word Processor to Give a WYSIWYG (What You See Is What You Get) Program. Users Can See What the Chart Looks Like Before It Is Printed.
Decision Graphics, Inc. (Colorado).

DHMA Plotter. David L. Vernier. Dec. 1986. *Compatible Hardware:* Apple II+, IIe, IIgs. *Operating System(s) Required:* Apple DOS 3.3. *Memory Required:* 48k. *General Requirements:* Driven Harmonic Motion Analyzer avail. from PASCO Scientific.
disk $39.95 (ISBN 0-918731-18-6).
Collects, Analyzes & Graphs Data from The PASCO DRIVEN HARMONIC MOTION ANALYZER.
Vernier Software.

Di-Graph Scientific Plotting. *Items Included:* Bound manual. *Customer Support:* Free hotline - no time limit; 30 day limited warranty; updates are $5/disk plus S&H.
MS-DOS 2.0 or higher. IBM & compatibles (500k). $124.95-$174.95. *Nonstandard peripherals required:* Hard disk. *Addl. software required:* EGA, VGA, or Hercules.
Menu-Driven Scientific Plotting Package for Producing Presentation-Quality Graphs in a Variety of Formats. These Formats Include XY, Polar, 3-D Surface, & Contour Plots, As Well As Smith Impedance/Admittance Charts. Both Functions (2-D & 3-D) & Data from Standard ASCII Data Files May Be Plotted Either Separately or on the Same Graph. Extensive Control Is Provided for Labeling & Other Presentation Aspects.
Dynacomp, Inc.

Di-Man: Mandelbrot Fractal Graphics. *Items Included:* Bound manual. *Customer Support:* Free hotline - no time limit; 30 day limited warranty; updates are $5/disk plus S&H.
MS-DOS. IBM & compatibles (256k). $49.95-$89.95. *Nonstandard peripherals required:* Requires an 80386 (with an 80387 math coprocessor) or 80486 computer, 4Mb of total system RAM, VGA or compatible graphics capability, & a hard disk.
Fractal Graphics Package. It Is Menu-Driven, with Optional Mouse Support. 80-Bit Floating Point Precision Allows Magnification up to 10-14 Without Distortion. Magnification Can Be Run in a Near-Continuous Zoom Mode under User Control. Orbit Diagrams for Any Region Are Easily Obtained.
Dynacomp, Inc.

Di-Man Mandelbrot Fractal Graphics. *Items Included:* Full manual. No other products required. *Customer Support:* Free telephone support - no time limit. 30 day warranty.
MS-DOS 3.2 or higher. IBM & compatibles (512k). $49.95 compiled version; $89.95 compiled plus Source Code. *Optimal configuration:* 80386 (with an 80387 math coprocessor) or 80486, 4Mb of total system RAM, VGA or compatible graphics capability, & hard disk.
Exceptionally Fast & Easy-to-Use Fractal Graphics Package. Other Features Include: 175,000 Iterations per Second on a 33 MHz 80386; Diagrams Generated May Be Saved to Disk with Automatic Data Compression, & Recalled. File Output Can Be in TIFT Format for Import to Other Software; VGA Screen Resolution (640 x 480) Images May Be Printed in Color on a HP Paintjet. High Resolution (1920 x 1440) B&W Shaded Output Can Be Printed on HP Laserjet Plus Compatible Printers.
Dynacomp, Inc.

Di-Man: Mandelbrot Fractal Graphics. 1992. *Items Included:* Detailed manuals included with all Dynacomp products. *Customer Support:* Free telephone support to original customer - no time limit; 30 day limited warranty.
MS-DOS 3.2 or higher. IBM PC & compatibles (512k). $49.95 Compiled Version; $89.95 Compiled plus Source Code (Add $5.00 for 3 1/2" format; 5 1/4" format standard). *Optimal configuration:* IBM 80386 (with an 80387 math coprocessor) or 80486 computer, 4Mb of total system RAM, VGA or compatible graphics capability, & a hard disk.
An Exceptionally Fast & Easy-to-Use Fractal Graphics Package. It Is Menu-Driven, with Optional Mouse Support. 80-Bit Floating Point Precision Allows Magnification up to 10(14) Without Distortion. Magnification Can Be Run in a Near-Continuous Zoom Mode under User Control. The User Can Select the Colors (up to 16); Overlay with a Grid; Break a Run, Save the Current Work, & Resume Later, & More. Includes 40-Page Manual with Examples.
Dynacomp, Inc.

DIA-PLUS. *Operating System(s) Required:* UNIX or UNIX-like environments. *Memory Required:* 1000k.
contact publisher for price.
Provides Electronic Mail, Electronic Filing & Retrieving Capabilities Fully Integrated with Automated Office Facilities to View & Manage Personal Correspondence & Distributed Information. Services Are Performed Via Access to IBM's DISOSS, PERSONAL SERVICES/36, & Other Copies of DIA-PLUS on Peer Nodes Architecture. Programmatic Interface Feature Enables DISOSS Access to Be Easily Integrated with a Vendor's Office Automation, Enabling the User to Request Services via Formatted Mail Log & Status Information Online. Standard Rabbit Features Such As Online HELP Facilities, Soft Keyboard Configuration, & Profitable System Configuration Are Provided.
Rabbit Software Corp.

The Diagnosis of Pulmonary Embolus: A Clinician's Approach. Jeffrey R. Galvin. *Customer Support:* Toll-free technical support - no charge. In U.S. - 9AM-5PM EST 800-343-0064. In U.K. - 44(0)81-995-8242.
System 7.0 or higher. Apple Macintosh (4Mb). CD-ROM disk $175.00 Individual; $495.00 Institutional (ISBN 1-57276-006-0, Order no.: SE-006-001). *Nonstandard peripherals required:* CD-Rom drive.
This Multimedia Product Reviews the Diagnosis of Pulmonary Embolus Starting from the Patient Presentation & Finishing with a Discussion of the Proper Use & Interpretation of the Diagnostic Tests. This Course Covers Eight Chapters & Thirty Patient Cases.
SilverPlatter Education.

The Diagnosis of Pulmonary Embolus: A Clinician's Approach. Jeffrey R. Galvin. Mar. 1995. *Customer Support:* Toll-free technical support - no charge. In U.S. 9AM - 5PM EST 800-343-0064; in U.K. 44(0)81-995-8242.
System 7.0 or higher. Apple Macintosh (8Mb). CD-ROM disk $175.00, Individual, ,495.00 Institutional (ISBN 1-57276-006-0, Order no.: SE-006-002). *Nonstandard peripherals required:* CD-ROM drive.
Microsoft Windows 3.1. 386 IBM compatible PC (8Mb). CD-ROM disk $175.00, Individual, ,495.00 Institutional. *Nonstandard peripherals required:* CD-ROM drive (MPC Standard), 640x480 display wiht 256 colors, MPC Standard Soundboard & Speakers.
This Multimedia Product Reviews the Diagnosis of Pulmonary Embolus Starting from the Patient Presentation & Finishing with a Discussion of the Proper Use & Interpretation of the Diagnositc Tests. This Course Covers Eight Chapters & Thirty Patient Cases.
SilverPlatter Education.

Dial-Data. Version: 5.2. 1981. *Compatible Hardware:* IBM PC. *Operating System(s) Required:* MS-DOS. *Language(s):* BASIC (source code included). *Memory Required:* IBM 256k. *Items Included:* Manual, symbol lists.
$50.00 3.5" or 5.25" disk.
Financial Database That Allows User to Access Quotes on Stocks, Commodities, Options, Mutual Funds.
Global Market Information, Inc.

DIALBACK: Secures Dial-in Lines. Version: 2.2. 1991. *Compatible Hardware:* MicroVAX & VAX. *Operating System(s) Required:* VMS, MICROVMS. *Language(s):* Basic. *Memory Required:* 260k. *Items Included:* 1 year maintenance, quarterly newsletter. *Customer Support:* 6:00 a.m.-6:00 p.m. MST.
depending on CPU $673.00-$3036.00.
Enables Identification/Authentication of a Dial-in User & Location. It Requires User to Enter Identification Code Prior to Log-in. Looks up the User's Telephone Number, Hangs up, & Calls the User Back. Upon Code Re-Entry, Normal Log-in Takes Place . On NCSC List.
Raxco, Inc.

Diamond Hunter. *Compatible Hardware:* Atari 400, 800. *Language(s):* Atari BASIC. *Memory Required:* 48k.
disk $16.95.
Gather Diamonds from Maze of Caves.
Dynacomp, Inc.

Diascriptive Cloze Set Program: Diascriptive Cloze I-IV. Ron Buchter. 1995. *Items Included:* Diskettes, guides, documentation & binders. *Customer Support:* Toll free customer service Hot Line 1-800-645-3739 (9a.m. - 5p.m. Eastern Time) software guaranteed for two years.
System 6.07 or higher (2Mb); System 7.0 or higher (4Mb). Macintosh. 3.5" disk $249.00 (Order no.: DK21119).
Each Unit Has Thirty User-Paced CLOZE Passages, Grouped in Three Readability Levels. Teachers May Limit Students to Specific Readability Levels or Allow the Users to Select Any Story (Any Level) from a Menu. The Wide Range of Nonfiction Passages Uses the Modified (Multiple Choice) Format Which Parallels Many State Competency Tests. The Cloze Stories Are Content-Area Based with Literature, Science & Social Studies Themes.
Educational Activities Inc.

Diascriptive 2010 Reading Programs: Diascriptive II. Carol Buchter & Ron Buchter. 1995. *Items Included:* Diskette & teachers guide documentation & binder. *Customer Support:* Toll free customer service Hot Line 1-800-645-3739 (9a.m. - 5p.m. Eastern Time) software guaranteed for two years.
System 6.07 or higher (2Mb); System 7.0 or higher (4Mb). Macintosh. 3.5" disk $395.00 (Order no.: DK21050).
The Unique Management System Is Completely Automatic, Recording Each Students Progress & Remediating or Advancing the Student Through Each Strand Without Teacher Intervention. The Teacher Can Obtain Individual Scores, a Summary of Scores, or a Print Out of a Summary of All the Diagnostic Results by Typing a Simple Command. (Mac Version Includes Time on Task).
Educational Activities Inc.

Diascriptive 2010 Reading Programs: Diascriptive III. Carol Buchter & Ron Buchter. 1995. *Items Included:* Diskette & teachers guide documentation & binder. *Customer Support:* Toll free customer service Hot Line 1-800-645-3739 (9a.m. - 5p.m. Eastern Time) software guaranteed for two years.
System 6.07 or higher (2Mb); System 7.0 or higher (4Mb). Macintosh. 3.5" disk $335.00 (Order no.: DK21112).
The Unique Management System Is Completely Automatic, Recording Each Students Progress & Remediating or Advancing the Student Through Each Strand Without Teacher Intervention. The Teacher Can Obtain Individual Scores, a Summary of Scores, or a Print Out of a Summary of All the Diagnostic Results by Typing a Simple Command. (Mac Version Includes Time on Task).
Educational Activities Inc.

Diascriptive 2010 Reading Programs: Diascriptive IV. Carol Buchter & Ron Buchter. *Items Included:* Diskette & teachers guide documentation & binder. *Customer Support:* Toll free customer service Hot Line 1-800-645-3739 (9a.m. - 5p.m. Eastern Time) software guaranteed for two years.
System 6.07 or higher (2Mb); System 7.0 or higher (4Mb). Macintosh. 3.5" disk $335.00 (Order no.: DK21116).
The Unique Management System Is Completely Automatic, Recording Each Students Progress & Remediating or Advancing the Student Through Each Strand Without Teacher Intervention. The Teacher Can Obtain Individual Scores, a Summary of Scores, or a Print Out of a Summary of All the Diagnostic Results by Typing a Simple Command. (Mac Version Includes Time on Task).
Educational Activities Inc.

Diascriptive 2010 Reading Programs: Diascriptive I. Carol Buchter & Ron Buchter. 1994. *Items Included:* Diskette & teachers guide documentation & binder. *Customer Support:* Toll free customer service Hot Line 1-800-645-3739 (9a.m. - 5p.m. Eastern Time) software guaranteed for two years.
System 6.07 or higher (2Mb); System 7.0 or higher (4Mb). Macintosh. 3.5" disk $335.00 (Order no.: DK21111).
The Unique Management System Is Completely Automatic, Recording Each Students Progress & Remediating or Advancing the Student Through Each Strand Without Teacher Intervention. The Teacher Can Obtain Individual Scores, a Summary of Scores, or a Print Out of a Summary of All the Diagnostic Results by Typing a Simple Command. (Mac Version Includes Time on Task).
Educational Activities Inc.

Dicey's Song. Cynthia Wright. Apr. 1996. *Items Included:* Program manual. *Customer Support:* Free technical support.
School ver.. System 7.1 or higher. Macintosh (4Mb). 3.5" disk contact publisher for price (ISBN 1-57204-387-3). *Nonstandard peripherals required:* 256 color monitor, hard drive, printer.
Lab pack. System 7.1 or higher. Macintosh (4Mb). 3.5" disk contact publisher for price (ISBN 1-57204-363-6). *Nonstandard peripherals required:* 256 color monitor, hard drive, printer.
Site license. System 7.1 or higher. Macintosh (4Mb). 3.5" disk contact publisher for price (ISBN 1-57204-388-1). *Nonstandard peripherals required:* 256 color monitor, hard drive, printer.
School ver.. Windows 3.1 or higher. IBM/Tandy & 100% compatibles (4Mb). disk contact publisher for price (ISBN 1-57204-364-4). *Nonstandard peripherals required:* VGA or SVGA 640 x 480 resolution (256), mouse, hard drive, sound device.
Lab pack. Windows 3.1 or higher. IBM/Tandy & 100% compatibles (4Mb). disk contact publisher for price (ISBN 1-57204-389-X). *Nonstandard peripherals required:* VGA or SVGA 640 x 480 resolution (256), mouse hard drive, sound device.
Site license. Windows 3.1 or higher. IBM/Tandy & 100% compatibles (4Mb). disk contact publisher for price (ISBN 1-57204-365-2). *Nonstandard peripherals required:* VGA or SVGA 640 x 480 resolution (256), mouse, hard drive, sound device.
This companion for young adult literature is ideal for students who don't know how to start that book report, or give that needed summary. Gentle prompts throughout the guide section of the program include Warm-up Connections, Thinking about Plot, Quoting & Noting, Keeping a Journal, If I Were ---' Responding to Questions, Using Quotations, Taking a Personal View, Write to Others, & Write a Sequel.
Lawrence Productions, Inc.

The Dictator. May 1991.
DR DOS, PC-DOS/MS-DOS 3.X or 4.X, PC-MOS. 80x86 with Hayes or Hayes compatible modem (192k). disk $39.95 (ISBN 0-928407-04-7). *Addl. software required:* PROCOMM PLUS v2.0. *Networks supported:* NOVELL.
Automated Data Transfer System That Is Able to Call Multiple Computers (That Have Modems) & Then Upload or Download One or More Files to That Computer. Simple to Use, (Its Commands Are a Subset of PROCOMM PLUS v2.00) & Program. Supports Only the Functions Necessary to Send/Get Files from a Remote Site.
The COMPLETE Machine.

Dictionary, 2 diskettes. *Items Included:* Bound manual. *Customer Support:* Free hotline - no time limit; 30 day limited warranty; updates are $5/disk plus S&H.
MS-DOS. IBM & compatibles (360k). $9.95.
CP/M. $9.95.

Two-Disk Set of 44,000 Words Saved in Sequential Access, ASCII Format. Naturally, They Are in Alphabetical Order. They Can Be Used As the Database for Word Utilities & Games, among Other Things.
Dynacomp, Inc.

A Dictionary of the English Language. Samuel Johnson. Edited by Ann McDermott.
IBM. CD-ROM disk $295.00 (ISBN 0-521-55765-8).
Cambridge Univ. Pr.

Diet. *Compatible Hardware:* Apple II+, IIe, IIc; Franklin Ace. *Language(s):* Applesoft BASIC. *Memory Required:* 48k.
disk $24.95.
Investigates the Effect of Calories, Carbohydrates, Protein, & Lipids in a Diet. The User Enters a List of the Amounts & Types of Food Consumed in a Day, Age, Weight, Health, Physical Activity, & Sex. Analyzes the Information & Provides Ideas for Proper Nutrition & Losing or Gaining Weight.
Compuware.

Diet Analysis. *Customer Support:* 800-929-8117 (customer service).
MS-DOS. IBM/PS2. disk $79.99 (ISBN 0-87007-815-1).
Analyzes User's Diet in Terms of What Is Ingested As Well As Weight, Age & Sex. Will Make Recommendations for Improvements.
SourceView Software International.

Diet Analyzer. *Items Included:* Bound manual. *Customer Support:* Free hotline - no time limit; 30 day limited warranty; updates are $5/disk plus S&H.
MS-DOS. IBM & compatibles (256k). disk $49.95. *Nonstandard peripherals required:* One single-sided drive (minimum); printer supported but not necessary.
Makes It Easy for You to Review & Improve Your Eating Habits. You Simply Enter Foods & It Automatically Shows You 24 Nutrients for Each Food & Keeps Running Totals! Easily Look up Nutritional Information about Foods & Adjust That Information Based on Portion Sizes. Make Intelligent Menu Planning a Pleasure. Enter a Typical Menu & See How It Stacks up to What You Should Be Eating. Make a Little Adjustment Here or There until You Get It Right. Print Menus on Paper & Build a Library of Nutritionally Balanced Meals. Keep a Log of the Foods You Eat. Periodically Compare Your Average Daily Intake of 24 Nutrients with Your Targeted Goals. As You Insert, Adjust, or Delete Foods in the Work Sheet, All Nutrients & Totals Are Instantly & Automatically Updated. Nutritional Information May Be Displayed in Physical Units (e.g., Grams, Milligrams, etc.) or As Percent of Dietary Goal.
Dynacomp, Inc.

Dietary Intervention - Hypertension. 1988. *Compatible Hardware:* IBM PC & compatibles. *Operating System(s) Required:* MS-DOS. *Language(s):* BASIC. *Memory Required:* 512k.
1 unit module $225.00 (Order no.: RCS-8418).
Provides for Application of Concepts Related to Aspects of Dietary Intervention in the Control of Hypertension.
Educational Software Concepts, Inc.

Dietcare. *Operating System(s) Required:* PC-DOS/MS-DOS, OS/2. *Memory Required:* starter version-20Mb, full version-40000k. *Items Included:* Includes 3 days on-site training, 1-year warranty, & user manual. *Customer Support:* Free updates, enhancements & toll-free 800 lines for customers under warranty.
Version Starter. disk $8000.00.
Version 6000. 3.5" disk $12000.00.

Maintains Patient Information System. Prints Patient Cards, Menus, Nourishment Labels, & Scans Menus. Generates Tray Tickets for Selected Menu Items & Production Tallys.
Practorcare, Inc.

Dietician. *Compatible Hardware:* Apple Macintosh. *Memory Required:* 512k.
3.5" disk $94.95.
Nutritional Information.
ALsoft, Inc.

Differential Equations. *Compatible Hardware:* IBM PC. *Operating System(s) Required:* PC-DOS. *Language(s):* MBASIC (source code included).
disk $29.95.
Yields Numerical Solutions to Ordinary Differential Equations Given Suitable Initial Conditions.
Dynacomp, Inc.

Differential Equations Graphics Package. *Version:* 5. Aug. 1995. *Compatible Hardware:* IBM PC. *Operating System(s) Required:* PC-DOS/MS-DOS 3.1. *Language(s):* GWBASIC, BASICA.
disk $75.00.
20 Graphics Programs for Class Demonstrations of Major Topics in Differential Equations. They Show the Solutions & Effects of Changes on Initial Conditions & Other Parameters.
MatheGraphics Software.

Differential Equations with Parameter Estimation. 1992. *Items Included:* Detailed manuals included with all Dynacomp products. *Customer Support:* Free telephone support to original customer - no time limit; 30 day limited warranty.
MS-DOS 3.2 or higher. IBM PC & compatibles (512k). $379.95 Full System; $239.95 Full System, minus parameter fitting (Add $5.00 for 3 1/2" format; 5 1/4" format standard). *Optimal configuration:* IBM, MS-DOS 3.3 or higher, 640k RAM, graphics capability. A mouse & math coprocessor are supported, but not required.
Provides a Powerful Tool for Solving Systems of Differential Equations & Adjusting the Associated Parameters to Fit Experimental Data. It Addresses a Typical Problem Encountered with Process Modelling: the Physics of the Situation Suggests Possible Models, Expressed in Terms of Rate Equations, & Experimental Data Is Available to Help Determine What the Appropriate Model Is (& the Values of the Parameters). Includes a 145-Page Manual Containing Very Detailed Explanations, along with Numerous Examples.
Dynacomp, Inc.

Diffusion Model Library for LaPlace Transform Tools. *Items Included:* Bound manual. *Customer Support:* Free hotline - no time limit; 30 day limited warranty; updates are $5/disk plus S&H.
MS-DOS. IBM & compatibles (256k). disk $89.95. *Addl. software required:* Laplace Transform Tools.
Library of Diffusion Models for LAPLACE TRANSFORM TOOLS. It Covers Models for Both Mass Diffusion & Heat Transfer. Treated Are Diffusion Equations with First Order Depletion & General Source Terms, As Well As Coupled Two-Component Systems. The Boundary Constraints Include: Fixed Concentrations; Zero Flux; Evaporative Mass Loss; Finite Reservoir; & Even the Most General Mixed Boundary Condition.
Dynacomp, Inc.

Diffusion Model Library for Laplace Transform Tools. 1995. *Items Included:* Full manual. *Customer Support:* Free telephone support - 90 days, 30-day warranty.
MS-DOS 3.2 or higher. 286 (584k). disk $89.95. *Nonstandard peripherals required:* CGA/EGA/VGA.
This Is a Library of Diffusion Models for LAPLACE TRANSFORM TOOLS. It Covers Models for Both Mass Diffusion & Heat Transfer. Treated Are Diffusion Equations with First Order Depletion & General Source Terms, As Well As Coupled Two-Component Systems. The Boundary Constraints Include: Fixed Concentrations; Zero Flux; Evaporative Mass Loss; Finite Reservoir; & Even the Most General Mixed Boundary Condition.
Dynacomp, Inc.

Dig Dug. *Compatible Hardware:* Atari XL/XE.
ROM cartridge $19.95 (Order no.: RX8026).
Atari Corp.

Digestion Unit: Digestion, 3 disks. 1985. *Compatible Hardware:* Apple, IBM PC & compatibles. *Operating System(s) Required:* Apple DOS, MS-DOS. *Memory Required:* 48k.
disk $115.00 (Order no.: PMNC1A).
backup set $30.00.
Consists of Three Disks Dealing with the Subject of Digestion.
Aquarius Instructional.

Diggerbonk. *Compatible Hardware:* Atari 400, 800 with Atari BASIC, APX. *Memory Required:* cassette 16k, disk 32k. *General Requirements:* Joystick.
Atari APX. disk $24.95.
Atari 400, Atari 800. disk $19.95.
Single-Player Maze Game.
Dynacomp, Inc.

DiGiCAD. *Version:* 3.00. *Compatible Hardware:* IBM PC & compatibles. *Items Included:* Disks, manuals, hardware copy protection key. *Customer Support:* No charge.
First License. disk $3000.00.
Each Additional. disk $979.00.
CAD Software Used for Civil Engineering, Surveying, Mapping, Architectural & GIS Design.
Digital Matrix Services, Inc.

Digiday Electronic Daily Calendar: 365 Days of Classic Quotes. Sep. 1995. *Items Included:* Registration card, license envelope, CD-ROM, cardboard insert. *Customer Support:* Phone support, Fax back service, WWW site.
Microsoft Windows 3.1. 386 SX (4Mb). disk $12.99 (ISBN 1-888331-01-1, Order no.: DD-QU-01). *Optimal configuration:* 486 DX 66, 8Mb RAM, 256-color display.
A Line of Windows Software That Provides an Electronic Equivalent to the Popular Page-a-Day Paper Calendar. Each Day You Will Be Presented with an Inspirational Thought-Provoking or Humorous Quote. Also Includes Screen Savers, As Well As a Reminder & To-Do System & a Clock with Built-In Alarms.
Vision X Software, Inc.

Digiday Electronic Daily Calendar: 365 Days of Great Words to Know. Sep. 1995. *Items Included:* Registration card, license envelope, CD-ROM, cardboard insert. *Customer Support:* Phone support, Fax back service, WWW site.
Microsoft Windows 3.1. 386 SX (4Mb). disk $12.99 (ISBN 1-888331-02-X, Order no.: DD-WD-01). *Nonstandard peripherals required:* Sound board recommended. *Optimal configuration:* 486DX 66, 8Mb RAM, 256-color display.
A Line of Windows Software That Provides an Electronic Equivalent to the Popular Page-a-Day Paper Calendar. Each Day You Will Be Presented with a "Power Word" to Help Build Your Vocabulary. Also Includes Other Vocabulary Improvement Features As Well As a Reminder & To-Do System, & a Clock with Built-In Alarms.
Vision X Software, Inc.

TITLE INDEX

Digiday Electronic Daily Calendar: 365 Days of Off-the-Wallpaper. Sep. 1995. *Items Included:* Registration card, license envelope, CD-ROM, cardboard insert. *Customer Support:* Phone support, Fax back service, WWW site. Microsoft 3.1. 386 SX (4Mb). disk $12.99 (ISBN 1-888331-00-3, Order no.: DD-WP-01).
Optimal configuration: 486 DX 66, 8Mb RAM, 256-color display.
A Line of Windows Software That Provides an Electronic Equivalent to the Popular Page-a-Day Paper Calendar. Each Day You Will Be Presented with a Interesting Pattern or Texture That Is Sure to Jazz up Your Windows Desktop. Also Includes a Reminder & To-Do System As Well As a Clock with Built-In Alarms.
Vision X Software, Inc.

DigiMate: A Coordinate Point Digitizer Interface. Version: 2.5. Shirl A. Vonasek. Aug. 1990. *Items Included:* Manual w/tutorial example. *Customer Support:* 120 days free phone support; 1 yr unlimited (on all Simplicity Software), $249.00; 90 day moneyback guarantee.
PC-DOS/MS-DOS 3.0 or higher. IBM PC, XT, AT, PS/2 & compatibles (256k). disk $199.00, incl. manual (ISBN 0-932071-09-0).
Nonstandard peripherals required: 1 hard drive; Digitizer board capable of sending ASCII coordinates. *Optimal configuration:* Graphics card.
An Easy-to-Use, Menu-Driven Utility to Digitize Coordinate Map Points, Contours & End Area Cross Sections into an ASCII Coordinate Data File. The ASCII File Can Be Used with Coordinate Geometry, Contouring or CAD Programs. Also Computes Perimeter & Area of Closed Figures & Computes Volumes from Contour Maps or End Areas Cross Sections.
Simplicity Systems, Inc.

Digimax: Hardware. Version: 2.0. Apr. 1995. *Customer Support:* Tech support M-F, 9-4 CST free. Other thru the L. D. charges 612-425-0557. DOS or Amiga. 386 or higher (4Mb). disk $695.00.
3D Object Digitizer. Create Complex Quickly & Easily.
Impulse, Inc.

DigiScope. *Compatible Hardware:* Commodore Amiga.
3.5" disk $79.95.
Digital Oscilloscope Emulation.
ACDA Corp.

DIGIT. Version: 3.11. Nov. 1985. *Compatible Hardware:* IBM PC, PC XT, PC AT & compatibles. *Operating System(s) Required:* MS-DOS, PC-DOS. *Language(s):* BASIC. *Memory Required:* 512k. *General Requirements:* Digitizer, graphics display.
disk $500.00 (Order no.: DIGIT).
Reads Point Coordinates from a Digitizer & Allows the On-Screen Editing of the Point File Created. For Each Set of X,Y Coordinates, the Program Will Accept 1 or 2 Additional Values. The Z Values May Be Entered As Constants for Digitizing a Contour Map or As Unique Variables That Change at Each Data Point.
Geostat Systems International, Inc. (GSII).

Digital Building System. *Compatible Hardware:* Commodore Amiga.
3.5" disk $299.00.
Emulation & Instruction System for Digital Electronics. Users Build Circuits on the Hi-Res Screen by Picking Parts & Soldering Them Together. The Program Computes the Logic State of Each Pin of Every Part & Displays a Part's Wires in Different Colors, Depending on Its State of Activity. Circuits Can Also Be Repaired or Changed by Soldering & Desoldering Joints & Moving, Inserting, Deleting, or Rotating Parts. The Disk-Based Libraries Contain Multiple Input Logic Gates & The 74XX Series of Integrated Circuits. Libraries with Different Integrated Circuits Are Also Available, or Users Can Create Their Own Parts with the Accompanying CHIP EDITOR Program.
MicroMaster, Inc.

Digital Filter. *Compatible Hardware:* Apple II with Applesoft; IBM PC. (source code included). *Memory Required:* 128k.
disk $49.95, incl. manual.
Data Processing Program Which Teaches How to Design Filter Functions.
Dynacomp, Inc.

Digital Filter Design. *Compatible Hardware:* HP Series 200 Models 216/220, 226/236 Personal Technical Computers. *Language(s):* BASIC 2.0. *Memory Required:* 256k.
HP 216/220. 3-1/2" or 5-1/4" disk $500.00 ea. (Order no.: 98828A).
HP 226/236. 5-1/4" disk $500.00 ea.
Provides the Tools Necessary for Designing Digital Filters. Includes Routines for Designing Both Infinite Impulse Response (IIR) & Finite Impulse Response (FIR) Digital Filters. Also Included Are Routines for Transforming Analog Filter Functions, H(s), to Digital Filter Functions H(z). Once the Program Has Computed the Filter Coefficients, Both Magnitude & Phase Plots Are Available to Measure the Actual Performance of Those Filters.
Hewlett-Packard Co.

Digital Filter Design Tutorial. (Plane Analysis Ser.: No. 3). *Compatible Hardware:* Apple II, IBM. *Operating System(s) Required:* Apple DOS 3.2, 3.3, MS-DOS. *Language(s):* Applesoft BASIC, Machine. *Memory Required:* Apple 48k, IBM 128k.
disk $49.95.
Covers Transversal, Comb & Interpolation Filter.
Dynacomp, Inc.

Digital Gourmet Classic. Version: 2.6. *Customer Support:* Unlimited free technical support. Mac. Mac Plus or higher (2Mb). Contact publisher for price.
Contains over 1,000 Traditional & Contemporary Recipes - from Apple Pie to Zucchini - Stored on Computer Disk. The Recipes Are Compiled from a Variety of Sources & Acclaimed by Such Chefs As Hemit Tevin, Executive Chef of Fountainbleau Hilton. This Program Lets You Easily Find, Modify & Add Unlimited New Recipes; Create & Print Shopping Lists. Calculates Nutritional Information for Each Recipe & Ingredient, Including Calorie, Carbohydrate, Protein, & Fat Content; a Dictionary of Cooking Terms; a Help Section; & a Quick Print Option. You May Also Adjust Recipe Serving Sizes, Create & Print Shopping Lists & Recipes. Sophisticated Searching Features Allow You to Quickly Find Recipes of Your Choice.
TeleTypesetting Co.

Digital Gourmet Deluxe. Version: 2.6.2. Jan. 1994. *Items Included:* 4 disks or CD; instruction insert; lastest HyperCard Program. *Customer Support:* 30 days unlimited support; free technical support over the telephone.
Macintosh OS. Macintosh (2Mb). disk $149.00 (Order no.: FL3).
Teletypesetting.

Digital Gourmet Deluxe. Version: 2.6. *Customer Support:* Unlimited free technical support. Mac. Mac Plus or higher (2Mb). Contact publisher for price.
Now You Can Prepare Fabulous Gourmet Recipes Just Like the Pros! The Digital Gourmet Deluxe Is a Collection of All of the Cookbooks in the Award-Winning Digital Gourmet Series. Has the Same Features As the Classic Version & Contains an Additionl 5000 Specialty & International Cookbooks. Create Your Own Customized Cookbook. Prints Shopping List & Recipes. Includes Nutritional Information for Thousands of Foods. Each Specialty Book Typically Contains 500 Recipes. You May Add Recipes to Any of These Books or Simply Use the Empty Book to Keep Track of Your Own Recipes.
TeleTypesetting Co.

Digital Gourmet Deluxe. Version: 2.6.2. Jan. 1994. *Items Included:* 2 disks; instruction insert; lastest HyperCard Program. *Customer Support:* 30 days unlimited Support; free technical support over the telephone.
Macintosh (2Mb). disk $650.00 (Order no.: FL3).
(Order no.: FL3.5).
Teletypesetting Co.

DIGITAL SOUND GALLERY

Digital Image Processing (DIP), 2 disks. *Compatible Hardware:* Apple II; IBM PC. *Language(s):* Applesoft BASIC for Apple (source code included). *Memory Required:* Apple 48k, IBM 256k.
Set. $59.95.
Allows the User to Digitally Manipulate Images (15 Samples Are Supplied Including Pictures of Lincoln, Kirchoff & Saturn) to Remove Interference Noise, Improve Contrast, Sharpen & Generally Filter Images. The Experiment Menu Includes Processing Examples (Run with User's Parameters) for Overexposure or Underexposure, Noise, Interference, Double Exposure (the User Is Given 2 Different Double Exposure Pictures to Try to Rescue), & Poor Contrast. Each Image Can Be Manipulated in the Following Ways: Gamma Correction (User Chooses the Gamma), Inversion (Good for Making Slides), Histogram Correction, User-Supplied Nonlinear Contrast Correction (User Supplies the Table Lookup), & Digital Filtered (User Supplies the Filter Function).
Dynacomp, Inc.

Digital Music Mentor. David G. Peters. 1984. *Customer Support:* ECS offers technical support to registered users. Call (217) 359-7099. Other than the telephone call - technical support is no charge.
Windows 3.1. IBM. $39.95 single station/$200.00 network (Order no.: W-1481).
This Program Is a Terrific Addition to Classroom & Private Instruction. The Teacher Records Exercises/Tunes That Are to Be Studied. The Student Can Then Study Away from Class/Lesson Time by Hearing How the Piece Is to Sound & Then Be Given the Opportunity to Record Their Version of the Piece. The Teacher Can Then Review & Discuss Possible Problems & Ways to Better Expand on Musical Ideas.
Electronic Courseware Systems, Inc.

Digital Orchestrator Plus. Version: 2.0. Oct. 1995.
IBM. disk $159.95 (ISBN 1-888743-01-8).
Computer Music Sequencer/Editor/Arranger.
Voyetra Technologies.

Digital Sound Gallery, Vol. 1, 2 Vols. Feb. 1996. *Items Included:* 4 page instructional booklet, "Composer's Toolkit" software. *Customer Support:* Free customer support available Mon-Fri, 9-6 pm via telephone, fax, mail, BBS, e-mail. Windows 3.1x, Windows95 (8 Mb). IBM or compatible 486DX 2/66. disk $39.99 (ISBN 1-888743-03-4). *Nonstandard peripherals required:* Sound card, speakers or headphones. *Addl. software required:* "Digital Orchestrator Plus". *Optimal configuration:* IB or compatible

281

PC, windows 3.1x or Windows 95, (16 mb RAM) Pentium processor, sound card.
The "Digital Sound Gallery" is a collection of digital audio files in ORC format for use with Voyetra's "Digital Orchestrator Plus" software.
Voyetra Technologies.

Digital Sound Gallery, Vol. 2. Feb. 1996. *Items Included:* 4 page instructional booklet, "Composer's Toolkit" software. *Customer Support:* Free customer support available Mon-Fri, 9-6pm via telephone, fax, mail, BBS, e-mail.
Windows 3.1x, Windows 95 (8mb). IBM or compatible 486DX2/66. disk $39.99 (ISBN 1-888743-04-2). *Nonstandard peripherals required:* Sound card, speakers or headphones. *Addl. software required:* "Digital Orchestrator Plus". *Optimal configuration:* IBM or Compatibles, Windows 3.1x or Windows 95, (16mb RAM), Pentium processor, sound card.
The "Digital Sound Gallery" is a collection of Digital Audio files in ORC format for use with Voyetra's "Digital Orchestrator Plus" software.
Voyetra Technologies.

Digital System Design Using VHDL. Chin-Hwa Lee. Apr. 1993.
$15.00 examples diskette 3 1/2" (ISBN 1-882819-01-2).

DIGITALIS. Edward P. Hoffer & G. Octo Barnett. Dec. 1985. *Compatible Hardware:* Apple II; IBM PC, PCjr, PC XT, PC AT. *Operating System(s) Required:* MS-DOS 2.0 or higher. *Memory Required:* Apple 64k, IBM 128k. *General Requirements:* 2 disk drives for Apple; 80-column display for IBM PCjr.
Apple. disk $85.00 (ISBN 0-683-16808-8).
IBM. disk $85.00 (ISBN 0-683-16809-6).
Guides the User Step-by-Step Through the Basic & Clinical Pharmacology of This Important but Potentially Dangerous Cardiac Medication.
Williams & Wilkins.

DIGITIZE. *Version:* 7.0. *Items Included:* Manual. *Customer Support:* Free phone & mail support, 30-day money back guarantee.
MS-DOS. IBM PC, PC XT, PC AT & compatibles. disk $349.00. *Optimal configuration:* 386 with LaserJet II, dot matrix printers (Epson compatible).
Digitizing Software for Most Popular Digitizers. Print & Stream Modes Are Supported for ASCII Digitizers: Calcomp, GTCO, Houston Instruments, Kurta, Numonics, Summagraphics. Features Automatic Logarithmic-to-Linear & UTM-to-Lat/Long Conversions, Point Labeling, Screen Display & Auto Recall Calibration. Map Data Is Produced in Standard ASCII Format.
RockWare, Inc.

Digitze Digitizer Software Interface. *Items Included:* Full manual. No other products required. *Customer Support:* Free telephone support - no time limit. 30 day warranty.
MS-DOS 3.2 or higher. IBM & compatibles (512k). disk $339.95. *Optimal configuration:* IBM, MS-DOS 3.1 or higher, 512k RAM.
Macintosh. 3.5" disk $339.95. *Optimal configuration:* MAC SE or II with ADB (Apple Desktop Bus).
With DIGITIZE You May: Digitize Points, Lines, Polygons, & Continuously Connected Lines. Input Location Values in Any Coordinate System. Continuous Readout of the Sylus Location Is Shown on the Screen. Edit the Data As Entered (As Opposed to Postprocessing). Save the Data in Six Different, File Formats. Have Lengths, Perimeters, & Areas Automatically Calculated & Displayed. Automatically Calibrate Using Three Known Points. Convert Logarithmic-to-Linear or UTM-to-Long/Latitude Automatically. Append Files from Previous Sessions or Other Maps.
Dynacomp, Inc.

Dimensions. *Compatible Hardware:* Apple Macintosh Plus. *Memory Required:* 1000k.
Design Dimensions $1595.00.
RayTrace Dimensions $1495.00.
Render Dimensions $895.00.
DXF Interpreter $495.00.
VersaCAD Interpreter $295.00.
Presentation Toolkit $495.00.
Three-Dimensional Design, Modeling, Presentation & Animation Program.
Visual Information, Inc.

Dimensions Presenter.
Macintosh Plus (2Mb). disk $595.00.
Three-Dimensional Rendering, Presentation & Walk-Through Animation of Solid Surfaces with In-Betweening. Offers High-Quality Imaging & Animation Capabilities to CAD Users. Accepts Files from Powerful CAD Programs & Animates in Three Dimensions. Images Can Be Exported to Presentation Software or Sent to Film Recorder, Color Printer & Video Output Devices. Features Include: Key Frame Animation with In-Betweening Provides Smooth Frame Sequencing; Animation Can Be Created for Walkthroughs & Other Object Movements; 16 Light Sources Can Be Defined per Image; Many More Features Available.
Visual Information, Inc.

DINE Right for Windows. Darwin Dennison. Feb. 1992. *Items Included:* User's manual, food & activity records. *Customer Support:* Free technical support, 10-day money-back guarantee, telephone support.
Microsoft Windows 2.x, 3.x. IBM PC, XT, AT, PS/2 & compatibles (640k). disk $149.00. *Nonstandard peripherals required:* Microsoft or compatible mouse recommended. *Addl. software required:* Microsoft Windows. *Optimal configuration:* IBM AT or compatible, 640k, 4Mb hard disk space, Microsoft Windows 2.X, 3.X. *Networks supported:* Novell.
Lose Weight & Improve Your Health by Adjusting Your Food Choices & Portion Sizes to Meet Federal Dietary Guidelines. Diet/Recipe/Activity Analysis Can Be Printed in Chart, Graph & Message Form. Includes the DINE Database, Which Has No Missing Values & Contains 5600 Plus Brand Name, Generic & Fast Food Items, As Well As 194 Activities.
DINE Systems, Inc.

Dinner at Eight. *Compatible Hardware:* Apple Macintosh, IBM PC. *Items Included:* Mac 3 double or single-sided disks with program & 160 recipes; IBM 3 or 5 disks with program & recipes. *Customer Support:* 800-688-7466.
Dinner at Eight $49.95.
Recipe Collection & Filing System.
Rubicon Publishing.

Dino Eggs. (Series A).
All Apple IIs. disk $5.00. *Optimal configuration:* Apple II, joystick.
Commodore 64. disk $5.00.
When You Leaped Back in Time to the Mesozoic Era, You Accidentally Brought along a Case of 21st Century Measles & Contaminated All the Dinosaurs. They're Doomed - Unless You Can Carry Enough Dino Eggs Back to Your Time Warp! To Avoid Squirming Proto-Snakes, Crawling Protopedes & Falling Proto-Spiders, You Must Climb, Leap, Jump & Run All over the Cliffs Where the Dino Eggs Are Buried. If Dino Mom Catches You Taking Her Eggs, She'll Try to Stomp the Daylights Out of You. Can You Save Yourself by Building a Fire Before She Uses You for a Doormat.
Word Assocs., Inc.

Dino Match: A Mind-Building Game for Windows. *Version:* 2.0. David Carlson & James Lindly. Jul. 1994. *Items Included:* One bound manual, Registration card, FREE bag of candy - from Farley Candy Company. *Customer Support:* 90 days unlimited warranty on materials.
Windows 3.1. IBM & compatibles (4Mb). $39.95; Educational Discount 10%; Case of 28 Discount 30% (ISBN 1-885708-01-7, Order no.: MATCH). *Nonstandard peripherals required:* Sound Blaster or compatible sound card is optional, hard drive required. *Optimal configuration:* 486/33MHz, Windows 3.1, 4Mb RAM, Sound Blaster or compatible card, 6Mb free hard disk space.
Windows-Based Game for Children Ages 5-9. The Object of "Dino Match" Is to Help Derik the Dinosaur Rescue Books from Rex the Tyrannosaurus. The Game Consists of Ten Progressively Difficult Mazes & Memory Tasks. The Goal Is to Earn Enough Points to Make the "Dino Hall of Fame".
DynoTech Software.

Dino Numbers: A Math Game for Windows. *Version:* 2.0. Dec. 1994. *Items Included:* One 3 1/2" High Density diskette. *Customer Support:* 90 days unlimited warranty on materials. Technical support phone for registered users. America Online Account (DTGames aol.com).
Windows 3.1. 386 or higher (IBM & compatibles) (4Mb). disk $20.00 (ISBN 1-885708-03-3). *Nonstandard peripherals required:* Sound Blaster, or compatible, sound card (optional); Hard drive required (6Mb free space). *Addl. software required:* None - All drivers supplied & automatically installed by setup program. *Optimal configuration:* 486/33 MHz or higher; Windows 3.1; 4Mb RAM; Sound Blaster, or compatible, sound card; 6Mb free hard drive space.
Exciting Window-Based Math Game for Children. Includes Animation, Music, & Sound Effects. The Object of the Game Is to Collect Cows in a Haystack Maze. To Rescue Cows from Rex the Tyrannosaurus, Derik the Dinosaur Must Solve Arithmetic Problems. The Game Offers a Possible Combination of 30 Different Mazes.
DynoTech Software.

Dino Spell: A Spelling Game for Windows. *Version:* 2.02. Nov. 1994. *Items Included:* One 3 1/2" HD-DS diskette; Custom Word List Manager. *Customer Support:* 90 days unlimited warranty on materials. Technical support phone for registered users. America Online Account (DTGames aol.com).
Windows 3.1. 386 or higher (IBM & compatibles) (4Mb). disk $20.00 (ISBN 1-885708-02-5). *Nonstandard peripherals required:* Sound Blaster, or compatible, sound card (optional); Hard drive required (6Mb free space). *Addl. software required:* None - All drivers supplied & automatically installed by setup program. *Optimal configuration:* 486/33 MHz or higher; Windows 3.1; 4Mb RAM; Sound Blaster, or compatible, sound card; 6Mb free hard drive space.
Exciting Window-Based Spelling Game for Children. Includes Animation, Music, & Sound Effects. The Object of the Game Is to Collect Apples in a Maze. To Rescue Apples from Rex the Tyrannosaurus, Derik the Dinosaur Must Solve Various Spelling Challenges. The Game Offers a Possible Combination of 30 Different Mazes.
DynoTech Software.

Dino Trilogy: Three Educational Windows Games. *Version:* 2. Dec. 1994. *Items Included:* "Dino Match" (Memory Building) on 3 1/2" High Density diskette. "Dino Spell" (Spelling Practice) on 3 1/2" High Density diskette. "Dino Numbers"

TITLE INDEX

(Math Skills) on 3 1/2" High Density diskette. "Word List Manager" (Custom Spelling Lists) on diskette with "Dino Spell". *Customer Support:* 90 days unlimited warranty on materials. Technical support phone for registered users. America Online Account (DTGames aol.com).
Windows 3.1. 386 or higher (IBM & compatibles) (4Mb). disk $30.00 (ISBN 1-885708-04-1). *Nonstandard peripherals required:* Sound Blaster, or compatible, sound card (optional); Hard drive required (17Mb free space). *Addl. software required:* None - All drivers supplied & automatically installed by setup program. *Optimal configuration:* 486/33 MHz or higher; Windows 3.1; 4Mb RAM; Sound Blaster, or compatible, sound card; 17Mb free hard drive space.
Exciting Window-Based Educational Games for Children. Includes Animation, Music, & Sound Effects. The Object of the Games Is to Collect "Prizes" in Various Mazes. To Rescue the Items from Rex the Tyrannosaurus, Derik the Dinosaur Must Solve Assorted Challenges. The Set Offers a Possible Combination of 90 Different Mazes.
DynoTech Software.

Dino Wars. *Customer Support:* Back up disks available.
Amiga (512k). $39.95.
MS-DOS (512k). IBM PC & compatibles. $39.95.
Multiple Disks, Two Player Option. Interactive Strategy With Fully Animated Arcade Sequences & a Complete Dinosaur Encyclopedia. Choice of Five Different Board Set Ups.
DigiTek Software.

Dinosaur Adventure.
Contact publisher for price.
Knowledge Adventure, Inc.

Dinosaur Adventure (3-D).
MS-DOS 5.0 or higher, Windows 3.1 or higher. 386 processor or higher (4Mb). CD-ROM disk $69.95 (Order no.: R1123). *Nonstandard peripherals required:* CD-ROM drive. *Optimal configuration:* 386 processor operating at 16Mhz or higher, MS-DOS 5.0 or higher, Windows 3.1 or higher, 30Mb hard drive, mouse, VGA graphic adapter & VGA color monitor (SVGA recommended), 8Mb RAM, external speakers or headphones (with sound card) that are Sound Blaster compatible.
Macintosh (4Mb). (Order no.: 1123A). *Nonstandard peripherals required:* 14" color monitor or larger, CD-ROM drive.
An Interactive Multimedia Environment for Learning about Dinosaurs, Earth, Biology & Geology. Computer Images, Fully Narrated & Animated Sequences, Full-Color Photos & Full-Motion Video Bring Prehistoric Earth to Life. Includes a Complete Dinosaur Index Showing Museums Where Dinosaur Remains Can Be Seen Worldwide.
Library Video Co.

Dinosaur Discovery.
MS-DOS 5.0 or higher, Windows 3.1 or higher. 386 processor (4Mb). CD-ROM disk $39.95 (Order no.: R1020). *Nonstandard peripherals required:* CD-ROM drive. *Optimal configuration:* 386 processor operating at 16Mhz or higher, MS-DOS 5.0 or higher, Windows 3.1 or higher, 30Mb hard drive, mouse, VGA graphic adapter & VGA color monitor (SVGA recommended), 8Mb RAM, external speakers or headphones (with sound card) that are Sound Blaster compatible.
Macintosh (4Mb). (Order no.: R1020A). *Nonstandard peripherals required:* 14" color monitor or larger, CD-ROM drive.
Includes Illustrations, Descriptions, Facts, Pronunciations of over 150 Prehistoric Animals & Narrated Slide Shows.
Library Video Co.

Dinosaur Safari.
MS-DOS 5.0 or higher, Windows 3.1 or higher. 386 processor (4Mb). CD-ROM disk $29.95 (Order no.: R1021). *Nonstandard peripherals required:* CD-ROM drive. *Optimal configuration:* 386 processor operating at 16Mhz or higher, MS-DOS 5.0 or higher, Windows 3.1 or higher, 30Mb hard drive, mouse, VGA graphic adapter & VGA color monitor (SVGA recommended), 8Mb RAM, external speakers or headphones (with sound card) that are Sound Blaster compatible.
Macintosh (4Mb). (Order no.: R1021). *Nonstandard peripherals required:* 14" color monitor or larger, CD-ROM drive.
Take a Serious Look at Dinosaurs Through Illustrations, Descriptions & Facts Describing the Physical Characteristics, Behavior & Environment on All of the Scientifically Know & Accepted Species of Dinosaurs (Ages 8 & Up).
Library Video Co.

Dinosaur Safari: MAC Jewel Case. Michael Ratliff. Sep. 1993. *Items Included:* Registration card. *Customer Support:* Creative Multimedia Corporation warrants the CD-ROM disc & diskettes to be free from defects in materials & workmanship under normal use & service for a period of 90 days from date of purchase. Creative Multimedia Corporation offers Technical Support to customers as needed.
System Software 7.0 or higher. Macintosh Plus or higher (2Mb). CD-ROM disk $69.99 (ISBN 1-880428-18-0, Order no.: 10394). *Nonstandard peripherals required:* 13" or larger color monitor with 640x480 resolution & 8-bit display. CD-ROM extensions required. *Optimal configuration:* CD-ROM drive with 150k/second transfer rate, 380ms or less access rate recommended. *Networks supported:* All.
Blast Back Through Time on a Mesozoic Adventure - Travel Through Five Time Periods to 310 Locations, on All Parts of the Globe; See the Continents Drift over Time & Volcanoes Erupt; Use Radar to Find Well-Hidden Dinosaurs, or Mating Calls to Lure the Extremely Shy Ones; Capture up to 60 Live-Action, Animated Creatures in Their Environments on Film or Video; Bring Your Dinosaurs Back Alive, by Creating Flash Cards with Your Photo Images. Solid Science & Fantastic Fun.
Creative Multimedia Corp.

Dinosaur Safari: MAC Retail Box. Michael Ratliff. Sep. 1993. *Items Included:* Registration Card. *Customer Support:* Creative Multimedia Corporation warrants the CD-ROM disc & diskettes to be free from defects in materials & workmanship under normal use & service for a period of 90 days from date of purchase. Creative Multimedia Corporation offers Technical Support to customers as needed.
System Software 7.0 or higher. Mactinosh Plus or higher (2Mb). CD-ROM disk $69.99 (ISBN 1-880428-25-3, Order no.: 10519). *Nonstandard peripherals required:* 13" or larger color monitor with 640x480 resolution & 8-bit display. CD-ROM extensions required. *Optimal configuration:* A CD-ROM drive with 150k/second transfer rate, 380ms or less access rate recommended. *Networks supported:* All.
Blast Back Through Time on a Mesozoic Adventure - Travel Through Five Time Periods to 310 Locations, on All Parts of the Globe; See the Continents Drift over Time & Volcanoes Erupt; Use Radar to Find Well-Hidden Dinosaurs, or Mating Calls to Lure the Extremely Shy Ones; Capture up to 60 Live-Action Animated Creatures in Their Environments on Film or Video; Bring Your Dinosaurs Back Alive, by Creating Flash Cards with Your Photo Images. Solid Science & Fantastic Fun.
Creative Multimedia Corp.

DINOSAURS (MICROSOFT)

Dinosaur Safari: MPC Jewel Case. Michael Ratliff. Sep. 1993. *Items Included:* Registration card. *Customer Support:* Creative Multimedia Corporation warrants the CD-ROM disc & diskettes to be free from defects in materials & workmanship under normal use & service for a period of 90 days from date of purchase. Creative Multimedia Corporation offers Technical Support to customers as needed.
Microsoft Windows 3.1, MS-CDEX 2.2 or higher. 386SX or higher; hard drive with 1Mb free disk space. CD-ROM disk $69.99 (ISBN 1-880428-19-9, Order no.: 10429). *Nonstandard peripherals required:* SuperVGA resolution with 256 colors, Sound Card w/windows driver. CD-ROM drive w/150k/second transfer rate, 380ms or less access rate. *Networks supported:* All.
Blast Back Through Time on a Mesozoic Adventure - Travel Through Five Time Periods to 310 Locations, on All Parts of the Globe; See the Continents Drift over Time & Volcanoes Erupt; Use Radar to Find Well-Hidden Dinosaurs, or Mating Calls to Lure the Extremely Shy Ones; Capture up to 60 Live-Action, Animated Creatures in Their Environments on Film or Video; Bring Your Dinosaurs Back Alive, by Creating Flash Cards with Your Photo Images. Solid Science & Fantastic Fun.
Creative Multimedia Corp.

Dinosaur Safari: MPC Retail Box. Michael Ratliff. Sep. 1993. *Items Included:* Registration card. *Customer Support:* Creative Multimedia Corporation warrants the CD-ROM disc & diskettes to be free from defects in materials & workmanship under normal use & service for a period of 90 days from date of purchase. Creative Multimedia Corporation offers Technical Support to customers as needed.
Microsoft Windows 3.1, MS-CDEX 2.2 or higher. 386SX or higher, hard drive with 1Mb free disk space (4Mb). CD-ROM disk $69.99 (ISBN 1-880428-20-2, Order no.: 10395). *Nonstandard peripherals required:* SuperVGA resolution with 256 colors, Sound Card with Windows Drivers. CD-ROM drive with 150k/second transfer rate & 380ms or less access rate. *Networks supported:* All.
Blast Back Through Time on a Mesozoic Adventure - Travel Through Five Time Periods to 310 Locations, on All Parts of the Globe; See the Continents Drift over Time & Volcanoes Erupt; Use Radar to Find Well-Hidden Dinosaurs, or Mating Calls to Lure the Extremely Shy Ones; Capture up to 60 Live-Action, Animated Creatures in Their Environments on Film or Video; Bring Your Dinosaurs Back Alive, by Creating Flash Cards with Your Photo Images. Solid Science & Fantastic Fun.
Creative Multimedia Corp.

Dinosaurs (Microsoft).
Windows. IBM & compatibles. CD-ROM disk $59.95 (Order no.: R1310). *Nonstandard peripherals required:* CD-ROM drive. *Optimal configuration:* 386 processor operating at 16Mhz or higher, MS-DOS 5.0 or higher, Windows 3.1 or higher, 30Mb hard drive, mouse, VGA graphic adapter & VGA color monitor (SVGA recommended), 8Mb RAM, external speakers or headphones (with sound card) that are Sound Blaster compatible.
Macintosh (4Mb). (Order no.: R1310A). *Nonstandard peripherals required:* 14" color monitor or larger, CD-ROM drive.
Take Narrated, Guided Tours with Expert "Dino Don" Lessem, Watch Full-Motion Video from the PBS Series "The Dinosaurs!" or Explore Your Own Personal Dinosaur Dig. More Than 200 Articles & 1,000 Illustrations & Photos Make This a Complete, Exciting Journey into the World of Dinosaurs.
Library Video Co.

Dinosaurs: The Multimedia Encyclopedia.
MS-DOS 5.0 or higher, Windows 3.1 or higher. 386 processor or higher (4Mb). CD-ROM disk $49.00 (Order no.: R1124). *Nonstandard peripherals required:* CD-ROM drive. *Optimal configuration:* 386 processor operating at 16Mhz or higher, MS-DOS 5.0 or higher, Windows 3.1 or higher, 30Mb hard drive, mouse, VGA graphic adapter & VGA color monitor (SVGA recommended), 8Mb RAM, external speakers or headphones (with sound card) that are Sound Blaster compatible.
Macintosh (4Mb). (Order no.: R1124A). *Nonstandard peripherals required:* 14" color monitor or larger, CD-ROM drive.
This Interactive Guide Answers Almost Every Question People Ask about Dinosaurs. Uses Full-Color Video, Color Illustrations & Photos, & Animated Sequences to Show How Dinosaurs Lived & Died. Journey into the World of Dinosaurs.
Library Video Co.

Direct Connect. *Version:* 2.01. Randall Hughes. Jan. 1983. *Compatible Hardware:* IBM PC. *Operating System(s) Required:* MS-DOS, PC-DOS. *Language(s):* Pascal, Assembly. *Memory Required:* 128k. *General Requirements:* 2 disk drives.
disk $95.00.
Communications Package Designed to Access Other Databases & Computers. Features XMODEM Protocol for Data Transfer at up to 9600 Baud.
Direct-Aid, Inc.

Direct Information. *Version:* 1.5. Jan. 1990. *Items Included:* 1 manual, Cannon Zapshot camera, Cannon still video player, custom hardware. *Customer Support:* Installation & training, service contracts after 1 year warranty, telephone support, 24 hour service available.
MS-DOS 3.0 or higher, Optional Netware compatibility. 386 or 386SX processor (640K). contact publisher for price. *Optimal configuration:* Novell N. *Networks supported:* NOVELL.
Allows End User to Produce & Present a Multimedia Information System for Lobbies of Highrise Office Buildings. Intermixing of Computer Graphics & Still Video Enhance the Presentation of Tenant Location Information & the Location of Retail Shopping within the Building or Complex. Novell Compatible Software Allows System Updates from Building Management Office to Be Transmitted to Customer Station in Building Lobby.
KMS Systems, Inc.

Direct Mail. *Compatible Hardware:* Apple Macintosh. *Memory Required:* 512k.
Single user with Omnis 3 Plus Runtime. 3.5" disk $295.00.
Single user without Omnis 3 Plus Runtime. 3.5" disk $69.95.
Multiuser (requires Omnis 3 Plus). 3.5" disk $175.00.
Mailing List Management.
H&D Leasing.

Direct Observation Form Scoring Program - Apple II Version. *Version:* 2.2. Thomas M. Achenbach. 1986. *Items Included:* Detailed manual. *Customer Support:* Free telephone support with no time limit.
ProDOS. Apple II series (64k). disk $135.00 (ISBN 0-938565-02-8). *Optimal configuration:* Apple II with 64k & printer capable of 132-character lines if user wishes to print profiles.
Provides for Entry & Verification of Data from Direct Observation Form, Plus Scoring of Data on Profile for the Direct Observation Form. Up to Six DOFs Can Be Entered & Averaged per Subject, Plus Six for Each of Two Control Subjects. Mean Scores from Target & Control Subjects Will Be Displayed on Printed Profile & Stored in Computer File.
Univ. of Vermont, Dept. of Psychiatry.

Direct Observation Form Scoring Program - IBM PC Version. *Version:* 2.2.2. Thomas M. Achenbach. 1986. *Items Included:* Detailed manual. *Customer Support:* Free telephone support with no time limit.
MS-DOS. IBM PC & compatibles (512k). disk $135.00 (ISBN 0-938565-01-X). *Optimal configuration:* IBM PC compatible with 512k, & printer capable of 132-character lines if user wishes to print profiles.
Provides for Entry & Verification of Data from Direct Observation Form, Plus Scoring of Data on Profile for the Direct Observation Form. Up to Six DOFs Can Be Entered & Averaged per Subject, Plus Six for Each of Two Control Subjects. Mean Scores from Target & Control Subjects Will Be Displayed on Printed Profile & Stored in Computer File.
Univ. of Vermont, Dept. of Psychiatry.

Direct Plus. *Version:* 4.1. Mar. 1992. *Items Included:* One documentation manual. *Customer Support:* 60 days free support upon purchase. Annual maintenance & support - $600 single user, $900 multiuser. Includes tax updates, enhancements & telephone support.
DOS. IBM compatible (256k). $5000.00 single user; $7500.00 multiuser. *Networks supported:* Novell, LANtastic.
UNIX. IBM compatible (1Mb). $12,500.00.
Primary Applications Are: Sales, Scheduling, Dispatch, Rating, Billing, Accounts Receivable, Commission Driver Settlement, Job Profitability, Payroll (Salary, Hourly, Percentage, Mileage, or Flat Rate), Accounts Payable, General Ledger, Balance Sheet, Profit & Loss & Other Financial Statements, Fuel Tax, Driver Logs, Vehicle Maintenance, Electronic Data Interchange (EDI), Storage & Warehouse. Software Operates on Both DOS & UNIX Platforms.
Direct Systems, Inc.

The Director. *Version:* 2. *Compatible Hardware:* Commodore Amiga.
3.5" disk $129.95.
Professional Display & Animation Application. Provides the Following Features: Uses Any IFF Images, Any Resolution, & Any Number of Colors; Supports HAM & Overscan; Page Flip Full or Partial Screens; Fades, Dissolves, Wipes, Blits, Stencils; Digitized Soundtrack Module; Preload Images, Fonts, & Sounds up to the Memory Limit; Isolate Any Part of the Screen for Independent Control; Script-Based Structure; Keyboard & Mouse Interaction; Built-In Drawing Commands; Random Number Generator; Executes AmigaDOS Commands from the Script; Text String & File Input & Output. Not Copy Protected.
The Right Answers Group.

The Director Plus Modules. *Version:* 1.2. 1992. *Items Included:* One year of free telephone technical support, an operations manual in a 3-ring binder, the Runtime Version of Revelations. *Customer Support:* After the first year of free telephone technical support, additional technical support can be purchased if needed.
MS-DOS. IBM PC & compatibles (320k). Basic module avail. at no charge. *Networks supported:* Novell, IBM PC-NET, Banyan Vines, LAN Manager for MS-DOS, & most other DOS compatible networks.
Pathworks or Digital Equipment Corp.'s VMS. VAX (320k). Contact publisher for price. *Networks supported:* DECNET.
UNIX, SUNOS. SPARC Station. Contact publisher for price.
This Is a Modular Approach to Accident/Incident Record Keeping. The Basic Module Enables All Employee Accidents & Illnesses & Also Any Near Misses to Be Recorded. The Program Will Generate "The OSHA 200 Log", a "Daily First Aid Log", & a "Cases by Specific Sort Report." Additional Modules Can Be Purchased.
Pro-Am Software.

Directors Series. Sep. 1987. *Compatible Hardware:* Atari ST. *Memory Required:* 512k.
3.5" disk $79.95 (ISBN 1-55790-097-3, Order no.: 25925).
Professional Quality Color Drawing & Cell Animation Programs for Creating Special Effects.
Broderbund Software, Inc.

Directory. *Compatible Hardware:* IBM PC; Tandy 2000; TRS-80 Model II, Model III, Model 4, Model 12, Model 16.
contact publisher for price.
Derives a Complete Directory from Church Donation Information. Can Format As a Telephone or Select-Type Book with Three Column Pages, Alphabetization, Pagination, & First/Last Name Indicators.
Custom Data (New Mexico).

Directory of Free Computer Publications. Charles LaGasse. Jul. 1991. *Items Included:* Paperless-on line documentation. *Customer Support:* Free telephone support.
PC-DOS or MS-DOS 3.1 or higher. IBM compatible XT or higher (256k). disk $9.95 (ISBN 0-942199-01-4, Order no.: DFCP). *Optimal configuration:* 1 floppy disk (for installation), 1 hard disk (512k disk storage for files including indexes), Mono or color monitor, Printer (Generic printer supported, 15 CPI, Set Margins as appropriate). *Networks supported:* Single User.
A List of Free Computer Publications in Major Computer Subject Areas That Contains Listings of 200 Publications from over 150 Companies Including, Books, Catalogs, Magazines, Newsletters & Other Publication Types Covering Books, Careers, Communications, IBM PC, Software, UNIX & over 50 Other Subjects.
Computer Insights.

Directory of National Helplines. 1995. *Items Included:* Manual. *Customer Support:* One year of the CSAP is provided at n/c; 30 day no risk guarantee.
MS-DOS. IBM or compatibles (640k). disk $195.00 (ISBN 0-927875-67-5, Order no.: 1785). *Addl. software required:* Winnebago CIRC and/or CAT V 5.1 or higher. *Optimal configuration:* Same as Winnebago CIRC/CAT or Winnebago CAT, an additional 4Mb hard disk space per year. *Networks supported:* IPX or Netbios compatible.
3.5" disk $195.00 (ISBN 0-927875-66-7, Order no.: 1785).
An Aid to Locating Toll-Free Services Throughout the Country Offering Advice, Support, & Assistance to Persons in Need. More Than 600 Toll-Free Numbers Direct Users to Organizations That Specialize in Providing a Variety of Services. Also Included Are a Large Number of Travel Helplines for Assistance in Travel Plans.
Winnebago Software Co.

Directory of the State Legislature. Jul. 1989. *Items Included:* Spiral bound manual. *Customer Support:* 30-day money back guarantee.
MS-DOS (640k). IBM PC & compatibles. disk $29.95, per state (ISBN 0-945659-11-3). *Addl. software required:* Any database manager, spreadsheet or word processor.
MAC-DOS (500k). 3.5" disk $29.95, per state (ISBN 0-945659-12-1). *Addl. software*

required: Any database manager, spreadsheet or word processor.
Database of the Selected State Legislature, Including Name Address, Phone, Party & District Available for Each of 50 States. Usable with a Datafile for Database, Word Processor or Spreadsheet.
Gabriel Publishing Co.

Directory of the U.S. Congress. Jul. 1989. *Items Included:* Spiral bound manual. *Customer Support:* 30-day money back guarantee.
MS-DOS (640k). IBM PC & compatibles. disk $24.95 (ISBN 0-945659-10-5). *Addl. software required:* Any database manager, spreadsheet, or word processor.
3.5" disk $24.95 (ISBN 0-945659-10-5). *Nonstandard peripherals required:* MAC-DOS (50k). *Addl. software required:* Any database manager, spreadsheet, or word processor.
Data File for Database Word Processor or Spreadsheet of U.S. House & Senate. Includes Full Name, Address, Phone, Party, State, Committees, Subcommittees.
Gabriel Publishing Co.

Directory of U.S. Government Buying Offices. Apr. 1989. *Items Included:* Spiral bound manual. *Customer Support:* 30-day money back guarantee.
MS-DOS (640k). IBM PC & compatibles. disk $24.95 (ISBN 0-945659-05-9). *Addl. software required:* Any database manager, spreadsheet or word processor.
MAC-DOS (500k). 3.5" disk $24.95 (ISBN 0-945659-07-5). *Addl. software required:* Any database manager, spreadsheet or word processor.
Database of over 1000 Federal Buying Offices Giving Titles, Address Governmental Organization & Full Address. Usable with a Variety of Word Processors, Database Managers or Spreadsheets.
Gabriel Publishing Co.

Directory on Computer. *Version:* 3.0. Jan. 1992. *Items Included:* 3-ring binder manual. *Customer Support:* Unlimited via phone.
PC/MS-DOS 3.0 or higher. IBM & compatibles (640k). disk $1500.00 (ISBN 0-932599-09-5).
Database of Information from the DIRECTORY OF MAJOR MALLS. Information on Shopping Centers of at Least 250,000 Sq. Ft. in Gross Leasable Area, Ownership, Location, Management, Design, Tenant List, etc. for Each Center. Accompanied by Interactive Custom Software Program. Capable of Creating Reports & Mailing Labels. ASCii, dBASE Files & Custom Sort Files Available.
JOMURPA Publishing, Inc.

DirLabel. *Customer Support:* 800-929-8117 (customer service).
MS-DOS. IBM/PS2. disk $29.99 (ISBN 0-87007-283-8).
Produces a Subscript Size Label Printout of Diskette Directories.
SourceView Software International.

DISASM. *Compatible Hardware:* Atari. *Language(s):* Assembly.
disk $24.95 (ISBN 0-936200-20-0).
cassette $24.95 (ISBN 0-936200-20-0).
General Purpose 6502 Disassembler & Boot File Copier. Completely Menu Driven & Self Prompting. Works with or Without Assembler/Editor Cartridge.
Blue Cat.

Disassembler. *Compatible Hardware:* TI 99/4A. *Operating System(s) Required:* DX-10. *Language(s):* Extended BASIC. *Memory Required:* 48k.

disk $18.95.
Utility Program Which Disassembles Assembly Language into Text, Data (Hex) or Code (Mnemonics). Also Disassembles CPU Memory Locations. Disassembled Output Can Be Displayed or Simultaneously Printed.
Eastbench Software Products.

Discipline Tracking System. *Version:* 8.01. 1994. *Items Included:* 1 full manual. *Customer Support:* $225/per year.
MS-DOS 6.2 or higher. IBM-PC 486 & compatibles (640k). disk $995.00. *Optimal configuration:* IBM-PC 486 or compatible w/ 4Mb of RAM, SVGA monitor & card, 3.5" HD floppy drive, DOS 5.0. *Networks supported:* Novell Netware, Artisoft Lantastic, Windows NT.
This System Tracks Disciplinary Infractions, Locations Where Problems Occur, Punishments, & the Teachers & Administrators Involved. In Addition This Is a Multi-Year System, Allowing You to Track a Student's Disciplinary History Throughout Their Stay at Your School. This System's Database Is Fully Integrated with All of Our Other Modules.
Applied Educational Systems, Inc.

DISCOTEST II. *Version:* 2. David C. Dale & Daniel D. Federman. Oct. 1984. *Compatible Hardware:* IBM PC & compatibles; Macintosh. *Operating System(s) Required:* Windows 3.1 or higher, MS-DOS or Macintosh System 6.0.7 or higher. *Memory Required:* IBM 640k, Macintosh 1000k. *Items Included:* The annual subscription includes a comprehensive user's guide & 8 new patient management cases. *Customer Support:* 1-800-643-4351.
Windows/DOS. disk $169.95 (ISBN 0-89454-003-3).
Macintosh. disk $169.95 (ISBN 0-89454-006-8).
Continuing Medical Education (CME) Test for Physicians on Diskette Which Consists of Eight Patient Management Problems. During One Year the User Can Earn up to 32 Category 1 CME Credits. Tests Can Be Re-Used for Self-Education.
Scientific American Medicine.

Discounted Cash Flow. *Compatible Hardware:* Apple, IBM PC, CP/M based machines. *Operating System(s) Required:* CP/M, MP/M, CP/M-86. *Language(s):* MBASIC. *Memory Required:* CP/M, MP/M & Apple 64k; CP/M-86 & IBM 128k. *General Requirements:* 2 disk drives, printer.
disk $49.00.
Calculates Present Value, Future Value, & Interest Rate. Compares the Results to Determine the Impact of Inflation.
Microsystems.

The Discoverers.
MS-DOS 3.1 or higher, Windows. 386 processor or higher, (640k). CD-ROM disk $39.95 (Order no.: R1181). *Nonstandard peripherals required:* CD-ROM drive. *Optimal configuration:* 386 processor or higher, MS-DOS 3.1 or higher, Windows 3.1 or higher, 20Mb hard drive, external speakers or headphones (with sound card) that are Sound Blaster compatible, VGA graphics & adapter, VGA color monitor.
Macintosh (4Mb). (Order no.: R1181A). *Nonstandard peripherals required:* 14" color monitor or larger, CD-ROM drive.
Study New & Old Discoveries with Archaeologists, Marine Biologists, Anthropologists & Astrophysicists. This Exciting Program Features an Extended Learning Module Containing Many Fascinating Easy-to-Do Classroom Projects (Ages 8 & Up).
Library Video Co.

Discovering Authors, 1995. *Version:* 2.0. Nov. 1995.
IBM. CD-ROM disk $500.00 (ISBN 0-8103-5101-3, Order no.: 101621).
Mac. CD-ROM disk $500.00 (ISBN 0-8103-5105-6, Order no.: 101936).
Author Biographies & Criticism. Single User Version.
Gale Research, Inc.

Discovering Jobs. Edited by Linda Thurn. Nov. 1995.
IBM. CD-ROM disk $495.00 (ISBN 0-8103-6473-5, Order no.: 102160).
Career Guidance Info, Job Descriptions, Single User.
Gale Research, Inc.

Discovering Music. Sep. 1995.
IBM. CD-ROM disk $79.95, incl. manual (ISBN 1-888743-00-X).
Computer Music Teaching CD-ROM.
Voyetra Technologies.

Discovering Psychology. *Version:* 2.1. C. M. Levy & M. Morgan. *Items Included:* 150 page of documentation. *Customer Support:* Free telephone support.
Apple II series, IBM PC & compatibles. disk $495.00.
Fifteen Programs Designed to Introduce Students to Classical Topics in Psychology in an Interesting Way. The Principal Purpose of These Programs Is to Show How Knowledge about Behavior Can Be Obtained in a Systematic, Objective Manner. After Working Through a Few Programs & Examining the Results, Students Should Have a Clear Understanding of the Empirical Method As It Applies to Specific Issues in Psychology.
Life Science Assocs.

Discovery. *Version:* 2.0. *Compatible Hardware:* Commodore Amiga.
$39.95.
Education Fun with Math, Spelling, & 19 Other Subjects.
Microillusions, Inc.

Discrete Probability I: Shape of Well-Known Distributions. Bruce E. Trumbo. 1983. *Compatible Hardware:* Apple II+, IIe, IIc. *Operating System(s) Required:* Apple DOS 3.3. *Language(s):* BASIC. *Memory Required:* 48k.
disk $50.00 (ISBN 0-933694-31-8, Order no.: COM 3106A).
Features Interactive Demonstrations with Graphics & Live Simulation Demonstrations. Interactive Access to a Variety of Computations Illustrate Statistical Analysis, Can Shift Focus from Computational Details to Models, Methods, Results & Consequences of Bad Data Points, etc.
COMPress.

Discrete Probability II: Simulations, Limit Theorems & Distribution Functions. Bruce E. Trumbo. 1983. *Compatible Hardware:* Apple II+, IIc, IIe. *Operating System(s) Required:* Apple DOS 3.3. *Language(s):* BASIC. *Memory Required:* 48k.
disk $50.00 (ISBN 0-933694-32-6, Order no.: COM 3107A).
Features Interactive Demonstrations with Graphics & Live Simulation Demonstrations. Interactive Hyper-Geometric Distributions Allow User to Select Parameter Values & See Mean, Variance, Probabilities & a Plot of Distribution. Graphic Display & Comparison Tables Show Approximations of Normal to Binomial, Binomial to Poisson.
COMPress.

DISDUP. *Compatible Hardware:* Atari 400, 800, 1200XL. *Operating System(s) Required:* DOS 2.0. *Language(s):* Machine. *Memory Required:* 24k.
disk $24.95 (ISBN 0-936200-21-9).
Designed to Copy Disk Sector Information. Allows User to Specify Single Sector, Range of Sectors, or All Sectors. Allows Copies to Be Made Without Read Verify.
Blue Cat.

disED. May 1990.
Amiga DOS 1.2 or higher. Amiga 1000, 500, 2000, 2500, or 3000 (512k). 3.5" disk $25.00.
A Very Small & Fast Text Editor with Full Menu & Mouse Support. Fully User Configurable. Multi-Tasking.
Dissidents.

Disilog. *Operating System(s) Required:* CP/M, SB-80. *Memory Required:* 64k.
disk $110.00.
Disassembler That Converts 8080/Z80 Machine Object Code into Zilog/Mostek Standard Assembly Language. Can Generate Source Output & List Output. Constructs a Cross-Reference Listing That Shows Label, Address, & Reference Type.
Lifeboat Assocs.

Disk Access Supervisor. *Compatible Hardware:* Apple II, II+. *Operating System(s) Required:* Apple DOS 3.2. *Language(s):* Applesoft II. *Memory Required:* 32k.
disk $24.95.
Allows User to Directly Manipulate Information Stored on the Disk.
Powersoft, Inc.

Disk Data Handler 64k. *Compatible Hardware:* TRS-80 Color Computer. *Language(s):* BASIC with Machine Language. *Memory Required:* 32k or 64k.
cassette $54.95.
Designed to Use the Full 64k of Machines in Which It Is Accessible, But Can Also Be Configured for a Standard 32k Machine. Uses the Standard ROM's - No Other Operating System Is Required. Serves As a Generalized Tool Which Allows Users to Design Disk Data Files for Their Own Specific Applications. Provides an On-Screen Editing Facility for Input & Updating of Data, a Capability for Selection & Sorting of Data, a Flexible Approach for Output of Reports on Screen or Printer, & an Ability to Output Information to Disk Files for Use by User Written Programs for Any Computational or Special Formatting Requirements.
Custom Software Engineering, Inc.

Disk Doctor. *Compatible Hardware:* Apple II, II+, IIe; Franklin Ace. *Operating System(s) Required:* Apple DOS 3.3. *Language(s):* BASIC. *Memory Required:* 32k.
disk $24.95.
Track-&-Sector Editor Lets User Read & Modify Apple Diskettes. Works on Diskettes Created by DOS 3.2, DOS 3.3, Pascal System, or Apple CP/M. Any Sector Can Be Displayed & Edited on the Screen. Includes Commands Which Allow Hard Copies of the Sector to Be Printed in 40 or 80 Column Format. Changes Can Be Character Data or Hex. Diskettes Can Be Tested & Verified.
Compuware.

Disk Double Entry. *Compatible Hardware:* TRS-80 Color Computer. *Language(s):* BASIC, Machine. *Memory Required:* 32k.
cassette $45.95.
Debit/Credit Transactions Entered in General Journal Format Are Used to Maintain Account Balances, Account Ledgers, Trial Balance Reports, Income Statements & Balance Sheets. Summary Reports May Be Produced up to 4 Levels of Subtotals. Designed So That Debits & Credits Are in Balance. Comments May Be Used.
Custom Software Engineering, Inc.

Disk Editor. *Compatible Hardware:* TRS-80.
contact publisher for price.
Instant Software, Inc.

Disk Library. *Compatible Hardware:* Apple II+. *Language(s):* Applesoft BASIC. *Memory Required:* 32k.
disk $24.95.
Allows the User to Locate Programs at a Rapid Rate. Features File Handling Capabilities That Permit the User to: List All Disk Titles in the Library; Add Program Names & Disk Titles to the Library; Delete Program Names & Disk Titles; Change Program Names, Program Location, & Disk Contents; List All Programs in the Library; & Search for a Program Alphabetically, by Disk Title, or by Program Name. Includes LIBRARY STARTER, Which Can Delete All Disk Library Text Files & Reformat the Disk for More Records.
Instant Software, Inc.

Disk Manager. *Compatible Hardware:* TI 99/4A. *Operating System(s) Required:* DX-10. *Language(s):* Extended BASIC. *Memory Required:* 48k.
disk $17.95.
Disk Catalog Program Which Displays Catalog Sorted by File Name. Size Parameters & Disk Names Are Also Displayed.
Eastbench Software Products.

Disk Manager. *Version:* 6.0. Apr. 1992. *Compatible Hardware:* IBM PC & compatibles, PC XT, PC AT, PS/2, 386, 486 or compatibles. *Operating System(s) Required:* PC-DOS/MS-DOS 2.0 & higher. *Memory Required:* Installation 640K, Device Driver 3k-7k, Dynamic Drive Overlay 4k. *Customer Support:* Technical support via phone.
disk 349.00-375.00.
Uses latest ASHRAE Residential & ACCA Manual "J" Procedures to Calculate Residential/Condominium Light Commercial Cooling/Heating Loads, Annual Energy Requirements & Operating Costs. Has direct access to ARI Equipment Data Disk Allows Comparison of Different Equipment Selections & Fuels. Accepts User Inputs of Commercial Construction Materials as Well as Calling the Complete ACCA List of Materials Automatically. Handles Heat Pumps, Multizone Systems, Mobile Homes, Cathedral Ceilings, Building Rotation, Radiant or Hot Air Heating; R-values to R-57. Gives Air CFM or Baseboard Heating Requirements. Saves Job General Data & Equipment Specifications for Late Use. Bin Method for Energy. Automatic Weather & Bin Data for 900 Cities. State-of-the-Art Full-Fuction Interactive Prompted Input Screens with Windows, Use of Mouse, Pop-up Calulator, Defaults,
Ontrack Computer Systems, Inc.

Disk Manager Mac & Kits. *Version:* 4.0. Jan. 1995. *Items Included:* Detailed manual. *Customer Support:* Technical support via telephone, Internet & BBS.
Macintosh System 6 & above. Supports Mac Plus & newer Macintosh Models including Power Macs. 3.5" disk $69.95.
Easily Installs & Completely Prepares Virtually Any SCSI or IDE Disk Drive, Read/Write Optical or Floptical Device for Use in Any Apple Macintosh Computer. User Can Verify & Partition Automatically, or with Product's Custom Installation Features, Tailor Device to Fit Specific Needs. Speeds Data Transfer Rate. Comes with Collection of Data Protection & Maintenance Utilities. Allows Users to Create Partitions up to 4 Gigabytes When Using System 7.5. Hardware Installation Kits Also Available. Includes Power Mac & SCSI Manager 4.3 Support.
Ontrack Computer Systems, Inc.

Disk Manager-N. *Version:* 3.12. May 1991. *Compatible Hardware:* IBM PC & compatibles, PC XT, PC AT, PS/2. *Operating System(s) Required:* Novell Netware. *Memory Required:* 128k. *General Requirements:* Novell Netware. *Customer Support:* Technical support via telephone, Internet & BBS.
disk $319.95.
Complete Hard Disk Drive Installation Package That Will Initialize, Partition, & Prepare Virtually Any Hard Disk Drive for Use in a NetWare 2.x File Server. Automates the Installation Process, & Safeguards Your Data Against Damage or Inaccessibility.
Ontrack Computer Systems, Inc.

Disk Master. *Customer Support:* 800-929-8117 (customer service).
MS-DOS. Apple II. disk $49.99 (ISBN 0-87007-830-5).
Keep a Complete & Detailed Catolog of User's Diskette Collection. Menu-Driven & Easy to Use.
SourceView Software International.

Disk Optimizer. *Version:* 5.0. Oct. 1985. *Compatible Hardware:* IBM PC & compatibles. *Operating System(s) Required:* PC-DOS/MS-DOS 2.0 or higher. *Memory Required:* 128k. *Customer Support:* 9:00 AM to 5:30 PM EST - (603) 644-5555.
disk $49.95.
Restores "Like New" Speed to Drive. The Reason it's Slowing Down is DOS Takes the Buckshot Approach to Storing Files' Fragments. In a Few Minutes, Disk Optimizer Can Reverse the Aging Process & Give Disk the Same Zip it Had When it Was New. The New Disk Optimizer Will Also Recover Accidentally Formatted Disks.
SoftLogic Solutions.

Disk Optimizer for Windows. Jul. 1993. *Items Included:* One manual, diskettes, & registration card. *Customer Support:* Telephone support available from 9:00am to 5:30pm EST - 603-644-5555.
DOS 3.3 or higher. IBM PC, XT, AT, PS/2 & compatibles or clone (480k Windows RAM). disk $49.95. *Addl. software required:* Windows 3.1 or higher.
New Disk Optimizer for Windows Is the Tune up for Your Hard Drive That Goes to Work When You Stop. Runs under Windows & Uses Spare Time When You're Not Working to Clean up the File Fragmentation That Can Slow down Your Hard Disk & Make Windows & All Your Programs Go Slower. Your Files Will Always Be Loading & Saving As Fast As Possible. Works When You Don't to Clean up the Mess That DOS Can Make of Your Disk.
SoftLogic Solutions.

Disk Ranger - Ranger Reader. *Version:* 4.7.1. *Compatible Hardware:* Apple Macintosh 512KE. $59.95, incl. both programs & pin-feed labels.
Hard & Floppy Disk Catalog & Label Utility.
Graham Software Co.

Disk Scope. *Compatible Hardware:* TRS-80 Model I. *Memory Required:* 32k.
disk $24.95 (Order no.: 139RD).
Locate Files on Disks, Display Track & Sector in Hexidecimal & ASCII, Gain Access to Any File by Constructing a Suitable Password.
Instant Software, Inc.

Disk-Tape Exchange. *Compatible Hardware:* TRS-80.
contact publisher for price.
Instant Software, Inc.

TITLE INDEX

Disk Technician. Version: 4. Eric Grasshoff & Norman Ivans. May 1990.
MS-DOS/PC-DOS (512k). disk $99.95 (ISBN 0-929594-06-1, Order no.: D3/5).
Disk Diagnostic & Recovery Software. Eliminates Data Drag, Brings Dead Disks Back to Life, Predicts Crashes, Recovers Data, Restores Down Systems, Prevents & Repairs Problems, Tests & Resets Interleave for Optimal Performance.
Disk Technician Corp.

Disk Technician Advanced. Version: 6. Eric Grasshoff & Norman Ivans. Sep. 1989.
MS-DOS/PC-DOS (512k). disk $149.95 (ISBN 0-929594-05-3, Order no.: DA3/5).
Disk Diagnostic & Recovery Software. Eliminates Data Drag, Brings Dead Disks Back To Life, Predicts Crashes, Recovers Data, Restores Down Systems, Prevents & Repairs Problems, Tests & Resets Interleave for Optimal Performance.
Disk Technician Corp.

Disk Technician Advanced: Automated A1 Software System. Eric Grasshoff & Norman Ivans. Jul. 1988. Operating System(s) Required: PC-DOS/MS-DOS.
disk $189.95 (Order no.: DT3-5).
3.5" disk $189.95 (Order no.: DT3-5/3).
Maintains Data, Keeps Programs up & Running, Prevents Power Problems from Damaging Data, Predicts Imminent Hardware Failure Before Data Is Lost & Speeds-Up Hard Disk System. No Technical Skills Needed.
Disk Technician Corp.

Disk Technician: Automated A1 Software System. Version: 2.0. Eric Grasshoff & Norman Ivans. Nov. 1987. Operating System(s) Required: PC-DOS/MS-DOS. Memory Required: 256k.
disk $99.95 (Order no.: DTI-4).
Maintains Data, Keeps Programs up & Running, Prevents Power Problems from Damaging Data, Predicts Imminent Hardware Failure Before Data Is Lost. No Technical Skills Needed.
Disk Technician Corp.

Disk Technician Gold. Aug. 1991.
PC/MS-DOS. IBM PC & compatibles (512k).
disk $149.95 (ISBN 0-929594-07-X).
Hard Disk Utility That Finds & Repairs Hard Disk Problems in the Background of Other Programs, Unattended. No Technical Skills Are Required. Once Installed, No Further User Intervention Is Required. A Memory-Resident Device Driver Provides Real-Time Error Detection, Repair, Data Recovery, Hardware Failure Prediction, Systems Diagnostics & Virus Prevention. Separate, Menu-Driven Program Provides Interleave Resetting, Nondestructive LLF & Manual Tests.
Disk Technician Corp.

Disk Technician +. Version: 2.0. Eric Grasshoff & Norman Ivans. Nov. 1987. Operating System(s) Required: PC-DOS/MS-DOS. Memory Required: 384k.
disk $129.95 (Order no.: DT2-4).
Maintains Data, Keeps Programs up & Running, Prevents Power Problems from Damaging Data, Predicts Imminent Hardware Failure Before Data Is Lost. No Technical Skills Needed.
Disk Technician Corp.

Disk Technician Pro. Eric Grasshoff & Norman Ivans. Sep. 1989.
MS-DOS/PC-DOS (512k). disk $99.95 (ISBN 0-929594-04-5, Order no.: DP3/5).
Disk Diagnostic & Recovery Software. Eliminates Data Drag, Brings Dead Disks Back to Life, Predicts Crashes, Recovers Data, Restores Down Systems, Prevents & Repairs Problems, Tests & Resets Interleave for Optimal Performance.
Disk Technician Corp.

Diskeeper. Version: 7.0. Aug. 1994. Items Included: Free Disk Analysis Utility which reports on the conditon of the disk. Free Companion Program "Control Master" which allows the monitoring & limiting of the system resources available to DISKEEPER/Plus. Users Guide & Quick Start Guide are both available in Bookreader online documentation format at no additional charge. Customer Support: 90 day warranty. Annual support & update service: 15% of the price for Single-Use License for the same CPU size. Faxed or written SPR handling. Yearly telephone support: 24 hour/7 days a week telephone support is an additional $750.00. Must have Annual Support & Update service.
VMS. DEC VAX & Alpha AXP machines (600 to 800 pages). $320.00 to $13,200.00 VAX; $2000.00 to $7105.00 Alpha AXP. Optimal configuration: DEC VAX/VMS or Alpha AXP running VMS. Networks supported: All Digital Equipment Corp.-supported cluster configurations including LAVC, CI, FDDI, DSSI, & mixed-interconnect.
Customized Online Disk Defragmenter Which Improves System Speed & Performance by Consolidating Fragmented Files & Spaces on the Disk. This reduces the System Slows & Resource Waste Which Result from Having to Retrieve & Store Fragmented Files. Using DISKEEPER Results in Disks That Are "Well Kept".
Executive Software.

Diskeeper Performance Edition. Jul. 1993. Items Included: Free Disk Analysis Utility which reports on the conditon of the disk. Free Companion Program "Control Master" which allows the monitoring & limiting of the system resources available to DISKEEPER. Customer Support: 90 day warranty. Annual support & update service: 15% of the price for Single-Use License for the same CPU size. Faxed or written SPR handling. Yearly telephone support: 24 hour/7 days a week telephone support is an additional $750.00. Must have Annual Support & Update service.
Open VMS. DEC VAX (700 to 900 pages). $400.00 to $16,500.00. Optimal configuration: Open VMS VAX.
Comprised of the Online Disk Defragmenter DISKEEPER in Combination with Fragmentation Controller. Consolidates Fragmented Files & Spaces on the Disk for Faster Read I/O. Fragmentation Controller Speeds Write I/O by Intercepting File Creations & Extensions & Modifying Them on the Way to the Disk. Performance Is Improved at Both Ends of the Operation.
Executive Software.

Diskette Cookbook Series. Version: 2.0. Compatible Hardware: IBM PC, PCjr, PC XT, PC AT. Items Included: 25 cookbooks. Customer Support: Yes.
disk $20.00.
most cookbooks $6.00 ea.
Transcription to Disk of 25 of the Most Popular Cookbooks. Users Can Search, Scale, & Print Recipes. Hard Disk Search Is Supported. User Can Create a Cookbook.
Vanilla Software.

Diskette Inventory System. Compatible Hardware: Atari 400, 800. Language(s): Atari BASIC. Memory Required: 24k.
disk $21.95.
Provides a Method for the User to Determine the Location of Single or Multiple Copies of Programs or Data Files in a Diskette Collection.
Dynacomp, Inc.

Diskette Manager II. Version: 2.X. Feb. 1985. Compatible Hardware: IBM PC & compatibles, PC XT, PC AT. Operating System(s) Required: PC-DOS 2.X, 3.X. Memory Required: 128k. General Requirements: 2 disk drives.
disk $79.95.
Library Program for Diskette Management with All the Features of DISKETTE MANAGER Plus an Additional File Management Feature Which Allows User to Generate a Complete Cross-Reference Report Between Files & Diskettes. Searches May Be Made Using Any Combination of DOS Wild Card Conventions.
Lassen Software, Inc.

Diskette Manager Plus. Version: 1.X. Oct. 1983. Compatible Hardware: IBM PC & compatibles, PC XT, PC AT with IBM or Epson Graftrax Plus printer & 2 disk drives. Operating System(s) Required: PC-DOS 2.x or 3.x. Memory Required: 128k. General Requirements: 2 disk drives; IBM or Epson Graphtrax Plus printer.
disk $59.95.
Library Program for Diskette Management. Prints Labels Containing Diskette Name, File Names, up to 8 Lines of Comments, & Storage Status of Each Diskette. Catalog File Is Constructed with Label Information, File Size & Storage Dates. Printed Reports Are Available in 4 Formats.
Lassen Software, Inc.

DiskExpress II. Version: 2.04.
DOS 6.0 or higher. Macintosh 512k, 512e, Plus, XL (1Mb). 3.5" disk $39.95.
Improves the Performance of the Macintosh Disk Drive. Gathers All the Pieces of Files Distributed in Blocks Across the Disk & Puts Them into Contiguous Blocks. All Unused Blocks Are Also Placed Together So That MacServe Users Will No Longer Encounter the "Disk Too Fragmented" Message When Attempting to Create New Volumes. Also Finds Media & Directory Errors, Recovers Missing Blocks, Compacts the Desktop File, & Secures Deleted Data. Supports Floppy & Hard Disks with Either MFS & HFL Formats.
ALSoft, Inc.

DISKGUISE. Jun. 1985. Operating System(s) Required: CP/M 2.2. Memory Required: 24k.
disk $38.00 (ISBN 0-924945-03-6, Order no.: 003).
Allows Files (Including Overlay Files) to Be Found Automatically on Different Drives &/or User Areas. Allows Swapping of Disk-Drive Names, & Transforming User Areas into Stand-Alone Disk-Drives.
Logic Assocs.

Disklock. Items Included: Manual. Customer Support: Free, toll call.
System 4.1 or higher. Mac Plus or higher. 3.5" disk $189.00.
Locks Macintosh Disks, Files & Folders with 3 Levels of Security.
Fifth Generation Systems, Inc.

Diskmap. Michael Wagner. Compatible Hardware: TRS-80.
disk $29.95.
Produces a Listing of Disk Space Allocation by Granule, & Produces a Listing of All Granules Allocated to Each Data File.
Blue Cat.

DiskMaster. Mar. 1988. Compatible Hardware: Commodore Amiga. Memory Required: 512k. 3.5" disk $49.95.
File Management Program Offering User the Ability to View & Manipulate up to 80 Files & Directories. Copy, Move, Rename & Print File Without Keying AmigaDOS into the CLI.
Progressive Peripherals & Software, Inc.

Diskmizer. Version: 1.1. Items Included: 1 manual & license PAK.
VMS 5.0 & higher. Digital VAX Family. $349.00-$30,000.00. Networks supported: Decnet, VAX

Cluster.
Uses Patented Real-Time Data Compression Technology, Proven in over 500,000 Installations Worldwide, That Works Quietly in the Background, Transparently & Automatically Compressing & Decompressing Data As Needed by Your Applications. Doubles the Storage Capacity of Your Computer's Hard Disk. Speed & Average Compression Ratio Rivals the Performance of Expensive Hardware Devices & in Many Cases Will Actually Improve the Performance of Your Hard Disk System.
Intersecting Concepts.

DISKPAK. *Compatible Hardware:* Atari 1200XL. *Operating System(s) Required:* Atari DOS 2.0. *Language(s):* Machine. *Memory Required:* 48k.
disk $24.95 (ISBN 0-936200-22-7).
Allows User to Store Files on the Sections of Boot Disks Which Are Normally Unused.
Blue Cat.

DiskQuick. Harry Bruce & Gene Hite. *Compatible Hardware:* Apple IIe, IIc, IIgs. *Operating System(s) Required:* Apple DOS 3.3. *Memory Required:* 128k.
disk $29.50.
Disk Drive Emulator. Creates a RAM Disk, Making the Apple Think a Disk Drive Is Connected to Slot 3.
Beagle Brothers.

Diskworld. *Compatible Hardware:* Apple Macintosh. *Memory Required:* 512k.
3.5" disk $9.95.
Monthly Software Subscription Filled with a Variety of Software of Value to Macintosh Users.
Softdisk, Inc.

Dispatch Management (a Part of ABECAS). *Version:* 3.3. *Customer Support:* On site training unlimited support services for first 90 days & through subscription thereafter.
MS-DOS, PC-DOS 3.x or higher. Contact publisher for price. *Nonstandard peripherals required:* Hard disk (30Mb); 132-column printer. *Networks supported:* Novell, NTNX, 10-Net, Unix, Xenix, Turbo DOS (Multi-User version for all).
Records Called Loads, Generates Dispatching Equipment & Assigns Loads to Equipment for Trips. 3-Way Screen Shows Loads, Equipment & Other Data. Loads & Equipment Can Be Organized by Various User-Selected Data Factors. Options Include Carrier/Area Use Search, Driver Trip Log Data, Driver Summary Hours, Safety Record & Customer Inquiry. Multiple Jobs Can Be Assigned Per Load. Mileage Tracked Automatically Through Pre-Entered Zip Codes.
Argos Software.

Dispatch Route Sales. *Customer Support:* 800-929-8117 (customer service).
MS-DOS. IBM/PS2. disk $1999.99 (ISBN 0-87007-676-0).
A Route Sales & Truck Inventory Control System for Larger & Smaller Size Route Sales Companies. Provides for Truck Reconcilliation & Sales Commission Reports. Produces a Route Performance Report, & Sales Analyses by Route, Product, District, & Line of Business As Well As by Customer. For Chain Stores, Dispatch Produces Sales Analysis for Each Individual Store & a Summary of the Chain in Total. This Is a Complete Accounting System That Includes Route Sales & Sales Analysis Systems, Accounts Receivable & Delinquent Accounts, Accounts Payable & Check Reconcilliation, General Ledger & Fixed Assets, Inventory Control & Open Order Reporting & Payroll.
SourceView Software International.

DisplayWrite 3 Tutorial. Troop & Woo. 1986. *Compatible Hardware:* IBM PC. *General Requirements:* Printer.
Template Diskette $29.95 (Order no.: W208-1).
Text/Workbook & Template Diskette Tutorial to Be Used with DisplayWrite 3.
South-Western Publishing Co.

DISTANL: Distribution Circuit Analysis. *Version:* 4.10. Dennis M. Levy. 1990. *Compatible Hardware:* IBM PC, PC XT, PC AT & compatibles. *Operating System(s) Required:* MS-DOS, PC-DOS. *Memory Required:* Without AUTOCAD interface, 410k, with AUTOCAD interface 540k. *General Requirements:* Hard disk, printer.
MS-DOS & PC-DOS. disk $5000.00 (ISBN 0-934795-00-2).
Provides a Means of Modeling & Analyzing a Utility's Primary Distribution System, Giving Utility Personnel the Information Necessary to Make Justifiable Operational & Planning Decisions. Facilitates Voltage & Loading Studies for Determining System Expansion Plans, Effect of a New Large Load, a Line Loss Analysis, a Power Factor Analysis & Fault Current Sectionalizing Studies.
Power System Engineering, Inc.

Distant Suns. *Version:* 2.0. 1990. *Items Included:* 1 manual. *Customer Support:* 90 days unlimited warranty; free telephone support.
Windows. IBM 386 25MHz & higher (4Mb). CD-ROM disk $69.95 (ISBN 1-886082-07-3, Order no.: DSW-295). *Optimal configuration:* 8Mb.
System 7. MAC (6Mb). CD-ROM disk $99.95 (ISBN 1-886082-08-1, Order no.: DSM-298). *Optimal configuration:* 8Mb.
Windows CD-ROM. 386 25 & higher (4Mb). CD-ROM disk $149.95 (ISBN 1-886082-09-X, Order no.: DSWCD-296). *Optimal configuration:* 486 & higher, 8Mb RAM.
System 7. MAC (4Mb). CD-ROM disk $149.95 (ISBN 1-886082-10-3, Order no.: DSMCD-299).
A Virtual Planetarium That Transports You Through Space & Time to Show You the Night Sky Exactly As It Appeared from Any Point in the Solar System, As Far Back As 4713 B.C. or As Far Forward As 10,000 A.D.
Virtual Reality Laboratories, Inc.

Distel. *Operating System(s) Required:* CP/M, SB-80. *Memory Required:* 64k.
disk $110.00.
Disassembler Which Converts 8080/Z80 Machine Code into Intel 8080 or PASM/TDL. Generates Source Output. Contructs a Cross-Reference Listing That Shows Label, Address & Reference Type.
Lifeboat Assocs.

Distributing. *Version:* 8A. Sep. 1993. *Compatible Hardware:* Altos, Radio Shack, IBM PC & compatible, UNISYS, NCR, IBM RT. *Operating System(s) Required:* PC-DOS/MS-DOS, Unix, Xenix; Novell, 3Com. *Language(s):* COBOL 85. *Memory Required:* Single user 1Mb, multi-user 5000k. *General Requirements:* Trac Line's Integrated Accounting software. *Customer Support:* Included with the support for the Integrated Accounting.
UNIX/XENIX, 3COM, Novell. disk $450.00.
MS-DOS. disk $800.00.
Offers Wholesaler Specialized Tasks above Basic Integrated Accounting. Activities Include: Ability to Run More Than One Company on the Same Accounting Software, Tracking & Maintaining Inventory at More Than One Warehouse or Internal Location, & Variable Pricing to Automatically Assign Customer Pricing Through 250 Different Pricing Routines. Icludes All Distribution Management Activities Special to the Wholesaler.
Trac Line Software, Inc.

Distribution Management System. Fisher Business Systems, Inc. *Compatible Hardware:* TI Professional. *Operating System(s) Required:* MS-DOS. *Memory Required:* 128k. *General Requirements:* Printer.
$99.00.
Includes Sales Order Entry, Purchase Management, Inventory Control, Billing, Accounts Receivable, Sales Commission Processing, Payroll, Accounts Payroll & General Ledger.
Texas Instruments, Personal Productivit.

District Attendance. *Version:* 8.00. 1992. *Items Included:* 1 full manual. *Customer Support:* 1 yr. maintenance $225.00.
MS-DOS 6.2 or higher. IBM-PC 486 & compatibles (640k). disk $995.00. *Nonstandard peripherals required:* 9600 Baud Modem. *Optimal configuration:* IBM-PC 486 w/4Mb RAM, SVGA monitor & card, DOS 6.2, 3.5" HD & 5.25" HD floppy drives, 200Mb hard drive. *Networks supported:* Novell Netware, Artisoft Lantastic, Windows NT.
The District Attendance System Is Used at the District or Superintendent's Office. Using a Modem, This System Will Download Daily Attendance Information & Student Data from All of the Schools in the District That Are Currently Using the Daily Attendance System. District Office Can Print Attendance Reports for the Entire District at Any Time after Importing Data from All of Its Schools.
Applied Educational Systems, Inc.

Ditch Hydraulics. 1980. *Compatible Hardware:* Apple II+. *Operating System(s) Required:* Apple DOS. *Language(s):* Applesoft BASIC (source code included). *Memory Required:* 48k.
disk $45.00.
Computes All Parameters of Any Ditch Hydraulics.
M.P.S. Co.

Diurnal Arc. *Compatible Hardware:* TI 99/4A with Extended BASIC. *Operating System(s) Required:* DX-10. *Language(s):* Extended BASIC. *Memory Required:* 48k.
cassette $16.95.
User Provides the Coordinates for Geographic Location & the Coordinates of Any Astronomical Body. Derives the Local Horizontal Coordinates for the Body Through Any Interval of the Sidereal Day.
Eastbench Software Products.

Diversi-DOS. *Compatible Hardware:* Apple II. *Operating System(s) Required:* Apple DOS 3.2, 3.3. *Language(s):* Applesoft BASIC. *Memory Required:* 48k.
disk $5.00.
documentation $3.00.
licensing fee $25.00.
Speeds up Disk Input/Output by a Factor of 3. Includes a Keyboard Buffer.
Dynacomp, Inc.

Diversified Computing Payroll. *Compatible Hardware:* AT&T 3B2; IBM PC & compatibles, PC XT, PC AT, System 36 PC. *Operating System(s) Required:* PC-DOS, UNIX. *Language(s):* BASIC (source code included). *General Requirements:* Wide carriage printer.
contact publisher for price.
Payroll Program.
Diversified Computing.

Diving Scorer. 1987. *Compatible Hardware:* IBM PC & compatibles. *Operating System(s) Required:* PC-DOS/MS-DOS. *Memory Required:* 128k. *Items Included:* Disk, instructions.
disk $49.95 (ISBN 0-926152-66-1).
Features Entry Registration, Scoring & Computation of Standings for Competitions at All Levels in Springboard & Platform Diving.
Persimmon Software.

TITLE INDEX

Divorce Planner. *Compatible Hardware:* IBM PC & compatibles. *Memory Required:* 512k. *General Requirements:* Free standing program.
$400.00 including taxes for one state.
$600.00 including taxes for several states.
Helps Lawyers & Financial Advisers Evaluate the Tax & Cash Flow Consequences of the Support Part of Divorce Agreements. Models Incorporate FICA & Federal Income Taxes, As Well As Those for 42 States & for New York City & Yonkers. Program Calculates Net Income & the Cash Available after Paying Support Payments, & Prints Report Showing the Parties' Interrelated Financial Figures.
FinPlan Co.

Divorce Yourself: The National No-Fault Divorce Kit. (The/Legal Self-Help Ser.). Daniel Sitarz. Oct. 1995.
IBM. 3.5" disk $12.95 (ISBN 0-935755-25-X).
Contains All of the Legal Forms & Documents Necessary to Obtain a No Fault Divorce in Any State.
Nova Publishing Co.

Divorce Yourself: The National No-Fault Divorce Kit. (Legal Self-Help Ser.). Daniel Sitarz. Apr. 1996.
IBM. 3.5" disk $12.95 (ISBN 0-935755-21-7).
Forms-On-Disk - Containing All of the Legal Forms Necessary to Obtain a No-Fault Divorce.
Nova Publishing Company.

DLB/Plus. *Version:* 4.0. Dec. 1989. *Items Included:* Media, Comb bound installation & user manual. *Customer Support:* 30 day support which includes toll free hot line; varies for one year thereafter.
VMS 4.7 or higher. DEC VAX family (256k). $300.00-$7500.00.
A Software Utility That Analyzes Disk File I/O & Lock Usage & Dynamically Tunes Operating Parameters on All VAX/VMS Systems. Also Prevents Disk Fragmentation.
Touch Technologies, Inc.

DLDIS: Disk-Based Labeling Disassembler. *Compatible Hardware:* TRS-80.
contact publisher for price.
Instant Software, Inc.

DME by Dagar. *Version:* 302. 1986. *Compatible Hardware:* Altos; IBM PC. *Operating System(s) Required:* MP/M-86, CP/M-86, MS-DOS, Concurrent DOS. *Memory Required:* 512k.
stand alone $5000.00.
option to Dagar Universal Pharmacy Software Package $3600.00.
Designed to Provide Inventory Control for Durable Medical Equipment. Also Includes Rental, Delivery, Sales, Inventory, & Fully Automatic Third Party Billing of Monthly Rental Charges. Available As Standalone Package or As Add-On to to DAGAR UNIVERSAL PHARMACY SOFTWARE PACKAGE.
Dagar-Software Development Corp.

DME-XPRESS. *Version:* 1.30. Sep. 1992. *Items Included:* Operator Manual, AcuCobol Runtime & Utilities. *Customer Support:* Monthly support $125.00 - support provided via telecommunications, documentation & on site visits. Support contract provides product enhancements at no additional charge.
Multi-user: Digital Research CCDOS 3.2 or higher; Single user: MS-DOS Version 3.3 or higher. IBM compatible 80X86 (2Mb). Platform dependent. *Nonstandard peripherals required:* Multiport board required for multi-user. *Optimal configuration:* IBM RISC System/6000, AIX Version 3.2, IBM 150Mb tape, IBM 3151; terminals as required, 132 column printer. *Networks supported:* DOS networks.

Designed to Facilitate the Process of Sales & Rentals of Durable Medical Equipment Products, File Claims by Paper & Electronically & Provide an Effective Method of Managing the Receivables Process. The Primary Goal of the System Is to Reduce the Time Between Service Rendered & Payment Received.
DataHouse, Inc.

dMERGE. Quality Computing Systmes, Inc. *Compatible Hardware:* TI Professional. *Operating System(s) Required:* MS-DOS, CP/M-86. *Memory Required:* 64k. *General Requirements:* dBASE II, printer.
$99.00.
dBASE II Utility Package That Allows Merger of dBASE II Data Files into a Document File on Disk & Prints the Merged Documents.
Texas Instruments, Personal Productivit.

DMP7 & DMP11 Pro. *General Requirements:* MIDI interface; Yamaha DMP7 or DMP11. Macintosh (1Mb). DMP11 $395.00.
DMP11 Pro $295.00.
Integrates Editors, Librarians & Intelligence Real-Time Controllers.
Digital Music Services.

DMS - III. *Compatible Hardware:* IBM PC, PC XT, PC AT, & compatibles, PS/2. *Operating System(s) Required:* PC-DOS/MS-DOS. *Language(s):* Compiled MBASIC. *Memory Required:* 256k. *General Requirements:* 2 floppy disk drives or hard disk.
disk $295.00.
Creates & Manages Databases. Menus Will Lead the User Through Computing Creation, & Allow User-Defined Procedures & Reports. Each New User Definition Will Automatically Redefine the Menu to Reflect the Changes. Uses Multiple Logical Operators for Record Selection, & Allows 60 Characters per Field, 60 Fields per Record, & up to 32,000 Records per File, Depending on Disk Capacity. Converses with a Variety of Word Processing Software, Such As WordStar.
Utility Billing Specialists.

dms4Cite: Document Management System for Citations. *Version:* 5.30. Eric Martz & Rudolph Jaeger. Jun. 1991. *Items Included:* Disks, manual & license agreement. *Customer Support:* Free telephone consultation during the first year followed by a $50 annual maintenance fee which includes updates.
MS-DOS. IBM PC & compatibles (640K). disk $295.00. *Nonstandard peripherals required:* Hard disk.
Personal Bibliographic Reference Management System. It Is Menu-Driven with Extensive On-Line Help to Assist in Building, Editing, Searching & Citing the World's Scientific Literature in Fields. Easily Formats References for Publication in Leading Scientific Journals. Accepts References & Abstracts Downloaded by Phone from Public Databases (e.g., National Library of Medicine), Chemical Abstracts, etc." Free Demo Disk Available.
Sidereal Technologies, Inc.

The DNA Inspector IIe. *Version:* 3.16. *Compatible Hardware:* Macintosh Plus, System 6 or 7. *General Requirements:* Hard disk. *Items Included:* 2 disks, manual, disk holder. *Customer Support:* Telephone support.
3.5" disk $345.00.
DNA Analysis Software.
Textco.

DNA Music. *Version:* 2.0. *Compatible Hardware:* Commodore Amiga. *Items Included:* Source code. *Customer Support:* Telephone support.
3.5" disk $19.95.
Music Based upon DNA Molecule.
Silver Software.

DOC IN THE BOX: THE MEDICAL SELF

DNA/RNA Builder. *Version:* 2.0. *Items Included:* Diskette & manual. *Customer Support:* Telephone inquiries.
MAC-DOS (1Mb). Macintosh, all models. disk $199.00.
Generate 3-D Perspective Views of Double or Single-Stranded DNA or RNA Starting with a Simple 1-Letter Sequence Listing. Program Includes Literature Structures for A, B, & C Helixes, or Define Your Own Helix & Base Dihedral Angles. Images May Be Printed or Pasted into Most Word-Processing Programs (Color Mac-II).
Atlantic Software.

DNS Crew Requirements Model. *Version:* 3.1. Jul. 1990. *Items Included:* Manual, source code in C. *Customer Support:* On site training & 1 year maintenance & phone support included. Extended maintenance $3000/year.
MS-DOS. IBM Compatible 386-387 or 486 computer (2Mb). $20,000.00 corporate license (Order no.: 913100). *Addl. software required:* Phar Lap Tools.
Product Simulates Crew Assignments Under Variations of Work Rules, Crew Districts, & Operating Plans, & Shows the Number of Crews & Total Work Units for Each Scenario.
DNS Assocs., Inc.

Do-It-Yourself Adventure Kit & Dormac's Castle. *Compatible Hardware:* TRS-80 Model I, Model III, Model 4 with Level II BASIC. *Language(s):* BASIC (source code included). *Memory Required:* 48k.
disk $29.95.
Enables Users to Build a Modestly Sized Adventure Program. Allows 94 Rooms with 4 Doors, 4 Key Rooms, 2 Disaster Rooms, Darkness Rooms, 15 Help Objects, 10 Treasures, Creatures, Traps, etc.
Dynacomp, Inc.

Doane/Equipment. *Version:* 4.2. *Compatible Hardware:* IBM PC & compatibles. *Memory Required:* 256k. *Customer Support:* 60/hr phone; modem.
disk $1995.00.
Equipment Management, Scheduling, & Recordkeeping System Designed to Help Control Equipment Costs. Will Alert the Users When the Next Maintenance Operation Will Take Place Based on a Recommended Schedule. The Program Maintains an Equipment & Parts Inventory with Purchase Summary, Reorder Report, & Parts-Use Summary. Can Be Integrated with a Cost Accounting System.
Doane Agricultural Services Co.

Doane System for Nurseries & Landscape. *Items Included:* Manual, workbook, demo information, & tutorial. *Customer Support:* $60 per hour for telephone support; 9% annual maintenance based on retail price software; 90 days free support; online help.
MS-DOS. IBM & compatibles (384K). modules start from $750.00 to complete turnkey systems for $11,000.00. *Networks supported:* Novell, Lantastic.
Accounting: Management Program Specially Designed for the Wholesale Nursery& Landscape Contractors. Includes Full Accounting, Inventory, Bidding & Job Costing. Written with Powerful Database Providing Easily Created Reports for Additional Information.
Doane Agricultural Services Co.

Doc in the Box: The Medical Self-Diagnosis Program. Jun. 1994. *Items Included:* Registration card, instruction sheet. *Customer Support:* 900 support number $2.00 per minute; limited 60 day warranty.
DOS. IBM PC & compatibles (192k). disk $9.95

(ISBN 1-57269-000-3, Order no.: 3202 42005). *Addl. software required:* DOS 2.1 or higher. *Optimal configuration:* Single floppy drive. Hard disk drive recommended.
The Best & Easiest-to-Use Medical Reference You Can Own. Simply Choose the Symptoms You Are Experiencing from the Program Tables. Logical Diagnosis & the Appropriate Recommended Treatment Approaches Will Appear on the Screen.
Memorex Products, Inc., Memorex Software Division.

Doc Monitor.
Macintosh Plus or higher. 3.5" disk $219.95.
Checks All Online Volumes for Old Documents to Offline Backup Media.
OITC, Inc.

Dock-It. *Compatible Hardware:* Commodore 64, 128. *General Requirements:* Standard EMG or Biofeedback EMG Sensor.
ROM cartridge $19.95 (Order no.: SOFC64-04-005).
By Using Two Muscle Groups, the Player Controls Four Different Space Ships & Docks Them. A Timing Mechanism Is in Operation During the Game Sequence & Can Be Adjusted to Suit Different Ability Levels. The Game Requires Muscle Coordination & Speed.
Bodylog.

Docket. *Version:* 2.0. Dec. 1988. *Operating System(s) Required:* PC-DOS/MS-DOS, OS/2, Windows. *Memory Required:* 2000k. *General Requirements:* Hard disk.
$495.00 to $1495.00.
System Automatically Generates the Calendar of Critical Dates (Obligations) for the Administration of Estates & Trusts. Recurring Obligations Are Generated Automatically & Due Dates Are Adjusted for Saturdays, Sundays & Holidays. The Calendars May Be Printed by Client, Responsible Party & Supervisor.
Computer Decisions Corp.

Docket & Multiuser Docket. *Version:* 4.0. 1993. *Compatible Hardware:* IBM PC & compatibles. *Operating System(s) Required:* PC-DOS; Networks such as Novell, Lantastic. *Customer Support:* 30 days' free support, 1 yr. maintenance $250.00.
disk $495.00.
$795.00 Multiuser Docket.
Time Management Software System for Attorneys. Produces Calendars of Appointments, Critical Dates, Deadlines & Things-to-Do with Self-Imposed Deadlines. Includes User-Defined Templates to Enter Series of Events. Account or Project Reports of Everything Docketed to Be Done on a Particular Case or Project Are Also Produced. Attorney Can Use the Quick Calendar Call up to Go Straight to His Current Calendar. Multiuser Docket Is Available for Networked Systems.
Micro Craft, Inc.

Docket Calendar/Critical Dates. *Version:* 2.5. 1985. *Compatible Hardware:* IBM PC, PC XT, PC AT & compatibles, PS/2. *Operating System(s) Required:* PC-DOS 2.1 or higher. *Language(s):* Pascal. *Memory Required:* PC-DOS 2.1 256k, PC-DOS 3.0 or higher 320k. *General Requirements:* 2 disk drives or hard disk.
disk $495.00-$795.00.
Supports up to 80 Attorneys. Will Keep Track of All Important Appointments & Deadlines, Including Perpetual Dates & Reminders. The "Macro" Facility Enables Users to Schedule up to Eleven Events Associated with a Single Event. Scheduling & Work Flow Can Be Sorted by Virtually Any Category & Printed Out or Displayed on the Monitor. Allows Unlimited Memoranda with Each Entry. Each Entry Is Checked to Make Sure That the Time-Keeper Assigned Is Available to Work on the Project.
CompuLaw, Ltd.

Docket Control-Calendaring. *Version:* 1.0. Jun. 1985. *Compatible Hardware:* IBM PC & compatibles. *Operating System(s) Required:* PC-DOS. *Language(s):* COBOL. *Memory Required:* 512k. *General Requirements:* Hard disk, printer. *Items Included:* Disks, manuals, 90 days of support. *Customer Support:* Direct from Morningstar.
disk $295.00 single-user; $395.00 multi-user.
Complete Appointment Scheduling Package Intended for Improved Time Management. Includes Report Generator for up to 99 Different "User Defined" Report Formats.
Morningstar Technology Corp.

Doctor. *Compatible Hardware:* TI 99/4A with Extended BASIC. *Operating System(s) Required:* DX-10. *Language(s):* Extended BASIC. *Memory Required:* 48k.
User Speaks with the "Doctor" to Obtain His Advice on a Host of Matters.
Eastbench Software Products.

Doctor Ami. Jun. 1990. *Customer Support:* 90 day defective warranty, free technical support at 215- 683-5609.
Amiga DOS. Amiga (512k). 3.5" disk $49.95.
An Amiga Memory & Hard Drive Diagnostic Utility That Performs Low-Level Tests on Your System Using an Elegant Interface with Simple Controls & Displays. Consists of Two Programs, Memory Doctor & Drive Doctor.
Free Spirit Software, Inc.

Dr. Chips. *Compatible Hardware:* Apple II, TRS-80.
disk $20.00.
cassette $15.00.
Computerized Psychoanalyst. Asks Questions, Helps Answer Them & Analyzes Dreams.
Instant Software, Inc.

Dr. Dobb's Essential HyperTalk Handbook. Michael Swaine. *Compatible Hardware:* Apple Macintosh.
book & disk $39.95 (ISBN 0-934375-99-2).
book only $24.95 (ISBN 0-934375-98-4).
Reference Covering Topics Such As the Object-Oriented Program on Which HyperTalk Is Based, the Move from Authoring to Scripting, Programming Style Considerations, Useful Components, & Interfacing to Other Languages. Included Is a Reference Section & a "Programmer's Peg Board," Which Is a Library of Reusable Components Such As Resources, Scripts, & Objects. All Programs Are Available on Disk.
M & T Bks.

Dr. Dobb's Toolbook of Forth, Vol. I. Edited by Marlin Ouverson. *Operating System(s) Required:* MS-DOS.
book & disk $39.95 (ISBN 0-934375-57-7).
book only $22.95 (ISBN 0-934375-10-0).
Collection of Useful Forth Programs & Tutorials Which Contains Expanded & Revised Versions of Dr. Dobb's Journal of Software Tools' Best Forth Articles, along with New Material. Contents Include: Mathematics in Forth, Modifications/ Extensions, Forth Programs, Forth - the Language, & Implementing Forth. There Are Also Appendixes That Will Help Users Convert fig-Forth to Forth-83. The Screens in the Book Are Available on Disk As ASCII Files in MS-DOS Format.
M & T Bks.

Dr. Dobb's Toolbook of Forth, Vol. II. Editors of Dr. Dobb's Journal. *Operating System(s) Required:* MS-DOS.
book & disk $45.95 (ISBN 0-934375-51-8).
book only $29.95 (ISBN 0-934375-41-0).
Anthology of Forth Programming Techniques & Development. Includes the Best Articles on Forth from Dr. Dobb's Journal of Software Tools, along with Material from Other Forth Experts. Topics Include: Forth Philosophy & Standards, Programming Windows, Extended Control Structures, the Design of a Forth Target Compiler, etc. The Screens in the Book Are Available on Disk As ASCII Files.
M & T Bks.

Dr. Dobb's Toolbook of 80286/80386 Programming. Edited by Phillip Robinson. *Operating System(s) Required:* MS-DOS.
book & disk $39.95 (ISBN 0-934375-53-4).
book only $24.95 (ISBN 0-934375-42-9).
Discussion of the 80x86 Family of Microprocessors. Features Opinions on the Environments, Operating Systems, Tricks, Clues, & Pitfalls of 80x86 Programming.
M & T Bks.

Dr. Dobb's Z80 Toolbook. David E. Cortesi. *Operating System(s) Required:* MS-DOS.
book & disk $40.00 (ISBN 0-934375-55-0).
book only $25.00 (ISBN 0-934375-07-0).
Contains Information Programmers Need in Order to Write Z80 Assembly Language Programs. Includes a Method of Designing Programs & Coding Them in Assembly Language, & a Demonstration of the Method Used in the Construction of Several Programs. Also Included Is an Integrated Toolkit of Subroutines for Arithmetic, String-Handling, & Control of the CM/M File System.
M & T Bks.

Dr. Dumont's Wild P.A.R.T.I. Michael & Muffy Berlyn. *Compatible Hardware:* IBM PC, Apple Macintosh.
IBM PC. disk $39.95 (Order no.: 01003).
Macintosh. 3.5" disk $39.95 (Order no.: 04003).
What If Your Mind Was Directly Hooked up to a Machine? Your Job Is to Teach This Machine How to See, Hear, & Perceive Reality. Then, What If You Discovered That the Machine Was Insane, & Its Insanity Began to Infect You? From the Designer Who Brought You Such Imaginative Hits As "Tass Times in Tonetown" & "Cyborg".
First Row Software Publishing.

Dr. HALO IV Imaging Pak. *Version:* 1.5. Sep. 1991. *Items Included:* Operation manual. *Customer Support:* 90-day warranty, technical support.
DOS. PS/2 & above or compatible (512k). $140.00 (Order no.: DH4). *Nonstandard peripherals required:* Graphics card.
Comprehensive Family of Graphics & Imaging Programs for Editing & Manipulating Images from Many Sources. Includes Sophisticated Paint Program; the Viewer File Conversion Utility; the Presents Slide Show Program; the Grab Screen Capture Utility; & a Font Editor for Customizing Users Own Fonts, Symbols or Logos.
Media Cybernetics, Inc.

Dr. Know. 1987. *Items Included:* 3 ring binder with program disk(s), teacher's guide & reproducible student worksheets. *Customer Support:* Phone support (805) 473-7383.
Apple II (128k). $59.95 single, $109.95 5-user, $159.95 10-user, $359.95 30-user (SL/Ntwk) (ISBN 0-917623-24-X). *Networks supported:* All.
Shows How a Computer Can Be Used to Simulate Thinking. Tool for Exploring the Potential for Artificial Intelligence (AI) in the

TITLE INDEX

Classroom & Will Help Students Keep up with the Latest Developments in Computer Technology. Includes Logic, Expert Systems, & Challenging Games.
Ventura Educational Systems.

Dr. LOGO. Digital Research. Jun. 1985. *Compatible Hardware:* TI Professional. *Operating System(s) Required:* CP/M-86, Concurrent CP/M-86. *Memory Required:* 128k. *General Requirements:* 2 disk drives.
$150.00.
Checks Command & Statement Syntax As Program Line Entered. Program Lines Translated into Condensed, Internal Line.
Texas Instruments, Personal Productivit.

Dr. Pascal. *Version:* 2.0. Nov. 1988. *Compatible Hardware:* IBM PC, IBM PS/2, DEC Rainbow, VAX, SPARC. *Operating System(s) Required:* PC-DOS/MS-DOS, VMS, UNIX. *Language(s):* Pascal. *Memory Required:* 512k. *Items Included:* 185 page manual.
disk $89.00 ea. for PC; VAX $800.00 plus; student pricing available.
IBM PC, PC-DOS. (ISBN 0-941897-00-1).
DEC Rainbow, MS-DOS. (ISBN 0-941897-02-8).
Programming System for Standard Pascal Which Integrates an Editor, an Interpreter, & a Visible Capability. By Showing the Inner Operation of a Running Program, Program Facilitates Understanding of Programming Concepts & Reduces Debugging Time.
Visible Software.

Dr. Ruth's Game of Good Sex. *Compatible Hardware:* Apple II+, IIe, IIc; Commodore 64/128; IBM PC & compatibles; Tandy 1000.
disk $29.95 ea.
Apple. (Order no.: 45852).
IBM. (Order no.: 45854).
Commodore. (Order no.: 45855).
One or More Adult Players Answer True-False or Multiple Choice Questions Relating to Each Other's Sexual Awareness.
Avalon Hill Game Co., The Microcomputer Games Div.

Dr. Solomon's Anti-Virus Toolkit. *Version:* 6.XX (updated monthly). Alan Solomon & United Kingdom - S&S International Staff. Jun. 1992. *Customer Support:* Free on-line support.
DOS 3.x or higher. PC/AT/or Microchanel. disk $149.95. *Networks supported:* All Novell & DOS based peer to peer. Any network accessed by a DOS workstation.
Windows, OS/2, Netware. Contact publisher for price.
Contact publisher for price, quarterly & monthly updates.
Offers the Most Comprehensive Treatment & Preventative Maintenance System Available to Combat Computer Virus Infections. Detects or Identifies All Known Viruses & Variants Including Stealth & Polymorphic Viruses - & Does So Quickly & Safely.
Ontrack Computer Systems, Inc.

Dr. Solomon's Audit. *Version:* 1.3. S&S International PLC. Mar. 1994. *Items Included:* Spiral bound manual. *Customer Support:* 12 months free technical support; thereafter 15% of purchase per annum.
MS-DOS & MS-Windows. 486 DX/33 IBM PC & compatibles (6Mb). $695.00 managers pack workstation license (Order no.: 714-840-4656). *Optimal configuration:* 486 DX/33 PC, 6Mb RAM, MS-DOS 3.1 & MS-Windows 3.1. *Networks supported:* Any DOS compatible network.
Provides Comprehensive Software Auditing Across Networks or on Standalone PCs to Enable System Administrators to Maintain an Accurate Record of Installed Licenses, Which in Turn Ensures That Your Organization Stays Within the Software Licensing Laws.
Computer Security Corp.

Dr. Solomon's RingFence. *Version:* 1.1. S&S International PLC. Mar. 1994. *Items Included:* Spiral bound manual. *Customer Support:* 12 months free technical support; thereafter 15% of purchase per annum.
MS-DOS, MS-Windows. Any PC with a hard disk (640k). $29.00 to $11.00 depending on quantity (Order no.: 714-840-4656). *Optimal configuration:* Any PC with a hard disk, DOS 3.1 or higher, 20k free disk space, 3k free memory for TSR. *Networks supported:* Novell 3.XX.
Stops Viruses Before They Start by Controlling Floppy Disks in, Out & Around Your Organization. Using Diskette Authorization & Optional Data Encryption, RingFence Ensures That Only Approved Diskettes Are Used & Confidential Data & Programs Are Secure.
Computer Security Corp.

Dr. Term Professional. *Compatible Hardware:* Commodore Amiga 500, 1000, 2000.
3.5" disk $99.95.
Telecommunications Program Which Provides XMODEM, YMODEM, & WXMODEM Protocols, Features 40 Different Macros Accessible from the Function Keys, Pull-Down Menus & a Script Language. Users Can Store Up to 300 Entries in a Phone Book, & Include Parameters with Each Entry. Provides Multi-Level Password Protection.
Progressive Peripherals & Software, Inc.

Dr. T's Sing-A-Long Around the World. Jun. 1994. *Items Included:* 36-page full-color songbook with lyrics to all songs in English & original language of each song. *Customer Support:* Free unlimited technical support.
Windows 3.1. IBM (386 or higher) (4Mb). CD-ROM disk $29.95 (ISBN 1-885769-01-6).
Nonstandard peripherals required: Sound card, CD-ROM drive.
Dr. T's Music Software, Inc.

Dr. T's Sing-a-Long Around the World. Sep. 1995. *Customer Support:* Telephone support - free (except phone charge).
Windows 3.1. IBM & compatibles (386 DX-20) (4Mb). CD-ROM disk $12.99 (ISBN 1-57594-006-X). *Nonstandard peripherals required:* 2x CD-ROM player, Sound Card, VGA monitor. *Optimal configuration:* 486 SX-33.
An Adventure in the Music & Culture of the World.
Kidsoft, Inc.

Dr. T's Sing-a-Long Around the World. Sep. 1995. *Customer Support:* Telephone support - free (except phone charge).
Windows 3.1. IBM & compatibles (386 DX-20) (4Mb). CD-ROM disk $12.99 (ISBN 1-57594-045-0). *Nonstandard peripherals required:* 2x CD-ROM player, Sound Card, VGA monitor. *Optimal configuration:* 486 SX-33.
An Adventure in the Music & Culture of the World. Blister Pack Jewel Case.
Kidsoft, Inc.

Dr. T's Sing-A-Long Kids' Classics. Dec. 1993. *Items Included:* 48-page full-color songbook with lyrics & musical score. *Customer Support:* Free unlimited technical support.
Windows 3.1. IBM (386 or higher) (4Mb). CD-ROM disk $29.95 (ISBN 1-885769-00-8).
Nonstandard peripherals required: Sound card, CD-ROM drive.
Dr. T's Music Software, Inc.

Dr. T's Sing-a-Long Kid's Classics. Sep. 1995. *Customer Support:* Telephone support - free (except phone charge).
Windows 3.1. IBM & compatibles (386 DX-20) (4Mb). CD-ROM disk $12.99 (ISBN 1-57594-007-8). *Nonstandard peripherals required:* 2x CD-ROM player, Sound Card, VGA monitor. *Optimal configuration:* 486 XS-33.
An Animated Karaoke for Kids.
Kidsoft, Inc.

Dr. T's Sing-a-Long Kid's Classics. Sep. 1995. *Customer Support:* Telephone support - free (except phone charge).
Windows 3.1. IBM & compatibles (386 DX-20) (4Mb). CD-ROM disk $12.99 (ISBN 1-57594-046-9). *Nonstandard peripherals required:* 2x CD-ROM player, Sound Card, VGA monitor. *Optimal configuration:* 486 SX-33.
An Animated Karaoke for Kids. Blister Pack Jewel Case.
Kidsoft, Inc.

The Doctor's Book of Home Remedies.
Macintosh. CD-ROM disk $39.95. *Nonstandard peripherals required:* CD-ROM drive.
Features Medical Information, Medical Alert, & Personal Interactive Checkup Section. Contains a Database of over 2000 Practical Cures, 25 Minutes of Full-Motion Video & Detailed Medical Illustrations.
Compton's NewMedia, Inc.

Doctor's Collections Manager & Bookkeeper. Larry Friedman & Steven Friedman. May 1989. *Items Included:* Diskettes, manual, book/folder, 8 1/2" x 11" pages of each application & Form. *Customer Support:* 30 day exchange or refund if package seals unopened.
MS-DOS (256k). IBM compatible. 5.25" disk $84.00 (ISBN 1-877766-04-6, Order no.: COLL-5). *Addl. software required:* Wordprocessor, Spreadsheet - Lotus 123 compatible. *Optimal configuration:* Form generator software.
3.5" disk $84.00 (ISBN 1-877766-05-4, Order no.: COLL-3).
$44.00, manual only (ISBN 1-877766-06-2, Order no.: COLL-M).
Step-by-Step Training Outlines. Preauth & Dual Insurance Organizer, Patient & Insurance Payments, Duties of Insurance Staff, Collection Forms & Letters, 4 Bills & Statements. Legal & Small Claims Steps, Checklists, collection & Accounts Receivable, Correspondences. BOOKKEEPING: Payroll Ledger, Monthly & Yearly Prod/Coll., Yearly TAX Planner, Chart of Accounts & Check Register, Petty Cash Receipts, Spreadsheets for Ease in TAX Prep. Not Copy-Protected.
On the Mark Computer Software Co.

Doctor's Computer Organizer. Larry Friedman & Steven Friedman. May 1989. *Items Included:* Diskettes, manual, book/folder, 8 1/2" x 11" pages of each application & form. *Customer Support:* 30 day exchange or refund if package seals unopened.
MS-DOS (256k). IBM compatible. $54.00 (ISBN 1-877766-07-0, Order no.: CHPT-5). *Addl. software required:* Work processor. *Optimal configuration:* Form generator program.
$54.00 (ISBN 1-877766-08-9, Order no.: CHPT-3).
$28.00, manual only (ISBN 1-877766-09-7, Order no.: CHPT-M).
One Page Reference Sheets on Each Computer Topic. Insert These Pages & Forms in Your Own OFFICE MANUAL! Customize Your Own Forms Using These As Guidelines. Easy to Read & with Pictures. Most Every Manual Is Dry & Dull, but NOT This Fun Manual! Reinforce Your Way of Programming! Be Professional with Your Time on

the Computer & the Training of Your Staff. Make the Doctor Appear to be the Computer Expert to the New Staff Member! Not Copy-Protected.
On the Mark Computer Software Co.

Doctor's Contacts & Filebox Address & Phone Manager. Larry Friedman & Steven Friedman. May 1989. *Items Included:* Diskettes, manual, book/folder, 8 1/2" x 11" pages of each application & form. *Customer Support:* 30 day exchange or refund if package seals unopened.
MS-DOS (256k). IBM compatible. $64.00 (ISBN 1-877766-11-9, Order no.: CONT-5). *Addl. software required:* Word processor, PC-FILE+ or PC-FILE:dB or dBASE III. *Optimal configuration:* 512k ram, hard disk.
$64.00 (ISBN 1-877766-11-9, Order no.: CONT-3).
$24.00, manual only (ISBN 1-877766-12-7, Order no.: CONT-M).
DATA BASES for: Friends, CPR Courses, Restaurants, Stores, Laboratories, Magazines & Subsriptions, Zip Codes, Area Codes, Foreign Friends, & More. HANDOUTS for Patients: Specialists - Surgeons, Orthodontists, Professionals, Resources, Video Lending Library, & More. These Most Useful Topics Are Easily Accessible. Why Reinvent the Wheel Yourself, Just Use These As Is, or Clone Them to Fit Your Exact Specifications. Not Copy-Protected.
On the Mark Computer Software Co.

Doctor's Demo Disk. Larry Friedman & Steven Friedman. May 1989. *Items Included:* Diskettes, manual, book/folder, 8 1/2" x 11" pages of each application & form. *Customer Support:* 30 day exchange or refund if package seals unopened.
MS-DOS (256k). IBM compatible. $14.00 (ISBN 1-877766-13-5, Order no.: DEMO-5). *Addl. software required:* Word Processor. *Optimal configuration:* PC-FILE+ or PC-FILE:dB or dBASE III.
$14.00 (ISBN 1-877766-14-3, Order no.: DEMO-3).
$14.00, manual only (ISBN 1-877766-15-1, Order no.: DEMO-M).
Doctor, Dentist, & Health Professionals- by Computer: Analyze 545 Fees; Employee Wages & Benefits; Reorder Supplies; Humor, Songs & Rhymes; Training & Organizational Aids for New Staff; Step-by-Step Outlines & Checklists; Inexpensive Recall System; Tray Set-ups & Color Coding; Inventory; Insurance Organizer; Menu Program; Management aids; Well-organized & Fast- reading. Customize & Create New Forms Easily. Samples Enclosed. Not Copy-Protected.
On the Mark Computer Software Co.

Doctor's Inventory Organizer. Larry Friedman & Steven Friedman. May 1989. *Items Included:* Diskettes, manual, book/folder, 8 1/2" x 11" pages of each application & form. *Customer Support:* 30 day exchange or refund if package seals unopened.
MS-DOS (256k). IBM compatible. $64.00 (ISBN 1-877766-29-1, Order no.: INV-5). *Addl. software required:* Word Processor, PC-FILE+ or PC-FILE:dB or dBASE III. *Optimal configuration:* 512k Ram, hard disk.
$64.00 (ISBN 1-877766-30-5, Order no.: INV-3).
$34.00, manual only (ISBN 1-877766-31-3, Order no.: INV-M).
INVENTORY LIST OF ITEMS OWNED: Data Base of All Your Equipment, Supplies & Leasehold. Search & Sort by Any Category, Item, etc.. Update Prices As Items Depreciate. INVENTORY CONTROL: Office Storage Locations, Short Items or Missing Items Need Replacing/Ordering. For Personal Items Owned at HOME, too! DOCUMENTATION & UPDATES: Insurance Purposes, Fire, Theft, Destruction, Death. Know What You Own & How Much It Is Worth. Not Copy-Protected.
On the Mark Computer Software Co.

Doctor's Legal Aid. Larry Friedman & Steven Friedman. Jul. 1989. *Items Included:* Diskettes, manual, book/folder, 8 1/2" x 11" pages of each application & form. *Customer Support:* 30 day exchange or refund if package seals unopened.
MS-DOS (256k). IBM compatible. $114.00 (ISBN 1-877766-32-1, Order no.: LEGL-5). *Addl. software required:* Word processor.
$114.00 (ISBN 1-877766-34-8, Order no.: LEGL-3).
manual only $74.00 (ISBN 1-877766-35-6, Order no.: LEGL-M).
EMPLOYEES: Benefits, Associates, Licenses, Tax Info, Progress Reviews, Duties & Jobs, Payroll, Interviewing. PATIENTS & INSURANCE: Financial Responsibility & Recourse, Estimates & Statements, Refunds, Collection, Release & Assignment. MALPRACTICE AIDS: Errors & Omissions, Contractual Obligations, Abandonment, Minors & Age of Consent, Credit & Loans, Literature. LIABILITY: Informed Consent, Charting, Malpractice Prevention, Record Keeping, Property, Torts. Fully Computerized. Not Copy-Protected.
On the Mark Computer Software Co.

Doctor's Master Menu. Larry Friedman et al. May 1989. *Items Included:* Diskette, manual, book/folder, 8 1/2" x 11" pages of each application & form. *Customer Support:* 30 day exchange or refund if package seals unopened.
MS-DOS (256k). IBM-compatible. $54.00 (ISBN 1-877766-75-5, Order no.: MENU-5). *Addl. software required:* Word processor. *Optimal configuration:* Graphics capability, color monitor. *Networks supported:* No.
$54.00 (ISBN 1-877766-76-3, Order no.: MENU-3).
$24.00 (ISBN 1-877766-77-1, Order no.: MENU-M).
Doctor, Dentist, & Health Professional Computer MENU Program. Use the Pre-defined Options or Customize Your Options from A to Z! Action Logo Screen with Colors, Dos & Utility Menu Included. Use Your Billing & Insurance Program as Choice B. Other Optional Programs: Reordering Supplies, Fee Schedule Analysis, Employee Analysis, Patient Handouts, Inventory, & More! Data Base, Spreadsheet, Word Processor, Modem, & Other Programs Available. Not Copy-Protected.
On the Mark Computer Software Co.

Doctor's Modem & Bulletin Boards. Larry Friedman & Steven Friedman. May 1989. *Items Included:* Diskettes, manual, book/folder 8 1/2" x 11" pages of each applications & forms. *Customer Support:* 30 day exchange or refund if package seals unopened.
MS-DOS (256k). IBM compatible. $74.00 (ISBN 1-877766-45-3, Order no.: MODM-5). *Nonstandard peripherals required:* Modem. *Addl. software required:* Word processor, modem software program.
$74.00 (ISBN 1-877766-46-1, Order no.: MODM-3).
$34.00, manual only (ISBN 1-877766-48-8, Order no.: MODM-M).
On-Line Computer Resource for Professionals, Bulletin Board Use on "the Home Office for Professionals". Downloading, Uploading, Conferencing for Dentists, Doctors, Lawyers, Accountants & Allied Health Professionals. Computer Hardware & Professional Software for under $100.00. Discounts on Modem, Mouse, Disks, Paper & Ribbons, Communication Software & SHAREWARE. Text, Spreadsheet & Data Base Files Available. Not Copy-Protected.
On the Mark Computer Software Co.

Doctor's Office Companion. *Version:* 4.02. 1985. *Compatible Hardware:* IBM PC. *Operating System(s) Required:* PC-DOS/MS-DOS 2.0 or higher. *Memory Required:* 192k. *General Requirements:* 20Mb harddisk, 132-column printer.
disk $995.00, incl. documentation.
Medical Billing Package Designed to Support 5500 Guarantors for a 1- to 5-Doctor Office. Patient Data Is Gathered for Printing of the HCFA 1500 Universal Insurance Form. Provides Insurance Billing & Allows Other Payments (Such As Cash) to Be Handled. Provides Accounts Receivable Aging Reports & Supports up to 1000 CPT Codes. When Reports Are Entered During Daily Transactions, a Corresponding Description Is Produced.
High Technology Software Products, Inc.

Doctor's Ordering Supplies System. Larry Friedman & Steven Friedman. May 1989. *Items Included:* Diskettes, manual, book/folder, 8 1/2" x 11" pages of each application & form. *Customer Support:* 30 day exchange or refund if package seals unopened.
MS-DOS (256k). IBM compatible. $94.00 (ISBN 1-877766-49-6, Order no.: ORDR-5). *Addl. software required:* Word processor, PC-FILE+ or PC-FILE:dB or dBASE III. *Optimal configuration:* 512k Ram, hard disk.
$94.00 (ISBN 1-877766-51-8, Order no.: ORDR-3).
$34.00, manual only (ISBN 1-877766-52-6, Order no.: ORDR-M).
Computerize the Tedious & Boring Task of Reordering Supplies. Compare 2 Supply House Prices Per Item. Printouts of All Your Suppliers, Products & Abbreviations. Customize Printouts with Your Letterhead. Data Base Includes Hundreds of Items Already Entered. dBase III Compatible Files, but Much Easier to Use PC-FILE:dB. Search for Items by Supplier, Category, Price, Last Ordered,etc. Don't Be Caught Without That Needed Supply for Your Patient! Not Copy-Protected.
On the Mark Computer Software Co.

Doctor's Prescription Organizer. Larry Friedman & Steven Friedman. Jul. 1989. *Items Included:* Diskettes, manual, book/folder, 8 1/2" x 11" pages of each application & form. *Customer Support:* 30 day exchange or refund if package seals unopened.
MS-DOS (256k). IBM compatible. $64.00 (ISBN 1-877766-79-8, Order no.: RX-5). *Addl. software required:* Word processor, PC-FILE+ or PC-FILE:dB or dBASE III. *Optimal configuration:* 512 Ram, hard disk.
$64.00 (ISBN 1-877766-80-1, Order no.: RX-3).
$24.00, manual only (ISBN 1-877766-82-8, Order no.: RX-M).
DRUG INVENTORY: Data Base of Over 200 Commonly Prescribed Medicines. Search & Sort by Category, Item, Use, etc. Update Information From Your Current PDR on Medicines. INDICATIONS/USES: Access Medical Info Within Seconds. See Summaries of Uses & Abuses of Medicines. DOCUMENTATION: Save the Doctor's Time in Prescribing. Know What You Use, & How to Prescribe These Medicines. An Innovative Way to Review Medicines, Keep Current, & Be Aware of the Drugs Your Patients Are Taking. Not Copy-Protected.
On the Mark Computer Software Co.

Doctor's Psychology Manual. Larry Friedman & Steven Friedman. Jul. 1989. *Items Included:* Diskettes, manual, book/folder, 8 1/2" x 11" pages of each application & form. *Customer Support:* 30 day exchange or refund if package seals unopened.
MS-DOS (256k). IBM compatible. $64.00 (ISBN 1-877766-53-4, Order no.: PSYCH-5). *Addl.*

software required: Word processor.
$64.00 (ISBN 1-877766-54-2, Order no.: PSYCH-3).
$34.00, manual only (ISBN 1-877766-55-0, Order no.: PSYCH-M).
Doctors & Health Professionals Computer Generated Forms Data Bases. The Game of Family Life First Time Presented Anywhere. Psychology Profiles & Paramerers. Memory Files. Resume Building Blocks Enclosed for Applications & Jobs. Training Manual & Organizational Aid for New Clients. Step-by-Step Outlines for Procedures. Well-Organized & Fast-Reading. Customize & Create New Forms Easily. Not Copy-Protected.
On the Mark Computer Software Co.

Doctor's Real Estate Analyzer. Larry Friedman & Steven Friedman. Jul. 1989. *Items Included:* Diskettes, manual, book/folder, 8 1/2" x 11" pages of each application & form. *Customer Support:* 30 day exchange or refund if package seals unopened.
MS-DOS (256k). IBM compatible. $94.00 (ISBN 1-877766-59-3, Order no.: RE-5). *Addl. software required:* Word processor, Lotus 123 or compatible spreadsheet; PC-FILE+ or PC-FILE:dB or dBASE III. *Optimal configuration:* 512k Ram, hard disk.
$94.00 (ISBN 1-877766-60-7, Order no.: RE-3).
$44.00, manual only (ISBN 1-877766-61-5, Order no.: RE-M).
SPREADSHEETS: New Property Analysis, Pricing & Commissions, Monthly & Yearly Cash Estimates, Your Personal Balance Sheet & Income Statement for the Bank, & More. DATA BASES: Location, Location, Location. Know What the Tax Assessor & Owners Paid for Their Properties. Understand the Realty Market in Your Area. Spot a Bargain When You See It. FORMS/DOCUMENTS/LETTERS: Use These Standard Forms & Customize for Your Own Use. Keep the Legal Expenses & Escrow Expenses in Check. Learn Too! Not Copy-Protected.
On the Mark Computer Software Co.

DocuCalc. *Version:* 6.12. L. A. Chapman. Sep. 1982. *Compatible Hardware:* IBM PC, PC XT, PC AT & compatibles, PS/2; DEC Rainbow; Texas Instruments; Wang. *Operating System(s) Required:* PC-DOS or MS-DOS. *Language(s):* Compiled BASIC. *Memory Required:* 192k. *Customer Support:* Yes.
disk $95.00.
Allows Review of LOTUS 1-2-3, Release 1, 1A or 2.0 & SYMPHONY, Release 1.0, 1.1, Model Formulas in Several Grid Layouts, or One per Line Sequenced by Row or Column. Before Changing a Cell, DocuCalc's Cross-Reference Report Can Tell Which Other Cells Refer to It. Circular References Can Be a Sign of a Major Error in a Model, Program Tells Which Cells Are Involved. Use with LOTUS 1-2-3 & SYMPHONY.
Micro Decision Systems (Pennsylvania).

DocuLiner. Advanced Software, Inc. *Compatible Hardware:* IBM PC, PC XT, PC AT & compatibles. *Operating System(s) Required:* PC-DOS/MS-DOS 2.10 or higher; Novell, 3Com, or other compatible Netbios networks. *Customer Support:* 60 days toll-free.
disk $149.00, single users.
$695.00, 5 network stations.
Enables Users to Compare & Mark the Revisions in Legal Documents Including Contracts, Wills, Briefs, etc. The Program Will Detect & Highlight Changes in Documents in Any Four Ways: Split Screen Display, Printed Redlined Draft, Redlined File on Disk, or a Summary Report Referencing Each Revision by Line & Page Number. Changes & Deletions Can Be Marked by Several Methods, Including Bold & Strike Out Marks. Documents Compared Can Be Created by Different Word Processors, Including WORPERFECT 4.2 & 5.0, WORD, MULTIMATE, WORDSTAR, etc. Other Features Include: Ability to Track Insertions & Deletions of Any Size & Distance from the Origin; User Can Print Documents Directly, Without Having to Re-Run Their Word Processing Program.
CompuLaw, Ltd.

Document Administrator. *Version:* 2.0. *Operating System(s) Required:* PC-DOS 3.1.
10-user installation $2495.00.
additional workstations $150.00 ea.
Program Provides Document Administration on PC-Based Networks, Integrates a Variety of Applications Such As Microsoft Word, WordPerfect, Displaywrite & 1-2-3. Supports Automatic Document Numbering, Configurable Revision Tracking, Check-Out Protection to Prevent Simultaneous Editing, & the Ability to Maintain Forms & Boilerplate Items.
Augmentx.

Document Storage System (DSS). *Version:* 7.0. Jan. 1993. *Items Included:* 3 ring binder documentation, run time interpreter. *Customer Support:* Year support & upgrades - $120.00 per year. On-site install & training if desired - all expenses.
Macintosh OS. Macintosh (2.5Mb System 6.X, 4.0Mb System 7.X). $1299.95 single user; $1999.95. *Optimal configuration:* Macintosh with 030 or 040 processor, System 7.X, 4Mb RAM, fast hard drive, accelerated video, laser or dot matrix printer. *Networks supported:* 100% network interoperable.
DOS 5.X or higher & Windows. MS-DOS PC 386 or higher (4Mb). $1299.95 single user; $1999.95. *Addl. software required:* Windows. *Optimal configuration:* 386 or 486, DOS 5.X or higher, 4Mb RAM, fast hard drive, accelerated video, laser or dot matrix printer. *Networks supported:* 100% network interoperable.
Manages the Leasing of Warehouse Space Allotted to the Storage of Documents Using the Warehouse, Row, Shelf, Bin Model. Tracks Bins Leased, Availabilities, Receivables, Deposits & More. Allows Automatic Billing & Assesses Late Fees. Complete Line Item Control During Invoicing. Export Data to Other Program Supporting: DIF, SYLK, dBASE, LOTUS, ASCII. Multi-User & Cross Platform. 100% Network Interoperable.

Docupower!, 20 disks. Bob Stek. 1984. *Compatible Hardware:* IBM PC & compatibles. *Operating System(s) Required:* CP/M, MS-DOS, CP/M-86. *Language(s):* C. *Memory Required:* 64k. *General Requirements:* 2 disk drives, printer.
disk $149.00 ea.
CP/M. (ISBN 0-913733-04-0).
MS-DOS. (ISBN 0-913733-05-9).
Allows the Owner to Create New Text Using Boilerplates Made from the Original Text. Assembles by Number Selected Paragraphs, Sections, & Pages into an Indexed Resource File of Reusable Ideas. The Owner Can Pull the Numbered Text from This File to Create New Documents Such As Specification Sheets, Legal Papers, & Exams; the Owner's Original Word Processing Software Creates, Revises, & Formats Letters & Reports As Usual.
Computing!.

DocuSystem. *Version:* 6.2. NDX Corp. Jul. 1992. *Compatible Hardware:* Tandem. *Customer Support:* 800 number, free on-site training.
contact publisher for price.
An Integrated Documentation Search & Retrieval System Which Allows a Company to Store & Search Its Manuals, Catalogs, & Other Internal Documents As Well As Tandem's Technical Manual Set. DocuSystem Provides On-Line Access to the Most Up-to-Date Versions of the User's & Tandem's Documentation to All Employees in an Organization. Pre-Built Databases of the Most Current Manuals Are Available from NDX. DocuSystem Consists of Four Modules Allowing a Company to Put Together a System to Fit Their Needs. Modules Allow Users to Create Databases, Search & Retrieve Information, Print Information & Add Comments.
NDX Corp.

DOE - PC IV. *Version:* 1.0. Sep. 1992. *Items Included:* Manual, diskettes. *Customer Support:* 800-722-6154, 30 day money back guarantee, free telephone technical support.
Microsoft Windows 3.0 & 3.1. IBM PC AT, recommend 386 (4Mb). disk $695.00. *Addl. software required:* Microsoft Windows. *Networks supported:* IBM NetBIOS compatible.
Generates Optimal Experimental Designs from User-Specified Factors & Interactions in a Windows Interface. Designs Include Factorials, Central Composite, Box-Behneken & Plackett-Burman Having up to 128 Runs with 3-Factor Quadratic Interactions. Factor Effects, Variance or Contrast Analyses Can Be Done on Individual or Grouped Data with Missing, Repeated or Added Runs with ANOVA & Graphical Outputs.
Quality America, Inc.

DOG: Disk OrGanizer. *Version:* 3.20. *Compatible Hardware:* IBM PC & compatibles. *Operating System(s) Required:* DOS 2.0 or higher. *Memory Required:* 128k, recommended 640k. *Customer Support:* 707-961-1632, 10 AM-6 PM PST/PDT.
$30.00 Shareware registration.
Shareware Defragmenter & Disk Packer. Allows User to Write Command Files That Will Organize Files in Any Sequence or Arrangement or User May Select from Preset Options: Fast Mode, Directory Order, Packed Order & Fragmented Order. Not Copy Protected.
Soft GAMs Software.

DogPak. *Version:* 1.06. Gordon Waite. Jan. 1994. *Customer Support:* Unlimited telephone support.
MS-DOS. 286 (640k). disk $102.99 (ISBN 0-934777-14-4).
A Database & Handicapping Program for Greyhound Racing Fans. Past Performance Data Available via Racing Greyhounds BBS.
Pico Publishing.

Dolphin's Pearl. (Creative Pastimes Ser.). John O'Neil. *Compatible Hardware:* Atari, Commodore 64.
Atari. disk $29.95 (ISBN 0-8359-1417-8).
Commodore 64. disk $39.95 (ISBN 0-8359-1418-6).
Players Have to Live, Act & Feel Like a Dolphin Does in Order to Seek Out & Find a Pearl Hidden in Dolphin Lore. It All Takes Place in a Underwater-World Dream Environment.
Prentice Hall.

Domes of Kilgari. *Compatible Hardware:* TRS-80.
contact publisher for price.
Instant Software, Inc.

Domestic Relocation Gross-Up Procedure. *Version:* 10.0. Jan. 1995. *Items Included:* Complete documentation less than 25 pages. *Customer Support:* Free hotline support, 1-day training $850.00 plus travel expenses, annual maintenance fee $395.00.
PC-DOS (256k). IBM PC & compatibles. disk $495.00. *Addl. software required:* Lotus 1-2-3 ver 2.X or greater.
Produces Substitute IRS Form 4782, Along with Providing the Gross-Up for Federal, State, Local & FICA Taxes. Handles Multiple & Split Year

Moves. Also Allows Users to Define Their Own Specific Fields & Determine Which Fields to Grossed-Up or Not Grossed-Up.
The Hessel Group, Inc.

Domestic Relocation Tracking System (DRTS). Version: 9.0. Jan. 1996. Items Included: Complete documentation less than 70 pages. Customer Support: Free hotline support, 1-day training $850 plus travel expenses.
DOS 3.1 or higher or Windows (640k). IBM PC & compatibles. disk $1895.00.
Database Tracking System Designed for the Corporate Relocation Professional. Can Track Infinite Number of Relocation Events & Provide Ad Hoc Reporting. Can Additionally Calculate Precise Gross-Up Needed (& Produce IRS Substitute Form 4782) to Make the Transferee Whole, While Considering All Federal, State, Local & FICA Taxes.
The Hessel Group, Inc.

Dominion-Tank Police, Vol. I. Apr. 1995. Customer Support: Dedicated voice mail phone number; will respond back to consumer.
Windows 3.1 or higher; Macintosh. IBM or 100% compatible 486SX 25MHz (4Mb); 68030/68040 Color Mac System 7.1 or higher (4Mb). CD-ROM disk $14.99 (ISBN 1-57339-006-2, Order no.: ROMI2932CT). Nonstandard peripherals required: 2X CD-ROM drive.
Exciting, Action-Oriented Animation from Japan As the Tank Police Battle the Curvacious Cat Sisters & the Half-Human, Half-Cyborg Gang Leader Buaku.
Image Entertainment.

Dominion-Tank Police, Vol. II. Apr. 1995. Customer Support: Dedicated voice mail phone number; will respond back to consumer.
Windows 3.1 or higher; Macintosh. IBM or 100% compatible 486SX 25MHz (4Mb); 68030/68040 Color Mac System 7.1 or higher (4Mb). CD-ROM disk $14.99 (ISBN 1-57339-007-0, Order no.: ROMI2933CT). Nonstandard peripherals required: 2X CD-ROM drive.
The Exciting Animated Adventures of the Tank Police Continue in Newport City, 2010. The Ruthless Buaku Gang Is Still at Large & Still Dedicated to Stealing That Ever So Precious Commodity; the Urine of Healthy People.
Image Entertainment.

Dominion-Tank Police, Vol. III. May 1995. Customer Support: Dedicated voice mail phone number; will respond back to consumer.
Windows 3.1 or higher; Macintosh. IBM or 100% compatible 486SX 25MHz (4Mb); 68030/68040 Color Mac System 7.1 or higher (4Mb). CD-ROM disk $14.99 (ISBN 1-57339-008-9, Order no.: ROMI2934CT). Nonstandard peripherals required: 2X CD-ROM drive.
The Vicious Buaku Gang Has Changed Its Tactics. Now They Are Out to Steal an 80-Year Old Painting of Buaku Himself - the Last Known Artwork Created While the World Was Still Healthy.
Image Entertainment.

Dominion-Tank Police, Vol. IV. May 1995. Customer Support: Dedicated voice mail phone number; will respond back to consumer.
Windows 3.1 or higher; Macintosh. IBM or 100% compatible 486SX 25MHz (4Mb); 68030/68040 Color Mac System 7.1 or higher (4Mb). CD-ROM disk $14.99 (ISBN 1-57339-009-7, Order no.: ROMI2935CT). Nonstandard peripherals required: 2X CD-ROM drive.
At Long Last We Learn the Truth about Buaku's Origin. Could There Be Something Noble in the Efforts of This Half-Human, Half-Cyborg? Find Out in the Action Packed Conclusion of the Classic Series.
Image Entertainment.

Domino. Compatible Hardware: Apple II; IBM PC. Language(s): Applesoft BASIC for Apple. Memory Required: Apple 48k, IBM 128k. General Requirements: Graphics card for IBM. disk $29.95.
The Computer Takes the Place of 1 of the Players in the Traditional Game of Dominoes. Uses Graphics to Simulate the Playing Table.
Dynacomp, Inc.

Dominoes. General Requirements: Commodore Amiga.
3.5" disk $24.95.
Board Game.
Polygon Software Corp.

Don Quixote. Feb. 1995. Items Included: CD-ROM booklet. Customer Support: Free technical support via phone as of release date.
MPC/Windows. 386.25 or higher IBM compatible (4Mb). CD-ROM disk $29.95 (ISBN 1-885784-13-9, Order no.: 1189). Optimal configuration: MPC CD-ROM player, S-VGA graphics card (640x480x256 colors) with compatible monitor, MPC compliant sound card, mouse, Windows 3.1.
Cervantes' Don Quixote Explores the Wisdom of All Ages. See Don Quixote Set Forth to Rid the World of Evil Using Truth & Honor As His Lance & Sword. Follow the Story of a Man on a Quest. Understand the Discovery. Vivid Illustrations, Lively Music & Powerful Narration Combine to Create an Engaging Multimedia Story.
Technology Dynamics Corp.

Don Scott's Professional Selling the Computer Course, 72 Page Selling G. Operating System(s) Required: PC-DOS 2.0. Memory Required: 128k. Items Included: Don Scott's Guide to Professional Selling.
disk $89.00, incl. shelf case & bklt.
Group Sales Training Program. Includes Simulated Practice Sessions.
Bureau of Business Practice.

Donations Tracking. Version: 7.1. Apr. 1991. Items Included: Step-by-Step Instruction manual. Customer Support: Free support by phone, FAX, correspondence, or modem. On-site training and/or installation, $229.00 per day plus expenses..
MS/PC DOS 3.0 or higher. PC, 286, 386, 486; Tandy 3000 or higher (640k). disk $995.00 (Order no.: 1301). Nonstandard peripherals required: Interface to Touch-Tone requires our voice digitization board. Programs without Touch-Tone interface do not require nonstandard peripherals, boards. Optimal configuration: 386SX computer with a fast hard disk & our telephone interface board. Networks supported: Novell.
High Speed Daily Receipts. Prints Journal. Posts to Donor Records. Prints Receipts. Powerful Select & Store Allows Labels, Letters, Lists of Any Segment of the Database. Boolean Set Can Be Refined Until the Exact Population Is Extracted. Customized for Each Client.
Robert H. Geeslin (Educational Programming).

Donkey Kong. Compatible Hardware: Atari XL/XE.
ROM cartridge $19.95 (Order no.: RX8031).
Atari Corp.

Donkey Kong, Jr. Compatible Hardware: Atari XL/XE.
ROM cartridge $19.95 (Order no.: RX8040).
Atari Corp.

Donor Records. Version: 5.5. Jan. 1996. Customer Support: 30 days free; annual support contract.
PC-DOS/MS-DOS, Windows. IBM or comatible (640k). $1250.00.
Maintains Donor Name & Address Data. Tracks Gifts, Pledges, In-Kind Contributions. Prints Lists, Mailing Labels, or Exports to Word Processing. Virtually Unlimited Selection Criteria.
Executive Data Systems, Inc. (Georgia).

Donor Room. Compatible Hardware: Apple Macintosh 512K. General Requirements: Hard disk or external disk drive.
3.5" disk $4995.00.
Blood & Donor Tracking System.
Interactive Network Technologies, Inc.

Donormaster II. Version: 3.0. Jul. 1988. Compatible Hardware: IBM RS 6000, Sequant UNISYS, Intel80X86, Moto680x0, Sun Sparc, any SCO Unix compatible system. Operating System(s) Required: DOS, UNIX, XENIX, Novell, AIX, SUN OS. Language(s): UX BASIC & C-ISAM. Memory Required: 1000k. General Requirements: Printer. Customer Support: 800 no., user grp., documentation, updates.
$1795.00 & up. Networks supported: Most LAN environments.
Complete Fund Raising System for Non-Profit Development Professionals. Comprehensive Donor Management, Gift Processing, Planned Gifts, Pledges, Matching Gifts, Word Processing, & Reporting Functions.
Master Systems.

DonorPerfect. Version: 4.0. Starkland Systems. Apr. 1986. Items Included: Documentation & manuals, disks, 120 day support/warranty. Customer Support: 120 days full support with system, on-site training available, 1 yr maintenance $350. Free user groups & quarterly newsletters.
PC-DOS/MS-DOS. IBM PC & compatibles, XENIX (512k). disk $2295.00 single user; $3895.00 multi-user. Optimal configuration: 286 or 386, MS-DOS, 640, printer, word processor, 40Mb hard disk. Depends on size of database. 150,000 records - 386, 486, 80Mb-200Mb HD. Networks supported: Any dBASE III & LANPack, e.g., Novell, 3COM, PC-Link, GTE, LANtastic.
Windows System 6 or higher. Macintosh (512k). 3.5" disk $2295.00 single user; $3895.00 multi-user.
Automates the Administrative Tasks of Any Fundraising Office. Maintains Donor & Prospect Records, Automates Mailings & Lists & Provides Unlimited Summary & Statistical Reporting. The Package Contains a Complete Pledge Maintenance & Reminder System & Provides Comprehensive Gift Processing. Designed for Both the Novice & Experienced User.
SofterWare, Inc.

Doodle Drawer. Compatible Hardware: Atari 400, 800. Language(s): Atari BASIC. Memory Required: 16k.
disk $18.95.
"Paint" Using Atari Joystick.
Dynacomp, Inc.

Doom - Shareware. Customer Support: All of our products are unconditionally guaranteed.
DOS. CD-ROM disk $9.95 (Order no.: DOOM-SHARE). Nonstandard peripherals required: CD-ROM drive.
The Shareware Version of Id Software's Doom 1.
Walnut Creek CDRom.

Doom - Toolkit. Customer Support: All of our products are unconditionally guaranteed.
DOS. CD-ROM disk $19.95 (Order no.: DOOM-TOOLKIT). Nonstandard peripherals required: CD-ROM drive.
500 Ready to Run Levels, Articles, & More for Doom 1.
Walnut Creek CDRom.

TITLE INDEX

Dorland's Electronic Medical Speller. Reference Software International Staff. Oct. 1992. *Items Included:* License, installation card, disks. *Customer Support:* Free support at these toll numbers: DOS (801) 228-9918, Windows (801) 228-9919.
DOS. IBM PC & compatibles (500k). disk $89.00. *Nonstandard peripherals required:* Must use WordPerfect 5.0 or 5.1 to work! Compatibility with WP 6.0. *Addl. software required:* WordPerfect 5.0 or 5.1. *Optimal configuration:* 500k of hard disk space. *Networks supported:* Network ready.
Windows. IBM PC & compatibles (500k). disk $89.00. *Nonstandard peripherals required:* WordPerfect 5.1 or 5.2 for Windows. *Addl. software required:* WordPerfect 5.1 or 5.2 for Windows. *Networks supported:* Network ready.
Includes over 140,000 Medical Terms from 58 Fields in the Medical Profession for: Transcription of Patient Charts, Referral Letters, Writing of Articles for Medical Journals, & for Any Other Medically-Related Transcription Needs. The Medical Speller Works Inside the Spellers of WordPerfect for Windows or DOS.
WordPerfect Corp.

DOS/Windows Secrets. Steven Ross.
disk $24.80, incl. 184p. text (ISBN 0-929321-18-9).
WEKA Publishing, Inc.

DOS BOSS. Bert Kersey & Jack Cassidy. Aug. 1984. *Compatible Hardware:* Apple II, II+, IIe, IIc, IIgs. *Operating System(s) Required:* Apple DOS 3.3. *Language(s):* Machine, BASIC. *Memory Required:* 48k.
disk $24.00.
DOS 3.3 Enhancer. Enables the User to Rename Apple DOS Commands & Error Messages. The Change Feature May Be Appended to Any or All of the User's Programs So That Anyone Using the User's Disks (Booted or Not) on Any Apple Will Be Reminded DOS the Way the User Designed It. Catalogs May Also Be Customized.
Beagle Brothers.

DOS Buttons. Jun. 1994. *Customer Support:* By telephone or fax, normally no charge, 30 day money-back guarantee.
MS-DOS 5.0 for development system, 3.0 for target system. IBM 286 or higher (1Mb development, 196k target). disk $99.95 (ISBN 0-929392-23-X). *Addl. software required:* MS or Borland C Plus Plus.
Helps You Quickly Create Buttons, Bars, On-Screen Calculators & Keyboards Without Running Windows. It Results in a Small Amount of Run-Time Code That Is Designed to Be Used with Embedded Applications with Touch Screens, Mice, Trackballs, or Other Pointing Devices. You Define the Button Locations, Sizes, Colors, & Labels. Make Single-Action or Double-Action Buttons, or Even "Radio Buttons". Display Bars (Thermometers) Let You Input or Display Data. Source Code Included. Use MS or Borland C Plus Plus.
Annabooks.

DOS Customizer. *Compatible Hardware:* Apple.
contact publisher for price.
Instant Software, Inc.

DOS Enhanced Debug. Manuel J. Alvarez, II. *Compatible Hardware:* IBM PC, PCjr, PC XT, PC AT, Portable PC. *Operating System(s) Required:* DOS 1.10, 2.00, 2.10, 3.00, 3.10. *Memory Required:* 128k. *General Requirements:* IBM Monochrome Display, IBM Color Display, or TV (two can be used simultaneously).
disk $24.95 (Order no.: 6276594).
Assists User in Developing Programs by Providing a Controlled Full-Screen Environment. User Can Display & Alter Memory Code, or Any Register, As Well As Run All or Part of the Program to Diagnose Any Problems. Traces the Addresses of the Last 288 Instructions Executed & Allows for Single Keystroke Running or Single Stepping of the Program. Also Assembles 8086/88 Code Directly into Memory & Displays HEX & ASCII Files Without Loading Them into Memory.
Personally Developed Software, Inc.

The DOS Enhancer. *Compatible Hardware:* Apple II.
contact publisher for price.
S&H Software.

DOS File Tracker. Barry N. Shiffrin. *Compatible Hardware:* IBM PC, PC XT, PC AT, Portable PC. *Operating System(s) Required:* PC-DOS 2.00, 2.10, 3.00, 3.10. *Memory Required:* 128k. *General Requirements:* 2 disk drives, IBM Display; IBM Graphics Printer recommended; fixed hard disk optional.
disk $19.95 (Order no.: 6276518).
Reads & Catalogues Disk Directories. At User's Request, a Listing of All Files, or a Listing of Selected Files Can Be Displayed or Printed. Each File in the Catalog Can Be Identified with User's Comments, a Security Classification Can Be Added to Selected Files, & Files Can Be Grouped by Type. Prints Diskette Labels & Comment-Identifying Inserts.
Personally Developed Software, Inc.

DOS File View. Jack Botner. *Compatible Hardware:* IBM PC, PCjr, PC XT, PC AT, Portable PC, 3270 PC. *Operating System(s) Required:* PC-DOS 2.00, 2.10, 3.00, 3.10. *Memory Required:* 128k.
disk $19.95 (Order no.: 6276593).
Allows User to Look at Files in Detail Without the Need of a File Editor, Eliminating Potential Data Destruction When Reviewing Files. User Can Search for Specific Words or Characters, Read Large Files in 64k Segments, Choose ASCII or HEX Displays, Assign Program Commands to Any Function Key, & Choose Screen Colors to View Files When Using a Color Display.
Personally Developed Software, Inc.

DOS Help! *Version:* 6.2. Apr. 1994. *Items Included:* One page instruction sheet. *Customer Support:* Telephone support; 30 day money back guarantee.
DOS 2.0 or higher. IBM PC & compatibles (64k). disk $49.95.
Hypertext Substitute for the Printed DOS Manual.
Flambeaux Software, Inc.

DOS Helper. *Compatible Hardware:* Apple II, II+, IIe, IIc; Franklin Ace. *Operating System(s) Required:* Apple DOS 3.3. *Language(s):* BASIC, Machine. *Memory Required:* 48k. *Customer Support:* Help at (305) 977-0686.
disk $29.95.
Utility Program Designed for Enhancing the Operating System. Disk Sectors Can Be Read, Searched, Modified, Rewritten. DOS Commands & Error Messages Can Be Changed. Catalogs Can Be Alphabetized & Deleted, Files Can Be Restored.
The Professor Corp.

DOS Memories. Dick Balonek. *Compatible Hardware:* IBM PC, PC XT, PC AT, Portable PC. *Operating System(s) Required:* PC-DOS 2.00, 2.10, 3.00, 3.10. *Memory Required:* 128k. *General Requirements:* IBM Display or Enhanced Color Display.
disk $34.95 (Order no.: 6276607).
Enables User to Save DOS Screens to a File for a Permanent Record of Computer Usage, Assign Multiple DOS Commands (up to 256 Characters to a Single Key), Scroll the Display in Any Direction, Recall Previously Entered Commands, Lock the Display to Prevent Messages from Scrolling, Use Profiles to Define Colors, Keys, & Output Buffer Size, Display 43 Lines with an IBM Enhanced Graphics Adapter.
Personally Developed Software, Inc.

DOS Merge 286. *Compatible Hardware:* IBM PC AT. *Operating System(s) Required:* Microport System V/AT. *Customer Support:* 30 day installation warranty.
$275.00.
Allows DOS & Unix to Run Concurrently.
Microport, Inc.

DOS Merge 386. *Compatible Hardware:* 80386 AT-bus microcomputers with Microport System V/386. *Operating System(s) Required:* Microport System V/386. *Customer Support:* 30 day installation warranty.
$399.00.
Allows Concurrent Operation of Multiple DOS & Unix Program.
Microport, Inc.

DOS Partner. *Compatible Hardware:* IBM PC & compatibles. *Memory Required:* 128k.
disk $39.95.
File Management Utility Program Designed to Copy & Delete Files.
Allied Computer Group.

DOS Power Tools, 2nd Edition Revised for DOS 5.0: Techniques, Tricks & Utilities. Paul Somerson. *Items Included:* Three 5.25" disks. *Customer Support:* Phone number available for technical support, 212-492-9832; free disk replacement within 90 days of purchase.
PC-DOS. IBM PC & compatibles. disk $49.95 (ISBN 0-553-35464-7).
The All-Time Bestselling Book/Disk Package Has Been Revised & Updated for DOS 5.0. Covers: DOS Versions 2 Through 5, Optimizing DOS Configurations for Windows, 386/486 Class Memory Management, Sophisticated Batch File Techniques. Three Disks Contain More Than 100 All-New DOS 5.0 Utilities to: Automate Hard Disk Management, Streamline Screen/Printer Control. Somerson Is a Bestselling Author & Noted PC Expert.
Bantam Bks., Inc.

DOS Shell. Timothy Purves. Mar. 1986. *Compatible Hardware:* Atari ST. *Operating System(s) Required:* TOS.
3.5" disk $39.95 (ISBN 0-923213-12-0, Order no.: AT-DOS).
Mimics the MS-DOS Command Format for Users Who Do Not Need a Graphics Interface. Global File Names Let Users Copy or Delete Multiple Files with a Single Command. Wild Cards & Batch Files Are Also Available. Some of the Commands Featured Include: Dir; Change, Make, Remove; Path; Tree; Type; Check Disk; Copy, Rename, Delete; Pipe, Filter, Redirection.
MichTron, Inc.

DOS-2-DOS. *Compatible Hardware:* Commodore Amiga.
3.5" disk $55.00.
File Transfer MS-DOS & Atari ST to & from Amiga. Reads & Writes 5.25" or 3.25" MS-DOS Disks, Atari ST Disks (GEM Format), & Converts ASCII File Line Editing Characters.
Central Coast Software.

DOS Windows. *Compatible Hardware:* Sun 386i, Sun 386i Sun OS, Sun 386i workstation. *Operating System(s) Required:* UNIX, Sun OS, SunView.
$7990.00.
Allows Multiple DOS Applications to Run Under Control of Sun OS & the SunView Windowing System.
Sun Microsystems Inc.

DosNet. *Version:* 3.3. James W. Moody. Dec. 1991. *Items Included:* Manual, if not OEM version. *Customer Support:* Free phone, other support by agreement.
DOS386. 8088 thru 80486 CPU's (640k). $99.95 (ISBN 0-924626-03-8). *Optimal configuration:* 386 4Mb RAM. *Networks supported:* DosNet.
PC-DOS/MS-DOS. 8088 thru 80486 CPU's.
MS-DOS Compatible Networking System for Use on the IBM PC & Clone Computers. It Is Simple to Use, Has Access Security & a Simple Installation. Networking DOS386 Links Two Computers or Hundreds of Computers in a Client Server Configuration. Uses Popular Ethernet or Arcnet Network Cards.
Intelligent Machines.

DOSPLUS 2.0. *Compatible Hardware:* TRS-80 Model II, Model 12, Model 16. *Language(s):* BASIC.
disk $249.95.
Operating System Featuring a Global Program Editor & a BASIC Array Sort.
Blue Cat.

DOSPLUS 3.4. *Compatible Hardware:* TRS-80 Model I, Model III.
disk single or double density $149.95.
Disk Operating System for TRS-80. Options Include BASIC Array Sort, Controlled Screen Input, & Tape/Disk - Disk/Tape Utility.
Instant Software, Inc.

DOSPLUS 3.5. *Compatible Hardware:* TRS-80 Model I, Model III. *Operating System(s) Required:* TRSDOS. *Language(s):* BASIC.
disk $149.95.
Provides Faster More Reliable Backup, Reduced Disk Access Time, DOS Command Repeat, Single Disk Model III File Conversion & Complete Device Routing.
Blue Cat.

DOSPLUS 4.0. *Compatible Hardware:* TRS-80 Model I, Model III, Model 4.
disk $199.95.
Conversion Utility Programs Which Allow Model I & Model III Software to Be Run.
Blue Cat.

DOSShell. *Compatible Hardware:* IBM PC XT. *Operating System(s) Required:* MS-DOS. *Memory Required:* 92k.
contact publisher for price.
Disk Utility & Operating System Aid.
Tom Sheldon Publishing.

DOStamer. 1986. *Compatible Hardware:* TRS-80. *Operating System(s) Required:* TRSDOS 6.X, MS-DOS. *Memory Required:* 64k.
TRS-DOS. disk $69.95 (Order no.: D4TAMER).
MS-DOS. disk $69.95 (Order no.: DMDTAMER).
The Alternate Source.

DosUtils. *Version:* 3.1. May 1991. *Compatible Hardware:* IBM PC, XT, AT, EISA, PS/2 & compatibles, ST506 (RLL & MFM), ESDI, SCSI & IDE/AT interface hard disk drives. *Operating System(s) Required:* PC-DOS. *Memory Required:* 128k. *Customer Support:* Technical support via telephone, Internet & BBS.
disk $99.95.
A Collection of Expert Performance, Diagnostic, Repair, & Data Recovery Programs Designed for Easy Maintenance & Effective Management of Your Hard Disk Drive. Provides File Recovery Tools Including Undelete, & Will Perform Non-Destructive Low-Level Formats, Diagnostics, Performance Tests, & More.
Ontrack Computer Systems, Inc.

DOS386. *Version:* 2.99. James W. Moody. Jun. 1989. *Items Included:* Manual, if not OEM version. *Customer Support:* Free phone, other support by agreement.
DOS386 (27k). 8088 thru 486 (64k). $59.95 for the basic pkg. (ISBN 0-924626-01-1). *Optimal configuration:* 386 4Mb RAM. *Networks supported:* DosNet.
MS-DOS Compatible 8088 Thru 80486
Operating System Intended for Use on the IBM PC & Clone Compatible Computers. The Source Is Written in Assembler & Is Small in Size. When the System Is 27k in Size, It Has a Small Shell, the DOS Kernel, & No Network.
Intelligent Machines.

Dot Matrix & Laser Printer Utilities. *Items Included:* Full manual. No other products required. *Customer Support:* Free telephone support - no time limit. 30 day warranty.
MS-DOS 3.2 or higher. IBM & compatibles (512k). disk $19.95.
Extensive Collection of Utilities for Both Dot Matrix & Laser Printers. The Utilities Include Pop-Up Printer Configuration, Screen Dumps, & Font Down-Loading. These Utilities Come on Two Disks. A Printed 65-Page Documentation Package Is Included.
Dynacomp, Inc.

Dot Matrix & Laser Printer Utilities. 1992. *Items Included:* Detailed manuals are included with all DYNACOMP products. *Customer Support:* Free telephone support to original customer - no time limit; 30 day limited warranty.
MS-DOS 3.2 or higher. IBM PC & compatibles (512k). $19.95 (Add $5.00 for 3 1/2" format; 5 1/4" format standard). *Optimal configuration:* IBM, 256k RAM, MS-DOS 2.0 or higher, & a CGA or equivalent.
An Extensive Collection of Utilities for Both Dot Matrix & Laser Printers. The Utilities Include Pop-Up Printer Configuration, Screen Dumps, & Font Down-Loading. Several Screen Dump Programs Are Available: Hercules to Toshiba P1340, 1351; CGA to Okidata; & the Venerable GRAFTRAX. A Printed 65-Page Documentation Package Is Included.
Dynacomp, Inc.

Double Agent: For Making & Breaking Secret Codes. Timothy P. Banse. Sep. 1987. *Compatible Hardware:* IBM PC & compatibles. *Operating System(s) Required:* PC-DOS, MS-DOS. *Memory Required:* 64k.
disk $29.95 (ISBN 0-934523-17-7).
Scrambles Memos, Letters & Spreadsheets So No One but User Can Read Them. Can Be Used to Crack Someone Else's Secret Codes. Operates with Algorithm Similar to One Used by Green Berets & Central Intelligence Agency.
Middle Coast Publishing.

Double-Deck Pinochle. *Compatible Hardware:* TRS-80 Model I, Model III, Model 4 with BASIC; IBM PC. *Memory Required:* TRS 48k, IBM 128k.
disk $29.95.
cassette $19.95.
Fast-Paced Pinochle.
Dynacomp, Inc.

Double Dragon. *Customer Support:* 90 day warranty.
MS-DOS 2.1 or higher. IBM (512K). disk $14.99. *Nonstandard peripherals required:* Requires CGA, EGA, Tandy or VGA graphics.
Atari ST (512K). 3.5" disk $14.99.
Amiga. 3.5" disk $14.99.
Commodore 64 (64K). disk $14.99. *Nonstandard peripherals required:* Joystick required.
The Highest Acclaimed Martial Arts Game of All Time is Available for Your Computer at Home. Join in Deadly Combat with the Savage Street Gang of the Infamous Shadow Boss. Use Whatever Weapons Come to Hand As You Pursue the Gang Through the Slums, Factories, & Wooded Outskirts of the City.
Virgin Games.

Double Reed Fingerings. Anne Miller. 1985. *Compatible Hardware:* Apple IIplus, IIe, IIc, IIGS; Commodore 64, 128; IBM PC. *Operating System(s) Required:* Apple DOS 3.3, PC-DOS 3.3 or higher. *Language(s):* QuickBasic. *Memory Required:* Apple 48k, Commodore 64k, IBM 640k. *Customer Support:* Yes.
Apple. disk $39.95 (ISBN 0-942132-57-2, Order no.: A-1177).
Commodore 64. disk $39.95 (ISBN 0-942132-58-0, Order no.: C-1177).
IBM. disk $39.95.
A Drill-&-Practice Tutorial on Problem Fingerings for the Oboe & Bassoon. Users Are Given Musical Examples to Review the Forked F, Left-Hand E-Flat, Half Hole, or the Octave Keys (Oboe) & the Whisper Key, Half Hole, Alternate G-Sharp, or Alternate A-Sharp (Bassoon) Fingerings. The User May Select a Fingering Problem to Review & the Number of Problems. User Feedback Is Given, & a Record Is Retained for the Instructor.
Electronic Courseware Systems, Inc.

Double Switch. *Items Included:* Instruction manual. *Customer Support:* Free Telephone support.
DOS/Windows 95. IBM & compatibles (8Mb). Contact publisher for price. *Nonstandard peripherals required:* CD-ROM drive.
MAC. Macintosh (4Mb). Contact publisher for price. *Nonstandard peripherals required:* CD-ROM drive.
Saturn. Sega Saturn. Contact publisher for price.
Digital Pictures, Inc.

Double-Take. *Version:* 2.1. Mark Simonsen. *Compatible Hardware:* Apple II, II+, IIe, IIc, IIgs. *Operating System(s) Required:* Apple DOS 3.3, ProDOS. *Language(s):* Machine. *Memory Required:* DOS 3.3 48k, ProDOS 64k.
disk $34.95.
Designed for Cataloging & Scrolling in Both Directions. Reports All Variables with Values & Line Numbers. Features Include a Memory-Resident Hexadecimal Converter, Free Disk Space, Instant Program Statistics, etc.
Beagle Brothers.

Double Up. John Higgins & Muriel Higgins. *Compatible Hardware:* IBM PC, Apple IIe, IIc, IIgs. *Operating System(s) Required:* MS-DOS. *Memory Required:* Apple 64k, MS-DOS 256k. *General Requirements:* 1 disk drive or hard disk, printer, color or mono monitor. *Items Included:* Program with 25 reading passages, authoring system. *Customer Support:* 800-654-8715 full lifetime guarantee.
single site license disk $69.95 (ISBN 0-940503-18-2).
site license disk $139.95 (ISBN 0-940503-28-X).
Takes One or Two Sentences & Puts Words in Alphabetical Order. User Puts Them Back, Two Words at a Time. Provides Text Entry, Score Keeping, Print Functions.
Research Design Assocs., Inc.

DoubleDOS. *Version:* 5.5. Mar. 1984. *Compatible Hardware:* IBM PC, PC XT, PC AT, PS/2, & compatibles. *Operating System(s) Required:* PC-DOS/MS-DOS 2.0 or higher. *Memory Required:* 256k. *Customer Support:* 9:00 AM to 5:30 PM EST - (603) 644-5555.
$69.95.
Multi-Tasking Lets User Do Twice the Work with PC, Instead of Waiting. Lets User Print, Plot, Communicate in the Background, While Running Another Program in the Foreground. Support for Direct Screen Writers & EGA! Supports 1 Megabyte of LIM EMS 4.0.
SoftLogic Solutions.

Douglas CAD/CAM Layout Systems: Printed Circuit Board Design & Manufacturing. *Compatible Hardware:* Apple Macintosh Plus or higher.
layout system software $95.00.
layout with print option $395.00.
layout with print & plot option $525.00.
Family of Products for Electronic Design & Manufacturing. Supports Conventional Assembly Procedures & Surface Mount Technology As Well As Solder Masks & Screen Layers. Flexible Software Accepts Variety of Grids, Pads, Holes & Trace Widths. Accept Pads up to 0.400 in Size. Provides Layout Area of 32" by 32", 50 Levels of Magnification & Grid Sizes down to 0.001 Inch.
Douglas Electronics.

Douglas CAD/CAM Professional System: Integrated CAD-CAM for Electronic Design & Manufacturing.
Macintosh Plus or Higher. disk Professional Layout, MacSpice $1500.00 ea. *Addl. software required:* Gerber File Creator, Gerberlin, Drill Tape Creator, MacSpice.
disk Autorouter $700.00 ea.
disk Gerberlin or Gerber File Creator $250.00 ea.
disk Drill Tape Creator $150.00.
disk $1500.00 ea. Schematic.
disk professional system Demo $25.00.
Fully Integrated Engineering Tool That Takes User from Schematic Drawing to Final Routed Board. Consists of Three Programs: Professional Layout Has All Features of Douglas CAD/CAM Plot Program Plus Full Color Support, Unlimited Multilayers & Integration with Other Two Programs Via Parts List; Schematic Includes Digital Simulation, Bussing, User-Definable Devices & Net List Generation; AutoRouter Is a Command-File Driven Multipass Router That Will Handle up to 16 Layers. Upon Board Layout Completion, Users Can Transfer Files to Douglas CAD/CAM Facility where Photoplots and/or Prototype Boards Can Be Produced. Conversion, Drill Tape Creation & Analog Simulation Software Constitute Add-Ons to the Package.
Douglas Electronics.

Dow Jones Market Analyzer PLUS. *Version:* 2.0. 1989-1991. *Compatible Hardware:* Mac Plus, Classic, SE, SE/30, LC, II, IIx, IIci, IIcx, IIsi or IIFX, Superdrive or hard drive required. *Operating System(s) Required:* MS-DOS 3.1, PC-DOS 3.1 & higher. *Memory Required:* 640k. *General Requirements:* Mac: Printer, modem, color monitor for color charting. *Items Included:* Manual, reference card & disks. *Customer Support:* (609) 452-1511.
disk $499.00.
Macintosh (2Mb). 3.5" disk $149.00.
Technical Analysis Program That Collects Historical Quotes for Stocks, Bonds, Treasury Issues, Options, Mutual Funds, Market Indexes & Commodities from Dow Jones. Creates Bar, Comparison, Relative Strength & Point & Figure Charts. Analysis Tools Are Moving Averages, Trendlines, Oscillators & Volume Indicators. User-Defined & over 30 Ready-to-Use Formulas Include Moving Average Convergence-Divergence, Wilder Relative Strength, Directional Movement, Stochastics, Williams %R, Bollinger Bands & More. The Technical Screening Reports Compare Current Price Volume to Past Activity & Point Out Stocks with the Greatest Profit Potential. The Macintosh Version Includes Candlestick Charting & Strategy Testing. The IBM Version Includes Portfolio Management.
Dow Jones Information Services.

Dow Jones Spreadsheet Link. *Version:* 2.0. Oct. 1992. *Compatible Hardware:* IBM PC, PC XT, AT, PS/2. *General Requirements:* Modem, Lotus 1-2-3, Microsoft Excel, or Quattro Pro. *Items Included:* Manual & disks. *Customer Support:* 609-452-1511.
5.25" or 3.5" disk $149.00.
Communications/Utility Program That Automatically Downloads Data from Dow Jones News/Retrieval & Formats It to Lotus 1-2-3, Microsoft Excel, or Quattro Pro Spreadsheets.
Dow Jones Information Services.

Dow Jones Spreadsheet Link. Dow Jones & Co., Inc. *Compatible Hardware:* HP 150 Touchscreen, HP 110 Portable.
3.5" disk $250.00 (Order no.: 45511D).
Connects the Dow Jones News/Retrieval to the LOTUS 1-2-3, MULTIPLAN, or VISICALC Spreadsheet. Information Is Moved Directly into the Customized Spreadsheet. Once the Information Has Been Received, It Can Be Immediately Processed. Includes an Automatic Log-On Feature. Designed for Investors, Credit & Money Managers, Financial Analysts, & Strategic Planners.
Hewlett-Packard Co.

Down to Earth Business Software. *Version:* 3.3. May 1991. *Operating System(s) Required:* Unix; MS-DOS; VMS, LANS, Netware, AIX, ULTRIX, A/UX. *Items Included:* Full set manual; user guide; installation notes. *Customer Support:* 60 days free with purchase; 1% list price per month thereafter: 24-hour installation hotline, 11-hour daily phone support, nationwide dealer network, bulletin board, 2 newsletter, user group.
$400.00-$2000.00 per module depending on hardware.
13 Comprehensive Business Modules; One-Key "Help" at Each Prompt; FIND Key; Shortcuts; Windows. Separate or Integrated: GL, AP, AR, Payroll, Inventory, Purchase Order, Sales Analysis, Order Entry, Item/Resource Scheduling, Report Writer, Job Cost, Bill of Materials.
DISC (California).

DownHill Challenge. *Compatible Hardware:* Apple IIgs; Atari ST; Commodore 64; Amiga; IBM PC & compatibles; Tandy. *Memory Required:* Commodore 64k; Apple, IBM, Tandy 256k; Atari 512k.
Commodore. disk $24.05.
Apple. disk $29.95.
IBM, Tandy. disk $29.95.
Atari, Amiga. 3.5" disk $29.95.
Ski-Racing Simulation.
Broderbund Software, Inc.

DOWNLD. *Compatible Hardware:* Atari 400, 800, 12000XL. *Operating System(s) Required:* Atari DOS 2.0. *Language(s):* Machine. *Memory Required:* 48k.
disk $24.95 (ISBN 0-936200-23-5).
Controls Baud Rate & Tape Leader Time. Provides Cassette File Verification.
Blue Cat.

The Downloader. *Version:* 3.5. *Items Included:* User manuals. *Customer Support:* Full technical support at (801) 265-9998.
PC-DOS 2.0 or higher. IBM PC, PC XT, PC AT, PS/2 & compatibles. contact publisher for price. *Nonstandard peripherals required:* Hard drive (2 floppies or 1 hard & 1 floppy); Hayes 1200, 2400, 9600 or compatible modem for CompuServe, Dial/Data, Dow Jones, MarketScan, DBC Signal.
A Powerful Stock Market Data Collection Program for Historical & End-of-Day Price Quotes from the Following Vendors: CompuServe, DBC Signal, Dial/Data, Dow Jones, & MarketScan. Features Include 1,200, 2, 400, or 9,600 Baud Rate, Unattended Operation, Complete Mouse Support & a Graphical User Interface with Dialog Boxes, Auto-Dial & Redial, Simple-to-Create Keyboard Macros for Complete Program Automation, Custom Modem Configurations, & a Built-In Telephone Director for Vendor Numbers. Has the Ability to Export Data into ASCII & LOTUS 1-2-3 File Formats, As Well As Convert Data from Other Popular Investment Software Formats. A CompuServe, DBC Signal, & Dial/Data Version Are Available Separately.
Equis International.

The/DownLoader-Dial/Data. *Version:* 3.5. *Compatible Hardware:* IBM PC, PC XT, PC AT, PS/2, & compatibles. *Operating System(s) Required:* PC-DOS 2.2 or higher. *Memory Required:* 512k. *General Requirements:* 2 disk drives or hard disk, Hayes Smartmodem 1200 or compatible. *Items Included:* User Manual. *Customer Support:* Full technical support at (801) 265-9998.
A Data Collection Program Designed for Use with MetaStock or ComputTrac/PC Technical Analysis Software. The Dial/Data Version Collects Historical Price & Volume Data from Dial/Data's Extensive Database of Stock Market Data. Program Features Include Auto-Dial, Auto Re-Dial, Auto-Log on & Collection, Update All or Some Securities, 300/1200/2400/9600 Baud Speed, Add & Delete Securities, On-Screen Help Window.
Equis International.

DPIPE: Waste Drainage Pipe Sizing. *Items Included:* Manual. *Customer Support:* Toll free telephone support.
IBM PC & compatibles (256k). disk $295.00.
Calculates Optimal Pipe & Vent Sizes for Sanitary Building Drain Systems with up to 400 Pipe Sections. Program Follows Exact Methodology Described in the ASPE Databook. Existing Drainage Systems Can Also Be Analyzed Because DPIPE Allows the Designer to Fix the Size of Any Pipe Sections.
Elite Software Development, Inc.

dProgrammer. *Compatible Hardware:* IBM PC & compatibles. *Operating System(s) Required:* CP/M, CP/M-86, MS-DOS, PC-DOS. *Language(s):* DBASE II (source code included). *Memory Required:* 300k. *General Requirements:* 2 disk drives or hard disk.
$295.00.
Allows User to Create an Application Which Is Tied Together by Menus, & Uses Data Stored in Files to Define the Application. Program Is Menu-Driven & Password Protected, & Allows User to Define Their Own Lists & Reports. Users Can Produce a Variety of Data Entry & Display Programs & Can Utilize the Menu Structure to Add Complex Programs, Written in dBASE II, Which Perform Special Functions.
Sensible Designs.

DR Graph. Digital Research. Jun. 1984. *Compatible Hardware:* TI Professional. *Operating System(s) Required:* CP/M-86, Concurrent CP/M-86. *Memory Required:* 192k. *General Requirements:* 3-plane graphics board, color plotter.
$295.00.
Creates Business Charts, Graphs or Both, 4 Type Styles, Control Size & Color of Type. Possible to Write Comments on Graphs.
Texas Instruments, Personal Productivit.

Drafix CAD Professional. *Version:* 3.0. *Items Included:* CD-ROM with 5,000 symbols, 250 floor plans, hundreds of sample drawings. *Customer Support:* Free customer support on-line 816-891-8418, Compuserve Library.
IBM PC 386 or 486 (2Mb). CD-ROM disk $495.00. *Nonstandard peripherals required:* Mouse. *Addl. software required:* Windows 3.1

or higher.
Lets User Divide Screen into Four Independent Views, Each of Which Can Show a Portion of a Drawing. Windows Can Be Linked So That a Change in One Is Reflected in the Others. Supports Third-Party Developers Through Drafix Graphic Language; This Offers Extensions for Interfacing with with Database, Function Definition & Menu Modification. Lets User Annotate Images with Text or Numeric Values for Easy Creation of Job Estimates or Invoices. Visual Symbols Display Lets User View a Picture of a Symbol. Associative Dimensioning Facilties Automatically Redraw All Dimensions Linked to an Entity When It Is Changed. Includes Symbol Library with Optional Libraries Available. Compatible with Other Applications Including AutoCAD & Excel.
Foresight Resources Corp.

Drafix CAD Ultra. *Version:* 4.2. Nov. 1988. *Compatible Hardware:* PC-DOS/MS-DOS. *Memory Required:* 640k. *General Requirements:* Mouse or digitizer; EGA, VGA, or Hercules graphics adapter. *Customer Support:* Free customer support on-line 816-891-8418, Compuserve Library.
disk $395.00.
2-D Program for General Purpose Drafting with Automatic Associative Dimensioning. Can Turn Drawings into Usable Database & Spreadsheet Information. Includes General Symbols Library & CADapult. A Conversion Utility That Allows Users to Move Information to Lotus 1-2-3, dBASE, Word Processors & Other Database & Spreadsheet Programs.
Foresight Resources Corp.

Drafix Network Symbols Library. *Version:* 1.0. Jul. 1991. *Customer Support:* Free tech support at 816-891-8418 to registered users.
MS-DOS. IBM XT, AT, & higher (1Mb). disk $150.00. *Addl. software required:* Drafix Windows CAD.
Predrawn Symbols for LAN Equipment & Cabling.
Foresight Resources Corp.

Draft Master Software Series: California Business Incorporations. *Version:* 1.2C. 1988. *Items Included:* A user's manual which includes instructions on operating the program & a Tutorial to Introduce a New User to the Program's Features. An Attorney's Manual Containing Illustrations of the Forms & Explanations of the Legal Consequences of the Use of the Forms. *Customer Support:* Free hotline support through an 800 number.
MS-DOS or PC-DOS version 2.0 or higher. IBM XT, AT, PS/2 or compatibles with hard disk (512K). disk $395.00 (Order no.: 638). *Addl. software required:* Recommended to be used with a Word Processing program.
This Menu-Driven Document Assembly Program Enables the User to Produce Custom-Drafted Documents to Incorporate a Business in California. The Package Includes over 50 Forms, Such As Articles of Incorporation, Bylaws, Resolutions for Corporate Organization, & Notices & Minutes of Meetings of Directors & Shareholders.
Matthew Bender & Co., Inc.

Draft Master Software Series: California Deposition & Discovery on Disk. *Version:* 1.2. J. N. DeMeo (Editorial Consultant). 1988. *Items Included:* A user's manual which includes instructions on operating the program & a tutorial to introduce a new user to the program's features. *Customer Support:* Free hotline support through an 800 number.
MS-DOS or PC-DOS version or higher. IBM XT, AT, or PS/2 or compatible with hard disk (512K). disk $495.00 (Order no.: 905). *Addl. software required:* Rcommended to be used with a Word Processing program.
This Menu-Driven Document Assembly Program Enables the User to Draft the Forms from Matthew Bender's "California Deposition & Discovery" Set , Including a Wide Variety of Discovery Forms, Such As Motions, Applications, & Orders Relating to Depositions, Interrogatories, Requests for Admissions, etc.
Matthew Bender & Co., Inc.

Draft Master Software Series: California Marital Settlement Agreement. *Version:* 1.2C. Marshall S. Zolla (Editorial Consultant). 1988. *Items Included:* A user's manual which includes instructions on operating the program & a tutorial to introduce a new user to the program's features. An attorney's manual containing illustrations of the forms & explanations of the legal consequences of the use of the forms. *Customer Support:* Free hotline support through an 800 number.
MS-DOS or PC-DOS version 2.0 or higher. IBM XT, AT or PS/2 or compatible with hard disk (512K). disk $495.00 (Order no.: 908). *Addl. software required:* Recommended to be used with a Word Processing system.
This Menu-Driven Document Assembly Program Enables the User to Draft Both Simple & Complex Marital Settlement Agreements under California Law. Comprehensive in Coverage, the System Includes Provisions for Property Division, Support, Custody, & Other Areas. Also Includes Prenuptial Agreements & Co Habitation Agreements.
Matthew Bender & Co., Inc.

Draft Master Software Series: California Personal Injury. *Version:* 1.2c. William D. Gibbs (Editorial Consultant). 1988. *Items Included:* A user's manual which includes instructions on operating the program & a tutorial to introduce a new user to the program's features. Two Attorney's Manuals Containing Illustrations of the Forms & Explanations of the Legal Consequences of the Use of the Forms. *Customer Support:* Free hotline support through an 800 number.
MS-DOS or PC-DOS version 2.0 or higher. IBM XT, AT, PS/2 & compatibles with hard disk (512K). disk $495.00 (Order no.: 912). *Addl. software required:* Word Processing program recommended.
This Menu-Driven Document Assembly Program Enables the User to Draft a Complaint & over 120 Other Related Forms for Use Prior to Trial in a Personal Injury or WrongfulDeath Action in California. Some Areas Covered Include Client Intake, Attorney-Client Agreements, Claims, the Complaint, Service of Process, & Judgment Before Trial.
Matthew Bender & Co., Inc.

Drafting the Federal Complaint, 1991. Roger C. Park. *Compatible Hardware:* IBM PC & compatibles, Macintosh. *Memory Required:* 128k. *Items Included:* Booklet of background materials. Macintosh. 3.5" disk $79.00 (Order no.: K984). IBM PC & compatible. $ 79.00 3.5" or 5.25" disk (Order no.: K985).
Learning Package for Litigators & Trial Skill Trainers. May Be Used for Self-Instruction & In-House Training & Is Designed to Refresh & Strengthen New or Unpracticed Skills. Will Help Practice the Skills of Drafting a Federal Complaint. It Will Take the Student Through the Jurisdictional Allegations & Factual Counts of a Federal Court Complaint. Under Constant Questioning by the Computer, the Student Is Asked to Evaluate the Merits of Various Paragraphs in a Complaint & to Assess Their Vulnerability to a F.R.C.P. 12(b)(6) Motion to Dismiss. The Program Consists of Three Principal Sections: Jurisdictional Allegations, Factual Allegations, & Ethical Considerations. As the Users Proceed Through the Program, Numerous Drafting & Pleading Pointers & Professional Responsibility Issues Are Raised & Explained until They Arrive at a Model Federal Complaint.
American Law Institute.

Drafting Wills & Trust Agreements on CAPS. Robert P. Wilkins & Capsoft Development Corporation. Jun. 1992. *Items Included:* 2 3-ring binders, 2 volume drafting guide with commentary entitled Drafting Wills & Trust Agreements: A Systems Approach, newsletter "News from DWTA". *Customer Support:* Unlimited telephone access to toll-free technical support line during normal business hours is included with price of programs & subsequent updates. Training at customer's site is available starting at $600 for 4 hours. Training also available from author, Bob Wilkins, at the RPW Learning Center in South Carolina.
PC-DOS/MS-DOS 3.1 or higher. IBM PC & 100% compatibles (640k). disk $895.00. *Addl. software required:* WordPerfect Version 5.0 or higher. *Optimal configuration:* 12 CPI printer, hard disk. *Networks supported:* Novell A-Netware, AT&T Starlan, & Banyan Vines.
Powerful, Sophisticated Document Assembly Program for Total Decision-Making Control over Dozens of Clause Options & Forms Covering Every Family Estate Planning Need. Drafts Simple Wills, Long Form Wills with Testamentary Trusts, Revocable Trusts Agreements, Codicils, Pour-Over Wills, & Trust Amendments. Modify Clauses, Temporarily or Permanently, for Maximum Flexiblity.
Shepard's/McGraw-Hill, Inc.

Drafting Wills & Trust Agreements on CAPS. Robert P. Wilkins & Capsoft Development Corporation Staff. Jun. 1992. *Items Included:* 2 3-ring binders, 2 volume drafting guide with commentary entitled Drafting Wills & Trust Agreements: A Systems approach, newsletter "News from DWTA". *Customer Support:* Unlimited telephone access to toll-free technical support line during normal business hours is included with price of programs & subsequent updates. Training at customer's site is available starting at $600 for 4 hours. Training also available from author, Bob Wilkins, at the RPW Learning Center in South Carolina.
PC-DOS/MS-DOS 3.1 or higher. IBM PC & 100% compatibles (640k). disk $895.00. *Addl. software required:* WordPerfect Version 5.0 or higher. *Optimal configuration:* 12 CPI printer, hard disk. *Networks supported:* Novell A-Netware, AT&T Starlan, & Banyan Vines.
Powerful, Sophisticated Document Assembly Program for Total Decision-Making Control over Dozens of Clause Options & Forms Covering Every Family Estate Planning Need. Drafts Simple Wills, Long Form Wills with Testamentary Trusts, Revocable Trusts Agreements, Codicils, Pour-Over Wills, & Trust Amendments. Modify Clauses, Temporarily or Permanently, for Maximum Flexibility.
Shepard's/McGraw-Hill, Inc.

Draftsman DXF. *Version:* 5.0. Shirl A. Vonasek & Mark D. Floan. Jun. 1987. *Items Included:* Manual with tutorial. *Customer Support:* 120 days free phone support; 90 day moneyback guarantee.
MS-DOS 3.0 or higher (640k). IBM PC & compatibles. disk $249.00, incl. manual (ISBN 0-932071-07-4). *Nonstandard peripherals required:* 1 hard drive. *Addl. software required:* Any DXF-capable CAD.
A Coordinate Data File Interface Program to Generic CADD Ver. 5.0 or Higher or Any DXF-

Capable CAD. Provides a Menu-Driven Drawing Editor Which Uses Coordinate Data to Construct Drawing Files. Supports Many Third Party COGO Data File Formats.
Simplicity Systems, Inc.

Dragnet. Version: 2.0. Compatible Hardware: IBM 286 or 386. Operating System(s) Required: PC-DOS/MS-DOS 2.0 or higher. General Requirements: Hard disk, MicroSoft Windows. disk $145.00.
Text Retrieval Program Capable of Searching the Full Text of Files.
Access Softek.

Dragonblast. Compatible Hardware: Atari 400, 800 with Atari BASIC. Memory Required: disk 48k.
disk $21.95.
Dragon Protects Castle from Exploding Worms & Killer Comets.
Dynacomp, Inc.

Dragons of Flame. U.S. Gold. Customer Support: Technical support line: (408) 737-6850 (11am-5pm, PST); 14 day money back guarantee & 30 day exchange policy.
DOS 2.11 or higher. disk $39.95. Nonstandard peripherals required: Requires a color monitor & a graphics adaptor (i.e., CGA, EGA, Tandy 16-color).
Workbench. Amiga (512k). 3.5" disk $39.95.
Atari ST (512k). 3.5" disk $39.95.
Commodore 64/128 (64k). disk $29.95. Optimal configuration: Commodore 64/128 with a copy program (to make back-up disks) & a joystick.
Control up to Ten Companions, One at a Time. Objective: Rescue Slaves Held by the Ravaging Dragonarmies in the Foul Fortress of Pax Tharkas. Each Companion Has Different Specialized Skills. Use Them Wisely Along the Way to Evade Evil Draconian Patrols. Keep One Step Ahead of the Malevolent Dragonarmies While Battling Dragons, Giant Wasps, Griffins, Wraiths, Xombies, & Scores of Other Monsters! Action Happens in Real Time & in Colorful Animation.
Strategic Simulations, Inc.

Dragonstrike. Westwood Associates. Customer Support: Technical support line: (408) 737-6850 (11am-5pm, PST); 14 day money back guarantee/30 day exchange policy.
DOS 2.11 or higher. IBM PC & compatible (512k). disk $49.95. Nonstandard peripherals required: Requires a color monitor & a graphics adaptor (i.e., CGA, EGA, Tandy 16-color, VGA).
Commodore 64/128 (64k). disk $39.95.
Workbench. Amiga (512k). disk $49.95.
This First Ever Dragon Combat Simulator Lets You Ride the Mighty Dragons of Krynn into Fierce Combat. As You Progress Through 3 Different Orders of the Knighthood, You Will Gain Bigger & More Powerful Dragon Mounts to Ride in Over 20 Different Missions! Battling Alongside Other Good Dragons, You Will Fight Enemy Dragons As Well As Wyverns, Ships, Archers, & Flying Citadels. For One Player.
Strategic Simulations, Inc.

Drainage Pipe Sizing: DPIPE. Oct. 1988. Compatible Hardware: IBM PC, PC XT, PC AT & compatibles. Memory Required: 256k.
3.5" or 5.25" disk $295.00.
Calculates Optimal Pipe & Vent Sizes for Sanitary Building Drain Systems with up to 400 Pipe Sections. Existing Drainage Systems Can Also Be Analyzed Because Program Allows the Designer to Fix the Size of Any & All Pipe Sections. Besides Sizing Reports, DPIPE Can Also Print a Complete Bill of Materials Showing Both Labor & Material Costs. Pipes Are Automatically Sized in Accordance with the BOCA Code. However, Program Has Provision for Sizing Pipes Using Codes Different from BOCA. Allows Users to Define & Maintain As Many Sizing Code Files As Necessary. Contains Built-In Data Concerning Fixtures, Pipe Materials & Pipe Fittings. Allows the User to Maintain Various Material Files, & Each Material File Can Contain up to 96 Different Fixtures, 72 Pipe Fittings, & 16 Material Types.
Elite Software Development, Inc.

DrainCalc. Version: 4.5. Stephen J. Langlinais & Mark D. Floan. Jun. 1989. Items Included: Manual with tutorial. Customer Support: 120 days free phone support; 90 day moneyback guarantee.
MS-DOS 2.1 or higher (384k). IBM PC & compatibles. disk $295.00 incl. manual (ISBN 0-932071-08-2). Nonstandard peripherals required: 2 floppy drives or 1 floppy & 1 hard drive.
Provides Analysis & Design Functions for Open Channel Hydraulics, Culvert Design & Storm Sewer Design Using Standard Engineering Formulas As Well As the Soil Conservation Service (SCS) Curves.
Simplicity Systems, Inc.

Drakkhen.
MS-DOS 3.2 or higher. IBM PC/XT/AT & compatibles (512K). contact publisher for price. Addl. software required: CGA, EGA required.
Kickstart 1.2 or higher. Amiga 500/1000/2000 (512K). contact publisher for price. Nonstandard peripherals required: 1 disk drive, color monitor required.
You Hve Been Chosen to Lead Your Hand-Picked Band of Four Brave Adventurers on a Treacherous Journey. Your Quest is to Reclaim the Mystical Jewels from Eight Dragon Princes, Resurrect the Great Dragon & Restore the Primeval Realm, the Souce of All Magic in the Universe.
Data East U.S.A., Inc.

Draw-Forms. Compatible Hardware: Apple Macintosh. Memory Required: 512k. General Requirements: ImageWriter or LaserWriter.
3.5" disk $59.95.
MACDRAW Business Forms.
Data Management Assocs. of New York, Inc.

Draw Poker. Compatible Hardware: TI 99/4A with Extended BASIC.
write for info. disk or cassette.
Card Game Played Against Computer. You & Computer Are Given a Bankroll of $5,000.00. Your Hand Is Dealt with All 5 Cards Showing & Computer's Hand Is Dealt Face Down.
Texas Instruments, Personal Productivit.

Drawbase. Version: 1.7. Compatible Hardware: IBM PC & compatibles. Memory Required: 640k. General Requirements: Hard disk. Customer Support: $900 per year.
$2995.00 to $4995.00.
CAD Program for Architecture Featuring 3-D Capabilities, Macro Facilities, Text Editor, Walls, Wall Opening, Insert Object, Construction Geometry, Architectural Symbols, Space Accounting, On-Line Help & User-Customizable, Integrated Database. Manager Links Are Available to Lotus 1-2-3 & Symphony. Imports & Exports IGES & .DXF File Formats. Can Import ASCII Text Files into Drawing. Technical Phone Support Available.
CADworks, Inc.

Drawbridge. Version: 5.0. May 1992. Operating System(s) Required: PC-DOS/MS-DOS. Memory Required: 384k. General Requirements: Graphics card, mouse (optional). Items Included: Disk, manual. Customer Support: 30 days phone support.
disk $189.00 (ISBN 0-922394-14-8).
Allows Interactive Design of Graphic Displays. Object-Oriented Graphics Editing Allows Control over Attributer of Individual Graphics Objects. Once the Graphic Has Been Created, the Program Is Automatically Written to Recreate It As an ASCII File of Source Code Calls to the Graphics Library. Supports Borland BGI, Genus GX, MetaWindow & Microsoft Graphics Libraries.
Courseware Applications, Inc.

Drawing Discovery.
Apple II (48k). 3.5" disk $29.99 (Order no.: 1227).
3.5" disk $39.99, incl. backup disk (Order no.: 1227B).
Creativity Software Designed to Allow Children to Produce Their Own Designs & Drawings Using a Keyboard. Will Support Color & a Joy Stick. Provides for Saving the Pictures & Recalling Them from the Disk. Very Useful for Teaching Art & Design Concepts. Designed Specifically to Encourage the Creativity of Children, It Has Been Used Extensively with Young Children Because of Its Untimed, Unhurried, Open-Ended, Non-Threatening, & Non-Competitive Nature.
Trillium Pr.

Drawing Gallery. Compatible Hardware: HP 150 Touchscreen.
3.5" disk $345.00 (Order no.: 45411A).
Helps User Create Word & Picture Graphics, Such As Organization Charts, Process-Flow Diagrams, & Text Charts. Provides Electronic Templates & Other On-Screen Drawing Aids. Includes a Library of Ready-Made Pictures & Text to Add to the Graphics.
Hewlett-Packard Co.

Drawing Table. Compatible Hardware: Apple IIgs, Macintosh 512K or higher. Memory Required: 512k. General Requirements: Color monitor recommended, Macintosh needs 2 800k drives or hard disk.
$129.95.
Create Detailed Flowcharts, Diagrams, Floor Plans, Architectural Drawings or Any Line Drawing in Multiple Colors. Includes a Library of Geometric Shapes & Symbols Which Can Be Positioned in the Drawing in Any Size, Pattern, or Color. Graphics Can Be Moved Individually or in Groups & Overlapped Without Erasing the Work Beneath. Type Fonts Are Also Included. Features Built-In Horizontal & Vertical Rulers.
Broderbund Software, Inc.

DrawingMaster Plus (Model 52224).
Macintosh. $14,995.00.
High-Performance D-Size Plotter Using Direct-Imaging Technology to Produce Superior Quality One- or Two-Color (Black & Red) Drawings on Roll-Feed Media 24 Inches Wide. Performance Specifications Include Normal Resolution of 200 DPI at Media Travel Speed of 2 IPS. Qualplot Mode Doubles Resolution in Media Travel Axis & Halves Plotting. Quickplot Mode Produces Plotting Speed of 3.5 IPS & Halves Resolution in Media Travel Axis.
CalComp, Inc.

DrawPower 3D (AutoCAD). Version: 3.0. 1990. Items Included: Documentation. Customer Support: Available at additional cost.
PC-MS/DOS. 386 or higher (8Mb). disk $3500.00. Networks supported: Novell.
Used for Architectural Quality Drawing. Automates Casework Drafting & Design. It Can Handle All Architectural Chores from Drawing Plan & Elevation Walls to Placing Casework in Both Views. Allows the User to Customize the

Casework to Their Specifications. Utilizing a Built-In Computer-Aided-Drafting Package, the Standard Features Are at User's Disposal Including Snaps, Zooms & Various Editing Features. The 3D Model Uses AutoCAD Release 13 for Windows.
Pattern Systems International, Inc.

Dream Machine Laserstack. *Items Included:* 2 Floppy discs, user's guide. *Customer Support:* M-F 9 AM-5 PM Pacific Time (213) 451-1383.
Macintosh Plus, SE, II or Portable (1 Mb). 3.5" disk $59.95. *Nonstandard peripherals required:* Videodisc player, monitor & cables; Dream machine I or Dream machine II videodisc. *Addl. software required:* Hype.
Attain Immediate Access to Any of 286 Computer-Generated Motion Picture Sequences via This Combined LaserStack Index to Both Volumes of Dream Machine. Navigate & Access Works via Title, Source, Type, Purpose, Motion, Rendering or Modeling Technique. An Illustrated Glossary Reinforced by Select Sequences from the Disc, Explains & Demystifies Computer Graphics Terminology.
The Voyager Co.

Dreidel Drama. *Compatible Hardware:* Apple II+, IIe, IIc. *Language(s):* BASIC, Machine. *Memory Required:* 48k.
disk $19.95.
Holiday Program Which Features the 3 Following Dreidel Games: Regular Dreidel; Dreidel 1000; & Forty-Four Candles.
Davka Corp.

DREP. Computer College. *Compatible Hardware:* TI Professional. *Operating System(s) Required:* CP/M-86, MS-DOS. *Language(s):* DBASE II. *Memory Required:* 64k. *General Requirements:* Winchester hard disk, printer.
$1295.00.
Data Base/File Management Program Designed for Manufacturing or Sales Organizations.
Texas Instruments, Personal Productivit.

Dress Shop. *Version:* 1.5. Nov. 1991. *Items Included:* 5.25" & 3.5" disks, 1 hinged perfect bound user guide, 1 warranty card & 1 page read me paper. *Customer Support:* 800 number customer support; 90 day maintenance; 90 day money back guarantee.
PC-DOS 2.11 or higher. IBM PC/XT/AT or compatible (640k). disk $99.95. *Optimal configuration:* Epson or IBM compatible dot matrix printer; narrow or wide carriage.
Software Allows User to Print Out Custom Fitted Patterns (Slopers). User Enters 13 Key Measurements into Computer, Program Does All the Calculating. User Chooses from 29 Garments & Printer Prints Out Panels Which When Taped Together Make a Full-Sized Pattern.
Livingsoft, Inc.

Drexel Plot. *Compatible Hardware:* Apple Macintosh. *Operating System(s) Required:* Finder 4.1, 5.3.
3.5" disk $11.00.
Graphing Application That Allows the User to Enter up to Four Paired Sets of Data & Place up to Four Lines on the Same Graph. Users Can Select the Range, Increments, & Axis Origin for the Graph & the Number of Decimal Places for the Numbers on the Grid.
Kinko's.

Drill-Mate. *Version:* 2.0.
MS-DOS. IBM 386 or higher (2Mb). $3000.00. *Addl. software required:* PRODUCT PLANNER required for some versions. *Networks supported:* Novell Net Ware.
Automatically Creates & Draws Drilling & Routing Instructions for Custom-Sized Parts. User Can Automatically Change the Position of All Machining Relative to a Predetermined Point. Uses "Parametric Design" to Allow the Drilling Template to Be Re-Sized once the Part Size & Thickness Is Given. Template Log Keeps Track of Programs.
Pattern Systems International, Inc.

Drill Report. *Version:* 2.6. Jan. 1990. *Items Included:* User manual. *Customer Support:* Free phone support.
Macintosh Plus or higher (2Mb). 3.5" disk $135.00 (Order no.: DR-1). *Addl. software required:* Hypercard 2.0 or higher. *Optimal configuration:* Macintosh &/or higher, 2Mb RAM, hard disk. *Networks supported:* Appletalk.
Password Protected Fire Service DataBase Used to Keep Track of Training & Drill Schedules, Supports Grading & Calculates Grade Averages for Final Reports & Summaries. System 7.0 Savvy.
Sound Advice, Inc.

Drive Cleaner. *Version:* 1.1. Oct. 1992. *Items Included:* 3M brand disk drive cleaning kit. *Customer Support:* 11-5 Mon-Fri Eastern Time (904) 576-9415 or online through AppleLink, America Online, GEnie, CompuServe.
Macintosh 6.0.2 or higher including System 7. Macintosh. 3.5" disk $34.95, SRP (Order no.: DCM). *Optimal configuration:* Macintosh 6.0.2 or higher.
Effectively & Safely Cleans Any Macintosh 3.5" Disk Drive. Includes Free 3M Corp. Head Cleaner (Recommended by Apple Computer) & Software for the Best Cleanings.
Seven Hills Software Corp.

Drive Rocket. *Version:* 2.0. Jul. 1993. *Customer Support:* Technical support via telephone, Internet & BBS.
DOS & Windows. IBM PC AT, 386, 486, Pentium & Compatibles. disk $39.95. *Optimal configuration:* Recommended for IDE (AT interface) hard disk drive models that support the read/write multiple commands & are larger than 80Mb in capacity.
This New Device Driver Increases the Rate at Which Most IDE Drives Transfer Data So That Your Hard Disk Drive Processes at the Maximum Performance Level. Now Includes a Fast Disk Driver for Windows.
Ontrack Computer Systems, Inc.

DriveAlyne. *Customer Support:* 800-929-8117 (customer service).
MS-DOS. Commodore 128; CP/M. disk $49.99 (ISBN 0-87007-495-4).
Uses a Dysan Digital Diagnostic Diskette to Check the Alignment of 8" Drives, Including Spindle Centering, Radial Head Alignments, & Azimuth Alignments. For Computers with Western Digital Controller Chip.
SourceView Software International.

Drol. Aik Beng. *Compatible Hardware:* Atari 400, 800, XL series; Commodore 64.
disk $34.95 ea.
Atari. (Order no.: ATDSK-130).
Commodore. (Order no.: COMDSK-243).
Offers: Airborne Turkeys That Cook up into Thanksgiving Roast When Zapped; Overweight, Hopping Monsters That Toss Lightning Bolts; Scorpions; Lizards; a Magnet-Tossing Witch Doctor & More. Players Take on the Task of Pursuing a Red-Headed Girl & Her Propeller-Beanied Brother Who Have Wandered Away from Their Home. Mesmerized by the Spell of a Witch Doctor, the Children Drift Aimlessly Through the Scrolling Underground Corridors of an Ancient Civilization. A Rocket Backpack, Protective Laser Gun & Wide-Screen Radarscope Are Provided to Help the Player Rescue Them.
Broderbund Software, Inc.

DROPIN. John Higgins & Muriel Higgins. May 1992. *Items Included:* Manual & disk. *Customer Support:* Lifetime warranty; customer service hotline (800-654-8715).
MS-DOS 2.0 or higher. IBM & compatibles (256k). Single copy $49.95; Site License $139.95 (ISBN 0-940503-89-1, Order no.: IBM 650). *Optimal configuration:* EGA color monitor. *Networks supported:* Yes.
A Word Puzzle Generator - Takes a Short Text, Between 25 & 220 Characters (i.e. Roughly Between Five & Fifty Words) & Arranges the Characters in a Grid, Like a Crossword Grid. The Task Is to Reconstruct the Original Passage by "Dropping In" the Appropriate Letter into Its Correct Position. May Be Used with Beginners or Advanced Learners.
Research Design Assocs., Inc.

DRP Addresses. *Version:* 9. May 1996. *Items Included:* Portfolio spreadsheet worksheet. *Customer Support:* Yes.
Macintosh (1Mb). 3.5" disk $35.00 (ISBN 0-9623179-4-2). *Addl. software required:* Excel & Works, Word Processor.
IBM PC & compatibles (640k). disk $35.00 (ISBN 0-9623179-5-0). *Addl. software required:* Excel & Works, Word Processor.
Directory of Dividend Reinvestment Stocks. Includes Name, Ticker, Exchange, Industry of, & Complete Address & Phone Number.(This is an Expanded Version of "DRP Stocks"). Can Be Used as Mailmerge.
S.A.M. Designs.

DRP Addresses. *Version:* 1994-7. Suzanne Mitchell. Jun. 1994. *Items Included:* Dividend Achievers List, Portfolio Mgmt for spreadsheet. *Customer Support:* No fees - phone or online thru Prodigy, America onLine (AOL) or EWorld (Apple).
Macintosh 6.08 or higher. Macintosh (Apple) (1Mb). 3.5" disk $35.00 (ISBN 0-9623179-4-2, Order no.: DRP ADDRESSES 7-94). *Addl. software required:* Word processor, Excel 2.2 or other spreadsheet program.
MS-DOS. IBM & compatibles (4Mb). disk $35.00 (ISBN 0-9623179-4-2, Order no.: DRP ADDRESSES-7-94). *Addl. software required:* Lotus 1-2-3 V2.3, Quattro, word processor or Excel. *Optimal configuration:* 5 1/4 HD disk or 3 1/2 HD disk.
Disk Lists over 1200 Stocks with Exchange, Ticker, Address, Industry. Also Stocks That Can Be Purchased Direct, Discounts, IRAS, ADRS. Helpful Dividend Reinvestment Advice.
S.A.M. Designs.

DRP Stocks. *Version:* 7. Jun. 1994. *Items Included:* Portfolio spreadsheet worksheet. *Customer Support:* Yes.
Macintosh (1Mb). 3.5" disk $15.00. *Addl. software required:* Excel & Works, Word Processor.
IBM PC & compatibles (640k). disk $15.00.
Directory/Database of Dividend Reinvestment Stocks. Name, Ticker, Exchange & Category List Text on DRP Investing, Hints, Addresses of Interest & Direct Investing.
S.A.M. Designs.

Drug Actions in Hypertension. (Health Care Professional Ser.).
MS-DOS 2.1 or higher. IBM PC & compatibles. disk $39.95 (Order no.: 6HCP).
Describes Peripheral Adrenergic Inhibitors, Angiotensin-Converting Enzyme Inhibitors, Calcium Channel Blockers & Calcium Entry-Blocking Drugs, Including Mechanism of Action, Side Effects & Individual Characteristics. Helps in the Development of Plans for Choosing an Agent for an Individual Patient & Deciding Which Medication Is Most Likely to Cause a Given

Adverse Effect. Explains Effects of Calcium Entry-Blocking Drugs on Heart Disease & Cardiac Arrythmias.
Cardinal Health Systems, Inc.

Drug Culture Monopoly. Thomas J. Rundquist. Jun. 1995. *Items Included:* Manual includes Drug Slang Glossary, Michigan Criminal Law, Foreword, Paper Version of Game (Hard copy), Play Money, Bust & Luck Cards, Game Board Sheet, Psychological Analysis of Drug Culture. *Customer Support:* By Fax, by phone, by mail at no charge.
PC Windows (3.1), DOS 5, 386 PC (minimum). IBM PC & compatibles (2Mb). disk $30.50 (ISBN 1-884239-05-6). *Optimal configuration:* 386 PC or higher with 4Mb RAM.
Monopoly Style Game of Criminal Drug Activities Designed by Addicts. Real Life Events Described. Meant to Be Based on the Criminals Lives.
Nova Media, Inc.

Drug Interactions Advisor. Robert W. Hogan. Jan. 1986. *Compatible Hardware:* Apple IIe or IIc; IBM PC. *Memory Required:* 128k. *General Requirements:* 80-column text card for Apple.
Apple program disk $99.50 (ISBN 0-683-16820-7).
Apple datc disk $49.95 (ISBN 0-683-16821-5).
IBM program disk $99.50 (ISBN 0-683-16836-3).
IBM data disk $49.95 (ISBN 0-683-16821-5).
Designed to Allow Rapid Retrieval of Critical Information about Interactions among Commonly Prescribed Drugs. Accesses a Database of Nearly 500 Generic & over 1300 Trade Mark Drugs with Potential Interactions for up to 12 Drugs at a Time. The Data Disk Will Be Updated Semiannually.
Williams & Wilkins.

Drug Master Plus. Oct. 1994. *Compatible Hardware:* IBM PC XT, PC AT, & compatibles. *Operating System(s) Required:* MS-DOS 3.0 or higher. *Language(s):* QuickBASIC. *Memory Required:* 640k. *General Requirements:* Hard disk. *Customer Support:* Updated 3 times a year for $95/yr.
$99.95.
Drug Information System with a Database Covering over 4200 Drugs, Selected for Clinical Relevance & Usefulness. Includes Detailed Text on Drug-Drug Interactions, GI Side Effects, Drug-Food/Nutrient/Alcohol Interactions, Drug-Laboratory Interactions, & More. Allows Drug-Drug Interacting Testing on One to Twenty Drugs. Also Includes a Relational Patient Database That Includes Patient Name, ID #, Sex, Age, Drugs, & Medication Allergies. Potential Allergies Are Flagged During the Drug Selection Process. Printout Is Suitable for Inclusion in the Medical Record.
Rapha Group Software, Inc.

Druid. Nov. 1995. *Customer Support:* Free hint line service available 4:00-8:00p.m. (EST) weekdays, 12:00-4:00p.m. (EST) weekends & holidays. Technical support on weekdays 9:00a.m.-5:00p.m. (EST), 30-day warranty with dated proof of purchase. After 30-day warranty expires, $12.50 replacement fee applied.
PC-DOS/MS-DOS. 486/33 MHz (4Mb). CD-ROM disk $64.95 (ISBN 0-926846-81-7). *Nonstandard peripherals required:* Double speed CD-ROM drive, SVGA, 265-color, sound blaster.
Druid Is a Fully Animated & Interactive Action Adventure That Features an Easy Point-&-Click Interface & High Resolution SVGA Graphics. And Don't Forget Your Axe! Arriving upon the World of Navan, You'll Discover a Realm of Astral Creatures, Psionics, Politics & Magic That Are Unparalleled in Any Adventure Game. Spanning Five Islands & over 40 Hours of Play, Druid Succeeds in Combining a Graphically Rich Gaming Environment with a Well-Developed Story & an Effortless Interface.
Sir-Tech Software, Inc.

Drum Studio. *Compatible Hardware:* Commodore Amiga. *Customer Support:* Backup disk available.
3.5" disk $14.95.
Non-Intuition Percussive Composition Program.
DigiTek Software.

DS Backup Plus. *Compatible Hardware:* Tandy 1000, 1200, 3000. *Memory Required:* 256k. *General Requirements:* Hard disk.
disk $79.95.
Backup Utility Which Runs Faster Than the Backup Utility That Comes With MS-DOS. Also Comes With SPEEDBAK, a Separate Program That Makes Backups Even Faster but Doesn't Work With All Compatibles.
Design Software.

DS-Concrete. *Compatible Hardware:* Apple Macintosh 512KE, PLUS, SE, SE/30, II, IIcx, IIx. *General Requirements:* 800K disk drive or hard disk; Microsoft Excel. *Customer Support:* Free technical support, 30-day money back guarantee.
3.5" disk $195.00.
HyperCard demo avail.
Concrete Beam Analysis & Design Rectangular Column & Rectangular Spread Footing Programs for Engineering.
Daystar Software, Inc.

DS: Display Window. Ken Berry. *Operating System(s) Required:* MS-DOS.
disk $39.95, incl. manual (ISBN 0-934375-32-1).
Contains the Programs Necessary to Control the Operator Console in the Tele Operating System, & Will Work with Any Memory-Mapped Hardware. Included Are Functions to Create & Delete Virtual Displays, & Functions to Overlay a Portion of a Virtual Display on the Physical Display. Features BIOS-Level Drivers for a Memory-Mapped Display, Window Management Support, etc.
M & T Bks.

DS-DOS Plus 2.11. Tim Purves. *Compatible Hardware:* Sanyo MBC 555. *Memory Required:* 200k.
disk $49.95 (ISBN 0-923213-25-2, Order no.: SA-DS2).
MS-DOS 2.11 Enhancement with Other Utilities Included.
MichTron, Inc.

DS Optimize. *Version:* 1.10C. *Compatible Hardware:* IBM PC & compatibles. *Operating System(s) Required:* DOS 3.0 or higher. *Memory Required:* 256k.
disk $69.95.
Menu-Driven Hard Disk Defragmenter & Packer. Not Copy Protected.
Design Software.

DS-Steel2D. *Compatible Hardware:* Apple Macintosh, PLUS, SE, SE/30, II, IIcx, IIx. *General Requirements:* 800k disk drive or hard disk; Microsoft Excel. *Customer Support:* Free technical support, 30-day money back guarantee.
3.5" disk $295.00.
demo avail.
Engineering Program That Designs Steel Frames & Trusses According to the 1989 ASD AISC Code. Features AISC Standard Shapes, User-Customizable Shapes & Stress Check Calculation. Design Data May Be Read from Frame Mac Text Files or Entered Manually.
Daystar Software, Inc.

DS-Wood. *Compatible Hardware:* Apple Macintosh, PLUS, SE, SE/30, II, IIcx, IIx. *General Requirements:* 800K disk drive or hard disk; Microsoft Excel. *Customer Support:* Free technical support, 30-day money back guarantee.
3.5" disk $195.00.
HyperCard demo avail.
Engineering Program That Designs Wood Frames & Trusses According to the 1985 AITC Code. Design Information May Be Read from Frame Mac Text Files or Entered Manually. Features AITC Stress Check Calculation, Including Major & Minor Axis Bending Stress, Tension & Compression Stress & Horizontal Shear Stress.
Daystar Software, Inc.

DSA Signature Software. *Version:* 1.2. 1991. *Items Included:* Users Guide. *Customer Support:* Free telephone support, Users Guide & on-line help.
MS-DOS. IBM PC, XT, AT, PS/2 & compatibles (256k). $149.95 single unit commercial; $74.95 single unit government (Order no.: DSA SIGNATURE). *Optimal configuration:* 512k RAM. *Networks supported:* All.
Sun/SunOS, HP-US, DEC ULTRIX/OSF. Sun/UNIX, HP, DEC (256k). $187.45 single user commercial; $93.50 single user government (Order no.: DSA SIGNATURE - SUN). *Optimal configuration:* 512k RAM. *Networks supported:* All.
site licenses & quantity discounts avail.
Implementation of Digital Signature & Secure Hash Algorithms That Provides Verification That Documents Exchanged Between Correspondents Have Not Been Modified & That They Have Come from the Purported Sender. Allows User to Attach Digital Signature to a Document Using Private Key, & Anyone May Validate That Signature Using Signer's Public Key.
Information Security Corp.

D.S.D. - Direct Store Delivery Physical Inventory: Telxon PTC-710. *Version:* 2.70. Oct. 1995. *Items Included:* Manuals. *Customer Support:* Initial training provided on site by dealer repr. All on going support provided by modem & telephone.
MS-DOS 6.0. Telxon PTC-710 & PS/2 3865X (512k). $800.00 & cost of Telxon. *Addl. software required:* Computerized Daily Book V5.0 or higher. *Networks supported:* Netware Lite & LANtastic.
Permits All Deliveries to Be Scanned via Telxon PTC-710 Then Uploaded to Daily Book Where a Purchase Invoice Is Created Automatically. The Operator Audits the Margins, etc. & Accepts a Payment Method at Which Time the A/P & Inventory Are Updated. Physical Inventory Program Permits Inventory to Be Downloaded to Telxon PTC-710. The System Prints Exception Reports & Adjusts Book to Actual Value.
Service Station Computer Systems, Inc.

DSD80: Debugger. Jan. 1985. *Operating System(s) Required:* CP/M. *Memory Required:* 32k.
disk $115.00 (Order no.: 191).
SLR Systems.

DSTAT: Software for the Meta-Analytic Review of Research Literatures. *Version:* 1.10. Blair T. Johnson. 1989. *Items Included:* 1 manual. *Customer Support:* Free technical support; 90 days limited warranty.
MS-DOS. IBM & compatibles (640k). disk $99.95, incl. documentation (ISBN 1-56321-136-X).
3.5" disk $99.95, incl. manual (ISBN 1-56321-137-8).
documentation $9.95 (ISBN 1-56321-138-6).
demo disk $10.00 (ISBN 1-56321-139-4).
3.5" demo disk $10.00 (ISBN 1-56321-131-9).
This Software Package Was Written to Aid

Meta-Analysts As They Review the Studies Comprising Research Literatures.
Lawrence Erlbaum Assocs. Software & Alternate Media, Inc.

DTP Advisor, 2 disks. Sep. 1988. *Compatible Hardware:* Apple Macintosh. *Memory Required:* 1024k. *General Requirements:* Hard disk; printer recommended.
disk $79.95 (Order no.: 33555).
HyperCard Application That Contains a Graphic Arts & Design Advisor/Tutorial & a Graphic Arts Project Management System.
Broderbund Software, Inc.

D.Tree. *Version:* 1.1. 1989. *Memory Required:* 256k. *Items Included:* 128-page spiral bound monograph.
disk $180.00 (ISBN 0-89189-280-X, Order no.: B-68-9-025-20).
Teaches Decision Analysis by Means of Decision Tree Construction; Provides Methods for Examining Role of Laboratory Examination in Patient Care & Comparison of Expected Costs & Benefits.
ASCP Pr.

Dual Currency Aware. *Version:* 2.32. *General Requirements:* Hard disk drive.
Macintosh Plus or higher. 3.5" disk $1995.00.
General Ledger, Accounts Receivable, Accounts Payable.
Database International, Inc.

Duct Design - DD4M. *Version:* 07/1991. 1979. *Compatible Hardware:* IBM PC & compatibles. *Operating System(s) Required:* MS-DOS, PC-DOS. *Language(s):* Compiled & Assembly Language. *Memory Required:* 448k. *Customer Support:* Technical hotline, "Lifetime" support at no charge.
$265.00.
Air Duct Design - DD4M (New Update) Uses Static Regain, Constant Velocity & Equal Friction Methods of ASHRAE 1985, Independently or Together, to Design Air Ducts. Handles up to 1000 Duct Sections & Paths. Automatic Screens for 100-plus ASHRAE-Listed Fittings. Prints Schedule of Fittings & Duct Sections for Job. Super-Fast; Fully Compiled. Graphical Presentation of Air Pressures Throughout System. Fully Prompted with Latest State-of-the-Art Full-Function Input Screens with Windows, Defaults, Error Checking etc. Menu Driven. English Units.
MC2 Engineering Software.

Duct System Design. *Items Included:* Bound manual. *Customer Support:* Free hotline - no time limit; 30 day limited warranty; updates are $5/disk plus S&H.
MS-DOS. IBM & compatibles (256k). full system $249.95.
demo disk $5.00.
Interactively Sizes Air Duct Systems Using the Static-Regain, Constant-Velocity, or Equal-Friction Methods of ASHRAE, Either Independently or Together. Includes These Features: Calculates Pressure Required at Blower & the Drop in Each Section & Path; Handles Round, Rectangular, & Oval Ducts with Variable Roughness - Galvanized, Fiberglass, or Flexduct; Allows Mixed Use of the Three Sizing Methods - Static Regain for Trunks & Main Branches, & Equal Friction for Runouts (for Example); Altitude & Humidity Corrected; Calculates Path & Section Drops As Inputs Are Made - Sizes of Sections & Settings of Dampers May Be Reviewed & Changed So As to Balance the Path Drops During the Design Process; Prints Out Losses (in Detail) for Straight Sections & for Each Fitting, & Prints Out a List of Duct & Fitting Requirements; Handles Exhaust As Well As Blowing Applications.
Dynacomp, Inc.

DUCTSIZE: Static Regain & Equal Friction. *Items Included:* Manuel. *Customer Support:* Free toll free telephone support.
IBM PC & compatibles (256k). disk $495.00.
Calculates Optimal Duct Sizes Using Static Regain, Equal Friction, or Constant Velocity Methods. Based on the 1989 ASHRE Handbook of Fundamentals & the SMACNA HVAC Systems Duct Design Manual.
Elite Software Development, Inc.

Duden: Das Herkunftsworterbuch, Vol. 1. *Version:* 1.1.
80386 (4Mb). CD-ROM disk $59.95 (ISBN 3-411-06781-0, Order no.: 067810). *Addl. software required:* Microsoft Windows 3.1 or higher (mouse recommended). *Networks supported:* IBM 2.4Mb.
20,000 Entries.
Langenscheidt Pubs., Inc.

Duden: Das Stilworterbuch, Vol. 2. *Version:* 2.0.
80386 (4Mb). CD-ROM disk $59.95 (ISBN 3-411-06581-8, Order no.: 06581-8). *Addl. software required:* Microsoft Windows 3.1 or higher (mouse recommended). *Networks supported:* IBM.
Combines Grammar & Vocabulary As the Ultimate Reference Work on the Correct Usage of the German Grammar. More Than 100,000 Samples, Sentences, Idioms & Idiomatic Expressions.
Langenscheidt Pubs., Inc.

Duden: Das Worterbuch Medizinischer Fachausdruke. *Version:* 1.1.
80386 (4Mb). CD-ROM disk $69.95 (ISBN 3-411-06771-3, Order no.: 067713). *Addl. software required:* Microsoft Windows 3.1 or higher (mouse recommended). *Networks supported:* IBM 2Mb.
37,000 Entries.
Langenscheidt Pubs., Inc.

Duden: Die Deutsch Rechtschreibung, Vol. 1. *Version:* 1.1.
80386 (4Mb). CD-ROM disk $59.95 (ISBN 3-411-06700-4, Order no.: 067004). *Addl. software required:* Microsoft Windows 3.1 or higher (mouse recommended). *Networks supported:* IBM.
115 Entries, Includes the 79 Item German Spelling Reform Slated to Be Enacted by 1997.
Langenscheidt Pubs., Inc.

Duden: Dt. Universal WB, Duden Oxford GWB, Englisch. *Version:* 1.1.
80386 (4Mb). CD-ROM disk $179.95 (ISBN 3-411-06922-8, Order no.: 069228). *Addl. software required:* Microsoft Windows 3.1 or higher (mouse recommended). *Networks supported:* IBM 2Mb.
260,000 Entries & Usage Examples, 450,000 Eng-Ger-Eng Translations.
Langenscheidt Pubs., Inc.

Duden Multimedia: Mein Ertes Lexikon (for Pre-Readers).
80386 (4Mb). CD-ROM disk $105.95 (ISBN 3-411-06761-6, Order no.: 067616). *Addl. software required:* Microsoft Windows 3.1 or higher (mouse recommended). *Networks supported:* IBM 2Mb.
Features Words, Definitions, Pictures, & 30 Different Comprehension Games.
Langenscheidt Pubs., Inc.

Duden PC Bibliothek: Das Bedeutungsworterbuch, Vol. 10.
IBM compatible PC (2.7Mb). 3 disks $59.95 (ISBN 3-411-06861-2, Order no.: 068612). *Addl. software required:* Microsoft Windows Version 3.1 (mouse recommended).
75,000 Entries.
Langenscheidt Pubs., Inc.

Duden PC Bibliothek: Das Fremdworterbuch, Vol. 5. *Version:* 1.1.
IBM compatible PC (3.5Mb). 4 disks $59.95 (ISBN 3-411-06844-2, Order no.: 06844-2). *Addl. software required:* Microsoft Windows Version 3.1.
50,000 Entries, 100,000 Definitions, 300,000 Grammar, Pronunciation & Etymological Clarifications.
Langenscheidt Pubs., Inc.

Duden PC Bibliothek: Die Sinn und Sachverwandten Worter, Vol. 8.
IBM compatible PC (2.9Mb). 3 disks $59.95 (ISBN 3-411-06851-5, Order no.: 068515). *Addl. software required:* Microsoft Windows Version 3.1 (mouse recommended).
82,000 Entries.
Langenscheidt Pubs., Inc.

Duden: Redewendungen und Sprichwortliche Redensarten, Vol. 11.
80386 (4Mb). CD-ROM disk $59.95 (ISBN 3-411-06871-X, Order no.: 06871X). *Addl. software required:* Microsoft Windows 3.1 or higher (mouse recommended). *Networks supported:* IBM 2Mb.
10,000 Entries.
Langenscheidt Pubs., Inc.

Duden: Richtiges und Gutes Deutsch, Vol. 9. *Version:* 1.1.
80386 (4Mb). CD-ROM disk $59.95 (ISBN 3-411-06791-8, Order no.: 067918). *Addl. software required:* Microsoft Windows 3.1 or higher (mouse recommended). *Networks supported:* IBM.
Trouble Spots in the German Language.
Langenscheidt Pubs., Inc.

Duden: Zitate und Ausspruche, Vol. 12.
80386 (4Mb). CD-ROM disk $59.95 (ISBN 3-411-06881-7, Order no.: 068817). *Addl. software required:* Microsoft Windows 3.1 or higher (mouse recommended). *Networks supported:* IBM 2Mb.
Quotations & Famous Sayings from Classical Times Through Modern Advertising Jargon, Organized According to Topic.
Langenscheidt Pubs., Inc.

Due Date*Plus: Duedate Monitoring. *Version:* 2.2. Oct. 1994. *Items Included:* Manual & 6 months free maintenance (technical support & updates). *Customer Support:* Annual maintenance (technical support & updates) fee of $150 (after first six months); 90 days warranty; telephone training available for $75/hr.; conferences.
DOS 3.1 or higher. IBM & compatibles. Contact publisher for price. *Networks supported:* Novell, Novell-Lite, Lantastic.
*May Be Used As a Stand-Alone or May Be Interfaced with Version 2 of TB*Plus (Professional Time & Billing). Insures Meeting Important Deadlines by Tracking Any Duedates - Tax, Accounting, Auditing, Payroll & Others. The Program Can Automatically Track Extensions & Recurring Projects.*
UniLink.

Due Process. *Items Included:* Manual.
MS-DOS (256k). IBM PC & compatibles. contact publisher for price. *Nonstandard peripherals required:* Telephone line with RJ-11 jack. *Addl. software required:* IBM BASIC compiler.
DBASE III System Which Supports Process Server Industry. Tracks Pending Services, Current & Past Due Charges by Invoice User. Maintains Check List, Produces Forms & Produces a Variety of Reports on Clients, Employees & Account Receivable Status.
Management Systems, Inc.

TITLE INDEX

The Duel: Test Drive II - The Collection.
Customer Support: 90 days limited warranty, customer support phones: (408) 296-8400, hours: M-F 8-5 pm.
CGA & HERC 384k; EGA & TGA 512k. PC only. $49.95.
T2MC - Macintosh 512k, Plus, SE, IIx, IIcx, IIci (800k drive, 1Mb memory, B&W only). 3.5" disk $54.95.
The World's Two Fastest (200 mph) Production Cars, the Porsche 959 vs. the Ferrari F40 Race Head-to-Head Through Picturesque Scenery. Optional Car & Scenery Disks Are Available to Create Your Own Combinations of Landscapes & High Performance Cars.
Accolade, Inc.

DUMP: Hex-ASCII Memory Dump. Dick Rettke. Jan. 1979. *Compatible Hardware:* Apple II, II+, IIe, IIc, IIgs. *Operating System(s) Required:* Apple DOS, ProDOS. *Language(s):* Machine. *Memory Required:* 32k.
disk $9.95 (ISBN 0-926567-01-2, Order no.: DUMP).
Used for Debugging.
Rettke Resources.

Dungeon Master. *Compatible Hardware:* Atari ST, Commodore Amiga, Apple IIgs. *Memory Required:* Atari & Commodore 1Mb, Apple 1250k.
3.5" disk $39.95.
Real-Time Fantasy Role-Playing Adventure.
FTL Games.

Dungeon Masters Assistant, Vol. I: Encounters, 2 disks. Paul Murray et al. 1988. *Compatible Hardware:* Apple II, II+, IIe, IIc, Commodore 64/128, IBM PC or compatible, Amiga. *Memory Required:* Apple-64k, C/64-64k, IBM-256k, Amiga-512k. *Items Included:* Rulebook. *Customer Support:* 14 day money back guarantee/30 day exchange policy; tech support line: (408) 737-6800 (11:00 - 5:00 PST); customer service: (408) 737-6800 (9:00 - 5:00 PST).
disk $29.95.
Utility Program Designed to Help Dungeon Masters Generate Encounters For AD&D Campaigns. With Thousands of Separate Encounters, Monsters & Characters Provided, It Can Reduce Game Prep Time by Several Hours Per Session. Over 1000 Encounters & Over 1300 Monsters & Characters, Including All Monsters From the AD&D Monster Manuals I & II. Monster Records & Encounter Printouts Total Several Hundred Pages.
Strategic Simulations, Inc.

Dungeon Masters Assistant, Vol. II: Characters & Treasures. Al Escudero & James Ward. *Customer Support:* Technical support line: (408) 737-6850 (11am-5pm, PST); 14 day money back guarantee/30 day exchange policy. DOS 2.11 or higher. IBM PC & compatible (384k). disk $29.95.
Commodore 64/128 (64k). disk $29.95.
Workbench. Amiga (512k). 3.5" disk $29.95.
Apple II (64k). disk $29.95.
A Utility Program Designed to Help Dungeon Masters Generate Characters & Treasures for AD&D Campaigns. No Longer Is it Necessary to Spend Hours Populating a Town or Dungeon with Player Characters or Henchmen. Speed up Your Game Immeasurably by Generating Detailed Player or Non-Player Characters, & Large Treasure Hoards, in Moments! Every Facet of Character Generation, From Languages & Spell Lists to Class & Racial Abilities, Is Accounted for. All Character Classes, Including Multi-Class Characters, Can Be Rolled up in a Snap & Will Appear on Ready-Made Character Sheets with Pertinent In formation. Sheets Can Be Printed for Instant Use.
Strategic Simulations, Inc.

Dungeon of Danger. Adrian Vance. Oct. 1985. *Compatible Hardware:* Apple II. *Operating System(s) Required:* Apple DOS. (source code included). *Memory Required:* 48k.
disk $9.95 (ISBN 0-918547-29-6).
illustration files on the disk avail.
Fantasy Adventure Game Which Takes Place in "The Age of Magic". Requires Strategy to Win. Not Copy Protected.
AV Systems, Inc.

Duns Market Manager. Jan. 1986. *Compatible Hardware:* IBM PC & compatibles, PC XT. *Operating System(s) Required:* PC-DOS. *Memory Required:* 512k.
disk write for info.
Data Base Management System Created for Marketing Managers Seeking to Increase Their Productivity While Saving Time. Builds a System of Marketing Information Allowing User to Store, Combine, & Retrieve a Virtually Unlimited Level of Detail on Prospects from Data Bases of Marketing Information & Activities, As Well As Create Two Dozen Customized Management Reports. Interfaces with LOTUS 1-2-3 & MULTIMATE, & Communicates with Dun & Bradstreets's On-Line Search & Screening Services.
Dun & Bradstreet Credit Services.

Duns Print/PC. Apr. 1987. *Compatible Hardware:* IBM PC & compatibles. *Operating System(s) Required:* PC-DOS. *Memory Required:* 512k. *General Requirements:* Hard disk, modem.
disk $190.00.
Telecommunications Package for Connecting to D & B's On-Line Services. Stores Each Report in Uniquely-Named File. Features Comprehensive File Management Module.
Dun & Bradstreet Credit Services.

DunsPlus. *Version:* 2A. DunsPlus, Inc. Dec. 1985. *Compatible Hardware:* IBM PC, PC XT, PC AT. *Operating System(s) Required:* PC-DOS 2.1, 3.1. *Memory Required:* 256k. *General Requirements:* 2 disk drives or hard disk.
disk at quantity one $250.00.
Integrated Microcomputing System for Business Professionals in Large Corporate Environments. Integrates LOTUS 1-2-3, MULTIMATE or DISPLAYWRITE Word Processing, DBASE III, & Western Union Electronic Mail. Can Be Customized to the Individual User's Needs. Communications Capabilities Include 3270 & Async Terminal Emulation & PC-to-PC File Transfer, As Well As Enhanced Access to Public Databases.
Dun & Bradstreet Computing Services.

DUSC: Disk Utility Sort Catalog. Dick Rettke. Sep. 1979. *Compatible Hardware:* Apple II, II+, IIe, IIc, IIgs. *Operating System(s) Required:* Apple DOS 3.2, 3.3. *Language(s):* Machine. *Memory Required:* 32k.
disk $9.95 (ISBN 0-926567-03-9, Order no.: DUSC).
High Speed Sort of DOS Catalog into Ascending Alpha Sequence.
Rettke Resources.

Dust Emissions: Dustcon & Stockpile Software. F. W. Parrett. 1992. *Items Included:* Dustcon suite of programs; Stockpile suite of programs; review explaining all aspects of dust emissions. *Customer Support:* Fax.
MS-DOS 2.1 or higher. IBM PC & compatibles (640k). software pkg. $224.00 (ISBN 1-56252-227-2).
Contains Two Major Suites of Dust Emission Programs. DUSTCON Provides a Simple Modeling Approach Based on Gaussian Distribution Equations to Calculate, & to Plot, Dust Deposition Rates from Open-Cut Mines, Stockpiles or Quarries, in up to 16 Compass Directions from the Source of the Dust. Stockpile Suite Calculates Dust Emissions from Coal Stockpiles Using the Modeling Equations Developed at the Warren Springs Laboratory in the UK. The Review Covers Dust in Mining, Quarrying, & Bulk Handling of Material.
Computational Mechanics, Inc.

Dutch Foreign Direct Investment in the United States 1974-1994. May 1995. *Items Included:* Spiral bound manual. *Customer Support:* Unlimited telephone support.
MS-DOS 6.0/Windows 3.1 or higher. PC Clone 486 or higher (4Mb). disk $125.00 (ISBN 1-878974-09-2). *Addl. software required:* Database Versions are available for MS Access 2.0, Excel, Lotus, Paradox, Foxpro, & dBASE. *Optimal configuration:* PC clone with MS-DOS 6.0/Windows 3.1 or higher. Must have MS Access 2.0, or Excel, or Lotus or Paradox or Foxpro or dBASE.
Database of All Dutch Foreign Direct Investment Transactions in the United States 1974-1994.
Jeffries & Associates, Inc.

Duxbury Braille Translator. *Version:* IBM PC 7.9, MAC 8.8. Jun. 1991. *Compatible Hardware:* Apple Macintosh, IBM PC & compatibles, VAX/VMS, PDP-11/RSX, NCR Tower/Unix. *Operating System(s) Required:* PC-DOS/MS-DOS 2.1 or higher. *Language(s):* C. *Memory Required:* Macintosh, 1024k, others 512k. *General Requirements:* 1 floppy disk drive & hard drive with 2Mb available. *Items Included:* Disks, print manuals, Braille manuals. *Customer Support:* Free unlimited by telephone, 1 year access to Bulletin Board.
0 $495.00 single-user license.
Translates Print to Braille & Vice Versa. Foreign Languages & Math Available. The IBM PC Version Includes a Special Bridge for WORDPERFECT Files.
Duxbury Systems, Inc.

Dvorak's Guide to PC Connectivity. John C. Dvorak et al. Jun. 1992. *Items Included:* Three 5.25" disks. *Customer Support:* Phone number available for technical support, 212-492-9832; free disk replacement within 90 days of purchase.
IBM PC & compatibles. disk $49.95 (ISBN 0-553-35335-7).
This Book/Disk Package Is the Definitive & Complete Resource on Mixing & Matching Hardware, Software, Text & Graphics. There Has Never Been a Book Like It! Chapter Topics: Serial/Parallel/Network/Modem Connections, Components, Peripherals, Software Applications, Disks, File Formats, Networks. The Disks Contain LANtastic Networking Software, Word Forward, HiJaak File Conversion Software, & Much More! Dvorak Is an Internationally Known Columnist, Industry Commentator, & Bestselling Author.
Bantam Bks., Inc.

Dvorak's Guide to PC Games. John C. Dvorak & Peter Spear. *Items Included:* Two 5.25" disks. *Customer Support:* Phone number available for technical support, 212-492-9832; free disk replacement within 90 days of purchase.
IBM PC & compatibles. disk $29.95 (ISBN 0-553-35144-3).
This Is the Ultimate Buyer's Guide to PC Games. Covers Hundreds of Commercial & Shareware Titles Including: Tetris, Wizardry, SimCity. Includes Hardware Requirements, Tips, Tricks, & "Insider Secrets". Dvorak's Own Game Rating System Is Included. The Two Disks Contain Ready-to-Run Versions of the Authors' Favorite Games.
Bantam Bks., Inc.

DVT: Database Visualization Tool. *Items Included:* 3-ring bound manual, tutorial. *Customer Support:* Free unlimited technical support.
PC or MS-DOS 3.0 or higher. IBM PC & compatibles (560k). $490.00.
Visualizes Databases in 2- & 3-Dimensional Graphics, Using Both Numeric & Non-Numeric Data. Includes a Programmed Decision System That Evaluates Data & Suggests Graph Types (Plots, Histograms, Pie Charts, Bar Charts, Box Plots, Surface Diagrams, etc.) That Best Illustrate the Database.
IntelligenceWare, Inc.

DX11 & TX81Z Pro. *General Requirements:* MIDI Interface; Yamaha TX802 or TX81Z tone generator.
Macintosh (1MB). DX11 Pro $139.00.
TX81Z Pro $139.00.
Integrated Editors/Librarians.
Digital Music Services.

DX7 II & TX802 Pro. *General Requirements:* MIDI interface Yamaha DX7 II or TX802 synthesizer.
Macintosh 512KE or higher. $199.00, DX7 II Pro.
TX802 Pro $249.00.
Integrated Editors/Librarians.
Digital Music Services.

DX7 Voicing Program. *Compatible Hardware:* CX5M & other MSX systems.
contact publisher for price (Order no.: YRM 103).
Displays All DX7 Voice Parameters on the Video Monitor & Allows Programming from the Computer Keyboard. Voice Parameters Are Displayed in Graphs.
Yamaha Corp. of America.

Dynabase Database Program. *Compatible Hardware:* IBM. *Memory Required:* 128k.
disk $49.95.
Database Package Which May Be Configured by the User.
Dynacomp, Inc.

Dynabase Database Program. *Items Included:* Full manual. No other products required.
Customer Support: Free telephone support - no time limit. 30 day warranty.
MS-DOS 3.2 or higher. IBM & compatibles (512k). disk $39.95.
Easy-to-Use Database Package Which May Be Configured by the User. The Program Utilizes Sequential Access Techniques to Eliminate the Requirements of Setting Limits on the Size of Any Field, & to Make the Most Efficient Use of Available Disk Space. The Program Functions Have Been Structured Around the File Access Method to Provide the Least Amount of Delay.
Dynacomp, Inc.

The Dynacomp Battle Trilogy: Leipzig 1813, Waterloo 1815, Shiloh 1862, 3 games.
Compatible Hardware: Atari 400, 800.
Language(s): Atari BASIC (source code included).
Memory Required: 48k. *General Requirements:* Joysticks.
Disk set. $79.95.
Dynacomp, Inc.

DynaFORTH. *Compatible Hardware:* CP/M based machines with MBASIC. *Language(s):* FORTH (source code included). *Memory Required:* 48k.
disk $74.95.
8" disk $76.45.
8080 Assembly Language Implementation of the FigFORTH 8080 Version 1.1 Language.
Dynacomp, Inc.

DynaKey.LIB.
IBM PC & compatibles. disk $169.00.
Makes Mailing Lists More Efficient to Enter, & Reduces Keystrokes, Translates Abbreviations & Adds Missing Punctuation. Program Runs in Two Ways: Clipper Language Program Expands Abbreviations & Adds Missing Punctuations & Casing. Conversion of Downloaded Data into Presentable Name Is Also Possible.
Peoplesmith Software.

Dynamic & Continuous Distillation. *Items Included:* Full manual. No other products required. *Customer Support:* Free telephone support - no time limit. 30 day warranty.
MS-DOS 3.2 or higher. IBM & compatibles (512k). disk $2899.95. *Addl. software required:* Steady State Continuous Distillation.
DCD Solves Your Distillation & Control System Modeling Problems with Excellent Design & Troubleshooting Capabilities. It Models Continuous Columns by Solving the Necessary Differential Equations Derived from the Column & Control Loop Dynamics. To Use DCD, You Need STEADY STATE CONTINUOUS DISTILLATION Which Provides the Steady-State Solution That Is the Starting Point in the Dynamic Simulation.
Dynacomp, Inc.

Dynamic System Analyzer: Linear & Nonlinear Systems. 1995. *Items Included:* 150-page manual. *Customer Support:* Free telephone support - 90 days, 30-day warranty.
MS-DOS 3.2 or higher. 286 (584k). disk $74.95. *Nonstandard peripherals required:* CGA/EGA/VGA.
Students Can Explore 22 Common Physical Systems - Including More Than 30 Different Scenarios - & View the Results Simultaneously in Graphs & Animations. Numerical Tables of Variables Are Easily Accessed. Systems Include One- & Two-Dimensional, Orbital, Harmonic, & Chaotic Motion, As Well As Electrical Phenomena.
Dynacomp, Inc.

Dynamic Tape Accelerator. *Version:* 3.1. *Compatible Hardware:* DEC VAX. *Operating System(s) Required:* VMS. *Items Included:* Media & documentation. *Customer Support:* 30 days included, toll-free hotline.
$1000.00-$3500.00.
Eliminates Tape I/O Bottlenecks Transparently, & Regulates the Flow of Data from the Computer to the Tape Drive.
Touch Technologies, Inc.

Dynamics. 1985. *Items Included:* Manual with theory, sample runs, program listings in BASIC. *Customer Support:* Free phone, on-site seminars.
MS-DOS. IBM (128k). disk $110.00.
Macintosh. Macintosh. 3.5" disk $110.00.
22 Programs That Solve Problems in Rigid Body Dynamics with Graphical Display of Solutions. Follows Same Sequence Used in Most Textbooks on Dynamics. Includes Programs for Vector Operations, Motion in Plane Polar Coordinates, Harmonic Motion, Friction & Viscosity, Systems of Particles, Inertias & Centers of Mass, Impulse-Momentum, Numerical Integration of Equations of Motion, Work/Energy Collisions, Energy Surfaces & Gradients, Angular Momentum, Translation & Rotation, Gyroscopes, Rotating Coordinate Systems, Coriolis Acceleration, Kepler's Laws, Vectors & Transformations.
Kern International, Inc.

Dynamics & Vibration Analysis. 1995. *Items Included:* Full manual. *Customer Support:* Free telephone support - 90 days, 30-day warranty.
MS-DOS 3.2 or higher. 286 (584k). disk $599.95. *Nonstandard peripherals required:* CGA/EGA/VGA.
A Computerized Form of the Book, Formulas for Natural Frequency & Mode Shape, by Robert D. Blevins. It Provides a Summary of Formulas & Principles for Analyzing the Vibration of Hundreds of Structural & Fluid Systems.
Dynacomp, Inc.

Dynamics Device Drivers. *Compatible Hardware:* TRS-80 Model I.
disk $24.95 (Order no.: 199RD).
cassette $19.95 (Order no.: 0228R).
Allows Users to Reprogram Their Keyboard, Video Display, & Printer to Customize the Commands Their Computer Sends to Its Components.
Instant Software, Inc.

Dynamind Neural Network Processor. *Items Included:* Full manual. No other products required. *Customer Support:* Free telephone support - no time limit. 30 day warranty.
MS-DOS 3.2 or higher. IBM & compatibles (512k). disk $169.95. *Optimal configuration:* 286, 386, or 486 PC, 640k RAM, DOS 3.0 or higher & an EGA or VGA monitor. A mouse & math coprocessor are supported, but optional.
Combines an Elegant Interface with Exceptional Power to Give You a Full-Featured Tool for Creating, Training, & Implementing Neural Networks. Comprehensive Documentation & Numerous Examples Take You Step-by-Step Through a Neural Network Solution.
Dynacomp, Inc.

DynaPerspective. *Version:* 2.0. Sep. 1990. *Items Included:* Manual; 5 diskettes. *Customer Support:* 30-days unlimited warranty.
MS-DOS. IBM compatibles (640k). disk $995.00. *Optimal configuration:* 386; MS-DOS 4.0; extended memory.
Macintosh II (2Mb). 3.5" disk $995.00. *Nonstandard peripherals required:* Hard disk, high resolution color RGB monitor, 8 bit expanded RAM color graphics board.
Three-Dimensional Modeling & Design Presentation Program That Can Stand Alone or Enhance CAD Drafting Systems. Models Are Built from Flexible Geometric Primitives with User-Defined Dimensions. Also Includes DynaPerspective Parts Library, RAM-Based Speed with the Macintosh II's Floating Point Accuracy, Wire-Frame Modeling, Surface Rendering, 3-Point Perspective View Control, Light Source Shading & Surface Transparency Capabilities, DXF Format Import/Export, PICT & PICS File Save Capability, 3 Color Palette Modes & Instantaneous On-Screen Color Display. Create Fly bys/Walk Throughs of Model. Save As High Speed Animations for Play Back at Near Video Speeds.
Dynaware USA, Inc.

Dynaword Document Creator. *Items Included:* Bound manual. *Customer Support:* Free hotline - no time limit; 30 day limited warranty; updates are $5/disk plus S&H.
MS-DOS. IBM PC & compatibles (128k, 360k). disk $59.95.
Word Processor.
Dynacomp, Inc.

Dyno-Quest. 1989-1991. *Items Included:* Disk(s), user's guide, poster, coloring book, warranty card, swap coupon. *Customer Support:* 90 day unlimited warranty; 800 toll free number, 800-221-7911, 8:00 a.m.-5:00 p.m. Arizona time; Updates $10.
Macintosh System 6 or higher. Macintosh (1Mb monochrome, 2Mb color). 3.5" disk $69.99 (ISBN 1-55772-270-6, Order no.: 0302).
Optimal configuration: 2Mb color monitor, Macintosh LC. *Networks supported:* Digicard.
MS-DOS. IBM, Tandy, MS-DOS compatible

TITLE INDEX

(128k). disk $49.95 (ISBN 0-918017-05-X, Order no.: 0301). *Nonstandard peripherals required:* VGA or CGA card. *Optimal configuration:* 128k, color monitor, VGA card. *Networks supported:* Velan, Novell, Digicard.
DOS. Apple II, Apple IIe, Apple IIGS, Apple II Plus (48k). disk $49.95 (ISBN 0-918017-04-1, Order no.: 0300). *Optimal configuration:* Apple II, printer, color monitor, 48k. *Networks supported:* Digicard.
Takes You to the Age of Dinosaurs & Encourages Strategic Thinking & Exploration of Alternatives. While Increasing One's Knowledge of Dinosaurs, You Also Strengthen Problem-Solving Techniques & Your Planning & Organizational Skills. Can Be Customized to Individual Needs with CHALLENGE UPGRADE. Ages 9 to Adult.
Mindplay.

E-VENIX/386. *Customer Support:* VenturCom has four levels of support. Prices start at $200.00 per year. In addition, there are three courses which are held several times each year.
IBM PC compatible. This includes any Intel based ISA or EISA computer (2Mb). $300.00. *Networks supported:* Ethernet - TCP/IP.
Is USL Unix Ruggedized for Data Acquisition & Control. It's the Only Embedded & ROMable Unix OS That Delivers Guaranteed Real Time Unix. Developers Can Build on over 3,000 Off-the-Shelf Applications & Use the Same Powerful & Familiar Operating System for Development & Target Systems. E-Venix's New Automatic Start-Up & Fault Tolerance Features Have Greatly Expanded the Horizons of Unix Applications.
VenturCom.

E-Z-CRP: Capacity Requirements Planning System. *Version:* 11.0. Jun. 1986. *Compatible Hardware:* IBM PC & compatibles. *Operating System(s) Required:* MS-DOS. *Language(s):* C-BASIC. *Memory Required:* 128k. *General Requirements:* E-Z-MRP Material Requirements Planning System, printer, hard disk. *Customer Support:* 1 year free telephone support & upgrades.
disk $1295.00.
Accepts Work Center Definitions & Standard Routings for Manufactured Parts. Calculates the Day-by-Day Utilization of Each Work Center's Capacity Based On: Work Center Capacity; User-Defined Routings; & Total Manufacturing Requirements As Calculated by E-Z-MRP. Allows Users to Determine Over- & Under-Utilization of Work Centers, & Adjust Their Manufacturing Schedules Accordingly.
Alliance Manufacturing Software.

E-Z-Lab. *Version:* 11.0. Jan. 1988. *Compatible Hardware:* IBM PC & compatibles. *Memory Required:* 128k. *General Requirements:* 132-colmun printer. *Customer Support:* 1 year free telephone support & upgrades.
disk $695.00.
Labor Distribution & Job Cost System. Provides Users with Job Costing & Accounting of Direct & Indirect Labor Dollars. Takes Information from Employee Timecards & Then Calculates the Actual Direct Labor & Burden Dollars Charged to the Job on the Wage & Burden Rates That Were Entered in the Employee File.
Alliance Manufacturing Software.

E-Z MRP Junior: Material Requirements Planning System for Small Manufacturers. *Version:* 11.0. Feb. 1990. *Items Included:* Complete user's manual, plus the following software packages: (1) BMP: Bill of Materials Plus (2) E-Z-MRP Material Requirements Planning (3) E-Z-CRP Capacity Requirements Planning. *Customer Support:* 1 year free phone-in support & upgrades.
MS-DOS. IBM PC & compatibles (64k). disk $980.00. *Optimal configuration:* MS-DOS microcomputer, hard disk, standard printer, 128k memory.
Identical to the Full E-Z MRP in Every Respect Except One: Where E-Z MRP Will Accept to 32,000 Part Numbers Per Data Base, the Program Is Limited to 500 Parts. It Includes BMP, E-Z MRP, & E-Z CRP (See Listings Elsewhere in This Guide).
Alliance Manufacturing Software.

E-Z-MRP: Material Requirements Planning System. *Version:* 11.0. C. R. Smolin. Nov. 1984. *Compatible Hardware:* IBM PC & compatibles. *Operating System(s) Required:* MS-DOS. *Language(s):* C-BASIC. *Memory Required:* 128k. *General Requirements:* Hard disk, printer. *Customer Support:* 1 year free telephone support & upgrades.
disk $1995.00.
Materials Requirements Planning System Designed to Run on Microcomputers & Operates in Tandem with Another Smolin Product - BILL OF MATERIALS PLUS (BMP) - & Unlike Other MRP Systems, Requires No Other On-Line Applications. While Providing Many of the Features & Benefits Normally Seen Only in Mainframe MRP Systems, Its User-Oriented Approach to Data Entry & Report Generation Can Cut the Normal 18-Month MRP Implementation Cycle to 3 Weeks.
Alliance Manufacturing Software.

E-Z-PI: Physical Inventory System. *Version:* 11.0. Dec. 1990. *Items Included:* Complete user's manual for all company products. *Customer Support:* First year free phone-in support; $50/year thereafter.
DOS based. IBM PC & compatibles (64k). disk $495.00. *Addl. software required:* E-Z-MRP. *Optimal configuration:* Hard disk & 132-column printer.
Assists in Taking Physical Inventory by Tracking up to 20 Inventory Locations. It also Transfers Results to the E-Z-MRP Database with an Optional Audit Trail to The DAUDIT System. Flexible Reporting Includes: On-Hand/Actual/Variance, Missing & Duplicate Tags, & Exception Reporting. E-Z-PI Allows Multiple Data Entry Operators, & Custom Tag Printing is Available.
Alliance Manufacturing Software.

E-Z Pilot II: Training Package. May 1985. *Compatible Hardware:* Apple II+, IIe, IIc. *Operating System(s) Required:* Apple DOS 3.3. *Language(s):* BASIC, LOGO. *Memory Required:* 64k. *General Requirements:* Printer.
$219.95, incl. 1 author disk, 1 tutorial disk, 1 48k sample disk, 1 64k sample disk, 25 student reference cards, an instr's. manual, & a technical handbk. (Order no.: 21-10).
add'l. student manuals (set of 10) $40.00 (Order no.: 21-30).
back-up disk $10.00.
Programming Language Similar to BASIC but Easier to Learn.
Hartley Courseware, Inc.

E-Z Plot. Peter Theis. 1984. *Compatible Hardware:* Apple II, II+, IIe, IIc. *Operating System(s) Required:* Apple DOS 3.3. *General Requirements:* Printer & Grappler+ Printer Interface Card.
disk $34.50 (ISBN 1-55797-039-4, Order no.: AP2-AG82).
Designed to Create Graphic Pictures & Lettering Designs. Graphics Can Be Created, Changed, Saved, Loaded, & Printed. Can Be Used for Title Pages, Teacher Demonstrations, Pictures for Programs & Games, Logos, & Other Uses. An E-Z PLOT Picture Takes Approximately 34 Sectors of Disk Memory.
Hobar Pubns.

E-Z-PO: Purchase Order Module. *Version:* 11.0. Jun. 1993. *Items Included:* Full User's Manual. *Customer Support:* 1 yr. free phone-in support.
PC-DOS/MS-DOS. IBM PC & compatibles (128k). disk $695.00. *Addl. software required:* E-Z-MRP. *Networks supported:* Yes.
Add-On Module to the E-Z-MRP Material Requirements Planning System. Allows the User to Create, Maintain, & Print Purchase Orders, Using a Vendor Name & Address File. System Offers a Forms Design Program Which Allows the User to Place the 30 User-Definable Data Fields Wherever Desired, Accommodating Pre-Printed Forms. Also Automatically Generates Sequential Printed Forms. Also Automatically Generates Sequential Purchase Order Numbers, Transfers P.O. Line Item Details Automatically to the E-Z-MRP Supply Side File, & Maintains On-Hand Inventory Balances Through a Built-In Receiving Function.
Alliance Manufacturing Software.

Eadweard Muybridge Laserstack. *Items Included:* 1 floppy disk, instruction booklet. *Customer Support:* M-F 9 AM-5 PM Pacific Time (213) 451-1383.
Macintosh Plus, SE, II or Portable (1 Mb). 3.5" disk $59.95. *Nonstandard peripherals required:* Videodisc player, monitor & cables. *Addl. software required:* HyperCard 1.2.2 or higher.
An Electronic Index to Muybridge's Encyclopedic Work Featuring an In-Depth Biography & a Discussion of Muybridge's Lasting Influence on Art & Motion Pictures.
The Voyager Co.

Eagle Point Advantage Series for AutoCAD & MicroStation. *Version:* 1315. Oct. 1995. *Items Included:* On-line help, manuals, 30-day free tech support. *Customer Support:* On-line help, manuals, 30-day free tech support.
DOS, UNIX, Sun, Windows, Windows NT. 486, Pentium (16Mb). $495.00-$2495.00 per module. *Addl. software required:* AutoCAD or MicroStation. *Optimal configuration:* 323, Pentium.
Offers AutoCAD, MicroStation Based or Standalone Modules. Operating Systems Include, UNIX, SUN, DOS, WINDOWS & WINDOWS NT. All Products Designed to Expedient Design Process for Civil Engineers, Surveyors, Landscape Architects, Architects, Builders, GIS Managers, & Environmental Planners. Free Demo Diskettes Available.
Eagle Point Software.

Ear Challenger Windows. Chris Alix. *Customer Support:* 90 day warranty against defective software.
Windows 3.1 (Microsoft) DOS 5.0. IBM 386 or 486 (2Mb). disk $39.95 (Order no.: W-1419). *Nonstandard peripherals required:* VGA display minimum.
A New Windows Game to Assist with Tonal Memory. One or Two-Player Games Test the User's Abilities to Hear & Remember a Series of Tones. Very Colorful & a Lot of Fun for All Ages. MIDI Not Required, but May Be Used with Any Windows Compatible MIDI or Sound Device.
Electronic Courseware Systems, Inc.

Ear Training - A Technique for Listening. *Version:* 2.0. Jan. 1989. *Compatible Hardware:* Apple II, II+, IIe. *Memory Required:* 48k. *General Requirements:* Applesoft language card, MM1 Music Board or S.A.M. DAC Board, speakers or headphones.
disk $195.00.
Provides a Set of Interactive Drill Sessions for the Principle Topics: Melodic Dictation, Rhythm Dictation, Harmonic Dictation, Melody Error Drills, Rhythm Error Drills, Harmony Error Drills, Harmonic Function Drills & Interval Drills.
Wm. C. Brown Pubs.

Earl Weaver Baseball. *Compatible Hardware:* Commodore Amiga, IBM PC.
Commodore Amiga. 3.5" disk $49.95.
IBM. 3.5" disk $39.95.
Electronic Arts.

Earl Weaver Baseball Data Disk. *Compatible Hardware:* Commodore Amiga.
3.5" disk $19.95.
Data on 1986 Major-League Teams.
Electronic Arts.

Early Bird. Gregory A. Fay. Nov. 1991. *Items Included:* One IBM disk (5.25" or 3.5"), one spiral bound manual, promotional material. *Customer Support:* Unlimited technical support via mail, telephone or CompuServe (all is free). 30 day money back guarantee.
MS-DOS or PC-DOS version 2.1 or higher. IBM compatible (200k). $30.00 (ISBN 0-9629699-0-7). *Optimal configuration:* Hard disk, 512k RAM, any printer.
Full-Featured Reminder Program Featuring Simple or Complex Reminders, Desktop Calendar & Scan (AUTOEXEC) Modes, Color Pull- Down/Pop-Up Menus, Context Sensitive On-Line Help, Alarm, DOS Shell, Mouse Support, File Commands, Selectable Group Printing, User Definable Classes, Notice, Print/Display Options & Special Effects.
Allan Computer Products.

Early Learning English. Jan. 1994. *Items Included:* Program on CD-ROM, CD Booklet, & Registration Card. *Customer Support:* Free unlimited customer support via telephone.
Macintosh System 7.0 or higher. Macintosh LC or higher (4Mb). CD-ROM disk $249.00 (ISBN 1-57268-072-5, Order no.: 49100). *Nonstandard peripherals required:* 12 inch monitor or larger; CD-ROM drive. *Optimal configuration:* 5Mb RAM.
Our Early Learning CD-ROM Programs Are Designed to Establish a Foundation of Basic Reading, Writing, & Math Skills. Stories, Audio, Graphics, & Animation Encourage Students to Participate in the Learning Process. These Programs Will Help Students Develop the Self-Esteem & Self-Expression, Which Are Vital to Future Academic Success.
Conter Software.

Early Learning Math. Jan. 1994. *Items Included:* Program on CD-ROM, CD Booklet, & Registration Card. *Customer Support:* Free unlimited customer support via telephone.
Macintosh System 7.0 or higher. Macintosh LC or higher (4Mb). CD-ROM disk $249.00 (ISBN 1-57268-074-1, Order no.: 49300). *Nonstandard peripherals required:* 12 inch monitor or larger; CD-ROM drive. *Optimal configuration:* 5Mb RAM.
Our Early Learning CD-ROM Programs Are Designed to Establish a Foundation of Basic Reading, Writing, & Math Skills. Stories, Audio, Graphics, & Animation Encourage Students to Participate in the Learning Process. These Programs Will Help Students Develop the Self-Esteem & Self-Expression, Which Are Vital to Future Academic Success.
Conter Software.

Early Learning Spanish. Jan. 1994. *Items Included:* Program on CD-ROM, CD Booklet, & Registration Card. *Customer Support:* Free unlimited customer support via telephone.
Macintosh System 7.0 or higher. Macintosh LC or higher (4Mb). CD-ROM disk $249.00 (ISBN 1-57268-073-3, Order no.: 49200). *Nonstandard peripherals required:* 12 inch monitor or larger; CD-ROM drive. *Optimal configuration:* 5Mb RAM.
Our Early Learning CD-ROM Programs Are Designed to Establish a Foundation of Basic Reading, Writing, & Math Skills. Stories, Audio, Graphics, & Animation Encourage Students to Participate in the Learning Process. These Programs Will Help Students Develop the Self-Esteem & Self-Expression, Which Are Vital to Future Academic Success.
Conter Software.

Early Math. (The/Talking Tutor Ser.).
Windows. IBM & compatibles. CD-ROM disk $44.95 (Order no.: R1024). *Nonstandard peripherals required:* CD-ROM drive. *Optimal configuration:* 386 processor or higher, MS-DOS 3.1 or higher, 20Mb hard drive, 640k RAM, external speakers or headphones (with sound card) that are Sound Blaster compatible, VGA graphics & adapter, VGA color monitor.
Macintosh (4Mb). (Order no.: R1024A). *Nonstandard peripherals required:* 14" color monitor or larger, CD-ROM drive.
This Outstanding Series Uses Puzzles, Exciting Stories, Color-Animation & Music to Teach the Basics (Ages 3-6).
Library Video Co.

Early Music Skills - MIDI. Lolita Walker Gilkes. 1985-94. *Compatible Hardware:* Apple II Plus, IIe; Atari ST; Commodore 64, 128; IBM PC & compatibles; IBM PC Windows; Macintosh. *Operating System(s) Required:* Apple DOS 3.3, Macintosh System 6.0.3-7.1, PC-DOS 3.3 or higher, Windows 3.1. *Language(s):* QuickBasic. *Memory Required:* Apple 48k, Commodore 64k, IBM 640k, Macintosh 512k. *General Requirements:* Internal MIDI card, MIDI compatible music keyboard or synthesizer, Macintosh requires external MIDI interface. Windows compatible MIDI or sound device optional. *Customer Support:* Yes.
disk $39.95 (ISBN 1-55603-023-1).
Macintosh. 3.5" disk $59.95.
Tutorial & Drill for the Beginning Music Student. Covers Four Basic Music Reading Skills: Recognition of Line & Space Notes, Understanding of the Numbering System for Musical Staff, Visual & Aural Identification of Notes Moving up & down, & the Recognition of Notes Stepping & Skipping up & Down.
Electronic Courseware Systems, Inc.

Earth Coupled Pipe Loop Sizing: ECA. Version: 1.24. Aug. 1988. *Compatible Hardware:* IBM PC, PC XT, PC AT & compatibles. *Memory Required:* 256k.
3.5" or 5.25" disk $495.00.
Elite Software Development, Inc.

Earth Observatorium: Mission to Planet Earth. Jun. 1995. *Customer Support:* Free 30 day technical support, 90 day warranty.
Mac 7.0. Mac II (8Mb). CD-ROM disk $39.00 (ISBN 1-885237-04-9). *Nonstandard peripherals required:* 16 or 24 bit video suggested. *Addl. software required:* Quicktime included.
Windows 3.1/NT/95. 486 (8Mb). (Order no.: 103-001). *Nonstandard peripherals required:* Suggest 16 or 24 bit video board, mouse, CD-ROM.
Contains over 13,000 Images of Earth & Radar Images. Maps, Video, Audio & Text Help Explain NASA's Mission to Planet Earth Program. Search Capabilities Included.
Rocky Mountain Digital Peeks.

An Earth with One Spirit: Stories from Around the World for the Child Within Us All CD. Mike Pinder. Dec. 1995.
IBM. CD-ROM disk Contact publisher for price (ISBN 1-888057-06-8).
Mike Pinder, Singer, Songwriter of The Moody Blues, Narrates Seven Uplifting & Imaginative Stories or Myths for Children over a Musical Atmosphere Created by Mike Pinder. The Third of a Series of Three Spoken Word Albums for Children. Also "A Planet with One Mind" & "An People with One Heart".
One Step Records.

Earthwords for Alien Dinosaurs Super Media.
80386 (4Mb). CD-ROM disk $34.95 (ISBN 0-88729-798-6, Order no.: 297986). *Addl. software required:* Microsoft Windows 3.1 or higher (mouse recommended). *Networks supported:* IBM.
Same As Superplanetary Version with the Addition of Voice. Four Languages on One Disk (English, Fr., Span., Jap.).
Langenscheidt Pubs., Inc.

Earthwords for Alien Dinosaurs Superplanetary.
80386 (4Mb). CD-ROM disk $29.95 (ISBN 0-88729-799-4, Order no.: 297994). *Addl. software required:* Microsoft Windows 3.1 or higher (mouse recommended). *Networks supported:* IBM.
10 Language Games Each with 10 Levels of Difficulty. 17 Languages on 1 Diskette (Eng., Fr., Span., Ger., Ital., Port., Greek, Deutch, Polish, Russian, Hungarian, Czech, Turk., Hebrew, Chinese, Korean, Japanese).
Langenscheidt Pubs., Inc.

Earthwork. 1980. *Compatible Hardware:* Apple II+. *Language(s):* Applesoft BASIC (source code included). *Memory Required:* 48k.
disk $180.00.
manual only $16.00.
Based on End Area, Computes Cuts, Fills, Top Soil or Unsuitable Material Removal & Structural Fill. These Quantities Are Listed in Square Feet of Areas & Accumulated Volumes in Cubic Yards per Cross Section. Includes Routines That Let User Balance the Cuts & Fills, to Repeat the Cross Sections, to Change or Modify the Cross Section Data, Road Template, etc.
M.P.S. Co.

Earthwork. 1989. *Compatible Hardware:* IBM PC & compatibles. *Operating System(s) Required:* PC-DOS/MS-DOS. *Language(s):* QBASIC. *Customer Support:* Telephone assistance.
disk $47.00, incl. user guide.
disk $127.00, incl. source code.
Handles Any Number of Stations with Station Equations & Roadbed Template Exceptions Including Ditches (Widths & Profile), Slope Schedule & Shrinkage Factor. Superelevation May Be Developed by Rotation about Centerline or Median Edge. Output Includes Earthwork Summaries or Roadbed Coordinates. Input Is Prompted from the User & Is Free-Format.
Systek, Inc. (Mississippi).

Earthworm Jim. *Items Included:* Installation Guide.
IBM PC. Contact publisher for price (ISBN 0-87321-022-0, Order no.: CDD-3114).
Activision, Inc.

EASE 2. *Compatible Hardware:* H-P 9000, DEC VAX, Sun, Macintosh, IBM.
contact publisher for price.
Static & Dynamic Structural Analysis Program Well Suited for the Analysis of Building Systems. It Performs Static, Modal, Response Spectrum & Time History Analysis. Data Structures Provide for Such Items As Base Isolation, Rigid Floor Diaphragms & Beam Rigid End Zones. The Program Includes Graphic Sub-Systems for Developing Models from Architectural Drawings & for Visualizing Results Based on the Topology or on Cartesian Coordinates.
Engineering/Analysis Corp.

TITLE INDEX

East Asian Text Processing. *Customer Support:* All of our products are unconditionally guaranteed.
DOS, Windows, Unix. CD-ROM disk $39.95 (Order no.: EAST ASIAN). *Nonstandard peripherals required:* CD-ROM drive.
Utilities to View, Edit & Output East Asian Languages.
Walnut Creek CDRom.

East Meets West Nutrition Planner. *Items Included:* 5.25" or 3.5" diskettes, 10 page installation/operation manual. *Customer Support:* Telephone customer support at no charge available M-F 9:00-5:00 Pacific time.
MS-DOS. IBM compatible (512k). $49.95 retail (ISBN 0-923891-04-8, Order no.: MS1).
Optimal configuration: Hard disk recommended.
Find the Nutritional Value of One Meal or Save & Keep Track of Meals over Days, Weeks, Months, Years. Identify & Balance Requirements for Vitamins, Minerals, Proteins, Carbohydrates & Fats. Add Foods to the Already Extensive Database of Japanese & Western Foods, & Save Personal Meal Histories for an Unlimited Number of People.
Ishi Press International.

Eastern European Library. *Version:* 5.0. *Items Included:* Manual, reg. card. *Customer Support:* Free phone support.
PC or compatible. disk $149.00 (Order no.: PC098).
6.02 & higher. Macintosh. 3.5" disk $149.00 (Order no.: M098).
26 PostScript & TrueType Fonts Which Support Albanian, Croatian, Czech, German, Hungarian, Polish, Romanian, Slovak, Slovenian & English.
Casady & Greene, Inc.

Eastwood. Oct. 1995. *Customer Support:* Toll-free technical support, on-line, fax back.
Windows 95. 486/66 or higher (8Mb). CD-ROM disk under $50.00 (ISBN 1-888104-00-7, Order no.: 7-14120-70904-9). *Nonstandard peripherals required:* 2x CD-ROM drive.
Optimal configuration: 486/66 w/8Mb RAM, 2x CD-ROM drive, 16-bit color running Windows 95.
The Double CD-ROM Eastwood Allows Fans to Revel in the Exploits of Their On-Screen Legend & Get to Know the Man Behind the Legend. Including Movie Clips, Interviews, Memorabilia & More.
Starwave Corp.

Easy Access. *Items Included:* Bound manual. *Customer Support:* Free hotline - no time limit; 30 day limited warranty; updates are $5/disk plus S&H.
MS-DOS. IBM & compatibles (256k). disk $29.95. *Nonstandard peripherals required:* 1 disk drive; Hayes or compatible modem; printer supported but not required.
Communications Program Which Allows a Computer User at a Remote Location to Call up Another Computer (Running EASY ACCESS) & Send or Receive Data Files or Programs of Any Type. Allows Several Levels of Security. The Manager of the Host System Can Determine Which Users Can Send, Receive, or Kill Files. The System Manager Can Also Determine Which Disk Drives Are Available to the Remote Users. Read from & Write to All Disk Drives & Subdirectories. Keeps a Log of All Files Sent, Received, or Killed, As Well As the Time & Date of the Action & the User Involved. Also Supports the Popular XMODEM File Transfer Protocol.
Dynacomp, Inc.

Easy Accounts Payable. *Compatible Hardware:* B-20 series, B-22. *Operating System(s) Required:* BTOS. *Language(s):* BASIC. *Memory Required:* 256k.
disk $895.00.
Applications Product Which Meets General Ledger Requirements & Provides Accounting Control of Cash Disbursements. Capabilities Include the Following: Adds or Deletes Vendor Information, Generates a Variety of Printed Reports, & Allows User to Post Invoices, Print Checks Directly at Workstation, & Query Vendor & Department Status.
Burroughs Corp.

Easy Accounts Receivable. *Compatible Hardware:* B-20 Series, B-22. *Operating System(s) Required:* BTOS. *Language(s):* BASIC. *Memory Required:* 256k. *General Requirements:* Printer.
disk $895.00.
Provides Functions Necessary for Management & Control of Receivables. Allows User to Post Cash Receipts, Credit Memos, Invoices, Assess Service Charges on Past Due Accounts, etc. Records Accounts Due & Collected. Features Include Multiple Company Capacity, Balance Forward or Open Item Processing, & Multiple Age. Reports Include Summary Age Analysis, Credit Limit, & Activity List.
Burroughs Corp.

Easy Alarms. *Version:* 2.5. *Items Included:* Manual, sample calendars. *Customer Support:* Free technical support.
Mac 6.04 or higher. Macintosh (1Mb). 3.5" disk $49.00. *Optimal configuration:* System 7.0.
Calendar, Reminder & To-Do List Manager for the Macintosh.
Nisus Software, Inc.

Easy Business Cards for Windows. 1995.
MS-DOS, version 5.0 or higher. IBM-compatible 386. disk $29.95. *Nonstandard peripherals required:* 3 1/2 available disk space.
Microsoft Windows, version 3.1 or higher, supported laser or ink-jet printer.
Easy Business Cards for Windows is Claris' new solution for creating professional-quality business cards using a PC & printer. Within minutes, users can select from 29 PaperDirect business card paper designs & more than 290 professionally developed business card styles to create a business image that is "just right" for their needs.
Claris Corporation.

Easy Calc. *Compatible Hardware:* TRS-80 Model I, Model III. *Memory Required:* 48k.
disk $49.95.
Enter & Save a Series of Calculations That Can Be Executed with One Keystroke. Handles up to 600 Figures.
Instant Software, Inc.

Easy-Checking. *Compatible Hardware:* Apple Macintosh 512KE. *General Requirements:* External disk drive, ImageWriter, Omnis 3 Plus. 3.5" disk $99.00.
Checking System.
Technology with Ease, Inc.

Easy-Checking+. *General Requirements:* External disk drive, ImageWriter, LaserWriter.
Macintosh Plus or higher (1Mb). 3.5" disk $195.00.
Checking System for Business.
Technology with Ease, Inc.

Easy Com Easy Go. *Version:* 1.01. Oct. 1984. *Compatible Hardware:* Apple II+, IIe, IIc. *Operating System(s) Required:* ProDOS. *Language(s):* Assembly. *Memory Required:* 64k.
$119.00.
Features Unattended Sending & Receiving of Files, Integrated Word Processor, Auto Log-In & Keyboard Macros.
Transend Corp.

Easy Computing Greatest Hits, 6 disks. Jul. 1988. *Operating System(s) Required:* PC-DOS/MS-DOS. *Language(s):* BASICA/GW-BASIC. *Memory Required:* 256k. *General Requirements:* CGA card, color monitor. 3.5" or 5.25" disk $29.95 (ISBN 0-917765-25-7, Order no.: GH).
Collection of over 55 Games & Business/Educational Applications & 50 Tutorials Pertaining to DOS & BASIC Programming Published in "Easy Computing" Magazine 1986/1987.
D & M Software Pubs.

Easy-D-Scout: Defensive Football Scouting System. Jan. 1995. *Compatible Hardware:* Apple II, IBM PC. *Operating System(s) Required:* Apple DOS 3.3, MS-DOS 5.0 or higher, Windows 3.1, Windows 95. *Memory Required:* Apple II 64k, IBM compatible 640k.
Apple II. disk $49.50 (Order no.: FB-03).
IBM PC. disk $99.00 (Order no.: FB-04).
Features Complete Play-by-Play, Defensive Front Tendencies, Defensive Coverage Tendencies, Hole Vulnerability Graphics, Pass Zone Vulnerability Graphics, Down & Distance Tendencies, Hash Mark Tendencies, Blitz Tendencies, etc.
Comp-U-Sports, Inc.

Easy Dealer. Credit Control Computers. *Compatible Hardware:* TI Professional. *Operating System(s) Required:* MS-DOS. *Language(s):* MBASIC. *Memory Required:* 192k. *General Requirements:* Winchester hard disk, printer.
$2000.00.
Complete Car Sales Package for Dealer. From Writing Sales Contracts to Accounts Receivable System.
Texas Instruments, Personal Productivit.

EASY: Estate & Trust Fiduciary Accounting System. *Version:* EZ96. Dec. 1995. *Compatible Hardware:* IBM & compatibles. *Operating System(s) Required:* DOS, Windows. *Memory Required:* 2000k. *General Requirements:* Hard disk. *Customer Support:* Telephone/modem support $1000 (annual).
$3500.00.
Produces Fiduciary Accountings for Estates & Trusts, in National Standard & State Formats, Client Summaries, Supporting Schedules, 706 Worksheets, Client Financial Statements, & 1041 Expense Data. Includes an Automatic Double-Entry General Ledger, Bank & Cash Reconciliations, Inventory & Investment Tracking, & Office-Wide Management Reports. Options Include the Docket System Which Automatically Generates the Calendar of Events for Estates & Trusts.
Computer Decisions Corp.

Easy Expert. May 1988. *Compatible Hardware:* IBM PC compatibles. *Memory Required:* 512k. 3.5" or 5.25" disk $49.95.
User Can Create Questions, Decision Rules & Conclusions Using a Menu-Driven Editor for up to 5 Different Rule Domains. User Can Create a Run-Time Program That Can Be Used By Customers, Students, Sales Representatives, Managers, Technicians Or Any Intended User.
Park Row Software.

Easy Extra. *Version:* 1.5. *Compatible Hardware:* IBM PC & compatibles. *Memory Required:* 256k, for DOS 3.0, 3.1, & some IBM PC compatibles 320k. *General Requirements:* Hard disk recommended. *Items Included:* Easy Mail.
disk $129.00.
Enables the User to Access the Computers Main Functions in Three Keys. Features Pop-Up Editing Menu, Spelling Checker & a Command for Restoring Deleted Text. Includes Easy Mail, Which Helps User Manage Mailing Lists & Create

Customized Mailings Automatically. Insert Lotus Spreadsheet Files Directly into Documents, with No Added Steps.
WordStar International, Inc.

Easy General Ledger. *Compatible Hardware:* B-20 Series, B-22. *Operating System(s) Required:* BTOS. *Language(s):* BASIC. *Memory Required:* 256k. *General Requirements:* Printer.
disk $895.00.
Designed to Meet General Accounting/Reporting Needs. Consists of Five Basic Functions: Entering, Maintaining, Reporting, Updating & Period-End Processing of General Ledger Information. Includes Multiple Companies, Straight Line Budgeting, General Journal Posting & Other Features. Reports Include Chart of Accounts, Financial Statements, & Transaction Tracking.
Burroughs Corp.

Easy Inventory Control. *Compatible Hardware:* B-20 Series, B-22. *Operating System(s) Required:* BTOS. *Language(s):* BASIC. *Memory Required:* 256k. *General Requirements:* Printer.
disk $895.00.
Menu-Driven System Which Provides the Basis for an Inventory Control System. Allows User to Monitor Incoming & Outgoing Stock Movement & Accomplishes Basic Stock Control Through a Series of Operating Reports. Features Include Multiple Companies, Costing Methods, & Real-Time Transaction Entry.
Burroughs Corp.

Easy Landlord. *Version:* 1.5. Feb. 1994. *Items Included:* Program, Demonstration Data, Tutorial, Users Manual, NEBS Forms Catalog. *Customer Support:* There is currently no charge for Easy Landlord support. Our customer support personnel may be reached from 8:30am to 5:30pm CST, Monday through Friday at (214) 713-6370. Customer support is also available via fax at (214) 713-6308. Customer support is also available on Compuserve.
DOS. IBM PC & compatibles (640k). disk $69.95 (Order no.: (800)925-5700). *Addl. software required:* DOS 5.0 or higher. *Optimal configuration:* VGA color monitor, 1Mb RAM, Hewlett Packard or compatible laser printer, DOS 5.0 or higher.
Macintosh. Macintosh Plus or higher (2Mb). 3.5" disk $69.95 (Order no.: (800)925-5700). *Addl. software required:* System Software version 7.0 or higher. *Optimal configuration:* Macintosh II, 4Mb RAM, VGA color monitor, System 7 software, laser printer.
Microsoft Windows 3.1. IBM PC & compatibles, 386 processor or higher (4Mb RAM). disk $69.95 (Order no.: (800)925-5700). *Addl. software required:* DOS 5.0 or higher, Windows 3.1 or higher. *Optimal configuration:* 486DX 60MHz PC, 8Mb RAM, Windows 3.1, DOS 6.0, Hewlett Packard or compatible laser printer, VGA color monitor.
An Information Management System for Effective Managing up to 50 Total Units. Whether You Operate in DOS, Windows, or Macintosh, Easy Landlord Helps You Quickly Automate Every Face of Your Property Management Business. Will Save You Time, Money & Paperwork. Can Generate Reports for Individual or Consolidated Properties. Makes Sure Your Books Are Accurate & Balanced. Its Double-Entry Accounting System Includes General Ledger, Accounts Payable, & Tenant Receivables & May Be Set up on Either a Cash or Accrual Basis. Complete Time-Consuming Tasks in a Flash, & with Increased Accuracy. Recurring Transactions, Checkbook Reconciliation, Computer Generated Checks, Tenant Billing & Late Notices Are Only a Few of the Features That Will Allow You to Spend Your Time on More Cash Oriented Tasks.
Outlook Software, Inc.

Easy Loans. *Version:* 1.05. Mar. 1993. *Items Included:* 1 manual, 1 set diskettes, warranty, software license agreement. *Customer Support:* Free telephone support on 214-713-6370 or FAX support on 214-713-6308.
DOS 3.3 or higher; Windows 3.1 or higher. IBM compatible 286 or higher (640k). disk $39.95 (Order no.: 800-925-5700).
DOS 3.3 or higher; Windows. IBM compatible 286 or higher (2Mb). disk $39.95 (Order no.: 800-925-5700). *Addl. software required:* Microsoft Windows 3.0 or higher.
Complete Loan Schedules Quickly & Easily. Car Loans or Adjustable Rate Mortgages. Compare or Combine Different Financing Scenarios. Solve for the Unknown Variable - Interest Rate, Loan Amount, Term of Loan, Payment Amount, or Input All the Variables & Print a Loan Schedule. Budget Worksheet for Maximum Qualifying Mortgage Amount.
Good Software Corp.

Easy Money - Easy Money PLUS. *Version:* 4.6. Nov. 1988. *Compatible Hardware:* IBM PC & compatibles, PC XT, PC AT. *Operating System(s) Required:* MS-DOS. (source code included). *Memory Required:* EZ Plus 640k, Easy Money 640k. *General Requirements:* Lotus 1-2-3 Release 2.X or Quattro Pro (optional); Lotus 1-2-3 Release 2.3 or higher for EZ Plus. *Customer Support:* User manual, telephone support.
disk $375.00 Easy Money; $500.00 EZ Plus.
Integrated Program for Personal Financial Planning Including Tax, Estate, Insurance, Retirement & Investments. Designed for Use by Financial Planners, Insurance Agents, CPA's, Bank & Investment Advisors.
Money Tree Software.

Easy Order Entry-Invoicing. *Compatible Hardware:* B-20 Series, B-22. *Operating System(s) Required:* BTOS. *Language(s):* BASIC. *Memory Required:* 256k. *General Requirements:* Printer.
disk $895.00.
Helps Small Businesses to Manage Costs, Sales, Inventory & Accounts Receivable. Handles Invoicing & Order Entry Including Updates of Customer Accounts & Stock Records (If Inventory System Is Installed). Records Orders & Amount Due for Collection, & Creates Pick Tickets, Invoices, & Credit Memos. Provides Reports & Inquiries, Optional Interface to General Ledger, Miscellaneous Stock Items, & Other Features.
Burroughs Corp.

Easy Pieces SA. *General Requirements:* External disk drive or hard disk drive; ImageWriter II or LaserWriter.
Macintosh with (1Mb). 3.5" disk $3995.00.
Distributor Order Processing for Advertising Specialty Industry.
Technology with Ease, Inc.

Easy Presentation Graphics. *Version:* 2.04. *Compatible Hardware:* IBM PC & compatibles. *Memory Required:* 640k. *General Requirements:* CGA, EGA, VGA, LCD or Plasma display. *Customer Support:* Free unlimited tech support for 1 year.
disk $89.95.
Business Graphics Program Which Allows Users to Choose from 12 Different Charts, to Manipulate Spreadsheet Information into a Business Chart. Imports Data from SYLK, DIF, ASCII, .WK1 & .WKS Files.
Brown Bag Software.

Easy Public Institutions Payroll. *Compatible Hardware:* B-20 Series, B-22. *Operating System(s) Required:* BTOS. *Language(s):* BASIC. *Memory Required:* 256k. *General Requirements:* Printer.
disk $2900.00.
Payroll System Designed to Aid Public Institutions in Performing Payroll & Providing Reports to State & Federal Governments. Calculates Earnings, Deductions & Taxes. Includes Simple Checkwriting, Automated Reporting & Real-Time Updating of Information. Allows Multiple Payroll Cycles, Addition of User-Coded Routines, & Provides Links to Other Programs & Files.
Burroughs Corp.

Easy Record. Paul McLeod. *Compatible Hardware:* Atari ST, Sanyo. *General Requirements:* GEM, C compiler.
Atari. 3.5" disk $79.95.
Sanyo. 5-1/4" disk $199.95.
C Programmer's Utility Enables Users to Implement the Features of a Binary-Indexed Record Director (BIRD) to Maintain a Model of Their File Set-Up at Any Time. Handles up to 16 Files at One Time with up to 8 Key Fields for Major Classes & 8 Fields under Each Key for Minor Classes, & 65,000 Individual Records under Each File. Compilers Tested Include: Alcyon C, Digital Research C, Lattice C, & Megamax C on the Atari ST, & Lattice C on the IBM PC.
MichTron, Inc.

Easy ROR. 1996. *Items Included:* Manual. *Customer Support:* Free telephone hotline support 7 days a week.
MS-DOS. 8086 (IBM PC) (640k). disk $89.00.
Windows. 80286 ("286") (2Mb). disk $89.00.
Exact Calculation of Internal & Time-Weighted Rate of Return for Single or Composite Portfolios over Any Time Period Using Only Deposit, Withdrawal, & Tax Information. Designed for Investors & Money Managers Needing Accurate, Expedient Means of Calculating Portfolio Performance. Annual & Annualized Cumulative Returns Can Be Calculated According to Asset Allocation Both Before or after Taxes and/or Fees. Time-Weighted AIMR Methods May Include Daily Valuation, Modified Dietz & Modified BAI. Retains All Client Data for Any Number of Portfolios, Graphs Portfolio Activity, & Exports Data Files to Spreadsheets.
Hamilton Software, Inc.

EASY!ROUTE II: Amusement Route Management System. 1987. *Operating System(s) Required:* PC-DOS. *Memory Required:* 256k.
disk $595.00 (ISBN 0-928353-01-X).
Video Game Management System Assists the Small to Medium-Sized Operator in Controlling Routes of Less Than 500 games. Prints Documents for Cash Collections & Monitors Pick up/Delivery of Equipment. Other Reports Analyze Shortages, Revenue Trends by Game & Location, Complete History of Collections, & Game Movements.
Southland Assocs.

Easy Sales - ASI. *Compatible Hardware:* Apple Macintosh Plus. *General Requirements:* External disk drive; ImageWriter; Omnis 3 Plus.
3.5" disk $1200.00.
Designed to Satisfy the Unique Needs of Advertising Specialty Distributors. Automates & Simplifies the Routine Paperwork Associated with Processing Sales Orders in a Way That Maintains the Look of Commonly Used Forms Within the Industry.
Technology with Ease, Inc.

Easy Scout. Nick Interdonato. Jan. 1996. *Compatible Hardware:* Apple II, IIc; IBM PC. *Operating System(s) Required:* Apple DOS 3.3, MS-DOS 5.0 or higher, Windows 3.1, Windows 95. *Language(s):* Clipper, FoxPro. *Memory Required:* Apple II 64k, IBM compatible 640k.
Apple. disk $49.50 (ISBN 0-928065-00-6, Order

no.: FB-01).
IBM. disk $49.50 (Order no.: FB-02).
Football Scouting System. Reports Include: Play-by-Play, Down & Distance, Formation, Hash Mark, Field Position & Motion Tendencies.
Comp-U-Sports, Inc.

Easy Slider. *Version:* 3.0. *General Requirements:* Macintosh II for color output; or any Macintosh with HFS.
3.5" disk $149.95.
Slide Creation Software.
Management Graphics, Inc.

Easy Street. Jan. 1992. *Items Included:* Disk(s), user's guide, poster, coloring book, warranty card, swap coupon. *Customer Support:* 90 day unlimited warranty; 800 toll free number, 800-221-7911, 8:00 a.m.-5:00 p.m. Arizona time; Updates $10.
Macintosh System 6 or higher. Macintosh (1Mb monochrome, 2Mb color). 3.5" disk $69.99 (ISBN 1-55772-361-3, Order no.: 8302). *Optimal configuration:* 2Mb color monitor, Macintosh LC. *Networks supported:* Digicard.
MS-DOS. IBM, Tandy, MS-DOS compatible (128k). disk $49.99 (ISBN 1-55772-065-7, Order no.: 8301). *Nonstandard peripherals required:* VGA or CGA card. *Optimal configuration:* 128k, color monitor, VGA card. *Networks supported:* Velan, Novell, Digicard.
DOS. Apple II, Apple IIe, Apple IIGS, Apple II Plus (48k). disk $49.99 (ISBN 1-55772-018-5, Order no.: 8300). *Optimal configuration:* Apple II, printer, color monitor, 48k. *Networks supported:* Digicard.
Award Winning Easy Street Is a Playful Adventure & the Key to Building Reading, Math & Problem-Solving Skills. This Lifelike Adventure with Digitized Speech Takes Youngsters down Easy Street Where They Purchase the Goodies from 48 Words on Their Shopping List While Keeping One Eye Out for Knuckles, the Pesky Gorilla. Ages 3 to 9.
Mindplay.

EASY TABLE: An Operation Manual. *Version:* 10.89. Apr. 1990. *Items Included:* 1 120-page operation manual. *Customer Support:* On-site training: $200/1 day; $380/2 days; $560/3 days; $740/4 days; $920/5 days. Telephone support: $200/year (limited phone calls); $500/year (unlimited).
Any operating system that can run with TEX, eg., UNIX, DOS, VMS, etc. (640K). $150.00 - $1500.00 (ISBN 0-9624854-0-3). *Addl. software required:* Any TEX version.
An Application Table Software Program Designed for the TEX Typesetting System. It Relies on Templates in Order to Execute the Formats That You Specify. Multi-Spanner Headings, Row Spanners, Horizontal & Vertical Rule Styles, Automatic Decimal Alignment, & Automatic Table-Breaking Across Pages Are Some of Its Main Features.
Khanh Ha.

Easy Time & Billing. *Version:* 1.02. Jan. 1993. *Items Included:* 1 manual, 1 set diskettes, warranty, software license agreement. *Customer Support:* Free telephone support on 214-713-6370 or FAX support on 214-713-6308.
DOS 3.3 or higher. IBM compatible 286 or higher (1Mb). disk $69.95 (Order no.: 800-925-5700). *Addl. software required:* Microsoft Windows 3.0 or higher.
Powerful Tool for Time Tracking & Billing. Gives Control over Time & Billing Tasks. Log & Track Time, Expenses, & Charges. Record Work in Process. Create Invoices. Print Invoices for Clients. Track Payments per Invoice & Customer. Evaluate Your Time Management & Cash Flow. Keep Track of Customer Payment History.
Good Software Corp.

Easy Working: The Filer. *Compatible Hardware:* Apple IIgs, IIe, IIc; Commodore 64/128; IBM PC, PC AT. *Memory Required:* Commodore 64k, Apple 128k, IBM 384k. *General Requirements:* DOS 2.0 or higher. *Customer Support:* (617)494-1220, 494-1221.
3.5" or 5.25" disk $9.95.
Multi-Purpose Program Designed to Simplify the Storage, Selection, & Reporting of Information. Allows Users to Maintain or Create Mailing Lists, Inventories, Club Memberships, or Other Types of Information. Integrates with EASY WORKING: THE WRITER & EASY WORKING: THE PLANNER.
Spinnaker Software Corp.

Easy Working: The Planner. *Compatible Hardware:* Apple IIe, IIc; Commodore 64/128; IBM PC, PC AT. *Memory Required:* Commodore 64k, Apple 128k, IBM 384k. *General Requirements:* DOS 2.0 or higher. *Customer Support:* (617)494-1220, 494-1221.
3.5" or 5.25" disk $9.95.
Electronic Spreadsheet. Can Be Used for Mathematical Calculations, Budgeting, Tax Calculation, Expense Reports, Financial Statements, etc. Integrates with EASY WORKING THE WRITER & EASY WORKING THE FILER.
Spinnaker Software Corp.

Easy Working: The Writer. *Compatible Hardware:* Apple IIe, IIc; Commodore 64/128; IBM PC, PC AT. *Memory Required:* Commodore 64k, Apple 128k, IBM 384k. *Customer Support:* (617)494-1220, 494-1221.
3.5" or 5.25" disk $9.95.
Word Processing Features Allow Creation of Letters & Reports. Includes 100.000 Word Spellchecker. Editing Functions Include Insert, Delete, Cut, Paste, & Copy. Integrates with EASY WORKING THE WRITER & EASY WORKING THE PLANNER.
Spinnaker Software Corp.

EasyCAD 2. *Version:* 2.72. *Compatible Hardware:* IBM PC & compatibles. *Customer Support:* Free customer support for registered users.
disk $199.00.
CAD Program for Mechanical Engineering & Architecture Featuring User-Definable Symbols, Scripts, Automatic Area Calculation, Macro Facilities, Text Editor, & On-Line Help. Imports & Exports. DXF File Formats. Technical Phone Support Available.
Evolution Computing.

EasyData: NH Business & Professional Directory on Disk. Northwood Corp. Mar. 1992.
5Mb hard drive. IBM compatible. disk $495.00.
Database of 36,000 NH Businesses, Contact Names, & Addresses Which Can Be Sorted by City (or County) & by Business Classification. Information Can Be Downloaded to Mailing Labels, Marketing Sheets, or an ASCII Comma Delimited Format.
Tower Publishing.

EASYDIJ. *Version:* 8.5. May 1995. *Compatible Hardware:* IBM PC, XT, AT, PS2. *Operating System(s) Required:* MS-DOS 3.3 or higher. *Memory Required:* 512k. *General Requirements:* Disk drive. *Items Included:* Illustrated user manual. *Customer Support:* Free 30-day telephone support.
$390.00 (ISBN 0-945851-41-3). *Nonstandard peripherals required:* Any Digitizer Tablet.
Menu-Driven Coordinate Management & Measuring Program for the IBM PC, PS2 Using Any Digitizing Tablet. Product Writes the Digitized Drawing Coordinates or Measured Data into an ASCII, DBF & DXF Lotus, File. It Can Display the Data As Points or Lines on the Monitor.
Geocomp, Ltd.

EASYEST LX. Apr. 1991. *Items Included:* User's manual, three 5.25" low density disks & two 3.5" high density disks, one DAS driver, & EASYFC conversion utility for converting files to ASCII or binary format. *Customer Support:* 90 days no-charge technical support.
DOS 2.0 or higher. IBM PC/AT/XT & 100% compatibles (640k) - including PS/2 & 386-based computers in real mode. disk $995.00 (ISBN 0-924729-18-X, Order no.: EZTLX). *Nonstandard peripherals required:* Math co-processor, Microsoft or compatible mouse, color monitor w/EGA or VGA adapter, data acquisition board, LIM expanded memory & hard disk with 1.5Mb free. *Optimal configuration:* 386 computer with mouse, VGA card, & color monitor.
An Icon-Driven Data Acquisition Program with Analysis, Graphics, & Record/Playback Functions. EASYEST LX Is a Platform for Automating Tests & Experiments. Supports over 100 Printers & Plotters.
Keithley Asyst.

EasyFlow. *Version:* 6.0. May 1989. *Compatible Hardware:* IBM PC & compatibles, PS/2. *Operating System(s) Required:* PC-DOS/MS-DOS 2.0 or higher. *Language(s):* Assembly. *Memory Required:* 512k. *General Requirements:* CGA/EGA/VGA or Hercules monochrome compatible adapter card.
disk $149.95, incl. manual.
update $60.00.
Full-Screen Graphics Program Dedicated to Flowcharts & Organization Charts, & Data Flow Programs, Allows Modification & Updating. Features Supported Include: Automatically Centered Text. Text Formatting Controls Allow Users to Over-Ride the Automatic Formatting Where Desired; Lines Are Created by Specifying the Starting & Ending Points; Editing Facilities Allow Shapes or Entire Rows & Columns of Shapes to Be Inserted or Deleted; Large Chart Size (up to 16 Shapes Wide & 16 Shapes High) Allows Handling of Very Large Flowcharts & Organization Charts; Charts Can Be Larger Than the Screen; Works with All Printers; 20 Standard Flowcharting Data Flow & Organizational Shapes Includes; Common Shapes Supplied in 3 Sizes; 175 Page Manual with Examples; Context-Sensitive HELP Facility; Any Number of Titles Can Be Placed on a Chart.
HavenTree Software, Ltd.

EasyKey Visual Keyboard. *Items Included:* Users manual, 3 1/4" disk. *Customer Support:* One-year warranty. Customer support by telephone.
Windows 3.0. PC 286 (2Mb). disk $59.00. *Nonstandard peripherals required:* Pointing device - mouse, light pen, VGA.
An On-Screen Keyboard That Floats on Top of the Program in Any Windows Application & Allows User to Type via Alternative Input Device. Works in Conjunction with Inkwell Systems' PCPRO LIGHT PEN SYSTEM & TELEWAND. Features 25 Keyboard Layouts, Different Size Keyboards, & Can Create Unlimited Macro Panels.
Inkwell Systems.

EasyPost Insurance Agency Management System. Advanced Business Systems, Inc. *Compatible Hardware:* TI Professional. *Operating System(s) Required:* MS-DOS. *Memory Required:* 256k. *General Requirements:* Printer.
$3600.00.
Designed to Meet Marketing, Accounting & Management Information Needs of the Property & Casualty Insurance Agency.
Texas Instruments, Personal Productivit.

EasySAA.
IBM PC & compatibles (640k). EasySAA $500.00, Infront $1500.00.
Application Generator Which Develops DOS User Interfaces That Are Upwardly Compatible with OS/2 While Complying with IBM's SAA Common User Access. Produces Front-End Interfaces for 3270 Mainframe Applications. Also Supports Peer-to-Peer & Mixed 3270/Peer-to-Peer Applications. Generator Combines Editing, Compiling, Debugging & Testing in One Environment. Can Automatically Produce Prototype Applications with Color, Menu Placement, Help & Keyboard Handling. Includes a Code Library & Is Object Based. Objects Supported Include Procedures, Windows, Dialog Boxes & More. Requires Infront or Infront/HPO, Multi Soft's Development System.
Multi Soft, Inc.

EasySales Pro.
Information Unlimited Software (IUS). Mar. 1984. Compatible Hardware: TI Professional. Operating System(s) Required: MS-DOS. Memory Required: 128k. General Requirements: Winchester hard disk, printer. $495.00.
Professional Prospect Management System.
Texas Instruments, Personal Productivit.

Easyscreen-PC.
Version: 2.0. Feb. 1984. Compatible Hardware: IBM PC & compatibles. Operating System(s) Required: PC-DOS/MS-DOS 1.1, 2.0. Language(s): Microsoft BASIC, Compiled & Interpretive (source code included). Memory Required: DOS 1.1 64k, DOS 2.0 128k.
disk $189.95.
Electronic Filing & Reporting System or Application Development Tool. Allows User to Draw Screen Layouts on Display Screen. Screens May Be Used to Process Data in Full Screen or "Block Mode" Allowing Total Freedom of Cursor Movement & Data Input. Includes Multiple Data Types, Screen Attributes, Screen Overlays, Simple Windowing & Screen Processing Interrupts.
Prodata, Inc. (Idaho).

EasyShare.
Version: 2.07. May 1992. Items Included: User manual, sample definition files. Customer Support: 30 day money back guarantee, telephone support.
DOS 3.0 or higher. IBM PC, AT, PS/2 & compatibles (28 or 36k). disk $240.00.
Agent System, Which Is a TSR Program That Imitates a User to Any Program. Automates Processes by Controlling the Execution of Other Programs. Product Can Control Complicated PC to Mainframe Sessions & Works with Both IBM & Asynchronous Terminal Emulators. Supports HLLAPI. Transfers Data Between Any Two Applications by "Rekeying" It As a User Would. Supports Full Range of Functions, Logic & Branching to Control Program Execution. Uses a Defination File Based upon Functions & Tables Rather Than a Script Language.
Adisoft.

EasyShow 2 for Windows.
Version: 2.0. Windows. IBM. Contact publisher for price.
The Ultimate Authoring Program Designed to Get the Best Out of Your VideoShow Equipment & to Minimize Time & Effort. Easily Convert Charts from Bar to Pie or from Line Graph to Bar Chart at the Click of a Button. Create Dazzling Video Effects in Record Time. Simple Pull down Menus Give Access to Powerful Automatic Functions. Import High Quality Photographs & Clip Art Using Any of the Following Formats BMP, GIF, TIF, PCX & TGA. Always Directly Linked to GPC's ImageProcessor for Superior Quality Photographic Image Capture, Positioning & Compression. Can Output Images to Any Windows-Supported Printer. Control Font, Size, Color, Justification, Shadows, Bullets (over 210 to Choose from), Pauses or Frame Styles.
General Parametrics Corp.

EasyWriter I System Legal.
Information Unlimited Software (IUS). Jun. 1984. Compatible Hardware: TI Professional. Operating System(s) Required: MS-DOS. Memory Required: 128k. General Requirements: Printer.
contact publisher for price.
Personal Integrated Word Processing, Spell-Checking & Mail-Merge System.
Texas Instruments, Personal Productivit.

EasyWriter I System Medical.
Information Unlimited Software. Jun. 1984. Compatible Hardware: TI Professional. Operating System(s) Required: MS-DOS. Memory Required: 128k. General Requirements: Printer.
contact publisher for price.
Personal Integrated Word Processing, Spell-Checking (Over 20,000 Medical Terms) & Mail-Merge System.
Texas Instruments, Personal Productivit.

EasyWriter II System.
Information Unlimited Software. Compatible Hardware: TI Professional. Operating System(s) Required: MS-DOS. Memory Required: 128k. General Requirements: 2 disk drives, printer.
$395.00 (Order no.: TI P/N 2311505-0001).
Integrated Word Processing System, Includes Spell-Checking & Mail-Merge.
Texas Instruments, Personal Productivit.

EasyWriter II System Legal.
Information Unlimited Software. Feb. 1984. Compatible Hardware: TI Professional. Operating System(s) Required: MS-DOS. Memory Required: 128k. General Requirements: 2 disk drives, printer.
contact publisher for price.
Integrated Word Processing System, Includes EASYSPELLER II (Over 20,000 Legal Terms) & EASYMAILER II.
Texas Instruments, Personal Productivit.

The Eating Machine.
Barbara S. Thorne. Aug. 1983. Compatible Hardware: Apple II+, IIe, IIc. Operating System(s) Required: Apple DOS 3.2, 3.3. Language(s): BASIC. Memory Required: 48k.
disk $19.98, incl. bklt. (ISBN 0-87190-022-X).
Scientific & Factual Program Designed for Healthful Diet Management & Nutritional Planning. Handles Nutritional Intake of up to 20 Persons for up to 7 Days.
Muse Software.

Eating the Chocolate Elephant: Take Charge of Change Through Total Process Management.
Mark D. Youngblood. Apr. 1994. Customer Support: A tear-out card in book will provide this info.
$24.95 ea. (ISBN 1-57187-002-4, Order no.: RM3140 (BOOK ONLY)).
Provides Framework to Achieve Significant & Sustained Performance Improvement Through Total Process Management, Which Integrates the Best of Business Process Reengineering, Total Quality Management & Benchmarking into a Single Solution. The Seven-Part Total Process Management Method Is Presented in a Logical & Easily Understood Manner. Also Available Is the Total Process Management Toolkit, Which Includes a WIN Compatible Flowcharting Program, ABC FlowCharter 3.0.
Micrografx, Inc.

EAZY PC.
D. Kenyock. Mar. 1984. Compatible Hardware: IBM PC. Operating System(s) Required: PC-DOS. Language(s): BASIC. Memory Required: 128k.
disk $99.00.
Menu Creation System.
Aquidneck Data Corp.

EBASIC with Starbase 3.2.
Compatible Hardware: CP/M based machines, IBM. Memory Required: CP/M 48k, IBM 128k.
disk $39.95.
8" disk $42.45.
Programming Language with Most of the Standard Features of Microsoft BASIC.
Dynacomp, Inc.

Ebonstar.
Compatible Hardware: Commodore Amiga.
3.5" disk $24.95.
Arcade Space Game up to 4 players.
Microillusions, Inc.

ECA-2: Electronic Circuit Analysis.
Version: 2.65. 1994. Operating System(s) Required: MS-DOS, PC-DOS. Language(s): C. Memory Required: 256k. General Requirements: Hard disk, coprocessor, printer, graphics display. Items Included: 5.25" disk, user's manual. Customer Support: 30 day unlimited warranty; 1 yr maintenance with 2 updates min. $175.00.
Eval. kit $45.00 ECA-2 $775.00 demo N/C (ISBN 0-927449-52-8, Order no.: E2PM).
High Performance Interactive Analog Circuit Simulator, with AC, DC, Transient, Fourier, Worst-Case, & Monte Carlo Analysis. Components Allowed Are Resistors, Capacitors, Inductors, Batteries, Diodes, Transistors, Oscillators, Voltage & Current Sources, Transmission Lines, Voltage Controlled Components (Modulators), & User Created Macro Models. Component Variables Can Include Tolerance, Temperature Coefficient, Bandwith, Leakage, Q & Non Linearities (Continuous, Expressed As a Polynomial, or Piecemeal with Breakpoints). Analysis Can Sweep Voltage, Time, Temperature or Frequency for a Range of Values of One or Several Components. The Following Parameters May Be Calculated: Node or Branch Output May Be Tabular or Graphic -- Bode Plots, DC Transfer & Transient Timing Diagrams of up to 4 Different Parameters. The User Defined Graphics Operate in Real Time Allowing the User to Interrupt & Redefine Circuit Speeding up the Iterative Design Process.
Tatum Labs, Inc.

ECA-2.
Version: 2.31. Compatible Hardware: Apple Macintosh. Memory Required: 512k. Items Included: disk, user's manual. Customer Support: 30 day unlimited warranty. 1 yr. service $175.00.
3.5" disk $775.00 (ISBN 0-927449-12-9).
Analog Circuit Simulation Program.
Tatum Labs, Inc.

Echo: Environment Controller.
Timothy Purves. Jun. 1986. Compatible Hardware: Atari ST, IBM PC. Memory Required: 512k. General Requirements: GEM, X-10 controler units, X-10 power house.
Atari. 3.5" disk $39.95.
IBM. 5-1/4" disk $39.95 (ISBN 0-923213-11-2, Order no.: AT-ECH).
Software/Hardware Combination Enables the ST to Control Electric Appliances. Can Regulate Thermostats, Dim Incandescent Lights, & Has a Timer Program That Takes Weekends & Holidays into Account. Uses X-10 Remote Plug-In Modules, Being Completely Wireless.
MichTron, Inc.

Echos - MIDI.
Reid Alexander. Customer Support: 90 day warranty against defective software.
DOS 3.3 or higher. IBM (640k). disk $79.95 (Order no.: MI-1383). Nonstandard peripherals required: MIDI interface, MIDI keyboard.
System 6.0.7 - System 7.1. Macintosh (1Mb). 3.5" disk $99.95 (Order no.: MAC-1383). Nonstandard peripherals required: MIDI interface, MIDI compatible music keyboard.

TITLE INDEX

Focuses on Strengthening Sight Reading Skills As Well As Rhythm & Note Rading Accuracy. The Student Is Able to Implement the Concepts of Sightreading Through the "Echoing" of More Than 15 Musical Examples. This Program Also Allows the Student to Look at Two Separate Pieces of Music & Identify Which Piece Is Being Played.
Electronic Courseware Systems, Inc.

Echos II. Reid Alexander. 1991. *Customer Support:* ECS offers technical support to registered users. Call (217) 359-7099. Other than the telephone call - technical support is no charge.
DOS 3.3 or higher. IBM (640k). $79.95 single station/$400.00 network (Order no.: MI-1384). *Nonstandard peripherals required:* MIDI keyboard, Roland MPU-401, MIDI interface or 100% compatible.
This Sequel to Echos Is Designed to Strengthen Music Sightreading Skills at the Keyboard. It Incorporates Tuneful Musical Examples in Keys Ranging from 2 Sharps & Flats to 6 Sharps & Flats, in Both Major & Minor Keys. All Musical Examples Are First Heard & Then the Student Has Three Opportunities to Correctly Play Each Example. Any Missed Notes Are Highlighted for Quick Recognition. This Program Also Contains Additional Sightreading "Flashes". Four Correctly Played Flashes Are Then Arranged in Various Combinations to Challenge the Student When Playing Longer Musical Examples. Requires MIDI.
Electronic Courseware Systems, Inc.

ECM Turing Machine. *Items Included:* Bound manual. *Customer Support:* Free hotline - no time limit; 30 day limited warranty; updates are $5/disk plus S&H.
Apple (48k). disk $49.95. *Nonstandard peripherals required:* One disk drive.
Simplest Operational Model of the Formal Definition of Computation. Has Only Five Instructions, but Can Compute Anything Computable (Within the Constraints of Available Memory).
Dynacomp, Inc.

ECMLink. Sep. 1994. *Items Included:* One modem, copy of Carbon Copy Plus software. *Customer Support:* Thirty days of free support.
MS-DOS; Microsoft Windows. IBM PC & compatibles (8Mb). $10,000.00 & up. *Optimal configuration:* 120Mb hard disk; payer communicaitons hardware & software; printer; 14.4 baud modem; 2Mb Video RAM.
Enables Providers to Submit UB92s, HCFA-1500s, & Other Forms Directly to All of Their State Payers, Eliminating Any per Bed/Claim Fees. On-Site Provider & Payer Specific Edits Allow Correct Claims to Be Submitted to Payers the First Time. Secondary Billings & Billing Date Posting Can Be Automated. System Is PC-Based.
Learned-Mahn.

Eco East Africa: A Virtual Simulation Game. Viridis. Apr. 1995. *Customer Support:* Free 800 Number Technical Support.
Windows. PC with 486SX 33MHz or higher (8Mb). disk $59.95 (ISBN 1-884899-13-7). *Optimal configuration:* PC with 486/25MHz or higher, 8Mb RAM, Windows 3.1 or higher, double-speed CD-ROM drive, 256 color VGA card or higher, Sound Blaster 16 or compatible sound card, stereo headphones or speakers.
A Virtual Simulation Game That Recreates the Natural Environment of the East African Plains Through Photo-Realistic Animation, Beautifully Composited Landscapes & Natural Sound. Users View Breathtaking Images of Africa, Observe Animal Behaviors & Experience the Changing Seasons. Additionally Users Can Assume the Role of Warden in a Fictional Game Park & Participate in the Interactive Experience of Managing the Parks Delicate Ecosystem.
IVI Publishing, Inc.

Ecological Linguistics Fonts. *Compatible Hardware:* Apple Macintosh. *Memory Required:* 1000k.
Bitmap base systems $35.00 to $60.00.
Apple Script Manager systems for Arabic, Japanese, Korean, Greek, & Chinese $60.00. to 120.00 Laser base systems for Roman or Greek based alphabets $90.00.
Laser base systems for other alphabets $120.00 to $500.00.
Features Various Complex Alphabets of Asia & Eastern Europe. Allows Alphabetical Sorting & Indexing, Automatic Transliteration, & Custom Modifications. LaserFonts Include European Times, VietnamTimes, MideastTimes, IndicTimes, GreekTimes, IPATimes, Russian, Cyrillic, Thai, Khmer, Arabic, Hebrew, Armenian, Georgian, etc. Bitmap Fonts Include European, Right-to-Left Scripts, Vertically Written Alphabets, Tibetan, North India, South India, Southeast Asia, Syllabaries, Japanese & Chinese Characters, Mayan Hieroglyphs, Egyptian Hieroglyphs, & Sign Language Writing.
Ecological Linguistics.

ECOMAP: A Global View of Major Terrestrial Ecosystems. *Version:* 1.10. Roger Cox & Kathy Cox. Feb. 1992. *Items Included:* Printed installation instructions. *Customer Support:* Free support by mail or phone to registered users.
MS-DOS 2.0 or higher. IBM PC & compatibles (640k). Single-user copy $19.95; Site licenses start at $70.00 (Order no.: EMAP-PC5 (5.25"); EMAP-PC3 (3.5")). *Nonstandard peripherals required:* Graphics adapter: CGA, EGA, VGA or Hercules color or monochrome graphics monitor. *Optimal configuration:* 640k RAM, EGA or VGA graphics with color monitor, printer.
System 6 or 7. Macintosh (1Mb). Single-user copy $19.95; Site licenses start at $70.00 (Order no.: EMAP-MAC). *Addl. software required:* HyperCard 2.0 or higher.
An Interactive Display Program Using a Database of All Major Land-Based Ecosystems, Digitized on a Global Grid. User Can View Any of 14 Major Ecosystems, or Groups of Ecosystems, on the Entire Planet or a Single Continent. Unlike Most Maps, the Emphasis Is on Earth & Its Biological Communities.
Save the Planet Software.

Econograph II.
IBM PC (256k). Contact publisher for price. *Addl. software required:* Graphics card.
Computer Based Learning Package Consisting of Nine Interactive Tutorial Lessons Including Supply & Demand, Money Expansion, AS/AD, Keynesian Cross Analysis, Supply Under Perfect Competition, & Monopoly.
Dryden Press.

Econometrics. *Version:* 10.0. (Professional Ser.). 1989. *Compatible Hardware:* Apple Macintosh, IBM PC & compatibles. *Memory Required:* 512k. *Items Included:* Disks, book, program instructions. *Customer Support:* Telephone.
disk $145.00 (ISBN 0-920387-24-1).
Topics Covered Are Statistical Distributions & Statistical Inference; Multilinear Regression, Including Weighted Regression Models, Ridge Regression, Splines, Logit Analysis; Models Using Sets of Simultaneous Equations; Models Based on Time-Series, Including Autocorrelation, Seasonal Models, Lagged Variables, the Cochran-Orcutt Correction for Autocorrelation in Residuals, the Durbin-Watson Statistic. A Full Set of File Transfer Programs Is Included So That Data Can Be Transferrred to & from Popular Spreadsheets.
Lionheart Pr., Inc.

ECONOMICS: WHO'S GOT THE GOODS

Economic & Hedonic Damages System. Charles W. de Seve. Sep. 1990. *Items Included:* Disk case, documentation, disks. *Customer Support:* Unlimited 800 telephone line support.
MS-DOS 2.1 or higher. IBM & compatibles (640k). disk $199.95. *Optimal configuration:* IBM, 640k RAM, 20Mb hard disk drive, color monitor.
Using Statistical Data & Formula, the Software Calculates Damages Based on the Specifics of a Personal Injury or Wrongful Death Case. Users Can Access a Preliminary Assessment of Losses. The Software Measures the Economic Damages According to the Procedures for Determining Economic & Hedonic Damages.
Anderson Publishing Co.

Economic Insulation Sizing. *Items Included:* Full manual. No other products required. *Customer Support:* Free telephone support - no time limit. 30 day warranty.
MS-DOS 3.2 or higher. IBM & compatibles (512k). disk $419.95. *Optimal configuration:* IBM, MS-DOS 3.3 or higher, 512k RAM, hard drive & CGA/EGA/VGA (or higher) graphics capability.
demo disk $5.00.
EIS Will Help You to Easily & Quickly Select the Insulation Thickness That Provides the Lowest Total Installation & Operating Cost over the System Life for Both Piping & Equipment. Supports Both U.S. & S.I. Units.
Dynacomp, Inc.

Economic Loss Program. *Customer Support:* 1 year.
IBM PC & compatibles (256k). disk $59.95.
Calculates Present Value of Future Losses, Allowing for Selection of Inflation Rate & Investment Percentage Rate.
Lawyers Software Publishing Co.

Economics: Principles & Applications. Henry Billings & Linda Hancock. Nov. 1994. *Items Included:* Software program guide. *Customer Support:* Customer support is available through our toll-free number 800-328-1452, ask for Technical Support. Free on-site training is also available through the same number.
DOS. IBM & compatibles (256k). 5.25" disk $285.00 (ISBN 0-8219-1092-2, Order no.: 95509G). *Nonstandard peripherals required:* Color graphics card. *Optimal configuration:* Color monitor & printer. *Networks supported:* Not designed for networks, but can be installed to a network.
DOS. IBM & compatibles (256k). 3.5" disk $285.00 (ISBN 0-8219-1096-5, Order no.: 95509H). *Nonstandard peripherals required:* Color graphics card. *Optimal configuration:* Color monitor & printer. *Networks supported:* Not designed for networks, but can be installed to a network.
The Program Includes Nine Disks Which Offer an Interactive Simulation. They Include Review & Tests for the Textbook.
EMC Publishing.

Economics: Who's Got the Goods? (Micro Learn Tutorial Ser.). *Customer Support:* Free telephone support.
Macintosh (2Mb). Single copy, $44.95; Lab pack/5, $115.00; Network v., $249.00 (ISBN 0-939153-21-1).
Tutorial Teaches Basic Economic Concepts, Including Scarcity, Factors of Production, Goods, Services, Opportunity Cost, Types of Systems, Factor & Product Markets, Supply & Demand. Tables & Graphs Are Amply Used to Develop Understanding. Tutorial & test mode gives explanations for every answer, choice, correct & incorrect. Complete scorekeeping system.
Word Assocs., Inc.

ECONRISK. Ellis International Services, Inc. Jan. 1984. *Compatible Hardware:* IBM PC, PC XT, PC AT & compatibles. *Operating System(s) Required:* PC-DOS, MS-DOS. *Language(s):* FORTRAN. *Memory Required:* 640k. *General Requirements:* Printer.
disk $2995.00 (Order no.: ECONRISK). *Comprehensive Economic Evaluation System Designed to Help Determine the Economic Viability of a Project. In Addition to Producing Risk, Sensitivity, & Threshold Price Analyses, the Program Computes Discounted Cash Flow Rate of Return (DCFROR), Net Present Value (NPV), & Profit/Loss Using Corporate Book Accounting.*
Geostat Systems International, Inc. (GSII).

ECOORD: Fuse & Breaker Coordinator. Jul. 1989. *Items Included:* Bound user manual. *Customer Support:* Unlimited toll-free telephone support 800-648-9523.
MS-DOS (384k). IBM PC, PC XT, PC AT, AT 286 & 386. disk $995.00 (Order no.: 800-648-9523). *Nonstandard peripherals required:* CGA, EGA, VGA or Hercules graphics monitor; Epson or LaserJet printer; HP or Houston Intrument plotter.
Aids in Selective Coordination of Circuit Breakers & Fuses by Providing Instantaneous Review of Time-Circuit Curves in Proposed Electrical Protection System. Supplied with Library of over 200 Protection Devices from Various Manufacturers. Designer Can Define up to 35,000 Additional Devices. Up to 24 Drawings Can Be Plotted per Project. Includes Ability to Plot on K & E Graph Paper, & Create AutoCAD DXF Files.
Elite Software Develpoment, Inc.

Ed-U-Games Cultural Literacy Edition. Dec. 1988. *Items Included:* Disk & documentation. *Customer Support:* Phone support as necessary.
Macintosh (1Mb). 3.5" disk $29.95 (Order no.: EDG-USA). *Optimal configuration:* Mac+ with 1Mb of memory.
An Object-Oriented Educational Game Includes Game Driver Which Will Run Other Editions. Covers Material from the Cultural Literacy List.
Solar Systems Software.

Ed-U-Keep II: Professional Record Keeping System for Educators. *Version:* 3.01B. Greg M. Taylor. 1988. *Items Included:* Camera-ready "sign-in form" included coding system manual; 5.25" & 3.5" disks included. *Customer Support:* 90 day free support; $150.00/year renewable.
IBM MS-DOS 3.1 or higher (640k) Windows. IBM PC, XT, AT, PS/2 & compatibles. disk $950.00 single-user; $1250.00 multi-user. *Optimal configuration:* 80286 or 80386, 40Mb hard disk, VGA monitor.
disk $1250.00 Novell version.
Provides Detailed Information on Employee Training Quickly & Easily. Provides Deficiency Reports. Tracks Licensing Requirements. Designed to Handle Small to Large Organizations (from 50 Employees to 10,000 Employees). Demonstration Disk Available.
Edukeep Co., The.

ED-U-KEEP 2000 for Windows. Feb. 1996. *Items Included:* Users manuals, runtime access. *Customer Support:* 1 year support $150.00 renewable, first 90 days free.
Windows 3.1 or Windows 95. 486-SX (8Mb). $1595.00 single user.
Microsoft Workgroups or NT. 486DX (8Mb). $1995.00 & up, client-server.
Provides Detailed Information on Employee Training. Deficiency Reports, Standard Reports, & a Report Writer Is Included. Sophisticated Yet Easy to Use. An Invaluable Management Tool for Maintaining Compliance. Free Demo Available.
The Edukeep Co.

The Eddie Cantor Radio Show, 1942-1943. Eddie Cantor. 1994.
IBM. CD-ROM disk Contact publisher for price (ISBN 1-887958-04-5).
Gari Brian.

EDG C Front End. *Items Included:* Full source code, full internal documentation. *Customer Support:* 1 year of maintenance included in license price; additional maintenance available at additional cost.
UNIX, VMS. Depending on sublicensing rights, $15,000.00-$100,000.00 up.
Designed for Compiler Developers Who Wish to Build a C Compiler or a C Source Analysis Tool. It Supports Both ANSI & K&R C, & Features Rapid Compilation, Full Error Checking, & a High-Level Tree-Structured Intermediate Form. Host & Target Computer Characteristics Are Configurable, Allowing Use in a Variety of Environments & As a Cross-Compiler.
Edison Design Group.

EDG C++ Front End. *Items Included:* Full source code, full internal documentation. *Customer Support:* 1 year of maintenance included in license price; additional maintenance available at additional cost.
UNIX, VMS. Depending on sublicensing rights, $30,000.00-$100,000.00 up.
Designed for Compiler Developers Who Wish to Build a C Plus Plus Compiler or a C Plus Plus Source Analysis Tool. It Supports the C Plus Plus Language As Defined by the Annotated C Plus Plus Reference Manual, Also Most Features in the Emerging C Plus Plus Standard. ANSI C & K&R C Are Also Supported. It Features Rapid Compilation, Full Error Checking, & a High-Level Tree-Structured Intermediate Form. Host & Target Computer Characteristics Are Configurable, Allowing Use in a Variety of Environments & As a Cross-Compiler.
Edison Design Group.

EDG FORTRAN Front End. *Items Included:* Full source code, full internal documentation. *Customer Support:* 1 year of maintenance included in license price; additional maintenance available at additional cost.
UNIX, VMS. Depending on sublicensing rights, $15,000.00-$100,000.00 up.
Designed for Compiler Developers Who Wish to Build A FORTRAN Compiler or a FORTRAN Source Analysis Tool. It Supports the FORTRAN 77 Language & Popular Extensions, & Features Rapid Compilation, Full Error Checking, & a High-Level Tree-Structured Intermediate Form. Host & Target Computer Characteristics Are Configurable, Allowing Use in a Variety of Environments & As a Cross-Compiler.
Edison Design Group.

EDI - EDGE - LAN. *Version:* 5.2. Jun. 1993. *Items Included:* One User Manual; Reference Cards; On-line help & on-line tutorial. *Customer Support:* Toll-free hotline support & software updates ($1500/year).
MS-DOS. IBM PC & compatibles (640k). disk $5000.00 (Order no.: 125200). *Optimal configuration:* DOS 3.0 or higher, 640k RAM, 40Mb disk, Hayes compatible modem.
Provides Standalone & Unattended Operation in a LAN Environment; Supports All Public U.S. & International Standards & All Networks. Also Includes User-Friendly Tools for EDI Mapping, & for Customizatiton of Screens, Flatfiles for Interfacing, & Print Formats. QUICK FORM Feature Provides System-Generated Formats Automatically. Spanish Version Also Available.
DNS Assocs., Inc.

EDI - ENTRY. *Version:* 5.2. Jun. 1993. *Items Included:* One User Manual (264 pages); Reference Cards; On-line help & on-line tutorial. *Customer Support:* Maintenance - including toll-free hotline support, $350/year.
MS-DOS. IBM PC & compatibles (640k). disk $1250.00 (Order no.: 215200). *Optimal configuration:* DOS 3.0 or higher, 640k RAM, 40Mb disk, Hayes compatible modem. *Networks supported:* All public networks.
Easily-Installed, Inexpensive Product Designed for Companies with Limited EDI Requirements, or for Situations in Which Centralized Control Is Desired. Provides Standalone or Unattended Operation; Supports All Standards & All Networks. Utilizes Pre-Configured Transactions & New Mapping Acquired from DNS or from an EDI/EDGE User.
DNS Assocs., Inc.

EDI/EDGE. *Version:* 5.2. Jun. 1993. *Items Included:* All published ANSI & TDCC, EDI standards. *Customer Support:* Toll free hotline support & software updates ($500.00 annual fee).
MS-DOS (640k). $2500.00 3.5" or 5.25" disk (Order no.: 115200). *Optimal configuration:* DOS 3.0 or higher, 640k RAM, 40Mb disk, Hayes compatible modem.
Provides Stand Alone & Unattended Operation; Supports All Public U.S. & International Standards & All Networks. Also Includes User-Friendly Tools for EDI Mapping, & for Customization of Screens, Flat Files for Interfacing, & Print Formats; QUICKFORM Feature Provides System-Generated Formats Automatcially. Spanish Version Also Available.
DNS Assocs., Inc.

EDI EDGE. *Version:* 5.1. Aug. 1992. *Items Included:* 2 manuals, quick reference guide. *Customer Support:* Maintenance - including hotline, $600-$2100/yr.; Training - $500 class, Custom installation, on-site training, consulting - $1000/day.
UNIX. IBM RS/6000. Contact publisher for price (Order no.: 135100). *Optimal configuration:* UNIX 5.3, 4Mb RAM, 60Mb disk, Hayes compatible modem.
UNIX. RS/6000.
Provides Stand Alone & Unattended Operation; Supports All Public U.S. & International Standards & All Networks. Also Includes User-Friendly Tools for EDI Mapping & for Customization of Screens, Flat Files for Applciations Interface, & Print Formats. QUICKFORM Feature Provides System-Generated Formats Automatically.
DNS Assocs., Inc.

EDI: Electronic Data Interchange. *Customer Support:* Free telephone & BBS Technical support.
MS/PC DOS; Concurrent DOS, Xenix, Unix. IBM PC/XT/AT & compatibles; IBM PS/2 (512k). single user $995.00, +039. *Networks supported:* Novell, Lantastic, Banyan VINES; all NETBIOS compatible.
multi user or network $1295.00.
The Order Entry EDI Interface utility allows INMASS/MRP user to upload ASCII format order files, customer files, & address files from other sources to the INM/MRP Order Entry Module.
INMASS/MRP.

Edifice. *Customer Support:* 800-929-8117 (customer service).
MS-DOS. IBM/PS2. disk $1999.99 (ISBN 0-87007-693-0).
A Project (Job) Cost Control Package Designed for Companies That Need to Control Costs by Projects. An Accounting Package for Construction

TITLE INDEX

& Engineering Companies. Product Contains the Following Systems: Project Cost Control, Accounts Receivable & Delinquent Accounts, Accounts Payable & Fixed Asset, Inventory Control & Open Order Reporting, & Payroll. Key Features Include: Controlling Inventories at the Warehouse & by Projects; Daily Material Transfer Reports; Forecasting of Hours & Costs by Project & Phase; Comparison of Actual Costs To Budgeted Amounts; Active & Completed Project Reports; Equipment; Sub-Contractor & Other Charges Registers; Cost Detail Reports by Project & Phase; Labor Cost Distribution by Project; Automatically Pays Meal & Car Allowances; Cost Detail Reports by Labor, Overhead, Materials, Equipment, Subcontractor & Other Charges. Provides for Project Billing.
SourceView Software International.

Edit Lister. *Compatible Hardware:* Apple Macintosh.
3.5" disk $900.00.
Video Editor.
Max 3, Inc.

Edit Worx: Video Editing & Production Management. *Items Included:* Software only to control videotape & videodisc machine control & video frame grabbing. *Customer Support:* On-Site training by dealer reps, regular upgrades, worldwide BBS, telephone support.
Macintosh IIx (4Mb). approx. $3495.00, call for exact price (Order no.: EDIT WORX). *Optimal configuration:* 100Mb (or more) hard disk, color display, videotape machines. *Networks supported:* Appletalk.
Allows Novice or Expert Video Editor to Catalog, Edit & Assemble Videoproducts. Uses Simple Iconic Image of Video Segment As Building Block, Allowing Users to Prepare & Assemble Their Products by Arranging Blocks in Sequence. Once Sequence Is Defined, System Will Automatically Assemble Final Product from Source Material.
Specialized Computer Systems.

EDIT-32. *Items Included:* 1 spiral bound manual. *Customer Support:* $60.00 for telephone consultation, updates $20.00, documentation $20.00.
PC/MS-DOS or compatible OS version 3.3 or higher. IBM PC PS/2 or compatible (640k). disk $185.00.
Screen-Oriented Text Editor Which Offers "GoldKey" Style Editing. DOS Users May Define Keys to Be DOS Compatible. Advanced Features Include Multi-File Editing with Windowing, a Powerful Command Language with Numeric Manipulation & Additional Execution, "Teach" Cap ability & Regular Expression Pattern Sebdubg.
S & H Computer Systems, Inc.

EDIT 2000. *Version:* 1.4. 1991. *Items Included:* Full documentation included. *Customer Support:* Technical telephone support at no charge.
UNIX SVR3/SVR4, QNX 2.15, QNX 4, LynxOS Windows. Microcomputer 80386/486 (512k). $395.00. *Optimal configuration:* Intel 80386/486, 1Mb RAM, Interactive/SCO UNIX-rcc compiler.
UNIX SVR3/SVR4, QNX 2.15, QNX 4, LynxOS. Microcomputer 80386/486 (256k). $395.00.
The Editor Brings Modern Editing Facilities to the UNIX/QNX Operating System, Giving Programmers a More Productive Environment. Principal Features Include Multiple File Editing, Cutting & Pasting Between Buffers, Compile, Undo & Redo, Brace Matching, & Online Help. Editing Multiple Files in Multiple Windows Saves Time & Effort, Especially on Large Projects. Cutting & Pasting Between Files Makes Moving Code Easier, Saving Time & Errors. Undo & Redo Operations Let You Fix Miskeys One Keystroke at a Time. Parenthesis & Bracket Matching Help C & C Plus Programmers. View & Edit Complex Expressions. Online Help & User-Configurable. Keystrokes Help Make It Easy to Learn to Use the Editor. These & Other Editing Features Combine to Make EDIT 2000 a Powerful Tool for Programming Development.
Computer Innovations, Inc.

EDITBAS. *Version:* 2.0. 1989.
PC/MS-DOS (384k). IBM PC & compatibles. $29.95.
A Memory Resident Extension to Interpreted Basic's Editor. Pop it up from Within Basic & Instantly Renumber All or Any Portion of Program; Move or Copy a Routine; & Cross Reference a Line(s), Variable, Keyword Token or String Literal.
Educational Micro Systems, Inc.

Editor-Assembler. *Compatible Hardware:* TI 99/4A.
contact publisher for price (Order no.: PHM 3055).
Allows User to Program in TMS 9000 Assembly Language.
Texas Instruments, Personal Productivit.

Editor/Librarian for Yamaha TX81Z.
Compatible Hardware: Commodore Amiga.
3.5" disk $79.00.
MIDITALK.

EDIX. *Version:* 8. May 1987. *Compatible Hardware:* AT&T 3B; IBM PC, PC AT; NCR Tower; Sun; DEC VAX. *Operating System(s) Required:* MS-DOS, UNIX, XENIX, VMS. *Language(s):* C. *Memory Required:* 512k.
IBM PC. disk $195.00.
AT&T, Multiuser XENIX, SUN. disk $425.00.
Full Screen Editor Featuring Multiple Windows (4) & Buffers (12) Where User Can Use up to Four Windows at a Time for Comparing Drafts or for Moving or Copying Text from One Document to Another. Also Offers Search & Replace Capability & User Customization by Means of a Macro Definition Facility.
Emerging Technology Consultants.

EDM Macro Editor. *Compatible Hardware:* TRS-80 Model I, Model III. *Memory Required:* 48k. *General Requirements:* 2 disk drives. $49.95.
The Alternate Source.

EDM: The Programmable File Editor.
Compatible Hardware: TRS-80. *Language(s):* BASIC, Machine, Assembly, Macro.
disk $99.95, incl. documentation & hot-line support.
documentation $25.00.
Gives Mini & Mainframe Editing Capability to TRS-80 Systems.
The Alternate Source.

EdScheme: A Modern Lisp. *Version:* 3.4. May 1991. *Items Included:* 128 page users guide & reference manual. *Customer Support:* 60 day warranty, unlimited telephone support.
IBM PC & compatibles (384k). disk $49.95 (ISBN 0-9628745-4-X).
Atari ST/Mega (512k). disk $49.95 (ISBN 0-9628745-5-8).
Macintosh (512k). 3.5" disk $49.95 (ISBN 0-9628745-6-6).
Scheme Interpreter That Runs from Floppy or Hard Drive. Fast & Efficient Incremental Optimizing Compiler. Features Include Color-Coded Expressions, Turtle Graphics, an Integrated Editor with Automatic Parenthesis-Matching & Support for Functional Programming Techniques & Object Oriented Programming.
Schemers, Inc.

EDUCLIP IMAGES FIVE: EDUCATIONAL

EDT+. *Version:* 6.0. Jun. 1993. *Items Included:* 1 bound EDT & reference guide. *Customer Support:* 30-day money-back guarantee; free customer service & updates for 60 days; annual maintenance plans available.
MS-DOS, UNIX or Windows. IBM PC, XT, AT & compatibles, Sun, HP, SGI, Digital UNIX. $300.00 & up.
Emulation of VAX EDT. Word-Processing Package with ASCII Import/Export Capabilities. Features Automatic Backup of Files & UNDO Command, Column Cut/Paste, Split Screen Windows, Supports 132 Column Mode. Allows User to Simultaneously Edit 80 Files. Based on the VAX/EDT by Digital Equipment Corporation. Supported EVE/TPU Capabilities.
Boston Business Computing, Ltd.

Education Applications of the Wise-III. *Version:* 1.010. Charles L. Nicholson & Charles L. Alcorn. Mar. 1996. *Customer Support:* Free unlimited phone support.
Windows 3.X, Windows 95. 286 (4Mb). disk $249.50 (Order no.: W-1090). *Nonstandard peripherals required:* Printer.
Intelligence & Learning Ability Test. The Program Will Give You a Full Report, with Appropriate Remedial Activities Suggested.
Western Psychological Services.

The Education Disc. Mar. 1995. *Customer Support:* Telephone support, 30 day money back guarantee.
DOS 3.1 or higher or Windows 3.1. IBM PC & compatibles. Contact publisher for price (ISBN 1-886770-05-0). *Optimal configuration:* VGA, Sound card, mouse recommended.
A Collection of over 1500 Educational Programs, Most of Which Will Run from the CD-ROM. Includes Games, Language, Math, Spelling, Music, Biology, Astronomy & More.
Neon Publishing.

Education Management II. *Compatible Hardware:* TRS-80 Model III.
contact publisher for price.
Educational Programming, Inc.

Education Works. *Items Included:* Browser/launcher/installer front end software. *Customer Support:* 90 day warranty, free call back technical support.
System 6. Color Mac (4Mb). CD-ROM disk $9.95. *Nonstandard peripherals required:* CD-ROM drive. *Networks supported:* Apple File Sharing.
Windows 3.1. IBM 386 (4Mb). CD-ROM disk $9.95. *Nonstandard peripherals required:* CD-ROM drive.
BeachWare.

Educational Media Locator. (Media Locator Ser.). Pref. by Walt Carroll. 1996.
IBM & compatibles. 3.5" or 5.25" disk $125.00 (ISBN 0-88367-510-2).
Electronic Book.
Olympic Media Information.

EduClip Images Five: Educational Borders. Jan. 1995. *Items Included:* Manual with index of all borders. *Customer Support:* 30 day return policy if materials returned in resaleable condition. Free telephone support.
MS-DOS, Windows. IBM & compatibles (Hard drive). disk $39.95 (ISBN 0-918187-53-2, Order no.: DBMEDU5). *Addl. software required:* Any application that accepts EPS format.
Macintosh. Macintosh (Hard drive). 3.5" disk $39.95 (ISBN 0-918187-48-6, Order no.: DMCEDU5). *Addl. software required:* Any application that accepts EPS format.
This Collection of Educational Borders Includes

Curriculum Areas - Music, Art, Science, Etc. School Lockers, Certificates, Numbers, Languages, Holidays, Sports & Other Miscellaneous Items. Extra Bonus Included Is Non-Border Forms Such As a Blank Calendar & Assignment Sheets. Requires Compatible Page Layout, Word Processing, Drawing or Paint, Presentation Programs That Accept EPS Format. For Both IBM & Macintosh. Guide Includes Index of All Borders.
Teach Yourself by Computer Software, Inc.

EduClip Images Four - Technology, Math, Science. Sep. 1994. *Items Included:* 1 guide. MAC, MS-DOS, Windows. Macintosh, IBM & compatibles. disk $39.95 (ISBN 0-918187-47-8, Order no.: DMCEDU4 (MACINTOSH); DBMEDU4 (IBM)). *Optimal configuration:* Hard drive.
Includes Hard to Find Clip Art for Technology, Math, & Science Curriculum Areas. Images Range from Simple Tools & Levers to Resources & Machines, Lab Equipment & Experiments to Math Symbols. Some Examples Include: Anthropods, Bunsen Burner, Molecules, Gears, Renewable Raw Materials, Screw Heads, Levers, Joints, Pulleys, Geometric Shapes & More. Guide Shows Suggested Uses & Samples for Handouts, Worksheets, Newsletters As Well As an Index of All the Images Created. Requires Compatible Page Layout, Word Processing, Drawing or Presentation Applications. Macintosh Formats: EPS, PICT, & PAINT; IBM Formats: EPS & TIF.
Teach Yourself by Computer Software, Inc.

EduClip Images 1 - Sports, Holidays, School Items. Jan. 1991. *Items Included:* Diskettes, index & manual.
Macintosh. disk $39.95 (ISBN 0-918187-44-3). *Addl. software required:* Any program that accepts EPS, TIF, PAINT, PICT.
MS-DOS, MAC. IBM & compatibles. disk $39.95 (ISBN 0-918187-49-4). *Addl. software required:* Any program that accepts EPS, TIF, PAINT, PICT.
Collection of of Clip Art for Educators - Disks Include School Items, Nature, Sports, Holidays. Art Can Be Used for Handouts, Worksheets, Newsletters. Includes Holidays, School Items, Curriculum Items. Graphics Can Be Separated. Macintosh Formats: EPS, PAINT, PICT. IBM Format: EPS, TIF.
Teach Yourself by Computer Software, Inc.

EduClip Images 2 - Initials & Numbers with Graphics. Jan. 1992. *Compatible Hardware:* IBM PC & compatibles; Macintosh family. Macintosh. disk $39.95 (ISBN 0-918187-45-1). IBM. disk $39.95 (ISBN 0-918187-50-8). Collection of Initial Caps & Numbers with Art. Graphics Can Be Separated from Alphabet or Numbers for Individual Use in Handouts, Worksheets, Newsletters & Other Classroom & School Materials. Macintosh Format: EPS, PAINT, PICT. IBM Format: EPS, TIF.
Teach Yourself by Computer Software, Inc.

EduClip Images 3 - Curriculum Logos, Social Studies, Sports, Holidays. Jun. 1993. *Items Included:* Diskettes, index & manual.
Macintosh. 3.5" disk $39.95 (ISBN 0-918187-46-X). *Addl. software required:* Any program that accepts EPS, Pict, Paint.
MS-DOS, MAC. IBM & compatibles. disk $39.95 (ISBN 0-918187-51-6). *Addl. software required:* Any program that accepts EPS, TIF.
Collection of Education Clip Art Includes Logo Designs for Each Curriculum Area, i.e. Math, Social Studies, Music etc., Social Studies Events, Holidays. The Graphics Can Be Separated to Create More Images for Individual Use in Handouts, Worksheets, Newsletters & Other Classroom & School Material. Macintosh Format: EPS, PAINT, PICT. IBM Format: EPS, TIF.
Teach Yourself by Computer Software, Inc.

Edutainment Trivia! John Girard. Jan. 1995. *Customer Support:* Telephone support, 30 day money back guarantee.
DOS 3.1 or higher. IBM & compatibles (512k). Contact publisher for price (ISBN 1-886770-00-X). *Nonstandard peripherals required:* VGA.
Four Trivia Games for PC Compatibles. Uses VGA Graphic & Soundblaster Cards. Includes Four Additional Strategy Games for a Total of Eight Games on Each CD-ROM. All Games Run from the CD.
Neon Publishing.

EdWord. *Version:* 3.1. Jun. 1992. *Items Included:* 1 set of documentation, 5 reference cards. *Customer Support:* First year of maintenance free, 15% annual maintenance fee, unlimited phone support, training available for additional fee.
VM/CMS, MVS (T80, CICS), VSE/CISC, XA/ESA. IBM & compatible mainframes. $2480.00-$11,340.00 Annual; $6200.00-$28,350.00 Perpetual.
PC-Like Word Processor That Is Easy to Learn & Support. Offers Pull-Down Menus, Pop-Up Windows, Prefix Commands & Natural Language Word Commands. It Includes a Thesaurus & Spell Checker. EdWord Supports Popular Printer Drivers & Can Be Integrated with Trax's Mainframe Spreadsheet, ESS, or with Existing Systems to Maximize Flexibility.
Trax Softworks, Inc.

EdWordVision. *Version:* 3.1. Jun. 1992. *Items Included:* 1 set of documentation, 5 reference cards. *Customer Support:* First year of maintenance free, 15% annual maintenance fee, unlimited phone support, training available for additional fee.
VM/CMA. IBM & compatible mainframes. $4480.00-$13.340 Annual; $11,200.00-$33.350.00 Perpetual.
EdWordVision Is an Intuitive Editor for PROFS & OfficeVision & Can Co-Exist with or Replace the Current Editor for These Systems. Supports All OfficeVision Menus & Author Profiles for Consistency & Familiarity. It Includes Pull-Down Menus, English-Like Word Commands, Resettable PF Keys, Online HELP, Spell Checker, & Laser Printer Support.
Trax Softworks, Inc.

EDX. Michael Schulze. 1984. *Compatible Hardware:* TRS-80 Model I, Model III, Model 4. *Operating System(s) Required:* TRSDOS 6.0.
Model I, Model III. disk $29.95.
Model 4. disk $39.95.
Text Processing & Formatting Program Which Features a Key That Tells the Computer to Start "Learning" Your Keystrokes. 128 Keystrokes Can Then Be Remembered & Executed with One Keystroke.
The Alternate Source.

EE Designer III. *Version:* 1.8. *Compatible Hardware:* IBM PC, PC XT, PC AT, PS/2. *Operating System(s) Required:* MS-DOS, PC-DOS. *General Requirements:* Hard disk, color graphics, mouse. *Items Included:* Comprehensive Software System. *Customer Support:* Included. disk $3495.00, includes: schematic capture, circuit simulation, PCB layout, artwork generation, libraries, & documentation (Order no.: EE03). CAE/CAD Integrated Software Package for Electrical Engineers. Enables Users to Perform Circuit Design, Schematic Capture, Circuit Simulation & Printed Circuit Board Design.
Team Visionics Corp.

EGA Paint 2005: Graphics Generation-Editing. *Items Included:* Bound manual. *Customer Support:* Free hotline - no time limit; 30 day limited warranty; updates are $5/disk plus S&H.
MS-DOS 2.0 or higher. IBM & compatibles (348k). disk $49.95. *Nonstandard peripherals required:* EGA board (or compatible); supports (though not needed) Microsoft Mouse, Mouse Systems Mouse, etc.
Was Designed to Be Used with the Enhanced Graphics Adapter (EGA). With EGA PAINT, User Can Create Graphics, Capture Screens from Other Programs, Merge Graphics & Text, etc. It Is Perfect for Designing Logos, Laying Out Floor Plans, Preparing Charts & Ad Copy, etc. Features: Screen Capture; Full Screen Editing; High Res EGA; Supports PC QUICK ART; Fill, Pour, Airbrush, Smooth, Stretch, Skew, Grid, Arc, Ellipse, Pallette, Zoom, etc., Commands; Text Processor; Image Library; EGA Slide.
Dynacomp, Inc.

EGA Paint 2005: Graphics Generation-Editing. 1992. *Items Included:* Detailed manuals are included with all DYNACOMP products. *Customer Support:* Free telephone support to original customer - no time limit; 30 day limited warranty.
MS-DOS 3.2 or higher. IBM PC & compatibles (512k). $49.95 (Add $5.00 for 3 1/2" format; 5 1/4" format standard). *Optimal configuration:* IBM, 348K RAM, MS-DOS 2.0 or higher & an EGA board or compatible. Supports Microsoft Mouse, Mouse Systems Mouse, etc.
Designed to Be Used with the Enhanced Graphics Adapter (EGA). Features: Screen Capture; Full Screen Editing; High RES EGA; Supports PC Quick Art; Fill, Pour, Airbrush, Smooth, Skew, Grid, Arc, Ellipse, Pallette, Zoom; Text Processor; Image Library; EGA Slide. Includes an Excellent 200-Page Bound Manual.
Dynacomp, Inc.

Egg Production Pricing. Feb. 1982. *Compatible Hardware:* IBM PC & compatibles. *Operating System(s) Required:* MS-DOS 3.0 or higher. *Language(s):* BASIC (source code included). *Memory Required:* 256k. *Customer Support:* Telephone.
disk $135.00.
Reports by Gradeout or by Flock the Value & Percentages of Each Gradeout. Also Computes Commission for Growers.
Locus Systems.

Egg Roll. *Compatible Hardware:* Commodore 64, 128. *General Requirements:* Standard or Biofeedback EMG sensor.
ROM cartridge $19.95 (Order no.: SOFC64-03-002).
Muscle Coordination & Control Game in Which Electrical Signals from the Muscles Control the Progress of Eggs Rolling Down Ramps.
Bodylog.

EGGPRO (Windows & DOS). *Version:* 2.0. 1993. *Items Included:* User's Guide. *Customer Support:* Free technical support.
MS Windows 3.0 or higher. IBM PC & compatibles (384k). disk $195.00. *Optimal configuration:* IBM PC compatible computer with MS Windows 3.0 or higher, 384k RAM, 80-column printer. *Networks supported:* Novell.
PC-DOS/MS-DOS. IBM PC & compatibles (384k). disk $195.00. *Optimal configuration:* IBM PC compatible computer with MS-DOS, 384k RAM, 80-column printer. *Networks supported:* Novell.
Minimizes the Cost of Feeding Laying Chickens While Maintaining Adequate Nutrient Intake for Peak Commercial Egg Production. Calculates Nutrient Requirements Based on Temperature, Body Weight, Daily Weight Change, Consumption, Percent Production, Feather Score, Net Case Weight & Age of Flock. Used with MIXIT-2 Plus, It Includes 5 Energy, 2 Methionine, & 1 Lysine Equations & Factors to Modify These Equations.
Agricultural Software Consultants, Inc.

TITLE INDEX

EGWord. Version: 6.0. Nov. 1989. Compatible Hardware: Apple Macintosh. Memory Required: 2000k. Items Included: EGBridge front-end processor.
3.5" disk $499.00.
Japanese Word-Processing Software. Includes 80,000 Kanji Word Dictionary, Automatic Kana-Kanji Character Conversion, Romaji & Kana Input Modes, & Various Font Styles. MacPaint Compatible & English Word-Processing Capability.
Qualitas Trading Co.

eHOP: Electronic Handbook of Probability.
Oct. 1993. Items Included: User's Manual (32pp). Customer Support: Unlimited telephone support.
MS-DOS 3.3 Plus. IBM PC/AT, 486 Recommended (4Mb). disk $69.00. Addl. software required: MS Windows 3.1.
Reference for 28 Distributions, Including 3 Non-Central. Solves for P Values, Percentage Points & Distribution Parameters. Extremely Accurate & Very Fast. Lots of Graphs & Technical Information. Short (5 Minute) Learning Curve.
Crunch Software Corp.

Eigen Analyzer. Compatible Hardware: IBM PC & compatibles. Memory Required: 256k.
disk $49.95.
Designed to Facilitate Finding the Real & Complex Eigen Values of Any Real Matrix. Matrix Data & Eigen Value Results Can Be Saved on Disk for Later Recall & Editing As ASCII Files.
Dynacomp, Inc.

Eight Ball. Sep. 1986. Compatible Hardware: Atari ST. Operating System(s) Required: TOS. Memory Required: 512k.
3.5" disk $39.95 (ISBN 0-923213-38-4, Order no.: AT-EIG).
Mouse-Controlled Graphic Billiard Game.
MichTron, Inc.

Eight-User Thoroughbred/OS. Compatible Hardware: IBM PS/2. Memory Required: 512k.
disk $1695.00.
Available for Models 50, 60, & 80. Multi-User, Multitasking Operating System Follows a Three-User Version Previously Introduced.
Thoroughbred.

Eighthink: The Visual Thinking Tool for the 90s. Version: 2.02. Compatible Hardware: Apple Macintosh family. Memory Required: 2000k. Items Included: User guides/sample model templates. Customer Support: Technical support free to registered users.
3.5" disk $695.00.
Model-Building & Simulation Tool. User Can Graphically Construct Business Model & Test Hypothetical Situations to Facilitate Decision Making.
High Performance Systems, Inc.

8088 Tutor Monitor: IBM PC-8088 Assembly Language Programming. Richard E. Haskell. May 1986. Compatible Hardware: IBM PC. Operating System(s) Required: PC-DOS 1.1 or higher. Memory Required: 64k.
disk $20.00 (ISBN 0-938273-11-6, Order no.: DI112).
manual $25.00.
Used to Load & Examine Any Disk File, Disassemble Any 8088 Code, Debug EXE Files, Examine & Change Memory, Set Breakpoints & Single Step Instructions.
Rehi Bks.

8080/Z80 MetaFORTH Cross Compiler.
Operating System(s) Required: CP/M, CDOS. Memory Required: 48k.
disk $450.00.
Cross-Compiler Utility Program.
Inner Access Corp.

87 Software Pak. Version: 6.1. Oct. 1985. Compatible Hardware: IBM PC. Operating System(s) Required: PC-DOS. Language(s): Microsoft Quick BASIC, IBM BASIC Compiler, IBM FORTRAN or Pascal version 1.0 (source code included).
$180.00.
Contains Intel 8087 Numeric Processor Chip & Software Needed to Make the 8087's High Speed & High Accuracy Usable in an IBM PC. Performs All Calculation in an Extended Precision Format, 80 Bits or 18 Decimal Digits. Contains 68 Operations Including: Addition, Subtraction, Multiplication, Division, Square Root, Trigonometric, Exponential, Logarithmic. Source Code Allows for Other Functions to Be Added. Its Libraries Work with the Compiler. Included Are a Set of Matrix Manipulation Routines & a Fast Fourier Transform Routine.
Hauppauge Computer Works.

EIS Toolkit. Oct. 1989. Items Included: ENCORE! Plus (Financial Modeling Software) & its 4 volume user manual. The EIS Toolkit 2 volume user manual. Upon request FEROX MICROSYSTEMS, Inc. will supply our EIS manual in an electronic format for easy editing & additions. This allows the user to have a custom manual specific to their EIS application. Customer Support: Free telephone support, in-house or on-site training available. Charges depend on training desired & number of participants. Consulting available System Design $1200.00/day; Programming, Jr. Consultant $600.00/day, Sr. Consultant $1200.00/day.
MS-DOS 2.0 or higher. IBM PC or compatibles. $2395.00 (includes ENCORE! Plus).
Nonstandard peripherals required: Hard disk required, mouse recommended. Addl. software required: ENCORE! Plus. Networks supported: Novell, 3COM, Token Ring.
Comes Fully Loaded with a Set of Logic & Functions for Calculating & Reporting, Using Your Data or is Easily Modified to Fit Your Specific Needs. Accepts Data from Accounting Systems, Spreadsheets, ENCORE! Models or Outside Databases. Provides Exception Reporting, Drill-Down Logic, Explanatory Messages, Automated Monthly Reporting, Charting & Trend Analysis.
Ferox Microsystems, Inc.

EIVAN - An Interactive Orbital Trajectory Planning Tool. NASA Ames Research Center. May 1989. Items Included: Source code. Customer Support: Limited telephone support from COSMIC.
Macintosh. $50.00 Program; $12.00 documentation (Order no.: ARC-12365). Addl. software required: Microsoft Excel.
COSMIC.

ELCAD: Intelligent Computer Aided Design Software Package. Items Included: 3 spiral bound manuals. Customer Support: 90 days unlimited warranty; subsequent maintenance $1,200 & up annually; training $500.00 per day.
MS-DOS. IBM AT & compatibles (640k). $10,500.00 & up. Optimal configuration: Hi-Resolution Monitor, Video Board, Plotter, Mouse. Networks supported: Novell, Lantastic.
Unix. HP 9000 (2Mb). contact publisher for price. Optimal configuration: Plotter, Mouse, Hi-Resolution Video.
VMS. DEC. contact publisher for price. Optimal configuration: Plotter, Mouse, Hi-Resolution Video.
Intelligent CAD Graphics Package Which Greatly Simplifies Design & Modification Because Logical Information As Well As Graphical Information Is Known to the Software Package. Broad Spectrum of Cross Compatibility with Other Well-Known CAD Packages on the Graphics Level.
Howard W. Myers & Assocs.

ELECTRIC WEBSTER

Electra-Find. Version: 3.3. Sep. 1985. Compatible Hardware: CP/M based machines; Epson QX-10; IBM PC, PC XT; Kaypro 2, Kaypro 4; Morrow MD2, MD3; MS-DOS based machines. Operating System(s) Required: CP/M-80, PC-DOS, MS-DOS. Memory Required: 64k.
disk $49.00, incl. manual.
Finds, Retrieves, & Extracts Text Material from Groups of Files Produced by a Word Processor. Does Boolean Phonetic, & Wild Card Searches. Any Amount of Text Material Can Be Retrieved Automatically.
O'Neill Software.

The Electric Address Book. (The IMSI Home Library). International Microcomputer Software, Inc. Compatible Hardware: Commodore 64; IBM PC, PCjr.
disk $39.95.
IBM PC. (ISBN 0-13-248634-2).
IBM PCjr. (ISBN 0-13-248642-3).
Commodore 64. (ISBN 0-13-248626-1).
Replaces the Rolodex, Cardtray, & Paper Address Book with a Single Diskette.
Prentice Hall.

Electric Machinery Examples. Version: IBM. S. Umans. Aug. 1985. Compatible Hardware: IBM PC. Memory Required: 64k. General Requirements: CGA card, color monitor. Items Included: 2 disks & documentation in folder.
$34.28, set (ISBN 0-07-831327-9).
Provides Eight Interactive, Multi-Dimensional Examples of Topics Covered in the Text "Electric Machinery", 4th ed., by Fitzgerald.
McGraw-Hill, Inc.

Electric Pencil. Michael Shrayer. Compatible Hardware: TRS-80. Operating System(s) Required: NewDOS, TRSDOS, DOSPLUS, MultiDOS.
disk $89.95 (ISBN 0-936200-24-3).
cassette $79.95.
Character Oriented Word Processor, Which Facilitates the Movement of Text. Everything Appears on the Screen As It Occurs.
Blue Cat.

Electric Pencil PC. Compatible Hardware: IBM PC. Operating System(s) Required: PC-DOS 1.0, 1.1, 2.0. Memory Required: 48k. General Requirements: Monochrome or color display, printer.
disk $29.95.
2-Keystroke Commands Execute "Control Commands" Such As Search & Replace, Insert, Delete, etc. Function Keys Are Definable up to 16 Keystrokes of Any Key Combination. Underlined & Bold Characters Appear That Way on the Screen.
Blue Cat.

Electric Pencil PC Tutor. Compatible Hardware: IBM PC.
disk $29.95 (ISBN 0-936200-40-5).
Provides 63 HELP Screens for Instant Assistance. Requires ELECTRIC PENCIL PC to Operate.
Blue Cat.

The Electric Tarot. Gerald J. Schueler. May 1984. Compatible Hardware: IBM PC & compatibles. Memory Required: 256k.
$24.95 ea. (ISBN 0-87542-714-6).
Atari disk. (ISBN 0-87542-987-4).
Displays Each Card "Drawn" by Your Interaction with the Computer with Meanings & Interpretation. Print-Out Capabilities in Program. Uses Major Arcana Only.
Llewellyn Pubns.

Electric Webster. Phil Manfield. 1983. Compatible Hardware: Tandy Model 1000, 2000; TRS-80 Model I, Model III, Model 4; IBM

PC & compatibles. *Operating System(s) Required:* PC-DOS/MS-DOS, CP/M. *Language(s):* Assembly.
TRS-80 Model I, III, 4. disk $89.95.
TRS-80 w/Correcting Feature. $99.99.
TRS-80 Hyphenation. $32.49.
TRS-80 Grammar & Style Checker. $32.49.
CP/M, PC-DOS, Tandy w/Correcting Feature, Hyphenation & Grammar. $129.55.
Spelling Checker That Offers Hyphenation Feature & a Grammar & Style Checker. Detects Words Spelled Incorrectly & Displays the Correct Spellings. If the User Guesses at the Correct Spelling, the Program Will Check the Guess Before the Correction Is Made. Once All Corrections Have Been Indicated, Each Error Will Be Corrected Whenever It Occurs in the Text. The Hyphenation Feature Allows the User to Insert Discretionary Hyphens into a Document to Make End-of-Line Hyphenation Automatic. With the Grammar & Style Checker the User Can Look for 22 Types of Grammatical Errors, Including Double Negatives & Wordy Phrases.
Cornucopia Software.

Electrical. *Compatible Hardware:* Aegis, HP-UX, HP/Apollo, OS Sun, DEC work stations, VMS, Ultrix. *Items Included:* Documentation. *Customer Support:* Maintenance, training; 800 number. contact publisher for price.
Electronic-Design Package. Includes Schematic Circuit-Wiring Layout.
Auto-Trol Technology Corp.

Electrical Contractor Calculator. 1995. *Items Included:* Full manual. *Customer Support:* Free telephone support - 90 days, 30-day warranty. MS-DOS 3.2 or higher. 286 (584k). disk $19.95. *Nonstandard peripherals required:* CGA/EGA/VGA.
ECC Is a Menu-Driven Calculator for Electrical Contractors. It Handles Voltage Drops for a Given Load & Line; Required Wire Sizes; Cable & Conduit Selection; Box Fill; Zonal Cavity Lighting; & More. All of These Calculations Can Be Done by Hand, or Obtained from Tables. However, ECC Is Faster & Easier to Use.
Dynacomp, Inc.

Electrical Engineering Library. *Compatible Hardware:* TI 99/4A.
disk or cassette - contact publisher for price.
Library of Tools Commonly Used by Electrical Engineers, Including Filter Design, Root Locus, Smith Chart & Phase-Locked Door.
Texas Instruments, Personal Productivit.

Electrical Engineering Series, 2 disks. *Compatible Hardware:* Apple II, II+. *Language(s):* Applesoft II. *Memory Required:* 32k.
Set. $74.95 (Order no.: 10031).
Covers a Variety of Aspects of Electrical Engineering.
Powersoft, Inc.

Electro Bits. *Compatible Hardware:* Apple Macintosh. *General Requirements:* Hard disk or external disk drive; MacPaint, SuperPaint, FullPaint or compatible program. *Items Included:* Diskette & manual. *Customer Support:* Complete telephone support, 90-day warranty.
3.5" disk $24.95.
demo disk $5.00.
Circuit Graphics. A Collection of over 200 Electronic Elements & over 40 Microcomputer Template Symbols to Draw Circuit Diagrams & Flow Charts. Elements & Symbols Are Indexed into the Following Libraries: Amplifiers, Audio, Capacitors, Filters, Flip-Flops, Flow Charts, Gates, Integrated Circuits, Miscellaneous, Resistors & Semiconductors. Program Is Available in English or Spanish, As Well As in PictureBase Format or HyperCard Stack.
Medina Software, Inc.

Electro-Services Weather Fax. *Version:* 7.0. Jan. 1996. *Compatible Hardware:* IBM PC & compatibles. *Operating System(s) Required:* PC-DOS/MS-DOS, VGA graphics. *Memory Required:* 2000k. *Items Included:* ESC-102 hardware. *Customer Support:* telephone support.
$479.00 3.5" or 5.25" disk, incl. ESC 102 hardware card (ISBN 0-923854-03-7, Order no.: ESC102).
Series of Programs to Acquire, Display & Enhance Satellite Image Data from U.S. & Foreign Weather Satellites.
Satellite Data Systems, Inc.

The Electronic Astrologer: Reveals Your Horoscope. Rique Pottenger & Maritha Pottenger. Aug. 1995. *Items Included:* Manual (12 pages). *Customer Support:* Free tech support available by phone to registered owners for one year.
Windows 3.1. 386 PC (4Mb). Contact publisher for price. *Networks supported:* Any that Windows does.
Easily Calculate Horoscopes with Latitude, Longitude & Time Change Information Built In. User Enters Date, Place & (Optional) Time of Birth. Comprehensive Interpretations (40-50 Pages) on Screen or Printed. Extensive Help. Click on Any Part of the Horoscope for More Information or Personalized Reading.
A C S Publications.

Electronic BillBoard. *Customer Support:* 800-929-8117 (customer service).
MS-DOS. Apple II. disk $59.99 (ISBN 0-87007-426-1).
Has a Graphics Display of Color Patterns Intermixed with Customer Messages of any Duration. Great for Unattended Display in Trade Shows or Retail Stores.
SourceView Software International.

The Electronic Breadboard. *Compatible Hardware:* Apple, II+; TRS-80 Model I, Model III. *Language(s):* Applesoft BASIC. *Memory Required:* 32k.
disk $59.95.
cassette $49.95.
Aids in the Design Analysis of Analog Circuits & May Be Used to Evaluate Voltage, Impedance, Currents, & the Frequency Response of Any Circuit As Well As Many Other Applications. By Entering Sample Circuits & Determining Frequency Responses, Students Verify Electrical Theory. A Tutorial Is Included. Can Be Utilized by Audio Component Repair Technicians, Electrical Engineers, Students of Electronics, & Electricians.
Instant Software, Inc.

Electronic Builder. June Wright. 1989. *Items Included:* 1 manual. *Customer Support:* 1-800 Help Line.
DOS 3.3 or DOS 5.0. IBM PS/2 Models or compatibles (640k). Contact publisher for price; part of KIDWARE 2 PLUS package. *Nonstandard peripherals required:* VGA graphics board & monitor, IBM speech adapter card or Digispeech, M-Audio, or Soundblaster, external speaker, mouse; Powerpad optional. *Addl. software required:* DOS 3.3, DOS 5.0 & software associated with mouse. *Optimal configuration:* One IBM PS/2 Model 25 or Model 30 with 640k RAM, color display (MCGA or VGA), one 720k 3.5" disk drive, IBM Speech Adapter, one IBM Proprinter or Star Micronics color printer & one external, keyboard, IBM mouse, DOS 3.3 & DOS 5.0. *Networks supported:* Novell, ICLAS.
Creates Abstract Designs by Combining Different Sized Shapes & Colors. Printout Pictures. Teachers Can Build Designs for Children to Reconstruct.
Mobius Corp.

Electronic Clipper. Aug. 1989. *Items Included:* Image Quest electronic indexing system; Options - a monthly creative supplement with layout suggestions & manipulation ideas; Printed pictorial index; File binder for disks; Binder for options & indexes. *Customer Support:* Free technical support via telephone to customers.
Macintosh (2Mb). CD-ROM disk Monthly subscription is $67.50 per month. *Addl. software required:* Page layout or draw program that accepts EPS or TIFF files. *Optimal configuration:* Macintosh computer with a hard drive & a PostScript compatible printer device or phototypesetter.
IBM or compatibles 640k. CD-ROM disk Monthly subscription is $67.50 per month. *Addl. software required:* Page layout or draw program that accepts EPS or TIFF files. *Optimal configuration:* IBM or compatible with 640k memory & a PostScript compatible printer device or phototypesetter.
Monthly General Purpose Art & Idea Service Featuring Quality Graphics & Creative Ideas for Electronic Design Projects. Includes Seasonal Graphics, Symbolic & Stylized Art & Photos, Borders, Mortices, Textures & Other Design Elements Plus a Full Color Graphic Monthly. Includes EPS & TIFF Graphic Files with Artistic Styles & Techniques Such As Airbrush, Stipple, Gray Scale & More. Product Is Available on 3.5" Disk, 5.25" Disk or CD-ROM.
Dynamic Graphics, Inc.

Electronic Disk ROM. *Compatible Hardware:* HP 86A/87.
ROM cartridge $195.00 (Order no.: 00087-15012).
Structures User RAM As If It Were a Disk, Thus Increasing Program Chaining Speed & Disk Information Access. Also Allows the Computer to Utilize a 10Mb Winchester Disk.
Hewlett-Packard Co.

Electronic Easel. June Wright. 1989. *Items Included:* 1 manual & 1 overlay. *Customer Support:* 1-800 Help Line.
DOS 3.3, DOS 5.0. IBM PS/2 Model 25 or 30 & compatibles (640k). Contact publisher for price; part of KIDWARE 2 PLUS package. *Nonstandard peripherals required:* VGA graphics board & monitor, IBM speech adapter card or Digispeech, M-Audio, or Soundblaster, external speaker, mouse; Powerpad optional. *Addl. software required:* DOS. 3.3, DOS 5.0 & software associated with mouse. *Optimal configuration:* One IBM PS/2 Model 25 or Model 30 with 640k RAM, color display (MCGA or VGA), one 720k 3.5" disk drive, IBM Speech Adapter, one IBM Proprinter or Star Micronics color printer & one external, keyboard, IBM mouse, DOS 3.3 & DOS 5.0. *Networks supported:* Novell, ICLAS.
Shows How Colors Mix to Form New Colors. Children Can Paint Pictures & Make Printouts.
Mobius Corp.

Electronic Grade Book. *Version:* 8.01. 1994. *Items Included:* 50 full manuals (1 per teacher). *Customer Support:* $225.00/per year for 1 school no limit on number of teachers.
MS-DOS 6.2 or higher. IBM-PC 486 & compatibles (640k). disk $995.00. *Optimal configuration:* IBM-PC 486 or compatible w/ 4Mb RAM, SVGA monitor & card, 3.5" HD floppy drive, DOS 6.2. *Networks supported:* Novell Netware, Lantastic, Windows NT.
This System Allows Teachers to Enter Daily Grades & Have the Program Calculate Term, Semester & Final Grades. Once All of the Grades Have Been Entered They Can Be Downloaded to the Grade Reporting System to Be Included on Report Cards. Grades Can Be Transferred on Floppy Disks or over a Network.
Applied Educational Systems, Inc.

TITLE INDEX

An Electronic Holmes Companion. Robert J. Stek. Dec. 1987. *Compatible Hardware:* Apple Macintosh; IBM PC & compatibles. *Operating System(s) Required:* MS-DOS/PC-DOS. *Memory Required:* 384k. *General Requirements:* Hard disk.
IBM. disk $59.95 (ISBN 0-945317-00-X, Order no.: MS-1).
IBM. 3.5" disk $59.95 (ISBN 0-945317-01-8, Order no.: MS-2).
Macintosh. 3.5" disk $59.95 (ISBN 0-945317-02-6, Order no.: MAC-1).
ASCII Text of All Sherlock Holmes Stories by Sir A. Conan Doyle with Text Search/Retrieval & Literary Analysis Programs.
PsyLogic Systems.

Electronic IV. Nov. 1987. *Compatible Hardware:* IBM PC. *Memory Required:* 384k. *General Requirements:* Graphics card; Generic CADD or First CADD. *Customer Support:* Unlimited technical support to registered users.
IBM. disk $74.95 (ISBN 1-55814-032-8, Order no.: F1004).
IBM. 3.5" disk $74.95 (ISBN 1-55814-033-6, Order no.: T1004).
(ISBN 1-55814-035-2, Order no.: X1004).
(ISBN 1-55814-038-7, Order no.: W1005).
180 Pre-Drawn CADD Symbols of Electronic TTL Components.
Autodesk, Inc.

Electronic Mail. *Compatible Hardware:* IBM PC & compatibles, PC XT, PC AT. *Operating System(s) Required:* MOS. (source code included). *Memory Required:* 4 users 256k, 9 users 512k.
$995.00, incl. basic system.
Provides Inter-Terminal Communications & Interfaces to THE SOURCE, DOW JONES, & TIME NET. User Transmits Mail to Another User on the System. The Mail Is Stored until the Addressee Returns to the System, at Which Time Notification Is Made That Mail Is Waiting.
Hurricane Systems, Inc.

Electronic Office System (EOS). *Operating System(s) Required:* IRIS.
$2000.00 (Order no.: EOS01).
Dictionary. $500.00 (Order no.: EOS02).
manual $60.00 (Order no.: A-0024).
installation manual $12.00 (Order no.: A-0026).
Comprises Several Software Packages Including Word Processing, Electronic Mail & Electronic Calendar.
Point 4 Data Corp.

Electronic Print Media Service. Sep. 1992. *Customer Support:* Free technical support via phone.
Macintosh. CD-ROM disk Monthly membership $89.50. *Nonstandard peripherals required:* Hard disk, PostScript compatible printer device or phototypesetter, compatible CD-ROM reader/drive. *Addl. software required:* Page layout or draw program that accepts EPS files & TIFF files.
Windows 3.0. IBM PC & compatibles (640k). CD-ROM disk Monthly membership $89.50. *Nonstandard peripherals required:* PostScript compatible printer; CD-ROM reader/driver. *Addl. software required:* Page layout or draw program that accepts EPS & TIFF files.
Monthly General Purpose Art & Idea Service Featuring Quality Graphics & Creative Ideas for the Widest Variety of Visual Applications for Electronic Design Projects. Each Monthly Collection Includes Seasonal Graphics, Symbolic & Stylized Art & Photos, Borders, Mortices, Textures & Other Design Elements, Food Art, a Full Color Graphic Monthly, Plus Illustrations of People Involved in a Variety of Business, Recreational & Social Situations. Electronic Print Media Service Is Electronically Indexed in Image QUEST for Identification & Retrieval of Images at Computer Speed. A Printed Pictorial Index Is Also Provided As Well As Tearsheet, a Monthly Supplement Providing Idea Starters, Layout Design Suggestions Specific to the Images in Each Monthly Issue. Includes EPS & TIFF Graphic Files Offering Great Variety in Artistic Styles & Techniques. Storage Units Are Provided for Discs & Indexes.
Dynamic Graphics, Inc.

Electronic Rolodex. 1985. *Compatible Hardware:* Apple II, II+, IIc. *Operating System(s) Required:* Apple DOS 3.3. *Memory Required:* 48k. *General Requirements:* Applesoft in ROM.
$49.95.
Computerized Card File. Optional 1 to 15 Line Cards. Programmed for Small, Large, or 3 x 5 Cards. All Information Stored Alphabetically. No Sort Ever Needed. Keeps Track of Printed Files So a Hard Copy of Updates May Be Printed.
Nikrom Technical Products, Inc.

Electronic Spreadsheet Applications for Cost Accounting. 1989. *General Requirements:* Lotus 1-2-3.
IBM/Tandy. contact publisher for price (ISBN 0-538-80116-6, Order no.: AE81B8).
IBM PS/2. contact publisher for price (ISBN 0-538-80253-7, Order no.: AE81B8H88).
Text-Workbook & Template Diskette Package Covering the Use of Spreadsheets in Cost Accounting Contains: (A) Short Tutorial on Lotus; (B) 20 Plus Problems Illustrating Common Cost Accounting Concepts (C) Instruction for Constructing Templates to Solve Other Problems.
South-Western Publishing Co.

Electronic Spreadsheet Applications for Intermediate Acctg. 1988. *General Requirements:* Lotus 1-2-3.
IBM/Tandy. contact publisher for price (ISBN 0-538-40120-6, Order no.: 02A3).
IBM PS/2. contact publisher for price (ISBN 0-538-40122-2, Order no.: 02A38).
Text-Workbook & Template Diskette Package for Use with any Intermediate Accounting Text. Enables Students to Learn Intermediate Accounting Concepts Utilizing Lotus 1-2-3.
South-Western Publishing Co.

Electronic Spreadsheet System (ESS). *Version:* 5.1. Jun. 1992. *Items Included:* 1 set of documentation, 5 reference cards. *Customer Support:* First year of maintenance free, 15% annual maintenance fee, unlimited phone support, training available for additional fee.
VM/CMS, MVS (CICS, TSO, XA, ESA), VSE/CICS. IBM & compatible mainframes. $3100.00-$14,180.00 Annual; $7750.00-$35,440.00 Perpetual.
Powerful PC-Like Spreadsheet That's Easy to Learn & Use. ESS' Size Is Virtually Unlimited. It Is Compatible with Popular Macro Languages & Graphics Packages. Can Access Most Mainframe Files & Read & Write Lotus 1-2-3 Files. Has DB2 & SQL/DS Interfaces. Works with Trax's Word Processor, EdWord, & Existing Systems.
Trax Softworks, Inc.

Electronic Typewriter. *Version:* 2.0. Dec. 1986. *Operating System(s) Required:* CP/M-80, MS-DOS. *Memory Required:* 64k. *General Requirements:* Printer. *Items Included:* Manual/disk/warranty card. *Customer Support:* 18 month via telephone.
disk $29.00.
Converts Any Computer & Printer into a One Line Memory Electronic Typewriter with Settable Margins, Tabs, Line Spacing, etc.
Micro-Art Programmers.

ELEMENTARY SCIENCE: THE HUMAN BODY

Electronic Watershed Management Reference Manual. Philip R. Chernin et al. Oct. 1995. *Customer Support:* Printable bug sheet.
DOS 3.1 or higher, MS Windows 3.1 or higher, Single CD ROM drive. 386 or higher (6Mb). $295.00-$375.00 (ISBN 0-9648877-0-3, Order no.: 90695). *Nonstandard peripherals required:* Sound card for video, audio. *Optimal configuration:* 8Mb RAM, Quad Speed CD ROM drive.
Watershed Management Information from 84 Water Utilities. Descriptions of 102 Best Management Practices (BMPs). Descriptions of Watershed Management Related Programs in Every State & the Federal Government.
AWWA Research Foundation.

Electronic Whole Earth Catalogue. Sep. 1988. *Compatible Hardware:* Apple Macintosh. *Memory Required:* 1024k.
contact publisher for price (Order no.: 33655).
Runs under HyperCard.
Broderbund Software, Inc.

Electronic Woodcuts & Holiday Clip Art. *Compatible Hardware:* Apple Macintosh. *General Requirements:* MacPaint.
3.5" disk $39.95.
Collection of Ornate Pictorials. Contains 200 Items Which Include Borders & Ornaments Suitable for Creating Unique Holiday Displays.
Bitmap, Inc.

Electronics Design Calculator. *Compatible Hardware:* TRS-80 Model I, Model III. *Memory Required:* 16k.
cassette $14.95 (Order no.: 0204R).
Computes Complex Calculations Including Formulas for Reactance, Resonant Frequency, Resistors & Capacitors in Parallel & Series.
Instant Software, Inc.

Electronics Engineer Assistant. *Compatible Hardware:* Apple II, Commodore PET. *Memory Required:* 8-32k.
Apple. disk $19.95 (Order no.: 0267AD).
PET. cassette $14.95 (Order no.: 0085P).
Analyzes Problems in Network Analysis & Microstrip Design.
Instant Software, Inc.

The Electrophysiology System. 1981. *Compatible Hardware:* IBM PC XT, PC AT, PS/2 Model 30. *Operating System(s) Required:* MS-DOS, PC-DOS. *Language(s):* C. *Memory Required:* 640k.
contact publisher for price.
Designed to Provide the Clinical & Research Electrophysiologist with Applications That Allow for Faster Interpretation of Electrophysiology Study Results.
Trinity Computing Systems, Inc.

Elementary Computer Literacy System. *Compatible Hardware:* Apple II.
contact publisher for price.
National Business Institute.

Elementary Science: The Human Body. Dec. 1995. *Customer Support:* Telephone support - free (except phone charge).
Windows 3.1. IBM & compatibles (386 DX-20) (4Mb). CD-ROM disk $12.99, Jewel (ISBN 1-57594-088-4). *Nonstandard peripherals required:* 2X CD ROM player, sound card, VGA monitor. *Optimal configuration:* 486 SX-33.
CD-ROM disk $12.99, Blister.
Journey with the Invisible Man to Find Out How the Human Body Works As He Visits the Doctor. The Invisible Man Shows You All the Different Bones & Organs in Your Body, While He Explains How They All Work Together.
Kidsoft, Inc.

Elementary Science: The Human Body. Feb. 1996. *Customer Support:* Telephone support - free (except phone charge).
Windows 3.1. IBM compatible 386 DX-20 (4Mb). CD-ROM disk $12.99 (ISBN 1-57594-101-5). *Nonstandard peripherals required:* 2x CD-ROM, sound card, VGA monitor. *Optimal configuration:* 486, SX-33.
Learn How the Human Body Works, about Bones & Organs. Blister Pack.
Kidsoft, Inc.

Elementary Science: The Human Body. Dec. 1995. *Customer Support:* Telephone support - free (except phone charge).
Windows 3.1. IBM & compatibles (386 DX-20) (4Mb). CD-ROM disk $12.99 (ISBN 1-57594-088-4). *Nonstandard peripherals required:* 2X CD-ROM player, sound card, VGA monitor. *Optimal configuration:* 486 SX-33.
Journey with the Invisible Man to Find Out How the Human Body Works As He Visits the Doctor. The Invisible Man Shows You All the Different Bones & Organs in Your Body, While He Explains How They All Work Together. Jewel Case.
Kidsoft, Inc.

Elementary Signer: Elementary Signer. 1987. *Compatible Hardware:* Apple II series, Apple IIgs, Macintosh; IBM PC & compatibles. *Memory Required:* Apple II series 48k, Apple IIgs 48k, IBM PC & compatibles 256k, Macintosh 512k. *General Requirements:* 2 disk drives for talking version, CGA card for IBM.
Apple II series Talking. disk $99.95.
Apple II series Silent. disk $79.95.
Apple IIgs Talking. disk $99.95.
Apple IIgs Silent. disk $79.95.
IBM PC & compatibles. 3.5" or 5.25" disk $79.95.
Macintosh Talking. 3.5" disk $99.95.
Macintosh Silent. 3.5" disk $79.95.
Allows Users to Practice ASL Sign Language. 1600 Signs Displayed on Screen When Equivalent English Word Is Selected. User Controls Speed, Can Stop Action of Sign, Repeat Signs, Turn Captions on & Off. Words Selected from Any of the 16 Data Disks Can Be Stored on User's Disk for Replay. Learning Comprehension Feature Tests Knowledge of Selected Signs; Allows Three Guesses & Keeps Score.
E&IS SignWare.

Elements of Mathematics. Ray E. Zubler & Susan L. Sarapata. *Customer Support:* 90 day warranty against defective software.
DOS 3.3. Apple II (48k). disk $49.95 (Order no.: A-1111).
DOS 3.3 or higher. IBM (640k). disk $49.95 (Order no.: I-1111).
This Program Includes Two Lessons & a Test in the Addition of Simple & Complex Fractions. The First Lesson Deals with the Reduction & Addition of Fractions & Mixed Numbers Having Common Denominators, Using Graphics (Pie Slices) for Illustration. The Second Lesson Moves to Problems Having Unlike Denominators. Test Results are Stored in a File Which Is Accessible to Both the Student & Instructor.
Electronic Courseware Systems, Inc.

Elements of Medical Terminology. *Compatible Hardware:* IBM PC, PC XT, PC AT.
disk $49.95.
College Level Drill & Practice in Medical & Anatomical Terminology. 25 Lessons Teach Combining Forms, Roots, Suffixes & Prefixes. These Word Elements Are Combined to Provide a Vocabulary. New Words Can be Understood by Recognition of Their Parts. Review Section Eliminates the Need to Retake Individual Lessons. Handles up to 200 Students & Keeps Track of Each Student by an Identifier.
Applied MicroSystems, Inc. (Georgia).

Elements of Music. John M. Eddins & Robert L. Weiss, Jr. *Customer Support:* 90 day warranty against defective software.
DOS 3.3. Apple II (48k). disk $99.95 (Order no.: A-1107).
DOS 3.2 or higher. IBM (640k). disk $99.95 (Order no.: I-1107). *Nonstandard peripherals required:* CGA card & monitor minimum.
System 6.0.2 - System 7.1. Macintosh (1Mb). 3.5" disk $99.95 (Order no.: MAC-1107).
Elements of Music Is an Entry-Level Music Program for Use by Children or Adults. Random Drills, Either Timed or Untimed, Are Provided for Naming Both Major & Minor Key Signatures & Naming Notes from a Musical Staff or from a Keyboard.
Electronic Courseware Systems, Inc.

Elements Plus. *Version:* 2.1. 1987. *Items Included:* Atoms, a HyperCard stack giving a history of atom discoveries. *Customer Support:* Free phone support.
MAC-DOS (1Mb). 3.5" disk $20.00. *Addl. software required:* HyperCard. *Optimal configuration:* System 6.0.2.
Periodic Table of the Elements. Shows Density, Melting & Boiling Points, Oxidation Numbers, Atomic Number & Weight, Chemical Symbols, Electron Shells, Color & Element Descriptions, Crystal Symmetry, Alchemy Symbols, & More.
Flight Engineering.

Eleven Rule Greyhound. Ronald D. Jones. 1985. *Compatible Hardware:* Apple II; Commodore 64; IBM PC; TRS-80 Model I, Model III, Color Computer. *Operating System(s) Required:* CP/M. *Memory Required:* 64k.
disk $59.95 ea. (Order no.: D006).
Apple. (ISBN 1-55604-102-0).
CP/M. (ISBN 1-55604-103-9).
IBM. (ISBN 1-55604-106-3).
disk or cassette $59.95.
Commodore. (ISBN 1-55604-104-7).
Color Computer. (ISBN 1-55604-105-5).
Model I & Model III. (ISBN 1-55604-107-1).
Analyzes 11 Most Important Factors. Suited for Recreational Greyhound Handicappers.
Professor Jones Professional Handicapping Systems.

1120 Corporation. *Items Included:* Manual. *Customer Support:* Free 90 day maintenance.
PC-DOS, MS-DOS 2.0 or higher. IBM PC-XT, IBM PC-AT or compatible (512k). disk $189.00.
2nd year renewal $89.00.
Spreadsheet Similar to IRS Layout for Tax Preparation.
Profitime, Inc.

1120S Subchapter S Corporation. *Items Included:* Manual. *Customer Support:* Free 90 day maintenance.
PC-DOS, MS-DOS 2.0 or higher. IBM PC-XT, IBM PC-AT or compatible (512k). disk $189.00.
$89.00 2nd year renewal.
Spreadsheet Similar to IRS Layout for Tax Preparation.
Profitime, Inc.

The 1120 Solution, 3 disks. *Version:* 99.3. Jan. 1990. *Compatible Hardware:* IBM PC XT & compatibles, PC AT, PS/2. *Operating System(s) Required:* PC-DOS/MS-DOS 2.X or higher. *Language(s):* Pascal. *Memory Required:* 512k. *General Requirements:* Hard disk. *Customer Support:* Unlimited free.
disk $895.00.
renewal $495.00.
Facilitates In-House Preparation & Printing of 1120 & 1120S Corporate Tax Returns & Related Transmittal Letters.
Creative Solutions, Inc. (Michigan).

1120 TAX ASSEMBLY. *Version:* 3.02. *Compatible Hardware:* Altos Series 5-15D, Series 5-5D, 580-XX, ACS8000-XX; Burroughs B20-3 with 2 disk drives; DEC Rainbow 100 with 2 disk drives, Rainbow 100+ with 10Mb hard disk; IBM PC with 2 disk drives, PC XT, PC AT, IBM compatibles; Kaypro 11/IV with 2 disk drives, Kaypro 10; Xerox 820 with 2 disk drives; ZILOG MCZ-250. *Operating System(s) Required:* CP/M, MP/M, CP/M-86/80, PC-DOS, MS-DOS.
License fee unit. $1500.00 (Order no.: 1120).
License fee site. $2250.00.
Maintenance unit. $500.00.
Maintenance site. $750.00.
Designed to Interface with PRE-AUDIT. Facilitates the Preparation of the U.S. Corporation Income Tax, Form 1120 Through Line 30, Taxable Income after Net Operating Loss Deductions. Also Prepares Three Five-Year History Reports: M1 Timing Differences, M2 Permanent Differences, Retained Earnings (Appropriated & Unappropriated).
Coopers & Lybrand.

Elite Accounting System: ELITEAR, ELITEAP, ELITEGL, ELITEPA, ELITEWP. Arthur Hayward. Jan. 1984. *Operating System(s) Required:* MS-DOS. *Language(s):* RMCOBOL. *Memory Required:* 128k. *General Requirements:* 2 disk drives, 132-column printer.
Set. $155.00.
disk $45.00 ea.
Provides 5 MultiCompany-MultiUser Integrated or Stand Alone Packages with Features That Can Be Altered by the Flag Settings. The General Ledger Package May Be Used for Fund Accounting in Schools, Municipalities, etc. Programs Are Menu Driven with Files Updated in Real Time. Files Are Indexed, Requiring No Sorting.
Elite Systems, Inc.

Elite Mail for Windows or DOS: Direct Mail Planning Tool. Jan. 1993.
PC-DOS/MS-DOS. Any PC clone (384k). disk $69.00. *Addl. software required:* Windows 3.0 or higher, DOS 2.1 or higher.
A Planning Tool for Direct Mailings. Gives User the Total Cost for Every Mailing, Lets User "Goal-Seek" to Meet Specific Profit Objectives, & Performs "What If" Calculations on Key Mailing Decisions. Helps Avoid Low-Profit or No-Profit Mailings. Can Pay for Itself.
Elite Software.

Elite-Menu: Fast Program Access with File Security. Nov. 1991. *Items Included:* Disk & manual.
PC-DOS/MS-DOS 2.0 or higher. IBM or clone (256k). disk $39.00 (Order no.: ELMEN-01). *Optimal configuration:* One 5.25" or 3.5" floppy drive, one hard drive, 256k RAM, & 2k RAM resident shell for program. *Networks supported:* Novell, 3COM.
Provides an Easy Organization of PC Programs via Custom Menus That Provide Single-Key Access to Any Program, Password Security to Protect Un-Authorized Hard-Drive Access, & Automatic Logging of Programs Used (Who, When, How Long). Lets Non-DOS Users Access Any PC. Designed for Home or Office Applications.
Elite Software.

The Elite System. May 1981. *Compatible Hardware:* AT&T 3B2, AT&T 6386, Compaq 386. *Operating System(s) Required:* UNIX, XENIX. *Memory Required:* 1024k. *General Requirements:* Hard disk, printer, modem. *Customer Support:* 90 day warranty. A Customer support contract is available on an annual basis. This includes unlimited telephone support, remote diagnostics, updates & new releases to the software.

TITLE INDEX

contact publisher for price.
Time Billing, Accounting, Docketing & Calendaring System Developed Specifically for Law Firms. Performs All Accounting Functions, As Well As a Host of Other Tasks Essential to a Law Firm Operation. Other Features Include Integrated Trust Accounting & Retainer Handling, Integrated Folder Control, & Integrated Docket & Calendar Control. Word Processing, Litigation Support, & On-Line Research Are Available.
Elite Data Processing.

Elite-Xfer: Color Computer File Transfer Utility. *Version:* 1.1. Dec. 1991.
PC-DOS/MS-DOS. Any PC compatible (180k). disk $39.95. *Optimal configuration:* Standard PC color or B&W display.
Lets Any MS-DOS Computer Read Color Computer Disks. Freely Transfer Both Binary & ASCII Files to MS-DOS, & Back. Works with All PC Floppy & Hard Drives. Formats Color Computer Disks on Any PC in 15 Seconds. Helps Fix Bad Color Computer Disks & Expands the Usage of Your Color Computer Disk Files.
Elite Software.

Eliza. *Version:* 3.1. *Compatible Hardware:* IBM PC & compatibles. *Operating System(s) Required:* PC-DOS/MS-DOS. *Memory Required:* 256k. *General Requirements:* Hard disk recommended. *Items Included:* 32 pg. Thinking Software catalog.
3.5" or 5.25" disk $34.95.
Includes the Original ELIZA with Source Code in Turbo Prolog.
Thinking Software, Inc.

Eliza: The Computer Psychotherapist. *Version:* 3.0. Steve Grumette. 1982. *Compatible Hardware:* Apple II, II+, IIc, IIe; Commodore 64; CP/M based machines; IBM PC. *Operating System(s) Required:* PC-DOS, MS-DOS, Apple DOS, CBM DOS, CP/M. *Language(s):* BASIC (source code included). *Memory Required:* 48k. disk $45.00 ea.
MS-DOS, PC-DOS. (Order no.: 9001).
Apple DOS. (Order no.: 9002).
Commodore 64 DOS. (Order no.: 9003).
Commodore 64 DOS. (Order no.: 9004).
Full Implementation of the Classic Artificial Intelligence Demonstration Program.
Artificial Intelligence Research Group.

Eliza II. *Compatible Hardware:* IBM PC. *Operating System(s) Required:* MS-DOS. *Memory Required:* 128k.
disk $19.95.
Artificial Intelligence Program.
Dynacomp, Inc.

Elvira II: The Jaws of Cerberus. Sep. 1991.
Items Included: Catalog, copy protection device, manual, & proof of purchase card. *Customer Support:* Technical support 408-296-8400, Bulletin Board (modem) 408-296-8800 (settings: 300, 1200, 2400 baud; 8 data; no parity; 1 stop bit).
IBM DOS 2.1 or higher; EGA, VGA, MCGA (640k). IBM PC, AT, & compatibles.
Recommended: 10 MHz or higher & AT class machine. $59.95. *Optimal configuration:* Hard drive mandatory. Mouse, graphics card & sound board.
Find Elvira, the Owner of Black Widow Productions, Among Three Movie Back Lots (A Graveyard, Haunted House, & Catacombs) with Monsters of Gothic Horror. Fight a Cataclysmic Battle of Magic & Might with a Nether-World Entity of Awesome Dimension & Fury to Rescue Her.
Accolade, Inc.

Elvira: Mistress of the Dark. Nov. 1990. *Items Included:* Catalog, copy protection device, manual, proof of purchase card, & warranty card. *Customer Support:* Technical support 408-296-8400, 90 day limited warranty.
IBM DOS 2.1 or higher, Tandy-DOS (640k).
IBM PC, XT, AT (10 MHz Plus) & compatible; Tandy 1000, 3000, 4000 (hard drive required). IBM $59.95. *Optimal configuration:* Hard drive, mouse, graphics card, & sound board.
Amiga Kickstart 1.2 or 1.3 (1mb). Amiga 500/1000/2000. $59.95. *Optimal configuration:* Hard drive, mouse.
Atari ST (512k). Atari ST 520/1040, no E or FM Models. $49.95. *Optimal configuration:* Hard drive, keyboard, mouse.
Horror-Movie Realism in an Enormous Castle. Battle Ghoulish Warriors in Hand-to-Hand Combat, Use Spell-Book to Mix Potions & Ward off Evil Spirits, & Find Six Keys to Unlock a Secret Chest.
Accolade, Inc.

The Elysian Fields. Mark Novembrino. Nov. 1985. *Compatible Hardware:* Apple II+, IIe, IIc, IIgs. *Memory Required:* 64k.
disk $39.95.
lab packs avail.
Educational-Entertainment Software.
American Eagle Software, Inc.

EM-8086. Lifeboat Associates. *Compatible Hardware:* TI Professional. *Operating System(s) Required:* MS-DOS. *Memory Required:* 64k. $200.00.
Allows Software for 8-Bit Machines to Run on Systems Using MS-DOS Without Modification of User Program.
Texas Instruments, Personal Productivit.

EM4105-Plus. *Version:* 5.40-2.52. Sep. 1987. *Compatible Hardware:* IBM PC, PC XT, PC AT & compatibles. *Memory Required:* 400k. *Customer Support:* Unlimited phone support.
disk $379.00 (Order no.: EM4105).
Emulates a Tektronix 4105 Color Graphics Terminal. PC May Be Used As a Color Graphics Work Station to Run MSC GRASP, PATRAN, SUPERTAB, SAS GRAF, 20-20, DI-3000, RS-1, PLOT-10, etc. Includes All Features of EM320 Plus Text-over-Graphics, 16 Colors from a Palette of 64, LocalPan & Zoom, Hard Copy, HP Plotter Support, Tektronix Setup Commands, & Graph Save & Recall.
Diversified Computers Systems.

Embedded TCP IP & NFS. *Customer Support:* VenturCom provides four levels of support priced from $200.00 per year.
E-VENIX. IBM PC compatibles. This includes all Intel based ISA & EISA computers (2Mb). $100.00. *Networks supported:* Ethernet.
Now Available for Embedded Applications. Now You Can Embed These Networking Systems You Have Relied Upon in the Past. Provides a Host Based Network Protocol Suite & NFS Provide a Networked File Sharing System.
VenturCom.

Embroidery Expert. *Version:* 3.0. *General Requirements:* Designer's Edge. *Items Included:* Computer, tablet or scanner, software, interface equipment. *Customer Support:* Technical support & 5 days training included, lifetime updates at approximately $25.00 each.
Macintosh II, IIx, IIcx (2k). 3.5" disk $17,000.00. $30,000.00-$35,000.00 complete system.
Offers Color Stitch Display, Rapid Stitch Generation & a Variety of Stitch Fills, Enabling a Designer to Produce Quality Work Quickly & Accurately. Stitches Can Be Inserted, Deleted, Repositioned, Mirrored or Duplicated. Size & Density of Stitches Created As Objects Can Be Increased or Decreased. Artwork Can Be Scanned or Digitized into the Computer.
Graphic Applications, Inc.

EMERGE: EMERGENCY DEPARTMENT

Embroidery Plus. *Version:* 2.0. *Compatible Hardware:* Apple Macintosh, Macintosh Plus, SE, II, IIx, IIcx. *General Requirements:* Designer's Edge. *Items Included:* Macintosh Plus, Designer's Edge, Digitizing Tablet, Embroidery Plus. *Customer Support:* Technical support & 3 days training included, lifetime updates at approx. $25.00 each.
3.5" disk $8200.00.
complete systems start at $15,000.00 to $21,000.00.
Allows the User to Generate & Display Stiches Automatically. Stitches Can Be Inserted, Deleted, Repositioned Mirrored or Duplicated. The Program Allows the User to Read, Punch & Translate Between Barudan, Eltac, Tajima, Marco, Melco & Ultramatic Formats. Artwork Can Be Scanned or Digitized into the Computer.
Graphic Applications, Inc.

Embryo Transfer. Agri-Management Services, Inc. *Compatible Hardware:* TI Professional. *Operating System(s) Required:* MS-DOS. *Memory Required:* 64k. *General Requirements:* Printer. $995.00.
Allows Recipients Synchronized with the Donor, Accurate Recording of Deposit of Each Embryo, Recording of Treatments & Problems, Billing of Owners of Donors & Preparing of Breed Transfer Reports.
Texas Instruments, Personal Productivit.

Embryo Transfer Management. *Compatible Hardware:* IBM PC, PC XT & compatibles. $1000.00.
Farm Management Systems of Mississippi, Inc.

EMCI: Electronic Media Claims Interface. *Version:* 4.0. Jan. 1988. *Items Included:* One modem, copy of Carbon Copy Plus software. *Customer Support:* Thirty days of free support.
MS-DOS. IBM PC & compatibles (2Mb). $21,000.00 & up. *Optimal configuration:* 120Mb hard disk; payer communications hardware & software; printer, 9600 baud modem.
Enables Providers to Submit UB92s, HCFA-1500s, & Other Forms Directly to Payers, Eliminating Any per Bed/Claim Fees. On-Site Provider & Payer Specific Edits Allow Correct Claims to Be Submitted to Payers the First Time. Secondary Billings & Billing Date Posting Can Be Automated. System Is PC-Based.
Learned-Mahn.

EMC2/TAO. *Version:* 3.4. Jun. 1991. *Items Included:* User, Administrator, Installation Guides. *Customer Support:* Toll free-24 hour phone support, first year free maintenance - 18% of then current price 1 yr. thereafter, all user/support manuals.
DOS/VSE, MVS, MVS/ESA, MVS/XA, VM, VM/CMS, OS/400, MS-DOS, OS/2, Windows 3.0. IBM System/370/390 architecture, IBM AS/400, IBM PC & compatibles (512k mainframe, 400k LAN). $1100.00 25 users LAN; $5000.00 AS/400; $30,000.00 mainframe. *Networks supported:* LAN Manager, LAN Server, NetBIOS, IPX, Netware 3.X, Pathworks, Windows, TC/PIP, Banyon VINES.
Enterprise-Wide Electronic Mail & Office Automation Communication System, That Runs on the Mainframe, Midrange, & LAN Alike. Features Include Bulletin Boards, File Folders, Calendaring, Conferencing, Mailing Lists, & Mail Forwarding. Also Offers Many Gateways Such As X.400, SNADS, MHS, SMTP, FAX, & More.
Fischer International Systems Corp.

Emerge: Emergency Department Classification & Information Systems. *Operating System(s) Required:* PC-DOS. *General Requirements:* 2 disk drives, printer.

319

contact publisher for price.
Utilizes an Objective Patient Classification Methodology to Provide Emergency Department Managers & Health Systems Administrators with Essential Clinical, Staffing & Operational Data.
Medicus Systems Corp.

Emergency Transfusion. Byron A. Myhre & Henry M. Taylor. May 1987. *Compatible Hardware:* IBM PC & compatibles, PCjr, PC XT, PC AT. *Operating System(s) Required:* PC-DOS/MS-DOS 2.XX. *Language(s):* BASIC (source code included). *Memory Required:* 128k.
disk $47.00, incl. documentation (ISBN 0-89189-240-0, Order no.: 68-5-001-20).
The User Is Shown the Serologic Reaction of Ten Donor Bloods. Several of These Have Problems with Blood Group Antibodies, Inconsistency of Serum, & Cell Typing in the ABO Systems. The User Must Solve Each of These Problems & Determine Which Patient Gets What Blood.
ASCP Pr.

EMF: Electromagnetic Fields. 1995. *Items Included:* Full manual. *Customer Support:* Free telephone support - 90 days, 30-day warranty. MS-DOS 3.2 or higher. 286 (584k). disk $69.95. *Nonstandard peripherals required:* CGA/EGA/VGA.
This Fully Interactive Software Tool Encourages Rapid, Qualitative Exploration of Electric & Magnetic Fields - a Notoriously Abstract Topic - & Will Help Your Students Gain an Intuitive Understanding of Force Fields, Gauss's Law, Ampere's Law, & the Concept of Flux.
Dynacomp, Inc.

EM4105. *Version:* 5.40-2.52. Jan. 1988. *Compatible Hardware:* IBM PC, PC XT, PC AT & compatibles; PS/2. *Operating System(s) Required:* PC-DOS/MS-DOS 2.0 or higher. *Memory Required:* 350k. *Customer Support:* Unlimited phone support.
disk $359.00.
Tektronix 4105/4107 Terminal Emulator Also Emulates the Tektronix 4010/4014 Terminals, the DEC VT320, VT220, VT102, VT100 & VT52 Terminals & VT640 Retrographics. Supports Local Picture Files, Plotter, Local Pan & Zoom, High Resolution Hard Copy, DOS Hot Key, On-Line Help, & All Features of EM320.
Diversified Computers Systems.

EMIS: Editor & Machine Interface for CNC. 1995. *Items Included:* Full manual. *Customer Support:* Free telephone support - 90 days, 30-day warranty.
MS-DOS 3.2 or higher. 286 (584k). disk $149.95. *Nonstandard peripherals required:* CGA/EGA/VGA.
A Low Cost Editor & Machine Interface System for Computerized Numerical Control. It Provides Features for Both Developing CNC Programs, As Well As Communicating with the Machine Tool. Open-Ended & May Be Used for Other CNC Machines by Simply Creating the Appropriate Dictionary. A Fully Annotated Bridgeport Library Is Provided.
Dynacomp, Inc.

EMPATH. 1991. *Items Included:* User manual, software diskette available in 5.25" & 3.5". DOS, UNIX. All PC's & IBM compatibles. Contact publisher for price.
Allows UNIX Operating System Users to Link PCs to a UNIX Server. The PC Can Act As a Dumb Terminal but Allows for DOS to UNIX or UNIX to DOS File Transfer of Files. The User Can Hot Key from DOS to UNIX & Back. Also Allows for Attached Printing & Multiple Sessions. PC Print Screen from UNIX, Full Color Support, Baud Rates from 110 to 38400 & Modem Support.
LDS, Inc.

Emperor's New Clothes. Technopop Staff. Dec. 1994.
Windows 3.1 386 Enhanced Mode. IBM & 100% compatibles 386 or higher (4Mb). CD-ROM disk Contact publisher for price (ISBN 1-885932-06-5). *Nonstandard peripherals required:* 640 x 480 256 VGA, mouse, MPC CD-ROM. *Optimal configuration:* 8Mb RAM Sound Card.
System 7.0 or higher. 68020 MAC (25Mb). CD-ROM disk Contact publisher for price (ISBN 1-885932-07-3). *Nonstandard peripherals required:* Color monitor, CD-ROM.
The Delightful Children's Fairy Tale by Hans Christian Andersen. In This Interactive Storybook, Children Click on Humorous "Hot Spots" Each with Its Own, Humorous & Entertaining Animations.
Trimark Interactive.

Employ-EASE. Jun. 1984. *Operating System(s) Required:* MS-DOS. *Memory Required:* 256k. *General Requirements:* Hard disk.
$13,000.00.
Comprehensive Turnkey Human Resources Management System. Manages Information Such As Benefits, Compensation, Performance, EEO/AA Training & Development with an Ad Hoc Reporting Feature for Customized Reports & the Sentry 3000 Optical Mark Reader for Ease of Data Entry & Conversion.
National Computer Systems, Inc.

Employee Application Resume Rating & Categorizing Scale: EARRCS. Thomas J. Rundquist. *Customer Support:* By Fax, e-mail, & phone "no charge".
Windows 3.1. PC IBM & compatibles (2Mb). disk $50.00 (ISBN 1-884239-07-2). *Optimal configuration:* 4MB RAM 486DX33. *Networks supported:* Novell, LANS.
Allows an Employer to Rate & Categorize Employment Applicants per Their Resume and/or Application in a Simple & Organized Fashion. Employers Can by Simply Having the Prospective Employee Fill Out the Two Page Form & Returning It to the Future Employer Be Able to Process & Build a Data Bank of Thousands of Resumes for Quick & Easy Retrieval for Specific Job Openings. Various Criteria Can Be Entered into the Variables Section for Customized Searches or Rating.
Nova Media, Inc.

Employee Management System: Reduce Employee Turnover. *Version:* 4.3. Dennis Drew. May 1985. *Compatible Hardware:* IBM PC & compatibles. *Operating System(s) Required:* PC-DOS 2.0 or higher, MS-DOS 2.0 or higher. *Memory Required:* 256k. *General Requirements:* Printer.
disk $95.00 (ISBN 0-924122-00-5).
Helps Decrease Employee Turnover by Opening Communications. Aids Managers in Hiring the Right People for the Right Job. Designed to Help Employees Feel Valuable & Help Motivate Them to Achieve Maximum Productivity.
Dennis Drew.

Employee Policy Manual On-a-Disk. *Items Included:* Full manual. No other products required. *Customer Support:* Free telephone support - no time limit. 30 day warranty.
MS-DOS 3.2 or higher. IBM & compatibles (512k). disk $199.95. *Optimal configuration:* IBM, word processor which can read WordPerfect, MS Word, or ASCII text files.
Macintosh. 3.5" disk $199.95. *Optimal configuration:* Macintosh, MS Word 3.1 or MacWrite 4.5 text file compatible word processor.
Creating a Policy Manual Can Take Weeks of Research & Writing, & You May Even Overlook Critical Issues That Could Cost You Dearly. Wish It Was Already Written? It Is! Why Start from Scratch? EMPLOYEE POLICY MANUAL Makes That Tedious Job As Easy As Filling in the Blanks! Just Read the Files with Your Favorite Word Processor. Contains over 110 Policies, Including: Employee Selection, Medical Interviews, Smoking Policy, Compensation, Employee Benefits, Employee Expenses & Much More.
Dynacomp, Inc.

Employee Scheduling & Labor Costing. 1985. *Compatible Hardware:* IBM PC. *Operating System(s) Required:* MS-DOS, networks. (source code included). *Memory Required:* 256k. *General Requirements:* 2 disk drives, printer.
disk $500.00 (ISBN 0-922121-10-9, Order no.: ES918).
Advanced Analytical/CharterHouse.

Employee Scheduling System. 1989. *Memory Required:* 512k.
PC-DOS/MS-DOS. disk $395.00.
Facilitates the Assignment of Work Shifts & Days Off to Employees. Allocates Full/Part-Time Employees Based on Minimum Staffing Levels, or in Proportion to Workload Levels. Identifies Scheduling Conflicts, Prepares As Much of Schedule As Possible Based on Specified Constraints, & Facilitates Completion of Schedule by Designer. Prints Daily Rosters in Calendar Form.
Computing Power Applied.

Empower. *Version:* 3.0. Feb. 1994. *Items Included:* Spiral bound manuals & on-line help; Run Time Version of MS Access; Source Code Provided. *Customer Support:* 30 days unlimited warranty; maintenance 1 1/2% per month of license fee; training packages available; customization of software available, hotline included.
Windows 3.X; Windows for PEN; NT; UNIX. IBM compatible PC (4Mb). Individual $795.00 ea.; Network starts 5K; site license available. *Optimal configuration:* 4Mb RAM; 300Mb disk storage; 486 processor/33Mhz. *Networks supported:* Novell, Workgroups, NT.
Next Generation of Account Information Managers Designed to Supply the Sales Force with the Information Necessary to Efficiently Manage Their Sales Territories. Incorporates Modules for Sales Contact Management, Appointment Scheduling, Tax Management & Expense Reporting As Well As Providing Sales Order History, Quote History, Competitive Activity, Sales Forecasting, Sales Correspondence, Pre-Order Entry, Pricing Inquiries, Tickler Files, Sales Notes, Lost Business Reporting, & Call Activity Reporting.
MIT Group, Inc.

EMU/470 Data General Terminal Emulator for IBM Micros & Personal Computers. *Version:* 5.0. Jan. 1989. *Items Included:* Operator's manual. *Customer Support:* Free telephone support.
PC-DOS or MS-DOS (384k). IBM or compatible. disk $249.00. *Nonstandard peripherals required:* Any com port or modem, graphics adapter (EGA, VGA, CGA, MCGA, or Herc.). *Optimal configuration:* 384k, DOS2+, VGA/EGA/CGA/MCGA/Herc., any com port or modem, (EGA/VGA for D470C).
A Color Graphics Terminal Emulator That Runs on IBM PCs or PC Compatibles & EMUlates the DG Dasher Terminals VT100, VT320, TEK4010, D411, W640, D462 As Well As the D470C. It Supports Text, Binary, XMODEM, YMODEM, & Kermit File Transfers. Automatic Dialing, Logon, & Logoff Functions Are Provided. Runs Stand Alone or under CEO Connection. It Has Compressed Mode of 135 Characters Per Line on

Any Graphics Adapter. Communication Rates from 300-38400 bps Selectable. All 12 Function Keys on the IBM Enhanced Keyboard (All 15 on the Dasher) Are Usable. All Four COM Ports Available under PC-DOS 3.3 & 4 Usable. Break Key Sends True Break Signal. Multi-Tiered Menu System for Easy System Control Without Consuming Key-Codes.
Rhintek, Inc.

EMU-TEK. Version: 3.0. 1982. Compatible Hardware: IBM PC, PC XT, PC AT & compatibles. Operating System(s) Required: PC-DOS/MS-DOS 2.0 or higher. Memory Required: 256k. Customer Support: One year free telephone support.
disk $295.00.
Five Plus. disk $495.00.
EMU-TEK for Windows. disk $995.00.
4200 Plus. disk $950.00.
Communications Program Featuring Full TEKTRONIX Terminal Emulation & an Alternate Mode for Text-Only Operations.
FTG Data Systems.

EMU 220. Version: 2.20. Rainer McCown. Jan. 1984. Compatible Hardware: Data General, IBM PC & compatibles. Operating System(s) Required: DOS. Language(s): Assembly. Memory Required: 64k. General Requirements: Modem. Items Included: Manual for operation. Customer Support: Free telephone support.
write for info.
Terminal Emulator for IBM PCs Emulating the Data General Dasher 200 Series Terminals.
Rhintek, Inc.

Emulator-86. Lifeboat Associates. Compatible Hardware: TI Professional. Operating System(s) Required: MS-DOS. Memory Required: 64k. General Requirements: 2 disk drives.
$75.00.
Permits All TI Computer Software to Run under Both MS-DOS & CP/M-86 Operating Systems.
Texas Instruments, Personal Productivit.

Emulator 86. Compatible Hardware: IBM PC. Operating System(s) Required: MS-DOS, PC-DOS, SB-86. Memory Required: 64k.
disk $75.00.
Enables Users to Run Software Written for CP/M Systems on DOS Systems. Also Enables Users to Fully Integrate & Mix Programs.
Lifeboat Assocs.

EM320-DOS. Version: 5.40. Apr. 1986. Compatible Hardware: IBM PC, PC XT, PC AT & compatibles, PS/2. Operating System(s) Required: PC-DOS/MS-DOS 2.0 or higher. Memory Required: 256k. Customer Support: Unlimited phone support.
disk $199.00.
Full VT320 Emulator for the IBM PC Family. Emulates the DEC VT320, VT102, VT100 & VT52 Terminals. Supports 132 Columns, Color Graphics, Downloadable Character Sets, Softkeys, DOS Hot Keys, User-Defined Keys, Local Printer, File Transfer, Automated Modem Dialer, Command/Script Files, WordPerfect Mode.
Diversified Computers Systems.

EM320 for Windows. Version: 2.13. Sep. 1991. Items Included: 2 perfect bound manuals. Customer Support: Unlimited phone support. DOS/Windows. 386 or higher (4Mb). disk $229.00 (Order no.: EM320-WIN-3A). Networks supported: Pathworks, TCP/IP including LAN Workplace & Winsock, Int14, BAPI, UB XNS.
A Windows Application That Turns Your PC into a VT320/220 Terminal. Supports DECnet, TCP/IP, or Serial Connections. Advanced Features Includes Toolbars, DDE Support, 48 Line Display, 132 Column Display, a Modem Dialer, Definable Keyboard, a Multi-Instance Interface, Command Language, & Xmodem & Kermit File Transfer.
Diversified Computers Systems.

EM340 for Windows. Version: 2.13-1.04. Feb. 1994. Items Included: 3 perfect bound manuals. Customer Support: Unlimited phone support. DOS/Windows. 386 or higher (4Mb). disk $359.00 (Order no.: EM340-WIN-3A). Networks supported: Pathworks, TCP/IP including LAN Workplace & Winsock, Int14, BAPI, UB XNS.
A Windows Application That Turns Your PC into a VT340/VT320 & Tektronix 4014 Graphics Terminal. Supports DECnet, TCP/IP, or Serial Connections. High Resolution ReGIS, Sixel & Tektronix Display & Printing Capabilities Are Provided. Includes All of the EM320 for Windows Product Features.
Diversified Computers Systems.

EM4010. Version: 5.40-3.07. Jan. 1985. Compatible Hardware: IBM PC, PC XT, PC AT & compatibles, PS/2. Operating System(s) Required: PC-DOS/MS-DOS 2.0 or higher. Memory Required: 330k. Customer Support: Unlimited phone support.
disk $249.00.
Tektronix 4010/4014 Terminal Emulator. Also Emulates the DEC VT320, VT220, VT102, VT100, & VT52 Terminals. Supports Local Picture Files, High Resolution Hard Copy, Plotter, VT640 Retrographics, DOS Hot Key, On-Line Help.
Diversified Computers Systems.

Enable OA. Version: 4.0. Customer Support: Free technical support to registered users for 30 days; free electronic support via Enable BBS, GEnie, CompuServe (registered users).
DOS 3.3 Plus or OS/2. 8086, 8088, 80286, 80386, 80486, IBM PS/2 & compatibles (640k). disk $795.00. Networks supported: Banyan Vines, Novell, IBM LAN Server.
SCO UNIX System V (3.2.2) or Interactive UNIX (3.2).
80386 Plus (6Mb). disk $795.00.
DOS/OS2 & UNIX Platform Support. Relational Database, 3-D Spreadsheet, Business Graphics, Communications & Comprehensive WP Support Including Outline, Toc, Macros, Page Preview, Thesaurus, Spell Checker (Optional Grammar Checker). All Modules Tightly Integrated System Using Common Interface, Simplifying Information Sharing Across Modules. LAN-Ready or Stand-Alone.
Enable Software, Inc.

Enable Office. Sep. 1992. Customer Support: Unlimited telephone technical support for registered users - free; unlimited electronic support via Enable BBS, GEnie & CompuServe - free; 90-day warranty; enhanced support plans, $59-$149/year.
DOS 3.3-5.0 or OS/2 1.2, 1.3. 8086, 8088, 80286, 80386, 80486, IBM PS/2 & compatibles (640k). SRP $995.00. Networks supported: Novell, Banyan & IBM LAN Server.
A Four-User Workgroup Version of Enable 4.5 Which Allows Access to All Enable Tools & Modules, As Well As Including Higgins Mail & Higgins Group Productivity Software - Which Provides Scheduling, Calendar Capabilities & E-Mail for a Workgroup. Users Can Share Files, As Well As Communicate & Remotely Check Each Other's Schedules.
Enable Software, Inc.

Enable 4.5. Version: 4.5. Apr. 1992. Items Included: 2 binders with reference documentation, test-drive, template, benefits & privileges booklet. Customer Support: Unlimited telephone technical support for registered users - free; unlimited electronic support via Enable BBS, GEnie & CompuServe - free; 90 day warranty; enhanced support plans, $59-$149/year.
DOS 3.3-5.0 or OS/2 1.2, 1.3, 2.0. 8086, 8088, 80286, 80386, 80486, IBM PS/2 & compatibles (640k). SRP $795.00. Networks supported: LANtastic 4.1; 10Net 5.0; Novell NetWare Lite 1.0; Novell NetWare 286 1.5, 2.2; Novell NetWare 386 3.11; IBM LAN Server 1.2, 1.3; Banyan Vines 4.11; Moses PromiseLAN (2-user); Moses ChosenLAN (4-user).
A LAN-Based (or Stand-Alone) "Integrated" Word Processing, Database, Spreadsheet, Business Graphics, Communications Package Which Offers Significant Import/Export Flexibility; Links to Higgins Electronic Mail & Higgins Productivity Software; Relational Database, & Productivity Tools Such As Calendar & Calculator.
Enable Software, Inc.

Encephalon. Version: 2.0. G. Banks. 1981. Compatible Hardware: Apple II, IIc; Basis 6402; Franklin Ace. Operating System(s) Required: Apple DOS 3.3. Language(s): BASIC (source code included). Memory Required: 48-64k.
disk $39.00 (ISBN 0-914555-08-1).
Practice Neurologic Examination & Diagnosis on Simulations Constructed from the Findings of Actual or Hypothetical Patients. User Ventures a Diagnosis, after Which the Simulator Presents the Correct Diagnosis with a Brief Discussion of the Case.
Andent, Inc.

Enchanter. Dave Lebling & Marc Blank. 1983. Compatible Hardware: Apple II+, IIe, IIc; Macintosh; Atari 400, 800, 1200, ST; Commodore 64/128, Amiga; DEC Rainbow; IBM PC & compatibles, Kaypro II; Texas Instruments, TI 99/4A; TRS-80 Model I, Model III, Color Computer. Operating System(s) Required: MS-DOS, CP/M.
Apple II, Macintosh, Amiga, DEC, IBM. disk $29.95.
Atari XL/XE, Commodore 64/128. $24.95.
Kaypro, TI-99/4A, TI Professional, TRS-80. $14.95.
You Are a Novice Magician Sent into Single-Handed Combat with a Dark & Fierce Power. Worldly Weapons Will Avail You Naught, for Your Foe Is the Evil Warlock Who Holds Sway over the Kingdom. To Defeat Him, You'll Need to Use All the Cunning You Can Muster, along with Spells Acquired on Your Way. If You Succeed, You'll Be Elevated to a Seat in the Illustrious Circle, If You Fail... But One Does Not Speak of Such Things.
Activision, Inc.

Enchanter. Infocom. Compatible Hardware: HP 150 Touchscreen, HP 110 Portable.
3.5" disk $39.95 (Order no.: 92243UA).
You Are an Apprentice Magician Whom Fate Has Chosen to Combat a Dark & Fierce Power. Worldly Weapons Avail You Nought, for Your Foe Is the Evil Warlock Who Holds Sway over the Land. To Defeat Him, You Will Have to Match Your Skills As a Necromancer Against His, Using Spells You Have Learned from Your Masters in the Circle of Enchanters & Others You Will Acquire As You Proceed on Your Quest. If You Succeed, You Will Be Elevated to a Seat in the Illustrious Circle; If You Fail... but One Does Not Speak of Such Things.
Hewlett-Packard Co.

Enchanter Trilogy. Compatible Hardware: Commodore Amiga.
3.5" disk $29.85.
Enchanter, Sorcerer, & Spellbreaker.
Activision, Inc.

Encore! Plus. *Version:* 2.0. Feb. 1991. *Compatible Hardware:* IBM-PCs or Compatibles. *Operating System(s) Required:* MS-DOS 2.0 or higher. *Language(s):* Pascal. *Memory Required:* 640k. *General Requirements:* Hard disk. *Items Included:* 4 volume user manual, one year maintenance agreement; includes free software updates & unlimited telephone support. *Customer Support:* Free telephone support. Both training & consulting available on a fee bases.
$895.00.
Financial Analysis, Planning, Consolidations, Reporting & Graphics System. As a Modeling Tool, Its Primary Use Is for Financial Projections & Budgeting. In Addition, Program Functions As a Systems Development Tool for Financial Reporting Systems. Allows User to Create Menus, Specify Data Input Screens, Produce Reports, Create Graphs & Automate an Application. Also Includes Features Such AS Goal Seeking, Regression, & Monte Carlo Simulations. Mouse Support Has Been Added to Facilitate Executive Information System (EIS) Development, with Drilldown, Color Exception Reporting & Trend Analysis.
Ferox Microsystems, Inc.

Encrypt. *Version:* 1.01. Mar. 1989. *Customer Support:* 90 day warranty against defects in disk manufacture, immediate replacement of defective media.
MS-DOS/PC-DOS 3.1 or higher (256k). IBM PC/XT/AT/PS2 compatible. disk $34.95. *Optimal configuration:* PC/AT or PS/2, hard disk, EGA or VGA graphics, 640k, one floppy drive.
Program Which Easily Allows the User to Encode & Password Protect Text Files Which Are Confidential. Also Able to Protect an Entire Diskette. Uses Powerful Data Encryption Scheme Virtually Impossible to Break.
Thinking Software, Inc.

Encumbrance Accounting. May 1990. *Items Included:* User guide, technical reference manual. *Customer Support:* Training included with purchase. Hot-line & remote diagnostic service included with maintenance.
VAX/VMS (2Mb). Digital VAX. $109,000.000 up.
An Integrated Solution to the Budgetary Control & Fund Accounting Requirements of Small Governments, School Districts, Not-for-Profit Enterprises, Private Industry & Other Public Agencies. Transactions in RossPO, RossAP & RossGL Initiate "Fund Availability Checking" in RossEA Which Ensures That Budget Appropriation Amounts Are Not Exceeded.
Ross Systems, Inc.

Encyclopedia of Associations CD-ROM 95-1. (Global Access: Associations Ser.). Jul. 1995.
IBM CD ROM. CD-ROM disk $1095.00 (ISBN 0-7876-0221-3, Order no.: 008562).
90,000 National, International, & Regional, State, & Local Associations.
Gale Research, Inc.

Encyclopedia of Associations: National 95 IBM CD ROM. (Discovering Associations Ser.). Edited by Karin Koek. Dec. 1995.
IBM CD ROM. CD-ROM disk Contact publisher for price (ISBN 0-7876-0025-3, Order no.: 108713).
22,600 National Associations.
Gale Research, Inc.

Endgame Software: Mathematical Go Endgames. Raymond Chen. May 1994. *Items Included:* Book "Mathematical Go Endgames" by Berlekamp & Wolfe (234 pages). User guide for software. *Customer Support:* Telephone customer support at no charge.
MS-DOS 3.2 or higher. IBM & compatibles (640k). disk $59.95, incl. book, "Mathematical Go Endgames" (Order no.: GS26). *Nonstandard peripherals required:* Mouse, EGA or VGA graphics. *Optimal configuration:* 640k RAM, Mouse, VGA graphics.
Applies Combinatoric Game Theory to Go Endgame Positions. Software Implements All Example Problems from Text, Playing Either Side with Mathematical Precision. Software Calculates & Displays All Mathematical Values, Including Intermediate Values. When Playing First, Software Can Defeat Even Top Level Professional Go Players.
Ishi Press International.

Endler Multidimensional Anxiety Scales (EMAS). *Version:* 3.010. Norman S. Endler et al. *Customer Support:* Free unlimited phone support.
Windows 3.X, Windows 95. 286 (4Mb). disk $150.00 (Order no.: W-1058). *Nonstandard peripherals required:* Printer.
Three Related Self-Report Measures That Allow Greater Precision in Assessing & Predicting Anxiety Across Situations - & Measuring Treatment Response. They Can Be Used with a Wide Range of People, Including Adolescents, Adults, Clinical Patients, the Elderly - Anyone Who Reads at an Eighth-Grade Level or Higher.
Western Psychological Services.

Endlink. *Version:* Mac 2.0, PC 2.0. *General Requirements:* Endnote-Plus. *Items Included:* Disk, manual. *Customer Support:* Free phone support.
Macintosh 512ke or higher, IBM PC & compatibles. 3.5" disk $99.00.
Allows Users to Import References from Online Services Directly into EndNote.
Niles & Assocs., Inc.

Endnote Plus: Enhanced Bibliographic Software. *Version:* 2.0. Apr. 1993. *Items Included:* 1 user manual, program diskettes. *Customer Support:* Free phone support.
Windows 3.1 or higher. XT & higher (512k). disk $299.00. *Optimal configuration:* Mouse supported but not required.
Macintosh System 4.2 or higher. Macintosh (512k or higher). 3.5" disk $299.00.
A Reference Database & Bibliography Maker. Including Faster Searching, Customizeable Sorting, & a Journal Abbreviations Table. Users Can Use the "AND", "OR", & "NOT" Connectives for True Boolean Searching. Builds Bibliographies Automatically in the User's Word Processor in Any Bibliographic Style (e.g. MLA, APA, Science). Includes More Than 300 Bibliographic Styles.
Niles & Assocs.

Energy Audit. *Compatible Hardware:* TRS-80 Model I, Model III. *Memory Required:* 16-32k.
disk $75.00 (Order no.: 0052RD).
cassette $49.95 (Order no.: 0089R).
Analyzes Building Material Costs, & Answers Other Important Home Energy Conservation Questions on the Dollars & Sense Level.
Instant Software, Inc.

ENERGY: Commercial Energy Analysis. *Items Included:* Manual. *Customer Support:* Free toll free telephone support.
IBM PC & compatibles (256k). disk $695.00.
Calculates Monthly & Annual Operating Costs on Buildings Having as Many as 1000 Zones & 100 Air Handling Systems.
Elite Software Development, Inc.

Energy Consumption for Heating & Cooling in Commercial Buildings & Economic Analysis of Alternatives - EN4M. Aug. 1990.
Compatible Hardware: IBM PC & compatibles. *Operating System(s) Required:* MS-DOS, PC-DOS. *Language(s):* Compiled & Assembly Language. *Memory Required:* 256k. *Customer Support:* Technical hotline, "Lifetime" support at no charge.
$650.00-$995.00.
Energy Consumption & Economic Analysis - EN4M (New Update) Uses Enhanced ASHRAE Modified Bin Energy Calculation Procedure to Estimate Monthly/Yearly Building Energy Consumption at Any World-Wide Location. Exception Flexibility in Specifying Loads & Operating Schedules. Economic Analysis of User-Specified Energy-Saving Options. Fully Compiled. Fast (10 Sec. per Run), Interactive, Prompting. Will Compare Eight Alternates at One Time. Extensive Manual with Worksheeting & Examples. English Units Only.
MC2 Engineering Software.

Energy Monitor: Energy Use Monitoring System. *Compatible Hardware:* Apple II; TRS-80 Model I, Model III. *Operating System(s) Required:* TRSDOS. *Memory Required:* 48k.
TRS-80 Model III. disk $245.00 (ISBN 0-201-15603-2).
Apple II. disk $245.00 (ISBN 0-201-15601-6). manual $10.00.
Tracks Energy Use Within a Single School or an Entire School System. Includes a Set of 6 Reporting Formats, & Provides Analysis of Building Energy Use on a Month-by-Month Basis by Fuel Type & Complete Records of Electric Bills, Gas Bills, Oil Bills or Any Other Metered or Non-Metered Fuel.
Addison-Wesley Publishing Co., Inc. (School Division).

Energy Owl. Raymond W. Merry. Jun. 1986. *Compatible Hardware:* IBM PC. *Operating System(s) Required:* MS-DOS. *Memory Required:* 128k.
disk $99.95 (ISBN 0-936561-23-8, Order no.: EOWL).
Program to Track Energy Usage & Cost for Single or Multiple Facility Businesses. Includes Budgeting. Tracks up to 5 Energy Determining Factors, Such As Occupancy, Heating Degree Days, etc. Can Work for Any Type of Energy.
Rays Computers & Energy.

Engagement Management Templates. *Compatible Hardware:* ALTOS Series 5-15D, Series 5-5D, 580-XX, ACS8000-XX; DEC Rainbow 100 with 2 disk drives, Rainbow 100+ with 10Mb hard drive; IBM PC with 2 disk drives, PC XT, IBM compatibles; Kaypro 11/IV with 2 disk drives, Kaypro 10; Xerox 820 with 2 disk drives; ZILOG MCZ-250. *Operating System(s) Required:* CP/M, MP/M, CP/M-86/80, PC-DOS, MS-DOS.
contact publisher for price (Order no.: EMT).
Time Management Budget. (Order no.: TMB).
Individual Time Management Summary. (Order no.: ITMS).
Time Management Overview. (Order no.: TMO).
Series of Interrelated Spreadsheets Designed to Facilitate More Effective Budgeting, Work Scheduling, Time Reporting, Time Control, Fee Negotiations, & Billings.
Coopers & Lybrand.

Engagement Manager. *Version:* 1.2. Nov. 1991. *Items Included:* 1 wiro-bound manual. *Customer Support:* Free for the first 3 months; $95 annual fee after that.
DOS 3.1 or higher. 100% IBM compatible PC (490k). disk $195.00 nonmember; $175.50 AICPA member. *Optimal configuration:* 100% IBM compatible PC, DOS 3.1 or higher, 640k RAM, printer capable of printing condensed or compressed.
Project Management System for Accountants.

TITLE INDEX

THE ENGINEER'S COMPANION MECHANICAL

This Practice Management Tool Creates Budgets or Proposals, Records Time & Expenses, Analyzes/Revises Estimates to Complete, Allows User to Modify the Budget & Print Reports. These Reports Allow User to Track Budget Variances, Time Statistics, Over- or Under-Budget Areas, Delays, Staff Hours & Numerous Other Key Engagement Areas.
American Institute of Certified Public Accountants.

Engincomp. *Version:* IBM. Chapra-Canale. Jul. 1986. *Compatible Hardware:* IBM PC. *Memory Required:* 256k. *General Requirements:* CGA card. *Items Included:* 1 disk & user's manual in folder.
$27.24, set (ISBN 0-07-831320-1).
Includes Three Computational Programs Needed by Engineers & Scientists: Spreadsheets, Descriptive Statistics Program & Line-Graph Generator.
McGraw-Hill, Inc.

Engineering Collection, No. 2. *Items Included:* Full manual. No other products required. *Customer Support:* Free telephone support - no time limit. 30 day warranty.
MS-DOS 3.2 or higher. IBM & compatibles (512k). disk $239.95.
Collection of Various Programs for Analyzing Specific Applied Engineering Problems. The Calculations Provided Are: Conveyor Belt Calculations, Geometric Properties of Sections, Volumes of Various Solids, Counter Flow Heat Exchanger, Capacity of Conical/Triangular Storage Piles, Heat Loss from Insulated Piping, Estimating Air Consumption & More.
Dynacomp, Inc.

Engineering Collection, No. 2. 1992. *Items Included:* Detailed manuals are included with all DYNACOMP products. *Customer Support:* Free telephone support to original customer - no time limit; 30 day limited warranty.
MS-DOS 3.2 or higher. IBM PC & compatibles (512k). $239.95 (Add $5.00 for 3 1/2" format; 5 1/4" format standard). *Optimal configuration:* IBM, MS-DOS 2.0 or higher & 640k RAM. Printer is supported but not necessary.
A Collection of Various Programs for Analyzing Specific Applied Engineering Problems. Calculations Provided Are: Conveyor Belt Calculations; Geometric Properties of Sections; Volumes of Various Solids; Counter Flow Heat Exchanger; Heat Loss from Insulated Piping; Pressure Loss Through Valves; Friction Head Loss in Pipes; Capacity of a Flat/Trough Belt; Developed Length of Pipe Bends; Horsepower for Screw Conveyor & 20 More.
Dynacomp, Inc.

Engineering Collection, No.1. *Compatible Hardware:* IBM. (source code included). disk $39.95, incl. manual.
Contains 10 Programs: Antenna Plot, Bode Plot, Convolution, Fourier Plot, Number Conversion, Reactor Simulation, Control System Simulation, SPlot, PPlot & SCPlot.
Dynacomp, Inc.

Engineering Collection VIII: The Energy Analyst. 1995. *Items Included:* Full manual. *Customer Support:* Free telephone support - 90 days, 30-day warranty.
MS-DOS 3.2 or higher. 286 (584k). disk $369.95. *Nonstandard peripherals required:* CGA/EGA/VGA.
An Extensive Collection of Independent Engineering Applications Collected Together into One Large Package. Each Module in the Collection Is Complete, Interactive, Self-Prompting, & Menu-Driven. You Are Led by the Hand at Each Step. Both the Input Data & the Results May Be Easily Printed in a Form Ready for Inclusion in Reports. Calculations Include: Insulation Economics, Shell & Tire Exchangers, Combustion Analysis, Piping Pressure Drop, Cogeneration Economics, Steam Surface Condenser, Cooling Tower, Condenser-Tower, Pipe Network, Steam Heater, Steam Turbine, Gravity Drain Flow, Heat Recovery Steam Generator, Gas Compressor, Gas Turbine, Boiler Chimney, Nozzle & Orifice Flow, Flash Tank Heat Recovery, Centrifugal Pump, Fan, Duct Design, Psychrometrics, Steam Properties, Desuperheater, Space Heating Load.
Dynacomp, Inc.

Engineering Collection VI: Fluid, Mechanical, Energy & Cost Calculations. 1995. *Items Included:* Full manual. *Customer Support:* Free telephone support - 90 days, 30-day warranty.
MS-DOS 3.2 or higher. 286 (584k). disk $99.95. *Nonstandard peripherals required:* CGA/EGA/VGA.
An Extensive Compilation of Practical Engineering Calculations for Industrial & Manufacturing Applications. It Is Fully Menu-Driven, Internally Documented, & Is Exceptionally Easy-to-Use. The Categories Covered Include: Length, Volume, Weight, & Power Conversions. Speed, Acceleration, & Force Calculations. Ohm's Law, DC/Single-Phase/Three-Phase Motor Calculations.
Dynacomp, Inc.

Engineering Collection 4: Fluid, Mechanical Energy & Cost Calculations. *Items Included:* Full manual. No other products required. *Customer Support:* Free telephone support - no time limit. 30 day warranty.
MS-DOS 3.2 or higher. IBM & compatibles (512k). disk $99.95.
Extensive Compilation of Practical Engineering Calculations for Industrial & Manufacturing Applications. Categories Covered Include: Length, Volume, Weight, & Power Conversions; Speed, Acceleration, & Force Calculations; Ohm's Law, DC/Single-Phase/Three-Phase Motor Calculations & More.
Dynacomp, Inc.

Engineering Collection 4: Practical Engineering Calculations. *Items Included:* Full manual. No other products required. *Customer Support:* Free telephone support - no time limit. 30 day warranty.
MS-DOS 3.2 or higher. IBM & compatibles (512k). disk $99.95.
Collection of over 40 Solutions to Common Engineering Problems. It Is Fully Menu-Driven. Subjects Covered Include: Wall Thicknesses for Pipes & Shells under Pressure. Fluid Flow Through Pipes & Orifices. Air Flow in Ducts, Minimum Duct Wall Thicknesses. Horsepower to Maintain Flow Rates & Heads. Horsepower fcr Screw, Belt, Apron, & Pan Conveyors. Chain & Belt Calculations & More.
Dynacomp, Inc.

Engineering Collection 7: Metal Fabrication - Machining. *Items Included:* Full manual. No other products required. *Customer Support:* Free telephone support - no time limit. 30 day warranty.
MS-DOS 3.2 or higher. IBM & compatibles (512k). disk $99.95. *Optimal configuration:* IBM, MS-DOS 3.2 or higher, 640k RAM. Printer is supported, but not required.
Targeted at Fabrication Situations in Which Certain Common, But Often Tedious Calculations Are Required Before a Job Can Be Undertaken. Subjects Covered Include: Tight/Slack-Side & Effective Tensions for a V-Belt. V-Belt Length Required for a Given Configuration. Lathe Turning Calculations: Rate of Removal, Feed Rate, Cutting Time, Depth of Cut, Required HP, Spindle Torque. Milling & Drilling Calculations (Similar to above) & More.
Dynacomp, Inc.

Engineering Sketchpad. *Items Included:* Bound manual. *Customer Support:* Free hotline - no time limit; 30 day limited warranty; updates are $5/disk plus S&H.
MS-DOS. IBM & compatibles (128k). disk $29.95. *Nonstandard peripherals required:* IBM graphics board; two disk drives; printer; option included of using 8087 math coprocessor for increased speed. *Addl. software required:* Graphics screen dump program to prepare hard copy of drawings.
Graphics Program for Engineers, Technicians, Architects, Interior Designers, or Anyone Who Frequently Uses a Straight-Edge, Compass, & Templates to Make Drawings for Documentation & Explanation. Draws on a 5,000-Point Cartesian Coordinate System to Allow the Preparation of Easily-Read Drawings (Transistors, Resistors, Desks, etc.). These Stored Drawings Can Be Rotated, Mirrored, Inverted, Expanded, or Contracted Before Being Included in a New Drawing. In Addition, Structures May Be "Dragged about" to Simplify Positioning Them.
Dynacomp, Inc.

Engineering Tool Kit. *Version:* 6.0. *Compatible Hardware:* Apple Macintosh; Windows. *Memory Required:* 1000k. *Items Included:* Sprial bound manual. *Customer Support:* Free telephone support.
3.5" disk $119.00.
Engineering Program Featuring Data, Graphics, Statistics & Regression Analysis.
Sof-Ware Tools.

Engineers Aide II: Mechanical. *Items Included:* 100 page manual. *Customer Support:* Free.
MS-DOS (640k). IBM or compatibles. disk $895.00. *Networks supported:* Novell.
Macintosh (1Mb). disk $695.00.
Integrated Package of Eight Programs for Mechanical Engineers, Includes Engineering Drawings, Engineering Calculations, Design Specifications, Unit Conversions, Conveyor Sizing, Mechanical Drive Sizing, Mechanical Shape Analysis, & Shaft Alignment Analysis.
Epcon.

Engineer's Aide I: Process. *Compatible Hardware:* Apple Macintosh Plus, IBM PC & Compatibles. *Items Included:* 150 page manual. *Customer Support:* Free.
English or metric version $695.00.
professional version $1195.00.
Integrated Package of 9 Programs for Process Engineers.
Epcon.

The Engineer's Companion Mechanical Engineering Analysis. *Items Included:* Full manual. No other products required. *Customer Support:* Free telephone support - no time limit. 30 day warranty.
MS-DOS 3.2 or higher. IBM & compatibles (512k). disk $139.95. *Optimal configuration:* IBM, MS-DOS 2.0 or higher, 512k RAM, & CGA/EGA/VGA or compatible graphics capability. Hard disk or a high density disk drive is highly recommended.
$19.95 manual.
A Must for Every Engineer Involved in the Mechanical Design of Structures for Supporting, Bracing, & Containment. It Is a Powerful, Extensive, & Sophisticated Collection of over 100 Engineering Calculations Aimed Specifically at Designing & Analyzing the Torsional Deflection & Stress Associated with Various Bars & Tubes; Thermal Stress & Deflection of Bars & Plates; Contact Deformation & Stress Between Spheres, Parallel & Crossed Cylinders, & More.
Dynacomp, Inc.

The Engineer's Companion: Mechanical Engineering Analysis. 1992. *Items Included:* Detailed manuals included with all Dynacomp products. *Customer Support:* Free telephone support to original customer - no time limit; 30 day limited warranty.
MS-DOS 3.2 or higher. IBM PC & compatibles (512k). $199.95 Complete package, incl. both manuals (Add $5.00 for 3 1/2" format; 5 1/4" format standard). *Optimal configuration:* IBM, MS-DOS 2.0 or higher, 512k RAM, & CGA/EGA/VGA or compatible graphics capability. A hard disk or a high density disk drive is highly recommended.
$39.95 310-page applications manual only.
A Must for Every Engineer Involved in the Mechanical Design of Structures for Supporting, Bracing, & Containment. It is a Powerful, Extensive, & Sophisticated Collection of over 100 Engineering Calculations Aimed Specifically at Designing & Analyzing the Torsional Deflection & Stress Associated with Various Bars & Tubes; Thermal Stress & Deflection of Bars & Plates; Contact Deformation & Stress Between Spheres, Parallel & Crossed Cylinders, & More.
Dynacomp, Inc.

Engines for Education. Roger C. Schank & Chip Cleary. 1995. *Customer Support:* Free technical support, 90-day limited warranty.
Mac. CD-ROM disk $29.95 (ISBN 1-56321-189-0).
The CD-ROM along with the Book, Describes How Using Computers Can Provide Motivating Environments for Learning.
Lawrence Erlbaum Assocs. Software & Alternate Media, Inc.

English As a Second Language (ESL): After the Auction. 1994.
Windows or Macintosh. 3.5" disk $69.95, teacher's ed. (ISBN 1-882949-95-1, Order no.: 10042101ND).
CD-ROM disk $39.95 (ISBN 1-882949-96-X).
An English Language Learning Software Product That Is Extremely Easy-to-Use Allowing Students to Choose One of Three Levels of Grammatical Complexity & View Text of the Dialogue As It Is Spoken. "After the Auction" Presents the Drama of a Typical Day at Your Local American Community Center. The Story Features Characters from Diverse Cultural Backgrounds Joining Together to Resolve Realistic, Everyday Conflicts Through Understanding & Cooperation.
Paragon Media.

English SAT I. (Micro Learn Tutorial Ser.). *Items Included:* Booklet (includes dictionary). *Customer Support:* Free telephone support.
MAC. MS-DOS. IBM, Macintosh (2 Mb), Apple II series, (48k), Commodore 64. 5.25" disk, $39.95 (Lab pack/5 $99.00). 3.5" disk, $44.95 (Lab pack/5 $115.00). Apple, Ibm or Macintosh network, $249.00 (ISBN 1-57265-036-2).
DOS. (ISBN 0-939153-83-1).
APP. (ISBN 0-939153-53-X).
Study Aid for the Verbal Portion of the SAT Test, Containing Sections on Antonyms, Analogies, Sentence Completions, Reading Comprehension & grammar. Tutorial modes gives explanations for all answer choices, correct & incorrect. Test mode included.
Word Assocs., Inc.

English SAT II. (Micro Learn Tutorial Ser.). *Items Included:* Study guide & SAT word dictionary. *Customer Support:* Free telephone support.
MAC. DOS. IBM or compatibles, Macintosh (2 Mb), Apple II series (48k), Commodore 64. 5.25" disk, $39.95 (Lab pack/5 $99.00). 3.5" disk, $44.95 (Lab pack/5 $115.00). Apple, IBM or Macintosh network, $249.00 (ISBN 1-57265-039-7).
APP. (ISBN 0-939153-87-4).
Study Aid for the Verbal Portion of the SAT Test, Concentrating on Root Words As Basis for SAT Success. Select Topics by 1) Root Words or by 2) Topics (Antonyms, Analogies, Sentence Completion or Reading Comprehension). Tutorial mode gives explanations for every answer, choice, correct or incorrect. Test mode included.
Word Assocs., Inc.

English Series. Ray E. Zubler & David Dolman. 1986. *Customer Support:* ECS offers technical support to registered users. Call (217) 359-7099. Other than the telephone call - technical support is no charge.
DOS 3.3. Apple. $495.00 single station/$2475.00 network (Order no.: A-1120). *Networks supported:* AppleShare/Apple Talk.
DOS 3.2 or higher. IBM. $495.00 single station/$2475.00 network (Order no.: I-1120). *Networks supported:* Novell.
A Comprehensive Set of English Grammar Lessons Which Includes Instruction & Drills on Irregular Verbs, Helping Verbs, Verb Conjugation, Verb Tenses, Transformations, Passive & Active Verbs, Participles, Infinitives, Prepositions, Mass & Count Nouns, Determiners, Demonstratives, Conjunctions, & Simple vs. Present Progressive Verbs. Additional Features Include Records of Student Scores, Monitoring of Student Progress, & Adjustment of the Lesson Difficulty Levels. A Printed Workbook Accompanies the Set.
Electronic Courseware Systems, Inc.

Enhanced BASIC. *Compatible Hardware:* TRS-80 Model I. *Memory Required:* 16k.
cassette $24.95 (Order no.: 0077K).
Adds Features to Level II BASIC - Direct Use of Hexadecimal & Octal Constants, Enhanced String Handling Capabilities, & Ability to Call up to 10 Machine Language Subroutines from BASIC.
Instant Software, Inc.

Enhanced Chartist. *Items Included:* Complete manual. *Customer Support:* 1 yr. maintenance $495.00.
Mac II series (2Mb). $2590.00.
Real-Time Charting & Technical Analysis.
Roberts-Slade, Inc.

Enhanced Finite Element Analysis - ST10MB. *Version:* 01/1985. 1981. *Compatible Hardware:* IBM & compatibles. *Operating System(s) Required:* MS-DOS, PC-DOS. *Memory Required:* MS-DOS 256k. *Customer Support:* Technical hotline, "Lifetime" support at no charge.
disk $995.00.
Enhanced to Include 3-D Plate Problems, Shear Walls, & Anisotropic Materials. Accumulates Material Weights, & Takes Thermal Stresses for any Elements. Has Out-of-Core Solution Module Available for Large Problems. SI Metric or English Units.
MC2 Engineering Software.

Enhanced Gold Dog Analysis. Ronald D. Jones. 1984. *Compatible Hardware:* Apple II; Commodore 64; IBM PC; TRS-80 Model I, Model III, Color Computer. *Operating System(s) Required:* CP/M. *Memory Required:* 64k.
disk $199.95 ea.
Apple. (ISBN 1-55604-060-1, Order no.: D002).
CP/M. (ISBN 1-55604-061-X, Order no.: D002).
IBM. (ISBN 1-55604-064-4, Order no.: D002).
disk or cassette $199.95.
Commodore. (ISBN 1-55604-062-8, Order no.: D002).
Color Computer. (ISBN 1-55604-063-6, Order no.: D002).
Model I & Model III. (ISBN 1-55604-065-2, Order no.: D002).
Full-Featured Greyhound Analysis Which Uses a Combination of Speed & Class Based upon the Grade of the Race. Track Records & Kennel Ratings Are Maintained on a Data Base, Initializing the System for a Specific Track. Master Bettor Evaluates Scores & Every Betting Combination of the Top 5 Dogs Which Are Printed on the Printer and/or Video.
Professor Jones Professional Handicapping Systems.

Enhanced Gold Dog with Track Management. Ronald D. Jones. 1984. *Compatible Hardware:* Apple; Commodore; IBM; TRS-80 Model I, Model III, Color Computer. *Operating System(s) Required:* CP/M. *Memory Required:* 64k.
disk $279.90 ea.
Apple. (ISBN 1-55604-066-0, Order no.: D012).
CP/M. (ISBN 1-55604-067-9, Order no.: D012).
Commodore. (ISBN 1-55604-068-7, Order no.: D012).
Color Computer. (ISBN 1-55604-069-5, Order no.: D012).
IBM. (ISBN 1-55604-070-9, Order no.: D012).
Model I & Model III. (ISBN 1-55604-071-7, Order no.: D012).
Greyhound Analysis Which Uses a Combination of Speed & Class Based upon Grade of the Race. Track Records & Kennel Ratings Are Maintained on a Data Base, Initializing the System for a Specific Track. Master Bettor Evaluates Scores & Every Betting Combination of the Top 5 Dogs Are Given. Provides Edge & Helps Eliminate Losing Money with Winning Dogs. Track Management Is Designed to Keep Records on All Dogs Running at a Track.
Professor Jones Professional Handicapping Systems.

Enhanced Gold Horse - Thoroughbred. Ronald D. Jones. 1983. *Compatible Hardware:* Apple II; Commodore 64; IBM PC; TRS-80, Color Computer; CP/M machines. *Memory Required:* 64k.
Apple. disk $199.95 (ISBN 1-55604-006-7).
CP/M. disk $199.95 (ISBN 1-55604-007-5).
IBM. disk $199.95 (ISBN 1-55604-010-5).
Commodore. disk or cassette $199.95 (ISBN 1-55604-008-3).
Color Computer. disk or cassette $199.95 (ISBN 1-55604-009-1).
TRS-80. disk or cassette $199.95 (ISBN 1-55604-011-3).
Adds to the "GOLD" EDITION's Features a Complete MASTER BETTOR System Integrated onto the Same Disk.
Professor Jones Professional Handicapping Systems.

Enhanced Gold Quarterhorse. Ronald D. Jones. 1983. *Compatible Hardware:* Apple II; Commodore 64; IBM PC; TRS-80 Model I, Model III, Color Computer. *Operating System(s) Required:* CP/M. *Memory Required:* 64k.
disk $169.95 ea.
Apple. (ISBN 1-55604-048-2, Order no.: Q002).
CP/M. (ISBN 1-55604-049-0, Order no.: Q002).
IBM. (ISBN 1-55604-052-0, Order no.: Q002).
disk or cassette $169.95 ea.
Commodore. (ISBN 1-55604-050-4, Order no.: Q002).
Color Computer. (ISBN 1-55604-051-2, Order no.: Q002).
Model I & Model III. (ISBN 1-55604-053-9, Order no.: Q002).
Complete Quarterhorse Analysis Designed for the Close Finishes Involved in This Type of Race. Designed Around Intricate "Speed" Ratings but Includes All Handicapping Variables. Fine Tuning to Specific Area & Track Gives a Prediction of the Finish. Has Master Bettor Which Evaluates Scores & Every Betting Combination of the Top 5 Horses Is Printed on the Printer and/or Video.
Professor Jones Professional Handicapping Systems.

TITLE INDEX

ENTERPRISE NETWORK SIMULATION TOOLBOX

Enhanced Gold Thoroughbred with Track Management. Ronald D. Jones. 1984. *Compatible Hardware:* Apple II; Commodore 64; IBM PC; TRS-80 Model I, Model III, Color Computer. *Operating System(s) Required:* CP/M. *Memory Required:* 64k.
disk $279.90 ea.
Apple. (ISBN 1-55604-012-1, Order no.: H012).
CP/M. (ISBN 1-55604-013-X, Order no.: H012).
Commodore. (ISBN 1-55604-014-8, Order no.: H012).
Color Computer. (ISBN 1-55604-015-6, Order no.: H012).
IBM. (ISBN 1-55604-016-4, Order no.: H012).
Model I & Model III. (ISBN 1-55604-017-2, Order no.: H012).
Full-Featured Thoroughbred Analysis Designed for the Professional & Serious Novice. Designed to Evaluate All Relevant Factors & Variables & Give a Accurate Prediction of the Finish. Can Fine Tune to a Specific Track & Has Master Bettor Which Evaluates Scores. Every Betting Combination of the Top 5 Horses Is Printed on the Printer or Video. Track Management Is Designed to Keep Records on All Horses Running at a Track.
Professor Jones Professional Handicapping Systems.

Enhanced Lottery/Lotto Analysis. Ronald D. Jones. 1986. *Compatible Hardware:* Apple II; Commodore 64; IBM PC; TRS-80 Model I, Model III, Color Computer. *Operating System(s) Required:* CP/M. *Memory Required:* 64k.
disk $129.95 ea.
Apple. (ISBN 1-55604-162-4, Order no.: L003).
CP/M. (ISBN 1-55604-163-2, Order no.: L003).
Commodore. (ISBN 1-55604-164-0, Order no.: L003).
Color Computer. (ISBN 1-55604-165-9, Order no.: L003).
IBM. (ISBN 1-55604-166-7, Order no.: L003).
Model I & Model III. (ISBN 1-55604-167-5, Order no.: L003).
Helps Predict 3- & 4-Digit Numbers for Lottery & Expands to 5- & 6-Digit Numbers for Lotto Using Demitrov's Latest 6 Digit Theory. Gives User Ability to Track All Forms of Lottery & Lotto & Compile the Most Probable Sets of Numbers Based on the Past. All "Mechanical" Systems Evoke Bias Which Can Be Statistically Evaluated & Isolated with Program.
Professor Jones Professional Handicapping Systems.

Enhanced Master Harness Handicapper with Track Management. Ronald D. Jones. 1985. *Compatible Hardware:* Apple II; Commodore 64; IBM PC; TRS-80 Model I, Model III, Color Computer. *Operating System(s) Required:* CP/M. *Memory Required:* 64k.
disk $279.90 ea.
Apple. (ISBN 1-55604-192-6, Order no.: T012).
CP/M. (ISBN 1-55604-193-4, Order no.: T012).
Commodore. (ISBN 1-55604-194-2, Order no.: T012).
Color Computer. (ISBN 1-55604-195-0, Order no.: T012).
IBM. (ISBN 1-55604-196-9, Order no.: T012).
Model I & Model III. (ISBN 1-55604-197-7, Order no.: T012).
Initialize System with Track Records, Drivers, Trainers on Data Base System. Evaluates All Relevant Variables & 5 Accurate Prediction of Finish. Features National Tracks with Variance Table on Data Base. Master Bettor Evaluates Scores & Every Betting Combination Is Printed on Printer or Video. Track Management Is Designed to Keep Records on All Horses Running at a Track.
Professor Jones Professional Handicapping Systems.

Enhanced Structural & Finite Element Analysis. *Items Included:* Bound manual. *Customer Support:* Free hotline - no time limit; 30 day limited warranty; updates are $5/disk plus S&H.
MS-DOS. IBM & compatibles (256k). full system $899.95.
demo disk $5.00.
Solves Two-Dimensional & Three-Dimensional Problems of Six Types: Plane Frames; Space Frames; Space Trusses; Floor Grids; Rods & Membranes; 3-D Plates.
Dynacomp, Inc.

EnLIGHT Multimedia Milling Curriculum. Jan. 1994. *Items Included:* Three spiral bound manuals. *Customer Support:* 800/221-2763, No charge.
MS-DOS version 5.0 or higher. IBM & compatibles (2Mb). $595.00 1st copy; $200.00 additional copies (ISBN 0-941791-07-6, Order no.: CAM-7111, CAM-7131). *Nonstandard peripherals required:* Sound blaster sound card & speakers. *Optimal configuration:* 486 DX/2 66MHz 8Mb RAM, sound blaster card & speakers, mouse, SVGA monitor & adapter card.
An Interactive Teaching Package That Exposes Students to Practical Machining Applications & Processes.
Light Machines Corporation.

EnLIGHT Multimedia Turning Curriculum. Jan. 1994. *Items Included:* Three spiral bound manuals. *Customer Support:* 800/221-2763, No charge.
MS-DOS version 5.0 or higher. IBM & compatibles (2Mb). $595.00 1st copy; $200.00 additional copies (ISBN 0-941791-06-8, Order no.: CAM-7101, CAM-7121). *Nonstandard peripherals required:* Sound blaster sound card & speakers. *Optimal configuration:* 486 DX/2 66MHz 8Mb RAM, sound blaster card & speakers, mouse, SVGA monitor & adapter card.
An Interactive Teaching Package That Exposes Students to Practical Machining Applications & Processes.
Light Machines Corporation.

EnPlot. *Version:* 3.12. 1991.
Windows 3.0. IBM PC & compatibles. disk $399.00. *Nonstandard peripherals required:* Supports PostScript & PCL compatible printers.
Windows 3.0 Application That Analyzes Raw Material & Makes Presentation -Quality Charts & Graphs. Supports Semi-Log or Log-Log Scales with Grids on or off, Tick marks in or out & More. Performs Automatic Scaling, Multicolor Overlays, & 3-D Plots.
ASM International.

ENS Electronic News Service. *Compatible Hardware:* IBM PC, PC XT. *Operating System(s) Required:* PC-DOS. *Language(s):* C. *Memory Required:* IBM PC 64k, PC XT 128k. *Customer Support:* For more information, phone 202-467-4900 (Susan Carroll).
contact publisher for price.
Allows Access to Electronic News Service Which Provides: Analysis of All Major Government Economic & Financial Reports on Date of Release, Weekly Consensus Survey of Foreign Exchange Rates; Daily Outlook on Foreign Exchange; Dr. Michael K. Evans' Daily Economic Outlook Report, Weekly Updates on Macroeconomic Sector, Extensive Forecasts, the U.S. Economy, Daily Reports on the Credit Market & the Stock Market & Other Information.
Evans Economics, Inc.

Enterprise. *Version:* 1.1. Dec. 1990. *Items Included:* Six user manuals; One Administrator's Guide. *Customer Support:* 60 days free; 1 year maintenance contract $395.00.
DOS 3.1 plus networks. IBM compatibles (640k). $695.00 for 6 users. *Networks supported:* Novell, IBM, Microsoft, SITKA, Lantastic.
A Real-Time Multi-User Scheduling & Messaging for Office- Wide Management with Automatic Conflict Checking & Meeting Maker to Compare Multiple Calendars. Integrates To-Do Lists, Task Delegation, Client & Account-Project Management, Card File, Phone List, Quick Memo & Hot Keys for Electronic Document Transfer.
Chronos Software, Inc.

Enterprise Network Simulation Toolbox: Broadcast Wan-Lan Simulation. Jan. 1996. *Items Included:* Sample input & output files & users manuals on disk. *Customer Support:* Assistance in formulative inputs & understanding outputs, price free or variable.
MS-DOS. IBM PC (8Mb). disk $4500.00 (Order no.: 840). *Nonstandard peripherals required:* Math coprocessor. *Addl. software required:* FORTRAN Compiler & Linker. *Optimal configuration:* Source code can be compiled & linked for execution on any Machine with a FORTRAN compiler & linker.
Performs Discrete Event Simulations of Wide Area Broadcast Networks & Bus-Based Local Area Networks. Source Code Versions of 840 Are Available in ADA(841), BASIC(842), "C" (843), PASCAL(844), MODULA-2(845), FORTRAN(846), & COBOL(847). Each of the Seven Versions Is Available Individually or Collectively at a Significantly Reduced Price. The 840 Source Code Versions Are Intended to Facilitate the Development of Simulation Models in the Language of the User's Choice & to Support Courses in Simulation Model Development & Comparative Programming Languages.
Cane Systems.

Enterprise Network Simulation Toolbox: Network Link-by-Link Simulation. Jan. 1996. *Items Included:* Sample input & output files & users manuals on disk. *Customer Support:* Assistance in formulative inputs & understanding outputs, price free or variable.
MS-DOS. IBM PC (8Mb). disk $4500.00 (Order no.: 811). *Nonstandard peripherals required:* Math coprocessor. *Addl. software required:* FORTRAN Compiler & Linker. *Optimal configuration:* Source code can be compiled & linked for execution on any Machine with a FORTRAN compiler & linker.
A Discrete Event Simulation Tool That Is Quite Similar to Product 810. Simulates the Network One Link at a Time. Can Model Any & All Known Protocols, Including, but Not Limited to: TCP/IP, X.25, SNA, 802.3, 802.4, 802.5, 802.6, SDLC, HDLC, BSC, DATAGRAM Packet Switching, VIRTUAL CIRCUIT Packet Switching, MESSAGE Switching, & CIRCUIT Switching Networks. This Tool Will Accommodate Any Number & Any Combination of Full Duplexed, Half Duplexed & Simplex Circuits & Any Number of Message Priorities. It Generates Special Intermediate Data Files Which Allow the User to Develop Input for Animation & Static Graphics Packages of His Choice. This Product Is Supported by Product 408.
Cane Systems.

Enterprise Network Simulation Toolbox: Network Link Simulation. Jan. 1996. *Items Included:* Sample input & output files & users manuals on disk. *Customer Support:* Assistance in formulative inputs & understanding outputs, price free or variable.
MS-DOS. IBM PC (8Mb). disk $4500.00 (Order

no.: 810). *Nonstandard peripherals required:* Math coprocessor. *Addl. software required:* FORTRAN Compiler & Linker. *Optimal configuration:* Source code can be compiled & linked for execution on any Machine with a FORTRAN compiler & linker.
A Discrete Event Simulation Tool That Can Model Any & All Known Protocols, Including, but Not Limited to: TCP/IP, X.25, SNA, 802.3, 802.4, 802.5, 802.6, SDLC, HDLC, BSC, DATAGRAM Packet Switching, VIRTUAL CIRCUIT Packet Switching, MESSAGE Switching, & CIRCUIT Switching Networks. This Tool Will Accommodate Any Number & Any Combination of Full Duplexed, Half Duplexed & Simplex Circuits & Any Number of Message Priorities. It Generates Special Intermediate Data Files Which Allow the User to Develop Input for Animation & Static Graphics Packages of His Choice.
Cane Systems.

Enterprise Network Simulation Toolbox: Network Path Simulation. Jan. 1996. *Items Included:* Sample input & output files & users manuals on disk. *Customer Support:* Assistance in formulative inputs & understanding outputs, price free or variable.
MS-DOS. IBM PC (8Mb). disk $4500.00 (Order no.: 820). *Nonstandard peripherals required:* Math coprocessor. *Addl. software required:* FORTRAN Compiler & Linker. *Optimal configuration:* Source code can be compiled & linked for execution on any Machine with a FORTRAN compiler & linker.
A Discrete Event Simulation Tool That Can Model Any & All Known Protocols, Including, but Not Limited to: TCP/IP, X.25, SNA, 802.3, 802.4, 802.5, 802.6, SDLC, HDLC, BSC, DATAGRAM Packet Switching, VIRTUAL CIRCUIT Packet Switching, MESSAGE Switching, & CIRCUIT Switching Networks. This Tool Will Accommodate Any Number & Any Combination of Full Duplexed, Half Duplexed & Simplex Circuits & Any Number of Message Priorities. It Generates Special Intermediate Data Files Which Allow the User to Develop Input for Animation & Static Graphics Packages of His Choice.
Cane Systems.

Enterprise Network Simulation Toolbox: Network Response Time Simulation. Jan. 1996. *Items Included:* Sample input & output files & users manuals on disk. *Customer Support:* Assistance in formulative inputs & understanding outputs, price free or variable.
MS-DOS. IBM PC (8Mb). disk $4500.00 (Order no.: 830). *Nonstandard peripherals required:* Math coprocessor. *Addl. software required:* FORTRAN Compiler & Linker. *Optimal configuration:* Source code can be compiled & linked for execution on any Machine with a FORTRAN compiler & linker.
A Discrete Event Simulation Tool That Can Model Any & All Known Protocols, Including, but Not Limited to: TCP/IP, X.25, SNA, 802.3, 802.4, 802.5, 802.6, SDLC, HDLC, BSC, DATAGRAM Packet Switching, VIRTUAL CIRCUIT Packet Switching, MESSAGE Switching, & CIRCUIT Switching Networks. This Tool Will Accommodate Any Number & Any Combination of Full Duplexed, Half Duplexed & Simplex Circuits & Any Number of Message Priorities. It Generates Special Intermediate Data Files Which Allow the User to Develop Input for Animation & Static Graphics Packages of His Choice.
Cane Systems.

Entertainer Kit. *Compatible Hardware:* Atari XL/XE.
ROM cartridge $24.95 (Order no.: KX7101).
Atari Corp.

Entertainment Digest, Vol. I. Apr. 1995. *Items Included:* Special bonus offer & chance to win free software. *Customer Support:* Phone 201-845-3357, Fax 201-845-4638, Compuserv 76605.1506, Genie C. Niehoff, American Online C. Niehoff, Internet 76605.1506 Compuserv. COM, Fido Netmail Andy Schmidt 1:2604/511.
Windows version 3.1 or higher. IBM PC or compatible (2Mb). disk $29.95 (ISBN 1-885936-00-1). *Optimal configuration:* IBM or compatible, 4Mb RAM, 386 or higher, VGA high resolution with 256 colors & sound card. *Networks supported:* Windows NT & Windows for WorkGroups.
Complete Game Library - Offering You Games of Skill & Chance That Are Fun for the Whole Family! Whether You Are Seven or Seventy, Entertainment Digest Has the Games to Play Again & Again. For Even More Excitement, Check Out the Other Entertainment Digest Volumes.
Argos Gameware.

Entomorph MAC: Plague of the Darkfall. Dec. 1995. *Items Included:* 32 page rulebook. *Customer Support:* 30 day limited warranty.
System 7 or higher, MAC LC 475, 68040 or higher. MAC, Power Mac CD-ROM 25MHz or higher. CD-ROM disk $59.95 (ISBN 0-917059-34-4, Order no.: 012371). *Nonstandard peripherals required:* Requires 20Mb of hard drive space, 256 color monitor required. *Optimal configuration:* Requires 8Mb RAM.
A Fantasy Role Playing Adventure That Takes Place in the World of Aden. Grisly Combat with a Variety of Deadly Attack Options. Presented in State-of-the-Art High Resolution Graphics.
Strategic Simulations, Inc.

Entrapment. *Compatible Hardware:* TI 99/4A. contact publisher for price (Order no.: PHT6101).
Command the Space Ship That Patrols the Earth's Atmosphere & Protect the Earth from Attack.
Texas Instruments, Personal Productivit.

The Entrepreneur's Financial Workplate. *Version:* 2.0. (The Entrepreneur's Workplate Ser.). May 1984. *Operating System(s) Required:* IBM PC & compatibles. *Language(s):* 1-2-3 (source code included). *Memory Required:* 256k. *General Requirements:* 2Mb free on hard drive, Lotus 1-2-3 Release 2.0 or higher.
disk $49.95, incl. manual (Order no.: ENT-84010).
Provides 7 Templates for Profit & Loss, Income Statement, Cash Flow, & Balance Sheet Analyses. Designed to Help Users to Develop a Business Plan or Analyze the Financial Position of Their Company.
Riverdale Systems Design, Inc.

The Entrepreneur's Inventory Workplate. *Version:* 2.0. (The Entrepreneur's Workplate Ser.). Jan. 1985. *Compatible Hardware:* IBM PC & compatibles. *Operating System(s) Required:* MS-DOS. *Language(s):* 1-2-3 (source code included). *Memory Required:* 256k. *General Requirements:* 2Mb free on hard drive, Lotus 1-2-3 Release 2.0 or higher.
disk $49.95, incl. manual (Order no.: ENT-85080).
Helps User to Devise Corporate Inventory Strategy by Systematically Studying the Cost Components of, & Demand for, Inventory, So That Customer Service & Goodwill Are Maintained at Minimal Cost. Users Can Develop an Inventory Price List & Sales Log, Allowing Them to Respond to Customer Queries. Users Can Also Control Inventory & Measure Performance, Conduct Period & Year-to-Date Valuation, Profitability, & Economic Analysis.
Riverdale Systems Design, Inc.

The Entrepreneur's Marketing Workplate. *Version:* 2.0. (The Entrepreneur's Workplate Ser.). Jun. 1985. *Compatible Hardware:* IBM PC & compatibles. *Operating System(s) Required:* MS-DOS. *Language(s):* 1-2-3 (source code included). *Memory Required:* 256k. *General Requirements:* 2Mb free on hard drive, Lotus 1-2-3 Release 2.0 or higher.
disk $49.95, incl. manual (Order no.: ENT-85050).
Set of 10 Templates Designed to Help the User Answer Questions Concerning a Product's Market Potential, Performance, & Optimal Pricing Strategies. User Can Also Track Advertising Dollars, Gauge the Effectiveness of Ads, & Create a Message Schedule.
Riverdale Systems Design, Inc.

The Entrepreneur's Personnel Workplate. *Version:* 2.0. (The Entrepreneur's Workplate Ser.). Jan. 1985. *Compatible Hardware:* IBM PC & compatibles. *Operating System(s) Required:* MS-DOS. *Language(s):* 1-2-3 (source code included). *Memory Required:* 256k. *General Requirements:* 2Mb free on hard drive, Lotus 1-2-3 Release 2.0 or higher.
disk $49.95, incl. manual (Order no.: ENT-85040).
Provides Templates Which Are Necessary to Track Payroll, Analyze Employee Expense, Attendance & Performance Records, or Produce Client Billing Records. Includes Model Which Helps Forecast Personnel Supply & Demand or Analyze Salary Budgets & Staffing Levels. An Employee Directory Can Also Be Generated, Listing Hiring Date, Position, Salary, Phone Extension, & Other Data.
Riverdale Systems Design, Inc.

The Entrepreneur's Sales Workplate. *Version:* 2.0. (The Entrepreneur's Workplate Ser.). Jun. 1985. *Compatible Hardware:* IBM PC & compatibles. *Operating System(s) Required:* MS-DOS. *Language(s):* 1-2-3 (source code included). *Memory Required:* 256k. *General Requirements:* 2Mb free on hard drive, Lotus 1-2-3 Release 2.0 or higher.
disk $49.95, incl. manual (Order no.: ENT-85060).
Tool to Help User Manage a Sales Effort. A Sales Order Database Is Created from Which Sales Forecasts & Performance Analyses Can Be Completed. Other Functions Include: a Customer/Prospect List, Sales Compensation Analysis, Sales Plan/Time Allocation Model, & Staffing Levels.
Riverdale Systems Design, Inc.

Entrypoint. Datalex. *Compatible Hardware:* TI Professional. *Operating System(s) Required:* MS-DOS. *Memory Required:* 128k. *General Requirements:* 2 disk drives, printer.
development $1450.00.
operator $1000.00.
Screen-Oriented Data Entry Software.
Texas Instruments, Personal Productivit.

Entrypoint for Windows. *Version:* 1.94. 1993. *Items Included:* Application Development/Imaging software & a comprehensive user's guide. *Customer Support:* Toll-free technical support hotline, electronic bulletin board, classes, quarterly newsletter.
MS-DOS 3.1 or higher, MS Windows 3.0 or higher, 1886 enhanced mode. 80386 CPU (4Mb). Contact publisher for price. *Optimal configuration:* 40Mb hard disk.
Application Development/Imaging System That Provides Development Tools for Designing Customized Data Entry Screens with Editing, Data Validation, & Export Options. Data Entry Workstation Features Include Immediate Error Detection & Flagging, Re-Key Verification, Data Retrieval & Validation from Lookup Tables, the

TITLE INDEX

Ability to Access Images, & the Ability to Use OCR/ICR Software for the Automatic Insertion of Data into Fields & for Verification of That Data. Interfaces with Standard Communications Products & Commercial Networks.
DATALEX.

Entrypoint 90. Version: 1.4. 1988. Compatible Hardware: IBM PC XT, PC AT, PS/2 & compatibles. Operating System(s) Required: PC-DOS/MS-DOS. Language(s): Microsoft C. Memory Required: 512k. General Requirements: Hard disk recommended. Items Included: Software for application development & data entry. Customer Support: Toll-free hotline, electronic bulletin board, award-winning manuals, quarterly newsletter, classes.
$1075.00 developer module; $725.00 workstation module. Networks supported: IBM PC-NET, Ethernet, 3COM, StarLAN, Token-Ring, IBM LAN Manager, Novell Netware, Banyan VINES & others.
Package for Developing Customized PC Data Entry Systems for Business Applications Such As Accounting, Payroll, Inventory, Market Research, Personnel, Clinical Trials & Litigation Support. Includes Extensive Editing & Error Checking Capabilities, Plus Automatic Export Options. Features Full-Screen Editor for Designing Data Entry Screens & Menu-Driven Edit Implementation. Replacement for Expensive Key-to-Disk Systems. Features Include: Accumulators, Audit Trails, Auto Dup, Auto Save, Checkdigits, Communications, Data Reformatting, Editing, Error Checking, Export Options, Help Screens, LAN Module, Operator Statistics, Password Protection, Scanner Support, Table Lookup, Text Fields, Trail Verification, Turnkey Systems, 24-Hour Electronic Bulletin Board, 800 Hotline.
DATALEX.

Entrypoint 90/Plus. Version: 1.4. Jan. 1991. Items Included: Five manuals that contain complete documentation. Customer Support: Toll-free technical support hotline, electronic bulletin board, training, manuals, quarterly newsletter.
DOS 2.0 or higher. IBM PC or compatible (512k for developing applications, 256k for data entry). $3500.00 dependent on concurrent usage. Networks supported: IBM PC-NET, Ethernet, 3COM 3 Plus, StarLAN, Token.Ring, IBM LAN Manager, Novell Netware, Banyan VINES & others.
Same Features As Entrypoint 90 Plus an Audit Trail Facility for Recording Changes to Data, a Program for Reformatting Batches after Changes Are Made to an Application, a Program for Printing Forms, & a Program for Viewing Data Across Batches or Exporting the Data in a Format Compatible with Standard Databases. Also Includes a Customizable User Interface, a Program for Integrating External "C" Routines into Applications, & an Application Converter. Ideal for Clinical Trials Applications.
DATALEX.

Environmental Abstracts. Items Included: Quarterly Updates.
disk
An International clearinghouse of information on topics from global warming to gasoline prices - drawn from core academic & professional journals, government reports, patents, & grey literature with little or no distribution.
Congressional Information Service.

The Environmental Manager: TEM. Version: 2.10. Items Included: Application Platform ("C-Power"), 3-hole notebook-style user manual for each module, non-copy-protected software. Customer Support: Free one day on site training, free one year maintenance, free one year telephone support, free access to modem bulletin board, quarterly newsletter..
MS-DOS version 2.1 or higher (640k). IBM PC or compatible. $1240.00 to $2000.00 per module. Optimal configuration: IBM AT, color monitor, 640k RAM & 20Mb hard disk. Networks supported: Novell LAN.
Environmental Software Designed for Comprehensive, Integrated Use. Modular Design Allows User to Customize System to Their Needs. Modules Include: Environmental Audit, Air Emissions, Wastewater Monitoring, Groundwater Monitoring, Operational Journal, Incident Reporting, Permit Tracking, MSDS Management, Waste Management, Hazardous Waste Manifesting, Chemical Waste Inventory, Task Management, & Storage Tanks. In Addition, a New Module Is Being Developed to Handle SARA Reporting. System Has a Powerful Query Module Utilizing SQL, & Good Reporting Features. Many Modules Also Feature Complicated Statistics.
Environmental Telesis & Controls, Inc.

Environmental Views Series CD-ROM. Thomas Detwyler. Dec. 1994. Items Included: 30-day refund policy, customer support - phone M-F, 8-5 EST, 715-344-6060.
Windows. 8086 or higher CPU (4Mb). $49.95 each title. Optimal configuration: 8086 or higher CPU, 4Mb RAM, MS-Windows 3.1 or higher, VGA graphics board with 256 colors or higher & compatible monitor, mouse or other pointing device, CD-ROM drive.
DOS & Macintosh. Macintosh (2Mb). $49.95 each title. Optimal configuration: 2Mb RAM, graphics board with 256 colors & compatible monitor, CD-ROM drive, & application software that can read .TIF or .BMP or .TGAFiles.
First Five Titles: Endangered Species, Fossil Fuels, Renewable Energy, Soil Erosion & Conservation, & Wetlands. Every Title Contains over 100 Full-Color, Digital Photos - Each with a Substantive Explanatory Caption Frame. Photos from Around the World. Includes a Windows Presentation Program to Sort & Sequence Images & Captions, Add Comments, Play & Save Slide-Shows, etc.
Optilearn, Inc.

ENVISION. Version: 4.3. Feb. 1992. Items Included: Manuals, training video. Customer Support: Hotline, maintenance, upgrades.
Macintosh, MS-DOS Windows 3.1. Quadra, Power PC 486 (16Mb). 3.5" disk $1995.00. Nonstandard peripherals required: 24-bit color, or 8-bit color card, standard. Optimal configuration: Mac IIci, scanner, printer, 19" monitor/24-bit color card. Networks supported: All Mac compatible.
Applies 3D Surface Detail to 2D Images. Allows High Resolution Rendering of Any Image. Drape Cloth Upholstery on Car Seats, Wrap Textures Around Objects, Apply Marble Facades to Buildings - Create Photo-Realistic Images Prior to Making Sample Products or Prototypes. Works Effectively for Soft or Hard Surfaces in a Variety of Industries Including Graphics, Entertainment, Industrial Design, Interiors & Architecture, Automotive & Aerospace.
ModaCAD, Inc.

EOS Accounting: Record-Keeping & Accounting System, 8 disks. Version: 4.0. Jan. 1993. Operating System(s) Required: MS-DOS, Novell, IBM OS/2. Items Included: Sales order, purchase order, job cost.
disk $895.00 ea.
General Ledger.
Accounts Receivables.
Accounts Payable.
Payroll.
Inventory.
Complete Accounting System with Accounts Receivable, Accounts Payable, General Ledger, Order Entry, Purchase Order, Payroll & Inventory Control. Provides Standard Balance Sheet & Income Statement by Department or by Individual Job.
Computer Age, Inc.

EOS Construction Job Costing. Version: 4.0. Jan. 1993. Items Included: Data dictionary; complete system flow charts; installation guidelines. Customer Support: 3 hours free setup & support; 6 months maintenance; support $75.00 per hour billed in 1 tenth hour increments.
DOS, Novell, OS/2. IBM & compatibles (640k). $4000.00-$12,000.00 (Order no.: EOS JOB COST). Addl. software required: Knowledge Man, Runtime or development system. Optimal configuration: IBM, 386, 2Mb RAM. Networks supported: Novell, OS/2.
OS/2. IBM & compatibles (4Mb). $4000.00-$12,000.00 (Order no.: EOS JOB COST OS/2). Addl. software required: Knowledge Man, Runtime or Development System. Networks supported: Novell, OS/2.
Job Cost Accounting Program Designed for Efficient Data Entry. One Point Designed for GL, AP, AR, INV, Payroll Card Reader Interface for Job Cost & Payroll Transactions Extensive Union Support. Extensive Rebill Support.
Computer Age, Inc.

EOS Manufacturing: Manufacturer Accounting. Jan. 1987. Compatible Hardware: IBM PC & compatibles. Operating System(s) Required: MS-DOS, Novell, OS/2. Memory Required: 640k. General Requirements: Hard disk, color monitor, printer.
Novell. disk $8000.00 (Order no.: MFG/SYS).
MS-DOS. disk $5000.00 (Order no.: MFG/SYS).
(Order no.: MFG/SYS).
Complete & Integrated Software System for Job Shops & Manufacturers. Includes General Ledger, Accounts Payable, Accounts Receivable, Purchase Order, Inventory, Bill of Materials, Material Requirements Planning, & Job Costing, AIAG Barcode & EDI.
Computer Age, Inc.

EPA Emissions Analysis Above-Ground Storage Tanks. Items Included: Full manual. No other products required. Customer Support: Free telephone support - no time limit. 30 day warranty.
MS-DOS 3.2 or higher. IBM & compatibles (512k). full system $589.95, ,5.00 demo disk.
Make the Required EPA Storage Tank Emissions Calculations Quickly & Easily with This Time-Saving Tool. Retrieves the Appropriate Factors, from Its Database & Performs the Calculations Required to Estimate Organic Liquid Storage Tank Emissions According to the Procedures Described in EPA Publication AP-42, "Compilation of Air Pollutant Emission Factors," Section 4.3, "Storage or Organic Liquids." Calculates the Breathing Losses & the Working Losses for Fixed-Roof Tanks, & the Rim Seal Losses & Withdrawal Losses for Internal & External Floating-Roof Tanks.
Dynacomp, Inc.

EPA's Sampling & Analysis Methods Database, Vols. 1-3. Version: 2.0. Edited by Lawrence H. Keith. Sep. 1995.
DOS 2.0 or higher, hard drive with 1.5 mb of memory. IBM or compatible microcomputer. 3.5" disk $250.00 (ISBN 0-87371-418-0).
Lewis Publishers.

EPI Info. Version: 5.01B. Andrew G. Dean et al. Oct. 1991. Customer Support: Telephone & information hotline for tech. support, 404-728-0545 - 5 days per week.

EPLAN/TPLAN: INDIVIDUAL EDUCATION -

PC-DOS/MS-DOS 2.0 or higher. IBM PC/XT/AT or compatible. disk $35.00.
Develop Questionnaires Adding Optional Range Checking, Legal Values, Automatic Coding, Skip Patterns, Repeat Fields. Creates Rational File Systems, Links Several Questionnaires, Produces Lists, Frequencies & Multidimensional Tables. Performs Chi-Square, Mantel-Haenszel & Fisher Tests, Crude & Stratified Odds Ratios & Relative Risks, Confidence Intervals, Means, One-Way Anova & Kruskal-Wallis Tests, etc. Graphics-Histograms, Bar, Line & Pie Charts. Import Fixed Length, Comma Delimited, dBASE, Lotus 1-2-3 Files. Export Files in 12 Formats.
USD, Inc.

EPLAN/TPLAN: Individual Education - Transition Plan. 1994. *Items Included:* User's manual, system disks (3), database disks (1). *Customer Support:* Free telephone support for 12 months after purchase.
  MS Windows. IBM PC or compatibles (6Mb). disk $275.00 (ISBN 1-888333-08-1).
    Nonstandard peripherals required: Mouse, color monitor. *Optimal configuration:* 13Mb of available space on hard disk drive.
  Macintosh System 7.0. Macintosh (9Mb). 3.5" disk $275.00 (ISBN 1-888333-09-X).
    Nonstandard peripherals required: Mouse, color monitor. *Optimal configuration:* 15Mb of available space on hard disk drive.
Interactive Environment for IEP (Individual Education Plan) Development. It Consists of Menus & Buttons of Functional Options. System Uses a Window-Based Visual Interface to Display Mouse-Selectable Choices to the User. Calls TPLAN (Transition Planning) to Assist in Making Decisions in Areas Including Education, Employment, etc. to Fulfill Almost All a Student's Transition Needs. Contains Service Provider Database for State by Subarea (County, Parish, Borough).
Analysis & Simulation, Inc.

EPLAN/TPLAN: Individual Education - Transition Plan. 1994. *Items Included:* User's manual (6 - three (3) each of EPLAN & TPLAN), system disks (9 - three each of EPLAN & TPLAN), database disks (3). *Customer Support:* Free telephone support for 12 months after purchase.
  MS Windows. IBM PC or compatibles (6Mb). disk $760.00, site license (ISBN 1-888333-10-3). *Nonstandard peripherals required:* Mouse, color monitor. *Optimal configuration:* 13Mb of available space on hard disk drive.
  Macintosh System 7.0. Macintosh (9Mb). 3.5" disk $760.00, site license (ISBN 1-888333-11-1). *Nonstandard peripherals required:* Mouse, color monitor. *Optimal configuration:* 15Mb of available space on hard disk drive.
Interactive Environment for IEP (Individual Education Plan) Development. It Consists of Menus & Buttons of Functional Options. System Uses a Window-Based Visual Interface to Display Mouse-Selectable Choices to the User. Calls TPLAN (Transition Planning) to Assist in Making Decisions in Areas Including Education, Employment, etc. to Fulfill Almost All a Student's Transition Needs. Contains Service Provider Database for State by Subarea (County, Parish, Borough).
Analysis & Simulation, Inc.

EPLAN: Individual Education Plan. 1994. *Items Included:* User's manual, system disks (2). *Customer Support:* Free telephone support for 12 months after purchase.
  MS Windows. IBM PC or compatibles (4Mb). disk $180.00 (ISBN 1-888333-06-5).
    Nonstandard peripherals required: Mouse, color monitor. *Optimal configuration:* 10Mb of available space on hard disk drive.
  Macintosh System 7.0. Macintosh (4Mb). 3.5" disk $180.00 (ISBN 1-888333-04-9).
    Nonstandard peripherals required: Mouse, color monitor. *Optimal configuration:* 10Mb of available space on hard disk drive.
Interactive Environment for IEP (Individual Education Plan) Development. It Consists of Menus & Buttons of Functional Options. System Uses a Window-Based Visual Interface to Display Mouse-Selectable Choices to the User.
Analysis & Simulation, Inc.

EPLAN: Individual Education Plan. 1994. *Items Included:* User's manual (3), system disks (6 - two (2) for each copy). *Customer Support:* Free telephone support for 12 months after purchase.
  MS Windows. IBM PC or compatibles (4Mb). disk $490.00, site license (ISBN 1-888333-07-3). *Nonstandard peripherals required:* Mouse, color monitor. *Optimal configuration:* 10Mb of available space on hard disk drive.
  Macintosh System 7.0. Macintosh (4Mb). 3.5" disk $490.00, site license (ISBN 1-888333-05-7). *Nonstandard peripherals required:* Mouse, color monitor. *Optimal configuration:* 10Mb of available space on hard disk drive.
Interactive Environment for IEP (Individual Education Plan) Development. It Consists of Menus & Buttons of Functional Options. System Uses a Window-Based Visual Interface to Display Mouse-Selectable Choices to the User.
Analysis & Simulation, Inc.

EPRINT. *Customer Support:* 800-929-8117 (customer service).
  MS-DOS. Commodore 128; CP/M. disk $29.99 (ISBN 0-87007-412-1).
A Versatile Machine Language Printer Forms Control Program for CP/M Computers (8080 or Z80). It Allows the Owner of the MX80 or Other Epson Printer to: 1) Set the Printer Options Without Having to Run Individual Programs Every Time User Wants Change a Form, & 2) Exploit All of the Hardware Set Features of the MX80. Controlled by a Menu & Includes the Following Selections: Select, Page Width, Single or Double Striking or Characters, Emphasized or Normal Printing, Line Spacing, Forms Length, Horizontal Tabs, Vertical Tabs, & Forms Change.
SourceView Software International.

EPS Exchange. *Items Included:* Complete documentation. *Customer Support:* Telephone & BBS.
  MAC O/S. Apple Macintosh Family (2Mb). $149.00. *Addl. software required:* Aldus Freehand & Adobe Illustrator 88 or 3.0. *Optimal configuration:* Macintosh, 2Mb RAM, Freehand & Illustrator 88 or 3.0.
Altsys Corp.

EPS Linker. Thomas B. Stevens & Edward M. Glassgow. May 1991. *Items Included:* Manual. *Customer Support:* Telephone technical support for an annual fee of $50.00.
  Macintosh 6.05. Macintosh Classic (1Mb). Single User $30.00; Site Terms $90.00 (Three manual & disk sets-Additional sets $10.00 each). *Nonstandard peripherals required:* Hard drive. *Addl. software required:* HyperCard 2.0 or higher. *Optimal configuration:* Macintosh SE 30.4Mb RAM 80Mb hard drive, system 6.07 Hypercard 2.0.
Links all EPS Directories & Appointment Calendars to the SHARP WIZARD Electronic Organizer. Works with EPS PERSONAL MANAGER, EPS TEACHER'S ASSISTANT, EPS SCHOOL ADMINISTRATOR'S ASSISTANT & EPS SCHOOL MANAGER.
Executive Productivity Systems.

EPS Personal Manager System. *Version:* V.2.0. Thomas B. Stevens & Edward M. Glassgow. Mar. 1990. *Items Included:* Manual. *Customer Support:* Telephone technical support for an annual fee of $50.00.
  Macintosh 6.05. Macintosh Classic (1Mb). Single User $79.00; Site Terms $249.00 (Three manual & disk sets, Additional manuals $25.00 each). *Nonstandard peripherals required:* Hard drive. *Addl. software required:* HyperCard 2.0 or higher. *Optimal configuration:* Macintosh SE 30.4Mb RAM, 80Mb Hard drive, system 6.07 Hypercard 2.0.
Consists of Two Shells. The Scheduling Shell: Includes an Automated Daily, Weekly & Monthly Appointment Calendar System, Expandable Calendars into the Twenty-First Century, a Year at a Time. Manages to Do Lists, Birthday & Anniversary Reminders, & Events Automatically. The Information Shell: Includes Automated Dialing & Call Tracking, Tracking & Totaling of Expenses & Mileage, Client Tracking Timing & Billing, Memo & Note Preparation, Address Book, Secure Password Protection for Confidential Information, Direct Linkage to Programs & Documents, On-Line Help, Incredible Cross-Shell Search Capabilities, & Many Other Features. Unique Open Ended Calculation Fields Allow You to Enter Comments & Notations As You Track Your Expenses.
Executive Productivity Systems.

EPS Records Management System: The Central Filling Solution. *Version:* V.1.0. Thomas B. Stevens & Edward M. Glassgow. Jan. 1990. *Items Included:* Manual. *Customer Support:* Telephone Technical Support for an annual fee of $50.00.
  Macintosh 6.05. Macintosh Classic (1Mb). disk $149.00, Additional manuals ,20.00 each. *Nonstandard peripherals required:* Hard drive. *Addl. software required:* HyperCard 2.0 or higher. *Optimal configuration:* Macintosh SE 30.4Mb RAM, 80Mb hard drive, system 6.07 Hypercard 2.0. *Networks supported:* Appletalk, AUX. Ethernet.
Designed To Track & Maintain Paper Files, Media, or Any Form of Documentary Information in a Systematic, Organized Manner. Product Uses a Coding System To Locate & Keep Track of Paper Files, Computer Files & Disks, Maps, Photographs, Oversized Documents & Any Other Information in Any Format. Product Is a Network or Stand-Alone System.
Executive Productivity Systems.

Epsilon Programmer's Editor. *Version:* 6.0. *Compatible Hardware:* IBM PC, PC XT, PC AT & compatibles. *Operating System(s) Required:* PC-DOS/MS-DOS, OS/2, UNIX, XENIX. (source code included). *Memory Required:* 256K. *Items Included:* 235 Page manual. *Customer Support:* Telephone.
  disk $250.00.
Program Editor Which Provides C Language Support & Fixes Errors While the Compiler Runs. Also Includes Multiple Windows & Unlimited File Size.
Lugaru Software, Ltd.

EpsWord. *Customer Support:* 800-929-8117 (customer service).
  MS-DOS. IBM/PS2. disk $79.99 (ISBN 0-87007-421-0).
Enhances WordStar Print Menu & Print Options to Include Features of Graftrax-Plus.
SourceView Software International.

EQL (English Query Language). *Compatible Hardware:* IBM PC XT, PC AT, PS/2. *Memory Required:* 640k. *General Requirements:* PC/Focus 3.0 program.
  disk $246.00.
Natural-Language Interface for PC/Focus. Will Access DBASE III & DBASE III Plus Files.
Information Builders, Inc.

TITLE INDEX

Equation Solver. Compatible Hardware: TI 99/4A. Operating System(s) Required: DX-10. Language(s): Console BASIC. Memory Required: 16k.
disk or cassette $19.00.
Interactive Program Finds the Solution to Any F(X)=0 Form Equation. The Interval Within Which a Solution Must Be Found, the Number of Iterations & the Tolerance of the Solution Can Be Specified.
Eastbench Software Products.

The Equator II: Equation Evaluation & Plotting. 1992. Items Included: Detailed manuals included with all Dynacomp products. Customer Support: Free telephone support to original customer - no time limit; 30 day limited warranty.
MS-DOS 3.2 or higher. IBM PC & compatibles (512k). $79.95 (Add $5.00 for 3 1/2" format; 5 1/4" format standard). Optimal configuration: IBM, MS-DOS 2.1 or higher, CGA, EGA, or VGA graphics capability, 512k RAM, & two floppy drives (or one floppy & a hard disk).
A Personalized, Menu-Driven Mathematical Equation Storage, Evaluation, & Plotting System. It Allows You to Not Only Save Your Equations in a Menu-Organized Manner, but Also Allows You to Document the Variables & Parameters Used. You May Evaluate Expressions at Points or over Ranges to Create Tables, Graphs, or Disk Files. Includes a Clearly-Written 80-Page Manual, As Well As Numerous Examples on Disk.
Dynacomp, Inc.

The Equator 2: Equation Evaluation & Plotting. Items Included: Full manual. No other products required. Customer Support: Free telephone support - no time limit. 30 day warranty.
MS-DOS 3.2 or higher. IBM & compatibles (512k). disk $79.95. Optimal configuration: IBM, MS-DOS 2.1 or higher, CGA, EGA, or VGA graphics capability, 512k RAM, & two floppy drives for one floppy & a hard disk. Can be used with 360k drives, although 720k or higher drives are recommended.
Personalized, Menu-Driven Mathematical Equation Storage, Evaluation, & Plotting System. It Allows You to Not Only Save Your Equations in a Menu-Organized Manner, but Also Allows You to Document the Variables & Parameters Used.
Dynacomp, Inc.

Equil: Chemical Equilibrium Calculations for Solutions. Items Included: Bound manual. Customer Support: Free hotline - no time limit; 30 day limited warranty; updates are $5/disk plus S&H.
MS-DOS 3.1 or higher. IBM & compatibles (640k). disk $239.95. Nonstandard peripherals required: Two floppy drives (or one floppy & a hard disk); CGA, EGA, or compatible graphics (for screen graphics); supports 80x87 math coprocessor.
Interactively Solves Aqueous Chemical Equilibrium Problems. User Specifies the Solution Properties (e.g., pH, Ionic Strength, Solution Components), & EQUIL Will Search Its Chemical Equilibrium Database for the Appropriate Reactions. It Then Constructs Mass Balance Relationships. The Results May Be Presented in the Form of pH Titration Curves, Complex Formation Curves, or Species Concentration Diagrams, As Appropriate. Solutions Saturated with Respect to More Than One Solid Phase Can Be Treated, & Systems Consisting of More Than 60 Species May Be Modeled. Publication-Quality Graphs May Be Printed on Most Dot Matrix Printers, As Well As PostScript & HPGL Devices.
Dynacomp, Inc.

Equilibrium. Compatible Hardware: Apple Macintosh. General Requirements: Microsoft BASIC 2.0.
3.5" disk $28.00.
Chemical Equilibrium Calculation Program.
E & M Software Co.

Equilibrium Flash Calculations. Items Included: Full manual. No other products required. Customer Support: Free telephone support - no time limit. 30 day warranty.
MS-DOS 3.2 or higher. IBM & compatibles (512k). disk $679.95.
Calculates All Types of Two-Phase Flash Problems. Includes a Physical Property Database. Performs Bubble & Dew Point Calculations As Well As Rigorous Flash Analysis with or Without Heat Transfer into the System. Uses U.S., SI, & Metric Units. Includes a Complete & Detailed Manual Which Describes All Procedures.
Dynacomp, Inc.

EquiMac. Version: 1.3. Compatible Hardware: Apple Macintosh. General Requirements: Hard disk. Items Included: Two floppy disks & manual with binder & slipcase. Customer Support: Unlimited support-customer pays for call.
3.5" disk $695.00.
Horse & Horse Farm Management.
Equine Computer Software.

Equinox-Solstice. Compatible Hardware: TI 99/4A with Extended BASIC module. Operating System(s) Required: DX-10. Memory Required: 48k.
cassette $14.95.
Equinox & Solstice Times Are Computed for Any Year.
Eastbench Software Products.

EQUIPD: The Equipment Management System. Version: 1.1. Eleanor Turino. Mar. 1986. Compatible Hardware: IBM PC & compatibles. Operating System(s) Required: MS-DOS 2.0 or higher. Memory Required: 128k. General Requirements: Hard disk.
disk $195.00 (ISBN 0-938213-00-8).
Design to Manage Equipment Purchased, Leased or Rented by Corporations, Schools & Other Organizations.
Berkshire Software Co.

Equipment & Supply Dealer Package. Agri-Management Services, Inc. Compatible Hardware: TI Professional. Operating System(s) Required: MS-DOS. Memory Required: 64k. General Requirements: Printer.
$1495.00.
Inventory Program Tied to Order Entry Routine Tied to Receivables Program.
Texas Instruments, Personal Productivit.

Equipment Boss: Equipment Tracking. Version: 5.0. Mar. 1993. Items Included: Chapter of documentation. Customer Support: Same as Construction Management Software.
PC-DOS. IBM-PC, PC AT, PS/2 (640k). Contact publisher for price. Nonstandard peripherals required: 20Mb hard disk. Addl. software required: Construction Management Software. Networks supported: Novell.
Controls the Safety & Profitability of Equipment. Fully Integrated with CMS Accounting & Job Costing. Does IRS Accepted Depreciation, Maintenance Schedules, Equipment Reports, Calculates Cost of Ownership, & Posts Costs from Payroll, A/P & Direct. Maintenance Records, Cost Types & Masterfile of Common Costs Are All User Definable.
(Small System Design), Inc.

EQUIPMENT SCHEDULER

Equipment Inventory. Compatible Hardware: TRS-80 Model I, Model III. Operating System(s) Required: TRSDOS. Language(s): BASIC. Memory Required: 16k.
disk or cassette $64.95.
Lets Users Keep Expense Records on over One Hundred Pieces of Equipment by Purchase Date, Serial Number, Description, & Purchase Cost.
Duane Bristow Computers, Inc.

Equipment Maintenance (a Part of ABECAS). Version: 3.3. Jan. 1989. Customer Support: On site training unlimited support services for first 90 days & through subscription thereafter.
PC/MS-DOS 3.x. IBM PC & compatibles. Contact publisher for price. Nonstandard peripherals required: Hard disk (30Mb or higher); 132 column printer.
User Can Track Equipment & Manage Its Maintenance, Permits & Records. Master Record Provides Data on Each Item, Broken Down by Power Units, Trailers, & Other Items. Allows Details Such as Type, Cost, etc. to Be Entered & Tracked. Maintenance Schedules & Licenses May Also Be Tracked. Summary & Detail on Each Repair Order May Be Maintained in History File. Repair Order Interfaces with CA Supplies Inventory & Allows Allocation of Supplies to Repair Orders. Multi-User Version Available for Novell, NTNX, 10-Net, Unix/Xenix, Turbo DOS & Maintenance Worksheets, Government Reporting & Others.
Argos Software.

Equipment Rental Software. 1980. Compatible Hardware: IBM PC, PC XT, PC AT & compatibles. Operating System(s) Required: MS-DOS. Language(s): BASIC (source code included). Memory Required: 640k.
disk $499.00 (Order no.: LSC-2001).
Lizcon Computer Systems.

Equipment Sales & Rental Software. Operating System(s) Required: MS-DOS. Memory Required: 640k. General Requirements: Hard disk, printer.
Single user. disk $499.00 (Order no.: LSC2017). Multi-user (Novell). $799.00.
Equipment Rental Software in Both Single User & Multi-User Formats Capable of Keeping Track of Customer Information As to Rental History & Checks Expiration Date of Credit Cards. Features Daily Sales Receipts, Reports & Summary of Transactions by Individual Sales Clerk. Keeps Track of Inventory During Invoice Generation, Reservations & Returns. Items Can Be Traced by Item Code, Customer Code or Sales Receipts Number. Security Deposits Received & Returned Are Reported.
Lizcon Computer Systems.

Equipment Scheduler. Version: II. 1992. Items Included: Complete instructions in 3 ring binder. Customer Support: 1 year free replacement of damaged disks, free unlimited telephone customer support.
MS-DOS. IBM-PC, XT, AT, PS-2 or compatible (512k). disk $189.00 (ISBN 1-55812-099-8). Addl. software required: None.
Enter All Equipment. Enter Scheduling Details. Search & Print by Day, Week or Month. You Will See Instantly What Has to Be Where & When It Has to Be There. Generate Various Reports: All Equipment by Type, Condition, Location & Use. Enter a Name or Department to Find Out What They Use & When. Blank "User Fields" Let You Enter Other Searchable Details. This Program Does It All ... Except Push the Equipment Down the Hall.
Right On Programs.

ERA/Link. Version: 2.0. 1992. Customer Support: Sixty days of free support.
MS-DOS. IBM PC & compatibles (1Mb). $4000.00 & up. Optimal configuration: 20Mb hard disk; payer communicaitons hardware & software; printer; 9600 baud modem.
Receives Remittance Advice Data Directly from Payers, Lock Boxes, & Collection Agencies. Additional Modules Enable Automation of Payment Posting & Secondary Billing. System is PC-Based.
Learned-Mahn.

Eric The Unready. Items Included: Disks, game manual, package insert, warranty card, product catalog. Customer Support: Toll free technical assistance (1-800-658-8891). Computer operated pre-recorded hint line (1-900-776-5583) $.75 1st min., $.50 each additional min. Hint book $9.95 plus s/h.
MS-DOS 3.3 or higher. IBM & compatible (640k). disk $59.95. Optimal configuration: IBM PC 80386 with 640k RAM & SVGA/VGA adapter & monitor, Microsoft compatible mouse & Soundblaster compatible soundcard.
Comedy/Fantasy, Eric The Unready Searches the Magical Kingdom of Torus to Find the Kidnapped Princess.
Legend Entertainment Company.

ERMASOFT Easy Fonts. Compatible Hardware: PC-DOS. Memory Required: 25-80k. Customer Support: (818) 707-3818.
disk $79.95.
3.5" disk $79.95.
A RAM-Resident Utility to Allow Users to Select Fonts for Downloading to Laser Printers. Converts Fonts into Landscape Mode. Provides Font Inventory Reports, & Monitors Memory.
ERM Assocs.

Ernie's Big Splash. Compatible Hardware: Commodore 64, IBM PC & compatibles.
disk $9.95.
Maze Builder Which Develops Planning, Predicting & Problem-Solving Skills.
Hi Tech Expressions, Inc.

Ernie's Magic Shapes. Compatible Hardware: Atari XL, XE; Commodore 64; IBM PC & compatibles.
disk $9.95.
Shape & Color Matching Game.
Hi Tech Expressions, Inc.

Escape from Management Hell. Robert Gilbreath. May 1995. Items Included: For Windows/MPC - QuickTime for Windows 2.01 (on the CD-ROM); For Macintosh - QuickTime 2.0 & Sound Manager (also on the CD-ROM). Customer Support: Free online support on America online using key word Zelos; Toll free number 1-800-345-6777; 90 day money back guarantee.
Windows/MPC; Macintosh. 386, 33MHz, double speed CD-ROM drive (8Mb); Macintosh 68030, 25MHz (8Mb). CD-ROM disk $29.95 (ISBN 1-883387-11-6). Nonstandard peripherals required: 640x480, 256 color display, Microsoft compatible mouse, SoundBlaster compatible 16 bit sound card; 13" 256 color monitor. Addl. software required: DOS 5.0 or higher, Microsoft Windows 3.1, QuickTime for Windows 2.01; System 7.0, QuickTime 2.0, Sound Manager.
Learn to Avoid Classic Management "Sins" in This Entertaining & Practical Tool for Business Managers. In This CD-ROM, Adapted from the Critically Acclaimed Book by Robert Gilbreath, Twelve Executives Are Summoned to Satan's Inquisition & Recount Their Management Pitfalls Through Imaginative Parables, Teaching Critical Insights & Management Wisdom for the '90s.
Zelos.

Escape from Volantium. Compatible Hardware: Atari 400, 800. Language(s): Atari BASIC. Memory Required: 16k. General Requirements: Joystick.
disk $19.95.
Escape an Alien World. Kill Guards & Maneuver Your Ship Through a Maze.
Dynacomp, Inc.

Escrow Exec. Version: 1.9. Jan. 1985. Operating System(s) Required: PC-DOS, MS-DOS. Memory Required: 128k.
disk $399.95.
Maintains Multiple Client/Customer Ledgers with Transactions & Balances Within a Single Checking Account. Prints Checks, or Allows for Handwritten Check Entry. Warns User if Client Balance Is Insufficient for Check. System Is Single Entry Type, Like a "One-Write" Manual System.
Data Source One, Inc.

Eshkolit.
IBM PC & compatibles. disk $34.95.
Nonstandard peripherals required: CGA, EGA or VGA display.
Hebrew Alphabet Game. Includes "What's Next?" Where Player Tries to Guess a Hidden Letter, & "Three's Company", a Timed Game Where Player Enters the Letter Following Three Consecutive Letters.
Davka Corp.

ESP. Version: 1.8. Mar. 1987. Compatible Hardware: IBM PC, Epson. Memory Required: 128k.
disk $100.00, incl. manual.
audio cassette instr. $15.00.
Full-Screen Text & Program Editor with an End Formatter & EQS Mathematical Typing Package. Includes Other Utility Programs (e.g. Print Utilities), On-Screen Demo, & Help Files. Features Single-Stroke Function Keys, Simple Word Commands, User-Defined Keys & Profiles, & Line-Drawing/Graphics Commands. END Adds Page Breaks, Page Number, Headers & Footers (All Adjustable), Performs Utility Services Such As Underlining, Implements Printer Features Such As Italics & Boldface, Half-Line Spacing Mode, & Footnotes. EQS Produces Greek & Other Special Symbols & Facilitates Super- & Subscripts. EQS Includes Special Instructions & Graphic Patterns for Mathematics on IBM/Epson-Compatible Printers, a Program for Converting Mathematical Symbols into Printer Instructions, & Keystroke Definitions.
Software Resources.

ESP - Accounting System. Customer Support: On site installation & training available.
Macintosh (4Mb). $750.00 plus a one time $250.00 per user license fee. Addl. software required: ESP - Sales & Office Management. Integrates with Time Management, Sales & Office Management, Estimating & Proposal Creation System, Inventory & Payroll Modules.
Designed to Handle All Your Bookkeeping Needs, with One Special Difference. Designed So That the Charting Decisions Are Determined During System Setup. From That Point on Very Little Bookkeeping Experience Is Needed for Daily Operations. There Is an Abundance of Detailed Ledgers, an Audit System That Leaves Nothing to the Imagination. The User-Direct Report System Offers Three Separate Default Formats for an Unlimited Number of Reports. The Finance Module Keeps Track of All Active & Inactive Bank Accounts As Well As Transactions. An Invoice Payable May Be Assigned to One Account with a Secondary Association & Job Costing May Be As Detailed As You Require. Printing Checks Is Accomplished with a Point & Click. Accounts Receivable Can Automatically Create Invoices from Jobs, Inventory or on the Fly.
CORGROUP Computer Operations Resource Group.

ESP - Estimating & Proposal Creation System. Customer Support: On site installation & training available.
Macintosh (4Mb). $325.00 plus a one time $250.00 per user license fee. Addl. software required: ESP - Sales & Office Management. Integrates with Time Management, Sales & Office Management, Accounting, Inventory & Payroll Modules.
Designed to Create Proposals Organizing Information to Fit Specific Requirements. Information May Be Stored with All Explanations & Cost Factors in a Global Library Making It Available for Future Proposals. Cost Factors May Be Tied to Inventory, Employee or Outside Contractors for Automatic Price Updating. Users May Connect Time Directly to Individual Cost Factors of an Estimate/Proposal or on a Time & Material Job, Create the Cost Factor. A Proposal May Be Changed to a Contract Automatically, Contracts to Invoices & Invoices to Account Posting. Print Work Orders Organized by Groups & Subgroups. Include Task Explanations, Do Percentage Modifications, Scheduling & When Used in Conjunction with ESP Accounting; Get Full Job Cost Analysis. Complete a Material List with Options to Include Vendors, Costs & Charges. Create a Billing Schedule with up to Six Progress Billings. Print Options Allow for Use of Form Documents, Custom or a Combination of Both.
CORGROUP Computer Operations Resource Group.

ESP: (Employee Stock Purchase). Version: 3.0. Language(s): Turbo Pascal. Memory Required: 512k. General Requirements: Hard disk. Customer Support: Application & technical telephone support, system training; updates & enhancements.
MS-DOS 3.1 or higher. IBM PC & compatibles. license $5000.00. Networks supported: LANS. $995.00 # annual service fee.
Automates Qualified (423b) Employee Stock Purchase Plan Administration. Supports Multiple Distributions under a Single Offering , Fixed or Rolling Offering Periods. Purchase Limitations & Calculates Purchase Price Based on Plan Parameters. Allows Import of Employee Data & Contributions. Reports Satisfy SEC, IRS & Internal Reporting Requirements.
ShareData (California).

ESP (Executive Sensory Perception). Version: 3.0. Items Included: Manual included with binder & slipcase, day binder for convenient transfer of information. Customer Support: On site installation & training services are available as well as customizing to specific needs.
Macintosh (4Mb). $1975.00 Set, plus a one time $250.00 license fee per additional user. Nonstandard peripherals required: Hard disk drive. Networks supported: Data Club.
Fully-Integrated Business Management System Available in Single or Multi-User Versions. System Is Designed to Meet Diverse Accounting, Customer Service, Sales, Inventory & Time Management Needs. The Basic ESP System Includes a Single User License, Time Management, Sales & Office Management, Estimating & Proposal Creation System, Accounting & Inventory & Purchase Order System. (ESP Payroll System May Be Purhcased Separately).
CORGROUP Computer Operations Resource Group.

ESP Inventory & Purchase Order System. Customer Support: On site installation & training available.
Macintosh (4Mb). $325.00 plus a one time $250.00 per user license fee. Addl. software required: Sales & Office Management.

TITLE INDEX

Integrates with ESP - Time Management, Sales & Office Management & Estimating & Proposal Creation System modules.
Controls the Movement & Timing of Inventory. Designed to Organize Supplies into Groups & Subgroups & to Maintain Information Such As: Cost, Charge, Unit Size, Stock, Supplier, & on Order Status. Features a Low Inventory Status System & Maintains Additional Information, Including Graphics, on Inventory; Such As Other Goods or Service Required with the Use of an Item. With Optional Fonts, Print Bar Code Labels. Subsystem Allows the User to Organize Inventories of Non-Resale Items Such As Assets & Price Only Lists. Users Can Create & Post Purchase Orders or Retain for Addition & Future Posting. Features the Ability to Review & Print the Purchase History of Any Given Item.
CORGROUP Computer Operations Resource Group.

ESP Office & Time Management. *Customer Support:* On site installation & training available.
Macintosh (4Mb). $325.00 plus a one time $250.00 per user license fee.
Key Feature Is Ability to Organize Information in Such a Way As to Make It Readily Available to Many People & Projects. Provides the Means to Handle Vast Amounts of Information in a Relaxed Manner. Organize Your Client, Vendor, Contract & Employees. Each Main Record May Have Any Number of Associated Records. Organize Information into Groups & Subgroups. All Communications May Be Recorded - Know What Letter Was Written & When. Keep Time & Date Stamped Notes on Conversations & Enter Automatic Follow up Reminders for Anytime Now or in the Future. Program Will Even Dial the Phone & Log the Call As Well As Tell Users the Time Zone. Simple Appointment Insertion into Your Appointment Book, Labels & Mass Mailing Are All Automatic. Includes ESP Time Management. Integrates with ESP - Time Managment, Estimating & Proposal Creation System, Accounting, Inventory & Purchase Order & Payroll Modules.
CORGROUP Computer Operations Resource Group.

ESP Payroll System. *Customer Support:* On site training & installation available.
Macintosh (4Mb). $1500.00 plus a one time $250.00 per user license fee. *Addl. software required:* ESP - Sales & Office Management.
Integrates with ESP - Time Managment, Sales & Office Management, Accounting & Estimating & Proposal Creation system modules.
Designed to Accurately Calculate Your Employee Payroll & Withholdings. Entries May Be As Detailed As You Require. Select the Proper Workers Compensation Code for Each Entry or Let the Default Stand. Users Enter from One per Pay Period to Any Number Required per Day. A Report & Tracking System Allows for Detailed Information on the Time Aspect on Any Job, Period or Employee Including True Hourly Costs. Track Payments Due on Workers Compensation. Print 8109 Reports, 941, 940 & W2's. Combined with ESP - Estimating & Proposal Creation System, Users May Connect Time Directly to Individual Cost Factor of an Estimate/Proposal or Create the Cost Factor on a Time & Material Job. State Specific Modules Are Sold Separately.
CORGROUP Computer Operations Resource Group.

ESP: Precognition, Clairvoyance & Telepathy. *Version:* 2.0. 1990. *Operating System(s) Required:* IBM. *Language(s):* BASIC (source code included). *Memory Required:* 48k.
disk $40.00.
One of the 15 Units of the "Discovering Psychology" Program. Runs Extrasensory Perception (ESP) Experiments Using Randomized Selection of Stimuli. User Predicts Item in a Series That Will Appear on Screen. Trial-by-Trial Feedback Is an Option. Analyses Include Raw Data Tables, Descriptive Statistics & Single Subject Test of Significance. Can Be Used by High Schools, Colleges, & Individuals.
Life Science Assocs.

ESP Test Researcher & Ancient Oracles PC.
Jan. 1996. *Items Included:* Instruction handbook.
DOS or Windows. PC (640k). disk $19.90 (ISBN 1-56087-130-X). *Optimal configuration:* Min. 286, DOS or Windows 3.1, 2k RAM.
A Dynamic PC Computer Program, That Provides Scientific Proof of ESP. Includes Three Simplified Training Programs for Reading Runes, Dice & Playing Cards. A Serious ESP & Research Program Where You Can Conduct Many Psychic Experiments Including Clairvoyance & Psychokinesis.
Top of the Mountain Publishing.

Espionage at International Electronics: Exploring WordPerfect. *Version:* 3.1. Steve Corder et al. 1996. *Items Included:* 1 disk, 1 teacher book, 70 pp.; 1 student activity text, 120 pp. Additional copies of activity text available for $10.95; 10 or more copies, each $9.95.
Customer Support: Call 1-800-341-6094 for free technical assistance, 30 day approval policy, money back guarantee.
Macintosh. 3.5" disk $69.95 (ISBN 0-8251-2781-5, Order no.: 0-27815). *Addl. software required:* WordPerfect 3.1.
Windows. IBM & compatibles. disk $69.95 (ISBN 0-8251-2782-3, Order no.: 0-27823). *Addl. software required:* WordPerfect 6.0.
Send Your Students on a Secret Mission to Find Out Who Stole the Files from International Electronics. This Flexible, Ready-to-Use Simulation Is a Motivating Way for Students to Sharpen Their WordPerfect Skills & to Begin Using Computer Applications As Problem-Solving Tools.
J. Weston Walch Pub.

ESPN & Pop Warner Interactive Football. Oct. 1995. *Items Included:* Brochure, warranty card, & license agreement. *Customer Support:* Unlimited telephone technical support - first 10 minutes free, $1.00 per minute thereafter.
DOS 5.0 or higher & Windows 3.1. IBM PC & 100% compatibles. CD-ROM disk $59.95 (ISBN 1-882284-33-X, Order no.: STF-01-MXC). *Nonstandard peripherals required:* SVGA video board sound card, CD-ROM.
Learn How to Improve Your Game with Expert Advice.
Intellimedia Sports.

ESPN Baseball: Hitting. Apr. 1994. *Items Included:* CD-ROM disc w/manual, brochures, warranty card & registration card. *Customer Support:* Free, unlimited technical support via 1-800 number.
3DO Player. CD-ROM disk $59.95 (ISBN 1-882284-14-3, Order no.: SBB-01-3DO).
The Hitting Title Demonstrates Correct Mechanics Such As the Stride & Launch Position, Swinging under Control & Adjusting to Pitches. Also Included Are the Mental Aspects of Hitting, Bunting, Rules of the Game, Hitting Drills, & Much More.
Intellimedia Sports.

ESPN Golf Lower Your Score with Tom Kite: Shotmaking. Apr. 1994. *Items Included:* CD-ROM disc w/manual, brochures, warranty card, & registration card. *Customer Support:* Free, unlimited technical support via 1-800 number.
3DO player. CD-ROM disk $79.95 (ISBN 1-882284-10-0, Order no.: SGK-01-3DO).
Provides Golfing Theories That Can Help Anyone Learn to Play a More Consistent Game. Shotmaking Includes Stroke Saving Shots, Sand Shots, Shots from Trouble & Games Around the Green. A Question & Answer Feature Called "Ask the Pro" Allows You to Get Score-Improving Advice from Kite & Sports Psychologist Dr. Bob Rotella on All Aspects of the Game.
Intellimedia Sports.

ESPN Interactive Baseball Playing the Field.
Jun. 1995. *Items Included:* Brochure, warranty card, & license agreement. *Customer Support:* Unlimited telephone technical support - first 10 minutes free, $1.00 per minute thereafter.
DOS 5.0 or higher & Windows 3.1. IBM PC or 100% compatible (8Mb). CD-ROM disk $59.95 (ISBN 1-882284-32-1, Order no.: STB-01-MXC). *Nonstandard peripherals required:* SVGA Video Board, Sound Card, CD-ROM.
Learn How to Improve Your Game with Expert Advice from Two Professionals - Ron Frasier & Tommy Lasorda.
Intellimedia Sports.

ESPN Interactive Golf: Tom Kite Shotmaking.
Version: 2.0. Sep. 1995. *Items Included:* Brochure, warranty card, & license agreement. *Customer Support:* Unlimited telephone technical support - first 10 minutes free, $1.00 per minute thereafter.
DOS 5.0 or higher & Windows 3.1. IBM PC or 100% compatible (8Mb). CD-ROM disk $59.95 (ISBN 1-882284-21-6, Order no.: SGK-01-MXC). *Nonstandard peripherals required:* SVGA Video Board, Sound Card, CD-ROM.
Learn How to Imiprove Your Game with Expert Advice from Golf's All Time Highest Money Winner - Tom Kite.
Intellimedia Sports.

ESPN Interactive Soccer: Skills & Strategies by Intelliplay. Aug. 1994. *Items Included:* CD-ROM disc w/manual, brochures, warranty card, & registration card. *Customer Support:* Free, unlimited technical support via 1-800 number.
MS-DOS 5.0 or higher, Windows 3.1. IBM PC & 100% compatible (4Mb). CD-ROM disk $69.95 (ISBN 1-882284-63-1, Order no.: SSO-02-MPC). *Nonstandard peripherals required:* CD-ROM w/150k transfer rate, 16 bit SVGA card w/512k VRAM memory. *Addl. software required:* Microsoft Windows 3.1. *Optimal configuration:* MPC Level 2 compliant machine.
An Interactive Personalized Coaching & Instruction Disc. You'll Learn: Basic Skills Including Fundamental Kick, Trap, Heading & Throwing Skills That All Players Need. Goalkeeping Instruction by Tony Meda on Positioning, Catching, Dives, & Ball Distribution. Offensive & Defensive Play - Covering Transitions, Channeling Press, Team Balance, Playing off the Ball & Much More.
Intellimedia Sports.

ESPN Let's Go Skiing. Oct. 1994. *Items Included:* Manual, brochure, warranty card & license registration. *Customer Support:* Free, unlimited technical support via 1-800 number.
3DO. 3DO. $59.95 SRP (ISBN 1-882284-64-X, Order no.: SSK-01-3DO).
Learn How to Ski More Effectively with ESPN's Interactive Sports Instruction Title.
Intellimedia Sports.

ESPN Let's Play Baseball. Jun. 1994. *Items Included:* CD-ROM disc w/manual, brochure, warranty card, & registration card. *Customer Support:* Free, unlimited technical support via 1-800 number.
MS-DOS 5.0 or higher, Windows 3.1. IBM PC & 100% compatible (4Mb). CD-ROM disk

$49.95 (ISBN 1-882284-59-3, Order no.: SBO-01-MPC). *Nonstandard peripherals required:* CD-ROM w/150k transfer rate, 16 bit SVGA card w/512k VRAM memory. *Addl. software required:* Microsoft Windows 3.1. *Optimal configuration:* MPC Level 2 compliant machine. 3DO system. CD-ROM disk $49.95 (ISBN 1-882284-58-5, Order no.: SBO-01-3DO). *Ozzie Smith, All-Star Shortstop & 13-Time Gold Glove Winner, Teaches You a Variety of Techniques That Can Help You Become a Complete & Winning Ballplayer. In Let's Play Baseball, "The Wizard of Oz" Shows You How to Perform All the Fundamentals That Add up to Game Winning Results.*
Intellimedia Sports.

ESPN Let's Play Baseball. Aug. 1994. *Items Included:* CD-ROM disc w/manual, brochures, warranty card, & registration card. *Customer Support:* Free, unlimited technical support via 1-800 number.
System 6.07 or higher. Macintosh with 68030/33 MHz or higher (4Mb). CD-ROM disk $49.95 (ISBN 1-882284-72-0, Order no.: SBO-01-MAC). *Nonstandard peripherals required:* Monitor support for 256 or more colors.
An Interactive, Personalized Coaching & Instruction Disc. You Will Learn Fundamental & Advanced Baseball Skills.
Intellimedia Sports.

ESPN Let's Play Beach Volleyball. Sep. 1994. *Items Included:* Instruction booklet, CD-ROM, warranty card, registration. *Customer Support:* Free technical support via 1-800 number.
300 Platform. CD-ROM disk $49.99 (ISBN 1-882284-68-2, Order no.: SBV-01-300).
Learn the Fundamentals As Well As the More Advanced Subjects on How to Improve Your Volleyball Game.
Intellimedia Sports.

ESPN Let's Play Beach Volleyball. Aug. 1994. *Items Included:* CD-ROM disc w/manual, brochure, warranty card & registration card. *Customer Support:* Free, unlimited support via 1-800 number.
MS-DOS 5.0 or higher. IBM PC or 100% compatible. CD-ROM disk $49.95 (ISBN 1-882284-68-2, Order no.: SBV-01-MPC). *Nonstandard peripherals required:* CD-ROM with 150k transfer rate, 16 bit SVGA card w/ 512k VRAM memory. *Addl. software required:* Microsoft Windows 3.1. *Optimal configuration:* MPC level 2 compliant machine.
Teaches the Fundamentals of the Game As Well As How to Improve Your Score.
Intellimedia Sports.

ESPN Let's Play Beach Volleyball. Aug. 1994. *Items Included:* CD-ROM disc w/manual, brochures, warranty card, & registration card. *Customer Support:* Free, unlimited technical support via 1-800 number.
System 6.07 or higher. Macintosh with 68030/33 MHz or higher (4Mb). CD-ROM disk $49.95 (ISBN 1-882284-26-7, Order no.: SBV-01-MAC). *Nonstandard peripherals required:* Monitor support for 256 or more colors.
An Interactive, Personalized Coaching & Instruction Disc. You Will Learn the Basics of Fundamental Volleyball As Well As Advanced Topics.
Intellimedia Sports.

ESPN Let's Play Soccer. Jun. 1994. *Items Included:* CD-ROM disc w/manual, brochures, warranty card, & registration card. *Customer Support:* Free, unlimited technical support via 1-800 number.
MS-DOS 5.0 or higher, Windows 3.1. IBM PC & 100% compatible (4Mb). CD-ROM disk

$49.95 (ISBN 1-882284-62-3, Order no.: SSO-01-MPC). *Nonstandard peripherals required:* CD-ROM w/150k transfer rate, 16 bit SVGA card w/512k VRAM memory. *Addl. software required:* Microsoft Windows 3.1. *Optimal configuration:* MPC Level 2 compliant machine. 3DO multiplayer. CD-ROM disk $49.95 (ISBN 1-882284-60-7, Order no.: SSO-01-3DO).
Great Soccer Instruction from World-Class Players John Harkes & Mia Hamm Help You Build Winning Soccer Skills at Your Pace. Play Better Defense - Learn the Basic Defensive Stance, How to Channel the Attack, Apply Pressure, Give Cover Help, Achieve Team Balance, & Make Good Decisions on the Field. Play Better Offense - Learn the Three Laws of Offense, How & When to Get Wide, Receive the Ball, Get Deep & Create Team Balance. This Program Shows You Just How Its Done, with Top-Quality Live Action Coaching - Plus Skill Building Drills You Can Practice on Your Own.
Intellimedia Sports.

ESPN Let's Play Soccer. Aug. 1994. *Items Included:* CD-ROM disc w/manual, brochures, warranty card, & registration card. *Customer Support:* Free, unlimited technical support via 1-800 number.
System 6.07 or higher. Macintosh with 68030/33 MHz or higher (4Mb). CD-ROM disk $49.95 (ISBN 1-882284-70-4, Order no.: SSO-01-MAC). *Nonstandard peripherals required:* Monitor support for 256 or more colors.
An Interactive, Personalized Coaching & Instruction Disc. You Will Learn Fundamental & Advanced Soccer Skills.
Intellimedia Sports.

ESPN Let's Play Tennis. Sep. 1994. *Items Included:* CD-ROM, manual, instruction booklet, brochures. *Customer Support:* Free, unlimited technical support via 1-800 number.
MS-DOS 5.0 or higher. IBM PC & 100% compatibles (4Mb). CD-ROM disk $49.95 (ISBN 1-882284-56-9, Order no.: STE-01-MPC). *Nonstandard peripherals required:* CD-ROM w/15k transfer ate, 16 bit SVGA card w/512k VRAM memory. *Addl. software required:* Microsoft Windows 3.1. *Optimal configuration:* MPC Level 2 compliant machine.
3DO machine. 3DO machine. CD-ROM disk $49.95 (ISBN 1-882284-54-2, Order no.: STE-01-3DO).
Puts You onto the Court with Former U.S. Open Champion Tracy Austin Plus Grand Slam Champions & ESPN Commentators Cliff Drysdale & Fred Stolle. These Top Professionals Use Step-by-Step, Live-Action Instruction to Help You Execute Better Strokes - & Teach You the Essentials of Successful On-Court Strategy.
Intellimedia Sports.

ESPN Let's Play Tennis. Sep. 1994. *Items Included:* CD-ROM disc w/manual, brochures, warranty card, & registration card. *Customer Support:* Free, unlimited technical support via 1-800 number.
System 6.07 or higher. Macintosh with 68030/33 MHz or higher (4Mb). CD-ROM disk $49.95 (ISBN 1-882284-71-2, Order no.: STE-01-MAC). *Nonstandard peripherals required:* Monitor support for 256 or more colors.
An Interactive, Personalized Coaching & Instruction Disc. You Will Learn Fundamental & Advanced Tennis Skills.
Intellimedia Sports.

ESPN Lower Your Score with Tom Kite: The Full Swing & Putting. Oct. 1994. *Items Included:* Manual, warranty card, response card. *Customer Support:* Free unlimited technical support via 1-800 line.
DOS 5.0 or higher. IBM PC & 100%

compatibles (5Mb). disk $69.95 (ISBN 1-882284-51-8, Order no.: SGK-02-MPC). *Addl. software required:* Windows 3.1, MPC compliant. *Optimal configuration:* SVGA with 16.7 million colors.
Interactive Sports Instruction Disc Designed to Improve Your Golf Game with Advice from Tom Kite. This Set Focuses on the Full Swing & Putting.
Intellimedia Sports.

ESPN Winning Hoops with Coach K. Jan. 1995. *Items Included:* Instruction booklet, manual, warranty card, brochure. *Customer Support:* Free, unlimited technical support via 1-800 line.
DOS 5.0 or higher. IBM & 100% compatibles (4Mb). disk $49.99 (ISBN 1-882284-36-4, Order no.: SBK-02-MAC). *Nonstandard peripherals required:* 16 bit sound card, SVGA video card with minimum 256 colors. *Addl. software required:* Windows 3.1 MPC compliant. *Optimal configuration:* MPC level 2 compliant machine.
Learn Fundamentals As Well As Advanced Game Winning with Professional Coaching from Coach K.
Intellimedia Sports.

ESQ-1. *Version:* 6.1. 1980. *Compatible Hardware:* IBM PC & compatibles, PC XT, PC AT, PS/2. *Operating System(s) Required:* MS-DOS. *Language(s):* CBASIC. *Memory Required:* 256k. *Customer Support:* Yearly support contract $500.00.
disk $1595.00.
Suited for the Attorney Who Works at Home or at the Office. Contains Accounts Receivable, Invoices & Multiple Time/Billing Rates.
KIS Computer Corp.

Essays on Cyberspace & Electronic Education. Paul Levinson. 1990.
DOS. Any type of IBM (64k). $19.95 (ISBN 1-56178-008-1).
DOS-Hypertext. Must run DOS 2 or higher (128k). $19.95 (ISBN 1-56178-025-1).
MAC. Any Type of Macintosh (64k). $19.95 (ISBN 1-56178-026-X).
Anthology of Essays on: Impact of Computer Telecommunications or Education, Evolution of Technology, Human Development of Outer Space, Impact of Media upon Human Thought & Cognition.
Connected Editions, Inc.

Essential Data Duplicator 4 (EDD 4). *Version:* 4.9. *Compatible Hardware:* Apple II, II+, IIe, IIc, IIgs, III (in emulation mode).
$29.95.
Copy Program Available for Backing up Uncopyable or Copy-Protected Disks. Features a High-Resolution Graphic DISK SCAN Option to Help Locate Information on a Disk, A CERTIFY DISK Option for Certifying Blank Disks, & an EXAMINE DISK DRIVE Option to Help Disk Run Properly.
Utilico.

Essential Data Duplicator 4 Plus (EDD 4 Plus). *Version:* 4.9+. *Compatible Hardware:* Apple II, II+, IIe, IIgs.
$129.95.
Copy Program Similar to EDD 4, but Also Includes a Hardware Interface Card for Greater Copying Power.(Duodisk, Platinum, & Unidisk 5.25" Disk Drive Owners Need Our $15 Cable Adapter).
Utilico.

Essex. Bill Darrah & William Mataga. *Compatible Hardware:* Apple II+, IIe, IIc, Macintosh; Atari 400, 800, XL, XE Series, 520 ST; Commodore 64; IBM PC & compatibles, PC XT, PCjr. *General*

TITLE INDEX

Requirements: 2 disk drives for Atari 400, 800, XL & XE Series.
disk $44.95 ea.
Apple II+, IIe & IIc. (Order no.: APDSK-1222).
Atari 520 ST. (Order no.: ATDSK-2291).
IBM. (Order no.: IBMDSK-4222).
Macintosh. 3.5" disk $44.95 (Order no.: MACDSK-5222).
Commodore. disk $39.95 (Order no.: COMDSK-3222).
Atari 400, 800, XL & XE Series. disk $39.95 (Order no.: ATDSK-2222).
Electronic Novel Featuring a Parser with over a 1200-Word Vocabulary & a Continuously Changing Real-Time Universe. Program Is an Intergalactic Search & Rescue Aboard the Starship "Essex" As It Races to Save the One Scientist Capable of Stopping the Destruction of the Universe. The Professor Has Been Forced to Crash-Land on an Isolated Planet Inhabited by Carnivorous Hamster People, the Vile Vollchons & Other Unknown Horrors.
Broderbund Software, Inc.

Estamore: Cost Estimating for Single Family Housing. *Items Included:* Bound manual. *Customer Support:* Free hotline - no time limit; 30 day limited warranty; updates are $5/disk plus S&H.
MS-DOS 2.1 or higher. IBM & compatibles (256k). disk $99.95. *Nonstandard peripherals required:* Printer supported.
Cost Estimator for Single Family Residences. Starts from the Concept Level, with Refinement As Desired. Once the Parameters You Deem Important Are Specified, Their Values Are Stored for Use in Future Estimates. Real Estate Agents Can Use ESTAMORE As a Sales Tool for Helping Clients Understand the Value of Their Selection & the Effect of Specific Requirements. Contractors Can Quickly Provide Ball Park Estimates & Refine Them for Bids. Lenders, Insurance Agents, & Appraisers Can Use ESTAMORE to Establish Values for Existing (Replacement Value) & New Houses. Prints Summary Reports, or Detailed Breakdown Reports by Category (Detail Sheets).
Dynacomp, Inc.

Estate Forecast Model. Sep. 1985. *Items Included:* Owners manual/software documentation & data gathering forms. *Customer Support:* Customer service is provided to all customers free of charge for 30 days after the purchase date. After that time, maintenance may be purchased at $150 per year.
IBM DOS. IBM compatible (640k). disk $695.00 Stand Alone Version (ISBN 0-943293-00-6).
Networks supported: Novell, Lantastic & Banyan.
Estate Forecast Model (EFM) Visually Explains the Concepts of Estate Planning, & Demonstrates Where the Need for Planning Exists. It Requires Minimal Data Entry & Allows the Planner to Develop & Compare "What If" Scenarios. Has 13 Different Scenarios; 706-Style Recap Reports; Calculates for All 50 States, Has Built-In Text Explanations; & Calculates Probate Expenses.
ViewPlan, Inc.

Estate Maximizer. Stephan R. Leimberg & Joseph Coluzzi. Mar. 1994. *Customer Support:* 30-day money-back guarantee, telephone support, facsimile service.
DOS. 386 or higher speed personal computer. disk $249.00. *Addl. software required:* Lotus 2.3 or higher. *Optimal configuration:* IBM PC or compatible system, 2Mb RAM, expanded memory driver DOS version 3.0 or higher, Lotus 123 version 2.3 or higher.
Windows. 386 or higher speed personal computer. disk $249.00. *Addl. software required:* Lotus or Excel for Windows. *Optimal configuration:* IBM PC or compatible system, 4Mb RAM, expanded memory driver, Windows version 3.0 or higher, Excel or Lotus 123 for Windows.
Unique Myth Breaker: The Only Way to Know If the Client Is Better off Paying Federal Estate Taxes at the First Death or Second Death. May Save Hundreds of Thousands of Dollars! Powerful Information Presented in Professionally Designed Reports.
Dynamic Financial Logic Corp.

Estate Planning Tools. *Version:* 9.00. Mar. 1992. *Operating System(s) Required:* PC-DOS/MS-DOS 2.0 or higher. *Language(s):* Pascal. *Memory Required:* 448k. *Items Included:* User manual & 12 months of maintenance coverage. *Customer Support:* 1-800-367-1040, Annual maintenance contract: $99.00.
3.5" or 5.25" disk $249.00.
Covers Tools & Techniques of Estate Planning As well As Business Valuation, Present Value & Future Value Calcs in 49 Areas. Includes GRATs, GRUTs, GRITs, Split Interests, Private Annuities, Charitable Remainder Trusts, Sec. 6166 Installments, Sec. 303 Stock Redemptions.
CCH ACCESS Software.

Estate Practice Assistant. Donald H. Kelley & Konrad Schmidt, III. Sep. 1991. *Items Included:* 1 perfect-bound manual, tri-annual newsletter "Subscriber News". *Customer Support:* Unlimited telephone access to toll-free technical support line during normal business hours is included with price of programs & subsequent updates. Training at customer's site is available starting at $600 for 4 hours.
PC-DOS/MS-DOS 3.1 or higher. IBM PC & 100% compatibles (640k). disk $350.00.
Optimal configuration: 12 CPI printer, hard disk. *Networks supported:* Novell A-Netware, AT&T Starlan, & Banyan Vines.
*1) Estate Planning: Calculates Federal Estate Tax (Includes Flow Chart) & Affects of Gifts/Growth; Calculates Split Interest Trusts, GRITs & QPRTs.
2) Form 706 Preparation: Calculates Annuity or Life Interest; Calculates S303 & S6166 Eligibility & Marital Legacy Funding. 3) Estate Administration: Calculates Estate Tax Attributable to IRD: Calculates S6166 Dispositions & Amortization; Calculat6s Form 706A.*
Shepard's/McGraw-Hill, Inc.

Estate Practice Assistant. Donald H. Kelley & Konrad Schmidt, III. Sep. 1991. *Items Included:* 1 perfect-bound manual, tri-annual newsletter "Subscriber News". *Customer Support:* Unlimited telephone access to toll-free technical support line during normal business hours is included with price of programs & subsequent updates. Training at customer's site is available starting at $600 for 4 hours.
PC-DOS/MS-DOS 3.1 or higher. IBM PC & 100% compatibles (640k). disk $350.00.
Optimal configuration: 12 CPI printer, hard disk. *Networks supported:* Novell A-Netware, AT&T Starlan, & Banyan Vines.
*1) Estate Planning: Calculates Federal Estate Tax (Includes Flow Chart) & Affects of Gifts/Growth; Calculates Split Interest Trusts, GRITs & OPRTs.
2) Form 706 Preparation: Calculates Annuity or Life Interests; Calculates S303 & S6166 Eligibility & Marital Legacy Funding. 3) Estate Administration: Calculates Estate Tax Attributable to IRD; Calculates S6166 Dispositions & Amortization; Calculates Form 706A.*
Shepard's/McGraw-Hill, Inc.

Estate Resource. *Version:* 3.96. 1996. *Compatible Hardware:* IBM PC. *Operating System(s) Required:* PC-DOS 3.1 & higher. *Memory Required:* 250k. *General Requirements:* Hard disk.
disk $795.00, incl. manual.
Financial Modelling of Estate Planning Strategies. Accesses Basic Data on Clients Assets, Form of Ownership & Structure of Wills. Determines Taxable Estate & Property Distribution. Includes Software for Basic & Advanced Estate Plans, As Well As Business Valuation Software, Social Security Benefits Calculation & More.
Benefit Analysis.

Estate Tax Planner. Harry S. Chud. May 1983. *Compatible Hardware:* IBM PC & compatibles, PC XT, PC AT. *Operating System(s) Required:* MS-DOS. (source code included). *Memory Required:* 64k. *Customer Support:* Free telephone Support.
disk $100.00.
Estate Planning Program Which Follows the IRS Form 706 for Both Input of Assumptions & Calculation of Results. Determines the Estate Tax on a Specific Set of Facts & These Facts Can Be Changed at Will to Determine the Change in the Estate Tax. The Program Can Help in Preparation of IRS Form 760 As the Results Section Follows the Form 706 by Line Number. It Also Can Determine Whether Trusts Can Help in Reducing the Estate Tax. Automatically Computes Most Tax Limitations. Play "What If", Make Changes or Additions. Recalculates & Selects the Lowest Tax Option. Input & Calculation Section Follows Forms. Can Modify, Use Graphics, Print Hard Copies, Scroll & Review & Unlimited Back-Up.
Accounting Professionals Software, Inc.

ESTAX. A. L. Moses. Nov. 1983. *Compatible Hardware:* IBM PC, PC XT, PC AT. *Operating System(s) Required:* PC-DOS 2.0. *Language(s):* BASIC (source code included). *Memory Required:* 384k.
IBM PC, PC XT, AT 386. disk $99.00.
disk $298.00.
Provides Estate Tax Projections for a Married Couple, Using 8 Different Marital Deduction Formulae, User Hypothetical Years of Death & User Supplied Inflation Factor. Takes into Account Scheduled Changes in Tax Rates & Credits.
Professional Data Corp.

Estimate. *Version:* 6.0. Jul. 1992. *Compatible Hardware:* IBM. *Operating System(s) Required:* MS-DOS. *Language(s):* QuickBASIC (source code included). *Memory Required:* 512k. *Items Included:* Manual/programs/installation support. *Customer Support:* Personal telephone contact.
$4500.00.
Estimates Costs of Labor, Materials & Purchases for Printing Jobs.
Printers Software, Inc.

Estimate: Job Cost Estimating System. *Version:* 2.2. Gerald E. Johnson. Jan. 1984. *Compatible Hardware:* Altos, IBC, Onyx, Seiko. *Operating System(s) Required:* Oasis. *Language(s):* BASIC. *Memory Required:* 64k. *General Requirements:* 2 disk drives, printer.
disk $1500.00 (ISBN 0-922660-01-8).
Multi-Function Program for Construction Cost Estimating. Designed for Use by Architects, Engineers, Contractors or Other Professionals Associated with the Construction Industry. Estimates Job Costs from Labor, Materials, Equipment, Fixed Quotes & Sub-Contracts. Detailed & Summarizec' Reports Are Formatted for Presentation.
Business Design Software.

Estimated Tax Penalties Calculator. *Version:* 4.01. Jul. 1992. *Items Included:* User manual, 12 months of maintenance coverage. *Customer Support:* Free telephone support: 1-800-367-1040, Annual maintenance contract: $39.00.
PC-DOS/MS-DOS 2.0 & higher. IBM PC &

ESTIMATING 4 CONSTRUCTION

compatibles (640k). disk $99.00 (Order no.: 1695).
Used for Quickly Calculating Estimated Tax Penalty Owed the IRS for Underpayments by Individuals & Corporations. Can Be Used for Prior Years or for Planning Future Estimated Payments. Fully Considers Rules under Code Sec. 6654(d)(1) & 6655(3)(B). Calculations Include Adjusted Seasonal Method, Annualized Income Worksheet, SE Tax Worksheet, 2210, 2220.
CCH Access Software.

Estimating 4 Construction.
Macintosh Plus or higher. 3.5" disk $1500.00.
Construction Take-Off & Estimating System.
Software Constructors, Inc.

The Estimator. *Customer Support:* 800-929-8117 (customer service).
MS-DOS. IBM/PS2. disk $99.99 (ISBN 0-87007-776-7).
A General Estimation Program Designed by an Architect, & Is Based on the Synthesis III Relational Database Management System. Designed for Use in Construction Estimation, & Efficiently Welds Ideas of a Spreadsheet & Data Together.
SourceView Software International.

The Estimator. *Version:* 1.1. Jun. 1990. *Items Included:* Disks, manual, sample data. *Customer Support:* 90 days free telephone support.
DOS version 3.0 or later. IBM & compatibles (512k). $795.00.
Combines Useful Features from Spreadsheets, Database Managers, & Word Processors into One Specialized Software Package for the Construction Estimator. Helps Builders & Contractors Perform Take-Offs, Produce Bids & Print Detailed Purchasing Lists. Features Include Unlimited Capacity for Items & Assemblies, Tracking of Subcontracts & Automatic Interface to YARDI's CONSTRUCTION ACCTG.
Yardi Systems.

Estimator Plus. *Compatible Hardware:* Apple Macintosh. *Memory Required:* 512k. *General Requirements:* Second floppy disk drive or hard disk; printer; Omnis 3 Plus.
3.5" disk $495.00.
Estimating & Job Cost Program.
Microserve, Inc.

ESTMAT 2000. *Version:* 1.20. 1978. *Items Included:* Getting started manual, primer, system guide, security booklet, installation guide. *Customer Support:* Through Dealer.
MS-DOS or PC-DOS. IBM & compatibles (640K). $5295.00 - $9495.00. *Nonstandard peripherals required:* Probe Box/Dallas Key. *Networks supported:* Novell.
Menu-Driven Estimating System Uses a Probe Device to Take-Off Quantities from Blueprints. Offers Built-in Branch Feeder & Switchgear Assemblies, Which Can Be Taken Off with a Single Key Stroke.
Software Shop Systems, Inc.

ETABS. *Version:* 5.4. *Items Included:* Complete set of program documentation, including User & Verification manuals. *Customer Support:* 1 year maintenance, 15% of program price.
MS-DOS. IBM PC AT or compatible (1Mb). $3000.00-$6000.00. *Optimal configuration:* 4MB RAM, 100Mb hard disk.
A Series of Large Capacity Computer Programs Specifically Developed for Three-Dimensional Analysis & Design of High-Rise & Low-Rise Buildings. Can Analyze Moment Frame, Braced Frame or Shear Wall Buildings, or Combinations of These.
Computers & Structures, Inc.

Etch-A-Sketch Magic Screen Machine. Sep. 1995. *Items Included:* Pocket Etch-A-Sketch toy, manual, CD ROM. *Customer Support:* 1 yr. free tech. support.
Windows 3.1 or higher. PC (4Mb). CD-ROM disk $29.95 (ISBN 1-888280-01-8, Order no.: 1501). *Addl. software required:* Windows. *Optimal configuration:* 386/25 or higher CD-ROM, Windows 3.1 or higher, 4Mb RAM, hard disk, VGA 256 color monitor.
Includes Six Engaging Computer Toys That Develop Essential Skills. Kids Are Challenged to Think & Be Creative. Each Unique Computer Toy Comes with All Kinds of Fun Push-Buttons, Switches, & Knobs That Lets Kids Develop & Build Skills in an Open, Exploratory, & Interactive Way.
Screen Magic, Inc.

Ethermail Server Kit. ThreeCom Corp. Feb. 1984. *Compatible Hardware:* TI Professional. *Operating System(s) Required:* MS-DOS 2.1, EtherShare Server Kit. *Memory Required:* 256k. *General Requirements:* Winchester hard disk, Etherlink.
$750.00 (Order no.: TI P/N 2239859-0001).
Facilitates Interoffice Communications by Sending Messages Through the Network Electronically.
Texas Instruments, Personal Productivit.

Etherprint Server Kit. ThreeCom Corp. Feb. 1984. *Compatible Hardware:* TI Professional. *Operating System(s) Required:* MS-DOS 2.1, EtherShare Server Kit. *Memory Required:* 256k. *General Requirements:* Winchester hard disk, Etherlink.
$500.00 (Order no.: TI P/N TI 2239865-0001).
Allows Many Users to Share the Same Printer by Queuing Printing Requests.
Texas Instruments, Personal Productivit.

Etherseries User Kit. ThreeCom Corp. Feb. 1984. *Compatible Hardware:* TI Professional. *Operating System(s) Required:* MS-DOS 2.1, EtherShare running in network. *Memory Required:* 128k. *General Requirements:* Etherlink (if Ethermail, running 192k RAM).
$96.00 (Order no.: TI P/N 2242853-0001).
Interconnects Computers into a Resource Sharing Local Area Network.
Texas Instruments, Personal Productivit.

Ethershare Server Kit. ThreeCom Corp. Feb. 1984. *Compatible Hardware:* TI Professional. *Operating System(s) Required:* MS-DOS 2.1. *Memory Required:* 256k. *General Requirements:* Winchester hard disk, Etherlink.
$500.00 (Order no.: TI P/N 2239853-0001).
Allows Many Users to Share Fixed Disk Resources in a Network.
Texas Instruments, Personal Productivit.

The Etiology of Cancer. *Version:* 2. Nadine Small. *Customer Support:* Toll-free technical support - no charge. In U.S. - 9AM-5PM EST 800-343-0064. In U.K. - 44(0)81-995-8242.
Microsoft Windows Version 3.1. 386 IBM - Compatible PC (4Mb). CD-ROM disk $175.00 Individual, $495.00 Institutional (ISBN 1-57276-003-6, Order no.: SE-003-002). *Nonstandard peripherals required:* MPC Standard CD-ROM player 640 x 480 display with 256 colors, MPC standard soundboard & speakers.
System 7.0 or higher. Apple Macintosh (4Mb). CD-ROM disk $175.00 Individual, $495.00 Institutional (Order no.: SE-003-002). *Nonstandard peripherals required:* CD-ROM drive.
This Multimedia Accelerated Learning Tutorial Addresses the Environmental & Genetic Causes of Cancer. It Combines Text, Graphics, Animation, & Clinical Images into an Interactive Format. Contains Chapters on: Introduction,

SOFTWARE ENCYCLOPEDIA 1996

Multistage Process of Carcinogenesis, Chemical Carcinogens, Initiation & Promotion of Tumors, Radiation, DNA Repair, DNA Tumor Viruses, RNA Tumor Viruses, Oncogenes & Proto-Oncogenes, Tumor Suppressor Genes, Colorectal Cancer As a Model for Multi-Stage Process of Carcinogenesis, Invasion & Metastasis.
SilverPlatter Education.

The Etiology of Cancer. *Version:* 2.0. Nadine Small. Aug. 1993. *Customer Support:* Toll-free technical support - no charge. In U.S. 9AM - 5PM EST 800-343-0064; in U.K. 44(0)81-995-8242.
System 7.0 or higher. Apple Macintosh (4Mb). CD-ROM disk $175.00, Individual, ,495.00 Institutional (ISBN 1-57276-003-6, Order no.: SE-003-002). *Nonstandard peripherals required:* CD-ROM drive.
Microsoft Windows, Version 3.1. 386 IBM-Compatible PC (4Mb). CD-ROM disk $175.00, Individual, ,495.00 Institutional. *Nonstandard peripherals required:* MPC Standard CD-ROM player, 640x480 display with 256 colors, MPC Standard Soundboard & speakers.
This Multimedia Accelerated Learning Tutorial Addresses the Environmental & Genetic Causes of Cancer. It Combines Text, Graphics, Animations & Clinical Images into an Interactive Format. Contains Chapters on: Introduction, the Multistage Process of Carcinogenesis, Chemical Carcinogens, the Initiation & Promotion of Tumors, Radiation, DNA Repair, DNA Tumor Viruses, RNA Tumor Viruses, Oncogenes & Proto-Oncogenes, Tumor Suppressor Gene, Colorectal Cancers As a Model for Multi-Stage Process of Carcinogenesis, Imasient Metas.
SilverPlatter Education.

ETOOLS: Electric Tools. *Items Included:* Manual. *Customer Support:* Toll free telephone support.
MS-DOS. IBM-PC & compatible (256k). disk $99.00.
Allows the Calculation of Eight Common Electrical Design Tasks Including: Wire Sizing, Conduit Sizing, Voltage Drop Calculations, Short Circuit Analysis, & Residential Panel Sizing, & the Quick Look-Up of Common Electrical Formulas & NEC Tables.
Elite Software Development, Inc.

Entreby System 2000. *Version:* 9.5. Sep. 1982. *Compatible Hardware:* IBM PC & compatibles. *Operating System(s) Required:* MS-DOS 3.30. *Language(s):* Pascal. *Memory Required:* 512k. *General Requirements:* Hard disk, printer.
disk $4950.00.
Business System Capable of Performing Manual Billing Functions. Generates Mailing Labels, Including Labels for Mass Mailings, & Itemizes Yearly Prescription Expenditures. Provides a Drug Profile for Each Customer, & Accesses Patient & Doctor Information. Provides Pricing Formulas, Prints Prescription Labels, Generates Receipts, & Monitors Drug Interactions.
Etreby Computer Co., Inc.

Euchre. *Compatible Hardware:* Atari 400, 800. *Language(s):* Atari BASIC. *Memory Required:* disk 48k. *General Requirements:* Joystick.
disk $19.95.
Traditional Card Game.
Dynacomp, Inc.

Eureka: The Solver. *Compatible Hardware:* Apple Macintosh; IBM PC & true compatibles; PC XT, PC AT, 3270 PC, Portable PC. *Operating System(s) Required:* PC-DOS/MS-DOS 2.0 or higher. *Memory Required:* IBM 384k, Macintosh 512k.
$99.95 (ISBN 0-87524-181-6).
Problem-Solving Program for Scientists, Engineers, Financial Analysts, & Students. Using

Pull-Down Menus & a Full-Featured Text Editor, Users Can Solve Most Problems in Algebra, Trigonometry, or Calculus. Can Also Graph a Function & Generate a Report. Includes Built-In Functions for Logarithmic, Exponential, Statistical, & Financial Calculations. Features Context-Sensitive Help, 8087 Math Coprocessor Support, & an On-Screen Calculator.
Borland International, Inc.

EuroFonts Video, 8 disks. *Compatible Hardware:* Commodore Amiga. *Items Included:* 3 manuals, reference charts, utilities, color ref. *Customer Support:* Phone support 206-733-8342.
3.5" disk $164.95.
High Quality, Antialiased Video Fonts. Three Formats: Set of Toaster Conversions, Broadcast Titler & Toaster Paint Sizes Range 30-120 Pixels High. Fonts Include Upper & Lower Case & Symbols. 2 to 6 Sizes Each. Utilities, Keycharts & Extensive Docs. Described in September 1991 AmigaWorld. Supports English, German, French, Spanish, Italian, Portuguese, Scandinavian, Latvian, Polish, Albanian & Others.
CLASSIC CONCEPTS Futureware.

European Challenge: Test Drive II Scenery Disk - The Collection. Feb. 1990. *Items Included:* Catalog, copy protection device, manual, proof of purchase card. *Customer Support:* Technical support 408-296-8400, 90 day limited warranty.
Amiga-Kickstart 1.2 or 1.3, Apple IIGS-Pro DOS 16 (512k). Amiga 500, 1000, 2000, Apple IIGS. $21.95. *Addl. software required:* The Duel: Test Drive II. *Optimal configuration:* Hard drive, keyboard, joystick, & graphics card.
Commodore (64k). $14.95. *Addl. software required:* The Duel: Test Drive II. *Optimal configuration:* Hard drive, keyboard, joystick, & graphics card.
IBM DOS 2.1 or higher, Tandy-DOS (384-CGA, MGA 512k EGA, Tandy 16 color). IBM PC, XT, AT, PS/2 models 25, 30, 50, 60, Tandy 1000 series, 3000, 4000. $21.95. *Addl. software required:* The Duel: Test Drive II. *Optimal configuration:* Hard drive, keyboard, joystick, & graphics card.
Car Driving Simulation. Some of the Toughest & Most Beautiful Roads in Europe: From the Northern Plains to the Central Mountains to the Southern Coasts.
Accolade, Inc.

European R & D Plus. *Items Included:* Annual Updates.
CD-ROM disk $1595.00 for 1 year (Order no.: RDB110).
Comprising both The Directory of European Research & Development & Who's Who In European Research & Development," European R & D Plus is the only work to cover both commercial & academic research & development activities in all scientific disciplines. It spans 36 Western & Eastern European countries (including all the European former Soviet republics), & profiles over 20,000 research facilities & 100,000 senior researchers, research managers, & consultants.
Bowker-Saur.

EuroScript. *Version:* 2.0. Nov. 1993. *Items Included:* User manual, Keyboard Layout Chart, Keycap Sticker Sheet. *Customer Support:* Free telephone support, defective disks replaced.
Macintosh. Macintosh (1Mb). 3.5" disk $49.95. *Addl. software required:* Any Word Processor. *Optimal configuration:* 4Mb RAM & a hard drive.
Use Your Own Standard Macintosh Fonts to Type French, German, Spanish, Portuguese, Danish, Norwegian, Swedish, Frisian, & Breton. Uses Regular Keys to Produce the Special Characters.
Linguist's Software, Inc.

EuroScript Text Converter. *Version:* 3.0. Oct. 1993. *Items Included:* User manual, Keyboard Layout Chart, Keycap Sticker Sheet. *Customer Support:* Free telephone support, defective disks replaced.
Macintosh. Macintosh (1Mb). 3.5" disk $79.95. *Addl. software required:* Any Word Processor. *Optimal configuration:* 4Mb RAM & a hard drive.
If You Type Phonetically on a Text-Mode Computer & Transfer That Text to a Mac, You Can Use Our Program EuroScript Text Converter to Convert the Files into the EuroScript-Controlled Language. Makes Cross-Platform File Transfer Possible. Available Only As an Upgrade to Another Full-Priced EuroScript Product.
Linguist's Software, Inc.

EuroSlavic. *Version:* 2.0. 1995. *Items Included:* User's manual; keyboard layout chart; keycap sticker sheet. *Customer Support:* Free telephone support, defective disks replaced free.
Macintosh. Macintosh (1Mb). 3.5" disk $99.95. *Addl. software required:* Any word processor.
$50.00 each additional typeface family when ordered at the same time.
Professional-Quality, Hinted, Type-1 & TrueType EuroSlavicLS Font in Plain, Bold, Italic, & Bold-Italic Styles with Polished Bitmaps in 10, 12, 14, 18, & 24-Point Sizes. Fonts Follow the Same Layout As Apple Central European (CE) Fonts. EuroSlavic Includes All the Characters for Typing in Albanian, Croatian, Czech, English, Estonian, French, German, Hungarian, Italian, Latvian, Lithuanian, Polish, Portuguese, Romanian, Slovak, & Slovenian. Also Gives You the Option of Nine National Keyboard Layouts: Croatian, Czech, French, German, Hungarian, Polish, Romanian, & Slovak, Plus a U.S. Keyboard with All of the Characters of the Eastern European Languages. Every Keyboard Is Able to Access Every Character in the SuroSlavicLS Font.
Linguist's Software, Inc.

EuroSlavic for Windows. Sep. 1994. *Items Included:* User's manual; keyboard layout chart; keycap sticker sheet. *Customer Support:* Free telephone support, defective disks replaced free.
Windows. IBM or compatibles (4Mb). disk $99.95. *Addl. software required:* MS Windows 3.1X or ATM.
Each additional typeface family when ordered at the same time $50.00; EuroSlavic Professional $249.95.
Features National Standard Keyboard Layouts for Croatian, Czech, French, German, Hungarian, Polish, Romanian, & Slovak Languages. Has the Characters & Accents for All Slavic Languages That Use the Roman Alphabet, with Most Accented Characters Available Without Typing Overstriking Accents. Contains Professional-Quality, Hinted, Plain, Bold, Italic, & Bold-Italic Styles (Except Chan Includes Plain Only) in Both TrueType & Type-1 Formats. For All Windows 3.1-Compatible Applications. Type-1 Works with ATM & Windows 3.1. WordPerfect for Windows Users Typing Overstriking Characters (Instead of Composite Characters) Must Upgrade to Version 6.0a or Newer.
Linguist's Software, Inc.

Evaluation of Obstructive Lung Disease by Pulmonary Function Testing. 1985. *Compatible Hardware:* Apple II+, IIe, IIc; IBM PC & compatibles. *Operating System(s) Required:* Apple DOS 3.3, MS-DOS. *Language(s):* BASIC. *Memory Required:* Apple 48k, IBM 512k.
disk $200.00 (Order no.: PIP-81304).
Identifies the Changes in Pulmonary Function Tests, Specifically Spirometry, Flow-Volume Loops, Lung Volumes, Single Breath Diffusion, & Cardio-Pulmonary Exercise, That Are Pathognomonic of Chronic Obstructive Pulmonary Disease (COPD). The Learner Will Identify the Presence of COPD & Classify Its Severity Based on the Results of Test Data Provided. The Learner Also Will Identify the Pulmonary Function Changes Seen in Asthma, Bronchitis, & Emphysema.
Educational Software Concepts, Inc.

Even More Incredible Machine. Sep. 1995. *Customer Support:* Telephone support - free (except phone charge).
Windows 3.1. IBM & compatibles (386 DX-20) (4Mb). CD-ROM disk $12.99 (ISBN 1-57594-009-4). *Nonstandard peripherals required:* 2x CD-ROM player, Sound Card, VGA monitor. *Optimal configuration:* 486 SX-33.
160 Brain-Twisting Puzzles.
Kidsoft, Inc.

Even More Incredible Machine. Sep. 1995. *Customer Support:* Telephone support - free (except phone charge).
Windows 3.1. IBM & compatibles (386 DX-20) (4Mb). CD-ROM disk $12.99 (ISBN 1-57594-048-5). *Nonstandard peripherals required:* 2x CD-ROM player, Sound Card, VGA monitor. *Optimal configuration:* 486 SX-33.
160 Brain-Twisting Puzzles. Blister Pack Jewel Case.
Kidsoft, Inc.

Event Log. Charles F. Cicciarella. Sep. 1991. *Items Included:* Staple bound user's guide, run time files of Microsoft Basic Professional Development System. *Customer Support:* Customer can call for technical assistance, no charge 704-398-1309. 90 days warranty on media only.
MS-DOS 2.11 or higher. IBM PC & compatibles (256k). disk $99.00 (ISBN 0-926152-71-8, Order no.: 71).
Mouse Driven System for Data Collection & Analysis for Observational Studies. Data Is Collected by Pointing with the Mouse on a Grid of Cells Representing Behaviors or Events Defined by the User. Each Cell in an Array of up to 10 X 10 May Be Used As a Counter & a Timer.
Persimmon Software.

Everybody's Planner. *Compatible Hardware:* Apple II series, IBM & all compatibles. *Memory Required:* Apple 64k, IBM 640k. *General Requirements:* Graphics card, mouse or paddles. *Items Included:* Manual. *Customer Support:* No charge telephone tech support.
Apple. 3.5" or 5.25" disk $99.95 (ISBN 0-939377-02-0, Order no.: 2010-011).
IBM. disk $99.95 (ISBN 0-939377-04-7, Order no.: 2010-312).
Create Project Plans & Flowcharts. Includes Two Complete Programs. Features Include Pull-Down Menus, Current & Alternate Calendars, Seven Text & Graphics Reports. Activation Feature Uses Color to Depict Flow Sequences.
Abracadata, Ltd.

Everybody's Planner. *Version:* 2.3.
DOS 3.0 or higher. disk $99.95 (Order no.: 74473420130 1). *Optimal configuration:* DOS, 640k, DOS 3.0 or higher, mouse & hard drive recommended.
Apple II (64k). disk $99.95.
A Simple & Effective Project Manager. With This Program Users Can Create Critical-Path-Based P.E.R.T. Charts, Graphs, & Project Scheduling Calendars for Projects up to 9 Years Long. Included in This Package Is a Free Flowcharts Program Which Uses 19 Rotatable Flowchart Shapes, & an Activation Feature for Using Color to Depict Flow Sequences.
Abracadata, Ltd.

Everybody's Planner: Scheduling & Flowcharting. *Items Included:* Bound manual. *Customer Support:* Free hotline - no time limit; 30 day limited warranty; updates are $5/disk plus S&H.
 MS-DOS 2.1 or higher. IBM & compatibles (256k). disk $99.95. *Nonstandard peripherals required:* CGA card; printer supported.
 Apple (64k). disk $99.95. *Nonstandard peripherals required:* Supports (though not necessary) paddles, mouse, & joystick; printer supported.
Tool for Planning & Graphically Depicting a Wide Range of Projects & Processes. Broken down into Two Major Functions; Scheduling & Flowcharting. Scheduling Features Include: Graphic Representations of Projects with Critical Path Plus Early & Late Start & Finish Dates; Sets up Current & Alternate Calendars, Work Sheet Templates, on/off Day Switches; Charts Resource & Task Slack Times; Full Editing Capability, Pull-Down Menus, Help Screens; Seven Reports - Task Charts, Resource Charts, Task Reports, Expense Reports, Task Costing, Resource Allocation Analysis/Resource Summary, & Project Summary; Handles Plans up to 5 Years Long (Through 2014), & Schedules up to 6 Full Screens. The Flowcharting Features Include: 20 Flowchart Shapes Which Can Be Rotated & Scaled to 9 Different Sizes; Small, Normal, & Bold Text Insertion, Vertical or Horizontal; Full Editing, Including Area Moves; Colored Activation Lines That Show the Flow; Unlimited Chart Size.
Dynacomp, Inc.

The Everything You Wanted to Know about Sports Encyclopedia.
 MS-DOS 3.1 or higher, Windows 3.1 or higher. 386 processor or higher (4Mb). CD-ROM disk $39.95 (Order no.: R1316). *Nonstandard peripherals required:* CD-ROM drive. *Optimal configuration:* 386 processor operating at 16MHz or higher, MS-DOS 5.0 or higher, Windows 3.1 or higher, 30Mb hard drive, mouse, VGA graphic adapter & VGA color monitor (SVGA recommended), 4Mb RAM, external speakers or headphones (with sound card) that are Sound Blaster compatible.
Produced in Cooperation with "Sports Illustrated for Kids," This Program Gives Children the Opportunity to Learn about Sports History, Master the Rules & Regulations of Any Sport, Check Out Stats & Play a Trivia Game to Test Sports Knowledge.
Library Video Co.

Everywhere U. S. A. Travel Guide. Dec. 1993. *Items Included:* User Guide. *Customer Support:* 30 day warranty.
 Windows. IBM & compatibles (4Mb). disk $19.95 (ISBN 1-885638-05-1). *Nonstandard peripherals required:* Sound Board.
A Comprehensive Resource of Travel Information Covering Every State & Region in the Country. This 2 CD-ROM Disc Set Contains More Than 6,000 Thousand Photos & over 80 Minutes of Full Motion Video Detailing More Than 3,000 Attractions & Events Throughout the U.S. Each Activity is Accompanied with an Up-to-Date Description, Address, Phone Number, Hours & Locator Map.
Deep River Publishing, Inc.

Evidence for the Litigator, 1991. Roger C. Park. Nov. 1991. *Items Included:* Booklet of background materials.
 IBM PC & compatible (128k). disk $79.00 (Order no.: K988).
 Macintosh (128k). 3.5" or 5.25" disk $79.00 (Order no.: K989).
Learning Package for Litigators & Trial Skill Trainers. May Be Used for Self-Instruction or In-House Training & Is Designed to Refresh & Strengthen New or Unpracticed Skills. Measures the Lawyer's Knowledge of the Federal Rules of Evidence & Ability to Recognize Evidentiary Questions. Using Vignettes & Trial Transcripts, the Exercise Simulates the Trial of a Personal Injury Case. The User Plays the Role of Judge &, under Steady Questioning by the Computer, Rules on Trial Counsel's Objections to the Admissibility of Particular Evidence. The Practitioner Is Then Asked to Justify These Rulings by Giving Reasons for Admitting or Excluding the Evidence in Question. The Exercise Provides a Survey of Evidence, Covering Such Topics As Hearsay, Opinion Evidence, Objections to Form, & the Best Evidence Rule.
American Law Institute.

The Evolution of Technology. David G. Hays. 1991.
 DOS. Any type of IBM (64k). $12.95 (ISBN 1-56178-016-2).
 DOS-Hypertext. Most run DOS 2 or higher (128k). $12.95 (ISBN 1-56178-015-4).
 MAC. Any type of Macintosh (64k). $12.95 (ISBN 1-56178-016-2).
Scholarly Monograph on History of Inventions from the Dawn of Humanity Through the 20th Century.
Connected Editions, Inc.

The Ewe-Ram Productivity System. *Compatible Hardware:* Commodore 64, 128; IBM PC & compatibles. *Operating System(s) Required:* MS-DOS, PC-DOS. *Language(s):* BASICA.
 disk $45.00.
IN-TEC Equipment Co.

Examinator: Simulation of the MS Windows Certified Professional Examinations. May 1993. *Items Included:* Guide & Owner's manual. *Customer Support:* 30-day limited warranty.
 Windows 3.1. IBM & compatibles (1Mb). disk $89.00 (ISBN 0-9635203-0-X). *Nonstandard peripherals required:* Printer optional, mouse optional. *Optimal configuration:* Windows 3.1, mouse.
Prepares Users to Become Certified by Microsoft Corporation & Thus Recognized As Windoes Experts. Certification Benefits Include a License from Microsoft to Use Windows Logo in One's Advertisements & Promotions, Including Business Cards, Letterhead, Circulars, Brochures, Yellow-Page Advertisements, Mailing, Banners, Resumes, & Invitations.
Transcender Corp.

The Examiner: Item Banking & Examination Administration. *Version:* 2.40. Stanley R. Trollip & Gary C. Brown. Jul. 1992. *Customer Support:* 1 year free maintenance; subsequent maintenance at $150.00/year.
 MS-DOS. IBM PC compatible (512k). $1195.00. *Optimal configuration:* 80286/80386 640k RAM, 1Mb extended, 1 floppy, 1 hard disk, DOS 3.1 or higher. *Networks supported:* Any network using standard DOS calls.
System of Programs for Development & Administration for All Types of Tests. Holds up to 99,000 Items Per Item Bank, with Unlimited Number of Item Banks. Sophisticated Classification Scheme. Delivers Both On-Line & Paper Tests, Including Graphics. Supports Scanners for Scoring & Stores Statistics for Examinee Records & Item Analysis. IBM PC Based.
The Examiner Corp.

ExampleKrafter. *Compatible Hardware:* Apple Macintosh. *Memory Required:* 512k. *General Requirements:* ImageWriter, LaserWriter or Linotronic.
 3.5" disk $49.95.
Musical Typesetting Software.
MusiKrafters Music Services.

Excel-Japanese. *Version:* 2.2J. Microsoft Corp. 1989. *Items Included:* User's manual & reference manual in Japanese. *Customer Support:* Telephone technical support.
 Macintosh KanjiTalk 6.0.7 or higher. Macintosh. 3.5" disk $699.00.
Japanese Version of Powerful Spreadsheet/Database Application; Includes All Excel 2.2 Features Plus Ability to Sort by Japanese & Assign Japanese Names to Fields & Values.
Qualitas Trading Co.

Excelsior Quiz 2. Jan. 1992. *Items Included:* Perfect-bound manual, installation sheet, on-line tutorial. *Customer Support:* Telephone support, newsletter.
 MS-DOS 3.3 or higher. IBM PC & compatibles. disk $155.00 (ISBN 1-878401-25-4). *Nonstandard peripherals required:* 2 disk drives. *Addl. software required:* Word processor. *Networks supported:* MS Netbios compatible (Novell, 3-COM, Vianet, etc.).
 System 6.08 or higher. Macintosh. 3.5" disk $155.00 (ISBN 1-878401-26-2).
Item Bank Management Program for Test Questions & Test Generation in a Windows-Like Environment. Features Include Question Formatting & Graphics with Some Word Processors, Choosing or Omitting Specific Questions, Selective Testing Based on Various Criteria, Generating Matching Answer Sheets & Answer Keys, & Sorting Questions on Exams.
Excelsior Software, Inc.

Exchange Calculator. *Compatible Hardware:* Apple Macintosh.
 contact publisher for price.
Calculates Diabetic Exchanges.
MFE Assocs.

Exciting Experiences of Love. *Version:* 2.0. Rob Reinish. Aug. 1995. *Items Included:* CD, instruction booklet. *Customer Support:* 801-253-2522.
 Windows 3.1, Windows 95. PC (4Mb). CD-ROM disk $29.95 (ISBN 1-887867-01-5). *Nonstandard peripherals required:* CD-ROM drive. *Optimal configuration:* 8 Mb, Sound card, True Color monitor.
Developed to Encourage Communication & Intimacy Between Loving Couples. Uses Text Display Voice, Music, Graphics & the Presentation Logic to Guide Players Through a Broad Range of Romantic & Sensuous yet Tasteful Adventures.
Relationship Software, LLC.

Exciting Experiences of Love. Sep. 1995.
 CD-ROM disk $29.95 (ISBN 1-887867-01-5, Order no.: EE20SC).
Relationship Software, LLC.

eXclaim! RealTime Spreadsheet. *Version:* 0.9. *Items Included:* 1 spiral bound manual. *Customer Support:* Installation support up to 60 days. Maintenance after 60 days is 25% of product price. (These terms are flexible since product is still in beta version).
 UNIX, XENIX. Most computers (UNIX). From $1850.00 per CPU.
X Windows, Realtime Spreadsheet Provides Spreadsheet Analysis of Continuously Updated Prices from RealTime Datafeeds. Monitors Price & Analysis, Generates Alert Messages, Makes Calls to SQL Databases in Historical Data, & Export Results to Other Applications. Provides Advanced X Features Including Mouse Control, Pull-Down Menus, Dialog Boxes & X Graphics. File, Function & Marco Compatible with LOTUS 1-2-3.
UniPress Software, Inc.

TITLE INDEX

eXclaim! Spreadsheet. *Version:* 0.9. *Items Included:* 1 spiral bound manual. *Customer Support:* Installation support free up to 60 days. Maintenance after 60 days is 25% of product price. (These terms are flexible since product is still beta version).
UNIX, XENIX. Most computers (SUN, DEC, IBM, MP, Sony, DataGeneral, SCO, Apollo, etc).
Priced from $695.00 per CPU.
X Window Spreadsheet Compatible with LOTUS 1-2-3 Files, Macros & Functions. Offers a Full Complement of Math, Statistical & Logical Functions. With the Mouse Users Can Control the Cursor, Invoke Commands, Select All Regions, Change Column Widths & Heights, Paste Range & Function Names. Pull Down Menus, Dialog Boxes. Business Graphics Included, Displayed in X Windows.
UniPress Software, Inc.

Exec-Amort - Loan Amortizer Plus. *Version:* 2.06. Feb. 1987. *Compatible Hardware:* IBM PC, PC XT, PC AT, PS/2 & true compatibles. *Operating System(s) Required:* PC-DOS/MS-DOS 2.12 or higher. *Memory Required:* 205k. *Customer Support:* Yes.
IBM. 3.5" or 5.25" disk $149.95 (ISBN 0-929800-00-1, Order no.: EC5.25 OR EC3.5).
Novell. 3.5" or 5.25" disk $450.00 (ISBN 0-929800-01-X, Order no.: ECN5.25 OR ECN3.5).
Provides Full Loan Amortization Calculations & Reports. Performs Prepaid Interest Calculations, 360 Day, 365 Day & Actual/360 Day Interest Calculations. Permits User Definable Rounding for: Interest & APR/IRR/Yield Computations. Also Provides Odd Period Calculations & an Extra Payment System. User Friendly Features Include: Menu Selection, Consistent Terminology, & Data Entry Format, Full Text & Number Editing Capabilities, Context Sensitive Help Screens, & Save & Load Client Information to/from Disk.
Electrosonics.

EXECPLAN. *Version:* 3.33. Feb. 1996. *Compatible Hardware:* IBM PC, PC XT, PC AT & compatibles. *Memory Required:* 640k. *General Requirements:* Hard disk, 5.0Mb. *Customer Support:* 30 day guarantee, 90 day free support & maintenance; $695/yr; phone support, all updates & new version releases (20% early pymt. discount).
disk $1995.00.
Comprehensive, Fully Integrated, Versatile Personal Financial Planning System for Use by Professional Financial Planners. Features Include: Thorough Implementation of Federal Income Taxes, Specific State Income Tax Implementation, Financial Profiles Projected up to 100 Years with Full Reports Available for Each Year, Complete Estate Planning, Cash Management Simulation, Investment Planning, Capital Needs Analysis. Over 106 Reports with Integrated Text Reporting & Full Dynamic Report Customization & Education & Special Funding Analysis. Interfaces for Data Transfer with DBCAMS. Runs As DOS Program Using Windows Environment; Also Fully Integrated Graphics Program Included.
ExecPlan, Inc.

EXECUSTAT, 4 disks. *Version:* 3.0. Apr. 1992. *Compatible Hardware:* IBM PC & compatibles, PC XT, PC AT. *Operating System(s) Required:* DOS 2.0 or higher. *Memory Required:* 640k. *General Requirements:* Hard disk with 4Mb RAM, mouse support avail. *Items Included:* Full documemtation including tutorials. *Customer Support:* No current charges for support.
$375.00.
Integrated Data Analysis & Graphics Package Designed for Use by Non-Experts. Covers Basic Statistics, Exploratory Data Analysis, Regression, Plotting, Estimation & Forecasting, Quality Control. Useful in Market Research, Financial Analysis, Sales Forecasting, Quality Assurance. Features: Statistical Interpreter, Which Explains Results of Numerical Calculations in Simple Terms; Modern User Interface; 350 Page Hypertext Help System.
Strategy Plus, Inc.

Execution Time Profiler. *Compatible Hardware:* HP series 200, series 300. *Language(s):* BASIC (source code included).
$195.00, incl. 10 other utilities.
Prints out the Percentage of Total Program Execution Time Which Is Used by Each Line of a Program. Also Includes: UNIVPLOT, a Graph Plotting Program, COMPARE, Which Compares 2 Versions of the Same Program & Prints out Their Differences, CRUNCH, Which Reduces Files on Disk to Their Minimum Length, CALENDAR, Which Prints a Calendar for Any Modern Year, & RNDGRAPH, Which Produces Graphic Designs Based on the Random Number Generator.
James Assocs.

Executive Alert System. *Compatible Hardware:* IBM PC. *Memory Required:* 64k.
disk $250.00.
Designed to Provide Decision Support for the Executive That Tracks Various Key Indicators of Company Performance. Allows User to Do Projections & Year-to-Date Totals. The Completed Information Is Printed or Displayed in Numbers or Bar Charts. Contains 26 Pre-Defined Indications, but Allows User to Replace or Add More.
Lifeboat Assocs.

Executive Assistant. Mark Haley. Jun. 1985. *Compatible Hardware:* AT&T; Compaq; HP Vectra; IBM PC & compatibles, PCjr, PC XT, PC AT; ITT, NCR; Tandy; TeleVideo; Zenith. *Operating System(s) Required:* PC-DOS. *Memory Required:* 384k. *General Requirements:* 300/1200 baud Hayes or compatible modem for MCI Mail or AT&T Mail.
disk $150.00.
Word-Processor, Database Manager, Appointment Calendar, with Added Communications Features (Includes a Sign-On for MCI Mail). Together These Services Turn PC into a Communication Device: Users Can Send Regular or Electronic Mail, Telexes or Overnight Mail, or Can Use the Word Processor to Type Memos & Print Them on Their Printer or LaserJet. Memos Can Be Printed at User's Desk or Be Sent Anywhere with MCI MAIL.
Analytical Software, Inc.

Executive Challenge: OPT Thoughtware. Creative Output, Inc. Sep. 1986. *Compatible Hardware:* IBM & compatibles. *Memory Required:* 128k.
Regular version. disk $89.95 (ISBN 0-88427-064-5).
Advanced version. disk $200.00.
Manufacturing Simulation Complete with Inventory Fluctuation Through Finished Goods. Includes Documentation, Clues & Quiz. Shows How to Increase Profits Through Better Control of Manufacturing. Based on the Optimized Production Technology Principles of Manufacturing.
North River Pr., Inc.

Executive Chess. *Customer Support:* 800-929-8117 (customer service).
MS-DOS. IBM/PS2. disk $79.99 (ISBN 0-87007-450-4).
An Easy-to-Operate, Graphics Oriented Chess Game.
SourceView Software International.

EXECUTIVE PHONE DIRECTORY

Executive Computing in BASIC: The IBM Personal Computer. Peter Mears. Edited by Paul Becker. Jun. 1984. *Compatible Hardware:* IBM PC.
disk $39.95, incl. bk. (ISBN 0-03-064129-2).
Reinforcement Exercises & Problems to Expedite the Learning of BASIC Programming Concepts.
Dryden Pr.

Executive Cursor Control: Joystick Support Software. Jeff Pack. 1984. *Compatible Hardware:* IBM Plug compatible. *Operating System(s) Required:* MS-DOS 2.0 or higher. *Memory Required:* 64k.
disk $39.95 (Order no.: 820024).
Combined with the Kraft Precision Joystick Provides User with a Rapid & Convenient Method of Cursor Movement. The Program Lets User Move the Cursor Across the Screen or Scroll down Through Lines of Data. User Can Duplicate Any Individual Key or Command Keystrokes by Assigning Them to the Joystick Buttons. Experienced Users Will Find That the Joystick Buttons Can Be Assigned a Different Function Within Each Program Directory.
Kraft Systems Co.

Executive Health Expert. *Version:* 4.01. *Compatible Hardware:* IBM PC & compatibles. *Operating System(s) Required:* PC-DOS, MS-DOS. *Memory Required:* 256k. *General Requirements:* Hard disk recommended. *Items Included:* 32 pg. Thinking Software catalog.
3.5" or 5.25" disk $34.95.
Helps Users Assess Their Health. The Ten Categories Available Include: Heart Problems, Respiratory Problems, General Health, Sexual Problems, Emotional Problems, etc. There Are Over 3500 Rules in the Knowledge Base. Consultations Average from 15 to 30 Minutes & Users Are Advised to Consult a Doctor When Professional Help Is Required.
Thinking Software, Inc.

Executive Interface. Gerald E. Johnson. Oct. 1985. *Operating System(s) Required:* OASIS. *Memory Required:* 64k. *General Requirements:* 2 disk drives or hard disk.
disk $350.00 (ISBN 0-922660-03-4, Order no.: EIS-1085).
Menu-Driven Program That Interfaces with the User's CPU. All Functions Are Handled by Number Choice.
Business Design Software.

Executive Mastery Accounting. *Customer Support:* 800-929-8117 (customer service).
MS-DOS. IBM/PS2. disk $299.99 (ISBN 0-87007-660-4).
A Full Featured General Accounting System. Allows User to Make Changes & Additions to the Source Code. Includes Full Source Code & Documentation on Several Disks, GL, AP, AR, Fixed Assets, Inventory & Payroll.
SourceView Software International.

Executive MemoMaker. *Compatible Hardware:* HP 150 Touchscreen.
3.5" disk $245.00 (Order no.: 45418A).
Assists the Business Professional in Creating Letters, Memos, & Reports. Includes a Merged Graphics Feature Allowing User to Position Graphics Right Next to Text Without Cutting & Pasting. Also Includes MEMOSPELLER Which Finds Misspellings & Suggests Corrections.
Hewlett-Packard Co.

Executive Phone Directory. Charles W. Evans. *Compatible Hardware:* IBM PC, PCjr, PC XT, PC AT, Portable PC, 3270 PC with IBM Display & Asynchronous Adapter, Autodialing Modem (optional for automatic dialing). *Operating System(s) Required:* DOS 1.10, 2.00, 2.10, 3.00,

3.10. *Memory Required:* 128k.
disk $34.95 (Order no.: 6276528).
Designed for Office & Personal Phone Use. Can Be Used for Locating Phone Numbers, for Generating Specialized Mailing Lists, or for Automatic Dialing. Accepts up to Eight Separate Directories (Each up to 500 Entries), or Can Accept an 8000 Entries Directory Produced with EXECUTIVE PHONE DIRECTORY BUILD YOUR OWN.
Personally Developed Software, Inc.

Executive Phone Directory Build Your Own. Charles W. Evans. *Compatible Hardware:* IBM PC, PC XT, PC AT, Portable PC, 3270 PC. *Operating System(s) Required:* DOS 1.10, 2.00, 2.10, 3.00, 3.10. *Memory Required:* 128k. *General Requirements:* Executive Phone Directory (Message Feature optional); 2 disk drives or hard disk recommended.
disk $149.95 (Order no.: 6276524).
Takes Data from a Variety of Input Files & Collates & Indexes Information to Put It into the Directory Format Specified by User. Directory Size Is Limited Only by Diskette Size (about 8000 Entries on a 360k Formatted Floppy).
Personally Developed Software, Inc.

Executive Phone Directory with Message Feature. Charles W. Evans. *Compatible Hardware:* IBM PC, PCjr, PC XT, PC AT, Portable PC. *Operating System(s) Required:* DOS 2.10, 3.00, 3.10. *Memory Required:* 128k. *General Requirements:* IBM Display, IBM Personal Computer Cluster Adapter, Asynchronous Adapter, modem (auto-dialing optional), IBM Cluster program; IBM Matrix Printer optional.
disk $39.95 (Order no.: 6276533).
Offers All the Directory Services of EXECUTIVE PHONE DIRECTORY Plus a Phone Message Generation & Forwarding Function. Phone Messages Received at One Terminal Can Be Dialed Automatically As the User Edits His/Her Own Message List.
Personally Developed Software, Inc.

Executive Phone-Mailer. *Items Included:* Bound manual. *Customer Support:* Free hotline - no time limit; 30 day limited warranty; updates are $5/ disk plus S&H.
MS-DOS 2.1 or higher. IBM & compatibles (128k). disk $49.95. *Nonstandard peripherals required:* Parallel printer port; two double-density disk drives, or one drive & a hard disk.
Database System for Maintaining Addresses & Phone Numbers. In Addition to the Normal Address Information, User Can Include Company Name, Home & Office Phone Numbers (Including Area Codes), & a One-Line Comment. User Has Flexibility in Setting Both the Address "Field" Widths As Well As Label Width (One-Up or Two-Up Labels) & Spacing. Labels Can Be Printed Alphabetically by Name, by Selected City or State, by Area Code, or in ZIP Code Order. Multiple Labels for a Selected Person Can Also Be Printed.
Dynacomp, Inc.

Executive Plus. *Customer Support:* 800-929-8117 (customer service).
MS-DOS. IBM/PS2. disk $99.99 (ISBN 0-87007-383-4).
An Integrated Package That May or May Not Reside in RAM, Includes a 500 Line Word Processor with a Full Set of Editing Functions. Works Closely with Notebase. Mailmerges with Customizable Information in th Rolodex. Full Function Calculator & Calender are Included. Task Management is Simplified by Enabling the Customixable Recording of Important Activities Data under Each Rolodex Entry, or Directly. Encryption of Files is an Additional Feature for the Security Minded.
SourceView Software International.

Executive Search System. *Version:* 96.1. *Compatible Hardware:* IBM PC & compatibles. *Operating System(s) Required:* PC-DOS/MS-DOS 2.0 or higher, Windows 3.0 or higher. *Memory Required:* 384k.
disk $150.00, one issue.
$400.00 annual subscription (six issues).
Consists of a Database & Windows or DOS Software That Mergers User's Personalized Cover Letter with the Names & Addresses of Approximately 5000 Recruitment Firms. Users Can Print Cover Letters, Envelopes, & Mailing Labels. Firms Can Be Selected by Industry, Geographical Location, & Job Category. Database Updated 6 Times per Year.
Custom Databanks, Inc.

Executive Writeone System. *Compatible Hardware:* B-20 series, B-22. *Operating System(s) Required:* BTOS. *Language(s):* PL/M, Assembly. *Memory Required:* 256k. *General Requirements:* Printer.
disk $500.00.
Designed to Provide Basic Editing Capabilities for Single or Multiple Users. Performs Word Processing Functions, Create, Edit, View & Print. Provides Automatic Text Formatting, Rapid Text Entry, Insertion, Deletion, Movement & Copying of Text, & Additional Functions. Print Capabilities Include: Number of Copies to Be Printed, Option to Print Individual Pages, & Direct or Spooled Printing.
Burroughs Corp.

The Executive's Guide to the IBM PC: BASIC Programming & VisiCalc. *Compatible Hardware:* IBM PC.
disk $39.95.
Demonstrates Business Programming for Accounts Receivable, General Ledgers, etc. & Provides Applications & Instructions on How to Get Started.
Prentice Hall.

The Executive's Market Decision Kit. May 1989. *Items Included:* User manual & software tutorials. *Customer Support:* 30 day money back guarantee, free phone support, on line tutorials & help in software.
DOS or O/S2 (256k). IBM PC, XT, AT, PS/2 or compatibles. $299.00 (US & Canada), $349.00 (International). *Nonstandard peripherals required:* CGA, EGA, VGA, or Hercules graphics board. *Addl. software required:* Lotus 1-2-3 release 2, 2.01, 2.2, or 3. *Optimal configuration:* IBM PCAT, DOS 2.1 or higher, 640k RAM, EGA board, 1-2-3 release 2 or higher. *Networks supported:* All that are supported by Lotus 1-2-3.
Helps Business Executives to Select Target Markets, Price Products, Evaluate Proposed Advertising Programs, & Prioritize Sales Leads for Ensuring Efficient Use of Sales Resources.
Successware.

Executive's Time Value. 1982. *Compatible Hardware:* MS-DOS based machines; IBM. *Language(s):* Microsoft BASIC.
disk $45.00 (Order no.: 258).
Takes the Executive Through a Self-Analysis of His/Her Own Priorities & Computes Cost of Efforts.
Resource Software International, Inc.

Exodus for the Macintosh. *Version:* 4.0. *Items Included:* Free Networking Software for DECNET & TCP/IP Networks. *Customer Support:* 90-day unlimited technical support.
Macintosh Plus or higher. 3.5" disk $295.00.
X Window Display Server.
White Pine Software, Inc.

ExoSquad: Interactive MovieBook. *Version:* 1.5. Nov. 1995. *Items Included:* Manual, registration card, promotional flyers. *Customer Support:* Phone technical support - toll call.
Windows 3.1 or higher. 386/33 or higher (8Mb). CD-ROM disk $29.95 (ISBN 1-57303-027-9). *Nonstandard peripherals required:* Sound card, CD-ROM drive. *Optimal configuration:* 486/33 with 8Mb RAM, Win 3.1 or higher 2X CD-ROM drive, SVGA monitor.
An Exclusively Licensed Computer Adventure/ Activity Book for Children. The Story of the ExoSquad Is Told in a 50-Page "History" Book Loaded with Interactive Animations, Movies, Sounds, & Educational Activities. There Is an Area Where Kids Can Design Their Own E-Frames, & the ExoFleet Center That Introduces "Cadets" to the Basics of Flight Through Creating Their Own Paper Airplanes with Official ExoFleet Insignias.
Sound Source Interactive.

The Exotic Garden: The Ultimate Guide to Growing Plants. Dec. 1993. *Customer Support:* Phone support.
Windows 386SX or higher, Windows 3.1 or higher (2Mb). CD-ROM disk $34.95 (ISBN 1-884076-01-7, Order no.: 408-464-1552). *Nonstandard peripherals required:* MPC1 compatible sound board (optional) MPC4 CD-ROM players, mouse. *Optimal configuration:* 486 or higher, 4Mb RAM, sound board.
Users Can Learn Thousands of Helpful Growing Tips & View High Quality, Color Photographs of Bromeliads, Cacti, Ferns, Herbs & Edibles, Orchids, Palms, & Other Flowering & Foliage Ornamental Plants. Explore Time Lapse Cinematography of Flowers, Seed & Fruit Development. Novices Can Access the Step-by-Step Basics to Growing Indoor Plants; While Experts Can Investigate More Detailed Information & Access Latin Names. Intended for Any Plant Enthusiast, Users Can Conduct Searches with the Option of Four Different Search Paths. Enhance Your Indoor/Outdoor Environment with The Exotic Garden - the Ultimate Guide to Growing Plants.
VT Productions, Inc.

Expanded Pharmacy Software. *Version:* 110D. 1985. *Compatible Hardware:* Altos; IBM. *Operating System(s) Required:* MP/M-86, CP/M-86, MS-DOS, Concurrent CP/M, Concurrent DOS. *Memory Required:* 512k.
$4000.00.
Enhanced Version of STANDARD PHARMACY SOFTWARE PACKAGE Which Provides Retail Pharmacies with a Single Entry, Menu-Driven System That Handles up to 50 Third Party Plans, & Provides Labels, Receipts, Patient Profiles, Bilingual Label Instructions Daily, & Narcotics Reports. Also Handles up to 10 Different Pricing Plans & Provides Flags for Interactive Drugs. Can Be Upgraded to the Universal System.
Dagar-Software Development Corp.

Expedition. *Version:* 4.1. May 1993. *Operating System(s) Required:* PC-DOS/MS-DOS. *Memory Required:* 640k. *Customer Support:* First year free telephone support & upgrades. Additional years at 20% purchase price.
disk $2500.00.
Organizes Information for Construction & Engineering Contract Control. Prepares Transmittals, Correspondence, Tracks Submittals, Change Orders, Bids, Material Deliveries & Requisitions for Payment. Also Creates Reports, Meeting Minutes & Dunning Letters. Links Issues for Quick Review & Retrieval of Information. Multi-User.
Primavera Systems, Inc.

Expense Account Manager. *Version:* 3.0. *Compatible Hardware:* IBM PC & compatibles. *Operating System(s) Required:* MS-DOS 2.0 & later. *Memory Required:* 420k. *General Requirements:* Printer.
disk $99.00.
Designed to Organize & Track Travel & Entertainment Expenses. Benefits Business Executives & Individual Professionals Such As Corporate Managers, Attorneys, Accountants, Salesmen, Consultants, Physicians, & Anyone Else Whose Business Takes Them out of the Office for Periods of Time. Specific Features Include Entry & Correction of Travel/Entertainment Expenses, Reminders of Expenses That Are Often Overlooked, Prompting for Specific Information Required by the IRS, & Budget Projections. Automatically Reconciles Travel Advances & Tracks Reimbursements. An Interface to LOTUS 1-2-3 & Other Spreadsheets Provided to Allow Additional Reporting of the Expense Data. Provides for Foreign Currency Conversion & Graphs of Spending. Prints Pocket Recording Sheets to Record Expenses As They Are Incurred. Change the Definitions of the Expense Items, Budget Lines, & Subtotals Without Any Computer Programming.
Adaptive Software.

Expense Management. *Compatible Hardware:* TRS-80 Model III.
contact publisher for price.
Citation Systems.

Expense Report! *Version:* 1.01. Aug. 1992. *Items Included:* Manual. *Customer Support:* 30 day money back guarantee, free telephone.
DOS 3.0. IBM PC & compatible (512k). $90.00 single user. *Networks supported:* Novell, PC LAN, Vines.
Eliminates Manual Expense Reports. Works on Notebooks to Networks. Features: Flexible Charge Codes & Expense Types, Handles Cash Advances, Personal Expenses on a Corporate Card, Reconcilement, Third Party Billing, Updates Your G/L, Calendar & Calculator, User Customizable Help & Very Easy to Learn.
Adisoft.

Expense-Track-II. *Version:* 2.00. Kailash Chandra. Jun. 1984. *Compatible Hardware:* IBM PC, PCjr, PC XT, PC AT & compatibles. *Operating System(s) Required:* PC-DOS/MS-DOS. *Language(s):* Compiled BASIC. *Memory Required:* 256k.
disk $69.95 (ISBN 0-918689-04-X).
Prints Checks, & Various Summary Reports & Gives Running Totals.
Sapana Micro Software.

Experimental Methods in Psychology. Gustav Levine & Stanley Parkinson. *Customer Support:* Free technical support, 90-day limited warranty.
IBM. 3.5" disk Contact publisher for price (ISBN 1-56321-144-0).
5.25" disk Contact publisher for price (ISBN 1-56321-145-9).
cloth book $39.95 (ISBN 0-8058-1438-8).
Test Bank Disk to Compliment Book of the Same Title. Focuses on the Experimental Methods & the Associated Terminology Encountered in the Research Literature of Psychology.
Lawrence Erlbaum Assocs. Software & Alternate Media, Inc.

Experimental Statistics. *Version:* 10.0. (Professional Ser.). 1989. *Compatible Hardware:* Apple Macintosh, IBM PC & compatibles. *Memory Required:* 512k. *Items Included:* Disks, book, program instruction. *Customer Support:* Telephone.
disk $145.00 (ISBN 0-920387-00-4).
This General-purpose Statistics Package Covers the Following Major Topics: Distributions & Sampling, Statistical Inference, Regression Analysis, the Design of Experiments & the Analysis of Variance. The Full-size Book Describes the Background & Usage of Statistics, with Examples; Program Instructions Cover Specific Details of the More Than Sixty Computer Programs Included in the Package. Specific Topics Included: Sampling Distributions, the Application of the Central Limit Theorem, Sampling (Including Sampling Distributions & How to Calculate the Sample Size in an Experiment), the Normal Distributions & Those Distributions Based on It (t, Chi-Square, & F), Inverse & Non-central Distributions, Statistical Inference & Hypothesis Testing (Including Non-parametric Testing), Type I & Type II Errors, Regression Analysis (Including Simple Linear & Multilinear Regression, & Regression Using Orthogonal Arrays for Parameter Design). The 28 Programs on Analysis of Variance Cover All Major Type.
Lionheart Pr., Inc.

ExperLink.
Macintosh 512K or higher. 3.5" disk $500.00.
Symbolic 3600 Link to ExperLisp.
ExperTelligence.

ExperLogo. *Version:* 2. *Compatible Hardware:* Apple Macintosh.
3.5" disk $95.00.
Version of LOGO Which Utilizes "Bunnies" Rather Than the Usual "Turtles" to Perform Tasks.
Expertelligence.

Expert Choice. *Version:* 8.0. Ernest H. Forman et al. 1985-1994. *Compatible Hardware:* IBM PC & compatibles. *Operating System(s) Required:* PC-DOS 5.0 or higher. *Language(s):* BASIC, Assembly. *Memory Required:* 640k. *Customer Support:* Telephone.
disk $495.00 (Order no.: BE).
demo disk $10.00.
Executive Decision Support System for the Professional to Be Used for Complex Problem Solving That Has Multiple Criteria, Alternatives, Scenarios & Game Players. Also Helps Justify to Others Why a Decision was Made. Uses Include: Resource Allocation, Employee Evaluation, Procurement, Policy Decisions, & Research & Development.
Expert Choice, Inc.

Expert Ease. *Items Included:* Bound manual. *Customer Support:* Free hotline - no time limit; 30 day limited warranty; updates are $5/disk plus S&H.
MS-DOS. IBM PC, PC/XT (256k). disk $395.00.
Decision Tree Analysis Tool. It Creates an Expert System of Your Own Design, Using Your Own Specialized Knowledge. Once Your Expert System Is Created, a Non-Expert Can Use the System to Obtain the Same Result or Decision That You Would Have Made. Also Allows You to Analyze & Refine Your Own Decision-Making Process. No Programming Is Required - Just Type in Examples of Previous Decisions. Creates a Decision Tree Based on Rules It Derives from Your Examples, Automatically Eliminating Redundancies & Alerting You to Any Inconsistencies. You Can Add Text in Your Own Words to Fit the People Who Will Be Using Your Expert System. And You Can Expand, Modify, or Refine Your System Any Time.
Dynacomp, Inc.

Expert 87. *Compatible Hardware:* IBM PC & compatibles. *Operating System(s) Required:* PC-DOS/MS-DOS. *Memory Required:* 256k. *General Requirements:* Hard disk recommended. *Items Included:* 32 pg. Thinking Software catalog.
5.25" or 3.5" disk $495.00.
Expert System Generator & Decision Support System. Supports the Development of Consensual Expert Systems, Representing the Combined Viewpoints of As Many As 25 Experts, All Addressing the Same Problem from the Perspective of Their Own Individual Expertise.
Thinking Software, Inc.

Expert System Six Pack. *Version:* 1.01. *Compatible Hardware:* IBM PC & compatibles. *Operating System(s) Required:* PC-DOS, MS-DOS. *Memory Required:* 256k. *General Requirements:* Hard disk recommended. *Items Included:* 32 pg. Thinking Software catalog.
5.25" or 3.50" disk $129.95.
Package Includes: ESIE, Rulemaker, Inference, Expert, XXXPERT, Impshell, Plus a User's Guide with Rulebase Examples.
Thinking Software, Inc.

Expert System Tutorial. *Items Included:* Bound manual. *Customer Support:* Free hotline - no time limit; 30 day limited warranty; updates are $5/disk plus S&H.
MS-DOS. IBM & compatibles (256k). disk $29.95. *Nonstandard peripherals required:* Printer required.
Expert Systems Are Artificial Intelligence (AI) Programs Which Record Your Expertise in a Particular Subject Area So That Non-Experts Can Then Make Decisions (Based on Your Knowledge) by Simply Answering Computer-Generated Questions. This Particular System Allows User to Troubleshoot (a Stand-Alone Automobile Engine Repair Expert Is Included As an Extended Example), or Do a "Needs Analysis". Low-Cost Way to Examine This Type of Product to See If the Procedure Is Applicable to Your Situation. In Many Cases, EST Itself May Be Sufficient for Your Needs. (DYNACOMP Also Has RESIDENT EXPERT for Real Estate, HANSEN-PREDICT for Large Procedures Like Employee Interviews, & EXPERTISE for General Purpose Use.) Here Are Some Typical Uses for EST: Troubleshooting of Automobiles, Electronics, & Plumbing; Choosing Players for Sports; Figuring Cheapest Shipping Means in a Mailroom, etc.
Dynacomp, Inc.

Experteach-III. Apr. 1988. *Operating System(s) Required:* PC-DOS/MS-DOS. *Memory Required:* 512k.
disk $129.95 (ISBN 0-945877-01-3, Order no.: EXP3-1872).
Provides a Comprehensive Introduction to System Technology. Includes Interactive & Graphic Tutorials & Exercises Which Teach Each Component of System Technology. Topics Covered Include Inference Methods, Logic, Frames, Inheritance, Knowledge Representation, Knowledge Acquisition & Validation.
IntelligenceWare, Inc.

EXPERtIMENTAL DESIGN. *Version:* 3.2. Ramon Olivero et al. Oct. 1986. *Compatible Hardware:* IBM PC & compatibles, PC XT, PC AT. *Operating System(s) Required:* PC-DOS/MS-DOS 2.1 or higher. *Language(s):* Turbo Pascal. *Memory Required:* 256k. *Items Included:* Manual, 3.5" diskette. *Customer Support:* Free telephone support to registered users.
disk $295.00 (ISBN 0-932651-14-3).
Expert System That Determines the Statistical Requirements of Projects & Suggests the Most Appropriate of 13 Experimental Designs.
Statistical Programs.

Exploratory Data Analysis. *Version:* 10.0. R. Stevenson. Jun. 1989. *Items Included:* Disks, book, program instructions. *Customer Support:* Telephone support.

MS-DOS (512k). IBM PC & compatibles. 3.5" disk $145.00 (ISBN 0-920387-05-5).
Macintosh. 3.5" disk $145.00.
Descriptive Statistical Techniques Are Primarily Graphical. It Is Useful to Calculate Things, but It Is Essential to Inspect the Data Before Entering into Intensive Numerical Analysis. Product Is Graphics-Oriented & Makes Use of EDA Techniques. User Can Examine Data with Letter-Value Displays, Stem & Leaf Displays & Boxplots; Also When Fitting Data to a Line User Can Run a Resistant Line Through Data Points As Well As Carry Out Regression Calculations. Analysis of Variance Is Complemented by Median Polish & the Preparation of Coded Tables. Distribution of Data Points Can Be Checked by Drawing Rotograms. Program Set Includes Crosstabulations, Distributions, Regressions, & Sensitivity Analysis. Graphics & File Transfer Is Included at No Extra Charge.
Lionheart Pr., Inc.

Explore America! Jul. 1995. *Items Included:* User guide, registration card. *Customer Support:* 30 day warranty, free technical support.
Windows. 386 with 3Mb avail. hard drive space (4Mb). CD-ROM disk $14.95 (ISBN 1-885638-15-9). *Nonstandard peripherals required:* SVGA, display, audio board, CD-ROM drive, Microsoft CD-ROM extensions 2.2 or higher.
Multimedia Tour of the United States Takes the Curious Traveler to More Than 3,000 Attractions Including Festivals, Theaters, Museums, Historic Sites, Baseball Teams & Much More. Video, Sound, & More Than 6,000 Colorful Photos Highlight the Best the U.S. Has to Offer, & Up-to-Date Descriptions, Addresses, Phone Numbers, Hours, & a Locator Map Help You Get to the Destination of Your Choice.
Deep River Publishing, Inc.

Exploring America's National Parks. *Version:* 2.0. 1995. *Items Included:* Operating manual. *Customer Support:* Free telephone technical support 1-800-850-7272.
DOS 3.1, Windows 3.1. 33Mhz 80486DX (4Mb). CD-ROM disk $49.95 (ISBN 1-884014-60-7). *Nonstandard peripherals required:* CD-ROM drive, VGA video/display at 256 colors, Soundblaster compatible audio board. *Addl. software required:* Microsoft CD-ROM extensions 2.2. *Optimal configuration:* 8Mb dual speed CD-ROM.
System 6.07. 68030 processor or higher, Color Macintosh (256 Plus color display, 13" monitor). CD-ROM disk $49.95 (ISBN 1-884014-61-5). *Nonstandard peripherals required:* CD-ROM drive, mouse. *Optimal configuration:* 8Mb, dual speed CD-ROM drive.
Updated Database of over 230 National Parks with Photography by David Muench & Full Motion Video of the Larger Parks <end>
Multicom Publishing, Inc.

Exploring America's National Parks. *Version:* 2.0. Aug. 1995. *Items Included:* Operating manual. *Customer Support:* Free technical support (800) 850-7272.
DOS 3.1, Windows 3.1; Macintosh. 33MHz 80486DX VGA video/display at 256 colors (4Mb); Macintosh System 6.07 68030 processor or higher (256 Plus color display). CD-ROM disk $59.95 (ISBN 1-884014-69-0). *Nonstandard peripherals required:* CD-ROM drive.
An Interactive Database of over 230 National Parks Featuring the Photography of David Muench As Well As the Full Range of Multimedia Options.
Multicom Publishing, Inc.

Exploring America's National Parks: Mac-MPC Book Bundle. *Version:* 2.0. Oct. 1995. *Items Included:* Operating manual, catalog, registration card. *Customer Support:* Free technical support 206-622-5530.
DOS 3.1, Windows 3.1, Windows 95; Macintosh. 486SX 25MHz or higher (8Mb RAM); 68030 processor System 7.1 or higher (8Mb RAM). CD-ROM disk Contact publisher for price (ISBN 1-884014-76-3). *Addl. software required:* Double speed CD-ROM drive.
An Upgrade to National Parks of America. This CD Brings the User Information on All 230 National Parks. This CD Contains Video on the Most Popular Parks & a Search Function That Allows the User to Search for the Park(s) That Best Fit the Specifics They Are Searching For. This CD-ROM Comes Bundled with a Beautiful Book, National Parks of America.
Multicom Publishing, Inc.

Exploring America's National Parks: Stand-Alone (Hybrid). *Version:* 2.0. Aug. 1995. *Items Included:* Operating manual, catalog, registration card. *Customer Support:* Free technical support 206-622-5530.
DOS 3.1, Windows 3.1, Windows 95; Macintosh. 486SX 25MHz or higher (8Mb RAM); 68030 processor System 7.1 or higher (8Mb RAM). CD-ROM disk $59.95 (ISBN 1-884014-69-0). *Addl. software required:* Double speed CD-ROM drive.
An Interactive Database of over 230 National Parks Featuring the Photography of David Muench As Well As the Full Range of Multimedia Options.
Multicom Publishing, Inc.

Exploring Ancient Cities. Jun. 1994.
Mac: System 7.0, 13-inch monitor (256 or better colors) (6Mb). CD-ROM disk $59.95 (ISBN 1-57047-011-1, Order no.: AC). *Nonstandard peripherals required:* CD-ROM drive (double speed recommended).
CPU with 486/33 MHz or higher processor (8Mb). CD-ROM disk $59.95. *Nonstandard peripherals required:* CD-ROM drive (double speed recommended).
This CD Brings Articles from Scientific American to Multimedia Format. Readers Can Explore Teotihuacan (Mexico); Pompeii (Italy); Petra (Jordan); Four of Crete's Bronze Age Palaces, & Other Sites. Readers Will Have Access to Interactive Maps, Video, Photography, Sound, Narration, & Text, Video & Photo Export.
Sumeria, Inc.

Export by Mail. Jan. 1995. *Customer Support:* Unlimited telephone support.
MS-DOS 6.0/Windows 3.1 or higher. PC Clone 486 or higher (4Mb). disk $15.00 (ISBN 1-878974-26-2). *Addl. software required:* MS Windows 3.1 or higher. *Optimal configuration:* PC clone with MS-DOS 6.0/Windows 3.1 or higher. 4Mb of hard disk storage recommended.
Multimedia Tutorial Which Installs in MS Windows 3.1 or Higher. Steps You Through an Overview of Exporting by Mail in about 30 Minutes.
Jeffries & Associates, Inc.

Export To Win! Jan. 1990. *Items Included:* Provided with each simulation is a manual describing the various simulation decisions & a facilitators guide that explains simulation set-up & terminology. *Customer Support:* Included in all licensing agreements is a service contract that entitles licensees to a Train-the-Trainer program & an 800 support phone number.
PC/MS-DOS 2.0 & higher. IBM PC/XT/AT & compatibles (640k). disk $149.95. *Nonstandard peripherals required:* 2 disk drives &/or hard disk.
Simulated Export Department for Gaining a Better Understanding of the International Marketplace.
Strategic Management Group, Inc.

Exporting Guide for Business. *Compatible Hardware:* Apple Macintosh Plus. *Memory Required:* 1000k. *General Requirements:* HyperCard. *Customer Support:* Free.
3.5" disk $159.95.
Exporting Guide. Topics Covered Include: Export Strategies, Export Advice, Market Research, Methods of Exporting & Channels of Distribution, etc.
Milum Corp.

Express. *Compatible Hardware:* Apple Macintosh, IBM PC.
Stand-alone. disk $99.00.
Bundled with Omnis 3. $575.00.
Application Development Front-End for the OMNIS 3 PLUS Relational Data Base Running on the Macintosh. Package Will Enable OMNIS 3 Users to Develop a Working Database by Defining the Files & Fields after Which Automatically Generates All Screens, Menus, & Reports.
Blyth Software, Inc.

Express. Apr. 1992. *Items Included:* Instruction manual, student activity book. *Customer Support:* 60-day warranty; telephone assistance.
MS-DOS. IBM & compatibles (128k). disk $75.00 (ISBN 1-880967-09-X).
$725.00 Site License.
Designed to Provide Activities to Reinforce the Written Communication Skill. Provides a Review of Grammer, Rules of Writing, etc., Leading the User to the Development of Sentences, Paragraphs, Business Letters, Memos, & Reports.
LHR Assocs.

Express Check. *Version:* 4. Dec. 1989. *Items Included:* Disks, printed manual. *Customer Support:* One year free technical support.
MS-DOS. IBM & compatibles (320k). disk $34.95.
Menu Driven Checkbook Management System Geared for Home & Small Business Users. Screens Graphically Resemble Actual Checks, ATM's & Deposits, Making It Very Intuitive to Use. Features Include Checkwriting to Any Check Format, Check Register, Budget Code Totals, Monthly Budget Code Averages, Simple Reconciliation & More.
Expressware Corp.

ExpressCalc. *Version:* 4. Dec. 1988. *Items Included:* Disks, printed manual. *Customer Support:* One year free technical support.
IBM & compatibles (512k). disk $59.95.
Simplified Way to Use a Spreadsheet Program. Good for the Person Who Needs Number Crunching Without a Lot of Extras. Features Include Replicate, Move, Look-Up Tables, Windows, Powerful Field Formatting etc.
Expressware Corp.

ExpressForm. *Compatible Hardware:* Apple Macintosh. *Memory Required:* 512k.
3.5" disk $94.95.
Screen & Forms Manager.
Evolutionary Commercial Systems.

ExpressGraph. Aug. 1986. *Items Included:* Disk, printed manual. *Customer Support:* One year technical support.
IBM & compatibles (256k). disk $29.95. *Nonstandard peripherals required:* IBM or EPSON Graphics printer required, CGA color monitor.

TITLE INDEX

Produces Bar Charts, & Line Graphs. Numerical Information May Be Typed in Directly or May Be Imported From Other Applications Such As Express Check, File Express & Express Calc.
Expressware Corp.

Expressionist. Version: 3.2. Compatible Hardware: Apple Macintosh, Windows. Items Included: 1 disk, 1 manual. Customer Support: 519-747-2505.
3.5" disk $159.00.
Application &/or Desk Accessory Which Enables Users to Develop Mathematical Equations from Within an Application.
Waterloo Maple, Inc.

EXPRFR. 1982. Compatible Hardware: IBM PC & compatibles. Operating System(s) Required: MS-DOS. Language(s): BASIC (source code included). Memory Required: 128k.
disk $395.00.
Designed for External Pressure, Calculations Based on Outside Diameters. Curve Values Built into Program. Handles Carbon Steel & Stainless Steel. These Calculations Apply to Cylinders, Cones & Elliptical-Spherical-Flanged & Dished & Flat Heads.
Technical Research Services, Inc.

EXSELL. Version: 3.053. Mar. 1992. Compatible Hardware: IBM PC & compatibles, networks. Operating System(s) Required: MS-DOS. Memory Required: 512k. General Requirements: Hard disk recommended, modem for autodialing. Items Included: Software, manual (180 pages +), 30 days telephone support. Customer Support: $85 annually, unlimited telephone.
disk $149.00. Addl. software required: Sec under Network Software applies to single user also.
Organizes the Client or Prospect Database & Provides Instant Access to a Variety of Stored Information: a Customer Profile, Contact History, Comment File, 4 User Definable Histories & 26 User Definable Codes. In Addition to the Basic Client Information (Name, Company Name, 2 Addresses & Phone Numbers) the Customer Profile Includes 26 User Definable Codes As Well As a Next & Last Contact Date. A Tickler File Reminds User When to Make Scheduled Calls, While Providing a Method for Updating the Status of Each Individual. Contains a Built-In Word Processor. Demo Disk Available.
Excalibur Sources, Inc.

EXSELL (LAN). Version: 3.053. Mar. 1992. Items Included: 200 page manual; program diskettes. Customer Support: 30 days free telephone support; 1 year unlimited telephone support $250; on-site training-design-implementation-consulting available.
Novell ELS, ELS II, Advanced Netware, Netbio s, Lanis. Novell, netbios compatible file servers & (1-5 users) $150.00. Addl. software required: EXMPORT needed to import & export ASCII data files. Networks supported: Novell (all Levels), Netbios compatible LANS.
Automated Multi-User System That Is Designed to Turn a LAN into an Integrated Sales, Prospect, & Telemarketing Solution. Features a Contact Profile with More Than 60 Fields, Including 2 Addresses & Phone Numbers; 26 User Definable Fields & 4 Multiline Unlimited Histories. Autodialer, Tickler, Follow-Up, Lead Fulfillment, Complete Reporting, Help & Telephone Directory.
Excalibur Sources, Inc.

EXSYS EL: Expert System Development Package. Version: 1.0. Compatible Hardware: IBM PC, PC XT, PC AT. Operating System(s) Required: MS-DOS. Language(s): C. Items Included: Manual. Customer Support: Unlimited free telephone support.

Development package. Development System for IBM PC $175.00.
Runtime License for IBM PC (does NOT include editor) $500.00.
both Editor & Runtime License for IBM PC $600.00.
Human Decision Making Capability on a PC, Workstation, or Mini-Computer. Produces Knowledge-Based Expert Systems Using IF-THEN-ELSE Production Rules. There Is No Programming Knowledge Required of the Expert System Developer. Using This Product, Any Body of Knowledge, No Matter How General, Can Be Developed into a Decision-Making Expert System. This Is a Limited Student Version.
Exsys, Inc.

Exsys Professional-Expert Systems Development Tool. Version: 3.0. Operating System(s) Required: MS-DOS, VAX/VMS, Unix, OS/2 PM, Microsoft-Windows, OSF/MOTIF, Macintosh. Items Included: Manual, video tape tutorial. Customer Support: Unlimited free telephone support, training.
$995.00 & up.
Provides Features Such As a Command Language with the Power to Completely Define the Expert System's Exact Method of Execution, & an Array Function Which Lends the Power of Table/Frame-Based Knowledge Representation. Also Includes an Unlimited Hypertext Capability. Automatic Unattended Validation of Knowledge Base. Invisibly Embeds & Easily Interfaces to Other Applications, Databases & Process Control Software.
Exsys, Inc.

Extend. Version: 3. Compatible Hardware: Apple Macintosh series, including Power Macintosh & PC compatibles. General Requirements: Apple Macintosh O/S, Windows 3.1, Windows 95, Windows NT. Items Included: Generic, Discrete Event, Engineering, & Plotter Libraries. Customer Support: Free customer support, free newsletter. $695.00.
Increase Productivity & Quality, Support Decisions, & Justify Costs with EXTEND. Before Implementing Changes, Model Existing Processes in EXTEND, or Design & Build New Processes or Systems in EXTEND, Then Save Time & Resources by Experimenting with "What-If" Model Scenarios. Ideal Tool for Modeling Industrial & Commercial Operations, Engineering Processes, Scientific Experimentation, & for the Reengineering of Business Processes.
Imagine That, Inc.

Extend.
Windows 3.1. PC 386 or higher (8Mb). disk $695.00.
MacOS 6.0.7 or higher. Macintosh (4Mb). 3.5" disk $695.00.
Easy-to-Use, Powerful Desktop Tool for Continuous, Discrete Event, & Combined Simulations. This Dynamic Simulation Environment Even Lets You Modify or Create Blocks Using Its Integrated Compiled Language & Dialog Editor. Extend Models Consist of Customizable, Iconic Blocks Which User Can Select from a Menu & Place on a Model Worksheet. Connect Blocks with the Mouse to Show Data Flow, Set Appropriate Parameters in the Dialog Boxes.
Imagine That, Inc.

Extend-a-Name Plus. Version: 3.10. General Requirements: Lotus 1-2-3, Symphony, Microsoft Word, WordStar 4 or WordPerfect 4 & 5, 5.1 requires DOS 3.0 or later, hard disk. Customer Support: to registered users.
IBM PC & compatibles, PS/2 (45k or 5k with EMS installed). $89.00.
Allows User to Append Current DOS File Names or Create New Ones; Names Can Be up to 60

EXTEND PLUS MANUFACTURING

Characters Long. The Extended Names Can Include Any Special Characters, Including Spaces & Punctuation. Lets User Organize Files into Libraries Within Subdirectories, & from Within an Application, Lets User Perform DOS Routines Such As Copying, Deleting & Naming Files.
World Software Corp.

Extend Plus BPR: Business Process Reengineering. Version: 3. Items Included: Extend simulation engine with additional libraries of blocks for reengineering business processes & statistical analysis. Customer Support: Free technical support, free newsletter.
Apple Macintosh O/S, Windows 3.1, Windows 95, Windows NT. Apple Macintosh series, including Power Macintosh & PC compatibles. $990.00.
Business Process Reengineering Tool That Supports Systems Analysis Techniques. A Flow Charting Interface Is Integrated with the EXTEND Simulation Engine to Model Business Processes. Used for Planning & Decision Support, Operations & Production Systems, Cycle Time Reduction, Continuous Improvement, Human Performance Modeling, Activity-Based Costing, & Productivity & Quality Improvement.
Imagine That, Inc.

Extend Plus BPR: Business Process Reengineering.
Windows 3.1. PC 386 or higher (8Mb). disk $990.00.
MacOS 6.0.7 or higher. Macintosh (4Mb). 3.5" disk $990.00.
Business Process Reengineering Tool That Supports Systems Analysis Techniques. A Flow Charting Interfaces Is Integrated with the EXTEND Simulation Engine to Model Business Processes. Used to Model Organizational Change, Analyze New Processes for Technology Insertion, Provide Metrics for Strategic Planning, Reduce Cycle Time, & for Productivity & Quality Improvement.
Imagine That, Inc.

Extend + Manufacturing. Version: 3. Items Included: Extend simulation engine with additional libraries of blocks for industrial & commercial modeling & statistical analysis. Customer Support: Free customer support; free newsletter.
Apple Macintosh O/S, Windows 3.1, Windows 95, Windows NT. Apple Macintosh series, including Power Macintosh & PC compatibles. $990.00.
Dynamic Modeling Tool for Simulating Discrete Industrial & Commercial Processes. Combines EXTEND with Two Specialized Libraries of Blocks for Manufacturing & Statistics. Assists in the Prediction of System Bottlenecks, Determination of Buffer Lengths, Build Times, & Process Timing So Costs Can Be Justified Before Resources Are Committed, Options Can Be Analyzed, & Operating Procedures Documented.
Imagine That, Inc.

Extend Plus Manufacturing.
Windows 3.1. PC 386 or higher (8Mb). disk $990.00.
MacOS 6.0.7 or higher. Macintosh (4Mb). 3.5" disk $990.00.
Dynamic Modeling Tool for Simulating Discrete Industrial & Commercial Processes. Combines EXTEND with Two Specialized Libraries of Blocks for Manufacturing & Statistics. Assists in the Prediction of System Bottlenecks, Determination of Buffer Lengths, Build Times, & Process Timing So Costs Can Be Justified Before Resources Are Committed, Options Can Be Analyzed, & Operating Procedures Documented.
Imagine That, Inc.

EXTENDED BASIC

Extended BASIC. *Compatible Hardware:* TI 99/4A.
contact publisher for price (Order no.: PHM 3026).
BASIC with the Following Enhancements: Multi-Statement Lines, IF-THEN-ELSE Statements, Direct Screen Accessing, Program Chaining.
Texas Instruments, Personal Productivit.

Extended BASIC Programming. *Compatible Hardware:* IBM PC, PC XT, Portable PC. *Operating System(s) Required:* PC-DOS 2.00, 2.10, 3.00, 3.10. *Memory Required:* 128k.
disk $34.95 (Order no.: 6276625).
Enhances the Functions of IBM BASIC Compiler (Version 1.00).
Personally Developed Software, Inc.
  BASIC Memory Extender. Alan J. Testani. *Enables Users to Write BASIC Programs That Contain More Than 64k of Data. Also Automatically Handles All Functions Necessary to Manage the Data Outside of BASIC. Numbers Can Be Stored in Arrays up to 64k in Size with Each Array Holding up to 32,678 Integers, 16,384 Single-Precision Numbers, or 8192 Double-Precision Numbers.*
  UnNumber. Peter A. Lewis. *Lets Users Remove Unreferenced Line Numbers from BASIC Files, Which Enables Them to Develop Programs Using the BASIC Interpreter (Where Changes Can Be Easily Made), Then Convert Them So They Can Be Compiled under the BASIC Compiler's/N Parameter. Also Checks How Many Lines Are Deleted from the Program.*

Extended Payments. (Service Management Ser.). 1996.
DOS, Unix. IBM PC. disk contact publisher for price.
The "Extended Payments" feature of FasTrak enables your firm to automate the installment programs you are offering to your customers.
Core Software, Inc.

Extra! Entry Level. *Version:* 1.30. Sep. 1991. *Compatible Hardware:* IBM PC & compatibles, PS/2. *Operating System(s) Required:* PC-DOS/MS-DOS. *Memory Required:* 36k. *General Requirements:* Runs on Attachmate, IBM, IRMA 3270 coax or SDLC adapters. *Items Included:* Documentation. *Customer Support:* Toll-free technical support hot-line.
3.5" or 5.25" disk $275.00 (Order no.: P6100). *Networks supported:* NetBios.
Basic 3270 Micro-to-Mainframe Terminal Emulation Software for IBM PC's, PS/2's & Compatibles. Works With Coax, Remote Modem or LAN. Includes File Transfer, Screen Print & Application Program Interfaces.
Attachmate Corp.

Extra! Extended for DOS. *Version:* 3.0. Aug. 1992. *Items Included:* Documentation. *Customer Support:* Toll-free technical support hotline.
PC-DOS, MS-DOS 3.0. IBM PC & compatibles, PS/2. 3.5" or 5.25" disk $425.00. *Networks supported:* NetBios, IPX.
3270 Emulation Product. Takes Advantage of Low Memory Consumption & LIM 4.0 EMS Support. Lets You Transfer Files Without Interrupting Your PC Application Using IBM-Standard Send/Receive (IND$FILE) File Transfer, DISOSS PS/CICS Transfer, or TSO/CMS Editor Transfer. Works with up to Four Active Host Sessions Concurrently. Provides 3287 Printer Emulation. Choose Between Light Pen or Mouse for Input. Universal Connectivity Allows You to Choose Coax, LAN Gateway, SDLC, or ADLC Connection. Lets You Use Any NETBIOS or IPX-Compatible LAN Adapter, Including IBM Token Ring.
Attachmate Corp.

EXTRA! for Macintosh. *Version:* 1.2. Aug. 1993. *Items Included:* User's Manual. *Customer Support:* Toll-free technical support hot line, provided at no charge for life of product.
Macintosh System 6.04 or higher. Macintosh (1Mb). 3.5" disk $425.00. *Networks supported:* AppleTalk.
Provides Powerful Yet Simple Workstation to Host Connectivity. 3270 Terminal Emulation with Multiple Sessions Is Provided. Mainframe Session Screens May Be Scaled, Colored & Independently Positioned. Background Batch File Transfer Is As Simple As Point & Click. File Transfer Types Supported Are IBM's IND$FILE for VM/CMS, MVS/TSO & CICS. OV/MVS Import/Export Is Also Supported. 3287 Printer Emulation Support Gives End Users the Flexibility & Power to Print Their Mainframe Applications at Their Local and/or LAN Attached Printers. EXTRA! Provides Graphical Keyboard Remapping & a SmartPad Keypad. Light Pen Is Supported. EXTRA! Connectivity Is via Coax DFT, 802.2 over Token Ring or Appletalk LAN Connections May Be Shared with PC's via the Attachmate Gateway Multiple Protocol Support.
Attachmate Corp.

EXTRA! for OS-2. Jun. 1993. *Items Included:* 3 manuals which include Using Extra!; Quick Installation Guide; Host Automation Utilities Guide. 3 disks-2 program, 1 Host Automation Utilities. 1 Keyboard Templates Book. *Customer Support:* 1. Free customer support for the life of the product - or - 2. Special software support called "Central Support Agreement" which provides 1.) Automatic product upgrades 2.) Dedicated central support toll-free number 3.) Software status reports 4.) Product information updates 5.) Customer support bulletins 6.) Automated FaxBark System 7.) Attachmate BBS, price varies depending on number of workstations.
IBM Os/2 2.0 or 2.1. 386 or higher (8Mb). disk $425.00 (Order no.: P8300). *Optimal configuration:* 486 or higher, 12Mb RAM, 200Mb hard drive (These are optional needs of the operating system). *Networks supported:* IBM NETBIOS & DLC, Novell (IPX/SPX) Netware Requestor.
Provides Our Customers with a Full Featured 3270 Emulation Product under OS/2. Product Highlights Include 3270 Terminal & Printer Emulation, Universal Connectivity, Multiple Sessions in Sizable Windows, Smart Pad, Hotspots, Macros, LAN Compatible Host Automation Utilities, Light Pen Support, File Transfer, Copy/Paste, & Print Screen.
Attachmate Corp.

EXTRA! for Windows. *Version:* 3.3. Mar. 1992. *Items Included:* Documentation. *Customer Support:* Toll-free technical support hotline.
PC-DOS, MS-DOS 3.0 or higher. IBM PC's & compatibles (1Mb). disk $425.00. *Addl. software required:* Windows 3.1. *Networks supported:* NetBios, DLL (802.2), IPX, TCP/IP, Banyan.
High-Performance Communication Product for 3270 Host Access. Provides an Easy-to-Use, Full Featured 3270 Emulator, Fast File Transfer, Printer Emulator, & a Robust Connectivity Engine That Can Be Used to Create Mission-Critical Client/Server Applications to the Host. Highly Flexible & Extendible, It Provides a Wealth of Automation Options That Make Integrating and/or Interacting with Mainframe Information Easier Than Ever. Universal Connectivity Allows Users to Choose from Coax, TN3270, Full SNA Remote Access via SDLC or ADLC, & LAN Connectivity via the Attachmate Gateway Option, Novell NetWare for SAA, & IBM Gateway Systems Utilizing IPX, NetBIOS, or IEEE 802.2 As the Transport Mechanism.
Attachmate Corp.

Extra K. Mark Simonsen & Alan Bird. Mar. 1986. *Compatible Hardware:* Apple II, II+, IIe, IIc, IIgs. *Operating System(s) Required:* Apple DOS 3.3, ProDOS. *Language(s):* Machine, BASIC. *Memory Required:* 128k.
disk $39.95.
The Disk Contains Several Programs That Let User Utilize up to 128k of Memory. Will Store Variables, Strings, Arrays, & Data in Apple's Extra 64k of Memory. Allows Chaining of Programs. Allows Dividing the Memory into Two 64k Banks, So That Users Can Have Two Sets of Programs in Memory at Once & Switch Between Them at Will. Other Features Provide the Ability to Make Fast Disk Copies, Compare Two Disks, Create High-Speed Animation & Window Effects, Use the Extra Memory As an Electronic Notepad.
Beagle Brothers.

Extra K. *Version:* 1.10. *Compatible Hardware:* IBM PC & compatibles. *Memory Required:* 9k. *General Requirements:* Lotus Symphony 1.1, 1.2, 2.0, 2.2. *Customer Support:* Free unlimited.
disk $79.95.
Memory-Management Product for Lotus Symphony Allows Users to Unload the Four Nonspreadsheet Portions of Symphony, Freeing Up to 94k of Memory for Users' Worksheet. Users Can Choose to Unload One or More of the Four Nonspreadsheet Environments: Word Processing, Communications, Form Entry, & Graphics. Depending on the Combination, Users Can Free Between 35k & 94k for Spreadsheet. Symphony Users with Expanded Memory Can Free Up to 21,000 More Cells for Their Worksheets Symphony 2.2 users get Significant Expanded Memory Management Improvements.
Lerman Assocs.

Extra! 3270 Gateway Option. *Version:* 3.0. 1992. *Compatible Hardware:* IBM PC & compatibles. *Operating System(s) Required:* PC-DOS/MS-DOS. *Memory Required:* 256k. *General Requirements:* LAN, remote modem, coax token ring interface coupler, Attachmate Extra! connectivity software. *Items Included:* Documentation. *Customer Support:* Toll-free technical support hot-line.
3.5" or 5.25" disk $50.00 (Order no.: P6400).
$50.00 3.5" or 5.25" disk, incl. AppleTalk (Order no.: P6400F).
The 3270 Gateway Option Is a Flexible Multi-Platform & Simultaneous Multi-Protocol LAN-to-Mainframe Connectivity Product. Supports LAN-Connected IBM PC & PS/2 & Compatible Workstations Running DOS, Windows, & Macintosh Workstation Platforms. Provides Coax-DFT, SNA/SDLC Links, & Token Ring (802.2) Protocols to the Mainframe. LAN Protocols Supported Include IBM NETBIOS, 802.2 (TIC), IPX, AppleTalk, & Asynchronous Remote Communication.
Attachmate Corp.

EY/FastPlan. *Version:* 4.0. Aug. 1987. *Compatible Hardware:* IBM PC & compatibles. *Memory Required:* 640k. *General Requirements:* Lotus 1-2-3 Releases 1A or higher. *Items Included:* Software; 200 page manual. *Customer Support:* 9am-5pm, CST, M-F; (800) 421-0004. $99.00.
Financial Model Produces Five-Year Annual & Quarterly Projections of Cash Flow, Income, Manufactured Inventory, Balance Sheets, & Key Ratios. Color Graphic Review of Borrowing Levels & Limits, Cash Flow, & Valuation.
Ernst & Young.

Eye Chart Generator. *Compatible Hardware:* Apple Macintosh.
3.5" disk $14.95.
Displays & Prints Standard Eye Charts. Each Chart Is Somewhat Different. For Distance Vision Testing Only.
Sher-Mark Products, Inc.

TITLE INDEX

Eye Play 2. *Version:* 2.0. *Compatible Hardware:* Commodore Amiga. *Customer Support:* Telephone support.
3.5" disk $19.95.
Build Computer Art from 36 Graphic Routines.
Silver Software.

Eyewitness Encyclopedia of Science.
Windows. IBM & compatibles. CD-ROM disk $69.95 (Order no.: R1195). *Nonstandard peripherals required:* CD-ROM drive. *Optimal configuration:* 386 processor operating at 16MHz or higher, MS-DOS 5.0 or higher, Windows 3.1 or higher, 30Mb hard drive, mouse, VGA graphic adapter & VGA color monitor (SVGA recommended), 4Mb RAM, external speakers or headphones (with sound card) that are Sound Blaster compatible.
This Encyclopedia Contains Entries Organized into Five Major Categories: Chemistry, Mathematics, Physics, Life Sciences, & Who's Who of Science. This Program, along with a Quick-Access Index, Links Common Principles to Different Areas of Science, Clearly Explaining the Integration of Science & Technology into Everyday Life (Ages 10 & Up).
Library Video Co.

EZ Backup. *Customer Support:* Free, unlimited. MS/PC-DOS 3.0 or higher. IBM PC XT, AT, PS/2 & compatibles (256k). disk $99.00.
Software System for Backing up Hard Disks onto Ordinary 5.25" or 3.5" Floppy Disks. Keeps Track of the Disks You Used, & Allows Incremental Backup to Speed up Daily Backup Operations.
EKD Computer Sales & Supplies Corp.

EZ-Backup. *Compatible Hardware:* Commodore Amiga.
3.5" disk $49.95.
File Backup Utility Manages Data on Backup Disk.
EZ Soft.

EZ Barcode III: Bar Code Printer. 1995. *Items Included:* Full manual. *Customer Support:* Free telephone support - 90 days, 30-day warranty. MS-DOS 3.2 or higher. 286 (584k). $269.95-$389.95. *Nonstandard peripherals required:* CGA/EGA/VGA.
Prints All Standard Bar Codes Including Code 39, UPC, EAN, Interleaved 2 of 5, Code 128 & Many More. It Is Also Certified by the U.S. Postal Service to Print POSTNET for Bulk & Business Reply Mail. With WYSWYG Screen Formats & Mouse Support, EZ BARCODE III Offers Fine Control of Bar Code Density, Wide-to-Narrow Ratios, Bar & Space Widths, Typestyles & More.
Dynacomp, Inc.

EZ Barcode II: Bar Code Printer. 1995. *Items Included:* Full manual. *Customer Support:* Free telephone support - 90 days, 30-day warranty. MS-DOS 3.2 or higher. 286 (584k). disk $139.95. *Nonstandard peripherals required:* CGA/EGA/VGA.
Provides a Variety of Features for a Wide Range of Bar Code Printing Needs. These Features Include: Prints Code 39 (up to 40 Characters), Interleaved Code 2 of 5 & UPC Version A; Supports Most Dot Matrix & HP LaserJet (& Compatible) Printers; Variable Bar Code Height (0.1" to 1"), Margin, Distance Between Bar Codes; Multiple Columns of Bar Codes on a Single Line; Automatic Incrementing; Print Text Files Generated by Other Programs, or Use Built-In Entry & Editing Utilities; Print Text Beneath Bar Code; 1-999 Copies; Multi-Pass Printing.
Dynacomp, Inc.

EZ-BLUMNOTE. *Customer Support:* Free, unlimited.
MS/PC-DOS 3.0 or higher. IBM PC XT, AT, PS/2 & compatibles (512k). disk $149.00.
Allows User to Print Julius Blumberg Inc. No. 1000N Serial Notes & No. B2000 Corporate Serial Notes with Ease. Legal & Business Professionals Know That Manual Entry of These Serial Notes Is Repetitious & Time Consuming. Calculates & Print the Required Number of Serial Notes on Any HP-Compatible Laser Printer.
EKD Computer Sales & Supplies Corp.

EZ CALC. *Version:* 1.33. Apr. 1986. *Compatible Hardware:* Atari ST. *Memory Required:* 512k. disk $49.95 (Order no.: RS22).
Spreadsheet Program Incorporating Mouse Control & Pull down Menus for Ease or Use. Also Has Built-In Note Pad Feature & 10-Key Calculator.
Royal Software.

EZ-CAM. *Version:* 5.0. *Compatible Hardware:* IBM AT, PS/2. *General Requirements:* 80287/387, color EGA, VGA or super VGA. *Items Included:* EZ-Mill, EZ-Utils, EZ-Build & manuals. *Customer Support:* 800 No. hotline, BBS & fax.
disk $3000.00.
$5995.00 with computer & printer.
Computer-Aided Manufacturing System That Creates Programs for CNC Milling, Turning Centers & Wirecut EDM.
Bridgeport Machines, Inc.

EZ-Camp. *Version:* 13.0. Jun. 1982. *Compatible Hardware:* IBM PC & compatibles. *Operating System(s) Required:* PC-DOS/MS-DOS. *Language(s):* BASIC. *Memory Required:* 512k. *General Requirements:* Hard disk.
disk $990.00-$3495.00 (ISBN 0-926937-00-6).
Micro-Based System Designed to Automate the Administrative Functions of Camps & Conference Centers. Incorporates Several Sub-Modules Which Include Word Processing, Accounting, Camper & Counselor Databases, Transportation Coordination, Bunklist Management, & Canteen Management. Features Completely Integrated Functionality with an Approach Designed for Both New & Experienced Users.
SofterWare, Inc.

EZ-Care. *Version:* 13.0. Oct. 1985. *Compatible Hardware:* IBM PC & compatibles. *Operating System(s) Required:* PC-DOS/MS-DOS. *Language(s):* BASIC. *Memory Required:* 512k. *General Requirements:* Hard disk.
disk $895.00-2500.00 (ISBN 0-926937-10-3).
Designed to Automate the Administrative Functions of Child Care Centers & Day Schools. Incorporates Several Sub-Models Which Include Registration & Data Management Accounts Receivable, Cash Receipts, Accounts Payable, Payroll, General Ledger, Computerized Time-Clock, Scheduling & Attendance Management. Features Integrated Functionality with a Consistent Approach Designed for Both New & Experienced Users.
SofterWare, Inc.

EZ-dBASE. *Compatible Hardware:* TRS-80 Model III, Color Computer.
contact publisher for price.
Blanton Software Service.

EZ-EST. *Version:* 1.2. Jan. 1989. *Items Included:* Manual, 2 - lumber templates, 1 - residential remodeling template. *Customer Support:* Free non-collect telephone, 1-year free update.
MC-DOS/PC-DOS 2.1 or higher (320k). IBM or compatible PC XT, AT 386 mono CGA, EGA, VGA. $85.00. *Optimal configuration:* At EGA or VGA 640k hard disk printer.
Individualized Estimating Program.
Construction Concepts.

EZ LANGUAGE JAPANESE: THE SIMPLE

EZ-INSTALL Installation Aid. *Version:* 5.0. May 1987. *Items Included:* 2 bound manuals; 3 diskettes. *Customer Support:* Free phone support; 60 day money-back guarantee.
MS-DOS, PC-DOS 2.1 or higher. IBM PC or compatible (256k). disk $249.00.
OS/2. IBM PC or compatible. 3.5" disk $349.00.
Provides the PC Developer a Tool for Building Comprehensive, Thorough Installation Routines for Applications & Software Products. Can Modify CONFIG.SYS, AUTOEXEC.BAT, Compresses Files, etc.
The Software Factory, Inc.

EZ Language French: The Simple Vocabulary & Pronunciation Tutor. *Items Included:* 1 user manual. *Customer Support:* Tech support, 60-day money-back guarantee.
Windows 3.1 or higher. IBM compatible 386 or higher (2Mb). CD-ROM disk $29.95 (ISBN 0-924677-21-X). *Nonstandard peripherals required:* PC speaker or Sound Blaster compatible sound card, mouse, recommended CD-ROM drive.
An Innovative Language Tutor That Takes Full Advantage of Your PC to Create a Multimedia Learning Atmosphere. Words Are Displayed with Colorful, Descriptive Graphics to Stimulate Word-to-Object Associations. The Program Uses the Built-In PC Speaker or Any Sound Blaster-Compatible Sound Card to Let You Hear the Native Language Speaker Properly Say the Word or Phrase. Available on CD-ROM Only.
IMSI (International Microcomputer Software, Inc.).

EZ Language German: The Simple Vocabulary & Pronunciation Tutor. *Items Included:* 1 user manual. *Customer Support:* Tech support, 60-day money-back guarantee.
Windows 3.1 or higher. IBM compatible 386 or higher (2Mb). CD-ROM disk $29.95 (ISBN 0-924677-22-8). *Nonstandard peripherals required:* PC speaker or Sound Blaster compatible sound card, mouse, recommended CD-ROM drive.
An Innovative Language Tutor That Takes Full Advantage of Your PC to Create a Multimedia Learning Atmosphere. Words Are Displayed with Colorful, Descriptive Graphics to Stimulate Word-to-Object Associations. The Program Uses the Built-In PC Speaker or Any Sound Blaster-Compatible Sound Card to Let You Hear the Native Language Speaker Properly Say the Word or Phrase. Available on CD-ROM Only.
IMSI (International Microcomputer Software, Inc.).

EZ Language Italian: The Simple Vocabulary & Pronunciation Tutor. *Items Included:* 1 user manual. *Customer Support:* Tech support, 60-day money-back guarantee.
Windows 3.1 or higher. IBM compatible 386 or higher (2Mb). CD-ROM disk $29.95 (ISBN 0-924677-24-4). *Nonstandard peripherals required:* PC speaker or Sound Blaster compatible sound card, mouse, recommended CD-ROM drive.
An Innovative Language Tutor That Takes Full Advantage of Your PC to Create a Multimedia Learning Atmosphere. Words Are Displayed with Colorful, Descriptive Graphics to Stimulate Word-to-Object Associations. The Program Uses the Built-In PC Speaker or Any Sound Blaster-Compatible Sound Card to Let You Hear the Native Language Speaker Properly Say the Word or Phrase. Available on CD-ROM Only.
IMSI (International Microcomputer Software, Inc.).

EZ Language Japanese: The Simple Vocabulary & Pronunciation Tutor. *Items Included:* 1 user manual. *Customer Support:* Tech

support, 60-day money-back guarantee.
Windows 3.1 or higher. IBM compatible 386 or higher (2Mb). CD-ROM disk $29.95 (ISBN 0-924677-25-2). *Nonstandard peripherals required:* PC speaker or Sound Blaster compatible sound card, mouse, recommended CD-ROM drive.
An Innovative Language Tutor That Takes Full Advantage of Your PC to Create a Multimedia Learning Atmosphere. Words Are Displayed with Colorful, Descriptive Graphics to Stimulate Word-to-Object Associations. The Program Uses the Built-In PC Speaker or Any Sound Blaster-Compatible Sound Card to Let You Hear the Native Language Speaker Properly Say the Word or Phrase. Available on CD-ROM Only.
IMSI (International Microcomputer Software, Inc.).

EZ Language Russian: The Simple Vocabulary & Pronunciation Tutor. *Items Included:* 1 user manual. *Customer Support:* Tech support, 60-day money-back guarantee.
Windows 3.1 or higher. IBM compatible 386 or higher (2Mb). CD-ROM disk $29.95 (ISBN 0-924677-23-6). *Nonstandard peripherals required:* PC speaker or Sound Blaster compatible sound card, mouse, recommended CD-ROM drive.
An Innovative Language Tutor That Takes Full Advantage of Your PC to Create a Multimedia Learning Atmosphere. Words Are Displayed with Colorful, Descriptive Graphics to Stimulate Word-to-Object Associations. The Program Uses the Built-In PC Speaker or Any Sound Blaster-Compatible Sound Card to Let You Hear the Native Language Speaker Properly Say the Word or Phrase. Available on CD-ROM Only.
IMSI (International Microcomputer Software, Inc.).

EZ Language Spanish: The Simple Vocabulary & Pronunciation Tutor. *Items Included:* 1 user manual. *Customer Support:* Tech support, 60-day money-back guarantee.
Windows 3.1 or higher. IBM compatible 386 or higher (2Mb). CD-ROM disk $29.95 (ISBN 0-924677-20-1). *Nonstandard peripherals required:* PC speaker or Sound Blaster compatible sound card, mouse, recommended CD-ROM drive.
An Innovative Language Tutor That Takes Full Advantage of Your PC to Create a Multimedia Learning Atmosphere. Words Are Displayed with Colorful, Descriptive Graphics to Stimulate Word-to-Object Associations. The Program Uses the Built-In PC Speaker or Any Sound Blaster-Compatible Sound Card to Let You Hear the Native Language Speaker Properly Say the Word or Phrase. Available on CD-ROM Only.
IMSI (International Microcomputer Software, Inc.).

EZ Language: The Simple Vocabulary & Pronunciation Tutor. *Items Included:* 1 user manual. *Customer Support:* Tech support, 60-day money-back guarantee.
Windows 3.1 or higher. IBM compatible 386 or higher (2Mb). CD-ROM disk $69.95 (ISBN 0-924677-11-2). *Nonstandard peripherals required:* PC speaker or Sound Blaster compatible sound card, mouse, microphone optional, CD-ROM drive.
An Innovative Language Tutor That Takes Full Advantage of Your PC to Create a Multimedia Learning Atmosphere. Words Are Displayed with Colorful, Descriptive Graphics to Stimulate Word-to-Object Associations. The Program Uses the Built-In PC Speaker or Any Sound Blaster-Compatible Sound Card to Let You Hear the Native Language Speaker Properly Say the Word or Phrase. Six Different Languages: French, Spanish, Italian, German, Russian, & Japanese. Available on CD-ROM Only.
IMSI (International Microcomputer Software, Inc.).

EZ Ledger. *Version:* 3.0a. 1993. *Compatible Hardware:* IBM PC, PC XT; Apple IIe, IIgs, IIc. *Language(s):* Turbo PASCAL. *Memory Required:* 640k. *General Requirements:* Hard disk, printer. *Items Included:* Disks, Complete illustrated instructions binder. *Customer Support:* Technical 8:30-4pm M-F telephone no charge.
disk Apple $99.00, IBM $149.00 (Order no.: EZ).
Simple Ledger Program for Libraries. Allows User to Keep Track of Budgeted Items. Budget & Budget Balance Are Displayed on Screen or Printer.
Right On Programs.

EZ-Log. 1985. *Compatible Hardware:* IBM PC & compatibles. *Memory Required:* 512k. *General Requirements:* Printer that runs at least 200 CPS. 3.5" or 5.25" disk $495.00.
Radio & Traffic Billing System.
The Management.

EZ Mail. *Compatible Hardware:* TRS-80 Model III, Color Computer.
contact publisher for price.
Blanton Software Service.

EZ-PrintSet. *Version:* 1.2. *Compatible Hardware:* IBM PC & compatibles, PS/2. *General Requirements:* Lotus 1-2-3 release 2.x. *Customer Support:* Free telephone support (not toll-free). 3.5" or 5.25" disk $49.95.
Allows User to Produce Many Reports from One Spreadsheet Without Having to Reset Printer Information. User Can Change All Spreadsheet Print Settings on One Screen, & Name & Store Print Settings for Various Ranges in a Worksheet. Can Be Used with Any Printer.
Lichtman Industries.

EZ-Rx System. Jan. 1984. *Compatible Hardware:* IBM PC with 80Mb+ hard disk. *Operating System(s) Required:* MS-DOS. *Language(s):* Compiled MBASIC. *Memory Required:* 1000k. *Customer Support:* $50/month.
disk $1495.00.
Includes Mainframe Features & Interfaces with Accounts Receivable, Inventory Control, & Third-Party Billing. Stores Thousands of New Prescriptions on a Patient Before Filling the Profile & Requiring a Deletion (or a New Profile). Multiple Fee Schedules Selected by Patient or Drug, Alpha Lookup of Patients, Drugs, & Accounts. Full OBRA 90 Data & Electronic Claims Support.
Signature Software Systems, Inc.

EZ Text, 2 disks. Jul. 1983. *Operating System(s) Required:* CP/M.
CP/M. 8" disk $19.95.
CP/M. 5.25" 40 TRK disk $19.95.
CP/M. 5.25" 80 TRK disk $19.95.
Full Screen Editor That Displays a Command Line & Text. Single Letter Commands Switch Modes. Block, Move, Read & Write Are Supported.
Elliam Assocs.

EZDSX: Z80 Disassembler. Zee Microwave. Jun. 1984. *Operating System(s) Required:* CP/M-80. *Memory Required:* 48k.
disk 40 TPI $24.95 (ISBN 0-923875-35-2).
disk 80 TPI $24.95 (ISBN 0-923875-36-0).
8" disk $24.95 (ISBN 0-923875-34-4).
Non-Interactive Two Pass Disassembler Will Convert a CP/M-80 COM File into a Z-80 Assembly Language Source File with Pseudo Ops. Synthetically Generates Labels.
Elliam Assocs.

EZDT: Z80 Dynamic Debugger. Zee Microwave. Jun. 1984. *Operating System(s) Required:* CP/M-80. *Memory Required:* 48k.
disk 40 TPI $22.95 (ISBN 0-923875-29-8).
disk 80 TPI $22.95 (ISBN 0-923875-30-1).
8" disk $22.95 (ISBN 0-923875-28-X).
Allows User to Dump, Test, Debug, Disassemble, Set Break Points, Modify & Trace Z-80 Assembly Language Programs. Additional Commands Are Provided to Convert Input to Decimal, HEX, & ASCII; Display First & Next Disk Directory Blocks; Set Number of Display Lines; Memory Test over Address Range & Display Stack Contents.
Elliam Assocs.

EZMENU.
MS-DOS 3.0 or higher (512k). disk $19.95.
A "Menu Maker" Program That Requires Hard Drive. Allows User to Execute All Programs on Hard Drive by Selecting Them from a Screen Menu. Adding, Deleting, & Modifying Program Selections on the Menu Is Simplified. Not Memory Resident, Therefore All Computer's Memory Is Available to the Program Selected From Menu.
Blanton Software Service.

EZRes: Memory Resident Bar Code Printing. 1995. *Items Included:* Full manual. *Customer Support:* Free telephone support - 90 days, 30-day warranty.
MS-DOS 3.2 or higher. 286 (584k). disk $139.95. *Nonstandard peripherals required:* CGA/EGA/VGA.
A Memory-Resident Application Which Prints Bar Codes upon Demand. You Activate & Deactivate Bar Code Printing by Sending Special Characters to the Printer. Upon Activation, Subsequent Characters or Words Are Printed in the Corresponding Bar Code Format. This Meant That You May Prepare Mixed Text & Bar Code Output Using Almost Any Word Processor or Text-Producing Program.
Dynacomp, Inc.

EZSCRIP. *Compatible Hardware:* TRS-80 Model III, Color Computer.
contact publisher for price.
Blanton Software Service.

EZSCRIP PLUS. *Compatible Hardware:* TRS-80 Model III, Color Computer.
contact publisher for price.
Blanton Software Service.

EZTOUCH. *Items Included:* 1 program diskette, 1 manual. *Customer Support:* Free telephone support for registered users, (510) 845-2110.
MS-DOS/PC-DOS 2.0 or higher. IBM PC & compatibles (256k). disk Developer version $195.00. *Nonstandard peripherals required:* Touch screens from: Dale Electronics, Carroll Touch, Pewrsonal Touch, Elographics.
runtime $50.00.
Stand-Alone, All-in-One Tool to Program Touch-Sensitive Hardware Systems. Enables Users to Control Touch Frames, Independent of Programming Language or Application, Without Having to Create Software "Drivers", Procedures or Functions. Communicates Touch Choices to Any Applicaiton Program Through the Keyboard Buffer.
Software Science, Inc.

EZX-11. *Version:* 2.00. *Items Included:* Spiral bound manual.
disk $150.00.
Version of the Census X-11 Seasonal Adjustment Procedure. It Provides a Fully Menu & Dialog Driven Interface to the Full X11 Procedure, Including Both Quarterly & Monthly Adjustment, Trading Day & Holiday Adjustments. Adjust Series One At a Time or Build a Batch File for Automatic Adjustment of Hundreds of Series. Output Can Be Sent to a Printer, a File, or Suppressed for Batch Runs. Also Offers a Number of Important Data Preparation

TITLE INDEX

Procedures, Such As Interpolation, Compaction, Benchmarking & Splicing. Other Recent Additions to the Package Include Forecasting Using Exponential Smoothing & Spectral Techniques & High-Quality Graphics. It Can Import Data in ASCII Formats & Also Directly From Lotus or dBase III on the PC & Excel (Saved as WKS) on the Macintosh. While Designed to Work Closely with the RATS Econometrics Package, It Can Also Be Used As a Stand-Alone Program.
Estma.

E3M: Short Circuit Current & Voltage Drop Calculation. *Version:* 06/1996. 1980. *Language(s):* Compiled Assembly Language. *Memory Required:* 448k. *Customer Support:* Technical hotline, "Lifetime" support at no charge. MS-DOS/PC-DOS. IBM & compatible. $745.00. *Short Circuit Current Voltage Drop & - E3M (New Update) Uses per-unit Procedures to Calcuate Symmetric, AsymmeDrop & Power Factor - E3M (New Update) Uses per-unit Procedures to Calculate Symmetric, Asymmetric, Instantaneous & Other 3-Phase & 1-Phase Bolted Fault Currents, Voltage Drops & Power Factor Throughout in Mixed Resistive & Reactive Circuits. Carries Disk Files of Equipment Data in All Commercial Sizes for 30 Different Equipment Types Including Wire, Bus, Fuses, Breakers, Switches, Transformers, Rotating Machines, Overhead Wire, etc. Special Pop-Up Screens To Help with Wire & Cable Sizing. Handles 700 Fault Loc with Fully Prompting, Latest State-of-the-Art Input Screens with Windows, Defaults, Error Checking, Nearly 100 "Help" Messages. English Units.*
MC2 Engineering Software.

F/A-18 Intercepter. *Compatible Hardware:* Commodore Amiga.
3.5" disk $19.95.
Racing Simulation.
Electronic Arts.

F & I Billing System. Jan. 1981. *Compatible Hardware:* Tandy 1000. *Operating System(s) Required:* MS-DOS. *Language(s):* BASIC, FOXPRO. *Memory Required:* 640k. *General Requirements:* Hard disk, 10Mb min.
disk $4000.00.
Designed for Automobile Dealers, Calculates Monthly Payments, & Prints All Retail Delivery Forms. Leasing, Inventory, Sales Analysis, & Credit Bureau Interface Are Also Available.
American Systems Corp.

F-BASIC. *Version:* 4.0. *Compatible Hardware:* Commodore Amiga. *Items Included:* System disk, sample programs disk, user's manual.
3.5" disk $99.95.
Enhanced Compiled BASIC Language.
Delphi Noetic Systems.

F-BASIC System SLDB. *Version:* 4.0. *Compatible Hardware:* Commodore Amiga. *Items Included:* System disk, user's manual.
3.5" disk $60.00.
Source-Level Debugger Companion to F-BASIC.
Delphi Noetic Systems.

F-Chart 1-2-3. *Version:* 1A. Mar. 1983. *Compatible Hardware:* IBM PC with Lotus 1-2-3. *Operating System(s) Required:* PC-DOS 2.0. (source code included). *Memory Required:* 256k.
disk $100.00.
demo $10.00.
manual only $20.00.
Calculates Solar Heating System Performance Using Methods Presented in "Solar Heating Design by the F-Chart Method". SI Units Are Used.
E. Jessup & Assocs.

F-15 Strike Eagle. Sid Meier. *Compatible Hardware:* Apple II+, IIe, IIc; Atari ST; Commodore 64, 128; IBM PC, PCjr; Tandy. *Items Included:* Manual. *Customer Support:* Free customer service, (410) 771-1151, Ext. 350.
disk $19.95.
3-D Fighter Combat Includes: Airborne Radar, Air to Air Missiles, Surface to Air Missile Defense, Ground Target Bombing, Full Aerobatics & Multiple Combat Scenarios.
MicroProse Software.

F40 Pursuit Simulator. Jun. 1989.
MS-DOS (512k). disk $44.95. *Optimal configuration:* EGA board.
Amiga 500, 1000, 2000 (512k). 3.5" disk $44.95. *Nonstandard peripherals required:* Joy stick.
Atari ST 520, 1040, ST2, ST4 (512k). 3.5" disk $44.95. *Nonstandard peripherals required:* Color monitor.
Commodore 64, 128 (64k). $39.95.
Race Against the Clock in Four States of America. Avoid Being Busted by the Policemen or Crashing into the Road Blocks. Find the Best Way on the Real Mapped Highways.
Titus Software Corp.

F-19 Stealth Fighter. 1987. *Compatible Hardware:* Commodore 64/128, IBM PC; Amiga. *Items Included:* Manual, keyboard overlay, maps. *Customer Support:* Free customer service, (410) 771-1151, Ext. 350.
Commodore. disk $19.95.
IBM. 3.5" or 5.25" disk $69.95.
Amiga. 3.5" disk $59.95.
Jet Fighter Simulation Featuring 3-D Graphics. Spectacular Visuals in the Plane That Radar Doesn't See. Secret Missions in U.S. Navy Stealth Fighter.
MicroProse Software.

F77Lib. *Customer Support:* 800-929-8117 (customer service).
MS-DOS. Commodore 128; CP/M. disk $49.99 (ISBN 0-87007-496-2).
Provides the Missing Pieces in the INTRINSIC Function Library of CP/M Operating Systems to Create a Full FORTRON 77 Library of Real & DOUBLE PRECISION Functions of Maximum Practical Accuracy. The Most Benefit Can Be Seen with Microsoft FORTRAN & BASIC Compilers. Among Functions Addressed are SIN, SINH, TANH, LOG2, Square Root, & Double Precision Products. Source Code & Manual Included. Creates Full Library of Real & Double Precision Numbers for the Intrinsic Function Library for Full Fortran 77 Standards.
SourceView Software International.

F-Trans. Ron Holyer. Apr. 1984. *Compatible Hardware:* CP/M-80 or MS-DOS compatibles; IBM PC & compatibles. *Operating System(s) Required:* CP/M-80, MS-DOS, PC-DOS. *Language(s):* Assembly. *Memory Required:* CP/M 32k, DOS 64k.
disk $59.95.
Communication Utility Allows Files to Be Transferred Between CP/M-80 & MS-DOS Computers Regardless of System & Disk Format Differences, Including Connecting Serial Ports of Computer. Custom-Made Cables Available. Allows Multiple-File Transmitting with Single Command.
Generic Computer Products, Inc. (GCPI).

f(Z) Complex Variable Graphics. 1992. *Items Included:* Detailed manuals are included with all DYNACOMP products. *Customer Support:* Free telephone support to original customer - no time limit; 30 day limited warranty.
MS-DOS 3.2 or higher. IBM PC & compatibles (512k). $39.95 2 diskettes (standard version); $49.95 2 diskettes (8087 version) (Add $5.00 for 3 1/2" format; 5 1/4" format standard). *Optimal configuration:* IBM, 320k RAM, 2 360k drives (or 1 floppy & 1 hard disk), MS-DOS 2.0 or higher, & a color graphics card.
CVG Is an Interactive, Educational, Computer-Graphics Package Designed to Aid in the Study of Functions of a Complex Variable. CVG Can Graph Rational Functions, Exp(z), Log(z), & the Riemann Zeta Function. CVG Can Compose, Add, Subtract, Multiply, Divide, Differentiate, & Integrate Functions. You Can Also Draw on Either the Complex Plane or on the Riemann Sphere.
Dynacomp, Inc.

F-15 Strike Eagle II. 1989. *Items Included:* Manual, keyboard summary card. *Customer Support:* Free customer service, 1-410-771-1151, Ext. 350.
80286. IBM PC, PC XT, PC AT, PS/2; Tandy 1000/3000. disk $54.95 (ISBN 1-55884-013-3). *Optimal configuration:* IBM or compatible 286; CGA, EGA, MCGA, VGA monitor; DOS 2.1 or higher.
Up-Date of the Classic Game of Aerial Combat. Solid-Filled Polygon-Based 3-D Graphics Generate Incredible Visual Detail. Smooth, Fast Animation. Four Levels of Difficulty. Streamlined Weapons Console. Multiple "Camera" Angles for a View of the Best Action.
MicroProse Software.

F-15 Strike Eagle II: Operation Desert Storm Scenario Disk. 1991. *Items Included:* Manual, poster. *Customer Support:* Free customer service, 1-410-771-1151, Ext. 350.
80286. IBM PC, PC XT, PC AT, PS/2; Tandy 1000/3000. disk $29.95 (ISBN 1-55884-144-X). *Optimal configuration:* IBM or compatible 286; CGA, EGA, MCGA, VGA; DOS 2.1 or higher.
Scenario Disk for F-15 Strike Eagle II, Must Own F-15 II. Eight Historically-Based Operation Desert Storm Missions. New North Cape & Central Europe "Worlds". Night Combat Capability. Spectacular New 3-D Graphics & Breathtaking Sounds.
MicroProse Software.

F-15 Strike Eagle III. Sep. 1992. *Items Included:* Manual, keyboard overlay. *Customer Support:* Free customer service, 1-410-771-1151, Ext. 350.
80386 required, 16MHz, hard disk required, DOS 5.0, VGA, Joystick, sound card. IBM & most compatibles (640k). disk $79.95 (ISBN 1-55884-205-5). *Optimal configuration:* 386, 16MHz, hard disk, DOS 5.0, VGA, Joystick, sound card.
Revolutionary New Visual System Combining 3-D Polygon & Sprite Graphics Technologies Provides an Unpresidented Level of Detail & Richness of Visual Experience. Two Player Capability via Modem. Most Authentic & Functional Cockpit Ever Presented in a Flight Simulation. Streamlined Dogfighting Enhances Playability.
MicroProse Software.

F-117A Nighthawk Stealth Fighter 2.0. *Version:* 2.0. 1991. *Items Included:* Manual, keyboard overlay. *Customer Support:* Free customer service, 1-410-771-1151, Ext. 350.
80386, 16MHz required. IBM 386 & most compatibles (640k). disk $79.95 (ISBN 1-55884-141-5). *Optimal configuration:* VGA/MCGA graphics, joystick or mouse, DOS 3.0 or higher.
Pilot America's Radar-Elusive Jet. Theaters Include Persian Gulf, Central Europe, Cuba, North Korea, Libya, Vietnam & More. Great Sound Package. Spectacular Night Graphics & Special Night HUD Features. Realistic Cockpit & In-Plane Graphics. More Advanced Weapons, Dramatic Explosions & More Challenging Enemy Artificial Intelligence.
MicroProse Software.

Faast-3. *Version:* 3.3D. Jan. 1996. *Items Included:* One user manual, 300 plus pgs. *Customer Support:* Phone support free; update service at extra cost (from $300.00).
PC-DOS/MS-DOS 2.1 or higher. PC or compatible 8086/8087/8088 (512k). $995.00 & up. *Optimal configuration:* VGA & 8087; pen plotter or hi-res dot printer or laser (HP).
PC-DOS/MS-DOS 3.3 or higher. 80386, 80486 or Pentium (80387 optional) (3Mb). $1662.00 & up. *Optimal configuration:* VGA; pen plotter, hi-res dot printer, HP laser.
VAX VMS 4.4 or higher. VAX 11/725 or higher. $3499.00 & up. *Optimal configuration:* Tek graphics, pen plotter.
Intergraph CLIX. Intergraph Clipper. $3499.00 & up.
SUN OS 4.1.3. SUN Sparc. $3499.00 & up.
Solves Fluid Flow Problems for Piping Design. Features Graphic Display of Piping As Well As Graphic Display of Results. Integral Graphics with Full Interactive Error Detection & Recovery.
Faast Software.

Fabmaster. *Version:* 4.D.5. Fabmaster. Jul. 1991. *Items Included:* User documentation. *Customer Support:* Included in purchase price: 6 month warranty, 1 year maintenance for 10% of list price, 3 day training course available.
MS-DOS. PC-AT (1Mb). $19,500.00 (Order no.: FBMSTR). *Optimal configuration:* PC-AT 386/486 DOS 5.0, 1Mb RAM fast, 40Mb drive, VGA graphics printer. *Networks supported:* Novell, Ethernet, VAX, NFS.
Integrated PC-Based Software Module for Programming Assembly & Test Machines. Reads in Popular PCB CAD Formats & Converts Them to a Neutral Database. Graphically Displays Boards on Screen. Allows Search & Selection of Data for Output to Target Machine Output Formats Are Generated Automatically.
Team Visionics Corp.

FABS. Lifeboat Associates. *Compatible Hardware:* TI Professional. *Operating System(s) Required:* MS-DOS. *Language(s):* Assembly. *Memory Required:* 64k. *General Requirements:* 2 disk drives.
$150.00.
Allows User to Program Fast, Active B-Tree, Multi-Path Structures.
Texas Instruments, Personal Productivit.

FABS PLUS. *Version:* 4.6B. Aug. 1991. *Items Included:* Spiral-bound manual, disk with programs. *Customer Support:* Technical support by Phone (813-961-7566) or Fax (813-963-6180).
PC-DOS/MS-DOS 2.1 or higher, Windows. IBM or compatible (128k). disk $195.00 (Single User) $295.00 (Network). *Addl. software required:* Programming Languages: C, Basic, Pascal, Fortran, Cobol.
OS/2 1.1 or higher. IBM or compatible (2Mb). 3.5" disk $195.00 (single user) $295.00 (Network). *Addl. software required:* Programming Languages: C, Basic, Pascal, Fortran, Cobol. *Networks supported:* LAN-Manager & all Net-Bios compatible.
A BTREE Subroutine, Maintains Key Files for FAST Data Retrieval in Large Data Files. Use As Either Memory Resident or Linked Directly. Network Version for Networks Support DOS File Locking. Record Access Less Than One-Half Second from Extremely Large Files. Millions of Records Permitted. Occupies Approximately 23k Including All Buffers. High Speed Re-Indexing Program. Key Files Maintained Dynamically & Require No Sorting. 20 Files Open Concurrently.
Computer Control Systems, Inc.

FACC II. *Compatible Hardware:* Commodore Amiga.
3.5" disk $34.95.
Disk Performance Enhancer.
Elastic Reality, Inc.

FaceIt. *Compatible Hardware:* Apple Macintosh.
3.5" disk $100.00.
Adds Macintosh Interface to Programs Written in Basic, C, Fortran, Pascal & Others.
FaceWare.

Faces. 1990. *Items Included:* manual.
IBM PC or compatible (512k). disk $39.95.
MAC Plus or higher (1Mb). $44.95. *Networks supported:* AppleTalk.
Amiga Kickstart 1.2 or higher (512k). $39.95.
Stack the Falling Blocks of Face Segments of the Famous & Not-so-Famous in the Proper Order to Make Complete Faces. Swap the Pieces, Flip Them, & Drop Them into Place. "To Rotate Shakespear's Nose or Not to Rotate Shakespeare's Nose, That is the Question." Picture This If You Will - Joan of Arc's Nose on Napoleon's Mouth. What a Combination! Rack up the Scores by Making Perfect or Mixed Faces, but Remember There Are no Points for "Double Chins" in This Game! When You Create a Perfect Face, Your Opponent Gets a Stack of Face Pieces Dumped onto His Screen.
Spectrum HoloByte.

Faces of Summer. (Photopaedia Ser.: Vol. 2). Feb. 1995. *Items Included:* Warranty/registration card, game manual. *Customer Support:* Technical Support Number: 1-800-734-9466, 90 days limited warranty.
Windows 3.1; Macintosh System 7 or higher. IBM 33MHz i80486DX (8Mb); Macintosh 16MHz 68030 or higher, 25MHz 68LC040 or higher (5Mb). CD-ROM disk $59.99 (ISBN 1-888158-06-9). *Nonstandard peripherals required:* Double-speed CD-ROM drive. *Addl. software required:* MS-DOS 5.0 or higher.
This 400 Photo Collection, Including a Number Not Before Published Are Taken by Koichi Inakoshi, One of Japan's Premier Photographers. Inakoshi Captures Fleeting Moments in His Journey Around the Globe in His Photos of Summer. Also Included Is a Biographical Sketch & an Autobiographical Essay by the Artist.
Synergy Interactive Corp.

Facilities Scheduler. *Customer Support:* 800-929-8117 (customer service).
MS-DOS. Apple II. disk $149.99 (ISBN 0-87007-702-3).
Computerizes the Scheduling of Discrete Events in up to 999 Locations. Examples Are Classrooms, Motorpool Vehicles, Equipment Usage, Janitorial Services, Salespersons on a Route, Office Building Suites, & Conference Rooms in Large Organizations. All Scheduling May Be Handled Through One Central Location & Printouts Dispersed to Key Locations. Users Schedule, Inquire About, & Find Available Rooms, Display Information on Screen or Printer & Delete Records. There Is Immediate Detection & Reporting of Scheduling Conflicts, & Selective Printing of Scheduled Activities.
SourceView Software International.

Facilities Scheduling: Room Reservations. *Version:* 7.1. Aug. 1991. *Items Included:* Step-by-Step instruction manual. *Customer Support:* Free support by phone, FAX, correspondence, or modem. On-site training and/or installation, $229.00 per day plus expenses.
MS/PC DOS 3.0 or higher. PC, 286, 386, 486; Tandy 3000 or higher (640k). disk $995.00 (Order no.: 7001). *Nonstandard peripherals required:* Interface to Touch-Tone requires our voice digitization board. Programs without Touch-Tone interface do not require non-standard peripherals, boards. *Optimal configuration:* 386SX computer with a fast hard disk & our telephone interface board. *Networks supported:* Novell.
Reserves Rooms, AV Equipment, Training Supplies. Quickly Find Open Room, Schedule Repetitive Meetings, etc. Prints Great Many Lists. Customized for Each Client.
Robert H. Geeslin (Educational Programming).

Facility Master. *Customer Support:* 800-929-8117 (customer service).
MS-DOS. IBM/PS2. disk $699.99 (ISBN 0-87007-700-7).
Schedules Rooms & Equipment for up to 1000 Rooms in Ten Building, up to 8000 Serialized Pieces of Equipment & 99,999 Pieces of Non-Serialized Equipment Per Minor Category, in Ten Magor Categories Each with Ten Minor Categories. Will Produce a Variety of Reports Helpful for the Management of Any Group of Buildings.
SourceView Software International.

Facility Scheduler, 2 disks. Mar. 1986. *Compatible Hardware:* IBM PC & compatibles. *Operating System(s) Required:* MS-DOS 2.0 or higher. *Language(s):* Pascal. *Memory Required:* 256k. *Items Included:* 1 manual. *Customer Support:* Free support & user newsletters.
$300.00.
Designed to Handle the Scheduling of Facilities for Organizations or Individuals. Single or Multiple Events May Be Scheduled. Conflicts in Date, Time & Facility Are Checked for & Printed. Prints Monthly Calendar for All Events or for a Specified Organization and/or Facility. Prints Letters, Labels, Lists & Allows Users to Create Their Own Reports or Letters. Also Billing for Use of Facilities.
Parish Data Systems, Inc.

Facility Series: FL-I (Industrial); FL-O (Office-Commercial). *Compatible Hardware:* Unix Sun, Aegis; HP-UX, HP Apollo; DEC Ultrix. *Items Included:* Documentation. *Customer Support:* Maintenance plan, training, 800 number. contact publisher for price. *Addl. software required:* Series 5000.
Packages Are Interactive Facility, Furniture, & Equipment Tracking Systems for Planning, Designing & Managing Industrial Plants & Office Facilities. As the Facility Layout is Created, a Model is Defined Automatically That Stores Information About the Plant Equipment, Office Area, Furnishings, Manufacturing Processes & Office Equipment in a Relational DBMS.
Auto-Trol Technology Corp.

Fact-Stractor. Bio-Grammatical Engineering. Aug. 1986. *Compatible Hardware:* Apple Macintosh, IBM PC. *Memory Required:* 512k.
IBM version 1. disk $99.00 (Order no.: FS-I1).
IBM version 2. disk $199.00 (Order no.: FS-I2).
Macintosh version 1. 3.5" disk $99.00 (Order no.: FS-M1).
Macintosh version 2. 3.5" disk $199.00 (Order no.: FS-M2).
Natural Language Processor Which Reads English ASCII Text Files. Version 1 Creates Printed Summaries of the Processed Text. Version 2 Uses the Information to Build a Database Which May Be Used by Other Database Management Programs.
Hexcraft, Inc.

Factmatcher: Search & Find. 1983. *Compatible Hardware:* IBM PC, PC XT, PC AT. *Operating System(s) Required:* MS-DOS 2.0. *Memory Required:* 256k. *General Requirements:* Hard disk.
disk $1600.00.
International Technology Group, Inc.

Factor Extractor. *Version:* 3.21. Jan. 1987. *Compatible Hardware:* IBM PC, PC XT, PC AT & compatibles. *Operating System(s) Required:* MS-DOS, PC-DOS. *Language(s):* C. *Memory Required:* 640k. *General Requirements:* Hard disk. *Customer Support:* 800, BBS, FAX, Optional Training.
disk $495.00.
Identifies & Prioritizes Which Input Variables (up to 100) Determine Process Output Quality. Tells the User Exactly What Factors Must Be Controlled to Produce a High Quality Product.
Stochos, Inc.

FACTORIAL-DESIGN. *Version:* 2.1. Sridhar Seshdari & Stanley N. Deming. 1989. *Items Included:* Manual, 3.5" diskette. *Customer Support:* Free telephone support to registered users.
MS-DOS. IBM PC/XT/AC & compatibles (384k). disk $295.00 (ISBN 0-932651-19-4).
Program for Using Full 2-Level Factorial Designs to Investigate 2-, 3-, & 4-Factor Systems. Acquires Data to Fit a First-Order Polynomial Model with 2-Factor Interaction Terminals.
Statistical Programs.

Factory Manager. 1989.
DOS. 486 (128k). Contact publisher for price. *Nonstandard peripherals required:* Printer.
Provides Information for Parts Cost for Quotations Using Machine Cost Labor Rates Overhead Rates & Burden Factors. Job Costing, Accounts Receivable Inventory, Time Tickets Bills of Material & Job Routings Are Also Included.
Zeltner Assocs., Inc.

FACTS. *Version:* 6.4. *Compatible Hardware:* IBM RS/6000, IBM PC & compatibles, most 286 & 386 platforms. *Memory Required:* 512k. *General Requirements:* Hard disk, 100Mb. *Customer Support:* Telephone support 8:00-7:00 EST. Contact publisher for price.
Full-Function, Integrated Software System for Wholesalers/Distributors Composed of Accounts Receivable, Sales Orders, Inventory Control, Purchase Orders, Sales Analysis, Accounts Payable, General Ledger, Payroll, Office Automation, & Report Writer. A System of Automated & Manual Controls & Procedures Combining to Control Inventory Levels, Increase Service Levels, & Maximize Turns. Available under Various Platforms Including: UNIX, XENIX, DOS, AIX, & Most Networks. Features Include: Multi-Company, Multi-Bank & Warehouse, Multiple Pricing & Costing Schemes, Rapid Data Access for Larger Files, & Input Validation.
Software Solutions, Inc.

Facts & Faces of U.S. Presidents. *Compatible Hardware:* Apple Macintosh Plus. *Memory Required:* 1000k. *General Requirements:* 800k disk drive; HyperCard. *Items Included:* Disk, manual. *Customer Support:* 800 phone support.
3.5" disk $49.50.
Provides Facts on Presidents.
Visatex Corp.

Facts & Figures. *Version:* 3.1. Sep. 1985. *Compatible Hardware:* IBM PC & compatibles. *Operating System(s) Required:* PC-DOS, MS-DOS. *Language(s):* COBOL, Assembler. *Memory Required:* 256k. *General Requirements:* Graphics capabilities. *Customer Support:* Yearly or hourly fee.
disk $295.00 (Order no.: FF20).
Provides Query Capability Against User-Supplied Data or Management Summary Data Extracted from CRS Accounting Applications (or Both). Output Is in Bar Graph & Line Report Format.
Computer Related Services, Inc.

Facts on File - Public Library Database. *Version:* 5.1. 1994. *Items Included:* Manual. *Customer Support:* One year of CSAP is provided at N/C; 30 day no risk guarantee.
MS-DOS. IBM & compatibles (640k). 5.25" disk $1025.00 (ISBN 0-927875-48-9, Order no.: 1710). *Addl. software required:* Winn CAT, Winn Informational Database subscription Item No. 1770 for $299.00. *Optimal configuration:* An additional 25Mb of hard disk space annually; other configurations same as Winn CAT. *Networks supported:* Netbios or IPX compatible.
3.5" disk $1025.00 (ISBN 0-927875-47-0, Order no.: 1710).
Winnebago CIRC/CAT Supports Full Text Informational Public Library Database Records. Facts on File Is a Concise Source of the News & Current Events As Reported in Major U.S. & International Newspapers & Magazines, Indexed for Instant Retrieval. This Provides for One-Step Searching from the Winn CAT Program. Updates Are Distributed Monthly with an Annual Subscription Fee.
Winnebago Software Co.

Facts on File-College Library Database. *Version:* 5.1. 1994. *Items Included:* Manual. *Customer Support:* One year of CSAP is provided at N/C; 30 day no risk guarantee.
MS-DOS. IBM & compatibles (640k). 5.25" disk $1025.00 (ISBN 0-927875-50-0, Order no.: 1720). *Addl. software required:* Winn CAT V. 5.1 or greater, Winn Informational Database subscription Item No. 1770 for $299.00. *Optimal configuration:* An additional 25Mb of hard disk space annually; other configurations same as Winn CAT. *Networks supported:* Netbios or IPX compatible.
3.5" disk $1025.00 (ISBN 0-927875-49-7, Order no.: 1720).
Winnebago CIRC/CAT Supports Full Text Informational College Library Database Records. Facts on File Is a Concise Source of the News & Current Events As Reported in Major U.S. & International Newspapers & Magazines, Indexed for Instant Retrieval. This Provides for One-Step Searching from the Winn CAT Program. Updates Are Sent Out Monthly & an Annual Subscription Is Required.
Winnebago Software Co.

Facts on File-School Library Database. *Version:* 5.1. 1994. *Items Included:* Manual. *Customer Support:* One year of CSAP is provided at N/C; 30 day no risk guarantee.
MS-DOS. IBM & compatibles (640k). 5.25" disk $825.00 (ISBN 0-927875-42-X, Order no.: 1700). *Addl. software required:* Winn CAT, Winn Informational Database subscription Item No. 1770 for $299.00. *Optimal configuration:* An additional 25Mb of hard disk space annually; other configurations same as Winn CAT. *Networks supported:* Netbios or IPX compatible.
3.5" disk $825.00 (ISBN 0-927875-41-1, Order no.: 1700).
Winnebago CIRC/CAT Supports Full Text Informational Database Records Which Includes a School Library Database. Facts on File Is a Concise Source of the News & Current Events As Reported in Major U.S. & International Newspapers & Magazines, Indexed for Instant Retrieval. This Provides for One-Step Searching from the Winn CAT Program. Updates Are Distributed Monthly with an Annual Subscription Fee.
Winnebago Software Co.

Factuary. Oct. 1994. *Items Included:* Software Documentation/Owners Manual & Quick Reference Card. *Customer Support:* Customer Service is provided to all customers free of charge for 30 days after the purchase date. After that time, maintenance may be purchased at $95 per year.
Microsoft Windows. IBM & compatibles (3Mb). $349.00 Stand Alone Version (ISBN 0-943293-08-1). *Addl. software required:* Windows version 3.0 or higher. *Optimal configuration:* Mouse. *Networks supported:* Novell, Lantastic & Banyon.
Factuary Performs Actuarial Calculations for Use in Estate Tax Planning.
ViewPlan, Inc.

Faculty-Staff Attendance Manager. *Items Included:* Bound manual. *Customer Support:* Free hotline - no time limit; 30 day limited warranty; updates are $5/disk plus S&H.
MS-DOS. IBM & compatibles (128k). disk $229.95. *Nonstandard peripherals required:* Two disk drives; printer.
Apple (64k). disk $229.95.
Handles the Attendance Records for up to 500 School Employees, Both Faculty & Other Staff Members. It Manages 12 Kinds of Absences, Including (but Not Limited to): Professional Days; Personal Days; Jury Duty; Tardies. It Also Accumulates & Subtracts Absences from the Individual's Cumulative Number of Days Available, Including Half Days. Various Reports Are Provided, Including: Monthly for Entire Year; by Department, ID Number, or Alphabetically; Days Staff Members Were Absent; Reasons for the Absences; Percentages of Absences, per Individual or for All Employees; Absentees on a Particular Day; Monday Absences or All Friday/Monday Absences; Individual Attendance Record for Any Staff Member.
Dynacomp, Inc.

The Faery Tale Adventure. *Compatible Hardware:* Commodore Amiga; IBM; C64. $49.95.
Participate in the Adventures of Three Brothers As They Travel Through a Faery Land Full of Vicious Monsters, Enchanted Princesses, Fearsome Dragons, & Even a Kindly Wood Cutter or Two. Over 20 Thousand Animated Screens.
Microillusions, Inc.

Fair & Square. Nan Holcomb & Jane Steelman. Oct. 1993. *Items Included:* Directions on use of the program, registration card. *Customer Support:* 90 days limited warranty, replacement disks for fee of $10.00 & proof of purchase.
6.07. MAC LC (2Mb). 3.5" disk $29.95 (ISBN 0-944727-20-4). *Optimal configuration:* MAC LC, System 7.1, 4Mb RAM.
Kevin Wants to Play & Win or Lose Fair & Square. User Can Read Kevin's Story by Clicking a Button on the Screen or Use a Switch to Hear the Story Read Word by Word or Sentence by Sentence As the Text Is Highlighted in Color of Choice.
Jason & Nordic Pubs.

FairCom ODBC Driver. *Version:* 1.5. Dec. 1995. *Customer Support:* Free, unlimited technical support by phone of FAX from 9am to 5pm CST for 3 months from purchase date. 24-hour access to e-mail facilities. Annual support program includes full unlimited technical support; automatic priority shipment of all upgrades/fixes & free subscription to technical publication.
Windows 3.1, Windows 95, Windows NT. IBM. disk $59.00, per node. *Networks supported:* TCP/IP.
Allows Direct, Easy Access to C-Tree Plus Files from ODBC Compliant Applications. Contains All Logic Necessary to Handle Requests from a Front-End Application. DLL Design Supports Three Modes of C-Tree Plus: Single/Multi-User Non-Server & Client/Server. Support: Full Core/

FAIRCOM SERVER

Level 1 ODBC Standard; Some Level 2. Meets/ Exceeds Requirements of Most ODBC-Compliant Applications.
FairCom Corp.

FairCom Server. Version: 6.05.26A. Items Included: 1 perfect bound installation guide. Customer Support: Free, unlimited technical support by phone or FAX from 9am to 5pm CST for 3 months from purchase date. 24-hour access to e-mail facilities. Annual support program includes full unlimited technical support; automatic priority shipment of all upgrades/fixes & free subscription to technical publication.
Unix. Motorola 88OPEN. disk $1495.00 1-5 users; $2395.00 6-125 users; $3795.00 125 users; call publisher for unlimited users. Networks supported: TCP/IP & Shared Memory.
Sun OS 4.1, Solaris 2.0. Sun Sparc. disk $1495.00 1-5 users; $2395.00 6-125 users; $3795.00 125 users. Networks supported: TCP/IP, Shared Memory, Message Queues.
AIX. IBM RS6000. disk $1495.00 1-5 users; $2395.00 6-125 users; $3795.00 125 users. Networks supported: TCP/IP, Shared Memory, Message Queues.
HP 9.XX. HP9000. disk $1495.00 1-5 users; $2395.00 6-125 users; $3795.00 125 users. Networks supported: TCP/IP, Shared Memory, Message Queues.
DOS. disk $1495.00 1-5 users; $2395.00 6-125 users; $3795.00 125 users. Networks supported: NetBIOS compatible networks & Novell Netware.
Unix; AT&T, SCO, Interactive, QNX, Lynx, Linux, Apple AUX. disk $1495.00 1-5 users; $2395.00 6-125 users; $3795.00 125 users. Networks supported: TCP/IP, Shared Memory.
OS/2. disk $1495.00 1-5 users; $2395.00 6-125 users; $3795.00 125 users. Networks supported: NetBIOS compatible networks & Novell Netware SPX.
High-Performance, Multi-Threaded, Transaction Processing Server. Features Include: Heterogeneous Networking; File Mirroring; Industrial Quality Transaction Processing, Including Full Commit & Rollback; Intermediate Save Points; Complete Logging; Automatic Log Management; Restart/Disaster Recovery; User Passwords; Access Security & On-Line Administration; Deadlock Detection/Resolution; Read/Write Locks at Record/Individual Key Level; More.
FairCom Corp.

FairCom Server. Version: 6.05.26A. Dec. 1995. Items Included: 1 perfectbound administrator's guide. Customer Support: Free, unlimited technical support by phone of FAX from 9am to 5pm CST for 3 months from purchase date. 24-hour access to e-mail facilities. Annual support program includes full unlimited technical support; automatic priority shipment of all upgrades/fixes & free subscription to technical publication.
Windows 95. IBM (4Mb). 5 user $745.00; 12 user $1495.00; 125 user $2395.00. Networks supported: TCP/IP; Netbios.
Windows NT. IBM (4Mb). 5 user $745.00; 12 user $1495.00; 125 user $2395.00. Networks supported: TCP/IP; Netbios; Shared Memory.
NLM (4Mb). 5 user $745.00; 12 user $1495.00; 125 user $2395.00. Networks supported: SPX.
High-Performance, Multi-Threaded, Transaction Processing Server. Features Include: Heterogeneous Networking, File Mirroring, Industrial Quality Transaction Processing, Including Full Commit & Rollback; Intermediate Save Points; Complete Logging; Automatic Log Management; Restart/Disaster Recovery; User Passwords; Access Security & On-Line Administration; Deadlock Detection/Resolution; Read/Write Locks at Record/Individual Key Level; More.
FairCom Corp.

Falcon. Version: 3.0. 1991. Items Included: manual. Customer Support: phone support. IBM PC compatible (640k). disk $69.95.
The Original Falcon F-16 Fighter Simulation was Acclaimed for Its Realism. Now, Falcon 3.0 Takes This Authenticity to the Edge. The Flight Models Are Real. The Terrain Is Real. The Radar & Weapons Systems Are Real. The Threats Are Real. No Phony Weapons or Magic Bullets Here...Just the Best Civilian F-16 Simulation Available. You Don't Just Play Falcon 3.0, You Strap Yourself in & Get Ready for Battle.
Spectrum HoloByte.

Falcon: F-16 Fighter Simulation. Version: IBM 1.03, Mac 2.2, Amiga 1.2, Atari ST 1.2, Tandy 1.0. 1987. Compatible Hardware: Apple Macintosh Plus, Macintosh SE, Macintosh II; Atari 520-1040ST; Atari Mega 2/4; IBM PC, PC XT, PC AT & compatibles; Tandy 1000. Macintosh SE/30. Macintosh Portable, MAC IIx, MAC IIcx, MAC IIci; Amiga 500, Amiga 1000, 2000, 2500, & Tandy 1000A/EX/SX/HX/TX. Operating System(s) Required: PC-DOS/MS-DOS; Amiga Kickstart 1.2 or above. Memory Required: IBM 256k; Tandy 384k; Macintosh 1Mb; Amiga, IBM AT, Tandy 512k.
IBM AT. disk $59.95 (ISBN 0-928784-20-7).
Apple Macintosh. disk $59.95 (ISBN 0-928784-19-3).
Atari. 3.5" disk $49.95 (ISBN 0-928784-21-5).
Amiga. disk $49.95.
Tandy. disk $29.95.
Simulation of Combat Action in an "F-16A Fighting Falcon". Players Engage Enemy MiG's in Dogfight Battles or Can Play Against One Another by Connecting Two Computers. Features Sound & Digitized Airplane Images, "Radar" Mechanisms, & Four Alternating Heads-Up Displays.
Spectrum HoloByte.

Falcon MC. Nov. 1992.
MAC. Color MAC 6.05 or higher 4Mb). 3.5" disk $69.95.

Falconian Invaders. Compatible Hardware: Commodore 64.
contact publisher for price (Order no.: C-1510).
3-D Arcade Space Game.
Creative Equipment.

FAMAS (Financial Analysts Management & Authoring System). Version: 3.23. Items Included: Product diskettes, technical manual, report calculations, quick reference guide, system manager's guide, three-ring book in box. Customer Support: 1) 30-day free trial period, 2) $750/copy maintenance fee includes tool-free support, upgrades, & product newsletter, 3) On-site training $1,200/day.
MS-DOS 3.3 or higher. IBM PC or compatibles, 286 or higher (490k). disk $2900.00 & up depending on # locations. Optimal configuration: Hard disk, printer. Networks supported: All.
Provides for Historical Analysis, Industry Comparisons, Covenant Tracking, Trends, Ratios, Various Cash Flow & Cash Flow Variance Analysis, Long- & Short-Term Projections, Consolidations, Budget-to-Actual Analysis, Narrative Credit Write-Up Reports, Financial Performance Ratio Score.
Crowe, Chizek & Co.

Family Banking. 1984. Compatible Hardware: Apple II, II+, IIe, IIc; Franklin Ace. Operating System(s) Required: Apple DOS 3.3. Language(s): BASIC, Machine. Memory Required: 48k. Customer Support: Help at (305) 977-0686.
Disk set. $49.95, incl. manual (ISBN 0-87284-008-5).
Keeps Track of Family Banking & Obtain Detailed Reports of Personal Finances.
The Professor Corp.

The Family Budget. Compatible Hardware: Apple. (source code included).
disk $34.95.
Dynacomp, Inc.

Family Budget Analysis. Customer Support: 800-929-8117 (customer service).
MS-DOS. IBM/PS2. disk $79.99 (ISBN 0-87007-814-3).
Provides a Detailed Analysis of a Family Budget & Provides Suggestions on Methods of Improving the Budget.
SourceView Software International.

Family Cash Planning. Compatible Hardware: Apple II, II+, IIe, IIc; Franklin Ace. Operating System(s) Required: Apple DOS 3.3. Language(s): BASIC, Machine. Memory Required: 48k. Customer Support: Help at (305) 977-0686.
Disk set. $69.95, incl. manual (ISBN 0-87284-009-3).
Personal Financial Management Program.
The Professor Corp.

Family Connections. Version: 4.0. 1992. Operating System(s) Required: PC-DOS/MS-DOS. Memory Required: 640k. General Requirements: Hard disk. Customer Support: 60-day unlimited warranty, toll free phone.
3.5" or 5.25" disk $59.00 (ISBN 0-917169-34-4).
Display/Print Ordered Columnar Reports, Charts, Family Group Sheets, Biographies, Relationships, & Calendar. Data Entry via Grid Like Spread Sheets. Accepts Data from the Mormon's P.A.F. Software, & Other GEDCOM Supported Software Including from Family Roots. Exports GEDCOM.
Quinsept, Inc.

Family Doctor: MAC Jewel Case. Version: 3. Sep. 1993. Items Included: Registration card. Customer Support: Creative Multimedia Corporation warrants the CD-ROM disc & diskettes to be free from defects in materials & workmanship under normal use & service for a period of 90 days from date of purchase. Creative Multimedia Corporation offers Technical Support to customers as needed.
System Software 6.0.7 or higher. Macintosh Plus or higher (2Mb). CD-ROM disk $79.99 (ISBN 1-880428-21-0, Order no.: 10434). Addl. software required: CD-ROM extensions. Optimal configuration: Color requires color display with 32-bit QuickDraw. Networks supported: All.
Now in Its Third Edition, This Family Medical Reference Has Already Sold over 100,000 Copies. Combines Full-Color Illustrations, Text, Sound, Animation & Video, to Provide Answers to Questions about the Family's Health & Well-Being. Answers to More Than 2,000 Commonly Asked Questions, Written in Friendly Style for Easy to Use by Everyone, Animated First Aid Section, Anatomy Section with Video Explains How the Body System Works, Comprehensive Prescription Drug Guide, Images Linked to Questions for Reference & More.
Creative Multimedia Corp.

The Family Doctor: MAC Retail Box. Version: 3. Sep. 1993. Items Included: Registration Card. Customer Support: Creative Multimedia Corporation warrants the CD-ROM disc & diskettes to be free from defects in materials & workmanship under normal use & service for a

period of 90 days from date of purchase. Creative Multimedia Corporation offers Technical Support to customers as needed.
System Software 6.0.7 or higher. Macintosh Plus or higher (2Mb). CD-ROM disk $79.99 (ISBN 1-880428-28-8, Order no.: 10521). *Addl. software required:* CD-ROM extensions. *Optimal configuration:* Color requires color display with 32-bit QuickDraw. *Networks supported:* All.
Now in Its Third Edition, This Family Medical Reference Has Already Sold over 100,000 Copies. Combines Full-Color Illustrations, Text, Sound, Animation & Video, to Provide Answers to Questions about the Family's Health & Well-Being. Answers to More Than 2,000 Commonly Asked Questions, Written in Friendly Style for Easy to Use by Everyone, Animated First Aid Section, Anatomy Section with Video Explains How the Body System Works, Comprehensive Prescription Drug Guide, Images Linked to Questions for Reference & More.
Creative Multimedia Corp.

Family Doctor: MPC Jewel Case. *Version:* 3. Sep. 1993. *Items Included:* Registration card. *Customer Support:* Creative Multimedia Corporation warrants the CD-ROM disc & diskettes to be free from defects in materials & workmanship under normal use & service for a period of 90 days from date of purchase. Creative Multimedia Corporation offers Technical Support to customers as needed.
Microsoft Windows 3.1. 386SX PC or higher (2Mb). CD-ROM disk $79.99 (ISBN 1-880428-22-9, Order no.: 10430). *Optimal configuration:* SuperVGA resolution Monitor with 256 colors; CD-ROM Drive with 150kb second transfer rate & 380 access rate recommended. *Networks supported:* All.
Now in Its Third Edition, This Family Medical Reference Has Already Sold over 100,000 Copies. Combines Full-Color Illustrations, Text, Sound, Animation & Video, to Provide Answers to Questions about the Family's Health & Well-Being. Answers to More Than 2,000 Commonly Asked Questions, Written in Friendly Style for Easy to Use by Everyone, Animated First Aid Section, Anatomy Section with Video Explains How the Body System Works, Comprehensive Prescription Drug Guide, Images Linked to Questions for Reference & More.
Creative Multimedia Corp.

Family Doctor: MPC Retail Box. *Version:* 3. Sep. 1993. *Items Included:* Registration card. *Customer Support:* Creative Multimedia Corporation warrants the CD-ROM disc & diskettes to be free from defects in materials & workmanship under normal use & service for a period of 90 days from date of purchase. Creative Multimedia Corporation offers Technical Support to customers as needed.
Microsoft Windows 3.1. 386SX PC or higher (2Mb). CD-ROM disk $79.99 (ISBN 1-880428-23-7, Order no.: 10438). *Nonstandard peripherals required:* Sound Card with Windows Driver. *Optimal configuration:* SuperVGA resolution Monitor with 256 colors; CD-ROM drive with 150kb/second transfer rate & 380 access rate recommended. *Networks supported:* All.
Now in Its Third Edition, This Family Medical Reference Has Already Sold over 100,000 Copies. Combines Full-Color Illustrations, Text, Sound, Animation & Video, to Provide Answers to Questions about the Family's Health & Well-Being. Answers to More Than 2,000 Commonly Asked Questions, Written in Friendly Style for Easy to Use by Everyone, Animated First Aid Section, Anatomy Section with Video Explains How the Body System Works, Comprehensive Prescription Drug Guide, Images Linked to Questions for Reference & More.
Creative Multimedia Corp.

Family Fortune. *Version:* 3.3. Mar. 1990. *Items Included:* Computer concepts, finance concepts. IBM & compatibles (640k). disk $39.95 (ISBN 0-918065-45-3, Order no.: FF). *Nonstandard peripherals required:* Hard disk drive & any printer.
Make Decisions, Control Finances & Stay Organized. Contains 10 Programs Including: Electronic Checkbook, Financial Planner, Budgeting & More.
FAMware.

Family Heritage File. *Version:* 4.0. *Compatible Hardware:* Apple Macintosh. *Memory Required:* 512k. *Items Included:* 1 disk & instruction manual (183 pages). *Customer Support:* Telephone (no charge); mail.
3.5" disk $149.00 (Order no.: 75815-300).
Easy to Use & Comprehensive Genealogical Software System for Personal or Professional Use.
Starcom Microsystems.

Family Links. *Version:* 1.3. P. J. Vorenberg. Jun. 1991. *Items Included:* Disks & Manual (20 pp). *Customer Support:* 60 day unlimited warrantee, toll free phone.
MS-DOS/PC-DOS. IBM & compatibles (256k). $35.00 (ISBN 0-917169-37-9). *Nonstandard peripherals required:* Requires hard disk Mac & MS-DOS only.
Macintosh. $35.00 (ISBN 0-917169-38-7).
ProDOS. Apple. $35.00 (ISBN 0-917169-39-5).
Exchange Data Between Lineages/Family Roots & Many Other Software Programs from Other Companies. Submit Data in GEDCOM Form to Mormons. Use Also to Reorganize a Data Base. Family Links Is Included with All New Purchases of Version 3 Family Roots & Lineages.
QuinSept, Inc.

Family Medical Advisor. 1983. *Compatible Hardware:* Apple II, Commodore 64, IBM PC. *Memory Required:* 64k.
disk $38.00.
Analyzes Overt Symptom Data & Identifies the Most Probable Cause of Illness. Compares Symptoms Entered to a Glossary of Nearly 10,000 Terms, Analyzes Resulting Data, & Diagnoses the Condition from a Database of 200 Specific Medical Ailments. Also Identifies the Effects of Substance Abuse & Poisons.
Navic Software.

Family Origins. *Version:* 2.5. Parsons Technology. Aug. 1993.
3.5" disk Contact publisher for price (ISBN 1-57264-040-5).
Parsons Technology.

Family Origins for Windows. Parsons Technology. Aug. 1993.
3.5" disk Contact publisher for price (ISBN 1-57264-041-3).
Parsons Technology.

Family Reunion. *Version:* 4.0. Apr. 1993. *Compatible Hardware:* IBM PC, PC XT, PC AT & compatibles. *Operating System(s) Required:* PC-DOS/MS-DOS 3.0 or higher. *Language(s):* MicroSoft C. *Memory Required:* 640k.
disk $39.95 (Order no.: FR). *Nonstandard peripherals required:* Hard disk drive, color/graphics display & any printer, 540k available.
For Home Use or Professionals. Tracks Living Relatives As Well As Genealogical Research via Pedigree Charts. Features Group Sheets, Descendant Charts, Birthday Charts, Address Labels, Text, Indexes, Searches, etc.
FAMware.

Family Roots. *Version:* 3. S. C. Vorenberg. 1982-92. *Operating System(s) Required:* Apple DOS or ProDOS, Finder. *Language(s):* Applesoft BASIC, C. *Memory Required:* Apple II Plus, IIe, Commodore 64 64k; Macintosh 2 Mb; Apple ProDOS, Commodore 128 128k. *General Requirements:* 132-column printer recommended. *Customer Support:* 60-day unlimited warranty, toll-free phone.
Commodore 128. disk $114.00 (ISBN 0-917169-26-3).
Commodore 64. disk $114.00 (ISBN 0-917169-17-4).
Apple ProDOS. disk $129.00 (ISBN 0-917169-11-5).
Macintosh. disk $129.99 (ISBN 0-917169-41-7).
Menu-Driven Integrated Package for Beginner to Advanced Geneaologist. Consists of Nine Main Programs Including: EDIT, Which Stores Basic Family Information for Each Member Including Birth & Death, Parents, Children, & Marriages; FREEFORMS & STRUCTURES, Which Prints Two Types of Descendants Charts & Four Types of Pedigree Charts; PERSONS, Which Prints All Information on One Person in Single Page Format; GROUPS, Which Also Prints Two Types of Family Group Sheet; MANAGER, Which Allows User to Configure the System & Define the Forms; SEARCH, Which Examines Data Stored by EDIT, Finding Information User Requests; LISTS, Which Prints Alphabetized or Numerically Ordered Lists of Names for Selected Individuals, Including Surnames That Sound Alike; WORDS, Which Allows Storage of Longer Notes or Supplemental Information That Does Not Fit into Basic Categories. Utilities Generate Address Lists, Reassign ID's, Reallocate Database Storage, & Provide Additional Functions.
Quinsept, Inc.

Family Roots. *Version:* 4.3. S. C. Vorenberg & P. Maddox. Oct. 1993. *Items Included:* Manual. *Customer Support:* 60-day unlimited warranty, toll-free phone.
PC-DOS/MS-DOS/OS2. IBM & compatibles (640k). disk $129.00 (ISBN 0-917169-42-5). *Optimal configuration:* 486 with 4Mb RAM, MS-DOS 6.2, color monitor, laser or inkjet printer, hard disk.
Data Entry by Person, Standard Genealogy Facts Plus 30 Optional Fields. Print Descendants Charts, Descendancy Reports, Ancestor Charts (4 Different Styles), Family Group Sheets (User-Definable, 24 Styles Supplied), Biographies, Sorted Lists, Relationship Diagram, Addresses. Parameters Allow Extensive Changes to Information & Layout of Printouts. Print Books with Page Index of Names. Export to Word Processor. Functions to Resize & Restructure Data Included. Search & Replace. Mouse Optional, Pull Down Menus, 2 Printers Supported, GEDCOM Import & Export.
QuinSept, Inc.

Family Ties. *Version:* 1.16. 1986. *Compatible Hardware:* Apple Macintosh 512k; CP/M based machines; IBM PC & compatibles. *Operating System(s) Required:* CP/M, MS-DOS PC-DOS. *Language(s):* Compiled BASIC. *Memory Required:* 64k.
disk $55.00.
demo disk $17.00.
Genealogy Program to Organize All Your Names, Dates & Places.
Computer Services.

Family Tree. *Items Included:* Bound manual. *Customer Support:* Free hotline - no time limit; 30 day limited warranty; updates are $5/disk plus S&H.
Commodore 64. disk $19.95.
Specialized Genealogy Data Base System for Recording & Analyzing Family Histories. It Can

FAMILY TREE MAKER DELUXE: CD EDITION

Accept, Edit, & Store Data for 500 Individuals & Provide Either Screen or Printer Reports. Features Include: Year Search; Name Search; Family Search; Alphabetical Sort & List; Vital Statistics. For Four-Generation Displays, an 80-Column Printer Is Required.
Dynacomp, Inc.

Family Tree Maker Deluxe: CD Edition. *Version:* 2.0. Oct. 1994. *Items Included:* 1 perfect bound manual, 1 CD-ROM disk, 1 registration card. *Customer Support:* 30 day money back guarantee, free technical support. MS-DOS. 386 or higher IBM PC or compatible (4Mb). CD-ROM disk $69.99 (ISBN 1-886914-01-X, Order no.: FTD20R0000). *Nonstandard peripherals required:* Microsoft or compatible mouse, VGA or better display, CD-ROM drive, hard drive with 7Mb free. *Addl. software required:* Windows 3.1. *Optimal configuration:* 386 or higher IBM PC or compatible with MS-DOS, Windows 3.1, 8Mb of RAM, 10Mb free space on hard drive, printer, mouse, CD-ROM drive, VGA display.
Organizes Family Information & Automatically Creates Family Trees, Birthday & Anniversary Calendars, Mailing Labels, Cards, Name Tags & Hundreds of Reports. Stores Information Including Photos & Video Clips in a Multimedia "Scrapbook." Includes 100 Million Names from the 1700's to 1900's U.S. Census & a Research "How To" Guide.
Banner Blue Software, Inc.

Family Tree Maker for Windows. *Version:* 2.0. Aug. 1994. *Items Included:* 1 perfect bound manual, 2 3.5" disks, 1 registration card. *Customer Support:* 30 day money back guarantee, free technical support. MS-DOS. 386 or higher IBM PC or compatible (4Mb). disk $54.99 (ISBN 1-886914-00-1, Order no.: FTW20R3500). *Nonstandard peripherals required:* Microsoft or compatible mouse, VGA or better display, CD-ROM drive, hard drive with 7Mb free. *Addl. software required:* Windows 3.1. *Optimal configuration:* 386 or higher IBM PC or compatible with MS-DOS, Windows 3.1, 8Mb of RAM, 10Mb free space on hard drive, printer, mouse, CD-ROM drive, VGA display.
Just Enter Information about Parents, Children & Marriages, Family Tree Maker Organizes Family Information & Automatically Creates Ancestor Trees, Descendant Trees, Birthday & Anniversary Calendars, Mailing Labels, Cards, Name Tags & Hundreds of Reports. Store Family Information Including Photos, Scanned Images, & Video Clips in an Electronic Multimedia "Scrapbook".
Banner Blue Software, Inc.

FamilyCare Software. *Version:* 1.05. Oct. 1988. *Compatible Hardware:* Apple Macintosh, IBM PC & compatibles. *Items Included:* Disk(s) & 40 page users guide. *Customer Support:* Unconditional 30 day money back guarantee. 90 day replacement period for faulty diskettes. Free technical support - (800)426-8426.
Apple Macintosh (512k). 3.5" disk $99.00.
IBM PC & compatibles (256k). disk $99.00.
Models the Diagnostic Process Used by Physicians to Help Parents Pinpoint & Treat Their Children's Medical Problems (Birth to Fifteen). After Answering Questions About All Related Symptoms, the Parent Receives Recommendations for Home Treatment, Medications, or for Professional Medical Attention.
Lundin Laboratories, Inc.

Famous Charts: Graphic Astrology. Jul. 1994. *Customer Support:* Free unlimited phone support. System 6.07 or higher, System 7 Savvy.
Macintosh (1Mb). 3.5" disk $59.50, package.
Timed Charts of the World's Most Famous Personalities. Three Collections Spanning Various Categories of Interest with at Least 400 Charts in Each Collection. Includes Source Notes. For Use with Io Series Program.

FAMOUS: Farm Management Accounting System. *Version:* 5.6. 1996. *Compatible Hardware:* Systems compatible with OS. *Operating System(s) Required:* Novell, MS-DOS, UNIX, Windows, NT, other networks. *Language(s):* ACUCOBOL. *Memory Required:* 640k. *Items Included:* Operator's manual for each application purchased. *Customer Support:* 90 days unlimited support, annual support fee thereafter. On-site training available (travel expense extra).
$750.00 to $4300.00.
Designed As an Agricultural Computer System with AG Payroll, Crop Costing, Accounts Payable, & General Ledger with Financial Statements. Payroll & Accounts Payable Automatically Update Crop Costs & General Ledger.
Holm-Dietz Computer Systems, Inc.

FAMOUS: Produce System. *Version:* 5.6. *Items Included:* Operator's manual for each application purchased. *Customer Support:* 90 days unlimited support, annual support fee thereafter. On-site training available (travel expense extra).
MS-DOS, AIX, SCO UNIX, NOVELL, Windows NT. Systems compatible with O/S above. $1000.00-$20,000.00. *Addl. software required:* COBOL runtime.
IBM compatibles.
Designed As an Accounting System for Produce Packers, Shippers, Wholesalers & Brokers. Provides Inventory Control (Pallets, Lots, Pools); Order Entry (Confirmations, Bills of Lading); Specialized Invoicing (Delivered Sales, Consignments); Receivable Processing; & Grower Settlement (Actual, Average or Pool Prices Minus Grower Charges).
Holm-Dietz Computer Systems, Inc.

Fancy Font. *Version:* 3.0. Sep. 1982. *Compatible Hardware:* IBM PC & compatibles. *Operating System(s) Required:* MS-DOS 2.0 or higher. *Memory Required:* 256k. *General Requirements:* 2 disk drives, printer.
disk $180.00.
demo disk $10.00.
Provides Fonts in Sizes from 8 to 40 Points Including Roman, Bold, Italic, Script & Old English. Print High Quality Fonts on Dot Matrix or HP LaserJet & Printer. Add-On Fonts Available in 6-72 Points.
SoftCraft, Inc. (Wisconsin).

Fancy Programming in Applesoft. 1982. *Compatible Hardware:* Apple IIe.
disk $30.00.
Teaches How to Recover a Program & How to Input Data Without Stopping a Program. Also, Shows How to Save an Applesoft Program As a Binary File.
Prentice Hall.

Fancy Word. *Version:* 3.0. *Compatible Hardware:* IBM PC & compatibles. *Operating System(s) Required:* PC-DOS, MS-DOS. *Memory Required:* 192k. *General Requirements:* Microsoft Word. Epson, Toshiba, Laser Jet or compatible printer.
disk $140.00.
Enables MICROSOFT WORD Users with a Dot Matrix or Laser Printer to Print Their Documents in Near Typeset Quality. Standard Font Styles Include: Roman, Sans Serif, Bold, Italic, Script, Old English, etc. in 10 to 24 Point Sizes. Optional Fonts Can Be from 6 to 72 Points.
SoftCraft, Inc. (Wisconsin).

SOFTWARE ENCYCLOPEDIA 1996

FANII Software Program. *Version:* 4.3. Jun. 1989. *Compatible Hardware:* IBM PC, PC XT, PC AT. *Operating System(s) Required:* DOS 2.0. *Language(s):* C. *Memory Required:* 256k. *General Requirements:* Hard disk.
disk $1495.00 (Order no.: 1046-05).
Statistical Process Control (SPC) Data Base That Stores & Analyzes SPC Data Collected by DataMyte Collectors in the Factory Area Network. Reports Generated Include X-Bar & R, X-Bar & Sigma, Histogram, Capability, Cusum & Data Reports. File Management Allows the User to Save, Copy, Delete or Edit Data Files or Translate FAN Data Files to Popular Speadsheet Format. Can Also Be Used to Set up DataMyte Data Collectors.
DataMyte Corp.

FANSI-Console: The Integrated Console Utility. *Version:* 4.0. Mark Hersey. Mar. 1991. *Compatible Hardware:* IBM PC & compatibles, PC AT. *Operating System(s) Required:* PC-DOS 2.0 or higher. *Memory Required:* 128k. *Items Included:* User manual & technical manual.
3.5" or 5.25" disk $119.95 (ISBN 0-933737-01-7).
Improvements over Standard Console Driver. Speed up Screen Writing. Increased Type Ahead. Additional ANSI X3.64 Commands Beyond ANSI.SYS. Compatibility with Most Programs. Auto Screen Disable During Inactivity Scroll Recall. Eliminate Screen Blinking on Some Adapters. Increased Typeamatic Rate. More Memory for Keyboard Macros Than ANSI.SYS. One Finger Pausing. Support for 50 Line Displays. VT100 Emulation. Keyboard Induced Break Points.
Hersey Micro Consulting, Inc.

FANSIM: Frequency ANalysis & SYnthesys. *Version:* 2.4. *Items Included:* Manual. *Customer Support:* Technical support, no fee, by telephone. IBM & compatibles. Corporate $445.00 (Order no.: FSP). *Addl. software required:* Works with or without co-processor.
$119.00 Personal.
Academic $395.00.
Frequency Analysis & Synthesis on up to 2k Records. Allows FFT Operations, Windowing, Transfer Functions, Time & Special Function Generation, Curve Fitting, Bode Plots. Limited License Version.
Tutsim Products.

FANSIM: Frequency Domain Analysis & Simulation. *Items Included:* Bound manual. *Customer Support:* Free hotline - no time limit; 30 day limited warranty; updates are $5/disk plus S&H.
MS-DOS 2.0 or higher. IBM & compatibles (384k). $39.95-$349.95. *Nonstandard peripherals required:* 80x87 math coprocessor; CGA, EGA, or Hercules graphics (or equivalent).
Offers Full System Simulation in the Frequency Domain. Inputs May Be Either Time or Frequency Data Functions. Time Data Functions May Be Tabular Results Saved on Disk from TUTSIM Simulations, Real Measured Responses, or Data Generated Internally in FANSIM. FFT Techniques Convert Time Responses to Spectral Functions. Other Spectral Data May Be Generated from Polynomial Forms, or from Pole/Zero Descriptions. There Are 40 Functions Available to Manipulate Spectral Data. Time Domain Data May Be Compared to Determine the Spectral Transfer Function (Especially Useful with TUTSIM Output Data Files Where the Model Is Excited with the TUTSIM "Chirp" Function). Functions May Be Cascaded or Used Open-Loop or Closed-Loop. Some Analyses May Use the Various Correlation Functions.
Dynacomp, Inc.

TITLE INDEX

Fantasy Fest. DreamForge, Micro Magic Inc. Staff et al. Sep. 1994. *Items Included:* 4 manuals & 2 data cards. *Customer Support:* 30 day limited warranty.
DOS 5.0 or higher. IBM PC & compatibles with CD-ROM drive, Hard drive & mouse (4Mb). CD-ROM disk $39.95 (ISBN 0-917059-20-4, Order no.: 062221). *Optimal configuration:* 386/33 or higher.
A Compilation Product Which Includes 2 Titles from Our Advanced Dungeons & Dragons Line: Dungeon Hack & Unlimited Adventures. As Well As 2 Products from Our Dungeons & Dragons Line: Fantasy Empires & Stronghold.
Strategic Simulations, Inc.

Fantasy Football. Fantasy Sports Properties Staff. Aug. 1995. *Items Included:* Set up instruction sheet. *Customer Support:* (503) 639-6863.
DOS 5.0. IBM PC 386 or higher (640k). disk $7.95 (ISBN 1-887783-02-4, Order no.: 4100-1003). *Optimal configuration:* IBM PC 386 or higher, 640k RAM, EGA, VGA, or CGA, DOS 5.0.
A Football Statistical Program to Allow Users to View Historical Game Records & Attempt to Predict Future Results.
Entertainment Technology.

Fantasy General. Midnight Software. Mar. 1996. *Items Included:* 64 page manual. *Customer Support:* 30 day limited warranty.
PC-DOS CD-ROM 5.0 or higher. 386/40 (8Mb). CD-ROM disk $69.95 (ISBN 0-917059-49-2, Order no.: 05240-1). *Nonstandard peripherals required:* 1Mb SVGA card, CD drive, 2X, sound blaster family & 100% compatibles. *Optimal configuration:* 486/50, uncompressed hard drive.
Recruit Mystical Creatures. Find Heroes, Aquire Magical Items, Cast Spells. Choose from over 120 Fantasy Units. Build an Army & Lead It Well. Choose to Be Any of Four Different Heroes & Battle the Shadow Lord & His Minions Across Five Continents.
Strategic Simulations, Inc.

Fantavision. Scott Anderson. *Compatible Hardware:* Apple II+, IIe, IIc, IIgs. *Memory Required:* Apple II+, IIe, IIc 64k; Apple IIgs 256k. *General Requirements:* Mouse, Apple Graphics Tablet, KoalaPad, or joystick.
Apple II+, IIe, IIc. disk $49.95 (Order no.: APDSK-41).
Apple IIgs. 3.5" disk $59.95 (ISBN 0-922614-74-1, Order no.: 25152).
Graphics & Animation Program Which Allows User to Draw Stick Figures, Solid Shapes, Lines, Faces, Bodies, the Moon, & the Stars Using a Mouse, Graphics Tablet, Joystick or KoalaPad. The Computer Will Create up to 64 Drawings for Every One User Draws, Automatically Producing Cell Animation-Style Movement & Special Effects.
Broderbund Software, Inc.

Fantavision - IIgs. *Compatible Hardware:* Apple IIgs. *Memory Required:* 256k. *General Requirements:* External disk drive.
3.5" disk $59.95 (Order no.: ALDSK-501).
Redesigned Version to Take Advantage of Apple IIgs' Capabilities. Offers a Library of Digitized Sound. Will Print Color Images on the IMAGEWRITER II. Generates "In-Between" Frames. Accepts Other Hi-Res Backgrounds.
Broderbund Software, Inc.

Farm. June Wright et al. 1990. *Items Included:* 1 manual. *Customer Support:* Training workshop - $2,000-two days on site. 1-800 Help Line.
DOS 3.3, DOS 5.0. IBM PS/2 Model 25, 30, 30/286 & compatibles (640k). Contact publisher for price; part of KIDWARE 2 PLUS package. *Nonstandard peripherals required:* VGA graphics board & monitor, IBM speech adapter card or Digispeech, M-Audio, or Soundblaster, external speaker, mouse; Powerpad optional. *Addl. software required:* DOS. 3.3, DOS 5.0 & software associated with mouse. *Optimal configuration:* One IBM PS/2 Model 25 or Model 30 with 640k RAM, color display (MCGA or VGA), one 720k 3.5" disk drive, IBM Speech Adapter, one IBM Proprinter or Star Micronics color printer & one external, keyboard, IBM mouse, DOS 3.3 & DOS 5.0. *Networks supported:* Novell, ICLAS.
Build a Farm by Selecting among Various Animals, Props, & Multi-Cultural Characters. Make Printouts of Farm Scenes & Write Stories.
Mobius Corp.

Farm Accounting. *Customer Support:* 800-929-8117 (customer service).
MS-DOS. IBM/PS2. disk $199.99 (ISBN 0-87007-658-2).
A Complete Ranching & Farming Accounting System - Including GL, AP, AR, & Payroll - with Special Inventory Features for Tracking the Genealogy of Breeding Stock. Includes Expenses Journal, Sales Journal, Five Profit & Loss Formats, Trial Balance, Check Register, Cash Requirement Forecast, Net Worth Reporting, Depreciation Schedules, Total Account Flexibility & Unofficial Closing or Trial Closing. Allows the User to Extract Profit & Loss Information, Net Worth, Future Cash Requirements & Check Registers So User Can Control & Analyze Costs, Identify Profit Centers & Locate Problem Areas.
SourceView Software International.

Farm Accounting System. Merle W. Wagner. 1983. *Compatible Hardware:* Apple II Plus, IIe, IIc; IBM. *Memory Required:* 48k, 640k. *General Requirements:* Monochrome monitor, printer.
disk $49.95 (ISBN 0-922900-37-X, Order no.: CFA-910).
Single Entry Accounting System Designed to Store a Complete Year's Records on 1 Data Disk.
Cherrygarth, Inc.

Farm Accounting System: FAS. *Version:* 3.55. Farmhand Computer Systems. 1980. *Compatible Hardware:* IBM PC & compatibles, PC XT, PC AT, PS/2. *Operating System(s) Required:* MS-DOS, PC-DOS. *Language(s):* FORTRAN. *Memory Required:* 512k. *Items Included:* Manual. *Customer Support:* 1 hour per package purchased.
$495.00 5.25" or 8" or 3.5" disk.
Complete Financial Management Tool for the Farmer. By Entering Checks Written & Deposits Made, FAS Prints Detailed Breakdowns of Income & Expense by Farm Operation &/or by Enterprise, Also Allows You to Write Checks for Purchases.
MCC Software (Midwest Computer Ctr. Co.).

Farm Biz. *Version:* 1A. Jul. 1994. *Items Included:* 350 page perfect bound manual. *Customer Support:* 30 days free after 1st call.
MS-DOS 3.3 or higher. IBM & compatibles (640k). $149.00 Retail; School Prices $89.00 to $103.00 (ISBN 0-918709-61-X, Order no.: FARM BIZ). *Optimal configuration:* Hard disk with 12Mb free. *Networks supported:* Novell, PC LAN.
A Cash Accounting System Providing Comprehensive Financial Reports Focusing on Taxes & Enterprise Profitability. Monthly Transactions Provide Concurrent On-Screen Checkbook Balancing with Vendors, & Pull-Down Menus. Cashflow Plans, Sales & Enterprise Statement Analysis, Crop Break Evens, Profit & Loss Statements & Networth Statement Are Just a Few of the Reports Featured.
Specialized Data Systems, Inc.

FARM MANAGEMENT SERIES

Farm Budget Planning System, 3 disks. Merle W. Wagner. 1982. *Compatible Hardware:* Apple II+, IIe, IIc. *Memory Required:* 48k. *General Requirements:* Printer.
disk $49.95 (ISBN 0-922900-36-1, Order no.: CFB-900).
Involves Cropping System, Livestock System, Labor & Capital Returns, Debt Repayment Capacity Balance Sheet, Income Taxes & Social Security, Income & Debt Principal Repayment.
Cherrygarth, Inc.

Farm Business Analysis. David Melberg. 1983. *Compatible Hardware:* Apple II series. *Operating System(s) Required:* Apple DOS 3.3. *Memory Required:* 48k. *General Requirements:* Printer.
disk $34.50 (ISBN 1-55797-153-6, Order no.: AP2-AG403).
Will Help Analyze the Crop Profitability on a Farm, Methods for Buying Land, & How to Calculate the Projected Corn Yield. Will Calculate the Breakeven Rent Value per Acre & the Profit per Acre at Various Prices. Production Cost per Acre Will Be Shown with How the Production Cost will Change with Different Yields.
Hobar Pubns.

Farm Credit Plan. *Version:* 1.2. Feb. 1988. *Operating System(s) Required:* MS-DOS, BTOS. *Memory Required:* 1000k. *General Requirements:* 80Mb hard disk.
disk $3500.00.
Designed to Allow the Computer User to Handle Credit Card Transactions, Tracking the Receivable & Prorating a Percentage Back to the Store of Purchase. Works Well with a Bank Handling the Processing for Various Implement Type Dealers. The Source Code Can Be Purchased to Customize the Software for Specific Needs.
CMV Software Specialists, Inc.

Farm Database Financial Analysis & Records. Duane Bristow. *Compatible Hardware:* TRS-80, Model I, Model III. *Operating System(s) Required:* TRSDOS. *Language(s):* BASIC. *Memory Required:* 48k. *General Requirements:* Printer.
disk $195.00.
$5.00, instructions.
Keeps Income & Expense Records for Farmers. Can Be Adapted to Suit Others.
Duane Bristow Computers, Inc.

Farm Enterprise Analysis. Duane Bristow. *Compatible Hardware:* TRS-80 Model I, Model II. *Operating System(s) Required:* TRSDOS. *Language(s):* BASIC. *Memory Required:* 48k.
disk $69.95.
$5.00, incl. instruction & sample print-out.
Breakeven Cost Analysis per Unit of Production & Total for Farm of up to Ten Enterprises. User Defines Enterprises & Inputs & Allocates Fixed Expenses & Land Cost.
Duane Bristow Computers, Inc.

Farm Management Series. *Compatible Hardware:* IBM & compatibles. *Operating System(s) Required:* DOS. *Language(s):* Pascal. *Memory Required:* 640k. *General Requirements:* 1 drive & hard disk.
disk write for info.
Cash Flow & Income Planning Tool Using Either User-Input Data or Data Generated by the AG Finance Accounting System. Generates a Profit/Cost Report & a Cash Flow Report for the Coming Production Year. The User Can Alter Any or All of the Cost & Cash Flow Items or Revenue to Perform Breakeven Analysis & to Evaluate Cash Flow Issues. Ratio Analysis.
Countryside Data, Inc.

Farm Sense. *Version:* JC-2.5. Apr. 1994. *Items Included:* 240 page perfect bound manual. *Customer Support:* 30 days free after 1st call. Money back guarantee.
 MS-DOS 2.1 or higher. IBM & compatibles (512k). $44.95 Retail; School Prices $22.50 to $27.00 (ISBN 0-918709-25-3, Order no.: FARM SENSE). *Networks supported:* Novell, PC LAN.
Specially Designed Chart of Accounts for Farming Gets Beginners off to a Fast Start. No Debits, Credits or Accounting Knowledge Needed. 240 Page Manual. Income Statements with Budget Forecasts, Cashflow & Schedule F Reports.
Specialized Data Systems, Inc.

Farm Simulator. Duane Bristow. *Compatible Hardware:* TRS-80. *Operating System(s) Required:* TRSDOS. *Language(s):* BASIC.
 disk $34.95.
 cassette $19.95.
Allows Farmer to Simulate & Forecast Farm Finances Year-by-Year.
Duane Bristow Computers, Inc.

The Farmers Home Property Management System. *Version:* 9.2. Oct. 1994. *Items Included:* User manual; 30 day warranty period; 30 day support. *Customer Support:* Annual maintenance agreement. Included: unlimited telephone and/or modem support. Free new version, updates, documentation, input on future enhancements, plus special offers on new products (15% of license fee or minimum $600.00).
 Microsoft DOS 3.3 or higher. IBM & compatibles (386sx) (640k). $3495.00-$11,495.00 (based on number of projects & network). *Optimal configuration:* 486 or higher, DOS 5.0 or higher, GA color monitor, laser printer, 3.5" disk drive, 120Mb HD. *Networks supported:* Novell, Lantastic.
A Comprehensive, PC Based Accounting System, Designed Especially for Property Management. It Integrates a Complete FmHA 515 Forms Processing Module Through Tenant Certifications & Project Worksheets with Powerful Management Control of Your Residential Property Through Its Tenant Database.
Classic Real Estate Systems, L.L.C.

Farrow-Finish Hog Production: Decision Aid. Merle W. Wagner. 1982. *Compatible Hardware:* Apple II Plus, IIe, IIc; IBM. *Memory Required:* 48k, 640k. *General Requirements:* Printer.
 disk $29.95 (ISBN 0-922900-17-5, Order no.: CFD-445).
Budget Analysis for a Complete Hog Operation; 26 Data Entries, 10 Calculations.
Cherrygarth, Inc.

FAS - Fixed Assets. *Version:* 7.0. *Customer Support:* Support subscription, 900 number.
 DOS/Network, UNIX. IBM PC & compatibles. $795.00-$995.00.
Comprehensive Fixed Asset Accounting System That Enables Tax & Financial Managers to Maintain Auditable Records on All of Their Fixed Assets. The Program Maintains up to Five Depreciation Schedules for Each Asset & Provides Complete Tax & Financial Reporting Necessary for Federal Tax Filing, Financial Statement Reporting, & General Ledger Posting.
RealWorld Corp.

FAS: Fixed Asset System. *Version:* 7.0. Jan. 1991. *Items Included:* Manual. *Customer Support:* 30 day free trial, 30 day money back guarantee, 1 year maintenance - $300.00 (includes annual update), seminars, Oo-site training & customizations.
 DOS. IBM & compatibles (640k). disk $795.00.
 Optimal configuration: Any IBM compatible equipped with DOS 3.0 or higher & a hard drive.
Fixed Asset Database for Depreciation Calculation & Inventory Management. Features All IRS & GAAP Accepted Depreciation Methods. The System Calculates up to 5 Sets of Depreciation Schedules Including Federal, State, Internal, AMT & ACE. Also Has 17 Standard Reports Including FASB96.
Best Programs.

FAS 2000. *Version:* 1.0. Jun. 1991. *Items Included:* Manual - guide to depreciation. *Customer Support:* 30 day free trial, 30 day money back guarantee, 1 year maintenance - $395.00 (includes annual update), seminars, on-site training & customizations.
 DOS. IBM & compatible (640k). Single User $1495.00, Network $1995.00. *Optimal configuration:* 386-25 MHz, 2Mb RAM, disk cache, math coprocessor. *Networks supported:* Novell Netware 286 & 386.
Fixed Asset Database for Depreciation Calculation & Inventory Management. Provides Tax & Financial Information Necessary for Tax Filings Financial Statement Reporting & General Ledger Posting. Offers Capabilities Such As Maintenance Schedule Tracking, Lease Administration & Bar Code Inventory Technology. Seven Sets of Depreciation Schedules Including Federal, State, Internal, AMT & ACE Are Supported.
Best Programs.

FASB13. *Compatible Hardware:* Altos Series 5-15D, Series 5-5D, 580-XX, ACS8000-XX; IBM PC with 2 disk drives, PC XT, & compatibles; Xerox 820 with 2 disk drives; ZILOG MCZ-250. *Operating System(s) Required:* CP/M, MP/M, PC-DOS, MS-DOS.
 contact publisher for price (Order no.: FASB13).
Named After the Financial Accounting Standard Board Statement 13, with Which It Is in Accordance. Actually an Editor Whose Function Is to Create a Data File Suitable for Input into One of Coopers & Lybrand's Four Lease Programs (SASE$13, SASR$13, LESSEE, & LESSOR) on the General Electric Time-Sharing Network (GEISCO), for Subsequent Processing.
Coopers & Lybrand.

Faser-Energy Accounting: FASER. Steven Hines. Jul. 1987. *Compatible Hardware:* IBM PC & compatibles. *Operating System(s) Required:* CP/M, CP/M-86, MS-DOS, PC-DOS. *Language(s):* MBASIC. *Memory Required:* MS-DOS 256k. *General Requirements:* 2 disk drives, printer.
 disk $795.00.
 8" disk $795.00.
 demo disk $38.00.
Accounting System for Energy Reporting That Performs Energy Accounting of Non-Residential Buildings. Uses Systematic Tracking & Analysis of Energy Consumption & Costs in an Effort to Better Manage & Control Energy Conservation Measures & Utility Budgets. By Compiling a Data Base of Historical & Current Data. It Can Be Used to Analyze Trends, Spot Potential Problems, Provide Reports & Graphs, Calculate Energy Dollar, & Backup All Energy Management.
Elite Software Development, Inc.

FASER Energy Accounting: Fast Accounting System for Energy Reporting. *Version:* 9. Steven D. Heinz. Oct. 1993. *Compatible Hardware:* IBM PC & compatibles, 286 or higher. *Operating System(s) Required:* PC-DOS/MS-DOS 3.3 or higher. *Memory Required:* 640k. *General Requirements:* hard disk. *Items Included:* Software; documentation; free support.
 disk $1950.00-$12,000.00 based on size of using organization.
Utility Bill Tracking, Reporting Analysis. Used by School Districts, Universities, Municipalities, Military, & Corporations to Systematically Track & Analyze Energy Usage & Costs. Performs Automatic Adjustments for Weather & Billing Period Variances. Spots Meter & Billing Errors. Allows Spreadsheet Entry of Monthly Utility Bills. Also Incorporates Budgeting Option & Tracks Units of Production. Maintains Complete Historical Records of Costs & Usage. Verifies Monthly Bills, Performs Rate Schedule Analysis & Prints Multi-Year Reports & Graphs.
OmniComp, Inc.

FAST. *Compatible Hardware:* IBM PC & compatibles, PC XT, PC AT. *Operating System(s) Required:* DOS 2.0 or higher. *Memory Required:* 384k. *General Requirements:* Hard disk.
 contact publisher for price.
Designed to Streamline User's Audit, Review, Compilation & Tax Engagements.
FAS, Inc.

Fast! Advantage. *Version:* 2.01. *Items Included:* Complete documentation. *Customer Support:* Toll-free support (prices vary); hands-on regional seminars & on-site training (prices vary).
 MS-DOS. IBM or 100% compatible (640k). disk $395.00. *Optimal configuration:* 80286, 80386, 80486-based PC, 640k RAM, with 510k of free RAM. *Networks supported:* Novell.
A Complete Trial Balance Workpaper Tool That Helps Accountants Complete Everything from the Detail Account Analysis to Lead Schedules, Trial Balance Worksheet, & Final Financial Statements. Includes a "Shoebox" Transaction Entry System That Arranges Unorganized Records into a Meaningful Set of Accounting Reports. Imports Client Data from over 75 Packages.
Prentice Hall Professional Software.

Fast EDI. *Version:* 1.1. Apr. 1993. *Items Included:* User manual, on-line help & on-line tutorial.
 MS-DOS. IBM PC & compatibles (640k). disk $349.95 (Order no.: 311100). *Optimal configuration:* DOS 3.0 or higher, 640k RAM, 10Mb disk, Hayes compatible modem. *Networks supported:* Any one public network.
Low-Priced Product Designed for Companies That Need a Quick, Inexpensive EDI Capability to Begin the Exchange of Information Electronically with Their Trading Partners Using a PC.
DNS Assocs., Inc.

Fast File. *Compatible Hardware:* IBM PC.
 contact publisher for price.
Enables the IBM PC to Write Its Own Programs. Fully Integrated Applications Systems Are Generated. Features Include: File Security, File Definition, File Maintenance, Report Writing, Search/Inquiry, Calculations, Menu-Driven.
Information Analysis, Inc.

Fast-Finance. *Compatible Hardware:* IBM PC.
 contact publisher for price.
Swiftware Corp.

Fast-Flex Pro. *Version:* 1.11. *Compatible Hardware:* IBM PC & compatibles. *Memory Required:* 640k. *Items Included:* Online documentation including sample legal forms & documents to set up a functioning cafeteria benefit plan. *Customer Support:* Written & telephone questions answered promptly at no charge. Reduced-price annual updates, 30-day money-back guarantee.
 $995.00 per pkg.
Complete Administration of IRC Section 125 Flexible Benefit Plans & Section 401(k) Savings Plans. Features Include Discrimination Testing, Take-Home Paycheck Comparisons, Tax Savings

TITLE INDEX

Analysis, Automatic Reimbursement Check Printing, Automatic Salary Reduction Posting, Bank Statement Reconciliation & Extensive Reporting Capabilities. Menu-Driven Program Requires No Special Computer or Accounting Knowledge. Interfaces with Most PC-Based Payroll Software. Unlimited Companies & Divisions Can Be Administered.
Interval Software.

Fast-Flex Pro Network: The Flexible Spending Plan Administration Kit. *Version:* 1.11. Ronald R. Durtschi & Steven R. Skabelund. Mar. 1996. *Items Included:* Complete 140 page manual with sample employee & employer enrollment forms, plan legal description, & copyable enrollment software to demonstrate tax savings to potential plan participants. *Customer Support:* Thirty-day money-back guarantee. Unlimited customer support for software operation. Complete legal support at competitive rates for modifying sample plan document or other customization.
DOS 3.1 or higher w/ Lantastic, Netware, etc. IBM compatibles (640k). disk $3995.00. *Addl. software required:* None required, but exports to Wordperfect 5.1 for fancy reports. Can also export to any spreadsheet. *Optimal configuration:* Hard disk on each network machine preferred. Printer highly recommended. Supports laser printer.
Complete Accounting, Reporting, Discrimination Testing, & Reimbursement Check Printing for IRC Sec. 125 & Sec. 401(K) Flexible Benefit Plans. Includes Copyable Enrollment Software & Forms & a Sample Plan Legal Description to Help Any Company Set up a Functioning, IRS-Qualified Plan. Handles Unlimited Companies & Divisions. Also Tracks Employee 401(K) Account Balances. Enables Multiple Users to Administer Any Company's Flexible Spending & 401(K) Plans Simultaneously. No Limit or Number on Network Nodes.
Interval Software.

Fast Fourier Transform. *Compatible Hardware:* TI 99/4A. *Operating System(s) Required:* DX-10. *Language(s):* Console BASIC. *Memory Required:* 16k.
$15.00, incl. demo disk.
Calculates the Transform of Complex or Real Data Where the Number of Points Is a Power of 2. Results Are Displayed in Complex Pairs & in Magnitude/Angle Form.
Eastbench Software Products.

Fast Fourier Transform Master. *Compatible Hardware:* Apple, IBM, TRS-80. *Items Included:* Bound manual. *Customer Support:* Free hotline - no time limit; 30 day limited warranty; updates are $5/disk plus S&H.
$49.95-$57.95.
Two Versions Are Available: SINGLE PRECISION for "Run of the Mill" Analysis; DOUBLE PRECISION for Exacting Analysis. The Size of the Array Processed Is Limited Only by Available RAM. All of the Transforms Are Performed "in Place". This Saves Memory. And All of the Transforms Can Be Performed with Hanning Windowing. Also, Inverse Transforms Can Be Computed.
Dynacomp, Inc.

Fast Fourier Transform Master. 1992. *Items Included:* Detailed manuals are included with all DYNACOMP products. *Customer Support:* Free telephone support to original customer - no time limit; 30 day limited warranty.
MS-DOS 3.2 or higher. IBM PC & compatibles, Apple, TRS-80 (512k). $49.95-$57.95 (Add $5.00 for 3 1/2" format; 5 1/4" format standard).
FFT Master Is Presently the Most Popular of the MATH MASTER Series Because of the Need for a Truly Fast FFT & One That Has the Features This Has. For Speed, Consider the Following 26 Seconds (IBM Version) for a 1024-Point Single-Precision Real Transform! Two Versions of FFT MASTER Are Available: Single Precision for "Run of the Mill" Analysis. Double Precision for Exacting Analysis. The Size of the Array Processed Is Limited Only by Available RAM. All of the Transforms Are Performed "in Place". And All of the Transforms Can Be Performed with Hanning Windowing. Also, Inverse Transforms Can Be Computed.
Dynacomp, Inc.

Fast Fourier Transform Tutorial. (Plane Analysis Ser.: No. 1). *Compatible Hardware:* Apple II with Applesoft, IBM PC. *Operating System(s) Required:* Apple DOS 3.2 or 3.3; MS-DOS. (source code included). *Memory Required:* Apple 48k, IBM 256k.
disk $39.95.
Menu-Driven, Graphics Oriented Educational Program Designed for Both Classroom Use & Self Instruction.
Dynacomp, Inc.

Fast Load. *Compatible Hardware:* Commodore 64. *Memory Required:* 64k.
disk $40.00.
Arcade Game.
Epyx, Inc.

Fast Track Schedule: Simple Scheduling. Impassive Power. *Version:* 4.0. Nov. 1995. *Items Included:* Manual, diskettes, essentials booklet. *Customer Support:* Free, unlimited technical support, 30 day money back guarantee.
Windows 3.1, Windows 95, Windows NT. 386DX microprocessor (2Mb). 3.5" disk $299.00 (Order no.: 1014001000121). *Nonstandard peripherals required:* 4Mb hard disk space.
System 7.0 or higher. Macintosh, Power Maintosh, MacPlus (2Mb). (Order no.: 1014001000111). *Nonstandard peripherals required:* 4Mb hard disk space.
Draw Bars to Enter Dates or Type Dates to Draw Bars. Easy Formatting, Stored Layouts, Control Palette, On-Line Help, Page Options, Page Preview, Page Stamps, Paste in Graphics, Paste in Logos. File Transperance...Create Files with Either the Macintosh or Windows Version & Effortlessly Convert Them to the Other, Providing the Most Dynamic, Cross-Platform Project Scheduling Solution. Scheduled, Revised, & Actual Dates, Customizable Work Calendar.
AEC Software.

FASTAR. *Version:* 2.0. Jan. 1987. *Items Included:* User manual, administrator's manual. *Customer Support:* Free telephone support; installation support; technical support & training. Fees vary according to extent of support required.
MS-DOS 3.0 or higher. IBM PC/XT/AT, 386, 486 & compatibles. $50,000.00 headquarter site fee. *Networks supported:* 3Com, Banyan Vines, IBM PC LAN, IBM Token Ring, Novell Netware.
15% license renewal fee per year.
Based on Concept of Using Financial Schedules for Data Entry, & Reporting, it Provides: Lotus 1-2-3 Data Entry Using Existing Spreadsheets; Straightforward Rules Using Cell/Range Based Logic; 1-2-3 Production Reporting; Management Reports; Ad-hoc Query Capabilities; Analysis Using 1-2-3 Reports.
IMRS, Inc.

FASTAT. *Compatible Hardware:* Apple Macintosh Plus or higher, IBM PC, 286 or higher & compatibles. *Memory Required:* 1000k, Mac II 2000k, DOS 640k. *General Requirements:* Hard disk, 68881 coprocessor supported. *Items Included:* Documentation. *Customer Support:* Free technical support.
3.5" disk $495.00.
For People Who Don't Have a Strong Background in Statistics. The Program Can Handle Summary Statistics, One- & Multiple-Way Tables, Chi-Square, Pearson & Spearman Correlations, Regression, Nonparametric Tests, Analysis of Variance & Covariance, Series Transformation & Smoothing, Forecasting, & Principal Components & Common Factor Analysis. Can Also Be Used to Create Two- & Three-Dimensional, Full-Color Scatterplots, Line Plots, Bubble Plots, Regression & Confidence Intervals, Influence Plots, Probability Plots, Scatterplot Matrices, Histograms, Cumulative Histograms, & Other Graphs for Presentations. Includes Built-In Text & Data Editors. Can Handle up to 150 Variables & Unlimited Cases.
Systat, Inc.

Fastback Plus. *Version:* 3.1. *Compatible Hardware:* IBM PC, PC XT, PC AT. *Operating System(s) Required:* PC-DOS, MS-DOS 2.0 or higher. *Memory Required:* 330k. *Customer Support:* 504-291-7283.
disk $189.00 (Order no.: FB01).
Hard Disk Backup (& Restore) Software Utility. A 10Mb Hard Disk Can Be Backed up on Floppies in Less Than 4 Minutes on a PC AT. Automatically Formats the Floppy As It Saves the Data. Can Use Both Drives on a Dual Drive System. Cataloging Feature Provides Rapid Lookup of Archived Data & Prevents Accidental Overwriting.
Fifth Generation Systems, Inc.

Fastback PLUS. *Version:* 3.0.
System 4.2 (512k). Mac 512E. disk $189.00.
Adds Data Compression, Enhanced Device Support, Multifinder Compatibility, Network File Transfer & Macro Support to Fastback Plus. Offers Three Data Compression Choices: No Compression, Save Time or Save Disk. Devices Supported Include HFS Devices, Bernoulli Cartridges & ANSI Tape Devices.
Fifth Generation Systems, Inc.

FASTC. *Compatible Hardware:* IBM PC & compatibles; PC XT, PC AT. *Operating System(s) Required:* DOS 2.0 or higher. *Memory Required:* 384k.
contact publisher for price.
Converts Labor-Intensive Clerical & Mathematical Procedures into Completely Automated Functions.
FAS, Inc.

FastCAD. *Version:* 2.72. *Compatible Hardware:* IBM PC & compatibles. *Language(s):* Assembly. *General Requirements:* 8087, 80287, 80387 math co-processor 80486 DX; CGA, EGA, or Hercules Graphics Adapter; mouse or digitizer. $795.00.
CAD Software Featuring Pull-Down Menus, Text Editor Allowing Customization of Menus & Creation of Special Features, Multiple Drawing Windows, & Cross-Hatching, As Well As All Other Standard Capabilities Expected from a CAD Package.
Evolution Computing.

FastCAD 3D. *Version:* 2.72. Jul. 1990. *Items Included:* FastCAD 2D program, tutorial, & reference manual FasCAD RenderMan program 3D manual. *Customer Support:* Free technical support for registered users.
MS-DOS/PC-DOS 2.10 or higher. IBM PC, AT, PS2, 386 or 486 & compatible. disk $1495.00. *Optimal configuration:* LIMS/expanded memory required for hidden surface removal, 8087, 80207, 80387 math coprocessor or 80486 DX - for FastCAD RenderMan, 4Mb RAM (above DOS) & Targa 16/24/32/ or Vista Video card.

FASTEAM DISKETTE (TEMPLATES): TQM

Solves Problems Such As Hidden Surface Removal, Smooth On-Screen Animation, & Adding a Third Dimension Without Having to Type the Elevation. FasCAD RenderMan Accepts Three-Dimensional Geometry Produced by FasCAD, Along with Specified Light Sources & Surface Appearances, Then Creates a Photo-Realistic Image.
Evolution Computing.

FasTeam Diskette (Templates): TQM Templates for Work Teams. Susan B. Hardwicke. Apr. 1994. *Customer Support:* TQM consulting & training - fees vary according to services needed & facilitating. WordPerfect for Windows. disk $25.00. *Diskette Available As Separate Item but Also Sold in Conjunction with "FASTEAM" Workbook for TQM Work Teams. Diskette Supplies Templates of Surveys, Flowcharts, Meeting Action Item Forms, Meeting Agenda Forms, Team Attendance Forms, Team Milestones, Sample Mission & Vision Forms, Team Evaluation Form, Concensus Decision-Making, Team Progress Data, Team Behaviors, etc.*
Total Quality Innovators.

Faster-Raster. Geophysical Consulting & Computer Applications. *Compatible Hardware:* TI Professional. *Operating System(s) Required:* MS-DOS, MS-FORTRAN. *Memory Required:* 64k. *General Requirements:* 3-plane graphics, 8087 co-processor, color monitor. $150.00 (Order no.: TI88, TI87). *Library of CALCOMP Compatible Graphics Primitive Subroutines, Callable from MS-FORTRAN.*
Texas Instruments, Personal Productivit.

FASTG. *Compatible Hardware:* IBM PC & compatibles, PC XT, PC AT. *Operating System(s) Required:* DOS 2.0 or higher. *Memory Required:* 384k. *General Requirements:* Hard disk. contact publisher for price. *The Fund Accounting Version of Fast.*
FAS, Inc.

FastHelp. *Items Included:* Manual. *Customer Support:* Free telephone support. IBM, IBM PS/2 & compatibles (64K). disk $79.95. *Addl. software required:* Lotus 1-2-3. *Interactive, Context-Sensitive Help System That Runs Concurrently with Lotus 1-2-3. Become an Expert with Lotus without Ever Picking up a Manual. By Pressing the F1 Key, FastHelp Will Help User Through Any of 33 Lotus Functions, Step-by-Step While User Works in Spreadsheet.*
ComTrain, Inc.

FastLabel. *Version:* 1.2.4. *Compatible Hardware:* Apple Macintosh. *Memory Required:* 512k. *Items Included:* Manual, disk, warranty. 3.5" disk $79.95. *Nonstandard peripherals required:* Printers - Laser or Image Writer. *Labeling Software; Allows Users to Manage a Wide Range of Labeling Chores, from Mailing Lists to Disk Labels, from Envelopes & Price Tags to VCR Labels.*
Vertical Solutions.

FastPak Mail. *Compatible Hardware:* Apple II series & other CP/M-based systems; IBM PC & compatibles. *Operating System(s) Required:* CP/M, PC-DOS/MS-DOS, 2.0 or higher. *Memory Required:* IBM 256k. $29.00 to $39.00. *Database for Managing Mailing Lists, Form Letter Generation, Label Printing, & Other Related Activities. Its Lists Can Contain As Many As 65,000 Names. Can Sort Files by Last Name, Company Name, ZIP Code, or Reference Code. Lists Created with Other Programs Can Be Directly Transferred Without Retyping.*
DHA Systems & Software.

FastPlan III. *Version:* 1.15. Judd Kessler. May 1982. *Compatible Hardware:* IBM PC & compatibles. *Operating System(s) Required:* PC-DOS, MS-DOS. *Memory Required:* 640k. *General Requirements:* Hard disk. *Items Included:* 3 ring binder & slipcase. *Customer Support:* 30-day moneyback guarantee, annual $495.00 includes tax updates & toll-free technical support. disk $1995.00 Network plus $295.00 per optional module (Capital needs, Time & Billing, Blotter & Commission, Graphics, Text Library). *Networks supported:* All Netbios compatible: Novell, Lantastic, etc. *Data Base Management & Tax & Financial Planning System Designed to Keep Track of a Financial Planner's Clients & All of the Clients' Investments. Includes Tickler System, Phone Dialer & Automatic Downloading of Securities Prices.*
Abacus Data Systems, Inc.

FasTracs. Apr. 1993. *Items Included:* Reference manual. *Customer Support:* Unlimited free telephone support, free BBS. DOS/Windows. PC (2Mb). disk $179.95. *Addl. software required:* Windows 3.1 or higher. *Easy to Use Project Manager That Produces Nine Status Reports & Four Different Gantt Charts. Also Produces Org Charts. Offers a Drag-and-Drop Interface, Is Completely Customizable by the User, & Can Be Learned in Less Than One Hour. Operates in Both English & German.*
Applied MicroSystems, Inc.

FasTracs. *Version:* 2.0. May 1993. *Customer Support:* Free telephone support; free computer BBS. MS-DOS, Windows (2Mb). disk $179.95. *Addl. software required:* Windows 3.1 or higher. *Easy-to-Use Project Manager Monitoring up to 10,000 Tasks in Every Project. Drag-and-Drop Interface & Completely User-Configurable. Showing Planned vs. Actual Performance, It Produces 9 Status, Loading, & Cost Reports, 4 Different Gantt Charts in Addition to Organizational Charts. Operates in German & English.*
Applied MicroSystems, Inc. (Georgia).

Fastrak. *Version:* 2.3. *Compatible Hardware:* IBM PC & compatibles. *Memory Required:* 640k. *General Requirements:* Hard disk. $300.00 to $1500.00 per module. *Financial/Accounting Software. Posts Recurring Transactions, Automatic Posting from Other Modules, Report Format User Definable, Ability to Jump Modules, Reports Comparative Statements, Links with External Software, Password Access, Audit Trail, Error Recovery, Automatic Back-Up for Each Module, Log off Out-of-Balance, Reject Erroneous Account Numbers, On-Line Help & Source Code Available.*
Core Software, Inc.

FasTrak Accounting. *Version:* 2.3. Nov. 1983. *Compatible Hardware:* IBM PC Network. *Operating System(s) Required:* SCO UNIX, DOS. *Memory Required:* 640k. disk $2000.00. *Adds Accounts Payable & Accounts Receivable to the General Ledger. The Open Item Accounts Receivable Facilitates Recording of Sales, Returns, Credit Memos, & Payments Received from Customers. Reports Include: Statements, Aging, Cash Receipts by Type, Check Distribution, & Payment History by Invoice. The Open Item Accounts Payable Module Includes Reports Showing Cash Requirements, & Invoice Selection for Automatic Check Distribution Among Invoices. This Module Can Be Integrated to a Specialized Application Developed in DataFlex.*
Core Software, Inc.

SOFTWARE ENCYCLOPEDIA 1996

FasTrak: Accounting with Inventory & Order Entry. *Version:* 2.3. May 1985. *Compatible Hardware:* IBM PC Network, Wang L10. *Operating System(s) Required:* SCO UNIX, DOS. *Memory Required:* 640k. disk $700.00. *Supplements All the Features Discussed under the FASTRACK Accounting Package with a Retail Inventory Control & Order Entry System. Inventory Control Includes Price Lists of Current & Discontinued Stock, Reorder & Value Reports, Physical Inventory Worksheets, Sales Analysis Reports by Salesperson (Computes Commission) & Customer. Order Entry Includes Conversion of a Quote to an Order, Backorder Editing, Backorder Listings by Customer & Stock Number, Picking List by Location, & Packing Slip.*
Core Software, Inc.

FasTrak: Accounting with Serialized Inventory. *Version:* 2.3. May 1985. *Compatible Hardware:* IBM PC Network, Wang L10. *Operating System(s) Required:* SCO UNIX, DOS. *Memory Required:* 640k. disk $3200.00. source code avail. per module $100.00. *Supplements the Features Discussed under the FASTRAK Accounting with Inventory Package with a Special Tracking System for Big Ticket Items. The Following Information Is Stored for Each Item: Vendor's ID, Vendor's Invoice Number, Wholesale Price, Freight Allocation, Date Received, Customer's ID, Date Sold, & Retail Price. In-Stock Serialized Items Also Store a Status Code & Condition Code. Other Reports Include Location Lists, Sorts of Items from a Vendor & Serialized Sales Analysis by Vendor & Customer.*
Core Software, Inc.

FasTrak: General Ledger with Report Writer. *Version:* 2.3. Nov. 1983. *Compatible Hardware:* IBM PC Network, Wang L10. *Operating System(s) Required:* SCO UNIX, DOS. *Language(s):* DatFlex. disk $700.00. source code avail. per module $100.00. *Allows up to 98 Profit Centers. Includes a Trial Balance Report & Transaction Audit Trails by Journal & Account Number, etc. Financial Statements Include Balance Sheet, 1 Dept. P&L, 3 Dept. P&L, & Consolidated P&L. User Can Define the Headings, Sub-Headings, Subtotals, Spacing Between Sections & Page Breaks, & the Order of Appearance of Each COA Number. Up to 9 Levels of Sub-Totals & Accumulations Across the Entire Chart of Accounts Are Accommodated.*
Core Software, Inc.

FasTrak: Service Management Series, 4 modules. Dec. 1985. *Compatible Hardware:* IBM PC Network, Wang L10. *Operating System(s) Required:* SCO UNIX, DOS. *Language(s):* DataFlex. *Memory Required:* 640k. disk $2100.00. source code avail. per module $100.00. *Suitable for Almost Any Organization Which Fixes Other's Equipment. Features Management (Tracks PM Scheduling, Machine History, & Technician's Time; Invoices for Billable Work), Contract Processing (Invoices for Contracts, Accommodates Metering, Does Auto-Renewals, Provides Expiration Lists, & Profitability Reports), Dispatch/Depot Tracking. The Latter Is Primarily Composed of One Configuration from Which the Operator Can Perform All Dispatching & Repair Tracking Functions.*
Core Software, Inc.
  Dispatching - Depot Tracking.
  Contract Processing.

TITLE INDEX

Service Management.
Service Parts.

FasTrak 2.32: Service Management Software.
Items Included: Documentation. *Customer Support:* Free 90-day warranty also offer customization, training, telephone support & BBS contact care for pricing information.
Ms-DOS, MS-Windows NT, Windows NT. 386. disk
FasTrak Service Management software is part of an on-line, multi-user integrated system. The system is developed in Dataflex & the Service Management module offers submodules including service dispatching, Corporate Customer Dispatching & Service Contract Processing. It includes work order processing (service invoicing), technician time usage analysis, preventative maintenance (PM) for customers, cyclical billing for contracts, renewals, expiration lists & profitability analysis. All work done under a contract is entered as a work order, & the details are compared to the revenue generated by the contract. Changes made in one file automatically appear where appropriate on other terminals in a multi-user system. Users can customize the system by defining service areas, service type codes, pay codes, & by entering technician information. Other FasTrak modules include Inventory Control & Accounting.
Core Software Inc.

FastStart Legal: For WordPerfect (Versions 5.0 & 5.1). *Items Included:* Small manual. *Customer Support:* Free Telephone support.
IBM PC & PS/2 & compatibles (256K). disk $350.00 single user; multi user available.
Networks supported: Novell, 3Com, IBM Token Ring, Banyan Vines.
Training Program for WordPerfect. The Program is Disk-Based, So It's on Computer & Available Whenever Needed. Law Office Application.
ComTrain, Inc.

FastStart Plus: For dBASE IV. *Items Included:* Small manual. *Customer Support:* Free telephone support.
IBM PC, PS/2 or compatible (256K). single user $150.00 - $250.00; multi user available.
Networks supported: Novell, IBM Token Ring, 3Com, Banyan Vines.
Training Programs Which Run on Computer. Designed to Make User More Productive with Software Application. Actually Simulates the Application User is Learning. No More Manuals! No More Classes.
ComTrain, Inc.

FastStart Plus: For DOS (2.01 to 3.3 or Release 5.0). *Items Included:* Small manual. *Customer Support:* Free telephone support.
IBM PC, PS/2 & compatibles (256K). single user $150.00-$275.00; multi user available.
Networks supported: Novell, IBM Token Ring, 3Com, Banyan Vines.
Training Programs Which Run on Computer. Designed to Make User More Productive with Software Application. Actually Simulates the Application User is Learning. No More Manuals! No More Classes.
ComTrain, Inc.

FastStart Plus: For Lotus 1-2-3 (rel. 2.01, 2.2 & 2.3). *Items Included:* Small manual. *Customer Support:* Free telephone support.
IBM PC, PS/2 & compatibles (256K). single user $150.00 - $250.00; multi user available.
Networks supported: Novell, IBM Token Ring, 3Com, Banyan Vines.
Training Programs Which Run on Computer. Designed to Make User More Productive with Software Application. Actually Simulates the Application User is Learning. More more Manuals! No More Classes.
ComTrain, Inc.

FastStart Plus: For WordPerfect (ver. 4.2, 5.0, 5.1). *Items Included:* Small manual. *Customer Support:* Free telephone support.
IBM PC, PS/2 or compatible (256K). single user $150.00 - $250.00; Multi User Available.
Networks supported: Novell, IBM Token Ring, 3Com, Banyan Vines.
Training Program Which Runs on Computer. Designed to Make User More Productive with Software Application. Actually Simulates the Application User is Learning. No More Manuals! No More Classes.
ComTrain, Inc.

FastTrack. *Version:* 2.0. Mark Rohrbough. Oct. 1990. *Items Included:* Complete, easy-to-use documentation. *Customer Support:* Free full year of customer support from time of purchase.
DOS 2.0 or higher (640k). IBM PC, XT, AT, PS/2, 386 & 100% compatibles. disk $149.95 (ISBN 1-877855-02-2). Optimal configuration: IBM compatible, hard disk, 640k RAM.
Provides Everything to Easily Track & Communicate with People. Incorporates Benefits of a Data Base, Mail List, & Word Processor. Tracks All Pertinent Information Including Categories & Notes. Sorts. Prints Labels, Rosters, Phone Book, Rolodex. Write Letters, Postcards & Then Mail Merge. Bulk Mail Sort. Import/Export to Other Programs. Dials Phone.
SoftServe Pr.

FastTrack Schedule. *Version:* 4.0. *Items Included:* Manual, 3.5" diskettes, essentials booklet. *Customer Support:* Free & unlimited technical support (703) 450-2318.
Windows 3.1, Windows 95, Windows NT. 386DX microprocessor or higher. 3.5" disk $299.00.
Macintosh, Power Macintosh.
Scheduling Software Takes Full Advantage of Windows 95 Capabilities As Well As a Completely Redesigned Interface. In Addition to New 32-Bit Technology, Windows 95 Functionality Includes OLE 2.0, Send Mail Capability, Drag & Drop, Long Filenames, UI Shell Support, Universal Naming Conventions, Uninstall, & Windows 95 Common Dialogs & Property Sheets. Includes User Interface Improvements Such As Integrated Layouts, Template & Preference Enhancements, Context-Sensitive On-Line Help, & the Industry's First Use of Context-Sensitive Tool Tips along with the More Powerful Bubble/Balloon Help for Toolboxes, Palettes, & All Dialog.
AEC Software.

FastTrax. *Version:* 4.0. *Compatible Hardware:* IBM PC & compatibles. *Operating System(s) Required:* PC-DOS 2.0 or higher. *Memory Required:* 800k expanded memory may be required over 85Mb; most hard drives 512k. *Customer Support:* (510) 525-3510, 24-hours. disk $70.00.
Disk Defragmenting Utility That Speeds Disk Access & Reclaims Wasted Space. Fast, Safe & Can Handle Any Size DOS Disk, Including Partitions Larger Than 1Gb, Hard Disks with More Than 1024 Cylinders, & Any Combination of Files, Directories, Directory Levels, Clusters & File Sizes. Unique "In-Cylinder" Technique Places Most Files Within Disk Cylinder Boundaries, Reducing Track-to-Track Seeks. MakeTrax (Included) Allows Placement of Files, Directories & Free Space for Best Performance. Offers Batch Operation & Power Failure Protection.
FastTrax International.

FastWire II. *Compatible Hardware:* IBM PC, PC XT, PS/2. *Memory Required:* 360k.
disk $129.95.
Utility for Laptop to Desktop Communication That Enables Users to Transfer Files from a Laptop to an IBM PC, or from an XT to a PS/2. Supports Three Command Modes-Split Screen, Form, & Command.
Rupp Brothers.

Fastword. *Compatible Hardware:* IBM PC, PC XT & compatibles.
disk $250.00-$495.00.
demo pkg. with manual.
Features Include: Search & Replace, Wordwrap, Horizontal Scrolling, Centering, Fill Justify, Automatic Paragraph Reformat & Pagination. A Block of Text Can Be Inputted, Moved, Duplicated, Saved, or Removed. All Settings May Be Saved with User's Text. Each Document Contains Its Own Margins, Tabs, Search/Replace Strings & Printer Formats.
Schmidt Enterprises.

FAS2000. Best Solutions, Inc. Staff. *Customer Support:* Support subscription, 900 number.
DOS. IBM & compatibles. $1595.00; Network version $2059.00.
Power, Flexibility, Control & Comprehensiveness via Enhanced Audit Schedules, Income Tax Reports, & Easier Access to Key Asset Information. Retains the Same Ease of Use As FAS, yet Provides Users with the Benefit of Being Able to Completely Customize Asset Management to Fit Their Needs. Also Includes Automatic Asset Transfer & Partial Disposal Capabilities.
RealWorld Corp.

Fatcat. Alan Bird. *Compatible Hardware:* Apple II, II+, IIe, IIc, IIgs. *Operating System(s) Required:* Apple DOS 3.3.
disk $34.95.
Disk Library Program. Reads All DOS 3.3 & ProDOS File Names into One or More "Master Catalog" Files for Sorting, Searching, & Printing. The Catalog Can Be Updated at Any Time by Simply Reading in New or Altered Disks. The SORTCAT Utility Lets Users Sort Catalogs & Move File Names to Any Position. The File Comparer Will Compare Any Two AppleSoft Files & Print the Non-Matching Lines on the Screen. Will Allow Changing of the Disk Volume Number.
Beagle Brothers.

Fax Modems & Online Services. Margarette Dornbusch. Edited by Steve Bender.
disk $24.80, incl. 160p. text (ISBN 0-929321-19-7).
WEKA Publishing, Inc.

FaxBuilder. Nov. 1990. *General Requirements:* 640k RAM, hard disk. *Items Included:* User's Manual. *Customer Support:* 800 number for registered users.
MS DOS 3.3 & higher. IBM & compatibles (640k). disk $49.95. Optimal configuration: Mouse.
Produces FAX Documents, Such As Cover Sheets, That Truly Reflect Your Business. This Easy to Use Product Lets You Quickly Create Cover Pages for Normal & Unique FAX Situations. Built in Database Allows You to Retrieve Customer Information Instantly & Automatically Fills in the Cover Sheet for You. It's As Simple to Use As Point & Click.
Unison World.

FaxFacts. *Items Included:* Fully descriptive manual. *Customer Support:* Three months of free support following initial purchase. Additional 1 year periods available at current rate. 60 day guarantee.
MS-DOS 3.0 or later. IBM PC/AT or compatible machine with hard disk (640k). $3000.00 & up. *Nonstandard peripherals required:* Hayes JT-Fax 9600 Fax Board(s), or Brooktrout 111 or

112 Fax Board(s), or Gamma Fax CP Fax Board(s), Dialogic D20 or D40 Voice Board(s). *Addl. software required:* Hijaack PS, GoScript Plus.
Fax Image Retrieval System Provides a Means of Delivering Fax Images to a Caller at a Remote Fax Machine. Images Can Be Received Through a Caller Initiated Fax Transmission or Through a Network User/System Operator Initiated Fax Transmission. System Configuration Allows for Same Call & Call-Back Fax Image Delivery, Fax Broadcasting, Fax MailBox, Credit Card Charge-per-Fax, IVR/Questions Box, Direct Faxing from Windows.
Copia International, Ltd.

FB Pro. *Compatible Hardware:* Apple Macintosh. *Memory Required:* 512k. *General Requirements:* MIDI Interface; Yamaha FB-01 Tone Generator.
3.5" disk $129.00.
Integrated Editor-Librarian Software Package Designed for the Yamaha FB-01 Synthesizer.
Digital Music Services.

FC: Fire Control. Nov. 1982. *Compatible Hardware:* IBM PC. *Operating System(s) Required:* MS-DOS. *Memory Required:* 640k. *General Requirements:* Hard disk.
disk contact publisher for price.
Used in Conjunction with Notifier CMS-100 Fire Alarm System, Generates a Response to an Alarm for Security Personnel. Printed History & Diagnostics Allow Management of Fire Alarm System.
KMS Systems, Inc.

FCEU: File Compress & Encryption Utility. Ron Holyer. Sep. 1986. *Compatible Hardware:* IBM PC. *Operating System(s) Required:* PC-DOS, MS-DOS. *Memory Required:* 128k. *General Requirements:* Hard disk.
disk $39.95.
File Compression & Encryption Utility Which Compresses Disk Files up to 50% of Their Original Size. Also Provides File Security Since Compressed Files Cannot Be Read or Executed Without Expanding the Files. Optional File Passwords May Be Used. A Permanent File Erase Option Is Included to Make It Impossible to Recover Sensitive Data Once It Has Been Deleted. Supports Wild Cards in File Names So That Groups of Files Can Be Processed with a Single Command.
Generic Computer Products, Inc. (GCPI).

FeatureFormat. *Operating System(s) Required:* CP/M, MS-DOS.
disk $49.00.
Professional Version. $99.00.
Preprogrammed Key Definition Program Designed to be Used with WordStar. Enables User to Turn Rarely-Used Keys into Function Keys. The Professional Version Also Permits User to Record Any Sequence of Keystrokes, Including WORDSTAR Commands, & to Play them Back by Pressing the "=" Key.
Powersoft, Inc.

FED: Font Editor. 1990. *Items Included:* Documentation included on diskette.
MS-DOS (640k). PC, XT, AT or compatible. disk $99.00 (ISBN 0-938245-57-0).
Creates a Graphic Pixel by Pixel Representation of a Character & Permits the User to Change It by Filling & Blanking Pixels of Choice. The User Controls the Character Box & Such Parameters As Offset & Pitch. Existing Characters May Be Changed, & New Characters Created. Characters Can Be Lifted from Different Fonts or Borrowed from the Same Font To Be Used As Substitutes for Existing or Missing Characters & As Starting Points for Further Editing. Reflections of Characters Are Also Supported.
Inverted-A, Inc.

Federal Estate Tax Returns: Calculation & Preparation. Mark R. Gillett & Elizabeth G. Gillett. Jun. 1985. *Compatible Hardware:* IBM PC. *Operating System(s) Required:* PC-DOS/MS-DOS 3.1 or higher. *Memory Required:* 640k. *General Requirements:* Hard disk.
disk $950.00.
*Calculates & Prepares Federal Estate Tax Return Form 706 & Associated Schedules. Also Performs the Following Functions: Interrelated Calculations When Federal Estate or State Death Taxes Are Payable Out of Property Which Qualifies for Either the Marital or Charitable Deduction; Permits the Estate to Elect Special Use Valuation under IRC *2032A, & Prepares the Notice of Election & Agreements; Automatically Prepares a Checklist Informing the Preparer of Additional Forms or Documents That Must Be Submitted with Form 706; Calculates Marital Deduction Funding under Formula Clauses; Checks for Errors in Input, & Checks to See If the Return Is Internally Consistent; State Modules Available.*
Shepard's/McGraw-Hill, Inc.

Federal Estate Tax Returns: Calculation & Preparation. Mark R. Gillett & Elizabeth Gillett. Jun. 1985. *Items Included:* 1 perfect-bound manual, tri-annual newsletter "Subscriber News". *Customer Support:* Unlimited telephone access to toll-free technical support line during normal business hours is included with price of programs & subsequent updates. Training at customer's site is available starting at $600 for 4 hours.
PC-DOS/MS-DOS 3.1 or higher. IBM PC & 100% compatibles (640k). disk $950.00. *Optimal configuration:* 12 CPI printer, hard disk. *Networks supported:* Novell A-Netware, AT&T Starlan, & Banyan Vines.
Calculates/Prints Form 706 & Associated Schedules. 1) Calculates Interrelated Deductions, Marital Deductions, Charitable Deductions, & Special Use Valuations under S2032A. 2) Performs Interrelated Calculations When Federal or State Taxes Are Payable Out of Marital/Charitable Deduction Property. 3) Performs Interrelated Interest Calculations, Including S6166. Calculates Estate's Residue for Each Residual Beneficiary. State Modules Available.
Shepard's/McGraw-Hill, Inc.

Federal Gift Tax Returns: Calculation & Preparation. Mark R. Gillett & Elizabeth G. Gillett. Jan. 1994. *Items Included:* 1 perfect-bound manual, tri-annual newsletter "Subscriber News". *Customer Support:* Unlimited telephone access to toll-free technical support line during normal business hours is included with price of programs & subsequent updates. Training at customer's site is available starting at $600 for 4 hours.
PC-DOS/MS-DOS 3.1 or higher. IBM PC & 100% compatibles (640k). disk $490.00. *Optimal configuration:* 12 CPI printer, hard disk. *Networks supported:* Novell A-Netware, AT&T Starlan, & Banyan Vines.
Calculates & Prints Form 709, Associated Schedules A, B, & C. Instantly Recalculates the Tax Every Time You Edit the Form, Letting You Explore Various Taxing Scenarios. Performs Interrelated Net Gift Calculations, Automatically Splits Gifts Between Husband's & Wife's Returns, & Calculates Interest on Underpayments & Overpayments.
Shepard's/McGraw-Hill, Inc.

Federal Gift Tax Returns: Calculation & Preparation. Mark R. Gillett & Elizabeth G. Gillett. Jan. 1991. *Items Included:* 1 perfect-bound manual, tri-annual newsletter "Subscriber News". *Customer Support:* Unlimited telephone access to toll-free technical support line during normal business hours is included with price of programs & subsequent updates. Training at customer's site is available starting at $600 for 4 hours.
PC-DOS/MS-DOS 3.1 or higher. IBM PC & 100% compatibles (640k). disk $490.00. *Optimal configuration:* 12 CPI printer, hard disk. *Networks supported:* Novell A-Netware, AT&T Starlan, & Banyan Vines.
Calculates & Prints Form 709, Associated Schedules A, B, & C. Instantly Recalculates the Tax Every Time You Edit the Form, Letting You Explore Various Taxing Scenarios. Performs Interrelated Net Gift Calculations, Automatically Splits Gifts Between Husband's & Wife's Returns, & Calculates Interest on Underpayments & Overpayments.
Shephard's/McGraw-Hill, Inc.

Federal Income Tax Planning for 1990 & 1991. Eugene J. Aubert. Feb. 1991. *Items Included:* 3 5.25" disks or 2 3.5" disks plus 31-page manual on disk. *Customer Support:* Provided on limited basis over telephone.
PC-DOS 2.0 or higher (256k). IBM PC, XT, AT or compatible. disk $20.00 (ISBN 0-929416-03-1). *Addl. software required:* Lotus 1-2-3 or compatible. *Optimal configuration:* 1 floppy drive & 1 hard-disk drive.
Two Programs, Three Examples Plus Worksheets & Manual. Runs with Lotus 1-2-3. Includes One 1990 Income Tax Software For Tax Due 4/15/91, & One 1991 Income Tax Software To Estimate Withholding & Tax Payments Due 4/16, 6/15, 9/15/91 & 1/15/92. Facilitates Tax Planning To Minimize Tax Bite, Establish Amount of Withholding & Quarterly Payments To Avoid IRS Penalty & Maximize Portfolio Income. Ask Those "What If" Questions & See the Effect on the Bottom Line.
Advanced Financial Planning Group, Inc.

Federal Income Taxes. Version: 1995. Feb. 1995. *Items Included:* Complete instructions included, on disk. *Customer Support:* 90 days free support.
MS-DOS, Windows 3.1. IBM & compatibles (620k). $79.95 Plus $3.50 S&H (Order no.: 1994). *Addl. software required:* Lotus 1-2-3 Version 4.0 or higher. *Optimal configuration:* IBM compatible, MS-DOS Rel. 5.0 or higher, Windows 3.1, 8Mb RAM, printer (preferably laser or ink jet).
Prepares Federal Forms 1040, Schedules A, B, C, D, E, F, R, SE, EIC & Forms 2119, 2441, 3903, 4214 & 6251. Macro Controlled Input to Fill in 77 Line Data Input Form. Prints Returns in Approved IRS Format.
Compiled Systems.

Federal JobLink: The Complete SF 171 & Supportive Forms Package. Version: 2.1. Jan. 1991. *Compatible Hardware:* Apple Macintosh. *Memory Required:* 512k. *General Requirements:* MacDraw (specify I or II). *Customer Support:* Correspondence & telephone.
3.5" disk $62.95 (ISBN 0-9624552-1-0).
Complete Package of Application Forms & Information for Persons Seeking Employment in the Federal Government. Reference Book Describes Procedures for Obtaining Ratings & Serves As Source for Completing Applications. Forms & Answers Are Printed in One Step. Each Form Appears on Screen for Easy Completion & Updating. Result Is Near-Typeset-Quality Application.
Multisoft Resources.

FEDTAX92: Federal Income Tax Calculator. Nov. 1990. *Memory Required:* Lotus 1-2-3 192k, Symphony 384k. *General Requirements:* Lotus 1-2-3 or Symphony.
disk $35.00 ea.
Lotus 1-2-3. (Order no.: FEDTAX85-I).

Symphony. (Order no.: FEDTAX85-S).
Designed to Project Tax Position. Individual Tax Information Can Be Easily Entered into the Template & Tax Status Is Immediately Calculated.
Easy-As, Inc.

Feed Plant Management. Agri-Management Services, Inc. *Compatible Hardware:* TI Professional. *Operating System(s) Required:* MS-DOS. *Memory Required:* 64k. *General Requirements:* Printer.
$1995.00.
Designed for the Operation of a Feed Mill Regardless of Its Complexity or Simplicity. Bags, Bulk or Combination.
Texas Instruments, Personal Productivit.

Feedback Linear Systems Simulator. *Items Included:* Bound manual. *Customer Support:* Free hotline - no time limit; 30 day limited warranty; updates are $5/disk plus S&H.
MS-DOS 2.0 or higher. IBM & compatibles (256k). disk $99.95. *Nonstandard peripherals required:* Color graphics card (e.g., CGA, EGA, Hercules).
Linear Control-Systems Analysis Package. The Control System under Study Is Described by the Various Poles, Zeroes, & Gains. FEEDBACK Then Calculates the Open- & Closed-Loop Gain, Open-Loop Phase, & Error Responses As a Function of Frequency. Also Provided Are the Gain & Phase Margin (for Stability). In Addition, the Transient Responses to Impulse, Step, Ramp, or Pulse Inputs Are Available.
Dynacomp, Inc.

Feedlot & Swine Finish Floor Management. Agri-Management Services, Inc. *Compatible Hardware:* TI Professional. *Operating System(s) Required:* MS-DOS. *Memory Required:* 64k. *General Requirements:* Printer.
$495.00.
Management System for the Feedlot on an Individual Pen Basis.
Texas Instruments, Personal Productivit.

The Feeling's Mutual. Stuart James. 1994. *Items Included:* Disk & manual.
MS-DOS & Windws. disk $60.00 (ISBN 1-885837-10-0).
Macintosh. 3.5" disk $60.00 (ISBN 1-885837-11-9).
Investment Software.
Interpretive Software Inc.

Feith Document Database: Document Storage & Retrieval System. *Version:* 3.1. Aug. 1992. *Items Included:* Manual & on-line help. *Customer Support:* All support options are available on a per install basis. Training is included with the original install.
UNIX platform with PCs running DOS 3.0 & Windows 3.1. 386 PCs. Contact publisher for price. *Networks supported:* Ethernet, Token Ring, TCP/IP, Novell.
Stores & Maintains All Document Needs. Including Any Size Document up to E-Size Drawings, Workflow, FAX Input/Output, Multimedia Annotation, Computer Output to Laser Disk (C.O.L.D.), Optical Character Recognition, Security, Magnification & Many Other Features.
Feith Systems & Software, Inc.

Fellow Travellers. Sharon Lerch. 1990.
DOS. Any type of IBM (64k). $8.95 (ISBN 1-56178-002-2).
MAC. Any type of Macintosh (64k). $8.95 (ISBN 1-56178-019-7).
Collection of Original Short Stories; Fiction.
Connected Editions, Inc.

The Fellowship of the Ring: A Software Adventure. J. R. R. Tolkien. *Compatible Hardware:* Apple IIe, IIc; Commodore 64, 128; IBM PC, PCjr.
contact publisher for price.
Based on J. R. R. Tolkien's Fantasy Novel. The Package Contains Two Complete, Consecutive Adventures with Over 100 Graphic Locations, Which Allow Users to See Middle-Earth Through the Eyes of Frodo, Sam, Merry, & Pippin. User Can Assume the Role of Any One of These Characters, or Play with up to Three Friends, Each of Whom Can Become a Different Hobbit.
Addison-Wesley Publishing Co., Inc.

FEMG: A Finite Element Mesh Generator. *Compatible Hardware:* Apple Macintosh. *Memory Required:* 512k.
3.5" disk $20.00.
Interactive Finite Element Mesh Generator & Editor for Engineers.
Kinko's.

Ferrari Formula One. *Compatible Hardware:* Commodore Amiga.
3.5" disk $19.95.
Racing Simulation.
Electronic Arts.

Fertilizer Plant Management. Agri-Management Services, Inc. *Compatible Hardware:* TI Professional. *Operating System(s) Required:* MS-DOS. *Memory Required:* 64k. *General Requirements:* Printer.
$1995.00.
Designed for the Operation of a Fertilizer Plant Operation Regardless of Its Complexity or Simplicity. Bags, Bulk or Combination.
Texas Instruments, Personal Productivit.

Fetchit. *Version:* 1.23. Kent Ochel & Jerry Spencer. Oct. 1989. *Items Included:* Tutorial. *Customer Support:* Unlimited free technical support at (512) 251-7541.
MS/PC-DOS 3.1 or higher. IBM PC, XT, AT & compatibles (512K). disk $79.95. *Nonstandard peripherals required:* Hard disk required. *Networks supported:* LAN.
Finds Any Text from Any Source & Transfers Selected Portions Directly to Word Processor. Can Search for Any Text & Show Which Files Contain the Text User Is Looking for. Also Views Files in HEX or ASCII & Displays Information from Computer Memory.
Business Resource Software.

FFA Leadership Record. Gary Sande. 1986. *Compatible Hardware:* Apple II series, IBM PC & compatibles. *Operating System(s) Required:* Apple DOS 3.3, PC-DOS 2.0 or higher. *Memory Required:* Apple 48k, IBM 128k. *General Requirements:* 2 disk drives, printer.
Apple. disk $74.50 (ISBN 1-55797-188-9, Order no.: AP2-AG524).
IBM. disk $74.50 (ISBN 1-55797-189-7, Order no.: IBM-AG524).
Menu-Driven Program Which Allows the FFA Members to Record, Categorize & Maintain an Ongoing Record of Their Leadership Activities. Information Is Recorded in the Same Manner & Format As the American Farmer Degree & FFA Proficiency Award Applications Forms. Information May Be Recorded & Updated on a Regular Basis During the Entire Seven Possible Years of FFA Membership. The Information Is Stored on the Student's Personal Leadership Data Disk & a Printout Is Available at Any Time.
Hobar Pubns.

Fiber Optic Design. Palais & Johnson. 1990. *Items Included:* Manual with theory, sample runs, program listings in BASIC. *Customer Support:* Free phone, on-site seminars.
MS-DOS. IBM (128k). disk $85.00.
10 Programs for Design of Fiber Optic Systems & Devices, Including Attenuation, Waveguides, Modes, Optical Fibers, Light Source Coupling, Optical Time Domain Reflectometer, Simulator, Digital Fiber Optic Communication System, Fiber Optic Weight Sensor, Fiber Optic Gyroscope.
Kern International, Inc.

Fiber Optic Technology: An Overview. Dec. 1994. *Items Included:* User manual. *Customer Support:* Free technical support & a 30-day warranty (1-800-521-CORE).
MS-DOS. IBM & compatibles (512k). 3.5" disk $199.00 (ISBN 1-57305-016-4). *Nonstandard peripherals required:* High-density 3.5" disk drive; VGA color monitor. *Addl. software required:* MS-DOS version 3.3 or higher. *Optimal configuration:* IBM (512k), MS-DOS version 3.3 or higher, VGA color monitor, keyboard, Microsoft compatible mouse (optional).
Fiber Is Used in Telecommunication Systems for Long Haul Transmission on Land & Across Seas, to Carry Many Simultaneous Telephone Conversations. Fiber Is Also Used in Applications Such As Links Between Computers & High-Resolution Video Terminals, Medical Imaging, & Between Computers & Peripheral Devices. Its Versatility & Virtually Unlimited Band Width Provide for Today's Hi-Speed Services & Carry Us Well into the Future for Transport of Services Yet Undiscovered.
Bellcore.

FictionMaster: For Novelists & Short Story Writers. *Version:* 1.1. Sol Stein. Feb. 1994. *Items Included:* Manuals. *Customer Support:* Help is available at no charge Monday - Friday, 9:00 am to 5:00 pm, eastern time, 914 762-1255.
DOS 2.0 or higher. IBM & compatibles. disk $299.00 (ISBN 1-879584-24-7).
Mac Plus or higher, System version 6.0.5 or higher. Macintosh. 3.5" disk $299.00 (ISBN 1-879584-25-5).
Advanced Program for Novelists & Short Story Writers That Enables Them to Transfer Writing from Their Word Processor into the Program, Improve It & Solve Existing Problems under the Guidance of Sol Stein, & Then To Transfer It Back into Their Word Processor. Comes in Four Parts: Creating Memorable Characters, Developing Page-Turning Plots, The Dialogue Doctor, & Overcoming Obstacles to Publication. Deals with Such Matters As How to Show a Story Instead of Telling It, How to Move Flashbacks into the Present, How to Handle Point of View, & 54 Other Subjects. Program Is Designed So That It Can Be Used by Talented Beginners As Well As Professionals. Stein Is the Author of Nine Successful Novels & Is an Award-Winning Teacher. He Has Also Edited Such Successful Writers As James Baldwin, Jack Higgins, Elia Kazan, & Lionel Trilling.
The WritePro Corp.

Fiduciary Accounting for Trusts & Estates. Mark R. Gillett et al. Nov. 1986. *Compatible Hardware:* IBM PC. *Operating System(s) Required:* PC-DOS/MS-DOS 3.1 or higher. *Memory Required:* 640k. *General Requirements:* 12 cpi printer.
disk $875.00.
Allows for the Maintenance & Updating of Each Client's Trust or Estate & Facilitates the Preparation of Reports to the Courts, Beneficiaries, & Other Interested Parties. Offers the Following Features: Reports Meeting the Demands of the National Fiduciary Accounting Standards; Direct Access via Modem to the Current & Historic Pricing of Traded Securities & Bonds; Predefined Chart of Accounts Allowing for Each Upkeep of Assets, Liabilities, Income, &

Expenses; Built-In Docket Control System; Business Reports Including Schedule of Assets & Liabilities, Income Statement, Trial Balance, Cash Receipts Journal, Cash Disbursements, General Journal, Bank Account, Reconciliation, & Depreciation Reports; Transfer of Information to FEDERAL ESTATE TAX RETURNS: CALCULATION & PREPARATION; Florida, New York & Virginia Modules Available.
Shepard's/McGraw-Hill, Inc.

Fiduciary Accounting for Trusts & Estates. Mark R. Gillett et al. Nov. 1986. *Items Included:* 1 perfect-bound manual, tri-annual newsletter "Subscriber News". *Customer Support:* Unlimited telephone access to toll-free technical support line during normal business hours is included with price of programs & subsequent updates. Training at customer's site is available starting at $600 for 4 hours.
PC-DOS/MS-DOS 3.1 or higher. IBM PC & 100% compatibles (640k). disk $825.00.
Optimal configuration: 12 CPI printer, hard disk. *Networks supported:* Novell A-Netware, AT&T Starlan, & Banyan Vines.
Generate National Fiduciary Accounting Standards Reports, Price Securities On-Line, & Customize the Chart of Accounts. Group Assets Together for Financial/Income Statements & Use in Conjunction with Shepard's Federal Estate Tax Returns or Fiduciary Accounting for Trusts & Estates. Design Reports with the Custom Report Generator. State Modules Available.
Shepard's/McGraw-Hill, Inc.

Fiduciary Income Tax Returns: Calculation & Preparation. Mark R. Gillett et al. Feb. 1989. *Items Included:* 1 perfect-bound manual, tri-annual newsletter "Subscriber News". *Customer Support:* Unlimited telephone access to toll-free technical support line during normal business hours is included with price of programs & subsequent updates. Training at customer's site is available starting at $600 for 4 hours.
PC-DOS/MS-DOS 3.1 or higher. IBM PC & 100% compatibles (640k). disk $575.00.
Optimal configuration: 12 CPI printer, hard disk. *Networks supported:* Novell A-Netware, AT&T Starlan, & Banyan Vines.
Calculates/Prints Form 1041, & Associated Schedules, Calculates Interrelated Calculations Such As Forms 1041ES, 1041T, 2210, 4797, 4835, 4952, 8582, & 8656. Calculates Interest on Underpayments & Overpayments, Allocates Tax Attributes among the Beneficiaries Based on Either Percentage or Actual Distribution, Automatically Transfers Income Information Already Entered into Fiduciary Accounting for Trusts & Estates, State Modules Available.
Shepard's/McGraw-Hill, Inc.

Fiduciary Income Tax Returns: Calculation & Preparation: Core Program, Laser Versions (HP, HP Center Piece, Canon LBP-8II & Xerox 4045). Mark R. Gelett et al. Feb. 1989. *Customer Support:* Training is available starting at $600.00 for 4 hours, first year maintenance is available at no charge with the purchase of a new package or revision.
MS/PC-DOS 3.1 or higher (500k). Core package $575.00.
This Program Calculates & Prepares Form 1041 & Supporting Schedules & Has a Gateway to Fiduciary Accounting for Trusts & Estates Which Permits the Transfer of Income Information for Ease of Preparation to Form 1041. State Modules Available.
Shepard's/McGraw-Hill, Inc.

Field File Program. 1985. *Compatible Hardware:* Apple II+, IIe, IIc; IBM PC, PCjr. *Memory Required:* Apple 48, IBM 64k.
Apple. disk $79.95 (Order no.: AP AG211).
IBM. disk $79.95 (Order no.: IBM AG211).
Allows the Producer to Keep a Record of Each Field in Each Farm He Operates. Stores All Information Pertinent to the Field, Including Acres, Yield, Comments, All Inputs. Includes Soil Test & Recommendations.
Micro Learningware.

Field Manager. *Version:* 2.0. Apr. 1994. *Customer Support:* 30 day free support - 1 year support (all products of CDI - $200).
DOS. IBM & compatibles (640k). disk $199.00.
Optimal configuration: DOS 3.3 or higher.
DOS. 808 - 286 Version on request 386-486 versions as well (640k). disk $199.00.
Provides for Tracking of Chemical & Fertilizer Applications by Field & Farm. ASCS Map & Farm Numbers. Crop Planting & Harvest Info. Weather Record's Can Be Maintained. Helps to Meet EPA Tracking Requirements & Environment Conditions. Lots of Comment Area to Help Record Unique or Special Situations. Applicator EPA Number & Emergency Phone Numbers of Chemical or Fertilizer Manufacturers You Use.
Countryside Data, Inc.

Field Manager. Apr. 1994. *Items Included:* Manuals, blank forms, binder. *Customer Support:* On line screen helps - support package 6 months/12 months options - $50-$100 - Digitizing maps - per farm basis - additional charges.
MS-DOS - Mapping requires Windows. IBM & compatibles (2Mb). disk $199.00. *Addl. software required:* Windows - if using Mapping add on option. *Optimal configuration:* 4Mb-8Mb - 386 or higher - hard drive.
Track Chemicals for EPA Requirements. Record Fertilizer, Chemical, Crops, Weed & Insects. Record Weather Info. Soil Test, Tissue Tests & Moisture. Extensive Comments Areas. Field Records Tie to ASCS Maps. Mapping Program Available for Windows Uses. Records Harvest & Planting Information for Full Crop & Field Management.
Countryside Data, Inc.

Field Manager. *Version:* Updated 1991 for IBM compatible. *Compatible Hardware:* IBM PC & compatibles. *Operating System(s) Required:* MS-DOS 3.1 & higher. *Language(s):* Compiled BASIC. *Memory Required:* 640k. *General Requirements:* Printer: Hard disk. *Items Included:* Program disk & manual. *Customer Support:* 30 minutes free; Pay-per-call at $1.95/minute.
disk $495.00, $45.00, trial size.
manual $20.00.
Field Record Database That Provides Detailed Records of Every Field's Production History Including Soil Test, Yields, Costs, Business & Information. Also Provides Breakeven Analysis on a Field-by-Field Basis Using Projected or Actual Yields, Prices, & Costs. The Reporting Feature Allows User to Design Reports & Output to a Printer.
Harvest Computer Systems, Inc.

FieldMouse. 1983.
$175.00.
MSC Technologies, Inc.

Fields & Operators. Martin Lapidus. Mar. 1989. Windows. IBM PC & compatibles (512k). disk $135.00 (ISBN 0-943189-03-9).
Macintosh (512k). disk $135.00 (ISBN 0-943189-04-7).
Animates Surfaces, Vector Fields, Differential Operators, Differential Geometry, All in Two or Three Dimensions.
Lascaux Graphics.

1541/1571 Drive Alignment. Oct. 1986. *Items Included:* Manual with diagrams explaining how to adjust drive alignment. *Customer Support:* Free technical support at 215-683-5699.
CBM (64k). Commodore 64. 3.5" disk $34.95.
CBM (128k). Commodore 128. 3.5" disk $34.95.
Reports Alignment Condition of Disk Drive As User Performs Adjustments.
Free Spirit Software, Inc.

50 Classic Business Contracts. *Version:* 2.0. Dec. 1988. *General Requirements:* 800k disk drive.
Macintosh 512K or higher (1Mb). 3.5" disk $49.95.
Collection of 50 Copy & Edit Business Contracts. Titles Include: Partnership Agreement, Power of Attorney, Equipment Rental, Employment Agreement, etc. Legal Definitions are Available for Many of the Terms Within Individual Contracts.
Milum Corp.

51 Ready to use Engineering Programs. *Version:* 6.0. Jan. 1990. *Items Included:* Reference manual & formula book. *Customer Support:* Free product/technical support available over the phone.
MS-DOS/PC-DOS. IBM XT/AT/386 & compatibles (640k). disk $245.00.
51 Programs, Designed by Professional Engineers from Various Engineering Curriculums Such As: Mathematics, Hydraulics, Machine Design, Structures, etc. These Are Routinely Used Programs & Eliminate the Need to Search Through Handbooks & Textbooks. Reduces Calculating Hours & Eliminates Errors.
Unik Assocs.

57 Cookbooks CD-ROM: Thousands of the World's Greatest Recipes. Oct. 1996. *Items Included:* Instruction booklet.
DOS & Windows 3.1. PC (2k). CD-ROM disk $29.90 (ISBN 1-56087-125-3). *Optimal configuration:* 386, Windows 3.1 2k.
57 Cookbook Files Covering Everything You Wanted to Know about Cooking. Tens of Thousands of Recipes & a Master Program to Index, Search, & Even Make a Shopping List - Instantly at Your Fingertips. Bonus Programs on Diets, Health & Nutrition.
Top of the Mountain Publishing.

5250 Local Gateway. 1988. *Compatible Hardware:* IBM PC, PC XT, PC AT & compatibles, PS/2 Model 25, PS/2 Model 30, PS/2 Model 50, PS/2 Model 60, PS/2 Model 70, PS/2 Model 80. *Operating System(s) Required:* PC-DOS/MS-DOS 3.0 or higher. *Memory Required:* Gateway 60k, PC Node 91k. *General Requirements:* Local 5250 adapter. *Items Included:* Software, hardware, modem. *Customer Support:* Free, 800-642-5888.
3.5" or 5.25" disk $1995.00.
Alllows PC to Function As a Local Gateway into a NETBIOS-Compatible Local Area Network. Routes All 5250 Data & Handles the NETBIOS Interface Between the Gateway & Workstation Nodes. LAN Workstations, As Gateway Nodes, Process the Same Information & Produce the Same Results As If They Were Real IBM 5250 Display or Printer Devices. IBM PC AT or PS/2 Recommended for Maximum Performance. Network Interface Is Configurable at Runtime for Increased Efficiency. Supports Native IPX/SPX (Novell), Banyan VINES, or IBM NETBIOS.
Micro-Integration Corporation.

5250 Remote AutoSync. 1988. *Compatible Hardware:* IBM PC & compatibles, PS/2. *Operating System(s) Required:* PC-DOS/MS-DOS. *Memory Required:* 158k. *General Requirements:* The host modem must

have the same modem protocol but does not need AutoSync. At 1200 baud, any 212A modem that operates synchronously will work. At 2400 baud, any V.22 or V.22 bis modem that can connect to a Hayes will work. At 4800 and 9600 baud, a Hayes V9600 modem that uses V.32 half duplex must be used. *Items Included:* Software, manual. *Customer Support:* Free, 800-642-5888.
3.5" or 5.25" disk $495.00.
Supports the Hayes AutoSync Feature of High Speed Hayes Modems. Allows the Use of a Standard Asynchronous Port on PC or PS/2 to Run Remote IBM 5250 Applications, Which Is Standard on All 5250 Remote Products. Allows System/3X Communications Without Communications Hardware Adapters.
Micro-Integration Corporation.

The Fighting Irish: The History of Notre Dame Football. Oct. 1995. *Customer Support:* 800 number (free), online support forums.
Windows 486SX, 25MHz; Macintosh. IBM & compatibles (8Mb); Performa 550 (33MHz 68030) (8Mb). CD-ROM disk $39.95 (ISBN 1-57595-006-5). *Nonstandard peripherals required:* Double-speed CD-ROM drive, Super VGA color card capable of 256 color display, "SoundBlaster" compatible sound card; Double-speed CD-ROM drive.
The History of Notre Dame Football: Every Player, Every Team, Every Year of Football - with the Legends, Big Games, Statistics for All Americans, Awards, & Records. Facts, Fictions, & Folklore. Over 1,000 Photos, 30 Minutes of Video, Statistics. Trivia Game.
Macmillan Digital U. S. A.

File Alert for Windows NT. *Version:* 1.0. Dec. 1993. *Items Included:* Installation & instruction booklet, and a help-text manual included on the CD itself. *Customer Support:* 90 day money back guarantee.
Microsoft Windows NT. Intel, MIPS, or Alpha AXP PC's. $99.00 per node.
32-Bit Application That Automatically Detects File Corruption from All Possible Sources. Instantly Reports Data Corruption from Sources Such as Worn-Out Hard Disks, Power Failure, User Error, or Software Defects.
Executive Software.

File-Buster. *Version:* 5.1. *Operating System(s) Required:* CP/M. *Language(s):* Assembly 8080. *Memory Required:* 24k.
disk $29.95.
manual $15.00.
Disk Updating System That Lets User Tag File Names That Are Listed Alphabetically & Copy Tagged Files to Another Disk. Files Can Also Be Erased in the Same Way, but Program Gives User a Second Chance to Change His Mind Before Erasing. File Sizes & Remaining Disk Space Can Be Displayed. Allows User to Rename Existing Files.
Elliam Assocs.

File Conversion Utility. John Hall. *Compatible Hardware:* IBM PC, PCjr, PC XT, PC AT, Portable PC, 3270 PC. *Operating System(s):* PC-DOS 2.00, 2.10, 3.00, 3.10. *Memory Required:* 128k.
disk $29.95 (Order no.: 6276629).
Eliminates Manual Preparation of PC File Data for "Import" by LOTUS 1-2-3 or SYMPHONY Spreadsheet Programs. Converts Selected Rows & Columns of Data from a PC ASCII File for Spreadsheet Use or into a New PC File Customized to User's Specifications. User Is Asked to Respond to Simple Questions or Instructions on Sequentially Presented Segments of the Original PC File Data. Responses Can Be Saved for Future Use with Later or Similar Versions of PC File Data or for Batch Processing.
Personally Developed Software, Inc.

The File Converter. 1984. *Compatible Hardware:* Commodore 64. *Memory Required:* 20k.
disk $39.95, incl. instr's. manual on disk.
Allows Files Created in Any Data Base to Be Read or Transferred from One Data Base to Another. Allows Transfer of Text Files from One Word Processor to Another. Any Program, Sequential or Relative File May Be Converted to Another Type.
Applied Technologies, Inc.

File Director. Steve Brecker & Even Gross. *Items Included:* Manual. *Customer Support:* Free, toll call.
System 4.1 or higher. Mac 512k. 3.5" disk $129.00.
Alternative Interface for the Macintosh That Organizes Work By Project & Provides DA for Easier Copying, Moving & Deleting. It Also Provides DA Phone RPN Calculators & Calendar Programs.
Fifth Generation Systems, Inc.

File Edit. *Version:* I. Niels Immerkaer. Aug. 1984. *Compatible Hardware:* Heath-Zenith, IBM PC & compatibles. *Operating System(s) Required:* PC-DOS, MS-DOS. *Language(s):* Assembly. *Memory Required:* 128k.
disk $39.95.
File Dump/Patch; Full-Screen Editing Format. File Contents Displayed by Logical Blocks Within File. Data Displayed in ASCII & Hex Formats (Either by Selecting a Specific Block or Searching for Specified Data Values). Makes Patches to Binary Program Files.
Generic Computer Products, Inc. (GCPI).

File-80. *Compatible Hardware:* HP 86/87 Personal Computers with dual disk drive. *Memory Required:* 128k.
disk $270.00 (Order no.: 82824A).
Solution-Oriented File Management System Designed to Provide a Method of Managing Files & Producing Output (Records, Labels, Letters) from Information in the Files.
Hewlett-Packard Co.

File Express. *Version:* 5. *Items Included:* Disks, printed manual. *Customer Support:* Free one year technical support.
MS-DOS 2.0 or higher. IBM & compatibles (512k). disk $99.00 (ISBN 1-878012-05-3).
Complete Full Featured Flat File Database Program. Completely Menu Driven with a Powerful Formula Handler for Greater Flexibility. Features Include Mailing Labels, Reports, Global Search & Replace, Search for Duplicates, Quick Labels, Record Selection etc.
Expressware Corp.

File Force. *Version:* 1.2.2. *Compatible Hardware:* Macintosh. *Items Included:* 5 Disks. *Customer Support:* 90 Days free maintenance, free unlimited technical support.
3.5" disk $395.00.
Data Management for Novices & Experts. Users Can Employ Templates or Create a Personalized System for Entering Data, Even a Mirror Image of Existing Paperwork System. Users Can Also Do Instant Searches & Sorts, Rapid Updates, & Quick & Detailed Columnar Reports; Create Form Letters & Address Labels with Intuitive, Built-In Editors; & Allow Several Users Access to the Same Files Simultaneously. For Additional Power System Can Be Upgraded to ACIUS's 4th Dimension.
ACIUS, Inc.

File-It! *Compatible Hardware:* IBM PC, PC XT, PC AT, PC compatibles; DEC; AT&T. *Operating System(s) Required:* PC-DOS, MS-DOS, UNIX, XENIX.
contact publisher for price.

Interactive File Manager for Business Professionals & Casual Users Who Want to Build, Use, & Maintain Simple Applications Such As Tracking Prospects, Producing Mailing Labels, & Controlling Inventories. It Is Menu-Driven, Using Ring Menus to List Options at the Top of the Screen. On-Line Help Is Available at Any Time. Users Can Easily Create Databases, Design Reports, or Perform On-Line Searches.
Relational Database Systems, Inc.

File Manager. *Compatible Hardware:* HP 85 with Plotter/Printer ROM (HP 00085-15002), ROM Drawer (HP 82936A), HP-IB interface (HP 82937A), Mass Storage ROM (HP 00085-15001), Disk Memory (HP 82900 series, 9121D/S, 9134A, 9135A, or 9895A); HP 86/87 with modem (HP 82950A), dual disk drive. *General Requirements:* 16k Memory Module (HP 82903A), plotter (HP 7225B with HP 17601A module, HP 9872C, or HP 7470A), Advanced Programming ROM (HP 00087-15005).
$200.00 ea.
HP 85. (Order no.: 88103A).
HP 86/87. (Order no.: 88104A).
Allows User to Create & Enter Data into a File Structure & Then Perform Searching, Sorting, Reporting, & Plotting Functions. Handles up to 1000 Records of 1000 Bytes Each (File Size Dependent on the Mass Storage Capacity); Data Can Be Translated to a String Data File for Use with Other Software Such As VisiCalc PLUS.
Hewlett-Packard Co.

File Plus. *Version:* 2.0. Sep. 1989. *Compatible Hardware:* IBM PC & compatibles. *Operating System(s) Required:* MS-DOS. *Language(s):* BASIC. *Memory Required:* 256k. *Customer Support:* Customer support available.
disk $29.95.
Filing System with Sub-Heading Capability & an Open Format. Alphabetical Index & Cross References.
D W N.

File Transfer. Oct. 1983. *Compatible Hardware:* IBM PC with Kronos TimeKeeper System, Text Editor. *Operating System(s) Required:* DOS 1.1, 2.0, 2.1. *Memory Required:* 192k.
contact publisher for price (Order no.: SD-04016-000).
Batch Processing Program That Allows Transfer of Information Between KRONOS TIMEKEEPER (Computerized Timeclock) & an IBM PC. Allows Creation of Command Files to Poll TimeKeeper & Produce & Store Reports from One or Multiple TIMEKEEPER Systems on Disk.
Kronos, Inc.

File Xfer. Mel Tainiter. *Compatible Hardware:* IBM PC & compatibles, PC XT. *Operating System(s) Required:* DOS 2.0 or higher. *Memory Required:* 170k. *General Requirements:* 2 disk drives.
disk $65.00 (ISBN 0-934577-00-5).
Assists in the Transfer of Data from a Variety of Commonly Used File Formats Including Those Used in Current Best Selling Software Packages for Business.
Softext Publishing Corp.

File Zero.
Macintosh 512KE. 3.5" disk $35.95.
Overwrites Selected Files Prior to Deleting the File.
OITC, Inc.

File Zero INIT. *Version:* 2.3.
Macintosh 512KE. 3.5" disk $59.95.
An Addition to the Macintosh Operating System That Transparently Overwrites All Files Prior to an Application Commanded Delete.
OITC, Inc.

Filebase. Version: 8.0. Jan. 1989. *Operating System(s) Required:* CP/M, MS-DOS, PC-DOS. *Memory Required:* 64k.
CP/M. disk $99.00 (ISBN 0-923775-00-5).
PC-DOS/MS-DOS. $99.00 (ISBN 0-923775-01-3).
Variable-Length Fields Data Manager. Provides Comma Delimited Format for Letter-Merge Programs Such As MAILMERGE, MULTIMATE, WORDPERFECT, DISPLAYWRITE & WORD. Creates Subset Files, & Includes Built-In Computation & Report Generation. Sorts on Embedded Last Names & Zips. Functions As File Processor for Existing Files.
EWDP Software, Inc.

FileBase. Version: 6.5. 1995. *Items Included:* Manuals, customization. *Customer Support:* Free on-site training, 90 days free support, maintenance at 15% on annual basis, hourly.
DOS, Windws (all versions), Unix. 386 (500k). disk $3000.00. *Nonstandard peripherals required:* Bar code reader, SVGA.
A File Room Management System with a Customizable Database for Tracking Every File, Folder, or Other Document in Your Office. Uses Your Computer's E-Mail to Send Messages for Creating & Requesting Files, Updating Their Status, etc. Information Can Be Entered Via Keyboard, or by Placing Bar-Code Labels on Each File & Scanning Them with a Portable Bar Code Reader, Turning Your File Room into a True Check-In/Check-Out Center. Bar-Code Data is Automatically Uploaded for Providing Up-to-the-Minute Information on Every File. "Notes" Can Keep Track of Where a File Is, Where It Was, Who Has It, Who Had It, Who Needs It Now, & More. Determine Which Files Are in Which Office by Scanning the Office Bar Code, & Then Each File in That Office. Create Your Own File Room Reports with FileBase's Report Writer.
Synaptec Software, Inc.

FileCommand II. Glenn E. Huff. *Compatible Hardware:* IBM PC, PCjr, PC XT, PC AT, Portable PC with IBM Display. *Operating System(s) Required:* PC-DOS 2.00, 2.10, 3.00, 3.10. *Memory Required:* 128k.
disk $19.95 (Order no.: 6276658).
Allows User to Sort & Scroll Through the Directories, Issue Many DOS Commands at Once (up to 63 Characters), Redefine Keys, Set Screen Colors, Issue DOS Commands to Multiple Files, & Invoke with One Keystroke.
Personally Developed Software, Inc.

FileFinder. Oct. 1990. *Customer Support:* On-line help.
DOS. IBM PC compatibles (100k). disk $69.00
 (Order no.: FILEFINDER). *Networks supported:* Yes.
A Handy, Fast Utility That Lets You Locate a File by Name or by Something Inside the File.
Thunderstone Software/Expansion Programs International, Inc.

FileMagic. *Compatible Hardware:* Apple Macintosh. *Memory Required:* 512k.
3.5" disk $99.95.
Macintosh System Enhancement That Speeds up the Selection of Files & Folders by Extending the Standard Dialog Box Presented by the Open & Save Commands Available in Most Application Programs.
Magnus Corp.

FileMaker Pro. Version: 3.0. 1996.
System 7.0 or higher. Macintosh or Power Macintosh (4-8Mb). 8" disk $199.00. *Networks supported:* Apple Talk, IPX/SPX or TCP/IP Networking for multi-user file sharing.
Windows. IBM (8-16 Mb).
For Windows 95 or NT 3.51: 8Mb RAM (16Mb RAM) for Windows NT 3.51).
FileMaker Pro for Macintosh & Windows, is now offering relational capabilities, yet retaining its legendary simplicity. It runs on Windows 95, Windows NT, Power Macintosh CPU's & 680X0 Macintosh CPU's & is the only cross-platform database that is multi-user & network ready out-of-the box.
Claris Corporation.

FileMaker Pro Server. Version: 3.0. 1995.
System 7.1 or higher. Power Macintosh (68030 or greater). 3.5" disk $999.00.
System 7.1 or higher.
FileMaker Pro Server 3.0 is a high performance database engine that dramatically accelerates FileMaker Pro operations over AppleTalk, IPX/SPX & now TCP/IP networks. With it's unique 'multi-protocol' support, FileMaker Pro Server can host files for Apple Talk IPCX/SPX & TCP/IP guests simultaneously. Additionally FileMaker Pro Server 3.0 is written to take advantage of Open Transport TCP/IP networking, which gives users the benefit of native PowerMac Networking.
Claris Corporation.

FileMaker Pro 3: Training on CD. Quay2 Multimedia. Apr. 1996.
IBM. CD-ROM disk $49.95 (ISBN 0-201-88622-7).
Peachpit Pr.

Filemaster. Version: 2.2. Jul. 1993. *Customer Support:* 90 day warranty. Annual support & update service: 15% of the price for Single-Use License for the same CPU size. Faxed or written SPR handling. Yearly telephone support: 24 hour/7 days a week telephone support is an additional $750.00. Must have Annual Support & Update service.
Open VMS. DEC VAX & Alpha AXP (1,400 for installation). $320.00 to $13,200.00. *Optimal configuration:* DEC VAX or Alpha AXP, running Open VMS.
Provides Easier File & Disk Management for OpenVMS VAX & Open VMS Alpha AXP Systems with an Easy to Use PC Style Graphical Interface. Increase Productivity by Providing Full View of the Directory Tree, Recovery of Wasted Disk Space, Finding Files Fast, & the Integration of All System applications into an Easy, Menu-Based Interface. Allows Management of Large Disk Farms with Ease.
Executive Software.

Filemax. J. B. Rose. Mar. 1987. *Compatible Hardware:* Data General. *Operating System(s) Required:* RDOS/ICOBOL.
disk $250.00.
Tells Users When It Is Time to Reorganize Their File(s).
Infodex, Inc.

FileMover. *Compatible Hardware:* IBM PC & compatibles, PC XT, PC AT.
disk $59.95.
Provides Most of the Features of Big U's FileMover Plus the Ability to Back up Entire Subdirectories & Alphabetize & Rearrange File Names in Any Order.
Beagle Brothers.

FilePac. DBI Software Products. *Compatible Hardware:* TI Professional. *Operating System(s) Required:* MS-DOS, CP/M. *Memory Required:* 64k. *General Requirements:* Printer.
$150.00.
Creates Files & Generates Simple Reports.
Texas Instruments, Personal Productivit.

FilePad. Version: 1.5. Feb. 1996. *Items Included:* Users manual. *Customer Support:* Technical support.
Newton (1Mb). disk $89.00.
The First General Purpose Flat-File Database for the Newton. Users Can Create Customized Databases to Track Inventory, Conduct Surveys & Take Sales Orders by Incorporating Text, Paragraph Fields, Radio Buttons, Check Boxes, Poplists & Borders into User-Defined Layouts.
HealthCare Communications.

FilePro Plus. Version: 3.0. Sep. 1985. *Compatible Hardware:* IBM PC AT & compatibles, PS/2; AT&T, DEC, Tandy, Hewlett Packard, UNISYS, NCR. *Operating System(s) Required:* UNIX, XENIX, MS-DOS, PC-DOS. *Memory Required:* single-user 256k, multi-user 512k. *General Requirements:* Hard disk.
MS-DOS & PC-DOS. disk $995.00.
XENIX & UNIX. disk or cartridge $1595.00.
Application Development System with Relational Data Base Manager. Offers Full Screen Editor & Built-In Maintenance Features. Applications & Data Are Portable Between XENIX/UNIX, DOS & LAN's. Filepro Plus Includes: Custom Menu Generator. Report & Forms Generator, Screen Generator, Screen Creation, New Browse Look-Up Windows & an On-Line Tutorial. File-Pro Plus Can Handle over 16 Million Records per File & Provides File Import/Export Capabilities.
Small Computer Co., Inc.

FilePro 16. Version: 3.0. Howard Wolowitz. 1984. *Compatible Hardware:* IBM PC, PC XT, PC AT, & compatibles; Tandy 3000, 4000, 5000. *Operating System(s) Required:* MS-DOS, PC-DOS, OS/2, UNIX, XENIX. *Language(s):* Assembly, C. *Memory Required:* 256k. *General Requirements:* Hard disk.
MS-DOS, PC-DOS. disk $495.00.
UNIX, XENIX. disk $995.00.
Relational DBMS/Application Developer Featuring User-Defined Menus/Field Types & Password Security. Supports up to 16 Million Records per File with up to 999 Fields per Record. Up to 10 Files Can Be Open at One Time. Users Can Add to & Revise Their System at Any Time Without Having to Change Data. Files Can Be Transferred Between MS-DOS/PC-DOS & UNIX/XENIX Microcomputers.
Small Computer Co., Inc.

FilePro 16 Plus Network. *Compatible Hardware:* IBM PC & compatibles. *Operating System(s) Required:* DOS 3.0 or higher. *Memory Required:* 512k. *General Requirements:* NetBIOS-compatible LAN. Hard disk recommended.
$1495.00 per 5 users.
$100.00 each additional user.
Networked Database-Management System. The LAN Version Features Automatic Record Locking & Transparent Conversion of Single-User Programs.
Small Computer Co., Inc.

Filer Finder: Index to Information Management Software for Microcomputers. Version: 3.0. Gregg Shadduck & Jeanette Sullivan. Jul. 1990. *Compatible Hardware:* MS-DOS based computers. *Operating System(s) Required:* MS-DOS 2.0. *Memory Required:* 512k. *General Requirements:* 2 disk drives or hard drive.
disk $34.50 (ISBN 0-935975-00-4).
Focuses on Management of Textual Data with Microcomputers, That Is Storing, Indexing, Manipulating, & Retrieving Textual Information. Over 400 Pieces of Software Are Described & Made Accessible by a Series of Descriptive Menus.
Shadduck & Sullivan.

TITLE INDEX

Files, 2 diskettes. *Items Included:* Bound manual. *Customer Support:* Free hotline - no time limit; 30 day limited warranty; updates are $5/disk plus S&H.
MS-DOS 2.0 or higher. IBM PC, XT (256k). $69.95. *Nonstandard peripherals required:* 2 disk drives (or a hard disk); color or monochrome monitor; printer supported.
Provides All the Integrated Software Tools the Typical Professional, Manager, or Entrepreneur Needs to Work Quickly & Efficiently. The Program Features the Following: It's a Database Manager; It's a Spreadsheet; It's a Word Processor; It's a Calculator; It's a Report Generator; It's a Graphics Generator; It Provides Trending; It Provides Statistics; It's a Critical-Path Model Generator. In Addition - User Can Edit BASIC Programs or Assembly-Language Source Code Using the Word Processor; Transfer ASCII Files in or Out; Convert from Almost Any Units to Any Other Units; Display the Sum, Average, etc., of the Entire File; Store Multiple Files in Memory & Manipulate Them Just As You Would Data in a Calculator. All Files of All Types Fit Together in a Common Master List of Relations. Once User Sets the Margin, Spacing, or Any Format Value, the Value Acts in the Logical Way on Graphs & Data-File Displays.
Dynacomp, Inc.

Filling Out Job Applications. Feb. 1996. *Items Included:* Program manual. *Customer Support:* Free technical support, 90 day warranty.
Single user. System 7.1 or higher. Mac, 16 MHz rating, 68030 or better processor (LC II or higher) (5Mb). 3.5" disk $99.95 (ISBN 1-57204-097-1, Order no.: APM152). *Nonstandard peripherals required:* 256 color monitor, 13" or larger.
Lab pack. System 7.1 or higher. Mac, 16 MHz rating, 68030 or better processor (LC II or higher) (5Mb). 3.5" disk $199.00 (ISBN 1-57204-118-8, Order no.: APM152LPK). *Nonstandard peripherals required:* 256 color monitor, 13" or higher.
Site license. System 7.1 or higher. Mac, 16MHz rating, 68030 or better processor (LC II or higher) (5Mb). 3.5" disk $399.00 (ISBN 1-57204-120-X, Order no.: WIN152SITE). *Nonstandard peripherals required:* 256 color monitor, 13" or higher.
Single user. Windows 3.1 or higher. IBM 386 (8Mb). disk $99.95 (ISBN 1-57204-098-X, Order no.: WIN152). *Nonstandard peripherals required:* 256 color monitor, sound card, mouse. *Addl. software required:* SVGA graphics.
Lab pack. Windows 3.1 or higher. IBM 386 (8Mb). disk $199.00 (ISBN 1-57204-119-6, Order no.: WIN152LPK). *Nonstandard peripherals required:* 256 color monitor, mouse, sound card. *Addl. software required:* SVGA graphics.
Site license. Windows 3.1 or higher. IBM 386 (8Mb). disk $399.00 (ISBN 1-57204-121-8, Order no.: WIN152SITE). *Nonstandard peripherals required:* 256 color monitor, mouse, sound card. *Addl. software required:* SVGA graphics.
Takes the student through the process of filling out a job application form.
Lawrence Productions, Inc.

Film Writing, 3 disks. Robert Pirosh. May 1985. *Compatible Hardware:* Apple IIc, IIe. *Memory Required:* 64k.
disk $69.00 ea.
Covers the Essentials of Successful Screenwriting, Including How to Develop a Story Structure Visually.
The Software Teacher, Inc.

Disk 1. Writing Visually.
(ISBN 0-928781-17-8, Order no.: AP-22).
Covers: Conflict; Character Identification; & Premise.
Disk 2. Developing a Script.
(ISBN 0-928781-18-6, Order no.: AP-23).
Covers: Theme; Spade Work: Thinking Things Out First; Character Motivations; Creating Surprise; & Building Action.
Disk 3. Script Formats.
(ISBN 0-928781-19-4, Order no.: AP-24).
Covers: Step Outline; Screen Treatment; & Screenplay Format.

FILMPATH: Audio Visual Scheduling. *Version:* 4.00. Jesse Tarshis & Ken Youngstrom. 1985. *Compatible Hardware:* IBM PC, PC XT, PC AT, & compatibles. *Operating System(s) Required:* PC-DOS/MS-DOS, Novell, NETBIOS. *Language(s):* DBXL & Quicksilver. *Memory Required:* 640k. *General Requirements:* Hard disk, printer. *Items Included:* Software, documentation. *Customer Support:* Toll free technical support.
$795.00 - $995.00.
Menu Driven Database System Which Allows Schools or Libraries to Catalog & Schedule Audio-Visual Items, Equipment & Facilities, Maintain a Database of Users, Schedule Items, & Keep Track of Usage for Reporting Purposes & Collection Development.
Alpine Data, Inc.

Filter Analysis. *Compatible Hardware:* Apple II with Applesoft, IBM PC. *Operating System(s) Required:* Apple DOS 3.2 or 3.3.
disk $29.95.
cassette $29.95.
Calculates the Effective Attenuation of an Electrical Filter Composed of Passive Elements. Results Available in Several Forms.
Dynacomp, Inc.

Filter Analysis: Passive Filter Evaluation. 1992. *Items Included:* Detailed manuals included with all Dynacomp products. *Customer Support:* Free telephone support to original customer - no time limit; 30 day limited warranty.
MS-DOS 3.2 or higher. IBM PC & compatibles (512k). $29.95 (Add $5.00 for 3 1/2" format; 5 1/4" format standard). *Optimal configuration:* IBM, 256k.
Evaluates the Attenuation Characteristics of Filters Composed of Passive Elements. The Results of the Analysis May Be Displayed Either Graphically or in Tabular Form, Showing Attenuation in Decibels Versus Log-Frequency, & Phase Versus Log-Frequency. Element Descriptions & Placements Are Easily Described. Includes 32-Page Manual.
Dynacomp, Inc.

Final Assembly. *Compatible Hardware:* Atari 400, 800. *Language(s):* Atari BASIC. *Memory Required:* disk 32k. *General Requirements:* Joystick.
disk $19.95.
Assemble Rockets.
Dynacomp, Inc.

Final Draft. *Compatible Hardware:* IBM PC & compatibles. *Memory Required:* Without thesaurus 128k, with thesaurus 256k. *General Requirements:* Hard disk.
disk $195.00.
Includes a Thesaurus That Offers a Wide Selection of Synonyms & Antonyms. Also Enables the User to Restore a Backup File, Print, Spell Check, Create a Table of Contents, Delete a File or Change Document Drive Destination.
CYMA/McGraw-Hill.

Final Legacy. *Compatible Hardware:* Atari XL/XE. ROM cartridge $19.95 (Order no.: RX8067).
Atari Corp.

Final Mission. *Customer Support:* Back up disks available.
Amiga (512k). $14.95.
Avoid Dangerous Mines, Traps & Energy Fields as You Dig & Climb Your Way Through 350 Different Levels of Graphics, Sound & Programming.
DigiTek Software.

The Final Word. *Compatible Hardware:* IBM PC & compatibles with 2 disk drives & printer. *Operating System(s) Required:* PC-DOS, MS-DOS, CP/M, CP/M-86, XENIX. *Language(s):* C. *Memory Required:* 64-128k.
disk $300.00.
Word Processor Designed to Handle Large Document Production. Can Edit & Display More Than One File at a Time. Features Automatic Generation of the Table of Contents, Indices, Footnotes, Chapter Section Numbering, Multiple Buffers & Windows, & Command Sets. Sections of Text Can Be Transferred Between Buffers, Deleted, or Restored. Provides Automatic Protection Against System Crashes & Interruptions. The 160 Different Commands Are Organized in a Logical Series of Menus. Special Formatting Commands Produce Output That Is Spatially & Typographically Arranged into Chapter Title, Enumerated Indented Lists, Sub-Heads, & Cross-References. User Can Edit Documents Larger Than the Main Memory.
Mark of the Unicorn.

Finally! Modules. *Compatible Hardware:* IBM PC & compatibles. *Operating System(s) Required:* PC-DOS/MS-DOS. *Language(s):* QuickBASIC. *General Requirements:* FINALLY! library & QuickBASIC 3.0 or 4.0.
disk $99.00.
Enables Users to Add Pull-Down Windows, Horizontal Menus, Pop-Up Help Screens, Input Screens, & Directory Messages to Their Compiled BASIC Programs.
Komputerwerk.

Finally! Subroutines. *Compatible Hardware:* IBM PC & compatibles. *Operating System(s) Required:* PC-DOS/MS-DOS. *Language(s):* QuickBASIC, TurboBASIC (source code included). *General Requirements:* QuickBASIC or TurboBASIC.
disk $99.00.
Includes a Library File for Linking to Programs Compiled with the BRUN Option. Also Includes Routines for Date Manipulation, Math, Graphics, Hardware Interface, Sorting, & Keyboard Control. Among the Math Routines Are Trigonometric Functions Not Found in BASIC; Number Base Conversions; Programs to Calculate the Average, Minimum, & Maximum Values of an Array.
Komputerwerk.

Finally! Xgraf. *Compatible Hardware:* IBM PC & compatibles. *Operating System(s) Required:* MS-DOS. *Language(s):* QuickBASIC. *General Requirements:* QuickBASIC 4.0 or 4.5.
disk $125.00.
Extended Graphics Kernel for Compiled BASIC. Allows Quick Manipulation of Graphics, Screen Packing, Zooming, File Saving/Loading, & Importing Screens from Other Packages.
Komputerwerk.

Finalsoft Executive: Groupware for Windows. *Version:* 1.2. Jan. 1992. *Items Included:* 1 bound user manul, 1 applications guide (how to use our product to solve your problems). *Customer Support:* 90 days free at (305) 477-2750,

FINANCE

Through CompuServe Windows Forum. DOS/Windows 3.0 & 3.1. 80286 (1Mb RAM). 1 user $99.00; 6 user $445.00; 10 user $695.00; 20 user $1198.00. *Nonstandard peripherals required:* Hard disk, mouse recommended. *Addl. software required:* DOS & MS Windows. *Optimal configuration:* 386 with 80Mb hard disk, 4Mb RAM & mouse. *Networks supported:* Novell, LANtastic, Banyan, LAN Manager, 10Net & Other NetBIOS Networks capable of running Windows.
Workgroup Productivity Solution, Providing an Economical, Fully Integrating Personal & Group Scheduler, Full Featured MHS E-MAIL Quick Letter Writer with Hypertext, a dBASE Compatible Database, Electronic Agenda, Calendar, to Do Lists & Directory.
Finalsoft Corp.

$Finance. *Version:* 3.5. *Operating System(s) Required:* CP/M, MS-DOS. *Language(s):* Quick Basic. *Memory Required:* 64k. *Items Included:* Manual, disk & warranty card. *Customer Support:* 18 month via telephone.
disk $79.00.
demo disk & manual $20.00.
Menu-Driven Accounting Program for Personal Finances, Account Manager Which Will Write &/or Post Checks to the Check Register, Record Bank Charges & Deposits, Reconcile the Checking Account to the Bank Statement & Provide a Listing of All Transactions in Both Printed & Disc File Form.
Micro-Art Programmers.

Finance Charge & Insurance Premium Rebates. *Version:* 1249B. *Compatible Hardware:* Sharp ZL-6100 system, ZL-6500 System. *Language(s):* Sharp Microcode.
$400.00.
Computes Finance Charge Rebates & Insurance Premium Rebates by 2 Methods: Actuarial & Rule-of-78's. Also Amortizes Simple-Interest Loans by the Exact Number of Days Between Payments to Find the Simple-Interest Payoff Amount. Provides a Calendar-Year Actuarial Interest Summary for IRS Tax Reporting Purposes.
P-ROM Software, Inc.

Finance I. *Customer Support:* 800-929-8117 (customer service).
MS-DOS. Apple II. disk $79.99 (ISBN 0-87007-259-5).
Provides Appreciation, Depreciation & Amortization Schedules on Screen or Printed. Computes NPV, FV, & Other Finance Measures are also Included.
SourceView Software International.

Finance Manager. *Customer Support:* 800-929-8117 (customer service).
MS-DOS. Apple II. disk $49.99 (ISBN 0-87007-821-6).
IBM PC, PS/2. disk $49.99 (ISBN 0-87007-820-8).
A Complete Home Finance System, Pefect for Planning, Budgeting & Organizing Tax Records. Provides Six Practical Money Management Modules. Comfortable to Use with Online Help Screens Available at Any Time, Sample Files & a "Quick Tour" Tutorial. Provides the Forms to Fill in & Lists the Options in a Special Message Window; Allows up to 35 Automatic Transactions to Save Time Paying Bills; 100 Different Income, Expenses, Tax & Balance Sheet Categories & up to 32 Tax Fields. Has a Financial Calculator So User Can Analyze Borrowing, Saving & Investment Decisions; Create an Amortization Table to Display Principal & Interest Payments on a Loan. Defines up to 32 Fields; Keeps a Running Total of Taxable Amounts; Retrieves Information Quickly at Tax Time. Will Do Planning & Budgeting.
SourceView Software International.

Finance Models. Apr. 1982. *Compatible Hardware:* Apple II, IIe; IBM PC, PCjr, PC XT; TRS-80 Model III. *Operating System(s) Required:* TRSDOS, CP/M, CP/M-86. (source code included). *Memory Required:* Apple 48k, all others 64k. *General Requirements:* VisiCalc, SuperCalc, Multiplan, or Lotus 1-2-3.
disk $59.95.
Contains Spreadsheet Templates Which Format Cash Budget Projections for Loans. Provides the "What If?" Calculations Available in Spreadsheets, As Well As Breakeven Sales, Cash Budget, Proforma Balance Sheet & Income Statements, Depreciation Tables, Financial Ratio Formulas, & Net Present Worth Analysis.
Software Models.

Finance Projections. *Compatible Hardware:* IBM PC, Apple II, II+, IIe; Atari 400, 800; Columbia; Compaq; Commodore CBM 8096; Franklin Ace; Fujitsu; HP 150 Touchscreen; LNW 80; Sharp PC 5000; Sperry; Tandy 2000; TI Professional; TRS-80 Model I, Model II, Model III, Model 4, Model 12, Model 16; Wang. *Operating System(s) Required:* CP/M. *Memory Required:* 48k. *General Requirements:* General Requirements: Visicalc, Supercalc, Multiplan or Lotus 1-2-3.
disk $59.95.
Software Models.

FinanceMaster Personal Finance & Budgeting. *Items Included:* Bound manual. *Customer Support:* Free hotline - no time limit; 30 day limited warranty; updates are $5/disk plus S&H.
MS-DOS 2.0 or higher. IBM & compatibles (512k). full system $89.95. *Nonstandard peripherals required:* One floppy (or mini) & one hard disk; supports both color & monochrome monitors.
manual only $10.00.
Personal Finance System for the Individual Who Wishes to Control & Analyze His or Her Financial Activities Using the Power of a Computer. It Is Menu-Driven, with On-Line Help Screens, a Pop-Up Calculator, & Data Windows. Requires No Accounting Knowledge. Reduces the Time Spent Paying Bills by Remembering Recurrent Expenses (e.g., Periodic Rents), Maintaining Check Registers, Printing Checks (Any Format, Including Payee Address, If Desired. Amounts Are Automatically Printed As Words). Keeps Accurate Records of Cash, Checkbook Balances, Savings Accounts, Credit Cards (with Transaction Record). Storage Capacity Is Virtually Unlimited. Sets up Budget with Comparisons (e.g., Bar Charts) Showing Budgeted & Actual Expenses & More.
Dynacomp, Inc.

Financer Super. *Compatible Hardware:* IBM PC, PC XT. *Operating System(s) Required:* PC-DOS, MS-DOS. *Memory Required:* 256k.
disk $49.95.
Utility Program Which Helps with Financial Calculations. Includes Present Value of a Future Amount, Simple/Compound Interest, Future Value of a Present Amount, Amortization Schedule, Day-of-the-Week, Daysek, Days Between Dates, Term of an Installment Loan & Present Value of a Series of Payments.
Zephyr Services.

Financial. *Version:* Series V. *Operating System(s) Required:* DOS, Novell & Lantastic Networks. *Items Included:* Software & manuals. *Customer Support:* 800 number telephone support, Bulletin Board services, remote support, product enhancements available.
Prices start at $2000.00.
Single-Source Computer System Covering: the Spectrum of Loan Activities, from Application to Commitment to Closing. Capable of Tracking the Pipeline, Operating from One or Many Workstations, & Exchanging Information On-Line with Other Computers. Programs Include: Loan Qualification, Loan Application, Forms Generation, HMDA & 1098 Reporting & Tracking.
Sulcus Law Management Services, Inc.

Financial Accounting Package. *Version:* 93.12. (Profit Ser.). *Compatible Hardware:* IBM 386 & compatibles, Novell, Unix. *Operating System(s) Required:* PC-DOS/MS-DOS. *Language(s):* BASICM (source code included). *Memory Required:* 512k. *General Requirements:* 20Mb hard disk for IBM.
IBM 386 & compatibles. disk $995.00 (Order no.: FAP3).
Novell & Unix. disk $1495.00 (Order no.: FAP3).
General Ledger Package That Includes Reversing & Recurring Entries, Trial Balance Input, Consolidations, Departmentals, & Budgets. Produces All Necessary Financial Statements from Balance Sheet & Income Statement to Statements of Changes to YTD General Ledger.
Crosstech Systems, Inc.

Financial Analysis Template. *Version:* 2.01. Nov. 1988. *Compatible Hardware:* IBM PC & compatibles. *Memory Required:* Lotus 1-2-3 256k, Symphony 512k.
$199.00.
Five Programs Include Income-Property Analysis (up to 15 Years), Amortization Schedules, Break-Even Analysis, Cash-Flow Analysis, & Compound-Interest Calculation.
R. H. Miller & Assocs.

The Financial Analyst. *Version:* 1.0. Apr. 1983. *Compatible Hardware:* IBM PC with color graphics adapter. *Operating System(s) Required:* DOS. *Memory Required:* 128k. *General Requirements:* Printer recommended.
disk $225.00, incl. Boardroom Graphics.
demo disk $25.00.
Menu-Driven Planning Tool for Small or Large Businesses. Will Create Five Year Plans or Financial Analyses Including Income Statement, Balance Sheet & Cash Flow. Can Be Purchased Separately or Integrated into a Problem-Solving Tool.
Analytical Software, Inc.

Financial Analyst. *Compatible Hardware:* Apple II, II+, IIe, IIc. (source code included). *Memory Required:* 48k.
disk $9.95 (ISBN 0-918547-17-2).
Includes 18 Programs for Analyzing Any Aspect of an Investment, Loan, Note, etc. Will Produce Loan Amortization Tables, Future Value of Investments, Withdrawals, Minimum Investment for an Income, Income from Investments, Effective Interest, Annual Depreciation, Salvage Value, Commercial Discount Paper, Loan Principal, Balloons, etc.
AV Systems, Inc.

Financial & Interest Calculator. *Version:* 90.01. *Compatible Hardware:* Apple Macintosh, Apple II Series, IBM PC's & PS/2.
3.5" or 5.25" disk $89.00.
Retirement Plan IRR, Loan Amortization Schedules, etc. Internal Rate of Return Calculations, Fixed & Increasing Annuities, Annual Percentage Rates (APR).
Larry Rosen Co.

Financial Calculator. *Compatible Hardware:* HP 150 Touchscreen.
3.5" disk $39.95 (Order no.: 45423A).
Simulates the HP-12C Business Calculator. In Addition to the HP-12C's Computing & Programming Power, User Can Copy All Programs & Registers onto Files & Recall Them at Will. Results Can Be Transferred to VisiCalc or Lotus 1-2-3.
Hewlett-Packard Co.

TITLE INDEX

Financial Calculator. 1987. *General Requirements:* Lotus 1-2-3.
IBM/Tandy. contact publisher for price (ISBN 0-538-40631-3, Order no.: 03F3).
Text & Template Diskette Package that Provides a Tool for Analysis & Demonstrates how Computers can Solve Financial Problems. Eliminates Computation Time.
South-Western Publishing Co.

Financial Cookbook: A Consumer's Guide.
Kaczmarski. 1986. *Compatible Hardware:* Apple IIe, IIc; Commodore 64; COMPAQ Portable, DESKPRO, IBM PC; Tandy 1000. *Operating System(s) Required:* PC-DOS 2.1 & higher. *Memory Required:* 64k.
disk $42.50 (Order no.: H-48).
Consists of 32 "Recipes" Which Analyze Savings, Mortgage, & Others Financial Topics. Displays a Statement of the Best Financial Decision & Gives a Summary & Rationale for Its Calculations.
South-Western Publishing Co.

Financial Decisions. May 1985. *Compatible Hardware:* IBM PC & compatibles, PC XT, PC AT. *Operating System(s) Required:* PC-DOS 1.1, 3.0, 3.3, MS-DOS. (source code included). *Memory Required:* 128k. *General Requirements:* Hard disk. *Customer Support:* Free telephone Support.
disk $100.00.
Spreadsheet Program with 15 Built-In Functions.
Accounting Professionals Software, Inc.

Financial Decisions. *Version:* 3.0. *Compatible Hardware:* Apple Macintosh.
3.5" disk $65.00.
Excel Templates.
GenMicronics.

Financial Decisions. *Compatible Hardware:* HP 85, 86/87.
data cartridge, 3-1/2" or 5-1/4" disk $95.00 ea.
HP 85. (Order no.: 82803A).
HP 86/87. (Order no.: 82833A).
Designed to Assist User in Evaluating Financial Decisions. Programs Include: Compound Interest, Loan Amortization, Discounted Cash Flow, Depreciation, Interest Conversions, Bonds, Notes, Breakeven Analysis, & Odd-Days Interest.
Hewlett-Packard Co.

Financial Healthcheck for Windows. *Version:* 1.1. May 1994. *Items Included:* Manual.
Windows. IBM (4Mb). Contact publisher for price (ISBN 1-885364-03-2). *Addl. software required:* Windows 3.1. *Optimal configuration:* IBM 486/386; Windows 3.1; 4Mb RAM; mouse, color monitor.
Wave Communications, Inc.

Financial Independence. Multisoft Corp.
Compatible Hardware: IBM PC & compatibles; Tandy. *Operating System(s) Required:* MS-DOS 2.0 or higher. *Memory Required:* 256k.
disk $149.00 (ISBN 0-922614-75-X, Order no.: 32210).
Contains Four Main Modules: Tax Estimator, Budget Manager, Stock Manager, & Goal Analyzer. May Be Used to Keep Track of User's Personal Budget, Investment Goals, & Cash Balances. Features Automatic Updating from One Module to Another, On-Screen Menus & Prompts, Automatic Reports, etc.
Broderbund Software, Inc.

Financial Learning System. Sep. 1990. *Items Included:* Workbook material.
PC-DOS/MS-DOS 2.0 or higher. IBM PC/XT/AT, PS2 & compatibles; Apple Macintosh (384k for IBM; 512k for Mac). disk $149.95. *Nonstandard peripherals required:* 2 disk drives and/or a hard disk.
Computer Simulation Challenges the User to Manage a Company, Making the Decisions to "Grow" the Business. Features a Highly Realistic Competitive Environment Which Gives the User "Real World" Experience. Extensive Tutorial, Analysis & Consulting Screens Are Included To Assist User. Accompanying Workbook Materials Include Financial Theory & Practice, Examples of Financial Reporting, & Practice Exercises in Financial Application.
Strategic Management Group, Inc.

Financial Learning System. Aug. 1990. *Items Included:* Provided with each simulation is a manual describing the various simulation decisions & a facilitators guide that explains simulation set-up & terminology. *Customer Support:* Included in all licensing agreements is a service contract that entitles licensees to Train-the-Trainer program & an 800 support phone number.
PC/MS-DOS 2.0 & higher. IBM PC/XT/AT & compatibles (256k). disk $300.00. *Nonstandard peripherals required:* 2 disk drives &/or a hard disk.
Dynamic Self-Study Business System of a Competitive Industry Which Includes a Financial Simulation.
Strategic Management Group, Inc.

Financial Management for Small Businesses.
Jan. 1989. *Compatible Hardware:* Apple Macintosh Plus, Macintosh SE, Macintosh II; IBM PC & compatibles. *Memory Required:* Macintosh 1Mb, IBM 512k. *General Requirements:* Hard disk, printer; Excel 1.5 or Lotus 1-2-3 2.01.
Excel/Macintosh. 3.5" disk $69.95 (ISBN 1-55571-036-0).
Lotus/IBM. disk $69.95 (ISBN 1-55571-053-0).
Software/Workbook Package That Gives Users Knowledge on How to Use Financial Analysis to Help Run Their Business. Users Learn How to Evaluate Their Company's Financial Management, Develop a Financial Operating Plan, or Go after a Business Loan or Venture Capital. The Software Generates over 25 Different Graphs a Reports to Chart a Company's Financial Picture, Showing Users How to Interpret What They See.
Oasis Pr.

Financial Management System. *Compatible Hardware:* MS-DOS based machines. (source code included). *Memory Required:* 128k.
disk $149.95, incl. instr. bk.
Financial Analysis Package.
Dynacomp, Inc.

Financial Management Techniques. *Version:* 1.1. *Items Included:* Combination package contains 3-ring binder edition of "Financial Managements Techniques for Small Business" by Arthur R. DeThomas ISBN 1-55571-320-3. *Customer Support:* Free technical support over phone; limited warranty.
DOS 3.0 or higher. IBM & compatibles (640k). disk $99.95 (ISBN 1-55571-319-X, Order no.: FMTSSS/A31). *Nonstandard peripherals required:* Hard disk with 1.5Mb free space, EGA or VGA monitor.
DOS 3.0 or higher. IBM & compatibles (640k). disk $129.95, incl. bk. (ISBN 1-55571-320-3, Order no.: FMT1BS/A31). *Nonstandard peripherals required:* Hard disk with 1.5Mb free space, EGA or VGA monitor.
Designed to Help You Get a Better Picture of Your Businesses Economic Health by the Timely Monitoring of Your Financial Standing. Automatically Calculates 61 Ratios & Other Indicators. Includes Graphing & Forecasting. Combination Package Recommended for People Needing to Gain Understanding of Financial Information.
Oasis Pr., The.

FINANCIAL PLANNING: LONG RANGE

Financial Management Tools for Small Business. Arthur R. DeThomas & Gary Ambrosino. *Items Included:* comprehensive workbook. *Customer Support:* 15 day unlimited warranty - telephone technical.
DOS 2.1 or higher. IBM (512K). 3.5" or 5.25" disk $99.95. *Nonstandard peripherals required:* Hard disk or 2-360K floppy drives or 1-720K floppy drive. *Addl. software required:* Lotus or a compatible spreadsheet.
Software Program That Incorporates Extensive Spreadsheets & a Comprehensive Workbook to Help the Small Business in the Areas of Financial Management. It Guides the Business Person Through Sales Forecasting, Sales Analysis, Accounts Receivable Management, Accounts Payable Management, Inventory & Control Management.
Oasis Pr.

The Financial Manager. *Version:* 4.0. 1989. *Compatible Hardware:* IBM PC & compatibles. *Operating System(s) Required:* MS-DOS 2.18. *Memory Required:* 512k.
disk $1495.00.
demo disk $25.00.
Designed to Provide Farmers with Financial & Production Management Analysis Capabilities.
Farm Management, Inc.

Financial Navigator. *Version:* 5.0. *Compatible Hardware:* IBM PC & compatibles. *Memory Required:* 512k. *Customer Support:* $35.00 for 1 month, $250.00 unlimited calls, includes upgrade. $495.00.
Personal Accounting & Financial Management System Designed for Individuals with Complex Finances. Includes Investment Tracking & Reporting Capabilities, & Check Printing. Also Features Automatic Pricing for Marketable Securities & Automatic Transactions for Unrealized Gains & Losses.
Financial Navigator International.

Financial Needs for Retirement. *Version:* 2.0. *Compatible Hardware:* IBM PC & compatibles. *Memory Required:* program requires 60k. *General Requirements:* Lotus 1-2-3 release 2+ *Items Included:* Instruction manual. *Customer Support:* 708-246-3365.
$49.00.
Projects Year-by-Year Financial Status for 25 Years into Retirement. Inputs Include Investment Assets, Average Returns, Tax Rates, Current Living Needs, Social Security, Pensions, Earnings, IRA Type Withdrawals. Inflation Rates, etc. User Can Determine If Moves are Necessary or Permitted in Order to Live Happily Ever After: Retire or Keep Working, Get Higher Yielding Investments, Change Lifestyle, Make More Gifts or Donations, & Future Estate Size for Will & Trust Planning. What-If Trials Are Calculated Immediately.
V. A. Denslow & Assocs.

Financial Pak. *Version:* 2. David Powers. Jul. 1985. *Compatible Hardware:* IBM PC & compatibles. *Operating System(s) Required:* PC-DOS, MS-DOS. *Language(s):* BASIC, Pascal. *Memory Required:* 128k.
disk $149.00.
Can Be Used for Mutual Fund Analysis, Loan Amortizations, Annuity Investments. MUTUAL FUND Provides Effective Buy/Sell Advice Using Average-Cost Basis; LOAN AMORTIZATION Handles Most Fixed-Rate Loan Situations; ANNUITY INVESTMENT Provides Information for Deposit Plans (IRAs).
Generic Computer Products, Inc. (GCPI).

Financial Planning: Long Range Economic Forecast, International GNP, Valuation.
Richard R. Sylvester. Aug. 1993. *Customer*

Support: Purchase money back if not satisfactory. MS-DOS. IBM PC & compatibles (640k). disk $49.50 (ISBN 0-932010-69-5). *Addl. software required:* Lotus 1-2-3 version 1A or higher or Excel.
Spreadsheet Formats for LOTUS 1-2-3 or EXCEL Allows Forecast of United States GDP to Year 2015, Using Data Base from 1945. Input for Unemployment Rate & Government Budget Allows Prediction of Budget Deficit. Valuation Formats for Real Property, Corporate Equity, & Intangible Values. On 3.5" Diskette with 1.2Mb of Program Material.
Ph.D. Publishing Co.

Financial Planning System. Fisher Business Systems, Inc. *Compatible Hardware:* TI Professional with printer. *Operating System(s) Required:* MS-DOS. *Memory Required:* 128k. $1500.00.
Combines Personal Income Tax Module & Investment Analysis Module to Form an Integrated Financial System.
Texas Instruments, Personal Productivit.

Financial Planning TOOLKIT. *Version:* 5.0. Stephan R. Leimberg & Robert T. LeClair. Jun. 1995. *Items Included:* 250-page refererence manual. *Customer Support:* 30-day money-back guarantee, 1-year service contract for $89, telephone support, facsimile service.
PC-DOS (256k). IBM PC, PC XT, PC AT & compatibles. disk $249.00.
Financial Planning Programs Covering 49 Different Calculations in Investments, Real Estate, Insurance, Budgeting, Net Worth Calculations & Projections, Retirement Planning, Educational Funding & More.
Leimberg & Leclair, Inc.

Financial Planning Tools. *Version:* 3.10. Stephan R. Leimberg & Robert T. LeClair. Jul. 1992. *Items Included:* User manual, 12 months of maintenance coverage. *Customer Support:* Free telephone support: 1-800-367-1040, Annual maintenance contract: $99.00.
PC-DOS/MS-DOS 2.0 & higher. IBM PC & compatibles (512k). disk $249.00 (Order no.: 1691).
Performs 49 Different Financial Planning Calculations in Seven Essential Areas: Investments, Inflation, Real Estate, Insurance, Net Worth, Financial Goals & Budgeting. Calculate Internal Rate of Return, College Funding Needs, Mortgage Amortization, Home Refinancing Breakeven, Insurance Needs, Required IRA Withdrawals, Much More.
CCH Access Software.

Financial Planning, 1996. Richard R. Sylvester. Jan. 1996. *Customer Support:* Telephone consultation 10 minutes no charge; $250 per hour thereafter.
DOS. 286 (800k). 3.5" disk $450.00 ea. (set of 4) (ISBN 0-932010-96-2). *Addl. software required:* Lotus 1-2-3.
Detailed Calculation Formats for Financial & Economic Issues, Such As: Valuation of a Business, Affordability of a Proposed New Residence, Lease Rates, Interest vs. Principal, Real Property Value, Transfer Pricing, Calculation of 20-Year Forecast for GNP & Stock Market Trends, & Supporting Problem Formats for Rapid Solution of Complex Economic Issues.
Ph.D. Publishing Co.

Financial Ratio Calculations. 1982. *Compatible Hardware:* IBM PC & compatibles. *Language(s):* Microsoft BASIC.
disk $45.00 (Order no.: 266).
Interactively Records Data Elements & Calculates Key Financial Ratios Such As Current Ratio, Acid Test Ratio, Current Liabilities to Owners, (Shareholders) etc.
Resource Software International, Inc.

Financial Ratios. *Version:* 1.0. 1984. *Compatible Hardware:* IBM PC & compatibles, PC XT, PC AT. *Operating System(s) Required:* PC-DOS 2.X, 3.X. *Memory Required:* 128k.
$34.95.
Provides Ratio Analysis of Financial Statements. User Selects Ratios from a Menu & Then Program Asks for Facts Needed to Compute the Ratios. A Report Can Be Printed.
Lassen Software, Inc.

Financial Reporting. *Version:* 3.03. *Items Included:* Complete documentation. *Customer Support:* Toll-free support (prices vary); hands-on seminars & on-site instruction (price varies); computer-based tutorial.
MS-DOS. IBM or 100% compatible (44k). disk $995.00. *Addl. software required:* System Manager. *Optimal configuration:* 80286, 80386, or 80486-based PC, 640k RAM. *Networks supported:* Novell.
Features Quick Client Setup & Easy Transaction Entry. Flexible Report Presentations & a Full Complement of Financial Statements Are Ready to Use Without Special Formatting. Can Copy Chart of Accounts, Financial Statements, & Other Setup Information from the Master or Another Client's File.
Prentice Hall Professional Software.

Financial Statement Analyzer. *Version:* 5.0. Oct. 1994. *Compatible Hardware:* IBM PC & compatibles. *Operating System(s) Required:* MS-Windows 3.1. *Memory Required:* 256k. $99.00.
Menu-Driven Worksheet Application for MS-Excel 5.0. Analyzes up to Five Periods of Financial Statements & Produces Projected Pro Forma Statements Based on Two or Three-Year Averages of Historical Data. Includes Reports on Common-Size Balance Statements to Assets, Liabilities, & Sales; Common-Size Operating Statements to Sales; & Operating-Cash-Flow & Cash-Flow Analyses. Also Includes an RMA H-Score Bankruptcy Predictor.
Weston & Muir.

Financial Systems. *Customer Support:* Software warranty; 24 hours, 7 days a week; 800 number; hardware/software staging; training & seminars; documentation; system personalization; consulting services.
DSM, OpenVMS, DOS, AIX, MSM, OSF/1, HP-UX. DEC, IBM & HP platforms (2Mb). contact publisher for price.
Streamline the Core Functions for Maintaining Control of Detailed Financial Reporting in the Medical Laboratory: General Ledger, Accounts Receivable & Billing, Accounts Payable, Materials Management, Payroll, Fixed Assets & Electronic Claims. These Functions Are Fully Supported by Comprehensive Reporting & Management Analysis Capabilities.
ANTRIM Corp.

Financial Templates for Small Business. *Customer Support:* 15 day unlimited warranty, telephone technical support.
IBM PC, XT, AT, PS/2 & compatibles (512k). disk $69.95 (ISBN 1-55571-052-2). *Nonstandard peripherals required:* Hard disk or two floppy disk drives.
Macintosh. 3.5" disk $69.95 (ISBN 1-55571-051-4). *Addl. software required:* Microsoft Excel 2.0.
Multi-Purpose Templates Which Are Ready to Use with & Lotus 1-2-3 or PSI Research Spreadsheet Program Available Through PSI Research/The Oasis Press. Handles the Financial Calculations for the Following Four Workbooks (Also Available Through PSI Research/The Oasis Press): The Loan Package; Develop Your Business Plan; Venture Capital Proposal Package;
Negotiating the Purchase or Sale of a Business. Takes the Drudgery Out of Calculating Financial Reports & Performing "What-If" Scenarios for Business. Use the Results for Better Internal Monitoring & Planning & for Completing External Financial Proposals to Lenders, Venture Capitalists & More.
Oasis Pr.

Financial Templates for Small Business. *Customer Support:* Free technical support over phone; limited warranty.
DOS. IBM & compatibles. disk $69.95 (ISBN 1-55571-321-1, Order no.: FTMPSTMP31). *Addl. software required:* LOTUS 1-2-3 or EXCEL.
Macintosh. Macintosh. 3.5" disk $69.95 (ISBN 1-55571-322-X, Order no.: FTMPSTMP3M). *Addl. software required:* LOTUS 1-2-3 or EXCEL.
Provides over 35 Templates. They Are Recommended for Individuals with Some Basic Experience and/or Knowlege of Lotus or Excel. Excellent Tool for Planning & Analyzing Your Business.
Oasis Pr., The.

Financial Utilities Pack. *Compatible Hardware:* Apple Macintosh.
3.5" disk $29.95.
Financial Analysis.
Brainstorm Development, Inc.

Financier - Loan Escrow Servicing. *Customer Support:* Software & hardware maintenance contracts available.
MS-DOS. IBM & compatibles. $9995.00. *Nonstandard peripherals required:* 640k RAM, DOS 3.3 or higher, IBM compatible, laser printer (HPLJT). *Networks supported:* Novell.
A Sophisticated, Easy-to-Use Loan Escrow System. The System Provides Calculations & Reports Necessary for Escrow, As Well As a Complete Set of Uniformly Designed Documents Which Are Typeset & Computer Spaced. Basic Information Is Entered Only Once. Complete APR Calculator. Creates Selling Reports.
Applied Business Software, Inc.

Financier/CAL - Financial Calculator. *Customer Support:* Software & hardware maintenance contracts available.
MS-DOS. IBM & compatibles. $995.00. *Optimal configuration:* 640k RAM, DOS 3.3 or higher, laser printer (HPLJT). *Networks supported:* Novell.
Turns the Computer into a Complete Financial Calculator & Allows the User to Obtain Answers to Complex Calculations. For Each Calculation, an Entire Screen of Information & Instruction Is Displayed, Guiding the User Through Every Entry, Prints Amortization Schedules Either Gross or Net Yield to the Investor, Includes a "What-If" Loan Negotiation Tool.
Applied Business Software, Inc.

Financier/CMO - Collateralized Mortgage Obligation. *Items Included:* Manuals. *Customer Support:* Software & hardware maintenance contracts available.
MS-DOS. IBM & compatibles. $5995.00. *Optimal configuration:* 640k RAM, DOS 3.3 or higher, IBM compatible, laser printer (HPLJT). *Networks supported:* Novell.
Simple Idea for Predictable Investing with High Yield Potential. There Is a Lot of Tracking Involved with the CMO, & It's Virtually Impossible to Do Manually. Your Existing Clients Will Be Able to Choose an Alternative to the Traditional Mortgage Investments. You Can Offer Small Investors an Uncommonly High Yield for a Short Term Investment.
Applied Business Software, Inc.

Financier/DRE - Department of Real Estate Annual Report. *Customer Support:* Software & hardware maintenance contracts available. MS-DOS. IBM & compatibles. $1295.00.
Optimal configuration: 640k RAM, DOS 3.3 or higher, IBM compatible, laser printer (HPLJT). *Networks supported:* Novell.
Automates the Production of the Annual Report to the Department of Real Estate. It Uses the Information Entered in Financier/TDS, Eliminating Duplication of Data. Makes the Calculations & Analysis Required by D.R.E. & Produces the "Mortgage Loan/Trust Deed Annual Report," along with a DRE Master File Listing.
Applied Business Software, Inc.

Financier/PSS - Partnership Servicing. *Items Included:* Manuals. *Customer Support:* Software & hardware maintenance contracts available. MS-DOS. IBM & compatibles. $5995.00.
Optimal configuration: 640k RAM, DOS 3.3 or higher, IBM compatible, laser printer (HPLJT). *Networks supported:* Novell.
Quickly & Efficiently Maintains All the Records Related to the Servicing of Both Growth & Income Partnerships. As New Loans Are Purchased, Principal Reductions Are Made, or Loans Are Paid Off, the Share Value of Each Partnership Changes.
Applied Business Software, Inc.

Financier-Trust Deed Servicing.
disk $7995.00. *Networks supported:* Novell.
Complete Ledger Card Maintained on Each Trustor's Account Containing a Detailed History of Every Payment Made & How It Was Disbursed. Investor Portfolio Maintained for Each Investor Showing All Trust Deeds Owned Either in Whole or in Part, Initial Investment, Interest Rate, Principal Balance, etc. Other Comprehensive Histories on Checks Issued to a Particular Lender, Loan Servicing Business & Underlying Loans. Includes Complete Trust Accounting & Trust Account to Bank Reconciliation.
Applied Business Software, Inc.

FinCalc. *Version:* 2.0. Jan. 1988. *Compatible Hardware:* IBM PC & compatibles. *Memory Required:* As a worksheet application 168k; as an add-in 7k. *General Requirements:* Lotus 1-2-3 releases 2 & 2.01.
3.5" or 5.25" disk $59.95.
upgrade policy & site licenses avail.
Performs Time-Value-of-Money & Cash Flow Analyses. Emulates Hewlett-Packard HP-12C Calculator's Financial Functions, Calculating Interest Rates, Number of Payment Periods, Present Value, Payments, & Future Value for Fixed Amount Payments. Also Calculates Cash Flow for IRR, NPV, & NFV For Varying Payments, Accommodating As Many As 2,000 Flows. Contains Enhanced Financial @Functions & Generates Amortization Tables That Include Payment Dates & Annual Summaries.
Spreadsheet Solutions Corp.

Find It. May 1986. *Compatible Hardware:* Apple IIe, IIc, IIgs.
$50.00.
Multi-Level Program Designed to Aid in Retraining Visual/Spatial Skills, Such As Figure-Ground & Visual Closure. Also Useful with Goal Areas of Memory, Attention & Concentration in Cognitive Rehabilitation, & Special Education. Consists of 10 Levels in a Graded Hierarchy. The Simplest Level Has 3-5 Background Lines of the Same Color with a Familiar Figure of a Different Color Placed on Top (Multiple Choice Responses Are Used). The Highest Level Has 50 Background Lines of Various Colors with a Figure Placed on Top & Requires That the Name of the Object Be Entered.
Greentree Group, Inc.

Find-It. *Operating System(s) Required:* CP/M. *Memory Required:* 48k.
disk $2500.00.
Designed As a File Management System for the User Without Programming Experience. Allows One to Construct & Use Textual Data Files, Initiate & Conclude Searches & Prepare Individualized Reports.
Wang Laboratories, Inc.

Find It Quick. *Compatible Hardware:* TRS-80 Model I, Model III. *Memory Required:* 32k.
disk $49.95 (Order no.: 0258RD).
Keep Track of Articles, Memos, & Client Lists with This Personal Librarian.
Instant Software, Inc.

FindFile. *Version:* 2.0. Jul. 1990. *Items Included:* Documentation. *Customer Support:* Phone support, free.
DOS 2.0 or higher. IBM PC or compatible (40k). disk $15.00.
Search & Locate Any Given File Name on Disk Drives (Including Network Drives). Locate Similar & Exact Names Automatically.
SK Data, Inc.

FINDISK-III. Nov. 1983. *Compatible Hardware:* IBM PC; TRS-80 Model I, Model II, Model III, Model 4, Model 12, Model 16. *Operating System(s) Required:* TRSDOS, NewDOS, PC-DOS. *Memory Required:* 48k. *General Requirements:* Line printer.
TRS-80 Model II, 12, 16. disk $25.00.
TRS-80 Model I, Model III, Model 4. disk $20.00.
IBM. disk $25.00.
Reads Files from Disks, Prints Disk Labels, Compiles Sorted Master List of Files, Their Size & Location.
Documan Software.

Findit. *Compatible Hardware:* North Star with North Star BASIC or CP/M & MBASIC. (source code included). *Memory Required:* 48k.
disk $19.95.
Enables Users to Locate a Variety of Calendar Information, Including Phone Numbers, Birthdays, & Addresses.
Dynacomp, Inc.

Findswell. *Version:* 2.2. Jun. 1987. *Compatible Hardware:* Apple Macintosh. *Memory Required:* 512k.
3.5" disk $29.95 (ISBN 0-940331-03-9).
File Locator - Hard Disk Organizer.
Working Software, Inc.

Finest Hour. *Version:* 5.1. Mar. 1993. *Operating System(s) Required:* PC-DOS/MS-DOS. *Memory Required:* 640k. *Customer Support:* First year free telephone support & upgrades. Additional years at 20% purchase price.
disk $4000.00.
Manages High Intensity, Short Duration Projects Including Shutdowns, Turnarounds, Retrofits, & Outages. Integrates Scheduling, Resource Management & Cost Control & Creates Tabular & Graphic Reports & Presentation Bar Charts & Network Logic Diagrams for Precedence & Arrow Networks. Activities May Be Assigned to Any of 31 Separate Calendars to Facilitate Managing Projects with Varying Shifts & Work Weeks. Includes On-Screen Updating & Review of All Project Details.
Primavera Systems, Inc.

FingerSpeller. 1983. *Compatible Hardware:* Apple II series, Apple IIgs, Macintosh; IBM PC & compatibles. *Memory Required:* Apple II 48k, Macintosh 512k, IBM 256k. *General Requirements:* Color Graphics Card for IBM.
Apple II Talking. disk $49.95.
Apple II Silent. disk $39.95.
Apple IIgs Talking. disk $49.95.
Apple IIgs Silent. disk $39.95.
Macintosh Talking - Requires MacinTalk. 3.5" disk $49.95.
Macintosh Silent. 3.5" disk $39.95.
IBM Silent. disk $19.95.
Provides User with an American Sign Language Manual Alphabet Keyboard. ASL Handshape of the Letter Appears by Pressing Any Key. Displays Individual Letters or Spells Words up to 30 Letters Long at User Selected Speeds. Learning Comprehensive Mode Allows Use to Be Tested from a Group of Words Already Programmed into Software or Create Personal File of Words to Be Stored or Used. Apple II & Apple IIgs Versions Are Copy Protected.
E&IS SignWare.

FingerZoids. *Version:* 5.0. A. Tolu-Honary. 1992. *Items Included:* Manual, warranty registration forms. *Customer Support:* 90 days replacement of any defective merchandise. After 90 days $10 per disk for replacing any defective or damaged diskette. Original copy must be returned along with $10 cost of replacement.
Any Macintosh DOS. Macintosh Plus & higher (512k). 3.5" disk $49.95.
Any version Apple DOS. All types Apple II series (128k). disk $49.95.
Manual Alphabet (Hand Letter Configurations) Drop from the Sky and the User Has to Press the Keys Corresponding to Each Letter to Shoot Them down or Lose Gunners. Several Waves & Letter Attack Are Provided, Each at Faster Speed. Very Challenging & Improves Receptive Skills for Finger-Spelling.
E&IS SignWare.

Finishing Feeder Cattle: Decision Aid. Merle W. Wagner. 1982. *Compatible Hardware:* Apple II+, IIe, IIc, IBM. *Memory Required:* 48k, 640k. *General Requirements:* Printer.
disk $29.95 (ISBN 0-922900-16-7, Order no.: CFD-335).
Program Can Be Modified to Fit a Particular Course on Farming Operation by Anyone Familiar with the Apple. Includes Student & Course Name, Date & Instructor's Comments for Entry Information, & the Number of Market Animals Sold, Average Weight, & Average Price per Pound for Income Information. The Feed Costs Can Include Corn & Price per Bushel, Silage & Price per Pound. Other Costs Can Include Veterinary & Medicine, Marketing, Power, Fuel, Equipment Repair, Labor, Miscellaneous, Interest on Cattle Investment, Taxes & Insurance & Number of Cattle Purchased.
Cherrygarth, Inc.

Finishing Feeder Lambs: Decision Aid. Merle W. Wagner. 1982. *Compatible Hardware:* Apple II Plus, IIe, IIc; IBM. *Memory Required:* 48k, 640k. *General Requirements:* Printer.
disk $29.95 (ISBN 0-922900-20-5, Order no.: CFD-557).
Lambs Purchased by the Head & Finished to Any Weight. 23 Data Entries; 10 Calculations.
Cherrygarth, Inc.

Finishing Feeder Pigs Decision Aids. Merle W. Wagner. 1982. *Compatible Hardware:* Apple II Plus, IIe, IIc; IBM. *Language(s):* BASIC. *Memory Required:* 48k, 640k. *General Requirements:* Printer.
disk $29.95 (ISBN 0-922900-18-3, Order no.: CFD-446).
back-up disk $9.95.
manual $19.95.
Can Be Customized to Fit a Particular Course or Farming Operation. Calculations Include: Gross Income, Total Feed Cost, Total Direct Cost,

Income Minus Direct Cost, Investment Overhead, Total Expense, Total Expense per Pound of Market Hog, Net Return to Management, Net Return to Labor-Management, Rate Earned on Investment.
Cherrygarth, Inc.

Finite Element Analysis. Simha & Hsu. 1986. *Items Included:* Spiral manual contains theory, sample runs, source code in FORTRAN. *Customer Support:* Free phone.
MS-DOS. IBM (640k). disk $120.00. *Addl. software required:* FORTRAN, Halo Graphics.
A Book/Disk Package for 2 Dimensional Stress, Heat Transfer & Dynamic Analysis Using Finite Elements. Three Programs Include: Elas for Stress, Heat for Heat Transfer & Vibe for Dynamic Analysis Including Stress Wave Propagation. Output Shows Stress & Temperature Contours.
Kern International, Inc.

Finite Element Analysis - ST10M. *Version:* 06/1986. 1981. *Operating System(s) Required:* MS-DOS, PC-DOS. *Language(s):* Compiled. *Memory Required:* 256k. *Customer Support:* Technical hotline, "Lifetime" support at no charge.
$895.00.
Finite Element Analysis - ST10M Solves for Nodal Displacements, Forces & Reactions in Plane Frame, Space Frame, Space Truss, Floor Grid, & Rod/Membrane Problems. Unlimited Point & Distributed Loads, Material Types, Restrained Nodes, May Be Specified. Rigid or Pinned Joints. Auto Set-up & Preprocessor (Grid Generator) for Plane Frames. SI Metric & English Units.
MC2 Engineering Software.

FinPlan-10. *Compatible Hardware:* Apple Macintosh. *Memory Required:* 512k. *General Requirements:* Excel.
3.5" disk $195.00.
Tax Planning & Cash Flow Report Created & Used by Financial Planning Professionals.
Softflair, Inc.

FIPS: Financial Planning Simplified. *Compatible Hardware:* IBM PC, PCjr, PC XT. *Operating System(s) Required:* MS-DOS, PC-DOS 1.1. *Memory Required:* 128k. *General Requirements:* Color monitor, printer.
disk $195.00, incl. documentation.
demo disk $30.00, incl. documentation.
Helps Create Financial Plans in the Areas of Financial Independence, Educational Funding, Personal Cash Flow, Estate Taxes, & Personal Income Tax.
Antech, Inc.

Fire & Forget. *Compatible Hardware:* Commodore Amiga.
3.5" disk $39.95.
3 Levels of 6 Conflicts; 1 or 2 Players per Team.
Titus Software Corp.

FIRE: Fire Sprinkler Hydraulic Calculations. *Items Included:* Manual. *Customer Support:* Toll free telephone.
IBM PC & compatibles (256k). disk $1250.00.
Performs Hydraulic Calculations on Fire Sprinkler Systems in Exact Accordance with the Latest Standards Set by the NFPA. Handles Tree, Grid, & Hybrid Systems with up to 1200 Sprinklers.
Elite Software Development, Inc.

Fire Hose Records. 1992. *Items Included:* Detailed manuals are included with all DYNACOMP products. *Customer Support:* Free telephone support to original customer - no time limit; 30 day limited warranty.
MS-DOS 3.2 or higher. IBM PC & compatibles (512k). $395.00 (Add $5.00 for 3 1/2" format; 5 1/4" format standard). *Optimal configuration:* IBM, 384k RAM, MS-DOS 2.0 or higher. Hard disk is recommended, but not necessary. Supports both monochrome & color displays, as well as an 80-column or wider printer.
demo disk $10.00.
Automates the Collection & Reporting of Fire Hose Data. You Simply Fill in the Blanks on the Screen Using Service Test Data Gathered from Field Tests. Print a Hose Repair Order If Needed. The Results of the Current Inspection Plus up to 14 Past Inspections Are Stored on Disk. You Can Track Failed Service Tests, Maintenance, Repairs, Damage, & Removal of Hose from Service. Quickly Provides Up-to-Date Reports. Includes Manual Describing Operation, Master Data Forms, & a Demonstration Diskette.
Dynacomp, Inc.

Fire Power. (One-on-One Ser.). *Compatible Hardware:* Commodore 64, Amiga; Apple IIgs; IBM.
$24.95.
Arcade Style Tank Game Featuring Digitized Sounds & Music, Realistic Graphics, & Fast Action.
Microillusions, Inc.

Fire Reporter. *Version:* 2A. Jan. 1986. *Compatible Hardware:* IBM PC XT. *Operating System(s) Required:* DBASE III. *Memory Required:* 256k.
disk $125.00.
Module for dBASE III That Is Designed to Provide the User with Information Regarding a Firecall, While the Fire Companies Are Enroute to the Scene of a Fire.
Software Lab East.

Fire Sprinkler Design. *Version:* 4.0. William W. Smith. Sep. 1988. *Compatible Hardware:* IBM PC & compatibles. *Operating System(s) Required:* PC-DOS/MS-DOS. *Language(s):* CB-80. *Memory Required:* MS-DOS 256k. *General Requirements:* 2 disk drives, printer.
disk $995.00.
8" disk $695.00.
3.5" disk $695.00.
demo disk $38.00.
documentation $25.00.
Designed to Perform Hydraulic Calculations on Fire Sprinkler Systems in Accordance with the Latest Standards Set by the National Fire Protection Association (NFPA 13). Handles Tree & Grid Systems with up to 1200 Sprinklers for MS-DOS Based Computers & 68 Sprinklers for CP/M Computers, Reports List GPM Water Flow & Velocity Through All Pipe Sections, the GPM Water Flow & Residual Pressure at Each Sprinkler Head, the Pressure Losses Incurred in Each Pipe Section Due to Both Friction & Elevation Changes, the Maximum System Demand Pressure, & the Total Water GPM Demanded by the System.
Elite Software Development, Inc.

Fire Sprinkler Grid Design. *Items Included:* Bound manual. *Customer Support:* Free hotline - no time limit; 30 day limited warranty; updates are $5/disk plus S&H.
MS-DOS. IBM & compatibles (448k). full system $949.95. *Nonstandard peripherals required:* 80-column (or wider) dot matrix printer.
demo disk $5.00.
Follows NFPA Standards (Meeting Underwriter's Requirements) to Automatically Set up & Evaluate Fire Sprinkler Systems of the Grid Type. It Handles Regular or Irregular Systems, Sets up Pipe Numbering, & Recommends Pipe Sizes Throughout the System. It Prints a Semi-Log Water Graph in NFPA Format & a Schematic Diagram Showing the Design Area. Printed Outputs Are Suitable for Direct Presentation to Underwriters.
Dynacomp, Inc.

Fire Sprinkler Grid System Design - HP4M. *Version:* 07/1990. 1981. *Operating System(s) Required:* MS-DOS, PC-DOS. *Language(s):* Compiled & Assembly. *Memory Required:* 448k. *Customer Support:* Technical hotline, "Lifetime" support at no charge.
$995.00.
Fire Sprinkler Grid System Design - HP4M (New Update) Uses NFPA Methods to Design Fire Sprinkler Systems of the Grid Type. Highly Automated, Automatically Numbers Pipes & Nodes. Handles Regular or Irregular Systems. Prints Semi-Log Water Graph, Schematic Diagram & Other Outputs Ready for Presentation to Underwriters. Prints List of Pipe & Fitting Requirements. Automatic Pipe Diameters, Fitting Equivalent Lenghts, Design Area, Remote Head Location. State-of-the-Art Full-Function Interactive Prompted Input Screens with Windows, Defaults, Error Checking, Function Keys, Color or B/W, etc. Fully Compiled. Powerful, Shortcut Inputs (Five Minutes for a Regular System), Fast Solution. English & SI Metric Units.
MC2 Engineering Software.

Fire Sprinkler System Design. *Items Included:* Bound manual. *Customer Support:* Free hotline - no time limit; 30 day limited warranty; updates are $5/disk plus S&H.
MS-DOS. IBM & compatibles (256k). full system $229.95. *Nonstandard peripherals required:* 80-column (or wider) printer.
demo disk $5.00.
Interactively Works with the Designer to Develop Fire Sprinkler Systems of the Tree & Loop Types. It Employs the NFPA Formulas & Calculation Procedures to Produce Printouts in the NFPA "Manual 13" Format, Ready for Presentation to Underwriters for Approval.
Dynacomp, Inc.

Fire Sprinkler Tree System Design - HP6M. *Version:* 04/1989. 1984. *Compatible Hardware:* IBM PC & compatibles. *Operating System(s) Required:* MS-DOS, PC-DOS. *Language(s):* Compiled Assembly. *Memory Required:* 448k. *Customer Support:* Technical hotline, "Lifetime" support at no charge.
disk $245.00.
Fire Sprinkler Tree & Loop System Design - HP6M (New Update) Uses NFPA Methods to Design Fire Sprinkler Systems of the Tree Type. Fast, Convenient, Fully Compiled. Prints Semi-Log Water Graph, Detailed Outputs Ready for Presentation to Underwriters. Prints List of Pipe & Fitting Requirements. Automatic Pipe Diameters, Fitting Equivalent Lengths, State-of-the-Art Full-Function Interactive Prompted Input Screens with Windows, Defaults, Error Checking, Function Keys, Color or B/W, etc. Powerful, Shortcut Inputs. English & Metric Units.
MC2 Engineering Software.

Fired Heater. *Version:* 2. Jun. 1988. *Compatible Hardware:* IBM PC. *Language(s):* BASIC. *Memory Required:* 256k.
disk $200.00 ea.
IBM PC. (Order no.: 02-011).
Rates & Checks Fired Heater Performance for Existing Heater Design. Program Addresses the Radiant Section & Average & Maximum Front Face Flux, Film Temperature, Tube Metal Temperature (Clean or Coked), Film Coefficient, Overall Efficiency, etc. Along with Defining a Radiant Geometry, Number of Tubes, Tube Length, etc. Program Handles Vertical Cylindrical & Vertical Tube Type Furnaces, 1 Side Fired or 2 Side Fired. Correction Section Analysis Includes Short Bank & Extended Surfaces. Analysis Is Both Thermal & Geometric. Extended Surfaces Handled Are Serrated for Solid Fins, Studs, & Bare Tube.
Information Resource Consultants.

TITLE INDEX

Firefighter.
MS-DOS 3.1 or higher, Windows 3.1 or higher. 386 processor or higher (4Mb). CD-ROM disk $29.95 (Order no.: R1264). *Nonstandard peripherals required:* CD-ROM drive. *Optimal configuration:* 386 processor operating at 16MHz or higher, MS-DOS 5.0 or higher, Windows 3.1 or higher, 30Mb hard drive, mouse, VGA graphic adapter & VGA color monitor (SVGA recommended), 4Mb RAM, external speakers or headphones (with sound card) that are Sound Blaster compatible.
Macintosh (4Mb). (Order no.: R1264A). *Nonstandard peripherals required:* 14" color monitor or larger, CD-ROM drive.
Beyond the Alarms, Sirens & Flames of This Startlingly Realistic, Always Thrilling Program, There Is Important Information That Teaches Life-Saving Rules of Fire Safety & Prevention, & Explanations of Firefighting Gear & Trucks.
Library Video Co.

FirePlan. *Version:* 2.6. *Compatible Hardware:* Apple Macintosh Plus or higher, system 7.0 (2Mb). *Memory Required:* 2000k. *General Requirements:* Hard disk; HyperCard 2.0 or higher. *Items Included:* User manual. *Customer Support:* Free phone support.
3.5" disk $395.00.
Database for Fire Prevention, Pre-Planning, CAD.
Sound Advice, Inc.

The Firm. Jun. 1995. *Items Included:* User Manual on disk. *Customer Support:* 90 Days.
DOS 3.1 or higher. 286 or higher. disk $499.95 - $4999.95 (ISBN 0-933735-03-0). *Networks supported:* All that Clarion Supports.
A System for Tracking Clients & Case Management.
Tin Man Software.

FirmMerge. Sheila V. Malkani & Michael F. Walsh. Nov. 1994.
IBM. disk $28.95 (ISBN 0-9637970-4-2).
MAC. 3.5" disk $28.95.
Provides an Inexpensive & Easy Way to Contact Hundreds of Firms, While Maintaining Complete Control over Your Job Search. With a Few Simple Clicks on Your Computer, This Sophisticated Software Generates Mail-Merge Letters & Mailing Labels at the Firms You Choose. Just Select the Cities & Practice Areas in Which You Are Interested & the Software Does the Rest. In No Time, You Can Send Out Hundreds of Letters. The Most Efficient Tool for Landing a Job at the Firm of Your Choice.
Mobius Pr.

First ACT! Oct. 1991. *Customer Support:* Free to registered users.
DOS 3.1 or higher. IBM & compatibles (640k). disk $79.95.
Entry-Level Contact Manager. Integrates a Contact Database, Calendar Manager, Pre-Defined Report Generator, & a Word Processor. Has an Intuitive User-Interface & Customizable Pop-Up Windows Throughout to Minimize Keystrokes Required for Data-Entry. Offers Core Contact Management Features to the First-Time, Small Business, & Home Office User.
Contact Software International, Inc.

1st Aid Kit. *Version:* 2.7. *Compatible Hardware:* Apple Macintosh, Macintosh XL, Macintosh 512k. *Items Included:* Recovery software & 300 page troubleshooting guide.
3.5" disk $99.95.
Helps Users Resolve Any Macintosh Problem - from Difficulties with Printing Documents to Recovering Data from Damaged Disks (Including Hard Disks). Included Is a Clearly Written 300 Page Troubleshooting Guide Which List Many Different Error Conditions, Helps Users Track down Solutions, Presents a Step-by-Step Recovery Process, & Shows How to Avoid Future Problems. The Software is Not Copy Protected.
1st Aid Software.

First Aid Try & Buy. CyberMedia Staff. *Items Included:* The package includes a 3.5" diskette, a mini-manual & a Try & Buy Brochure.
MS Windows 3.1 or higher. IBM PC & compatibles, 386 or higher. disk $39.99 (ISBN 1-57548-006-9). *Addl. software required:* First Aid for Windows users requires 3Mb hard disk.
An Application That Provides Instant Support for the Microsoft Windows Environment & for Applications Which Run in This Environment.
IBM Software Manufacturing Solutions (ISMS).

1st BBS-II. *Items Included:* Manual, license agreement entitling free user support. *Customer Support:* 90-day limited warranty, free support for registered users.
AppleTalk & System 6/7 compatible. Macintosh (1Mb). 3.5" disk $129.00. *Optimal configuration:* Macintosh Plus or higher, 1Mb of RAM, Modem speeds up to 38,400 bps & V.32 & V.42 bis are supported.
Powerful Data Communications System, & Links Together Macintoshes, & DOS Machines, Which Have Modems or Are Connected to an AppleTalk Network. Remote Users Would Have the Ability to Access Databases, Transfer Files & E-Mail Capability. 1stBBS-II Would Prove Invaluable for Companies with Branches in Many Different Cities. All Remote Users Would Have the Ability to Access Databases, Such As a Customer Address List, Price List, Inventory, etc. & to Send Private E-Mail Messages with Files Attached. Registered Owners Are Licensed to Make an Unlimited Number of Copies of the MAC or DOS Version of the Remote Modules. Program Is Designed to Minimize Online Time & Expense by Allowing Users to Perform Many of Their Tasks While Offline. Host Module Is Password Protected & Maintains an Activity Log.
1st Desk Systems, Inc.

1st-Class. *Version:* 2.5. 1990. *Items Included:* Complete technical reference manual; user guides; tutorials, quick reference.
OS/2, MS-DOS, VMS. IBM PC, XT, AT & compatibles PCs. 3.5" or 5.25" disk $2495.00.
An Integrated, Multi-Platform Knowledge Base System That Extends Conventional Data Processing Practices to Knowledge Base Applications. Enables Programmers to Apply the Four Key Methodologies, Forward Chaining, Backward Chaining, Hypothetical Reasoning & Object-Oriented Programming to Reach a Conclusion or Recommendation. The Added Advantage of Natural Language Facility Speeds Development by Writing Rules in English. The Powerful Graphical Developer & User Interfaces Simplify & Enhance the Delivery of Knowledge Base Applications.
AICorp.

1st Class Fusion. *Version:* 2.15. Jul. 1987. *Compatible Hardware:* IBM PC & compatibles, PS/2; VAX under VMS. *Operating System(s) Required:* PC-DOS/MS-DOS 2.0 or higher. *Memory Required:* 512k. *Items Included:* Free runtime. *Customer Support:* Free telephone support, disk tutorials on request.
5.25" disk $1495.00 (3.5" disk upon request).
Enables a User with No Programming Experience to Capture an Expert's Body of Knowledge & Make It Useable to Others As a Basis for Decisions. Data Can Be Entered in Either a Spreadsheet Format or a Direct "Decision Tree" That Provides a Graphic Representation of the User's Logic. Additional Graphics Facilities Enable Users to Capture & Display Screens from Other Programs. Product Also Contains Code Generators, a Math Calculator, & a dBASE III Interface for Direct Access to Data Stored in .DBF Files. There Is an Unlimited Run-Time License with No Royalties.
1st Class Expert Systems, Inc.

FIRST DAYS ON THE JOB

1st Class HT (Hypertext). *Version:* 2.10. Mar. 1989. *Compatible Hardware:* IBM PC, PC XT, PC AT, PS/2, & compatibles. *Operating System(s) Required:* PC-DOS/MS-DOS, OS/2. *Memory Required:* 512k. *Items Included:* Free runtime. *Customer Support:* Free telephone support, disk tutorials on request.
5.25" disk $2495.00 (3.5" disk on request).
Combination Expert System Shell/Hypertext Authoring System. Allows Developing Hypertext Systems That Give Advice During & at the Conclusion of an Expert System Consultation, with the "Browsing" Ability That Hypertext Allows. In Addition, Lets the Hypertext System Control the Operation of the Expert System So That What the User Does During Browsing Can Affect the Rest of the Consultation. Includes Free Run-Time License.
1st Class Expert Systems, Inc.

A First Course in Factor Analysis. *Version:* 2. Andrew L. Comrey & Howard B. Lee. 1992. *Customer Support:* Free technical support, 90-day limited warranty.
IBM Mainframe. disk $6.00 (ISBN 1-56321-100-9).
IBM Mainframe. 3.5" disk $6.00 (ISBN 1-56321-101-7).
DOS - PC Program. disk $6.00 (ISBN 1-56321-102-5).
DOS - PC Program. 3.5" disk $6.00 (ISBN 1-56321-103-3).
DOS - Expanded PC Program. disk $6.00 (ISBN 1-56321-146-7).
DOS - Expanded PC Program. 3.5" disk $6.00 (ISBN 1-56321-147-5).
This Is an Electronic Version of a Book Which Examines Confirmatory Factor Analysis & Structural Equation Modeling.
Lawrence Erlbaum Assocs. Software & Alternate Media, Inc.

A First Course in Grammar & Usage for Psychology & Related Fields: Electronic Edition. John E. Bellquist. 1994. *Customer Support:* Free technical support, 90-day limited warranty.
IBM DOS. 3.5" disk $12.00 (ISBN 1-56321-141-6).
IBM DOS. 3.5" disk $25.00, incl. paper bk. (ISBN 1-56321-142-4).
A Style & Usage Guide Outlined in the Book That Runs "Online" Alongside Users Word Processors.
Lawrence Erlbaum Assocs. Software & Alternate Media, Inc.

First Days Cumulative Index, 1955-1991. Margaret Monty. Dec. 1992.
IBM. disk $14.95 (ISBN 1-879390-12-4).
IBM. 3.5" disk $14.95 (ISBN 1-879390-14-0).
MAC. 3.5" disk $14.95 (ISBN 1-879390-13-2).

First Days on the Job. Feb. 1996. *Items Included:* Program manual. *Customer Support:* Free technical support, 90 day warranty.
Single user. Windows 3.1 or higher. IBM 386 (8Mb). disk $99.95 (ISBN 1-57204-153-6, Order no.: WIN454). *Nonstandard peripherals required:* 256 color monitor, sound card, mouse. *Addl. software required:* SVGA graphics.
Lab pack. Windows 3.1 or higher. IBM 386 (8Mb). disk $199.00 (ISBN 1-57204-155-2, Order no.: WIN454LPK). *Nonstandard peripherals required:* 256 color monitor, sound card, mouse. *Addl. software required:* SVGA graphics.

Site license. Windows 3.1 or higher. IBM 386 (8Mb). disk $399.00 (ISBN 1-57204-157-9, Order no.: WIN454SITE). *Nonstandard peripherals required:* 256 color monitor, sound card. *Addl. software required:* SVGA graphics.
Single user. System 7.1 or higher. Mac, 16 MHz rating, 68030 or better processor (LC II or higher) (5Mb). 3.5" disk $99.95 (ISBN 1-57204-152-8). *Nonstandard peripherals required:* 256 color monitor, 13" or larger.
Lab pack. System 7.1 or higher. Mac, 16 MHz rating, 68030 or better processor (LC II or higher) (5Mb). 3.5" disk $199.00 (ISBN 1-57204-154-4, Order no.: APM454LPK). *Nonstandard peripherals required:* 256 color monitor, 13" or larger.
Site license. System 7.1 or higher. Mac, 16 MHz rating, 68030 or better processor (LC II or higher) (5Mb). 3.5" disk $399.00 (ISBN 1-57204-156-0, Order no.: APM454SITE). *Nonstandard peripherals required:* 256 color monitor, 13 or larger.
Covers filling out forms, introductions, training programs, where to park, manners & other topics.
Lawrence Productions, Inc.

First Encounter: The Ultimate Earthling Challenge. John Besnard. 1987. *Compatible Hardware:* Apple II series. *Memory Required:* 48k.
3.5" disk $29.95.
Alien Arcade Adventure Game. Player Is Challenged by a Mysterious Intelligence & Must Pass the Alien Academy in Orbit I.Q. Test by Solving Forty-Eight Separate Tests of Mind & Reflex. But in Order to Solve the Games & Puzzles, Player Must Learn An Alien Language & Alphabet in Order to Comprehend the Rules.
Softdisk, Inc.

First Food Cost Expert.
IBM PC, PC XT, PC AT, PS/2 & compatibles (256k). 3.5" or 5.25" disk $750.00.
Menu-Driven Food Cost Control Expert Program.
First Food Cost Expert.

First Opinion. *Version:* 2.1. Jun. 1986. *Compatible Hardware:* IBM PC. *Operating System(s) Required:* PC-DOS. *Language(s):* Quicksilver. *Memory Required:* 640k. *General Requirements:* Printer. *Customer Support:* Toll free telephone support.
$595.00.
Assists the Office Staff in Selecting the Best of Ten Categories for In-Depth Questioning When Interviewing Patients for Chief Complaint. Uses a Sorting Algorithm That Picks a Highly Probable Diagnostic Label & the Appropriate Physician for Referral. Considers Over 8000 Symptom Matches in 250 Diseases.
SRC Systems, Inc.

First Over Germany. John Gray. *Items Included:* Rulebook. *Customer Support:* Technical support line: (408) 737-6850 (11am-5pm, PST); 14 day money back guarantee/30 day exchange policy.
Commodore 64/128 (64k). disk $49.95.
DOS 2.11 or higher. IBM PC & compatible (384k). disk $59.95. *Nonstandard peripherals required:* Requires a color monitor & a graphic adaptor (i.e., CGA, EGA).
This Game System Allows You to Join the 306th Bombardment Group on 25 Real-Life Combat Missions Over the Death-Filled Skies of Nazi Europe. Hand Pick Your Ten Crew Members to Fly Your Very Own B-17 Flying Fortress. Start Out Flying Training Missions in Utah to Raise Your Crew's Efficiency & Experience. This User-Friendly Flight Simulator Gives You the Feel of Flying a Real B-17. You & Your Crew Must Deal with Flak, Mechanical/Engine Failures, Fuel Usage, Bailing Out, & Falling Out of Formation. You Engage Enemy Fighters in Realistic Animated Combat.
Strategic Simulations, Inc.

First Steps Counting & Thinking Games. Yoon-Jung Kim Choi. 1995. *Items Included:* CD-ROM, user guide. *Customer Support:* 90 day warranty from date of purchase.
Windows 3.1 or Win 95. 386SX 16MHz (4Mb). disk $29.95 (Order no.: 60600). *Addl. software required:* Windows compatible soundcard. *Optimal configuration:* Hard drive with minimum 386SX/16MHz, SVGA display.
Lab Pack $85.00 (Order no.: 60612).
System 6.0.7. Macintosh (2Mb for Sys 6.0.7, 4Mb for Sys 7.0). 3.5" disk $29.95 (Order no.: 40600).
Lab Pack $85.00 (Order no.: 40612).
Sound Efffects & Speech, Counting & Skill Building Exercises.
Optimum Resource, Inc.

First Steps Counting & Thinking Games. Yoon-Jung Kim Choi. 1995. *Items Included:* CD-ROM, user guide. *Customer Support:* 90 day warranty from date of purchase.
Windows 3.1 or Win 95. 386SX 16MHz (4Mb). CD-ROM disk $29.95 (Order no.: 50600). *Nonstandard peripherals required:* MSCDEX 2.2 or higher, MPC compatible CD-ROM drive. *Addl. software required:* Windows compatible soundcard. *Optimal configuration:* Hard drive with minimum 386SX/16MHz, SVGA display.
CD-ROM disk $85.00, Lab Pack (Order no.: 50612).
System 6.0.7. Macintosh (2Mb for Sys 6.0.7, 4Mb for Sys 7.0). CD-ROM disk $29.95 (Order no.: 50600). *Nonstandard peripherals required:* CD-ROM drive.
CD-ROM disk $85.00, Lab Pack (Order no.: 50612).
Sound Efffects & Speech, Counting & Skill Building Exercises.
Optimum Resource, Inc.

1st Word. *Compatible Hardware:* Atari ST. 3.5" disk $49.95 (Order no.: DS5029).
Atari Corp.

FirstAid for Writers. Sol Stein. Mar. 1992. *Items Included:* Manual. *Customer Support:* Help is available to registered customers at no charge Monday-Friday, 9:00 am to 5:00 pm, 914-762-1255.
MS-DOS 2.0 or higher. IBM PC & compatibles (512k). disk $299.00 (ISBN 1-879584-15-8, Order no.: 7 28923 01018 9).
System 4.1 or higher (System 7 compatible). Macintosh (512k). disk $299.00 (ISBN 1-879584-18-2, Order no.: 7 28293 01014 1).
Enables Writer to Import Nonfiction & Fiction Writing Problems Without Retyping, Fix Everything That Needs Fixing under Guidance, See the Evidence of Improvement on Screen, & Then Export Work Back to Work Processor. Divided into Five Modules That Can Be Accessed Independently: Gearing up - Helps Solve Problems Writers Can Experience Before Starting to Work; Quickfix - Helps with Turning on the Engine, Description, Advanced Characterization, Suspense, Tension, Pace; Intervention - Covers Architectural Suspense, Erotic Writing, Point of View, Flashbacks; Nonfiction - How to Make Nonfiction As Interesting & Enjoyable As Fiction; Refresher - Shows What to Do First When Revising, the Eight Other Major Steps to Undertake Before a General Revision. Program Can Also Be Used As Advanced Tutorial. Developed by Sol Stein, Prize-Winning Author-Editor, Creator of WritePro.
The WritePro Corp.

1stBase-II. 1984. *Items Included:* Manual, lesson plan. *Customer Support:* 800 support, 800 BBS line, 30 day money back guarantee.
Mac OS. Macintosh (1Mb). 3.5" disk $179.00 (Order no.: 800-522-2286). *Optimal configuration:* MAC SE/30, 2.5Mb RAM, System 6.08 or higher. *Networks supported:* ATALK, Ethernet.
Automated, Programmable Relational Database. Create Files of Your Own Design, Enter & Edit Data, Sort Multiple Fields, & Produce Reports from Single or Relationally Joined Files. Macro Programming, 40 Plus Functions Which Allows Arithmetic Computing with Function Analysis on up to 100 Derived Fields Using IF-THEN-ELSE Logical Arguments. Up to 5-Across Labels & Simple Mail Merge Functions Are Supported. Reports with Multiple Line Headings Can Include up to 100 Derived Fields & Can Be Saved As Text. Featuring Ease of Use & Setup, Supports up to 2 Billion Records, Blueprint Lockout, Time & Date Calculations, 255 Characters per Field, 255 Fields per Record. Allows Custom User Interfaces in 1stVUE or HyperCard. Macros Are Saved As Documents at the Finder to Allow Automated Processes to Be Run from HyperCard.
1st Desk Systems, Inc.

1stPort-II. 1985. *Items Included:* Manual. *Customer Support:* 800 support, 800 BBS line, 30 day money back guarantee.
Mac OS. Macintosh (1Mb). 3.5" disk $79.00 (Order no.: 800-522-2286). *Optimal configuration:* MAC SE/30, 2.5Mb RAM, System 6.08 or higher. *Networks supported:* ATALK, Ethernet.
File Conversion Program. A Datafile & Spreadsheet Reformatter Used to Convert & Reformat Almost Any Datafile from Almost Any Source, Formatted or Unformatted: Mainframes, Minis, PCs, Macintoshes, Bar Codes, Electronic Scales, Data Acquisition Devices, etc. Contains the Unique "Movable Column Boundary Screen" That Can Create or Change Field Boundaries in Formatted or Unformatted File Structure. Conversions Supported Include DIF, SYLK, Flat, Tab-Delimited, Comma-Delimited, 1stDESK & User Defined Custom Formats. Field Renaming & Definition of Type & Length Made Unique Use of the Macintosh's Graphics Capability. Also Contains MacroAccess to Automate Commands Defined by Users As Icons at the Finder & Linked Together to Trigger Repetitive Steps.
1st Desk Systems, Inc.

1stVue-II. Jan. 1994. *Items Included:* Manual, lesson plan. *Customer Support:* 800 support, 800 BBS line, 30 day money back guarantee.
Mac OS. Macintosh (2Mb). 3.5" disk $179.00 (Order no.: 800-522-2286). *Optimal configuration:* MAC SE/30, 2.5Mb RAM, System 6.08 or higher. *Networks supported:* ATALK, Ethernet.
Provides the Tools Required for Users to Set up Applications via Forms & Files. Form Completion & Multi-User Database That Includes a Unique Graphic Forms Interface with Multimedia Capability. Designed for Use with 1stBASE-II, a Relational Database & Report Generator. Features Patented Fuzzy Find over Weighted Fields, & MacroAccess Command Icon System Automation. Supports 12 Different Kinds of Data Filters Including Documents, Sounds, Pictures & QuickTime Movies. Database Is Automatically Generated Based on the Form's Attributes. Numerous Display & Entry Filters Provide Users with an Efficient Way of Entering & Displaying All Their Business Information.
1st Desk Systems, Inc.

The FIS-CAL Accounts Payable System. *Version:* 7.6. Dec. 1990. *Compatible Hardware:* IBM PC & compatibles. *Operating System(s)*

TITLE INDEX

Required: DOS, XENIX, UNIX. *Language(s):* C. *Memory Required:* 4000k.
DOS. $595.00.
UNIX, XENIX. $795.00.
Account Payable Check Writing, Partial Payments, Flexible Aging of Payables, Bank Reconciliation, Payments Made by Due Date & Special Cycle, Automatic Posting to General Ledger, On-Line Inquiry, Variety of Reports.
Fiscal Systems, Inc.

The FIS-CAL Accounts Receivable System.
Version: 7.6. Dec. 1990. *Compatible Hardware:* IBM PC & compatibles. *Operating System(s) Required:* DOS, UNIX, XENIX. *Language(s):* C. *Memory Required:* 4000k.
DOS. $595.00.
UNIX, XENIX. $795.00.
Open Item or Balance Forward by Customer, Table Driven Sales Tax for up to 999 Tax Areas, Customer Billing with Discount Computed, Flexible Aging of Account Balances, Special Statement Cycles, On-Line Inquiry, Variety of Reports.
Fiscal Systems, Inc.

Fis-Cal Business System: FIS-CAL Point-of-Sale Manager's Workstation Software. *Version:* 3.0. Jul. 1994. *Operating System(s) Required:* Xenix. *Memory Required:* 4000k.
Xenix. $1695.00 (Order no.: XPOS073).
Links to FIS-CAL POS-2000 Point-of-Sale Terminals to Provide Management Control. Broad Range of Capabilities & Reports Available. Operates on a PC; Complete Hardware/ Software Package Available.
Fiscal Systems, Inc.

The FIS-CAL General Ledger System. *Version:* 7.6. Dec. 1990. *Compatible Hardware:* IBM PC & compatibles. *Operating System(s) Required:* DOS, XENIX, UNIX. *Language(s):* C. *Memory Required:* 4000k.
DOS. $595.00.
XENIX, UNIX. $795.00.
The Chart of Accounts May Be Arranged to Fit the Company's Needs. The User Defines the Format & Content of Financial Reports, i.e. Balance Sheet, Income Statement & Special Reports. Detailed Transaction Posting from A/R, A/P, Sales Order & Purchase Order Processing & Inventory/Point of Sale.
Fiscal Systems, Inc.

The FIS-CAL Inventory Control System.
Version: 7.6. Dec. 1990. *Compatible Hardware:* IBM PC & compatibles. *Operating System(s) Required:* DOS, UNIX, XENIX. *Language(s):* C. *Memory Required:* 4000k.
DOS. $595.00.
UNIX, XENIX. $795.00.
Up to 16 Characters, up to 6 Levels of Quantity Price Breaks, Records Serial Numbers, Supports Sub-Assemblies, Variety of Reports.
Fiscal Systems, Inc.

The FIS-CAL Payroll System. *Version:* 7.62. Dec. 1993. *Compatible Hardware:* IBM PC & compatibles. *Operating System(s) Required:* DOS, UNIX, XENIX. *Language(s):* C. *Memory Required:* 4000k.
DOS. $595.00.
UNIX, XENIX. $795.00.
Piecework Payroll, Tips Deemed Wages, Commissions, Multiple Pay Rates & Cost Centers per Employee per Day Period, Deduction for 401(k) Retirement, Accurate Vacation Time & Sick Leave. Up to 99 Employee Deductions & 99 Benefits per Employee; Pay Periods May Be Daily, Weekly, Bi-Weekly, Semi-Monthly, Monthly, or Quarterly.
Fiscal Systems, Inc.

The FIS-CAL Purchase Order Processing System. *Version:* 7.6. Dec. 1990. *Compatible Hardware:* IBM PC & compatibles. *Operating System(s) Required:* DOS, UNIX, XENIX. *Language(s):* C. *Memory Required:* 4000k.
DOS. $595.00.
UNIX, XENIX. $795.00.
Supports Standard Orders for Selector Vendors, Processing Stocked & Non-Stocked Items, On-Line Inquiry to P.O. Status & Stock Status, Prints Purchase Orders upon Entry or All Together at a Later Time, Provides Information on Vendors - Discounts, Past Performance, Lead Time, & Minimum Order Requirements.
Fiscal Systems, Inc.

The FIS-CAL Sales Order Processing System.
Version: 7.6. Dec. 1990. *Compatible Hardware:* IBM PC & compatibles. *Operating System(s) Required:* DOS, XENIX, UNIX. *Language(s):* C. *Memory Required:* 4000k.
DOS. $595.00.
UNIX, XENIX. $795.00.
Automates Taking Orders, Shipping, & Billing of Customers, Prints Quotations, Acknowledge & Elements, Shipping Notes, Invoices, On-Line Inquiry for Order Status, Stock Status, Customer Status, Partial Shipments & Partial Invoices.
Fiscal Systems, Inc.

Fit & Trim. D. Abbott. 1983. *Compatible Hardware:* Apple II, IIc, IIe; Basis 6502; Franklin Ace. *Operating System(s) Required:* Apple DOS 3.3. *Language(s):* BASIC (source code included). *Memory Required:* 48-64k.
disk $39.00 (ISBN 0-914555-20-0).
Graded Weight Control/Exercise System for Weight Loss. Records Multi-Individual; Compares Various Time Increments.
Andent, Inc.

Fitness Analyst. *Version:* 5.4a. May 1992. *Items Included:* User manual, Dr Neimans's book - Fitness & Sports Medicine. Canadian Standardized Test of Fitness Kit. *Customer Support:* Free Tech/Nutrition help. 8-5 PST Monday - Friday. Training available, call for information (503) 585-6242. Customer satisfaction guaranteed. Replacement disks or money back for 45 days.
IBM PC & compatible (640k). disk $695.00 or pay $4.00 per time, 25 min. purchase ($100.00).
Fitness Testing & Training Software. Personalized Fitness Appraisal. Professional System. Tests Are Based on the Latest Research. Evaluations of: ACSM Medical Symptom & Status, Cardiac/ Stroke Risk Analysis, Fitness Appraisals, & Exercise Prescription. Compare to National Norms. Select from over 50 Tests. Receive Dr. Neiman's Book, Fitness & Sports Medicine & Canadian Standardized Test of Fitness Kit, Free with Purchase. Free Demo Available.
ESHA Research.

Fitness Manager. *Version:* 4.30b. *Items Included:* Complete bound instruction guide. *Customer Support:* Free support for first 60 days, 1 year toll-free support, $295.00.
DOS. IBM & compatibles. $795.00-$1495.00.
Optimal configuration: 486, 4Mb memory, fast hard disk. *Networks supported:* LANtastic, Novell.
"Manager Friendly" Software Will Automatically Bill Members Using 15 Cent EFT, Laser Printed Bank Drafts, Credit Cards or Statement. Full Accounting for Contracts, Dues, Payments, Aging & More. Track Prospects & Guest, Front Counter Check-Ins, & Employee Commissions. Prints Barcoded Membership Cards. Includes Scheduling Calendars & Employee Timeclock.
Aphelion, Inc.

FIVE YEAR PERSONAL DIARY

Fitness Master. Aug. 1993. *Items Included:* User manual. *Customer Support:* Free telephone support, customer satisfaction guarantee.
MS-DOS 3.2.1 or higher. IBM PC & compatibles (640k). disk $29.95. *Optimal configuration:* 2 drives; hard disk recommended. CGA, EGA, or VGA monitor.
Computerized Diary to Record Your Fitness Activity Using the Aerobic Point System. Covers 37 Sports. Analyze & Plot Points, Distance, Pace, Time, Heart Rate & Weight. Also Includes Personal Fitness Evaluation, Running & Cycling Training Plans, Tailored Weight Control Program, Numerous Fitness Tips & Checklists & Much More. Easy to Use with Pull-Down Menus & On-Line Help. Print to Dot-Matrix or Laser Printers.
Bridget Software Co.

The Five A's. *Items Included:* manuals. *Customer Support:* 90 days unlimited warranty.
MS-DOS Macintosh. contact publisher for price.
Networks supported: Virtually all LAN & AppleShare.
Financial Management & Accounting System Designed Industry Specific. Includes Job Tracking, Job Costing, Time Sheets, P.O. to Vendors, Traffic Scheduling, Job Estimating, A/P, A/R, & G/L. Reporting Offers User Compatibility with Virtually All Spread Sheet & Word Processing Software.
Quinn Essentials, Inc.

5 Ft. 10 Pak Special Edition. *Items Included:* Installation & user instruction; upgrade coupons.
CD-ROM disk Contact publisher for price.
Sirius Publishing, Inc.

5000 Plus Image Library. Alfred J. Heyman. *Items Included:* License agreement & registration card. *Customer Support:* 1-900-420-5005, $3.00 per minute.
Windows 3.1. IBM & compatibles (2.0Mb). CD-ROM disk $59.00 MSRP (ISBN 0-9634008-2-7). *Nonstandard peripherals required:* CD ROM drive. *Optimal configuration:* 386, 20MHz, 4Mb RAM.
Over 5000 Images on One CD ROM for Use with Presentation Software, Includes Powerful Search Engine.
Cascom International, Inc.

Five Weeks to Winning Bridge. *Items Included:* Bound manual. *Customer Support:* Free hotline - no time limit; 30 day limited warranty; updates are $5/disk plus S&H.
MS-DOS 2.0 or higher. IBM & compatibles (128k). disk $45.95.
Contains 35 Lessons Which Cover the Entire Game of Bridge: Bidding, Declarer Play, Defense, & Bridge Etiquette. It Provides an Extensive Treatment of the Play of the Cards, Including Opening Leads, Defensive Signalling, & Deceptive Play. It Then Presents Bidding Conventions Used by the Experts. And Finally, There Is Material on Bridge Ethics & Etiquette.
Dynacomp, Inc.

5 Weeks to Winning Bridge. *Compatible Hardware:* IBM PC & compatibles.
$39.95.
Teaches Users the Game of Bridge.
Great Game Products.

Five Year Personal Diary. Feb. 1985. *Compatible Hardware:* IBM PC, PC XT, PC AT. *Operating System(s) Required:* PC-DOS 2.0 & higher. *Memory Required:* 64k. *General Requirements:* Printer. RAM disk recommended.
disk $40.00.
one year diary $10.00.
A Page-a-Day Diary for Any Year, Starting with 1985. Enter up to 960 Characters of Text for Each Day.
Robert L. Nicolai.

Fixed Asset Inventory. *Compatible Hardware:* AT&T 3B2; IBM PC & compatibles, PC XT, PC AT, PC 36. *Operating System(s) Required:* DOS, UNIX. *Language(s):* BASIC (source code included). *Memory Required:* 512k. *General Requirements:* Wide-carriage printer.
contact publisher for price.
Meets All Requirements in Accordance with the Accounting & Reporting System Design Manual for Montana School Districts. All Types of Depreciation Will Be Provided for & Are User Defined.
Diversified Computing.

Fixed Asset Management Accounting System. *Version:* 7.0. *Operating System(s) Required:* PC-DOS/MS-DOS, Windows. *Language(s):* C. *Memory Required:* 640k. *Customer Support:* $325.00 ($425.00, multi-user) annual support.
single user $695.00.
multi-user $995.00.
Single User Plus "True" Multi-User Version with "Transaction Logging" for Networks. Entire Life History of Asset Depreciation Calculated During Data Entry & Available for View. Prior/Future Year Reporting Including ITC & Recaptures. Unlimited Number of Short Years. Up-to-Date with Tax Law Through Current Year. Up to Eight Sets of Books Per Asset. Checks MACRS "40% Rule" During Data Entry. Checks All Limits During Data Entry. Complete Insurance Reporting System. Built-In Capabilities for Consolidated Reports for Multiple Companies at No Extra Charge. An Optional "SQL" Report Writer for User Defined Reports.
E. F. Haskell & Assocs.

The Fixed Asset Package. J. Gary Bishop, Jr. May 1979. *Compatible Hardware:* Data General, IBM PC & compatibles. *Operating System(s) Required:* AIX, AOS/VS, Lantastic, MS-DOS, Multiuser DOS, Novell, RDOS, XENIX. *Language(s):* ICOBOL, COBOL, ICHOST (source code included). *Memory Required:* 256k. *Customer Support:* Yes, on-site training, seminars, toll-free number.
contact publisher for price (ISBN 0-926356-02-X).
source code avail.
Multi-Company, Multi-Location, Multi-Expense Center Reporting of Asset Depreciation. Book & Tax Record Computation, Investment Tax Credit Summary, Automatic Journal Preparation, & Roll-Over of Assets from Year to Year. Optional Deletion of Fully Depreciated Assets Is Included. Current Year Acquisition/Disposal Reports, Depreciation Projections, Individual Asset Inquiry, & Replacement Cost Reports Are Available. System Was Designed, Written, & Supported by a Certified Public Accountant.
Program Systems, Inc.

Fixed Asset System. *Version:* 5.0. 1984. *Compatible Hardware:* IBM PC & compatibles. *Operating System(s) Required:* PC-DOS 2.0. *Memory Required:* 256k. *General Requirements:* Printer.
disk $695.00, incl. manual.
Recordkeeping Program That Allows Complete Records of Property & Equipment for Insurance Companies, State & Local Governments, IRS, & Business Auditors. Automatically Calculates Modified ACRS & 16 Other Types of Depreciation & Investment Tax Custodian, Manufacturer, etc.
Best Programs.

Fixed Assets. *Version:* 5.1. Nov. 1990. *Items Included:* User guide, technical reference manual. *Customer Support:* Training included with purchase. Hot-line & remote diagnostic service included with maintenance.
VAX/VMS (2Mb). Digital VAX. $25,000.00.
An Online Assets System Offering Comprehensive Accounting Control Over Acquisition, Maintenance, Transfer, & Retirement of Corporate Assets. Fixed Assets Includes a Complete Set of Standard Reports & the Capability for Extended Asset Analysis Through a Powerful, Online Inquiry Language.
Ross Systems, Inc.

Fixed Assets & Depreciation. *Version:* 4.0. 1983. *Compatible Hardware:* IBM PC. *Operating System(s) Required:* MS-DOS, PC-DOS 1.1, 2.0. *Language(s):* MBASIC (source code included). *Memory Required:* 128k.
disk $500.00.
Provides Automatic Calculation of Depreciation. Features: Multiple Depreciation Methods, Multiple Formats, Investment Tax Credit Calculation. Interfaces to G/L & Client Write-Up.
CharterHouse Software Corp.

Fixed Assets-Depreciation. Pro Software, Inc. *Compatible Hardware:* TI Professional. *Operating System(s) Required:* MS-DOS. *Memory Required:* 64k.
$295.00.
Separate Book & Tax Calculations; 13 Depreciation Methods Including ACRS; Incorporated 1983 TEFRA-ITC Rulings; Multi-Company, Multi-Division.
Texas Instruments, Personal Productivit.

Fixed Assets: FA. *Version:* 5.8. May 1993. *Language(s):* C, COBOL & DIBOL. *General Requirements:* Depends on the specific configuration. *Customer Support:* Full service, update service; by arrangement.
VMS, Open VMS. DEC VAX Series, DEC Alpha AXP. $2500.00-$15,000.00.
Features Depreciation Calculations by ACRS, ACRSL, ACRS for Low Income Housing; Straight Line, 200%, 150%, & 125% Declining Balance Methods, Sum of the Years' Digits, & Units of Production. Other Features Include: User-Defined Asset Codes; Book, Tax, or Other (for State Use) Depreciation Ledger, or up to All Three Ledgers, for Each Asset; Depreciation Method Changes, Added Values, & Added Life Calculations; Asset History Kept for Each Asset Including Maintenance Expenses, Location Changes, & Retirement Information; Optional Automatic Change to Straight Line from Declining Balance Methods; On-Line Help-Text. Reports Include Depreciation Schedules, Asset Listings, a Book/Tax Comparison, Projected Depreciation, Asset History, Retirement Reports, Investment Credit Recapture Reports, & Property Tax & Insurance Reports.
Compu-Share, Inc.

Fixed Assets Management. 1992.
MS/PC DOS, Concurrent DOS, Xenix, Unix. IBM PC/XT/AT & compatibles, IBM PS/2 (512k).
single user or multi-user $695.00. *Networks supported:* Novell, Lantastic, Banyan VINES, all NETBOIS compatible.
"Fixed Assets Management" will quickly & accurately calculate all depreciation schedules for each corporate asset. Separate calculations may be done for Book, Federal Tax, & State Tax Schedules. "Fixed Assets Management" operates as a standalone program or as a direct interface to the INMASS/MRP General Ledger module.
INMASS MRP.

Fixed Assets Relief. *Version:* 1.1. Aug. 1993. *Items Included:* Bound manual. *Customer Support:* Free telephone, fax, modem for 1 yr. Maintenance $199 per year.
DOS 3.1 or higher. IBM PC, XT, 286, 386, 486, 586, PS/2. disk $795.00. *Optimal configuration:* IBM compatible computer with HP compatible laser printer. *Networks supported:* Novell, Lantastic, 3COM.
Supports a Very Comprehensive Menu of Depreciation Calculation As Well As Providing Extensive Fixed Asset Management Reports. Supports 6 Depreciation Books per Asset. Easily Customized for Maximum Productivity. Handles over 32,000 Assets.
Micro Vision Software, Inc.

Fixed Geometry Calculations. *Items Included:* Full manual. No other products required. *Customer Support:* Free telephone support - no time limit. 30 day warranty.
MS-DOS 3.2 or higher. IBM & compatibles (512k). disk $289.95.
These Additional Calculations May Be Added Directly to Your Current Copy of INSTRUCALC. For Specialized Flow Meters (for Both Gases & Liquids) You Can Size: Integral Flow Orifice Assemblies (Quadrant & Square Edge), Target Meters (.5 to 4 Inch), Elbow Flowmeters (All Sizes), Wedge Flowmeters (1 to 4 Inch), Chemical Seal Wedge Flowmeters (1 to 12 Inch), & Vortex Flowmeters (1 to 8 Inch). This Is a Handy Addition for INSTRUCALC Users Who Work with These Particular Devices.
Dynacomp, Inc.

FL/2B. *Version:* 2.8. May 1990. *Compatible Hardware:* IBM PC, PC XT, PC AT, PS/2. *Operating System(s) Required:* MS-DOS. *Language(s):* QuickBASIC. *Memory Required:* 640k. *General Requirements:* EGA, VGA or Hercules card.
$849.00.
Extension of Fairline/1 3-10 Master Curves with 3-10 Vertices Each & Free Orientation in Space. Generates OFE-Compatible Offset Files & Computes Upright Hydrostatics on Any Waterline. Screen Display of Component Curves, Lines, Planes or Perspective View.
AeroHydro, Inc.

Flag Race. *Compatible Hardware:* TRS-80 Model I, Model III.
disk $24.95.
Player Tries to Race a Car Through a Maze & Reach All the Flags Before Being Caught & Killed by Drone Cars.
Blue Cat.

Flak. *Compatible Hardware:* Apple II+, IIe, Macintosh. *Language(s):* Assembly. *Memory Required:* Apple II+, IIe 48k; Macintosh 128k.
disk $34.95.
Puts User in the Pilot's Seat of an Advanced AGX Hypersonic Fighter.
Funsoft, Inc.

Flare. John Migliavacca. Dec. 1983. *Compatible Hardware:* IBM PC with printer. *Operating System(s) Required:* DOS. *Language(s):* BASIC. *Memory Required:* 256k.
disk $125.00 (ISBN 0-917405-02-1).
Calculates Performance of a Hydrocarbon Flare by API RP-521 Methods. Determines Tip Diameter Based on Fraction of Sonic Velocity, Heat Generated, Flame Length & Flame Deflection by Wind & Steam Requirement for Smokeless Burning.
Techdata.

Flare Network Analysis. *Items Included:* Full manual. No other products required. *Customer Support:* Free telephone support - no time limit. 30 day warranty.
MS-DOS 3.2 or higher. IBM & compatibles (512k). disk $289.95.
Targeted Directly at Engineers Who Wish to Design Safe & Economical Flare Network Systems. FNA Quickly Calculates Pressure Drop, Velocity, & Diameter for Each Pipe in the Network, As Well As Optimum Pipe Sizes & Pressure & Velocity Profiles. Supports Both U.S. & Metric Units.
Dynacomp, Inc.

TITLE INDEX

Flare Network Analysis. 1992. *Items Included:* Detailed manuals included with all Dynacomp products. *Customer Support:* Free telephone support to original customer - no time limit; 30 day limited warranty.
MS-DOS 3.2 or higher. IBM PC & compatibles (512k). $289.95 (Add $5.00 for 3 1/2" format; 5 1/4" format standard). *Optimal configuration:* IBM, MS-DOS 2.0 or higher, 256k RAM, two floppy drives (or one floppy & a hard disk), & CGA or compatible graphics capability.
Targeted Directly at Engineers Who Wish to Design Safe & Economical Flare Network Systems. Even Very Complex Networks May Be Easily Modeled. Quickly Calculates Pressure Drop, Velocity, & Diameter for Each Pipe in the Network, As Well As Optimum Pipe Sizes & Pressure & Velocity Profiles. Both U.S. & Metric Units.
Dynacomp, Inc.

Flash! *Items Included:* Software & documentation. *Customer Support:* Toll Free technical support; 1st year maintenance free, thereafter 30% current list price. Contact vendor.
DOS 02/2, MACS, TSO, CICS, VM/CMS. IBM PC/XT/AT, IBM M/F, Macintosh. $9500.00 maintenance included for first year. *Networks supported:* LAN, ASYNC, SDLC.
An Advanced File Compression/Decompression Software System Designed for Use with IBM Compatible Micro-Mainframe File Transfer Systems. Compresses & Decompresses File Data for Transmission Between the PC & the Mainframe, & Then Expands the File to Original Size. Transmission Time & Costs Typically Reduced by up to 90%. Mainframe-to-Mainframe Version Also Available.
Telepartner International.

Flash Com. *Compatible Hardware:* Apple II; IBM PC, PCjr; Sanyo; TRS-80.
contact publisher for price.
Includes: Electronic Mailing & Messaging, Mailing List Manager, Utilities, Store & Forward Capabilities, Forms Manager & Business Forms & Letter Package.
Omni Computer Systems, Inc.

Flash, the Disk Accelerator. *Version:* 10. *Compatible Hardware:* IBM PC & compatibles. *Operating System(s) Required:* PC-DOS/MS-DOS 2.0 or higher. *Memory Required:* 256k. *General Requirements:* 2 disk drives or hard disk.
disk $69.95.
upgrade $25.00.
Disk Caching Software. Allows Users to Merge Conventional, Extended, & Expanded Memory into a Single Cache & Will Save Different Cache Configurations. Users May Request That Certain Frequently Accessed Files Stay Permanently in Cache. Package Also Includes a RAM Disk Which Automatically Sizes Itself to Fit the Data Loaded, Leaving the Rest of the Memory Pool to FLASH. Will Prevent Rebooting Before a Write Has Been Executed.
Software Matters.

FlashCrypt.
Macintosh 512KE or higher. 3.5" disk $249.00.
File Encryption.
Magnus Corp.

Fleet Check. *Compatible Hardware:* Commodore Amiga.
contact publisher for price.
Enhances Word Processing Software by Providing an Integrated Dictionary & Thesaurus. Documents Can Be Checked While They Are Typed or When Completed. Features: 90,000 Word Dictionary, Window Where Correct Spellings Are Suggested, Thesaurus with both Synonyms & Antonyms. Users Can Add up to 10,000 of Their Own Words. The Whole Program Is Memory Resident. Compatible with Most Major Word Processors.
Professional Software, Inc.

Fleet Control. *Items Included:* Bound manual. *Customer Support:* Free hotline - no time limit; 30 day limited warranty; updates are $5/disk plus S&H.
MS-DOS 2.1 or higher. IBM & compatibles (128k). disk $199.95. *Nonstandard peripherals required:* 132-column printer; dual 360k drives, or one 360k drive & a hard disk.
Will Help You Reduce the Operating Costs for Your Fleet of Vehicles. Menu-Driven & Includes These Databases: Vehicle Lookup Database; Gasoline Database; Repairs Database; Year-to-Date Costs Database; Preventive Maintenance Database. Preventive Maintenance Schedules Can Be Printed for Any Vehicle in the Vehicle Database for Any Given Time Frame.
Dynacomp, Inc.

Fleet Filer. *Compatible Hardware:* Commodore 64, 128.
disk $39.95.
Menu-Driven Database That Handles up to 50,000 Records with 20 Text or Numeric Fields. Also Sorts Records & Input/Output Information to FLEET SYSTEM 2+, 4 & Most Major Word Processors.
Professional Software, Inc.

Fleet Management System. *Version:* 1.1. Sep. 1988. *Items Included:* Documentation provided on diskette. *Customer Support:* Toll number provided. No charge for support provided by phone.
MS & PC-DOS. IBM PC/XT & compatibles. $75.00. *Nonstandard peripherals required:* None. *Optimal configuration:* IBM XT hard disk, MS-DOS, 512k Ram, 80 column printer.
Program Is Designed to Help Law Enforcement Agencies Control & Analyze Their Vehicle Gas Usage & Repair Costs. It Can Be Easily Modified for Use by Transportation Providers.
MicroServices, Inc.

Fleet Street Publisher. *Version:* 3.0. Mirrorsoft. Jul. 1989. *Items Included:* Spiral-bound manual.
TOS (512k). Atari ST. disk $249.95. *Optimal configuration:* 1Mb RAM.
Professional, Low-Cost Alternative to Typesetting & Artwork Services.
MichTron, Inc.

Fleet System 2+. *Compatible Hardware:* Commodore 64, 128. *Memory Required:* 64k. disk $59.95.
Word Processing/Check Spelling Software. Word Processor's Features Include Built-In 80-Column Display, Horizontal Scrolling During Typing, Centering, Indenting, Math Functions, Headers, Footers, Page Numbering, Search & Replace. Spell Checker Has a 90,000 Word Dictionary with up to 10,000 "Custom" Words to Be Included by the User. Has a "Vocabulary Feedback" Feature Providing Users with Information on the Number of Words Used, Number of Unique Words, Number of Times Each Word Appears, etc.
Professional Software, Inc.

Fleet System 3. *Compatible Hardware:* Apple IIe, IIc; Commodore 128. *Operating System(s) Required:* ProDOS. *Memory Required:* Apple 128k.
Commodore. contact publisher for price.
Apple. disk $79.95.
All of FLEET SYSTEM 2's Features Plus Integrated Thesaurus.
Professional Software, Inc.

Fleet System 4. *Compatible Hardware:* Commodore 128. *General Requirements:* RGB or 80-column composite color monitor.
disk $79.95.
backup disk $15.00.
Combines a Word Processor (with Dictionary & Thesaurus) with a Data Base.
Professional Software, Inc.

Fleetmax.
Microsoft Windows 3.1 or higher. 386/40MHz (8Mb). Contact publisher for price. *Nonstandard peripherals required:* 20Mb hard disk space, 16-color VGA monitor, Microsoft mouse or compatible pointing device. *Networks supported:* Novell Netware.
Offers over 32 Predefined Reports. The Foxfire Query/Report Generator Unlocks Fleetmax's Unlimited Data Tracking & Monitoring Technology to Provide Blazing-Fast Reports & Graphics in Literally Any Format, for Literally Any Purpose. Offers Total Control of All Critical Data - & Foxfire Puts It at Your Fingertips, in Any Configuration, Instantly. Create Your Own Wizards - & Create Real Control, Unlimited Control.
Creighton Manning.

Fleetmax for Windows. *Version:* 1.3. Nov. 1995. *Items Included:* User manual, Foxfire! Manual w/Professional Version. *Customer Support:* $195.00-$695.00 annual maintenance fee allows user to free upgrades & unlimited telephone support.
Windows 3.1 or higher. 80386 required, 80486 recommended & Pentium. $995.00 Professional version, higher for more than 2 simultaneous users; $595.00 Standard version (for standalone only). *Networks supported:* Most PC Networks.
Schedules & Forecasts Preventive Maintenance, Provides Exception Reports & Tells user Before Work Must be Done. Automatically Deducts Parts from Inventory & Updates P/M, Performs Repair Cost Analysis & P/M History. Tells You Where & When Parts are Used & When to Reorder, & Monitor Fuel Costs & Inventory.
Creighton Manning, Inc.

FLEX (Forward-Chaining Logical EXpert) System Toolkit. *Version:* 1.2. *Compatible Hardware:* IBM PC, PC XT, PC AT, PC compatibles. *Memory Required:* 512k. *General Requirements:* Prolog/MacProlog. *Items Included:* License/disk/documentation. *Customer Support:* Comprehensive customer support service.
IBM PC. disk $395.00.
Macintosh. disk $495.00.
Forward/Backward Chaining, Frames, Objects & Rules, Menus, Dialogues, Icons & Graphics.
Quintus Computer Systems, Inc.

Flex/Hybrid System. *Compatible Hardware:* IBM PC & compatibles.
disk $6200.00.
Electronic-Design Program Includes Interfaces to the Manufacturing Process.
Infinite Graphics, Inc.

Flex-i-Term. *Customer Support:* 800-929-8117 (customer service).
MS-DOS. Apple II. disk $79.99 (ISBN 0-87007-639-6).
A Machine Language Terminal Program That Operates the Terminal During Timesharing Operations. May be Modified for a Variety of Interaction Environments Through the Use of a Configurator. The Advantage of This Package Is That One Program Integrates Video, Keyboard, Modem & Output Devices into an Easily Controllable Package.
SourceView Software International.

FLEX-RATE+. *Version:* 7.1. 1985. *Compatible Hardware:* IBM PC & compatibles, PC XT, PC AT. *Operating System(s) Required:* MS-DOS 5.0 Plus. *Language(s):* Compiled BASIC, Assembly. *Memory Required:* 2000k.
disk $3000.00, Single user.
disk $4500.00, Local Area.
disk Wide Area $8750.00.
Adds the Ability to the LOANLEDGER+ Environment to Charge Interest on the Basis of Actual Days Elapsed between Scheduled Payments at a Different Rate for Each Day. Prints Calendar of Interest Rates for the Year. 99 Indexes Available.
Dynamic Interface Systems Corp.

Flex-Screen. *Version:* 2.0. *Compatible Hardware:* IBM PC, PC XT, PC AT; uses floppy or hard disk drive. *Operating System(s) Required:* MS-DOS; NOVELL. *Language(s):* BASIC, MS Quick BASIC. *Memory Required:* 640k. *Customer Support:* Toll-free telephone & modem.
$2495.00-$3995.00.
Accounts Receivable & Billing System for Clubs & Member Associations.
Ernest A. Jonson & Co.

Flex Type. *Version:* 2.1B. Mark Simonsen. Nov. 1984. *Compatible Hardware:* Apple II, II+, IIe, IIc, IIgs. *Operating System(s) Required:* Apple DOS 3.3. *Language(s):* Machine, BASIC. *Memory Required:* 48k.
disk $29.50.
Variable Hi-Res Text Utility. Allows Users to Combine Hi-Res & Text Without Special Commands. Produces Compressed & Expanded Text Type. Text Is Displayed in Normal 40 Columns, 20-Column Expanded, or 56- & 70-Column Compressed Characters.
Beagle Brothers.

FlexeLint. *Version:* 5.0. 1990. *Items Included:* Full Documentation included. *Customer Support:* Technical telephone support at no charge.
UNIX SVR3/SVR4. Microcomputer Intel 80386/486/Pentium. $395.00.
A C Source Code Analysis Facility That Can Analyze Your C Programs, to Help You Find Both Bugs & Portability Problems. FlexeLint for UNIX Is Computer Innovations' Port of the Popular PC-Lint Product from Gimpel Software. Both Traditional (K&R) & Modern (ANSI) C Dialects Are Supported. FlexeLint Will Analyze C Programs & Report on Bugs, Glitches, & Inconsistencies. It Works Across Multiple Source Modules, Providing Inter-File Cross Checks & Reports That C Compilers Miss. Diagnostics for Use of Macros, Typedefs, Declarations, etc. Help in Reorganizing Large Bodies of Code into Manageable Pieces, by Pointing Out Which Objects Are Used Globally & Locally. Reporting Is User-Customizable, to Adapt to Individual Preferences.
Computer Innovations, Inc.

FlexeLint for C/C Plus Plus. *Version:* 7.0. Jan. 1996. *Operating System(s) Required:* UNIX, VAX VMS, Ultrix, Sun O.S., Apollo, OS-9, IBM VM-MVS, QNX. *Memory Required:* 640k. *General Requirements:* K&R C compiler. *Items Included:* Software & reference manual. *Customer Support:* Fax & telephone tech support included.
3.5" or 5.25" MS-DOS disk $998.00 & up.
Diagnostic Facility for C & C Plus Plus. Will Find Bugs, Glitches & Inconsistencies That a Compiler Working on One Module at a Time Will Miss. Is Distributed in "Shrouded Source" Form. It Requires Only K & R C to Compile. Will Find Inconsistent Declaration, Argument/Parameter Mismatches, Uninitialized Variables, Unaccessed Variables, Variables Assigned but Not Used, Suspicious Macros, Indentation Irregularities, Function Recursion, Unusual Expressions, Printf-Scanf Irregularities & More. Provides for Strong Type Checking Based on Typedefs. Fully Customizable: All Error Messages Can Be Selectively Inhibited; Size of Scalars Can Be Altered; Format of Error Messages Can Be Adjusted; etc.
Gimpel Software.

FlexeLint for the QNX Operating System. *Version:* 5.0. Jan. 1992. *Customer Support:* Telephone technical support 10 a.m. - 5 p.m. (EST), Monday through Friday.
QNX (2.15D), QNX 4. $295.00, per single node. *Optimal configuration:* FlexeLint requires QNX version os.2.15D, an 80286-80486 CPU, & at least 512Kb of memory. More memory will be used by FlexeLint for larger programs.
Full-Featured Lint Facility That Has Been Designed to Report Errors & Potentially Hazardous Constructs in C Source Code. Helps Locate Bugs Earlier in the Software Development Process. Multi-Module Cross Checking is Also Available. The User Has Control Over the Analysis Process. Output Can Be Customized to Suit Individual Programming Styles.
Computer Innovations, Inc.

Flexibility-Plus. *Version:* 4.05. Jun. 1991. *Compatible Hardware:* Data General. *Operating System(s) Required:* R-DOS, AOS-VS, AOS, AOS-WS. *Language(s):* Extended BASIC (source code included). *Memory Required:* 64k. *Items Included:* Manuals, source code, programmers reference manual, computerized training module. *Customer Support:* Continuing support agreements available.
DG Desktop. $4500.00, incl. manual.
DG MV4 & MV6. $11,000.00, incl. manual.
DG NOVA, Eclipse, MV4DC. $8000.00, incl. manual.
DG MV 8. $15,000.00, incl. manual.
DG MV 10. $17,500.00, incl. manual.
Completely Integrated, Menu-Driven Accounting System with 12 Major Modules. System Is Parameter Driven, Permits Data Verification, & Provides Complete Audit Trail. Includes Operator's Manual, Computerized Training Module, & "Programmers Reference Manual".
JTW Computer Systems, Inc.

Flexidraw. *Version:* 5.5. Jul. 1987. *Compatible Hardware:* Commodore 64, SX64, 128.
disk $34.95, incl. manual, key overlay.
Enables Users to Produce Computer Graphics Ranging from Simple Free-Hand Sketches to Technical Drawings. Features Include: Multiple Line Widths for Free-Hand Sketching, Rubberbanding, or Point-to-Point Drawing; Automatic Shapes, Ten Font Styles in Three Sites; Ooops/Undo; Two Separate Workscreens, & Library of Symbols. Supports Light Pens, Joysticks, Touch Pad, & Mouse. Light Pens Sold Separately.
Inkwell Systems.

Flexifont. Jun. 1985. *Compatible Hardware:* Commodore 64, SX64, 128.
disk $29.95.
Enables User to Create, Edit, Verify, & Save Letters, Symbols, or Patterns. Interfaces with FLEXIDRAW. Package Includes 33 Font Styles, Font Capture Program, File Mover Program, & FLEXIDRAW Filer. Light Pen or Menu Driven.
Inkwell Systems.

Flexitext. *Items Included:* Bound manual. *Customer Support:* Free hotline - no time limit; 30 day limited warranty; updates are $5/disk plus S&H.
MS-DOS. IBM & compatibles (128k). disk $29.95.
Comprehensive & Versatile Text Management Utility. It Even Gives You the Ability to Transport Text Files from One Word Processor to Another. With fLEXITEXT User Can: Sort Files Using up to 16 Keys, All with Independent Order & Attributes; Encrypt/Decrypt Using Your Own Key; Change to Upper or Lower Case; Turn off High Bits; Translate to ASCII; Convert One Character to Another; Add a Character after Another (e.g., Add Line Feeds to All Carriage Returns); Remove Specific Characters (e.g., Hard Carriage Returns). The Manual Includes Many Examples, As Well As a Discussion of Word Processor File Structures.
Dynacomp, Inc.

FlexNet. *Compatible Hardware:* IBM PC AT. *Operating System(s) Required:* FlexOS.
$250.00.
Networking Resource Manager for FlexOS. Includes an Electronic Mail Utility - a Server/Requester to IBM PC LAN & FlexOS Functionality Supported Across the Network.
Digital Research, Inc.

FlexOS 386.
An 80386-based system under MS-DOS. $1600.00-$2995.00.
Includes Systems Builder's Kit 58K. Features Real-Time OS, DOS Support.
Digital Research, Inc.

FlexQL. *Version:* 2.0. *Items Included:* Documentation for the Report Writer & the SQL engine. *Customer Support:* Free business hour toll support lines; CompuServe Forum; 90 Media warranty.
DOS 6.22 & higher, UNIX. IBM PC & compatibles (500k), various UNIX. disk multi-user $595.00. *Networks supported:* Novell, IBM, 3Com, AT&T.
disk single-user $295.00.
Multi-File Relational Report Writer & SQL Engine Can Access Data Stored in Many Different File Formats As Well As Being Able to Export Data to Them.
Data Access Corp.

FlexShare Database Server. *Version:* 6.02. Jun. 1989. *Customer Support:* Telephone, Fax, telex, electronic mail & support. Training classes.
Macintosh (1Mb). 3.5" disk $695.00. *Nonstandard peripherals required:* Hard disk. *Addl. software required:* Multi-user requires AppleTalk & one of the following: AppleShare, Tops, or FlexShare; FlexShare &/or AppleShare require dedicated Macintosh.
Speeds Flexware Database Performance over AppleTalk. Normally, Accounting Systems Access a Shared Database by Having Each Computer Read Through the "Index" Portions of the Database in Order to Find the Record They Need. This Means That the Network Can Become Jammed with the Transmission of Indexes, & Performance in a Large Network Is Poor. With FlexShare, the Computer That Holds the Database Does the Search Locally & Returns the Requested Record. As a Result, Users Receive the Information They Need Faster & the Load on the Network is Cut. Performance May Be Improved by a Factor of 30 to 80 in Larger Networks. Requires Either a Dedicated Computer or Can Co-Exist with AppleShare on the Same Computer.
Microfinancial Corp./FLEXWARE.

FLEXWARE Accounts Payable. *Version:* 6.02. Jun. 1989. *Customer Support:* Telephone, Fax, telex, electronic mail & support. Training classes.
Macintosh (1Mb). 3.5" disk $895.00. *Nonstandard peripherals required:* Hard disk. *Addl. software required:* Multi-user requires AppleTalk & one of the following: AppleShare, Tops, or Flexware; FlexShare &/or AppleShare require dedicated Macintosh.
Designed to Maintain Vendor Information & to Receive Vendor Invoices, Calculate Invoice Due

Dates & Discounts, Distribute Invoices to Appropriate General Ledger Accounts, Write Checks at the Optimum Time, & Provide Management Reports Including Cash Forecasting Reports. Features Include Manual & Void Checks, Multiple Bank Accounts, Unlimited Distribution, Automatic Payment Recommendation with Complete Control of What is Paid, Credit Memos, Recurring Payments, Easy Tracking of What Invoices Each Check Paid, What Checks Were Used to Pay Each Invoice, etc., Reconciliation, Checks by Number & Vendor, One-Time Vendor Processing, Agings, 1099 Vendor Processing, Paid History Remains as Long as Needed. On-Line Help with Learn Mode. System is Multi-user, Multi-Company, Multi-Department, Modifiable, with Complete Audit Trails & Can Be Fully Integrated to Other Flexware Modules.
Microfinancial Corp./FLEXWARE.

FLEXWARE Accounts Receivable. Version: 6.02. Jun. 1989. *Customer Support:* Telephone, Fax, telex, electronic mail & support. Training classes.
Macintosh (1Mb). 3.5" disk $895.00.
 Nonstandard peripherals required: Hard disk. *Addl. software required:* Multi-user requires AppleTalk & one of the following: AppleShare, Tops, or FlexShare; FlexShare &/or AppleShare require dedicated Macintosh.
System Designed to Provide Instant Access to Sales History & Credit Status. Decreases Time Spent Preparing Invoices & Statements & Can Improve Average Collection Time. Features Include a Variety of Invoice Formats, Summary Invoice to Full Inventory Update with Automatic Pricing & Description, Unlimited Ship-to Addresses, Credits, Void Checks, Manual & Recurring Invoices, Statements, Deposits, Agings, Auto or Manual Credit Apply, Paid Items Remain as Long as User Chooses, Open Item or Balance Forward, Partial Payments, Calculations for Discount Tax & Finance Charges, & On-line Help & Learn Mode. System Is Multi-User, Multi-Company, Multi-Department, Modifiable, with Complete Audit Trails & Can Be Fully Integrated to Other Flexware Modules.
Microfinancial Corp./FLEXWARE.

FLEXWARE Application Development System. 1979. *Compatible Hardware:* Apple Macintosh; Corvus Concept; DEC Vax; IBM PC & compatibles, PC XT, PC AT; Pinnacle; Stride. *Operating System(s) Required:* MS-DOS, UCSD p-System. *Language(s):* Pascal (source code included). *Memory Required:* 256k. *General Requirements:* 2 disk drives or hard disk.
contact publisher for price.
Can Be Used for Both Vertical Market Software Package Development & for Custom Programming. Data May Be Shared Between FLEXWARE Applications & Many Spreadsheets, Databases, Graphics Packages, Word Processors, & Other Packages. FLEXWARE Applications Support Both Local & Remote Access.
Microfinancial Corp./FLEXWARE.

FLEXWARE Database Development System. Version: 6.02. Jun. 1989. *Customer Support:* Telephone, FAX, telex, electronic mail support. Training classes.
Macintosh (2.5Mb). disk $3400.00. *Nonstandard peripherals required:* Hard disk. *Addl. software required:* Multi-user requires AppleTalk & 1 of the following: AppleShare, Tops or FlexShare; Flex and/or AppleShare require dedicated Macintosh.
A Fourth-Generation Database Language Designed to Create High-End Multi-User Applications. Includes Interpreter, Screen-Change Facilities, Database Definitions, Reports, Sequential Processor Programs, Speed Utilities & Data Insertion/Extraction Facilities. Also Contains a Number of High Level Programs & Utilities, Including an Automatic Application Documentor, to Aid Developers.
Microfinancial Corp./FLEXWARE.

FLEXWARE General Ledger. Version: 6.02. Jun. 1989. *Customer Support:* Telephone, Fax, telex, electronic mail & support. Training classes.
Macintosh (1Mb). 3.5" disk $895.00.
 Nonstandard peripherals required: Hard disk. *Addl. software required:* Multi-user requires AppleTalk & one of the following: AppleShare, Tops, or FlexShare; FlexShare &/or AppleShare require dedicated Macintosh.
Designed to Record a Company's Financial Transactions, Receive Information from Other Accounting Applications, & Maintain Records for Management Reports & Financial Statements. Entries Are Made into User-Defined Journals & Then Posted to Ledgers. System Provides for Recurring Journal Entries, Audit Trails, & Mid-Period Financials & Trial Close. Features Include 12 or 13 Accounting Periods; Standard & User-Defined Financial Statements & Chart of Account; Comparisons to Budgets &/or Previous Years; Account Number Validation; Up-to-The Minute Financial Status; Prior Periods Do Not Have to Close to Begin New Period, Keep Detail As Long As Desired, Copy Chart of Accounts Between Companies, with On-Line Help & Learn Mode. System Is Multi-User, Multi-Company, Multi-Department, Modifiable, with Complete Audit Trails & Can Be Fully Integrated to Other Flexware Modules.
Microfinancial Corp./FLEXWARE.

FLEXWARE Integrated Accounting System. 1979. *Compatible Hardware:* Apple Macintosh; Corvus Concept; DEC VAX; IBM PC & compatibles, PC XT, PC AT; Pinnacle; Stride. *Operating System(s) Required:* MS-DOS, UCSD p-System. *Language(s):* Pascal (source code included). *Memory Required:* 256k.
contact publisher for price.
Microfinancial Corp./FLEXWARE.

FLEXWARE Inventory. Version: 6.02. Jun. 1989. *Customer Support:* Telephone, Fax, telex, electronic mail & support. Training classes.
Macintosh (1Mb). 3.5" disk $895.00.
 Nonstandard peripherals required: Hard disk. *Addl. software required:* Multi-user requires AppleTalk & one of the following: AppleShare, Tops, or FlexShare; FlexShare &/or AppleShare require dedicated Macintosh.
Designed for Managers to Balance Inventory Levels Between Adequate Stock to Meet Sales or Usage Requirements Without Excess Investment in Inventory. Allows User to Record All Inventory Movement: Orders, Receipts, Sales, Issues, Transfers, Adjustments, & More for Multiple Locations. One Level of Component or Bill of Material Inventory Management Is Also Supported. Features Include 9 Price Levels, LIFO, FIFO, Weighted Average, & Standard Cost, Purchase Source Analysis, Full Part History, Physical Adjustments,Individual Item Tracking; Tracking by Product, Class & Inventory Category; Part Number Cross Reference; & On-Line Help. System Is Multi-User, Multi-Company, Multi-Department, Modifiable, with Complete Audit Trails & Can Be Fully Integrated to Other Flexware Modules.
Microfinancial Corp./FLEXWARE.

FLEXWARE Job Costing. Version: 6.02. Jun. 1989. *Customer Support:* Telephone, Fax, telex, electronic mail & support. Training classes.
Macintosh (1Mb). 3.5" disk $995.00.
 Nonstandard peripherals required: Hard disk. *Addl. software required:* Multi-user requires AppleTalk & one of the following: AppleShare, Tops, or FlexShare; FlexShare &/or AppleShare require dedicated Macintosh.
Integrated Cost Accumulation Module. Costs Accrued Through Payroll, Accounts Payable, Accounts Receivable, General Ledger, & Inventory are Detailed & Summarized in Job Costing. Can Be Used in Conjunction with Flexware Accounts Receivable (Customer Credits & Invoices), Flexware Payroll (Labor Distribution), Flexware Accounts Payable (Purchases of Material, Subcontracts, & Equipment Rental), Flexware General Ledger (General & Administration, & Other Miscellaneous Costs), Flexware Inventory (Transfers from Stock to Job Site), or As a Stand-Alone Cost Tracking System. Provisions are Made to Establish Jobs & to Designate Certain Jobs for Internal Company Use for Equipment & Cost Center Accounting. Also Contains Estimating Capability. Jobs May Be Segregated into As Many As 4 Levels of Detail, with Phase Being the Highest Level. Other Available Levels Include Subphase, Line, & Item. Different Jobs May Use Different Estimating Structures, Depending Upon Unique Needs.
Microfinancial Corp./FLEXWARE.

FLEXWARE Order Processing. Version: 6.02. Jun. 1989. *Customer Support:* Telephone, Fax, telex, electronic mail and support. Training classes.
Macintosh (1Mb). 3.5" disk $795.00.
 Nonstandard peripherals required: Hard disk. *Addl. software required:* Requires Flexware Inventory & Flexware Accounts Receivable Systems; Multi-user requires AppleTalk & one of the following: AppleShare, Tops, or Flexware; Flexware &/or AppleShare require dedicated Macintosh.
Enters, Records, Processes, & Reports Sales Orders Entered at the Moment an Order Is Taken. Will Automatically Post Customer Accounts in the Flexware Accounts Receivable Module & Update Product Records in the Flexware Inventory Module. As Orders from Customers Are Entered, Inventory Status is Shown & Automatically Reserved. Shippers Are Printed; Then Orders Are Filled. When Shipped, the Order Is Recalled & an Invoice Is Automatically Created After Any Necessary Changes Are Made. Features Include: Backorder Tracking; Instant Update & Inquiry of Customer Status; Reference to Orders by Customer; Payment Terms Vary by Customer; Credit Memo Processing; Credit Limit Checking; Credit Hold Protection; Reservation of Inventory; Tax Calculation; & On-line Help.
Microfinancial Corp./FLEXWARE.

FLEXWARE Payroll. Version: 6.02. Jun. 1989. *Customer Support:* Telephone, Fax, telex, electronic mail & support. Training classes.
Macintosh (1Mb). 3.5" disk $895.00.
 Nonstandard peripherals required: Hard disk. *Addl. software required:* Multi-user requires AppleTalk and one of the following : AppleShare, Tops, or FlexShare; FlexShare &/or AppleShare require dedicated Macintosh.
Designed to Maintain Employee & Pay Information. Processes Salaried or Hourly Employees with Flexible Time-Card Entry Using a Variety of Pay Rates to Calculate Their Net Pay. System Calculates a Variety of Voluntary & Tax Deductions with User Definable Tax Tables, for State & Federal, to Arrive at a Net Pay. System Produces Checks with Stubs, Pay Registers, & Federal Quarterly & Annual Reports. Maintains Personnel Information, One Time Pay & Deductions, Advances & Pay Adjustments, Manual & Void Checks, Bonuses & Commissions, % of Gross & 401K Deductions, Union Requirements, Variety of Time Card Formats, Restore Program to Easily Re-Do Payroll, W2, 940, 941 Processing, Pay Grades, Any Frequencies, (Weekly, Monthly, etc.), Multiple

Bank Accounts, & On-Line Help. Multi-User, Multi-Company, Multi-Department, Modifiable, with Complete Audit Trails & Can Be Fully Integrated to Other Flexware Modules.
Microfinancial Corp./FLEXWARE.

FLEXWARE Point of Sale. *Version:* 6.02. Oct. 1989. *Customer Support:* Telephone, Fax, telex, electronic mail & support. Training classes.
Macintosh (1Mb). disk $695.00. *Nonstandard peripherals required:* Hard disk. *Addl. software required:* Requires Flexware General Ledger, Accounts Receivable, & Inventory modules; Multi-user requires Apple-Talk & 1 of the following: AppleShare, Tops or FlexShare; FlexShare and/or AppleShare require dedicated Macintosh.
System for Recording Sales in a Retail, Wholesale or Service Environment. Includes Cash, Credit, On-Account Sales, Price Lookup or Full Perpetual Inventory, Multiple Cash Drawer Control, Sales on 4" Receipt Printer or Full Sized Invoices, Bar Code Compatibility, Multi-Level Pricing, Discounts, Tax Calculation, Full Inventory Management, Extensive Security, Daily Sales Report, Daily Credit Report, Sales Report by Date, Product Categories, & Salesperson, Price Lists, Stock Status, Reorder Reports, Parts Lists.
Microfinancial Corp./FLEXWARE.

FLEXWARE Purchasing. *Version:* 6.02. Jun. 1989. *Customer Support:* Telephone, Fax, telex, electronic mail & support. Training classes.
Macintosh (1Mb). 3.5" disk $795.00.
Nonstandard peripherals required: Hard disk. *Addl. software required:* Multi-user requires AppleTalk & one of the following: AppleShare, Tops, or FlexShare; FlexShare &/or AppleShare require dedicated Macintosh.
Designed to Help Reduce Costs of Purchasing, Insure Adequate Inventory Levels, & Minimize Inventory Investment. On-hand Quantities are Monitored, Triggering Purchase Recommendations or Automatic Ordering. POs are Printed & Tracked & Vendor Analysis Can Help Determine the Best Sources, Based on Delivery Times, Price & Other Data. Once Inventory is Received, Backorders are Tracked, POs Cleared & Inventory is Updated. Can Be Run Alone but for Maximum Benefit, Should Be Integrated with Flexware Inventory & Flexware Accounts Payable. Featured Include: Stocked, Special Orders, Blanket Orders & Releases, Automatic Ordering from Inventory Based on Reorder Quantity & Levels with Overrides, Purchase Order Printing, Purchase Source Analysis, Receipt Processing, Outstanding Item Analysis, On-Line Help. System is Multi-User, Multi-Company, Multi-Department, Modifiable, with Complete Audit Trails & Can Be Fully Integrated to Other Flexware Modules.
Microfinancial Corp./FLEXWARE.

FLEXWARE Sales Analysis System. 1979. *Compatible Hardware:* Apple Macintosh; Corvus Concept; DEC VAX; IBM PC & compatibles, PC XT, PC AT; Pinnacle; Stride. *Operating System(s) Required:* MS-DOS, UCSD p-System. *Language(s):* Pascal (source code included). *Memory Required:* 256k.
contact publisher for price.
Provides Sales Analysis by Product, Product Category, Customer, Salesperson & Commission Analysis.
Microfinancial Corp./FLEXWARE.

FLEXWARE Spreadsheet. 1979. *Compatible Hardware:* Apple Macintosh; Corvus Concept; DEC Vax; IBM PC & compatibles, PC XT, PC AT; Pinnacle; Stride. *Operating System(s) Required:* MS-DOS, UCSD p-System. (source code included). *Memory Required:* 256k. *General Requirements:* 2 disk drives or hard disk.
contact publisher for price.
Spreadsheet Program That Interfaces Directly to the Flexware Database Where All the Applications Are Stored. User Just Enters the Name in the Cell. Selection Criteria & Ranges May Also Be Specified.
Microfinancial Corp./FLEXWARE.

FLGH. 1982. *Compatible Hardware:* IBM PC & compatibles. *Operating System(s) Required:* MS-DOS. *Language(s):* BASIC. *Memory Required:* 128k.
$395.00.
Calculates the Stresses for Integral, Hub-Type Flanges with Configuration & Design Conditions Given. Also Calculates Maximum Allowable Working Pressure for a Given Design. Curve Values F, F (FL) & V (VL) Are Calculated Within the Program.
Technical Research Services, Inc.

FLGL. 1982. *Compatible Hardware:* IBM PC & compatibles. *Operating System(s) Required:* MS-DOS. *Language(s):* BASIC. *Memory Required:* 128k.
$275.00.
Calculates the Stresses for Loose-Type Flanges, with Configuration & Design Conditions Given. Also Calculates Maximum Allowable Working Pressure.
Technical Research Services, Inc.

Flight Master. *Customer Support:* 800-929-8117 (customer service).
MS-DOS. IBM/PS2. disk $139.99 (ISBN 0-87007-591-8).
For Pilots Flying any Type of Aircraft & for FBO's Air Taxi, & Charter Operators. Consists of 17 Individual Programs. Calculates Weight & Balance Data for any Type Aircraft with up to 10 Seats. Uses Forecast Winds Aloft for up to Nine Altitudes, Calculates Range & Endurance Data for Differnt Consumables & Flight Level Conditions.
SourceView Software International.

Flight of the Intruder. *Version:* 1.2. 1990. *Items Included:* manual. *Customer Support:* phone support.
IBM PC or compatible (640k). disk $59.95.
  Optimal configuration: 5.25 or 3.5 disk drive.
As You Catapult off the USS Shiloh, Know That You Are Headed for Intense Air Combat over North Vietnam. Flight of the Intruder Transports You Back to 1972 & Operation Linebacker. Fly into Hostile North Vietnamese Territory Accompanied by As Many As Seven Friendlies in Your Choice of A-6 Intruder or F-4 Phantom II. Select from Thirteen Sequential Operations Based on Stephen Coonts' Novel, Flight of the Intruder, or Act As Commander Air Group & Design Your Own Missions.
Spectrum HoloByte.

Flight Path. *Compatible Hardware:* TRS-80.
contact publisher for price.
Instant Software, Inc.

Flight Plan. *Items Included:* Bound manual. *Customer Support:* Free hotline - no time limit; 30 day limited warranty; updates are $5/disk plus S&H.
MS-DOS. IBM & compatibles (256k). disk $59.95.
General-Aviation Package Which Provides Pilots, Instructors, & Fixed-Base Operators with: Flight-Planning Checklist for Recording Airport, Communications, Weather, & Special-Use Airspace Data & Notices to Airmen; Weight-&-Balance Computations for Specific 2- & 4-Place Aircraft & Typical Rental Aircraft; Navigation Computations - Magnetic Course, Magnetic Heading, Ground Speed, Leg Time, & Total Distance & Time for up to Nine Legs (Unlike Some Programs, FLIGHT PLAN Allows Direct Routing & Does Not Depend on Specific Navigational Facilities & Their Operational Status); Kneeboard-Size Flight Log Showing Checkpoint, Distance, True Air Speed, Altitude, Magnetic Course, Magnetic Heading, Ground Speed, Leg Time, & Total Distance & Time, with Space for Noting Compass Error, Actual Time, Navigational Aids, & Preflight & Inflight Recalculations, & More.
Dynacomp, Inc.

Flight Plan. *Version:* 3.0. *Items Included:* 70-page spiral bound manual, Airport & Navaid databases. *Customer Support:* Telephone support.
Macintosh II, SE30, 2.5Mb. disk $129.95 (Order no.: 20-1500). *Addl. software required:* Microsoft Excel version 2.2 or later. *Optimal configuration:* Hard disk.
(Order no.: 20-1400).
Complete Flight Planning Package. With Airport & Naval Information Available, User Can Quickly Prepare VFR, IFR, LORAN & RNAV Flight Plans. Databases Include Every U.S., Latin American, South American & Australian Airport That Has at Least One Paved Runway.
IGS International.

Flight Plan. *Customer Support:* 800-929-8117 (customer service).
MS-DOS. Apple II. disk $79.99 (ISBN 0-87007-443-1).
Computes Complex Private or Commercial Flight Plans. Headings & Distances are Computed Using Turn Radius of Aircraft. The Flight Plan Computes Fuel Burned, Fuel Remaining at Each Turn Point, Uses Forecast Wind to Correct Headings & Speed.
SourceView Software International.

Flight Simulator. *Compatible Hardware:* Apple II with Applesoft; IBM PC. (source code included). *Memory Required:* 48k, except IBM 128k.
disk $19.95.
Take-Off, Fly, Navigate & Land an Airplane.
Dynacomp, Inc.

Flight Simulator: Scenery Disk #7. *Compatible Hardware:* Atari ST, Commodore Amiga, IBM PC & compatibles.
3.5" disk $29.95.
Southeastern US Scenery for Use with Flight Simulator.
SubLOGIC.

Flight Simulator: Scenery Disk #11. *Compatible Hardware:* Atari ST, Commodore Amiga, IBM PC & compatibles.
3.5" disk $29.95.
Flight Simulator Scenery Disk.
SubLOGIC.

Flintstones Coloring Book: Spanish Version. Nov. 1994. *Items Included:* Soft cover, stapled manual & registration card. *Customer Support:* Free customer service via our 800 number. Unlimited warranty on disk replacement.
System 6.0.7 or higher. Any 256 color capable MAC (4Mb). 3.5" disk $14.95 (ISBN 1-888046-79-1, Order no.: ISF1009). *Nonstandard peripherals required:* 4Mb hard disk space req.; high density drive req. & 13" monitor or larger.
Windows 3.1 or higher, 386 or higher. IBM, Tandy & 100% compatibles (4Mb). disk $14.95 (ISBN 1-888046-80-5, Order no.: ISF1012). *Nonstandard peripherals required:* 256 colors or higher. *Optimal configuration:* Latest drives video cards: Trident, Diamond, ATI, Orchid, Headlands. Sound boards: Audio Spectrum & Sound Blaster.
Interactive Coloring Book with 30 Coloring Pictures, Featuring the Flintstones Characters.
Image Smith, Inc.

TITLE INDEX

Flip-Ello. *Compatible Hardware:* IBM PC. *Operating System(s) Required:* MS-DOS. *Language(s):* Compiled BASIC. *Memory Required:* 64k.
contact publisher for price.
Plays the Popular Board Game Known Commonly by the Names "Othello" & "Reversi". Game Allows the Player to Play the Computer or Use the Computer As an Automatic Playing Board.
Resuba Digital Systems.

Flip Side. K. Olsen & P. Hollyer. Nov. 1985. *Compatible Hardware:* Atari ST, Sanyo 550, IBM PC with GEM. *Operating System(s) Required:* TOS. *Memory Required:* 512k.
Atari. 3.5" disk $29.95 (ISBN 0-923213-10-4, Order no.: AT-FLI).
Reversi-Type Board Game Enables Users to Customize Play at the Beginning of Each Game. Can Be Played Against the Computer, a Human Opponent, or the Computer Can Play Against Itself. Six Levels of Play Are Available. Computer Can Help by Showing All Available Moves, Suggest a Move, Switching Sides with the Player. Users Can Edit the Board for Creating Their Own Training Problems.
MichTron, Inc.

Flipper. *Version:* 4.0. John S. Smith. Mar. 1990. *Items Included:* Print & braille documenation. *Customer Support:* Telephone support.
MS-DOS (128k). disk $495.00. *Nonstandard peripherals required:* Speech synthesizer.
Screen Access Utility to Provide Voice Output to Most MS-DOS Applications Programs.
Raised Dot Computing, Inc.

Flipsketch. *Compatible Hardware:* Atari 400, 800. *Language(s):* Atari BASIC. *Memory Required:* disk 24k. *General Requirements:* Joystick.
disk $23.95.
Low Resolution Graphics Program Which Allows the Creation of an Unlimited Number of Screens, 24 Colors, & Slow to Rapid Animation.
Dynacomp, Inc.

The Flo Series, 3 pts. *Version:* 5. 1992. *Compatible Hardware:* IBM PC & compatibles. *Operating System(s) Required:* Windows 3.1 or Windows 95. *Language(s):* C. *Memory Required:* 1500k. *Items Included:* 5 manuals, 1 tutorial, 4 User's Guides. *Customer Support:* 90 days free, 1 yr. $150.
disk $1895.00.
Integrated Series of Programs to Assist in the Entire Process of Piping Design.
Engineered Software, Inc.
Pt. 1. Piping Network Design & Analysis. $1495.00.
Consists of PIPE-FLO Pipeline Database Program.
Pt. 4. Pump-Flo for Pump Design & Selection. $245.00.
Design Tool for Use in Evaluation of Centrifugal Pumps for a Specific Piping Project.
Pt. 5. Con-Flo for Controlvalve Sizing. $195.00.
Design Utility for the Sizing of Control Values According to Instrument Society of America Standards.
Pt. 6. Ori-Flo Office Utility Program. $195.00.
Design Utility for Flat Plate Metering Orifices.

Flo-Stat. *Version:* 2.0. *Items Included:* Manual & Disk. *Customer Support:* Free.
Macintosh Plus. 3.5" disk $195.00.
Entry Level Statistical Analysis, Mapping, & Graphics Package That Includes a Maplink Feature for Linking Rows in a Statistical Worksheet with Objects in a Map, Such as Counties or Cities, for Visualizing Analyzed Data. Program Also Lets User Link Data to Maps or Pictures Created in MacDraw, Superpaint, or Canvas, & Any Other Application That Supports the Mac Clipboard. Program Can Create Numerous Types of Charts & Graphs from Data, Including Worksheets from Excel & Tab Delimited ASCII.
Senecio Software, Inc.

Flo-Stat: An Elementary Statistics, Mapping Graphics System. *Version:* 2.0. Jerry W. Wicks & Jose L. Pereira de Almeida. 1995. *Items Included:* 1 3 1/2" diskette & 1 staple-bound manual. *Customer Support:* Phone support.
Macintosh II class machines or higher, System 6. 0.7 minimum. Macintosh (1Mb). 3.5" disk $20.00 (ISBN 1-884386-00-8).
A Powerful Statistical Analysis & Graphics Package Designed for Use in the Educational & Business Setting. Its Ease of Use & Basic Statistical Routines Make It Ideal for a First Semester Statistics Course. Flo-Stat's Data Importing & Exporting Capabilities, Business Graphics, Industry-Standard Tabular Output, & Ability to Manipulate Moderately Large Data Files, Makes It the Ideal Analytic Tool for a Wide Range of Research Needs.
Senecio Software, Inc.

FLOATING-RATE+. *Version:* 7.1. Feb. 1987. *Items Included:* Complete 3-ring binder manual with room for updates, help screens behind all input stages. *Customer Support:* On-site training, unlimited telephone support & all new enhancements throughout the year.
MS-DOS 5.0 & higher (2Mb). IBM XT/AT, PS/2 & compatibles, IBM System 36, 38 & AS400MS. single-user $3000.00; Local Area Network $4500.00; Wide Area Network $10, 500.00. *Nonstandard peripherals required:* Boards; dot matrix printer, 132-column-wide carriage. *Addl. software required:* LOANLEDGER+ *Networks supported:* Novell, 3-Com, IBM PC NET.
Flexible Tool for Users Whose Rates Can Vary on a Daily Basis. Interest Is Calculated from Receipt Date to Receipt Date. Includes 99 Different Indices, Rate Floors & Ceilings. Produces Calendars of Rates for Each Day of the Year. Lets User Adjust Payments & Late Charge Amount As Required.
Dynamic Interface Systems Corp.

Flock Service Report. *Version:* 5.3. Feb. 1984. *Compatible Hardware:* IBM PC & compatibles. *Operating System(s) Required:* MS-DOS 3.0 or higher. *Language(s):* BASIC (source code included). *Memory Required:* 128k. *Customer Support:* Telephone.
disk $30.00.
Shows Weekly, Monthly, or Yearly Results. An Unlimited Number of Flocks Can Be Compared with Breeder Standards & with Each Other. Provides Information on the Following Topics: Expected Egg Production, Actual Egg Production, Expected Feed Cost per Dozen, Actual Feed Cost per Dozen, Expected Feed Consumption, Expected Feed Conversion, Actual Feed Conversion. Also Includes Totals for Brown Egg Birds, Totals for White Egg Birds, Totals by House Type, & Totals for All Birds.
Locus Systems.

FloCurve. *Version:* .02. P. L. Mariam. Jan. 1985. *Compatible Hardware:* IBM PC & compatibles, PC XT, PC AT. *Operating System(s) Required:* PC-DOS/MS-DOS 2.X, 3.0. *Memory Required:* 256k. *General Requirements:* Printer.
disk $49.95 (ISBN 0-935509-02-X, Order no.: 5200).
Prints a Flow Versus Differential Pressure Chart to Allow the User to Determine the Flow Given the Differential Pressure or the Differential When the Flow Rate Is Known. Calculates the Differential Pressure Generated from 100% Flow Rate to 8% Flow Rate.
FlowSoft, Inc.

Floor Display. *Items Included:* Installation Guide.
IBM. Contact publisher for price (ISBN 0-87321-023-9, Order no.: FDP-3075).
Activision, Inc.

Floor Plan Designer: The Do-It Yourself Architectural & Landscape Design Tool. Oct. 1994. *Items Included:* Registration card, instruction sheet. *Customer Support:* 900 support number $2.00 per minute; limited 60 day warranty.
Windows. IBM PC & compatibles (4Mb). disk $9.95 (ISBN 1-57269-010-0, Order no.: 3202 42275). *Addl. software required:* Windows 3.1 or higher. *Optimal configuration:* 4Mb RAM, SVGA or higher monitor, hard disk required, use any mouse.
Be Your Own Architect or Landscape Planner When You Have All the Tools. This Easy-to-Use Software Lets You Create Your Next Home or Update Your Current One.
Memorex Products, Inc., Memorex Software Division.

Floor Planning. *Version:* 8A. Sep. 1993. *Compatible Hardware:* PC-DOS, Xenix, Unix; 3COM, Novell, IBM RT, Unisys, NCR. *Language(s):* COBOL 85. *Memory Required:* Multi-user 3Mb or higher, single user 1000k. *General Requirements:* Integrated Accounting & the Purchase Order module. *Customer Support:* Included with the support for the Integrated Accounting.
Single user. disk $495.00.
Multi user. disk $620.00.
Provides Accurate Records on Serialized Items, Their Locations, Dates Received & Sold, & Vendor's Supplying Them. There Are Several Methods for Adding Serial Number Data for Items in Inventory. May Be Entered When Receiving Serialized Items Against a Purchase Order or Against an Existing Receiving Number. Has an Inventory Item/Serial Number Search Function. Records Receiving Number, Date Received Purchase Order Number & Vendor.
Trac Line Software, Inc.

Florida Corporation Formation Package & Minute Book. Wyman N. Bravard. May 1986. *Compatible Hardware:* IBM PC & compatibles. *Operating System(s) Required:* PC-DOS 2.0 or higher. *Memory Required:* 256k.
disk $39.95, incl. manual (ISBN 1-55571-009-3).
WORDSTAR-Compatible Word Processing Program Is Provided on the Disk, Together with the Text Files from the Book, Which Include All Letters, Bylaws, Articles of Incorporation & Other Forms Included in the Book.
Oasis Pr.

FlourTrac. Greg Griffith et al. *Items Included:* FlourTrac manual, communications software. *Customer Support:* On/site training, phone modem & telephone support, custom programming, 1 year support ($1,500.00).
MS-DOS, OS/2 (640k). IBM PC or compatible 286 to 386 processor, 16Mhz, 80Mb hard drive. $20,000.00. *Nonstandard peripherals required:* 2400 baud modem. *Optimal configuration:* MS-DOS 3.3 or greater, 640k RAM, 60Mb hard drive, 20Mhz, 386 processor. *Networks supported:* Novel Netware, IBM Token Ring, 3Comm, ATT Starlan, Alloy NTNX.
A Complete Commodity Accounting System for the Flour Milling Industry. FlourTrac Tracks Commodities from Contracting Through Delivery

FLOW

& Settlement. *Reporting Functions Include: Settlements & Checks, Daily Position Report, Vendor History Flour Mixes & Grind, Optional Lot Accounting & Mix Cost, Flour Invoicing.*
Vertical Software, Inc.

Flow. Oct. 1989. *Items Included:* Instruction included on disk. *Customer Support:* 90 days unlimited warranty.
MS-DOS, Windows 3.1. IBM XT, AT or compatible (512k). disk $49.95 plus $3.50 S&H (Order no.: 1074). *Addl. software required:* Lotus 1-2-3 Version 4.0 or higher. *Optimal configuration:* IBM AT, 640k RAM.
Cash Flow Analysis Listing Sources of Cash & Areas of Expenditure.
Compiled Systems.

Flow: Idea Processor. *Version:* 2.0. Sep. 1988. *Compatible Hardware:* Commodore Amiga. *Memory Required:* 512k. *Items Included:* disk & manual. *Customer Support:* Phone-in support available free of charge.
$99.95.
Idea (Outline) Processor That Allows Users to Interactively & Creatively Organize & Arrange Facts, Information, & Ideas into a Useful Format. Fully Supports All Features of the Amiga from Multitasking to Windows & the Mouse. Useful for Organizing Writing, Appointments, Presentations, or Categorizing & Finding Important Information. Works with PROWRITE, a Multi-Font Color Graphics Word Processor.
New Horizons Software.

Flow Master. *Customer Support:* 800-929-8117 (customer service).
MS-DOS. IBM/PS2. disk $299.99 (ISBN 0-87007-267-6).
Aids in th Analysis & Design of Piping Systems. Designed to Afford Analysisof One Individual Pipe, or a Network of up to a Thousand Pipes. Addresses the Problem of Incompressible, Steady Flow Through a Cylindrical Pipe of Uniform Cross Section.
SourceView Software International.

FLOWEL: Flow Element Sizing & Documentation. *Version:* 2.0. Nov. 1988. *Compatible Hardware:* IBM PC & compatibles. *Operating System(s) Required:* MS-DOS. *Language(s):* Compiled Advanced BASIC. *Memory Required:* 256k.
disk $595.00, incl. manual (ISBN 0-87664-903-7, Order no.: I903-7).
Performs Detailed Flow Element Sizing Calculations for Flow Element Bores for Orifice Plate Flange Taps, Pipe Taps, Corner Taps, Flow Nozzles, & Venturi Tubes.
Instrument Society of America (ISA).

Flowmaster: Pipes, Ditches & Open Channels. 1995. *Items Included:* Full manual. *Customer Support:* Free telephone support - 90 days, 30-day warranty.
MS-DOS 3.2 or higher. 286 (584k). $95.00-$495.00. *Nonstandard peripherals required:* CGA/EGA/VGA.
The Sister-Product to DYNACOMP's OPEN CHANNEL FLOW. Analyzes the Flow in Pipes, Ditches, or Channels, & Is Ideal for Most Common Sizing Calculations. Easy-to-Use. It Computes Flows & Pressures Based on Several Well-Known Formulas Such As Darcy-Weisbach (Colebrook-White), Manning's, Jutter's, & Hazen-Williams.
Dynacomp, Inc.

FLPROP. *Version:* 4.0. 1994. *Compatible Hardware:* IBM PC, PC XT, PC AT & compatibles, PS/2. *Operating System(s) Required:* PC-DOS/MS-DOS, Windows 3.1. *Language(s):* BASIC, Pascal, C. *Memory Required:* 4000k. *General Requirements:* Printer recommended. *Items Included:* Program disk & user manual. *Customer Support:* Free telephone support.
disk $149.00, incl. manual (ISBN 0-932507-00-X, Order no.: IBM-101).
Calculates Properties of Petroleum Products. Converts Specific Gravity to API & Vice Versa. Converts Viscosity from SSU/SSF to Centistokes. Calculates Viscosity & Gravity of Blended Products & at Various Temperatures & Bulk Moduli.
Systek (California).

Fludware: Lighting 2 Axis Point by Point. *Items Included:* Complete manual. *Customer Support:* Free toll-free telephone support; optional updates available at nominal charge.
MS-DOS. IBM PC & compatible (256k). disk $595.00.
Calculates Light Levels on Uniform Grid Points in Both Vertical & Horizontal Planes. Lighted Areas Can Be Indoor or Outdoor & Can Be Gridded in up to 1,600 Points. Demo Available.
Elite Software Development, Inc.

FLUENT. *Version:* 4.4. 1996. *Language(s):* FORTRAN. *Items Included:* Maintenance, documentation, training.
UNIX, VMS, HP-UX, Vulcan, Primos, Aegis, MVS/TSO, VM/CMS (8MB). Convex, Cray; DECstation, 11/780, MicroVAX, VAX 8000; HP; IBM; Masscomp; Prime; Solbourn; Sun 3, 4; SGI. contact publisher for price.
Solves Both Steady-State & Transient Navier-Stokes Equations Using Finite Volume Method in 2-D or 3-D Geometries. Fluent Models Laminar & Turbulent Flows in Stationary or Rotating Frames Using the Two Equation K-Epsilon Model, RNG Model, or the Reynolds Stress Model. Predicts Radiative & Convective Heat Transfer, Isothermal Flows or Flows with Heat Transfer, Reactive Flows with Chemical Species, Gases Laden with Dispersed Phase, Droplets (with or Without Evaporation and/or Combustion), Flow Through Porous Media, & Buoyancy Driven Flows, Menu-Driven Interface for Problem Setup & Output of Results Permits Grid Generation in Body-Fitted or Regular Coordinates & Does Not Require Knowledge of Computer Programming.
Fluent, Inc.

Fluent. *Version:* 4.4.
Windows 3.1, Windows 95 or Windows/NT. 486 or Pentium-based PC. Contact publisher for price.
A Computational Fluid Dynamics Package Ideally Suited for Modeling Turbulent Fluid Flow & Heat Transfer Problems with or Without Chemical Reactions. Has State-of-the-Art Physical Models & Special Features Required by Uses in the Power Generation, Environment, Materials Processing, Chemical Processing & Petrochemical Industries. Includes a True CAD Preprocessor for Geometry Modeling & Mesh Generation & Import/Modification of Models from Other CAD/CAE Software. Two Solver Modules, for Structured & Unstructured Meshes, Provide Unmatched Flexibility & Power in Terms of Mesh Type, Numerical Methods & Physical Models. A Modern Graphical User Interface, Convenient Model Definition Toolkits & Powerful 3D Graphics Make Possible Easy Model Building, Solution & Postprocessing.
Fluent, Inc.

Fluent/UNS. *Version:* 4.0.
AIX 3.2.5. IBM RS6000 UNIX workstations. Contact publisher for price.
A Computational Fluid Dynamics Package Ideally Suited for Modeling Turbulent Fluid Flow & Heat Transfer Problems in & Around Complex Geometries Encountered in Automotive Applications. Provides Unparalleled Mesh Flexibility since Triangular, Quadrilateral, Tetrahedral, Hexahedral, Prismatic & Other Element Shapes Can All Be Utilized. Includes a True CAD Preprocessor for Geometry Modeling & Mesh Generation & Import/Modification of Models from Other CAD/CAE Software. State-of-the-Art Numerical Methods & Physical Models for Automotive Flows Are Provided Within the Framework of a Solver Capable of Utilizing Fully Unstructured & On-the-Fly Solution Adaptive Meshes. A Modern Graphical User Interface, Convenient Model Definition Toolkits & Powerful 3D Graphics Make Possible Easy Model Building, Solution & Postprocessing.
Fluent, Inc.

Fluent Laser Fonts: True Type Starter Set. Jun. 1991. *Customer Support:* Free phone support.
Macintosh. 3.5" disk $29.95 (Order no.: M091).
22 True Type Typefaces & a 6 Month Subscription Offer to Publish Magazine.
Casady & Greene, Inc.

Fluid/Gas Flow Collection I: Steam, Gas, Liquid, & Paper Stock. 1995. *Items Included:* Full manual. *Customer Support:* Free telephone support - 90 days, 30-day warranty.
MS-DOS 3.2 or higher. 286 (584k). disk $949.95. *Nonstandard peripherals required:* CGA/EGA/VGA.
Composed of the Following Six Gas/Fluid Flow Modules: Steam I Will Either Size a Steam Line Based on Criteria, or Give the Pressure Drop Through a Line That Has Been Sized. Steam II Allows You to Preliminarily Pre-Size All the Lines in a Steam System When the Steam Temperature & Steam Pressure Are the Only Two Things Actually Known. Liquid Piping I Allows You to Preliminarily Pre-Size All the Lines in a Liquid Piping System Based on a Maximum Velocity. Liquid Piping II Assists the Piping Designer in Preliminarily Sizing Pulp & Paper Stock Lines. All Theory Is Based on the University of Maine's Correlation of Brecht & Heller Data. Liquid Piping III Assists Piping Designers in Sizing Stock Lines Using the Method Outlined in the TAPPI Technical Information Sheet (TIS) 408-4. Gas System Piping Allows User to Preliminarily Pre-Size All the Lines in a Gas System When the Temperature, Pressure, Specific Gravity, & Viscosity Are the Only Things Known.
Dynacomp, Inc.

Fluid Mechanics Programs for the IBM PC. *Version:* IBM. D. B. Olfe. Nov. 1986. *Compatible Hardware:* IBM PC. *Memory Required:* 64k. *General Requirements:* CGA card. *Items Included:* 1 disk & documentation.
disk $26.36 (ISBN 0-07-831114-4).
Provides Flow Visualization Using Computer Graphics, & Organizes Problem Solutions into Computer Programs. Extends the Material Included in White: FLUID MECHANICS by Providing Computed Solutions to Problems Not Worked Out in the Textbook.
McGraw-Hill, Inc.

FLX-I-SORT. *Operating System(s) Required:* CP/M, 2.2. *Memory Required:* 32k. *Customer Support:* 800-929-8117 (customer service).
MS-DOS. contact publisher for price.
Performance Oriented Disk File Sort, Designed for Efficient Memory & Disk Storage Usage.
SourceView Software Internstional.

Flying Fortress B-17. Aug. 1992. *Items Included:* Manual, keyboard summary, poster. *Customer Support:* Free customer service, 1-410-771-1151, Ext. 350.
80286 minimum, 80386 recommended. IBM PC, AT, PS/2 or 100% compatibles (640k). disk $69.95 (ISBN 1-55884-191-1). *Optimal*

TITLE INDEX

configuration: VGA/MCGA graphics, DOS 3.0 or higher, 5.0 recommended. Keyboard or joystick recommended.
Accurately Recreates the Hazards & Challenges of Piloting This Legendary Aircraft on Bombing Missions over Occupied Europe. Authentic Flight Dynamics, Ordnance & the Ability to Take Control of Any Crew Position Will Provide Hours of Entertainment. Customize Your B-17 with Authentic Nose Art. Fully Functional, Completely Authentic Cockpit.
MicroProse Software.

FM Music Composer. *Compatible Hardware:* CX5M & other MSX systems.
contact publisher for price (Order no.: YRM 101).
User Generates an On-Screen Music Staff onto Which They "Write" Notes by Entering Them from the Computer Keyboard or Directly from the Music Keyboard. Up to Eight Parts Can Be Entered & Each Part Can Be Assigned a Different "Instrument".
Yamaha Corp. of America.

FM Music Macro. *Compatible Hardware:* CX5M or other MSX systems.
contact publisher for price (Order no.: YRM 104).
Allows Users to Incorporate Musical Voices into Their BASIC Programs. Adds a Special Set of Commands to BASIC, Permitting Control of the Digital FM Voice Generator.
Yamaha Corp. of America.

FM Voicing Program. *Compatible Hardware:* CX5M & other MSX systems.
contact publisher for price (Order no.: YRM 102).
Gives User Control over the CX5M Digital FM Voice Generator to Edit & Alter the Pre-Programmed Voices or Create New Ones.
Yamaha Corp. of America.

Focal Point II. Nov. 1989.
Macintosh Plus, SE or II. disk $199.95 (Order no.: ID-183). *Nonstandard peripherals required:* Hard disk.
User Can Keep Track of Appointments, Tasks & Activities with the Linked Daily & Monthly Calendars & To-Do List. Schedule Recurring Appointments with One Simple Entry & Set an Alarm to Alert You Ahead of Time. Plan, Execute & Track Projeacts, with Ease & Efficiency. Create Proposal, Then Turn It into a Complete Set of Project Specifications. Automatic Merging of Milestones into Your To-Do List. Print Out Calendars, Task Lists, & over 60 Other Reports in Multiple Formats, Including Three Popular Organizer Sizes.
10.0.

FOCTALK. *Version:* 2.0. May 1987. *Memory Required:* 512k. *General Requirements:* Modem or IRMA Card.
$450.00.
Stand-Alone Micro-to-Mainframe Link That Enables Users of Hard Disk Based Systems to Specify, Access & Transfer Data from Mainframe File or Database Acessible Through the Use of FOCUS Report Writer (Residing on the Mainframe). Allows Files to Be Created on the PC for Transfer to the Mainframe, As Well As the Building of FOCUS Report Requests on the PC for Execution on the Mainframe. Executed Reports Can Be Downloaded to the PC in Either ASCII, DIF or LOTUS PRN Formats. Features Include LINK Communications Facility. TABLETALK, FILETALK & TED (the Full-Screen Editor).
Information Builders, Inc.

Focus. *Version:* 5.2. *Compatible Hardware:* DEC MicroVAX, VAX 8978.
MicroVAX 2000. $6800.00.
VAX 8978. $155,700.00.
Read-only Interfaces. $900.00-$10,000.00.
Read-Write. $1,695.00-$18,925.00.
Includes Full Application Development Capabilities for SQL Databases. Also Features Read & Update Interfaces.
Information Builders, Inc.

Focus. *Compatible Hardware:* IBM PC AT, PS/2 & compatibles, Sun, Apollo, Pyramid, NCR Tower, Motorola 6000, AT&T 3B2, Unix System V. *Operating System(s) Required:* MS-DOS/PC-DOS 2.0 or higher.
DOS version. $1295.00.
Unix version. $450.00 to $50,000.00.
4GL Database-Management System.
Information Builders, Inc.

Focus for Unix 4GL/DBMS. *Compatible Hardware:* Unix & compatibles.
$1,000.00 to $15,850.00.
Includes SQL Translator & Networking Enhancements. Allows SQL Statements to Generate Requests Against Focus Databases & Sequential Files. Enhancements Include Remote File System Support, & Bidirectional File Transfer & Application Portability Between Unix Machines, Between Unix-Based Computers & Personal Computers, & Between Unix-Based Computers & Mainframes.
Information Builders, Inc.

Focus 4GL/DBMS. *Version:* 5.2. *Compatible Hardware:* DEC VAX.
MicroVAX 2000 $6800.00.
VAX 8978 cluster $15,570.00.
Includes ModifyTalk, a New Automatic Application Generator, Integration with the DEC All-In-One Office Automation Package, & a New Application Migration Facility.
Information Builders, Inc.

Focus Interface. *Compatible Hardware:* DEC VAX.
$1750.00 to $8500.00.
Ability to Link a Focus 4GL/DBMS with an Ingres Relational Database Management System from Relational Technology. Allows the Relational Joining of Ingres Tables to DBMS, Rdb, RMS, Sybase, Oracle & Focus Files. Also Allows All Focus Reporting, Graphics, Spreadsheet & Data Analysis Capabilities to Transparently Access Data Stored in Ingres Databases.
Information Builders, Inc.

Fogle Accounts Payable. *Version:* 3.03. Jan. 1985. *Compatible Hardware:* IBM PC, PC XT, PC AT, PS/2. *Operating System(s) Required:* PC-DOS. *Language(s):* Compiled BASIC. *Memory Required:* 512k. *General Requirements:* Fixed disk. *Items Included:* Reference manual, tutorial manual. *Customer Support:* Phone/modem support included first year, nominal fee thereafter.
disk $400.00 (ISBN 0-924068-12-4, Order no.: AP1).
Payable System Including Invoice Management (Entry, Purchase Journal, Aging Report, Hold/Partial Payment, Recurring Payments, & Check Writing), Vendor Management & Ability to Print Checks for One-Time Vendor. Handles Early Payment Discounts.
Fogle Computing Corp.

Fogle Accounts Receivable. *Version:* 3.0. Jun. 1985. *Compatible Hardware:* IBM PC, PC XT, PC AT, PS/2. *Operating System(s) Required:* PC-DOS. *Language(s):* Compiled BASIC. *Memory Required:* 512k. *Items Included:* Reference manual. *Customer Support:* Phone/modem support included first year, nominal fee thereafter.
disk $400.00 (Order no.: AR1).
Manages Receivable, Prints Invoices & Aging Reports, & Handles Late Charges & Early Payment Discounts.
Fogle Computing Corp.

Fogle General Ledger. *Version:* 3.03. Apr. 1982. *Compatible Hardware:* IBM PC, PC AT, PC XT, PS/2. *Operating System(s) Required:* PC-DOS. *Language(s):* Compiled BASIC. *Memory Required:* 512k. *Items Included:* Reference manual. *Customer Support:* Phone/modem support included first year, nominal fee thereafter.
disk $400.00 (ISBN 0-924068-07-8, Order no.: GL1).
Features Full Screen Data Entry (8 Debits & 8 Credits on Screen at the Same Time), Repeating Transactions, Comparison to Month by Month Budget & to Last Year's Data.
Fogle Computing Corp.

Fogle Payroll. *Version:* 3.03. Jan. 1985. *Compatible Hardware:* IBM PC, PC AT, PC XT, PS/2. *Operating System(s) Required:* PC-DOS. *Language(s):* Compiled BASIC. *Memory Required:* 512k. *Items Included:* Reference manual. *Customer Support:* Phone/modem support included first year, nominal fee thereafter.
disk $500.00 (ISBN 0-924068-13-2, Order no.: PA1).
Payroll System Featuring Employee Record Management, Multiple Distribution of Employee's Wage Expense, Computation of All Withholdings, Allows Other Deductions, Payroll Register, Payroll Summary, Pay History (Month, Quarter, Year), Check Writing (One Employee, by Department, by Pay Period), & Generates Information for Form 941 & W-2's.
Fogle Computing Corp.

FolderBolt for Windows: Integrated Security for Windows Directories. Sep. 1993. *Items Included:* Manual. *Customer Support:* Free, unlimited technical support, 90 day warranty.
MS-DOS 5, Windows 3.1. disk $99.00.
Protects Your Folders/Directories with a Password. Create Completely Locked Folders, Read-Only Folders, or Password-Protected Drop Box Folders. No One Without the Password Can Open, Duplicate, Delete, or Move Them. File Encryption, from the Fastest (LightningCrypt) to the Most Rigorous (Triple DES), Also Included. Administrator Override Available.
Kent Marsh Ltd.

FolderBolt: Integrated Security for the Macintosh Desktop. *Version:* 1.02. Apr. 1991. *Items Included:* Manual. *Customer Support:* Free, unlimited technical support, 90 day warranty. Macintosh System 6.04 or higher. Macintosh (512k). 3.5" disk $129.95.
Protects Your Folders (Including Your System Folder) with a Password. Create Completely Locked Folders, Read-Only Folders, or Password-Protected Drop Box Folders. No One Without the Password Can Open, Duplicate, Delete, or Move Them. Can Unlock All Your Folders at Once & Re-Lock Them on Shutdown. Also Generates a Complete Audit Trail of Failed Attempts. Combine FolderBolt with Other Security Products from Kent Marsh Ltd. for Comprehensive Protection Second to None.
Kent Marsh Ltd.

Follow-Up. *Version:* 2.1. *Compatible Hardware:* IBM PC, PC XT, & compatibles. *Operating System(s) Required:* PC-DOS/MS-DOS 2.0 & higher. *Language(s):* Pascal, Assembly. *Memory Required:* 256k. *General Requirements:* 2 disk

FONE*DATA

drives, printer; hard disk recommended. *Customer Support:* (802) 672-5194.
disk $495.00.
Provides a Method for Tracking Information about Current or Prospective Customers, Clients & Members of Organizations. Direct Word Processor Capability, Report Generation, Tickler Generation, & Multiple Levels of Sorts on Data, Translation Facility for Languages Other Than English.
CompuCepts, Inc.

Fone*Data. Aug. 1993. *Items Included:* Diskettes & manual. *Customer Support:* Toll free product information line, technical support-unlimited at no charge; 30 day money back.
DOS 3.0 or higher. IBM & compatibles. $495.00; single update $150.00; Automatic update $95.00; updates every 6 mos. *Addl. software required:* Database or Data Reading Program. *Optimal configuration:* 386/486 5Mb hard drive space free.
Provides a Cross-Reference of Zip Code to Area Code/Prefix. The Database Provides a Latitude & Longitude of Each Area Code & Prefix. There Are Three Zip Codes Listed with Each Record, Each A Zipcode Associated W/That AC/Prefix MSA & County FIPS Codes Are Also Provided.
Mailer's Software.

FONE800: Your Toll-Free Telecommunications Resource. *Version:* 3.1. Jul. 1994. *Items Included:* Document included with package, manual on disk. *Customer Support:* Phone support, promotion item & site license(s), upgrade discounts.
MS-DOS 3.3 or higher, PC-DOS, DR-DOS, MS Windows. PC & compatibles (286 or higher) & DOS equipped MACs, Workstations (640k). disk $34.95 (ISBN 1-884384-11-0, Order no.: 11164). *Optimal configuration:* PC 640k RAM, hard disk, MS-DOS 3.3 or higher, color monitor.
A System for Storing, Updating, & Placing Toll-Free ("800") Telephone Calls. The Major Function Is to Collect & Organize a Library of Personal, Information, Consumer, & Health Related "800" Telephone Numbers. Menu-Driven Program Can Even Dial the Number Thru a Modem Equipped Computer. Although the Program Comes with a Sample Data Base of over 4000 Entries of Toll-Free Numbers, the User Can Add, Delete, & Update, the Data Base to Conform to Their Individual Personal Tastes & Requirements.
Eugene L. Woods, PE.

FONE800: Your Toll-Free Telecommunications Resource. *Version:* 2.1. Jul. 1994. *Items Included:* Document included with package, manual on disk. *Customer Support:* Phone support, promotion item & site license(s), upgrade discounts.
MS-DOS 3.3 or higher, PC-DOS, DR-DOS, MS Windows. PC & compatibles (286 or higher) & DOS equipped MACs, Workstations (640k). disk $34.95 (ISBN 1-884384-10-2, Order no.: 11164). *Optimal configuration:* PC 640k RAM, hard disk, MS-DOS 3.3 or higher, color monitor.
A System for Storing, Updating, & Placing Toll-Free ("800") Telephone Calls. The Major Function Is to Collect & Organize a Library of Personal, Information, Consumer, & Health Related "800" Telephone Numbers. Menu-Driven Program Can Even Dial the Number Thru a Modem Equipped Computer. Although the Program Comes with a Sample Data Base of over 4000 Entries of Toll-Free Numbers, the User Can Add, Delete, & Update, the Data Base to Conform to Their Individual Personal Tastes & Requirements.
Eugene L. Woods, PE.

FONE: Manage Communication Costs. *Version:* 6.3. Aug. 1994. *Items Included:* Document included with package, manual on disk. *Customer Support:* Phone support, promotion item & site license(s), upgrade discounts.
MS-DOS 3.3 or higher, PC-DOS, DR-DOS, MS Windows. PC & compatibles (286 or higher) & DOS equipped MACs, Workstations (640k). disk $49.95 (ISBN 1-884384-01-3, Order no.: 11163). *Optimal configuration:* PC 640k RAM, hard disk, MS-DOS 3.3 or higher, color monitor.
This Full-Featured Program Handles Everything from Address Labels, to a Handy Appointment Calendar, to Maintaining a FASTFONE List of Frequently Called Numbers, to Providing an On-Screen Note Pad for Each Contact Entry in the Data Base. Cost-Time Records Can Be Obtained Without a Modem, or Will Dial Your Calls Thru Your Modem.
Eugene L. Woods, PE.

FONE: Manage Communication Costs. *Version:* 6.2. Aug. 1993. *Items Included:* Document included with package, manual on disk. *Customer Support:* Phone support, promotion item & site license(s), upgrade discounts.
MS-DOS 3.3 or higher, PC-DOS, DR-DOS, MS Windows. PC & compatibles (286 or higher) & DOS equipped MACs, Workstations (640k). disk $49.95 (ISBN 1-884384-00-5). *Optimal configuration:* PC 640k RAM, hard disk, MS-DOS 3.3 or higher, color monitor.
This Full-Featured Program Handles Everything from Address Labels, to a Handy Appointment Calendar, to Maintaining a FASTFONE List of Frequently Called Numbers, to Providing an On-Screen Note Pad for Each Contact Entry in the Data Base. Cost-Time Records Can Be Obtained Without a Modem, or Will Dial Your Calls Thru Your Modem.
Eugene L. Woods, PE.

FONE900: Your Audiotex Cost Management Resource. *Version:* 2.1. Mar. 1994. *Items Included:* Document included with package, manual optional. *Customer Support:* Phone support, site license, upgrade discounts.
MS-DOS/PC-DOS, DR-DOS, MS Windows. PC & compatibles (286 or higher) & DOS equipped MACs, Workstations (640k). disk $35.00 (ISBN 1-884384-21-8, Order no.: 11229). *Optimal configuration:* PC 640k RAM, hard disk, MS-DOS 3.3 or higher, color monitor.
A Comprehensive Telephone Call Pricing Data Base Program That Calculates the Approximate Cost of AUDIOTEX Calls Before Placed, Displays On-Going Call Cost in Real Time, & Serves As a Powerful Business-Personal Directory Management Tool. The Major Function of the Program Is to Collect & Organize a Library of Personal, Informational, Consumer, & Health Related "900" Telephone Numbers. Menu-Driven Program Can Even Dial the Number Thru a Modem Equipped Computer. Comes with Example Data Base of Audiotex Entry Types That the User Can Modify, Add to, Delete, & Update, to Conform to Their Individual Personal Tastes & Requirements.
Eugene L. Woods, PE.

FONE900: Your Audiotex Cost Management Resource. *Version:* 1.1. Mar. 1993. *Items Included:* Document included with package, manual optional. *Customer Support:* Phone support, site license, upgrade discounts.
MS-DOS, PC-DOS, DR-DOS, MS Windows. PC & compatibles (286 or higher) & DOS equipped MACs, Workstations (640k). disk $35.00 (ISBN 1-884384-20-X). *Optimal configuration:* PC 640k RAM, hard disk, MS-DOS 3.3 or higher, color monitor.
A Comprehensive Telephone Call Pricing Data Base Program That Calculates the Approximate Cost of AUDIOTEX Calls Before Placed, Displays On-Going Call Cost in Real Time, & Serves As a Powerful Business-Personal Directory Management Tool. The Major Function of the Program Is to Collect & Organize a Library of Personal, Informational, Consumer, & Health Related "900" Telephone Numbers. Menu-Driven Program Can Even Dial the Number Thru a Modem Equipped Computer. Comes with Example Data Base of Audiotex Entry Types That the User Can Modify, Add to, Delete, & Update, to Conform to Their Individual Personal Tastes & Requirements.
Eugene L. Woods, PE.

FONE: Your Call Pricing Program of Choice. *Version:* 6.3. Aug. 1994. *Items Included:* Telecommunications information file, & extensive help file via main menu selection & F1 Hot Key field help. *Customer Support:* Mailing list for updates/new software: telephone support plus super discounts on updates & other software products for registered users; limited warranty.
DOS 3.3 or higher. IBM PC & compatibles (640k). disk $49.95 (ISBN 1-884384-01-3). *Nonstandard peripherals required:* Hard disk. *Optimal configuration:* PC/PC compatible, DOS 5.0, 640k, hard disk.
USA & International Telcom Users! Have You Ever Wondered "Ahead of Time" What It Would Cost to Make a Phone Call? FONE Provides You with the Answer As Well As "Real Time" Phone/FAX Call Pricing by Showing Accumulated Charges On-Screen During Your Call. FONE Will Save You Money by Telling You the Best Time to Place Your Call at the Lowest Rate. Over 130 Countries Are Available for International Calls. If You Have a Modem, You Can Auto-Dial from a Customizable On-Line Directory (Now with Auto Redial). Other Features Include Area Code Look-Up, WATS Service, & Much More. Use FONE Sample Rates or Your Own Point-to-Point Rates. This Sophisticated, Menu-Driven Program Is Elegant & Very Easy to Use. Report(s): Print Call Log, Estimated Bill, Address Labels, & More.
Eugene L. Woods, PE.

FONE800: Your Personal Toll-Free Data Base. *Version:* 3.1. May 1994. *Items Included:* Where to find 800 numbers file, 4000 sample DB file, & help file. *Customer Support:* Mailing list for updates/new software; telephone support plus super discounts on updates & other software products for registered users; limited warranty.
DOS 3.3 or higher. IBM PC & compatibles (640k). disk $34.95 (ISBN 1-884384-11-0). *Nonstandard peripherals required:* Hard disk. *Optimal configuration:* PC/PC compatible, DOS 5.0, 640k, hard disk.
USA & International Telcom Users! Trying to Find a Toll-Free 800 Number? Don't Touch That Phone! 800 Information Could Be a Keystroke Away. If You've Ever Called Long Distance Only to Learn Later That You Could Have Called an 800 Number, FONE800 Will Save You a Bundle. This Database of over 4000 Toll-Free Numbers Gets You Started & Can Be Easily Added to & Modify. Sorted by Categories Just Like Your Regular Phone Book, the Number You Need Is Quickly Located. There's Even a Brief Description of the Company. Have a Modem? Let FONE800 Dial the Number for you! A Memo Pad Keeps Track of Your Conversation, & a Hot Key Shows Your Previous Conversation Notes. Requires a 720k or Higher Floppy Drive & a Hard Disk.
Eugene L. Woods, PE.

FONE900: Your Personal AUDIOTEX Data Base. *Version:* 2.1. Nov. 1993. *Items Included:* Where to find 900 numbers file, sample data base, & help file. *Customer Support:* Mailing list

TITLE INDEX

FONTOGRAPHER

for updates/new software; telephone support plus super discounts on updates & other software products for registered users; limited warranty. DOS 3.3 or higher. IBM PC & compatibles (640k). disk $35.00 (ISBN 1-884384-21-8). Nonstandard peripherals required: Hard disk. *Optimal configuration:* PC/PC compatible, DOS 5.0, 640k, hard disk.
Many Companies Now Have 900 Phone Numbers, & We All Know How Much It Costs to Dial Them. Or Do We? Now You Can Track Every 900 Call from This Custom Database. FONE900 Calculates the Charges Before You Call, Then Monitors Call Duration & Cost. Also Features a Time/Date-Stamped Memo Pad, Optional Modem Dialing, & a Sample Database That Easily Expands to Hold All Your 900 Numbers.
Eugene L. Woods, PE.

Font/DA Juggler Plus. *Items Included:* 51-page user manual. 33-page utilities manual. *Customer Support:* Telephone support 713-353-1510, 90-day repair or replacement of faulty manual or defective disk.
Mac-DOS 5.0 or higher (512k). Macintosh 512KE or higher. disk $59.95. *Networks supported:* Most AppleTalk including AppleShare, TOPS & MacServe.
Font/Desk Accessory (DA)FKey/Sound Utility. Greatly Extends Power of Macintosh by Giving User Access to Hundreds of Fonts, DAs, FKeys & Sounds Simultaneously. System Resources Remain in Font/DA Mover or FKey/Sound Mover Files & Are Opened by Font/DA Juggler Plus. Features 100% MultiFinder Compatibility, Font Compression, DA List, Font List, Sound List, User-Definable Hot Keys & Much More.
ALSoft, Inc.

Font Downloader & Editor. *Compatible Hardware:* Apple II+, IIe, & compatibles; Franklin Ace. *Operating System(s) Required:* Apple DOS 3.3. *General Requirements:* Printer, parallel printer card.
disk $39.00.
User Can Design Special Types of Custom Characters, Foreign Language Symbols, Math or Electronic Symbols. Fonts for ProWriter, Apple Dot-Matrix, & Apple ImageWriter Are Provided. Additional Fonts Are Available on Separate Font Library Disks.
Micro-W Distributing, Inc.

Font Effects. *Version:* 1.2. *Compatible Hardware:* IBM PC & compatibles.
disk $95.00.
Utility Which Enables Users to Process Bit-Mapped Fonts in the SoftCraft or HP SoftFonts Format, SoftCraft EDF File, or Aldus/Microsoft Windows TIFF Format. Users Can Add Special Effects Such As Shadows, Outlines, Contours, or Patterns.
Softcraft, Inc. (Wisconsin).

Font Factory GS. *Version:* 1.3. Wilfried Ricken. Jul. 1989. *Items Included:* Extra font disk. *Customer Support:* 11-5 Mon-Fri EST 904-576-9415 or on-line through AppleLink, America Online, GEnie & CompuServe.
GS/OS (768k). Apple IIGS. 3.5" disk $39.95 (Order no.: 4030). *Optimal configuration:* Apple IIGS, 768k memory, 2 3.5" disk drive, monitor & printer.
A Font Editor That Can Be Used to Change Fonts or Create New Fonts, Symbols or Pictures That Can Be Used With Word Processing, Desktop Publishing & Drawing Programs. Compatible Programs Can Run on Any Apple II as Long as They Support "Standard IIGS Fonts".
Seven Hills Software Corp.

Font Mechanic. Mark Simonsen & Jon Simonsen. Dec. 1985. *Compatible Hardware:* Apple II, IIe, IIc, IIgs. *Operating System(s) Required:* Apple DOS 3.3, ProDOS. *Language(s):* Machine, BASIC. *Memory Required:* DOS 3.3 48k, ProDOS 64k. *General Requirements:* Shape Mechanic program.
disk $29.95.
Companion to SHAPE MECHANIC & BEAGLE SCREENS Disks. It Gives 30 New Fonts, Plus a Set of Utilities for Manipulating Shape Fonts As Well As Fonts from Other Sources. Users Are Allowed to Convert Non-Shape Table Fonts from Disks Like Apple's DOS TOOL KIT, HIGHER TEXT, HIGHER FONTS, the PENGUIN Disks, BEAGLE GRAPHICS, etc. Users Can Change the Horizontal &/or Vertical Dimensions of a Font for Special Emphasis or Special Effects.
Beagle Brothers.

Font Solution Pack. *Version:* 2.0. May 1988. *Customer Support:* Free technical support (phone toll only).
PC- or MS-DOS 3.1 or higher (512k). IBM PC, AT or compatible. disk $495.00. *Addl. software required:* Ventura Publisher, Aldus PageMaker, or Microsoft Windows; or Microsoft Word, WordPerfect, or OfficeWriter.
Package to Provide, Create, Customize, Add Special Effects to, & Install Bitmap Soft Fonts for the Most Popular PC Desktop Publishing Packages & Word Processors & HP LaserJet Series II Compatibles.
SoftCraft, Inc. (Wisconsin).

Font Special Effects Pack. Aug. 1988. *Customer Support:* Free technical support (phone toll only).
PC- or MS-DOS 3.1 or higher (512k). IBM PC, AT or compatible. disk $295.00. *Addl. software required:* Ventura Publisher, Aldus PageMaker, or Microsoft Windows; or Microsoft Word, WordPerfect, or OfficeWriter.
Package to Provide, Customize, Add Special Effects to, & Install Bitmap Soft Fonts for the Most Popular PC Desktop Publishing Packages & Word Processors & HP LaserJet Series II Compatibles.
Softcraft, Inc. (Wisconsin).

Font Works for Macintosh. *Items Included:* Browser/installer/launcher front end software. *Customer Support:* 90 day warranty, free call back technical support.
System 6. Any Mac. CD-ROM disk $9.95. *Nonstandard peripherals required:* CD-ROM drive. *Networks supported:* Apple File Sharing.
BeachWare.

Fontagenix. *Compatible Hardware:* Apple Macintosh. *General Requirements:* Image Writer. Fontagenix I, II, III (Valfonts Collection) or IV. 3.5" disk $39.50 ea.
All four. 3.5" disk $139.50.
Fontagenix I Is a Collection of 11 Bitmap (Dot Matrix) Fonts. Fontagenix II Is a Collection of 11 Bitmap Fonts. Fontagenix III (Valfonts Collection) Is a Collection of 12 Biptmap Fonts. Fontagenix IV Is a Collection of 13 Bitmap Fonts.
Devonian International Software Co.

Fontastic Plus. *Version:* 2.0. *Compatible Hardware:* Apple Macintosh. *Items Included:* Disk, user guide. *Customer Support:* Yes, telephone & BBS.
3.5" disk $99.95.
Specialized Bitmap Font Editor Designed to Create New Fonts & Typefaces or Customize Different Character Sets. User Can Create Bitmapped Logos, Foreign Characters, Clip Art & Custom Fonts. Scaling (up to 127 Points High), Rotation, Styling, & Editing Capabilities Make Font & Graphic Design Easier. Includes Such Features as Kerning Pairs & Fractional Character Widths; Allows for Printing on QuickDraw Printers. Also Has Integrated Font Mover.
Altsys Corp.

FontFiddler: Kerning Editor. Jul. 1993. *Items Included:* Manual, registration card. *Customer Support:* Free support.
Windows 3.1. IBM PC & compatibles (2Mb). disk $99.95 (ISBN 1-879464-05-5). *Addl. software required:* TrueType, PostScript Type 1. *Optimal configuration:* 486 33Mz with 4Mb RAM & a hard disk. *Networks supported:* Ethernet.
Ares Software Corp.

FontGen V.1. 1993. *Compatible Hardware:* IBM PC. *Operating System(s) Required:* MS-DOS 2.X or higher. *Memory Required:* 520k. *General Requirements:* Laser printer. *Items Included:* VS laser word processor tool kit, font selection, manuals. *Customer Support:* Telephone (no charge), FAX/Mail/BBS.
$295.00.
Font Editor/Generator for High Speed Precision Design of Fonts, Special Symbols, & Logos at 300 or 600 dpi Resolution. Features On-Line Help, Pop-Up Menus, WYSIWYG Display, Single Keystroke Commands, Rubberbanded Design Tools, Preview Editing, & Global Function. Supports Mouse & Several Scanners. Now Supports Seven Different Font Formats.
VS Software.

Fontina. *Version:* Boston. Aug. 1991. *Customer Support:* Toll-free tech support hotline.
Macintosh System 6 or System 7. Macintosh (512k). 3.5" disk $69.96. *Optimal configuration:* Macintosh 512k or higher.
Improves All Macintosh Font Menus, Replacing Conventional Scrolling Menus with Fast, Productive Multi-Column Tables. Groups Related Fonts Together, Displays Samples of Selected Fonts, & Is Compatible with All Macintosh Software.
Eastgate Systems, Inc.

FontMonger. *Version:* 1.0.4. Apr. 1991. Macintosh & Windows 3.0. 3.5" disk $99.95 (Order no.: FM1000).
Provides Type Format Conversion in Any Direction, Among PostScript Type 1, Type 3, & TrueType Fonts. It Converts Type to Adobe Illustrator or EPS Files, So User Can Combine Graphics & Type, Then Install the Results Back Into a Font. Type Modification Abilities Include Access to Unencoded Characters, Generating Custom Oblique Characters, Generating Superior & Inferior Characters, & Generating En & EM Fractions.
Ares Software Corp.

FontMonger Windows. Apr. 1992. *Items Included:* Dual media - 3.5" & 5.25" disks included; manual. *Customer Support:* Technical support available.
Microsoft Windows 3.0 or higher. IBM 286, 386, 486, & compatibles. disk $149.95 (ISBN 1-879464-01-2). *Addl. software required:* Windows, outline fonts in TrueType, Intellifont, PostScript Type 1, PostScript Type 3, or Nimbus Q format.
Bridges Competing Font Technologies by Letting Desktop Publishers Convert Between Adobe PostScript Type 1 & Type 3, Intellifont, Nimbus Q & TrueType (for Windows 3.1). Converted Fonts Can Be Saved for IBM PC & compatibles, Macintosh & NeXT Computers. Product Allows User to Modify Character Outlines with Built-In Drawing Tools or Generate Customized Typefaces & Characters Such As Obliques, Fractions & Small Caps. Copy & Paste Characters to Create a New Font.
Ares Software Corp.

Fontographer. *Version:* 3.5. *Compatible Hardware:* Macintosh; IBM PC & compatible; NeXT workstations. *Memory Required:* 1000k.

Items Included: Manual, tutorial, unlimited technical support, five free fonts, complimentary copy of STYLE MERGER (an Altsys utility that merges styled fonts into one font family). *Customer Support:* Telephone & BBS support.
3.5" disk $495.00.
Provides the Means to Develop Professional Typographic Character Sets. As a Specialized Graphics Editor, Product Gives User the Ability to Produce POSTSCRIPT Language Fonts for the Macintosh, IBM PC, & NeXT Workstations As Well As TRUETYPE Fonts for the Macintosh & PC. Designers Can Also Modify Existing Typefaces, Incorporate POSTSCRIPT Artwork, Automatically Trace Scanned Images, & Utilize Flexible Tools to Create Designs from Scratch. New Features Include: Freehand Drawing Tool Which Allows for Professional & Precise Inline & Outline Drawing with Either the Mouse or Alternate Input Methods Such As Pressure Sensitive Pen Systems & Digitizing Tablets; Calligraphic Pen Tool Which Allows the Creation of Calligraphic Fonts with the Mouse, Pressure-Sensitive Pens, or Digitizing Tablets; Variable-Weight Pen Tool; Font Interpolation; Change Weight; Multiple Master Font Technology; Hint Editing.
Altsys Corp.

FontPack Plus. *Compatible Hardware:* Commodore 64, 128. *Operating System(s) Required:* GEOS or GEOS 128.
disk $29.95.
Collection of 53 Fonts for Use with GEOS Applications.
Berkeley Softworks.

Fontpak. *Compatible Hardware:* Apple II+, IIe, IBM PC, PC XT. *Operating System(s) Required:* Apple DOS 3.3; PC-DOS/MS-DOS 2.0 or higher. *Language(s):* Assembly. *Memory Required:* 512k.
disk $25.00 ea.
Companion Volumes to the FONTRIX Graphics Software Package (Which Is Required in Order to Use Them) & Range in Their Thematic Organization from Standard & Decorative Typefaces to Special Applications, Including Arts, Sciences, Engineering, Design & Foreign Languages.
Data Transforms, Inc.

FontPrint. Delmer D. Hinrichs. Jun. 1985. *Compatible Hardware:* IBM PC & compatibles; TRS-80 Model I. *Operating System(s) Required:* MS-DOS, TRSDOS. *Language(s):* Compiled BASIC (source code included). *Memory Required:* TRS-DOS 48k, MS-DOS 128k. *General Requirements:* Epson, Gemini, or IBM 9-pin dot-matrix graphics printer. *Items Included:* Disk & instructions. *Customer Support:* Free.
TRS-DOS. disk $10.00.
IBM. disk $15.00.
Prints Text Files from the Corresponding Hinrichs Software Word Processors. Output Is in Any of 10 Special Graphic Fonts, Including Script. Options Include: Proportional Spaced, Justified, Double Strike, Underline, & Overstrike.
Hinrichs Software.

Fontrix (Apple). *Version:* 1.55. Duke Houston & Steve Boker. Aug. 1984. *Compatible Hardware:* Apple II+, IIe, IIc, IIgs, III (in emulation). *Operating System(s) Required:* Apple DOS 3.3. *Language(s):* C & Assembly. *Memory Required:* 64K.
Apple. disk $95.00.
Fontpak. additional 10-font disk $25.00 ea.
Graphics & Typesetting Program Gives Users the Ability to Mix Text & Graphics on a Workspace Formatted to Fill an Entire Printed Page by Using Virtual Graphics. Package Includes Three Menu-Driven Programs: THE GRAPHIC WRITER Contains All the Tools for Typesetting, Drawing, & Painting on the Graphics Workspace. Typesetting Is Done from the Keyboard. THE FONT EDITOR Is Used for Editing Existing Fonts or Creating New Ones, One Character at a Time, Each Character Being Assigned a Key on the Keyboard. THE GRAPHIC PRINTER Dumps Single Screen & Extended Screen Graphics to Most Popular Dot Matrix, Ink Jet, & Laser Printers. All Integrated Programs Are Menu-Driven.
Data Transforms, Inc.

Fontrix (IBM). *Version:* 3.0. *Compatible Hardware:* IBM PC & true compatibles, PCjr, PC XT, PC AT. *Operating System(s) Required:* PC-DOS/MS-DOS 2.0, 2.1, 3.0, 3.2, 3.3. *Memory Required:* 640k. *General Requirements:* CGA, EGA, VGA, or Hercules card.
disk $155.00.
Fontpak. 10-font disk $25.00 ea.
Graphics & Typesetting Software Package Which Enables Users to Generate Presentation-Quality Type & Illustrations, & Print Them on over 60 Different Dot Matrix, Ink Jet, & Laser Printers. Has the Ability to Create Images Larger Than the Display Screen by Using Disk Storage As Virtual Memory & Allowing the Display to Scroll in All Four Directions Through a Bit-Mapped Graphics Workspace Which Can Be 23 Times the Area & Resolution of One Screen (up to 115 Times with a Hard Disk). Package Includes Three Integrated Programs: THE GRAPHIC WRITER Commands & Coordinates the Virtual Graphic Workspace, Allowing Typesetting & Graphic Creation to Occur; THE FONT EDITOR Is a Program for Editing Existing Fonts or Creating New Ones One Character at a Time, Each Character Being Assigned to a Key on the Keyboard; THE GRAPHIC PRINTER Dumps Single-Screen & Extended-Screen Graphics to Most Popular Printers.
Data Transforms, Inc.

Fonts & Borders. *Compatible Hardware:* IBM PC & compatibles. *General Requirements:* 2 disk drives or hard disk; PrintMaster Plus. *Customer Support:* 510-748-6938.
$39.95 ea.
Provides 20 New Borders & 20 New Fonts to Be Used with PrintMaster Plus. Includes Additional 'Upgrade Disk' Which Provides Owners of Original PrintMaster with a Free Copy of PrintMaster Plus.
Unison World.

Foo Castle. Sep. 1995. *Customer Support:* Telephone support - free (except phone charge). Windows 3.1. IBM & compatibles (386 DX-20) (4Mb). CD-ROM disk $12.99 (ISBN 1-57594-010-8). *Nonstandard peripherals required:* 2x CD-ROM player, Sound Card, VGA monitor. *Optimal configuration:* 486 XS-33.
Exciting & Educational Point & Click Adventure Kids Will Love.
Kidsoft, Inc.

Foo Castle. Sep. 1995. *Customer Support:* Telephone support - free (except phone charge). Windows 3.1. IBM & compatibles (386 DX-20) (4Mb). CD-ROM disk $12.99 (ISBN 1-57594-049-3). *Nonstandard peripherals required:* 2x CD-ROM player, Sound Card, VGA monitor. *Optimal configuration:* 486 SX-33.
The Exciting & Educational Point & Click Adventure Kids Will Love. Blister Pack Jewel Case.
Kidsoft, Inc.

Fooblitzky. *Compatible Hardware:* Apple II+, IIe, IIc; Atari XL/XE; IBM PC & compatibles. *Memory Required:* Atari 48k; Apple & IBM 128k.
disk $39.95.
Multiplayer Strategy Game. Players Must Find Four Secret Items in the City of Fooblitzky. Secret Objects Change Every Time the Game Is Played. Includes Four Workboards, Four Markers, & Two Sets of Rules.
Activision, Inc.

Food & Wine's Wine Tasting. 1994.
386 or higher. CD-ROM disk $59.95. *Nonstandard peripherals required:* CD-ROM drive.
Macintosh. CD-ROM disk $59.95. *Nonstandard peripherals required:* CD-ROM drive.
Program Teaches the Basics of Wine Judging and Other Areas of Wine Culture.
Times Mirror Multimedia.

Food & Wine's Wine Tasting: An Interactive Experience. Ehrlich Multimedia Staff. Oct. 1994. System 7.0.1. Mac II CX or higher (4Mb). CD-ROM disk $59.95 (ISBN 1-885551-01-0). *Nonstandard peripherals required:* CD-ROM (2x speed min). *Optimal configuration:* 8Mb RAM strongly recommended.
Windows 3.1. Any MPC Level II (4Mb). CD-ROM disk $59.95 (ISBN 1-885551-00-2). *Optimal configuration:* 8Mb strongly recommended.
Intended to Help Refine Taste Preferences & Appreciation of Wine for Novices & Connoisseurs Alike. At the Heart of the Program Are Interactive Tastings of 48 Wines Selected by Steven Olson, a Wine Expert. Users Learn about Wine Making & How it Effects Taste, Color & Aroma. Includes Data Bases of Growing Regions & Grape Varietals.
Times Mirror Multimedia.

The Food Processor, Basic: Nutrient Analysis. *Version:* 5.03. Bob Geltz & Betty Geltz. Sep. 1992. *Compatible Hardware:* IBM PC & compatibles, Macintosh. *Operating System(s) Required:* PC-DOS/MS-DOS. *Language(s):* Pascal. *Memory Required:* IBM 384k, Macintosh 512k. *General Requirements:* 2 floppy disk drives, or hard disk, printer. *Items Included:* Book - The Food Finder-Food Sources of Vitamins & Mineral. *Customer Support:* Training available, telephone assistance, menu & recipe analysis service.
disk $295.00 ea., include manual & Food Finder, Food Sources of Vitamins & Minerals.
IBM. (ISBN 0-940071-04-5, Order no.: 84002).
For Menus, Recipes, Daily Intakes. Calculate Personalized Nutrition Recommendations & 7 Day Fitness Plans with 200 Activities. Excesses/Deficiencies in Numeric/Graphic Forms. Choose from Various Reports. Export to Word Processor or Use Text Editor. Includes 3000 Foods, but Expandable to over 11,000. Analyzes for 37 Nutrients Including Fats, Cholesterol, Sugar, & Caffeine. Preview Nutrient Breakdown Window. High/Low Search by Nutrient Weight Loss/Gain Adjustments. Compiled from Handbook 8 & over 575 Scientific Sources. Exchanges-For Help with Special Diets. Free Demo Disk Available.
ESHA Research.

The Food Processor Plus. *Version:* 5.03. *Compatible Hardware:* IBM. *Items Included:* Food finder book. *Customer Support:* Free demo disk, telephone assistance, menu/recipe analysis service available.
3.5" disk $495.00.
Nutrition & Diet Analysis. 7-Day Fitness Profile Capability W/200 Activities. Menu Planner, Spreadsheet & Other Reports, Text Editor, 9,700 Foods, 105 Nutrients, High-Low Search, Weight Gain/Loss, Unlimited Profile Capability.
ESHA Research.

TITLE INDEX

Food Service Cluster, 21 disks. 1985. *Compatible Hardware:* Apple, IBM PC & compatibles. *Operating System(s) Required:* Apple DOS, PC-DOS/MS-DOS. *Memory Required:* 48k.
Set. $450.00.
Job Related Reading Programs Providing: Reading Skills Essential for Success in Vocational Classes, Reading Skills Necessary to Ensure Continuous On-the-Job Success, Pre- & Post-Assessment Data.
Aquarius Instructional.
 Words of Package Information, 3 disks.
  $70.00 (Order no.: APPLE PM181, IBM-BM281).
  Three Lessons Which Teach the Vocabulary Related to Package Information.
 Words for Preparation & Service, 6 disks.
  $135.00 (Order no.: APPLE PM182, IBM BM282).
  Six Lessons Which Teach the Vocabulary Related to Food Preparation & Service.
 Words of Safety & Sanitation, 4 disks.
  $95.00 (Order no.: APPLE PM183, IBM BM283).
  Four Lessons Which Teach the Vocabulary Related to Food Service Safety & Sanitation.
 Words of Kitchen Equipment & Tools, 4 disks.
  $95.00 (Order no.: APPLE PM184, IBM BM284).
  Four Lessons Which Teach the Vocabulary Related to Kitchen Equipment & Tools.
 Words of Food Service Abbreviation, 4 disks.
  $95.00 (Order no.: APPLE PM185, IBM BM285).
  Four Lessons Which Teach the Vocabulary Related to Food Service Abbreviations.

Foodserve. *Operating System(s) Required:* PC-DOS/MS-DOS, OS/2. *Memory Required:* 256k. *Items Included:* Includes up to 5 days on-site training, 1-year warranty, & user manual. *Customer Support:* Free updates, enhancements, & toll-free 800 lines for customers under warranty.
3.5" or 5.25" disk $5000.00-$15000.00.
Management Tool for a Food Service Operation. Provides Cost Capability at Recipe, Menu, Cycle Levels. Features Production Reports, Procurement, Inventory, Labor Analysis, Cost, & Budget.
Practorcare, Inc.

FoodTrack/InnaTrack. 1983. *Operating System(s) Required:* UNIX/VS. *Memory Required:* 4000k.
contact publisher for price.
Complete, Integrated On-Line Manufacturing/Distributing System Geared to the Light & Medium Manufacturing Industries.
Draves & Barke Systems, Inc.

Football. *Version:* I. David Powers. Oct. 1983. *Compatible Hardware:* IBM PC & compatibles. *Operating System(s) Required:* PC-DOS, MS-DOS. *Language(s):* Compiled BASIC. *Memory Required:* 64k. *General Requirements:* CGA card, optional joystick.
disk $24.95, incl. documentation & software registration form.
Fast-Action One- or Two-Player Game in Which Players Play Offense Against Computer-Controlled Defense. You Can Run, Pass or Punt the Ball, & Even Try for a Field Goal. Keeps Statistics, Time, & Score. Nine Skill Levels Are Available.
Generic Computer Products, Inc. (GCPI).

Football. *Compatible Hardware:* TI 99/4A with PLATO interpreter solid state cartridge.
contact publisher for price (Order no.: PHM 3009).
Computer Simulation of Football Based on Actual Professional Football Statistics.
Texas Instruments, Personal Productivit.

Football Addition. Ronald D. Jones. 1985. *Compatible Hardware:* Apple; Commodore; IBM; TRS-80 Model I, Model III, Color Computer. *Operating System(s) Required:* CP/M. *Memory Required:* 64k.
disk $149.95 ea.
 Apple. (ISBN 1-55604-126-8, Order no.: F003).
 CP/M. (ISBN 1-55604-127-6, Order no.: F003).
 Commodore. (ISBN 1-55604-128-4, Order no.: F003).
 Color Computer. (ISBN 1-55604-129-2, Order no.: F003).
 IBM. (ISBN 1-55604-130-6, Order no.: F003).
 Model I & Model III. (ISBN 1-55604-131-4, Order no.: F003).
Football Prognosis Programs Designed to Predict Team Scores, Over-Under, Non-Bets, & Regular Bets. Data Can Be Entered for Entire Season or for Previous Week Only. Data Base Gives the Option of Storing 100 Teams & All the Data Necessary to Professionally Predict Game Outcomes with or Without Using the Point Spread. "Team Strength Rating" Based on Win/Loss Ratio Designed to Isolate "Ripe" Opportunities & Provide a Second Option. Cumulative Yearly and/or Last 4 Weeks Evaluated at Any Point in Season.
Professor Jones Professional Handicapping Systems.

The Football Book. *Customer Support:* 800-929-8117 (customer service). MS-DOS. Commodore 64. disk $49.99 (ISBN 0-87007-544-6).
Stores, Retrieves, & Evaluates an Extensive Amount of Data Compiled From Regular Season National Football League Games. The 1981, 1982, 1983, & 1984 Seasons are Provided on the Diskette. Menu-Driven with Ten Available Options: Initialize, Input Data, Review Games, Compare Teams, Plot Data, Week Schedule, Team Schedule, Standings, Point Spreads, & Predictions. All Options But the First Generate Hard Copies. Several Seasons' Worth of Data Can be Placed on a Single Diskette Making This a Very Compact & Readily Availble Storage Place for Most Team Statistics. Produces Gambling Odds Based on Detailed Team Stats Input by the User.
SourceView Software International.

Football Forecaster. *Compatible Hardware:* Apple II+. *Language(s):* Applesoft BASIC. *Memory Required:* 32k.
disk $24.95.
Keeps Updated Records of All NFL Teams Each Season, & Predicts Winners & Point Spreads Each Week. User Types in the Game Scores Each Week, Receives Screen Displays &/or Printouts of Current League Standings, Team Status & Next Week's Winners.
Instant Software, Inc.

Football Guide, 1994. *Version:* 94.2 S. Jim Dalton. May 1994. *Customer Support:* Money back if not satisfied; exhchange disk for new one with results to date; answer all questions by mail or phone.
IBM or compatibles, MS-DOS. IBM & compatibles (640k). disk $15.00, Shareware (Order no.: 1994 OR 1995 FOOTBALL GUIDE). Optimal configuration: 486-DX2 66Hz (runs faster) & hard drive.
An Easy-to-Use Guide to the 1994 NFL Football Season! Contains the Season's Schedules & Computes Standings Based on the Results of Games (Entered in an Easy-Enter Format). The FBG Predicts the Winners of Games Based on Previous Results. Players Compete Against the FBG in the OFFICE POOL.
DALTONWARE.

Football Master. *Customer Support:* 800-929-8117 (customer service). MS-DOS. IBM/PS2. disk $49.99 (ISBN 0-87007-798-8).
A Game of College Football Strategy Which Lets User Call the Plays Just As the Coach of a Major College Team Would. This Is Not an Arcade Game & Quality Has Not been Sacrificed to Bring You Arcade Graphics. Complete Stats Are Included for Top 20 & Big Ten Teams for 1985, 1986, 1987 & Provision is Made for the User to Set up Databases for Any Other Teams.
SourceView Software International.

Football-Picks. David Powers. May 1984. *Compatible Hardware:* IBM PC & compatibles. *Operating System(s) Required:* PC-DOS, MS-DOS. *Language(s):* BASIC. *Memory Required:* 64k. *General Requirements:* Printer.
disk $24.95.
Allows User to Make Predictions about NFL Games with an Assist from His Personal Computer. Relies Solely on Computer-Generated Predictions or Combine Program Results with Other Factors Such As User's Own Judgement. Uses Information Found in Newspapers. Does Not Require Predictions of Each & Every Game to Obtain Results.
Generic Computer Products, Inc. (GCPI).

Football Predictor with Data Base. Ronald D. Jones. 1984. *Compatible Hardware:* Apple; Commodore; IBM; TRS-80 Model, Model III, Color Computer. *Operating System(s) Required:* CP/M. *Memory Required:* 64k.
disk $99.95 ea.
 Apple. (ISBN 1-55604-120-9, Order no.: F002).
 CP/M. (ISBN 1-55604-121-7, Order no.: F002).
 Commodore. (ISBN 1-55604-122-5, Order no.: F002).
 Color Computer. (ISBN 1-55604-123-3, Order no.: F002).
 IBM. (ISBN 1-55604-124-1, Order no.: F002).
 Model I & Model III. (ISBN 1-55604-125-X, Order no.: F002).
Football Prognosis Programs Designed to Predict Team Scores, Over-Under, Non-Bets, Regular Bets. Handicapper Has Choice of Entering Data for the Entire Season or for Only the Previous Week. Data Base Version Gives the Option of Storing 100 Teams & All of the Data Necessary to Professionally Predict Game Outcomes with or Without Using the Point Spread.
Professor Jones Professional Handicapping Systems.

Football Predictor Without Data Base. Ronald D. Jones. 1984. *Compatible Hardware:* Apple; Commodore; IBM; TRS-80 Model I, Model III, Color Computer. *Operating System(s) Required:* CP/M. *Memory Required:* 64k.
disk $49.95 ea.
 Apple. (ISBN 1-55604-114-4, Order no.: F001).
 CP/M. (ISBN 1-55604-115-2, Order no.: F001).
 IBM. (ISBN 1-55604-118-7, Order no.: F001).
 disk or cassette $49.95 ea.
 Commodore. (ISBN 1-55604-116-0, Order no.: F001).
 Color Computer. (ISBN 1-55604-117-9, Order no.: F001).
 Model I & Model III. (ISBN 1-55604-119-5, Order no.: F001).
Football Prognosis Programs Designed to Predict Team Scores, Over-Under, Non-Bets, Regular Bets & Super Bets.
Professor Jones Professional Handicapping Systems.

Football Records. Merle W. Wagner. 1983. *Compatible Hardware:* Apple II Plus, IIe, IIc; IBM. *Memory Required:* 48k, 640k. *General Requirements:* Printer.
disk $49.95, incl. manual (ISBN 0-922900-42-6,

Order no.: CFS-820).
Useful for Any Number of Teams, Players or Games. 16 Offensive Entries. 16 Defensive/Kicking Entries. Different Data Disk for Each Team.
Cherrygarth, Inc.

Football Simulation. Adrian Vance. Oct. 1985. *Compatible Hardware:* Apple II. *Operating System(s) Required:* Apple DOS. *Memory Required:* 48k.
disk $9.95 (ISBN 0-918547-27-X).
Simulates a Football Game to Teach Strategy & Plays. Not Copy Protected.
AV Systems, Inc.

The Football Statbook. 1985. *Operating System(s) Required:* MS-DOS, PC-DOS. *Memory Required:* 256k. *General Requirements:* Printer.
disk $79.00.
Maintains & Prints Game, Year-to-Date, & Lifetime Football Stats.
RJL Systems.

Football Statistics. Version: 93-1. Sep. 1993. *Compatible Hardware:* Macintosh, IBM PC & compatibles. *Operating System(s) Required:* Macintosh, PC-DOS/MS-DOS 2.1. *Language(s):* BASIC. *Memory Required:* Macintosh 2Mb, IBM 512k. *General Requirements:* 1 HD 3 1/2 disk drive, 80-column printer with compressed print.
Macintosh. disk $59.95 (ISBN 0-922526-20-6).
IBM. (ISBN 0-922526-31-1).
Keeps a Complete Set of Offensive, Defensive, & Kicking Statistics Both for Individual Players & the Team. Reports Are Printed for Current Game & for Season-to-Date.
Big G Software.

FOR. *Compatible Hardware:* Cromemco Systems. *Operating System(s) Required:* UNIX. *Language(s):* FORTRAN 77. *Memory Required:* 2048k.
$2995.00.
8" disk write for info.
Full Implementation of ANSI-Standard FORTRAN 77.
Cromemco, Inc.

For Mice Only!: Three Beatrix Potter Mouse Tales. Beatrix Potter. May 1995. *Items Included:* Online information in a "Readme.Wri" File. *Customer Support:* 24 hour Voicemail & FAX.
Windows. Multimedia PC (4Mb). CD-ROM disk $19.95 (ISBN 1-887323-02-3). *Nonstandard peripherals required:* CD-ROM drive, sound card. *Optimal configuration:* Windows 3.1 or higher, CD-ROM drive, sound card, 4Mb RAM or higher, VGA monitor: 640x480/256 colors, 3.5Mb hard drive space, processor rec: 486SX or higher.
Three Beatrix Potter Mouse Tales: "The Tale of Two Bad Mice;" "The Tale of Mrs. Tittlemouse;" "The Tale of Johnny Town-Mouse." Includes the Original Color Illustrations, Complete Spoken & Written Texts, Glossary of Difficult & Unfamiliar Words, Biography of Beatrix Potter, Guide to Using the CD-ROM.
Field Multimedia.

For Rabbits Only!: Three Beatrix Potter Rabbit Tales. Beatrix Potter. May 1995. *Items Included:* Online information in a "Readme.Wri" File. *Customer Support:* 24 hour Voicemail & FAX.
Windows. Multimedia PC (4Mb). CD-ROM disk $19.95 (ISBN 1-887323-01-5). *Nonstandard peripherals required:* CD-ROM drive, sound card. *Optimal configuration:* Windows 3.1 or higher, CD-ROM drive, sound card, 4Mb RAM or higher, VGA monitor: 640x480/256 colors, 3.5Mb hard drive space, processor rec: 486SX or higher.
Three Beatrix Potter Rabbit Tales: "The Tale of Peter Rabbit;" "The Tale of Benjamin Bunny;" "The Tale of the Flopsy Bunnies;" Includes the Original Full Color Illustraions, Complete Spoken & Written Texts, Glossary of Difficult & Unfamiliar Words, Biography of Beatrix Potter, Guide to Using the CD-ROM.
Field Multimedia.

For Squirrels Only!: Two Beatrix Potter Squirrel Tales. Beatrix Potter. May 1995. *Items Included:* Online information in a "Readme.Wri" File. *Customer Support:* 24 hour Voicemail & FAX.
Windows. Multimedia PC (4Mb). CD-ROM disk $19.95 (ISBN 1-887323-00-7). *Nonstandard peripherals required:* CD-ROM drive, sound card. *Optimal configuration:* Windows 3.1 or higher, CD-ROM drive, sound card, 4Mb RAM or higher, VGA monitor: 640x480/256 colors, 3.5Mb hard drive space, processor rec: 486SX or higher.
Two Beatrix Potter Squirrel Tales: "The Tale of Timmy Tiptoes;" "The Tale of Squirrel Nutkin." Includes the Original Color Illustrations, Complete Spoken & Written Texts, Glossary of Difficult & Unfamiliar Words, Biography of Beatrix Potter, Guide, & "Nutkin's Riddles" Game.
Field Multimedia.

For-Winds. *Compatible Hardware:* IBM PC, PC XT, PC AT & compatibles. (source code included).
disk $89.95.
Gives the FORTRAN Programmer the Capability of Generating up to 255 Windows on the Screen. Each Window Can Be Individually Scrolled, Moved, Sized, Generated, & Removed.
Alpha Computer Service.

FORCE. *Operating System(s) Required:* IRIS. $3000.00.
user manual $30.00 (Order no.: A-0023).
1A System Development guide $7.00 (Order no.: X-0200).
Source Code Generation System That Generates Independent, Documented & Totally Transportable IRIS Business BASIC Programs That Are Fully-Commented & Error-Free.
Point 4 Data Corp.

The Force: Construction Estimating Program. *Compatible Hardware:* IBM PC & compatibles. *Memory Required:* 320k. *General Requirements:* Hard disk.
disk $125.00.
The Evaluator. disk $50.00.
Construction Concepts.

Force VII. *Compatible Hardware:* Apple II; Commodore 64/128. *Memory Required:* 64k. *General Requirements:* Joystick Optional.
Apple. disk $19.95 (ISBN 0-88717-201-6, Order no.: 15953-43499).
Commodore. disk $19.95 (ISBN 0-88717-200-8, Order no.: 15951-43499).
Game in Which User Chooses Soldier to Confront Alien & When. Each Member of the Force Fights Alone, Facing Fatigue, Hunger, Strange Environs, & a Deadly & Numberless Enemy.
IntelliCreations, Inc.

ForComment, 4 disks. Elk Software Development Corp. *Compatible Hardware:* AT&T 6300, 6300 Plus; Compaq Portable, Portable II, Deskpro 286; Epson Equity I, II, III; IBM PC, PC XT, PC AT; Leading Edge Models M, D, AT; Zenith 150, 160. *Operating System(s) Required:* PC-DOS/MS-DOS 2.0 or higher; IBM PC & most Novell & 3Com networks. *Memory Required:* 256k.
disk $199.00 (ISBN 0-922614-76-8, Order no.: 50010).
Network/Workgroup version. $999.00 (ISBN 0-922614-90-3, Order no.: 50110).
Will Enable up to 15 Reviewers, Using Their Own Computers, to Make Comments & Suggest Revisions of User's Texts. Each Comment Is Automatically Stamped with the Reviewer's Initials & the Date, Creating an Audit Trail. Then, FORCOMMENT Will Automatically Collate All the Comments. THE FORCOMMENT File Can Be Sent to Reviewers via Network, via Modem, or by Passing Disks. Includes a Built-In Mini-Word Processor for Writing Short Documents. Works Directly with Formatted Word Processing Files from WordStar, MutliMate, & WordPerfect As Well As ASCII Files from Any Other Leading Word Processors, Spreadsheets, or Data Bases.
Broderbund Software, Inc.

ForeCalc. Version: 1.05. *Items Included:* (2) 5.25" disks or (1) 3.5" disk. *Customer Support:* telephone support (617) 484-5050; license agreement registration card update information.
IBM PC XT, PC AT & compatibles, PS/2. disk $149.00.
ForeCalc is a Forecasting Add-In Designed for People Who Use Lotus 1-2-3 or Symphony. User Specifies Historical Data & Program Generates Forecasts. Designed for Users Without Prior Knowledge of Statistics. Incorporates Exponential Smoothing Models to Create Forecasts & to Choose Best Statistical Technique. User Can Also Choose From Four Techniques: Simple, Holt, Winters & Custom. Results Can Be Saved & Graphed.
Business Forecast Systems, Inc.

Forecast. Version: 3.2. Gerald E. Johnson. Jan. 1985. *Compatible Hardware:* Altos; IBC; Onyx; Seiko. *Operating System(s) Required:* Oasis. *Language(s):* BASIC. *Memory Required:* 64k. *General Requirements:* Printer.
disk $500.00 (ISBN 0-922660-00-X).
Multi-User Oriented, Structured Financial Analysis System Designed to Project Operating Budgets, Calculate Cash Flow, & Determine Cash Surplus.
Business Design Software.

Forecast Express: Forecast Management System. Version: 3.2. Apr. 1990. *Items Included:* Manual & diskette. *Customer Support:* Free installation & technical support; limited warranty.
MS-DOS. IBM PC (512K). disk $295.00.
Nonstandard peripherals required: Hard drive required.
Assists in Defining & Analyzing Financial Goals. Prints a Complete Set of Automatically Updated Financial Statements. Linked to Revenue, Department Expense, & Loan Amortization Schedules (Included). The Forecast Management System Analyzes Forecasting Logic, Cash Requirements, Revenue & Cost of Sales, Department Budgets, Loan Amortization, & More.
JIAN Tools for Sales.

Forecast Master Plus. Version: 1.16. *Items Included:* 3 5 1/4" disks or 2 3 1/2" disks. *Customer Support:* Telephone support (617) 484-5050; registration card user manual, applied statistical forecasting book license agreement.
IBM PC & compatibles (640k). disk $695.00.
Nonstandard peripherals required: Hard disk drive; math coprocessor.
Intended for the Professional Business Forecaster Familiar with Complicated Forecasting Models. User Can Choose from Eight Forecasting Models, Ranging from Exponential Smoothing & Box-Jenkins to Multivariate State Space & Variable Parameter Regression. User Can Factor Variables Into Models Such As Advertising & Seasonal Fluctuations.
Business Forecast Systems, Inc.

TITLE INDEX

FOREFRONT CONSTRUCTION MANAGEMENT

Forecast Plus. *Version:* 2.1. Dec. 1984. *Compatible Hardware:* IBM PC, PC XT, PC AT & compatibles. *Operating System(s) Required:* PC-DOS, MS-DOS, CP/M. *Language(s):* Compiled BASIC. *Memory Required:* 192k. *General Requirements:* 2 disk drives, printer. disk $595.00, incl. user's manual. manual $30.00. demo disk & manual $50.00. *Data Manager, Exploratory, & Forecasting Package. Data Management Includes Data File Creation & Editing, Algebraic Transformations, Trading-Day Adjustments, Lags & Differencing. Exploratory Graphic Features Include Time Plots, 4253HT Smoothing, Box Plots, Aggregate Box Plots, Spread vs. Level Plots, & Autocorrelation Functions. Forecasting Procedures Include Simple Moving Averages, Single Exponential Smoothing, Double Exponential Smoothing, Harrison's Harmonic Smoothing, Holt's Two Parameter Smoothing, Brown's Quadratic Exponential Smoothing, Winter's Seasonal Smoothing, SABL Robust Decomposition, Census X-11 Decomposition, Regression Trend Analysis, Multiple Trend Analysis, Generalized Adaptive Filtering, & Box-Jenkins Analysis.* StatPac, Inc.

Forecast Pro. *Version:* DOS 2.0, Windows 1.1. *Items Included:* License agreement, registration card. *Customer Support:* (617) 484-5050. MS-DOS/PC-DOS. IBM PC & compatibles. disk $595.00. Windows, DOS. 3.5" or 5.25" disk $595.00. *A Complete Stand Alone Package Designed for the Average Business Person. A Built-in Exput System Analyzes Data & Recommends the Appropriate Technique. The Program Provides Automatic Fitting Routines & Exput Guidance Obliviating the Need for a Background in Statistics. Package Uses Exponential Smoothing, Box Jenkins & Dynamic Repression Models.* Business Forecast Systems, Inc.

Forecaster. *Customer Support:* 800-929-8117 (customer service). MS-DOS. Apple II. disk $79.99 (ISBN 0-87007-336-2). *a Program Which Allows Seasonal & Economic Factor Indices to Be Used in Conjunction with a Variety of Smoothing Techniques, Including Both "Soft" & "Hard" Smoothing.* SourceView Software International.

Forecasting. *Compatible Hardware:* HP Series 200: Models 216/220, 226/236 Personal Technical Computers with BASIC 2.0. *Memory Required:* 180k. HP 216/220. 3-1/2" or 5-1/4" disk $500.00 ea. (Order no.: 98818A). HP 226/236. 5-1/4" disk $500.00. *Allows Time-Series Data to Be Analyzed, Smoothed, Forecasted, & Plotted Using a Variety of Statistical Techniques.* Hewlett-Packard Co.

Forecasting. Dec. 1988. *Customer Support:* Free telephone & BBS Technical support. MS/PC DOS, Concurrent DOS, Xenix, Unix. IBM PC/XT/AT & compatibles, IBM PS/2 (512k). single User $695.00. *Nonstandard peripherals required:* Hard disk, 132 column printer. multiuser $695.00. Unix & Xenix $1495.00. *The Forecasting Module of INMASS II, MC Software's Integrated Manufacturing Software Package, Provides a Tool for Preparing Statistical Forecasts. Historical Information Is Retained from the Other Modules Such As Inventory & Sales Order Entry & Subjected to a Variety of Statistical Processes to Arrive at Production & Sales Projections.* INMASS/MRP.

Forecasting. *Customer Support:* Free telephone & BBS technical support. MS/PC DOS, Concurrent DOS, Xenix, Unix. IBM PC/XT/AT & compatibles; IBM PS/2 (512k). disk single user or multi-user $695.00. *Networks supported:* Novell, Lantastic, Banyan VINES, all NETBOIS compatible. *This integrated manufacturing softpackage provides a tool for preparing statistical forecasts. Historical information is retained from the other modules such as Inventory & Sales Order Entry & subjected to a variety of statistical processes to arrive at production & sales projections.* INMASS/MRP.

Forecasting & Time-Series. *Version:* 10.0. (Professional Ser.). 1989. *Compatible Hardware:* Apple Macintosh, IBM PC & compatibles. *Memory Required:* 512k. *Items Included:* Disks, book, program instructions. *Customer Support:* Telephone. disk $145.00 (ISBN 0-920387-02-0). *Covers the General Methods of Analysis of Time-Series & the Forecasting Techniques Based on Those Methods. All Types of Time-Series Are Considered, Those with Trends, Seasonality & Periodicity, Autoregressive, & So Forth. Examples of Time-Series Used Range from Stock Prices & a Utilities Index to Population Series. Elaborate Data Entry & Transformation Facilities Are Provided. Time-Series Analysis Covers the Study of Periodicity, Correlation & Cross-Correlation, Autoregression, & Fast Fourier Transforms. Forecasting Techniques Range from Simple Methods Such As Moving Average Smoothing & Exponential Smoothing, Through Autoregression & Regression Models, to Box-Jenkins Techniques. Two Independent Box-Jenkins Models Are Provided; a Three-Parameter Model Which Can Handle Non-Stationary Series, & an Approximate ARIMA # (3,1,2) Model. Simple Transfer Function Modeling Is Included.* Lionheart Pr., Inc.

The Forecasting Edge Box-Jenkins Automated Time Series Forecasting. *Items Included:* Full manual. No other products required. *Customer Support:* Free telephone support - no time limit. 30 day warranty. MS-DOS 3.2 or higher. IBM & compatibles (512k). disk $99.95. *Menu-Driven Package Which Applies the Sophisticated Box-Jenkins Time-Series Forecasting Method in an Automated Manner Which Is Very Easy to Use, As Well As Surprisingly Accurate. The Analysis Is Particularly Well-Suited to Data Which a Cyclical Component, Such As Sales, the Stock Market, & Similar Seasonal Processes. The 156-Page Manual Has the Same Emphasis As the Software: Ease-of-Use. There Is Little Discussion of Theory (That Can Be Found in Text Books). Instead, Each Option Is Described in Detail, with Examples.* Dynacomp, Inc.

The Forecasting Edge: Box-Jenkins Automated Time Series Forecasting. 1992. *Items Included:* Detailed manuals included with all Dynacomp products. *Customer Support:* Free telephone support to original customer - no time limit; 30 day limited warranty. MS-DOS 3.2 or higher. IBM PC & compatibles (512k). $99.95 (Add $5.00 for 3 1/2" format; 5 1/4" format standard). *Optimal configuration:* IBM, MS-DOS 2.0 or higher, 256k RAM, CGA/EGA/VGA or compatible graphics for line graphs. An 80-column or wider printer & math coprocessor are supported, but not necessary. *A Menu-Driven Package Which Applies the Sophisticated Box-Jenkins Time-Series Forecasting Method in an Automated Manner Which Is Very Easy to Use, As Well As Surprisingly Accurate. The Analysis Is Particularly Well-Suited to Data Which a Cyclical Component, Such As Sales, the Stock Market, & Similar Seasonal Processes. The 156-Page Manual Has the Same Emphasis As the Software: Ease-of-Use. There Is Little Discussion of Theory (That Can Be Found in Text Books). Instead, Each Option Is Described in Detail, with Examples.* Dynacomp, Inc.

Forecasting Software System. *Compatible Hardware:* Apple II, II+, IIe, IIc; IBM PC & compatibles, PC XT. *Operating System(s) Required:* PC-DOS 2.0 or higher. disk $295.00. *Designed to Meet the Exacting Needs of Virtually All Areas of Forecasting Including Business, Finance & Manufacturing.* Softext Publishing Corp.

FOREFRONT Construction Management System: Accounts Payable. *Version:* 5.0. Sep. 1995. *Items Included:* Source code, training manuals. *Customer Support:* Annual software support includes: toll-free hotline, fax, software trouble-shooting, minor bug fixes, regularly scheduled DCI software upgrades & enhancements, & general information on maximizing the benefits of your system. MS-DOS, Novell, UNIX, XENIX, Windows. IBM compatible (4Mb; 8Mb recommended). Contact publisher for price. *Addl. software required:* McDonnell Douglas PRO-IV Runtime. *Networks supported:* Novell. *Schedules Payments & Provides Immediate Analysis of All Vendor Accounts Balances. Advanced Reporting Provides the Information Needed to Track Vendor Accounts & Effectively Manage Purchase Discounts to Reduce Interest Expense & Increase Profits. Recurring Invoices Are Automatically Recorded, & Credit Memos Are Easy to Prepare. Invoices to Be Paid Can Be Selected by Vendor, Payment Date & Type of Vendor. Manual Checks Are Quick & Easy to Record, & If a Check Is Issued in Error, the System Automatically Reverses the Payment, Reopens the Invoices, Adjusts Vendor Records & Corrects the General Ledger Accounts.* Dexter & Chaney, Inc.

FOREFRONT Construction Management System: Accounts Receivable. *Version:* 4.2. Sep. 1994. *Items Included:* Source code, training manuals. *Customer Support:* Annual software support includes: toll-free hotline, fax, software trouble-shooting, minor bug fixes, regularly scheduled DCI software upgrades & enhancements, & general information on maximizing the benefits of your system. MS-DOS, Novell, UNIX, XENIX. IBM compatible (4Mb; 8Mb recommended). Contact publisher for price. *Addl. software required:* McDonnell Douglas PRO-IV Runtime. *Networks supported:* Novell. *Sets up Jobs As Contracts, Allowing Several Contracts for Each Customer. The Contract Has All the Information to Automatically Print Draw Requests in the Industry-Standard Format. The System Also Allows for Standard Time & Material Invoicing with Special Tax Reporting for Local & State Governments. The Cash Receipts Entry Allows for Non-Accounts Receivable Deposits So the System Can Even Print Deposit Slips. Finance Charges & Statements Can Also Be Automatically Calculated for Late Payers. The Accounts Receivable Module Also Includes Complete Change Order Tracking from the Owner. The System Is Fully Integrated with Forefront General Ledger & Job Cost.* Dexter & Chaney, Inc.

FOREFRONT Construction Management System: Equipment Control.
Version: 5.0. Sep. 1995. *Items Included:* Source code, training manuals. *Customer Support:* Annual software support includes: toll-free hotline, fax, software trouble-shooting, minor bug fixes, regularly scheduled DCI software upgrades & enhancements, & general information on maximizing the benefits of your system.
- MS-DOS, Novell, UNIX, XENIX, Windows. IBM compatible (4Mb; 8Mb recommended). Contact publisher for price. *Addl. software required:* McDonnell Douglas PRO-IV Runtime. *Networks supported:* Novell.

Provides All Necessary Information to Track All the Costs Against Equipment, & All the Revenue Generated by Using or Renting Equipment. The Rental Revenue Can Be Tracked Separately for Each Equipment Code & Separately for Hourly, Daily, Weekly or Monthly. Various Reports & On-Line Inquiry, Which Show the Revenue & Costs per Hour, Alert Management to Potential Problems Before They Become Too Costly. Monthly Costs Such As Depreciation, Insurance & Licensing Can Be Automatically Calculated & Posted to Each Equipment Code. Equipment Control Is Integrated with Other Modules in the Forefront Construction Management Series.
Dexter & Chaney, Inc.

FOREFRONT Construction Management System: Esti-Link.
Version: 5.0. Sep. 1995. *Items Included:* Source code, training manuals. *Customer Support:* Annual software maintenance includes: toll-free hotline, fax, software trouble-shooting, minor bug fixes, regularly scheduled DCI software upgrades & enhancements, & general information on maximizing the benefits of your system.
- MS-DOS. IBM & compatibles (4Mb). Contact publisher for price. *Addl. software required:* McDonnell Douglas PRO-IV Runtime. *Networks supported:* Novell.
- Novell. IBM & compatibles (4Mb). Contact publisher for price. *Addl. software required:* McDonnell Douglas PRO-IV Runtime. *Networks supported:* Novell.
- UNIX/XENIX, MS-DOS, Novell, Windows. IBM & compatibles, IBM RS/6000, AT&T, Bull, HP9000, NCR (Varies). Contact publisher for price. *Addl. software required:* McDonnell Douglas PRO-IV Runtime.

Esti-Link Allows FOREFRONT Users to Load Job Estimates Directly from Widely Used Construction Estimating Systems into the Job Cost System. This Saves Time & Assures Accuracy in Setting up New Jobs.
Dexter & Chaney, Inc.

FOREFRONT Construction Management System: Fixed Assets.
Version: 5.0. Sep. 1995. *Items Included:* Source code, training manuals. *Customer Support:* Annual software support includes: toll-free hotline, fax, software trouble-shooting, minor bug fixes, regularly scheduled DCI software upgrades & enhancements, & general information on maximizing the benefits of your system.
- MS-DOS, Novell, UNIX, XENIX, Windows. IBM compatible (4Mb; 8Mb recommended). Contact publisher for price. *Addl. software required:* McDonnell Douglas PRO-IV Runtime. *Networks supported:* Novell.

Handles the Following Depreciation Methods: Accelerated Cost Recovery System; Straight-Line Declining Balance; & Sum-of-the-Year Digits. The System Tracks Vital Information about Fixed Assets, Including User-Defined Asset Code Description & Serial Number, Date Capitalized & the Asset Location. Fixed Assets Aids the Determination of Replacement in Order to Maximize Investment & Provides Salvage Amounts, Even for Fully Depreciated Assets. Fixed Assets Is Integrated with Other Modules in the Forefront Construction Management System.
Dexter & Chaney, Inc.

FOREFRONT Construction Management System: General Ledger.
Version: 5.0. Sep. 1995. *Items Included:* Source code, training manuals. *Customer Support:* Annual software support includes: toll-free hotline, fax, software trouble-shooting, minor bug fixes, regularly scheduled DCI software upgrades & enhancements, & general information on maximizing the benefits of your system.
- MS-DOS, Novell, UNIX, XENIX, Windows. IBM compatible (4Mb; 8Mb recommended). Contact publisher for price. *Addl. software required:* McDonnell Douglas PRO-IV Runtime. *Networks supported:* Novell.

Provides the Ability to Print or Display up to Four Years of Data at Any Time, & Prior-Year Entries Will Automatically Update Current-Year Balances. A Special Feature, the Financial Report Writer, Allows Customized Income Statements & Balance Sheets to Be Developed Easily & Also Fully Supports Departmental & Consolidated Statements. Monthly, Quarterly & Yearly Reports Can Be Generated for Revenue & Expense Analysis. Comparisons with Prior Years & Budgets Are Easily Maintained. G/L Is Integrated with All Other Modules in the Forefront Construction Management System.
Dexter & Chaney, Inc.

FOREFRONT Construction Management System: Inventory Control.
Version: 5.0. Sep. 1995. *Items Included:* Source code, training manuals. *Customer Support:* Annual software support includes: toll-free hotline, fax, software trouble-shooting, minor bug fixes, regularly scheduled DCI software upgrades & enhancements, & general information on maximizing the benefits of your system.
- MS-DOS, Novell, UNIX, XENIX, Windows. IBM compatible (4Mb; 8Mb recommended). Contact publisher for price. *Addl. software required:* McDonnell Douglas PRO-IV Runtime. *Networks supported:* Novell.

Offers the Flexibility to Use Multiple Warehouses & an Unlimited Number of Items. The User-Defined Alphanumeric Item Code Can Be Defined up to 15 Characters, with Multi-Level Pricing. Quantity Breaks, Customer Special Pricing & Promotional Discounts Can Easily Be Built into the Pricing Structure. The Physical Inventory System Facilitates Counting Inventory & Provides Effective Reporting of Any Variances. Assortment Processing Offers the Convenience to Turn a Group of Raw Items into a Single Finished Item. The Reorder Report, with Six Months of Sales Information, Will Serve As an Essential Tool in Planning Purchases.
Dexter & Chaney, Inc.

FOREFRONT Construction Management System: Info-Link.
Version: 5.0. Sep. 1995. *Items Included:* Source code, training manuals. *Customer Support:* Annual software maintenance includes: toll-free hotline, fax, software trouble-shooting, minor bug fixes, regularly scheduled DCI software upgrades & enhancements, & general information on maximizing the benefits of your system.
- MS-DOS, Novell, Windows. IBM & compatibles (4Mb). Contact publisher for price. *Addl. software required:* McDonnell Douglas PRO-IV Runtime. *Networks supported:* Novell.
- Novell. IBM & compatibles (4Mb). Contact publisher for price. *Addl. software required:* McDonnell Douglas PRO-IV Runtime. *Networks supported:* Novell.
- UNIX/XENIX. IBM & compatibles, IBM RS/6000, AT&T, Bull, HP9000, NCR (Varies). Contact publisher for price. *Addl. software required:* McDonnell Douglas PRO-IV Runtime.

Info-Link Links the Data Contained in the FOREFRONT Construction Management System with Standard Windows Productivity Software (e.g., Microsoft Access, Excel & Word, & Lotus 1-2-3). User's Can Pull Accounting & Project Management Information from FOREFRONT to Create Spreadsheets, Graphics, Documents, & Other Tools.
Dexter & Chaney, Inc.

FOREFRONT Construction Management System: Order Processing.
Version: 5.0. Sep. 1995. *Items Included:* Source code, training manuals. *Customer Support:* Annual software support includes: toll-free hotline, fax, software trouble-shooting, minor bug fixes, regularly scheduled DCI software upgrades & enhancements, & general information on maximizing the benefits of your system.
- MS-DOS, Novell, UNIX, XENIX, Windows. IBM compatible (4Mb; 8Mb recommended). Contact publisher for price. *Addl. software required:* McDonnell Douglas PRO-IV Runtime. *Networks supported:* Novell.

Highly Flexible Order Entry Process Handles Stock & Non-Stock Items, Partial Shipments & Backorders, Drop Shipments, Discounts & Credit Memos with Ease. After an Order Is Entered, a Sales Order & Picking Sheet Can Be Printed, along with a Packing List & Shipping Labels. When Shipments Are Made, Confirmed Orders Automatically Create Invoices. Tracking Backorders Is No Longer a Problem. Practical Reports Detailing Pending Orders Help Target Potential Problems & Fill Orders More Efficiently. Sales Tax Reports & Commission Reports Can Be Printed on Demand for Any Date-Range Stored on the System.
Dexter & Chaney, Inc.

FOREFRONT Construction Management System: Preventive Maintenance.
Version: 5.0. Sep. 1995. *Items Included:* Source code, training manuals. *Customer Support:* Annual software maintenance includes: toll-free hotline, fax, software trouble-shooting, minor bug fixes, regularly scheduled DCI software upgrades & enhancements, & general information on maximizing the benefits of your system.
- MS-DOS, Novell, UNIX, XENIX, Windows. IBM & compatibles (4Mb). Contact publisher for price. *Addl. software required:* McDonnell Douglas PRO-IV Runtime. *Networks supported:* Novell.
- Novell. IBM & compatibles (4Mb). Contact publisher for price. *Addl. software required:* McDonnell Douglas PRO-IV Runtime. *Networks supported:* Novell.
- UNIX/XENIX. IBM & compatibles, IBM RS/6000, AT&T, Bull, HP9000, NCR (Varies). Contact publisher for price. *Addl. software required:* McDonnell Douglas PRO-IV Runtime.

Preventive Maintenance Allows Maintenance Tasks (I.E., Oil Changes) & Schedules to Be Set for Equipment. Schedules May Be Based on Usage on Jobs, Elapsed Time, Both, or a Fixed Date. Reports Indicate Equipment Needing Service & Parts & Labor Required. A Detailed Record Is Made of Each Service.
Dexter & Chaney, Inc.

FOREFRONT Construction Management System: Purchase Order.
Version: 5.0. Sep. 1995. *Items Included:* Source code, training manuals. *Customer Support:* Annual software support includes: toll-free hotline, fax, software trouble-shooting, minor bug fixes, regularly scheduled DCI software upgrades & enhancements, & general information on maximizing the benefits of your system.
- MS-DOS, Novell, UNIX, XENIX, Windows. IBM compatible (4Mb; 8Mb recommended). Contact publisher for price. *Addl. software required:* McDonnell Douglas PRO-IV Runtime. *Networks supported:* Novell.

Allows the Contractor to Control Purchases by

TITLE INDEX

FOREFRONT CONSTRUCTION MANAGEMENT

the Project Managers. It Allows Inquiry or Reports for All Purchases Sorted by Vendor, Job or Item. The Purchase Order System Is Fully Integrated with the Job Cost System to Immediately Track the Total Dollar Amount Committed to the Job & Phase. This Gives the Contractor the Power to Spot Potential Cost Overruns As the Orders Are Being Placed. The System Is Integrated with the Accounts Payable System So the Accounting Control Is There to Automatically Track the Difference Between Ordered & Invoiced Amounts.
Dexter & Chaney, Inc.

FOREFRONT Construction Management System: Sales Analysis. *Version:* 5.0. Sep. 1995. *Items Included:* Source code, training manuals. *Customer Support:* Annual software support includes: toll-free hotline, fax, software trouble-shooting, minor bug fixes, regularly scheduled DCI software upgrades & enhancements, & general information on maximizing the benefits of your system.
 MS-DOS, Novell, UNIX, XENIX, Windows. IBM compatible (4Mb; 8Mb recommended). Contact publisher for price. *Addl. software required:* McDonnell Douglas PRO-IV Runtime. *Networks supported:* Novell.
Pulls Together Information Needed to Effectively Monitor Sales Efforts. Every Line of Each Invoice & Credit Memo Issued by Forefront Order Processing Is Recorded in Sales Analysis. Accumulating This Data Is Time-Consuming & Expensive; Instead, Forefront Does the Work Automatically. The System Tracks Customers, Customer Types, Items Sold, Category Volumes, Salespeople, Commissions & More. Reports May Be Printed, Sorted & Summarized As Needed, & Any Date Range Stored in the System May Be Chosen. Forefront Sales Analysis Reports Include Unit & Dollar Amounts, Cost of Goods Sold & Gross Margins Including Percentages.
Dexter & Chaney, Inc.

FOREFRONT Construction Management System: Service Contracts. *Version:* 5.0. Sep. 1995. *Items Included:* Source code, training manuals. *Customer Support:* Annual software support includes: toll-free hotline, fax, software trouble-shooting, minor bug fixes, regularly scheduled DCI software upgrades & enhancements, & general information on maximizing the benefits of your system.
 MS-DOS, Novell, UNIX, XENIX, Windows. IBM compatible (4Mb; 8Mb recommended). Contact publisher for price. *Addl. software required:* McDonnell Douglas PRO-IV Runtime. *Networks supported:* Novell.
Promotes Greater Management Control over Service Contract Revenues & Costs. The System Generates the Initial Contract Proposal & the Executed Contract, Schedules the Contract Visits for the Year, Creates the Work Orders for the Scheduled Visits & Performs the Billing Automatically. Service Contracts Provides the Information Through Inquiry & Reporting to Evaluate the Profits of Certain Contracts. Service Contracts Is Integrated with Other Modules in the Forefront Construction Management System.
Dexter & Chaney, Inc.

FOREFRONT Construction Management System: Small Tools. *Version:* 5.0. Sep. 1995. *Items Included:* Source code, training manuals. *Customer Support:* Annual software support includes: toll-free hotline, fax, software trouble-shooting, minor bug fixes, regularly scheduled DCI software upgrades & enhancements, & general information on maximizing the benefits of your system.
 MS-DOS, UNIX, XENIX, Windows. IBM compatible (4Mb; 8Mb recommended). Contact publisher for price. *Addl. software required:* McDonnell Douglas PRO-IV Runtime. *Networks supported:* Novell.
Provides Contractors with Information on Where & How Much Their Small Tools Are Costing Them. The System Provides a Fast & Efficient Method for Logging Either Who or What Job Is Checking Out the Tools. When the Tools Are Returned, They Are Automatically Assigned to the Shop Location until They Are Issued Again. A Billing Rate May Be Established for Each Tool & a Billing Report Produced by Job, Which Can Be Entered in Forefront Job Cost. Inquiry Screens Are Available to Immediately Track the Tools Which Have Been Assigned. Small Tools Is Integrated with Other Modules in the Forefront Construction Management System.
Dexter & Chaney, Inc.

FOREFRONT Construction Management System. *Version:* 5.0. Sep. 1995. *Items Included:* Source code, training manuals. *Customer Support:* Annual software support includes: toll-free hotline, fax, software trouble-shooting, minor bug fixes, regularly scheduled DCI software upgrades & enhancements, & general information on maximizing the benefits of your system.
 MS-DOS, Novell, UNIX, XENIX, Windows. IBM compatible (4Mb; 8Mb recommended). Contact publisher for price. *Addl. software required:* McDonnell Douglas PRO-IV Runtime. *Networks supported:* Novell.
Fully Integrated Package Designed for the Construction Industry. It Provides a Complete Solution for Tracking a Job from Beginning to Completion. The 20 Modules Include Job Costing, Payroll, Accounts Payable/Subcontract Management, Accounts Receivable/Billing, General Ledger, Equipment Control, Preventive Maintenance, Fixed Assets, Purchase Order, Work Order, Small Tools, Service Contracts, & Time & Material Billing. Forefront Is Written in Pro-IV, a Fourth-Generation Language from McDonnell Douglas Information Systems.
Dexter & Chaney, Inc.

FOREFRONT Construction Management System: Job Cost. *Version:* 5.0. Sep. 1995. *Items Included:* Source code, training manuals. *Customer Support:* Annual software support includes: toll-free hotline, fax, software trouble-shooting, minor bug fixes, regularly scheduled DCI software upgrades & enhancements, & general information on maximizing the benefits of your system.
 MS-DOS, Novell, UNIX, XENIX, Windows. IBM compatible (4Mb; 8Mb recommended). Contact publisher for price. *Addl. software required:* McDonnell Douglas PRO-IV Runtime. *Networks supported:* Novell.
Manages Costs of Labor, Material, Equipment & Sub-Contracted Costs for Each Construction Job. The System Allows for Unlimited Cost Types Within a Job & Phase, Inquiry for Reviewing Projected Cost to Complete, & Detail Transactions Immediately on the Screen; & It Permits Completion Percentages to Be Entered or Calculated Automatically. The System Verifies Input Data, & Allows Transaction Entries to Be Edited & Corrected Prior to Posting. The System Creates Audit Trails for Accounting Purposes, & Posting Programs Automatically Produce Journals. Job Cost Is Integrated with Other Modules in the Forefront Construction Management System.
Dexter & Chaney, Inc.

FOREFRONT Construction Management System: Payroll. *Version:* 5.0. Sep. 1995. *Items Included:* Source code, training manuals. *Customer Support:* Annual software support includes: toll-free hotline, fax, software trouble-shooting, minor bug fixes, regularly scheduled DCI software upgrades & enhancements, & general information on maximizing the benefits of your system.
 MS-DOS, Novell, UNIX, XENIX, Windows. IBM compatible (4Mb; 8Mb recommended). Contact publisher for price. *Addl. software required:* McDonnell Douglas PRO-IV Runtime. *Networks supported:* Novell.
Manages All Aspects of Payroll Control & Reporting for the Contractor. It Provides Data Required by Union & Organizations Including Fringes & Multiple Pay Rates & Includes a Certified Payroll Report. The System Tracks Important Changes to the Employee Master Record Such As Dates of Hire, Re-Hire, Termination, Last Rate Change & Last Review. Information Regarding Vacation, Holiday & Sick Hours with Optional Accrual per Pay Period Are Automatically Tracked. In Addition, Full Payroll Burdens Are Distributed to Job Cost & General Ledger. Payroll Is Integrated with Other Modules in the Forefront Construction Management System.
Dexter & Chaney, Inc.

FOREFRONT Construction Management System: Time & Materials-Billing. *Version:* 5.0. Sep. 1995. *Items Included:* Source code, training manuals. *Customer Support:* Annual software support includes: toll-free hotline, fax, software trouble-shooting, minor bug fixes, regularly scheduled DCI software upgrades & enhancements, & general information on maximizing the benefits of your system.
 MS-DOS, Novell, UNIX, XENIX, Windows. IBM compatible (4Mb; 8Mb recommended). Contact publisher for price. *Addl. software required:* McDonnell Douglas PRO-IV Runtime. *Networks supported:* Novell.
Efficiently Calculates & Prepares a T & M Bill. The T & M System Is Integrated with Job Cost, Purchase Order, Inventory & Payroll to Automatically Accumulate All the Billing Amounts from the Actual & Committed Costs for Each Job. Billings May Be Produced As Soon As the Costs Have Been Committed, Eliminating the Need to Wait for Each Cost Type or Job Total. Multiple Billing Formats Are Available for Each Job, & All the Line Items Can Be Modified Even after the Bill Has Been Automatically Created. The Bill Can Be Printed & Transferred to the Forefront Accounts Receivable System Without Any Duplication of Entry.
Dexter & Chaney, Inc.

FOREFRONT Construction Management System: Work Order. *Version:* 5.0. Sep. 1995. *Items Included:* Source code, training manuals. *Customer Support:* Annual software support includes: toll-free hotline, fax, software trouble-shooting, minor bug fixes, regularly scheduled DCI software upgrades & enhancements, & general information on maximizing the benefits of your system.
 MS-DOS, Novell, UNIX, XENIX, Windows. IBM compatible (4Mb; 8Mb recommended). Contact publisher for price. *Addl. software required:* McDonnell Douglas PRO-IV Runtime. *Networks supported:* Novell.
Provides a Complete Billing System for Service Calls. This System Allows a User to Enter the Work Order As Soon As It Is Called in & Immediately Dispatch a Ticket or Blank Order Form. Once Work Is Completed, the System Allows the User to Enter Unlimited Descriptions of the Work Performed & Any Additional Work That May Be Required. Makes Entering Labor & Materials Very Efficient, & Because the Invoice Amounts Are Totalled on the Screen, a User Can Check Work Immediately. A Completed Work Order or Invoice Can Be Printed As Soon As the Entry Is Complete.
Dexter & Chaney, Inc.

Foreign Direct Investment in the United States. Jan. 1995. *Customer Support:* Unlimited telephone support.
MS-DOS 6.0/Windows 3.1 or higher. PC Clone 486 or higher (4Mb). disk $15.00 (ISBN 1-878974-24-6). *Addl. software required:* MS Windows 3.1 or higher. *Optimal configuration:* PC clone with MS-DOS 6.0/Windows 3.1 or higher. 4Mb of hard disk storage recommended.
Multimedia Tutorial Which Installs in MS Windows 3.1 or Higher. Steps You Through an Overview of Foreign Direct Investment in the United States in about 30 Minutes.
Jeffries & Associates, Inc.

Foreign Exchange Dealer Support System: FXAT. *Version:* 6.1. Dec. 1995. *Items Included:* Users manual, complete documentation, installation assistance, re-installation if accidentally destroyed. *Customer Support:* 1st year Alpha Plus support is free, subsequent years are optional & cost about 20% of the software price, includes telephone technical assistance, free updates with new releases, conferences, training & user seminars.
MS-DOS 5.0 or higher (640k), Windows 3.X or higher, Novell Netware. 100% IBM (386 & up) compatibles. $16,000.00 with discounts for multiple user systems. *Networks supported:* Novell-Token Ring, Advanced Network.
Automates & Manages All Information Flows Associated with Foreign Currency Trading Including Front Office Information Flow & Automated Input into Backoffice Accounting. Installation on Individual Micros or Novell Networks. Handles Multi-Legged Transactions. Integrated Money Market & FOREX Systems Are Available.
Alphametrics Corp.

Foreign Exchange Software. *Version:* 2.0. Albert Bookbinder. Aug. 1993. *Compatible Hardware:* IBM PC. *Operating System(s) Required:* MS-DOS. *Language(s):* BASIC. *Memory Required:* 64k. *Items Included:* Handbook. *Customer Support:* Telephone support.
disk $144.00 (ISBN 0-916106-12-8).
Forecasts & Evaluates Price, Risk, & Return on Exchange of Foreign Currencies in International Trade or Investment. Includes 11 Interactive Programs for Foreign Currency Exchange. Programs Included Are: Moving Average, Exponential Moving Average, Exponential Smoothing for Forecasting, Monthly Seasonal Index, Monthly Link Relatives, Multiple Correlation, Multilateral Foreign Exchange & Value, Bilateral Foreign Exchange & Value, Real Interest Rate & Foreign Exchange, Arbitrage-Conversion, & Arbitrage-Reverse Conversion.
Programmed Pr.

Foreign Exchange Trading System. (International Finance Ser.). Spot Systems, Inc. Staff. Sep. 1983. *Compatible Hardware:* IBM PC, PC XT, PC AT, PS/2, 386, 486 & compatibles. *Operating System(s) Required:* MS-DOS 3.0 & higher, Windows. *Language(s):* Compiled BASIC. *Memory Required:* 640k. *General Requirements:* Hard disk.
Base System. Contact publisher for price.
Networks supported: LAN-Novell, Token Ring.
Analytical Tool That Can Improve Trading Decisions, While Providing the Accounting & Operation Support for the Trading Function. Trading Personnel Have Access to Real Time Information on Foreign Exchange Contracts, Rates, & Positions. Management Can Obtain Profitability Data & Reports on Compliance with Credit & Position Limits. System Includes the Analysis of Customer Limits, Position Including Consolidation of Customer Parent/Subsidiary Relationship. Detailed Analysis with Breakeven Calculations Is Provided. Generates General Ledger Entries Using User-Defined Accounting Tables. Additional Features: Foreign Processing of Spot, Forward, & Options Contracts; Processing of Other Foreign Currency Cash Flows; Revaluation of Contracts to Changing Spot & Forward Rates, & Reporting of Payment Instructions. Includes Report Writer. Automatic Interface to Swift & Spot Systems Multi-Currency GL. Both Stand-Alone & Network Versions Are Available.
Spot Systems, Inc.

Foreign Fonts Edition. *Compatible Hardware:* Apple Macintosh. *General Requirements:* ImageWriter.
3.5" disk $69.50.
Collection of 22 Bitmap Fonts. Most of the Fonts Have Functional Single-Stroke Accenting Keys for Use with Special Accents, Diacritics, Aspiration Signs & Vowel Symbols.
Devonian International Software Co.

Foreign-Language Fonts. *Compatible Hardware:* Apple Macintosh; IBM or compatibles. *General Requirements:* ImageWriter or LaserWriter. *Items Included:* 800k disk, user's manual, keyboard chart. *Customer Support:* Telephone support, defective disks replaced free.
$49.95 to $149.95.
ImageWriter & LaserWriter Fonts for over 270 Languages.
Linguist's Software, Inc.

Foreign Language Library: Teacher Authored Games in French, German, Russian, Spanish, Italian. *Version:* 3.3. Jul. 1984. *Items Included:* Mini-brochure with instructions & foreign language alphabets/fonts. *Customer Support:* Back-up disks - $10, free correction or repair of software.
DOS 3.3. Apple II Series. each author $29.95 (Order no.: FL-FRE, FRENCH; FL-GER, GERMAN; FL-ITA, ITALIAN; FL-RUS, RUSSIAN; FL-SPA, SPANISH). *Networks supported:* Contact Schoolhouse for info.
each game $19.95 (Order no.: INFL-1 SHARK; INFL-2 PUTT PUTT; INFL-3 AUTO SHOP; INFL-4 ALIENS; INFL-5 CHICKEN RACE; INFL-6 TICKY TACKY TOE).
all 6 games $99.95 (Order no.: INFL-X 6 GAMES).
Games with Animation & Fun; Teacher Provides Drill Material. All Alphabets & Accent Marks Provided Automatically. Available in French, German, Russian, Spanish, & Italian.
Interkom.

Foreign Language Word Processing. Mar. 1984. *Compatible Hardware:* Apple II, II+, IIe, IIc. *Operating System(s) Required:* Apple DOS 3.3. *Memory Required:* 48k.
disk write for info.
Simplified Foreign Language Word Processing with All Alphabets & Diacritical Marks.
Interkom.
English Word Pro.
  disk $34.95 (Order no.: IN-WP).
French Word Pro.
  disk $44.95 (Order no.: FRE-WP).
German, Spanish, Italian, & French Word Pros.
  disk $44.95 (Order no.: GER-WP/SPA-WP/ITA-WP/FRE-WP).
Russian Word Pro.
  disk $49.95 (Order no.: RUS-WP).

Forensic Provider. *Compatible Hardware:* Macintosh SE; IBM PC AT. *General Requirements:* Hard disk, printer. *Customer Support:* 6 months free.
Single user (multiuser upon request). 3.5" disk $950.00.
Demo disk. $25.00.
Forensic Medical Billing System.
Mark Kalish.

Foresight: Decision Support System. *Version:* 7.2. 1991. *Items Included:* Multiple volume user, systems & operations manuals. *Customer Support:* On-site installation/technical training, free user training in Atlanta, GA offices; hot line support, release/enhancements, newsline publication (all part of six (6) months product support program).
PC-DOS/MS-DOS 2.0 or higher, MVS, VSE. IBM PC & compatibles, IBM mainframes. contact publisher for price. *Nonstandard peripherals required:* 80287 Coprocessor Asynchronous Communications Port (if using mainframe file transfer). *Optimal configuration:* Minimum of 5Mb hard disk. *Networks supported:* Novell.
Corporate Planning, Financial Modeling, Forecasting, Reporting System with Multi-Level Consolidation, Goal Seeking, "What-If" Analysis, Risk Analysis, Worksheet Generation. Built-In Interface to Other Files/Subroutines.
COMPRO.

Forest Fire. *Compatible Hardware:* Atari 400, 800. *Language(s):* Atari BASIC (source code included). *Memory Required:* 24k. *General Requirements:* Joystick.
disk $18.95.
cassette $14.95.
Simulation Game.
Dynacomp, Inc.

Forest Fire Dispatcher. Duane Bristow. *Compatible Hardware:* TRS-80 Model I, Model III. *Operating System(s) Required:* TRSDOS. *Language(s):* BASIC.
contact publisher for price.
Simulation in Which User Is Forester in Charge of a Ranger District until Rain Ends the Forest Fire Season. How Many Acres Can Be Saved & at What Cost.
Duane Bristow Computers, Inc.

Forest Inventory Analysis. Duane Bristow. *Compatible Hardware:* TRS-80 Model III. *Language(s):* BASIC.
disk $54.95.
cassette $34.95.
Allows Professional Foresters to Analyze Data Collected by Forest Inventory Sampling Procedures.
Duane Bristow Computers, Inc.

Forest Sample Database. *Compatible Hardware:* TRS-80 Model III, Model 4. *General Requirements:* 2 disk drives.
$350.00.
Set of 2 Programs for Professional Foresters to Allow Development of a Database from Either Variable Radius Plots or Fixed Radius Plots.
Duane Bristow Computers, Inc.

Forestar Accounts Payable/Purchase Order Tracking System. *Version:* 7.0. 1991. *Items Included:* Multiple volume user, systems & operating manuals. *Customer Support:* Free on-site installation/technical training, free user training in Atlanta, GA offices; hot line support, release/enhancements, newsline publication (all part of six (6) month product support program).
DOS MVS. IBM 9370 through 3090, ES 9000 series. contact publisher for price. *Addl. software required:* CICS, VSAM.
On-Line, Realtime, Multicompany Processing with Automatic Recurring Payments, Automatic Discount Calculations, Standard Costing, Duplicate Invoice Screening, Multi-Bank Processing, Check Reconciliation, One-Time Vendors, Automatic PO/Receipt/Invoice Matching, 1099 Reporting, Cash Requirements Analysis, NOTEPAD, Advanced On-Line Data Entry & Inquiry.
COMPRO.

Forestar Accounts Receivable/Sales Analysis System. Version: 6.0. 1990. Items Included: Multiple volume user, systems & operations manuals. Customer Support: Free on-site installation/technical training, free user training in Atlanta, GA, hot line support, release/ enhancements, newsline publication (all part of six (6) months product support program).
DOS MVS. IBM 9370 through 3090, ES 9000 series. contact publisher for price. Addl. software required: CICS, VSAM.
On-Line, Realtime, Multicompany Processing for Open Item/Balance Forward Accounts, Realtime Cash Application, User-Controlled Terms, Discounts, Service Charges, Dunning Messages. Credit Holds, Disputed Invoice Flag, NOTEPAD, Advanced On-Line Data Entry & Inquiry. Powerful Sales Analysis Module with Comparative Analysis/Reporting by Customer, Product, Salesperson.
COMPRO.

Forestar Fixed Assets Systems. Version: 7.0. 1991. Items Included: Multiple volume user, systems & operations manuals. Customer Support: Free on-site installation/technical training, free user training in Atlanta, GA Offices, hotline support, release/enhancements, newsline publication (all part of six (6) months product support program).
DOS MVS, MS-DOS. IBM 370 through 3090, ES 9000 series, IBM PC. contact publisher for price. Addl. software required: CICS, VSAM.
On-Line, Realtime Multicompany Processing, Dual Book & Tax Accounting, Including ADR, ACRS, TEFRA, TRA of 1984, 1985, & 1986 Including AMT & ACE. Automatic ITC & Recapture Calculations, Inventory Tracking, Insurance Revaluation, Automatic Depreciation Projection (FASB 96).
COMPRO.

Forestar General Ledger/Financial Reporting System. Version: 7.0. 1990. Items Included: Multiple volume user, systems & operating manuals. Customer Support: Free on-site installation/technical training, free user training in Atlanta, GA offices, hotline support, release/ enhancements, newsline publication (all part of six (6) month product support program).
DOS MVS. IBM 9370 through 3090, ES 9000 series. contact publisher for price. Addl. software required: CICS, VSAM.
Comprehensive On-Line, Realtime, Multicompany Processing, Including Automatic Consolidations with Eliminations, Standard & Custom Reporting, Responsibility Reporting, Project/Product Tracking, Inter/Intra Company Allocations, Multiple Fixed/Variable Budgets, Automatic Accrual Reversals, Recurring Vouchers, Advanced On-Line Data Entry & Inquiry, & Download to PC's. Fully Integrated with All Other COMPRO Systems.
COMPRO.

Forgetful Freddy. Jan. 1994. Items Included: Program on CD-ROM, CD Booklet, & Registration Card. Customer Support: Free unlimited support via telephone.
Macintosh System 7.0 or higher. Macintosh LC or higher (4Mb). CD-ROM disk $49.00 (ISBN 1-57268-041-5, Order no.: 49002). Nonstandard peripherals required: 12 inch monitor or larger; CD-ROM drive. Optimal configuration: 5Mb RAM.
Helps Children Learn to Make Lists, Use a Calendar, & Develop Memory Skills.
Conter Software.

Forlib-Plus. Compatible Hardware: IBM PC, PC XT, PC AT & compatibles.
disk $69.95.
Supports Graphics, Interrupt Driven Communication, Program Chaining, & File Handling/Disk Support. A FORTRAN Coded Subroutine Is Included Which Will Plot Data on the Screen Either in Linear/Linear, Log/Linear, Linear/Log, or Log/Log on the Appropriate Grid. Versions Available For Microsoft, Supersoft, Ryan McFarland, IBM Professional, Lahev, & IBM FORTRAN.
Alpha Computer Service.

Form Letter Module. Ed Zaron. Mar. 1981. Compatible Hardware: Apple II, II+, IIe, IIc. Operating System(s) Required: Apple DOS 3.2, 3.3. Language(s): Assembly. Memory Required: 48k.
disk $19.98 (ISBN 0-87190-005-X).
Allows Creation of Personalized Letters in Mass Mailings.
Muse Software.

Form Letter Writer. Apr. 1986. Compatible Hardware: IBM PC, PC XT, PC AT. Operating System(s) Required: PC-DOS/MS-DOS. Language(s): Compiled BASIC. Memory Required: 128k. General Requirements: Printer.
routine only $25.00 (must be used with note pad); full program $50.00.
Creates Mail Order File Used by Another Program (Note Pad) in Writing Form Letters.
Robert L. Nicolai.

Form 1099 Generator. Version: 9.1. 1995. Compatible Hardware: IBM PC & compatibles. Operating System(s) Required: MS-DOS 2.1. Language(s): C (source code included). Memory Required: 128k. General Requirements: Hard disk or 2 floppy drives.
disk $200.00.
manual $25.00.
Generates 1099 Forms for Clients. Accommodates Several Clients on Single Disk, & Stores over 500 Payee Records per Density Disk & 1000 on Double-Sided Disk. Automatically Sets up File Space for New Client Payee Records. New Payees Can Be Added & Payments Can Be Input at Any Time. Payee Records Are Updated Immediately, & Any Item May Be Changed. All Active Payees Are Retained in File for Following Year. Program Automatically Configures to User's Terminal. Prints List of All Payees, Payee Payment Records, & Payee Mailing Labels, Form 1099 & Client Disk Index. Prints on Continuous Forms in Multiple Copies, & Forms Can Be Used in Window Envelopes.
Omni Software Systems, Inc. (Indiana).

The Form 1099 Printer. Version: 7.1. 1995. Items Included: Complete operating manual. Customer Support: Unlimited telephone support.
MS-DOS. IBM PC or compatible (256k). $50.00. Optimal configuration: IBM PC or compatible, 256k RAM, printer. Networks supported: Novel, Unex.
Produces Professional Looking 1099 & W-2 Forms from Information Which Is Entered Only One Time. Programs Are Updated with the Latest IRS Requirements. High Quality Input Screens Allow Easy Entry & Editing of Reporting Information. All Data Is Saved on Disk to Enable the User Fast, Efficient Yearly Conversion of Client & Payee Information. Form 1099-MISC, DIV, INT & Form W-2.
Omni Software Systems, Inc. (Indiana).

Formall. Items Included: Manual, sample forms. Customer Support: Free telephone support Mon-Fri 9-5 EST.
MS-DOS 2.0 or higher (512k). IBM PC, PC XT, PC AT, PS/2 & compatibles. contact publisher for price. Optimal configuration: Hard-drive-based microcomputer, daisy wheel on laser printer. Networks supported: Novell.
Produces Business Forms in Minutes. User Can Select Desired Form from 26-Item Menu. Also Produces Labels, Writes Checks & Prints Shipping Documents.
North Winds.

Formbuster. Version: 2.0. 1994. Items Included: 1 manual. Customer Support: 90 days unlimited warranty; free telephone support.
Windows. IBM 386 (4Mb). disk $99.95 (ISBN 1-886082-06-5, Order no.: FBW-550). Nonstandard peripherals required: Fax modem & scanner optional. Optimal configuration: 8Mb. Networks supported: Not directly.
A Form Filler That Makes Form Filling Less Time Consuming. Can Extract Information from Any Windows Database Without Typing a Word. Developes Its Own Database As You Fill It Out. This Product Thinks for Itself. And The More You Use It the Smarter It Gets.
Virtual Reality Laboratories, Inc.

Formlet. 1979. Compatible Hardware: IBM PC; TRS-80 Model I, Model II, Model III, Model 12, Model 16. Operating System(s) Required: TRSDOS, PC-DOS. Memory Required: 48-64k. TRS-80 Model, Model III. disk $47.95.
IBM PC. disk $47.95.
TRS-80 Model III, Model 12, Model 16. 8" disk $47.95.
Prepares Form Letters from a Selection of Pre-Written & Stored Stock Paragraphs. Stores Such Letters on Disk & Allows Users to Select among Them at Will. Users Can Intermix Fresh Text or Add Stock Paragraphs at Any Time.
Contract Services Assocs.

Formlet. Compatible Hardware: IBM PC; TRS-80 Model II, Model III, Model 12, Model 16. Operating System(s) Required: Scripsit 1.0, 2.0. contact publisher for price.
Creates a Complete or Select List of Names from Database of Church Donations Program for Insertion into Form Letters. Must Be Used in Conjunction with ELECTRIC PENCIL.
Custom Data (New Mexico).

The Forms Designer. Compatible Hardware: IBM PC. Operating System(s) Required: PC-DOS. Memory Required: 128k. General Requirements: 2 disk drives.
disk $195.00.
Creates Input Screen Formats for IBM PC Programs. Allows Programmers to Write Data-Entry Modules, with Extensive Screen Formatting & Error-Trapping. Consists of 3 Parts: a Form Editor, Run-Time Subroutines, & a Data-Entry Program. Among the Subroutines Included Are Utilities to Clear the Screen, Display the Input Form, Display a Message at the Top of the Form, Read a Field & Write to a Field.
BIT Software, Inc.

Forms Foundry. 1983. Compatible Hardware: Apple II series, Apple III. Operating System(s) Required: SOS, Apple DOS 3.3. Language(s): Applesoft. Memory Required: 48k. General Requirements: Tractor-feed printer.
disk $99.95.
Print Invoices/Sales Receipts, Purchase Orders & Debit & Credit Memos on Generic Forms or Plain Paper. Does Not Contain Its Own Data Base.
American Eagle Software, Inc.

Forms 4: Form Fill in Program, 3 programs. Sep. 1987. Operating System(s) Required: CP/M, CP/M-80, MS-DOS, PC-DOS. Language(s): MBASIC, ZBASIC. Memory Required: CP/M 64k, MS-DOS & PC-DOS 256k. General Requirements: Printer.
disk 40 TPI $49.95 (ISBN 0-923875-41-7).
disk 80 TPI $49.95 (ISBN 0-923875-42-5).
8" disk $49.95 (ISBN 0-923875-40-9).

manual only $10.00.
Group of Programs That Takes the Work out of Filling in the Same Form over & over Again with Different Data. These Programs Allow User to Handle Any Kind of Form. Word Processing-Type Control Keys Available When Entering Data. Can Be Used with External File. Field Editing Included.
Elliam Assocs.

Forms in Flight 2. *Compatible Hardware:* Commodore Amiga.
3.5" disk $119.00.
Three-D Drawing & Animation with Phong Shading.
Micro Magic.

Forms in Flight: 3D Drawing & Animation.
Compatible Hardware: Commodore Amiga. *Memory Required:* 1024k.
3.5" disk $79.00.
Features Include: Library Objects; Surface of Revolution; Red/Blue Stereo Images; Plotter Support (HP-GL); Dynamic Memory Allocation; Hidden Line Removal; Unattended Frame Generation; Surface Extrusions; Interchangeable 2D/3D Drawing; Independent Object Modification; Splines, Polygons, Free-Hand; Complex Object Nesting & Motion; Partial Object Rendering Capability; Copy (Mirror, From-To, Rotation, Dynamic); Variable Shading; Real Time Playback; Dynamic Observer Movement & Perspective Control (Rotate, Pan, Roll, Magnify, Move In/Out, Movable Look Point; & Overscan/PAL Support.
Micro Magic.

Forms-Kit. *Version:* 3.0. David Powers. Jul. 1985. *Compatible Hardware:* IBM PC & compatibles. *Operating System(s) Required:* MS-DOS, PC-DOS. *Language(s):* BASIC, Pascal (source code included). *Memory Required:* 64k. *General Requirements:* 80-column printer.
disk $49.95.
Data Entry Kit for the Terminal. Contains Its Own Editor to Create Screen Forms. Can Be Used for Both Random & Sequential Access File Structures. Sample Program Provided, Shows Ease-of-Use & Convenience of Data Entry Modifications.
Generic Computer Products, Inc. (GCPI).

Forms Management Toolkit. 1987. *Compatible Hardware:* IBM PC & compatibles, PC XT, PC AT. *Operating System(s) Required:* PC-DOS/MS-DOS 2.0 or higher. (source code included). *Memory Required:* 512k. *General Requirements:* Video adapter.
$79.95.
Lets User Enter a "Picture" of How the Form Will Look on the Screen. Displays the Form & Handles All User Input (Including Editing & Cursor Movement). The Routines Automatically Check Fields for Correct Format, Print Error Messages, & Ask the User to Re-Enter Fields until They Are Correct. Other Features Include: Support for All IBM PC Characters; Lets User Defines Any Number of "Exit Keys"; Provides Fields for Phone Numbers, Zip Codes, Social Security Numbers, Dates in Various Formats, Numeric, Integer, Integer Range, Free-Format, & Fixed Format Fields.
True BASIC, Inc.

Forms Master. *Compatible Hardware:* HP 150 Touchscreen.
3.5" disk $295.00 (Order no.: 45443A).
Can Be Used with Microsoft Pascal, Compiled BASIC, or FORTRAN to Create Application Interfaces. A Special Forms Editor Allows User to Create Screens with Enhancements Such As Boldface, Inverse Video, Italics, Blinking, & Underlining. Protection, Setting Tab Order, & Acceptable Characters Can Be Defined for Any Field.
Hewlett-Packard Co.

Forms 2. *Compatible Hardware:* Apple II; IBM RT PC. *Operating System(s) Required:* CP/M, UNIX, Apple DOS 3.3, SOS. *Language(s):* COBOL. *Memory Required:* Apple 64k.
IBM. disk $200.00.
disk $400.00.
Programming Tool Designed to Speed the Creation of Programs Involving Interactive Screen-Handling. Allows the Programmer to "Paint" a Form on the Screen, Just As It Should Appear to the User at Run-Time, & Generates COBOL Source Code. No Programming Experience Is Needed.
Micro Focus, Inc. (California).

Forms2000 for Windows Reference Manual: General Manager's Handbook. *Version:* 2.0. Clinton A. Kleinsorge. Feb. 1995. *Items Included:* 510 page Manual bound in three-ring binder with 2 diskettes of over 100 Quattro Pro & WordPerfect Software Templates. *Customer Support:* Free telephone support.
Microsoft Windows 3.1. IBM PC & compatibles (4Mb). disk $279.00 (ISBN 0-9644900-0-5).
Addl. software required: WordPerfect for Windows 6.0 & QuattroPro for Windows 5.0. *Optimal configuration:* 3 1/2 diskette and/or Hard drive (8Mb).
Condensed from Years of Hands-On Experience, This Professionally Designed Collection of Business Forms & Software Templates for Financial Management, Marketing Management, Personnel Management, Recruiting Management, & Project Management, Gives Instant Access to Virtually Every Form That Will Ever Be Needed to Run a Service Industry Company.
Diamond Group.

The Forms: WordPerfect Version. *Version:* 2.1. Sep. 1991. *Items Included:* 1 spiral-bound manual, macros to replace company name & company logo. *Customer Support:* Free.
MS-DOS 3.0. IBM PC (512k). $139.00 plus $49.00 for optional logo. *Nonstandard peripherals required:* Hewlett-Packard LaserJet Series II/III & compatibles. *Addl. software required:* WordPerfect DOS 5.1. *Networks supported:* All.
Eighty-Nine Business & Office Forms Developed in WordPerfect 5.1 Customized with Your Company Name & Address & Optional Company Logo. Includes Ten "Shell" Forms. Make Your Own Alterations in Seconds. Fill in the Forms on the Screen & Then Print on Your HP LaserJet Series II/III or Compatible Laser Printer.
Top Banana, Inc.

FormsProgrammer.
Macintosh (512k). disk $99.00.
Programmer's Utility That Enables Rapid Production of Custom Designed Output, Both to Screen Display & to Printer. Consists of Two Parts: Graphics Design Program & Programming Source Code Generator, Graphics Section Permits User to Draw Desired Output onto Screen Using Familiar Macintosh Drawing Tools. Source Code May Be Generated in Several Versions of Pascal & C Languages. End Result Is Source Code File Containing All Code Required to Draw Output As Single Procedure. Graphics Files Created by Program May Be Saved & Used Later to Modify Output. May Be Used by HyperCard Users to Produce Custom Output.
OHM Software.

FormTool Small Business Edition: Create Forms, Easily. *Items Included:* 80 Pre-Designed Forms & User Manual. *Customer Support:* Tech support.
Windows 3.1 or higher. IBM PC compatible 386 or higher (2Mb). disk $49.95 (ISBN 0-924677-29-5). *Optimal configuration:* VGA monitors recommended.
Specially Created Forms Package for the Forms Design & Usage Needs of the Small Business or Home Office. This Program Delivers Form Design & Fill-In Features at a Price You Can't Afford to Miss. Design with Easy-to-Use Drawing Tools.
IMSI (International Microcomputer Software, Inc.).

The Formula Plus G.A.S. Lifeboat Associates. *Compatible Hardware:* TI Professional. *Operating System(s) Required:* MS-DOS. *Memory Required:* 64k. *General Requirements:* 2 disk drives.
$595.00.
Texas Instruments, Personal Productivit.

FormZ. *Version:* 2.1. Oct. 1987. *Compatible Hardware:* IBM PC & compatibles. *Operating System(s) Required:* PC-DOS/MS-DOS 2.1 or higher. *Language(s):* PROLOG. *Memory Required:* 512k. *Customer Support:* No charge, M-F 9-5 EST.
disk $149.95.
Forms Processing Application That Can Store Information to Database Files, Called Libraries That Can Be Accessed to Complete Other Forms. Integrates Word Processing, Data Processing, & Math Calculations.
North Winds.

Forte Twinax. *Compatible Hardware:* IBM PC & compatibles. *Memory Required:* 256k.
disk $895.00.
Communication Link Between Personal Computers & IBM System 34, 36, or 38 Computers over Twinax Cables. Allows a PC to Emulate an IBM Model II, 5291, or 5292 Model I Terminal Accessing a System 34/36/38, or a Remote Attachment Through a Modem to an IBM 5294 Workstation Controller or an IBM 5251 Model 12. Permits up to Four Concurrent Host Sessions (Including a 5250 Printer Session) to Operate in the Background Mode, & Lets Users Switch Between Emulation & DOS. IBM Applications Supported Are DisplayWrite 36, Attachment 36, & File Support Utility.
Forte Communications, Inc. (California).

FORTH-32. *Compatible Hardware:* IBM PC. *Operating System(s) Required:* PC-DOS 1.0, 1.1, 2.0. *Memory Required:* PC-DOS 1.0, 1.1 64k; PC-DOS 2.0 96k.
contact publisher for price.
Segment Sensing Language Which Makes Segment Boundaries Transparent to Programmer. Features Intermixed 16- & 32-Bit Addressing Modes with Fig-FORTH & FORTH-79 Compatibility, As Well As Full Screen Editor, DOS Interface, Decompiler, Graphics, Assembler, Case Verb, Debug, User Controlled I/O with Communications to Three Parallel & Two Serial Ports, & Video Monitor Interface. Includes Quest Package Builder Utility Which Transforms User-Developed Programs into Marketable Software Packages by Building Condensed, Executable Image on Disk with Only Those FORTH Verbs Which Are Needed.
QuesTech, Inc.

FORTHCOM: Communications Module.
Compatible Hardware: IBM PC, PC XT, PC AT, PS/2; TRS-80 Model I, Model III, Model 4. *Operating System(s) Required:* MMSFORTH. *Language(s):* MMSFORTH (source code included). *Memory Required:* 32k. *General Requirements:* Modem.
disk $49.95.
Menu-Driven Communications Program in MMSFORTH That Permits a Wide Variety of RS-232 & Telephone Communication Activities. May Be Preset to Various Settings from 110 to 2400 Baud (Up to 19,200 Baud for Some Sub-Routines). Used with Two FORTHCOM Systems,

It Supports Extra Efficient Data Compression, Error-Checking & Auto-Retry. (Nearly as Efficient) Xmodem Protocol with Any Other Computer. Integrates with Other MMSFORTH Applications Such As DATAHANDLER, DATAHANDLER-PLUS, FORTHWRITE, GENERAL LEDGER, etc.
Miller Microcomputer Services.

FORTHWRITE. *Compatible Hardware:* IBM PC, PC XT, PC AT, PS/2; TRS-80 Model I, Model III, Model 4. *Language(s):* MMSFORTH (source code included). *Memory Required:* 48k.
disk $99.95.
Word Processor Which Features On-Line Help Screens & Screen Prompts. Provides Ability to Imbed Additional Printer Control Characters. Supports Text Indents & Outdents, Relative Margin Settings, & Permits Block & Document "Includes" Anywhere in Text. Has Print-to-Disk Option & Full-Proportional Support of Appropriate Printers with Tabbing. "Include" Feature Allows Documents to Be Chained Internally. Multiple Documents Can Be Chained at Printout. Integrates with Other MMSFORTH Applications Such As DATAHANDLER, DATAHANDLER-PLUS, FORTHCOM, etc.
Miller Microcomputer Services.

FORTRAN. Microsoft, Inc. *Compatible Hardware:* HP 150 Touchscreen.
3.5" disk $350.00 (Order no.: 45449A).
Provides Part of a Complete Program Development Environment on the Touchscreen. Allows Users Who Desire a High-Level Language to Implement Compute-Bound Applications While Maintaining Code Transportability. The Package Is a Subset of the ANSI X3.1978 Standard & Features a 3-Pass Compiler.
Hewlett-Packard Co.

FORTRAN Optimizing Compiler. *Version:* 4.0. *Compatible Hardware:* IBM PC & compatibles, PC XT, PC AT. *Memory Required:* 320k, recommended 512k.
contact publisher for price.
Redesigned to Take Advantage of the Optimizer & Code Generator Features of MICROSOFT C COMPILER Version 4.0. Compiler Time Switches Let User Choose the Level of Optimization. Supports a Wide Range of Math Libraries & Runs with or Without 8087/80287 Co-Processor. By Default, the Program Uses the Instruction Set for the 8086/8088 Processor. By Turning on a Switch Option When Compiling, Programs Can Take Advantage of the More Powerful Instruction Sets of 80186/80188/80286 Processors. The MICROSOFT CodeView Debugger Is Included in the Package.
Microsoft Pr.

FORTRAN Scientific Subroutine Library. *Version:* 2.0. *Compatible Hardware:* IBM PC & compatibles. *Language(s):* FORTRAN (source code included). *Memory Required:* 256k. *Customer Support:* 212-850-6788/6194.
disk $575.00 (ISBN 0-471-51499-3).
Consists of More Than 100 Pretested & Precompiled Mathematical & Statistical Subroutines Supplied on Disk As a Linkable Library & As a Source Code. More Than 400 Pages of Documentation Are Included. The Subroutines Cover Formulas for: General Statistics, Probability, Analysis of Variance, Regressions, Matrices, Interpolations, Fourier Analysis, Cross Tabulations, Differential Equations, Roots of Biquadratic Equations, Function Evaluation, Systems of Equations, Time Series Analysis, etc.
John Wiley & Sons, Inc.

FORTRAN Scientific Subroutine Package. *Compatible Hardware:* IBM PC, PC XT, PC AT & compatibles. (source code included).
disk $295.00.
Includes Approximately 100 FORTRAN Subroutines Falling Under the Following Categories: Matrix Storage & Operations, Correlation & Regression, Design Analysis (ANOVA), Discriminant Analysis, Factor Analysis, Eigen Analysis, Time Series, Nonparametric Statistics, Distribution Functions, Linear Analysis, Polynomial Solutions, & Data Screening.
Alpha Computer Service.

FORTRAN 77. *Version:* 3.1. Mar. 1991. *Items Included:* Documentation & implementation notes. *Customer Support:* Limited phone support - n/c, Technical BBS - n/c, Annual update - $300.00.
UNIX. Motorola Delta 88k systems, all OCS/BCS compliant systems. $2000.00. *Optimal configuration:* 8Mb Ram, hard disk.
UNIX. Data General Avion, Motorola, Tectronix, Opus, Everex. $2000.00.
Every 88K & Opus 88K. $2000.00.
Full ANSI 77 Optimizing Mainframe Caliber Compiler for M 88000 Based Systems. Most VAX/VMS, IBM/VS, HP & Cray Extensions. Also MIL-STD 1753 & Some FORTRAN.
Absoft Corp.

FORTRAN to BASIC Syntax Translator. *Compatible Hardware:* HP 9000 Series 200, 300, 9845, 520. *Language(s):* BASIC.
disk $495.00.
Translates Programs Written in FORTRAN into Almost Ready-to-Run BASIC.
James Assocs.

FORTRAN Tools for AppMaker. *Version:* 1.5.2. Apr. 1991. *Items Included:* FORTRAN tools manual. *Customer Support:* Free unlimited phone support.
Macintosh. Macintosh Plus or higher. 3.5" disk $150.00 (Order no.: M1000). *Nonstandard peripherals required:* Hard drive with 5Mb free space. *Optimal configuration:* 4Mb.
Application Generator for Software Development.
Language Systems Corp.

FORTRAN Tutor. (Private Tutor Ser.). Thomas K. Brown. *Compatible Hardware:* IBM PC, PCjr, PC XT, PC AT, Portable PC, 3270 PC. *Memory Required:* 128k. *General Requirements:* Double-sided disk drive, IBM Display; also requires IBM Private Tutor 1.00, 2.00, or IBM Private Tutor Presenter 1.10.
disk $19.95 (Order no.: 6276567).
Package of 6 Lessons for Engineers & Scientists. Includes Arithmetic Operations, I/O Operations, Program Control, Arrays & Using Data Files.
Personally Developed Software, Inc.

FORTRAN 77. *Version:* 4.1. Jul. 1985. *Compatible Hardware:* Sundance 16; C5002, C8002A. *Operating System(s) Required:* UNIX. *Language(s):* C. *Memory Required:* 256k.
disk $500.00.
Compiler System That Supports Most ANSI 66 FORTRAN & FORTRAN 77 Dialects. This Package Has Extended FORTRAN Language (EFL) & Ratfor Preprocessors. The Compilers & Libraries Are Fully Compatible with the UNIX Operating System.
Digital Research, Inc.

FORTRAN-77. *Compatible Hardware:* TRS-80 Model II, Model 16; Tandy 6000. *Operating System(s) Required:* CP/M. *Language(s):* Assembly, C. *Memory Required:* CP/M 68k, TRS-80 & Tandy 256k.
$25.00.
manual only $25.00.
Full Mainframe-Quality ANSI FORTRAN-77 Which Allows Access to Full 68000 Memory. Includes a Run-Time Library, Plus Intrinsic Functions for High Throughput. Has Ability to Call Routines Written in Assembly or 'C', & Handles 6 Data Types (Integer, Real, Double Precision, Complex, Character & Logical). Includes a Language Compiler, Code Generator, & Module Linker to Produce 68000 Code.
TriSoft.

Fortune Telling. *Compatible Hardware:* IBM PC; TRS-80 Model I Level II, Model III, Model 4, Tandy 1000. *Operating System(s) Required:* TRSDOS. *Language(s):* BASIC. *Memory Required:* 16k.
disk or cassette $19.95.
Ask Computer a Question & Receive an Answer.
Viking, Inc.

Fortune Telling with Dice & Numerology. 1992. *Items Included:* Detailed manuals are included with all DYNACOMP products. *Customer Support:* Free telephone support to original customer - no time limit; 30 day limited warranty.
MS-DOS 3.2 or higher. IBM PC & compatibles (512k). $19.95 (Add $5.00 for 3 1/2" format; 5 1/4" format standard). *Optimal configuration:* IBM, 128k RAM, run with either monochrome or graphics.
Fortune Telling with Dice May Not Be One of the Most Familiar Ways of Reading the Future, but It Is One of the Simplest. The Software Does All of the Table Look-Ups. All You Have to Do Is Throw the Dice, Either on the Screen (Computer Simulation) or on the Table (with Real Dice). The System Allows You Three Different Ways of Casting Your Future: Short-Term General Forecast; Short-Term Specific, & Long-Term. A Dozen Subject Areas Are Covered.
NUMEROLOGY Uses the Most Common Method for Describing Aspects of Your Inner Self from Your Name, Either Common or Birth, & Your Birth Date. It Gives You a Basic Makeup Analysis & Allows You to Look into Your Future to Find Compatibilies Involving People, Places, & Lucky Numbers.
Dynacomp, Inc.

Forword Word Processor. *Compatible Hardware:* IBM PC & compatibles. *Operating System(s) Required:* PC-DOS, MS-DOS. *Memory Required:* 256k. *General Requirements:* 2 disk drives, graphics (mono or color), ECI proprietary language board.
disk $395.00.
circuit board $495.00.
Multilingual Word Processor for Use with ECI's Various Language Boards. A Full Function Package Allowing the Interspersing of Foreign & English Text on the Same Line.
Eastern Computers, Inc. (ECI).

FotoMan Camera for the Computer with FotoTouch Gray Image Editing Software. Oct. 1991. *Items Included:* 2 manuals; docking stand for computer interface; FotoMan camera. *Customer Support:* 7 day-a-week phone support; limited lifetime warranty.
IBM AT or higher (for Windows to run effectively) Windows OS (1Mb). disk $799.00.
Accepts Digital Images Captured by the FotoMan Digital Camera & Downloaded into the Computer by Means of the Serial Port. Offers Gray Scale Editing & Sophisticated Image Manipulation, Including Flip, Rotate, Resize, Deskew, & Other High-End Functions. Images Can Be Stored in All Popular Graphics Fill Formats & Exported into a Number of Desktop Publishing & Word Processing Applications.
Logitech, Inc.

FotoROM: The Superior Photo Collection on CD-ROM. WEKA Publishing.
CD-ROM. CD-ROM disk $199.00 (ISBN 0-929321-09-X).
Photo Collection on CD-ROM. Computer Images; Basework 200 Images, Supplements 60 Images.
WEKA Publishing, Inc.

Foundation Graphics Toolbox. *Version:* 1.1. *Compatible Hardware:* Apple Macintosh, Tandem Computers. *Memory Required:* 2000k. *General Requirements:* Tandem mainframe. *Items Included:* Sample application, user manual. *Customer Support:* Training, hotline, consulting.
contact publisher for price.
Macintosh Graphics in Tandem Computer Applications.
Menlo Business Systems, Inc.

Foundation Vista. *Version:* 4.8. *Compatible Hardware:* Apple Macintosh. *Memory Required:* 2000k. *Items Included:* User guide, sample application design, Page Maker templates. *Customer Support:* Training, hotline, consulting, design review.
contact publisher for price.
SQL-Oriented Analysis & Design Tool. Supports Data Flow Diagrams, Entity Relationship, Program Structure, Form Design Editors with Central Design Repository.
Menlo Business Systems, Inc.

Foundation Vista Translator. *Version:* 1.3. *Items Included:* User guide. *Customer Support:* Training, hotline, consulting, design review.
Macintosh (1Mb), Tandem Mainframe. contact publisher for price.
Interfaces Compiled Vista Designs with the Tandem Environment.
Menlo Business Systems, Inc.

Foundry & Die Cast Management System.
1982. *Compatible Hardware:* IBM & compatibles. *Operating System(s) Required:* MS-DOS. *Language(s):* BASIC. *Memory Required:* 128k. *General Requirements:* Printer.
contact publisher for price.
Provides Information for Molding, Scrap, Net Good Castings, Heats Poured & Other Data. Includes Order Entry, Inventory Control, Production Scheduling, Order Backlog, Order Acknowledgment, Automatic Invoicing, Sales Analysis & Commissions, & Selling Price Changes.
Zeltner Assocs., Inc.

Four Crystals of Trazere.
DOS Version 3.1 or higher. IBM PC or 100% compatibles (512k). disk $24.95. *Optimal configuration:* IBM PC or 100% compatibles; DOS Version 3.1 or higher; 512k free memory; 256-color VGA, EGA, Tandy, CGA, AdLib, Soundblaster, Roland; full mouse support.
Enter a Land of Enchantment Gone Bad in This Fantasy Role-Playing Game. The Good Citizens of Trazere Have Been Mysteriously Mutated into Monsters. Your Band of Four Must Discover the Cause & Reverse the Horrible Transmogrification.
Software Toolworks.

4D Write. *Version:* 1.0.3. 1991. *Customer Support:* 90 Days free maintenance, free unlimited technical support.
Macintosh Plus or higher (1Mb). 3.5" disk $295.00.
Word Processing Module Designed for Integration into 4th Dimension (Software Program). Provides Word Processing Capabilities, Document Processing, Basic Database Publishing, Document Tracking, Hot Links with Other Modules, & Procedural Control Between Product & 4th Dimension.
ACIUS, Inc.

Four Footed Friends. (Vroombooks Ser.). T-Maker Co. Staff.
Contact publisher for price (ISBN 0-918183-02-2).
Children's Software.
T/Maker Co., Inc.

Four Footed Friends. *Version:* CD-Mac. (Vroombooks Ser.). T-Maker Company.
Macintosh. Contact publisher for price (ISBN 0-918183-04-9).
Children's Software.
T/Maker Co., Inc.

Four Footed Friends. *Version:* CD-Windows. (Vroombooks Ser.). T-Maker Company.
Windows. Contact publisher for price (ISBN 0-918183-05-7).
Children's Software.
T/Maker Co., Inc.

4.4 BSD Lite. *Customer Support:* All of our products are unconditionally guaranteed.
Unix. CD-ROM disk $39.95 (Order no.: LITE). *Nonstandard peripherals required:* CD-ROM drive.
UCB 4.4 BSD-Lite Distribution, Source Code Only (Not for Export).
Walnut Creek CDRom.

4.4 BSD Lite (Export). *Customer Support:* All of our products are unconditionally guaranteed.
Unix. CD-ROM disk $39.95 (Order no.: LITE-EXPORT). *Nonstandard peripherals required:* CD-ROM drive.
UCB 4.4 BSD-Lite Distribution, Source Code Only.
Walnut Creek CDRom.

400D-RPG Development Tools for DOS.
Version: 1.1. Sep. 1994. *Items Included:* User manual (3 volume set) plus Lattice 400D Quick Start Guide. *Customer Support:* 90 days free technical support. Annual maintenance fee available for 750.00.
PC-DOS/MS-DOS or DR-DOS 5.0 or higher, 4Mb hard disk space, 2Mb of memory, 80386, 80486, Pentium. First yr. license fee 2495.00; 675.00 ea. additional programmer; Maintnance fee: 750.00.
DOS-Based RPG/400 Development Environment That Lets You Offload RPG Development to a PC & Recover Important AS/400 System Resources. And with Faster Compilations & Superior Debugging Tools, Lattice 400D Increases Programmer Productivity. Provides All the RPG Development Tools Needed to Create RPG Programs for the AS/400: an RPG Compiler (V2R3-Compatible); DDS Compilers for Physical, Logical, Display, & Printer Files; a Full-Screen Editor (SED); Screen Design Aid (SDA); & an Interactive Source-Level Debugger (Lattice CodeProbe (CPR)). New Versions 1.1: Network Support; Improved Memory Management; Increased Support of DOS keywords - Including WINDOWS Keywords; & Increased Subfile Support.
Lattice, Inc.

400 Developer Desktop. *Version:* 3.0. Mar. 1985. *Items Included:* Documentation. *Customer Support:* Technical support via fax, Bulletin Board System (BBS) or CompuServe. 10 days free telephone support after 1st initial call.
Windows NT Client. PC 386 (8Mb). disk $750.00.
OS/2 Warp. PC 386 (8Mb). disk $750.00.
A Comprehensive Software Package That Allows AS/400 Programmers to Develop, Test & Run RPG-400 Applications on a Single Desktop or Home PC. The Product Supports the AS/400 Features PDM, SEU, SDA, DDS, CL & Query Replicated on the PC. Includes the Fastest RPG Compiler Available, As Well As an Interactive Debugger to Further Increase Productivity. Generated & Tested Source Code Is Transportable to the AS/400.
California Software Products, Inc.

400 Enterprise System. *Version:* 3.0. Feb. 1996. *Items Included:* Documentation. *Customer Support:* Technical support (first year included) via telephone, fax, Bulletin Board System (BBS) or CompuServe.
Windows NT. PC 386 (8Mb). from $5750.00 for 10 users. *Nonstandard peripherals required:* AS/400 connection.
OS/2 Warp. PC 386 (8Mb). $5750.00 for 10 users. *Addl. software required:* AS/400 connection.
The Fastest & Least Expensive Way to Benefit from the Increased Speed & Optimization of Resources Provided by Client/Server. Current AS/400 Applications Are Recompiled, Using Existing AS/400 Hardware & PC Workstations, to Create a Native PC Client System That Runs on the PC Client Sharing the Data Files on the AS/400 Server. Can Also Be Used to Move Development Tasks of Editing, Compiling, & Testing (DDS, RPG, CL, etc.) to the PC Client While the Source Libraries Remain on the AS/400. This Is the Most Economical & Effective Way of Increasing the Productivity of Your AS/400.
California Software Products, Inc.

400 Professional System. *Version:* 3.0. Jan. 1992. *Items Included:* Documentation. *Customer Support:* Technical support via telephone, fax, Bulletin Board System (BBS), CompuServe. First 30 days free telephone support.
Windows NT. PC 386 (8Mb). $3500.00 development system; from $350.00/user for system services.
OS/2 Warp. PC 386 (8Mb). $3500.00 development system; from $350.00/user for system services.
A Comprehensive Software Package That Allows Users to Migrate AS/400 RPG400 Applications to PCs & PC Networks. The Development Tool-Set & System Support of the AS/400 (RPGC, DDS, PDM, SEU, SDA, CL, QUERY, etc.) Are Replicated on the PC to Allow On-Going Maintenance of Migrated Applications. Provides the Ideal Platform for Distributing RPG400 Applications to a New User Base.
California Software Products, Inc.

4-In-One: Easy But Fun. *Compatible Hardware:* Commodore Amiga.
3.5" disk $14.95.
SlotCars, CircuitMania, ShufflePuzzle, Follow.
Polyglot Software.

Four Toes. *Compatible Hardware:* Apple II with Applesoft. *Operating System(s) Required:* Apple DOS 3.2, 3.3. *Memory Required:* 48k.
disk $18.95.
3-Dimensional Game. Object of the Game Is to Get 4 Markers in One of 76 Possible Rows.
Dynacomp, Inc.

Fourier Analysis & Synthesis. Jun. 1985. *Compatible Hardware:* IBM PC & Compatibles; TRS-80 Model I Level II, Model III, Model 4. *Operating System(s) Required:* TRSDOS, MS-DOS. *Language(s):* BASIC, Compiled BASIC (source code included). *Memory Required:* TRS-80 disk 32k, MS-DOS 128k. *Items Included:* Disk & instructions. *Customer Support:* Free.
disk $10.00.
MS-DOS (uses 80x87, if available). disk $15.00, uses 80x87, if available.
Used to Determine Cyclic Variation in Data. Cycles Can Be Used to Predict Data. Data Can Be Stored on Disk. Results Are in Graphics or Tables & Can Be Viewed on Screen or Printed.
Hinrichs Software.

TITLE INDEX

Fourier Analysis Forecaster. *Items Included:* Bound manual. *Customer Support:* Free hotline - no time limit; 30 day limited warranty; updates are $5/disk plus S&H.
MS-DOS. IBM & compatibles (128k or 512k). $99.95-$169.95.
CP/M (64k). disk $99.95.
Stock Market Analysis. Procedures Used Are Equally Well Suited to Cyclic Data in General. Typical Uses: Stock & Commodity Cycle Identification, Forecasting; Sales Forecasting - Separating the Trends from Seasonal Cycles, "Deseasonalizing"; Engineering Analysis of Mechanical Impulses to Determine Resonant Frequency & Damping Factor; Fitting General Spectral Data to Find Laplace Transform (& Thereby Poles & Zeroes).
Dynacomp, Inc.

Fourier Analyzer. (Fourier Transform Ser.: No. 1). *Compatible Hardware:* Apple II with Aplesoft; IBM PC. (source code included). *Memory Required:* 48k, except IBM 128k.
disk $19.95, incl. manual.
Scientific Program Which Can Be Applied to Examine the Frequency Spectrum Characteristics of Defined Duration Signals, Such As Groups of Pulses.
Dynacomp, Inc.

Fourier Toolkit Transform, Correlation, Filtering, & Time Series Analysis. *Items Included:* Full manual. No other products required. *Customer Support:* Free telephone support - no time limit. 30 day warranty.
MS-DOS 3.2 or higher. IBM & compatibles (512k). disk $129.95. *Optimal configuration:* IBM, MS-DOS 3.1 or higher, 640k RAM, CGA/EGA/VGA, Hercules, or PC3270 (or compatible) graphics capability.
The Ultimate "Scientific Pocket Calculator" for Doing Frequency Spectrum & Correlation Analysis. Engineers, Scientists, Statisticians, Economists, Stock/Commodity Market Analysts, Mathematicians, & Students May Quickly, Easily, & Conveniently Transform Data to & from the Frequency Domain, As Well As Perform Many of the Standard Time Series Calculations.
Dynacomp, Inc.

Fourier Transform Series, 3 disks. *Compatible Hardware:* Apple II with Applesoft; IBM PC. *Memory Required:* 48k, except IBM 128k.
Disk set. $79.95.
Frequency Spectrum Series.
Dynacomp, Inc.

4th Dimension. *Version:* 3.0. Sep. 1992. *Compatible Hardware:* Macintosh Plus, SE, IIx or higher. *Memory Required:* 1000k. *General Requirements:* System 6.0.3 or higher. *Customer Support:* 90 Days free maintenance, unlimited free technical support.
3.5" disk $895.00. *Networks supported:* AppleShare, TOPS, 3Com, Novell; $125.00 Single User.
demo disk $20.00.
$395.00 Run-Time version for 4 users.
Database Management System Featuring Structured & Free-Form File Types, Automatic Indexing, Split/Merge Files, Multi-User Access, Built-In Programming Language, Built-In Editor, Debugging Facilities, Run-Time Version, Graphics Editor, Forms-Generation Ability & On-Disk Tutorial. Offers a Maximum of 511 Fields per Record, 32,767 Characters per Field, 16 Million Records per File & 468 Characters per Record. Imports & Exports Comma-Delimited & Delimited by User-Chosen Delimiters ASCII, DIF & SYLK File Formats. Interfaces with BASIC, Pascal, C, COBOL, FORTRAN & Assembler Languages.
ACIUS, Inc.

4xFORTH. *Compatible Hardware:* Atari ST. *Items Included:* 2 Diskettes & manual.
3.5" disk $69.95, incl. manual.
upgrade from 4xFORTH Level 1 $20.00.
Comes with GEM Interface Including All VDI & AES Calls. Package Includes Editor, Assembler, Floating Point, Binary Save, Royalty Free Turnkey, Forth Accelerator, LineA, Stream Files, etc.
The Dragon Group, Inc.

FoxBASE+. *Version:* 2.10. *Compatible Hardware:* IBM PC & compatibles. *Operating System(s) Required:* MS-DOS 2.0 or higher. *Items Included:* 3 manuals, 5 disks. *Customer Support:* Free & unlimited phone support (toll number).
Single-user. disk $395.00.
unlimited runtime $500.00.
A Relational Database Management System for MS/PC-DOS Systems. Fully Compatible with dBASE III PLUS, Allowing Existing dBASE Applications to Run Unchanged. Combines the Flexibility of "Dot-Prompt" Programming with the Speed & Security of Compiled Code.
Microsoft Pr.

FoxBASE+/LAN. *Version:* 2.10. *Compatible Hardware:* IBM PC & compatibles. *Operating System(s) Required:* DOS 3.1 or higher. *Memory Required:* 390k. *General Requirements:* NetBIOS compatible network software. *Items Included:* 3 manuals, 5 disks. *Customer Support:* Free & unlimited phone support (toll number).
$595.00 per network server.
$700.00 LAN Runtime.
Networked Database-Management System Featuring Automatic File & Record Locking. Not Copy Protected; No Maximum Number or Networked User's Copy. dBASE III PLUS compatible. Fast Execution Speed.
Microsoft Pr.

FoxBASE+/Mac. *Version:* 2.01. *General Requirements:* Hard disk drive; System 4.2 or higher; Finder 6.0. *Items Included:* 4 manuals. 2 disks. *Customer Support:* Free & unlimited phone support (toll number).
Macintosh Plus or higher (1Mb). Single-User $495.00, Multi-User $695.00.
royalty-free Run-Time version $300.00.
Combines the Power & Maturity of the dBase Language with an Accessible Interface Relational Database Management System for the Apple Macintosh. Runs Existing dBase III PLUS & FoxBASE & DOS Applications Without Change. Provides Windows, Menus, Buttons, Mouse Support & Other Elements of the Standard Mac Interface. Up to 200 Times Faster Than Other Macintosh Database Management Products.
Microsoft Pr.

FoxBASE+/386. *Version:* 2.10. *Compatible Hardware:* 80386-based PCs. *General Requirements:* 80287 or 80387 coprocessor, 2Mb of RAM. *Items Included:* 3 manuals, 5 disks. *Customer Support:* Free & unlimited phone support (toll number).
$595.00.
$500.00 Unlimited Runtime.
DBASE III PLUS Work-Alike for 80386 Machines. Uses Extended Memory for Fast Performance.
Microsoft Pr.

FoxGraph. *Compatible Hardware:* IBM PC, PC XT, PC AT & compatibles, PS/2. *Operating System(s) Required:* DOS 2.1 or higher. *Memory Required:* 640k. *General Requirements:* Hard disk, Hercules, CGA, EGA, VGA, or Super EGA graphics adapter & monitor. *Items Included:* 1 manual, 3 disks. *Customer Support:* Free & unlimited phone support (toll number).
$295.00.
Graphics Development Package Capable of Creating Two- & Three-Dimensional Business & Scientific Graphs. Its Data Manager Can Support up to 4096 Data Cells for Plotting. Allows Users to Create Plots up to 36" by 48", or Generate IMG Files for VENTURA PUBLISHER & Tag Image File Format Files. Suports Laser Printer & PostScript Output Devices.
Microsoft Pr.

FoxPro. *Version:* 2.0. *Items Included:* 4 manuals, 4 disks. *Customer Support:* Free & unlimited phone support (toll number).
IBM PC XT (512k). $795.00, FoxPro/LAN $1295.00, Distribution Kit $500.00, Library Construction Kit $500.00.
The Fastest Relational Database System Available for PC Compatibles. Allows User to Open up to 25 Databases at Once. Includes Pull-Down Menus, Scroll Bars, Zoomable Windows, Support for Color & a Mouse, String Fields Store up to 64k & Memo Fields Store Unlimited Amount of Data. Memo Fields Can Handle Binary Data. Non-Procedural Operations & Mac-Like Interface Make It Easy for Beginners to Use. View Window Lets User Define Databases & Relationships, Complex Labels, Reports, Screens, Menus & Queries Can Be Created Without Programming. On-Screen Preview of Report & Labels. LAN Version Also Available.
Microsoft Pr.

FoxPro 2.0 Power Tools. Malcolm C. Rubel. *Items Included:* Two 5.25" disks. *Customer Support:* Phone number available for technical support, 212-492-9832; free disk replacement within 90 days of purchase.
IBM PC & compatibles. disk $54.95 (ISBN 0-553-35294-6). *Addl. software required:* FoxPro 2.0.
This Book/Disk Package Provides FoxPro Developers/Programmers with Abundant Insights into Programming Techniques & over 300 Ready-to-Use FoxPro 2.0 Utilities to Be Directly Linked to Users' Applications. Utilities Include: Screen/ Menu Tools, Context-Sensitive Help Development Systems, Printer Control/Report Generation. Malcolm Rubel Is a Well-Known Expert on Database Systems & Author of Bantam's dBASE IV Power Tools.
Bantam Bks., Inc.

Fractal Attraction: A Fractal Design System for the Macintosh. Kevin D. Lee & Yosef Cohen. Oct. 1991. *Items Included:* 1 Macintosh disk, 72 page user manual. *Customer Support:* Free customer support available through software developer (i.e., Kevin Lee).
System Software 6.0 or higher. MacPlus or higher (1Mb). 3.5" disk $53.00 (ISBN 0-12-440740-4, Order no.: 1-800-321-5068).
Macintosh Application with Which One Uses Iterated Function Systems (IFS) to Design Fractals. In a Draw-Like Window, the User Manipulates Transformations by Pointing, Clicking, & Dragging. The Corresponding Equations Are Shown in a Spreadsheet-Type Window, & the Resulting Fractal Is Generated in a Third Window.
Academic Pr., Inc.

Fractal Ecstasy. Jun. 1993. *Items Included:* User Guide. *Customer Support:* 30 day warranty.
Windows. IBM & compatibles (4Mb). disk $14.95 (ISBN 1-885638-03-5).
An Exciting Exploration of More Than a Thousand Spectacular Full Clor, Full Screen Fractal Images with Animation, & Dozens of Motion Video Fly-Throughs Using the Video for Windows Format. Zoom in & Out & Experience Fractals in Motion or Make Your Own Designs with Our Unique Fractal Generating Program, "Fractal Creator", Watch the Results Unfold.
Deep River Publishing, Inc.

FRACTAL FRENZY

Fractal Frenzy. *Customer Support:* All of our products are unconditionally guaranteed.
All Systems. CD-ROM disk $39.95 (Order no.: FRACTAL). *Nonstandard peripherals required:* CD-ROM drive.
2000 Beautiful Images Plus Programs to Create Your Own.
Walnut Creek CDRom.

Fractal Music. *Version:* 2.0. *Compatible Hardware:* Commodore Amiga. *Items Included:* Source code. *Customer Support:* Telephone support.
3.5" disk $19.95.
Music & Graphics Based upon Fractal Math.
Silver Software.

Fractal Programming in C. Roger T. Stevens. Aug. 1989. *Items Included:* All source code to reproduce fractals available on disk.
MS-DOS. IBM PC & compatibles. disk $24.95 (ISBN 1-55851-037-0). *Nonstandard peripherals required:* EGA or VGA & color monitor. *Addl. software required:* Turbo C, Quick C or Microsoft C compiler.
disk $39.95, incl. book (ISBN 1-55851-038-9).
Hands-On Reference That Enables Users to Program Fractal Curves. Discussed Are the Von Koch Snowflake, Gosper Curve & Dragon Curves. 100 Black-&-White Fractals & 32 Full-Color Fractals Are Illustrated. All Source Code Available on Disk.
M & T Bks.

Fractals. *Version:* 3.3. *Compatible Hardware:* Apple Macintosh. *Memory Required:* 1024k. *Items Included:* Diskette & manual. *Customer Support:* Telephone.
3.5" disk $49.95.
Fractal Graphics Program. Generate Views of Mandelbrot & Julia Sets. (Color MacII) Zoom Capability.
Atlantic Software.

Fractalscope, 2 diskettes. *Items Included:* Bound manual. *Customer Support:* Free hotline - no time limit; 30 day limited warranty; updates are $5/disk plus S&H.
Apple (64k). $29.95. *Nonstandard peripherals required:* Two drives; graphics printer supported (you must supply screen dump utility).
Menu-Driven Package Which Will Allow User to Create Fractal Images Surrounding the Mandelbrot Set. Features Include Three Resolution Modes, Zoom, & Printable Image Files. A Vector-Trace Mode Is Available to Graphically Record the Relative Size, Quadrant, & Vector of Each Iteration. However, You Do Not Have to Know Any Mathematics to Be Able to Experiment.
Dynacomp, Inc.

Fractionation Tray Design & Rating. *Items Included:* Full manual. No other products required. *Customer Support:* Free telephone support - no time limit. 30 day warranty.
MS-DOS 3.2 or higher. IBM & compatibles (512k). full system $389.95.
demo disk $5.00.
Designs New As Well As Rates Existing Fractionation Trays for Tray Liquid-Vapor Loadings. It Also Performs Rigorous Tray Efficiency Calculations. All Analyses May Be Made for Valve, Bubble Cap, & Sieve Trays. You May Try Numerous Feasible Tray Configurations in Only a Few Minutes to Find the Optimal Design and/or Rating.
Dynacomp, Inc.

Frame Relay: A Technical Overview. Dec. 1994. *Items Included:* User manual. *Customer Support:* Free technical support & a 30-day warranty (1-800-521-CORE).
MS-DOS. IBM & compatibles (512k). 3.5" disk $199.00 (ISBN 1-57305-017-2). *Nonstandard peripherals required:* High-density 3.5" disk drive; VGA color monitor. *Addl. software required:* MS-DOS version 3.3 or higher. *Optimal configuration:* IBM (512k), MS-DOS version 3.3 or higher, VGA color monitor, keyboard, Microsoft compatible mouse (optional).
This Course begins with an Exploration of the Evolution of Information Processing & Why This Evolution Leads Us to a Need for a New Networking Infrastructure. Then, the Basic Technical Characteristics & Trade-Offs Between Frames & Cells Are Explained. A Discussion of Frame Relay Technology Examines Both the Frame Format Details & the Transmission Aspects Involved. Finally, Frame Relay Services, Standards, & Alternatives Are Explained.
Bellcore.

Frame-Up. *Version:* 1.5. Tom Weishaar. 1984. *Compatible Hardware:* Apple II, II+, IIe, IIc, IIgs. *Operating System(s) Required:* Apple DOS 3.3. *Language(s):* Applesoft BASIC. *Memory Required:* 48k.
disk $29.50.
Apple Presentation Program. Allows User to Create Displays from Low & High Resolution & Text Frames. Frames Can Be Advanced or Reversed with a Single Key Command. Features Include a Reference Chart, On-Screen Menus & a Bidirectional Scrolling Catalog. A Text Screen Editor Allows the User to Produce Black & White Text Frames. The User Can Also Type Titles & Comments on the Screen While a Presentation Is in Progress.
Beagle Brothers.

FRAMER: Display Document Files. *Version:* 2.2. 1983. *Operating System(s) Required:* VMS, MICROVMS. *Language(s):* Basic. *Memory Required:* 330k.
Included with CNTRL.
Converts Session-Oriented Logs to a Printable Format. Allows User to Imbed Converted Log Files in User Documentation. Converts Logs to a Variety of Formats (E.G, LN03, Generic, etc.). Lets User Define Personal Format.
Raxco, Inc.

Framework Fonts. *Compatible Hardware:* Apple Macintosh. *Memory Required:* 512k.
3.5" disk $79.95.
Border & Frame Fonts for PostScript Devices. These Downloadable Laser Fonts Can Be Printed on Any PostScript Printer & In Any Font Size That an Application Allows.
Data Management Assocs. of New York, Inc.

Framework IV. *Compatible Hardware:* IBM PC. *Memory Required:* 640k. *General Requirements:* 10Mb hard disk.
disk $695.00.
LAN version $995.00.
Integrated Package Featuring Word Processing, Spreadsheet, Database, Graphics, Communications, Outlining & Electronic Mail. Includes Context Switching, Mail/Merge Database Link, Built-In Language in All Modules, 32,000 by 32,000 Spreadsheet Matrix Size & Context-Sensitive On-Screen Help. Pastes Spreadsheet Sections & Graphics into Word-Processing Files with Dynamic Linking of Spreadsheets & Graphics to Word-Processing Files. Unlimited Number of Spreadsheets Linked; Number of Database Tables Linked in One Query Is Limited by Memory. Unlimited Number of Files Edited Simultaneously. Imports & Exports Framework II, dBASE III, Display Write, WordStar, MultiMate, WordPerfect, WK1, WKS, SYLK & Other File Formats.
Borland International, Inc.

Le Francais Vivant One. Ariane-Cathy Culot et al. *Items Included:* Software program guide. *Customer Support:* Customer support is available through our toll-free number 800-328-1452, ask for Technical Support. Free on-site training is also available through the same number.
MS-DOS. IBM & compatibles (256k). 3.5" disk $315.00 (ISBN 0-8219-1232-1, Order no.: 95324H). *Nonstandard peripherals required:* CGA or better graphics adaptor. *Optimal configuration:* Color monitor & printer. *Networks supported:* Not designed for networks, but can be installed to a network.
MS-DOS. IBM & compatibles (256k). 5.25" disk $315.00 (ISBN 0-8219-0595-3, Order no.: 95324G). *Nonstandard peripherals required:* CGA or better graphics adaptor. *Optimal configuration:* Color monitor & printer. *Networks supported:* Not designed for networks, but can be installed to a network.
Apple PRODOS. Apple IIe or higher (128k). disk $315.00 (ISBN 0-8219-0596-1, Order no.: 95324F). *Nonstandard peripherals required:* 80-column card for 64k Apple II's. *Optimal configuration:* Color monitor & printer. *Networks supported:* Not designed for networks, but can be installed to a network.
Designed to Review, Drill, & Apply the Vocabulary, Structures, & Cultural Information Presented in the Textbook in an Easy-to-Use Interactive Environment.
EMC Publishing.

Le Francais Vivant Two. Ariane-Cathy Culot et al. *Items Included:* Software program guide. *Customer Support:* Customer support is available through our toll-free number 800-328-1452, ask for Technical Support. Free on-site training is also available through the same number.
MS-DOS. IBM & compatibles (256k). 3.5" disk $295.00 (ISBN 0-8219-1233-X, Order no.: 95333H). *Nonstandard peripherals required:* CGA or better graphics adaptor. *Optimal configuration:* Color monitor & printer. *Networks supported:* Not designed for networks, but can be installed to a network.
MS-DOS. IBM & compatibles (256k). 5.25" disk $295.00 (ISBN 0-8219-0808-1, Order no.: 95333G). *Nonstandard peripherals required:* CGA or better graphics adaptor. *Optimal configuration:* Color monitor & printer. *Networks supported:* Not designed for networks, but can be installed to a network.
Apple PRODOS. Apple IIe or higher (128k). disk $295.00 (ISBN 0-8219-0949-5, Order no.: 95333F). *Nonstandard peripherals required:* 80-column card for 64k Apple II's. *Optimal configuration:* Color monitor & printer. *Networks supported:* Not designed for networks, but can be installed to a network.
Designed to Review, Drill, & Apply the Vocabulary, Structures, & Cultural Information Presented in the Textbook in an Easy-to-Use Interactive Environment.
EMC Publishing.

Frankenstein. *Version:* 1.5. Feb. 1995. *Items Included:* BookWorm Student Reader (diskette). *Customer Support:* 30 day MBG. Technical support (toll call) - no charge.
System 7.0 or higher. Macintosh (5Mb). CD-ROM disk $29.95 (ISBN 1-57316-028-8, Order no.: 16163). *Nonstandard peripherals required:* CD-ROM drive, 12" color monitor. *Optimal configuration:* 13" color monitor recommended.
Windows 3.1 or higher. IBM compatible (MPC) 386 DX (4Mb). CD-ROM disk $29.95. *Nonstandard peripherals required:* Standard multimedia compatible CD-ROM. *Optimal configuration:* 8Mb RAM recommended, 256 color monitor recommended.
One of the Most Enduring Horror Stories of All

TITLE INDEX

Time, Frankenstein Has Held Readers Spellbound since Its First Publication in 1818. This Edition Includes Complete Unabridged Text & In-Depth Discussions of the Many Differences Between Hollywood's Popularized View of the Tale & Mary Shelley's Darker, Deeper Original. Features Complete Sound Allowing the User to Listen to All or Part of Each Work.
Communication & Information Technologies, Inc. (CIT).

Frankenstein & Selected Works of Poe, Vol. 4. Version: 1.5. Feb. 1995. *Items Included:* BookWorm Student Reader (diskette). *Customer Support:* 30 day MBG. Technical support (toll call) - no charge.
System 7.0 or higher. Macintosh (5Mb). CD-ROM disk $59.95 (ISBN 1-57316-036-9, Order no.: 19004). *Nonstandard peripherals required:* CD-ROM drive, 12" color monitor. *Optimal configuration:* 13" color monitor recommended.
Windows 3.1 or higher. IBM compatible (MPC) 386 DX (4Mb). CD-ROM disk $59.95. *Nonstandard peripherals required:* Standard multimedia compatible CD-ROM. *Optimal configuration:* 8Mb RAM recommended, 256 color monitor recommended.
Complete Text of Frankenstein As Well As an In-Depth Discussion of Hollywood's View of the Tale & Mary Shelley's Darker, Deeper Original. Poe Features Selected Works Including The Raven, Anabel Lee, & Others. Both Contain Complete Sound Allowing the User to Listen to All or Part of Each Work.
Communication & Information Technologies, Inc. (CIT).

Franklin Big League Baseball Encyclopedia: HRS-100. Jun. 1992. *Items Included:* Four 5" floppy disks, two 3.5" disks, one printed manual.
MS-DOS. IBM PC or compatible (640k). disk $99.99 (ISBN 0-945731-88-4). *Optimal configuration:* MS-DOS 3.1 or higher.
Instant Search & Retrieval on Statistical Baseball Information. Includes Batting & Pitching Stats for Every Player Ever to Play in the Major Leagues. Also Includes Player Biographical Data, As Well As Year by Year Team & Individual Stats. Unique Stats May Be Created via a Number of Different Search Criteria.
Franklin Electronic Pubs., Inc.

Fraternal Software: Complete Membership Management. Version: 2.0. Open Door Software Division. 1992. *Items Included:* Manual. *Customer Support:* On-site training available - $200.00/day plus per diem; Customization $50.00/hr, maintenance on customized copies $100.00/month.
DOS. IBM & compatibles (512k). disk $69.00 (ISBN 1-56756-010-5, Order no.: OD200I).
Macintosh. 3.5" disk $69.00 (ISBN 1-56756-011-3, Order no.: OD210M).
State of the Database Art Software Application Handling Basic Accounting Features, Member Information, Fines, Dues, & Demerits for Any Membership Organization. Works Well with Multiple Organizational Management Software. Addresses the Needs of National Chapters As Well As Local Member Information System Needs in an Integrated Package. Allows for Electronic Transfer of Information.
Advantage International.

Freakin' Funky Fuzzballs. Nov. 1990. *Items Included:* 11-page manual, two 5.25" diskettes, one 3.5" diskette, one-page eyechart. *Customer Support:* 30-day warranty free replacement if proof of purchase indicating purchase date is provided. If over 30-day warranty, please provide $12.50 replacement fee. Customer support help line hotline available Monday through Friday 4:00 PM to 8:00 PM & 12:00 noon to 4:00 PM weekends & holidays.
MS-DOS. IBM PC & 100% compatibles. disk $19.95 (ISBN 0-926846-58-2, Order no.: RC30107000). *Nonstandard peripherals required:* Optional: Hard disk drive, Roland MT32 or AdLib sound cards. Requires: 2 disk drives of any combination. *Optimal configuration:* IBM PC 100% compatibles, combination of any 2 disk drives, minimum memory: 384k CGA, 512k EGA, 640k VGA, Optional hard disk drive.
An Arcade-Style, Graphic Adventure Pits the Player, As a Majestic Fuzzball, Against an Ever-Moving, Always-Chasing Enemy. As the Player Maneuvers the Fuzzball, the Floor Begins to Disappear Which May Make Travel Difficult. However, by Building the Fuzzball's Vitality & Strength, the Player Can Hope to Triumph to the Next Level. Of Course, As the Fuzzball Moves from Floor to Floor It May Pick up Many Goodies Along the Way: Magical Wands, Protective Armor, & Shields, Healing Potions, etc. Freakin' Funky Fuzzballs Guarantees Fun & a Lot of it. As Your Strategy Develops, So Will Your Points Progress. As the Player, You'll Find It Hard to Stop Playing. You Just Know & Are Certain of It, That You Could Have Made It Further ... & If You Do It One More Time, You Will Make It Further.
Sir-Tech Software, Inc.

Freaky Friday. Intentional Education Staff & Mary Rodgers. *Items Included:* Program manual. *Customer Support:* Free technical support, 90 day warranty.
School ver.. Mac System 7.1 or higher. Macintosh (4Mb). 3.5" disk contact publisher for price (ISBN 1-57204-347-4). *Nonstandard peripherals required:* 256 color monitor, hard drive, printer.
Lab pack. Mac System 7.1 or higher. Macintosh (4Mb). 3.5" disk contact publisher for price (ISBN 1-57204-323-7). *Nonstandard peripherals required:* 256 color monitor, hard drive, printer.
Site license. Mac System 7.1 or higher. 256 color monitor, hard drive, printer. 3.5" disk contact publisher for price (ISBN 1-57204-348-2).
School ver.. Windows 3.1 or higher. IBM/Tandy & 100% compatibles (4Mb). disk contact publisher for price (ISBN 1-57204-324-5). *Nonstandard peripherals required:* VGA or SVGA 640x480 resolution (256), mouse, hard drive, sound device.
Lab pack. Windows 3.1 or higher. IBM/Tandy & 100% compatibles (4Mb). disk contact publisher for price (ISBN 1-57204-349-0). *Nonstandard peripherals required:* VGA or SVGA 640x480 resolution (256), mouse, hard drive, sound device.
Site license. Windows 3.1 or higher. IBM/Tandy & 100% compatibles (4Mb). disk contact publisher for price (ISBN 1-57204-350-4). *Nonstandard peripherals required:* VGA or SVGA 640x480 resolution (256), mouse, hard drive, sound device.
This companion for young adult literature is ideal for students who don't know how to start that book report, or give that needed summary. Gentle prompts throught the guide section of the program include Warm-up Connections, Thinking about Plot, Quoting & Noting, Keeping a Journal, If I Were ———' Responding to Questions, Using Quotations, Taking a Personal View, Write to Others, & Write a Sequel.
Lawrence Productions, Inc.

Freddy's Rescue Roundup. D. P. Leabo & Arlen V. Strietzel. *Compatible Hardware:* IBM PC, PCjr, PC XT, Portable PC with IBM Color Display, one double-sided disk drive, joystick (optional). *Operating System(s) Required:* DOS 2.00, 2.10, 3.00, 3.10. *Memory Required:* IBM PCjr 256k, all others 128k.
disk $19.95 (Order no.: 6276511).
Freddy, the Maintenance Man Has to Clean All 25 Levels of the Cliff Dwellings Park Which Is about to Reopen. While Removing the Roadrunners, He Must Watch Out for the Park's Robots Which Have Gone Berserk, Compacting Anyone They Can Find.
Personally Developed Software, Inc.

Frederik Pohl's GATEWAY. *Items Included:* Game manual, hint book, warranty card. *Customer Support:* Toll-free technical assistance (1-800-658-8891). Computer operated pre-recorded Hint Line (1-900-776-5583), $.75 first minute, $.50 each additional minute. Self-guiding Hint Book with choice of hints or answers ($9.95 plus s/h).
MS-DOS 3.3 or higher. IBM PC & compatibles (640k). 3.5" disk $59.95 (ISBN 1-880520-05-2, Order no.: GW-3). *Optimal configuration:* IBM PC 80286 or 80386 with 640k RAM & VGA adapter & monitor.
5.25" disk $59.95 (ISBN 1-880520-07-9, Order no.: GW5DD).
Fast Paced Mystery Thriller Which Challenges Player to Discover the Secrets of the Heechee World Before Those Secrets Destroy the Universe.
Legend Entertainment.

FReditor. Version: 1.5. *Items Included:* User manual. *Customer Support:* Telephone support.
Macintosh 512K or higher. 3.5" disk $99.95.
Fortran Editor for the Macintosh. Handles Files up to 32,000 Lines. Has Special Functions, Such as Multiple Windows, GREP Search & Replace, Custom Autowrap, On-Screen Column Markers, & the Ability to Generate Tables for Export to Spreadsheets.
Battelle.

Free & Reduced Planner. *Operating System(s) Required:* PC-DOS/MS-DOS, OS/2. *Memory Required:* 256k. *General Requirements:* 5 Mb on hard Disk. *Items Included:* Includes 6-month warranty, user manual. *Customer Support:* Free updates, enhancements, & toll-free 800 lines for customers under warranty.
3.5" or 5.25" disk $2500.00.
School Food Service Provides Free, Reduced, & Pre-Paid Meal Plans. Features Meal Application Module Which Offers Free & Reduced Applications for National School Lunch Program & Sales Module Which Offers All Sales & Meal Count Data for State & Federal Reimbursements. Interfaces with Practorcare POS System & Student Verification System.
Practorcare, Inc.

Free Willy 2: The Adventure Home. Version: 1.5. (Interactive MovieBook Ser.). Jul. 1995. *Items Included:* Manual, registration card, promotional flyers. *Customer Support:* Phone technical support.
Windows 3.1 or later. 386/33 or higher (4Mb). CD-ROM disk $29.95 (ISBN 1-57303-022-8). *Nonstandard peripherals required:* Sound card, CD-ROM drive. *Optimal configuration:* 486/33 with 8Mb RAM, Win 3.1 or later, 2X CD-ROM drive, SVGA monitor.
Interactive MovieBooks are Exclusively Licensed Computer Story/Activity Books for Children Ages 4 & up. These CD-ROMs Combine the Fun of Movies with the Educational Value of a Book. Movies Come Alive with Video Clips, Pictures, Sound Effects, Animation & Other Surprises. Computer Puzzles, Games, Mazes, & Many Other Learning Activities Are Included.
Sound Source Interactive.

FreeBSD. *Customer Support:* All of our products are unconditionally guaranteed.
Unix. CD-ROM disk $39.95 (Order no.: BSD).
   Nonstandard peripherals required: CD-ROM drive.
Full 32-Bit Unix Operating System for Intel PCs (Revision).
Walnut Creek CDRom.

Freecopy, Freeformat, Freemode, etc. Apr. 1984. *Compatible Hardware:* IBM PC & compatibles; Compaq; Tandy 2000; DEC Rainbow. *Operating System(s) Required:* MS-DOS 1.25, 2.0, 2.1, PC-DOS 1.0, 1.1, 2.0, 2.1. *Language(s):* Assembly (source code included). *Memory Required:* 64k.
disk $25.00, incl. user's guide.
Squire Buresh Assocs., Inc.

FreeForm Debugger. *Version:* 5.1. *Items Included:* Software manual. *Customer Support:* One full year support, updates & hot line telephone support.
MS-DOS, XENIX, UNIX. IBM PC & compatible & all UNIX machines. $2200.00 & up.
Converts Your Computer into a Complete 68000 Development Station. Debugs All Members of the Motorola 68000 Family, Including the 68302 & the Entire CPU32 Line of Microcontrollers. Full Source-Level Display of Both Code & Data Are Supported. No Emulator Is Required. Controls Your Application Directly Through Any Available Serial Port, by Communicating with a Small Target Monitor Program That We Supply You. The FreeForm User Interface Is Easy to Learn & Yet Also Provides a Complete Debugging Language for Support of Complex Debugging Capabilities.
Software Development Systems, Inc.

FREEFORM(R). *Version:* 7.0. Sep. 1989. *Compatible Hardware:* AT&T 385; IBM PC, PC XT; Victor 9000; Alpha Micro; DEC VAX: 3B2; Fortune Fortune 32:16; Cadmus, Sun Worksations, Macintosh. *Operating System(s) Required:* MS-DOS, UNIX, VMS, ULTRIX. *Language(s):* C. *Memory Required:* 320k.
IBM. disk $1500.00.
VAX/VMS, ULTRIX, UNIX, AT&T. cassette $1800.00 ea.
Application Development Package Designed to Run with Related Database Servers (Terdata, S4base, XDB Nucleus, PC Oracle) Provides Screen Handler, Report Writer & Applications Generator Which Is Designed to Reside on a Wide Variety of Host Computers Communicating with Above Servers. Any Application Developed on One Host Runs Unchanged on Any Other Host Computer.
Dimension Software Systems, Inc.

Freelance Graphics for Windows. *Items Included:* Adobe Type Manager & 13 fonts.
Windows 3.0 or higher. 286, 386, or 486 IBM or COMPAQ PCs (2Mb). disk $129.00.
   Nonstandard peripherals required: Hard disk, mouse, EGA, VGA or 8514A.
Presentation Software Program to Create Handouts, Slides, Overheads & Other Presentation Material. Features Include: SmartMasters, a Set of 60 Professional Looking Design Sets That Allow User to Choose a "Look" That Will Include Page Design, Font, Type Size, & Color; Outliner, to Organize & Introduce Changes into the Text; Page Sorter, to Review Presentation on the Screen; & Smart Charting Which Allows User to Select from 96 Pre-Defined Charts & Graphics, Takes the Data & Automatically Composes the Chart, Adding Color, & Inserting Legends. 500 Full Color Images from the Freelance Symbol Gallery are Available. Imports Data & Text from Lotus 1-2-3 & Ami Pro.
Lotus Development Corp.

Freelance Maps Facts. *Compatible Hardware:* IBM PC, PC XT, PC AT, 3270 PC. *Memory Required:* IBM PC, PC XT, PC AT 384k; 3270 PC 512k. *General Requirements:* Freelance Plus. *Libraries of Map Symbols to Be Used with FREELANCE PLUS.*
Lotus Development Corp.
   Continents & Countries.
   $145.00.
      Contains Boundaries & Labels for the Continents & Countries of the World. Also Contains Boundaries & Names for the Canadian Provinces. Allows Map Viewing from a Global or Continent Perspective.
   U. S. Counties.
   $145.00.
      Contains County Boundaries & Names for All 50 States.
   U. S. 3-Digit Zip Codes.
   $145.00.
      Contains 3-Digit Zip Code Boundaries & Codes for All 50 States.
   U. S. Major Cities & MSAs (Metropolitan Statistical Areas).
   $145.00.
      Contains Names & Placement Markers for: Top U.S. Cities Ranging in Population from 150,000 to 1,000,000; State Capitals for All 50 States. Also Contains Boundaries for the Top 50 Cities & 150 MSAs.
   U. S. Complete Set.
   $395.00.
      Includes All the U.S. Sets. Also Includes U.S. Congressional District Boundaries for All 50 States.

Freelance Plus. *Version:* 3.0. *Compatible Hardware:* IBM PC, PC XT, PC AT, PS/2 Models 30/50/60, 3270 PC; other Lotus-certified compatibles. *Memory Required:* IBM PC, PC XT, PC AT 384k; 3270 PC 640k. *General Requirements:* Hercules Graphics Card, CGA, or EGA. Output deviecs: plotters - HP7470A, HP7550A, Calcomp M84; IBM XY/749; Houston Instruments DMP-29; printers - Epson FX-80, MX-80, RX-80; Genicom 3304; HP LaseJet, LaserJet Plus; IBM Color Graphics Printer, Color JetPrinter, Graphics Printer-5152002, Proprinter, Quietwriter Model 2; IDS Prism 132; Okidata Microline 82 or 92; Toshiba P351; image recorders - Polaroid Palette (320k memory), Matrix MVP, Videoshow 150/160. Optional input devices: Microsoft Mouse, Mouse Systems PC Mouse, Summagraphics SummaSketch Tablet, Kurta Series One Tablet. Output options: paper, transparencies, 35mm slides.
5-1/4" or 3-1/2" disks $495.00.
demo package $10.00.
Offers a Solution for Creating Visual Communications for Business. Combines the Capabilities to Create Various Graphics: Standard Business Charts, Chart Editing, Diagrams, Word Charts, Freehand Drawings, Symbols, & Maps. Includes Many Features Provided in CAD Programs, Including Single Point Editing, Grids, Rulers, Zoom, Rotate, a Full-Screen Cross-Hair, & Other Tools for Creating Graphics. Employs the LOTUS User Interface. Users Can Import Files from 1-2-3, SYMPHONY, & GRAPHWRITER for Customization & Export Files to MANUSCRIPT to Combine Text & Graphics. May Be Used in Combination with a Desktop Publishing or Word Processing Program. Libraries of Map Symbols That Can Be Incorporated into Communications Created with FREELANCE PLUS Are Available.
Lotus Development Corp.

Freeze Frame. Bill Dunlevy & Ken Olson. 1985. *Compatible Hardware:* Sanyo 555. *Memory Required:* 128k. *General Requirements:* Dot matrix printer.
disk $39.95.
Prints Pictures or Screen Information & Saves Screen Image to Disk for Later Printing.
MichTron, Inc.

Freight Bill Accounting (a Part of ABECAS). *Version:* 3.3. Jan. 1989. *Customer Support:* On site training unlimited support services for first 90 days & through subscription thereafter. Contact publisher for price.
Generates Freight Bills and/or Invoices for Most Types of Freight Handlers & Brokers, Including LTL, Truckload, Delivery, Dump, Tank & Agricultural. Shipper, Consignee & Customer Information Saved As Freight Bills Are Entered. Mileage Between Shipper & Consignee Is Saved When First Entered & Will Repeat Automatically. Freight Bill Information May Be Entered Such As Purchase Order Number, Bill of Lading Number, Load Number, Load Date, Freight Bill Date. etc. Also, Alternative Screen Is Provided to Allow Entry of Additional Information on Each Load for Analysis Purposes, Such As Driver, Truck, Trailer, Commodity, Origin, Destination, Unloaded Mileage, Hours & More. Line Detail Entry Is Simplified Through Use of Pre-Defined Charge Codes That Provide Descriptions, Handle the Accounting, Indicate Whether PUC Taxable or Not, Hazardous or Not & More. Delivery Receipts, Freight Bills, Manifests & Consolidated Invoices (Statements) May Be Printed.
Argos Software.

French Advance Variation: Electronic Chessbook. *Version:* 2. Nikolic. 1995. *Items Included:* Book & disk with 500 or more games (over 200 annotated). *Customer Support:* Telephone support by appointment.
MS-DOS 2.0 or higher (512k). 3.5" disk $25.00, incl. softcover text. *Nonstandard peripherals required:* Mouse, graphics, 3 1/2" drive.
Atari ST (520k). Atari. disk $25.00.
   Nonstandard peripherals required: Monocrhome monitor DS/DD drive.
Authoritative Introduction to & Analysis of an Important Chess Opening.
Chess Combination, Inc.

French Foreign Direct Investment in the United States 1974-1994. May 1995. *Items Included:* Spiral bound manual. *Customer Support:* Unlimited telephone support.
MS-DOS 6.0/Windows 3.1 or higher. PC Clone 486 or higher (4Mb). disk $125.00 (ISBN 1-878974-07-6). *Addl. software required:* Database Versions are available for MS Access 2.0, Excel, Lotus, Paradox, Foxpro, & dBASE. *Optimal configuration:* PC clone with MS-DOS 6.0/Windows 3.1 or higher. Must have MS Access 2.0, or Excel, or Lotus or Paradox or Foxpro or dBASE.
Database of All French Foreign Direct Investment Transactions in the United States 1974-1994.
Jeffries & Associates, Inc.

Frequency Domain Filtering Tutorial. (Engineering Tutorial Ser.: No. 9). *Compatible Hardware:* Apple II with Applesoft; IBM PC. *Operating System(s) Required:* Apple DOS 3.2, 3.3. (source code included). *Memory Required:* Apple 48k, IBM 256k.
disk $39.95.
Dynacomp, Inc.

Frequent Flyer Calculator. *Compatible Hardware:* Apple Macintosh. *Memory Required:* 1000k.
3.5" disk $44.95.
Used to Plan Trips to Maximize Flight & Bonus Mileage; Keeps Track of Accumulated Flight & Bonus Mileage.
IGS International.

Friendly Finder. 1987. *Compatible Hardware:* IBM PC & compatibles; PC XT, PC AT. *Operating System(s) Required:* PC-DOS/MS-DOS 2.0 or higher for IBM PC, PC XT; PC-DOS/MS-DOS 3.0 or higher for IBM PC AT. *Memory Required:*

TITLE INDEX

80k.
disk $99.00.
dBASE Search Utility. Will Perform "Fuzzy" Searches, Providing up to 16 Close Matches for Each Search. Features the Capability of Integrating Fields Found into Other Applications.
Proximity Technology, Inc.

Friendly Writer with Friendly Speller. *Version:* 3.4. Michael D. Yaw et al. Feb. 1984. *Compatible Hardware:* IBM PC, PC XT, PC AT, PCjr; Compaq; Corona. *Operating System(s) Required:* PC/MS-DOS 2.0 or higher. *Language(s):* Assembly. *Memory Required:* 128k. *Customer Support:* 24hr hot line.
disk $89.95.
Includes 70,000 Word Dictionary/Spell Checker. All Functions & Commands from Setting Margins to Moving or Inserting Block of Text, Can Be Executed with a Single Keystroke. Features Include: User-Defined Letter Format, Automatic Left-Right Justification, Cursor Control, Underlining, Move, Insert, Delete, Letter Recall by Name or Date, Classification.
FriendlySoft, Inc.

FriendlyRider Speller. *Version:* 3.4. May 1988. *Compatible Hardware:* IBM PC & compatibles. *Memory Required:* 128k.
contact publisher for price.
Word-Processing Package with ASCII Import/Export Capabilities. Features Undo Command & 70,000-Word User-Expandable Spelling Checker. Writer & Speller on One Disk.
FriendlySoft, Inc.

FriendlyWare. *Version:* 2.2. *Operating System(s) Required:* PC-DOS/MS-DOS 2.0 or higher. *Memory Required:* 128k.
disk $89.95.
Personal Word Processor Designed for the Secretary or Writer Who Needs Documents That Do Not Require Extensive Formatting. Includes Menus & On-Line Help Screens As Well As a Feature for Searching a Particular Word or Group of Words from the User's Descriptive Names in the Directory of Letters.
Friendlysoft, Inc.

Friendlyware Checkbook. *Version:* 2.1. Aug. 1989.
IBM PC, PC XT, PC AT, PS/2 (384k). PC-DOS, MS-DOS, OS/2. disk $49.95 (ISBN 0-918605-06-7).
Easy-to-Use Program Which Allows User to Manage Personal or Small Business Checking Accounts. Also Used for Tax Recordkeeping, Expense Recordkeeping & Can Be Used for Budgeting. Handles Multiple Accounts, Prints Checks & Reports. Able to Generate over 160 Different Reports Relating to All Transactions on Account, Expenses, Tax-Deductible Items, etc.
Friendlysoft, Inc.

FriendlyWare PC Arcade. *Version:* 3.3. Michael D. Yaw et al. Mar. 1983. *Compatible Hardware:* IBM PC, PC XT, PC AT, PCjr; Compaq; Corona. *Operating System(s) Required:* DOS 2.0 or higher. *Language(s):* Assembly. *Memory Required:* 128k.
disk $29.95.
Includes 10 Games Written in Text Mode So That They Can Be Played on Both a Monochrome & Color Monitor. Games Include: ASCII Man, Gorilla, Robot War, Hopper, Starfighter TX-16, Eagle Lander, Shooter, PC Derby, Bug Blaster, & Brick Breaker. Features Sound off/on & Pause Keys.
FriendlySoft, Inc.

Fright Night. Steve Bak & Pete Lyon. Apr. 1989. Amiga (512k). disk $39.95.
Play Role of Jerry Dandridge While Searching House Looking for Bloodsucking Fun.
MichTron, Inc.

Frog Master. *Compatible Hardware:* Atari 400, 800. *Memory Required:* 16k. *General Requirements:* Joysticks.
disk $21.95.
High-Concentration Game with Arcade Features.
Dynacomp, Inc.

Frogger. *Compatible Hardware:* TRS-80 Model I, Model III.
contact publisher for price.
Cornsoft Group.

From the Mixed-up Files of Mrs Basil E. Frankweiler. Intentional Education Staff & Elaine Konigsburg. Apr. 1996. *Items Included:* Program manual. *Customer Support:* Free technical support, 90 day warranty.
School ver.. System 7.1 or higher. Macintosh (4Mb). 3.5" disk contact publisher for price (ISBN 1-57204-283-4). *Nonstandard peripherals required:* 256 color monitor, hard drive, printer.
Lab pack. System 7.1 or higher. Macintosh (4Mb). 3.5" disk contact publisher for price (ISBN 1-57204-259-1). *Nonstandard peripherals required:* 256 color monitor, hard drive, printer.
Site license. System 7.1 or higher. Macintosh (4Mb). 3.5" disk contact publisher for price (ISBN 1-57204-284-2). *Nonstandard peripherals required:* 256 color monitor, hard drive, printer.
School ver. Windows 3.1 or higher. IBM/Tandy & 100% compatibles (4mb). disk contact publisher for price (ISBN 1-57204-285-0). *Nonstandard peripherals required:* VGA or SVGA 640 x 480 resolution (256), mouse, hard drive, sound device.
Lab pack. Windows 3.1 or higher. IBM/Tandy & 100% compatibles (4Mb). disk contact publisher for price (ISBN 1-57204-285-0). *Nonstandard peripherals required:* VGA or SVGA 640 x 480 resolution (256), mouse, hard drive, sound device.
Site license. Windows 3.1 or higher. IBM/Tandy & 100% compatibles (4Mb). disk contact publisher for price (ISBN 1-57204-261-3). *Nonstandard peripherals required:* VGA or SVGA 640 x 480 resolution (256), mouse, hard drive, sound device.
This companion for young adult literature is ideal for students who don't know how to start that book report, or give that needed summary. Gentle prompts throughout guide section of the program include Warm-up Connections, Thinking about Plot, Quoting & Noting, Keeping a Journal, If I Were ———' Responding to Questions, Using Quotations, Taking a Personal View, Write to Others, & Write a Sequel.
Lawrence Productions, Inc.

Front Desk. Jan. 1989. *Compatible Hardware:* Apple Macintosh. *Memory Required:* 1000k. *General Requirements:* HyperCard.
3.5" disk $250.00.
Designed to Manage the Front Desk of a Weekly or Smaller Daily Newspaper. Features Advertising, Billing, Classified Ad Management, Billing & Typesetting, News & Editorial Typesetting Using News Flow Technology.
Random Access.

Front Desk: 104 Rooms. *Version:* 1.1. John Leib. *Items Included:* User's manual. *Customer Support:* Intial customization, telephone support, on-site training & support negotiable.
DOS 3.1 or higher. IBM & compatibles (640k). $650.00 per installation. *Nonstandard peripherals required:* Hard disk desirable. *Optimal configuration:* Computer, DOS, 640k RAM, Epson dot-matrix impact printer or compatible, hard disk.
Hotel Management System That Provides Features Including Reservations, Registrations & Billing Needs, & Hotel Status Reports.
Front Desk Systems.

Front Desk: 600 Rooms. *Version:* 2.0. John Leib. *Items Included:* User's manual. *Customer Support:* Intial customization, telephone support, on-site training & support negotiable.
DOS 3.1 or higher. IBM & compatibles (640k). $2000.00 single user; $2500.00 multi user. *Nonstandard peripherals required:* Hard disk with 5Mb free. *Optimal configuration:* Computer, DOS, 640k RAM, Epson-compatible dot-matrix impact printer, hard disk. *Networks supported:* All Whose File-Protection Features Can Be Disabled & Which Attaches Drives of Other Computers.
Hotel Management System That Provides Features Including Reservations, Registrations & Billing Needs; Night Audit & Hotel Status Reports; & Instant Pop-Up Context-Sensitive Help Screens, Room-Availability Screens, & Hotel Guest List Screens. Optional Interface for Telephone Call Accounting & Optional Cash Drawer.
Front Desk Systems.

Front Office. *Version:* 2.0, 4.6. Oct. 1986. *Items Included:* User manual, Runtime version of Omnis 3. *Customer Support:* 90 days free phone support, after 90 days $80.00 per month multi user & $60.00 per month single user; training at customer site $1000.00 & $1500.00 for single & multi user respectively plus travel expenses.
Mac Plus (1Mb), Mac OS, V6 & V7. $2895.00 single user, $3495.00 multiuser. *Optimal configuration:* Mac 030 V, 2Mb RAM, 80Mb hard drive, Imagewriter. *Networks supported:* Novell, Appletalk.
Offers Fast, Accurate Patient & Insurance Billing for All the Complex Requirements of Today's Small to Medium Sized Medical Offices. Designed for Various Practices, Whether They Are Pediatricians, Optometrists, General Practitioners. Billing Transactions Can Be Entered Quickly, Superbills Printed, & Claims Processed with Only a Few Key Strokes. Features Pop up Lists of Account Numbers for Patients, Procedure & Diagnostic Codes for Fast & Easy Data Entry.
Systec Computer Services.

FrontEnd. *Version:* 2.084. *Compatible Hardware:* Apple Macintosh. *Memory Required:* 512k.
3.5" disk $180.00.
Macintosh Mainframe Communications with User Interface Utility for Host Software; Data General D210, 0410 & VT 100 Terminal Emulation.
Kaz Business Systems.

FS: The File System. Ken Berry. *Operating System(s) Required:* MS-DOS. *General Requirements:* SK: The System Kernel (M&T Publishing, Inc.).
disk $39.95, incl. manual (ISBN 0-934375-65-8).
Supports MS-DOS Disk File Structures & Serial Communication Channels. Provides Complete Documentation for Installing & Using FS. Features a Telecommunications Support Facility That Allows a Common Set of Functions to Handle Both Disk Files & Telecommunications.
M & T Bks.

F77L-EM/32. *Version:* 5.1. May 1993. *Operating System(s) Required:* PC-DOS & Phar-Lap 386 PIPE Character on ASCII keyboard DOS-Extender. *Memory Required:* Extended 2000k. *Items Included:* Manuals, Editor, Debugger, Profiler, Make, Library Manager, Video Graphics, Linker, Make Utility. *Customer Support:* Free telephone, BBS, CompuServe & newsletters.
disk $795.00.
32-Bit FORTRAN Compiler That Gives Users the Ability to Port Programs As Large As 4Gb (Gigabytes) on 80386/486 Computers. Full ANSI 77 Standard & On-Line Debugger/Profiler, Multi-Lingual Error Messages in English, Dutch, French, German, Italian & Spanish. Includes Phar-Laps's 386 DOS-Extender.
Lahey Computer Systems, Inc.

F77L-Lahey-FORTRAN. Version: 5.0. Jun. 1991. Compatible Hardware: IBM PC & compatibles. Operating System(s) Required: PC-DOS, MS-DOS. Language(s): FORTRAN. Memory Required: 256k. Items Included: Manuals, Editor, Graphics, Profiler, Linker, Debugger, Library Manager, Make Utility. Customer Support: Free telephone, BBS, CompuServe & newsletters.
disk $595.00, incl. manual (Order no.: F77L).
Full ANSI(X3.9-1978) FORTRAN Standard with Additional Features. Compatible with Third Party Software. Includes Source On-Line Debugger, Large Arrays, Namelist, & Other Popular Extensions, Editor's Choice PC Magazine. Multilingual error messages in English, Dutch, French, German, Italian & Spanish.
Lahey Computer Systems, Inc.

FTK-File Management System. Operating System(s) Required: UNIX, XENIX, DOS. Language(s): Sculptor 4GL.
contact publisher for price.
File Management System & File/Time Keeping System for Attorneys. Includes Customer Billing, Recording of Proper Time of Clients & Cases, & Information Processing & Recording.
Universal Data Research, Inc.

Fuel Tax Specialist. Compatible Hardware: Apple Macintosh.
Single user with Runtime Omnis 3 Plus. 3.5" disk $2400.00.
Multiuser (Requires Multiuser Omnis 3 Plus). 3.5" disk $2900.00.
Calculates Fuel Taxes for Trucking Businesses.
H&D Leasing.

Full Screen Forms Display (A). Compatible Hardware: IBM PC. Operating System(s) Required: MS-DOS. Language(s): BASIC (source code included). Memory Required: 64k.
disk $60.00.
Provides a Table-Driven Way of Using Full Screen Displays via Prompts to the User. Features Tables Which Extend the Capabilities of Extended BASIC Programs.
Computer Systems Consultants.

Full Screen Inventory-MRP (A). Compatible Hardware: IBM PC. Operating System(s) Required: MS-DOS. Language(s): BASIC (source code included). Memory Required: 64k.
disk $110.00.
Designed for Small Inventories. Keeps Files in Alphabetical Order, Locates &/or Prints Items in Back Order or Items Below Minimum Stock Levels & Produces File in Item or Vendor Order. Material Requirement Planning (MRP) Capability Is Included for Manufacturing Environments.
Computer Systems Consultants.

Full Screen Mailing List (A). Compatible Hardware: IBM PC. Operating System(s) Required: MS-DOS. Language(s): BASIC (source code included). Memory Required: 64k.
disk $105.00.
Designed for Simple Mailing Lists, the File Is Maintained in Alphabetical Order. User May Locate All Records Which Match (Using Either a Partial or the Full Name) in Fields Such As Name, City, State or Zip Code.
Computer Systems Consultants.

FullAuthority: The Intelligent Table of Authorities Generator. Version: 3.0. May 1988. Compatible Hardware: IBM PC & compatibles, Wang VS. Operating System(s) Required: PC-DOS/MS-DOS 2.0 or higher. General Requirements: Printer. Customer Support: Extended support & upgrade program.
disk $160.00.
Eliminates Re-Reading, Cross-Referencing, Alphabetizing, & Other Tasks Associated with Preparing a Table of Authorities. Automatically Locates, Alphabetizes, Corrects Common Citation Errors, & Creates a Formatted Table of Authorities. Reads Citations in a Variety of Forms, Including Those in Bluebook & California Citation Formats. Automatically Sorts Each Located Cite into Case, Statute, Book & Law Review, or Other Citation Categories. Prepares Each Cite to Be Included in the Table of Authorities by Correcting Various Errors Found Within the Cite. May Be Printed Through Any Major Word-Processing Program.
Jurisoft.

FULMAP. Compatible Hardware: Atari. Language(s): BASIC. Memory Required: 4k.
disk $39.95 (ISBN 0-936200-19-7).
cassette $39.95 (ISBN 0-936200-19-7).
Machine Language Cross Reference Utility for BASIC Programmers. Provides Variable Cross Reference, a Cross Reference of the Constants Used, & a Map of the Line Numbers Used in a BASIC Program.
Blue Cat.

Fun & Games. Compatible Hardware: Atari 400, 800. Language(s): Atari BASIC (source code included). Memory Required: 24k. General Requirements: Joystick.
disk $12.95.
Includes 4 Educational Programs: Jumble, Guessit, Possible & Leapfrog.
Dynacomp, Inc.

Fun & Games on the PCjr. J. Edward Volkstorf. 1985. Compatible Hardware: IBM PCjr. Operating System(s) Required: PC-DOS 2.1. Language(s): Cartridge BASIC (source code included). Memory Required: 64k.
bk. $14.95 (ISBN 0-13-332461-3).
disk contact publisher for price.
One-Player & Multi-Player Games That Teach Game Design & Programming.
Prentice Hall.

Fun City. Customer Support: 800-929-8117 (customer service).
MS-DOS. IBM/PS2. disk $39.99 (ISBN 0-87007-562-4).
A Variety of Games Including Roulette & Trivia.
SourceView Software International.

Function Graphs & Transformations-Vector Analysis. Compatible Hardware: Apple II, II+. Language(s): Applesoft II, Machine. Memory Required: 32k.
disk $34.95 (Order no.: 10029).
Permits Visual, Intuitive, & Experiential Approach to Topics Such As Algebra, Trigonometry, & Analytic Geometry. Can Serve As Vehicle for Integrating Complementary Intuitive & Analytic/Symbolic Approaches Such As Intuition & Visualization, & for Strengthening Symbol Manipulation Skills. Uses Apple II High Resolution Graphics Capabilities to Draw Detailed Graphs of Functions Which User Defines. Program Can Also Be Used to Process Electrical Phase & Force Vectors. Converts from Polar to Cartesian System, & Converted Coordinates Can Be Plotted Automatically.
Powersoft, Inc.

Function Point Manager. Customer Support: Client Support Program: $250 with initial purchase, $350 late renewal.
Microsoft Windows 3.1 or higher. 386SX or higher (4Mb). disk $1500.00. Nonstandard peripherals required: Hard disk.
A Complete, PC-Based Tool That Supports Function Point Analysis (FPA) - a Technique for Measuring the Size of Software Projects. The Tool Provides an Intuitive Graphical Interface That Enables You to Enter Information about the Functional Components of an Application, Then Uses This Information to Perform the Function Point Calculations. Provides Its Users with a Central Repository for Function Point Analysis Data. Supports the Methodology & Standards Created by the International Function Point Users Group (IFPUG) Whose Primary Objective Is to Ensure Counting Consistency Within the IS Community.
ABT Corp.

Functional Harmony - MIDI: Basic Chords. Vincent Oddo. 1987. Compatible Hardware: Apple II+, IIGS, IIe; Atari ST; IBM PC; Macintosh plus or higher. Operating System(s) Required: Apple DOS 3.3, Macintosh System 6.0.3-7.1, PC-DOS/MS-DOS 3.3 or higher. Language(s): QuickBasic. Memory Required: Apple 48k, IBM 640k, MAC 512k. General Requirements: Roland MPU & MIDI interface card; MIDI-compatible music keyboard; amplifier; headphones or other audio monitoring systems. CGA card for IBM. Passport MIDI can be substituted for the Roland MPU & MIDI interface card for Apple. Macintosh requires external MIDI interface.
disk $39.95 ea.
Apple. Macintosh. 3.5" disk $50.00 only avail. in a set (ISBN 1-55603-051-7, Order no.: MA-1239).
IBM. (ISBN 1-55603-052-5, Order no.: MI-1239).
Atari. (ISBN 1-55603-065-7, Order no.: MST-1239).
Designed to Help Develop Facility in Harmonic Anaylsis in a Drill-&-Practice Format. Contains Four Quizzes Which Allow the User to Practice Analyzing Chords in Major or Minor Keys & in Root Positions or Inversions. Also Features Student Record-Keeping Which Allows the Instructor to Select the Numbers of Problems Presented for Each Student. When Using MIDI, the Chord Displayed Will Play Through the Audio Device to Help Facilitate Chord Identification.
Electronic Courseware Systems, Inc.

Functional Harmony: Basic Chords. Vincent Oddo. 1987. Compatible Hardware: Apple II+, IIe, IIc, IIGS; IBM PC. Memory Required: Apple 48k, IBM 640k. General Requirements: Color graphics card for IBM.
disk $39.95 ea.
Apple. (ISBN 1-55603-047-9, Order no.: A-1231).
IBM. (ISBN 1-55603-048-7, Order no.: I-1231).
Designed to Help Develop Facility in Harmonic Analysis in a Drill-&-Practice Format. Contains Four Quizzes Which Allow the User to Practice Analyzing Chords in Major or Minor Keys & in Root Positions or Inversions. Also Features Student Record Keeping Which Allow the Instructor to Select the Numbers of Problems for Each Quiz.
Electronic Courseware Systems, Inc.

Functions. Items Included: Bound manual. Customer Support: Free hotline - no time limit; 30 day limited warranty; updates are $5/disk plus S&H.
MS-DOS. IBM & compatibles (256k). disk $39.95. Nonstandard peripherals required: Color graphics card; printer supported. Addl. software required: BASICA.
Commodore 64. disk $29.95.
May Be Used in a Defined Interval to Find the Roots, Maxima & Minima, the Integral, Derivatives, & to Plot a Graph of a Function. The Function May Be Either an Expression or a Finite Power Series (Polynomial) Read from a Disk File. The Expression May Be up to 1,000 Characters Long & Is Easily Entered from the Keyboard. The Power Series May Have up to 50 Terms. User May Predefine Any Recurrent Constants, & Specify the Error Bound for the Results.
Dynacomp, Inc.

TITLE INDEX

Fund Accountant. *Version:* 7.0. *Compatible Hardware:* Altos, Bull, IBM, UNISYS. *Items Included:* Documentation. *Customer Support:* Available/contract.
contact publisher for price.
Multi-Fund Budgetary Accounting System for Non-Profit Organizations.
Computer Center.

Fund Accounting. *Version:* 450.3. Feb. 1986. *Compatible Hardware:* IBM PC & compatibles. *Operating System(s) Required:* MS-DOS, PC-DOS. *Language(s):* QuickBASIC. *Memory Required:* 512k. *General Requirements:* Hard disk. *Items Included:* System diskettes, users guide, training tutorial. *Customer Support:* Telephone; annual contracts available.
$650.00 to $750.00.
A Not-for-Profit Equivalent of General Ledger. It Is Designed Especially for Civic Service, Religious, Educational, & Governmental Organization's Financial Condition Is Reported Through Printed Budgets, Monthly & Year-to-Year Expense Itemizations, & Encumbrances. Users Can Use up to 20 Positions to Design Account Numbers That Comply with State & Local Regulations. Flexible Reporting Allows Users to Determine Which Funds to Include in Each Report. Reports Can Be Printed for Organization's Months, Quarters, & Fiscal Year, & for Fiscal Year. Transactions Include Journal Posting, Cash Receipts, & Cash Disbursements. Fund Accounting Can Be Used with IMS A/P, A/R & Payroll Systems. Runs Single User or Multi-User on Many Networks.
International Micro Systems, Inc.

Fund Accounting 4+. *Version:* 8.1. *Compatible Hardware:* 80386-based PCs, Unix System V. *Operating System(s) Required:* Unix V or SCO Xenix V. *Items Included:* G/L; A/R; A/P; P/O; Check Reconciliation; Inv; P/R; O/E & Lynx. *Customer Support:* Toll free per hour: $75.00.
$1995.50.
Includes Modules for General Ledger, Accounts Payable, & Purchase Order; Check Reconciliation; Payroll & Lynx.
Cougar Mountain Software, Inc.

Fund Accounting One Plus. *Version:* 8.1. *Compatible Hardware:* IBM PC & compatibles. *Memory Required:* 640k. *General Requirements:* Hard disk. *Items Included:* G/L; A/P; P/R; P/O; Check Reconciliation; Lynx (ASCII file converter). *Customer Support:* Toll free per hour: $75.00.
$599.50 per package.
Financial/Accounting Software. Posts Recurring Transactions, Automatic Posting from Other Modules, Report Format User Definable, Reports Comparative Statements, Ability to Jump Modules, Wild Card, Links with External Software Programs, Audit Trail, Error Recovery, Log off Out-of-Balance, Reject Erroneous Account Numbers, On-Line Help & Source Code Available.
Cougar Mountain Software, Inc.

Fund Accounting Software Series. *Version:* 3.6, 5.5. 1994-95. *Compatible Hardware:* IBM & compatibles. *Operating System(s) Required:* PC-DOS/MS-DOS, Windows. *Language(s):* COBOL. *Memory Required:* 640k. *Customer Support:* 30 days free, annual support contract. $300.00-$850.00.
manual & demo disk $50.00.
Designed for Non-Profit Organizations. Provides All Major Financial Statements. Compatible with United Way Chart of Accounts.
Executive Data Systems, Inc. (Georgia).

Fund Accounting 2+. *Version:* 8.1. *Compatible Hardware:* IBM PC & compatibles, DOS Network version. *Operating System(s) Required:* MS-DOS/PC-DOS 2.0 or higher. *Items Included:* Includes modules for G/L; A/P; P/R; P/O; Check reconciliation & Lynx. *Customer Support:* Toll free per hour: $75.00.
disk $1199.95.
Includes Modules for General Ledger, Accounts Receivable & Accounts Payable.
Cougar Mountain Software, Inc.

Fundamentals of Heat Transfer. 1995. *Items Included:* Full manual. *Customer Support:* Free telephone support - 90 days, 30-day warranty. MS-DOS 3.2 or higher. 286 (584k). disk $599.95. *Nonstandard peripherals required:* CGA/EGA/VGA.
Minimal Training Is Needed - Just Follow the Menus. You Can Start Solving Sophisticated Problems Immediately. Features: Analyze Many Different Design Alternatives in Minutes. Backsolve to Optimize Your Design. Provides Good Alternative to Finite Element Analysis. Automatically Converts Units. Perform Table Look-Ups with Linear/Cubic Interpolation.
Dynacomp, Inc.

Fundamentals of IBM PC Assembly Language. Al Schneider. Feb. 1984. *Compatible Hardware:* IBM PC. *Operating System(s) Required:* PC-DOS. *Language(s):* BASIC. *Memory Required:* 64k.
disk $35.50, incl. bk. (ISBN 0-8306-5057-1, Order no.: 5057C).
Shows How the Assembly Language Can Overcome the Limitations Offered by BASIC & How Users Can Also Use Assembly Subroutines along with Their BASIC Programs.
TAB Bks.

Fundamentals of Protocols. Jul. 1995. *Items Included:* User manual. *Customer Support:* Free technical support & a 30-day money back guarantee.
MS-DOS. IBM & compatibles (640k). 3.5" disk $395.00 (ISBN 1-57305-020-2). *Nonstandard peripherals required:* High-density 3.5" disk drive; VGA color monitor. *Addl. software required:* MS-DOS version 3.3 or higher. *Optimal configuration:* IBM (640k), MS-DOS version 3.3 or higher, VGA color monitor, keyboard, Microsoft compatible mouse.
This Is a 3-Hour Computer-Based Training Program That Addresses the Need for Protocols in the Data Communications World & Also Shows Its Relationship to the OSI Reference Model.
Bellcore.

FundMaster: Activity Fund Accounting. *Version:* 2.0. Kenneth Temkin et al. Jan. 1994. *Items Included:* 1 saddle stitched manual. *Customer Support:* Free customer support telephone line.
Macintosh (System 6 or 7). Any Macintosh computer (2Mb System 6, 4Mb System 7). 3.5" disk $99.99 (ISBN 0-932743-02-1). *Optimal configuration:* Printer (optional). (Windows Version Being Beta Tested).
An Accounting Program for Keeping Track of Fundraising Activities at Schools, Churches & Non-Profit Organizations. Reports Each Day's Transactions, Provides Up-to-the-Minute Balances, & Prints Out a Trial Balance & Monthly Statements. Requires No Formal Accounting Background.
School Management Arts, Inc.

Funds Smart. Jun. 1988. *Items Included:* Operators manual. *Customer Support:* On site training, telephone support, first year maintenance free, annual maintenance after 1st year $500.
PC-DOS/MS-DOS. IBM Micros & compatibles (640). Monthly lease, initial customization. *Networks supported:* Novell, Banyan, etc.
A Complete Accounting & Management System for Purchased & Sold Federal Funds. Accounting for Clients, Accrual, Cash, GL, Customized for Confirmations, Tickets, Data Sheets. Over 40 Standard Reports Plus a Report Writer, Average Rates & Balances, Policy Control, Broker Fees Reconciliation, Direct & Broker Trades.
Wall Street Consulting Group.

Fundware. *Version:* 4.4. *Compatible Hardware:* IBM PC, PC XT, PC AT & compatibles; NecAstra; XENIX/UNIX. *Operating System(s) Required:* MS-DOS, XENIX, UNIX, LANs. *Language(s):* COBOL. *Memory Required:* 640k. *General Requirements:* Printer.
module $695.00-$1595.00.
Contains the Following Functions: General Ledger, Accounts Payable, with Encumbrance, Utility Billing, Accounts Receivable, Budget Forecasting, Payroll/Personnel, Fixed Asset Depreciation. Features Include: All Systems Update to General Ledger, Due-To/Due from Accounting, Unlimited Years of Data Can Be Stored On-Line, Transactions Are Edited On-Line, All Transactions Are Updated to the Database. Multi-User Version Runs on XENIX & All LANs. Minicomputer & UNIX Versions & AIX Versions Also Available.
American Fundware, Inc.

Fundwatch. *Items Included:* Bound manual. *Customer Support:* Free hotline - no time limit; 30 day limited warranty; updates are $5/disk plus S&H.
MS-DOS 2.0 or higher. IBM & compatibles (128k). disk $39.95. *Nonstandard peripherals required:* Graphics card; graphics printer necessary for printed plots.
Menu-Driven Tool Created to Simplify Evaluation & Comparison of Various Common Investments Including Mutual Funds, Stocks, Bonds, & Many Commodities Such As Energy & Precious Metals. Designed to Allow Home Investors to Seriously Evaluate Such Investments Inexpensively & Quickly Without Requiring a Modem or a Costly Data Network Subscription. Although Especially Suited for the Fast-Growing Market of Mutual Funds, FUNDWATCH Can Be Used to Evaluate Virtually Any Type of Capital Growth or Income Oriented Instrument, Including Market Averages Such As the Dow Jones Industrial Average.
Dynacomp, Inc.

FUNDWATCH PLUS. *Version:* 2.0. 1995. *Compatible Hardware:* IBM PC. *Operating System(s) Required:* PC-DOS/MS-DOS 2.0; Windows Version requires Windows 3.0. *Memory Required:* Windows 2Mb, PC-DOS/MS-DOS 128k. *Customer Support:* Hotline.
3.5" or 5.25" disk $29.00, incl. manual.
Simplifies Evaluation & Comparison of Various Common Investments Including Mutual Funds, Stocks, Market Indices, & Many Commodities. Annualizes Total Returns, Analyzes Volatility, Evaluates Trends, Creates Comparative Graphics Including Performance, Moving Averages & Relative Strength, & Maintains Basic Portfolio Information for an Unlimited Number of Funds. User Enters Share Prices on a Weekly Basis, & Dividend & Share Distributions As They Occur.
Hamilton Software, Inc.

Funeral Directors Management & Accounting System. *Version:* 4.0. May 1982. *Language(s):* C. *Memory Required:* 512k. *Customer Support:* BBS, FAX, 800-VOICE.
Windows, Win 95. PC AT & compatibles (2Mb). disk $1895.00.
Allows Storage of Complete Case Information. Case Can Be Retrieved & Updated at Any Time. Prints All Government Forms, Veterans Forms, Social Security Forms, Death Certificates, etc. Information Is Automatically Sent to Other Accounting Functions Which Includes Accounts Payable, Accounts Receivables & General Ledger. Payroll & Inventory Management Systems Are Also Available.
Davidson Software Systems.

Funny Fruit Faces. Jul. 1994. *Items Included:* Parent's Guide. *Customer Support:* (904) 576-9415 11-5 ET M-F, online at AppleLink, American Online, CompuServe, eWorld, GEnie. Mac 6.0.5 or higher. Macintosh (2Mb). 3.5" disk $49.95, SRP (ISBN 0-931277-19-1, Order no.: FFFM). *Optimal configuration:* Macintosh running 6.0.5 or higher, 2Mb RAM, mouse.
Provides Thousands of Face Making Combinations for Endless Hours of Fun. Voice & Graphics Guide Kids Through the Game So They Can Enjoy Playing Independently. Using Just the Mouse, Kids Create Fruits with Expressions, Arms, Hats & Many Other Features. Kids Can View Their Fruits On-Screen, or Print Them.
Seven Hills Software Corp.

FunPlot. *Compatible Hardware:* Apple Macintosh. 3.5" disk $15.00.
Function Plotter & Calculus Demonstrator.
Kinko's.

FunPlot-3D. *Compatible Hardware:* Apple Macintosh. 3.5" disk $25.00.
Three-Dimensional Graphics Program for Representing Functions of Two Variables.
Kinko's.

Fuse & Breaker Coordination - E4M. *Version:* 09/1989. 1982. *Operating System(s) Required:* MS-DOS, PC-DOS. *Language(s):* Compiled. *Memory Required:* 256k. *Customer Support:* Technical hotline, "Lifetime" support at no charge. $295.00.
Coordination, Fuse, Breaker, & Wire - E4M Uses the Buss Up-Over-&-Down Method to Coordinate Electrical Fuses & Breakers to Wire for Proper Operating Sequence. On-Board Data Files. Highly Enhanced Screens, Interactive. Detailed Printout of Inputs & Outputs. Fully Compiled. SI Metric or English Units.
MC2 Engineering Software.

Fuse-Circuit Breaker-Wire Coordination Analysis. *Items Included:* Bound manual. *Customer Support:* Free hotline - no time limit; 30 day limited warranty; updates are $5/disk plus S&H.
MS-DOS. IBM & compatibles (256k). full system $269.95.
demo disk $5.00.
Uses the Buss Up-Over-&-Down Method for Coordination of Electrical Fuses & Breakers to Wire for Proper Operating Sequence in Commercial & Industrial Distribution Systems. Handles Circuits of up to 5,000 Devices (MS-DOS Version/Hard Disk).
Dynacomp, Inc.

Fusion Network Software. *Version:* 3.3. *Compatible Hardware:* LAN Controllers, 3COM Ethernet, DECnet, Western Digital Ethernet. *Language(s):* C. *Memory Required:* 512k.
contact publisher for price.
Provides File Transfer, Remote Program Execution & Virtual Terminal Capabilities Between IBM PC, VAX, 68000 & 8086 Processors on the Same Ethernet Local Local Area Network. Compatible with LAN Controllers from a Variety of Vendors (3COM, Western Digital). Supports Ethernet, Token-Ring, & RS232 Links. Can Run TC P/IP & XNS Protocols Separately or Concurrently.
Network Research Corp.

Future Classics Collection. Curt Toumanian. Feb. 1990.
$39.95.
Five Video Games on One Disk. Includes Diskman, Blockalanche, Lost 'N Maze, Tankbattle, & Diet Riot.
LIVE Studios, Inc.

Future Damage & Present Value Calculator. *Version:* 1990. *Customer Support:* 1 year.
disk $89.50.
Estimates Future Lost Earnings Based on Percentage of Disability, Age, Gender, Race, Educational Status, Interest Rate & Annual Earnings.
Lawyers Software Publishing Co.

FutureWave. *Operating System(s) Required:* PC-DOS/MS-DOS, OS/2. *Memory Required:* 256k. *General Requirements:* 132-column printer & 20Mb hard disk recommended.
3.5" or 5.25" disk $2995.95.
Complete System for the Management of the Medical Office. Package Includes Accounts Receivable, Paper & Electronic Claim Form Processing, General Ledger, Payroll Processing, Accounts Payable, Word Processing, Spreadsheet Analysis, Appointment Handling & Office Administration. System Automatically Handles up to Ten Users.
CMA Micro Computer.

FYI 3000 Plus. *Compatible Hardware:* IBM PC & compatibles. *Operating System(s) Required:* PC-DOS/MS-DOS.
disk $195.00.
Text Database Replacing FYI 3000. In Addition to FYI 3000's Searching & Retrieving Text Information Features It Adds the Following: Hard Disk Pathway Support, Allowing up to 12 DOS Pathways per Database with up to 100 Files per Path; Full Boolean & Truncated Searching Giving User Control over AND/OR/NOT/XOR with Infinitely Nested Parentheses & Truncation of Search Words; the Maximum Entry Size Has Been Increased from 500 to 1000 Words. Other New Features Give User the Ability to Define Their Own Entry Style, Customize the Program Defaults, Select the Order of Retrieval, etc.
Software Marketing Assocs.

F(Z) Complex Variable Graphics, 2 diskettes. *Items Included:* Bound manual. *Customer Support:* Free hotline - no time limit; 30 day limited warranty; updates are $5/disk plus S&H.
MS-DOS 2.0 or higher. IBM & compatibles (320k). $39.95-$49.95. *Nonstandard peripherals required:* Two 360k drives (or one floppy & one hard disk).
Interactive, Educational, Computer-Graphics Package Designed to Aid in the Study of Functions of a Complex Variable. Can Graph Rational Functions, Exp(z), Log(z), & the Riemann Zeta Function. Besides These Primitive Functions, CVG Can Compose, Add, Subtract, Multiply, Divide, Differentiate, & Integrate Functions.
Dynacomp, Inc.

G & G GL: Client Write-Up. Grover Cunningham. Apr. 1983. *Operating System(s) Required:* CP/M-80, CP/M-86, MP/M-80, MP/M-86, PC-DOS, MS-DOS. *Language(s):* CBASIC. *Memory Required:* CP/M-80 64k; CP/M-86, MS-DOS & PC-DOS 128k. *Customer Support:* Free telephone support.
disk $495.00 ea. (ISBN 0-917791-01-0).
Keep Accounting Records of Any Business Which Keeps Records for Several Clients.
Best Programs.

G & G 1040. Jan. 1983. *Operating System(s) Required:* CP/M, CP/M-86, MP/M-80, MP/M-86, PC-DOS, MS-DOS. *Language(s):* CB-80, CB-86. *Memory Required:* CP/M-80 64k, CP/M-86 128k. *Customer Support:* Free telephone support.
disk $300.00 (ISBN 0-917791-00-2).
Compute & Prepare IRS Form 1040 & Related Schedules.
Best Programs.

G & G 1065: Partnership Return. Grover Cunningham. Aug. 1985. *Operating System(s) Required:* CP/M-80, CP/M-86, MP/M-80, MP/M-86, PC-DOS, MS-DOS. *Language(s):* CBASIC. *Memory Required:* 8-bit 64k, 16-bit 128k. *General Requirements:* Hard disk recommended. *Customer Support:* Free telephone support.
disk $300.00 (Order no.: 00-3).
Tax Preparation Software. Supports All Appropriate IRS Forms, Multiple Schedules, & All Supporting Schedules.
Best Programs.

G & G 1120: Corporation Return. Grover Cunningham. Aug. 1985. *Operating System(s) Required:* CP/M-80, CP/M-86, MS-DOS, PC-DOS. *Language(s):* CBASIC. *Memory Required:* 8-bit 64k, 16-bit 128k. *Customer Support:* Free telephone support.
disk $300.00 ea. (Order no.: 00-4).
Tax Preparation Software. Supports All Appropriate IRS Form, Multiple Schedules, & All Supporting Schedules.
Best Programs.

G & G 1120S: Sub Chapter S Corporate. Grover Cunningham. Aug. 1985. *Operating System(s) Required:* CP/M-80, CP/M-86, MP/M-80, MP/M-86, PC-DOS, MS-DOS. *Language(s):* CBASIC. *Memory Required:* 8-bit 64k, 16-bit 128k. *Customer Support:* Free telephone support.
disk $300.00 (Order no.: 00-5).
Tax Preparation Software That Supports All Appropriate IRS Forms, Multiple Schedules, & All Supporting Schedules.
Best Programs.

G/Async Gateway. *Operating System(s) Required:* PC-DOS/MS-DOS. *Memory Required:* Gateway 256k, Workstation 384k. *Items Included:* Hardware, software, modem cable. *Customer Support:* One-year warranty, toll-free telephone support (permanent).
disk $1595.00 (Order no.: 8800-5761).
Provides a Modem Pool of up to Four Concurrent Modem Connections. Up to Four Products May Be Installed in the Gateway PC for a Total of Sixteen Available Connections. Each LAN User Has Access Through the Gateway to Dial or Dedicated Links, Eliminating the Need for Individual Modems & Telecommunications Lines. Features Intelligent Coprocessor Board with Four Ports, Installed in One PC on the LAN.
Gateway Communications, Inc.

G-NETIX. *Items Included:* Two manuals. Crash course manual, technical supplement. Floppies or CD depending on format chosen.
Windows CD-ROM (4Mb or more extended memory). CD-ROM disk $69.95 (Order no.: 06013). *Optimal configuration:* Windows 3.1, 386/25 MHz or higher. SVGA card (Windows Accelerator recommended) CD-ROM drive. Optional: Windows compatible sound card.
Windows Floppy (4Mb or more extended memory). disk $59.95 (Order no.: 06012). *Optimal configuration:* Windows 3.1, 386/25 MHz or higher. SVGA card. (Windows Accelerator recommended) Optional: Windows compatible sound card.
Macintosh CD-ROM (4Mb). CD-ROM disk $69.95 (Order no.: 06023). *Optimal configuration:* System 6.07 or higher, CD-ROM drive, hard disk.
Macintosh Floppy (4Mb). 3.5" disk $59.95 (Order no.: 06022). *Optimal configuration:* System 6.07 or higher, hard disk.
A Genetic Engineering Simulation Game. The Human Population on Earth Was Destroyed by a Plague. As a Biologist in Space with Genetic Materials, the Player Must Try to Recreate the Human Species. During the Growth, the Embryo Mutates & the Player Must Try to Correct the Mutation.
ISM, Inc.

TITLE INDEX

G. P. L. E: Global Program Line Editor. *Version:* 4.1. Neil Konzen. Nov. 1985. *Compatible Hardware:* Apple II, II+, IIe, IIc, IIgs. *Operating System(s) Required:* Apple DOS 3.3, ProDOS. *Language(s):* Machine, BASIC. *Memory Required:* DOS 3.3 48k, ProDOS 64k.
disk $49.95.
Allows for Simple Program Editing. Includes Global Editing with Search & Replace. User Can Automatically Move the Cursor to a Particular Point in a Program. Compatible with Many Beagle Brothers' Software Packages.
Beagle Brothers.

G-Poll: Gilbarco Interface. *Version:* 4.1D. Jun. 1995. *Items Included:* Manuals & diskette. *Customer Support:* 1st year support via modem. MS-DOS. IBM PS/2 or compatibles (640k). disk $1525.00. *Optimal configuration:* DOS 3.3, 640k RAM, Hard Disk, (Serial Card 25 Pin) G-Poll. *Networks supported:* PC LAN.
Program Scheduler Activates Poller At Selected Times Throughout Day. Request Function Gets Sales Data. Program Function Allows User to Program POS Device from PC. This Allows PLU/SKU Price Changes As Well As Pump Price Changes. The Posting Function Places All Data into the Computerized Daily Book. Accepts Data from CRIND Units & Scanners.
Service Station Computer Systems, Inc.

G/Remote Bridge 64. *Version:* 1.5. Jun. 1989. MS-DOS (512k). IBM PC, PC XT, PC AT, PS/2 & compatibles. disk $2495.00 (Order no.: 88006740). *Networks supported:* Novell Netware 2.0 or higher.
Allows Any Novell Netware (v2.xx) Local-Area Network (LAN) to Be Remotely Bridged to Another. Allows Complete NetWare Transparency. User in Tokyo Can Contact File Servers in London, Madrid or Chicago. Features Coprocessor Board for Peak Protocol Conversion. May Be Used in Non-Dedicated Mode. Single-User Version Also Available.
Gateway Communications, Inc.

G/SNA Gateway. *Version:* 4.0. *Operating System(s) Required:* PC-DOS/MS-DOS. *Memory Required:* Workstation 85k. *General Requirements:* LAN System, Novell NetWare or IBM NETBIOS. *Items Included:* Gateway communications coprocessor board; modem cable software. *Customer Support:* One-year warranty, toll-free technical support (permanent).
disk $2995.00 (Order no.: 8838-6150).
Provides up to 128 Logical Connections to IBM Host Via One Physical Connection. Features Intelligent Coprocessor Board Installed in One PC on the LAN. Other PCs on the LAN Communicate Through the Gateway to the Host System.
Gateway Communications, Inc.

G-Spell. *Version:* 4.00. Gordon Waite. 1988. *Compatible Hardware:* IBM PC. *Operating System(s) Required:* MS-DOS 2.0 or higher. *Language(s):* C. *Memory Required:* 512k. *General Requirements:* Hard disk.
disk $9.95 (ISBN 0-934777-01-2).
Spelling Checker That Uses a 90,000-Word Dictionary to Proofread Documents. Allows User to Customize Dictionary to User's Specific Application by Adding Words or Jargon to Create User's Own Customized Dictionary. Can Proof Any Text File.
Pico Publishing.

G-Whiz. *Version:* 1.03. Aug. 1985. *Compatible Hardware:* IBM PC; 1 floppy disk drive & hard disk. *Operating System(s) Required:* MS-DOS 2.0 or higher. *Memory Required:* 128k.
disk $9.95 (ISBN 0-934777-00-4).
Helps Manage Files on Hard Disk or Diskettes. User Can Copy, Move, Delete, or Print Selected Files; Sort Files on Either File Name or Extension; & Look at File Sizes. On-Line Help Screens & Documentation Provide Quick Reference.
Pico Publishing.

G/X25 Gateway. *Operating System(s) Required:* PC-DOS/MS-DOS. *Memory Required:* Workstation 190k. *General Requirements:* LAN System, Novell NetWare or IBM NETBIOS. *Items Included:* Communications coprocessor board, Gateway software, modem cable, terminal emulation.
disk $1895.00.
Allows Multiple Concurrent Minicomputer & Mainframe Connections for up to Sixty-Four Users. The Gateway Functions As a Packet Assembler-Disassembler, Providing Multiple Connections Via One Physical Connection Using the Worldwide Standard X.25 Protocol. Features Intelligent Coprocessor Board with Two Ports, Installed on One PC on the LAN.
Gateway Communications, Inc.

Gadget. Oct. 1994. *Items Included:* Warranty/registration card, game manual. *Customer Support:* Technical Support Number: 1-800-734-9466, 90 days limited warranty.
Macintosh 7.0 or higher. 25MHz 68030 or higher; 33MHz 68LC040 or higher recommended (4Mb). CD-ROM disk Contact publisher for price (ISBN 1-888158-00-X). *Nonstandard peripherals required:* Double speed CD-ROM. *Addl. software required:* Adaptability to QuickTime 1.6.1. *Optimal configuration:* 640 x 480 dots/256 colors; mouse.
Windows 3.1. 33MHz i486 or higher (8Mb). CD-ROM disk $79.99 (ISBN 1-888158-01-8). *Nonstandard peripherals required:* Double-speed CD-ROM drive, 8bit 22KHz PCM sound reproduction (equivalent to Sound Blaster). *Optimal configuration:* MS-DOS 5.0 or higher; CD-ROM Extensions Ver 2.2 or higher; 3Mb plus open area in hard disk; 640 x 480 dots/256 colors (SVGA); mouse.
Windows 95 & 3.1. 33MHz 486 or higher (8Mb). CD-ROM disk $79.99 (ISBN 1-888158-02-6). *Nonstandard peripherals required:* Double-speed CD-ROM, 8bit 22KHz PCM sound reproduction (equivalent to Sound Blaster), mouse. *Addl. software required:* MS-DOS 5.0, Microsoft Windows 3.1 or Windows 95, CD-ROM Extensions Ver 2.2 or higher. *Optimal configuration:* 3Mb or more in open area; 640x480 dots/256 colors (SVGA).
This Mystery Adventure Takes Place on a Locomotive in a Retro-Future World. Information & Clues Are Provided in Every Setting & by Other Passengers. While Making the Rounds of Seven Stations, a Museum & an Observatory, You Put Together a Collection of Gadgets That Solve the Mystery.
Synergy Interactive Corp.

GageTrol: Gage Calibration & GR&R Software System. *Version:* 3.602. Jul. 1993. *Items Included:* Operations manual. *Customer Support:* Telephone support, BBS support, FAX support.
3.1 or higher. IBM & compatibles (640K). $795.00 (Order no.: GIBM-000). *Networks supported:* All PC Networks.
Provides Complete Record Keeping for All Gages, & Replaces Cumbersome Card Files. The Program Allows Sorting & Listing by Criteria Like Gage Name, Date Next Study Is Due, & Customer. Control Charts for Calibration Measurements (Showing Wear Trends) & GR & R Test Values Are Produced Along with Gage Performance Curves.
Hertzler Systems, Inc.

GageTrol NET: GR & R Software System Network Version. *Version:* 3.602. Jul. 1993. *Items Included:* Operations manual. *Customer Support:* Telephone support, BBS support, FAX support.
DOS 3.1 or higher. IBM PC & compatibles (640K). disk $2995.00 (Order no.: GIBM-300). *Networks supported:* All PC Networks.
Network Version of the GageTrol Single User System. Enter, Retrieve, & Analyze Gage Data Simultaneously at Workstations Throughout Plant. Unique Security Rights, Passwords, & Configurations Settings for Each User. A Single Database Eliminates the Time Lag Between Data Entry & Analysis, Reducing Response Time to Problem Areas.
Hertzler Systems, Inc.

Gaither: Restaurant POS System. *Version:* 2.5. Oct. 1993. *Customer Support:* 24 hour/7 days per week.
DOS. PC (4Mb). Contact publisher for price. *Optimal configuration:* DOS 4Mb RAM. *Networks supported:* Novell.
A Touch Screen Restaurant Management System - Includes Logic for All Types of Restaurants.
National Guest Systems Corp.

Galactic Battles. *Compatible Hardware:* Commodore 64. *Memory Required:* 32k. *General Requirements:* Joystick.
disk $19.95.
Space Arcade Game.
Dynacomp, Inc.

Galactic Conqueror. Mar. 1989.
MS-DOS (256k). IBM or compatibles. $44.95.
Amiga 500, 1000, 2000 (512k). 3.5" disk $44.95. *Nonstandard peripherals required:* Joy stick.
Atari ST 520, 1040, ST2, ST4 (512k). 3.5" disk $44.95. *Nonstandard peripherals required:* Color monitor.
Strategy Action Game. Pacify the 416 Planets of the Galaxy. Find the Best Strategy for Not Being Overwhelmed by the Enemy.
Titus Software Corp.

Galactic Invasion. (One-on-One Ser.). *Compatible Hardware:* Commodore Amiga. $24.95.
Arcade Style Game Featuring Digitized Sounds & Music, Realistic Graphics, & Fast Action.
Microillusions, Inc.

Galax Attax. *Compatible Hardware:* TRS-80 Color Computer, TDP-100.
contact publisher for price.
Spectral Assocs.

Galaxian. *Compatible Hardware:* Atari XL/XE. ROM cartridge $16.95 (Order no.: CXL4024).
Atari Corp.

Galaxy. *Version:* 3.0. *Compatible Hardware:* IBM PC & compatibles. *Memory Required:* 512k. *General Requirements:* EGA, 43-line EGA, CGA or VGA. *Items Included:* Manual, 3.5" & 5.25" disks, reg card, updates to next major version. *Customer Support:* Free to registered users.
disk $99.95.
Includes Microlytics SpellFinder 100,000 Word Dictionary & WordFinder 220,000 Word Thesaurus. Mouse Support, Multiple Windows, Pull Down Menus, Dialog Boxes, & Context-Sensitive Help. Multiple Fonts, Micro-Justification, Proportional Spacing.
OmniVerse Software Corp.

Galaxy Patrol. *Compatible Hardware:* HP 86/87. *Memory Required:* 64k.
3-1/2" or 5-1/4" disk $39.00 ea. (Order no.: 92248FA).

As the Captain of an Interceptor Craft on the Fringes of the Galaxy You Are Patrolling the Galactic Border, Repelling Any Alien Incursion You Discover.
Hewlett-Packard Co.

Gale Business Resource, 1995, Pt. 1. Edited by Karin Koek. Sep. 1995. *Items Included:* 2 disks.
IBM. CD-ROM disk $79.95, annual subscription (ISBN 0-8103-9044-2, Order no.: 108874).
Gale Business Resources Allows You Fast Electronic Access to Every U.S. Industry with a Four-Digit SIC Code - As Well As 208,000 American Companies Within These Industries. It Also Includes SEC Reports for Fortune 1,000 Companies, All Current U.S. Industrial Outlook Data, Market Share Reports, Products & Brands, Ranking, Company Histories, Industry Profiles, Statistics & Much More.
Gale Research, Inc.

Gale Business Resource, 1995, Pt. 2. Edited by Karin Koek. Feb. 1996. *Items Included:* 2 disks.
IBM. CD-ROM disk $79.95, annual subscription (ISBN 0-8103-9045-0, Order no.: 151553).
Gale Business Resources Allows You Fast Electronic Access to Every U.S. Industry with a Four-Digit SIC Code - As Well As 208,000 American Companies Within These Industries. It Also Includes SEC Reports for Fortune 1,000 Companies, All Current U.S. Industrial Outlook Data, Market Share Reports, Products & Brands, Ranking, Company Histories, Industry Profiles, Statistics & Much More.
Gale Research, Inc.

Gale Business Resource, 1995, Pt. 3. (Business Resource IBM CD ROM Ser.). May 1996. *Items Included:* 2 disks.
IBM CD ROM. CD-ROM disk $79.95, annual subscription (ISBN 0-7876-0217-5, Order no.: 109113).
Gale Business Reources Allows You Fast Electronic Access to Every U.S. Industry with a Four-Digit SIC Code - As Well As 208,000 American Companies Within These Industries. It Also Includes SEC Reports for Fortune 1,000 Companies, All Current U.S. Industrial Outlook Data, Market Share Reports, Products, & Brands, Rankings, Company Histories, Industry Profiles, Statistics & Much More.
Gale Research, Inc.

Gale Business Resource, 1995 Box. (Business Resource IBM CD ROM Ser.). Edited by Karin Koek. Aug. 1996. *Items Included:* 2 disks.
IBM CD ROM. CD-ROM disk $79.95, annual subscription (ISBN 0-7876-0218-3, Order no.: 109114).
Gale Business Reources Allows You Fast Electronic Access to Every U.S. Industry with a Four-Digit SIC Code - As Well As 208,000 American Companies Within These Industries. It Also Includes SEC Reports for Fortune 1,000 Companies, All Current U.S. Industrial Outlook Data, Market Share Reports, Products, & Brands, Rankings, Company Histories, Industry Profiles, Statistics & Much More.
Gale Research, Inc.

Gale Career Guidance System. (Career for Business CD Package DOS Ser.). Edited by Linda Thurn. Sep. 1995.
IBM. $6995.00 single user; $8995.00 network (ISBN 0-7876-0300-7, Order no.: 109238).
Contains Career Guidance Info, & Data on Potential Employers.
Gale Research, Inc.

Gale Career Guidance System. *Version:* Expanded. (Career for Business CD Package DOS Ser.). Edited by Linda Thurn. Sep. 1995.
IBM. $4995.00 single user; $6262.00 network (ISBN 0-7876-0495-X, Order no.: 109527).
Contains Career Guidance Info, & Data on Potential Employers & Self Assessment Module to Match Jobs to an Individual's Interest & Abilities.
Gale Research, Inc.

Gale Career Guidance System. Edited by Linda Thurn. Oct. 1995.
IBM. disk $6995.00 (Order no.: 109532).
Contains Information on over 1200 Jobs Divided into 250 Categories. Also Includes Information on over 220,000 Potential Employers & Electronic Access to the Government Career Guides: Occupational Outlook Handbook & Dictionary of Occupational Titles.
Gale Research, Inc.

GALENUS: Disease Processor. *Version:* 1.5. Oct. 1990. *Customer Support:* Toll free telephone support.
MS-DOS 3.1. IBM PC. disk $2995.00.
Combines a Medical Encyclopedia with a Patient Chart System to Introduce a New Concept in Clinical Management. Named for the Ancient Medical Logician, This Application Functions on All PC-DOS Personal Computers. Database of 1265 Disease Titles with Their ICD-9 Codes. Peripheral Databases Hold Each Category of Clinical Management Terminology: Symptoms, Signs, Laboratory Tests, Specialty Tests & Therapies. One Relational Database Contains 20,000 Plus Links Between the Diseases & Every Appropriate Manifestation (Symptoms, Signs, etc.). A Second Relational File Correlates 7000 Plus Links Between the Diseases & Every Appropriate Intervention (Therapies).
SRC Systems, Inc.

The Gallery Collection. *Version:* 2.0. *Compatible Hardware:* IBM PC & compatibles; Hewlett-Packard Vectra, Touchscreen. *Operating System(s) Required:* PC-DOS 2.1 or higher. *Memory Required:* 384k.
disk $695.00.
Presentation Graphics Package Consisting of Two Separate Applications: Charting Gallery & Drawing Gallery. Features Ability to Export Graph & Text Files, Text Annotation Capabilities & Two Clip-Art Libraries, Which Include a Basic Collection of Artwork, Borders & Lettering & the Business Management Portfolio, a Collection of Graphics, Forms, Maps & Symbols. Not Copy Protected.
Hewlett-Packard Co.

Gallery Picture Library, Vol. II. *Compatible Hardware:* HP 150 Touchscreen.
3.5" disk $95.00 (Order no.: 45433A).
Expands the DRAWING GALLERY's Selection of Pictures by Providing More Than 200 Ready-Made Drawings for Enhancing Charts & Drawings. Includes Pictures of Buildings & Vehicles, As Well As Cartoons, & a Wide Range of Other Images. Also Includes Two Additional Electronic Templates: Floorplan & Mapping. Images Can Be Used Directly with the EXECUTIVE MEMOMAKER.
Hewlett-Packard Co.

Gambler's Game Pak. *Customer Support:* 800-929-8117 (customer service).
MS-DOS. Apple II. disk $59.99 (ISBN 0-87007-061-4).
Several Gambling Games, Including Roulette, Blackjack, Red Dog & Dice.
SourceView Software International.

Games Disc '95. Mar. 1995. *Customer Support:* Telephone support, 30 day money back guarantee.
DOS 3.1 or higher or Windows 3.1. IBM PC & compatibles (512k). Contact publisher for price (ISBN 1-886770-03-4). *Optimal configuration:* VGA, Sound card, mouse recommended.
A Collection of over 1500 Games, Most of Which Can Be Run from the CD-ROM. Includes Educational Programs, 3D Games, Arcade Games, Adventure Games & Many More.
Neon Publishing.

Game Pack II. *Items Included:* Installation Guide.
IBM. Contact publisher for price (ISBN 0-87321-086-7, Order no.: MS2-3032).
Activision, Inc.

Game Pack II. *Items Included:* Installation Guide.
IBM PC. Contact publisher for price (ISBN 0-87321-087-5, Order no.: CDD-3032).
Activision, Inc.

Game Pack Three. Mar. 1993.
DOS. IBM. 3.5" or 5.25" disk $49.95 (Order no.: 111289; 111290).
Get Ten Mind Bending Pulse Quickening Games Packed into a Single Compact Disc! Includes The Chessmaster 2100, The Software Toolworks Robot Tank, Beyond the Black Hole, Life & Death, Gin King/Cribbage King, Checkers, Loopz, Puzzle Gallery, Life, & More. A Must Have for the Serious Gamester.
Software Toolworks.

Game Pak One.
IBM. disk $39.95.
Buckle up for Chuck Yeager's Advanced Flight Trainer, Airplane Factory, The Hunt for Red October, Chessmaster 2000, Life & Death. A $205 Value.
Software Toolworks.

Game Works for Macintosh. *Items Included:* Browser/installer/launcher front end software. *Customer Support:* 90 day warranty, free call back technical support.
System 6. Mac Plus (2Mb, 4Mb in System 7). CD-ROM disk $9.95. *Nonstandard peripherals required:* CD-ROM drive. *Optimal configuration:* 8Mb RAM. *Networks supported:* Apple File Sharing.
BeachWare.

Games. *Compatible Hardware:* HP 85.
data cartridge, 3-1/2" or 5-1/4" disk $95.00 ea. (Order no.: 82818A).
Provides a Way to Become Familiar with the Keyboard & Operation of the HP 85 Personal Computer.
Hewlett-Packard Co.

Games, Games, & More Games. *Version:* 3. Pat Palmer & Roger Palmer. Jun. 1982. *Compatible Hardware:* TRS-80 Model II, Model 12, Model 16; Tandy 6000. *Operating System(s) Required:* TRSDOS. *Language(s):* BASIC (source code included). *Memory Required:* 64k.
disk $25.00 (Order no.: 4726-1).
Includes Crazy Eights, Stocks & Bonds, Castle Keep & 10 More. Games Are for 1-6 Players.
Palmer & Palmer.

Games, Graphics & Sound for the IBM PC.
Dorothy Strickland. *Compatible Hardware:* IBM PC. *Operating System(s) Required:* DOS, UCSD p-System. *Language(s):* BASIC, Pascal, FORTRAN.
disk $64.95, incl. bk. (ISBN 0-89303-470-3).
disk $40.00 (ISBN 0-89303-471-1).
UCSD p-System. disk $30.00 (ISBN 0-89303-472-X).
Turn Sound & Graphics Techniques into Animation.
Brady Computer Bks.

Games in English. Sep. 1995. *Customer Support:* Telephone support - free (except phone charge).

TITLE INDEX

Windows 3.1. IBM & compatibles (386 DX-20) (4Mb). CD-ROM disk $12.99 (ISBN 1-57594-011-6). *Nonstandard peripherals required:* 2x CD-ROM player, Sound Card, VGA monitor. *Optimal configuration:* 486 SX-33.
Interactive Games in English.
Kidsoft, Inc.

Games in English. Sep. 1995. *Customer Support:* Telephone support - free (except phone charge).
Windows 3.1. IBM & compatibles (386 DX-20) (4Mb). CD-ROM disk $12.99 (ISBN 1-57594-050-7). *Nonstandard peripherals required:* 2x CD-ROM player, Sound Card, VGA monitor. *Optimal configuration:* 486 SX-33.
Interactive Games in English. Blister Pack Jewel Case.
Kidsoft, Inc.

Games in French. Sep. 1995. *Customer Support:* Telephone support - free (except phone charge).
Windows 3.1. IBM & compatibles (386 DX-20) (4Mb). CD-ROM disk $12.99 (ISBN 1-57594-012-4). *Nonstandard peripherals required:* 2x CD-ROM player, Sound Card, VGA monitor. *Optimal configuration:* 486 SX-33.
Interactive Games in French.
Kidsoft, Inc.

Games in French. Sep. 1995. *Customer Support:* Telephone support - free (except phone charge).
Windows 3.1. IBM & compatibles (386 DX-20) (4Mb). CD-ROM disk $12.99 (ISBN 1-57594-051-5). *Nonstandard peripherals required:* 2x CD-ROM player, Sound Card, VGA monitor. *Optimal configuration:* 486 SX-33.
Interactive Games in French. Blister Pack Jewel Case.
Kidsoft, Inc.

Games in German. Sep. 1995. *Customer Support:* Telephone support - free (except phone charge).
Windows 3.1. IBM & compatibles (386 DX-20) (4Mb). CD-ROM disk $12.99 (ISBN 1-57594-013-2). *Nonstandard peripherals required:* 2x CD-ROM player, Sound Card, VGA monitor. *Optimal configuration:* 486 SX-33.
Interactive Games in German.
Kidsoft, Inc.

Games in German. Sep. 1995. *Customer Support:* Telephone support - free (except phone charge).
Windows 3.1. IBM & compatibles (386 DX-20) (4Mb). CD-ROM disk $12.99 (ISBN 1-57594-052-3). *Nonstandard peripherals required:* 2x CD-ROM player, Sound Card, VGA monitor. *Optimal configuration:* 486 SX-33.
Interactive Games in German. Blister Pack Jewel Case.
Kidsoft, Inc.

Games in Japanese. Sep. 1995. *Customer Support:* Telephone support - free (except phone charge).
Windows 3.1. IBM & compatibles (386 DX-20) (4Mb). CD-ROM disk $12.99 (ISBN 1-57594-014-0). *Nonstandard peripherals required:* 2x CD-ROM player, Sound Card, VGA monitor. *Optimal configuration:* 486 SX-33.
Interactive Games in Japanese.
Kidsoft, Inc.

Games in Japanese. Sep. 1995. *Customer Support:* Telephone support - free (except phone charge).
Windows 3.1. IBM & compatibles (386 DX-20) (4Mb). CD-ROM disk $12.99 (ISBN 1-57594-053-1). *Nonstandard peripherals required:* 2x CD-ROM player, Sound Card, VGA monitor. *Optimal configuration:* 486 SX-33.
Interactive Games in Japanese. Blister Pack Jewel Case.
Kidsoft, Inc.

Games in Spanish. Sep. 1995. *Customer Support:* Telephone support - free (except phone charge).
Windows 3.1. IBM & compatibles (386 DX-20) (4Mb). CD-ROM disk $12.99 (ISBN 1-57594-015-9). *Nonstandard peripherals required:* 2x CD-ROM player, Sound Card, VGA monitor. *Optimal configuration:* 486 SX-33.
Interactive Games in Spanish.
Kidsoft, Inc.

Games in Spanish. Sep. 1995. *Customer Support:* Telephone support - free (except phone charge).
Windows 3.1. IBM & compatibles (386 DX-20) (4Mb). CD-ROM disk $12.99 (ISBN 1-57594-054-X). *Nonstandard peripherals required:* 2x CD-ROM player, Sound Card, VGA monitor. *Optimal configuration:* 486 SX-33.
Interactive Games in Spanish. Blister Pack Jewel Case.
Kidsoft, Inc.

Games Pack I & II. *Compatible Hardware:* Apple II with Applesoft; IBM PC. (source code included). *Memory Required:* Apple 48k, IBM 128k.
disk $19.95.
Cross-Section of Traditional Computer Games.
Dynacomp, Inc.

Games II. *Compatible Hardware:* HP 85.
data cartridge, 3-1/4" or 5-1/4" disk $95.00 ea. (Order no.: 82819A).
Graphic, Arcade-Type Games to Provide Entertainment & to Familiarize User with the Keyboard & General Operation of the HP 85 Personal Computer.
Hewlett-Packard Co.

Games-200. *Compatible Hardware:* HP Series 200 Models 216/220, 217 Personal Technical Computers. *Memory Required:* 512k.
3.5" disk $49.00 (Order no.: 45475B).
Challenge Your Computer with Two Games. ROBOTANK: Can Your Tank Survive the Attacking Army of Enemy Tanks? CRIBBAGE: Play the Computer in One-, Two-, Three-, or Four-Handed Games.
Hewlett-Packard Co.

GANTT LAB MANAGER. Version: 1.2d. Mar. 1988. *Compatible Hardware:* IBM PC & compatibles, PC XT, PC AT. *Operating System(s) Required:* PC-DOS/MS-DOS 2.0 or higher. *Language(s):* Compiled BASIC. *Memory Required:* 256k. *General Requirements:* 2 floppy disk drivers or hard disk, 132-column printer or laser printer. *Items Included:* Diskette(s), manual, quick reference guide, template instructions. *Customer Support:* Telephone support for registered owners.
disk $395.00, incl. manual & reference guide.
optional template disk $40.00.
Database & Graphics Tool for Laboratory Management Which Allows Users to Plan & Track Day-to-Day Workload & Lab Q.A. Activities; to Schedule Equipment Use, Calibration, & Servicing; to Manage Lab Projects & Inventories; & to Optimize Use/Productivity of Personnel, Facilities, Material, Time, & Money, Exports ASCII to Spreadsheets, Word Processors, Telecommunications Software, etc.
Gantt Systems, Inc.

GANTT-PACK: Work Processor. Version: 3.4d. 1988. *Compatible Hardware:* IBM PC & compatibles, PC XT, PC AT. *Operating System(s) Required:* PC-DOS/MS-DOS 2.0 or higher. *Language(s):* Compiled BASIC. *Memory Required:* 256k. *General Requirements:* 2 floppy disk drives or hard disk, 132-column printer or laser printer. *Items Included:* Diskette, manual, quick reference guide, sample file on disk. *Customer Support:* Telephone support for registered owners.
disk $225.00, incl. documentation, manual & reference guide.
User-Customizable (No Programming Required) Database & Planning, Scheduling, Project Tracking/Control, & Resource Management Tool. Stores Files That Show Tasks, Assignments, Personnel, Costs, & Timetables, & Saves Multiple Versions of Plans. Features Gantt Timeline Graphics & Milestone Charts. Exports ASCII Files to Spreadsheets, Word Processors, Telecommunications Software, etc.
Gantt Systems, Inc.

GANTT SAMPLE LOG. Version: 1.1d. Mar. 1988. *Compatible Hardware:* IBM PC & compatibles, PC XT, PC AT. *Operating System(s) Required:* PC-DOS/MS-DOS 2.0 or higher. *Language(s):* C Compiled BASIC. *Memory Required:* 256k. *General Requirements:* 2 floppy disk drives or hard disk, 132-column printer or laser printer. *Items Included:* Diskette & manual. *Customer Support:* Telephone support for registered owners.
disk $395.00, incl. documentation.
Database Tool for Logging, Tracking, Retrieving, & Reporting on Samples. Stores Data on Source & Type of Sample, Dates/Times Logged in & out, Test Method(s) Used, Personnel/Equipment Involved, Key Test Results, Cross-Reference to Lab, Notebook Page, & Storage Location, Exports Files to Spreadsheets, Telecommunications Software, Programs for Statistical Analysis, & User's BASIC Programs. Interfaces with GANTT LAB MANAGER for Sample Scheduling & Tracking.
Gantt Systems, Inc.

Garage Keeper Inventory Control & Invoicing System: Garage Keeper I. *Operating System(s) Required:* MS-DOS. *Language(s):* FORTRAN, Assembler, C. *Memory Required:* 512k. *Customer Support:* telephone, BBS, Fax & remote modem support.
disk $500.00.
Inventory Control, Invoicing, Accounting & Service Management System for Independent Garages, Automotive Specialty Shops & Small Dealerships. Helps User Organize Inventory & Prints Copies of Customer Invoices.
Computer Assistance, Inc.

Garage Keeper System III. Version: 3.2. Nov. 1992. *Operating System(s) Required:* MS-DOS. *Memory Required:* 512k. *Customer Support:* telephone, BBS, fax & remote modem.
disk $1750.00.
Does All Paperwork for an Independent Auto Repair Shop. Includes Accounting & Service Management Programs in Addition to Invoicing, Order Entry & Inventory Control Functions.
Computer Assistance, Inc.

Garage Keeper 500. Version: 1.1. Mar. 1994. *Customer Support:* telephone, BBS, fax & remote modem support.
PC-DOS, NetBios, Novell (640k). disk $3500.00 to $12,495.00 (Order no.: GK500).
Provides for Unlimited Point of Sale/Service Workstations. Tracks Customers, Vehicles, Services, Inventory, Mechanics, Vendor & Receivables. Priced by Number of Users.
Computer Assistance, Inc.

GarageKeeper. Computer Assistance, Inc. *Compatible Hardware:* TI Professional. *Operating System(s) Required:* MS-DOS. *Memory Required:* 64k. *General Requirements:* Printer.
$3000.00.
Inventory Control & Invoicing System for Automotive Repair Garages & Other Job Shops.
Texas Instruments, Personal Productivit.

Garbo. *Customer Support:* All of our products are unconditionally guaranteed.
DOS, Mac. CD-ROM disk $29.95 (Order no.: GARBO). *Nonstandard peripherals required:* CD-ROM drive.
337 MB of PC Plus 135 MB Mac Programs.
Walnut Creek CDRom.

Garden Master. *Customer Support:* 800-929-8117 (customer service).
MS-DOS. IBM/PS2. disk $79.99 (ISBN 0-87007-657-4).
Database That Keeps Track of Where User Plants Garden Vegetables, in Terms of Season, Dates, & Plot Location. Includes Calculator, Calendar, & a Database of Recipes.
SourceView Software International.

Gardening Gift Pack. 1995. *Items Included:* Operating manual. *Customer Support:* Free telephone technical support 1-800-850-7272.
DOS 3.1, Windows 3.1; Macintosh. 33Mhz 80486DX, VGA video/display at 256 colors (4Mb); Macintosh, System 6.07, 68040 processor or higher (4Mb). CD-ROM disk Contact publisher for price (ISBN 1-884014-64-X). *Nonstandard peripherals required:* CD-ROM drive. *Optimal configuration:* 8Mb, Dual speed CD-ROM.
Multicom Publishing, Inc.

GARMANAGER I. *Compatible Hardware:* IBM PC, PC XT. *Operating System(s) Required:* MS-DOS, PC-DOS. *Memory Required:* 256k. *General Requirements:* 132-column printer.
disk $3000.00.
Asset & Liability Management Package for Financial Institutions Which Gives Reports on Treasury Balances & Maturities for Five Years, & Non-Treasury for Thirty Years.
Distributed Planning System Corp.

GAS. *Version:* .14. P. L. Mariam. Jan. 1984. *Compatible Hardware:* IBM PC & compatibles, PC XT, PC AT. *Operating System(s) Required:* PC-DOS/MS-DOS 2.X, 3.0. *Memory Required:* 256k. *General Requirements:* Printer.
disk $499.95 (ISBN 0-935509-03-8, Order no.: 5100).
Computes the Beta Ratio, Flow, or Differential Pressure for Gas Flows Using American Gas Association (AGA) Equations. Allows User to Enter the Supercompressibility Factor (Fpv), Compressibility Factor (Zf) or Can Calculate the Supercompressibility Factor Based upon the Specific Gravity, Temperature, & Pressure of the Fluid. Built-In Pipe Data to Prevent Errors in Looking up the Actual Inside Diameter of Pipe by Specifying the Nominal Pipe Size & Schedule.
FlowSoft, Inc.

Gas Man. James H. Philips. 1984. *Compatible Hardware:* Apple II, II+. *Language(s):* Applesoft. *General Requirements:* 2 game controls.
contact publisher for price (ISBN 0-201-05798-0).
Enables User to Simulate a Variety of Clinical & Hypothetical Situations, & Test & Compare Anesthetic Administration Techniques.
Addison-Wesley Publishing Co., Inc.

GASMAN: Understanding Anesthesia Uptake & Distribution. James H. Philip. Oct. 1990. *Items Included:* Tutorial Text with 30 exercises teaching the basic concepts of inhalation anesthetic administration.
System 4.1 or higher. Macintosh (512k). 3.5" disk $245.00 (ISBN 0-9628045-0-9). *Nonstandard peripherals required:* None. *Addl. software required:* None. *Networks supported:* Tops, Appletalk.
Site license $635.00.
Computer Simulation & Text That Teaches Uptake & Distribution of Inhalation Anesthetics Graphic Displays Simulate the Delivery of Anesthesia Gases to the Body Compartments of a 70-kg Subject.
Med Man Simulations.

GasMap: Gallium Arsenide Model Analysis Program. Michael Golio. Mar. 1991. *Items Included:* 50 page ring-bound user's manual.
IBM PC compatible. Contact publisher for price (ISBN 0-89006-533-0, Order no.: C1533).
GasMap Is a Set of Two Computer Programs That Efficiently Extract Model Parameter Values for Microwave MESFET Devices. Data Produced by This Program Can Be Used in Both Small & Large Signal Commercially Available Circuit Simulation Packages. It Is Also Very Useful for Evaluating the Merits of Different Large Signal Models.
Artech Hse., Inc.

GASMOD: Gas Pipeline Simulation. *Version:* 3.8. Shashi Menon. Dec. 1995. *Items Included:* User manual with sample problems. *Customer Support:* Free telephone support.
PC-DOS/MS-DOS, Windows 3.1, Windows 95. IBM PC, XT, AT, PS/2 & compatibles (4Mb). disk $1995.00 (ISBN 0-932507-67-0, Order no.: 767). *Optimal configuration:* IBM compatible with DOS 5.0 or higher with 8Mb RAM, floppy disk, hard disk, color monitor, printer.
Gas Pipeline Hydraulic Simulation Considering Flow Deliveries/Injections along Pipeline with Multiple Compressor Stations. Calculates Pressures & Horsepowers Required. English & Metric Units. Easy to Use Pull-Down Menus & On-Line Help.
Systek (California).

GATE. *Version:* 1.1. Dec. 1993. *Items Included:* Manual. *Customer Support:* (904) 576-9415 11-5 ET M-F, online at AppleLink, American Online, CompuServe, eWorld, GEnie.
Mac 6.0.7 or higher. Macintosh (4Mb). 3.5" disk $49.95, SRP (ISBN 0-931277-20-5, Order no.: GTM). *Nonstandard peripherals required:* 640 x 480 display with 256 colors. *Optimal configuration:* Macintosh with 6.0.7 or higher, 4Mb RAM, joystick, 640 x 480 display with 256 colors.
Blends the Excitement of Arcade Action with the Intrigue of Adventure Gaming to Cook up a Brain-Teasing Challenge That Includes Smooth Animation, Stimulating Musical Scores & Sound Effects. Escape the Castle's Dungeon, Battle Fearsome Enemies, Solve Puzzling Riddles, & Defeat Your Captor to Restore Peace & Tranquility to the Land.
Seven Hills Software Corp.

GATO: World War II Submarine Simulation. *Version:* Commodore & Atari 1.00; Apple 1.3. Mar. 1984. *Compatible Hardware:* Apple IIe, IIc, Laser 128, Franklin Ace 500, 2100, 2200; Atari 520/1040ST, Mega 2/4; Commodore 64/128. *Memory Required:* Apple II & Atari 512k, TOS in ROM; Commodore 64k.
IBM PC. contact publisher for price (ISBN 0-928784-00-2).
Apple II. disk $14.95 ea. (ISBN 0-928784-01-0).
Atari. disk $14.95 (ISBN 0-928784-05-3).
Commodore. disk $14.95 (ISBN 0-928784-03-7).
Simulation of World War II Submarine on a Patrol Mission. Features 3-D Perspective, 9 Levels of Difficulty, Day & Night Missions, & Morse Code Messages.
Spectrum HoloByte.

GB-Analytic. *Version:* 1.2. *Compatible Hardware:* IBM PC, PC XT, PC AT, 386, 486. *Memory Required:* 128k. *General Requirements:* CGA, EGA, MCGA or Hercules Graphics or VGA. *Items Included:* Documentation. *Customer Support:* Free technical support.
disk $200.00 (ISBN 0-945830-02-5).
Presentation-Graphics Package for On-Screen Slide Shows. Chart-Making Features Include Line, Text, Scatter, Max/Min, Spline, Linear Trend, Logarithmic Trend & Exponential Trend Charts. Provides 16 User-Selectable Colors, 1 Typeface & 1 Font Size. Outputs to PostScript Printer, HP LaserJet, Dot-Matrix Printer, Film Recorder, Plotter, Color Ink-Jet Printer & Thermal Printer. Captures Data from Other Applications While They Are Running. Also Features On-Screen Help & GB Analytic, a RAM-Resident Utility That Displays Graphs of the Data in Other Applications.
New England Software, Inc.

GB-STAT. *Version:* 2.0. Mar. 1989. *Items Included:* Documentation. *Customer Support:* Free technical support.
MS-DOS/PC-DOS 2.0 or higher (512k). IBM PC, PC XT, PC AT, PS/2, 3270 & true compatibles. disk $399.95 (ISBN 0-945830-03-3). *Nonstandard peripherals required:* CGA, EGA, MCGA, VGA or Hercules graphics.
Statistical Analysis Data Management/Graphics Package. Program is Menu-Driven, Handles Missing Data, & Has Flexible Data Entry. User Can Graph Both Data & Statistical Results. Varied File Import Functions with Automatic Conversions Let User Perform Statistical Analyses of Data Taken from Virtually all Leading Programs. Imports Lotus PRN, ASCII, & DIF files.
New England Software, Inc.

GB-Stat Statistics As Graphs. *Items Included:* Full manual. No other products required. *Customer Support:* Free telephone support - no time limit. 30 day warranty.
MS-DOS 3.2 or higher. IBM & compatibles (512k). disk $279.95.
Menu-Driven Statistical Analysis Package with an Emphasis on Graphical Presentation. According to PC Week, GB-STAT "Is a Statistical Bulldozer on a Par with Such Heavyweight Packages As SPSS..." As You Can See from the Accompanying Sample Graphics Displays, GB-STAT Is a High Quality Product. It Is Also Exceptionally Easy to Use.
Dynacomp, Inc.

GB-Stat: Statistics As Graphs. 1992. *Items Included:* Detailed manuals are included with all DYNACOMP products. *Customer Support:* Free telephone support to original customer - no time limit; 30 day limited warranty.
MS-DOS 3.2 or higher. IBM PC & compatibles (512k). $349.95 (Add $5.00 for 3 1/2" format; 5 1/4" format standard). *Optimal configuration:* IBM, MS-DOS 2.0 or higher, 512k RAM, two floppy disk drives (or one floppy & a hard disk), & CGA, EGA, MCGA, VGA, Hercules or compatible graphics capability. Supports an 80x87 math coprocessor. Supports most printers & plotters.
A Menu-Driven Statistical Analysis Package with an Emphasis on Graphical Presentation. Capabilities: DATA I/O: Data Entry Can Be from the Keyboard or from/to ASCII, DIF, or Lotus PRN Files; Chart Types: X-Y; Double Y; Log; Scatter; Spline; Error Bar; Trend Line/Log/ Exponential; High-Low; Step; Column; Bar; Line; Mixed; & More. Automatic Statistical Graphs. Nonparametric Procedures; T-Tests & Anovas; Multivariate Statistics; Regression Analysis; Descriptive Statistics; Data Distributions.
Dynacomp, Inc.

GCLISP: Golden Common LISP. *Version:* 1.1. 1984. *Compatible Hardware:* Compaq; DEC Rainbow; IBM PC, PC XT, PC AT, & true PC compatibles; Wang. *Operating System(s)*

TITLE INDEX

GED STUDIES

Required: PC-DOS/MS-DOS 2.0 or higher. *Language(s):* LISP. *Memory Required:* 640k. *General Requirements:* Hard disk, 640k, 8087 co-processor, CGA card, mouse, & printer are recommended.
disk $495.00 (ISBN 0-917589-02-5).
Extensive Subset of COMMON LISP, Supporting More Than 400 LISP Primitives. Advanced Features Include Co-Routines for Multi-Tasking, Macros for Code Clarity, Streams for I/O, Closures for Object-Centered Programming, & Multiple-Value-Returning Functions for Efficiency. The Package Includes: the GCLisp Interpreter, the GMACS Editor, the San Marco LISP Explorer, the On-Line Help System. Also Included Are: LISP, 2nd Edition by Winston & Horn; The Common LISP Reference Manual; & the Golden Common LISP User's Manual.
Gold Hill, Inc.

GCLISP 286 Developer. *Compatible Hardware:* Compaq Portable 286, Deskpro; IBM PC AT & true compatibles. *Operating System(s) Required:* PC-DOS/MS-DOS 3.0 or higher. *Memory Required:* DOS-accessible memory 512k, extended memory 2000k. *General Requirements:* 2.7Mb hard disk; 640k base memory & 15Mb additional memory, 80287 numeric co-processoor, professional graphics adapter/display, mouse, & printer recommended.
GCLisp 286 Developer. $1195.00.
HALO Graphics. $250.00.
Programming Environment for GCLisp-Based Applications That Require Extended Memory & Faster Execution. The DEVELOPER Features: Can Address up to 15Mb RAM; Applications Run 15 Times Faster Than GOLDEN COMMON LISP in the Interpreted Mode; the Subset of COMMON LISP Includes Lexical & Dynamic Scoping, Transcendental Functions, Full LISP Package Facility, Macro Definition & Expansion, Time/Room Measurement Functions, & Some ZETALISP-Based Extensions. Has Full Compatibility with VAX COMMON LISP Environment of VMS/VAX & with COMMON LISP Environment on Symbolics 3600-Series Machines. The HALO Software Library Provides User with Point, Line, Arc, Circle, & Ellipse Functions. Advanced Functions Include Hatch Style, Pattern Fills, & Dithering Commands. DEVELOPER Package Also Includes: GCLisp LM Interpreter & LM Compiler, GMACS Editor, San Marco LISP Explorer, On-Line Help System, User Guide & References, Programming Examples, & GCLisp Debugger.
Gold Hill, Inc.

GCLrun, 2 disks. *Compatible Hardware:* IBM PC AT or true compatibles for development machine; IBM PC or true compatibles for end-user machine. *Operating System(s) Required:* PC-DOS/MS-DOS 3.0 for the development machine, PC-DOS/MS-DOS 2.0 or higher for the end-user machine. *Memory Required:* 512k. *General Requirements:* Same as for the CLisp 286 Developer for development machine.
contact publisher for price.
Creates an Executable File from a Compiled GCLisp Program. Accepts Any Error-Free Compiled Output from the 286 DEVELOPER. Programs Written in Lattice C or Microsoft C Can Be Built into the Application Runtime.
Gold Hill, Inc.

GD&T-E-BOD: Electronic Book on Disk. *Version:* 1.0. Sam Levy. Sep. 1991. *Items Included:* 3 "D" ring binder manual. *Customer Support:* Hotline.
Apple MAC 6.2 or 7.0. Apple MAC. $23.00 (ISBN 1-883467-03-9, Order no.: IGTI50).
Addl. software required: Microsoft Excel 3.0.
The Book Itself Is New. It Begins by Detailing the Difference Between U.S., Canadian & European Interpretations & Theories & Develops the Entire GD&T System Using the U.S.A. Theories As the Basis. Prior to the Discourse on Geometric Tolerancing, We Learn of Gladman's Papers & How He Energized the Mini Revolution Toward Geometric Tolerancing. Each Major Concept & Symbol Is Broken down & Explained Eventually Leading to the Logic of Why the Mechanics of the System Is Necessarily the Way It Is. Stepped Analysis Is Used in Positional Calculations. An Entire Section Is Devoted to Metric & Customary "Limits & Fits"; the Geometric Tolerances Are More Graphic Than the Usual Explanations. Fun Reading - Great CAD Graphics.
International Geometric Tolerancing Institute, Inc.

Gear Calculations. *Compatible Hardware:* IBM PC or compatible. *Operating System(s) Required:* MS-DOS. *Language(s):* UX-Basic (source code included).
contact publisher for price.
Provides Gear Cutting Parameters for Most Gears.
Comcepts Systems.

Geardesign. *Items Included:* Bound manual. *Customer Support:* Free hotline - no time limit; 30 day limited warranty; updates are $5/disk plus S&H.
MS-DOS. IBM & compatibles (256k). $599.95 set; $229.95 ea.
Three-Volume Set of Programs to Calculate the Best Spur, Helical, & Bevel Gears for a Given Application. Menus Guide User Through the Entire Design Process to Find the Minimum Size of New Gears, Optimization of Replacement Gears, & Allowable Loading.
Dynacomp, Inc.

GED Assessment. Jan. 1994. *Items Included:* Program on CD-ROM, CD Booklet, & Registration Card. *Customer Support:* Free unlimited customer support via telephone.
Windows 3.1 or higher running under DOS 5.0 or higher. 386 SX (4Mb RAM; 500k low Dos Mem; 6Mb free disk space). CD-ROM disk $249.00 (ISBN 1-57268-059-8, Order no.: 11100). *Nonstandard peripherals required:* Sound card (either: Sound Blaster - 8, 16, PRO; Media Vision ProAudio Spectrum; or Microsoft Sound System); MPC compatible CD-ROM drive; VGA monitor; & microphone. *Optimal configuration:* 25 MHz 386 SX.
A Battery of Computerized, Criterion-Referenced Tests Test Designed to Meet the Assessment Needs of Programs Preparing Students to Take the Officie GED Exam. Tests in Each of the Five GED Subject Areas Are Provided.
Conter Software.

GED Literature. Jan. 1994. *Items Included:* Program on CD-ROM, CD Booklet, & Registration Card. *Customer Support:* Free unlimited customer support via telephone.
Windows 3.1 or higher running under DOS 5.0 or higher. 386 SX (4Mb RAM; 500k low Dos Mem; 6Mb free disk space). CD-ROM disk $249.00 (ISBN 1-57268-061-X, Order no.: 11102). *Nonstandard peripherals required:* Sound card (either: Sound Blaster - 8, 16, PRO; Media Vision ProAudio Spectrum; or Microsoft Sound System); MPC compatible CD-ROM drive; VGA monitor; & microphone. *Optimal configuration:* 25 MHz 386 SX.
Designed to Improve Functional Literacy, Offering You a Comprehensive High School Equivalency Reading Course. The Course Is Specifically Designed for Use by Students Preparing to Take the Reading Portion of the GED Test, As Well As Participants in Alternative Education, At-Risk, & Adult Education Programs.
Conter Software.

GED Math. Jan. 1994. *Items Included:* Program on CD-ROM, CD Booklet, & Registration Card. *Customer Support:* Free unlimited customer support via telephone.
Windows 3.1 or higher running under DOS 5.0 or higher. 386 SX (4Mb RAM; 500k low Dos Mem; 6Mb free disk space). CD-ROM disk $249.00 (ISBN 1-57268-060-1, Order no.: 11101). *Nonstandard peripherals required:* Sound card (either: Sound Blaster - 8, 16, PRO; Media Vision ProAudio Spectrum; or Microsoft Sound System); MPC compatible CD-ROM drive; VGA monitor; & microphone. *Optimal configuration:* 25 MHz 386 SX.
A Comprehensive Program of Study Designed to Meet the Needs of High School Remediation, Adult Education, & GED Programs. The GED Math Program Covers Six Major Instructional Areas: Numbers, Probability & Statistics, Interpreting Data, Operations, Geometry, & Algebra.
Conter Software.

GED Science. Jan. 1994. *Items Included:* Program on CD-ROM, CD Booklet, & Registration Card. *Customer Support:* Free unlimited customer support via telephone.
Windows 3.1 or higher running under DOS 5.0 or higher. 386 SX (4Mb RAM; 500k low Dos Mem; 6Mb free disk space). CD-ROM disk $249.00 (ISBN 1-57268-062-8, Order no.: 11103). *Nonstandard peripherals required:* Sound card (either: Sound Blaster - 8, 16, PRO; Media Vision ProAudio Spectrum; or Microsoft Sound System); MPC compatible CD-ROM drive; VGA monitor; & microphone. *Optimal configuration:* 25 MHz 386 SX.
These Programs Are Comprehensive, High School Science Course Designed to Support Mainstream Instruction, As Well As Prepare Student for Taking the Science Portion of the GED Test. Four Major Instructional Areas Are Covered: Physics, Chemistry, Biology, & Earth Science. The GED Science Program Reinforces Logical Thinking Strategies, Study Skills, & Test-Taking Strategies in Addition to Content.
Conter Software.

GED Social Studies. Jan. 1994. *Items Included:* Program on CD-ROM, CD Booklet, & Registration Card. *Customer Support:* Free unlimited customer support via telephone.
Windows 3.1 or higher running under DOS 5.0 or higher. 386 SX (4Mb RAM; 500k low Dos Mem; 6Mb free disk space). CD-ROM disk $249.00 (ISBN 1-57268-063-6, Order no.: 11104). *Nonstandard peripherals required:* Sound card (either: Sound Blaster - 8, 16, PRO; Media Vision ProAudio Spectrum; or Microsoft Sound System); MPC compatible CD-ROM drive; VGA monitor; & microphone. *Optimal configuration:* 25 MHz 386 SX.
A Comprehensive Course Designed to Support What Students for Taking the Social Studies Portion of the GED Test. Major Instructional Areas Include: American History, Political Science, Economics, Geography, & Behavioral Science.
Conter Software.

GED Studies. Jan. 1994. *Items Included:* Program on CD-ROM, CD Booklet, & Registration Card. *Customer Support:* Free unlimited customer support via telephone.
Windows 3.1 or higher running under DOS 5.0 or higher. 386 SX (4mb RAM; 500K low DOS Mem; 6Mb free disk space). CD-ROM disk $799.00 (ISBN 1-57268-077-6, Order no.: 91005). *Nonstandard peripherals required:* sound card (either; Sound Blaster - 8.16, PRO; Media Vision ProAudio Spectrum; or Microsoft Sound System); MPC compatible CD-ROM drive; VGA monitor; & microphone. *Optimal configuration:* 25 MHz 386 SX.

GED Writing

This Program Provides Instructions in the Five Areas Tested in the Official GED Test: Math, Literature, Science, Social Studies, & Writing. This Program Could Also Be Used in Alternative Education, At-Risk, & Adult Education Programs. Conter Software.

GED Writing. Jan. 1994. *Items Included:* Program on CD-ROM, CD Booklet, & Registration Card. *Customer Support:* Free unlimited customer support via telephone.
Windows 3.1 or higher running under DOS 5.0 or higher. 386 SX (4Mb RAM; 500k low Dos Mem; 6Mb free disk space). CD-ROM disk $249.00 (ISBN 1-57268-064-4, Order no.: 11105). *Nonstandard peripherals required:* Sound card (either: Sound Blaster - 8, 16, PRO; Media Vision ProAudio Spectrum; or Microsoft Sound System); MPC compatible CD-ROM drive; VGA monitor; & microphone. *Optimal configuration:* 25 MHz 386 SX.
The Writing Program Is a Comprehensive Program Addressing Skills in Grammar, Punctuation, Composition, Spelling & Dictionary Usage. In Addition, the Course Provides Comprehensive, Age-Appropriate Keyboarding Instruction. The Course Is Designed to Complement Classroom Instruction or to Be Used As Part of a GED Program.
Conter Software.

Gee Bee Air Rally. *Compatible Hardware:* Commodore Amiga.
3.5" disk $39.95.
Airplane Race.
Activision, Inc.

GeeWiz: Wizard Maker. *Version:* 2.0. Philip Rodgers, Jr. Jan. 1996. *Items Included:* User's manual, software on 3.5" floppy disks. *Customer Support:* 90 days free support.
Windows 3.X, 95, or NT. 486DX2-66MHz (8Mb). disk $89.00. *Nonstandard peripherals required:* VGA. *Addl. software required:* Visual Basic 4.0 Pro.
Visual Basic 4.0 OLE Add-In Makes Wizards for Applications. Also Makes Wizards That Automate VB Tasks. Wizards Can Generate Code, API's & Constants, & Code to Respond to User Input. View Code As It's Built. Save Code, Copy It, or Link to Code Windows. Includes over Ten Wizards.
Resolutions Now.

Gel-Pro Analyzer. May 1995. *Items Included:* Manual, Gel-Pro disks, copy protection key. *Customer Support:* 90 day unlimited warranty.
Windows 3.1. 386, 256 colors (8Mb). disk $2499.00.
A Comprehensive, Easy-to-Use Software Application That Provides Automated Support for Gel-Analysis & Quantification Functions. Designed for Molecular Biologists Involved in Gel & Protein Research. Gel-Pro's User Interface Is Written in Standard Molecular Biology Terms & Follows Conventional Laboratory Protocols. It Fits Seamlessly into the Lab Routine, Improving Through-Put, Minimizing Ambiguity, & Increasing Repeatability. Also Provides a Wide-Range of Experiment Management Functions for Storage & Retrieval of Images. In Addition to User Notations & Lab Notes, These Functions Provide Logs of Specific Experiments & Record Parameters for Future Repetitions.
Media Cybernetics, L. P.

GEM Artline. *Compatible Hardware:* IBM PC. *Operating System(s) Required:* PC-DOS 3.0 or higher. *General Requirements:* EGA, CGA, VGA or Hercules graphics, hard disk, mouse.
contact publisher for price.
Graphics Desktop Publishing Package Which Emphasizes Typography & Drawing. User Can Draw Freehand, or Trace Scanned Imgaes Imported from Other Packages. Design & Text Can Be Rotated, Shadowed, Patterned, Stretched, & Scaled. Includes Libraries of Typefaces & Clip Art That Can Be Enhanced or Modified. Built-In Tools Can Be Used to Draw Curves, Lines, Ellipses, Polygons, & Other Shapes.
Digital Research, Inc.

The GEM Collection. *Compatible Hardware:* IBM PC, PC XT, PC AT, PC compatibles with appropriate graphics capability & a pointing device (mouse).
disk $199.00.
Includes GEM DESKTOP, an Environment Allowing the User to Take Advantage of Windows, Menus, & Icons; GEM WRITE, a Word Processing Program Based on VOLKSWRITER DELUXE by Lifetree Software, Inc.; & GEM PAINT Including the Tools to Add Pictures, Titles & Diagrams with a Variety of Paintbrushes & Pencils, Shapes, Patterns, Type Styles, & Type Sizes.
Digital Research, Inc.

GEM Desktop Publisher. *Compatible Hardware:* IBM PC & true compatibles, PS/2. *Operating System(s) Required:* GEM.
disk $395.00.
Enables Users to Combine Text & Graphics in the Same Document. Its Features Includes: WYSIWYG; Insert, Delete, Rearange, & Merge Text & Graphics; Automatic Reformatting; Automatic Text Flow Around Graphic Rectangles; Style Sheets; Automatic Scaling of Graphics; Multiple Fonts in Multiple Sizes, Colors, & Styles; Import Text & Commands from Other Word Processors; Page Numbers, Headers, & Footers; Compatibility with Other GEM Applications & Numerous Output Devices.
Digital Research, Inc.

GEM Draw. *Compatible Hardware:* IBM PC & compatibles. *Operating System(s) Required:* PC-DOS, MS-DOS. *Memory Required:* 320k. *General Requirements:* Mouse recommended.
disk $249.00, incl. GEM Desktop & manual.
Digital Research, Inc.

Gem Draw Plus. *Compatible Hardware:* AT&T 6300; IBM PC, XT, AT, 3270, 384 (DOS 2.X, 3.X).
disk $299.00.
Digital Research, Inc.

GEM 1st Word Plus. *Compatible Hardware:* IBM PC & compatibles. *Memory Required:* 512k. $199.00.
Able to Combine Text, Illustrations, Graphs, Charts & Maps in One Document. Decimal Tabulation, Personal Style Sheets & Mouse or Keyboard Driven Block Operations Are Included. Bold, Italic & Underlined Text Are Displayed On-Screen.
Digital Research, Inc.

GEM Graph. *Version:* 2.0. *Compatible Hardware:* IBM PC & compatibles. *Operating System(s) Required:* DOS 2.0 or higher. *Memory Required:* 384k. *General Requirements:* 2 disk drives, graphics adapter. Hard disk recommended.
disk $249.00.
Business Graphics Package That Runs in the GEM Desktop Environment. Supports Lotus 1-2-3, DIF & ASCII File Formats. Users Can Access 8 On-Screen Colors & 18 Predefined Patterns. Not Copy Protected.
Digital Research, Inc.

The Gem of Zephyrr. *Version:* 1.6.1. Apr. 1988. *Compatible Hardware:* Apple IIgs, II series; IBM PC & compatibles. *Memory Required:* Apple II series 64k, Apple IIgs 256k, IBM 512k.
Apple II series. 3.5" disk $24.95 (ISBN 0-916163-92-X).
Apple II series. (ISBN 0-916163-94-6).
Apple IIgs. 3.5" disk $24.95 (ISBN 1-55616-011-9).
IBM. disk $24.95 (ISBN 1-55616-036-4).
IBM. 3.5" disk $24.95 (ISBN 1-55616-040-2).
Adventure Game.
DAR Systems International.

GEM Presentation Team. *Version:* 2.0. *Compatible Hardware:* IBM PC XT. *Operating System(s) Required:* PC-DOS 2.0 or Concurrent DOS 386 2.0 or higher. *Memory Required:* 512k. *General Requirements:* Hard disk.
disk $495.00.
Presentation Graphics Package for On-Screen Slide Shows. Chart-Making Features Include Bar, Line, Text, Pie, Organization, Symbol, 3-D, Map, Area & Flow Charts; Multiple Charts on One Screen; & Free Positioning of Charts, Labels & Titles on Screen. Provides 16 User-Selectable Colors, 9 Typefaces & 6 Font Sizes. Outputs to PostScript Printer, HP Laserjet, Dot-Matrix Printers, Film Recorder, Plotter, Color Ink-Jet Printer & Phototypesetter. Imports GEM, IMG, WKS, WK1, DIF, CSV & PRN File Formats. Also Features Bitstream Fontware Installation Kit, GEM Desktop Calculator, Clock, 6 Alignment Types, 36 Fill Patterns, 17 Line Types, Copy, Flip Horizontal & Vertical & 9 Text Chart Templates.
Digital Research, Inc.

GEM WordChart. *Compatible Hardware:* IBM PC & compatibles.
contact publisher for price.
Digital Research, Inc.

GEM/3: Graphics Environment Manager. *Compatible Hardware:* IBM PC & compatibles. *Operating System(s) Required:* PC-DOS 3.X.
contact publisher for price.
Graphics User Interface Which Is Faster Than the Previous Release. Supports Both EGA & VGA Display Modes. Includes Nine Standard Fonts & Provides Support for Laser Printer, Including Selecting Paper Trays.
Digital Research, Inc.

GEMIDEX: PC Data Entry. *Version:* G5, G7. 1989-93. *Compatible Hardware:* IBM PC & compatibles. *Operating System(s) Required:* MS-DOS 3.0 or higher. *Language(s):* BASIC, Assembly. *Memory Required:* 640k.
disk $750.00 (ISBN 0-918709-20-2, Order no.: DEXSUP).
disk $400.00 (ISBN 0-918709-22-9, Order no.: DEXOPR).
Contains 029 Key Pad, Supervisor Tutorial, On-Line Help, Built-In File Transfer, Character-by-Character Checking, Key Verify & Batch Balance.
Specialized Data Systems, Inc.

GEMini Atari. *Customer Support:* All of our products are unconditionally guaranteed.
Atari. CD-ROM disk $39.95 (Order no.: GEMINI). *Nonstandard peripherals required:* CD-ROM drive.
616 MB of Atari St, TT, Falcon Plus Lynx & Jaguar.
Walnut Creek CDRom.

Gems of the Word. *Version:* 1.1. 1989. *Items Included:* Manual. *Customer Support:* 30 day money back guarantee. Free telephone support - you pay only for the call.
6.0.5 or higher (7.0 compatible). MAC Plus or higher (1Mb). 3.5" disk $39.95. *Nonstandard peripherals required:* 800k drive, hard drive.
A Bible Program That Everyone Can Enjoy! Gives You an Easy to Access Database of over 2000 of the Best Loved, Most Often Quoted Bible

Passages, Organized Under More Than 150 Different Topics. Offers a Start-Up Program to Give You a "Verse of the Day" Personalized to Your Interest. The Simple Gems of the Word DA Is Great for Customizing Greeting Cards, Letters, Church Bulletins & Other Correspondence. Available in King James Version or New International Version.
Beacon Technology, Inc.

GemStar. Customer Support: 800-929-8117 (customer service).
MS-DOS. IBM/PS2. disk $1999.99 (ISBN 0-87007-729-5).
Designed for the Unique Inventory Control Needs of Jewelry Stores. Tracks Items Sold but Not Restocked, Items to be Reordered, & the Current Value of Gold. Uses Modula 10 Check Digit item Numbers for Increased Security.
SourceView Software International.

Gene Construction Kit. Version: 1.17. Robert Gross et al. Mar. 1990. Items Included: Manual, sample files, enzyme lists, standard vectors. Customer Support: Free phone support.
Mac Plus, System 6 & 7. $1245.00. Optimal configuration: Mac Quadra, color monitor, 4mBytes RAM.
$845.00 academic price (degree granting institutions).
Allows Graphic Manipulation of DNA Sequences & Sophisticated Plasmid Drawing Capabilities. It is Ideal for Managing Complex Construction Projects & for Generating High Quality Illustrations. Provides an Electronic Notebook for the Project & Functions as a Database.
Textco.

Genealogical Data Base System: GDBS. Version: 2.0. 1991. Operating System(s) Required: Apple ProDOS, MS-DOS 3.0 or higher. Language(s): Applesoft BASIC, Assembly & QuickBASIC. Memory Required: Apple 48k, MS-DOS 512k. Items Included: 5 disks for Apple, 4 for MS-DOS. Customer Support: By phone, newsletter, mail & on-line services.
Apple II, II+, IIe, IIc. disk $99.95.
IBM PC, & compatibles. disk $69.95.
Designed to Enable Users to Enter, Store, Sort, & Maintain Genealogical Information. Printed Products Include Five Kinds of Pedigree & Descendants Charts, Family Group Sheets, Assorted Alphabetical & Numerical Listings, & Soundex Codes. Charts Are Stored in Text Files for Immediate Reproduction/Transmission to Other Computers Via Modem. As Many As Nine Paragraphs of User-Defined Information or Text Can Also Be Entered for Each Person in the Data Base. Utilities Enable Initializing, & Copying; Displaying Free Space on Disks; Sorting, Copying, Locking, & Unlocking Data Records on Disks for Transmission/Reception via Modem. Word Processing Capabilities Are Also Available.
Data Base System.

General Accounting. Compatible Hardware: Apple Macintosh, Macintosh Plus.
3.5" disk $3000.00.
Accounts Receivable, Accounts Payable, General Ledger.
Advanced Data Systems, Inc.

General Accounting. Version: 90.. Jan. 1994. Compatible Hardware: DEC, IBM PC & Compatibles, RS6000. Language(s): Progress 4GL. Memory Required: 1000k. Customer Support: 90 days free.
$1000.00 per module. Addl. software required: Progress 4GL.
General Ledger-Financial Statements, Accounts Receivable, Accounts Payable, Payroll, Inventory Control, Customer Order Processing, Purchase Orders, Fixed Assets, & Job Cost.
Automation Resources Corp.

General Accounting. Version: 6.1. Items Included: Disks, manual, sample data. Customer Support: 90 days of free telephone support.
IBM PC, XT, AT, PS/2 & compatibles (640k). disk $495.00. Nonstandard peripherals required: Hard disk or dual floppy drive.
General Ledger Program That Can Be Used in Conjunction with Yardi Construction Accounting, Payroll Accounting, or As a Stand Alone Program. Features Include Automated Check Writing, Departmental Accounting & Budget Comparisons. Menu Driven with On-Screen Help, Password Security.
Yardi Systems.

General Accounting Business Packages.
contact publisher for price. Networks supported: Novell.
Complete Line of Accounting Packages: Accounts Receivable, Accounts Payable, Payroll, General Ledger, Inventory, Order Entry, Checkbook Management. All Packages Work Alone, or in an Integrated Way, So Entries Made in One Program Automatically Update the Necessary Data in Other Programs.
Applied Business Software, Inc.

General Accounting System. 1984. Compatible Hardware: IBM PC or compatibles with 20Mb hard disk, 132-column printer. Operating System(s) Required: PC-DOS. Memory Required: 640k. Items Included: GL, AP, AR, Payroll, Master Menu ($200.). Customer Support: 8-5; 5 days/week.
subsystem pkg. $895.00.
Integrated Accounting Package Includes Accounts Payable/Receivable, Payroll, & General Ledger, Master Menu.
Nelson Data Resources, Inc.
  Accounts Payable.
    Designed to Assist in the Management of Cash Flow, Vendor Analysis, & the Payment of Bills. Invoice Entries Are Listed & Can Be Corrected Before Being Put into the Outstanding Invoice File. User Can Take Discounts, Make Partial or Full Payments, & Apply Credit Memos. Computer-Printed Checks Can Pay Multiple Invoices per Vendor. Manually Written Checks Can Be Entered into the Computer & Applied Against Outstanding Payables.
  Accounts Receivable.
    Designed to Help Company to Manage Customer Credit & Collection. Determines Current Customer Balances & Prints Overdue Accounts. Handles Hundreds of Customers & Pertinent Data Including Year-to-Date Charges, Date of Last Payment, & Aging Reports. User Can Add, Correct, Delete, Display, or Print Customer Information. Outstanding Invoices Report Prints All Open Invoices by Customer. Report Lists Original Invoice Amount, Balance Due, & Accumulated Interest for Each Unpaid Invoicee. Statements of Account Which Show Balance Due for All Unpaid Invoices Can Be Printed for All or for Individual Customers. User Can Enter Partial Customer Payments, Overpayment, Credit Memos, & Adjustments. All Information Is Stored for Later Reference. Journal Entries Can Be Generated for Automatic Update of General Ledger. Complete Audit Trails Are Provided. Monthly Transaction Report Shows All Activity by Customer in Date Order.
  Master Menu.
    Creates a Common Menu for all Software (Including Non-NDR Software) That Has Been Installed on Users' Computer. In Addition, the Utilities Functions Enable Users to Backup Data, Restore Files, Set up Security Codes, Change Companies, Install New Programs, etc. Without Using any System-Level Computer Commands.
  Payroll.
    Allows Firm to Compensate Employees for Their Services & Accumulate Data Useful in Filing Tax, Union, & Management Reports. Handles Active or Inactive Employees, & Permits User to Add Employee Records & Change Tax Tables, Addresses, Wage Rates, & Other Background Information. Hourly Entries for Regular, Overtime, Vacation, & Sick Hours Are Listed & Corrected Before Being Posted to Employee Master File. Employer Can Pay Employees Weekly, Biweekly, Monthly, Semimonthly, or in Any Combination. Stores Wages & Salaries for Regular, Overtime, & Special Income & Permits Special Payrolls to Be Run. Automatically Calculates Federal & State Taxes, As Well As Other Deductions, from Gross Wages. Journal Entries Can Be Generated for Automatic Update of General Ledger System. Complete Audit Trails Are Provided.

General Business. Mar. 1982. Compatible Hardware: IBM PC & compatibles; Tandy 4000, 3000, 5000. Operating System(s) Required: MS-DOS, PC-DOS, XENIX. Language(s): DBASE III Plus, IV & FOXBASE, FOXPRO. Memory Required: 640k.
contact publisher for price.
General Accounting & History of Records for Medical Laboratory.
Trionics.

General Engineering Software. Compatible Hardware: IBM PC, PC XT; Commodore. Operating System(s) Required: MS-DOS. Language(s): BASIC. Memory Required: 64k.
disk $195.00.
Includes Programs Such As: Fitting Circles into Squares; Geometric Properties of Section: Volumes of Various Solids; Quadratic Equation; Convert FPM into RPM; Heat Exchanger; Friction Head Loss in Pipe; Heat Loss; Hydraulics; Centrifugal Pump Head; Bridge Brakes; etc.
Unik Assocs.

General Homesteader. Compatible Hardware: Commodore 64, 128; IBM PC & compatibles. Operating System(s) Required: MS-DOS, PC-DOS. Language(s): BASICA.
disk $45.00.
IN-TEC Equipment Co.

General Ledger. Version: 14.0. (Accounting Software Ser.). Aug. 1993. Compatible Hardware: IBM PC & compatibles. Operating System(s) Required: PC-DOS/MS-DOS 3.X & up. Language(s): MegaBASIC. Memory Required: 640k. General Requirements: Hard disk, wide-carriage printer. Customer Support: (203) 790-9756.
disk $295.00, Network Option ,300.00 more. manual $50.00.
Features Entry & Maintenance of General Ledger & Journal Accounts. Automatic Tie-In to Receivables, Payables, & Payroll. Includes, Trial Statements, Combined & Comparative Statements, Custom Statements, & Register. "Finance Package" Computes Mortgage, Loan, & Lease Info. Extended Ledger Feature Tracks Previous & Budget Figures. Depreciation Option Tracks Fixed Assets, Calculates Depreciation Using A.C.R.S. or Regular Depreciation Tables.
Applications Systems Group (CT), Inc.

General Ledger. (Service Management Ser.). 1996.
DOS, Unix. IBM PC. disk contact publisher for price.
FastTrak's "General Ledger" has two options. The first option is the full G/L which gives the user various features. The second option G/L

GENERAL LEDGER

Transaction Creation, will only create G/L transactions which can be exported for other applications to use.
Core Software, Inc.

General Ledger. Compatible Hardware: IBM PC, PC XT, PC AT & compatibles. Memory Required: 256k. Customer Support: Toll free telephone.
disk $995.00.
Ernest A. Jonson & Co.

General Ledger. Version: 2.0. 1989. Language(s): C. General Requirements: Hard disk, 132-column printer. Items Included: Disks & manuals. Customer Support: Free.
MS-DOS, PC-DOS, Concurrent DOS, Unix, Xenix. All IBM compatibles. single-user $795.00. Networks supported: Novell & Microsoft. multi user, unix, xenix $995.00.
demo disk with manual $20.00.
The Central Component of the Business Software Series. Transactions May Be Posted Directly or Are Automatically Posted from Other MC Modules. Allows Posting to Prior Periods, Prior Year Comparisons, Recurring Transactions, Auto Reversing Transactions.
INMASS/MRP.

General Ledger. Version: 450.3. 1978. Compatible Hardware: IBM PC & compatibles. Operating System(s) Required: MS-DOS, PC-DOS. Language(s): QuickBASIC. Memory Required: 512k. General Requirements: Hard disk. Items Included: System diskettes, users guide, training tutorial. Customer Support: Telephone; annual contracts available.
$395.00 to $495.00.
Designed to Provide Small to Medium-Sized Businesses & Accounting Service Companies with an Accounting System Capable of Processing & Reporting Basic Financial Data. Extensive Error Checking Done at Time of Entry. Primary Reports Include Balance Sheet, Income Statement, Trial Balance, & General Ledger List. Journals Generated by System Include Cash Receipts & Cash Disbursements. Monthly & Year-to-Year Budgets Are Entered Through Spreadsheet-Like Controls That Allow User "What-If" Analysis Before Budgets Are Finalized. The System Can Process up to 99 Independent Companies, with Division &/or Departmental Accounting. General Ledger Interfaces with IMS Accounts Payable, Accounts Receivable, Payroll, & Inventory Control Systems. The System May Be Run Single User or Multi-User on Many Networks.
International Micro Systems, Inc.

General Ledger. Version: 6.10. 1977. Compatible Hardware: IBM PC & compatibles, PC XT, PC AT, PS/2. Operating System(s) Required: MS-DOS, PC-DOS. Language(s): FORTRAN. Memory Required: 640k. Items Included: Manual. Customer Support: 1 hour per package purchased.
5-1/4" or 8" or 3-1/2" disk $495.00.
Fully Auditable, Journal Driven, Double Entry System That Creates a Detailed Non-Destructive Audit Trail. Designed to Automate a User's Current General Ledger System. Can Be Expanded to Accommodate New Accounting Formats. Also Provides for Divisionalized Reporting, with Automatic Consolidation of Divisions.
MCC Software (Midwest Computer Ctr. Co.).

General Ledger. Version: 3.3. (Integrated Manufacturing & Financial System Ser.). Compatible Hardware: VAX, IBM PC. Operating System(s) Required: MS-DOS, Novell, Micro/VMS, VAX/VMS, UNIX. Language(s): DIBOL. MS-DOS. single-user $750.00.
DEC PDP-11/VAX. $1500.00 multi-user.
Accepts Interfaced Transactions from Other Modules, Allows Journal Entries, & Maintains Revenues & Costs for Company, Division, Department & Account. Reports Actual to Budgeted Revenues, Costs, & Profitability by Current Month, Year-to-Date, & Prior Year. Schedules Can Be Produced to Show Breakdowns of Sales, Cost of Sales, Depreciation, Cash in Bank, Overhead, & Asset Inventory Control.
Primetrack.

General Ledger. Version: 5.12. Jun. 1990. Items Included: User guide, technical reference manual. Customer Support: Training included with purchase. Hot-line & remote diagnostic service included with maintenance.
VAX/VMS. Digital VAX (2Mb). $36,000.00 up.
A Comprehensive General Ledger/Financial Management System, Providing Online Access to Accounting Data. Users Can Customize All Aspects of the System, Including Account Format, Data Types, & Report Formats. Predefined Inquiries Provide Easy, Fast Access to All Accounting Information. Tight Integration to AP, PO, AR, FA, Payroll & Distribution Systems Provides User with a Complete Solution.
Ross Systems, Inc.

General Ledger. Walter Wheeler. 1985. Compatible Hardware: IBM PC & compatibles; Gimex. Operating System(s) Required: MS-DOS, PC-DOS, OS9. Memory Required: 64k. General Requirements: 2 disk drives. Items Included: Manual. Customer Support: Yes.
IBM. disk $695.00 (Order no.: G/L).
Smoke Signal. disk $695.00.
Double Entry General Ledger That Is Used for Both Large & Small Business Applications. Can Be Used As Stand Alone or Integrated with Accounts Receivable, Accounts Payable, & Payroll Modules. Transactions Are Entered into Various Journals & Balanced Prior to Posting to the General Ledger. Complete Audit Trails Are Printed Along with Standard Financial Reports.
Trend Computer Systems.

General Ledger (a part of ABECAS). Version: 3.3. Jan. 1989. Customer Support: On site training unlimited support services for first 90 days & through subscription thereafter.
PC/MS-DOS 3.x or higher. IBM PC & compatibles. Contact publisher for price. Nonstandard peripherals required: Hard disk; 132 column printer.
Supports Multiple Companies with As Much Detail & History As Desired. Two Ledgers Are Maintained Concurrently. One on a Cash Basis & One on an Accrual Basis. Reports May Be Generated on Either Basis. User May Define Department (up to 8 Characters) & Chart of Accounts (Also up to 8 Characters) As Required. GL Postings Provide Complete Audit Trail of All Spreadsheets. All or Selected Transactions Can Be Saved to Historical Transactions File. Analysis Report Available for Both Current Month & Historical Transactions. Journal Transactions May Be Entered for Prior Periods, Prior Years or As Repeating or Reversing Entries. Ledger Balances & Monthly History Maintained in Master File by Account. Multi-User Version Available for Novell, NTNX, 10-Net, Unix/Xenix, Turbo DOS, & Others.
Argos Software.

General Ledger by Profit Center. Duane Bristow. Compatible Hardware: TRS-80 Model III. Operating System(s) Required: TRSDOS. Language(s): BASIC. Memory Required: 48k. General Requirements: 2 disk drives.
disk $195.00.
Maintains a Database of 3000 Transactions per Disk, Keeps Totals by Account, Profit Center, Vendor, & Bank Account.
Duane Bristow Computers, Inc.

General Ledger-Client Write-Up. Occupational Computing Co., Inc. Compatible Hardware: TI Professional. Operating System(s) Required: MS-DOS. Memory Required: 128k. General Requirements: Printer.
$750.00.
Allows User-Controlled Formatting of Financial Statements.
Texas Instruments, Personal Productivit.

General Ledger-Cost Accounting (a Part of ABECAS). Version: 3.3. Operating System(s) Required: MS-DOS. Customer Support: On site training unlimited support services for first 90 days & through subscription thereafter.
contact publisher for price.
Provides a Cash-Basis & Accrual-Basis General Ledger. Maintains a Separate Set of Cost Accounting Records from the Same Entries. Other Features & Functions Include: Departmental Accounting Support. Full Budgeting & Prior Year Comparisons, Track Crops, Lots, Equipment, Projects, Work Orders, or Jobs, Detailed Records Maintained by Activity & Account, Annual & Monthly Budgets Supported. Several Summary Reports Can Be Generated.
Argos Software.

General Ledger File. Sep. 1987. Compatible Hardware: IBM PC & compatibles. Memory Required: 256k. General Requirements: Lotus 1-2-3 Release 2/2.01 or higher. Customer Support: Free telephone support.
$49.00.
Designed for Small Businesses, Automates the Posting of Receipts & Disbursements to a General Ledger. Automatically Totals & Prints Monthly & Year-to-Date Net-Profit or Loss Statements. Expense-Range Headings Are Modifiable.
Reco, Inc.

The General Ledger for Professionals & General Ledger-M. Version: 7.0. (Legal & Professional Ser.). 1992. Compatible Hardware: IBM PC & compatibles. Operating System(s) Required: PC-DOS/MS-DOS; Networks such as Novell, Lantastic. Customer Support: 30 days' free support, 1 yr. maintenance $250.00.
disk $995.00.
General Ledger System for All Professionals Who Bill for Their Time & Services. Specially Designed for Professionals Such As Attorneys, Accountants, Psychiatrists, Consulting Engineers, & Others Using the Cash Method of Accounting. Will Record Professional Fees & Costs Out of Fee for Each Billing Professional in a Firm. Interfaces with VERDICT to Automatically Produce Posting Registers of Expenses Paid for Clients & Clients' Payments. General Ledger-M Is Available for Networked Systems.
Micro Craft, Inc.

General Ledger: Module 2. Version: 7.11. Jeff Gold. Jul. 1991. Items Included: Perfect-bound manuals. Customer Support: 90 days toll-free technical phone support; each additional year $150.
MS-DOS 3.1 or higher (384k). IBM PC, PC XT, PC AT, PS/2 & compatibles. disk $295.00. Addl. software required: System Manager. Networks supported: PC-LAN, 3COM, Novell, Lantastic.
Handles up to 9998 Accounts in the User-Defined Chart of Accounts. Maintains a Financial History of the Previous 12 Months. Transactions Can Be Posted to Prior or Future Months. Entries Are Posted Automatically to the General Ledger. Various Reports Are Available in Several Different Formats.
Manzanita Software Systems.

TITLE INDEX

General Ledger Multiple Company Reporting & Posting.
$175.00 ea.
Edits Unposted G/L Journal Transactions; Copies & Prints Chart of Accounts to a New Company & for a Range of Companies; Prints G/L & Journal for a Range of Companies & Periods; Prints G/L & Activity for a Range of Companies & Periods; Prints Trial Balance for a Range of Companies; Prints Financial Statements for a Range of Companies; Prints Income Statements for a Range of Periods; Posts Journal to Master for a Range of Companies.
Advanced Concepts, Inc.

General Ledger Rev. 3.05. *Compatible Hardware:* IBM PC. *Operating System(s) Required:* PC-DOS. *Language(s):* Compiled BASIC. *Memory Required:* 640k. *General Requirements:* 1 disk drive. *Customer Support:* available for quarterly support & enhancement fee.
$700.00.
General Ledger Package in a Client Write up Style. Supports Multiple Cost Centers. Has the Ability to Produce Comparative Reports for Budget & Prior Period, As Well As the Ability to Produce Bar & Line Graph.
Datacount, Inc.

General Ledger Software to Accompany FINANCIAL ACCOUNTING, 7th Edition. Ernest I. Hanson et al. Mar. 1993.
IBM. instr's. software 5.25" $16.00 (ISBN 0-03-097516-6).
instr's. software 3.25" $16.00 (ISBN 0-03-097515-8).
Dryden Pr.

General Ledger Software to Accompany PRINCIPLES OF ACCOUNTING, 6th Edition. Ernest I. Hanson et al. Mar. 1993.
IBM. problems software $13.50 (ISBN 0-03-097444-5).
problems software $13.50 (ISBN 0-03-097443-7).
Dryden Pr.

General Ledger System Jr. *Version:* 8. May 1981. *Items Included:* Binder with documentation. *Customer Support:* 1 yr. maintenance $65 includes phone support, newsletter & enhancements released during the year for the user's computer.
DOS Ver. 3.1 or higher. IBM PC & compatibles (384k). disk $250.00. *Nonstandard peripherals required:* Hard drive. *Optimal configuration:* Hard drive, printer.
Designed for Any Type of Business or Personal Use. Provides for User Defined Chart of Accounts & Financial Statements. Allows up to 99 Departments/Profit Centers. Financials Can Be Maintained on the Cash or Accrual Method. Includes Budgets. Designed for Use As a Cash Basis When Integrating with TABS III Jr or Profit$ource.
Software Technology, Inc.

General Ledger System-M Jr. *Version:* 8. May 1981. *Items Included:* Binder with documentation. *Customer Support:* 1 yr. maintenance $85 includes phone support, newsletter & any enhancements released during their maintenance period for their computer at no charge.
DOS Ver. 3.1 or higher. IBM PC & compatibles (384k). disk $350.00. *Nonstandard peripherals required:* Hard drive. *Optimal configuration:* Hard drive & printer. *Networks supported:* Novell, IBM PC Network & compatibles.
True Multi-User Version of GLS Jr Allowing up to 10 Workstations to Make or Retrieve General Ledger Information. Integrates with STI's TABS III-M Jr & Accounts Payable System-M Jr.
Software Technology, Inc.

General Radiology: An Interactive Compendium. Stephen Baker. Oct. 1994.
Mac/Windows PC (5Mb). disk $200.00 (ISBN 1-56815-038-5). *Optimal configuration:* PC Windows 3.1.
Mosby Multi-Media.

General Statistics. *Compatible Hardware:* HP 85, 86/87.
HP 85. data cartridge, 3-1/2" or 5-1/4" disk $95.00 ea. (Order no.: 82804A).
HP 86/87. da. 3-1/2" or 5-1/4" disk $95.00 (Order no.: 82834A).
Set of Statistical Routines for Data Evaluation. Includes Simple & Paired Sample Analysis, Test Statistics, Continuous & Discrete Distribution, & Multiple Linear Regression.
Hewlett-Packard Co.

General Thermal Analyzer. NASA Johnson Space Center. 1986. *Compatible Hardware:* IBM PC. *Operating System(s) Required:* PC-DOS. *Language(s):* BASIC (source code included). *General Requirements:* 2 disk drives.
disk $50.00 (Order no.: MSC 21140).
Solves Transient & Steady-State Thermal Problems. The User Models the Thermal Problem in Terms of a Resistance & Capacitance Network. The User Defines the Network, Writes His/Her Own Variable Block, & Has Available Most of the Options Associated with Thermal Analyzer Programs Written for Mainframe Computers. Relax Network Provisions for Zero Capacitance Nodes, One Way Conductors for Fluid Flow Simulation, & Bivariate Data Interpolation Are Some of the Features Included.
COSMIC.

Generations, the Genealogy Program. Jan. 1988. *Compatible Hardware:* TRS-80 Model III, Model 4; IBM PC & compatibles. *Operating System(s) Required:* TRSDOS. *Memory Required:* TRS-80 64k, IBM 192k.
cassette $29.95.
Created by & for Genealogists. Ancestor Tracing, Statistical Data Bank, Pedigree Charts.
Micro-80, Inc.

The Generator: The Universal Test Data Generator. *Version:* 2.0. Sep. 1994. *Items Included:* (1) One manual with 3.5" disk. *Customer Support:* Telephone support - free.
MS-DOS 5.0 & higher, Optional versions: Windows, UNIX, OS/2, OS/400. PC AT & higher (4Mb). $169.00 copy; volume discounts avail. (ISBN 0-9643722-1-5). *Optimal configuration:* 386/33 or higher with 4Mb RAM, 80Mb HD or higher.
Developed to Enable the Application Developer to Fully Test His Handiwork, by Giving Him the Ability to Produce Test Data That Looks & Acts Exactly Like the Production Data That Will Ultimately Pass Through His Application. And, by Producing the Data in Sufficient Quantities, He Can Simulate Actual Production Loads.
Mach One Software, L.L.C.

Generic CADD. *Version:* 6.0. *Operating System(s) Required:* PC-DOS/MS-DOS 2.0 or higher. *Memory Required:* 640k. *General Requirements:* Two floppy disks and/or 10 Mb hard disk. Graphics card: Hercules, CGA, EGA, VGA, ATT 6300. *Items Included:* Includes Dot Plot & Desk Convert. *Customer Support:* 60 day money back guarantee, unlimited technical support to registered users.
disk $495.00 (Order no.: F0603).
Two-Dimensional Design & Drafting Package. Offers the Professional Enhanced Capabilities Required for Daily Production Work Including Hatches & Fills, High Speed Dynamic Drag, Linear & Angular Dimensioning & a Macro Command Language.
Autodesk, Inc.

Generic CADD for the Macintosh. *Version:* 2.0. *General Requirements:* Accelerator board, hard disk, & math co-processor recommended. *Customer Support:* 60 day money back guarantee, unlimited technical support to registered users.
Apple Macintosh, Macintosh II, SE, Plus (1Mb). 3.5" disk $495.00.
True Computer-Aided Design & Crafting for the Business & Entry-Level CADD User. User Can Make Drawings with a Complete Set of Simple Objects Including Points, Lines, Circles, Arcs, Ellipses, & Bezier & Spline Curves. Symbol Libraries Includes 2300 Predrawn Standard Symbols That Conform to Industry Guidelines. Includes a Mac to MS-DOS Translator Utility, the Ability to Save Files in PICT or EPS Format, the Ability to Open a PICT File Without Using the Clipboard, & a Select All Capability. Drawings Have Floating-Point Precision to 16 Decimal Places. Users Can Place Objects on 256 Layers, Rotate Them on Any Angle, & Change Their Scales.
Autodesk, Inc.

Generic 3D. *Version:* 1.1. *Items Included:* In-depth tutorial.
MS-DOS 2.1 or higher (640k). IBM PC, PC XT, PC AT, PS/2 & compatibles. $349.00; preview $9.95. *Nonstandard peripherals required:* Graphics display with resolution of at least 640 by 200; EMS memory & math coprocessor recommended.
Three-Dimensional CAD Program Includes Two Navigational Aids: Color-Coded Cursor with X, Y & Z Labels; Cursor Tracking Rather than Coordinate Specification. Features Include Rubber Banding, Dynamic Dragging, Layer Hiding & Grid Snapping. Available Views Include Isometric, Oblique, 2D Flat & Perspective. Compatible with Generic CADD Drawing Files.
Autodesk, Inc.

Generis Data Retrieval System. *Items Included:* Bound manual. *Customer Support:* Free hotline - no time limit; 30 day limited warranty; updates are $5/disk plus S&H.
MS-DOS 2.0 or higher. IBM & compatibles (256k). disk $29.95. *Nonstandard peripherals required:* Printer supported (80 columns or wider), but optional.
MBASIC 5.2 or higher. CP/M (64k). disk $29.95.
Atari (48k). disk $29.95.
Commodore 64 (64k). disk $29.95.
Cross-Indexing System Which May Be Used to Store & Retrieve Information According to Keywords. Originally Designed to Index Journal Articles, It Can Be Equally Well Applied to Record Collections, Recipe Files, etc.
Dynacomp, Inc.

Genesis: Nutrition Analysis-Labeling Software: Nutrient Analysis Labeling Aid. *Version:* 4.14. Elizabeth S. Hands & Robert B. Geltz. Jan. 1991. *Items Included:* Manual; The Food Finder - Food Sources of Vitamins & Minerals; additional information & list of foods & codes. *Customer Support:* Free 30-day preview; telephone assistance, menu/recipe analysis service available - quote per job; training available - quote per job.
PC-DOS & MS-DOS. IBM (640k). disk $995.00 (Order no.: 70049).
Food Analysis Program for 105 Nutrients, 9,700 Foods & Ingredients & Expandable. This "Lab in Your Computer" Assists with Analyses for Meeting Nutrition Labeling Requirements. Has over 50 Functions to Assist with Formulation Development & Information Management. Calculate Cost, Percent of USRDA, Nutrient Excesses & Deficiencies, & Adjust # for Water Loss. Figures Nutrient Ratios & Nutrient Totals.

Quick Food/Ingredient Search. Export Analyses to Word Processing. Data from USDA Handbook 8 & 560 Additional Scientific Sources. Reduces Lab Analysis Costs. Provides Quick Turn-Around on Information for Marketing. Saves Time & Money. Add Your Formulations.
ESHA Research.

Genesis: The Adventure Creator. *Compatible Hardware:* Apple II with Applesoft. *Operating System(s) Required:* Apple DOS 3.2, 3.3. *Memory Required:* 48k.
disk $49.95.
Create, Edit & Play Your Own Adventure Games.
Dynacomp, Inc.

GENESIS The Third Day. *Version:* 1.0. Jun. 1991. *Items Included:* 1 spiral bound manual 2 diskettes.
Amiga DOS. Amiga (1Mb). $149.95. *Addl. software required:* Expansion disks available, they include U. S. locations such as Yosemite, Grand Canyon Mt St. Helen & more. *Optimal configuration:* 3Mb recommended.
Recreates Any Landscape on Your Computer with This Fractal Landscape Generator or Make Your Own Landscapes. Animation Support with Tweeving Allows You to Ply Through Any Landscape. Supports, U. S. G. S. Information. Visit Any U. S., Moon or Mars Location Without Leaving the Room.
Microillusions, Inc.

GenGen. *Compatible Hardware:* IBM PC & compatibles. *Operating System(s) Required:* MS-DOS, CP/M-80, CP/M-86. *Language(s):* CB-86. *Memory Required:* 64k. *General Requirements:* IBM or Epson Graphics compatible printer (MX, FX, RX, LQ, or EX).
disk $395.00.
General Purpose Text, OCR, & Barcode Label Generating System. Provides Text Sizes from 1/8" to 1", Allowing Labels to Be Created for Most Applications, Including AIAG, LOGMARS, & HIBC. Allows User Total Control of Placement & Size of All Text & Code 39 Barcode.
KDA Systems.

Genifer. *Version:* 3.0. Jan. 1986. *Compatible Hardware:* IBM PC & compatibles. *Operating System(s) Required:* PC-DOS/MS-DOS 2.0 or higher. *Memory Required:* 640k. *General Requirements:* 2 720k disks (hard disk recommended). *Customer Support:* First 60 days free, then $89 per year.
disk $395.00 (ISBN 0-922698-05-8).
dBASE Application Generator. Developers Can Interactively Create Screens, Menus, Reports, & Prototype Applications. Uses a Data Dictionary to Keep Database Definitions Together, Produces Structured Source Code, Which Allows Maintenance & Modification. Directly Supports dBASE III Plus. Optional Templates for dBASE IV Clipper, FoxPro Quicksilver, dbXL, & FoxBASE+, Arago Single & Multi-User.
Bytel Corp.

Genium MSDS Collection on CD-ROM. Sep. 1994. *Items Included:* Acrobat Exchange LE. *Customer Support:* 30 day satisfaction guarantee.
MS-Windows. IBM PC & compatibles (4Mb). CD-ROM disk $449.00 plus $159.00/year updating service (Order no.: (518) 377-8854). *Nonstandard peripherals required:* CD-ROM player.
Macintosh System 7.0. Macintosh or Power Macintosh.
Contains over 900 Genium-Developed Material Safety Data Sheets. Each MSDS Profile's a Chemical's Potential Hazards Including Material Identification; Ingredients; First Aid; Fire Fighting; Accidental Release; Handling & Storage; Physical Data; Fire & Explosion; Stability & Reactivity; Health Hazards; Spill, Leak & Disposal; Personal Protection; Transport; & Regulatory Data.
Genium Publishing Corp.

Genline PC. *Version:* 5.41. *Compatible Hardware:* IBM PC & compatibles. *Items Included:* Everything for line-by-line generation, tracing, & standard box libraries. *Customer Support:* Toll-free number, updates, yearly contracts.
disk $10,000.00.
CAD Program Designed for the Box-Manufacturing Industry.
Genline CAD/CAM Systems.

GENL3D. *Version:* 2.0. Apr. 1986. *Compatible Hardware:* IBM PC, PC XT, PC AT & compatibles. *Operating System(s) Required:* MS-DOS, PC-DOS. *Language(s):* FORTRAN. *Memory Required:* 512k. *General Requirements:* Printer, plotter.
disk $1000.00 (Order no.: GENL3D).
Imposes User-Specified Boundaries Within a 2D/3D Block Reserve Model. The Limits Closed Polygons with Any Number of Vertices & Can Be of a Geologic, Mining, or Property Type. They Can Be a Level or Section or a Series of Equally Spaced Level or Section Planes of the Block Model. Each Polygon Is Identified with a Level or Section Index & a Type Index Such As Rock Code, Pit Expansion or Slope Number.
Geostat Systems International, Inc. (GSII).

Genstat. *Version:* 5. *Items Included:* 1 Genstat manual, 1 reference summary, 1 procedures library, users & installers notes. *Customer Support:* 90 days free maintenance, additional maintenance is available.
DOS 3.1, Windows NT. IBM PC & compatibles, IBM 80306. $750.00-$2675.00. *Addl. software required:* IBM PC & compatibles require a math co-processor.
Leading Edge Statistical Package Providing Major Standard Analyses Plus Advanced Capabilities for Procedures Such As REML & Other Design of Experiment Work. May Be Used in Either Command or Interactive Menu Mode & Is Easily Customized.
Numerical Algorithms Group, Inc.

Gensystems. *Compatible Hardware:* TRS-80 Model I, Model III.
contact publisher for price.
Armstrong Genealogical Systems.

Genterm/ADM3. *Version:* 2.04. Apr. 1986. *Compatible Hardware:* IBM PC, PC XT, PC AT, PS/2's & compatibles. *Operating System(s) Required:* PC-DOS 2.0, MS-DOS 2.0 or higher. *Language(s):* Assembly. *Memory Required:* 256k. *General Requirements:* Modem.
disk $79.95 (Order no.: GTADM3).
Provides Full Lear-Sigler ADM3A & ADM31 Emulation Including Block & Character, Protected Field & Two-Screen Modes. Includes Keyboard Redefinition, Programmable Macro Keys, 100 On-Line Help Screens, & Save Screen to Disk. Communications Package Provides XMODEM & Kermit File Transfers, Capture Data to Disk/Printer, Selectable Flow Control, & Line-by-Line & ASCII File Transfers.
Information Analysis Systems Corp.

Genterm/3101. *Version:* 2.02. Apr. 1986. *Compatible Hardware:* IBM PC, & compatibles, PC XT, PC AT, PS/2. *Operating System(s) Required:* MS-DOS 2.0, PC-DOS 2.0 or higher. *Language(s):* Assembly. *Memory Required:* 256k. *General Requirements:* Modem.
GT3101. disk $79.95.
Provides Full IBM 3101 Emulation Including Block & Character, Transparent, & Program Modes. Includes Keyboard Redefinition, Programmable Macro Keys, Save Screen to Disk, & 100 On-Line Help Screens. Communications Package Provides XMODEM & Kermit File Transfers, Capture Data to Disk/Printer, Selectable Flow Control, & Line-by-Line & ASCII File Transfers.
Information Analysis Systems Corp.

GenTerm/TV9. *Version:* 2.02. IAS Corp. Apr. 1986. *Compatible Hardware:* IBM PC, PC XT, PC AT, PS/2. *Operating System(s) Required:* MS-DOS 2.0 or higher. *Language(s):* Assembly. *Memory Required:* 256k. *General Requirements:* Modem.
disk $79.95 (Order no.: GTTV9).
Provides Full Televideo 950 Emulation, Including Host Programmable Function Keys, Screen Message Area & Status Line. Includes Keyboard Redefinition, Programmable Macro Keys, Save Screens to Disk, & 100 On-Line Help Screens. Communications Package Provides XMODEM & Kermit File Transfers, Capture Data to Disk/Printer, Selectable Flow Control, & ASCII & Line-by-Line File Transfers.
Information Analysis Systems Corp.

GeoCalc.
GEOS. Commodore 64. disk $49.95.
GEOS. Commodore 128. disk $69.95.
Apple II. disk $69.95.
Spreadsheet for Tracking & Analyzing Numerical Data. Users Can Create Their Own Formulas & Perform Calculations for Anything from Simple Geometry to Cost Projections. Availabe in 80 Columns for Commodore 128.
Berkeley Softworks.

geoChart. *Items Included:* 9 chart types, 14 formats to display axes label values, 32 marker patterns, comprehensive manual with over 115 graphics. *Customer Support:* 90-day warranty, customer support (1) Q-link telecommunications network, (2) direct phone lines.
Commodore 64 or 128 (64k). $29.95. *Nonstandard peripherals required:* Mouse or joystick. *Addl. software required:* GEOS or GEOS 128.
Gives Numerical Data Visual Impact. Import Data from GEOS-Based Applications to Enhance Business Reports or Graphically Display Home Budget Analyses. Then, Copy Chart to GeoWrite, GeoPaint or GeoPublish. For Complex Business Plans or School Reports.
Berkeley Softworks.

GEOCONTOUR. *Version:* 4.1. Feb. 1984. *Compatible Hardware:* IBM PC, PC XT, 3270 PC. *Operating System(s) Required:* MS-DOS. *Language(s):* FORTRAN. *Memory Required:* 256k. *General Requirements:* Graphics card, plotter. *Items Included:* Manual, disks. *Customer Support:* Telephone support, 30 day warranty.
$700.00 Large version.
Plots Contours for an Arbitrary Set of Data. User Inputs Coordinates & Known Values at Each Coordinate Together with Desired Contour Values. Uses Linear Interpolation to Locate & Draw Contour Lines. Plots on Screen, Pen Plotter, & Printer.
GEOCOMP Corp.

Geodynamics Multimedia Database. 1992. *Items Included:* Teacher's guide. *Customer Support:* Toll free assistance.
PC-DOS/MS-DOS, Windows. IBM PC, PS/2 & compatibles (640k). disk $136.00 stand alone version (ISBN 1-56348-114-6, Order no.: GS-M100). *Nonstandard peripherals required:* Hard disk, color monitor, mouse recommended, graphics card. *Optimal configuration:* PS/2 or compatible, hard disk, 3.5" drive, color monitor & mouse. *Networks supported:* All.
Windows. disk $160.00 stand alone version (ISBN 1-56348-192-8, Order no.: GS-W100).
System 6.X & 7.X. Macintosh (512k). disk $145.00 stand alone version (ISBN 1-56348-195-2, Order no.: GS-H100). *Optimal configuration:* All models with hard disk & Mouse, CD-ROM drive. *Networks supported:* All.
Windows for PC. PC & compatibles (1Mb). disk $275.00 (ISBN 1-56348-198-7, Order no.: GS-

C100). *Optimal configuration:* PC, hard drive, color monitor CD drive, mouse. *Networks supported:* All.
Comprehensive Resource with Extensive Data on 1,500 Volcanoes & 89,000 Earthquakes. Has the Capability to Plot Sites of Earthquakes & Volcanoes on Maps of the Entire World; a Hemisphere; a Particular Geologic Region; or Any Area Chosen. Excellent for Plate Tectonics Investigation.
E.M.E.

GeoFile. *Operating System(s) Required:* GEOS.
Commodore 64. disk $49.95.
Commodore 128. disk $69.95.
Apple II. disk $69.95.
Database Manager Which Enables Users to Sort, Edit, & Prioritize Data. Available in 80 Columns for Commodore 128.
Berkeley Softworks.

GEOFLOW. *Version:* 4.0. Mar. 1984. *Compatible Hardware:* IBM PC, PC XT, PC AT, 3270 PC. *Operating System(s) Required:* MS-DOS. *Language(s):* FORTRAN. *Memory Required:* 256k. *Customer Support:* Technical support, 30 day warranty.
$800.00.
Solves 2-Dimensional Steady State Seepage Problems. Solves Confined & Unconfined Flow Problems.
GEOCOMP Corp.

GEOGRAF Level One. *Version:* 5.0. Jun. 1990. *Items Included:* User manual, graphics utilities diskette. *Customer Support:* 30 day warranty, technical support, 90 day free upgrade.
MS-DOS. IBM PC & compatibles (256k). disk $149.00. *Nonstandard peripherals required:* Graphics card. *Addl. software required:* Compiler.
Graphics Library of Subroutines & Functions Which Are Callable from Inside a Program. User Can Create Custom Graphs & Charts Using Any of 13 Different Fonts & Several Line Types. Product Is Device Independent. Supports C, BASIC.
GEOCOMP Corp.

Geographical Dictionary.
Apple Macintosh. 3.5" disk $29.95. *Addl. software required:* Spellswell, Lookup, MicroSoft Works 2.0 or Mindwrite 2.0, Expert Writer, Expert Publisher, QuickLetter, Resume Maker.
Supplemental Dictionary for Use with Spellswell, Lookup, Microsoft Works 2.0 & MindWrite 2.0, QuickLetter, Expert Writer, Expert Publisher & Resume Maker. Contains Correct Spellings of over 30,000 Cities, States, Countries, Provinces & Bodies of Water from All over the Globe.
Working Software, Inc.

Geometric Positioning & Tolerancing: Geometric Positioning & Tolerance. Dec. 1987. *Compatible Hardware:* IBM PC. *Memory Required:* 512k. *General Requirements:* 2 Disk drives, graphics card, Generic CADD. *Customer Support:* Unlimited technical support to registered users.
disk $34.95 (ISBN 1-55814-096-4, Order no.: F1900).
3.5" disk $34.95 (ISBN 1-55814-097-2, Order no.: T1900).
120 ANSI & International Standard Symbols for Geometric Positioning & Tolerancing.
Autodesk, Inc.

Geometric Principles of CAD Graphics. Apr. 1992. *Items Included:* Spiral manual contains theory, sample runs. *Customer Support:* Free phone, on-site seminars.
MS-DOS. IBM (128k). disk $96.00. Macintosh. Any Macintosh. 3.5" disk $96.00.
This Is a Book/Disk Package That Shows How to Write Software to Carry Out Various CAD Graphics Operations in 2 & 3 Dimensions. Includes Bezier Curves, Comic Sections, 2 & 3 Dimensional Shapes.
Kern International, Inc.

Geometry. Jan. 1994. *Items Included:* Program on CD-ROM, CD Booklet, & Registration Card. *Customer Support:* Free unlimited support via telephone.
Windows 3.1 or higher running under DOS 5.0 or higher. 386 SX (4Mb RAM; 500k low Dos Mem; 6Mb free disk space). CD-ROM disk $49.00 (ISBN 1-57268-023-7, Order no.: 53103). *Nonstandard peripherals required:* Sound card (either: Sound Blaster - 8, 16, PRO; Media Vision ProAudio Spectrum; or Microsoft Sound System); MPC Compatible CD-ROM drive; VGA monitor; & microphone. *Optimal configuration:* 25MHz 386 SX.
High School Math for Windows. These Programs Offer Interactive Instruction for High-School-Aged Students. These CD-ROMs Contain Interactive Lessons Which Parallel the Pre-Algebra Concepts Taught in Eighth & Ninth Grades. Algebra 1 Reinforces Major Algebraic Concepts Your Child Must Master in School. Individual CD-ROMs for Geometry, Algebra 2, & Trigonometry Complement Programs for Grades Nine Through Twelve.
Conter Software.

Geometry. Jan. 1994. *Items Included:* Program on CD-ROM, CD Booklet, & Registration Card. *Customer Support:* Free unlimited customer support via telephone.
Windows 3.1 or higher running under DOS 5.0 or higher. 386 SX (4Mb RAM; 500k low Dos Mem; 6Mb free disk space). CD-ROM disk $249.00 (ISBN 1-57268-057-1, Order no.: 13102). *Nonstandard peripherals required:* Sound card (either: Sound Blaster - 8, 16, PRO; Media Vision ProAudio Spectrum; or Microsoft Sound System); MPC compatible CD-ROM drive; VGA monitor; & microphone. *Optimal configuration:* 25 MHz 386 SX.
High School Math for Windows: These Programs Offer Interactive Instruction for High-School-Aged Students. These CD-ROMs Contain Interactive Lessons Which Parallel the Pre-Algebra Concepts Taught in Eighth & Ninth Grades. Algebra 1 Reinforces Major Algebraic Concepts Your Child Must Master in School. Individual CD-ROMs for Geometry, Algebra 2, & Trigonometry Complement Programs for Grades Nine Through Twelve.
Conter Software.

Geometry: Concepts & Proofs. (Micro Learn Tutorial Ser.). *Items Included:* Teaching manual including tests. *Customer Support:* Free telephone support.
MAC. IBM, Macintosh (2Mb), Apple II series, (48k). 5.25" disk $39.95 (Lab pack/5 $99.00). 3.5" disk, $44.95 (Lab pack/5 $115.00). Apple, IBM or Macintosh network, $249.00 (ISBN 1-57265-030-3).
DOS. (ISBN 0-939153-66-1).
APP. (ISBN 0-939153-73-4).
Algebraic Problem-Solving Techniques Are applied to Angles, Angle Bisectors, Complements/Supplements, Altitude & Median, Triangle Sum, Properties, Proofs of Isosceles & Congruent Triangles. Topics Can Be Used Sequentially or By Difficulty Level. Emphasis Is on the First Half of a One Year Course. Tutorial mode gives explanations for every answer choice, correct & incorrect. Test mode included.
Word Assocs., Inc.

Geometry: Planely Simple. (Micro Learn Tutorial Ser.). *Items Included:* Manual includes tests, puzzles & worksheets. *Customer Support:* Free telephone support.
MAC. IBM, Macintosh (2Mb), Apple II series, (48k), Commodore 64. 5.25" disk, $39.95 (Lab pack/5 $99.00). 3.5" disk, $44.95 (Lab pack/5 $115.00). Apple, IBM or Macintosh network, $249.00 (ISBN 0-939153-24-6).
DOS. Macintosh. Single copy, $44.95; Lab pack/5, $115.00; Network v., $249.00 (ISBN 0-939153-49-1).
Balances Abstract Concepts & Practical Applications of Plane Geometry. Lessons on Geometric Figures with a Review of Lines & Angles. Examines Triangles, Quadrilaterals, & Other Polygons. Strong Emphasis on Problem-Solving & Applications, Including Perimeter, Circumference, Areas of Polygons & Circles. Tutorial mode gives explanations for every answer choice, correct or incorrect. Test mode included.
Word Assocs., Inc.

Geometry: Right Triangles. (Micro Learn Tutorial Ser.). *Items Included:* Teacher's manual. *Customer Support:* Free telephone support.
MAC. IBM, Macintosh, (2Mb), Apple II series, (48k). 5.25" disk, $39.95 (lab pack/5 $99.00). 3.5" disk, $44.95 (Lab pack/5 $115.00). Apple, IBM or Macintosh, $249.00 (ISBN 1-57265-033-8).
DOS. (ISBN 0-939153-88-2).
Interactive Tutorial Teaches All Real Number Manipulations of Square Roots, Pythagorean Theorem & Triples, Ratios & Calculations of 45-45-90 & 30-60-90 Triangles, Altitude to the Hypotenuse; Introduces Trignometry; Provides Practice in Word Problems. Aid for College Entrance Exam Preparation. Tutorial mode gives explanations for all answer choices, correct or incorrect. Test mode included.
Word Assocs., Inc.

Geometry Toolkit. 1995. *Items Included:* Book & software (teacher's manual). *Customer Support:* Technical support available - no charge; free upgrading.
System 7.0 or higher. Mac LC or higher (1Mb). $79.95 school; $129.95 5-user; $179.95 10-user; $379.95 30-user (ISBN 1-57116-014-0).
Build a Basic Understanding of Important Geometry Concepts Using This Highly Interactive Educational Tool. Simulates Geometric Models & Learning Devices to Engage Students in Meaningful Learning Experiences. Concepts Developed Include Patterns, 3-Dimensional Solids, Shapes & Constructions. Comprehensive Instructional Guide with Reproducible Worksheets Included.
Ventura Educational Systems.

Geometry, Vol. 1: Basic Geometrical Notions. 1995. *Items Included:* Full manual. *Customer Support:* Free telephone support - 90 days, 30-day warranty.
MS-DOS 3.2 or higher. 286 (584k). disk $44.95. *Nonstandard peripherals required:* CGA/EGA/VGA.
Measurement, Postulates, Transformations.
Dynacomp, Inc.

Geometry, Vol. 2: Introduction to Plane & Space Geometry. 1995. *Items Included:* Full manual. *Customer Support:* Free telephone support - 90 days, 30-day warranty.
MS-DOS 3.2 or higher. 286 (584k). disk $44.95. *Nonstandard peripherals required:* CGA/EGA/VGA.
Arc, Polygons, Areas, Volume, & More.
Dynacomp, Inc.

GEOPAL+. Version: 7.0. Items Included: Manual. Customer Support: Free phone & mail support, 30-day money back guarantee.
MS-DOS. IBM PC, PC XT, PC AT & compatibles. disk $195.00. Nonstandard peripherals required: EGA or VGA card. Optimal configuration: 386 Machine with LaserJet II, dot matrix printers (Epson compatible).
Comprises 15 Geological Tools, Including Periodic Chart, Map Thickness, Geologic Time Scale, Drilling Thickness & Igneous Rock Classification.
Rockware, Inc.

geoProgrammer. Items Included: GeoAssembler, geoLinker, geoDebugger, over 400 pages of documentation. Customer Support: 90-day warranty, customer support (1) Q-link telecommunications network (2) direct phone lines.
Commodore 64 or 128 (64k). $69.95. Addl. software required: GEOS.
This Complete Assembly Language Development Package Gives the User Power to Create Complex GEOS Applications with Icon, Menu & Window Interfaces. GeoProgrammer Provides an Ideal Learning Environment for Assembly Language Programming.
Berkeley Softworks.

geoPublish. Items Included: Graphics grabber to import graphics from Newsroom, Print Shop, & PrintMaster clip art, library over 25 tools & 32 patterns. Customer Support: 90-day warranty, customer support via Q-link telecommuncations network & by direct phone lines to company.
Commodore 64 or 128 (64k). $49.95. Nonstandard peripherals required: Mouse or joystick. Addl. software required: GEOS or GEOS 128.
Apple II (128k). $99.95. Nonstandard peripherals required: Mouse or joystick.
Ideal for Creating One Page Flyers, Sophisticated Newsletters, Greeting Cards Or 7' x 9' Posters, geoPublish Is a Revolutionary Desktop Publishing Package. Place Graphics Anywhere, Enlarge Text to 192 Points, Create Vertical Text, Smooth & Resize Graphics & More.
Berkeley Softworks.

George Plimpton's Great Speaker's File of Stories Jokes & Anecdotes. 1985. Compatible Hardware: IBM, Apple IIe.
$29.50, incl. manual.
Computerized File of Humor, Anecdotes, Ad Libs. Index by Subject & Words. Can be Used for Personal Speech Preparation.
Bureau of Business Practice.

George Shrinks.
MS-DOS 3.1 or higher, Windows 3.1 or higher. 386 processor or higher (4Mb). CD-ROM disk $39.95 (Order no.: R1190A). Nonstandard peripherals required: CD-ROM drive. Optimal configuration: 386 processor operating at 16MHz or higher, MS-DOS 5.0 or higher, Windows 3.1 or higher, 30Mb hard drive, mouse, VGA graphic adapter & VGA color monitor (SVGA recommended), 4Mb RAM, external speakers or headphones (with sound card) that are Sound Blaster compatible.
Macintosh (4Mb). (Order no.: R1190B). Nonstandard peripherals required: 14" color monitor or larger, CD-ROM drive.
This Beautifully Crafted Interactive Program Is Based on the Award-Winning Book by William Joyce. Award-Winning Illustrations, Read-Aloud Narration, Original Music, Sing-Along Songbook, Sound Effects & a Simple Interface Make This a Valuable Addition for Any School or Library (Ages 3-7).
Library Video Co.

GEOS: Graphic Environment Operating System. Version: 2.0. General Requirements: Mouse or joystick. Items Included: DeskTop, diskTurbo, geoPaint, geoWrite, & desk accessories.
Commodore 64. disk $59.95, incl. deskTop, diskTurbo, geoPaint, geoWrite, & Desk Accessories.
Commodore 128. disk $69.95.
Apple II. disk $69.95.
Provides Commodore Owners with a Graphics-Based User Interface. The Integrated DiskTurbo Software Improves 1541's Disk Drive Performance 5 to 7 Times. Can Be Divided into 4 Areas: Two Functional Aspects (deskTop & Desk Accessories) & Two Applications (geoPaint & geoWrite).
Berkeley Softworks.
  deskTop.
    Graphic Interface Making File Organization & Management Easier.
  geoPaint.
    Full-Featured Color Graphics Drawing & Painting Program. The Pointer Will Operate Any of the 14 Graphic Tools & Shapes in the Drawing Menu.
  geoWrite.
    Easy-to-Use "What-You-See-Is-What-You-Get" Word Processor. Users May Choose from 5 Different Fonts in Many Different Styles & Point Sizes. Documents May Contain up to 64 Pages.
  Desk Accessories.
    Utilities That Can Be Accessed While in Any GEOS Application. These Include an Alarm Clock, a Notepad, a Four-Function Calculator, & Photo & Text Albums Which Store Pictures & Phrases to Be Pasted into Applications. The Preference Manager Enables Users to Establish Parameters for Mouse Speed, Date, Time, & Background Color.

GeoSight Professional. Version: 4.3. Mar. 1991. Items Included: GS report, report generation utility, GS plot, plotting utility, Gateway software, bound manual. Customer Support: 120 day free phone support, 1 yr. maintenance, $500.00, on-site training & installation available.
MS-DOS 3.0 or higher (512k). IBM PC, AT, (286 or 386) or compatible. $1850.00. Nonstandard peripherals required: 80287 math co-processor, EGA graphics or equivalent, color monitor.
Geographic Information System Which Allows for Allocation or Reallocation of Territories or Geographic Areas. Used to Allocate Territories to Sales People, Distribution Centers, Customer Service Centers. Also Permits Detailed Analysis of Sales & Marketing Patterns.
Sammamish Data Systems, Inc.

GEOSIN. Version: 4.1. Jan. 1984. Compatible Hardware: IBM PC, PCjr, PC XT, PC AT, 3270 PC. Operating System(s) Required: MS-DOS. Language(s): FORTRAN. Memory Required: 128k. Customer Support: Technical support, 30 day warranty.
$900.00.
Reduces, Stores, Prints, & Plots Data from Slope Indicator Readings. Program Performs Standard Calculations to Determine Horizontal Movement, Remove Bad Readings from Calculations, & Correct Rotation.
GEOCOMP Corp.

GEOSLOPE. Version: 5.0 & 5.1. Aug. 1983. Compatible Hardware: IBM PC, PC XT, PC AT, 3270 PC. Operating System(s) Required: MS-DOS. Language(s): FORTRAN. Memory Required: 256k. Customer Support: Technical support, 30 day warranty.
disk $970.00 Version 5.0; $1950.00 Version 5.1.
Determines Factor of Safety for Potential Slip Surfaces. Capabilities for Circular, Block & Irregular Surfaces.
GEOCOMP Corp.

GeoView: Contour Mapping & Analysis. Version: 3.0. Items Included: loose leaf manual in binder. Customer Support: One year free upgrades on software & manual to registered owners. Technical support directly from this office to registered owners is free. AppleLink address: D2261.
Macintosh Plus or higher. single-user license $595.00; for multiuser site licensing, educational institutions, & non-profit organizations, contact publisher for price.
Contour Mapping & Analysis Application That Creates Contour Maps from X, Y & Z Data. Data Input Is in Standard ASCII Text Format. Data Field Consists of Site Name, X Coordinate, Y Coordinate & Z Value. Data Point Locations Can Be in Either Latitude or UTM Input with One Z Value per Record & up to 5000 Records per Map. Some Types of Maps Created Are Contour, Three-Dimensional, Base, Trend Surface in color & Overlay. Features Include Multiple Dynamic Windows, Draggable Maps & Easy-to-Use Options.
Computer Systemics.

German & Russian Practice. 1992. Items Included: Detailed manuals are included with all DYNACOMP products. Customer Support: Free telephone support to original customer - no time limit; 30 day limited warranty.
MS-DOS 3.2 or higher. Apple. $27.95 (Add $5.00 for 3 1/2" format; 5 1/4" format standard).
Side One of This Disk Contains German Sentences & Words in a Hangman Game. Side Two Contains Russian with a Simple Method for Learning the Cyrillic Alphabet.
Dynacomp, Inc.

German Foreign Direct Investment in the United States 1974-1994. May 1995. Items Included: Spiral bound manual. Customer Support: Unlimited telephone support.
MS-DOS 6.0/Windows 3.1 or higher. PC Clone 486 or higher (4Mb). disk $125.00 (ISBN 1-878974-08-4). Addl. software required: Database Versions are available for MS Access 2.0, Excel, Lotus, Paradox, Foxpro, & dBASE. Optimal configuration: PC clone with MS-DOS 6.0/Windows 3.1 or higher. Must have MS Access 2.0, or Excel, or Lotus or Paradox or Foxpro or dBASE.
Database of All German Foreign Direct Investment Transactions in the United States 1974-1994.
Jeffries & Associates, Inc.

Gestetner Integration Manager. Compatible Hardware: Apple Macintosh.
contact publisher for price.
Integrates MACWRITE, MACPAINT, MACDRAW, PAGEMAKER, & VERSASCAN, Allowing Switching Between Applications & Providing an On-Line Help File.
Gestetner Corp.

Get It Free on the Internet: The Penny-Pincher's Guide to Online Bargains. Tracey Winters. Apr. 1996. Items Included: A 64-page companion booklet that reviews web sites & includes instructions on how to use the software. Customer Support: Access to the Go!Guides web site & FAQ, customer support by email at help goguides.com.
Macintosh System 7.0 or higher. Macintosh (4Mb). 3.5" disk $12.99 (ISBN 1-57712-012-4). Nonstandard peripherals required: Modem 14.4 or faster. Addl. software required: Internet account & connection. Optimal configuration: Macintosh System 7.0 or higher, at least 4Mb of RAM, at least 2Mb of free disk space, color monitor, 14.4 or 28.8 modem, Internet account.
Windows 3.1 or Windows 95. IBM or compatible

TITLE INDEX

(4Mb). disk $12.99. *Nonstandard peripherals required:* 14.4 or 28.8 modem. *Addl. software required:* Internet account. *Optimal configuration:* IBM-compatible running Windows 3.1 or Windows 95, at least 2Mb free space on hard drive, at least 4Mb RAM, color monitor, 14.4 or 28.8 modem, Internet account.
Online Shopping Is the Great New Internet Adventure. In Get It Free on the Internet, You'll Discover What You Can Get for Free, How to Get It, & What to Be Wary Of.
Motion Works Publishing.

Get the News on Usenet: Using Newsgroups to Join the Conversation, Which Is Always in Progress. Karl Mamer. Apr. 1996. *Items Included:* A 64-page companion booklet that reviews web sites & includes instructions on how to use the software. *Customer Support:* Access to the Go!Guides web site & FAQ, customer support by email at help goguides.com.
Macintosh System 7.0 or higher. Macintosh (4Mb). 3.5" disk $12.99 (ISBN 1-57712-001-9). *Nonstandard peripherals required:* Modem 14.4 or faster. *Addl. software required:* Internet account & connection. *Optimal configuration:* Macintosh System 7.0 or higher, at least 4Mb of RAM, at least 2Mb of free disk space, color monitor, 14.4 or 28.8 modem, Internet account.
Windows 3.1 or Windows 95. IBM or compatible (4Mb). disk $12.99. *Nonstandard peripherals required:* 14.4 or 28.8 modem. *Addl. software required:* Internet account. *Optimal configuration:* IBM-compatible running Windows 3.1 or Windows 95, at least 2Mb free space on hard drive, at least 4Mb RAM, color monitor, 14.4 or 28.8 modem, Internet account.
With This Kit You'll Find Out What Newsgroups Are All about - & Even Join in the Conversation, Which Is Always in Progress.
Motion Works Publishing.

Get Your Affairs In Order. 1986. *Compatible Hardware:* Apple II series; IBM PC. *Memory Required:* Apple 48k; IBM 64k.
Apple. disk $29.95 (ISBN 0-917729-57-9, Order no.: AP950).
IBM. disk $29.95 (ISBN 0-917729-58-7, Order no.: 1950).
Documents the State of User's Financial Affairs & Organizes Personal Affairs in a Step-by Step manner. Allows User to Input, Save, Edit & Print a Hard Copy of Key Data.
Compu-Tations, Inc.

Getaway: Laptop Entertainment Six Pack. Version: 1.02. Jan. 1992. *Items Included:* System profile utility to diagnose system performance. *Customer Support:* Telephone or mail support, no toll-free number.
DOS 2.1. PC/XT/AT, Hercules/CGA/EGA/VGA/DCGA. disk $39.95 (Order no.: 1600ST). *Optimal configuration:* 386, VGA, mouse.
6 Easy-to-Play Games. Cascade (Dice), Stuffin the Briefcase (Puzzle), Dominos, Solitaire, Totem (Logic), Word Salad. Supports All Graphic Display Modes. Designed to Optimize LCD Screen Performance. System Profile Feature Shows CPU, Screen, Mouse Performance. Plays from one 720k Disk or Install to Hard Drive.
Epyx, Inc.

Getaway Windows: Windows Entertainment 6-Pack. *Items Included:* User's Guide & 3 diskettes 3.5. *Customer Support:* 90-day warranty - customer support 8:30-5:30 PST (415) 368-3200.
DOS/Microsoft Windows 3.0 or higher. IBM PC & compatibles, VGA, SVGA, EGA, hard disk (2Mb). disk $39.95 (Order no.: 16105T). *Addl. software required:* Microsoft Windows 3.0 or higher. *Optimal configuration:* Hard disk, mouse, Windows 3.1 or MPC compatbile sound card.
Easy-to-Play Windows Entertainment. Cascade (Dice), Stuffin the Briefcase (Puzzle), Dominos, Solitaire, Totem (Logic) & Word Salad. Supports All Graphic Display Modes...Have a Great Multimedia "Coffee Break"! WARNING: Can Be Addictive. Enjoy the Digitized Sound & Animated Color Grpahics.
Epyx, Inc.

Getaway Windows: Windows Entertainment 6-Pack. *Items Included:* User's guide & 3 diskettes 3.5. *Customer Support:* 90 day warranty, customer service available 8:30-5:30 PST (415) 368-3200.
DOS/Microsoft Windows 3.0 or higher. IBM PC & compatibles, VGA, SVGA, EGA, hard disk (2Mb). disk $39.95 (Order no.: 16105T). *Addl. software required:* Microsoft Windows 3.0 or higher. *Optimal configuration:* Hard disk, mouse, Windows 3.1 or MPC compatible sound-card.
6-Pack of Easy-to-Play Windows Entertainment. Cascade (Dice), Stuffin the Briefcase (Puzzle), Dominos, Solitaire, Totem (Logic) & Word Salad. Supports All Graphic Display Modes...Have a Great Multimedia "Coffee Break"! "WARNING Can Be Addictive" Enjoy the Digitized Sound & Animated Color Graphics.
Everbright Software.

GetMemo. *Compatible Hardware:* Apple Macintosh Plus.
3.5" disk $35.00.
Add-On for McMax Database That Enables Users to Output Memo Fields.
JPL Assocs.

Getting Started with Quality Management. Howard Gitlow. Jan. 1994. *Customer Support:* Unlimited support.
Contact publisher for price.
This Interactive Software Application Provides a Road Map to Help You to Get the Leadership of Your Organization Started with the Practice of Quality Management. It Provides Valuable Information on How to Avoid Most of the Common Pitfalls. It Maintains an Extensive Database & Produces Reports.
LearnerFirst.

Gettysburg. Sep. 1993. *Customer Support:* Free technical support - Call/Fax/Mail, Phone: 305-567-9996, Fax: 305-569-1350.
Windows 3.1 or higher. 386 SX, 386DX or higher (2Mb). disk $49.95. *Nonstandard peripherals required:* 3 1/2 floppy disk drive, mouse. *Optimal configuration:* 4Mb RAM, Windows-compatible sound card & speakers.
Change the Course of History with the Recreation of the Battle at Gettysburg. Users Can Take Command of Union or Confederate Troops in the Monumentous Battle. Play General Lee or Meade Against a Simulator That Takes into Account Terrain, Troop Morale & Stamina, Ammunition, & Aim.
SWFTE International, Ltd.

Gettysburg Multimedia Battle Simulation. SWFTE Staff & Turner Interactive Staff. Mar. 1994. *Customer Support:* Free technical support - Call/Fax/Mail, Phone: 305-567-9996, Fax: 305-569-1350.
Windows 3.1. 386 SX or higher (2Mb). CD-ROM disk $69.95. *Nonstandard peripherals required:* CD-ROM drive, VGA graphics card, mouse. *Optimal configuration:* 4Mb RAM, SVGA graphics recommended, sound card.
The Battle of Gettysburg Comes to Life with Scenes from the Turner Pictures' Movie "Gettysburg." Leading Civil War Historian Delivers Battlefield Commentary & Video Clips Highlight the Famous Battle. Users Take Command of Union or Confederate Troops to Relive the 3-Day Battle, or Change History.
SWFTE International, Ltd.

Gettysburg: The Turning Point. David Landrey & Chuck Kroegel. 1986. *Compatible Hardware:* Apple II, II+, IIe, IIc, III; Atari 400, 800, 1200; Commodore 64, 128, Amiga; IBM PC. *Language(s):* Machine, compiled BASIC. *Memory Required:* Atari 48k, Apple 64k, IBM 128k. *Items Included:* rulebook, mapcard. *Customer Support:* 14 day money back guarantee/30 day exchange policy; tech support line: (408) 737-6850 (11:00 -5:00 PST); customer service: (408) 737-6800 (9:00 - 5:00 PST).
disk $59.95.
Recreates the Battle in Detail. Includes Ammunition Points, Fatigue Rules, Every Artillery Man & Combat That Is Resolved down to Each Soldier.
Strategic Simulations, Inc.

GFA Artist. *Compatible Hardware:* Atari ST. *Memory Required:* 1000k. *General Requirements:* TOS in ROM, color monitor.
3.5" disk $79.95.
Users Can Create Animation Sequences Up to 20,000 Frames Long. Enables Users to Incorporate Text Into Pictures Using Any of the 4 Fonts Provided. Users Can Also Create Their Own Fonts With the Font Editor Module. Allows the Creation of a Cycling Color Effect. Users Can Create Their Own Fill Patterns, & Merge Multiple Film Files. Two Modes Are Provided: Low-Res & Low-Res Static, Which Uses Over 1000 Colors Simultaneously. Users Can Work in Both Modes at the Same Time, Combining Multiple Palettes.
MichTron, Inc.

GFL Championship Football. *Compatible Hardware:* Commodore Amiga.
3.5" disk $44.95.
Arcade Football Game.
Activision, Inc.

GFlow: Fluid Mechanics Software. Busnaima. 1987. *Items Included:* Spiral manual contains theory, sample runs. *Customer Support:* Free phone, on-site seminars.
MS-DOS. IBM (128k). disk $140.00. *Addl. software required:* BASIC.
Solves 20 Isothermal, Incompressible Flow Problems Using Mavier Stokes Equations Solved via Finite Differences Based on Marker & Cell Method. Uses Cartesian or Cylindrical Coordinates. Boundary Conditions Can Be No Slip, Free Slip, Outflow, Inlet, Moving. Obstacles Can Be Placed in the Flow Field. Transient & Steady State Solutions, Output Includes Numerical Data Describing Flow Field Plus Graphical Display of Flow Vectors.
Kern International, Inc.

Ghost Gobbler. *Compatible Hardware:* TRS-80 Color Computer, TDP-100.
contact publisher for price.
Spectral Assocs.

Ghost Town. *Compatible Hardware:* TI-99/4A.
disk or cassette - contact publisher for price.
Texas Instruments, Personal Productivit.

Ghostprinter Printer-to-Disk Spooler. *Items Included:* Full manual. No other products required. *Customer Support:* Free telephone support - no time limit. 30 day warranty.
MS-DOS 3.2 or higher. IBM & compatibles (512k). disk $9.95. *Optimal configuration:* IBM, MS-DOS 2.1 or higher, 4k RAM.
Handy Memory-Resident Utility Which Redirects Printer Output to a Disk File. It Can Be Used in

Situations in Which the Application Requires a Printer, but None Is Currently Available; for Compactly Archiving Printer Output; for Spooling Printer Output to Disk for Later Printing; for Importing Printer Output to Wordprocessors; for Saving Text Screens to Disk (Using the PrtScr Key); etc.
Dynacomp, Inc.

GhostWriter 128. *Customer Support:* 800-929-8117 (customer service).
MS-DOS. Commodore 128; CP/M. disk $49.99 (ISBN 0-87007-836-4).
The Prime Word Processor & Spelling Checker for the Commodore 128 Computer. It Runs in C128 "Fast Mode," Includes an 80-Column Window, & a 30,000-Plus Spelling Checker. User Can Make Instant Changes on the Screen & See Exactly What Will Print. A Thorough Manual Is Included with "How-to" Guides & Command Reference Sections to Aid Even the First-Time User. Features Include an 80/40 Column Viewscreen Window with Space for up to 240 Self-Formating Columns. Works with OmniWriter Files & Other Popular Productivity Packages. Does Not Work in CP/M Mode.
SourceView Software International.

The Gibbs System. *Version:* 4.2. *Compatible Hardware:* Macintosh Plus or higher. *General Requirements:* Hard disk recommended. *Items Included:* Documentation. *Customer Support:* Free On-Site Training, Free phone support, 90-days unlimited warranty.
3.5" disk $7000.00 approx.
Computer-Aided Design & Manufacturing. Package Modules All Components to Take User from Initial Design Through the Actual Generation & Downloading of a Numerical Control Program for Controlling NC/CNC Machines.
Gibbs & Assocs.

Gif Galore. *Customer Support:* All of our products are unconditionally guaranteed.
All Systems. CD-ROM disk $39.95 (Order no.: GIF). *Nonstandard peripherals required:* CD-ROM drive.
Over 5000 Beautiful Gif Images in Dozens of Categories.
Walnut Creek CDRom.

GiftMaker Pro. *Version:* 5.0. Aug. 1994. *Items Included:* Complete operations guide (manuals); Quarterly newsletter. *Customer Support:* 60 day money back guarantee; annual support agreement - provides unlimited telephone support & free upgrades; cost-$690 per year.
Macintosh. All Macintosh & PC with Windows 3.1. $2990.00 single user $3990.00 multi-user (2-5 users); additional users over 5, $1000.00 15 users. *Addl. software required:* Word Processing. *Networks supported:* TOPS, Appleshare, NetWare, Data Club, System 7.1 File Sharing.
MS-DOS/Windows 3.1. IBM PC or compatible 386 or 486 machine (4Mb). $2990.00 single user; $3990.00 multi-user (2-5 users); additional users, over 5, $99.00. *Addl. software required:* Word Processing. *Networks supported:* Netware, Lantastic.
Mail List, Membership & Fund-Raising Management Program Designed for Large, Full Time Development Departments. It Has All Advanced Features Needed by Today's Fundraising Professionals Including: Complete Biographical Information; Searchable Free-Form Notes; Advanced Membership Module; Complete Pledge & Donation Tracking; Ad Hoc Report Generator; Flexible Output Options; Complete Mailing Label Sections; Auto Mail Merge & Much More.
Campagne Assocs., Ltd.

Giga Games II. *Customer Support:* All of our products are unconditionally guaranteed.
DOS, Windows. CD-ROM disk $39.95 (Order no.: GAMES2). *Nonstandard peripherals required:* CD-ROM drive.
494 MB of the Newest Shareware & Freeware Games in Many Categories.
Walnut Creek CDRom.

GigaGames. *Customer Support:* All of our products are unconditionally guaranteed.
DOS, Windows. CD-ROM disk $39.95 (Order no.: GIGAGAMES). *Nonstandard peripherals required:* CD-ROM drive.
3000 DOS & Windows Games in Many Categories.
Walnut Creek CDRom.

Gin Rummy. *Compatible Hardware:* Apple, C-64, IBM. *Items Included:* Bound manual. *Customer Support:* Free hotline - no time limit; 30 day limited warranty; updates are $5/disk plus S&H. disk $19.95.
A Match for the Best Gin Rummy Players Around. This Program Is for One Player Against the Computer. It Allows Knocking, Laying off, & All Standard Game Conventions.
Dynacomp, Inc.

GINO: General Interactive Optimizer. Judith Liebman. *Compatible Hardware:* IBM PC, PC XT, PC AT. *Memory Required:* 256k.
disk $700.00 (ISBN 0-89426-050-2).
Brings the Power of Nonlinear Programming to Users Without Computer Programming Skills.
Boyd & Fraser Publishing Co.

GIS World Source CD 1996. Edited by Gayle K. Rodcay.
IBM. CD-ROM disk $149.95 (ISBN 1-882610-24-5).
GIS (Geographic Information Systems) Listings: Computer Industry-Directories; Computer Engineering; Computer Software; Geography-Methodology; Mapper-Computer System.
GIS World, Inc.

GL - Rdb Financial Management System: GL - Rdb. *Version:* 6.0. 1993. *Items Included:* User's Guides & other documentation are included. *Customer Support:* Full service, update service; by quotation.
OpenVMS. DEC VAX Series & DEC Alpha AXP. disk $5000.00-$30,000.00. *Optimal configuration:* Alpha, VAX & LAN. *Networks supported:* Pathworks, OS-2, Lan Manager, Netware & Macintosh.
Most Cost-Effective, Full-Featured Accounting Software on Alpha AXP/VAX Systems. Offers Highly Flexible Chart of Accounts Design & Changes En Masse. Easily Produces Virtually Any Financial Report. Backed by a Full Suite of Accounting, Human Resources/Payroll, & Distribution Software.
Compu-Share, Inc.

GL*Plus (General Ledger). *Version:* 6.35. Oct. 1990. *Compatible Hardware:* IBM PC & compatibles. *Operating System(s) Required:* PC-DOS/MS-DOS 3.1. *Memory Required:* 640k. *Items Included:* Documentation manual; Quick Start Users Guide. *Customer Support:* 6 months toll free telephone support & updates, 90 day unlimited warranty; annual maintenance (support & updates) $150.00.
$1695.00 multi-client/multi-user.
$795.00 single user.
Includes: Multiple Master Chart of Accounts, Flexible Report Formatting, Spreadsheet Interface, Departmental & Sub Dept. Financial Statements, Fully Integrated & up to 10 Digit Account Numbers.
UniLink.

GLAS Acquisitions Module: Graphical Library Automation Systems. 1996. *Items Included:* Spiral bound reference & tutorial style manual. Quick reference summary. *Customer Support:* Turn-key vendor: hardware, peripherals, hardware/software support contracts, toll free phone & Internet Access to product support, & training.
Windows 3.1X, Windows NT, Windows for Workgroups, Windows 95. 486 (8Mb). 3.5" disk $2950.00, GSA & School pricing avail. (ISBN 0-929795-45-8). *Nonstandard peripherals required:* SVGA. *Networks supported:* Novell, Banyon, Microsoft Network, IBM LANtastic.
Windows-Based Library Automation Software That Provides Journal, Report & Monograph Ordering & Claim Letters, Collection Maintenance, & Allocation of Costs Are All a Part of This Module. Also Provides Searching & Multi-User Options. Orders Online with Ebsco, Majors, Dawson, & the Information Store & Readmore. Entries Automatically Transfer Appropriate Data to the Cataloging & Serial Modules. 65,000 Titles.
Data Trek, Inc.

GLAS Cataloging Module: Graphical Library Automation Systems. 1996. *Items Included:* Spiral bound reference & tutorial style manual. Quick reference summary. *Customer Support:* Turn-key vendor: hardware, peripherals, hardware/software support contracts, toll free phone & Internet Access to product support, & training.
Windows 3.1X, Windows NT, Windows for Workgroups, Windows 95. 486 (8Mb). 3.5" disk $2950.00, GSA & School pricing avail. (ISBN 0-929795-42-3). *Nonstandard peripherals required:* SVGA. *Networks supported:* Novell, Banyon, Microsoft Network, IBM LANtastic.
Windows-Based Library Automation Software Providing Streamlined Data Entry. Print Cross-Reference Reports for Authors, Subjects, or Added Entries. Bibliographic Searching Through Boolean Logic Statements on Most Elements of Database. Generate New Book List, Shelf List, Spine & Book Labels, & Reports by Author, Circulation & Acquisitions Modules. Modules Sold Independently. 65,000 Titles.
Data Trek, Inc.

GLAS Circulation Module: Graphical Library Automation Systems. 1996. *Items Included:* Spiral bound reference & tutorial style manual. Quick reference summary. *Customer Support:* Turn-key vendor: hardware, peripherals, hardware/software support contracts, toll free phone & Internet Access to product support, & training.
Windows 3.1X, Windows NT, Windows for Workgroups, Windows 95. 486 (8Mb). 3.5" disk $2950.00, GSA & School pricing avail. (ISBN 0-929795-43-1). *Nonstandard peripherals required:* SVGA. *Networks supported:* Novell, Banyon, Microsoft Network, IBM LANtastic.
Windows-Based Library Automation Software Providing Check-In, Check-Out, Hold & Renewal. Overdue Reports & Notices, & Fine Payments Are Generated along with Borrower Reports Listing. Title, Cost, & Due Date for Holdings Out to Any Particular Borrower or Borrowers. A Full Complement of Management Reports, a Reserve Collection Management Option, & Inventory Options Provide Comprehensive Circulation Service. Reserve Collection Management Option & Inventory Options. Also Offers Full Bar Code Support. Integrates with Cataloging & Serials Modules. 65,000 Titles.
Data Trek, Inc.

GLAS Databridge Module: Graphical Library Automation Systems. 1996. *Items Included:* Spiral bound reference & tutorial style manual. Quick reference summary. *Customer Support:* Turn-key vendor: hardware, peripherals, hardware/software support contracts, toll free phone & Internet Access to product support, & training.
Windows 3.1X, Windows NT. 486 (8Mb). 3.5" disk $1195.00, GSA & School pricing avail. (ISBN 0-929795-46-6). *Networks supported:* Novell, Banyon, Microsoft Network, IBM LANtastic.
Transfers Bibliographic Data Stored in MARC Formats from MARCIVE, OCLC & CD-ROM & More to ACQUISITIONS, CATALOGING, & CIRCULATION Modules. Eliminates the Chores of Keyboard Entry into the Graphical Library Automation System for Those Records Which Are Already Available in Machine-Readable Formats, Minimizes Initial Cataloging & the Export Functions Allow Users to Share Records with Other Sites or Institutions.
Data Trek, Inc.

GLAS EasySearch Utility: Graphical Library Automation Systems. 1996. *Items Included:* Spiral bound reference & tutorial style manual. Quick reference summary. *Customer Support:* Turn-key vendor: hardware, peripherals, hardware/software support contracts, toll free phone & Internet Access to product support, & training.
Windows 3.1X, Windows NT. 486 (8Mb). 3.5" disk $395.00, GSA & School pricing avail. (ISBN 0-929795-47-4). *Nonstandard peripherals required:* SVGA. *Networks supported:* Novell, Banyon, Microsoft Network, IBM LANtastic.
Gives Your Library a Quick & Simple Way to Search Your GLAS System Online. Specify Your Own Search Strategies Using Boolean Searching Techniques or Browse on a Specific Index. Search by Title, Author, Subject, Call Number, Series, Added Entry or ID Number in the GLAS Cataloging Module, or Search by Title, Subject or Acronym in the GLAS Serials Module.
Data Trek, Inc.

GLAS Serials Module: Graphical Library Automation Systems. 1996. *Items Included:* Spiral bound reference & tutorial style manual. Quick reference summary. *Customer Support:* Turn-key vendor: hardware, peripherals, hardware/software support contracts, toll free phone & Internet Access to product support, & training.
Windows 3.1X, Windows NT, Windows for Workgroups, Windows 95. 486 (8Mb). 3.5" disk $2950.00, GSA & School pricing avail. (ISBN 0-929795-44-X). *Nonstandard peripherals required:* SVGA. *Networks supported:* Novell, Banyon, Microsoft Network, IBM LANtastic.
Windows-Based Library Automation Software Providing Check-In, Routing, Slip Maintenance, & Production, Arrival Tracking, Issue Production, Claims Alert, & Form Printing, & Renewal Alerts. Claims Online with Ebsco, Dawson, Information Store, Majors, & More. Reports Include Budget & Projection, Status of Missing Issues, & Serials Catalog along with Claim Letter Printing, a History File Is Also Maintained & Boolean Searching. Integrates with Acquisitions & Circulation. 65,000 titles.
Data Trek, Inc.

Glasnost Cyrillic Library Two. *Version:* 4.1. 1992. *Items Included:* Manual, reg. card. *Customer Support:* Free phone support.
PC or compatibles. disk $149.00 (Order no.: PC083).
6.02 & higher. Macintosh. 3.5" disk $149.00 (Order no.: M083).
17 PostScript & TrueType Fonts Which Support Russian, Byelorussian, Serbian, Ukrainian, Bulgarian, Macedonian, & English.
Casady & Greene, Inc.

Glaxxons.
contact publisher for price.
Mark Data Products.

Gleanings: Uncollected Poems of the Fifties.
David Ignatow. Aug. 1994. *Items Included:* Descriptive instructions. *Customer Support:* Free by phone.
Apple/MAC. MAC (516k). 3.5" disk $9.00 (ISBN 1-887638-02-4). *Optimal configuration:* Hypertext Viewer supplied.
Windows. PC compatible (516k). disk $9.00 (ISBN 1-887638-00-8). *Optimal configuration:* Hypertext Viewer supplied.
MS-DOS - ASCII. All platforms (516k). disk $9.00 (ISBN 1-887638-04-0). *Addl. software required:* Any Word processor.
A Hypertext Collection of More Than 120 Poems, Many Previously Unpublished, by a Major American Poet.
GRIST On-Line.

Glider. *Version:* 4.0. John Calhoun. Aug. 1991. *Customer Support:* Free phone support.
Macintosh. 3.5" disk $49.95 (Order no.: M104).
Fly the Glider from Room to Room & Try to Get Past the Wildest Obstacles You've Ever Seen, Including Mysterious Copters, Air Vents, & the Dreaded Paper Shredder! Each One of the 60 Rooms Holds a New Surprise. Get Past Them All & Fly Out of the House. Use the Room Editor to Create Your Own Version of Obstacle-Filled Rooms.
Casady & Greene, Inc.

Glider Pro. John Calhoun. Sep. 1994. *Items Included:* Manual, 2 disks, reg. card. *Customer Support:* Free phone support, 90 MBG.
Macintosh (2Mb). 3.5" disk $49.95. *Optimal configuration:* System 7 or higher.
Long-Awaited Sequel to Glider 4.0. Now Fly the Paper Airplane Right Out of the Old Home, over Meadows, Thru Mailboxes, etc. until You Find & Possess the Magic Stars & Reach Your Ultimate Destiny. Family Entertainment.
Casady & Greene, Inc.

GLIM. *Version:* 4.0. *Items Included:* 2 manual set, users & installers notes. *Customer Support:* 90 days free maintenance; additional support is available.
DOS. Apple Macintosh (512k plus, XL). $468.00-$588.00. *Addl. software required:* Optional co-processor.
Mac OS. IBM PC & compatibles (256k). $600.00-$2340.00.
Original Generalized Linear Interactive Modelling Software. Extremely Popular in Life Expectancy & Meantime Between Failure Studies. Contains Model Options Including Cox Hazard Analysis, Contigency Tables, Survival Models & More in a Powerful Command Language Shell.
Numerical Algorithms Group, Inc.

Global Commander. *Compatible Hardware:* Commodore 64/128, Amiga, Atari ST, IBM PC & compatibles. *Memory Required:* Commodore 64/128 64k; Amiga, Atari, IBM 512k. *General Requirements:* Joystick Optional.
Commodore 64/128. disk $29.95 (ISBN 0-88717-214-8, Order no.: 16152-43499).
Amiga. 3.5" disk $39.95 (ISBN 0-88717-216-4, Order no.: 16152-43499).
Atari. 3.5" disk $39.95 (ISBN 0-88717-233-4, Order no.: 16159-43499).
IBM. disk $39.95 (ISBN 0-88717-233-4, Order no.: 16154-43499).
In the Role of Global Commander of the Satellite Defense & Espionage Network, Player Has 4 Goals: Establish Close Working Relationships with Individual Countries; Promote Good Relations Between Each Country & Its 15 Fellow United Nuclear Nations Member Countries; & Make Sure That the Economic & Military Balance Is Maintained. Player Controls SDI Satellites, Troop Placements, & Spy Networks in Order to Determine the Actions of Each Superpower.
IntelliCreations, Inc.

Global Information Access & Management. Jan. 1995. *Customer Support:* Unlimited telephone support.
MS-DOS 6.0/Windows 3.1 or higher. PC Clone 486 or higher (4Mb). disk $15.00 (ISBN 1-878974-25-4). *Addl. software required:* MS Windows 3.1 or higher. *Optimal configuration:* PC clone with MS-DOS 6.0/Windows 3.1 or higher. 4Mb of hard disk storage recommended.
Multimedia Tutorial Which Installs in MS Windows 3.1 or Higher. Steps You Through an Overview of Global Information Access & Management in about 30 Minutes.
Jeffries & Associates, Inc.

Global LAB Color: HSI Color Image Processing. Sep. 1990. *Items Included:* Complete hardcover manual. *Customer Support:* 1 year unlimited warranty.
$1995.00 (Order no.: SP0226-CG). *Optimal configuration:* PC AT (386 or higher), PC-DOS 3.0 or higher, VGA display card, external RGB monitor, Microsoft mouse, 40Mb or higher hard drive, 1.5Mb or higher of extended memory.
24-Bit HSI/RGB Color Image Processing & Analysis Application for Scientist, Engineers, & Researchers. Capabilities Include Image Segmentation Based on Color, Histogram & Line Profile Analysis, Spatial Measurements, Filtering, & Color Manipulation. Macros Are Available to Automate Operation. Frame Grabbers Are Supported for Image Capture from Video Sources.
Data Translation.

Global Lab Data Acquisition. *Version:* 3.0. Jun. 1991. *Items Included:* Complete hardcover manual, tutorial. *Customer Support:* 1 year unlimited warranty, free technical support.
DOS 3.0 or higher (512k). PC/XT, PC/AT or PS/2 with microchannel. $1285.00 (Order no.: SP0147). *Nonstandard peripherals required:* Data translation DT2801, DT2821, DT2831, DT3831 or DT2812 series data acquisition board. *Optimal configuration:* Mouse, printer, hard drive with at least 3.5Mb free space, 512k of memory.
High Performance Data Acquisition, Display & Analysis Software. The Package Supports Continuous Gap-Gree Data Acquisition at Speeds up to 250 KHz. The Statpack Signal Processing Module Performs Digital Signal Processing, Digital Filtering, Statistical, Trigonometric, Logical & Mathematical Processing Operations. The Graphpack Printing Module Produces Hardcopy Output of Data.
Data Translation.

Global LAB Image: Image Processing for Microsoft Windows. Jun. 1991. *Items Included:* Complete hardcover manual, tutorial documents. *Customer Support:* 1 year unlimited warranty, 90 days free technical support.
Microsoft Windows 3.1 or higher & MS-DOS (consult factory for version). PC AT 80386-based or higher. $2495.00 (Order no.: SP0550-CW). *Nonstandard peripherals required:* Data translation frame grabber board, any Windows compatible 4 or 8 bit graphics adapter (8-bit required for single monitor

operation w/out frame grabber), compatible monitor. *Optimal configuration:* PC AT (80386 or 80486), Microsoft Windows 3.1 or higher, 4Mb RAM, MS-DOS (consult factory for version), Windows compatible mouse minimum of 5Mb free space on hard drive.
An Image Processing & Analysis Application for Scientists, Engineers, & Researchers. Capabilities Include Automatic Object Counting & Measurement, Spatial & Intensity Measurement, Filtering, & Frequency Domain Processing. Interpreted C Programming Can Be Used to Add Functions to the Application. Frame Grabbers Are Supported for Image Capture from Video Cameras or VCRs.
Data Translation.

Global Limits Reporting System. (International Finance Ser.). May 1984. *Compatible Hardware:* IBM PC, PC XT, PC AT, PS/2, 386, 486 & compatibles. *Operating System(s) Required:* MS-DOS 3.0 or higher, Windows. *Language(s):* Compiled BASIC. *Memory Required:* 640k. Base System. Contact publisher for price.
Networks supported: LAN-Novell, Token Ring.
Provides Exception Reporting by Country & Customer Head Office. Limits Can Be Established for Different Transaction Categories by Time Period. Includes Trader Inquiry Subsystem Providing On-Line Country & Customer Limits, Outstandings, & Availability Information. Outstanding Information from Other Sites May Be Captured, Thus Providing Full Global Exposure & Outstandings Control.
Spot Systems, Inc.

Global Portfolio System (GPS). *Version:* 3.0. *Items Included:* Documentation. *Customer Support:* Dial-in hot line, in-person.
UNIX. Most hardware platforms (16Mb). Call vendor for details. *Networks supported:* All major networks.
Utilizes the INGRES Relational Data Base Product & Is Offered on a Wide Variety of Hardware (UNIX) Platforms. Provides the Client with Extensive Multi-Currency Capability As Well As Total Flexibility in the Way in Which the System Operates. Targeted to Large Money Management Firms, As Well As Those Smaller Firms with International Requirements, Rapid Growth, or the Desire to Utilize the Most Flexible Technology Available.
DST Belvedere.

Glockenspiel C++. *Version:* 2.0. *Items Included:* C++ user's guide. *Customer Support:* Maintenance available, call for pricing.
UNIX, VMS. Apple MAC II A/UX, HP9000/3xxx & 4xx, Motorola, DG AViiON, Unisys/Convergent, DEC VAX, DECstation, IBM RS/6000, Sun-4 SPARC. Starts at $1400.00.
UNIX. Sun-3, Sun-4 (SPARC), IBM RS/6000, DECstation, HP/Apollo 9000/3xx, HP 9000/4xx, Motorola, AViiON, 386 UNIX. Starting at $1400.00.
VMS. DEC VAX, VAXstation, MicroVAX. Starting at $1400.00.
A Proprietary Implementation of the C++ Language with Support for Either AT&T's Specification of Version 1.2 or 2.0. Is Implemented As a Translator Pre-Compiler to the Host Compiler. The Translator Emits C Code Which Compiles As Usual. completely Compatible with AT&T's C++ Translator v.2.0. Also Continues to Support Version 1.2. Full Compatibility with Existing C Programs Is also Maintained.
Oasys, Inc.

GLOWS Client Accounting System, 5 modules. *Version:* 4.2. Apr. 1988. *Compatible Hardware:* Altos; AT&T 3B2; IBM PC & compatibles. *Operating System(s) Required:* DOS, XENIX, UNIX. *Language(s):* Busines BASIC (source code included). *Memory Required:* 1000k. *Customer Support:* Annual phone support $400/yr; per call by charge card $100/hr.
Entire system. $3500.00, incl. all modules.
Write-Up Package. $1995.00, incl. Client's Write-Up General Ledger & Financial Report Generator.
Audit package. $1995.00, incl. Audit General Ledger & Financial Report Generator.
A Multi-User, Multi-Client Package Designed for the Practicing Accountant. System Features Include: a Sophisticated General Ledger; Full Sub-Accounting Capabilites; Clean Audit Trail; Ability to Copy Similar Information from Company to Company; User Designed Menus; & Flexible, User Defined Financial Report Formatting.
Orion Microsystems, Inc.
 GLOWS Audit System.
  $695.00.
 GLOWS After-the-Fact (Post-Facto) Payroll.
  $495.00.
  Fully Integrated with General Ledger; Allows up to 7 State & Local Taxes; Automatic Preparation of Continuation Sheets; 941 Worksheet with Depository Requirements Calculated; Employee Ledger Cards; Preparation of W-2's; Reporting by Month, Quarter or Year-to-Date.
 GLOWS Fixed Asset System.
  $695.00.
  Features Pre-1981, TEFRA, or TRA Methods Current Year's Depreciation Can Be Reviewed & Automatically Recomputed; Automatic Flagging & Conversion to Straight-Line When Applicable; Investment Credit & Depreciation Recapture; Checks for Balance of Fixed Asset Schedule to General Ledger Control.
 GLOWS 1099 System.
  $295.00.
 GLOWS Write-Up System.
  $695.00.

GLOWS Practice Management System: GLOWSPM. *Version:* 4.2. Apr. 1989. *Compatible Hardware:* Altos; AT&T 382; IBM & compatibles. *Operating System(s) Required:* XENIX, DOS, UNIX. *Language(s):* Business BASIC (source code included). *Customer Support:* Annual phone support $400/yr. per call by credit card $100/hr.
$1995.00.
History Option. $595.00.
GLOWSPM & History Option. $2500.00.
Provides an Open-Time Work-in-Process System. Billable Time & Expenses Are Captured to Ascertain Staff Productivity Levels. Includes an Open-Invoice Accounts Receivable System, Job Scheduling & Job Costing Which Allows Tracking of Open Jobs or Matters Broken down into As Many As 99 Component Phases. HISTORY OPTION Provides Historical Analysis of Production for Estimates on Jobs & Analysis of Performance.
Orion Microsystems, Inc.

Glowsap. *Version:* 4.2. Feb. 1989. *Items Included:* Manual. *Customer Support:* Annual phone support $400/year, per call by credit card $100/hour.
Xenix, Unix, DOS. Altos, ATT, IBM PC & compatibles. disk $495.00. *Addl. software required:* Business Basic. *Networks supported:* Novell, 3Com, Banyan.
Multi-User, Multi-Client Package. Allows Entry & Payment of Vouchers Based on Date Due or Discount Date & Prints the Accounts Payable Checks. System Features Include Cash or Accrual Basis, Checkwriting for Non-Vendor & Also for Non-Voucher Payments, Use of Multiple Cash & Accounts Payable Accounts & Vouchers Created Automatically for Recurring Monthly Payments.
Orion Microsystems, Inc.

Glowsar. *Version:* 4.2. Feb. 1989. *Items Included:* Manual. *Customer Support:* Annual phone support $400/year, per credit card call $100/hour.
Xenix, Unix, DOS. Altos, ATT, IBM PC & compatibles. disk $695.00. *Addl. software required:* Business Basic. *Networks supported:* Novell, 3Com, Banyan.
Multi-User, Multi-Client Package. Invoices May Be Created for Cash Sales, As Hand Invoices, from Sales Orders or Input Directly for Regular Invoices. Features Include Unlimited Goods & Services Codes Each with up to Five Prices & Designated if Subject to Tax or Commissions; Also Calculates Sales Commissions Based on Gross or Net Sales.
Orion Microsystems, Inc.

Glowspr. *Version:* 4.2. Feb. 1989. *Items Included:* Manual. *Customer Support:* Annual phone support $400/year, per call by credit card $100/hour.
XENIX, UNIX. Altos, ATT, IBM PC & compatibles. disk $695.00. *Addl. software required:* Business Basic. *Networks supported:* Novell, 3Com, Banyan.
Multi-User, Multi-Client Package, Generates Automatic Payroll Lists, Calculates Taxes & Prints Payroll Checks. Features Include up to 99 Divisions Each Having up to 99 Departments; up to 30 Wage & Miscellaneous Deductions per Payroll; up to 7 State & Local Taxes per Payroll; Tax Rates Held in Easily Modified Tables.
Orion Microsystems, Inc.

GLS (General Ledger System). *Version:* 8. May 1981. *Compatible Hardware:* IBM PC, PC AT & compatibles. *Operating System(s) Required:* DOS Ver. 3.1 or higher. *Language(s):* MBASIC. *Memory Required:* 384k. *Items Included:* Binder with documentation. *Customer Support:* 1 yr. maintenance, $108.00, entitles users to phone support, quarterly newsletters & enhancements made available for their computer during the year at no charge.
disk $500.00.
demo disk $35.00.
maintenance fee (optional) $108.00.
Designed for Any Type of Business or Personal Use. Provides for User-Defined Chart of Accounts & Financial Statement Formats. Allows up to 99 Departments/Profit Centers That Can Be Consolidated. Financials Can Be Maintained on Either Cash or Accrual Method. Designed for Cash Basis When Integrating with TABS III, TABS III-M or Profit$ource. Allows Budgets. When Integrated with STI's APS Unpaid Invoices Can Be Posted & Unposted by Using a Menu Selection.
Software Technology, Inc.

GLS-M (General Ledger System-M). *Version:* 8. May 1981. *Compatible Hardware:* IBM PC & compatibles. *Operating System(s) Required:* DOS Ver. 3.1 or higher; Novell Netware or IBM PC Network software. *Memory Required:* 384k. *General Requirements:* Hard disk. *Items Included:* Binder with documentation. *Customer Support:* 1 yr. maintenance, $144.00, entitles users to phone support, quarterly newsletters & enhancements made available for their computer during the year at no charge.
disk $700.00.
maintenance fee (optional) $144.00.
demo disk $35.00.
True Multi-User Version of GLS Allowing up to 200 Terminals to Enter or Retrieve General Ledger Information. Integrates with TABS III-M & APS-M.
Software Technology, Inc.

TITLE INDEX

GM-SYS: Gravity-Magnetics Modeling Software. Version: 3.04. 1989-93. *Items Included:* Manual. *Customer Support:* Six-month renewable service contract included with license; service contract includes telephone support, software & manual updates, bug fixes, technical notes; training available (fee).
  MS-DOS. IBM & compatibles (470k). $1680.00 & up depending on options (Order no.: 101). *Nonstandard peripherals required:* Math coprocessor. *Optimal configuration:* 386 EGA/VGA RAM 640k, mouse/digitizer.
  UNIX. Sun SPARC (Sun OS 4.1.X) (3Mb excluding UNIX, Windows, etc.). $9500.00 and up (Order no.: 201). *Addl. software required:* Motif or Open Windows 3.0. *Optimal configuration:* Sun SPARC, Motif 1.2, Maximum RAM, Sun OS 4.1.2. *Networks supported:* Standard UNIX environment.
  Constructs 2-D or 2.75-D (Optional) Models, Computes Gravity and/or Magnetic-Model Responses, Permits Editing & Revision of Models to Test Geologic Hypotheses. This Interactive, Forward or Simultaneous/Inversion (Optional) Modeling Software Includes up to 125 Bodies, 5, 100 Vertices & 500 Observation/Calculation Points per Model. Models & Data Entered by Digitizer, from Files or by Hand. Cross-Sections Generated on Plotters or Line Printers.
  Northwest Geophysical Assocs., Inc.

GMAT: Exam Preparation Series, 6-8 disks. *Compatible Hardware:* Apple; AT&T; Franklin Ace; IBM PC, PCjr; Tandy; Zenith.
  Complete Series. $299.95 (ISBN 0-918349-04-4, Order no.: GMAT).
  Gold Label. $349.95.
  Covers All Areas of the Graduate Management Admissions Test Including Reading Comprehension, Verbal Ability, Writing Ability, Analysis of Business Situations, Mathematics & Problem Solving. Data Sufficiency Uses SCL to Customize Individual Study Plans. Provides Unlimited Drill & Focused Practice.
  Krell Software Corp.

GNU. *Customer Support:* All of our products are unconditionally guaranteed.
  Unix. CD-ROM disk $39.95 (Order no.: GNU). *Nonstandard peripherals required:* CD-ROM drive.
  250 MB of GNU Software for Unix for Both SunOS & Solaris.
  Walnut Creek CDRom.

Go Fish. *Compatible Hardware:* Apple II with Applesoft; IBM PC. *Language(s):* BASIC (source code included). *Memory Required:* 48k.
  disk $18.95.
  Classic Children's Card Game.
  Dynacomp, Inc.

Go4000 Advanced Computer Go. *Items Included:* Full manual. No other products required. *Customer Support:* Free telephone support - no time limit. 30 day warranty.
  MS-DOS 3.2 or higher. IBM & compatibles (512k). disk $29.95. *Optimal configuration:* IBM, MS-DOS 3.2 or higher, 512k RAM, & graphics capability.
  Advanced GO Player for the Thinking Person. You May Select Multiple Skill Levels, Choose Handicap Levels (Even or 2-9, Either Player), & Save/Reload Games in Progress. There Is Also a Set of Saved Championship Games for Tutorial Purposes. Included Are 12 Game Modules Which Implement over 30 Game Tactics for Beating the Human Player.
  Dynacomp, Inc.

Goal Rush. Version: 4.X. Don Cahill. Dec. 1995. *Customer Support:* Maintenance contract with free annual upgrade.
  MS-DOS. XT, AT, etc. (640k). $595.00 plus $59.00 each user kit (manual, Goal Mine Library, Prospector bk., disk); Spanish option $1250.00 additional (ISBN 0-941457-05-2). *Optimal configuration:* Printer.
  Macintosh 6.04. Mac Plus, SE, etc. (1Mb). $595.00 plus $59.00 each user kit (manual, Goal Mine Library, Prospector bk., disk); Spanish option $1250.00 additional (ISBN 0-941457-06-0). *Optimal configuration:* Printer.
  IEP Planners Can Prepare Pages of Learning Goals & Objectives for a Handicapped Student in Minutes. Thousands of Different Page Formats. Goals & Objectives Library on Disk Can Be Edited & Expanded. Progress Reports Keyed to IEP Objectives. Available in English & Spanish. Multi-User License Standard.
  IEP Pubs.

Goal Solutions. Version: 2.30. Dec. 1986. *Compatible Hardware:* IBM PC & compatibles. *Memory Required:* 64k. *General Requirements:* Lotus 1-2-3 Release 2 & 2.01, Symphony Releases 1, 1.01, 1.1, & 1.2.
  $99.95.
  Assists in the Decision-Making Process to Achieve As Many As 25 Specified Goals, Solving Them Simultaneously. Areas of Application Include Financial Analysis, Budget Planning, Marketing, & Personal Financial Planning.
  Enfin Software Corp.

Goal Solutions-Plus. Version: 2.30. Aug. 1987. *Compatible Hardware:* IBM PC & compatibles. *Memory Required:* 320k. *General Requirements:* Lotus 1-2-3 Releases 2 & 2.01, Symphony Releases 1, 1.01, 1.1, & 1.2.
  $195.00.
  Assists in the Decision-Making Process to Achieve As Many As 50 Goals with As Many As 50 Variables. Helps Assign Priorities to Conflicting Goals. Allows Hierarchical Budget Calculations with Proportional Allocation of Budget to Multiple Accounts. Performs Impact & Sensitivity Analyses with As Many As 25 Variables & Sorts Variables by Descending Impact & Sensitivity.
  Enfin Software Corp.

Goferwinkel's Adventure. Feb. 1995. *Items Included:* CD-ROM booklet. *Customer Support:* Free technical support via phone as of release date.
  MPC/Windows. 386.25 or higher IBM compatible (4Mb). CD-ROM disk $29.95 (ISBN 1-885784-04-X, Order no.: 1226). *Optimal configuration:* MPC CD-ROM player, S-VGA graphics card (640x480x256 colors) with compatible monitor, MPC compliant sound card, mouse, Windows 3.1.
  Macintosh. Macintosh (4Mb). CD-ROM disk $29.95 (ISBN 1-885784-27-9, Order no.: 1263). *Optimal configuration:* CD-ROM drive, color monitor with 256 plus colors, system version 6.07 or higher.
  Journey with Goferwinkel in His Exciting Comic Book Adventure. Help Him Restore Peace & Happiness in the Lavender Land As He Finds His Way Home. Give Advice When He Faces Perplexing Dilemmas! Goferwinkel's Adventure Offers a Fantasy World with Technological Twists & an Exciting Story That You Join Through Multimedia Interactivity.
  Technology Dynamics Corp.

GoFonts. *Items Included:* Disks, manual. *Customer Support:* Technical support by telephone: (619) 450-4600; FAX: (619) 450-9334; BBS (619) 450-9370.
  PC-DOS/MS-DOS (640k). IBM PC & compatibles. Write for info - Plus Collection (ISBN 1-878388-04-5). *Nonstandard peripherals required:* Hard disk.
  Write for info - Starter Collection (ISBN 1-878388-07-X).
  Write for info. Emphasis Collection (ISBN 1-878388-08-8).
  Write for info - Corporate I.D. Collection (ISBN 1-878388-09-6).
  Includes over 2000 PostScript Compatible Outline Intelligent Fonts That Can Be Installed in Word Processing & Desktop Publishing Programs. GoScript PostScript Language Interpreter Then Translates the Generated Print Files & Uses These Fonts to Print Them on Most Laser, Inkjet & Dot Matrix Printers.
  LaserGo, Inc.

Gold Dog Analysis. *Compatible Hardware:* Apple; Commodore 64; IBM; TRS-80, Color Computer; CP/M based machines.
  Apple. disk $149.95 (ISBN 1-55604-054-7).
  CP/M. disk $149.95 (ISBN 1-55604-055-5).
  IBM. disk $149.95 (ISBN 1-55604-058-X).
  Commodore. disk or cassette $149.95 (ISBN 1-55604-056-3).
  Color Computer. disk or cassette $149.95 (ISBN 1-55604-057-1).
  TRS-80. disk or cassette $149.95 (ISBN 1-55604-059-8).
  Professional Greyhound Analysis System Which Can Evaluate All Variables. Tracks Records & Kennel Ratings Are Maintained on a Data Base, Initializing the System for a Specific Track.
  Professor Jones Professional Handicapping Systems.

Gold Harness Handicapper. Ronald D. Jones. 1984. *Compatible Hardware:* Apple; Commodore; IBM; TRS-80 Model I, Model III, Color Computer. *Operating System(s) Required:* CP/M. *Memory Required:* 64k.
  disk $159.95 ea.
  Apple. (ISBN 1-55604-180-2, Order no.: T001).
  CP/M. (ISBN 1-55604-181-0, Order no.: T001).
  Commodore. (ISBN 1-55604-182-9, Order no.: T001).
  Color Computer. (ISBN 1-55604-183-7, Order no.: T001).
  IBM. (ISBN 1-55604-184-5, Order no.: T001).
  Model I & Model III. (ISBN 1-55604-185-3, Order no.: T001).
  Initialize the System with Track Records & Drivers & Trainers on Data Base System. Trotter/Pacer Analysis Is Designed to Evaluate All Relevant Variables & Give Accurate Prediction of the Finish. Serves to Eliminate False Favorites While Illustrating True Contenders. Also Features National Tracks with Variance Table on Data Base.
  Professor Jones Professional Handicapping Systems.

Gold Rush. Adrian Vance. Oct. 1985. *Compatible Hardware:* Apple II. *Operating System(s) Required:* Apple DOS. (source code included). *Memory Required:* 48k.
  disk $9.95 (ISBN 0-918547-26-1).
  illustration files on the disk avail.
  Simulates This Historical Event in Mid-19th Century America. Puts the Player in That Time Period with Decisions to Make & Things to Do. Not Copy Protected.
  AV Systems, Inc.

Golden Music. *Items Included:* Source code. *Customer Support:* Free by phone.
  Amiga DOS 1.2 or higher (512k). contact publisher for price. *Optimal configuration:* Standard Amiga with 512k RAM or more.
  Plays Music Based on the Golden Mean from Mathematics.
  Silver Software.

The Golden Pyramid. Aug. 1987. *Compatible Hardware:* Commodore Amiga. *Operating System(s) Required:* Workbench 1.2 or higher.

Memory Required: 512k.
3.5" disk $13.95.
Computer Game Show Complete with a Speaking Game Show Host. Tests Users' Knowledge of People, Places, Things, Song Titles, Nursery Rhymes, Characters, Phrases, Quotations, Movie Titles, etc. On-Screen Gadgets Control All Aspects of Game Play. The Host Utilizes a Random Speech Process to Insure Interesting Conversation Throughout the Game Play. For up to Five Players per Game. Free of Charge.
Micro Entertainment.

Golden Retriever 2.0. Version: 4.1. Compatible Hardware: IBM PC, PC AT, PC XT, & compatibles. Memory Required: 128k.
disk $99.00.
Document & Text Retrieval Program That Can Locate Exact Matches & Similar Text Patterns on a Hard Disk or Network Drives. No Indexing or Pre-Processing is Required.
SK Data, Inc.

The Golden Voyage. Compatible Hardware: TI 99/4A.
write for info. disk or cassette.
Texas Instruments, Personal Productivit.

Goldilocks Gamebook. Customer Support: Free, unlimited.
System 6 Mac. 030 Mac, 256 colors (4Mb). CD-ROM disk $24.95. Nonstandard peripherals required: Sound card, CD-ROM drive.
Windows 3.1 PC. 486 PC (4Mb). Nonstandard peripherals required: Any Windows supported sound card, CD-ROM drive.
Beautifully Illustrated & Animated, Interactive Version of the Classic Goldilocks & the Three Bears Story. Presents the Story in over 30 Interactive Screens. You Can Have the Story Read to You While You Watch the Bears Discover What Goldilocks Has Been up To. Or You Can Navigate Through the Story Yourself & Discover the World of Goldilocks. Throughout the Story You Can Also Choose to Play One of the Seventeen Separate Games That Relate to Specific Scenes & Encounters. Help Baby Bear Rebuild His Broken Chair, Help Randy Raccoon Decide Where to Plant His Trees or Help the Bears Clean up the Kitchen by Putting Their Porridge Bowls Away. Interactive Story & Educational Game Collection for Kids Ages 2 to 102.
BeachWare.

GoldMine. Version: 2.5.
Windows. Contact publisher for price.
Contact Management-Based Groupware for the Enterprise.
ELAN Software Corp.

Goldrunner II. Microdeal. Apr. 1988. Compatible Hardware: Atari ST. Memory Required: 512k.
3.5" disk $39.95.
Fifty Years Have Passed Since the Death of Earth & the Subsequent Exodus to the Ring Worlds of Triton. Defeated, the Few Hostile Piraes Who Remained Were Forced to Seek Refuge in Ancient Buildings with a Daring Surprise Attack They Have Captured Rescue the Defense Robots. Player Must All of the Robots & Save Humanity.
MichTron, Inc.

Goldspread Statistical. Items Included: Bound manual. Customer Support: Free hotline - no time limit; 30 day limited warranty; updates are $5/disk plus S&H.
MS-DOS 2.0 or higher. IBM & compatibles (384k). disk $79.95. Nonstandard peripherals required: Graphics capability (CGA, EGA, Hercules, or compatible); 80-column (or wider) printer for printed reports, or a dot matrix printer for printed reports & graphs (software will operate without a graphics card & printer, but graphics & printed reports will not be available).
Integrated System with Extensive Spreadsheet, Data Management, & Statistical Features. In Addition, GOLDSPREAD Can Read & Write Lotus 1-2-3 Files. It Includes All Lotus Functions, & Is Upwards Compatible with Lotus Commands. Also, GOLDSPREAD Macros Are a Superset of the Corresponding Lotus Macros.
Dynacomp, Inc.

GoldWorks II.
IBM PC & compatibles. disk $8900.00.
Macintosh II (8Mb). disk $7900.00. Nonstandard peripherals required: 15 Mb free disk space.
System Building Tool That Combines Windows with a Graphics Layout Tool, a Knowledge Representation System & a Menu Interface. Supports Integrated Forward & Backward Chaining for Large Production Applications. Also Interfaces to C, dBASE III, Lotus 1-2-3, Windows Draw, Hypercard & ASCII Formatted Disks.
Gold Hill, Inc.

Golf Classic-Battling Bugs. (Skillbuilders Ser.). William Kraus. 1982. Compatible Hardware: Apple II family. Operating System(s) Required: Apple DOS 3.3. Language(s): BASIC, Assembly. Memory Required: 48k. Items Included: Teacher's guide, reproducible worksheets. Customer Support: 800-Service.
disk $34.95 (ISBN 0-88335-362-8, Order no.: SMP02).
disk $49.95, incl. backup (Order no.: SMP02). $75.00 Lab pk. 5 add'l. copies of same disk.
GOLF - Up to Four Players Can Tee off for 18 Holes. Each Player Determines the Angle That the Golf Ball Should Be Hit & the Distance It Must Travel to the Hole. Comes in Two Apple Versions, 48k & 128k (Includes More Obstacles & Greater Challenges). BATTLING BUGS - A Row of "Negative" Bugs Faces a Row of "Positive" Bugs. The Two Rows March Toward Each Other until the Colliding Bugs Disappear. Players Must Add the Correct Number of Bugs to Each Row to Combat the Survivors.
Milliken Publishing Co.

Golf Handicapper: Slope Index System. Items Included: Bound manual. Customer Support: Free hotline - no time limit; 30 day limited warranty; updates are $5/disk plus S&H.
MS-DOS 2.0. IBM & compatibles (256k). disk $39.95. Nonstandard peripherals required: Two floppy disk drives (or one floppy & a hard disk); 80-column (or wider) printer.
Commodore 64. disk $39.95. Nonstandard peripherals required: Commodore 1525 (or compatible) printer.
Database Designed Specifically for Golfers. It Computes the Handicap Index for Each Player Based on the USGA Slope System. Records Are Easily Entered, Stored, Retrieved, & Edited.
Dynacomp, Inc.

Golf Handicapping. Version: 1.95. Compatible Hardware: PC/AT, PS/2. Operating System(s) Required: MS-DOS, XENIX, UNIX, Windows, NT. Language(s): Visual BASIC. Memory Required: 4000k. General Requirements: Hard disk. Customer Support: Toll free hotline. Contact publisher for price.
Allows Six Handicap Types, Including USGA, USGA Handicap Index & Trend Handicap. Score Entry Is Simple, Can Be Done by the Golfer or Golf Shop Staff, As Total Score or Hole-by-Hole. Automatically Adjusts for Equitable Stroke Control, Based on Golfer's Handicap. Hole-by-Hole Averages & Ringer Scores Maintained for Reference. Reports Include Individual Handicap Cards, Posting Sheets, Master Printouts, Monthly Summaries, Etcetera. Interfaces with COSMOS' Tournament Management System & Proshop Management System for Billing.
Cosmos International, Inc.

Golf Handicapping System. Version: 7.2. 1984. Compatible Hardware: Apple Macintosh, IBM PC & compatibles. Memory Required: 512k. General Requirements: Hard disk, high density floppy recommended. Items Included: Documentation, 3.5" or 5.25" program diskettes. Customer Support: Extended telephone support is available for a fee.
$125.00.
Calculates Slope on 18 Hole Basis Using USGA Rules. Handicap Cards Available. Current 1994 USGA Rules Dealing with Equitable Stroke Control & Tournament Rounds Included.
Lake Avenue Software.

Golf League Secretary. Sep. 1992. Items Included: User's guide. Customer Support: 800 phone number defect support.
MS-DOS 2.1 or higher (256k). IBM PC, PS/2 & MS-DOS compatibles. $44.95. Optimal configuration: MS-DOS Compatible w/256k, 1 diskette drive, printer.
Full Function Statistics Manager for All Sizes of Golf Leagues. Maintains Statistics on Teams & Individuals in 9 & 18 Hole Golf Leagues. Produces Weekly League Standings Sheets, Maintains Golfer Handicaps, Average Scores, Best & Worst Scores. Report May be Output to Screen or Attached Printer.
Mighty Byte Computer, Inc.

Golf Pro. Compatible Hardware: Atari 400, 800. Language(s): Atari BASIC (source code included). Memory Required: 48k. General Requirements: Joystick.
disk $21.95.
Golf Simulation.
Dynacomp, Inc.

Golf Resort Diskettes. Version: 2.01. May 1990. Items Included: User's guide. Customer Support: Telephone support: $2.00/min (Master Card, Visa).
MS-DOS/PC-DOS 2.0 or higher. IBM XT, AT, PS/2 (all models) & compatibles (512k). disk $12.50 (Order no.: RD).
Each Diskette Features Information from Major Golf Resort Areas Throughout the U.S. Including Descriptions of the Area, Major Resorts, & Courses. Highlighted Information Includes: Rates & Fees, Architects, Rankings, Golf Pro, & Electronic Scorecards. Data Sheets & Mailing Labels May Be Printed for Each Resort & Course. Additionally, Mailing Lists May Be Created.
Focus/2000, Inc.

Golf Simulation. Adrian Vance. Oct. 1985. Compatible Hardware: Apple II. Operating System(s) Required: Apple DOS. (source code included). Memory Required: 48k. Items Included: Miniature & regulation golf game simulations.
disk $9.95 (ISBN 0-918547-25-3).
illustration files on the disk avail.
Simulates a Golf Game to Teach Strategy & Club Selection Skills. Not Copy Protected.
AV Systems, Inc.

Golf the Series: The Full Swing. Nov. 1995. Customer Support: 60 Day Limited Warranty.
Windows. PC Compatible (4mg). CD-ROM disk $59.95 (ISBN 1-887209-30-1). Addl. software required: Windows 3.1. Optimal configuration: 80486/33 mhz PC with MPC compatible sound card, mouse, speakers, color VGA monitor, 8 Bit VGA adapter (256 colors), 4 MB Ram (8 MB or greater preferred), CD-ROM Drive, 6 MB or greater free disk space, MS DOS 5.0 or later & Windows 3.1.

TITLE INDEX

"The Full Swing" Is Your Own Interactive Instruction on CD-ROM. The Detailed Fundamentals & Mechanics Are Presented Using Photos, Images, Videos, Graphics, & Animation to Enhance the Actual Audio Lessons As They Are Being Presented. Gary Smith, Your Instructor, Is One of the Top Teaching Pros in the Nation.
Spirit of St. Louis Software Co.

Golf Time Reservation System. *Version:* 1.95. Jan. 1987. *Items Included:* Manuals. *Customer Support:* On-site training, 24 hour support line.
MS-DOS, Windows. 386, 100Mb hard drive (4Mb). Contact publisher for price. *Optimal configuration:* Pentium, 16Mb RAM, Windows, 200 plus Mb hard drive. *Networks supported:* Novell Netware, Netware Lite.
A Multi-National, Multi-Lingual, Multi-Currency Tee Reservation System for Use in the Golf Industry. Helps Manage the Play on a Single Course or for a Full, Regional Area. Provides Starter Sheets, Billing Reports, Sales Forecasts, Daily & Weekly Review, & Travel Agent Commissions.
Cosmos International, Inc.

Golf Tournament Management System.
Version: 1.95. Jan. 1984. *Items Included:* Software manual. *Customer Support:* 35-day, no-cost, toll-free support; annual support option; on-site training option..
MS-DOS, UNIX, XENIX, Windows, NT. PS/2 & compatibles (4Mb). Contact publisher for price. *Optimal configuration:* IBM compatible, ISA/EISA, 80386 with 4Mb RAM, Windows, Visual BASIC. *Networks supported:* Novell Netware.
SCO XENIX/UNIX, Windows, NT, MS-DOS. PS/2 (4Mb). Contact publisher for price. *Optimal configuration:* IBM compatible, ISA/EISA, 80386 with 4Mb RAM, SCO UNIX O/S or Windows.
MS-DOS, Windows, NT, XENIX, UNIX. Intel 386-486, Pentium (4Mb). Contact publisher for price. *Optimal configuration:* Pentium, Windows.
Establishes Tournaments with Teams of One to Five Golfers, Within the Teams, Better Balls of One, Two, Three, Four or Five May Be Used. Scoring Methods Include Match Play, Stroke, Stroke - Best Ball, Scramble, Pinehurst, Handiway. Uses USGA or Trend Handicap. Chicago (Quota) & Peoria. Team Pairings Can Be Computer-Generated, Based on Handicap, or Manual. Then Score Cards & Cart Cards Can Be Printed. Betting on the Tournament Can Include Parimutuel or Calcutta. Entry Fees, Big Skins & Cart Charges Can Be Tracked & Posted to the Club or Pro Shop Management Systems.
Cosmos International, Inc.

Golf Tournament Scoring. *Version:* 7.2. Jul. 1984. *Compatible Hardware:* IBM PC & compatibles, Apple Macintosh. *Operating System(s) Required:* PC-DOS, MS-DOS. *Language(s):* DBASE III Plus/dB IV, Fox BASE. *Memory Required:* 512k. *General Requirements:* Hard disk recommended. *Customer Support:* Extended telephone support available for $75/hour.
$125.00.
source code $200.00.
Processes Tournament Scores by Golfer for Generating Reports for Winners of Competition/Low Gross, Low Net, Partners Best Ball, Big Skins, Little Skins, Unlimited Partner's Competition. Includes Random Pairing (As Used in PGA ProAM Tournaments). Golfers Can Use a Handicap or Have Computer Calculate a Handicap Based on That Round (Calloway); Automatically Converts Slope Index to Handicap for Course Tournament Is Being Played On.
Lake Avenue Software.

Golfer's Database. *Compatible Hardware:* Atari 400, 800 with Atari BASIC. (source code included). *Memory Required:* 32k.
disk $29.95.
Designed to Keep Track of Golf Scores, Number of Putts, Greens Hit, Courses Played, Course Rating & Other Statistics.
Dynacomp, Inc.

GolfMaster/2000. *Version:* 2.01. Apr. 1990. *Items Included:* Spiral-bound user's guide, self training tutorial & tutorial data. *Customer Support:* Telephone support: $2.00/min (Master Card, Visa).
MS-DOS/PC-DOS 2.0 or higher. IBM XT, AT, PS/2 (all models) & compatibles (512k). disk $59.50 (Order no.: GM2000).
Calculate & Retain Golf Match Results for Day & Season. Match, Medal, & Quota Point Play. Automatic Presses, Skins, & Greenies. Computerized Scorecards Include Ratings & Slopes As Well As Hole-by-Hole Yardages, Par & Handicap Information for up to Three Sets of Tees. Golfer Handicapping per USGA Handicapping Manual & Procedures.
Focus/2000, Inc.

Goliath: Computer GO for the Macintosh. *Version:* 3.0. Jan. 1993. *Items Included:* User guide. *Customer Support:* Telephone customer support at no charge.
System 6.0 or higher. Macintosh (1Mb). 3.5" disk $59.95 (ISBN 0-923891-37-4, Order no.: GS24). *Optimal configuration:* 68030 CPU or higher, 2Mb RAM or higher.
Strongest Commercially Available GO Playing Program. Includes Multiple Difficulty Levels, 9-13-19 Line Boards, Handicap 2-9 Stones, Save/Restore Game, Optional Display of Tactical Analysis, Territory, Life & Death Status of Groups, & Ladders. Unlike Most Other Computer GO, Goliath Has a Good Sense of Shape & Rarely Makes a Big Mistake.
Ishi Press International.

Gomoku II. *Compatible Hardware:* Atari 400, 800. *Language(s):* Atari BASIC. *Memory Required:* 16k. *General Requirements:* Joystick.
disk $18.95.
Ancient Oriental Game.
Dynacomp, Inc.

Goodness-of-Fit. Sep. 1985. *Compatible Hardware:* IBM PC & compatibles, PC AT, PC XT. *Operating System(s) Required:* PC-DOS, MS-DOS, CP/M. *Language(s):* Compiled BASIC. *Memory Required:* 192k.
disk $195.00, incl. manual.
manual $35.00.
demo disk & manual $50.00.
Interactive Regression Package for Professional Researchers, Scientists, & Economists. Contains Multiple Regression, Probit Regression, Principal Components Analysis & Multicollinearity Diagnostics. Data Manager Contains Programs to Enter, Edit, Print, Merge, Transform, & Reformat Data Files. Files May Contain up to 30 Variables & 1000 Records. Transformations Can Be Performed Using Standard Algebraic Equations Including Special Commands for Trigonometric Functions, Differencing, Paging, Sorting, & Creating Dummy Variables. All Data Files (Including Residuals) Are Stored in Sequential ASCII Format & Are Compatible with Most Other Programs.
StatPac, Inc.

GoPAC Module (Graphical Online Public Access Catalog): Library Automation System. 1992. *Items Included:* 3 ring bound reference style manual, including a quick reference summary & diskette. *Customer Support:* Data Trek Inc. is a turn-key vendor supplying software, hardware, peripherals, hardware/software contracts, toll-free phone & Internet access to product support, installations, training, refresher training, user groups & bi-monthly technical newsletter.
Microsoft Windows 3.0 or higher, MS-DOS. 386SX or compatibles, VGA monitor (2Mb). 3.5" or 5.25" disk $495.00 (school discount, multiple purchase discount & GSA pricing available) (ISBN 0-929795-18-0). *Nonstandard peripherals required:* 1 floppy & 1 hard disk drive, printer. *Addl. software required:* Data Trek's Professional Series or Manager Series OPAC module, & Cataloging module. *Optimal configuration:* 486 computer, 4Mb RAM. *Networks supported:* Novell, IBM, Banyan, 3COM, PathWorks.
Combines the Latest Windows Technology with Data Trek's Innovative Searching Engine. Graphical Online Public Access Catalog Provides an OPAC That Is Simple to Use, Yet Powerful Enough for the Most Advanced Searcher. Unites the Features of Manager Series or Professional Series OPAC with Easy-to-Use, Point-and-Click Searching. As Items Are Checked in or Out, Manager Series or Professional Series OPAC (Required to use GoPAC) Shows Status Changes Immediately.
Data Trek, Inc.

GoScribe. *Items Included:* 5.25" or 3.50" diskettes, installation/operation pamphlet. *Customer Support:* Telephone customer support at no charge available M-F 9:00-5:00 Pacific time.
MS-DOS. IBM compatible (512k). $59.95 retail (ISBN 0-923891-22-6, Order no.: GS12). *Optimal configuration:* Supports EGA, CGA & Hercules graphics, mouse optional.
Program Records, Edits & Plays Back GO GAMES. Includes Complete Commenting Capabilities, Variations & Annotation. Construct Problems or Record Games for Later Study or Comment by a Stronger Player. User's PC Is the Platform for Playing Through Games Stone by Stone & Exploring Variations. Designed to Playback Our Pre-Recorded Game Collections.
Ishi Press International.

GoScript. *Version:* 4.0. Nov. 1991. *Items Included:* Disks, manual, license agreement. *Customer Support:* Technical support by telephone: (619) 450-4600; FAX: (619) 450-9334; BBS (619) 450-9370.
PC-DOS/MS/DOS (640k). IBM PC & compatibles. disk $149.00 (ISBN 1-878388-00-2). *Nonstandard peripherals required:* Hard disk.
PostScript Language Interpreter with 13 Scalable Fonts. Translates PostScript Text & Graphic Print Files Generated by Most Major Word Processing & Desktop Publishing Programs into a Form Most Printers (Laser, Inkjet & Dot Matrix) Can Print.
LaserGo, Inc.

GoScript Plus. *Version:* 4.0. Nov. 1991. *Items Included:* Disks, manual, license agreement. *Customer Support:* Technical support by telephone: (619) 450-4600; FAX: (619) 450-9334; BBS (619) 450-9370.
PC-DOS/MS-DOS (640k). IBM PC & compatibles. disk $299.00 (ISBN 1-878388-01-0). *Nonstandard peripherals required:* Hard disk.
Printing Utility Software for the IBM PC. PostScript Language Interpreter with 35 Scalable Fonts. Translates PostScript Text & Graphic Print Files Generated by Most Major Word Processing & Desktop Publishing Programs into a Form Most Laser, Inkjet, & Dot Matrix Printers Can Print.
LaserGo, Inc.

GoScript Select. Version: 4.0. Nov. 1991. Items Included: Manual, diskettes. Customer Support: Technical support by telephone: (619) 450-4600; FAX: (619) 450-9334; BBS (619) 450-9370. PC, MS-DOS 3.0 or higher. IBM PC/XT, AT, PS/2 & compatible (640k). disk $99.00 (ISBN 1-878388-10-X). Nonstandard peripherals required: Fixed disk.
Printing Utility Software for the IBM PC. PostScript Language Interpreter with 13 Scalable Fonts for Use with Hewlett-Packard LaserJet & Deskjet Printers. It Translates PostScript Print Files Generated by Most Major Word Processing & Desktop Publishing Programs into a Form the HP Printers Can Print.
LaserGo, Inc.

The Gourmet Computer Cookbook. Constance Curtin & Nolen Provenzano. 1988. Customer Support: ECS offers technical support to registered users. Call (217) 359-7099. Other than the telephone call - technical support is no charge.
DOS 3.3. Apple. disk $29.95 (Order no.: A-1226).
DOS 3.2 or higher. $29.95 single station/$150.00 network (Order no.: I-1226).
Contains Features Such As Print Outs of Ingredients, Procedures, & Shopping Lists, As Well As Recommendations of Substitutes for Hard-to-Find Ingredients. An Automatic Calculation Feature Calculates Ingredients Based on the Number of Servings Selected.
Electronic Courseware Systems, Inc.

Gourmet Gift Pack. 1995. Items Included: Operating manual. Customer Support: Free telephone technical support 1-800-850-7272. DOS 3.1, Windows 3.1; Macintosh. 33Mhz 80486DX, VGA video/display at 256 colors (4Mb); Macintosh, System 6.07, 68030 processor or higher (4Mb). CD-ROM disk Contact publisher for price (ISBN 1-884014-63-1). Nonstandard peripherals required: CD-ROM drive. Optimal configuration: 8Mb, Dual speed CD-ROM.
Multicom Publishing, Inc.

GPS-II (Graphics Printer Support). Version: 9.0. 1985. Compatible Hardware: IBM PC & compatibles. Operating System(s) Required: MS-DOS, PC-DOS 2.1 or higher. Memory Required: 512k. General Requirements: Hard disk, 132-column printer.
$495.00.
Converts Standard PMS-II & RMS-II Network Diagrams, Bar Charts, Graphs & Histograms into High Quality, Graphic Presentations, Without Expensive Mainframe/Plotters. Prints Diagrams, Graphs & Histograms Sideways & Provides a Time-Series, Zone Headed Network Diagram for Easy to Follow Network Logic on Many Dot Matrix Printers. Subsystem to PMS-II.
North America MICA, Inc.

GPSS/PC. Version: 2.0. May 1986. Compatible Hardware: IBM PC, PC XT, PC AT, PS/2 & compatibles. Operating System(s) Required: PC-DOS/MS-DOS 2.0 or higher. Memory Required: 512k. Items Included: 2 manuals, security software. Customer Support: 1 year free with telephone hotline (800 number).
$1495.00 economy version, incl. tutorial manual & reference manual.
$1995.00 full version.
EMS version $2400.00.
Full Powered Version of GPSS, the General Purpose Simulation System. Fully Interactive Allowing the User to Alter the Structure & Values Within a Running Simulation. Built-In Features Include Keystroke Error Prevention, Command Recognition & Automatic Spacing. Includes Animation of Simulations & 5 other Graphics Windows Through Which a Running Simulation Can Be Viewed. Also Includes Access to FORTRAN via HELP Blocks.
Minuteman Software.

GPSS/PC Animator. Version: 1.02. Nov. 1988. Compatible Hardware: IBM PC, PC XT, PC AT, PS/2. General Requirements: EGA with 256k, AutoCAD version 9 or 10; 640k RAM. Items Included: Manual & software. Customer Support: 1 year - no extra charge.
disk $995.00 (Order no.: 2009).
Works in Conjunction with AutoCAD to Produce a Realistic Animated View of a Simulation. This Software Is a Postprocessor to Enhance the 2D Character Graphic Animations Produced by the GPSS/PC Software Giving Them 3D Realism & Control Via AutoCAD.
Minuteman Software.

Grade Out Analysis. 1982. Compatible Hardware: IBM PC & compatibles. Operating System(s) Required: MS-DOS 3.0 or higher. Language(s): BASIC (source code included). Memory Required: 256k. Customer Support: Telephone.
disk $30.00.
Enter Gradeouts for Life of the Flock, Program Prints Them out & Accumulates Percent by Gradeout Category.
Locus Systems.

Grade Reporting System. Version: 8.01. 1981. Items Included: 1 full manual. Customer Support: 90 days unlimited warranty; unlimited technical support via telephone for $225/system per year. MS-DOS. IBM or compatible (640k). disk $995.00. Optimal configuration: MS-DOS 6.2 or higher, 15Mb including data, of space on a hard drive (to include all 5 systems). Networks supported: Novell, LANtastic, Windows NT.
This System Enters Student Grade Data Using an Optical Scanner or Keyboard, Then Produces a Multi-Copy Scholarship Report Complete with Parent Name & Address, Thus Facilitating Mailing If Necessary. Daily Attendance Information Is Automatically Transferred to Be Printed on Final Reports. Transcripts & a Variety of Other Reports May Be Printed.
Applied Educational Systems, Inc.

GRAF-X Plus. Feb. 1987. Items Included: 3 manuals, 3 diskettes. Customer Support: 1 year free phone support, 1 year maintenance $500.00.
DOS 3.3. 80286 w/coprocessor, EGA, 7Mb HD, HD Floppy (1Mb). disk $9995.00 (ISBN 1-887777-08-3). Optimal configuration: 486, 4Mb RAM, DOS 6.X, VGA, 15"-17" monitor, laser printer, dual monochrome monitor.
An Advanced CAM System. Part Geometry, Toolpath & Machining Parameters Are Described in GRAFX Language & Are Graphically Displayed (the System Allows Interactive Editing). G-Code Is Produced Using Post Processors, Then Downloaded Through the DNC Communications Module to Machine, Tape, etc. It Includes a User-Modifiable Macro Library, Full Logic (Looping, Branching, Subroutines) & True Family of Parts Capability.
Datacut, Inc.

Grafeas. Version: 3.1. May 1991. Compatible Hardware: IBM PC & compatibles. Memory Required: 512k. Customer Support: One month free support.
disk $399.00.
Multilingual Word Processing Package (24 Languages Available) with ASCII Import/Export Capabilities. Features UNDO Command & Outlining Capabilities. Allows User to Simultaneously Edit 2 Files. Mail/Merge Capabilities Include Sorting & Selecting.
Apollon Engineering, Inc.

Grafix. Compatible Hardware: TRS-80 Model I with Level II BASIC. Memory Required: 16k. disk $19.95.
Draw Graphics with Cursor & Save As a String Variable in BASIC Program.
Dynacomp, Inc.

GRAFX II. Feb. 1990. Items Included: 2 manuals, 3 diskettes. Customer Support: 1 year free phone support, 1 year maintenance $500.00.
DOS 3.3. 80286 w/coprocessor, EGA, 7Mb HD, HD Floppy (2Mb). disk $4995.00 (ISBN 1-887777-04-0). Nonstandard peripherals required: Mouse. Optimal configuration: 486, 4Mb RAM, DOS 6.X, VGA, 15"-17" monitor, laser printer.
An NC/CAD/CAM System Incorporating an Advanced, Easy to Use, Graphic User Interface. Geometry Is Created Using the Full-Featured, Integrated CAD Front End. Machining Parameters Are Accessed & ToolPath Generated in the CAM Module. G-Code Is Produced Using Post Processors, Then Downloaded Through the DNC Communication Module Directly to Machine, Tape, etc.
Datacut, Inc.

GRAFX II: Limited Edition. May 1994. Items Included: 2 manuals, 3 diskettes. Customer Support: 60 day free phone support, 1 year maintenance $500.00.
DOS 3.3. 80286 w/coprocessor, EGA, 7Mb HD, HD Floppy (2Mb). disk $1495.00 (ISBN 1-887777-06-7). Nonstandard peripherals required: Mouse. Optimal configuration: 486, 4Mb RAM, DOS 6.X, VGA, 15"-17" monitor, laser printer.
An NC/CAD/CAM System Incorporating an Advanced, Easy to Use, Graphic User Interface. Geometry Is Created Using the Full-Featured, Integrated CAD Front End. Machining Parameters Are Accessed & ToolPath Generated in the CAM Module. G-Code Is Produced Using Post Processors, Then Downloaded Through the DNC Communication Module Directly to Machine, Tape, etc.
Datacut, Inc.

Grain Clerk. Items Included: Grain Clerk operators manual, communications software. Customer Support: 60 days free customer support, 1 yr. maintenance, $600.00, 60 days limited warranty, phone modem & telephone support, training available.
MS-DOS, OS/2 (640k). IBM PC or compatible. disk $6500.00. Optimal configuration: MS-DOS 3.3 or higher, 60Mb hard drive, 20 MGHz, 386 processor/486 processor. Networks supported: Novel Netware.
MS-DOS 3.3 or higher (512k). IBM XT or compatible. contact publisher for price. Nonstandard peripherals required: 30Mb hard drive, 2400 Baud Modem.
A Complete Grain Accounting System That Tracks Grain from the Time of Contract, Thru Delivery, Storage & Settlement. Storage & Discounts Are Automatically Calculated & Subtracted from the Settlement & Checks. Complete Reporting Functions Including: Contract Reporting, Settlements, Daily Position Reports, Customer History & Hedge Reporting.
Vertical Software, Inc.

GrainTrac. Version: 4.1. Jun. 1989. Compatible Hardware: IBM PC. Operating System(s) Required: PC-DOS. Language(s): Compiled BASIC. Memory Required: 640k. Items Included: GrainTrac manual, communications software. Customer Support: On-site installation & training is available; Telemodem & telephone support.
disk $9500.00.
Commodity Accounting Program for Commodity Traders, Elevators, Flour Millers, Co-Ops, River Terminals, & Sub-Terminals.
Vertical Software, Inc.

TITLE INDEX

The Grammar of Ornament, Compact Edition.
Bruce D. Hubbard et al. Nov. 1995. *Items Included:* Extensive color manual, color guide to the 2,300 designs in the CD. *Customer Support:* Installation & operation suppmts. provided free M-F 9-5, PST. CD has an unlimited warranty. 20% restocking fee is charged for damaged returns. Wholesale, retail, mail-order & site license discounts available.
Mac OS 7.0 or higher. Macintosh II (3Mb). CD-ROM disk $99.00 (ISBN 1-887721-00-2). *Nonstandard peripherals required:* 16 bit graphics controller card, 1x CD-ROM, 15" color display, 4Mb hard disk space. *Optimal configuration:* 24 bit graphics controller card, 17 or 19" color display, 8Mb application RAM, 2x CD-ROM.
Windows 3.1, Windows 95. IBM PC & compatibles (4Mb). CD-ROM disk $99.00. *Nonstandard peripherals required:* 16 bit graphics controller card, 1x CD-ROM, 15" color display, 4Mb hard disk space. *Optimal configuration:* 24 bit graphics controller card, 2x CD-ROM, 8Mb application RAM, 17 or 19" color display.
This Beautiful Reproduction of the 1865 Quarto Edition on CD-ROM Features 2,300 Designs from Cultures & Epocs Worldwide. The Text & Art Are Hyper-Linked Together & May Be Freely Copied. Elegantly Packaged, It Includes an Extensive Color User Manual & a Design Guide. For Windows & Mac.
Direct Imagination.

The Grammar of Ornament, Professional Artist's Edition. Bruce D. Hubbard et al. Nov. 1995. *Items Included:* Extensive user guide, color guide to all 3,000 plus designs on the CD, color guide to EPS designs. *Customer Support:* Installation & operation suppmts. provided free M-F 9-5, PST. CD has an unlimited warranty. 20% restocking fee is charged for damaged returns. Wholesale, retail, mail-order & site license discounts available.
Mac OS 7.0 or higher. Macintosh II (3Mb). 3.5" disk $199.00 (ISBN 1-887721-01-0). *Nonstandard peripherals required:* 16 bit graphics controller card, 1x CD-ROM, 15" color display, 4Mb hard disk space. *Optimal configuration:* 24 bit graphics controller card, 17 or 19" color display, 8Mb application RAM, 2x CD-ROM.
Windows 3.1, Windows 95. IBM PC & compatibles, 33MHz 486 (4Mb). disk $199.00. *Nonstandard peripherals required:* 16 bit graphics controller card, 1x CD-ROM, 15" color display, 4Mb hard disk space. *Optimal configuration:* 24 bit graphics controller card, 2x CD-ROM, 17 or 19" color display, 66MHz 486 or higher.
Based on the Masterpiece of All Chromolithographic Books, the CD Has over 3,000 Designs from Cultures Worldwide. The Text & Designs (Folio Edition, High Resolution Scans) Are Hyper-Linked Together. 160 Designs Are Available in EPS for Immediate Use. Includes Extensive User Manual, a Complete Design Guide & an EPS Design Guide.
Direct Imagination.

Grammatik. *Version:* 5. Reference Software International Staff. 1992. *Items Included:* License, user's guide, rule designer guide, network admin. guide, quick reference card, disks. *Customer Support:* Free support at Toll Number: DOS 801-228-9918, Windows 801-228-9919, Macintosh 801-228-9917.
DOS 3.0 or higher. IBM PC & compatibles (640k). $99.00 SRP. *Optimal configuration:* 1.6Mb hard disk space required, 286 or higher. *Networks supported:* Network ready.
Windows 3.0 or higher & DOS 3.1. IBM PC & compatibles (286 or higher) (2Mb). $99.00 SRP. *Optimal configuration:* 286 or higher computer, mouse, hard disk, 2.2Mb of hard disk space required. *Networks supported:* Network ready.
Macintosh System 6.0.3 or higher. Mac Plus or higher (2Mb). $99.00 SRP. *Optimal configuration:* 2Mb of hard disk space required. *Networks supported:* Network ready.
Proofreads Writing for Thousands of Errors in Grammar, Style, Spelling, Usage, & Punctuation. The Program Highlights Errors, Offers Advice, & Lets Users Make Corrections Instantly. Users May Choose from One of Ten Writing Styles or Customize Grammatik to Fit the User's Personal Writing Needs.
WordPerfect Corp.

Grammatik Mac. *Version:* 2.0. *Customer Support:* 30 day money back guarantee.
3.5" disk $50.00.
Will Bail User Out of any Grammatical Error. Can Detect Thousands of Grammar, Style, Usage, Punctuation, & Spelling Errors. Tells the Problem(s), & Suggest the Correction(s). New Features Include Additional Customizing Options & Support for Networks & Color Monitors.
Reference Software International.

Grammatik UNIX. *Version:* 1.0. *Items Included:* Manual.
UNIX/SCO Xenix. SCO Xenix 286/386 SCO Unix System V/386 (1.2Mb). $495.00 multi-user only. *Addl. software required:* word processor.
Grammar & Style Checker for SCO Xenix/UNIX System V, Proofreads Your Writing for Thousands of Errors in Grammar, Style, Usage, Punctuation, & Spelling. Provides Direct Support for Microsoft Word, WordPerfect, SCO Lyrix, & Troff/Nroff Style Files.
Reference Software International.

Grammatik V. *Version:* 2.0. Jul. 1988. *Compatible Hardware:* IBM PC, PC AT, PC XT, PS/2. *Operating System(s) Required:* PC-DOS/MS-DOS. *Memory Required:* 512k. *General Requirements:* Hard disk. *Customer Support:* 30 day money back guarantee, free technical support to all registered users.
disk $90.00.
Provides Proofreading for Errors in Grammar, Style, Usage, Spelling, & Punctuation. Interactive Showing of Suspected Problems, Offers Suggestions for Improvements, & Edits Document Immediately. Can Detect Errors Such As: Incomplete Sentences, Subject/Verb Agreement Problems, Incorrect Word Usage, Double Negatives, Incorrect Possessives, Split Infinitives & Transposed Letters.
Reference Software International.

Grammatik Windows 2.0. *Version:* 2,0. Apr. 1991. *Items Included:* manual. *Customer Support:* free technical support for all registered users; 30 day money back guarantee.
Microsoft Windows. IBM compatible (1Mb). $99.00 single; $245.00 multi-user. *Addl. software required:* DOS, word processor. *Networks supported:* All networks that use file-locking, ie Novell, 3Com, Banyan Vines etc.
Grammar & Style Checker for Microsoft Windows, Proofreads Your Writing for Thousands of Errors in Grammar, Style, Spelling, Usage, & Punctuation. Works from Within Three Windows Word Processors & Provides Direct Support for Numerous Windows & DOS- Based Word Processor.
Reference Software International.

Grand Prix Circuit. *Customer Support:* 90 day warranty, phone: (408) 296-8400 hrs: M-F 8-5 pm.
PC-DOS 2.1 or higher; Tandy-DOS. IBM PC with CGA/Hercules (384k), IBM with EGA/Tandy 16 color (512k). $24.95.
Commodore (64k). $29.95.
Amiga-Kickstart 1.2 or 1.3 (512k). $24.95.
Apple IIGs, 512k, ProDOS 16. disk $44.95.
Macintosh 512k, 512ke, Plus, SE, II. 3.5" disk $49.95.
Experience the Power & Glamour of Racing Formula One Cars on the Grand Prix Circuit. Climb into the Cramped Quarters of a Formula One Race Car As You Compete Against World-Class Drivers on the Official Grand Prix Circuit. The Actual Grand Prix Circuit Tracks Await You - Each with Its Own Overpasses, Treacherous Tunnels, Snake-Like Curves & Corners, & Pulse Pounding Pit Stops. Rack up Enough Points on the Circuit & You'll Become the World's Best Driver.
Accolade, Inc.

Grand Slam Bridge.
IBM. disk $59.95.
Features Computer Plays With Cue Bids, Weak 2 Bids, 5 Card Majors, Blackwood, Stayman, Gerber, PreEmpts, etc. Hands Can Be Saved for Future Replay. Will Deal Random Hands or Users Can Design Their Own. The Computer Will Provide Bid & Play Hints. Any Combination of Computer & People Can Play. Features Realistic Card Table Display.
Electronic Arts.

Grandmaster Championship Chess. Jun. 1995. *Items Included:* Manual, catalog. *Customer Support:* Tech support - customer pays for call.
Windows. IBM 386/33 PC or compatible, 486 recommended (4Mb); partial install w/1Mb hard drive, DOS 5.0). CD-ROM disk $44.00 (ISBN 1-57519-010-9). *Addl. software required:* CD-ROM player (double speed drive recommended) & software. *Optimal configuration:* VGA, SVGA, 256 color recommended. Mouse required, Sound Blaster, AdLib, General MIDI & any Windows compatible card. *Networks supported:* Mode/Network.
Macintosh. System 7.0 or higher (4Mb, 1Mb hard drive space for optimal install). CD-ROM disk $44.00. *Addl. software required:* CD-ROM double speed drive. *Optimal configuration:* Sound Manager 2.0 (for music).
Designed to Include Features Which Will Appeal to Both the Novice & Experienced Player Feature Set Includes: a Powerful New Engine Animated Tutorials & Network & Modem Play. Multiple Boards & Chess Sets & a Selection of MIDF Music.
IntraCorp/Capstone.

GrandView. *Version:* 2.0. *Compatible Hardware:* IBM PC & compatibles. *Operating System(s) Required:* PC-DOS/MS-DOS 2.0 or higher. *Memory Required:* 256k. *Items Included:* full retail, 3 disks, 2 manuals.
disk $147.50.
Uses Outline Structure As its Basic Format for Entering & Organizing Information. Features Include After-theFact Category Assignments, Multiple Windows, & Macros.
Symantec Corp.

Grantmaster. *Version:* 1.1. *Items Included:* Documentation in 3-ring manual. *Customer Support:* 800 number, user group, documentation, updates.
DOS, UNIX, XENIX, Novell, AIX, SunOS. MOTO680X0, ATT, IBM RS/6000, NCR, UNISYS, INTEL 80X80. Contact publisher for price. *Addl. software required:* Donormaster II. *Networks supported:* Most LAN environments.
Complete Software System for Managing the Grant Making Process. Tracks Grant Applications from Date of Receipt Throughout the Evaluations

Process, & Provides Easy Status Reports along the Way. Once a Grant Is Approved, the System Will Schedule & Track Payments Due, Providing Cash Flow Projections, Compliance Requirements, Past Due Payments, & More. An Interface to Word Processing Is Standard, So Communications to Any Segment of the Database Is Quick & Easy. Designed to Organize & Simplify the Entire Grant Management Process, Enabling Foundation Managers to Focus on Their Mission, Not Paperwork & Administration Details.
Master Systems.

Grants: Financial Grant Management Forms. *Version:* 1.1. Feb. 1992. *Items Included:* 1 bound manual. *Customer Support:* Free.
MS-DOS 3.0. IBM PC (512k). disk $295.00. *Nonstandard peripherals required:* Hewlett-Packard LaserJet Series II or III or compatible. *Addl. software required:* WordPerfect DOS 5.1. *Networks supported:* All.
Six Financial Federal Grant Management Forms Developed in WordPerfect 5.1, Which May Be Retrieved, "Filled in" & Then Printed on an HP II/III or Compatible Laser Printer. All Columnar Math Functions Accomplished Automatically. The Forms May Be Readily Modified to Conform to Government Changes.
Top Banana, Inc.

Grantseeker's F.I.N.D: Florida Information Network Database. *Version:* 2.5. Jan. 1996. *Items Included:* One spiral-bound manual, one mid-year data update, free customer support. *Customer Support:* 30 day limited warranty, unlimited phone support, limited on-site training. 5 dollars for demo. diskette. DOS based. 80286, IBM-PC. disk $395.00. *Nonstandard peripherals required:* Laserjet & printer, EGA video system, h.d. floppy drive (640k) 7 Mb free hard disk space.
F.I.N.D. is The Tool for grant searching. This comprehensive program includes detailed profiles of over 3,500 federal, state & private grant programs available for grantseekers. It drastically reduces research time & allows the user to take full advantage of a wide-range of available grant programs.
Florida Funding Publications.

Graph-in-the-Box Executive. *Version:* 1.17. Jan. 1990. *Items Included:* Documentation, manual & Getting Started Booklet. *Customer Support:* Free technical support.
MS-DOS 2.0 or higher. IBM PC/AT, PS/2 or compatibles. 3.5" & 5.25" disk $299.95.
Memory-Resident Program That Captures Data & Text Directly from the Screen of Virtually Any Software Program, Then Manipulates, Displays & Prints it As a Graph or Chart. Features Include Bar, Pie, Organizational Charts, & 57 Data-Manipulation Functions.
New England Software, Inc.

Graph-in-the-Box Executive: Professional Graphics & Charting. 1995. *Items Included:* Full manual. *Customer Support:* Free telephone support - 90 days, 30-day warranty.
MS-DOS 3.2 or higher. 286 (584k). disk $269.95. *Nonstandard peripherals required:* CGA/EGA/VGA.
demo disk $5.00.
An Advanced Outgrowth of the Original GRAPH-IN-THE-BOX, Which More Than 300,000 People Are Currently Using. It Has Been Called "The World's Most User-Friendly Program" by Personal Computing Magazine. This Endorsement Is Important to Remember So That You Will Not Be Frightened by the EXECUTIVE's Wide Array of Features. Here Is a Partial List of Those Features: 15 Different Chart Types - Line; Line Area; Step; Step Area; Scatter; Vertical Bars; Horizontal Bars (Normal Overlapped, Paired, Cluster); Trend Lines (Polynomial, Logarithmic, Exponential); Spline, Hi-Low; Mixed; Pie; Linked Pie; XY; Text Charts; Organizational Charts. Large Data Matrix - 15 Variables, 500 Points per Variable (up to 1000 Points Total). Flexible Data Entry - from Keyboard; from ASCII, DIF, GIX, GIB, & GIA Files; Capture Data & Text Produced on the Screen from Other Software.
Dynacomp, Inc.

Graph-in-the-Box Release 2. *Version:* 2.2. Nov. 1988. *Compatible Hardware:* IBM PC, PC XT, PC AT, 3270 PC, PS/2, true compatibles. *Operating System(s) Required:* MS-DOS 2.0 or higher. *Memory Required:* 128k. *General Requirements:* Math co-processor; CGA, EGA, VGA, MCGA, & Hercules cards supported. *Items Included:* Documentation. *Customer Support:* Free technical support.
disk $139.95, incl. user's guide (ISBN 0-945830-00-9).
Memory-Resident Graphics Program. To Create a Graph, User Runs Cursor over the On-Screen Data & Chooses from Column, Bar, Pie, Scatter, Filled/Not Filled, Stacked/Not Stacked, Colors, & Textures. Graphs Can Be Printed on Any Popular Dot Matrix Printer As Well As HP Plotters, Laserjet Printers & Compatibles. Release 2 Adds Features Such As Full Page Printout, Multiple Charts per Page, Batch Printing, File Merge, Slide Show Presentation. Creates HPGL & PostScript Files. Compatible with VENTURA PUBLISHER & PAGEMAKER. Not Copy Protected. Can Be Run Non-Resident.
New England Software, Inc.

Graph Master (IBM). Jun. 1987. *Compatible Hardware:* IBM PC & compatibles. *Memory Required:* 256k. *General Requirements:* CGA, EGA, or VGA card.
disk $39.95.
Translates Data & Ideas into Graphs & Pictures. Produces Text, Bar, Line, Area, Up-Down, Scatter, Regression, & Freehand Charts or Graphs. Features Complete Graphic & Data Editing Involving Text Insertion, Lines, Circles, Boxes, Copy/Move, Multiple Fonts, Fill Patterns, Pixel Editing, etc. Plots Math Functions. Allows Control over Titles, Subtitles, Footnotes, Legends, Labels, Grid Lines, Scaling. Output to Dot-Matrix or Laser Jet Printer or Disk. Also Performs Statistical Analysis.
Bridget Software Co.

Graph Scientific Plotting & Data Transformation. *Items Included:* Bound manual. *Customer Support:* Free hotline - no time limit; 30 day limited warranty; updates are $5/disk plus S&H.
MS-DOS 3.1 or higher. IBM & compatibles (640k). disk $139.95. *Nonstandard peripherals required:* Two floppy disk drives (or one floppy & a hard disk); graphics capability; almost all dot matrix printers are supported.
Package for Preparing Publication-Quality X-Y Plots. Data May Be Entered from the Keyboard or a Data File, Plotted on Screen, Edited, Transformed, Annotated, Archived, & Reproduced in High Resolution on Almost All Dot Matrix Printers (Including PostScript Printers & HPGL Plotters).
Dynacomp, Inc.

Graph Scientific Plotting & Data Transformation. *Items Included:* Full manual. No other products required. *Customer Support:* Free telephone support - no time limit. 30 day warranty.
MS-DOS 3.2 or higher. IBM & compatibles (512k). disk $139.95.
Low-Cost Package for Preparing Publication-Quality X-Y Plots. Data May Be Entered from the Keyboard or a Data File, Plotted on Screen, Edited, Transformed, Annotated, Archived, & Reproduced in High Resolution on Almost All Dot Matrix Printers (Including PostScript Printers & HPGL Plotters). Transformation Operations Include Log, Exp, Reciprocal, Square, Square-Root, Addition, Multiplication, Division, As Well As Integration or Differentiation of Calculated Curves. Transformations May Be Cascaded.
Dynacomp, Inc.

Graphic Analysis Package. 1982. *Compatible Hardware:* IBM PC, PC XT & compatibles. *Operating System(s) Required:* PC-DOS, MS-DOS. *Language(s):* BASIC (source code included). *Memory Required:* 256k.
disk $450.00.
Becomes an Electronic Planimeter When Used with Any GTCO DIGI-PAD. Areas of Irregular Polygons, Perimeters & Distances Can Be Measured.
GTCO Corp.

The Graphic Exchange. *Compatible Hardware:* Apple IIgs. *Operating System(s) Required:* ProDOS 8. *Memory Required:* 768k.
3.5" disk $49.95 (ISBN 0-927796-37-6, Order no.: 271).
Users Can Pass Virtually Any Apple II Graphics Image Between Different Application Programs. Allows Users to Take a PRINT SHOP Graphic & Convert It to a Super Hi-Res Image. Newsroom Art Can Be Used in DAZZLE DRAW & MACPAINT Disks Can be Used As a Source of Clip Art.
Roger Wagner Publishing, Inc.

The Graphic Programmer. Adrian Vance. Feb. 1984. *Compatible Hardware:* Apple II, II+, IIe, IIc. *Operating System(s) Required:* Apple DOS. *Language(s):* Applesoft BASIC (source code included). *Memory Required:* 48k.
disk $19.95, incl. manual & audio cassette tutorial (ISBN 0-918547-02-4).
Course in Graphic Programming. Programs Include a Shape Table Writer, Graphing Systems, 3D Simulating/Translating Techniques & Systems, & Automatic Drawing. Most Routines Are Plotting, Graphing & Drawing Routines for Teaching at Any Level. All Programs Are Linear, Modular, Listable, Modifiable & Copyable.
AV Systems, Inc.

Graphic Screen Print Program: GSPR. *Compatible Hardware:* TRS-80 Color Computer with dot matrix printer. *Language(s):* Extended Color BASIC, Machine. *Memory Required:* 16k.
line printer $7.95.
Non-Radio Shack Printers or DMP 110/120. $9.95.
Takes Graphics Screen Developed with BASIC Program & Dumps to Printer. Screen Image May Be Shifted Right or Left, Print Normal or Reverse.
Custom Software Engineering, Inc.

Graphical Analysis. *Version:* MS-DOS. 1988. *Items Included:* 40-page manual. *Customer Support:* Telephone support; newsletter.
MS-DOS. IBM compatible, XT, AT, PS/2 (320k). disk $39.95 (ISBN 0-918731-25-9, order no.: GA-IBM). *Nonstandard peripherals required:* CGA or Hercules Graphics. *Optimal configuration:* 320k RAM.
Plots Well-Labeled Graphs of Experimental Data. After Data Is Entered, Modified Versions of the Graph (e.g., with the X-Axis Data Squared Before Plotting) May Be Quickly Drawn to Help in the Search for the Relationship Between the Variables. Semi-Log & Log-Log Graphs Can Be Made. The Linear Regression "Best Fit" Line Can Be Included on the Graph. Graphs May Be Printed. Data Files Created Can Be Transferred to & from Lotus 1-2-3 or Microsoft Works.
Vernier Software.

TITLE INDEX

Graphical Analysis III. David L. Vernier. 1986-1988. *Compatible Hardware:* Apple II+, IIe, IIc, IIgs; IBM PC PC XT PC AT PS/2. *Operating System(s) Required:* Apple ProDOS, MS-DOS. *Memory Required:* Apple 64k, IBM 256k. *General Requirements:* CGA card (IBM only). Apple. disk $29.95 (ISBN 0-918731-17-8). IBM. disk $29.95 (ISBN 0-918731-25-9).
Plots Well-Labeled Graphs of Experimental Data. After Data Is Entered, Modified Versions of the Graph (e.g., with the X-Axis Data Squared Before Plotting) May Be Drawn to Help in the Search for the Relationship Between the Variables. Semi-Log & Log-Log Graphs Can Be Made. The Linear Regression "Best Fit" Line Can Be Included on the Graph. Data Tables May Be Edited, Printed, or Saved on Diskette. Copies of the Graphs May Be Made on a Printer. Compatible with AppleWorks.
Vernier Software.

Graphical Approaches to Multivariate Data Analysis. Bruce E. Trumbo. 1985. *Compatible Hardware:* Apple II+, IIe, IIc. *Operating System(s) Required:* Apple DOS 3.3. *Language(s):* BASIC. *Memory Required:* 48k. disk $50.00 (ISBN 0-933694-34-2, Order no.: COM 3104A).
COMPress.

Graphical Regression Analysis. Version: 3. Sep. 1995. *Compatible Hardware:* IBM PC; Apple II. *Operating System(s) Required:* DOS 3.1. *Language(s):* GWBASIC, BASICA. *Memory Required:* 16k. disk $30.00.
Graphics Program That Performs Univariate Regression Analysis. Displays the Resulting Scatter Plot & Regression Line. Allows for Editing of Data to See Effects of Changes on the Line, the Correlation Coefficient & the Standard Error of the Estimate.
MatheGraphics Software.

Graphics Are Easy. John Brewer. 1984. *Items Included:* Installation instruction, reference, & teacher's cards. *Customer Support:* ECS offers technical support to registered users. Call (217) 359-7099. Other than the telephone call - technical support is no charge.
DOS 3.2 or higher. IBM. disk $99.95 (Order no.: I-1229).
An Introductory Graphics Programming Course Using BASIC & the IBM-PC, TANDY PC, or PC-Compatibles. The Program Presents All of the Graphics Statements & Techniques for Their Use. An Electronic Bookmark Records Progress & Provides Quick Access to Where Each User Was in the Program. The Program Consists of Three Diskettes: PROGRAM, SUPPORT, & GAME & Three User CARDS.
Electronic Courseware Systems, Inc.

Graphics BASIC. *Customer Support:* 800-929-8117 (customer service).
MS-DOS. Commodore 64. disk $49.99 (ISBN 0-87007-843-7).
Enhances User's Commodore 64's BASIC with Additional Graphics, Sprites, Sound, Animation & Utility Commands Using Easy to Understand English Words. Features Include: High Resolution Commands--HIRES, MULTI, DOT, LINE, BOX, CIRCLE, FILL & SCALE. Built-In Sprite Editor with Over 20 Commands. Interrupt Driven Precision Provides "Invisible" Background Operation. 1 to 3 Voice Fully Automated Background Sound. 4 Waveforms to VIC 1525 Printer. Programmable Function Keys. Disk or Cassette Interface. Joystick Control. Scroll & Roll Screen in any Direction. Error Detection & More. Manual Included.
SourceView Software International.

Graphics Charts & Graphs. Rick Frye. disk $14.80, incl. 160p. text (ISBN 0-929321-20-0).
WEKA Publishing, Inc.

Graphics Conversion & Printing Utilities. *Items Included:* Full manual. No other products required. *Customer Support:* Free telephone support - no time limit. 30 day warranty.
MS-DOS 3.2 or higher. IBM & compatibles (512k). two disks $19.95.
This Set of Utilities Is Aimed Specifically at Converting Between Different Pictorial File Formats, Viewing, & Transforming Graphics Files into Halftone & Dithered B&W Formats for Printing. Depending on the File Size, 512K to 640K Is Required.
Dynacomp, Inc.

Graphics Conversion & Printing Utilities. 1992. *Items Included:* Detailed manuals included with all Dynacomp products. *Customer Support:* Free telephone support to original customer - no time limit; 30 day limited warranty.
MS-DOS 3.2 or higher. IBM PC & compatibles (512k). $19.95 2 disks (Add $5.00 for 3 1/2" format; 5 1/4" format standard).
This Set of Utilities Is Aimed Specifically at Converting Between Different Pictorial File Formats, Viewing, & Transforming Graphics Files into Halftone & Dithered B & W Formats for Printing. Depending on the File Size, 512K to 640K Is Required. Included Is a 40-Page Manual.
Dynacomp, Inc.

Graphics Converter Gold for Windows. Mar. 1995. *Items Included:* Users Guide, ClipArt images on CD-ROM. *Customer Support:* Tech support 60-day money-back guarantee.
Windows 3.1 or higher. IBM PC & compatibles. disk $69.95 (ISBN 0-924677-31-7). *Optimal configuration:* 4Mb RAM, 6Mb hard disk space. *Networks supported:* Netware, MS Workgroups.
Comprehensive File Conversion & Graphics Management Software for Windows. Converts Graphic Images from over 70 Formats in Seconds. Built-In Cataloging, Image Editing & Screen Capture.
IMSI (International Microcomputer Software, Inc.).

Graphics Development Toolkit for DOS. Version: 2.2. *Operating System(s) Required:* PC-DOS 2.0 or higher. *Language(s):* Compiled BASIC, FORTRAN, Pascal, C, Macro-Assembly, Assembly. *Customer Support:* phone/FAX. $795.00.
Provides Software Developers with a Complete Graphics Development Environment for the IBM PC Family & Compatibles. With Its Extensive & Growing Set of Drivers for Displays, Printers, Plotters & Input Devices It Removes from the Applications Developer the Burden of Supporting the Ever Increasing Number of New Peripherals (Over 300 Supported). The C Library of Graphics Routines Speeds Development of Interactive Graphics Applications Such as Business Graphics, Computer-Aided Design & Desktop Publishing. Applications Can Be Written in a Device Independent Manner; No Change to the Application Program is Required to Take Advantage of New Device Drivers. Includes Language Binding for Versions of C, Pascal, FORTRAN, BASIC Compiler & Macro Assembler.
Graphic Software Systems, Inc.

Graphics Editor 200. *Compatible Hardware:* HP Series 200: Models 216/220, 226/236, 217/237. *Memory Required:* 768k. disk $445.00 (Order no.: 45537B).
Create Charts & Diagrams, Organization Charts, Block Diagrams, & Text Charts by Combining Graphics with Text. Its User Interface Is Organized into a "Drawing Board" of Multiple Windows: One to Draw on, One for a Command Menu, & More for Status & Prompting. Output Can Be Directed to HP TECHWRITER Document Processing Software As Well As Printers & Plotters. Input Can Be by Keyboard, Mouse or Digitizer.
Hewlett-Packard Co.

Graphics for Engineering Math. Version: 2. Sep. 1995. *Compatible Hardware:* IBM PC. *Operating System(s) Required:* MS-DOS. *Language(s):* GWBASIC. *Memory Required:* 16k. disk $60.00.
6 Graphics Programs for Class Demonstrations in Engineering Math. Included in the Study Are Solutions of Differential Equations, Approximation of Functions & Motion.
MatheGraphics Software.

Graphics for the Apple. 1983. *Compatible Hardware:* Apple II. *Operating System(s) Required:* Apple DOS 3.3. *Language(s):* BASIC (source code included). *Memory Required:* 48k. disk $50.00, incl. guide (Order no.: 203-AD).
Explains How to Write Fast & Simple Two- & Three-Dimensional Graphics Software. The Self-Teaching Guide Features Applications for Science, Education, & Business. Includes 61 Step-by-Step Tutorial Programs.
Kern International, Inc.

Graphics for the IBM PC. *Compatible Hardware:* IBM PC, PC XT, compatibles. *Operating System(s) Required:* PC-DOS 2.0. *Language(s):* BASIC. *Memory Required:* 64k. disk $50.00, incl. guide (Order no.: 202-ID).
Explains How to Write Two & Three-Dimensional Graphics Software. The Self-Teaching Guide Features Applications for Science, Education & Business. The Package Also Includes 61 Step-by-Step Tutorial Programs.
Kern International, Inc.

Graphics Gallerias 1/11. 1987. *Items Included:* Two 4-disk packages of clip art disks w/ Flexidraw & Doodle formats installation/usage manual, printed reference manual. *Customer Support:* 90 day warranty.
Commodore 64, 64C, 128 or SX64. $32.00, for both sets. *Addl. software included:* Flexidraw. *Optimal configuration:* 1802/1902 monitor, Flexidraw, Flexifont, Graphics Integrator 2.
Artistic Shortcuts for Creating Graphic Expression. Each Galleria Contains 15-20 Pages of Clip Art & Illustrations (Similar to Templates) for Simple Cut & Paste Integration into User's Graphics. All Flexidraw Compatible.
Inkwell Systems.

The Graphics Gallery. *Compatible Hardware:* IBM PC, PC XT, PC AT.
contact publisher for price.
Aids Users in Creating Presentation-Quality Graphics on Their PC's. Works with LOTUS 1-2-3, Transforming Its Graphs into Customized Presentations Enhanced with Color, Text, & Illustrations. Also Works with the Leading Desktop Publishing Packages. Gives Users a Flexible Choice of Output: Overhead Transparencies Produced by an HP Plotter, 35mm Slides, or Printed Output on Laser Printers.
Hewlett-Packard Co.

The Graphics Generator: Business & Technical Applications for the IBM PC. Version: 1.06. Larry J. Goldstein. *Compatible Hardware:* IBM PC. *Language(s):* BASIC. *Memory Required:* 64k. *General Requirements:* CGA card, Epson MX-80 with GrafTrax-80.
disk $195.00 (ISBN 0-89303-266-2).
Takes Data Directly from VisiCalc Worksheet &

Transforms Columns of Figures into Graphs. User Can Produce Bar Charts, Line Graphs, Pie Charts, & Line Functions.
Brady Computer Bks.

Graphics Integrator. *Version:* II. Oct. 1985. *Compatible Hardware:* Commodore 64, SX64, 128.
disk $29.95.
Converts Picture Files from One Graphics Package for Use in Another. Provides Word Processor Compatible Output with Packages Having an External File Input Capability, Allowing Integration of Text & Pictures. Can Be Used for Printing Pictures from Graphics Programs Not Currently Supporting Printer Drivers. Creates Stand-Alone Picture Files That Can Be Entered As BASIC. Allows User to Create Picture Slide Shows in 4 Different Formats.
Inkwell Systems.

The Graphics Link Plus. *Version:* 2.0B. *Compatible Hardware:* IBM PC. *Customer Support:* 1:00 pm to 4:00 pm EST or via BBS or Fax anytime.
disk $149.00.
Bridges the Gap Between Graphics Program with Incompatible File Formats. Handles All Popular & Many Not-So-Popular Bit-Mapped File Formats in Use by Graphics Programs Today. Works with 1 to 8 Bit Color, Gray-Scale or Black & White Graphics. Converts & Captures DOS or Windows Based Graphics Screens for Importation into Other Applications. Also Has a Scaling Option to Allow User to Create Any Size Graphic Image the Application Calls for & Batch Printing of Graphic Images to Industry Standard Printing.
TerraVision, Inc.

Graphics Master. *Customer Support:* 800-929-8117 (customer service).
MS-DOS. Apple II. disk $49.99 (ISBN 0-87007-771-6).
A Complete Graphics System, Which Includes a Shape Editor & Several Graphics Utilities.
SourceView Software International.

Graphics Presentations. *Compatible Hardware:* HP 85 with 16k Memory Module (HP 82903A), HP-IB Interface (HP 82937A), ROM Drawer (HP 82936A), plotter/printer ROM (HP 00085-15002), & plotter (HP 7225B with HP 17601 Module, HP 9872C, or HP 7470A); HP 86/87 with ROM Drawer (HP 82936A), plotter/printer ROM (HP 00085-15002), & plotter (HP 7225B with HP 17601 Module, HP 9872C, or HP 7470A). *General Requirements:* 230k, BASIC 3.0, & plotter for HP Series 200 Models 216/200, 226/236, 217/237.
HP 85. data cartridge, 3-1/2" or 5-1/4" disk $240.00 ea. (Order no.: 82801A).
HP 86/87. 3-1/2" or 5-1/4" disk $240.00 ea. (Order no.: 82831A).
HP 216/220, 226/236. 3-1/2" or 5-1/4" disk $750.00 ea. (Order no.: 98815A).
HP 217/237. 3-1/2" or 5-1/4" disk $750.00 ea. (Order no.: 98815A).
Helps User Prepare Charts & Overhead Slides for Management Reports, Meetings, Customer Presentations, etc. Text & Illustrations Can Be Prepared Without Programming by Responding to a Series of Questions That Generate Text, Pie, Bar or Line Charts.
Hewlett-Packard Co.

Graphics Programming in C. Roger T. Stevens. *Operating System(s) Required:* MS-DOS. *General Requirements:* Turbo C or Microsoft C compiler.
book & disk $39.95 (ISBN 1-55851-019-2).
book only $24.95 (ISBN 1-55851-018-4).
Details the Fundamentals of Graphics Programming for the IBM PC Family & Compatibles. Includes Discussions of ROM BIOS, VGA, EGA, & CGA Capabilities; the Use of Fractals; Methods of Displaying Points on the Screen; & Better Algorithms for Drawing & Filling Lines, Rectangles, Polygons, Ovals, Circles, & Other Shapes.
M & T Bks.

Graphics Programming on the IBM Personal Computer. J. Edward Volkstorf, Jr. 1984. *Compatible Hardware:* IBM PC. *Operating System(s) Required:* PC-DOS 1.1, 2.0. *Language(s):* BASIC. *General Requirements:* Color capability for about half the programs.
disk $34.95, incl. bk. (ISBN 0-13-363219-9).
Introduction to Graphics Programming in BASIC.
Prentice Hall.

Graphics Programs for the IBM PC. Robert J. Traister. 1983. *Compatible Hardware:* IBM PC. *Operating System(s) Required:* PC-DOS. *Memory Required:* 64k.
disk $40.50, incl. bk. (ISBN 0-8306-5020-2, Order no.: 5020C).
TAB Bks.

Graphics Scrapbook. *Compatible Hardware:* Apple II & compatibles, Commodore 64/128, IBM PC & compatibles.
contact publisher for price.
Collection of Pictures That Can Be Used with THE PRINT SHOP or PrintMaster, or CREATE A CALENDAR. Each Disk Includes over 100 Pictures. Titles Currently Available Are SCHOOL SCRAPBOOK, SPORTS SCRAPBOOK, & OFF THE WALL SCRAPBOOK.
Epyx, Inc.

Graphics Server for Actor 4.0. 1991. Windows. IBM PC, XT, AT & compatibles. $299.00.
Supports ACTOR 4.0, Allowing User to Add Full-Color Graphs & Charts to Applications. Program Offers Nine Graph Types & Several Statistics Functions. Graphics Server Is a DLL.
Pinnacle Publishing Inc.

Graphics Supermarket with Source Code. *Compatible Hardware:* Apple IIgs. *Memory Required:* 512k.
3.5" disk $149.95 (ISBN 0-939377-26-8, Order no.: 4020-412).
Automatically Takes Shapes, Patterns Icons or Entire Scenes That the User Creates & Translates into Assembly & C Source Code. The Source Code Can Then Be Used in Programs with No Licensing Fees Required. Can Also Use Images Created with Other Programs. Other Features Include 4096 Colors, Color Printing, Zoom Editing, Pull-Down Menu or Icon Control of Features.
Abracadata, Ltd.

Graphics Transformer. *Version:* 2.1. Oct. 1993. *Operating System(s) Required:* MS-DOS. *Customer Support:* 30 day unconditional guarantee, unlimited free phone support BBS, 415-454-2893.
DOS 3.0 or higher (640k). IBM PC, XT, AT, PS/2, 386, 486, & compatibles with hard drive (512k). contact publisher for price (Order no.: SGP01).
Allows User to Convert Most Popular Graphics File Formats, Such As Those Used By Ventura Publisher, PageMaker, PC Paintbrush, AutoCAD, Dr HALO, WordPerfect & More. It Supports Raster to Raster, Vector to Raster, & Vector to Vector Conversions & Has a Screen Capture Mode.
IMSI (International Microcomputer Software, Inc.).

The Graphics Warehouse.
Any Macintosh. 3.5" disk $20.50.
Bit-mapped art.
Showker Graphic Arts & Design.

Graphics Works.
MS-DOS 5.0 or higher. IBM 386 or higher (4Mb). disk $295.00 (Order no.: GW2L10ENG). *Addl. software required:* Windows 3.1. *Optimal configuration:* 8Mb RAM, CD-ROM drive.
Features Innovative & Easy-to-Use Products That Let You Quickly & Painlessly Edit Photos, & Create Charts, Graphs, Drawings, & Presentations. Includes: WINDOWS DRAW, PHOTOMAGIC, WINCHART, WINDOWS ORGCHART, SLIDESHOW, 10,000 Clip Art Images, 1,000 Stock-Quality Photos, 30 Special Effects, an ImageBrowser, & More Than 150 TrueType Fonts.
Micrografx, Inc.

GraphicWriter III. *Version:* 1.1. Gary Crandall & David Hecker. Aug. 1991. *Compatible Hardware:* Apple IIgs. *Memory Required:* 768k. *General Requirements:* Printer. *Items Included:* Fonts & clip art. *Customer Support:* 11-5 Mon-Fri EST 904-576-9415 or on-line through AppleLink, America Online, GEnie & CompuServe.
3.5" disk $149.95.
Desktop Publishing Program That Can Do up to Four Columns of Text, Graphics & Paint on the Same Page. Can Import BITMAP Files from Other Graphic Programs.
Seven Hills Software Corp.

Graphing Package. *Compatible Hardware:* TI-99/4A.
disk or cassette - contact publisher for price.
Provides Plotting Techniques Such As Cartesian & Polar, Scatter & XYZ Plots.
Texas Instruments, Personal Productivit.

GraphMaster. *Version:* 2.0. Jul. 1988. *Compatible Hardware:* IBM PC & compatibles. *Operating System(s) Required:* PC-DOS/MS-DOS. *Memory Required:* 256k. *General Requirements:* CGA, EGA or VGA.
disk $49.95.
Allows User to Translate Data into Graphic Pictures, Including Bar, Line, Pie, Scatter & Text Charts. Features Screen Painting; Box, Circle & Line Drawing; Correlation & Regression Analysis & Curve Fitting.
Zephyr Services.

GraphPack. *Compatible Hardware:* Apple Macintosh. *General Requirements:* Microsoft FORTRAN, DCM FORTRAN or Language Systems FORTRAN.
3.5" disk $70.95.
Fortran Plotting Package for Scientific & Technical Work.
Lipa Software.

GraphPak Professional. *Version:* 3.0. *Compatible Hardware:* IBM PC & compatibles. *Operating System(s) Required:* PC-DOS/MS-DOS. *Language(s):* BASIC. *Memory Required:* 256k. *Customer Support:* 8:30-5:30 EST.
disk $149.00.
Collection of BASIC Routines for Displaying Business & Scientific Line, Bar, & Pie Charts Automatically from Within the Programs. Enables Users to Create 3-D Charts with Manual or Automatic Scaling, Titles & Legends in Any Style or Size, As Well As Scrolling & Windowing in Graphics. Comes with a Font Editor for Customizing Character Sets. Source Code Is Included. Available in Separate Versions for Microsoft QUICKBASIC & SPECTRA Publishing's PowerBASIC. Not Copy Protected.
Crescent Software.

TITLE INDEX

GraphPlan. Chang Laboratories. *Compatible Hardware:* HP 150 Touchscreen.
3.5" disk $300.00 (Order no.: 45467A).
Integrates a Financial Spreadsheet with Graphics. The Spreadsheet Features Are Invoked via a Single-Stroke Command Menu. Features One-Touch Graphics Capabilities, Which Allow the User to Create Graphics Directly from the Spreadsheet with a Single Touch-Driven Command. Also Includes a Report Generator, Ranking & Sorting Capabilities. Integrates with MICROPLAN.
Hewlett-Packard Co.

GraphPlay. Laurence Harris. 1993. *Items Included:* Disk & manual. *Customer Support:* Unlimited technical support for registered users.
Macintosh. Macintosh, System 7 users need min. of 2.5Mb (500k). 3.5" disk $50.00 single copy price (ISBN 0-534-20586-0, Order no.: 800-354-9706). *Optimal configuration:* Macintosh Plus or higher model with 500k Mb of memory in addition.
$400.00 plus $10.00 per CPU site license (ISBN 0-534-20587-9).
Developed to Help Students Gain an Understanding of the Relationship Between a Function in Algebraic Form & Its Graph. Because GraphPlay Only Examines Functions of Certain Predefined Types, It Has the Advantage of 1) Text Written on the Screen the Way Books Are Written, 2) Speed & 3) Can Anticipate Unusual Situations & Handle Them with Appropriate Responses. Simple to Use. Function Parameters Are Controlled via the Mouse or Keyboard. All Functions That Students Study Are Built in, So the Student Won't Have to Dream up Functions, Ranges, or Values If They Don't Know How.
Brooks/Cole Publishing Co.

GraphPower. 1994. *Items Included:* Book & software (teacher's manual). *Customer Support:* Technical support available - no charge; free upgrading.
System 7.0 or higher. Mac LC or higher (1Mb). $79.95 school; $129.95 5-user; $179.95 10-user; $379.95 30-user (ISBN 1-57116-000-0). *Networks supported:* Yes.
A Comprehensive Tool for Creating Graphs & Helping Students Learn to Analyze Data. Begin by Setting up Your Data in a Table & Then Instantly View a Variety of Graph Forms. Graph Forms Include Pictograph, Vertical Bar Graph, Horizontal Bar Graph, Line Graph, Circle Graph, & Box & Whisker Graph. Features an Integrated Database, Built-In Statistical Functions, 9 Levels of Tutorials for Grades K-8, Animated Draw Tools, a Comprehensive Teacher's Guide & Reproducible Student Activity Sheets. Grade Levels K-8.
Ventura Educational Systems.

Graphtrix. *Version:* 1.3. *Compatible Hardware:* Apple II, II+, IIe. *Operating System(s) Required:* Apple DOS 3.3. *Language(s):* Applesoft. *Memory Required:* 64k.
disk $65.00.
Menu-Driven Screen Dump for Apple Hi-Res Graphics. Screen Dump Installable into & Callable by User's Own Applesoft Program. Recommended as a Screen Dump for Apple Logo Graphics.
Data Transforms, Inc.

Graphwriter Basic Set. Graphics Communications, Inc. *Compatible Hardware:* HP 150 Touchscreen.
3.5" disk $395.00 (Order no.: 45484A).
Produces Presentation Graphics Through Pre-Defined Formats. Users Can Produce Pie, Bar, Line Text, Scatter, Regression, & Bar-Line Charts - Either on Paper or Transparencies. Provides a Context-Sensitive HELP Key.
Hewlett-Packard Co.

Grasp. *Version:* 4.0. *Compatible Hardware:* IBM PC & compatibles. *Operating System(s) Required:* PC-DOS 2.0 or higher. *Memory Required:* 512k. *General Requirements:* CGA, EGA, VGA or MCGA display. *Items Included:* Capture Utility, Paint Program, Animation Programming Graphic Image printing Utility, Compiler Utility, The Graphics Link+ *Customer Support:* Unlimited 503-488-0224.
$349.00.
Desktop Animation Package That Can Produce Animated Sequences That Shift Image Coordinates, Adjust: the Palette, Produce Sounds & Branch to Other Scripts or Outside Programs. Commands Can Be Incorporated into C, BASIC, Turbo Pascal & Other Shell Programs. Not Copy Protected.
Paul Mace Software.

Gravitator Plus. Jul. 1988. *Compatible Hardware:* IBM PC & compatibles. *Operating System(s) Required:* PC-DOS/MS-DOS. *Memory Required:* 256k. *General Requirements:* CGA card or EGA/VGA with CGA emulation.
disk $89.95.
Calculates the Gravitational Forces on Astronomical Bodies Such As Stars & Planets & Determines Their Orbits. Allows The User to Set up Systems, Watch Them Evolve & Vary the Orientation, Scale & Angle of View.
Zephyr Services.

Grav2D.
Macintosh 512K or higher. 3.5" disk $100.00.
Two-Dimensional Gravity Modeling Program.
Rockware Data Corp.

GRCCOM/Quest. *Version:* 6.3. Apr. 1985. *Compatible Hardware:* IBM PC & compatibles. *Operating System(s) Required:* PC-DOS, MS-DOS. *Language(s):* FORTRAN. *Memory Required:* 512k.
contact publisher for price.
Allows Access to GRC's Resource Database Which Contains More Than 7 Million MARC Records. With Software Developed Specifically for Clerical Personnel, a Library Can Establish Its Own Database by Creating & Matching Records As Well As Modifying Them to Reflect Local Data. Formatted Screens & Error Detection Help Assure Error-Free Conversion of Cataloging to a Machine-Readable Database. Once the Database Is Established, a Library Can Produce CDM or CD-ROM Catalogs.
GRC International, Inc.

Great Chefs-Master Collection. *Compatible Hardware:* Apple II+, IIe, IIc, IIgs, Macintosh; Atari ST; Commodore 64, 128; IBM PC.
Set. $39.95.
disk $39.95 ea.
Vol. A-F.
Vol. G-N.
Vol. O-Z.
Includes Nearly 600 Recipes from the PBS Television Series "Great Chefs" Comes Complete with its own Database Manager; or Increase Power with Micro Kitchen Companion.
Concept Development Assocs., Inc.

Great Chefs of PBS Master Collection, Vols. I, II & III. *Compatible Hardware:* Apple II series (64k); Atari ST; C-64; Macintosh (512k); IBM (128k). *Items Included:* Bound manual. *Customer Support:* Free hotline - no time limit; 30 day limited warranty; updates are $5/disk plus S&H.
disk $59.95.
The Only Complete Collection of "Great Chefs" Recipes, Cooking Tips, & Anecdotes from the Acclaimed PBS Television Series. Includes Easy-to-Follow Directions & Wine Recommendations for Each Dish. There Are 825 Entries from over 100 Top-Name Cooks. Includes All New GREAT CHEFS OF THE WEST.
Dynacomp, Inc.

GREAT PAINTINGS RENAISSANCE TO

The Great Game. *Items Included:* Installation Guide.
IBM PC. Contact publisher for price (ISBN 0-87321-077-8, Order no.: CDD-3110).
Activision, Inc.

Great Gantt! *Version:* 1.3. Nov. 1989. *Items Included:* Software & documentation. *Customer Support:* Support & update service, $50.00; update only, $25.00.
Macintosh Plus, SE, II. 3.5" disk $195.00.
Will Provide High Quality Output from Mac Project Files & ASCII Text Files. The Charts Will Be Entirely Configurable by the User & Can Be Sent to a Supported Output Device or to a PICT File. Each Configuration Can Be Saved to Disk So That It Can Be Reused with Different Schedules.
Varcon Systems.

The Great International Paper Airplane Construction Kit. Neosoft, Inc. May 1985. *Compatible Hardware:* Apple II+, IIe, IIc, Macintosh; Commodore 64, 128; IBM PC, PC XT, PC AT. *Operating System(s) Required:* PC-DOS 2.0 or higher for IBM. *Memory Required:* Apple II 64k, Macintosh 128k. *General Requirements:* Printer. MousePaint program recommended for Apple II; KoalaPad recommended for Commodore; CGA card for IBM; ImageWriter printer for Macintosh.
Apple II. disk $39.95 (ISBN 0-671-61129-1).
Commodore. disk $39.95 (ISBN 0-671-61127-5).
IBM. disk $39.95 (ISBN 0-671-61128-3).
Macintosh. 3.5" disk $39.95 (ISBN 0-671-55297-X).
Set of Paper Airplane Templates & a Library of Airplane Graphics. Select One of over a Dozen Designs, Embellish the Wings & Fuselage with Aeronautical Art, Print the Creation on the Imagewriter Printer, Fold & Fly. Based on THE GREAT INTERNATIONAL PAPER AIRPLANE BOOK.
Brady Computer Bks.

Great Naval Battles II: Guadal Canal 1942-43. Sep. 1995. *Items Included:* CD in jewel case. *Customer Support:* 30 Day Limited Warranty.
DOS 5.0 or higher. PC CD (4Mb). CD-ROM disk $9.95 (ISBN 0-917059-31-X, Order no.: 062541). *Optimal configuration:* 486/33.
Naval Simulation.
Strategic Simulations Inc.

Great Naval Battles, Vol. III: Fury in the Pacific. Zero Software Inc. Staff. Feb. 1995. *Items Included:* 1 128 page perfect bound manual & 1 data card. *Customer Support:* 30 day limited warranty.
DOS 5.0 or higher. IBM PC compatible with CD-ROM, Hard drive & Mouse (4Mb). CD-ROM disk $69.95 (ISBN 0-917059-24-7, Order no.: 062241). *Nonstandard peripherals required:* 512 SVGA card & VESA driver. *Optimal configuration:* Requires 14Mb of hard drive space, uncompressed hard drive recommended, 386/33 required, 486/33 recommended.
From SSI's Advanced Simulator Series Encompassing the Entire Pacific Theater of WWII. Provides a First-Person View of All Ships, As Well As an Eagle's Eye View of Tactical Situation Maps.
Strategic Simulations, Inc.

Great Paintings Renaissance to Impressionism: The Frick Collection. Robb Lazarus et al. Jun. 1994. *Items Included:* Instruction manual, upgrade card (if available). *Customer Support:* Call-in, 1-800, fax back & on-line support are available at no charge for the lifetime of the disk.
Macintosh with 68030 processor or higher.
Macintosh, double speed CD-ROM drive

423

(8Mb). CD-ROM disk $79.95 (ISBN 1-886664-02-1). *Nonstandard peripherals required:* 24-bit graphics card strongly recommended, Quick Time Movie.
Windows 3.1 or higher. Windows System 3.1 or higher (8Mb). CD-ROM disk $79.95 (ISBN 1-886664-03-X). *Nonstandard peripherals required:* 24-bit graphics card strongly recommended.
View the Masterpieces of the "Frick Collection" in New York, One of the Preeminent Collections of Western Painting. The Collection Spans from the Early Renaissance to Nineteenth Century & Features over 138 Works by Artists Such As Piero della Francesca, Titian, Rembrandt, Vermeer, & Monet.
Digital Collections, Inc.

Great Paintings Renaissance to Impressionism: The Frick Collection: Jewel Case. Robb Lazarus et al. Jun. 1994. *Items Included:* Instructional manual, upgrade card (if available). *Customer Support:* Call-in, 1-800, fax back & on-line support are available at no charge for the lifetime of the disk.
Macintosh with 68030 processor or higher (8Mb). CD-ROM disk $49.95 (ISBN 1-886664-33-1). *Nonstandard peripherals required:* Double speed CD-ROM drive, 24-bit graphics card strongly recommended.
Windows 3.1 or higher (8Mb). CD-ROM disk $49.95 (ISBN 1-886664-34-X). *Nonstandard peripherals required:* 24-bit graphics card strongly recommended.
Digital Collections, Inc.

Great Plains Accounting Series: Accounts Payable. *Version:* 5.35. Mar. 1986. *Compatible Hardware:* Apple Macintosh, Macintosh II, Macintosh Plus, Macintosh SE; IBM PC & compatibles. *Operating System(s) Required:* PC-DOS 3.1 or higher. *Language(s):* Turbo Pascal, C. *Memory Required:* 1000k.
disk $795.00.
Accommodates up to 32,767 Vendors. Simplifies Cash Management, Allowing User to Take Advantage of Best Terms & Supplier Discounts. Prints Cash Requirement Report & Checks.
Great Plains Software.

Great Plains Accounting Series: Accounts Receivable. *Version:* 5.35. Mar. 1986. *Compatible Hardware:* Apple Macintosh II, Macintosh Plus, Macintosh SE; IBM PC & compatibles. *Operating System(s) Required:* PC-DOS 2.0 or higher. *Language(s):* Turbo Pascal, MPW Pascal. *Memory Required:* 1000k.
disk $795.00.
Stores up to 32,767 Customers. Features Up-to-Date Information Including Profit by Customer, Type, Salesperson, & State. Balances Are Automatically Checked Against Credit Limits. Full or Partial Payments Can Be Added, & Cash Can Be Applied to All Specific Invoices.
Great Plains Software.

Great Plains Accounting Series: General Ledger. *Version:* 5.35. Mar. 1986. *Compatible Hardware:* Macintosh II, Macintosh Plus, Macintosh SE; IBM PC & compatibles. *Operating System(s) Required:* DOS 3.1 or higher for IBM. *Language(s):* Turbo Pascal, C. *Memory Required:* 1000k.
disk $795.00.
Stores up to 32,767 Accounts & up to 999 Profit Centers. Transactions Are Traced Through the Use of Audit Trails. Also Provided Are Various Reports, & Comparisons Between Last Year's, Current & Year-to-Date Figures.
Great Plains Software.

Great Plains Accounting Series: Inventory. *Version:* 5.35. Jul. 1986. *Compatible Hardware:* IBM PC & compatibles; Apple Macintosh Plus, SE, II. *Operating System(s) Required:* PC-DOS 3.1 or higher for IBM. *Language(s):* Turbo Pascal, C. *Memory Required:* 1000k.
disk $795.00.
Accommodates up to 6000 Inventory Items with Part Numbers of up to 15 Characters. Offers "Component Maintenance" for Tracking Light Production/Assembly Work. Supports FIFO, LIFO & Weighted Average Inventory Valuation Methods. Offers up to 36 Locations per Inventory Item, Each with a "Bin Location". Handles Inventory Transfers from One Location to Another. Prints Price Lists with up to 3 Price Levels & 3 Quantity Breaks. Calculates up to 5 Taxes per Customer. Allows "Book-to-Physical" Adjustments of Inventory Records. Calculates Total Quantity-on-Hand, Quantity-on-Order, Quantity-in-Stock & Reorder Points. Handles Serial Numbered Inventory Items & Generates a Variety of Reports Such As: Inventory Item List, Purchase Receipts Report, Stock Status Report, & Physical Inventory Checklist.
Great Plains Software.

Great Plains Accounting Series: Network Manager. *Version:* 5.35. Oct. 1986. *Compatible Hardware:* Apple Macintosh II, SE, & Plus; IBM PC & compatibles. *Language(s):* Turbo Pascal. *Memory Required:* 1024k. *General Requirements:* Hard disk, printer.
disk $995.00.
Great Plains Network Manager Allows Several People to Use the Great Plains Accounting Series at One Time When Using a Local Area Network. It Provides Program-, File- & Record-Level Lockouts to Allow Simultaneous Workstation Activity While Assuring the Integrity of Accounting Information. Network Manager Supports Cash Drawers & Printers at Each Workstation, & It Can Be Added to a Single-User Accounting System at Any Time, Without the Need to Re-Enter Data or Restructure the System. Additional Workstations Can Be Added at Any Time. Network Manager is Part of the Great Plains Accounting Series, a Full-Featured Multi-Module Accounting System. The Series Also Includes General Ledger, Accounts Receivable, Accounts Payable, Payroll, Inventory, Purchase Order, Order Entry with Point of Sale, Job Cost & Executive Advisor.
Great Plains Software.

Great Plains Accounting Series: Order Entry with Point of Sale. *Version:* 5.35. Jul. 1986. *Compatible Hardware:* IBM PC & compatibles; Apple Macintosh Plus, SE, II. *Operating System(s) Required:* PC-DOS 3.1 or higher for IBM. *Language(s):* Turbo Pascal, C. *Memory Required:* 1000k.
disk $795.00.
Allows Non-Inventoried Items to Be Sold. Back Order Report Allows User to Review All Backorders & Recalls Customer Status on Backordered Products. Handles up to 4 Credit Card Types. Prints User Defined Picking Tickets. Calculates Commissions As Percentage of Actual Cost or Current Cost. Handles Cash & Account Sales, Returns, Quotes, Repayments & Deposits. Provides a Point of Sale Mode, & Can Be Linked to Cash Drawer to Serve As a Cash Register. Prints a Variety of Reports Including: Back Order Report, Open Order Report, Sales Analysis Report, & Customized Point of Sale Invoices.
Great Plains Software.

Great Plains Accounting Series: Payroll. *Version:* 5.35. Mar. 1986. *Compatible Hardware:* Apple Macintosh II, SE, Plus; IBM PC & compatibles. *Operating System(s) Required:* PC-DOS 3.1 or higher for IBM. *Language(s):* Turbo Pascal, C. *Memory Required:* 1000k.
disk $795.00.
Payroll Module Allows for up to 32,767 Employees, Depending upon Disk Storage Space. Features Eight Payroll Periods, 20 Pay Types, 20 Deductions & 5 Tax Withholdings. Supports Multiple States with a Tax Table Available for All 50 States. Prints W-2 Statements & 941 Preparation Reports.
Great Plains Software.

Great Plains Accounting Series: Purchase Order. *Version:* 5.1. Mar. 1987. *Compatible Hardware:* IBM PC & compatibles; Apple Macintosh Plus, SE, II. *Operating System(s) Required:* PC-DOS 3.1 or higher for IBM. *Language(s):* Turbo Pascal, C. *Memory Required:* 512k.
disk $795.00.
Allows Purchase Orders to Be Entered, Edited & Deleted, & Updates Inventory When Registered. Prints Individual or a Specific Range of Customer Defined Purchase Orders, Also Handles "Changed Orders". Handles 4 Types of Purchase Orders: Regular, Recurring or "Standing" Orders, Drop-Ship & Blanket. Allows Manual or Automatic Removal of Filled or Completed Orders. Allows Items Not Set up As Part Numbers to Be Entered into the System. Handles Shipment or Invoice Only Transactions, Partial Shipments, & One-Time Items Not in Inventory. Provides Vendor Analysis Based on Purchase Order History. Updates Quantities on Order & on Hand When Integrated with Inventory. Handles Due Dates, Ship Dates, & Items Received in Fractional Units. Prints a Variety of Reports Such As: Open Order Report, Receivings Report, Serial Number Aging Report, Backorder Fill Report, Purchase Order History & Vendor Analysis Report.
Great Plains Software.

Great Plains Accounts Receivable. Great Plains Software. Jan. 1984. *Compatible Hardware:* TI Professional with printer, Winchester second drive. *Operating System(s) Required:* MS-DOS. *Memory Required:* 256k.
$495.00.
Maintains Up-to-Date Customer Information. Integrates with Other Modules.
Texas Instruments, Personal Productivit.

Great Plains Executive Advisor. *Version:* 5.1. (Great Business Accounting Ser.). Mar. 1988. *Compatible Hardware:* Apple Macintosh, IBM PC & compatibles. *Operating System(s) Required:* Mac-System 3.2 or higher/Finder 5.3 or higher, PC-DOS/MS-DOS. *Memory Required:* Macintosh 1Mb, IBM 512k. *General Requirements:* 20Mb hard disk.
disk $595.00.
Helps Firms Spot Trends, Evaluate Performance & Compare Activity from Month to Month. Provides a Graphic Analysis of Company Finances, As Well As Vendor, Customer, Employee Purchases, Sales & Order Information. Offers More Than 75 Ratios & Business Performance Measures to Display Liquidity, Profitability, Activity, Coverage & Stock Ratios. Allows Users to Make Period-by-Period Comparisons Between Business's Current Performance & Previous Year, Budget & Industry Average Indexes to Show Cyclical Variations During a Business Year & More Accurately Reflect How Well Business Is Doing. Exception Reporting Capabilities Lets Users Spotlight Their Best Customers, Largest Outstanding Balance, & Top Employees. Color Codes Graphics for Dynamic Reports, Offers Flexible Report Formatting, Allows Users to Generate Reports & Ratios Showing Only the Range of Accounts, Customer & Vendors Desired.
Great Plains Software.

TITLE INDEX

Great Plains Import Manager. Version: 5.1. Compatible Hardware: IBM PC & compatibles. Memory Required: 512k. General Requirements: 20Mb hard disk.
disk $495.00.
Great Plains Software.

Great Plains Report Maker Plus. Version: 5.1. (Great Plains Accounting Ser.). May 1987. Compatible Hardware: IBM PC & compatibles. Language(s): Turbo Pascal. Memory Required: 512k. General Requirements: Hard disk, printer. Customer Support: Report design service available.
disk $495.00.
Great Plains Software.

Great Plains Software Accounts Payable. Great Plains Software. Jan. 1984. Compatible Hardware: TI Professional. Operating System(s) Required: MS-DOS. Memory Required: 256k. General Requirements: Winchester hard disk, printer.
$495.00.
Improves Cash Control by Tracking Total Invoices Received from Vendors & Minimum Order Amounts.
Texas Instruments, Personal Productivit.

Great Plains Software General Ledger. Great Plains Software. Jan. 1984. Compatible Hardware: TI Professional with printer, & Winchester second drive. Operating System(s) Required: MS-DOS. Memory Required: 256k.
$495.00.
Financial Accounting & Management System. Eliminates Unnecessary Re-Entry of Information & Allows for Tracing of Transaction Through Comprehensive Audit Trails.
Texas Instruments, Personal Productivit.

Great Plains Software Payroll. Great Plains Software. Jan. 1984. Compatible Hardware: Texas Instruments. Operating System(s) Required: MS-DOS. Memory Required: 256k.
$495.00, incl. module.
Texas Instruments, Personal Productivit.

The Great Quake of '89 Hypercard Stack. Items Included: 2 floppy discs, user's guide. Customer Support: M-F 9 AM-5 PM Pacific Time (213) 451-1383.
Macintosh Plus, SE, II or Portable. 3.5" disk $49.95. Nonstandard peripherals required: Videodisc player, monitor & cables; the Great Quake of '89 videodisc. Addl. software required: HyperCard 1.2.2. or higher.
Immediately Recall Specific Earthquake Footage, Print Transcripts of Supplementary Information, or Customize & Play Back Video Sequences in Any Order Using ABC News Interactive's Special Documentary Maker.
The Voyager Co.

Great Restaurants, Wineries & Breweries. 1994. Customer Support: 30 day warranty. Windows. optical disk $14.95.
Takes the User on a Tour of Many of the Nation's Best Restaurants, Wineries, & Microbreweries. More Than 4000 Photographs & Menus Showcase Great Dining & Drinking Establishments. Also Offered Are Hundreds of Recipes from the Nation's Best Chefs Allowing Users to Prepare Specialities at Home. Users Can Also Search & Select Restaurants, Breweries, & Wineries by City & State or Find Them Highlighted on Regional or Local Maps.
Deep River Publishing, Inc.

Great Restaurants, Wineries, & Breweries. Jul. 1994. Items Included: User Guide. Customer Support: 30 day warranty.
Windows. IBM PC & compatibles (4Mb). disk $39.95 (ISBN 1-885638-07-8). Nonstandard peripherals required: Sound Board.
This Program Takes Users on a Tour of the Nation's Best Eating & Drinking Establishments. More Than 4,000 Photographs, Menus & Recipes Showcase over 1,400 Restaurants, Wineries & Breweries. Provides Information about Opening Hours, Prices & House Specialties. Users Can Search & Select Restaurants, Wineries, & Breweries by City or State & Find Them Highlighted on Regional Maps.
Deep River Publishing, Inc.

Greek-Hebrew Text for Windows. Feb. 1996. Items Included: Disks, marketing literature, order form, registration card. Customer Support: 30 day money back guarantee; limited replacement warranty on diskettes defective at time of purchase; free telephone technical support.
Windows 3.1 or higher. IBM 386/486 or 100% compatible (4Mb, 8Mb recommended). 3.5" disk $49.95 (ISBN 1-56514-121-0). Addl. software required: Biblesoft's PC Study Bible. Optimal configuration: 3.5, 1.44Mb disk drive for installation, 2Mb hard drive space; mouse or pointer device recommended.
A Complete Greek & Hebrew Text for Use with the PC Study Bible.
Biblesoft.

Greek History & Culture. John Kallas.
IBM. disk $29.99 (Order no.: 6059).
disk $39.99, incl. backup disk (Order no.: 6059B).
Apple II. 3.5" disk $29.99 (Order no.: 6040).
3.5" disk $39.99, incl. backup disk (Order no.: 6040B).
Software Games on the History, Art, & Culture of Ancient Greece. Contains Four or Five Different Games. The Games Are Designed for One, Two, or Three Players. Players Are Given a Question & Challenged to Spell the Correct Answer Letter by Letter. Points Are Assigned by Letter & for Answering the Entire Word Correctly. The Answer Is Reinforced with Information. This Is Sophisticated Material in an Enjoyable Format.
Trillium Pr.

Greek Mythology. John Kallas.
IBM. disk $29.99 (Order no.: 6032).
disk $39.99, incl. backup disk (Order no.: 6032B).
Apple II. 3.5" disk $29.99 (Order no.: 6024).
3.5" disk $39.99, incl. backup disk (Order no.: 6024B).
Software Games on the History, Art, & Culture of Ancient Greece. Contains Four or Five Different Games. The Games Are Designed for One, Two, or Three Players. Players Are Given a Question & Challenged to Spell the Correct Answer Letter by Letter. Points Are Assigned by Letter & for Answering the Entire Word Correctly. The Answer Is Reinforced with Information. This Is Sophisticated Material in an Enjoyable Format.
Trillium Pr.

Greek New Testament for Windows. Version: 1.6. Sep. 1992. Items Included: User's manual. Customer Support: Free telephone support; defective disks replaced free.
Windows. IBM or compatibles (4Mb). disk $59.95. Addl. software required: MS Windows or ATM. Optimal configuration: 4Mb RAM & 386.
Entire Text of the Greek New Testament, the Authoritative UBS 4th Edition Licensed to Linguist's Software by the United Bible Societies, Derived in Part from the Machine Readable Text Created by Timothy & Barbara Friberg at the U. of Minn.
Linguist's Software, Inc.

Greek New Testament with Grammatical Tags for Windows. Version: 1.3. Sep. 1992. Items Included: User's manual. Customer Support: Free telephone support; defective disks replaced free.
Windows. IBM or compatibles (2-4Mb). disk $79.95. Addl. software required: MS Windows or ATM. Optimal configuration: 4Mb RAM & 386.
UBS Greek New Testament, 4th Edition Derived, in Part, from the Machine-Readable Text Created by Timothy & Barbara Friberg, at the University Computer Center, University of Minnesota with Grammatical Tags Included.
Linguist's Software, Inc.

Greek Old Testament for Windows. Version: 1.3. Sep. 1992. Items Included: User's manual. Customer Support: Free telephone support; defective disks replaced free.
Windows. IBM or compatibles (2-4Mb). disk $59.95. Addl. software required: MS Windows or ATM. Optimal configuration: 4Mb RAM & 386.
UBS Septuagints, Ed. A. Rahlfs, Including Sinaiticus, Alexandrinus, Vaticanus & Theodotion, Derived from the TLG Machine-Readable Text.
Linguist's Software, Inc.

Greek Old Testament with Grammatical Tags for Windows. Version: 1.1. May 1993. Items Included: User's manual. Customer Support: Free telephone support; defective disks replaced free.
Windows. IBM or compatibles (4Mb). disk $79.95. Addl. software required: MS Windows or ATM. Optimal configuration: 4Mb RAM & 386.
Entire Text of Alfred Rahlfs' Septuagint (Including the Full Text of Codex Sinaiticus, Alexandrinus, Vaticanus, & Theodotion Where They Differ Substantially) Licensed to Linguist's Software by the Deutsche Bibelgesellschaft, Derived from the Machine Readable Text Created by the Thesaurus Linguae Graecae, U. Calif. Irvine. Includes Grammatical Tags & Dictionary Forms.
Linguist's Software, Inc.

The Greek Transliterator. Version: 6.1. Kent Ochel & Bert Brown. Oct. 1989. Items Included: Tutorial disk; 3-ring binder with manual. Customer Support: Unlimited free technical support (512) 251-7541.
Any DOS or Windows. IBM PC; XT; AT & compatible (512k). disk $99.95.
Any Macintosh. 3.5" disk $99.95.
(NIV or KJV) Provides the Serious Bible Student with Tools Necessary to Study the New Testament in the Original Language. Strong's Reference Numbers Are Assigned to the English Text & a Dictionary Gives the Greek Transliteration, Word Origin & Derivations. VERSE SEARCH Is required.
Bible Research Systems.

Grenn Hills C++. Version: 2.1. Jul. 1991. Items Included: Manuals. Customer Support: Maintenance available, call for pricing.
UNIX VMS. Sun 4, RS/6000, DECstation (2Mb). $1000.00 & up.
A True C++ Compiler That Supports Native & Embedded Systems Development. Compiles with AT&T C++ Versions 2.0 & 2.1. The Compiler Utilizes Advanced Optimizing Techniques Including Inlining, Loop Unrolling & Register Caching, Compiles Kernighan & Ritchie C Code & Supports the ANSI C Standard.
Oasys, Inc.

Green Recipe. Compatible Hardware: IBM PC. Operating System(s) Required: MS-DOS.
contact publisher for price.
Determines Best Fertilizer Mix at Least Cost for Given Crop & Field.
Comcepts Systems.

Greenleaf ArchiveLib. *Version:* 2.0. Feb. 1996. *Language(s):* C, C Plus Plus, Visual Basic, Delphi. *Items Included:* 2 paperback manuals. *Customer Support:* Telephone technical support; free online technical support; quarterly newsletter.
DOS, Windows 3.X, Windows 95, Windows NT, OS/2. 80X86 compatibles (640k). disk $279.00. *Addl. software required:* C Plus Plus compiler.
Provides the Developer a Set of Classes & Functions to Compress & Store ASCII & Binary Data into an Archive for Storage, As Well As to Retrieve & Expand the Stored Data from the Archive. Data Is Compressed & Expanded Using a Proprietary Algorithm. Uncompressed Data Can Be Situated in a File or a Memory Buffer. Designed to Be Flexible for Handling Any Type of Data That Developers Require. The Series of Classes & Functions in ArchiveLib Is Geared to the C Plus Plus Programmer, but Maintains Language Independence. It Contains a Variety of Functions to Add, Replace, Delete, Update & Retrieve Objects of Compressed Data Within the Archive. Available As a DLL for Access to Windows Developers. Includes Source Code & Is Royalty Free. Supports Most Popular Plus Plus Compilers.
Greenleaf Software, Inc.

Greenleaf Comm Plus Plus. *Version:* 3.0. Jun. 1995. *Items Included:* 2 paperback manuals, source code. *Customer Support:* Telephone technical support; free technical BBS; quarterly newsletter.
DOS, Windows 3.X, Windows 95, Windows NT, OS/2. 80X86 compatibles (512k). disk $279.00. *Addl. software required:* C Plus Plus compiler.
Will Accommodate Interrupt-Driven, Circular Buffered Service for 35 Ports at Baud Rates to 115,200 Baud. As a C Plus Plus Communication Library, It Provides a Hierarchy of Classes Which Give the Programmer Simple Access & Control of Serial Communications. Classes Are Provided for: Serial Port Controls, Modem Controls, File Transfer Protocols & Calculation of Check Values. In Addition to This, There Are Classes That Support Hardware Dependent Features. These Classes Are Derived from an Abstract Base Class. Features Include Support for Hayes Smartmodems, CompuServe B Plus, XMODEM, YMODEM, ZMODEM, Kermit, XON/XOFF for VT52 & VT100 (Subset) Terminal Emulation. Support Is Included for MSDOS, Microsoft Windows, & OS/2. Automated Installation Procedure & Examples Are Included. No Royalties.
Greenleaf Software, Inc.

Greenleaf CommLib Level 2. *Version:* 5.2. Jun. 1995. *Language(s):* Assembly, C, Visual Basic. *Items Included:* Source code, manual, reference guide. *Customer Support:* Phone support, 24-hour BBS, newsletter.
IBM PC & compatibles. $359.00.
Asynchronous Communication Library. Supports CompuServe B Plus, Xmodem, Ymodem, Zmodem, Kermit, & ASCII File Transfer Protocols, XON/XOFF, RTS/CTS (Request to Send/Clear to Send), DTR/DSR (Data Terminal Ready/Data Set Ready) Handshaking, & FIFOs on 16550 UARTS; DOS, 286 & 386 DOS Extenders, Windows 3.1 & Windows NT Supports Multiport Non-Intelligent & Intelligent Boards, 35 Ports, 115, 200 Baud.
Greenleaf Software, Inc.

Greenleaf DataWindows. *Version:* 3.0. Jul. 1992. *Compatible Hardware:* IBM PC & compatibles, PS/2. *Operating System(s) Required:* PC-DOS/MS-DOS, 386 protected mode. *Language(s):* C, Assembly (source code included). *Memory Required:* Minimum 512k, recommended 640k. *Items Included:* Manual, reference guide, newsletter. *Customer Support:* Telephone support, 24 hour online BBS.
disk $350.00, DOS & 386.
Windows, Data Entry, & Menus Library for C Programmers. Provides Device Independence & Overlaid Windows with Screen Management. Includes Greenleaf MakeForm (Enables Developers to Design Screens & Alter the Screens after the Program Is Finished Without the Need for Compiling or Linking). Supports 286 & 386 DOS Extenders, Mouse in Menus & Dialog Boxes.
Greenleaf Software, Inc.

Greenleaf Financial Mathlib. *Version:* 1.10. 1990. *Compatible Hardware:* IBM PC & compatibles, PS/2. *Memory Required:* 512k. *Items Included:* Manual, 1 year subscription newsletter. *Customer Support:* Telephone support, 24 hour online BBS.
3.5" or 5.25" disk $395.00.
Brings Exact Representation of Decimal Numbers, Plus Complete Business & Financial Applications Functions to the C Language. Includes Business Functions Such As: Compound Interest, Internal Rate of Return, Cash Flow Analysis, Bond Calculations, Amortization, Statistics, Trig., Array Processing & Print Flexibility. Accuracy to 18 Decimal Digits, with Complete Control over Rounding & Truncation. Comprehensive Error Detection System. Includes Online Help System.
Greenleaf Software, Inc.

Greenleaf MakeForm. *Version:* 2.0. *Compatible Hardware:* IBM PC & compatibles, PS/2. *Operating System(s) Required:* PC-DOS/MS-DOS. *General Requirements:* Greenleaf DataWindows 3.0 or higher. *Items Included:* Manual, reference guide. *Customer Support:* Telephone support, 24-hour online BBS, newsletter.
PC-DOS/MS-DOS. Included w/ Greenleaf DataWindows.
Enables Developers to Design Screens & Alter the Screens After the Program Is Finished Without the Need for Compiling or Linking.
Greenleaf Software, Inc.

Greenleaf SuperFunctions. *Version:* 1.1. *Compatible Hardware:* IBM PC & compatibles. *Operating System(s) Required:* PC-DOS/MS-DOS. *Items Included:* Manual, reference card. *Customer Support:* Telephone support, 24-hour online BBS, newsletter.
disk $299.00.
Includes 360 Functions for C Programmers: Advanced DOS & Interrupt Functions; Expanded Memory (EMM) Interface; Microsoft Mouse Interface Functions; Keyboard Functions; Logical Windows Setup Functions, Write Data to Windows, Cursor Control, Clear, Move & Scroll, Video Attribute Controls; Menu Functions; Date Functions Utility, Get System Date, Set System Date, ASCII String Dates, Julian Date Support, SFTIMEDATE Support, Conversions, Dates for Database Use, Adding Days to Date, Comparing Dates; CMOS Timer & Alarm; Project Scheduling; Time Functions Get System Date, Set System Date, ASCII String Time Output, Scanning ASCII String Time, SFTIMEDATE Support, Format Conversions, Time Formats for Database Use, Adding Minutes to Time, Comparing Times.
Greenleaf Software, Inc.

Greenleaf Viewcomm. *Version:* 3.0. 1991. *Operating System(s) Required:* PC-DOS/MS-DOS. *Items Included:* Manual, cables. *Customer Support:* Telephone support, 24 hour online BBS.
3.5" or 5.25" disk $399.00.
All the Features of a Dedicated Serial Data Analyzer. Users Can See What Is Happening on the RS-232 Serial Port in Detail. Monitor Mode Examines Data Flow Between a Pair of Communicating Devices, Capturing Data, Status & Mode Signals to a Buffer or Disk File & Displaying It. Source Code Lets Users Intervene: Send Data to Either Device from the Keyboard or File or Both While Observing Responses. Baud Rates up to 115200. View Data in ASCII, EBCDIC, HEX, Octal, Decimal, or Binary, with Graphics for the Non-Printable Codes. Utility Functions Include Push to DOS.
Greenleaf Software, Inc.

Greetingware Christmas Medley: Electronic Xmas Gift-Card. *Version:* 2. Aug. 1984. *Compatible Hardware:* IBM PC, PCjr, PC XT, PC AT. *Operating System(s) Required:* PC-DOS 2.0 or higher. *Language(s):* Compiled Advanced BASIC. *Memory Required:* 128k.
disk $9.95, incl. operating instructions (ISBN 0-933631-00-6, Order no. 84101).
Displays a Christmas Greeting Which Is Accompanied by Jingle Bells. 6 Popular Sing-Along Carols, Each with Pitch Aid, Unusual Arrangements & Several Verses Are Included. A Bouncing Star Synchronizes Words & Music on Monitor. Continuous Version Which Plays Unattended, Is Available.
Roxbury Research, Inc.

Greetingware Do-It-Yourself Kit: GW Promotional Kit. *Version:* 2. Dec. 1984. *Compatible Hardware:* IBM PC, PC XT, PC AT. *Operating System(s) Required:* PC-DOS 2.0 or higher. *Language(s):* Compiled Advanced BASIC. *Memory Required:* 128k. *General Requirements:* 2 disk drives.
disk $24.95 (ISBN 0-933631-04-9, Order no.: 84105).
Designed for Personal or Corporate Promotions. Allows Licensee to Create GW Christmas or Birthday Sing-Along Gift/Card Disks with Any Desired Displayable Greetings. Kit Includes a Character Processing Greeting Inserter.
Roxbury Research, Inc.

Greg Norman's Shark Attack: The Ultimate Golf Simulator. *Customer Support:* 90 day warranty.
MS-DOS 2.1 or higher. IBM (512K). disk $39.99. Nonstandard peripherals required: CGA, EGA, Tandy or VGA Graphics required. Atari St (512K). 3.5" disk $39.99.
Amiga (512K). 3.5" disk $39.99.
Golf Simulation with Realistic Three-Dimensional Graphics. There Are 5 Game Types & You Can Design Your Own Swing & Other Features.
Virgin Games.

Greggway HVAC-PC. *Version:* 4.0. *Compatible Hardware:* IBM PC & compatibles. *Memory Required:* 640k.
disk $685.00.
Computerized Estimating System for the Air Conditioning Contractors. Labor & Material Costs for Low Pressure, High Pressure, Welded, Duct Board, Round & Square Duct.
Tallysheet Corp.

Greggway PIPE-PC. *Version:* 4.2. Oct. 1995. *Compatible Hardware:* IBM PC & compatibles. *Memory Required:* 640k.
disk $585.00.
Computerized Estimating System for Piping/Plumbing Contractors. Provides Six Sets of "Starter" Tables with over 1300 Items. Users May Create Their Own Tables.
Tallysheet Corp.

Greyhound Professional Series Analysis Module. Ronald D. Jones. Jul. 1986. *Compatible Hardware:* Apple; Commodore; IBM; TRS-80 Model I, Model III, Color Computer. *Operating*

System(s) Required: CP/M. Memory Required: 64k.
disk $249.95 ea.
Apple. (ISBN 1-55604-240-X, Order no.: PD01).
CP/M. (ISBN 1-55604-241-8, Order no.: PD01).
Commodore. (ISBN 1-55604-242-6, Order no.: PD01).
Color Computer. (ISBN 1-55604-243-4, Order no.: PD01).
IBM. (ISBN 1-55604-244-2, Order no.: PD01).
Model I & Model III. (ISBN 1-55604-245-0, Order no.: PD01).
Up to 11 Races on Each Dog Can Be Evaluated to Provide Results. Full Screen & Faster Input Makes for Quicker Entry. Artificial Intelligence Is Used to Learn More about Favored Factors. Contains Complete Betting Mode Holding Tanks for Late Scratches & Entries; Track Record Adjustor & Multi-Track Modules. Complete "Help" Functions Available.
Professor Jones Professional Handicapping Systems.

Greyhound Professional Series Database Manager. Ronald D. Jones. Jul. 1986. *Compatible Hardware:* Apple; Commodore; IBM; TRS-80 Model I, Model III, Color Computer. *Operating System(s) Required:* CP/M. *Memory Required:* 64k.
disk $449.95 ea.
Apple. (ISBN 1-55604-252-3, Order no.: PD03).
Commodore. (ISBN 1-55604-253-1, Order no.: PD03).
CP/M. (ISBN 1-55604-254-X, Order no.: PD03).
Color Computer. (ISBN 1-55604-255-8, Order no.: PD03).
IBM. (ISBN 1-55604-256-6, Order no.: PD03).
Model I & Model III. (ISBN 1-55604-257-4, Order no.: PD03).
Essential Data on Every Dog Can Be Saved in a Data Base to Be Used in Conjunction with the Analysis Module. Includes Storage of Last 10 Races of All Dogs on Disk, Attains Higher Win Percentage Due to More & Better Information, Automatic Storage of Races & Complete Printouts of Previous Races.
Professor Jones Professional Handicapping Systems.

Greyhound Professional Series Factor Value Multiple Regression Module. Ronald D. Jones. Jul. 1986. *Compatible Hardware:* Apple; Commodore; IBM; TRS-80 Model I, Model III, Color Computer. *Operating System(s) Required:* CP/M. *Memory Required:* 64k.
disk $349.95 ea.
Apple. (ISBN 1-55604-246-9, Order no.: PD02).
CP/M. (ISBN 1-55604-247-7, Order no.: PD02).
Commodore. (ISBN 1-55604-248-5, Order no.: PD02).
Color Computer. (ISBN 1-55604-249-3, Order no.: PD02).
IBM. (ISBN 1-55604-250-7, Order no.: PD02).
Model I & Model III. (ISBN 1-55604-251-5, Order no.: PD02).
Provides Fast Multiple Regression Analysis, Deriving the Most Precise Weighting Formula Available. Includes Manual Factor Weighting Ability, Complete Multiple Regression of Target Races, a Holding Tank Link to Bet Module, As Well As True Low Level Artificial Intelligence.
Professor Jones Professional Handicapping Systems.

Greyhound Track Record Adjustor. Ronald D. Jones. 1985. *Compatible Hardware:* Apple; Commodore; IBM; TRS-80 Model I, Model III, Color Computer. *Operating System(s) Required:* CP/M. *Memory Required:* 64k.
disk $29.95 ea.
Apple. (ISBN 1-55604-108-X, Order no.: DOTA).
CP/M. (ISBN 1-55604-109-8, Order no.: DOTA).
Commodore. (ISBN 1-55604-110-1, Order no.: DOTA).
Color Computer. (ISBN 1-55604-111-X).
IBM. (ISBN 1-55604-112-8, Order no.: DOTA).
Model I & Model III. (ISBN 1-55604-113-6, Order no.: DOTA).
Graduated Records Can Be Stored on All Grades. Designed to Eliminate the Problem with Speed Errors in Lower Grade Dogs Due to "A" Track Records.
Professor Jones Professional Handicapping Systems.

GRiD Debug. *Version:* 3.2. Nov. 1987. *Compatible Hardware:* IBM PC XT, PC AT & compatibles. *Operating System(s) Required:* MS-DOS 3.2 or higher. *Memory Required:* 110k. *General Requirements:* InterGRiD Operating Environment.
$500.00 includes GRidDevelop, GRiDWrite, development utilities & libraries.
Stand-Alone Source-Code & Symbolic Debugger. Reads Intel File Formats. Compatible Languages Are Intel Pascal, PLM, Assembly, FORTRAN & Mark Williams C. Supports 8086 Instruction Set, Intel Overlays, Remote Debugger, 43-Line Mode & 50-Line Mode. Features Full Screen Interface; Code & Register Values Windows Display; & Procedure Name Entry/Exit, Source Code Line, Assembly Code Line & Timing Breakpoint Types. Also Includes Resident/Non-Resident Mode, On-Line Help, Window Capability, Environment Save, Access to OS Information & Network Debugging.
GRiD Systems Corp.

GRIDDER. *Version:* 2.3. Mar. 1986. *Compatible Hardware:* IBM PC, PC XT, PC AT & compatibles. *Operating System(s) Required:* PC-DOS, MS-DOS. *Language(s):* FORTRAN. *Memory Required:* 512k. *General Requirements:* Printer.
disk $500.00 (Order no.: GRIDDER).
Imposes a Grid or Mesh over the Data Sets for the Current & Proposed Topography of an Excavation Area. The Program Completes Inverse Distance to a Power Estimation of Both Data Sets, Providing the Calculation Base for VOLUME.
Geostat Systems International, Inc. (GSII).

GRiDPrint/GRiDPlot/GRiDFile/GRiDWrite/GRiDMaster/GRiDPaint/GRiDTask. *Compatible Hardware:* GRiD Compass Computer; GRiDCase Computer Family. *Operating System(s) Required:* GRID-OS, MS-DOS. *Language(s):* Pascal, PL/M, FORTRAN, C, BASIC, COBOL. *Memory Required:* 256k.
contact publisher for price.
Management Tools Which Format Documents & Generate Graphs. Desk Organizer & Application Developer.
GRiD Systems Corp.

GRiDReformat. *Compatible Hardware:* GRiD Compass Computer; GRiDCase Computer Family. *Operating System(s) Required:* GRiD-OS, MS-DOS. *Memory Required:* 256k.
disk $100.00.
Allows GRiD Computer User to Utilize Data from Virtually Any Source - Another Computer System, Databases, PC's.
GRiD Systems Corp.

GRIDZO. *Version:* 7.0. *Items Included:* Manual. *Customer Support:* Free phone & mail support, 30-day money back guarantee.
MS-DOS. IBM PC, PC XT, PC AT & compatibles. $379.00. Nonstandard peripherals required: EGA or VGA card. *Optimal configuration:* 386 machine, LaserJet II, dot matrix printers (Epson compatible).
Gridding/Contouring Package Including Inverse Distance Gridding Algorithm, Control Point Filtering, Automatic Grid Dimensioning, Contour Smoothing, Irregular Contour Spacing, Contour Masking, Labeling, Cluster Point Compensation. 10 Gridding Algorithms, Mathematical & Statistical Functions.
RockWare, Inc.

Gridzo Contour & Perspective Mapper. *Items Included:* Full manual. No other products required. *Customer Support:* Free telephone support - no time limit. 30 day warranty.
MS-DOS 3.2 or higher. IBM & compatibles (512k). disk $469.95. *Optimal configuration:* IBM, MS-DOS 3.0 or higher, 640k RAM, 10Mb hard disk space, & CGA/EGA/VGA or Hercules monochrome graphics. Math coprocessors are supported, but not required.
Macintosh. 3.5" disk $459.95. *Optimal configuration:* Macintosh, 1Mb RAM & supports large screens, color displays, & a math coprocessor.
Powerful General-Purpose Contour & Three-Dimensional Perspective Mapper. It Is Specifically Applicable to Terrain Mapping & Other Geological Uses, but Is Also Well-Suited for Use in the Areas of Mathematics, Engineering (Civil, Mining, Modeling), & Science. Its Very High Data Capacity (32000) Points, Coupled with Extensive Analysis Features, Make It the Top-of-the-Line Product in Surface Mapping.
Dynacomp, Inc.

Grocery. Duane Bristow. *Compatible Hardware:* TRS-80 Model I, Model III. *Operating System(s) Required:* TRSDOS. *Language(s):* BASIC. *Memory Required:* 48k.
TRS-80 Model III. disk $34.95.
cassette $19.95.
Stores & Lists up to 700 Grocery Items. Selects Items User Needs & Gives Print Command to Produce Shopping List.
Duane Bristow Computers, Inc.

Grossman Accounting Software: for the Agribusiness Industry. *Customer Support:* Free on site training; first 6 months support free; yearly support is 13% percent of cost of software; modem support; phone support; classroom training & "user group" meetings.
IBM PC (2Mb). Contact publisher for price. Networks supported: Novell primarily.
Totally Integrating Accounting Software for Commodities Firms, Grain Terminals, Grain Elevators, Feed Manufacturers, Seed Companies, & Agribusiness Retailers. Packages Include All General Accounting, Grain Purchases, Grain Sales, Feed Manufacturing, Patronage, Production Scheduling, Futures/Options & Hedging/Basis Analysis.
Grossman & Assocs., Inc.

Grover's Animal Adventure. *Compatible Hardware:* Commodore 64, IBM PC & compatibles.
disk $9.95.
Teaches Children Different Animal Environments.
Hi Tech Expressions, Inc.

Grow. Clifford Schorer. Sep. 1995. *Items Included:* Spiral bound work book, spiral bound textbook. *Customer Support:* 90 days warranty.
Macintosh. Mac (8Mb). 3.5" disk $79.95 (ISBN 0-9643690-0-1). *Addl. software required:* Microsoft Excel.
IBM (compatible) Windows. IBM & compatibles (8Mb). disk $79.95 (ISBN 0-9643690-1-X). *Addl. software required:* Microsoft Excel.
Financial Accounting Computer Software Program Designed to Help Growing Companies Analyze Their Business & Perform Better. This Management System Does the Following: Identifies Problems & Opportunities; Measures

Solvency, Efficiency, Profitability & People Performance; Compares Results with Previous Periods; Provides Action Plans for Growing Profits; Generates Management Reports.
Connect, Inc.

Grower Accounting (a Part of ABECAS). Version: 3.3. Customer Support: On site training unlimited support services for first 90 days & through subscription thereafter.
PC/MS-DOS 3.x. IBM PC & compatibles. Contact publisher for price. Nonstandard peripherals required: Hard disk (30Mb or higher); 132 column printer.
Allows User to Define Growers, Receive Raw Product & Process/Pack into Finished Products by Size, Label & Product. Updates Inventory Management Module. Sub-Lots/Pallets/Bins May Be Tracked & Shipments May Be Entered. Charges May Be Calculated Based on Raw Processed or Shipped Product. Advances & Charges May Also Be Tracked. Numerous Management Reports Are Available As Well As Specific Grower Reporting. This Module Requires That Inventory Management, Accounts Receivable, & Sales Order Modules As Well As Lot/Size Detail Options Be Present. Multi-User Version Available for Novell, NTNX, 10-Net, Unix/Xenix, Turbo DOS, & Others.
Argos Software.

Growing Dairy Calves Decision Aids. Merle W. Wagner. 1982. Compatible Hardware: Apple II Plus, IIe, IIc; IBM. Language(s): BASIC. Memory Required: 48k, 640k. General Requirements: Printer.
disk $29.95 (ISBN 0-922900-14-0, Order no.: CFD-224).
back-up disk $9.95.
manual $19.95.
Can Be Modified to Fit a Particular Course or Farming Operation. Calculations Include: Gross Income, Total Feed Cost, Total Direct Cost, Income Minus Direct Cost, Investment Overhead, Total Expense, Total Expense per Pound of Calf Sold, Net Return to Management, Net Return to Labor/Management, Rate Earned on Investment.
Cherrygarth, Inc.

The Growth Search System. Version: 96.1. Customer Support: Free telephone support.
MS-DOS or Windows 3.0 or higher (384k). $250.00, for any one issue.
$700.00, for annual 6-issue subscription.
Consists of a Windows or DOS Software Plus Database of Names & Addresses of Approximately 2600 of the Fastest Growing U.S. Companies. Users Can Print Cover Letters, Envelopes & Mailing Labels. Firms Can Be Selected by Investment Preferences with Respect to Industry, Geography, Number of Employees, Dollar Sales. Database Updated 6 Times per Year.
Custom Databanks, Inc.

GRX 300-400.
Macintosh SE, II. disk GRX-300 $4995.00. Nonstandard peripherals required: Connecting cable.
disk GRX-400 $6495.00.
GRX-300 Is an Eight-Pen Drafting Plotter Featuring Paper Size of ANSI A to ANSI D Cut Sheet, Maximum Plotting Area of 33.5 by 22 Inches, Plotting Speed of 24 Inches per Second & Resolution of 0.78125 Microns. GRX-400 Is an Eight-Pen Drafting Plotter Featuring Paper Size of ANSI A to ANSI E Cut Sheet, Maximum Plotting Area of 43.5 by 33.5 Inches, Plotting Speed of 24 Inches per Second & Resolution of 0.78125 Microns. Other Features Include Custom VLSI Chip for the Micro-Step System, Custom CPU for Pen Carousel Optimization, Optional 1Mb Buffer & More.
Roland Digital Group.

GS Numerics. Version: 1.8. Items Included: Users manual. Customer Support: 319-927-6537.
GSOS 5.0.2. Apple IIGS (1Mb). 3.5" disk $99.95. Nonstandard peripherals required: Disk drive.
Educational Mathematics Program with Emphasis on Basic Algebra & Trigonometry, the Building Blocks of Calculus & Other Higher Math. Special Emphasis Is Directed Toward Analyzing Polynomials, Trigonometric Functions & the Exponential Functions. Analysis Can Be Done Either Analytically or Graphically, Allowing User to See the Forms of Functions, Without the Time Intensive Labor Required to Draw Graphs by Hand. Features Include: Scientific Calculator, Polynomial Operations, Non-polynomial Functions, x-y Data Analysis, Systems of Linear Equations, Matrix Operations, File Operations, Graphics, & More.
Spring Branch Software, Inc.

GSS*CGM. Version: 3.0. Language(s): C, FORTRAN. Customer Support: phone/FAX.
MS-DOS. IBM PC & compatibles, PS/2. $495.00.
ANSI (American National Standards Institute) Standard That Uses Compact Data Codes to Describe Graphics Primitives, Attributes & Text in a Picture. Many Applications Can Save Graphics As CGM Files; for Example, Lotus Freelance, Ashton-Tate Applause & Harvard Graphics. Interpreter Option Is Available. Programmers Can Now Create Interactive Graphics Applications for Cut & Paste. Interpreter Can Read & Display CGM Files Regardless of Origin. User Can Exchange Metafiles from One Application to Another, Transmit Them Via Modem, & Recreate Them. Supports Binary, Clear Text, & Character Encoded Formats. User Can Develop Graphics Applications That Can Read CGM Files from Other Applications Without CGM Format Translation. OS/2 Version Supports Both Microsoft C & Microsoft FORTRAN.
Graphic Software Systems, Inc.

GSS-Toolkit Kernel System. Version: 2.14. Operating System(s) Required: PC-DOS 2.0 or higher. Language(s): FORTRAN, C. Memory Required: 512k. General Requirements: 360k floppy disk; floating point processor (recommended); serial or parallel ports for peripherals (optional).
disk $795.00.
International Standards Organization Has Adopted the Graphical Kernel System (GKS) As the Standard Programmer Interface to Graphics Functions. GSS-Toolkit Is a Library of GKS-Conforming Functions for Microcomputers. A Linkable Subroutine Library, Kernel System Is a Programming Tool. User Includes Calls to High-Level Graphics Routines in the Application Source File, & Then Compiles the Program. External References Generated by the Graphics Subroutine Calls Are Satisfied When the Compiled Application Module Is Linked with the Kernel System Graphic Library.
Graphic Software Systems, Inc.

Guderian. Compatible Hardware: Apple II+, IIe, IIc; Atari 800/XL/XE; Commodore 64/128. General Requirements: Joystick.
disk $30.00 ea., incl. rulebook & planning map. Apple. (Order no.: 48152).
Atari & Commodore. (Order no.: 48193).
Simulates the German Army's Invasion of Russia in 1941. The German Player Must Master Blitzkrieg Tactics to Encircle & Overrun Soviet Divisions & Drive Deep Enough into Russia to Make the Capture of Moscow Possible. There Is a Solitaire Option Allowing the Player to Take Command of Either the German or Soviet Armies As Well As to Overrun Attacks, Supply Rules, Soviet Leaders, Rail Movement, & Optional Reinforcements. For One or Two Players.
Avalon Hill Game Co., The Microcomputer Games Div.

Guide Professional Publisher. Version: 3.5. Compatible Hardware: IBM PC AT, XT, PS/2 & compatibles. Operating System(s) Required: MS-DOS, MS-Windows 2.x & higher. Memory Required: 640k. General Requirements: Mouse, graphics board PC, hard disk required. Items Included: Disks, set-up & user manuals. Customer Support: 8:00 to 4:00 PST, Monday through Friday.
IBM PC. Contact publisher for price.
The Industry's Most Complete System for Electronic Publication Development & Distribution. This System Includes a Comprehensive Set of Tools to Manage High-Volume Production of Interactive Publications. Includes Both the Software & Support Necessary to Automate the Conversion of Existing Documents, While Creating a Custom, Interactive Environment for the User. GPP Is a Collection of Automated Conversion Filters, Flexible Authoring Tools & Powerful Tools to Manage Text, Images & Multimedia Information. In Addition, It Provides Automatic Indexing, Advanced Table Management, Oversized Image Handling & Custom Scripting Options. Includes a Bundled Run-Time License That Lets You Distribute Electronic Publications to an Unlimited Number of Users Without Additional Incremental Cost.
InfoAccess, Inc.

Guide to Building Products from Builder Magazine, 1996. Builder Magazine Staff. Aug. 1995. Items Included: 8-page booklet - How to Play the CD & System Requirements. Customer Support: Fax support line (415) 322-0962.
Macintosh; Windows. Macintosh 68030 processor or higher, Systems 6.07 or higher (6Mb); Windows system must meet the MMPC Level II standards. CD-ROM disk $39.95 (ISBN 0-9647983-0-1). Addl. software required: Quicktime 2.0 or higher, CD.
A Building Products Buyer's Guide on CD-ROM. Electronic Desktop Reference Guide That Lists 10,000 Building Products from 2,100 Manufacturers. Product Information Includes Address, Phone & Fax Number of Manufacturer, Product Photo & Description, Advertisement or Video. Run on Multi-Media Capable PC's with Windows or Macintosh Computers.
Hanley-Wood, Inc.

Guide to the Holy Land for Mac & Windows. (Historical Travel Guides Ser.). Theodorich. Edited by Ronald G. Musto & Eileen Gardiner. Apr. 1996.
Windows. IBM. disk $20.00 (ISBN 0-934977-56-9).
Macintosh. 3.5" disk $20.00 (ISBN 0-934977-46-1).
Twelfth-Century Guide to the Holy Land on Diskette with Photographs, Plans, Maps, & Views That Supplement the Original Guide with an Electronic Guide to the Monuments with Special Emphasis on Jerusalem. Includes bibliography, Introduction, & Notes.
Italica Pr.

Guide to Wide Area Networks: A Step-by-Step Introduction. 1995. Customer Support: 30 day no risk guarantee.
IBM. disk $9.95 (ISBN 0-927875-59-4, Order no.: 7470).
Comprehensive Guide Which Explains the Different Means of Connectivity with a Wide Area Network. The Guide Includes Definitions of the Different Type of Networks, Cabling, etc. It Includes Many Diagrams to Aid in Determining Which Setup Best Meets Your Needs & Assists with the Terminology.
Winnebago Software Co.

TITLE INDEX

GuideView. Jun. 1991. *Items Included:* 1 manual; 1 program diskette; at least 1 set of data diskettes. *Customer Support:* 30-day money-back guarantee; on-line tutorial, "Help Text Banner" on screens, help menu, & detailed reference guide. DOS 3.1 or higher. IBM or 100% compatible (640k). Single user program $105.00, single user data disk $85.00 (ISBN 1-56433-089-3). *Optimal configuration:* IBM or 100% compatible personal computer, color monitor or monochrome, printer, 5.25"/3.5" floppy drive, 640k RAM, DOS 3.1 & higher, hard disk. *Networks supported:* Novell & compatibles. Computer-Based Search & Retrieval System That Enables Users to Immediately Access Information Contained in the PPC Guides. It Allows Users to Perform "Key Word", Searches and/or Generalized Searches. Retrieved Information Can Be Printed Directly Through GuideView.
Practitioners Publishing Co.

GuideWare. *Version:* 4.0. Sep. 1992. *Items Included:* 1 manual; 1 program diskette; at least 1 set of data diskettes. *Customer Support:* 30-day money-back guarantee; on-line tutorial, "Help Text Banner" on screens, help menu, & detailed reference guide. DOS 3.1 or higher. IBM or 100% compatible (640k). Single user program $105.00, single user data disk $85.00 (ISBN 1-56433-074-5). *Optimal configuration:* IBM or 100% compatible personal computer, 640k RAM, DOS 3.1 or higher, color or monochrome monitor, printer, 5.25"/3.5" floppy drive. *Networks supported:* Novell & compatibles. Computer-Based System That Enables Users to Print and/or Customize the Practice Aids Contained in PPC Guides. These Practice Aids Can Be Customized Using GuideWare's Guide Editor or WORDPERFECT 5.0 & 5.1.
Practitioners Publishing Co.

The Guinness Disc of Records, 1993.
IBM CD-ROM. CD-ROM disk $99.95 (Order no.: 111311).
MPC. CD-ROM disk $99.95 (Order no.: 111307).
MAC CD-ROM. CD-ROM disk $99.95 (Order no.: 111309).
Explore the Fastest, Easiest-to-Use Collection of Achievements & Accomplishments, Failures & Flops, Ever Assembled for CD-ROM. This Single Source Is the Most Authoritative Reference on Every Topic - Perfect for Trivia Buffs, Teachers, Writers & Researchers. It's a Gold Mine of Fascinating Information That Will Entertain for Hours on End.
Software Toolworks.

Guitar Master. *Version:* 2.1. Jan. 1991. *Items Included:* User's manual; demo program available for $5.00.
IBM PC, XT, AT, PS/2 & compatibles. disk $49.95.
Teaches User How to Play Any Standard MIDI File Format Song Using a Computerized Graphical Guitar. Also Can Calculate, Display & Print Hundreds of Different Scale & Chord Charts. User Can Create Custom Scale & Chord Charts Using the Edit Option, Turning Notes on & off & Adding Custom Fingerings. Custom Charts Can Be Saved as Image Files & Later Recalled. Product Handles Any Type of Alternative Tuning as Well as Providing Support for Four Fretboard Notations Ranging from Simple Dots to the Actual Note Value. With a Roland MPU-401 Attachment, Product Becomes a 64 Track Sequencer Capable of Recording, Playing or Overdubbing to Any Track.
Spartan Software Systems.

Gulf Strike. Jun. 1983. *Compatible Hardware:* Apple II+, IIe, IIc; Atari 800/XL/XE; Commodore 64/128; IBM PC & compatibles; Tandy 1000. *Memory Required:* 64-128k. *General Requirements:* Joystick; CGA card for IBM.
disk $30.00 ea.
IBM. (Order no.: 44954).
Commodore, Atari. (Order no.: 44993).
Commodore, Apple. (Order no.: 44994).
Simulates the Effect of a Soviet Invasion of Iran Sometime in the Near Future. The Soviet Player Has Tank Armies, Mechanized Units, & Infantry Rolling Across the Iranian & Afghanistan Borders, Submarines, Destroyers, & Aircraft Carriers in the Persian Gulf, & Command of the Iraqi Forces Currently at War with Iran. The United States Player Has His Armed Forces & French & British Expeditionary Forces.
Avalon Hill Game Co., The Microcomputer Games Div.

Gumball Rally Adventure. *Compatible Hardware:* IBM. *Memory Required:* 128k.
disk $19.95.
Racing Game in Which You Draw Your Own Map to Make It to the Finish Line.
Dynacomp, Inc.

Gunship. 1986. *Compatible Hardware:* Atari ST; Commodore 64/128; IBM PC, PC XT, PC AT; Amiga. *Items Included:* Manual, keyboard overlay. *Customer Support:* Free customer service, (410) 771-1151, Ext. 350.
IBM, Atari ST. $19.95.
Commodore 64. disk $39.95.
Amiga. 3.5" disk $54.95.
AH-64 APACHE Attack Helicopter Simulation. User Sits in the Cockpit Wearing the "Integrated Helmet Targeting System" (IHTS). Search & Destroy, Rescue, & Covert Missions Are Available. Features 3-Dimensional Graphics & Joystick Control.
Microprose Software.

Gunship 2000. Sep. 1991. *Items Included:* Manual, keyboard overlay. *Customer Support:* Free customer service, 1-410-771-1151, Ext. 350.
80286, 10MHz, hard disk required. IBM AT, PS/2; Tandy & most compatibles (640k). disk $69.95 (ISBN 1-55884-121-0). *Optimal configuration:* Joystick recommended. Supports most VGA/MCGA graphics; supports IBM, Tandy, Roland, Adlib cards.
Multi-Helicopter Combat Simulation. Take Total Command of a Full Troop of America's Most Powerful & Versatile Rotor Craft. Theaters Include the Persian Gulf & Central Europe. Topographical 3-D Graphics Provide Uncanny Realism. Digitized Speech. Multiple Mission Profiles.
MicroProse Software.

Gunship 2000: Islands & Ice Scenario Disk. *Version:* VGA only. Aug. 1992. *Items Included:* Manual. *Customer Support:* Free customer service, 1-410-771-1151, Ext. 350.
80286, 12MHz, hard disk required. Not a stand alone, must use Gunship 2000. IBM & most compatibles (640k). disk $39.95 (ISBN 1-55884-122-9). *Optimal configuration:* MCGA/VGA, Joystick recommended; Adlib, Roland, Sound Blaster; IBM, ATI stereo.
Renew the Challenge & Excitement Originally Experienced When You Took Command of Your Original Gunship. Mission Builder Lets You Create the Types of Challenges You Enjoy the Most. New Theaters in Antarctica & the Philippine's. Better Sound Card Support, Expanded Database of Targets, Air & Artillery Close Support. The Most Realistic Multi-Helicopter Simulation Yet.
MicroProse Software.

Gunshoot. *Customer Support:* Back up disks available.
Amiga (512k). $14.95.
Shoot the Criminals, But Avoid the Civilians. Includes 12 Characters, One or Two Player Mode, & Digitized Sound.
DigiTek Software.

GURU. *Version:* 6.0. Jan. 1996. *Compatible Hardware:* IBM PC XT, PC AT, PS/2 & compatibles; LAN. *Operating System(s) Required:* PC-DOS, OS/2. *General Requirements:* 10Mb hard disk. Expanded memory supported. *Items Included:* Documentation, 1 yr customer support. *Customer Support:* 1 year included.
Contact publisher for price.
AI System That Integrates Expert System & Natural Language Capabilities with Productivity Tools Like Data Base Management, Spreadsheet, & Graphics. Rule Set Manager Is Menu-Driven & Supports an Unlimited Number of Rules Which Are a Series of IF-THEN Statements Experts Use to Analyze a Problem. Rules Can Employ Any of GURU's Facilities, Allowing Users to Build AI Systems.
Micro Data Base Systems, Inc. (MDBS).

Gus & the Cyberbuds Go to the Kooky Carnival. Modern Media Venture Staff. Sep. 1995. *Customer Support:* Telephone support - free (except phone charge).
Windows 3.1. IBM & compatibles (386 DX-20) (4Mb). CD-ROM disk $12.99 (ISBN 1-57594-020-5). Nonstandard peripherals required: 2x CD-ROM player, Sound Card, VGA monitor. *Optimal configuration:* 486 SX-33.
Interactive Learning Adventure - Explore the Zany Environments of the Kooky Carnival Jam Packed with Animations, Activities & Super Fun Games.
Kidsoft, Inc.

Gus & the Cyberbuds Go to the Kooky Carnival. Modern Media Venture Staff. Sep. 1995. *Customer Support:* Telephone support - free (except phone charge).
Windows 3.1. IBM & compatibles (386 DX-20) (4Mb). CD-ROM disk $12.99 (ISBN 1-57594-059-0). Nonstandard peripherals required: 2x CD-ROM player, Sound Card, VGA monitor. *Optimal configuration:* 486 SX-33.
Interactive Learning Adventure - Explore the Zany Environments of the Kooky Carnival Jam Packed with Animations, Activities & Super Fun Games. Blister Pack Jewel Case.
Kidsoft, Inc.

Gus & the Cyberbuds Sing, Play & Paint A-Long. Sep. 1995. *Customer Support:* Telephone support - free (except phone charge).
Windows 3.1. IBM & compatibles (386 DX-20) (4Mb). CD-ROM disk $12.99 (ISBN 1-57594-017-5). Nonstandard peripherals required: 2x CD-ROM player, Sound Card, VGA monitor. *Optimal configuration:* 486 SX-33.
Baskets of Fun Painting & Singing with Gus & the Cyberbuds.
Kidsoft, Inc.

Gus & the Cyberbuds Sing, Play & Paint A-Long. Sep. 1995. *Customer Support:* Telephone support - free (except phone charge).
Windows 3.1. IBM & compatibles (386 DX-20) (4Mb). CD-ROM disk $12.99 (ISBN 1-57594-056-6). Nonstandard peripherals required: 2x CD-ROM player, Sound Card, VGA monitor. *Optimal configuration:* 486 SX-33.
Baskets of Fun Painting & Singing with Gus & the Cyberbuds. Blister Pack Jewel Case.
Kidsoft, Inc.

Gus Goes to Cyber Town. Sep. 1995. *Customer Support:* Telephone support - free (except phone charge).
Windows 3.1. IBM & compatibles (386 DX-20) (4Mb). CD-ROM disk $12.99 (ISBN 1-57594-019-1). *Nonstandard peripherals required:* 2x CD-ROM player, Sound Card, VGA monitor. *Optimal configuration:* 486 XS-33.
Interactive Learning Game with Lots of Music & Fun.
Kidsoft, Inc.

Gus Goes to Cyber Town. Sep. 1995. *Customer Support:* Telephone support - free (except phone charge).
Windows 3.1. IBM & compatibles (386 DX-20) (4Mb). CD-ROM disk $12.99 (ISBN 1-57594-058-2). *Nonstandard peripherals required:* 2x CD-ROM player, Sound Card, VGA monitor. *Optimal configuration:* 486 SX-33.
Interactive Learning Game with Lots of Music & Fun. Blister Pack Jewel Case.
Kidsoft, Inc.

Gus Goes to Cyberopolis. Modern Media Ventures Staff. Sep. 1995. *Customer Support:* Telephone support - free (except phone charge).
Windows 3.1. IBM & compatibles (386 DX-20) (4Mb). CD-ROM disk $12.99 (ISBN 1-57594-018-3). *Nonstandard peripherals required:* 2x CD-ROM player, Sound Card, VGA monitor. *Optimal configuration:* 486 XS-33.
Interactive Learning Adventure - from the Aquarium to the Subway, Kids Have Endless Opportunities to Observe, Experiment & Learn.
Kidsoft, Inc.

Gus Goes to Cyberopolis. Sep. 1995. *Customer Support:* Telephone support - free (except phone charge).
Windows 3.1. IBM & compatibles (386 DX-20) (4Mb). CD-ROM disk $12.99 (ISBN 1-57594-057-4). *Nonstandard peripherals required:* 2x CD-ROM player, Sound Card, VGA monitor. *Optimal configuration:* 486 SX-33.
Interactive Learning Adventure - from the Aquarium to the Subway, Kids Have Endless Opportunities to Observe, Experiment & Learn. Blister Pack Jewel Case.
Kidsoft, Inc.

Gus Goes to Cyberopolis. Jan. 1996. *Customer Support:* Telephone support - free (except phone charge).
System 7 or higher. 256 color capable Macintosh (8Mb). CD-ROM disk $12.99 (ISBN 1-57594-104-X). *Nonstandard peripherals required:* 2X CD ROM drive, 640/480 resolution monitor.
The Title Features the Return of Gus, the Lovable Dog Who Accompanies You on Your Journey Through Cyberopolis. There Are Six Exciting Environments for Children to Explore, Each Providing a Positive & Entertaining Experience. While Exploring Each Environment Children Search for the Elusive CyberBuds, Enlightened & Intriguing Characters Who Reveal Interesting Habits of Information.
Kidsoft, Inc.

Gus Goes to CyberStone Park. Dec. 1995. *Customer Support:* Telephone support - free (except phone charge).
Windows 3.1. IBM & compatibles (386 DX-20) (4Mb). CD-ROM disk $12.99, Jewel (ISBN 1-57594-080-9). *Nonstandard peripherals required:* 2X CD ROM player, sound card, VGA monitor. *Optimal configuration:* 486 SX-33.
CD-ROM disk $12.99, Blister.
Travel with Gus to CyberStone Park, a Colonial Wilderness Chock Full of Fun Places to Explore. Children Will Meet Ranger Jackie & Ranger Rick & Learn How to Safely Enjoy Time in the Wilderness.
Kidsoft, Inc.

Gus Goes to Cyberstone Park. Feb. 1996. *Customer Support:* Telephone support - free (except phone charge).
Windows 3.1. IBM compatible 386 DX-20 (4Mb). CD-ROM disk $12.99 (ISBN 1-57594-093-0). *Nonstandard peripherals required:* 2x CD-ROM, sound card, VGA monitor. *Optimal configuration:* 486, SX-33.
Travel, Exploration, Wilderness Safety. Blister Pack.
Kidsoft, Inc.

Gus Goes to CyberStone Park. Dec. 1995. *Customer Support:* Telephone support - free (except phone charge).
Windows 3.1. IBM & compatibles (386 DX-20) (4Mb). CD-ROM disk $12.99 (ISBN 1-57594-080-9). *Nonstandard peripherals required:* 2X CD-ROM player, sound card, VGA monitor. *Optimal configuration:* 486 SX-33.
Travel with Gus to CyberStone Park, a Colonial Wilderness Chock Full of Fun Places to Explore. Children Will Meet Ranger Jackie & Ranger Rick & Learn How to Safely Enjoy Time in the Wilderness. Jewel Case.
Kidsoft, Inc.

Gusher. *Version:* 5. 1982. *Compatible Hardware:* IBM PC. *Operating System(s) Required:* MS-DOS 2.0 or higher. *Language(s):* IBM UCSD p-System. *Memory Required:* 256k. *General Requirements:* 2 disk drives, printer.
disk $3000.00, incl. documentation.
Designed to Eliminate Common Accounting Problems Which an Oil & Gas Operator Might Encounter. Lists Revenue & Working-Interest Owners, Vendors, Vendor Invoices, Amounts to Be Paid, & Amounts to Be Billed.
High Technology Software Products, Inc.

Guying: Guying & Anchoring. *Version:* 2.0. Dennis M. Levy. Oct. 1983. *Compatible Hardware:* IBM PC & compatibles, PC XT, PC AT. *Operating System(s) Required:* MS-DOS, PC-DOS. *Memory Required:* 70k. *General Requirements:* 2 disk drives, printer.
disk $300.00 (ISBN 0-934975-03-7).
Provides Field Engineer with the Means to Determine Proper Guying & Anchoring of Distribution of Transmission Lines. Calculates Total Forces to Be Guyed, Minimum Number of Guys That May Be Used & Determines Minimum Guy Lead. Suitable for Grade B or C Construction & Angle or Deadend Pole. Safety Factors Are Used in Accordance with National Electric Safety Codes.
Power System Engineering, Inc.

GW-BASIC. Microsoft, Inc. *Compatible Hardware:* HP 150 Touchscreen, HP 110 Portable.
3.5" disk $395.00 (Order no.: 45450D).
Gives All the Standard Microsoft BASIC Commands &, in Addition, Includes Graphics Commands, Data Communication, Access to Sub-Directories, Keyboard & Timer Event Trapping, & a Full Screen Editor.
Hewlett-Packard Co.

GW-Convert. Dennis Allen. *Compatible Hardware:* TRS-80 Model 4. *Operating System(s) Required:* CP/M. *Language(s):* BASIC.
$99.95, incl. manual.
Collection of Programs & Subroutines Designed to Translate IBM BASIC Programs for Execution on the TRS-80 Model 4 (in the 4 Mode Only). Graphics Conversion Requires the Radio Shack or Grafix Solution High-Resolution Board. Programming Hints & Tips Are Included, & Several Functions & Subroutines May Be Merged with Model 4 Programs & Sold Without Royalty. Programs That Use the IBM Communication Protocol May Also Require a BASIC Compiler to Execute Properly.
The Alternate Source.

GW HVAC-PC. *Version:* 4.2. Sep. 1991. *Operating System(s) Required:* PC-DOS/MS-DOS. *General Requirements:* Hard disk.
disk $685.00.
Estimates the Sheet Metal Labor & Material Cost for Construction.
Tallysheet Corp.

GW Pipe-PC. *Version:* 4.0. Sep. 1991. *Operating System(s) Required:* PC-DOS/MS-DOS. *Memory Required:* 640k. *General Requirements:* Hard disk.
disk $585.00.
Calculates Piping & Plumbing Cost Estimates for New Construction.
Tallysheet Corp.

GWBasic Total Well Production Systems Optimization Manual: GWBasic TWPSOM Software. *Version:* 2.0. *Items Included:* 6 volume set containing 16 three ring binder manuals, 31 program disks, & 19 graphic disks running Harvard Graphics, Run time version of DOS, GWBASIC Interpreter. *Customer Support:* 30 days limited warranty & disclaimer.
PC-DOS/MS-DOS 3.0 or higher. IBM PC, PC XT, PC AT, PS/2 series, OS/2 systems, & compatibles (640k) & hard disk required with at least 11Mb of unused disk space. 6 volume manual & diskette set $4995.00 (3.5" or 5.25" diskettes) (ISBN 1-881433-03-X). *Nonstandard peripherals required:* 80 column & 132 column HP laser jets & HP compatible printers. *Addl. software required:* Harvard Graphics 2.3 or higher.
Problem Solving Book on Total Well Production Systems Optimization from Reservoir to Separator & Pipeline Using TWPSOM Program with Applications from Economic Analysis to Engineering & Operations to Reservoir Simulation. Includes Thousands of Illustrations, Nodal System Curves, Charts, Sample Problems for Each Program, Input/Output Listings, Variables, Flowcharts, GWBASIC Program Listings. Shows You How the Methods & Personal Computing Techniques Can Work to Solve Complex Petroleum Production Engineering Problems & Provide Engineers with a Faster Approach to the Optimization Process.
Amanat U. Chaudhry.

Gymnastics. *Compatible Hardware:* Apple II, II+, IIe, IIc; Commodore 64. *Memory Required:* 64k.
$45.00 ea. (Order no.: INT 0016A).
Apple. (Order no.: INT0016A).
Commodore. (Order no.: INT0016C).
Allows the User to Score a Gymnastics Tournament As It Occurs & Also Keep Track of the Progress of Competition. Handles Both Men's & Women's Competition. Printed Reports Include: Team Standings, Individual Team Breakdown, Event Summary, & All-Around Summary. Designed to Be Used on Site As a Tournament Takes Place, & to Minimize the Time Required for Typing in of Data & Printing of Reports. Statistical Program Enables the Coach to Enter Competition Data for Each Team Member for an Entire Season. Printed Reports Include: One-Person Summary, Team Summary, & Team Breakdown. Program Can Also Track Qualifying Scores for Post-Season Tournaments for Individuals & Teams.
Intellectual Software.

Hail to the Chief. *Compatible Hardware:* Apple II, II+, IIe; Atari 800, 1200XL; Franklin Ace; TRS-80 Model III, Model 4. *Operating System(s) Required:* Apple DOS 3.3, TRSDOS. *Language(s):* BASIC. *Memory Required:* 48k.
disk $24.95.
Simulation Game with Objective of Being Elected President. Taxes & Unemployment Are Some of

the 10 Issues Which Must Be Taken into Account When Planning Campaign Strategy & Fund Raising. There Are 4 Models in the Product & 10 Levels of Difficulty Within Each Model. More Involved Models Take into Account Factors Like Campaign Finance, Spending Limits & Incumbency.
Compuware.

Hair Shaping, 3 disks. 1987. *Compatible Hardware:* Apple II, IIc, IIe; IBM PC & compatibles. *Operating System(s) Required:* Apple DOS; PC-DOS/MS-DOS. *Memory Required:* 48k.
Apple. disk $195.00 (ISBN 0-87354-276-2, Order no.: CSMT4A).
IBM. 3.5" or 5.25" $195.00.
Features Hair Shaping, Facial Shapes, Hair Styling Techniques, Roller/Pincoils.
Aquarius Instructional.

Hakotev. *Version:* 1.2. Mar. 1993. *Items Included:* 1 manual, Hebrew key cap stickers, function template. *Customer Support:* 30 days money-back guarantee, free telephone support.
Windows 3.1. IBM & compatibles (1Mb). disk $495.00. *Nonstandard peripherals required:* Windows requirements. *Addl. software required:* Windows 3.1. *Networks supported:* NetWare.
Premiere Hebrew Multilingual Word Processor for Windows. Includes 26 Hebrew True Type fonts As Well As Fonts for All Eastern & Western European Languages Including Russian & Greek. Distinctive Features Include Columns, Exporting Hebrew to Other Windows Apps, Easy to Use, All Diacritical & Cantillation Markings & Bilingual Documentation & Help.
Hakotev Systems.

Halftone Computer. W. Andrew Bear. 1984. *Compatible Hardware:* Apple II series. *Operating System(s) Required:* Apple DOS 3.3. *Memory Required:* 48k. *General Requirements:* Printer.
disk $34.50 (ISBN 1-55797-205-2, Order no.: AP2-IE653).
Enables the Student to Compute Halftone Exposures by Simply Typing in the Density Values & Basic Exposure Time. The Information Necessary for Running the Program Includes; Basic Highlight Density for Screen; Main Exposure in Seconds; Basic Shadow Density for Screen; & Basic Flash Exposure in Seconds. All This Information Comes from User's Test Negative. User Inputs the Data & the Computer Will Provide the Correct Setting for the Camera.
Hobar Pubns.

Halley's Comet. Oct. 1985. *Compatible Hardware:* Apple II, II+, IIe, IIc. (source code included). *Memory Required:* 48k.
disk $9.95 (ISBN 0-918547-16-4).
illustration files on disk avail.
Includes Programs to Determine When & Where to Look to Find Halley's Comet. Will Generate a Star Map That Can Be Saved to Disk & Printed with Appropriate Software, Graphic Outputing Routine Not Included. Teaches the Structure, Function & Origin of Comets. Gives the History of This Comet As Well As Background on Comets in General.
AV Systems, Inc.

Halley's Comet Locator. *Customer Support:* 800-929-8117 (customer service).
MS-DOS. IBM/PS2. disk $39.99 (ISBN 0-87007-154-8).
Provides Information in the Form of Star Maps & Text Displays on How to Find & Observe Halley's Comet.
SourceView Software International.

Halo Imaging Library. *Version:* 1.4. Apr. 1993. *Items Included:* 2 spiral bound manuals. *Customer Support:* 30-day money back guarantee, 90-day warranty, free technical support.
DOS 5.0, Windows. IBM PC & compatibles (4Mb). disk $599.00. *Addl. software required:* C Compiler, Windows 3.1. *Optimal configuration:* DOS 5.0 Intel 386, 8Mb; Windows 3.1 in Protected Mode, ANSI compatible C compiler.
SOLARIS. SPARC (8Mb). disk $999.00. *Addl. software required:* ANSI compatible C compiler. *Optimal configuration:* SOLARIS 1.X, X11R4/5 Motif, SPARC compiler C 2.0.1, SPARC, 8Mb.
OS/2. IBM 386. disk $599.00. *Addl. software required:* Presentation Manager, C compiler. *Optimal configuration:* OS/2 2.0, PM, IBM C Set/2 1.0, Intel 386, 19Mb.
System 6 MAC. Motorola 68020. 3.5" disk $599.00. *Addl. software required:* C compiler. *Optimal configuration:* Macintosh system 7, Symantec THINK C 5.0 or Apple MPW C V3.2, Motorola 68020, 8Mb.
Multi-Platform Toolkit for Adding Imaging Capabilities to Applications. Create & Manage Virtual Images; Convert from One Image Class to Another, Enhance Images Using Histogram Equalization, Brightness, Contrast & Gamma Adjustments; Add Effects Including: Blur, Sharpen, Despeckle, Edge Enhance, & More; Overlay Images; Perform Spatial Transformations. Read & Write Image Files.
Media Cybernetics, Inc.

Halstead Russell Neuropsychological Evaluation System. *Version:* 1.015. Elbert W. Russell & Regina I. Starkey. *Items Included:* Kit includes manual, 10 recording booklets. *Customer Support:* Free unlimited phone support with a toll free number.
Windows 3.X, Windows 95. IBM or 100% compatible. disk $395.00 (Order no.: W-1072 5.25"; W-1073 3.5"). *Nonstandard peripherals required:* VGA monitor & graphical adaptor. *Optimal configuration:* 80836SX, DOS 5.0, color VGA monitor, hard disk with one Mb of free disk space, printer.
Comprehensive, Integrated, & Flexible Approach to Neuropsychological Assessment. Uses 22 Tests Drawn from the Halstead Battery or Incorporated from Clinical Practice in Order to Cover a Specific Cognitive Function. Takes Raw Scores from These Tests, Corrects Them for Age & Education, & Converts Them to Scaled Scores.
Western Psychological Services.

HAM Package. *Compatible Hardware:* Apple II, Commodore PET. *Memory Required:* 32k.
Apple. disk $19.95 (Order no.: 0176AD).
PET. cassette $14.95 (Order no.: 0054P).
Set of 3 Programs: Basic Electronic Formulas, Dipole Antenna & Yagi Antenna.
Instant Software, Inc.

Hamlet & MacBeth, Vol. 1. *Version:* 1.5. Feb. 1995. *Items Included:* BookWorm Student Reader (diskette). *Customer Support:* 30 day MBG. Technical support (toll call) - no charge.
System 7.0 or higher. Macintosh. CD-ROM disk $59.95 (ISBN 1-57316-033-4, Order no.: 19001). *Nonstandard peripherals required:* CD-ROM drive, 12" color monitor. *Optimal configuration:* 13" color monitor recommended.
Windows 3.1 or higher. IBM compatible (MPC) 386 DX (4Mb). CD-ROM disk $59.95. *Nonstandard peripherals required:* Standard multimedia compatible CD-ROM. *Optimal configuration:* 8Mb RAM recommended, 256 color monitor recommended.
This Volume Contains Two of Shakespeare's Best Known Tragedies. This BookWorm Edition Features Complete Background Information, a Fully Annotated Text with All Difficult Passages Explained, & Extensive Literary Discussions Drawn from the World's Best Scholars. Beautifully Illustrated with Pictures from Stage Performances & Art Masterpieces.
Communication & Information Technologies, Inc. (CIT).

Handbook of Latin American Studies, CD-ROM: 1936-1994, Vols. 1-53. Library of Congress Staff & Dolores M. Martin. Feb. 1996.
DOS. IBM-PC. CD-ROM disk $150.00 (ISBN 0-292-74690-3).
University of Texas Pr.

Handbook of Research in Language Development Using Children. Jeffrey L. Sokolov & Catherine E. Snow. 1994. *Customer Support:* Free technical support, 90-day limited warranty.
Mac. 3.5" disk $5.00 (ISBN 1-56321-157-2).
IBM DOS. 3.5" disk $5.00 (ISBN 1-56321-158-0).
cloth book $89.95 (ISBN 0-8058-1185-0).
paper book $32.50 (ISBN 0-8058-1186-9).
The Disk Contains Transcription Data As a Companion to the Book. It Offers Examples of Computer Research in Action As Well As Tutorials for the Creative Application of the Tools Provided by the Child Language Data Exchange System.
Lawrence Erlbaum Assocs. Software & Alternate Media, Inc.

Handheld Calculator Programs for Rotating Machinery Equipment Design, 4 disks. *Version:* Apple; IBM. L. Fielding. 1985. *Compatible Hardware:* Apple II+, IIe, IIc; IBM PC. *Items Included:* 4 disks & manual.
Apple Set. $750.00, incl. manual (ISBN 0-07-079368-9).
IBM Set. $750.00, incl. manual (ISBN 0-07-079369-7).
25 Programs Deal Specifically with Vibration Analysis, Fluid Dynamics Design, & Mechanical Design, & Includes All Programs from Fielding's Book: HAND-HELD CALCULATOR PROGRAMS FOR ROTATING EQUIPMENT DESIGN.
McGraw-Hill, Inc.

Handicapper II. *Compatible Hardware:* Apple II with Applesoft; IBM PC. (source code included). *Memory Required:* 48k, IBM 128k.
disk $49.95.
Handicapping Scheme Designed for Thoroughbred Races of Lengths 6, 6 1/2 or 7 Furlongs.
Dynacomp, Inc.

Hands-On Math, Vol. 1. 1993. *Items Included:* Book (teacher's manual) & software. *Customer Support:* Technical support available - no charge; free upgrading.
System 7.0 or higher. Mac LC or higher (1Mb). $59.95 school; $109.95 5-user; $159.95 10-user; $359.95 30-user (ISBN 0-917623-52-5).
DOS 3.3, ProDOS. Apple IIe or higher (640k for DOS 3.3, 128kfor ProDOS). $59.95 school; $109.95 5-user; $159.95 10-user; $359.95 30-user (ISBN 0-917623-33-9).
DOS 3.1 or higher. IBM PC or 100% compatibles (512k). $59.95 school; $109.95 5-user; $159.95 10-user; $359.95 30-user (ISBN 0-917623-55-X).
Simulates the Use of Six Manipulative Devices: Rods, Number Tiles, Counters, Chip-Trading, Geoboard, & Tangrams. For Each Device a Playground Program Provides the Child with an Opportunity to Freely Explore & Discover Important Mathematical Concepts, & an Exercise Reinforces Essential Concepts. Children Learn Number Concepts, Basic Operations, Fractions & Many Other Math Concepts by Moving Objects

on the Screen. Teachers Can Use the Program to Present Mathematical Ideas in a Structured Way by Following the Lessons Suggested in the Manual. Grade Levels K-8.
Ventura Educational Systems.

Hands-On Math, Vol. 2. 1993. *Items Included:* Book (teacher's manual) & software. *Customer Support:* Technical support available - no charge; free upgrading.
System 7.0 or higher. Mac LC or higher (1Mb). $59.95 school; $109.95 5-user; $159.95 10-user; $359.95 30-user (ISBN 0-917623-89-4).
DOS 3.3, ProDOS. Apple IIe or higher (640k for DOS 3.3, 128kfor ProDOS). $59.95 school; $109.95 5-user; $159.95 10-user; $359.95 30-user (ISBN 0-917623-35-5).
Simulates the Use of Five Manipulative Devices: Two Color Counters, Color Tiles, Mirrors, Attribute Blocks & Base Ten Blocks. The Active Learning Program Provides Students with an Opportunity to Investigate a Variety of Important Mathematical Ideas. In Addition to the Exploratory Environments, Interactive Drill & Practice Type of Programs Reinforce Learning & Measure Progress. Teacher's Guide & Reproducible Student Worksheets. Grade Levels K-8.
Ventura Educational Systems.

Hands-On Math, Vol. 3. 1993. *Items Included:* Book (teacher's manual) & software. *Customer Support:* Technical support available - no charge; free upgrading.
System 7.0 or higher. Mac LC or higher (1Mb). $59.95 school; $109.95 5-user; $159.95 10-user; $359.95 30-user (ISBN 0-917623-14-2).
DOS 3.3, ProDOS. Apple IIe or higher (640k for DOS 3.3, 128kfor ProDOS). $59.95 school; $109.95 5-user; $159.95 10-user; $359.95 30-user (ISBN 0-917623-36-3).
Focuses on the Use of Six Math Instructional Techniques: a Hundreds Chart, Graphing Activities, a Number Balance, Dominoes, Line Design & Fraction Bars. The Playground for Each Technique Allows the Student to Explore & Discover Math Concepts. The Exercises Are Aimed at Providing the Student with Specific Activities to Practice Working with Concepts & to Help in Mastering Objectives. Teacher's Guide & Reproducible Student Worksheets. Grade Levels K-8.
Ventura Educational Systems.

Handweavers' Input Program for the Commodore 64. May 1985. *Compatible Hardware:* Commodore 64. *Operating System(s) Required:* DOS 1541. *Language(s):* BASIC. *Memory Required:* 64k. *General Requirements:* Color monitor. *Customer Support:* Telephone or mail support.
disk $15.00, incl. instr. bklt. (ISBN 0-9608406-2-1).
Tool for Weavers to Use When Planning New Weaving Patterns - The Drawdown Shows on the Screen, & Can Use up to 16 Colors. Changes Can Be Made Easily, Enabling the Weaver to Experiment with a Variety of Loom Threadings, Treadlings & Color Sequences.
Herbi Gray.

Handwriting Analyst. *Version:* 4.0. *Items Included:* Manual, plastic guide, input form, disk. *Customer Support:* Unlimited 800 support line (free); 30 day unlimited warranty.
Macintosh. 3.5" disk $79.95.
Apple II. disk $79.95.
IBM PC. disk $79.95.
Constructs Personality Profiles from Signatures & Handwriting Samples.
Wintergreen Software.

Handwriting & Numerology, 2 diskettes. *Items Included:* Bound manual. *Customer Support:* Free hotline - no time limit; 30 day limited warranty; updates are $5/disk plus S&H.
MS-DOS 2.0 or higher. IBM & compatibles (256k). $19.95. *Nonstandard peripherals required:* Graphics capability.
Contains Three Personal Packages: HANDWRITING Gives a Personality Analysis Based on Thirteen Handwriting Characteristics; NUMEROLOGY Uses Your Name & Birthdate to Give a Profile of Desires, etc.; BIORHYTHM Gives the Classic Charts Based on Your Birthdate.
Dynacomp, Inc.

Hangman. *Compatible Hardware:* TI 99/4A. contact publisher for price (Order no.: PHM3037).
Players Try to Figure Out the Mystery Word.
Texas Instruments, Personal Productivit.

Hangman. Charles Platt.
IBM. disk $29.99 (Order no.: 1421).
disk $39.99, incl. backup disk (Order no.: 1421B).
A Sophisticated & Elegant Version of This Classic Word/Vocabulary/Spelling Game. Gives the Player a Range of Choices from Four- to Nine-Letter Words with Six Levels of Difficulty. The Program Comes Loaded with Words Chosen for Gifted Middle School Students, but It Is Easy to Change the Words in Memory. The Program Keeps Track of Each Player & Does Not Give the Same Word Twice to a Player. Keeps Track of up to 40 Players & Their Scores. An Excellent Educational Game, Very Useful for Foreign Languages, Specialized Vocabulary, Names, As Well As English Vocabulary.
Trillium Pr.

Hansen-Predict. *Items Included:* Bound manual. *Customer Support:* Free hotline - no time limit; 30 day limited warranty; updates are $5/disk plus S&H.
MS-DOS 2.0 or higher. IBM & compatibles (256k). disk $199.95. *Nonstandard peripherals required:* Printer supported, but optional.
Self-Learning, General Purpose "Expert" System. It Is an Artificial Intelligence (AI) Software Package Which Allows User to Impart Knowledge to the Computer in a Way That Allows the Computer to Predict Future Outcomes of Situations Based on the Information Available at That Time.
Dynacomp, Inc.

HarbourMaster. *Version:* 6.0. Mar. 1982. *Compatible Hardware:* IBM PC, PC XT, PC AT, PS/2. *Operating System(s) Required:* PC-DOS. *Language(s):* Compiled BASIC. *Memory Required:* 512k. *General Requirements:* Fixed disk. *Items Included:* Reference manual. *Customer Support:* Phone/modem support included first year, nominal fee thereafter.
disk $600.00 (ISBN 0-924068-06-X, Order no.: HA1).
Manages a Marina. Includes General Ledger, Automatic Billing & Accounts Receivable.
Fogle Computing Corp.

Hard Disk Toolkit. Aug. 1991. *Customer Support:* Free technical support.
Macintosh (1Mb). 3.5" disk $199.95. *Nonstandard peripherals required:* SCSI hard disk. *Optimal configuration:* Mac+ or later. *Networks supported:* AppleShare, Tops.
Replaces Hard Disk's Native Installer. Provides True SCSI Partitioning, Extensive Diagnostics, Password Protection & High-Performance SCSI Drivers, System 7 Compatible, Supports SC512.
FWB Software, Inc.

Hard Disk Utilities-Optical Disk Utilities. *Version:* 2.33. May 1991. *Items Included:* Manual included. Also includes Mounter control panel for mounting/unmounting partitions from the Apple menu. And, a startup document (init) is included for working with removable disk drives. *Customer Support:* Free technical support for the software, by mail, FAX, & phone, to registered users.
Macintosh System Software 6.0.5 or higher. Macintosh Plus or higher (1Mb). Hard Disk Utilities $99.95; Optical Disk Utilities $129.95. *Nonstandard peripherals required:* Hard disk (SCSI drive) read/write optical (Optical Disk Utilities). *Optimal configuration:* System Software 6.0.7 or higher (System 7 compatible). *Networks supported:* AppleShare, TOPS, System 7 FileSharing.
Format, Partition, & Mount over 150 Different Kinds of Hard Disks for Use on the Macintosh. Optical Disk Utilities Works with 7 Different Kinds of Read/Write Optical Drives. Partitions Can Be Password Protected. Can Make the Necessary Patitions for A/UX. System 7 Compatible.
Diversified I/O, Inc.

Hard Drive Turbo Kit. Dave Clemens & Timothy Purves. Dec. 1988. *Compatible Hardware:* Atari ST. *Memory Required:* 512k. *General Requirements:* Hard drive.
3.5" disk $59.95.
Includes Backup, Tuneup & M-Cache.
MichTron, Inc.

HardBall!
IBM PC. disk $14.95.
Commodore Amiga, 64/128. disk $24.95.
Apple Macintosh. 3.5" disk $29.95.
Plays As a Field-Action Game, a Manager-Strategy Game, or Both. Watch Curveballs Actually Drop over the Plate, Listen to the Umpire Yell "Strike Three" (Amiga Only), or Consult the Manager's Screen for a Key Substitution. You Can Position the Infield & Outfield to Match the Batter's Style or Game Situation.
Accolade, Inc.

Hardball II. Oct. 1989. *Items Included:* Catalog, copy protection device, manual, proof of purchase card, & warranty card. *Customer Support:* Technical support 408-296-8400, 90 day limited warranty, Bulletin Board (modem) 408-296-8800 (settings: 300, 1200, 2400 baud; 8 data; No parity; 1 stop bit).
IBM DOS 2.1 or higher. IBM PC, XT, AT & compatibles (512k): CGA, EGA, HERC/TGA (640k). $29.95. *Optimal configuration:* Hard drive, keyboard, joystick, graphics card, & sound board.
Tandy 16-color (640k). Tandy 1000 series, 3000, 4000. $29.95. *Optimal configuration:* Hard drive, keyboard, joystick, graphics card, & sound board.
Macintosh (1Mb B&W, 2Mb Color). Macintosh Plus, II, IIx, IIfx, IIci, IIcx, IIsi, IIIc, SE, SE/30, Portable, Classic. $54.95. *Optimal configuration:* Hard drive, keyboard, joystick, graphics card, & sound board.
Baseball Game with Effortless Gameplay, Authentic Graphics, & Relism. More Major League Ballparks, Features, Options, Choices, Playability & True-to-Ballplayer Animation Than the Original.
Accolade, Inc.

Hardy Cross Network Analysis. *Items Included:* Bound manual. *Customer Support:* Free hotline - no time limit; 30 day limited warranty; updates are $5/disk plus S&H.
MS-DOS. IBM & compatibles (256k). full system $229.95. *Nonstandard peripherals required:* 80-column (or wider) printer.

demo disk $5.00.
Uses the NFPA Pressure Drop Equations to Derive Solutions to Water Distribution Systems (the Hardy Cross Method). It Is Applicable to the Design of Large Problems Such As Municipal Water & Fire Sprinkler Distribution Systems. It Balances Large Systems Rapidly, to a Degree of Accuracy Specified by the User. HCNA Calculates Hydraulically Balanced Flows & Pressure Drops in Each Pipe Section, & Provides Tabular Displays of All Inputs & Outputs.
Dynacomp, Inc.

Hardy Cross Water Distribution System Analysis - HP3M. *Version:* 08/1995. Mar. 1991. *Compatible Hardware:* IBM PC & compatibles. *Operating System(s) Required:* MS-DOS, PC-DOS. *Language(s):* Compiled. *Memory Required:* 256k. *Customer Support:* Technical hotline, "Lifetime" support at no charge. $245.00.
Hardy Cross Water Distribution System Analysis - HP3M Uses NFPA (Hazen-Williams) Pressure Drop Equations to Perform a Hardy Cross Solution of Water Distribution Systems with 900 Pipes, Unlimited Loops with Common Pipes & Unlimited Numbers of Inflows & Outflows of Fixed GPM. Any Type of Pipe May Be Used. Fast Solution, Tracked on Screen for User. Menu Driven, Fully Prompted & Compiled. Tabular Review & Change of Inputs. SI Metric or English Units.
MC2 Engineering Software.

Harmonic Analyzer. (Fourier Transform Ser.: No. 3). *Compatible Hardware:* Apple II with Applesoft; IBM PC. (source code included). *Memory Required:* 48k, IBM 128k.
disk $29.95, incl. manual.
Specific to Repetitive Wave Forms (Cyclic Processes).
Dynacomp, Inc.

Harmonic Motion Workshop. 1982. *Compatible Hardware:* Apple II, II+, IIe; Franklin Ace 1000. *Language(s):* Applesoft BASIC. *Memory Required:* 48k.
disk $75.00, incl. documentation.
Visually Presents Simple & Damped Harmonic Motion. An Object Is Placed in Harmonic Motion on Screen. By Using the Keyboard, the Student Can Alter Such Variables As the Phase, Amplitude, & the Damping Factor. The Student Will Then See the Effect Made on the Movement of the Object. The Instantaneous Velocity & Acceleration Vectors, Kinetic & Potential Energy Values, & a Corresponding Object in Circular Motion Can Also Be Displayed While the Object Is in Motion.
High Technology Software Products, Inc.

Harmonic Progressions. Vincent Oddo. 1991. *Customer Support:* 90 day limited warranty against defective or damaged disks.
DOS 3.3 or higher. IBM PC (512k). disk $200.00 (ISBN 1-55603-332-X, Order no.: MI-1338). *Nonstandard peripherals required:* CGA minimum. *Optimal configuration:* Need MIDI interface & MIDI compatible music keyboard. *Networks supported:* Novell, Corvus.
System 6.0.3-System 7.1. Macintosh Plus or higher (512k). 3.5" disk $200.00 (ISBN 1-55603-333-8, Order no.: MAC-1338). *Optimal configuration:* External MIDI device, MIDI compatible music keyboard. *Networks supported:* AppleTalk, Novell, Corvus.
Improves Skills in Functional Harmony Analysis. Studies Include Root Position Chords, Inverted Chords & V7, Embellishing 6/4 Chords & V7, & Cadence Patterns. Each Area Includes Practice Analyzing Chords, Harmonic Dictation, & Aural Identification. Record Keeping Included.
Electronic Courseware Systems, Inc.

Harmony. *Compatible Hardware:* Apple Macintosh. *General Requirements:* Hard disk.
3.5" disk $5495.00.
Industrial Data Acquisition & Control.
Darvish Systems.

Harness Handicapper. *Items Included:* Bound manual. *Customer Support:* Free hotline - no time limit; 30 day limited warranty; updates are $5/disk plus S&H.
MS-DOS. IBM & compatibles (128k). disk $59.95. *Nonstandard peripherals required:* Printer.
Apple (48k). disk $59.95.
Guides You Step-by-Step Through the Analysis of Each Horse's Past Performance Chart in Your Track Program by Means of a Series of Easy to Follow Screen Prompts, Questions, & Menus. The Output Is a Graded Line of Numerical Ratings Displayed on Your Printer. The Author Is a Professional Handicapper with More Than 35 Years' Experience in Both Thoroughbred & Harness Racing & Is a Member of the U.S. Harness Writers' Association.
Dynacomp, Inc.

Harpoon. *Compatible Hardware:* Commodore Amiga.
3.5" disk $44.95.
Naval Task-Force War Simulation.
360, Inc.

Harpoon II. *Items Included:* Manual. *Customer Support:* Technical Support - N/C.
Macintosh. 68020 Processor (4.5Mb). CD-ROM disk $56.00 (ISBN 1-57519-004-4, Order no.: 990060). *Nonstandard peripherals required:* CD-ROM. *Addl. software required:* CD-ROM driver. *Optimal configuration:* Color Macintosh 6Mb free memory, System 7, CD-ROM drive, 68040 processor. At least 6Mb free hard drive space.
Currently Being Used by the U.S. Military for Training, Harpoon II Is Set to Blow You Out of the Water with: BattleSet 1-Global Conflicts, 15 Realistic Contemporary Scenarios. Actual Footage of Weapons Launching & Hitting Targets; Sensor Communications Models Simulate Contemporary Electronic Warfare; Military-Style Vector Maps in Full Color; VAST Database Containing Technical Specs, Photos, & Illustrations for Hundreds of Ships, Subs, & Aircraft. Toolbar Buttons Allow You to Command Your Forces with the Click of a Mouse.
IntraCorp/Capstone.

Harpoon II Battleset, No. 2: WestPac. *Items Included:* Installation instruction card, catalog, warranty card. *Customer Support:* 90 day limited warranty. Free phone support Mon. thru Fri. - 9AM to 6PM.
Macintosh System 7. Color Mac 12" monitor or higher, 68020 processor, 5Mb hard drive (4.5Mb). 3.5" disk $39.95 (ISBN 1-57519-007-9, Order no.: 854060). *Addl. software required:* Harpoon II Macintosh. *Optimal configuration:* 68040 processor, 6Mb free memory.
WestPac Battleset Includes 15 New Scenarios in the Western Pacific Including China, Japan, North & South Korea, Russia & More! With over 100 New Platforms & Photos WestPac Lets You Control the Pacific Rim.
IntraCorp/Capstone.

Harpoon II Battleset, No. 3: Cold War. *Items Included:* Installation instructions, catalog, warranty card. *Customer Support:* Limited 90 day warranty. Free phone support Mon. thru Fri. - 9AM to 6PM.
Macintosh System 7. Color Mac 12" monitor or higher, 68020 processor, 5Mb hard drive (4.5Mb). 3.5" disk $39.95 (ISBN 1-57519-006-0, Order no.: 990022). *Addl. software required:* Harpoon II Macintosh. *Optimal configuration:* 68040 processor, 6Mb free memory.
The Duel Between the Eagle & the Bear Continues with Cold War Battleset. 15 New Scenarios Time Line in the Mid 1980's, over 100 New Platforms & a Database Adjusted for the Era Keeps the Cold War Alive for You to Rewrite History.
IntraCorp/Capstone.

Harrison's CD-ROM - Harrison's Plus. Jun. 1995.
MAC/Windows. CD-ROM disk $195.00 (ISBN 0-07-026896-7).
CD-ROM disk $395.00, Harrison's Plus (ISBN 0-07-864134-9).
Harrison's Plus Includes on One CD the Full Text, Tables & Illustrations of Harrison's Principles of Internal Medicine, 13/E Linked to the 1995 U.S. Pharmacopeial Drug Information for the Health Care Professional & Selected Medline Abstracts. Plus Two Free Updates to the Drug Information Within the First 12 Months of Purchase. Harrison's CD-ROM Includes the Complete Harrison's, 13/E & Selected Medline Abstracts.
Health Professions Div./McGraw-Hill, Inc.

Harry & the Haunted House. (Living Book Ser.). Marc Schlichting.
MS-DOS 5.0 or higher, Windows 3.1 or higher. 386 processor or higher (4Mb). CD-ROM disk $49.95 (Order no.: R1188). *Nonstandard peripherals required:* CD-ROM drive. *Optimal configuration:* 386 processor operating at 16MHz or higher, MS-DOS 5.0 or higher, Windows 3.1 or higher, 30Mb hard drive, mouse, VGA graphic adapter & VGA color monitor (SVGA recommended), 4Mb RAM, external speakers or headphones (with sound card) that are Sound Blaster compatible.
Macintosh (4Mb). (Order no.: R1188). *Nonstandard peripherals required:* 14" color monitor or larger, CD-ROM drive.
Highly Interactive Animated Stories for Children That Have Hundreds of Beautiful Animations & Have Received Countless Awards. In English & Spanish.
Library Video Co.

Harry Helio. *Compatible Hardware:* Commodore 64, 128. *General Requirements:* COMET (Computerized Muscle Exerciser & Trainer).
ROM cartridge $29.95 (Order no.: SOFC64-04-007).
disk $19.95 (Order no.: DISC64-11-007).
For Performing Isometric Exercises. By Pushing or Pulling on the COMET, User Flies a Helicopter over Obstacles. The Game Assesses User's Strength, & Then Using a Video Game Format, Guides User Through a Strength Training Technique.
Bodylog.

HAS (Health Assistance System). *Compatible Hardware:* TRS-80 Model II, Model 16.
contact publisher for price.
Robert Bloom.

Hay-Pasture Production: Decision Aid. Merle W. Wagner. 1982. *Compatible Hardware:* Apple II Plus, IIe, IIc; IBM. *Operating System(s) Required:* Apple DOS 3.3, MS-DOS 2.0. *Language(s):* BASIC. *Memory Required:* 48k, 640k. *General Requirements:* Printer.
disk $29.95 (ISBN 0-922900-12-4, Order no.: CFD-113).
Costs Covered Include: Machinery Operation & Depreciation, Interest, Grain Storage & Drying, Taxes & Land Management, Return on Land/Cash Rent, Labor, Fencing & Water, Fertility Credit. Calculations Include: Total Fertilizer, Herbicide, & Insecticide Costs; Total Cost Except Management; Total Direct Cost; Gross Return

per Acre; Income Minus Direct Cost; Management Return; Labor/Management & Land Management Return; Total Seed & Seeding Cost.
Cherrygarth, Inc.

HCFA2522 Simulator. *Compatible Hardware:* Altos Series 5-15D, Series 5-5D, 580-XX, ACS8000-XX; IBM PC with 2 disk drives, PC XT, IBM compatibles; Xerox 820 with 2 disk drives; Zilog MCZ-250. *Operating System(s) Required:* CP/M, MP/M, PC-DOS, MS-DOS.
contact publisher for price.
Hospitals & Skilled Nursing Facilities Can Explore Reimbursement Strategies on a Microcomputer Thus Reducing Time-Sharing Expenses. Edits Data, So If the User Chooses to Run MedPlan on the GE System, the Generated Reports Will Be Valid & Suitable for Filing. Worksheets Produced by the Simulator Itself, However, Are Not Approved for Filing with Fiscal Intermediaries. Data Must Be Transferred onto Official 2552 Forms, or Run Through MedPlan.
Coopers & Lybrand.

H.C.I. Phone Biller. *Version:* 2.0. Oct. 1988. *Operating System(s) Required:* PC-DOS/MS-DOS. *General Requirements:* 20Mb on hard disk.
$7800.00.
Billing System for Long Distance Phone Calls. Handles Domestic & International Calls, Credit Card Calls, up to 240 Rate Tables, Organization by Project Codes, & Other Chargeback/Charge Distribution Plans.
Hershey Consultants, Inc.

HD Back-Up. *Version:* 2.0. Jan. 1986. *Compatible Hardware:* Apple Macintosh, Macintosh XL under MacWorks.
3.5" disk $49.95.
Back-Up Utility That Can Copy All Data from Hard-Disk Drives & Other Peripherals to Floppy Disks.
PBI Software, Inc.

HD 20 & 30 Back-Up.
Macintosh. 3.5" disk $49.95.
Performs Floppy Disk Backups Globally, Incrementally by File & by Folder.
PBI Software, Inc.

HDC FirstApps. May 1990. *Items Included:* User's guide. *Customer Support:* Technical support available by phone, free 1st six months.
Microsoft Windows version 3.0 or higher running on MS-DOS 3.x or higher. Microsoft Windows compatible personal computer (30k). disk $99.95. *Optimal configuration:* 386/486 Microsoft Windows compatible computer, Microsoft Windows 3.0 or higher, 4Mb RAM, VGA or higher res. monitor, house.
Set of Nine MicroApps (Pop-up Utilities) for Microsoft Windows That Customize & Enhance the Windows System. The Nine MicroApps Allows User to Do Everything from View Their System Memory Usage Graphically in Three Windows Modes to Put an Interactive Calendar in Their Background.
HDC Computer Corp.

HDC Windows Express. *Version:* 3.0. May 1990. *Items Included:* User's guide, editor & installation guide. *Customer Support:* Technical support available by phone, free first six months.
Microsoft windows 3.0 or higher running on MS-DOS 3.x or higher. Microsoft Windows compatible personal computer (35k). disk $99.95. *Optimal configuration:* 386/486 MS Windows compatible computer, MS Windows 3.0 or higher, 4MB RAM, VGA or higher res. monitor, mouse.
Menu System for the Microsoft Windows Workstation. Windows Express Allows Users to Group Applications into Flexible, Hierarchical Folders. Other Important Features Include: Network Compatibility, System Security, Password Protection, Full-Color Icons with a Powerful Editor, & Quick Keys.
HDC Computer Corp.

HDCopy. *Version:* 4.58. 1985. *Operating System(s) Required:* MS-DOS, PC-DOS. *Memory Required:* 64k. *General Requirements:* Hard disk. disk $200.00 (Order no.: 404001).
Allows Software Protected with PADLOCK II or SAFEGUARD DISK to Run on a Hard Disk Without the Protected Floppy in Drive A. It Provides Totally Safe, Easy-to-Install/Uninstall Hard Disk Protection. Each Time Product Is Executed Successfully, the Installation Counter (Which Is Part of the Fingerprint) Is Decremented. When the Count Reaches Zero, Product Will Not Allow An Additional Hard Disk to Be Protected until a Previous Hard Disk Fingerprint Is Uninstalled.
Glenco Engineering, Inc.

HDIS: CP/M 8080 Disassembler. Hall Associates. Feb. 1983. *Operating System(s) Required:* CP/M-80. *Memory Required:* 64k. *General Requirements:* 2 disk drives.
disk 40 TPI $49.95 (ISBN 0-923875-47-6).
disk 80 TPI $49.95 (ISBN 0-923875-48-4).
8" disk $49.95 (ISBN 0-923875-46-8).
Multi-Pass Disassembler Which Produces Source Code with No Human Assistance. HDIS Produces Labeled, Correctly Disassembled Source Automatically, As Well As Automatically Shifting Between Instruction & Data Disassembly During Creation of the Source Code & Finds Unlabeled Character Strings.
Elliam Assocs.

HDLC/SDLC COMPAC. *Compatible Hardware:* IBM PC, PC XT. *Operating System(s) Required:* PC-DOS. *Language(s):* C. *Memory Required:* 64k.
disk $695.00.
Allows Communication Through a Frontier Technologies Advanced Communication Board.
Frontier Technologies Corp.

HDP: Highway Design Program. *Version:* 1.22. Jul. 1991. *Compatible Hardware:* IBM PC, PC XT, PC AT, & true compatibles. *Operating System(s) Required:* MS-DOS, PC-DOS. *Memory Required:* 640k. *General Requirements:* Hard disk, printer. *Items Included:* Manual, 120-day free maintenance. *Customer Support:* 1 year maintenance for $200.
$595.00.
Performs Calculations & Operations for Highway & Railway Design, Computes Earthwork Quantities & Produces Complete Plots of Roadway Design & Earthwork Characteristics. Also Computes Volumes of Excavated Material Using a Digital Terrain Model (DTM). Both Bath & Interactive Processing Capabilities Are Available. Interfaces to Most Popular Micro-Based CAD Programs.
Research Engineers.

HDPRTCT. *Customer Support:* By phone Mon-Fri 8:30 AM-5:30 PM CST.
MS-DOS. IBM PC, PC XT, PC AT. disk $99.00 (Order no.: 432003).
.EXE Program That Provides End User with Method of Transferring Floppy Disk Fingerprint to Hard Disk. Allows Program Protected with PC PADLOCK to Run on Hard Disk Without Requiring Protected Key Disk in Drive A. PADLOCK Will Automatically Look for Hard Disk Fingerprint If Default Drive Is Hard Disk. If No Fingerprint Is Found PADLOCK Will Check for Fingerprint in Drive A. System Can Be Set to Allow More Than One Hard Disk to Be Protected at a Time.
Glenco Engineering, Inc.

Head Coach: Football Simulation. *Version:* 2.0. *Compatible Hardware:* Commodore Amiga.
3.5" disk $49.95.
Provides the Following Features: Instant Replays with Slow Motion Option; Shows Status While Game Is in Progress; Player Injuries & Substitutions; Create Defensive Alignments; Returns Fumbles & Interceptions; Call Blocking Assignments; Display Jersey Number or Player Strength; Computer Can Run Both or Neither Teams; Create Weather - Wind, Sun, Rain, or Snow; Choose Stadium Type, Name, & Surface.
MicroSearch.

Head Trauma. 1982. *Compatible Hardware:* Apple II+, IIe, IIc; IBM PC & compatibles. *Operating System(s) Required:* MS-DOS, Apple DOS 3.3. *Language(s):* BASIC. *Memory Required:* Apple 48k, IBM 512K.
disk $200.00 (Order no.: CCS-8222).
Presents the Case of a Motor Vehicle Accident Victim with Increased Intracranial Pressure Secondary to a Subdural Hematoma. Areas Tested Include ABG Interpretation, Management & Recognition of Increased ICP, Knowledge of Cerebral Perfusion Pressure & Bronchial Hygiene.
Educational Software Concepts, Inc.

Headliner. *Version:* 1.51. 1988. *Items Included:* Spiral bound user's guide. *Customer Support:* Free telephone support.
PC-DOS/MS-DOS 2.1 or higher. IBM PC & compatibles (256k). disk $195.00. *Optimal configuration:* 1Mb of free hard disk space.
Provides Marketing & Promo Writers with Tools for Writing Effective Titles, Headlines, Subheadings, Bullets, Slogans, Jingles & Other Promotional Expressions. Edits, Retrieves & Substitutes Words/Phrases in 25 Databases Containing 50,000 Expressions.
The Namestormers.

Headliner. *Compatible Hardware:* IBM PC, PC XT. *Memory Required:* 256k.
$24.95.
Print Banners & Signs on Any 80 or 132 Column Printer in Letters up to 13" High (Smaller Sizes, Too). Any Length Headline. For Parties, Kids, Offices, Stores.
Zephyr Services.

Health Care (Nursing Home) Patient Billing. *Compatible Hardware:* DECmate, PDP 11-23. *Operating System(s) Required:* COS-310, MICRO-RSX. *Language(s):* DIBOL-83. *Customer Support:* One year support.
disk $10,000.00, incl. user's guide (Order no.: 85-14).
Provides Complete Billing, Receivable Accounting, & Contractual Allowance Cost Reporting to Serve the Needs of Facilities Providing Nursing Care to Both Private & Subsidized Patients at All Skill Levels. Features Include Individual Patient History Cards Detailing Charges & Credits. Each Card Reports Census Day Totals for Each Patient Provider.
Corporate Consulting Co.

Health Care: Patient Management. Jul. 1988. *Compatible Hardware:* IBM PC & compatibles. *Operating System(s) Required:* PC-DOS/MS-DOS. *Memory Required:* 640k. *General Requirements:* IBM PC or AT compatible monitor, 80/132-column printer.
3.5" or 5.25" disk $500.00.
Designed to Track Patient's Needs, the Resources That Meet Those Needs & the Caseworkers Who Watch over Each Patient.
Rambow Enterprises.

Health Med. *Compatible Hardware:* Commodore Amiga.
3.5" disk $99.00.
Gives Comprehensive Medical Information.
Lee Software.

TITLE INDEX

HEALTH Planning & Administration CD-ROM Database. Aug. 1992.
MS Windows 3.1 or higher. IBM & compatibles (4Mb). CD-ROM disk $495.00-$695.00; Networks $1995.00 & up. *Nonstandard peripherals required:* Magnetic or CD-ROM, using ISO 9660. *Optimal configuration:* IBM & compatibles, 80386 or higher, 4Mb RAM, 20Mb hard disk, mouse, MS Windows 3.1 or higher.
System 6.0.7 or higher. Apple Macintosh (3Mb). CD-ROM disk $495.00-$695.00; Networks $1995.00 & up. *Optimal configuration:* Apple Macintosh Plus or higher, 3Mb RAM, System 6.0.7 or higher.
HEALTH Is an Electronic Reference Database to the Published Literature on Health Care Delivery. Contains Bibliographic References Published by the U.S. National Library of Medicine since 1975, Covering Health Care Planning & Health Care Delivery Systems. The Database Contents, Now Including more than 600,000 References & Abstracts, Are Distributed on CD-ROM (Compact Disc, Read-Only Memory) Optical Disc. Knowledge Finder Search-&-Retrieval Software Makes Searching of the HEALTH Database Easy, Effective & Fast. After the User Types a Phrase or Sentence Describing the Information Needed, It selects the References in the Database That Appear to Best Match the Request, & Presents Them in Order of likely relevance. The HEALTH Database Covers Materials Published since 1975.
Aries Systems Corp.

Health Specialist. 1984. *Items Included:* User manual, reports. *Customer Support:* License agreement. Maintenance fee $65.00 per month; additional rates are provided according to activity involved; includes: analysis & design, programming, data entry, training, telephone training & assistance, hardware installation & repair, & disaster recovery.
MS-DOS environment. IBM PC & compatibles (640k). contact publisher for price. *Networks supported:* Novell.
Designed to Maintain the Complicated Paper Work Involved in Managing a Health Facility. It Separates & Yet Consolidates the Physician Services, Hospital Services, Physician Information, Hospital Information, Employer/Client Records, & Third Party Administration. Also Available Are: CPT-4 Codes, ICD-9 Codes, Regional Length of Stay for DRG Classifications, & Valid UB-82 Classifications.
Evolution, Inc.

Healthcare Media Locator. (Media Locator Ser.). Pref. by Walt Carroll. 1996.
IBM & compatibles. 3.5" or 5.25" disk $145.00 (ISBN 0-88367-506-4).
Electronic Book.
Olympic Media Information.

Healthlines: Programs for Optimal Well-Being. Robert S. Gold. May 1987. *Compatible Hardware:* Apple IIe, IIc. *Memory Required:* 128k.
complete 10 disk package $400.00 ea. (ISBN 0-697-01411-8).
Master Program $100.00 ea.
individual content disk $40.00 ea.
Health Education Software That Can Be Purchased As a Package or As Individual Units in Any Combination. The First Diskette Contains Introductory Material, an Initial Health Risk Appraisal Program, & a Personal Goal Setting Program for Each of the 9 Subsequent Content Disks (Which Can Be Purchased Independently). A Teacher Utility Diskette Is Free to Purchasers of the Complete Set.
Wm. C. Brown Pubs.

HealthMaster. *Customer Support:* 800-929-8117 (customer service).
MS-DOS. Apple II. disk $69.99 (ISBN 0-87007-058-4).
Commodore 64. disk $59.99 (ISBN 0-87007-593-4).
IBM PC; PS/2. disk $99.00 (ISBN 0-87007-569-1).
Analyzes User's Physical Characteristics & Produces a Scheduled Maintenance Diet Program Aimed Specifically at User's Goals & Needs. There are Several Models for Athletes & Non-Athletes. Calculates Lean Body Mass & Ideal Weight, & Allows for a Longitude Database of Statistics. Will Project Weight Loss or Gain, Given a Level of Exercise Regime & Calorie Intake.
SourceView Software International.

HealthPay. 1991. *Items Included:* Modem & communications software included. *Customer Support:* Customer Documentation - user's guide, promotional materials, custom forms & information brochures, extended support services.
MS-DOS. IBM PC & 100% compatibles (640k). disk $7500.00.
Automates the Collection of Self-Pay & Co-Pay Patient Payments by Allowing Healthcare Providers to Automatically Deduct Payments from Customer's Checking & Savings Account.
Learned-Mahn.

Hear Today...Play Tomorrow: Find That Tune, Ear Training Skills, Descending-Ascending Intervals, Melodic Dictation (Beginner), Melodic Dictation (Intermediate), 5 disks.
Penny Pursell. 1986. *Compatible Hardware:* Apple II+, IIe, IIc; Commodore 64, 128; IBM PC & compatibles. *Operating System(s) Required:* Apple DOS 3.30, PC-DOS/MS-DOS. *Language(s):* QuickBasic. *Memory Required:* Apple 48k, IBM 640k. *General Requirements:* CGA card for IBM.
disk $199.95, ea. set (ISBN 1-55603-061-4).
Apple set. (ISBN 1-55603-021-5, Order no.: A-1180).
Commodore set. (ISBN 1-55603-022-3, Order no.: C-1180).
IBM set. (ISBN 1-55603-061-4).
Series of Aural-Visual Exercises Designed to Improve Ear Training & Music Reading Skills. In EAR TRAINING SKILLS the User Must Identify & Notate Intervals or Simple Melodies Produced by the Computer. FIND THAT TUNE Shows Three Melody Lines from Familiar Music & Plays One of the Excerpts for the User to Correctly Identify. In DESCENDING/ASCENDING INTERVALS the User Identifies & Notates Intervals Played by the Computer. The Beginning Level of Melodic Dictation Allows the User to Complete Portions of Familiar Melodies by Filling in the Missing Notes. The Intermediate Level of This Program Presents Complex Melodies for the User to Complete. All Programs Have Varying Difficulty Levels & Retain Student Records for the Instructor.
Electronic Courseware Systems, Inc.

Hearing Management System, Industrial Safety System. *Language(s):* COBOL.
contact publisher for price.
Corporate Safety & Health Systems.

The Hearsay Rule & Its Exceptions, 1991.
Roger C. Park. *Memory Required:* 128k. *Items Included:* Booklet of background materials.
Macintosh. 3.5" disk $79.00 (Order no.: K986).
IBM PC & compatibles. $79.00 3.5" or 5.25" disk (Order no.: K987).
Learning Package for Litigators & Trial Skill Trainers. May Be Used for Self-Instruction & In-House Training & Is Designed to Refresh & Strengthen New or Unpracticed Skills. Based upon the Federal Rules of Evidence, It Features Vignettes & Trial Transcripts from a Slip-&-Fall Case & a Bank Robbery Case to Illustrate, in Context, the Kind of Hearsay Evidence Objections Likely to Occur in Practice. The Program Is Divided into Three Parts: the First Part Examines Individual Hearsay Exceptions Through Case Vignettes; Part Two Uses a Trial Transcript of a Bank Robbery Case; & Part Three Features a Trial Transcript of a Slip-&-Fall Case to Raise Evidence.
American Law Institute.

Hearts. Loki Eng. Nov. 1984. *Compatible Hardware:* Apple Macintosh. *Operating System(s) Required:* Mac. *Language(s):* Pascal. *Memory Required:* 128k.
disk $29.95 (ISBN 0-917963-02-4).
Heart Card Game.
Artsci, Inc.

Hearts 2.0. *Compatible Hardware:* Atari 400, 800 with Atari BASIC. (source code included). *Memory Required:* 48k.
disk $19.95.
2-Handed Version Which Includes 3-Card Passing, & Shooting the Moon. Provides Sound & Graphics.
Dynacomp, Inc.

Heat & Mass Transfer Equilibrium Calculations. *Items Included:* Full manual. No other products required. *Customer Support:* Free telephone support - no time limit. 30 day warranty.
MS-DOS 3.2 or higher. IBM & compatibles (512k). disk $289.95.
Performs Equilibrium Calculations for Flash & Drying Stages, Dew-Point & Bubble-Point Temperatures/Pressures, & Condensation & Vaporization Curves. Included on Disk Are the Chemical Properties of 400 Compounds (34 Entries per Compound). You May Also Add up to 400 More of Your Own. Uses Metric Units.
Dynacomp, Inc.

Heat & Mass Transfer: Equilibrium Calculations. 1992. *Items Included:* Detailed manuals included with all Dynacomp products. *Customer Support:* Free telephone support to original customer - no time limit; 30 day limited warranty.
MS-DOS 3.2 or higher. IBM PC & compatibles (512k). $279.95 (Add $5.00 for 3 1/2" format; 5 1/4" format standard). *Optimal configuration:* IBM, MS-DOS 2.0 or higher, 192k RAM.
Performs Equilibrium Calculations for Flash & Drying Stages, Dew-Point & Bubble-Point Temperatures/Pressures, & Condensation & Vaporization Curves. Included on Disk Are the Chemical Properties of 400 Compounds (34 Entries per Compound). You May Also Add up to 400 More of Your Own. Uses Metric Units.
Dynacomp, Inc.

Heat Exchanger. *Version:* 2. Jun. 1988. *Compatible Hardware:* IBM PC. *Language(s):* BASIC. *Memory Required:* 256k.
disk $300.00 ea.
IBM PC. (ISBN 0-931821-34-7, Order no.: 02-071).
Based on Tube Side & Shell Side Physical Properties, Tube Size, Mass Flowrates, Material Constants, & Initial Tube Side Pass & Shell Length, Program Determines Average Physical Properties, LMTD, Area, Overall Coefficient, Number of Tubes per Pass, Shell Diameter, Tube & Shell Side Flow Parameters. Unspecified Terminal Temperature & Tube & Shell Side Pressure Drop. Handles Liquid or Gas & 9 Flow Conditions on Tube Side & 7 Flow Conditions on Shell Side; Including Boiling & Condensation Regimes. Shell Side & Tube Side Pressure Drops

Are Calculated. Sensible & Latent Heat Transfer Duty Is Calculated Based on Physical Property Input. Program Features Optimization Routine on Tube Side with Tube Length or Tube Diameter & on Shell Side with Baffle Spacing.
Information Resource Consultants.

Heat Exchanger Design Shell-&-Tube. *Items Included:* Full manual. No other products required. *Customer Support:* Free telephone support - no time limit. 30 day warranty.
MS-DOS 3.2 or higher. IBM & compatibles (512k). disk $949.95.
A Totally Integrated Package Which Will Give You Quick First-Pass Designs & Reliable Cost Estimates for Standard Heat Exchanger Projects. It Gives You an Overview for 15 Different Type of Exchangers with Respect to Both Mechanical & Thermal Designs. These Designs Conform with Industry, TEMA, & ASME Standards. HED Provides Cost & Weight Estimations As Well As an On-Line Units Conversion Utility. Included Are Data Files Containing the Physical Properties for 500 Compounds (the User May Add up to 100 More). Uses U.S. & Metric Units.
Dynacomp, Inc.

Heat Exchanger Design: Shell-&-Tube. 1992. *Items Included:* Detailed manuals included with all Dynacomp products. *Customer Support:* Free telephone support to original customer - no time limit; 30 day limited warranty.
MS-DOS 3.2 or higher. IBM PC & compatibles (512k). $989.95 (Add $5.00 for 3 1/2" format; 5 1/4" format standard). *Optimal configuration:* IBM, MS-DOS 3.0 or higher, 256k RAM, a hard disk, CGA or compatible graphics.
A Totally Integrated Package Which Will Give You Quick First-Pass Designs & Reliable Cost Estimates for Stranded Heat Exchanger Projects. It Gives You an Overview for 15 Different Types of Exchangers with Respect to Both Mechanical & Thermal Designs. These Designs Conform with Industry, TEMA, & ASME Standards. Provides Cost & Weight Estimations As Well As an On-Line Units Conversion Utility. Uses U.S. & Metric Units.
Dynacomp, Inc.

Heat Exchanger Network Analysis Single-Phase, Shell-&-Tube. *Items Included:* Full manual. No other products required. *Customer Support:* Free telephone support - no time limit. 30 day warranty.
MS-DOS 3.2 or higher. IBM & compatibles (512k). disk $2899.95. *Optimal configuration:* IBM, MS-DOS 3.3 or higher, 512k RAM, hard disk, graphics capability, & a printer.
Optimizes the Operation & Design of Heat Exchanger Networks by Quickly Analyzing Various Possible Arrangements. It Calculates the Heat & Material Balances for Hydrocarbon Systems Involving Complex Networks of Heat Exchangers, Heaters, Flash Drums, Crude Desalters, & Other Equipment. It Rigorously Calculates the Heat Transfer Coefficients & the Pressure Drops in Single-Phase Exchangers, Using the Industry-Wide Accepted Stream-Analysis Method.
Dynacomp, Inc.

Heat Exchanger Network Optimizer. *Items Included:* Full manual. No other products required. *Customer Support:* Free telephone support - no time limit. 30 day warranty.
MS-DOS 3.2 or higher. IBM & compatibles (512k). disk $279.95.
Will Help You to Financially Optimize Network Configurations for Grass-Roots or Retro-Fit Applications. The Default Values for the Economic Factors, Such As Limiting Exchange Geometry (Maximum Diameter & Length), Base Capital Cost, Capital Cost Exponent, Minimum LMTD Correction Factor, etc., May All Be Varied to Match the Specific Design at Hand. The Base Capital Cost May Be in Any Currency. The Algorithm Used Is Based on Minimum Utility Consumption, Operating Within User-Defined Constraints. Uses U.S. or Metric Units.
Dynacomp, Inc.

Heat Exchanger Network Optimizer. 1992. *Items Included:* Detailed manuals included with all Dynacomp products. *Customer Support:* Free telephone support to original customer - no time limit; 30 day limited warranty.
MS-DOS 3.2 or higher. IBM PC & compatibles (512k). $279.95 (Add $5.00 for 3 1/2" format; 5 1/4" format standard). *Optimal configuration:* IBM, MS-DOS 2.0 or higher, 256k RAM, two floppy drives (or one floppy & a hard disk).
HENCO Will Help You to Financially Optimize Network Configurations for Grass-Roots or Retro-Fit Applications. The Default Values for the Economic Factors, Such As Limiting Exchange Geometry (Maximum Diameter & Length), Base Capital Cost, Capital Cost Exponent, Minimum LMTD Correction Factor, etc., May All Be Varied to Match the Specific Design at Hand. Uses U.S. or Metric Units.
Dynacomp, Inc.

Heat Loss. *Compatible Hardware:* Apple; IBM. *Memory Required:* 48k, IBM 128k.
disk $59.95.
Uses ASHRAE Methods to Calculate Heat Losses Through Various Parts of a Building.
Dynacomp, Inc.

Heat Transfer Analysis. Aug. 1983. *Compatible Hardware:* Apple II+, IBM PC. *Operating System(s) Required:* PC-DOS, Apple DOS 3.3. *Language(s):* BASIC (source code included). *Memory Required:* Apple 48, IBM 128k. *Customer Support:* Telephone.
Apple. $200.00.
IBM. $250.00.
Calculates Heat Flow & Interface Temperatures Through Wall Sections of up to 10 Layers. Contains Standard Refractory K-Value Tables That Can Be Changed. User Inputs Estimated Hot & Cold Face Temperatures, Material Codes, & Thicknesses. Enhanced IBM Version Calculates Heat Transfer Through Walls or Cylinders, Using One of the Five Subprograms.
PEAS (Practical Engineering Applications Software).

Heat Transfer Software. *Version:* IBM. A. D. Kraus. Jul. 1986. *Compatible Hardware:* IBM PC & compatibles. *Memory Required:* 256k. *Items Included:* Disk & documentation.
disk $27.24 (ISBN 0-07-831344-9).
Solves Such Heat Transfer Problems As Fin Evaluations, Conduction & Convection Correlations.
McGraw-Hill, Inc.

Hebrew - Signs, Banners, & Greeting Cards. Sep. 1987. *Operating System(s) Required:* PC-DOS/MS-DOS. *Memory Required:* 128k. *General Requirements:* CGA, EGA or VGA; printer; & The Printshop software by Broderbund.
disk $9.99 (ISBN 0-9621501-7-7).
Will Print Signs, Banners, & Greeting Cards in Hebrew.
Bellmore Software.

Hebrew CalendarMaker. *General Requirements:* CalendarMaker program (CE Software). Macintosh Plus or higher. 3.5" disk $34.95.
Designed to Be Used with CE Software's CALENDARMAKER to Generate Hebrew Dates, Torah Portions, & Jewish Holidays. Includes 15 Pictures for Monthly Calendars, & 24 Judaic Icons for Individual Dates.
Davka Corp.

Hebrew DAvka. *Items Included:* Manual, Hebrew keyboard stickers.
Macintosh Plus or higher. 3.5" disk $69.95.
Desk Accessory Which Allows You to Insert Small Amounts of Hebrew into Most Standard Macintosh Applications.
Davka Corp.

Hebrew Enhancement of First Word Plus. *Version:* 2.3. Jun. 1988. *Compatible Hardware:* Atari ST. *Memory Required:* 512k. *General Requirements:* First Word Plus 2.00.
3.5" disk $179.00.
Bilingual, Bidirectional Hebrew/English Word Processing with First Word Plus. Allows Hebrew/English on Same Line.
Specialized Software.

Hebrew LaserWriter Fonts. *Compatible Hardware:* Macintosh Plus or higher.
3.5" disk $50.00 ea.
Fonts for PostScript Printers. Can Be Used with Davka's Hebrew Word Processors or with Any Other Left-to-Right English Program.
Davka Corp.

Hebrew Scriptures (BHS) for Windows. *Version:* 1.2. Sep. 1992. *Items Included:* User's manual. *Customer Support:* Free telephone support; defective disks replaced free.
Windows. IBM or compatibles (4Mb). disk $59.95. *Addl. software required:* MS Windows or ATM. *Optimal configuration:* 4Mb RAM & 386.
Complete Text in Hebraica Format of the Biblio Hebraica Stuttgartensia Old Testament, 1967/77 Deutsche Bibelgesellschaft, Derived from the Michigan-Claremont BHS Machine-Readable Text, Revised under the Coordination of Richard E. Whitaker with Special Support from the CCAT.
Linguist's Software, Inc.

The Hebrew Transliterator. *Version:* 6.1. Kent Ochel & Bert Brown. Oct. 1989. *Items Included:* Tutorial Disk; 3-ring binder with manual. *Customer Support:* Unlimited free technical support at (512) 251-7541.
Any DOS or Windows. IBM PC; XT; AT; or compatibles (512k). disk $99.95.
Any Macintosh. 3.5" disk $99.95.
(NIV or KJV) Provides the Serious Bible student with Tools Necessary to Study the Old Testament in the Original Language. Strong's Reference Numbers Are Assigned to the English Text & a Dictionary Gives the Hebrew Transliteration, Word Origins & derivations. VERSE SEARCH Is required.
Bible Research Systems.

HEC-1. *Version:* 4.0. U.S. Army Corps of Engineers. Sep. 1990. *Compatible Hardware:* AT&T PC 6300; Compaq; IBM PC, PC XT. *Operating System(s) Required:* PC-DOS, MS-DOS. *Memory Required:* 640k. *General Requirements:* Hard disk, 8087 co-processor for IBM. *Items Included:* Manual.
disk $295.00.
HEC-1 and HEC-2. $495.00 incl. manual.
Flood Hydrograph Package. Simulates the Surface Runoff from a River Basin. The Model Components Include the Stream Network, Runoff Characteristics, River Routing, Reservoir Routing, & Several Other Components.
Research Engineers.

HEC-2. Feb. 1992. *Compatible Hardware:* AT&T PC 6300; Compaq; IBM PC, PC XT. *Operating System(s) Required:* PC-DOS, MS-DOS. *Memory Required:* 640k. *Items Included:* Manual.
disk $295.00.
Water Surface Profile Program. Calculates Water Surface Profiles for a Defined Channel Including Losses Due to Bridges, Expansions & Contractions

TITLE INDEX

in the Channel. Either Subcritical or Supercritical Flow Conditions May Be Analyzed. Utilities Included Are PLOTEC-2, REORDER, & EDIT. PLOTEC-2 Reads HEC-2 Data Files & Plots the Cross Sections of the Defined Channel. REORDER Reverses the Order of Cross-Sections in the HEC-2 Data File. EDIT Is a Text Editor.
Research Engineers.

The Heist. (Series A).
All Apple IIs. disk $5.00. *Optimal configuration:* Apple II, joystick.
Commodore 64. disk $5.00. *Optimal configuration:* Commodore 64, joystick.
Join Forces with the World's Greatest Super-Agent to Brave the Unknown Terrors of International Espionage, & Test Your Strategy & Cunning Against Overwhelming Odds! Your Mission Is to Infiltrate a Museum That's Actually a Front for a Criminal Organization...& Heist All the Art in Your Search for a Top-Secret Microfilm. You Must Maneuver Carefully Through 96 Different Rooms Fiendishly Boobytrapped with a Multitude of Deadly Dangers. Leap Recklessly from Moving Platforms, Evade Man-Eating Robots, Dodge Tons of Falling Boxes & Monstrous Stompers - & Maybe You'll Succeed. Maybe.
Word Assocs., Inc.

Helical Spring Design. T. Boronkay & T. Youtsey. 1985. *Compatible Hardware:* Apple II, IBM PC. *Operating System(s) Required:* Apple DOS 3.3, PC-DOS 2.0. *Language(s):* BASIC (source code included).
disk $110.00.
Menu-Driven Program for the Design & Analysis of Helical Springs.
Kern International, Inc.

Hell on Disk: An Interactive Tour of the Infernal Otherworld. Eileen Gardiner. Aug. 1996.
Windows. IBM. CD-ROM disk $25.00 (ISBN 0-934977-61-5).
Macintosh. CD-ROM disk $25.00 (ISBN 0-934977-60-7).
A Compilation of Texts & Images on the History of Hell.
Italica Pr.

Hello Master. *Customer Support:* 800-929-8117 (customer service).
MS-DOS. Apple II. disk $49.99 (ISBN 0-87007-791-0).
Users Can Own the Source Code to Virtually Every Version of HELLO Available for the Apple II Running Under DOS 3.3. Versions That Provide a Variety of Menu Structures & Selection Procedures Which Save Work & Hardship. Hours of Fun & Valuable Programming.
SourceView Software International.

HELMSMAN for Windows. *Version:* 3.2. Nov. 1992.
IBM PC & compatibles (3Mb). $50,000.00 site license. *Optimal configuration:* IBM PC & compatibles (mouse & SVGA monitor recommended). Windows 3.1 Network compatible with all major LANs, 3Mb/workstation; 8Mb/LAN file server. Disk space required: 60Mb/Workstation, 500Mb/LAN file server.
A Windows Based PC/LAN Management Reporting Database. The System Automates the Entire Month/Quarter/Year-End Closing Process from the Collection of Financial Data Through the Consolidation Process to the Production of Boardroom Quality Financial Reports. Open Architecture Allows All Popular PC Software Products to Access Its Data. There Is a Very Tight Integration with Excel & Lotus Spreadsheets. The System Is Designed to Allow Financial Analysts & Executives to Easily Design Their Own Applications & Reports Using Simple Visual Commands. There Is a Sophisticated "Drill-Down" Feature That Allows the User to Quickly Access Supporting Financial Data for an Unlimited Number of Levels. Other Applications That HELMSMAN Supports Are: Budgeting, Financial Analysis, Strategic Planning, & Access to Historical Data. The System Is Also Available on DOS.
Helmsman Corp.

Help One Student to Succeed (HOSTS) Language Arts: A Diagnostic-Prescriptive-Structured Mentoring Instructional Delivery System. *Version:* 4.0. Jun. 1994. *Items Included:* 1 SDT Kit, 1 IRI Book, 1 Responding to Literature Book, 1 4.0 Computer Manual & Software, 1 Resource Index Notebook, 2 Program Manuals with Program Manual Sample Folders, 1 Expandable File Folder, 2 Administrator Handbooks, 1 HOSTS video, 2 Packages (50 ea. pack) Student Profile Cards, 2 Mentor Recruitment & Training Kits with Mentor Kit Sample Folders, 1 each of three promotional brochures, 1 Student Folder Make-It Kit, 1 Trademark Guidelines Packet, 1 Hand Scoring Assessment Set, 1 Scoring Keys Set, 1 Assessment Administration Manual, 1 Group Profile Card, 1 set ROI File Folders. *Customer Support:* Free on-site training.
Macintosh 6.0 or higher. Macintosh SE or higher (4Mb). Contact publisher for price (ISBN 1-886010-00-5). *Optimal configuration:* Macintosh Performa, 5Mb RAM, Stylewriter II printer, Macintosh Operating System Version 7.1, 40Mb hard disk. *Networks supported:* AppleTalk, EtherNet.
HOSTS Has Compiled a Computerized Database of over 7,000 Titles of High Quality Resource Materials Cross-Referenced to Learning Objectives & Student Learning Style & Indexed for Instruction. Teachers Access the Database to Prepare Individualized Lesson Plans. The HOSTS Concept Utilizes One-on-One Tutorials with Volunteers Who Provide Personalized Instruction Two or More Hours Each Week.
Hosts Corp.

Helpdesk 1. *Version:* 2.0. Aug. 1993. *Customer Support:* On-Line help under Windows; 42 page user guide; disk based training tutorial.
Windows, MS-DOS. PC 386 or 486 (8Mb). disk $3995.00 to $14,995.00 plus optional extras. *Addl. software required:* MS-DOS & MS-Windows or Windows for Workgroups. *Optimal configuration:* 20Mb HDD, 486DX33 with 8-16 Mb RAM, Mouse, VGA monitor. *Networks supported:* Netware (Novell), Lantastic (Artisoft), & Microsofts: LanManager, Windows NT, & Windows for Workgroups.
Caller Support System for Assisting Internal Callers with PC & Terminal Related Problems & Another Version Is Used by Manufacturers Who Sell & Support Products. System Includes 12 Data Bases: Call Tracking, Asset Tracking, Return Material System, Repair Records, Serial Number Records, Problems/Solutions Records, Caller Master Records, On-Site Dispatch Records, Configuration Records, & Product Master Records.
Bullseye Systems.

HelpDir: File Manager. *Version:* 2.0. Feb. 1992. *Items Included:* 34 page manual.
MS-DOS. IBM PC, PC XT, PC AT, 386, 486 (256k). disk $9.95 (ISBN 0-911827-12-9, Order no.: 7802). *Optimal configuration:* MS-DOS computer, 1 disk drive, 1 hard drive.
File & Directory Management Utility. It Makes Everyday File Management Chores a Snap. A Must for Every MS-DOS and/or Windows User. Complete Range of File Management Utilities: Change, Copy, Move, Erase, Rename & Sort Files & Directories by Pressing a Key or Clicking the Mouse. Search for Any File on Your Floppy Disk or Hard Disk. Read, Edit & Print Files. Start Programs Directly from the File Manager or from a Built-In Menu Program. "Chain" Document Files to the Related Application Program. Object Oriented Operation. Integrated Full-Feature Text Editor.
Elcomp Publishing, Inc.

HELU Accounts Payable. *Version:* 7.0. Wallace L. Rankin. Jan. 1987. *Operating System(s) Required:* MS-DOS, UCSD p system. *Language(s):* Pascal. *Memory Required:* 256k. *General Requirements:* 2 disk drives or hard disk. disk $199.00.
Accounting Program for Small Businesses Designed to Produce Data Manipulation & Sorting. Vendor File Maintenance & Interactive Entry of Expense Vouchers & Disbursements Are Provided. Prints Accounts Payable, Monthly Summary, & Checks. Expense Journal & Disbursements Journal Are Printed on Request.
Helu Software Corp.

HELU General Ledger. *Version:* 7.0. Jan. 1987. *Operating System(s) Required:* ZDOS, MS-DOS, UCSD p-System. *Language(s):* Pascal. *Memory Required:* 256k.
disk $199.00.
Accounting Program for Small Businesses Designed to Produce Rapid Data Manipulation & Sorting. Other Modules Are Integrated to Make a Complete Accounting System. Adjustments to Entry Journals Insure Auditability. Prints Chart of Accounts, Monthly Trail Balance & Journals. Some Additional Reports Are Current Balance Sheet & Year-to-Date Income Expense.
Helu Software Corp.

HELU Payroll. *Version:* 7.0. Jan. 1987. *Operating System(s) Required:* UCSD p-System, MS-DOS. *Language(s):* Pascal. *Memory Required:* 256k.
disk $199.00.
Accounting Program for Small Businesses Designed to Produce Rapid Data Manipulation & Sorting. Includes Complete Employee File Maintenance, Time Records, Ability to Print Paychecks on Pre-Printed Check Forms, Produce W-2 & Periodically Required Tax Reports. Upon Request, Will Print Alphabetical Employee Summary.
Helu Software Corp.

Hematology VideoReview. Emmanual C. Besa. Aug. 1994. *Items Included:* User manual, quick-start sheet, Keyboard Utilities, Quicktime extension, & Microsoft Multimedia Viewer (Windows version) or HyperCard (Macintosh version). *Customer Support:* Free, unlimited technical support via our toll-free number (1-800-945-4551).
Macintosh. Macintosh with a hard drive (2Mb). 3.5" disk $220.00 (ISBN 1-57349-063-6). *Nonstandard peripherals required:* Level 3 NTSC videodisc player with RS-232 interface & connector cable, video monitor. *Addl. software required:* System 7.0 or higher, Slice of Life VI videodisc. *Networks supported:* All LANs.
Windows. IBM compatible with 80286 or higher processor, a hard drive & a mouse (2Mb). disk $220.00 (ISBN 1-57349-254-X). *Nonstandard peripherals required:* Level 3 NTSC videodisc player with RS-232 interface & connector cable, video monitor. *Addl. software required:* MS-DOS 3.3 or higher, Windows 3.1 or higher, Slice of Life VI videodisc. *Networks supported:* All LANs.
A Complete Teaching & Review Program in Hematology. Provides Clear & Comprehensive Coverage of Key Topics in Hematology, with Direct Links to Related Images from the University

of Utah's Slice of Life VI Videodisc (Available Separately) & Image-Based Testing of the Materials Covered for Self-Evaluation.
Keyboard Publishing, Inc.

The Herbalist CD-ROM. *Version:* 2. David Hoffmann. 1994. *Items Included:* Startup manual, registration card. *Customer Support:* Telephone assistance for installation. Lifetime media (CD-ROM) replacement (exchange).
- Windows 3.1 or higher. PC or compatible (4Mb). CD-ROM disk $49.95 (ISBN 1-886649-00-6). *Nonstandard peripherals required:* CD-ROM drive. *Addl. software required:* Windows 3.1 or higher. *Optimal configuration:* 256 color monitor, 4Mb RAM, MPC standard sound card. *Networks supported:* Not tested - site licenses available.
- Macintosh 6.0.4 or higher. Macintosh (6Mb). CD-ROM disk $49.95 (ISBN 1-886649-01-4). *Nonstandard peripherals required:* CD-ROM drive. *Optimal configuration:* 256 color monitor. *Networks supported:* Not tested - network lic. avail. from publisher.
- DOS 3.1 or higher. PC (512k). CD-ROM disk $49.95 (ISBN 1-886649-17-0). *Networks supported:* Not tested - lic. avail.

Herbal Medicine Text Includes Data & Citations on 200 Medicinal Herbs. Color Photos on 190 Herbs. Narration by the Author. Music Search Software - Available for Windows & Macintosh.
Hopkins Technology.

Hercules Graphics Utilities. *Items Included:* Full manual. No other products required. *Customer Support:* Free telephone support - no time limit. 30 day warranty.
- MS-DOS 3.2 or higher. IBM & compatibles (512k). two disks $9.95.

This Is an Interesting Set of Graphics Utilities Which We Have Assembled from Public-Domain & Shareware Sources. They Are Designed for Owners of IBM Computers Having Hercules Graphic Cards. The Three Most Important Utilities on These Diskettes Are a Graphics Screen-to-Disk Capture System; an IBM CGA Emulator (Which Allows IBM CGA Programs to Operate with a Hercules Card); & a 180 Column by 43 Line File Display Utility.
Dynacomp, Inc.

Herdsman. AgraData, Inc. *Compatible Hardware:* TI Professional. *Operating System(s) Required:* MS-DOS, CP/M-86. *Memory Required:* 128k. *General Requirements:* 2 disk drives, printer. $1795.00.
Dairy Herd Management Program. Generate 50 Reports to Organize Rounds, Record Herd Activity to Facilitate Data Entry & Assist in Getting Daily Chores Done.
Texas Instruments, Personal Productivit.

The Hermitage Art Treasures Tour. Intersoft, Inc. Jan. 1996. *Items Included:* Registration card. *Customer Support:* Tel 360-650-0534, 90 limited warranty.
- Windows. 386DX, 8-bit (4Mb). CD-ROM disk $49.95 (ISBN 1-57307-000-9). *Networks supported:* Yes.

Interactive Tour of the State Hermitage Museum.
Cascade Marketing International, Inc.

The Hermitage, Vol. 2: The Winter Palace. State Hermitage Museum Staff & J.V. Intersoft Staff. Jun. 1994. *Items Included:* 20 page written manual. *Customer Support:* 90 day money back guarantee, customer support phone 206-650-0534 free.
- DOS V3.3 or higher, Windows compatible. IBM or compatible (640k). 5.25" VGA disk $99.95 (ISBN 1-57307-013-0). *Optimal configuration:* DOS V3.3 or higher, IBM or compatible (286, 386, 486, Pentium) mouse, VGA/SVGA monitor, 640k RAM, 9Mb free hard drive space. *Networks supported:* Novell.
- 5.25" SVGA disk $99.95 (ISBN 1-57307-014-9). *Optimal configuration:* IBM or compatible, DOS V3.3 or higher, mouse, SVGA monitor, 640k RAM, 15Mb hard disk free space.
- 3.5" VGA disk $99.95 (ISBN 1-57307-011-4). *Optimal configuration:* IBM or compatible, DOS V3.3 or higher, mouse, VGA/SVGA monitor, 640k RAM, 9Mb hard disk free space.
- 3.5" SVGA disk $99.95 (ISBN 1-57307-012-2). *Optimal configuration:* IBM or compatible, DOS V3.3 or higher, mouse, SVGA monitor, 640k RAM, 15Mb hard disk free space.
- $79.95 CD-ROM Version (ISBN 1-57307-015-7).

A Historical Architectural Tour of Russia's Winter Palace, St. Petersburg.
Cascade Marketing International, Inc.

Heroes of the Lance, 2 disks. 1988. *Memory Required:* Commodore 64/128 64k, IBM 256k, Atari ST & Amiga 512k. *Customer Support:* 14 day money back guarantee/30 day exchange policy; tech support line: (408) 737-6800 (11:00-5:00 PST); customer service: (408) 737-6800 (9:00-5:00 PST).
- Commodore 64/128. disk $29.95.
- Atari ST, Amiga, IBM. disk $39.95.

Re-Creates the Epic Battle Between Good & Evil on the World of Krynn. You Control Eight Companions, Each With Different Specialized Attributes & Skills. Guide These Brave Adventurers Deep Into the Treacherous Ruins of the Temple Xak Tsaroth to Retrieve the Precious Disks of Mishakal.
Strategic Simulations, Inc.

HES MON 64. *Customer Support:* 800-929-8117 (customer service).
- MS-DOS. Commodore 64. disk $39.99 (ISBN 0-87007-845-3).

A Machine Language Monitor Program for Assembly Language Programmers. Allows the User to Search for, Display, Compare & Transfer Values at Specific Memory Locations. The User Can Assemble or Disassemble Blocks of Code. Essential for Debugging Assembly Language Programs. It Features Forward & Reverse Scrolling, "Hunt" & "Walk", & Output to Disk, Tape, Screen or Printer.
SourceView Software International.

Hewlett-Packard ColorPro Graphics Plotter. *Compatible Hardware:* Apple Macintosh.
- 3.5" disk $1295.00.

Eight-Pen Desktop Plotter Which Requires Thirty Party Software to Drive It. Fonts Are Limited to an Optional Graphics Enhancement Cartridge That Requires Some BASIC Programming.
Hewlett-Packard Co.

Hex. *Compatible Hardware:* Atari ST with joystick, Commodore Amiga.
- 3.5" disk $39.95.

Strategy Game. Change 19 Hexagonal Blocks to Green Before the Computer-Controlled Opponents (Some Using Magic, Some Just Brute Force) Change Them to Purple. Each of the 12 Opponents Employs a Different Strategy.
Mark of the Unicorn.

HFS Locator Plus. *Version:* 2.03. *Compatible Hardware:* Apple Macintosh.
- 3.5" disk $39.95.

HFS Utility Which Supports File Search by Name or Date, Creates Folders, & Transfers Files Between Folders.
PBI Software, Inc.

HGRAM. *Version:* 1.1. Sep. 1985. *Compatible Hardware:* IBM PC, PC AT, PC XT & compatibles. *Operating System(s) Required:* MS-DOS, PC-DOS. *Language(s):* FORTRAN. *Memory Required:* 320k. *General Requirements:* Printer, plotter.
- disk $1250.00 (Order no.: HGRAM).

Plots Histograms of Composited Geologic or Mining Values & Computes the Statistics of Their Distribution. Also Plots Both the Relative & Cumulative Frequency Curves of One or Two Variables.
Geostat Systems International, Inc. (GSII).

Hi-Res Graphics Utilities. *Compatible Hardware:* Apple II. *Language(s):* Applesoft II. *Memory Required:* 32k.
- disk $24.95 (Order no.: 10034).

High-Resolution Shapes May Be Drawn Using the Shape Table.
Powersoft, Inc.

Hi-Res Plus. *Compatible Hardware:* Apple II+. *Language(s):* Applesoft BASIC. *Memory Required:* 48k.
- disk $49.95.

Add Sound Effect to Programs That Zoom, Zing, Crackle, Whistle, Buzz, etc. Mix Graphics & Text for Visual Effects, Overstrike on Characters, Expand the Text Window, Reverse Screeen Images Changing Black to White & White to Black, Roll the Screen in a Continuous Wrap-Around, Scroll the Screen up, down, Right, or Left. Remedy ON ERR Problems & Debug Programs. Use Commands in a BASIC or Machine Language Program to Show File after File of Graphic/Text Screen. Compatible with PLE.
Instant Software, Inc.

Higgins Mail. *Version:* 2.5. 1993. *Items Included:* Documentation, quick reference template, registration card. *Customer Support:* Free technical support (unlimited), electronic support via Enable BBS, on-site education programs at charge.
- DOS 3.3 Plus, OS/2 1.1 or higher. 8086, 8088, 80286, 80386, 80486, IBM PS/2 & compatibles (287k). 8-user starter kit $295.00; 4-user exp. kit $149.00; 12-user exp. kit $349.00; 20-user exp. kit $495.00; 100-user exp. kit $1995.00. *Nonstandard peripherals required:* Intel Satisfaxion board for FAX Gateway. *Optimal configuration:* 640k equipped system. *Networks supported:* Banyan Vines 4.11; LANtastic 4.1; 10Net 5.0; Novell Lite 1.0; Novell 286 1.5 & 2.2; Novell 386 3.11; IBM LAN Server 1.2, 1.3; Moses PromiseLAN & ChosenLAN.

Comprehensive E-Mail Support for LAN-Based Workgroups (& Remote Laptop or Stand-Alone Users) Providing: Message or "Conversation" History; Distribution Lists; Message Confirmation; Text/Spreadsheet/Graphics File Enclosures; Hot Key Access to Other DOS Applications; FAX Support; Encryption; 2-Password Security; Multiple Gateway Support. Flexible System Administration Capabilities, Concurrent with General Use.
Enable Software, Inc.

Higgins Productivity. *Version:* 2.5. 1993. *Items Included:* Documentation, quick reference template, on-line tutorial. *Customer Support:* Free, unlimited technical support; unlimited electronic support via Enable BBS; on-site education available at charge.
- DOS 3.3 Plus. 8086, 8088, 80286, 80386, 80486 IBM PS/2 & compatibles (327k). 8-user LAN kit $695.00; 4-user exp. kit $349.00; 12-user exp. kit $995.00. *Nonstandard peripherals required:* Intel Satisfaxion board for FAX Gateway. *Optimal configuration:* 640k equipped system. *Networks supported:* Banyan Vines 4.11; LANtastic 4.1; 10Net 5.0; Novell Lite 1.0; Novell 286 1.5 & 2.2; Novell 386 3.11; IBM LAN Server 1.2, 1.3; Moses

TITLE INDEX

PromiseLAN & ChosenLAN.
Includes All Capabilities of Higgins Mail Plus: Group Scheduling, To-Do Lists, Expense Reporting, etc. Allows Users to Designate "Shared Resources" or "Shared Information Areas" (e.g. Competitive Information or Conference Rooms) Accessible by Designated Users with Ability to View, Update, Print, Based on Authority Level.
Enable Software, Inc.

High C/C Plus Plus 386 Compiler. Version: 3.2. Customer Support: Free technical support for registered users.
DOS, Windows, Windows NT, OS/2, Solaris, UNIX SUR4, AIX. 80386, 80486 & Pentium. $795.00 - $895.00.
Create 32 Bit Protected Mode DOS Applications or 32 Bit Windows Applications & Dynamic Link Libraries (DLLS) Using High C/C++. Includes Source Level Debugger with Local & Global Descriptor Table Viewers.
MetaWare, Inc.

High C-286. Version: 1.6. Compatible Hardware: IBM PC & compatibles. Operating System(s) Required: DOS. Memory Required: 1000k. General Requirements: Hard disk.
disk $495.00.
16 Bit C Compiler Featuring D4S Service Functions, & Low Level Keyboard Input. Compilation Is an Added-Step Process. Supports Math Coprocessor & Technical Hot Line & Microsoft C, MASM, & LINK-Compatible.
MetaWare, Inc.

High Per Form. Version: 2.01. May 1991.
disk write for info.
United Systems Software Corp.

High Performance Level II COBOL. Version: 2.6. Compatible Hardware: IBM PC & compatibles. Memory Required: 64k. General Requirements: Hard disk.
disk $325.00.
COBOL Compiler Meeting Level 2 Requirements in All Categories, Nucleus, Table Handling, Sequential I/O, Relative I/O, Indexed I/O, Sort/Merge, Library, Debug & Interprogram Communications for a High Federal Standard Level. Compilation Is an Added Step Process. Features a Math Coprocessor & Supports Technical Hot Line.
Micro Focus, Inc. (California).

High Performance Level II COBOL with animator. Version: 2.6. Compatible Hardware: IBM PC & compatibles. Memory Required: 64k. General Requirements: Hard disk.
disk $495.00.
COBOL Compiler Meeting Level 2 Requirements in All Categories, Nucleus, Table Handling, Sequential I/O, Relative I/O, Indexed I/O, Sort/Merge, Library, Debug & Interprogram Communications for a High Federal Standard Level. Features Animator & Math Coprocessor. Supports Technical Hot Line.
Micro Focus, Inc. (California).

HighPerForm Appraisal Processor. Version: 2.01. Compatible Hardware: IBM PC, PC XT, PC AT. Operating System(s) Required: MS-DOS. Memory Required: 640k. General Requirements: HD disk drives, Epson compatible printer, HP Laser compatible, Brothel. Items Included: Disk, manual. Customer Support: 6 month free: Annual Fee.
disk $549.00.
Allows the Residential Appraiser to Save & Re-Use Standard Appraisals; Enter Words & Phrases with a Single Keystroke; Instantaneously Calculate All Adjustments & Totals on the Screen; Print Custom-Tailored Bills; & More. Use to Fill in Forms for Appraisal of Residential, Condominium, Land, Employee Relocation, Short-Form, Residential Income, VA/FHA Properties & Other Forms.
United Systems Software Corp.

Highrise. (Micro Learn Learning Games Ser.). Apple II (48k); Commodore 64. disk $14.95.
Optimal configuration: Apple II, 48k, Commodore 64, 1 drive.
Entertaining Educational Game with Movable Shapes Arranged in Columns. Player Has Barnaby Pick up Shapes & Move Them to a Platform, Hoisting Them One at a Time to Construct a Building. Blocks Must Balance or the Building Falls. On Completion of a Balanced Building, Barnaby Climbs to the Top & Starts the Next Level. Game Has 24 Levels, Marked by Increasingly Complex Shapes & Fewer Columns to Choose From. Develops Planning Skills, Eye-Hand Coordination, Shape Perception & Logic. Extremely Interactive; Removable Time Clock; Records Highest Scores.
Word Assocs., Inc.

Highrise. (Series B). Joe Calabrese.
All Apple IIs. $15.00 (ISBN 1-57265-060-5).
Optimal configuration: Apple II, keyboard.
Apple. $15.00.
This Arcade-Type Game Develops Planning Skills, Logic, Eye-Hand Coordination & Shape Perception. Select Blocks of Various Shapes & Sizes from Five Chutes. Load Them onto a Springboard, in Any of Five Positions - & Flip Them Up. Plan Correctly, & You'll Build a Balanced Tower or Building. On Completion of a Balanced Building, Barnaby Climbs to the Top & Starts the Next Level. Stack Them Wrong, & They Come Crashing Down. It's a Race Against Time, with 24 Levels of Increasingly Complex Shapes & Fewer Columns to Choose From. In the Instructional Mode, You Can Turn the Timing off, so the Player Can Progress at His Own Speed. Extremely Interactive.
Word Assocs., Inc.

Highrise Math. (Micro Learn Learning Games Ser.). Customer Support: Free telephone support.
Apple II (48k). $39.95 (Lab pack/5 $99.00) (ISBN 0-939153-34-3). Optimal configuration: Apple II, 48k, 1 drive.
Combines the Award-Winning Highrise Game with an Educational Game Designed to Stimulate Math, Logic, Planning & Perceptual Skills. Select One or More Arithmetic Operations at an Easy or Tough Level. Construct a Valid Math Statement (" 1 Plus 1" or "2.1 x 4 - 1") That Equals Your "Goal" Number for the Level. In Other Words, the Game Gives You the Answer, & You Supply the Problem. Build Your Tower of Numbers High & Watch Barnaby Climb to the Next Level of Difficulty.
Word Assocs., Inc.

HighStyle. Version: 1.01. Compatible Hardware: IBM PC & compatibles. Memory Required: 256k. Items Included: User manual.
$375.00.
Desktop-Publishing Package Including Such Page-Formatting Features As Text Flotation, Automatic Pagination, Automatic Numbering of Pages, Automatic Columning, Cropping, Hyphenation, Justification, Kerning & Leading. Supports ASCII Word Processing; GEM Draw, Lotus, Monographics Plus & Other Graphics Programs; CGA Graphics Card; & Laser Printers. Also Includes Style Sheets.
Lattice, Inc.

HiJaak for DOS. Version: 2.1. Compatible Hardware: IBM PC. Items Included: User's manual. Customer Support: 30 day money back guarantee; 800 number tech support.
$189.00 3.5" or 5.25" disk.
Provides the Ability of Converting Graphics Images from One Format to Another & Grabbing Data from the Screen or from LaserJet Output. Some 60 Plus Formats Are Supported Including: Amiga, DXF, GEM, IMG, WMF, CGM, BMP, TGA, DRW, & WPG (WordPerfect) CompuServe, HP LaserJet, InSet/HiJaak, LOTUS, Macintosh, PC PAINTBRUSH, POSTSCRIPT (Destination Only), 34 Custom TIFF Flavors, Text. Also Supported Are the Following Graphics Screens (Source Only): CGA, EGA, VGA, Hercules, & Some 20 Graphics Cards. Designed for Desktop Publishing. Also a Variety of 24 FAX Formats.
InSet Systems, Inc.

HiJaak Graphics Suite. Version: 3.0. Sep. 1994. Items Included: 5 manuals, 15 3.5 disk, 1 CD-ROM. Customer Support: 30 day unlimited warranty, OEM inquiries encouraged, Concurrent use license, GSA listing available, free tech support (not toll free).
Microsoft Windows Version 3.1 w/46Mb HD space available. IBM PC & compatibles (4Mb). CD-ROM disk Contact publisher for price (Order no.: 721177006151). Optimal configuration: 486 w/8Mb, Windows 3.1.
Networks supported: Novell Netware.
Includes Upgraded HiJaak PRO & HiJaak Browser. New Additions Are HiJaak Smuggler, HiJaak TouchUp & Micrografx DRAW. Browser Allows Better Organization, Keywording, Automatic Cataloging & Searching by Keywords & Attributes. PRO with IGOR (Intelligent Graphics Object Recognition) Converts Raster to Vector Graphics File Formats Using Either Centerline or Outline Techniques & Gives Access to Tolerance Settings, Undither & Speak Removal. Smuggler Uses Thumbnails to Visually Import Virtually Any Graphics File, All from Within Any Application That Supports Pasting Graphics from the Windows Clipboard. TouchUp Enhances Raster Graphics with Text, Color, Special Effects, & Much More. Nearly Every Commonly Used Editing Tool Is Available. Micrografx DRAW Boosts Vector Graphics with Drawing Tools, Object Manipulation, Line Styles & Other Special Effects.
InSet Systems, Inc.

Hillsfar. Apr. 1989.
IBM PC & compatibles (384k). Version 1.2 $49.95 one 3.5" & two 5.25" disks. Nonstandard peripherals required: CGA, EGA & Tandy 16 color graphic mode supported by IBM.
Commodore 64, 128 (64k). Version 1.3 $39.95.
Atari ST (512k). Version 1.1 $39.95.
Amiga (512k). 3.5" disk $39.95.
Fantasy That Combines Best of Role-Playing Adventures & Fast-Paced Action Games. Explore City of Hillsfar & Discover a Quest (There Are Many Possible Ones). Transfer Your Favorite Character from the Pool of Radiance or Curse of the Azure Bonds or Create One from Scratch. Your Quest Will Keep You Constantly on the Move. Fight in the Arena, Run Mazes, Pick Locks & More. Think Fast, Move Fast. These Minigames Happen in Real Time.
Strategic Simulations, Inc.

Hinsch Time Planner. Sep. 1992. Items Included: User's guide. Customer Support: Free telephone support, 60 day money-back warranty.
DOS/Windows 3.1. IBM compatible (4Mb). disk $129.00. Optimal configuration: Supports pen, if available.
A Calendar with Project Management & Time-Tracking Features, Such As Timelines & Cost-Period Graphs. Unlike Ordinary Calendar Programs, It Can Add up Times & Expenses.
H. M. Hinsch & Co., Inc.

HIPS. *Compatible Hardware:* UNIX. *Items Included:* Source code. *Customer Support:* Telephone hotline.
$2995.00.
Image Processing Package Which Handles Sequence of Images in the Same Way That It Handles Single Frames for Simple Image Transformations, Filtering, Convolution, Fourier & Other Transformation Processing etc. Also Includes Libraries, All Source & On-Line Documentation.
SharpImage Software.

HiQ. *Items Included:* Software, documentation. *Customer Support:* Toll-free technical support, training, field seminar, user group meetings.
Mac OS-compatible with System 7. Macintosh or Power Macintosh, 68020 processor or higher, floating point coprocessor (5Mb). 3.5" disk $695.00. *Optimal configuration:* 68020 or higher processor & a floating point coprocessor. 5Mb RAM, (8Mb recommended).
Object-Based Numerical Analysis & Data Visualization Software Package. It Gives Scientists & Engineers an Integrated Graphical Environment for Solving Real-World Math Problems. HiQ Has More Than 600 Mathematical Functions, Report Generation Capabilities, Interactive Three-Dimensional Graphs, A Scripting Language, a Compiler, & a Set of Application-Specific "Problem Solvers." Problem Solvers Generate HiQ-Script Programs, Which Users Can Modify for Custom Applications.
National Instruments.

HiScore Database. *Compatible Hardware:* Atari 400, 800. *Language(s):* Atari BASIC (source code included). *Memory Required:* cassette 16k, disk 24k.
disk $16.95.
Designed to Maintain Game Score Records.
Dynacomp, Inc.

HiSoft BASIC. HiSoft. Nov. 1988. *Memory Required:* 512k. *General Requirements:* Atari ST. 3.5" disk $79.95.
BASIC Programming Language with Stand-Alone Compiler. Features Include Interactive GEM Editor, Modern Structured Language, Total Support for GEM, BIOS, XBIOS; Single & Double Precision Numbers.
MichTron, Inc.

HiSoft BASIC Professional. HiSoft. Nov. 1988. *Compatible Hardware:* Atari ST, Commodore Amiga. *Memory Required:* 512k.
3.5" disk $159.00.
For the More Advanced User. Many Unique Features Including Additional Libraries, Commands & The Ability to Program Desk Accessories.
MichTron, Inc.

HiSoft C Interpreter. Jun. 1989.
TOS (512k). Atari ST. disk $99.95.
User Can Learn C Using Program. Since This Is an Interpreter, Not a Compiler, It Lets User Develop, Debug & Test Programs in a Simple Environment.
MichTron, Inc.

HiSoft Dev Pac. HiSoft. *Compatible Hardware:* Atari ST; Commodore Amiga. *Language(s):* Assembly. *Memory Required:* 512k.
3.5" disk $99.95.
Includes a Full 68000 Macro Assembler, a Complete Screen Editor & a Diassembler & Debugger.
MichTron, Inc.

Histcon. Robert D. Loevy. May 1985. *Compatible Hardware:* Apple II, IBM PC.
disk $95.00.
Apple. (ISBN 0-13-388992-0).
IBM. (ISBN 0-13-389024-4).
Prentice Hall.

HISTO. *Version:* 2.3. May 1984. *Compatible Hardware:* IBM PC, PC XT, PC AT, & compatibles. *Operating System(s) Required:* PC-DOS, MS-DOS. *Language(s):* FORTRAN. *Memory Required:* 512k. *General Requirements:* Printer.
disk $800.00 (Order no.: HISTO).
Prints the Histograms of up to 20 Variables for Unlimited Amounts of Data. The Relative & Cumulative Histograms Can Be Computed in Real & Logarithmic Space.
Geostat Systems International, Inc. (GSII).

Histogram Plot. *Version:* 2.0. J. McFarland. 1981. *Compatible Hardware:* Apple II, IIc, IIe; Basis 6502; Franklin Ace. *Operating System(s) Required:* Apple DOS 3.3. *Language(s):* BASIC (source code included). *Memory Required:* 48k.
Apple. disk $39.00 (ISBN 0-914555-09-X).
Statistics Package Displays or Prints-Out: Raw Data, Computed Data, Mean, Median, Standard Deviation, Expected Cell Frequencies, Actual Cell Limits & Frequencies, & Chi-Square Goodness of Fit Calculations.
Andent, Inc.

Histology QuizBank, Vol. 1. Stephen W. Downing. Aug. 1994. *Items Included:* User manual, quick-start sheet, Keyboard Utilities, & Microsoft Multimedia Viewer (Windows version) or HyperCard (Macintosh version). *Customer Support:* Free, unlimited technical support via our toll-free number (1-800-945-4551).
Macintosh. Macintosh with a hard drive (2.5Mb). 3.5" disk $199.00 (ISBN 1-57349-230-2).
Addl. software required: System 7.0 or higher. *Networks supported:* All LANs.
Windows. IBM compatible with 80286 or higher processor, a hard drive & a mouse (2Mb). disk $199.00 (ISBN 1-57349-233-7). *Addl. software required:* MS-DOS 3.3 or higher, Windows 3.1 or higher. *Networks supported:* All LANs.
Over 300 Multiple-Choice Questions Covering All Areas of Histology, with Detailed Feedback & Direct Links to Related Materials Appearing in the Histology TextStack.
Keyboard Publishing, Inc.

Histology QuizBank, Vol. 2. Matthew G. Kestenbaum et al. Aug. 1994. *Items Included:* User manual, quick-start sheet, Keyboard Utilities, & Microsoft Multimedia Viewer (Windows version) or HyperCard (Macintosh version). *Customer Support:* Free, unlimited technical support via our toll-free number (1-800-945-4551).
Macintosh. Macintosh with a hard drive (2.5Mb). 3.5" disk $199.00 (ISBN 1-57349-236-1).
Addl. software required: System 7.0 or higher. *Networks supported:* All LANs.
Windows. IBM compatible with 80286 or higher processor, a hard drive & a mouse (2Mb). disk $199.00 (ISBN 1-57349-239-6). *Addl. software required:* MS-DOS 3.3 or higher, Windows 3.1 or higher. *Networks supported:* All LANs.
Over 500 Multiple-Choice Questions Covering All Areas of Histology, with Detailed Feedback & Direct Links to Related Materials Appearing in the Histology TextStack.
Keyboard Publishing, Inc.

Histology TextStack. Junqueira, Carneiro & Kelley Staff. Aug. 1994. *Items Included:* User manual, quick-start sheet, Keyboard Utilities, & Microsoft Multimedia Viewer (Windows version) or HyperCard (Macintosh version). *Customer Support:* Free, unlimited technical support via our toll-free number (1-800-945-4551).
Macintosh. Macintosh with a hard drive (2.5Mb). CD-ROM disk $280.00 (ISBN 1-57349-064-4).
Nonstandard peripherals required: CD-ROM player required, 256-color monitor recommended. *Addl. software required:* System 7.0 or higher. *Networks supported:* All LANs.
Windows. IBM compatible with 80286 or higher processor, a hard drive & a mouse (2Mb). CD-ROM disk $280.00 (ISBN 1-57349-134-9).
Nonstandard peripherals required: CD-ROM player required, 256-color monitor recommended. *Addl. software required:* MS-DOS 3.3 or higher, Windows 3.1 or higher. *Networks supported:* All LANs.
The Complete Text with All Tables, Figures, Diagrams, & Color Illustrations from Appleton & Lange's Basic Histology by Junqueira, Carneiro, & Kelley. Includes a Collection of Tools for Searching, Capturing & Manipulating Data of Interest.
Keyboard Publishing, Inc.

Histology Video Review. Matthew G. Kestenbaum & Frank J. Wilson. Aug. 1994. *Items Included:* User manual, quick-start sheet, Keyboard Utilities, & Microsoft Multimedia Viewer (Windows version) or HyperCard (Macintosh version). *Customer Support:* Free, unlimited technical support via our toll-free number (1-800-945-4551).
Macintosh. Macintosh with a hard drive (2.5Mb). 3.5" disk $220.00 (ISBN 1-57349-069-5).
Nonstandard peripherals required: Level 3 NTSC videodisc player with RS-232 interface & connecting cables, video monitor. *Addl. software required:* System 7.0 or higher, Slice of Life V or VI. *Networks supported:* All LANs.
Windows. IBM compatible with 80286 or higher processor, a hard drive & a mouse (2Mb). 3.5" disk $220.00 (ISBN 1-57349-227-2).
Nonstandard peripherals required: Level 3 NTSC videodisc player with RS-232 interface & connecting cables, video monitor. *Addl. software required:* MS-DOS 3.3 or higher, Windows 3.1 or higher, Slice of Life V or VI. *Networks supported:* All LANs.
A Complete Electronic Course in Basic Histology. Includes 20 Complete Chapters in Human Histology, a Comprehensive Image-Based Self-Testing Module, & References to More Than 1,000 Related Images from the Slice of Life Videodisc (Available Separately). Also Includes Powerful Features That Facilitate Fast, Easy Searching, Tagging, Manipulating, & Saving of Information Interest, & a Tool for Building Interactive Electronic Lessons.
Keyboard Publishing, Inc.

Histology VideoIndex. Stephen W. Downing. Aug. 1994. *Items Included:* User manual, quick-start sheet, Keyboard Utilities, & Microsoft Multimedia Viewer (Windows version) or HyperCard (Macintosh version). *Customer Support:* Free, unlimited technical support via our toll-free number (1-800-945-4551).
Macintosh. Macintosh with a hard drive (2.5Mb). 3.5" disk $300.00 (ISBN 1-57349-067-9).
Nonstandard peripherals required: Level 3 NTSC videodisc player with RS-232 interface & connecting cables, video monitor. *Addl. software required:* System 7.0 or higher, Histology: A Photographic Atlas videodisc. *Networks supported:* All LANs.
Windows. IBM compatible with 80286 or higher processor, a hard drive & a mouse (2Mb). disk $300.00 (ISBN 1-57349-244-2). *Nonstandard peripherals required:* Level 3 NTSC videodisc player with RS-232 interface & connecting cables, video monitor. *Addl. software required:* MS-DOS 3.3 or higher, Windows 3.1 or higher, Histology: A Photographic Atlas videodisc. *Networks supported:* All LANs.
Descriptive Captions for All the Images on Histology: A Photographic Atlas (Available Separately), a Videodisc Collection of More Than 7,000 Color Photographs As Seen Through a Light Microscope.
Keyboard Publishing, Inc.

TITLE INDEX

Historical Collections of Louisiana.
MS-DOS (5Mb). IBM & compatibles. CD-ROM disk $50.00. *Nonstandard peripherals required:* CD-ROM drive.
Electronic Publication of an Old & Extremely Rare Multivolume Collection of Documents Dealing with the European Conquest of the Mississippi Valley. CD-ROM Text Appears in Word Perfect 5.1 Format & Is Key-Word Searchable.
Louisiana State University Press.

History of Computing: An Encyclopedia of the People & Machines That Made Computer History. *Version:* 1.15. Mark Greenia. Jan. 1996. *Items Included:* Includes printed instructions, install program & help screens. *Customer Support:* Free 90-day Tech Support via Internet E-mail to Lexikon2-aol.com.
Windows 3.1 or Windows 95. IBM PC & compatibles 80386 (4Mb), VGA color. 3.5" disk $25.00 (ISBN 0-944601-64-2, Order no.: HOC).
A Full Windows-Based Encyclopedia on Diskettes. Over 1,000 Pages of Information Covering Early Counting Methods, Typewriters, Early Calculators, Early Digital Computers, & Microcomputers. Includes Computer Company Profiles, Biographical Sketches of Computer Pioneers, Computer Glossary & Dictionary of over 7,000 Terms, & 100 Digitized Photos of Early Machines & Pioneers. Full Hypertext Support. Self-Running, Easy to Use. Includes Install Program & Help Utility.
Lexikon Services.

HISTORYMAKER IV. *Version:* 3.0. Galen B. Cook. Jun. 1986. *Compatible Hardware:* IBM PC & compatibles. *Operating System(s) Required:* PC-DOS. *Memory Required:* 640k. *General Requirements:* Hard disk. *Customer Support:* Toll free telephone support.
disk $995.00.
This Product Is a Complete, Clinical Record System for Physician's Office or Other Outpatient Service Areas. Maintains an Electronic Medical Chart on All Patients According to S.O.A.P. Format & Requires Virtually No Keyboard Input from the Physician in the Process.
SRC Systems, Inc.

Hit Disks, Vol. 1, 4 disks. Microdeal. Nov. 1988. *Compatible Hardware:* Atari ST, Commodore Amiga. *Memory Required:* 512k.
3.5" disk $49.95.
Four Arcade Games in One Package. Karate Kid II, Goldrunner, Jupiter Probe & Slaygon. Demo Available for Slaygon Only.
MichTron, Inc.

The Hitchhiker's Guide to the Galaxy. Douglas Adams & Steve Meretzky. Oct. 1984. *Compatible Hardware:* Apple II, II+, IIe, IIc; Macintosh; Atari 400, 800, 800XL, 1200XL, ST; Commodore 64/128, Plus 4, Amiga; IBM; Mindset; Tandy 2000; TI 99/4A, TI Professional; TRS-80 Model I, Model III, Color Computer. *Operating System(s) Required:* MS-DOS 2.0, CP/M.
disk $39.95.
Atari XL/XE, Commodore 64/128. $34.95.
Galactic Adventure Adapted from Douglas Adams' Best-Selling Novel. Playing the Role of Arthur Dent, You'll Be Part of Every Twist & Turn of the Plot (Which Is Not Necessarily Similar to That of the Book), the Object Being, According to the Authors, to "Stay Alive, Don't Panic, & Have a Good Time." Package Contains: a "Don't Panic" Button, Authentic Fluff, Megadodo Publications Sales Brochure for the Latest Model of THE HITCHHIKER'S GUIDE, Official Destruct Orders for Your Home...& Planet, a Microscopic Space Fleet, & No Tea.
Activision, Inc.

The Hitchhiker's Guide to the Galaxy. Infocom. *Compatible Hardware:* HP 150 Touchscreen, HP 110 Portable.
3.5" disk $39.95 (Order no.: 92244BA).
You Are Arthur Dent, & a Bulldozer Is Preparing to Level Your House Even As an Alien Space Fleet Is Preparing to Level Your Planet. So What Else Is Left but to Grab a Pint of Bitters for the Road & Join Ford Prefect, Trillian, Zaphod Beeblebrox & Marvin on a Cosmic Jaunt into the Outer Reaches Where Anything Can - & Does - Happen. And Don't Forget Your Towel!
Hewlett-Packard Co.

HIV Tracking System. *Customer Support:* 24 hour/day, 7 day/week.
MS-DOS, Novell Netware/Turbo Pascal (language). IBM PC & compatibles (640k & 3mb extended). $50,000-$150,000. *Networks supported:* Novell Netware.
Records Demographic & Testing Data for Anonymous & Identified Patients. One Thousand Levels of Security Are Provided for Each Record Information Field. Instrument Data Is Transmitted Directly. Object Oriented Designer Records Allow Each Installation to Customize the Demographic & Testing Data Tracked by the System. Screens, Workflow, & Reports Are All Definable by Each Installation.
LCI.

HiWire II. *Version:* 2.2r0. *Items Included:* Comprehensive manual & tutorial in 3-ring binder & case. *Customer Support:* 30-day money back guarantee; free customer support on toll-free number & bulletin-board-system (BBS).
MS-DOS 3.0 & higher. IBM PC, PC-XT, PC-AT, PS/2; Compaq; 100% compatibles, NEC-9801 (640k). $995.00.
CAD Tool for Electronics Designers Who Create Schematics & Printed-Circuit-Board Layouts. Features Include: Menu-Driven Operation from a Mouse or Keyboard, Support for LIM & XMS Memory, Simultaneous Display & Editing MUltiple Files, Easy Component Creation & Modification, Ratsnesting, Variable Inch & Metric Grids. Display Adapters Supported Include CGA, EGA, VGA, Super-VGA, & Hercules. Output Drawings to Dot-Matrix printers, Pen-Plotters, HP & PostScript Laserprinters, & Photoplotters.
Wintek Corp.

HMSL. *Version:* 4.2. *Compatible Hardware:* Commodore Amiga; Macintosh. *Customer Support:* BBS, updates, etc..
Amiga version. 3.5" disk $95.00.
Macintosh version. 3.5" disk $95.00.
Hierarchical Music Specification Language.
Frog Peak Music.

Hobbes OS/2 Archived. *Customer Support:* All of our products are unconditionally guaranteed.
OS/2. CD-ROM disk $29.95 (Order no.: HOBBES). *Nonstandard peripherals required:* CD-ROM drive.
3000 OS/2 Programs Including Utilities, Service Packs & More.
Walnut Creek CDRom.

Hobbes Ready-to-Run. *Customer Support:* All of our products are unconditionally guaranteed.
OS/2. CD-ROM disk $39.95 (Order no.: R2RHOBBES). *Nonstandard peripherals required:* CD-ROM drive.
Thousands of OS/2 Programs All Ready to Run Right off the CD.
Walnut Creek CDRom.

Hockey Drome. *Items Included:* Installation Guide.
IBM PC. Contact publisher for price (ISBN 0-87321-024-7, Order no.: CDD-3111).
Activision, Inc.

Hodge Podge. 1992. *Items Included:* Detailed manuals are included with all DYNACOMP products. *Customer Support:* Free telephone support to original customer - no time limit; 30 day limited warranty.
MS-DOS 3.2 or higher. IBM PC & compatibles, Apple, C-64, Atari, TRS-80 (512k). $19.95 2 diskettes plus manual (Add $5.00 for 3 1/2" format; 5 1/4" format standard).
A Computer "Happening" for Children from Ages 18 Months to Seven Years & Older. Program Consists of Many Cartoons, Animations, & Songs Which Appear When Any Key on the Computer Is Pressed. Each Key Provides Something Different for the Child to Explore, from Apples to Zigzags. With an Adult Present the Child Can Be Told about Magnets, Numbers, Musical Notes, Animals, up & down, Color, & Much, Much More. When Alone the Child Will Be Kept Endlessly Amused by the Color, Sound, & Wonderful Pictures Displayed.
Dynacomp, Inc.

Hog Manager. *Compatible Hardware:* IBM PC & compatibles. *Operating System(s) Required:* MS-DOS 1.1 & higher. *Language(s):* Compiled BASIC. *Memory Required:* 256k. *General Requirements:* 132-column printer. *Items Included:* Program disk & manual. *Customer Support:* 30 minutes free; Pay-per-call at $1.95/minute.
disk $595.00, incl. manual.
manual $20.00.
demo $45.00.
Pork Production Record Keeping System. Special Feature Allows User to Define Management Options & Performance Observations to Record Whatever Information Is Most Relevant. Up to 12 Management Events Can Be Scheduled & Reported by Sow Group. Reports Can Be Sorted with Subtotals, Averages, & Ratios Printed at Each Level.
Harvest Computer Systems, Inc.

Hog Production Records. Merle W. Wagner. 1981. *Compatible Hardware:* Apple II Plus, IIe, IIc; IBM. *Operating System(s) Required:* Apple DOS 3.3, MS-DOS 2.0. *Language(s):* BASIC. *Memory Required:* 48k, 640k. *General Requirements:* Printer.
disk $49.95, incl. manual (ISBN 0-922900-04-3, Order no.: CFR-444).
Income/Expense Information for a Complete Hog Operation. 400 Sows per Data Disk. Breeding & History Available for Each Sow.
Cherrygarth, Inc.

Hole-in-One Miniature Golf. *Customer Support:* Back up disks available.
Amiga DOS (512k). Commodore Amiga. disk $39.95.
Atari ST (512k). disk $29.95.
MS-DOS (256k). Apple/MAC, IBM PC & compatibles. disk $34.95.
Commodore 64/128 (64k). disk $29.95.
Uses (Point & Click) Mouse Interface to Provide Game Levels for All Ages. Up to Four Players. 5 Courses, 90 Holes. Extra Courses Available for Amiga & IBM PC.
DigiTek Software.

Hole-In-One Miniature Golf, Extra Course Disk 3. *Customer Support:* Back up disks available.
Amiga (512k). $19.95.
MS-DOS (256k). IBM PC & compatibles. $19.95.
Includes Three Extra Courses With 54 More Exciting Holes. Fight Gravity, Magnetism, & Disappearances in This Extra Course for the Original Hole-in-One Miniature Golf.
DigiTek Software.

Hollywood Hijinx. Dave Anderson. Jan. 1987. *Compatible Hardware:* Apple II, II+, IIe, IIc, Macintosh; Atari XL/XE, ST; Commodore 64, 128, Amiga; DEC Rainbow; IBM PC & compatibles; TI Professional.
Apple II, Macintosh, Atari ST, Amiga, DEC, IBM. disk $39.95.
Atari XL/XE, Commodore 64/128. $34.95.
You Play the Starring Role in One of Hollywood's Zaniest "B" Movies. Comes with a Copy of "Tinselworld" Magazine, an Autographed Photo of Uncle Buddy (the Producer), a Letter from Aunt Hildegarde, & a Lucky Palm-Tree Swizzle Stick.
Activision, Inc.

Holman Bible Dictionary for Windows. Parsons Technology. Mar. 1994.
3.5" disk Contact publisher for price (ISBN 1-57264-005-7).
Parsons Technology.

HoloCAD: Holographic Computer Aided Design. Version: 1.3. Jan. 1995. *Items Included:* Manual. *Customer Support:* Applications, custom printer drivers.
Workbench 1.3 or higher. Any Amiga (1Mb). 3.5" 880k disk $100.00 (Order no.: AHC). *Nonstandard peripherals required:* 35mm camera, high-resolution film, RGB filters. *Optimal configuration:* Dot-addressable graphics printer (dye-sub 16M color best),1Gb hard disk drive, 1Mb Plus CHIP RAM, tungsten-halogen lamp recommended.
MS-DOS 5.0 or higher. PC-286 or higher (1Mb). 3.5" 720k or 5.25" 1.2M disk $125.00 (Order no.: PHC). *Nonstandard peripherals required:* 35mm camera, high-resolution film, RGB filters. *Optimal configuration:* Dot-addressable graphics printer (dye-sub 16M color best), 1GB hard disk drive, 512k or higher VGA, tungsten-halogen lamp recommended.
3D Vector, Scaler Drawing Gadgets: Scale, Rotate, Translate Objects, View. Wire-Frame, Solid Model; Hidden Line, Surface Removal; Transparency Levels. Add 2D Image to Background. Make Real 3D Color Holograms!
United ProCom Systems.

Home Appraiser. *Items Included:* Bound manual. *Customer Support:* Free hotline - no time limit; 30 day limited warranty; updates are $5/disk plus S&H.
MS-DOS. IBM & compatibles (256k). disk $59.95.
Designed to Estimate Potential Market Value of Real Property. It Is Intended Primarily for Individual Homeowners & Prospective Home Buyers. It Allows User to Approximate the Effects of Various Physical, Economic, & Territorial Factors Which Have Some Degree of Impact on the Overall Value of Property. Supply Selected Information about the House (or Condo) & the Computer Provides a Depreciated Value & a "Bottom Line" Estimate of Projected Market Value.
Dynacomp, Inc.

Home Budget Manager. *Compatible Hardware:* HP 86/87. *Memory Required:* 96k.
3-1/2" or 5-1/4" disk $69.00 ea. (Order no.: 92248EA).
Helps Users Monitor & Control Their Household Budget. Allows Users to: Record Income & Expenses in Their Own Format; Create a Budget Which Corresponds to Their Customized Expenses, Then Compare Their Outlays Against the Budget; Enter Checks into Multiple Expense Categories; Record Autoteller, Bank Charge, & Cash Expense Entries; Flag & Track Tax Exempt Income & Expenses; & Create Reports & Graphs.
Hewlett-Packard Co.

Home Budget-II. *Compatible Hardware:* TI 99/4A. *Operating System(s) Required:* DX-10. *Language(s):* Console BASIC. *Memory Required:* 16k.
disk or cassette $29.95.
Maintains a Monthly (Periodic) Record of Income & Expenditures. User Defines Own Categories. 3 Items Are Shown in the Budget Area: Category, Funds Allotted & Actual Expenses for Any Given Period. Data on Cash Flow Is an Optional Feature. All Data Can Be Routed to a Printer.
Eastbench Software Products.

Home Budget-III. *Compatible Hardware:* TI 99/4A with Extended BASIC. *Operating System(s) Required:* DX-10. *Language(s):* Extended BASIC. *Memory Required:* 48k.
cassette $29.95.
Maintains a Monthly (Periodic) Record of Income & Expenditures. User Defines the Categories. 3 Items Are Shown in the Budget Area: Category, Funds Allotted & Actual Expenses for Any Given Period. Data on Cash Flow Is an Optional Feature. All Data Can Be Routed to a Printer. Cassette-Based Extended BASIC Version of HOME BUDGET.
Eastbench Software Products.

Home Budget-IV. *Compatible Hardware:* TI 99/4A. *Operating System(s) Required:* DX-10. *Language(s):* Extended BASIC. *Memory Required:* 48k.
disk $29.95.
Disk-Based Version of HOME BUDGET Maintains a Monthly (Periodic) Record of Income & Expenditures. User Defines the Categories. 3 Items Are Shown in the Budget Area: Category, Funds Allotted & Actual Expenses for Any Given Period. Data on Cash Flow Is an Optional Feature. All Data Can Be Routed to a Printer.
Eastbench Software Products.

Home Budgetor. *Customer Support:* 800-929-8117 (customer service).
MS-DOS. Apple II. disk $59.99 (ISBN 0-87007-061-4).
Helps Plan User's Budget & Keep Personal Finances Accurate & up to Date, It Also Analyzes Budget -- Professionally. Streamlines the Drudgery of Account Updating & Balancing so User Can Spend More Time Where It Counts -- Analyzing & Pinpointing Cash Flows. The Basic Goal Is to Help the Individual or Small Businessperson Plan & Balance a Budget. This Includes Three Steps: First Users Enter the Projected Income & Expenses Over Monthly & Yearly Time Periods. Second, Enter the Actual Income & Expenses for Each Month. Third, the System Compares the Projected & Actual Figures.
SourceView Software International.

Home Doctor. *Items Included:* Bound manual. *Customer Support:* Free hotline - no time limit; 30 day limited warranty; updates are $5/disk plus S&H.
MS-DOS. IBM & compatibles (128k). disk $39.95. *Nonstandard peripherals required:* One disk drive.
Commodore 64 (64k). disk $39.95.
Works in Two Steps. First You Choose a General Category from a Scrolling Alphabetical List of Problems (e.g., Abdomen, Swollen). Then You Are Asked a Series of Yes/No Questions. If a Diagnosis Is Determined, You Are Then Given Advice As to a Course of Action.
Dynacomp, Inc.

Home Energy Conservation. J. Chandler. Nov. 1984. *Compatible Hardware:* Apple II, IBM-PC (640k). *Language(s):* BASIC. *Memory Required:* 128k.
Apple. disk $60.00, incl. tchr's. guide (ISBN 0-923820-15-9, Order no.: EC-A402).
IBM. disk $65.00, incl. tchr's. guide.
Finds & Tracks Household Energy Consumption, & Explores Conservation Methods. Uses Spreadsheet Techniques.
EME Corp.

The Home Filing Manager. *Compatible Hardware:* Atari XL/XE. *Operating System(s) Required:* AOS. *Language(s):* BASIC. *Memory Required:* 16k.
disk $24.95.
General Purpose Electronic Filing Card for Home Use. Sorts by Title or by Key Word or Phrase. Items May Also Be Flagged for Later Use. Permits Lines, Words, or Characters to Be Inserted into File Text.
Atari Corp.

Home Finance Management. Apr. 1982. *Compatible Hardware:* Apple II, II+, IIe; Atari 400, 800; Columbia; Commodore CBM 8096; Compaq; Franklin Ace; Fujitsu; HP 150 Touchscreen; IBM PC, PC XT; LNW 80; Sharp PC 5000; Sperry; Tandy 2000; TI Professional; TRS-80 Model I, Model II, Model III, Model 4, Model 12, Model 16; Wang. *Operating System(s) Required:* CP/M, CP/M-86, MS-DOS, PC-DOS. (source code included). *Memory Required:* 48k. *General Requirements:* 2 disk drives, printer; also requires VisiCalc, SuperCalc, MultiPlan, or Lotus 1-2-3.
disk $39.95.
Collection of Spreadsheet Templates Designed to Aid in the Managing of the Family Budget. Templates Help Create a Personal Budget for the Year & a Shopping List, & Determine What the Monthly Payments Will Be When Purchasing a Home. Also Helps Determine How Much a Family Can Save Using an IRA Savings Account, & Creates the Totals Needed on the IRS Schedule A Form.
Software Models.

Home Financial Decisions. *Compatible Hardware:* TI Home Computer. *Memory Required:* 32k.
contact publisher for price (Order no.: PHM 3006).
Step-by-Step Guide Answers Financial Questions.
Texas Instruments, Personal Productivit.

Home Health Agency Cost Report System. *Compatible Hardware:* Altos Series 5-15D, Series 5-5D, 580-XX, ACS8000-XX; IBM PC with 2 disk drives, PC XT, IBM compatibles; Xerox 820 with 2 disk drives; ZILOG MCZ-250. *Operating System(s) Required:* CP/M, MP/M, PC-DOS, MS-DOS.
contact publisher for price (Order no.: HCFA1728).
Prepares or Verifies Medicare Cost Reimbursement Reports for Home Health Agencies According to HCFA Requirements for Forms HCFA1728-81 for Periods Beginning on or After December 5, 1980. Determines Reimbursements & Evaluating Rate Structures for Medicare Audits. Reimbursements Are Computed under Title XVIII (Medicare).
Coopers & Lybrand.

Home Improvement 1-2-3. 1995. *Items Included:* Operating manual. *Customer Support:* Free telephone technical support 1-800-850-7272.
DOS 3.1, Windows 3.1. 33Mhz 80486DX, VGA video/display at 256 colors (4Mb). disk $59.95 (ISBN 1-884014-68-2). *Nonstandard peripherals required:* CD-ROM drive, Sound Blaster compatible audio board. *Addl. software required:* Microsoft CD-ROM extensions 2.2. *Optimal configuration:* 8Mb, Dual speed CD-ROM.
DOS 3.1, Windows 3.1. 33Mhz, 80486DX (4Mb). disk $49.95 (ISBN 1-884014-66-6).

TITLE INDEX

HOME

Nonstandard peripherals required: CD-ROM drive, Sound Blaster compatible audio board. *Optimal configuration:* 8Mb, Dual speed CD-ROM.
System 6.07. 68030 processor or higher Color Macintosh (256 plus colors, 13" monitor) (4Mb). 3.5" disk $49.95 (ISBN 1-884014-67-4). *Nonstandard peripherals required:* CD-ROM drive. *Optimal configuration:* 8Mb, dual speed CD-ROM.
Multimedia Home Improvement Guide.
Multicom Publishing, Inc.

Home Improvement 1-2-3: Hybrid Kit. Sep. 1995. *Items Included:* Operating manual, catalog, registration card. *Customer Support:* Free technical support 206-622-5530.
DOS 3.1, Windows 3.1, (8Mb RAM); Macintosh. 486SX 25MHz or higher (8Mb RAM); 68030 processor System 7.1 or higher (8Mb RAM). CD-ROM disk Contact publisher for price (ISBN 1-884014-75-5). *Addl. software required:* Double speed CD-ROM drive.
Covers All Aspects of Home Remodeling, Decorating & Repair. More Than 2000 Full Color Illustrations, 75 Full Color Photographs, Clear Step-by-Step Instructions for All Do It Yourself Projects. Time & Difficulty Estimates for All Projects & Straight Forward Safety Tips.
Multicom Publishing, Inc.

Home Improvement 1-2-3: Mac-MPC Kit. Oct. 1995. *Items Included:* Operating manual, catalog, registration card. *Customer Support:* Free technical support 206-622-5530.
DOS 3.1, Windows 3.1, Windows 95; Macintosh. 486SX 25MHz or higher (8Mb RAM); 68030 processor System 7.1 or higher (8Mb RAM). CD-ROM disk Contact publisher for price (ISBN 1-884014-75-5). *Addl. software required:* Double speed CD-ROM drive.
A Compilation of over 250 Do-It-Yourself Projects. Each Area in the Main Interface of the Program Corresponds to a Chapter in the Book. For Example, There Are Sections on Plumbing, Heating, Electrical, Floors, etc. Contains over 30 Minutes of Video & Advice from the Experts at the Home Depot.
Multicom Publishing, Inc.

The Home Inspection Business from A to Z On-Site Checklist: The Narrative Checklist the Other's Don't Have! *Version:* 3. Guy Cozzi. Jan. 1995. *Customer Support:* Fees have not yet been determined for customer support. This will be determined by the sales volume of the product.
All operating systems. All computers that use word processor programs. 3.5" disk Contact publisher for price (ISBN 1-887450-12-2). *Addl. software required:* Any word processor computer program that can read ASCII text.
All operating systems. All computers that use word processor programs. 5.25" disk Contact pubisher for price (ISBN 1-887450-13-0). *Addl. software required:* Any word processor computer program that can read ASCII text.
The Text on This Computer Disk Is an On-Site Checklist That Can Be Used to Evaluate Any House or Condo. The On-Site Checklist Is Filled Out by the Home Inspector at the Site to Note Any Repair Problems or Safety Hazards.
NeMMaR.

The Home Inspection Business from A to Z Report Writing Document. *Version:* 3. Guy Cozzi. Jan. 1995. *Customer Support:* Fees have not yet been determined for customer support. This will be determined by the sales volume of the product.
All operating systems. All computers that use word processor programs. 3.5" disk Contact publisher for price (ISBN 1-887450-10-6). *Addl. software required:* Any word processor computer program that can read ASCII text.
All operating systems. All computers that use word processor programs. 5.25" disk Contact pubisher for price (ISBN 1-887450-11-4). *Addl. software required:* Any word processor computer program that can read ASCII text.
The Text on This Computer Disk Is a Report Writing Document That Can Be Used to Send Narrative Home Inspection Reports to Clients. The Report Writing Document Is Filled Out by the Home Inspector Based upon the On-Site Evaluatoins Made of Any House or Condo.
NeMMaR.

The Home Insurance Inventory. *Compatible Hardware:* IBM. (source code included). *Memory Required:* 128k.
disk $29.95.
Inventory Program Especially Designed for Valuable Collections & Household Inventory Records.
Dynacomp, Inc.

Home Insurance Protector. *Compatible Hardware:* IBM. *Memory Required:* 128k.
disk $29.95.
Keeps an Inventory of Personal Possessions.
Dynacomp, Inc.

Home Inventory. Andrew Bear. 1985. *Compatible Hardware:* Apple II series; IBM PC & compatibles; TRS-80 Model III, Model 4. *Operating System(s) Required:* Apple DOS 3.3, MS-DOS, TRSDOS. *Memory Required:* Apple & TRS-80 48k, IBM 64k. *General Requirements:* Printer; 2 disk drives for TRS-80.
Apple. disk $37.00 (ISBN 1-55797-177-3, Order no.: AP2-AG509).
IBM. disk $43.50 (ISBN 1-55797-179-X, Order no.: IBM-AG509).
Designed to Help Keep Track of User's Personal Inventory. The Printouts Will Be Useful in Maintaining a Record of Inventory Items, Values & Descriptions. Will Allow User to Add, Subtract & Update Inventory Records.
Hobar Pubns.

Home Inventory Management. *Compatible Hardware:* Commodore 64. *General Requirements:* 1541 disk drive, printer.
disk $14.95.
Maintains Records of Location, Item, Date Purchased, Cost, Description & Optional Field for Each Item. Holds 1400 Records per Disk. Prints Reports by Record ID or Location. Will Give Total Value & Sub-Values of Inventory by Room.
Raymond L. Reynolds.

Home Inventory Manager. Jul. 1991. *Items Included:* direction manual. *Customer Support:* 30 minutes free; Pay-per-call at $1.95/minute.
MS-DOS. PC compatible (512k). disk $79.00.
This Program Keeps Track of What You Own, Where Its Kept, & How Much Its Worth. The Detail Inventory Report Lists All The Information on Each Item You Own. The Inventory Summary Report Includes Only the Major Information on Each Item. Use It with Insurance Agents & Police. The Report Can List Items Alphabetically or by Room with Sub-Totals for Cost & Value.
Harvest Computer Systems, Inc.

Home Library Catalog. 1996.
100% on-screen prompts; 100% menu driven. disk $99.00.
Home Library Catalog is the perfect program to catalog, maintain & manage a book collector's books, records, videos, magazines or other print or non-print media. Easy to install, learn & use, the efficient, affordable program is the perfect way to catalog, search, locate & organize books & other media.
RIGHT ON PROGRAMS.

Home Management Unit, 3 disks. 1986. *Compatible Hardware:* Apple II, IIc, IIe; TRS-80. *Operating System(s) Required:* Apple DOS, TRSDOS. *Memory Required:* 32k.
Apple. disk $115.00 (ISBN 0-87354-279-7, Order no.: HCA333).
TRS-80. disk $115.00 (Order no.: HCT333).
back-up set included.
Features Reading Product Labels, Reading Warnings & Monthly Bills.
Aquarius Instructional.

Home Management 2. *Items Included:* Bound manual. *Customer Support:* Free hotline - no time limit; 30 day limited warranty; updates are $5/disk plus S&H.
MS-DOS. IBM & compatibles (256k). disk $19.95. *Nonstandard peripherals required:* Graphics capability & printer supported, but not necessary.
Automate All Checking & Record-Keeping Chores, Plan a Budget, Keep Track of Your Stock Portfolio & Analyze Its Performance Against the Dow Jones Industrial Average, Amortize Loans, & Much More. The Checking Account & Budget Features Include: Multiple Accounts, 54 User Defined Expense Categories; 30 User Defined Deposit Categories; Completely Menu-Driven - No Special Commands to Learn. The Loan Function Prints Amortization Tables Including Payment Number, Year, Periodic Payment, Payment Interest, Total Interest, Payment Principle, Total Principle, & Balance Due.
Dynacomp, Inc.

Home Money Manager. Adrian Vance. Oct. 1985. *Compatible Hardware:* Apple II. *Operating System(s) Required:* Apple DOS. (source code included). *Memory Required:* 48k.
disk $9.95 (ISBN 0-918547-35-0).
illustration files on the disk avail.
Keyboard Operated Personal Budgeting System. Not Copy Protected.
AV Systems, Inc.

Home Planetarium. *Compatible Hardware:* Atari ST.
3.5" disk $29.95 (Order no.: DS5007).
Atari Corp.

Home Purchase. 1978. *Compatible Hardware:* Apple II; IBM PC & compatibles; TRS-80, Tandy. *Operating System(s) Required:* MS-DOS, Apple DOS. *Language(s):* BASIC. *Memory Required:* 48k.
disk $75.00.
Designed to Aid Home Buyers, Sellers, Investors, & Realtors in Making Decisions When Buying, Selling, & Comparing Properties.
Realty Software.

Home School CD-ROM: Two Hundred Ninety-Nine of the Best Educational Shareware Computer Programs. Jan. 1996. *Items Included:* Instruction booklet.
DOS & Windows 3.1. PC (2k). CD-ROM disk $29.90 (ISBN 1-56087-112-1). *Optimal configuration:* 386, Windows 3.1 2k.
Over 300 Educational Programs to Instruct Children in an "Entertaining" Manner. Covers: Geography, History, Science, Math, Reading & Spelling Tutors. Teach Your Young Children at Home! Also Great for Adults to Help Pass the G.E.D. Test.
Top of the Mountain Publishing.

Home, Sweet Home. Jan. 1994. *Items Included:* Program on CD-ROM, CD Booklet, & Registration Card. *Customer Support:* Free unlimited customer support via telephone.
Macintosh System 7.0 or higher. Macintosh LC or higher (4Mb). CD-ROM disk $39.00 (ISBN 1-57268-088-1, Order no.: 20881). *Nonstandard*

HOME

peripherals required: 12 inch monitor or larger; CD-ROM drive. *Optimal configuration:* 5Mb RAM.
Windows 3.1 or higher running under DOS 5.0 or higher. 386 SX (6Mb RAM; 500k low Dos Mem; 6Mb free disk space). CD-ROM disk $39.00 (Order no.: 20881). *Nonstandard peripherals required:* Sound card (either: Sound Blaster - 8, 16, PRO; Media Vision ProAudio Spectrum; or Microsoft Sound System; MPC compatible CD-ROM drive; VGA monitor; & microphone. *Optimal configuration:* 25 MHz 386 SX.
This Program Is an Engaging, Interactive Learning Experience. Students Meet a New Friend Named Dominique, Whose Family Is Moving to a New House. With the Help of Sound, Graphics, & Animation, Young Readers Learn Many New Things along the Way. Students Explore & Learn New Vocabulary at Their Own Pace.
Conter Software.

Home, Sweet Home. Jan. 1994. *Items Included:* Program on CD-ROM, CD Booklet, & Registration Card. *Customer Support:* Free unlimited customer support via telephone.
Windows 3.1 or higher running under DOS 5.0 or higher. 386 SX (4Mb RAM; 500k low Dos Mem; 6Mb free disk space). CD-ROM disk $39.00 (ISBN 1-57268-089-X, Order no.: 21881). *Nonstandard peripherals required:* Sound card (either: Sound Blaster - 8, 16, PRO; Media Vision ProAudio Spectrum; or Microsoft Sound System; MPC compatible CD-ROM drive; VGA monitor; & microphone. *Optimal configuration:* 25 MHz 386 SX.
This Program Is an Engaging, Interactive Learning Experience. Students Meet a New Friend Named Dominique, Whose Family Is Moving to a New House. With the Help of Sound, Graphics, & Animation, Young Readers Learn Many New Things along the Way. Students Explore & Learn New Vocabulary at Their Own Pace.
Conter Software.

Home, Sweet Home. Jan. 1994. *Items Included:* Program on CD-ROM, CD Booklet, & Registration Card. *Customer Support:* Free unlimited customer support via telephone.
Macintosh System 7.0 or higher. Macintosh LC or higher (4Mb). CD-ROM disk $39.00 (ISBN 1-57268-090-3, Order no.: 22881). *Nonstandard peripherals required:* 12 inch monitor or larger; CD-ROM drive. *Optimal configuration:* 5Mb RAM.
This Program Is an Engaging, Interactive Learning Experience. Students Meet a New Friend Named Dominique, Whose Family Is Moving to a New House. With the Help of Sound, Graphics, & Animation, Young Readers Learn Many New Things along the Way. Students Explore & Learn New Vocabulary at Their Own Pace.
Conter Software.

HomeFiler.
Apple II. $39.95, Lab pack/5 $99.00. *Optimal configuration:* Apple II, 2 drives.
Simplified Data Base for the First-Time Users and/or Students. Streamlined Menus & Help Screens to Manage Information Quickly & Easily. Easy-to-Follow Instructions & Numerous Screen Prompts Help User to Store & Sort Data & to Print Reports. Good Student Introduction to Data-Base Concepts & to Organize & Manipulate Information. On-Screen Tutorial.
Word Assocs., Inc.

The Homeowner. *Items Included:* Bound manual. *Customer Support:* Free hotline - no time limit; 30 day limited warranty; updates are $5/disk plus S&H.
MS-DOS. IBM & compatibles (256k). disk $39.95.

Can Help Owners of Single Homes (Who Do Repairs & Renovations Themselves) & Owners of Rental Property (Who Do Repairs & Maintenance on a Regular Basis to Several Properties) Save Money & Be Better Organized.
Dynacomp, Inc.

Homeowners. *Compatible Hardware:* IBM PC. *Operating System(s) Required:* CP/M, MP/M, MS-DOS, PC-DOS. *Language(s):* Machine. *Memory Required:* 56k.
disk $750.00.
File System for the Insurance Agent Who Markets Casualty Insurance. Policy Information for the Home Insured Can Be Stored, & Other Types of Insurance That the Client Might Have with the Agency Can Be Flagged. Features Include Template Searches, Combines an Agent's Active, Hold & Cancelled File into One File, & Interfaces with Word Processing.
Lansing Computer Assocs., Inc.

HomeStyles' HomeDesigns Multimedia Encyclopedia: 1,001 Best-Selling Home Plans on CD-ROM. *Version:* 1.1. 1995.
IBM. CD-ROM disk $19.95 (ISBN 1-56547-054-0).
Contains 1,001 Top Selling Home Plans from 50 of North America's Best Designers & Architects. Includes an Easy-to-Use Interface Which Lets You Select Homes That Fit Your Lifestyle & Budget. Hot Buttons Allow You to View Front Elevations of Homes, Floor Plans & Spec Information for All 1,001 Plans. Also Included Are State-of-the-Art Interactive Floor Plans Which Let You Explore Interior & Exterior Views of the Home in 3D Plus over 200 Color Images of Top Home Designs.
HomeStyles Publishing & Marketing, Inc.

HomeStyles' HomeDesigns Multimedia Encyclopedia: 3,003 Best-Selling Home Plans on CD-ROM. *Version:* 2.0. Jan. 1996. *Items Included:* 2 CD-ROMs.
IBM. CD-ROM disk $34.95 (ISBN 1-56547-055-9).
Contains 3,003 of the Country's Hottest Selling Home Plans in a Variety of Styles & Sizes, All Drawn by Top-Rated Architects & Designers. Also Includes the Latest in Special Multi-Media Functions Like a Virtual Reality Tour of the Consumer Home of the Year, Clips from Videographic Home Tour Videos, Interactive Floor Plans & Color Images of Homes.
HomeStyles Publishing & Marketing, Inc.

Hometime Weekend Home Projects: Your Interactive Guide to Home Improvement. Hometrends Inc. Staff & Hometime Video Publishing Staff. Sep. 1994. *Customer Support:* Free 800 Number Technical Support.
Windows. PC with 486SX 25MHz or higher (8Mb). disk $39.95 (ISBN 1-884899-15-3). *Optimal configuration:* 486SX 25MHz or higher PC, 8MB RAM, double-speed CD-ROM drive, VGA Plus 640x480 monitor displaying 256 colors, MS-DOS 5.0 or higher, Windows 3.1 MS-DOS CD-ROM Extensions (MSCDEX 2.2 or higher), stereo headphones or speakers, 1MB free hard disk space for installation, mouse or compatible positioning device, 16-bit sound card (100% Sound Blaster compatible), Accelerated 8-bit video card.
Macintosh. Color capable Macintosh (8Mb). disk $39.95 (ISBN 1-884899-29-3). *Optimal configuration:* Color capable Macintosh (LCIII, CI, VX, FX, Quadra, Performa 400/600 Powerbook with color video out), 8Mb RAM, System 7.1 or higher, 13" color monitor, hard disk, double-speed CD-ROM drive, stereo headphones or speakers, mouse.
Do-It-Yourselfer's & Fans of the Public Television Show Hometime Will Want to Own This Helpful Home Improvement Program. Twelve Topic Areas

SOFTWARE ENCYCLOPEDIA 1996

Are Featured, Including Building a Deck, Wallpapering, Painting & Much More. Dean Johnson, the Host of Hometime, Provides Expert Advice & Clear Instructions. Includes over 60 Minutes of Video & Unique Calculator Feature.
IVI Publishing, Inc.

Hometown Demographics. 1992. *Items Included:* Detailed manuals are included with all DYNACOMP products. *Customer Support:* Free telephone support to original customer - no time limit; 30 day limited warranty.
MS-DOS 3.2 or higher. IBM PC & compatibles, Apple, Commodore 64 (512k). $148.00 2 diskettes plus manual (Add $5.00 for 3 1/2" format); 5 1/4" format standard). *Optimal configuration:* Apple IIc or IIe, IBM PC or PCjr, or a Commodore 64 (or C-128 in the C-64 mode). A printer is supported but optional.
Demographic Surveys of One's Home Town, a Common Part of Local History Projects, Can Be Completed Quickly & Easily. The Computer Is Used to Store 12 Categories of Data, Including Age, Gender, Marital Status, Ethnic Origin, Employment, & Residence. Nine Blank Categories Are Available to Save Data for Additional Items Designed by the Students. Comes with a Thorough Step-by-Step Guide, Teachers' Notes, & Learning Objectives.
Dynacomp, Inc.

Hometown U. S. A. *Version:* Macintosh 1, MS-DOS 2.0. 1988-1992. *Items Included:* Manual for particular machine; Ideas book - full of ways to use the program. *Customer Support:* Phone support.
MS-DOS. IBM compatible (256k). disk $39.95. *Nonstandard peripherals required:* Graphics card.
Apple Macintosh. Macintosh (512k). 3.5" disk $39.95. *Addl. software required:* A point program that reads "MacPaint" file.
Allows the User to Design & Build 3-D Model Buildings, the Size of HO Railroad. The Templates Can Be Edited by Adding Windows & Doors As Well As Fill Patterns for Siding.
Publishing International.

HomeVentory. Jul. 1988. *Compatible Hardware:* IBM PC & compatibles. *Memory Required:* 256k.
disk $24.95.
Creates an Inventory of Household Items. The User Enters Descriptions, Prices, Purchase Date, Serial Numbers or Other Identification for Items in Each Room.
Zephyr Services.

Honey Bunch. *Version:* 6.2. *Compatible Hardware:* IBM PC & true compatibles, PC XT, PC AT, Portable PC. *Memory Required:* 128k. *General Requirements:* TDT multiprotocol adapter or UDS Syncup modem. *Items Included:* User manual. *Customer Support:* 1 year free, except for long distance return call charges & Fax info. $499.00 - $4995.00.
Allows the IBM PC to Emulate VIP 78xx/77xx Sync/Async Terminals for All HONEYWELL Bull Mainframes. Operates at up to 9600 Baud Speed Providing Full Emulation & File Transfer. Features: Hot Key, RTS/CTS Parametrable, Installable on the Hard Disk, Transparent Printing, CALL USING for Local Program Interface, Status Line. Can Gateway Either Sync or X.25. CGI Pac Base Interface. Windows 3 & DOS Compatible.
TDT Group, Inc.

Honey Hunt: Bright Beginning Series. *Compatible Hardware:* TI 99/4A with Milton Bradley MBX Expansion System.
contact publisher for price (Order no.: PHM3156).
Help Our Little Bee Find Flowers, but Beware of Spiders & Dragon-Flies. Includes Music, Graphics & Speech Synthesis.
Texas Instruments, Personal Productivit.

TITLE INDEX

The Honeymooners. Michael Breggar & MicroMosaics. Feb. 15/1989. *Compatible Hardware:* IBM PC; Commodore 64/128, Amiga.
IBM PC. disk $39.95 (Order no.: 01008).
Amiga. 3.5" disk $39.95 (Order no.: 06008).
Commodore 64/128. disk $29.95 (Order no.: 05008).
Mutilateral Role-Playing Comedy.
First Row Software Publishing.

Hoops. *Compatible Hardware:* IBM PC & compatibles. *Operating System(s) Required:* PC-DOS/MS-DOS 2.0 or higher. *Memory Required:* 256k. *General Requirements:* CGA, EGA, or VGA card.
disk College or Pro version $60.00.
both versions $100.00.
annual update $30.00.
Basketball Simulation Game That Allows Users to Match Over 600 College Teams Selected From the Last 49 Years. The Game's Focus is on the Strategy. As the Game is Played, the Computer Displays the Text of the Game's Play-by-Play Action, the Game Scoreboard, Function Key Options, Player Box Scores, Which Are Updated Instantly During the Game. Users Can Have the Computer Coach Both Teams, or Play Against the Computer or Another Player. Eight Speed Selections are Available. When Coaching a Team, Users Choose the Starting Lineup, the Offensive & Defensive Sets, When to Stall, When to Intentionally Foul, & When to Yank a Player When He's Fatigued or in Foul Trouble. Users Can Also Change Strategy Over the Course of the Game & Toggle Between Screens for an In-Depth Look at the Other Team's Current Stats. Other Options Include a Pro & College Shot Clock, the Three-Point Shot, Home or Neutral Court Setting, & Color.
Hoops.

HOOPS. *Items Included:* Documentation & first year's technical support. *Customer Support:* Available.
X-DOS, Windows, Macintosh. $2100.00.
3-D Graphics Interactive Development System.
Ithaca Software.

Hopper. *Compatible Hardware:* Atari 400, 800. *Language(s):* Atari BASIC. *Memory Required:* 48k. *General Requirements:* Joystick.
disk $17.95.
Action Arcade Game.
Dynacomp, Inc.

Horary Astro Clock: M-65H. 1984. *Compatible Hardware:* IBM PC. *Memory Required:* 128k.
disk $50.00 (ISBN 0-925182-38-9).
Maintains an Updated Chart on the Screen.
Matrix Software.

HORIZON - TWO SERIES: General Ledger, Accounts Payable, Property Management. Version: 3C. 1993. *Items Included:* Documentation on each module is included in the price. *Customer Support:* Annual Support Agreements are available & include product enhancements & telephone support. 90 days unlimited telephone support to start. Price varies depending on modules. On-site training is available at $600.00 per day plus expenses.
PC-DOS/MS-DOS 5.0 or higher; Novell Netware 3.11 or higher. 386/486 (4Mb). Single User $3000.00-$18,000.00. *Optimal configuration:* 386/486, 4Mb, 110Mb or higher, VGA Monitor, wide carriage printer, HP Laser Jet II, IID, IIP, III, IIID, IIIP, IIISI, IV for MICR Check Writing. *Networks supported:* Novell Netware/Windows for Workgroups.
Menu-Driven, Full-Screen Edit with Pop-Up Windows, Point & Shoot Accounting Package for Professional Property Management Firms. First Property Management System to Be Lease Driven. Accounts Receivable Meets the Needs of Residential (Apartments or Condos), Retail, Commercial or Industrial Tenants. Modules Include Lock Box, On-Site Marketing Tracking, Remote & Local Property Management, Tenant Improvement Tracking, Operating Expense Escalations, CAM, Percentage Rent Reconciliation. General Ledger System Provides Cash & Accrual in the Same Set of Books, 12-Month Trend Ledgers, Cash Flow & Budget Forecast, Remote-Site Accounts Payable.
Execudata, Inc.

HORIZON - TWO SERIES: Job Cost, General Ledger, Accounts Payable. Version: 3C. 1993. *Items Included:* Documentation on each module is included in the price. *Customer Support:* Annual Support Agreements are available & include product enhancements & telephone support. 90 days unlimited telephone support to start. Price varies depending on modules. On-site training is available at $600.00 per day plus expenses.
PC-DOS/MS-DOS 5.0 or higher; Novell Netware 3.11 or higher. 386/486 (4Mb). Single User $3000.00-$18,000.00. *Optimal configuration:* 386/486, 4Mb, 110Mb or higher, VGA Monitor, wide carriage printer, HP Laser Jet II, IID, IIP, III, IIID, IIIP, IIISI, IV for MICR Check Writing. *Networks supported:* Novell Netware/Windows for Workgroups.
Menu-Driven, Full-Screen Edit with Pop-Up Windows, Point & Shoot Accounting System for Builder/Developers Developing Any Type of Project. In Addition to the Standard General Ledger & Accounts Payable Applications, Development/Construction Costs Are Tracked & Analyzed Through a Variety of Reports Including: Construction Budget, Job Cost Analysis (Cost per Square Foot), Budget Variance (Original Compared to Revised Budget), Change Order Log (History of All Charges), Loan Draw Request by Lender Category. The Commitment Control System Tracks Payments Against Contracts & Payments Against Change Orders Separately. Allows User to Distinguish Between Various Types of Commitments (Contracts, Work Orders & Purchase Orders).
Execudata, Inc.

Horizon Accounting. Version: 6.0. FMS, Harvest Computer. *Items Included:* Notebook, manual. *Customer Support:* Available.
MS-DOS 3.1 or higher & Windows. IBM PC, XT, AT or compatible (640k). contact publisher for price. *Optimal configuration:* 1 floppy, hard drive, 80 column printer.
An Accounting Program That Allows User to Track Cost of Production by Enterprise, Monitor Expenses Compared to Budgets, Track Inventory, Payables & Receivables As Well As Compiling Financial Trends. Single Entries That Are Automatically Debited & Credited to the Correct Accounts. Books Are Always in Balance.
Farmer's Software Assn.

Horizon Accounting. Version: 6. *Compatible Hardware:* IBM or compatible. *Operating System(s) Required:* MS-DOS 3.1 or higher. *Language(s):* Compiled BASIC. *Memory Required:* 640k. *General Requirements:* Printer. *Items Included:* Program disk & manual. *Customer Support:* 30 minutes free; Pay-per-call at $1.95/minute.
disk $625.00.
demo disk $45.00.
Double-Entry Farm Accounting System. Figures All Debits & Credits & Automatically Posts to the Appropriate Accounts. Up to 350 Accounts Can Be Included, Identified with Names or Number Codes. Handles Multiple Checking Accounts, As Well As Open Accounts, Notes, & Savings Accounts. Program Is Not Copy Protected.
Harvest Computer Systems, Inc.

Horizon Accounting. Version: 6. *Compatible Hardware:* IBM or Compatible. *Operating System(s) Required:* MS-DOS 3.1 or higher. *Memory Required:* 640k. *General Requirements:* Hard disk, printer. *Items Included:* Program disk & manual. *Customer Support:* 30 minutes free; Pay-per-call at $1.95/minute.
disk $625.00.
demo disk $45.00.
Updated from Version 3 for MS-DOS Hard Disk. Special Features Include 46 Macros That Can Be Invoked from a Menu or with a Mouse, Can Add Vendors During Entries, Income Statement Showing 12 Months Side-by-Side, & More to Enhance the Program & Its Capabilities.
Harvest Computer Systems, Inc.

Horizon Inventory. *Compatible Hardware:* IBM PC & compatibles. *Operating System(s) Required:* MS-DOS 3.1 & higher. *Language(s):* Compiled BASIC. *Memory Required:* 640k. *Items Included:* Program disk & manual. *Customer Support:* Pay-per-Call at $1.95/minute.
disk $195.00, incl. manual.
manual $20.00.
demo disk $45.00.
Calculates Grain & Livestock Inventory, Figures Resale Deductions, & Prints Detailed Management Reports.
Harvest Computer Systems, Inc.

Horizon Invoicing. Version: 2. Aug. 1991. *Items Included:* Manual in 3 ring binder. *Customer Support:* 30 minutes free; Pay-per-call at $1.95/minute.
MS-DOS 3.1 or higher. IBM AT, 386, or 486 compatible (640k). disk $325.00. *Addl. software required:* Horizon Accounting Small Business Version.
For Businesses with Accounts Receivables. Sales Invoices Are Entered Quickly & Easily. Customer Addresses, etc. Automatically Looked Up. Shipping Charges & Sales Taxes Calculated Automatically. Back-Ordered Items Monitored. Reports- Daily Sales, Sales Reports Sub-Totaled in Different Ways, Item Reports, Customer Credit History. Prints Invoices, Labels, Customer Lists, etc.
Harvest Computer Systems, Inc.

Horizon Nine Keys Personality Profile. John H. Richards. Aug. 1994.
MS-DOS. IBM & compatibles (1Mb). Single Profile $5.95 (ISBN 1-885802-65-X).
MS-DOS. IBM & compatibles (1Mb). Five Profiles $24.45 (ISBN 1-885802-66-8).
MS-DOS. IBM & compatibles (1Mb). Ten Profiles $39.45 (ISBN 1-885802-67-6).
MS-DOS. IBM & compatibles (1Mb). 25 Profiles $74.45 (ISBN 1-885802-68-4).
Horizon Nine Keys Publishing.

Horizon Order/Inventory. Version: 4. *Items Included:* Program disk & manual. *Customer Support:* 30 minutes free; Pay-per-call at $1.95/minute.
MS-DOS 3.1 & higher. IBM PC & compatibles (640k). disk $650.00. *Nonstandard peripherals required:* Hard disk. *Optimal configuration:* 80386 or higher computer, MS-DOS 3.1 or higher (640k).
Looks up Prices, Addresses, Terms & Discounts for Invoices. The System Can Print Invoices, Packing Slips, & Shipping Labels Individually or in a Batch. Invoiced Items Are Automatically Subtracted from Inventory & Back-Ordered Items Are Tracked. User Can Monitor the Number Ordered, Sold, & on Hand of Each Item. Reports Include: Daily Sales Report, Counter Payments for Customers Who Pay Their Bills in Person, Item History Report, Customer Credit History Reports.
Harvest Computer Systems, Inc.

Horizon Payroll: For IBM. Version: 5. Items Included: Program disk & manual. Customer Support: 30 minutes free; Pay-per-call at $1.95/minute.
 MS-DOS 3.1 & higher. IBM PC & compatibles (448k). disk $350.00. Nonstandard peripherals required: Hard drive. Optimal configuration: 80286 computer 3.1 or higher 640k.
 demo disk $45.00.
 Complete Payroll System. Keeps Details & Prints Reports at Any Time, Tracks Vacation & Sick Days, Uses Any Number of In & Out Times; Can Use Even 10 Different Commissions, Prints Out W-2 Forms, Different Labor Accounts, a Mouse or Color Monitor.
 Harvest Computer Systems, Inc.

Horizon Preceptions: Crop, Inventory, Orders, Modules. Jan. 1996. Items Included: Notebook, manual, disks. Customer Support: Available.
 MS Windows. 386-486 preferred (4Mb). Contact publisher for price. Nonstandard peripherals required: Mouse, VGA.
 An Accounting Program That Allows User to Track Cost of Predictions by Enterprises, Monitor Expenses Compared to Budgets, Track Inventory, Payable & Receivables As Well As Compiling Financial Trends. Single Entries That Are Automatically Debited & Credited to the Correct Accounts. Books Are Always in Balance.
 Farmer's Software Associaton.

Horizon Two Series: General Ledger, Accounts Payable, Job Cost. Version: 2A. 1979. Items Included: Documentation & education for three (3) people included in price. Additional training is available at $560.00 per day plus expenses. Customer Support: Annual support agreements are available & include product enhancements & telephone support. Price varies depending on modules.
 DOS 3.x or higher or Novell Netware 2.1 or higher. IBM & compatibles (640k). Single User $3000.00-$14,000.00; Multi-User $4000.00-$18,000.00. Optimal configuration: IBM or 100% compatible; 640k; 30Mb; color monitor; wide carriage printer/parallel port. Networks supported: Novell Netware.
 Menu-Driven, Full Screen Edit Accounting System for Builder/Developers Developing Any Type of Project. In Addition to the Standard General Ledger & Accounts Payable Applications, Development/Construction Costs Are Tracked & Analyzed Through a Variety of Reports Including: (1) Construction Budget; (2) Job Cost Analysis (Cost Per Square Foot); (3) Budget Variance (Original Compared to Revised Budget); (4) Change Order Log (History of All Changers); & (5) Loan Draw Requests by Lendor Category.
 Execudata.

Horizon Two Series: General Ledger, Accounts Payable, Property Management. Version: 2A. 1979. Items Included: Documentation & education for three (3) people included in price. Additional training is available at $560.00 per day plus expenses. Customer Support: Annual support agreements are available & include product enhancements & telephone support. Price varies depending on modules.
 DOS 3.x or higher or Novell Netware 2.1 or higher. IBM & compatibles (640k). Single User $3000.00-$14,000.00; Multi-User $4000.00-$18,000.00. Optimal configuration: IBM or 100% compatible; 640k; 30Mb; color monitor; wide carriage printer/parallel port. Networks supported: Novell Netware.
 Complete Menu-Driven Accounting Package for Professional Property Management Firms. The General Ledger System Provides a Departmentalized Chart of Accounts (Including Balance Sheet Items) Plus Monthly & Year-to-Date General Ledgers. Accounts Receivable Meets the Needs of Residential (Apartments or Condos), Commercial or Industrial Rentals. Reports Include: (1) Tenant Status (Rent Roll Including Future Tenants); (2) Vacancy Analysis; (3) Tenant Receipts Balance Due; (4) Tenants Eligible for Rent Increases; (5) Tenant Invoicing; (6) Tenant Payment History; (7) Cash Receipts Worksheet; (8) Automatic Three-Day Notice Generation & Common Area Maintenance Percentage Calculations; (9) Lease Abstract; & (10) Tenant Profile Information.
 Execudata.

Horizon-2 Series: Job Cost General Ledger, Accounts Payable. Version: 2C. 1986. Items Included: Documentation & Education for two people included in price. On-site training is available at $600.00 per day plus expenses. Customer Support: Annual support agreements are available & include product enhancements & telephone support. Price varies depending on modules.
 DOS 3.x or higher or Novell Netware 2.1 or higher. IBM & compatibles (640k). Single user $3000.00-$14,000.00; Multi-user $4000.00-$18,000.00. Optimal configuration: IBM or compatible 640k; 40Mb or higher; color monitor; wide carriage printer/parallel port. Networks supported: Novell Netware.
 Menu-Driven, Full Screen Edit Accounting System for Builder/Developers Developing Any Type of Project. In Addition to the Standard General Ledger & Accounts Payable Applications, Development/Construction Costs Are Tracked & Analyzed Through a Variety of Reports Including: Construction Budget; Job Cost Analysis (Cost Per Square Foot); Budget Variance (Original Compared to Revised Budget); Change Order Log (History of All Charges); Loan Draw Request by Lender Category. The Commitment Control System Tracks Payments Against Contracts & Payments Against Change Orders Separately. Allows You to Distinguish Between Various Types of Commitments (Contracts, Work Orders & Purchase Orders).
 Execudata.

Horizon-2 Series: Property Management, General Ledger, Accounts Payable. Version: 2C. 1986. Items Included: Documentation & education for two people included in price. On-site training is available at $600.00 per day plus expenses. Customer Support: Annual support agreements are available & include product enhancements & telephone support. Price varies depending on modules.
 DOS 3.x or higher or Novell Netware 2.1 or higher. IBM or compatibles (640k). Single user $3000.00-$14,000.00; Multi-user $4000.00-$18,000.00. Optimal configuration: IBM or compatible 640k; 40Mb or higher; Color monitor; wide carriage printer/parallel port. Networks supported: Novell Netware.
 Complete Menu-Driven Accounting Package for Professional Property Management Firms. The General Ledger System Provides a Departmentalized Chart of Accounts (Including Balance Sheet Items) Plus Monthly & Year-to-Date General Ledgers. Accounts Receivable Meets the Needs of Residential (Apartments or Condos), Commercial or Industrial Rentals. Reports Include: Tenant Status (Rent Roll Including Future Tenants); Vacancy Analysis; Tenant Receipts Balance Due; Tenants Eligible for Rent Increases; Tenant Invoicing; Tenant Payment History; Cash Receipts Worksheet; Automatic 3-Day Notice Generation & Common Area Maintenance Percentage Calculations; Lease Abstract; & Tenant Profile Information.
 Execudata.

Horoscope Program: M-1. Compatible Hardware: Commodore 64, PET, VIC-20.
 disk or cassette $30.00.
 Calculates a Complete Natal Chart with House System of User's Choice.
 Matrix Software.

Horoscopics Plus. Jun. 1983. Compatible Hardware: IBM PC, PC XT. Operating System(s) Required: PC-DOS, MS-DOS. Memory Required: 256k. General Requirements: Printer.
 disk $59.95.
 Performs Astronomical Calculations to Determine Exact Sky Conditions for Date of Birth. Using These Results, a Horoscope Chart Is Printed Which Shows the Zodiac Constellations Relative to the Earth, & Plots the Positions in the Sky of the Sun, Moon & All 8 Other Planets. The Program Then Prints a Table of 8 Astronomical Parameters (i.e. Geocentric Longitude, Distance from Earth, etc.) for the Sun, Moon & Planets. An Astrological Reading Is Printed Based on the Positions of the Sun (Sun Sign), Moon (Moon Sign) & Each Planet. The Readings Is Done According to Traditional Astrological Interpretations. Also Provides a Table for Determining the Ascendant Sign, Depending on Time of Birth & Associated Astrological Interpretation. Includes an Analysis of the Conjunctions & Oppositions for the Date of Birth.
 Zephyr Services.

Horror in Hocking County. Don Canaan. 1989. IBM PC. 5.25" or 3.5" disk $7.95 (ISBN 0-9622875-0-4).
 True Crime Dale Johnston "Satanic" Murders in Logan, OH. This Edition Is "Republished" & contains All Original Illustrations & Photographs. Contains a Proprietary Reading Program for Text & Illustrations.

Horse Farm Management. Agri-Management Services, Inc. Compatible Hardware: TI Professional. Operating System(s) Required: MS-DOS. Memory Required: 64k. General Requirements: Printer.
 $995.00.
 Provides Management & Financial Information on an Individual Basis.
 Texas Instruments, Personal Productivit.

Horse Show Management. Agri-Management Services, Inc. Compatible Hardware: TI Professional. Operating System(s) Required: MS-DOS. Memory Required: 64k. General Requirements: 2 disk drives, printer.
 $495.00.
 Does Entire Secretarial Work for the Horse Show Down to Final Report for the Association.
 Texas Instruments, Personal Productivit.

Horticopia: Perennials & Annuals. Jun. 1995. Items Included: CD-ROM, users guide. Customer Support: 30 day warranty, free technical support by telephone or E-Mail.
 Windows 3.0. 386 or higher (4Mb). disk $89.00 (ISBN 1-887215-01-8). Nonstandard peripherals required: MPC2 compliant. Optimal configuration: Dual speed CD-ROM, 8Mb RAM, Windows 3.1, color printer.
 Features More Than 1500 Full Color High Quality Photographs of 650 Different Perennials & Annuals with Cultural Information on Many of the Plants. A Click & Point Graphical Interface Provides Plant Information by Name or Attribute with Dynamic Selection Feedback; Slide Show Capabilities; & Audio for Scientific Pronunciation.
 Desops, Ltd.

Horticopia Trees, Shrubs & Groundcovers. Jan. 1996. Items Included: CD-ROM, users guide. Customer Support: 30 day warranty, free technical support by telephone, fax, e-mail.

TITLE INDEX

Windows 3.1 & Windows 95. 486 or higher (8Mb). CD-ROM disk $90.00 (ISBN 1-887215-02-6). *Nonstandard peripherals required:* MCCII compliant. *Optimal configuration:* Dual speed CD-ROM, 8Mb RAM, Windows 3.1, 24 bit color, sound card.
Features More Than 3000 Full Color High Quality Photographs of 1000 Different Trees, Shrubs & Groundcovers with Cultural Information on Many of the Plants. A Click & Point Graphical Interface Provides You Plant Information by Name or Attribute with Dynamic Selection Feedback; Slide Show Capabilities; & Audio for Scientific Pronunciation.
Desops, Ltd.

The Hospital Financial Workplate. (The Hospital Workplate Ser.). Jul. 1985. *Compatible Hardware:* IBM PC XT & compatibles. *Operating System(s) Required:* MS-DOS. *Language(s):* 1-2-3 (source code included). *Memory Required:* 320k. *General Requirements:* Lotus 1-2-3 Release 2.0 or higher, 5Mb free on hard drive.
disk $395.00, incl. manual (Order no.: HCA-85050).
Provides the Templates & Formulas Necessary for the Analysis of the Financial Positions of the Hospital. Performs Profit & Loss, Income Statement, Cash Flow, & Balance Sheet Analyses. Enables User to Project Departmental & Operating Budgets, Conduct Variance Analysis, Study Salary & Labor Hours, Analyze Budgeted & Actual DEG Performance, or Evaluate the Feasability of Establishing a Preferred Provider Organization.
Riverdale Systems Design, Inc.

Hospital Management System. Version: 4.0. *Compatible Hardware:* IBM PC or compatibles, Novell Network, RS/6000. *Language(s):* Dataplex. *Memory Required:* 640k. *Items Included:* ADT, Billing, A/R, Medical Records, Inventory, Order Entry, Insurance Processing, General Ledger, Accounts Payable, Payroll. *Customer Support:* 8 - 5, M - F.
$14,800.00.
Computerized Bookkeeping System Specifically Designed for Small Hospitals. Programs Form a Comprehensive Patient Billing & Financial Management System. Applications Include: Patient Admission & Inquiry; Patient Billing; Accounts Receivable; General Ledger; Master Menu; Accounts Payable; Payroll; & General Ledger Link to Lotus 1-2-3. Medical Records, Third Party Logs, DRG Grouper & Encoder Also Available.
Nelson Data Resources, Inc.

The Hospital Market Workplate. (The Hospital Workplate Ser.). Jul. 1985. *Compatible Hardware:* IBM PC XT & compatibles. *Operating System(s) Required:* MS-DOS. *Language(s):* 1-2-3 (source code included). *Memory Required:* 320k. *General Requirements:* Lotus 1-2-3 Release 2.0 or higher, 5Mb free on hard drive.
disk $395.00, incl. manual (Order no.: HCA-85010).
Performs 2 Functions: the Analysis of Demographic Variables & the Identification of a Hospital's Service Area. Demographic Indices of Health Care Are Presented to Gauge Hospital Performance & Identify Any Need for Health Care Services. The Hospital Service Is Identified & Analyzed, Providing the Framework to Anticipate Future Needs for Health Care Programs.
Riverdale Systems Design, Inc.

The Hospital Medical Staff Workplate. (The Hospital Workplate Ser.). Jul. 1985. *Compatible Hardware:* IBM PC XT & compatibles. *Operating System(s) Required:* MS-DOS. *Language(s):* 1-2-3 (source code included). *Memory Required:* 320k. *General Requirements:* Lotus 1-2-3 Release 2.0 or higher, 5Mb free on hard drive.
disk $395.00, incl. manual (Order no.: HCA-85020).
Enables User to Monitor Staff Composition Trends for Significant Changes & to Identify Sub-Optimal Utilization of Medical Staff Members. Sorts Physicians by Various Characteristics & Uses Statistics. Other Analyses Identify the Regionwide Availability of Physician Manpower & Project the Need of Additional Physicians at the Facility under Various Scenarios.
Riverdale Systems Design, Inc.

The Hospital Space Planning Workplate. (The Hospital Workplate Ser.). Jul. 1985. *Compatible Hardware:* IBM PC XT & compatibles. *Operating System(s) Required:* MS-DOS. *Language(s):* 1-2-3 (source code included). *Memory Required:* 320k. *General Requirements:* Lotus 1-2-3 Release 2.0 or higher, 5Mb on hard drive.
disk $295.00, incl. manual (Order no.: HCA-85040).
Aids in the Operational Planning Within a Hospital for Each Department's Space Needs. Current Use Levels Are Surveyed to Determine How the Hospital's Space Is Being Put to Use. Past, Present, & Future Ratios of Products per Square Foot Are Studied & Compared to Guides.
Riverdale Systems Design, Inc.

Hospital Staff Scheduler. 1992. *Items Included:* Complete instructions in 3-ring binder. *Customer Support:* Unlimited telephone support no charge; free replacement of damaged disks.
MS-DOS. IBM PC, XT, AT, PS/2 & compatibles (512k). disk $289.00 (Order no.: HOSP).
The Way to Know Who Will Be on, "On Call" & "In the House" on a Particular Day, During a Particular Time or for a Particular Shift. Easy to Enter, Alter, Print & Read. Enter Departments & Staff Members Just Once. Enter Holidays, Vacation Days, Conference Days & Other "Special" Days. Then, Schedule Staff Easily & Efficiently. Check to See Who Is Available for a Particular Date for a Particular Location. Know Immediately Who Is Available & Who Is Not. Print Reports by Department, Staff Member or Date. Maintain Records in the Data Base for As Long As You Want. Delete When Ready.
p.r.n. medical software.

The Hospital Utilization Workplate. (The Hospital Workplate Ser.). Jul. 1985. *Compatible Hardware:* IBM PC XT & compatibles. *Operating System(s) Required:* MS-DOS. *Language(s):* 1-2-3 (source code included). *Memory Required:* 320k. *General Requirements:* Lotus 1-2-3 Release 2.0 or higher, 5Mb on hard drive.
disk $395.00 (Order no.: HCA-85030).
Analyzes Historical Hospital Utilization Trends & Projects Future Use. Inpatient, Ambulatory-Care, & Ancilliary Services Can All Be Studied. Also Includes Special Detailed Studies Covering the Use of & Projected Need for Selected Tertiary Services Such As Radiation Therapy, C+ Scanning, & Neonatal Programs.
Riverdale Systems Design, Inc.

Host Graphics Option for DOS. Version: 2.0. May 1990. *Customer Support:* Documentation. PC/MS-DOS. IBM PC, PS/2 & compatibles. disk $695.00. *Nonstandard peripherals required:* 85/4/A Adapter to Access 85/4/A. *Addl. software required:* Attachmate Extra! Extended. *Networks supported:* NetBios.
Takes Full Advantage of the PC's Inherent Flexibility & Ease-of-Use While Providing Full IBM Mainframe-Graphics Terminal Capabilities. Emulation So Precise That the Mainframe Thinks It's Attached to a 3170-G Terminal. Offers Support for Both Programmed Symbol Graphics (S3G) & Vector Graphics (All Points Addressable), Including 8514A Compatibility. Takes Advantage of EMS Memory. Provides Text-Graphics Plane Compatibility & Support for Text & Graphics Cursors.
Attachmate Corp.

Host Graphics Option for Windows. Version: 1.01. Jul. 1992. *Items Included:* User's manual. *Customer Support:* Toll-free technical support hot line, provided at no charge for life of product. PC-DOS/MS-DOS 3.0 or higher. IBM 286, 386 (3Mb). disk $695.00. *Addl. software required:* EXTRA! for Windows. *Networks supported:* NETBIOS, IPX, 802.2.
Allows PCs Running Microsoft Windows to Emulate the Function of an IBM 3179-G Mainframe Graphics Terminal. Supports All Windows Features Including All Windows-Installed Pointing & Output Devices. Provides Text/Graphics Plane Compatibility, Interactive Image Manipulation, & Accurate Image Display, Including an Option That Preserves the Correct Aspect Ratio for a Given Window Size.
Attachmate Corp.

Host 35-70. Jun. 1984. *Compatible Hardware:* IBM PC & compatibles. *Operating System(s) Required:* PC-DOS 1.1, 2.0, 2.1. *Memory Required:* 192k.
Host 35. contact publisher for price (Order no.: SD-04041-000).
Host 70. contact publisher for price (Order no.: SD04042-000).
Menu-Driven Packages That Facilitate Interactive Communications over an Error-Protected Line Between an IBM PC & a TIMEKEEPER System. Accesses Labor Cost Data, Allows Schedule of Employees, & Access Management Reporting. Storage & Printout of Data Is Facilitated Through Program.
Kronos, Inc.

HOT. Executive Systems, Inc. Sep. 1986. *Operating System(s) Required:* PC-DOS/MS-DOS 2.0 or higher. *Memory Required:* 256k.
3.5" or 5.25" disk $75.00 (ISBN 0-937867-87-X, Order no.: HOT).
Comprehensive Menu Development System. Includes Menu Maker & Several Internal Functions That Allow the User to Create a Complete Turnkey System. In Addition There Are Also Several Pop-up Utilities to Increase Productivity.
XTree Co.

Hot & Cool Jazz. *Compatible Hardware:* Commodore Amiga.
3.5" disk $29.95.
Music Data Disk.
Electronic Arts.

Hot Runtime Module. Sep. 1987. *Operating System(s) Required:* PC-DOS/MS-DOS 2.1 or higher. *Memory Required:* 256k. *General Requirements:* Hard disk.
$49.95.
Contains Basic HOT programs & a Developer That Transfers the Additional Customized Files & Distributes the Unit to a Work Station. Also Includes a Packet of Quick Reference Cards for the Optional HOT Pop-Up Services.
XTree Co.

HOTDIJ. Version: 3.0. Apr. 1991. *Operating System(s) Required:* MS-DOS 2.0 or higher. *Memory Required:* Application plus 99k. *Items Included:* User manual. *Customer Support:* Free 30-day telephone support.
license fee $335.00 (ISBN 0-945851-18-9).
Stay Resident Digitizing & Measuring Utility for Entering Data into Any PC-DOS/MS-DOS Software Program with a Digitizer.
Geocomp, Ltd.

Hotdij. *Version:* 4.0. *Items Included:* Complete documentation. *Customer Support:* Free 30-day telephone support.
  IBM PC & compatibles (59k). disk $335.00.
  Optimal configuration: IBM PC & compatibles 35k, 5 1/4" floppy disk drive & a RS-232 port.
  demo disk $40.00 incl. user manual.
Software Utility Program That Directs Measured & Coordinate Data from the Digitizer into Most IBM PC Programs. Makes Data Appear As If You Entered It from the Keyboard. Allows User to Place Scaled Line Length, Area, & Coordinate Data Directly into Spread Sheets, Word Processors, Data Bases, & Most Other PC/MS DOS Programs. Adds Control Characters to the Digitizer Coordinates That Help Guide Your Data into Well Organized Columns on the Monitor. The Program Automatically Adjusts for Scale & Drawing Placement. For Measured Data, the User Can Set the Map Scale. You Can Also Adjust Hotdij for the Resolution of the Tablet.
Geocomp, Ltd.

Hotel Control System (HCS). *Version:* 8.00. 1983. *Compatible Hardware:* IBM PC, PC XT, PC AT & compatibles. *Operating System(s) Required:* MS-DOS 2.0. *Language(s):* Compiled Basic. *Memory Required:* 640k. *General Requirements:* 2 disk drives, printer.
  $2500.00 to $5000.00 single-user.
  $5000.00 to $8000.00 multi-user.
  evaluation kit $95.00.
  demo Kit $95.00.
Reservations/Accounting System for Motels/Hotels. Includes: RESERVATIONS, FRONT DESK, GROUP & COMPANY BILLING & GUEST HISTORY. GENERAL LEDGER, & ACCOUNTS PAYABLE Are Optional. Full Range of Reports & Statements Are Provided Including Night Audit Reports, Maid Scheduling, & Financial Statements for Individual Cost Centers, As Well As Consolidated Statements, Accounts Receivable Reports, Confirmations, Checkout Statements, etc.
Resort Data Processing, Inc.

HotFax. *Version:* 2.0. Jul. 1993. *Items Included:* 1 spiral-bound manual; addendum. *Customer Support:* 60 days free technical support (phone); BBS.
  DOS 3.0 or higher. IBM PC, XT, AT or true compatibles (2Mb). disk $149.95. *Nonstandard peripherals required:* Class 1, Class 2, SendFax or Intel Satisfaxtion Fax/Data Modem.
Full Featured Easy to Use Fax & Data Communication Product with Optical Character Recognition (OCR) for DOS. Combined with a Send/Receive or Send Fax Modem, HotFax Is All You Need to Send Laser Quality Faxes, Communicate with Remote Computers & Provide Fax Host & Data Host Access.
Smith Micro Software, Inc.

HotLine. *Version:* 2.25. *Items Included:* 1 spiral bound manual. *Customer Support:* 60 day free phone; BBS.
  DOS 3.0 or higher. IBM XT, AT, PS/2 or true compatibles (525k). disk $69.95. *Nonstandard peripherals required:* Hayes AT or compatible Modem.
  Microsoft Windows 3.0 or higher. IBM AT, PS/2 or compatibles (286 or higher) (1Mb). Contact publisher for price. *Nonstandard peripherals required:* Hayes AT or compatible modem.
High-Performance Personal Telephone Management Memory Resident (TSR) Program for Your PC. Pop-Up HotLine from Within Any Application. Create Unlimited Business & Personal Phonebooks in dBASE III Format, Take Notes on the Handy Notepad As You Talk, Look up Cities Area-Codes & Have HotLine Auto-Dial the Selected Contact for You. Comes with Your Choice of AT&T's Tool Free Numbers or the American Business Directory.
Smith Micro Software, Inc.

Houdini. *Version:* 3.0. *Compatible Hardware:* IBM PC & compatibles. *Memory Required:* 384k. disk $89.00.
Integrated Software Package Featuring Word-Processing, Database & Graphics Modules. Includes Context Switching, Built-In Language in All Modules & Context-Sensitive On-Screen Help. Edits 2 Files Simultaneously & Links 2500 Database Tables in One Query. Imports & Exports ASCII File Formats.
MaxThink, Inc.

A House Divided: The Lincoln-Douglas Debates. Dec. 1994. *Items Included:* CD-ROM, booklet, registration card. *Customer Support:* Support by Fax No. (415-358-5556).
  Windows 3.1 or Macintosh System 7.0 or higher. Apple Macintosh or 386, 486 or Pentium-based MPC Level II (5Mb). CD-ROM disk $35.00 (ISBN 0-9644452-0-4). *Nonstandard peripherals required:* CD-ROM drive, audio board, speakers, & 256 color video display. *Addl. software required:* Quicktime 2.0 or Quicktime for Windows 2.0 (included on CD). *Optimal configuration:* Macintosh w/256 color 13" monitor, 5Mb RAM, double speed CD-ROM drive or MPC Level II multimedia computer (386 or higher) 5Mb RAM, Windows 3.1, double speed CD-ROM drive, 256 color monitor, audio board & speakers.
Examines the Issues That Precipitated the Civil War. You'll Find Video Reenactments, Photos, Music, Political Cartoons, Slave Narratives, & Text That Tell the Story of the Crisis. Additional Resources Include Games, a Summary of the Debates, the Full Text of the Debates, & a Teacher's Guide.
Grafica Multimedia, Inc.

House Keeper. R. Alan Carl. Sep. 1985. *Operating System(s) Required:* PICK. *Memory Required:* 512k.
  $295.00 (Order no.: MICRO).
  $595.00 (Order no.: MINI).
Keeps Software Well Organized & Free of Unnecessary or Outdated Programs, Procedures, & Data Files. Inspects an Entire System & Produces a Complete Set of System Documentation.
Automation Consultants.

House Manager, Scorekeeper. *Operating System(s) Required:* CP/M. *Language(s):* Microsoft BASIC, C-BASIC. *Memory Required:* 64k.
  multi-league $495.00.
  single league $50.00.
Microsystems.

House of Cards. *Customer Support:* 90 day warranty.
  MS-DOS 2.1 or higher. IBM (256K). 3.5" disk $12.99; 5.25" disk $9.99. *Nonstandard peripherals required:* CGA, EGA, VGA or Tandy Graphics required.
Now You Can Enjoy Six Computerized Versions of Your All-Time Favorite Card Games. Play Two-Handed Bridge, Hearts, Spades, Cribbage, Pinochle or Gin Rummy Against the Ultimate Strategist - Your Own Computer. You Can Even Customize the Play by Selecting Such Options As Game Limit & Point Systems.
Virgin Games.

The House of Dies Drear. *Items Included:* Program manual. *Customer Support:* Free technical support, 90 day warranty.
  School ver.. System 7.1 or higher. Macintosh (4Mb). 3.5" disk contact publisher for price (ISBN 1-57204-246-X). *Nonstandard peripherals required:* 256 color monitor, hard drive, printer.
  Lab pack. System 7.1 or higher. Macintosh (4Mb). 3.5" disk contact publisher for price (ISBN 1-57204-222-2). *Nonstandard peripherals required:* 256 color monitor, hard drive, printer.
  Site license. System 7.1 or higher. Macintosh (4Mb). 3.5" disk contact publisher for price (ISBN 1-57204-247-8). *Nonstandard peripherals required:* 256 color monitor, hard drive, printer.
  School ver.. Windows 3.1 or higher. IBM/Tandy & 100% compatibles (4Mb). disk contact publisher for price (ISBN 1-57204-223-0). *Nonstandard peripherals required:* VGA or SVGA 640 x 480 resolution (256), mouse, hard drive, sound device.
  Lap pack. Windows 3.1 or higher. IBM/Tandy & 100% compatibles (4mb). disk contact publisher for price (ISBN 1-57204-248-6). *Nonstandard peripherals required:* VGA or SVGA 640 x 480 resolution (256), mouse, hard drive, sound device.
  Site license. Windows 3.1 or higher. IBM/Tandy & 100% compatibles (4Mb). disk contact publisher for price (ISBN 1-57204-224-9). *Nonstandard peripherals required:* VGA or SVGA 640 x 480 resolution (256), mouse, hard drive, sound device.
This companion for young adult literature is ideal for students who don't know how to start that book report, or give that needed summary. Gentle prompts throughout the guide section of the program include Warm-up Connections, Thinking about Plot, Quoting & Noting, Keeping a Journal, If I Were ———' Responding to Questions, Using Quotations, Taking a Personal View, Write to Others, & Write a Sequel.
Lawrence Productions, Inc.

The House of 60 Fathers. Intentional Education Staff & Mundart Sejong. *Items Included:* Program manual. *Customer Support:* Free technical support, 90 day warranty.
  School ver.. System 7.1 or higher. Macintosh (4Mb). 3.5" disk contact publisher for price (ISBN 1-57204-231-1). *Nonstandard peripherals required:* 256 color monitor, hard drive, printer.
  Lab pack. System 7.1 or higher. Macintosh (4Mb). 3.5" disk contact publisher for price (ISBN 1-57204-233-8). *Nonstandard peripherals required:* 256 color monitor, hard drive, printer.
  Site license. System 7.1 or higher. Macintosh (4Mb). 3.5" disk contact publisher for price (ISBN 1-57204-233-8). *Nonstandard peripherals required:* 256 color monitor, hard drive, printer.
  School ver.. Windows 3.1 or higher. IBM/Tandy & 100% compatibles (4Mb). disk contact publisher for price (ISBN 1-57204-208-7). *Nonstandard peripherals required:* VGA or SVGA 640 x 480 resolution (256), mouse, hard drive, sound device.
  Lab pack. Windows 3.1 or higher. IBM/Tandy & 100% compatibles (4Mb). disk contact publisher for price (ISBN 1-57204-233-8). *Nonstandard peripherals required:* VGA or SVGA 640 x 480 resolution (256), mouse, hard drive, sound device.
  Site license. Windows 3.1 or higher. IBM/Tandy & 100% compatibles (4Mb). disk contact publisher for price (ISBN 1-57204-209-5). *Nonstandard peripherals required:* VGA or SVGA 640 x 480 resolution (256), mouse, hard drive, sound device.
THis companion for young adult literature is ideal for students who don't know how to start that book report, or give that needed summary. Gentle prompts throughout the guide section of the program include Warm-up Connections, Thinking about Plot, Quoting & Noting, Keeping a Journal, If I Were ———' Responding to Questions, Using Quotations, Taking a Personal View, Write to Others, & Write a Sequel.
Lawrence Productions, Inc.

Household Budget Management. *Compatible Hardware:* TI Home Computer. *Memory Required:* 32k. *General Requirements:* cassette or disk data storage system.
contact publisher for price (Order no.: PHM 3007).
Helps Set Budget & Keep Records. Provides Graphic Analysis & Tables.
Texas Instruments, Personal Productivity Products.

Household Cash Planner: A Planning Guide to Household Finances. Jun. 1994. *Items Included:* Registration card, instruction sheet. *Customer Support:* 900 support number $2.00 per minute; limited 60 day warranty.
DOS. IBM PC & compatibles (640k). disk $9.95 (ISBN 1-57269-002-X, Order no.: 3202 42095). *Addl. software required:* DOS 3.0 or higher. *Optimal configuration:* Single floppy drive.
Plan & Anticipate Your Expenses & Have the Cash You'll Need. Easy to Follow Help Screens Make Financial Planning Easy.
Memorex Products, Inc., Memorex Software Division.

Household Expenses Profile. *Customer Support:* 800-929-8117 (customer service).
MS-DOS. Apple II. disk $39.99 (ISBN 0-87007-861-5).
Helps to Maintain a Working Household Budget by Profiling User's Expenses.
SourceView Software International.

Household Inventory System. *Version:* 1.3. Thomas Gleiter. Oct. 1988. *Compatible Hardware:* IBM PC & compatibles. *Operating System(s) Required:* PC-DOS/MS-DOS. *General Requirements:* Hard disk & printer recommended. *Items Included:* software diskette, demo diskette. *Customer Support:* Unlimited.
disk $29.95 (ISBN 0-9622124-0-7, Order no.: HIS525).
Organizes & Indexes Personal Property by Room of the Home & Category of Item. Also Records Details of Homeowner's Insurance Policy with Agent Name, Address, Phone, & Coverage Amounts for House & Personal Property. Contains Explanations of Homeowner's Insurance, Tips on Saving on Premiums, etc.
Gleiter Computer Services, Inc.

Household-Inventory-Track-I. *Version:* 2.00. Kailash Chandra. 1983. *Compatible Hardware:* IBM PC, PCjr, PC XT & compatibles. *Operating System(s) Required:* PC-DOS 1.1, 2.0, 2.1. *Language(s):* Compiled BASIC. *Memory Required:* 256k.
disk $45.95 (ISBN 0-918689-02-3).
Menu-Driven Household Inventory System. Also Inventory & Fixed Asset Control for Small Businesses.
Sapana Micro Software.

Housing Assistance Pac. DBi Software Products. *Compatible Hardware:* TI Professional. *Operating System(s) Required:* MS-DOS, CP/M-86. *Memory Required:* 64k. *General Requirements:* Printer.
$600.00.
Reduces Paperwork & Amount of Time Needed to Manage H.U.D. Projects.
Texas Instruments, Personal Productivit.

Hoverforce. Mar. 1991. *Items Included:* Catalog, copy protection device, manual, proof of purchase card, & warranty card. *Customer Support:* Technical support 408-296-8400, 90 day limited warranty, Bulletin Board (modem) 408-296-8800 (settings: 300, 1200, 2400 baud; 8 data; no parity; 1 stop bit).
IBM DOS 2.1 or higher, Tandy-DOS (640k). IBM PC, XT, AT, & compatibles, Tandy 1000 series, 3000, 4000. $49.95. *Optimal configuration:* Hard drive, keyboard, mouse, joystick, graphics card, & sound board.
Amiga-Kickstart 1.2, 1.3 or 2.0 (512k). Amiga 500, 1000, 2000. $49.95. *Optimal configuration:* Keyboard, mouse, joystick, graphics card, & sound board.
Interdict Supply Runs & Terminate the New Breed of Criminal Called Alterants As the Ultimate Bio-Warrior. Strapped into a Hard-Firing, Hyper-Fast Urban Assault Skimmer, You Are the Best of the "Public Enforcers" Known As the Red Wasp Unit.
Accolade, Inc.

How To Create Multimedia. 1994.
Macintosh. CD-ROM disk $29.95. *Nonstandard peripherals required:* CD-ROM drive.
Focus is on Using Multimedia for Presentations. Includes Tips & Royalty-Free Graphics & Videos. Also Includes Copy of COMPEL P.E. from Asymetrix.
Jasmine Multimedia Publishing.

How to Create Your Own Computer Bulletin Board. Lary L. Myers. Aug. 1983. *Compatible Hardware:* Apple IIe, II+; TRS-80 Model I, Model III, Model 4. *Operating System(s) Required:* TRSDOS, Apple DOS. *Memory Required:* 32-48k.
disk $35.50 ea., incl. bk.
TRS-80 Model I. (ISBN 0-8306-5041-5, Order no.: 5041C).
Model III & Model 4. (Order no.: 5077C).
Shows How Anyone Can Design & Implement an Effective CBB. Included Are Actual Programs & Complete Explanations.
TAB Bks.

How to Form Your Own New York Corporation, Computer Edition. Anthony Mancuso. *Items Included:* Disk & 272-page manual. *Customer Support:* Free technical support Monday-Friday, 9-5 PST; unlimited money back guarantee.
PC/MS-DOS 2.0 or higher. IBM PC & compatibles. 5.25" & 3.5" disks $69.95 (ISBN 0-87337-089-9).
Macintosh. 3.5" disk $69.95 (ISBN 0-87337-091-0).
Provides Legal Documentation for Businesses Wishing to Incorporate in New York.
Nolo Pr.

How to Form Your Own Texas Corporation, Computer Edition. Anthony Mancuso. *Items Included:* Disk & 240-page manual. *Customer Support:* Free technical support Monday-Friday, 9-5 PST; unlimited money back guarantee.
PC/MS-DOS 2.0 or higher. IBM PC & compatibles. 5.25" & 3.5" disks $69.95 (ISBN 0-87337-092-9).
Macintosh. 3.5" disk $69.95 (ISBN 0-87337-094-5).
Provides Legal Documentation for Businesses That Wish to Incorporate in Texas. This Software Package Contains All the Instructions, Tax Information & Forms One Needs to Incorporate, Including the Certificate of Incorporation, Bylaws, Minutes & Stock Certificates; Full Instructions on How to Incorporate a New or Already Existing Business; Complete Information on Meeting S Corporation Tax Status; Federal Tax Reform Act Rates & Rules, etc. All Organizational Forms Are on Disk.
Nolo Pr.

How to Get on the Internet: Finding, Installing, & Using Internet Connection Software to Get Online. Laurie Drukier & Kim Schrader. Apr. 1996. *Items Included:* A 64-page companion booklet that reviews web sites & includes instructions on how to use the software. *Customer Support:* Access to the Go!Guides web site & FAQ, customer support by email at help goguides.com.
Macintosh System 7.0 or higher. Macintosh (4Mb). 3.5" disk $12.99 (ISBN 1-57712-000-0). *Nonstandard peripherals required:* Modem 14.4 or faster. *Addl. software required:* Internet account & connection. *Optimal configuration:* Macintosh System 7.0 or higher, at least 4Mb of RAM, at least 2Mb of free disk space, color monitor, 14.4 or 28.8 modem, Internet account.
Windows 3.1 or Windows 95. IBM or compatible (4Mb). disk $12.99. *Nonstandard peripherals required:* 14.4 or 28.8 modem. *Addl. software required:* Internet account. *Optimal configuration:* IBM-compatible running Windows 3.1 or Windows 95, at least 2Mb free space on hard drive, at least 4Mb RAM, color monitor, 14.4 or 28.8 modem, Internet account.
This Guide Tells You Everything You Need to Know about Finding, Installing, & Using Internet Connection Software to Get Online.
Motion Works Publishing.

How to Implement ISO 9000. Lawrence A. Wilson. Apr. 1994. *Items Included:* The entire set of 1992 ISO 9000 standards is integrated into the application. *Customer Support:* Unlimited support.
Contact publisher for price.
This Interactive Software Application Helps You Understand & Prepare for ISO 9000 Registration. It Personalizes the Process by Providing Information You Need Specifically for Your Organization. It Breaks the Complex Registration Process into Simple, Step-by-Step Activities. The Standards Are Tailored to Your Needs & Guides Through the Writing of Your Quality Manual.
LearnerFirst.

How to Publicize High Tech Products & Services. Daniel S. Janal. Feb. 1991.
MS-DOS. IBM PC & compatibles (256k). disk $24.95.
A Hands-On Guide with Worksheets, Sample Materials & Proven Strategies to Gain Publicity for Products & Services.
Ten-K Pr./Janal Communications.

How to Publish on the Internet: Build Your Own Home Page on the World Wide Web. Maureen Nicholson & Michael Hayward. Apr. 1996. *Items Included:* A 64-page companion booklet that reviews web sites & includes instructions on how to use the software. *Customer Support:* Access to the Go!Guides web site & FAQ, customer support by email at help goguides.com.
Macintosh System 7.0 or higher. Macintosh (4Mb). 3.5" disk $12.99 (ISBN 1-57712-003-5). *Nonstandard peripherals required:* Modem 14.4 or faster. *Addl. software required:* Internet account & connection. *Optimal configuration:* Macintosh System 7.0 or higher, at least 4Mb of RAM, at least 2Mb of free disk space, color monitor, 14.4 or 28.8 modem, Internet account.
Windows 3.1 or Windows 95. IBM or compatible (4Mb). disk $12.99. *Nonstandard peripherals required:* 14.4 or 28.8 modem. *Addl. software required:* Internet account. *Optimal configuration:* IBM-compatible running Windows 3.1 or Windows 95, at least 2Mb free space on hard drive, at least 4Mb RAM, color monitor, 14.4 or 28.8 modem, Internet account.
This Is Your Guide to Joining the Digital Revolution by Building Your Own Home Page on the World Wide Web.
Motion Works Publishing.

How to Use Apple IIe: Skill Builder Series.
Compatible Hardware: Apple IIe. *Operating System(s) Required:* Apple DOS. *Memory Required:* 128k.
disk $49.95 (ISBN 0-922274-48-7).
Interactive Simulation Tutorial Which Teaches Users How to Operate the Apple IIe.
American Training International, Inc.

How to Use dBase III Plus. *Version:* III Plus. Patricia A. Menges. 1986. *Items Included:* Quick Reference Guide, audio tapes, practice disk. *Customer Support:* 30 day-right of return; Editorial support for course content/exercises.
DOS. IBM. disk $175.00 (ISBN 0-917792-36-X, Order no.: 302). *Addl. software required:* dBase III Plus.
Self-paced training in using dBase III Plus to create, edit, get reports from & use for analysis of databases.
OneOnOne Computer Training.

How to Use dBase 4. *Version:* V.2. Jacqueline Jonas. 1989. *Items Included:* Quick Reference Guide, audio tapes, practice disk. *Customer Support:* 30 day-right of return; Editorial support for course content/exercises.
DOS. IBM & compatibles. disk $175.00 (ISBN 0-917792-65-3, Order no.: 304). *Addl. software required:* dBase IV.
Self-paced training in using dBase IV to use, edit, create, get reports from & query databases.
OneOnOne Computer Training.

How to Use Excel for Windows. *Version:* 5. B. Alan August. 1994. *Items Included:* Data disk, quick reference guide. *Customer Support:* Call with questions about taking the course or course exercises.
Windows. IBM. disk $175.00 (ISBN 1-56562-043-7).
Self-Studio, Audio-Based Course for Excel 5 Teaches Creating, Editing, Printing, Spreadsheets; Includes Creating Formulas, Using Functions & Simple Graphs & Macros.
OneOnOne Computer Training.

How to Use Freelance Windows. *Version:* 2.X. Natalie B. Young. 1992. *Items Included:* Data disk, quick reference guide. *Customer Support:* Call with questions about taking the course or course exercises.
Windows. IBM. disk $175.00 (ISBN 1-56562-036-4).
Self-Studio, Audio-Based Course for Lotus Freelance for Windows Teaches Creating, Editing, Saving, Printing Presentations & Slide Shows.
OneOnOne Computer Training.

How to Use Harvard Graphics for Windows.
Natalie B. Young. 1992. *Items Included:* Data disk, quick reference guide. *Customer Support:* Call with questions about taking the course or course exercises.
Windows. IBM. disk $175.00 (ISBN 1-56562-048-8).
Self-Studio, Audio-Based Course for Harvard Graphics for Windows Teaches Creating, Editing, Printing, Running Presentations & Slide Shows.
OneOnOne Computer Training.

How to Use Harvard Graphics 3.0. *Version:* 3.0. Jacqueline Jonas & Natalie B. Young. 1992. *Items Included:* Quick Reference Guide, audio tapes, practice disk. *Customer Support:* 30 day-right of return; Editorial support for course content/exercises.
DOS. IBM & compatibles. disk $175.00 (ISBN 1-56562-003-8, Order no.: 606). *Addl. software required:* Harvard Graphics 3.0.
Self-paced training in creating presentations, drawings & slideshows with HG3.
OneOnOne Computer Training.

How to Use Internet Email: Installing & Using Eudora to Get the Most Out of Electronic Mail. Michael Hayward. Apr. 1996. *Items Included:* A 64-page companion booklet that reviews web sites & includes instructions on how to use the software. *Customer Support:* Access to the Go!Guides web site & FAQ, customer support by email at help goguides.com.
Macintosh System 7.0 or higher. Macintosh (4Mb). 3.5" disk $12.99 (ISBN 1-57712-002-7). *Nonstandard peripherals required:* Modem 14.4 or faster. *Addl. software required:* Internet account & connection. *Optimal configuration:* Macintosh System 7.0 or higher, at least 4Mb of RAM, at least 2Mb of free disk space, color monitor, 14.4 or 28.8 modem, Internet account.
Windows 3.1 or Windows 95. IBM or compatible (4Mb). disk $12.99. *Nonstandard peripherals required:* 14.4 or 28.8 modem. *Addl. software required:* Internet account. *Optimal configuration:* IBM-compatible running Windows 3.1 or Windows 95, at least 2Mb free space on hard drive, at least 4Mb RAM, color monitor, 14.4 or 28.8 modem, Internet account.
Get the Most Out of Electronic Mail by Following the Instructions in This Guide for Installing & Using Eudora.
Motion Works Publishing.

How to Use Lotus Freelance Plus. *Version:* 3.0. Jacqueline Jonas. 1989. *Items Included:* Quick Reference Guide, audio tapes, practice disk. *Customer Support:* 30 day-right of return; editorial support for course content/exercises.
MS-DOS. IBM & compatibles. disk $175.00 (ISBN 0-917792-48-3, Order no.: 604). *Addl. software required:* Freelance Plus.
Self-paced training in creating, editing, running presentations with Freelance.
OneOnOne Computer Training.

How to Use Lotus One-Two-Three. *Version:* 2.3. Janice Rinehart. 1991. *Items Included:* Quick Reference Guide, audio tapes, practice disk. *Customer Support:* 30 day-right of return; Editorial support for course content/exercises.
DOS. IBM & compatibles. disk $175.00 (ISBN 0-917792-92-0, Order no.: 240). *Addl. software required:* Lotus 1-2-3 2.3.
Self-paced training in using 1-2-3 2.3 to create, edit, print spreadsheets, graph from spreadsheets data, create & use simple databases macros.
OneOnOne Computer Training.

How to Use Lotus One-Two-Three for Windows. *Version:* 1.X. Charles R. Wolf. 1992. *Items Included:* Quick Reference Guide, audio tapes, practice disk. *Customer Support:* 30 day-right of return; Editorial support for course content/exercises.
DOS/Windows. IBM & compatibles. disk $175.00 (ISBN 0-917792-99-8, Order no.: 250). *Addl. software required:* Lotus 1-2-3 for Windows.
Self-paced training for using 1-2-3 1.0 for Windows to create, edit, print spreadsheets, graphs, construct simple databases & macros.
OneOnOne Computer Training.

How to Use Lotus 1-2-3 for DOS. *Version:* 3.4. Charles R. Wolf. 1993. *Items Included:* Data disk, quick reference guide. *Customer Support:* Call with questions about taking the course or the course exercises.
DOS. IBM. disk $175.00 (ISBN 1-56562-026-7).
Self-Studio, Audio-Based Course for Lotus 1-2-3 Teaches Creating, Saving, Editing, Printing Spreadsheets; Includes Creating Formulas, Using Functions Creating Simple Graphs & Macros.
OneOnOne Computer Training.

How to Use Lotus 1-2-3 for Windows. *Version:* 5. Charles R. Wolf. 1994. *Items Included:* Data disk, quick reference guide. *Customer Support:* Call with questions about taking the course or the course exercises.
Windows 5. IBM. disk $175.00 (ISBN 1-56562-061-5).
Self-Studio, Audio-Based Course for Lotus 1-2-3 Teaches Creating, Saving, Editing, Printing Spreadsheets; Includes Creating Formulas, Using Functions Creating Simple Graphs & Macros.
OneOnOne Computer Training.

How to Use Microsoft Access for Windows 95. *Version:* 7. Kimi Nance. 1996. *Items Included:* Data disk, quick reference guide. *Customer Support:* Call with questions about taking the course or course exercises.
Windows 95. IBM. disk $175.00 (ISBN 1-56562-071-2).
Self-Studio, Audio-Based Course for Access for Windows 95 Teaches Creating Modifying Printing Tables, Forms & Reports; Covers Queries & Creating Simple Macros.
OneOnOne Computer Training.

How to Use Microsoft Access for Windows. *Version:* 2. Natalie B. Young. 1995. *Items Included:* Data disk, quick reference guide. *Customer Support:* Call with questions about taking the course or course exercises.
Windows. IBM. disk $175.00 (ISBN 1-56562-059-3).
Self-Studio, Audio-Based Course for Access for Windows Covers Creating & Modifying Database Tables Forms & Reports; Covers Queries, Importing Graphics, Creating Macros & Much More.
OneOnOne Computer Training.

How to Use Microsoft Excel for Windows 95. *Version:* 7. B. Alan August. 1996. *Items Included:* Data disk, quick reference guide. *Customer Support:* Call with questions about taking the course or course exercises.
Windows. IBM. disk $175.00 (ISBN 1-56562-069-0).
Self-Studio, Audio-Based Course for Excel for Windows Teaches Creating, Editing, Printing Spreadsheets; Includes Writing Formulas, Using Functions, Recording Simple Macros & Creating Graphs.
OneOnOne Computer Training.

How to Use Microsoft Windows 3.0. *Version:* 3.0. Jacqueline Jonas. 1991. *Items Included:* Quick Reference Guide, audio tapes, practice disk. *Customer Support:* 30 day-right of return; Editorial support for course content/exercises.
DOS/Windows. IBM & compatibles. disk $175.00 (ISBN 0-917792-87-4, Order no.: 126). *Addl. software required:* Microsoft Windows 3.0.
Self-paced training for Windows 3.0 operating environment; covers navigating the window system, Windows Write, Paintbrush, Calculator, notepad & other utility applications, as well as file management.
OneOnOne Computer Training.

How to Use Microsoft Windows 3.1. *Version:* 3.1, 3.11. Charles R. Wolf & Jacqueline Jonas. 1992. *Items Included:* Quick Reference Guide, audio tapes, practice disk. *Customer Support:* 30 day-right of return; Editorial support for course content/exercises.
DOS/Windows. IBM & compatibles. disk $175.00 (ISBN 1-56562-004-6, Order no.: 132). *Addl. software required:* Microsoft Windows 3.1.
Self-paced training for Windows 3.1 operating environment; covers navigating Windows, File Manager, Program Manager, Windows Write, Paintbrush, calculator, Notepad, games, & much more.
OneOnOne Computer Training.

TITLE INDEX

How to Use Microsoft Word. *Version:* 5.5. Sally Hargrave. 1991. *Items Included:* Quick Reference Guide, audio tapes, practice disk. *Customer Support:* 30 day-right of return; Editorial support for course content/exercises.
  DOS. IBM & compatibles. disk $175.00 (ISBN 0-917792-95-5, Order no.: 434). *Addl. software required:* Microsoft Word 5.5.
Self-paced training in creating, editing, printing, merge printing a variety of documents.
OneOnOne Computer Training.

How to Use Microsoft Word for Windows. *Version:* 6.X. Christine Reid & Sally Hargrave. 1992. *Items Included:* Quick Reference Guide, audio tapes, practice disk. *Customer Support:* 30 day-right of return; Editorial support for course content/exercises.
  DOS/Windows. IBM & compatibles. disk $175.00 (ISBN 1-56562-011-9, Order no.: 440). *Addl. software required:* Microsoft Word for Windows.
Self-paced training in creating, editing, printing, merge printing a variety of documents.
OneOnOne Computer Training.

How to Use Microsoft Word for Windows. *Version:* 2.X. Sally Hargrave & Christine Reid. 1991. *Items Included:* Quick Reference Guide, audio tapes, practice disk. *Customer Support:* 30 day-right of return; Editorial support for course content/exercises.
  DOS/Windows. IBM & compatibles. disk $175.00 (ISBN 0-917792-94-7, Order no.: 436). *Addl. software required:* Microsoft Word for Windows.
Self-paced training in creating, editing, printing, merge printing a variety of documents.
OneOnOne Computer Training.

How to Use Microsoft Word for Windows 95. *Version:* 7. Deborah Paulsen. 1991. *Items Included:* Data disk, quick reference guide. *Customer Support:* Call with questions about taking the course or the course exercises.
  Windows 95. IBM. disk $175.00 (ISBN 1-56562-068-2).
Self-Studio, Audio-Based Course for WinWord 7, Teaches Creating, Saving, Editing, Merging, Printing a Variety of Documents.
OneOnOne Computer Training.

How to Use Microsoft Word Mac. *Version:* 5.X. Christine Reid. 1991. *Items Included:* Quick Reference Guide, audio tapes, practice disk. *Customer Support:* 30 day-right of return; Editorial support for course content/exercises.
  Apple System. Macs. disk $175.00 (ISBN 1-56562-005-4, Order no.: 442). *Addl. software required:* Microsoft Word Mac.
Self-paced training for creating, editing, printing, merge printing a variety of documents.
OneOnOne Computer Training.

How to Use Microsoft Word Mac. *Version:* 5.x. Christine Reid. 1991. *Items Included:* Data disk, quick reference guide. *Customer Support:* Call with questions about taking the course or the course exercises.
  Microsoft Word 5.x. MAC. 3.5" disk $175.00 (ISBN 1-56562-005-4).
Self-Studio, Audio-Based Course for Word 5.x Mac, Teaches Creating, Saving, Editing, Printing, Merge Printing a Variety of Documents.
OneOnOne Computer Training.

How to Use Microsoft Word PC. *Version:* 5.5. Sally Hargrave. 1991. *Items Included:* Data disk, quick reference guide. *Customer Support:* Call with questions about taking the course or the course exercises.
  Microsoft Word 5.5. IBM PC. disk $175.00 (ISBN 0-917792-95-5).

Self-Studio, Audio-Based Course for Word PC, Creating a Variety of Documents Creating, Saving, Editing, Printing, Merge Printing.
OneOnOne Computer Training.

How to Use MS-DOS. *Version:* 6.x. Charels R. Wolf. 1992. *Items Included:* Data disk, quick reference guide. *Customer Support:* Call with questions about taking the course or the course exercises.
  MS-DOS 6. IBM. disk $175.00 (ISBN 1-56562-021-6).
Self-Studio, Audio-Based Course for Essential Features of MS-DOS.
OneOnOne Computer Training.

How to Use MS-DOS 5. *Version:* 5.X. Charles R. Wolf. 1991. *Items Included:* Quick Reference Guide, audio tapes, practice disk. *Customer Support:* 30 day-right of return; Editorial support for course content/exercises.
  DOS. IBM & compatibles. disk $175.00 (ISBN 0-917792-73-4, Order no.: 120). *Addl. software required:* MS-DOS.
Self-paced training for MS-DOS 5 operating system software; covers all essential, most special features of the system.
OneOnOne Computer Training.

How to Use Novell Netware. *Version:* 3.x. Karen Hannum & Delta Group. 1992. *Items Included:* Data disk, quick reference guide. *Customer Support:* Call with questions about taking the course or the course exercises.
  Novell NetWare 3.x. IBM. disk $225.00 (ISBN 1-56562-002-X). *Networks supported:* Novell.
Self-Studio, Audio-Based Course for End User & Administrator Features of Novell NetWare, Version 3.XX.
OneOnOne Computer Training.

How to Use Novell NetWare 286 & SFT. *Version:* 2.X. Pinnacle Communications, Inc. Staff. 1991. *Items Included:* Quick Reference Guide, audio tapes, practice disk. *Customer Support:* 30 day-right of return; Editorial support for course content/exercises.
  DOS. IBM & compatibles. disk $225.00 (ISBN 0-917792-88-2, Order no.: 154). *Addl. software required:* Novell NetWare.
Self-paced training for NetWare; comes with disk simulation of NetWare environment; covers new users in first 2 tapes - logon & logging off, navigating the menu system, becoming comfortable with NetWare environment; tapes 3 & 4 are for supervisors & cover security, rights, printing. Simulation includes Filers, Session, Syscon, PConsole.
OneOnOne Computer Training.

How to Use PageMaker 5 for Mac, Pt. I. *Version:* 5. Natalie B. Young. 1994. *Items Included:* Data disk, quick reference guide. *Customer Support:* Call with questions about taking the course or the course exercises.
  MAC. 3.5" disk $175.00 (ISBN 1-56562-037-2).
Self-Studio, Audio-Based Course for PageMaker Desktop Publisher, Teaches Essential Features to Create a Variety of Documents.
OneOnOne Computer Training.

How to Use PageMaker 5 for Mac, Pt. II. *Version:* 5. Natalie B. Young. 1994. *Items Included:* Data disk, quick reference guide. *Customer Support:* Call with questions about taking the course or the course exercises.
  MAC. 3.5" disk $175.00 (ISBN 1-56562-038-0).
Self-Studio, Audio-Based Course for PageMaker 5 for the Mac Teaches the Story Editor & Other Intermediate Features.
OneOnOne Computer Training.

How to Use PageMaker 5 for Windows, Pt. I. *Version:* 5. Linda K. Schwartz. 1994. *Items Included:* Data disk, quick reference guide. *Customer Support:* Call with questions about taking the course or the course exercises.
  Windows. IBM. disk $175.00 (ISBN 1-56562-034-8).
Self-Studio, Audio-Based Course for PageMaker Desktop Publisher, Teaches Essential Features to Create a Variety of Documents.
OneOnOne Computer Training.

How to Use PageMaker 5 for Windows, Pt. II. *Version:* 5. Linda K. Schwartz. 1994. *Items Included:* Data disk, quick reference guide. *Customer Support:* Call with questions about taking the course or the course exercises.
  Windows. IBM. disk $175.00 (ISBN 1-56562-035-6).
Self-Studio, Audio-Based Course for PageMaker 5 for Windows Teaches Story Editor & Intermediate Features of the Software.
OneOnOne Computer Training.

How to Use PageMaker Mac. *Version:* 3 & 4. Linda K. Schwartz & Natalie B. Young. 1991. *Items Included:* Quick Reference Guide, audio tapes, practice disk. *Customer Support:* 30 day-right of return; Editorial support for course content/exercises.
  Apple System. Macintoshes. disk $195.00 (ISBN 1-56562-000-3, Order no.: 514). *Addl. software required:* PageMaker Mac.
Self-paced training in using PageMaker Mac version to create, edit & print a variety of desktop published documents; also includes Story Editor.
OneOnOne Computer Training.

How to Use PageMaker PC: With Story Editor. *Version:* 4. Linda K. Schwartz. 1991. *Items Included:* Quick Reference Guide, audio tapes, practice disk. *Customer Support:* 30 day-right of return; Editorial support for course content/exercises.
  DOS/Windows. IBM & compatibles. disk $195.00 (ISBN 0-917792-85-8, Order no.: 516). *Addl. software required:* PageMaker PC.
Self-paced training in using PageMaker to create a variety of desktop published documents, also includes Story Editor.
OneOnOne Computer Training.

How to Use Paradox. *Version:* 2. B. Alan August. 1990. *Items Included:* Quick Reference Guide, audio tapes, practice disk. *Customer Support:* 30 day-right of return; Editorial support for course content/exercises.
  DOS. IBM & compatibles. disk $175.00 (ISBN 0-917792-42-4, Order no.: 308). *Addl. software required:* Paradox.
Self-paced training in using Paradox to create, edit, query & get reports from a database.
OneOnOne Computer Training.

How to Use Paradox for Windows. *Version:* 5. B. Alan August. 1994. *Items Included:* Data disk, quick reference guide. *Customer Support:* Call with questions about taking the course or course exercises.
  Windows. IBM. disk $175.00 (ISBN 1-56562-058-5).
Self-Studio, Audio-Based Course for Paradox for Windows Teaches Creating & Modifying Databases, Forms & Reports; Covers Queries, Printing, & Importing Data.
OneOnOne Computer Training.

How to Use Paradox for Windows. *Version:* 1-4.X. Karen Hannum & B. Alan August. 1992. *Items Included:* Data disk, quick reference guide. *Customer Support:* Call with questions about taking the course or course exercises.

Windows. IBM. disk $175.00 (ISBN 1-56562-047-X).
Self-Studio, Audio-Based Course for Paradox for Windows, Creating, Editing, Modifying Databases & Tables; Creating & Editing Forms & Reports, Printing Database Objects; Queries & Creating Databases from Scratch.
OneOnOne Computer Training.

How to Use PowerPoint for Windows. *Version:* 4. Natalie B. Young. 1994. *Items Included:* Data disk, quick reference guide. *Customer Support:* Call with questions about taking the course or course exercises.
Windows. IBM. disk $175.00 (ISBN 1-56562-057-7).
Self-Studio, Audio-Based Course for PowerPoint 4, Teaches Creating, Editing, Printing Slides; Creating & Modifying Slide Shows, Graphs & Charts.
OneOnOne Computer Training.

How to Use PowerPoint for Windows 95. *Version:* 7. Kimi Nancy & Natalie B. Young. 1996. *Items Included:* Data disk, quick reference guide. *Customer Support:* Call with questions about taking the course or course exercises.
Windows 95. IBM. disk $175.00 (ISBN 1-56562-070-4).
Self-Studio, Audio-Based Course for PowerPoint 7, Teaches Creating, Editing, Printing Slides & Slide Shows; Running Slide Shows with Transitions, Creating & Printing Graphs & Organization Charts.
OneOnOne Computer Training.

How to Use QuarkXPress. *Version:* 2.X-3.1. Karen L. Zorn & Kathy M. Berkemeyer. 1990. *Items Included:* Quick Reference Guide, audio tapes, practice disk. *Customer Support:* 30 day-right of return; Editorial support for course content/exercises.
Macintosh System. Macs. disk $175.00 (ISBN 0-917792-76-9, Order no.: 512). *Addl. software required:* QuarkXPress.
Self-paced training in using Quark to create, edit & print a variety of desktop published documents.
OneOnOne Computer Training.

How to Use Quattro Pro. *Version:* 2 & 3. B. Alan August. 1990. *Items Included:* Quick Reference Guide, audio tapes, practice disk. *Customer Support:* 30 day-right of return; Editorial support for course content/exercises.
DOS. IBM & compatibles. disk $175.00 (ISBN 0-917792-79-3, Order no.: 234). *Addl. software required:* Quattro Pro.
Self-paced training for creating, editing, printing, graphing spreadsheet data; covers all essential & many special features of the software, including macros.
OneOnOne Computer Training.

How to Use Quattro Pro for Windows. *Version:* 6. Patricia A. Menges. 1995. *Items Included:* Data disk, quick reference guide. *Customer Support:* Call with questions about taking the course or course exercises.
Windows. IBM. disk $175.00 (ISBN 1-56562-060-7).
Self-Studio, Audio-Based Course for Quattro Pro Teaches Creating, Saving, Editing, Printing Spreadsheets; Writing Formulas, Using Functions, Creating Simple Macros & Graphs.
OneOnOne Computer Training.

How to Use Quattro Pro for Windows. *Version:* 5. Patricia A. Menges. 1995. *Items Included:* Data disk, quick reference guide. *Customer Support:* Call with questions about taking the course or course exercises.
Windows. IBM. disk $175.00 (ISBN 1-56562-044-5).
Self-Studio, Audio-Based Course for Quattro Pro Teaches Creating, Saving, Editing, Printing Spreadsheets; Writing Formulas, Using Functions, Creating Simple Macros & Graphs.
OneOnOne Computer Training.

How to Use UNIX & XENIX. David Levin. 1990. *Items Included:* Quick Reference Guide, audio tapes, practice disk. *Customer Support:* 30 day-right of return; Editorial support for course content/exercises.
UNIX. UNIX-compatible PC or mini. disk $225.00 (ISBN 0-917792-49-1, Order no.: 122). *Addl. software required:* UNIX; XENIX.
Self-paced training for Unix & Zenix operating system; includes instruction for file management, vi editor, all essential & many special features of the system.
OneOnOne Computer Training.

How to Use Windows 95. Charels R. Wolf. 1995. *Items Included:* Data disk, quick reference guide. *Customer Support:* Call with questions about taking the course or the course exercises.
Windows 95. IBM. disk $175.00 (ISBN 1-56562-076-3).
Self-Studio, Audio-Based Course for Essential Features of Windows 95; Explore Control Panels, Desktop, Installing Hardware & Software & Much More.
OneOnOne Computer Training.

How to Use WordPerfect. *Version:* 5.0 & 5.1. Gayle Jensen & Sally Hargrave. 1989. *Items Included:* Quick Reference Guide, audio tapes, practice disk. *Customer Support:* 30 day-right of return; Editorial support for course content/exercises.
DOS. IBM & compatibles. disk $175.00 (ISBN 0-917792-57-2, Order no.: 428). *Addl. software required:* WordPerfect.
Self-paced training in creating, editing, printing & merge printing a variety of documents.
OneOnOne Computer Training.

How to Use WordPerfect for Windows. *Version:* 5.2. Sally Hargrave & Deborah Paulsen. 1992. *Items Included:* Quick Reference Guide, audio tapes, practice disk. *Customer Support:* 30 day-right of return; Editorial support for course content/exercises.
DOS/Windows. IBM & compatibles. disk $175.00 (ISBN 0-917792-99-8, Order no.: 438). *Addl. software required:* WordPerfect for Windows.
Self-paced training for creating, editing, printing, merge printing a variety of documents.
OneOnOne Computer Training.

How to Use WordPerfect for Windows. *Version:* 6.1. Kimi Nance & Sally Hargrave. 1995. *Items Included:* Data disk, quick reference guide. *Customer Support:* Call with questions about taking the course or course exercises.
Windows. IBM. disk $175.00 (ISBN 1-56562-064-X).
Self-Studio, Audio-Based Course for WordPerfect 6.1 Teaches Creating, Saving, Editing, Printing & Merge Printing a Variety of Documents; Includes Spell Check & Grammatik.
OneOnOne Computer Training.

How to Use Your PC/AT. *Compatible Hardware:* IBM PC & compatibles. *Operating System(s) Required:* PC-DOS/MS-DOS 2.0 or higher. *Memory Required:* 256k.
disk $75.00.
Guide User on How to Operate Their Computer.
American Training International, Inc.

How to Use Your PC/XT. *Compatible Hardware:* IBM PC & compatibles. *Operating System(s) Required:* PC-DOS/MS-DOS 2.0 or higher. *Memory Required:* 256k.
disk $49.95.
Guide User on How to Use Their Computer.
American Training International, Inc.

How to Use Your PS/2. 1988. *Compatible Hardware:* IBM PC & compatibles. *Operating System(s) Required:* PC-DOS/MS-DOS 2.0 or higher. *Memory Required:* 256k.
3.5" or 5.25" disk $75.00 (Order no.: A-16).
Helps First-Time PC Users Become Familiar with Their Computer's Basic Features.
American Training International, Inc.

How to Write a Business Plan. *Version:* 1.75. Max Fallek & Rueben Bjerke. Sep. 1992. *Items Included:* Two spiral bound manuals. Manual I - How to Write a Business Plan Use & Instruction Manual. Manual II - Manual on What Is a Business Plan, How to Use & How to Write. *Customer Support:* Company provides toll free 800 number of unlimited Customer Support. Full warranty for 90 days on software.
PC-DOS/MS-DOS; Apple Macintosh. IBM & compatibles; Apple Macintosh (512k). disk $125.00 (ISBN 0-939069-42-3). *Networks supported:* Novell, 3COM.
Software Package Prepares All of the Narrative for a Business Plan Including Executive Summary, Marketing, Advertising & Sales Plans, Production Plan, R&D, Finance Plan & Method, Key Personnel, Advisors, Competition & All Other Sections. Also Prepares Cash Flow, Profit & Loss & Balance Sheet Spreadsheets for Three Years. Includes Sample Business Plan.

HP AdvanceWrite Plus. *Compatible Hardware:* Hewlett-Packard, IBM PC & compatibles. *Memory Required:* 640k. *General Requirements:* Hard disk.
disk $710.00.
Designed to Replace HP ADVANCEWRITE III Software. New Features Include the Ability to Integrate Graphics & Scanned Images into Documents, Fill Out Paper Forms, & Perform Mathematical Equations.
Hewlett-Packard Co.

HP Plotter Emulator. *Items Included:* Full manual. No other products required. *Customer Support:* Free telephone support - no time limit. 30 day warranty.
MS-DOS 3.2 or higher. IBM & compatibles (512k). disk $9.95.
HPGL Output Is Widely Used in Graphics Software Such as AutoCAD, Generic CADD, MathCAD, SAS, MICROCADAM, Schema, & More. The HP PLOTTER EMULATOR Can Print & Display the Associated Plotfiles. It Has Native Mode Drivers for Epson & NEC Compatible 9- & 24-Pin Dot Matrix Printers; HP Laserjet, Deskjet, & PaintJet; IBM 9- & 24-Pin Proprinters; Quietwriter 2 & 3; & the LaserPrinter. Includes 26-Page Printed Manual.
Dynacomp, Inc.

HP Softfonts. *Compatible Hardware:* IBM PC & compatibles.
disk $200.00, ea. typeface.
Font Libraries. Typefaces Available Include: Century Schoolbook, Headline Typefaces, ITC Garamond, Letter Gothic, Prestige, Elite, TmsRmn/Helv, Zaph Humanist.
Hewlett-Packard Co.

HP TechWriter. *Compatible Hardware:* HP Series 200 Models 216/220, 226/236, 217/237 Personal Technical Computers with I/O PROM. *Memory Required:* 512k.
HP 216/220, 226/236. 3-1/2" or 5-1/4" disk

$795.00 ea. (Order no.: 98819A).
HP 217/237. 5-1/4" disk $795.00 ea.
Document Editor That Eliminates the Need for a Technical Professional to "Cut & Paste" Pictures into Memos & Documents. Accepts Pictures from Any Graphics Editor Capable of Producing Plot Files. Allows the User to Reference These Processed Plot Files from a Document, View Both Text & Pictures on the Screen As They Should Appear in the Document, & Produce a Hard Copy of the Document. Supported Graphics Editors Include: Project Management (Rev. B), Graphics Presentations (Rev. D), Statistics Library (Rev. B), & EGS/200.
Hewlett-Packard Co.

HP-UX BASIC. *Compatible Hardware:* HP Series 200 HP-UX the Integral PC. *Operating System(s) Required:* UNIX.
3.5" disk $295.00 (Order no.: 82860J).
Lets Users Take Advantage of the Graphics & I/O Capability of the Integral PC. Users Can Also Call Routines Written in C for Further Expandability.
Hewlett-Packard Co.

HP-UX C Compiler. *Compatible Hardware:* HP Series 200 HP-UX the Integral PC. *Operating System(s) Required:* UNIX.
3.5" disk $295.00 (Order no.: 82857J).
Standard C Compiler Including the MC68000 Assembler Libraries & on/off Documentation.
Hewlett-Packard Co.

HP-UX Development System. *Compatible Hardware:* HP Series 200 HP-UX the Integral PC. *Operating System(s) Required:* UNIX.
3.5" disk $495.00 (Order no.: 82856J).
Provides the Capabilities & Features Normally Expected with a Single-User UNIX Operating System. Includes File System Management, Program Preparation, Text Processing, & Communications.
Hewlett-Packard Co.

HP 48SX Engineering Mathematics Library. John F. Holland. Aug. 1992. *Items Included:* 1 ROM card, 656 page user manual. *Customer Support:* Free customer support available through software developer (i.e., John F. Holland).
ROM card for the HP48SX calculator. disk $149.95 (ISBN 0-12-352380-X, Order no.: 1-800-321-5068).
Consists of a ROM Card Which Provides 1109 User Programmable Commands & Thousands of Complex Functions Covering the Spectrum of Applied & Engineering Mathematics. MATHLIB Has a User-Friendly Interface via a Special System of 34 Menus.
Academic Pr., Inc.

HPAC Details. Oct. 1988. *Operating System(s) Required:* PC-DOS/MS-DOS. *Memory Required:* 640k. *General Requirements:* AutoCAD version 10 or higher.
3.5" or 5.25" disk $250.00.
demo disk $10.00.
A Drawing Library of Details Commonly Used in Project HVAC & Plumbing Drawings. These Details Can Be Retrieved, Modified, & Inserted Using AutoCAD Release 10 or 11. Details Include Control Diagrams, Ductwork, Piping, Pumps, Fans, Chiller, Boiler, AC Units, Plumbing, Water Heaters, etc. More than 100 Details are Available in DWG Format. A Manual Illustrates Each Detail & Drawing Filename.
E. Jessup & Assocs.

HPGL Spooler. Jun. 1990. *Items Included:* Reference manual, product registration form. *Customer Support:* Free unlimited phone support. Macintosh (1Mb). 3.5" disk $195.00. *Optimal configuration:* Macintosh, hard disk. *Networks supported:* Appletalk, TOPS.
Utility That Allows Un-Attended Plotting of Single or Multiple HPGL Language Files to Plotters with Roll-Feed, or Automatic Sheet Feed Options. Users Can Queue Lists of Files for Plotting. Lists are Then Saved for Replotting Undated Drawings. This Effectively Creates an Archive That is Always Available. The Spooler Also Runs in a Background Mode under MultiFinder, Leaving the Computer Free to Proceed with Other Important Current Work.
Forthought, Inc.

HPIPE: Hydronic Pipe Sizing. *Items Included:* Manual. *Customer Support:* Toll free telephone support.
IBM PC & compatibles (256k). disk $395.00.
Sizes Pipe & Simulates Flow Conditions for Pipe Networks, Including Chilled & Hot Water Piping Systems. Systems Can Range from Simple to the Most Complex, & Any Non-Compressible Fluid is Allowed. Built-in Library Data for Many Different Pipe Materials, Valves, Fittings, Pumps, & Coils are Supplied with Program.
Elite Software Development, Inc.

HRVantage. *Items Included:* Implementation workbook. *Customer Support:* Toll-free technical support, documentation, usergroups & conferences, client training, data conversion, implementation & customization assistance - prices vary.
Windows 3.1, PC-DOS/MS-DOS. IBM, PS/2 & compatibles. Contact publisher for price. *Nonstandard peripherals required:* 20Mb minimum hard disk & 30Mb disk drive. *Addl. software required:* Microsoft Access. *Networks supported:* Microsoft LAN Manager, Novell Netware, Banyan Vines.
Designed Using the Industry-Standard Technology of MICROSOFT's ACCESS Database Management System. Provides Comprehensive HR Management. Total Functionality Is Achieved Through Easy Data Entry & Retrieval, Advanced Data Analysis Features, Unlimited History Tracking & the Most Powerful Reporting Capabilities Available in a Graphic Environment. System Navigation Is Easy, As Mouse Interaction Allows the User to Simply Point to Information for Most Reports, Queries & Analyses. Measure the Pulse of Your Organization & Put Issues into Perspective in Just Minutes with This Intuitive System. A User-Friendly Graphic Environment Visually Prompts the User with Buttons, Tool Bars, Pull down Menus & Point & Click Selection Options.
SPECTRUM Human Resource Systems Corp.

HRVantage for Client/Server. Dec. 1995. *Customer Support:* Toll-free technical support, documentation, on-site training, users groups, users conferences, data conversion, implementation & customization assistance - prices vary.
File Server: Windows NT 3.51, SQL Server for Windows NT 6.0, Workstation: Microsoft Access 2.0, Windows 95 or Windows NT (Server: 96Mb, Workstation 32Mb). Pentium (dual recommended. CD-ROM disk Contact publisher for price. *Addl. software required:* Windows for Workgroups, 3.11.
A Full-Featured, Visually Oriented System That Accesses, Analyzes, & Graphically Presents Enterprise - Wide Information. By Utilizing a Microsoft Access Front-End & a Microsoft SQL Server Back End, HRVantage Delivers on the Promises of Intelligently Distributed, Scalable Computing Within a Balanced & Fully Integrated Environment. Enables Organizations to Quickly & Easily Generate Complex Queries, Colorful Graphical Analyses & Attractive Reports with Point & Click Ease.
SPECTRUM Human Resource Systems Corp.

HTML Template Master CD. Christopher D. Watkins & Erica Sadun. May 1995. *Items Included:* Simple instructions/licenses. *Customer Support:* Technical support, 30 day unlimited warranty, site license available.
Windows 3.1; Mac System 6. IBM PC or compatible (4Mb); Mac Quadra or higher (4Mb). CD-ROM disk $39.95 (ISBN 1-886801-06-1). *Nonstandard peripherals required:* CD drive.
Nonstandard peripherals required: CD drive. This CD-ROM Teaches HTML Coding Through On-Line Templates & Clip Art. Create Logos, Home-Pages, & Other Designs via Point & Click. Multiplatform (MAC & Windows). General Instructions & Tutorial for Anchors, Bookmarks, Images, Etc.
Charles River Media.

Huang's I Ching. (Ancient Arts Ser.). Kerson Huang. *Compatible Hardware:* Apple II with Applesoft, Apple II+, IIe, IIc, III. *Operating System(s) Required:* Apple DOS. *Memory Required:* 48k. *Items Included:* Manual. *Customer Support:* Free phone support.
disk $49.95 (ISBN 0-87199-031-8).
Casts & Interprets Single or Multiple I Ching Hexagrams; Has Short I Ching Tutorial.
Astrolabe, Inc.

Huang's I Ching 2000. Kerson Huang. 1987. *Compatible Hardware:* IBM PC & compatibles. *Memory Required:* 128k. *General Requirements:* Printer. *Items Included:* Manual. *Customer Support:* Free phone support.
disk $49.95 (ISBN 0-87199-064-4).
Allows User to Cast & Interpret the Hexagram of the Moment with Its Changing Lines. Optional Printout Includes User's Questions & I Ching's Answer. The Revised Version Includes a New Translation from the Original Chinese, Plus a Modern Commentary. Also Includes a Tutorial on the I Ching.
Astrolabe, Inc.

Huckleberry Finn & Tom Sawyer, Vol. 3. Version: 1.5. Feb. 1995. *Items Included:* BookWorm Student Reader (diskette). *Customer Support:* 30 day MBG. Technical support (toll call) - no charge.
System 7.0 or higher. Macintosh (5Mb). CD-ROM disk $59.95 (ISBN 1-57316-035-0, Order no.: 19003). *Nonstandard peripherals required:* CD-ROM drive, 12" color monitor. *Optimal configuration:* 13" color monitor recommended.
Windows 3.1 or higher. IBM compatible (MPC) 386 DX (4Mb). CD-ROM disk $59.95. *Nonstandard peripherals required:* Standard multimedia compatible CD-ROM. *Optimal configuration:* 8Mb RAM recommended, 256 color monitor recommended.
Huckleberry Finn & Tom Sawyer, Two of America's Favorite Characters Are Together in This Volume Featuring Mark Twain. Rendered Directly from the Original Manuscript. Includes the Original Illustrations. Features Complete Sound Allowing the User to Listen to All or Part of Each Work.
Communication & Information Technologies, Inc. (CIT).

Hugh Johnson's Wine Cellar: A Wine & Food Companion. Brandon Ross & Wetzel Reid. Feb. 1987. *Compatible Hardware:* IBM PC, PC XT, PC AT. *Operating System(s) Required:* PC-DOS 2.0 or higher for IBM PC, PC XT; PC-DOS 3.0 or higher for IBM PC AT. *Memory Required:* 256k. *General Requirements:* 2 disk drives; printer recommended.
disk $69.95 (ISBN 0-671-61992-6).
Provides a Master List of More Than 1000 Wines from All over the World That Can Be Searched

According to Various Criteria. Contains Vintage Charts That Give Advice on Optimum Drinking Years for Various Wines & Show the Qualities of Vintages Dating Back to 1928.
Brady Computer Bks.

The Human Brain: Neurons. Aug. 1986. *Compatible Hardware:* Apple II, II+, IIe, IIc, IIgs. *Memory Required:* 64k.
$49.95.
Neuronal Structure, Types of Neurons, Electrical Potentials, Synaptic Transmission, & Neurotransmitters Are Reviewed.
Biosource Software.

Human Resources Management & Imaging System: HR. *Version:* 5.8. May 1993. *Customer Support:* 90 days initial service, full & update service by quotation.
DEC VMS, Open VMS. source code by quotation.
Applies Imaging Technology to Human Resources Management. An Electronic Employee File Instantaneously Recalls Images to the Screen: Applications, Photographs, Forms, Licenses, Claims, etc. Tracks Attendance, Benefits, Events, Reviews, Salaries. Comprehensive Internal & Government Reporting, Interface with Payroll Management, More.
Compu-Share, Inc.

Human Resources Management System: HRMS. Sep. 1985. *Operating System(s) Required:* MS-DOS. *Memory Required:* 512k.
disk $18,500.00.
Integrates Micro-Based Personnel Software with Mainframe Payroll Processing to Provide a Leading Edge Human Resources Management Solution for Companies with 100 to 5,000 Employees. Integrates with CDBC's Payroll-4 Service Through Use of ORCHESTRATOR, Its Mainframe Micro Link Software. LAN Capability.
Control Data Business Management Services.

Human Resources Simulation for Lotus 1-2-3. 1989.
IBM PC. contact publisher for price (ISBN 0-538-07834-0, Order no.: G838).
IBM PS/2. contact publisher for price (ISBN 0-538-07836-7, Order no.: G8382).
Supplemental Package that Provides Students with Decision-Making Experience with Commonly Encountered Situations in a Typical Human Resources Information System. Setting is "Metro Hospital." Problems & Exercises Portray the Pros & Cons of Such a System. An Intro. to the Basics of Lotus 1-2-3 is Provided in the Student Book.
South-Western Publishing Co.

Humble Expert System Shell. *Version:* 2.0. *Compatible Hardware:* Apple Macintosh Plus. *Memory Required:* 1000k. *General Requirements:* Hard disk drive; Smalltalk-80 Programming Environment.
3.5" disk $395.00.
Expert System Development Tool for the Smalltalk-80 Programming Environment.
Xerox Corp.

HUMBUG. *Compatible Hardware:* Motorola 6800/6809/68000 CPUs. *Language(s):* Assembly (source code included).
contact publisher for price.
Debugging Tool for 68000, 6800 & 6809-Based Systems.
Star-K Software Systems Corp.

Hummingbird Laboratory System. Jan. 1986. *Compatible Hardware:* IBM PC & compatibles. *Operating System(s) Required:* MS-DOS/Novell Netware. *Language(s):* TurboPascal. *Memory Required:* 4000k. *General Requirements:* 40Mb hard disk. *Customer Support:* 24 hours, 7 days a week.
Single user. $10,000.00-$20,000.00.
Multi-user. $15,000.00-$75,000.00.
Includes Expanded Patient Reports, Cumulative Summary Reports, Windows Functions, Billing Module, Management Reports, & Modules for All Lab Departments.
LCI.

The Hunt for Red October. *Compatible Hardware:* Apple II, IIgs, Macintosh; Commodore 64/128, Amiga; Atari ST; IBM PC & compatibles. *Memory Required:* Apple II 128k; Commodore 64k; IBM, Atari, Amiga, Apple IIgs, Macintosh 512k. *General Requirements:* Joystick or mouse.
Apple. 3.5" disk $39.95 (ISBN 0-88717-244-X, Order no.: 16200-43499).
Commodore 64/128. disk $39.95 (ISBN 0-88717-220-2, Order no.: 16201-43499).
Commodore Amiga. 3.5" disk $49.95 (ISBN 0-88717-217-2, Order no.: 16202-4399).
IBM. 3.5" or 5.25" disk $49.95 (ISBN 0-88717-219-9, Order no.: 16204-43499).
Atari. 3.5" disk $49.95 (ISBN 0-88717-218-0, Order no.: 16209-43499).
Apple IIgs. 3.5" disk $49.95 (ISBN 0-88717-245-8, Order no.: 16205-43499).
Apple Macintosh. 3.5" disk $49.95 (ISBN 0-88717-246-6, Order no.: 16207-43499).
Direct from the Pages of Tom Clancy's Best-Selling Novel Comes the Ultimate Submarine Combat Simulation. The Games Options Are Icon-Driven & Allow Commander-Friendly Control of the Red October.
IntelliCreations, Inc.

The Hunt for Red October.
IBM & compatibles. 3.5" or 5.25" disk $24.95. *Optimal configuration:* IBM PC, XT, AT; CGA, EGA; hard disk; keyboard, joystick or mouse.
Macintosh (1Mb). 3.5" disk $24.95. *Optimal configuration:* Macintosh Plus, SE; 1Mb, 800k drive; hard disk; mouse.
Test Your Brilliance in Stealth, Evasion & Navigation As Commander of the Red October, in the Ultimate Submarine Simulation Game.
Software Toolworks.

Hunt the Wumpus. *Compatible Hardware:* TI-99/4A with PLATO interpreter solid state cartridge.
contact publisher for price (Order no.: PHM 3023).
A Hunt in a Hidden Maze of Caverns & Twisted Tunnels. Seek Out the Lair of the Wumpus While Avoiding Perils along the Way.
Texas Instruments, Personal Productivit.

The Hunter. *Compatible Hardware:* IBM PC & compatibles. *Operating System(s) Required:* PC-DOS/MS-DOS. *Memory Required:* 256k. *General Requirements:* Hard disk recommended. *Items Included:* 32 pg. Thinking Software catalog.
3.5" or 5.25" disk $29.95.
Can Search for a File on a Hard Disk by File Name or by File Contents. Allows Users to Enter a Starting Directory. Scans Through a 80Mb Hard Disk in Less Than Three Minutes.
Thinking Software, Inc.

HUPBEN: Hospital & University Personal Benefits System. *Version:* 4.3. Mar. 1987. *Items Included:* User manual. *Customer Support:* 90 days unlimited support after installation & training, ongoing support & maintenance $450/yr.
PC-DOS (512k). PC AT & compatibles. $3000.00, network $4000.00 (ISBN 0-928246-03-5). *Nonstandard peripherals required:* Hard disk. *Addl. software required:* "PC Anywhere" for remote support. *Optimal configuration:* Mono or color monitor; 640k RAM; DOS 3.30. *Networks supported:* Novell.
Multi-User Hospital & University Personnel Benefits Management System. Designed for a Large Department at Hospital of University of Pennsylvania & Tracks All Employees by Title & Position, Produces an Historical Position & Title "Tenure Track" Report As Well As Classic Minority Reports. Also Contains a Salary Source Porgram for Each Employee & Allows Personnel Administrator to Track up to Twenty Salary Sources per Employee.
HEL Custom Software, Inc.

Hustle. *Compatible Hardware:* TI 99/4A. contact publisher for price (Order no.: PHM3034).
Direct a Snake-Like Object to Hit Targets While Avoiding Your Opponent, the Edge of the Screen & Yourself.
Texas Instruments, Personal Productivit.

HVAC Design. *Customer Support:* 800-929-8117 (customer service).
MS-DOS. Apple II. disk $199.99 (ISBN 0-87007-521-7).
Calculates & Designs an HVAC System Based on ASHRAE Methods. CLTD, CLF, Radiant Heat, Timed Lag of Internal & External Sensible Loads Can be Calculated for Whole Buildings up to 30 Rooms.
SourceView Software International.

HVAC Tools: A Collection of HVAC Utilities. Jun. 1989. *Items Included:* Bound user manual. *Customer Support:* Unlimited toll-free telephone support (800) 648-9523.
MS-DOS (256k). IBM PC, PC XT, PC AT AT 286, 386. disk $149.00. *Optimal configuration:* Hard disk (20Mb); color monitor. *Networks supported:* All networks supported.
Allows Quick Calculation of 11 Common HVAC Design Tasks. These Include Duct Sizing, Wire Sizing, Three-Way Coil Interpolation, Mixed Air & State Point Psychometrics, Fan Curve & Cost Analysis, U-Factor Calculations. Refrigeration Line Sizing, Hydraulic Pipe Sizing, & Quick Look-Up of Common HVAC Formulas & Conversion Factors. Minimal Input Required; One Key Produces Formatted Reports. Many Functions Can Be Made Memory Resident.
Elite Software Development, Inc.

Hyatt Legal Services: Home Lawyer. *Version:* 2.0. Joel Hyatt & OverDrive Systems. Feb. 1990. *Items Included:* Reference manual. *Customer Support:* Free technical support (216) 292-3410, 9:00 - 6:00 PM, M-F.
DOS 2.0 or higher. IBM PC & compatibles (256K). disk $49.95. *Optimal configuration:* Hard disk.
Lets User Create Change or Update 16 of the Most Frequently Needed Legal Documents. Included Are: General & Medical Power of Attorney, Residential Lease, Independent Contractor Agreement, Last Will & Testament (Which is Valid in Every State Except Louisiana), Bill of Sale & More.
Meca Ventures, Inc.

HyBase (DBMS for Mac). *Version:* 3.0 & 3.0N. Jun. 1991. *Compatible Hardware:* Apple Macintosh. *Memory Required:* 2000k minimum; recommended 4000k. *General Requirements:* Hard disk; HyperCard software. *Items Included:* manual, diskettes & DEMO.
$450.00 Version 3.0, Single User.
$2000.00 & up, Version 3.0N (1 server & 3 clients).
A Complete Database Programming Environment. Its Client/Server Architecture Includes Full Object-Oriented Features for Development Modularity & Ease of Maintenance, Together with Popular SQL

TITLE INDEX

Features, Such As Select. Features Flexible Data Models That Combine the Best Features of Relational, SQL & Object-Oriented Technology. It Supports Multiple Front-Ends, Such As HyperCard, SuperCard, Plus, etc. It Handles Various Kinds of Data Objects, Such As Integers, Strings (with No Length Restriction), Dates, CRSR, PICT Resources or Even Objects That a User Creates. A Report Writer, Together with a Client API for "C" or Pascal, Are Also Provided.
Answer Software Corp.

Hydrant Flow Records. *Items Included:* Bound manual. *Customer Support:* Free hotline - no time limit; 30 day limited warranty; updates are $5/disk plus S&H.
MS-DOS 2.0 or higher. IBM & compatibles (256k). full system $295.00. *Nonstandard peripherals required:* Hard disk recommended, but not necessary; supports both monochrome & color displays, as well as an 80-column (or wider) printer.
demo disk $10.00.
Automates the Preparation of Hydrant Flow Test Reports & the Associated Record Keeping. Just Fill in the Screen Blanks Using Your Flow Test Data. Then, by Simply Pressing a Key, You Can Calculate Individual Flows from Each Hydrant, Total Test Flow, & Flows at Other Pressures. Other Features Include: Hydrant History Reports; Calculates Flow at Residual Pressure; Automatically Scaled Flow Versus Pressure Graph.
Dynacomp, Inc.

Hydraulic Pipe Design. *Items Included:* Bound manual. *Customer Support:* Free hotline - no time limit; 30 day limited warranty; updates are $5/disk plus S&H.
MS-DOS. IBM & compatibles (256k). full system $139.95. *Nonstandard peripherals required:* 80-column (or wider) printer.
demo disk $5.00.
Interactively Sizes Pipes for Hydraulic (H20) Systems Which Do Not Have Interconnected Loops. It Calculates Pressure Drop, Velocity, & Volume for Each Pipe Section & Recommends the Correct Pipe Size for the Normal Velocity Range. User May Override the Recommendation for Retrofit Work, to Eliminate Odd Sizes, etc.
Dynacomp, Inc.

Hydraulic Pipe Design - HP2M. *Version:* 09/1995. 1979. *Compatible Hardware:* IBM PC & compatibles. *Operating System(s) Required:* MS-DOS, PC-DOS. *Language(s):* Compiled. *Memory Required:* 256k. *Customer Support:* Technical hotline, "Lifetime" support at no charge. $145.00.
Hydraulic Pipe Design - HP2M Uses Standard Velocity Tables, NFPA & ASHRAE Pressure Drop Equations to Size Pipes for Hydraulic Systems. Highly Automated; Fully Prompted & Compiled. Menu Driven. SI Metric or English Units.
MC2 Engineering Software.

Hydro-Metallurgical Fundamentals: Metropro. Jul. 1984. *Compatible Hardware:* IBM PC & compatibles. *Language(s):* BASIC. *Memory Required:* 64k.
disk $25.00.
IBM PC. (ISBN 0-931821-02-9, Order no.: 07011).
Seven Programs Cover Slurry Calculations, Slurry Distribution, Screen Distribution, & Hydrocyclones. Slurry Calculations Calculates Pertinent Property Data for Slurries: Specific Gravity, Percent Volume, GPM Slurry & Water Based On Ore Specific Gravity & Rate. Slurry Distribution Calculates "Overs" & "Unders" for Open Circuit or Closed Circuit Screen Configurations Including Recirculating Load.
Information Resource Consultants.

Hydro-Metallurgical Leaching Process Equipment: Hydropro. *Version:* 2. Jan. 1988. *Compatible Hardware:* IBM PC. *Language(s):* BASIC. *Memory Required:* 64k.
disk $50.00.
IBM. (ISBN 0-931821-06-1, Order no.: 01-141).
Three Programs Cover Slurry Pressure Drop, Thickener Sizing, & Extraction & Leaching. Slurry Pressure Drop Calculates Two Phase Vehicle Pressure Drop for Heterogeneous Slurry Flow in Pipes. This Is an Interactive Program with Slurry Viscosity Trial Input Until Closure. Full Vehicle & Slurry Conditions Are Outputted. Thickener Sizing Calculates Diameter, Compression Zone & Center Well Depth Plus Compression Zone & Underflow Stream Property Data Based on Typical Free Settling & Compression Thickener Test Data. Extraction/Leaching Calculates Extract and Feed Forward Stream Data and Determines the Number of Units for Batch Leaching, Continuous Leaching with Constant Underflow, Constant Overflow & Continuous Counterflow Leaching with Variable Underflow.
Information Resource Consultants.

Hydro-Pack. *Version:* 6.0. Jan. 1990. *Items Included:* Reference manual & formula book. *Customer Support:* Free product/technical support available over the phone.
MS-DOS/PC-DOS. IBM XT/AT/386 & compatibles. disk $245.00.
Package Provides 26 Engineering Programs, Designed by Professional Engineers, in Areas Such As: Hydraulics, Structures, Mathmatics, etc. These Are Programs Routinely Used in Organizations Dealing with Fluids & Gases. These Programs Can Eliminate the Time Lost Searching for Formulas in Handbooks & Textbooks. They Reduce Calculating Hours & Eliminate Errors.
Unik Assocs.

Hydro-Pack Hydraulics Analysis. *Items Included:* Bound manual. *Customer Support:* Free hotline - no time limit; 30 day limited warranty; updates are $5/disk plus S&H.
MS-DOS 2.0 or higher. IBM & compatibles (640k). disk $239.95. *Nonstandard peripherals required:* Printer supported, but not necessary.
A Collection of Hydraulic Engineering Programs for Analyzing Specific Hydraulics Problems. Some Calculations Provided Are: Pressure Loss Through Valves; Friction Head Loss in Pipes; Fluid Pressure on a Piston; Speed of an Actuator; Work & Power; Horsepower & Torque; Hydraulic Systems; Centrifugal Pump Head & More.
Dynacomp, Inc.

HYDRO-1. *Version:* 3.0. Apr. 1990. *Compatible Hardware:* IBM PC, PC XT, PC AT, PS/2. *Operating System(s) Required:* MS-DOS. *Language(s):* QuickBASIC. *Memory Required:* 640k.
$795.00.
Hydrostatics & Intact Stability. Calculates Equilibrium Flotation Planes for Any Symmetric Vessel at Arbitrary Loadings & Heel Angles. Equilibriates Trim As Well As Sinkage. Cycles Through Waterlines or Heel Angles Automatically to Generate Data for Curves Form & Cross Curves of Stability.
AeroHydro, Inc.

HYDRO-2. *Version:* 3.0. Apr. 1990. *Compatible Hardware:* IBM PC, PC XT, PC AT, PS/2. *Operating System(s) Required:* MS-DOS. *Language(s):* QuickBASIC. *Memory Required:* 640k.
$1295.00.
Damaged Stability & Floodable Length. In Addition to HYDRO-1 Capabilities, Allows Flooding of Any Combination of Transverse Compartments, with Specified Permeabilities. Automates Calculation of Floodable Length from Section Areas.
AeroHydro, Inc.

Hydrodata Monthly Summary GIS. May 1994. *Items Included:* Bound Documentation, License. *Customer Support:* Unlimited telephonic support. On-Site by contract.
Designed for use with ESRI software. System configuration for software use varies: DOS, Windows, UNIX. CD-ROM disk $995.00 (ISBN 1-884632-01-7). *Addl. software required:* ArcView, ArcInfo, PC ArcInfo, ArcCAD.
Summary Statistical Analyses on over 74,000 Daily Meteorological Observations at over 31,000 Observation Stations. USGS WATSTORE Daily Streamflow Data Is the Basis for Statistical Summaries. Native ArcInfo, ArcView, & ArcCAD Data Sets. We Are an ESRI Authorized ArcData Publisher.
Hydrosphere Data Products, Inc.

Hydrodata STORET GIS. Oct. 1994. *Items Included:* Bound Documentation, License. *Customer Support:* Unlimited telephonic support. On-Site by contract.
Designed for use with ESRI software. System configuration for software use varies: DOS, Windows, UNIX. CD-ROM disk $995.00 (ISBN 1-884632-02-5). *Addl. software required:* ArcView, ArcInfo, PC ArcInfo, ArcCAD.
Summary Statistical Analyses for More Than 700,000 Measurement Stations Nationwide. Entire Record of Water Quality Observations. US EPA STORET Data Is the Basis for Statistical Summaries. Native ArcInfo, ArcView, & ArcCAD Data Sets. We Are an ESRI Authorized ArcData Publisher.
Hydrosphere Data Products, Inc.

Hydrodata USGS Daily Values. *Version:* 5.0. Jan. 1993. *Items Included:* Bound Documentation, License. *Customer Support:* Unlimited telephonic support. On-Site by contract.
DOS. IBM-PC or compatible 20 mg Hard Drive (512k). CD-ROM disk $995.00, Subscribe ,495.00 year one, ,250.00 future years (ISBN 1-884632-06-8). *Nonstandard peripherals required:* CD-ROM Drive. *Addl. software required:* MS Extention 2.0 Plus or substitute. *Optimal configuration:* 640k RAM, 20mg Hard Drive Math Coprocessor.
USGS WATSTORE Daily Streamflow Values for over 100 Years at Gauging Stations in All 50 States. Access via Our Proprietary Data Retrieval Software. Includes Some Climatological & Water Quality Data.
Hydrosphere Data Products, Inc.

Hydrodata USGS Peak Values. *Version:* 4.0. Jan. 1993. *Items Included:* Bound Documentation, License. *Customer Support:* Unlimited telephonic support. On-Site by contract.
DOS. IBM-PC or compatible 20 mg Hard Drive (512k). CD-ROM disk $995.00, Subscribe ,495.00 year one, ,250.00 future years (ISBN 1-884632-07-6). *Nonstandard peripherals required:* CD-ROM Drive. *Addl. software required:* MS Extention 2.0 Plus or substitute. *Optimal configuration:* 640k RAM, 20mg Hard Drive Math Coprocessor.
USGS WATSTORE Peak Streamflow Values for over 100 Years at Gauging Stations in All 50 States. Access via Our Proprietary Data Retrieval Software. Flood Flow & Ranking Information. National Coverage One Disc.
Hydrosphere Data Products, Inc.

Hydropac 2 Storm Drainage Design. *Items Included:* Full manual. No other products required. *Customer Support:* Free telephone support - no time limit. 30 day warranty.
MS-DOS 3.2 or higher. IBM & compatibles (512k). disk $495.00. *Optimal configuration:* IBM, MS-DOS 3.2 or higher, 640k RAM, & hard drive. Printer is optional.
Includes All of the Analyses Needed for Storm

Drainage Design, Sediment Basin Sizing & Detention Basin Sizing (Including Grade & Vertical Curve Calculations). Further, Can Transfer Storm Sewer Profiles & Hydraulic Gradients to AUTOcad Using HYDROpac's DXF Files. This Takes the Work Out of Storm Drainage Computation & Profile Generation for Site, Roadway & Subdivision Design. Comprehensive & Well-Tested.
Dynacomp, Inc.

Hydroworks: Hydraulic & Pneumatic Schematics. *Items Included:* Bound manual. *Customer Support:* Free hotline - no time limit; 30 day limited warranty; updates are $5/disk plus S&H.
MS-DOS 2.0 or higher. IBM & compatibles (384k). disk $849.95. *Nonstandard peripherals required:* Two disk drives (or a floppy & a hard disk); parallel printer port; CGA or EGA (or equivalent) with a color monitor; Microsoft (or compatible) mouse.
Package for Drawing Hydraulic or Pneumatic Schematics. Features an Extensive Symbol Library of Common Power Unit Arrangements, Directional Control Valves, Check Valves, Regulators, Filters, Cylinders, Accumulators, & Discrete Components. Completed Schematics Are Generated by Interconnecting the Desired Library Elements with Flow or Pilot Lines. Components May Be Moved, Copied, Deleted, Mirrored, or Rotated.
Dynacomp, Inc.

Hyper-Action. *Compatible Hardware:* Apple Macintosh Plus. *General Requirements:* Hard disk drive; HyperCard.
3.5" disk $94.50.
Professional Information Manager Used to Consolidate & Bring Order & Control to a User's Daily Personal, Sales & Business Activities.
Multi Soft, Inc.

Hyper Estimator. *Version:* 1.1. Oct. 1988. *Compatible Hardware:* Apple Macintosh Plus or higher. *General Requirements:* Hard disk drive; HyperCard provided with program. *Items Included:* HyperCard, user manual. *Customer Support:* Free phone support (toll call).
3.5" disk $95.00.
with Hyper-Remodeler $145.00.
Designed for Architects, Builders or Homeowners Who Are Planning Residential Construction Projects. The Program Finds the Approximate Cost of Additions, New Construction or Total Rehabilitation Work.
Turtle Creek Software.

Hyper Remodeler. *Version:* 1.1. Apr. 1989. *Items Included:* HyperCard included with program, user manual included. *Customer Support:* Free phone support (toll call).
Apple Macintosh (1Mb). Plus, Classic, SE, SE/30 or any II. $95.00 or $145.00 if combined with Hyper.Estimator. *Nonstandard peripherals required:* Hard disk required. *Addl. software required:* HyperCard - provided with program. *Optimal configuration:* Hard disk required - any size is OK.
Estimates Construction Costs for Residential Remodeling Projects. Handles Dimensions on a Room by Room Basis. Designed for Builders, Architects or Homeowners.
Turtle Creek Software.

HyperACCESS/5. *Version:* 3.0. Aug. 1992. *Compatible Hardware:* IBM PC, PC XT, PC AT, PS/2, 386, & PC compatibles; Zenith Z-100 (separate version). *Operating System(s) Required:* PC-DOS/MS-DOS 2.0 or higher or OS/2. *Language(s):* C. *Memory Required:* 350k. *Items Included:* Manual. *Customer Support:* 30 day money back guarantee.
DOS $99.95.
DOS & OS/2 Combo Pack $199.00.
ISDN $199.00.
Communications Package. Has the Capability to Adapt Itself to User's Computer & Modem Characteristics. Enables Users to Link to Mainframes, Minis, Micros, or RS-232C Devices. Emulates VT-52, VT-100/102, TeleVideo 925/950, IBM 3101, H-19, & TTY Terminals. Supports up to 19,200 Baud & Transfers Files Using Kermit, XMODEM (CRC or Checksum), YMODEM, & Other ASCII Protocols. Features Mouse Support & Provides Protection Against Viruses. Features Remote Access Capabilities. Can Also Be Set for Unattended Operations, Allowing Authorized Callers To Use the PC without Description.
Hilgraeve, Inc.

HyperAlarms. *Compatible Hardware:* Apple Macintosh Plus. *General Requirements:* HyperCard.
3.5" disk $10.00.
Alarm Clock.
Poor Mans Software.

HyperAtlas. *General Requirements:* HyperCard. Macintosh Plus or higher. 3.5" disk $99.00.
Graphic Interface for Geographically Based Data.
Cartesia Software.

HyperBible: The Computerized Chain Reference Tool. *Compatible Hardware:* Apple Macintosh Plus, SE, SE30, II, IIcx. *Memory Required:* IBM PC's Using Windows 2Mb for Windows; MAC 1000k. *Items Included:* HyperCard (MAC) ToolBook (PC). *Customer Support:* Free, you pay for call 719-594-4884.
King James Version. $199.00. *Nonstandard peripherals required:* Hard disk (9Mb).
New International Version. $199.00.
Computerized Bible Study. Based on the Thompson Chain Reference Bible. Features of the Book Include Topical Cross Referencing with More Than 100,000 Topical References; Pre-Selected Topics for Bible Studies; General Index of More Than 7,000 Topics & Names; Archaeology Information, Electronic Atlas & Pronunciation Assistance.
Beacon Technology, Inc.

HyperCard Authoring Tool for Presentations, Tutorials & Information Exploration. *Version:* 2.0. Dennis Myers & Annette Lamb. Jan. 1990. *Items Included:* Diskette with stack shells & graphics (practice stacks). *Customer Support:* No support provided.
Macintosh Plus, SE, II & IIcx (1Mb). disk $49.95.
Training Program to Show How to Use Apple's HyperCard to Prepare Intructional Materials & Presentations. Discusses Educational Theory As Well As Incorporating Multimedia Such As CD-ROM, Video, Scanners & Digitized Sound.
Career Publishing, Inc.

HyperCard (Mac) Creativity Tool: Student Version for Writing, Organizing & Multimedia. *Version:* 2.0. Annette Lamb & Dennis Myers. 1991. *Customer Support:* Instructor's guide, site license, & student diskette. System 6.0.5 or higher. Macintosh Plus (with two 3.5" drives), Classic, SE, II, IIcx, IIsi (2Mb). Handbook/Workbook $39.95 (ISBN 0-89262-326-8). *Nonstandard peripherals required:* Hard drive recommended.
Instructor's Guide $50.00 (ISBN 0-89262-328-4).
Student Diskette Site License $39.95 (Order no.: CP-HCCTSL).
Provides Step-by-Step Instruction in the Use of HyperCard Version 2.0 As a Personal & Academic Productivity Tool. Also Contains Step-by-Step Instructions on How to Incorporate Technologies Such As Graphics, Scanners, Sound, Laserdiscs, & Compact Discs. Includes Practice Exercises.
Career Publishing, Inc.

HyperCELL, 1995: A Hypermedia Presentation of Cell Biology. Gene R. Williams. Aug. 1994. System 6.0.7 or higher. Macintosh SE, Classic, LC & all members of the II family (2Mb). $1000.00 first year annual site license agreement; $500.00 per year for renewals (ISBN 0-8153-1901-0). *Optimal configuration:* Macintosh, SE, Classic, LC, & all members of the II family, 2Mb RAM, 15Mb hard disk space, System 6.0.7 or higher, HyperCard version 2.1 or higher & a Home stack.
Windows, DOS 3.1 or higher. $1000.00 first year annual site license agreement; $500.00 per year for renewal. *Optimal configuration:* Windows, DOS 3.1 or higher, Microsoft Windows version 3.1 or Microsoft Windows version 3.0 & Multimedia Extensions to Windows, VGA graphics adapter & monitor, Mouse (Microsoft or compatible), 3.5" (1.44M) or 5.25" (1.2M) disk space drive, 24Mb of hard disk space, 4Mb RAM.
A Powerful Cell Biology Teaching Program Consisting of Text, Graphics, & Animated Diagrams That Has Three Major Advantages over Traditional Teaching Approaches: 1. Its Easy-to-Follow Animated Diagrams Illuminate & Clarify Kinetic Cellular Processes That Are Otherwise Difficult for Students to Grasp from Lectures or Textbooks. 2. Its Hypermedia Learning Environment Conveys a Sense of the Complex Interrelationships That Govern Cell Systems. 3. Its Extensive Annual Updates Keep It Close to the Cutting Edge of the Discipline.
Garland Publishing, Inc.

Hyperchem for Windows. *Version:* 2. Mar. 1992. *Items Included:* Three 3-hole punched manuals, 2 perfect bound manuals, forms, binders. *Customer Support:* Provided by local dealers.
MS/PC-DOS 3.1 or higher. IBM 386, 486 & compatibles (4Mb RAM). $3500.00 SRP (ISBN 1-56444-010-9). *Nonstandard peripherals required:* 20Mb available hard disk space; 80387 or 80487 math coprocessor; MS compatible mouse; VGA or better color monitor with VGA or better graphics adapter. *Addl. software required:* MS Windows 3.0 or higher.
Integrates Graphics, Modeling, & Computational Capabilities to Give User Access to the Benefits of Computer-Aided Molecular Design.
Autodesk, Inc.

HyperChen for Windows: Upgrade Pack 1.2 MB Version. *Version:* 3. Hypercube, Inc. Apr. 1993. *Items Included:* 3 3-hole punched manuals & binder; 3 perfect bound manuals; media. *Customer Support:* Support provided by local dealers.
PC-DOS/MS-DOS V3.1 or higher. IBM 386/486 or compatibles; minimu 20k available hard disk space (4Mb). disk $3500.00 SRP (ISBN 1-56444-705-7). *Nonstandard peripherals required:* 80387 or 80487 math co-processor, MS compatible mouse, VGA or higher color monotir with VGA or higher. *Addl. software required:* MS Windows 3.0. *Optimal configuration:* IBM or compatible 486 6Mb RAM, 40Mb hard disk, 80486 math co-processor; VGA color monitor & graphics adapter, MS Windows, MS Mouse.
Windows-Based Scientific Software Providing the Ability to Build, Manipulate & Study 3D Molecular Structures on a PC & Use the Data & Graphical Output with Other Windows Applications.
Autodesk, Inc.

TITLE INDEX

HyperChen for Windows: Upgrade Pack 1.44 MB Version. *Version:* 3. Hypercube, Inc. Apr. 1993. *Items Included:* 3 3-hole punched manuals & binder; 3 perfect bound manuals; media. *Customer Support:* Support provided by local dealers.
PC-DOS/MS-DOS V3.1 or higher. IBM 386/486 or compatibles; minimu 20k available hard disk space (4Mb). disk $3500.00 SRP (ISBN 1-56444-704-9). *Nonstandard peripherals required:* 80387 or 80487 math co-processor, MS compatible mouse, VGA or higher color monotir with VGA or higher. *Addl. software required:* MS Windows 3.0. *Optimal configuration:* IBM or compatible 486 6Mb RAM, 40Mb hard disk, 80486 math co-processor; VGA color monitor & graphics adapter, MS Windows, MS Mouse.
Windows-Based Scientific Software Providing the Ability to Build, Manipulate & Study 3D Molecular Structures on a PC & Use the Data & Graphical Output with Other Windows Applications.
Autodesk, Inc.

HyperChen for Windows: 1.2 MB Version. *Version:* 3. Hypercube, Inc. Apr. 1993. *Items Included:* 3 3-hole punched manuals & binder; 3 perfect bound manuals; media. *Customer Support:* Support provided by local dealers.
PC-DOS/MS-DOS V3.1 or higher. IBM 386/486 or compatibles; minimu 20k available hard disk space (4Mb). disk $3500.00 SRP (ISBN 1-56444-702-2). *Nonstandard peripherals required:* 80387 or 80487 math co-processor, MS compatible mouse, VGA or higher color monotir with VGA or higher. *Addl. software required:* MS Windows 3.0. *Optimal configuration:* IBM or compatible 486 6Mb RAM, 40Mb hard disk, 80486 math co-processor; VGA color monitor & graphics adapter, MS Windows, MS Mouse.
Windows-Based Scientific Software Providing the Ability to Build, Manipulate & Study 3D Molecular Structures on a PC & Use the Data & Graphical Output with Other Windows Applications.
Autodesk, Inc.

HyperChen for Windows: 1.2 MB Version. *Version:* 3 (Locked). Hypercube, Inc. Apr. 1993. *Items Included:* 3 3-hole punched manuals & binder; 3 perfect bound manuals; media. *Customer Support:* Support provided by local dealers.
PC-DOS/MS-DOS V3.1 or higher. IBM 386/486 or compatibles; minimu 20k available hard disk space (4Mb). disk $3500.00 SRP (ISBN 1-56444-700-6). *Nonstandard peripherals required:* 80387 or 80487 math co-processor, MS compatible mouse, VGA or higher monotir with VGA or higher. *Addl. software required:* MS Windows 3.0. *Optimal configuration:* IBM or compatible 486 6Mb RAM, 40Mb hard disk, 80486 math co-processor; VGA color monitor & graphics adapter, MS Windows, MS Mouse.
Windows-Based Scientific Software Providing the Ability to Build, Manipulate & Study 3D Molecular Structures on a PC & Use the Data & Graphical Output with Other Windows Applications.
Autodesk, Inc.

HyperChen for Windows: 1.44 MB Version. *Version:* 3. Hypercube, Inc. Apr. 1993. *Items Included:* 3 3-hole punched manuals & binder; 3 perfect bound manuals; media. *Customer Support:* Support provided by local dealers.
PC-DOS/MS-DOS V3.1 or higher. IBM 386/486 or compatibles; minimu 20k available hard disk space (4Mb). disk $3500.00 SRP (ISBN 1-56444-703-0). *Nonstandard peripherals required:* 80387 or 80487 math co-processor, MS compatible mouse, VGA or higher color monotir with VGA or higher. *Addl. software required:* MS Windows 3.0. *Optimal configuration:* IBM or compatible 486 6Mb RAM, 40Mb hard disk, 80486 math co-processor; VGA color monitor & graphics adapter, MS Windows, MS Mouse.
Windows-Based Scientific Software Providing the Ability to Build, Manipulate & Study 3D Molecular Structures on a PC & Use the Data & Graphical Output with Other Windows Applications.
Autodesk, Inc.

HyperChen for Windows: 1.44 MB Version. *Version:* 3 (Locked). Hypercube, Inc. Apr. 1993. *Items Included:* 3 3-hole punched manuals & binder; 3 perfect bound manuals; media. *Customer Support:* Support provided by local dealers.
PC-DOS/MS-DOS V3.1 or higher. IBM 386/486 or compatibles; minimu 20k available hard disk space (4Mb). disk $3500.00 SRP (ISBN 1-56444-701-4). *Nonstandard peripherals required:* 80387 or 80487 math co-processor, MS compatible mouse, VGA or higher color monotir with VGA or higher. *Addl. software required:* MS Windows 3.0. *Optimal configuration:* IBM or compatible 486 6Mb RAM, 40Mb hard disk, 80486 math co-processor; VGA color monitor & graphics adapter, MS Windows, MS Mouse.
Windows-Based Scientific Software Providing the Ability to Build, Manipulate & Study 3D Molecular Structures on a PC & Use the Data & Graphical Output with Other Windows Applications.
Autodesk, Inc.

HyperComposer. *General Requirements:* Two 800K disk drives or hard disk drive; System 4.2 or later (not compatible with System 6.0); Finder 5.3 or later; HyperCard 1.2.1 or later.
Macintosh Plus or higher (1Mb). 3.5" disk $69.95.
Sound & Music Toolkit for HyperCard.
Addison-Wesley Publishing Co., Inc.

HYPERCROSS. *Compatible Hardware:* TRS-80 Model I, Model III, Model 4. *Operating System(s) Required:* CP/M, MS-DOS.
Will Format a Disk Readable by CP/M or MS-DOS (PC-DOS) on a TRS-80 Model I, Model III or Model 4, Depending on Version. Files Can Then Be Copied to the Newly Formatted Diskette & Read Directly on MS-DOS or CP/M Machine.
The Alternate Source.
  HYPERCROSS2-A: CP/M.
    disk $49.95 ea.
    Model I. (Order no.: D1HYCA).
    Model III. (Order no.: D3HYCA).
    Model 4. (Order no.: D4HYCA).
    Supports the Creation & File Transfer to Most Popular CP/M Formats Only.
  HYPERSROSS2-B: PC.
    disk $49.95 ea.
    Model I. (Order no.: D1HYCB).
    Model III. (Order no.: D3HYCB).
    Model 4. (Order no.: D4HYCB).
    Supports the Creation & File Transfer to Most Popular MS-DOS Formats Only.
  HYPERCROSS2-C: XT-70.
    disk $99.95 ea.
    Model I. (Order no.: D1HYCC).
    Model III. (Order no.: D3HYCC).
    Model 4. (Order no.: D4HYCC).
    Suproots the Creation & File Transfer to Most Popular Formats for Both CP/M & MS-DOS (PC-DOS).
  HYPERCROSS2-D: XT-130.
    disk $129.95 ea.
    Model I. (Order no.: D1HYCD).
    Model III. (Order no.: D3HYCD).
    Model 4. (Order no.: D4HYCD).
    Supports over 130 Different CP/M & MS-DOS Popular & Not-So-Popular Diskette Formats. "Deluxe" Version Includes Maximum Support for TRS-80 System.

Hyperdom. *Compatible Hardware:* TRS-80 Model I, Model III, Model 4 with Level II BASIC. (source code included). *Memory Required:* 48k.
disk $18.95.
Dominoes-Type Game.
Dynacomp, Inc.

HyperEngine. *Compatible Hardware:* Apple Macintosh. *Memory Required:* 512k.
3.5" disk $125.00.
Developer Tool That Opens Stacks Within Applications.
Symmetry Corp.

Hyperfile. *Version:* 4.0. *Compatible Hardware:* IBM PC & compatibles, PS/2. *Operating System(s) Required:* MS-DOS, OS/2, UNIX, Windows, Windows for Work Groups, Windows NT. *Memory Required:* 640k.
$195.00 business version.
$995.00 network version.
Intelligent Filing for Windows Text Database System, Unlimited Record Size, Unlimited Records per File. Supports Boolean Searches, & Searches Can Be Directed to a Specific Field or Other Qualifier. Also Features the Ability to Build Own Data Files; Run in Background, As a Desk Accessory & with MultiFinder; Imports, Exports & Appends ASCII Files; Supports Multiple Users; & Looks at File, Record & Item Level.
All Easy Software Corp.

HYPERFILE: Windows Filing Software. *Customer Support:* 90 days free phone support.
MS-DOS 2.0 or higher. IBM PC, XT, AT, PS/2 & compatibles (640k). $495.00 Business version; $999.00 Network version.
Allows User to Set Up Files Similar to Any Professional Office. Requires No Programming. Allows Fast Filing & Retrieval of Hard to Manage Files. May Be Used with Optical Scanners. Will Store Files from Most Popular Programs, i.e., Word, Wordstar, Word Perfect, Lotus, dBase, CAD/CAM etc. Runs under Microsoft Windows. Generates Reports in Any Format. Security Capabilities Include User IDs & Passwords Which Can Be Set Up to Provide Multiple Level Database Security Protection. Will Also Store, Keyword, & Retrieve GRAPHICS files.
All Easy Software Corp.

Hyperfont. Mike Ostendorf. Feb. 1989.
TOS (512k). Atari ST. disk $49.95.
User Designs & Edits Fonts for DTP.
MichTron, Inc.

Hypergate Writer.
Macintosh Plus or higher. 3.5" disk $395.00.
A Professional Tool for Writing Hypertext & Hypermedia Documents. Designed to Support Deeply Intertwined Hypertext, Not Just Stacks of Cards or Scrolling Documents. Includes Key Navigation Tools, Such As Thumb Stacks, Book Marks & Margin Notes & Introduces True Hypertext Index Tools.
Eastgate Systems, Inc.

HyperGene. *Items Included:* Spiral-bound manual. *Customer Support:* Free technical support (504) 649-0484.
OS 6.0 or higher (1Mb). Macintosh Plus or higher. $89.95 (Order no.: 4079). *Addl. software required:* HyperCard.

Genealogy Program That Keeps Track of Relatives by Blood-Line or Marriage. Maintain, Store & Display Information Such As Alias, Spellings, Landholdings, Military History, Artifacts, Documentation, Bibliographies, & Family Anecdotes. Ancestors & Descendents Can Be Viewed or Printed in Tree Format From Any Subject's Point of View.
CompServCo.

HyperHebrew. *Compatible Hardware:* Macintosh Plus or higher. *General Requirements:* HyperCard.
3.5" disk $39.95.
Introduces Hebrew Language Basics.
Davka Corp.

Hyperion. *Version:* 1.5. Jul. 1991. *Items Included:* Reference guide. *Customer Support:* Free telephone support. Training, installation support - varied pricing.
MS-DOS/PC-DOS, MS Windows, Windows NT. 386, 486 & compatibles; DEC Alpha; MIPS RISC. $125,000.00 headquarter site fee. *Nonstandard peripherals required:* VGA Monitor. *Addl. software required:* Microsoft Windows 3.X. *Optimal configuration:* 386 computer or higher with DOS 3.X, 4Mb RAM, VGA, Windows 3.X, mouse. *Networks supported:* 3COM, Banyan Vines, IBM PC LAN, IBM TokenRing, Novell Netware.
Comprehensive Corporate-Wide Business & Financial Reporting Capabilities Within a Graphical Environment. PC-LAN Based, It Combines Sophisticated Functionality with the Convenience, Architectural Advantages, & Productivity Benefits of Microsoft Windows. Collects, Consolidates, & Reports Business Information at Both Corporate & Departmental Levels.
IMRS, Inc.

HyperLibrary. *Version:* 2.0.3. *Compatible Hardware:* Apple Macintosh Plus or higher. *General Requirements:* Hard disk drive; Printer; HyperCard 1.2. *Items Included:* 1 program disk and 1 user's manual. *Customer Support:* Unlimited by mail or FAX.
3.5" disk $15.00.
Reference Tool. Features Include: Online Help, a Precise Description of the Dewey Decimal System, Unprecedented Online Notes Section That Allows a User to Clip Certain Information & Save It for Later, a Large & Diverse Library of Biographical Sources, a Date-Time Stamping Feature for the Online Note Cards Section, a Standard Keyword Search Function, etc.
Friedman Computing & Publishing.

HyperSearch. *Version:* 1.1.3. *Compatible Hardware:* Apple Macintosh. *Memory Required:* 1000k. *General Requirements:* Two 800k disk drives or hard disk; HyperCard.
3.5" disk $119.95.
Flexible Searching System Designed Specifically for Use with HyperCard. Features Various Search Options, Including Boolean Operators, Instant Searching, etc.
Discovery Systems.

HyperSeder. *Compatible Hardware:* Apple Macintosh Plus. *General Requirements:* HyperCard.
3.5" disk $39.95.
Takes User Through the Steps of the Passover Seder, Explaining the Reasons Behind the Various Seder Customs & Showing Them How to Conduct Their Own Passover Seder.
Davka Corp.

HyperShopper. *Compatible Hardware:* Apple Macintosh Plus. *Memory Required:* 1000k. *General Requirements:* Two 800k disk drives or hard disk; Hypercard. *Customer Support:* 8-5 M-F Pacific Time.
3.5" disk $19.95.
Database That List Products from More Than 1, 000 Mail Order Companies.
Camtronics Software.

HyperSift. *Memory Required:* 256k.
PC-DOS 2.0 or higher. IBM. $75.00. *Nonstandard peripherals required:* askSam textbase.
Stand Alone Application with All the Reporting & Retrieval Capabilities of Its Parent Program, the askSam Textbase. Designed for End Users of askSam Textbases Who Use Them for Reference & Reporting with No Need for Modification. Allows Users to Retrieve & Report (But Not Alter) Information in an askSam Textbase. Capabilities Include Executing Stored Programs, Backtracking Through a List of Past Queries, & Printing Reports. Provides an Effective Method of Distributing Textbases to a Large Number of People.
askSam Systems.

HYPERSTAT: Macintosh Hypermedia for Analyzing Data & Learning Statistics. David M. Lane. Jul. 1993. *Items Included:* Two Macintosh disks, 128 page user manual. *Customer Support:* Free customer support available through software developer (i.e., David Lane).
Macintosh System 6.0.5 or higher (1Mb RAM, 2Mb RAM recommended). 3.5" disk $39.95 (ISBN 0-12-436130-7, Order no.: 1-800-321-5068). *Addl. software required:* Hypercard 2.1 or higher, or Hypercard Player 2.1 or higher.
Unique Hypermedia Software Package for the Macintosh. Serves As an Integrated Combination of a Program for Data Analysis, a Hypertext in Statistics, & a Set of Interactive Simulation/Data Analysis Exercises Called "Explorations." It Is Both a Statistics Book That Can Do Calculations & a Statistical Analysis System with a Tremendous Amount of On-Line Help.
Academic Pr., Inc.

Hyperstudio. *Version:* 2.0. May 1993. *Items Included:* Spiral bound User Reference & Tutorial Manual, Sprial bound Hyperlogo Manual, ProDOS Extension. *Customer Support:* Telephone support (619) 442-0522 x13.
System 6.0.8. Macintosh Plus (2Mb). 3.5" disk $199.95, single user (ISBN 0-927796-41-4, Order no.: MRW-023). *Optimal configuration:* Color Macintosh, System 7, 4Mb RAM. *Networks supported:* AppleShare, Novell.
Easy to Use Creative Multimedia Authoring Tool That Does Not Require Knowledge of Scripting of Programming to Use.
Roger Wagner Publishing, Inc.

HyperStudio (IIgs). *Version:* 3.1J. *Compatible Hardware:* Apple IIgs. *Memory Required:* 1000k. *Items Included:* Reference Manual, Tutorial Manual, Sound Digitizing Board, Microphone. *Customer Support:* Phone 619-442-0522 x13.
3.5" disk $199.95 (ISBN 0-927796-39-2, Order no.: GRW-017).
Easy to Use Creative Multimedia Authorizing System.
Roger Wagner Publishing, Inc.

HyperTalk Language Toolkit. *Version:* 4.0. *Customer Support:* Free.
Macintosh Plus or higher. 3.5" disk $495.00.
Allows HyperTalk to Be Embedded into Software Application Products.
Abraxas Software, Inc.

Hypertension Management. Edward P. Hoffer & G. Octo Barnett. Jul. 1985. *Compatible Hardware:* Apple II with 2 disk drives; IBM PC, PCjr with 80 column display, PC XT, PC AT. *Operating System(s) Required:* MS-DOS 2.0 or higher. *Memory Required:* Apple 64k, IBM 128k.
IBM. disk $85.00 (ISBN 0-683-16803-7).
Apple. disk $85.00 (ISBN 0-683-16802-9).
Concentrates on Long Term Management of Hypertension Using Antihypertensive Drugs & Therapies.
Williams & Wilkins.

Hypertensive Emergencies. Edward P. Hoffer & G. Octo Barnett. May 1985. *Compatible Hardware:* Apple II IBM PC, PCjr, PC XT, PC AT. *Operating System(s) Required:* MS-DOS 2.0 or higher. *Memory Required:* Apple 64k, IBM 128k. *General Requirements:* 80-column display; 2 disk drives for Apple.
IBM. disk $85.00 (ISBN 0-683-16801-0).
Apple. disk $85.00 (ISBN 0-683-16800-2).
Features a Series of Simulated Emergencies Involving Patients with Severe and/or Complicated Hypertension.
Williams & Wilkins.

Hypertext. *Compatible Hardware:* IBM PC & compatibles. *Operating System(s) Required:* PC-DOS/MS-DOS. *Memory Required:* 256k. *General Requirements:* Hard disk recommended. *Items Included:* 32 pg. Thinking Software catalog.
3.5" or 5.25" disk $29.95.
Written in HYPERTEXT, Contains a Full Listing & Explanation of the Business Possibilities of This Technology.
Thinking Software, Inc.

Hypertext '87 Digest. *Compatible Hardware:* Apple Macintosh.
3.5" disk $10.00.
Hypertext Document.
Eastgate Systems, Inc.

Hyperwedding Planner. *Version:* 1.1. Oct. 1988. *Compatible Hardware:* Apple Macintosh. *Memory Required:* 1000k. *General Requirements:* Printer, Hypercard.
contact publisher for price.
Database for Planning Weddings. Tracks Guests Invited, Addresses, Table Numbers, Gifts Received, Thank-You's Sent. Generates Labels & Several Different Reports. Also Has Search Functions & Essential Data File (Caterer, Band, Florists, etc.). Features a User-Friendly Rolodex-Type Interface.
Specialized Software.

Hyperworks. *Version:* 1.75. Paul Pearson & Christopher Watson. Sep. 1989. *Items Included:* Manual, ResCopy, ResEdit, & HyperCard software, ShowDialog software (currently included with non-commercial license pre-paid), limited licensing of external resources. *Customer Support:* Limited warranty for 90 days for defective media, Professional version has limited technical support (telephone).
Apple Macintosh (2Mb). $99.95; Professional $149.95. *Nonstandard peripherals required:* Hard disk drive.
Contains Script Tools, Object Tools, Stack Tools, External Resources Stack, Several Practice Stacks. A Supplemental Development Environment & Collection of Integrated Programming Utilities for Apple's Hypercard. Features Include the Workdesk, Script Processor, Resource Installer, Code Cleaner, Optimizer, Updater, Studio ICON, & Studio MENU. Over 30 New Externals.
Hyperworks Software Design & Development.

HyperX. *Version:* 2.0. *Compatible Hardware:* Apple Macintosh Plus. *General Requirements:* Two 800k disk drives or hard disk drive; HyperCard.

3.5" disk $49.95.
Features Include Graphic Rule Map; Integrated Help System & Expanded Tutorial; Forward & Backward Chaining Inference Engine; Attribute Value Pairs & Import & Export Rules As Text & Fact Demons.
Millennium Software.

HYPERZAP. *Compatible Hardware:* TRS-80.
disk $49.95 (Order no.: D8HZAP).
Will Create, Modify & Backup Part or All of Any Floppy Disk.
The Alternate Source.

Hypnosis. *Version:* 2.0. E. Neiburger. 1979. *Compatible Hardware:* Apple II, IIc, IIe; Basis 6502; Franklin Ace; IBM PC, PC XT, PC AT. *Operating System(s) Required:* Apple DOS 3.3, MS-DOS 3.1. *Language(s):* BASIC (source code included). *Memory Required:* 48k.
disk $50.00 (ISBN 0-914555-10-3).
Utilizes Photo-Optic & Acoustic Sensory Stimulation to Induce & Potentiate Hypnotic States.
Andent, Inc.

I Ching: Canon of Change. *Items Included:* Bound manual. *Customer Support:* Free hotline - no time limit; 30 day limited warranty; updates are $5/disk plus S&H.
MS-DOS. IBM & compatibles (256k). disk $49.95. *Nonstandard peripherals required:* Printer supported, but not necessary.
Apple. disk $49.95.
The New Translation of the I Ching Used in This Program Aims to Restore the Original Face of the Book As It Was Written Three-Thousand Years Ago. To That End, the Findings of Modern Archeology & Scholarship Have Been Used to Help Decipher the Meaning of Words & Phrases in the Chinese Original.
Dynacomp, Inc.

I-EMP: Interactive Engineering Math Pack. Richard F. Warriner. Dec. 1984. *Compatible Hardware:* IBM PC, PC XT, PC AT. *Operating System(s) Required:* MS-DOS. *Language(s):* MS-BASIC (source code included). *Memory Required:* 96k.
disk $65.00, incl. manual (ISBN 0-927814-01-3, Order no.: IEMP).
Series of Mathematics Programs Applicable to Engineering Analysis.
R. F. Warriner Assocs.

I/O EXPRESS. *Version:* 2.0. Dec. 1991. *Items Included:* Free Data Caching Analysis Utility which reports on direct I/O counts & hit rates. *Customer Support:* 90 day warranty. Annual support & update service: 15% of the price for Single-Use and/or Cluster License Fees for every node of the cluster. Faxed or written SPR handling. Yearly telephone support: 24 hour/7 days a week telephone support is an additional $750.00. Must have annual support & update service.
VMS V5.0 & higher. VAX. $480.00 to $19,800.00. *Optimal configuration:* DEC VAX/VMS. *Networks supported:* All Digital Equipment Corp.-supported cluster configurations including LAVC, CI, FDDI, DSSI & mixed-interconnect.
A Software Data Caching Product That Improves Response Time & Can Eliminate Input/Output Bottlenecks on Digital's VAX/VMS Systems. It Uses Excess Host Memory, When Available, to Store Frequently Used Data Blocks from the Disk. These Blocks Can Then Be Read Almost Instantly from Memory, Thus Avoiding Time-Consuming Disk Access.
Executive Software.

I/O ROM. *Compatible Hardware:* HP 85, 86/87.
HP 85. ROM cartridge $195.00 (Order no.: 00085-15003).
HP 86/87. (Order no.: 00087-15003).
Provides Input/Output Commands That Enhance the HP Series 80 BASIC Language Capability.
Hewlett-Packard Co.

I. O. Silver. Brad Wihelmsen. *Compatible Hardware:* Apple II, II+, IIe, IIc, IIgs. *Operating System(s) Required:* Apple DOS 3.3.
disk $29.95.
Hi-Res Strategy/Arcade Game.
Beagle Brothers.

I-TAS: Interactive Thermal Analysis System. *Version:* 2.0. Richard F. Warriner. Apr. 1984. *Compatible Hardware:* IBM PC & compatibles. *Operating System(s) Required:* MS-DOS, PC-DOS. *Language(s):* Not applicable; compiled code. *Memory Required:* 256k. *General Requirements:* Printer.
disk $450.00, incl. manual (ISBN 0-927814-00-5, Order no.: ITAS).
manual $30.00.
Network-Type, Finite Difference Program for Engineers Which Solves Heat Transfer Problems. Obtains Steady State & Transient Solutions for Diffusion, Arithmetic, & Boundary Nodes with Conduction, Convection, & Radiation Connectors. Boundary Temperatures & Heat Flow Rates May Be Functions of Time. Interactive Option Simplifies Input Procedure.
R. F. Warriner Assocs.

I to Z. *Operating System(s) Required:* CP/M. *Language(s):* Assembly 8080. *Memory Required:* 16k.
disk $50.00, incl. source code.
Translates Intel 8080 to Zilog Z-80 Assembler Mnemonics & Processes Z80 & 8080 Pseudo-Ops for M80.
Aton International, Inc.

IACCT: Base Accounting & Database, 2 disks. *Version:* 5.0. Harold L. Reed. Aug. 1991. *Compatible Hardware:* Any machine running MS-DOS. *Operating System(s) Required:* PC-DOS/MS-DOS 3.3 or higher. *Language(s):* Clipper. *Memory Required:* 640k. *General Requirements:* Hard disk, printer.
$249.50 (ISBN 0-924495-00-6).
An Integrated, Interactive, Natural Language Accounting, Database & Mail System for Professionals or Service Organizations. It Is a Natural Language System That Can Be Treated As a Clerk or Administrative Assistant for a Professional or Service Organization. IACCT Knows Accounting, Based on General Accounting Rules, But It Departs from Old Paper Ledger Based Bookkeeping Systems. The New System Makes It Practical to Have an Accounting Program That Does All Accounting, Including Payroll, with an English Language Command Structure & Still Leave Room for Database Management, Letter Writing & Mail Capabilities.
IDEA Computers, Inc.

IAP Supplement. *Version:* 8A. Sep. 1993. *Compatible Hardware:* PC-DOS, Xenix, Unix, 3COM & Novell machines using R/M cobol runtime version 2.0 or higher. *Memory Required:* Multi-user 1Mb or higher, single user 500k. *General Requirements:* Integrated accounting. *Customer Support:* Included with the support for the Integrated Accounting.
Single user. disk $1120.00.
Multiuser. disk $1245.00.
Designed for Companies Such as Those in Catalog Sales Whose Order Processing Needs are More Complex-Shipping Items on the Same Order from Different Sources, Printing & Filling Orders Many Times in One Day, & Processing Huge Numbers of Orders Very Quickly. Shipments on the Same Order: You Can Ship Individual Items from Different Warehouses. You Can Also Ship Line Items from the Current Warehouse or Drop Ship Others from the Vendor.
Trac Line Software, Inc.

IAS-H: Insurance Agent System-Health. *Version:* 1.1. Jan. 1985. *Compatible Hardware:* IBM PC with 2 disk drives. *Operating System(s) Required:* DOS 2.1 or higher. *Language(s):* Compiled BASIC. *Memory Required:* 128k. *Items Included:* User Manual. *Customer Support:* 30 days warranty.
disk $595.00.
Compares Different Health Policies on a Spreadsheet Basis, Using up to 25 Medical & 10 Dental Benefits. Calculations of Client Premiums for Specific Carriers Are Also Provided. Handles Commission Accounting of Amounts Due from Various Carriers & Provides Overdue Reminders & Cash-Flow Summaries. User Maintains a Personal Data Base of Carriers & Clients, Limited Only by Disk Size.
International Logic Corp.

IBM LinkWay Authoring Tool for Presentations, Tutorial, & Information Exploration. Annette Lamb. 1993. *Items Included:* Handbook/workbook contains folder shells, graphics, fonts & video drivers. Includes 3 1/2" diskette. *Customer Support:* Technical support from editorial staff.
IBM PS/1 or PS/2, PC/XT, AT & compatibles (2Mb). $49.95 handbook/wkbk. (ISBN 0-89262-353-5). *Nonstandard peripherals required:* Mouse. *Optimal configuration:* Two diskette drivers or one diskette drive & one hard disk. 2Mb RAM, 20Mb hard disk, 1. 44Mb diskette drive.
$50.00 instr's. guide (ISBN 0-89262-356-X).
Design & Develop Effective, Efficient & Appealing Computer-Based Instructional Material. The Entire Instructional Process from Planning & Pretesting Through Instruction & Evaluation Is Done on the Computer.
Career Publishing, Inc.

IBM LinkWay Creativity Tool for Writing, Organizing, & Multimedia. Annette Lamb. 1992. *Items Included:* Handbook/workbook with student disektte. Diskette contains shells, graphics, fonts & video drivers. *Customer Support:* Technical support from editorial staff.
MS-DOS 2.1 or higher. IBM PS/2, PC/XT, AT & compatibles (512k). $39.95 handbook/wkbk. (ISBN 0-89262-353-5).
$50.00 instr's. guide (ISBN 0-89262-356-X).
Step-by-Step Instruction in the Use of LinkWay As a Personal & Academic Productivity Tool. Learn to Create Interactive Reports & Presentations. Write Scripts & Use Files to Make Folders Run Properly.
Career Publishing, Inc.

IBM PC: An Introduction to the Operating System, BASIC Programming & Applications. 1984. *Compatible Hardware:* IBM PC.
disk $25.00.
Updated Version for the Introductory Book for the IBM PC. Includes Two Chapters That Emphasize the Importance of Structuring & Planning Programs. Also Gives Information on Debugging Programs.
Prentice Hall.

IBM PC-Apprentice: Dollars & Sense, Tutorial Workbook. 1984. *Compatible Hardware:* IBM PC & compatibles.
disk $34.95, incl. bk. (ISBN 0-13-452863-8).
Enables Students to Gain Familiarity with Business Software Before They Enter the Business

World, & Offers Business Users a Hands-On Tutorial for Mastering Software That They Either Own Already, or Are Considering Buying.
Prentice Hall.

IBM PC-Apprentice: Easybusiness System General Ledger, Tutorial Workbook. 1984. *Compatible Hardware:* IBM PC & compatibles.
disk $34.95, incl. bk. (ISBN 0-13-452905-7).
Enables Students to Gain Familiarity with Business Software Before They Enter the Business World, & Offers Business Users a Hands-On Tutorial for Mastering Software That They Either Own Already, or Are Considering Buying.
Prentice Hall.

IBM PC-Apprentice: FORTRAN-77-Beginning, Tutorial Workbook. 1984.
disk $34.95, incl. bk. (ISBN 0-13-452889-1).
Enables Students to Gain Familiarity with Business Software Before They Enter the Business World, & Offers Business Users a Hands-On Tutorial for Mastering Software That They Either Own, or Are Considering Buying.
Prentice Hall.

IBM PC-Apprentice: Open Access, Tutorial Workbook. 1984. *Compatible Hardware:* IBM PC & compatibles.
disk $44.95, incl. bk. (ISBN 0-13-452947-2).
Enables Students to Gain Familiarity with Business Software Before They Enter the Business World, & Offers Business Users a Hands-On Tutorial for Mastering Software That They Either Own Already, or Are Considering Buying.
Prentice Hall.

IBM PC-Apprentice: SuperCalc III, Tutorial Workbook. 1984.
disk $34.95, incl. bk. (ISBN 0-13-452970-7).
Enables Students to Gain Familiarity with Business Software Before They Enter the Business World, & Offers Business Users a Hands-On Tutorial for Mastering Software That They Either Own Already, or Are Considering Buying.
Prentice Hall.

IBM PC-Apprentice: UCSD Pascal-Beginning, Tutorial Workbook. 1984.
disk $34.95, incl. bk. (ISBN 0-13-452988-X).
Enables Students to Gain Familiarity with Business Software Before They Enter the Business World & Offers Business Users a Hands-On Tutorial for Mastering Software That They Either Own Already, or Are Considering Buying.
Prentice Hall.

IBM PC Assembly Language Tutor. Richard Haskell. Feb. 1985. *Compatible Hardware:* IBM PC, Compaq, Columbia. *Operating System(s) Required:* PC-DOS. *Memory Required:* Compaq & Columbia 128k; PC-DOS 360k.
disk $24.95 (ISBN 0-13-448662-5).
Introduction to Assembly Language Programming & Interfacing Using Tutor Monitoring.
Prentice Hall.

IBM PC 8080 Assembly Language Tutor.
Compatible Hardware: IBM PC.
disk $34.95.
Teaches 8088 Assembly Language. Also Covers Computer Memory, 8088 Arithmetic, Branching Instructions, Addressing Modes, Graphics, Interrupts & Subroutines. Displays Memory & Register Contents, Permitting Users to See the Effect Each Program Statement Has.
Prentice Hall.

IBM PC Graphics. John C. Craig & Jeff Bretz. 1984. *Compatible Hardware:* IBM PC. *Operating System(s) Required:* PC-DOS. *Language(s):* BASIC. *Memory Required:* 128k.
disk $32.95, incl. bk. (ISBN 0-8306-5113-6, Order no.: 5113C).
Collection of Programs Covering a Variety of Subjects. Provides Numerous Graphics Techniques. Designed to Expand Programming Knowledge.
TAB Bks.

IBM PC XT Assembly Language: A Guide for Programmers. 1983. *Compatible Hardware:* IBM PC.
disk $35.00.
Teaches How to Create & Run Assembly Programs & the Entire Instruction for the 8088 Microprocessor.
Prentice Hall.

IBM PC XT Graphics Book. John Fowler. May 1984. *Compatible Hardware:* IBM PC, PC XT. *Operating System(s) Required:* PC-DOS 1.1, 2.0.
disk $29.95, incl. bk. (ISBN 0-13-448416-9).
bk. $14.95 (ISBN 0-13-448408-8).
BASIC Programs for Graphics Creations.
Prentice Hall.

IBM Superzap. *Compatible Hardware:* IBM PC. *Operating System(s) Required:* DOS.
disk $149.95 (ISBN 0-936200-49-9).
Disk Data Recovery & Modification Program. Reads & Writes Any Sector on a Disk. Commands Can Be Executed by Entering the Name of the Command or by Pressing a Control Key Combination.
Blue Cat.

Icarus. *Items Included:* 100-page manual. *Customer Support:* 800-929-8117 (customer service).
MS-DOS. IBM/PS2. disk $499.99 (ISBN 0-87007-742-2).
A Scientific Equation Solver & Graphic Software Package. Designed to Be Fast & Accurate in the Most Complex Function Analysis. It Will Calculate One or Two Independent Variable Functions of Whatever Complexity, Used Like a Pocket Calculator or Using the ICARUS Macro Language Instructions. It Will Read, Modify & Store the Numerical Values of the Calculated Functions. Retrieve from Disk or Manually Input Experimental Data. Plot in 2D, 3D or Both the Numerical Data Using All of the Graphic Transformations Like Translations, Scaling, Rotations, etc. Will Load & Store Plots from & to Disk, Build Animated Sequences for Demonstrations, Advertising or Situations Such As Lectures. Is Fully Menu Driven. All of the Commands & the Options Are Displayed in 3 Menus, or Work in Command Mode. Supports the Numeric Co-Processor Chip, & Can Be Called from Microsoft Windows. Able to Print Images on Printer or Modify Them Through Windows' PAINT.
SourceView Software International.

Icarus87. *Customer Support:* 800-929-8117 (customer service).
MS-DOS. IBM/PS2. disk $499.99 (ISBN 0-87007-743-0).
A Scientific Equation Solver & Graphic Software Package. Designed to be Accurate in the Most Complex Function Analysis. Supports the Numeric Co-Processor Chip, & Can be Called from Microsoft Windows. Supports the 8087 Faster Calculations. A 100-Page Manual is Provided.
SourceView Software International.

ICC-Intercom 102-FileXpress: Burroughs Term Emulation & File Transfers. Version: 4.0. 1983. *Compatible Hardware:* IBM PC & compatibles; Burroughs B20/B25; Wang. *Operating System(s) Required:* MS-DOS, CTOS. *Memory Required:* 192k.
IBM, Wang. disk $375.00.
Burroughs. cassette $695.00.
Terminal Emulation & File Transfers for Connecting Micros to All Burroughs Mainframes.
Intercomputer Communications Corp.

ICC-Intercom 500/600: Sperry Terminal Emulation Mapper File Transfers, SDF File Tranfers. Version: 2.95. 1983. *Compatible Hardware:* AT&T 6300; IBM PC & compatibles, PC XT, PC AT; Olivetti; Sperry PC, Wang PC; Zenith. *Memory Required:* 192k. *General Requirements:* Hard disk; ICC/DataXpress mainframe software for Sperry.
IBM, Sperry, AT&T, Zenith. disk Emulation & File Transfer $525.00.
Mainframe software for file transfer. disk $995.00.
Terminal Emulation & File Transfer for Connecting Micros to All Sperry Mainframes. It Also Downloads/Uploads MAPPER Files & Automatically Reformats Them for Use in Lotus, WordStar etc. SDF Files Can Also Be Transferred.
Intercomputer Communications Corp.

ICD-9-CM 1996 Codes on Disk. Oct. 1995.
disk $129.95 (ISBN 1-57066-038-7).
The 1996 International Classification of Diseases Official Diagnostic Codes & Revisions on Disk with Softcover Volume.
Practice Management Information Corp.

Ice. Jun. 1991. *Items Included:* 200 page perfect bound manual, reference card. *Customer Support:* 60-day money back guarantee, free technical support.
DOS 2.1 or higher. IBM & compatibles (80k). $99.99. *Addl. software required:* Lotus 1-2-3 R 2.2 or 2.3. *Networks supported:* Network compatible.
Add-In for 1-2-3 R 2.2 & 2.3. Allows Spreadsheet Users to Distribute Custom, Tamper-Proof Applications to Other 1-2-3 Users Conveniently. With 73 New Macro Keywords. Users Have the Tools to Secure Macros & Formulas & Develop Spreadsheets That Look Like a Stand-Alone Application.
Baler Software Corp.

ICHIEFS Communication Network. *Items Included:* User manual, telephone directory. *Customer Support:* 1-88-2-MACNET.
MacNet. Macintosh. 3.5" disk $74.95. *Optimal configuration:* Modem, dedicated phone line, printer.
PCMacNet. IBM. disk $99.95. *Addl. software required:* Microsoft Windows for IBM. *Optimal configuration:* Modem, dedicated phone line, printer.
An Electronic Mail & Bulletin System. Offers Fire Service Information in the Areas of Training, Legislation & Workshop Conferences. Users Can Access Various Fire Awareness Organizations Through the System.
International Assn. of Fire Chiefs.

ICMS: Integrated Cash Management System. Oct. 1979. *Compatible Hardware:* IBM PC with modem. *Operating System(s) Required:* MS-DOS, PC-DOS. *Language(s):* Pascal. *Memory Required:* 512k. *General Requirements:* Modem, hard disk.
$3,000.00-$46,000.00.
Produces Worksheets, Forecasts, Portfolios, Cash Ledger & Customized Reports for Treasury & Accounting Departments. Captures Bank, Treasury & Accounting Data & Converts into a Common Format. Modules Include Capture & Conversion, Borrowing & Investments, Cash Ledger, Proof of Cash, Worksheet, & Forecast. CASH LEDGER Maintains an Audit Trail of Transactions, & Calculates Balances for Each Account, Operating Unit & Total Corporate Cash Position. PROOF OF CASH Verifies the Accuracy of the Data Base. WORKSHEET Reconciles Balances & Provides Same-Day Forecasting Automatically Updated with Actual Reported Figures. FORECASTS Projects Transactions, Investments, Borrowings, Balance Positions, & Average Collected Compensation.
ICMS.

TITLE INDEX

Icon Design System. *Compatible Hardware:* HP 150 Touchscreen with 9111A graphics tablet (optional).
3.5" disk $99.00 (Order no.: 45311A).
Developed for Programmers Using Pascal, BASIC, GW-BASIC, & Lattice C. Features HP Touch Function Key Menus, On-Line Help, & Pre-Written Routines to Integrate Icons into Pascal, BASIC, or Lattice C. For Simple Graphics Editing It Features Free Drawing & Graphics Commands to Create & Refine Icons. Also Proves the Following Functions: Polygon Fill in Nine Patterns, Grid Overlays for Touch Field Programming, & the Ability to Move, Scale & Mirror Icons.
Hewlett-Packard Co.

Icon-It! Pro. *Version:* 3.0. *Compatible Hardware:* Macintosh Plus, Macintosh SE, Macintosh II & up.
3.5" disk $129.00.
Allows Users to Assign Familiar Pictures to Represent Menu Items, Desk Accessories, Fkeys, & EXCEL or TEMPO Macros. Elimates the Necessity to Check Menus or Memorize Keyboard Commands. Includes Templates for Popular Programs, & Allows Users to Create Their Own Icons with a Built-In Editor. Provides On-Line Help. Not Copy Protected. Supports Color.
Olduvai Corp.

Icon Manial. *Version:* 1.02. David Ransen. *Items Included:* 1 diskette, manual, promo materials. *Customer Support:* Free tech support to registered users.
System 7. Color capable Macintosh (2.5Mb). Retail: $69.95; Street: $44.95 (Order no.: 94627 00033).
The Ultimate Package for Icon Customization. Features Include: Large Icon Collection, Easy to Use Interface, Icon Editor, Thumbnailing, Modification of System Icons.
Dubl-Click Software.

Iconic Query. *Version:* 1.4f. Mar. 1993. *Items Included:* Manuals. *Customer Support:* 1 year free on-line tech support.
Windows 3.1 or higher. IBM PC & compatibles (3Mb). disk $290.00. *Networks supported:* LAN.
A Breakthrough Program That Uses Icons & the New What-You-See-Is-What-You-Ask Method to Access Database Systems. It Introduces Several Innovations at Once Including Iconic GUI's, Hypertext & 3D Data Graphics. Users Can Browse a Database, Get Answers, & Create Reports & Graphs Immediately Without Learning a Query Language.
IntelligenceWare, Inc.

Iconix PowerTools. *Compatible Hardware:* Apple Macintosh, UNIX. *Memory Required:* 512k. *Items Included:* One of 10 modules, for object-oriented & structured analysis & design. An integrated, multi-user suite of CASE tools that can be custom-combined to fit the needs of individual projects. *Customer Support:* Telephone/Maintenance contracts available.
3.5" disk $1495.00 ea.
Software Productivity Improvement.
ICONIX Software Engineering, Inc.

IConSys: Interim Construction Lending System. *Version:* 9.02. *Items Included:* 8 1/2" X 11" hard-cover manual. *Customer Support:* 90-day free telephone support; optional annual maintenance, $500; On-site training & other services available; 30-day limited guarantee.
MS-DOS 3.3X or higher. IBM PC/XT, AT, PS/2 & compatibles (640K). disk single user $3500.00. *Networks supported:* Novell, 3-Com, Token Ring.
A Construction Loan Tracking & Fund Control System. Disburse on Demand, in Periodic Draws, or Based upon Percent Complete. Uses Existing Check Forms.
Weston & Muir.

ICX-File Transporter. *Version:* 3.1. Rick Hollinbeck. Mar. 1980. *Compatible Hardware:* Zenith, IBM, Apple, Kaypro, North Star, Sanyo, Epson, Compupro, DEC, Altos, NEC. *Operating System(s) Required:* CP/M-80. *Language(s):* C (source code included). *Memory Required:* 64k.
8" disk $89.00.
CP/M to ISIS-II File Transfer Package Which Facilitates Complete Manipulation of Single Density ISIS-II Disks.
Western Wares.

IDAC-A-Stac. *Compatible Hardware:* Apple Macintosh Plus. *Memory Required:* 1000k. *General Requirements:* 2 800k disk drives or hard disk; IDAC-1000 peripheral; HyperCard.
3.5" disk $75.00.
Data Acquisition System.
IDAC, Inc.

IDAC-Chrome. *Compatible Hardware:* Apple Macintosh.
3.5" disk $2495.00.
Chromatography System.
IDAC, Inc.

Idea Generator. *Version:* 2.2. *Compatible Hardware:* IBM PC & compatibles. *Operating System(s) Required:* PC-DOS/MS-DOS. *Memory Required:* 256k. *General Requirements:* Hard disk recommended. *Items Included:* 32 pg. Thinking Software catalog.
5.25" or 3.5" disk $195.00.
Uses a Series of Seven Techniques Designed to Clarify Users' Thinking, Focus Their Efforts, & Help Them Come up with New Solutions to Their Problems. Users Set up the Problem & Map Their Goal. Package Includes the Book "The Art of Creative Thinking".
Thinking Software, Inc.

The Idea Generator Plus. *Version:* 3.1. 1990. *Compatible Hardware:* Hard disk or 2 disk drives. *Operating System(s) Required:* PC-DOS/MS-DOS 2.0 or higher. *Memory Required:* 256k. *Items Included:* Manual, Book "The Art Of Creative Thinking". *Customer Support:* Telephone hotline.
3.5" disk $79.95 (ISBN 0-928615-01-4, Order no.: 140).
Problem Solving & Creativity Enhancing Program. Guides the User Through a Three-Step Process to Think up New Ideas & Then Evaluate Them. Useful for Writing Proposals & Reports, Developing Plans, & Even Group Brainstorming.
Experience in Software, Inc.

The Idea Generator Plus: Structured Brainstorming. *Items Included:* Bound manual. *Customer Support:* Free hotline - no time limit; 30 day limited warranty; updates are $5/disk plus S&H.
MS-DOS 2.0 or higher. IBM & compatibles (256k). disk $89.95. *Nonstandard peripherals required:* Printer recommended. *Addl. software required:* Compatible with READY! & THINK-TANK.
Useful for Anyone Who Needs to Solve Problems - Whether You Are a Plant Manager, Marketing Specialist, Lawyer, or a Trainer. Presents a Structured Step-by-Step Approach to Problem Solving. User Moves Through Three Stages: Problem Statement, Idea Generation, & Evaluation. Each Stage Will Help You Clarify Your Thinking. At the End, You Will Have Solutions & Thoughts That Come From You, but Through the Computer.
Dynacomp, Inc.

Idea-Tree. *Version:* 2.1. *Compatible Hardware:* IBM PC & compatibles. *Operating System(s) Required:* MS-DOS, OS/2. *Memory Required:* 192k. *General Requirements:* 2 floppy disk drives or a hard disk, modem.
$99.00.
Multi-Topic BBS System. Offers Public & Private Message Areas, Each with File Transfer Capability, XMODEM, Data Base, DOS Interface, etc.
Protosoft.

IDIS: The Information Discovery System. *Version:* 2.0a. Sep. 1991. *Items Included:* Manuals. *Customer Support:* 1 year free on-line tech support.
Windows 3.1 or higher. IBM PC & compatibles (4Mb). disk $1900.00.
Automatically Analyzes Databases. It Decides What to Look at, Generates Hypotheses, Discovers Hidden & Unexpected Patterns, Rules of Knowledge, in Addition to Graphs & Anomalies Waiting to Be Uncovered. Results Are Displayed in a Hypermedia Environment. IDIS Interfaces with Oracle, DB2, dBASE, & Sybase.
IntelligenceWare, Inc.

IDM-C1. *Version:* 2.0. 1981. *Operating System(s) Required:* CP/M 2.2. *Language(s):* Compiled MBASIC. *Memory Required:* 56k.
8" disk $169.00 (Order no.: 806).
Interactive Data Manager.
Micro Architect, Inc.

IDM-IV. 1980. *Compatible Hardware:* TRS-80 Model I, Model III, Model 4. *Operating System(s) Required:* TRSDOS. *Language(s):* BASIC (source code included). *Memory Required:* 32k.
disk $69.00.
$15.00, manual.
Database/Report System.
Micro Architect, Inc.

IDM-V. 1980. *Compatible Hardware:* TRS-80 Model I, Model III. (source code included). *Memory Required:* 48k. *General Requirements:* 2 disk drives.
disk $99.00.
$10.00, manual.
Database/Report System with Enhancements.
Micro Architect, Inc.

IDM-X. 1981. *Compatible Hardware:* IBM PC; TRS-80 Model II. *Operating System(s) Required:* TRSDOS, PC-DOS, CP/M 2.2. *Language(s):* BASIC (source code included). *Memory Required:* 64k.
disk $99.00.
manual $25.00.
Database Management System with Built-In Sort/Merge Package.
Micro Architect, Inc.

IDRC/rpm Software. Nov. 1988. *Operating System(s) Required:* PC-DOS/MS-DOS. *Memory Required:* 512k. *Customer Support:* 90 days free unlimited, training available.
contact publisher for price.
Keeps Inventory of Leased & Owned Properties. Maintains Complete Property Data, Including Terms of Lease or Property Value, Lease Options, Space Allocation, Insurance, Taxes, Utilities, Services Provided, Financial Information, Zoning Information, Deed & Purchase Information. Provides Full Report Generation.
Conway Data, Inc.

IEPSystem/Bonanza. *Version:* 6.9A. Donald Cahill. Aug. 1994. *Customer Support:* Annual maintenance, $120; Options: on-site training.
MS-DOS. IBM XT, 286, 386 etc. (640k). $1995.00 plus $69.00 ea. user kit (manual, ref.

library, disk) (ISBN 0-941457-01-X). *Optimal configuration:* Printer.
Macintosh 6.04. Mac Plus & higher (1Mb). $1995.00 plus $69.00 ea. user kit (manual, ref. library, disk) (ISBN 0-941457-03-6). *Optimal configuration:* Printer.
Prepares IEPs (Individual Education Plans) for Handicapped Students & Progress Reports in English. Library of Goals, Objectives, Criteria, etc. (5000 Plus) on Disk Can Be Edited & Expanded. Adaptable to All State Regulations. Multi-User License Standard. Price Includes Custom Programming of IEP Document Format.
IEP Pubs.

If/Then. *Version:* 1.03. *Compatible Hardware:* IBM PC & compatibles. *Operating System(s) Required:* PC-DOS, MS-DOS. *Memory Required:* 256k. *General Requirements:* Lotus 1-2-3 software. Hard disk recommended. *Items Included:* 32 pg. Thinking Software catalog.
5.25" or 3.5" disk $99.00.
Introduction to Artificial Intelligence Using a Guidebook & LOTUS 1-2-3 Spreadsheets. Users Learn How to Apply the Major Concepts of AI Such As Forward & Backward Chaining.
Thinking Software, Inc.

If You Give a Mouse a Cookie. Laura J. Numeroff & Felicia Bond.
Macintosh (4Mb). CD-ROM disk $39.95 (Order no.: R1303A). *Nonstandard peripherals required:* 14" color monitor or larger, CD-ROM drive.
This Program Invites Children to Read, Color, Sing & Follow Their Favorite Mouse from One Fun-Filled Project to Another. This Interactive Storybook Contains Excellent Graphics, Animations, Activities & Page-by-Page Narrations (Ages 3-7).
Library Video Co.

IFDS Graphics Presentation System. Jan. 1983. *Compatible Hardware:* IBM PC, PC XT & compatibles. *Operating System(s) Required:* PC-DOS, MS-DOS. *Language(s):* Compiled BASIC. *Memory Required:* 128k. *General Requirements:* HP 7470A X-Y Plotter; color monitor recommended.
IBM. disk $499.00.
Creates 30 Color Graphs Based on Client Data Base & Analyses Generated by IFDS Software.
IFDS, Inc.

IFDS Professional Series/2. 1979. *Compatible Hardware:* IBM PC, PC XT & compatibles. *Operating System(s) Required:* PC-DOS, MS-DOS. *Language(s):* Compiled BASIC. *Memory Required:* 640k.
disk $1100.00.
Integrated Package Designed for Use by Professionals in Creating Personal Financial & Tax Plans for Clients. Analyses Include Correct Financial Position, 5-Year Tax Planning, & Educating Children.
IFDS, Inc.

IFDS Professional Series/3. *Version:* 2.1. 1979. *Compatible Hardware:* IBM PC, PC XT & compatibles. *Operating System(s) Required:* PC-DOS, MS-DOS. *Language(s):* Compiled BASIC. *Memory Required:* 640k.
disk $1650.00.
Designed for Use by Professionals to Create a Personal Financial & Tax Plan Covering All Investments & All Aspects of Financial Planning.
IFDS, Inc.

IFDS Word Processing Interface. Jan. 1983. *Compatible Hardware:* IBM PC, PC XT & all compatibles. *Operating System(s) Required:* PC-DOS, MS-DOS. *Language(s):* Compiled BASIC. *Memory Required:* 128k. *General Requirements:* Word Processing software capable of handling ASCII Files.
disk $199.00.
Allows User to "Print" to a Word Processing File in Order to Manipulate Data or Change Output Formats Created by Any IFDS Software.
IFDS, Inc.

IFF Image Resource Library. *Compatible Hardware:* Commodore Amiga.
3.5" disk $99.95.
Benchmark Module 2.
Avant-Garde Software.

IFPS-Personal. Execucom Systems Corp. *Compatible Hardware:* TI Professional with 2 disk drives. *Operating System(s) Required:* MS-DOS. *Memory Required:* 256k.
$3000.00.
Combines the Non-Procedural Modeling Power of IFPS with the Use of a Spreadsheet.
Texas Instruments, Personal Productivit.

IHOME: Home Accounting/Data Base. *Version:* 5.0. Harold L. Reed. Aug. 1991. *Compatible Hardware:* IBM PC. *Operating System(s) Required:* PC-DOS/MS-DOS 3.3 or higher. *Language(s):* Clipper. *Memory Required:* 640k. *General Requirements:* hard Disk, printer.
disk $149.50.
An Integrated, Interactive, Natural Language Accounting, Database & Mail System for Home Use. It Is a Natural Language System That Can Be Treated As a Clerk or Friend for a Household. IHOME Knows Accounting, Based on General Accounting Rules, But It Departs From Old Paper Ledger Based Bookkeeping Systems. The New System Makes It Practical to Have an Accounting Program That Does All Accounting with an English Language Command Structure & Still Leave Room for Database Management, Letter Writing & Mail Capabilities.
IDEA Computers, Inc.

Illumilink. Jun. 1990. *Items Included:* Manual, hardware, 2 3.5" disks. *Customer Support:* 90 day warranty.
Amiga. 3.5" disk $100.00.
An Illumi Mouse Box Containing an InfraRed Receiver & Transmitter, Plus a Phone Jack for a Wireless Telephone. The Phone Becomes a Remote Amiga Command Center. Built-in DTMF Tone Mute Allows the Phone to Work as a Microphone, Too. Make Pop-up Amiga Screen Duplicates of User Favorite IR Remote Controllers. Output for Separate IR LEDS. Also Included, MIDISynergy III with Source Code, Turns MIDI Notes into IR Commands for MIDI Coordinated Audio Visual Equipment Shows.
Geodesic Pubns.

Illustrations. (Studio Ser.). *Items Included:* Visual index, user's guide. *Customer Support:* Free & unlimited technical support to registered users; 60 day money-back guarantee.
Macintosh. Macintosh (Minimum required for program with which you want to use ClickArt). 3.5" disk $99.95. *Nonstandard peripherals required:* PostScript compatible printer. *Addl. software required:* Any desktop publishing, word processing or works application that accepts EPS files.
Windows V.3.0 or higher. IBM PC & compatibles (Minimum needed for application with which you will use ClickArt). 3.5" disk $99.95. *Addl. software required:* Any desktop publishing, word processing or works application that accepts CGM or WMF files.
MS-DOS V.3.3 or higher. IBM PC & compatibles (Minimum needed for application with which you will use ClickArt). 3.5" disk $99.95. *Addl. software required:* Any desktop publishing, word processing or works program that accepts WMF or CGM files.
Over 175 Images! Highest-Quality Full-Color Images Available; Ready-to-Use, or Changed in Appropriate Drawing Program; Designed in Full-Color (CMYK); Ready for Color Separations & Commercial Printing; Produced to Print in Detailed Greyscale on Black & White Printers.
T/Maker Co., Inc.

ILS-Interactive Laboratory System. *Compatible Hardware:* DEC PC.
contact publisher for price.
Consists of More Than 80 Interactive Signal Processing Programs. Provides Waveform Display & Editing, Digital Filtering, Spectral Analysis, & Data Acquisitions. Applications Include: Noise & Vibration Analysis, Speech, Biomedical, Acoustic, & Radar Signals.
Signal Technology, Inc.

ILS-PC 1. *Compatible Hardware:* IBM PC, PC XT. $1495.00.
Signal Processing Program That Provides Data Acquisition Support, Waveform Display & Editing, Digital Filtering, & Spectral Analysis. Applications Include Noise & Vibration, Speech, Seismology, Acoustics, Sonar, Radar, Bio-Medicine, etc.
Signal Technology, Inc.

ILS-SKY. *Compatible Hardware:* DEC Micro/PDP-11. *General Requirements:* Graphics terminal, modem. *Items Included:* Helpline.
contact publisher for price.
Signal Processing Program That Integrates to the SKYMNK Array Processor from SKY Computers, Inc. Applications Include: Speech, Noise & Vibrations, Seismology, Acoustics, Biology, Sonar, Radar, Medicine, & Simulation.
Signal Technology, Inc.

I'm Hiding. (Bright Beginning Ser.). *Compatible Hardware:* TI-99/4A.
contact publisher for price (Order no.: PHM3155).
Hide-&-Seek with Bugs Playing Peek-A-Boo in a Crayon Box. Bugs Give Clues & Key Pad Lets Youngsters Deduce Hiding Places. Includes Graphics & Speech Synthesis.
Texas Instruments, Personal Productivit.

I'm No Accountant: Business Journal Template for LOTUS 1-2-3. *Version:* 1.65. Aug. 1991. *Items Included:* manual, disk, license. *Customer Support:* 12 month help & written support.
MS-DOS 2.x or higher. IBM PC, XT, AT or compatible (512k). $30.00 per user (ISBN 0-932289-46-0, Order no.: INA). *Addl. software required:* LOTUS 1-2-3 version 2.01, 2.2 or 2.3. *Optimal configuration:* 640k RAM & 512k EMS, printer.
1-2-3 Template for Cash Flow, Single Entry Accounting Which is Menu Driven to Provide Full Screen Entry of Payments, Deposits & Salary, Bank Statement Reconciliation, Query by Account Number, Summary by Account Number, Printed Reports, Removable Help, & Direct Access to the Data with LOTUS 1-2-3.
Microsmith Computer Technology.

I'm Out - Screen Saver - Business Version. *Version:* 1.96. Nov. 1996. *Items Included:* Manual, 3 3.5" diskettes. *Customer Support:* One year free technical support, 30 day unlimited warranty.
Windows 3.1. 80286(AT), (512k). 3.5" disk $39.95.
The Only Screen Saver That Works for You. Yes, It Displays Pretty Pictures, Just Like Other Screen Savers, but I'm Out Does More! You Can Leave a Customized Message for Others & Others Can Leave Private Messages for You. Let People Know Where You Are, & When You,ll Be Back Or Use I'm Out to Remind Yourself of an Important Meeting.
PSG-HomeCraft Software.

TITLE INDEX

I'm Out - Screen Saver - Personal Version.
Version: 1.96. Nov. 1995. *Items Included:* Manual, 3 3.5" diskettes. *Customer Support:* One year free technical support, 30 day unlimited warranty.
Windows 3.1. 20286(AT), (512k). 3.5" disk $39.95.
The Only Screen Saver That Works for You. Yes, It Displays Pretty Pictures, Just Like Other Screen Savers, But I'm Out Does More! You Can Leave a Customized Message for Others & Others Can Leave Private Messages for You. Let Your Family Know Where You Are & When You, Il Be Back, Or Use I'm Out to Remind Yourself of an Important Appointment.
PSG-HomeCraft Software.

Image Maker. Mike Medvedovsky. 1985. *Compatible Hardware:* IBM PC; NEC APC III. *Operating System(s) Required:* PC-DOS 3.2. *Language(s):* QuickBasic. *Memory Required:* 640k. *General Requirements:* CGA card for IBM. disk $79.95 ea. (ISBN 1-55603-013-4).
IBM PC. (ISBN 1-55603-013-4, Order no.: I-1151).
NEC APC III. (ISBN 1-55603-020-7, Order no.: N-1151).
Character Set Editor. Allows the Novice As Well As the Experienced Computer Programmer a Method for Creating Character Sets. Program Options Allow the Character Sets to Be Converted into Formats Usable by BASIC. Characters Can Be Created with As Many As 3 Colors & Sizes Varying up to 45 by 45 Pixels. Each Character Set Can Hold As Many As 150 Characters.
Electronic Courseware Systems, Inc.

Image-Pro Plus. *Version:* 1.3. Aug. 1995. *Items Included:* Copy protect key, 2 bound manuals. *Customer Support:* 30-day money back guarantee, 90-day warranty, free technical support & maintenance for one year.
DOS 3.1, Windows 3.1. IBM PC 386 & compatibles (2Mb). disk $2999.00.
Nonstandard peripherals required: VGA or SuperVGA. *Optimal configuration:* IBM PC 386, Windows 3.1, 4Mb, laser printer, frame grabber.
Quantitative Image Analysis Software for Black & White, Gray Scale, & 24-Bit Color Images. Comprehensive Counting, Sizing, Statistical & Image Enhancement Functions Make Image-Pro Plus an Ideal Tool for Research & Industrial Applications Where Analysis of an Image Can Help to Understand Processes, Make Comparisons, or Identify Microscopic Objects.
Media Cybernetics, Inc.

Image-Pro Plus. *Version:* 2.0. Jan. 1996. *Items Included:* CD-ROM, copy protection key, welcome brochure, device notes, Auto-Pro Quick Reference Guide. *Customer Support:* Free technical support for one year with purchase, 90 day unlimited warranty.
Windows 95/Windows NT. 386, 640x480x256 (8Mb). CD-ROM disk $2999.00.
Designed for Windows 95. Utilizing 32-Bit Technology, This Program Provides Fast & Accurate Image Processing & Analysis Solutions to Researchers & Scientists Who Are Working with More Powerful Operating Systems Such As Win 95 & Win/NT. Provides Users with Easier Software Installation, Improved & Easier to Use Draw, Text, & Fill Tools, a New Image Database for Image Storage, & a Highly Interactive Screen Painting Which Allows for Visual Adjustments in Brightness, Contrast, Gamma, & Psuedocolor.
Media Cybernetics, L. P.

Image Word-Graphics Processor. *Operating System(s) Required:* CP/M. *Language(s):* Z80 Assembly. *Memory Required:* 64k.
disk $149.00, incl. documentation.
Combines a Word Processing Program with Many of the Features of a Graphics Program. Using Function Keys at the Top of the Keyboard, Graphics Such As Flow Charts & Bar Graphs Can Be Created. The Word Processing Capabilities Include Bold Face Type & Proportional Spacing in Addition to Normal Editing Functions.
MicroArt Corp.

Imagebank EPS Maps.
Any Macintosh. 3.5" disk $79.99.
Encapsulated PostScript Maps.
DigiTech Systems.

Imagebank Professional ClipArt Images. *Compatible Hardware:* Apple Macintosh.
3.5" disk $29.95.
Series of Clip Art Images That Can Be Ordered by Subject.
DigiTech Systems.

ImageBuilder. *Version:* 2.1. *Compatible Hardware:* IBM PC & compatibles. *Operating System(s) Required:* PC-DOS/MS-DOS 3.0 or higher. *Memory Required:* 512k. *General Requirements:* CGA, EGA, VGA, or Hercules card. *Items Included:* Symbol Library.
disk $149.00.
Users Can Create Slide & Overhead Transparencies on the IBM PC. Offers the Ability to Design Bar, Line, Pie, & Organization Charts, along with Diagrams, Word Slides & Drawings. Images Can Be Sent via Modem to MAGICorp's Slide Service & Have Slides & Transparencies Delivered Overnight. New Features Added to this Version Include Image Export & Special Effects. The Export Capability Lets Users Send High Resolution Graphics to Desktop Publishing Programs. The Graphics Are Exported in Object-Oriented Form. Two Special Effects Added to Version 2.1 Include Sweep & Curved Text. Sweep Creates Text Spirals, Text Zooms, Color Spectrums, & Shading Effects. The CurvedText Function Creates Text along a Curve.
ImageBuilder Software, Inc.

ImageBuilder. *Compatible Hardware:* IBM PC XT. *Memory Required:* 512k.
disk $99.00.
Presentation Graphics Package for On-Screen Slide Shows. Graphics & Chart-Making Features Include Object Rotation, Image Reduction & Enlargement, Zoom & Undo Commands & Picture/Symbol Library; Bar, Line, Pie, Text, Organization, Scatter & Flow Charts; Histograms; Multiple Charts on One Screen; & Free Positioning of Charts, Labels & Titles on Screen. Provides 100,000 User-Selectable Colors, Designable Palettes, 4 Typefaces & Scalable Font Sizes. Outputs to PostScript Printers, Dot-Matrix Printers, Film Recorders & Integrated Link to Service Bureau. Imports CGM, PIC, ASCII, WKS, WK1 & dBASE III PLUS File Formats. Also Features On-Screen Help, Shading, Drop Shadows, Distortion, Bursts & Sweeps.
TriDos Software Pubs.

ImageKey. 1991. *Items Included:* One set of manuals. *Customer Support:* Customer support required. 15% per annum.
OS/2 2.X. 486 Processor, 8514 VGA, SVGA or XGA Adapter (16Mb). Development System $15,500.00. *Optimal configuration:* OS/2 2.X, 16Mb RAM, 60Mb hard drive, 486 processor. *Networks supported:* Novel NetWare, IBM LAN Server, LAN Manager, LAN Requester.
Combines the Capabilities of a Full Featured, Production Data Entry System with State-of-the-Art OCR/ICR Technology. Regardless of Whether the Data Is Recognized with or by Human Operators, It Will Be Subjected to Extensive Edits & Validation Procedures. The Flexibility & Power Make It the Ideal High-Volume, Production Oriented Front-End for a Wide Variety of Major Vendor Image Systems.
Southern Computer Systems, Inc.

ImageKit Cities Disk, No. 7. May 1995. *Items Included:* CD-ROM booklet. *Customer Support:* Free technical support via phone as of release date.
Macintosh. System 6.07 or higher, 68020 processor, CD-ROM drive (4Mb). CD-ROM disk $249.00 (ISBN 1-885784-39-2, Order no.: 1393). *Optimal configuration:* System 7.0 or higher, 68030 processor, 8Mb of application RAM, 16 or 24 bit monitor, double-speed CD-ROM drive.
Has 120 High Resolution (300 DPI) Images of City Skylines, Industrial Textures, Architectural Items, & Many More. ImageKit Is a 10 CD Library of Imagery Created for Digital Imaging Artists by Digital Imaging Artists. All Images Are Royalty Free with Extensive Keywording & Cross-Referencing Within Browser Software for the MAC Average Image Size: 10"x6.5", File Size: 16-18 MB; Pixel Dimensions: 3000x2000.
Technology Dynamics Corp.

ImageKit Earth Disk, No. 6. May 1995. *Items Included:* CD-ROM booklet. *Customer Support:* Free technical support via phone as of release date.
Macintosh. System 6.07 or higher, 68020 processor, CD-ROM drive (4Mb). CD-ROM disk $249.00 (ISBN 1-885784-38-4, Order no.: 1386). *Optimal configuration:* System 7.0 or higher, 68030 processor, 8Mb of application RAM, 16 or 24 bit monitor, double-speed CD-ROM drive.
Contains 120 High Resolution (300 DPI) Images of Our Beautiful Planet. Images Include Majestic Mountains, White Desert Sands, Rock Formations, Natural Textures, & Much More. ImageKit Is a 10 CD Library of Imagery Created for Digital Imaging Artists by Digital Imaging Artists. All Images Are Royalty Free with Extensive Keywording & Cross-Referencing Within Browser Software for the MAC Average Image Size: 10"x6.5", File Size: 16-18 MB; Pixel Dimensions: 3000x2000.
Technology Dynamics Corp.

ImageKit Foliage Disk, No. 5. May 1995. *Items Included:* CD-ROM booklet. *Customer Support:* Free technical support via phone as of release date.
Macintosh. System 6.07 or higher, 68020 processor, CD-ROM drive (4Mb). CD-ROM disk $249.00 (ISBN 1-885784-37-6, Order no.: 1379). *Optimal configuration:* System 7.0 or higher, 68030 processor, 8Mb of application RAM, 16 or 24 bit monitor, double-speed CD-ROM drive.
Holds 120 High Resolution (300 DPI) Images of Exotic Flowers, Towering Trees, & Lots More. ImageKit Is a 10 CD Library of Imagery Created for Digital Imaging Artists by Digital Imaging Artists. All Images Are Royalty Free with Extensive Keywording & Cross-Referencing Within Browser Software for the MAC Average Image Size: 10"x6.5", File Size: 16-18 MB; Pixel Dimensions: 3000x2000.
Technology Dynamics Corp.

ImageKit Illustrations Disk, No. 2. May 1995. *Items Included:* CD-ROM booklet. *Customer Support:* Free technical support via phone as of release date.
Macintosh. System 6.07 or higher, 68020 processor, CD-ROM drive (4Mb). CD-ROM disk $179.00 (ISBN 1-885784-34-1, Order no.: 1348). *Optimal configuration:* System 7.0 or higher, 68030 processor, 8Mb of application

RAM, 16 or 24 bit monitor, double-speed CD-ROM drive.
Contains 120 High Resolution (300 DPI) Illustrations Ranging from Basic Illustrated Textures to Meticulous 3-D Renderings. ImageKit Is a 10 CD Library of Imagery Created for Digital Imaging Artists by Digital Imaging Artists. All Images Are Royalty Free with Extensive Keywording & Cross-Referencing Within Browser Software for the MAC Average Image Size: 8.5" x6.4", File Size: 3.5 MB; Pixel Dimensions: 1280x960.
Technology Dynamics Corp.

ImageKit Miscellaneous Disk, No. 10. May 1995. *Items Included:* CD-ROM booklet. *Customer Support:* Free technical support via phone as of release date.
Macintosh. System 6.07 or higher, 68020 processor, CD-ROM drive (4Mb). CD-ROM disk $249.00 (ISBN 1-885784-42-2, Order no.: 1423). *Optimal configuration:* System 7.0 or higher, 68030 processor, 8Mb of application RAM, 16 or 24 bit monitor, double-speed CD-ROM drive.
Contains 120 High Resolution (300 DPI) Images of Those Hard to Find Images Such As Brilliant Fireworks & Flickering Flames. ImageKit Is a 10 CD Library of Imagery Created for Digital Imaging Artists by Digital Imaging Artists. All Images Are Royalty Free with Extensive Keywording & Cross-Referencing Within Browser Software for the MAC Average Image Size: 20" x6.5", File Size: 16-18 MB; Pixel Dimensions: 3000x2000.
Technology Dynamics Corp.

ImageKit Objects Disk, No. 8. May 1995. *Items Included:* CD-ROM booklet. *Customer Support:* Free technical support via phone as of release date.
Macintosh. System 6.07 or higher, 68020 processor, CD-ROM drive (4Mb). CD-ROM disk $179.00 (ISBN 1-885784-40-6, Order no.: 1409). *Optimal configuration:* System 7.0 or higher, 68030 processor, 8Mb of application RAM, 16 or 24 bit monitor, double-speed CD-ROM drive.
Showcases 336 High Resolution (300 DPI) Images Ranging from Computers to Food. Objects Are Against White Background with Corresponding Mask Files. ImageKit Is a 10 CD Library of Imagery Created for Digital Imaging Artists by Digital Imaging Artists. All Images Are Royalty Free with Extensive Keywording & Cross-Referencing Within Browser Software for the MAC Average Image Size: 6"x6.5", File Size: 10 MB; Pixel Dimensions: 2300x1500.
Technology Dynamics Corp.

ImageKit People Disk, No. 9. May 1995. *Items Included:* CD-ROM booklet. *Customer Support:* Free technical support via phone as of release date.
Macintosh. System 6.07 or higher, 68020 processor, CD-ROM drive (4Mb). CD-ROM disk $179.00 (ISBN 1-885784-41-4, Order no.: 1416). *Optimal configuration:* System 7.0 or higher, 68030 processor, 8Mb of application RAM, 16 or 24 bit monitor, double-speed CD-ROM drive.
Contains 291 High Resolution (300 DPI) Images of People Shot with Your Specific Stripping Needs in Mind...with Corresponding Mask Files. ImageKit Is a 10 CD Library of Imagery Created for Digital Imaging Artists by Digital Imaging Artists. All Images Are Royalty Free with Extensive Keywording & Cross-Referencing Within Browser Software for the MAC Average Image Size: 5"x9", File Size: 10 MB; Pixel Dimensions: 1900x2700.
Technology Dynamics Corp.

ImageKit ScreenRez. May 1995. *Items Included:* CD-ROM booklet. *Customer Support:* Free technical support via phone as of release date.
Macintosh. System 6.07 or higher, 68020 processor, CD-ROM drive (4Mb). CD-ROM disk $149.95 (ISBN 1-885784-32-5, Order no.: 1324). *Optimal configuration:* System 7.0 or higher, 68030 processor, 8Mb of application RAM, 16 or 24 bit monitor, double-speed CD-ROM drive.
This Disc Contains All 1597 Images from the Entire 10 CD ImageKit Set in Screen Resolution (72 DPI) for Effortless Manipulation, Quick Comping & Impressive Multimedia Design. All ScreenRez Images Are Royalty Free. Image Elements Are Categorized by Illustrations, Skies, Water, Foliage, Earth, Cities, Objects, People, & Miscellaneous.
Technology Dynamics Corp.

ImageKit Skies Disk, No. 3. May 1995. *Items Included:* CD-ROM booklet. *Customer Support:* Free technical support via phone as of release date.
Macintosh. System 6.07 or higher, 68020 processor, CD-ROM drive (4Mb). CD-ROM disk $249.00 (ISBN 1-885784-35-X, Order no.: 1355). *Optimal configuration:* System 7.0 or higher, 68030 processor, 8Mb of application RAM, 16 or 24 bit monitor, double-speed CD-ROM drive.
Contains 120 High Resolution (300 DPI) Images of Swirling Clouds, Sizzling Sunsets, & Much More. ImageKit Is a 10 CD Library of Imagery Created for Digital Imaging Artists by Digital Imaging Artists. All Images Are Royalty Free with Extensive Keywording & Cross-Referencing Within Browser Software for the MAC Average Image Size: 10"x6.5", File Size: 16-18 MB; Pixel Dimensions: 3000x2000.
Technology Dynamics Corp.

ImageKit Ten CD Set. May 1995. *Items Included:* CD-ROM booklet. *Customer Support:* Free technical support via phone as of release date.
Macintosh. System 6.07 or higher, 68020 processor, CD-ROM drive (4Mb). CD-ROM disk $1295.00 (ISBN 1-885784-33-3, Order no.: 1331). *Optimal configuration:* System 7.0 or higher, 68030 processor, 8Mb of application RAM, 16 or 24 bit monitor, double-speed CD-ROM drive.
This Set Features over 1500 Professionally Acquired Royalty-Free Images & the Software Tools to Access Them Immediately. ImageKit Was Designed by Digital Imaging Professionals for Digital Imaging Professionals. A Perfect Collection of Usable Imagery That Provides Thousands of Image Elements Categorized by Illustrations, Skies, Water, Foliage, Earth, Cities, Objects, People, & Miscellaneous.
Technology Dynamics Corp.

ImageKit Water Disk, No. 4. May 1995. *Items Included:* CD-ROM booklet. *Customer Support:* Free technical support via phone as of release date.
Macintosh. System 6.07 or higher, 68020 processor, CD-ROM drive (4Mb). CD-ROM disk $249.00 (ISBN 1-885784-36-8, Order no.: 1362). *Optimal configuration:* System 7.0 or higher, 68030 processor, 8Mb of application RAM, 16 or 24 bit monitor, double-speed CD-ROM drive.
Houses 120 High Resolution (300 DPI) Images Ranging from Rippling Waves to Roaring Waterfalls. ImageKit Is a 10 CD Library of Imagery Created for Digital Imaging Artists by Digital Imaging Artists. All Images Are Royalty Free with Extensive Keywording & Cross-Referencing Within Browser Software for the MAC Average Image Size: 10"x6.5", File Size: 16-18 MB; Pixel Dimensions: 3000x2000.
Technology Dynamics Corp.

ImageLink Module: Library Automation System. 1993. *Items Included:* 3 ring bound reference style manual, including a quick reference summary & diskette. *Customer Support:* Data Trek Inc. is a turn-key vendor supplying software, hardware, peripherals, hardware/software contracts, toll-free phone & Internet access to product support, installations, training, refresher training, user groups & a technical newsletter.
PC-DOS/MS-DOS, Windows 3.0 or higher. 386 or compatible; VGA monitor (4Mb). 3.5" or 5.25" disk Contact publisher for price (ISBN 0-929795-22-9). *Nonstandard peripherals required:* 1 floppy & 1 hard disk drive, printer. *Addl. software required:* Data Trek's GOPAC, OPAC, & Cataloging modules. *Optimal configuration:* 486 computer, 8Mb RAM. *Networks supported:* Novell, IBM, 3COM, Banyan, LANtastic, PathWorks, Windows NT, NetWare.
Uses the Latest Technology to Import & Link Scanned Images Such As Photos, Maps, Graphics or Illustrations to Records in Your Database. User May Link an Unlimited Number of Images to Any Record. Uses Sophisticated Compression Techniques to Conserve Disk Space. Compatible with Graphical Library Automation System, Manager Series & Professional Series Product Lines. Once Images Are Imported & Linked, They Are Automatically Available to Be Viewed in GOPAC.
Data Trek, Inc.

ImagEntry. *Version:* 2.1. Jun. 1995. *Items Included:* Reference manual, user manual, keyboard template, decals. *Customer Support:* 90 day maintenance, Customer Care Plan Subscription at 15%, telephone support, trianing (scheduled & on-site), consulting.
DOS. 386/16 (2Mb), VGA. disk $1000.00 (Order no.: IE2.1).
Viking Software Services, Inc.

ImagEntry. *Version:* 3.0. Mar. 1996. *Items Included:* Reference manual, user manual, keyboard template, decals. *Customer Support:* 90 day maintenance, Customer Care Plan Subscription at 15%, telephone support, trianing (scheduled & on-site), consulting.
DOS. 386/16 (2Mb), VGA. disk $1100.00 (Order no.: IE3.0).
Viking Software Services, Inc.

ImagEntry. Apr. 1996. *Items Included:* Reference manual, user manual, keyboard template, decals. *Customer Support:* 90 day maintenance, Customer Care Plan Subscription at 15%, telephone support, trianing (scheduled & on-site), consulting.
Windows 3.11 or Windows 95. 486/25 (4Mb), VGA. disk $1200.00 (Order no.: IEW1.0).
Viking Software Services, Inc.

Images - Thermal. *Version:* 3.0. Jul. 1994. *Items Included:* User's manual. *Customer Support:* 12 mos. additional maintenance available.
MS-DOS (640k). IBM PC, XT, AT, PS/2 or compatibles. $795.00.
Performs Two & Three-Dimensional Heat Transfer Analyses for Complex Engineering Structures. Performs Steady-State Conduction, Convection & Radiation Analysis. 3000 Nodes.
Celestial Software, Inc.

Images-AISC. *Version:* 5.0. Jul. 1994. *Compatible Hardware:* IBM PC & compatibles. *Operating System(s) Required:* MS-DOS. *Language(s):* BASIC, Assembly. *Memory Required:* 640k. *Items Included:* User's manual.
$395.00.
Tests Structural Members for Compliance with American Institute of Steel Construction Codes.

TITLE INDEX

Stresses Are Determined & Compared Against Code Requirements. Menu-Driven; Utilizes User Prompts.
Celestial Software, Inc.

Images With Impact! Accents & Borders 1.
General Requirements: 2 MB of RAM; page-layout; PostScript or phoyotypesetter.
Macintosh Plus or higher. 3.5" disk 5 800K disks $129.00,.
Over 250 Historical, Natural, Contemporary Geometric & Seasonal Design Elements.
3G Graphics.

Images with Impact! Business 1. Compatible Hardware: Apple Macintosh; IBM PC & compatibles. Memory Required: 1000k. General Requirements: PostScript Laser Printer. Items Included: User manual. Customer Support: 800-456-0234.
3.5" disk $129.95.
Collections of High Resolution PostScript Clip Art Stored in EPS Format. Contains More Than 170 Illustrations & Symbols Created with Adobe Illustrator & Contained on Four 800k Disks. Images Are Strictly Business Related with Sections Devoted to Computers, Occupational Icons, People Doing Business, Communications, Aerospace, Public Symbols, Display Framers & Business Phrases. System Is Resolution Independent & Will Print at the Maximum Resolution of the PostScript Output Device Chosen. Provides an Extensive User's Guide Containing Many Examples of Ways to Use Images. A Pictorial Index Shows Where Each Image Is Located & How It Is Organized. The Number of Useful Images Can Be Almost Doubled If Used in Conjunction with Adobe Illustrator or Aldus Freehand or Corel Draw. Many of the Individual Graphics Pieces Can Be Lifted & Used Separately.
3G Graphics.

Images with Impact! Graphics Symbols 1.
Compatible Hardware: Apple Macintosh; IBM PC & compatibles. General Requirements: PostScript printer. Items Included: User manual, pictorial index. Customer Support: 800-456-0234.
3.5" disk $99.95.
Product Is First in Series. Requires Program That Reads Encapsulated PostScript (EPS) Files. Imaginative, Lighthearted Drawings in Categories Devoted to Display, Frames, Graphic Series, Multigraphics, Portfolio & Symbols. Images Are Resolution Independent & Will Print at the Maximum Resolution of the Output Device Chosen. Number of Useful Images Will Increase Greatly If Adobe Illustration, Freehand, or Corel Draw Is Used.
3G Graphics.

Images-2D. Version: 4.0. Jul. 1990. Compatible Hardware: IBM PC & compatibles. Operating System(s) Required: MS-DOS. Language(s): BASIC, Assembly. Memory Required: 640k. General Requirements: Printer. Items Included: User's manual.
Static $195.00; Dynamic $395.00.
Determines Response to Any Static Loads Including Deadweight, Imposed External Loads & Thermal Expansion. Automatically Generates Gravity or Deadweight Loads. Summarizes Stresses, Loads & Reactions in a Report Format on Standard Sized Paper. Deflected Shapes Can Be Plotted on the Screen & Exaggerated to Aid User in Understanding Structure Behavior.
Celestial Software, Inc.

Images-3D. Version: 3.0. Jul. 1994. Compatible Hardware: IBM PC, PC XT, PS/2 or compatibles. Operating System(s) Required: MS-DOS. Language(s): FORTRAN, BASIC, Assembly, C. Memory Required: 640k. General Requirements: Printer. Items Included: User's manual.
$795.00-$1395.00.
Performs Three-Dimensional Static Modal & Dynamic Analyses for Modeling Complex Engineering Structures & Systems. Performs Stress Analysis & Gives Results of Loads, Deflection, & Stresses. 18000 DOF, 3000 Nodes.
Celestial Software, Inc.

ImageStation. Version: 5.6. Sep. 1991. Customer Support: 90 day support & free upgrade; 1 Time Upgrade, $99.00; 1 year maintenance, $199.00.
DOS 2.0 or higher, Unix (XWindows/Motif), Xenix. IBM PC or compatibles (640k), DG Aviion, RS/6000, Intergraph 2000. disk $1795.00, TARGA. Nonstandard peripherals required: SVGA, TARGA 16/24/32/PLUS, Illuminator 16, RealVision 16E. Addl. software required: Memory Manager preferable. Optimal configuration: Videographics board, 4Mb RAMs, 60Mb hard drive.
disk $695.00, SVGA.
Design, Drawing, & Graphing Package Which Extends Over a Range of Different Platforms. Program Also Has Direct Support for a Number of Scanners & Outputs to a Number of Color Thermal Printer & Film Recorders.
Yale Graphics.

ImageStudio. Compatible Hardware: Apple Macintosh Plus, Macintosh SE, Macintosh II. General Requirements: External disk drive recommended. Supports any PostScript-compatible printer.
3.5" disk $495.00.
Image Processing Software. Manipulates Gray-Level Information of Images Generated by High Resolution Scanners, Allowing Users to Generate Camera-Ready Output. Images Can Be Stored in a Variety of Formats for Incorporation into Page Design Software Applications, Including READY SET GO! 4.0 (Letraset).
Letraset USA.

ImageVAULT. Jun. 1994. Items Included: User manual. Customer Support: Free phone technical support via 1-800 number.
Macintosh. Macintosh (4Mb). CD-ROM disk Contact publisher for price (ISBN 1-57600-016-8). Optimal configuration: Macintosh, 4Mb free space drive, 8-bit video & monitor, Photo CD-capable CD-ROM drive.
Windows. 386 IBM PC & compatibles (4Mb). Optimal configuration: 386 IBM PC & compatibles, 4Mb free space hard drive, 12Mb Windows swap file, VGA adapter & compatible monitor, CD-ROM ZA drive Mode 2.
Any other system which meets the requirements for viewing Kodak Photo CD such as Panasonic 3DO, Philips CD-I, etc.
Collection of Royalty-Free Stock Photography.
Digital Impact, Inc.

ImageVAULT Pro. Jun. 1994. Items Included: User manual. Customer Support: Free phone technical support via 1-800 number.
Macintosh; Windows. Macintosh (4Mb); IBM 386 or compatible (4Mb). CD-ROM disk $149.95 (ISBN 1-57600-017-6, Order no.: 50601). Nonstandard peripherals required: CD-ROM drive.
Collection of Royalty-Free Stock Photography.
Digital Impact, Inc.

ImageVAULT, Vol. 1: General Interest. Jun. 1994. Items Included: User manual. Customer Support: Free phone technical support via 1-800 number.
Macintosh; Windows. Macintosh (4Mb); IBM 386 or compatible (4Mb). CD-ROM disk $149.95 (ISBN 1-57600-016-8, Order no.: 50501). Nonstandard peripherals required: CD-ROM drive.
Collection of Royalty-Free Stock Photography.
Digital Impact, Inc.

IMAN: I MANUFACTURE

Imaginator. Sep. 1995. Customer Support: Telephone support - free (except phone charge).
Windows 3.1. IBM & compatibles (386 DX-20) (4Mb). CD-ROM disk $12.99 (ISBN 1-57594-021-3). Nonstandard peripherals required: 2x CD-ROM player, Sound Card, VGA monitor. Optimal configuration: 486 SX-33.
The Pick It, Cut It, Paste It, Record It, Paint It, You Make It - Creativity Tool for Kids.
Kidsoft, Inc.

Imaginator. Sep. 1995. Customer Support: Telephone support - free (except phone charge).
Windows 3.1. IBM & compatibles (386 DX-20) (4Mb). CD-ROM disk $12.99 (ISBN 1-57594-060-4). Nonstandard peripherals required: 2x CD-ROM player, Sound Card, VGA monitor. Optimal configuration: 486 SX-33.
The Pick It, Cut It, Paste It, Record It, Paint It, You Make It - Creativity Tool for Kids. Blister Pack Jewel Case.
Kidsoft, Inc.

Imagine. Version: 4.0. Nov. 1995. Items Included: 352 manual spiral bound. Customer Support: Tech support free of charge M-F 10am-4pm CST 1-612-425-0557.
1.3 or higher on Amiga/PC-DOS. Commodore Amiga (4k), PC 386 or higher with Math Chip (4Mb). disk $895.00 (Order no.: 3.0 AMIGA). Optimal configuration: Accelerated machine 8Mb & hard drive.
5.0 or higher DOS. PC or compatible (4k). disk $695.00 (Order no.: 3.0 PC). Nonstandard peripherals required: SVGA card. Addl. software required: DOS. Optimal configuration: 386 or higher with matching SVGA card, hard drive 8Mb or more.
A Complete 3D Ray Tracing & Rendering Animation Package. Imagine Lets You Make Flying Logos to Complete Character Animations. The Only Limitation Is Your Imagination.
Impulse, Inc.

Imaging for DataEase (IFD). Version: 1.15. Feb. 1992.
DOS 3.2 or higher. IBM PC & compatible. $995.00 Single User Version. Nonstandard peripherals required: Scanner, video or still camera.
Program That Allows Complete Integration of Documents, Images & Text within DATAEASE Relational Database Applications. Program Supports Crucial File Compression Standards to Alleviate Disk Storage Limitations That Can Become a Problem When Capturing & Storing Images. Also Provided Are Drivers for the Hewlett Packard ScanJet 11C & Fujitsu M309x Series Scanners, & Interfaces for Optical Disk Drives Operating on a Single User Workstation or Local Area Network (LAN). Compatible with DATAEASE 4.2 & 4.5.
Solana Software International.

IMAN: I Manufacture, 2 disks. Version: 5.0. Harold Reed. Aug. 1991. Compatible Hardware: IBM PC. Operating System(s) Required: PC-DOS/MS-DOS 3.3 or higher. Language(s): Clipper. Memory Required: 640k. General Requirements: Hard disk, printer.
$449.50 (ISBN 0-924495-02-2).
Integrated, Interactive, Natural Language Accounting, Database & Mail System for Those Who Build Products. It Is a Natural Language System That Can Be Treated As a Clerk or Administrative Assistant. IMAN Knows Accounting, Based on General Accounting Rules, But It Departs from Old Paper Ledger Based Bookkeeping Systems. The New System Makes It Practical to Have an Accounting Program That Does All Accounting, Including Payroll, with an English Language Command Structure & Still Leave Room for Database Management, Letter Writing & Mail Capabilities.
IDEA Computers, Inc.

IMC Quest. Jan. 1986. *Operating System(s) Required:* MS-DOS, PC-DOS. *Memory Required:* 256k.
  disk Single user $199.95.
  disk Multi user $399.95.
Business & Personal Directory, Note Pad, Simple Word Processor & Calendar. Allows for 99 Locations & Contacts per Entry, Foreign & U.S. Address Formats, Inquiry & Printing. Prints Mailing Labels, Envelopes of Any Size, Directory List, File Cards, Letters, Appointments, Notes & Rolodex Cards.
Information Management Corp.

Immunology QuizBank, Vol. 1. Ivan W. Roitt & Peter Delves. Oct. 1994. *Items Included:* User manual, quick-start sheet, Keyboard Utilities, & Microsoft Multimedia Viewer (Windows version) or HyperCard (Macintosh version). *Customer Support:* Free, unlimited technical support via our toll-free number (1-800-945-4551).
  Macintosh. Macintosh with a hard drive (2.5Mb). 3.5" disk $220.00 (ISBN 1-57349-195-0). *Addl. software required:* System 7.0 or higher. *Networks supported:* All LANs.
  Windows. IBM compatible with 80286 or higher processor, a hard drive & a mouse (2Mb). disk $220.00 (ISBN 1-57349-196-9). *Addl. software required:* MS-DOS 3.3 or higher, Windows 3.1 or higher. *Networks supported:* All LANs.
Over 500 Multiple-Choice Questions Covering All Areas of Immunology, with Detailed Feedback & Direct Links to Related Materials Appearing in the Immunology TextStack.
Keyboard Publishing, Inc.

Immunology TextStack. Ivan W. Roitt. Oct. 1994. *Items Included:* User manual, quick-start sheet, Keyboard Utilities, & Microsoft Multimedia Viewer (Windows version) or HyperCard (Macintosh version). *Customer Support:* Free, unlimited technical support via our toll-free number (1-800-945-4551).
  Macintosh. Macintosh with a hard drive (2.5Mb). CD-ROM disk $280.00 (ISBN 1-57349-190-X). *Nonstandard peripherals required:* CD-ROM player required, 256-color monitor recommended. *Addl. software required:* System 7.0 or higher. *Networks supported:* All LANs.
  Windows. IBM compatible with 80286 or higher processor, a hard drive & a mouse (2Mb). CD-ROM disk $280.00 (ISBN 1-57349-192-6). *Nonstandard peripherals required:* CD-ROM player required, 256-color monitor recommended. *Addl. software required:* MS-DOS 3.3 or higher, Windows 3.1 or higher. *Networks supported:* All LANs.
The Complete Text with All Tables, Figures, Diagrams, & Color Illustrations from Essential Immunology by Ivan W. Roitt. Includes a Collection of Tools for Searching, Capturing & Manipulating Data of Interest.
Keyboard Publishing, Inc.

IMPACT. *Version:* 5.57. 1991. *Items Included:* User guide documentation included. *Customer Support:* Toll-free telephone support as part of annual maintenance.
  MS-DOS 3.2 or higher plus Microsoft CD-ROM extensions 2.0 plus & CD-ROM Extensions 2.0 plus, 2 CD-ROM drives, VGA color monitor, MNP level 5 2400 bps modem. IBM PC XT, AT, 386 or 100% compatible microcomputer (640k). CD-ROM disk write for info. *Nonstandard peripherals required:* One or more CD-ROM drives. Hard disk and/or modem required for some modules. *Optimal configuration:* IBM compatible 286 PC, 640k RAM, MS-DOS 3.2. *Networks supported:* LANtastic ethernet - information on others on request.
A CD-ROM Based Library Public Access Catalog System, Operating on IBM Compatible Microcomputers Equipped with CD-ROM Drives. The Library's Bibliographic Database in Machine Readable Form Is Mastered on CD-ROM by Auto-Graphics & Accessed Using the System's Retrieval. Modular Architecture Includes Separate Modules for Location Based Searching, Cataloging & Interlibrary Loan. The System Administration Module Lets Individual Workstations Be Customized in Many Ways. The Search Interface Is Designed to Be Self-Teaching & User Oriented.
Auto-Graphics, Inc.

IMPACT. May 1993. *Items Included:* Free zipcodes database, 400 page manual. *Customer Support:* 1 year free technical support & BBS access.
  DOS 3.0; DOS 3.1 for multi-user. IBM PC, XT, AT or compatibles (524k). $189.95 single user; $289.95 multi-user; $69.95 Lite; $79.95 Laptop. *Optimal configuration:* 16 MHz 286 or higher, DOS 5.0, 2Mb or higher, disk cache or 18ms hard disk. *Networks supported:* All networks supported.
Fully Customizable Contact Management System. Features a Unique Group & Folder Structure Which Allows the End-User to Design Multiple Work Environments. Features a Completely Customizable Data Entry Interface, Telemarketing System, a Comprehensive Scheduling System, a Report, Label & Mail-Merge Designer & Generator.
Talon Software, Inc.

The Impersonator. *Version:* 2.0. Randall Hughes. Sep. 1985. *Compatible Hardware:* IBM PC, PC AT, PC XT. *Operating System(s) Required:* MS-DOS, PC-DOS. *Language(s):* Pascal & Assembly. *Memory Required:* 192k.
  disk $175.00.
Asynchronous Communications Tool & Terminal Emulator. Preconfigured Emulations for ADM-3A; VT 52/100; IBM 3101 Model 10, 20; Hazeltine Espirit & 1510; TeleVideo 912/950; NCR 7900 & TTY. Contains a Built-In Programming Language for Designing Additional Terminal Emulations. Features X-Modem Protocol, Window Support, Ability to Remember Complex Logon Procedures & Transfer of Files.
Direct-Aid, Inc.

The Importer: Import Distribution System. Apr. 1987. *Operating System(s) Required:* Unix, Xenix. *Memory Required:* 512k. *General Requirements:* 2 disk drives, printer, modem. $5,000-$150,000.
Includes Order Entry with A/R, A/P with LCs & Discount Acceptances, G/L, & Report Writer.
Dataverse Corp.

Impossible Mission. *Compatible Hardware:* Commodore Amiga.
  3.5" disk $39.95.
Arcade, Action Strategy Game.
Epyx, Inc.

Impressionism & Its Source. Feb. 1995. *Items Included:* CD-ROM booklet. *Customer Support:* Free technical support via phone as of release date.
  MPC/Windows. 386.25 or higher IBM compatible (4Mb). CD-ROM disk $49.95 (ISBN 1-885784-04-X, Order no.: 1134). *Optimal configuration:* MPC CD-ROM player, S-VGA graphics card (640x480x256 colors) with compatible monitor, MPC compliant sound card, mouse, Windows 3.1.
Interact with Outstanding Art from the Impressionist Movement. View over a Thousand Full-Color Paintings & Drawings Done in Oil, Gauche, Watercolor, Pastel & Other Media. Study the Works of Monet, Renoir, Cezanne & Their Contemporaries. Gain Insight into the Use of Bright Colors & Light That Give Impressionism Its Distinct Look.
Technology Dynamics Corp.

Imprimis. Mar. 1995. *Customer Support:* Toll-free 800 line, support & assistance center, emergency 24-hour support, modem support & diagnostics, etc. Provided as part of our support & assistance program - 15% annual fee - basic on total software license fees - training on-site - $800 per day plus expenses.
Contact publisher for price.
Tangible Vision, Inc.

IMRS Forms. *Operating System(s) Required:* PC-DOS/MS-DOS 3.0 or higher, MS Windows. *Memory Required:* 4000k. *General Requirements:* Hard disk. *Items Included:* User & administrator guides. *Customer Support:* Installation support; training; telephone support.
  $40,000.00 per headquarter site fee.
  15% annual renewal fee.
PC-Based Collection & Management System That Completely Automates Numeric & Textual Data Collection Requirements Throughout a Corporation. System Is Customizable for Variety of Applications, Including Tax Reporting, Inventory Control, Sales Tracking, & Scheduled Financial Data Collection.
IMRS, Inc.

IMRS OnTrack. *Version:* 2.0. Oct. 1989. *Memory Required:* 2Mb EMS & 640k. *Items Included:* Administrator's guide, quick reference card. *Customer Support:* Free hotline, Training, Installation support - varied pricing.
  DOS 3.0 or higher, MS Windows. IBM PC/XT/AT, 386, 486 & compatibles. $60,000, including 10 users. *Nonstandard peripherals required:* VGA; Windows pointing device. *Networks supported:* 3COM, Banyan Vines, IBM PC LAN, Novell Netware, IBM Token Ring.
Information Access & Delivery System That Accesses & Organizes Data from Any Corporate Source & Graphically Presents It to Corporate Users. Incorporates Open Architecture Design for Easy Integration with Other Corporate Systems & Provides Easy Access to Popular Analysis Tools. Uses Windows Fonts, Pointing Devices, & Printers. Integrates All Types of Data into One Environment.
IMRS, Inc.

IMSI Mouse - Combo: PS-2 & Serial. *Version:* 2.0. *Items Included:* Custom - Mouse Pad, Adapter & CursoramaPlus. *Customer Support:* Tech support.
  Windows 3.1 or higher. IBM PC & compatibles Serial or PS/2. disk $69.95 (ISBN 0-924677-32-5). *Optimal configuration:* Serial or PS/2.
Both Serial & PS/2. It's Ideal Pointing Device for Any Graphics or Mouse-Driven Software. Three Button Ergonomic Shaped Mouse That Is 100% MS, & Mouse Systems Compatible. IMSI Uses Dynamic Resolution Technology Which Allows for Precise control over the Speed of the Cursor on the Screen. 42000 DPI.
IMSI (International Microcomputer Software, Inc.).

IMSI Publisher. *Version:* 3.0. Jun. 1992. *Items Included:* Manual, Clip Art diskette (150 images), Image 72 manual & diskette (painting program), extra courier typeface diskette. *Customer Support:* 30-day unconditional guarantee, unlimited free telephone support, BBS.
  MS-DOS. 286 (640k). disk $99.95 (Order no.: SIP30). *Nonstandard peripherals required:* Graph. *Optimal configuration:* 386 with 40Mb hard disk, VGA adapter, mouse.
DOS-Based DTP Program Ideal for the Creation of Small to Medium-Sized Documents -

TITLE INDEX

Brochures, Newsletters, Memos, Invitations, Custom Letters, Reports. Strong Suite of Built-In Word Processing Features Like a Thesaurus, SpellChecker & Find & Replace Clip Art Also Included.
IMSI (International Microcomputer Software, Inc.).

In-CAD. *Compatible Hardware:* Apple Macintosh II.
3.5" disk $2495.00.
True Solids Modeler for Mechanical Design, Engineering, Drafting, Analysis, & Manufacturing. Combines Constructive Solid Geometry Capabilities with a WYSIWYG Interace. The Program Differentiates Between Material & Voids. Building-Block Primitives & Boolean Operations Are Used to Add & Subtract Material & Users Can View Models from any Direction with Hidden Lines Removed, Shaded, or Sectioned. Other Capabilities Include Dimensioning, Splines, User-Definable Text Fonts & Cross Hatch Patterns, Full Geometry Creation & Editing, Subfigures for Library Parts & Components, User-Definable Attributes & Grouping, Labeling with Balloons & Automatic Incrementing, Variable Width Lines, & a Programming Language. Features an IGES Translator for Importing & Exporting Files Between Other CAD Systems. A Translator Is Also Included for AutoCAD DXF Files.
Infinite Graphics, Inc.

In-Out. *General Requirements:* Hard disk drive; HyperCard.
Macintosh Plus or higher. 3.5" disk $69.95.
In/Out Office Tracking System.
Milum Corp.

In Search of Spot. (Math Blaster Ser.: Episode 1).
Windows. IBM & compatibles. CD-ROM disk $59.95 (Order no.: R1223). *Nonstandard peripherals required:* CD-ROM drive. *Optimal configuration:* 386 processor operating at 16Mhz or higher, MS-DOS 5.0 or higher, Windows 3.1 or higher, 30Mb hard drive, mouse, VGA graphic adapter & VGA color monitor (SVGA recommended), 4Mb RAM, external speakers or headphones (with sound card) that are Sound Blaster compatible.
This Program Teaches Problem-Solving & Mental Math Skills in the Context of an Exciting Adventure Game. Features over 50,000 Different Problems in Nine Key Subject Areas (Ages 6-12).
Library Video Co.

In the Promised Land, 5 disks. *Compatible Hardware:* Commodore Amiga.
3.5" disk incl. book $89.95.
Bible Studies for Adults.
Micro-Ed.

InBox. *Version:* 3.0. *Compatible Hardware:* Apple Macintosh; IBM PC. *Memory Required:* Mac-312k, IBM-345k. *Items Included:* Client software for up to 20 users; DOS or Mac administration software. *Customer Support:* (415) 769-9669.
disk $329.00.
20 User Electronic Mail & File Transfer.
Sitka Corp.

InBox. *Version:* 2.0. Apr. 1987. *Compatible Hardware:* Apple Macintosh, IBM PC. *Operating System(s) Required:* AppleTalk local area network. *Memory Required:* 512k.
InBox/MAC Personal Connection. 3.5" disk $125.00.
InBox/PC Personal Connection. 3.5" disk $195.00.
InBox Starter Kit. 3.5" disk $350.00.
Desktop Communications Package. Can Be Used on APPLETALK & NETBIOS LANs to Transfer Spreadsheet, Word Processing, Database, Graphics, Publishing, & Other Files from Macintosh to Macintosh, Macintosh to PC (& Vice Versa), & from PC to PC. Also Allows Users to Create, Send, & Receive Memos & Phone Messages While Running Other Applications. Supports Multiple Message Centers for Larger Networks.
Think Technologies.

Inc. Magazine's How to Really Start Your Own Business. Inc. Magazine Staff. Sep. 1994. *Items Included:* For Windows/MPC - QuickTime for Windows 1.1.1 (on the CD-ROM); For Macintosh - QuickTime 1.6.1, Sound Manager (on the CD-ROM). *Customer Support:* Free online support on America online using key word Zelos; Toll free number 1-800-345-6777; 90 day money back guarantee.
Windows/MPC; Macintosh. 386, 33MHz, single speed CD-ROM drive (8Mb); 68030, 25MHz Macintosh compatible single speed CD-ROM drive (8Mb). CD-ROM disk $29.95 (ISBN 1-883387-14-0). *Nonstandard peripherals required:* 640x480, 256 color SVGA monitor, Microsoft compatible mouse, SoundBlaster compatible sound card; 13" 256 color monitor. *Addl. software required:* DOS 5.0 or higher, Microsoft Windows 3.1, QuickTime for Windows 1.1.1; System 7.0, Quicktime 1.6.1, Sound Manager.
Get Inside Tips from the Founders of Crate & Barrel, Celestial Seasonings, David's Cookies, Pizza Hut, & Others! Learn How They Turned Their Dreams into Successes - & Apply Them to Your Own Business. Save Time & Money So You Can Turn Your Entrepreneurial Dreams into Reality.
Zelos.

Income & Expense Report: Non-Profit Organizations. *Compatible Hardware:* TI 99/4A. *Operating System(s) Required:* DX-10. *Language(s):* Extended BASIC. *Memory Required:* 48k.
cassette $39.95.
Accounting System Using the Fund Account Method. Up to 200 Income or Expense Categories Can Be Allocated for up to 20 Different Funds. 20 Different Bank Accounts Can Be Maintained. Generates Monthly Treasurer's Report.
Eastbench Software Products.

INCOME II: Integrated Company Management. *Version:* 2.0. 1989. *Compatible Hardware:* Altos; Compupro; Compaq; Fujitsu; Heath-Zenith; HP; IBM PC, PC XT, PC AT; NEC; Tandy. *Operating System(s) Required:* MS-DOS, PC-DOS, Concurrent DOS, Unix, Xenix; Novell & Microsoft networks. *Language(s):* C. *Memory Required:* 640k. *General Requirements:* Hard disk, & 132-column printer. *Items Included:* Disks & manual. *Customer Support:* Through VARs, support contracts available.
single-user per module $695.00.
multi-user per module $995.00.
Payroll single-user $995.00.
Payroll multi-user $1295.00.
Unix, Xenix $1495.00.
Integrated Set of Modules Including A/P, A/R, G/L, Inventory, Order Entry, Purchase Order, & Payroll. Designed to Cut Inventories & Increase Productivity in Small & Medium Companies. INMASS/MRP.
 Accounts Payable.
  Maintains a Flexible Chart of Accounts. Reports Include 3-Column Balance Sheet, Income Statement, Trial Balance, etc.
 Accounts Receivable.
  Supports Balance Forward or Open-Item Accounting. Applies Credit Memos, Automatically Calculates Service Charges & Monthly Bills. Prints Invoices, Statements, & Mailing Labels.
 General Ledger.
  Automatically Pays Expenses. Applies Open Credit Memos & Permits Partial Payments. Reports Include Cash Requirements, Payment Preview, Check Register; Prints Mailing Labels.
 Inventory.
  Controls a Perpetual Inventory. Provides Average, Standard, LIFO & FIFO Costing. Reports Include Reorder, Valuation, Activity, Physical Inventory Worksheet, Standard Costing Variation, Spares Usage, ABC Analysis. Prints Price List, Bin Labels.
 Order Entry.
  Records & Controls Customer Orders. Backorders Items Not in Stock or Reduces the Order to Match Inventory. Calculates Sales Commissions. Prints Order Acknowledgements, Packing Lists, Invoices.
 Purchase Order.
  Creates Orders & Tracks Receipts. Provides Vendor Performance Analysis Report.
 Payroll.
  Tracks Payroll for Company.

Income Property Analysis. 1978. *Compatible Hardware:* Apple II+, IIe, III; CP/M based machine; IBM PC & compatibles; TRS-80, Tandy. *Operating System(s) Required:* MS-DOS, Apple DOS. *Language(s):* BASIC. *Memory Required:* 48k.
disk $75.00.
Provides a Financial Analysis of Income Producing Property. Up to 4 Loans May Be Entered, Rents, Vacancy Factor, Taxes, Insurance, Utilities, Repairs, Legal Costs, Management Expense, & Any Other Monthly Expenses Are All Taken into Account in the Calculation of Total Cash Necessary to Purchase, Leverage Achieved, Gross Income Multiple, & the Loan to Value Ratio.
Realty Software.

Income Statement System. *Compatible Hardware:* Apple II, II+. *Language(s):* Applesoft II. *Memory Required:* 48k. *General Requirements:* Printer.
disk $49.95 (Order no.: 10002).
Menu Driven System Contains 8 Programs.
Powersoft, Inc.

Incorporate Your Business: The National Corporation Kit. (The/Small Business Library). Daniel Sitarz. Oct. 1996.
IBM. 3.5" disk $12.95 (ISBN 0-935755-23-3).
Forms-On-Disk - Containing All of the Legal Forms Necessary to Incorporate a Business in Any State.
Nova Publishing Company.

Incredible Image Pak 2000: ClickArt. *Items Included:* Visual index, user's guide. *Customer Support:* Free & unlimited technical support to registered users; 60 day money-back guarantee.
Macintosh. Macintosh, System 6.0.7 or higher (1Mb). 3.5" disk or CD-ROM $159.95. *Addl. software required:* Any word-processing, desktop publishing or works program that accepts graphics.
Windows MS-DOS. IBM PC & compatibles. 3.5" disk or CD-ROM $159.95. *Addl. software required:* Any word processing, desktop publishing or works program that accepts graphics.
Over 2000 Images! Full-Color Images; Ready-to-Use, or Changed in Appropriate Drawing Program; Designed in Full-Color (CMYK); Produced to Print in Detailed Greyscale on Black

& White Printers; Includes the ClickArt Trade Secret - Images Traded to Every Popular Graphics Format, Guaranteed to Work with All Popular Applications.
T/Maker Co., Inc.

The Incredible Journey. Sheila Burnford. Apr. 1996. *Customer Support:* Free technical support, 90 day warranty.
School ver.. System 7.1 or higher. Macintosh (4Mb). 3.5" disk contact publisher for price (ISBN 1-57204-177-3). *Nonstandard peripherals required:* 256 color monitor, hard drive printer.
Lab pack. System 7.1 or higher. Macintosh (4Mb). 3.5" disk contact publisher for price (ISBN 1-57204-178-1). *Nonstandard peripherals required:* 256 color monitor, hard drive, printer.
Site license. System 7.1 or higher. Macintosh (4Mb). 3.5" disk contact publisher for price (ISBN 1-57204-179-X). *Nonstandard peripherals required:* 256 color monitor, hard drive, printer.
School ver.. Windows 3.1 or higher. IBM/Tandy & 100% compatibles (4Mb). disk contact publisher for price (ISBN 1-57204-180-3). *Nonstandard peripherals required:* VGA or SVGA 640 x 480 resolution (256), mouse, hard drive, sound device.
Lab pack. Windows 3.1 or higher. IBM/Tandy & 100% compatibles (4Mb). disk contact publisher for price (ISBN 1-57204-181-1). *Nonstandard peripherals required:* VGA or SVGA 640 x 480 resolution (256), mouse, hard drive, sound device.
Site license. Windows 3.1 or higher. IBM/Tandy & 100% compatibles (4Mb). disk contact publisher for price (ISBN 1-57204-182-X). *Nonstandard peripherals required:* VGA or SVGA 640 x 480 resolution (256), mouse, hard drive, sound device.
This companion for young adult literature is ideal for students who don't know how to start that book report, or give that needed summary. Gentle prompts throughout the guide section of the program include Warm-up Connections, Thinking about Plot, Quoting & Noting, Keeping a Journal, If I Were———' Responding to Questions, Using Quotations, Taking a Personal View, Write to Others, & Write a Sequel.
Lawrence Productions, Inc.

The Incredible Toon Machine. Sep. 1995. *Customer Support:* Telephone support - free (except phone charge).
Windows 3.1. IBM & compatibles (386 DX-20) (4Mb). CD-ROM disk $12.99 (ISBN 1-57594-030-2). *Nonstandard peripherals required:* 2x CD-ROM player, Sound Card, VGA monitor. *Optimal configuration:* 486 XS-33.
An Outstanding Cartoon Construction Game for Puzzle Lovers.
Kidsoft, Inc.

The Incredible Toon Machine. Sep. 1995. *Customer Support:* Telephone support - free (except phone charge).
Windows 3.1. IBM & compatibles (386 DX-20) (4Mb). CD-ROM disk $12.99 (ISBN 1-57594-069-8). *Nonstandard peripherals required:* 2x CD-ROM player, Sound Card, VGA monitor. *Optimal configuration:* 486 SX-33.
An Outstanding Cartoon Construction Game for Puzzle Lovers. Blister Pack Jewel Case.
Kidsoft, Inc.

Incredible Toon Machine. Jan. 1996. *Customer Support:* Telephone support - free (except phone charge).
System 6.0.7 or higher. 256 color capable Mac with 68030 processor (4Mb). CD-ROM disk $12.99 (ISBN 1-57594-113-9). *Nonstandard peripherals required:* 2X CD ROM drive, mouse, 640/480 resolution monitor.
Enter a World Where Pinwheels & Dynamite, Cartoon Characters & Cheese, Even Gravity & Air Pressure Can Be Manipulated for Those Who Love Fiendishly Fun Puzzles.
Kidsoft, Inc.

Incredible Toon Machine. Feb. 1996. *Customer Support:* Telephone support - free (except phone charge).
System 6.0.7 or higher. 256 color Mac with 68030 processor (4Mb). CD-ROM disk $12.99 (ISBN 1-57594-113-9). *Nonstandard peripherals required:* 2x CD-ROM drive, mouse, 640/480 resolution monitor.
Enter a World Where Pinwheels & Dynamite, Cartoon Characters & Cheese, Even Gravity & Air Pressure Can Be Manipulated for Those Who Love Fiendishly Fun Puzzles.
Kidsoft, Inc.

Index Cards for IBM PC/XT/AT. *Version:* 1.1. 1989. *Items Included:* 16 page manual. *Customer Support:* 90 days unlimited warranty.
MS-DOS 2.X - 4.X & 5.0. IBM PC/XT/AT, PS/2 or compatibles (256k). disk $19.95 (Order no.: 9504).
This Program Package Will Give User Indexcards on Computer. User Search for & Select by an Entry. Each Entry is a Keyword! Logical & Allows to Search for Combinations of Keywords. Thousands of Possible Applications. Index Cards 8x32 - 245 Characters per Index Card, Index Cards 16x32 - 512 Characters per Index Card, Index Cards 16x64 - 1024 Characters per Index Card.
Elcomp Publishing, Inc.

INDEX+: Instrument Index. *Version:* 2.0. 1987. *Compatible Hardware:* IBM PC & compatibles. *Operating System(s) Required:* MS-DOS. *Language(s):* Compiled BASIC with Assembler. *Memory Required:* 512k.
disk $595.00, incl. manual (ISBN 0-87664-906-1, Order no.: 1906-1).
Finds, Sorts, Displays, & Prints Instrument Tag Numbers.
Instrument Society of America (ISA).

Individual Retirement Account. *Compatible Hardware:* Altos Series 5-15D, Series 5-5D, 580-XX, ACS8000-XX; DEC Rainbow 100 with 2 disk drives, Rainbow 100+ with 10MB hard disk; IBM PC with 2 disk drives, PC XT, IBM compatibles; Kaypro 11/IV with 2 disk drives, Kaypro 10; Xerox 820 with 2 disk drives; ZILOG MCZ-250. *Operating System(s) Required:* CP/M, MP/M, CP/M-86/80, PC-DOS, MS-DOS.
contact publisher for price (Order no.: IRA).
Template Designed to Analyze Investments in Either IRS or Keogh Plan Accounts. Calculates the Gross Residual Value & Present Value of an Investment in an IRA Resulting from a Rollover from Another Type of Retirement Plan. Also Produces a Schedule Showing Deposits, Earnings, Distribution & Annual Balance for a 15 Year Period.
Coopers & Lybrand.

Individual Training for Lotus 1-2-3. *Version:* 2.2. Jan. 1990. *Memory Required:* 128k. *Items Included:* 2 diskettes, 1 reference manual. *Customer Support:* Call Individual Software (90 days).
3.5" or 5.25" disk $69.95.
Computer-Based Tutorial on Lotus 1-2-3. Provides Interactive Lessons on Work-Sheet Basics, Menus, Formulas, Formats Range Commands & More. Also Covers Graphics, Databases & Expert Topics.
Individual Software.

Individual Training for PageMaker. *Version:* 4.0. *Compatible Hardware:* Macintosh. *Customer Support:* Call Individual Software (90 days).
3.5" disk $69.95.
Computer-Based Tutorial on PageMaker. Runs Side-by-Side with PageMaker Under Multifinder. Covers Mac-Basics, Running PageMaker, Placing Text & Graphics. Rulers & Toolbox Functions, Autoflow, Plus Design Topics & Expert Information.
Individual Software.

Individual Training for Project Management. Nov. 1985. *Compatible Hardware:* IBM PC & compatibles. *Operating System(s) Required:* PC/MS-DOS 2.0 or higher. *Memory Required:* 128k. *Items Included:* 2 diskettes, reference manual. *Customer Support:* Call Individual Software (90 days).
3.5" or 5.25" disk $69.95 (Order no.: 1009).
Teaches the Most Commonly Used Project Management Techiques of Critical Path Method (CPM), Program Evaluation & Review Techniques (PERT), & Gantt Charts. The User Is Guided Through an Introduction to Project Management Which Outlines the Key Elements of Planning Scheduling, Budgeting, & Controlling. Lessons Include How to Construct a Project Network, Assign Calendar, Identify Milestones, & Update a Project Plan.
Individual Software.

The Individualist: Computer Box. Todd Rundgren. Jul. 1995. *Items Included:* 1 manual. *Customer Support:* 30 day limited warranty.
MAC System 7.1 or higher; Windows 3.1 or higher. MAC w/68040 or any Power Mac (8Mb); IBM 486SX 25MHz or higher, Pentium compatible (8Mb). CD-ROM disk $16.95 (ISBN 1-887739-02-5, Order no.: 7-14774-30012-8). *Nonstandard peripherals required:* Double speed CD-ROM drive.
Enhanced Audio CD Which Consists of 10 Original Songs & 10 Interactive Graphical Environments That Plays in Standard Audio CD Players & MAC & PC CD-ROM Drives.
ION.

The Individualist: Jewel Case. Todd Rundgren. Jul. 1995. *Items Included:* 1 manual. *Customer Support:* 30 day limited warranty.
MAC System 7.1 or higher; Windows 3.1 or higher. MAC w/68040 or any Power Mac (8Mb); IBM 486SX 25MHz or higher, Pentium compatible (8Mb). CD-ROM disk $16.95 (ISBN 1-887739-01-7, Order no.: 7-14774-20012-1). *Nonstandard peripherals required:* Double speed CD-ROM drive.
Enhanced Audio CD Which Consists of 10 Original Songs & 10 Interactive Graphical Environments That Plays in Standard Audio CD Players & MAC & PC CD-ROM Drives.
ION.

Indoor Soccer. *Compatible Hardware:* TI 99/4A with PLATO interpreter solid state cartridge.
contact publisher for price (Order no.: PHM 3024).
Computer Version of Five-on-a-Side Soccer, Including Passes, Shots, Interceptions, Saves & Tackles.
Texas Instruments, Personal Productivit.

InduScript Text Converter. *Version:* 3.0. Jun. 1993. *Items Included:* User manual, Keyboard Layout Chart, Keycap Sticker Sheet. *Customer Support:* Free telephone support, defective disks replaced.
Macintosh. Macintosh (1Mb). 3.5" disk $79.95. *Addl. software required:* Any Word Processor. *Optimal configuration:* 4Mb RAM & a hard drive.
If You Type Phonetically on a Text-Mode

TITLE INDEX

Computer & Transfer That Text to Your Mac You Can Use Our Program InduScript Text Converter to Convert Your Whole Folder of Files Which You Have Typed into Any of the InduScript-Controlled Languages.
Linguist's Software, Inc.

Industrial Strength Payroll. Version: 2.31. Jul. 1993. Items Included: Comprehensive manual in deluxe cloth binder & slipcase. Optional forms creation software available for those with laser printer & "T" cartridge. Customer Support: 2 hours no cost support to registered owners during 1st 6 months. Thereafter $60.00/hr with no minimum. Optional tax table service $45.00/tax year. Optional continuous program maintenance $75.00/tax year.
PS-DOS/MS-DOS 2.1 or higher. IBM PC, XT, AT, PS/2 or 100% compatible micro-computer (640k). $245.00 (ISBN 1-877915-07-6, Order no.: 1065 (5.25"), 1063 (3.50")). Nonstandard peripherals required: Printer capable of printing 132 characters in condensed or normal mode, OR Helwett-Packard Laserjet series II or 100% compatible laser. Optimal configuration: 640k, hard disk, DOS 3.3.
Option MICR Encoding $315.00 single user, $475.00 site (ISBN 1-877915-08-4).
Automate a Weekly, Bi-Weekly, Semi-Monthly & Monthly Payroll for a Maximum of 30,000 Employees per Client. Handles up to 999 Separate Companies. It Is a Multi-State Program Able to Process Three States in the Same Company File. Accommodates Hourly, Salaried & 1099 Personnel. Allows Payroll Frequencies to Be Mixed. Provides Eight User-Definable Earnings Categories Plus Tips & 12 Automatic, User-Definable Deductions. Records After-the-Fact Payroll. Calculates Federal, FICA, Medicare & Backup Withholdings. Any Employee Can Have Taxes Withheld for Two States, Two Disabilities & Two Cities Concurrently. Maintains Personnel History Data & Completes W-2s, W-3s, 940s, 941s, 942s, 943s, 1096s & 1099-MISCs Using an Impact or Laser Printer. Prints Monthly & Quarterly Wage & Other Reports Including FUTA & SUTA Information in Both Generic & State Specific Formats. Files W-2s & 1099s Magnetically. Prints Paychecks & Vouchers with Y-T-D As Well As Current Payroll Information on the Stubs.
Phoenix Phive Software Corp.

Industry Norms & Key Business Ratios on Diskette. Compatible Hardware: IBM PC & compatibles. Operating System(s) Required: PC-DOS. Language(s): BASIC. Memory Required: 512k.
disk write for info.
Available for More Than 800 Lines of Business in Both One & Three Year Editions. By Simply Selecting the Industry of His Choice, the User Can Compare the Financial Status of His Customers & Prospects to Their Industry Peers, Identify an Account's Business Strengths & Weaknesses. With the Three Year Edition an Industry's Unique Trends Can Be Pinpointed Instantly.
Dun & Bradstreet Credit Services.

Inertia. Version: 3.2 1. Sep. 1988. Items Included: manual, training guide. Customer Support: 317-469-4140.
MS-DOS 3.0 or higher. IBM PC & compatibles (640K). $10,000.00.
MAC O/S 6.0. MAC IIcx 5Mg RAM & color graphics. 3.5" disk $3000.00.
Engineering Modeling, Analysis & Design System Using Finite Element Techniques. Includes InSolid, InThermal, InDynamic, InMotion, InSpring, InFrame, InProp, InTruss, InBeam, CADLink.
Modern Computer Aided Engineering, Inc.

Infection Control. Items Included: Manuals, training exercises, quick reference guide.
IBM PC, XT, AT, & compatibles; PS/2. contact publisher for price.
Management Reporting from Any Angle.
Beechwood Software.

Infemed: Medical Management - Macintosh. Apr. 1986. Compatible Hardware: Apple Macintosh. Memory Required: 512k.
contact publisher for price.
Medical Management System Which Is Easy to Learn Because It Resembles the Pegboard System.
Infeld Software.

Infidel. Michael Berlyn. 1983. Compatible Hardware: Apple II, Macintosh; Atari XL/XE, ST; Commodore 64, Amiga; CP/M-based machines; IBM PC; Kaypro; TI Professional; TRS-80 Model I, Model III. Operating System(s) Required: CP/M, MS-DOS. Memory Required: 32k.
disk $14.95.
You Are Marooned by Your Followers in the Heart of the Deadly Egyptian Desert. A Searcher of Fortune by Trade, You've Come Here in Search of a Lost Pyramid & Its Untold Reaches. Now You Must Locate & Gain Entry to the Tomb, Decypher Its Hieroglyphs, & Unravel Its Mysteries One by One. Death Will Lick at Your Heels As You Race to the Shattering Climax of This Match of Wits Between You & the Most Ingenious Architects, Builders, & Assassins of All Time & the Ancient Egyptians.
Activision, Inc.

Infidel. Infocom. Compatible Hardware: HP 150 Touchscreen, HP 110 Portable.
3.5" disk $44.95 (Order no.: 92243WA).
You Are Marooned by Your Followers in the Heart of the Deadly Egyptian Desert. A Searcher of Fortune by Trade, You've Come Here in Search of a Lost Pyramid & Its Untold Reaches. Now You Must Locate & Gain Entry to the Tomb, Decypher Its Hieroglyphs, & Unravel Its Mysteries One by One. Death Will Lick at Your Heels As You Race to the Shattering Climax of This Match of Wits Between You & the Most Ingenious Architects, Builders, & Assassins of All Time - the Ancient Egyptians.
Hewlett-Packard Co.

InfiNit. Compatible Hardware: IBM PC & compatibles.
disk $13,000.00.
Net-List Extraction Program for Automating Testing in the PC Board Manufacturing Process.
Infinite Graphics, Inc.

Info-Mac V. Customer Support: All of our products are unconditionally guaranteed.
Mac. CD-ROM disk $49.95 (Order no.: INFO-MAC). Nonstandard peripherals required: CD-ROM drive.
10,000 Mac Files: Demos, Hypercards, Games, Programs, More.
Walnut Creek CDRom.

INFO/MASTER. Version: 2.2. Items Included: Manuals. Customer Support: Annual renewal fee 20% of purchase price/yr..
MVS/ESA, MVS/XA, MVS/SP; VM/SP, VM/HPO, VM/XA; DOS/VSE, DOS/VSE/SP; FUJITSU MSP, FUJITSU/FSP; IBM System/370 & System/390 (and compatibles). $15,000.00-$34,000.00. Addl. software required: VTAM. Networks supported: IBM SNA.
Part of the ASM Product Line, This Offers a Repository Data Base for Network & Systems Information, & a Facility for Developing & Customizing Applications Such As Problem, Change & Configuration Management. Through Its Integration with the Other ASM Components, the Program Facilitates Automated Recovery Procedures in Response to a Failure in the Network or Systems.
Sterling Software.

Info Trust: Client Information Trust. Version: 2.2. (Electronic Data Banking Ser.). R. E. Baker & Prema Nakra. Aug. 1992. Compatible Hardware: IBM 486-based Pentium, Digital Alpha. Operating System(s) Required: MS-DOS, Windows 3.X, 95 & NT. Language(s): Clarion. Memory Required: 512k. General Requirements: Hard drive, printer, modem. Items Included: In Trust Text, work sheets & user manual. Customer Support: 90 day unlimited warranty, extended maintenance, bulletin board, $125.00 per year, including annual updates.
disk $495.00 ea.
Windows 3.X. (ISBN 0-931755-36-0, Order no.: FS 230/2).
Windows 95. (ISBN 0-931755-37-9, Order no.: FS 230/3).
Windows NT. (ISBN 0-931755-38-7, Order no.: FS 230/4).
Implements Client Information Trust. Enables Legal & Financial Professionals to Collect Vital Information & Prepare Key Document Records, i.e., Wills, Estate Plans, Financial Plans for Banking in Secured Numbered Accounts in Info Trust Data Banking Center. On-Line Data Storage Provides Clients with Swift & Easy Retrieval of Vital Records & Documents at Anytime from Anywhere in the World.
Ellington Duval, Inc.

Info Trust: Personal Information Trust. Version: 2.2. (Electronic Data Banking Ser.). Prema Nakra & Robert E. Baker. Aug. 1992. Operating System(s) Required: MS Windows, MS-DOS. Language(s): Clarion/DBL. Memory Required: 512k. Items Included: Text & worksheets, user's manual. Customer Support: 90 day unlimited warranty.
disk $149.00.
Windows 95 & NT. (ISBN 0-931755-18-2, Order no.: FS 130/4).
(ISBN 0-931755-19-0, Order no.: FS 130/5).
Creates a Private Information Trust. Enables Individuals to Collect, Organize & Record Vital Data, Information & Documents. Financial, Legal & Personal Records for Electronic Vaulting in the Info Trust Data Baking Center. Secure, On-Line, Data Storage Allows Swift Access & Easy Retrieval at Any Time from Anywhere in the World. Safeguarding Individual & Joint Information Trust Accounts.
Ellington Duval, Inc.

InFoCAD. Version: 8.0. 1992. Items Included: Media, documentation. Customer Support: Maintenance (includes updates, new releases, & documentation) 10% of software per year; support (includes a toll free number) 5% of software per year.
UNIX work stations & servers including: DG/UX, AIX, ULTRIX, Sun OS, HP/UX. $5000.00 - $12500.00 depending on platform. Networks supported: TCP/IP.
UNIX (24Mb RAM, 330Mb disk). Sun, SPARC Dec Risc, IBM Risc, DGAvision, IBM. Volume discounts available. Networks supported: TCP/IP Ethernet.
Completely Integrated GIS/CADD/COGO Software Product Packaged in a Modern Production-Oriented, Graphical User Environment. Product's Foundation Is a Graphical-Relational Database Management System Which Serves as the Basis for Utilities Which Provide Functionality Ranging from Map Generation with Surveying Accuracy to Complex Spatial Analysis & Thematic Mapping.
Digital Matrix Services, Inc.

InFoCASE. *Version:* 8.0. 1992. *Items Included:* Media & documentation. *Customer Support:* Maintenance (includes updates, new releases & documentation) 10% of software per year. Support (includes a toll free number) 5% of software per year.
UNIX including: HP/UX, DG/UX, SunOS, ULTRIX, AIX, & SCO. UNIX Workstations, servers, & PCs including: HP, DG, SUN, DEC, IBM, & IBM PC compatibles (24Mb). $500.00 per license; volume discounts avail. *Networks supported:* TCP/IP.
InFoCAD's Highly Intuitive, "Push Button," Object Oriented CASE Management System Which Provides Information to Operators, Supervisors, & Managers. It Tracks Everything That Comprises an Activity, Project, Staff Assignment or Department's Progress. Management Information Is Presented in the Form of Reports, Graphs, Pie & Bar Charts, & Histograms.
Digital Matrix Services, Inc.

InfoCheck: Custom Test Maker, Designer. *Items Included:* Installation guide & diskettes. *Customer Support:* Toll-free, fee-free, technical support on the product title & the underlying application.
Windows 3.1 or higher. IBM PC & compatibles. disk $160.00. *Nonstandard peripherals required:* VGA.
Part of an Integrated Curriculum of Computer-Based Training & Testing Products. Contains 50 Pre-Made Questions. The Administrator Has the Option to Add Custom Made Questions, & Also Select/Deselect Questions. Contact InfoSource for More Information.
InfoSource, Inc.

InfoCheck: Databases Access 2.0 for Windows Fundamentals & Intermediate. *Items Included:* Installation guide & diskettes. *Customer Support:* Toll-free, fee-free, technical support on the product title & the underlying application.
Windows 3.1 or higher. IBM PC & compatibles. disk $160.00. *Nonstandard peripherals required:* VGA.
Part of an Integrated Curriculum of Computer-Based Training & Testing Products. Contains 50 Pre-Made Questions. The Administrator Has the Option to Add Custom Made Questions, & Also Select/Deselect Questions. Contact InfoSource for More Information.
InfoSource, Inc.

InfoCheck: Designer. *Items Included:* Installation guide & diskettes. *Customer Support:* Toll-free, fee-free, technical support on the product title & the underlying application.
Windows 3.1 or higher. IBM PC & compatibles. disk $200.00. *Nonstandard peripherals required:* VGA.
Testing Software That Enables You to Create up to 30 Multiple Choice Questions per Test. Administrator Has Various Administrative Options Which Include: Select/Deselect Questions, All User Messages, Single User Messages, & Much More. Contact InfoSource for More Information.
InfoSource, Inc.

InfoCheck: Graphics & Presentations, PowerPoint 4.0 for Windows Fundamentals. *Items Included:* Installation guide & diskettes. *Customer Support:* Toll-free, fee-free, technical support on the product title & the underlying application.
Windows 3.1 or higher. IBM PC & compatibles. disk $160.00. *Nonstandard peripherals required:* VGA.
Part of an Integrated Curriculum of Computer-Based Training & Testing Products. Contains 50 Pre-Made Questions. The Administrator Has the Option to Add Custom Made Questions, & Also Select/Deselect Questions. Contact InfoSource for More Information.
InfoSource, Inc.

InfoCheck: Operating Environements Windows 3.1 Fundamentals, Windows 95 Fundamentals. *Items Included:* Installation guide & diskettes. *Customer Support:* Toll-free, fee-free, technical support on the product title & the underlying application.
Windows 3.1 or higher. IBM PC & compatibles. disk $160.00. *Nonstandard peripherals required:* VGA.
Part of an Integrated Curriculum of Computer-Based Training & Testing Products. Contains 50 Pre-Made Questions. The Administrator Has the Option to Add Custom Made Questions, & Also Select/Deselect Questions. Contact InfoSource for More Information.
InfoSource, Inc.

InfoCheck: Spreadsheets, Excel 5.0 for Windows Fundamentals & Intermediate, Lotus 1-2-3 Rel. 5 for Windows Fundamentals & Intermediate. *Items Included:* Installation guide & diskettes. *Customer Support:* Toll-free, fee-free, technical support on the product title & the underlying application.
Windows 3.1 or higher. IBM PC & compatibles. disk $160.00. *Nonstandard peripherals required:* VGA.
Part of an Integrated Curriculum of Computer-Based Training & Testing Products. Contains 50 Pre-Made Questions. The Administrator Has the Option to Add Custom Made Questions, & Also Select/Deselect Questions. Contact InfoSource for More Information.
InfoSource, Inc.

InfoCheck: Word Processing Word 2.0 for Windows, Word 6.0 for Windows Fundamentals & Intermediate, WordPerfect 6.1 for Windows Fundamentals & Intermediate. *Items Included:* Installation guide & diskettes. *Customer Support:* Toll-free, fee-free, technical support on the product title & the underlying application.
Windows 3.1 or higher. IBM PC & compatibles. disk $160.00. *Nonstandard peripherals required:* VGA.
Part of an Integrated Curriculum of Computer-Based Training & Testing Products. Contains 50 Pre-Made Questions. The Administrator Has the Option to Add Custom Made Questions, & Also Select/Deselect Questions. Contact InfoSource for More Information.
InfoSource, Inc.

Infocom: Science Fiction Collection. *Items Included:* Installation Guide.
IBM PC. Contact publisher for price (ISBN 0-87321-029-8, Order no.: CDD-3097).
Activision, Inc.

Infodex. *Compatible Hardware:* Commodore 64. *Operating System(s) Required:* PC-DOS, MS-DOS, CP/M. *Customer Support:* 800-929-8117 (customer service).
MS-DOS. contact publisher for price.
Electronic Rotary Card Filing & Maintenance System That Catalogs & References Information in a Variety of Ways.
SourceView Software International.

InfoIMAGE. *Version:* 8.0. Sep. 1992. *Items Included:* Media & documentation. *Customer Support:* Maintenance (includes updates, new releases & documentation) 10% of software per year. Support (includes a toll free number) 5% of software per year.
UNIX including: HP/UX, DG/UX, SunOS, ULTRIX, AIX, & SCO. UNIX workstations, servers, & PCs including: HP, DG, SUN, DEC, IBM, IBM PC compatibles (24Mb). $2500.00; volume discounts avail. *Networks supported:* TCP/IP.
A Fully Integrated Image Module Which Offers InFoCAD Users the Ability to Calibrate, Rectify to Real World Coordinates, & Display Raster Images of Any Size or Resolution. Also Integrates Imagery into the GIS Database Environment, Thereby Allowing Users to Efficiently Manage Images Through InFoCAD's G-RDBMS As Well As Perform On-Screen Digitizing. An Ideal, Low-Cost, Easy to Use, Image Management & Document Retrieval System.
Digital Matrix Services, Inc.

Infomanager. (The IMSI Home Library). International Microcomputer Software, Inc. (IMSI). Oct. 1984. *Compatible Hardware:* Commodore 64, IBM PC, PCjr.
disk $39.95 ea.
IBM PC. (ISBN 0-13-464132-9).
IBM. (ISBN 0-13-464140-X).
Commodore. (ISBN 0-13-464124-8).
Record Manager System That Stores, Retrieves & Updates. Suitable to Any Data That Needs Organization & Upkeep.
Prentice Hall.

InfoMapper: Information Resources Management Online Support System. *Version:* 1.2. Jul. 1992. *Items Included:* User manual, project manager's guide, instructor's guide, demo disk (optional; available separately), system administrator's guide. *Customer Support:* Tech support arrangements available. Terms & conditions upon request. Installation assistance & information management orientation training available. Ongoing consulting/support.
MS-DOS 3.3 or higher. IBM or compatible PCs or Networks; Apple; DEC; AT&T (640k). disk $595.00 (ISBN 0-9606408-4-3). *Networks supported:* BANYAN, Novell, Others.
Foreign language version upgrade $100.00.
Identifies, Profiles, & Inventories All Manual & Automated Information Resource Entities, Any Organization. Produces Internally or Acquires Externally, Brings in to the Enterprise, Stores, Uses & Re-Uses. Uses Standard & Universally Applicable Taxonomics. Released As RunTime Version of dBASE IV for PCs, Networks, UNIX, VAX & Macintosh. Also Available in French, German, Spanish.
Information Management Pr., Inc.

Infominder. *Compatible Hardware:* Commodore Amiga.
3.5" disk $89.95.
Hierarchical Data Retrieval System.
Byte by Byte.

INFOQUEST Services Software: Student Services Software - Educational. *Version:* 4.0. Open Door Software Division. 1989. *Items Included:* Manual. *Customer Support:* On-site training available - $200.00/day, plus per diem; Customization available, $50.00/hr; Maintenance on customized copies, $100.00/month.
IBM & compatible (512k). disk $999.00 (ISBN 1-56756-006-7, Order no.: OD100I).
3.5" disk $750.00 (ISBN 1-56756-007-5, Order no.: OD130M).
Student Services Software Which Includes BOOKMATE (a Service Linking Buyers & Sellers of Books to Negotiate Their Own Prices. Students Can Buy Books for Less from Other Students at Prices They Choose), CLASSMATE (a Referral System for Notes, Tests, & Tutors), KEYMATE (a Numbered Key Chain Tracking System for Returning Lost or Misplaced Keys to Students), RIDEMATE (a Computer Ride-Sharing Service) & TEACHMATE (a Teacher Evaluation & Student/Faculty Opinion Polling Service).
Advantage International.

Inforcom: Adventure Collection. *Items Included:* Installation Guide.
IBM PC. Contact publisher for price (ISBN 0-87321-028-X, Order no.: CDD-3096).
Activision, Inc.

TITLE INDEX

INFORMATIONAL DATABASES

Inforcom: Comedy Collection. *Items Included:* Installation Guide.
IBM PC. Contact publisher for price (ISBN 0-87321-026-3, Order no.: CDD-3094).
Activision, Inc.

Inforcom: Fantasy Collection. *Items Included:* Installation Guide.
IBM PC. Contact publisher for price (ISBN 0-87321-027-1, Order no.: CDD-3095).
Activision, Inc.

Inforcom: Mystery Collection. *Items Included:* Installation Guide.
IBM PC. Contact publisher for price (ISBN 0-87321-025-5, Order no.: CDD-3098).
Activision, Inc.

Informa. Abacus Data, Inc. *Compatible Hardware:* TI Professional. *Operating System(s) Required:* CP/M-86, MS-DOS. *Memory Required:* 192k. *General Requirements:* Printer.
$795.00 (Order no.: INFORMA 15).
Full Relational Database Management System & Automatic Programming System.
Texas Instruments, Personal Productivit.

Informal Reading. Eunice Insel & Ann Edson. 1994. *Items Included:* Diskette & teachers guide & binder. *Customer Support:* Toll free customer service Hot Line 1-800-645-3739 (9a.m. - 5p.m. Eastern Time) software guaranteed for two years.
Mac 6.0 Plus. Macintosh (4Mb). 3.5" disk $59.95 (Order no.: DK28070).
Determines a Quick Placement Level for All Your Students! Validated by over 3000 Students, This Test Places Each Student in an Instructional Reading Range Through Grade 12. Automatically Administrated, Scored, & Managed.
Educational Activities Inc.

Information Center: Strategies & Case Studies.
Shaku Atre. Jul. 1986.
contact publisher for price.
Provides Pragmatic Solutions That Can Be Translated to Accommodate Specific Orgaizational Needs.
Atre Software, Inc.

Information Management (IMPac). *Compatible Hardware:* HP 85 with Plotter/Printer ROM (HP 00085-15002), 16k memory module (HP 82903A), plotter (HP 7225B with HP 17601A module, HP 9872C, or HP 7470A), ROM Drawer (HP 82936A, HP-IB interface (HP 82937A), mass storage ROM (HP 00085-15001), disk memory (HP 82900 series, 9121D/S, 9134A, 9135A, or 9895A).
3-1/2" or 5-1/4" disk $115.00 ea. (Order no.: 82817A).
System for List Management. Each Record Can Be 20 to 1024 Bytes Long. Fields Can Be Defined As Alphanumeric, Numeric-Only, & Dollars. Includes Create, Update, Search, & Extend Routines, Plus a Querying System, Report Writer, & Graphics Capability.
Hewlett-Packard Co.

Information Manager/6000 for Justice. *Items Included:* Software license, installation, basic orientation. *Customer Support:* Services contract, modem support, travel extra.
IBM RISC System 6000 (all), Alpha Micro (all), Most UNIX; PC's & LAN's. Contact publisher for price.
Integrated Information Management System for County Courthouses, Sheriffs, Municipal Courts & Police Agencies. Encompasses All Offices Involved in the Administration of Justice; Available in Modules or As a Complete System.
Earl R. Hunt & Assoc., Inc.

Information Manager/6000 for Law Firms. Jun. 1986. *Items Included:* Software license, installation, base orientation. *Customer Support:* Services contract; training included (travel extra); software license; installation; basic orientation.
IBM RISC System 6000 (all), Alpha Micro (all), UNIX (most). Contact publisher for price.
A Results-Based Multi-User, Integrated Client Manager, Time & Billing, Docketing, Financial, Litigation, & Word Processing System. Helps Manage Firms up to 100 Lawyers.
Earl R. Hunt & Assoc., Inc.

Information Rainbow. *Version:* 1.1. Mar. 1994. *Items Included:* Developer's guide, hardware key, seven disks of examples. *Customer Support:* 1 yr. no charge - 2nd yr. on $295.00 per copy.
Macintosh. Quadra 605 (8Mb), 160Mb disk, 14" monitor. 3.5" disk $2500.00, additional copies depending on quantity ,500.00-,1500.00 (Order no.: IR-US01). *Addl. software required:* Painting, drawing, word processing, sound editing (used to create content materials). *Optimal configuration:* Quadra 650, 17" touch-screen monitor, 12Mb Memory, 500Mb disk, CD ROM. *Networks supported:* Appletalk, Ethernet.
Allows User to Create an Interactive Information System Without Programming. By Placing Pictures, Sounds, Text, Video Clips, & Documents into Folders on the Hard Disks a Public Information System Can Be Created Overnight. Applications Such As Wayfinding, Assisting in the Purchase Decision, Surveys, Welcoming Guests, Dialing the Phone, & Dispensing Maps, Coupons, or Other Printed Materials Are Supported. Built-In Attract Loop May Be Used for Advertising or Sponsor Recognition.
First Wave.

Information Support Systems. *Customer Support:* Software warranty; 24 hours, days a week; 800 number; hardware/software staging; training & seminars; documentation; system personalization; consulting services.
DSM, OpenVMS, DOS, AIX, MSM, OSF/2, HP-UX. DEC, IBM & HP platforms (2Mb). contact publisher for price.
ANTRIM Corp.

Information Support Systems. *Customer Support:* Software warranty; 24 hours, days a week; 800 number; hardware/software staging; training & seminars; documentation; system personalization; consulting services.
DEC VAX, Alpha AXP, DECStation & PC Platforms using OpenVMS, DSM, OSF/1 or DOS; IBM RISC System 6000 under AIX, Micronetic MUMPS, or DOS; HP9000 under HP-UX. DEC, IBM & HP platforms (2Mb). contact publisher for price.
Augments the Processing Capabilities of Each Applications Software Offered for the Medical Laboratory. OnlineLab Application Electronically Unites Laboratories with Physician Offices They Serve. Report Writer: Query Requests, Information Retrieval from Antrim's Systems, Data Formatting for Reporting, & Disposition of Reports to Other Applications, Terminals, and/or Printers. Optical Disk Archiving: Downloads Data from the Laboratory's Host Computer & Reformats Data for Long-Term Storage. Later, It Provides Rapid Access to Archived Information & Expedient Reporting of Information to Terminal, Export Files, Printers & FAX Machines. Hand Held Terminals: Automates Data Collection at the Source, Providing Accountability for When Tasks Are Completed. Data Collected Is Uploaded Easily & Quickly into Antrim's Systems for Subsequent Processing & Reporting.
ANTRIM Corp.

Information Systems for Attorneys: Series 500, 600. Jan. 1987. *Compatible Hardware:* IBM PC, PC AT, PC XT & PS/2. *Operating System(s) Required:* PC-DOS/MS-DOS 3.1 or higher. *Language(s):* BASIC, C. *Memory Required:* 256k. *General Requirements:* Hard disk, printer.
contact publisher for price.
Computer-Based Method of Managing Law Office Information. Provides Five Systems to Address the Legal Practice & Financial Management Requirements of the Law Firm or Corporate Law Department. Series 500 Modules Are Designed for Single-User PCs, While Series 600 Modules Are Designed for Networked PCs. Modules from Both Series May Be Combined.
Manac-Prentice Hall Software, Inc.

Information Systems for Attorneys: Series 900, 1000. Oct. 1986. *Compatible Hardware:* IBM System/36. *Operating System(s) Required:* SSP. *Language(s):* RPG II, C. *Memory Required:* 512k. *General Requirements:* Hard disk, printer.
contact publisher for price.
Computer Based Method of Managing Law Office Information. The Wide Range of Systems (13) Addresses the Unique Requirements of a Law Firm or Corporate Law Department As Well As the Preferences of Individual Attorneys. The OMNILAW Module Ties Together All Law Office Automation.
Manac-Prentice Hall Software, Inc.

Information Systems for Attorneys: Series 2000. Jun. 1988. *Compatible Hardware:* IBM AS/400. *Operating System(s) Required:* OS/400. *Language(s):* RPG III & RPG 400. *General Requirements:* 9404/9406 CPU, Driver 230; PTF level or GA c8190110 & SF00252.
contact publisher for price.
Provides a Computer-Based Method of Managing Law Office Information. Addresses the Requirements of Larger Law Firms & Corporate Law Departments As Well As the Preferences of Individual Attorneys. The OMNILAW Module Ties Together All Law Office Automation.
Manac-Prentice Hall Software, Inc.

Informational Databases. 1994. *Customer Support:* 1 year free customer support including 800 support & our 2 hour call-back guarantee.
MS-DOS (Foots on File). IBM PC & compatibles (25Mb per year per database). Facts on File School Library Database $525.00; Public Library Database $725.00; College Library Database $725.00; Winnebago Informational Database 1 year subscription $299.00.
MS-DOS (UM1). IBM PC & compatibles (Resource/One Select 75Mb/year; Resource/One 200Mb/year; PA Library 500Mb/year. Resource/One Select $625.00; Resource/One $1095.00; PA Library $1995.00; Winnebago Informational Database Subscription for UMI $299.00 per year.
Software Creates a Seamless Interface Between Winnebago CAT or (CIRC/CAT) on the Databases. CAT Users Can Access the Library Materials & Database Listings in the Same Online Catalog Search. You Can View, Add, & Delete Records from Your Informational Databases. Foots on File & UMI Databases Are Available.
Winnebago Software Co.

Informational Databases. Apr. 1994. *Items Included:* Included in the IBM CIRC/CAT 3 ring binder manual of 428 pages. *Customer Support:* Guaranteed 2 hr call-back; 1st year of support included with program purchase; toll-free 1-800 number; modem support; program updates & manual revisions; replacement program disks if necessary; subscription to the WUG Letter, 30 day money back guarantee.
MS-DOS. IBM or compatible PC-Based computer, DOS 3.0 or higher (640k). $525.00

INFORMIX

Facts on File 3.5" (School Library Database); $725.00 ea. (Public Library or College Library Database); $299.00 (Information Database Subscription) (ISBN 0-927875-39-X, Order no.: 1700 (SCHOOL LIBRARY); 1710 (PUBLIC LIBRARY); 1720 (COLLEGE LIBRARY); 1770 (INFORMATION DATABASE SUBSCRIPTION)). *Nonstandard peripherals required:* Epson or compatible printer with tractor feed, barwand, & keyboard. Additional hard drive space anywhere between 25Mb to 200Mb depending on database. *Optimal configuration:* 486 or higher processor, MS-DOS 5.0 or higher, 1Mb RAM, 2Mb hard disk space for every 1,000 MARC records in database. *Networks supported:* Winnebago LAN, Novell, ICLAS, & LANtastic.
$625.00 Resource One Select 3.5" UMI (Proquest) Database; $1095.00 Resource One 3.5" UMI (Proquest) Database; $1995.00 PA Library 3.5" UMI (Proquest) Database; $299.00 UMI Informational Database Subscription (ISBN 0-927875-41-1, Order no.: 1730 (RESOURCE ONE SELECT PROQUEST); 1740 (RESOURCE ONE PROQUEST); 1750 (PA LIBRARY); 1760 (INFORMATIONAL DATABASE SUBSCRIPTION)).
Gives Patrons & Staff Access Through the On-Line Catalog to More Than One Database & Gives Them the Benefit of One-Stop Searching. The Databases That Are Available Are Facts on File & UMI's Resource One & Resource One Select. You Can Print or Display Text Records.
Winnebago Software Company.

INFORMIX. *Operating System(s) Required:* UNIX.
contact publisher for price.
Collection of Programs Designed to Help Users Build Database Applications.
BBN Software Products Corp.

Informix. Sep. 1984. *Compatible Hardware:* IBM PC, PC XT, PC AT. *Operating System(s) Required:* UNIX. XENIX, MS-DOS. *Language(s):* C. *Memory Required:* 128k.
contact publisher for price.
Integrated, Relational Database Management System with a Built-In Module Designed for Menu-Driven Operation. Features Include Menu-Driven User Interface; Unrestricted, Logical File Placement & Access; Reconstructs Data to Suit User's Need.
Relational Database Systems, Inc.

Informix-ESQL/Ada. *Compatible Hardware:* Apple Macintosh II; A/UX.
3.5" disk $1600.00.
Enables Programmers to Embed SQL Statements into Ada Programs.
Informix Software.

Informix-ESQL/C.
IBM PC & compatibles. disk $595.00.
A/UX. Macintosh II. disk $1095.00.
Free-Form, Command & Menu-Driven Database-Management System Featuring Help Screen, Automatic Indexing & Split/Merge Files. Offers a Maximum of 32K Fields per Record, Characters per Field & Characters per Record; Unlimited Indexes per File; & up to 8 Active Indexes. (The Number of Records per File Is Limited to Disk Space.) Allows User to Revise Field Descriptions at Will.
Informix Software, Inc.

INFORMIX-ESQL/C. *Compatible Hardware:* IBM, PC, PC XT, PC AT, PC compatibles; DEC; AT&T. *Operating System(s) Required:* PC-DOS, MS-DOS, UNIX, XENIX. *Language(s):* C.
contact publisher for price.
Offers Two Sets of Complementary Tools for Highly Specialized Applications: SQL - the Industry Standard Database Language Imbedded in C & Programming Tools Allowing User to Call C Functions & Using Special C Library Routines While Working in INFORMIX-SQL.
Relational Database Systems, Inc.

Informix-4GL. *Compatible Hardware:* DEC VAX. *Operating System(s) Required:* VMS.
$4,300.00 & up.
Informix's C-ISAM, an Industry Standard Indexed Sequential Access Method for Unix, Available for VMS. C-ISAM, Which Uses B+ Tree Indexes for Data Retrieval, Is Compatible with Informix's Front-End Database Tools.
Informix Software, Inc.

Informix-4GL. *Operating System(s) Required:* PC-DOS/MS-DOS, OS/2, PC LAN, VMS, Unix.
IBM. disk $995.00.
Macintosh. 3.5" disk $2400.00.
Database Management System Provides On-Screen Help, Free-Form & Structured File Definition, Automatic Indexing, Split & Merge Files, Built-In Editor, Debugging Facilities, Compiler Included with Rapid Development System, & Run-Time Version Available. Features Unlimited Fields per Record; 32,000 Characters in Field; Unlimited Records per File; 32,000 Characters in Record; Unlimited Indexes per File; & up to 120 Bytes of Active Files. Offers 88 Commands, 28 Functions, Limited by Memory with the Number of Lines per Command Field & Variables. Offers Comma-Delimited ASCII Data-Import/Export Capabilities. Languages Include C, COBOL, & Ada.
Informix Software, Inc.

Informix-4GL Rapid Development System & Interactive Debugger. *Compatible Hardware:* IBM PC, PS/2. *Operating System(s) Required:* DOS.
$1495.00 per package.
Provides DOS Programmers with an Environment for Developing & Simultaneously Debugging SQL-Based Database Applications. The Product Eliminates the Need for a C Compiler by Compiling 4GL Code into a Pseudo-Code, Which Is Run by a P-Code Runner Within the Product.
Informix Software, Inc.

Informix SQL. *Version:* 2.0. Jun. 1980. *Compatible Hardware:* Altos. *Operating System(s) Required:* XENIX.
disk $995.00.
Allows Users to Query the Database & Create New Relations Through English-Like Query Statements Interactively. Other Features Include: Automated Functional Menus, Custom Screen Design, Total Format Control, Response & Data Protection.
Altos Computer Systems.

Informix-SQL. *Compatible Hardware:* Apple Macintosh, IBM PC & compatibles.
IBM. disk $795.00.
Macintosh. 3.5" disk $1600.00.
Free-Form, Command & Menu-Driven Database-Management System Featuring Help Screen, Automatic Indexing & Split/Merge Files. Offers a Maximum of 32K Fields per Record, Characters per Field & Characters per Record; Unlimited Indexes per File; & up to 8 Active Indexes. Allows User to Revise Field Descriptions at Will.
Informix Software, Inc.

INFORMIX-SQL. Feb. 1985. *Compatible Hardware:* IBM PC, PC XT, PC AT, PC compatibles; DEC; AT&T. *Operating System(s) Required:* PC-DOS, MS-DOS, XENIX, UNIX. *Language(s):* C. *Memory Required:* UNIX, Vax, XENIX 128k; MS-DOS, PC-DOS 192k.
IBM, MS-DOS. disk $795.00.
UNIX, XENIX. disk $1600.00.
Integrated, Relational Database Management System with 4 Built-In Modules Designed for Menu-Driven Operation. Features Include Menu-Driven User Interface; Unrestricted, Logical File Placement & Access; Reconstruction of Data to Suit User's Need; Query Module; Audit Trails; Accesses Files Through C-ISAM B Tree Method. Provides Security.
Relational Database Systems, Inc.

InfoScan.
disk $49.95 (Order no.: D8INFO).
Combines the Features of a Word Processor, Data Base Manager & Information Retrieval & Display Utility, & Is Usable with a Wide Variety of Data Situations.
The Alternate Source.

InfoSelect. *Version:* 1.12. Dec. 1989. *Customer Support:* 30 day money back guarantee, customer support (201)342-6518.
PC/MS-DOS. IBM PC & compatibles (7k). disk $99.95.
Optionally RAM Resident Personal Information Manager Providing Quick Retrieval of Notes, Ideas, Plans, Contacts etc.
Micro Logic Corp.

InFoTERM. *Version:* 8.0. Sep. 1992. *Items Included:* Media & documentation. *Customer Support:* Maintenance (includes updates, new releases & documentation) 10% of software per year. Support (includes a toll free number) 5% of software per year.
UNIX including: HP/UX, DG/UX, SunOS, ULTRIX, AIX, & SCO. Standard ASCII Terminal. $1000.00 depending on platform; volume discounts avail. *Networks supported:* TCP/IP.
Non-Graphic Database Manager Which Provides InFoCAD Users with Cost-Effective Data Entry, Manipulation, & Retrieval of InFoCAD Databases from Any Standard ASCII Terminal. Allows Users to Compose & Execute Non-Graphical Data Queries, Store New & Edit Existing Records, & Quickly & Easily Create Custom Formatted Reports.
Digital Matrix Services, Inc.

InFoTRACE. *Version:* 8.0. Sep. 1992. *Items Included:* Media & documentation. *Customer Support:* Maintenance (includes updates, new releases & documentation) 10% of software per year. Support (includes a toll free number) 5% of software per year.
UNIX including: HP/UX, DG/UX, SunOS, ULTRIX, AIX, & SCO. UNIX workstations, servers, & PCs including: HP, DG, SUN, DEC, IBM, IBM PC compatibles (24Mb). $10,000.00; volume discount avail. *Networks supported:* TCP/IP.
A Fast, Efficient, Cost-Effective, User-Assisted Raster to Vector Conversion Tool Specifically Designed to Lower the Cost of Data Conversion in a Production-Oriented Environment. Fully Integrated into InFoCAD Thereby Making an Ordinary User a Full-Fledged GIS Operator Who Can Produce Large Amounts of Accurate Data in a Short Amount of Time.
Digital Matrix Services, Inc.

InFoTRAN. *Version:* 8.0. Sep. 1992. *Items Included:* Media & documentation. *Customer Support:* Maintenance (includes updates, new releases & documentation) 10% of software per year. Support (includes a toll free number) 5% of software per year.
UNIX including: HP/UX, DG/UX, SunOS, ULTRIX, AIX, & SCO. UNIX workstations, servers, & PCs including: HP, DG, SUN, DEC, IBM, IBM PC (24Mb). $5000.00 depending on platform; volume discounts avail. *Networks supported:* TCP/IP.
A Complete Object-Oriented Programmer's Toolkit Which Enables Programmers to Use

InFoCAD As the Foundation for Custom Tailored Applications Which Compile & Link with the Core Software. The Combination of InFoCAD, InFoTRAN Calls, & FORTRAN & C Routines Gives Programmers the Edge in Developing Sophisticated, Spacially-Oriented Applications.
Digital Matrix Services, Inc.

InFoVIEW. *Version:* 8.0. Sep. 1992. *Items Included:* Media & documentation. *Customer Support:* Maintenance (includes updates, new releases & documentation) 10% of software per year. Support (includes a toll free number) 5% of software per year.
UNIX including: HP/UX, DG/UX, SunOS, ULTRIX, AIX, & SCO. UNIX Workstations, servers, & PCs including: HP, DG, SUN, DEC, IBM, & IBM PC compatibles (24Mb). $779.00-$2779.00 depending on configuration; discount with InFoCASE purchase. *Networks supported:* TCP/IP.
Low Cost Version of InFoCAD Which Is Limited Only by the Inability to Edit Graphics. InFoVIEW Is an Ideal Product for Companies That Perform Large Amounts of Database Editing, Analysis, & Reporting & No Graphic Editing. May Also Be Configured with Database Editing and/or Imaging Functionality.
Digital Matrix Services, Inc.

Infront. *Compatible Hardware:* IBM PC & compatibles. *Memory Required:* 640k.
disk $1500.00.
Application Development System Which Allows Users to Build a PC Application That Runs in Front of an Existing Mainframe Application without Changing Any Mainframe Code. Includes a Screen Capture Module for Converting 3270-Type Screen Images into PC-Based Forms. Features a Form Generator Program for Editing the Captured Screen Image & a Fill-in-the-Blanks Component That Supports the Definition of Common Attribute Settings & Editing Functions.
Multi Soft, Inc.

Ingram Books In Print Plus. 1995. *Items Included:* Weekly Updates. *Customer Support:* Information & Assistance Hotline; Electronic Bulletin Board.
DOS 3.1 or higher. IBM 286 or higher (565k). CD-ROM disk $1300.00 for 1 year. *Nonstandard peripherals required:* Hard disk (10 Mb free space); CD-ROM player running under DOS extensions 2.0 or later.
Adds Weekly Title by Title Updates of the Ingram Book, Audio, & Video Inventories Along with the Ingram Electronic Ordering System to the Books In Print Plus Database. Special Ingram Format Displays Ingram's Retail Price, Title Code, Subject Code, & Return Code, Along with Warehouses' Stock Status, On-Hand, On-Order Quantities, & Greenlight Availability.
R.R. Bowker.

Ingram Books In Print Plus: with Book Reviews. 1995. *Items Included:* Weekly Updates. *Customer Support:* Toll free support hotline & electronic bulletin board.
DOS 3.1 or later. IBM 286 or higher and compatibles (535k). CD-ROM disk $1800.00. *Nonstandard peripherals required:* CD-ROM player running under MS-DOS Extensions 2.0 or later; Hard disk (minimum 10 Mb free space).
Weekly Updates Provide Up-to-the Minute Inventory & New Product Information For Eight Ingram Warehouses & "Greenlight" Titles - Including Audio, Video & Print Materials Not Eligible For the Books In Print Database. Special Ingram Format Displays Ingram's Retail Price, Title Code, Subject Code, & Return Code, Along with Warehouses' Stock Status, On-Hand, On-Order Quantities & Greenlight Availability. Includes Full Text Reviews From 12 Esteemed Book Reviewing Media.
R. R. Bowker.

INGRES. *Version:* 4.0. Dec. 1985. *Compatible Hardware:* DEC MicroVAX I, II; HP 9000/500, 9000/300. *Operating System(s) Required:* VMS, Ultrix, HP/UX. *Memory Required:* 1000k.
MicroVAX I, HP 9000/300. primary (supported) license $7500.00.
supplemental (unsupported) license $4000.00.
MicroVAX II, HP 9000/500. $15,000.00 primary (supported) license.
supplemental (unsupported) license $7500.00.
All micros. annual maintenance & update fee $4000.00.
update fee only $2000.00.
Full-Function Integrated Relational Database Management & Applications Development System Available for Mainframe, Mini, & Microcomputers. Offers a Choice of Either the QUEL or SQL Query Languages. Fourth Generation Language, DSL for Application Development, & Screen-Based Visual Programming Tools for Development of Interactive Queries, Graphs, & Reports.
Relational Technology.

Initial Network Topology Toolbox: Array Shortest Path Initial Topology Generator. Jan. 1996. *Items Included:* Sample input & output files & users manuals on disk. *Customer Support:* Assistance in formulating inputs & understanding outputs, price free or variable.
MS-DOS. IBM PC (8Mb). disk $1199.00 (Order no.: 305). *Nonstandard peripherals required:* Math coprocessor. *Addl. software required:* FORTRAN Compiler & Linker. *Optimal configuration:* Source code can be compiled & linked for execution on any machine with a FORTRAN compiler & linker.
Given an Input Topology, Either an Existing One or One Generated by Product 301, This Tool Generates an Initial Topology Using the Techniques of Shortest Paths. The User Then Molds the Initial Topology into the Final Topology. This Product Should Only Be Used When the User's Computer System Can Handle Very Large Link Arrays, e.g., 999,000 Links. In the Event That Handling Large Arrays Is a Problem, the User Should Use Product 306, Which Replaces Link Arrays with Random Files.
Cane Systems.

Initial Network Topology Toolbox: Generator of Networks with Required Nodal Connectivity. Jan. 1996. *Items Included:* Sample input & output files & users manuals on disk. *Customer Support:* Assistance in formulating inputs & understanding outputs, price free or variable.
MS-DOS. IBM PC (8Mb). disk $309.00 (Order no.: 309). *Nonstandard peripherals required:* Math coprocessor. *Addl. software required:* FORTRAN Compiler & Linker. *Optimal configuration:* Source code can be compiled & linked for execution on any Machine with a FORTRAN compiler & linker.
This Tool Generates a Network Topology That Has the Nodal Connectivity Specified by the User, Where Nodal Connectivity Is the Minimum Number of Nodes That Must Be Removed in Order to Disconnect a Network into 2 or More Networks.
Cane Systems.

Initial Network Topology Toolbox: Input Network Topology Generator. Jan. 1996. *Items Included:* Sample input & output files & users manuals on disk. *Customer Support:* Assistance in formulating inputs & understanding outputs, price free or variable.
MS-DOS. IBM PC (8Mb). disk $499.00 (Order no.: 301). *Nonstandard peripherals required:* Math coprocessor. *Addl. software required:* FORTRAN Compiler & Linker. *Optimal configuration:* Source code can be compiled & linked for execution on any machine with a FORTRAN compiler & linker.
Given a Set of N Nodes & the Vertical & Horizontal Coordinates for Each Node, This Product Generates a Maximally Connected Topology of N(N-1) Links & Link Distances. The Primary Purpose Is to Generate an Input Topology for Products 302-308.
Cane Systems.

Initial Network Topology Toolbox: Minimum Distance Spanning Tree Initial Topology Generator. Jan. 1996. *Items Included:* Sample input & output files & users manuals on disk. *Customer Support:* Assistance in formulating inputs & understanding outputs, price free or variable.
MS-DOS. IBM PC (8Mb). disk $375.00 (Order no.: 302). *Nonstandard peripherals required:* Math coprocessor. *Addl. software required:* FORTRAN Compiler & Linker. *Optimal configuration:* Source code can be compiled & linked for execution on any machine with a FORTRAN compiler & linker.
Given an Input Topology, Either an Existing One or One Generated by Product 301, This Tool Generates an Initial Topology Using the Techniques of Minimum Spanning Trees, Where a Spanning Tree Is a Subnetwork Containing All the Network Nodes & a Subset of Links Such That There Is Exactly One Path Between Each Pair of Nodes. A Minimum Distance Spanning Tree Is a Spanning Tree in Which the Sum of the Link Distances Is a Minimum. The User Then Molds the Initial Topology into the Final Topology.
Cane Systems.

Initial Network Topology Toolbox: Minimum Links Topology Generator. Jan. 1996. *Items Included:* Sample input & output files & users manuals on disk. *Customer Support:* Assistance in formulative inputs & understanding outputs, price free or variable.
MS-DOS. IBM PC (8Mb). disk $350.00 (Order no.: 308). *Nonstandard peripherals required:* Math coprocessor. *Addl. software required:* FORTRAN Compiler & Linker. *Optimal configuration:* Source code can be compiled & linked for execution on any Machine with a FORTRAN compiler & linker.
Given an Input Topology, Either an Existing One or One Generated by Product 301, This Tool Generates an Equivalent Topology with a Minimum Number of Links. The User Then Molds It into the Final Topology.
Cane Systems.

Initial Network Topology Toolbox: Min-Max Spanning Tree Initial Topology Generator. Jan. 1996. *Items Included:* Sample input & output files & users manuals on disk. *Customer Support:* Assistance in formulating inputs & understanding outputs, price free or variable.
MS-DOS. IBM PC (8Mb). disk $350.00 (Order no.: 304). *Nonstandard peripherals required:* Math coprocessor. *Addl. software required:* FORTRAN Compiler & Linker. *Optimal configuration:* Source code can be compiled & linked for execution on any machine with a FORTRAN compiler & linker.
Given an Input Topology, Either an Existing One or One Generated by Product 301, This Tool Generates an Initial Topology Using the Techniques of Min/Max Spanning Trees, Where a Spanning Tree Is a Subnetwork Containing All the Network Nodes & a Subset of Links Such That There Is Exactly One Path Between Each Pair of Nodes. A Min/Max Spanning Tree Is a Spanning Tree in Which the Weight, e.g., Distance, Cost, etc., of the "Heaviest" Link Is a Minimum. The User Then Molds the Initial Topology into the Final Topology.
Cane Systems.

Initial Network Topology Toolbox: Minimum Weight Spanning Tree Initial Topology Generator. Jan. 1996. *Items Included:* Sample input & output files & users manuals on disk. *Customer Support:* Assistance in formulating inputs & understanding outputs, price free or variable.
MS-DOS. IBM PC (8Mb). disk $375.00 (Order no.: 303). *Nonstandard peripherals required:* Math coprocessor. *Addl. software required:* FORTRAN Compiler & Linker. *Optimal configuration:* Source code can be compiled & linked for execution on any machine with a FORTRAN compiler & linker.
Given an Input Topology, Either an Existing One or One Generated by Product 301, This Tool Generates an Initial Topology Using the Techniques of Minimum Spanning Trees, Where a Spanning Tree Is a Subnetwork Containing All the Network Nodes & a Subset of Links Such That There Is Exactly One Path Between Each Pair of Nodes. A Minimum Weight Spanning Tree Is a Spanning Tree in Which the Sum of the Link Weights, e.g., Cost, Is a Minimum. The User Then Molds the Initial Topology into the Final Topology.
Cane Systems.

Initial Network Topology Toolbox: Random File Shortest Path Initial Topology Generator. Jan. 1996. *Items Included:* Sample input & output files & users manuals on disk. *Customer Support:* Assistance in formulating inputs & understanding outputs, price free or variable.
MS-DOS. IBM PC (8Mb). disk $1199.00 (Order no.: 306). *Nonstandard peripherals required:* Math coprocessor. *Addl. software required:* FORTRAN Compiler & Linker. *Optimal configuration:* Source code can be compiled & linked for execution on any machine with a FORTRAN compiler & linker.
Given an Input Topology, Either an Existing One or One Generated by Product 301, This Tool Generates an Initial Topology Using the Techniques of Shortest Paths. The User Then Molds the Initial Topology into the Final Topology. This Product, Which Is Virtually Identical to Product 305, Should Be Used When the User's Network Has a Large Number of Links, e.g., 999,000, & His Computer System Cannot Handle Very Large Arrays.
Cane Systems.

Initial Network Topology Toolbox: Random Initial Network Topology Generator. Jan. 1996. *Items Included:* Sample input & output files & users manuals on disk. *Customer Support:* Assistance in formulative inputs & understanding outputs, price free or variable.
MS-DOS. IBM PC (8Mb). disk $165.00 (Order no.: 307). *Nonstandard peripherals required:* Math coprocessor. *Addl. software required:* FORTRAN Compiler & Linker. *Optimal configuration:* Source code can be compiled & linked for execution on any Machine with a FORTRAN compiler & linker.
Given an Input Topology, Either an Existing One or One Generated by Product 301, This Tool Generates Random Initial Topologies by Randomizing the Input. The User Then Selects One of the Resulting Topologies & Molds It into the Final Topology.
Cane Systems.

Ink Trapping Computer. James Tenorio. 1984. *Compatible Hardware:* Apple II series. *Operating System(s) Required:* Apple DOS 3.3. *Memory Required:* 48k. *General Requirements:* Printer.
disk $21.50 (ISBN 1-55797-209-5, Order no.: AP2-IE657).
Will Calculate the Percentage of Ink Trapping Efficiency for a Two-Color Combination Using Process Colors. Densitometer Readings Should Be Taken Ahead of Time & Then Entered into the Program.
Hobar Pubns.

inLARGE. *Version:* 2.0. *Compatible Hardware:* Apple Macintosh Plus or higher.
3.5" disk $195.00.
Image-Enlarging Software Utility for People with Low Vision. Includes a Variety of User-Modifiable Features: Magnification Level, Size of Magnified Area, Automatic Panning, Color Inversion, Cursor Tracking.
Berkeley Systems, Inc.

Inmagic DB/SearchWorks. Sep. 1995. *Items Included:* User manual. *Customer Support:* 45 days free, $300/yr. thereafter.
Windows 3.1. 80486. 3.5" disk $395.00 single user; $1450.00 5 user.
A Read-Only Version of Inmagic DB/TextWorks Textbase Software. Features Include Integrated Image Management, (Color & Black-&-White), Customizable Menu Screens, User-Definable Online Help, & Report Writer with Drag-&-Drop Layout & Formatting.
Inmagic, Inc.

Inmagic DB/TextWorks. *Version:* 1.1. Jun. 1995. *Items Included:* User manual, run-time version of the software. *Customer Support:* 45 days free, $300/yr. thereafter.
Windows 3.1. 80486 (8Mb). 3.5" disk $795.00 single user; $2900.00 5 user.
Windows-Based Textbase Software - Database Software Optimized to Handle Text. Features Include Unlimited Length Text Fields, Rapid Text Searching, WYSIWYG Report Writer, Full Text Import, & Relational-Like Database Linking, & Integrated Image Management.
Inmagic, Inc.

INMAGIC Image. May 1993. *Items Included:* Documentation & sample database with images. *Customer Support:* 45 days of free support in U.S., technical support contract $300/year.
DOS. DOS compatible (500k). disk $1750.00 single user license. *Optimal configuration:* 386 or above, HP Laserjet IV, Mass storage device, DOS 3.1 or higher. *Networks supported:* Novell, Banyan, Lantastic & other DOS networks.
Combines a Flexible & Easy-to-Use Database Management System with Low-Cost, Non-Proprietary Image Management. Create, Store, Retrieve, & Print Records with Fields That Are Unlimited & Variable in Length. With the Press of a Key Display or Print Images That Are Seamlessly Linked to the Record. Requires No Specialized Hardware or Software. Supports TIFF Format.
Inmagic, Inc.

INMAGIC Plus. *Version:* 1.0. Aug. 1992. *Compatible Hardware:* IBM PC & compatibles; DEC VAX, MicroVAX. *Operating System(s) Required:* MS-DOS 3.1 or higher. *Customer Support:* Free for 45 days after purchase, for microcomputer $300 yr.
IBM PC. disk $795.00.
Text Database-Management System with Unlimited Characters per Field, Unlimited Characters per Record, 75 Fields per Record & Unlimited Records per File. Boolean Searches, & Searches Can Be Restricted to Specific Field or Other Qualifier. Also Features Ability to Build Own Data Files & to Import & Export ASCII Test Files. Includes a Powerful Report Designer Which Creates a Variety of Printed Output. New Prompted Searching, Proximity Searching, & Full Text Capabilities.
Inmagic, Inc.

INMASS II: Integrated Manufacturing Software Series. *Version:* 2.0. 1989. *Compatible Hardware:* Altos; Compupro; Compaq; Fujitsu; Heath-Zenith; HP; IBM PC, PC XT, PC AT; NEC; Tandy. *Operating System(s) Required:* MS-DOS, PC-DOS, Concurrent DOS, Unix, Xenix, Novell & Microsoft networks. *Language(s):* C. *Memory Required:* 640k. *General Requirements:* Hard disk, 132-column printer. *Items Included:* Disks & manuals. *Customer Support:* Through VARs, support contracts available.
single-user $995.00.
multi-user $1295.00.
Unix, Xenix $1495.00.
Integrated Package for Manufacturers. Modules Include Inventory, Bill of Materials, Job Costing, Work-in-Process, Material Requirements Planning, Order Entry, Purchasing, Forecasting & Bar Coding. Integrates with Income II. Can Be Downloaded Through ASCII Files to Work with Other Software.
INMASS/MRP.

INMASS-MRP. 1996. *Customer Support:* free telephone & BBS technical.
MS/PC DOS; Concurrent DOS, Xenix, Unix. IBM PC/XT/AT & compatibles, IBM PS/2 (512k). $795.00-$1095.00 per module for single-user version; $995.00-$1595.00 multi-user version. *Networks supported:* Novell, Lantastic, Banyan VINES; all NETBOIS compatible.
INMASS/MRP is an integrated, modular package for manufacturers designed for manufacturers designed to prove better tracking control, improved purchasing, time-phased material requirements planning, & cost-effective production. Modules include: Inventory, Bill of Materials, Purchasing, Sales Order Entry. Customer Histories. Vendor Histories, Sales Contract Management, Job Cost/Work in Process, Material Requirements Planning (MRP), Bar Coding, Forecasting, Payroll, Accounts Payable, Accounts Receivable, General Ledger, IQ Report Writer.
INMASS/MRP.

Inn Control System (ICS). *Version:* 8.0. 1988. *Items Included:* Reference manual. *Customer Support:* $500.00 a day for on-site training; yearly support contract 10% of purchase price ; 24 hour, 365 day support contract available.
MS-DOS. IBM PC, XT, AT & compatibles (640K). $895.00 - $1395.00 single user; $2495.00 - $4495.00 multi user. *Nonstandard peripherals required:* Printer. *Networks supported:* Novell.
Reservations/Accounting System for Motels/Hotels. Including Reservations, Front Desk, Group & Company Billing & Guest History. General Ledger & Accounts Payable Are Optional. Full Range of Reports & Statements Are Provided, Including Night Audit, Maid Scheduling, Financial Statements, Accounts Receivable, Confirmations & Folios.
Resort Data Processing, Inc.

InnaTrack/FoodTrack. 1983. *Operating System(s) Required:* UNIX/VS. *Memory Required:* 4000k.
contact publisher for price.
Complete & Fully Integrated On-Line Manufacturing/Distributing Company Toward Primarily Directed Toward Light & Medium Manufacturing Industries.
Draves & Barke Systems, Inc.

INNCharge. May 1993. *Items Included:* Video training tapes along with documentation. *Customer Support:* Start up training & continued customer support. Video training.
MAC LCIII or higher with System 6.05 or higher.
MAC LCIII or higher (4Mb). 3.5" disk $2995.

TITLE INDEX

00 single unit; $4995.00 up to 15 units. *Addl. software required:* Helix runtime comes with system.
System for Creating Sales & Catering Contracts for Meetings & Conventions. Tracks Dates, Logs Meetings, Keeps Records of All Aspects of the Event. Creates Drawings for Set-Up Showing Table, Chair, Riser, A-V, & etc. Layouts. Multi-User System That Can Support up to 30 Users.
MacAcademy.

InnServ B&B HyperGuide. *Compatible Hardware:* Apple Macintosh Plus. *General Requirements:* Two disk drives or hard disk; HyperCard.
3.5" disk $15.95.
Bed & Breakfast & Country Inn Database.
InnServ Co.

Innstar Hotel-Restaurant Management System. *Compatible Hardware:* IBM 386, 486, 586. *Operating System(s) Required:* PC-DOS, Novell. *Language(s):* C & MACRO Assembly. *Memory Required:* 1000k. *Customer Support:* 24 hours, 7 days a week.
contact publisher for price.
Handles up to 600 Rooms & Posts Room & Tax for 300 Rooms in Only 2 Minutes. Provides Management for: Reservations, Front Desk, Telephone, Housekeeping, Building Maintenance Control, Night Audit, Restaurant Cashier, Restaurant Pre-Check, Back Office Accounting, Sales, Catering & Marketing Departments.
National Guest Systems Corp.

INPAC Customer-Client Tracking. *Items Included:* Bound manual. *Customer Support:* Free hotline - no time limit; 30 day limited warranty; updates are $5/disk plus S&H.
MS-DOS 3.0 or higher. IBM & compatibles (512k). disk $99.95. *Nonstandard peripherals required:* Two drives (or a hard disk); printer supported, but not required.
Automate & Control Data about Customers, Clients, Leads, & Accounts. It Allows User to Enter a Virtually Unlimited Number of Leads (Customers, Clients, etc.) While Maintaining a History of All Contacts & the Sales Made to Each One. Each Day It Will Show You the Calls & Appointments You Need to Make. Keeps Track of Appointments, Prints Your Letters, & Much More.
Dynacomp, Inc.

INPRFR. *Compatible Hardware:* IBM PC. *Operating System(s) Required:* MS-DOS. *Language(s):* BASIC. *Memory Required:* 128k.
disk $320.00.
Designed for Internal Pressure, Calculations Based on Inside & Outside Diameter for Thickness Required, Maximum Pressure & Actual Stress. These Calculations Apply to Cylinders, Cones & Elliptical-Spherical-Flanged & Dished & Flat Heads.
Technical Research Services, Inc.

Inputed Interest. *Compatible Hardware:* Altos Series 5-15D, Series 5-5D, 580-XX, ACS8000-XX; Kaypro 11/IV with 2 disk drives, Kaypro 10; Xerox 820 with 2 disk drives; ZILOG MCZ-250. *Operating System(s) Required:* CP/M, MP/M.
contact publisher for price (Order no.: APB21$).
Evaluates a Note Subject to the Following Conditions: Note Is Noninterest-Bearing, Note Has Stated Rate Different from Rate of Interest for Debt at Time of Transaction, Payment of Part or All Interest Is Deferred. When the Face Amount of Such a Note Does Not Represent the Face Amount at the Time of Exchange, It Calculates the Present Value of the Note & Amortizes the Discount or Premium As Interest Expense, or Income, over the Life of the Obligation. This Calculation Involves the "Interest Method" in Accordance with Opinion 21 of the Accounting Principles Board.
Coopers & Lybrand.

Inquire - Report Writer. *Customer Support:* Free telephone & BBS technical support.
MS/PC DOS; Concurrent DOS, Xenix, Unix. IBM PC/XT/AT & compatibles; IBM PS/2 (512k). single user $1095.00, +039. *Networks supported:* Novell, Lantastic, Banyan VINES; all NETBIOS compatible.
multi-user or network $1595.00.
"Inquire" is an extremely powerful Report Generator. IT allows the user to create custom reports containing information that is not provided as a standard part of the INMASS/MRP system. It allows each user to pull date from different program files selectively.
INMASS/MRP.

Inquiry Action Express: Salesman's Marketing & Management. *Compatible Hardware:* Data General; IBM PC XT, PC AT & compatibles. *Operating System(s) Required:* AOS, RDOS, Super DOS, PC-DOS/MS-DOS. *Language(s):* Business BASIC (source code included). *Memory Required:* 64k.
IBM. disk $2495.00.
Data General. disk or tape $895.00-$2495.00.
Mailing List, Inquiry Fulfilment, Follow-Up, Telemarketing Multi-User, Individualized Mailings & Word Processing.
QAX International Systems Corp.

The Ins & Outs of Diets Multimedia Diet Education. *Items Included:* Full manual. No other products required. *Customer Support:* Free telephone support - no time limit. 30 day warranty.
MS-DOS 3.2 or higher. IBM & compatibles (512k). disk $99.95.
Physicians Can Improve Patient Education, Satisfaction, & Compliance All at the Same Time. Patients Learn (at Their Own Pace) Effecitve Strategies to Lose Weight & Maintain Weight Loss. They Are Provided with a Simple, Well-Organized Approach to Understanding the Behaviors That Lead to Weight Gain. They Are Instructed How to Control Their Diets & Behavior, & How to Begin an Exercise Program. Reinforcement Is Provided with a Nine-Page Synopsis of the Lesson to Take Home for Review. This System Was Designed by a Primary Care Physician & Has Been Office-Tested (with Rave Reviews).
Dynacomp, Inc.

Insertion Order. Dec. 1987. *Compatible Hardware:* IBM PC & compatibles.
$69.50.
Uses Advertisement Cost & Frequency to Compute Gross & Net Costs & Agency Commission & Prints Insertion Order.
Compu-Literate.

Inside AutoCAD Disk: 6th Edition. Aug. 1990.
IBM PC & compatibles. disk $14.95 (ISBN 1-56205-030-3).
Support Disk for the 6th Edition of Inside AutoCAD Covering Release 10 Through 11. Contains Drawings, Menus, & Macros Included in the Book.
New Riders Publishing.

Inside MapInfo. *Version:* 4.0. Larry Daniel et al.
DOS/Windows, Windows NT, Windows 95, UNIX, Mac. CD-ROM disk $49.95, incl. 500 pg. pap. bk. (ISBN 1-56690-088-3, Order no.: 2007).
Contains Everything You Need to Know about MapInfo in a Comprehensive Tutorial, with Data-Specific Case Studies Relevant to Business, Financial, & Resource Management Applications. CD-ROM Includes Sample Consumer Demographic, Boundary, Market Segmentation, & Other Data from Leading Commercial Data Providers.
High Mountain Pr., Inc.

Inside the IBM PC: Access to Advanced Features & Programming Techniques. Peter Norton. *Compatible Hardware:* IBM PC.
disk $65.00 (ISBN 0-89303-559-9).
disk $79.95, incl. bk. (ISBN 0-89303-558-0).
Inside Look at the Microprocessor, Operating System, PC-DOS & ROM.
Brady Computer Bks.

Inside Trac. *Version:* 2.0. Nov. 1986. *Compatible Hardware:* IBM PC, PC XT, PC AT, PS/2 & compatibles. *Operating System(s) Required:* PC-DOS 2.X-3.X. *Language(s):* MicroSoft C. *Memory Required:* 256k. *General Requirements:* Printer.
disk $59.00 (ISBN 0-924354-10-0, Order no.: HG10).
Professional Time & Billing System Designed for Use by CPA's, Attorney's & Consultants. Works Like a "Pop-Up" Program.
Hawkeye Grafix.

INSIGHT. *Compatible Hardware:* TRS-80. *Operating System(s) Required:* TRSDOS 6.x. *Memory Required:* 64k.
disk $19.95 (Order no.: D4INST).
Features Tutorial Help for the Beginner, Supports EQU Libraries, Disassemblies Larger Than a Single Diskette & Many Other Features. Interacts with the 6.x DEBUG Utility.
The Alternate Source.

Inspiration. *Version:* 4.0. Nov. 1991. *Compatible Hardware:* Apple Macintosh. *Memory Required:* 1000k. *General Requirements:* Hard disk. *Items Included:* Manual with tutorials, idea book. *Customer Support:* Free customer support to registered customer.
3.5" disk $295.00.
For Brainstorming, Creative Thinking, Planning & Organizing; Combines Easy-to-Use Visual Diagraming & Powerful Outlining. Two Views of the Same Information, a Visual Freeform View & a Structured Outlining Textual View. Based on the Concepts of Mindmapping & Clustering Inspiration. Integrates Right & Left Brain Functions Providing a Powerful Tool for Creative Thinking.
Inspiration Software, Inc.

INSTALL OWNER'S MANUAL. *Version:* 3.2. Eric J. Heflin & Larry Hastings. May 1992. *Customer Support:* All support is free, but not toll free. BBS, FAX, Voice Mail (9:00am-5:00pm), CompuServe.
MS-DOS, OS/2, Windows. IBM & compatibles (200k). disk $249.95 (ISBN 1-56747-000-9). *Optimal configuration:* 350k, MS-DOS 4.0 & higher, OS/2 1.1 & higher, & Windows 3.1. *Networks supported:* All.
A Set of Tools That Automates the Installation of Any Product Distributed on Diskettes or CD-ROM. INSTALL Is Configured Using a Script File (Which Is an Easy-to-Learn "Installation Language") That Gives You Complete, Precise Control over the Installation Process. Handles All End-User Errors, Reduces Disk Costs by Compressing Data, Detects the Target Computer's Environment, Modifies System Files, & Updates Prior Versions. Full Source Code, No Royalties, & a 30 Day Money-Back Guarantee.
Knowledge Dynamics.

Installment Loan Payment. 1982. *Compatible Hardware:* Intel & compatibles. *Operating System(s) Required:* MS-DOS. *Language(s):* Microsoft BASIC.
disk $65.00 (Order no.: 257).
Manages Detailed Principal & Interest Data by Installments.
Resource Software International, Inc.

475

Installment Sales. *Compatible Hardware:* Altos Series 5-15D, Series 5-5D, 580-XX, ACS8000-XX; DEC Rainbow 100 with 2 disk drives, Rainbow 100+ with 10MB hard disk; IBM PC with 2 disk drives, PC XT, IBM compatibles; Kaypro 11/IV with 2 disk drives, Kaypro 10; Xerox 820 with 2 disk drives; ZILOG MCZ-250. *Operating System(s) Required:* CP/M, MP/M, CP/M-86/80, PC-DOS, MS-DOS.
contact publisher for price (Order no.: IS).
Planning Tool That Can Help Analyze Installment Sale or Lump Sum Sale Alternatives. Under the Lump Sum Sale, the Package Compares the After-Tax Earnings of the Lump Sum Payment to the After-Tax Earnings under the Installment. Also Computes the Net Present Value & the Compounded Future Value of the Income Streams under Each Option. Provides Four Payment Methods: Combined Level Payment, User-Defined Level Principal Payment, User-Defined Combined Level Payment, Balloon Payment. Also Generates Four Reports: Tax Analysis Report, Lump Sum Payment vs. Installment Sales, Financing Schedule Report, & Input Data/Ratio Report.
Coopers & Lybrand.

Instant-C. *Version:* 5.2. Aug. 1992. *Compatible Hardware:* IBM PC & compatibles. *Operating System(s) Required:* PC-DOS/MS-DOS 3.0 or higher, DR DOS. *Language(s):* C. *Memory Required:* 4000k. *Customer Support:* Telephone & BIX support, 508-653-6006; BIX mail: rational.
disk $495.00.
C Language Incremental Compiler in a Complete Development Environment. Includes an Integrated Editor, Browser, Compiler, Interpreter, Linker, & Debugger. Gives Programmers Access to 16Mb of Extended Memory on an 80386/486 PC.
Rational Systems, Inc.

Instant ImageTalk. *Compatible Hardware:* Apple Macintosh. *Memory Required:* 1000k. *General Requirements:* Panasonic videodisc recorder-player; composite video monitor; EEOC stillframe encoder/decoder system; HyperCard.
3.5" disk $35,000.
Audio-Video Production System.
Royal Recovery Systems, Inc.

Instant Install with Keys Please! *Compatible Hardware:* IBM PC or compatible; Columbia; Compaq; IBS; North Star Dimension; Leading Edge; ITT XTRA; Tandy 2000. *Operating System(s) Required:* MS-DOS, CP/M-80, PC-DOS, CP/M 3.0, TurboDOS. *Language(s):* CB-80 & Assembly. *Memory Required:* 56-128k.
$69.95.
Assigns All 140 WORDSTAR Editor & Dot Commands to the Function Keys on CRT Keyboards for Text Editing.
Precision Software Products.

Instant Job Winning Letters. William S. Frank.
disk $39.95 (ISBN 1-884087-01-9).
CareerLab Bks.

Instant Keyboard Fun I - MIDI. Nancy Poffenberger. 1985. *Compatible Hardware:* Apple II+, IIe; Commodore 64, 128. *Operating System(s) Required:* Apple DOS 3.3. *Language(s):* QuickBasic. *Memory Required:* Apple 48k, Commodore 64k. *General Requirements:* MIDI Interface card; MIDI-compatible music keyboard or synthesizer.
disk $39.95 ea., Incl. book.
Apple. (ISBN 1-55603-036-3, Order no.: MA-1179).
Commodore. (ISBN 1-55603-037-1, Order no.: MC-1179).
Consists of 26 Songs the User Plays on a Synthesizer Keyboard. The User Does Not Have to Be Able to Read Music - Just Note Names Shown on the Screen, Then Press the Correct Labeled Key on the Keyboard. At the End of Each Song, the Percentage of Correctly Played Notes Is Given. Words to Popular Tunes Are Displayed with the Corresponding Note Names. The User Has the Option of Hearing the Tune Any Time During the Program.
Electronic Courseware Systems, Inc.

Instant Pages. *General Requirements:* Epson or HP LaserJet Printer.
PC-DOS 2.1 or higher (256K). disk $49.95.
Creates & Fills In Forms, Organization Charts, Calendars & Multicolumn Newsletters.
Electronic Arts.

Instant Recall. *Version:* 2.0. Jun. 1992. *Items Included:* Cross-indexed manual with tutorial; Quick reference card. *Customer Support:* Free telephone technical support - unlimited; FAX support; On-line context-sensitive help.
MS-DOS DOS 2.1 or higher (DOS 3.0 or higher & hard disk for memory resident mode). IBM PC, XT, AT, PS/1, PS/2 or compatible (512k). disk $129.00. *Optimal configuration:* IBM PC or compatible.
Manages Deadlines, Appointments, Tasks, Notes, Addresses, Phone Numbers, Pops-Up over Software at Touch of a Key. Offers Alarms, Conflict Checking, Follow-Up Dates, Dialer, Mouse Support, 30 Text Pages per Item. Search by Text, Date, Topic, Priority, Person Assigned. Mail Merge, Pop-Up Calculator. Automatic Reconciliation. Prints Calendars & Reports to Fit Paper Organizer Systems. Top Rated by InfoWorld (Recommended Product 8.7 Score) & PC Magazine (Editors' Choice Award).
Chronologic Corp.

Instant Recall OFFICE. Jun. 1992. *Items Included:* Cross-indexed manuals with tutorial; network systems manager's manual, quick reference cards. *Customer Support:* Free telephone tech support - unlimited. FAX support. On-line context sensitive help.
DOS Version 3.1 or higher (25k RAM BR). IBM PC, PC XT, PC AT, PS/1, PS/2 & compatibles (512k). 2 users $249.00; 5 users $495.00; 10 users $795.00; 20 users $1495.00; 50 users $2995.00; 100 users $4995.00. *Optimal configuration:* Approximately 1Mb of disk space for program, help, & utility files. At least 200k of disk space for each user's data. *Networks supported:* Novell Netware (Version 2.15 or higher), Netware Lite, Banyan Vines, IBM LAN Manager, Microsoft LAN Manager, 3COM, LANtastic, & Other NetBIOS compatible networks.
Offers Group Scheduling, Task Tracking, Contact Management, Note Organization, Electronic Messaging & Flexible Information Sharing. It Reconciles Changes Between Network & Portables & Prints Professional Quality Reports. Provides Pop-Up Alarms, Automatic Conflict-Checking, Advance/Overdue Notice, Hassle-Free Mail/Merge. Reads Banyan StreetTalk & Novell Bindery for Easy Installation & Maintenance.
Chronologic Corp.

Instant Replay Professional (IRPRO). *Version:* 3.1. 1994. *Items Included:* Mystro Paint Program, Animation Programs, Royalty Free Compiler, Screen Grabbers, Visual Scripting Tools, DOS Based Software Memorization Package. Includes 521 page Users Manual, with hands on exercises. *Customer Support:* Available 8am to 5pm, MST, full 30 day guarantee, first 2 hours free telephone technical support, then $75.00 per hour.
MS-DOS. IBM PC & compatible (640k). $795.00 packages available. *Optimal configuration:* IBM compatible 286, 386, 486, MS-DOS, 640k, VGA Adapter, Mouse, 40Mb Plus Hard Drive. *Networks supported:* Coding is network independent, will support LAN, Novell, & others.
A "Multimedia Systems Manager" Designed for Authoring Tutorial, CBT Courseware, Diskette Based Software Ads, & Computer Based Professional Presentations. Serves As the Systems Manager for Incorporating DOS Based Software, Audio, Video, Graphics, Animations, Special Effects, & Compressed Video into Your Presentation. Supports RealSound, Which Requires No Special Hardware on the Playback PC. Has the Ability to Control a Laserdisc Player, Managing "What" & "How" Material Is Accessed & Presented. A Variety of Audio & Graphics Boards Are Supported, Managed & Sold by IRPRO. Touchscreens Are Also Supported. A Royalty Free Distribution Compiler Is Also Included. Supports a Mouse. Requires a Hard Disk. Comes with Both 4.25" & 3.5" Diskettes. Full 30 Day Guarantee.
Instant Replay Corp.

Instant Terminal. *Compatible Hardware:* IBM PC, PC XT, PC AT, PS/2.
$49.95.
Terminal Emulation Program. Terminals Emulated Include the Following: ADDS; DEC VT52, VT100, VT102, VT220; Data General D200, D410; Hewlett-Packard 2622A; IBM 3101; Televideo 910, 921, 925, 950; TI; Wyse 50. Transfers Files Using Nine Transfer Protocols.
Softronics, Inc.

InstaPlan. *Version:* 3. *Compatible Hardware:* IBM PC & compatibles. *Operating System(s) Required:* PC-DOS/MS-DOS 2.0 or higher. *Memory Required:* 640k. *Items Included:* Tracker option. *Customer Support:* Free.
disk $249.00.
Enables Users to Develop a Plan Interactively & Turn It into a Presentation. Outlines Can Have up to 11 Levels & They Are Automatically Indented. Information Can Be Output in Tabular, Gantt, & Presentation Form. After the User Assigns the Work, the Program Will Automatically Summarize What It Will Cost & How Many People Will Be Needed. Up to 600 Activities Can Be Assigned on a 640k PC. Includes Desktop Presentation Facilities That Create Overhead Slides, Proposals, & Handouts on the IBM PROPRINTER or GRAPHICS PRINTER, EPSON & Compatibles, & HP LaserJet PLUS.
Micro Planning International.

Institute of Management International Databases Plus. *Customer Support:* Annual Updates.
MS-DOS. IBM or compatibles. disk $1395.00 1 year (Order no.: IMB110).
This compilation of multimedia information contains seven databases & comes equipped with fulltext document delivery facilities for journals from the Institute of Management as well as for Management Working Papers from the University of Warwick library.
Bowker-Saur.

The Institutional Real Estate Investor, Junior: For Individual Ownerships, 3 disks. Dewitt Smith. Sep. 1986. *Compatible Hardware:* IBM PC & compatibles. *General Requirements:* Hard disk, printer, Lotus 1-2-3 Release 1A or 2.
$195.00.
demo disk $20.00.
Decision Support Tool for Professional Investment Analysis of Commercial or Residential Multi-Tenant Buildings. Reports & Graphs Available for Display or Printing Include: 10 Year Proforma & Cash Flow, Optimum Sales, Analysis, Analysis of Benefits, ROI, Net Cash Flow, Breakeven & Loan Coverage. Completely Menu-Driven & Fully Updated for the Tax Reform Act of 1986, Including Phase-In Rules.
Jewell ComputerEase.

TITLE INDEX

Instrucalc. *Items Included:* Full manual. No other products required. *Customer Support:* Free telephone support - no time limit. 30 day warranty.
MS-DOS 3.2 or higher. IBM & compatibles (512k). $679.95-$879.95.
Features: ControlValveSizing - Liquid Flow; Gas/Vapor Flow; Two-Phase Flow; Flow Element Sizing - Orifice Plate, Flange Taps (Liquid Gas/vapor); Orifice Plate, Pipe Taps (Liquid, Gas/Vapor); Orifice Plate, Corner Taps (Gas/Vapor); Flow Nozzle & Venturi (Liquid, Gas/Vapor); Universal Calcuation, Liquid; Pitot Tubes - Restriction Orifice Plates (Liquid, Gas/Vapor); Rotameters (Liquid, Gas/Vapor); Pressure Relief Device Sizing - Relief Valves (Liquid, Gas, Steam, Entrapped Liquid in Heat Exchange/Pipeline, Fire Size); Tank Vents; Safety Heads (Liquid/Gas Relief). Includes a 280-Page Manual.
Dynacomp, Inc.

Instrucalc. *Version:* 3.1. Stanley Thrift. Mar. 1994. *Items Included:* Manual. *Customer Support:* 30 day money-back guarantee.
DOS 3.1 (256k). disk $895.00; upgrade $225.00 (Order no.: 429). *Optimal configuration:* Printer optional. *Networks supported:* Multiple copy discounts available.
Size Control Valves, Orifice Plates, Pilot Tubes, & Relief Devices Quickly & Accurately. You Can Then Produce Data Sheets for the Calculated Items & Prepare Instrument Summaries. You Can Use the Data Sheets As a Database for Generating Reports. Choose Any Combination of Engineering Units, Including U.S., SI, & User-Generated Units, & Easily Switch Units in the Midst of a Calculation. New Version Includes a Waterhammer Program.
Gulf Publishing Co.

INSTRUCTOR. *Version:* 1.2-7. 1987. *Items Included:* Manuals (system, reference & installation), 1 year maintenance, quarterly newsletter. *Customer Support:* 6am-6pm, MST.
MicroVMS & VMS 4.6 & higher. MicroVAX & VAX (250k). Included with CNTRL.
Allows Support Staff to Train New or Existing Users Easily. It Also Enables the Trainer to Demonstrate Interactively Any Program, Utility or Application on Unlimited Terminals Simultaneously. With the Optional ATTEND Module, Students Can Join the Demonstration from Remote Sites, Join a Demonstration in Progress, Communicate with the Trainer.
Raxco, Inc.

Instructor's Manual on WordPerfect 5.1 to Accompany FINANCIAL ACCOUNTING, 7th Edition. Ernest I. Hanson et al. Mar. 1993.
IBM. disk $16.00 (ISBN 0-03-098233-2).
3.5" disk $16.00 (ISBN 0-03-098232-4).
Dryden Pr.

Instructor's Manual on WordPerfect 5.1 to Accompany PRINCIPLES OF ACCOUNTING, 6th Edition. Ernest I. Hanson et al. Feb. 1993.
IBM. disk $13.50 (ISBN 0-03-098235-9).
3.5" disk $13.50 (ISBN 0-03-098234-0).
Dryden Pr.

Instructor's Manual to Accompany FINANCIAL ACCOUNTING, 7th Edition. Ernest I. Hanson et al. Mar. 1993.
IBM. disk $16.00 (ISBN 0-03-097461-5).
3.5" disk $16.00 (ISBN 0-03-097460-7).
MAC. 3.5" disk $16.00 (ISBN 0-03-097462-3).
Dryden Pr.

Instructor's Manual to Accompany PRINCIPLES OF ACCOUNTING, 6th Edition. Ernest I. Hanson et al. Mar. 1993.
IBM. disk $13.50 (ISBN 0-03-097440-2).
3.5" disk $13.50 (ISBN 0-03-097439-9).
Dryden Pr.

Instrument Specification Data Sheets. *Items Included:* Full manual. No other products required. *Customer Support:* Free telephone support - no time limit. 30 day warranty.
MS-DOS 3.2 or higher. IBM & compatibles (512k). disk $289.95.
Helps Engineers Compile Consistent Data Sheets Efficiently & Easily. Produces & Tracks Multiple-Page ISA-Style Data Sheets for Any Number of Projects. Comes with a Master File of Ready-to-Use Data Sheets for a Variety of Instruments. Datasheets Can Be Printed, Individually or Collectively, Directly to a Printer or to a Printer File. Includes Complete & Detailed Manual Which Describes All Procedures.
Dynacomp, Inc.

Instruwire: Electrical & Instrument Wiring Design & Documentation. Continental Controls. Oct. 1986. *Compatible Hardware:* IBM PC, PC XT, PC AT & compatibles. *Operating System(s) Required:* PC-DOS/MS-DOS 3.1. *Language(s):* Assembly, C, FORTRAN. *Memory Required:* 512k. *General Requirements:* Graphics card, 2Mb hard disk space. *Customer Support:* 30 day money-back guarantee.
disk $995.00, incl. 80-page manual (ISBN 0-87201-427-4).
Can Be Used to Design & Document Wiring Schedule for PLC, Distributed Micro-Processor-Based Controllers, Discrete Analog Controllers, & Other Similar Systems. This System Reduces Drafting Work for Construction & for Updating Drawings After Project Installation, from 50% to 70%. Allows Rapid Update of Electric & Instrument Wiring Documentation After the Construction Phase of the Project. Construction Wiring Documentation Can Be Stored & Retrieved by Any Criteria. The Wiring Schedule, from Field Devices to Control Systems Is Shown Diagrammatically in the Loop Diagrams Output by the Program. Errors Are Minimized or Eliminated Through Internal Checking Capabilities. Features Include Checking & Reporting Capabilities for Wiring Data. Will Accommodate I/O Lists & Equipment Configurations for Most Vendor Equipment. Provides Documentation in the Form of Component Indexes.
Gulf Publishing Co.

Insurance. *Compatible Hardware:* IBM PC, Tandy 2000, Kaypro. *Operating System(s) Required:* TRSDOS, CP/M, PC-DOS. *Language(s):* BASIC. *Memory Required:* 64k.
disk $750.00.
Prepares Official Insurance Blanks for New Automobile Policies for the State of New Jersey. Calculates Rates & Limitations & Print the Filled-Out Forms. Each Company Has a Slightly Different "Official" Form. Prepares Bills for Renewals According to Their Due Dates.
Computer Technical Services of New Jersey.

Insure. *Compatible Hardware:* IBM PC. *General Requirements:* Hard disk.
contact publisher for price.
Allows the User to Integrate Agency Functions Including: Accounting Procedures, Claims Processing, Word Processing, General Ledger & Customer File Retrieval.
Prodata, Inc. (Idaho).

Inte-Print. Stan Leeson. Jan. 1987. *Compatible Hardware:* IBM PC & compatibles. *Operating System(s) Required:* PC-DOS, MS-DOS. *Memory Required:* 128k. *General Requirements:* Hard disk, printer.
disk $49.95.
Menu-Driven Program Which Allows Users to Combine Text from Their Word Processor with Pictures of Their Choice, in One Document. Works with a Variety of Drawing Programs, & Allows Flexibility in Custom Editing As Well As Versatility in Picture Producing. Can Be Used in Conjuction with Many Word Processors, As Well As Many Dot Matrix Printers. Currently Supports over 30 Printers. Provides 6 Pre-Defined Sizes for Picture Drawing, but Horizontal & Vertical Parameters May Be Customized.
Generic Computer Products, Inc. (GCPI).

INTEGRATED MANUFACTURING SYSTEM

Integrated Accounting. *Version:* 8A. Sep. 1993. *Compatible Hardware:* IBM PC & compatibles, NCR, UNISYS, Radio Shack, Altos, IBM RT. *Operating System(s) Required:* PC-DOS/MS-DOS, Unix, Xenix, 3COM, NOVELL, AIX. *Language(s):* COBOL 85. *Memory Required:* Multi-user 3Mb or higher, single user 1000k. *General Requirements:* At least 60Mb hard disk, 132-column printer & RM Cobol 2.0 or higher. *Customer Support:* $860.00 per year for 30 minutes per month.
XENIX/UNIX, 3Com, Novell, AIX. disk $1010.00.
MS-DOS. disk $1872.00.
Combines Accounts Receivable, Accounts Payable, General Ledger, Inventory Control, Sales Orders, Sales Analysis, Salesforce Management, Serial Number Tracking, List Management, Billing, & Purchasing. Provides Up-to-the-Minute Reporting Throughout the Entire System. Each Transaction Automatically Posts & Updates the Necessary Areas of the Software System. Designed As a Multi-User System, but Can Be Used Single-User As Well. Expands with Add-On Vertical Modules for Specific Businesses Such As Retailing, & Wholesaling.
Trac Line Software, Inc.

Integrated Accounting on Microcomputers. 1987. *Memory Required:* Apple 64-256k, IBM 128-256k. *General Requirements:* 80-column card is required to run Q30026 on the Apple IIe.
Apple II Series, IIgs. contact publisher for price (ISBN 0-538-51025-0, Order no.: Q30026).
PC-DOS/MS-DOS. write for info. (ISBN 0-538-51026-9, Order no.: Q30027).
OS/2. write for info. (ISBN 0-538-51066-8, Order no.: Q30067).
Text-Workbook & Diskette Packages Covering General Ledger, Depreciation, Accounts Receivable, Accounts Payable, Financial Statement Analysis, & Payroll.
South-Western Publishing Co.

Integrated Accounting Package for TRSDOS 2.0. *Version:* 2.0. 1981. *Operating System(s) Required:* TRSDOS 2.0. *Language(s):* BASIC (source code included). *Memory Required:* 64k.
disk module $149.00 ea. (Order no.: 607-610).
hard disk version $199.00.
Modules: Accounts Receivable, Accounts Payable, Payroll, General Ledger.
Micro Architect, Inc.

Integrated Financial Management-General Accounting. *Version:* System VI. 1981. *Operating System(s) Required:* PC-DOS, MS-DOS. *Language(s):* Microsoft BASIC 6.0 compiler. *Memory Required:* 640k. *General Requirements:* 132-column printer.
disk $4380.00 (Order no.: 4).
Designed for Architectural & Engineering Firms with up to 500 Employees & 3000 Active Projects. Integrates the Accounting Functions of Payroll, Accounts Payable, Accounts Receivable & General Ledger with the Features Necessary for Effective Management & Billing of Projects.
Micro Mode, Inc.

Integrated Manufacturing System. *Version:* 4.0. *Compatible Hardware:* VAX; IBM PC & compatibles. *Operating System(s) Required:* MS-DOS, VMS, UNIX, Novell. *Language(s):* DIBOL (source code included). *Memory Required:* 32k. *General Requirements:* 2 disk drives, printer.
disk $1000.00.

Designed for Manufacturers Who Ship to Customer Order. Applications Include: Order Entry/Invoicing, Quotations, Bills of Material/ Routing, Inventory/Purchasing, Job Cost, Production Planning, Shop Floor Control, Material Requirements Planning, Tool Inventory, Direct Marketing, Factory Data Collection, Communications System, All Finanical Word Processing & Electronic Spreadsheet. Applications Can Be Run Individually or Integrated As a Complete System.
Primetrack.

Integrated Project Management System (IPMS). *Version:* 3.1. *Compatible Hardware:* IBM PC XT, PC AT, PS/2. *Operating System(s) Required:* DOS, MVS, SSP, OS/400. *Memory Required:* 512k.
$3000.00 single user.
$6000.00 up to 5 users.
$1000.00 graphics package option.
Project-Management Package Featuring Automatic Resource Leveling, Context-Sensitive On-Screen Help, Task-by-Task Data-Entry Style, LAN-Specific Version, Multi-User File Reading & Writing, 120,000 Activities & Disk Method of Data Storage. 10 Level Work Breakdown Structure. 999 Resources Leveled Simultaneously. Specifies Individual Calendars for a Resource & Produces Resource Distribution Histograms. Automatically Draws PERT Charts. Eight Simultaneous Criteria Can Be Used to Select Activities; Four Simultaneous Fields Can Be Used to Sort Activities. Interfaces with Artemis, MAPPS, Project/2 & Tellaplan Software Without Additional Programming.
Timephaser Corp.

Integrated Structural Design. *Items Included:* Documentation with examples for user to follow. *Customer Support:* Update program available-15% of package price. 30 day unlimited warranty.
contact publisher for price.
Completely Integrated Frame, Truss, Beam & Column Design Software Provides Simple Solutions To Complex Problems. Although Complex Finite Elements Techniques Are Used, No Formal Training Is Needed. Many Solutions May Be Completed in Less Than Thirty Seconds. A Material Library Is Included Which Contains All AISC Steel Specifications for Immediate Reference. Another Material May Be Added as Required. Unknown Section Properties Are Also Calculated on Demand to Simplify Design Process (CAD Interface Available).
Engineering Software Co.

Integrity Master: Anti-Virus - Data Integrity System. *Version:* 1.43c. Wolfgang Stiller. Apr. 1993.
DOS 2.0 or higher, also works with OS/2. IBM compatible PC (256k). $35.00; or $189.00 for IM "Pro" version (Order no.: 1-800-622-2793 OR 708-397-1221). *Optimal configuration:* Hard disk not required but suggested for best use. *Networks supported:* All, supported via DOS workstations.
Easy to Use Data Integrity, Security, & Virus Protection. Protects Against Much More Than Just Viruses. Hardware Glitches, Software Bugs, Even Deliberate Sabotage Are Detected. If a Virus Strikes, Integrity Master Identifies It by Name & (Unlike Other Programs) Also Identifies Any Damage Caused by the Virus.
Stiller Research.

Intelligent Backup. *Version:* 2.2Q. *Compatible Hardware:* IBM PC & compatibles. *Memory Required:* 320k.
disk $149.95.
This Programs is Menu Driven. Its Functions That Can Be Initiated By Single-Key Designations, &
The Color Can Be Customized. The Program Can Handle Only 200 Directories Until Users Have to Increment The Memory in an Awkward Manner.
Sterling Software Co.

Intelligent Report System (IRS). *Version:* 3.0. *Compatible Hardware:* IBM PC & compatibles. *Customer Support:* 90 day unlimited warranty, yearly maintenance plans available.
disk $795.00. *Addl. software required:* Requires SSP's PROMIS, project management software system.
Advanced Report Writing Package for the SSP's PROMIS Project-Manangement System. Enables the User to Display or Print Reports Based on Any Data Within the PROMIS Database. Custom Report Writer Offers An Artificial Intelligence Based Query Language, Data Transfer Capability & a Built-In Business Graphics Utility.
Cambridge Management Systems, Inc.

Intellimaint. Sep. 1993. *Items Included:* Manual. *Customer Support:* 1 year maintenance: 10% of package price. Pkg. price: Ranges between $2995.00 & $15,000.00.
MS-DOS/Windows 3.1. IBM compatible PC with 386 or higher processor (4Mb). starts at $2995.00. *Nonstandard peripherals required:* Windows compatible mouse. *Networks supported:* LAN, Novell or compatible.
Windows Based CMMS Package Designed to Help the Engineer Schedule, Track, & Control Maintenance Activities. Also Organizes Vast Amounts of Information That Deal with Personnel, Equipment, Spare Parts, Time, & Costs. State of the Art Options Include Networking, Bar Coding, & Graphics, Interface Available. Total Productive Maintenance, & Total Quality Management Concepts Included. Saves Time, Money, & Is Easy to Use.
Intelligent Manufacturing Solutions, Inc.

Intellipath.
contact publisher for price.
Educational Computer-Based Information System for Pathologists. State-of-the-Art PC Technology Combines Comprehensive Atlas of Videodisc Photomicrographs with Expert System Software. System Responds to User to Form Probable Differential Diagnoses.
ASCP Pr.

Intelliplay Cowboy Casino. Feb. 1994. *Items Included:* Learn to Play Poker book, warranty card, CD-ROM containing software, & brochure of other Intelliplay products. *Customer Support:* Free, unlimited technical support via 1-800 number.
MS-DOS 5.0 or higher, Windows 3.1. IBM PC & 100% compatibles (4Mb). CD-ROM disk $59.95 (ISBN 1-882284-05-4, Order no.: SCC-01-MPC). *Nonstandard peripherals required:* CD-ROM with 150k transfer rate, 16 bit SVGA card w/512k RAM memory. *Addl. software required:* Microsoft Windows 3.1. *Optimal configuration:* MPC Level 2 Compliant machine.
Helps Master the Rules & Fundamentals of Several Variations of Poker. Play Poker with Five Hilarious Wild West Characters in a Full Motion Video Simulation of a True Saloon Game. Learn 5-Card Draw, 5-Card Stud, 7-Card Stud, Texas Hold'em & More. With Cowboy Casino Learning Has Never Been This Much Fun.
Intellimedia Sports.

IntelliPlay Cowboy Casino. Apr. 1994. *Items Included:* CD-ROM disc w/manual, brochures, warranty card, & registration card. *Customer Support:* Free, unlimited technical support via 1-800 number.
3DO player. CD-ROM disk $49.95 (ISBN 1-882284-11-9, Order no.: SCC-01-3DO).
Helps Master the Rules & Fundamentals of Several Variations of Poker. Play Poker with Five Hilarious Wild West Characters in a Full Motion Video Simulation of a True Saloon Game. Learn 5 Card Draw, 5 Card Stud, 7 Card Stud, Texas Hold'em & More. With Cowboy Casino Learning Has Never Been This Much Fun.
Intellimedia Sports.

IntensiveNet. 1982. *Compatible Hardware:* IBM PC XT, PC AT, PS/2 Model 30. *Operating System(s) Required:* MS-DOS. *Language(s):* C. *Memory Required:* 640k.
contact publisher for price.
Patient Data Management System That Uses Monitor-Lab-Produced Data to Provide a Condensed Evaluation of the Patient's Condition & Identify Status Changes. May Be Interfaced to On-Line Vital Signs Monitor.
Trinity Computing Systems, Inc.

Interactive Appointments. *Customer Support:* 800-929-8117 (customer service).
MS-DOS. Apple II. disk $99.99 (ISBN 0-87007-439-3).
A 31-Day Calendar is Kept for a Maximum of 14 Scheduled Appointments per Day. The Calendar Keeps Track of Four Data Elements for Each Appointment: the Appointment Time, Name of Person Scheduled for the Appointment, with One Full Line of General Information About the Appointment & Who Made the Appointment.
SourceView Software International.

Interactive Bibliography. *Customer Support:* 800-929-8117 (customer service).
MS-DOS. IBM/PS2. disk $99.99 (ISBN 0-87007-474-1).
Written by an Eminent UC-Berkeley Scientist. Allows the Preparation of Bibliographies. Allows up to 100 Characters for Authors, 200 Characters for Titles, up to 65 Spaces for Keywords & Handle up to 99999 Reference Numbers. User May Annotate Each List with up to 400 Characters of Text.
SourceView Software International.

Interactive-C. Nov. 1985. *Operating System(s) Required:* MS-DOS 2.0 or higher. *Memory Required:* 256k.
disk $249.00 (Order no.: 75-1131).
Consists of Fully-Integrated Interpreter, Full-Screen Editor, Symbolic Debugger, Command Processor "Shell", & Execution Profiler. Permits Learning & Debugging "C" Programs 10 Times Faster Than Traditional Methods.
IMPACC Assocs., Inc.

Interactive Catalog. *Customer Support:* 800-929-8117 (customer service).
MS-DOS. IBM/PS2. disk $199.99 (ISBN 0-87007-563-2).
Allows a Company to Catalog its Product Line in up to 110 Hierachical Classification Groups & Index up to 1100 Products. It Supports Multiple Disk Collections, Hard Disks, & Hierarchical Directories. Program Automatically Allows Users to Screen for Different Types of Product Availabilies, Select Purchases of Sales Literature, Demos & Fully Functional Products, & Automatically Generates a Purchase Order. There are Several Main Files Reserved for Information on the Company. Will Work on Both XT & AT Systems. A Multi Level Serialization of Diskettes & Purchase Orders are Generated. Allows Multiple Levels of Rebates or Commissions.
SourceView Software International.

Interactive Cluster Analysis: Multidimensional Statistics. *Items Included:* Bound manual. *Customer Support:* Free hotline - no time limit; 30 day limited warranty; updates are $5/disk plus S&H.
MS-DOS. IBM & compatibles (256k). disk

TITLE INDEX

$59.95. *Nonstandard peripherals required:* CGA (or equivalent) graphics capability; hard disk (or two floppies); Epson MX/RX/FX or IBM Prowriter (or compatible) dot matrix printer supported; ten-fold speed increase possible if math coprocessor present.
Generic Tool for Classifying Members of a Test Population Using Non-Hierarchical Clustering Analysis Techniques.
Dynacomp, Inc.

Interactive Cobol Generator. *Customer Support:* 800-929-8117 (customer service).
MS-DOS. Commodore 128; CP/M. disk $199.99 (ISBN 0-87007-307-9).
Automatic CODE Generator for RM Cobol, with Data Dictionary.
SourceView Software International.

Interactive Cobol Generator (IBM). *Customer Support:* 800-929-8117 (customer service).
MS-DOS. IBM/PS2. disk $399.99 (ISBN 0-87007-308-7).
A Programming Tool for the R/M Cobol Programmer. Provides a Tool With Which the Programmer Can Create Applications & Try Them Without Having to Worry about Throwing out Long Hours to Coding Effort.
SourceView Software International.

Interactive Computer Library to Accompany Production & Operations Management.
Norman Geither. Edited by Anne Smith. *Compatible Hardware:* IBM PC & compatibles; Apple II; TRS-80.
contact publisher for price (ISBN 0-03-064123-3).
Provides a Set of Completely Interactive FORTRAN 77 Programs for POM Problem Solving.
Dryden Pr.

Interactive Data Extraction & Analysis.
Version: 4.11. *Compatible Hardware:* IBM PC & compatibles. *Memory Required:* 640k. *General Requirements:* 2.5Mb of free hard disk space. *Items Included:* 1 perfect bound user manual. *Customer Support:* 1-800-265-IDEA.
$1300.00 Nonmember.
$1170.00 for AICPA members.
Auditing Utility Lets User Transfer & Reformat Mainframe, Minicomputer, & Incompatible PC Data for PC. Through the Utility, User Can Utilize & Summarize Data, Browse Through Files, Display Graphs, & Print Customized Reports.
American Institute of Certified Public Accountants.

The Interactive Diabetic Cookbook. *Items Included:* Bound manual. *Customer Support:* Free hotline - no time limit; 30 day limited warranty; updates are $5/disk plus S&H.
MS-DOS. IBM & compatibles (128k). disk $69.95. *Nonstandard peripherals required:* Two floppy drives (or one floppy & one hard disk).
Software Package Which Assists in All Aspects of Meal Planning & Recipe Selection to Control Diabetes. For Individual As Well As Institutional Use. Includes over 200 Recipes from the Mary Jane Finsand Series of Diabetic Cookbooks. You Can Also Add Your Own Recipes.
Dynacomp, Inc.

The Interactive Encyclopedia. *Version:* 3.0.
386 or higher (2Mb). CD-ROM disk $149.95.
Nonstandard peripherals required: CD-ROM drive, DAC, ADC, music Synthesizer, VGA.
Upgrade $49.95.
Completely Redesigned with 256 Color Pictures & an Interface That Is Easier to Use with Instant Access to Any Category in the Encyclopedia, from Videos to Sound, Articles to Maps.
Compton's NewMedia, Inc.

Interactive Financial Accounting. *Version:* 3.0. *Compatible Hardware:* DEC Micro VAX II, IBM PC AT. *Operating System(s) Required:* PC-DOS, UNIX, VMS. *Language(s):* SQL, RPT, C (source code included). *Memory Required:* 640k. *General Requirements:* Hard disk.
IBM. contact publisher for price.
VAX. contact publisher for price.
Financial Accounting System Using the ORACLE Database Management System. Runs under All Operating Systems Which Run ORACLE.
Avalon Software.

Interactive Fly Fishing School. May 1995. *Items Included:* CD-ROM with online documentation. *Customer Support:* Unlimited free technical support via 1-800 number.
DOS 6.0 or higher. IBM or 100% compatibles (4Mb). disk $59.95 (ISBN 1-882284-31-3, Order no.: SFFO1MXC). *Nonstandard peripherals required:* Fully MPC compliant or Multimedia ready. *Optimal configuration:* MPC Level 2 for IBM compatible machines.
Macintosh System 7. Macintosh (4Mb). 3.5" disk $59.95 (Order no.: SFFO1MXC). *Nonstandard peripherals required:* Fully MPC compliant or Multimedia Ready.
Learn the Secrets of Fly Fishing from the Pros Who Starred in the Movie "A River Runs Through It".
Intellimedia Sports.

The Interactive Guide to Soccer. 1995.
Windows or Macintosh. CD-ROM disk $64.95 (ISBN 1-882949-91-9, Order no.: 96009102ND).
The Complete Guide to Soccer at Your Fingertips! Learn Basic Fundamentals of the Sports along with the History, Rules, & Game Specifics. A Wonderful Tool for Officials, Referees, Coaches & Novice Players. Each CD-ROM demonstrates Basic Skills Using Live Game Situations, Then Brakes Them down Further into Learning Components with Drills & Technique Tips.
Paragon Media.

The Interactive Guide to Soccer. Jan. 1995.
IBM. CD-ROM disk $64.95 (ISBN 1-882949-91-9, Order no.: 96009-102ND).
Paragon Media.

The Interactive Guide to Volleyball. 1994.
Windows or Macintosh. CD-ROM disk $64.95 (ISBN 1-882949-90-0, Order no.: 96009101ND).
The Complete Guide to Volleyball at Your Fingertips! Learn Basic Fundamentals of the Sports along with the History, Rules, & Game Specifics. A Wonderful Tool for Officials, Referees, Coaches & Novice Players. Each CD-ROM demonstrates Basic Skills Using Live Game Situations, Then Brakes Them down Further into Learning Components with Drills & Technique Tips.
Paragon Media.

Interactive Manufacturing Control. *Version:* 8.0. Feb. 1988. *Compatible Hardware:* DEC Micro VAX II, IBM PC AT. *Language(s):* SQL, RPT (source code included). *Memory Required:* 640k. *General Requirements:* Hard disk.
IBM. contact publisher for price.
VAX. contact publisher for price.
Manufacturing Control Using the ORACLE Database Management System - Complete MAP II Capability.
Avalon Software.

Interactive Multiple Prediction. *Version:* 2.0.
Allan Easton. Jun. 1985. *Compatible Hardware:* IBM PC. *Operating System(s) Required:* PC-DOS 1.1. *Language(s):* QUICK BASIC. *Memory Required:* 128k. *General Requirements:* 2 disk drives or hard drive. *Customer Support:* Free hotline.
IBM PC (Rev. 1.2). $69.95, incl. 8087 support.
IBM PC (Rev. 1.0, 2 DSDD). $69.95.
manual $10.00.
Multiple, Linear Regression Program That Accepts As Input a Data-Set Made up of One Criterion Variable & M-1 Predictor Variables.
Mathematical Software Co.

INTERACTIVE QUESTIONNAIRE ANALYSIS:

Interactive Multiple Prediction: Multiple Linear Regression. *Items Included:* Bound manual. *Customer Support:* Free hotline - no time limit; 30 day limited warranty; updates are $5/disk plus S&H.
MS-DOS 2.0 or higher. IBM & compatibles (256k). disk $69.95. *Nonstandard peripherals required:* CGA graphics capability (or equivalent); two floppies (or a floppy & a hard disk); printer supported.
Multiple Linear Regression Package Which Will Handle up to 1000 Samples (Data Points) with 79 Independent Variables. It Calculates the Multiple Regression Coefficients, Beta Weights, R, R2, along with the Usual Standard Error Estimates (Sigma, Chi-Square, Residuals, etc.). Features Include: Provisions for Cross-Validation Studies; Choice of Full (All Variables) or Stepwise Forward Multiple Regression; A Quick Statistical Test to Determine Which Univariate Transformation Is Likely to Be the Most Productive.
Dynacomp, Inc.

Interactive Options. *Customer Support:* 800-929-8117 (customer service).
MS-DOS. IBM PC, PS/2. disk $179.99 (ISBN 0-87007-437-7).
Apple II. disk $79.99 (ISBN 0-87007-439-3).
A Tool Used to Analyze & Evaluate Combinations of Stock Options Contracts. Enables the Average Investor to Profit from Option Trading Without the Large Risks Normally Associated with Options. Once Data on a Stock Is Entered, the Computer Reports an Implied & Assumed Stock Volatility & Long/Short Information. A Graphic Display Is Provided on a Variety of Measures, Which Are All Controlled Through an Easy to Use Menu System.
SourceView Software International.

Interactive Questionnaire Analysis. Aug. 1989.
Items Included: Spiral bound 80-page manual. *Customer Support:* Free hotline.
MS-DOS, PC-DOS (256k). IBM PC & compatibles & Macintosh 68030. $169.95. *Addl. software required:* DOS Master or Windows. *Optimal configuration:* VGA & printer.
Tool for Analyzing Questionnaire & Survey Responses. Suitable for Social, Psychological, Political, Business, Economic, Health or Physical Sciences. User Can Draw Inferences from Masses of Empirical Data Derived Derived from Multiple Measurements (or Responses) from a Test Population. Accommodates Metric Data Set Consisting of up to 150 Columns & 1000 Rows. Consists of Five Major Parts: Data Entry & Editing; Raw Data Manipulation & Analysis; Multivariate Analysis of Questionnaire Data; Search for Surrogate Variables; Miscellaneous Procedures.
Mathematical Software Co.

Interactive Questionnaire Analysis: Questionnaire Response Statistics. *Items Included:* Bound manual. *Customer Support:* Free hotline - no time limit; 30 day limited warranty; updates are $5/disk plus S&H.
MS-DOS 2.0 or higher. IBM & compatibles (512k). disk $99.95. *Nonstandard peripherals required:* CGA (or equivalent) graphics; two

floppy disk drives (or one floppy & a hard disk); math coprocessor supported (though not necessary), as well as a printer.
Macintosh (1Mb). 3.5" disk $99.95.
Nonstandard peripherals required: Two 800k disk drives (or a hard disk).
Analytic Tool for Analyzing Questionnaire & Survey Responses. It Is Applicable to the Social, Psychological, Political, Business, Economic, Health, or Physical Sciences, As Well As Marketing or Public-Opinion Research. Data Analysis Includes One, Two, Three & Four Variable Statistics, Transformations, & 2- or 3-Way Cross-Tabulations. Also Available Are Multiple Factor Analysis (Factor Extraction, Factor Rotation, Factor Score), & Cluster Analysis (for Identifying "Types" among the Cases); Manifold-Match, Euclidian Distance, Profile-Matching.
Dynacomp, Inc.

Interactive Source Debugger. *Items Included:* Bound manual. *Customer Support:* Free hotline - no time limit; 30 day limited warranty; updates are $5/disk plus S&H.
MS-DOS 2.0 or higher. IBM & compatibles (256k). disk $49.95. *Addl. software required:* BASIC or BASICA (IBM), or GWBASIC (compatibles).
Interactive Debugging & Maintenance Tool for Developing BASIC Programs. At Any Program Break, Various Debugging Options Are Available. User Can List & View Any Part of the Program, Display the Value of Any Variable, Change the Value of Any Variable, & Branch to Any Line of the Program & Continue from There On. Additionally, Breaks Can Be Set at Preselected Lines. Breaks Can Also Be Set at the Occurrence of Specified Conditions. Selected Parts of the Program May Be Run under the Debugger While the Rest of the Program Is Executed Normally.
Dynacomp, Inc.

Interactive StatPak. *Customer Support:* 800-929-8117 (customer service).
MS-DOS. Commodore 128; CP/M. disk $399.99 (ISBN 0-87007-515-2).
Complete Statistical System for Parametric & Non-Parametric Statistics. Supports ASCII, System Data & Matrix Datafiles. Includes Data Smoothing.
SourceView Software International.

Interactive Stock. *Customer Support:* 800-929-8117 (customer service).
MS-DOS. Commodore 128; CP/M. disk $49.99 (ISBN 0-87007-436-9).
IBM PC, PS/2. disk $99.99 (ISBN 0-87007-044-4).
A Menu-Driven Package of Mathematical & Statistical Routines for Making Specific Buy & Sell Decisions in the Stock, Commodities & Options Market. It Is a Complete System Intended for Optimization of "Tuning" of These Methods, Indications of Appropriate Buy & Sell Signals on a Daily Basis, & Creation/Validation of Relevant Price History Files. Interactive Stock Includes the Moving Average Method, the Max/Min Methods, the Average Down/Sell up Methods, the Correlation Method. Interactive Stock Computers Commissions for Commodities on a Flat-Rate Basis & for Stocks & Options on a Rough Percentage Basis. The Menu Structure Lends Itself Readily to Experimenting on a Single Piece File with Different Techniques.
SourceView Software International.

Interactive Warranty. *Customer Support:* 800-929-8117 (customer service).
MS-DOS. IBM/PS2. disk $99.99 (ISBN 0-87007-026-6).
A Warranty Generation Program That May be Used by Programmers or Users as a Front End Access Module That Automatically Generates a Questionnaire on the Origination of the Sale, & Allows the Generation of an Identity & Password Screen Prior to Execution. Includes Provision for Generating & Requiring a Password for Program Access. Cuts Down on Pirating of Programs Without Copy Protection, & Increases the Response Rate for Warranty Registrations. Makes Program Secure from Casual Inspection.
SourceView Software International.

Interactive Waveform Analysis: Fourier Series Decomposition, Filtering & Reconstruction.
Items Included: Bound manual. *Customer Support:* Free hotline - no time limit; 30 day limited warranty; updates are $5/disk plus S&H.
MS-DOS. IBM & compatibles (256k). disk $59.95. *Nonstandard peripherals required:* CGA (or equivalent) graphics capability; hard disk (or two floppies); Epson MX/RX/FX or IBM Prowriter (or compatible) dot matrix printer is supported; ten-fold speed increase possible if math coprocessor is present.
Provides Researchers with an Easy-to-Use Tool for Studying Periodic Functions. The Procedures Include: Fourier Analysis (Sine/Cosine Series Coefficients); Fourier Synthesis (with Noise) of Periodic Waveforms Using Series; Data & Frequency Spectrum Graphical Displays; Data Smoothing; Block Filtering (Time & Frequency Domain Responses); Combining of Data Sets; Resonance Simulation; Derivative Computation & Display; Paired Cross-Correlation; Data Reconstruction from Transform; & More.
Dynacomp, Inc.

InterBridge. *Version:* 1.12. *Compatible Hardware:* Apple Macintosh. *Memory Required:* 256k. *General Requirements:* AppleTalk network; IBM requires Apple, Centram Systems West, or Tangent Technologies AppleTalk PC Cards. *Items Included:* System guide, 7 Quick Reference cards, 800k diskette & power supply. *Customer Support:* 8:00AM - 8:00PM EST, Monday through Friday.
$799.00.
Network Bridge Which Connects Separate AppleTalk Networks. Enables Users on One Network to Share All Services & Devices of the Other.
Hayes Microcomputer Products, Inc.

Interceptor. *Compatible Hardware:* TRS-80 Model I, Model III.
disk $24.95.
Intercept Waves of Renegade Robot Spacecraft to Get Back to Your Mothership in Order to Refuel & Launch on Your Mission to Save the Federated Planets.
Blue Cat.

InterChange. *Version:* 3.0. *Compatible Hardware:* Commodore Amiga.
3.5" disks $129.95.
Enables Users to Share Objects Between Formats Such As Lightwave, Imagine, Turbo Silver, Sculpt, VideoScape, PAGErender, Vista Dems, AutoCAD DXF, 3D Studio, Wavefront, CAD-3D & Imagemaster ISHAPES.
Syndesis Corp.

InterChange for Windows. *Customer Support:* Unlimited technical support, sample conversions, free bug fixes, upgrade for minimal cost.
Windows, Windows 95 or Window NT (8 extra). disk $495.00.
Enables User to Convert Between 40 Popular 3D File Formats, Such As 3D Studio, Lightwave, AutoCAD DXF, Wavefront, VRML, etc. Preserves Geometry, Surface Information, Hierarchy & Rotational Centers & More. Converts a Single File or Batch Files.
Syndesis Corp.

The Interest Analyzer. *Version:* 2.26. Michael D. Jones. Mar. 1993. *Items Included:* 1 manual. *Customer Support:* 90 day warranty, notification of major updates.
MS-DOS. IBM PC, XT, AT & compatibles (512k). disk $25.00. *Optimal configuration:* 386 or higher, printer capable of condensed print - 15CPI or higher, hard drive.
Produces Professional Scheduler & Illustrations for Savings, Annuities, Loans, Mortgages & Depreciation. Flexible with Variable Deposits, Withdrawals, Payments, Interest Rates, & Compound Methods. Tax Analysis, COLA, Loan Acceleration. Solve for Calculators. Save & Restore Multiple Clients. Side by Side Comparisons. Illustration Detail Is Monthly - Annual, Calendar or Fiscal.
Insight Software Solutions.

Interest Expense Estimator. *Compatible Hardware:* Altos Series 5-15D, Series 5-5D, 580-XX, ACS8000-XX; DEC Rainbow 100 with 2 disk drives, Rainbow 100+ with 10MB hard disk; IBM PC with 2 disk drives, PC XT, IBM compatibles; Kaypro 11/IV with 2 disk drives, Kaypro 10; Xerox 820 with 2 disk drives; ZILOG MCZ-250. *Operating System(s) Required:* CP/M, MP/M, CP/M-86/80, PC-DOS, MS-DOS.
contact publisher for price.
Created to Assist the Auditor in Performing Reasonableness Tests of Interest Expense. Estimates Current-Year Interest Expense Based on Prior-Year Relationships. This Analytical Tool Helps the Auditor Determine the Nature & Extent of Other Substantive Test of Interest Expense.
Coopers & Lybrand.

Interest-NDL-Form 2210 Calculators. *Items Included:* Manual for CPE credit. *Customer Support:* Free support 1 year.
MS/PC-DOS (640k). IBM PC, PC XT, PC AT & compatibles. stand-alone $95.00; software with questionnaire $195.00. *Addl. software required:* Lotus 1-2-3.
Program Allows User to Calculate Interest for Deficiencies, Refunds & Tax-Motivated Interest; Also Calculate NOL for Both Regular & Amount Tax & Form 2210.
Accounting Professionals Software, Inc.

Interest-Only-Balloon-Payment Loan. *Compatible Hardware:* Sharp ZL-6100 system. *Language(s):* Sharp Microcode.
$400.00.
Computes & Discloses Loans Where Interest Is Paid on the First of Each Month & the Principle at Maturity. Interest Is Computed Using an Actual Calendar. An Origination Fee Can Be Charged.
P-ROM Software, Inc.

Interest Only Installment Loan. *Compatible Hardware:* Sharp ZL-6100 System. *Language(s):* Sharp Microcode.
$400.00.
Computes & Discloses Simple-Interest Monthly Installment Loans in Which the Borrower First Pays Some Number of Interest Only Payments Before Starting Principal & Interest Payments. Includes Provisions for an Origination Fee & Any Other Prepaid Charges & Prepaid Odd-Day Interest.
P-ROM Software, Inc.

INTERE$Tplus. *Version:* 7.1. 1985. *Compatible Hardware:* IBM PC & compatibles, PC XT, PC AT. *Operating System(s) Required:* MS-DOS 3.3 or higher. *Language(s):* Compiled BASIC, Assembly. *Memory Required:* 2000k. *Customer Support:* On site training, unlimited telephone support & all.
disk $3000.00 single.
disk $4500.00 local area network.
disk $10,500.00 wide area network.

Adds Balloons, Interest-Only, Commercial, & Partially Amortizing Loans to the LOANLEDGER+ Environment. Features Include: Simple Interest, Mortgage Style, Adjustable Rate, Maturity Aging, & Principal Payment at Maturity.
Dynamic Interface Systems Corp.

Interest Rate Calculation. 1982. *Compatible Hardware:* MS-DOS based machines. *Language(s):* Microsoft BASIC.
disk $65.00 (Order no.: 256).
Calculates Actual Interest Rate in Compliance with Regulation Z of Truth in Lending Act.
Resource Software International, Inc.

Interest Rate Risk Analyzer-Regulatory Performance Monitor: IRRA-RPM. Jul. 1990. *Items Included:* Spiral-bound manual. *Customer Support:* 1 yr. maintenance, $500.00.
MS-DOS 3.3. 286 IBM compatible (640k). IRRA/MVM $1695.00. *Optimal configuration:* 386-DX or higher, MS-DOS 5.0. *Networks supported:* Novell.
User Defined Chart of Accounts. Enter Balances & Rates for Rate Sensitive Assets & Liabilities by Maturity/Repricing Periods IRRA Computes Scheduled Amortization & Applies Either Prepayment or Decay Rate Assumptions That You Provided. IRRA Figures Your Gap Position, the MVM Calculates Your Market Value. MVM Computes Both Market Value of Portfolio Equity & Estimates Net Interest Income.
Farin & Assocs.

InterFont. *Version:* 1.2. *Compatible Hardware:* Commodore Amiga 500, 1000, 2000.
3.5" disk $119.95.
Font Editor That Lets Users Create Fonts That Can Be Used in Three-Dimensional Animation & Modeling Programs Such as Sculpt 3D, VideoScape 3D, Turbo Silver, & Forms in Flight. Can Also Be Used to Make Structured Clip Art for Gold Disk's Professional Page Desktop Publishing Program. Twenty Pre-Made Serif & Sans-Serif InterFonts Are Included with the Package. Users Can Also Create Their Own Custom Shapes in up to Sixteen Colors. The Package Also Includes Syndesis's InterFont Designer, Which Can Be Used to Trace over Any Amiga Bitmap Font & Create InterFonts. Includes InterChange, Syndesis' Object Conversion Utility.
Syndesis Corp.

InterFont Upgrade. *Compatible Hardware:* Commodore Amiga.
3.5" disk $79.95.
Creates 3D Font Objects for 3D Modeling Programs. This Upgrade Available for InterChange Owners.
Syndesis Corp.

Interim Reporting System. *Version:* 8.01. 1986. *Items Included:* 1 full manual. *Customer Support:* 90 days unlimited warranty; unlimited technical support via telephone for $225/system per year.
MS-DOS. IBM or compatible (640k). disk $995.00. *Optimal configuration:* MS-DOS 6.2 or higher, 15Mb of space on a hard drive (to include all 5 systems). *Networks supported:* Novell, LANtastic.
A Progress Report Used Between Grading Periods. Enter Teacher Comments Using an Optical Scanner or Keyboard. This Report Is Printed on a Dual Copy Form, & May Be Sent to All Students, or Only Selected Students.
Applied Educational Systems, Inc.

Interleaf Publisher. *Version:* 3.6. *Language(s):* C Language. *Items Included:* Software, documentation. *Customer Support:* Free telephone support for 90 days followed by paid tel. sup., bulletin board, newsletter, user groups, maintenance training contract.
Apple Macintosh II (5Mb); 2Mb with Virtual Version 2.0.2 (Connectix). version 3.6 $995.00.
IBM PS/2 Model 70, 80 (2Mb), 8036-based machines. version 1.1 995.00.
Fully Integrated Text-&-Graphic Electronic Publishing Application Suited for Both Short & Long Documents. Publisher Provides Full Word Processing, Extensive Graphics Capabilities & Automated Page Layout. Users Can Share Docs with No Loss of Text or Graphics.
Interleaf, Inc.

Interlibrary Loan Control. *Version:* 3.0a. 1993. *Items Included:* Complete illustrated instructions. *Customer Support:* 1 year free replacement of damaged disks, free unlimited telephone customer support.
MS-DOS. IBM-PC, XT, AT, PS-2 or compatible (512k). disk $189.00 (ISBN 1-55812-096-3). *Addl. software required:* None.
Network version $439.00.
Windows version $229.00.
Windows Network version $439.00.
For All Libraries That Make or Fill Interlibrary Loans. Enter Names of Libraries & Requests. Computer Prints Out Forms (Based on ALA Format & Saving You the Cost of Purchasing Expensive Forms). Personalize the Form for Your Library. Print Reports on Loans by Month & Year. Keeps Statistics on Loans. Makes It Easy to Make & Maintain Loans.
Right On Programs.

Interlibrary Loan Manager.
DOS 5 or Win 3.1 (640K). DOS $189.00; DOS Network 439.00; Windows 229.00; Windows Network 439.00.
This program makes it a simple matter to enter & track all incoming & outgoing loans. Enter those libraries from which you borrow or to which you Loan. The information remains in the database to be recalled as needed.
Right on Programs.

Interlinear Transliterated Bible. Nov. 1994. *Items Included:* Disks, marketing literature, order form. *Customer Support:* No fee for customer support: 30 day money back guarantee, limited replacement warranty on diskettes defective at time of purchase, free telephone technical support.
PC-DOS/MS-DOS 3.1 or higher & Windows 3.1 or higher. IBM 386/486 or 100% compatibles; also XT/AT/286 for DOS (640k DOS or 4Mb Windows). 3.5" disk $59.95 (ISBN 1-56514-028-1). *Addl. software required:* Biblesoft's PC Study Bible, New Exhaustive Strongs & King James Version text. *Optimal configuration:* 3.5", 1.44Mb disk drive for installation, 5Mb hard drive space; mouse or pointer device recommended.
Interlinear Transliterated Bible with Lexicon Definitions from Thayer's & Brown-Driver-Briggs. Enables User to Conduct Word & Definition Searches of Greek & Hebrew Words Without User Having Prior Knowledge of Original Languages.
Biblesoft.

intermail. *Compatible Hardware:* Apple Macintosh, IBM PC & compatibles. *Operating System(s) Required:* AppleTalk network.
1-4 users $299.95.
5-10 users $499.95.
11-20 users $749.95.
21-250 users $949.95.
demo disk $10.00.
Integrated Desktop Communications Solution That Enables Users to Compose & Send Notes, Memos, Phone Messages, Graphics, Reminders, & Files of Any Type to Other Users in the Office or to Remote Computers. Works from Within Other Applications.
Internet.

Intermediate Statistics: A Modern Approach. James P. Stevens. 1991. *Customer Support:* Free technical support, 90-day limited warranty.
DOS. 3.5" disk Contact publisher for price (ISBN 1-56321-094-0).
5.25" disk Contact publisher for Price (ISBN 1-56321-093-2).
cloth book $65.00 (ISBN 0-8058-0491-9).
paper book $29.95 (ISBN 0-8058-0492-7).
Along with This, the Author Fully Integrates Two of the Major Statistical Packages, SAS & SPSSX.
Lawrence Erlbaum Assocs. Software & Alternate Media, Inc.

Intermediate Word. *Version:* 5.1. Dec. 1992. *Items Included:* 90-minute audio cassette with instructions, practice disk with lesson files & examples, Quick Reference Card, Extra Practice Card. *Customer Support:* Free technical support 800-832-2499, 100% satisfaction guarantee.
Macintosh Plus, SE or II. 3.5" disk $39.95 (ISBN 0-944124-11-9). *Optimal configuration:* Microsoft Word 5.1, Mactinosh Plus, SE or II, 2 disk drives, or 1 disk drive plus a hard disk, printer, mouse & cassette tape recorder.
Personal Training for Microsoft Word 5.1. Learn to Create Form Letters & Other Print Merge Documents, Number Lines & Sort Records, & Create & Format Tables.
Personal Training Systems.

Internal Funds Tracking & Commissary: Correction Administration System. *Version:* 3.0. Palladium Software Corp. Aug. 1992. *Operating System(s) Required:* MS-DOS Windows, NT Server. *Language(s):* Level 5. *Memory Required:* 4000k.
disk $7000.00 ea.
Windows. (ISBN 0-931755-77-8, Order no.: CJ 400/3).
Windows 95. (ISBN 0-931755-78-6, Order no.: CJ 400/4).
Windows NT. (ISBN 0-931755-79-4, Order no.: CJ 400/5).
Provides Order Taking, Order Tracking, Delivery of Commissary Products; Maintains Automated Perpetual Inventory & Maintains Up-to-Date Record of Inmate Fund Availability; with Full Reporting System.
Ellington Duval, Inc.

Internal Rate of Return. 1982. *Compatible Hardware:* MS-DOS based machines. *Language(s):* Microsoft BASIC.
disk $40.00 (Order no.: 261).
Calculates IRR on Capital Investments.
Resource Software International, Inc.

International Classification of Diseases: ICD - Latest Revision. 1995. *Items Included:* Full manual. *Customer Support:* Free telephone support - 90 days, 30-day warranty.
MS-DOS 3.2 or higher. 286 (584k). $199.95-$299.95. *Nonstandard peripherals required:* CGA/EGA/VGA.
This Versionn of the ICD-9 Is Unquestionably the Best on the Market. It Is Produced by Coders for Coders. Its Overwhelming Popularity Is Proven by the Sheer Numbers Sold. The Addendum & the Update Material for Volumes 1 & 2 Are Prepared under Contract with the National Center for Health Statistics. Also, Volume 3 Is Produced under Contract with the Health Care Financing Administration (HCFA). These Contracts Mean That You Are Getting Official, Accurate, & High Quality ICD-9s.
Dynacomp, Inc.

International Gran Prix. Richard Orban. 1981. *Compatible Hardware:* Apple II, II+, IIe. *Operating System(s) Required:* Apple DOS 3.2, 3.3. *Language(s):* Assembly. *Memory Required:* 48k.

disk $9.98 (ISBN 0-87190-012-2).
Simulates Automobile Racing on the Courses of the Grand Prix Circuit.
Muse Software.

International Language Quick Look. Jan. 1995. *Customer Support:* Unlimited telephone support. MS-DOS 6.0/Windows 3.1 or higher. PC Clone 386 or 486 or higher (4Mb). disk $15.00 (ISBN 1-878974-23-8). *Addl. software required:* MS Windows 3.1 or higher. *Optimal configuration:* PC clone with MS-DOS 6.0/Windows 3.1 or higher.
International Language Vocabulary for the MS Windows Cardfile. Includes Separate Cardfiles for French, German, Spanish, Italian, Dutch, & Romanized Japanese.
Jeffries & Associates, Inc.

International Loan/Deposit Accounting System. (International Finance Ser.). Spot Systems, Inc. Staff. Mar. 1984. *Compatible Hardware:* IBM PC, PC XT, PC AT, PS/2, 386, 486 & compatibles. *Operating System(s) Required:* MS-DOS 3.0 & higher, Windows. *Language(s):* Compiled BASIC. *Memory Required:* 640k. *General Requirements:* Hard disk.
Base System. Contact publisher for price.
 Networks supported: LAN-Novell, Token Ring. *Analytical Tool That Can Improve Trading Decisions While Providing the Accounting & Operations Support for the Trading Function. Trading Personnel Have Access to Real-Time Information on Money Market, Outstanding Loans, Deposits, DDA, CD, & Foreign Currency Accounts, Rates & Positions. Management Can Obtain Profitability Data & Reports on Compliance with Credit & Position Limits. Tracks Customer Limits & Outstandings & Consolidates Customer Parent/Subsidiary Relationship. Provides a Detailed Cashflow Analysis for 60 Months Forward Including Calculations of Gaps & Effective Yields. Also Reports on Payment Instructions for Contracts Reaching Value & Maturity Date & Generates General Ledger Entries Through a User-Defined Accounting Interface. Both Stand-Alone & Network Versions Are Available. Includes Report Writer.*
Spot Systems, Inc.

International Metallic Materials Cross-Reference. ToData Computer Systems Staff. Sep. 1993. *Items Included:* Runtime version of Paradox. *Customer Support:* 30 day satisfaction guarantee.
 Microsoft Windows version 3.1 or higher. IBM PC & compatibles (4Mb). disk $399.00 (Order no.: (518) 377-8854).
Companies That Operate Internationally May Have Obligations That Require Purchasing or Specifying Metallic Materials in Specification Systems & Materials Designations Unfamiliar to Them. This Cross-Reference Is a Guide to Engineers & Procurement Personnel for Easy Recognition of Metallic Materials Designations That Are Equivalent to Each Other on the Basis of Chemical Composition.
Genium Publishing Corp.

International Problem Solving Using Logo. Heinz-Dieter Boecker et al. 1991. *Customer Support:* Free technical support, 90-day limited warranty.
 IBM DOS. 3.5" disk $14.95 (ISBN 1-56321-069-X).
 Mac. 3.5" disk $14.95 (ISBN 1-56321-068-1). cloth book $120.00 (ISBN 0-8058-0305-X). paper book $55.00 (ISBN 0-8058-0306-8).
This Companion Disk to the Book Helps Explore the Importance & Value of Interactive Problem Solving.
Lawrence Erlbaum Assocs. Software & Alternate Media, Inc.

International Recipes: World of Exciting Cuisines at Your Fingertips. Oct. 1994. *Items Included:* Registration card, instruction sheet. *Customer Support:* 900 support number $2.00 per minute; limited 60 day warranty.
 Windows. IBM PC & compatibles (2Mb). disk $9.95 (ISBN 1-57269-011-9, Order no.: 3202 42255). *Addl. software required:* Windows 3.1 or higher. *Optimal configuration:* VGA or higher monitor, hard disk required, use with any mouse.
An Entire World of Outstanding Cuisine Is at Your Fingertips. Remarkable Library of over 300 Recipes Can Be Cross-Indexed with Your Favorite Ingredient.
Memorex Products, Inc., Memorex Software Division.

International Soccer. Microdeal. Jun. 1988. *Compatible Hardware:* Atari ST; Commodore Amiga. *Memory Required:* 512k. *General Requirements:* Amiga leatherneck 4-player adapter for more than two players.
 Atari ST. 3.5" disk $39.95, (demo avail.).
 Amiga. 3.5" disk $39.95.
Arcade Game in Which Players Can Select Team Colors, Wind, Rain, & Night Play Options.
MichTron, Inc.

International Software Sales General Ledger. International Software Sales, Inc. *Compatible Hardware:* TI Professional with printer & 2 disk drives. *Operating System(s) Required:* MS-DOS. *Memory Required:* 64k.
 $995.00.
Interactive with A/R, A/P, Inventory & Payroll. Allows Direct Posting to G/L Accounts Using One-Sided Entry Method.
Texas Instruments, Personal Productivit.

International Standard Bible Encyclopedia. Feb. 1996. *Items Included:* Disks, marketing literature, order form, registration card. *Customer Support:* 30 day money back guarantee; limited replacement warranty on diskettes defective at time of purchase; free telephone technical support.
 Windows 3.1 or higher. IBM 386/486 or 100% compatible (4Mb, 8Mb recommended). 3.5" disk $79.95 (ISBN 1-56514-117-2). *Addl. software required:* Biblesoft's PC Study Bible. *Optimal configuration:* 3.5, 1.44Mb disk drive for installation, mouse or pointer device recommended.
An Extensive Encyclopedia of Articles Covering Bible Words & Concepts to Be Used As an Add-On to the PC Study Bible Originally Published As a 5-Volume Series with Each Article Written by Respected Scholars in the Assigned Topic.
Biblesoft.

International Teller System. 1986. *Compatible Hardware:* IBM PC, PC XT, PC AT, PS/2, 386, 486 & compatibles. *Operating System(s) Required:* MS-DOS, Windows. *Memory Required:* 640k. *General Requirements:* Hard disk, printer.
Base system. Contact publisher for price.
 Networks supported: LAN-Novell, Token Ring. *Provides for Sale & Purchase of Foreign Currency & Dollar Drafts, Traveller's Checks, Wires & Buying/Selling of Currency. Buying & Selling Rates for Each Transaction Type Are Set by User at Beginning of Day. Calculates Fees According to User-Created Fee Table. Produces Drafts, Customer Receipts, SWIFT Draft Advices (MT110), SWIFT Wires (MT100, MT202). Interfaces to SPOT SYSTEMS MULTI-CURRENCY GL. Corporate & Correspondent Draft/Wire Remote Issuance Option Available. Remote Teller Option Also Available.*
Spot Systems, Inc.

The Internet Business Guide: Essential Online Resources. Douglas Grant et al. Apr. 1996. *Items Included:* A 64-page companion booklet that reviews web sites & includes instructions on how to use the software. *Customer Support:* Access to the Go!Guides web site & FAQ, customer support by email at help goguides.com.
 Macintosh System 7.0 or higher. Macintosh (4Mb). 3.5" disk $12.99 (ISBN 1-57712-005-1). *Nonstandard peripherals required:* Modem 14.4 or faster. *Addl. software required:* Internet account & connection. *Optimal configuration:* Macintosh System 7.0 or higher, at least 4Mb of RAM, at least 2Mb of free disk space, color monitor, 14.4 or 28.8 modem, Internet account.
 Windows 3.1 or Windows 95. IBM or compatible (4Mb). disk $12.99. *Nonstandard peripherals required:* 14.4 or 28.8 modem. *Addl. software required:* Internet account. *Optimal configuration:* IBM-compatible running Windows 3.1 or Windows 95, at least 2Mb free space on hard drive, at least 4Mb RAM, color monitor, 14.4 or 28.8 modem, Internet account.
What's Online for Your Business? The Internet Business Guide Explains What Resources & Benefits Await You.
Motion Works Publishing.

Internet Family Guide: Resources for Learning & Playing Online. Meredith B. Woodward. Apr. 1996. *Items Included:* A 64-page companion booklet that reviews web sites & includes instructions on how to use the software. *Customer Support:* Access to the Go!Guides web site & FAQ, customer support by email at help goguides.com.
 Macintosh System 7.0 or higher. Macintosh (4Mb). 3.5" disk $12.99 (ISBN 1-57712-009-4). *Nonstandard peripherals required:* Modem 14.4 or faster. *Addl. software required:* Internet account & connection. *Optimal configuration:* Macintosh System 7.0 or higher, at least 4Mb of RAM, at least 2Mb of free disk space, color monitor, 14.4 or 28.8 modem, Internet account.
 Windows 3.1 or Windows 95. IBM or compatible (4Mb). disk $12.99. *Nonstandard peripherals required:* 14.4 or 28.8 modem. *Addl. software required:* Internet account. *Optimal configuration:* IBM-compatible running Windows 3.1 or Windows 95, at least 2Mb free space on hard drive, at least 4Mb RAM, color monitor, 14.4 or 28.8 modem, Internet account.
This Smart Cyberguide Has the Best Internet Resources for Families. It's Packed with Links to Online Games, Parenting Support Groups, Suggestions for Arts & Crafts, Homework Help, & That's Just the Beginning.
Motion Works Publishing.

The Internet for Everybody. *Version:* 1.0.1. Point Productions Staff. Jan. 1995. *Customer Support:* Free technical support (508) 879-0006 (9-5 EST).
 Windows; Macintosh. 486 or higher, 33MHz (8Mb); Mac 68030 (4Mb). CD-ROM disk $49.95 (ISBN 1-887246-00-2). *Nonstandard peripherals required:* Sound card, CD-ROM drive, 256 color display. *Addl. software required:* Quicktime (supplied on CD-ROM).
Learn about the Internet the Easy Way! This Comprehensive Disc Shows You What to Type & Exactly How the Computer Screens Look & Act When You Get Online. With over Two Hours of Live Video Including High Resolution Screen Shots, Internet Expert, Dick Rubinstein, Takes You on a Guided Tour of the Internet with Stops along the Way to Explain Both Basics & Advanced Concepts.
CD Solutions, Inc.

TITLE INDEX

Internet Info. *Customer Support:* All of our products are unconditionally guaranteed.
DOS, Unix. CD-ROM disk $39.95 (Order no.: INET). *Nonstandard peripherals required:* CD-ROM drive.
Newest Collection of Internet Related Documents Including FTPs, RFCs, FAQs.
Walnut Creek CDRom.

Internet Marketing, Print & Electronic Publishing Software CD-ROM. Jan. 1996. *Items Included:* Instruction booklet.
DOS & Windows. PC (2k). CD-ROM disk $29.90 (ISBN 1-56087-117-2). *Optimal configuration:* 386, Windows 2k.
DOS & Windows 3.1. IBM & compatibles (4 disks) 3.5" (2k). disk $39.87 (ISBN 1-56087-112-1). *Optimal configuration:* 386 Windows 3.1 2k.
57 Complete Shareware Programs to Write, Paste-Up, Publish & Market Your Books, Reports, Catalogs, CD-ROMs & PC Disks. Featuring: Interactive Multimedia, Electronic Publishing & Internet Marketing. Includes EAN Barcode Generator, DataBase Program, Office Tracker, Accounting & Inventory Programs, Plus 42 Other Great Complete Office Software.
Top of the Mountain Publishing.

The Internet Media Guide: News & Entertainment in Cybersapce. Richard Pinet. Apr. 1996. *Items Included:* A 64-page companion booklet that reviews web sites & includes instructions on how to use the software. *Customer Support:* Access to the Go!Guides web site & FAQ, customer support by email at help goguides.com.
Macintosh System 7.0 or higher. Macintosh (4Mb). 3.5" disk $12.99 (ISBN 1-57712-010-8). *Nonstandard peripherals required:* Modem 14.4 or faster. *Addl. software required:* Internet account & connection. *Optimal configuration:* Macintosh System 7.0 or higher, at least 4Mb of RAM, at least 2Mb of free disk space, color monitor, 14.4 or 28.8 modem, Internet account.
Windows 3.1 or Windows 95. IBM or compatible (4Mb). disk $12.99. *Nonstandard peripherals required:* 14.4 or 28.8 modem. *Addl. software required:* Internet account. *Optimal configuration:* IBM-compatible running Windows 3.1 or Windows 95, at least 2Mb free space on hard drive, at least 4Mb RAM, color monitor, 14.4 or 28.8 modem, Internet account.
In This Internet-Junkie's Joyride Through Cyberspace, You'll Find Everything from the New York Times & Project Gutenberg to National Public Radio, Newsgroups & Media Education.
Motion Works Publishing.

Internet Navigation Simulator: An Interactive Tutor-on-Disk. James Potter. Sep. 1995. *Items Included:* Instruction booklet, Bonus: over 50 hours free time on Compuserve, America Online, Genie.
DOS. PC (640k). disk $49.90 (ISBN 1-56087-081-8). *Optimal configuration:* 286 DOS 640k RAM.
Windows 3.1. PC (2k). disk $49.90 (ISBN 1-56087-135-0). *Optimal configuration:* 386 Windows 3.1 2k.
User Can Quickly Learn to Test-Drive the Internet Superhighway Without the Cost or Stress of Going On-Line. Extremely Easy to Use: Just Follow the Prompts...It Shows You How to Create, Send & Accept Electronic Mail over the Internet, How to Use Indexes Including Archie, WWW, Gopher.
Top of the Mountain Publishing.

Internet Simulator CD Package. Christopher D. Watkins & Stephen R. Marenka. Jul. 1995. *Items Included:* 30 page users manual. *Customer Support:* Technical support, 30 day unlimited warranty, site license available.
MS-DOS; Macintosh; Windows 3.1 or 95. IBM & compatibles (640k); Macintosh Performa, Quadra, Power PC (640k). CD-ROM disk $39.95 (ISBN 1-886801-02-9). *Nonstandard peripherals required:* CD drive.
This CD-ROM Will Enable Users to Browse the Internet Without Logging On. The CD Will Teach The User to Access Mosaic, Research User Groups, Use E-MAIL & FTP. Simulates on Line Access to IP Connected PCs & MACs. Discusses Firewalls & Internet Security, File Compression & Archiving. Internet Resource Guide Included.
Charles River Media.

Internet Simulator CD Package. Christopher D. Watkins & Stephen R. Marenka. Jul. 1995. *Items Included:* 30 page users manual. *Customer Support:* Technical support, 30 day unlimited warranty, site license available.
MS-DOS; Macintosh; Windows 3.1 or 95. IBM & compatibles with CD drive (640k); Mac with CD drive, Performa, Quadra, Power PC (640k). CD-ROM disk $39.95 (ISBN 1-886801-02-9). *Nonstandard peripherals required:* CD-drive.
Will Enable Users to Browse the Internet Without Logging On. The CD Will Teach the User to Access Mosaic, Research User Groups, Use E-Mail & FTP. Simulates on Line Access to IP Connected PCs & MACs. Discusses Firewalls & Internet Security, File Compression & Archiving. Internet Resource Guide Included.
Charles River Media.

Internet Travel Guide: Practical Business & Adventure Resources. Meredith B. Woodward. Apr. 1996. *Items Included:* A 64-page companion booklet that reviews web sites & includes instructions on how to use the software. *Customer Support:* Access to the Go!Guides web site & FAQ, customer support by email at help goguides.com.
Macintosh System 7.0 or higher. Macintosh (4Mb). 3.5" disk $12.99 (ISBN 1-57712-007-8). *Nonstandard peripherals required:* Modem 14.4 or faster. *Addl. software required:* Internet account & connection. *Optimal configuration:* Macintosh System 7.0 or higher, at least 4Mb of RAM, at least 2Mb of free disk space, color monitor, 14.4 or 28.8 modem, Internet account.
Windows 3.1 or Windows 95. IBM or compatible (4Mb). disk $12.99. *Nonstandard peripherals required:* 14.4 or 28.8 modem. *Addl. software required:* Internet account. *Optimal configuration:* IBM-compatible running Windows 3.1 or Windows 95, at least 2Mb free space on hard drive, at least 4Mb RAM, color monitor, 14.4 or 28.8 modem, Internet account.
The Smart Cyberguide Gives You Up-to-the-Minute Resources to Inform & Inspire Your Travel Dreams.
Motion Works Publishing.

Internet Video Starter Kit. 1994. *Items Included:* 2-30 minute videos. *Customer Support:* 30 day no risk guarantee.
$149.00 (ISBN 0-927875-57-8, Order no.: 9500).
Comprehensive Workbook along with 2 30-Minute Videos Show You How to Connect to the Internet, Select a Provider, Use E-Mail, Search with "Gophers", Transfer Files, etc. With Performance Rights Included, Allows You to Circulate and/or Use This Kit As An Educational Resource So Your Patrons & Students Can Also Learn to Navigate the Internet.
Winnebago Software Co.

The Internet Watch Dog. Algorithm, Inc. Staff. *Customer Support:* Free technical support, 30 day limited warranty, site licenses available.
Windows 3.1 or higher. IBM & compatibles (4Mb). disk $24.95 (ISBN 1-886801-49-5). *Optimal configuration:* PC or compatible; 386 or higher; Windows 3.1 or higher, 3.5" disk drive.
Monitors Internet Usage by Capturing Screenshots at Intervals Set by the User. Loaded onto the Hard Drive, the Watch Dog Enables Parents or Employers to Control Internet Usage Without "Blocking" Addresses or URLs.
Charles River Media.

The Internet Watch Dog. Algorithm, Inc. Staff. Dec. 1995. *Customer Support:* Free technical support, 30 day limited warranty, site licenses available.
Windows 3.1 or higher. IBM & compatibles (4Mb). disk $24.95 (ISBN 1-886801-49-5). *Optimal configuration:* PC or compatible; 386 or higher.
Monitors Internet Usage by Capturing Screenshots at Intervals Set by the User. Loaded onto the Hard Drive, the Watch Dog Enables Parents or Employers to "Control" Internet Usage Without "Blocking" Addresses or URLs.
Charles River Media.

Interpersonal Styles Inventory. Version: 1.013. Maurice Lorr & Richard P. Youniss. *Customer Support:* Free unlimited phone support with a toll free number.
DOS 3.0 or higher. IBM or 100% compatible (512k). disk $195.00 (Order no.: W-1050 5.25"; W-1051 3.5"). *Optimal configuration:* Hard drive with 1Mb free disk space, printer.
Comprehensive Assessment of Interpersonal Functioning. Designed for Individuals 14 Years & Older, the ISI is a Self-Report Inventory That Gives the Administrator a Very Accurate Indication of the Way an Individual Relates to Others.
Western Psychological Services.

Interpolation. Version: 3. Sep. 1995. *Compatible Hardware:* IBM PC.
disk $25.00 ea.
Graphical Portrayal of Interpolation. Program Will Construct the Interpolating Polynomial Based on up to 20 Different Points. It Will Draw the Points, Graph the Polynomial, Print-Out the Expression for the Polynomial & Allow Predictions Based on It.
MatheGraphics Software.

Intersolv Q&E. Version: 6. Aug. 1994. *Compatible Hardware:* IBM PC AT & compatibles. *Memory Required:* 2000k. *Items Included:* Software & users guide. *Customer Support:* 30 days free support.
$499.00.
Queries, Edits Data & Imports into User's Current Application. Provides Common User Interface for over Thirty (30) Databases, Including DB2, SQL Server, SYBASE, Netware SQL, Ingres, XDB, SQL Base, Btrieve, Oracle, dBASE, Paradox, ASCII Text Files, IBM SQL/DS & Excel. Additional Features Include Graphical Drag-&-Drop Forms Designer, Query Builder Customizable Icon Bar with Scripts, Fill-in-the-Blank Queries & Report Writer.
Intersolv.

Intersolv Q&E. Version: 5.0. Nov. 1992. *Items Included:* 500-page manual, product literature. *Customer Support:* Free 30 day technical support w/paid programs available, on-site or off-site training.
OS/2 2.1 or higher. PC, IBM PS/2, PC/AT & compatibles (2Mb). disk $495.00 (Order no.: QSV5001-50). *Optimal configuration:* 1Mb min memory, 4Mb disk.
OS/2 2.1 or higher. IBM PS/2, PC/AT & compatibles. disk $495.00 (Order no.:

QSV3001-50). *Optimal configuration:* 2Mb RAM.
Allows Endusers to Build Sophisticated Queries Generate Professional Reports, Develop Custom Forms That Feature Query by Example, & Link Data into Other Business Applications. Data Warehousing Capabilities Provide Meaningful Data Sets from Which Users Can Create Ad-Hoc Queries. Supports 20 Plus Databases & ODBC. Absolutely No Programming Required. Q&E for OS/2 Supports ALLBASE, Btrieve, Clipper DB2, DB2/2, DB2/6000, dBASE, Excel, FoxBase, FoxPro, Gupta SQLBase, Image/SQL, Informix, Ingres, Microsoft, SQL Server, Netware SQL, Oracle, Paradox, Progress, SQL/400, SQL/DS Sybase System 10, Sybase SQL Server 4, Teradata, Text Files & XDB.
Intersolv.

Intertools. *Items Included:* C Cross Compilers, Cross Assemblers, Source Level Cross Deluggers. *Customer Support:* Telephone technical support, training, user documentation.
PC-DOS 3.1 or higher (260k). IBM PC & compatibles, Sun, Apollo, HP 9000, Dec VAX. $1975.00-$14,800.00.
Unix, VAX Ultirx, VAX VMS, MS-DOS. contact publisher for price.
Software Toolkit Consists of Optimizing ANSI C Compiler, Assembler, Cross-Debugger & Utilities Library. Toolkit Supports Embedded Systems Development, & Macro Cross Assembler Provides Interface Between Assembly Language & C. PassKey Debugger (See Listing) Gives Realtime Diagnostics in C or Assembly Language. Utility Programs Include Linker, Locator, Formatter, Librarian, Symbol Lister & Symbol Mapper. Produces Code for the 68000, 8086, NEC V Series, Am 29000, TMS 340, V60-V70 & the 96002.
Intermetrics Microsystems Software, Inc.

Intex Bond Calculations. *Version:* 2.5. Mar. 1989. *Customer Support:* 30 day money back guarantee; technical support (phone).
MS-DOS. IBM. disk $495.00 & up.
Provides Accurate Functions Which Compute Yield, Price, Duration, Convexity, Horizon Return, & Many Other Key Bond Calculations for a Variety of Domestic & International Bonds. Also Handles Odd Coupon, Step Coupon, & PIK Coupon Bonds, As Well As Bonds with Sinking Fund Provisions. International Version Computes Bond Calculations for More Than 16 Countries. Works with Lotus 1-2-3 for Windows 4.X & Excel.
Intex Solutions, Inc.

Intex CMO Analyst. *Version:* 2.1E. 1993. *Customer Support:* Telephone support N/C.
MS-DOS (Windows 3.1 under MS-DOS). IBM PC compatible, XT, AT. Contact publisher for price. *Addl. software required:* Lotus 1-2-3 Windows 4X or Excel.
First & Only Spreadsheet-Based CMO Portfolio Analysis Program. As an Add-In to Lotus 1-2-3 or Microsoft Excel for Windows, CMO Analyst is an Open System That Lets Users Define & Model Any CMO, from Simple to Complex, in Unlimited Ways. At the Core of CMO Analyst Is Intex's Complete & Highly Accurate Database of CMO Deal Models, Enhanced Continually with New Deals & Updates of Seasoned Deals. Using the Many " functions" Provided, Users Can Easily Analyze Individual Tranches or Entire CMO Portfolios, & at the Same Time Utilize All the Tools Provided by the Spreadsheet Itself for Charting, Sensitiviy Analysis, Vector Analysis & Much More. Among the Hundreds of Calculations Provided Are Price, Yield, Duration & Weighted Average Life, Recent PSA, Tranche Cashflow, Current Tranche Factor & More.
Intex Solutions, Inc.

Intex Mortgage-Backed Calculations. *Version:* 3.1.4. *Items Included:* Manual & diskette. *Customer Support:* Free technical support, 30 day money back guarantee.
MS-DOS. IBM PC, XT, AT, PS/2 or 100% compatible. disk $495.00. *Addl. software required:* Lotus 1-2-3.
Computes All Key MBS Calculations, Factoring in Considerations Such As Prepayment Rates, Delay Days & Service Costs Which Can Significantly Impact Your Results. You Enter These Functions into Your Spreadsheet or Database with Just a Few Simple Commands. Offers a Choice of Three Different Versions. The Basic Version Offers a CPR Prepayment Model; the Advanced Version Provides CPR, PSA & FHA Models, & Support for ARMs; the Excess Servicing Version Adds Calculations for Institutions Which Issue MBS Instruments.
Intex Solutions, Inc.

Intext. *Version:* 3.32. *Compatible Hardware:* IBM PC & compatibles. *Memory Required:* 512k. *Items Included:* Manual, reference card, keyboard layout card(s). *Customer Support:* yes.
with two languages $195.00.
with three languages $250.00.
Intext '2L2' Chinese Word Processor. $395.00.
Multilingual Word Processing Application Which Lets Users Work with More Than One Language at the Same Time. When the User Needs to Switch from One Language to Another, the Keyboard Is Automatically Reconfigured at the Touch of a Function Key. Menus, Help Messages, & Manuals Are Available in the Respective Languages. To Identify the Position of Foreign Characters on the Keyboard Layout Guides, Stickers, Key Caps, or Keyboards with LCD's Can Be Used (Supports HoHe Computer Technology's LCD Keyboard). Supported Languages Include: Arabic, Chinese, Czeckoslovakian, Danish, Dutch, American & British English, Farsi, French, French Canadian, Finnish, Gaelic, German, Greek, Hebrew, Icelandic, Italian, Macedonian, Norwegian, Polish, Portuguese, Romanian, Russian, Spanish, Swedish, Turkish, Urdu, & Serbo-Croatian.
Intex Software Systems International, Ltd.

Intimacy. 1993. *Items Included:* 56 page manual. *Customer Support:* Full telephone support - free.
PC-DOS/MS-DOS. IBM PC, XT, AT, PS/1, PS/2 & compatibles (192k). disk $69.95 (ISBN 0-933281-10-2). *Optimal configuration:* 1 disk drive or hard disk, printer.
Program Provides a Valuable Way to Explore Romantic Relationships Using the Science of Numerology. The Highly Insightful Reports Produced by This Program Are Full of Practical Suggestions That Can Help Couples to Have Stronger, More Meaningful Partnerships. The 6 to 8 Page Reports Include 7 Important Topics That Show the Dynamics at Work in a Relationship.
Widening Horizons, Inc.

InTouch NSA - Network Security Agent. *Items Included:* AXP computer system comes preloaded with Intouch NSA, 1 spiral manual. *Customer Support:* 30 days free support, 1 yr. - 15% of list price. Training avail. on site or at TTI...price varies.
Contact publisher for price.
Complete Ethernet LAN Monitoring & Unauthorized Use Detection Device. Monitor All Users, Set Violation Rules, No-Impact to System Load. Protect Systems from Internal Crime.
Touch Technologies, Inc.

Intra Day Analyst. *Version:* 2.4. 1981. *Compatible Hardware:* Apple; IBM PC, PC XT, PC AT & compatibles.
contact publisher for price.
Turns an IBM PC or Compatible into a Real-Time, On-Line Technical Analysis Workstation. Displays Variable Length Bar Charts with Accompanying Studies Chosen by User. Up to 50 Different Stocks or Futures Can Be Followed & More Than 60 Different Charts Can Be Drawn. Is Fully Supported by Full-Time Telephone Assistance.
Intra Day Analyst.

Intra Day Analyst/PC, 2 disks. Jul. 1987. *Compatible Hardware:* IBM PC XT, PC AT & compatibles. *General Requirements:* 2 disk drives or hard disk, CGA card, supported live quote machine.
disk $1600.00 (ISBN 0-944173-01-2).
Graphic Technical Analysis Package for Real Time Investment Market Data. Includes Commodity Stock Trading & Forecasting Stock Market.
CompuTrac, A Telerate Co.

IntroCAD. *Version:* 2.0. Jan. 1988. *Compatible Hardware:* Commodore Amiga 500, 1000, 2000. *Memory Required:* 512k.
3.5" disk $79.95.
Enables Users to Draw Lines, Boxes, Circles, & Arcs, & Provides Erase, Move, Clone, Size, Rotate, Set Line, & Point Edit Functions. Users Can Adjust Text Size, Select X & Y Axes, & Zoom in on Multiple Levels of a Drawing. Supports Isometric & Projection Gridding & Provides a Snap-to-Grid Function. Can Produce Ellipses, Rectangles, & Stretched & Reversed Text. Can Also Maintain a Parts Library.
Progressive Peripherals & Software, Inc.

Introducing C. *Version:* 1.13. 1985. *Compatible Hardware:* IBM PC, PC XT, PC AT. *Operating System(s) Required:* PC-DOS 2.0. *Language(s):* C. *Memory Required:* 192k.
$125.00, incl. demo disk, color graphics & C function library (ISBN 0-923167-00-5).
Combines a Self-Paced Manual with a C Interpreter. Presents Such "C" Concepts As Standard K&R Syntax & Operators, Full Structures & Unions, Arrays, & Pointers & Data Types. Designed for Both Casual & Professional Programmers.
Computer Innovations, Inc.

Introduction to Behavioral Objectives. *Version:* 2.0. Yoder. 1992. *Compatible Hardware:* IBM PC. *Memory Required:* 128k.
disk $145.00, incl. user's guide (Order no.: 64-71817).
Deals with the Basic Theory Behind the Concept of Writing Behavioral Objectives As Part of the Documentation of Nursing Process.
J. B. Lippincott Co.

Introduction to Cardiothoracic Imaging. C. Carl Jaffe et al. Nov. 1993. *Items Included:* Software supplied on CD-ROM disc, User's Manual.
Macintosh. Macintosh II or Quadra with minimum of 13 inch 256-color display (8Mb). CD-ROM disk $149.00 (ISBN 1-884012-02-7, Order no.: 93-002). *Nonstandard peripherals required:* CD-ROM drive to load software. *Optimal configuration:* Macintosh IIci, fx, LC, or Quadra with 13 inch or larger color monitor, 8Mb RAM, with CD-ROM drive. *Networks supported:* AppleShare.
A Comprehensive Multimedia Introduction to Diagnostic Imaging of the Chest & Cardiopulmonary System. The Software Incorporates Anatomy References, Extensive Information on Imaging Techniques, Diagnostic Image Findings, & over 70 Case Presentations. Included Are MRI, CT, Radiography, Echocardiography, & Other Cardiothoracic Imaging Techniques, & Cardiac Auscultation.
Yale Univ., Schl. of Medicine, Ctr. for Advanced Instructional Media.

TITLE INDEX

Introduction to Economics. Jan. 1990. *Items Included:* Teacher's manual/user's guide.
DOS 2.0 or higher. IBM (256k). 5.25" disk $280.00 (ISBN 0-8219-0650-X, Order no.: 95500G). *Nonstandard peripherals required:* Color graphics adapter.
Apple DOS 3.3. Apple IIc or IIe (128k). disk $280.00 (ISBN 0-8219-0640-2, Order no.: 95500F).
Eight Diskette Program That Covers Micro & Macroeconomics Concepts in Tutorial & Simulations. Users Can Invest in the Stock Market, Open & Manage a Business, Learn Basic Economic Concepts & Terminology.
EMC Publishing.

Introduction to Nursing Diagnosis. *Version:* 2.0. Marianne E. Yoder. 1992. *Compatible Hardware:* IBM PC. *Language(s):* PC PILOT, SuperPILOT. *Memory Required:* 64k.
disk $145.00.
Tutorial Includes: Define Nursing Diagnosis, Compare & Contrast It Against a Medical Diagnosis, Identify the 3 Components of a Nursing Diagnosis, Describe How It Relates to the Nursing Process, Differentiate Between Appropriate & Inappropriate Nursing Diagnoses.
J. B. Lippincott Co.

Introduction to Nursing Orders. *Version:* 2.0. Yoder. 1992. *Compatible Hardware:* IBM PC. *Memory Required:* 128k.
disk $145.00, incl. user's guide (Order no.: 64-71841).
Covers the Basic Concept of Writing Nursing Orders As Part of the Documentation of the Nursing Process.
J. B. Lippincott Co.

Introduction to Patient Data. *Version:* 2.0. Yoder. 1992. *Compatible Hardware:* IBM PC. *Memory Required:* 128k.
disk $145.00, incl. user's guide (Order no.: 64-73326).
Computer Assisted Tutorial on the Data Collection Phase of the Nursing Process.
J. B. Lippincott Co.

Introduction to Radiopharmacy. (Nuclear Medicine -- Radiopharmacy Ser.). Ann M. Stevens. 1996.
DOS 3.1 or higher. IBM or compatible (512k). disk $150.00 (Order no.: MIS9021).
Nonstandard peripherals required: VGA.
This tutorial describes the production of medically useful radionuclides by reactor & cyclotron & discusses the characteristics (decay mode, carrier state, specific activity) of reactor & cyclotron produced radionuclides.
Educational Software Concepts, Inc.

Introduction to the Daylight Ephemeris.
Compatible Hardware: TI 99/4A with Extended BASIC module. *Operating System(s) Required:* DX-10. *Language(s):* Extended BASIC. *Memory Required:* 48k.
cassette $17.95.
Introduction to the DAYLIGHT EPHEMERIS PROGRAM. Defines Terms & Includes Examples & Instructions.
Eastbench Software Products.

Introduction to Translations. Jul. 1994. *Items Included:* User manual. *Customer Support:* Free technical support & a 30-day warranty (1-800-521-CORE).
MS-DOS. IBM & compatibles (512k). 3.5" disk $395.00 (ISBN 1-57305-004-0). *Nonstandard peripherals required:* High-density 3.5" disk drive; EGA color monitor. *Addl. software required:* MS-DOS version 3.3 or higher.
Optimal configuration: IBM (512k), MS-DOS version 3.3 or higher, VGA color monitor, keyboard, Microsoft compatible mouse (optional).
A Computer-Based Training (CBT) Course That Provides an Introduction to Important Fundamental Concepts That Relate to Initiating & Preparing Translations for Transmissoin of Local & Toll Calls over a Switching Network. This Is a Stand-Alone Course but It is Also a Helpful Prerequisite for More Advanced Training Relating to Establishing & Maintaining Translations Information.
Bellcore.

Introduction to Turbo Pascal: A Tutorial. Dec. 1988. *Operating System(s) Required:* PC-DOS/MS-DOS. *Memory Required:* 256k. *General Requirements:* CGA, EGA, or VGA; color monitor.
disk $51.95 (ISBN 0-9621501-0-X).
Teaches Programming in Turbo Pascal, Turtle Graphics & Procedures with Parameters Are Included. Includes Management Feature.
Bellmore Software.

Introductory Calculus. 1992. *Items Included:* Detailed manuals are included with all DYNACOMP products. *Customer Support:* Free telephone support to original customer - no time limit; 30 day limited warranty.
MS-DOS 3.2 or higher. IBM PC & compatibles (512k). $179.95 (Add $5.00 for 3 1/2" format; 5 1/4" format standard).
Differentiation of Algebraic Functions; Maxima/Minima-Part 1; Maxima/Minima-Part 2; Relative Rates-Part 1; Relative Rates-Part 2; Integration of Algebra Fns; Differentiation of Trig Functions; Integration of Trig Fns; Integration: Planar Areas; Integration: Volumes; Integration: Arc Lengths; Integration: Surface Areas.
Dynacomp, Inc.

Introductory Chemistry I. 1992. *Items Included:* Detailed manuals are included with all DYNACOMP products. *Customer Support:* Free telephone support to original customer - no time limit; 30 day limited warranty.
MS-DOS 3.2 or higher. IBM PC & compatibles (512k). $59.95 (Add $5.00 for 3 1/2" format; 5 1/4" format standard).
Calorimetry; Specific Heat Capacity; Fusion/Vaporization; Specific Gas Laws; General Gas Law; Faraday's Law; Gram Molecular Mass; Mole Concept; Symbols & Valences; Names of Compounds; Formulas of Compounds; Gas Law Analysis; Calorimetry Analysis.
Dynacomp, Inc.

Introductory Chemistry II. 1992. *Items Included:* Detailed manuals are included with all DYNACOMP products. *Customer Support:* Free telephone support to original customer - no time limit; 30 day limited warranty.
MS-DOS 3.2 or higher. IBM PC & compatibles (512k). $59.95 (Add $5.00 for 3 1/2" format; 5 1/4" format standard).
Molarity Concept; Normality Concept; Molality Concept; Mass/Mass Problems; Mass/Volume Problems; Volume/Volume Problems; Stoichiometry Problems; Percent Concentration; pH Concept; Electrochemical Cells; Chemistry I Analysis; Chemistry II Analysis; Stoichiometric Analysis.
Dynacomp, Inc.

Introductory Editor. David N. Smith. *Compatible Hardware:* IBM PC, PCjr, PC XT, PC AT, Portable PC, 3270 PC. *Operating System(s) Required:* PC-DOS 2.00, 2.10, 3.00, 3.10. *Memory Required:* 128k. *General Requirements:* IBM Matrix Printer recommended.
disk $19.95 (Order no.: 6276589).
Allows User to Create Documents or Letters, Print Drafts, & Modify Any ASCII File. Displays Files of up to 1500 Lines in Length & 254 Characters in Width. Files Containing up to 50,000 Characters Can Be Edited. Allows User to Copy, Move, & Delete Blocks of Lines, Split & Join Lines, Use Programmable Keys, Search & Locate Strings of Data, & Print Drafts of Documents.
Personally Developed Software, Inc.

Introductory Lectures on Data Parallel Computing. Edited by Panagiotis Metaxas.
IBM. CD-ROM disk $35.00 (ISBN 1-56881-059-8).
Contains Eight Invited Lectures That Focus on Data-Parallel Computing, the Major Programming Paradigm of Parallelism Today. The Lectures Are Interactive & Span Three Areas of Parallel Computing: Programming Languages, Algorithms, & Research Topics. They Can Be Used As Tutorials, & As Reference in an Introductory Course on Parallel Computation. Each Lecture Contains a Quicktime Movie of the Speaker Delivering the Talk, Composed of the Transparencies Used During the Lecture Synchronized with the Voice of the Speaker. It Also Contains Information about the Speaker & Additional Materials, Like Animations, Videos, Programs & Software That Help the Understanding of the Lecture. The Code for Building the Parallaxis-III Compiler & Information on How to Get the NESL Compiler Is Also Included. A Simple & Intuitive Interface Helps Navigating Through the Contents of the CD-ROM.
AK Peters, Ltd.

Introductory Physics I. 1992. *Items Included:* Detailed manuals are included with all DYNACOMP products. *Customer Support:* Free telephone support to original customer - no time limit; 30 day limited warranty.
MS-DOS 3.2 or higher. IBM PC & compatibles (512k). $59.95 (Add $5.00 for 3 1/2" format; 5 1/4" format standard).
Linear Kinematics; Projectile Motion; Momentum & Energy; Inclined-Plane Analysis; Inelastic Collision; Centripital Force; Pulley Systems-Machines; Calorimetry; Specific Heat Capacity; Fusion/Vaporization; Vector Analysis I; Vector Analysis II; Projectile Analysis; Calorimetry Analysis.
Dynacomp, Inc.

Introductory Physics II. 1992. *Items Included:* Detailed manuals are included with all DYNACOMP products. *Customer Support:* Free telephone support to original customer - no time limit; 30 day limited warranty.
MS-DOS 3.2 or higher. IBM PC & compatibles (512k). $59.95 (Add $5.00 for 3 1/2" format; 5 1/4" format standard).
Specific Gas Laws; General Gas Laws; Thermodynamics I; Thermodynamics II; Transverse Waves; Longitudinal Waves; Mirrors & Lenses; Refraction of Light; Series Circuits; Parallel Circuits; Series/Parallel Circuits; Electric Fields; Photoelectric Effect; Internal Reflection; Gas Law Analysis; Optics Analysis.
Dynacomp, Inc.

Intruder Alert. *Compatible Hardware:* Atari 400, 800. *Language(s):* Atari BASIC (source code included). *Memory Required:* 16k.
disk $19.95.
Escape the "Dreadstar" in Order to Save the Federation.
Dynacomp, Inc.

IN2CAD. Mar. 1986. *Compatible Hardware:* IBM PC, PC AT, PC XT & compatibles. *Operating System(s) Required:* PC-DOS, MS-DOS. *Language(s):* FORTRAN. *Memory Required:* 512k. *General Requirements:* AutoCad.
disk $700.00 (Order no.: IN2CAD).

Conversion Program Which Formats Any Geostat Plot File to One Compatible with the AutoCAD System. This Graphics Display System Will Help Enhance Plots with Geologic Labels, Cultural Labels, Seam Correlations & Haul Roads. A Professional Can Also Use the Graphics to Layer Options for Different Departmental Applications.
Geostat Systems International, Inc. (GSII).

INV-V. 1981. *Compatible Hardware:* TRS-80 Model I, Model III, Model 4. *Operating System(s) Required:* TRSDOS. *Language(s):* BASIC (source code included). *Memory Required:* 48k.
disk $110.00.
manual $10.00.
Advanced Inventory System Accesses Items by a 9-Digit Alphanumeric Key.
Micro Architect, Inc.

INV-X. *Version:* 4.0. 1981. *Compatible Hardware:* IBM PC; TRS-80 Model II. *Operating System(s) Required:* TRSDOS, PC-DOS, MS-DOS. *Language(s):* BASIC. *Memory Required:* 64-128k.
disk $199.00.
manual $25.00.
Inventory Control System with a Sort/Merge Package.
Micro Architect, Inc.

Invasion. Excalibur. Oct. 1987. *Compatible Hardware:* Atari ST. *Memory Required:* 512k. *General Requirements:* Color monitor.
3.5" disk $29.95.
Designed to Improve Basic Typing, Spelling & Math Skills. Users Destroy Invading Strings of Characters by Typing Them in Sequence As They Descend upon the City. If an Invader String Makes It to The City Before Being Typed Buildings Will Blow Up. User Can Create, Add or Modify Content of Game.
MichTron, Inc.

Inventory.
$345.00 ea.
Pricing Based upon Customer Price Code.
Multi-Location Inventory.
Fractional Inventory.
Fifty Character Description.
Unit Price for Each Inventory Item Is Based Upon a Price Code Assigned to Each Customer.
Advanced Concepts, Inc.

Inventory. *Version:* 14.0. (Accounting Software Ser.). Aug. 1993. *Compatible Hardware:* IBM PC & compatibles. *Operating System(s) Required:* MS-DOS, PC-DOS 3.X & up. *Language(s):* MegaBASIC. *Memory Required:* 640k. *General Requirements:* Hard disk, wide carriage printer. *Customer Support:* (203) 790-9756.
disk $295.00, Network Option ,300.00 more.
manual $50.00.
Allows Entry of Inventory & Inventory Updates; Prints Price Tags & Inventory Labels. Automatic Update of Inventory Due to Sales, Orders, Returns, Receipts. Tie-In Available to Invoicing, Order Entry, Purchasing, Point of Sale, & Bill of Materials. Reports Include Physical Inventory Form, Cost vs. Price Analysis. Sales Analysis Reports Available. Vendor Cross Reference Available. Inventory Records Include Vendor, Location Product & Price Codes, On-Hand, on Order, Backorder Quantity & Reorder Limit for Specific Listing.
Applications Systems Group (CT), Inc.

Inventory. *Compatible Hardware:* Apple Macintosh Plus, SE, II. *General Requirements:* Hard disk; FileMaker II (Pro); ImageWriter I, II; LaserWriter optional. *Items Included:* Bar code software, hardware & documentation; includes some customizing; Bar code printing software.

Customer Support: Free telephone support.
1995.00 Software.
350.00 Bard code reader.
Bar-Code System. Allows User to Conduct an Inventory Audit by Scanning Bar Codes Assigned to the Names of Employees, Warehouses, Bin Numbers & Inventory Items. Bar code printing.
Computext.

Inventory. (Service Management Ser.).
DOS, Unix. IBM PC. disk contact publisher for price.
Handles up to 999 difference stocking locations, such as warehouses, trucks, or technician cases. Minimum quantities, bin locations, & physical inventory parameters are stored for each stocking location.
Core Software, Inc.

Inventory. *Version:* 2.0. 1989. *Compatible Hardware:* Altos; Compupro; Compaq; Fujitsu; Heath-Zenith; HP; IBM PC, PC XT, PC AT; NEC; Tandy. *Operating System(s) Required:* MS-DOS, PC-DOS, Concurrent DOS, Unix, Xenix; Novell & Microsoft networks. *Language(s):* C. *Memory Required:* 640k. *General Requirements:* Hard disk, 132-column printer. *Items Included:* Disks & manuals. *Customer Support:* Through VARs, support contracts available.
disk single-user $995.00.
multi-user $1295.00.
Unix, Xenix $1495.00.
demo disk & manual $20.00.
Provides LIFO, FIFO, Standard & Average Costing. Works with Order Entry Program to Track up to 20 Price Levels/Items. Produces Reorder, Activity, Standard Costing Variation & Other Reports. Prints Bin Labels & Price Lists. Multiple Location Within a Warehouse & Multiple Warehouse Item Tracking.
INMASS/MRP.

Inventory. *Version:* 10.0. *Compatible Hardware:* Apple Macintosh, IBM PC & compatibles. *Memory Required:* 512k. *Items Included:* Disks, book, program instructions. *Customer Support:* Telephone.
disk $145.00.
Inventory Management.
Lionheart Pr., Inc.

Inventory. ADS Software, Inc. *Compatible Hardware:* TI Professional, IBM, CP/M-86. *Operating System(s) Required:* MS-DOS. *Memory Required:* 128k. *General Requirements:* 2 disk drives.
$485.00 (Order no.: SY P/N T012-005).
Provides Up-to-the-Minute Analysis of Inventory Stock Levels, Product Sales Performance & Profitabilty on an Item-by-Item Basis.
Texas Instruments, Personal Productivit.

Inventory, 5 modules. May 1983. *Compatible Hardware:* IBM PC, PC XT, PC AT. *Operating System(s) Required:* PC-DOS. *Language(s):* COBOL. *Memory Required:* 192k. *General Requirements:* 2 disk drives.
$1600.00-$3750.00.
Five Modules Include: the Inventory Control Module Provides Stock Status, Re-Order & Transaction Reporting; the Secondary Location Module Can Support Any Number of Secondary Sites; the Pick List Module Generates Material Picking Lists; the Cycle Counting Module Calculates Stock Room Accuracy; & the Historical Usage Module Reports Usage Monthly, Year-to-Date, & Annually.
Twin Oaks, Inc.

Inventory. *Memory Required:* 56k.
contact publisher for price.
Group of Programs Includes Tracking Information for Each Piece of Inventory, Reporting, & Bill of Materials.
Universal Data Research, Inc.

Inventory Accounting. *Compatible Hardware:* IBM PC & compatibles, PC XT, PC AT. *Operating System(s) Required:* MOS. *Memory Required:* 4 users 256k, 9 users 512k.
$995.00, incl. basic system.
Includes Customer Master File, Purchase Order System, Long Item Codes, Discounts, States Tax, Invoices, Daily Sales Analysis, Reports, Inventory Item List, Movement Report & Buying Guide.
Hurricane Systems, Inc.

Inventory Accounting. *Version:* 6.70. Jan. 1988. *Operating System(s) Required:* PC-DOS/MS-DOS. *Memory Required:* 640k. *General Requirements:* Hard disk, MCC's Accounts Receivable System. *Items Included:* Manual. *Customer Support:* 1 hour per package purchased.
3.5" or 5.25" disk $695.00.
Complete One-Entry System. Order Entry Function Automatically Produces Work or Sales Orders, Confirms the Order, Prints the Invoice, Updates the Inventory on-Hand & Creates All Accounting Journal Entries. Orders Are Then Posted to A/R Where Customer Aging, Sales Analysis & Commission Reporting Are Updated.
MCC Software (Midwest Computer Ctr. Co.).

Inventory & Gold Adjustment. *Compatible Hardware:* IBM PC; Tandy 1200.
contact publisher for price.
Cen-Tex Data Systems, Inc.

Inventory Control. *Version:* 2.3. May 1984. *Compatible Hardware:* Intel 80286, 80386, 80486, etc.. *Operating System(s) Required:* MS-DOS, Novell, THEOS, UNIX, Win 95, Win/NT. *Language(s):* BASIC. *Memory Required:* 44k.
disk $1995.00.
Provides Receipt & Shipment Tracking. Keeps Records of Allocations to Customers or Work in Progress. Provides Flexibility of Ordering Methods.
COMPASS.

Inventory Control. *Items Included:* Bound manual. *Customer Support:* Free hotline - no time limit; 30 day limited warranty; updates are $5/disk plus S&H.
MS-DOS 2.0 or higher. IBM & compatibles (128k). disk $59.95. *Nonstandard peripherals required:* Two disk drives (or one floppy & a hard disk), & an 80-column (or wider) printer.
Will Allow User to Value All Inventory Items at Either the Average Cost or the Last Price Paid. It Will Sort into Descending Order & Print the Total Inventory Value. In Addition, Besides the Normal Functions of Adding & Deleting On-Hand Amounts, INVENTORY CONTROL Will Give You the Option of Printing Summary Information for All Parts of the System, or Detailed Information on a Selected Part Basis. Other Features Include the Option to Print a Historical Report Showing the Usage or Sales for All Parts over the Past 12 Months on a Month-by-Month Basis. The Documentation Includes a Complete Set of Program Listings for Those Who May Wish to Customize the Package.
Dynacomp, Inc.

Inventory Control.
DOS Network. IBM & compatibles. Contact publisher for price.
Inventory Control Which Allows for Tiered Discounts, Promotions, Volume Discounts, Multiple Warehouses. FIFO or AUG Costing, Manufacturing, Order Entry, Contracting, Purchase Orders, & Many Other Features. Integrates to All Other Grossman Systems.
Grossman & Assocs., Inc.

TITLE INDEX

Inventory Control. Version: 7.0. Wallace L. Rankin. Jan. 1987. *Operating System(s) Required:* UCSD p-System, MS-DOS. *Language(s):* Pascal. *Memory Required:* 256k. $199.00.
Accounting Program for Small Businesses Designed to Produce Rapid Data Manipulation & Sorting. Complete Inventory Control System with Master File Maintenance Is Included. Provides Updates of Current Stock & Order Status Reports, along with Stock Item Listings. Reports Regarding Inventory Analysis & Transactions Are Available upon Request.
Helu Software Corp.

Inventory Control. 1996. *Customer Support:* Free telephone & BBS technical support.
MS/PC DOS, Concurrent DOS, Xenix, Unix. IBM PC/XT/AT & compatibles, IBM PS/2 (512k). singer-user $1095.00. *Networks supported:* Novell, Lantastic, Banyan VINES; all NETBIOS compatible.
multi-user or Network $1595.00.
THE INMASS/MRP Inventory program is one of the mose powerful inventory programs available for microcomputers. It is an extremely flexible system being used by manufacturers, distributors, retailers & other businesses maintaining perpetual inventory. It provided many sophisticated features which go beyond those typically found in microcomputer inventory software. It allows them master copying, user-definable decimal percision, alternate costing methods, unit of measure conversions, cycle counting, unlimited inventory items, multiple warehouses & unlimited locations within each warehouse for each stock item. It also supports multiple stock items per location user-defined "Hold" locations for testing or inspection (non-nettable).
INMASS/MRP.

Inventory Control. Version: 4.5. 1992. *Compatible Hardware:* IBM PC & compatibles, PC XT, PC AT, 386, 486, Pentium, PS/2. *Operating System(s) Required:* PC-DOS/MS-DOS 3.X, 4X, 5X, 6X, Windows 3.1, Windows 95. *Language(s):* BASIC, C, Assembler. *Memory Required:* 640k. *General Requirements:* Stand-alone or 4Mb Network file server. *Customer Support:* 90 day warranty, onsite training, telephone support.
disk $995.00.
Tracks Inventory Status, Analyzes Data for Profitability, Reports Valuation, Computes Selling Prices, Interfaces with Billing & Order Entry, Job Costing, Bill of Materials Processing.
LIBRA Corp.

Inventory Control. Version: 2.0. May 1987. *Items Included:* Comprehensive Manual in 3 ring cloth binder & slipcase. *Customer Support:* 2 hours no cost support to registered users during first six months. Service contracts available thereafter at a cost of $60.00 per hour with no minimum.
PC/MS-DOS 2.1 or higher (256k). IBM PC, XT, AT, PS/2 & 100% compatible micro computers. $145.00 (ISBN 1-877915-00-9, Order no.: 1-877915-00-9). *Optimal configuration:* HARD Disk.
Designed to Manage an Inventory of up to 3200 Items on a Hard disk System, 1800 Items with 2 Double-Sided Disk Drives or 800 Items on a Single Double-Sided Disk Drive. It Provides 19 Inventory Categories: Item Number, Description, Unit of Measure, Class, Weight, Location, Vendor Name, Vendor Number, Cost, Retail Price, Reorder Quantity, Minimum Level, Allocation, on Order, on Hand, Order Date, Month & Year-to-Date Sold & Year-to-Date Returned. Produces the Following Reports, All of Which Can Be Customized with 7 Levels of Searching & up to 2 Levels of Sorting: Inventory Status, Inventory Value, Below Minimum Level Report, Retail Price List, Physical Inventory List, Inventory Planning Report, Shelf & Package Labels, Profit Report & Inventory Master List. Also Generates Purchase Orders on Forms or Plain Paper.
Phoenix Phive Software Corp.

Inventory Control. Version: 6.3. 1995. *Operating System(s) Required:* MS-DOS, XENIX. *Language(s):* Compiled BASIC. *Memory Required:* 256k. *General Requirements:* Hard drive, printer. *Items Included:* Manual, disk, demo. *Customer Support:* Free phone support for 90-days; $25.00 per call after.
disk $200.00 (ISBN 0-918185-23-8).
3.5" or 5.25" disk $200.00.
Interactive Stock Control System with Full Integration to Both Invoicing & General Ledger System.
Taranto & Assocs., Inc.

Inventory Control. BPI Systems, Inc. *Compatible Hardware:* TI Professional. *Operating System(s) Required:* MS-DOS. *Language(s):* MBASIC. *Memory Required:* 128k. *General Requirements:* Winchester hard disk, color monitor, printer.
$395.00 (Order no.: TI P/N 2311448-0001).
Provides Current Information on Inventory. Tracks Minimum Quantities & Back Ordered Merchandise.
Texas Instruments, Personal Productivit.

Inventory Control & Cost Analysis for Restaurants. *Compatible Hardware:* IBM PS/2, PC AT with floppy disk drive, 1 hard drive & printer. *Operating System(s) Required:* MS-DOS. *Language(s):* MBASIC. *Memory Required:* 256k. *Customer Support:* First 30 days free; $250.00/year toll free; auto update: $200/year. contact publisher for price.
demo disk $50.00.
Restaurant Management System That Can Help Place Orders After a Physical Count. User Can Create & Cost Out New Menus While the Program Does the Calculations. Provides Reports for Control & Inventory & Helps Handle Problems Such As Theft of Inventory, Overportioning of Ingredients, Inflation of Ingredient Costs, Selling More Low Profit Items Than High Profit, etc.
Computer Aid Corp.

Inventory Control & General Ledger.
Macintosh Plus or higher. $250.00 each; $400.00 both programs.
Night Club Accounting System.
Black Banana, Inc.

Inventory Control & Menu Analysis. Jan. 1982. *Compatible Hardware:* IBM PC & compatibles. *Operating System(s) Required:* PC-DOS. *Memory Required:* 256k. *General Requirements:* 1 disk drive & hard disk, printer. *Customer Support:* $250.00/year toll free.
Inventory Control. disk $1700.00.
Menu Analysis. disk $2200.00.
Designed to Reduce Food Costs & Answer Such Questions As: What Is Food Cost & Profit for Your Key Menu Items? Is Your Number One Selling Item's Food Cost Too High? What Is Your Most Important Food/Liquor Item? Helps Reduce Inventory on Hand & Overstocking. Handles 998 Inventory Items & 480 Menu Items on Sub-Recipes per Restaurant. Liquor Cost Is Computed Separately.
Computer Aid Corp.

Inventory Control: IC. Version: 5.8. May 1993. *Language(s):* Dibol & C, COBOL. *General Requirements:* Depends on specific configuration. *Customer Support:* Full service, update service; by quotation.
VMS. DEC VAX Series, DEC Alpha AXP. disk $3500.00-$15,000.00.
source code by quotation.
Layered Product, Using OE ORDER ENTRY & RE RECEIVABLES MANAGEMENT As a Base. The Combination of These Three Packages Provides the User with Complete Information Required for Maintaining Inventory Records, Placing Orders, Invoicing & Updating Accounts Receivable Information, Automatic Inventory Costing, & Incremental Inventory Accounting.
Compu-Share, Inc.

Inventory Control Program. Version: 7. *General Requirements:* Hard disk drive & printer recommended.
Macintosh 1Mb; IBM with Windows. 3.5" disk $295.00.
Keeps Track of Inventories for Wholesale, Distribution, & Retail Businesses; Many Special Versions.
S & J Enterprises.

Inventory Control with Purchasing. Version: 450.2. 1978. *Compatible Hardware:* IBM PC & compatibles. *Operating System(s) Required:* MS-DOS, PC-DOS. *Language(s):* QuickBASIC. *Memory Required:* 512k. *General Requirements:* Hard disk. *Items Included:* System diskettes, users guide, training tutorial. *Customer Support:* Telephone; annual contracts available.
$395.00 to $495.00.
Designed to Enter & Print Purchase Orders, Blanket Purchase Orders; Monitor Merchandise on Order by Item Number, Vendor, & Due Date. Reports Past Due Orders. Automatically Adjusts Inventory Balances & Unit Cost When Merchandise Received. Reports Include Vendor Master List, Inventory Valuation, Stock Status with Buy Flags, Order Desk Availability, & Gross Margins at Three Pricing Levels. Interfaces with IMS Order Processing & General Ledger Systems. Number of Vendors, Items, & Transactions Limited Only by Disk Capacity. Runs Single User or Multi-User on Many Networks.
International Micro Systems, Inc.

Inventory Management. Version: 4.50. 1978. *Compatible Hardware:* IBM PC & compatibles, PC XT, PC AT, PS/2. *Operating System(s) Required:* MS-DOS, PC-DOS. *Language(s):* FORTRAN. *Memory Required:* 320k. *Items Included:* Manual. *Customer Support:* 1 hour per package purchased.
5-1/4" or 8" or 3-1/2" disk $495.00.
Standard Features Include Part Master Maintenance of 2500 Parts per Diskette, Each with a Maximum 8-Digit Part Number, On-Line Order Entry & Maintenance for up to 950 Active Orders, Automatic Calculation of Inventory Journal Entries, Maintenance of Purchase Receipts, Inventory on Order, & Items on Back Order.
MCC Software (Midwest Computer Ctr. Co.).

Inventory Management (a Part of ABECAS). Version: 3.1. Jan. 1989. *Customer Support:* On site training unlimited support services for first 90 days & through subscription thereafter.
PC/MS-DOS 3.x. IBM PC & compatibles. Contact publisher for price. *Nonstandard peripherals required:* Hard disk (30Mb or higher); 132 column printer.
Provides Full-Featured Inventory System. Interfaces with Sales Order Processing, Purchase Order Processing & Grower Accounting Modules. Supports up to Four Price Levels, & Four Discount Levels for Each Item. Price of Each Item May Be Based on One of Five Pricing Methods. Items Produced & Used Are Both Tracked Separately. Shipping/Care Instructions May Be Associated with Each Inventory Item Through a Code. Cross-Reference Listing of User's Products to those of Other Vendors' Also Available. Summary Month-to-Date, Year-to-Date & Prior

INVENTORY MANAGEMENT SYSTEM

Year Information Maintained. Multi-User Version Available for Novell, NTNX, 10-Net, Unix/Xenix, Turbo DOS & Others.
Argos Software.

Inventory Management System. *Items Included:* Bound manual. *Customer Support:* Free hotline - no time limit; 30 day limited warranty; updates are $5/disk plus S&H.
MS-DOS. IBM & compatibles (256k). disk $99.95.
Updates the Inventory Based on Current Period Transactions. Summarizes Revenues & Quantities of Sales, Orders Placed, & Goods Received. Details Current Purchasing Needs. Calculates Potential Profit Based on Inventory, Overhead, & Expected Sales. Shows the Number of Periods of Supply That the Current Inventory Level Represents. Evaluates Inventory Wholesale Costs, Retail Values, & Cost of Goods on Order. Provides Sales Forecasting. Highlights Parts Currently Overstocked.
Dynacomp, Inc.

Inventory Master. *Version:* 4.0. Aug. 1985. *Compatible Hardware:* Atari 800, 800XL, ST. *Memory Required:* 64k.
Atari 800, 800XL. disk $89.95.
Atari ST. disk $179.95.
Royal Software.

Inventory-Plus. *Version:* 5.6. 1994. *Items Included:* Complete operating manual. *Customer Support:* Unlimited telephone support.
MS-DOS. IBM PC or compatible (256k). $195.00. *Optimal configuration:* IBM PC or compatible, 256k RAM, printer. *Networks supported:* Novel, Unex.
Designed for the First Time Computer User Which Offers Detailed Control Over All Aspects of Inventory Operations. Developed for the Small Retailer, Contractor, or Other Small Business Owner Who Needs a Tight Inventory Control System to Reduce Revenue Tied up in Stock. Has an Integrated Accounts Receivable System Which Automatically Posts Quantities Sold to the Proper Inventory Account.
Omni Software Systems, Inc. (Indiana).

Inventory Pro - Plus. *Version:* 5.11. Feb. 1991. *Items Included:* full documentation with tutorial. *Customer Support:* 90 day free unlimited phone support, optional extended support plans are available that include free upgrades.
MS-DOS 3.0 or higher. IBM or compatible (640k). disk $195.00 Pro; $395.00 Plus. *Networks supported:* Novell compatible, Net BIOS.
$295.00 Pro network; $695.00 Plus network.
A Fully Featured Inventory Program That Integrates with Recipe Writer Pro for Foodservice Inventory Maintenance, Counting, & Management. Designed for Foodservice Inventory & Links Directly with the Recipe Writer Pro. Information Stored Includes Ingredient Name, Order Unit, Recipe Unit, Vendor, Reorder Points, Current Inventory, & Vendor Name. Performs Inventory Extensions & Reports Inventory Levels & Values Instantly. Count Sheets Are Printed, with Inventory Sorted Alphabetically or by Location to Facilitate Counting. There Are Screens for Entering the Counts That Increment Inventory Totals with Each Entry. New Plus Level Module Adds Purchase History, Vendor Comparison, & Theoretical Actual & Variance Usage Reporting. Available Interfaces to Popular Accounting Packages.
At Your Service Software, Inc.

Inventory System: !Assetrac - Bar Code Asset. *Items Included:* User/procedural manual, !Barsoft reference manual, 30 day start-up support. *Customer Support:* Annual telephone support $395.00, on-line (modem/emulation) support $695.00.
IBM PC AT, 386 & Compatibles (256k). disk $1750.00. *Addl. software required:* !Assetrac IRL for hand-held (portable) scanner.
Automates Asset & Equipment Inventory Through Bar Code & Portable Data Collection Terminals with Bar Code Scanners. All Software Is Completely Menu Driven. User Can Modify or Add Screens, Fields Reports & Labels. Complete System Support Available.
ASAP Systems.

Inventory with Point of Sale. Great Plains Software. Jan. 1984. *Compatible Hardware:* TI Professional. *Operating System(s) Required:* MS-DOS. *Memory Required:* 256k. *General Requirements:* Winchester hard disk, printer. $595.00, incl. module.
Allows up to 30,000 Part Numbers, 3 Quantity Breaks & 5 Price Levels for Each Break.
Texas Instruments, Personal Productivit.

Inverse Fast Fourier Transform Tutorial. *Items Included:* Bound manual. *Customer Support:* Free hotline - no time limit; 30 day limited warranty; updates are $5/disk plus S&H.
MS-DOS. IBM & compatibles (128k). disk $39.95. *Nonstandard peripherals required:* Color graphics card.
Apple (48k). disk $39.95.
Useful to Engineers & Scientists Who Wish to Learn about the IFFT, Its Operation, & the General Ability to Reconstruct Signals (Time Functions) from Their Discrete Fourier Transforms. The Documentation Is Broken into Two Parts. The First Part Deals with the Theory of the Fourier Transform Pair in General, the Discrete Fourier Transform (DFT), the Fast Fourier Transform (FFT), & Frequency Domain Filtering. Many Graphical Examples Are Included Throughout. The Second Part Relates to Operating the Program. To Run the Program, Just Follow the Prompts. You Can Specify Various Standard Signals (or Your Own) & the Sampling Interval. Up to 128 Points May Be Specified (or Loaded from Disk). Or You Can Specify the Harmonics (up to 64) Directly. User May Also Specify the Filter or Use a Pole/Zero Description. Real & Imaginary Coefficients May Be Used.
Dynacomp, Inc.

Invest Now! *Version:* 2.0 Pro. *Compatible Hardware:* IBM PC & compatibles. *Memory Required:* 128k.
$195.00.
Memory-Resident Stock & Option Analysis Program That Analyzes the Buying of Calls & Puts, Writing Naked & Covered Calls & Writing Naked Puts. Also Determines a Stock's Return from Dividends & Realized/Unrealized Profit or Loss. User Can Input Actual Brokerage Fees or Have the Program Provide Typical Commission Rates on Trades. The Package Computes Simple & Annual Returns on Investments & Applies Necessary Margin Requirements Where Applicable.
Emerging Market Technologies, Inc.

Investimator: Investment Analysis Worksheets. *Version:* 2.0. May 1990. *Compatible Hardware:* IBM PC & compatibles, Macintosh. *Items Included:* Manual & diskette. *Customer Support:* Free installation & technical support; limited warranty, call JIAN 415-941-9191.
$139.00. *Addl. software required:* Spreadsheet-Lotus 1-2-3 version 2.01 or compatible for PC; any SYLK compatible spreadsheet for the Macintosh.
Collection of Spreadsheets That Evaluate Alternatives for Business & Real Estate Investment Opportunities. Comparative Analysis Spreadsheets Include Equipment Lease vs. Buy, Simple Business Acquisition, Franchise Purchase, Multi-Unit Real Estate Purchase, Mortgage Refinancing, & Fixed vs. Variable Mortgage & Mortgage Qualification. Provides Supporting Evidence for Justifying a Financial Decision.
JIAN Tools for Sales.

The Investing Advisor. *Compatible Hardware:* IBM. *Language(s):* MS-DOS. *Memory Required:* 128k.
disk $49.95.
Facilitates Investment Buying & Selling Decisions, Tracks Long & Short Term Trends, Price-Trend Analysis & Buy/Sell Rules. Tracks 64 Long, 64 Short Term Investments.
Dynacomp, Inc.

Investment Analysis. *Version:* 3.31/R2. Nov. 1987. *Compatible Hardware:* IBM PC, PC XT, PC AT, PS/2 & compatibles. *Operating System(s) Required:* MS-DOS, PS-DOS. *Language(s):* CBASIC, C. *Memory Required:* 128k. *General Requirements:* 2 disk drives.
disk $295.00.
Performs Income/Expense Analysis & Cash Flow Analysis for Holding Periods of up to 25 Years. Tax Reform Act of 1986 Features Included.
Berge Software.

Investment Analysis with Your Microcomputer. Leslie E. Sparks. 1983. *Compatible Hardware:* TRS-80 Model III, Model 4. *Operating System(s) Required:* TRSDOS. *Language(s):* BASIC. *Memory Required:* 32k.
disk $37.50, incl. bk. (ISBN 0-8306-5049-0, Order no.: 5049C).
An Exploration of Investment Theory & Computer Usage.
TAB Bks.

Investment Analyzer. *Customer Support:* 800-929-8117 (customer service).
MS-DOS. Apple II. disk $79.99 (ISBN 0-87007-812-7).
This Program Calculates all of the Necessary Stats to Make That Decision. Several Analytical Methods are Employed.
SourceView Software International.

Investment Club I. *Compatible Hardware:* Commodore 64, IBM PC, TI 99/4A Home Computer. *Language(s):* Extended BASIC.
TI. disk $69.95 (Order no.: 231XD).
IBM, Commodore. contact publisher for price.
River City Software, Inc.

Investment Club II. *Compatible Hardware:* IBM PC, Commodore 64, TI 99/4A Home Computer. *Language(s):* Extended BASIC.
TI. disk $79.95 (Order no.: 232XD).
IBM, Commodore. contact publisher for price.
River City Software, Inc.

Investment Evaluator. Dow Jones & Co., Inc. Feb. 1984. *Compatible Hardware:* TI Professional. *Operating System(s) Required:* MS-DOS. *Memory Required:* 128k. *General Requirements:* Printer.
$150.00 (Order no.: TI P/N 2311490-0001).
Tool for Gathering, Organizing & Analyzing Portfolio Information.
Texas Instruments, Personal Productivit.

Investment Expert. *Version:* 2.03. *Compatible Hardware:* IBM PC & compatibles. *Operating System(s) Required:* PC-DOS, MS-DOS. *Language(s):* Turbo PROLOG. *Memory Required:* 256k. *General Requirements:* Hard disk recommended. *Items Included:* 32 pg. Thinking Software catalog.
3.5" or 5.25" disk $34.95.
Part of the IMPSHELL EXPERT SYSTEM. Queries for Information on Current Economic Indicators, & Then Suggests the Best Investment Vehicle.
Thinking Software, Inc.

TITLE INDEX

Investment IRR Analysis (after Taxes) for Stocks, Bonds, & Real Estate. *Version:* 92.7. *Compatible Hardware:* Apple Macintosh, Apple II series, IBM PC & PS/2. *General Requirements:* MicroSoft Excel, Multiplan, AppleWorks, Lotus Jazz, Lotus 1-2-3, Claris Works, or MicroSoft Works.
3.5" or 5.25" disk $89.00.
Detailed Cash Flow Analysis of Investments; Calculates Internal Rate of Return Before & After Reinvesting After-Tax Cash Flows.
Larry Rosen Co.

INVESTMENT-MASTER. *Version:* II. David Powers. Jan. 1985. *Compatible Hardware:* IBM PC & compatibles. *Operating System(s) Required:* MS-DOS, PC-DOS. *Language(s):* Pascal. *Memory Required:* 64k.
disk $49.95.
Program to Handle Lump Sum & Annuity Investment Calculations. Handles Deposit/Withdrawal Annuities. Can Be Used for Deposit Saving Plans, Mutual Funds & IRA's.
Generic Computer Products, Inc. (GCPI).

Investment Software. *Version:* 1.2. Albert Bookbinder. Apr. 1983. *Compatible Hardware:* Apple II, Macintosh; Commodore 64; DEC; IBM PC; Kaypro; Sanyo; TRS-80. *Operating System(s) Required:* CBM, CP/M, Macintosh, MS-DOS, TRS-DOS. *Language(s):* BASIC (source code included). *Memory Required:* 32k. *Items Included:* Handbook. *Customer Support:* Telephone support.
disk $119.95 (ISBN 0-916106-06-3).
Includes 50 Interactive Programs Which Forecast & Evaluate Price, Risk, & Return on Stocks, Bonds, Options, Futures, & Foreign Exchange. Programs Compose the Following Six Packages: Statistical (20 Programs), Bonds (12 Programs), Stocks (6 Programs), Options (6 Programs), & Commodities & Futures (3 Programs).
Programmed Pr.

Investment Tax Analyst. *Compatible Hardware:* IBM PC. *Memory Required:* 192k.
$60.00.
Year Round Tax Planning Tool Lists the Advantages & Disadvantages of Every Investment Move.
AIS Microsystems.

Investment Tax Credit Options. *Compatible Hardware:* Altos Series 5-15D, Series 5-5D, 580-XX, ACS8000-XX; DEC Rainbow 100 with 2 disk drives, Rainbow 100+ with 10MB hard disk; IBM PC with 2 disk drives, PC XT, IBM compatibles; Kaypro 11/IV with 2 disk drives, Kaypro 10; Xerox 820 with 2 disk drives, ZILOG MCZ-250. *Operating System(s) Required:* CP/M, MP/M, CP/M-86/80, PC-DOS, MS-DOS.
contact publisher for price (Order no.: ITC).
Designed for Clients Faced with the Option of Classifying Certain Property As Research & Development Property (Three Years) or As Other Property (Five Years). Calculates the Discounted Present Value of the Tax Benefits & the After-Tax Cash Cost of Acquiring Property in the New Three-Year & Five-Year ACRS Classes. Various Assumptions Can Be Considered by Factoring in Such Variables As the Inflation Rate & the Overall Income Tax Rate Paid by the Business in Various Years.
Coopers & Lybrand.

InvestNet. Jan. 1986. *Compatible Hardware:* Compaq 286; IBM Micros & compatibles. *Memory Required:* 640k. *General Requirements:* Hard disk, modem, file server, network software. *Customer Support:* Onsite training, telephone support.
contact publisher for price. *Networks supported:* Novell, Banyan, etc.

Multiuser Product Designed for Complete Accounting & Analysis for a Bank Investment Department. Includes Liability Management for Repurchase Agreements, Jumbo Certificates of Deposit, Commercial Paper, Fed Funds; Bond Investment; Account Safekeeping; Dealer, Desk; & Cash Management.
Wall Street Consulting Group.

The Investor. *Version:* 1.14. David Lange & David Craig. Jan. 1986. *Compatible Hardware:* Apple Macintosh, Macintosh XL, Macintosh Plus, Macintosh SE, Macintosh II. *Memory Required:* 512k.
disk $150.00.
Designed to Take Full Advantage of MAC's Power & User Interface. Accommodates All Types of Securities. Buys, Sells, Short Sells, Dividends, Interest, Cash Accounting & Margin Are Covered. Quotes May Be Updated Manually or via DJNR. Over a Dozen Reports & Graphs Illustrate Portfolio Performance.
P3, Inc.

Investor. Zocco. 1987. *Compatible Hardware:* IBM PC, PS/2. *Memory Required:* 128k. *General Requirements:* 2 disk drives, master program necessary to run template disks.
contact publisher for price.
Individual disk. (ISBN 0-538-06400-5).
Master disk. (ISBN 0-538-06405-6).
write for info. txt. wkbk. (ISBN 0-538-06400-5, Order no.: F40).
Integrated Ivestment Portfolio Management.
South-Western Publishing Co.

The Investor's Accountant. *Version:* 4.0. 1996. *Items Included:* 219 page bound manual. *Customer Support:* Free telephone support.
DOS 2.0. IBM PC, PS/2 (512k). disk $395.00.
Optimal configuration: should have hard disk drive.
Powerful System Provides Comprehensive Maintenance, Analysis & Reporting for an Unlimited Number of Separate Portfolios Containing Any Type of Investment or Asset. Tracks Performance of Investments Individually & by Type, Automatically Adjusting Basis & Incorporating Proceeds from Dividends, Option Writing, Return of Capital, Stock Splits, Mergers, etc. Calculates Portfolio-Specific Internal Rate of Return, ROI, YTD Tax Liability, & Prints IRS Schedules B & D. Provides Automatic "Sweep" Transferring, Foreign Currency Conversions, Global Updating of Securities, Price Range & Other Market Event Alerts, & Portfolio Merging. Provides Tracking, Graphing, & Analysis of Individual Securities. Allows Both Manual & Automatic Price Updating (Allowing Numerous On-Line Sources), Retains an Unlimited Number of Transactions, & Holds Personal Information for Each Account.
Hamilton Software, Inc.

The Investor's Portfolio. *Version:* 1.2. Oct. 1988. *Customer Support:* 60 days free customer support for registered owners.
DOS 3.3 or higher (640k). IBM PC/XT/AT, PS/2. $795.00 to $995.00.
Has Portfolio Management, Analysis, Report, & Communications Programs. Keeps Track of Almost Any Security & Transaction, Including Spreads, Shorts, Open Orders, Zero Coupon Bonds, Etc. Calculates Return on Investment. Prints IRS Schedule B & D; Over 30 Standard Reports. Automatic Updating of Security Prices by Modem. IBM PC/XT/AT or PS/2, 640K, Hard Disk.
Savant Software, Inc.

InView. *General Requirements:* Panorama.
Macintosh Plus or higher. $650.00, with Panorama.
$400.00, without Panorama.
Photography Management.
HindSight.

INVOICER

Invisible Tricks Toolbox. (Toolbox Ser.: No. 5). *Compatible Hardware:* Apple II series. *Memory Required:* 64k.
disk $39.95 (ISBN 0-927796-36-8, Order no.: 182).
Adds Commands with Effects Only Visible to the Programmer. Commands Like Named GOTO, GOSUB, & IF-THEN-ELSE Can Be Added to Any Applesoft Program. Ability to Add & Delete Toolbox Commands While the Program Is Running.
Roger Wagner Publishing, Inc.

Invoice & List It for Excel: Time & Billing System. *Version:* 2. Jan. 1992. *Items Included:* Instructions. *Customer Support:* Free phone support.
Macintosh (1Mb). 3.5" disk $49.95. *Addl. software required:* Microsoft Excel 2.2a or higher.
This Is an Invoice System That Automatically Calculates the Input Data, & a Macro That Creates an Invoice List. Creating the Invoice List Is Done by Running the Macro Which Lists the Input Data from the Invoice & Keeps a Running Total of the Invoices. A Macro Is Also Included That Lists the Customer's Address & Phone Number for a Customer Data Base or Mailing List; Which Can Be Saved As Text & Print Merged with Microsoft Word Merge Features for Printing Mailing Lists. Also Included Is a Statement Form That Automatically Calculates the Input Data. Complete Forms May Be Printed on a Laser or Impact Printer; Or You May Use a Custom Multi-Purpose, Continuous, & Laser Forms. Custom Form Ordering Information Included.
Freemyers Design.

Invoice Billing-Order Entry & Sales Analysis. *Version:* 3.5. May 1984. *Compatible Hardware:* Intel 80286, 80386, 80486, etc.. *Operating System(s) Required:* MS-DOS, Novell, THEOS, UNIX, Win 95, Win/NT. *Language(s):* BASIC. *Memory Required:* 44k.
disk $1695.00.
Provides Invoice Entry, Acknowledgment, Invoicing Cycle, Billing & Automatic Update of Receivables, & Sales Analysis Features.
COMPASS.

Invoice Writer. 1981. *Items Included:* Manual. *Customer Support:* 90-day warranty for defective products, toll-free telephone support.
Apple DOS 3.3 (48k). Complete Apple II series. disk $64.95. *Optimal configuration:* Printer.
Prepares Invoices on Plain Paper. Holds About 80 Invoices, Editing, Discounts, Taxes & Maintains Accounts Receivable if Desired by User. Form Design Permits Use of Window Envelopes.
Information Intelligence, Inc.

InvoiceM. *Compatible Hardware:* TRS-80 Model I, Model III, Model 4. *Operating System(s) Required:* TRSDOS. *Language(s):* BASIC (source code included). *Memory Required:* 32k. *General Requirements:* 2 disk drives, Radio Shack Inventory Control System.
disk $39.00.
Allows Creation of Invoices on Plain Paper from Radio Shack's ICS Data Files. When User Enters Stock Number & Quantity, Program Computes & Prints Totals.
Computer/Business Services.

InvoiceR. *Compatible Hardware:* TRS-80 Model I, Model III, Model 4. *Operating System(s) Required:* TRSDOS. *Language(s):* BASIC (source code included). *Memory Required:* 32k. *General Requirements:* 2 disk drives, Radio Shack Inventory Control System.
disk $65.00.

THE INVOICER-PLUS

Produces Either Plain-Paper NEBS Form #9040 Invoices from Radio Shack Inventory System #26-1553. Reduces Inventory & Allows for Discounts & Sales Tax.
Computer/Business Services.

The Invoicer-Plus. Version: 8.0. Sep. 1995. Compatible Hardware: IBM PC with 2 disk drives or hard disk. Operating System(s) Required: PC-DOS 2.1. Language(s): C (source code included). Memory Required: 128k.
disk $250.00.
General Billing Program for Accountants, Lawyers, Doctors, Consultants, or Any Small Business That Sells a Number of Different Products or Services. Includes a Built-In Accounts Receivable Program That Automatically Forwards Unpaid Balances to the Next Billing Period.
Omni Software Systems, Inc. (Indiana).

The Invoicer with Accounts Receivable. Version: 3.0. Jul. 1990. Compatible Hardware: IBM PC. Operating System(s) Required: PC-DOS/MS-DOS 2.0. Memory Required: IBM 384k. General Requirements: 2 disk drives or hard disk, printer. Customer Support: 60 days free phone support.
disk $149.00 (Order no.: AR).
Produces Invoices, Statements, Past Due Notices, Labels, Shipping Labels, Rolodex Cards & Reports. Options Include Open Item or Balance Forward, Finance Charge Capability, Multiple-Taxing Ability. Reports Include Aging, Activity Collection, Master Customer & Stock List, Posting Report, etc. Allows Free Format Typing on Invoices. Suited for Service, Product or Professional Billing. Save & Recall Entire Invoice.
MiccaSoft, Inc.

The Invoicer with Sales Tracking/Inventory. Version: 2.0. Jul. 1990. Compatible Hardware: IBM PC. Operating System(s) Required: PC-DOS/MS-DOS 2.0. Memory Required: IBM 384k. General Requirements: 2 disk drives or hard disk, printer. Customer Support: 60 days free phone support.
disk $149.00 (Order no.: IC).
Suited for Service, Product or Professional Sales Tracking & Billing. Produces Invoices, Picking Tickets (Optional), Labels, Address Labels, Rolodex Cards & Reports. Reports Include By-Month Sales & Purchases Reports, Current Inventory Levels, Reorder Report, Retail Price List, Master Account & Billing Item Lists, Gross Sales/On Hand Reports, etc. Tracks Unit & Dollar Amounts of Sales & Purchases by Month.
MiccaSoft, Inc.

Invoices & Sales Slips. 1990. Items Included: Manual.
MS-DOS 2.X - 4.2. IBM PC/XT/AT & PS/2 or compatibles (256K). disk $19.95 (Order no.: 9505).
The Program Allows User to Keep Track of Deliveries Made to Customers. Everytime Merchandise Is Shipped to a Customer User Writes a Delivery Note to Accompany the Shipment. The Delivery Notes Are Saved on Disks, with Address, Item Numbers, Descriptions, & Quantities Shipped. After a Certain Period, for Example at the End of Each Month, User Loads the Delivery Notes from the Disk, Calculates the Totals, & Prints Them Out As Invoices to Be Sent to Customers.
Elcomp Publishing, Inc.

Invoicing with Accounts Receivable & Inventory. ADS Software, Inc. Compatible Hardware: TI Professional. Operating System(s) Required: MS-DOS. Memory Required: 128k. General Requirements: 2 disk drives, printer. $895.00.
Designed for Small/Medium Business with "Post" Billing Requirements.
Texas Instruments, Personal Productivit.

InvoicIt. Version: 1.42. General Requirements: Hard disk drive; MacMoney 4.0. Items Included: User manual & sample forms packet. Customer Support: 310-338-0155; mail: E-mail services.
Macintosh Plus or higher. 3.5" disk $79.95.
Invoicing & Accounts Receivable.
Survivor Software Ltd.

Invomax: Inventory Profit Optimizer. Items Included: Bound manual. Customer Support: Free hotline - no time limit; 30 day limited warranty; updates are $5/disk plus S&H.
MS-DOS 2.0 or higher. IBM & compatibles (256k). $49.95-$59.95. Nonstandard peripherals required: Monochrome & CGA graphics are supported; printer supported, but optional.
Inventory Optimizer Which Helps You Structure Your Inventory System to Maximize the Overall Profit Picture. The Variables Considered by INVOMAX (& Stored in Disk Files) Are: Projected Sales Rate; Inventory Capital Investment Interest; Storage Expenses; Order Lead Times; Re-Order Level; Re-Order Period; Sales Price per Unit; Cost per Unit.
Dynacomp, Inc.

InVue. Compatible Hardware: Apple Macintosh. 3.5" disk $199.95.
Client Data, Billing & Business Management Template.
HindSight.

InWord. Version: 1.01. Compatible Hardware: IBM PC. General Requirements: Lotus 1-2-3 Release 2.x.
disk $99.95.
Full-Function Word Processor Running Inside 1-2-3. Allows Users to Move Text into the Spreadsheet or to Move Spreadsheet Data into a Document. Provides the Ability of Creating "Live Links" Directly to Data in the Spreadsheet, So That a Change in the Spreadsheet Will Automatically Show up in the Document. Features Include Mail Merge, Automatic Word Wrap & Paragraph Re-form, Horizontal Scrolling, Search & Replace, Cut & Paste, Cursor Movement by Word, Sentence, or Paragraph, etc. Documents Can Be Formatted with Headers, Footers, Page Numbers, Tab Stops, Indents, Hanging Indents, As Well As Left, Right, Center, or Full Justification. Supports Printing with Bold, Underlined, & Italic Text, & Mixed Typefonts & Pitch.
Funk Software.

Io Atlases: Graphic Astrology. ACS Publications & Times Cycles Research. Apr. 1995. Items Included: Documentation. Customer Support: Free unlimited phone support.
System 6.07 or higher, System 7 Savvy. Macintosh (1Mb). 3.5" disk $195.00 ea. or $295.00 package.
American & International Atlas Modules Provide You with Instant Access to Longitudes, Latitudes & Date Sensitive Time Zone Information for over a Quarter Million Cities in the World. No More Wasting Hours of Precious Time Researching ESSENTIAL Chart Data in Large Volumes of Complex Tables Set in Tiny Type. Just Click & in Seconds Data Is Entered & Calculated.

Io Edition: Graphic Astrology. Version: 2.1. Apr. 1995. Items Included: Manual with boxed slipcover & free Glyphs desk accessory. Customer Support: Free unlimited phone support.
System 6.07 or higher, System 7 Savvy. Macintosh (1Mb). 3.5" disk $295.00.
Sophisticated Calculation & Charting Program for Use by Those Who Do Not Need an Interpretation. Tropical, Sidereal & Heliocentric Zodiac Systems. Calculates Natal, Sunrise, Harmonics, Transit Search, Composite, Relationships, & Synastry Charts; Solar & Lunar Returns Plus Seven Different Progressions. Plus Many Other Features That Make It the Tool of Choice for Professional Astrologers & Students.
Time Cycles Research.

Io Forecast: Graphic Astrology. Version: 2.1. Apr. 1995. Items Included: Manual with boxed slipcover & free Glyphs desk accessory. Customer Support: Free unlimited phone support.
System 6.07 or higher, System 7 Savvy. Macintosh (1Mb). 3.5" disk $249.50.
Powerful Transit Interpreter That Produces Amazingly Accurate Predictions for a Fascinating Look into Your Future. Ideal for Novice Astrologers. Ease of Use Allows Even Those Who Do Not Study Astrology to Benefit from a Personalized Transit Interpretation. Fully Editable for Those That Wish to Customize Interpretations.

Io Horoscope: Graphic Astrology. Version: 2.1. Apr. 1995. Items Included: Manual with boxed slipcover & free Glyphs desk accessory. Customer Support: Free unlimited phone support.
System 6.07 or higher, System 7 Savvy. Macintosh (1Mb). 3.5" disk $249.50.
Full Featured Natal Chart Interpreter. Produces 18-20 Page Interpretations & an Introduction to Astrology. The Ideal Starting Point for Novice Astrologers. Ease of Use Allows Even Those Who Do Not Study Astrology to Benefit from a Personalized Natal Interpretation. Fully Editable Text.

Io Relationship: Graphic Astrology. Version: 2.1. Apr. 1995. Items Included: Manual with boxed slipcover & free Glyphs desk accessory. Customer Support: Free unlimited phone support.
System 6.07 or higher, System 7 Savvy. Macintosh (1Mb). 3.5" disk $249.50.
Highly Revealing Interpreter Which Takes a Detailed Look at Personal & Business Relationships. Ideal for Novice Astrologers. Ease of Use Allows Even Those Who Do Not Study Astrology to Benefit from a Personalized Relationship Interpretation. Relationship, Composite & Synastry Interpretations Well-Written & Fully Editable.

IONET Plus LAN Operating System. Version: 5.1. Mar. 1993. Items Included: Software, full documentation, 3.50", 5.25" diskettes. Customer Support: Free Technical support 8AM - 8PM EST. Reseller certification program available.
DOS 3.1. IBM PC & compatibles (128k). 2-User Base Pack $198.00; 5-User $445.00; 10-User $789.00; 100-User $1999.00. Nonstandard peripherals required: Any LAN adapters with NDIS drivers. Optimal configuration: 640k, printers.
Provides a Cost Effective, Simple & Quick to Use Workgroup Networking Solution for Small & Medium-Sized Businesses. Supports DOS 6.0, Windows 3.1. Supports Many Networking Applications Such As Chat, E-Mail & Others.
Tiara Computer Systems.

IONOPROP: Ionospheric Propagation Assessment. May 1991. Items Included: 120 Page User's Manual.
IBM PC & compatibles. disk $150.00 (ISBN 0-89006-565-9).
Program That Computes Maximum Usable Frequency (MUF) & Lowest Usable Frequency (LUF) for a User Defined Sunspot Number (or 10.7-cm flux) & X-Ray Flux.
Artech Hse., Inc.

IpsoFacto Litigation Support System. Version: 2.5. Robert Tripodi. May 1993. Items Included: User's manual (250 pages approximately), Program diskette, Warranty Registration Form. Customer Support: 90-day free telephone

support (8:00 a.m. to 5:00 p.m. EST). Free demo disk available. Low-cost upgrades available to registered users. On-site training services available for a fee.
MS-DOS version 3.0 or higher. IBM PC-XT, AT, PS/2 & true compatibles (640k). $995.00 single-user copy; site licenses available. *Optimal configuration:* Hard disk, 400k of "free memory," Performance is improved with additional memory, including EMS. *Networks supported:* All major networks, including Novell NetWare, Banyan Vines, Microsoft LAN Manager, etc.
High-Speed, Full Text Search & Retrieval Program for Disk-Based Documents. Designed Specifically for Managing Legal Style Text Files, Such As Transcripts, It Provides a Full Set of Features for Querying Documents, Extracting & Annotating Text, & Collecting Attorney Notes in Ordered Form.
Signum Microsystems, Inc.

IPSS: Interactive Population Statistical System. *Version:* 03/1989. *Compatible Hardware:* Apple Macintosh Plus, Macintosh SE, Macintosh II, Quadras. *Language(s):* Think Pascal, Consular assembler. *Memory Required:* 1000k. *General Requirements:* 2 800k disk drives or hard disk. 68020/68030 processor & 68881/68882 math co-processor for IPSS II. Works with any overhead projector compatible with Macintosh. *Items Included:* Manual & Program Data Disks. *Customer Support:* Free.
IPSS. 3.5" disk $295.00.
IPSS II. $395.00.
Graphics-Based Demographic Package for Business Marketers, Demographers, & Educators. Demographic Measures of the Program Include: Total Births; Child Mortality; Child/Woman Ratio; Crude Birth & Death Rate; Total Deaths; Age Dependency Ratios; Population Doubling Timing; Life Expectancy at Birth; Etc. Allows Users to Create Population Pyramids, Bar & Line Graphs, Three-Dimensional Population Pyramids, & Lexis Surface & 100 Percent Surface Graphics. Can Be Used to Paste Graphics Directly into Spreadsheet or Word Processing Programs & Automatically Convert Them to Numerical Data. All Tabular & Graphics Output Can Be Printed or Saved to Disk as MacDraw or MacPaint Files.
Senecio Software, Inc.

I.Q. Quest. Nov. 1990. *Customer Support:* Phone support, free with return of warranty card. Damage disk warranty, free with return of warranty card.
PC-DOS/MS-DOS. IBM & compatibles (640k). 3.5" or 5.25" disk $59.95. *Optimal configuration:* PC or Compatible, 640k RAM, color monitor, hard drive.
An Integrated Educational Package. It Contains Spelling, Mathematics, Geography & History Sections. It Comes with Assignment Writer to Create Reports, Stories, Letters & Essays. The Family Financial is an Added Bonus to the Parents That Will Supply Answers to "What If" Type Questions.
VITREX Corp.

IQ Report Writer. *Version:* 7. 1995. *Items Included:* Manuals, registration card, license. *Customer Support:* Support & training available from dealers or from vendor for a fee. Telephone support & training (on site or at our facilities) to users for a fee.
MS-DOS, UNIX. IBM XT/AT PS/2, Tandy & compatibles, Altos. disk $795.00-$995.00. *Addl. software required:* System Kit (one per installation). *Optimal configuration:* Hard disk, 132 column printer.
XENIX; IBM 286/386 AT/Tandy compatibles 286/386. disk $895.00. *Addl. software required:* System kit (one per installation).

Optimal configuration: Hard disk, 132 column printer.
UNIX. *Addl. software required:* System kit (one per installation). *Optimal configuration:* Hard disk, 132 column printer.
Networks-Novell. IBM & compatibles. disk $695.00. *Addl. software required:* System kit (one per installation). *Optimal configuration:* Hard disk - 132 column printer.
Provides the Tools Needed to Design & Print Custom Reports & Graphs from RealWorld Data Files. This Comprehensive Package Provides for Reports & Graphs Which Can Be Designed & Created from All RealWorld Packages; & Serves As a Bridge Between RealWorld Files & Popular Spreadsheet, Database, Word Processing & Graphics Packages.
RealWorld Corp.

IQ Test for Windows. Nov. 1994. *Customer Support:* Free unlimited customer support.
Windows. 386 (4Mb). disk $14.95 (ISBN 1-886031-03-7, Order no.: 11004). *Optimal configuration:* 486 33MHz, 8Mb RAM, Sound card, color monitor.
A Multimedia Version of an IQ Test to Be Taken at Home for Fun.
Virtual Entertainment, Inc.

IQLISP. *Version:* 1.8.5. Sep. 1989. *Compatible Hardware:* IBM PC,. *Operating System(s) Required:* PC-DOS 2.0, 3.0, MS-DOS. *Language(s):* Assembly/Lisp. *Memory Required:* 192k.
IBM PC. disk $270.00, incl. manual (Order no.: IQLISP-IBM).
Implementation of LISP for Microcomputers. Designed for Research & Development. Features Macros, Multiple Display Windows, Graphics, 8087 Support & Parser Control. Brings Expert Systems, Rapid Prototyping, & Natural Language Interfaces Within the Reach of the IBM PC User. A Compiler Is Included As Well As an Interpreter. Source for the Compiler Is Included.
Integral Quality, Inc.

The IRA Investment Analyzer. *Version:* 1.1. Apr. 1988. *Customer Support:* One-year money back guarantee, unlimited phone support.
MS-DOS 2.0 or higher (320k). IBM PC & compatibles. disk $149.95. *Optimal configuration:* Monitor, printer.
Demonstrates Benefit of Making Non-Deductible IRA Contributions. Calculates After-Tax Growth of Investment Held Outside An IRA, & Compares This Result to Same Investment Held in an IRA Account. Includes 45 Years of Analysis & Handles Full Range of Partial IRA Deductibility.
Winning Strategies, Inc.

I.R.A. Selector. *Customer Support:* 800-929-8117 (customer service).
MS-DOS. IBM/PS. disk $99.99 (ISBN 0-87007-044-4).
Helps to Determine What Persons Should Have What Types of Individual Retirement Accounts. Various Types of Investment May Be Selected.
SourceView Software International.

IRETAIL: With Product Inventory, 2 disks. *Version:* 5.0. Harold L. Reed. Aug. 1991. *Compatible Hardware:* IBM PC. *Operating System(s) Required:* PC-DOS/MS-DOS 3.3 or higher. *Language(s):* Clipper. *Memory Required:* 640k. *General Requirements:* Hard disk, printer. $349.50 (ISBN 0-924495-01-4).
An Integrated, Interactive, Natural Language Accounting, Database & Mail System for Those Who Sell Products. It Is a Natural Language System That Can be Treated As a Clerk or Administrative Assistant. IRETAIL Knows Accounting, Based on General Accounting Rules, But It Departs from Old Paper Ledger Based Bookkeeping Systems. The New System Makes It Practical to Have an Accounting Program That Does All Accounting, Including Payroll, with an English Language Command Structure & Still Leave Room for Database Management, Letter Writing, & Mail Capabilities.
IDEA Computers, Inc.

IRIS. *Operating System(s) Required:* CP/M-86, MP/M-86, MS-DOS.
contact publisher for price.
Optometric Practice Management System Offering Multi-User Micro Computer Configuration & Incorporating Patient Records & Recall, Accounts Receivable, Order Entry, Inventory, Accounts Payable & General Ledger Sub-Systems.
Continental Business Computers, Inc.

IRIS Explorer: Visualization. *Version:* 3.0. Mar. 1995. *Items Included:* Documentation. *Customer Support:* Customer support includes updates & enhancements, access to our technical support via fax, phone or email. $600 for 4 concurrent users.
IBM AIX, DEC Alpha OSFI, SGI IRIX, HP HPUX, Sun OS 4.1.3, Sun Solarios, Cray Unicos (32Mb), NT. $4000.00 for 4 concurrent users (Order no.: IRIS EXPLORER). *Nonstandard peripherals required:* Graphics boards required. *Optimal configuration:* 32Mb RAM, 100Mb swap, 100Mb disk.
An Object Oriented Visual Programming System for Data Visualization, Animation, Manipulation & Analysis, Designed for Scientists & Engineers to Create Applications for Displaying & Analyzing Complex Multi-Dimensional Datasets Interactively, Often Without Any Programming at All. It is Both Powerful & Easy to Use.
Numerical Algorithms Group, Inc.

IRIS*FLANGE: Design of bolted flange connections. *Version:* 2.81. Nov. 1991. *Items Included:* User manual & Hardware Lock Device for copy protection. *Customer Support:* Maintenance, enhancement & support $250.00 per year.
DOS 3.0 or higher (550k). IBM PC AT, PS/2 & compatibles (286, 386, 486). $1995.00 (ISBN 0-87201-405-3). *Nonstandard peripherals required:* Math coprocessor, EGA graphics & color monitor. *Optimal configuration:* Hard disk.
Design or Analyze Flanged Connections. Program Calculates Flange Stresses, Maximum Allowable Pressure, or Flange Thickness for a Given Flange Geometry. Program Includes Several Internal Databases: ASME Section VIII Allowable Stresses for 100 Common Materials As Well As 12 Bolting Materials; Appendix 2 Gasket Factors, Seating Stresses & Materials; Appendix 2 Shape Constants & Flange Factors: Bolt Cross Section Areas; ANSI B16.5, API-605, & MSS SP-44 Flange Standards Including Dimensions, Sizes & Pressure Classes.
Engineering Design Analysis Consultants, Inc.

IRIS (Interactive Real-Time Information System). *Compatible Hardware:* Point 4 Data Corp. MARK 2T, MARK 3/3T, MARK 5, MARK 8, MARK 9.
MARK 2T,3/3T,5,8. $3000.00
MARK 9. $3500.00, incl. mapping.
R8 program listing. $450.00.
R7 program listing. $800.00.
R8 installment & configuration manual $45.00 (Order no.: S-0009).
R8 operations manual $18.00 (Order no.: S-0010).
R8 user manual $20.00 (Order no.: S-0011).
R7.3 user reference manual $22.00 (Order no.: S-0004).
R7.3 manager reference manual $20.00 (Order no.: S-0003).
Multi-User Operating System Designed for the

Business Environment. High-Speed, Multi-Tasking Capabilities. Supports up to 72 Users on a Single System with Scheduling of Work, Multi-Level Security Protection & a Data Management System. Features a Business BASIC Orientation.
Point 4 Data Corp.

IRIS*NOZZLE: Local stress analysis due to external loading per WRC-107. *Version:* 1.81. Nov. 1991. *Items Included:* User manual & hardware lock device for copy protection. *Customer Support:* Maintenance, enhancement & support $300.00 per year.
DOS 3.0 or higher (550k). IBM PC AT, PS/2 & compatibles (286, 386, 486). $2495.00 (ISBN 0-87201-408-8). *Nonstandard peripherals required:* Math coprocessor, EGA graphics & color monitor. *Optimal configuration:* Hard disk.
Calculates Localized Primary & Secondary Membrane Stresses, Secondary Bending & Peak Stresses & Primary General Membrane Stress Due to Internal Pressure. Program Includes Several Internal Databases Such As: ASME Section VIII, Division 1 Allowable Stress for 100 Common Materials; ASME Section 2 Design Fatigue Curves for the above Materials; WRC-107 Charts for Cylindrical & Spherical Shells. It Also Includes Menus to Specify Attachments, Shell Types, Orientation of Vessel Axis, Materials, & Forces & Moments. Data Entry Is Quick & Easy Using Spreadsheet-Style Input for Geometric & Loading Data for Attachments under Consideration.
Engineering Design Analysis Consultants, Inc.

IRIS*VESSEL: Pressure Design & Analysis per ASME Sec VIII, Div. 1. *Version:* 1.81. Nov. 1991. *Items Included:* User manual & Hardware Lock Device for copy protection. *Customer Support:* Maintenance, enhancement & support $925.00 per year.
DOS 3.0 or higher (550k). IBM PC AT, PS/2 & compatibles (286, 386, 486). $6995.00 (ISBN 0-87201-409-6). *Nonstandard peripherals required:* Math Coprocessor, EGA graphics & color monitor. *Optimal configuration:* Hard disk.
Design New or Analyze Existing Vertical & Horizontal Vessels. Program Does ASME Code Calculations, Wind & Seismic Calculations, Zick Analysis, Nozzle Reinforcement, Skirt Base Ring & Chair Design, English, SI or Metric Units Capability. Program Includes Several Internal Databases: ASME Section VIII, Division 1 Appendix 5; ANSI B16.5, API-605, & MSS SP-44 Flange Pressure Ratings: ANSI A58.1 & UBC, Wind & Seismic Factors.
Engineering Design Analysis Consultants, Inc.

IRMA: Investment Records Management Aid. *Compatible Hardware:* IBM PC. *Memory Required:* 256k.
disk $49.95.
Tool for Those Interested in Financial, Tax, & Investment Planning. Available Functions Include: Cash Income Forecast for Any Month, Annual Income Distribution by Month, Cost-Versus-Value Summaries, History of Investment Activity, Capital Gain/Loss Summaries, Income Totals by Investment & by Type, Percentage Distribution of Portfolio by Category, & Investment Value Comparisons Between Dates.
Dynacomp, Inc.

IRMAcom-RJE. *Compatible Hardware:* IBM PC & compatibles. *General Requirements:* IRMAcom board.
contact publisher for price.
Provides 2780/3780 RJE Workstation Emulation in BSC Environments. Lets PC Act As a Workstation Display & Lets a Parallel or Serial Printer Attached to PC Emulate a Workstation Printer, Including Forms Control Capabilities. Provides Support for RJE Console & Operator Selectable Output Devices (Printers & Disks), & Allows for Transfer of Both Text & Binary Data. Fully Compatible with IBM's 2780/3780 Standards, Thus Allowing the Possibility of Communicating with Non-IBM Computers Which Support 2780/3780 RJE Communications.
Digital Communications Assocs.

IRMAcom-3270. *Compatible Hardware:* IBM PC. *Memory Required:* 192k. *General Requirements:* IRMAcom board.
contact publisher for price.
Provides 3274 or 3276 Emulation in SNA Environments. Lets PC Act As a 3278 Terminal, & Lets Multiple Parallel or Serial Printers Attached to PC Emulate 3287 or 3289 System Printers in LU1 or LU3 Modes, While Maintaining 3270 Communications Link. Both ASCII & EBCDIC Line Transmission Are Supported. Includes Software to Let User Reassign 3270 Key & Key Sequence Locations on PC Keyboard.
Digital Communications Assocs.

IRMAcom-3270B. *Compatible Hardware:* IBM PC. *General Requirements:* IRAMcom board.
contact publisher for price.
Provides 3271 or 3275 Emulation in BSC Environments. Lets PC Act As a 3278 Terminal, & Lets Multiple Parallel or Serial Printers Attached to PC Emulate 3284, 3286, or 3288 System Printers. Shift Between Terminal Mode & PC Mode, While Maintaining 3270 Communications Link. Both ASCII & EBCDIC Line Transmission Are Supported. Includes Software to Let User Reassign 3270 Key & Key Sequence Locations on PC Keyboard.
Digital Communications Assocs.

IRMAcom-3770. *Compatible Hardware:* IBM PC. *General Requirements:* IRMAcom board.
contact publisher for price.
Provides 3770 RJE Workstation Emulation in SNA Environments. Lets PC Act As a Workstation Display & Lets a Parallel or Serial Printer Attached to PC Emulate a Workstation Printer, Including Formatted Printing Capabilities. Provides Support for Either ASCII or EBCDIC Transmission Lines & Allows for Transfer of Both Text & Binary Data. Supports Multiple Selectable Devices & Job Files & Is Fully Compatible with SNA 3770 Standard, Thus Allowing the Possibility of Communicating with Non-IBM Computers Which Support SNA 3770 RJE Communications.
Digital Communications Assocs.

IRMAlink DBX-CICS. *Compatible Hardware:* IBM PC. *Operating System(s) Required:* PC-DOS/MS-DOS 2.0. *General Requirements:* IRMAline or IRMAlette board; IBM mainframe running under DOS/VSE & CICS, MVS & CICS, or OS/VS1 & CICS.
contact publisher for price.
Advanced Data File Transfer & Security System That Enables DP Managers to Retain Total Control of Mainframe Database While Giving PC & Data Center Users Access to Specific Data They Need. Automatically Converts Data Between Popular Mainframe Formats & Formats the PC Can Read & Use (Such As BASIC, DIF, Record, PRN, CSV). Both Text & Binary Data Can Be Transferred.
Digital Communications Assocs.

IRMAlink FT-TSO. *Compatible Hardware:* IBM PC with IRMA board (or IRMAlette & IRMAline) & IBM mainframes running under MVS/TSO.
contact publisher for price.
Transfers Files Between PC's with IRMA & IBM Mainframes Running under MVS/TSO. Handles Transfer of Both Binary & Text Files & Supports Both Fixed & Partitioned Datasets with Either Fixed or Variable Record Formats. Supports International Character Sets & Lets User Specify Character Set to Use in Transfers.
Digital Communications Assocs.

IRMA2. *Compatible Hardware:* IBM PC, PC XT, PC AT; PS/2 Models 30/50/60/80.
contact publisher for price.
Terminal Emulation Software Allowing PC-to-Mainframe Link.
Digital Communications Assocs.

Iron Angel of the Apocalypse. Feb. 1995. *Items Included:* Warranty/registration card, game manual. *Customer Support:* Technical Support Number: 1-800-734-9466, 90 days limited warranty.
3DO. disk $59.99 (ISBN 1-888158-08-5).
In a Tower High above a Desolate City, a Mad Scientist Pursues His Experiments. His Mission...to Create the Ultimate Killing Machine & Purge the World. All That Remains Is the Last Piece of Equipment for Tetsujin. The Assimilation Process Is Underway & You Have Been Chosen.
Synergy Interactive Corp.

Iron Angel of the Apocalypse: The Return. Dec. 1995. *Items Included:* Warranty, registration card, game manual. *Customer Support:* Technical support number: 1-800-734-9466, 90-day limited warranty.
3DO. IBM. CD-ROM disk $57.99 (ISBN 1-888158-14-X).
Tetsujin Has Been Resurrected, & Your Mind Is Now Bonded Mechanized Body. The Clandestine SCR Organization Has Given You Life. The Golden Android Has Returned to Take Revenge Against You. Battle Past Motoids Bent on Your Destruction, or Humanity Is Doomed!
Synergy Interactive Corp.

Iron Angel of the Apocalypse: The Return. Dec. 1995. *Items Included:* Warranty/registration card, game manual. *Customer Support:* Technical support number: 1-800-734-9466, 90-day limited warranty.
3DO. CD-ROM disk $47.99 (ISBN 1-888158-14-X).
Tetsujin Has Been Resurrected, & Your Mind Is Now Bonded Mechanized Body. The Clandestine SCR Organization Has Given You Life. The Golden Android Has Returned to Take Revenge Against You. Battle Past Motoids Bent on Your Destruction, or Humanity Is Doomed.
Synergy Interactive Corp.

Iron Blast Furnace. *Version:* 2. Sep. 1988. *Compatible Hardware:* IBM PC. *Language(s):* BASIC. *Memory Required:* 512k.
disk $400.00 ea.
IBM PC. (ISBN 0-931821-30-4, Order no.: 06-301).
IBM PS/2.
Based on % Weight Composition of Ore, Pellets, Sinter, Flux, Coke, Injected Fuels, Hot Metal & Basicity. Program Computes: Charge Balance Calculation, Complete Material Balance with Element & Compound Distribution to Hot Metal, Slag, Blast Furnace Gas, Thermal Balance, Optimization Based on Active Carbon Program. Handles 3 Ores, Pellets, Sinter, 2 Fluxes, Cole, & 2 Injected Fuels. Program Also Checks Burden for Self Fluxing Conditions.
Information Resource Consultants.

Iron Helix. Jun. 1993.
MAC. Color Classic or higher w/CD-ROM drive (4Mb). CD-ROM disk $99.95.

Ironclads. *Compatible Hardware:* CP/M based machines with MBASIC. *Operating System(s) Required:* CP/M. *Language(s):* Machine. *Memory Required:* 48k.
disk $29.95.
8" disk $32.45.
Simulation of Naval Strategy & Tactics Between Steam & Wind-Driven Warships.
Dynacomp, Inc.

TITLE INDEX

Irregular Skip Loan. Version: 2258A. May 1987. Compatible Hardware: Sharp ZL-6500 System. Language(s): Compiled BASIC.
$1000.00.
Computes the Level Payment for Loans with an Irregular Monthly Payment Schedule with Life Insurance & an Origination Fee. Computes the APR & Prints an Entire Amortization Schedule Showing the Loan Data & the Life Insurance Premium for Each Payment.
P-ROM Software, Inc.

IRS Factors Calculator. Version: 3.01. Robert J. Doyle & Stephan R. Leimberg. Nov. 1991. Items Included: User manual on disk, 12 months of maintenance coverage. Customer Support: Free telephone support: 1-800-367-1040, Annual maintenance contract: $27.00.
PC-DOS/MS-DOS 2.0 & higher. IBM PC & compatibles (320k). disk $69.00 (Order no.: 1685).
Computes the Value of Annuities, Life Estates & Remainders for Terms of Years, One & Two Lives under IRS Methods. Designed to Handle GRATs & GRUTs, GRITs with Reversions. Handles Changing Monthly AFR Rates. Formerly ALR Plus.
CCH Access Software.

IRS-InterestCalc. Version: 2.1. Dec. 1987. Compatible Hardware: IBM PC & compatibles. Memory Required: 384k.
$149.95.
Calculates the Interest on IRS Tax Deficiencies & Refunds, Including the 120% Rate for Tax-Motivated Transactions. Verifies Penalties & Interest on Penalties, Including Fraud, Negligence, Failure to File & Pay, Substantial Understatement of Tax, & Valuation Overstatements. Allows User to Update Interest Rates. Accommodates As Many As Three Interim Payments of Tax & Interest.
Winning Strategies, Inc.

ISA Dictionary on Disk: Electronic Dictionary of Measurement & Control. Oct. 1994. Items Included: Operating instructions.
DOS/Windows 3.X. PC compatible (4Mb). disk $115.00 (ISBN 1-55617-529-9, Order no.: 529-9). Optimal configuration: IBM 386, 4Mb RAM, 3 1/2 disk drive, 5Mb space available on hard drive, color VGA monitor.
Serves As an Electronic Version of the ISA Dictionary of Measurement & Control. Users Can Quickly Access over 12,000 Terms & Definitions & 150 Symbols. The Dictionary Was Authored Using the Microsoft Multimedia Viewer Authoring Tool.
Instrument Society of America (ISA).

ISA Standards Library CD-ROM: Guidelines for Quality & Safety. Sep. 1994. Items Included: Manual.
DOS/Windows. PC Compatible. CD-ROM disk $650.00 (ISBN 1-55617-531-0, Order no.: 531-0). Nonstandard peripherals required: CD-ROM drive. Optimal configuration: IBM 386/25M, Color VGA monitor, CD-ROM drive, 5Mb available hard drive space.
Now ISA Standards & Recommended Practices Are Available As Hypertext CD-ROM Product. Over 3000 Pages of Standards on One CD. Fully Text-Searchable. Hyperlinks Let You Find the Information You Need in Seconds.
Instrument Society of America (ISA).

Isaac Asimov's Library of the Universe. Jan. 1996. Customer Support: Telephone support - free (except phone charge).
System 6.0.5 or higher. 256 color capable Mac with a 68030 processor (4Mb). CD-ROM disk $12.99 (ISBN 1-57594-112-0). Nonstandard peripherals required: 2X CD ROM drive, 640/480 resolution monitor.
Blast off into the Solar System & Explore the Stars, Planets & the Sun. Learn about the "Seas" That Exist on the Moon. Then Blast off into Space to Meet Some of the First Astronauts.
Kidsoft, Inc.

Isaac Asimov's Library of the Universe: The Solar System. Dec. 1995. Customer Support: Telephone support - free (except phone charge).
Windows 3.1. IBM & compatibles (386 DX-20) (4Mb). CD-ROM disk $12.99, Jewel (ISBN 1-57594-089-2). Nonstandard peripherals required: 2X CD ROM player, sound card, VGA monitor. Optimal configuration: 486 SX-33.
CD-ROM disk $12.99, Blister.
Blast off into the Solar System & Explore the Stars, Planets & the Sun. Learn about the "Seas" That Exist on the Moon. Then Blast off into Space to Meet Some of the First Astronauts.
Kidsoft, Inc.

Isaac Asimov's Library of the Universe: The Solar System. Dec. 1995. Customer Support: Telephone support - free (except phone charge).
Windows 3.1. IBM & compatibles (386 DX-20) (4Mb). CD-ROM disk $12.99 (ISBN 1-57594-089-2). Nonstandard peripherals required: 2X CD-ROM player, sound card, VGA monitor. Optimal configuration: 486 SX-33.
Blast off into the Solar System & Explore the Stars, Planets & the Sun. Learn about the "Seas" That Exist on the Moon, Then Blast off into Space to Meet Some of the First Astronauts. Jewel Case.
Kidsoft, Inc.

Isaac Asimov's: The Solar System. Feb. 1996. Customer Support: Telephone support - free (except phone charge).
Windows 3.1. IBM compatible 386 DX-20 (4Mb). CD-ROM disk $12.99 (ISBN 1-57594-102-3). Nonstandard peripherals required: 2x CD-ROM, sound card, VGA monitor. Optimal configuration: 486, SX-33.
Explore the Stars, Planets & the Sun. Learn about Seas That Exist on the Moon. Meet Some of the First Astronauts. Blister Pack.
Kidsoft, Inc.

ISAR, 10 modules. Version: 2.0.
$29.95, incl. manual (Order no.: D8ISAR). Designed for Data Storage & Retrieval, & Assists with a Variety of User-Defined Reports.
The Alternate Source.

ISDN: A Closer Look. Oct. 1994. Items Included: User manual. Customer Support: Free technical support & a 30-day warranty (1-800-521-CORE).
MS-DOS. IBM & compatibles (512k). 3.5" disk $199.00 (ISBN 1-57305-001-6). Nonstandard peripherals required: High-density 3.5" disk drive; VGA color monitor. Addl. software required: MS-DOS version 3.3 or higher.
Optimal configuration: IBM (512k), MS-DOS version 3.3 or higher, VGA color monitor, keyboard, Microsoft compatible mouse (optional).
Provides a Concise Yet Thorough Understanding of ISDN - Its Architecture & Applications. This Self-Paced Training Course Enables You to Learn Both the Terminology & Technology Associated with ISDN. The Computer-Based Course Brings New Life to Learning - Presenting the Topics with Colorful Graphics. You'll Even Be Able to Gauge Your Progress by Taking the Challenging Exercises of the Completion of Each Section.
Bellcore.

ISDN Loop Qualification & Extension: An Overview. Jul. 1995. Items Included: User manual. Customer Support: Free technical support

ISLAND OF THE BLUE DOLPHINS

& a 30-day money back guarantee.
MS-DOS. IBM & compatibles (640k). 3.5" disk $295.00 (ISBN 1-57305-056-3). Nonstandard peripherals required: High-density 3.5" disk drive; VGA color monitor. Addl. software required: MS-DOS version 3.3 or higher.
Optimal configuration: IBM (640k), MS-DOS version 3.3 or higher, VGA color monitor, keyboard, Microsoft compatible mouse.
This Is a 2-Hour Computer-Based Training Program Describing the ISDN Digital Subscriber Loop & the Various Problems & Benefits Associated with Analog & Digital Transmission.
Bellcore.

ISDN Sales Planning: An Overview. Jul. 1995. Items Included: User manual. Customer Support: Free technical support & a 30-day money back guarantee.
MS-DOS. IBM & compatibles (640k). 3.5" disk $295.00 (ISBN 1-57305-018-0). Nonstandard peripherals required: High-density 3.5" disk drive; VGA color monitor. Addl. software required: MS-DOS version 3.3 or higher.
Optimal configuration: IBM (640k), MS-DOS version 3.3 or higher, VGA color monitor, keyboard, Microsoft compatible mouse.
This Is a 2-Hour Computer-Based Training Program Describing How to Sell Products That Utilize ISDN & It Also Gives Case Studies & Current Application Information to Help Design a Sales Strategy.
Bellcore.

ISE-ISIS II Emulator. Version: 5.5. Rick Hollinbeck. 1980. Compatible Hardware: Altos, Apple II, DEC, IBM PC, Kaypro, Zenith. Operating System(s) Required: CP/M-80, C-DOS, MS-DOS. Language(s): MAC Assembly (source code included). Memory Required: 64k.
disk $89.00.
8" disk $89.00.
Emulates the ISIS-II System Calls for Testing ISIS Programs under CP/M. A Paged Memory Version Emulates a Full 64k ISIS Configuration.
Western Wares.

IS4: Hotel Property Management System. Version: 1.3. Feb. 1994. Customer Support: 24 hour/7 days per week.
Windows. PC (8Mb). Contact publisher for price.
Optimal configuration: Windows 12Mb RAM. Networks supported: Novell.
Windows Based Hotel System Programmed in FOXPRO. Designed for Large Hotels with Sophisticated Management Needs.
National Guest Systems Corp.

Ishido: The Way of Stones. Aug. 1990. Items Included: Catalog, copy protection device, manual, proof of purchase card, & warranty card. Customer Support: Technical support 408-296-8400, 90 day limited warranty, Bulletin Board (modem) 408-296-8800 (Settings: 300, 1200, 2400 baud; 8 data; no parity; 1 stop bit).
IBM DOS 2.1 or higher, Tandy-DOS, (512k), Tandy EGA, MCGA, CGA, Hercules. IBM PC, XT, AT, & compatibles; Tandy 1000 series, 3000. $24.95. Optimal configuration: Hard drive, keyboard, mouse, & graphics card.
Macintosh (1Mb, 800k drive (B&W), 2Mb hard drive color). Macintosh Plus, 512ke, II, IIx, IIfx, IIci, IIcx, SE, SE/30, Portable. $54.95. Optimal configuration: Hard drive, keyboard, mouse, & graphics card.
Strategy Game.
Accolade, Inc.

Island of the Blue Dolphins. Intentional Education Staff. Items Included: Program manual. Customer Support: Free technical support, 90 day warranty.
School ver.. Mac System 7.1 or higher.

493

Macintosh (4Mb). 3.5" disk contact publisher for price (ISBN 1-57204-338-5). *Nonstandard peripherals required:* 256 color monitor, hard drive, printer.
- Lab Pack. Mac System 7.1 or higher. Macintosh (4Mb). 3.5" disk contact publisher for price (ISBN 1-57204-314-8). *Nonstandard peripherals required:* 256 color monitor, hard drive, printer.
- Site license. Mac System 7.1 or higher. Macintosh (4Mb). 3.5" disk contact publisher for price (ISBN 1-57204-339-3). *Nonstandard peripherals required:* 256 color monitor, hard drive, printer.
- School ver.. Windows 3.1 or higher. IBM/Tandy & 100% compatibles (4Mb). disk contact publisher for price (ISBN 1-57204-315-6). *Nonstandard peripherals required:* VGA or SVGA 640x480 resolution (256), mouse, hard drive, sound device.
- Lab pack. Windows 3.1 or higher. IBM/Tandy & 100% compatibles (4Mb). disk contact publisher for price (ISBN 1-57204-340-7). *Nonstandard peripherals required:* VGA or SVGA 640x480 resolution (256), mouse, hard drive, sound device.
- Site license. Windows 3.1 or higher. IBM/Tandy & 100% compatibles (4Mb). disk contact publisher for price (ISBN 1-57204-316-4). *Nonstandard peripherals required:* VGA or SVGA 640x480 resolution (256), mouse, hard drive, sound device.

Lawrence Productions, Inc.

ISOPOLY. *Version:* 3.33. Feb. 1986. *Compatible Hardware:* IBM PC, PC AT, PC XT & compatibles. *Operating System(s) Required:* PC-DOS, MS-DOS. *Language(s):* FORTRAN. *Memory Required:* 512k. *General Requirements:* Printer, plotter.
disk $2500.00 (Order no.: ISOPOLY).
Flexible, High Quality Contouring Program That Accurately Maps the Results of Geostatistical Estimation Techniques. Working with Any Rectangular or Square Grid of Data, ISOPOLY Will Contour the Estimates for Each Grid Point. For Large Maps, the Program Automatically Splits the Data into Bands Which Can Be Assembled.
Geostat Systems International, Inc. (GSII).

IS-SPICE/386. *Customer Support:* Free.
An 80386-based system under MS-DOS. $386.00.
Macintosh. 5.25" or 3.5" disk $95.00.
Analog Circuit Simulator.
INTUSOFT.

IT. *Version:* 1.0.1r7. Feb. 1989. *Items Included:* 363-page user manual. *Customer Support:* Telephone support, defective disks replaced free.
Macintosh (1Mb). 3.5" disk $199.95.
Gives Linguists, Literary Scholars, Translators & Anthropologists a Tool for Developing a Body of Annotated Interlinear Text. Keeps Word & Morpheme Annotations Aligned Vertically with Their Base Form & Saves Annotations in On-Line Lexical Database. Inserts Previous Annotations Automatically When Unambiguous (up to 22 Kinds of Annotation per Analyzed Text).
Linguist's Software, Inc.

ITC: (Investor Tracking Capability). *Version:* 2.1. Aug. 1986. *Compatible Hardware:* IBM PC & compatibles, multi-user acces with LANS. *Operating System(s) Required:* MS-DOS 3.1 or higher. *Language(s):* TURBO PASCAL. *Memory Required:* 512k. *General Requirements:* Hard disk. *Customer Support:* Application & technical telephone support; system training; updates & enhancements.
IBM PC & compatibles. license $5000.00.
annual service fee $995.00.

Tracks Shareholder Information & Generates Stock Certificates. Processes Common Stock & Preferred Stock Issuances, Transfers, Conversions Redemptions, Dividends & Stock Splits. Maintains Shareholder Information & Allows User to Comply with SEC & IRS Reporting Requirements.
ShareData (California).

Item Inventory & Tracking. *Version:* 2.0. 1995. *Items Included:* Complete illustrated instructions. *Customer Support:* 90 days free replacement of damaged disks, free unlimited telephone customer assistance.
DOS (640k). $349.00; Network $989.00.
Windows (640k). $359.00; Network $999.00.
Inventory & Tracking Program That Includes Complete Record Keeping for All Repairs & Loans (with Search or Reporting). Macro Feature Allows Duplication of Any Item with One Key Stroke. Open Ended. Search & Print by 17 Fields. 4 User Defined Fields. 5 Line Notes Fields. All on Screenprompts & Menu Driven.
Right On Programs.

Item Master & Control File. May 1983. *Compatible Hardware:* IBM PC, PC XT, PC AT. *Operating System(s) Required:* PC-DOS. *Language(s):* COBOL. *Memory Required:* 192k. *General Requirements:* 2 disk drives.
disk $875.00.
Five Levels of Engineering Classification May Be Used Including Prototype, Limited Production, Full Production, Replacement, & Obsolete. Product Family Code Is Used for Report Classification. Item's Control Code Can Be Master Scheduled, Material Planning, Re-Order Point, or Non-Controlled. Item's Procurement Code Can Be Purchased, Manufactured, Phantom, or Descriptive. Can Be Used to Switch from Real-Time to Batch Processing.
Twin Oaks, Inc.

ITEX-ALIGN. *Version:* 2.0. *Items Included:* documentation, demonstration guide, 1 program. *Customer Support:* 90-day warranty, upgrade programs available.
MS-DOS (640k). OEM $2250.00, end-user $4500.00. *Nonstandard peripherals required:* ITI frame grabber. *Addl. software required:* ITEX. *Optimal configuration:* 25 MHz 386/486 PC AT with 80387 math coprocessor.
A High-Speed, Gray-Scale Pattern Recognition Software Package Used in PC AT-Based Vision Systems for Precision Searching to Sub-Pixel Accuracy & Repeatability. Used in Automated Assembly & Inspection Applications to Perform Searching, Alignment, Registration, Guidance, & Tracking. The Software Is Ideally Suited for Automated Semiconductor & PCB Manufacturing Processes That Include Wafer Probing, Pick-and-Place, Wire/Die Bonding, X-Ray Inspection, Wafer Dicing, Alignment/Exposure, Film Thickness Metrology, Screen Printing, Ink Dot Recognition, & Multi-Layer PCB Registration.
Imaging Technology, Inc.

ITGAUSS. *Version:* 1.2. Jun. 1983. *Compatible Hardware:* IBM PC, PC XT, PC AT & compatibles. *Operating System(s) Required:* PC-DOS, MS-DOS. *Language(s):* FORTRAN. *Memory Required:* 512k. *General Requirements:* Printer.
disk $750.00 (Order no.: ITGAUSS).
Transforms the SIM3 or SIM3C Model Back into the Original Histogram Distribution. The Model Is Defined by the Expansion of a Transformation Function with Hermite Polynomials. This Expansion Is Derived by TGAUSS Using Experimental Data Distributed According to the Required Model. Statistics, Variograms, Maps, & a Sorted List of the Transformed Values Can Be Produced by ITGAUSS.
Geostat Systems International, Inc. (GSII).

It's a Bird's Life. Dec. 1995. *Customer Support:* Telephone support - free (except phone charge). Windows 3.1. IBM & compatibles (386 DX-20) (4Mb). CD-ROM disk $12.99, Jewel (ISBN 1-57594-079-5). *Nonstandard peripherals required:* 2X CD ROM player, sound card, VGA monitor. *Optimal configuration:* 486 SX-33.
CD-ROM disk $12.99, Blister.
Explore 60 Beautifully Illustrated & Animated Scenes to Play Games, Puzzles, & Other Interactive Activities. Children Will Learn about World Geography, Rain Forest, Clouds, & Birds.
Kidsoft, Inc.

It's a Bird's Life. Feb. 1996. *Customer Support:* Telephone support - free (except phone charge). Windows 3.1. IBM compatible 386 DX-20 (4Mb). CD-ROM disk $12.99 (ISBN 1-57594-092-2). *Nonstandard peripherals required:* 2x CD-ROM, sound card, VGA monitor. *Optimal configuration:* 486, SX-33.
Explore 60 Beautifully Illustrated & Animated Scenes to Play Games, Puzzles & Other Interactive Activities. Children Will Learn about Word Geography, Rain Forests, Clouds, & Birds.
Blister Pack.
Kidsoft, Inc.

It's a Bird's Life. Dec. 1995. *Customer Support:* Telephone support - free (except phone charge). Windows 3.1. IBM & compatibles (386 DX-20) (4Mb). CD-ROM disk $12.99 (ISBN 1-57594-079-5). *Nonstandard peripherals required:* 2X CD-ROM player, sound card, VGA monitor. *Optimal configuration:* 486 SX-33.
Explore 60 Beautifully Illustrated & Animated Scenes to Play Games, Puzzles, & Other Interactive Activities. Children Will Learn about World Geography, Rain Forest, Clouds, & Birds.
Jewel Case.
Kidsoft, Inc.

It's Legal. *Version:* 2.0. Feb. 1990. *Compatible Hardware:* IBM or compatible. *Memory Required:* 512k. *Items Included:* Spiral-bound manuals. *Customer Support:* Free, unlimited technical support.
DOS 2.0. disk $69.00.
Creates Simple, Living Wills, Certificates of Guardianship, Promissory Notes, General & Special Powers of Attorney, Residential & Commercial Leases. Upgrade Also Includes Durable Health Care Power of Attorney, Consumer & Credit Letters, Consulting Agreements, & Bill of Sale.
Parsons Technology.

It's My Business (with Simplex). *Compatible Hardware:* IBM PC & compatibles. *Operating System(s) Required:* MS-DOS 1.0, 1.1, 2.0, 2.1. *Memory Required:* 128k.
disk $695.00.
Free-Form Relational DBMS. Accesses Its Database Through English-Language Constructs. Supports Floating Point Mathematics for up to 19-Digit Accuracy. Accepts up to 65,535 Records per File with up to 256 Fields per Record. Unlimited Number of Files Can Be Open at One Time.
QuesTech, Inc.

It's Only Rock 'N Roll. *Compatible Hardware:* Commodore Amiga.
3.5" disk $29.95.
Instant Music Songs.
Electronic Arts.

Its-Writer. *Version:* 1.8. *Compatible Hardware:* IBM PC & compatibles for DOS, UNIX-base. *Operating System(s) Required:* PC-DOS/MS-DOS 2.10 or higher. *Memory Required:* 128k. *Items Included:* Language, hard

TITLE INDEX

copy manual, on-line documentation. *Customer Support:* Phone support to registered users.
disk $150.00.
What Was Comprehension Comes As Sample Program. Includes a Programming Language with Which to Design & Implement Interactive Text Systems & Tutorial, CAI, or Other Menued Interfaces, with WYSIWYG Approach. (Companion to Metamorph).
Thunderstone Software/Expansion Programs International, Inc.

I.V. Meds for Kids: Basic Nursing Procedures. *Version:* Apple. California State University. Dec. 1985. *Compatible Hardware:* Apple II, II+, IIe, IIc. *Memory Required:* 64k.
disk $54.95 (ISBN 0-07-831028-8).
Students Implement a Doctor's Order for a Pediatric IV Medication in a Step-by-Step Manner, Making the Decisions Necessary in Planning the Safe Administration of Medication to Children.
McGraw-Hill, Inc.

IWS: Integrated Work Station. *Compatible Hardware:* IBM PC, PC XT, PC AT, Ps/2. *Operating System(s) Required:* MS-DOS. *Memory Required:* 256k. *General Requirements:* Hard disk.
IWS Development package. disk $850.00.
IWS Shell/MS-DOS. disk $195.00.
The End-User Shell Interfaces Applications Programs As Menu Choices. The Set of Desktop Applications Includes: Scratchpad, Calculator, Calendar with Appointment Scheduler, Reminders, & Clock. All Applications Are Available on the Pop-Up Menu.
XYZT Computer Dimensions, Inc.

IXL: The Discovery Machine. *Customer Support:* Free phone tech support.
IBM PC & compatibles. 3.5" or 5.25" disk $490.00. *Nonstandard peripherals required:* Hard disk; CGA or EGA.
Discovers Hidden Patterns & Unexpected Relationships in Large Databases. Combines Artificial Intelligence & Statistics to Analyze User Database & Produces Easy-to-Read Rules. Reads Databases in a Variety of Formats & Produces Logical Statements & Rules Which Provide Insight for Decision Making.
IntelligenceWare, Inc.

J-Forth Professional. *Version:* 2.0. *Compatible Hardware:* Commodore Amiga. *Items Included:* 2 disks & manual.
3.5" disk $180.00.
32 Bit, Subroutine Threaded, Interactive Forth Programming Language That Supports Forth '83, '79, & FIG Standards. Package Includes Compiler, Assembler, Source Level Debugger, Target Compiler for Standalone Applications, Full Amiga Library & Structure Support, Local Variables, IFF Toolbox, Example Programs, Tutorials, & an Object Oriented Dialect.
Delta Research.

J. K. Lasser's Your Money Manager. J. K. Lasser Tax Institute. Oct. 1986. *Compatible Hardware:* Apple II+, IIe, IIc, Macintosh; Commodore 64, 128; IBM PC, PCjr, PC XT. *Memory Required:* Commodore 64k; Apple, Macintosh & IBM 128k. *General Requirements:* Printer recommended.
Apple. disk $89.95 (ISBN 0-671-53208-1).
IBM. disk $89.95 (ISBN 0-671-53207-3).
Commodore. disk $69.95 (ISBN 0-671-53211-1).
Macintosh. disk $99.95 (ISBN 0-671-53209-X).
Features Transaction Windows for Recording Checks, Deposits, & Regular & Irregular Payment Records; Full Allocation of All Transactions, for Both Record-Keeping & Tax Purposes; a Four-Function Calculator; Preparation & Printing of Reports on the User's Financial Position; Selection of Graphs for Instant Analysis of Current & Projected Trends. Information Can Be Transferred in a Single Step to J. K. LASSER'S YOUR INCOME TAX.
Brady Computer Bks.

Jack Nicklaus Course Designers Clip Art, Vol. 1. *Items Included:* Catalog, copy protection device, manual, proof of purchase card. *Customer Support:* Technical support 408-296-8400, 90 day limited warranty.
IBM DOS, 2.1 or higher, Tandy-DOS (512k). IBM PC, XT, AT, & compatibles, Tandy 1000 series. $19.95. *Addl. software required:* Exclusively for use with Jack Nicklaus' Unlimited Golf & Course Design. *Optimal configuration:* Hard drive installable, keyboard, mouse, graphics card, & sound board.
Ready-to-Play at Desert Highlands Golf Course, the Pride of Arizona. More Than 50 Finished Objects Including Trees, Golf Carts, Rocks, Buildings, etc. Three New Land Plots: Seaside Vista, Lush Parkland, & Desert. Eight New Scenic Backgrounds Including Mountains, Seashore & Parkland.
Accolade, Inc.

Jack Nicklaus' Greatest 18 Holes of Golf. *Compatible Hardware:* IBM PC, Tandy, Macintosh.
IBM, Tandy. disk $24.95.
Macintosh. 3.5" disk $59.95.
Play Against a Computerized Jack Nicklaus.
Accolade, Inc.

Jack Nicklaus Presents: The Great Courses of the U.S. Open. Jan. 1991. *Items Included:* Catalog, copy protection device, manual, proof of purchase card, & warranty card. *Customer Support:* Technical support 408-296-8400, 90 day limited warranty.
IBM DOS 2.1 or higher (640k). Apple IIGS; Amiga 500, 1000, & 2000. $14.95. *Addl. software required:* Either Jack Nicklaus' Greatest 18 Holes of Major Championship Golf or Jack Nicklaus' Unlimited Golf & Course Design or Signature Edition. *Optimal configuration:* Hard drive, keyboard & mouse.
IBM PC, XT, AT, & compatibles; Tandy 1000 series.
Addl. software required: Either Jack Nicklaus' Greatest 18 Holes of Major Championship Golf or Jack Nicklaus' Unlimited Golf & Course Design. *Optimal configuration:* Hard drive, & mouse.
Pebble Beach, California: The One & Only. If You Don't Know About Pebble & the U.S. Open, You Don't Know Golf. Nicklaus Won His Third Open Title Here in 1972. Ten Years Later, Tom Watson Barely Edged Jack with a Death-Defying Chip into the 17th Hole. Oakmont, Pennsylvania: Home of Nearly 200 Bunkers. Jack Calls It "Maybe the Toughest Course in the World." Talk About Tradition. Six U.S. Opens, Three PGAs. Springfield, New Jersey: Aristocratic, Elegant. Site of Three Opens. Jack Won Here in '67, Then Again in '80, Tying Bobby Jones & Ben Hogan for Most U.S. Open Victories.
Accolade, Inc.

Jack Nicklaus Presents the International Course Disk. 1989. *Items Included:* Manual. *Customer Support:* 90 day warranty; (408) 296-8400, 8am-5pm, M-F; Bulletin Board (408) 296-8800 (Bulletin Board settings: 300, 1200, 2400 baud; 8 data; no parity; 1 stop bit).
DOS 2.1 or higher. IBM PC, XT, AT, + 100% compatibles, Tandy 1000 series, 2000, 3000 (384k). disk $21.95.
Commodore 64/64c/128, 64k. disk $14.95.
Macintosh (1Mb). 3.5" disk $21.95.
Amiga 500, 1000, 2000, (512k). 3.5" disk $21.95.
Apple IIgs (512k). disk $21.95.
Jack Nicklaus' 18 Holes of Major Championship Golf Add-On Disk.
Accolade, Inc.

Jack Nicklaus Presents the Major Championship Courses of 1989. *Customer Support:* 90 Days limited warranty.
IBM PC/Tandy. $14.95.
Contains: U.S. Open Championship June 15-18; Oak Hill Country Club, Rochester, NY; British Open Championship, July 20-23, Royal Troon Golf Club, Troon, Scotland; PGA Championship, August 10-13, Kemper Lakes Golf Club, Hawthorn Woods, IL. Add on Disk to Jack Nicklaus' Greatest 18 Holes of Major Championship Golf.
Accolade, Inc.

Jack Nicklaus Presents the Major Championship Courses of 1990. 1990. *Items Included:* Manual. *Customer Support:* 90 day warranty; (408) 296-8400, 8am-5pm, M-F; Bulletin Board (408) 296-8800 (Bulletin Board settings: 300, 1200, 2400, 2400 baud; 8 data; no parity; 7 stop bit).
DOS 2.1 or higher. IBM PC, XT, AT, + 100% compatibles, Tandy 1000 series, 2000, 3000 (384k). disk $14.95.
Add-On Disk to Jack Nicklaus' 18 Holes of Major Championship Golf.
Accolade, Inc.

Jack Nicklaus Presents the Major Championship Courses of 1991. Apr. 1991. *Items Included:* Catalog, copy protection device, manual, proof of purchase card, & warranty card. *Customer Support:* Technical support 408-296-8400, 90 day limited warranty.
IBM DOS 2.1 or higher (640k). IBM PC, XT, AT, & compatibles. $14.95. *Addl. software required:* Either Jack Nicklaus' Greatest 18 Holes of Major Championship Golf or Jack Nicklaus' Unlimited Golf & Course Design or Signature Edition. *Optimal configuration:* Hard drive, & mouse.
Optimal configuration: Hard drive, & keyboard.
U.S. Open Championship: Hazeltine National Golf Club, Chaska, Minnesota - Designed by Robert Trent Jones. British Open Championship: Royal Birkdale Golf Club, Southport, England - Englands Finest Links & Six-Time Site of the British Open. PGA Championship: Crooked Stick Golf Club, Carmel, Indiana - Features the Trademark Pot Bunkers & Scottish Mounding of Legendary Designer Pete Dye.
Accolade, Inc.

Jack Nicklaus' Unlimited Golf & Course Design. Jun. 1990. *Items Included:* Catalog, copy protection device, manual, proof of purchase card. *Customer Support:* Technical support 408-296-8400, 90 day limited warranty, Bulletin Board (modem) 408-296-8800 (settings: 300, 1200, 2400 baud; 8 data; no parity; 1 stop bit).
IBM DOS 2.1 or higher, Tandy-DOS. IBM PC, XT, AT & compatibles; Tandy 1000 series, 3000, 4000 (512k). $44.95. *Optimal configuration:* Hard drive, keyboard, mouse, graphics card, & sound board.
This Simulation Captures the Complete Golf Experience. From Sculpting Landscape to Playing Magnificent, Finished Courses - This Is Truly Golf from the Ground up.
Accolade, Inc.

Jack's Adventures Beyond the Beanstalk. Apr. 1996. *Customer Support:* 90 days unlimited warranty.
Mac. Macintosh 68030 (8Mb). CD-ROM disk Contact publisher for price. *Addl. software*

JAGGED ALLIANCE

required: Quicktime 2.0.
Windows. 486/DX 33 (8Mb). *Addl. software required:* Video for Windows V1-1D/Quicktime for Windows 2.0.
Hosted by Disney's Jim Varney, Jack's Adventures Is a Rollicking Interactive Journey Through the World Beyond the Beanstalk. Join Jack & His Wacky Friends As They Combine Their Talents to Defeat Eek the Evil Sorceress. Jack's Adventures Is the First Children's Title to Feature 2D, 3D, & Full Motion Video.
Global MediaNet Corp.

Jagged Alliance. Ian R. Currie. *Customer Support:* Free hint line service available 4:00-8:00 p.m. (EST) weekdays, 12:00-4:00 p.m. (EST) weekends & holidays. Technical support - weekdays 9:00 a.m. to 5:00 p.m. (EST) 30-day warranty with dated proof of purchase. After 30-day warranty expires, $12.50 replacement fee applied.
PC-DOS/MS-DOS. IBM PC/100% compatibles (4Mb). CD-ROM disk Contact publisher for price (ISBN 0-926846-74-4). *Optimal configuration:* CD-ROM version - 4Mb RAM, CD-ROM drive, 15Mb free hard disk space, 80486/33 or higher, PC/MS-DOS 5.0 or 6.X, mouse, sound card.
PC-DOS/MS-DOS. IBM PC/100% compatibles. disk $59.95 (ISBN 0-926846-73-6). *Optimal configuration:* 3.5" diskette version.
Strategic Role-Playing Simulation - Choose & Control a Team of 8 Mercenaries from More Than 50 Personalities to Assist You in Regaining Control of Metavira a Remote Island in the South Atlantic. Provides 3D Modeled Animations, Realistic Overhead Perspectives, Cinematic Sequences, Digitized Sound Effects & Musical Score.
Sir-Tech Software, Inc.

Jagged Alliance. Apr. 1996. *Customer Support:* Free hint line service available 4:00-8:00p.m. (EST) weekdays, 12:00-4:00p.m. (EST) weekends & holidays. Technical support on weekdays 9:00a.m.-5:00p.m. (EST), 30-day warranty with dated proof of purchase. After 30-day warranty expires, $12.50 replacement fee applied.
MS-DOS. IBM PC 486/33 MHz (8Mb). CD-ROM disk Contact publisher for price (ISBN 0-926846-85-X). *Nonstandard peripherals required:* Double speed CD-ROM drive, DOS 5.0 or 6.X, SVGA, sound blaster.
The Intense Challenge of Single & Multiplayer Tactical Strategic Combat Gets Personal in Deadly Games. Featuring a Unique New Approach, Deadly Games Offers Completely Flexible Game Play. Whether It Be Single or Multiplayer, Campaign Play or Single Scenarios, Each Battle Promises to Be Packed with Action, Loaded with Personality, & Jammed with Excitement. To Top It off, Deadly Games Features New, More Deadly Weapons to Take on Tougher Opponents (Your Friends), & Single-Player Battles Against up to 32 Computer Enemies. Offering Intense Excitement Against Superb Computer AI & Game Play Against Intelligence & Unpredictability of a Live Opponent, Deadly Games Is One of the Most Creative & Flexible Gaming Environments Around.
Sir-Tech Software, Inc.

Jam Session, 3 disks. Bogas Productions. Oct. 1987. *Compatible Hardware:* Apple Macintosh. *Memory Required:* 512k.
$49.95 (ISBN 1-55790-122-8, Order no.: 12155).
Music Performance Program That Enables Anyone to Perform Professional Sounding Music Without Having Any Musical Background or Knowledge.
Broderbund Software, Inc.

James & the Giant Peach. Intentional Education Staff & Roald Dahl. *Items Included:* Program manual. *Customer Support:* Free technical support, 90 day warranty.
School ver.. System 7.1 or higher. Macintosh (4Mb). 3.5" disk contact publisher for price (ISBN 1-57204-225-7). *Nonstandard peripherals required:* 256 monitor, hard drive, printer.
Lab pack. System 7.1 or higher. Macintosh (4Mb). 3.5" disk contact publisher for price (ISBN 1-57204-201-X). *Nonstandard peripherals required:* 256 monitor, hard drive, printer.
Site license. System 7.1 or higher. Macintosh (4Mb). 3.5" disk contact publisher for price (ISBN 1-57204-226-5). *Nonstandard peripherals required:* 256 monitor, hard drive, printer.
School ver.. Windows 3.1 or higher. IBM/Tandy & 100% compatibles (4Mb). disk contact publisher for price (ISBN 1-57204-202-8). *Nonstandard peripherals required:* VGA or SVGA 640 x 480 resolution (256), mouse, hard drive, sound device.
Lab pack. Windows 3.1 or higher. IBM/Tandy & 100% compatibles (4Mb). disk contact publisher for price (ISBN 1-57204-227-3). *Nonstandard peripherals required:* VGA or SVGA 640 x 480 resolution (256), mouse, hard drive, sound device.
Site license. Windows 3.1 or higher. IBM/Tandy & 100% compatibles (4Mb). disk contact publisher for price (ISBN 1-57204-203-6). *Nonstandard peripherals required:* VGA or SVGA 640 x 480 resolution (256), mouse, hard drive, sound device.
This companion for young adult literature is ideal for students who don't know how to start that book report, or give that needed summary. Gentle prompts throughout the guide section of the program include Warm-up Connections, Thinking about Plot, Quoting & Noting, Keeping a Journal, If I Were————' Responding to Questions, Using Quotations, Taking a Personal View, Write to Others, & Write a Sequel.
Lawrence Productions, Inc.

Janet & Judy's Mission from Planet N. Sep. 1995. *Items Included:* 4 page fold out instruction manual included in Jewel Case package. *Customer Support:* Call tech service support - 805-497-8865 between 8:00AM - 5:00 PM.
Windows 3.1. 486/66MHz, 8Mb RAM, Sound card 16 bit, CD-ROM speakers, mouse. CD-ROM disk $39.99 (ISBN 0-9648640-0-2). *Optimal configuration:* Video - SVGA 256 colors 640x480.
A Learning Adventure Game for Children Ages 6-11. Janet & Judy Are Aliens on Their Very First Mission - to Deliver a Special Package to the President. But...They Lose the Package. Along Your Journey Looking for the Lost Package, You Can Explore Exciting Places in the U.S., Collect a Souvenir from Each State, See Wildlife, Play Video Games & Listen to Janet & Judy's Great Music.
Cherrystone Productions, Inc.

JANUS-Ada AdaVid. Jan. 1988. *Operating System(s) Required:* VHS. *Language(s):* JANUS/Ada (source code included).
disk $995.00.
Ada Tutorial (Video Instruction for Beginners) with Janus Extended Tutorial (Intermediate Level Tutorial: Written, with Example Programs).
RR Software, Inc.

The JANUS-Ada B-Pak Tools Kit: Development Package. *Version:* 2.1.3. Jan. 1990. *Compatible Hardware:* IBM PC, XT, AT, 386, 486. *Operating System(s) Required:* MS-DOS, PC-DOS, SCO UNIX, interactive

SOFTWARE ENCYCLOPEDIA 1996

UNIX. *Language(s):* JANUS/Ada. *Memory Required:* 1000k.
disk $700.00.
S-Pak (Systems Package). $4500.00, incl. source to runtime.
Includes All Runtime Libraries Offerd by RR Software Including 8087 Support, & Trig Functions. Contains: Assemblers, Compilation Tool, Disassembler, Efind, Linker, Profiler, & Syntax Checker. None Is Available Separately.
RR Software, Inc.

JANUS-Ada Compiler. *Version:* 2.1.3. Jan. 1990. *Compatible Hardware:* IBM PC, PC XT, PC AT & compatibles. *Operating System(s) Required:* MS-DOS 3.1, SCO UNIX, Interactive UNIX. *Language(s):* JANUS/Ada (source code included). *Memory Required:* 1000k.
Set. $360.00, incl. compiler, linker, & example programs.
Multi-Pass Compiler Which Produces JANUS/Ada Relocatable Files from JANUS/Ada Source. Code Is ROMable & Reentrant. Full Ada Syntax.
RR Software, Inc.

JANUS-Ada Cross Compilers. (source code included). *Memory Required:* 1000k.
contact publisher for price.
System Requirements Dependent on Host/Target Configuration Chosen.
RR Software, Inc.

The JANUS-Ada Pascal to Ada Translator (PASTRAN). *Version:* 2.0. *Compatible Hardware:* Compaq, Eagle, IBM PC, XT, AT Kaypro II, Seequa, 386, 486 & DEC VAX. *Operating System(s) Required:* MS-DOS, PC-DOS, VMS. *Memory Required:* 640k. *General Requirements:* Hard disk.
disk $10,000.00.
Takes Programs Written in Standard Pascal & Converts Them to JANUS/Ada Programs, or Ada, by Users Option. Most Pascal Features Are Translated, & Untranslated Features Are Flagged in Output Source Code.
RR Software, Inc.

JapanEase, Vol. 1: Katakana. Ayumi Software. Oct. 1990. *Items Included:* User's guide, Katakana writing practice sheets.
Mac OS 6.0.5 or higher. Macintosh 512k or higher (1Mb). 3.5" disk $99.95. *Addl. software required:* HyperCard 2.0 or higher.
Japanese Language Learning Tool: HyperCard Application That Teaches the Japanese Katakana Alphabet, 300 Vocabulary Words, 50 Basic Expressions & How to Say Time, Dates, Numbers, etc. Provides Native-Speaker Pronunciation & Amusing Animations & Graphics.
Qualitas Trading Co.

JapanEase, Vol. 2: Hiragana Grammar. Ayumi Software. May 1992. *Items Included:* User's guide, Hiragana writing practice sheets.
Mac OS 6.0.5 or higher. Macintosh 512k or higher (1Mb). 3.5" disk $99.95. *Addl. software required:* HyperCard 2.0 or higher.
Japanese Language-Learning Tool; HyperCard Application That Teaches Japanese Grammar, Vocabulary, & the Hiragana Alphabet; Provides Native-Speaker Pronunciation, a Bilingual On-Line Dictionary & 30 Essential Phrases.
Qualitas Trading Co.

Japanese Foreign Direct Investment in the United States 1974-1994. May 1995. *Items Included:* Spiral bound manual. *Customer Support:* Unlimited telephone support.
MS-DOS 6.0/Windows 3.1 or higher. PC Clone 486 or higher (4Mb). disk $125.00 (ISBN 1-878974-06-8). *Addl. software required:* Database Versions are available for MS Access 2.0, Excel, Lotus, Paradox, Foxpro, & dBASE.

TITLE INDEX

Optimal configuration: PC clone with MS-DOS 6.0/Windows 3.1 or higher. Must have MS Access 2.0, or Excel, or Lotus or Paradox or Foxpro or dBASE.
Database of All Japanese Foreign Direct Investment Transactions in the United States 1974-1994.
Jeffries & Associates, Inc.

Javelin PLUS. *Version:* 2.06. *Compatible Hardware:* IBM PC & compatibles. *Operating System(s) Required:* PC-DOS 2.0 or higher. *Memory Required:* 512k. *General Requirements:* 2 disk drives. Hard disk & graphics monitor recommended.
disk $695.00.
trial pack $35.00.
A Flexible, Easy-to-Use System for PC-Based Modeling. It Provides the Intuitive User Interface & Power of Spreadsheet with Superior Automatic Documentation Features. Multiple Views Allow Users to Summarize Their Model on Any Number of Spreadsheets & Graphs, or to Zoom in on Individual Line Items via Tables or Graphs. Model Logic Is Automatically Documented by a List of Formulas, Input Assumptions, & Model Results, As Well As a Diagram of How Formulas Are Related to Each Other; All Modeling Errors Are Summarized in One View. Includes a 175-Year Calendar; Over 140 Functions for Modeling. Data May Be Imported from or Exported to Lotus 1-2-3 Spreadsheets, Plus a Full Macro Language for Programming Turn-Key Applications.
Javelin Products Group.

Jazz. *Version:* 1A. Apr. 1986. *Compatible Hardware:* Apple Macintosh 512e. *Memory Required:* 512k. *General Requirements:* 2 disk drives or hard disk.
3.5" disk $395.00.
Offers Integration Between Its Stand-Alone Functions: Spreadsheet, Word Processing, Graphics, Data Management & Communications. Its HotView Feature Allows Users to Include Graphs, Database Files, & Worksheets into Their Word Processing Documents. If a Change Is Made to the Original Information, the Word Processing Document Will Be Automatically Updated. Also Offers "Cut & Paste" Capability Between JAZZ Functions & Other MACINTOSH Products. Fully Compatible with the MACINTOSH OFFICE, the APPLETALK Network, & the LASERWRITER Printer.
Lotus Development Corp.

Jazz Greats. Feb. 1995. *Items Included:* CD-ROM booklet. *Customer Support:* Free technical support via phone as of release date.
MPC/Windows. 386.25 or higher IBM compatible (4Mb). CD-ROM disk $49.95 (ISBN 1-885784-31-7, Order no.: 1301). *Optimal configuration:* MPC CD-ROM player, S-VGA graphics card (640x480x256 colors) with compatible monitor, MPC compliant sound card, mouse, Windows 3.1.
Explore the Mythical World of Jazz. Experience Popular Jazz Tunes, Entertaining Text, Emotional Artist Performances & Intriguing Discussion Videos Focusing on the Evolution of Jazz Music. Immerse Yourself in the Lives of These Top Jazz Legends. Delve into the Music, History & Influences of the Early Jazz Age.
Technology Dynamics Corp.

Jazz Greats: From Louis Armstrong to Duke Ellington (Jewel). *Items Included:* CD-ROM booklet. *Customer Support:* Free technical support via phone as of release date.
MPC/Windows. 386MHz or higher (4Mb). CD-ROM disk $39.95 (ISBN 1-885784-67-8, Order no.: 1304). *Optimal configuration:* MPC CD-ROM player, S-VGA graphics card (640x480x256 colors) with compatible monitor, MPC compliant sound card, mouse, Windows 3.1 or higher, Windows 95 compatible.
Explore the Roots of the Early Jazz Era. Experience Artist Performance Videos, over 15 Jazz Tunes, Intriguing Expert Discussions, Photographs & Narrative. Includes Duke Ellington's "Take the "A" Train," Art Tatum's "Tea for Two," Billie Holiday's "Fine & Mellow & More!" In French, German, Spanish & English on One Disc.
Technology Dynamics Corp.

JCM: Job Cost Management. *Version:* 2.2. May 1984. *Compatible Hardware:* IBM PC & compatibles. *Operating System(s) Required:* PC-DOS 2.0 or higher. *Language(s):* COBOL, Assembly. *Memory Required:* 256k. *Customer Support:* Hourly or yearly fees.
disk $595.00, incl. user's guide (Order no.: JCM).
demo disk free (Order no.: PRI.JCM).
Developed to Assist in the Management & Control of Various Types of Jobs & Projects. Provides an Orderly, Efficient Report System to Monitor One or Many On-Going Projects. Capabilities of the System Include Budgeting, Scheduling, Analysis Reporting Between Budgeting, & Actual Costs Incurred.
Computer Related Services, Inc.

Jericho. *Compatible Hardware:* Apple II+, IIe, IIc. *Language(s):* BASIC, Machine. *Memory Required:* 48k.
disk $9.95.
The Object of the Game Is to Knock Down the Walls of Jericho While Firing with Blasts on Joshua's Horn. When the Walls Have Been Knocked Down, a New Set of Walls Will Be Displayed. Any Time a Wall Is Destroyed, the Player Receives an Extra Warrior, but the Arrows Shoot More Intensely with Each New Wall.
Davka Corp.

Jerusalem Stores.
Windows 3.0 or higher. IBM PC or compatibles. disk $24.95 (Order no.: I888). *Optimal configuration:* IBM PC or compatibles, color monitor.
Challenges User to Match Rows of Falling Stones According to the Hebrew Letters Imprinted on Them. The Game Is Surrounded by Full-Color Scenes of Jerusalem That Change As You Move up to Different Playing Levels.
Davka Corp.

Jet Fighter II; Earth Invasion. Velocity Development & Three DI. Jan. 1996. *Items Included:* Set-up instruction sheet. *Customer Support:* 310-403-0043.
DOS for Jet Fighter; Win 3.1 or higher, DOS 5.0 for Earth Invasions. IBM PC. disk $12.95 (ISBN 1-887783-15-6, Order no.: 5100-2003). *Optimal configuration:* Jet Fighter: 386 or higher, 640k RAM, DOS 2.1 or higher, VGA/ EGA/CGA, Supports but does not required Adlib, Soundblaster, Analog joystick & mouse; Earth Invasion: Win 3.1 or higher, DOS 5.0 or higher, 4Mb HD, joystick, mouse or keyboard, VGA or SVGA, soundblaster, Adlib or Pro, Audio Spectrum compatible.
Jet Fighter Is an Air Combat Simulation Game. Earth Invasion Is a Space Game Whereas the Game Player Battles Against Aliens from Other Planets.
Entertainment Technology.

Jetfighter II. Velocity Development Corp. Staff. Aug. 1995. *Items Included:* Set up instruction sheet. *Customer Support:* (503) 639-6863.
DOS. IBM PC. disk $7.95 (ISBN 1-887783-00-8, Order no.: 5300-1002). *Optimal configuration:* IBM PC 386 or higher, 640k RAM, DOS 2.1 or higher, VGA/EGA/CGA/supports but does not require AdLib, Soundblaster, Analog joystick & mouse.
Air Combat Simulation Game.
Entertainment Technology.

JetFighter: The Ultimate Combat Flight Simulator. Jun. 1994. *Items Included:* Registration card, instruction sheet. *Customer Support:* 900 support number $2.00 per minute; limited 60 day warranty.
DOS. IBM PC & compatibles (640k). disk $9.95 (ISBN 1-57269-001-1, Order no.: 3202 42085). *Addl. software required:* DOS 2.0 or higher. *Optimal configuration:* Single floppy drive. Hard disk drive recommended, supports joystick.
True-to-Life Cockpit Controls & Death-Defying In-Air Encounters Makes the Experience Almost Too Real.
Memorex Products, Inc., Memorex Software Division.

Jewel Accounting System. Heritage Computing, Inc. *Compatible Hardware:* TI Professional. *Operating System(s) Required:* MS-DOS. *Memory Required:* 128k. *General Requirements:* Winchester hard disk, printer.
Set. $4875.00.
Fully Integrated Accounting System.
Texas Instruments, Personal Productivit.
General Ledger.
$975.00.
Accounts Payable.
$525.00.
Accounts Receivable with Billing & Inventory.
$850.00.
Accounts Receivable with Inventory.
$425.00.
Payroll.
$525.00.
Order Entry.
$425.00.
Job Cost.
$725.00.
Manufacturing.
$425.00.

JForth. *Compatible Hardware:* Commodore Amiga 500, 1000, 2000. *Memory Required:* 512k. *General Requirements:* External floppy drive recommended.
3.5" disk $99.95.
Software Development Environment Based on the Forth '83 Standard. The Forth Interest Group (FIG) & Forth-79 Standards Are Also Supported. Contains an Interpreter & a Compiler in One Language, Which Lets Users Compile Programs from the Keyboard. Utilizes "JSR-Threading" to Tie Together Compiled Programs & Programs Are Interactively Debugged Immediately Following Compile. Special Toolboxes Simplify Development & Users Can "Turnkey" & Distribute Completed Applications Without Royalties. Utilities Provided Include a 68000 Assembler & Disassembler, Search & Sort Routines, Local Variables, & Floating Point. Amiga Structures & Constants Are Predefined in ".J" Files Corresponding to the ".H" Files Used in C & Amiga Library Routines Are Called by Name. An Object Oriented Development Environment Is Also Included.
Delta Research.

JigSaw. Graham Dawson & Bernadette Brady. Jan. 1994. *Items Included:* 108-page manual. *Customer Support:* Free phone support.
Windows 3.1, Windows 95. 386 (2Mb, 4Mb recommended). disk $250.00 (ISBN 0-87199-130-6). *Nonstandard peripherals required:* VGA. *Addl. software required:* None, but a chart-casting program such as Solar, Fire, Nova, Chartwheels or Blue Star is

recommended.
Helps Astrologers Put the Pieces Together When Working with Groups of Charts. Has 3 Modules: "Rectification" Analyzes Charts of Life Events to Aid in Finding the Correct Birth Time; "Family Patterns" Analyzes Charts from Medium-Sized Groups to Find the Common Degree Areas, Aspects & Midpoints; & "Research" Analyzes Larger Groups of Charts for Any of a Wide Variety of Astrological Factors.
Astrolabe, Inc.

Jigsaw-It, Jr. Dynaware Staff. Sep. 1995. *Customer Support:* Telephone support - free (except phone charge).
Windows 3.1. IBM & compatibles (386 DX-20) (4Mb). CD-ROM disk $12.99 (ISBN 1-57594-022-1). *Nonstandard peripherals required:* 2x CD-ROM player, Sound Card, VGA monitor. *Optimal configuration:* 486 XS-33.
Electronic Jigsaw Puzzle.
Kidsoft, Inc.

Jigsaw-It, Jr. Dynaware Staff. Sep. 1995. *Customer Support:* Telephone support - free (except phone charge).
Windows 3.1. IBM & compatibles (386 DX-20) (4Mb). CD-ROM disk $12.99 (ISBN 1-57594-061-2). *Nonstandard peripherals required:* 2x CD-ROM player, Sound Card, VGA monitor. *Optimal configuration:* 486 SX-33.
Electronic Jigsaw Puzzle. Blister Pack Jewel Case.
Kidsoft, Inc.

Jigsaw! The Ultimate Electronic Puzzle.
Compatible Hardware: Apple IIgs, IBM, Amiga. *Items Included:* Manual & catalog. *Customer Support:* 90-day money back guarantee, 30-day preview policy for schools with purchase order number, $7.50 for back-ups, free replacement of damaged disk if under warranty.
3.5" disk Version 1 (11/1988) $39.95. *Optimal configuration:* RGB monitor.
PC-DOS/MS-DOS 2.0 or higher. disk Version 2 (03/1989) $39.95. *Nonstandard peripherals required:* CGA/EGA/VGA monitor.
Designed to Maximize the Performance of User's High Graphics Computer with Jigsaw Which Has Over 20 Puzzle Images for All Ages Ranging from Famous Places, Art Masterpieces, the Alphabet & Animals to Nature. Allows Users to Import Graphics Created from Other Popular Graphics Programs, Such as PAINTWORKS GOLD or DELUXE PAINT II & Turn Them into Puzzles to Play With. Select from 4 Levels of Game Complexity: 60 Pieces (the Ultimate Challenge), 40 Pieces (Standard Level), 15 Pieces (Level to Get Acquainted with the Program), 8 Pieces (Easiest Level).
Compton's NewMedia.

JMACS: Job Manufacturing & Accounting Control System. Jan. 1986. *Compatible Hardware:* IBM PC, PC AT & compatibles, Wang. *General Requirements:* Hard disk, printer.
PC. disk $4500.00-$6500.00 (ISBN 0-942915-01-1, Order no.: JMACS/VS).
IBM. disk $4500.00-$6500.00 (ISBN 0-942915-00-3, Order no.: JMACS/PC).
Material Requirements Planning & Job Costing System for Machining & Fabrication Environments. Designed to Fill the Computerization Needs for the Job Shop Manufacturer. Interfaces to MCBA & Real World Accounting System. Handles Customer Order Processing, Purchasing, Inventory, Bill of Materials, Plant Reporting, Job Costing & Security. Custom Enhancements Are Available.
Infosource Management, Inc.

JMI Portable C Library. *Version:* 2.1. Mar. 1986. *Compatible Hardware:* DEC; IBM; Intel; Motorola, any system with a standard C compiler. *Language(s):* C (source code included).
$5000.00, incl. manual.
manual only $25.00.
Portable Library Designed for Implementing ROMable Systems, Sharing Functions among Several Processes, & Restarting Memory-Resident Systems Without Reloading.
JMI Software Consultants, Inc.

JMP Statistical Discovery Software. *Version:* 3.1.5. *Items Included:* Documentation included. *Customer Support:* Two years technical support, training available.
Mac Plus or higher, Power Mac, Windows 3.1, Windows NT, Windows 95. $695.00, quantity & degree-granting disccounts available (ISBN 1-55544-450-4).
A Statistical Discovery Tool for Data Exploration & Experimentation Designed for Windows & Macintosh. Statistics Are Presented in a Graphical Way So That They Can Be Visually Understood & Can Give the Most Insight. JMP Also Provides Tools for Quality Improvement i.e. Quality Control Charts & Statistics, Including Shewhart & Pareto Charts. The Software Also Includes Design of Experiments Capabilities for Continuous Improvement in Products & Processes.
SAS Institute, Inc.

Job Attitudes: Assessment & Improvement.
Feb. 1996. *Items Included:* Program manual. *Customer Support:* Free technical support, 90 day warranty.
Single user. System 7.1 or higher. Mac, 16 MHz rating, 68030 or better processor (LC II or higher) (5Mb). 3.5" disk $99.95 (ISBN 1-57204-103-X, Order no.: APM151). *Nonstandard peripherals required:* 256 color monitor, 13" or larger.
Lab pack. System 7.1 or higher. Mac, 16 MHz rating, 68030 or better processor (LC II or higher) (5Mb). 3.5" disk $199.00 (ISBN 1-57204-130-7, Order no.: APM151LPK). *Nonstandard peripherals required:* 256 color monitor, 13" or larger.
Site license. System 7.1 or higher. Mac, 16 MHz rating, 68030 or better processor (LC II or higher) (5Mb). 3.5" disk $399.00 (ISBN 1-57204-132-3, Order no.: APM151SITE). *Nonstandard peripherals required:* 256 color monitor, 13 or larger.
Single user. Windows 3.1 or higher. IBM 386 (8Mb). disk $99.95 (ISBN 1-57204-104-8). *Nonstandard peripherals required:* 256 color monitor, mouse, sound card. *Addl. software required:* SVGA graphics.
Lab pack. Windows 3.1 or higher. IBM 386 (8Mb). disk $199.00 (ISBN 1-57204-131-5, Order no.: WIN151LPK). *Nonstandard peripherals required:* 256 color monitor, sound card, mouse. *Addl. software required:* SVGA graphics.
Site license. Windows 3.1 or higher. IBM 386 (8Mb). disk $399.00 (ISBN 1-57204-133-1, Order no.: WIN151SITE). *Nonstandard peripherals required:* 256 color monitor, sound card, mouse. *Addl. software required:* SVGA graphics.
Discusses attitudes appropriate to the vast majority of employment situations.
Lawrence Productions, Inc.

Job Boss. *Version:* 5.0. Jul. 1991. *Items Included:* pre-installation guide, installation guide, & documentation. *Customer Support:* Support Contract entitles user to 1 year of free telephone support, use of Bulletin Board (computerized information exchange), menu changes, periodic updates, & company name additions; price of service contract depends on software purchased; training, installation, available.
PC-DOS. IBM PC, PC XT, PC AT, PS/2 (640k). disk $995.00. *Nonstandard peripherals required:* 20 Mb hard disk. *Optimal configuration:* Language - Basic. *Networks supported:* Novell.
Estimating & Scheduling Package That Allows Estimates, Bids, & Job Budgets to be Created Using Templates, Master Cost Book, Assemblies, & Activities, & Produces a CMP Scheduling for Each Job. May Be Integrated with CMST Plus.
SSD (Small System Design), Inc.

Job Control. *Version:* 6.0. Jul. 1992. *Compatible Hardware:* IBM PC. *Operating System(s) Required:* MS-DOS. *Language(s):* QuickBASIC (source code included). *Memory Required:* 512k. *Items Included:* Manual/programs/installation support. *Customer Support:* Personal telephone contact.
$6000.00.
Tracks Cost & Location of Printed Jobs in Graphic Arts Manufacturing.
Printers Software, Inc.

Job Cost. *Version:* 14.0. (Accounting Software Ser.). May 1993. *Compatible Hardware:* IBM PC & compatibles. *Operating System(s) Required:* MS-DOS, PC-DOS 3.X & up. *Language(s):* MegaBASIC. *Memory Required:* 640k. *General Requirements:* Hard disk, wide carriage printer. *Customer Support:* (203) 790-9756.
$495.00, Network Option ,500.00 more.
manual $50.00.
Features Entry & Maintenance of Shop Orders & Automatic Posting of Accounts Payable & Payroll Data to Job Cost. Tie-In to Union Payroll, Tracks Union Information (eg. Fringe Benefits). Produces Union Reports. Allows Comparision of Estimate vs. Actual Costs, Entry of % Completion on Jobs for Over-Run Reporting.
Applications Systems Group (CT), Inc.

Job Cost. *Version:* 5.1. *Compatible Hardware:* IBM PC & compatibles.
disk $995.00.
Job Cost Accounting Module Includes Estimating, Cost Tracking, Billing & Reporting Functions. New Features Include Selection Windows & a Copy Feature That Allows Sections from an Existing Estimate to Be Copied into a New File. Also Multi User Capabilities with Record-Level Locking.
Great Plains Software.

Job Cost Accounting: JOBCOST. *Version:* 3.0. William W. Smith. Jul. 1982. *Compatible Hardware:* Apple II; DEC Rainbow, DEC VT180; Hewlett-Packard; IBM PC; Kaypro; Morrow; North Star; Osborne; Superbrain; TRS-80 Model I, Model III; Vector Graphics; Victor; Zenith. *Operating System(s) Required:* CP/M, CP/M-86, MS-DOS, PC-DOS. *Language(s):* CB-80 (source code included). *Memory Required:* CP/M 64k, MS-DOS 256k. *General Requirements:* 2 disk drives, printer.
disk $495.00.
8" disk $495.00.
3.5" disk $495.00.
demo disk $38.00.
Method of Keeping Track of Both Hourly & Direct Costs Associated with Completing Projects. There Is Provision for 75 Employees & 700 Active Projects. Each Project Can Have 15 Hourly Cost Categories & 5 Direct Costs Allocated to Each Job. Total of 15 Reports Are Provided. Reports Include Monthly, Quarterly, & Current to Date Total Job Costs, Detailed Employee Costs, Employee Summary Costs, Monthly Job Summaries, Client Receivables, Monthly Overhead Costs, & a Cash Flow Summary.
Elite Software Development, Inc.

Job Cost Accounting Software. *Version:* 6.5. RealWorld Corp. 1990. *Compatible Hardware:* Altos, 3086; IBM PC, PC XT, PC AT & compatibles. *Operating System(s) Required:*

TITLE INDEX

JOB COSTING

DOS, UNIX, XENIX, Novell NetWare. *Language(s):* MicroFocus & RM Cobol. *Memory Required:* 640k. *General Requirements:* Hard disk, printer. *Items Included:* User Manual. *Customer Support:* Support subscription available for fee, 900 number.
IBM. $795.00-$995.00.
UNIX, XENIX Networks. $795.00-$995.00.
RealWorld Job Cost Provides the Tools Needed to Track Costs, Income, Profits, etc., Related to Specific Jobs & Sub-Jobs. Job Cost Features Include Tracking Budgets Against Actual Costs Incurred; Detailed On-Line Inquiry; & Printing of Numerous Reports Such As Job Status, Job Performance, Job Profitability & Cost Category Analysis.
RealWorld Corp.

Job Cost Accounting System. 1986. *Compatible Hardware:* PC & compatibles, PS/2, RS/6000, System 36. *Operating System(s) Required:* AIX, MS-DOS, SSP. *Language(s):* BASIC (source code included). *Memory Required:* IBM 512k, RS/6000 8Mb, S/36 256k. *General Requirements:* 120Mb hard disk, printer, RS/6000 320Mb.
$5000.00-$18,000.00.
Accounting & Control System. Provides Estimating Order Entry, Job Cost, Payroll, A/P, A R & G/L & Miscellaneous Reports for Subcontractors or General Contractors.
Steppenwolff Corp.

Job Cost Estimator. Pro Software, Inc. *Operating System(s) Required:* MS-DOS. *Memory Required:* 64k.
$500.00.
System Stores Description, Cost, etc. for Common Construction Components. Produces Both Summary & Detail Estimates.
Texas Instruments, Personal Productivit.

Job Cost I. *Compatible Hardware:* Apple Macintosh Plus.
3.5" disk $1995.00.
Designed for Manufacturers Who Build Products to Order.
Advanced Data Systems, Inc.

Job Cost II. *Compatible Hardware:* Apple Macintosh Plus.
3.5" disk $6000.00.
Designed for Manufacturers Who Produce or Build Products to Order.
Advanced Data Systems, Inc.

Job Cost: JC. *Version:* 5.8. May 1993. *Language(s):* Dibol & C, COBOL. *General Requirements:* Depends on specific configuration. *Customer Support:* Full service, update service; by quotation.
VMS. DEC VAX Series, DEC Alpha AXP. disk $2500.00-$15,000.00.
Layered Package That Requires the GENERAL LEDGER SYSTEM & the ACCOUNTS PAYABLE SYSTEM As a Base. These Three Packages Work Together to Provide the User with a Complete Method of Posting Job Cost Information to Projects & Cost Centers.
Compu-Share, Inc.

Job Cost Management System. *Version:* 4.0. Dec. 1993. *Items Included:* Sample data, full manual. *Customer Support:* Free installation support (via phone) first 30 days; FAX & Bulletin Board: free, with response within 1-3 days; Phone support: 1 year, unlimited calls, 1-5pm M-F $150/year; Training is available from 3rd party.
DOS 3.3 or higher. PC compatibles/clones (2Mb). disk $399.00 (Order no.: JCMS 4.0). *Addl. software required:* Recommend an expanded memory manager; must have Advanced Accounting 4.03. *Optimal configuration:* Intel 486 or clone, DOS 5.0, 4Mb RAM, 386 MAX memory manager, Novell 3.12 network (for multiuser). *Networks supported:* Any NetBIOS compatible network; recommend Novell or LANtastic.
A Fully Featured Cost Accounting System Add-On to Advanced Accounting 4.03. Allows Creation of Estimates & Conversion of Estimates to Jobs. Tracks All Tasks & Costs. Extensive Reporting, Including Variance Analysis. Multiple Pay Rates for Employees. Can Be Run 'Standalone' or Fully Integrated with Other Accounting System Modules (e.g. Payroll). Source Code Is Available.
Business Tools Software.

Job Cost System. R. Alan Carl. 1979. *Operating System(s) Required:* CP/M, MS-DOS, PC-DOS, Pro-IV, PICK. *Memory Required:* 64-128k.
disk $595.00.
tape $2000.00.
Provides the Small Business with a Reliable Means of Tracking Actual vs. Estimated Costs & Measuring Profitability on a Job-by-Job Basis.
Automation Consultants.

Job Cost-Work-in-Process. *Version:* 2.0. 1989. *Compatible Hardware:* Altos; Compupro; Compaq; Fujitsu; Heath-Zenith; HP; IBM PC, PC XT, PC AT; NEC; Tandy. *Operating System(s) Required:* MS-DOS, PC-DOS, Concurrent DOS; Unix, Xenix; Novell & Microsoft networks. *Language(s):* C. *Memory Required:* 640k. *General Requirements:* Hard disk & 132-column printer. *Items Included:* Disks & manuals. *Customer Support:* Through VARs, support contracts available.
single-user $995.00.
multi-user $1295.00.
Unix, Xenix $1495.00.
demo disk & manual $20.00.
Compares Estimated & Actual Costs of Ongoing Jobs.
INMASS/MRP.

Job Cost: Work-in-Process. 1996. *Customer Support:* Free telephone & BBS technical support. MS/PC DOS, Concurrent DOX, Xenix; Unix. IBM PC/XT/AT & compatibles, IBM PS/2 (640k). $995.00. *Networks supported:* Novell, Lanstastic, Banyan VINES; all NETBOIS compatible.
"Job Cost/Work In Process" is a job costing tool for improving productivity in the Manufacturing environment. It adds analysis of the efficiency & accuracy of materials handling. Reports show standard & actual cost variances & budget vs. actual comparisons. It prints WIP job tickets or issue listings for work orders. This module interfaces with the INMASS/MRP complete series of modules for manufacturing companies including Bill of Materials, Inventory, Payroll & MRP/as well as all INMASS/MRP financial & manufacturing modules.
INMASS/MRP.

The Job Coster Automatic Job Estimating. *Items Included:* Bound manual. *Customer Support:* Free hotline - no time limit; 30 day limited warranty; updates are $5/disk plus S&H.
MS-DOS 2.0 or higher. IBM & compatibles (384k). disk $149.95. *Nonstandard peripherals required:* 80-column (or wider) printer.
demo disk $10.00.
Aimed at the Contractor Who Has Little Knowledge of Computers, & Little Time or Inclination to Study User's Manuals. Maintain a Master Parts List Which Contains the Descriptions & Costs of the Common Parts & Other Items. Create a Job Estimate Which Includes the Parts, Labor, Fees, Taxes, & Other Cost Items. Print a Job Summary Which Shows the Total Costs, the Prices Charged to the Customer, & the Profit Margins. Parts May Be Added/Deleted & Costs Changed at Will. Print a Professional-Looking Customer Estimate/Invoice to Be Presented to Your Customer. The Estimate or Invoice May Be Easily Modified to Reflect Changes Which Occur As the Work Progresses or Is Finished. Print a Parts Order List Which Can Be Given to Your Supplier.
Dynacomp, Inc.

The Job Coster Automatic Job Estimating. *Items Included:* Full manual. No other products required. *Customer Support:* Free telephone support - no time limit. 30 day warranty.
MS-DOS 3.2 or higher. IBM & compatibles (512k). disk $149.95.
demo disk $10.00.
User May: Maintain a Master Parts List Which Contains the Descriptions & Costs of the Common Parts & Other Items That You Use on Most of Your Jobs. Parts Are Organized into Categories, with Default Discounts/Markups for Each Category; Create a Job Estimate Which Includes the Parts, Labor, Fees, Taxes, & Other Cost Items; Print a Job Summary Which Shows the Total Costs, the Prices Charged to the Customer, & the Profit Margins. Parts May Be Added/Deleted & Costs Changed at Will; Print a Professional-Looking Customer Estimate/Invoice to Be Presented to Your Customer; Print a Parts Order List Which Can Be Given to Your Supplier.
Dynacomp, Inc.

The Job Coster: Automatic Job Estimating. 1992. *Items Included:* Detailed manuals included with all Dynacomp products. *Customer Support:* Free telephone support to original customer - no time limit; 30 day limited warranty.
MS-DOS 3.2 or higher. IBM PC & compatibles (512k). $149.95 Full Package (Add $5.00 for 3 1/2" format; 5 1/4" format standard). *Optimal configuration:* IBM, MS-DOS 2.0 or higher, 384k RAM, & an 80-column or wider printer.
demo disk $10.00.
Aimed at the Contractor Who Has Little Knowledge of Computers, & Little Time or Inclination to Study User's Manuals. With THE JOB COSTER You May: Maintain a Master Parts List Which Contains the Descriptions & Costs of the Common Parts & Other Items That You Use on Most of Your Jobs. Create a Job Estimate Which Includes the Parts, Labor, Fees, Taxes, & Other Cost Items. Print a Job Summary Which Shows the Total Costs, the Prices Charged to the Customer, & the Profit Margins. Print a Professional-Looking Customer Estimate/Invoice to Be Presented to Your Customer. Print a Parts Order List Which Can Be Given to Your Supplier.
Dynacomp, Inc.

Job Costing. *Version:* 5.8. 1978. *Compatible Hardware:* IBM PC. *Operating System(s) Required:* MS-DOS, PC-DOS 1.1, 2.0. *Language(s):* MBASIC (source code included). *Memory Required:* 128k.
PC-DOS & UNIX. disk $1000.00.
Provides Detailed Job Costs with Optional Interfaces from Payroll for Labor Costs & A/P for Material Costs. Features: Sorts, Job Cost Reports by Job, Department & Category Budget vs. Actual Costs.
CharterHouse Software Corp.

Job Costing. *Version:* 3.3. (Integrated Manufacturing & Financial System Ser.). *Compatible Hardware:* UNIBUS/VAX; IBM PC. *Operating System(s) Required:* MS-DOS, Novell, Micro/VMS, VAX/VMS, UNIX. *Language(s):* DIBOL.
MS-DOS. $750.00 single-user.
DEC PDP-11/VAX. $1500.00 multi-user.

JOB COSTING

Creates Production Information for Each Job. Calculates Estimated Costs & Quantities of Materials, Labor, & Overhead. Actual Costs Are Then Accumulated for Jobs As They Move Through Work-in-Process. Interfaces to GENERAL LEDGER to Maintain Asset Inventory Account.
Primetrack.

Job Costing. Version: 1.1-3.1, 3.4. Jun. 1982. Compatible Hardware: IBM PC. Operating System(s) Required: MS-DOS. Language(s): Compiled BASIC. Memory Required: 384k.
disk $300.00.
demo disk $50.00.
Designed to Keep Track of Costs Based on a Budget, Percent Complete & Actual Charges to Date. Allows up to 100 Cost Categories As Primary Division, 15 for a Secondary Division & 10 for Totals & Tracking Figures. Single Projects Can Be Combined to Show a Total Report for a Company's Total Activities. Daily Entries Are Entered Against Categories to Monitor PO's, Bids, Invoices, Draws & Payments. Monthly Reports Can Be Run to Compare Entries Against the Budget & Show Variances in Dollars & Percentages of Completion for Accurate Forecasting.
Rambow Enterprises.

Job Manager. Compatible Hardware: IBM PC, PC XT, PC AT. Memory Required: 256k. General Requirements: Hard disk.
disk $5475.00.
Designed for the Job Shop Manufacturer. Includes Accounts Payable, Accounts Receivable, General Ledger, Job Costing, & Payroll.
Business Computer Consultants/Merrill Street Software.

Job Planner (a Part of ABECAS). Customer Support: On site training unlimited support services for first 90 days & through subscription thereafter.
MS-DOS, PC-DOS. Contact publisher for price.
Nonstandard peripherals required: Hard disk (30Mb); 132-column printer. Networks supported: Novell, NTNX, 10-Net, Unix, Xenix, Turbo DOS (Multi-User version for all).
Allows User to Estimate or Plan As Many Jobs As Necessary. Estimates May Be Based on Pre-Defined Standard Costs. Handles Budgets/Estimates for up to 18-Month Periods. Various Reports Are Available for Both Individual Jobs & Job Summaries.
Argos Software.

Job Readiness Series. Feb. 1996. Items Included: Program manual. Customer Support: Free technical support, 90 day warranty.
Single user. System 7.1 or higher. Mac, 16 MHz rating, 68030 or better processor (LC II or higher) (5Mb, 2.5Mb free hard drive space). 3.5" disk $329.00 (ISBN 1-57204-095-5, Order no.: APM150). Nonstandard peripherals required: 256 color monitor, 13" or larger.
Lab pack. System 7.1 or higher. Mac, 16 MHz rating, 68030 or better processor (LC II or higher) (5Mb, 2.5MB free hard drive space). 3.5" disk $796.00 (ISBN 1-57204-114-5, Order no.: APM150LPK). Nonstandard peripherals required: 256 color monitor, 13" or larger.
Site license. System 7.1 or higher. Mac, 16 MHz rating, 680301 or better processor (LC II or higher) (5Mb, 2.5Mb free hard drive space). 3.5" disk $1596.00 (ISBN 1-57204-116-1, Order no.: APM150SITE). Nonstandard peripherals required: 256 color monitor, 13" or larger.
Single user. Windows 3.1 or higher. IBM 286 (8Mb). disk $329.00 (ISBN 1-57204-096-3). Nonstandard peripherals required: 256 color monitor, mouse, sound card. Addl. software required: SVGA graphics.
Lab pack. Windows 3.1 or higher. IBM 286 (8Mb). disk $796.00 (ISBN 1-57204-115-3, Order no.: WIN150LPK). Nonstandard peripherals required: 256 color monitor, mouse, sound card. Addl. software required: SVGA graphics.
Site license. Windows 3.1 or higher. IBM 286 (8Mb). disk $1596.00 (ISBN 1-57204-117-X, Order no.: WIN150SITE). Nonstandard peripherals required: 256 color monitor, mouse, sound card. Addl. software required: SVGA graphics.
The Job Readiness Series consists of four programs - "Successful Job Interviewing", "Job Attitudes:" "Assessment & Improvement," "Filling Out Job Applications", & "Resumes Made Easy." The goal of these programs is to familiarize the student with the elements of a successful job search. Successful Job Interviewing shows students how to conduct themselves properly during an interview. Job Attitudes Assessment & Improvement discusses attitudes appropriate to the vast majority of employment situations. Filling Out Job Applications takes the student through the process of filling out a job application form. Resumes Made Easy explains the different parts of the resume & why resumes are necessary.
Lawrence Productions, Inc.

Job Shop/Manufacturing.
MS-DOS, Unix, Xenix (512k). IBM PC, PC XT, PC AT & Compatible mini/micros. contact publisher for price.
Integrated Shop Control System Includes Estimating, Bill of Materials, Work-in-Process, etc. Options Include Multi-State Payroll & Tracking of up to 6 Cost Centers.
Universal Data Research, Inc.

Job Success Series. (Job Success Ser.).
single user. Windows 3.1 or higher. IBM 386 or higher (8Mb). disk $329.00 (ISBN 1-57204-096-3, Order no.: WIN450). Nonstandard peripherals required: 256 color monitor, sound card, mouse. Addl. software required: SVGA graphics.
Lab pack. Windows 3.1 or higher. IBM 386 or higher (8Mb). disk $796.00 (ISBN 1-57204-115-3, Order no.: WIN450LPK). Nonstandard peripherals required: 256 color monitor, sound card, mouse. Addl. software required: SVGA graphics.
site license. Windows 3.1 or higher. IBM 386 or higher (8Mb). disk $1596.00 (ISBN 1-57204-117-X, Order no.: WIN450SITE). Nonstandard peripherals required: 256 color monitor, sound card, mouse. Addl. software required: SVGA graphics.
single user. System 7.1 or higher. Mac, 16 MHz rating, 68030 or better processor (LC II or higher) (5Mb). 3.5" disk $329.00 (ISBN 1-57204-095-5). Nonstandard peripherals required: 256 color monitor, sound card, mouse.
Lab pack. System 7.1 or higher. MAC, 16 MHz rating, 68030 or better processor (LC II or higher) (5Mb). 3.5" disk $796.00 (ISBN 1-57204-114-5). Nonstandard peripherals required: 256 color monitor, sound card, mouse.
Site license. System 7.1 or higher. MAC, 16 MHz rating, 68030 or better processor (LC II or higher) (5Mb). 3.5" disk $1596.00 (ISBN 1-57204-116-1). Nonstandard peripherals required: 256 color monitor, sound card, mouse.
The Job Success Series consists of four programs, "First Days on the Job," "Your Personal Habits," Your Work Habits," & "Looking Good." The goal of these programs is to make the student more comfortable when they do land that first job. First Days on the Job covers filling out forms, introductions, training programs, where to park, manners & other topics. Your Personal Habits guides the students through personal habits that make people effective on their job. Topics include punctuality, hygiene & getting along with others. Your Work Habits emphasizes the importance of dependability & being a team player. Looking Good helps students gain valuable insights into dressing right for a variety of entry-level jobs.
Lawrence Productions, Inc.

Job Tracker. Items Included: Manual.
IBM PC & compatibles (256k). contact publisher for price.
System Designed to Track Time & Billing Information for Service Firms. Collect Hours Worked on a Job by Specific Employees, Broken Down by Client Task & Date. Reimbursement Charges Are Also Maintained by System.
Management Systems, Inc.

Jobmaster. Compatible Hardware: IBM PC. Memory Required: 128k.
disk $99.95.
Designed for Supervisors, Managers & Engineers Who Are Responsible for Managing Small Production & Assembly Programs.
Dynacomp, Inc.

JobSketch. Version: 2.0. Aug. 1991. Compatible Hardware: IBM PC & compatibles, Macintosh. Items Included: Manual & diskette. Customer Support: Free installation & technical support: limited warranty, call JIAN 415-941-9191.
$159.00. Addl. software required: Word Processor for PC's: PCWrite, Microsoft Word, etc. (Text comes in an ASCII file format). For Macintosh: MacWrite 4.5 or higher or Microsoft Word 3.01 compatible.
Addl. software required: Word Processor: MacWrite 4.5 or higher or Microsoft Word 3.01 compatible.
Provides 255 Job Descriptions on Diskette. Define Employees' Positions & Available Positions by Simply Editing the Prewritten Descriptions to Clarify Specifically the Jobs in the Company.
JIAN Tools for Sales.

JobTime Plus: Production Scheduling System. Version: 2.xx. Paul Wyman. Oct. 1986. Compatible Hardware: IBM PC, PC XT, PC AT, PS/2, 386, 486. Operating System(s) Required: PC-DOS, MS-DOS. Memory Required: 1000k. General Requirements: Hard disk, printer. Items Included: Updates for one year. Customer Support: Phone support, remote modem support, on-site consulting available.
Contact publisher for price (Order no.: JTP). Production Scheduling System. This Established Finite Capacity Scheduling System Is Simulation-Based. Experience Includes Installations with Seven Years of Operating History & a Large & Diverse User Base. JTP Is Used to Schedule Applications Ranging from Nuclear Fuel Production to Small Job Shops. JTP Includes Many Advanced Features, Some of Which Are: Multi-Color 3D Graphics to Assist in Decision Making (i.e. Variable Capacity over Time vs. Corresponding Queue in Work Centers), User-Defined Reporting, Automatic JiT Calculation of All Jobs, Mouse Controlled Scheduling Board, 14 Different Scheduling Rules Plus Option of User-Defined Rule, Minimization of Changeover (Setup). JTP Operates Stand Alone & Is Easy to Interface with Other Hardware/Software Systems.
JobTime Systems, Inc.

Jockey Competition Option Module. Items Included: Manual, catalog, update card. Customer Support: Always free over the phone, disks replaced free for first 30 days, disks

replaced for $10.00 after 30 days.
Commodore 64, 128. $14.95.
Amiga 500, 1000, 2000 (512k). $14.95.
Choose Which Horses You'll Ride to Victory Against 14 Computer Opponents. Stats Are Continuously Updated & Maintained. Works with All TRACK Disks.
SportTime Computer Software.

Joe Blade. *Customer Support:* Back up disks available.
Amiga (512k). $14.95.
Atari ST (512k). $14.95.
Mission: Rescue Six World Leaders Being Held Hostage by Terrorist Leader Crax Bloodfinger. Fight Perilous Dangers, Decode Six Explosive Bombs, Collect Cell Keys, Ammo, & Food for Survival. Color Graphics.
DigiTek Software.

Joe Spreadsheet Statistical. *Compatible Hardware:* IBM PC & compatibles; Macintosh. *Items Included:* Spiral bound manual featuring six tutorials.
Contact publisher for price.
Commercial Quality Financial Spreadsheet Which Is a LOTUS Work-a-Like. 8190 Rows & 256 Columns. Statistical Package Includes 30 Statistical @ Functions & a Set of Commands That Will Generate ANOVA, Descriptive & Rank Statistics, Hypothesis, & Non-Parametric Tests. Built-In Cell Annotator Allows "Post-It" Notes To Be Added To Cells & To Cell Ranges.
Dryden Pr.

Joey Software for Dental Office Management. *Version:* 3.3. *Compatible Hardware:* Apple Macintosh, Macintosh Plus, SE, SE/30, II, IIx & IIcx. *General Requirements:* Hard disk, ImageWriter. *Items Included:* Reference manual. *Customer Support:* Toll-free telephone, first 6 months support free.
$3295.00 single user; $4295.00 multi-user.
Dental Office Management.
CompuDent, Inc.

John C Dvorak's PC Crash Course & Survival Guide. Peter Harrison et al. Mar. 1990. *Items Included:* 150-lesson, self-paced typing tutor, directory listing program, MODEM simulation program, self-mastering test, exercises. *Customer Support:* Unlimited free technical telephone/FAX support.
DOS 2.0 or higher. IBM PC & compatibles (256k). 3.5" or 5.25" disk $34.95 (ISBN 1-878322-06-0, Order no.: DVCC-3 (3.5" DISK); DVCC-5 (5.25" DISK)). *Optimal configuration:* IBM-PC, Monitor, keyboard, 256k RAM, 2 floppy disk drives. *Networks supported:* NETBIOS compatible LANs.
Beginner's Introduction to DOS, Computers, & Computing. It Teaches the User How to Buy, Use & Live in Harmony with IBM PC, XT, AT & PS/2, Computers Plus Compatibles. Includes a Chapter on the History of Computers, Starting & Operating a Computer, How to Access Electronic Databases, Helpful Advice on Where to Buy Computers & Peripherals, a List of Trade Words & Jargon with Definitions.
Scandinavian PC Systems, Inc.

John Madden Football. Robin Antonick & John Madden. Mar. 1989. *Items Included:* Manual or ref card. *Customer Support:* Customer hint hotline (415) 572-9560.
Apple II (64k). $49.95 (Order no.: 1397).
 Optimal configuration: Joystick, keyboard.
IBM. disk $49.95.
Real Players, Action, Philosophy, Plays, Coaching Decisions, & Statistical Models.
Electronic Arts.

Jokes & Quotes. Michael L. Wester. Jan. 1995. *Customer Support:* Telephone support, 30 day money back guarantee.
DOS 3.1 or higher. IBM & compatibles (384k). Contact publisher for price (ISBN 1-886770-02-6). *Optimal configuration:* EGA & mouse recommended.
A Collection of over 10,000 Jokes & Quotes on CD-ROM. No Sexually Explicit or Vulgar Material. Over 60 Categories. Runs from the CD, No Installation.
Neon Publishing.

Jonathan Pond's Personal Financial Planner. Jonathan Pond. Feb. 1994. *Items Included:* On-line doc/help. *Customer Support:* No charge for support. Toll number 617-225-2136, calls received after working hours will be returned within 12 hrs. Support questions can be asked/answered on Compuserve.
MS Windows 3.1 or higher. IBM compatible 386 or higher, 4Mb free hard disk, 256 color SVGA/VGA monitor or higher (4Mb). disk $39.95 (ISBN 1-57317-001-1, Order no.: V-POND-0002). *Optimal configuration:* 8Mb RAM, 486 machine, Windows 3.1 running enhanced mode, VESA local bus.
Creates a Customized Financial Plan by Analyzing User's Personal Data Entererd into Interactive Worksheets. The Mixture of Pond's Expert Advice & Software Technology Gives Users the Knowledge & Tools to Construct a Lifetime Financial Plan. Issues Discussed Include Spending, Saving, Budgeting, Borrowing, Record Keeping, & More.
Vertigo Development Group.

Jonathan Pond's Personal Financial Planner. Jonathan Pond. Feb. 1994. *Items Included:* On-line doc/help. *Customer Support:* No charge for support, toll free number - 800-942-2848, toll number 617-225-2136, calls received after working hours will be returned in 12 hrs. Support questions can be asked on Compuserve.
MS Windows 3.1 or higher. IBM compatible 386 or higher, 4Mb free hard disk, 256 color SVGA/VGA monitor or higher (4Mb). CD-ROM disk $49.95 (ISBN 1-57317-002-X, Order no.: V-POND-0003). *Nonstandard peripherals required:* MPC compatible CD-ROM drive, sound board & speakers. *Optimal configuration:* 8Mb RAM, 486 machine, Windows 3.1 running enhanced mode, VESA local bus.
Creates a Customized Financial Plan by Analyzing User's Personal Data Entered into Interactive Worksheets. The Mixture of Interactive Software, Video, Text, & Sound Brings Mr. Pond & His Expertise Alive & Gives Users the Knowledge & Tools to Construct a Lifetime Financial Plan. Issues Discussed Include Spending, Saving, Budgeting, Borrowing, Record Keeping, & More.
Vertigo Development Group.

Jones Multimedia Encyclopedia: Your Guide to the Information Superhighway. Oct. 1995. *Customer Support:* Free 800 number.
Windows; Macintosh. CD-ROM disk Contact publisher for price. *Nonstandard peripherals required:* CD-ROM drive.
The First Encyclopedia on the Converging Industries of the Superhighway. The Encyclopedia Details the Industries, Technologies & People Responsible for Shaping Today's Infrastructure. Video, Audio, Illustrations, Diagrams, Animation, Articles & Essays Are Used to Bring the Information Superhighway to Life in a Comprehensive & Compelling Manner.
Jones Interactive Systems, Inc.

Jot It Down. *Compatible Hardware:* IBM PC & compatibles, PS/2. *Operating System(s) Required:* PC-DOS 2.1 or higher. *Memory Required:* 128k. *General Requirements:* Lotus 1-2-3, Symphony & compatible spreadsheets. $49.95.
Terminate & Stay Resident Utility That Keeps Track of Assumptions Behind Entries in Spreadsheet Cells. Up to 200 Notes per Spreadsheet by Date, Formula Value, or Label Can Be Saved.
Brady Computer Bks.

Journey to the Lair. Paul Benson. Mar. 1987. *Compatible Hardware:* Atari ST. *General Requirements:* Dragon's Lair video disc, laser disk player, special cable.
Dragon's Lair laser disk $29.95 (ISBN 0-923213-61-9).
video laser cable $29.95.
complete package $99.95 (Order no.: AT-JOU).
3.5" disk Journey to the Lair program $49.95.
Adapted from the Arcade Game "Dragon's Lair". You'll Help Dirk the Daring Save Princess Daphne.
MichTron, Inc.

Journey to the Planets. *Items Included:* Manual, registration card, flier describing all our titles, occasional promotional offers. *Customer Support:* Free telephone technical support.
DOS & Microsoft Windows 3.1. 12 MHz 80386SX. CD-ROM disk Contact publisher for price (ISBN 1-884014-20-8). *Nonstandard peripherals required:* MPC compatible. CD-ROM drive (680Mb) SVGA display, audio board, mouse, 486 DX processor. *Addl. software required:* Microsoft CD-ROM Extensions v.2.2.
Macintosh System 6.05. Color Macintosh (256 colors) (3.5Mb). CD-ROM disk Contact publisher for price (ISBN 1-884014-32-1). *Optimal configuration:* Single speed CD-ROM, 13" color monitor, 8 Mb RAM.
A Visual Showcase of the Solar System. Narrated Presentations of Diagrams, Animations, Hundreds of Photographs & Planetary Fly Overs Let You Explore the Surface of Mars & Other Planets.
Multicom Publishing, Inc.

Joust. *Compatible Hardware:* Atari XL/XE, ST.
Atari XL/XE. ROM cartridge $19.95 (Order no.: RX8044).
Atari ST. 3.5" disk $29.95 (Order no.: DS5026).
Atari Corp.

JoyMouse. Donald Roy. *Compatible Hardware:* IBM PC, PCjr, PC XT, PC AT, Portable PC. *Operating System(s) Required:* PC-DOS 2.00, 2.10, 3.00, 3.10. *Memory Required:* 64k. *General Requirements:* IBM Display, joystick.
disk $14.95 (Order no.: 6276606).
Allows a Joystick Connected to an IBM Game Control Adapter to Be Used for Cursor Movement. User Can Assign One of Nine Different Speeds for Cursor Movement, Choose One Speed for Either Horizontal or Vertical Movement, Assign Key Functions to Joystick Buttons, Redefine Joystick Buttons for Different Programs, etc.
Personally Developed Software, Inc.

Juggler. *Version:* 1.1. Jan. 1991. *Items Included:* Manual. *Customer Support:* 2 free hours; $60.00 per hour thereafter.
MS-DOS. IBM PC, XT AT, OS/2 & compatibles (640k). disk $99.00. *Networks supported:* Novell.
Data Manipulation Software That Will: Match, Merge & Sort ASCII or Column Binary Data Files; Randomize Records in Data Files; Sort Data by Picking Every Fourth Number Without

Duplication & Create a New File; Exchange Data Between Two Sets of Columns on the Same line of Data.
Analytical Computer Service, Inc.

The Juggler. Timothy Purves. Jan. 1988. *Compatible Hardware:* Atari ST. *Memory Required:* 512k.
3.5" disk $49.95.
Enables Users to Keep Up to 7 GEM Applications Resident in Memory. Recognizes Files with .PRG (Program), .TOS (Tramiel Operating System), & .TTP (TOS Takes Parameters) Extensions. Users can Switch Between .PRG Programs While They Are Running; .TOS & .TTP Applications Are Run to Completion Before any Action Can Be Taken.
MichTron, Inc.

Julie of the Wolves. International Education Staff & Jean C. George. Apr. 1996. *Items Included:* Program manual. *Customer Support:* Free technical support, 90 day warranty.
School ver.. System 7.1 or higher. Macintosh (4Mb). 3.5" disk contact publisher for price (ISBN 1-57204-237-0). *Nonstandard peripherals required:* 256 color monitor, hard drive, printer.
Lab pack. System 7.1 or higher. Macintosh (4Mb). 3.5" disk contact publisher for price (ISBN 1-57204-213-3). *Nonstandard peripherals required:* 256 color monitor, hard drive, printer.
Site license. System 7.1 or higher. Macintosh (4Mb). 3.5" disk contact publisher for price (ISBN 1-57204-238-9). *Nonstandard peripherals required:* 256 color monitor, hard drive, printer.
School ver.. Windows 3.1 or higher. IBM/Tandy & 100% compatibles (4Mb). disk contact publisher for price (ISBN 1-57204-214-1). *Nonstandard peripherals required:* VGA or SVGA 640 x 480 resolution (256), mouse, hard drive, sound device.
Lab pack. Windows 3.1 or higher. IBM/Tandy & 100 compatibles (4Mb). disk contact publisher for price (ISBN 1-57204-239-7). *Nonstandard peripherals required:* VGA or SVGA 640 x 480 resolution (256), mouse, hard drive, sound device.
Site license. Windows 3.1 or higher. disk contact publisher for price (ISBN 1-57204-215-X). *Nonstandard peripherals required:* VGA or SVGA 640 x 480 resolution (256), mouse, hard drive, sound device.
This companion for young adult literature is ideal for students who don't know how to start that book report, or give that needed summary. Gentle prompts throughout the guide section of the program include Warm-up Connections, Thinking about Plot, Quoting & Noting, Keeping a Journal, If I Were———' Responding to Questions, Using Quotations, Taking a Personal View, Write to Others, & Write a Sequel.
Lawrence Productions, Inc.

Julius Erving & Larry Bird Go One-on-One.
Compatible Hardware: Apple II, IIe, Macintosh; Atari 400, 800, 1200XL; Commodore 64, Amiga; IBM PC, PCjr, PC XT.
Apple, Atari, Commodore 64, IBM. disk $14.95. Amiga, Macintosh. 3.5" disk $19.95.
Electronic Arts.

Jumblezzz. 1987-1991. *Items Included:* Disk(s), user's guide, poster, coloring book, warranty card, swap coupon. *Customer Support:* 90 day unlimited warranty; 800 toll free number, 800-221-7911, 8:00 a.m.-5:00 p.m. Arizona time; Updates $10.
3.5" disk $49.95.
MS-DOS. IBM, Tandy, MS-DOS compatible (128k). disk $49.99 (ISBN 1-55772-068-1, Order no.: 6101). *Nonstandard peripherals required:* VGA or CGA card. *Optimal configuration:* 128k, color monitor, VGA card. *Networks supported:* Velan, Novell, Digicard.
DOS. Apple II, Apple IIe, Apple IIGS, Apple II Plus (48k). disk $49.99 (ISBN 0-918017-73-4, Order no.: 6100). *Optimal configuration:* Apple II, printer, color monitor, 48k. *Networks supported:* Digicard.
The Award Winning Word Attack Skills Program, Jumblezzz, Is a Fun Puzzle Game for Playing & Creating Scrambled Word Puzzles. Players Use the 150 Puzzle Library, with 50 Puzzles Each on 3 Difficulty Levels, to Practice Spelling Words. With CHALLENGE UPGRADE, Wordzzzearch Can Be Customized to Fit Individual Needs of Players. Ages 9 to Adult.
Mindplay.

Jump Jet. Oct. 1992. *Items Included:* Manual. *Customer Support:* Free customer service, 1-410-771-1151, Ext. 350.
80286, VGA, Adlib/Roland/Sound Blaster, hard disk required, Joystick, DOS 3.0 or higher. IBM AT, PS/2 & most compatibles (640k). disk $59.95 (ISBN 1-55884-224-1). *Optimal configuration:* 286, 16MHz, hard disk, 1Mb RAM, DOS 5.0, VGA, Joystick, sound card.
Complete Multiple Ground Attack & Close Air Support Missions While Mastering the Unique Flight Characteristics of the Harrier Aircraft. Unique Object Evolution System Enables Previously Destroyed Targets to Be Rebuilt. New Targets & Mission Assignments During Flight As Part of Dynamic Battlefield Environment.
MicroProse Software.

Jump Start Kindergarten.
MS-DOS 3.1 or higher, Windows. 386 processor or higher (640k). CD-ROM disk $54.95 (Order no.: R1325). *Nonstandard peripherals required:* CD-ROM drive. *Optimal configuration:* 386 processor or higher, MS-DOS 3.1 or higher, 20Mb hard drive, mouse, external speakers or headphones (with sound card) that are Sound Blaster compatible, VGA graphics & adapter, VGA color monitor.
This Complete, Fun, Curriculum-Based Program Teaches Math, Reading & Language Skills to Prepare Children for School. Inspire Children's Creativity with Activities, Games & Puzzles. Progress Is Recorded & Level of Difficulty Adapts to the Child's Current Learning Level (Ages 4-6).
Library Video Co.

Jumpsuit Color Program: Computerized Color Pattern Selection. *Version:* 1.1. Gary Peek. Feb. 1993. *Items Included:* Fabric samples, manual. *Customer Support:* Unlimited warranty, free telephone support.
MS-DOS. IBM (640k). disk $14.95 (ISBN 0-915516-88-8, Order no.: JSCOLOR). *Optimal configuration:* EGA or VGA color monitor.
Skydiving Jumpsuit Color Combinations May Be Viewed & Compared on the Screen. This Program Replaces Paper & Color Pencils.
Para Publishing.

Jungle Hunt. *Compatible Hardware:* Atari XL/XE. ROM cartridge $19.95 (Order no.: RX8049). Atari Corp.

Junior Encyclopedias: The Farm.
MS-DOS 5.0 or higher, Windows 3.1 or higher. 386 processor or higher (4Mb). CD-ROM disk $49.95 (Order no.: R1327). *Nonstandard peripherals required:* CD-ROM drive. *Optimal configuration:* 386 processor operating at 16MHz or higher, MS-DOS 5.0 or higher, Windows 3.1 or higher, 30Mb hard drive, mouse, VGA graphic adapter & VGA color monitor (SVGA recommended), 4Mb RAM, external speakers or headphones (with sound card) that are Sound Blaster compatible.
Children Can Visit the Farm for a Thrilling Adventure with First-Hand Opportunities for Discovery. Explore over 30 Places on a Farm with More Than 215 Animals, Plants, Tools & Machines That Are Defined & Explained in Detail.
Library Video Co.

Junior High Mathematics. 1992. *Items Included:* Detailed manuals are included with all DYNACOMP products. *Customer Support:* Free telephone support to original customer - no time limit; 30 day limited warranty.
MS-DOS 3.2 or higher. IBM PC & compatibles (512k). $179.95 (Add $5.00 for 3 1/2" format; 5 1/4" format standard).
Magic Squares (3 x 3); Multiplication; Division; Modular Arithmetic; Proportion Problems; Percentage Problems; Addition of Fractions; Subtraction of Fractions; Multiplication of Fractions; Division of Fractions; Mode, Median, & Mean; Bar Graph Analysis; Decimals I; Deicmals II; Verbal Problems.
Dynacomp, Inc.

Jupiter Mission 1999. Scott Lamb. Mar. 1984. *Compatible Hardware:* Commodore 64/128. *Language(s):* Assembly, BASIC. *General Requirements:* Joystick.
disk $35.00 (Order no.: 46355).
On Board the Space Beagle, Investigate the Source & Meaning of Radio Signals. You Must Deal with Meteor Showers, Science Probes, Alien Artifacts, & Navigating Your Spacecraft into a Rendezvous with Whatever Is Out There Beyond Jupiter.
Avalon Hill Game Co., The Microcomputer Games Div.

Jury Trial II. 1983. *Compatible Hardware:* Apple II, Commodore 64, IBM PC. *Operating System(s) Required:* Apple DOS 3.3, PC-DOS. *Memory Required:* 64k.
disk $49.00.
Murderers, Robbers, Kidnappers, Muggers, & Some Accused of Crimes Too Heinous to Mention, Are All Awaiting Trial on a Busy Court Docket. The Defendant Is Always Innocent until Proven Guilty, but the Jurors Vacillate Back & Forth As You & Your Opponent Examine & Cross-Examine Each Witness. Throughout the Trial the Computer Is the Judge-- Assigning Cases, Controlling the Proceedings, Ruling on Objections, Examining Evidence, & Passing Sentence, or Freeing the Defendant When the Verdict Is Read by the Jury Foreman. Justice Prevails When You Outwit Your Opponent with Devastating Courtroom Strategy, & the Jury Renders a Verdict in Your Favor, but Watchout - Your Opponent Can Appeal to a Higher Court & Try Again.
Navic Software.

Just Enough Pascal. *General Requirements:* Think Pascal; hard disk drive recommended. *Items Included:* 1 disk, 1 manual. *Customer Support:* (408) 372-8100.
Macintosh Plus or higher. 3.5" disk $75.00.
Add-On Learning Tool for Think Pascal Programming Environment.
Symantec Corp.

Just Grandma & Me. (Living Book Ser.). Mercer Mayer.
MS-DOS 5.0 or higher, Windows 3.1 or higher. 386 processor or higher (4Mb). CD-ROM disk $49.95 (Order no.: R1044). *Nonstandard peripherals required:* CD-ROM drive. *Optimal configuration:* 386 processor operating at 16MHz or higher, MS-DOS 5.0 or higher, Windows 3.1 or higher, 30Mb hard drive, mouse, VGA graphic adapter & VGA color monitor (SVGA recommended), 4Mb RAM,

TITLE INDEX

external speakers or headphones (with sound card) that are Sound Blaster compatible. Macintosh (4Mb). (Order no.: R1043). *Nonstandard peripherals required:* 14" color monitor or larger, CD-ROM drive. $35.00 Jewel case only (Order no.: R1044J). *Highly Interactive Animated Stories for Children That Have Hundreds of Beautiful Animations & Have Received Countless Awards. In English, Spanish & Japanese (Ages 3-8).*
Library Video Co.

JustEdit. Dave McManigal. *Compatible Hardware:* IBM PC, PCjr, PC XT, PC AT, Portable PC. *Operating System(s) Required:* PC-DOS 2.00, 2.10, 3.00, 3.10. *Memory Required:* 128k. *General Requirements:* IBM Matrix Printer optional.
disk $19.95 (Order no.: 6276590).
Data Manager That Can Be Used for Programming, Text Entry, etc. Serves As a Movable Window into the Text File. Each Line of Text Is Shown in Its Entirety So There Is No Need for Horizontal Scrolling. Vertical Scrolling Occurs on Text Line Boundaries under User's Direct Control. New or Revised Data Typed Anywhere on the Screen Is Used to Update the File Copy in Memory. Text Processing Commands Include: Insert, Delete, Split & Join Lines, Rename Files, & Load a New File at a Referenced Line. Also Allows Repeat, Search, & Replace Text Using the Program's Prefix/Suffix/Word-Bounded Operations. Files up to 64k Long Can Be Edited.
Personally Developed Software, Inc.

Jutland. May 1993. *Customer Support:* Free phone-in assistance with game-playing & technical questions.
MS-DOS 5.0. IBM PC compatible 386SX, 386DX, 486 (570k). CD-ROM disk $79.95. *Nonstandard peripherals required:* Supports 256 color VGA or VESA-compatible SVGA video cards. *Optimal configuration:* 640k RAM, 2Mb, EMS, SoundBlaster, 1Mb SVGA Video Card.
CD-ROM World War I Naval Simulation Multimedia Game with Digital Voice, Digital Video, High Degree of Historical Accuracy, Historical Manual & On-Line Help in Electronic Book Form on the CD. Studio Quality Music & Sound Effects.

Juvenile & Adult Probation Parole System. Version: 1.4. (Criminal Justice Ser.). Palladium Software Corp. Sep. 1992. *Language(s):* Level 5.
contact publisher for price.
Designed to Manage Juveniles & Adults, Provides Profile, Scheduling, & Accounting Procedures & Reports Vital to Tracking Clients on Release. A Comprehensive Case Management Program.
Ellington Duval, Inc.

K-Graph3. KUMA. Jun. 1989.
TOS (512k). Atari ST. disk $79.95.
Serves User's Graphic Presentation Needs & Assists in Decoding Masses of Numbers into Clear Visual Presentations.
MichTron, Inc.

K-TALK FileDISPATCHER: Data Aquisition & Gateway. Apr. 1986. *Compatible Hardware:* IBM PC, PC XT, PC AT. *Operating System(s) Required:* PC-DOS. *Memory Required:* 128k.
disk $400.00 (Order no.: FD100).
Designed to Transfer Files in the Background While a User Data Acquisition Program Runs in the Foreground. Both Programs Can Run Unattended. Also Allows a Microcomputer to Serve As a Gateway Between a Calling Computer & a Mainframe. Provides Error Checking/Error Correcting Using Cycle Redundancy Check; Remote Deletion & Renaming of Files; & Automatic Selection of Software Baud Rate on Auto Answer.
K-Talk Communications.

K-TALK FullFeatured. Version: 3.00. Apr. 1986. *Compatible Hardware:* IBM PC, PC XT, PC AT. *Operating System(s) Required:* PC-DOS. *Memory Required:* 128k. *General Requirements:* Modem.
disk $249.00 (Order no.: FF300).
Permits the Remote Transfer of Files from One Microcomputer to Another, in Attended or Unattended Modes, While in the Foreground or the Background; the Remote Transfer of Files with a Mainframe Using an Attended Microcomputer; & the Simultaneous Execution of a Program at Two Sites with Either Keyboard Controlling Both Sites. Features Include: Terminal Emulation, Automatic Protocol Switching; Support of Wild Cards, Ability to Send Messages During File Transfer, Automatic Selection of Software Baud Rate on Auto Answer, Sliding Window Protocol.
K-Talk Communications.

Kaa's Hunting. Feb. 1995. *Items Included:* CD-ROM booklet. *Customer Support:* Free technical support via phone as of release date. MPC/Windows. 386.25 or higher IBM compatible (4Mb). CD-ROM disk $29.95 (ISBN 1-885784-15-5, Order no.: 1219). *Optimal configuration:* MPC CD-ROM player, S-VGA graphics card (640x480x256 colors) with compatible monitor, MPC compliant sound card, mouse, Windows 3.1.
The Second of the Jungle Book Stories by Author Rudyard Kipling Tells More of the Adventures of the Boy Raised by Wolves. Follow Mowgli As He Befriends the Mischievous Bandarlog, the Monkey People. Watch His True Friends Enlist the Help of Kaa, the Great Rock Python, to Save Him from the People Without Honor.
Technology Dynamics Corp.

Kaboom, Jr. Sep. 1995. *Customer Support:* Telephone support - free (except phone charge). Windows 3.1. IBM & compatibles (386 DX-20) (4Mb). CD-ROM disk $12.99 (ISBN 1-57594-023-X). *Nonstandard peripherals required:* 2x CD-ROM player, Sound Card, VGA monitor. *Optimal configuration:* 486 SX-33.
Bring Your Computer to Life with Incredible Vivid Sound Effects.
Kidsoft, Inc.

Kaboom, Jr. Sep. 1995. *Customer Support:* Telephone support - free (except phone charge). Windows 3.1. IBM & compatibles (386 DX-20) (4Mb). CD-ROM disk $12.99 (ISBN 1-57594-062-0). *Nonstandard peripherals required:* 2x CD-ROM player, Sound Card, VGA monitor. *Optimal configuration:* 486 SX-33.
Bring Your Computer to Life with Incredibly Vivid Sound Effects. Blister Pack Jewel Case.
Kidsoft, Inc.

KaleidaGraph. Version: 3.0. Abelbeck Software Staff. 1993. *Items Included:* Documentation (Learning Guide & Reference Manual) & disks. *Customer Support:* Free to registered end-users 610-779-0522, fax 610-370-0548, Internet tech syynergy.com.
Macintosh System 6.0.5 & higher including 7.5. Macintosh 68k, Power Macintosh (1200k). $249.00 Retail - Educational pricing available (Order no.: SYNMAC333). *Optimal configuration:* 2Mb free RAM, 2Mb free on hard drive. *Networks supported:* Appleshare.
A Thoughtfully Designed Graphing Tool Providing Powerful Visual Displays & Analysis of Quantitative Information. Sixteen Graph Structures Are Provided for Plotting Large Amounts of Data (up to 32000 Points per Column) Using 20 Variables per Plot with Precise, Yet Flexible Control of Statistical Functions & Data Display Elements. Other Features Include Extensive Curve Fitting, Independent Upper & Lower Error Bars, 64 Colors on an Editable Palette & a Flexible Data Import Facility.
Synergy Software.

KANJI MOMENTS

Kaleidoscope. David M. Chess. *Compatible Hardware:* IBM PC, PCjr, PC XT, PC AT, Portable PC, 3270 PC with IBM Color Display. *Operating System(s) Required:* PC-DOS 1.10, 2.00, 2.10, 3.00, 3.10. *Memory Required:* 128k.
disk $14.95 (Order no.: 6276519).
Produces a Constantly Changing Pattern of Colorful Designs. User Can Control the Images by Changing the Pace or Freezing the Designs on the Screen. User Can Produce Original Designs by Altering the Parameters of the Program. Patterns Can Be Saved on Diskette.
Personally Developed Software, Inc.

Kalman Filtering Software. Version: 2. Dec. 1984. *Compatible Hardware:* IBM PC, PC AT. *Operating System(s) Required:* PC-DOS/MS-DOS 2.0 or higher. *Language(s):* QUICK BASIC-compiled. *Memory Required:* 128k. *General Requirements:* 2 disk drives.
disk $210.00 (ISBN 0-911575-31-6, Order no.: S-K2).
Design & Simulate Kalman Filters & Study Performance vs. Parameter Trade-Offs. Capabilities Include Ability to Design & Run a Kalman Filter/Smoother with Specified Gains Constant or Propagated on Simulated Observation Data, or on Actual Data for Specified Data Model, & Display Results. Test Noise Whiteness/Test Observability/Controllability/Plot Transfer Functions.
Optimization Software, Inc.

Kampfgruppe. Gary Grigsby. 1985. *Compatible Hardware:* Apple II, II+, IIe, IIc; Atari 400, 800, 1200; Commodore 64, Amiga; IBM. *Language(s):* BASIC, Machine. *Memory Required:* 48k.
$59.95.
Warfare Game in Which Opposing Regiment-Sized Forces Battle in Historical or Play-Created Scenarios. Each Unit Represents a Platoon of Tanks, Infantry, or Guns, & Resolves Combat down to Each Tank, Gun & Infantryman. Over 45 Different Vehicles Are Included, Each Rated for Front & Back Armor, Silhouette Size, Speed, Number of Machine Guns, Gun Range, Gun Penetration, Gun Accuracy, & Shell Size. Weapon Types Include: Tanks, Tank Destroyers, Assault Guns, Self-Propelled Artillery, Armored Cars, Halftracks, Trucks, Anti-Tank Guns, Howitzers, Mortars, Machine Guns, Field Artillery, Anti-Tank Rifles, Panzerfausts, Flamethrowers, Submachine Guns, & Rifles.
Strategic Simulations, Inc.

Kanji Moments. Oct. 1995. *Items Included:* One exercise book, one installation guide, & one registration card. *Customer Support:* 30 day money-back guarantee & free technical support. Microsoft Windows 3.1 or higher. IBM PC or compatibles (4Mb). CD-ROM disk $79.00 (ISBN 1-883653-09-6). *Nonstandard peripherals required:* Multimedia PC with CD-ROM drive (double-speed or higher) & SoundBlaster compatible soundcard. *Networks supported:* Any Local Area Network (LAN) software such as Novell Netware Lite or Personal Netware.
Multimedia Windows Based Program for the PC on CD-ROM for Learning Kanji. Consist of Sounds, Videos, Colorful Graphics & Animation.
BayWare, Inc.

Kanji Moments, Vol. 1. Nov. 1992. *Items Included:* 1 exercise book (spiral wrap bound), 1 installation guide (cardstock), 1 registration card. *Customer Support:* Free technical support. Microsoft Windows 3.1. IBM PC & compatibles (4Mb). CD-ROM disk $79.00 (ISBN 1-883653-05-3). *Nonstandard peripherals required:* Any Multimedia for the PC (MPC) compatible soundcards (Sound Blaster compatible).

503

Kanji Moments

Networks supported: Any (LAN) Local Area Network software such as Novell Netware Lite. *MultiMedia Windows Based for the PC on CD-ROM for Learning Kanji. Consists of Sound, Colorful Graphics, Animation.*
Bayware, Inc.

Kanji Moments, Vol. 1. Dec. 1995. *Items Included:* 1 exercise book (spiral wrap bound), installation guide, reg. card. *Customer Support:* Free technical support.
Microsoft Windows 3.1. PC 386 or higher (4Mb, 8Mb recommended). CD-ROM disk $79.00. *Nonstandard peripherals required:* 7Mb HD space, VGA/SVGA, MPC. *Networks supported:* Novell or any LAN software.
Picks up Where Power Japanese Leaves Off. Introduces 200 of the Ideographic Characters (Kanji) Used in the Japanese Language. These Characters Are Presented in the Form of Short Articles on Life & Culture in Japan. You Can Get the Translation, Japanese Phonetic Spelling (Furigana), & the Actual Stroke by Stroke Animation on Any Kanji Character by Just Clicking on It. The Same Goes for Any Japanese Word or Sentence. The Pronunciation of Any Sentence Is Also Just a Mouse Click Away. Comes with an Exercise Book.
Bayware, Inc.

Kanji Moments, Vol. 2. Nov. 1995. *Items Included:* 1 exercise book (spiral wrap bound), installation guide, reg. card. *Customer Support:* Free technical support.
Microsoft Windows 3.1. PC 486 (4Mb). CD-ROM disk $79.00 (ISBN 1-883653-07-X). *Nonstandard peripherals required:* MPC compatible sound card. *Networks supported:* Novell or any LAN software.
Covers 400 Additional Kanji Beyond What Is Covered in Volume One. The Characters Are Presented Through Articles on Life & Culture in Japan. Program Features Include an On-Line Reference, Instantaneous Translation of All Words & Phrases, Fully Animated Writing for All Kanji Characters, Discussions on Everyday Idioms & Grammar, As Well As All Sentences Accompanied by Sound. Comes with Extensive Exercise Book.
Bayware, Inc.

Karate Kid Part II. *Compatible Hardware:* Atari ST, Commodore Amiga. *General Requirements:* Color monitor.
3.5" disk $39.95.
Guide Daniel Through Fight after Fight Against Ever More Powerful Adversaries. Then Face the Evil Chozen Himself in the Castle of King Shohashi, Where You Must Discover the Secret of the Drum - or Die! But the Fight Isn't All: Catch Flies with Chopsticks & Break Ice with Your Bare Hand.
MichTron, Inc.

Karateka. Jordan Mechner. *Compatible Hardware:* Apple II+, IIe, IIc, IIgs; Atari 400, 800, XL, XE Series, ST; Commodore 64, 128; IBM PC & compatibles; Tandy. *Memory Required:* Apple & Atari XL/XE 48k, Commodore 64k, IBM & Tandy 128, Atari ST 512k. *General Requirements:* Joystick or keyboard.
Apple. disk $34.95 (Order no.: APDSK-39).
Atari 800/XL/XE & Commodore (one on each side). disk $14.95 (ISBN 1-55790-019-1, Order no.: 80230).
IBM & Tandy. disk $34.95 (Order no.: IBMDSK-217).
Atari ST. 3.5" disk $34.95 (ISBN 1-55790-018-3, Order no.: 10325).
Action Game in Which the Player Must Bypass Various Traps, Use His Martial Arts Skills to Overcome Opponents Who Get Stronger, & Avoid a Deadly Bird, In Order to Rescue a Princess in Distress. Features Smoothly Animated Characters & Scrolling Hi-Resolution Background.
Broderbund Software, Inc.

KASE:C Plus Plus for OS/2. *Version:* 2.1. Jul. 1994. *Items Included:* User's Guide, Tutorial. *Customer Support:* 30 days of support FREE; After then, one year of support costs 15% of the list price; Bulletin Board support FREE; CompuServe support FREE.
OS/2 2.1 or higher. Intel 80386 or higher (or compatible) (8Mb). $1495.00 list price. *Addl. software required:* OS/2 2.1 Toolkit; IBM's C Set Plus Plus compiler. *Optimal configuration:* 80486 system, 16Mb RAM, 10Mb working disk storage, VGA monitor, mouse, 3.5" disk drive.
The Object-Oriented Member of KASE Systems' Visual Design & Code-Generation Family of Tools. It Generates C Plus Plus Source Code & Is the Only Tool on the Market Today That Fully Supports IBM's User Interface Class Library. Allows You to Quickly & Easily Renovate Legacy Applications or Develop New Ones That Exploit Technologies Critical to Client/Server Environments.
KASE Systems.

KASE:VIP for OS/2. *Version:* 2.0. Mar. 1994. *Items Included:* User's Guide, Tutorial. *Customer Support:* 30 days of support FREE; After then, one year of support costs 15% of the list price; Bulletin Board support FREE; CompuServe support FREE.
OS/2 2.1 or higher. Intel 80386 or higher (or compatible) (4Mb). $1995.00 list price. *Addl. software required:* OS/2 2.1 Toolkit; IBM C Set 2 compiler. *Optimal configuration:* 80486 system, 12Mb RAM, 5Mb working disk storage, VGA monitor, mouse, 3.5" disk drive.
A Knowledge-Assisted Visual Design & Code-Generation Tool for Building GUI & Client/Server Applications. Will Generate All the Application Source Code Using the Patented Knowledge-Assisted Software Engineering (KASE) Technology. Applications Built Are Free of Run-Times & Royalties.
KASE Systems.

KASE:VIP for Windows. *Version:* 4.0. Apr. 1994. *Items Included:* User's Guide, Tutorial. *Customer Support:* 30 days of support FREE; After then, one year of support costs 15% of the list price; Bulletin Board support FREE; CompuServe support FREE.
MS-DOS 3.3 or higher; Microsoft Windows 3.1 or higher. Intel 80386 or higher (or compatible) (4Mb). $995.00 list price. *Addl. software required:* Microsoft Software Developer's Toolkit, Microsoft or Borland compiler. *Optimal configuration:* 80486 system, 8Mb RAM, 10Mb working disk storage, VGA monitor, mouse, 3.5" disk drive.
A Visual Design & Code-Generation Tool for Building GUI & Client/Server Applications. Will Generate All the Application Source Code Using the Patented Knowledge-Assisted Software Engineering (KASE) Technology. Applications Built Are Free of Run-Times or Royalties.
KASE Systems.

Katie's Farm. Feb. 1990. *Items Included:* Program manual. *Customer Support:* Free technical support 800-421-4157, 90 day warranty.
OS 5.0 or higher. Apple IIGS (1Mb). disk $39.95 (ISBN 0-917999-82-7).
Amiga DOS 1.3 or higher. Amiga (1Mb). disk $39.95 (ISBN 0-917999-98-3).
DOS 3.0 or higher. IBM (640k). disk $24.95 (ISBN 1-882848-59-4). *Nonstandard peripherals required:* Mouse recommended. Sound support strongly recommended - Sound Blaster, Covox, Tandy. *Networks supported:* I-Class.
System 6.0.5 or higher. Macintosh Plus, SE, SE30, Classic, LC, SI II (1Mb). 3.5" disk $24.95 (ISBN 0-917999-99-1).

In This "First Computer Activity" for Children Ages 2-5, an Endearing Preschooler, McGee, Takes Users along on a Visit to His Cousin Katie's Farm. Directing His Movements by Pointing & Clicking on the Icons at the Bottom of the Screen, Children Decide Whether McGee Will Feed the Chickens, Ride the Horse, or Pick Raspberries in the Garden. Katie's Farm Is an Excellent Way to Introduce Young Children to the Computer.
Lawrence Productions, Inc.

Kaywood Method. 1985. *Compatible Hardware:* IBM PC. *Language(s):* BASIC. *Memory Required:* 24k.
disk or cassette $199.99.
Handicapping Program.
COM-CAP.

KBLock. *Version:* 2.0A. 1990. *Items Included:* Manuals, 1 year maintenance, quarterly newsletter. *Customer Support:* 6am-6pm, MST. MicroVMS, VMS 4.6 & higher. MicroVAX, VAX (8k + 3k per on-line user). $303.00-$5436.00.
Used to Secure Unattended Logged-in Terminals. Users Can Lock Keyboard & Clear Screen with Keystroke -- Application Continues Uninterrupted in Background. Output is Buffered Until Terminal Is Unlocked. All Input Blocked Until the Normal Password is Entered.
Raxco, Inc.

KBMS: Knowledge Base Management System. *Version:* 404. 1990. *Items Included:* Complete technical reference manual; User's guides, tutorials, quick reference.
MVS/XA, MVS, VM, MS-DOS, VAX VMS & OS/2. IBM PCs & DEC VAX VMS, IBM maniframes. 3.5" disk OS/2 $7500.00.
disk MS-DOS $5000.00.
An Integrated Multi-Platform Knowledge Base System That Extends Conventional Data Processing Practices to Knowledge Base Applications. KBMS Enables Programmers to Apply the Four Key Methodologies: Forward Chaining, Backward Chaining, Hypothetical Reasoning, & Object-Oriented Programming to Reach a Conclusion or Recommendation. The Added Advantage of Natural Language Facility Speeds Development by Writing Rules in English. The Powerful Graphical Developer & User Interfaces Simplify & Enhance the Delivery of Knowledge Base Applications.
AICorp.

KC-TRUST: Trust Accounting System. Kelvin L. Crawford. Apr. 1986. *Compatible Hardware:* Burroughs B-20; IBM PC & compatible, PC XT, PC AT. *Operating System(s) Required:* CTOS, BTOS, MS-DOS, UNIX. *Language(s):* PDS-ADEPT PC (source code included). *Memory Required:* 640k. *Items Included:* Manual. $5000.00.
System Controls Include a Thorough Posting Errors (Real Time) Check Report with Daily Posting Journals to Provide for a Pre-Update Audit Trail & for Editing of Daily Posting Entries. Provides Automatic Descriptions During Posting. Major Posting Update Also Provides Posting Errors Report & Aborts Automatically If Posting Does Not Balance. Some of the Reports & Features Included Are: Income Statement/Balance Sheet, Court Report, Stock/Bond Holders List, Asset Maturity Map, Investment Portfolio Review, Excess Cash Report, General Ledger Detail Report, Automatic Posting of Dividend, Interest & Maturities, Automatic Computation of Capital Gain or Loss on Securities, Posting Descriptions Automatically Entered by System, Checkwriting, Fee Calculations, Distributions to Beneficiaries, Schedule D (Capital Gain or Loss), Dividend/Interest List, Update Market Values.
K.C. Data Program Services, Inc.

TITLE INDEX

KCS Level II.
Commodore Amiga. 3.5" disk $99.95.
Atari ST. 3.5" disk $69.95.
Program-Variations Generator & Master Editor. All Features of KCS 1.GA with the Additional Modules Mentioned Above. See KCS ST for Further Description.
Dr. T's Music Software, Inc.

KDS Development System. *Version:* 3.9. Barbara Wallace. Nov. 1994. *Compatible Hardware:* IBM PC, PC XT, PC AT, PS/2 & compatibles. *Operating System(s) Required:* PC-DOS 2.0 or higher. *Language(s):* Assembly. *Memory Required:* 640k. *General Requirements:* 2 disk drives. *Customer Support:* Telephone. On-site training optional at extra cost.
disk $1795.00.
Case-Based Expert System Shell. Generates up to 24,000 Rules per Frame from up to 256,000 Facts. Can Interface with Other Programs & Languages. Has a Menu Driven Graphics Interface. Has a Blackboard Which Allows for Use of Equations, Variables, etc. with High Numeric Accuracy.
KDS Corp.

KDS-VOX-PM. *Version:* 3.9. Barbara J. Wallace. Jan. 1995. *Items Included:* Loose-leaf manual (ca 275 pages) 30Mb of digital voice files. *Customer Support:* 3 days on-site training included (expenses extra). Annual support & up grades (optional) 10% of license fee. One year of telephone support included in basic license fee. 5 Run-Time licenses included at no extra charge.
OS/2 1.3 or higher. IBM AT or compatible with math chip (4mb). $15,000.00 basic license. Additional development systems $2500.00, additional run-time licenses $250.00 (Order no.: KDS/VOX). *Nonstandard peripherals required:* Dialogic 4/X board. *Optimal configuration:* Pentium-based PC compatible, 16Mb RAM, 150Mb hard disk boards as above. *Networks supported:* All we Know.
Frame-Based Expert System Which Interacts with End Users in Natural Speech. Supports up to 24 Simultaneous Users per PC. The Users Respond to Questions by Pressing Buttons on Any Touch-Tone Telephone. End Users Require No Computer, the System Can Be Accessed from Any Touch-Tone Telephone. Each Module Has a Capacity of 24,000 Rules & 256,000 Facts. Object-Oriented Blackboard with 500 Object Capacity. Can Also Produce & Run under DOS, Screen-Oriented Applications with or Without Graphics. 24 Hour Demonstration Line Phone Number Is 847-251-4975.
KDS Corp.

KEDIT. *Version:* 5.0. May 1992. *Operating System(s) Required:* PC-DOS 2.0 or higher, OS/2 1.3 or higher. *Memory Required:* 384k.
PC-DOS. $180.00 (ISBN 0-925126-00-4).
OS/2 (which includes DOS version). $210.00.
demo disk free.
Full-Screen Text Editor Compatible with XEDIT, IBM's VM/CMS Editor, Multiple-File Editing, Multiple Windows, Mouse Support, Block Operations, Redefinable Keys, Word Processing Functions, REXX Macros with Either Built-In REXX Subset, Personal REXX or IBM's OS/2 REXX, Undo/Redo, Online Help, File Locking, Macro Debugger, XMS & EMS Support.
Mansfield Software Group.

Keep on Trucking. *Compatible Hardware:* Apple Macintosh.
Single User with Runtime Omnis 3 Plus. 3.5" disk $1990.00.
Mutiuser (Requires MultiUser Omnis 3 Plus). 3.5" disk $2490.00.
Maintains Accounts Receivable, Payroll & Settlement Records for Interstate Trucking Businesses.
H&D Leasing.

Keep Your Cool: Manage Your Emotions. May 1994. *Customer Support:* Toll-free telephone number for technical support. 90 days warranty for defects in materials & workmanship.
Macintosh System 7.0. Macintosh with 68040 processor (5Mb). CD-ROM disk $49.95 (ISBN 1-886806-03-9). *Nonstandard peripherals required:* Double speed CD-ROM drive. *Addl. software required:* QuickTime (included on CD-ROM disc).
Microsoft Windows 3.1. PC compatibles; 486/33 MHz (runs slow on 386/25MHz) (8Mb). CD-ROM disk $49.95. *Nonstandard peripherals required:* 256 color display card (640x480); double speed CD-ROM drive. *Addl. software required:* QuickTime for Windows (included on CD-ROM disc).
Designed to Help You Manage Your Emotions by Choosing How You Feel. Helps You See What Triggers Your Emotions & Learn to Break Emotional Habits. This Highly Interactive CD-ROM Includes Video, Exercises, & Realistic Situations. It's for Anyone Who Gets Anxious, Frustrated, or Angry & Wants to Learn New Ways to Manage - Not Limit - Their Emotions.
Wilson Learning Corp.

KeepTrack Plus. *Version:* 2.1. Dan Finkelstein. May 1990. *Compatible Hardware:* IBM PC & compatibles. *Operating System(s) Required:* PC-DOS/MS-DOS 2.0 or higher. *Memory Required:* 384k. *Items Included:* 1 book-bound manual. *Customer Support:* Unlimited telephone support.
DOS. IBM & compatibles (384k). disk $99.00. 129.00 (05/1989).
Hard Disk Utility that Offers Fast & Usable Backup. Includes: a Graphic Organization Chart of Directories, Subdirectories & Files; Copy, Move, Rename, View & Delete Functions; Sort, Search & Protect Features. Makes Backup Diskettes with Identical File & Directory Structures As the Hard Disk.
The Finot Group.

Ken Elliott's Crapism Professional. *Version:* 2.0. Ken Elliott. Feb. 1995. *Items Included:* Manuals (2), 3.5" disk (free exchange for 5.25"). *Customer Support:* Limited phone support.
MS-DOS 3.2 or higher. IBM PC & compatibles (640k). disk $79.95 (ISBN 1-886070-05-9, Order no.: 9503). *Nonstandard peripherals required:* VGA or higher graphics.
Teaches Casino Craps. Place Any Bet Allowed in the Casino. Configure for Different Casino Conditions. High Speed Simulation of Most Betting Strategies to Test Systems. Extensive Graphical Statistical Display. The Interactive Portion of This Product Is Also Available Separately As Ken Elliiott's Crapism Interactive.
ConJelCo.

Ken Elliott's Crapsim Interactive. *Version:* 2.0. Ken Elliott. Feb. 1995. *Items Included:* 1 manual, 3.5" disk (free exchange for 5.25"). *Customer Support:* Limited phone support.
DOS 3.2 or higher. PC compatible (640k), VGA. Contact publisher for price (ISBN 1-886070-06-7, Order no.: 95031).
Teaches Casino Craps. Place Any Bet Allowed in the Casino Configure for Different Casino Conditions. Tutoring. This Is the Interactive Portion of CRAPSIM PROFESSIONAL.
ConJelCo.

Kevin the Kangaroo: Explore the Land down under with Your New Friend Kevin. *Items Included:* Pamphlet of instructions. *Customer Support:* Tech support, 60 day money-back guarantee.
Windows; Macintosh. IBM compatible 386SX or higher (4Mb); Mac LC or higher (2.5Mb). CD-ROM disk $39.95 (ISBN 0-924677-06-6).

KEYBOARD ARPEGGIOS-MIDI

Nonstandard peripherals required: Audio board, mouse, CD-ROM drive. *Addl. software required:* Video card 640x480 with 256 colors; Quicktime 2.0.
Explore the Australian Bush with Kevin the Kangaroo, Six Activities & Games Are Introduced by "Namatiira," the Young Aborigine, As You Learn about Kangaroos in the Australian Outback.
IMSI (International Microcomputer Software, Inc.).

Key Business Measures. *Compatible Hardware:* IBM PC. *Memory Required:* 256k. *General Requirements:* 2 disk drives, Lotus 1-2-3.
disk $100.00.
Converts Stored Financial Data into Active Management Information That Can Be Analyzed & Used. The User Can Create Custom Entries for Income Statements & Balance Sheets & the Program Automatically Generates Information for Established Financial Ratios & Other Performance Measures. Identify Current Status & Recent Trends & All Information Can Be Stored.
Prentice Hall.

Key Commander. *Compatible Hardware:* TRS-80 Model I, Model III. *Memory Required:* 16k.
cassette $29.95 (Order no.: 5027R).
Allows Easy Editing & Entry of Graphics into BASIC Programs.
Instant Software, Inc.

Key Matic. Jul. 1989.
OS/2 1.1 or higher. IBM PC & compatibles. disk $10.00 (ISBN 0-9615084-3-4, Order no.: KEY001).
Program Speeds up Keyboard by Setting Typematic Rate to 5, 10, 15, 20 or 30 Characters per Second. Typematic Delay Time Can Be Set to 250 or 500 Milliseconds. Uses Presentation Manager Dialog Boxes for User Input. Also Has Automatic Mode That Uses Either OS/2 Full-Screen Mode or OS/2 Windowed Mode.
J. B. Dawson.

Key Tag. *Version:* 1.15. *Customer Support:* By phone Mon-Fri 8:30 AM-5:30 PM CST.
MS-DOS. IBM PC, PC XT, PC AT & compatibles, PS/2. disk $200.00 (Order no.: 160002).
Stores Unique Company & Serialization Information, Preventing Deciphering & Reverse Engineering with an Unreadable 64-Bit Security Match. Random Number Generator Thwarts Piracy. Three Types Available: Standard Allows Software to Run for Unlimited Number of Executions; Coupon Allows Software to Run for a Certain Number of Times, Suitable for Trial-Based Sales & Leased Software; Read-Write Affords Programmer Ability to Read & Write 16-Byte String Variables Stored in System. Only Available for Programmer's Interface. Two Separate Routines Supplied- One for Reading & One for Writing.
Glenco Engineering, Inc.

Keyboard Arpeggios-MIDI. Reid Alexander. 1985-1986. *Compatible Hardware:* Atari ST; Apple II+, IIe; Commodore 64, 128; IBM PC & compatibles; Macintosh. *Operating System(s) Required:* Apple DOS 3.3, PC-DOS 3.3. *Language(s):* QuickBasic. *Memory Required:* Apple 48k, Commodore 64k, IBM 640k. *General Requirements:* Passport Designs MIDI card, MIDI-compatible music keyboard or synthesizer. CGA card for IBM.
disk $79.95 ea.
Apple. disk $79.95 ea. (ISBN 0-942132-61-0, Order no.: MA-1168).
Commodore 64. disk $79.95 ea. (ISBN 0-942132-62-9, Order no.: MC-1168).
IBM. disk $79.95 ea. (ISBN 1-55603-025-8,

Order no.: MI-1168).
Atari. disk $79.95 (ISBN 1-55603-066-5, Order no.: MST-1168).
This Program Reviews Keyboard Arpeggio Performance & Fingerings. It Is Presented in Five Parts: Instructions, Hand-over-Hand Triads (Major or Minor), Major Triads (Two Octaves), Minor Triads (Two Octaves), & a Final Quiz (Random Selection of All Forms). Computer Graphics Highlight the Presentation of the Notation, & Evaluation Feedback Is Stored in Student Records for the Instructor.
Electronic Courseware Systems, Inc.

Keyboard Blues - MIDI. G. David Peters. 1985-1986. *Compatible Hardware:* Atari ST; Apple II+, IIe; Commodore 64, 128; IBM PC & compatibles, Macintosh. *Operating System(s) Required:* Apple DOS 3.3, PC-DOS 3.3. *Language(s):* QuickBasic. *Memory Required:* Apple 48k, Commodore 64k, IBM 640k, MAC 512k. *General Requirements:* Passport Designs MIDI card, MIDI-compatible music keyboard or synthesizer, CGA card for IBM, External MIDI interface for Macintosh.
disk $79.95 ea.
Apple. disk $79.95 ea. (ISBN 0-942132-63-7, Order no.: MA-1158).
Commodore 64. disk $79.95 ea. (ISBN 0-942132-64-5, Order no.: MC-1158).
IBM PC. disk $79.95 ea. (ISBN 1-55603-032-0, Order no.: MI-1158).
Atari. disk $79.95 ea. (ISBN 1-55603-067-3, Order no.: MST-1158).
Macintosh 512. disk $99.95.
Presents Simple Chords & Introduces the User to the Twelve Bar Blues. The User Can Practice Playing & Hearing the Chord Changes, First with the Music & Then Without. The Drill-&-Practice Section Scores the User's Knowledge of the Simple Blues Chords. The User May Then Compose an Original Blues Solo with a Computer Accompaniment.
Electronic Courseware Systems, Inc.

Keyboard Chords - MIDI. G. David Peters. 1985-1986. *Compatible Hardware:* Atari ST; Apple II+, IIe; Commodore 64, 128; IBM PC & compatibles, Macintosh. *Operating System(s) Required:* Apple DOS 3.3, MAC System 6.3-7.1, PC-DOS 3.3. *Language(s):* QuickBasic. *Memory Required:* Apple 48k, Commodore 64k, IBM 640k, MAC 512k. *General Requirements:* Internal MIDI card, MIDI-compatible music keyboard or synthesizer, CGA card for IBM, External MIDI Device for MAC.
disk $79.95 ea. (ISBN 0-942132-65-3).
Apple. disk $79.95 ea. (ISBN 0-942132-65-3, Order no.: MA-1157).
Commodore 64. disk $79.95 ea. (ISBN 0-942132-66-1, Order no.: MC-1157).
IBM PC. disk $79.95 ea. (ISBN 1-55603-034-7, Order no.: MI-1157).
Atari. disk $79.95 ea. (ISBN 1-55603-068-1, Order no.: MST-1157).
Macintosh 512. disk $99.95 (ISBN 1-55603-295-1, Order no.: MAC-1157).
Composed of a Tutorial on Major, Minor, Diminished, & Augmented Chords; a Chord Spelling Drill; a Keyboard Drill; & a Test. The Tutorial Presents Qualities of Simple Chords. The Drill-&-Practice Programs Allow the User to Select the Inversion (Root 1st, or 2nd) & the Clef (Treble or Bass) for the Drill.
Electronic Courseware Systems, Inc.

Keyboard Extended Jazz Harmonies - MIDI. Joe Brownlee. *Compatible Hardware:* Atari ST; Apple II+, IIe; IBM PC & compatibles, Macintosh. *Memory Required:* Apple 48k, IBM 640k, MAC 512k. *General Requirements:* Roland MPU & MIDI interface card; MIDI-compatible music keyboard; amplifier, headphones or other audio monitoring systems. CGA card for IBM; Passport MIDI interface card can be substituted for the Roland MPU; MIDI interface card for Apple & External MIDI Interface for Macintosh.
disk $79.95 ea.
Apple. (ISBN 1-55603-043-6, Order no.: MA-1236).
IBM. (ISBN 1-55603-044-4, Order no.: MI-1236).
Atari ST. (ISBN 1-55603-069-X, Order no.: MST-1236).
Macintosh 512. disk $99.95 (ISBN 1-55603-307-9, Order no.: MAC 1236).
Sequel to JAZZ HARMONIES Designed to Help the Student Learn to Recognize, Identify & Build 9th, 11th & 13th Chords That Are Common in Jazz. The Lesson Contains Four Sections: Visual Chord Recognition, Aural Chord Recognition, Chord Symbol Drill, & Chord Spelling Drill. The Drills Allow the Students to Practice the Skills Until They Are Ready to Test Their Knowledge. Also Features Student Record Keeping to Allow the Instructor to Monitor Student Progress.
Electronic Courseware Systems, Inc.

Keyboard Fingerings. G. David Peters. 1987. *Customer Support:* ECS offers technical support to registered users. Call (217) 359-7099. Other than the telephone call - technical support is no charge.
DOS 3.3. Apple. disk $79.95 (Order no.: MA-1167). *Nonstandard peripherals required:* Internal MIDI interface, MIDI keyboard.
DOS 3.2 or higher. IBM. $79.95 single station/$400.00 network (Order no.: MI-1167). *Nonstandard peripherals required:* Roland MPU-401, MIDI interface or 100% compatible, MIDI keyboard. *Networks supported:* Novell.
Mac System 6.0.4 or higher. Macintosh. $79.95 single station/$400.00 network (Order no.: MAC-1167). *Nonstandard peripherals required:* MIDI interface & MIDI keyboard.
Designed to Review Standard & Special Fingerings for the Major, Natural Minor, & Harmonic Minor Scales. The Review Includes Instructions & Major & Minor Scale Review for Both the Right & Left Hands. The Computer Judges the Accuracy of the Scale Performance in Each Section & on the Final Test. Single Staves Are Used, with Treble for the Right-Hand Exercises & Bass for the Left-Hand. The Program Also Features Student Evaluation & Record Keeping. Requires MIDI.
Electronic Courseware Systems, Inc.

Keyboard Histology Series: Student Edition. Junqueira, Carneiro & Kelley Staff et al. Aug. 1994. *Items Included:* User manual, quick-start sheet, Keyboard Utilities, & Microsoft Multimedia Viewer (Windows version) or HyperCard (Macintosh version). *Customer Support:* Free, unlimited technical support via our toll-free number (1-800-945-4551).
Macintosh. Macintosh with a hard drive (2.5Mb). CD-ROM disk $169.00 (ISBN 1-57349-242-6). *Nonstandard peripherals required:* CD-ROM player required, 256-color monitor recommended. *Addl. software required:* System 7.0 or higher. *Networks supported:* All LANs.
Windows. IBM compatible with 80286 or higher processor, a hard drive & a mouse (2Mb). CD-ROM disk $169.00 (ISBN 1-57349-243-4). *Nonstandard peripherals required:* CD-ROM player required, 256-color monitor recommended. *Addl. software required:* MS-DOS 3.3 or higher, Windows 3.1 or higher. *Networks supported:* All LANs.
A Collection of Electronic Tools for Reference & Education in Histology. Includes: The Histology TextStack, the Complete Text with All Tables, Figures, Diagrams, & Color Illustrations from Appleton & Lange's Basic Histology by Junqueira, Carneiro, & Kelley. Histology QuizBank Volume 1, over 300 Multiple-Choice Questions Covering All Areas of Histology, with Detailed Feedback & Direct Links into Related Materials in the TextStack. Written by Stephen W. Downing. Histology QuizBank Volume 2, over 500 Additional Multiple-Choice Questions Covering All Areas of Histology, with Detailed Feedback & Direct Links into Related Materials in the TextStack. Written by Kestenbaum, Gibney, Matta & Wilson.
Keyboard Publishing, Inc.

Keyboard Immunology Series: Student Edition. Ivan W. Roitt & Peter Delves. Oct. 1994. *Items Included:* User manual, quick-start sheet, Keyboard Utilities, & Microsoft Multimedia Viewer (Windows version) or HyperCard (Macintosh version). *Customer Support:* Free, unlimited technical support via our toll-free number (1-800-945-4551).
Macintosh. Macintosh with a hard drive (2.5Mb). CD-ROM disk $169.00 (ISBN 1-57349-203-5). *Nonstandard peripherals required:* CD-ROM player required, 256-color monitor recommended. *Addl. software required:* System 7.0 or higher. *Networks supported:* All LANs.
Windows. IBM compatible with 80286 or higher processor, a hard drive & a mouse (2Mb). CD-ROM disk $169.00 (ISBN 1-57349-204-3). *Nonstandard peripherals required:* CD-ROM player required, 256-color monitor recommended. *Addl. software required:* MS-DOS 3.3 or higher, Windows 3.1 or higher. *Networks supported:* All LANs.
A Collection of Electronic Tools for Reference & Education in Immunology. Includes: The Immunology TextStack, the Complete Text with All Tables, Figures, Diagrams, & Illustrations from Essential Immunology by Ivan W. Roitt. Immunology QuizBank Volume 1, over 500 Multiple-Choice Questions Covering All Areas of Immunology, with Detailed Feedback & Direct Links into Related Materials in the TextStack. Written by Ivan W. Roitt & Peter Delves.
Keyboard Publishing, Inc.

Keyboard Intervals - MIDI. G. David Peters. 1985-1986. *Compatible Hardware:* Atari ST; Apple II+, IIe; Commodore 64, 128; IBM PC & compatibles; Macintosh. *Operating System(s) Required:* Apple DOS 3.3, MAC System 6.0.3-7.1, PC-DOS 3.3. *Language(s):* QuickBasic. *Memory Required:* Apple 48k, Commodore 64k, IBM 640k, MAC 512k. *General Requirements:* Internal MIDI card; MIDI-compatible music keyboard or synthesizer, color graphics card (IBM), External MIDI device - MAC.
disk $79.95 ea.
Apple. disk $79.95 ea. (ISBN 0-942132-69-6, Order no.: MA-1166).
Commodore 64. disk $79.95 ea. (ISBN 0-942132-70-X, Order no.: MC-1166).
IBM PC. disk $79.95 ea. (ISBN 1-55603-033-9, Order no.: MI-1158).
Atari. disk $79.95 ea. (ISBN 1-55603-071-1, Order no.: MST-1158).
disk $99.95 (ISBN 1-55603-305-2, Order no.: MAC-1158).
This Program Is Designed to Help Music Students Learn to Recognize & Play Major, Minor, Diminished, & Augmented Intervals. Users Must Be Able to Read Music & Play Notes on a Music Keyboard to Use This Lesson. The Program Is Composed of a Tutorial, an Interval Spelling Drill, a Keyboard Drill, & a Test. The Program Also Features Student Evaluation & Record-Keeping.
Electronic Courseware Systems, Inc.

Keyboard Jazz Harmonies - MIDI. Joe Brownlee. 1985-1986. *Compatible Hardware:* Atari ST; Apple II+, IIe; Commodore 64, 128; IBM PC & compatibles, Macintosh. *Operating System(s) Required:* Apple DOS 3.3, MAC

System 6.0.3-7.1, PC-DOS 3.3. *Language(s):* QuickBasic. *Memory Required:* Apple 48k, Commodore 64k, IBM 640k, MAC 512k. *General Requirements:* Internal MIDI card, MIDI-compatible music keyboard or synthesizer, CGA card for IBM, External MIDI device MAC.
disk $79.95 ea.
 Apple. disk $79.95 ea. (ISBN 0-942132-71-8, Order no.: MA-1154).
 Commodore 64. disk $79.95 ea. (ISBN 0-942132-72-6, Order no.: MC-1154).
 IBM PC. disk $79.95 ea. (ISBN 1-55603-035-5, Order no.: MI-1154).
 Atari. disk $79.95 ea. (ISBN 1-55603-072-X, Order no.: MST-1154).
 Macintosh 512. disk $99.95 (Order no.: MAC-1154).
Designed to Teach Chord Symbols, 7th Chord Recognition, & Chord Spelling. To Use This Lesson, a Basic Knowledge of Traditional Harmonies & Music Intervals Is Required. The Program Consists of a Tutorial, Four Drills, Four Quizzes, & a Final Quiz. The Final Quiz Has the Computer Play a Small Portion of a Jazz Tune, & the Student Must Give the Chord Symbol for Each Chord Change & Spell the Chord Using the Keyboard.
Electronic Courseware Systems, Inc.

Keyboard Kapers. Ray E. Zubler. *Customer Support:* 90 day warranty against defective software.
 System 6.0.4 - 7.1. Macintosh (1Mb). 3.5" disk $59.95 (Order no.: MAC-1159). *Optimal configuration:* Also requires MIDI interface & MIDI compatible music keyboard.
 DOS 3.3 or higher. IBM (640k). disk $39.95 (Order no.: MI-1159). *Nonstandard peripherals required:* CGA card & monitor minimum. *Optimal configuration:* Also requires MIDI interface & MIDI compatible music keyboard.
 DOS 3.3. Apple II (48k). disk $39.95 (Order no.: MA-1159). *Optimal configuration:* Also requires Internal MIDI interface & MIDI compatible music keyboard.
Consists of 3 Challenging Piano Keyboard Games. KEYBOARD CLUES Plots a Note on the Grand Staff & Requires That the Note Be Played on the Musical Keyboard. ?MYSTERY? NOTES Trains the Ear by Presenting One Note Visually & Aurally & Then Asks the User to Identify Other Notes Played by the Computer. KWIK KEYS Is a Timed Game Which Requires the Student to Play Back Notes Presented on the Screen As Quickly As Possible.
Electronic Courseware Systems, Inc.

Keyboard Kapers - MIDI. Ray E. Zubler. 1985-1986. *Compatible Hardware:* Atari ST; Apple II+, IIe; Commodore 64, 128; IBM PC & compatibles, Macintosh. *Operating System(s) Required:* Apple DOS 3.3, MAC System 6.0.3-7.1, PC-DOS 3.3. *Language(s):* QuickBasic. *Memory Required:* Apple 48k, Commodore 64k, IBM 640k, MAC 512k. *General Requirements:* Passport Designs MIDI card, MIDI-compatible music keyboard or synthesizer, CGA card for IBM, External MIDI device for Macintosh.
disk $39.95 ea.
 Apple. disk $39.95 ea. (ISBN 0-942132-73-4, Order no.: MA-1159).
 Commodore 64. disk $39.95 ea. (ISBN 0-942132-74-2, Order no.: MC-1159).
 IBM PC. disk $39.95 ea. (ISBN 1-55603-031-2, Order no.: MI-1159).
 Atari. disk $39.95 ea. (ISBN 1-55603-073-8, Order no.: MST-1159).
 Macintosh 512. disk $59.95 (ISBN 1-55603-294-3, Order no.: MAC-1159).
Consists of Three Games: "Keyboard Clues" Plots a Note on the Grand Staff & Requires That the Note Be Played on the Musical Keyboard; "?Mystery? Notes" Trains the Musical Ear by Presenting One Note Visually & Aurally & Then Asks the Student to Identify Other Note(s) Played by the Computer; "Kwik Keys" Is a Timed Game Which Requires the User to Play Back Notes Presented on the Computer Screen As Quickly As Possible.
Electronic Courseware Systems, Inc.

Keyboard Master. *Version:* 2.1. Jan. 1991. *Items Included:* User's manual; demo program available for $5.00.
 IBM PC, XT, AT & PS/2. disk $49.95.
Teaches User to Play Any Standard MIDI File Format Song Using a Computerized, Graphical Keyboard. Product Can Calculate, Display & Print Hundreds of Different Scale & Chord Charts. Can Also Create Custom Scale & Chord Charts Using the Edit Option, Turning Notes on & off & Adding Custom Fingerings. Custom Charts Can Be Saved as Image Files & Later Recalled. Provides Support for Four Keyboard Notations Ranging from Simple Dots to Actual Note Value. With a Roland MPU-401 Attachment, Product Becomes a 64 Track Sequencer Capable of Recording, Playing, or Overdubbing to Any Track.
Spartan Software Systems.

Keyboard Microbiology Series: Student Edition. John Sherris et al. Oct. 1994. *Items Included:* User manual, quick-start sheet, Keyboard Utilities, & Microsoft Multimedia Viewer (Windows version) or HyperCard (Macintosh version). *Customer Support:* Free, unlimited technical support via our toll-free number (1-800-945-4551).
 Macintosh. Macintosh with a hard drive (2.5Mb). CD-ROM disk $169.00 (ISBN 1-57349-209-4). *Nonstandard peripherals required:* CD-ROM player required, 256-color monitor recommended. *Addl. software required:* System 7.0 or higher. *Networks supported:* All LANs.
 Windows. IBM compatible with 80286 or higher processor, a hard drive & a mouse (2Mb). CD-ROM disk $169.00 (ISBN 1-57349-210-8). *Nonstandard peripherals required:* CD-ROM player required, 256-color monitor recommended. *Addl. software required:* MS-DOS 3.3 or higher, Windows 3.1 or higher. *Networks supported:* All LANs.
A Collection of Electronic Tools for Reference & Education in Microbiology. Includes: The Microbiology TextStack, the Complete Text with All Tables, Figures, Diagrams, & Color Illustrations from Appleton & Lange's Medical Microbiology, 3rd Edition, Edited by John Sherris. Microbiology QuizBank Volume 2, over 400 Multiple-Choice questions Covering All Areas of Microbiology, with Detailed Feedback & Direct Links into Related Materials in the TextStack. Written by Joseph Gots. Microbiology QuizBank Volume 3, over 400 Additional Multiple-Choice Questions Covering All Areas of Microbiology, with Detailed Feedback & Direct Links into Related Materials in the TextStack. Written by James Booth.
Keyboard Publishing, Inc.

Keyboard NAMEGAME. David Patch. *Customer Support:* 90 day warranty against defective software.
 DOS 3.3. Apple II (48k). disk $39.95 (Order no.: MA-1172). *Nonstandard peripherals required:* MIDI compatible music keyboard, Internal MIDI interface.
 DOS 3.3 or higher. IBM PC (640k). disk $39.95 (Order no.: MI-1172). *Nonstandard peripherals required:* CGA card & CGA monitor minimum, MIDI interface, MIDI compatible music keyboard.
 System 6.0.7 - 7.00. MAC (1Mb). 3.5" disk $59.95 (Order no.: MAC-1172). *Nonstandard peripherals required:* MIDI interface, MIDI compatible music keyboard.
A Drill-&-Practice Game Designed to Teach Note Position in the Treble & Bass Clef. Scoring Is Based on the Time It Takes to Play the Words Presented.
Electronic Courseware Systems, Inc.

Keyboard Note Drill - MIDI. John Eddins. 1985-86. *Compatible Hardware:* Atari ST; Apple II+, IIe; Commodore 64, 128; IBM PC & compatibles, Macintosh. *Operating System(s) Required:* Apple DOS 3.3, MAC System 6.0.3-7.1, PC-DOS 3.3. *Language(s):* QuickBasic. *Memory Required:* Apple 48k, Commodore 64k, IBM 640k, MAC 512k. *General Requirements:* Passport Designs MIDI card, MIDI-compatible music keyboard or synthesizer. CGA card for IBM.
disk $39.95 ea.
 Apple. disk $39.95 ea. (ISBN 0-942132-77-7, Order no.: MA-1155).
 Commodore 64. disk $39.95 ea. (ISBN 0-942132-78-5, Order no.: MC-1155).
 IBM PC. disk $39.95 ea. (ISBN 1-55603-029-0, Order no.: MI-1155).
 Atari. disk $39.95 ea. (ISBN 1-55603-075-4, Order no.: MST-1155).
 Macintosh 512. disk $59.95 (ISBN 1-55603-303-6, Order no.: MAC-1155).
Designed to Increase Speed in Identifying Notes Randomly Placed on the Bass or Treble Clef Staves. The Musical Keyboard Is Used to Allow for Selection of Correct Answers. Twenty Notes Must Be Identified to Complete Each Session. A Summary Score Is Presented at the End of Each Session. The Response Time Can Be Set to Adjust the Level of Difficulty.
Electronic Courseware Systems, Inc.

Keyboard Pathology Series: Student Edition. Cotran, Kumar & Robbins Staff & Robert D. Cardiff et al. Oct. 1994. *Items Included:* User Manual, quick-start sheet, Keyboard Utilites, & Microsoft Multimedia Viewer (Windows version) or HyperCard (Macintosh version). *Customer Support:* Free, unlimited technical support via our toll-free number (1-800-945-4551).
 Macintosh. Macintosh with a hard drive (2.5Mb). CD-ROM disk $199.00 (ISBN 1-57349-211-6). *Nonstandard peripherals required:* CD-ROM player required, 256-color monitor recommended. *Addl. software required:* System 7.0 or higher. *Networks supported:* All LANs.
 Windows. IBM compatible with 80286 or higher processor, a hard drive & a mouse (2Mb). CD-ROM disk $199.00 (ISBN 1-57349-212-4). *Nonstandard peripherals required:* CD-ROM player required, 256-color monitor recommended. *Addl. software required:* MS-DOS 3.3 or higher, Windows 3.1 or higher. *Networks supported:* All LANs.
A Collection of Electronic Tools for Reference & Education in Pathology. Includes: The Pathology TextStack, the Complete Text with All Tables, Figures, Diagrams, & Color Illustrations from W.B. Saunders' Robbins Pathologic Basis of Disease, 5th Edition, Written by Cotran, Kumar & Robbins. Pathology QuizBank Volume 2, over 1,300 Multiple-Choice Questions Covering All Areas of Pathology, with Detailed Feedback & Direct Links into Related Materials in the TextStack. Written by Robert D. Cardiff & Others.
Keyboard Publishing, Inc.

Keyboard Tutor. Vincent Oddo. 1987. *Compatible Hardware:* Apple II plus, IIe, IIc, IIgs; IBM PC; Macintosh System 6.0.3-7.1. *Memory Required:* Apple 48k, IBM 640k, MAC 512k. *General Requirements:* Color graphics card.
disk $39.95 ea.
 (ISBN 1-55603-297-8, Order no.: MAC-1230). $59.95 (ISBN 1-55603-050-9).
Presents a Series of Exercises for Learning

Elementary Keyboard Skills. The Exercises Include Practice in Knowing the Names of the Keys, Which Piano Keys Produce Which Notes, Matching Keys & Notes, Finding Whole Steps & Half Steps, & Other Important Keyboard Concepts. Each Lesson Allows the Student to Practice the Skills Until the "ESC" Key Is Pressed.
Electronic Courseware Systems, Inc.

Keyboard Tutor - MIDI. Vincent Oddo. *Compatible Hardware:* Atari ST; Apple II+, IIe; IBM PC & compatibles, Macintosh. *Operating System(s) Required:* Apple DOS 3.30, MAC System 6.0.3-7.1, PC-DOS/MS-DOS 3.3. *Language(s):* QuickBasic. *Memory Required:* Apple 48k, IBM 640k, MAC 512k. *General Requirements:* Internal MIDI interface card; MIDI compatible music keyboard; CGA card for IBM; External MIDI device for Macintosh.
disk $39.95 ea.
Apple. (ISBN 1-55603-053-3, Order no.: MA-1234).
IBM. (ISBN 1-55603-054-1, Order no.: MI-1238).
Atari. (ISBN 1-55603-077-0, Order no.: MST-1238).
Macintosh 512. disk $59.95 (ISBN 1-55603-297-8, Order no.: MAC-1238).
Presents a Series of Exercises for Learning Elementary Keyboard Skills. Includes Practice in Knowing the Names of the Keys, Which Piano Keys Produce Which Notes, Matching Keys & Notes, Finding Whole Steps & Half Steps, & Other Important Keyboard Concepts. Each Lesson Allows the Student to Practice the Skills Until the "ESC" Key Is Pressed. When Using the MIDI Option, the Program Requires the Student to Enter Notes on the Synthesizer Keyboard.
Electronic Courseware Systems, Inc.

Keyboarding Skill Development. *Version:* 3. 1994. *Memory Required:* Apple IIe & IIc 512k, IBM/Tandy 128-512, PS/2, Macintosh 512k.
Apple II series, IIgs. 5.25" disk Contact publisher for price (ISBN 0-538-61186-3, Order no.: Z387-3C).
Apple II series, IIgs. 3.5" disk Contact publisher for price (ISBN 0-538-62086-2, Order no.: Z388-1C).
DOS. 5.25" or 3.5" disk Contact publisher for price (ISBN 0-538-61187-1, Order no.: Z388-8C).
MAC. 3.5" disk Contact publisher for price (ISBN 0-538-62048-X).
20-Lesson Software Program Designed to Build Keyboarding Speed & Accuracy. Can Be Used with any Keyboarding Program.
South-Western Publishing Co.

KeyCap. *Version:* 2.11. Mar. 1990. *Items Included:* Approximately 25 pages of support documentation; license registration card. *Customer Support:* Free telephone support. MS-DOS or PC-DOS. IBM PC, XT, AT, PS/2 & compatibles (256K). 3.5" or 5.25" disk $149.95. *Addl. software required:* Ventura Publisher or other desktop publishing software.
PC Software Utility That Converts Documents from Xerox Memorywriter Electronic Typewriter Format to a Format That Is Ideal for Processing by Ventura Publisher. Keycap Allows User to Actually Insert the Xerox Typewriter Disk Into the PC. It Allows the Xerox Memorywriter to Become an Ideal Keystroke Capturing Device for Ventura. Menu-Driven.
Information Conversion Services, Inc.

KeyEntry III: PC-Based Software Data Entry System. *Version:* 6.0. 1992. *Compatible Hardware:* AT&T 6300; Compaq; IBM PC, PC XT, PC AT, PS/2; NCR PC. *Operating System(s) Required:* PC-DOS/MS-DOS, OS/2 Standard Edition. *Language(s):* Assembly; C. *Memory Required:* 640k. *Customer Support:* Customer Support Plan Available.
disk $395.00 - $995.00.
Complete demo package. $75.00.
Comprehensive Full-Function Software Data Entry System. With Complete Entry, Validation, Searching, Editing, & Verification Capabilities. Designs Data Entry Applications, Controls Data Flow & Monitors/Reports Operator Activity & Performance. Features a Complete Data Entry Language Subsystem & Extensive Security & Batch Control Functions. Used in a LAN, It Can Provide the Benefits of On-Line Terminals or Dedicated Systems Without Performance Degradation.
Southern Computer Systems, Inc.

KeyLISP: The Language (Apple II Edition). *Version:* 1.1a. Gerard Michon. May 1987. *Compatible Hardware:* Apple II. *Operating System(s) Required:* ProDOS. *Language(s):* Assembly, LISP. *Memory Required:* 64k. *General Requirements:* 80-column display recommended. *Items Included:* Package includes both 3.5" and 5.25" diskettes & 424 page bound manual. *Customer Support:* Technical hot-line.
disk $149.00 (ISBN 0-937185-00-0, Order no.: A2KLO1).
Implementation of the LISP Programming Language. In Addition to Symbolic Computations, It Supports Both Floating-Point & 'Infinite Precision' Arithmetic & Provides Many 'Exotic' Features (over 220 Functions). Documentation Includes a 424 Page Fully Indexed Manual, Tutorial, Glossary & Up-to-Date Bibliography.
XPrime Corp.

KEYMATE-RIDEMATE: Employee Services Software. Open Door Software Division. Apr. 1992. *Customer Support:* On site training available - $200.00/day, plus per diem; Customization available, $50.00/hr; Maintenance on customized copies, $100.00/month.
IBM & compatibles (512k). disk $99.00 (ISBN 1-56756-004-0, Order no.: OD400I).
Macintosh. 3.5" disk $99.00 (ISBN 1-56756-005-9, Order no.: OD410M).
Employee Services Application Providing Key Locator & Ride-Sharing Services for Employees. KEYMATE Is a Numbered Key Chain Tracking System for Returning Lost or Misplaced Keys to Employees. RIDEMATE Is a Computerized Ride-Sharing Service That Has Been Shown to Reduce Absenteeism, Promote Team Building, Reduce Parking Problems & Traffic Congestion.
Advantage International.

Keymates: A Color Keyboarding System. Mar. 1996. *Customer Support:* 1-800-824-5179 product information; 1-800-543-0453 technical support.
Windows 3.1 or higher. 486 SX 25MHz (4Mb). CD-ROM disk Contact publisher for price (ISBN 0-538-64735-3). *Nonstandard peripherals required:* Double speed CD-ROM, VGA 640x480, sound blaster or 100% compatible sound card.
Macintosh, 68030 (5Mb). *Nonstandard peripherals required:* Double speed CD-ROM, 256 colors.
A Typing Awareness Program Designed for Children Ages 5-8. It Is Color Coded & Provides Typing Activities While Reinforcing Language Arts Skills. Combines Bright, Color-Coordinated Handbands & Key Sticker with a Large Letter Color Computer Screen Display for Effective Learning by Young Children.
South-Western Publishing Co.

KeyNotes Associated Press Stylebook. *Version:* 2.0. *Compatible Hardware:* IBM PC & compatibles. *General Requirements:* Hard disk. $89.95.
Reference Guide for Writers.
Digital Learning Systems, Inc.

KeyNotes Financial Mathematics Handbook. Nov. 1989. *Customer Support:* Free, unlimited, 800 number.
MS-DOS. disk $99.95.
Memory Resident Formulas & Financial Concepts Explained in Detail.
Digital Learning Systems, Inc.

KeyNotes Writer's Handbook. *Version:* 2.0. *Compatible Hardware:* IBM PC & compatibles. *Operating System(s) Required:* PC-DOS 2.0 or higher. *General Requirements:* Hard disk. *Customer Support:* Free, unlimited - 30 day money back guarantee.
$79.95.
Memory Resident Utility. Includes a Language Style Guide; a Dictionary of Abbreviations, Foreign Expressions, Common Misspellings, & Signs & Symbols; & a Letter Writing Guide. Helps Users with Grammar, Punctuation, Forms for Business Correspondence, Organization & Style, Finding the Correct Word, Foreign Phrases, etc.
Digital Learning Systems, Inc.

Keys of the Wizard. *Compatible Hardware:* TRS-80 Color Computer, TDP-100.
contact publisher for price.
Spectral Assocs.

Keys to the Internet. Edited by Steven Ross. disk $24.80, incl. 160p. text (ISBN 0-929321-21-9).
WEKA Publishing, Inc.

Keysort & Data Edit Package. Duane Bristow. *Compatible Hardware:* TRS-80 Model I, Model III. *Operating System(s) Required:* TRSDOS. *Language(s):* BASIC. *Memory Required:* 48k. disk $75.00.
Package of 2 Programs for General Recordkeeping & Record Summaries.
Duane Bristow Computers, Inc.

Keyswap. *Version:* 4.0. Apr. 1987. *Compatible Hardware:* IBM PC. *Operating System(s) Required:* MS-DOS, PC-DOS. *Language(s):* Assembly. *Memory Required:* 64k.
disk $99.95.
Keyboard Macro Utility That Resides in Memory & Operates in the Background, Allowing User to Redefine the Output of Any Key or Keystroke Combination. Allows User to Create Context Sensitive Help Windows & Pick Selection Menus, with the DOS Window Feature, Can Load Two Programs at Once. Features Automatic Cut & Paste & Electronic Post-It Like Capability.
Maverick Software, Inc.

KeyWords: A Return to Readability. *Customer Support:* Free, unlimited.
MS/PC DOS 3.0 or higher. IBM PC XT, AT, PS/2 & compatibles (512k). disk $99.00. *Addl. software required:* WordPerfect 5.0/5.1. *Optimal configuration:* Any IBM PC XT, AT, PS/2 & compatibles.
180-Character Keyboard Symbol Set for WORDPERFECT. Helps You to Avoid Writing Misleading Documentation by Letting User Substitute Key-Like Symbols for Important Letters, Words, & Punctuation. Readers Will Understand Exactly What Keys to Press; for Example, Rather Than Displaying (RETURN), KeyWords Displays the Image of a Return Key in the Document.
EKD Computer Sales & Supplies Corp.

KI/Composer. *Version:* 5.0. Gary W. Krohm. Jul. 1990. *Items Included:* Program disks, manual, product registration card. *Customer Support:* 1 year software maintenance $395.00; training program $295.00; optional typesetter driver for Compugraphic Linotype or Autologic typesetter $495.00.

TITLE INDEX

DOS 3.10 or higher. IBM PC/AT/386/PS/2 & compatibles hard drive required. disk $895.00 (Order no.: KI5DOS). *Addl. software required:* Windows 3.1 or higher for preview only. *Optimal configuration:* 386 25MH+ with 2Mb RAM & +40Mb hard drive. *Networks supported:* Network File System, PC Net.
Sun OS 4.01 UNIX. Sun 3/60 Sun SPARC 8Mb. disk $895.00 (Order no.: KIUNIX). *Addl. software required:* News or OPEN Look. *Optimal configuration:* SPARC Server 1 with 24Mb RAM 660Mb DASD. (Order no.: KI5AIX).
Powerful Code Driven Typesetting Program That Will Operate on a Wide Variety of DOS & UNIX Based Computer Systems. Supports PostScript Output Devices & Older Typesetters from Autologic, Linotronic & Compugraphic. Editable Kerneling & Tracking Pairs. Support for As Many As 1800 Fonts. Fine Levels of Control in Typesetter Units. Full Ligature Support. Able to Position Rotate & Scale PostScript Files.
Krohm International, Ltd.

Kid McGee. Mar. 1994. *Items Included:* Program manual. *Customer Support:* Free technical support 1-800-421-4157, 90 day warranty.
Consumer. IBM or 100% compatible (1.5Mb). disk $29.95 (ISBN 1-882848-81-0, Order no.: 1B666). *Nonstandard peripherals required:* VGA or MCGA monitor. *Addl. software required:* Davidson's Kid Works2 or Broderbund's Kid Pix for DOS.
School ver.. IBM or 100% compatible (1.5Mb). disk $39.95 (ISBN 1-882848-82-9, Order no.: 1B666T). *Nonstandard peripherals required:* VGA or MCGA monitor. *Addl. software required:* Davidson's Kid Works2 or Broderbund's Kid Pix for DOS.
Lab pak. IBM or 100% compatible (1.5Mb). disk $99.95 (ISBN 1-882848-83-7, Order no.: 1B666LPK). *Nonstandard peripherals required:* VGA or MCGA monitor. *Addl. software required:* Davidson's Kid Works2 or Broderbund's Kid Pix for DOS.
network. IBM or 100% compatible (1.5Mb). 3.5" disk contact publisher for price (ISBN 1-882848-84-5, Order no.: 1B666NET). *Nonstandard peripherals required:* VGA or MCGA monitor. *Addl. software required:* Davidson's Kid Works2 or Broderbund's Kid Pix for DOS.
Site license. IBM or 100% compatible (1.52Mb). disk $399.00 (ISBN 1-882848-85-3, Order no.: 1B666SITE). *Nonstandard peripherals required:* VGA or MCGA monitor. *Addl. software required:* Davidson's Kid Works2 or Broderbund's Kid Pix for DOS.
consumer. MAC LC or above (1.5Mb). 3.5" disk $29.95 (ISBN 1-882848-86-1, Order no.: APM666). *Nonstandard peripherals required:* 256 color monitor highly recommended. *Addl. software required:* Davidsons' Kid Works2 or Broderbund's Kid Pix for DOS.
School ver.. MAC LC or above (1.5Mb). 3.5" disk $39.95 (ISBN 1-882848-87-X, Order no.: APM666T). *Nonstandard peripherals required:* 256 color monitor highly recommended. *Addl. software required:* Davidson's Kid Works2 or Broderbund's Kid Pix.
Lab pak. MAC LC or above (1.5Mb). 3.5" disk $99.95 (ISBN 1-882848-88-8, Order no.: APM666LPK). *Nonstandard peripherals required:* 256 color monitor highly recommended. *Addl. software required:* Davidson's Kid Works2 or Broderbund's Kid Pix.
network. MAC LC or above (1.5Mb). 3.5" disk contact publisher for price ISBN 1-882848-92-6, Order no.: APM666NET). *Nonstandard peripherals required:* 256 color monitor highly recommended. *Addl. software required:* Davidson's Kid Works2 or Broderbund's Kid Pix.
Let your child's imagination soar with "Kid McGee," featuring the colorful characters from "McGee No Words" Software Series. "Kid McGee" is additional clip art graphics for your existing kid works2 & Kid Pix programs. "Kid McGee" encourages creativity & imagenation through a variety of activities - coloring book, paint-by-number, disguises, complete-the-picture, background scenery, & mugshots. Best of all, there's no paint to clean Up! Also Includes: Mac LC or above (1.5Mb), 256 color monitor highly recommended; Davidson's Kid Works2 or Broderbund's Kid Pix; Site license; 03 #399.00; ISBN 1-882848-89-6; Order# APM666SITE.
Lawrence Productions, Inc.

Kid McGee II. Version: 2.0. 1996. *Items Included:* Program manual. *Customer Support:* Free technical support, 1-800-421-4157, 90 day warranty.
Consumer. Windows 3.1. IBM or 100% compatibles (1Mb RAM). disk $39.95 (ISBN 1-57204-403-9). *Nonstandard peripherals required:* 256 color in 640x480 mode, VGA or MCGA monitor, mouse.
School ver.. Windows 3.1. IBM or 100% compatibles (1Mb RAM). disk $49.95 (ISBN 1-57204-404-7). *Nonstandard peripherals required:* 256 color in 640x480 mode, VGA or MCGA monitor, mouse.
Lab pack. Windows 3.1. IBM or 100% compatibles (1Mb RAM). disk $129.95 (ISBN 1-57204-405-5). *Nonstandard peripherals required:* 256 color in 640x480 mode, VGA or MCGA monitor, mouse.
Site license. Windows 3.1. IBM or 100% compatibles (1Mb RAM). disk $699.00 (ISBN 1-57204-406-3). *Nonstandard peripherals required:* 256 color in 640x480 mode, VGA or MCGA monitor, mouse.
Let your child's imagination soar with Kid McGee, featuring the colorful characters from McGee NO WORDS Software Series. A self-contained electronic activity book for Windows, Kid McGee encourages creativity & imagination through a variety of activities - coloring book, paint-by-number, disguises, complete-the-picture, background scenery, & Mugshots. Best of all, there's no paint to clean up!
Lawrence Productions, Inc.

Kid Smarts: Learning Library, Alien Arcade, My Coloring Book. Merit Software Staff et al. Aug. 1995. *Items Included:* Set up instruction sheet. *Customer Support:* (503) 639-6863.
WIN. IBM PC. $14.95 Alien Arcade (ISBN 1-887783-06-7, Order no.: 5300-4002). *Optimal configuration:* IBM PC 386 or higher, Windows 3.1, V6A, 2Mb RAM, soundcard.
Windows. IBM PC. $14.95 My Coloring Book (Order no.: 5300-4002). *Optimal configuration:* IBM PC 386 or higher, Windows 3.1, VGA or higher, mouse, 4Mb RAM, soundcard, speaker.
DOS. IBM PC. $14.95 Learning Library (Order no.: 5300-4002). *Optimal configuration:* IBM PC 386 or higher, DOS 5.0, EGA/CGA/VGA, 1Mb RAM, Graphics card, speakers, CD-ROM EXT 2.1.
Includes Various Programs to Teach Children to Recognize Shapes, Colors, Learn to Count & Read Small Words. Children Also Learn to Color & Increase Dexterity Through Painting & Arcade Games.
Entertainment Technology.

KIDART: School Pac 1. Jan. 1993.
disk $159.95, Lab Pack (ISBN 1-883221-02-1).
disk $495.95, Network Edition (ISBN 1-883221-01-3).
disk $79.95, School Edition (ISBN 1-883221-00-5).
Imager, Inc.

KIDS ON SITE DEMO

KidDesk. Oct. 1992. *Items Included:* Manual. *Customer Support:* 30-day satisfaction guarantee, 90-day warranty, technical support.
Macintosh, System 6.0.7 or higher. Mac Plus or higher (1Mb for System 6.0.X, 2Mb for System 7.0). 3.5" disk $39.95. *Optimal configuration:* Macintosh with color monitor System 7, 4Mb RAM, equipped with microphone for sound input.
MS-DOS. IBM, Tandy or compatible (640k). disk $39.95. *Nonstandard peripherals required:* VGA or EGA. *Optimal configuration:* IBM, Tandy or compatible with color monitor, EGA or VGA, Sound Blaster with microphone for sound input.
Windows (4Mb). IBM or compatible. disk $39.95. *Nonstandard peripherals required:* VGA or EGA. *Optimal configuration:* IBM or compatible with color monitor, 4Mb RAM, VGA or EGA, Sound Blaster with microphone.
Colorful, Graphical Menuing Program, Allows Kids to Launch Their Own Programs but Prohibits Their Access to Any Other Files or Programs on the Hard Drive. Working Desktop Accessories, Including a Calendar, Calculator, Message Machine & Clock, Offer Children Hours of Fun on the Computer.
Edmark Corp.

KIDS - MIDI: Getting Ready to Play. Brenna Bailey. *Items Included:* 1 3-ring binder. *Customer Support:* 90 day warranty against defective software.
System 6.0.7 - 7.1. Macintosh (1Mb). 3.5" disk $79.95 (Order no.: MAC-1321). *Optimal configuration:* Also requires MIDI interface & MIDI compatible music keyboard.
DOS 3.3 or higher. IBM PC (640k). disk $79.95 (Order no.: MI-1321). *Optimal configuration:* Also requires MIDI interface & MIDI compatible music keyboard.
A Four Disk Series for the Very Young. ZOO PUPPET THEATER Reinforces Learning Correct Finger Numbers for Piano Playing; RACE CAR KEYS Teaches Keyboard Topography by Recognizing Solefege Syllables or Letter Names; DINOSAURS LUNCH Teaches Placement of Notes on Treble Staff; & FOLLOW ME Asks Users to Play Notes That Have Been Presented Aurally.
Electronic Courseware Systems, Inc.

Kids' Assembler. Aug. 1984. *Compatible Hardware:* Commodore 64. *Memory Required:* 64k.
disk $10.00 (ISBN 0-931145-01-5).
(ISBN 0-931145-00-7).
Beginner's Assembler Designed to Teach Young People How to Write Assembly Language Programs on the Commodore 64.
Sandlight Pubns.

Kids Classics. Version: 2.0. (Dr. T's Sing-A-Long Ser.). Jan. 1994. *Customer Support:* Free, unlimited.
Windows 3.1 or higher. IBM 386 or higher (4Mb). disk $24.95 (ISBN 1-884899-26-9).
Dr. T's Music Software, Inc.

Kids on Site. *Items Included:* Instruction manual. *Customer Support:* Free Telephone support.
DOS/Windows 95. IBM & compatibles (8Mb). Contact publisher for price. *Optimal configuration:* CD-ROM drive.
MAC. Macintosh (4Mb). Contact publisher for price. *Nonstandard peripherals required:* CD-ROM drive.
Digital Pictures, Inc.

Kids on Site Demo. *Items Included:* Instruction manual. *Customer Support:* Free Telephone support.
DOS/Windows 95. IBM & compatibles (8Mb).

Contact publisher for price. *Optimal configuration:* CD-ROM drive.
MAC. Macintosh (4Mb). Contact publisher for price. *Nonstandard peripherals required:* CD-ROM drive.
Digital Pictures, Inc.

Kid's Typing. (The/Talking Tutor Ser.).
Windows. IBM & compatibles. CD-ROM disk $44.95 (Order no.: R1026). *Nonstandard peripherals required:* CD-ROM drive. *Optimal configuration:* 386 processor or higher, MS-DOS 3.1 or higher, 20Mb hard drive, 640k RAM, external speakers or headphones (with sound card) that are Sound Blaster compatible, VGA graphics & adapter, VGA color monitor.
Macintosh (4Mb). (Order no.: R1026A). *Nonstandard peripherals required:* 14" color monitor or larger, CD-ROM drive.
This Outstanding Series Uses Puzzles, Exciting Stories, Color-Animation & Music to Teach the Basics (Ages 7-10).
Library Video Co.

Kid's Zoo. Sep. 1995. *Customer Support:* Telephone support - free (except phone charge). Windows 3.1. IBM & compatibles (386 DX-20) (4Mb). CD-ROM disk $12.99 (ISBN 1-57594-002-7). *Nonstandard peripherals required:* 2x CD-ROM player, Sound Card, VGA monitor. *Optimal configuration:* 486 SX-33.
Learn about Nature from the Cutest Creatures on the Planet.
Kidsoft, Inc.

Kid's Zoo. Sep. 1995. *Customer Support:* Telephone support - free (except phone charge). Windows 3.1. IBM & compatibles (386 DX-20) (4Mb). CD-ROM disk $12.99 (ISBN 1-57594-041-8). *Nonstandard peripherals required:* 2x CD-ROM player, Sound Card, VGA monitor. *Optimal configuration:* 486 SX-33.
Learn about Nature from the Cutest Creatures on the Planet. Blister Pack Jewel Case.
Kidsoft, Inc.

Kid's Zoo: A Baby Animal Adventure.
MS-DOS 3.1 or higher, Windows. 386 processor or higher (640k). CD-ROM disk $49.95 (Order no.: R1169). *Nonstandard peripherals required:* CD-ROM drive. *Optimal configuration:* 386 processor or higher, MS-DOS 3.1 or higher, 20Mb hard drive, external speakers or headphones (with sound card) that are Sound Blaster compatible, VGA graphics & adapter, VGA color monitor.
Macintosh (4Mb). (Order no.: R1169A). *Nonstandard peripherals required:* 14" color monitor or larger, CD-ROM drive.
Children Meet, Play with, Talk to & Learn about All Kinds of Baby Animals from the Tiny Butterfly to the Humongous Hippopotamus. Take a Closer Look at These Animals Using Picture Dictionaries, Talking Storybooks & Movie Clips.
Library Video Co.

KidSmarts: My Coloring Book Learning Library, Alien Arcade. Merit Software et al. Jan. 1996. *Items Included:* Set-up instruction sheet. *Customer Support:* 310-403-0043.
Alien Arcade & My Coloring Book: Windows; Learning Library: DOS. IBM PC. disk $14.95 (ISBN 1-887783-20-2, Order no.: 5200-3002). *Optimal configuration:* Alien Arcade: IBM PC 386 or higher, Windows 3.1, VGA, 2Mb RAM; My Coloring Book: IBM PC 386 or higher, Windows 3.1, VGA or higher, mouse, 4Mb RAM, soundcard, speaker; Learning Library: IBM PC 386 or higher, DOS 5.0, EGA/CGA/VGA, 1Mb RAM, Graphics card, speakers, CD ROM, Ext 2.1.
Includes Various Programs to Teach Children to Recognize Shapes, Colors, Learn to Count, &

Read Small Words. Children Also Learn to Color & Increase Dexterity Through Painting & Arcade Games.
Entertainment Technology.

KIDWARE 2 Plus Learning Center: (For Two Computer in One Classroom). John Rader et al. Jun. 1993. *Items Included:* One teacher's manual, one program manual, one Mother-Goose map & poster, one "I can Count the Petals of a Flower" poster & book, one Mouse Paint book, Big Red Barn book, one mouse pad, one microphone. *Customer Support:* Training workshop - 2,000.00-two days on-site, 1-800 help line.
DOS 3.3, DOS 5.0. IBM PS/2 Model 25 or 30 & compatibles (640k). For the optimal configuration: 2150.00. *Nonstandard peripherals required:* VGA graphics board & monitor, IBM speech adapter card, or Digispeech, M-Audio, or Soundblaster, External speaker, mouse. *Addl. software required:* DOS. 3.3, DOS 5.0 & software associated with mouse. *Optimal configuration:* One IBM PS/2 Model 25 or Model 30 with 640k RAM, color display (MCGA or VGA), one 720k 3.5" disk drive, IBM Speech Adapter, one IBM Proprinter or Star Micronics color printer & one External, keyboard, IBM mouse, Powerpad is optional DOS 3.3 & DOS 5.50. *Networks supported:* Novell, ICLAS.
Discovery Oriented Software for Young Children. An Educational Software Series Containing Eleven Software Programs for Children & Three Software for Teachers. Contains a License for Each Software Program to Be Used by Two Computer Stations in the Classroom. Comprehensive, Full-Curriculum Offering Supporting Developmental Education for early Childhood Programs. Also Used for Chilren with Special Needs.
Mobius Corp.

KIDWARE 2 Plus Single Station. John Rader et al. Apr. 1991. *Items Included:* Two manuals (teacher's, software guide), one Mother-Goose Map, one "I Can Count the Petals of a Flower" poster & book, one Mouse Paint book, Big Red Barn book, one mouse pad, one PowerPad, five overlays, one microphone, one serial cable. *Customer Support:* Training Workshop - $2,000-2 days on site, 1-800 Help Line.
DOS 3.3, DOS 5.0. IBM PS/2 & compatibles (640k). disk For the optimal configuration: $1195.00; School price 1195.00. *Nonstandard peripherals required:* VGA graphics board & monitor, IBM speech adapter card or Digispeech, M-Audio, or Soundblaster, external speaker, mouse. *Addl. software required:* DOS. 3.3, DOS 5.0 & software associated with mouse. *Optimal configuration:* One IBM PS/2 Model 25 or Model 30 with 640k RAM, color display (MCGA or VGA), one 720k 3.5" disk drive, IBM Speech Adapter, one IBM Proprinter or Star Micronics color printer & one external, keyboard, IBM mouse, Powerpad is optional DOS 3.3 & DOS 5.0. *Networks supported:* Novell, ICLAS.
Discovery Oriented Software for Young Children. An Educational Software Series Containing Eleven Software Programs for Children & Three Software for Teachers. Contains a License for Each Software Program. Comprehensive, Full-Curriculum Offering Supporting Developmental Education for Early Childhood Programs. Also Used for Children with Special Needs.
Mobius Corp.

Kinderama. Selena Studios Staff. Oct. 1995. *Customer Support:* Free on-line tech support at Selenaly-AOL.COM.
Windows. 486-66 processor, or Pentium preferred (8Mb). CD-ROM disk $14.95 (ISBN 1-55727-035-X, Order no.: KDCD01). *Optimal configuration:* 486-66 processor, or Pentium, with a minimum double speed CD-ROM, 1Mb video card required, Windows.
Al, the Dog, Has a Great Elfin Family He Takes Care of Despite the Fact That He Is Allergic to Humans. He Loves the Twins, Nick & Jade & Knack & Ruby. The Boys Are Great & Easy to Watch, but the Girls Have a Mischievous Steak & Wander off During One of His Allergy Attacks. Youngsters Must Help Al Locate the Girls in the Kinderama Forest. Along the Way They Will Learn Letter Identification, Counting, a Bit about Music, Classification, Discrimination, & Play Listening & Memory Games. There Are a Variety of Early Learning Activities to Keep Little Ones Busy & Happily Learning.
Unicorn Educational Software.

Kinetic Access II. Version: 1.60. *Items Included:* User's manual, security offices manual. *Customer Support:* Free unlimited telephone support, 3 months limited warranty.
MS-DOS 2.1 or higher. IBM & compatibles (256K). software only $165.00. *Nonstandard peripherals required:* Hard disk.
with card $195.00.
A Multi-Security Level PC Resource Control System. Provides 16 Security Levels, Each of Which May Have a Unique Set of Resource Permissions. Controls File & Directory Access, DOS Commands, System Devices, Printer & Communications Ports & System Interrupts. Provides for a Security Office, A Trusted User & a Backup User. Includes Privacy Key & Software Floppy Boot Protection. Options Include a Hardware Device Which Provides Absolute Floppy Boot Lock-Out.
Kinetic Corp.

Kinetic CADConvert. Version: 2.0. Jan. 1989. *Items Included:* User's guide, sample CAD files. *Customer Support:* Free unlimited telephone support; 3 months limited warranty.
MS-DOS 2.1 or higher. IBM & compatibles (256K). disk $99.95. *Addl. software required:* Any application capable of importing CGM; A CAD DXFfile.
Converts CAD Drawing Interchange Files (DXF) to Computer Graphics Metafiles (CGM). Converted Images Retain All Original Information Including Text, Colors, Line Types, Hatching Patterns & 3-D Perspective. The Resulting CGM File Can Be Imported into Any Application That Supports CGM, e.g.-Presentation Graphics & Desktop Publishing, for Enhancement & Merging with Text or Other Graphics.
Kinetic Corp.

Kinetic Collector/Macintosh. Jun. 1989. *Items Included:* Manual. *Customer Support:* Toll free tech service at no charge, 90 day warranty.
Macintosh (1Mb). Mac Plus, SE, SE/30, II, IIx, IIcx. $765.00 (Order no.: 1206605). *Nonstandard peripherals required:* Bio-Rad model 3550 microplate reader. *Networks supported:* AppleTalk Reader.
Kinetic Data Analysis Software for Use with the Bio-Rad Model 3550 Microplate Reader. Collects Absorbance Readings from Reader According to User Defined Protocol. Determines Kinetic Velocity for Each Well in Microplate. Saves Raw Data in Spreadsheet Compatible Files. Transfers Velocities to Microplate Manager/Macintosh Software for Further Analysis.
Bio-Rad Laboratories.

Kinetic Menu. Version: 2.50. *Items Included:* User's manual. *Customer Support:* Free unlimited telephone support, 30 months limited warranty.
MS-DOS 2.1 or higher. IBM & compatibles (256K). disk $39.95. *Nonstandard peripherals required:* Hard disk.

TITLE INDEX

An-Easy-to-Work-in Operating Environment. Set up 112 Applications Using Point-&-Shoot Selection. Run Any Application with Only 2 Keystrokes. Menu Entries Are Organized in Groups; Group Names & Menu Entries May be Real Word Rather Than Cryptic File Names or Computer Codes. Includes DOS Menu with Built-in Command HELP.
Kinetic Corp.

Kinetic Microlok. *Version:* 2.50. *Items Included:* User's manual. *Customer Support:* Free unlimited telephone support, 3 month limited warranty.
MS-DOS 2.1 or higher. IBM & compatibles (256K). software only $69.95. *Nonstandard peripherals required:* Hard disk.
w/EPROM $79.95.
w/Card $99.95.
Provides All-or-None Access Control for Stand-Alone PC's & LAN Nodes. Allows up to 16 Separate Users, Each with a Unique Password. Includes Software Floppy Boot Protection, Privacy Key, & a ScreenSaver. Options Include Two Forms of Encryption & a Hardware Device Which Provides Absolute Floppy Boot Lock-Out.
Kinetic Corp.

Kinetic U.S. Maps-3D. *Version:* 2.0. Jul. 1989. *Items Included:* Catalog of sample images. *Customer Support:* Free unlimted telephone support, 3 months limited warranty.
MS-DOS 2.1 or higher. IBM & compatibles (256K). disk $95.00. *Addl. software required:* Application capable of importing a CGM file.
A Set of 94 State, Regional & National United States Maps. Image Files Are Standard CGM & Are Compatible with a Wide Range of Word Processing, Desktop Publishing, Page Makeup & Presentation Graphics Software. Full Color, Three-Dimensional Map Image of Each Individual State & the Entire U.S. State Maps "Snap Together" Like Puzzle Pieces to Permit Construction of Regions of Adjacent States.
Kinetic Corp.

Kinetic Words, Graphs & Art. *Version:* 3.0. *Compatible Hardware:* IBM PC & compatibles. *Items Included:* Tutorial, reference manual, keyboard overlay, quick reference, installation guide. *Customer Support:* Free, unlimited.
disk $495.00.
Composed of Five Modules. Using Kinetic CAD Convert ($99.95), Users Can Work on Designs & Add Presentations Features.
Kinetic Corp.

King James Version. Jun. 1988. *Customer Support:* No fee is charged for our customer support: 30 day money back return guarantee; lifetime warranty on defective disk replacement; free telephone technical support.
PC or MS-DOS 2.0 or higher. IBM PC/XT/AT or compatible. 3.5" or 5.25" disk $49.95. *Addl. software required:* PC Study Bible. *Optimal configuration:* Hard disk with 1.5Mb hard disk space for each Bible version.
The Text of the King James Version of the Bible. Add-On Bible Version to Be Used with BIBLESOFT'S PC STUDY BIBLE.
Biblesoft.

King James Version. May 1993. *Customer Support:* No fee for customer support: (1) 30 day money back guarantee (2) Lifetime warranty replacement on defective disks (3) Free telephone technical support.
PC-DOS/MS-DOS 2.0 or higher. IBM PC, XT/AT/286/386/486 or 100% compatibles (640k). disk $49.95 (ISBN 1-56514-575-5). *Addl. software required:* PC Study Bible. *Optimal configuration:* Requires 5 1/4" 1.2Mb disk drive for installation & 3Mb of hard disk space. Mouse or pointer device recommended.
Text of the KING JAMES VERSION of the Bible. Add-On Bible Version to Be Used with BIBLESOFT'S PC Study Bible.
Biblesoft.

King James Version PC Study Bible King James Edition: PC Study Bible with Nave's - KJV. Sep. 1992. *Items Included:* One manual. *Customer Support:* No fee is charged for our customer support: 30 day money back return guarantee; lifetime warranty on defective disk replacement; free telephone technical support.
PC or MS-DOS 2.0 or higher. IBM PC/XT/AT or compatible. 3.5" or 5.25" disk $69.95. *Optimal configuration:* Hard disk with 3.5Mb hard disk space recommended.
Computerized Bible (with the Text of the King James Version of the Bible), Concordance, Word Processor & Naves Topical Bible. The Text of the American Standard Version of the Bible Will Be Added for $5.00 Once the Registration Card Is Received. Other Modules & Versions Can Be Added Later.
Biblesoft.

King James Version Text. May 1993. *Items Included:* Disks, marketing literature, order form. *Customer Support:* No fee for customer support: 30 day money back guarantee, limited replacement warranty on diskettes defective at time of purchase, free telephone technical support.
PC-DOS/MS-DOS 3.1 or higher or Windows 3.1 or higher. IBM 386/486 or 100% compatible (Windows); Also AT/XT/286 (DOS) (640k DOS or 4Mb Windows). 3.5" disk $39.95; $9.95 if purchased with the Interlinear Bible, Vines, Strong's or Treasury (ISBN 1-56514-243-8). *Addl. software required:* Biblesoft's PC Study Bible. *Optimal configuration:* 3.5" disk drive for installation & 1.5Mb of hard drive space, mouse or pointer device recommended.
The Text of The King James Verison of the Bible. This is an Add-On to the PC Study Bible.
Biblesoft.

King James Version Text. May 1993. *Items Included:* Disks, marketing literature, order form. *Customer Support:* No fee for customer support: 30 day money back guarantee, limited replacement warranty on diskettes defective at time of purchase, free telephone technical support.
PC-DOS/MS-DOS 3.1 or higher or MS Windows 3.0 or higher. 386/486 or 100% IBM compatible (Windows); Also AT/XT/286 (DOS) (640k DOS or 4Mb Windows). 5.25" disk $39.95; $9.95 if purchased with the Interlinear Bible, Vine's Expository Dictionary, Strong's or Treasury of Scripture Knowledge (ISBN 1-56514-575-5). *Addl. software required:* Biblesoft's PC Study Bible. *Optimal configuration:* Requires 5.25" 1.2Mb disk drive for installation & 1.5Mb of hard drive space, mouse or pointer device recommended.
The Text of the King James Verison of the Bible - an Add-On Bible Version to be Used with Biblesoft's PC Study Bible.
Biblesoft.

KingCOM. Mar. 1993. *Items Included:* User's guide, Getting Started pamphlet. *Customer Support:* Telephone support - free; OTC BBS - free; CompuServe Forum - free.
Microsoft Windows 3.1, MS-DOS. Any PC that will run Microsoft Windows 3.1 (4Mb). disk $50.00 (ISBN 1-883260-00-0). *Optimal configuration:* Microsoft Windows 3.1 and/or Windows for Workgroups, enough RAM to run Windows, communications software, modem or fax/modem. *Networks supported:* All PC networks with Windows 3.1 or higher.
Windows Communications Driver Replacement Which Manages How Your Communications Software, Such As Fax & Data Communications Packages, Vie for Ownership of Your Modem or Fax/Modem. Essentially Eliminates Device Contention Between Windows Communications Software & Serial Port Hardware.
OTC Corp.

KITCHEN & BREAKFAST ROOM PLANS

King's Indian Classical System: Electronic Chessbook. *Version:* 2. Edited by Genna Sosonko. Sep. 1994. *Items Included:* Book & disk with 500 or more games (over 200 annotated). *Customer Support:* Telephone support by appointment.
MS-DOS 2.0 or higher (512k). 3.5" disk $25.00, incl. softcover text (ISBN 0-917237-00-5). *Nonstandard peripherals required:* Mouse, graphics, 3 1/2" drive.
Atari ST (520k). Atari. disk $25.00. *Nonstandard peripherals required:* Monochrome monitor DS/DD drive.
Authoritative Introduction to & Analysis of an Important Chess Opening.
Chess Combination, Inc.

King's Indian Defense, 2 diskettes. *Compatible Hardware:* Apple II; Commodore 64; IBM. *Items Included:* Bound manual. *Customer Support:* Free hotline - no time limit; 30 day limited warranty; updates are $5/disk plus S&H.
$19.95.
Contains the Award-Winning COFFEEHOUSE CHESS MONSTER Chess Opponent Program. It Also Includes an Instructional Database on the Popular King's Indian Defense Opening System. There Is On-Screen Commentary As Well As Chessboard Graphic Animation Every Step of the Way. Examine All the Latest Analyses of the Major Variations, Including the Four-Pawns Attack, the Averbakh Variation, the Samisch Variation, & the Classical Variation, with Edited Commentary by Grandmaster Peter Biyiasis.
Dynacomp, Inc.

King's Quest I. Roberta Williams. *Compatible Hardware:* Apple IIe, IIc; Atari ST; Commodore Amiga; IBM PC, PCjr. *Memory Required:* 128k. disk $49.95 ea.
IBM. (Order no.: 31260102).
Atari. (Order no.: 16260102).
Amiga. (Order no.: 27260102).
Apple. (Order no.: 10260102).
Animated Adventure in Which Sir Graham Has Become King & Must Rescue a Captive Princess Somewhere in His Kingdom. Joystick &/or Keyboard Controls Move Sir Graham As He Walks, Jumps, Ducks, Swims, & Climbs Through 80 Screens.
Sierra On-Line, Inc.

Kiplinger's Simply Money. 1993. *Customer Support:* Support Agreement Available.
Windows. IBM PC & compatibles (4Mb). disk $69.99.
Graphically-Oriented Money Management System for Personal & Business Use. Tracks Checking, Savings, Mortgage, Credit Card, Asset, Liability, Investment & Payroll Accounts. Updates Stock Prices by Modem, Prints Personalized Checks, Budgets, Schedules Payments, Generates Reports & Graphs. Includes Transaction Reminders & Financial Advice from Kiplinger Washington Editors.
FourHome Productions.

Kirk's - Comm. *Customer Support:* All of our products are unconditionally guaranteed.
DOS. CD-ROM disk $39.95 (Order no.: KIRK'S - COMM). *Nonstandard peripherals required:* CD-ROM drive.
630 MB of Modem, BBS, & Other Communication Utilities.
Walnut Creek CDRom.

Kitchen & Breakfast Room Plans. *Version:* 1.2. Michael E. Nelson. 1995. *Items Included:* Complete instructions & plan book of layouts (symbol files). *Customer Support:* 30 day warranty.
DOS Version with CAD Program excepting DXF format. Any DOS computer w/CAD Program.

disk $49.95 (ISBN 1-886917-10-8). *Addl. software required:* CAD Program excepting DXF format.
Kitchen & Breakfast Room Plans, Symbols Files with 66 Layouts to Choose. DXF Format.
Nelson Michael E. & Assocs., Inc.

Kitchen Help. *Version:* 2.0. Charles E. Aylworth. Apr. 1986. *Compatible Hardware:* IBM PC & compatibles. *Operating System(s) Required:* PC-DOS/MS-DOS 2.0 or higher. *Language(s):* Pascal. *Memory Required:* 256k. *General Requirements:* 2 disk drives or hard disk, printer. disk $450.00 (ISBN 0-937973-07-6).
Calculates Estimated Food Costs Based on Sales Mix. Intended for Institutional & Large Scale Restaurants, Bakeries & Other Food Service. Handles 1000 Recipes, 8000 Ingredients Including Ingredients with Recipes, No Limit on Recipe Size. Recalculates Recipes for Different Batch Sizes. Performs Sales Analysis on Sales Mix.
Bottom Line Software.

Kitchen Sink. *Compatible Hardware:* TRS-80. write for info.
Instant Software, Inc.

Kittens to Cats.
Windows. CD-ROM disk $49.95 (ISBN 1-882949-93-5, Order no.: 91618108ND).
You Love Your Pet, & You've Made an Emotional & Financial Commitment to Seeing That It Grows up As Healthy & Happy. With This Interactive CD-ROM, You'll Learn the Techniques the Experts Use to Make Their Pets the Best They Can Be! An Easy-to-Use, VCR-Like Interface Guides You Through Each Important Stage of Your Pet's Life. Includes Free Video!
Paragon Media.

Kiwi POWER MENUS. Jun. 1992. *Items Included:* One diskette, 12 pg. manual & registration card. *Customer Support:* Free telephone support (non 1-800 number); 60-day full money back guarantee.
System 7 or higher. Macintosh. 3.5" disk $39.95 (ISBN 1-877777-03-X, Order no.: KPM10).
Networks supported: Appleshare, File Server.
Window & Document Management System for System 7. Responsive Way to Access the Contents of Folders Located in Your Apple Menu. This Utility Allows You to Organize Your Apple Menu in a More Structured Fashion, & User Can Efficiently Access Most Often Used Files.
Kiwi Software, Inc.

Kiwi POWER WINDOWS. *Version:* 1.5. Oct. 1991. *Items Included:* One diskette, 80 pg. manual & registration card. *Customer Support:* Free telephone support (non 1-800 number); 60-day full money back guarantee.
System 7 or higher. Macintosh. 3.5" disk $79.95 (ISBN 1-877777-02-1, Order no.: KPW15).
Networks supported: Appleshare, File Server.
Window & Document Management System for System 7. With Its Many Intelligent Window Layouts, You'll Maximize Use of Available Screen Space. And by Creating Work Sets, One Command Opens Multiple Documents, Applications, or Folders & Instantly Repositions Their Windows, Making Quick Work of Repetitive Tasks.
Kiwi Software, Inc.

KiwiEnvelopes! *Version:* 3.1. *Compatible Hardware:* Apple Macintosh. *Items Included:* Manual, registr. card. *Customer Support:* 60 day money back guarantee.
3.5" disk $49.95 retail (ISBN 1-877777-00-5).
Desk Accessory for Printing Envelopes. Specially Designed to Work with Word Processor.
Kiwi Software, Inc.

Klotski; Gemstorm. ZH Computer Corp. & Great Bear-Star Press. Jan. 1996. *Items Included:* Set-up instruction sheet. *Customer Support:* 310-403-0043.
Win 3.0, DOS for Klotski; DOS 3.0 or higher for Gemstorm. IBM PC. disk $12.95 (ISBN 1-887783-13-X, Order no.: 5100-2001). *Optimal configuration:* IBM PC, Windows 3.0 or higher, Mouse for Klotski; IBM PC, 256k RAM, CGA, keyboard for Gemstorm.
Logic & Skill Games.
Entertainment Technology.

Knight Force. Oct. 1989.
MS-DOS (512k). $44.95. *Optimal configuration:* EGA-VGA boards.
Amiga 500, 1000, 2000 (512k). 3.5" disk $44.95.
Atari ST 520, 1040, ST2, ST4 (512k). 3.5" disk $44.95. *Nonstandard peripherals required:* Color monitor.
Arcade Adventures Game. Defeat the Harmful Creatures of All Ages to Liberate the Princess.
Titus Software Corp.

Knights of the Sky. Nov. 1990. *Items Included:* Manual, key summary card, map. *Customer Support:* Free customer service, (410) 771-1151, Ext. 350.
IBM PC & compatibles (512k). 3.5" or 5.25" disk $59.95. *Nonstandard peripherals required:* Supports VGA/MCGA, EGA, CGA, Tandy 16-color (640k for VGA).
Become a World War I Flying Ace & Take to the Skies for Thrilling Aerial Dogfights Against Some of the Greatest Combat Pilots Ever - Including the Infamous Red Baron. Super 3-D Graphics Capture Every Heart-Pounding Moment; Intelligent Opponents & Challenging Scenarios Pose the Ultimate Test to Your Dogfighting Skills.
MicroProse Software.

Knitting Instruction. Sep. 1982. *Compatible Hardware:* Commodore 64, PET Series. *Language(s):* BASIC. *Memory Required:* 16k. disk $34.95.
Provides User with Instructions for Knitting Even the Most Complicated Patterns into a Sweater. Works More Accurately If User Can Enter the Gauge & Number of Stitches in a Pattern.
J.P. Programs.

Knockout. *Version:* 1.1. Sep. 1990. *Items Included:* Manual. *Customer Support:* 2 free hours of telephone support; $60.00 per hour thereafter.
MS-DOS. IBM PC, XT, AT, OS/2 or compatibles (640k). disk $250.00. *Networks supported:* Novell.
For Data Entry on PC's: 10 Key (Keypad) or Keyboard Entry, Enter Numeric & Alpha Data; Edit Data; Verify All or Parts of Data; Screen or Printed Display of Data; Add, Delete, Retrieve Respondents; Supervisor Management Reports; Marginal Counts; Data Output AS ASCII or Column Binary File.
Analytical Computer Service, Inc.

The Know It All Series. *Version:* 2.0. 1989. *Items Included:* Storage folder, user guide/teacher manual, 1 disk. *Customer Support:* Free telephone support.
Apple DOS 3.3. Apple II (128k). $49.95 per title. Set discounts for multiple titles (Order no.: KIA-A). *Optimal configuration:* Computer with printer.
MS-DOS. IBM or 100% compatible (256k). $49.95 per title. Set discounts for multiple titles (Order no.: KIA-I). *Nonstandard peripherals required:* CGA (minimum). *Optimal configuration:* Computer with minimum CGA capability & printer.
A Series of Eleven Titles: Five for Nutrition Education, Four for Health Education, & Two for Geography Education. All Titles Feature Three Familiar But Challenging Games. Each Title Includes an Editor, Enabling Educators to Create Their Own Games on Any Topic. All Titles Available Separately or in Sets.
DDA Software.

Knoware. *Version:* 2.1. Jan. 1986. *Compatible Hardware:* Apple II+, IIe; IBM PC & compatibles, PC XT. *Operating System(s) Required:* PC-DOS 1.1, 2.0; Apple DOS. *Language(s):* BASIC. *Memory Required:* Apple 64k, IBM 128k. *General Requirements:* CGA card.
disk $149.00 ea.
MS-DOS. (ISBN 0-924836-02-4).
Apple. (ISBN 0-924836-05-9).
Applications Programs Include: Introductory Spreadsheet for Data Analysis, Introductory Word Processor for Writing Letters & Memos, Introductory Database Manager for Maintaining Lists, Graphics Program for Making Bar & Pie Charts, Financial Analysis Programs for Investment Decisions.
Knoware Learning Systems, Inc.

Knowledge Finder. Oct. 1987.
MS Windows 3.1 or higher. IBM & compatibles (4Mb). CD-ROM disk $325.00-$2790.00. *Nonstandard peripherals required:* Magnetic or CD-ROM, using ISO 9660. *Optimal configuration:* IBM & compatibles, 80386 or higher, 4Mb RAM, 20Mb hard disk, mouse, MS Windows 3.1 or higher.
System 6.0.7 or higher. Apple Macintosh (3Mb). CD-ROM disk $325.00-$2790.00. *Optimal configuration:* Apple Macintosh Plus or higher, 3Mb RAM, System 6.0.7 or higher.
A Powerful Retrieval Tool for Accessing the Biomedical Literature, Designed for Use by Both Novice & Experienced Searchers. Knowledge Finder Databases, Prepared by the National Institutes of Health, Contain Descriptive Citations to Millions of Medical Journal Articles. Knowledge Finder, Which Runs on IBM & Compatible & Apple Macintosh Computers, Provides Easy, Economical & Power Access to the CD-ROM Databases. Uses Probabilistic Indexing & Retrieval Techniques, Representing the State-of-the-Art of Information Retrieval. Retrieved Citations Are Ranked in Likely Order of Relevance to the Searcher. As Well As Retrieving "Exact" Matches, It Finds Database Entries That Are "Close" to What the Searcher Requested.
Aries Systems Corp.

Knowledge Quest. Jan. 1989. *Items Included:* 2-page users guide. *Customer Support:* 30-day unlimited warranty, toll-free number 800-346-1930.
MS-DOS. IBM or compatible (256k). disk $24.95 (ISBN 1-888502-00-2, Order no.: KQI3). *Optimal configuration:* IBM or compatible hard drive, MS-DOS 2.0 or higher, 256k, CGA graphics, 3.5" drive.
PRO-DOS. Apple II (64k). disk $24.95 (ISBN 1-888502-01-0, Order no.: KQA5). *Optimal configuration:* Apple IIE or IIC, 64k, color, 1 5.25" drive.
Macintosh. Macintosh, color (2Mb). 3.5" disk $24.95 (ISBN 1-888502-02-9, Order no.: KQM3).
A Colorful, Highly-Interactive & Easy-to-Use Electronic Board Game for 1 Player, 2 Players or 2 Teams. In a Game, Players Score Points & Acquire Tokens by Correctly Answering 60 Multiple-Choice Questions Randomly Selected from a Pool of More Than 1,000 on Each Disk. Players Can Play a Complete Game or Quit at Any Time - High Score Wins.
CBE Services, Inc.

TITLE INDEX

KNOWLEDGEMAN

Knowledge Quest Essentials. Apr. 1990. *Items Included:* 2-page users guide. *Customer Support:* 30-day unlimited warranty, toll-free number 800-346-1930.
  MS-DOS. IBM or compatible (256k). disk $24.95 (ISBN 1-888502-03-7, Order no.: KQEI3). *Optimal configuration:* IBM or compatible hard drive, MS-DOS 2.0 or higher, 256k, CGA graphics, 3.5" drive.
  PRO-DOS. Apple II (64k). disk $24.95 (ISBN 1-888502-04-5, Order no.: KQEA5). *Optimal configuration:* Apple IIE or IIC, 64k, color, 1 5.25" drive.
  Macintosh. Macintosh, color (2Mb). 3.5" disk $24.95 (ISBN 1-888502-05-3, Order no.: KQEM3).
  A Colorful, Highly-Interactive & Easy-to-Use Electronic Board Game for 1 Player, 2 Players or 2 Teams. In a Game, Players Score Points & Acquire Tokens by Correctly Answering 60 Multiple-Choice Questions Randomly Selected from a Pool of More Than 1,000 on Each Disk. Players Can Play a Complete Game or Quit at Any Time - High Score Wins.
  CBE Services, Inc.

Knowledge Quest Human Body & Health. Jul. 1994. *Items Included:* 2-page users guide. *Customer Support:* 30-day unlimited warranty, toll-free number 800-346-1930.
  MS-DOS. IBM or compatible (256k). disk $24.95 (ISBN 1-888502-21-5, Order no.: KQHI3). *Optimal configuration:* IBM or compatible hard drive, MS-DOS 2.0 or higher, 256k, CGA graphics, 3.5" drive.
  PRO-DOS. Apple II (64k). disk $24.95 (ISBN 1-888502-22-3, Order no.: KQHA5). *Optimal configuration:* Apple IIE or IIC, 64k, color, 1 5.25" drive.
  Macintosh. Macintosh, color (2Mb). 3.5" disk $24.95 (ISBN 1-888502-23-1, Order no.: KQHM3).
  A Colorful, Highly-Interactive & Easy-to-Use Electronic Board Game for 1 Player, 2 Players or 2 Teams. In a Game, Players Score Points & Acquire Tokens by Correctly Answering 60 Multiple-Choice Questions Randomly Selected from a Pool of More Than 1,000 on Each Disk. Players Can Play a Complete Game or Quit at Any Time - High Score Wins.
  CBE Services, Inc.

Knowledge Quest Literature. Dec. 1993. *Items Included:* 2-page users guide. *Customer Support:* 30-day unlimited warranty, toll-free number 800-346-1930.
  MS-DOS. IBM or compatible (256k). disk $24.95 (ISBN 1-888502-15-0, Order no.: KQLI3). *Optimal configuration:* IBM or compatible hard drive, MS-DOS 2.0 or higher, 256k, CGA graphics, 3.5" drive.
  PRO-DOS. Apple II (64k). disk $24.95 (ISBN 1-888502-16-9, Order no.: KQLA5). *Optimal configuration:* Apple IIE or IIC, 64k, color, 1 5.25" drive.
  Macintosh. Macintosh, color (2Mb). 3.5" disk $24.95 (ISBN 1-888502-17-7, Order no.: KQLM3).
  A Colorful, Highly-Interactive & Easy-to-Use Electronic Board Game for 1 Player, 2 Players or 2 Teams. In a Game, Players Score Points & Acquire Tokens by Correctly Answering 60 Multiple-Choice Questions Randomly Selected from a Pool of More Than 1,000 on Each Disk. Players Can Play a Complete Game or Quit at Any Time - High Score Wins.
  CBE Services, Inc.

Knowledge Quest Mathematics. Jul. 1993. *Items Included:* 2-page users guide. *Customer Support:* 30-day unlimited warranty, toll-free number 800-346-1930.
  MS-DOS. IBM or compatible (256k). disk $24.95 (ISBN 1-888502-09-6, Order no.: KQMI3). *Optimal configuration:* IBM or compatible hard drive, MS-DOS 2.0 or higher, 256k, CGA graphics, 3.5" drive.
  PRO-DOS. Apple II (64k). disk $24.95 (ISBN 1-888502-10-X, Order no.: KQMA5). *Optimal configuration:* Apple IIE or IIC, 64k, color, 1 5.25" drive.
  Macintosh. Macintosh, color (2Mb). 3.5" disk $24.95 (ISBN 1-888502-11-8, Order no.: KQMM3).
  A Colorful, Highly-Interactive & Easy-to-Use Electronic Board Game for 1 Player, 2 Players or 2 Teams. In a Game, Players Score Points & Acquire Tokens by Correctly Answering 60 Multiple-Choice Questions Randomly Selected from a Pool of More Than 1,000 on Each Disk. Players Can Play a Complete Game or Quit at Any Time - High Score Wins.
  CBE Services, Inc.

Knowledge Quest Science. Jul. 1991. *Items Included:* 2-page users guide. *Customer Support:* 30-day unlimited warranty, toll-free number 800-346-1930.
  MS-DOS. IBM or compatible (256k). disk $24.95 (ISBN 1-888502-06-1, Order no.: KQSI3). *Optimal configuration:* IBM or compatible hard drive, MS-DOS 2.0 or higher, 256k, CGA graphics, 3.5" drive.
  PRO-DOS. Apple II (64k). disk $24.95 (ISBN 1-888502-07-X, Order no.: KQSA5). *Optimal configuration:* Apple IIE or IIC, 64k, color, 1 5.25" drive.
  Macintosh. Macintosh, color (2Mb). 3.5" disk $24.95 (ISBN 1-888502-08-8, Order no.: KQSM3).
  A Colorful, Highly-Interactive & Easy-to-Use Electronic Board Game for 1 Player, 2 Players or 2 Teams. In a Game, Players Score Points & Acquire Tokens by Correctly Answering 60 Multiple-Choice Questions Randomly Selected from a Pool of More Than 1,000 on Each Disk. Players Can Play a Complete Game or Quit at Any Time - High Score Wins.
  CBE Services, Inc.

Knowledge Quest Science Essentials. Dec. 1993. *Items Included:* 2-page users guide. *Customer Support:* 30-day unlimited warranty, toll-free number 800-346-1930.
  MS-DOS. IBM or compatible (256k). disk $24.95 (ISBN 1-888502-12-6, Order no.: KQSEI3). *Optimal configuration:* IBM or compatible hard drive, MS-DOS 2.0 or higher, 256k, CGA graphics, 3.5" drive.
  PRO-DOS. Apple II (64k). disk $24.95 (ISBN 1-888502-13-4, Order no.: KQSEA5). *Optimal configuration:* Apple IIE or IIC, 64k, color, 1 5.25" drive.
  Macintosh. Macintosh, color (2Mb). 3.5" disk $24.95 (ISBN 1-888502-14-2, Order no.: KQSEM3).
  A Colorful, Highly-Interactive & Easy-to-Use Electronic Board Game for 1 Player, 2 Players or 2 Teams. In a Game, Players Score Points & Acquire Tokens by Correctly Answering 60 Multiple-Choice Questions Randomly Selected from a Pool of More Than 1,000 on Each Disk. Players Can Play a Complete Game or Quit at Any Time - High Score Wins.
  CBE Services, Inc.

Knowledge Quest United States. Jul. 1995. *Items Included:* 2-page users guide. *Customer Support:* 30-day unlimited warranty, toll-free number 800-346-1930.
  MS-DOS. IBM or compatible (256k). disk $24.95 (ISBN 1-888502-24-X, Order no.: KQUSI3). *Optimal configuration:* IBM or compatible hard drive, MS-DOS 2.0 or higher, 256k, CGA graphics, 3.5" drive.
  PRO-DOS. Apple II (64k). disk $24.95 (ISBN 1-888502-25-8, Order no.: KQUSA5). *Optimal configuration:* Apple IIE or IIC, 64k, color, 1 5.25" drive.
  Macintosh. Macintosh, color (2Mb). 3.5" disk $24.95 (ISBN 1-888502-26-6, Order no.: KQUSM3).
  A Colorful, Highly-Interactive & Easy-to-Use Electronic Board Game for 1 Player, 2 Players or 2 Teams. In a Game, Players Score Points & Acquire Tokens by Correctly Answering 60 Multiple-Choice Questions Randomly Selected from a Pool of More Than 1,000 on Each Disk. Players Can Play a Complete Game or Quit at Any Time - High Score Wins.
  CBE Services, Inc.

Knowledge Quest World Geography. Jul. 1994. *Items Included:* 2-page users guide. *Customer Support:* 30-day unlimited warranty, toll-free number 800-346-1930.
  MS-DOS. IBM or compatible (256k). disk $24.95 (ISBN 1-888502-18-5, Order no.: KQGI3). *Optimal configuration:* IBM or compatible hard drive, MS-DOS 2.0 or higher, 256k, CGA graphics, 3.5" drive.
  PRO-DOS. Apple II (64k). disk $24.95 (ISBN 1-888502-19-3, Order no.: KQGA5). *Optimal configuration:* Apple IIE or IIC, 64k, color, 1 5.25" drive.
  Macintosh. Macintosh, color (2Mb). 3.5" disk $24.95 (ISBN 1-888502-20-7, Order no.: KQGM3).
  A Colorful, Highly-Interactive & Easy-to-Use Electronic Board Game for 1 Player, 2 Players or 2 Teams. In a Game, Players Score Points & Acquire Tokens by Correctly Answering 60 Multiple-Choice Questions Randomly Selected from a Pool of More Than 1,000 on Each Disk. Players Can Play a Complete Game or Quit at Any Time - High Score Wins.
  CBE Services, Inc.

Knowledge Server. Jun. 1988.
  MS Windows 3.1 or higher. IBM & compatibles (4Mb). CD-ROM disk $2195.00 & up. *Nonstandard peripherals required:* Magnetic or CD-ROM, using ISO 9660. *Optimal configuration:* IBM & compatibles, 80386 or higher, 4Mb RAM, 20Mb hard disk, mouse, MS Windows 3.1 or higher.
  System 6.0.7 or higher. Apple Macintosh (3Mb). CD-ROM disk $2195.00 & up. *Optimal configuration:* Apple Macintosh Plus or higher, 3Mb RAM, System 6.0.7 or higher.
  Uses the Knowledge Finder Literature Database Search System to Provide Access to Biomedical Literature Reference CD-ROM Databases Across Local Area AppleShare Networks. One or More Database Servers, Each Configured with One or More CD-ROM Databases, Can Be Accessed by Any Compatible IBM & Compatible or Macintosh Workstation Connected to the Network. A User at a Workstation Accesses the Database As Though It Was directly Connected to the Workstation. Knowledge Finder Is a Probabilistic Bibliographic Retrieval System That Simplifies End-User Searching, While Retaining the Power & Flexibilty Offered by Traditional Retrieval Systems.
  Aries Systems Corp.

KnowledgeMan. Micro Data Base Systems, Inc. *Compatible Hardware:* TI Professional. *Operating System(s) Required:* MS-DOS, CP/M-86. *Memory Required:* 192k. *General Requirements:* 2 disk drives, printer.
$500.00.
  Provides Broad Range of Information Processing Capabilities Managers & Professionals Need.
  Texas Instruments, Personal Productivit.

KnowledgePro Database Toolkit. *Version:* 1.20. *Compatible Hardware:* IBM PC & compatibles. *Operating System(s) Required:* MS-DOS. *Memory Required:* 350k. *Items Included:* Disk, manual. *Customer Support:* Phone, Fax, CompuServe.
disk $179.00.
Text Database-Management System That Accesses DBF Files Without Importing or Converting. Supports Boolean Searches, & Searches Can Be Restricted to a Specific Field or Other Qualifier. Also Features the Ability to Run in Background & Memory-Resident Modes: Import & Append ASCII, dBASE & Lotus Text Files.
Knowledge Garden, Inc.

KnowledgePro for DOS/DOS Gold. *Version:* 1.4. *Compatible Hardware:* IBM PC XT, PC AT. *Memory Required:* 512k. *Items Included:* Disks, manual/Royalty-Free Runtime incl. in Gold. *Customer Support:* Compuserve Forum, Phone Fax.
disk $195.00-$449.00.
Application Development Environment Which Combines the Features of an Expert System Shell & Those of a List Processing Language. Enables Programmers to Develop Applications Using DOS, Controls, External Programs.
Knowledge Garden, Inc.

KnowledgePro for Windows KPWin/KPWin Gold. *Version:* 2.51. *Items Included:* 2 disks, 2 manuals/Royalty-Free Runtime w/Gold. *Customer Support:* CompuServe Forum, Phone Fax.
MS Windows 3.X. IBM PC 286 (1Mb). disk $249.00-$549.00. *Optimal configuration:* Mouse & color & 386.
Tool for Rapid Creation of Windows Applications. The System Can Be Used by Programmers & Non-Programmers. Integrates Hypertext & Expert Systems. Interactive Design Tools Are Included. Supports DDE & DLC.
Knowledge Garden, Inc.

Kodak Precision Color Configure Users Guide: For Use with Aldus PhotoStyler. Aug. 1993. *Customer Support:* For customer service, product registration, upgrades, technical support, & CustomerFirst service plans, customers may call Aldus Customer Services at (206) 628-2320.
Macintosh. Contact publisher for price (ISBN 1-56026-261-3).
Aldus Corp.

Komstock's MapCalc. *Compatible Hardware:* Apple Macintosh, Macintosh Plus. *General Requirements:* Hard disk, ImageWriter, LaserWriter.
3.5" disk $1095.00.
Mapping Graphics System.
Komstock Co.

KONFIG. *Version:* 1.2. Aug. 1992. *Items Included:* Full documentation including User's Reference, System Administration manual & Install Guide & one (1) plot executive (e.g. PostScript, HP, CalComp, or Versatec). *Customer Support:* Maintenance plan, training, 1-800 number (customer help desk). Limited warranty for both hardware & software: 90 days to one year for software & new hardware, 30 days for used hardware.
SunOS, UNIX (16Mb). SPARCstation or SPARCserver with color monitor. Starter Kit, contact publisher for price (Order no.: V660). *Addl. software required:* Empress or Oracle relational database management software. *Optimal configuration:* SPARCstation 2; 32Mb memory; 600Mb disk; PostScript compatible laser printer. *Networks supported:* Ethernet, TCP/IP, SNMP.
Additional View/Update License, contact publisher for price (Order no.: V661).
View Only License, contact publisher for price (Order no.: V662).
NetTracker SNMP Interface $2000.00 (Order no.: V663).
Network Configuration & Asset Management System, Featuring Graphical Tools for Depicting a Network Including Logical, Physical, Facility & Device Views; RDBMS Technology for Documenting the Arrangement Connectivity & Descriptions of Devices; Tools for Network Design and/or Model Modification; & Interfaces to Leading Network Management Platforms.
Auto-Trol Technology Corp.

KPWin Plus Plus. *Version:* 1.50a. *Items Included:* Manual. *Customer Support:* Technical support - first 60 days free, annual $495.00 via phone, Fax, E-Mail; 30 days limited warranty; training available.
Windows (4Mb). disk $895.00. *Addl. software required:* Compiler (Microsoft or Borland). *Optimal configuration:* IBM 486 66 DXZ Windows 16 RAM.
This C Plus Plus Code Generation Utility Lets Developers Prototype Their Applications Using KPWin's Interactive Design Tools & Underlying Full-Featured OOP Language & Then Generate Readable, Efficient, Object-Oriented C Plus Plus. Supports Microsoft C/C Plus Plus 7.0, Visual C Plus Plus or Borland C Plus Plus Compilers. Includes a Complete Copy of KPWin.
Knowledge Garden, Inc.

KPWin SQLKIT. 1993. *Items Included:* Manual. *Customer Support:* Technical support - first 60 days free, annual $495.00 via phone, Fax, E-Mail; 30 days limited warranty; training available.
Windows (3.1 & 3.11) (4Mb). disk $399.00 (Order no.: SQL810). *Optimal configuration:* IBM 486 66 DXZ Windows 16 RAM. *Networks supported:* All.
This Add-In Tool for KPWin Provides Easy Access to Many Database Formats Using Standard Query Language (SQL) Calls. Databases Supported Include Oracle, SyBase, Informix, SQL Server & Many More. System Includes a Licensed Copy of the Q Plus E Library from Pioneer Software. Runtime Distribution of Applications Is Free.
Knowledge Garden, Inc.

Krell's GED Prep. *Version:* 1990. 1990. *Items Included:* 8 double sided disks & manual. *Customer Support:* Technical hotline at 800-245-7355; 30 day warranty on defect, 10 replacement of damaged disks.
Apple DOS. Apple (64k). disk $199.95 (ISBN 0-918349-57-5). *Networks supported:* Corvis.
MS-DOS. IBM PC & compatibles (64k). *Networks supported:* Novell.
This Product Prepares Test Takers for the New GED Exam. There Are 6 Areas of Study - Writing Skills, Social Studies, Reading Skills, Math, Science, & Literature & the Arts. The User Is Expected to Have an 8th Grade Reading & Math Skill. This Software Series Will Focus the User in on Topics Which Have Been Mastered & Those Topics Which Need Work. This Is a Goal Oriented Product.
Krell Software Corp.

KRIGE3. *Version:* 2.4. Oct. 1985. *Compatible Hardware:* IBM PC, PC XT, PC AT & compatibles. *Operating System(s) Required:* MS-DOS, PC-DOS. *Language(s):* FORTRAN. *Memory Required:* 512k. *General Requirements:* Printer.
disk $3000.00 (Order no.: KRIGE3).
Produces the Optimal Estimation of Blocks or Points from Known Sample Values. Utilizes a User-Specified Variogram Model to Estimate Two or Three Dimensional Areas. Produces a Regular Grid of Estimated Values & a Grid of the Standard Error of Estimation by Either Regular, Lognormal, or Indicator Kriging.
Geostat Systems International, Inc. (GSII).

KRIJAC. *Version:* 1.3. Jun. 1985. *Compatible Hardware:* IBM PC, PC XT, PC AT & compatibles. *Operating System(s) Required:* MS-DOS, PC-DOS. *Language(s):* FORTRAN. *Memory Required:* 512k. *General Requirements:* Printer.
disk $1500.00 (Order no.: KRIJAC).
Allows the Professional to Objectively Compare Different Variogram Models. The Analyst Can Then Select the One That Produces the Smallest Non-Biased Estimate Errors During the Kriging Process. Computes Estimation Errors by Kriging a Data Point with the Surrounding Data Points in the Test Area. The Analyst Controls the Location & Extent of the Test Area, the Size of the Kriging Matrix, & the Type of Variogram Model Used in the Validation.
Geostat Systems International, Inc. (GSII).

KRIREC. Sep. 1985. *Compatible Hardware:* IBM PC, PC XT, PC AT & compatibles. *Operating System(s) Required:* PC-DOS, MS-DOS. *Language(s):* FORTRAN. *Memory Required:* 512k. *General Requirements:* Printer, plotter.
disk $2500.00 (Order no.: KRIREC).
Computes Ore Recoveries in Blocks on a 3D Regular Grid Using Either Multigaussian or Disjunctive Kriging. These 2 Kriging Methods Allow the Perspective of Intra-Block Grade Distribution in the Estimation. With Both, KRIREC Computes Histograms & Variograms for Selected Mining Units, Which Can Be Sample Points, Blocks or the Entire Deposit.
Geostat Systems International, Inc. (GSII).

KRIVAR. *Version:* 1.32. Jun. 1984. *Compatible Hardware:* IBM PC, PC XT, PC AT & compatibles. *Operating System(s) Required:* MS-DOS, PC-DOS. *Language(s):* FORTRAN. *Memory Required:* 512k. *General Requirements:* Printer.
disk $1000.00 (Order no.: KRIVAR).
Interactive Kriging Program Which Allows the User to Determine If Further Sampling Is Needed & If So, Where. Utilizes a User-Specified Variogram & the Existing Data to Determine the Best Location to Sample Next. Locates the Spot That Yields the Greatest Reduction in the Total Sampling Variance. Serves As a Useful Tool for Planning Cost-Effective Sampling Strategies.
Geostat Systems International, Inc. (GSII).

Kronos Controller. Sep. 1985. *Compatible Hardware:* IBM PC, PC XT, PC AT. *Operating System(s) Required:* MS-DOS 1.0, 3.1 & PC-DOS 2.0, 3.0. *Memory Required:* 256k. *General Requirements:* Hard disk.
PC-DOS. $200.00 (Order no.: SD-00005-000).
MS-DOS. $200.00 (Order no.: SD-00005-000).
Menu-Driven Program That Provides Both Batch Processing & System Security for IBM PC, PC XT, & PC AT. User May Automatically Execute Programs or a Batch of Programs & Individually Program "Function Keys". Also Provides Password Hierarchy, Allowing Only Specified Employees Access to Tasks or Operating System.
Kronos, Inc.

Kroy Sign Studio.
Macintosh Plus or higher. Sign Studio Apprentice $349.00 to $649.00; Sign Studio Professional $2000.00 to $10,000.00.
Sign-Making Software.
Kroy, Inc.

TITLE INDEX

KSAM-PC. *Version:* 1.1. Aug. 1981. *Compatible Hardware:* IBM PC & compatibles. *Operating System(s) Required:* MS-DOS. *Language(s):* Microsoft BASIC, Compiled & Interpretive (source code included). *Memory Required:* 64k.
disk $89.95.
Provides Keyed or Indexed File Access from Microsoft BASIC. Data File Records Can Be Accessed by a Meaningful Key Field. Allows Partial or Generic Key Lookup, Duplicate Keys & Multiple Key Files. Multiple Access Levels for File Security. Key Can Be up to 249 Bytes & Data Records Can Be up to 32k Bytes.
Prodata, Inc. (Idaho).

KSIMS. *Compatible Hardware:* Apple Macintosh.
3.5" disk $21.50.
Simulation for Determining the Rate Law & the Reaction Rate of a Chemical Reaction.
Kinko's.

Kukulcan. Mark Giltzow. Nov. 1985. *Compatible Hardware:* Apple II+, IIe, IIc, IIgs. *Memory Required:* 64k.
disk $39.95.
Educational-Entertainment Software for the Gifted Child. Lab Packs Available.
American Eagle Software, Inc.

KWIKSTAT BASIC. *Version:* 4.1. Jun. 1995. *Compatible Hardware:* IBM PC. *Operating System(s) Required:* MS-DOS, PC-DOS. *Memory Required:* 512k. *Items Included:* Manual & disk. *Customer Support:* Yes.
$99.00.
Statistical Data Analysis Software Creates & Uses DBASE III Type Files. Includes Descriptive Statistics, T-Tests, Anova, Regression, Chi Square, Survival Analysis.
TexaSoft.

L-Zone. Feb. 1995. *Items Included:* Warranty/registration card, game manual. *Customer Support:* Technical Support Number: 1-800-734-9466, 90 days limited warranty.
Windows 3.1; Macintosh. IBM i80486SX or higher, 33MHz i80486DX recommended (8Mb); Macintosh System 7 or higher (8Mb). CD-ROM disk $69.99 (ISBN 1-888158-03-4). *Nonstandard peripherals required:* CD-ROM drive: double speed readout.
Complex Pathways, Futuristic Animation, & "Techno Jam" Music Create the Hyper-Automated City Built by the Mad Scientist. Clear the Traps Laid for You, Pass Through All the Zones, Only Then Will the Path to Planet Green Be Unveiled.
Synergy Interactive Corp.

Lab Partner. *Version:* 1.5. *Items Included:* Spiral bound manual. *Customer Support:* Free customer support.
Macintosh Plus or higher (1Mb), MS-DOS. 3.5" disk $500.00.
Experimental Design & Analysis.
Sof-Ware Tools.

Labcat. 1982. *Compatible Hardware:* IBM PC, PS/2. *Language(s):* Compiled C, BASIC. *Memory Required:* 640k. *General Requirements:* Hard disk, printer. *Items Included:* Software, user documentation. *Customer Support:* Toll-free user hotline; Labcat users' group; Training & Labcat newsletter.
disk $10,000 to $30,000.00 per module.
Family of 14 Software Modules for Automating Toxicology, Pathology & Genetic Toxicology Aspects of Animal Studies. Independent But Compatible Modules Cover Acute Toxicity, Eye Irritation, Skin Irritation, Bodyweights & Daily Observations, Food Consumption, Clinical Chemistry, Hematology, Ocular Toxicity, Organ Weights & Necropsy Records, Histopathology, Randomization Utility, Ames Test, CHO/HGPRT, Chromosome Aberrations, Mouse Lymphoma Tests & UDS.
Innovative Programming Assocs., Inc.

Label. *Compatible Hardware:* TRS-80 Model I, Model III. *Memory Required:* 16k.
cassette $24.95 (Order no.: 0168R).
Instead of Using Line Numbers Label Your BASIC Program Subroutines.
Instant Software, Inc.

Label Maker Version II. Oct. 1986. *Compatible Hardware:* IBM PC, PC XT, PC AT. *Operating System(s) Required:* PC-DOS/MS-DOS 1.1 or higher. *Language(s):* Compiled BASIC. *Memory Required:* 64k. *General Requirements:* Dot matrix printer. CGA card & color monitor recommended.
disk $50.00.
Types up to Five Lines of Text in Four Different Fonts & Three Different TypeFaces on Any One Across Label.
Robert L. Nicolai.

Label Planner. *Version:* 4.6. 1986.
MS-DOS. IBM 386 or higher. $500.00-$1000.00. *Nonstandard peripherals required:* Printer. *Addl. software required:* Cut Planner or Product Planner. *Networks supported:* Novell Net Ware.
Label Program That Never Needs a Computer Programmer to Make Changes or to Run It. Provides User with Labels for the Important Task of Keeping Track of Parts or Products. Labels Contain All the Information Neeeded. User Can Store Several Label Formats for Different Purposes. Also Available with Bar Coding.
Pattern Systems International, Inc.

Label Press: Label Printing Software Tamed. Allen Lubow. May 1994. *Items Included:* Disk containing a variety of templates including FED EX, K-MART, AIRBOURNE EXPRESS, AVERY LABELS, 188 p. manual. *Customer Support:* 30 days money back guarantee; tech support 718-369-2944 M-F 9:00AM-5:00PM EST.
System 6.0 (System 7.0 Rec.) works on System 7.1. MAC Plus or higher (2Mb). Label Press Thermal $795.00; Label Press Therman User $395.00 (ISBN 1-880773-19-8). *Optimal configuration:* System 7.x 2Mb RAM.
An Application Which Generates Bar Coded Labels for the Macintosh. Also Available for Thermal Printers. Comes with Hundreds of Industry Standard Templates As Well As 18 Bar Code Symbologies, Graphics Library, Data File Handling & Drawing Capabilities. Extremely Easy to Use.
Synex.

Labelets. Jun. 1986. *Compatible Hardware:* IBM PC & compatibles. *Memory Required:* 128k. *General Requirements:* Printer. *Customer Support:* Yes.
disk $24.95 (ISBN 0-929800-15-X, Order no.: LC5.25 OR LC3.5).
Makes Custom Labels to Sixty-Six Lines Long. Features Menu & Built-in Text Editor. Lets the User Print Labels, I.D. Labels, Price Tags, Notes etc. Customized Labels Using Printer Control Codes. Not a Mailing List Program.
Electrosonics.

Labels. Aug. 1989. *Items Included:* Instruction included on disk. *Customer Support:* 90 days unlimited warranty.
MS-DOS, Windows 3.1. IBM XT, AT or compatibles (512k). disk $29.95 plus $3.50 S&H (Order no.: 1071). *Addl. software required:* Lotus 1-2-3, Release for Windows 4.0 or higher. *Optimal configuration:* IBM AT, 640K RAM, Lotus 123 Rel. 2.2.
Automates the Printing of Labels from Lotus Data Base or by Importing dBASE III into Lotus.
Compiled Systems.

LABORATORY SYSTEMS

Labels. *Version:* 9.1. Jan. 1986. *Compatible Hardware:* DEC, VAX. *Operating System(s) Required:* VMS. *Language(s):* COBOL.
$1900.00.
Philip Lieberman & Assocs., Inc.

Labels & Envelopes Deluxe. *Version:* 3. *Compatible Hardware:* Apple Macintosh.
3.5" disk $45.00.
Label & Envelope Desk Accessory.
Eastgate Systems, Inc.

LABELS + FORMS. *Version:* 2.0. *Items Included:* Manual. *Customer Support:* Free by phone.
MS-DOS/PC DOS 2.0 or higher, & OS/2. IBM PC, XT, AT, PS/1, PS/2 & compatibles. disk $89.00.
Labels, Forms & Other Materials Printing Program. Prints on All Format Sheets. Can Put Serial Numbers in Printouts. Great for Printing Diskette Labels, Price Tags, Index Cards, Inventory Identification & Many Other Materials. Keeps a Printing History & Statistics for Better Inventory Management.
Highland Software, Inc.

LabelSoft. *Version:* 3.2010. Jul. 1991. *Compatible Hardware:* IBM PC & compatibles. *Operating System(s) Required:* PC-DOS/MS-DOS. *Memory Required:* 640k. *General Requirements:* 9 and 24-pin dot matrix printer, thermal printer, HP LaserJet II, III & compatible laser printer, graphics card. *Customer Support:* Free.
disk $259.00 to $595.00.
Computer Labeling Program. Produces Labels for a Variety of Uses Such As Product & Part Labels, Shelf & Bin Labels, Price Stickers, Production Control & Shipping Labels, & Barcode Symbologies.
Perrysburg Software Corp.

Laboratory in Cognition & Perception. C. M. Levy et al. 1982. *Compatible Hardware:* Apple II+, IIe, IIc. *Operating System(s) Required:* Apple DOS 3.3. *Language(s):* BASIC (source code included). *Memory Required:* 48k.
disk $155.00 ea., incl. student guide & instructor guide (Order no.: PSY224A).
$12.50 add'l student guide.
add'l instructor guide $10.00.
Exposes Students to a Variety of Phenomena, Theoretical Points of View, & Experimental Designs. The Package Demonstrates the Use of Between-Subject, Within-Subject, & Mixed Designs; Explores the Methodological Decisions of a Researcher, & Extends Students' Knowledge of Processes & Phenomena in Contemporary Human Experimental Psychology. The Experiments Simulated in the Package Include: Method of Constant Stimuli, Signal Detection, Span of Apprehension, Iconic Memory, Feature Detection, Pattern Interpretation, Retrieval from STM, Short-Term Forgetting, Comparing Visual & Semantic Information, Concept Learning, & Reasoning from Prose.
CONDUIT.

Laboratory Systems. *Customer Support:* Software warranty; 24 hours, days a week; 800 number; hardware/software staging; training & seminars; documentation; system personalization; consulting services.
DEC VAX, Alpha AXP, DECStations; PC platforms using OpenVMS, DSM, OSF/1, DOS; IBM RISC System 6000 under AIX, Micronetic MUMPS, or DOS; HP9000 under HP-UX. DEC, IBM & HP Platforms (2Mb). contact publisher for price.
Enables Interenterprise Operations, Promote Efficient & Successful Operations Management, & Ensure Adherence to Quality Control Standards. MultiSite Application Meets the Operational Needs of Multilaboratory, Regional Laboratory

Networks. *Application Addresses: Registration, Order Processing, Collection Scheduling, Specimen Transport, Worklist Processing, Results Processing, Results Reporting, Inquiry, & Management Reporting. General Laboratory Is Designed for Mid-Sized Laboratories. Application Addresses: Order Entry, Worklist Processing, Results Processing, Results Reporting, & Management Reporting. PCLab Application Is Designed for Small Laboratories. Provides Order Entry, Worklist Processing, Results Processing, Quality Control, Results & Management Reporting on a PC. Anatomic Pathology Application Addresses: Order Entry, Worklist Processing, Results Processing, Results Reporting, & Management Reporting.*
ANTRIM Corp.

LaBrow. Open Door Software Staff. *Customer Support:* Call for info.
DOS. IBM & compatibles. disk $24.99 (ISBN 1-56756-091-1, Order no.: OD10121).
A Powerful Database Management Utility Ideal for XBASE Developers. View Databases Through Any Index or Modify to Suit. Locate, Seek, Pack, Delete, & Completely Control Your Databases with This "Dangerous" Utility.
Advantage International.

Labsearch. 1988. *Compatible Hardware:* IBM PC & compatibles. *Operating System(s) Required:* PC-DOS/MS-DOS. *Memory Required:* 640k. *General Requirements:* 1.6Mb on hard disk. *Items Included:* 5 disks, manual.
disk $395.00 (Order no.: LS-1).
Allows Physician to Enter an Abnormal Lab Test, Indicate Whether It Is Abnormally High or Low, & Receive a List of All Possible Causes for the Abnormal Test Result. More Than One Test May Be Entered & Only Those Causes Common to Both Lists Will Be Received. Physician May Add to or Amend Database with All Coding Done Automatically. Printout Can Be Received at Any Time by Pressing One Key. Totally Menu Driven. Confirmation of Suspected Diagnosis Can Also Be Enter.
Golightly Cos.

LABTECH CONTROL. *Version:* 5.0. Sep. 1994. *Compatible Hardware:* IBM PC XT, PC AT 386/486, PS/2, or UNIX workstation. *Operating System(s) Required:* MS-DOS; ULTRIX-DEC, HP/UX-HP, AIX-IBM; Sun/OS-Sun, Interactive 386/ix-Interactive, VENIX-VenturCom, DOS Windows 3.1. *Memory Required:* UNIX or Windows 8Mb, DOS 640k. *General Requirements:* Hard disk, analog-digital hardware interface, graphics supported by Windows, 8Mb RAM. *Items Included:* Diskettes, documentation. *Customer Support:* 90 day free support. Support contract available after 90 days.
LABTECH CONTROL $1995.00; LABTECH CONTROLpro $3495.00 DOS or Windows versions.
CONTROL $3995.00; CONTROLpro $6495.00.
Menu & Icon-Driven Industrial Software That Can Be Configured As a SCADA (Supervisory Control & Data Acquisition) System for Process Monitoring. LT/CONTROL Supports an Extensive Library of Drivers for I/O Devices, for Plug-In Boards, Distributed I/O Systems, Single-Loop Controllers & PLCs. Features Include Alarm Monitoring, Annunciation & Logging; Multiple Screen Display; Real-Time Mathematical Calculations; Multiple Display Features, Including X-Y Graphs, Real-Time Trendlines, Digital Meters, Vertical & Horizontal Lines & Faceplates; & a Run-Time Operator Control Panel. Features Include PID Control for Process Control Features, Networking to Receive Data from Another Computer. Version 5 Is a Major Windows Enhancement.
Laboratory Technologies Corp.

LABTECH NOTEBOOK. *Version:* 8.01. Jul. 1994. *Compatible Hardware:* IBM PC & compatibles, DOS PC XT, PC AT, Windows 386/486, PS/2. *Operating System(s) Required:* MS-DOS 2.0 or higher, 5.0 recommended; Windows 3.1. *Memory Required:* Windows 8Mb, DOS 640k. *General Requirements:* 1 disk drive & hard disk; EGA or VGA card for real-time display capability; analog/digital hardware interface. *Items Included:* Diskettes, documentaiton. *Customer Support:* Free 90-days telephone support. Support contract available after 90 days.
LABTECH NOTEBOOK $495.00; LABTECH NOTEBOOKpro $995.00.
Menu & Icon-Driven General-Purpose Software Package for Data Acquisition & Control. Monitoring & Data Analysis Runs. Each Channel Can Be Set up with Different Characteristics. Calculated Channels Allow Mathematical, Statistical & Logical Calculations to Be Done in Real Time. Requires a Data Acquisition Hardware Interface. DOS or Windows Versions Available. NOTEBOOK Handles 100 Channels. NOTEBOOKpro Supports up to Five Screens, with up to 25 Windows per Screen. Allows up to Eight Stages per Channel for More Complex Scheduling of Data Acquisition. Up to 300 Blocks May Be Set up in NOTEBOOKpro. Bundled W/C-Icon Development Kit, Driver Toolkit, & C-Icon Development Kit for More Flexibility. NOTEBOOKpro Supports UNIX.
Laboratory Technologies Corp.

LabVIEW: Laboratory Virtual Instrument Engineering Workbench. 1986. *Compatible Hardware:* Apple Macintosh, Macintosh Plus, Macintosh SE, Macintosh II, IIx, IIcx, IIci, IIfx, Quadra, Power Macintosh; IBM PC AT & compatibles running Microsoft Windows 3.1; Sun Microsystems SPARCstation & compatibles; & Hewlett-Packard 9000 Series 700 workstations. *Language(s):* G. *Memory Required:* 8Mb RAM & 16Mb hard disk for PCs, & 24Mb main memory, 32Mb disk swap space, 12Mb disk space for Sun SPARCstations; Macintosh 4000k. *Items Included:* Software, documentation. *Customer Support:* Toll-free technical support, paid training, field seminars, user group meetings.
disk # starts at $1995.00.
Scientists & Engineers Use LabVIEW to Build Software Modules Called Virtual Instruments (Vis) Instead of Writing Cryptic Text-Based Programs. The Software Is a General-Purpose Programming Tool with Extensive Libraries for Data Acquisition, Instrument Control, Data Analysis, & Data Presentation. LabVIEW Is Available for PCs Running Microsoft Windows 3.1, Sun Workstations, Macintosh Computers, & HP 9000 Series 700 Workstations. Available Now.
National Instruments Corp.

LabWindows. *Version:* 2.3. 1989. *Items Included:* 5.25" or 3.5" floppies, 5 manuals, registration form, instrument library order form, co. short form catalog. *Customer Support:* Toll-free technical support, paid training, field seminars. Standard DOS. IBM PC, PC XT, PC AT & compatibles, PS/2 (640k). $695.00, Standard. *Nonstandard peripherals required:* GPIB Interface, data acquisition interface, graphics adapter (all optional). *Optimal configuration:* Hard disk.
Advanced $895.00.
LabWindows Is a Set of Software Tools & Libraries for Developing Programs in Microsoft C & QuickBASIC for Instrument Control, Data Acquisition, Analysis, & Presentation. Version 2.3 Features a New Code Builder User Interface, an Interactive Prototyping & Program Generation Utility to Help Users Automatically Design & Build Programs with Graphical User Interfaces.
National Instruments Corp.

The Labyrinth of Zyr. *Compatible Hardware:* Commodore PET with Commodore BASIC. *Memory Required:* 8k.
disk $21.95.
Find Your Way Through a Randomly Generated Labyrinth.
Dynacomp, Inc.

Ladder Network. *Compatible Hardware:* IBM. *Memory Required:* 128k.
disk $59.95.
Uses the Technique of Describing a Network As a Series of Cascaded Two-Ports.
Dynacomp, Inc.

LADPAQ: Labor & Delivery Productivity & Quality. *Operating System(s) Required:* PC-DOS. *General Requirements:* 2 disk drives, printer.
contact publisher for price.
Combines Proven Methodology with Computer Software to Support Management in the Labor & Delivery Department Including Surgical &/or Outpatient Procedures.
Medicus Systems Corp.

Lahey Fortran 90 (LF90). Aug. 1994. *Items Included:* Manuals, Editor, Debugger, Profiler, DOS-Extender, Librarian, MAKE Utility, Video Graphics, Linker. *Customer Support:* Free telephone, BBS, Newsletters, CompuServe.
MS-DOS 3.3 or higher. 386 w/Math coprocessor, 486, Pentium (8Mb). disk $895.00 (Order no.: 800-548-4778, 702-831-2500). *Optimal configuration:* Pentium w/8Mb RAM (or more).
This Professional Language System Combines Lahey's Award-Winning Fortran Compiler Design with Intel's Highly Optimized Code Generation Technology. LF90 Is Optimized for 386, 486, & Pentium PCs, Is a Full Implementation of the Fortran 90 Standard, & Contains an Interface to MetaWare High C.
Lahey Computer Systems, Inc.

Lahey Personal FORTRAN '77 (LP77). *Version:* 3.0. Jun. 1990. *Compatible Hardware:* IBM PC, PC XT, PC AT. *Operating System(s) Required:* MS-DOS 2.0 or higher. *Memory Required:* 256k. *Items Included:* Manual, Debugger, Editor, Video Graphics, Library Manager, Linker. *Customer Support:* Free telephone, BBS, CompuServe & newsletters.
disk $99.00.
Full Implementation of the FORTRAN '77 Standard (ANSI X3.9-1978). Targeted at the Educational Market & Professional Programmers Working with Smaller Applications (There Is a 64k Limit for Code Size). The LP77 TOOLKIT LIBRARY Is Available Separately.
Lahey Computer Systems, Inc.

Lake Avenue Accounting Collection. *Version:* 7.2. *General Requirements:* External disk drive or hard disk drive.
Macintosh 512K or higher (execpt Macintosh II). 3.5" disk $295.00.
Integrated Accounting.
Lake Avenue Software.

LAN Administrators Kit. *Compatible Hardware:* IBM PC & compatibles. *Operating System(s) Required:* PC-DOS/MS-DOS 2.0 or higher. *Memory Required:* 256k.
3.5" or 5.25" disk $75.00 (Order no.: L-50).
Provides a Roadmap with Easy-to-Follow Instructions on How to: Develop a Strategy for Administering a Local Area Network; Implement the Network into an Organization Efficiently & Effectively; Establish Administrative Controls for On-Going Operations of the LAN.
American Training International, Inc.

TITLE INDEX

LAN-DataCore. Software Connections, Inc. *Operating System(s) Required:* MS-DOS. *Memory Required:* 128k. *General Requirements:* Ethernet or Omninet.
single user $495.00.
Multi-User Relational Data Base Applications Development Tool for Local Area Networks.
Texas Instruments, Personal Productivit.

LAN-DataStore. Software Connections, Inc. *Operating System(s) Required:* MS-DOS. *Memory Required:* 192k. *General Requirements:* Ethernet or Omninet, color monitor.
Five-user version. $945.00.
Ten-user version. $1945.00.
single user $495.00.
Multi-User Relational Data Base Management Package Designed for the Network Environment.
Texas Instruments, Personal Productivit.

LAN Progress. *Version:* 4.2a. *Compatible Hardware:* IBM PC & compatibles. *Operating System(s) Required:* DOS 3.0 or higher. *Memory Required:* 512k. *General Requirements:* Hard disk.
$3000.00 for up to 16 users.
Networked Database-Management System. This Fourth Generation Development Tool Features a Powerful Language, Automatic Recovery & Transaction Processing. Dedicated Database Server Required for Network Use. Automatic & Programmable Record Locking Protect Shared Network Files. Not Copy Protected.
Progress Software Corp.

Lan Simulation Toolbox: IEE 802.5 Token Ring Simulation. Jan. 1996. *Items Included:* Sample input & output files & users manuals on disk. *Customer Support:* Assistance in formulative inputs & understanding outputs, price free or variable.
MS-DOS. IBM PC (8Mb). disk $4500.00 (Order no.: 910). *Nonstandard peripherals required:* Math coprocessor. *Addl. software required:* FORTRAN Compiler & Linker. *Optimal configuration:* Source code can be compiled & linked for execution on any Machine with a FORTRAN compiler & linker.
A Sophisticated Discrete Simulation Model of the IEEE 802.5 Token Ring Standard & 26 Variations Thereof. Performs a Robust Cumulative Probability Analysis of Queueing, Response Time, & Utilization Performance of Each Network Node, Link, & Path in Terms of 9 Statistics of Each Queueing, Response Time, & Utilization Performance Measures, Generating 1575 Types of Output.
Cane Systems.

LAN Troubleshooting Handbook. Mark A. Miller. Dec. 1989.
MS-DOS. IBM PC & compatibles. disk $24.95 (ISBN 1-55851-054-0).
MS-DOS. IBM PC & compatibles. disk $39.95, incl. book (ISBN 1-55851-056-7).
Technical Reference for the Systems Analyst Who Needs to Identify Problems & Maintain a LAN That Is Already Installed. Topics Include LAN Standards, the OSI Model, Network Documentation, LAN Test Equipment, Cable System Testing, ARCNet Troubleshooting, Ethernet Troubleshooting, StarLAN Troubleshooting, & Others.
M & T Bks.

Lancaster: The Teaching Partner for the Computerized Classroom. Nov. 1995. *Items Included:* 1 manual. *Customer Support:* Software support subscription includes quarterly newsletters, frequent free updates to the software, & 24-hour, 7-day a week technical support. Subscription is free the first year & $399/yr. afterwards.
Macintosh 7.1. Macintosh 040 (5Mb). CD-ROM disk $14.95 (Order no.: P1330(1)). *Networks supported:* Macintosh Network.
CD-ROM disk $4495.00 (Order no.: P1300(SITE)).
Gives Teachers a Tool to Teach with & Control Their Computerized Network. With Lancaster Teachers Can Restart & Shutdown Computers, Send & Retrieve Documents, Save Documents in Electronic Portfolios, Launch & Quit Applications, & More. Takes Full Advantage of Macintosh Ease-of-Use.
COMPanion Corp.

LanCD. *Version:* 3.2. Dec. 1995. *Customer Support:* 90 day warranty, installation, hotline support, hardware maintenance, software maintenance.
MS-DOS 3.3 or higher. 80386 or higher (8Mb). CD-ROM disk Contact publisher for price. *Nonstandard peripherals required:* 200k storage. *Networks supported:* IPX/SPX & SAP, Winsock, TCP/IP, Banyan Vines, NetBIOS/NetBEUI, Lan workplace for DOS, Windows for Workgroups.
Networking Software Features Include Multi-Platform, Multi-Protocol Support, FastCD Caching, Licensing Metering, Jukebox Support & Virtual Drive Mapping. Has Networking Solutions for the DOS, Windows, Windows NT, Windows 95 & Macintosh Markets.
Logicraft.

Lancer. *Compatible Hardware:* TRS-80 Color Computer. *Memory Required:* 32k. *General Requirements:* Joystick.
contact publisher for price.
Spectral Assocs.

Land Investor. *Compatible Hardware:* TRS-80 Model I, Model III.
contact publisher for price.
Realsoft, Inc. (Florida).

Land Survey Calculator. *Items Included:* Bound manual. *Customer Support:* Free hotline - no time limit; 30 day limited warranty; updates are $5/disk plus S&H.
MS-DOS 2.0 or higher. IBM & compatibles (128k). disk $19.95.
Program for Performing Many of the Calculations Related to Land Surveys. Using Your Deed, You May Find Lost Corners & Lines; Locate the Overgrown Stakes; Write Land Descriptions; Calculate Acreage; Plot Your Deed; Establish Test Plots; & More. Please Note That SURVEY May Require Some Equipment, Such As a Good Compass (& a Reference Line for Direction Calibration, Such As a Road), & a Measuring Tape.
Dynacomp, Inc.

LAND TRUST. *Customer Support:* Free on site training; free support first 6 months; yearly support is 13% of software cost; modem support; phone support; classroom training; "user group" meetings.
IBM PC & compatibles (2Mb). Contact publisher for price. *Networks supported:* Novell primarily.
Flexible Set of Programs Designed to Assist in Management of Land Trust Departments. System Provides Comprehensive & Accurate Means of Record Keeping While Allowing for Flexibility Required in Land Trust Operations.
Grossman & Assocs., Inc.

Landcadd Complete.
Mac II or IIx (4Mb). Site Planning & Landscape Design $995.00; Irrigation Design $795.00; CADD Construction Details $1185.00.
Programs Add Features to AutoCAD Release 11 or 12 for Land Planning & Landscape Design Customization. User Can Capture Screen Images of CAD Designs & Move Them into Other Applications Using the Clipboard. Site Planning & Landscape Design Module Is for Land Planners & Landscape Designers. Includes Symbols Library & Routines for Parking, Coordinate Geometry, Topography & Cut & Fill. Irrigation Design Helps with Irrigation Projects, & CADD Construction Details Provides More Than 650 Predrawn Landscape Details.
Landcadd, Inc.

The Landlord. *Version:* 3.15. Sep. 1991. *Items Included:* Manual. *Customer Support:* 30 days free software support. $75.00 automatic software updates as they are released during the six month term of the plan.
PC-DOS 3.1 or higher. IBM PC with hard disk or compatible (640k). disk $595.00.
Manages up to 100 Properties & 400 Rental Units. Features Automatic Calculation & Posting of Management Fees. System Contains Four Integrated Modules: Property Information System, General Ledger, Accounts Receivable & Accounts Payable. Produces over 50 Management & Financial Reports.
MIN Microcomputer Software, Inc.

The Landlord Plus. *Version:* 3.13. Jun. 1989. *Items Included:* Manual. *Customer Support:* 90 days limited warranty. 30 days free support. $75.00 to receive automatic updates during the six months of the plan.
PC-DOS 3.1 or higher. IBM PC with hard disk or compatible (384k). disk $295.00.
Cash Accounting System for Managing Ten or Fewer Properties & 100 or Fewer Rental Units. System Contains Four Integrated Modules: Property Information System, General Ledger, Accounts Payable & Accounts Receivable. Produces over 50 Timely & Accurate Reports.
MIN Microcomputer Software, Inc.

The Landmaster: Property Management Software. *Version:* 2.14. Jun. 1991. *Compatible Hardware:* IBM PC with hard disk or compatible. *Operating System(s) Required:* PC-DOS 3.1 or higher. *Language(s):* QuickBASIC. *Memory Required:* 640k. *General Requirements:* Novell Netware 2.00a or higher required for network version. *Items Included:* Manual. *Customer Support:* 30 days free software support. $75.00 automatic software updates as they are released during the six month term of the plan..
disk $1250.00.
Advanced Property Management System for Administration of Any Kind of Income Property. Includes Integrated G/L, A/P, A/R Modules That Function on a Cash or Accrual Basis.
MIN Microcomputer Software, Inc.

Landscape Library. *Version:* 2.0. *General Requirements:* PowerDraw or PowerCADD. *Items Included:* 3 diskettes, manual. *Customer Support:* free with registration.
Macintosh Plus or higher. 3.5" disk $79.00 (ISBN 1-878250-04-3).
Plan & Elevation View of Landscape Items, As Well As Family, Scientific & Common Names.
Engineered Software.

Landscape Plant Manager. *Items Included:* Bound manual. *Customer Support:* Free hotline - no time limit; 30 day limited warranty; updates are $5/disk plus S&H.
MS-DOS. IBM & compatibles (256k). disk $19.95.
Menu-Driven Plant Database from Which User Can Choose Plants Based on Various Landscape Planning Criteria. Included Is a Large File on Common Plants, Flowers, & Trees. You Can Also Add Your Own Information, Edit What Is There, & Search by Common or Scientific Name.
Dynacomp, Inc.

Landscape Plant Manager. 1992. *Items Included:* Detailed manuals are included with all Dynacomp products. *Customer Support:* Free telephone support to original customer - no time limit; 30 day limited warranty.
MS-DOS 3.2 (or higher). IBM PC & compatibles (512k). disk $19.95.
3.5" disk $24.95.
Menu-Driven Plant Database from Which You Can Choose Plants Based on Various Landscape Planning Criteria. Included Is a Large File on Common Plants, Flowers, & Trees. You Can Also Add Your Own Information, Edit What Is There, & Search by Common or Scientific Name. Includes a 60-Page Manual.
Dynacomp, Inc.

The Landscaper. Oct. 1983. *Compatible Hardware:* IBM compatible. *Operating System(s) Required:* PC-DOS. *Language(s):* BASIC. *Memory Required:* 64k.
disk $29.95.
Selects Plants from a List of Nearly 500, Based upon the Conditions Entered by the User. Selections Can Be Made for Type of Plant (Tree, Shrub, etc.), Evergreen/Deciduous, Drought Resistance, Season for Color, Shady Areas, Moisture Tolerance, Hilly/Sloping Terrain, & Extreme Sun/Heat. In the Hobby/Recreational Area, Home Gardening Problems Can Be Solved. In the Small Business Area, Landscape Contractors & Landscape Maintenance Companies Can Use This Program to Help in Custom Design & Maintenance of a Customer's Landscape. Nurseries Can Advise Customers, & a Computer Demo Can Be Set up As a Marketing Tool. In the Educational Area, Teachers & Professors Can Use This Product for Biology, Botany, Landscaping, or Horticulture Classes.
M. E. Fuller.

LANDSCAPER (Font Conversion Utility). 1989.
MS-DOS (256k). IBM PC, PC XT, PC AT & compatibles. disk $25.00 (ISBN 0-938245-56-2).
Converts HP Laserjet Fonts from Portrait to Landscape. Reads Portrait Soft Font Files & Creates Corresponding Landscape Font Files That Can Be Downloaded to Printer.
Inverted-A, Inc.

Landtech 86 Real Estate Closing System.
Version: 5.11. *Compatible Hardware:* IBM PC. *Customer Support:* $480.00/year, single user license.
$1495.00 single user license.
Designed to Do All Calculations & Prepare the Documents Necessary for Real Estate Settlements. The Package Prepares HUD, Pages 1 & 2, Buyer & Seller Closing Statements along with Checks & All Associated Disbursement Schedules. Also Included is a Complete Regulation Z APR Calculator. Full Forms Generator is Supplied for Preparing Deeds, Deeds of Trust, Mortgages & Other Instruments.
Landtech Data Corp.

Langenschedit PC Worterbuch Englisch.
PC compatible (512k). disk $350.00 (ISBN 3-468-90912-8, Order no.: 909128). *Addl. software required:* MS-DOS 2.11 or higher.
3.5" disk $350.00 (ISBN 3-468-90913-6, Order no.: 909136).
A Load & Stay Resident Program Featuring a 60,000 Entry German/English - English/German Dictionary with 125,000 Translations. Also Available in German/French & French/German.
Langenscheidt Pubs., Inc.

Langenschedits CD-ROM Bibliothek: PC Worterbuch Englisch, Duden Bedeutungsworterbuch, Meyers Grosses Hand Lexikon.
IBM compatible PC (512k). optical disk $179.95 (ISBN 3-468-90901-2, Order no.: 909012). *Addl. software required:* PC-DOS/MS-DOS Version 3.0 or higher, CD ROM drive, & text mode.
Contains Three Products: PC Worterbuch with 125,000 Translations, the Duden Dictionary of Contemporary German with a Basic Vocabulary of 16,000 Words & a Supplementary Vocabulary of 75,000 Words, Explanations, Grammar & Usage Examples, & Meyers Grosses Handlexikon, an Encyclopedia Containing 52,000 Headwords.
Langenscheidt Pubs., Inc.

Langenscheidt: Euroworterbuch Englisch.
IBM compatible PC (3-3.5Mb; CD-ROM 1Mb). 3 disks $39.95 (ISBN 3-468-90920-9, Order no.: 909209). *Addl. software required:* Microsoft Windows Version 3.1 or higher, Microsoft compatible mouse.
CD-ROM disk $39.95 (ISBN 3-468-90925-X, Order no.: 90925X).
45,000 Entries from the Fields of Economics, Politics, Culture & Travel.
Langenscheidt Pubs., Inc.

Langenscheidt: Euroworterbuch Franzosisch.
IBM compatible PC (3-3.5Mb; CD-ROM 1Mb). 3 disks $39.95 (ISBN 3-468-90921-7, Order no.: 909268). *Addl. software required:* Microsoft Windows Version 3.1 or higher, Microsoft compatible mouse.
CD-ROM disk $39.95 (ISBN 3-468-90926-8).
45,000 Entries form the Fields of Economics, Politics, Culture & Travel.
Langenscheidt Pubs., Inc.

Langenscheidt: Euroworterbuch Italienisch.
IBM compatible PC (3-3.5Mb; CD-ROM 1Mb). 3 disks $39.95 (ISBN 3-468-90922-5, Order no.: 909225). *Addl. software required:* Microsoft Windows Version 3.1 or higher, Microsoft compatible mouse.
CD-ROM disk $39.95 (ISBN 3-468-90927-6, Order no.: 909276).
45,000 Entries from the Fields of Economics, Politics, Culture & Travel.
Langenscheidt Pubs., Inc.

Langenscheidt: Euroworterbuch Spanisch.
IBM compatible PC (3-3.5Mb). 3 disks $39.95 (ISBN 3-468-90923-3, Order no.: 909233). *Addl. software required:* Microsoft Windows Version 3.1 or higher, Microsoft compatible mouse.
CD-ROM disk $39.95 (ISBN 3-468-90928-4, Order no.: 909284).
45,000 Entries from the Fields of Economics, Politics, Culture & Travel.
Langenscheidt Pubs., Inc.

Langenscheidt PC Bibliothek: 100 Musterbriefe Englisch.
IBM compatible PC (1.5Mb). 2 disks $27.95 (ISBN 3-468-90915-2, Order no.: 909152). *Addl. software required:* Microsoft Windows Version 3.1 or higher, Microsoft compatible mouse.
100 Sample Business Letters (Eng) Suitable for Use in Any Word Processing Program.
Langenscheidt Pubs., Inc.

Langenscheidt PC Bibliothek: 100 Musterbriefe Franzosisch.
IBM compatible PC (1.5Mb). 2 disks $27.59 (ISBN 3-468-90916-0, Order no.: 909160). *Addl. software required:* Microsoft Windows Version 3.1 or higher, Microsoft compatible mouse.
100 Sample Business Letters (Fr) Suitable for Use in Any Word Processing Program.
Langenscheidt Pubs., Inc.

Langenscheidt: Taschenworterbuch Englisch.
IBM compatible PC (5.5Mb). 4 disks $59.95 (ISBN 3-468-90902-0, Order no.: 909020). *Addl. software required:* Microsoft Windows Version 3.0 or higher, Microsoft compatible mouse.
CD-ROM disk $59.95 (ISBN 3-468-90903-9, Order no.: 909039).
120,000 Entries.
Langenscheidt Pubs., Inc.

Langenscheidt: Taschenworterbuch Franzosisch.
IBM Compatible PC (5Mb). 4 disks $69.95 (ISBN 3-468-90905-5, Order no.: 909055). *Addl. software required:* Microsoft Windows Version 3.0 or higher, Microsoft compatible mouse.
CD-ROM disk $69.95 (ISBN 3-468-90906-3, Order no.: 909063).
95,000 Entries.
Langenscheidt Pubs., Inc.

Langenscheidt's: (Basic Vocabulary) Grundwortschatz Englisch.
80386 (4Mb). CD-ROM disk $42.95 (ISBN 3-468-90850-4, Order no.: 908504). *Addl. software required:* Microsoft Windows 3.1 or higher (mouse recommended). *Networks supported:* IBM 1Mb.
3,000 Entries with Animation, Graphics, Sound & Memory Games, Usage Sentences, Preparation for Travel, and/or Advanced Language Examinations.
Langenscheidt Pubs., Inc.

Langenscheidt's: (Basic Vocabulary) Grundwortschatz Franzosisch.
80386 (4Mb). CD-ROM disk $42.95 (ISBN 3-468-90851-2, Order no.: 908512). *Addl. software required:* Microsoft Windows 3.1 or higher (mouse recommended). *Networks supported:* IBM 1Mb.
3,000 Entries with Animation, Graphics, Sound & Memory Games, Usage Sentences, Preparation for Travel, and/or Advanced Language Examinations.
Langenscheidt Pubs., Inc.

Langenscheidt's: (Basic Vocabulary) Grundwortschatz Italienisch.
80386 (4Mb). CD-ROM disk $42.95 (ISBN 3-468-90852-0, Order no.: 908520). *Addl. software required:* Microsoft Windows 3.1 or higher (mouse recommended). *Networks supported:* IBM 1Mb.
3,000 Entries with Animation, Graphics, Sound & Memory Games, Usage Sentences, Preparation for Travel, and/or Advanced Language Examinations.
Langenscheidt Pubs., Inc.

Langenscheidt's: (Basic Vocabulary) Grundwortschatz Spanisch.
80386 (4Mb). CD-ROM disk $42.95 (ISBN 3-468-90853-9, Order no.: 908539). *Addl. software required:* Microsoft Windows 3.1 or higher (mouse recommended). *Networks supported:* IBM 1Mb.
3,000 Entries with Animation, Graphics, Sound & Memory Games, Usage Sentences, Preparation for Travel, and/or Advanced Language Examinations.
Langenscheidt Pubs., Inc.

Langenscheidt's: Englisch Worterbuch Fur DOS - An Wender.
80386 (4Mb). CD-ROM disk $69.95 (ISBN 3-411-90910-2, Order no.: 909101). *Addl. software required:* Microsoft Windows 3.1 or higher (mouse recommended). *Networks supported:* IBM 1.5Mb.
60,000 Entries.
Langenscheidt Pubs., Inc.

Langenscheidt's: Euro-Set Englisch 1 Franzosisch - Italienisch - Spanisch.
80386 (4Mb). CD-ROM disk $99.95 (ISBN 3-411-90924-2, Order no.: 909241). *Addl. software required:* Microsoft Windows 3.1 or higher (mouse recommended). *Networks supported:* IBM 1Mb.
180,000 Entries, 4 Dictionaries (45,000 Entries Each) on One CD.
Langenscheidt Pubs., Inc.

Langenscheidt's: Handworterbuch Englisch for PC Windows & Mac.
80386 (4Mb). CD-ROM disk $179.95 (ISBN 3-468-90880-6, Order no.: 908806). *Addl. software required:* Microsoft Windows 3.1 or higher (mouse recommended). *Networks supported:* IBM 1Mb.
210,000 Entries, Grammar, Proper Names, Abbreviations, Usage Examples.
Langenscheidt Pubs., Inc.

Langenscheidt's: Handworterbuch Franzosish for PC Windows & Mac.
80386 (4Mb). CD-ROM disk $179.95 (ISBN 3-468-90881-4, Order no.: 908814). *Addl. software required:* Microsoft Windows 3.1 or higher (mouse recommended). *Networks supported:* IBM 1Mb.
210,000 Entries, Grammar, Proper Names, Abbreviations, Usage Examples.
Langenscheidt Pubs., Inc.

Langenscheidt's: Taschenworterbuch Englisch Mit Sprachausgabe.
80386 (4Mb). CD-ROM disk $99.95 (ISBN 3-411-90904-8, Order no.: 909047). *Addl. software required:* Microsoft Windows 3.1 or higher (mouse recommended). *Networks supported:* IBM 1Mb.
120,000 Entries with 5,000 Pronunciations, Ability to Add Own Entries.
Langenscheidt Pubs., Inc.

Langenscheidt's: Taschenworterbuch Russisch.
80386 (4Mb). CD-ROM disk $69.95 (ISBN 3-411-90908-0, Order no.: 90908X). *Addl. software required:* Microsoft Windows 3.1 or higher (mouse recommended). *Networks supported:* IBM 6Mb.
90,000 Entries.
Langenscheidt Pubs., Inc.

Language Collection. *Customer Support:* 800-929-8117 (customer service).
MS-DOS. IBM/PS2. disk $79.99 (ISBN 0-87007-582-9).
User Can Learn Numbers & Words in French, German, Spanish & Italian. Will Translate Monetary Figures, or Examine the Foreign Spelling of Words. Numbers from 0 to One Billion & Selected Common Words are Provided. All Words in English & a Specified Foreign Language May be Displayed at Once. All Numbers May be Displayed in English & a Specific Foreign Language or One at a Time.
SourceView Software International.

Language Drill. *Items Included:* Bound manual. *Customer Support:* Free hotline - no time limit; 30 day limited warranty; updates are $5/disk plus S&H.
MS-DOS. IBM & compatibles (128k). disk $39.95.
Apple (48k), does not include Swahili data files. disk $39.95.
Way to Rapidly Memorize Foreign Language Vocabulary. Using Either One of the Supplied Beginner's Lists (French, German, Spanish, Italian, Dutch, & Swahili), or a List Entered by the Student or Teacher, the User Is Drilled on Words Selected Randomly from the List. After an Incorrect (or Partially Correct) Answer Is Given, the Complete Correct Answer Is Displayed. Incorrect Responses Are Drilled More Frequently, Until They Have Been Correctly Translated Three Times in Succession.
Dynacomp, Inc.

Language Explorer. *Version:* 1.1. Aug. 1993. *Items Included:* Manual & 1 disk.
System 6.0.7 or higher. Color Macintosh, hard disk (1Mb). 3.5" disk $49.95 (ISBN 0-940081-70-9).
Windows 3.1. 386SX or higher. 3.5" disk $49.95 (ISBN 0-940081-75-X). *Nonstandard peripherals required:* Mouse, SVGA, sound card.
Macintosh & Windows. CD-ROM disk $49.95 (ISBN 0-940081-69-5).
Uses Fun Sounds & More Than 500 Animated Picture Tiles in 42 Topics to Build Your Vocabulary in English, French, German, & Spanish. Simply Select a Topic & a Language, Then Place the Tile in the Correct Frame. Level of Difficulty Is Adjustable for All Ages & Language Skills. Learn at Your Own Pace.
Nordic Software, Inc.

Language Extension System-Assembler. F. D. Wright. *Compatible Hardware:* IBM PC, PC XT, PC AT, Portable PC. *Operating System(s) Required:* PC-DOS 2.00, 2.10, 3.00, 3.10. *Memory Required:* 128k. *General Requirements:* 2 disk drives or hard disk; IBM Display; 8087 (80287 for PC AT) math co-processor; IBM Macro Assembler version 1.00.
disk $24.95 (Order no.: 6276584).
Allows User to Take Advantage of the 8087/80287 to Improve Program Accuracy & Speed. Accesses the Math Co-Processor from Assembly Language Programs, & Uses Macros to Include the 8087/80287 Opcodes.
Personally Developed Software, Inc.

Language Master. *Compatible Hardware:* Apple Macintosh; IBM PC & compatibles. *Memory Required:* 100k. *General Requirements:* 1.5Mb hard disk; Microsoft Word, MultiMate, Symphony, Lotus 1-2-3, Lotus Manuscript, Q&A, WordStar 2000, WordPerfect. *Customer Support:* Toll-free support.
$99.00.
Combines "Webster's Concise Electronic Dictionary" (a Full-Text 80,000 Word Dictionary with Definitions) & Webster's Electronic Thesaurus (40,000 Entries). The Two Reference Works Are Linked, Allowing Users to Access, for Example, a Synonym for a Word Used in a Dictionary Definition. If the Correct Spelling of the Word is Unknown, the System Will Respond to a Misspelled Entry with a List of Words That Are Phoenetically or Typographically Similar.
Proximity Technology, Inc.

The Language Pack. SilverSun Editorial Staff. Jul. 1995.
Windows, Macintosh. CD-ROM disk Contact publisher for price (ISBN 0-87779-455-3).
Includes the Full Text of Both Merriam-Webster's Collegiate Dictionary, Tenth Edition & the Harbrace College Handbook, Twelfth Edition Revised.
Merriam-Webster, Inc.

LANLink 5X. *Version:* 2.1. Rod Roark. *Items Included:* A 110 page user guide for installation, configuration & system operation. *Customer Support:* Three day on-site training program & three day workshop, contact TSL for pricing information.
PC/MS-DOS 2.0 or higher (40k server/satellite, 24k satellite computer). IBM PC & compatibles, XT, AT, PS/2. Two user starter kit $395.00, includes single user PC-MOS $195.00, server software $150.00, satellite software $100.00.
PC-MOS (32k server/satellite, 24k satellite computer). IBM PC & compatibles, XT, AT, PS/2. Two user starter kit $395.00, includes single user PC-MOS $195.00, server software $150.00, satellite software $100.00.
Allows a Parallel Data Transmission Rate of 3 Megabits Per Minute or Better Depending on Hardware. It Uses a Standard Parallel Port & Specialized Cabling to Communicate with the File Server & with Other Computers in a Workgroup. Also Supports Local Serial Communications up to 115,200 bps & Remote Communications Using Intelligent Serial I/O Boards (i.e. MAXPEED) at Speeds up to 19,200 bps. Requires Only 40k of RAM on the Server for Each Satellite Workstation on the Network. Supports Both PC-MOS & PC/MS-DOS in Any Combination on Both Servers & Workstations.
The Software Link, Inc.

LANLink Laptop. *Version:* 2.0. Rod Roark. *Items Included:* A user guide for installation, operating instructions & technical information. *Customer Support:* Three day on-site training program & three day workshop, contact BL for pricing information.
PC/MS-DOS & PC-MOS (40k). IBM PC & compatibles, AT, XT, PS/2. $139.95.
Laptop Connectivity Product That Does More Than Just File Transfer. Based on LANLink Technology, It Allows Laptops to Connect to Desktops for File Transfer, Program & Command Execution, Disk & Peripheral Sharing & Other LAN Functions. It is Compatible with PC-MOS, as Well as PC/MS-DOS Versions 2.0 & Later, Including PC-DOS 4.0.
The Software Link, Inc.

Lanscope. *Version:* 2.2B. *Compatible Hardware:* IBM PC & compatibles. *Operating System(s) Required:* Banyan Vines, Novell Advanced NetWare, PC-DOS/MS DOS 3.0 or higher. *Language(s):* Assembly, C. *Memory Required:* 640k. *General Requirements:* Network interface card & the shell or redirector of the LAN operating system at ea. workstation.
complete system $495.00.
Network Manager Which Combines Network Administration, Network & User Activity Reporting, Resource Management, Software License Metering, User Productivity Tools, & Workstation Menus. A Database Holds Information on Each User, Resource, & Workstation, Changes to the Network Being Implemented by Simply Making the Changes in the Database.
Connect Computer Co., Inc.

LANshadow. *Items Included:* Manuals. *Customer Support:* Free phone support.
MS-DOS. disk $695.00. *Networks supported:* Novell.
Novell Netware Full-Time On-Line Backup System. Ensures Against File Server Disaster by Providing a Second On-Line Backup Server in Case Anything Happens To the Primary File Server. If Active Server Fails, the Second "Shadow" Server Takes Over Immediately, Thereby Eliminating Costly Down-Time.
Network Management, Inc.

LANsmart Network OS. *Version:* 3.5. Jan. 1995. *Items Included:* 1 spiral bound manual, 1 installation guide, 2 5.25" diskettes, 1 warranty registration card. *Customer Support:* Free technical support (714) 455-1688.
DOS 3.0 or higher. IBM PC/XT/AT, PS/2 (2K). disk $395.00 (Order no.: LS-300).
Nonstandard peripherals required: D-Link industry standard Ethernet, token-ring, 10 Base or pocket LAN Adapters. *Networks supported:* Ethernet, 10 Base, Token-ring & pocket LAN Adapters.

LANTASTIC NETWORK OPERATING SYSTEM

Allows Users to Share Printers, Plotters, Disks, Files & CD ROMs. These Superior Functions Are Complimented with the Use of Only 2k of Memory. LANsmart May Be Used Stand-Alone or As a Supplement to Novell NetWare.
D-Link Systems, Inc.

LANtastic Network Operating System. Version: 5.0. *Compatible Hardware:* IBM PC & compatibles.
contact publisher for price.
Menu-Driven Networking Software Providing Electronic Mail & Networking & Security Management Tools.
Artisoft, Inc.

LANtastic Network Operating System. Version: 5.0. Feb. 1993. *Items Included:* Complete Guide to LANtastic manual & LANtastic Basics manual. *Customer Support:* Telephone technical support 602-670-7000. 24-Hour BBS 602-884-8648; Facts Fax 602-884-1397; Compuserve: Go Artisoft.
MS-DOS 3.1, 3.3-6.0. IBM PC, XT, AT & compatibles (40k server, 16k workstation). CD-ROM disk $99.00; $119.00 LANtastic/AI (single node); $659.00 (6-pack). *Nonstandard peripherals required:* Network Interface adapters.
Windows 3.1. IBM PC, XT, AT & compatibles (40k server, 16k workstation). CD-ROM disk $199.00; $139.00 LANtastic/AI (single node); $779.00 (6-pack). *Nonstandard peripherals required:* Network Interface adapters.
Peer-to-Peer Local Area Network That Connects up to 500 Users per Network. Provides Printer-, File-Sharing, Networking to CD-ROM, WORM, & OS/2 HPFS Drives. Includes Disk-Caching, Electronic Mail & Chat, Username & Password Protection. Access Control Lists, Time-of-Day Logins, & Audit Trails. Administration Features Include Remote Accounts, Global Resources, Remoter Server Management, & Batch Despooling.
Artisoft, Inc.

LANtrack. *Items Included:* Manuals. *Customer Support:* Free phone support.
MS-DOS (35k on server). disk $795.00. *Networks supported:* Novell.
Novell Netware Preventative Maintenance Tool Implemented As a Server VAP. As a Comprehensive Real-Time Server Monitoring Utility for Novell Networks, It Alerts Network Administrators to Potential Problems Before They Become Critical.
Network Management, Inc.

LANtrail. *Items Included:* Manuals. *Customer Support:* Free telephone support.
MS-DOS (5k). disk $595.00. *Networks supported:* Novell.
Novell Netware Audit Trail Utility with Flexible Reporting Features, Security Tracking & Disk Usage Tracking for Your Network & Local Drives. It Tracks Information on File Usage, Connection Usage & Bindery Changes.
Network Management, Inc.

LapCAD: Finite Element Modeler.
Macintosh Plus or higher (1Mb). disk $295.00. *Nonstandard peripherals required:* Hard disk drive (20Mb).
Simplifies Finite Element Modeling for MSC/Pal & MSC/Nastran. Finite Element Specific Formatting & Complex Geometric Computations Are Replaced with Simple Manipulation of Highly Visible Graphics. Built-In Features Include: Copying, Mirroring, Rotation, Translation, Expansion, Contraction, Deletion & Snapping Together, As Well As Linear & Circular Extrusion. Finite Element Features Such As Application of Physical Forces & External Forces & Constraints. These Can Be Echoed Graphically for Easy Verification.
LapCAD Engineering.

Laplace Transform Tools Numerical Inversion Utilities. *Items Included:* Full manual. No other products required. *Customer Support:* Free telephone support - no time limit. 30 day warranty.
MS-DOS 3.2 or higher. IBM & compatibles (512k). disk $239.95.
Implements a General (& Very Reliable) Technique for the Automatic Numerical Inversion of Laplace Transforms. F(s) Models Are Easily Entered from the Keyboard, & May Be Conveniently Stored & Recalled for Modification. Editing Is Simple. Functions Commonly Encountered (Such As Transcendentals & Hyperbolics) Are Available for Inclusion in the Model Description. Numerical Inversions Are Performed Quickly. Interactive Graphics Provide Publication-Quality Plotting of the Calculated Model Responses. You May Also Read ASCII Data Files & Plot Them for Comparison with Your Model.
Dynacomp, Inc.

LapLink Mac III. Version: 3.2. *Compatible Hardware:* Apple Macintosh system 5.0 or higher, IBM DOS 2.11 & above. *Items Included:* 3.5" & 5.25" Pc disks & 3.5" MAC disks; cable that supports 9 & 25 pin serial & DIN-8 MAC. *Customer Support:* (206) 483-8088.
3.5" disk $149.95.
Allows the Sharing of Files Between Macintosh & IBM, & Also Between Macintosh & Macintosh. PC to Macintosh Transfer Speed is over 115 kbps. SCSI DiskLink Connects a Macintosh Portable & Standard Macintosh. Modem Transfer Macintosh to PC or Macintosh to Macintosh. AppleTalk Transfers Also.
Traveling Software, Inc.

LapLink 4. Version: 4.0. *Compatible Hardware:* IBM PC/XT/AT/or PS/2 & compatibles. *Operating System(s) Required:* PC-DOS/MS-DOS 2.11 or higher. *Memory Required:* 440k. *Items Included:* 8' serial & parallel cables that support 9 & 25 pin serial & parallel ports. *Customer Support:* (206) 483-8088.
$169.95, incl. 5.25" disk, 3.5" disk, & 8' serial & parallel cables for connecting two computers.
Allows Users to Connect Any Combination of Two MS-DOS Computers in Order to Transfer Files over Modem or Cable. It Includes Easy to Use File Management Capabilities. Transmission Speed Can Be As High As 500,000 bps Through Parallel Mode.
Traveling Software, Inc.

Laptop UltraVision. Feb. 1991. *Customer Support:* Unlimited telephone support, 30 day money-back guaranty.
$69.95. *Nonstandard peripherals required:* Requires EGA or VGA screen. CGA type displays not supported.
A Unique Screen Enhancer for Today's Hottest Laptop & Notebook Systems. Lets User Choose from a Library of over 20 Screen Fonts, Adjust Grey Shades, Enlarge the Cursor, & See Extra Lines on Screen in a Host of Popular Applications. It Boosts Screen Writing Speed by As Much As 300%. Compatible with Portables from IBM, Compaq, Toshiba & Many Others.
Personics Corp.

Large-Integer Programming Subprograms (LIPS). *Compatible Hardware:* IBM PC & compatibles. *Language(s):* FORTRAN.
$80.00, incl. documentation.
Provides a Basic Set of Tools for Applications Which Need Very Large Integer Arithmetic.
Software Designs 2000.

SOFTWARE ENCYCLOPEDIA 1996

LAS AIMS: Agency Information & Management System for Independent Insurance Agents. Version: 2. 1985. *Compatible Hardware:* Unisys B20/B30 Series, Convergent Technologies AWS & IWS Series. *Operating System(s) Required:* CTOS, BTOS. *Language(s):* COBOL. *Memory Required:* 512k. *General Requirements:* 40Mb hard disk.
disk $4295.00, incl. initial license fee, installation & 2 days on-site training.
annual fee $840.00.
Integrated Policy Information, Billing, Accounting, Sales Analysis & Marketing.
LAS Systems, Inc.

LAS-FIMS: LAS Food Industry Management System for the Processed Food Industry. Version: 3. S. Lulla. 1984. *Compatible Hardware:* Unisys B20/B30 series, Convergent Technologies AWS, IWS & N-GEN series. *Operating System(s) Required:* BTOS, CTOS. *Language(s):* COBOL. *Memory Required:* 512k. *General Requirements:* 40Mb hard disk.
contact publisher for price.
Integrated Order Processing, Invoicing, Product Costing & Pricing, Raw Materials & Finished Products Inventory Control, Recipe Control, Sales Analysis & Reporting, Accounting System.
LAS Systems, Inc.

Las Vegas Keno. *Compatible Hardware:* IBM PC. *Language(s):* BASIC. *Memory Required:* 128k.
disk $19.95.
The Computer Is the Dealer & Calculates Payoffs, & the Player Bets on Which 20 Numbers Out of 80 the Dealer Will Draw.
Dynacomp, Inc.

Lascaux 1000: The Intelligent Calculator.
Martin Lapidus. Jun. 1987. *Operating System(s) Required:* MS-DOS, PC-DOS. *Memory Required:* 640k.
disk $39.00 (ISBN 0-943189-00-4).
Memory Resident Calculator That Operates with Units of Measurement along with Numbers. All Conversions Are Processed Automatically. It Also Allows the User to Maintain a List of Physical Constants That Can Be Instantly Entered into the Calculator.
Lascaux Graphics.

Laser Award Maker.
Macintosh Plus or higher (1MB). 3.5" disk $199.95.
Allows User to Produce Custom Designed Laser Quality Certificates, Awards, Diplomas, Announcements, Notices, Invitations, Coupons & Tickets. Program Offers Seven Categories: Business, Community, Education, Signs & Notices, Personal, Sports & General. User May Select Several Document Sizes, Vertical or Horizontal Formats, 20 Borders & Four Font Styles.
Baudville.

Laser Award Maker (IBM). *Items Included:* 1 spiral bound manual.
MS-DOS. IBM PC - XT, 286, 386, 486 or compatibles (640k). disk $199.00 (Order no.: 41935). *Nonstandard peripherals required:* Laser Printer (HP compatible). *Networks supported:* Novell 3COM etc, Network version needed.
Allows Users to Produce Custom Designed Laser Quality Certificates. Awards, Diplomas, Announcements, Notices, Invitations, Coupons, & Tickets. Program Offers 7 Distinct Categories: Business, Community, Education, Signs & Notices, Personal Sports & General, Also Includes 20 Borders & 4 Font Styles.
Baudville.

TITLE INDEX

Laser Bridge. Jan. 1988. *Items Included:* 1 spiral bound manual, 5.25" IBM diskette. *Customer Support:* 800 number, no charge.
DOS 2.1 or higher. IBM PC & compatibles (192k). disk $200.00. *Nonstandard peripherals required:* 1 floppy drive, monitor.
Processes Downloaded MARC Records from WLN's LaserCat CD-ROM Database & Translates Them into ASCII for Use with PC Database Management Programs Such As dBase, Rbase, PCFile, etc.
WLN.

Laser Cambodian. *Version:* 5.0. Nov. 1991. *Items Included:* User's manual, laminated keyboard layout chart. *Customer Support:* User's manual, keyboard layout chart, old U.S. keyboard mapping utility for System 7.0.
Macintosh (512k). 3.5" disk $99.95. *Addl. software required:* Any word processor.
ATM Compatible Type 1 & TrueType LaserWriter Cambodian Aksarjhar Font & Corresponding ImageWriter Fonts in 10, 12, 18, 24, 36, & 48 Point Sizes. Contains the Entire Set of Current Cambodian Characters, Including Overstrike Vowels & Diacritical Marks Which Can Be Placed over or under Any Letter & in Any Combination. Each Overstrike Character Has Automatic, Non-Deleting Backspacing for Fast Convenient Typing. Has Italic, Underline, Cutline, Shadow, Superscript, & Subscript Styles. Includes a Micro-Space Key for Minute Adjustments. AsiaScript Scripting System Allows the User to Type Combinations of Characters, Such As Subscripts, by Simply Typing the Spacebar. AsiaScript Includes Automatic Ligature Formation & Vowel Positioning.
Linguist's Software, Inc.

Laser Cycle. Cornerstone Computers Incorporated. *Compatible Hardware:* IBM PC. *Operating System(s) Required:* MS-DOS. *Memory Required:* 64k.
disk $39.95 (ISBN 0-89303-619-6).
Futuristic Race Game of Maneuvers & Counter-Maneuvers in Which Players Accelerate Their Laser Cycles Through Perilous Arenas. Player Must Ward off Deadly, Light-Seeking Attack Spheres While Completing Circuit to Become Champion of Champion Riders. Game Provides Sound & Light Effects As Player Progresses from Arena to Arena, Accumulates Points, & Advances in Rank by Skill Level among Circuit Riders.
Brady Computer Bks.

Laser Design! *Version:* 2. 1988.
IBM PC, PC XT, PC AT & compatibles (640k). disk $395.00. *Nonstandard peripherals required:* HP laser printer.
User Can Select Newsletter Design, Fill in Blanks on Screen, Feed in Word Processor Disks; Progam Calculates & Sets Type to Fit. Four-Page Newsletter Is Produced In 3.5 Minutes.
Computing!.

Laser Envelopes. *Version:* 3. Sep. 1990. *Compatible Hardware:* IBM PC & & compatibles. *Operating System(s) Required:* PC-DOS/MS-DOS 2.0 or higher, OS/2. *Language(s):* C. *Memory Required:* 65k. *Customer Support:* (818) 707-3818.
disk $59.95.
Format & Print Envelope Addresses Automatically for Printing on HEWLETT PACKARD, OKIDATA, MANNESMAN TALLY KYOCERA, & TOSHIBA Laser Printers, Panasonic & compatibles.
ERM Assocs.

Laser Fontpak, 2 vols. Dec. 1986. *Compatible Hardware:* IBM PC & compatibles. *Operating System(s) Required:* PC-DOS/MS-DOS. *General Requirements:* IBM Fontrix or Printrix.
disk $50.00.
Designed to Be Used with FONTRIX 2.8 or Later and/or PRINTIX 2.4 or Later. There Are Two Laser Font paks Each with 30 Fonts (5 Type Styles, with 6 Sizes of Each Style). May Be Used on Any Printer.
Data Transforms, Inc.

Laser Fonts. *Version:* 5.0. May 1986. *Compatible Hardware:* IBM PC & compatibles. *Operating System(s) Required:* PC-DOS, MS-DOS. *Memory Required:* 128k. *General Requirements:* HP, Canon, NCR, Tall Tree or compatible laser printers (printer must have download capability). contact publisher for price.
Downloads a Large Variety of Fonts, up to 72 Points in Size, into Laser Printer. Automatically Configures WORDPERFECT & MICROSOFT WORD to Fully Take Advantage of the Downloaded Fonts (Can Be Used with Other Word Processors That Can Access Soft Fonts). Allows Users to Include Graphics from LOTUS 1-2-3, PAINTBRUSH, & Scanners. Can Be Used with FANCY FONT or FANCY WORD to Speed Printing on Laser Printer. Package Includes a Starter Pack of Typefoundry-Quality Fonts Licensed from BITSTREAM.
SoftCraft, Inc. (Wisconsin).

Laser Georgian. *Version:* 4.0. May 1991. *Items Included:* English user's manual, keyboard layout chart, key caps sticker sheet. *Customer Support:* Telephone support, defective disks replaced free.
Macintosh (512k). 3.5" disk $99.95. *Addl. software required:* Any word processor.
TrueType & ATM-Compatible Type-1 LaserWriter TbilisiText & TbilisiCaps Fonts & Corresponding ImageWriter Fonts in 8, 9, 10, 12, 14 & 24 Point Sizes. Select Styles from the Style Menu: Italic, Underline, Outline, Shadow, Superscript, Subscript. Logical Layout Keyed to English Keyboard. Just Change Fonts to Go from Text to Caps.
Linguist's Software, Inc.

Laser IPA. *Version:* 8.0. Mar. 1987. *Items Included:* User manual, keyboard layout chart, keycap sticker sheet. *Customer Support:* Free telephone support, defective disks replaced.
Macintosh (1Mb). 3.5" disk $99.95.
5 International Phonetic Alphabet Outline Fonts with Polished Bitmap Screen Fonts. Plain & Bold TrueType & Type-1, ATM-Compatible, Hinted IPAKielSevens, IPAExtras & IPAKiel (All Times Style), TrueType & Type-1 IPAsans & Type-3 IPAplus (Both Helvetical Style). Contains All of the International Phonetic Alphabet Symbols & Diacritical Marks Plus over 200 Other Phonetic Symbols. 109 Overstrikes Can Go over Any Symbol, in Any Combination with Other Overstrikes & Understrikes. IPAExtras Has Raised Overstrikes to Go over Ascenders & Lowered Understrikes to Go under Descenders.
Linguist's Software, Inc.

Laser Laotian. *Version:* 4.1. Jun. 1991. *Items Included:* User's manual, keyboard layout chart. *Customer Support:* Telephone support, defective disks replaced free.
Macintosh (512k). 3.5" disk $99.95. *Addl. software required:* Any word processor.
ATM-Compatible, Type-1 LaserWriter & TrueType Laotian Font in Plain, Bold, Italic & Bold-Italic with Polished Plain Bitmap Fonts in 12, 18, 24, 36, & 48 Point Sizes. Two Keyboard Input Methods: 1) Traditional Laotian Layout, or 2) Logical Layout Keyed to English Keyboard. Vowels & Tone Marks Have Automatic Non-Deleting Backspacing. You Can Easily Mix in English Text. User's Manual & Keyboard Chart.
Linguist's Software, Inc.

LASER TECHFONTS

Laser Manager: Laser Printer Enhancements. *Items Included:* Bound manual. *Customer Support:* Free hotline - no time limit; 30 day limited warranty; updates are $5/disk plus S&H.
MS-DOS 2.1 or higher. IBM & compatibles (512k). disk $99.95. *Nonstandard peripherals required:* Hard disk & an HP LaserJet 500, 500 Plus, or Series II (or IID, IIP) or compatible printer.
Works with Existing Software to Improve the Quality of Your Printed Output. It Allows User to Print Spreadsheets, Documents, & Reports with Professional Typeset Quality from Existing Data Files.
Dynacomp, Inc.

Laser Manager: Laser Printer Enhancements. 1995. *Items Included:* Full manual. *Customer Support:* Free telephone support - 90 days, 30-day warranty.
MS-DOS 3.2 or higher. 286 (584k). disk $39.95. *Nonstandard peripherals required:* CGA/EGA/VGA.
Works with Existing Software to Improve the Quality of Your Printed Output. It Allows You to Print Spreadsheets, Documents, & Reports with Professional Typeset Quality from Existing Data Files. This Is Accomplished Directly, Without You Having to Transfer Files to a Desktop Publishing System or Confusing Word Processor. Best of All, the 63 Built-In Fonts Match Many of Those Used by Typesetters, Maintaining Both Consistency & Quality.
Dynacomp, Inc.

Laser Persian. *Version:* 2.0. 1992. *Items Included:* User's manual, keyboard layout chart, key caps sticker sheet. *Customer Support:* Telephone support, defective disks replaced free.
Any Macintosh that can run on System 6.0.7 (1Mb). 3.5" disk $99.95.
Bidirectional Word Processing. Automatic Contextualization & Ligature Formation. Includes Script Manager Compatible MiniWRITER Desk Accessory. For All Mac's (Except Those Requiring System 7.0) & Many Mac Programs. Vowel & Compound Vowel Overstrikes. Contains Persian System 6.0.7, Farsi Dialogue Boxes & Menus Plus System Switcher 1.1 for Hard Disk Switching to & from the Persian System. Add Any Fonts to the Persian System. Cursor Reliable in MiniWRITER & MacDraw, but Not in MacWrite & Ready, Set, Go! 4.0a (Both Right Justify OK) & MSWord (but Without Right Justification). Four Different Farsi ImageWriter Fonts, 3 Type-3 Laser Fonts, Arabic & Farsi Bitmap Fonts for English Systems. Farsi Alphabet Sorting. Gregorian, Lunar, & Solar Calendars.
Linguist's Software, Inc.

Laser Positive. *Version:* 3.0. *Items Included:* Computer, PostScript compatible laser printer, software, optional scanner. *Customer Support:* Technical support & 1 day training included, lifetime updates at cost of media & handling (approx. $25.00).
Apple Macintosh II, IIx, IIcx. complete systems $16,000.00 to $22,000.00; software only, $5000.00.
Designed for Screen Printers, Combining Lettering Design, Artwork Development, Color Separations & High Quality Laser Output. Features Include: Large Font Library, Interactive Text Manipulations, Built-In Drawing Tools, Adjustable Choke & Spread, Step & Repeat, Automatic Separations, Various Line Screens, & Option to Import, Edit & Color Separate Illustrator Files.
Graphic Applications, Inc.

Laser TechFonts. *Version:* 3.1. *Compatible Hardware:* Apple Macintosh. *Memory Required:* 512k. *Items Included:* Disks, user manual. *Customer Support:* Free telephone technical

LASER TERMINAL

support.
$139.00.
Font Package Featuring Mathematical, Scientific, Electronic, Analog & Digital Symbols.
Nisus Software, Inc.

Laser Terminal. *Compatible Hardware:* Apple Macintosh.
3.5" disk $20.00.
Terminal Emulator for Use with a Macintosh & VAX or Older Host Mainframe That Allows Files to Be Directed to a LaserWriter.
Kinko's.

Laser THAI. *Version:* 7.0. May 1988. *Items Included:* User manual, keyboard layout chart. *Customer Support:* Free telephone support, defective disks replaced.
Macintosh (1Mb). $99.95, per typeface; $299.95, all 8 typefaces.
ATM Type 1 PostScript & TrueType Fonts Are Available in Eight Quality Typefaces Compatible with All Macintosh Software with Font Menu Choices. The Vowels & Tone Markers Are Non-Deleting Backspacing Overstrikes. Wordwrap & Other Software Format Features Are Preserved. Now Includes AsiaScript Scripting System Which Allows the User to Type in the English System As If the Computer Were Operating in the Thai System. Simply Type the Consonant, the Vowel & Then the Tone Marker. Follows the Regular GatManee Keyboard Layout. Includes Corresponding Bit Map Fonts in at Least 24, 36, 48, & 60 Point. Requires No Special Keyboard. Their Type-1 & TrueType Fonts Will Print Properly Scaled at Any Size.
Linguist's Software, Inc.

Laser Tibetan. *Version:* 2.2. Jan. 1988. *Items Included:* User's manual, keyboard layout chart. *Customer Support:* Telephone support, defective disks replaced free.
Macintosh (1Mb). 3.5" disk $149.95. *Addl. software required:* Any word processor.
Type-1 & TrueType Tibetan Font & Type-3 Ornate Tibetan Font with Corresponding Bitmap Screen Fonts (Each in 12, 18, 24, 36, 48, 60, & 72 Point Sizes). All Style Options & Combinations Selectable from the Style Menu. Complete User's Manual & Keyboard Layout Chart. Use with Any Macintosh Compatible Software with Fonts Accessible from the Font Menu, e.g. Microsoft Word.
Linguist's Software, Inc.

LaserAmharic. *Version:* 3.0. Jul. 1994. *Items Included:* User manual, Keyboard Layout Chart, Keycap Sticker Sheet. *Customer Support:* Free telephone support, defective disks replaced.
Macintosh. Macintosh (1Mb). 3.5" disk $149.95. *Addl. software required:* Any Word Processor. *Optimal configuration:* 4Mb RAM & a hard drive.
ATM-Compatible Type-1 & TrueType AmharicLS Fonts in Plain, Bold, Italic, & Bold-Italic. Contains the Entire Ge'ez Script for Amharic & Tigrigna Characters. Simple Phonetic Input for All Characters.
Linguist's Software, Inc.

LaserArabic & Farsi. *Version:* 3.0. May 1989. *Items Included:* User manual, keyboard charts, key cap sticker sheet. *Customer Support:* Free telephone support, defective disks replaced.
Macintosh. Any Macintosh requires 1Mb RAM & a hard drive. 3.5" disk $99.95.
Four Type-1 & TrueType Fonts for Imagesetters & PostScript Printers. For Use with Macintosh Arabic System or Extensions. Only $49.95 When Purchased with Nisus.
Linguist's Software, Inc.

LaserArmenian. *Version:* 1.2. Apr. 1993. *Items Included:* User's manual, keyboard layout chart. *Customer Support:* Free telephone support; defective disks replaced free.
Any system. Macintosh (1Mb). 3.5" disk $99.95. *Addl. software required:* Any word processor. *Optimal configuration:* 4Mb RAM, hard drive.
ATM-Compatible, Type-1 & TrueType LaserWriter Armenian Font & Corresponding Polished Bitmap Fonts in 10, 12, 14, 18, & 24 Point Sizes. Select Styles: Italic, Underline, Outline, Shadow, Superscript, Subscript. Logical Layout Keyed to English Keyboard.
Linguist's Software, Inc.

LaserArmenian for Windows. *Version:* 2.0. Jul. 1992. *Items Included:* User's manual, keyboard layout charts, ANSI chart, keycap sticker sheet, & if needed, Keyboard Switcher utility, providing four characters per key in Windows. *Customer Support:* Free telephone support; defective disks replaced free.
Windows. IBM or compatibles (4Mb). disk $99.95. *Addl. software required:* MS Windows 3.1 or ATM. *Optimal configuration:* 4Mb RAM & 386.
Two Scalable Adobe Type Manager- (ATM-) Compatible, Type-1 & TrueType Armenian Fonts: Armenian & Armenian Vertical. TrueType Requires Microsoft Windows 3.1x; Also Works with Word 6 for DOS, WordPerfect 6.0b for DOS, & AutoCAD r.13. Type 1 Works with ATM & Windows; Also Works with OS/2 & AutoCAD r.12. WordPerfect for Windows Users Must Upgrade to Version 6.0a or Newer. Logical Keyboard Layout Keyed to English Keyboard. You Can Easily Mix English & Armenian Text.
Linguist's Software, Inc.

LaserBengali. *Version:* 1.4. Jun. 1993. *Items Included:* User's manual, keyboard layout chart. *Customer Support:* Free telephone support; defective disks replaced free.
Macintosh. Macintosh (1Mb). 3.5" disk $149.95. *Addl. software required:* Any word processor. *Optimal configuration:* 4Mb RAM, hard drive.
Professional-Quality, Hinted Bengali Type-1 & TrueType Font in Plain, Bold, Italic & BoldItalic Styles. InduScript Input Method Allows Easy, Phonetic Input of All Characters, Including Conjuncts. Includes Complete User's Manual & InduScript Phonetic Keyboard Chart. These Scaleable, Outline Fonts Display & Print at All Sizes.
Linguist's Software, Inc.

LaserBurmese. *Version:* 2.0. Apr. 1994. *Items Included:* User manual, Keyboard Layout Chart, Keycap Sticker Sheet, & a Micro-Space Key for minute adjustments. *Customer Support:* Free telephone support, defective disks replaced.
Macintosh. Macintosh (1Mb). 3.5" disk $99.95. *Addl. software required:* Any Word Processor. *Optimal configuration:* 4Mb RAM & a hard drive.
ATM-Compatible Type-1 & TrueType Burmese Font in Plain, Bold, Italic, & Bold-Italic with Corresponding Bitmap Screen Fonts in 12, 14, 18, 24, 36, & 48-Point Sizes. Burmese Contains the Entire Set of Current Burmese Characters, Including Overstrike Vowels & Diacritical Marks Which Can Be Placed over or under Any Letter & in Any Combination. Each of These Overstrike Characters Has Automatic Non-Deleting Backspacing. You May Select Other Styles from the Style Menu: Italic, Underline, Outline, Shadow, Superscript, & Subscript. They Are Compatible with Every Macintosh System & with All Standard Macintosh Software.
Linguist's Software, Inc.

LaserBurmese for Windows. *Version:* 1.1. Jul. 1994. *Items Included:* Keyboard Switcher utility, providing four charters per key in Windows, a user's manual, keyboard layout charts, ANSI chart & keycap sticker sheet. *Customer Support:* Free telephone support, defective disks replaced.
Windows. IBM & compatibles (4Mb). disk $99.95. *Addl. software required:* Microsoft Windows or ATM. WordPerfect for Windows 6.0 users must upgarde to 6.0a (free from WordPerfect Corp., as of 07/94) to type overstrikes. *Optimal configuration:* 4Mb RAM & 386.
Professional-Quality, Hinted, Scalable TrueType & Type 1 Fonts in Plain, Bold, Italic & Bold-Italic. LaserBurmese Contains the Entire Set of Current Burmese Characters, Including Overstrike Vowels & Diacritical Marks Which Can Be Placed over or under Any Letter & in Any Combination. Each of These Overstrike Characters Has Automatic Non-Deleting Backspacing. The Font Includes a Minispace for Minute Adjustments. TrueType Requires Microsoft Windows 3.1; Also Works with Word 6 for DOS, WordPerfect 6.0b for DOS & AutoCAD r.13. Type 1 Works with ATM & Windows; Also Works with OS/2 & AutoCAD r.12 & 13. WordPerfect for Windows Users Must Upgrade to Version 6.0a or Newer. A NeXT Version Is Available.
Linguist's Software, Inc.

LaserCambodian for Windows. *Version:* 3.4. Jun. 1992. *Items Included:* User's manual, keyboard layout chart, ANSI Table, keycap sticker sheet. *Customer Support:* Free telephone support; defective disks replaced free.
Windows. IBM or compatibles (4Mb). disk $99.95. *Addl. software required:* MS Windows or ATM. *Optimal configuration:* 4Mb RAM & 386.
Two Professional-Quality, Hinted Fonts in TrueType & Type 1 Formats: CambodianLS & CambodianLS Oblique. TrueType Requires Microsoft Windows 3.1; Also Works with Word 6 for DOS, WordPerfect 6.0b for DOS & AutoCAD r.13. Type 1 Works with ATM & Windows; Also Works with OS/2 & AutoCAD r.12 & 13. WordPerfect for Windows Users Must Upgrade to Version 6.0a or Newer. A NeXT Version Is Available. These Scalable Outline Fonts Display & Print at All Sizes. They Contain the Entire Set of Current Cambodian Characters, Including Overstrike Vowels & Diacritical Marks Which Can Be Placed over or under Any Letter & in Any Combination. Each of These Overstrike Characters Has Automatic Non-Deleting Backspacing for Fast Convenient Typing. Their Keyboard Layout Places Cambodian Sounds on Their Corresponding English Key. Keyboard Switcher Permits Accessing Four Characters per Key, Eliminating Most ANSI Codes.
Linguist's Software, Inc.

LaserCherokee. *Version:* 3.0. Jun. 1994. *Items Included:* User manual, Keyboard Layout Chart, Keycap Sticker Sheet, & Syllabary Chart. *Customer Support:* Free telephone support, defective disks replaced.
Macintosh. Macintosh (1Mb). 3.5" disk $99.95. *Addl. software required:* Any Word Processor. *Optimal configuration:* 4Mb RAM & a hard drive.
A High-Quality, Type-1 & TrueType Cherokee Font. Fully Scalable & ATM Compatible. Includes Hand-Polished Bitmaps in 12, 14, 18, & 24 Point Sizes. The Font Also Includes Times-Style English Characters. Simply Choose the Cherokee Font from the Font Menu & Select the Cherokee Keyboard Layout. Switch Instantly Between English & Cherokee by Pressing the Caps Lock Key. Logical, Syllabary-Style Input Allows the User to Type the Ohonetic Enlgish Syllabary to Produce the Characters.
Linguist's Software, Inc.

TITLE INDEX

LaserCherokee for Windows. *Version:* 1.1. Mar. 1994. *Items Included:* User manual, Keyboard Layout Chart, ANSI Chart, & Syllabary Chart. *Customer Support:* Free telephone support, defective disks replaced.
Windows. IBM & compatibles (4Mb). disk $99.95. *Addl. software required:* Microsoft Windows or ATM. *Optimal configuration:* 4Mb RAM & 386.
A High-Quality, Type-1 & TrueType Cherokee Font. Fully Scalable & ATM Compatible. TrueType Requires Microsoft Windows 3.1. Type 1 Works with ATM & Windows. The Font Also Includes Times-Style English Characters. Simply Choose the Cherokee Font from the Font Menu & Select the Cherokee Keyboard Layout. Switch Instantly Between English & Cherokee by Pressing the Hotkey. Logical, Syllabary-Style Input Allows the User to Type the Phonetic English Syllabary to Produce the Characters.
Linguist's Software, Inc.

LaserCoptic. *Version:* 3.1. Jan. 1993. *Items Included:* User's manual, keyboard layout chart. *Customer Support:* Free telephone support; defective disks replaced free.
Macintosh. Macintosh (1Mb). 3.5" disk $99.95. *Addl. software required:* Any word processor. *Optimal configuration:* 4Mb RAM, hard drive.
ATM Compatible Type 1 & TrueType Nag Hammadi-Style Coptic Fonts & Corresponding Polished Bitmap Fonts in 10, 12, 14, 18, & 24 Point Sizes. Contains the Entire Set of Coptic Characters, Including Letters Derived from Demotic & the Characters for Sahidic, Fayumic, Bohairic, & a Variety of Overstrike Bars & Dots & Special Coptic Diacritical Marks Which Can Be Placed over or under Any Letter & in Any Combination. Each of These Overstrike Characters Has Automatic Non-Deleting Backspacing for Fast Convenient Typing. The Logical Intuitive Keyboard Layouts Are Keyed to the English Keyboard with Coptic Sounds on Their Corresponding English Keys. You May Select Other Styles from the Style Menu: Italic, Underline, Outline, Shadow, Superscript, & Subscript. Compatible with Every Macintosh System, Including 7.0.1, & with All Standard Macintosh Software & Can Be Used in Conjunction with Any Other Language.
Linguist's Software, Inc.

LaserCoptic for Windows. *Version:* 2.1. Jan. 1993. *Items Included:* User's manual, keyboard layout chart, ANSI Table, keycap sticker sheet. *Customer Support:* Free telephone support; defective disks replaced free.
Windows. IBM or compatibles (4Mb). disk $99.95. *Addl. software required:* MS Windows or ATM. *Optimal configuration:* 4Mb RAM & 386.
Two TrueType & ATM-Compatible, Type 1 Hinted Nag Hammadi-Style Coptic Fonts. TrueType Requires Microsoft Windows 3.1; Also Works with Word 6 for DOS & WordPerfect 6.0b for DOS ($17.50 Upgrade from WordPerfect Corp. for 6.0 Users), AutoCAD r. 12; OS/2; NeXT (Available by Request). WordPerfect for Windows 6.0 Users Must Upgrade to 6.0a (Free from WordPerfect Corp., As of 7/94) to Type Overstrikes & Diacritical Marks. These Scalable Outline Fonts Display & Print at All Sizes. LaserCoptic Contains the Entire Set of Coptic Characters, Including Letters Derived from Demotic & the Characters for Sahidic, Fayumic, Bohairic, a Minispace, & a Variety of Overstrike Bars & Dots & Special Coptic Diacritical Marks Which Can Be Placed over or under Any Letter & in Any Combination. The Logical Intuitive Keyboard Layout Has Coptic Sounds on Their Corresponding English Keys.
Linguist's Software, Inc.

LaserCraft Images. *Compatible Hardware:* Apple Macintosh.
contact publisher for price.
Nikrom Technical Products, Inc.

LaserCree. *Version:* 3.0. 1995. *Items Included:* User's manual; keyboard layout chart; keycap sticker sheet. *Customer Support:* Free telephone support, defective disks replaced free.
Macintosh. Macintosh (1Mb). 3.5" disk $99.95. *Addl. software required:* Any word processor.
Professional-Quality, Hinted Cree Font in Both TrueType & Type-1 Formats, Has Plain, Bold, Italic & Bold-Italic Styles.
Linguist's Software, Inc.

LASerDEV. *Version:* 3.5. *Compatible Hardware:* IBM PC & compatibles, PC XT, PC AT. *Operating System(s) Required:* PC-DOS/MS-DOS 2.0 or higher. *General Requirements:* LaserJet or LaserJet Plus printer.
disk $295.00.
Software Device Driver Which Enables the HP LaserJet or LaserJet Plus Printers to Generate the Industrial & Retail Bar Code Symbologies. Users Can Print Bar Codes Intermixed with Text While Being Transparent to All the Native Commands of the LaseJet. Bar Code Symbologies Currently Supported Include CODE 39, UPC-A & Interleaved 2 of 5, CODE 49, CODE 128 with Others Available upon Request. High, Medium, & Low Bar Code Densities Are Supported.
Dataflow Technologies, Inc.

LaserFrench German Spanish. *Version:* 9.5. Dec. 1986. *Items Included:* User manual; Laminated keyboard layout chart; keycap sticker sheet. *Customer Support:* Free telephone support, detective disks replaced.
Macintosh (1Mb). 3.5" disk $99.95.
ATM-Compatible Type 1 & TrueType Romance Plain, Bold & Italic with Corresponding Polished ImageWriter Fonts for Use in MacWrite, Microsoft Word etc. Features 41 Overstrike Accents & Diacritical Mark Keys Each Having Automatic Non-Deleting Backspacing for Fast Typing over Any Letter or Symbol & in Any Combination. Complete with Laser-Adjusted Screen Fonts in 10, 12, 20, 24, 36 & 48 Point Sizes, Mini Space Bar, the LaserWriter Software, User's Manual, Laminated Keyboard Layout Chart. Style Variations: Plain, Italic, Underline, Shadow, Subscript, Superscript & Any Combination of These. Includes All European Languages Written in Roman Script As Well As Many African & American Indian Languages. Eurostriker allows you to type the accents & special characters of 21 European languages using only the semicolon & slash keys to produce the specaial characters. For example, all of the special characters or Romanian can be produced just by typing a semicolon after the special character.
Linguist's Software, Inc.

LaserGaelic. *Version:* 1.2. Apr. 1995. *Items Included:* User's manual; keyboard layout chart; keycap sticker sheet. *Customer Support:* Free telephone support, defective disks replaced free.
Macintosh. Macintosh (1Mb). 3.5" disk $99.95. *Addl. software required:* Any word processor.
Two Type-1 & TrueType Gaelic Fonts Including the Characters for Irish, Scottish & Manx Gaelic, Welsh, Breton, & Cornish. Logical, Easy-to-Use Layout Based on the Standard English Typewriter. Use Regular U.S. Keyboard or a Special Gaelic Keyboard Resource for Easy-to-Type Accented Characters.
Linguist's Software, Inc.

LaserGaelic for Windows. May 1995. *Items Included:* User's manual; keyboard layout chart; keycap sticker sheet. *Customer Support:* Free

LASERGEORGIAN PROFESSIONAL

telephone support, defective disks replaced free.
Windows. IBM or compatibles (4Mb). disk $99.95. *Addl. software required:* MS Windows 3.1X or ATM.
Professional-Quality, Hinted, Scalable Fonts in Both TrueType & Type 1 Formats: GaillimhLS Plain & GaelicLS Plain. For All Windows 3.1X-Compatible Applications. Type 1 Works with ATM & Windows; Also Works with OS/2 & AutoCAD R.12 & 13. WordPerfect for Windows Users Must Upgrade to Version 6.0a or Newer to Type Overstrikes. Includes Keyboard Switcher Windows Utility Providing Deadkeys & Four Characters per Key in Windows Applications. Fonts Alone Work in Word 6 for DOS, WordPerfect 6.0b for DOS, or Newer, AutoCAD R.12 & 13; OS/2; NeXT (Available by Request).
Linguist's Software, Inc.

Lasergenix: Sverdlovsk, Riverside, IPA, Newport News, Fontana, Fractional, Cracow, Chef Dijon, Bryansk. *Compatible Hardware:* Apple Macintosh. *General Requirements:* ImageWriter, LaserWriter, LaserWriter Plus.
3.5" disk $39.50.
LaserWriter Fonts - Cyrillic, Text & Graphics, Fractions, Eastern European, Cooking.
Devonian International Software Co.

LaserGeorgian. *Version:* 4.0. May 1991. *Items Included:* User's manual; keyboard layout chart; keycap sticker sheet. *Customer Support:* Free telephone support, defective disks replaced free.
Macintosh. Macintosh (1Mb). 3.5" disk $99.95. *Addl. software required:* Any word processor.
TrueType & ATM-Compatible Type-1 LaserWriter TbilisiText & TbilisiCaps Fonts & Corresponding ImageWriter Fonts in 8, 9, 10, 12, 14 & 24 Point Sizes. Select Styles from the Style Menu: Italic, Underline, Outline, Shadow, Superscript, Subscript. Logical Layout Keyed to English Keyboard or Standard Georgian Keyboard Layout Options. Just Change Fonts to Go from Text to Caps.
Linguist's Software, Inc.

LaserGeorgian for Windows. *Version:* 3.0. May 1992. *Items Included:* User's manual, keyboard layout chart. *Customer Support:* Free telephone support; defective disks replaced free.
Windows. IBM or compatibles (4Mb). disk $99.95. *Addl. software required:* MS Windows or ATM. *Optimal configuration:* 4Mb RAM & 386.
Two Scaleable Adobe Type Manager- (ATM-) Compatible, Type-1 & TrueType Georgian Fonts: TbilisiText & TbilisiCaps. TrueType Requires Microsoft Windows 3.1, & Works with Word 6 for DOS. Type 1 Works with ATM & Windows; Also Works with OS/2 & AutoCAD r.12. A NeXT Version Is Available. Keyboard Switcher with Two Keyboard Input Methods: 1) Traditional Georgian Layout, or 2) Logical Layout Keyed to English Keyboard. You Can Easily Mix English & Georgian Text. User's Manual, Keyboard Charts, & Keystickers.
Linguist's Software, Inc.

LaserGeorgian Professional. *Version:* 4.0. Mar. 1994. *Items Included:* User manual, Keyboard Layout Chart, Keycap Sticker Sheet. *Customer Support:* Free telephone support, defective disks replaced.
Macintosh. Macintosh (1Mb). 3.5" disk $199.95. *Addl. software required:* Any Word Processor. *Optimal configuration:* 4Mb RAM & a hard drive.
TrueType & ATM-Compatible Type-1 LaserWriter TbilisiText & TbilisiCaps Fonts & Corresponding ImageWriter Fonts in 8, 9, 10, 12, 14 & 24 Point Sizes, Plus Three More Headline Fonts: Batumi, Mtskheta, Telavi. Select Styles from the Style Menu: Italic, Underline, Outline, Shadow,

Superscript, Subscript. Logical Layout Keyed to English Keyboard or Standard Georgian Keyboard Layout Options. Just Change Fonts to Go from Text to Caps.
Linguist's Software, Inc.

LaserGeorgian Professional for Windows. *Version:* 3.0. Jan. 1994. *Items Included:* User manual, Keyboard Layout Chart, Keycap Sticker Sheet. *Customer Support:* Free telephone support, defective disks replaced.
Windows. IBM & compatibles (4Mb). disk $199.95. *Addl. software required:* Microsoft Windows or ATM. *Optimal configuration:* 4Mb RAM & 386.
Two Scaleable Adobe Type Manager-(ATM-) Compatible, Type-1 & TrueType Georgian Fonts: TbilisiText & TbilisiCaps Plus Three More Headline Fonts: Batumi, Mtskheta, Telavi. TrueType Requires Microsoft Windows 3.1, & Works with Word 6 for DOS. Type 1 Works with ATM & Windows; Also Works with OS/2 & AutoCAD r.12. A NeXT Version Is Available. Keyboard Switcher with Two Keyboard Input Methods: 1) Traditional Georgian Layout, or 2) Logical Layout Keyed to English Keyboard. You Can Easily Mix English & Georgian Text.
Linguist's Software, Inc.

LaserGlagolitic. Apr. 1995. *Items Included:* User's manual; keyboard layout chart; keycap sticker sheet. *Customer Support:* Free telephone support; defective disks replaced free.
Macintosh. Macintosh (1Mb). 3.5" disk $99.95.
Addl. software required: Any word processor.
A Pre-Cyrillic Russian Font. Professional-Quality, Hinted, Type-1 & TrueType Font.
Linguist's Software, Inc.

LaserGlagolitic for Windows. May 1995. *Items Included:* User's manual; keyboard layout chart; keycap sticker sheet. *Customer Support:* Free telephone support, defective disks replaced free.
Windows. IBM or compatibles (4Mb). disk $99.95. *Addl. software required:* MS Windows 3.1X or ATM.
Contains Professional, Hinted, Scalable TrueType & Type-1 Fonts. TrueType Requires Microsoft Windows 3.1; Also Works with Word 6 for DOS, WordPerfect 6.0b for DOS & AutoCAD R. 13. Type 1 Works with ATM & Windows; Also Works with OS/2 & AutoCAD R.12 & 13. WordPerfect for Windows Users Must Upgrade to Version 6.0a or Newer. A NeXT Version Is Available.
Linguist's Software, Inc.

LaserGo Type Commander TrueType Fonts for Windows 3.1: Blue Ribbon Collection. Apr. 1992. *Items Included:* Disks, installation instructions, license agreement. *Customer Support:* Free tech support by phone: 619-450-4600; by FAX: 619-450-9334; by BBS: 619-450-9370.
Windows 3.1. IBM & compatibles. Contact publisher for price (ISBN 1-878388-18-5, Order no.: TC-4040). *Nonstandard peripherals required:* Any printer, monitor or graphics card supported by Windows 3.1.
Ready-to-Use TrueType Scalable Screen & Printer Font Collection for Windows 3.1. The Blue Ribbon Collection (10 Fonts) Includes ITC AvantGarde, ITC Bookman, ITC Zaph Chancery Medium Italic & ITC ZaphDingbats. See & Print These Scalable Fonts on Any Printer, Monitor or Graphics Card Supported by Windows 3.1.
LaserGo, Inc.

LaserGo Type Commander TrueType Fonts for Windows 3.1: Harvest Collection. Apr. 1992. *Items Included:* Disks, installation instructions, license agreement. *Customer Support:* Free tech support by phone: 619-450-4600; by FAX: 619-450-9334; by BBS: 619-450-9370.
Windows 3.1. IBM & compatibles. Contact publisher for price (ISBN 1-878388-17-7, Order no.: TC-4030). *Nonstandard peripherals required:* Any printer, monitor or graphics card supported by Windows 3.1.
Ready-to-Use TrueType Scalable Screen & Printer Font Collection for Windows 3.1. The Harvest Collection (70 Fonts) Includes a Wide Assortment of Popular Faces, Plus Fun Novelty & Text Faces. See & Print These Scalable Fonts on Any Printer, Monitor or Graphics Card Supported by Windows 3.1.
LaserGo, Inc.

LaserGo Type Commander TrueType Fonts for Windows 3.1: Springtime Collection. Apr. 1992. *Items Included:* Disks, installation instructions, license agreement. *Customer Support:* Free tech support by phone: 619-450-4600; by FAX: 619-450-9334; by BBS: 619-450-9370.
Windows 3.1. IBM & compatibles. Contact publisher for price (ISBN 1-878388-16-9, Order no.: TC-4020). *Nonstandard peripherals required:* Any printer, monitor or graphics card supported by Windows 3.1.
Ready-to-Use TrueType Scalable Screen & Printer Font Collections for Windows 3.1. These Collections Include a Wide Assortment of Popular Faces, Plus Fun Novelty & Text Faces. See & Print These Scalable Fonts on Any Printers, Monitors & Graphics Cards Supported by Windows 3.1. The Springtime Collection Has 70 Typefaces.
LaserGo, Inc.

LaserGreek. *Version:* 18.0. May 1986. *Items Included:* User's manual; keyboard layout chart; keycap sticker sheet. *Customer Support:* Free telephone support, defective disks replaced.
Macintosh (1Mb). 3.5" disk $99.95.
5 Professional-Quality Fonts: TrueType & ATM-Compatible, Type-1 SymbolGreek in Plain, Bold, Italic & Bold-Italic with Polished Bitmaps Ranging from 9-48 Points; SymbolGreekP, Same As SymbolGreek but with a Tildeshaped Circumflex; Graeca Plain, Bold, Italic & Bold-Italic with Polished Bitmaps, & Greek Sans Plain, Bold, Oblique & Bold-Oblique, & an Uncial Font. Each Has 35 Accents, Breathing Marks, Iota Subscripts & Diereses with Automatic, Non-Deleting Backspacing over Any Symbol. All Have Nestle-Aland, UBS, Leiden & TLG Text Critical Symbols & Sigla & English, French, German Accents. Also Includes the Final Sigma Script Systems Which Automatically Changes Regular Sigmas to Final Sigmas According to Context.
Linguist's Software, Inc.

LaserGreek & Hebrew. *Version:* 12.6. Aug. 1993. *Items Included:* User manual, Keyboard Layout Chart, Keycap Sticker Sheets. *Customer Support:* Free telephone support, defective disks replaced.
Macintosh. Macintosh (1Mb). 3.5" disk $179.95.
Addl. software required: Any Word Processor.
Optimal configuration: 4Mb RAM & a hard drive.
Contains Everything in LaserGreek & LaserHebrew. $50 to Add LaserHebrew II.
Linguist's Software, Inc.

LaserGreek & Hebrew for Windows. *Version:* 4.5. Aug. 1993. *Items Included:* User manual, Keyboard Layout Chart, Keycap Sticker Sheet. *Customer Support:* Free telephone support, defective disks replaced.
Windows. IBM & compatibles (4Mb). disk $179.95. *Addl. software required:* Microsoft Windows or ATM. *Optimal configuration:* 4Mb RAM & 386.
Includes Everything in LaserGreek for Windows & LaserHebrew for Windows.
Linguist's Software, Inc.

LaserGreek for Windows. *Version:* 4.5. Mar. 1992. *Items Included:* User manual, keyboard layout chart, ANSI Table, keycap sticker sheet. *Customer Support:* Free telephone support; defective disks replaced free.
Windows. IBM or compatibles (4Mb). disk $99.95. *Addl. software required:* MS Windows or ATM. *Optimal configuration:* 4Mb RAM & 386.
Six Professional-Quality, Hinted, Scalable Fonts in Both TrueType & Type-1 Formats: SymbolGreek, SymbolGreekP, SymbolGreekPMono, Graeca, GreekSans, & UncialLS, with All but UncialLS & SymbolGreekPMono in Plain, Bold, Italic, & Bold-Italic Styles. Works with All Microsoft Windows 3.1x-Compatible Applications. Type 1 Works with ATM & Windows; Also Works with OS/2 & AutoCAD r.12 & 13. WordPerfect for Windows Users Must Upgrade to Version 6.0a or Newer. Includes Keyboard Switcher, a Utility Providing Four Characters per Key in Windows. Fonts Alone Work with Word 6 for DOS, WordPerfect 6.0b for DOS or Newer, & AutoCAD r.13. Has 35 Accents, Breathing Marks, Iota Subscripts & Diereses for Use in Any Combination to Overstrike Any Letter. Includes Nestle-Aland, UBS, Leiden & TLG Text-Critical Symbols & Sigla, Roman Alphabet, French & German Accents.
Linguist's Software, Inc.

LaserGreek, Hebrew & Phonetics. *Version:* 12.2. Sep. 1993. *Items Included:* User manual, Keyboard Layout Chart, Keycap Sticker Sheets. *Customer Support:* Free telephone support, defective disks replaced.
Macintosh. Macintosh (1Mb). 3.5" disk $249.95.
Addl. software required: Any Word Processor.
Optimal configuration: 4Mb RAM & a hard drive.
Includes Five of Our Most Popular Products: LaserGreek, LaserHebrew, LaserIPA, SemiticTransliterator, & TransRoman (a $499.75 Value). $50 to Add LaserHebrew II.
Linguist's Software, Inc.

LaserGuide: Patron Access Catalog. *Version:* 5.53. Jan. 1987. *Compatible Hardware:* IBM PC & compatibles, PS/2. *Memory Required:* 640k. *General Requirements:* Hard disk optional. *Customer Support:* Toll-free number.
contact publisher for price.
A Library's Cataloging Information Is Mastered on CD-ROM Discs & the LaserGuide Software Provides Patron Searching with New Features. Patrons May Perform Boolean Searches by Filling in AND, OR & NOT Windows. Resulting Matches Are Displayed Directly. The Library's Floor Plans Are Integrated into the Catalog. The Active Map Gives Patrons Directions to Selected Books. Searching Suggestions & Shelf Browsing Are Also Available. Instantly Updatable Using LaserMerge. Network License Available.
GRC International, Inc.

LaserGujarati. *Version:* 5.1. Sep. 1992. *Items Included:* User's manual, keyboard layout chart. *Customer Support:* Free telephone support; defective disks replaced free.
Macintosh. Macintosh (1Mb). 3.5" disk $149.95.
Addl. software required: Any word processor.
Optimal configuration: 4Mb RAM, hard drive.
Professional-Quality, Hinted Gujarati Type-1 & TrueType Font in Plain, Bold, Italic & BoldItalic Styles. InduScript Input Method Allows Easy, Phonetic input of All Characters, Including Conjuncts. Includes Complete User's Manual & InduScript Phonetic Keyboard Chart. These Scaleable, Outline Fonts Display & Print at All Sizes.
Linguist's Software, Inc.

TITLE INDEX

LaserGujarati for Windows. *Version:* 2.2. Nov. 1992. *Items Included:* User's manual, keyboard layout chart, ANSI charts, Keyboard Switcher utility providing four characters per key in Windows, & keycap sticker sheet. *Customer Support:* Free telephone support; defective disks replaced free.
Windows. IBM or compatibles (4Mb). disk $99.95. *Addl. software required:* MS Windows or ATM. *Optimal configuration:* 4Mb RAM & 386.
Professional-Quality, Hinted Gujarati Font in Both TrueType & Type 1 Formats in Plain, Bold, Italic, & Bold-Italic Styles. TrueType Requires Microsoft Windows 3.1; Also Works with Word 6 for DOS, WordPerfect 6.0b for DOS, & AutoCAD r. 13. Type 1 Works with ATM & Windows; Also Works with OS/2 & AutoCAD r.12 & 13. WordPerfect for Windows Users Must Upgrade to WordPerfect 6.0a or Newer. A NeXT Version Is Available. Includes a Transliterated Keyboard Layout with All Gujarati Characters. These Scalable Outline Fonts Display & Print at All Sizes.
Linguist's Software, Inc.

LaserGwich'in. 1995. *Items Included:* User's manual; keyboard layout chart; keycap sticker sheet. *Customer Support:* Free telephone support, defective disks replaced free.
Macintosh. Macintosh (1Mb). 3.5" disk $99.95. *Addl. software required:* Any word processor.
ATM-Compatible, Type-1 & TrueType Times-Style Gwich'In Font in Plain, Bold, Italic & Bold-Italic.
Linguist's Software, Inc.

LaserHebrew. *Version:* 15.0. Oct. 1986. *Items Included:* User's Manual, keyboard layout charts, keycap sticker sheet. *Customer Support:* Free telephone support, defective disks replaced.
Any Macintosh. 3.5" disk $119.95.
Type 1 & TrueType Hebraica (Polished 12, 18, 24, 36, 48 Point Bitmaps), Bethel, ScriptHebrew & AradLevelVI Fonts with English System Right-to-Left Macro. The Hebraica & Bethel Fonts Have All of the Vowel Points, Accents & Special Symbols for the Biblica Hebraica Stuttgartensia (Tanach/OT) Text, Including 99 Overstrikes with Automatic, Non-Deleting Backspacing for Fast Typing over Any Letter. Includes Uers's Manual, Key Charts & Keycap Sticker Sheet.
Linguist's Software, Inc.

LaserHebrew for Windows. *Version:* 5.3. Mar. 1992. *Items Included:* User's manual, keyboard layout chart, ANSI Table, keycap sticker sheet, & a right-to-left macro for Word for Windows. *Customer Support:* Free telephone support; defective disks replaced free.
Windows. IBM or compatibles (4Mb). disk $99.95. *Addl. software required:* MS Windows or ATM. *Optimal configuration:* 4Mb RAM & 386.
Four Professional-Quality, Hinted, Scalable TrueType & Type 1 Fonts: Hebraica, Bethel, ScriptHebrew & Arad Level VI for Inscriptional Hebrew. TrueType Requires Microsoft Windows 3.1; Also Works with Word 6 for DOS, WordPerfect 6.0b for DOS & AutoCAD R.13. Type 1 Works with ATM & Windows; Also Works with OS2 & Auto CAD R.12 & 13. WordPerfect for Windows Users Must Upgrade to WordPerfect 6.0a or Newer. A Next Version Is Available Includes Keyboard Layouts (Transliterated & Israeli) in Windows Applications. Has 100 Overstriking Vowel Points, Accents, Cantillation Marks, & Diacritical Symbols for Use in Any Combination to Overstrike Any Letter. Contains All Vowel Points, Accents, Dageshim, & Diacritical Marks That Occur in the Biblia Hebraica Stuttgartensia (Hebrew Scriptures - Tanach).
Linguist's Software, Inc.

LaserHebrewII. *Version:* 16.1. 1995. *Items Included:* User's manual; keyboard layout chart; keycap sticker sheet. *Customer Support:* Free telephone support, defective disks replaced free.
Macintosh. Macintosh (1Mb). 3.5" disk $99.95. *Addl. software required:* Hebrew System-compatible word processor & World Script I.
LaserHebrew Pro $149.95.
TrueType & Type-1 HebronII (Hebraica-Style) & Transliterate Fonts with Biblical Hebrew Resources for True Right-to-Left Text Entry & Line Wrap in Hebrew-Compatible Applications. Requires WorldScript I.
Linguist's Software, Inc.

LaserHindi Sanskrit. *Version:* 5.0. Apr. 1991. *Items Included:* User's manual, keyboard chart. *Customer Support:* Telephone support, defective disks replaced free.
Macintosh (512k). 3.5" disk $149.95. *Addl. software required:* Any word processor.
Professional-Quality, Hinted HindiSanskrit Type-1 & TrueType Font in Plain, Bold, Italic & BoldItalic Styles. InduScript Input Method Allows Easy, Phonetic Input of All Characters, Including Conjuncts. Separate Scripts Are Included for Hindi & Sanskrit Conjuncts. Includes Complete User's Manual & InduScript Phonetic Keyboard Chart. Scaleable, Outline Fonts Display & Print at All Sizes.
Linguist's Software, Inc.

LaserHindi Sanskrit for Windows. *Version:* 2.4. Jul. 1992. *Items Included:* User's manual, keyboard layout chart, ANSI Chart, keycap sticker sheet. *Customer Support:* Free telephone support; defective disks replaced free.
Windows. IBM or compatibles (4Mb). disk $99.95. *Addl. software required:* MS Windows or ATM. *Optimal configuration:* 4Mb RAM & 386.
Professional-Quality, Hinted TrueType & ATM-Compatible Type 1 HindiSanskrit Plain Font. Includes Keyboard Switcher Utility Providing Four Characters per Key in Windows. TrueType Requires Microsoft Windows 3.1; Also Works with Word 6 for DOS & WordPerfect 6.0b for DOS. Type 1 Works with ATM & Windows; Also Works with OS/2 & AutoCAD r.12. WordPerfect for Windows Users Must Upgrade to WordPerfect 6.0a. A NeXT Version Is Available. Vowels, Nasals, Vedic Accents, etc. Overstrike the Preceding to Give a Handwriting 'Feel'. All Accents & Overstrikes Have Automatic Non-Deleting Backspacing in Any Combination over Any Symbol. All Consonant Clusters Easily Available or Creatable. Mini-Headling Key for Careful Spacing of Difficult Groupings - Results Therefore Can Produce Camera-Ready Copy for Publishing. Can Easily Mix in English Text. Keyboard Switcher Permits Four Characters per Key in Windows. These Scaleable Outline Fonts Display & Print at All Sizes.
Linguist's Software, Inc.

LaserHulquminum. Jan. 1996. *Items Included:* User's manual; keyboard layout chart; keycap sticker sheet. *Customer Support:* Free telephone support, defective disks replaced free.
Macintosh. Macintosh (1Mb). 3.5" disk $99.95. *Addl. software required:* Any word processor.
Professional-Quality, Hinted HulquminumLS Times-Style Font in both TrueType & Type-1 Formats. HulquminumLS Comes in Plain, Bold, Italic, & Bold-Italic Styles. The HulquminumLS Font Contains All the Characters for English & Hul'qumi'num'. Also Has Many Overstriking Accents Which Can Be Used with Any Characters in Any Combination. EuroScript Scripting System Allows You to Type All the Special Characters of Hul'qumi'num' Using Only the Semicolon (for Underlines) & Slash (for Dieresis) Keys.
Linguist's Software, Inc.

LASERIPA FOR WINDOWS

LaserHulquminum for Windows. Jan. 1996. *Items Included:* User's manual; keyboard layout chart; keycap sticker sheet. *Customer Support:* Free telephone support, defective disks replaced free.
Windows. IBM or compatibles (4Mb). disk $99.95. *Addl. software required:* MS Windows 3.1X or ATM.
Professional-Quality, Hinted HulquminumLS Times-Style Font in Both TrueType & Type-1 Formats. Comes in Plain, Bold, Italic, & Bold-Italic Styles. The Font Contains All the Characters for English & Hul'qumi'num'. Also Has Many Overstriking Accents Which Can Be Used with Any Characters in Any Combination. TrueType Requires Microsoft Windows 3.1; Also Works with Word 6 for DOS, WordPerfect 6.0b for DOS & AutoCAD R. 13. Type 1 Works with ATM & Windows; Also Works with OS/2 & AutoCAD R.12 & 13. WordPerfect for Windows Users Must Upgrade to Version 6.0a or Newer. A NeXT Version Is Available.
Linguist's Software, Inc.

LaserInukititut. Jan. 1996. *Items Included:* User's manual; keyboard layout chart; keycap sticker sheet. *Customer Support:* Free telephone support, defective disks replaced free.
Macintosh. Macintosh (1Mb). 3.5" disk $99.95. *Addl. software required:* Any word processor.
Professional-Quality, Hinted InukititutLS Font in Both TrueType & Type-1 Formats. The Font Has Both English & Inukititut Characters in Plain, Bold, Italic & Bold-Italic Styles. EuroScript Scripting System Allows Easy Phonetic Input of the Entire Inukititut Syllabary. Also Includes an English Script for Typing Other Dialects with Easy Input.
Linguist's Software, Inc.

LaserInukititut for Windows. *Version:* 1.2. Sep. 1992. *Items Included:* User's manual; keyboard layout chart; keycap sticker sheet. *Customer Support:* Free telephone support, defective disks replaced free.
Windows. IBM or compatibles (4Mb). disk $99.95. *Addl. software required:* MS Windows 3.1X or ATM.
Professional-Quality, Hinted InukititutLS Font in Both TrueType & Type-1 Formats. The Font Has Both English & Inukititut Characters in Plain, Bold, Italic & Bold-Italic Styles. TrueType Requires Microsoft Windows 3.1; Also Works with Word 6 for DOS, WordPerfect 6.0b for DOS & AutoCAD R.13. Type 1 Works with ATM & Windows; Also Works with OS/2 & AutoCAD R.12 & 13. WordPerfect for Windows Users Must Upgrade to Version 6.0a or Newer. A NeXT Version Is Available.
Linguist's Software, Inc.

LaserIPA for Windows. *Version:* 4.1. Mar. 1992. *Items Included:* User's manual, keyboard layout charts, Keyboard Switcher for four characters per key, ANSI charts, & keycap sticker sheet. *Customer Support:* Free telephone support; defective disks replaced free.
Windows. IBM or compatibles (4Mb). disk $99.95. *Addl. software required:* MS Windows or ATM. *Optimal configuration:* 4Mb RAM & 386.
Professional-Quality, Hinted, Scalable International Phonetic Alphabet Fonts in Both TrueType & Type 1 Formats: Times-Style Regular & Bold IPAKielSeven, IPAExtra, IPAHighLow, & IPAKiel, Plus Regular Helvetica-Stype IPAsans. TrueType Requires Microsoft Windows 3.1; Also Works with Word 6 for DOS, WordPerfect 6.0b for DOS, & AutoCAD r.13. Type 1 Works with ATM with Windows; Also Works with OS/2 & AutoCAD r.12 & 13. WordPerfect for Windows Users Must Upgrade to Version 6.0a or Newer. A NeXT Version Is Available. The IPAKielSeven Font Includes All Currently-Approved IPA

Symbols & Diacritical Marks; the IPAKiel Font Includes All Kiel-Convention-Approved IPA Symbols & Diacritical Marks. These Overstrike Any Symbol in Any Combination with Other Overstrikes. All of Them Have Corresponding Raised Positions to Go over Ascenders, & Lowererd Positions to Go under Descenders, in IPAHighLow.
Linguist's Software, Inc.

Laserjet Printing Utilities. *Items Included:* Full manual. No other products required. *Customer Support:* Free telephone support - no time limit. 30 day warranty.
MS-DOS 3.2 or higher. IBM & compatibles (512k). disk $19.95.
This 3-Disk Set of Utilities Was Gleaned from Several Shareware & Public Domain Sources. It Contains Various Programs & Data Files Specifically Supporting the Hewlett-Packard LaserJet. Facilities Include: CGA & VGA Screen Dumps; Font Editing; 2-Up, 4-Up Page Printing (for Pamphlets); 66- & 88-Lines per Page Reformatting; Utilities to Select Cartridge Laser Fonts & Attributes; Program to Intercept Printer Output & Save It to a Disk File (Can Also Be Used with ASCII & Dot Matrix Printer Output); Font Downloading; Laserjet Emulation of Epson RX/FX/MX Printers (i.e., Programs Which Output to an Epson Printer Can Also Work with a LaserJet); Same for IBM Graphics Printer; Envelope Label Printer; Soft Font File Header Stripper; Utility to View Fonts on an EGA Screen; Utility to Convert HP Soft Fonts to Ventura; Many Font Libraries.
Dynacomp, Inc.

Laserjet Printing Utilities. 1995. *Items Included:* Full manual. *Customer Support:* Free telephone support - 90 days, 30-day warranty.
MS-DOS 3.2 or higher. 286 (584k). disk $19.95. Nonstandard peripherals required: CGA/EGA/VGA.
This 3-Disk Set of Utilities Was Gleaned from Several Shareware & Public Domain Sources. It Contains Various Programs & Data Files Specifically Supporting the Hewlett-Packard LaserJet. We Have Combined Them All into One Large Collection, & Have Prepared a Printed 40-Page Documentation Package Based on the Associated ".DOC" Files. Some of the Programs Are Well Described in the Manual; Others Are Not. Some Are Very Easy to Use; Others Require Some Experimentation to Get the Hang of Things.
Dynacomp, Inc.

LaserKannada. *Version:* 1.4. Jun. 1993. *Items Included:* User's manual, keyboard layout chart. *Customer Support:* Free telephone support; defective disks replaced free.
Macintosh. Macintosh (1Mb). 3.5" disk $149.95.
 Addl. software required: Any word processor. *Optimal configuration:* 4Mb RAM, hard drive.
Professional-Quality, Hinted Kannada Type-1 & TrueType Font in Plain, Bold, Italic & BoldItalic Styles. InduScript Input Method Allows Easy, Phonetic Input of All Characters, Including Conjuncts. Includes Complete User's Manual & InduScript Phonetic Keyboard Chart. These Scaleable, Outline Fonts Display & Print at All Sizes.
Linguist's Software, Inc.

LaserKorean. *Version:* 7.0. Oct. 1988. *Items Included:* User manual, keycap sticker sheet, keyboard layout charts. *Customer Support:* Free telephone support, defective disks replaced.
Macintosh. 3.5" disk $119.95.
Five ATM-Compatible, Type-1 & TrueType Korean Fonts: NewSeoul (Plain, Bold, Italic, Bold-Italic), NewJeju, Hilnchon, NewHiPusan, HiGwangju. Includes Laser Adjusted Polished Imagewriter Bit Map Fonts. For Use with All Major Macintosh Programs. The AsiaScript Scripting Program Allows the User to Use the Single-Byte Korean Fonts in the English System but with the Automatic Contextualization of the Korean System. The Korean Vowels & Consonants Are Automatically Placed in Proper Position As You Type. Easy to Learn, Easy to Use.
Linguist's Software, Inc.

LaserKorean for Windows. *Version:* 2.0. Jul. 1992. *Items Included:* User's manual, keyboard layout chart, ANSI Chart, keycap sticker sheet. *Customer Support:* Free telephone support; defective disks replaced free.
Windows. IBM or compatibles (4Mb). disk $99.95. *Addl. software required:* MS Windows or ATM. *Optimal configuration:* 4Mb RAM & 386.
Five ATM-Comaptible, Type-1 & TrueType Korean Fonts: NewSeoul (in Plain, Bold, Italic, Bold-Italic), NewJeju, Hilnchon, NewHiPusan, & HiGwangju. TrueType Requires Microsoft Windows 3.1, & Works with Word 6.0 for DOS, & WordPerfect 6.0b for DOS, or Newer. Type1 Works with ATM & Windows; Also Works with OS/2 & AutoCAD R.12. WordPerfect for Windows Users Must Upgrade to WordPerfect 6.0a, or Newer. A NeXT Version Is Available. The Keyboard Switcher Program Allows the User to Use the Single-Byte Korean Fonts in the English System, Similarly to Typing on a Korean Typewriter. Keyboard Switcher Eliminates ANSI Codes for Korean Letters. Initial, Middle, & Final Forms of Characters Are on a Single Key. Easy to Learn, Easy to Use.
Linguist's Software, Inc.

LaserKwakwala. Jun. 1995. *Items Included:* User's manual; keyboard layout chart; keycap sticker sheet. *Customer Support:* Free telephone support, defective disks replaced free.
Macintosh. Macintosh (1Mb). 3.5" disk $99.95.
 Addl. software required: Any word processor. Professional pkg. with Serif & Sans Serif Styles $149.95.
Professional-Quality, Hinted KwakwalaS Times-Style Font in Both TrueType & Type-1 Formats. Comes in Plain, Bold, Italic, & Bold-Italic Styles. The Font Contains All the Characters for English & Kwakwala. This Scalable, Outline Font Displays & Prints at All Sizes. EuroScript Scripting System Allows You to Type All the Accents & Special Characters of Kwakwala Using Only the Semicolon (Underline), Colon (Overcomma), & Slash (Underline/Overcomma) Keys. Single Combination Characters Are Formed Automatically As Soon As the Second Character in the Combination Is Typed. Composite Characters Can Be Easily Typed As Single or Separate Characters. The KwakwalaLS Font Has Been Arranged to Sort Kwakwala or English in Proper Alphabetical Order.
Linguist's Software, Inc.

LaserKwakwala for Windows. *Version:* 1.1. 1995. *Items Included:* User's manual; keyboard layout chart; keycap sticker sheet. *Customer Support:* Free telephone support, defective disks replaced free.
Windows. IBM or compatibles (4Mb). disk $99.95. *Addl. software required:* MS Windows 3.1X or ATM.
Professional pkg. with Serif & Sans Serif Styles $149.95.
Professional-Quality, Hinted KwakwalaLS Times-Style Font in Both TrueType & Type-1 Formats. Comes in Plain, Bold, Italic, & Bold-Italic Styles. The Font Contains All the Characters for English & Kwakwala. TrueType Requires Microsoft Windows 3.1; also Works with Word 6 for DOS, WordPerfect 6.0b for DOS & AutoCAD R.13. Type 1 Works with ATM & Windows; Also Works with OS/2 & AutoCAD R.12 & 13. WordPerfect for Windows Users Must Upgrade to Version 6.0a or Newer. A NeXT Version Is Available.
Linguist's Software, Inc.

LaserLaotian. *Version:* 4.1. Jun. 1991. *Items Included:* User's manual; keyboard layout chart; keycap sticker sheet. *Customer Support:* Free telephone support, defective disks replaced free.
Macintosh. Macintosh (1Mb). 3.5" disk $99.95.
 Addl. software required: Any word processor. LaserLaotian Professional $149.95.
ATM-Compatible, Type-1 LaserWriter & TrueType Laotian Font in Plain, Bold, Italic & Bold-Italic with Polished Plain Bitmap Fonts in 12, 18, 24, 36, & 48 Point Sizes. Two Keyboard Input Methods: 1) Traditional Laotian Layout, or 2) Logical Layout Keyed to English Keyboard. Vowels & Tone Marks Have Automatic Nondeleting Backspacing. You Can Easily Mix in English Text.
Linguist's Software, Inc.

LaserLaotian for Windows. *Version:* 2.4. Jul. 1992. *Items Included:* User's manual, keyboard layout chart. *Customer Support:* Free telephone support; defective disks replaced free.
Windows. IBM or compatibles (4Mb). disk $99.95 LaserLaotian; $99.95 LaserLaotian Sukanya; $149.95 for LaserLaotian Professional (which includes both fonts). *Addl. software required:* MS Windows or ATM. *Optimal configuration:* 4Mb RAM & 386.
Scalable Adobe Type Manager-(ATM) Compatible Type-1 & TrueType Laotian Font in Plain, Bold, Bold-Italic, & Italic Styles. TrueType Requires Microsoft Windows 3.1; Also Works with Word 6 for DOS & WordPerfect 6.0b for DOS. Type 1 Works with ATM & Windows; Also Works with OS/2 & AutoCAD r.12. WordPerfect for Windows Users Must Upgrade to WordPerfect 6.0a. A NeXT Version Is Available. Keyboard Switcher Permits Accessing Four Characters per Key, Eliminating Most ANSI Codes. Keyboard Switcher Has Two Keyboard Input Methods: 1) Traditional Laotian Layout, or 2) Logical Layout Keyed to English Keyboard. Vowels or Tone Marks Overstrike the Preceding Letter with Automatic Non-Deleting Backspacing. You Can Easily Mix English & Laotian Text.
Linguist's Software, Inc.

LaserLaotian Sukanya. *Version:* 4.1. Mar. 1994. *Items Included:* User manual, Keyboard Layout Chart, Keycap Sticker Sheet. *Customer Support:* Free telephone support, defective disks replaced.
Macintosh. Macintosh (1Mb). $99.59; $149.95 for LaserLaotian Professional which includes the LaserLaotian Laotian font. *Addl. software required:* Any Word Processor. *Optimal configuration:* 4Mb RAM & a hard drive.
ATM-Compatible, Type-1 LaserWriter & TrueType LaoSukanya Font in Plain, Bold, Italic & Bold-Italic with Polished Bitmap Fonts in 18, 24, 36 & 48 Point Sizes. Two Keyboard Input Methods: 1) Traditional Laotian Layout, or 2) Logical Layout Keyed to English Keyboard. Vowels & Tone Marks Have Automatic Non-Deleting Backspacing. You Can Easily Mix in English Text.
Linguist's Software, Inc.

LaserLittera. Mar. 1995. *Items Included:* User's manual; keyboard layout chart; keycap sticker sheet. *Customer Support:* Free telephone support, defective disks replaced free.
Macintosh. Macintosh (1Mb). 3.5" disk $99.95.
 Addl. software required: Any word processor. *Two Type-1 & TrueType Littera-Style Fonts with Polished Bitmaps in 10, 12, 14, 18, & 24-Point Sizes. Both Fonts Follow the Standard Layout for*

Macintosh Fonts. Gothic Littera Is a Font Style That Began in the Thirteenth Century As a Simplification of Letter Forms from the Earlier More Ornate Styles. It Was Popular in England, France, Germany, & Throughout Northern Europe.
Linguist's Software, Inc.

LaserLittera for Windows. May 1995. *Items Included:* User's manual; keyboard layout chart; keycap sticker sheet. *Customer Support:* Free telephone support, defective disks replaced free. Windows. IBM or compatibles (4Mb). disk $99.95. *Addl. software required:* MS Windows 3.1X or ATM.
Professional-Quality, Hinted, Scalable Font in Both TrueType & Type 1 Formats: LitteraLS Plain & LitteraScribe Plain. Gothic Littera Is a Font Style That Began in the Thirteenth Century As a Simplification of Letter Forms from the Earlier More Ornate Styles. It Was Popular in England, France, Germany, & Throughout Northern Europe. For All Windows 3.1X-Compatible Applications. Type 1 Works with ATM & Windows; Also Works with OS/2 & AutoCAD R.12 & 13. Includes Keyboard Switcher Windows Utility Providing Deadkeys & Four Characters per Key in Windows Applications. Fonts Alone Work in Word 6 for DOS, WordPerfect 6.0b for DOS, or Newer, AutoCAD R.12 & 13; OS/2; NeXT (Available by Request).
Linguist's Software, Inc.

LaserLogo Credit Card Symbol Font. *Compatible Hardware:* Apple Macintosh. *Items Included:* Disk & installation instructions. *Customer Support:* Via telephone.
3.5" disk $29.95.
Symbol Font Containing American Express, Visa & MasterCard Symbols.
George Monagle Graphics Partners.

LaserMalayalam. *Version:* 2.0. Nov. 1994. *Items Included:* User's manual; keyboard layout chart; keycap sticker sheet. *Customer Support:* Free telephone support, defective disks replaced free. Macintosh. Macintosh (1Mb). 3.5" disk $149.95.
Addl. software required: Any word processor. *Professional-Quality, Hinted Malayalam Type-1 & TrueType Font in Plain, Bold, Italic & Bold-Italic Styles. InduScript Input Method Allows Easy, Phonetic Input of All Characters, Including Conjuncts. Includes InduScript Phonetic Keyboard Chart. These Scaleable Fonts Display & Print at All Sizes.*
Linguist's Software, Inc.

LaserPaint. *General Requirements:* LaserWriter. Macintosh Plus or higher. 3.5" disk $495.00.
Complete Graphics Environment; Postcript Drawing, Bit Map & Text Editing.
LaserWare, Inc.

LaserPaint Color II: The Integrated Graphics Workshop. *Version:* 1.9. Apr. 1988. *Compatible Hardware:* Apple Macintosh II. *Memory Required:* 2000k. *General Requirements:* Color board.
3.5" disk $595.00.
Provides Drawing, Painting, Writing, & Paste-Up Capabilities. The Drawing Application Is a Full Featured PostScript Illustration Program. Painting Capabilities Include Full Editing of Imported Bit-Maps at 600dpi. Writing Features Include Runaround Text Justified Inside or Around Any Object, Full Kerning, & Full Editing. Color Separation Capabilities Include 4-Color Process or Line-Color, Performed Automatically on LaserWriter or Linotronic Printers, Printer's Registration Marks for Alignment, etc. Layout/Paste-Up Capabilities Include Multi-Page Working Surface, Configurable or Standard Column Guides, Automatic Printer's Registration Marks.
Produces Professional Quality Camera Ready Output. Imports Bit-Maps from Paint Programs; 300dpi Scanned Images in TIF Format; Text Files from Word Processors. Exports Pure PostScript Text Files; EPS, Encapsulated PostScript Files; & Edited, Enhanced, & Modified Bit-Maps.
LaserWare, Inc.

LaserPak. *Version:* 2.0. *Compatible Hardware:* IBM PC & compatibles. *Language(s):* Assembly, BASIC. *Memory Required:* 256k.
3.5" or 5.25" disk $149.00.
Enables the User to Draw Lines, Boxes, Circles, Symbols & Fill Patterns & Control & Download Fonts. Other Capabilities Include Graph Scales & Grids, Text Labeling. Also Includes a Symbol Editor That Can Be Used to Design & Manage Logos, Symbols, Clip-Art & Custom Fonts.
Crescent Software.

LaserPunjabi. *Version:* 2.0. Apr. 1993. *Items Included:* User's manual, keyboard layout chart, keycap sticker sheet. *Customer Support:* Free telephone support; defective disks replaced free. Macintosh. Macintosh (1Mb). 3.5" disk $99.95.
Addl. software required: Any word processor. *Optimal configuration:* 4Mb RAM, hard drive. *ATM-Compatible, Type 1 & TrueType Punjabi Font in Plain, Bold, Italic, & Bold-Italic Styles. Logical Phonetic Input & Automatic Overstriking Vowels Allow Fast, Convenient Typing of Punjabi. User May Select Other Styles from the Style Menu: Italic, Underline, Outline, Shadow, Superscript, & Subscript. Compatible with All Standard Macintosh Software & Can Be Used in Conjunction with Any Other Language.*
Linguist's Software, Inc.

LaserPunjabi for Windows. *Version:* 3.0. Aug. 1992. *Items Included:* User's manual, keyboard layout charts, ANSI chart & keycap sticker sheet. *Customer Support:* Free telephone support; defective disks replaced free.
Windows. IBM or compatibles (2-4Mb). disk $99.95. *Addl. software required:* MS Windows or ATM. *Optimal configuration:* 4Mb RAM & 386.
Contains Professional, Hinted, Scalable TrueType & Type-1 Fonts. TrueType Requires Microsoft Windows 3.1x; Also Works with Word 6 for DOS, WordPerfect 6.0b for DOS, & AutoCAD r. 13. Type 1 Works with ATM & Windows; Also Works with OS/2 & AutoCAD r.12. WordPerfect for Windows Users Must Upgrade to Version 6.0a or Newer. These Scalable, Outline Fonts Display & Print at All Sizes.
Linguist's Software, Inc.

LaserQuest. *Version:* 6.3. Jun. 1986. *Compatible Hardware:* IBM PC & compatibles, PS/2. *Operating System(s) Required:* PC-DOS, MS-DOS. *Language(s):* FORTRAN. *Memory Required:* 512k. *Customer Support:* Toll-free number.
CD-ROM disk contact publisher for price.
Uses CD-ROM Technology for Retrospective Conversions & On-Going Cataloging. GRC Resource Database Is Available on 7 CD-ROM Laser Discs Consisting of over 8 Million MARC Records with 2.0 Million Book Titles with Pre-1968 Inputs. For On-Going Cataloging, Bimonthly Cumulative Supplements Add Approximately 150,000 Titles with Each Edition. Access to All Formats in the Database Is by Title & Number (ISBN, etc.). Software Includes Formatted Screens, Keying Shortcuts, Error Detection & Allows Local Modifications & Original Cataloging for Database Building. Network Licenses Available.
GRC International, Inc.

LaserServe. *Version:* 1.1. *Compatible Hardware:* Apple Macintosh. *Memory Required:* 512k. *General Requirements:* AppleTalk.
3.5" disk $95.00.
Printer Management Utility. Allows Users to Submit Documents for Printing & Continue with Other Tasks. Decentralized Design Permits Single-User or Group Use. "Priority Service" Option Allows Prioritizing of Documents for Printing. "Pop-Up" Messages Indicate When Printing Is Complete. Does Not Require Hard Disk or Dedicated Server.
Infosphere.

LaserSinhalese. *Version:* 1.1. Oct. 1994. *Items Included:* User's manual; keyboard layout chart; keycap sticker sheet. *Customer Support:* Free telephone support, defective disks replaced free. Macintosh. Macintosh (1Mb). 3.5" disk $99.95.
Addl. software required: Any word processor. *Professional-Quality, Hinted Sinhalese Type-1 & TrueType Font in Plain, Bold, Italic & Bold-Italic Styles. InduScript Allows Easy, Phonetic Input of All Characters, Including Conjuncts.*
Linguist's Software, Inc.

LaserSpeed. *Version:* 1.5. May 1987. *Compatible Hardware:* Apple Macintosh. *Memory Required:* 20k.
3.5" disk $99.00.
pack of five $499.00.
Print Spooler for Use on Networks. Will Manage the Printing Order of up to 18 Documents. Compatible with PAGEMAKER, the TOPS Network, the MACSERVE File Server, & InBox Messaging Software.
Think Technologies.

LaserSyriac. *Version:* 1.2. Jun. 1993. *Items Included:* User manual, keyboard layout chart, keycap sticker sheet. *Customer Support:* Free telephone support, defective disks replaced. Macintosh. Macintosh (1Mb). 3.5" disk $99.95; $149.95 for LaserSyriac Professional (which includes LaserSyriac II). *Addl. software required:* Any Word Processor. *Optimal configuration:* 4Mb RAM & a hard drive.
Hinted Syriac (Estrangelo) Type-1 & TrueType Font with Vowels. For Use with the English System. Right-to-Left Macro (with AutoMac III, Included) Allows Right-to-Left Input in Most Applications (No Syriac Line Wrap). The Logical, Intuitive Keyboard Layouts Are Keyed to the English Keyboard with Syriac Sounds on Their Corresponding English Key. Includes a Micro-Space Key for Minute Adjustments.
Linguist's Software, Inc.

LaserSyriac. *Version:* 1.2. Jun. 1993. *Items Included:* User's manual; keyboard layout chart; keycap sticker sheet. *Customer Support:* Free telephone support, defective disks replaced free. Macintosh. Macintosh (1Mb). 3.5" disk $99.95.
Addl. software required: Any word processor. LaserSyriac Professional $149.95.
Hinted Syriac (Estrangelo) Type-1 & TrueType Font with Vowels. For Use with the English System. Right-to-Left Macro (with AutoMac III, Included) Allows Right-to-Left Input in Most Applications (No Syriac Line Wrap). The Logical, Intuitive Keyboard Layouts Are Keyed to the English Keyboard with Syriac Sounds on Their Corresponding English Key. Includes a Micro-Space Key for Minute Adjustments.
Linguist's Software, Inc.

LaserSyriac for Windows. *Version:* 1.3. Nov. 1993. *Items Included:* User manual, Keyboard Layout Chart, Keycap Sticker Sheet, & ANSI Table. *Customer Support:* Free telephone support, defective disks replaced.
Windows. IBM & compatibles (4Mb). disk $99.95. *Addl. software required:* Microsoft

Windows or ATM. *Optimal configuration:* 4Mb RAM & 386.
One Professional-Quality, Hinted Syriac Font with Vowels (EEstrangelo Plain) in Both TrueType & Type-1 Formats. TrueType Requires Microsoft Windows 3.1; Also Works with Word 6 for DOS & WordPerfect 6.0b for DOS ($17.50 Upgrade from WordPerfect Corp. for 6.0 Users), AudoCAD r.12; OS/2; NeXT (Available by Request). WordPerfect for Windows 6.0 Users Must Upgrade to 6.0a (Free from WordPerfect Corp., As of 7/94) to Type Overstrikes & Diacritical Marks. All 31 Vowel Points & Accents Are Automatic Overstrikes So That They May Be Placed in Any Order over Any Symbol. The Logical, Intuitive Keyboard Layouts Are Keyed to the English Keyboard with Syriac Sounds on Their Corresponding English Key.
Linguist's Software, Inc.

LaserSyriacII. Jan. 1996. *Items Included:* User's manual; keyboard layout chart; keycap sticker sheet. *Customer Support:* Free telephone support, defective disks replaced free.
 Macintosh. Macintosh (1Mb). 3.5" disk $99.95. *Addl. software required:* Hebrew System-compatible word processor & WorldScript I. LaserSyriac Professional $149.95.
TrueType & Type-1 Syrian (Estrangelo) Font. Also, HebronII & Transliterate Bitmap Fonts with Resources for Right-to-Left Text Entry & Line Wrap in Syriac-Compatible Applications Such As Nisus. Requires WorldScript I.
Linguist's Software, Inc.

LaserTamil. *Version:* 3.0. Oct. 1994. *Items Included:* User's manual; keyboard layout chart; keycap sticker sheet. *Customer Support:* Free telephone support, defective disks replaced free.
 Macintosh. Macintosh (1Mb). 3.5" disk $99.95. *Addl. software required:* Any word processor. LaserTamil Professional $149.95.
ATM-Compatible, Type-1 & TrueType Plain, Bold, Italic & Bold-Italic Tamil Font & Corresponding Bitmap Fonts in 12-, 14-, 18-, & 24-Point Sizes. You May Select Other Styles from the Style Menu: Underline, Outline, Shadow, Superscript, & Subscript. It Is Compatible with All Standard Macintosh Software & Can Be Used in Conjunction with Any Other Language. AsiaScript Scripting System Allows You to Type All Tamil Consonant-Vowel Combinations with Only Two Keys. Comes with Minispace Key for Fine Character Spacing.
Linguist's Software, Inc.

LaserTelugu. *Version:* 1.3. Jun. 1993. *Items Included:* User's manual, keyboard layout chart. *Customer Support:* Free telephone support; defective disks replaced free.
 Any system. Macintosh (1Mb). 3.5" disk $149.95. *Addl. software required:* Any word processor. *Optimal configuration:* 4Mb RAM, hard drive.
Professional-Quality, Hinted Telugu Type-1 & TrueType Font in Bold, BoldItalic, Condensed & CondensedItalic Styles. InduScript Input Method Allows Easy, Phonetic Input of All Characters, Including Conjuncts. Includes Complete User's Manual & InduScript Phonetic Keyboard Chart. These Scaleable, Outline Fonts Display & Print at All Sizes.
Linguist's Software, Inc.

LaserTewa. 1995. *Items Included:* User's manual; keyboard layout chart; keycap sticker sheet. *Customer Support:* Free telephone support, defective disks replaced free.
 Macintosh. Macintosh (1Mb). 3.5" disk $99.95. *Addl. software required:* Any word processor. *ATM-Compatible, Type-1 & TrueType Plain, Bold, Italic & Bold-Italic Tewa Fonts. Features 41 Overstrike Accents & Diacritical Mark Keys Each Having Automatic Non-Deleting Backspacing for Fast Typing over Any Letter or Symbol & in Any Combination.*
Linguist's Software, Inc.

LaserTewa for Windows. 1995. *Items Included:* User's manual; keyboard layout chart; keycap sticker sheet. *Customer Support:* Free telephone support, defective disks replaced free.
 Windows. IBM or compatibles (4Mb). disk $99.95. *Addl. software required:* MS Windows 3.1X or ATM.
 Each additional typeface family $50.00 when ordered at the same time; LaserTewa Professional $249.95.
Professional-Quality, Scalable, Hinted Fonts in Both TrueType & Type 1 Formats: LaserTewa Comes in Five Tyepstyles (Times-, Helvetica-, Palatino-, Garamond-, & Chancery-Styles), All in Plain, Bold, Italic, & Bold-Italic, (Except Chancery, Which Is in Plain Only). Includes All the Characters & Diacritics Needed to Type Tewa. The Diacritics Overstrike Any Symbol in Any Combination with Other Overstrikes. Includes ANSI Chart & Keyboard Switcher Utility, Providing Four Characters per Key in Windows. TrueType Requires Microsoft Windows 3.1; Also Works with Word 6 for DOS, WordPerfect 6.0b for DOS or Newer, & AutoCAD R.13. Type 1 Works with ATM & Windows; Also Works with OS/2 & AutoCAD R.12 & 13. WordPerfect for Windows Users Must Upgrade to Version 6.0a or Newer. A NeXT Version Is Available.
Linguist's Software, Inc.

LaserThai for Windows. *Version:* 2.0. Sep. 1993. *Items Included:* User manual, Keyboard Layout Chart, Keycap Sticker Sheet, & ANSI Charts. *Customer Support:* Free telephone support, defective disks replaced.
 Windows. IBM & compatibles (4Mb). $99.95 for first font; $50.00 for each additional font on the same invoice; $299.95 for LaserThai Professional for Windows which includes all 8 typefaces. *Addl. software required:* Microsoft Windows or ATM. *Optimal configuration:* 4Mb RAM & 386.
Eight Professional-Quality, Hinted Typefaces in Both TrueType & Type 1 Formats: Plain, Bold, Italic & Bold-Italic Styles. Includes Keyboard Switcher Windows Utility Providing Four Characters-per-Key in Windows Applications. Fonts Alone Work in Word 6 for DOS, WordPerfect 6.0b for DOS ($17.50 Upgrade from WordPerfect Corp. for 6.0 Users), AutoCAD r.12; OS/2; NeXT (Available by Request). WordPerfect for Windows 6.0 Users Must Upgrade to 6.0a (Free from WordPerfect Corp., As of 7/1994) to Type Overstrikes & Stress Marks. Keyboard Arranged According to Thai Standard GatManee Layout, Similar to a Thai Typewriter, That Works with Your U.S. Keyboard. Automatic Overstriking Characters Allow Vowels & Tones to Overstrike Preceding Consonant. Deadkeys Handle Combinations of Two Vowels & Tones on a Single Consonant. Word Wrap & Other Software Format Features Are Preserved.
Linguist's Software, Inc.

LaserTibetan. *Version:* 3.0. Jan. 1988. *Items Included:* User's manual; keyboard layout chart; keycap sticker sheet. *Customer Support:* Free telephone support, defective disks replaced free.
 Macintosh. Macintosh (1Mb). 3.5" disk $99.95. *Addl. software required:* Any word processor.
Type-1 & TrueType Tibetan Font & Type-3 Ornate Tibetan Font with Corresponding Bitmap Screen Fonts (Each in 12, 18, 24, 36, 48, 60 & 72 Point Sizes). All Style Options & Combinations Selectable from the Style Menu. Use with Any Macintosh Compatible Software with Fonts Accessible from the Font Menu, e.g. Microsoft Word.
Linguist's Software, Inc.

LaserTibetan for Windows. May 1994. *Items Included:* User manual, Keyboard Layout Chart, Keycap Sticker Sheet. *Customer Support:* Free telephone support, defective disks replaced.
 Windows. IBM & compatibles (4Mb). disk $99.95. *Addl. software required:* Microsoft Windows or ATM. *Optimal configuration:* 4Mb RAM & 386.
Scalable Adobe Type Manager-(ATM-) Compatible, Type-1 & TrueType Tibetan Font. TrueType Requires Microsoft Windows 3.1; Also Works with Word 6 for DOS & WordPerfect 6.0b for DOS. Type 1 Works with ATM & Windows; Also Works with OS/2 & AutoCAD r. 12. WordPerfect for Windows Users Must Upgrade to WordPerfect 6.0a. A NeXT Version Is Available. Keyboard Switcher Keyboard Input. You Can Easily Mix English & Tibetan Text.
Linguist's Software, Inc.

LaserTransliterator. *Version:* 10.0. Nov. 1986. *Compatible Hardware:* Apple Macintosh. *General Requirements:* External disk drive. *Items Included:* User's manual, laminated keyboard chart, key cap stickers. *Customer Support:* Telephone support, defective disks replaced free.
 3.5" disk $99.95.
LaserWriter Transliteration Software & 130 Languages.
Linguist's Software, Inc.

LaserTransliterator for Windows. *Version:* 2.0. Nov. 1993. *Items Included:* User manual, keyboard layout chart, keycap sticker sheet, & ANSI chart. *Customer Support:* Free telephone support, defective disks replaced.
 Windows. IBM & compatibles (4Mb). disk $99.95. *Addl. software required:* Microsoft Windows or ATM. *Optimal configuration:* 4Mb RAM & 386.
Includes 130 Languages. Type Accents Fast. Semitica Professional-Quality, Hinted Times-Style Plain, Bold, Italic, & Bold-Italic Styles in TrueType & Type 1 Formats. TrueType Requires Microsoft Windows 3.1; Also Works with Word 6 for DOS & WordPerfect 6.0b for DOS. Type 1 Works with ATM & Windows; Also Works with OS/2 & AutoCAD r.12. WordPerfect for Windows Users Must Upgrade to WordPerfect 6.0a. A NeXT Version Is Available. Featuers 58 Overstrike Accents & Diacritical Marks for Typing over Any Letter or Symbol & in Any Combination. The Transliteration Symbols of Hebrew, Arabic, Coptic, Greek (SBL System etc.), & Most Other Languages.
Linguist's Software, Inc.

LaserTurkish. Jan. 1996. *Items Included:* User's manual; keyboard layout chart; keycap sticker sheet. *Customer Support:* Free telephone support, defective disks replaced free.
 Macintosh. Macintosh (1Mb). 3.5" disk $99.95. *Addl. software required:* Any word processor. Serif & Sans Serif styles together $149.95.
Professional-Quality, Hinted TurkishLS Times-Style Font in Both TrueType & Type-1 Formats. TurkishLS Comes in Plain, Bold, Italic, & Bold-Italic Styles. The TurkishLS Font Contains All the Characters for English & Turkish, Matching the Apple Turkish Operating System Font. Four Keyboard Layouts Are Included, Two Following the Traditional Turkish Layout & Two Following the U.S. Layout.
Linguist's Software, Inc.

LaserUp! Draw. *Compatible Hardware:* Commodore Amiga.
 3.5" disk $99.95.
Screen-Drawing Package Duplicates PostScript.
S. Anthony Studios.

TITLE INDEX

LaserUp! Fonts 1. *Compatible Hardware:*
Commodore Amiga.
3.5" disk $39.95.
Fonts for LaserWriter.
S. Anthony Studios.

LaserUp! Plot. *Compatible Hardware:*
Commodore Amiga.
3.5" disk $49.95.
Aegis Draw Files to PostScript.
S. Anthony Studios.

LaserUp! Print. *Version:* 1.2. *Compatible Hardware:* Commodore Amiga.
3.5" disk $89.95.
Print Screen to LaserWriter, Color Separation.
S. Anthony Studios.

LaserUp! Utilities 1. *Compatible Hardware:*
Commodore Amiga.
3.5" disk $39.95.
IFF to PostScript Conversions.
S. Anthony Studios.

LaserVietnamese. *Version:* 6.0. Jul. 1990. *Items Included:* User's manual, laminated keyboard chart, keycap sticker sheet. *Customer Support:* Free telephone support, defective disks replaced.
Macintosh. $99.95 ea, ($249.95 all 5 faces).
Professional-Quality, Hinted Vietnamese Fonts in Both Type-1 & TrueType Formats. Types All Vietnamese Letters Quickly Without Using the Option Key or the Top Row of Keys. Comes with User's Manual, Keyboard Layout Chart, & Keycap Sticker Sheet. Includes Hundreds of Kerning Pairs for Automatic Kerning in Those Applications Which Support It. These Scaleable, Outline Fonts Print at All Sizes. Specify Times-Style, Helvetica-Style, Zaph Chancery-Style, Palatino-Style, or Garamond-Style, Also Specify for System 6 or 7.
Linguist's Software, Inc.

LaserVietnamese for Windows. *Version:* 3.0. Dec. 1992. *Items Included:* User's manual, keyboard layout chart. *Customer Support:* Free telephone support; defective disks replaced free.
Windows. IBM or compatibles (4Mb). disk $99. 95 ea. font; $249.95 for all five fonts. *Addl. software required:* MS Windows or ATM. *Optimal configuration:* 4Mb RAM & 386.
Five Professional-Quality, Hinted Vietnamese Fonts in Both TrueType & Type-1 Formats: Plain, Bold, Italic, & Bold-Italic (Except for VinaChan). Typeable on the Normal U.S. Keyboard. TrueType Requires Microsoft Windows 3.1; Type 1 Works with ATM & Windows. Automatic Overstriking Characters Allow Tones to Overstrike Preceding Consonant. Deadkeys Handle Combinations of Vowels & Tones on a Single Consonant. Word Wrap & Other Software Format Features Are Preserved. Comes with User's Manual, Keyboard Layout Chart, & Keycap Sticker Sheet. These Scalable, Outline Fonts Display & Print at All Sizes. Specify Times-Style, Helvetica-Style, Palatino-Style, Garamond-Style, or Zaph-Chancery Style.
Linguist's Software, Inc.

LaserYukon. *Version:* 1.2. Feb. 1995. *Items Included:* User's manual; keyboard layout chart; keycap sticker sheet. *Customer Support:* Free telephone support, defective disks replaced free.
Macintosh. Macintosh (1Mb). 3.5" disk $99.95.
Addl. software required: Any word processor. ATM-Compatible, Type-1 & TrueType Fonts. *Comes in Five Type Styles (Times-, Helvetica-, Palatino-, Garamond-, & Chancery-Styles), All in Plain, Bold, Italic, & Bold-Italic (Except Chancery, Which Is in Plain Only). Includes All the Characters & Diacritics Needed to Type the Following Athapascan Languages: Han, Gwich'in, Kaska, Northern Tutchone, Southern Tutchone, Tagish, Tanacross, Upper Tanana, Tahltan, & Plingit. The Diacritics Overstrike Any Symbol in Any Combination with Other Overstrikes.*
Linguist's Software, Inc.

LaserYukon for Windows. Mar. 1995. *Items Included:* User's manual; keyboard layout chart; keycap sticker sheet. *Customer Support:* Free telephone support, defective disks replaced free.
Windows. IBM or compatibles (4Mb). disk $99.95. *Addl. software required:* MS Windows 3.1X or ATM.
Each additional typeface family $50.00 when ordered at the same time; LaserYukon Professional $249.95.
Professional-Quality, Scalable, Hinted Fonts in Both TrueType & Type-1 Formats: Comes in Five Typestyles (Times-, Helvetica-, Palatino-, Garamond-, & Chancery-Styles), All in Plain, Bold, Italic, & Bold-Italic, (Except Chancery, Which Is in Plain Only). Includes All the Characters & Diacritics Needed to Type the Following Athapascan Languages: Han, Gwich'in, Kaska, Northern Tutchone, Southern Tutchone, Tagish, Tanacross, Upper Tanana, Tahltan, & Plingit. The Diacritics Overstrike Any Symbol in Any Combination with Other Overstrikes. Includes ANSI Chart & Keyboard Switcher Utility, Providing Four Characters per Key in Windows. TrueType Requires Microsoft Windows 3.1; Also Works with Word 6 for DOS, WordPerfect 6.0b for DOS or Newer, & AudoCAD R.12 & 13. Type 1 Works with ATM & Windows; Also Works with OS/2 & AutoCAD R.12 & 13. WordPerfect for Windows Users Must Upgrade to Version 6.0a or Newer. A NeXT Version Is Available.
Linguist's Software, Inc.

Lassie: Interactive MovieBook. *Version:* 1.5. Dec. 1994. *Items Included:* Manual, registration card, promotional flyers. *Customer Support:* Phone technical support.
Windows 3.1. 386SX 25MHz or higher (4Mb). disk $19.95 (ISBN 1-57303-012-0).
Nonstandard peripherals required: Sound card recommended. *Optimal configuration:* 486 or higher with 8Mb RAM, Windows, 3.1 or later, 15Mb free hard drive space available, sound card, 256 color monitor.
Interactive MovieBooks Are Exclusively Licensed Computer Storybooks for Children. Taken from the Movie Version, the Story Appears on the Computer in Book Form Which the Child Can Read, or, by Clicking the Mouse, Can Have Read to Them in a Boy's or Girl's Voice. Pictures Are Included Which by Clicking the Mouse, Turn into Short Clips from the Actual Movie.
Sound Source Interactive.

Last Resort. Nov. 1991. *Customer Support:* Free phone support.
DOS. IBM PC & compatibles. disk $49.95.
Saves All Your Typing in a Special File. If You Lose Something or Even Erase Part of a Document That You Never Saved, You Can Get It Back from This File. Also, for Technical Support Situations When You Have to Answer the Question "What Was the Last Thing You Did".
Working Software, Inc.

Last Resort: Typing Retrieval System. *Version:* 1.1. Apr. 1991. *Customer Support:* Free technical support at 408-423-5696.
Macintosh. Macintosh Plus & higher. 3.5" disk $49.95. *Nonstandard peripherals required:* Hard disk.
Helps Retrieve Typed Test When System Crashes or Text Is Lost for Various Reasons. Records Keystrokes That Are Typed & Saves Them on Hard Disk. Tool for Retrieving Text When Other Recovery Methods Have Failed. Keystrokes Are Saved in Time & Date Stamped Text Files for Easy Access.
Working Software, Inc.

LATTICE ES78 C DEVELOPMENT SYSTEM: MS

Lattice C Compiler. Lattice, Inc. *Compatible Hardware:* HP 150 Touchscreen, HP 110 Portable.
3.5" disk $495.00 (Order no.: 45452D).
Package Includes: Compiler, Linker, Librarian, Four Memory Modules, Numerous Library Functions, the Terminal Independence Package, etc. Includes "The C Programming Language" by Kernerghan & Ritchie.
Hewlett-Packard Co.

Lattice C Compiler for DOS & OS/2. *Version:* 6.06. *Compatible Hardware:* IBM PC & compatibles. *Operating System(s) Required:* PC-DOS/MS-DOS 2.1 or higher, OS/2 1.0 or higher. *Memory Required:* 512k. *General Requirements:* Hard drive. *Items Included:* User manuals; reference manuals, compiler library source code. *Customer Support:* Bulletin Board support; 30-day free technical support - subsequent support is available through a 900 number. FAX number available also.
disk $450.00.
Development System for Creating MS-DOS & OS/2 Programs. Provides All C Programming Tools Necessary Including: Lattice Optimizing C Compiler; CodePRobe Source-Level, Native, & Cross Debugger; Integrated, Programmable Screen Editor; DOS & OS/2 Overlay Linker; Full-Function Macro Assembler; Object Module Disassembler; Object Module Librarian; Make Librarian; & API Library & BIND Utility. Also Includes over 800 Library Functions Including Special Graphics, Database, Communications & Screen Management Libraries, Cross Reference Generator & More. 100% ANSI Compatible & Features More Than 100 Command Line Options That Allow User To Specify All Details of Compiler's Performance.
Lattice, Inc.

Lattice ES68K C Development System. *Version:* 5.10. Jan. 1989. *Items Included:* User manuals. *Customer Support:* Bulletin Board support; 30-day free technical support - subsequent support is available through a 900 number. FAX number available also.
MS-DOS 2.1 or higher, OS/2 1.0 or higher; 512k of memory. IBM PC & compatibles (512k). $900.00.
Offers a C Compiler with ROM Code Support, Including Scatter Loading of Segments & S Record Generation. Produces Fast, Efficient Code That Reduces the Need for Assembly Language Programming. Highly Efficient Library Routines Combined with Support for Register Variables & Built-In Functions Keep Your Programs Smaller While Providing New Levels of Speed, & the Global Optimizer Speeds Your Programs by up to 30 Percent. The Package Includes the Lattice C Compiler, Global Optimizer, Macro Assembler, More Than 140 Library Functions, Integrated Full Screen Editor (DOS & OS/2 Host Systems Only), Make Utility, Load Module Builder, C Cross Reference Generator, Object Module Utilities, File Management Utilities.
Lattice, Inc.

Lattice ES78 C Development System: MS-DOS to NEC uPD78310, uPD78312, or uPD78312-A Cross Development System. *Version:* 3.05. *Items Included:* User manuals. *Customer Support:* Bulletin Board support; 30-day free technical support - subsequent support is available through a 900 number. FAX number available also.
MS-DOS 2.1 or higher, OS/2 1.0 or higher. IBM PC & compatibles (256k). $1500.00.
Lattice MS-DOS to NEC Cross Development System 3.0 Is a Development System for NEC uPD78310, uPD78312 & uPD78312-A Series Microprocessors. The Lattice C Library Provides a Comprehensive Set of Useful Functions for Developing Programs for Stand-Alone ROM-

Based Systems. The Load Module Builder Can Produce a Binary Program, Which Is Translated to the Intel HEX Format That Is Suitable for Use in ROM Programming Systems. A Macro Assembler Is Also Supplied with the Package to Give the Programmer Full Control of the NEC Target Environment.
Lattice, Inc.

Lattice ES80 C Development System: MS-DOS to Zilog Z80 C Cross Development System. *Version:* 3.4. *Items Included:* User manuals. *Customer Support:* Bulletin Board support; 30-day free technical support - subsequent support is available through a 900 number. FAX number available also.
MS-DOS 2.1 or higher; 128k memory. IBM PC & compatibles (128k). disk $500.00.
Designed for Z80 Series Microcomputer Systems & Accepts Source Code Files That Are Written in C. The Package Produces Relocatable Machine Code in the Lattice Object Module Format, Which Can Be Combined into Larger Programs by the Lattice Load Module Builder LMBZ80 or Be Translated to the Microsoft L80 (REL) Format for Use by CP/M-80 Linkers. The Lattice C Library Provides a Comprehensive Set of Useful Subroutines for Developing Programs for the CP/M-80 Operating System. The Load Module Builder Can Produce a Program in Simple Binary Format or in the Intel HEX Format. A Macro Assembler As Well As Source Code for Many Library Functions Are Also Supplied with the Package to Give Programmers Full Control of the Target Environment.
Lattice, Inc.

Lattice RPG II Development System. *Version:* 4.02. Feb. 1986. *Compatible Hardware:* IBM PC. *Operating System(s) Required:* PC-DOS/MS-DOS 3.1 or higher. *Memory Required:* 512k. *General Requirements:* 2 disk drives or hard disk. Disk storage: 5Mb of disk space. *Customer Support:* 30 days free support; after 30 days users can purchase a 60-day support contract for $150.00 or yearly support for $500.00. Bulletin Board support; subsequent support is also available through a 900 number. FAX number available also.
complete development kit $1950.00.
This Is a Complete Programming Environment. It Supports System 36 SSP, Release 6.0 & Provides Language Extensions That Let a User Take Advantage of the PC Environment. It Provides the Tools & Utilities Necessary to Bring RPG II Programs & Programming to the PC. It Includes over 200 Programs, Files, & Samples (Including Lattice RPG II Compiler OCL Processor, Screen Design Aid, Source Entry Utility, Porting Utility, GSORT, Index File Utility, DOS Linker & Librarian, File Management Utilities). Comprehensive Documentation, Sample Files & Examples Are Also Included. There Are No Runtime License Fees Required for Applications Created with This Product. Also Included with Version 4.02: CALL/PARM Support; Networking Support; Superior Performance; Support for Programs with Data Areas Larger Than 64k.
Lattice, Inc.

Lattice 80286 C Development System for DOS & OS-2. *Version:* 6.05. *Items Included:* User manuals, reference manuals. *Customer Support:* Bulletin Board support; 30-day free technical support - subsequent support is available through a 900 number. FAX number available also.
MS-DOS 2.1 or higher, OS/2 1.0 or higher. IBM PC, PC XT, PC AT & compatibles, 80286 (512k). disk $495.00. *Optimal configuration:* Extended DOS applications require an IBM AT or compatible 80286 CPU to take advantage of up to 16Mb of extended memory. Hard drive.
Creates Programs That Break the 640k DOS Memory Barrier Without Breaking the Bank. The Royalty-Free Lattice DOS Extender Also Comes with the Package Which Means Users Can Create Applications That Use up to Approximately 16Mb of Memory & Distributes Them Without Paying Any Fees to Lattice or Another DOS Entender Vendor. Extended DOS Applications Require an IBM AT or Compatible 80286 CPU to Take Advantage of up to 16Mb of Extended Memory.
Lattice, Inc.

Law & Order: Litigation Support. Jan. 1986. *Operating System(s) Required:* PC-DOS, MS-DOS, CP/M, XENIX, UNIX, VMS. *Memory Required:* 512k. *General Requirements:* Hard disk.
disk $995.00 (Order no.: L&O).
Full Text Storage & Retrieval, Fully Indexed Fields for Document Number, Date, Key Words, to, from, Carbon Copied, Name Mentioned, Document Location. Attorney Comments Field & Unlimited Full Text for Document Field. Boolean Logic Searches by Date Range with and/or Operators. Attorney Comments Input Window While Viewing Full Text. Instant Return to Text Line Referenced in Attorney Comments.
Law Management Systems.

Law Enforcement Management: LEMS. Dec. 1984. *Compatible Hardware:* IBM PC. *Operating System(s) Required:* MS-DOS. *Memory Required:* 640k. *General Requirements:* Hard disk.
Records. disk $5000.00.
Jail. disk $5000.00.
Crime Analysis. disk $1800.00.
Personnel. disk $2500.00.
Equipment Maintenance. disk $1000.00.
Automates the Functions of a Police Department Including: Records Management, Jail Administration, Crime Analysis, Personnel Tracking & Equipment/Vehicle Maintenance in a Single Entry, Multi-User Program.
OCS/Syntax.

Law Firm Financial-G/L: Series 500 & 600. *Compatible Hardware:* IBM PC, PS/2.
contact publisher for price.
Provides Ability to Record Law Firm & Partnership Financial Data. Assists in Controlling Overhead, Cash Flow & Managing the Financial Progress of the Firm. Fully Integrated with the Client Financial System.
Manac-Prentice Hall Software, Inc.

Law Firm Financial Management: Series 900 to 2000. *Compatible Hardware:* IBM System/36, System/36 PC; AS/400.
contact publisher for price.
Provides Information to Assist with the Control of Overhead, Cash Flow & Profitability of the Firm. Traditional Financial Reports Are Available, Including a Trial Balance, Income Statement & Balance Sheet.
Manac-Prentice Hall Software, Inc.

Law Office Accounting & Timekeeping. Richard A. Bilancia. *Compatible Hardware:* TRS-80 Model 16, Tandy 6000, or any UNIX machine. *Operating System(s) Required:* UNIX, XENIX. *Language(s):* UNIFY (source code included). *Memory Required:* 384k.
8" disk $995.00.
manual $50.00.
Accounting, Timekeeping, Billing & Analysis System Written Using the Premier Relational Database Management System. Can Be Customized.
Computer Guidance & Support.

Law Office Management System. Contract Research Software Corp. *Operating System(s) Required:* MS-DOS. *General Requirements:* 2 disk drives, printer.
$2695.00.
Client Billing System. Features Time & Disbursements Accounting, Client Billing, Accounts Receivable & Management Reports.
Texas Instruments, Personal Productivit.

Law Search. *Version:* 2.0. Randall Hughes. 1983-1985. *Compatible Hardware:* IBM PC, PC XT, PC AT; TI Professional; Wang Professional. *Operating System(s) Required:* MS-DOS, PC-DOS. *Language(s):* C, Assembly. *Memory Required:* 192k.
disk $350.00.
Communications Program That Allows the User to Access WESTLAW Legal Database. Automatic Log-On with 1 Keystroke. Utilizes WESTLAW's Highlighting Scheme. Features Off-Line Query Building & Saving, On-Line Editing, a Built-In Thesaurus, the Ability to Save Information to Disk or Printer, an English Language Query Builder & Full Case Download to WordPerfect Format.
Direct-Aid, Inc.

Law Time Management. *Version:* 4.6. *Compatible Hardware:* IBM PC, PC XT. *Language(s):* Pascal. *Memory Required:* 192k. *General Requirements:* Printer. *Items Included:* 1 year free telephone support. *Customer Support:* Yearly support includes upgrades for $250.
$1500.00, incl. documentation.
demo & documentation $150.00.
documentation $25.00.
Provides Lawyers & Other Professionals with the Ability to Keep Track of Time & Expenses, Bill Clients for Services Performed, Record Cash Received & Manage Client Accounts Receivable.
Megamata, Inc.

LawBase. *Version:* 6.5. Sep. 1995. *Items Included:* Manual, Needs Analysis, tutorial. *Customer Support:* On site training $850.00 per day plus expenses. annual support - 15% per annum.
UNIX DOS Networks, Windows (all versions). All (256k). disk From $2000.00. *Networks supported:* Novell, Lantastic, Banyan, etc.
Computerized Case Management System That Increases the Productivity & Efficiency of the Entire Office. Allows Firms to Double Case Load with the Same Staff Size via the Integration of: Client Data-Base; Activity Files; Calendar; Diary & Tickler System; Document Generation; Conflict of Interest; Case Accounting; Search & Reports; & Automated Rolodex.
Synaptec Software, Inc.

LAWMAN Calendar: Calendar-Docket Control. Jun. 1991. *Compatible Hardware:* IBM PC. *Memory Required:* 256k.
disk $495.00.
Keeps Appointment Schedules for All Attorneys & Compares Appointments for First Available Free Time. Appointments Are Prioritized & Typed (Confirmed, Tentative, etc.). Allows Entry by Type of Event & Reports by Date Range, by Attorney, by Client & by Event.
Law Management Systems.

LAWMAN Case Management. *Items Included:* Manual. *Customer Support:* Free telephone support.
disk $795.00.
Organizes Typical Sequence of Events by Type of Law & Jurisdiction, Thereby Putting Order into Case Management. Versatile Program Produces Variety of Reports.
Law Management Systems.

TITLE INDEX

LAWMAN Conflict of Interest. Jun. 1991. Compatible Hardware: IBM PC.
disk $795.00.
Checks for Previous or Current Conflict by: Name, Case, Social Security Number, Federal Tax I.D. & Relationship (Client, Adversary, etc.).
Law Management Systems.

LAWMAN Document Manager. *Items Included:* Manual. *Customer Support:* Free telephone support.
disk $795.00.
User Can Track Documents in Library, Files or Computer System with This Fourth Generation Database Program. Documents Indexed by: Type of Law, Responsible Attorney, Date, Operator, Client/Matter, Location, Title & Searchable Free Form Text Field.
Law Management Systems.

LAWMAN Litigation Support. *Customer Support:* On-site with fee by arrangement.
disk $1495.00.
Fourth Generation Database Language Offering Speed, Power & Versatility. Features Unlimited Key Word Searches, Free Form Text Entry for Document & Attorney Comments, Searchable, Literal or Translate, Extensive & Comprehensive Reporting. Has Word Frequency Listing, & Error Correction. User Can Search Multiple Documents or Cases. Customization Possible.
Law Management Systems.

LAWMAN SST. *Items Included:* Manual. *Customer Support:* On-Site with fee by arrangement.
$1250.00 plus $200.00 per timekeeper.
Open Invoice, Premium Time Management & Billing Package. Comprehensive, Featuring Extensive Management Reports. Based on LAWMAN V Series. Has Versatility in Fee Charging & Application, Post, Unpost etc. Unlimited Editing & Prebilling Possible. Features Word Processing Interface. Has Integrated Calendar, Conflict & General Ledger.
Law Management Systems.

Lawman 7: Law Office Management System. Jun. 1991. *Operating System(s) Required:* PC-DOS, MS-DOS, CP/M, XENIX, UNIX, VMS. *Memory Required:* 512k. *General Requirements:* Hard disk. *Items Included:* Calendar, conflict of interest.
Lawman ELS. disk $995.00.
Lawman MLS. disk $1695.00.
Lawman VII. disk $2495.00.
The Database Concept Allows the Easy Generation of Custom Reports. Program Itself Can Be Customized upon Request.
Law Management Systems.

Lawn Service Routing & Accounting System. 1985. *Compatible Hardware:* DECmate, PDP 11-23. *Operating System(s) Required:* COS-310, MICRO-RSX. *General Requirements:* Hard disk.
disk $4375.00.
Combines Route Scheduling for Customer Service Contracts with Billing & Accounts Receivable to Serve the Special Needs of Lawn Care Companies. ROUTE SCHEDULING System Processes Customer Contracts Containing Specific Treatment Instructions for Five Seasons, & Organizes Customers into Routes for Servicing. OPERATIONS PLANNING Includes Printing Advance Service Notification Postcards with Address Labels, Daily Route Sheets for Treatment Teams, Check-Back Route Sheets, & Invoices. RECEIVABLE ACCOUNTING Includes Customer Statements Account Inquiry, Aged Trial Balance Reporting, & Cash Receipts Forecasting. System Connects to Corporate Consulting Company's GENERAL LEDGER.
Corporate Consulting Co.

LawPlan: Artificial Intel Database. *Version:* 2.1. Mar. 1991. *Items Included:* 2 manuals. *Customer Support:* On-site set up of database, manual; phone tech support.
MS-DOS, PC-DOS. IBM PC (512k). disk $3600.00. Optimal configuration: 640k, VGA, hard drive, 286 or 386 processor.
Database & Word-Processing Customized for the Law Office. A. I. Assistant Prepares Forms, Letters & Reports Based on Ordinary English Language Queries. Optional Speech Synthesis & Speech Command Modules.
Thinking Software, Inc.

Lawrence Productions' Discovering America. Aug. 1993. *Items Included:* Program manual. *Customer Support:* Free technical support 800-421-4157, 90 day warranty.
System 6.0.5 or higher. 3.5" disk $59.95 (ISBN 1-882848-50-0).
System 6.0.5 or higher. Macintosh (1Mb). $69.95 School Edition (ISBN 1-882848-51-9).
System 6.0.5 or higher. Macintosh (1Mb). $149.95 School Edition, Lab Pack (ISBN 1-882848-57-8).
PC-DOS/MS-DOS 3.0 or higher. IBM (640k). $59.95 3 1/2" disks (ISBN 1-882848-53-5). *Nonstandard peripherals required:* Microsoft mouse recommended, supports Ad Lib & Sound Blaster cards, hard drive.
PC-DOS/MS-DOS 3.0 or higher. IBM (640k). $59.95 5 1/4" disks (ISBN 1-882848-54-3). *Nonstandard peripherals required:* Microsoft mouse recommended, supports Ad Lib & Sound Blaster cards, hard drive.
PC-DOS/MS-DOS 3.0 or higher. IBM (640k). $69.95 School Edition, 3 1/2" disks (ISBN 1-882848-55-1). *Nonstandard peripherals required:* Microsoft mouse recommended, supports Ad Lib & Sound Blaster cards, hard drive.
PC-DOS/MS-DOS 3.0 or higher. IBM (640k). $69.95 School Edition, 5 1/4" disks (ISBN 1-882848-56-X). *Nonstandard peripherals required:* Microsoft mouse recommended, supports Ad Lib & Sound Blaster cards, hard drive.
PC-DOS/MS-DOS 3.0 or higher. IBM (640k). $149.95 School Edition, Lab Pack, 3 1/2" disks (ISBN 1-882848-57-8). *Nonstandard peripherals required:* Microsoft mouse recommended, supports Ad Lib & Sound Blaster cards, hard drive.
PC-DOS/MS-DOS 3.0 or higher. IBM (640k). $149.95 School Edition, Lab Pack, 3 1/2" disks (ISBN 1-882848-58-6). *Nonstandard peripherals required:* Microsoft mouse recommended, supports Ad Lib & Sound Blaster cards, hard drive.
You're a Spanish Explorer on an Awesome Expedition Through an Unknown Land. As You Venture Through Uncharted Wilderness You Will Battle Time, the Elements, & Who-Knows-What-Else. You Will Encounter Now-Extinct Indian Tribes, Bizarre Animals, Famous & Dangerous European Explorers, Ancient Ruins & Wonders Galore! Ages 8 & Older.
Lawrence Productions, Inc.

Lawsearch Plus: Natural Link Access to WESTLAW. Randall Hughes. Oct. 1985. *Compatible Hardware:* IBM PC, PC XT, PC AT; TI Professional. *Operating System(s) Required:* PC-DOS, MS-DOS. *Language(s):* C, Assembly. *Memory Required:* 512k.
disk $495.00.
Accesses WESTLAW Using Natural Language Interface. User Can Create Valid Queries in English. Features Off-Line Query Building & Saving; Built-In Thesaurus; On-Line Query Editing; Ability to Save Info to Disk or Printer; One Keystroke Log-On Access; & Full Case Downloading to WordPerfect Format.
Direct-Aid, Inc.

LawStar. *Customer Support:* 800-929-8117 (customer service).
MS-DOS. IBM/PS2. disk $1999.99 (ISBN 0-87007-388-5).
Full Fledged Accounting System for the Legal Profession. Includes Time Recording & Billing with Automatic Client Time Keeping, & Productivity by Attorney. Controls Work in Process, Produces a Prebilling Worksheet, & Provides for Selectivity in Billing. Includes Accounts Receivable, Accounts Payable, General Ledger, Payroll with 15 Types of Payments & 15 Types of Deductions, & Pre-Loaded State Tax Tables.
SourceView Software International.

LAWTRAC. *Compatible Hardware:* DEC VAX, IBM PC & compatibles, NBI minis, Wang PC. *General Requirements:* Hard disk.
Basic Package. $7995.00.
LAWTRAC Secretary. $3995.00.
LAWTRAC Lease. $3995.00.
Litigation & Project Management System, by Which Inside Counsel Can Budget Inside & Outside Litigation Costs (Both Time & Expenses) by Major Task or Event. It Also Keeps Track of the Calendar of Each Matter & Serves As a Docket Calendar for the Department. In Addition, It Keeps Track of Actual Costs & Events for Each Matter of the Project. Beyond This Basic Case Tracking Function, the System Offers Several Hundred User-Definable Categories with Which the Law Department Can Define Custom Data Bases about Its Cases, Projects, & Matters. All of These Data Fields Can Be Manipulated by a Report Writer to Allow Users to Customize the Content, Format, & Sequence of Data Reports. Multiple-User & Multiple-Site Arrangements Are Available.
Computer Power Group.

Lawyer Financial Management: Series 900 to 2000. *Compatible Hardware:* IBM System/36, System/36 PC; AS/400.
contact publisher for price.
Provides Information on Lawyer Time Worked, Time Billed, Fees Billed, Accounts Receivable & Cash Receipt Activity.
Manac-Prentice Hall Software, Inc.

Lawyer's WillWriter II. *Version:* 2.0. Aug. 1990. *Compatible Hardware:* Apple Macintosh; IBM PC & compatibles. *Operating System(s) Required:* PC-DOS, MS-DOS, ProDOS. *Language(s):* BASIC. *Memory Required:* Apple 64k, others 128k. *Items Included:* Software, manual, client interview forms. *Customer Support:* Available.
disk $250.00, incl. manual (ISBN 1-879530-01-5).
Helps Lawyers Prepare Wills & Trusts Quickly & Efficiently. Supply the Information, & the Program Puts the Information into Standard Will Trust Clauses & Prints them Out. When the Will Trust Needs to Be Updated, You Simply Rerun the Program.
Legisoft, Inc.

Laying Flock Production: Decision Aid. Merle W. Wagner. 1982. *Compatible Hardware:* Apple II Plus, IIe, IIc; IBM. *Operating System(s) Required:* Apple DOS 3.3, MS-DOS 2.0. *Language(s):* BASIC. *Memory Required:* 48k, 640k. *General Requirements:* Printer.
disk $29.95 (ISBN 0-922900-21-3, Order no.: CFD-667).
Budget Analysis for Egg Production. 17 Data Entries; 10 Calculations.
Cherrygarth, Inc.

Layman Probate Accounting. American Writers. Jun. 1991. *Operating System(s) Required:* PC-DOS, MS-DOS, CP/M, XENIX, UNIX, VMS. *Memory Required:* 256k. *General Requirements:* Hard disk.

disk $995.00 (Order no.: LAWPRO). Simplifies Probate Accounting by Requiring the User to Input Only Basic Accounting Data, with the Program Performing All of the Court Required Accounting, Production of Schedules, etc.
Law Management Systems.

LAYOUT. 1982. *Compatible Hardware:* IBM PC & compatibles. *Operating System(s) Required:* MS-DOS. *Language(s):* BASIC. *Memory Required:* 128k.
$105.00.
Provides Plate Layout for Concentric Cones & Ring Segments. Also Provides Nozzle Orientation for Cylindrical Vessels.
Technical Research Services, Inc.

Layout/CUA for DOS. *Operating System(s) Required:* PC-DOS. *Memory Required:* 640k. *General Requirements:* EASEL/DOS Development System.
$1900.00.
A Software Development Tool That Works with Easel/DOS Graphical Development tools, Which Can Create Applications That Automatically Comply with IBM's Common User Access Guidelines. Users Can Add Action & Scroll Bars, Pull-Down Menus, & Secondary Windows to DOS Application.
Easel Corporation.

Lazer Cycles. *Compatible Hardware:* Commodore 64.
contact publisher for price (Order no.: C-1506).
Trap Your Opponent Before You Are Trapped. Designed for 1 or 2 Players.
Creative Equipment.

LazyCalc. 1982. *Compatible Hardware:* TRS-80 Model I, Model III, Model 4. *Operating System(s) Required:* TRSDOS. *Language(s):* Z80 Assembly. *Memory Required:* 32k. *General Requirements:* Lazy Writer program.
disk $29.95.
Extension of LazyWriter. Does Adding, Subtracting, Multiplying & Dividing & Places Answers in Text.
Alpha Bit Communications, Inc.

LazyDoc. *Compatible Hardware:* TRS-80 Model I, Model III, Model 4. *Operating System(s) Required:* TRSDOS. *Language(s):* Z80 Assembly. *Memory Required:* 32k. *General Requirements:* Lazy Writer program.
disk $59.95.
Document Maker Which Allows User to Fill in Blanks When Printing up a Court Order or Judgement. Any Number of Standard Text Disks Can Be Prepared, Such As Court Orders, Contracts, Estate Planning.
Alpha Bit Communications, Inc.

LazyMerge. *Compatible Hardware:* TRS-80 Model I, Model III, Model 4. *Operating System(s) Required:* TRSDOS. *Language(s):* Z80 Assembly. *Memory Required:* 32k. *General Requirements:* Lazy Writer.
disk $44.95.
Allows User to Print Form Letters with the Name & Address Printed at Top of Each Letter. Custom Inserts May Also Be Printed into Body of the Letter. Works with a LAZY WRITER Mail List.
Alpha Bit Communications, Inc.

LazyTab. *Compatible Hardware:* TRS-80 Model I, Model III, Model 4.
$15.00.
Can Move Tabbed Items to New Settings & Align All Decimals.
Alpha Bit Communications, Inc.

LazyType. *Compatible Hardware:* TRS-80 Model I, Model III.
$29.95.
Allows Typing Letters Directly on Printer While Also As Input into Word Processor.
Alpha Bit Communications, Inc.

LazyWriter. *Version:* 3.5. David Welsh. 1985. *Compatible Hardware:* TRS-80 Model I, Model III, Model 4; MAX-80, or VID-80. *Operating System(s) Required:* TRSDOS, MultiDOS, LDOS, DOS-Plus. *Language(s):* Z80 Assembly. *Memory Required:* 32k.
disk $124.95, incl. manual.
Alpha Bit Communications, Inc.

LC Tracker. *Compatible Hardware:* IBM PC & compatibles, PS/2. *Memory Required:* 640k. *General Requirements:* Lotus 1-2-3 release 2/2.01.
Lotus 1-2-3 Template That Allows User to Record & Follow All Letters of Credit. Matches Loan & Letter-of-Credit Numbers Allowing User to Check Any Outstanding-Loan Balance. Produces Status Reports, Including Sales, Accounting, Shipping & Purchase Orders.
Karatz-Nogle Accountancy Corp.

LCA-1: Logic Circuit Analysis. *Version:* 1.30. Kim N. Leavitt. 1988. *Compatible Hardware:* IBM PC/MS-DOS. *Operating System(s) Required:* MS-DOS or PC-DOS. *Language(s):* C. *Memory Required:* 256k. *Items Included:* 5.25" disk, user's manual. *Customer Support:* 30 day unlimited warranty.
disk $195.00 (ISBN 0-927449-39-0, Order no.: LCPM).
Interactive or Batch Mode; Built-in, User Defined, Real-Time Graphics, Graphic or Tabular Output, Support for a Wide Variety of Graphics Adapters, Simple Abbreviated Commands, Quick Turnaround, Flexible Primitive Component Set, Design Rule Checks, Technology Specific Default Parameters, Loading, Record & Playback Commands, Macro Models, Multiple Input Signal Generators, Broad Selection of Probe Types, Bus Probes (Bin, Oct, Hex), Hierarchical Timing Specifications, & Comprehensive Support Inlcuding a 224 Page Manual. Demo Disk Available.
Tatum Labs, Inc.

LCFIL: L-C Filter Synthesis Program. *Compatible Hardware:* Apple Macintosh, IBM PC. *Operating System(s) Required:* MS-DOS. *Memory Required:* IBM 256k, Macintosh 512k. *General Requirements:* 2 disk drives or hard disk.
$195.00.
Stand-Alone Program for Electronic Engineers & Technicians Involved in the Design, Synthesis, &/or Analysis of L-C Filters. Expedites the Design & Analysis of Popular Families & Topologies. Provides Solutions for Passive Lowpass, Highpass, & Bandpass Filters. Can Design & Analyze Butterworth, Chebychev, Cauer, & Bessel Filters. Other L-C Filters May Be Analyzed. Users Can Specify Input Impedance & Inductors Q's, etc.
BV Engineering.

LeadMan: Lead Management Software. Open Door Software Staff. Mar. 1995. *Items Included:* Manual, video (when available). *Customer Support:* Call for info..
DOS. IBM & compatibles. disk $99.00 (ISBN 1-56756-079-2, Order no.: 005221). *Addl. software required:* DOS. *Optimal configuration:* IBM or compatible 486, 66MHz, 5Mb free space on hard disk, 4Mb RAM-3Mb Expanded Usable, VGA monitor, 3.5" HD floppy, keyboard, mouse, tape backup & uninterruptible power supply.
Windows. IBM & compatibles. disk $99.00 (ISBN 1-56756-080-6, Order no.: OD525W). *Addl. software required:* Windows. *Optimal configuration:* IBM or compatible 486, 66MHz, 5Mb free space on hard disk, 4Mb RAM-3Mb Expanded Usable, VGA monitor, 3.5" HD floppy, keyboard, mouse, tape backup & uninterruptible power supply.
Network Version. disk $599.00 (ISBN 1-56756-081-4, Order no.: OD530I). *Networks supported:* Novell Netware Lite.
A Comprehensive Software Application That Manages Prospect Leads. Designed for Telemarketing/Sales Professionals, Stock Brokers, or Anyone Else Interested in Qualifying Prospects. Speeds the Sales Cycle by Structuring the Process of Channeling Names from a List Through the Prospect Stage to the Client Stage. Automates the Old Shuffling Process of Prospect Lead Cards & Helps You Work Your Leads in 4 Easy Steps. LIST, TARGET, PROSPECT, CLIENT.
Advantage International.

Leaguebowl. Ron Gunn. 1994. *Compatible Hardware:* Commodore 64, 128; IBM PC & compatibles; Windows compatible. *Operating System(s) Required:* CBM DOS, DOS 2.1 or higher. *Language(s):* BASIC for C64, Compiled .EXE for IBM. *Memory Required:* CBM DOS 64k, IBM 350kk. *General Requirements:* Printer, color monitor. *Items Included:* 3 ring binder, 60 plus page manual, demo disk. *Customer Support:* 90 days. National "Help Network". Renewable 1 year warranty ($35).
Leaguebowl-48 (Commodore). disk $90.00 (Order no.: D048F).
Leaguebowl-28 (Commodore). disk $50.00 (Order no.: D028F).
LeagueBowl-PC2 (IBM). disk $50.00 (Order no.: D052I).
LeagueBowl-PC5. disk $90.00 (Order no.: D055I).
System of Programs Which Automatically Calculates All Phases of Bowling Score Records. Applies to All Types of Game Scoring. RECAPBOWL & ARCHIVEBOWL Can Be Run Only from This Program. LEAGUEBOWL 28 & 48 Are for Commodore 64, 128; LEAGUEBOWL PC2 & PC5 Are Designed for IBM PC & Compatibles. Contact Publisher for 16 Page Catalog Showing Sample Output.
Briley Software.

Learn about the Solar System & Halley's Comet. Ronald P. Millett. Nov. 1984. *Compatible Hardware:* Apple Macintosh. *Language(s):* MSBASIC. *Memory Required:* 128k.
contact publisher for price.
Includes Simulations of the Planets Rotating Around the Sun, Facts about the Planets (Available on Separate Display Pages), & an Interactive Test Program. Halley's Comet Is Simulated in Its Orbit Around the Sun.
Millett Software.

Learn Ten Foreign Languages CD-ROM. Jan. 1996. *Items Included:* Instruction booklet.
DOS & Windows 3.1. PC (2k). CD-ROM disk $29.90. *Optimal configuration:* 286, Windows 3.1 2k.
User Can Easily Learn 10 Languages. Read, Write & Speak Spanish, German, French, Japanese, Chinese, Russian, Croation, Vietnamese, Danish, Hebrew. Complete Programs That Include Flash Cards & Educational Language Games. Some Interactive Multimedia with Sound. Also Programs for Teaching Children Languages - Shareware.
Top of the Mountain Publishing.

Learn To Play Guitar.
MPC; 386 or higher, (2Mb). CD-ROM disk $49.95. *Nonstandard peripherals required:*

TITLE INDEX

CD-ROM drive, VGA, DAC, ADC, music synthesizer.
Teaches Beginning Through Intermediate Guitar, Including Fundamental Technique for Rock, Country, R & B, etc.
Cambrix Publishing Inc.

Learn to Speak Series (French or Spanish). *Version:* 4.0.2. Jul. 1994. *Items Included:* 360 page workbook/text with exercises for the language lessons. *Customer Support:* Registered users receive unlimited free technical support at 615-558-8270.
  Windows/MPC or compatible w/MPC Upgrade K.7. 80386DX/33 with MS-DOS 3.3 or higher (4Mb). CD-ROM disk $179.00. *Nonstandard peripherals required:* Sound Board, CD-ROM drive. *Addl. software required:* Windows 3.1.
  System 6.0.7 or higher, System 7 compatible. Macintosh 68030/25 or higher (4Mb). CD-ROM disk $179.00. *Addl. software required:* HyperCard 2.0.2 or higher.
An Entire Spanish (or French) Course Based Around Real-Life Situations. Extensive Digitized Video & Recordings of Native Speakers. Rigorous Vocabulary Exercises & Drills. Extensive Grammar & Pronunciation Drills. Recording Feature Allows User to Record & Listen & Compare Users Pronunciation with Native Speaker.
HyperGlot Software Co., Inc.

Learn to Use Windows 95. *Items Included:* 3.5" disks, user's guide. *Customer Support:* Toll free: 800-822-3522.
  Microsoft windows 3.1, windows for workgroups 3.11 or windows 95. 4 Mb RAM. 386 or Higher Windows Computer. 3.5" disk $14.95. *Nonstandard peripherals required:* 7mb free hard disk space, color VGA monitor, mouse.
Complete learning program for anyone who wants to take advantage of the Microsoft Windows 95 operating system.
Individual Software.

Learning Apple FORTRAN. Donald Geenen. 1986. *Compatible Hardware:* Apple II, II+, IIe, IIc. *Memory Required:* 64k. *General Requirements:* 2 disk drives, Apple FORTRAN. double-sided disk $20.00 (ISBN 0-88175-030-1).
Contains Material from Text "Learning Apple FORTRAN".
W. H. Freeman & Co. (Computer Science Press).

Learning DOS. *Compatible Hardware:* IBM PC & compatibles. *Operating System(s) Required:* MS-DOS. *Memory Required:* 256k.
  disk $49.95.
Interactive, On-Line Tutorial That Teaches the Essential DOS Operations. Not Copy Protected.
Microsoft Pr.

Learning English: Home & Family. Jan. 1994. *Items Included:* Program on CD-ROM, CD Booklet, & Registration Card. *Customer Support:* Free unlimited customer support via telephone.
  Macintosh System 7.0 or higher. Macintosh LC or higher (4Mb). CD-ROM disk $249.00 (ISBN 1-57268-079-2, Order no.: 40862). *Nonstandard peripherals required:* 12 inch monitor or larger; CD-ROM drive. *Optimal configuration:* 5Mb RAM.
  Windows 3.1 or higher running under DOS 5.0 or higher. 386 SX (6Mb RAM; 500k low Dos Mem; 6Mb free disk space). CD-ROM disk $249.00 (Order no.: 40862). *Nonstandard peripherals required:* Sound card (either: Sound Blaster - 8, 16, PRO; Media Vision ProAudio Spectrum; or Microsoft Sound System; MPC compatible CD- ROM drive; VGA monitor; & microphone. *Optimal configuration:* 25 MHz 386 SX.
This Program Is for Students in Grades Four Through Twelve Who Are Learning English. The Stories Help Students Acquire Vocabulary & Language Structure Using Familiar Locations. Language Patterns & Vocabulary Are Introduced in Naturally Occurring Contexts Based upon Themes & Situations. These Programs Combine Language Acquisition Approaches Including: Total Physical Response, Audio-Lingual, Natural, Communicative, & Direct Methods.
Conter Software.

Learning English: Neighborhood Life. Jan. 1994. *Items Included:* Program on CD-ROM, CD Booklet, & Registration Card. *Customer Support:* Free unlimited customer support via telephone.
  Macintosh System 7.0 or higher. Macintosh LC or higher (4Mb). CD-ROM disk $249.00 (ISBN 1-57268-078-4, Order no.: 40861). *Nonstandard peripherals required:* 12 inch monitor or larger; CD-ROM drive. *Optimal configuration:* 5Mb RAM.
  Windows 3.1 or higher running under DOS 5.0 or higher. 386 SX (6Mb RAM; 500k low Dos Mem; 6Mb free disk space). CD-ROM disk $249.00 (Order no.: 40861). *Nonstandard peripherals required:* Sound card (either: Sound Blaster - 8, 16, PRO; Media Vision ProAudio Spectrum; or Microsoft Sound System; MPC compatible CD- ROM drive; VGA monitor; & microphone. *Optimal configuration:* 25 MHz 386 SX.
This Program Is for Students in Grades Four Through Twelve Who Are Learning English. The Stories Help Students Acquire Vocabulary & Language Structure Using Familiar Locations. Language Patterns & Vocabulary Are Introduced in Naturally Occurring Contexts Based upon Themes & Situations. These Programs Combine Language Acquisition Approaches Including: Total Physical Response, Audio-Lingual, Natural, Communicative, & Direct Methods.
Conter Software.

Learning English: Primary. Jan. 1994. *Items Included:* Program on CD-ROM, CD Booklet, & Registration Card. *Customer Support:* Free unlimited customer support via telephone.
  Macintosh System 7.0 or higher. Macintosh LC or higher (4Mb). CD-ROM disk $249.00 (ISBN 1-57268-080-6, Order no.: 40863). *Nonstandard peripherals required:* 12 inch monitor or larger; CD-ROM drive. *Optimal configuration:* 5Mb RAM.
  Windows 3.1 or higher running under DOS 5.0 or higher. 386 SX (6Mb RAM; 500k low Dos Mem; 6Mb free disk space). CD-ROM disk $249.00 (Order no.: 40863). *Nonstandard peripherals required:* Sound card (either: Sound Blaster - 8, 16, PRO; Media Vision ProAudio Spectrum; or Microsoft Sound System; MPC compatible CD- ROM drive; VGA monitor; & microphone. *Optimal configuration:* 25 MHz 386 SX.
The Stories in This Program Are Designed to Support the Development of a Second Language in Primary Students. They Introduce Young Students to Stories, Songs, & Poems That Broaden Their Vocabulary Base, & to Concepts They Will Need to Acquire Essential to English Language Development. Instruction Emphasizes Exploration & Playing with Language.
Conter Software.

Learning English: Primary Rhymes. Jan. 1994. *Items Included:* Program on CD-ROM, CD Booklet, & Registration Card. *Customer Support:* Free unlimited customer support via telephone.
  Macintosh System 7.0 or higher. Macintosh LC or higher (4Mb). CD-ROM disk $49.00 (ISBN 1-57268-081-4, Order no.: 40864). *Nonstandard peripherals required:* 12 inch monitor or larger; CD-ROM drive. *Optimal configuration:* 5Mb RAM.
  Windows 3.1 or higher running under DOS 5.0 or higher. 386 SX (6Mb RAM; 500k low Dos Mem; 6Mb free disk space). CD-ROM disk $49.00 (Order no.: 40864). *Nonstandard peripherals required:* Sound card (either: Sound Blaster - 8, 16, PRO; Media Vision ProAudio Spectrum; or Microsoft Sound System; MPC compatible CD- ROM drive; VGA monitor; & microphone. *Optimal configuration:* 25 MHz 386 SX.
The Poems in This Program Address Phonemic Awareness, Provide an Opportunity to Experience the Cadence & Rhythm of the Language, & to Identify Letter-Sound Patterns.
Conter Software.

Learning Guitar Overnight. Dec. 1985. *Compatible Hardware:* Commodore 64. *Memory Required:* 64k.
  disk $39.95 (ISBN 0-931847-01-X, Order no.: 101CWA).
Teaches Basic Chords & How to Tune Guitars.
Chip Taylor Communications.

Learning LISP. Gnosis. Oct. 1983. *Compatible Hardware:* Apple II, II+, IIe; Franklin Ace. *Operating System(s) Required:* Apple DOS 3.3. (source code included). *Memory Required:* 32k, recommended 48k.
  disk $29.95, incl. bk. (ISBN 0-13-527839-2).
Tutorial Introduction to LISP, Language of Artificial Intelligence. Includes Elementary Examples of LISP Programs Used to Facilitate Learning of Language's More Abstract Concepts. Disk Containing Limited Implementation of LISP Is Available for Apple.
Prentice Hall.

Learning Styles Inventory. Richard M. Cooper & Jerry F. Brown. 1992. *Items Included:* Diskette & teachers guide & binder. *Customer Support:* Toll free customer service Hot Line 1-800-645-3739 (9a.m. - 5p.m. Eastern Time) software guaranteed for two years.
  Mac 6.0 Plus. Macintosh (4Mb). 3.5" disk $98.00 (Order no.: DK28092). *Nonstandard peripherals required:* Requires Hypercard 2.1 or higher.
Tabulation of Responses Is Done Automatically, Resulting in a Graph of the Student's Learning Style Preferences. The Inventory Can Be Administered to a Total Class Using Pencil/Paper & the Teacher Then Enters the Data on Computers.
Educational Activities Inc.

Learning Styles Inventory. *Version:* 2.010. Albert A. Canfield. *Customer Support:* Free unlimited phone support.
  MS-DOS 3.0 or higher (512k). IBM PC or 100% compatibles. 3.5" or 5.25" disk $185.00 (Order no.: W-1023 (5.25"); W-1041 (3.5")). *Optimal configuration:* Hard disk with one Mb free disk space, printer.
In Counseling Centers, Classrooms, & Industrial Training Programs, the LSI Is Used to Adapt Instructional Strategies to Learner Needs, to Design Alternative Curricula, to Help Individuals Select Courses or Work Environments Compatible with Their Learning Styles, & to Help Reduce Dropout Rates.
Western Psychological Services.

Learning Styles Inventory (LST). *Version:* 2.010. Albert A. Canfield. *Customer Support:* Free unlimited phone support.
  DOS 3.0 or higher. 286 (512k). 3.5" disk $185.00 (Order no.: W-1041).
Makes It Easier to Determine Which Learning Environments - & Which Instructors - Are Best for Particular Students.
Western Psychological Services.

The Learning System.
Apple II (48k). $50.00, Lab pack/5 $125.00. Optimal configuration: Apple II, 48k, 1 or 2 drives.
Create & Print Multiple Choice, Fill-In & Column-Match Tests, Lesson Material & Hints That Help Students Learn. The Student Takes the Exam in an Instruction or Test Mode via Computer or Tests Can Be Printed & Administered. The Instruction Mode Gives Hints & Provides Lesson Material; the Test Mode Tests the Students' Knowledge & Provides Scores. Separate Teacher's & Learner's Disks.
Word Assocs., Inc.

Learning to Sail. Customer Support: 800-929-8117 (customer service).
MS-DOS. Apple II. disk $69.99 (ISBN 0-87007-534-9).
Simulates a Fast 30 Foot Sailboat Sailing under Near Ideal Conditions Around a Plotted Course. Performance Is Rated & Can Be Compared Among Players. The Player Is Required to Actively Deal with Variables of Rudder, Mainsail, Jib, True Wind, Apparent Wind, & Magnitude.
SourceView Software International.

Lease-Buy Analysis. 1982. Compatible Hardware: MS-DOS based machines. Language(s): Microsoft BASIC, BASICA.
3.5" or 5.25" disk $55.00 (Order no.: 262).
Computes Tax Factors, Calculates & Prints Out Results in a Clear Detailed Comparative Manner.
Resource Software International, Inc.

Lease Oil & Gas Accounting Systems.
Compatible Hardware: MS-DOS.
contact publisher for price.
Provides: Revenue Distribution, JIB, AFE, AP, AR, Owner/User Tracking & Financial Statements.
Dykes Consulting, Inc.

The LeaseManag-r. Version: Fall, 1994. Sep. 1983. Compatible Hardware: 486 PC. Operating System(s) Required: DOS 6.0 or higher. Language(s): Clipper, dBASE III Plus compiled by C. Memory Required: 4000-8000k. General Requirements: 25Mb hard disk, 132 column printer. Items Included: Documentation, updates - two a year. Customer Support: User manuals, conference, workshop, telephone support, training.
disk $5000.00-$25,000.00 & up for base software - dependent on clients specific need.
Comprehensive Lease Administration & Accounting System. Highlights of the System Include: Collection & Cash Application, Separate G/L Interfaces to Host Systems, Flexible Payment Schedules, Electronic Funds Transfer, Depreciation.
LeaseTek, Inc.

Leasepur. Compatible Hardware: Altos Series 5-15D, Series 5-5D, 580-XX, ACS8000-XX; IBM PC, PC XT, PC AT (enhanced); Compaq with 2 disk drives; Compaq Plus with 10Mb hard disk; Hyperion with 2 disk drives; Chameleon Plus with 2 disk drives; Xerox 820 with 2 disk drives; Zilog MCZ-250. Operating System(s) Required: CP/M, MP/M, CP/M-86/80, PC-DOS, MS-DOS.
contact publisher for price.
Helps in the Decision-Making Process of Choosing Between Leasing or Purchasing Property or Equipment. User Supplies the Financial Data & the Program Produces Reports Comparing the Tax, Cash Flow & Overall Effects of Leasing & Purchasing. Also Produces Sensitivity Analyses That Measure the Effects of "What If" Changes to 7 Different Components of the Lease or Purchase: Down Payment, Estimated Salvage, Lease Payment Amounts, Annual Operating Costs, Cost of Capital, Marginal Capital Gains Rate & Financing Interest Rate.
Coopers & Lybrand.

LeaseStar 2000. Version: 2.0. Operating System(s) Required: PC-DOS/MS-DOS 3.1 or higher; Novell 3.11 or higher. Memory Required: 640k. General Requirements: 30Mb hard disk, modem, clock, LPT1, LPT2. Items Included: Sofware installation, training manuals, telephone support, promotional materials. Customer Support: Unlimited phone support, Mon-Fri, 9:00-6:00PM EST.
contact publisher for price.
Non-Recourse (Broker) Automotive Lease Processing System. Calculates Monthly Payment, Selling Price or Profit for up to 12 Funding Sources Simultaneously. Has Built in Rate & Residual Programs. Accesses All Major Credit Bureaus. Prints All Lease Contracts & Motor Vehicle Documentation. Provides Lease vs. Conventional Finance Comparisons to the Customer in a Non-Complex Manner.
Lease Star, Ltd.

Leasing Program. Compatible Hardware: Sharp ZL-6100 System, ZL-6500 System. Language(s): Sharp Microcode.
$400.00.
Computes: 6 Simple-Interest Types, "Money Factor" & Add-On Types. Computes Either the Monthly Payment or Available Lease Cap. Includes Provisions for Residual Values, Sales Tax & Non-Financed Monthly Charges. Also Available to Compute Ford Red Carpet Leases & GMAC Leases.
P-ROM Software, Inc.

The Least Cost Formulator. Version: 21.0. Jul. 1990. Compatible Hardware: IBM PC, PC XT, PC AT. Operating System(s) Required: PC-DOS, MS-DOS. Language(s): BASIC, FORTRAN. Memory Required: 640k. General Requirements: Hard disk, 80-column printer with form feed (compressed print), IBM BASIC compiler module BASRUN.EXE. Items Included: Software & manuals. Customer Support: 1 year & upgrades.
$4500.00-$25,000.00.
write for info. source code.
Designed for Companies That Prepare or Use Products That Require a Blend of Materials in Their Manufacture, Including: Processed Meat, Ice Cream, Yogurt, Nondairy Toppings, Processed Cheese, Animal Feeds, Fertilizer, Alloys, Fuels, Oils. Provides User with Linear Programming Without Assuming Knowledge of Mathematics or Programming. Determines Specific Amounts of Material Offered That Will Produce a Given Formulation at Minimum Cost While Meeting Applicable Regulatory Requirements & Quality Standards.
Resource Optimization, Inc.

Least Cost Network Design Toolbox: Least Cost Access Network Design. Jan. 1996. Items Included: Sample input & output files & users manuals on disk. Customer Support: Assistance in formulative inputs & understanding outputs, price free or variable.
MS-DOS. IBM PC (8Mb). disk $999.00 (Order no.: 502). Nonstandard peripherals required: Math coprocessor. Addl. software required: FORTRAN Compiler & Linker. Optimal configuration: Source code can be compiled & linked for execution on any Machine with a FORTRAN compiler & linker.
A Cost-Effective Way to Design Least-Cost Concentrator & Multiplexor Networks. The Outputs Generated by This Tool Include: 1. For Each Device, Whether the Device Is to Be Connected Directly with the Central Site or to a Specific Concentrator/Multiplexor; 2. For Each Tail Circuit: Circuit Length, the Monthly Circuit Cost, Monthly DCE Cost, & Monthly Concentrator Port Cost; 3. For Each Trunk Circuit: Circuit Length, Monthly Circuit Cost, Monthly DCE Cost, & Monthly Concentrator/Multiplexor Base Cost; 4. Candidate Concentrator Sites Not Selected; 5. Network Summary: Total Network Circuit Miles, Number of Concentrators & Multiplexors & Their Total Monthly Cost, Number of Trunk Circuit Miles & Their Monthly Cost, Number of Tail Circuit Miles & Their Monthly Cost, Total Monthly Trunk DCE Cost, Total Monthly Device DCE Cost, & Total Monthly Network Cost.
Cane Systems.

Least Cost Network Design Toolbox: Least Cost Multipoint Network Design. Jan. 1996. Items Included: Sample input & output files & users manuals on disk. Customer Support: Assistance in formulative inputs & understanding outputs, price free or variable.
MS-DOS. IBM PC (8Mb). disk $550.00 (Order no.: 501). Nonstandard peripherals required: Math coprocessor. Addl. software required: FORTRAN Compiler & Linker. Optimal configuration: Source code can be compiled & linked for execution on any Machine with a FORTRAN compiler & linker.
Many organizations Have a Central Computer to Which Terminals Are Attached. A Multipoint Circuit May Provide a Cost-Effective Technique for Connecting the Terminals to the Central Computer. However, the Computational Requirements for Evaluating All Possible Alternatives Render Manual Optimization Techniques Infeasible. The Multipoint Network Design Tool Is a Cost-Effective Way to Design a Minimum-Cost Multipoint Network. The Outputs Generated by This Tool Include: 1. Detailed Instructions on Device-Connection & the Length of the Circuit Required for Each Connection; 2. Network Characteristics: Total Circuit Length, Number of Attached Devices, Total Input Volume, Total Output Volume, & Number of Circuits. 3. Circuit Characteristics: Length of the Circuit, Number of Attached Devices, Input Volume, & Output Volume.
Cane Systems.

Least Cost Network Design Toolbox: Least Cost Trunking Network Design. Jan. 1996. Items Included: Sample input & output files & users manuals on disk. Customer Support: Assistance in formulative inputs & understanding outputs, price free or variable.
MS-DOS. IBM PC (8Mb). disk $299.00 (Order no.: 503). Nonstandard peripherals required: Math coprocessor. Addl. software required: FORTRAN Compiler & Linker. Optimal configuration: Source code can be compiled & linked for execution on any Machine with a FORTRAN compiler & linker.
The Network That Connects User Devices to Network Nodes Is Termed an Access Network, While the Network That Interconnects the Nodes Is Termed a Trunking Network. The Trunking Network Design Tool Is a Cost-Effective Way to Design Minimum Cost Trunking Networks. The Outputs Generated by This Tool Include: 1. Identification of the Nodes to Be Directly Connected; 2. The Distance Between Each Pair of Connected Nodes; & 3. Total Trunking Network Distance.
Cane Systems.

Least Cost Nutrition. Compatible Hardware: IBM System/23 PC, PC XT & compatibles.
$500.00.
Farm Management Systems of Mississippi, Inc.

Leather Goddesses of Phobos. Steve Meretzky. Aug. 1986. Compatible Hardware: Apple II, II+, IIe, IIc, Macintosh; Atari XL/XE, ST; Commodore 64, 128, Amiga; DEC Rainbow; IBM PC & compatibles; TI Professional.
Apple II, Macintosh, Atari ST, Amiga, DEC, IBM. disk $39.95.

TITLE INDEX

Atari XL/XE, Commodore 64/128. $34.95.
How Did You, a Regular at Joe's Bar in Upper Sandusky, Ohio, End up on a Martian Moon? You've Been Kidnapped by Minions of the Fiendish Leather Goddesses of Phobos, Who Are Plotting to Turn the Earth into Their Private Pleasure Palace. If You Succeed in Escaping Their Clutches, You'll Begin a Naughty, Bawdy, & Amusing Romp Across the Solar System. Your Mission Is to Collect the Materials You'll Need to Defeat the Leather Goddesses & Save Humanity from Their Dastardly Plan. It Has Three "Naughtiness" Levels to Please the Prude to the Lewd, & Male & Female Playing Roles.
Activision, Inc.

Leatherneck. Microdeal. May 1988. *Compatible Hardware:* Atari ST; Commodore Amiga. *Memory Required:* 512k. *General Requirements:* 4-player adapter for 3 & 4 player modes.
Atari ST. 3.5" disk $39.95, (Demo Avail.).
Amiga. 3.5" disk $39.95.
Arcade Action Game. Players Are Commando Warriors Entrenched in a Game of Skill & Survival As They Try to Rescue Their Captured Colleagues from the Corrupt Legions of the Evil Empire.
MichTron, Inc.

Ledgermaster: Client Write Up. *Version:* 4.4. Dec. 1993. *Compatible Hardware:* IBM PC, PC XT, PC AT. *Operating System(s) Required:* MS-DOS, PC-DOS. *Language(s):* COBOL. *Memory Required:* 256k. *Customer Support:* 30 days free, annual support contract.
$950.00.
manual & demo disk $35.00.
manual only $25.00.
Provides All Financial Statements & Supplementary Reports As Well As W-2's & 1099's. Designed for CPA's & Accounting Firms.
Executive Data Systems, Inc. (Georgia).

Legacy. *Version:* 1.0. *Items Included:* 90 day warranty, free unlimited telephone technical support. *Customer Support:* Free, toll-free. MS-DOS 3.2 or higher. IBM AT or compatible (80286 or 80386 CPU); PS/2 (640k). disk $495.00. *Nonstandard peripherals required:* 20Mb hard disk, EGA, Hercules or other Windows compatible display device, 2 or 3 button Windows compatible Mouse (serial or bus). *Networks supported:* Novell Netware, 3Com 3Plus Open, IBM PC LAN, Microsoft Networks.
Windows-Based Word Processing Program with Desktop Publishing Capabilities. Features Include Style Sheets, Search & Replace, Undo, Spell Checking, Thesaurus, Hyphenation, Table Generation, Location Dependency Between Document Components, & Automatic Index Generation. Users Can Specify Margins & Line Spacing Measurements in Inches, Centimeters, Points or Picas. Performs Automatic & User Controlled Kerning. Users Can Define Colors with Precision, Visually or Numerically Specifying Hue, Saturation & Intensity. Full Color Editing of Both Imported & Legacy Drawn Graphics. Compatible with Any Printer Supported under Microsoft Windows 3.0 or Higher.
NBI, Inc.

Legal. *Version:* Series V. *Operating System(s) Required:* DOS, Novell & Lantastic Networks. *Items Included:* Software & manuals. *Customer Support:* 800 number telephone support, Bulletin Board service, remote support, product enhancements available.
Prices start at $395.00.
Provides Fully Integrated, Interactive Series of Law Office Automation Functions Designed to Offer Billing to Management Capabilities to Sole Practitioners & Law Firms. Programs Include: Time & Billing, General Ledger, Trust Accounting, 1099 IRS Reporting, Tickler, Management Reports & Remote Batch.
SulcusLaw Management Services, Inc.

Legal Accounts Payable. *Version:* 4.0. 1984. *Compatible Hardware:* IBM PC & compatibles. *Operating System(s) Required:* PC-DOS. *Language(s):* COBOL. *Memory Required:* 526k. *General Requirements:* Hard disk, printer. *Items Included:* Disks, manuals, 90 days of support. *Customer Support:* Direct from Morningstar.
$295.00 single-user; $395.00 multi-user.
demo disk $50.00.
Provides One Time Document Handling for Law Office Accounting Procedures. As User Pays Bills Out of a General Operating Account, the Program Automatically Prints Checks & Check Register, Posts Entries to General Ledger & Bills Client for Any Advances.
Morningstar Technology Corp.

Legal Aide. *Compatible Hardware:* Apple Macintosh.
3.5" disk $799.95 to $3995.00.
Legal Time, Billing, & Office Management Package.
Interactive Network Technologies, Inc.

Legal Billing System, 2 disks. Jan. 1984. *Compatible Hardware:* IBM PC, PC XT; Morrow MD11. *Operating System(s) Required:* PC-DOS 2.0, CP/M 2.2, 3.0. *Memory Required:* 128k.
IBM PC XT. disk $1250.00 (ISBN 0-927607-00-X).
Morrow MD11. disk $995.00 (ISBN 0-927607-01-8).
CP/M 2.2. 8" disk $995.00 (ISBN 0-927607-02-6).
Allows Lawyers to Accurately Track All Time & Cost Transactions. Provides Reports Using an Unlimited Number of Descriptions.
Tri-L Data Systems, Inc.

Legal Billing II. *Version:* 2.56. Joe Marinello & Chris LeCroy. May 1987. *Compatible Hardware:* Apple Macintosh, IBM PC. *Memory Required:* 512k. *General Requirements:* Hard disk, printer. *Items Included:* Manual, disk. *Customer Support:* Free phone support.
IBM. disk $595.00 (Order no.: 336).
Macintosh. 3.5" disk $595.00 (Order no.: 366).
Designed for Small to Medium-Sized Firms. Provides All the Features of the Basic Program Plus the Following Enhancements: Full Trust Account Reporting; Archiving of Billed Services & Costs; Additional Billing Options; Ability to Handle More Employee & Activity Codes; Multi-User Option. Approved by the American Bar Association's Legal Technology Advisory Committee.
Satori Software.

Legal Billing II+. *Version:* 2.56. Joe Marinello & Chris LeCroy. May 1987. *Compatible Hardware:* Apple Macintosh, IBM PC. *Memory Required:* 512k. *General Requirements:* Hard disk, printer. *Items Included:* Manual, disk. *Customer Support:* Free phone support.
IBM. disk $995.00 (Order no.: 338).
Macintosh. 3.5" disk $595.00 (Order no.: 368).
Multi-User Version of Legal Billing II. Has a Security System Which Entails Using a Password. This Allows for the Ability to Enter Time at a Network System & Merge Batch Files.
Satori Software.

Legal Case Manager. Aug. 1992. *Items Included:* Comb-bound documentation, word processing module, report generator, automatic posting to Easy Alarms calendar/reminder system. *Customer Support:* Free telephone support (toll line), 30 day no-fault return policy.
Mac Plus or higher (2Mb). 3.5" disk $395.00 (Order no.: LCM). *Nonstandard peripherals required:* Hard disk required. *Addl. software required:* HyperCard 2.1 (included); System 6.0.5 or higher. *Optimal configuration:* 68030-based Mac; 4 plus Mb RAM; hard drive with 10Mb available.
Stores Client & Opposing Attorney Info, Police & Witness Names/Addresses, Doctors Names/Addresses, Client Medical Status, Medical Bills & Payments, Accident Info, Trial Checklist, Employment/Wage-Loss Data, Insurance Data, Discovery, Interrogatories, Deposition Summaries, Phone & Document Logs, Settlement Checklist, Domestic Relations Data. Built-In Word Processor Provides Quick & Easy Mail-Merge for Contact Letters, Requests for Information. Report Generator Supplies Convenient One Views.
De Novo Systems, Inc.

Legal Dictionary. *Compatible Hardware:* Apple Macintosh Plus. *Memory Required:* 1024k.
3.5" disk $49.95.
For Use with Spellswell. Contains More Than 20,000 Words & Abbreviations Specific to Work Done By Lawyers, Legal Secretaries, Law Enforcement Professionals, & Corporate Legal Departments.
Working Software, Inc.

The Legal Eagle. *Compatible Hardware:* Apple Macintosh.
Single user. 3.5" disk $995.00.
Multiuser. 3.5" disk $1295.00.
Customizable Time Cost/Disbursement Billing & Accounting Package.
Syscom, Inc.

Legal Insight. *Version:* 6. May 1991. *Compatible Hardware:* 386/486; AT&T, CCI/ICL, Data General, DEC, Hewlett-Packard, IBM RX/6000, MIPS, NCR Tower, Prime, Pyramid, Sun Microsystems, Unisys, Motorola, Convergent, Sequent, Compaq. *Operating System(s) Required:* UNIX. *Memory Required:* 2000k. *General Requirements:* Printer, modem, hard disk. *Customer Support:* Hotline support available; fully documented; on-site installation & training.
contact publisher for price.
Comprehensive Practice Accounting & Automation System. Fully Integrated Modules Include Time Management & Billing, Accounts Receivable, Accounts Payable, General Ledger & Trust Accounting, Contingency Accounting, Conflict Checking, Records Management, Cost Recovery Marketing, Collections & OCR Interface. UNIX DBMS & Integration to PC Networks. Integrates with Popular Office Automation Systems. Installations Nation-Wide & Canada.
Versys Corp.

Legal Ledger. *Version:* 2.2. Feb. 1987. *Compatible Hardware:* IBM PC, PC XT, PC AT. *Operating System(s) Required:* PC-DOS 2.1 or higher. *Language(s):* Pascal. *Memory Required:* PC-DOS 2.1 256k, PC-DOS 3.0 or higher 320k. *General Requirements:* Hard disk. *Customer Support:* 60 days toll-free.
disk $595.00.
Maintains & Performs: Built-In Check Writing (Client Disbursements & Cash Disbursements); Cash Disbursements Journal; Client Disbursements Journal; Cash Receipts Journal; General Journal; Chart of Accounts; Trial Balance; Income (P&L) Statement; Balance Sheet; Comparative Detailed & Consolidated Financial Statements. Integrates with the CLIENT MANAGEMENT SYSTEM. The "Customizer" Will Allow Users to Set All Colors & Sound.
CompuLaw, Ltd.

LEGAL-PRO BILLING & ACCOUNTS

Legal-Pro Billing & Accounts Receivable: Level 1. *Compatible Hardware:* IBM PC & compatibles. contact publisher for price.
Designed for Smaller Firms Who Wish to Automate Their Billing Function. Provides the Following Features: Integrated Cash, Retainer, Trust; Single Menu for Ease of Use; Aged A/R Report; Trust/Retainer Report; Pre-Bill Report; Reminder Messages on Bills; Summary Work in Process Report; Matter Status Inquiry on Screen; Unit Cost Disbursement Codes; User Defined Bill Formats; Alpha or Numeric Client Lists; Area of Law Tracking & Report Sorting Option; Easy-to-Use Facility for Bill Preparation.
Informatics Legal Systems, Inc.

Legal-Pro Billing & Accounts Receivable: Level 2. *Compatible Hardware:* IBM PC & compatibles. $995.00.
program maintenance $100.00, per yr.
Hotline Plus $150.00, per yr.
Designed for Firms That Are Working with a Small Budget, But Need to Be Able to Track the Productivity of Their Timekeepers on a Regular Basis. These Firms May Have up to 5 Timekeepers. In Addition to Level 1's Features, This System Includes: Full Attorney Productivity Reporting, Aged Work in Process Reports, Non-Billable Time Report, Interest Calculation on Past Due Accounts, File Control Listing, Client File Label Production for Listings.
Informatics Legal Systems, Inc.

Legal-Pro Billing & Accounts Receivable: Level 3. *Compatible Hardware:* IBM PC & compatibles. $1995.00.
program maintenance $200.00, per yr.
Hotline Plus $300.00, per yr.
Designed for Firms with Larger Staffs & Greater Client Requirements for Services. Includes All the Level 1 & 2 Features in Addition to: Pre-Bill Selection Criteria, Daily Reported Time Summary by Timekeeper, Multiple Time Batches, Client Level Billing, Billing & Payment Analysis.
Informatics Legal Systems, Inc.

Legal-Pro Billing & Accounts Receivable: Level 4. *Compatible Hardware:* IBM PC & compatibles. $2995.00.
program maintenance $300.00, per yr.
Hotline Plus $450.00, per yr.
Contains All Level 1-3 Features in Addition to: Attorney Classification (Associate, Partner, etc.), Client Ledger Card Printing for Full Client History, Attorney History Report by Client/Matter, Cash Receipts Register by Range, Write-Up/Down Analysis Report, Aged Accounts Receivable by Fee Arrangement Type.
Informatics Legal Systems, Inc.

Legal-Pro Checkwriting/Disbursements System. *Compatible Hardware:* IBM PC & compatibles. *General Requirements:* Legal-Pro Billing & Accounts Receivable module.
disk $950.00.
program maintenance $100.00, per yr.
Hotline Plus $150.00, per yr.
Similar to an Accounts Payable Program, but Tailored to the Law Office Environment. Can Be Integrated with All LEGAL-PRO Products. Will Handle All Five Major Sources of Checkwriting in a Law Firm: Check to a Vendor to Pay Offices Expenses, Check to a Vendor on Behalf of a Client, Checks Written from Trust or Retainer Accounts, Checks Written from Trust or Retainer Accounts to the Firm As a Result of Transferring Trust or Retainer Money in Bill Preparation, & Checks Written from Trust or Retainer Accounts to a Vendor on Behalf of a Client.
Informatics Legal Systems, Inc.

Legal-Pro Conflict of Interest System. *Compatible Hardware:* IBM PC & compatibles.
disk $495.00.
program maintenance $50.00, per yr.
Hotline Plus $75.00, per yr.
Will Provide Law Firms with Access to Any Potential Conflicts Based on a Wide Variety of Criteria. The System Can Be Used As a Stand-Alone Module or Can Be Used on the Same Computer As the Other Financial Modules. When the Client File Is Accessed, the CONFLICT SYSTEM Will Provide a Listing of All Clients in the BILLING SYSTEM That Have Not Had Any Conflict Names Added to Make Sure the Conflict Data Is Always Complete. Will Keep Track of Not Only Names, but Relationships As Well. All Inquiries Can Appear on the Screen with Full Scrolling Ability When Needed.
Informatics Legal Systems, Inc.

Legal-Pro Docket Control System. *Compatible Hardware:* IBM PC & compatibles.
disk $495.00.
program maintenance $50.00, per yr.
Hotline Plus $75.00, per yr.
Will Automate All Attorney & Staff Appointments. Designed to Be Integrated with the LEGAL-PRO BILLING & ACCOUNTS Module, but Can Be Operated As a Stand-Alone System As Well. When Used with the Billing Module, It May Use the Client & Matter Code Identification Already Established. Some Specific Features of the System Are: Can Keep Track of Dates by Reminder Dates or Critical Dates; Dates or Reminders Can Be Set Forward or Backward from the Event Date; Four Lines of Description Are Available per Docket Entry; All Docket Items Can Be Defined Automatically or Manually; Multiple Attorneys Can Be "Copied" Automatically by Entering Their Attorney Numbers on a Single Docket Item So That Individual Entries Are Not Required; Complete History of Any Docket Item Can Be Kept; Multiple Docket Entries Can Be Generated Automatically by Using Special Activity Codes Used by the Firm; Electronic Calendar Is Included.
Informatics Legal Systems, Inc.

Legal-Pro General Ledger System. *Compatible Hardware:* IBM PC & compatibles.
disk $950.00.
program maintenance $100.00, per yr.
Hotline Plus $150.00, per yr.
Provides Firms with the Ability to Produce Financial Statements on a Cash or Accrual Basis. May Be Used As a Stand Alone Module, or Can Be Directly Interfaced with All BILLING & ACCOUNTS RECEIVABLE Modules and/or the CHECKWRITING/DISBURSEMENTS Module.
Informatics Legal Systems, Inc.

Legal-Pro Remote Time Entry. *Compatible Hardware:* IBM PC & compatibles. *Operating System(s) Required:* MS-DOS.
disk $395.00.
program maintenance $50.00, per yr.
Hotline Plus $75.00, per yr.
Allows for Time Slip Entries to Be Made on a PC Other Than the One Being Used for the BILLING SYSTEM. Has the Same Screen Display Used in the Regular BILLING SYSTEM, the Only Difference in Operation Is That There Is No Immediate Validation of Client Matter or Attorney Numbers. These Will Be Verified Automatically During Input into the BILLING SYSTEM When the User Will Be Given the Opportunity to Correct Any Errors During Input Before Work Is Posted to Work in Process.
Informatics Legal Systems, Inc.

Legal-Pro Report Writer. *Compatible Hardware:* IBM PC & compatibles.
disk $495.00.

SOFTWARE ENCYCLOPEDIA 1996

program maintenance $50.00, per yr.
Hotline Plus $75.00, per yr.
Extracts Summary Information from the LEGAL-PRO BILLING & ACCOUNTS RECEIVABLE System for Use with Common Database Programs & LOTUS 1-2-3. The Firm Can Select Any of the 61 Data Elements Captured in the Billing Module. The System Allows Users to Select the Elements to Be Used & the Range of Values to Be Used for Each. Users May Also Use AND Logic or OR Logic Criteria.
Informatics Legal Systems, Inc.

Legal Reference Library. Richard R. Hammar.
IBM. CD-ROM disk $99.00 (ISBN 1-880562-21-9).
Christian Ministry Resources.

The Legal System - Series 1. *Version:* 6.5. Oct. 1983. *Compatible Hardware:* Altos, AT&T 38 Series, IBM PC & compatibles, NCR Tower, Sperry, Prime, NEC, CCI, All Networks. *Operating System(s) Required:* MS-DOS, XENIX, UNIX, DOS LANs. *Language(s):* COBOL. *Memory Required:* Per user - 256k. *General Requirements:* Hard disk, printer w/132-column print capability. *Items Included:* Complete documentation. *Customer Support:* 15 months of unlimited telephone support for only 25% of software cost. Other support arrangements are also available.
MS-DOS, XENIX, UNIX, DOS LANS, Windows (all versions). Starting at $1295.00.
Complete Time Billing, Accounting & Office Management Software for Law Firms & Similar Professional Offices. Basic System Includes Time Accounting, Accounts Receivable, Conflict Checking & Report & Statement Generation. Optional Modules Include Trust/Retainer Accounting, CheckWriter, Docket/Message Control, Management Reports, Remote Data Entry, & More. Installation, Training, Support & Documentation Also Available.
Synaptec Software, Inc.

Legal Text Analysis Tool: (LTAT). *Customer Support:* 90 days unlimited warranty; 1 year support & update contract-$100.00 Telephone support line.
Macintosh (2Mb). disk $495.00. *Addl. software required:* Hypercard. *Optimal configuration:* Mac Plus or Mac II, 2Mb RAM, 40+Mb disk.
Assists in the Preparation & Trial Phase of a Law Suit. Allows User to Search & Analyze Large Volumes of Text Data. Track, Search, & Report on Many Documents Simultaneously Involved With Litigation. Has Facilities for Building, Maintaining, & Printing Trial Hand Book. NOTE-IT Sub System Provides a Time Stamped Log of Each Attorney's Thoughts, Ideas, & Action Items As the Case Develops & Is Brought to Trial. Keeps Track of Document Name, Type, Location, & Date. Each Document Has an Issues Field. This Field Allows User to Categorize into Its Most Valuable Area in the Law Suit. Up to Eight Different Issues Per Document May Be Assigned. Each Summary Record & NOTE-IT Record Is Automatically Time Stamped As You Cut & Paste from the Original Document. Data Can Be Imported into This Product from Many Sources.
Products Diversified Interests.

The Legal Toolbox. *Compatible Hardware:* IBM PC & compatibles. *Operating System(s) Required:* PC-DOS/MS-DOS 2.0 or higher. $425.00.
CompareRite, CiteRite II, & FullAuthority, Three of Jurisoft's Productivity Programs, Are Grouped Together in One Package. CompareRite is a Redlining Program that Lets Users Compare Two Versions of a Document & Creates a Redlined Draft, Showing the Differences Between the Two. CiteRite II is a Citation Program that Checks

TITLE INDEX

Bluebook & California-Style Citations Without Requiring Text Markers to Indicate Where the Citations Occur. The Program Automatically Locates Citations in Legal Documents, Checks Them for Proper Form, & Reports any Errors. Can Be Operated as a Pop-Up Program that Checks Citations from Within a Word Processor. Full Authority Looks for Citations in Briefs & Arranges Them to Create a Formatted Table of Authorities. Lets Users Choose to Sort Them into Statute, Book, Law Review, or Other Cite Categories.
Jurisoft.

LegalEase: Legal Description Writer. Version: 1.5. Mark D. Floan & Shirl A. Vonasek. Aug. 1992. *Items Included:* Manual with tutorial. *Customer Support:* 120 days free phone support; 1 yr unlimited (on all Simplicity Software), $249.00; 90 day moneyback guarantee.
PC-DOS/MS-DOS 3.0 or higher. IBM PC, XT, AT, PS/2 & compatibles (512k). disk $99.00, incl. manual (ISBN 0-932071-14-7). *Addl. software required:* Survey Lite, Survey 4.0, or "Sight" Survey (COGO programs from Simplicity Systems, Inc.).
An Easy-to-Use Legal Description Writer/Processor for Use with Simplicity's COGO Programs. Using the COGO Routines Within SURVEY LITE, SURVEY 4.0, or "SIGHT SURVEY", the Metes & Bounds Description Can Be Checked for Accuracy with a Printed Precision Ratio & Tract Area. Legal Phrases Can Be User-Customized & an Editor Is Included for Adding Notes, Making Changes, etc. Descriptions Can Automatically Be Loaded into User's Own Word Processor.
Simplicity Systems, Inc.

Legalex. Version: 3.1. 1982. *Items Included:* User's reference manual. *Customer Support:* 6 mos. free telephone support, maintenance contracts available after free period. On-site training, price based on location.
MS-DOS. IBM PC, PC XT, & compatibles, PS/2 (512k). Single Station Version $395.00 to $995.00; Multi-User Version $2495.00 & up. *Nonstandard peripherals required:* Hard disk, printer. *Networks supported:* Novell Netware, IBM/3 COM LAN Manager, Banyon VINES.
Calendar/Docket That Allows User to Generate Single Dates or Calculate Sets of Related Dates Based on Timelines or Court Rules. Provides Timelines for Various Courts & User-Defined Timelines. Prints Calendar Reports & Offers Pop-Up Calendar for Entering Dates. Menu-Driven.
Computer Software for Professionals, Inc.

Legalmaster, 13 Modules. Feb. 1991. *Operating System(s) Required:* MS-DOS. *Memory Required:* 640k. *Items Included:* 700 page users Reference Manual. *Customer Support:* Six months unlimited telephone support - average response time 10 seconds.
MS-DOS. IBM PC, PC XT, PC AT. *Nonstandard peripherals required:* Hard disk, 195-column printer. *Networks supported:* Novell NetWare.
Law Firm Application Package.
Computer Software for Professionals, Inc.
  Module E. Docketing & Calendaring.
    disk $600.00.
    Permits the Entry of "Calendar Items" Such As Upcoming Events, Court Appearances, Filing Deadlines, Meetings, Hearings, etc. Includes Its Own Report Writer Permitting Event Listings Sorted by Date, Time, Attorney, Client, Matter, Location, Item Type, etc. Fully Integrated with the Time & Billing Modules.
  Module F. Working Attorney Revenue Distribution.
    disk $995.00.
    Permits Fee Receipts To Be Divided Among Attorneys Who Work on the Same Case/Matter.
  Module G. General Ledger Interface.
    disk $300.00.
    Allows User to Pass Data Keyed into Legalmaster into Any of Four Popular General Ledger Software Packages. Data Can Include Receipts, Billings, Adjustments, Trust (Retainer) Debits & Credits, & Reimbursable Expenses (Costs). These Transaction Types May Be Passed into Different G/L Accounts as a Function of "Type" (e.g., Fees, Costs, Finance Charges, Sales Taxes) When Relevant & Further by Area of Law, Responsible Attorney, Originating Attorney, Type of Client etc.
  Module I. Import Data Utility.
    disk $575.00.
    Allows Financial Transaction Data from Other Software, Such As Word Processing or Accounts Payable Packages or from Collection Devices, Such As Photocopy, Telephone Systems or Postage Meters, to Be Edited & Merged Within Legalmaster Files. This Module is Required for Uses of Legalmaster's Remote Transaction Data Entry Module (Module R).
  Module K. Conflict of Interest.
    disk $595.00.
    Designed to Help Avoid Potential Conflicts of Interest. Allows for the Storage of a Lengthy List of Names to Be Associated with Each Client &/or Matter & for These Names to Be Compared with the Names of the Principles of Any New Client. This Module is Fully Integrated with Legalmaster's Other Modules (Client & Matter Maintenance, Time & Billing, Docketing & Calendaring, MIRC, etc.) So That Data Relevant to More Than One Module Need Be Entered Only Once. Requires Modules A,B,D or Legalmaster Jr.
  Module R. Remote Transaction Data Entry.
    disk $550.00.
    Permits the Entry of Financial Transactions (Fees, Costs, Payment, etc.) from as Many Host-Compatible Workstations as Desired. Multiple Copies of the "Remote Entry Diskette May" Be Made As Desired. Up to 1000 Transactions May Be Entered in Any One "Batch" Through the Use of the Same User-Friendly Transaction Entry Screens As Are Used for Transaction Entry at the Workstation. Module "I" Is Required to Edit & Merge the Transaction Data from the "Remote Entry Diskettes" onto the Hard Disk at the Host Workstation.
  Module S. Security.
    disk $275.00.
    Provides Menu-Level, Function-Level & File-Level Security to All of Legalmaster's Application Modules Including Time & Billing, Reporting, Calendaring, Data Import, Data Export, History & Conflicts. Fully Interactive.

Legalmaster Conflicts Standalone: Conflicts of Interest. Version: 1993. 1993. *Items Included:* User's reference manual. *Customer Support:* 3 months free telephone support, maintenance contracts available after free period. On-site training, price based on location.
MS-DOS. IBM PC, PC XT & compatibles, PS/2 (550k). disk $895.00. *Nonstandard peripherals required:* Hard disk, printer. *Networks supported:* Novell.
Designed to Assist You in Determining If Individuals or Institutions Associated with a Prospective Client Are Involved with Any of Your Existing Cases. The Software Merely Compares One List of Names with Another & Displays or Prints Those That Match.
Computer Software for Professionals, Inc.

Legalmaster: Standard Version. 1995. *Items Included:* 700 page users reference manual. *Customer Support:* 6 months unlimited telephone support - average response time 10 seconds.
MS-DOS (640k). disk $4200.00. *Networks supported:* Novell NetWare.
Performs Time & Disbursement Accounting, Descriptive Billing, A/R, Retainer Trust Accounting, Custom Management Report Writer, Fee Splitting, & Historical Data Retention. Reports Included Are Pre-Bills, Statements in over 1000 Formats, Complete Audit Trails, Employees' Time Analysis, Permits User to Create His or Her Own Reports from Data Stored by Legalmaster. You Can Also Use the Built-In Report Writer to Get Lists of Unbilled Activity, Monthly Billings, Payments, Caselists, etc. Available in Five Separate Packages: S-2 (Limited to 2 Timekeepers), S-4 (Limited to 4 Timekeepers), S-8 (Limited to 8 Timekeepers), S-12 (Limited to 12 Timekeepers) & More Than 12 Timekeepers.
Computer Software for Professionals, Inc.

Legalmaster S4 Timekeepers. 1992. *Items Included:* User's reference manual. *Customer Support:* 3 mos. free telephone support, maintenance contracts available after free period. On-site training, price based on location.
MS-DOS. IBM PC, PC XT, PC AT, & compatibles, PS/2 (640k). disk $990.00. *Nonstandard peripherals required:* Hard drive & printer. *Networks supported:* Novell Netware.
S3 Performs Time Accounting, Disbursement Accounting, Descriptive Billing, Accounts Receivable, Retainer Trust Accounting, Management Reporting, Fee Splitting & Historical Data Retention; It Also Includes a Series of Report Writers. All Other Legalmaster Modules May Be Added to Legalmaster S, Including Docket Calendaring, Conflict of Interest, & Data Import (Primarily Used for Cost Recovery Devices Such As Photocopiers & Telephone Systems). Equivalent in Function to the Powerful $3700 Version of Legalmaster, This New Product Is for the Smaller Firm & Is Limited to Three Timekeepers (Tracks Time & Has Reporting Capabilities for up to Three Persons).
Computer Software for Professionals, Inc.

Legalmaster S8 Timekeepers. 1992. *Items Included:* User's reference manual. *Customer Support:* 3 mos. free telephone support, maintenance contracts available after free period. On-site training, price based on location.
MS-DOS. IBM PC, PC XT, PC AT, & compatibles, PS/2. disk $2000.00. *Nonstandard peripherals required:* Hard drive & printer. *Networks supported:* Novell Netware.
S6 Performs Time Accounting, Disbursement Accounting, Descriptive Billing, Accounts Receivable, Retainer Trust Accounting, Management Reporting, Fee Splitting & Historical Data Retention; It Also Includes a Series of Report Writers. All Other Legalmaster Modules May Be Added to Legalmaster S, Including Docket Calendaring, Conflict of Interest, & Data Import (Primarily Used for Cost Recovery Devices Such As Photocopiers & Telephone Systems). Equivalent in Function to the Powerful $3700 Version of Legalmaster, This New Product Is for the Smaller Firm & Is Limited to Six Timekeepers (Tracks Time & Has Reporting Capabilities for up to Six Persons).
Computer Software for Professionals, Inc.

LegalPad. Version: 3.0. 1993. *Customer Support:* 30 days' free support.
PC-DOS/MS-DOS. PC or PC-compatibles (640k). 495.00 for LegalPad for Verdict; $295.00 for LegalPad for TwinPak; site licensed.
Optimal configuration: Runs as a full memory-resident program or a 6k TSR, or non-memory resident.
Memory-Resident Program Which Integrates to Verdict or TwinPak. It Allows Remote Stations (Standalone Computers) to Make Batch Postings of Services, Expenses & Payments for the Verdict or TwinPak Billing System. It Includes a Timer/Poster, Batcher, Account Info, Notepad & Calendar.
Micro Craft, Inc.

LEGENDS & MYTHS

Legends & Myths. Luong Tam & Sara McKinnon. Nov. 1995. *Items Included:* Guide booklet with instructions, listing of stories & countries, & printed clues used in game.
Macintosh 7.1 or higher. Macintosh (color) (8Mb). CD-ROM disk $49.95 (ISBN 1-887107-02-9, Order no.: 02-9). *Addl. software required:* QuickTime included. *Optimal configuration:* Mac, 14" monitor, 256 color, double-speed CD-ROM drive.
Windows 3.1 or higher. Windows, MPC compatible (8Mb). *Addl. software required:* QuickTime included. *Optimal configuration:* Win: Super VGA, sound card, mouse, double-speed CD-ROM drive.
An Engaging Introduction to World Folklore for Ages 3 to Adult. Includes: Gallery - 170 Beautiful Children's Paintings Depicting the Folklore of 19 countries; Stories - 50 Legends & Myths, Read by Children; Puzzles - Electronic Jigsaw Puzzles, Made from Children's Art; Game - Discovering Treasure Objects Hidden in Magical Lands Help Players Solve Riddles & Word Puzzles about the Folk Tales. Activities Were Designed to Entertain & Help Build Basic Learning Skills. Picture Puzzles, Which Will Delight Children, Help Strengthen Eye-Hand Coordination Skills, While the Narrated Stories & Clues Call upon Listening & Memory Skills.
Opportune Pr.

Legends of Oz. *Items Included:* Manual, registration card, flier describing all our titles, occasional promotional offers. *Customer Support:* Free telephone technical support.
DOS & Microsoft Windows 3.1. 12 MHz 80386SX. CD-ROM disk Contact publisher for price (ISBN 1-884014-21-6). *Nonstandard peripherals required:* MPC compatible. CD-ROM drive (680Mb) SVGA display, audio board, mouse, 486 DX processor. *Addl. software required:* Microsoft CD-ROM Extensions v.2.2.
Macintosh System 6.05. Color Macintosh (256 colors) (3.5Mb). CD-ROM disk Contact publisher for price (ISBN 1-884014-33-X). *Optimal configuration:* Single speed CD-ROM, 13" color monitor, 8 Mb RAM.
The Complete Story of The Wonderful Wizard of Oz, As Well As Three New Adventures by Roger S. Baum. Contains Interactive Animation, Video Clips, Narration, & an OZ Game That Will Delight the Child in Everyone.
Multicom Publishing, Inc.

Legionnaire. *Compatible Hardware:* Apple II+, IIe, IIc, Commodore 64/128. *Memory Required:* 16-32k. *General Requirements:* Joystick.
disk $30.00 ea.
Real-Time Simulation of Tactical Ancient Combat Placing Player As Julius Caesar in Gaul, Outnumbered Against the Barbarian Hordes. Use the Cavalry to Decoy the Enemy, & Maneuver the Legions to Take Advantage of the Terrain. Shock Effects, Morale, & Fatigue Are Taken into Account.
Avalon Hill Game Co., The Microcomputer Games Div.

LEGO TC Logo Starter Pack. *Items Included:* Building set with model instructions for 8 different machines, three project booklets, teachers guide, reference guides, computer interface shot card. *Customer Support:* Free workshops & training in many locations, free toll-free information & technical support, free newsletter published 3 times per year.
IBM PC, P/S2 model 25 & model 30 & compatibles (256k). disk $515.00 (ISBN 0-914831-61-5, Order no.: 966). *Nonstandard peripherals required:* Color Graphics Adapter (CGA) card & color monitor. *Optimal configuration:* Any system with 256k, an open Industry Standard Architecture (ISA) slot (no microchannel systems), a CGA card & DOS 2.1 or higher.
Apple IIe, Apple IIgs & compatibles (64k). disk $485.00 (ISBN 0-914831-60-7). *Optimal configuration:* Any IIe or IIgs system with at least 64k, an open slot for a card & 5.25" disk drive.
Users Can Create Machines That Walk, Spin, Make Sounds & Model Real-Life Machines Such As Cars, Washing Machines, Merry Go Rounds, Traffic Lights, etc.
Lego Dacta.

Leipzig 1813. *Compatible Hardware:* Atari 400, 800. *Language(s):* Atari BASIC (source code included). *Memory Required:* disk 48k. *General Requirements:* Joystick.
disk $33.95.
1-Player Simulation of the 1st Day of Battle of Leipzig in Austria.
Dynacomp, Inc.

LEM Lander. *Compatible Hardware:* Apple II with Applesoft. *Memory Required:* 48k.
disk $16.95.
Simulation of Lunar Excursion.
Dynacomp, Inc.

Lenny's Multimedia Circus. Sep. 1995. *Customer Support:* Telephone support - free (except phone charge).
Windows 3.1. IBM & compatibles (386 DX-20) (4Mb). CD-ROM disk $12.99 (ISBN 1-57594-024-8). *Nonstandard peripherals required:* 2x CD-ROM player, Sound Card, VGA monitor. *Optimal configuration:* 486 XS-33.
Interactive Learning Adventures - Experience All That the Circus Has to Offer.
Kidsoft, Inc.

Lenny's Multimedia Circus. Sep. 1995. *Customer Support:* Telephone support - free (except phone charge).
Windows 3.1. IBM & compatibles (386 DX-20) (4Mb). CD-ROM disk $12.99 (ISBN 1-57594-063-9). *Nonstandard peripherals required:* 2x CD-ROM player, Sound Card, VGA monitor. *Optimal configuration:* 486 SX-33.
Interactive Learning Adventure - Experience All That the Circus Has to Offer. Blister Pack Jewel Case.
Kidsoft, Inc.

Lenny's Music Toons. Sep. 1995. *Customer Support:* Telephone support - free (except phone charge).
Windows 3.1. IBM & compatibles (386 DX-20) (4Mb). CD-ROM disk $12.99 (ISBN 1-57594-025-6). *Nonstandard peripherals required:* 2x CD-ROM player, Sound Card, VGA monitor. *Optimal configuration:* 486 XS-33.
Enter a Whole New World of Music Toon Adventures Where Music & Cartoons Come Alive Thru Interactive Animation.
Kidsoft, Inc.

Lenny's Music Toons. Sep. 1995. *Customer Support:* Telephone support - free (except phone charge).
Windows 3.1. IBM & compatibles (386 DX-20) (4Mb). CD-ROM disk $12.99 (ISBN 1-57594-064-7). *Nonstandard peripherals required:* 2x CD-ROM player, Sound Card, VGA monitor. *Optimal configuration:* 486 SX-33.
Enter a Whole New World of Music Toon Adventures Where Music & Cartoons Come Alive Thru Interactive Animation. Blister Pack Jewel Case.
Kidsoft, Inc.

Lenny's Time Machine. Sep. 1995. *Customer Support:* Telephone support - free (except phone charge).
Windows 3.1. IBM & compatibles (386 DX-20) (4Mb). CD-ROM disk $12.99 (ISBN 1-57594-026-4). *Nonstandard peripherals required:* 2x CD-ROM player, Sound Card, VGA monitor. *Optimal configuration:* 486 SX-33.
Travel Through Time in a Multimedia World of Games, Puzzles & Creative Adventures.
Kidsoft, Inc.

Lenny's Time Machine. Sep. 1995. *Customer Support:* Telephone support - free (except phone charge).
Windows 3.1. IBM & compatibles (386 DX-20) (4Mb). CD-ROM disk $12.99 (ISBN 1-57594-065-5). *Nonstandard peripherals required:* 2x CD-ROM player, Sound Card, VGA monitor. *Optimal configuration:* 486 SX-33.
Travel Through Time in a Multimedia World of Games, Puzzles & Creative Adventures. Blister Pack Jewel Case.
Kidsoft, Inc.

Leonard Nimoy Science Fiction. (The/Gold Collection: Vol. I). Jan. 1996. *Items Included:* CD-ROM & instruction card. *Customer Support:* 90 days unlimited warranty.
MAC. 68030 Processor (8Mb). Contact publisher for price. *Addl. software required:* Quicktime 2.0. *Optimal configuration:* 12Mb hard drive space.
Windows. 486/DX 33 (8Mb). Contact publisher for price. *Addl. software required:* Video for Windows V1-1D/Quicktime for Windows 2.0. *Optimal configuration:* 12Mb hard drive space.
A Compilation of 22 Science Fiction Works, Including 12 Complete Novels. Authors Include Jules Verne, H.G. Wells, Mary Shelley, Robert Louis Stevenson. Leonard Nimoy Is the Spokesman for the Project. A Portfolio of Original Artwork from the Various Periods Greatest Illustrators, Frank Kelly Freas & Ed Emshwiller. Real Time Videos Will Include Interviews with Renowned Experts, James Gunn & George Slusser.
Global MediaNet Corporation.

Leonard Nimoy Science Fiction. (The/Gold Collection: Vol. II). Jan. 1996. *Items Included:* CD-ROM & instruction card. *Customer Support:* 90 days unlimited warranty.
MAC. 68030 Processor (8Mb). Contact publisher for price. *Addl. software required:* Quicktime 2.0. *Optimal configuration:* 12Mb hard drive space.
Windows. 486/DX 33 (8Mb). Contact publisher for price. *Addl. software required:* Video for Windows V1-1D/Quicktime for Windows 2.0. *Optimal configuration:* 12Mb hard drive space.
A Compilation of 22 Science Fiction Works, Including 12 Complete Books. Authors Include Paul Anderson, Murry Leinster, David Osborn, Manly Wade Wellman, Bertram Chandler, Edgar Allen Poe. Leonard Nimoy Is the Spokesman. A Portfolio of Original Artwork from the Various Periods Greatest Illustrators, Frank Kelly Freas & Ed Emshwiller. Real Time Videos Will Include Interviews with Experts, James Gunn & George Slusser.
Global MediaNet Corporation.

LePrint. Version: 3.1. May 1989. *Compatible Hardware:* IBM PC, PC XT, PC AT & compatibles. *Operating System(s) Required:* PC-DOS 2.0 or higher, MS-DOS. *Memory Required:* 384k.
standard package $195.00, incl. 5 type styles.
extended package $495.00, incl. standard package plus 28 optional type styles.
add'l. type pkgs. (7 total) $75.00 ea.
Command-Based Desktop Publishing Software

TITLE INDEX

Package for Printing High Quality Text & Graphics. Thirty-Two Available Type Styles That Can Be Printed in Sizes Ranging from 4 Point to over 10 Inches Tall. Can Also Output Your Preferred Type Style in Obliqued, Condensed, Expanded or Outlined Form. Angled Text, Reversed Text & the Ability to Print Text in a Circle Are Just a Few of LePrint's Special Features. User Can See Document Exactly As It Will Be Printed with LePrint's WYSIWYG Preview Mode. Other Features Include: Automatic Reformatting, Multiple Columns, Hyphenation, Letter Pair Kerning, Variable Letter Spacing & Tracking. Also Allows for the Integration of Graphic Files. Supports Many Popular Word Processors & Any Non-Supported Processor That Can Create an ASCII File. Will Output to over 180 Dot Matrix Printers, Postscript Laser Printers & Non-Postscript Laser Printers.
LeBaugh Software Corp.

Les Manley: Lost in L.A. Sep. 1991. *Items Included:* Catalog, copy protection device, manual, & proof of purchase card. *Customer Support:* Technical support 408-296-8400, 90 day limited warranty.
IBM DOS 2.1 or higher (640k). IBM & compatibles, recommended; 8MHz AT class or faster. $59.95. *Optimal configuration:* Hard drive, keyboard, mouse, graphics card, & sound board.
Animated Graphic Adventure for Adults. To Unravel the Mystery of the Kidnapping of the Hippest Stars in Hollywood, Les Manley Must Scour La La Land - Sifting Through Out-of-Work Actors, Rock Stars & Gorgeous Babes.
Accolade, Inc.

LeScript. *Version:* 1.6. *Compatible Hardware:* IBM PC & true compatibles, PC XT; TRS-80 Model I, Model II, Model III, Model 4, Model 4P, Model 12, Model 16; Tandy 1000, 1200, 2000; Lobo MAX-80, LNW-80; LNW-TEAM; PMC-81; Holmes VID-80. *Operating System(s) Required:* MS-DOS 2.0 or higher, TRSDOS 1.3, 2.0, 2.3, 2.7, 2.8, 4.2, 6.0, 6.1, LDOS 5.1, LS-DOS 6.1, DOSPLUS 3.4 or 3.5, NEWDOS, NEWDOS/80, CP/M Plus 2.2 or 3.0. *Memory Required:* TRS-DOS 48k, MS-DOS 128k.
TRS-80 Model I, Model III; LNW-80, LNW-TEAM; Holmes VID-80; Lobo MAX-80. $129.95.
IBM PC, PC XT; Tandy 1000, 1200, 2000; TRS-DOS 2.0, 4.2; CP/M. $199.95.
Word Processor Featuring All the Basic Editing Functions. Can Handle ASCII, BASIC Program, EDTASM, Scriptsit, & VisiCalc Files. Other Features Include Form Letters, Chaining Files for Unattended Printing, Disk Directories, Special Characters Available from the Keyboard, & up to 55 Programmable Macro Keys with Text or Command Strings with No Limit on Length. Provides On-Line Help.
Anitek Software Products.

Lessons on Ada, 2 vols. Jun. 1983. *Compatible Hardware:* IBM PC, PC XT, PC AT, & compatibles. *Operating System(s) Required:* PC-DOS/MS-DOS 2.0 or higher. *Memory Required:* 150k.
disk $6000.00.
Features a Multi-User Interactive Computer-Aided Course in Ada Programming, Designed for Those with Previous Programming Experience. Provides a Core of Concepts Necessary for Students to Practice Ada Programming or to Begin Working on Actual Projects Using Modern Software Engineering Techniques. VOLUME I Introduces the User to the Ada Language & Modern Programming Techniques. VOLUME II Provides Elements for Advanced Programming.
Alsys, Inc.

LetraFont Type Library & LetraStudio.
Macintosh Plus or higher. LetraFont Typefaces $75.00.
LetraStudio software (includes four display typefaces) $495.00.
Display Typefaces & Type Customization Software.
Letraset USA.

Letraset Design Solutions. *Compatible Hardware:* Apple Macintosh.
contact publisher for price.
Letraset USA.

Letraset Design Templates. *Compatible Hardware:* Apple Macintosh. *Memory Required:* 512k.
3.5" disk $129.95.
Collection of over Forty Templates. Contains Page Layouts for Newsletters, Brochures, Catalogs, Envelopes & Other Applications. Each Template Comes in a Variety of Sizes & Styles & Can Be Used As is or Customized.
Letraset USA.

Letraset Type Library. *Compatible Hardware:* Apple Macintosh, Macintosh Plus. *Memory Required:* 2000k.
3.5" disk $75.00.
LetraStudio Software (Four Display Typefaces). 3.5" disk $495.00.
Display Typefaces & Type Customization Software.
Letraset USA.

LetraStudio. *Compatible Hardware:* Apple Macintosh.
contact publisher for price.
Letraset USA.

LetrTuck. *Compatible Hardware:* Apple Macintosh Plus.
3.5" disk $147.00.
Professional Letter Spacing. Gives Users Control over the Pre-Set Character Spacing Built into Desktop Publishing Software.
EDCO Services, Inc.

Let's Color: Coloring Book Software. Mar. 1996. *Items Included:* CD-ROM. *Customer Support:* 1-800-824-5179 product information; 1-800-543-0453 technical support.
Windows 3.1 or higher, DOS 3.3 or higher (4Mb). CD-ROM disk $29.50 (ISBN 0-538-64879-1). *Nonstandard peripherals required:* 256 color display.
Mac System 6.0.8 or higher. Color Macintosh, 256 colors (4Mb). CD-ROM disk $29.50 (ISBN 0-538-64877-5).
Let's Color Is a Multimedia Coloring Book Complete with Sounds, Textures & Patterns. Includes Dozens of Pictures Including Themes of Dinosaurs, the Rain Forest & More. Promotes Creative Expression. K-6.
South-Western Publishing Co.

Let's Do DOS Plus. *Version:* 2.0. Jul. 1992. *Items Included:* 3.5" & 5.25" program disks, saddle stapled manual.
MS/PC-DOS. IBM PC/X6/286/386/486 or higher & compatibles (256k RAM required). disk $19.95 (ISBN 0-9632069-0-7).
Program Allows User to Perform Basic DOS Functions without Having to Learn Complicated DOS Commands. User Simply Answers Clear On-Screen Questions. Information Screens Teach DOS Commands to Those Who Wish to Learn Them. An On-Line Glossary of DOS Terms Is Included.
Bridge Learning Systems.

Let's Go: The Budget Guide to Europe. 1994.
Macintosh. CD-ROM disk $49.95. *Nonstandard peripherals required:* CD-ROM drive.
Contains Historical Information about European Countries Including 100 Pictures of Countries, Cities, & Sights, Maps & Travel Essentials. Publisher Has Integrated a Language Section That Allows Users to Hear the Pronunciation of Key Names & Common Travel-Related Words in French, German, Italian, & Spanish. A Phone Book Section Provides Information for All Hotels, Restaurants & Museums Represented in the Disc.
Compton's NewMedia, Inc.

Let's Make a Wheel. *Items Included:* Bound manual. *Customer Support:* Free hotline - no time limit; 30 day limited warranty; updates are $5/disk plus S&H.
MS-DOS 2.0 or higher. IBM & compatibles (128k). disk $29.95.
Lottery Wheeling System. It Will Wheel All Possible Combinations to 59 Numbers & Wheel up to 100 Numbers in Abbreviated Systems.
Dynacomp, Inc.

Let's Play Monopoly. Greg Susong. Jan. 1984. *Compatible Hardware:* NEC 8201A; Radio Shack Model 100. *Memory Required:* 24k.
Radio Shack. cassette $29.95 (ISBN 0-932095-03-8).
NEC PC. cassette $29.95 (ISBN 0-932095-04-6).
Custom Software Engineering, Inc.

Let's Pretend: Our World Is a Playground. Mind Magic Productions. Nov. 1995. *Items Included:* Bonus value added Educational Picture-Dictionary Coloring Book (48 pages) adding definitions & Pronunciation to the 45 words introduced in the CD-ROM. *Customer Support:* 90 day warranty, tech. support available: (941) 355-3057.
Windows 3.1 or higher. IBM PC & compatibles (8Mb). CD-ROM disk $19.95 (ISBN 1-888489-00-6). *Nonstandard peripherals required:* CD-ROM drive. *Optimal configuration:* Printer - Color or gray scale, Double-speed CD-ROM drive.
Macintosh System 7.0 or higher. Macintosh LCIII or higher (68030/33 minimum) (8Mb). *Optimal configuration:* Color or gray scale printer, double speed CD-ROM drive.
Exciting Adventures of "Flash the Firefly" As He Travels from an Attic, to a Rain Forest, to an Ocean, & the Desert. Nine Stunning Screens with over 200 Original Animations, New Sound, Music & Humorous Actions to Delight & Educate Children. Includes Electronic Coloring Book with Print Option, Introduces 45 New Words As "Flash" Spells Them Out, & Contains Bonus Educational Picture-Dictionary Coloring Book Which Adds Pronunciation & Definitions to the Words Introduced in the CD-ROM.
Ringling Multimedia Corp.

Letterhead. Brian Lee et al. Jun. 1986. *Compatible Hardware:* Apple Macintosh; IBM PC, PC XT, PC AT. *General Requirements:* Graphics adapter for IBM.
Macintosh. 3.5" disk $79.95 (Order no.: MACDSK-5513).
IBM. disk $79.95 (Order no.: IBMDSK-4513).
Integrates Word Processing, an Address File, & Graphics Capabilities. On-Screen Windows Give User a Choice of Many Different Business & Personal Letter Formats, Plus a Wide Range of Typefaces. User May Design Letterhead & Stationery, Personalize Letters, Print Labels, & Add Graphics.
Broderbund Software, Inc.

Letterip. Jan. 1987. *Compatible Hardware:* LaserWriter printer Apple Macintosh; IBM PC & compatibles.

3.5" disk $75.00.
Customized PostScript Template Which When Downloaded to a PostScript Printer Translates a Text File into a Customized Business Letter That Can Include Letterhead.
Random Access.

LetterPerfect. *Version:* DOS 1.0, Macintosh 2.1. Jul. 1990. *Items Included:* Workbook, manual, templates. *Customer Support:* 800-541-5096 toll free calling & free support.
DOS 2.0 or higher. IBM PC & compatibles (330k). disk $149.00. *Optimal configuration:* Disk drives: One 720k or two 360k drives, hard disk space: 1.8mb. *Networks supported:* 10 Net, Novell Netware, IBM PC network, AT&T Start Group, Nexos, DNA, PC NOS, LN Smart, 3COM 3 Plus Open, TOPS 2.0, Vianet, grapevine.
Entry-Level Word Processor Compatible with WORDPERFECT 5.1. On-Line Help, Pull-Down Menus, & "Fast Key" Access to Features Make the Product Easy to Learn & Use. Familiar WORDPERFECT Function Keys Are Also Available. Runs Well on Machines with Limited Storage, Such As Battery-Powered Laptops. Features Include: 80,000-Word Speller, On-Screen Thesaurus, Graphics Integration, Font Support, Merge, Endnotes, Search, Print Preview, Macros, & Extensive Printer Support. When WORDPERFECT 5.1 Files Are Retrieved into LetterPerfect, All Codes Stay Intact, So Even 5.1 Features Not Included in LetterPerfect (e.g., Tables, Equations, Columns) Will Not Be Affected.
WordPerfect Corp.

LetterPerfect for Macintosh. *Version:* 2.1. Jul. 1992. *Items Included:* Certificate of license, reference manual, low-density disks 3.5".
Customer Support: 800-228-4144 7 a.m. - 6 p.m.; 801-226-5522 6 p.m. - 7 a.m..
Macintosh. Mac Plus or higher (1Mb for Sys 6; 2Mb for System 7). $149.00 SRP. *Optimal configuration:* Hard disk with 2.2Mb. *Networks supported:* Network ready.
A Streamlined Version of WordPerfect 2.1 for Macintosh & Contains All the Features Needed for Creating Everyday Memos, Letters & Reports. Features of This System 7 Savvy Program Include Columns, Graphics, Stationery, Merge, Speller, Thesaurus, Headers & Footers. Files Created with LetterPerfect Are Fully Compatible with WordPerfect for Macintosh.
WordPerfect Corp.

Lettertip. *Compatible Hardware:* Apple Macintosh, IBM PC & compatibles.
$75.00.
Customized PostScript Template Which, When Downloaded to a PostScript Output Device, Translates a Text File into a Customized Business Letter That Can Include Company Logos.
Random Access.

LetterWorks. Nov. 1988. *Items Included:* 500-page softcover book containing all the letters. *Customer Support:* Free phone support, no time limitation.
PC-DOS (256k). IBM-compatibles. disk $99.95 (ISBN 0-929543-01-7). *Addl. software required:* Any IBM-compatible word processor. Macintosh (128k). 3.5" disk $79.95 (ISBN 0-929543-02-5). *Addl. software required:* Any Macintosh word processor.
400 Business Model Business Letters, Proposals, Memos, Press Releases, & Other Business Documents. User Finds the Document He Wants in the LetterWorks Book & Calls it up from Within His Word Processor Using the LetterPower Disk Which Contains Text (ASCII) Files of All the Letters.
Round Lake Publishing Co.

Lettronics 731. *Compatible Hardware:* IBM PC, Apple IIe. *Operating System(s) Required:* CP/M.
contact publisher for price.
Electronic Mail System That Allows User to Edit Messages Using the Editor Provided. Messages May Be Sent & Received via Direct Distance Dialing, Any of the Available Electronic Mail Carriers, Telex, TWX Subscriber in the World via Western Union's EasyLink, or Similar Service Offered by RCA & TeleNet.
Satellite Technology & Research.

Level II COBOL. *Operating System(s) Required:* UNIX. *Language(s):* C, Machine.
contact publisher for price.
Mainframe-Level Compiler for ANSI'74 COBOL Programs. Designed for Business Applications.
BBN Software Products Corp.

Level II COBOL. *Operating System(s) Required:* XENIX, UNIX, CP/M, CP/M-86, MP/M, MP/M-86, PC-DOS, MS-DOS, RSX-11. *Memory Required:* 128k.
disk $1600.00.
Level II Compiler That Enables Microcomputers to Compile & Run Programs Written in ANSI'74 COBOL. Can Be Used to Execute Existing Mainframe COBOL Programs with Minimal Source Code Modification or to Develop New Applications for the Microcomputer Environment. Implements the ANSI '74 COBOL Standard to the 'High' Level Established by the U.S. Government & Includes All the Modules Defined by ANSI Standard, Except the Communication Module & the Report Writer. Tested & Validated by the Federal Compiler Testing Center.
Micro Focus, Inc. (California).

Level5. *Compatible Hardware:* DEC MicroVAX 2000, VAX 8800.
MicroVAX 2000 $4000.00.
$36000.00 VAX 8800.
Run-only versions are available from $1,600 to $14,400.
Interfaces to a Variety of Databases & Application Programs. Applications Developed in Level5 on the VAX Are Also Portable to Other Level5 Environments.
Information Builders, Inc.

Level5 Macintosh.
Macintosh Plus or higher (2MB). one-time fee $685.00.
unlimited usage site license $3000.00.
single run-time version $150.00.
Expert System Shell.
Information Builders, Inc.

Levinson Lyon Business Accounting Systems: A-R, A-P, G-L, Inventory. *Version:* 2.12. Jun. 1992. *Items Included:* 5 manuals, including jumpstart manual. *Customer Support:* Free 2 hrs. on-site training; 1 yr. maintenance, $191.40.
MS-DOS. IBM PC compatible (512k). disk $89.95 (Order no.: CSCLLB01). *Networks supported:* Novell NetWare, NetWare Lite, LANtastic, other Novell compatible.
Multi-Company, Multi-User - Supports Novell NetWare. Accounts Receivable, Billing & Inventory Control: Prints Invoices, Reduces Inventory, Posts to Customer Ledger, & Accumulates Sales Analysis in One Step; Generates a Gross Profit Analysis for Any Invoice, Any Salesperson, Any Territory, or Any Customer. Accounts Payable: Tracks Expenses, Prints Checks, 1099's; Uses Cash or Accrual Method of Accounting; Complete Bank Reconciliation. General Ledger: Produces Financial Reports for Any Period in the Two "Open" Years, up to 26 Periods - Interim Year-End Close Allows Processing to Continue While Awaiting Audit Adjustments.
CharterHouse Software Corp.

Levinson Lyon Data Link & Report Writer: D-L & R-W. *Version:* 2.12. Jun. 1992. *Items Included:* User manual. *Customer Support:* Free 2 hrs. on-site training; 1 yr. maintenance, $191.40.
MS-DOS. IBM PC compatible (512k). disk $79.95 (Order no.: CSCLLDL01). *Networks supported:* Novell NetWare, NetWare Lite, LANtastic, other Novell compatible.
Allows User to Transfer Levinson Lyon Data to Other Programs (Spreadsheets, Data Bases, Wordprocessors) or to Create Custom Reports. User Can Do Instant Queries on Data or, May Want to Perform Calculations on a Numeric Data Field. The Selected Data May Be Displayed on the Screen, Printed in a Standard Print Format, Graphed, Incorporated into a Custom Report or Transferred.
CharterHouse Software Corp.

Levinson Lyon Fixed Assets: F-A. *Version:* 2.12. Jun. 1992. *Items Included:* User manual.
Customer Support: Free 2 hrs. on-site training; 1 yr. maintenance, $191.40.
MS-DOS. IBM PC compatible (512k). disk $79.95 (Order no.: CSCLLFA01). *Networks supported:* Novell NetWare, NetWare Lite, LANtastic, other Novell compatible.
Fixed Assets, Continuously Updated since 1979, Provides for up to 34 Depreciation Methods & Current Requirements for Luxury Auto Cap. Designed for Use with Multiple Companies, the Software Can Process an Unlimited Number of Clients. The Program Even Automatically Determines Whether the Mid-Quarter Convention Applies & Adjusts Year-to-Date Depreciation in the Fiscal Year's Last Quarter. For Each Asset, the Depreciation Method, Life, Salvage, Type, Location, & Serial Number Can Be Set up Differently for Book, Federal, State, & Two Other Types of Side-by-Side Reporting - Including Alternative Minimum Tax.
CharterHouse Software Corp.

Levinson Lyon Manufacturing Inventory. *Version:* 2.12. Jun. 1992. *Items Included:* User manual. *Customer Support:* Free 2 hrs. on-site training; 1 yr. maintenance, $191.40.
MS-DOS. IBM PC compatible (512k). disk $79.95 (Order no.: CSCLLMF01). *Networks supported:* Novell NetWare, NetWare Lite, LANtastic, other Novell compatible.
Manufacturing Inventory Control Offers Integrated Control of Finished Goods, Subassemblies & Component Inventories, & Allows Costing Using a Multilevel, Indented Bill-of-Material Processor. Features Include: Inventory File Maintenance (20 Alphanumeric Part Key), Bill of Material File Maintenance, Product Cost Reporting, Production Activity Entry, Bill of Material Explosion & Update, Status of Commitment of Finished Goods and/or Component Inventories, Suggested Component Purchase Order Reports, Pick-Lists, Where-Used Reports. Prints Physical Inventory Worksheets, Item Labels, Price Lists, Component Inventory Valuations Using LIFO, FIFO (Unlimited Layers), or Average Cost. Ties in with Levinson Lyon O/E, A/R with Billing, P/O & G/L Systems.
CharterHouse Software Corp.

Levinson Lyon MICR Check Writer: MICR. *Version:* 2.12. Jun. 1992. *Items Included:* User manual. *Customer Support:* Free 2 hrs. on-site training; 1 yr. maintenance, $191.40.
MS-DOS. IBM PC compatible (512k). disk $79.95 (Order no.: CSCLLMI01). *Networks supported:* Novell NetWare, NetWare Lite, LANtastic, other Novell compatible.
With the New Laser MICR Check Writer Option for the Levinson Lyon Accounts Payable Software & a Laser Printer with MICR Capability, There Is No More Storing Boxes of Custom Checks for Multiple Bank Accounts and/or Multiple

TITLE INDEX

Companies/Clients. Print the Complete Check on Blank (Safety Paper) Stock, Including Company Logo, Bank Name & Logo, MICR Line, Check Form, Duplicate Copy, & Even the Signature, All in a Single Pass Through the Printer.
CharterHouse Software Corp.

Levinson Lyon Order Entry: O-E. Version: 2.12. Jun. 1992. Items Included: User manual. Customer Support: Free 2 hrs. on-site training; 1 yr. maintenance, $191.40.
MS-DOS. IBM PC compatible (512k). disk $79.95 (Order no.: CSCLLOE01). Networks supported: Novell NetWare, NetWare Lite, LANtastic, other Novell compatible.
Order Entry, in One Step, Prints Customer Workorders (Pick-Lists) & Shipping Labels, Commits Finished Goods Ordered, Updates Customer Orders & Backorders. Features Include: Open & Backorder Reports by Customer and/or Inventory Item, Order Profile by Customer or Item (On-Screen or Print), Selective Partial Billing on Previously Entered Orders with Automatic Backorders, Order Corrections. Shipment History/Search Provides Access to Invoiced Orders with Complete Information of Items/Prices Shipped. Ties in with Levinson Lyon A/R with Billing & Manufacturing Systems.
CharterHouse Software Corp.

Levinson Lyon Payroll: P-R. Version: 2.12. Jun. 1992. Items Included: User manual. Customer Support: Free 2 hrs. on-site training; 1 yr. maintenance, $191.40.
MS-DOS. IBM PC compatible (512k). disk $79.95 (Order no.: CSCLLPR01). Networks supported: Novell NetWare, NetWare Lite, LANtastic, other Novell compatible.
Payroll, Continously Updated since 1979, Provides for Full-Function Payroll, After-the-Fact Entry & Laser Printing of Yearly (W2) & Quarterly (941, DE3) Forms. Designed for Use with Multiple Companies, the Software Can Process an Unlimited Number of Clients. System Functions Include Automatic Computation of Withholdings (Federal, State, Local, FICA, SDI), Accumulation of: Group Totals for Workman's Compensation, 401k Data, Tips Reported, & 125 Deductions, FICA & Federal/State Withholding Deposit Check Computation & Printing, Quarterly (941, DE3DP, DE3B) & Yearly (W2) Tax Reports.
CharterHouse Software Corp.

Levinson Lyon Purchase Order: P-O. Version: 2.12. Jun. 1992. Items Included: User manual. Customer Support: Free 2 hrs. on-site training; 1 yr. maintenance, $191.40.
MS-DOS. IBM PC compatible (512k). disk $79.95 (Order no.: CSCLLPO01). Networks supported: Novell NetWare, NetWare Lite, LANtastic, other Novell compatible.
Purchase Order Module Offers Integrated Control of Goods & Services Being Ordered with Automatic Preparation of Accounts Payable Vouchers & Posting of Received Items to Inventory. Features Include: Purchase Order Form Printing (Identifying the Items Being Ordered by Your or Vendor No., the Time & Mode of Delivery, & the Expected/Negotiated Cost), On-Line Purchase Order Profile (by Vendor or Item), Open Purchase Order Reports (by Vendor, Buyer, or PO), Incoming Item Analysis Report in Date Requested Sequence (by Vendor, Buyer, or Your Item ID), Vendor Item Cross Reference Listing (20 Alphanumeric Item ID). Ties in with Levinson Lyon A/P & Inventory Systems.
CharterHouse Software Corp.

Levinson Lyon UPS Computerized Manifest: UPS. Version: 2.12. Jun. 1992. Items Included: User manual. Customer Support: Free 2 hrs. on-site training; 1 yr. maintenance, $191.40.

MS-DOS. IBM PC compatible (512k). disk $79.95 (Order no.: CSCLLUPS01). Networks supported: Novell NetWare, NetWare Lite, LANtastic, other Novell compatible.
UPS Module Eliminates the Need for Calculating & Handwriting Shipping Labels, COD Tags, & UPS Shipping Manifests. Integrated with Levinson Lyon Order Entry & Billing, There Is No Double Entry of Shipping Addresses or Freight Charges. In Addition, the Software Allows Manual Entry of Shipments Not Related to Orders or Invoices & It Meets Current UPS Certification Requirements. Low Cost Updates of Rate Tables Are Available.
CharterHouse Software Corp.

Lex Elite Word Processing/Database System. Version: 9D. Jul. 1990. Compatible Hardware: IBM PC & compatibles, VAX, NCR, Sequent. Operating System(s) Required: MS-DOS, UNIX, XENIX, VMS, RSX, TSX, RSTS. Memory Required: 512k. General Requirements: Hard disk. Items Included: User manual, tutorial, template, refcard. Customer Support: 30 days free 800 hotline, annual contracts available. $395.00 - $9995.00.
Word-Processor/Office Applications System with Built-In Database. All Lex Files Are 100% ASCII & All Aspects Are Customizable - Including Function Keys, Menus, Help Screens, Error Messages, Printer & Terminal Drivers & Database Reports & Forms. Features Include Spelling Checker, Thesaurus, Pull-Down Menus, Page Preview Pop-Up Help Windows & More.
Trajectory Software, Inc.

LexaSystem. Sep. 1992. Items Included: User manual.
Macintosh (2Mb). Contact publisher for price. Optimal configuration: 68030 chip preferred, 4Mb RAM, hard disk. Networks supported: AppleTalk, AppleShare.
Component Software Can Be Pieced Together to Form a Customized Law Practice Management System.
Xram Xpert Systems.

Lexegete A/B/C. Version: 4.0. Dec. 1995. Compatible Hardware: Apple Macintosh, IBM PC, PS/2 & compatibles. Operating System(s) Required: Mac DOS, PC-DOS/MS-DOS, OS/2, Windows 95. Memory Required: 1000k. Items Included: Binder, manual, PC-Write. Customer Support: 120 days warranty, free telephone support, upgrades-$15.00/volume.
3.5" disk $39.95, per volume (Order no.: LEX913). Nonstandard peripherals required: Mono Graphics Adaptor. Addl. software required: Clarisworks, MS-Word.
5-Megabyte Library of Lectionary Sermon Planning Tools for Matthew, Mark & Luke Based on the Common Lectionaries, Written by 70 Scholars & Pastors. Each File Includes Textual Setting, Analysis, Strategy, References, Worship Suggestions & Further Readings.
Tischrede Software.

Lexeqete: Matthew, Luke, & Mark. Compatible Hardware: Apple Macintosh, IBM PC. General Requirements: Clarisworks, Microsoft Word. 3.5" disk $39.95.
Lectionary Sermon Planning.
Tischrede Software.

Lexicographer: Multimedia Dictionary Authoring. Version: Commercial. Jan. 1996. Items Included: Lexicographer, Lexica, manuals & marketing. Customer Support: Email support - support abiogenesis.com, no charge; fax support - 360-733-6289, no charge; phone support - 360-650-9335, no charge; WWW support - http://www.portal.com/nabiogen, no charge.

LH ONLINE: ON-LINE PUBLIC ACCESS

MacOS 7.X (4Mb). 3.5" disk $299.99. Nonstandard peripherals required: Speech manager. Addl. software required: Word processor or text editor. Networks supported: Appletalk.
Powerful, Easy-to-Use Mac-Based Dictionary Authoring Software That Allows Authors & Publishers to Quickly Create Commercial Quality Computer Dictionaries with Graphics & Sound. Includes Lexica Dictionary-Viewing Software.
Abiogenesis Software.

Lexicographer: Multimedia Dictionary Authoring. Version: Academic. Jan. 1996. Items Included: Lexicographer, Lexica, manuals & reproducible teacher's guide with lesson plans. Customer Support: Email support - support abiogenesis.com, no charge; fax support - 360-733-6289, no charge; phone support - 360-650-9335, no charge; WWW support - http://www.portal.com/nabiogen, no charge.
MacOS 7.X (4Mb). 3.5" disk $249.99. Nonstandard peripherals required: Speech manager. Addl. software required: Word processor or text editor. Networks supported: Appletalk.
Powerful, Easy-to-Use Mac-Based Dictionary Authoring Software Designed for Teachers & High School/College Students to Create Electronic Dictionaries, Word Lists, & Indexes. Includes Lexica Dictionary-Viewing Software.
Abiogenesis Software.

LexiROM Meyers, Duden & Langenscheidt's. 80386 (4Mb). CD-ROM disk $299.95 (ISBN 3-411-06931-7, Order no.: 069317). Addl. software required: Microsoft Windows 3.1 or higher (mouse recommended). Networks supported: IBM 2Mb.
5 Reference Books on 1 CD: LexiROM Meyers Standard Lexikonin Drei Banden, Duden Band 1: Die Dt. Rechtschreibung, Duden Band 5: Das Frendworterbuch, Duden Band 8: Die Sinn-Und Sachverwandten Worter, Langenscheidts Taschenworterbuch Englisch. 450,000 Entries, 2,000 Pictures & Maps, 200 National Anthems, 50 Musical Examples, 50 Bird Calls, Numerous Animation & Video Clips.
Langenscheidt Pubs., Inc.

LH 'O': Library Helper 'Overdues'. Compatible Hardware: Apple II, II+, IIe, IIc. $69.00.
Comprehensive Record-Keeping System That Generates Overdue Notices. Eliminates Manual Title Drawer Searches & Hand Written Notices. Allows User to Sort by Record Number, Date, Name, Homeroom, Title, Author, DD Number or Fine.
SMS (Southern Micro Systems).

LH Online. Version: 1.0. Bob Pritchett & Jennifer Pritchett. Aug. 1991. Items Included: Manual. Customer Support: Free customer support.
MS-DOS. 8286 or higher (1Mb). A) single user $600.00; B) network version, 2-5 users $900.00; C) network version, 6 users $1200.00. Optimal configuration: 2MB memory; stacker co-processor. Networks supported: Novell & Lan Bios-compatible networks.
Searches All Author, Title, Subject, Publisher, & Note Fields Using Boolean Logic. Displays Fully Records in AACR2 Card Format. Produces Reports by Subject, Author, Title, Publisher, or Call Number, & Creates Author & Subject Authority Lists. Suitable for Small Libraries & Special Collections in Larger Libraries.
Scarecrow Pr., Inc.

LH Online: On-Line Public Access Catalog. 1992.
IBM AT 286, 386 & compatibles (1Mb). disk $600.00, Single User. Networks supported:

Novell & Lan Bios.
$900.00, Network Version.
$1200.00, Network Version (6 or more users).
Makes Simple or Complex Searches with Boolean Logic. Searches All Author, Title, Tracings, & Note Fields. Displays Records in AACR2 Card Format. Displays Full Record, Including Multiple Note Fields. Prints Reports by Subject, Author, Title, Call Number, or Publisher. Offers Multiple Report Formats. Prints Bibliographic Data for Patrons. Makes "See" & "See Also" Records. Creates Author & Subject Authority Lists. Accepts LIBRARIAN'S HELPER Data Disks, Microlif MARC Records & Keyboard Entry.
Scarecrow Pr., Inc.

Liaison.
Macintosh 512KE or higher. 3.5" disk $295.00.
Provides Dialup Access to & Universal Bridging of AppleTalk, EtherTalk, FlashTalk & ArcTalk.
Infosphere.

LibMan. *Customer Support:* 800-929-8117 (customer service).
MS-DOS. Commodore 128; CP/M. disk $49.99 (ISBN 0-87007-712-0).
Provides Several Unique Functions in an Integrated Operating Environment. First, it Is a General-Purpose Data Storage Which Helps User Better Manage & Control Data Resources. It Efficiently Stores ASCII & Non-ASCII Data File As Separate Members in a Library File, Using Indexed Table of Contents. You Can Assign a Password to the USERID to Help Protect User Files from Reading or Writing. Provides Data Security Through Access Control, Password Protection & Data Encryption. On a Hard Disk, Wordstar/Datastar Files Saved 87%, COM Files 68%, BAS Files 64%. To Improve Efficiency in Accessing Files, This System Provides Chronological Version Control of Files Within a Library, General Purpose Data Storage System Which Helps User to Better Manage & User Data Resources. It Efficiently Stores ASCII & ASCII & Non-ASCII Data Files as Separate Members in a Library File, Using an Indexed Table of Contents.
SourceView Software International.

LIBRA Accounts Payable. *Version:* 4.5. 1977. *Compatible Hardware:* IBM PC & compatibles, PC XT, PC AT, 386, 486, Pentium, PS/2. *Operating System(s) Required:* PC-DOS/MS-DOS 3.X, 4X, 5X, 6X, Windows 3.1, Windows 95. *Language(s):* BASIC, C, Assembler. *Memory Required:* 640k. *General Requirements:* Stand-alone or 2Mb Network file server. *Customer Support:* 90 day warranty, onsite training, telephone support.
disk $995.00.
Lets User Forecast with Future Aging & Tracks Activity with Vendors. Features Price File Aging, Multiple Payment Cycles, Generation Checks Including Laser Checks, 1099 Miscellaneous Income Reporting & Check Reconciliation. Optionally Handles Multi-Company Processing.
LIBRA Corp.

LIBRA General Ledger. *Version:* 4.5. 1977. *Compatible Hardware:* IBM PC & compatibles, PC XT, PC AT, 386, 486, Pentium, PS/2. *Operating System(s) Required:* PC-DOS/MS-DOS 3.X, 4X, 5X, 6X, Windows 3.1, Windows 95. *Language(s):* BASIC, C, Assembler. *Memory Required:* 640k. *General Requirements:* Stand-alone or 2Mb Network file server. *Customer Support:* 90 day warranty, onsite training, telephone support.
disk $995.00.
Accommodates Any Combination of Multiple Companies or Division Within Companies (Departments). Features User-Defined Chart of Accounts with Flexible Formatting of Financial Statements & Retention of Full Year's Detail. Allows User to Process Next Fiscal Year Prior to Closing Current Year, Preventing Bottlenecks in the Business Cycle. Custom Financial Statements.
LIBRA Corp.

LIBRA Payroll. *Version:* 4.5. 1978. *Compatible Hardware:* IBM PC & compatibles, PC XT, PC AT, 386, 486, Pentium, PS/2. *Operating System(s) Required:* PC-DOS/MS-DOS 3.X, 4X, 5X, 6X, Windows 3.1, Windows 95. *Language(s):* BASIC, C, Assembler. *Memory Required:* 640k. *General Requirements:* Stand-alone or 2Mb Network file server. *Customer Support:* 90 day warranty, onsite training, telephone support.
disk $1295.00.
Supports Any Combination of Weekly, Biweekly, Semi-Monthly & Monthly Pay Period Payrolls for Hourly & Salaried Employees. Supports up to 98 Companies per Data Base, Handles Skill Types, Worker's Compensation & Labor Distribution, EEOC, Quarterly Reports W2s & Magnetic Media W2s, Direct Deposit, Laserchecks, User Defined Deductions & Paytypes, 401ks & 125 Plans.
LIBRA Corp.

Librarian. *Version:* 6.1. Kent Ochel & Bert Brown. Aug. 1989. *Items Included:* Tutorial disk; 3-ring binder with manual. *Customer Support:* Unlimited free technical support at (512) 251-7541.
Any DOS or Windows. IBM PC; XT; AT & compatibles. disk $99.95.
Macintosh. 3.5" disk $99.95.
Allows the User to Create Permanent Indexes (Concordance) to the Bible Text. Once Created, These Indexes Allow the User to Gain Immediate Access to Verses in the Bible That Pertain to Specific Subject. VERSE SEARCH is required.
Bible Research Systems.

The Librarian. *Items Included:* Full manual. No other products required. *Customer Support:* Free telephone support - no time limit. 30 day warranty.
MS-DOS 3.2 or higher. IBM & compatibles (512k). disk $99.95.
User May Do Any of the Following with THE LIBRARIAN: Enter & Edit Items; Search for Specific Categories or Key Words in Any Field; List All Items in Your File; List All Retrieval Categories with Their Associated Items; List All Major Headings with Categories & Items Grouped Within; Alphabetize Anything Except the Abstracts; Set up Individual Disks to Handle Different Types of Items.
Dynacomp, Inc.

The Librarian. 1981. *Compatible Hardware:* Apple II Series. *Operating System(s) Required:* Apple DOS 3.3. *Language(s):* Applesoft BASIC (source code included). *Memory Required:* 48k.
disk $29.95.
demo disk $8.00.
Allows the User to Store Bibliographic Abstracts of Chapters of Books, Magazine Articles, Videotape Recordings, Songs, Recipes, Computer Programs, or Any Indexable Item Where an Abstract Is Desirable.
Professional Computerware.

Librarian List. *Compatible Hardware:* Apple II+, IIc, IIe; Franklin Ace; IBM PC, PC XT, PC AT. *Operating System(s) Required:* Apple DOS 3.3, MS-DOS 3.1. *Language(s):* BASIC (source code included).
disk $150.00.
Full Library System for the Smaller Institution That Includes Files for Books & Loans. Includes Journal Catalog, Want Lists, Staff Schedules, Text Editor, & Mail List Capabilities.
Andent, Inc.

The Librarian's Helper. *Version:* 5.0. Jennifer Pritchett & Fred Hill. 1991. *Compatible Hardware:* IBM PC & compatibles. *Operating System(s) Required:* PC-DOS/MS-DOS. *Language(s):* CB 86. *Memory Required:* IBM 256k. *General Requirements:* Printer. *Items Included:* Manual. *Customer Support:* Free telephone support.
disk $250.00 (ISBN 0-8108-2200-8).
update or reformat $30.00 (ISBN 0-8108-2045-5).
demo disk free (ISBN 0-8108-2046-3).
Stand-Alone, Menu-Driven Software Designed to Produce Catalog Cards & Labels for Spine, Book Pocket, & Circulation Cards in Conformity with AACR II Standards. Now Compatible with Laser Printers. The Save Feature Allows the Operator to Save the Material Input During a Session & Print It Out Later; Allows the Operator to Make Changes after a Set of Cards & Labels Has Been Produced & Print Out a New Set; Prints Acquisition Lists Sorted by Author, Title, or Call Number; & Allows Transfer of Data Saved on Disk to On-Line Catalogs & Database Programs.
Scarecrow Pr., Inc.

Library. *Compatible Hardware:* Apple Macintosh, Macintosh Plus, SE, II. *General Requirements:* Hard disk, ImageWriter I or II, LaserWriter. *Items Included:* Software for bar code reader communications & user's manual, some customizing included. *Customer Support:* Free telephone support.
3.5" disk (Software) $1995.00.
3.5" disk (Bar code reader) $350.00.
Bar-Code System.
Computext.

Library Assistant. Tom Sherer. 1985. *Compatible Hardware:* IBM PC compatible, THEOS compatible, UNIX compatible. *Operating System(s) Required:* THEOS, UNIX.
disk $10,000.00.
Automated Patron Services Featuring Volume Check-in/out, Volume Reservation, Fine Calculation/Collection, Usage Statistics, Phonetic Title, Subject, Author Search Capability, Electronic Catalog & OCLC Interface. Research Information Management/Phonetic Retrieval System Optional.
Comcepts Systems.

Library Border Book. Phil Bradbury. Sep. 1991. *Items Included:* Instructions & pictorial index and all illustrations. "Idea Station" booklet included. *Customer Support:* Unlimited free telephone support.
Macintosh. MAC Plus (1Mb). $49.95 (ISBN 1-879359-05-7, Order no.: 66.1). *Addl. software required:* Application which can import a graphic.
MS-DOS. PC or compatible (1Mb). $49.95 (ISBN 1-879359-06-5, Order no.: 66.2). *Addl. software required:* Any application which can import graphics. *Optimal configuration:* AT-class computer, 2Mb RAM, hard disk, encapsulated PostScript compatible programs.
Clip Art Borders & Headlines on Disk. Designed for Libraries, Schools & Non-Profit Organizations.
Library Educational Institute, Inc.

Library Information Management System: On-Line Catalog-Circulation. *Version:* 7.1. 1984. *Compatible Hardware:* IBM PC & compatibles; Tandy Model 3000. *Operating System(s) Required:* MS-DOS, PC-DOS. *Memory Required:* 640k. *General Requirements:* Hard disk. *Items Included:* Software & users guide. *Customer Support:* Custom modification available.
disk $995.00.
Librarian Enters Shelf Card Data, Patron ID Data. Computer Will Find Any Material (Book,

TITLE INDEX

Filmstrip, etc.) by Title, Author Subject, Accession Number, Call Number. Will Print a Full Set of Hard-Copy Cards, Patron Library Cards, Inventory Lists, BARCODES. Circulation by Barcode - Library Personnel Strikes Library Card & Patron Is Identified & Any Overdues or Fines Due Are Displayed, with All Other Books Out. Striking the Barcode in the Book Will Check It Out to the Patron. Check-In Is Similar - Just Strike the Barcodes.
Robert H. Geeslin (Educational Programming).

Library Management: Series 900 to 2000.
Compatible Hardware: IBM System/36, System/36 PC; AS/400.
contact publisher for price.
Record & Retrieve Library Card Catalogs.
Manac-Prentice Hall Software, Inc.

Library of ClipArt: Disk Version. Phil Bradbury. Nov. 1990. *Items Included:* One saddle stitched manual, pictorial index. *Customer Support:* Free unlimited telephone support.
Mac Plus or higher (1Mb). $79.95 per section; $319.80 complete 4-vol collection. *Addl. software required:* Any application which can import graphics.
MS-DOS. IBM PC, or compatible (2Mb). $79.95 per section; $319.80 complete collection. *Addl. software required:* Any application which can import graphics.
Library-Related Illustrations & Border Designs for Use As ClipArt. For Paste-up on Newsletter, Flyers, Posters, Bookmarks & Other Printed Publicity. Subjects Includes: Adults, Borders, Children, Announcers, Books, Audio-Visual, Bookmobile, Holiday, etc. Available in 4 Volumes: Spring, Summer, Fall, Winter or As a Complete Collection.
Library Educational Institute, Inc.

Library!: Personal Edition for Windows. Robert K. Haupt. Jun. 1995. *Items Included:* User's guide with glossary & index. *Customer Support:* 1-800 support available.
Windows. IBM PC & compatibles. disk $39.95 (ISBN 1-887494-02-2). *Addl. software required:* Windows.
An Easy-to-Use & Powerful Tool for Managing a Complete Printed Library: Documents, Books, Periodicals, Videotapes, Audiotapes, Computer Files, CD-ROMs, & Collections (e.g. Stamps, Comic Books, etc.).
Image Group International.

Library!: Personal Edition for Windows. Robert K. Haupt. Jun. 1995. *Items Included:* User's guide with glossary & index. *Customer Support:* 1-800 support available.
Windows. IBM PC & compatibles. disk $39.95 (ISBN 1-887494-02-2). *Addl. software required:* Windows.
An Easy-to-Use & Powerful Tool for Managing a Complete Printed Library: Documents, Books, Periodicals, Videotapes, Audiotapes, Computer Files, CD-ROMs, & Collections (e.g. Stamps, Comic Books, etc.).
SourceView Software International.

Library Subject Headings Data Base System.
Daniel D. Stuhlman. Jun. 1986. *Compatible Hardware:* IBM PC & compatibles. *Operating System(s) Required:* MS-DOS, Novell Network. *Memory Required:* 256k.
Novell Net.. contact publisher for price.
MS-DOS. disk $100.00 (ISBN 0-934402-20-5).
Data Base. disk $12.00 (ISBN 0-934402-22-1).
Stores & Retrieves Library Subject Headings. Can Also Be Used to Store Any Subject of 60 or Fewer Characters. Includes Library of Congress Subject Heading for Judaica.
BYLS Pr.

Library Symbol Clip Art. Phil Bradbury. Jun. 1993. *Items Included:* Instructions & Pictorial Index. *Customer Support:* Free unlimited telephone support.
Macintosh. MAC Plus (1Mb). $24.95 (ISBN 1-879359-07-3, Order no.: 300). *Addl. software required:* Program which can import graphic images.
MS-DOS. PC or compatibles (2Mb). $49.95 (ISBN 1-879359-08-1, Order no.: 300.1). *Addl. software required:* Program which can import graphics.
Clip Art Illustrations & Borders Featuring the National Library Symbol in over 80 Different Guises- e.g. Holding Flowers; Wearing a Safari Hat & Reading the Jungle Book; Talking on Telephone; with Cowboy Hat, etc.
Library Educational Institute, Inc.

Lien Writer. *Version:* 3.85. Frank W. Moore. Aug. 1992. *Items Included:* Diskettes & manual. *Customer Support:* 90 days unlimited; 1 yr. maintenance $100.00.
PC-DOS/MS-DOS 3.30 or higher. IBM PC/XT/AT or compatible (640k). disk $299.95 (Order no.: 6500). *Nonstandard peripherals required:* Printer, plain 8.5" x 11" paper. *Optimal configuration:* Any.
Will Do All of the Paperwork in the Mechanic's Lien Process, from Preliminary Notice to Any Form of Release to the Mechanic's Lien Itself for All 50 States.
Auctoritas Software.

Life & Death.
IBM. disk $24.95.
MAC. 3.5" disk $24.95.
Not for the Faint of Heart - or Clumsy of Wrist. You Hold a Human Life in Your Hands As You Cut into Living Flesh. Your Skill with the Scalpel While Monitoring On-Screen EKG, Pulse, Blood Pressure & Other Vital Signs Will Determine Whether Your Patient Goes to Recovery...or the Morgue. Watch Where You Make That Incision.
Software Toolworks.

Life & Death II: The Brain.
DOS. IBM & compatibles. disk $39.95.
Welcome to the Neurosurgery Wing, Doctor. It's the Ultimate Medical Adventure into the Depths & Mysteries of the Human Brain! Your Hectic Day Begins with X-Rays, CAT Scans, Ultra-Sound & MRIs, with Stunning Color Graphics & Digitized Sound. Only You Can Decide - Does Your Patient Need The Knife? Warning: Operate in Nightmare Mode & Things Could Get Completely Out of Hand.
Software Toolworks.

Life Cycle Analysis & Depreciation. *Compatible Hardware:* Apple, IBM.
$99.95.
Dynacomp, Inc.

Life Cycle Cost - LC2M. *Version:* 06/1987. 1979. *Compatible Hardware:* IBM PC & compatibles. *Operating System(s) Required:* MS-DOS, PC-DOS. *Language(s):* Compiled. *Memory Required:* 256k. *Customer Support:* Technical hotline, "Lifetime" support at no charge. $115.00.
Life Cycle Cost Analysis - LC2M Calculates Total Life Cycle Owning Cost by Summing the Present Worth of Annual Fuel, Power, Operating, Maintenance, & Major Overhaul Costs Over the Life of Equipment, Together with Initial Investment Costs. Separate Inflation & Discount Rates Allowed for Each Item. Fully Prompted & Compiled; Menu Driven. Rapid & Flexible. SI Metric or English Units.
MC2 Engineering Software.

LIFE CYCLE ECONOMICS PROGRAM

Life Cycle Cost Analysis. *Items Included:* Full manual. No other products required. *Customer Support:* Free telephone support - no time limit. 30 day warranty.
MS-DOS 3.2 or higher. IBM & compatibles (512k). disk $99.95.
demo disk $5.00.
Calculates the Total Life Cycle Cost of Owning a Piece of Equipment. It Factors in the Present Worth of Annual Fuel, Power, Operating, Maintenance, & Major Overhaul Costs, As Well As the Initial Investment. Separate Inflation & Discount Rates Are Allowed for Each Factor. Savings May Be Included As Negative Costs. Total Life Cycle Costs Savings by Category, & Total Cost per Unit of Capacity (e.g., BTU of Refrigeration) Are Displayed.
Dynacomp, Inc.

Life Cycle Cost Analysis. 1992. *Items Included:* Detailed manuals included with all Dynacomp products. *Customer Support:* Free telephone support to original customer - no time limit; 30 day limited warranty.
MS-DOS 3.2 or higher. IBM PC & compatibles (512k). $99.95 Full System (Add $5.00 for 3 1/2" format; 5 1/4" format standard). *Optimal configuration:* IBM, 256k RAM & an 80-column or wider printer.
demo disk $5.00.
LCCA Calculates the Total Life Cycle Cost of Owning a Piece of Equipment. It Factors in the Present Worth of Annual Fuel, Power, Operating, Maintenance, & Major Overhaul Costs, As Well As the Initial Investment. Separate Inflation & Discount Rates Are Allowed for Each Factor. Savings May Be Included As Negative Costs. Total Life Cycle Costs Savings by Category, & Total Cost per Unit of Capacity (E.G., BTU of Regrigeration) Are Displayed.
Dynacomp, Inc.

Life Cycle Cost Optimization for Piping Insulation. *Items Included:* Full manual. No other products required. *Customer Support:* Free telephone support - no time limit. 30 day warranty.
MS-DOS 3.2 or higher. IBM & compatibles (512k). disk $419.95. *Optimal configuration:* IBM, MS-DOS 3.1 or higher, 640k RAM, & CGA/EGA/VGA (or compatible) graphics capability.
INSULATION Will Save You Time & Money in Deciding on Piping Insulation. You May Select the Insulation Thicknesses That Provide the Lowest Total Installation & Operating Costs over the System Life for Both Piping & Equipment. This Menu-Driven Analysis Tool Comes with a Database of Manhours & Material Costs Which You May Modify for Particular Sites. You May Determine Thermal Losses Without Having to Input the Financial Entries in Order to Review Heat Loss Figures Without Regard to Cost.
Dynacomp, Inc.

Life Cycle Economics Program. *Version:* 2.0. Ricardo Cidale. Aug. 1984. *Compatible Hardware:* Apple II; DEC Rainbow, DEC VT180; Hewlett-Packard; IBM PC; Kaypro; Morrow; North Star; Superbrain; TRS-80 Model I, Model III; Vector Graphics; Victor; Zenith. *Operating System(s) Required:* CP/M, CP/M-86, PC-DOS, MS-DOS. *Language(s):* CB-80. *Memory Required:* CP/M 64k, MS-DOS 256k. *General Requirements:* 2 disk drives, printer.
disk $295.00.
8" disk $295.00.
3.5" disk $295.00.
demo disk $38.00.
Multiple Phased Life Cycle Economics Program That Uses the Net Present Value Method to Determine Lowest Cost among Project Alternatives. Allows User to Analyze Both Current & Projected Financial Needs by "Phasing" Alternatives over a Specified Period of Time.
Elite Software Development, Inc.

LIFE Goals. Version: 4.21. Oct. 1988. *Operating System(s) Required:* MS-DOS. *Memory Required:* 640k. *General Requirements:* Lotus 1-2-3. *Customer Support:* 1st 45 minutes free, $40/hr.
disk $695.00.
Financial Investments Analysis Program Allows Financial Planners & Agents to Produce Detailed Custom Financial Plans for Clients. Plans Can Run from 18 to 26 Pages & Contain Explanations & Analyses of the Client's Present & Desired Financial Goals. Included in the Generated Analyses Are: Financial Statements, Investment Performance, Monthly Budgeting Profiles, Effects of Inflation, College Funding Needs, Asset Diversification, Life Insurance Needs, Retirement Capital Needs, IRA's, Home Refinancing. In Addition, It Automatically Recalculates Federal Income Tax, Social Security, & Survivor Benefits.
Successful Money Management Software, Inc.

Life History Disk. Version: 4.0. *Compatible Hardware:* Apple Macintosh, Apple II, IBM. *General Requirements:* word processor. *Items Included:* 1 disk (Manual on disk). *Customer Support:* Telephone (no charge); mail.
3.5" disk $21.95.
Produces Superior Life Histories of Family Members.
Starcom Microsystems.

Life Insurance Planning. Version: 2.0. Floyd C. Henderson. Jun. 1983. *Compatible Hardware:* Atari 400, 800, 800XL, 1200 with Atari BASIC cartridge, Commodore 64; IBM PC, PC AT & compatibles. *Language(s):* BASIC (source code included). *Memory Required:* 48k.
disk $29.95 ea.
Commodore 64. (ISBN 0-917263-03-0).
Atari. (ISBN 0-917263-01-4).
Calculates Insurance Needs for Funeral Expenses, Living Expenses, & College Expenses. Accounts for Inflation in All Calculations.
Advanced Financial Planning.

Life Skills Math. (Micro Learn Tutorial Ser.). *Customer Support:* Free telephone support.
MAC. Macintosh (2Mb), Apple. 5.25" disk, $39.95; Lab pack/5, $99.00; 3.5" disks, $44.95, Lab pack/5, $115.00 Apple or Macintosh network $249.00 (ISBN 1-57265-051-6).
APP. $44.95, Labpack/5, $115.00, Network, Apple or Mac $249.00 (ISBN 0-939153-20-3).
MAC. (ISBN 1-57265-051-6).
Tutorial Teaches Students to Use Ratios, Proportions, Fractions, Decimals, Percent & Estimating in Everyday Life Situations, in the Context of Buying Food & Goods; Counting Calories, Grams of Fat, Vitamins; Figuring Discounts, Sales Tax, Tips, Interest on Charge Cards; & More. Tutorial mode gives explanations for all answer choices, correct & incorrect. Test mode included.
Word Assocs., Inc.

Life Style Analyzer. *Items Included:* Bound manual. *Customer Support:* Free hotline - no time limit; 30 day limited warranty; updates are $5/disk plus S&H.
MS-DOS. IBM & compatibles (256k). disk $49.95.
Evaluates Your Health Habits, Activities, Medical History, & Family Background to Identify Potential Health Problems.
Dynacomp, Inc.

LifeART Collections. Dec. 1989. *Items Included:* LifeART Transverter bonus utility either on 3.5" floppy or contained on CD-ROM 2-10 3.5" floppy image disks. Transverter manual. Image Galleries & Image Locator Guide (Mac Only). *Customer Support:* Tech support available at no additional charge by phone: (216) 382-1787

9AM-4PM EST. via CompuServe: 72410,2053.
Windows 3.0 MS-DOS 3.1. 386 or higher (4Mb). $99.00-$249.00. *Addl. software required:* Any application that supports graphics. *Optimal configuration:* 100Mz Pentium; 16Mb RAM; Windows 3.1.1; 32 bit color graphics card; 1Mb video RAM; CD-ROM drive; graphics accelerator card; 200Mb hard drive free space.
Macintosh System 6.0. Mac II or higher (4Mb). $99.00-$249.00. *Addl. software required:* Any application that supports graphics. *Optimal configuration:* System 7.1; 32 bit QuickDraw; CD-ROM drive, Power Mac; 16MbRAM; 32 bit graphic cards; graphics aqccelerator card; 200Mb hard drive free space.
MS-DOS 5.0. 386 25Mz Grayscale Monitor (4Mb). $99.00-$249.00. *Addl. software required:* Any application that supports 16 bit color graphics. *Optimal configuration:* 486 66Mz 8Mb RAM; Monitor w/256 color; graphics board; CD-ROM drive; 200Mb hard drive free space.
Collections of Professional-Level Computer Illustrations for the Medical, Emergency, Rescue, Education & Health Care Markets. Topics Include Detailed Anatomy, Scenes, Procedures, Techniques, Equipment & Symbols. Collections Contain up to 500 EPS Images That Can Be Used in Any Desktop Publishing, Presentation & Page Layout Application to Enhance Reports, Slides & Overheads, Pamphlets, Newsletters & More.
TechPool Studios.

LifeGuard. Oct. 1985. *Compatible Hardware:* Apple II, II+, IIe, IIc. (source code included). *Memory Required:* 48k.
disk $9.95 (ISBN 0-918547-18-0).
illustration files on disk avail.
Includes Programs to Predict Life Span, Determine Ideal Body Weight, Optimum Caloric Intake, Biorhythms, Detect Users' ESP, a Personality Test, & a Reaction Time Test & Analysis.
AV Systems, Inc.

LifeLines. Jul. 1988. *Compatible Hardware:* IBM PC & compatibles. *Operating System(s) Required:* PC-DOS/MS-DOS. *Memory Required:* 256k.
disk $39.95.
User Inputs Data on Ancestors from Distant Generations to Present. Generates Pedigree Charts, Descendants Charts, Marriage Lists & Alphabetical Listings. Includes Background on the Methods of Genealogy & References.
Zephyr Services.

Lifeplan. Version: 3.01. May 1989. *Customer Support:* 90 day warranty against defects in disk manufacture, immediate replacement of defective media.
MS-DOS/PC-DOS 3.1 or higher (256k). IBM PC/XT/AT/PS2 compatible. disk $34.95. *Optimal configuration:* PC/AT or PS/2, hard disk, EGA or VGA graphics, 640k, one floppy drive. *Networks supported:* Novell.
A Database Program for Improving Organization & Goal Accomplishment. Helps to Master Time Management in Daily Life. Main Menu Selections: Contacts, Calendar, Daily ToDo, Long Term Goals, Projects, Utilities.
Thinking Software, Inc.

Lighthouse Bibliography: Database. Version: 2.0. Mar. 1995. *Items Included:* 1 stitched manual. *Customer Support:* Telephone.
Microsoft Windows 3.1 & higher. PC or compatible 386SX or higher (4Mb). disk $59.95 (ISBN 0-9649980-0-9, Order no.: LHBIB 2.0). *Optimal configuration:* 486 computer, 4Mb RAM, VGA or SVGA monitor, graphics capable printer, 3.5 inch floppy 4Mb

of free hard disk space, Windows 3.1 OS.
A Computer Database & Retrieval Program of Information about Lighthouse Books, Magazines, & Sources. Contains over 4000 Entries. Has Search & Printing Capabilities.

Lighting Design. *Items Included:* Bound manual. *Customer Support:* Free hotline - no time limit; 30 day limited warranty; updates are $5/disk plus S&H.
MS-DOS. IBM & compatibles (256k). disk $449.95.
demo disk $5.00.
Uses the IES Room Cavity Maintained Lighting Level Method to Recommend the Number & Location of Fixtures Needed to Maintain a Desired Lighting Level in Building or Factory Projects.
Dynacomp, Inc.

Lighting Design - E5M. Version: 03/1991. 1979. *Operating System(s) Required:* MS-DOS, PC-DOS. *Language(s):* Compiled. *Memory Required:* 256k. *Customer Support:* Technical hotline, "Lifetime" support at no charge.
$495.00.
Lighting Design, Power Consumption - E5M Uses the IES Room Cavity Maintained Lighting Level Method to Recommend Number & Location of Fixtures Needed to Maintain the Desired Lighting Level in Building or Factory Projects. Automatically Prints Dimensioned Schematic Diagram of Suggested Layout. Also Gives Lighting Level Resulting from a User-Specified Number of a Desired Fixture. Fully Compiled. SI Metric opr English Units.
MC2 Engineering Software.

Lighting Fixture Program: LIGHT. Version: 4.0. May 1988. *Compatible Hardware:* IBM PC & compatibles. *Operating System(s) Required:* PC-DOS/MS-DOS. *Language(s):* CB-80. *Memory Required:* CP/M 64k, MS-DOS 256k.
disk $495.00.
demo disk $38.00.
Uses the IES Zonal Cavity Method to Calculate Fixture Requirements, Print a Lighting Fixture Schedule, & Provide an Energy Economics Report. Automatically Looks up & Interpolates for the Correct Coefficient of Utilization for Any Given Set of Room Conditions. Allows up to 500 Rooms per Project, & Each Room Can Have Three Different Lighting Fixtures. Allows User to Review, Revise, Add & Delete Fixtures from the Fixture Library. Also Allows User to Specify a Description, Cost, Watts Consumption, & a Manufacturer Name for Each Fixture in the Library.
Elite Software Development, Inc.

Lightning. *Compatible Hardware:* IBM PC, PC XT, PC AT.
disk copy protected $49.95.
not copy protected $89.95.
Accelerates Disk Access, Thus Saving Time for Loading & Saving Files. Loads with the DOS & Stays in the Background until a Disk Read/Write Operation Is Performed. Is Capable of Taking Full Advantage the ABOVE BOARD Memory for PCs with That Addition.
Lucid Corp.

Lightspeed. Oct. 1990. *Items Included:* Manual. *Customer Support:* Free customer service, (410) 771-1151, Ext. 350.
IBM PC or compatibles (640k). 3.5" or 5.25" disk (640k) $59.95. *Nonstandard peripherals required:* Supports VGA/MCGA, EGA, CGA, Tandy 16-color.
The Human Race Needs a New Home. Your Job: Explore Star Clusters, Find Suitable Worlds for Habitation & Negotiate with Aliens for Raw Materials, Resources & Treaties. But Space

Pirates Are Everywhere & Some Aliens Want Nothing But War. LIGHTSPEED Is The Alternate Universe You've Been Searching for.
MicroProse Software.

Lightspeed C 3.0. *Compatible Hardware:* Apple Macintosh Plus, Macintosh SE, Macintosh II, Macintosh IIx.
3.5" disk $175.00.
C Compiler Featuring MultiFinder Resource & Trap Support, 68020 & 68881 Code Generation, & Access to Color QuickDraw. Includes a Source-Code Level Debugger. On a Macintosh II, Debugger Output Can Be Directed to a Second Monitor.
Think Technologies.

Lightspeed Pascal. Aug. 1986. *Compatible Hardware:* Apple Macintosh. *Operating System(s) Required:* Macintosh System/Finder. *Language(s):* Pascal. *Memory Required:* 30-35k.
disk $125.00.
Enables Users to Create Their Own Standalone Macintosh Applications. Includes Text Editor, Compiler, Linker, Project Manager, & Intelligent Debuggers.
Think Technologies.

Lightyear. *Version:* 1.5. Lightyear, Inc. Jun. 1984. *Compatible Hardware:* IBM PC, PC XT, PC AT, & 100% compatibles. *Operating System(s) Required:* PC-DOS/MS-DOS 2.0 or higher. *Memory Required:* 192k. *General Requirements:* CGA monitor highly recommended. Operates on "A" or "C" drives only.
disk $99.00.
Helps Managers Combine Quantitative & Qualitative Factors into a Decision Model. Provides a Framework to Organize Information, Analyze Data & Evaluate Options.
Thoughtware, Inc. (Florida).

Li'l Men from Mars. *Compatible Hardware:* Atari 400, 800. *Language(s):* Atari BASIC (source code included). *Memory Required:* 24k.
disk $23.95.
1 Player Real Time Arcade Game.
Dynacomp, Inc.

Lime. *Version:* 3.0. Lippold Haken & Dorothea Blostein. 1993. *Items Included:* One spiral bound manual, one diskette.
Mac System 6-7.1. Macintosh (2Mb). 3.5" disk $295.00 (Order no.: MAC-1445). *Nonstandard peripherals required:* Postscript printer or Imagewriter. *Optimal configuration:* External MIDI interface, MIDI keyboard.
An Easy-to-Use Music Notation Package. Offers Real Time & Step Time Mini Input, Automatic Engraver Spacing, Score Optimization, Multiple Right & Left Staff Indenting, Lyrics Can Be Attached to Notes, Two Percussion Clefs, & Many Other Options.
Electronic Courseware Systems, Inc.

Limited Gold Dog Analysis. Ronald D. Jones. 1984. *Compatible Hardware:* Apple II; Commodore 64; IBM PC; TRS-80 Model I, Model III, Color Computer. *Operating System(s) Required:* CP/M. *Memory Required:* 64k.
disk $299.95 ea.
Apple. (ISBN 1-55604-072-5, Order no.: D003).
CP/M. (ISBN 1-55604-073-3, Order no.: D003).
Commodore. (ISBN 1-55604-074-1, Order no.: D003).
Color Computer. (ISBN 1-55604-075-X, Order no.: D003).
IBM. (ISBN 1-55604-076-8, Order no.: D003).
Model I & Model III. (ISBN 1-55604-077-6, Order no.: D003).
Uses Combination of Speed & Class Based upon the Grade of the Race. Track Records & Kennel Ratings Are Maintained on a Data Base Initializing the System for a Specific Track. Master Bettor Evaluates Scores & Everey Betting Combination of the Top 5 Dogs Are Given. Enables Handicappers to Assign Specific Values to the Racing Variables They Feel Are Important for Differences in Tracks & Different Types of Races.
Professor Jones Professional Handicapping Systems.

Limited Gold Dog with Track Management. Ronald D. Jones. *Compatible Hardware:* Apple; Commodore; IBM; TRS-80 Model I, Model III, Color Computer. *Operating System(s) Required:* CP/M. *Memory Required:* 64k.
disk $379.90 ea.
Apple. (ISBN 1-55604-078-4, Order no.: D013).
CP/M. (ISBN 1-55604-079-2, Order no.: D013).
Commodore. (ISBN 1-55604-080-6, Order no.: D013).
Color Computer. (ISBN 1-55604-081-4, Order no.: D013).
IBM. (ISBN 1-55604-082-2, Order no.: D013).
Model I & Model III. (ISBN 1-55604-083-0, Order no.: D013).
Uses Combination of Speed & Class Based on the Grade of the Race. Records Kennel Ratings Maintained on a Data Base, Initializing the System for a Specific Track. Master Bettor Evaluates Scores & Every Betting Combination of the Top Five Dogs Is Given. Limited Enables Handicappers to Assign Specific Values to the Racing Variables They Feel Are Important for Differences in Tracks & Different Types of Races. Track Management Is a Data Base Program Designed to Keep Records on All Dogs Running at a Track.
Professor Jones Professional Handicapping Systems.

Limited Gold Thoroughbred. Ronald D. Jones. 1984. *Compatible Hardware:* Apple II; Commodore 64; IBM PC; TRS-80, Color Computer; CP/M machines. *Memory Required:* 64k.
disk $299.95 ea.
Apple. (ISBN 1-55604-018-0).
CP/M. (ISBN 1-55604-019-9).
Commodore. (ISBN 1-55604-020-2).
Color Computer. (ISBN 1-55604-021-0).
IBM. (ISBN 1-55604-022-9).
TRS-80. (ISBN 1-55604-023-7).
Enables Professional Handicappers to Assign Specific Values to the Racing Variables They Feel Are Important. No Programming Experience Necessary.
Professor Jones Professional Handicapping Systems.

Limited Gold Thoroughbred with Track Management. Ronald D. Jones. 1984. *Compatible Hardware:* Apple II; Commodore 64; IBM PC; TRS-80 Model I, Model III, Color Computer. *Operating System(s) Required:* CP/M. *Memory Required:* 64k.
disk $379.90 ea.
Apple. (ISBN 1-55604-024-5, Order no.: H013).
CP/M. (ISBN 1-55604-025-3, Order no.: H013).
Commodore. (ISBN 1-55604-026-1, Order no.: H013).
Color Computer. (ISBN 1-55604-027-X, Order no.: H013).
IBM. (ISBN 1-55604-028-8, Order no.: H013).
Model I & Model III. (ISBN 1-55604-029-6, Order no.: H013).
Full-Featured Thoroughbred Analysis Designed for the Professional & Serious Novice. Designed to Evaluate All Relevant Factors & Variables & Give an Accurate Prediction of the Finish. Can Be Fine Tuned to a Specific Track. Master Bettor Evaluates Scores & Gives Every Betting Combination of the Top Five Horses. Handicappers Can Assign Specific Values to the Racing Variables They Feel Are Important. Track Management Is a Data Base Program Program Designed to Keep Records on All Horses Running at a Track.
Professor Jones Professional Handicapping Systems.

Limited Harness Handicapper. Ronald D. Jones. 1985. *Compatible Hardware:* Apple II; Commodore 64; IBM PC; TRS-80 Model I, Model III, Color Computer. *Operating System(s) Required:* CP/M. *Memory Required:* 64k.
disk $299.95 ea.
Apple. (ISBN 1-55604-198-5, Order no.: T003).
CP/M. (ISBN 1-55604-199-3, Order no.: T003).
Commodore. (ISBN 1-55604-200-0, Order no.: T003).
Color Computer. (ISBN 1-55604-201-9, Order no.: T003).
IBM. (ISBN 1-55604-202-7, Order no.: T003).
Model I & Model III. (ISBN 1-55604-203-5, Order no.: T003).
Full-Featured Harness Racing Analysis. Initialize System with Track Records, & Driver's & Trainers' Records on Data Base System. Evaluates All Relevant Variables & Gives Prediction of the Finish. Master Bettor Evaluates Scores, & Every Betting Combination of the Top Five Horses Is Printed on the Video or Printer. Limited Enables Handicappers to Assign Specific Values to the Racing Variables They Feel Are Important. Create Program Weight Based on a Particular Track for Maximum Win Percentage.
Professor Jones Professional Handicapping Systems.

Limited Harness Handicapper with Track Management. Ronald D. Jones. 1985. *Compatible Hardware:* Apple II; Commodore 64; IBM PC; TRS-80 Model I, Model III, Color Computer. *Operating System(s) Required:* CP/M. *Memory Required:* 64k.
disk $379.90 ea.
Apple. (ISBN 1-55604-204-3, Order no.: T013).
CP/M. (ISBN 1-55604-205-1, Order no.: T013).
Commodore. (ISBN 1-55604-206-X, Order no.: T013).
Color Computer. (ISBN 1-55604-207-8, Order no.: T013).
IBM. (ISBN 1-55604-208-6, Order no.: T013).
Model I & Model III. (ISBN 1-55604-209-4, Order no.: T013).
Full-Featured Harness Racing Analysis. Intialize System with Track Records, & Drivers' & Trainers' Records on Data Base System. Evaluates All Relevant Variables & Gives Prediction of the Finish. Master Bettor Evaluates Scores, & Every Betting Combination of the Top Five Horses Is Printed on the Video or Printer. Track Management Is a Data Base Program Designed to Keep Records on All Horses Running at a Track.
Professor Jones Professional Handicapping Systems.

LIMIT3. *Version:* 3.0. Mar. 1986. *Compatible Hardware:* IBM PC, PC XT, PC AT & compatibles. *Operating System(s) Required:* MS-DOS, PC-DOS. *Language(s):* FORTRAN. *Memory Required:* 512k. *General Requirements:* Printer, plotter.
disk $1000.00 (Order no.: LIMIT3).
Limits the Extent of Estimation by Creating a User-Defined Data Envelope. Only Values That Are Within the Area or Volume of Interest Are Used by the Estimation Programs, Thus Increasing Accuracy & Precision. The Program Will Also Define the Limits of a Block When the User Specifies the Cut-Off Values. It Applies Those Values Directly to the Grade of the Composites.
Geostat Systems International, Inc. (GSII).

LIMNEW. *Version:* 1.2. May 1985. *Compatible Hardware:* IBM PC, PC XT, PC AT & compatibles. *Operating System(s) Required:* MS-DOS, PC-DOS. *Language(s):* FORTRAN. *Memory Required:* 512k. *General Requirements:* Printer.
disk $500.00 (Order no.: LIMNEW).
Generates Screening Grids in a Set of Data to Limit the Extent of Calculation. In the VOLUMETRICS System, the Program Enables the Analyst to Calculate Cut & Fill for Just One Area of a Site. This Flexibility Allows the Analyst to Experiment with Different Topographic Models or Different Stages of a Site.
Geostat Systems International, Inc. (GSII).

LINDO: Linear Interactive & Discrete Optimizer. Linus Schrage. *Compatible Hardware:* Apple Macintosh; IBM PC, PC XT, PC AT. *Memory Required:* 320k.
disk $500.00 (ISBN 0-89426-090-1).
Optimizer That Includes Linear, Integer, & Quadratic Programming, More Than 50 Commands for Editing, Model Input, Optimization, & Sensitivity Analysis.
Boyd & Fraser Publishing Co.

The Line & the Shape Eater: An Interactive Adventure in New York City. *Version:* MPC1.0. MediaRight Technology & William Enco. Nov. 1992.
MPC compliant Windows 3.1. MPC (2Mb). CD-ROM disk $24.45 (ISBN 0-9637769-0-8). *Addl. software required:* Windows 3.1. *Optimal configuration:* 4Mb RAM, 386DX or higher processor.
CD-ROM Based, MPC Compliant, Children's Story. The Main Character, the Line, Introduces Children to Different Geometric Shapes & Their Roll in Art, Architecture & Every Day Life. Along the Way, the Evil Shape Eater Comes to Town. The Line Rallies the Cities Shapes to Act Cooperatively to Change the Evil Shape Eater into a Nice Creature. A Special Drawing Package Allows Children to Experiment with the Shapes They Learn About.
Cragsmoor Interactive, Inc.

Lineages. 1987. *Compatible Hardware:* Commodore 64/128. *Memory Required:* 64k. *Customer Support:* 60-day unlimited warranty.
$19.00, $29.00 (3 Levels) (ISBN 0-917169-23-9).
$49.00 (3 Levels) (ISBN 0-917169-24-7).
LINEAGES/STARTER-Stores Infomation for 570 People & Prints Lists, Descendants & Pedigree Charts on Standard Commodore Printer; LINEAGES/STANDARD- Does the Same but no Limit on Number of People & Can Print Address Lists & Person Sheets; LINEAGES/ADVANCED in Addition to Features of Lower-Priced Units Allows Custom Setup to Hardware, Prints Group Sheets, Performs Searches & Includes Line Editor.
Quinsept, Inc.

Lineages/Advanced. *Version:* 3.4. S. C. Vorenberg. Feb. 1990. *Customer Support:* 60-day unlimited warranty, toll-free phone.
ProDOS, Apple DOS 3.3, MS-DOS. Apple IIe, IIc, IIc+, IIgs (128k), IBM compatible. disk $59.00 (ISBN 0-917169-35-2).
Stores Information for Millions of People. Prints Lists, Pedigree Chart, Group Sheet. Also Descendants Charts & Limited Custom Setup. Includes Family Links.
Quinsept, Inc.

Lineages/Standard. *Version:* 3.4. S. C. Vorenberg. Feb. 1990. *Customer Support:* 60-day unlimited warranty, toll-free phone.
MS-DOS. IBM compatibles (128k). disk $32.00 (ISBN 0-917169-35-2).
ProDos. Apple IIe, IIc, IIc+, IIgs (128K). disk $32.00 (ISBN 0-917169-35-2).
Stores Information for Millions of People. Prints Lists, Pedigree Chart, Group Sheet on Standard Apple or IBM Printer. Includes Family Links.
Quinsept, Inc.

Linear Algebra. *Items Included:* Bound manual. *Customer Support:* Free hotline - no time limit; 30 day limited warranty; updates are $5/disk plus S&H.
MS-DOS. IBM & compatibles (256k). disk $39.95. *Nonstandard peripherals required:* Color graphics card; printer supported. *Addl. software required:* BASICA.
Commodore 64. disk $39.95.
Solves Simultaneous Linear Equations, Finds the Determinant or the Inverse of a Matrix, & Computes the Product, the Sum, or the Difference Between Two Matrices. It Also Has the Ability to Find the Real Eigenvalues. The Corresponding Eigenvectors Are Computed Using the Shifted Inverse Power Algorithm. For Further Efficiency, the Matrices Are First Transformed into Their Upper-Hessenberg Form.
Dynacomp, Inc.

Linear & Non-Linear Programming. *Version:* 10.0. *Compatible Hardware:* Apple Macintosh, IBM PC & compatibles. *Items Included:* Disks, book, program instruction. *Customer Support:* Telephone.
disk $145.00 (ISBN 0-920387-08-X).
Contains Two Linear Programming Programs, One Based on the SIMPLEX Algorithm, the Other Using a Monte Carlo Technique. General Purpose Quadratic & Non-Linear Programming Programs Are Implemented Using a Monte Carlo Technique. Special Problems Handled Include the Distribution & Transportation Problems, the Assignment Problem, & the Travelling Salesman Problem.
Lionheart Pr., Inc.

Linear Circuit Analysis: LINCAP. *Items Included:* Bound manual. *Customer Support:* Free hotline - no time limit; 30 day limited warranty; updates are $5/disk plus S&H.
MS-DOS 2.1 or higher. IBM & compatibles (256k). disk $39.95. *Nonstandard peripherals required:* Printer is supported.
Calculates the Gain, Phase, & Envelope Delay for AC-Equivalent Circuits Containing Resistors, Capacitors, Inductors, Op-Amps, & Both Bipolar & Field-Effect Transistors.
Dynacomp, Inc.

Linear Least Squares FORTRAN Subprogram. *Compatible Hardware:* IBM PC & compatibles. *Language(s):* FORTRAN.
$80.00, incl. documentation.
This Package of ANSI Standard Subprograms Provides the Foundation for a Variety of Applied Computations. Includes Singular Value Decompositions, Banded Least Squares, Constrained Least Squares & Householder's Method for Linear Least Square System.
Software Designs 2000.

Linear Ordinary Differential Equations. *Items Included:* Bound manual. *Customer Support:* Free hotline - no time limit; 30 day limited warranty; updates are $5/disk plus S&H.
MS-DOS. IBM & compatibles (256k). disk $49.95. *Nonstandard peripherals required:* Color graphics card; printer supported. *Addl. software required:* BASICA.
Commodore 64. disk $49.95.
Solves Boundary Value Problems Involving Linear Ordinary Differential Equations of Any Order, with Variable Coefficients. The Boundary Conditions May Also Be Equations Involving the Unknown Function & Its Derivatives, & the Evaluation Point May Be Different for Each One.
Dynacomp, Inc.

Linear Programmer. *Compatible Hardware:* Apple II with Applesoft; IBM PC. (source code included). *Memory Required:* 48k, IBM 128k.
disk $29.95.
Solves the Standard Linear Programming Inequality Problem.
Dynacomp, Inc.

Linear Programmer Minimax. *Items Included:* Bound manual. *Customer Support:* Free hotline - no time limit; 30 day limited warranty; updates are $5/disk plus S&H.
MS-DOS. IBM & compatibles (256k). disk $69.95.
Can Treat Over- & Under-Constrained Problems, Maximize an Objective Function, & Solve Simultaneous Linear Equations. It Uses the Fast & Efficient Khachian Algorithm to Obtain the Solution (or Nearest Solution) to the Matrix Inequality.
Dynacomp, Inc.

Linear Programmer Minimax. 1995. *Items Included:* Full manual. *Customer Support:* Free telephone support - 90 days, 30-day warranty.
MS-DOS 3.2 or higher. 286 (584k). disk $69.95. *Nonstandard peripherals required:* CGA/EGA/VGA.
LPM Is a More Powerful Version of DYNACOMP's LINEAR PROGRAMMER Which Can Treat Over- & Under-Constrained Problems, Maximize an Objective Function, & Solve Simultaneous Linear Equations. It Uses the Fast & Efficient Khachian Algorithm to Obtain the Solution (or Nearest Solution) to the Matrix Inequality.
Dynacomp, Inc.

Linear Programming. *Compatible Hardware:* HP 85, 86/87.
HP 85. data cartridge, 3-1/2" or 5-1/4" disk $95.00 ea. (Order no.: 82808A).
HP 86/87. 3-1/2" or 5-1/4" disk $95.00 ea. (Order no.: 82838A).
Solves a Variety of Optimization Problems Using a Modified Simplex Method That Incorporates Variable Bounds. Applications Include Chemical Blending, Production Scheduling, Profit Optimization, etc.
Hewlett-Packard Co.

Linear Programming Master. *Customer Support:* 800-929-8117 (customer service).
MS-DOS. Apple II. disk $69.99 (ISBN 0-87007-513-6).
Simplex Method, Allows 50 Constraints & 50 Variables to Minimize or Maximize Objective Function. Solves for Regular, Slack, Surplus & Dual Var.
SourceView Software International.

Linear Programming Subprograms in ANSI FORTRAN (LPSUBS). *Compatible Hardware:* IBM PC or compatibles. *Language(s):* FORTRAN.
$99.00, incl. documentation.
Provides the Subprograms Which Are the Heart of the Mathematics in the Popular LP-2000 LINEAR PROGRAMMING SYSTEM.
Software Designs 2000.

Linear Regression Master. *Customer Support:* 800-929-8117 (customer service).
MS-DOS. Apple II. disk $69.99 (ISBN 0-87007-514-4).
Solves Multiple Linear, Polynomial, Exponential & Geometric Models. Output Includes: Coefficients, T-Stat, F-Stat, R Squared, Anova Table, Durbin Watson & Residuals.
SourceView Software International.

Linear Systems Analysis. *Compatible Hardware:* HP Series 200 Models 216/220, 226/236 Personal Technical Computers with BASIC 2.0.

TITLE INDEX

Memory Required: 180k.
HP 216/220. 3-1/2" or 5-1/4" disk $500.00 ea. (Order no.: 98826A).
HP 226/236. 5-1/4" disk $500.00 ea.
Provides "Classical" Tools Needed for Analyzing Single-Input/Output Linear Systems. The Following Analysis Plots Are Available: Root Locus, Nyquist, Step Response, Impulse Response, & Bode. Linear Systems Can Be in the Form of a Control System Block Diagram or a Simple Transfer Function in Laplace (S) Notation.
Hewlett-Packard Co.

Linear Transient & AC Circuit Analysis. *Items Included:* Bound manual. *Customer Support:* Free hotline - no time limit; 30 day limited warranty; updates are $5/disk plus S&H.
MS-DOS 2.0 or higher. IBM & compatibles (256k). disk $99.95. *Nonstandard peripherals required:* CGA, EGA, or IBM/Epson (or compatible) printer.
Performs AC Response Calculations Giving Both Time & Frequency Domain Results. Circuit-Analysis Tool.
Dynacomp, Inc.

Linecost: Construction Material & Cost Estimating. *Version:* 2.4. Dennis M. Levy. 1990. *Compatible Hardware:* IBM PC, PC XT, PC AT & compatibles. *Operating System(s) Required:* MS-DOS, PC-DOS. *Memory Required:* 150k. *General Requirements:* 2 disk drives, printer (hard disk recommended).
disk $2000.00 (ISBN 0-934795-02-9).
Produces a Bill of Material from Electric Distribution Staking Information. Data Files Are Established with Material Items & Assembly Information As per Construction Specification for Transmission & Distribution. List of All Material Items & Construction Assemblies Are Printed. UNITADD, a Construction Assembly Unit Totaling Program, Provides the Means of Tabulating from Staking Sheets the Quantity of Each Type of Assembly Unit Used in a Construction Project.
Power System Engineering, Inc.

Lines, Boxes, etc. 1987. *Operating System(s) Required:* MS-DOS/PC-DOS. *Memory Required:* 128k.
IBM PC & compatibles. contact publisher for price.
Special Characters/Symbols for 9/24 Pin & Laser Printers.
M.A.P. Systems, Inc.

Lines Plus. C. R. Cowan. *Compatible Hardware:* IBM PC, PCjr, PC XT, PC AT, Portable PC, 3270 PC. *Operating System(s) Required:* PC-DOS 2.00, 2.10, 3.00, 3.10. *Memory Required:* 128k, PCjr with DOS 3.00 or 3.10 256k.
disk $19.95 (Order no.: 6276636).
Text Graphic Editor & Text Editor Create Drawings Composed of Lines, Boxes, & Arrows for Professional Reports. Users Can Label Parts of a Diagram, Try a Variety of Background Box Patterns; Use Different Text Alignments, & Choose Between Single & Double Lines. Options Are Available to Print, Save, Copy, Delete, or File a Copy. Sections of the Drawing Can Be Moved from One Part of the Screen to Another Area. Includes a Tutorial to Learn Basic Drawing Functions & Create Sample Drawings.
Personally Developed Software, Inc.

Lingerie International 100. Jun. 1994. *Items Included:* License agreement & registration card. *Customer Support:* 1-900-420-5005, $3.00 per minute.
Windows 3.1 or System 7. IBM & compatibles & Macintosh (2.0Mb). $39.00 MSRP (ISBN 0-9634008-6-X). *Nonstandard peripherals required:* CD ROM drive. *Optimal configuration:* 386, 20MHz, 4Mb RAM, VGA monitor with 256 colors.
One Hundred Photo CD Images with Corel Utilities for Image Conversion & Screensavers for Windows & Macintosh.
Cascom International, Inc.

Link Com. Feb. 1987. *Compatible Hardware:* IBM PC & compatibles. *Memory Required:* 128k. *Customer Support:* Yes.
disk $499.95 (ISBN 0-929800-14-1, Order no.: LINKCOM).
Utility Program That Allows Numerical Control Programs to Be Sent to CNC Equipment That Supports the DNC Link Protocol. Sold As a Site License. Interface to Boss 8 Using DNC Link Protocol.
Electrosonics.

Links 386 Pro. *Version:* DOS. *Items Included:* Manual. *Customer Support:* 90 days unlimited warranty, technical support line 1-800-793-8324.
386 SX/16mhz CPU. IBM PC or compatibles (2Mb). disk $69.95. *Nonstandard peripherals required:* Hard drive, Super VGA display, mouse. *Optimal configuration:* 386/33mhz CPU or higher, 8Mb RAM.
Golf Sports Simulation Program. Super VGA Graphics, Male/Female Golfers. Play with up to Eight Players Each with Individual Shirt Colors, Skill Level & Recorded Statistics. Player Can Record Individual Shot or Complete Game to Review or Play Against Another Player. Digitized Sound Track. Additional Add on Courses.
Access Software, Inc.

Linksware. Tracy Valleau. 1991. *Compatible Hardware:* Apple IIgs, Macintosh.
disk $189.00.
Allows the Creation of Hypertext & Hypermedia Links within Industry-Standard Files Such As WORD, WRITENOW, RTF & Others. "90 Second Learning Curve" Feature Allows User to Double Click on a Selected 'Hot-Word' & Then on a Selected Text, Graphic or Sound File, Creating a Permanent Link File for Easy Retrieval & Display. Keeping the Links in a Separate File Allows Editing to Be Done without Changing the Links or Files Themselves, & Allows Indexing of CD-ROMs.
Linksware Corp.

LinkUp 3270 Unisession for Windows. *Compatible Hardware:* IBM PC & compatibles. $295.00.
Allows IBM (or compatible) PCs & PS/2s to Emulate the IBM 3270 Terminal Family (Including Many 3472 Terminal Features). Includes IBM 3472 Compatible Host Addressable Print (HAP) Feature, CUT Emulation with 5 Session MLT Support, a Floating Keypad That Can Be Customized for up to 32 Mouse-Selectable Functions, Scalable Font & Window Sizing, Color Remapping, Copy & Paste Options, & File Transfer. HAP Enables a Direct Connection from the Controller to a PC-Attached Printer. Includes the DOS Emulation, Which Is the Same As ENS1C0. Requires a LinkUp 3270 Coax, M/Coax for Host Addressable Print & Display Emulation; IBM (or compatible) Adapter for Display Emulation Only.
Computer Logics, Ltd.

Linux. *Customer Support:* All of our products are unconditionally guaranteed.
Unix. CD-ROM disk $34.95 (Order no.: LINUX). *Nonstandard peripherals required:* CD-ROM drive.
Yggdrasil 1.1 Linux Operating System with X11 7 GNU.
Walnut Creek CDRom.

Linux Bible. *Customer Support:* All of our products are unconditionally guaranteed.
Unix. CD-ROM disk $39.95 (Order no.: LINUX BIBLE). *Nonstandard peripherals required:* CD-ROM drive.
764 Page Book of Everyting You Need to Know about Linux.
Walnut Creek CDRom.

LION (Library Information Online). *Version:* 3.00. 1991. *Compatible Hardware:* IBM PC & compatibles. *Operating System(s) Required:* MS-DOS, PC-DOS. *Memory Required:* 512k. *General Requirements:* Hard disk. *Customer Support:* 6 months telephone support free.
disk $750.00 to $1250.00 (ISBN 0-916625-13-3).
Public Access Catalog for Hard Disks & Networks, Suitable for Collections up to 500,000 Items; Keyword Searching & Boolean AND, OR & NOT in Author, Title, or Subject Field; Bibliographic Master Records up to 60,000 Characters; up to 960 Subject Descriptors.
Computer Assisted Library Information Co., Inc.

LION OPAC Inventory Module. *Version:* 3.00. 1992. *Compatible Hardware:* IBM PC & compatibles; Macintosh. *Customer Support:* 6 months telephone support free.
disk $300.00.
Module for Inventory Designed to be Used with CALICO's LION Online Public Access Catalog.
Computer Assisted Library Information Co., Inc.

The Lion, the Witch & the Wardrobe. Intentional Education Staff & C. S. Lewis. Apr. 1996. *Items Included:* Program manual. *Customer Support:* Free technical support, 90 day warranty.
School ver.. System 7.1 or higher. Macintosh (4Mb). 3.5" disk contact publisher for price (ISBN 1-57204-295-8). *Nonstandard peripherals required:* 256 color monitor, hard drive, printer.
Lab pack. System 7.1 or higher. Macintosh (4Mb). 3.5" disk contact publisher for price (ISBN 1-57204-271-0). *Nonstandard peripherals required:* 256 color monitor, hard drive, printer.
Site license. System 7.1 or higher. Macintosh (4Mb). 3.5" disk contact publisher for price (ISBN 1-57204-296-6). *Nonstandard peripherals required:* 256 color monitor, hard drive, printer.
School ver.. Windows 3.1 or higher. IBM/Tandy & 100% compatibles (4Mb). disk contact publisher for price (ISBN 1-57204-272-9). *Nonstandard peripherals required:* VGA or SVGA 640 x 480 resolution (256), mouse, hard drive, sound device.
Lab pack. Windows 3.1 or higher. IBM/Tandy & 100% compatibles (4Mb). disk contact publisher for price (ISBN 1-57204-297-4). *Nonstandard peripherals required:* VGA or SVGA 640 x 780 resolution (256), mouse, hard drive, sound device.
Site license. Windows 3.1 or higher. IBM/Tandy & 100% compatibles (4mb). disk contact publisher for price (ISBN 1-57204-273-7). *Nonstandard peripherals required:* VGA or SVGA 640 x 480 resolution (256), mouse, hard drive, sound device.
This companion for young adult literature is ideal for students who don't know how to start that book report, or give that needed summary. Gentle prompts throughout the guide section of the program include Warm-up Connections, Thinking about Plot, Quoting & Noting, Keeping a Journal, If I Were ———' Responding to Questions, Using Quotations, Taking a Personal View, Write to Others, & Write a Sequel.
Lawrence Productions, Inc.

LION-Union Catalog.
MS-DOS, PC-DOS (512k). IBM PC & compatibles. $750.00. *Optimal configuration:* Hard disk.
Module for Combined Databases for Use with LION Online Public Access Catalog.
Computer Assisted Library Information Co., Inc.

The Lion's Share. *Compatible Hardware:* Apple II+, IIe, IIc. *Memory Required:* 48k.
disk $14.95.
As a Military Spy for the Persians, Crack Your Way into the City of Babylon to Find Daniel & Then Have Your Persian Forces Attack the City.
Davka Corp.

LIP, the Loglan Interactive Parser, 2nd ed.
Version: 2.04. Robert A. McIvor et al. Jul. 1989. *Items Included:* Several pages of printed instructions. *Customer Support:* Occasional 5-day workshops $300-$500.
MS-DOS (65k). disk $50.00 (ISBN 1-877665-08-8).
MAC-DOS (90k). 3.5" disk $50.00 (ISBN 1-877665-09-6).
Produces Grammatical Analysis (Parse Tree/Sentence Diagram) of Any Sentence at Almost Any Level of Detail, As Well As Indicating Errors in Ungrammatical Sentences. Also Has the Facility of Parsing a Text File, Either Utterance by Utterance or All at Once. Useful for Loglan Writers, Teachers & Editors.
The Loglan Institute, Inc.

Liptocoe. Greg Gruse. *Compatible Hardware:* IBM PC, PCjr, PC XT, Portable PC, 3270 PC with IBM Color Display, one double-sided disk drive, joystick (optional).
disk $19.95 (Order no.: 6276569).
Guide Ractor (a Joystick or Keyboard Controlled Robot) Deeper into the Planet of Liptocoe. Race from Menacing Crawdites, & Avoid Death Mines While Collecting Enough Loons to Energize the Transporters - the Only Vehicles That Can Take You to Another Level of Adventure.
Personally Developed Software, Inc.

LIQPIPE: Pipeline Hydraulic Simulation.
Version: 3.5. Shashi Menon. Dec. 1995. *Items Included:* User manual with sample problems. *Customer Support:* Free telephone support.
PC-DOS/MS-DOS. IBM PC, XT, AT, PS/2 & compatibles. disk $1995.00 (ISBN 0-932507-66-2, Order no.: 766). *Optimal configuration:* IBM compatible with DOS 5.0 or higher with 4Mb RAM, floppy disk, hard disk, color monitor, printer.
Liquid Pipeline Hydraulic Simulation Considering Multiple Pumps in Series/Parallel on a Pipeline with Several Pump Stations. Calculates Pressures & Horsepower Required. Also Calculates Pump Impeller Trims Required to Reduce Energy Lost Due to Throttling. Easy to Use with Pull-Down Menus & On-Line Help. Uses Darcy Equation for Pressure Drop. English & Metric Units Due.
Systek (California).

LIQTHERM. *Version:* 3.6. 1994. *Compatible Hardware:* IBM PC, PC XT, PC AT & compatibles, PS/2. *Operating System(s) Required:* MS-DOS, PC-DOS. *Language(s):* BASIC. *Memory Required:* 640k. *Customer Support:* Free phone support.
IBM & compatibles. disk $495.00, incl. manual (ISBN 0-932507-35-2, Order no.: IBM-108).
demo disk $5.00.
Analyzes Hydraulics of Heated, Buried Liquid Pipeline, Taking into Account Heat Transfer with Surroundings. Calculates Pressures & Horsepower Required. Bare & Insulated Pipe Considered Viscosities Are Corrected for Pressure & Temperature. Frictional Heating Is Considered As Option. Calculates Heater Duty.
Systek (California).

Liquid-Liquid Extraction. *Items Included:* Full manual. No other products required. *Customer Support:* Free telephone support - no time limit. 30 day warranty.
MS-DOS 3.2 or higher. IBM & compatibles (512k). disk $579.95.
demo disk $5.00.
Determines the Material Balance, the Number of Theoretical Stages, & the Stage Efficiency in Extraction Operations. Provides an Up-to-Date Analysis of Liquid-Liquid Equilibria Behavior Using Proven Data. The Following Processes Represent a Few of the Typical Liquid-Liquid Extraction Cases That My Be Analyzed: Solvent Dewaxing (Lube Oils Using MEK-Toluene); Propane (Butane) Decarbonizing (FCCU Feed); Amine/Water Solvent with Stripping; Gasoline Sweetening Using Amine (DEA, MDEA, MEA, DGA, etc.). Includes Complete & Detailed Manual Which Describes All Procedures.
Dynacomp, Inc.

Liquid Pipeline Network Surge Analysis. *Items Included:* Full manual. No other products required. *Customer Support:* Free telephone support - no time limit. 30 day warranty.
MS-DOS 3.2 or higher. IBM & compatibles (512k). $3499.95 40 pipes; $4999.95 80 pipes.
Performs the Same Analysis As LIQUID PIPELINE SURGE ANALYSIS (Described Elsewhere), but for Networks Such As Liquid Gathering or Distribution Systems. Pressure Changes & Flow Rates in All Pipe Branches & at Every Time Step of the Simulation Are Calculated in Response to Closing Valves, Falling Pumps, Variable Boundary Pressures, Demands, & Other Upset Conditions Anywhere in the Network.
Dynacomp, Inc.

Liquid Pipeline Network Surge Analysis. 1992. *Items Included:* Detailed manuals included with all Dynacomp products. *Customer Support:* Free telephone support to original customer - no time limit; 30 day limited warranty.
MS-DOS 3.2 or higher. IBM PC & compatibles (512k). $1899.95 (Add $5.00 for 3 1/2" format; 5 1/4" format standard). *Optimal configuration:* IBM, MS-DOS 3.2 or higher, 640k RAM, a hard disk, & CGA or compatible graphics capability.
Performs the Same Analysis As LIQUID PIPELINE SURGE ANALYSIS, but for Networks Such As Liquid Gathering or Distribution Systems. Pressure Changes & Flow Rates in All Pipe Branches & at Every Time Step of the Simulation Are Calculated in Response to Closing Valves, Failing Pumps, Variable Boundary Pressures, Demands, & Other Upset Conditions Anywhere in the Network.
Dynacomp, Inc.

Liquid Pipeline Surge Analysis. *Items Included:* Full manual. No other products required. *Customer Support:* Free telephone support - no time limit. 30 day warranty.
MS-DOS 3.2 or higher. IBM & compatibles (512k). $1149.95 40 pipes; $1649.95 80 pipes. *Optimal configuration:* IBM, MS-DOS 3.3 or higher, 640k RAM & hard disk. Printer is supported.
Calculates Pressure & Flow Rates in Liquid Pipelines under Transient or Surge Conditions. You Can Model Pipes, Pumps, Valves, PRV's, Surge Tanks, Fittings, Leaks, Air Chambers, & Variable Supply/Delivery Pressures & Flow Rates. Pipe Elevations Are Included in the Specifications & Calculations. Up to 40 Pipe Sections Can Be Handled.
Dynacomp, Inc.

Liquid Pumping System Interactive Analysis & Balance. *Items Included:* Full manual. No other products required. *Customer Support:* Free telephone support - no time limit. 30 day warranty.
MS-DOS 3.2 or higher. IBM & compatibles (512k). disk $3999.95. *Optimal configuration:* IBM, MS-DOS 3.3 or higher, 640k RAM, hard disk & graphics capability.
demo disk $5.00.
Calculates the Discharge Head Required Regardless of the System's Complexity or Type of Pump Used. Calculating Discharge Head Requirements Is Complex Even When Only One Branch Is Involved, but LPSAB Handles up to 150 Branches & Will Automatically Balance All Branches with the Branch Requiring the Most Pump Head. Lets You Build a Model of the Piping System & Takes into Account Valves, Fittings, Control Valves, Equipment, & Other Nodes. Supports Both U.S. & S.I. Units.
Dynacomp, Inc.

LISA Plus: Library & Information Science Abstracts. 1995. *Items Included:* Quarterly Updates.
MS-DOS. IBM 286 or higher. CD-ROM disk 1450.00 for 1 year (Order no.: DLI110).
Offering fingertip control of past, present, & ongoing developments in librarianship & related fields.
Bowker-Saur.

LISCOMP. *Version:* 1.1. Bengt Muthen. 1993. *Customer Support:* Free technical support, 90 day limited warranty.
MS-DOS. IBM & compatibles. disk $210.00 (ISBN 1-56321-056-8).
3.5" disk $210.00 (ISBN 1-56321-057-6).
manual $35.00 (ISBN 1-56321-120-3).
Excellent Tool for Executing Advanced Analysis of Linear Structural Equations with a Comprehensive Measurement Model. Researchers Will Especially Appreciate the Ability to Combine Many Types of Variables, Estimators, & Analyses in a Single Program.
Lawrence Erlbaum Assocs., Software & Alternate Media, Inc.

LISP Database. *Compatible Hardware:* IBM PC & compatibles. *Operating System(s) Required:* PC-DOS/MS-DOS. *Memory Required:* 256k. *General Requirements:* Hard disk recommended. *Items Included:* 32 pg. Thinking Software catalog.
3.5" or 5.25" disk $29.95.
Includes a LISP Interpreter & Q&A, a Database Source Program That Can Be Modified by Users.
Thinking Software, Inc.

LISREL 8 & PRELIS 2: Comprehensive Analysis of Linear Relationships in Multivariate Data.
Karl G. Joreskog & Dag Sorbom. *Customer Support:* Free technical support, 90 day limited warranty.
MS-DOS. IBM & compatibles. 3.5" disk $575.00, Windows (ISBN 1-56321-140-8).
3.5" disk $495.00, DOS (ISBN 1-56321-148-3).
MAC. 3.5" disk $590.00 (ISBN 1-56321-112-2).
Extensively Revised & Updated, Offers an Impressive Array of New Facilities for Data Analysis Including Indirect & Total Effects & Their Standard Errors; Direct Specification of Mean Parameters; a Ridge Option for Handling Covariance & Correlation Matrices That Are Not Positive-Definitive; & Modification Indices for All Iterative Estimation Methods.
Lawrence Erlbaum Assocs., Software & Alternate Media, Inc.

List Handler. *Customer Support:* 800-929-8117 (customer service).
MS-DOS. Apple II. disk $59.99 (ISBN 0-87007-709-0).
Generalized Utility to Handle Lists of Objects, Names, Inventories, with Full Alphabetization & Searching, & Printing Out Lists by Category.
SourceView Software International.

TITLE INDEX

The List Manager. *Compatible Hardware:* HP 150 Touchscreen, HP 100 Portable.
3.5" disk $49.95 (Order no.: 35152D).
Organizing Tool Which Helps User to Maintain a Variety of "Listable" Data. Allows User to Collate Mail Lists for Organizations or Personal Lists for Phone Directories, Account Numbers, or Other Related Data. A Predefined Data Input Screen Prompts User for the Correct Data. Other Features Include User-Defined & Fixed-Format Report Generation, Data Retrieval, & Sorting & Printing Capabilities. Can Create Mail Merge Output Files for Use with the WRITER.
Hewlett-Packard Co.

List-N-Label. 1983. *Compatible Hardware:* Apple II; Commodore 64; IBM PC. *Memory Required:* 64k. *General Requirements:* Printer.
disk $12.00.
Mail List & Personnel Filing Program. Accepts up to 250 Entries with Name, Street, Address, City-State-Zip, Phone, & a Category Designator for Tagging & Sorting. Prints Mailing Labels. Lists & Labels May Be Sorted by Category.
Navic Software.

Listen!: A Music Skills Program. Vincent Oddo. 1985. *Compatible Hardware:* Apple II+, IIe, IIc, IIgs; Commodore 64, 128; IBM PC. *Operating System(s) Required:* Apple DOS 3.3, PC-DOS 3.3. *Language(s):* QuickBasic. *Memory Required:* Apple 48k, Commodore 64k, IBM 640k. *General Requirements:* CGA card for IBM.
disk $39.95 ea.
Apple. (ISBN 0-942132-81-5, Order no.: A-1164).
Commodore. (ISBN 0-942132-83-1, Order no.: C-1164).
IBM. (ISBN 0-942132-82-3, Order no.: I-1164).
Consists of Three Lessons Designed to Help Increase the Ability to Perceive & Identify Intervals, Basic Chords, & Seventh Chords. Each Lesson Reinforces Learning by Displaying the Correct Answers When an Incorrect Answer Is Given. A Score Page Offers Feedback on Knowledge of These Basic Music Skills.
Electronic Courseware Systems, Inc.

Listening to Users: Case Studies in Building Electronic Communities: 1992 Faxon Institute Annual Conference Proceedings. Jan. 1993.
MS-DOS 3.0 or higher. IBM or compatible PC w/hard drive (384k free memory, 640k recommended). disk $60.00 (ISBN 0-9631061-1-2).
Using a Hypertext Interface, the DOS-Based Conference Proceedings Includes Full Text of Many Papers Presented at the Conference As Well As the Exchanges & Related Ideas of over 50 Electronic Conference Participants. Users Can Zero-In on the Sections of Most Interest; Link to Related Material Throughout the Publication; Search for Any Term in the Text; Print Items of Particular Interest; Browse the Name Index.

Lister. *Customer Support:* 800-929-8117 (customer service).
MS-DOS. IBM/PS2. disk $99.99 (ISBN 0-87007-552-7).
System Designed to Produce Lists of Dollar Transactions, by Type of Transaction. Three Data Elements Are Entered: Transaction Dollar Amount, Transaction Key & Description. As Each Transaction Key & Dollar Amount Is Entered, the System Accumulates Summary Totals Based on the Key. There Is Online Help.
SourceView Software International.

LISTER: Alternative to Spread Sheets. Jun. 1990. *Compatible Hardware:* IBM PC. *Operating System(s) Required:* PC-DOS. *Memory Required:* 512k. *General Requirements:* 2 disk drives, printer.
disk $129.95 (Order no.: P100).
Summarizes Dollar Amounts into Sub-Categories Based on a Category Key. If Desired a Comment or Description of the Transaction Can Be Entered Alongside the Dollar Amount. May Be Used Like a Adding Machine, Enter a Number & a Grand Total is Displayed. If User Enters a Category Key, Next to the Number, a Sub-Total of All the Numbers with the Same Key is Displayed. The Category Key (up to 10 Characters) Does NOT Have to be Pre-Defined. Allows User to Scroll up/down the Multi-Line Input Screen, to Review or to Make Changes. User Can Sort Data, Print Reports, Merge Other Files, Consolidate Files; Analyze the Summary Totals, Sort Them, Add Descriptive Titles, & Print Reports. Has As Many As 500 Different Keys to Accumulate Sub-Totals on, Which Is Equivalent to Spread Sheet with 500 Columns. Sample Data Is Included.
State Business Systems, Inc.

LISTMAN: Telemarketing & Direct Mail List Management. *Version:* 1.1. Open Door Software Division. May 1992. *Items Included:* Manual. *Customer Support:* On-site training available, $200.00/day, plus per diem; Customization available, $50.00/hr; Maintenance on customized copies, $100.00/month.
IBM & compatible (512k). disk $99.00 (ISBN 1-56756-003-2, Order no.: OD5001).
Comprehensive Software Application That Tracks Large Lists of Potential Clients.
Advantage International.

Listmaster. *Operating System(s) Required:* CP/M.
contact publisher for price.
Practical Solutions, Inc.

Lite Editor. Cary Ravitz. *Compatible Hardware:* IBM PC, PCjr, PC XT, PC AT, Portable PC, 3270 PC. *Operating System(s) Required:* PC-DOS 2.00, 2.10, 3.00, 3.10. *Memory Required:* 128k, PCjr with DOS 3.00 or 3.10 256k.
disk $24.95 (Order no.: 6276637).
Full-Screen Editor Designed for Creating Outlines & Short Documents, & Editing Program Code. Users Can "Hide" Lines from the Screen, Making It Easy to Display Outlines of Their Text. Help Screens, Reference Cards, & Structured Code Can Be Displayed. Other Capabilities Include: Mark a Position & Return to It; Move, Copy, Overlay, & Delete Blocks of Text; Move or Copy Text Between Different Files; Shift Text Horizontally or Vertically. Flow Text with or Without Right Justification; Print Marked Areas of Text; Edit IBM Script/PC Files; Operate Functions Similar to SPF on Mainframe Terminals.
Personally Developed Software, Inc.

LITIDEX: Litigation Support/Document Management System. *Version:* IV. Michael Carr. Mar. 1986. *Compatible Hardware:* MS-DOS 3.1 compatible hardware. *Operating System(s) Required:* MS-DOS, UNIX. *Language(s):* F. *Memory Required:* 640k. *General Requirements:* Printer; 40Mb hard disk, modem & color monitor recommended.
MS-DOS version. disk $3400.00.
UNIX. disk write for info.
Automated Litigation Support Software Which Organizes & Categorizes Case-Related Documents. Features Rapid Indexing, As Well As Search & Retrieval of All Words & Phrases in Both Abstracts & Full Text Information.
MLSI.

Litigation & Resource Library: Series 500 & 600. *Compatible Hardware:* IBM PC, PS/2.
contact publisher for price.
Provides Ability to Collect & Index Data & Documents Related to Litigation Cases. Data Can Be Retrieved by Author, Recipient, Case Issue, or Source of Document. Provides Ability to Collect & Retrieve Library Publications, Attorney Work-Product & More with User-Defined Screen Capability.
Manac-Prentice Hall Software, Inc.

Litigation Express. *Version:* 1.01. Dec. 1984. *Compatible Hardware:* IBM or compatible. *Operating System(s) Required:* MS-DOS, PC-DOS. *Memory Required:* 320k. *Customer Support:* 412-397-8666.
disk $299.00.
Provides Automated Case Information Management for the Attorney. Can Be Used by the Practitioners, Law Firms, Corporations, & Governmental Agencies.
San Francisco Legal Systems.

Litigation Support. *Version:* 2.01. Jun. 1984. *Compatible Hardware:* IBM PC, PC XT, PC AT, & compatibles, PS/2. *Operating System(s) Required:* MS-DOS 2.0. *Language(s):* C. *Memory Required:* 512k. *General Requirements:* Printer. *Customer Support:* 90-day warranty; yearly software update & service $180.
disk $895.00.
In-House Evidentiary Research & Expert Witness Indexing System. Manages a Large Number of Documents and/or Witnesses Associated with a Case or Trial.
Data Law.

Litigation Support: Series 900 to 2000. *Compatible Hardware:* IBM System/36, System/36 PC; AS/400.
contact publisher for price.
All Case-Related Data Can Be Collected, Organized, Indexed & Retrieved As Required.
Manac-Prentice Hall Software, Inc.

Litigator & Litigator-M. *Version:* 4.0. 1992. *Compatible Hardware:* IBM PC & compatibles. *Operating System(s) Required:* PC-DOS/MS-DOS; Networks such as Novell, Lantastic. *Customer Support:* 30 days' free support, 1 yr. maintenance $250.00.
disk $395.00.
Litigation Support & File Management Practice System for Attorneys Who Try Cases in Court. Organizes a Case for Trial & Produces the Report Needed to Manage a Trial Practice. Information Covering Every Aspect of a Case Is Entered, from Witnesses to Documents to Settlement Negotiations. Reports Include: Case, Search & Sorted Reports. Also Runs Conflict of Interest Searches, Retrieves Past Efforts & Prints Active & Permanent Case & Client Lists & Reports. Integrates to Verdict & Docket for Conflict of Interest Searches. Litigator-M Is Available for Networked Systems.
Micro Craft, Inc.

Little Monster at School. (Living Book Ser.).
Mercer Mayer.
MS-DOS 5.0 or higher, Windows 3.1 or higher. 386 processor or higher (4Mb). CD-ROM disk $49.95 (Order no.: R1186). *Nonstandard peripherals required:* CD-ROM drive. *Optimal configuration:* 386 processor operating at 16MHz or higher, MS-DOS 5.0 or higher, Windows 3.1 or higher, 30Mb hard drive, mouse, VGA graphic adapter & VGA color

A LITTLE PAINTER

monitor (SVGA recommended), 4Mb RAM, external speakers or headphones (with sound card) that are Sound Blaster compatible. Macintosh (4Mb). (Order no.: R1186). *Nonstandard peripherals required:* 14" color monitor or larger, CD-ROM drive.
Highly Interactive Animated Stories for Children That Have Hundreds of Beautiful Animations & Have Received Countless Awards. In English & Spanish. Spend the Day with Little Monster As He Goes off to School to Learn about the ABCs, Numbers, Science & Other Subjects.
Library Video Co.

A Little Painter. *Version:* 1.2. Sep. 1995. *Items Included:* CD-ROM, Jewel Case, Installation Instructions. *Customer Support:* One year free technical support, 30 day unlimited warranty. Windows 3.1. 80286(AT), (512k). CD-ROM disk $29.95.
The Quality of the Images Make This Coloring Game Great Fun for Kids. Animated Images & Icons Make Using the Software Fun! Your Kids Will Create Pictures They'll Love to Show off to You, Neighbors, Friends, & Relatives. Your Refrigerator Will Be Covered with Pictures! Pictures Can Be Printed or Copied for Use with Other Programs.
PSG-HomeCraft Software.

Little Rascals. *Version:* 1.5. (Interactive MovieBook Ser.). Jul. 1995. *Items Included:* Manual, registration card, promotional flyers. *Customer Support:* Phone technical support. Windows 3.1 or later. 386DX 25MHz or higher (4Mb). CD-ROM disk $29.95 (ISBN 1-57303-020-1). *Nonstandard peripherals required:* Sound card, CD-ROM drive. *Optimal configuration:* 486 or higher with 8Mb RAM, Windows 3.1 or later, 15Mb free hard drive space available, sound card, 256 color monitor.
Interactive MovieBooks Are Exclusively Licensed Computer Story/Activity Books for Children Ages 4 & up. These CD-ROMs Combine the Fun of Movies with the Educational Value of a Book. Movies Come Alive with Video Clips, Pictures, Sound Effects, Animation & Other Surprises. Computer Puzzles, Games, Mazes, & Many Other Learning Activities Are Included.
Sound Source Interactive.

The Little Turtle. Vachel Lindsay. Oct. 1994. *Items Included:* Bound parent activity guide & user manual. *Customer Support:* Free 800# support for registered users; 90-day limited warranty.
System 7.0 or above. MAC LC 11 or above. 3.5" disk $49.95 (ISBN 1-57026-034-6). *Nonstandard peripherals required:* CD-Rom Drive, microphone (optional). *Optimal configuration:* MAC LC II, System 7, 4 mb RAM, color monitor, CD-ROM drive, hard drive, microphone (optional).
MPC Windows 3.1.1 (4 Mb). PC or compatible, 386 or above. *Nonstandard peripherals required:* CD-ROM drive, Soundblaster or 100% compatible, Audio card, Speakers, Microphone (optional). *Optimal configuration:* 386 PC or compatible, Windows 3.1.1, 4 mb RAM, CD-ROM drive, hard drive, soundblaster or 100% compatible, basic audio card, VGA graphics, & color monitor, mouse & speakers, microphone (optional).
"The Little Turtle" is a multi-media reading product for children ages 3-7 that features a story about a box turtle, context-based activities & a 240 word multimedia glossary, this CD-ROM product helps young children build pre-reading & beginning Reading skills.
Computer Curriculum Corporation.

Little Women. *Version:* 1.5. Feb. 1995. *Items Included:* BookWorm Student Reader (diskette). *Customer Support:* 30 day MBG. Technical support (toll call) - no charge.
System 7.0 or higher. Macintosh (5Mb). CD-ROM disk $29.95 (ISBN 1-57316-031-8, Order no.: 16166). *Nonstandard peripherals required:* CD-ROM drive, 12" color monitor. *Optimal configuration:* 13" color monitor recommended.
Windows 3.1 or higher. IBM compatible (MPC) 386 DX (4Mb). CD-ROM disk $29.95. *Nonstandard peripherals required:* Standard multimedia compatible CD-ROM. *Optimal configuration:* 8Mb RAM recommended, 256 color monitor recommended.
Louisa May Alcott's Novel Is Perhaps the Most Popular Girls' Story Ever Written. Among the Many Unique Features of This Edition Is the Text History Topic That Charts the Many Changes Alcott Made in the Course of the Work's Creation. Splendid Period Illustrations Are Also Featured. Features Complete Sound Allowing the User to Listen to All or Part of Each Work.
Communication & Information Technologies, Inc. (CIT).

Livestock Auction. Agri-Management Services, Inc. *Operating System(s) Required:* MS-DOS. *Memory Required:* 64k. $995.00.
Manages Multi-Transaction Operation, Regardless of Species, Size, Grouping, etc. Allows Detailed Animal Records & Financial Transaction Information on Each Animal.
Texas Instruments, Personal Productivit.

The Living Bible. May 1993. *Items Included:* Disks, marketing literature, order form. *Customer Support:* No fee for customer support: 30 day money back guarantee, limited replacement warranty on diskettes defective at time of purchase, free telephone technical support. PC-DOS/MS-DOS 3.0 or higher or Windows 3.1 or higher. 386/486 or 100% IBM compatible (Windows); Also AT/XT/286 (DOS) (640k DOS or 4Mb Windows). 3.5" disk $39.95 (ISBN 1-56514-223-3). *Addl. software required:* Biblesoft's PC Study Bible. *Optimal configuration:* 3.5" disk drive for installation & 1.5Mb of hard drive space, mouse or pointer device recommended.
The Text of The Living Bible - an Add-On to Be Used with Biblesoft's PC Study Bible.
Biblesoft.

The Living Bible. May 1993. *Items Included:* Disks, marketing literature, order form. *Customer Support:* No fee for customer support: 30 day money back guarantee, limited replacement warranty on diskettes defective at time of purchase, free telephone technical support. PC-DOS/MS-DOS 3.1 or higher or MS Windows 3.0 or higher. 386/486 or 100% IBM compatible (Windows); Also AT/XT/286 (DOS) (640k DOS or 4Mb Windows). disk $39.95 (ISBN 1-56514-565-8). *Addl. software required:* Biblesoft's PC Study Bible. *Optimal configuration:* Requires 5.25" 1.2Mb disk drive for installation & 1.5Mb of hard drive space, mouse or pointer device recommended.
The Text of The Living Bible - an Add-On Bible Version to Be Used with Biblesoft's PC Study Bible.
Biblesoft.

The Living Bible. May 1993. *Customer Support:* No fee for customer support: (1) 30 day money back guarantee (2) Lifetime warranty replacement on defective disks (3) Free telephone technical support.
PC-DOS/MS-DOS 2.0 or higher. IBM PC, XT/AT/286/386/486 or 100% compatibles (640k). disk $49.95 (ISBN 1-56514-565-8). *Addl. software required:* PC Study Bible. *Optimal configuration:* Requires 5 1/4" 1.2Mb disk drive for installation & 3Mb of hard drive space. Mouse or pointer device recommended.
Text of THE LIVING BIBLE. Add-On Bible Version to Be Used with BIBLESOFT'S PC Study Bible.

The Living Bible Add-On Module. Kenneth N. Taylor. Mar. 1990. *Customer Support:* No fee is charged for our customer support: 30 day money back return guarantee; lifetime warranty on defective disk replacement; free telephone technical support.
PC or MS-DOS 2.0 or higher. IBM PC/XT/AT or compatible. 3.5" or 5.25" disk $49.95. *Addl. software required:* PC STUDY BIBLE. *Optimal configuration:* Two 5.25" or 3.5" disk drives or a hard disk with 1.5Mb hard disk space for each Bible version. Hard drive recommended.
The Text of The Living Bible. Add-On Bible Version to Be Used with BIBLESOFT'S PC STUDY BIBLE.
Biblesoft.

Living Book Series.
MS-DOS 5.0 or higher, Windows 3.1 or higher. 386 processor or higher (4Mb). CD-ROM disk $399.60, Set (Order no.: R1042). *Nonstandard peripherals required:* CD-ROM drive. *Optimal configuration:* 386 processor operating at 16MHz or higher, MS-DOS 5.0 or higher, Windows 3.1 or higher, 30Mb hard drive, mouse, VGA graphic adapter & VGA color monitor (SVGA recommended), 4Mb RAM, external speakers or headphones (with sound card) that are Sound Blaster compatible. Macintosh (4Mb). (Order no.: R1042). *Nonstandard peripherals required:* 14" color monitor or larger, CD-ROM drive.
Highly Interactive Animated Stories for Children That Have Hundreds of Beautiful Animations & Have Received Countless Awards. 8 Volume Set.
Library Video Co.

Living TrustBuilder. *Version:* 3.1. Jul. 1992. *Compatible Hardware:* IBM PC & compatibles, Macintosh. *Items Included:* Manual & diskette. *Customer Support:* Free installation & technical support: limited warranty, call JIAN 415-941-9191.
$199.00. *Addl. software required:* PC's: word processor compatible with MS Word, WordPerfect, PCWrite, PFS First Choice, MS Works, WordStar & others. Macintosh: word processor, MacWrite 5.0 or MS Word 3.0 compatible.
Provides the Necessary Documents for Writing a Living Trust That Protects Financial Security. The Finished Document Addresses Issues Such As Cash Flow, Life Insurance Monies, Insulation Against Financial Attack, Income Taxes, & the Care of Surviving Children. The Finished Document Is Easily Customized & Ready for Legal Review.
JIAN Tools for Sales.

LMI FORTH-83 Metacompiler. *Version:* 3.1. Aug. 1994. *Compatible Hardware:* IBM PC & compatibles, PS/2. *Operating System(s) Required:* PC-DOS, MS-DOS, OS/2. *Language(s):* FORTH. *Memory Required:* 512k. $750.00.
Table-Driven Multi-Pass Forth-83 Compiler. Compiles Compact ROMable or Disk-Based Applications. Produces Headerless Code, Compiles from Intermediate States, & Performs Conditional Compilation. Cross-Compiles to 8080, Z80, 8086, 68000, 6502, 8051, 8096, 68HCII. There Is No License Fee or Royalty for Compiled Applications.
Laboratory Microsystems, Inc.

TITLE INDEX

LMserver. *Items Included:* User manuals. *Customer Support:* One year maintenance & customer telephone support with purchase.
UNIX, VAX/VMS. VAX, Masscomp, UNISYS 5030/5050, SUN 3, SUN 4, Honeywell XPS 100, NCR Tower, Harris MCX, UNISYS 5085/5095, Altos Plexus, AT&T3B2, Sequent, RS/6000, Motorola Delta, DEC 3100. contact publisher for price. *Addl. software required:* TCP/IP. *Optimal configuration:* Varies. *Networks supported:* Any MS-net or LAN Manager over TCP/IP or OSI.
Network Operating System Which Implements Microsoft's LAN Manager Protocol Specification. Allows Computers Running LAN Manager, LAN Server, PC Network, or Other Standards-Compatible Client Packages to Communicate with UNIX Computers. Provides for the Sharing of File, Print & Plot Resources, As Well as Client Control of Host Processes. Provides Sophisticated Interactive Network Administration & Management Utilities, as Well as Advanced Programming Tools for Distributed Application Development. Communicates with Clients Using Internet Standard TCP/IP Protocols Implementedf on Ethernet or Token-Ring Networks.
OCS/Syntax.

Load 1-2-3. *Version:* 2.0. Mar. 1984. *Compatible Hardware:* IBM PC & compatibles. *Operating System(s) Required:* PC-DOS 1.1, 2.0. (source code included). *Memory Required:* 640k. *General Requirements:* Lotus 1-2-3.
IBM. $120.00, incl. manual (ISBN 0-918627-00-1).
demo disk $10.00 (ISBN 0-918627-01-X).
manual only $20.00 (ISBN 0-918627-02-8).
Calculates Heating/Cooling Loads for Buildings Using ASHRAE Procedures. Heating Loads Are Calculated for Transmission Losses & Infiltration. Cooling Loads Are Calculated for Conduction, Solar, Internal Loads & Infiltration.
E. Jessup & Assocs.

LoadCalc. *Version:* 5.23. L. A. Chapman. Feb. 1982. *Compatible Hardware:* IBM PC & compatibles, PC XT, PC AT, PS/2; DEC Rainbow; Texas Instruments; Wang. *Operating System(s) Required:* PC-DOS/MS-DOS. *Language(s):* Compiled BASIC. *Memory Required:* 192k. *Customer Support:* Yes.
disk $175.00.
Converts Text or Print Files, Such As Those Downloaded from Another Computer, into Spreadsheet Files for LOTUS 1-2-3, VISICALC, MULTIPLAN, SUPERCALC or DIF, SYMPHONY, dBASE II, III, CHARTMAN.
Micro Decision Systems (Pennsylvania).

Loan Amortization. 1978. *Compatible Hardware:* Apple; IBM PC & compatibles. *Operating System(s) Required:* MS-DOS, Apple DOS. *Language(s):* BASIC. *Memory Required:* 48k.
disk $75.00.
Calculates the Loan Payment & Displays a Schedule of Loan Payments Including Dates, Payment Number, Payment, Principal Interest, & Loan Balance.
Realty Software.

Loan Amortization-Plus. *Version:* 4.2. 1995. *Items Included:* Complete operating manual. *Customer Support:* Unlimited telephone support.
MS-DOS. IBM PC or compatible (256k).
$125.00. *Optimal configuration:* IBM PC or compatible, 256k RAM, printer. *Networks supported:* Novel, Unex.
Complete Amortization Program Which Handles Regular Mortgage with Constant Interest Percentage on the Unpaid Balance, the Rule of 78's, Balloon Payments & Periodic Payments. Great for Preparing Amortization Schedules for Clients, Banks, Finance Companies, etc.
Omni Software Systems, Inc. (Indiana).

Loan Analysis. *Compatible Hardware:* IBM.
disk $29.95.
Dynacomp, Inc.

The Loan Arranger. David Marshall. 1985. *Compatible Hardware:* Apple II series. *Operating System(s) Required:* DOS. *Language(s):* BASIC. *Memory Required:* 48k. *General Requirements:* Printer.
disk $34.95 (ISBN 0-917729-66-8).
Evaluates Financing Alternatives & Effective Interest Rates As Well As Printing Loan Amortization Schedules.
Compu-Tations, Inc.

The Loan Arranger. *Compatible Hardware:* Atari 400, 800. *Language(s):* BASIC (source code included). *Memory Required:* 40k. *General Requirements:* Atari 810 disk drive, printer.
disk $29.95.
Designed to Help Keep Track of up to 25 Personal Loans.
Dynacomp, Inc.

The Loan Closer. *Version:* 2.3. Jun. 1984. *Compatible Hardware:* IBM PC, PC XT, PC AT. *Operating System(s) Required:* MS-DOS. *Language(s):* BASIC. *Memory Required:* 512k. *Items Included:* Manual, program disks. *Customer Support:* Phone, on-site training.
disk $3500.00.
Designed to Handle Any Type of Loan on the Market Today, Including All Fixed, Adjustable, Graduated & Interest-Only Payment Loans. Also Calculates Impounds, P&I, Taxes, Insurance, Fees, Odd Days Interest, Finance Charges, & Other Financial Information.
Contour Software, Inc.

Loan Express. *Version:* 1.0. Jun. 1991. *Items Included:* 150 page manual, Step-by-Step tutorial, data entry worksheet, automatic report writer, graphs. *Customer Support:* 1 year free support.
MS-DOS (640k). disk $195.00.
Helps You to Create Loan Proposals & Financial Business Plans Quickly. It Will Lead You Step-by-Step Through the Entire Loan Process & Will Offer Such Financing Options As; SBA Loans, Credit Lines, Leases, Asset Based Loans, Long Term Debt & Venture Capital. Automatically Produces 20-25 Page Written Proposal.
ValuSource.

The Loan Finder. *Version:* 3.0. May 1984. *Compatible Hardware:* IBM PC series, COMPAQ. *Operating System(s) Required:* MS-DOS. *Language(s):* BASIC. *Memory Required:* 512k. *Items Included:* manual, program disks. *Customer Support:* Phone, on-site training.
disk $450.00.
Prequalifies & Analyzes Prospective Borrowers & Their Ratios. Uses Prequalification Information to Search Through a List of Loan Types, Using Any Criteria Given, & Finds the Best Loan Available to the Borrower.
Contour Software, Inc.

Loan Handler. *Version:* 2.7. Feb. 1983. *Compatible Hardware:* IBM PC series, COMPAQ. *Operating System(s) Required:* MS-DOS. *Language(s):* BASIC. *Memory Required:* 512k. *Items Included:* Manual, program disks. *Customer Support:* Phone, initial on-site training.
disk $2250.00.
Processes Loan Applications, Verifications, Transmittal Summaries, Loan Submission Sheets, & Regulation Z Disclosures.
Contour Software, Inc.

Loan Manager. *Items Included:* 96 page manual. *Customer Support:* Free telephone support to registered users.

THE LOAN TRACKER

PC-DOS/MS-DOS 2.1 or higher. IBM PC PC XT, PC AT, PS/2 & compatibles. contact publisher for price.
Considers Points, Fees & Length of Time One Expects to Keep a Loan When Computing the Effective Interest Rate. Parameters Are Displayed on a Single Screen & Recalculated As Different Values Are Entered While Searching for the Best Deal. All Calculations Are Presented in Accordance with Established Banking Conventions.
Lassen Software, Inc.

Loan-Master. *Version:* 3.0. David Powers. Jan. 1985. *Compatible Hardware:* IBM PC & compatibles. *Operating System(s) Required:* MS-DOS, PC-DOS. *Language(s):* Pascal. *Memory Required:* 64k.
$49.95.
Loan Analysis Program to Handle Almost Any Type Fixed-Rate Loan Including Zero-Interest & "Balloon" Payments (Based on Years, Months, or Days). Useful for Analyzing Home or Auto Loans. Outputs Periodic or Annual Schedule, Ideal for Income Tax Purposes.
Generic Computer Products, Inc. (GCPI).

Loan-Pak. *Version:* 2.1. Robert P. King. Apr. 1983. *Operating System(s) Required:* PC-DOS 2.0, TurboDOS, CP/M-80, CP/M-86, MP/M II, MP/M-86. *Language(s):* CB 80, 86. *Memory Required:* 64k.
disk $79.95.
8" disk $79.95.
Loan Amortization Calculation & Schedule Printing Program.
Crownsoft Applications.

Loan Pricing & Profitability-Yield on Funds Used. *Compatible Hardware:* Sharp ZL-6100 System, ZL-6500 System. *Language(s):* Sharp Microcode.
$400.00.
Analyzes the Terms of a Commercial Loan Agreement & Computes the Yield the Bank Realizes on the Net Funds Used & Finds the Loan Interest Rate Required to Obtain a Yield. Takes into Account the Impact of Interest-Bearing Compensating Balances, Administrative Expenses & Credit & Maturity Risks.
P-ROM Software, Inc.

Loan Qualifier. *Version:* 1.5. *Compatible Hardware:* Apple Macintosh, Apple II, IBM-PC. *Memory Required:* 64k. *General Requirements:* Spreadsheet program such as EXCEL, Lotus 1-2-3, Appleworks; hard disk or two drives & printer. *Items Included:* 44 page manual with examples. *Customer Support:* 90 day unlimited warranty.
disk $99.00.
Assists in Qualifying Mortgage Prospects, Calculates Associated Costs & Generates a Loan Estimate Report.
Financial Microware.

Loan Sales/Purchase. 1978. *Compatible Hardware:* Apple; IBM PC & compatibles; Tandy. *Operating System(s) Required:* MS-DOS, Apple DOS. *Memory Required:* 48k.
disk $75.00.
Calculates Either the Present Value of a Loan Based on Required Percentage Return, or the Percentage Return Based on Price Paid for the Loan.
Realty Software.

The Loan Tracker. *Version:* 2.5. Jan. 1984. *Compatible Hardware:* IBM PC series, COMPAQ. *Operating System(s) Required:* MS-DOS. *Language(s):* BASIC. *Memory Required:* 512k. *Items Included:* Manual, program disks. *Customer Support:* Phone, initial on-site training.

LOANBASE DOCPREP II

disk $1000.00.
Follows the Current Status of Loans & Produces a Variety of Management Reports. Fully Integrated with THE LOAN HANDLER.
Contour Software, Inc.

LOANbase DocPrep II. *Version:* 2.5. Jul. 1993. *Items Included:* User manual, runtime version of FoxPro 2.5. *Customer Support:* Telephone, fax, on-site, bulletin board, 90 days with purchase of license. Annual support & update fees at one price.
  MS-DOS 6.X. IBM 386 & 486 (4Mb). $2995.00 Full system, Network; modules available. *Addl. software required:* JetForm JF-Merge needed for custom document design work only. *Optimal configuration:* 386-DX, 8Mb RAM, hard disk, HP Laserjet compatible. *Networks supported:* Novell Netware.
Loan Document Preparation for All Mortgage & Consumer Loan Closing Documents. Full Laser Printing Capability Included. Pop-Up Pull-Down Windows for Intuitive Access to Hundreds of Features. Imports Loan Data from Several Loan Origination Software Systems. Exports to Other Systems. Only Software Sold Which Is Used by Doc Prep Services. Currently Supports 900 Laser Loan Documents Used by 200 National Lenders. Most Users Learn This Software in One Day.
Lender Support Systems, Inc.

LOANbase III PLUS. *Version:* 4.6. Jan. 1987. *Compatible Hardware:* IBM PC & compatibles. *Operating System(s) Required:* MS-DOS 6.0, Novell NetWare. *Language(s):* Fox Pro Compiled Relational Database Utilizing xBASE compatible. *Memory Required:* 4000k. *General Requirements:* 386 DX hard disk; modem; HP Laser jet or dot matrix printer with 160 characters per line in compressed mode landscape. *Items Included:* User manual, telephone & FAX, 4 hrs. training. *Customer Support:* 90-day support, updates, limited warranty, custom data conversion.
  LOANbase III Entry Modules. disk $4000.00.
  LOANbase III Private Money Lender. disk $6000.00.
  LOANbase III PLUS Mortgage Banker Total Lender. $11,500.00.
  LOANbase III LAN Mortgage Banker Total Lender.
Loan Servicing/Accounting Software Package Designed for Lenders, Mortgage Bankers, Brokers, Banks, S&L's, Private Lenders, Thrifts, Credit Unions, & Consumer Finance Companies. Tracks, Displays, & Analyzes Borrower Payment Performance, Escrows/Impounds, Lender-Investor Portfolio Yield, Computes Principal, Interest Payment & Impound Escrow Distributions, Amortizes All Loan Types. Computes Late Charges, Fees, Automates NSF Reversals, Collections & Payoffs, Total Investor Accounting Included in Base System (LOANbase III). Links with Loan Processing Document Prep Systems. FHLMC, FNMA, & GNMA, & Private Investor Accounting. All Borrower & Investor Management Calculation Features Included.
Lender Support Systems, Inc.

LoanComp. 1979. *Compatible Hardware:* IBM PC; TRS-80 Model I, Model II, Model III, Model 4, Model 12, Model 16. *Operating System(s) Required:* TRSDOS, PC-DOS. *Memory Required:* 48-64k.
  disk $167.95.
Computes Interest & Principal Balances for Monthly, Annual & Loan Total Periods. Computes Payments Required to Amortize a Loan. Makes "True Annual Percentage Rate" Computation. Computes Annual Interest & Payoff Rebate According to the Rule of 78. Separate Section Analyzes Ordinary Annuities.
Contract Services Assocs.

LOANet. *Version:* 3.0. Jun. 1989. *Compatible Hardware:* IBM PC/XT, PS/2 & compatibles. *Operating System(s) Required:* MS-DOS 2.10 or higher. *Memory Required:* 640k. *Customer Support:* Toll-free phone service, 30 days unlimited warranty.
  write for info.
Interlibrary Loan & Electronic Mail System for Libraries Utilizing CD-ROM Discs Housing Appropriate Union Catalog Database for Group of Libraries in Network.
Library Systems & Services, Inc.

LoanLease Library.
  Macintosh 512KE or higher. 3.5" disk $69.95.
Loan Amortization System.
Softflair, Inc.

Loanledger+, 3 disks. *Version:* 7.1. 1983. *Compatible Hardware:* IBM PC & compatibles, PC XT, PC AT. *Operating System(s) Required:* MS-DOS, PC-DOS 3.3 & higher. *Language(s):* Assembly, BASIC, MS Compiled. *Memory Required:* 2000k. *General Requirements:* printer.
  disk $5500.00 ea. (ISBN 0-931813-01-8).
  disk Network $8250.00.
Services Mortgages; Consumer, Commercial & Construction & Revolving Credit Loans, for Mortgage Companies, Banks, Savings & Loans, Finance Companies, Thrifts, Credit Unions, Retail Stores & Private Lenders. Provides Accounting Management Reporting & an Array of Collection Tools. Performs Interest Calculations: Mortgage, Rule of 78's, Interest Only, Balloons, Adjustables. Produces Ledgers, Payment Books, Statements, Reminder & Collection Letters, Annual Closing Letters, 1099's, 1096's. Fully Inquiry Screens, Visual Verification Input. Reports Agings, Investor Accounting, Impounds Escrows, Yields, Cash Flow, Portfolio Risk/Exposure. Report Generator for ad hoc Database Reports Instantly. Projects Payoffs on Demand Notepad.
Dynamic Interface Systems Corp.

Local ACE - Authority Control Edit. *Version:* 1.3. 1994. *Items Included:* Manual. *Customer Support:* One year of CSAP is provided at N/C; 30 day no risk guarantee.
  MS-DOS. IBM & compatibles (640k). 5.25" disk $495.00 (ISBN 0-927875-46-2, Order no.: 1820). *Addl. software required:* Winn CIRC and/or CAT, Union CAT, PC Cardmaker. *Networks supported:* Netbios or IPX compatible.
  3.5" disk $495.00 (ISBN 0-927875-45-4, Order no.: 1820).
Lets You Ensure Your Material Database Is Uniform & Complete. You Can Add, Edit, & Delete the Bibliographic Information Contained in Multiple Records in One Editing Process. You Can Also Edit Call Numbers, Prefixes, Suffixes, Letter Capitalization, & Marc Tags.
Winnebago Software Co.

Local & Greenwich Sidereal Time. *Compatible Hardware:* TI 99/4A with Extended BASIC module. *Operating System(s) Required:* DX-10. *Language(s):* Extended BASIC. *Memory Required:* 48k.
  cassette $18.95.
Calculates Greenwich Mean Sidereal Time & Local Mean Sidereal Time in Hours, Minutes & Seconds When the User Provides the Geographic Longitude. Works for the Years 1975 to 2000.
Eastbench Software Products.

Local Area Networks: An Overview. Dec. 1994. *Items Included:* User manual. *Customer Support:* Free technical support & a 30-day warranty (1-800-521-CORE).
  MS-DOS. IBM & compatibles (512k). 3.5" disk $199.00 (ISBN 1-57305-012-1). *Nonstandard peripherals required:* High-density 3.5" disk drive; VGA color monitor. *Addl. software required:* MS-DOS version 3.3 or higher. *Optimal configuration:* IBM (512k), MS-DOS version 3.3 or higher, VGA color monitor, keyboard, Microsoft compatible mouse (optional).
In This Course, You Will Learn about the Topologies, the Components, & the Characteristics of the Various Technologies. It Is a Stand-Alone Course but Is Also a Helpful Prerequisite for More Advanced Training Related to Local Area Networking. The Training Will Take Approximately 1 to 2 Hours to Complete. It Is Training That Will Help You Understand Some of the On-Going Changes in Your Organization.
Bellcore.

Local Area Networks I: Fundamentals, Technologies & PCs. *Version:* 2.0. Edutrends, Inc. & Delphi, Inc. 1990. *Customer Support:* 30 day free phone support.
  MS-DOS (640k). IBM PC & 100% compatibles. disk $495.00 (ISBN 0-935987-39-8). *Nonstandard peripherals required:* CGA, EGA or VGA board with color monitor, Hercules graphics with monochrome monitor. *Optimal configuration:* Hard disk.
This Interactive CBT Course is Divided into Eight Broad Sections Including LAN Evolution to Revolution, the PCs Role in Communications, LAN Categories, Topology & Access Methods, Transmission Techniques & Media, LAN Standards, an Introduction to Resource Sharing, an Introduction to PC/LAN Products. Color Animated Graphics, on Line Glossary, Electronic Book Mark.
Edutrends, Inc.

Local Area Networks II: Resource Sharing, Interconnections & Products. *Version:* 2.0. Edutrends, Inc. & Delphi, Inc. 1990. *Customer Support:* 30 day free phone support.
  MS-DOS (640k). IBM PC/XT, AT, PS2 & 100% compatibles. disk $495.00 (ISBN 0-935987-40-1). *Nonstandard peripherals required:* CGA, EGA or VGA graphics board with color monitor or Hercules graphics with monochrome monitor. *Optimal configuration:* Hard disk.
Interactive Computer Based Training Course Focusing on Advanced LAN Topics Including LAN to LAN Interconnections & Resource Sharing Inter-LAN Alternatives Are Also Discussed. Several LAN Products Are Also Discussed in Detail. Edutrends Local Area Networks I CBT Course is a Prerequisite for LANS II. Different Types of Servers, Bridges & Gateways, LAN Operating Systems Are Also Covered. On-Line Glossary, Electronic Bookmark, Colorful Animated Graphics.
Edutrends, Inc.

Local 3270 DFT: 3270 Distributed Function Terminal. 1987. *Compatible Hardware:* IBM PC, PC XT, PC AT & compatibles, PS/2 Model 25, PS/2 Model 30, PS/2 Model 50, PS/2 Model 60, PS/2 Model 80. *Operating System(s) Required:* PC-DOS/MS-DOS 2.0 or higher. *Memory Required:* 256k. *General Requirements:* 3270 coax hardware adapter. *Items Included:* Software, hardware, manual. *Customer Support:* Free, 800-642-5888.
  3.5" or 5.25" disk $595.00.
Allows PC to Emulate a 3270 DFT (Distributed Function Terminal) Connected to an IBM 3174 or 3274 Control Unit. PC Can Connect to As Many As Five Simultaneous 3270 Sessions with the Mainframe. These Sessions Can Be LU-2 Keyboards/Displays, LU-3 Printers (3270 DS) or LU-1 Printers (SCS). Operates in Either BSC, SNA or Channel Attached Environments.
Micro-Integration Corporation.

TITLE INDEX

Local Expert: Where to Go, What to Do, How to Get There. *Version:* 1.02. 1994. *Items Included:* 3 free city mapsets: San Francisco, Washington, DC, Chicago; 35p. easy-to-read manual. *Customer Support:* Free unlimited technical support 1-800-999-6543 - 24 hrs. a day, 7 days a week. 30 day money-back guarantee. Customer service/orders/inquiries - 1-800-442-8887 - 24 hrs. a day, 7 days a week. Macintosh System Software 6.07 or higher. Macintosh (500k). 3.5" disk $99.00. *Nonstandard peripherals required:* High density 3.5" disks only. *Optimal configuration:* Comes with 8Mb of maps & data, but minimum requirement is 1.2Mb of hard disk space. (You can install the regions & cities that you want). Windows ver. 3.0 or higher (2Mb). 3.5" disk $99.00. *Nonstandard peripherals required:* High density 3.5" disks only. *Optimal configuration:* Comes with 8Mb of maps & data, but minimum requirement is 1.2Mb of hard disk space. (You can install the regions & cities that you want).
Your Personal Travel Guide That Combines Great Travel Tips with Detailed Maps. It's a Food Critic, Business Resource, Nightlife Review, & Sports Directory All Rolled into One. Includes U.S. & International Regional Maps, Lots of Fast, Easy-to-Use Mapping Tools, & Details for San Francisco, Washington, D.C., & Chicago. Over 100 Other Worldwide Cities Sold Separately.
Strategic Mapping, Inc.

Local Government Accounting System. *Compatible Hardware:* IBM PC, PC XT or compatibles. *General Requirements:* 40Mb hard disk, 132-column printer. *Items Included:* Master menu, General Ledger with Fund Accounting, Accounts Payable, Payroll, Utility billing, Accounts Receivable.
disk $9000.00.
Meets the Data Processing Requirements of Local Governments. Programs Cover Full Range of Accounting Needs Including Financial Reporting by Fund & Comparative Budgeting. Current & Historic Data Are Accessible with System. System Includes GENERAL LEDGER, UTILITY BILLING, ACCOUNTS PAYABLE, & PAYROLL Modules. The VEHICLE MAINTENANCE, WORD PROCESSING, DEPRECIATION, & SPREADSHEET Programs Can Be Added.
Nelson Data Resources, Inc.

Local Government-Education & Other Not for Profit Organizations. *Compatible Hardware:* IBM PC XT. *Operating System(s) Required:* MS-DOS. *Language(s):* Pascal. *Memory Required:* 512k. *General Requirements:* Printer, color display, color board adapter.
contact publisher for price.
National Computer Systems, Inc.

Local Governmental Administration: BA-GL, PAY, WILL, TAXES, VOTER. 1979. *Compatible Hardware:* AT&T 3B2; IBM PC & compatibles. *Operating System(s) Required:* PC-DOS, MS-DOS, UNIX. *Language(s):* BASIC (source code included). *Memory Required:* 256k. *General Requirements:* Wide carriage printer.
contact publisher for price.
Full Double Entry City/County Fund Accounting Based on GAAFR (Federal Standard) with Integrated Payroll Application. Also Includes: Utility Billing; Tax Billing; Tax Refunding; Voter Registration; Motor Vehicle; Fixed Assets; School District Accounting.
Diversified Computing.

Local Horizontal Coordinates. *Compatible Hardware:* TI 99/4A. *Operating System(s) Required:* DX-10. *Language(s):* BASIC. *Memory Required:* 48k.
cassette $16.95.
Computes the Horizontal Coordinates of Any Astronomical Body for Any Given Date.
Eastbench Software Products.

Local Sidereal Time. *Compatible Hardware:* TI 99/4A. *Operating System(s) Required:* DX-10. *Language(s):* Console BASIC. *Memory Required:* 16k.
cassette $16.95.
Calculates Local Mean Sidereal Time in Hours, Minutes & Seconds When the User Provides the Geographic Longitude. Works for the Years 1975 Through 2000.
Eastbench Software Products.

Local Space (Advanced Package): M-33. *Compatible Hardware:* Commodore 64, PET.
disk $50.00.
cassette $50.00.
Explores 5 Important Astrological Coordinate Dimensions.
Matrix Software.

Local Space & Coordinates: M-4. *Compatible Hardware:* Commodore 64, PET, VIC-20; TRS-80.
disk $30.00.
cassette $30.00.
Calculates Natal Chart & Presents Any of 5 Dimensions.
Matrix Software.

Local 3270. *Version:* 6.12. 1982. *Compatible Hardware:* IBM PC, PC XT, PC AT. *Operating System(s) Required:* MS-DOS, PC-DOS. *Language(s):* Assembly, Pascal. *Memory Required:* 128k. *Items Included:* Software, hardware, manual. *Customer Support:* Free, 800-642-5888.
$495.00.
Allows Bus-Based Microcomputers to Emulate 3278 Display Stations Using Existing Coaxial Networks. Allows User to Plug into Any IBM 3274 or 3276, Whether Local or Remote, BSC or SDLC. Keyboard Support Provides Full Emulation of IBM 4261 or 4627 EBCDIC Typewriter Keyboards. A Menu-Driven Configuration Program Allows User to Set Keyboard Definitions.
Micro-Integration Corp.

Local 3270. 1982. *Compatible Hardware:* IBM PC, PC XT, PC AT & compatibles, PS/2 Model 25, PS/2 Model 30, PS/2 Model 50, PS/2 Model 60, PS/2 Model 80. *Operating System(s) Required:* PC-DOS/MS-DOS 2.0 or higher. *Memory Required:* 135k. *General Requirements:* 3270 coax hardware adapter. *Items Included:* Software, hardware, manual. *Customer Support:* Free, 800-642-5888.
3.5" or 5.25" disk $495.00.
Allows PC to Function As Both a 3270 Terminal & a Desktop PC Workstation. Using the Hardware Adapter & Software Interface, a PC Can Be Plugged Directly into an IBM 3270 Control Unit or 3270 Display Adapter Using Existing Coaxial Cable.
Micro-Integration Corporation.

Local 5250. 1984. *Compatible Hardware:* IBM PC, PC XT, PC AT & compatibles, PS/2 Model 25, PS/2 Model 30, PS/2 Model 50, PS/2 Model 60, PS/2 Model 80. *Operating System(s) Required:* PC-DOS/MS-DOS 2.0 or higher. *Memory Required:* 64k. *General Requirements:* Local 5250 adapter. *Items Included:* Software, hardware, manual. *Customer Support:* Free, 800-642-5888.
3.5" or 5.25" disk $745.00.
Allows Users to Connect PC or PS/2 to an IBM 5251-12, 5294 Control Unit or Directly to a System/3X Minicomputer. The PC Can Then Process the Same Information & Produce the Same Results As If It Were a Real IBM 5250 Device with Attached Display Stations & Printers. Provides Support for up to 7 5250 Devices.
Micro-Integration Corporation.

Local 5250 for DOS, Windows, or OS-2. *Version:* DOS 4.05, OS/2 1.00 & Windows 1.02. 1984. *Operating System(s) Required:* PC-DOS. *Memory Required:* 128k. *Items Included:* Software, hardware, manual. *Customer Support:* Free, 800-642-5888.
$745.00 (ISBN 0-924465-24-7).
Designed to Allow Micros to Interface to IBM System 34, 36, 38 Computers or AS/400s via Locally Attached Twinaxial Cable Connections or an IBM 5291 Model 12 Control Unit/Display Station Combination. Allows a Personal Computer to Emulate an IBM 5250 Series Terminal As the Last Station on the Cable, As a "Pass-Through" Station, or As the Only Station. Display Devices Emulated Include the IBM 5251-11 & 5291-1 & -2 Monochrome Displays & the IBM 5292 Color Display. Supports Complete Screen Formatting & Display Attribute Handling for Emulation of the 5250 System 24-Line Display. Fully Emulates the 5250 Information Display System Typewriter Keyboard.
Micro-Integration Corp.

LOCIPRO: Root Locus Analysis. *Version:* 2. Jul. 1985. *Compatible Hardware:* Apple Macintosh; AT&T 6300; HP-125; IBM PC, PC jr, PC XT, PC AT, & compatibles; Tandy 1000, 1200, 2000; TI Professional; Xerox 820, 820-II, 860. *Operating System(s) Required:* PC-DOS/MS-DOS. *Language(s):* Compiled BASIC. *Memory Required:* IBM 256k, Apple 512k.
disk $195.00.
Root Locus Program Containing Integrated, Menu-Driven Routines Which Analyze Transfer Functions Derived from Block Diagrams of Linear Control Loop Systems. Users Enter the Transfer Function of Each Control Loop Block & the Program Computes the Composite Closed Loop Transfer Function. Root Movement As a Function of Gain Is Then Computed. Supports Free Format Input & Simple Editing. Files Are Fully Compatible with BVE's Signal Processing Program (SPP) Program to Perform Transient Analysis & PCPLOT & PLOTPRO Graphics Programs.
BV Engineering.

Lock & Key. *Customer Support:* 800-929-8117 (customer service).
MS-DOS. IBM/PS2. disk $99.99 (ISBN 0-87007-553-5).
Provides an Encoded Encryption Program Offering Security to the Users. With This System Present on User's Subdirectory, Merely Type "Encode" Followed by the Name of the File & the Code Phrase to Use in Encoding. If Desired, File Will Be Erased from the MS-DOS Directory, & Wiped from the Disk. To Decode, Just Type "Decode", the Name of the File, & the Code Phrase. The Code Phrase, May Be Any Length up to 250 Characters, Contain Letters in Upper and/or Lower Case, Numbers & Punctuation Allowing a Meaningful & Highly Unlikely Sentence to Be Used.
SourceView Software International.

LOCKBOX Interface. *Version:* 3.4. Oct. 1991. *Items Included:* Documentation included with package. *Customer Support:* Toll-free telephone support, local on-site or classroom training, consultation, & on-line help. Users can join one of many nationwide user groups. Annual updates & enhancement service available.
MS-DOS 3.1 or higher. IBM & compatibles 386 & higher. Priced by unit (ISBN 0-917391-00-4). *Addl. software required:* SKYLINE: The Property Management System. *Networks supported:* Novell.
Complete Link Between Bank Collection (LOCKBOX) Systems & SKYLINE: The Property Management System. Automates the Entire Cash Receipts Function. Using the Bank's LOCKBOX Service Prevents Misplaced, Delayed, or Stolen

Deposits & Speeds up Cash Flow. With This System, the Bank Transfers Collection Information Directly to SKYLINE Operating at the Management Office Ending Input Mistakes & Double Work. Gives User Total Detailed Cash Receipts, Tight Cash Control, & Helps with Speedy Collections, Data Accuracy & Maximum Staff Utilization.
The SOFTA Group, Inc.

Locomotion. Compatible Hardware: Atari 400, 800. Language(s): Atari BASIC. Memory Required: 32k. General Requirements: Joystick.
disk $23.95.
Arcade Game.
Dynacomp, Inc.

Lode Runner. Doug Smith. Compatible Hardware: Apple II+, IIe, IIc, IIgs, Macintosh; Atari 400, 800, XL, XE Series; Commodore 64, 128; IBM PC, & compatibles, PCjr, Tandy. Memory Required: Apple II & Atari 48k; Commodore 64k; IBM, Macintosh, Tandy 128k. General Requirements: Joystick for Apple II, Commodore, IBM, & Tandy; mouse for Macintosh.
Apple II. disk $34.95 (ISBN 0-922614-81-4, Order no.: 11450).
Macintosh. 3.5" disk $39.95 (ISBN 0-922614-82-2, Order no.: 11455).
disk $34.95 ea.
Commodore. (ISBN 0-922614-84-9, Order no.: 11430).
IBM & Tandy. (ISBN 0-922614-83-0, Order no.: 11410).
Atari. (ISBN 0-922614-85-7, Order no.: 11420).
Space Game in Which the Player Must Recapture Stolen Treasure from the Bungeling Empire by Maneuvering Through 150 Different Levels. Jumping, Running, & Drilling New Passageways with a Laser Pistol Are the Only Methods of Escape. Using the Game Generator User Can Move, Add, & Delete Ladders, Trap Doors, Floors, Gold Chests, & Enemies to Design Custom Playing Fields.
Broderbund Software, Inc.

Lode Runner Try & Buy. Sierra on Line Staff. Items Included: The package includes a 3.5" diskette, a mini-manual & a Try & Buy Brochure. MS-DOS 3.3 or higher. IBM (2Mb). disk $34.99 (ISBN 1-57548-003-4). Nonstandard peripherals required: Monitor card support.
It Is a Bounty Hunter's Game.
IBM Software Manufacturing Solutions (ISMS).

Lode Runner's Rescue. Josh Scholar. Compatible Hardware: Commodore 64. General Requirements: Joystick.
$29.95 (ISBN 0-922614-98-9, Order no.: 11130).
You Are Lode Runner's Daughter, Trying to Rescue Your Father from the Bungeling Empire. Run, Jump, Swim & Fight Your Way Through 46 Different Mazes on Your Way to His Prison Cell. Features 3-D Action, Altered Perspective Scrolling, & Includes a Game Generator That Lets You Construct & Save Your Own Maze Screens.
Broderbund Software, Inc.

LodeStar Plus. Version: 2.0. Jul. 1988. Compatible Hardware: IBM PC & compatibles. Operating System(s) Required: PC-DOS/MS-DOS 2.X, 3.X. Memory Required: 320k. General Requirements: CGA or EGA/VGA capability. Graphics printer and/or math co-processor optional.
disk $149.95.
Provides an Accurate, Variable Size View of the Sky for Any Date & Time for Any Location on Earth. Includes More Than 9000 Stars, All Messier Objects & the Sun, Moon & Planets. Simulates Daytime, Twilight & Night Sky & Can Automatically Plot & Track for Given Time Increments or Objects. User Can See Solar Eclipses, Planetary Conjunctions, Occultations & Transits, As Well As Scroll to Any Object to Re-Center Display, or Zoom in or Out.
Zephyr Services.

LOF: Lube, Oil & Filter. Items Included: Manual. Customer Support: 90 days, phone support.
DOS 3.1 or higher. IBM PC or compatible (640k). disk $295.00.
3, 6 & 12 Month LOF Reminder Postcards; Next LOF Date Computed & Available for Review; Fleet Reminder Reports; Customer Lists (Individual & Fleets); Minimum Hardware Required; Upgradeable to C.A.R.S. 1 Hour of Training Required.
Miramar, Ltd.

LogGen: Logmars Label Generating Software. Version: 1.6. Compatible Hardware: CP/M based systems; IBM PC & compatibles. Operating System(s) Required: MS-DOS, CP/M-80. Memory Required: 64k.
disk $345.00.
Produces Bar Code Labels Which Conform to MIL-STD-1189 & 129, the Military Standard Marking for Shipment & Storage, for Both the Exterior & Intermediate Labels. All Input Is Prompted on the Screen or Read from a Data File. Once Set up, the Data May Be Saved to a File & Retrieved As Required. Any Number of Labels May Be Repeated As Requested.
KDA Systems.

LOGGER. Version: 7.0. Items Included: Manual. Customer Support: Free phone & mail support, 30-day money back guarantee.
MS-DOS. IBM PC, PC XT, PC AT & compatibles. $599.00. Nonstandard peripherals required: EGA or VGA card. Optimal configuration: 386 with LaserJet II, dot matrix printer (Epson compatible).
Automatic Log Plotting for Lithologic Strip Logs. User-Customizable, Includes over 50 Formats: Coal, Petroleum, Mud Gas, Simple Lith Log, Hydrology & Geochemical. Up to 20 Columns of Quantitative Data May Be Plotted As Logarithmic or Linear Curves or Bar Histograms. 100 Symbols, Variable Scaling, Percentage Lithology & Porosity Included. Includes Cross Sections, Fence Diagrams, Base Mapping & Database Capabilities.
Rockware, Inc.

Logic Designer. Compatible Hardware: IBM. Operating System(s) Required: MS-DOS.
disk $49.95.
Dynacomp, Inc.

Logic Simulator. Compatible Hardware: Apple II with Applesoft, IBM PC. Operating System(s) Required: Apple DOS 3.2, 3.3; PC-DOS. Memory Required: Apple 48k, IBM 128k.
disk $49.95, incl. manual.
Provides 2 Ways to Test a Circuit Design.
Dynacomp, Inc.

Logic Simulator. 1995. Items Included: Full manual. Customer Support: Free telephone support - 90 days, 30-day warranty.
MS-DOS 3.2 or higher. 286 (584k). disk $49.95. Nonstandard peripherals required: CGA/EGA/VGA.
There Are Two Ways to Test a Circuit Design: Build a Prototype & Experimentally Examine All the Input/Output Conditions, or Probe the Circuit's Performance Using LOGIC SIMULATOR. The Latter Approach Is Faster & Less Expensive, As Well As Being More Amenable to Rapid Design Iterations. The Circuit Elements Which May Be Treated by LOGIC SIMULATOR Include the Following: Multiple Input AND, NAND, OR, NOR, EXOR & EXNOR Gates; Inverters; J-K & D Flip-Flops; One Shots.
Dynacomp, Inc.

Logic Tutor: Self-Instruction in Digital Switching Logic. Version: 1.20. M. H. Miller. Sep. 1990. Operating System(s) Required: Finder. Items Included: 3.5" Disk, User's Manual. Customer Support: 30 day unlimited warranty.
Macintosh. 3.5" disk $49.00 (ISBN 0-927449-15-3, Order no.: LTMC).
An Evolving Set of Six Graphic-Oriented Interactive Instructional Programs for the Study of Digital Switching Logic for Engineering Undergraduate Studies. Covering Such Topics as Combinational Logic, Logic Functions, Karnaugh Maps, Device Stimulations, e.g., Multiplexers, PLA's, etc., Flip-Flops & Counters, Digital Arithmetic, Base Conversions, Binary-Hexadecimal Addition, etc. Material Is Appropo for Anyone Learning Logic Circuits new, Teaching It, or as Refresher Material.
Tatum Labs, Inc.

Logical Patient Billing. Version: 4.000. Richard J. Ottenstein. Aug. 1993. Items Included: 3-ring binder containing a Tutorial & a Manual. Customer Support: Free unlimited phone support with a toll free number.
DOS 3.1 or higher. IBM or 100% compatible (80826 or higher) (512k). $295.00 Individual Version; $325.00 Group Practice Version (Order no.: W-1037 INDIVIDUAL VERSION; W-1039 GROUP PRACTICE VERSION). Optimal configuration: Hard disk with 2.3Mb free disk space for program, 3 kilobytes of additional disk space for each patient, printer. Available in 3.5" or 5.25" disks. A Computer Program That Handles Virtually All Patient Billing for Mental Health Practitioners. This Popular Program Automates the Hand Billing Procedures Used by Most Clinicians. Gives User the Speed & Accuracy of Computerized Billing - Without Changing the Way You Handle Patient Accounts. Developed by a Mental Health Practitioner, LPB Solves Virtually All Billing Problems.
Western Psychological Services.

Logical Reasoning: A Guide to Clear Thinking. Version: 2.0. Roderick A. Freeman. Jan. 1990. Items Included: Two booklets. Customer Support: 180 day warranty, customer support (619-464-4350) free.
DOS. IBM (540k). $32.95 (ISBN 0-9628332-0-7). Optimal configuration: VGA.
A Complete College-Level Course in Logic. Includes 12 Chapters, Each Chapter Contains a Tutorial & a Set of Practice Exercises. Five 1 1/2 Hour Examinations Are Also Provided.
University Quality software Co.

LogiQuest III. Software Products International (S.P.I.). Jan. 1984. Operating System(s) Required: MS-DOS. Memory Required: 192k. General Requirements: Printer, Winchester hard disk.
$395.00 (Order no.: TI P/N 2311414-0001).
Relational Database Management System That Interfaces with S.P.I.'s Other Program.
Texas Instruments, Personal Productivit.

Logistix. Compatible Hardware: Commodore Amiga.
3.5" disk $99.95.
Spreadsheet & Project Planner.
Precision, Inc.

Logit. General Requirements: Systat. Items Included: Documentation. Customer Support: Free technical support.
Macintosh Plus or higher. 3.5" disk $110.00.
IBM PC, 286 or higher & compatibles. 3.5" disk $150.00.
Logistic Regression for Binary & Multinominal Dependent Variables.
Systat, Inc.

TITLE INDEX

LOGO Data Toolkit. 1987. *Compatible Hardware:* Apple, Commodore 64. *Operating System(s) Required:* Apple Dos 3.3, ProDos. *Language(s):* Logo. *General Requirements:* Terrapin Logo, Commodore Logo or Logo Plus. *Customer Support:* Available. $49.95.
Provides Four Tool Programs for Data Acquisition, Manipulation, & Display. Compatible with TERRAPIN LOGO (Version 2.0 or Later), Commodore LOGO or LOGO Plus.
Terrapin, Inc.

LOGO Kit. *Compatible Hardware:* Atari XL/XE. ROM cartridge $49.95 (Order no.: KX7097).
Atari Corp.

Logo Plus. *Version:* 2.0. *Compatible Hardware:* Apple Macintosh. *Memory Required:* 4000k. *Customer Support:* Free Terrapin Times newsletter, technical tips, 90 day limited warranty.
3.5" disk $99.95.
3.5" disk 5 diskset $199.95.
3.5" disk 10 diskset $299.95.
3.5" disk 20 diskset $399.95.
Programming Language.
Terrapin, Inc.

Logos Bible Atlas.
Windows 3.1. IBM & compatibles (2Mb). disk $79.95 (Order no.: SW980-5F). *Optimal configuration:* Windows 3.1, 2Mb RAM & a minimum of 8 hard drive, requires mouse. Swap File strongly recommended.
3.5" disk $79.95 (Order no.: SW973-2F).
A Comprehensive Electronic Bible Atlas. It Features More Than 90 Subject Maps Covering the Entire Scope of Biblical History, As Well As Two Highly Detailed Geographic Site Maps (of Palestine & the Mediterranean Region) & a 3D Topographical Map, Built from Satellite Databases. All the Maps Are in Full Color & Vector-Based, Therefore Scalable & Printable or May Be Merged with Word Processing & Desktop Publishing. May Be Used Alone or in Conjunction with Other Logos Bible Software & Some Windows-Based Bible Programs Such As Quick Verse by Parsons.
Gospel Films Inc.

Logos Bible Clips. Gary Glover. *Items Included:* Full instructional video.
Windows 3.1 or higher, DOS 6.0 or higher. 386 or higher (2Mb). CD-ROM disk $119.95 (Order no.: CD931-7D). *Optimal configuration:* 386 or higher, Windows 3.1 or higher, DOS 6.0 or higher, CD-ROM drive, VGA monitor or higher, minimum 2Mb RAM, 5Mb hard drive space available, mouse recommended.
Complete Church Graphics Resource Kit. Everything You Need to Create Beautiful Graphics in This CD-ROM Artwork Library Containing 34 Full Color Backgrounds, 118 Biblical Situation Figures, & Hundreds of Props & Clips of Biblical Artwork to Make Your Graphic Imaging Projects Easy & Fun! All Images Are Vector Based & Can Be Used in Any Size, Color, & Configuration to Create Custom Posters, Flyers, Backgrounds, Transparencies, Banners, Church Bulletins, Coloring Pages, - Even Stand-Up Figures - & No Jagged Edges.
Gospel Films Inc.

Logos Bible Crosswords, Vol. 1.
IBM & compatibles (1Mb). disk $29.95 (Order no.: SW910-4F). *Optimal configuration:* 1Mb RAM & a minimum of 800k hard drive. Sound card required for sound effects, mouse recommended.
3.5" disk $29.95 (Order no.: SW903-1F).
A Collection of 200 Puzzles That Can Be Played Online or Printed Out. All of the Puzzles Are Color-Customizable & Have Numerous Clues with Bible References As Hints. Related Bible Verses Can Be Accessed from Logos Bible Software for Further Inspiration. Three Skill Levels Challenge Bible Knowledge from Beginning to Advanced Levels. Comes with Scribbles Font & Contains Sound Effects.
Gospel Films Inc.

Logos Bible Software Add-On Modules: ASV - American Standard Version (1901).
Windows 3.1, DOS 3.0. 386, 486, or Pentium (2Mb). disk $29.95 (Order no.: SW273-8E). *Optimal configuration:* 386, 486, or Pentium, 2Mb RAM, Windows 3.1, DOS 3.0, Sound card optional, allow approximately 11Mb hard drive.
3.5" disk $29.95 (Order no.: SW266-5E).
Add-On Modules Allow User to Turn the Basic Logos System into a Complete Biblical Reference Library. Different Translations along with Greek & Hebrew Texts Provide Deeper Insights into the Meaning of the Text; Reference Works Provide Valuable Information on the Bible & Its People, Places, & Times.
Gospel Films Inc.

Logos Bible Software Add-On Modules: BYZ Greek - The New Testament in the Original Greek According to the Byzantine-Majority Textform.
Windows 3.1, DOS 3.0. 386, 486, or Pentium (2Mb). disk $59.95 (Order no.: SW329-7E). *Optimal configuration:* 386, 486, or Pentium, 2Mb RAM, Windows 3.1, DOS 3.0, Sound card optional, allow approximately 11Mb hard drive.
3.5" disk $59.95 (Order no.: SW315-7E).
Add-On Modules Allow User to Turn the Basic Logos System into a Complete Biblical Reference Library. Different Translations along with Greek & Hebrew Texts Provide Deeper Insights into the Meaning of the Text; Reference Works Provide Valuable Information on the Bible & Its People, Places, & Times.
Gospel Films Inc.

Logos Bible Software Add-On Modules: BHS (Hebrew) - Biblia Hebraica Stuttgartensia.
Windows 3.1, DOS 3.0. 386, 486, or Pentium (2Mb). disk $59.95 (Order no.: SW441-2E). *Optimal configuration:* 386, 486, or Pentium, 2Mb RAM, Windows 3.1, DOS 3.0, Sound card optional, allow approximately 11Mb hard drive.
3.5" disk $59.95 (Order no.: SW427-7E).
Add-On Modules Allow User to Turn the Basic Logos System into a Complete Biblical Reference Library. Different Translations along with Greek & Hebrew Texts Provide Deeper Insights into the Meaning of the Text; Reference Works Provide Valuable Information on the Bible & Its People, Places, & Times.
Gospel Films Inc.

Logos Bible Software Add-On Modules: Greek 4-Pack - NA-UBS, BYZ, TR Scrivener's, TR Stephen's.
Windows 3.1, DOS 3.0. 386, 486, or Pentium (2Mb). disk $119.95 (Order no.: SW378-5E). *Optimal configuration:* 386, 486, or Pentium, 2Mb RAM, Windows 3.1, DOS 3.0, Sound card optional, allow approximately 11Mb hard drive.
3.5" disk $119.95 (Order no.: SW371-8E).
Add-On Modules Allow User to Turn the Basic Logos System into a Complete Biblical Reference Library. Different Translations along with Greek & Hebrew Texts Provide Deeper Insights into the Meaning of the Text; Reference Works Provide Valuable Information on the Bible & Its People, Places, & Times.
Gospel Films Inc.

LOGOS BIBLE SOFTWARE COLLECTION

Logos Bible Software Add-On Modules: NASB - New American Bible.
Windows 3.1, DOS 3.0. 386, 486, or Pentium (2Mb). disk $59.95 (Order no.: SW225-8E). *Optimal configuration:* 386, 486, or Pentium, 2Mb RAM, Windows 3.1, DOS 3.0, Sound card optional, allow approximately 11Mb hard drive.
3.5" disk $59.95 (Order no.: SW218-5E).
Add-On Modules Allow User to Turn the Basic Logos System into a Complete Biblical Reference Library. Different Translations along with Greek & Hebrew Texts Provide Deeper Insights into the Meaning of the Text; Reference Works Provide Valuable Information on the Bible & Its People, Places, & Times.
Gospel Films Inc.

Logos Bible Software Add-On Modules: NA-UBS Greek - The Greek New Testament.
Windows 3.1, DOS 3.0. 386, 486, or Pentium (2Mb). disk $59.95 (Order no.: SW308-4E). *Optimal configuration:* 386, 486, or Pentium, 2Mb RAM, Windows 3.1, DOS 3.0, Sound card optional, allow approximately 11Mb hard drive.
3.5" disk $59.95 (Order no.: SW301-7E).
Add-On Modules Allow User to Turn the Basic Logos System into a Complete Biblical Reference Library. Different Translations along with Greek & Hebrew Texts Provide Deeper Insights into the Meaning of the Text; Reference Works Provide Valuable Information on the Bible & Its People, Places, & Times.
Gospel Films Inc.

Logos Bible Software Add-On Modules: TR Scrivener's - Textus Receptus Scrivener's 1891 (Greek).
Windows 3.1, DOS 3.0. 386, 486, or Pentium (2Mb). disk $39.95 (Order no.: SW350-5E). *Optimal configuration:* 386, 486, or Pentium, 2Mb RAM, Windows 3.1, DOS 3.0, Sound card optional, allow approximately 11Mb hard drive.
3.5" disk $39.95 (Order no.: SW343-2E).
Add-On Modules Allow User to Turn the Basic Logos System into a Complete Biblical Reference Library. Different Translations along with Greek & Hebrew Texts Provide Deeper Insights into the Meaning of the Text; Reference Works Provide Valuable Information on the Bible & Its People, Places, & Times.
Gospel Films Inc.

Logos Bible Software Add-On Modules: TR Stephen's - Textus Receptus Stephenes 1550 (Greek).
Windows 3.1, DOS 3.0. 386, 486, or Pentium (2Mb). disk $39.95 (Order no.: SW364-5E). *Optimal configuration:* 386, 486, or Pentium, 2Mb RAM, Windows 3.1, DOS 3.0, Sound card optional, allow approximately 11Mb hard drive.
3.5" disk $39.95 (Order no.: SW357-2E).
Add-On Modules Allow User to Turn the Basic Logos System into a Complete Biblical Reference Library. Different Translations along with Greek & Hebrew Texts Provide Deeper Insights into the Meaning of the Text; Reference Works Provide Valuable Information on the Bible & Its People, Places, & Times.
Gospel Films Inc.

Logos Bible Software Collection.
DOS 3.1 or higher, Windows 3.1 or higher. 386, 486, or Pentium (2Mb). CD-ROM disk $49.95 (Order no.: CD946-5D). *Optimal configuration:* 386, 486, or Pentium, DOS 3.1 or higher, Windows 3.1 or higher, 2Mb RAM, VGA display, CD-ROM drive (double speed recommended), minimum 5Mb hard drive space, mouse required. Sound card optional.

LOGOS BIBLE SOFTWARE: KJV-ASV

CD-ROM disk $69.95, NRSV incl. Apocrypha (Order no.: CD904-8D).
Family Bible Software with Its Powerful Wordsearch & Custom Note-Taking Ability Provides the Basis for Family Bible Study in Both the King James Version & the American Standard 1901 Texts. The Logos New Nave's Topical Bible Makes over 100,000 Scripture References & More Than 20,000 Topics & Subtopics Available to Enhance Scripture Exploration. In His Time Is a Personal Information Mangaer Designed to Bring Greater Productivity, Fulfillment, & Organization into the Home & Office with an Array of More Than 28 Features to Help You Gain Control of Your Day-to-Day Activities. The One-Minute Bible Makes Daily Bible Reading & Devotionals Easy & Inspirational, While Bible Crosswords Tests Each Individual's Knowedge of Bible Events & Characters on Three Different Skill Levels. The Bible Screen Saver Randomly Displays Biblical Information On-Screen Throughout the Day.
Gospel Films Inc.

Logos Bible Software: KJV-ASV American Standard Verison.
Windows 3.1, DOS 3.0. 386, 486, or Pentium (2Mb). disk $149.95 (Order no.: SW008-5E). *Optimal configuration:* 386, 486, or Pentium, 2Mb RAM, Windows 3.1, DOS 3.0, Sound card optional, allow approximately 11Mb hard drive.
3.5" disk $149.95 (Order no.: SW001-8E).
An Easy-to-Use Yet Extremely Powerful Tool for Personal Bible Study. Logos Takes Full Advantage of the Windows Environment to Help Enrich Your Study by Eliminating Tedious Page-Flipping & Facilitating Deeper, Broader Research. Optional Add-On Texts & Reference Works Further Enhance Your Study.
Gospel Films Inc.

Logos Bible Software: KJV-NASB The New American Standard Bible.
Windows 3.1, DOS 3.0. 386, 486, or Pentium (2Mb). disk $159.95 (Order no.: SW036-0E). *Optimal configuration:* 386, 486, or Pentium, 2Mb RAM, Windows 3.1, DOS 3.0, Sound card optional, allow approximately 11Mb hard drive.
3.5" disk $159.95 (Order no.: SW029-8#).
An Easy-to-Use Yet Extremely Powerful Tool for Personal Bible Study. Logos Takes Full Advantage of the Windows Environment to Help Enrich Your Study by Eliminating Tedious Page-Flipping & Facilitating Deeper, Broader Research. Optional Add-On Texts & Reference Works Further Enhance Your Study.
Gospel Films Inc.

Logos Bible Software: KJV-NCV The New Century Version.
Windows 3.1, DOS 3.0. 386, 486, or Pentium (2Mb). disk $149.95 (Order no.: SW022-0E). *Optimal configuration:* 386, 486, or Pentium, 2Mb RAM, Windows 3.1, DOS 3.0, Sound card optional, allow approximately 11Mb hard drive.
3.5" disk $149.95 (Order no.: SW015-8E).
An Easy-to-Use Yet Extremely Powerful Tool for Personal Bible Study. Logos Takes Full Advantage of the Windows Environment to Help Enrich Your Study by Eliminating Tedious Page-Flipping & Facilitating Deeper, Broader Research. Optional Add-On Texts & Reference Works Further Enhance Your Study.
Gospel Films Inc.

Logos Bible Software: KJV-NIV The New International Version.
Windows 3.1, DOS 3.0. 386, 486, or Pentium (2Mb). disk $159.95 (Order no.: SW056-5E). *Optimal configuration:* 386, 486, or Pentium, 2Mb RAM, Windows 3.1, DOS 3.0, Sound card optional, allow approximately 11Mb hard drive.
3.5" disk $159.95 (Order no.: SW049-2E).
An Easy-to-Use Yet Extremely Powerful Tool for Personal Bible Study. Logos Takes Full Advantage of the Windows Environment to Help Enrich Your Study by Eliminating Tedious Page-Flipping & Facilitating Deeper, Broader Research. Optional Add-On Texts & Reference Works Further Enhance Your Study.
Gospel Films Inc.

Logos Bible Software: KJV-NKJV New King James Version.
Windows 3.1, DOS 3.0. 386, 486, or Pentium (2Mb). disk $149.95 (Order no.: SW084-0E). *Optimal configuration:* 386, 486, or Pentium, 2Mb RAM, Windows 3.1, DOS 3.0, Sound card optional, allow approximately 11Mb hard drive.
3.5" disk $149.95 (Order no.: SW077-8E).
An Easy-to-Use Yet Extremely Powerful Tool for Personal Bible Study. Logos Takes Full Advantage of the Windows Environment to Help Enrich Your Study by Eliminating Tedious Page-Flipping & Facilitating Deeper, Broader Research. Optional Add-On Texts & Reference Works Further Enhance Your Study.
Gospel Films Inc.

Logos Bible Software: KJV-NRSV The New Revised Standard Version.
Windows 3.1, DOS 3.0. 386, 486, or Pentium (2Mb). disk $149.95 (Order no.: SW070-0E). *Optimal configuration:* 386, 486, or Pentium, 2Mb RAM, Windows 3.1, DOS 3.0, Sound card optional, allow approximately 11Mb hard drive.
3.5" disk $149.95 (Order no.: SW063-8E).
An Easy-to-Use Yet Extremely Powerful Tool for Personal Bible Study. Logos Takes Full Advantage of the Windows Environment to Help Enrich Your Study by Eliminating Tedious Page-Flipping & Facilitating Deeper, Broader Research. Optional Add-On Texts & Reference Works Further Enhance Your Study.
Gospel Films Inc.

Logos Bible Software: KJV-RSV The Revised Standard Version.
Windows 3.1, DOS 3.0. 386, 486, or Pentium (2Mb). disk $149.95 (Order no.: SW042-5E). *Optimal configuration:* 386, 486, or Pentium, 2Mb RAM, Windows 3.1, DOS 3.0, Sound card optional, allow approximately 11Mb hard drive.
3.5" disk $149.95 (Order no.: SW035-2E).
An Easy-to-Use Yet Extremely Powerful Tool for Personal Bible Study. Logos Takes Full Advantage of the Windows Environment to Help Enrich Your Study by Eliminating Tedious Page-Flipping & Facilitating Deeper, Broader Research. Optional Add-On Texts & Reference Works Further Enhance Your Study.
Gospel Films Inc.

Logos Bible Software: KJV-The King James Version.
Windows 3.1, DOS 3.0. 386, 486, or Pentium (2Mb). disk $129.95 (Order no.: SW021-2E). *Optimal configuration:* 386, 486, or Pentium, 2Mb RAM, Windows 3.1, DOS 3.0, Sound card optional, allow approximately 11Mb hard drive.
3.5" disk $129.95 (Order no.: SW007-7E).
An Easy-to-Use Yet Extremely Powerful Tool for Personal Bible Study. Logos Takes Full Advantage of the Windows Environment to Help Enrich Your Study by Eliminating Tedious Page-Flipping & Facilitating Deeper, Broader Research. Optional Add-On Texts & Reference Works Further Enhance Your Study.
Gospel Films Inc.

Logos On-Line. *Compatible Hardware:* Apple Macintosh; IBM DOS, Windows, OS/2; NeXT; mini computers, mainframes. *General Requirements:* Inkjet or laser printer & supporting software. *Items Included:* User manual, printouts of images requested. *Customer Support:* free telephone support; free compatibility test disk. $150.00 up.
Custom Service Specializing in Rendering Company Logos & Symbols for Computer Use. Company Can Even Reproduce a Hand Written Signature or Custom Font. In Downloadable PostScript or TrueType Font Format, EPS File Format & Other IBM Vector Formats.
Software Complement.

LogoWriter Activities for Readers. Mar. 1990. *Items Included:* Direction sheets, teacher notes. *Customer Support:* Phone support, on-site training at current billing rate.
  Apple Prods. Apple IIe, Apple IIc, Apple IIGS (128k). $99.50 single classroom license; site licenses available (ISBN 0-9627047-0-9). *Addl. software required:* LogoWriter 2.0 or higher. *Optimal configuration:* Color monitor, color printer (both optional). *Networks supported:* Velan, AppleShare.
  MS-DOS. MS DOS compatible (256k). $99.50 single classroom license; site licenses available (ISBN 0-9627047-1-7). *Addl. software required:* LogoWriter 2.0 or higher. *Optimal configuration:* Color monitor, color printer (both optional). *Networks supported:* Novell, IBM.
Twenty-Five Activities Which Work in Conjunction with LOGOWRITER to Improve Reading & Writing Skills in Elementary School Children. Available (Fall 1991) for Apple IIe, Apple IIgs, IBM.
Compuco, Inc.

Looking Good. (Job Success Ser.). Feb. 1996. *Items Included:* Program manual. *Customer Support:* Free telephone support, 90 day warranty.
  Single user. Windows 3.1 or higher. IBM 386 (8Mb). disk $99.95 (ISBN 1-57204-109-9, Order no.: APM453). *Nonstandard peripherals required:* 256 color monitor, mouse, sound card. *Addl. software required:* SVGA graphics.
  Lab pack. Windows 3.1 or higher. IBM 386 (8mb). disk $199.00 (ISBN 1-57204-146-3, Order no.: APM453LPK). *Nonstandard peripherals required:* 256 color monitor, mouse, sound card. *Addl. software required:* SVGA graphics.
  Site license. Windows 3.1 or higher. IBM 386 (8Mb). disk $399.00 (ISBN 1-57204-148-X, Order no.: APM453SITE). *Nonstandard peripherals required:* 256 color monitor, mouse, sound card. *Addl. software required:* SVGA graphics.
  Single user. System 7.1 or higher. Mac, 16 MHz rating, 68030 or better processor (LC II or higher) (5Mb). 3.5" disk $99.95 (ISBN 1-57204-110-2, Order no.: WIN453). *Nonstandard peripherals required:* 256 color monitor, 13" or larger.
  Lab pack. System 7.1 or higher. Mac, 16 MHz rating, 68030 or better processor (LC II or higher) (5Mb). 3.5" disk $199.00 (ISBN 1-57204-147-1, Order no.: WIN453LPK). *Nonstandard peripherals required:* 256 color monitor, 13" or larger.
  Site license. System 7.1 or higher. Mac, 16 MHz rating, 68030 or better processor (LC II or higher) (5Mb). $399.00 (Order no.: WIN453SITE). *Nonstandard peripherals required:* 256 color monitor, 13" or larger.
Helps students gain valuable insights into dressing right for a variety of entry-level jobs.
Lawrence Productions, Inc.

TITLE INDEX

Lookup. Version: 2.4. Jul. 1987. Compatible Hardware: Apple Macintosh. Memory Required: 512k.
3.5" disk $59.95 (ISBN 0-940331-04-7).
Desk Accessory for Looking up the Spelling of Any Word, from Any Program. Includes a 93,000 Word Dictionary. Also Has "Beep-While-You-Type" Spelling Check.
Working Software, Inc.

Loom.
PC or compatible (640k). CD-ROM disk $79.95 (ISBN 0-7911-0674-8, Order no.: 110674).
Optimal configuration: PC or compatible, in DOS 3.1 or higher; Microsoft CD-ROM Extensions, 2.1 or higher; CD-ROM drive & software drivers; CD audio; keyboard, mouse or joystick; VGA 256-Colors.
Long after the Passing of the Second Shadow, When Dragons Ruled the Twilight Sky, Came the Age of the Great Guilds, Such As the Weavers. Over the Centuries, Their Craft Transcended the Limits of Physical Cloth, until They Wove the Very Fabric of Reality Itself. Help Young Bobbin Rescue His Guild from the Powers of Darkness...& You Just Might Save the Universe from an Unspeakable Catastrophe. Includes a Book of Spells for Intricate Spell-Casting System, Game & Audio Drama on CD-ROM, Detailed Animation & Special Effects, Cinematic Landscapes, Full Voice Dialog, & Orchestral Musical Performance. The Drama Is a 30 Minute Prequel to the Game, Produced at Lucasfilm's Academy Award-Winning Sprocket Sound Systems.
Software Toolworks.

The Loom & the Keyboard: Working Environment & Life on the Job. Gail S. Thomas. 1990.
DOS. Any type of IBM (64k). $8.95 (ISBN 1-56178-009-X).
DOS-Hypertext. Must run DOS 2 or higher (128k). $8.95 (ISBN 1-56178-028-6).
MAC. Any type of Macintosh (64k). $8.95 (ISBN 1-56178-027-8).
Scholarly Monograph Investigates & Compares Working Conditions in 19th Century Sweat Shops & People Who Work Behind Computer Terminals in 1980-1990's.
Connected Editions, Inc.

Lost & Found, Vol. 1.
MS-DOS 5.0 or higher, Windows 3.1 or higher. 386 processor or higher (4Mb). CD-ROM disk $39.95 (Order no.: R1163). *Nonstandard peripherals required:* CD-ROM drive. *Optimal configuration:* 386 processor operating at 16MHz or higher, MS-DOS 5.0 or higher, Windows 3.1 or higher, 30Mb hard drive, mouse, VGA graphic adapter & VGA color monitor (SVGA recommended), 4Mb RAM, external speakers or headphones (with sound card) that are Sound Blaster compatible.
Macintosh (4Mb). (Order no.: R1163). *Nonstandard peripherals required:* 14" color monitor or larger, CD-ROM drive.
Whimsical Riddles & Rhymes Are Clues As Children Explore These Colorful Programs to Find Lost Objects. Each Program Has 12 Interactive Areas to Explore, with Five Levels of Play to Teach Object & Letter Recognition & Problem Solving Skills (Ages 4-9).
Library Video Co.

Lost & Found, Vol. 2.
MS-DOS 5.0 or higher, Windows 3.1 or higher. 386 processor or higher (4Mb). CD-ROM disk $39.95 (Order no.: R1338). *Nonstandard peripherals required:* CD-ROM drive. *Optimal configuration:* 386 processor operating at 16MHz or higher, MS-DOS 5.0 or higher, Windows 3.1 or higher, 30Mb hard drive, mouse, VGA graphic adapter & VGA color monitor (SVGA recommended), 4Mb RAM, external speakers or headphones (with sound card) that are Sound Blaster compatible.
Macintosh (4Mb). (Order no.: R1338). *Nonstandard peripherals required:* 14" color monitor or larger, CD-ROM drive.
Whimsical Riddles & Rhymes Are Clues As Children Explore These Colorful Programs to Find Lost Objects. Each Program Has 12 Interactive Areas to Explore, with Five Levels of Play to Teach Object & Letter Recognition & Problem Solving Skills (Ages 4-9).
Library Video Co.

Lost & Found, Vol. 3.
MS-DOS 5.0 or higher, Windows 3.1 or higher. 386 processor or higher (4Mb). CD-ROM disk $39.95 (Order no.: R1339). *Nonstandard peripherals required:* CD-ROM drive. *Optimal configuration:* 386 processor operating at 16MHz or higher, MS-DOS 5.0 or higher, Windows 3.1 or higher, 30Mb hard drive, mouse, VGA graphic adapter & VGA color monitor (SVGA recommended), 4Mb RAM, external speakers or headphones (with sound card) that are Sound Blaster compatible.
Macintosh (4Mb). (Order no.: R1339). *Nonstandard peripherals required:* 14" color monitor or larger, CD-ROM drive.
Whimsical Riddles & Rhymes Are Clues As Children Explore These Colorful Programs to Find Lost Objects. Each Program Has 12 Interactive Areas to Explore, with Five Levels of Play to Teach Object & Letter Recognition & Problem Solving Skills (Ages 4-9).
Library Video Co.

Lost & Found Series.
MS-DOS 5.0 or higher, Windows 3.1 or higher. 386 processor or higher (4Mb). CD-ROM disk Set $119.85 (Order no.: R1336). *Nonstandard peripherals required:* CD-ROM drive. *Optimal configuration:* 386 processor operating at 16MHz or higher, MS-DOS 5.0 or higher, Windows 3.1 or higher, 30Mb hard drive, mouse, VGA graphic adapter & VGA color monitor (SVGA recommended), 4Mb RAM, external speakers or headphones (with sound card) that are Sound Blaster compatible.
Macintosh (4Mb). (Order no.: R1336). *Nonstandard peripherals required:* 14" color monitor or larger, CD-ROM drive.
Whimsical Riddles & Rhymes Are Clues As Children Explore These Colorful Programs to Find Lost Objects. Each Program Has 12 Interactive Areas to Explore, with Five Levels of Play to Teach Object & Letter Recognition & Problem Solving Skills (Ages 4-9). 3 Volume Set.
Library Video Co.

Lost Treasures. *Items Included:* Installation Guide.
IBM. Contact publisher for price (ISBN 0-87321-030-1, Order no.: ID-237).
Activision, Inc.

Lost Treasures. *Items Included:* Installation Guide.
IBM. Contact publisher for price (ISBN 0-87321-031-X, Order no.: PD-237).
Activision, Inc.

Lost Treasures. *Items Included:* Installation Guide.
IBM PC. Contact publisher for price (ISBN 0-87321-032-8, Order no.: CDD-3014).
Activision, Inc.

Lost Treasures Hintbook. *Items Included:* Installation Guide.
IBM. Contact publisher for price (ISBN 0-87321-091-3, Order no.: HBK-237).
Activision, Inc.

Lost Treasures II. *Items Included:* Installation Guide.
IBM PC. Contact publisher for price (ISBN 0-87321-034-4, Order no.: MSD-3015).
Activision, Inc.

Lost Treasures II. *Items Included:* Installation Guide.
IBM PC. Contact publisher for price (ISBN 0-87321-035-2, Order no.: CDD-3015).
Activision, Inc.

Lost Treasures II. *Items Included:* Installation Guide.
MAC. Contact publisher for price (ISBN 0-87321-033-6, Order no.: MAC-3015).
Activision, Inc.

The Lost Tribe. Sep. 1995. *Customer Support:* Telephone support - free (except phone charge).
Windows 3.1. IBM & compatibles (386 DX-20) (4Mb). CD-ROM disk $12.99 (ISBN 1-57594-035-3). *Nonstandard peripherals required:* 2x CD-ROM player, Sound Card, VGA monitor. *Optimal configuration:* 486 SX-33.
Modern Game of Strategy in a Pre-Historic World.
Kidsoft, Inc.

The Lost Tribe. Sep. 1995. *Customer Support:* Telephone support - free (except phone charge).
Windows 3.1. IBM & compatibles (386 DX-20) (4Mb). CD-ROM disk $12.99 (ISBN 1-57594-074-4). *Nonstandard peripherals required:* 2x CD-ROM player, Sound Card, VGA monitor. *Optimal configuration:* 486 SX-33.
Modern Game of Strategy in a Pre-Historic World. Blister Pack Jewel Case.
Kidsoft, Inc.

The Lost Tribe. Sep. 1992. *Items Included:* Program manual. *Customer Support:* Free technical support 800-421-4157, 90 day warranty.
PC-DOS/MS-DOS 3.0 or higher. IBM (610k). disk $39.95 (ISBN 0-917999-86-X). *Nonstandard peripherals required:* Microsoft mouse recommended, supports Ad Lib & Sound Blaster cards, hard drive.
System 5.0.4 or higher. Apple IIGS (1Mb). disk $49.95 (ISBN 1-882848-00-4).
System 6.0.5 or higher. Macintosh (1Mb). 3.5" disk $49.95 (ISBN 0-917999-85-1).
System 6.0.5 or higher. Macintosh (1Mb). $59.95 School Edition (ISBN 1-882848-01-2).
System 6.0.5 or higher. Macintosh (1Mb). $129.95 School Edition, Lab Pack (ISBN 1-882848-02-0).
System 5.0.4 or higher. Apple IIGS (1Mb). $59.95 School Edition (ISBN 1-882848-03-9).
System 5.0.4 or higher. Apple IIGS. $129.95 School Edition, Lab Pack (ISBN 1-882848-04-7).
Modern Game of Strageqy in a Prehistoric World. Children Ages 8 & Older Become Leaders of a Prehistoric Tribe Whose Home Has Been Destroyed by a Volcano. They Must Lead Their People to a New Home in a Distant Land. Along the Journey They Must Make Good Decisions, & Concentrate on Survival. Builds Decision Making & Leadership Skills. Great for Social Studies Classes.
Lawrence Productions, Inc.

The Lost Tribe. Sep. 1992. *Items Included:* Program manual. *Customer Support:* Free technical support 800-421-4157, 90 day warranty.
PC-DOS/MS-DOS 3.0 or higher. IBM (640k). $49.95 School Edition, 3 1/2" disks (ISBN 1-882848-05-5). *Nonstandard peripherals required:* Microsoft mouse recommended, supports Ad Lib & Sound Blaster cards, hard

LOT & SERIAL TRACKING

drive.
PC-DOS/MS-DOS 3.0 or higher. IBM (640k). $49.95 School Edition, 5 1/4" disks (ISBN 1-882848-06-3). *Nonstandard peripherals required:* Microsoft mouse recommended, supports Ad Lib & Sound Blaster cards, hard drive.
PC-DOS/MS-DOS 3.0 or higher. IBM (640k). $99.00 School Edition, Lab Pack, 3 1/2" disks (ISBN 1-882848-07-1). *Nonstandard peripherals required:* Microsoft mouse recommended, supports Ad Lib & Sound Blaster cards, hard drive.
PC-DOS/MS-DOS 3.0 or higher. IBM (640k). $99.00 School Edition, Lab Pack, 5 1/4" disks (ISBN 1-882848-08-X). *Nonstandard peripherals required:* Microsoft mouse recommended, supports Ad Lib & Sound Blaster cards, hard drive.
Modern Game of Stragegy in a Prehistoric World. Children Ages 8 & Older Become Leaders of a Prehistoric Tribe Whose Home Has Been Destroyed by a Volcano. They Must Lead Their People to a New Home in a Distant Land. Along the Journey They Must Make Good Decisions, & Concentrate on Survival. Builds Decision Making & Leadership Skills. Great for Social Studies Classes.
Lawrence Productions, Inc.

Lot & Serial Tracking. Version: 5.2. 1992. *Items Included:* User manual & reference manual, source code. *Customer Support:* 90 day warranty.
UNIX, VMS, DOS. 386, 486, IBM-compatible, Digital VAX. Contact vendor for price.
Networks supported: Novell.
Provides Full Traceability of Lot or Serial Controlled Items. Parts Are Tracked & Controlled from Purchasing to Inventory, to Manufacturing & Sales. Comprehensive Reports Are Included.
MCBA, Inc.

LOT: Lottery Analysis. *Compatible Hardware:* Apple II, Commodore 64, IBM PC, TRS-80, CP/M machines.
disk Lottery (3-4 digit) $79.95.
disk with Lotto (Max 99 digit) $99.95.
Statistical Comparison Program Designed to Detect Subtle Patterns in Winning Numbers & Digits.
Professor Jones Professional Handicapping Systems.

LOTS: Loan Origination Tracking System. *Compatible Hardware:* AS/400. *General Requirements:* Laser Printer for mortgage documents.
contact publisher for price.
Mortgage Origination System for Banks, Savings & Loans, Mortgage Brokers & Mortgage Bankers. Automates the Marketing, Processing & Closing of Mortgage Loans. Also Features Built-In Telemarketing.
Computer Consulting Ctr., Inc.

Lottery Leprechaun: A Software Guide for Selecting Numbers. Paul Rego. Oct. 1991. *Customer Support:* Free telephone support. 90 day trial period. Satisfaction guaranteed (or money back), for one year starting after trial period. (Entire product must be returned).
6.0.7 or higher. Macintosh (1Mb). $99.00 (ISBN 0-945876-06-8, Order no.: LL1). *Addl. software required:* HyperCard 2.0 or higher.
Helps User to Locate Numbers for Lotteries, Dog Racing, Horse Racing, etc. User Instructs the Software to Select Between One & Ten Numbers, Decides If Duplicate Numbers Are Allowed, & Determines the Range of Numbers Between 0 & 99.
Insight Data.

Lottery Winners' Secrets CD-ROM. Jan. 1996. *Items Included:* Instruction booklet.
DOS & Windows 3.1. PC (2k). CD-ROM disk $29.90 (ISBN 1-56087-118-0). *Optimal configuration:* 386, Windows 3.1 2k.
77 Exciting PC Shareware Computer Programs to Give You the Winning Edge. Includes: Chance Improver, Lottery Tracker & Analyzer, Total Lottery Management System, Lotto Simulation Game, Run Your Own Lottery...Even a Biorhythm Lottery Number Picker. Special Programs for WI, TX, OH, NJ, FL, WA, CA, Canada & Ireland.
Top of the Mountain Publishing.

Lotto-Five-Wheeler. Bob Nadler. Jan. 1994. *Items Included:* Instruction sheet. *Customer Support:* Phone support for 90 days.
PC-DOS/MS-DOS. Any IBM clone (256k). disk $29.95 (ISBN 0-933596-41-3).
This Program Takes As Input Numbers Significant to the Player, & Using These Numbers, Automatically Produces Any of Five Different Game "Wheels" (12x12, 14x23, 16x37, 18x56, or 22x100). Each Wheel Has a Mathematical Assurance of 3 of 4 of Winning Prize Money When Used in Five-Number Lotto Drawings. The User May Optionally Have the Program Select the Numbers to Be Wheeled. Wheels Generated Can Be Sent to the Screen or to a Printer.
F/22 Pr.

Lotto Master. *Items Included:* Bound manual. *Customer Support:* Free hotline - no time limit; 30 day limited warranty; updates are $5/disk plus S&H.
MS-DOS. IBM & compatibles (128k). disk $29.95. *Nonstandard peripherals required:* One drive; printer is supported & recommended.
Apple (48k). disk $29.95. *Nonstandard peripherals required:* Two drives.
Provides Support & Assistance to Today's Lottery Player. Its Data Base Allows User to Track Winning Numbers & Analyze Them for Projecting the Future. Can Be Customized for Any State Lottery; You Can Play & Track One or Several Different Lotteries. It Can Also Be Altered Should Your State Change the Lottery from 5/30 to 6/49 or Any Combination up to 9/99.
Dynacomp, Inc.

Lotto Wheeler. Version: 2.0. Bob Nadler. Apr. 1986. *Compatible Hardware:* Apple II+, IIc, IIe, IIgs; Atari 400, 800, 600XL, 800XL, 1200XL, 1400XL, 1450XLD, 65XE, 130XE; Commodore 64, 128; IBM PC XT, AT PCjr & compatibles. *Language(s):* Compiled Turbo Basic on PC-DOS/MS-DOS systems. *Memory Required:* 48k. *Items Included:* Users Manual. *Customer Support:* Yes.
disk $24.95 ea.
Apple. (ISBN 0-933596-32-4, Order no.: LW-AP).
Atari. (ISBN 0-933596-33-2, Order no.: LW-AT).
Commodore. (ISBN 0-933596-34-0, Order no.: LW-C).
IBM. (ISBN 0-933596-35-9, Order no.: LW-I).
Based on the Dimitrov Wheeling System, This Program Takes As Input Numbers Significant to the Player, & Using These Numbers, Automatically Produces any of Five Different Game "Wheels" (12 x 6, 12 x 42, 14 x 40, 16 x 38, or 18 x 42), Each has a Mathematical Assurance of 4 of 6 or greater of Winning Prize Money. Will Also, at the User's Option, Automatically Produce Wheels Using Numbers of Its Own Choosing. Numbers to Be Played Can Be Sent to Either the Screen or the Printer.
F/22 Pr.

Lotus Agenda. *Compatible Hardware:* IBM PC, PC XT, PC AT & compatibles, PS/2. *Operating System(s) Required:* PC-DOS 2.0 or higher. *Memory Required:* 640k. *General Requirements:* Hard disk.

disk $395.00.
Allows User to Monitor Complex Projects, Categorize Information Contained in Documents Such As Electronic-Mail Messages or Dow Jones News Retrieval Reports, & Export Information As ASCII Text Files.
Lotus Development Corp.

Lotus Demo & Exercise Set: Release 4. Aug. 1990. *Memory Required:* 120k. *Items Included:* 120 page manual & disk with more than 50 programs & over 200 macros.
3.5" or 5.25" disk $39.95.
Disk-Based Tutorial with Reference Book for LOTUS 1-2-3 Release 2.x & 3.x.
RJG Software & Training.

Lotus Express: PC Communications Software for MCI Mail. 1987. *Compatible Hardware:* IBM PC, PC XT, PC AT, PS/2 Models 30/50/60, Portable, Convertible; Compaq Portable, Plus, Deskpro; AT&T 6300. *Operating System(s) Required:* PC-DOS 2.0 or higher. *Memory Required:* PC-DOS 2.0, 2.1 256k; PC-DOS 3.0 or higher 320k; memory-resident configuration 640k. *General Requirements:* Hayes Smartmodem or true compatible. 3-1/2" version requires PC-DOS 3.2 for IBM PC, PC XT, PC AT, Convertible; PC-DOS 3.3 for PS/2. Hard disk recommended.
disk $100.00 (Order no.: 00-1757).
3.5" disk $100.00 (Order no.: 00-3167).
demo disk $5.00.
RAM Resident "Pop-Up" Utility Conducting Background Communications with the MCI Mail System. Supports up to Nine Mail Boxes per PC. Enables Users to Transfer 1-2-3 & Symphony Spreadsheet Files, As Well As Word Processing Documents, Telexes, & Electronic Mail. Data Is Routed Through the MCI Mail Network, Delivered to the PC, Downloaded, & Filed Without User's Assistance. The Program Will Check User's Electronic Mail at User-Specified Time Intervals.
Lotus Development Corp.

Lotus Graphwriter: Combination Set. *Compatible Hardware:* IBM PC, PC XT, PC AT; other Lotus-certified compatibles. *Memory Required:* 192k. *General Requirements:* Hercules or CGA card.
disk $495.00.
Menu-Driven, Stand-Alone Business Graphics Program That Offers a Collection of Pre-Defined Charts & Graphs for Business Presentations & Reports. Features 23 Different Types of Charts, Including Bar, Line, Combination, Pie, Text, Bubble, Organization, & Gantt Charts.
Lotus Development Corp.

Lotus Graphwriter II. *Compatible Hardware:* IBM PC, PC XT, PC AT, 3270 PC, PS/2. *Memory Required:* 512k. *General Requirements:* Hard disk; Hercules (monochrome), CGA, EGA, VGA, or MCGA (Multi-Color Graphics Array) card.
3-1/2" or 5-1/4" disk $475.00.
upgrade from Graphwriter $75.00.
Allows Users to Produce & Update Charts Created from Spreadsheets or Databases. Charts Created with GRAPHWRITER Can Be Linked to 1-2-3, Symphony, or dBASE Files. Then Data, Text, & Attributes Such As Line Color or Fill Pattern Can Be Determined by Values in the Spreadsheet or Database Files. This Version's Enhancements Include 1-2-3-Like User Interface, Direct Links to a Data Source, Automatic Updating & Output of Charts, the Ability to Place Multiple Charts on One Page, the Ability to View & Select Data from the Data Source, & Improved Chart Formats, File Handling, & Output Options.
Lotus Development Corp.

TITLE INDEX

Lotus HAL. *Compatible Hardware:* AT&T, Compaq, IBM PC & compatibles (except IBM PCjr, PC Convertible, or with 1-2-3 Release 1A on 3270 PC), other Lotus-certified compatibles. *Operating System(s) Required:* PC-DOS 2.0 or higher. *Memory Required:* 512k. *General Requirements:* 1-2-3 Release 1A, 2, or 2.01.
5-1/4" or 3-1/2" disk $150.00.
3-1/2" disk version for 5-1/4" disk registered users $30.00.
User Interface for Lotus 1-2-3. Its Vocabulary Includes English Words & Phrases & Users May Customize a Command Dictionary of Their Own. Simplifies the Process of Developing Macros & Enables Users to Test Them Before They Are Actually Used. Offers New Commands; for Example Users Are Enabled to Replace Items Anywhere in the Worksheet (Including Formulas) & Create Dynamic Links Between Cells in Multiple Worksheets.
Lotus Development Corp.

Lotus Manuscript. *Compatible Hardware:* IBM PC XT, PC AT, Portable; Compaq Portable, Portable II, Deskpro, Plus, 286; Hewlett Packard Vectra PC; AT&T 6300, 6300 Plus. *Operating System(s) Required:* PC-DOS 2.0 or higher. *Memory Required:* 512k, recommended 640k. *General Requirements:* Hard disk; IBM Graphics, Hercules, Hercules Plus, Hercules Graphics, Hercules Graphics Plus, CGA, or EGA card.
disk $495.00.
presentation disk $10.00.
Word Processor Targeted at Technical Writers. Users Are Able to Mix Text with Graphics from Lotus 1-2-3, Symphony, & Freelance Plus. Has the Capability to Import Diagrams & Scanned Images, As Well As Spreadsheets & Charts. The Integrated Outliner Will Enable Users to Move More Easily Through the Document. Because Documents Are Structured, Users Are Able to Globally Format an Entire Document or Format by Individual Sections. The "Document Compare" Feature Will Highlight Changes Between Revisions. Will Automatically Size & Generate Math Equations As Well As Upper & Lower Case Greek Symbols, Diacritical Marks, & Brackets. The "Print Formatter" Will Enable User to Control the Appearance of the Document (the Format Information Can Be Saved As a Template for Future Use). Supports Both Dot Matrix & Laser (Including PostScript) Printers.
Lotus Development Corp.

Lotus Measure. *Compatible Hardware:* IBM PC, PC XT, PC AT; Compaq Portable; HP Vectra PC. *Operating System(s) Required:* PC-DOS 2.0 or higher. *Memory Required:* 512k, hard disk configuration 640k. *General Requirements:* Hercules, CGA, or EGA card; 1-2-3 Release 2.0 or higher.
disk $495.00.
For Engineers & Scientists. Directly Collects Data into 1-2-3 for Analysis, Eliminating Middle Steps. Allows for a Broad Range of Product Applications by Supporting Popular Measurement Instruments Through IEEE-488 & RS-232-C Communication Buses, As Well As Aquisition Boards. Enables Direct Communication with More Than 8,000 Types of Instruments & Devices.
Lotus Development Corp.

Lotus 1-2-3. *Version:* Release 3. *Compatible Hardware:* IBM PC, PCjr, PC XT, PC AT, PS/2 Models 30, 50, & 60, Portable PC, Convertible, 3270, 3270/G, 3270/GX; Compaq Portable, Plus, Deskpro; AT&T 6300; DEC; other Lotus-certified compatibles. *Operating System(s) Required:* PC-DOS 2.0 or higher. *General Requirements:* IBM Utility program for PCjr; 3-1/2" disk version requires PC-DOS 3.2 for IBM PC, PC XT, PC AT & PC-DOS 3.3 for Convertible & PS/2.
3-1/2" or 5-1/4" disks $495.00.
This Release Has the Worksheet Expanded to 8192 Rows. Memory Management Is More Efficient, Allowing Data to Be Stored Anywhere on the Worksheet, & Can Address More Than 640k. Supports Intel's 8087/80287 Math Co-Processors. Comes with 40 New Macro Commands. Allows Users to Start Directly from a Hard Disk Without Putting the System Disk in the Floppy Disk Drive. DEC, Hewlett-Packard, & Wang Versions Available from Manufacturers.
Lotus Development Corp.

Lotus 1-2-3 Advanced Features. *Version:* 2.4. 1993. *Compatible Hardware:* IBM PC & compatibles. *Operating System(s) Required:* PC-DOS. *Memory Required:* 640k.
disk $29.95, incl. wkbk. (ISBN 0-935987-01-0).
Self-Study Guide Book & Data Disk Which Provides Step by Step Instructions. Designed for Those Who Already Know the Basic Commands. Emphasis Is on 1-2-3's Database Capabilities, Data Tables, Combining Files, Date Arithmetic & Macros. Lotus 1-2-3 Commands Covered Includes Date Arithmetic & Date Function, Data Query Find, Data Query Extract, AND/OR Criteria, Data Fill, Data Tables, Range Name Create, Range Value, File Combine, Macros, Windows & Protecting Cells, Worksheet Learn, Range Search. Final Project Evaluates Mastery. Must Be Used in Conjunctiom with Lotus 1-2-3, 2 or 2.2 Software.
Edutrends, Inc.

Lotus 1-2-3 for Everyone, Pt. I. *Version:* 2.4. 1993. *Compatible Hardware:* IBM PC & compatibles. *Operating System(s) Required:* PC-DOS, MS-DOS. *Memory Required:* 640k.
disk $29.95, incl. wkbk. (ISBN 0-935987-00-2).
Self-Study Guide Book & Data Disk Which Provides Step by Step Instructions. Provides Basic Instructions on the Lotus 1-2-3 Software Package. Emphasis Is on Integration of the Spreadsheet, Graphics & Database into an Integrated Worksheet. Lotus 1-2-3 Commands Covered Include Worksheet Insert, Delete, Column Width, Range Format, Label Prefix, Global vs. Range, Copy, Move, Printing, Saving & Retrieving Files, Absolute Cell Reference, Graphing & Sorting the Database, File Linking & Printing with Allways. Final Project Evaluates Mastery of Commands Covered. Must Be Used in Conjunction with Lotus 1-2-3, 2 or 2.2 Software.
Edutrends, Inc.

Lotus 1-2-3 for Marketing & Sales. Michael Laric & Ronald Stiff. Jun. 1984. *Compatible Hardware:* IBM PC. *Operating System(s) Required:* PC-DOS. *General Requirements:* Lotus 1-2-3.
disk $24.95, incl. bk. (ISBN 0-13-540956-X).
Shows How LOTUS 1-2-3 Can Be Applied to Marketing & Sales Analysis. Book Includes a Description of LOTUS 1-2-3 & Includes over 30 Spreadsheets.
Prentice Hall.

Lotus 1-2-3 for Windows: Add-in Development Kit. 1991. Windows. IBM PC & compatibles. $249.00.
Addl. software required: Lotus 1-2-3.
Allows User to Enhance Spreadsheet by Creating Custom @ Functions, New Macro Commands, & Custom User Interfaces That Can Be Launched from 1-2-3 Menus or SmartIcons. Add-ins Created with the Kit Are Windows DLLs That Provide a Direct Connection Between Custom C Code & 1-2-3 DLLs. Toolkit Includes Routines for Writing @ Functions That Comply with the 1-2-3 for Windows Core.
Lotus Development Corp.

LOTUS 1-2-3 FOR MACINTOSH

Lotus 1-2-3/G. *Operating System(s) Required:* OS/2. *General Requirements:* 386-based computer recommended.
disk $695.00.
upgrade from release 2.2 or 3 $75.00.
Incorporates the Features Found in Release 3 with New OS/2-Specific Features. Included Are True Three-Dimensional Worksheets, File-Linking Across Worksheets, & Database Enhancements, Such As the Ability to Perform Relational Database Joins.
Lotus Development Corp.

Lotus 1-2-3 Networker. *Version:* 2. *Compatible Hardware:* IBM PC & compatibles.
$2475.00 per package.
Enhances Access for up to Five Users Directly from the Network File Server by Eliminating the Need for Key Diskettes at Local PCs. Includes a 1-2-3-Add-In Which Locks Worksheet Files So That Only One User at a Time Can Make Changes While Providing Other Users with Read-Only Access.
Lotus Development Corp.

Lotus 1-2-3: Principles & Applications. 1990.
IBM PC. contact publisher for price (ISBN 0-538-80661-3, Order no.: DF69B8H81).
IBM PS/2. contact publisher for price (ISBN 0-538-80662-1, Order no.: DF69B8H88).
Text & Template Software Package Containing Instructions on Using Lotus 1-2-3. Includes Tutorials, Problems, Case Studies, & Exercises.
South-Western Publishing Co.

Lotus 1-2-3 Trainer's Kit: Parts I & II. 1993.
$480.00 ea. part.
site licensing avail.
Each Part Includes a Leader's Guide with Outline Master Disk, & 20 Student Guides. Designed for Classroom Instruction, Teaches How to Design Spreadsheets & Graphs, Enter & Edit Entries, & More.
Edutrends, Inc.

Lotus Report Writer. Sep. 1985. *Compatible Hardware:* IBM PC, PC XT, PC AT, Portable, 3270 PC; Compaq; AT&T 6300; other Lotus-certified compatibles. *Operating System(s) Required:* PC-DOS 2.0-3.1. *Memory Required:* 256k. *General Requirements:* 2 disk drives, Lotus 1-2-3 or Symphony database files.
disk $95.00.
demo disk $5.00.
Reads Files Created by 1-2-3 Release 1A & 2, & Symphony Release 1.0 & 1.1. The User Is Allowed to Change Field Names, Widths, & Formats, Insert Multiline Headers & Footers, Delete Unwanted Fields, & Sort on up to Four Levels. Can Also Do Common Calculations; Including Averages, Totals, Subtotals, Counts, & Minimums/Maximums. Customized Formats Can Be Saved for Generating Periodic Reports with Updated Information. Allows User to Create Custom Reports, Forms & Mailing Labels from 1-2-3 & Symphony Databases.
Lotus Development Corp.

Lotus 1-2-3 for Macintosh. 1992.
6.0.4 or higher. Macintosh Plus or higher (2Mb).
3.5" disk $495.00. *Nonstandard peripherals required:* Hard Drive.
Spreadsheet for Macintosh. Includes Recalc, Graphing Capability, 3-D Capability, Network-Administration Functions, Direct Interchange of Data Tables between Spreadsheet & Database Through Data Access Language (DAL) Linkage & Direct Command Linkage to dBase & Foxbase databases. Requires 3Mb RAM for System 7.
Lotus Development Corp.

Louis the Lion: Explore the African Savanna with Your New Friend Louis. *Items Included:* Pamphlet of instructions. *Customer Support:* Tech support, 60 day money-back guarantee.
Windows; Macintosh. IBM compatible 386SX or higher (4Mb); Mac LC or higher (2.5Mb). CD-ROM disk $39.95 (ISBN 0-924677-07-4). *Nonstandard peripherals required:* Audio board, mouse, CD-ROM drive. *Addl. software required:* Video card 640x480 with 256 colors; Quicktime 2.0.
Explore the African Savanna with Louis the Lion. Six Activities & Games Are Introduced by "Sambeke," the Young Masai, As You Learn about Lions in Their Natural Habitat.
IMSI (International Microcomputer Software, Inc.).

Louisville Behavior Checklist. *Version:* 2.010. Lovick C. Miller. *Customer Support:* Free unlimited phone support.
IBM PC & 100% compatibles, Apple. 3.5" or 5.25" disk (IBM); 5.25" disk (Apple); $170.00 (Order no.: W-1005 (5.25"); W-1032 (3.5"); W-1006 APPLE). *Optimal configuration:* DOS 3.0 or higher (512k), hard disk with one Mb of free disk space, printer.
Carefully Constructed, Well Standardized Inventory Assesses a Wide Range of Social & Emotional Behaviors Indicative of Psychopathological Disorders in Children & Adolescents.
Western Psychological Services.

Love Games. *Customer Support:* 800-929-8117 (customer service).
MS-DOS. IBM/PS2. disk $49.99 (ISBN 0-87007-854-2).
A Psychologically Based Matching Profile. Both User & One or More Persons Complete Simple but Penetrating Questions Which Match Users up with Ideal Type.
SourceView Software International.

LoveTies. *Version:* 1.0. Sheryl Canter. Oct. 1991. IBM PC & compatibles. 5.25" or 3.5" disk $89.95.
Astrology Software.
Permutations Software, Inc.

LoveTies. Sheryl Canter. Sep. 1991. *Items Included:* Manual with table of latitudes & longitudes. *Customer Support:* Technical support available by calling the company.
MS-DOS v.2.0 or higher. IBM-PC & compatibles (330k). 5.25" disk $89.95 (ISBN 0-9630781-5-1). *Optimal configuration:* Recommended: EGA or VGA graphics adapter, hard disk. 3.5" disk $89.95 (ISBN 0-9630781-3-5).
Does Individual Horoscopes & Chart Comparisons. The Comparison Report Is Oriented Towards Couples with Romantic Ties. Individual Report Runs about 5 Pages & the Comparison Report Is Another 5 Pages, Somewhat Less If Birthtimes Are Unknown. Astronomical Calculations Are Accurate to Within One Minute. The Program Is Fully Menu-Driven with Mouse Support, & Is Very Easy to Use. A Graphics Version of the Chart Wheel Can Be Viewed If EGA or VGA Is Available. All Reports Can Be Printed. On-Line Help Is Available.
Permutations Software, Inc.

Lower Cost of Market. *Compatible Hardware:* Altos Series 5-15D, Series 5-5D, 580-XX, ACS8000-XX; DEC Rainbow 100 with 2 disk drives, Rainbow 100+ with 10MB hard disk; IBM PC with 2 disk drives, PC XT, IBM compatibles; Kaypro 11/IV with 2 disk drives, Kaypro 10; Xerox 820 with 2 disk drives, ZILOG MCZ-250. *Operating System(s) Required:* CP/M, MP/M, CP/M-86/80, PC-DOS, MS-DOS.
contact publisher for price (Order no.: LCM).
Enables the Auditor to Complete Lower Cost of Market Tests for Inventory. Automatically Calculates: Total Book Value, Total, Total Net Realizable Value, Total Replacement Cost & Market Floor for Each Inventory Item, & Related Aggregate Totals for All Items Included in the Test, Excess, if Any of Cost over Market Value for Each Item & in the Aggregate.
Coopers & Lybrand.

LP-2000. *Compatible Hardware:* Apple II with Z80 Softcard or compatibles; IBM PC & compatibles. *Operating System(s) Required:* CP/M. *Memory Required:* Apple 64k, IBM 128k.
$299.00, incl. documentation set.
documentation only $25.00.
Employs Numerically Stable Mathematical Methods to Solve Linear Programming Problems. Provides Objective, Primal & Dual Solution Values, Reduced Costs & Constraint Values.
Software Designs 2000.

LPI-C. *Version:* 2.2 UNIX V.3 & V.4, 386/486. *Compatible Hardware:* 80386/486 & Pentium, Sparc. *Operating System(s) Required:* Unix. $595.00.
Full Conforming Implementation of ANSI Standard C. Compiler Offers an Integrated Preprocessor, Providing Fast Compilation Times, Cross-Language Calling, Component Architecture, & Extensive Error Messages. Provides Compatibility with Most CC Command Line Options, Allowing Existing Makefiles to Be Used Without Change. Comes Bundled with CodeWatch, a Powerful X/Motif Debugger.
Liant Software Corp.

LPI - C++. *Items Included:* Complete documentation set, including a User's Guide, Library Reference Manual, Quick Reference Guide, & Library Reference Manual, & Release Notes. *Customer Support:* 30-day warranty; additional support options available.
UNIX SVR3, SVR4. Intel 386/486. disk $1295.00.
SunOS. Sun SPARC. disk $1295.00.
LPI-C Plus Plus Is a True 32-Bit Compiler Implementation of C Plus Plus. It Is Compatible with CFront 1.2, 2.0, & 2.1, ANSI C, & Classic (K&R) C, & Includes a Complete Implementation of the 2.0 Iostream Library & a Complex Class Library. Supports Multiple Inheritance, Nested Types, Protected Derivations, Member Pointers, & Heap Management. Comes with CodeWatch, a Powerful Window-Based Source-Level Debugger. C Plus Plus Debugging Includes Full C Plus Plus Expression Evaluation, Class Browsing, & Easy Handling of Overloaded Functions.
Liant Software Corp.

LPI-COBOL. *Version:* 7.0. *Compatible Hardware:* 80386/486 & Pentium, Sparc. *Operating System(s) Required:* Unix.
$1295.00 & up.
Fully Implements the ANSI COBOL-85 & COBOL-74 Programming Language. Has Been Validated on Several Targets at the High Level, with No Discrepancies, & Is Also Fully X/Open Compliant. Powerful Run-Time Library Provides ISAM & SORT Functions. Cross Language Calling Allows Access to Several DBMS Packages, Through User-Provided C Routines. Comes Bundled with CodeWatch, a Powerful X/Motif Debugger.
Liant Software Corp.

LPI-FORTRAN. *Version:* 3.6 Unix 1.3, 386/486. *Compatible Hardware:* 80386/486 & Pentium, Sparc. *Operating System(s) Required:* Unix. $1295.00.
Full Implementation of the ANSI FORTRAN X3.9-1978 (FORTRAN-77) & MILSTD-1753. Provides Versatile Extensions That Ease the Transporting of Existing Applications to Other Systems, & Is Fully X/Open Compliant. High Performance Global Optimizer Offers Features Such As Global Optimization Across the Entire Compilation Unit, Function Inlining & Loop Unrolling. Includes the Following Floating-Point Coprocessor Support: Intel 80287 & Motorola 68881. Includes CodeWatch, a Powerful X/Motif Debugger.
Liant Software Corp.

LP77 Toolkit Library. *Version:* 3.0. *Compatible Hardware:* IBM PC, PC XT, PC AT. *General Requirements:* Lahey Personal FORTRAN '77 (LP77) software.
disk $49.00.
Library of 15 Additional Subroutines & Functions to Be Used with LP77 (Lahey Personal FORTRAN '77). Functions Provided Include DOS & BIOS Interrupt Handling, Stack Management for Assembly Language Routines, Bit Shifting, & DOS Command Execution.
Lahey Computer Systems, Inc.

Lqiud Pipeline Surge Analysis. 1992. *Items Included:* Detailed manuals included with all Dynacomp products. *Customer Support:* Free telephone support to original customer - no time limit; 30 day limited warranty.
MS-DOS 3.2 or higher. IBM PC & compatibles (512k). $969.95 (Add $5.00 for 3 1/2" format; 5 1/4" format standard). *Optimal configuration:* IBM, MS-DOS 2.0 or higher, 640k RAM, a hard disk, & CGA/EGA/VGA or compatible graphics capability.
Simulates the Transportation of Any Liquid Through a Pipeline under Unsteady or Upset Conditions. It Calculates the Transient Pressures & Flow Rates in a Linear Pipeline System & Includes Models for Pipes of Different Sizes & Characteristics, As Well As Models for Pumps, Various Valves, & Surge Tanks. You May Select up to 10 Modes at Which Pressures and/or Flows Rates Are to Be Calculated, Tabulated, & Plotted Against Time.
Dynacomp, Inc.

LS FORTRAN Professional. *Version:* 3.3. Jun. 1993. *Items Included:* 1 FORTRAN manual, MPW, 3 MPW manuals, Debugging Toolkit, TSiGraphics. *Customer Support:* Unlimited free technical support.
Macintosh. Mac LC & higher (6Mb). 3.5" disk $895.00 (Order no.: C3401).
FORTRAN 77 Compiler for Macintosh.
Language Systems Corp.

LS FORTRAN Standard. *Version:* 3.3. Nov. 1991. *Items Included:* MPW & 3 manuals, 1 Fortran manual. *Customer Support:* Free unlimited phone support.
Macintosh. Macintosh LC or Higher (6Mb). 3.5" disk $595.00 (Order no.: C3201). *Nonstandard peripherals required:* Hard drive with 5Mb free space.
Leading VAX-Compatible FORTRAN Compiler on the Macintosh. It Is a Validated ANSI FORTRAN 77 Compiler That Runs in Macintosh Programmer's Workshop (MPW). The Runtime Use Interface of Compiled FORTRAN Programs Is Fully Customizable by Programmers with Any Level of Macintosh Experience. A Full-Featured Scrolling Text Window with Complete MultiFinder Support Is Created Automatically.
Language Systems Corp.

LSC-2020 Fully Integrated Accounting Software. Ricardo M. Concepcion. 1985. *Compatible Hardware:* IBM PC, PC AT, PC XT & compatibles. *Operating System(s) Required:* MS-DOS. *Language(s):* BASIC. *Memory Required:* 640k. *General Requirements:* 2 disk drives & 20Mb hard disk.
disk $899.00 (Order no.: LSC-2020).

TITLE INDEX

Composed of General Ledger, Accounts Receivable, Inventory, Invoicing, Accounts Payable, & Payroll Programs. The General Ledger Consists of Cash Receipts Journal, Cash Disbursement Journal, & General Journal. It Provides Month-to-Date, Quarter-to-Date, & Year-to-Date Account Balances. The Ledger Provides Chart of Accounts & Prints Payroll Checks, & Checks for Vendors & Payees. The Program Generates Trial Balance, Balance Sheet & Income Statement. Features: Alphabetical Listing of Customers, Alphabetical Listing of Inventory, Product Ledger, Vendors & Suppliers, Accounts Receivable Ledger, A/R Aging Report, Accounts Payable Ledger, Cash Requirement Report, Cash Disbursement, General Journal, Employee List, Payroll Ledger, Cash Receipts Report, Trial Balance Report, Balance Sheet, & Income Statement.
Lizcon Computer Systems.

LSF: Least Square Curve Fitter. Sumar Corporation. 1984. *Compatible Hardware:* IBM PC. (source code included). *Memory Required:* 64k. *General Requirements:* 160k disk drive capacity, monochrome monitor with 80 columns.
disk $39.95 (ISBN 0-13-541227-7).
Explains Least Curve Fitting & How Engineers, Social Scientists, & Data Analysts Can Use This Program to Solve Equations on IBM PC. Documentation Provides Thorough Derivation of Equation Involved & Program Provides Software Routine for Deriving First, Second, or Third Degree Least Square Equations for User-Defined Data Sets.
Prentice Hall.

LSP: Logic Simulation Program. *Compatible Hardware:* Apple Macintosh, IBM PC & compatibles. *Memory Required:* IBM 256k, Macintosh 512k. *General Requirements:* Hard disk.
$150.00.
Stand-Alone Digital Logic Simulation Program. After Describing a Logical Circuit & Sequence of Binary Input Signals to the Program, LSP Will Compute the Resulting Binary Output Signals at Any (or All) Nodes of the Circuit to the Specified Times. The Output Is a Timing Diagram, or Tree Tables, Showing the Binary States of Each Selected Signal As a Function of Time.
BV Engineering.

LSQR. *Version:* 2.1. Sridhar Seshadri & Stanley N. Deming. 1989. *Items Included:* Manual, 3.5" diskette. *Customer Support:* Free telephone support to registered users.
MS-DOS. IBM PC/XT/AC & compatibles (384k). disk $295.00 (ISBN 0-932651-18-6).
A Matrix Least Squares for Fitting Linear Models to Data & Providing Regression Analysis Results for the Fitted Model.
Statistical Programs.

LT-Family of Software: Long Term Family of Software. *Compatible Hardware:* DEC PDP-11, VAX. *Operating System(s) Required:* PC-DOS, RSTS, Unix, VMS. *Language(s):* DBASE. *Items Included:* Training credits. *Customer Support:* Yes. write for info.
Integrated Modules for the Financial & Records Management of a Long Term Health Care Facility.
Roeing Corp.
 LT-Claims.
  Creates UB82 Electronic Claims for Payor Such As Medicaid, Medicare, & Other 3rd Party Payors. Flexible Format to Allow Payor Specific Format. Electronic Format Can Be Transmitted Via Modem, Tape, or Diskette.
 LT-CARE.
  Covers the Patient Data Base, All Receivables, Billings & Personal Funds for the Facility.
 LT-CHART.
  Automatically Produces the Physician, Treatment & Medication Orders. Allows Use of the Facility's Diagnosis System & the ICD9CM Coding Method.
 LT-PRX.
  Payroll/Personnel Module. Produces User-Defined Reports That Accumulate Costs by Nursing Units & Combine These Centers into Certification Levels for Analysis by Patient Day. Personnel Management Reports Assist in Planning for Evaluations, Establishing Benefit Eligibility or Other User-Defined Data.
 MEDREP.
  Facilitates the Preparation of Annual Government Cost Report. Automatically Extracts Data from the General Ledger & Payroll & Then Prints Cost Reports.
 Office Management.
  Includes 3 Components: Word Processing, Spreadsheet/Graphics & Compu-Trieve (Report Writer).
 Care Plan.
  Automated Plan of Care for a Facility's Patient Management Team. Reduces Labor Cost & Improves Accountability for Care.

LTB: Legal Time & Billing. Robert Hallem. Jul. 1984. *Compatible Hardware:* IBM PC compatibles. *Operating System(s) Required:* SCO UNIX, SCO XENIX. *Language(s):* C. *Memory Required:* 512k.
AT compatibles; UNIX. disk $1500.00, (demo disk 35.00) (ISBN 0-918103-01-0).
PC-DOS. disk $1500.00, (demo disk 35.00) (ISBN 0-918103-05-3).
Multi-User Timekeeping, Billing & Accounts Receivable System for up to 20 Timekeepers.
RTG Data Systems.

LTERM4. *Compatible Hardware:* TRS-80 Model 4. *Memory Required:* 64k.
disk $49.95 (Order no.: D4LTRM).
The Alternate Source.

L216. *Version:* 3.0. 1980. *Compatible Hardware:* TRS-80 Model I, Model III, Model 4. *Language(s):* Level II BASIC (source code included). *Memory Required:* 16k.
cassette $59.00.
replacement cassette $3.00.
manual $10.00.
Contains 11 Programs from Database Management to Sales Analysis.
Micro Architect, Inc.

Lucid Common LISP/DEC system. *Compatible Hardware:* Apollo, DEC VAX family, IBM RT PC, Prime 50 Series, Sun, Symbolics 3600 family. *Customer Support:* Full support.
contact publisher for price.
LISP Implementation Available for General-Purpose Computers. Language Implementation Provides All the Common LISP Functions. Package Includes an EMACS-Style Embedded Editor, a Windowing Facility, an Object-Oriented Programming Paradigm, & Complete Debugging Facilities.
Lucid, Inc.

Lucid Common LISP/386. *Customer Support:* Full support.
An 80386-based system under 386/ix or System V/386. $1895.00.
Integrated Common LISP Implementation.
Lucid, Inc.

Luck Everlasting. Natalie Babbit. Apr. 1996. *Items Included:* Program manual. *Customer Support:* Free technical support, 90 day warranty.
School ver.. System 7.1 or higher. Macintosh (4Mb). 3.5" disk contact publisher for price (ISBN 1-57204-165-X). *Nonstandard peripherals required:* 256 color monitor, hard drive, printer.
Lab pack. System 7.1 or higher. Macintosh (4Mb). 3.5" disk contact publisher for price (ISBN 1-57204-166-8). *Nonstandard peripherals required:* 256 color monitor, hard drive, printer.
Site license. System 7.1 or higher. Macintosh (4Mb). 3.5" disk contact publisher for price (ISBN 1-57204-167-6). *Nonstandard peripherals required:* 256 color monitor, hard drive, printer.
School ver.. Windows 3.1 or higher. IBM/Tandy & 100% compatibles (4Mb). disk contact publisher for price (ISBN 1-57204-168-4). *Nonstandard peripherals required:* VGA or SVGA 640x480 resolution (256), mouse, hard drive, sound device.
Lab pack. Windows 3.1 or higher. IBM/Tandy & 100% compatibles (4Mb). disk contact publisher for price (ISBN 1-57204-169-2). *Nonstandard peripherals required:* VGA or SVGA 640x480 resolution (256), mouse, hard drive, sound device.
Site license. Windows 3.1 or higher. IBM/Tandy & compatibles (4Mb). disk contact publisher for price (ISBN 1-57204-170-6). *Nonstandard peripherals required:* VGA or SVGA 640x480 resolution (256), mouse, hard drive, sound device.
This Companion for young adult literature is ideal for students who don't know how to start that book report, or give that needed summary. Gentle prompts throughout the guide section of the program include Warm-up Connections, Thinking about Plot, Quoting & Noting, Keeping a Journal, If Were ———' Responding to Questions, Using Quotations, Taking a Personal View, Write to Others & Write a Sequel.
Lawrence Productions, Inc.

Lucky Day-Lottery Number Report: M-197. John Townley. 1983. *Compatible Hardware:* Apple II+, IIe, IIc; Commodore 64, PET; IBM PC. *Language(s):* BASIC (source code included). *Memory Required:* 32k. *General Requirements:* 2 disk drives, printer.
disk $300.00 ea. (Order no.: M197).
Commodore 64. (ISBN 0-925182-17-6).
IBM. (ISBN 0-925182-18-4).
Apple. (ISBN 0-925182-19-2).
Uses Insights of Well-Known Numerology Author John Townley to Produce 2 Reports for Sale to Customers. Using Traditional Pythagorean Numerology, "Lucky Days" Reports Give a Monthly Summary of Days That Dovetail with Customers' Own Birthdate & Legal Name Numbers. "Lottery" Reports Give Personal Daily Numbers for Lotteries, Horse Races, etc.
Matrix Software.

Lumberman III. *Operating System(s) Required:* PC-DOS/MS-DOS, Unix, Xenix. *General Requirements:* DBL runtime license.
IBM. disk $4500.00.
Xenix, Unix. disk $7500.00.
Manages All Inventory Sales, Accounting & Ordering Functions for Both Stocking & Non-Stocking Distributors of Hard & Soft Woods. Industry Standard Units of Measure Utilized to Determine Costs, Margins & Inventory Status. Complete Integrated System Designed for Multi-User Applications.
MBA Computer Services, Inc.

Lumena. *Items Included:* manual. *Customer Support:* 30 days after purchase - free, return registration card within 30 days, additional 60 days free support, extended 12 month warranty

$395.00 (includes support & any update(s) during that period. Training at additional cost. MS—DOS. IBM PC AT, PS/2 & compatibles (4Mb). LUMENA Illuminator-PRO or Targa. *Nonstandard peripherals required:* 40 Mb hard drive, 1.2Mb floppy disk drive, serial port, Vista or Targa+ or various 16 or 32 bit videographics board, VGA & RGB monitors, digitizing tablet with stylus or mouse. *Optimal configuration:* 386 computer, 8Mb Memory, VGA & RGB monitors, pressure sensitive digitizing tablet, output device.
For Illuminator-PRO, Targa(Plus), Vista Boards & More. PC-Based 2D Color Graphics Design Program for the Creation & Production of High Impact Images. Offering over 250 Tools from a Palette of 32,000 or 16.7 Million Colors. 20 Special Effects Modes & Image Processing Capabilities. Input Accepted from Live or Recorded Video, Scanned Images, or Freehand Drawings. Output to Several Media Including Print, Slides or Videotape.
Time Arts, Inc.

Lump-Sum. *Version:* 2.1. Associates for International Research. Aug. 1995. *Customer Support:* No charge for telephone support. Annual upgrade/maintenance fee of $1,000. DOS. 386 (4Mb). disk $3500.00.
Database of Travel Costs for the United States & Canada. Primary Use Is to Calculate Lump-Sum Payments for Transferred Employees. Payment Is Used in Lieu of Direct Reimbursement for Homefinding, Temporary Living & Final Move Costs.
Hessel Group, The.

Lumpsum Distribution. *Compatible Hardware:* Altos Series 5-15D, Series 5-5D, 580-XX, ACS8000-XX; DEC Rainbow 100 with 2 disk drives, Rainbow 100+ with 10MB hard disk; IBM PC with 2 disk drives, PC XT, IBM compatibles; Kaypro II/IV with 2 disk drives, Kaypro 10; Xerox 820 with 2 disk drives; ZILOG MCZ-250. *Operating System(s) Required:* CP/M, MP/M, CP/M-80, CP/M-86, PC-DOS, MS-DOS.
contact publisher for price (Order no.: LUMPSUM).
Template Designed for Individual Financial Projections. Calculates the Discounted Present Value, Both Before & After Income Taxes, of the Alternative Distributions Schedules. Especially Useful for Individuals Approaching Retirement, Who Need to Decide How to Receive Their Retirement Plan Distributions.
Coopers & Lybrand.

Lunar Phases. *Compatible Hardware:* TI 99/4A. *Operating System(s) Required:* DX-10. *Language:* Extended BASIC. *Memory Required:* 48k.
cassette $16.95.
Eastern Standard Time Is Calculated for Each Lunar Phase. Any Other Time Zone Can Be Used with Modification to the Program.
Eastbench Software Products.

Lunar Rescue. Feb. 1988.
Mac 4.2 (1Mb). Micintosh Plus & SE. 3.5" disk $59.95 (Order no.: 0012).
A Space Adventure Incorporating Arcade-Style Action & Free-Market Trading Strategies. As You Transport Vital Supplies Between 26 Isolated Lunar Colonies, You Explore the Terrain & Debris Along the Supply Routes to Find Hidden Crystals. At Each Lunar Colony You Strategically Buy & Sell Commodities at the Robotic Trade Center. You Battle Against Out-of-Control Lunar Weaponry with Lasers, Space Cannons & Bombs & Defend Against Attacks with Decoys, Shields, Cloaking Devices & by Evasive Maneuvering.
XOR Corp.

Lunar Returns: M-8. *Compatible Hardware:* Commodore 64, PET, VIC-20.
disk $30.00.
cassette $30.00.
Calculates Exact Lunar Return. Lists Planets & Houses.
Matrix Software.

Lunar Rover Patrol. *Compatible Hardware:* Dragon Color Computer, MC-10, TRS-80 Color Computer, TDP-100. *Memory Required:* 32k. *General Requirements:* Joystick.
contact publisher for price.
Spectral Assocs.

Lunar Voyager. *Compatible Hardware:* TRS-80 Model I, Model III, Model 4 with Level II BASIC. *Memory Required:* 48k.
disk $23.95.
cassette $19.95.
Lunar Lander Graphics Simulation Game.
Dynacomp, Inc.

Luria-Nebraska Neuropsychological Battery (Adult & Child Forms). *Version:* 3.012. Charles J. Golden et al. *Customer Support:* Free unlimited phone support.
IBM PC & 100% compatibles. 3.5" or 5.25" disk $250.00 (Order no.: LNNB-ADULT W-1002 (5.25"), W-1030 (3.5")); LNNB-CHILD W-1002 (5.25"), W-1030 (3.5")). *Optimal configuration:* DOS 3.0 or higher (512k), hard disk with one Mb of free disk space.
Apple. 5.25" disk $245.00 (Order no.: W-1008).
Well-Known, Widely Used Test Battery Measures Broad Range of Neuropsychological Functions in Individuals 13 Years & Older. Children's Form Available for Use with 8 to 12-Year Olds. Computer Reports Generated by IBM Disk Include Both Scoring & Interpretation. Apple Disks Provide Scoring Only.
Western Pyschological Services.

The Lurking Horror. Dave Lebling. Jun. 1987. *Compatible Hardware:* Apple II, II+, IIe, IIc, Macintosh; Atari XL/XE, ST; Commodore 64, 128, Amiga; DEC Rainbow; IBM PC & compatibles; TI Professional. *Memory Required:* 48k.
disk $39.95.
Ever Since You Arrived at G.U.E. Tech, You've Heard Stories about the Creepy Old Campus Basements & Storage Rooms, Some So Ancient That They Contain Only Rotting Piles of Unidentifiable Junk. And You've Vowed Never to Set Foot in Any of Them. But Tonight, with a Blizzard Howling Around the Monolithic Buildings, Something Draws You Inexorably Downward. Suddenly, You're in a World That Rivals Your Most Hideous Visions. Shapes Emerge from the Dark Corners. Eerie Sounds Draw Closer. Slimy Passageways Lead to Sights so Horrifying That They Will Feed Your Nightmares for Weeks. You'll Face Ingenious Puzzles, Unique Characters, & Chilling Twists of Plot As You Explore the Ghastly Nether Regions of the Institute & Confront the Horror Lurking Below.
Activision, Inc.

LYNC: Telecommunications Software. *Version:* 5.0. Jan. 1980. *Compatible Hardware:* Action Computer; Actrix, Aftek-PC; Alspa; Altos; Apple II series, Apple Macintosh; Archives; AT&T PC; Bell-PC; BOS; Canon PC; Columbia; Compaq; Corona; Cromemco; Data General One; DEC Rainbow; Delta; Direct IPC; Discovery Systems; Durango; Eagle; Epson; Ericsson PC; Fujitsu Micro; IBM PC, PCjr, PC XT, PC AT; IMS; Intertec; ITT XTRA; Kaypro; Leading Edge; LOBO MAX-80; MAD Computer; Mitsubishi PC; Molecular; Morrow; Mugen; Multi Micro; NCR; NEC; North Star; Olivetti; Omikron; Onyx; Osborne 1; Otrona; Panasonic Sr. Partner; Paradise Computer; Pronto; Radio Shack; Sanyo; SD Systems; Sierra Data Systems; Sperry PC; Telecom; TeleVideo; Vector Graphics; Victor 9000; Wang PC; Xerox; Zenith; Zorba. *Operating System(s) Required:* Apple DOS, CP/M, CP/M-80, CP/M-86, MP/M-80, MS-DOS, PC-DOS, TurboDOS, Z-DOS. *Memory Required:* 64k. *General Requirements:* RS-232 cable, modem. *Customer Support:* Technical support services unlimited for registered users, 90 day warranty for disks. Phone No. 805-964-6767.
disk $195.00.
Automatic Communications Program That Lets Users Exchange Information & Data Between Their Microcomputer & Other Microcomputers, Minicomputers, Mainframes, Telex & Information Services. User Can Change Baud Rate, the Number of Times the Telephone Rings Before It Engages the Modem. Users Can Also Switch Between Full & Half Duplex, & Give Automatic Line Feeds Without Having to Leave LYNC & Reconfigure the Program. Macros Allow Automatic Log On/Off with Electronic Mail Services. Release 5.0 Has Encryption Added, the Message Being Descrambled by the Addressee with the Use of a Codeword. ASCII Conversion Command Allows Sending/Receiving 8-Bit Files.
Norton-Lambert Corp.

Lynngyde. *Customer Support:* 800-929-8117 (customer service).
MS-DOS. IBM/PS2. disk $39.00 (ISBN 0-87007-096-7).
A Playing Aid for Advanced Dungeons & Monsters Players, It Makes Playing the Game Faster, Easier & More Fun.
SourceView Software International.

Lynx. 1983. *Compatible Hardware:* IBM PC & compatibles. *Operating System(s) Required:* PC-DOS, MS-DOS, TurboDOS, MP/M. Networks including Novell, StarLAN, MultiLink Advanced, LANLink. *Memory Required:* 640k. *General Requirements:* Hard disk.
disk $99.50.
Takes Data from COUGAR MOUNTAIN Files & Translates It into a Format That Can Be Read by Other Programs (dBASE II, VISICALC, CALCSTAR, WORDSTAR), or the Reverse. Allows for Multi-Company Ledgers, Accounts Receivables, Inventories, Order Entries, Accounts, Payables, & Payrolls. Allows ASCII Data Files to Be Imported to or Exported from COUGAR MOUNTAIN Software. This Module Is Included in the Accounting Package.
Cougar Mountain Software, Inc.

Lyric Language French.
MS-DOS 5.0 or higher, Windows 3.1 or higher. 386 processor or higher (4Mb). CD-ROM disk $39.95 (Order no.: R1049). *Nonstandard peripherals required:* CD-ROM drive. *Optimal configuration:* 386 processor operating at 16MHz or higher, MS-DOS 5.0 or higher, Windows 3.1 or higher, 30Mb hard drive, mouse, VGA graphic adapter & VGA color monitor (SVGA recommended), 4Mb RAM, external speakers or headphones (with sound card) that are Sound Blaster compatible.
Macintosh (4Mb). (Order no.: R1049). *Nonstandard peripherals required:* 14" color monitor or larger, CD-ROM drive.
A Bilingual Multimedia Program with Full-Motion Video. An Innovative Way for Kids to Learn a Second Language Allowing Them to Record Their Voices As a Native Speaker's.
Library Video Co.

Lyric Language German.
MS-DOS 5.0 or higher, Windows 3.1 or higher. 386 processor or higher (4Mb). CD-ROM disk

TITLE INDEX

$39.95 (Order no.: R1222). *Nonstandard peripherals required:* CD-ROM drive. *Optimal configuration:* 386 processor operating at 16MHz or higher, MS-DOS 5.0 or higher, Windows 3.1 or higher, 30Mb hard drive, mouse, VGA graphic adapter & VGA color monitor (SVGA recommended), 4Mb RAM, external speakers or headphones (with sound card) that are Sound Blaster compatible.
Macintosh (4Mb). (Order no.: R1222).
Nonstandard peripherals required: 14" color monitor or larger, CD-ROM drive.
A Bilingual Multimedia Program with Full-Motion Video. An Innovative Way for Kids to Learn a Second Language Allowing Them to Record Their Voices As a Native Speaker's.
Library Video Co.

Lyric Language Series.
MS-DOS 5.0 or higher, Windows 3.1 or higher. 386 processor or higher (4Mb). CD-ROM disk $119.85, Set (Order no.: R1047). *Nonstandard peripherals required:* CD-ROM drive. *Optimal configuration:* 386 processor operating at 16MHz or higher, MS-DOS 5.0 or higher, Windows 3.1 or higher, 30Mb hard drive, mouse, VGA graphic adapter & VGA color monitor (SVGA recommended), 4Mb RAM, external speakers or headphones (with sound card) that are Sound Blaster compatible.
Macintosh (4Mb). (Order no.: R1047).
Nonstandard peripherals required: 14" color monitor or larger, CD-ROM drive.
A Bilingual Multimedia Program with Full-Motion Video. An Innovative Way for Kids to Learn a Second Language Allowing Them to Record Their Voices As a Native Speaker's. 3 Volume Set.
Library Video Co.

Lyric Language Spanish.
MS-DOS 5.0 or higher, Windows 3.1 or higher. 386 processor or higher (4Mb). CD-ROM disk $39.95 (Order no.: R1048). *Nonstandard peripherals required:* CD-ROM drive. *Optimal configuration:* 386 processor operating at 16MHz or higher, MS-DOS 5.0 or higher, Windows 3.1 or higher, 30Mb hard drive, mouse, VGA graphic adapter & VGA color monitor (SVGA recommended), 4Mb RAM, external speakers or headphones (with sound card) that are Sound Blaster compatible.
Macintosh (4Mb). (Order no.: R1048).
Nonstandard peripherals required: 14" color monitor or larger, CD-ROM drive.
A Bilingual Multimedia Program with Full-Motion Video. An Innovative Way for Kids to Learn a Second Language Allowing Them to Record Their Voices As a Native Speaker's.
Library Video Co.

Lyriq Crosswords: Crossword Magazine Edition. Oct. 1992. *Items Included:* User manual, 3 1/2" & 5 1/4" media, promotional offers. *Customer Support:* Free customer support via telephone.
DOS 3.1 & higher or Windows 3.0 & higher. IBM PC, PS/2 & 100% compatibles (512k). disk $29.95 (Order no.: 100). *Optimal configuration:* 512k RAM PC or PS/2 with hard disk; EGA or VGA screen resolution, mouse optional; DOS 3.1, Windows 3.0 or higher.
Electronic Crossword Puzzle Entertainment Product Featuring Name Brand Puzzles in Various Editions, e.g. Washington Post & Crossword Magazine. Others to Follow. Features Competition Play & Scoring, Multi-Player Capability, Printouts, Save-in-Progress, Hint & Help Modes. Zoom Mode Enlarges Puzzle for Easy Reading.
Lyriq International Corp.

Lyriq Crosswords: Washington Post Edition.
Oct. 1992. *Items Included:* User manual, 3 1/2" & 5 1/4" media, promotional offers. *Customer Support:* Free customer support via telephone.
DOS 3.1 & higher or Windows 3.0 & higher. IBM PC, PS/2 & 100% compatibles (512k). disk $29.95 (Order no.: 101). *Optimal configuration:* 512k RAM PC or PS/2 with hard disk; EGA or VGA screen resolution, mouse optional; DOS 3.1, Windows 3.0 or higher.
Electronic Crossword Puzzle Entertainment Product Featuring Name Brand Puzzles in Various Editions, e.g. Washington Post & Crossword Magazine. Others to Follow. Features Competition Play & Scoring, Multi-Player Capability, Printouts, Save-in-Progress, Hint & Help Modes. Zoom Mode Enlarges Puzzle for Easy Reading.
Lyriq International Corp.

Lyrix Word Processing System. Version: 6.0. Nov. 1982. *Compatible Hardware:* AT&T 6300+; IBM PC & compatibles, PC XT, PC AT. *Operating System(s) Required:* UNIX, XENIX. *Language(s):* C. *Memory Required:* 128k. *Items Included:* Manuals. *Customer Support:* 30-day warranty, hotline, newsletter, electronic bulletin board.
disk $595.00.
User-Configurable, Menu-Driven System Which Combines Text Editing, Formatting Capabilities, & Print-Time Commands. All Commands & Messages Can Be Re-Defined or Translated to a Foreign Language, with Support for Special Characters & Accents.
Santa Cruz Operation, Inc.

M-A-S 90 Accounting Software. Version: 2.0. *Items Included:* Complete documentation for each module purchased. *Customer Support:* Optional ClientCare support plans available - fee varies depending on installation.
DOS, Windows, Windows 95. 386 (4Mb). Contact publisher for price. *Networks supported:* Novell NetWare 3.11, 3.12, 4.1; Lantastic 6.0.
UNIX/XENIX. 386 (4Mb client, 8Mb server). Contact publisher for price.
Windwos NT Server 3.51. 386 (4Mb client, 8Mb server). Contact publisher for price. *Networks supported:* Windows NT workstation not supported.
The Most Complete Accounting Solution Available. With More Than 28 Modules, M-A-S 90 Systems Can Address General & Specialized Accounting Needs of Virtually Any Company, Regardless of Size, Industry or Operating System.
State Of The Art, Inc.

M.A.S. 90 EVOLUTION/2: Import Master.
Version: 1.1x. Mar. 1990. *Items Included:* User manuals; disk media, binder, slipcase. *Customer Support:* Free technical support to authorized resellers & consultants. End-user support provided for a fee - call publisher for pricing.
PC-DOS/MS-DOS. 286, 386, 486-based IBM, COMPAQ & compatibles (640k). disk $599.00. *Optimal configuration:* Operating system dependent. *Networks supported:* Novell, LANtastic.
SCO XENIX/UNIX. 286, 386, 486-based IBM, COMPAQ & compatibles (2Mb). Contact publisher for price. *Optimal configuration:* Operating system dependent. *Networks supported:* Novell, LANtastic.
UNIX. 286, 386, 486-based IBM, COMPAQ & compatibles (2Mb). Contact publisher for price. *Optimal configuration:* Operating system dependent. *Networks supported:* Novell, LANtastic.
Eliminates the Need for Manual Data Entry When Converting Data from Virtually Any File Format, Including ASCII, dBASE III Plus, DIF, & Lotus 1-2-3, into the M A S 90 EVOLUTION/2 Format. Import Master Removes the Barrier Between Your Current Accounting Software & M A S 90 EVOLUTION/2 Making the Conversion Process Painless, Economical, & Sensible.
State of the Art, Inc.

M.A.S. 90 EVOLUTION/2: Post Master. Version: 1.2x. Jun. 1990. *Items Included:* User manuals; disk media, binder, slipcase. *Customer Support:* Free technical support to authorized resellers & consultants. End-user support provided for a fee - call publisher for pricing.
PC-DOS/MS-DOS. 286, 386, 486-based IBM, COMPAQ & compatibles (640k). disk $199.00. *Addl. software required:* Library Master & Report Master. *Optimal configuration:* Operating system dependent. *Networks supported:* Novell, LANtastic.
SCO XENIX/UNIX. 286, 386, 486-based IBM, COMPAQ & compatibles (2Mb). Contact publisher for price. *Addl. software required:* Library Master & Report Master. *Optimal configuration:* Operating system dependent. *Networks supported:* Novell, LANtastic.
UNIX. 286, 386, 486-based IBM, COMPAQ & compatibles (2Mb). Contact publisher for price. *Addl. software required:* Library Master & Report Master. *Optimal configuration:* Operating system dependent. *Networks supported:* Novell, LANtastic.
Delivers Enhanced Office Productivity & Business Communication Capabilities, Allowing User to Achieve a Fully Automated Office. Post Master Combines Your M A S Accounting System with a Custom Database & Word Processor, to Generate Letters, Forms, Lists or Labels. Use It to Track Business Prospects, Generate Reminder Letters, or Even Produce a Direct-Mail Marketing Campaign.
State of the Art, Inc.

M/BANKER+. Version: 7.1. 1985. *Compatible Hardware:* IBM PC & compatibles, PC XT, PC AT. *Operating System(s) Required:* MS-DOS 5.0 & higher. *Language(s):* Compiled BASIC, Assembly. *Memory Required:* 2000k.
disk $3000.00.
disk $4500.00, Network.
Adds the Ability to Link Fractionalized/ Participating Investors to Any or All Loans in the LOANLEDGER+ Environment; up to 8,999 Investors on a Single Loan. Also Adds Many Reports, On-Screen Inquiry for Investors/Loans or Loans/Investors. Prints Checks & 1099's at End-of-Year. Produces FHLMC Reports.
Dynamic Interface Systems Corp.

M. C. Escher Screen Saver. Oct. 1995. *Items Included:* Soft cover, stapled manual & registration card. *Customer Support:* Free customer service via our 800 number, unlimited warranty on disk replacement.
Windows 3.1, 386 or higher. IBM, Tandy or 100% compatible (4Mb). disk $24.95 (ISBN 1-888046-89-9, Order no.: IS10225). *Nonstandard peripherals required:* Super VGA, sound card (100% sound blaster compatible), 4Mb hard disk space.
Drawings by M. C. Escher Animated for Use As a Screensaver for Computers.
Image Smith, Inc.

M-Disk. Timohty Purves. Nov. 1986. *Compatible Hardware:* Sanyo MBC 555. *Operating System(s) Required:* MS-DOS 1.25, 2.11. *Memory Required:* 128k.
disk $39.95 ea.
(ISBN 0-923213-26-0, Order no.: SA-MDI).
RAM Disk Software Program That Duplicates a Hardware Drive in Memory. Automatically Loads into GEM When the System Is Initialized. Users

Can Customize the Size of Memory Allocated to the RAM Disk. Useful to Single-Drive Owners, Making Two-Drive Operations Easier.
MichTron, Inc.

M-Master. *Compatible Hardware:* Apple II with Applesoft; IBM PC. (source code included). *Memory Required:* Apple II 48; IBM 128k.
disk $19.95.
Card Game Favored by Members of Mensa.
Dynacomp, Inc.

M/OS-80. *Memory Required:* 64k.
contact publisher for price.
CP/M Compatible, Floppy Disk Operating System for the MD or SD Series of the Microcomputer Board Systems.
Thomson Semi Conductors-Mostek Corp.

Mac A & D. *Version:* 5.0. 1995. *Items Included:* Product user's & tutorial manuals, sample documents & tutorials. *Customer Support:* 90 day telephone support with purchase & free newsletter update service - 18% annual. Onsite training available - contact vendor for cost.
Mac System 7 or UNIX/MAE. Macintosh (8Mb). $2995.00 copy, site license available. *Networks supported:* Appletalk.
A Complete CASE Solution for Structured Analysis & Design, Object-Oriented Analysis & Design, Real-Time Extensions, Task Design, Data Modeling, Screen Prototyping, Requirement Database & Global, Multi-User Data Dictionary & Code Generation.
Excel Software.

Mac-A-Mug. *Compatible Hardware:* Apple Macintosh. *Memory Required:* 512k.
3.5" disk $59.95.
Allows Users to Create an Almost Unlimited Number of Human Faces by Scrolling Through & Choosing from Hundreds of Individual Facial Features. Disks Contain Both Male & Female Features & Accessories & the Capability of Mixing the Two. Can Print Out a Face in a Number of Sizes, or the Output Can Be Copied into MacPaint for Further Enhancement.
Shaherazam.

Mac-A-Mug Pro. *Compatible Hardware:* Apple Macintosh. *General Requirements:* Hard disk, ImageWriter, LaserWriter.
3.5" disk $495.00.
Composite Human Faces.
Shaherazam.

Mac Aldus Home Publisher: Domestic. *Version:* 2.0. Nov. 1993. *Customer Support:* For customer service, product registration, upgrades, technical support, & CustomerFirst service plans, customers may call Aldus Customer Services at (206) 628-2320.
Macintosh. Contact publisher for price (ISBN 1-56026-286-9).
Aldus Corp.

The Mac Art Department. Tom Christopher.
Compatible Hardware: Apple Macintosh.
Memory Required: 128k. *General Requirements:* MacPaint; printer recommended.
3.5" disk $39.95, incl. manual (ISBN 0-671-54317-2).
Provides over 150 Reusable, Modifiable Images & Graphic Elements.
Brady Computer Bks.

Mac Art Library. *Version:* 1.1. *Compatible Hardware:* Apple Macintosh.
3.5" disk $39.95, per volume.
Variety-Pak $49.95.
entire library $250.00.
entire library in PictureBase format $275.00.
12-Disk Collection of Categorized Clip Art Which Includes Animals, Buildings, On the Farm, Flowers/Trees/Plants, Geography, Greeting Cards, Kitchen, People, Sports, Signs/Symbols/Borders, Tools, & Transportation.
Kentary, Inc.

Mac Best Sellers. *Items Included:* Installation Guide.
MAC. Contact publisher for price (ISBN 0-87321-088-3, Order no.: MAC-3041).
Activision, Inc.

Mac Bestsellers. *Items Included:* Installation Guide.
MAC. Contact publisher for price (ISBN 0-87321-089-1, Order no.: CDM-3041).
Activision, Inc.

Mac CARE. *Version:* 3.0. *Items Included:* Complete documentation, keycaps. *Customer Support:* 120 free support; 12% per year thereafter (includes annual updates).
Macintosh DOS 6.0 or higher. Macintosh (1Mb). 3.5" disk $1295.00.
Administrative System for Child Care Centers & Preschool. System Offers Facilities for Registration, Waiting List Management, Scheduling, Staff Information Management, Accounts Receivable.
SofterWare, Inc.

Mac ChartMaker: Domestic. Mar. 1994.
Customer Support: For customer service, product registration, upgrades, technical support, & CustomerFirst service plans, customers may call Aldus Customer Services at (206) 628-2320.
Macintosh. Contact publisher for price (ISBN 1-56026-276-1).
Aldus Corp.

Mac Church Assistant. *Compatible Hardware:* Apple Macintosh.
3.5" disk $199.00.
Church Member Management.
CP Software.

Mac Classic Art, Vol. 2: Domestic. Dec. 1992.
Customer Support: For customer service, product registration, upgrades, technical support, & CustomerFirst service plans, customers may call Aldus Customer Services at (206) 628-2320.
Macintosh. Contact publisher for price (ISBN 1-56026-156-0).
Aldus Corp.

Mac COBOL. *Compatible Hardware:* Apple Macintosh, Lisa 2 Series runnning under Macworks. *General Requirements:* External hard disk recommended.
contact publisher for price.
Fully Integrated High Level Certified ANSI 74 Compiler for the COBOL Programmer. Takes Full Advantage of the Features of the Apple Macintosh & Allows User to Switch Programming Tools with a Single Click of the Mouse & Get Instant Response Time.
Micro Focus, Inc. (California).

Mac COSA After Effects: Domestic. *Version:* 2.0. Jan. 1994. *Customer Support:* For customer service, product registration, upgrades, technical support, & CustomerFirst service plans, customers may call Aldus Customer Services at (206) 628-2320.
Macintosh. Contact publisher for price (ISBN 1-56026-266-4).
Aldus Corp.

Mac DateBook Pro: Domestic. *Version:* 2.01. Apr. 1993. *Customer Support:* For customer service, product registration, upgrades, technical support, & CustomerFirst service plans, customers may call Aldus Customer Services at (206) 628-2320.
Macintosh. Contact publisher for price (ISBN 1-56026-265-6).
Aldus Corp.

Mac EarthWorks. *Version:* 3.0. *Compatible Hardware:* Apple Macintosh. *Customer Support:* Unlimited by telephone.
Program. 3.5" disk $495.00.
Demo. 3.5" disk $25.00.
Earth Work; Calculates Cut & Fill Volumes.
MFE Assocs.

Mac Fetch: Domestic. Nov. 1992. *Customer Support:* For customer service, product registration, upgrades, technical support, & CustomerFirst service plans, customers may call Aldus Customer Services at (206) 628-2320.
Macintosh. Contact publisher for price (ISBN 1-56026-159-5).
Aldus Corp.

Mac Fetch: International English. *Version:* 1.2. Dec. 1993. *Customer Support:* For customer service, product registration, upgrades, technical support, & CustomerFirst service plans, customers may call Aldus Customer Services at (206) 628-2320.
Macintosh. Contact publisher for price (ISBN 1-56026-252-4).
Aldus Corp.

Mac Fetch Trial Version: Domestic. Dec. 1992.
Customer Support: For customer service, product registration, upgrades, technical support, & CustomerFirst service plans, customers may call Aldus Customer Services at (206) 628-2320.
Macintosh. Contact publisher for price (ISBN 1-56026-160-9).
Aldus Corp.

Mac FreeHand: Domestic. *Version:* 4.0. Nov. 1993. *Customer Support:* For customer service, product registration, upgrades, technical support, & CustomerFirst service plans, customers may call Aldus Customer Services at (206) 628-2320.
Macintosh. Contact publisher for price (ISBN 1-56026-190-0).
Aldus Corp.

Mac FreeHand: German. *Version:* 4.0. Mar. 1994. *Customer Support:* For customer service, product registration, upgrades, technical support, & CustomerFirst service plans, customers may call Aldus Customer Services at (206) 628-2320.
Macintosh. Contact publisher for price (ISBN 1-56026-193-5).
Aldus Corp.

Mac FreeHand: International English. *Version:* 4.0. Dec. 1993. *Customer Support:* For customer service, product registration, upgrades, technical support, & CustomerFirst service plans, customers may call Aldus Customer Services at (206) 628-2320.
Macintosh. Contact publisher for price (ISBN 1-56026-191-9).
Aldus Corp.

Mac FreeHand Japanese. *Version:* 3.0. May 1993. *Customer Support:* For customer service, product registration, upgrades, technical support, & CustomerFirst service plans, customers may call Aldus Customer Services at (206) 628-2320.
Macintosh. Contact publisher for price (ISBN 1-56026-134-X).
Aldus Corp.

Mac FreeHand Korean. *Version:* 3.0. May 1993. *Customer Support:* For customer service, product registration, upgrades, technical support, &

TITLE INDEX

CustomerFirst service plans, customers may call Aldus Customer Services at (206) 628-2320.
Macintosh. Contact publisher for price (ISBN 1-56026-135-8).
Aldus Corp.

Mac Gallery Effects User Manual. *Version:* 1.5. Apr. 1993. *Customer Support:* For customer service, product registration, upgrades, technical support, & CustomerFirst service plans, customers may call Aldus Customer Services at (206) 628-2320.
Macintosh. Contact publisher for price (ISBN 1-56026-184-6).
Aldus Corp.

Mac Grass. *Version:* 3.0. *Items Included:* Documentation, software, sample data. *Customer Support:* Available.
Apple Macintosh. $950.00. *Nonstandard peripherals required:* 80Mb hard disk.
Geographic Information System. Runs under A/UX.
Space Remote Sensing Center.

Mac II Tools. *Compatible Hardware:* Apple Macintosh II.
3.5" disk $59.00.
Extension of Basic MacForth Plus Programming for Color Graphics, 68020 Assembler, & 68881 Support.
Creative Solutions (Maryland).

Mac IntelliDraw: Domestic. *Version:* 2.0. Feb. 1994. *Customer Support:* For customer service, product registration, upgrades, technical support, & CustomerFirst service plans, customers may call Aldus Customer Services at (206) 628-2320.
Macintosh. Contact publisher for price (ISBN 1-56026-255-9).
Aldus Corp.

Mac LawnMan. *Compatible Hardware:* Apple Macintosh, Macintosh Plus. *General Requirements:* Hard disk; ImageWriter, LaserWriter.
3.5" disk $995.00.
Lawn Care Management & Accounting.
Nova R & D, Inc.

Mac Manager. Jun. 1984. *Compatible Hardware:* Apple Macintosh. *Memory Required:* 128k. disk $19.95.
Simulation Strategy Game. Simulation of Big-Business Management & Decision Making, Players Can Determine Through Their Decisions Whether They Go Boom or Go Bust.
Harvard Assocs., Inc.

Mac Menlo T65xx. *Version:* 4.0. *Compatible Hardware:* Apple Macintosh. *Memory Required:* 2000k. *Items Included:* User Guide. *Customer Support:* Hotline.
contact publisher for price.
Terminal Emulation; Tandem Mainframe, Built-In Macros, Multi-Session, File Transfer, Graphics, etc.
Menlo Business Systems, Inc.

Mac Minister. *General Requirements:* External disk drive or hard disk drive.
Macintosh or higher (512KE). 3.5" disk $69.00.
Communications & Expense-Management Tool for Ministers.
CP Software.

Mac 'n Med II Medical Office Management System. *Version:* 2k. *Compatible Hardware:* Apple Macintosh, Macintosh Plus. *General Requirements:* ImageWriter, LQ printer; hard disk. Single User. 3.5" disk $899.95.
Demo. 3.5" disk $25.00.
Medical Office Management System.
Somerville Assocs.

Mac 'n Med Spelling Checker. *Version:* 1.1. *Compatible Hardware:* Apple Macintosh, Macintosh Plus. *General Requirements:* Microsoft Word 4.0, Microsoft Write.
3.5" disk $29.95.
Medical Spelling Checker.
Somerville Assocs.

Mac On-Call. *Version:* 1.1. *Compatible Hardware:* Apple Macintosh. *General Requirements:* Hard disk.
3.5" disk $595.00.
Artificial Intelligence Diagnostic Knowledge Integrator.
IatroCom.

Mac PageMaker: Danish. *Version:* 5.0. Nov. 1993. *Customer Support:* For customer service, product registration, upgrades, technical support, & CustomerFirst service plans, customers may call Aldus Customer Services at (206) 628-2320.
Macintosh. Contact publisher for price (ISBN 1-56026-182-X).
Aldus Corp.

Mac PageMaker: Domestic. *Version:* 5.0. Jul. 1993. *Customer Support:* For customer service, product registration, upgrades, technical support, & CustomerFirst service plans, customers may call Aldus Customer Services at (206) 628-2320.
Macintosh. Contact publisher for price (ISBN 1-56026-172-2).
Aldus Corp.

Mac PageMaker: Dutch. *Version:* 5.0. Oct. 1993. *Customer Support:* For customer service, product registration, upgrades, technical support, & CustomerFirst service plans, customers may call Aldus Customer Services at (206) 628-2320.
Macintosh. Contact publisher for price (ISBN 1-56026-179-X).
Aldus Corp.

Mac PageMaker: Finnish. *Version:* 5.0. Dec. 1993. *Customer Support:* For customer service, product registration, upgrades, technical support, & CustomerFirst service plans, customers may call Aldus Customer Services at (206) 628-2320.
Macintosh. Contact publisher for price (ISBN 1-56026-181-1).
Aldus Corp.

Mac PageMaker: French. *Version:* 5.0. Sep. 1993. *Customer Support:* For customer service, product registration, upgrades, technical support, & CustomerFirst service plans, customers may call Aldus Customer Services at (206) 628-2320.
Macintosh. Contact publisher for price (ISBN 1-56026-174-9).
Aldus Corp.

Mac PageMaker: German. *Version:* 5.0. Sep. 1993. *Customer Support:* For customer service, product registration, upgrades, technical support, & CustomerFirst service plans, customers may call Aldus Customer Services at (206) 628-2320.
Macintosh. Contact publisher for price (ISBN 1-56026-175-7).
Aldus Corp.

Mac PageMaker: International English. *Version:* 5.0. Aug. 1993. *Customer Support:* For customer service, product registration, upgrades, technical support, & CustomerFirst service plans, customers may call Aldus Customer Services at (206) 628-2320.
Macintosh. Contact publisher for price (ISBN 1-56026-173-0).
Aldus Corp.

Mac PageMaker: Italian. *Version:* 5.0. Oct. 1993. *Customer Support:* For customer service, product registration, upgrades, technical support, & CustomerFirst service plans, customers may call Aldus Customer Services at (206) 628-2320.
Macintosh. Contact publisher for price (ISBN 1-56026-177-3).
Aldus Corp.

Mac PageMaker: Japanese. *Version:* 4.0j. Jun. 1992. *Customer Support:* For customer service, product registration, upgrades, technical support, & CustomerFirst service plans, customers may call Aldus Customer Services at (206) 628-2320.
Macintosh. Contact publisher for price (ISBN 1-56026-152-8).
Aldus Corp.

Mac PageMaker: Norwegian. *Version:* 5.0. Dec. 1993. *Customer Support:* For customer service, product registration, upgrades, technical support, & CustomerFirst service plans, customers may call Aldus Customer Services at (206) 628-2320.
Macintosh. Contact publisher for price (ISBN 1-56026-180-3).
Aldus Corp.

Mac PageMaker: Spanish. *Version:* 5.0. Oct. 1993. *Customer Support:* For customer service, product registration, upgrades, technical support, & CustomerFirst service plans, customers may call Aldus Customer Services at (206) 628-2320.
Macintosh. Contact publisher for price (ISBN 1-56026-178-1).
Aldus Corp.

Mac PageMaker: Swedish. *Version:* 5.0. Sep. 1993. *Customer Support:* For customer service, product registration, upgrades, technical support, & CustomerFirst service plans, customers may call Aldus Customer Services at (206) 628-2320.
Macintosh. Contact publisher for price (ISBN 1-56026-176-5).
Aldus Corp.

Mac Personal Class. *Version:* 2.0. *Compatible Hardware:* Apple Macintosh Plus. *Memory Required:* 1000k. *General Requirements:* Hard disk drive; HyperCard.
3.5" disk $59.00.
Personal Information Organizer Provides Users with the Ability of Recording Vital Personal Information. Can Be Custom Tailored to Fit Any Special Personal Needs. Categories Covered Include: Family Data, Personal Wills, Assets & Liabilities, Insurance Information, Important Documents, Burial Information, Ownership Certificates, Benefits, Real Estates & Investment Data.
Quadmation, Inc.

Mac Persuasion: Domestic. *Version:* 3.0. Feb. 1994. *Customer Support:* For customer service, product registration, upgrades, technical support, & CustomerFirst service plans, customers may call Aldus Customer Services at (206) 628-2320.
Macintosh. Contact publisher for price (ISBN 1-56026-213-3).
Aldus Corp.

Mac PressWise: Domestic. *Version:* 2.0. Mar. 1994. *Customer Support:* For customer service, product registration, upgrades, technical support, & CustomerFirst service plans, customers may call Aldus Customer Services at (206) 628-2320.
Macintosh. Contact publisher for price (ISBN 1-56026-279-6).
Aldus Corp.

Mac PressWise: French. Nov. 1992. *Customer Support:* For customer service, product registration, upgrades, technical support, & CustomerFirst service plans, customers may call Aldus Customer Services at (206) 628-2320.
Macintosh. Contact publisher for price (ISBN 1-56026-147-1).
Aldus Corp.

Mac PressWise: German. Nov. 1992. *Customer Support:* For customer service, product registration, upgrades, technical support, & CustomerFirst service plans, customers may call Aldus Customer Services at (206) 628-2320. Macintosh. Contact publisher for price (ISBN 1-56026-148-X).
Aldus Corp.

Mac Print to Video: Domestic. Sep. 1992. *Customer Support:* For customer service, product registration, upgrades, technical support, & CustomerFirst service plans, customers may call Aldus Customer Services at (206) 628-2320. Macintosh. Contact publisher for price (ISBN 1-56026-151-X).
Aldus Corp.

Mac TAG Teacher's Assistant Grader. *Version:* 2.04. *Items Included:* Disk, user manual. Macintosh or higher (512K). 3.5" disk $65.00.
Grade-Book Manager.
Nisus Software, Inc.

Mac-Tally. *Compatible Hardware:* Apple Macintosh. *Memory Required:* 1000k.
Site license available. 3.5" disk $145.00.
White Blood Cell Differential Counts. Site License Available.
Data Management Assocs. of New York, Inc.

Mac the Librarian. *Version:* 4.1. *Items Included:* Manual. *Customer Support:* First year free; 1 year maintenance, $225 (single user); $275 (multi-user); includes 800 number technical support & free updates.
Macintosh (4Mb). 3.5" disk Circ. $500.00, PAC $995.00, Card Printing $300.00 single user; Add $500.00 for multi-user (ea. 5 stations) (ISBN 0-929963-02-4, Order no.: MTLCIRC; MTL PAC; MTLCP). *Nonstandard peripherals required:* Barcode scanner (with circulation module). *Networks supported:* Appletalk-compatible, Ethernet.
3.5" disk Circ. $1000.00, PAC $1495.00, Card Printing $800.00 multi-user (Order no.: MTLCIRCMU; MTLPACMU; MTLCPMU).
Public Access Catalog (P.A.C.) with Optional Add-On Modules for Circulation & Card Production. Stand-Alone Circulation Module Available. Fully Integrated Library Management System Contains Authority Files for Authors, Subjects & Series. Stores & Imports Marc & MicroLIF Data.
Richmond Software Corp.

Mac-3000. *Compatible Hardware:* Apple Macintosh. *Memory Required:* 512k.
3.5" disk $150.00.
Hewlett-Packard 2392, DEC VT100 & IBM 3278 Terminal Emulation; File Transfers.
International Computer Consultants.

Mac TouchBase Pro: Domestic. *Version:* 3.01. Apr. 1993. *Customer Support:* For customer service, product registration, upgrades, technical support, & CustomerFirst service plans, customers may call Aldus Customer Services at (206) 628-2320. Macintosh. Contact publisher for price (ISBN 1-56026-263-X).
Aldus Corp.

Mac Transfer. *Compatible Hardware:* Apple Macintosh.
3.5" disk $60.00.
Apple II or IBM PC to Macintosh File Transfers.
Southeastern Software.

Mac TrapWise: Domestic. *Version:* 2.0. Mar. 1994. *Customer Support:* For customer service, product registration, upgrades, technical support, & CustomerFirst service plans, customers may call Aldus Customer Services at (206) 628-2320. Macintosh. Contact publisher for price (ISBN 1-56026-274-5).
Aldus Corp.

MAC-2-DOS Package. George E. Chamberlain. Aug. 1989. *Items Included:* An interface which plugs into the disk drive port on the Commodore Amiga, 1 user manual. *Customer Support:* 90 day unlimited warranty.
Amiga DOS 1.2 or higher. Commodore Amiga (512k). 3.5" disk $99.95. *Nonstandard peripherals required:* Macintosh compatible disk drive.
Combination of Hardware & Software That Enables Amiga Users to Transfer Amiga to & from the Macintosh Computer. System Transfers PostScript Files, ASCII Files, McBinary Files, Binary Files, & MacPaint Files to & from IFF. Users Have the Ability to Include a Macintosh Compatible Disk Drive Which Is Required When Using This Program.
Central Coast Software.

Mac TypeTwister: Domestic. Mar. 1994. *Customer Support:* For customer service, product registration, upgrades, technical support, & CustomerFirst service plans, customers may call Aldus Customer Services at (206) 628-2320. Macintosh. Contact publisher for price (ISBN 1-56026-257-5).
Aldus Corp.

MacAdios Manager II. *Version:* 1.5. *Items Included:* Manuals, documentation. *Customer Support:* Free technical support, upgrades.
Macintosh 512K, 512KE, Plus, SE, II, IIx. disk $890.00 (Order no.: GWL-MMII). *Nonstandard peripherals required:* MacAdios hardware.
General Purpose Data Acquisition Package. Performs FFT's & Inverse FFT's Spectrum Analysis, Statistical Analysis, Integration Differentiation, Histograms & Convolutions on Acquired Data.
GW Instruments, Inc.

MacAkkadian. *Version:* 4.6. Apr. 1987. *Items Included:* User's manual, keyboard layout chart. *Customer Support:* Free telephone support; defective disks replaced free.
Any system. Macintosh (1Mb). 3.5" disk $79.95. *Addl. software required:* Any word processor. *Optimal configuration:* 4Mb RAM, hard drive.
A Convenient Input System Plus the Complete Set of Neo-Assyrian Akkadian Signs in 12 & 24 Point High Quality Bitmap Fonts. MacAkkadian Contains All the Basic Akkadian Signs Listed in Rene Labat's Manual D'Epigraphie Akkadienne (5th Edition, 1976) & Rykle Borger's "Assyrisch-Babylonische Zeichenliste" (AOAT 33, 1978). It Contains More Than 740 Signs in Six Fonts, & Includes Significantly Oversized Cross Shaped Signs. The 12 Point Fonts Take up 75K & the 12 & 24 Point Fonts Together Take up 325K. Thus, an 800K Drive or Two 400K Drives Are Required for High Quality Printing. Any Macintosh Can Use the 12 Point Standard Quality Fonts.
Linguist's Software, Inc.

MacAnalyst. *Version:* 5.0. 1995. *Items Included:* Product manual, sample documents & tutorial. *Customer Support:* 90-day telephone support with product purchase, update service contract-18% annual fee, free newsletter.
MAC-OS, 7.0, UNIX/MAE. $995.00 MacAnalyst. *Optimal configuration:* Hard disk & ImageWriter or LaserWriter printer.
MacAnalyst/Expert $1595.00.
Site license available.
CASE Tool for Automating Industry Standard Analysis Techniques Including Data & Control Flow Diagrams, Real-Time Extensions, Process Specifications & Data Dictionary. Supports Data & Information Modeling Using Entity-Relationship Diagrams. Also Includes Object-Oriented Analysis & Requirement Database.
Excel Software.

MacAnatomy. *Memory Required:* 1000, recommended 2000k.
Macintosh Plus, Macintosh SE, Macintosh II. $95.00 per volume; 20% discount for schools. *Nonstandard peripherals required:* Hard disk recommended.
Complete Electronic Atlas of Human Anatomy in MacPaint Document Form.
MacMedic Pubns., Inc.

MacAnatomy Volumes 1-A. Dr. Robert Davis. May 1985.
Macintosh. disk $95.00. *Addl. software required:* MacPaint.
Atlas of Human Anatomy That Can Easily Be Modified & Incorporated into Teaching Material. Anatomical Details Are Presented As Line Drawings with Extensive Use of MacPaint Techniques for Emphasis. Useful for Students of Human Anatomy from High School to Medical School. Avaialble in Four Volumes. Can Be Ordered Singly or As a Complete Set.
MacMedic Pubns., Inc.

MacAppraiser. *Compatible Hardware:* Apple Macintosh, Macintosh Plus. *General Requirements:* ImageWriter, LaserWriter, hard disk.
3.5" disk $495.00.
URAR Report Processor.
Bradford & Robbins.

The MacArt Department. Tom Christopher. Apr. 1985. *Compatible Hardware:* Apple Macintosh. *Memory Required:* 128k.
disk $39.95, incl. bk. (ISBN 0-671-54317-2).
Offers Reusable Graphic Elements & a Manual That Explains How to Customize to Create Reports, Charts, Correspondence, etc. Contains over 100 Images Including: Household Objects, Borders, Travel Images, Food, Americana, Signs, Musical Instruments, etc.
Brady Computer Bks.

MacAstrologer. *Compatible Hardware:* Apple Macintosh.
3.5" disk $179.95.
Chart Design Program.
Full Phase Software.

MaCATI: Macintosh Assisted Telephone Interviewing. *Version:* 2.0. Jerry W. Wicks & Jose L. Pereira de Almeida. Nov. 1991. *Items Included:* Manual & disks, plus FLO-STAT statistical package & thesaurus & spell-checker software. *Customer Support:* Free phone support, on-site training & setup at cost.
MAC OS 6.0.7. Mac Classic II (2Mb). $3500.00 & up. *Nonstandard peripherals required:* Hard disk. *Networks supported:* AppleTalk & EtherTalk.
Complete Computer Assisted Telephone Interviewing (CATI) System Which Can Also Be Used for Computed Assisted Personal Interviewing & Disk by Mail Surveys. It Automates the Process of Questionnaire Editing, Skip Patterns, Data Collection & Data Processing Surrounding Large-Scale Survey Projects. MaCATI Is Simple to Learn & Use & Ideal for University Survey Research Centers, Market Research Companies, & Organizations Engaged in Telefund Drives & Telemarketing.
Senecio Software, Inc.

MacAuthorize. *Version:* 2.3. Feb. 1996. *Items Included:* 1 spiral bound manual, 1 diskette. *Customer Support:* 90 day free tech support, 90

TITLE INDEX

day warranty on materials.
Macintosh 6.0 or higher. Macintosh (128k). 3.5" disk $349.00 (Order no.: 401). *Optimal configuration:* Macintosh, 1Mb, hard drive, System 7.
Authorizes & Electronically Deposits Credit Card Sales. Sales May Be Authorized Individually, or Batched & Authorized All at Once. Eliminates the Need for Credit Card Terminals & Provides Many More Features. Supports Import, Export, AppleEvents & AppleScript Allowing Other Applications Access to Credit Authorization.
Neff Systems Group.

MacAuthorize - Hub. *Version:* 2.3. Feb. 1996. *Items Included:* Spiral bound manuals. *Customer Support:* 90 day free tech support, 90 day warranty on materials.
Macintosh System 7. Macintosh. Contact publisher for price. *Optimal configuration:* Macintosh Quadra or Workgroup Server, System 7, 1Mb RAM, hard drive, color monitor. *Networks supported:* LocalTalk or compatible.
Turns Your Macintosh Network into a Credit Authorization Network. It Eliminates All Your Credit Card Terminals by Integrating & Centralizing Credit Card Authorization. The Hub Can Service an Entire Network of Macintoshes Using One Modem to Communicate to the Bank Networks.
Neff Systems Group.

MacAuto. *Version:* 2.0. *Compatible Hardware:* Apple Macintosh.
3.5" disk $25.00.
Automotive Log Book.
Cra Z Software.

Macbeth. *Compatible Hardware:* Commodore 64/128.
disk $25.00 (Order no.: 47155).
Four Separate Graphic & Text Adventures Cover a Different Part of the Play... Two More Are Intertwined As You Help the Witches Assemble Their Evil Brew. Each Segment Has a Psychological Program in Which You & Shakespeare Delve into the Minds of Lord & Lady Macbeth. Includes Extensive Documentation.
Avalon Hill Game Co., The Microcomputer Games Div.

MacBible NIV or King James. *Compatible Hardware:* Apple Macintosh. *General Requirements:* ImageWriter, LaserWriter.
3.5" disk $129.00.
Twenty-Five Disk Volume of the King James Bible or the International Version.
Encycloware.

MacBits. *General Requirements:* ImageWriter or LaserWriter; MacPaint.
Any Macintosh. 3.5" disk $50.00.
Graphics/Clip Art; 1,000-Plus Iamges of 60 Native Macintosh Items Through System 2.0.
MacPoint Pubns.

MacBits Supplement.
Any Macintosh. 3.5" disk $100.00.
Clip Art; 1,500-Plus Images of 100 Native Macintosh Items Through System 2.0.
MacPoint Pubns.

MacBlast. *Compatible Hardware:* Apple Macintosh Plus, Macintosh SE, Macintosh II.
3.5" disk $195.00.
Emulates DEC VT-52, VT-100/200 & Other Terminals & Supports MultiFinder, Allowing Users to Switch Back & Forth Between Other Applications. Features Auto Dialing, Autolog to Remote Systems, Automated Modem Operations, & Includes BlastScript, a Programming Language That Lets Users Set up Repetitive Tasks or Scripts. Supports the MacBinary Standard & Uses a Proprietary Full-Duplex Protocol to Send Data in Both Directions at the Same Time. Can Send & Receive Binary Files, Text, & Console Commands. Operates Through RS-232 Ports with a Hard-Wired Link or Phone Line & Modem, or Over Asynchronous Links over Ethernet or AppleTalk Networks.
U.S. Robotics, Inc.

MacBraille. Bio-Grammatical Engineering. Mar. 1986. *Compatible Hardware:* Apple Macintosh. *Memory Required:* 128k.
3.5" disk $39.95 (Order no.: MB-1).
Allows Level 1 Braille to Be Printed on an Unmodified ImageWriter Printer. Font May Be Also Be Displayed on Screen for Editing by Sighted Users.
Hexcraft, Inc.

MacBurmese. *Version:* 1.4. Apr. 1989. *Items Included:* User's manual, keyboard layout chart. *Customer Support:* Free telephone support; defective disks replaced free.
Macintosh. Macintosh (1Mb). 3.5" disk $79.95. *Addl. software required:* Any word processor. *Optimal configuration:* 4Mb RAM, hard drive.
12- & 24-Point Bit Map & Screen Sizes, High Quality Printing. Logical, Easy-to-Use Layout Based on the Standard English Typewriter. User's Manual & Keyboard Layout Chart. Selected Directly from the Font Menu to Shift Instantly from English to Burmese in MACWRITE, MICROSOFT WORD & All Other Macintosh Word Processing Software. Full Style Options: Plain, Bold, Italic, Underline, Outline, Shadow, Superscript, Subscript & All Combinations.
Linguist's Software, Inc.

MacC-MacC Toolkit. *Version:* 6.0. Oct. 1984. *Compatible Hardware:* Apple Macintosh. (source code included). *Memory Required:* 512k. *Customer Support:* Free telephone support.
3.5" disk $425.00, incl. programmer's guide.
C Compiler & Support Library. Full Technical Support Is Provided. Mac II & SE Compatible.
Consulair Corp.

MacCad. *Items Included:* Spiral-bound manual. *Customer Support:* Free technical support (504) 649-0484.
OS 5.0 or higher (1Mb). Macintosh Plus or higher. $69.00 to $249.00. *Addl. software required:* MacDraw, MacDraft, MiniCad. *Optimal configuration:* Macintosh SE/30 or Mac II, 2Mb RAM.
MacCad Consists of a Variety of Templates Including Architectural, Electrical, Mechanical & Piping Symbols. Each Fully Documented Library Offers Vector Format Graphics Drawn to AIA, ANSI, & IEEE Standards. Requires MacDraw, MacDraft or MiniCad.
CompServCo.

McCAD EDS Electronic Design Systems. *Version:* 1.1. 1988. *Items Included:* User manual. *Customer Support:* initial 30-day free support, optional thereafter; annual maintenance $175.
Macintosh SE/SE 30 (2Mb). $1495.00 to $1995.00 (Order no.: EDS). *Optimal configuration:* Macintosh IIx, IIcx, (5Mb).
Offers Choice of Design Environments with Wide Range of System Configurations. Takes Designer Through Complete Cycle from Schematic Entry to Printed Circuit Board Design to Fabrication. Software Solutions Such As EDS-1 Offer a Single Integrated Design Environment. Stand-Alone Systems Such As PCB-1, PCB-ST & Schematics Offer Many Features of EDS-1. Systems Are Easy to Learn with Typical Learning Curves under 30 Minutes. They Include Wide Range of Output Device Drivers, & Support Imagewriter, Laserwriter, Linotronic, Houston Instrument & Hewlett-Packard Penplotters. Gerber Photo-Plotting Also Available. Independent Service Centers Provide High Quality Photo-Plots & Prototypes.
Vamp, Inc.

McCAD Software: Electronic & Printed Circuit-Board Design.
Macintosh Plus or higher. disk McCAD PCB-1 $395.00.
disk McCAD PCB-ST $995.00.
disk McCAD Schematics $495.00.
disk McCAD Shematics-DS, Gerber View $895.00 ea.
disk McCAD Gerber Translator $175.00.
disk McCAD EDS-1 (electronic design system) $1495.00.
disk McCAD EDS-2 (electronic design system) $1895.00.
Choice of Following Design Environments Is Offered: McCAD PCB-1, Stand-Alone Software Tool for Designing, Creating, Editing & Revising Printed Circuit-Board Art Work; McCAD PCB-ST, High-End Circuit Board Layout Package That Integrates with McCAD Schematics; McCAD Schematics, On-Line Multipaging Schematic Capture Package That Integrates with McCAD PCB-ST; McCAD Schematics-DS Consists of McCAD Schematics with Integrated Digital Function Simulator That Integrates with MCCAD PCB-ST; McCAD Gerber Translator, Converts Databases into Standard Format; McCAAD Gerber View, Converts Database Files into Circuit Design Database; McCAD EDS-1, Consists of Schematics, PCB-ST & Gerber Translator; McCAD EDS-2, Consists of EDS-1 with Digital Simulation Added.
Vamp, Inc.

MacCarols: The Christmas Disk. *Version:* x. Nov. 1987. *Compatible Hardware:* All Macintoshes except Macintosh II. *Memory Required:* 512k.
3-1/2" 400k disk $19.95.
3-1/2" 800k disk $29.95.
Plays & Sings a Selection of Popular Christmas Carols.
Park Row Software.

MACCFIRS. *Version:* 2.0. Jan. 1991. *Items Included:* Manuals. *Customer Support:* Free phone support.
MAC Systems 7.0 compatible. MAC Plus or higher (2Mb). $295.00-$495.00 (Order no.: MC-2.0). *Addl. software required:* Hypercard 2.0 or higher. *Optimal configuration:* MAC 68030 Processor, System 7.0, Hypercard 2.1, hard disk, 2Mb RAM. *Networks supported:* AppleTalk.
California Fire Incident Reporting System As Specified by the State Fire Marshal's Office, Incorporates All Error Corrections, with Pop-Up Menus for All Codes.
Sound Advice, Inc.

MacChemistry. *Compatible Hardware:* Apple Macintosh.
Site license availabe. 3.5" disk $145.00.
Templates; Electronic Storage Tray, Lab Set; Periodic Table.
Fortnum Software.

MacCherokee. *Version:* 1.4. Apr. 1989. *Items Included:* User's manual, keyboard layout chart. *Customer Support:* Free telephone support; defective disks replaced free.
Any system. Macintosh (1Mb). 3.5" disk $79.95. *Addl. software required:* Any word processor. *Optimal configuration:* 4Mb RAM, hard drive.
High-Quality Font in 12- & 24-Point Sizes for Cherokee. Logical, Easy-to-Use Layout Based on the Standard English Typewriter. With Complete User's Manual & Laminated Keyboard Layout

Sheet. Selected Directly from the Font Menu to Shift Instantly from English to Cherokee in MACWRITE or MICROSOFT WORD for Automatic Footnoting. Full Style Options: Plain, Bold, Italic, Underline, Outline, Shadow, Superscript, Subscript, & Combinations.
Linguist's Software, Inc.

MacChinese Cantonese. Version: 6.3. Sep. 1987. Items Included: User's manual. Customer Support: Telephone support, defective disks replaced free.
Macintosh (1Mb). 3.5" disk $99.95 (Add $60.00 for both Mandarin & Cantonese). Addl.
 software required: Microsoft Word thorugh 5.0.
Includes 4610 Traditional Chinese Characters for Use in Any English System (12 Pt), a 4610 Character Glossary for Microsoft Word (Through 5.0) with Pin Yin Input, & a HyperCard Player-Based Program for Typing All 4610 Characters with Pin Yin Input. HyperCard Player 2.1 & AutoMac III Macro Program Included. Includes User's Manual with a Complete Character Access Code List & an Electronic Version of the Code List for Quick, On-Screen Lookup in MS Word. All Style Options & Can Be Mixed with Any Other Fonts. Requires 2 Megs RAM.
Linguist's Software, Inc.

MacChinese Mandarin. Version: 6.3. Nov. 1987. Items Included: User's manual. Customer Support: Telephone support, defective disks replaced free.
Macintosh (1Mb). 3.5" disk $99.95 (Add $60.00 for both Cantonese & Mandarin). Addl.
 software required: Microsoft Word through 5.0.
Includes 4610 Traditional Chinese Characters for Use in Any English System (12 Pt), a 4610 Character Glossary for Microsoft Word (Through 5.0) with Pin Yin Input, & a HyperCard Player-Based Program for Typing All 4610 Characters with Pin Yin Input. HyperCard Player 2.1 & AutoMac III Macro Program Included. Includes User's Manual with a Complete Character Access Code List, & an Electronic Version of the Code List for Quick, On-Screen Lookup in MS Word. All Style Options & Can Be Mixed with Any Other Fonts. Requires 2 Megs RAM.
Linguist's Software, Inc.

MacChoro II with Map Animation. Items Included: Program, U.S. by state map & data files, example files. Customer Support: Telephone 90 days.
Macintosh Plus or higher. MacChoro & United States by state digital map $295.00.
additional file maps $50.00 ea.
Map Animation Program.
Image Mapping Systems.

MacChuck. Version: 1.5. Compatible Hardware: Apple Macintosh; IBM PC & compatibles. General Requirements: Mono or CGA Display Adapter; RS-232 serial cable.
3.5" disk $99.95.
PC Remote Control Program.
Vano Assocs., Inc.

MacChurch Data II. Compatible Hardware: Apple Macintosh. General Requirements: ImageWriter, LaserWriter.
3.5" disk $199.00.
Church Management, Funds, Contributions, Database; Forms.
Encycloware.

MacClade. Version: 3.0. Wayne Maddison & David Maddison. Nov. 1992. Items Included: 1 Perfect bound, 398 page manual. Customer Support: Free customer support via E-Mail.
System 4.1 or higher. Macintosh Plus or higher (2Mb). 3.5" disk $75.00 (ISBN 0-87893-491-X).
Computer Program for Graphic & Interactive Analysis of Phylogeny & Character Evolution . Systematists & other Evolutionary Biologists Can Use Its Flexible Analytical Tools To Examine Phylogenies or Interpret Character Evolution in a Phylogenetic Context.
Sinauer Assocs., Inc.

McCLint: C Programmer's McTool Series Tool 2. Version: 2.2. Aug. 1990. Customer Support: Free telephone support; 30 day unconditional money back guarantee.
System 5.2 or higher. Apple Macintosh (1Mb). 3.5" disk $149.95 (Order no.: MCTOOL2).
update $40.00.
C Source Code Analyzer (Lint) That Locates Unintended Programming Constructions &/or Latent Programming Mistakes in Multiple Files. It Identifies Function, Statement, Expression & Variable Type Errors Including Misplaced Semi-Colons, Operator Mixups & Incorrect Function Call Sequences. It Incorporates Powerful, Multi-Window Editing & C Source Code Highlighting System.
MMCAD Systems.

MacCoach: How to Use Your Macintosh, Vol. 1 & 2. (Training Power Ser.). Compatible Hardware: Apple Macintosh 512, Macintosh Plus. Operating System(s) Required: Apple DOS. Memory Required: 64k.
disk $49.95 (ISBN 0-922274-00-2, Order no.: A-30).
Interactive Simulation Tutorial on the Use of the Macintosh Computer. Contains Both Novice & Advanced Versions.
American Training International, Inc.

MacConcept. Version: 3.7.1. Items Included: Handbook, registration card, latest version on disk. Customer Support: 6 months free update.
Macintosh Classic or higher. disk $795.00.
 Optimal configuration: Macintosh with FPU recommended.
Demo. $39.00.
Conceptual Design System Allowing the Creation, Alteration & Animation of 3D Wire Frame Models. The Angle of View, Perspective & Scale Are Controlled by Using Dynamic Rotation & Other Viewing Options. It Can Interface Through PICT, IGES, DXF, Ford & GM. Data Output to ClarisCAD Is Also Included.
Klex Software, Inc.

MacConcord I (KJV). Version: 1.2. Compatible Hardware: Apple Macintosh. General Requirements: Hard disk; MacWrite, MicroSoft Word or compatible. Items Included: Diskette & manual. Customer Support: Complete telephone support, 90-day warranty.
3.5" disk $16.95 (Order no.: 48842-500).
New Testament Concordance. It Features a Series of Text Documents Containing A Library of More Than 10,000 References From the King James Bible. It Has Most Theological Topics & Other Subjects Pertaining to the Average Life.
Medina Software, Inc.

MacCourses. Compatible Hardware: Apple Macintosh.
contact publisher for price.
Golf Simulation Which Provides Additional Golf Courses for MACGOLF. Provides Four New 18-Hole, Par 72 Courses: Cedar Creek, Golden Sands, Thunder Ridge, & PCAI International.
Practical Computer Applications, Inc.

MacCourses. Nov. 1986.
Mac DOS 4.2 (512k). Macintosh 512k, Plus, SE. 3.5" disk $34.95 (Order no.: 8019). Addl. software required: MacGolf.
Four Additional 18-Hole Golf Courses for MacGolf.
XOR Corp.

McCPrint: C Programmer's McTool Series Tool No. 1. Version: 2.2. Aug. 1990. Customer Support: Free telephone support.
Apple Macintosh OS 5.2 or higher. Apple Macintosh (512k). 3.5" disk $99.95 (Order no.: MCTOOL1).
existing customer update charge $30.00.
Reformats/Beautifies C & C Plus Plus Source Code into a User Specified Format. Options Include Brace Placement, Comment Formats, Space Usage, Statement Alignment & More. If the User Does Not Like the Result, Simply Change the Options & Rerun. It Incorporates a Sophisticated Multi-Window Editing & Source Code Highlighting System.
MMCAD Systems.

MacDesigner. Version: 5.0. 1995. Customer Support: 90 day telephone support with product purchase; newsletter & update service contracts.
Macintosh System 7.0 or UNIX/MAE. Macintosh (8Mb) or UNIX with Macintosh Application Environment Software. $995.00 MacDesigner. $1595.00 MacDesigner/Expert.
Tool for Automating Structured & Object-Oriented Design Process. Includes Structure Charts, Object Communication Diagrams, Module Descriptions, Task Diagrams, Tree Diagrams, Data Dictionary & Requirement Database.
Excel Software.

MacDiet-Student Version. Compatible Hardware: Apple Macintosh.
MacDiet. 3.5" disk $25.00.
Expanded Database. 3.5" disk $35.00.
Performs Nutritional Data Manipulation.
Kinko's.

MacDINE Perfect. Darwin Dennison. Mar. 1992. Items Included: User's manual, food & activity records. Customer Support: Free technical support, 10-day money-back guarantee, telephone support.
Macintosh (1Mb). 3.5" disk $149.00.
 Nonstandard peripherals required: Hard drive.
 Optimal configuration: Macintosh with hard drive, 1Mb memory, 2Mb hard disk space.
 Networks supported: Ethernet, AppleTalk.
Lose Weight & Improve Your Health by Adjusting Your Food Choices & Portion Sizes to Meet Federal Dietary Guidelines. Diet/Recipe/Activity Analysis Can Be Printed in Chart, Graph or Message Form. Includes the DINE Database, Which Has No Missing Values & Contains 5600 Plus Brand Name, Generic, & Fast Food Items As Well As 194 Activities.
DINE Systems, Inc.

MacDisk Manager. Compatible Hardware: Apple Macintosh.
For printing disk info on tractor-feed inserts. 3.5" disk $29.95.
Complete kit (with pockets & inserts). 3.5" disk $49.95.
C-100 with cut inserts. 3.5" disk $23.95.
TF-100 Tractor-Feed Inserts. 3.5" disk $23.95.
Disk Identification Without Labels.
Weber & Sons, Inc.

MacDraft. Version: 4.0. Aug. 1985. Compatible Hardware: Macintosh family of computers with system 6.0.5 or higher; Power Macintosh compatible. Memory Required: 1500k. General Requirements: 1.5Mb RAM & a hard disk drive. Items Included: 576 page user reference manual & a tutorial. Customer Support: Telephone (510) 680-6818.
3.5" disk $449.00.
Provides a Full-Scaled, Multi-Layered Drafting Environment for Architectural/Engineering Design & Technical Illustration. It Offers a Complete Set of Easy to Use Drawing Tools, Including Linear, Radial & Angular Dimensions, Plus Special Tools

to Extend & Trim Lines, Create Perpendicular, Tangent & Parallel Lines, Fillets, Chamfers, Merge & Subtract Objects. For Increased Precision, MacDraft Provides Keyboard Editing & Placement of Objects. New Integrated Database Lets You Assign Data to Objects, Create Custom Reports & Link Them to Excel.
Innovative Data Design, Inc.

MacDraft for Windows. *Version:* 1.1a. Feb. 1992. *Items Included:* Reference manual. *Customer Support:* Call 510-680-6818 for free customer service & technical support.
Microsoft Windows 3.0 or higher which requires PC-DOS/MS-DOS Version 3.1 or higher. 286-based DOS compatible computer; EGA graphics adapter card & monitor; mouse or pointing device (1Mb of extended memory). disk $199.00. *Optimal configuration:* 386-based DOS-compatible computer with 2Mb extended memory; a hard disk with 2Mb free hard disk space; graphics adapter card such as VGA, Super VGA or compatible video graphics adapter & monitor, mouse.
Serious No-Nonsense Tool for Architectural & Engineering Design & Drafting, As Well As Technical Illustration. Incredibly Easy to Use, Powerful & Amazingly Precise, MacDraft Provides You with a Completely Scaled Drafting Environment Designed to Respond Quickly & Accurately to the Way You Think & Work. You Can Create Multi-Layered Drawings in Both English or Metric, While MacDraft's Auto Dimension Lines Are Displayed in the Units of Your Drawing.
Innovative Data Design, Inc.

MacDraw Pro. *Version:* 1.5. Jun. 1992.
System 6.0.5, Finder 6.1 or higher. Macintosh Plus or higher (2Mb). 3.5" disk $399.00.
Draw Package That Supports Creating & Editing Colors & Gradients. Has File Exchange Capabilities with Claris XTND Architecture, Tools for Greater Control over Text & Graphics, & On-Screen & Slide-Presentation Capabilities.
Claris Corp.

MacEdge 2. *Version:* 6.0. Jun. 1991. *Items Included:* Manual, registration card, Guide to Educators. *Customer Support:* 90 days unlimited warranty.
Macintosh (128k). 3.5" disk $49.95 (Order no.: T-051).
Macintosh Educational Software Product. Contains Eight Individual Applications Including Math & Reading. Covers Counting, Addition, Subtraction, Multiplication, Division, Matching, Phonetics, Alphabet, Word Groups, etc.
Think Educational Software, Inc.

MacElastic. *Version:* 1.1. Cooke, J.R. et al. Jan. 1987. *Compatible Hardware:* Apple Macintosh. *Memory Required:* 512k.
3.5" disk student $99.95.
3.5" disk professional $495.00.
Instructional Finite Element Analysis Program Crafted for the Novice User in Solving Equations of Classical Elasticity Theory.
Cooke Pubns.

MacEnvelope. Aug. 1991. *Compatible Hardware:* Apple Macintosh 512KE or higher. *General Requirements:* ImageWriter, LaserWriter, II, SC, NTX, LQ. *Items Included:* Manual, disk, registration card. *Customer Support:* Yes.
Macintosh System 7.0. 3.5" disk $79.95 (ISBN 1-880773-04-X).
Envelope Printing, Label Printing, Import & Export 1600 Names, Fonts, Styles, Sizes Graphics, Wide Area Postal Bar Coding Printed Automatically, Batch Printing, Sort by Zip, Sort Alphabetically, 150 Pre-Formatted Label Layouts, Desk Accessory Included.
Synex.

MacExpress. *Compatible Hardware:* Apple Macintosh Plus.
3.5" disk $195.00.
Instant Application & User Interface Manager, Development Tool.
ALsoft, Inc.

McFace Package. *Version:* 4.0. *Compatible Hardware:* Apple Macintosh. *Memory Required:* 512k. *Items Included:* Manual & 2 diskettes.
3.5" disk $169.00.
Stand-Alone Set of Code Resources That Add a Mac Interface to Programs Written in FORTRAN.
Tensor Laboratories.

MacFlow. *Version:* 4.0. *Items Included:* Manual. *Customer Support:* Free tech support to registered users.
Macintosh Plus or higher. 3.5" disk $295.00.
Flowchart Design & Development. System 7.5 Savvy. Power Mac Native.
Mainstay.

MacFORTH Plus. *Version:* 4.2.2. *Compatible Hardware:* Apple Macintosh. *Items Included:* 500-page manual, 3 disks. *Customer Support:* 203-498-7212.
3.5" disk $199.00.
Implementation of FORTH for the Macintosh. An Interactive Programming Language Environment Featuring Multi-Tasking, Built-In Assembler, Text Editor, High-Level Graphics, Toolbox Support, Royalty-Free Turnkey Compiler. Runs on All Macintoshes 512K or Greater.
Creative Solutions (Maryland).

MacForth 3-D Library. *Compatible Hardware:* Apple Macintosh. *General Requirements:* MacForth. *Customer Support:* 203-498-7212.
3.5" disk $25.00.
Graphics & Animation Extensions to MacForth Programming Language.
Creative Solutions (Maryland).

MacFortran. *Version:* 2.4. *Compatible Hardware:* Apple Macintosh. *Customer Support:* Hotline, BBS & BIX.
3.5" disk $295.00.
ANSI 77 Fortran Compiler with Debugger. No Limit on Code or Data Size. Includes Most VAX/VMS Extensions & Full Toolbox Support.
Absoft Corp.

MacFortran II. *Version:* 3.4. Aug. 1991. *Items Included:* Bundled with the complete release of MPW 3.2. 300 page illustrated manual with chapters devoted to use of the compiler with MPW tools, porting procedures, guide to options and optimizations. *Customer Support:* Free unlimited telephone support, 24 hour technical BBS, AppleLink.
Macintosh OS release 6.0.3 or higher. System 7.0 compatible. All Macintosh II series with FPU hardware (2Mb). $595.00 (Order no.: FAP3MAC2). *Optimal configuration:* Macintosh II with FPU hardware, 4Mb RAM, 6Mb free hard disk space.
VAX/VMS Compatible FORTRAN 77 Compiler for the Macintosh II Series. V3.1 Includes Most VAX/VMS Extensions Including STRUCTURE, UNION, MAP, & BYTE, All VAX Intrinsic Functions, & CRAY/Sun-Style POINTER. It Is Compatible with 68020/68030 CPU's & Includes a Threaded Math Library for Maximum Performance with 68040 Based Machines.
Absoft Corp.

MacFortran/020. *Version:* 2.4. *Compatible Hardware:* Apple Macintosh. *Customer Support:* Hotline & BBS, BIX.
3.5" disk $495.00.
68020/68881 Fortran 77 Compiler with Debugger. No Limit on Code or Data Size.
*Includes VAX/VMS, NAMELIST, Complex*16, MIL-STD-1753 Extensions. Full Toolbox Support & Extensive Documentation.*
Absoft Corp.

MacFunction. *Compatible Hardware:* Apple Macintosh. *Memory Required:* 1000k.
3.5" disk $79.95.
Features Multivariate Calculus.
True BASIC, Inc.

MacGaelic. *Version:* 3.3. Jun. 1989. *Items Included:* User's manual, keyboard layout chart. *Customer Support:* Free telephone support; defective disks replaced free.
Any system. Macintosh (1Mb). 3.5" disk $79.95. *Addl. software required:* Any word processor. *Optimal configuration:* 4Mb RAM, hard drive.
Irish, Scottish & Manx Gaelic, Welsh, Breton, & Cornish 12- & 24-Point Bit Map & Screen Sizes, High Quality Printing. Logical, Easy-to-Use Layout Based on the Standard English Typewriter. Not Copy Protected, User's Manual & Keyboard Layout Chart. Select Directly from the Font Menu to Shift Instantly from English to Gaelic, in All Macintosh Word Processing Software. Full Style Options: Plain, Bold, Italic, Underline, Outline, Shadow, Superscript, Subscript & All Combinations. Plus Ogham Font.
Linguist's Software, Inc.

MacGAMUT Instructor Disk. *Version:* 3.0. Ann K. Blombach. Jul. 1996. *Items Included:* Instructor guide furnished on disk. *Customer Support:* 30-day money-back guarantee of satisfaction; toll-free product support; instructor disk provided free to teachers whose students and/or institutions purchase 5 or more MacGAMUT 3.0 user disks.
Macintosh System 7 or higher. Mac II or higher (4Mb). 3.5" disk $10.00 (ISBN 1-886997-08-X, Order no.: ID30). *Nonstandard peripherals required:* None required, but MIDI keyboard may be used for input & output.
Allows Teachers to Reset Program Parameters for MacGAMUT 3.0 User Disks, Enabling Instructors to Restructure the Programs to Customize Them to Their Particular Course, Students, & Instructional Strategy.
MacGAMUT Music Software International.

MacGAMUT: Intervals, Scales, & Chords & Melodic Dictation Instructor Disk. *Version:* Chords 2.5, Melodic Dictation 2.0. Ann K. Blombach. Jun. 1995. *Items Included:* Instructor Guide furnished on-disk. *Customer Support:* 30-day money-back guarantee; toll-free product support; Instructor disk provided free to teachers whose students and/or institutions purchase 5 or more MacGAMUT User Disks.
Macintosh System 6 or higher. Macintosh Mac Plus or higher (2Mb). disk $10.00, free with orders of 5 or more User Disks BP2520 (ISBN 1-886997-06-3, Order no.: ID2520). *Nonstandard peripherals required:* None required, but MIDI keyboard may be used for input & output. *Optimal configuration:* Macintosh Mac Plus or higher computer, System 6 or higher, 2Mb RAM or more, MIDI keyboard, & MIDI interface.
Instructor Disk Allows Teachers to Reset Program Parameters for Both MacGAMUT: Intervals, Scales, & Chords 2.5 & MacGAMUT: Melodic Dictation 2.0, Enabling Instructors to Restructure the Programs to Customize Them To Their Particular Course, Students, & Instructional Strategy.
MacGAMUT Music Software International.

MacGAMUT: Intervals, Scales, & Chords & Melodic Dictation User Disk. *Version:* Chords 2.5, Dictation 2.0. Ann K. Blombach. Jun. 1995. *Items Included:* User Manual on disk. *Customer*

MACGAMUT USER DISK

Support: 30-day money-back guarantee; toll-free product support; Instructor Diskette for teachers allows them to reset program parameters as they wish for their students.
Macintosh System 6 or higher. Macintosh Mac Plus or higher (2Mb). 3.5" disk $30.00 (ISBN 1-886997-02-0, Order no.: BP2520). *Nonstandard peripherals required:* None required, but MIDI keyboard may be used for input & output. *Optimal configuration:* Macintosh Mac Plus or higher computer, System 6 or higher, 2Mb RAM or more, MIDI keyboard, & MIDI interface.
Combines Two Titles - MacGAMUT: Intervals, Scales, & Chords 2.5 & MacGAMUT: Melodic Dictation 2.0 - on a Single Disk.
MacGAMUT Music Software International.

MacGAMUT User Disk. Version: 3.0. Ann K. Blombach. Jul. 1996. *Items Included:* User guide furnished on disk. *Customer Support:* 30-day money-back guarantee of satisfaction; toll-free product support; instructor disk for teachers allows them to reset program parameters as they wish for their students.
Macintosh System 7 or higher. Mac II or higher (4Mb). 3.5" disk $35.00 (ISBN 1-886997-07-1, Order no.: MG30). *Nonstandard peripherals required:* None required, but MIDI keyboard may be used for input & output.
Unlimited Drill & Practice in Aural Skills Expected of Trained Musicians: Identifying & Notating Intervals, Scales, Chords, & Harmonic Progressions, & Notating Melodies from Dictation. User Enters Responses with Mouse or Optional MIDI Keyboard. Correct & Incorrect Responses May Be Compared Both Visually & Aurally.
MacGAMUT Music Software International.

McGee. Sep. 1989. *Items Included:* Program manual. *Customer Support:* Free technical support 800-421-4157, 90 day warranty.
OS 4.0 or higher. Apple IIGS (512k). disk $39.95 (ISBN 0-917999-74-6).
Amiga DOS 1.3 or higher. Amiga 500, 2000, 25000 (512k). disk $39.95 (ISBN 0-917999-95-9).
DOS 2.1 or higher. IBM/Tandy (640k). disk $24.95 (ISBN 0-917999-97-5). *Nonstandard peripherals required:* Mouse recommended. Sound support highly recommended - Sound Blaster, Covox, Tandy. *Networks supported:* λ.
System 6.0.5 or higher. Macintosh Plus, SE, SE30, Classic, LC, SI II (512k) 1M-color version. 3.5" disk $24.95 (ISBN 0-917999-96-7). *Networks supported:* λ.
In This "First Computer Activity" for Children Ages 2-5, an Endearing Preschooler, McGee, Invites Users to Take a Tour of His Home. Directing His Movements by Pointing & Clicking on the Icons at the Bottom of the Screen, Children Decide Whether McGee Will Play with Toys in His Room, Wake Mom in the Bedroom, Feed the Dog, & More! McGee Is a Great Way to Introduce Young Children to the Computer.
Lawrence Productions, Inc.

McGee at the Fun Fair. Feb. 1991. *Items Included:* Program manual. *Customer Support:* Free technical support 800-421-4157, 90 day warranty.
OS 5.0 or higher. Apple IIGS (1Mb). disk $39.95 (ISBN 0-917999-83-5).
Amiga DOS 1.3 or higher. Amiga (1Mb). disk $39.95 (ISBN 1-882848-60-8).
DOS 2.1 or higher. IBM/Tandy (640k). disk $24.95 (ISBN 1-882848-62-4). *Nonstandard peripherals required:* Mouse recommended. Sound support strongly recommended - Sound Blaster, Covox, Tandy.
System 6.0.5 or higher. Macintosh (1Mb). 3.5" disk $24.95 (ISBN 1-882848-61-6).
In This "First Computer Activity" for Children Ages 2-5, an Endearing Preschooler McGee, Invites Users to Go with Him & His Friend Tony to a Summer Fun Fair in the Park. Directing His Movements by Pointing & Clicking on the Icons at the Bottom of the Screen, Children Decide Whether McGee & Tony Will Buy Ice Cream, Play on the Slide or Fly a Kite. McGee at the Fun Fair Is a Fun Way to Introduce Young Children to the Computer.
Lawrence Productions, Inc.

McGee School Days. *Items Included:* Program manual. *Customer Support:* Free technical support (1-800-421-4157), 90 day warranty.
Consumer. Mac System 6.0.7 or higher. Macintosh LC or above (5Mb). 3.5" disk $59.95 (ISBN 1-57204-003-3, Order no.: CD555). *Nonstandard peripherals required:* 256 color monitor, mouse, CD-ROM.
School ed.. Mac System 6.0.7 or higher. Macintosh LC or above (5Mb). 3.5" disk $69.95 (ISBN 1-57204-004-1, Order no.: CD555T). *Nonstandard peripherals required:* 256 color monitor, mouse, CD-ROM.
Lab pack. 3.5" disk $149.95 (ISBN 1-57204-005-X, Order no.: CD555LPK).
Site license. Windows 3.1. IBM/Tandy & 100% compatibles (7Mb). disk $699.00 (ISBN 1-57204-006-8, Order no.: CD555SITE). *Nonstandard peripherals required:* VGA or SVGA 640 x 480 resolution, 256 color monitor, mouse, (Microsoft recommended), sound device, CD-ROM drive.
Consumer. Windows 3.1. IBM/Tandy & 100% compatibles (7Mb). disk $59.95 (ISBN 1-882848-93-4, Order no.: 1B555). *Nonstandard peripherals required:* VGA or SVGA 640 x 480 resolution, 256 color monitor, mouse, (Microsoft recommended), sound device, CD-ROM drive.
School ed.. Windows 3.1. IBM/Tandy & 100% compatibles (7Mb). disk contact publisher for price (Order no.: 1B555T). *Nonstandard peripherals required:* VGA or SVGA 640 x 480 resolution, 256 color monitor, mouse, (Microsoft recommended), sound device, CD-ROM drive.
Lab pack. Windows 3.1. disk $149.95 (ISBN 1-882848-95-0, Order no.: 1B555LPK). *Nonstandard peripherals required:* VGA or SVGA 640 x 480 resolution, 256 color monitor, mouse (Microsoft recommended), sound device, CD-ROM drive.
Site license. Windows 3.1. IBM/Tandy & 100% compatibles (7Mb). disk $699.00 (ISBN 1-882848-97-7, Order no.: 1B555SITE). *Nonstandard peripherals required:* VGA or SVGA 640 x 480 resolution, 256 color monitor, mouse (Microsoft recommended), sound device, CD-ROM drive.
Consumer. Mac System 6.0.7 or higher. Macintosh LC or above (5Mb). 3.5" disk $59.95 (ISBN 1-882848-98-5, Order no.: APM555). *Nonstandard peripherals required:* 256 color monitor, mouse, CD-ROM drive.
Give your child a head start in school with games that develop abilities in reading & math. Using the NO Words approach, children play classic games like, hopscotch & more. Children are ready for the first day of school with help from McGee & friends. Also includes; System 6.0.7 or higher; Macintosh LC or above (5Mb); 256 color monitor, mouse, CD-ROM drive; ISBN: 1-882848-99-3; Order # APM555T; price; $69.95; School ver. Lab pack; 1-57204-000-9 $149.95; Order # APM 555LPK; Site license; 1-57204-002-5; Order # APM555SITE; $699.00; Also includes; Windows 3.1; IBM/Tandy & 100% compatibles (7mb); 256 color monitor, mouse (Microsoft recommended), sound device, CD-ROM drive. Consumer, $59.95; ISBN 1-57204-036-x; Order # WIN555; School Ver. $69.95; ISBN 1-57204-037-8; Order # WIN555T; Lab pack $149.95; ISBN 1-57204-038-6; Order # WIN555LPK; Site license $699.00 ISBN 1-57204-040-8; Order # WIN555Site.
Lawrence Productions, Inc.

The McGee Series. Sep. 1992. *Items Included:* Program manual, School Edition also includes a Teacher's Activity Guide. *Customer Support:* Free technical support 800-421-4157, 90 day warranty.
DOS 2.1 or higher. IBM (640k). disk $44.95 (ISBN 0-917999-87-8). *Nonstandard peripherals required:* Mouse recommended, sound support, Sound Blaster, Covox, Tandy.
System 6.0.5 or higher. Macintosh (1Mb). 3.5" disk $49.95 (ISBN 0-917999-88-6).
System 6.0.5 or higher. Macintosh (1Mb). $59.95 School Edition (ISBN 1-882848-09-8).
System 6.0.5 or higher. Macintosh (1Mb). $129.00 School Edition, Lab Pack (ISBN 1-882848-10-1).
DOS 2.1 or higher. IBM (640k). $54.95 School Edition (ISBN 1-882848-11-X). *Nonstandard peripherals required:* Mouse recommended, Sound support strongly recommended - Sound Blaster.
DOS 2.1 or higher. IBM (640k). $99.95 School Edition, Lab Pack (ISBN 1-882848-12-8). *Nonstandard peripherals required:* Mouse recommended, Sound support strongly recommended - Sount Blaster.
This Award-Winning Preschool Series Is Designed to Be a Young Child's "First Computer Activity." Series Includes McGee, Katie's Farm, & McGee at the Fun Fair. Children Explore a House, a Farm, & a Fair in These Three Explorations for 2-5 Year Olds.
Lawrence Productions, Inc.

MacGolf. *Compatible Hardware:* Apple Macintosh.
$59.95.
3-D Golf Simulation with Fairways, Roughs, Bunkers, Water Hazards, Sand Traps, & Trees. Affords Users a Player's Eye View of the Course, in Any Direction, & an Aerial Overview of Each Hole. Gives Players Complete Control of Position, Ball Placement, Ball Speed & Direction, & Selection of All 14 Clubs. Includes Digitized Graphics & Sound.
Practical Computer Applications, Inc.

MacGolf. Dec. 1985.
Mac DOS 4.2 (512k). Macintosh 512k, SE, Plus. 3.5" disk $59.95 (Order no.: 6015).
3-D Graphic Simulation on Two Professionally-Designed 18-Hole Courses. Features Include Players' Skills Against Sand & Water Traps, Trees, Fairways, Roughs & Greens. Control Stance, Ball Placement & Direction, Club Choice, Swing & More. Accommodates up to Four Players.
XOR Corp.

MacGolf Classic. Jan. 1988.
Mac DOS 4.2 (1Mb). Macintosh Plus, SE, SE/30, II, IIx, IIcx. 3.5" disk $94.90 (Order no.: 7012). *Nonstandard peripherals required:* Color monitor.
Features Full-Screen Color Graphics with Sharp Screen Image Detail. Contains Original Two MacGolf Courses & Four Additional MacCourses, for a Total of 108 Holes. New Features Include Five Enlargement Options for Close-Up Viewing, Nine Practice Greens & Driving Range.
XOR Corp.

MacGospel (KJV)/HyperGospel. Version: 1.3. *Compatible Hardware:* Apple Macintosh. *General Requirements:* Hard disk or external disk drive; MacWrite, Microsoft Word or compatible; HyperCard. *Items Included:* 1 diskette & manual.

Customer Support: Complete telephone support, 90-day warranty.
3.5" disk $12.95 (Order no.: 48842-515).
demo disk $5.00.
Gospels of Matthew, Mark, Luke & John.
Medina Software, Inc.

McGraw-Hill Database. Feb. 1987. *Compatible Hardware:* Apple IIe, IIc, IIgs; Compaq; IBM PC; Tandy 1000. *Operating System(s) Required:* ProDOS, PC-DOS/MS-DOS 2.0 or higher. *General Requirements:* 2 disk drives or hard disk.
Apple. site license $250.00 (ISBN 0-07-838269-6).
IBM. site license $250.00 (ISBN 0-07-838244-0).
Can Be Used to Teach Database Management Applications or to Perform Simple Administrative Tasks. Offers a "Sort" Function to Reorder the Database in Ascending or Descending Order on a Field Chosen by the User, & a "Get" Function Which Searches the Database & Pulls out Those Records That Match a Pattern Specified by the User. The Program Provides a Maximum of 26 Fields for 250 Records, Depending on Individual Field Sizes. Fields May be Either Numeric or Alphanumeric.
Gregg/McGraw Hill.

McGraw-Hill Integrated Software: Spreadsheet, Database, Graphing, Word Processing. Sep. 1987. *Compatible Hardware:* Apple II, IBM PC. *Operating System(s) Required:* ProDOS, PC-DOS/MS-DOS 2.0 or higher. *General Requirements:* 2 disk drives or hard disk.
Apple. site license $829.00 (ISBN 0-07-838154-1).
Compaq, IBM, Tandy. site license $829.00 (ISBN 0-07-838143-6).
Teaching/Learning Tool Consisting of Four Program Modules That Can Be Used Independently or Integrated. Modules Are Word Processing, Spreadsheet, Database, & Graphing. Designed for Educational Use, the Series Contains Business-Like Capabilities Designed for Ease of Use. Features a Menu-Driven Format Common to All Four Modules, Two Tutorials, Help Screens, & a Student Manual Containing a Reference Section & Sample Exercises. Information Can Be Freely Moved among the Spreadsheet, Database, & Graphing Modules, & from These Modules to the Word Processing Module.
Gregg/McGraw-Hill.

McGraw-Hill Spreadsheet. Dec. 1986. *Compatible Hardware:* Apple IIe, IIc, IIgs; Compaq; IBM PC; Tandy 1000. *Operating System(s) Required:* ProDOS, PC-DOS/MS-DOS 2.0 or higher. *Memory Required:* 128k. *General Requirements:* 2 disk drives or hard disk.
Apple. site license $250.00, incl. user's guide (ISBN 0-07-838259-9).
IBM. site license $250.00, incl. user's guide (ISBN 0-07-838254-8).
Supports a Maximum of 26 Columns by 250 Rows, Depending on Cell Sizes. Allows Users to Input Appropriate Numeric & Alphanumeric Values, & the Program Then Automatically Performs Calculations Based upon Formulas Entered by the User. Provides Roll-Bar Menu Format, 2 Tutorials, & Help Screens. Can Be Used Independently or in Conjuction with Other Modules in the MCGRAW-HILL INTEGRATED SOFTWARE Series. Designed to Serve Most Educational Applications.
Gregg/McGraw-Hill.

McGraw-Hill Word Processing. Jul. 1987. *Compatible Hardware:* Apple IIe, IIc, IIgs; Compaq; IBM PC; Tandy 1000. *Operating System(s) Required:* ProDOS, PC-DOS/MS-DOS 2.0 or higher. *Memory Required:* 128k. *General Requirements:* 2 disk drives or hard disk.
Apple. site license $250.00 (ISBN 0-07-838165-7).
Compaq, IBM, & Tandy. site license $250.00 (ISBN 0-07-838169-X).
Performs the Basic Text Editing Functions plus Several More Advanced Functions - Justification, Headers & Footers, & Mail Merge for Personalized Letters. Allows Information Created Using the Spreadsheet, Database, & Graphing Modules to Be Moved into Word Processing Documents. Names & Addresses from the Database Can Also Be Merged into Word Processing to Personalize Letters. Graphs & Spreadsheets Can Be Included to Produce Business-Like Reports & Memos.
Gregg/McGraw-Hill.

MacGreek New & Old Testaments; MacHebrew Scriptures. *Version:* MacGreek NT 4.2, MacGreek OT 2.3, MacHebrew Scriptures 6.0. *Compatible Hardware:* Apple Macintosh. *General Requirements:* MacWrite or Microsoft Word; MacGreek or Laser Greek, MacHebrew or LaserHebrew. *Customer Support:* Telephone support, defective disks replaced free.
$59.95 ea.; tagged NT $79.95; & tagged LXX $99.95.
Greek New Testament; Text of the Alfred Rahlfs Edition of the LXX; Entire Text of the Biblia Hebraica Stutgartensia. The First Two Texts Are Also Available in a Version Which Includes the Grammatical Tags.
Linguist's Software, Inc.

MacGreek New Testament Dictionary. *Version:* 4.0. Nov. 1989. *Items Included:* User's manual. *Customer Support:* Telephone support, defective disks replaced free.
Macintosh (1Mb). 3.5" disk $49.95. *Addl. software required:* MacGreek or LaserGreek or MacGreek Hebrew & Phonetics; Microsoft Word 3 or 4.
List of Every Form of Every Word in the UBS Greek New Testament. User Specifies Word 3.0x or 4.0x. ASCII Word List File Included for Importing into Other Spelling Dictionaries.
Linguist's Software, Inc.

MacGridzo. *Version:* 3.3. *Compatible Hardware:* Apple Macintosh. *Memory Required:* 1000k.
3.5" disk $399.00.
Gridding/Contouring Package Includes 3 Gridding Algorithms, up to 32,000 Control Points, Smoothing & Labeling of Contour Intervals. 3-D Features Include Mesh Diagrams, Raised Contour Maps & Shaded Relief Maps. Solid Fill Color Plots, Proportional Symbol Maps, Grid Mathematics, & Trend Surface Capabilities Included.
RockWare, Inc.

MacHebrew Scriptures Converter. *Version:* 5.1. Oct. 1987. *Compatible Hardware:* Apple Macintosh. *Memory Required:* 512k. *Items Included:* 2 800k disks, user's manual, keyboard chart. *Customer Support:* Telephone support.
3.5" disk $79.95. *Addl. software required:* LaserHebrew or MacHebrew & MacHebrew Scriptures.
Creates 20 Optional BHS Text Formats: Vocalized/Consonantal; Hebrew/Transliterated; Masoretic or SBL; Morphological Divisions; for English or Hebrew Systems; BHS Lines or Verse Wrap. Includes Semitica Transliteration Font.
Linguist's Software, Inc.

MacHebrew Scriptures Dictionary. *Version:* 4.0. Jan. 1989. *Items Included:* 800k disk, user's manual, laminated keyboard charts. *Customer Support:* Telephone support.
Macintosh (1Mb). 3.5" disk $49.95. *Addl. software required:* MacHebrew or LaserHebrew or MacGreek Hebrew & Phonetics; Microsoft Word 3 or 4.
List of Every Word That Occurs in the MacHebrew Scriptures (BHS) for Spelling Checking in Microsoft WORD. User Specifies Word 3.0x or 4.0x Dictionary. Both Include ASCII Word List File for Importing into Other Spelling Dictionaries.
Linguist's Software, Inc.

MacHieroglyphics. *Version:* 3.7. Apr. 1986. *Items Included:* User's manual, laminated keyboard layout chart. *Customer Support:* Telephone support, defective disks replaced free.
Macintosh (512k). 3.5" disk $79.95. *Addl. software required:* Any word processor.
Over 1050 Characters in 8 Fonts Designed for Egyptologists & Students of Hieroglyphics. Contains All the Signs Shown in Gardiner's Egyptian Grammar 3 with Many Additions. Fonts Designed after the Standard Sign List of Gardiner. 234 Overstrike Keys for Composite Hieroglyphs. Diacritical Font Included Compatible with "New York" Font for Transliteration. Four "Lacuna Keys" for Showing Erasures (Two with Overstrike Capability). Proportioned Characters. Select Directly from the Font Menu of MacWrite or Microsoft Word. Now Compatible with FullWrite Professional! Letter Quality Printing in Laser 9, 10, 12, 14, 18 & 24 Point.
Linguist's Software, Inc.

Machine Engineering I. *Customer Support:* 800-929-8117 (customer service).
MS-DOS. IBM/PS2. disk $99.99 (ISBN 0-87007-257-9).
Includes Five Machinery Engineering Programs Complete with Graphics. C-Pump Functions Include Selection of Impeller Sizes for New Operating Points & Calculations of Seal Stability. C-Lect Selects Compressors. Hydhub Checks Torque Capability for Keyless Hydraulic Hubs. Gasmix Produces Gas Properties Used in Compressor Calculations for Given Gas Fractions. Metric Converts Between English & SI Units.
SourceView Software International.

Machine Shop. *Version:* 6.0. Jan. 1990. *Items Included:* refefence manual and formula book. *Customer Support:* Free product/technical support available over the phone.
MS-DOS/PC-DOS. IBM XT/AT/386 & compatibles (640k). disk $195.00.
Library of 21 Useful Engineering Programs from Various Engineering Curriculums Such As: Hydraulics, Structures, Mathematics, etc. These Are All Programs Routinely Used in a Machine Shop Environment. They Reduce Time Loss Due To Searching For Formulas in Handbooks & Textbooks. They Reduce Calculating Time & Eliminate Errors.
Unik Assocs.

Machinery Designers Library 1. Dec. 1992. *Items Included:* Manual, diskettes. *Customer Support:* Free with registration.
Macintosh. Macintosh Plus or higher (2Mb). 3.5" disk $79.00. *Addl. software required:* PowerDraw or PowerCADD.
Professionally Designed & Used Symbols Library for PowerDraw or PowerCADD. Contains over 1, 500 Fastener Symbols. Standard Screws & Fasteners Are Taken from ANSI Specs. This Is a Comprehensive Library Containing Bolts (Hex Head), Cap & Set Screws (Button/Flat Head Hex/TORX, Socket Head/TORX, Hex Socket Shoulder, Hex Socket Set), Machine Screws, Nuts, Washers & Combinations, Screw Ends & Threaded Holes. Each Symbol Is Available in Many Views & Sizes.
Engineered Software.

Machinery Designers Library 2. Dec. 1992.
Items Included: Manual, diskettes. *Customer Support:* Free with registration.
Macintosh. Macintosh Plus or higher (2Mb). 3.5" disk $79.00. *Addl. software required:* PoewrDraw or PowerCADD.
Professionally Designed & Used Symbols Library for PowerDraw Version 4.0. Contains over 1,200 Bearings Symbols. Nominal Dimensions Are Given in Commercial or ANSI Standards. This Is a Comprehensive Library Containing Precision Miniature Bearings, Dowel Pins, Drill Bushings, O-Ring/Grooves, Retaining Rings & Taper Pin Holes/Taper Pin Heads. Each Symbol Is Available in Many Views & Sizes.
Engineered Software.

Machinery Kinematics & Dynamics: MKAD.
Version: 3.0. May 1990. *Compatible Hardware:* IBM PC & compatibles. *Memory Required:* 256k. *General Requirements:* Hard disk, printer.
disk $695.00 (Order no.: MKAD).
General Purpose Computer Program for Kinematic & Dynamic Analysis of Planar Machinery. Models Open & Closed Mechanical Systems with Single or Multiple Degrees of Freedom. Models Are Built with Components Found in a Library Included in the Program. Nineteen Components Are Available. Models Mechanical Systems in Motion & Calculates the Position, Velocity & Acceleration of All Their Moving Parts. Forces & Torques Acting on & Within the System Are Calculated As Well. From a Given Set of Initial Conditions, the Motion of the System Can Be Integrated So That Its Behavior As a Function of Time Can Be Observed.
J. P. Axe.

Machinery Manager. *Version:* 4. Aug. 1989.
Items Included: manual in 3 ring binder. *Customer Support:* Pay-per-Call at $1.95/minute.
MS-DOS 3.1 or higher. PC compatible (448k). disk $195.00.
This Program Allows You to Analyze Maintenance & Repair Costs As Well As Have Easy Access to Equipment Information Such As Make, Model, Serial Number, Crankcase Capacity, Purchase Information, & Meter Readings. Be Reminded of Scheduled Maintenance Due. Print Cards to Keep in the Shop Detailing Maintenance & Repair History of All Equipment. Print Input Forms That You Can Use in the Shop to Note Repair & Maintenance Activities to Transfer to the Computer.
Harvest Computer Systems, Inc.

MacHorse. *Compatible Hardware:* Apple Macintosh. *Memory Required:* 512k. *General Requirements:* Hard disk.
3.5" disk $2500.00.
Horse-Management Program for Veterinarians, Breeders & Trainers.
Dapple Tech Computers.

MacHunter RMS. *Version:* 4.0. *Compatible Hardware:* Apple Macintosh or PowerBook.
Memory Required: 4000k. *General Requirements:* 40+Mb hard disk. *Items Included:* Omnis 7.0; Kiwi Envelopes. *Customer Support:* Service contract available for 15% of software price (single user: $395.00 per yr.).
$2600.000 single user (includes Run Time Omnis 7.0).
$1100.00 ea. addtl. user.
Comprehensive Recruitment-Management Information System Designed Specifically for Search Firms, Employment Agencies & In-House Employment Departments. Provides Candidate, Client & Requisition Search & Retrieval, Activity Tracking & Reporting. Also Included Are Integrated Productivity Tools: a Daily Planner & Time Management System, On-Line Rolodex with Automatic Phone Dialing Capability. Word Processing Features Include Text Processor, Mail Merge for Fast Production of Form Letters & Labels Plus an Individual Envelope Printing Utility.
MacHunter.

Mach386. 1990-92. *Items Included:* Mach 2.5 kernel, 4.3 BSD UNIX interface, GNU utilities from the Free Software Foundation, Networking (NFS & TCP/IP), X Window system, complete on-line documentation, optional Mach 3.0 microkernel add-on, optional MUI (Motif User Interface) add-on, optional DUI (DOS User Interface) add-on. *Customer Support:* Free 30-day installation support; dial-in autosupport at $150 per quarter or $500 annually.
Mach386. Common AT-bus IBM PC & compatibles. Complete system $995.00; options $195.00 ea. *Optimal configuration:* 100Mb of disk space & 8Mb of memory; an 80387 or 80287 floating-point processor chip recommended.
Mach-Based Binary Operating System Which Provides a 4.3 BSD UNIX Interface to i386/i486 Users. The System Runs on AT-Bus IBM PCs & compatibles. Besides Mach Abstractions & the 4.3 BSD Interface, the System Offers TCP/IP Networking, NFS, the X Window System, GNU Utilities, & Optional Mach 3.0 Microkernel, Motif User Interface, & DOS User Interface Modules.
Mount XINU.

Macindex. *Compatible Hardware:* Apple Macintosh.
3.5" disk $75.00.
Index to Published Information on the Macintosh with Various Appendix Listings.
MacPoint Pubns.

MacInn. *Version:* Single-user 1.4.7, Multi-user 2.0. *Compatible Hardware:* Apple Macintosh. *Memory Required:* 1000k. *General Requirements:* Hard disk drive, ImageWriter or LaserWriter. *Items Included:* Computer software, manual. *Customer Support:* 90 days, maintenance agreements available.
$895.00, Inn Version.
$450.00, B&B Version.
$1495.00, Multi-user version, starting price.
Lodging & Property Management Software for Inns, Hotels, Time-Share Condominiums & Conference Centers.
Eliot Software Co.

MacInstrain. *Version:* 2.5.
Macintosh Plus or higher. 3.5" disk $200.00.
Strain Analysis.
RockWare, Inc.

MacInstruments. *Version:* 1.05. *Items Included:* Manuals, documentation. *Customer Support:* Free technical support, upgrades.
Macintosh Plus, SE, II, IIx. 3.5" disk $790.00 (Order no.: GWL-INS).
Provides 4-Channel Emulation of Oscilloscope, Chart Recorder, Scrolling Strip Chart Recorder, & Scanline Recorder. Includes Zoom, Scroll or Pass Capabilities As Well As Simple Statistics.
GW Instruments, Inc.

Macintize. *Version:* 2.0. *Items Included:* 5.25" external disk drive, cables. *Customer Support:* Free telephone service.
Macintosh 512KE or higher. 3.5" disk $1495.00.
Transfers Compugraphic MCS-Coded Files to the Macintosh.
Mumford Micro Systems.

Macintosh Bar Code Printing Program. *Version:* 2.01. *Compatible Hardware:* Apple Macintosh. *General Requirements:* ImageWriter or LaserWriter.
3.5" disk $150.00.
free with purchase of bar-code reader.
Code 39 Label & Form Generation Program.
TPS Electronics.

The Macintosh Bible: Stax! Edition. *Compatible Hardware:* Apple Macintosh. *Memory Required:* 1000k. *General Requirements:* 2 800k floppy disk drives; HyperCard. Hard disk recommended. 3.5" disk $69.95.
Consists of Hint, Tips & Shortcuts for the Apple Macintosh.
Stax!.

The Macintosh Holmes Companion: The Digital Sherlock Holmes. *Customer Support:* Telephone or mail support.
Macintosh DOS (512k). $59.95. *Nonstandard peripherals required:* 800k disk drive. *Addl. software required:* MacWrite or similar word processing software. *Optimal configuration:* 1Mb of RAM, hard disk, MacWrite version 5.0.
These Disks Contain the Complete Set of Sherlock Holmes Stories - 56 Short Stories & 4 Novels. Stories Can Be Read, Analyzed, or Searches Made for Specific Words or Phrases Using MacWrite or Other Word Processor Software (Not Furnished). Useful for "Sherlockians", Researchers, Educators, or Other Interested Computer Users. This Edition is Authorized by Dame Conan Doyle & Also Includes Complete Calendars for 1850 - 1914; List of Baker Street Irregular Scion Societies; Purveyors of Holmes Books, Magazines, Items etc.; 100 Best Holmes References.
Baker Street Software.

Macintosh Pascal: Student's Diskette. L. A. Carmony & R. L. Holliday. 1985. *Compatible Hardware:* Apple Macintosh.
3.5" disk $20.00 (ISBN 0-88175-088-3).
Contains Material from Text: Macintosh Pascal.
W. H. Freeman & Co. (Computer Science Press).

Macintosh Pascal: Teacher's Diskette. L. A. Carmony & R. L. Holliday. 1985. *Compatible Hardware:* Apple Macintosh with Apple Macintosh Pascal, Version 1.0. *General Requirements:* Apple Macintosh with Apple Macintosh Pascal, version 1.0.
3.5" disk $20.00 (ISBN 0-88175-089-1).
Contains Material from Text: Macintosh Pascal.
W. H. Freeman & Co. (Computer Science Press).

Macintosh II A/UX Ada Compilation System & Toolset. *General Requirements:* 10Mb of disk space.
A/UX operating system. Macintosh II (4Mb). 3.5" disk $3095.00.
Toolset $800.00,.
Translates Source Programs Created on a Mac II Running A/UX Based on the MC68020, into Object Code That Executes on the Mac II Running A/UX. Products Include: Compiler (with High & Low Optimizers); Multi-Library Environment (Family Manager, Library Manager, Unit manager); Bunder, Which Combines Separately Compiled Ada Units into a Single Object Program; Run-Time Executive to Support Executing Ada Applications; & Full Documentation.
Alsys, Inc.

MacInventory. *Compatible Hardware:* Apple Macintosh. *Memory Required:* 512k.
MacInventory. 3.5" disk 495.00 to 7500.00.
Customized template. $250.00 to $5000.00.
Inventory Program for Retailing & Manufacturing.
MEAA, Inc.

MacIRMA API.
Macintosh SE or higher. 3.5" disk $195.00.
Application Programming Interface.
Digital Communications Assocs.

MacIRMA Graphics.
Macintosh SE or higher. hardware & software $1295.00.

TITLE INDEX

software upgrade $195.00.
Allows User to Access IBM Mainframe Computer Graphics Applications Through the MacIRMA Family of IBM 3270 Terminal Emulation Products.
Digital Communications Assocs.

MacKana & BASIC Japanese Kanji. *Version:* 3.2. Oct. 1984. *Items Included:* User's manual, keyboard layout chart. *Customer Support:* Free telephone support; defective disks replaced free.
Macintosh. Macintosh (1Mb). 3.5" disk $49.95. *Addl. software required:* Any word processor. *Optimal configuration:* 4Mb RAM, hard drive.
12 & 24 Point Japanese Font for All Systems on Any Macintosh. Includes All of the Hiragana & Katakana, Punctuation Marks, & 70 of the Most Commonly Used Kanji Including Numbers from 1-99,999. High Quality Printing in MACWRITE/PAINT or MICROSOFT WORD & All Programs for the Macintosh with a Font Menu. Simple Installation Instructions Are Included in the User's Manual. Transforms Your Keyboard to & from Japanese in a Second. Just Click on "Japanese" in the Font Menu. Japanese Appears on the Macintosh Monitor & Printouts. Style Variations Include Bold, Italic, Underline, Outline, Superscript, Subscript, Shadow. Logical Keyboard Design Makes for Ease of Use. Keyboard Layout Sheet Is Included. Requires Only 28k of Disk Space.
Linguist's Software, Inc.

Mackey-Saunders Data Collection: Contemporary American Horoscopes. *Version:* 1.x. Janice Mackey et al. Sep. 1990. *Items Included:* Manual. *Customer Support:* Free phone support.
MS-DOS, PC-DOS. IBM PC & MS-DOS compatibles (512k). 3.5" disk $50.00 (ISBN 0-87199-108-X). *Nonstandard peripherals required:* Hard disk. *Addl. software required:* Nova, Chartwheels I, Chartwheels II, Professional Natal Report, or other Nova-compatible program.
MacFinder. Macintosh (1Mb). 3.5" disk $75.00 (ISBN 0-87199-116-0). *Nonstandard peripherals required:* Hard disk. *Addl. software required:* Celeste I or Professional Natal Report.
Contains Horoscopes, Birth Data & Life-Event Dates of 600 20th-Century American Celebrities. All Birth Data Is Timed & from Birth Certificates. Charts Can Be Displayed on the Screen or Printed Out. Database Can Be Edited & Added to by the User.
Astrolabe, Inc.

MacKids Christmas Pack. *Version:* 1.0.3. Dec. 1991. *Items Included:* Manual & 3 diskettes.
System 6.0.5 or higher. Macintosh Plus or higher, (1Mb). 3.5" disk $39.95 (ISBN 0-940081-63-6).
Diverse Assortment of Games & Puzzles Charged with Holiday Cheer. More Than 15 Puzzles, Word Games, Memory Games & Other Activities for Kids of All Ages. Click on Any One of the Many Colorful Presents under the Carefully Decorated Christmas Tree to Start a New Game. Fun for the Whole Family.
Nordic Software, Inc.

MacKids Jungle Quest. *Version:* 1.1. Oct. 1992. *Items Included:* Manual & 3 diskettes.
System 6.0.8 or higher. Macintosh Plus or higher, hard drive (1Mb). 3.5" disk $39.95 (ISBN 0-940081-64-4).
Teaches Elementary Level Math in the Context of an Exciting Action/Adventure Game. Player Travels a Dangerous Path Through the Dark Jungles of a Far Off Land. Progress on the Quest to Free the King from the Evil Pygmies Is Dependent upon Correctly Solving Simple Math Problems. Lots of Sound & Color.
Nordic Software, Inc.

MacKids Preschool Pack. *Version:* 2.0. Jun. 1992. *Items Included:* Manual & 2 diskettes.
System 6.0.7 or higher. Macintosh Plus or higher (1Mb). 3.5" disk $39.95 (ISBN 0-940081-21-0).
Includes Six Colorful & Effective Learning Programs That Explore Letters, Numbers, Counting, Sequencing, Shapes, & Short-Term Memory. Voice & Sounds Reinforce Correct Responses. All Skill Levels Are Adjustable.
Nordic Software, Inc.

MacKids Word Quest. *Version:* 2.3. *Items Included:* Manual & 3 diskettes.
System 6.0.7 or higher. Macintosh Plus or higher, requires hard drive (1Mb) (2Mb with System 7). 3.5" disk $39.95 (ISBN 0-940081-22-9).
Adventure Game Using Sound & Animation to Teach Spelling. Player Explores Castles, Caves, & Words of an Enchanted Land in Search of 5 Magic Words. Many Words Must Be Spelled Correctly to Make Progress on This Quest. Words for Grades 1-6 Included.
Nordic Software, Inc.

MacKiss.
Macintosh 512K or higher. $495.00.
Software Driver for QMS Kiss, Big Kiss & Kiss Plus Laser Printers.
Laser Connection.

MacKojien. *Version:* 1.04. Ayumi Software. Feb. 1991. *Customer Support:* Telephone technical support.
Macintosh KanjiTalk 6.0.7 or higher. Macintosh (2Mb). CD-ROM disk $249.00. *Nonstandard peripherals required:* CD-ROM drive.
Prestigious Japanese Kojien Dictionary on CD-ROM for Macintosh; Includes Full Application & Desk Accessory Version; 200,000 Entry Words, 2000 Graphics, 234 Color Samples; Powerful Search Parameters.
Qualitas Trading Co.

Maclean. *Version:* 2.0. *Compatible Hardware:* Apple Macintosh. *Memory Required:* 512k. *General Requirements:* Hard disk, FileMaker Plus. *Items Included:* Cleaning Inventory File; Building Area Data File; Personnel Data File. *Customer Support:* (714) 770-5008.
3.5" disk $1700.00.
Building Cleaning & Maintenance Management Program.
Cleaning Management Institute/National Trade Pubns., Inc.

MacLinkPlus/Easy Open Translators. *Version:* 8.0. *Items Included:* Macintosh Easy Open from Apple. *Customer Support:* Phone technical support (free - toll number), 30 day MBG.
System 7 or higher. Macintosh Plus or higher (1Mb). 3.5" disk $109.00, SRP.
Macintosh & PC File Conversation Utility for Users Who Already Have Access to DOS/Windows Files. Translate Files Between Macintosh & PC Formats Right on the Mac Desktop. Thousands of High Quality Translation Combinations Including Word Processing, Spreadsheet, Database, & Graphics Applications. Macintosh Easy Open from Apple Included. Also Includes the Dataviz FileView Utility & an Internet Translation Kit.
DataViz, Inc.

MacLinkPlus/HP Palmtop. *Version:* 2.5. *Items Included:* Optional cable ($30). *Customer Support:* Free technical support line (203-268-0030) 9AM to 6PM Eastern.
6.0.7 & higher (Macintosh). Mac Plus or higher (1Mb). 3.5" disk $129.00.
HP95LX, 100LX, 200LX. Contact publisher for price.
Complete Solution for Translating, Transferring, or Backing up Files Between Your Palmtop & Mac. With a File Translation Library of over 100 Combinations, You Can Convert MEMO, LOTUS 1-2-3, APPOINTMENT BOOK, PHONE BOOK, NOTETAKER, & DATABASE Files to & from Popular Word Processing, Spreadsheet Database, & PIM File Formats for the Macintosh.
DataViz, Inc.

MacLinkPlus/PC Connect. *Version:* 8.0. *Items Included:* Macintosh PC Exchange, Macintosh Easy Open, Serial Cable. *Customer Support:* Free technical support line (203-268-0030) 9AM to 6PM Eastern.
Macintosh Plus or higher. 3.5" disk $199.00.
Transfer & Translate Files via Disk, Network or Included Cable. Thousands of Translation Combinations for Word Processors, Spreadsheets, Databases, & Graphics. Includes Macintosh Easy Open for "Double-Click" & "Drag & Drop" Translations. Also Includes Macintosh PC Exchange, Dataviz FileView & an Internet Translation Kit.
DataViz, Inc.

MacLinkPlus/Translators Pro. *Version:* 8.0. *Items Included:* Macintosh PC Exchange, Macintosh Easy Open. *Customer Support:* Free technical support line (203-268-0030) 9AM to 6PM Eastern.
Macintosh Plus or higher. 3.5" disk $149.00.
Convert PC Files into MAC Format with a "Double-Click." Convert Back to PC with a "Drag & Drop." Thousands of Translation Combinations for Word Processors, Spreadsheets, Databases, & Graphics. Includes Macintosh PC Exchange for Using DOS Disks in Your MAC. Multi-Packs/Site Licenses Available.
DataViz, Inc.

MacList. *Compatible Hardware:* Apple Macintosh. *Memory Required:* 512k.
3.5" disk $39.00.
Desk Accessory Database for Sorting & Searching Files.
Jam Technologies.

MacLocus. *Version:* 2.2. *Compatible Hardware:* Apple Macintosh. *Memory Required:* 512k. *Items Included:* 45 page user manual.
3.5" disk $75.00.
Design Tool Used by Engineers To Analyze Linear Control Systems. With Macintosh Interface Guidelines, It Allows User To Enter a System Description & Analyze It Using the Following Tools: Root Locus, Bode Plots, & Inverse LaPlace Transformations.
Riverdale Software, Inc.

MacLunchroom. *Version:* 5.03. *Compatible Hardware:* Apple Macintosh Plus, SE, II. *General Requirements:* 20Mb hard disk; ImageWriter or LaserWriter. *Items Included:* Software & Bar Code Reader.
3.5" disk $1390.00.
School Hot Lunch Recordkeeping Program.
T&M Systems, Inc.

MacManager. *Compatible Hardware:* Apple Macintosh.
3.5" disk $19.95.
Management Simulation.
Harvard Assocs., Inc.

MacMed. *Version:* 5.0. *Compatible Hardware:* Apple Macintosh IIsi, LC, MAC II, Plus, SE, SE 30. *General Requirements:* Hard disk; ImageWriter or LaserWriter. *Items Included:* Program 1 year software support & updates free. *Customer Support:* Full support $350.00/yr. after 1st year - upgrades only $200.00.
single user $2250.00.
multiuser $3450.00.
Medical Office Management.
NewHouse Medical Systems.

Macmillan Digital World Atlas. Oct. 1995. *Customer Support:* Free 800 number, Online forums.
Windows 486SX, 25MHz; Macintosh. IBM & compatibles (8Mb); LCIII/Performa 475 (8Mb). CD-ROM disk $39.95 (ISBN 1-57595-003-0). *Nonstandard peripherals required:* 256 color SVGA 640x480 res., double-speed CD-ROM drive, SoundBlaster compatible sound card; 256 color, 14" display, double speed CD-ROM. *Addl. software required:* Mac System 7.0, Quicktime 2.0.
Circumnavigate the Globe from Your Desktop Using the Most Elegant, Comprehensive, & Accurate Digital World Atlas Ever Produced. Physical, Political, & Satellite Maps; Hyperlinked Search Indexes; Powerful Locators, & Special Zoom Features Provide Instant Visual Access to More Than 150,000 Regions, States, Cities, & Bodies of Water.
Macmillan Digital U. S. A.

Macmillan Multimedia Dictionary for Children.
MS-DOS 5.0 or higher, Windows 3.1 or higher. 386 processor or higher (4Mb). CD-ROM disk $29.95 (Order no.: R1263). *Nonstandard peripherals required:* CD-ROM drive. *Optimal configuration:* 386 processor operating at 16Mhz or higher, MS-DOS 5.0 or higher, Windows 3.1 or higher, 30Mb hard drive, mouse, VGA graphic adapter & VGA color monitor (SVGA recommended), 4Mb RAM, external speakers or headphones (with sound card) that are Sound Blaster compatible.
Macintosh (4Mb). (Order no.: R1263A). *Nonstandard peripherals required:* 14" color monitor or larger, CD-ROM drive.
Based on America's Best-Selling Children's Dictionary, This Program Provides a Fun Way to Learn More Than 12,000 Words. Contains over 1,000 Vivid Pictures 400 Sound Effects, Bookmarks, Spoken Pronunciations, Word History & More (Ages 6-12).
Library Video Co.

Macmillan Visual Dictionary: Multimedia Edition. Sep. 1995. *Customer Support:* Free 800 number, Online forums.
Windows 486SX, 25MHz, double speed CD-ROM drive. IBM & compatibles (8Mb). disk $49.95 (ISBN 1-57595-000-6). *Nonstandard peripherals required:* Super VGA color card capable of 256 color display at 640x480; "SoundBlaster" compatible sound card.
Macintosh. Performa 550 (33MHz 68030) (8Mb). 3.5" disk $49.95. *Nonstandard peripherals required:* Color monitor capable of 256 color display at 640x480, double-speed CD-ROM drive. *Addl. software required:* System 7.1.
The Ultimate Resource for Visual Thinking - with Audio in Three Languages. 25,000 Fully Hyperlinked & Indexed Entries Pronounced in English, French, & Spanish; Contains 50 Animations & 3,500 Color Images.
Macmillan Digital U. S. A.

MacMohr. *Version:* 2.3. *Compatible Hardware:* Apple Macintosh. *General Requirements:* ImageWriter or LaserWriter.
3.5" disk $100.00.
Allows User to Program Graphic Displays of Mohr's Circles & Analytical Information Concerning Various Stress Parameters from Triaxial Compression Test Values.
RockWare, Inc.

MacMoney. *Version:* 4.02. Dec. 1993. *Compatible Hardware:* Apple, Macintosh Plus or higher. *Language(s):* PASCAL. *Memory Required:* 1000k. *General Requirements:* 2 disk drives recommended. *Items Included:* Manual, sample check pak. *Customer Support:* phone, mail, e-mail services.
3.5" disk $89.95.
Financial Record Keeping & Management Program. Exports Data to Other Programs, Imports Data from Other Programs Such As Quicken, Dollars & Sense, & Payroll by Aatrix. Prints Checks from Any Checkbook, & Performs Loan & Retirement Planning.
Survivor Software Ltd.

MacMovies.
Macintosh Plus or higher (512k). 3.5" disk $99.00.
Desktop Video Processing Package.
Beck-Tech.

MacNail. *Version:* 3.0. *Compatible Hardware:* Apple Macintosh Plus, Classic, SE, SE/30, LC or any II; IBM AT or PS/2 compatible. *Memory Required:* 1000k. *General Requirements:* Hard disk; Microsoft Excel. *Items Included:* User manual. *Customer Support:* Free phone support.
Apple Macintosh Plus, SE or II (1Mb). entire package $595.00; Also available as separate modules. *Nonstandard peripherals required:* Hard disk, Microsoft Excel.
IBM AT, PS/2 or compatibles (2Mb). *Nonstandard peripherals required:* Excel, Windows.
Construction Estimating, Scheduling & Job-Cost Accounting.
Turtle Creek Software.

MacNest. *Compatible Hardware:* Apple Macintosh.
3.5" disk $49.00.
Electronic Storage Tray.
Fortnum Software.

MacNFS: NFS Client for Macintosh. *Version:* 1.1. Jan. 1996. *Items Included:* Manual. *Customer Support:* 90 day warranty from time of purchase.
7.1 Macintosh or higher. 68020 (4Mb). 3.5" disk $249.00 (Order no.: TFS191). *Addl. software required:* Mac TCP/IP or Open Transport TCP/IP.
Allows the Macintosh User to Share Files on UNIX Machines Without Leaving the Convenience & Familiarity of Their Macintosh Desktop. Users Access Remote NFS Volumes Through the Standard "Chooser" Interface, & a NFS Mounted Volume Will Function Like a Local Disk. It's As Easy to Use As AppleShare.
Thursby Software Systems, Inc.

MacNumerics. Feb. 1991. *Items Included:* Two 3.5" 800k diskettes, 280 page users manual (three ring), warranty card. *Customer Support:* Telephone support (no charge); 90 day warranty.
system 6.0 or higher; system 7 compatible. Macintosh Plus, SE, Classic LC, SI, II (1 Mb). 3.5" disk $189.95. *Optimal configuration:* 6.0.7 classic with 1 mg RAM. *Networks supported:* AppleLink.
Mathematics Program Designed to Teach the Basic Tools of Mathematics. Includes Points, Graph Paper, Lines, Conic Sections, Polar Equations, Parametric Equations, Polynomials, Matrix Operation, Linear Systems, Unit Circle, X-Y Regression, Scientific Calculator, Unit Conversions & Periodic Chart. Graphs are Extensive. Graphs are Animated & Interactive, Clearly Demonstrating Solutions, Slopes, Roots, Areas of Integration & Areas between Curves. Includes Printing Program to Label, Describe, Save, Recall & Print any Program Screen on the Imagewriter, Stylewriter or Laserwriter Printer. Help & Showstep Screens.
Spring Branch Software, Inc.

MacNumerics Two. Dec. 1991. *Items Included:* One 1.4 meg diskette, 320 page spiral bound users manual. *Customer Support:* Telephone support - no charge; 90 day warranty.
6.0.7. Macintosh LC, SI or Color Macintosh-II (2 Mb). 3.5" disk $289.95. *Networks supported:* AppleLink.
Mathematics Program Used to Teach the Basic Tools of Mathematics. Tools Include Points, Graph Paper, Lines, Conic Sections, General Functions, Inequalities, Linear Programming, Systems of Linear Equations, Matrix Operations, Parametric Equations, Polar Equations, Polynomials, Trig Unit Circle, Vector Operations, X Y Regression, Scientific Calculator, Unit Conversions & Periodic Chart. Interactive & Animated Graphs Demonstrate Solutions, Slopes, Roots, Integral Areas & Areas Between Curves. Printing & Graph Labeling, Problem Explanation to Laserwriter, Stylewriter & Imagewriter.
Spring Branch Software, Inc.

MacNurse. *Compatible Hardware:* Apple Macintosh. *Memory Required:* 512k. *General Requirements:* External disk drive or hard disk; Multiuser Omnis 3 Plus.
single user with runtime $2500.00.
multiuser $3500.00.
Admission/Plan of Care System for Nursing Homes.
H&D Leasing.

MacNutriplan. *Compatible Hardware:* Apple Macintosh. *Memory Required:* 512k.
3.5" disk $75.00.
Diet-Nutrition Analysis.
NutriPlan.

Macola Accounting Software. *Version:* Progression Series 6.0. *Items Included:* Documentation provided in downsized binders, tutorial data. *Customer Support:* Four support plan options available ranging in price from $95.00 per pkg. to $3995.00 for an entire system.
IBM PC & compatibles (640k). $995.00 to $1595.00 per module. *Nonstandard peripherals required:* Hard disk. *Networks supported:* Novell TTS.
Program Consists of 21 Integrated Modules for Accounting, Distribution & Manufacturing. Posts Recurring Transactions, Automatic Posting from Other Modules, Report Format User Definable, Reports Comparative Statements, Ability to Jump Modules, Links with External Software Programs, Password Access, Encryption, Audit Trail, Error Recovery, Log off Out-of-Balance, Reject Erroneous Account Numbers & Source Code Available. All Components Include Commission on Cash Receipts.
Macola, Inc.

Macola Accounting Software: Accounts Payable (A-P). *Version:* Progression Series 6.0. *Compatible Hardware:* IBM PC, PC XT, PC AT, PC compatibles. *Operating System(s) Required:* MS-DOS. *Language(s):* Microfocus Cobol. *Items Included:* Documentation & tutorial data. *Customer Support:* Four support plan options available ranging in price from $95.00 per pkg. to $3995.00 for an entire system.
$995.00.
Functions Performed by the System Include: Entry of Basic Information About Every Vendor Users Do Business with; Enter All Day-to-Day A/P Transactions; On-Screen Viewing of Open Items in Vendor's Account; Print Report of Cash Needed to Pay A/P Open Items up Through Certain Date; Select Vouchers for Payment or Deferral, to Produce a Report of Checks to Be Printed, to Print the Computer Checks & Post the Payments to the Payments to the A/P Files, & to Print the Check Register for Manual, Prepaid & Computer-Printed Checks; Select Checks to Mark

As Paid, Then Print an Accounts Payable Check Reconciliation Report; Print Vendor Analysis Report & More.
Macola, Inc.

Macola Accounting Software: Accounts Receivable (A-R). *Version:* Progression Series 6.0. *Compatible Hardware:* IBM PC, PC XT, PC AT & compatibles. *Operating System(s) Required:* MS-DOS. *Language(s):* Microfocus Cobol. *Items Included:* Documentation & tutorial data. *Customer Support:* Four support plans available ranging in price from $95.00 per pkg. to $3995.00 for an entire system.
$995.00.
Functions Performed by the System Include: Entry of Basic Information about Customers Users Do Business with; Allows User to Enter Payments from Any Customer & Apply Those Payments to Customer's Account, As Well As Print a Report Telling User How Much the Customer Owes, & How Old These Owed Amounts are; On- Screen Viewing of the Transactions in a Customer's Account after a Specified Date. Print Statements Which List Customer Activity & Which Tell Them How Much They Owe the User. Print a Report Detailing Commissions Due to Each Salesperson. Print Six Sales Analysis Reports & More. Also, Service Invoice Processing.
Macola, Inc.

Macola Accounting Software: Assets & Depreciation (A-D). *Version:* Progression Series 6.0. *Compatible Hardware:* IBM PC, PC XT, PC AT, PC compatibles. *Operating System(s) Required:* MS-DOS. *Language(s):* Microfocus Cobol. *Items Included:* Documentation & tutorial data. *Customer Support:* Four support plans available ranging in price from $95.00 per pkg. to $3995.00 for an entire system.
$995.00.
Package Provides User with the Ability to Keep Track of a Company's Fixed Assets & to Calculate the Depreciation Costs for Those Assets. Incorporates Ace Depreciation & the Federal Tax Depreciation Method (ACRS, the Accelerated Cost Recovery System Defined into Law by the Economic Recovery Act of 1978) &, As Well, Offers Such a Wide Range of Traditional Depreciation Methods That the User Is Assured of Flexibility. Each Different Set of Data Related to the Company's Assets Is Called a Reporting Entity. It Is Necessary in the Present Package to Set up at Least Two Different Reporting Entities: the First Contains the Corporate Accounting of Each Asset, While the Second Is Set up to Accommodate the Depreciation Done for the Purpose of Filling Out Federal Tax Forms.
Macola, Inc.

Macola Accounting Software: Bill of Material Processor (BOMP). *Version:* Progression Series 6.0. *Compatible Hardware:* IBM PC, PC XT, PC AT, PC compatibles. *Operating System(s) Required:* MS-DOS. *Language(s):* Microfocus Cobol. *Items Included:* Documentation & tutorial data. *Customer Support:* Four support plans available ranging in price from $95.00 per pkg. to $3995.00 for an entire system.
$1595.00.
The Only Module the System Needs Is Inventory Management (I/M). Add a New Component to Product Structure. Change the Data Which Refers to the Relationship Between the Component & Its Parent. Inquire on a Product Structure Record. Delete a Component from a Product Structure. Replace an Obsolete Item with a Replacement Item in Places Where the Obsolete Item Appears As a Component. Copy a Product Structure for One Parent to a Different Parent with Automatic Resequencing.
Macola, Inc.

Macola Accounting Software: Customer Order Processing (COP). *Version:* Progression Series 6.0. *Compatible Hardware:* IBM PC, PC XT, PC AT, PC compatibles. *Operating System(s) Required:* MS-DOS. *Language(s):* Microfocus Cobol. *Items Included:* Documentation & tutorial data. *Customer Support:* Four support plans available ranging in price from $95.00 per pkg. to $3995.00 for an entire system.
$995.00.
For the Small to Medium Manufacturer/Distributor. Used in Performing the Basic & Standard Functions Necessary for a Company to Record, Track, Verify & Generally Handle Its Customer Orders. It Is Designed to Process Customer Orders from the Time They Are Entered Until They Are Billed. With Inventory Management (I/M), the System Can Handle the Computer Side of the Distribution Functions Except for Those Distributors Who Do Assembly Work to Create Final Products. For That BOMP Is Needed. When Entering Customer Orders in System, the Line-Items Are Allocated to Match the Order Quantity, Unless There Are Not Enough Available. In That Case, the User Has Several Entry-Time Options Including Partial Order, Back Order, etc.
Macola, Inc.

Macola Accounting Software: General Ledger (G-L). *Version:* Progression Series 6.0. *Compatible Hardware:* IBM PC, PC XT, PC AT, PC compatibles. *Operating System(s) Required:* MS-DOS. *Language(s):* Microfocus Cobol. *Items Included:* Documentation & tutorial data. *Customer Support:* Four support plans available ranging in price from $95.00 per pkg. to $3995.00 for an entire system.
$995.00.
The Program Is Designed for Producing Financial Statements, Primarily the Balance Sheet & the Profit & Loss Statement. Additional Financial Statements That Can Be Produced Are the Sources & Applications of Funds (SAF) Reports: Statement of Cash Flow, Changes in Financial Position, & Components of Working Capital. Allows User to Define & Change the Accounting Periods of Fiscal Year & to Define Current Accounting Period, As Well As Set up & Maintain the Chart of Accounts, Define Financial Entities of up to 36 Ranges of Profit Center Numbers. Financial Statements & Cost Reports Can Then Be Printed for Individual Financial Entities, Print a Trial Balance Showing Debit & Credit Entries, Define & Maintain Layouts (Formats) for Financial Statements. Also Transfer Data Directly from the Distribution File in the A/R, A/P, A/D, J/C, I/M or PR Package to the General Journal Transaction File.
Macola, Inc.

Macola Accounting Software: Inventory Management (I-M). *Version:* Progression Series 6.0. *Compatible Hardware:* IBM PC, PC XT, PC AT, PC compatibles. *Operating System(s) Required:* MS-DOS. *Language(s):* Microfocus Cobol. *Items Included:* Documentation & tutorial data. *Customer Support:* Four support plans available ranging in price from $95.00 per pkg. to $3995.00 for an entire system.
$995.00.
Allows User to Define Items in Inventory File. Keeps Track of Inventory Stocked at More Than One Location, Including the Quantity of the Item On-Hand, Allocated, & On-Order At Each Location. Prints Out Stock Status Information About a Selected Item or Range of Items by Location & Product Category, Including Three Reports: (1) Reordering Advice by Item; (2) Reordering Advice by Location; & (3) Reordering Advice by Vendor. Maintains a Convenient Table of Inventory Locations. Recalculates Vendor Level, Amounts of Safety Stock, & What the Recommended Minimum Order Amount Should Be for the Item, Based on the Actual Usage for the Period. As Well As a File of Valid Inventory Item Product Categories. Balances the LIFO/FIFO Layer File with the Master Inventory Item File.
Macola, Inc.

Macola Accounting Software: Payroll (PR). *Version:* Progression Series 6.0. *Compatible Hardware:* IBM PC, PC XT, PC AT, PC compatibles. *Operating System(s) Required:* MS-DOS. *Language(s):* Microfocus COBOL. *Items Included:* Documentation & tutorial data. *Customer Support:* Four support plans available ranging in price from $95.00 per pkg. to $3995.00 for an entire system.
$995.00.
Maintains Information About Employees; Earning Rates, Tax Information, Deductions, Period-to-Period, Quarter-to-Date & Year-to-Date Totals of Earnings, Taxes & Deductions. Generates the Time & Pay Transactions That Will Result in Employees Being Paid. Performs the Payroll Calculations. Automatically Prints Checks for Employees & Posts Earnings, Taxes & Deductions to Appropriate Accounts. Allows for Entry of Data About Manual, Non-Standard Transactions & Adjustments of Payroll Data. It Also Prints a Report of the Deductions & Earnings History; the Required Information to Fill Out the 941A Quarterly Payroll Report, Detailing What Employees Have Earned in the Quarter. Also Creates the SA Copy "A" File for Magnetic Media Reporting. Allows User to Print a Report That will Show P/R Expensed, A/P Expensed, & A/R Billed Against a Job, & Compares These to Budgeted Job Figures. Maintains a List of the Special Deductions & Earnings That Can Apply to An Employee's Pay.
Macola, Inc.

Macola Accounting Software: Purchase Order & Receiving (P-O). *Version:* Progression Series 6.0. *Compatible Hardware:* IBM PC, PC XT, PC AT, PC compatibles. *Operating System(s) Required:* MS-DOS. *Language(s):* Microfocus Cobol. *Items Included:* Documentation & tutorial data. *Customer Support:* Four support plans available ranging in price from $95.00 per pkg. to $3995.00 for an entire system.
$995.00.
Supports Three Types of Purchase Orders: Normal Orders, Blanket Orders & Releases Against Blanket Orders. The On-Line Entry & Editing of Purchase Orders Is Allowed. Prints Three Types of Purchase Orders. Also Carries a Brief Description of the Area to Where Material Should Be Transferred upon Receipt. Compares Receipt Date with Request Date & Displays a Warning If the Receipt Date Is Earlier Than the Request Date by a Margin Larger Than Company Policy Allows. Updates the Inventory File's Quantity On-Hand Immediately (On-Line). An Audit Trail Record Is Created to Keep Track of the Transaction. The Cash Requirements Projection Report Calculates the Amounts That Must Be Paid to Each Vendor over Four Periods (Which User Defines). Requires Macola's Inventory Management & Accounts Payable 5.02 Packages to Be Installed & Functioning.
Macola, Inc.

Macola Accounting Software: Report Writer (R-W). *Version:* Progression Series 6.0. *Compatible Hardware:* IBM PC, PC XT, PC AT, PC compatibles. *Operating System(s) Required:* PC-DOS. *Items Included:* Documentation & tutorial data. *Customer Support:* Four support plans available ranging in price from $95.00 per pkg. to $3995.00 for an entire system.
$895.00 single user; $1295.00 multi user.
Report Generating Program That Allows Users to Generate Their Own Reports Without the

Assistance of a Computer Programmer. Can Access Almost Every Data Field in Every File of the MACOLA ACCOUNTING SOFTWARE Packages. Reports Can Be Directed to Screen, Printer. Additionally, Users Can Send the Report Data to Database, Spreadsheet, or Graphics Packages.
Macola, Inc.

Macomo. Compatible Hardware: Apple Macintosh. Memory Required: 512k.
3.5" disk $185.00.
Software Development Cost & Schedule Estimation System.
OITC, Inc.

Macontrol. Compatible Hardware: Apple Macintosh. Memory Required: 512k. General Requirements: External disk drive.
3.5" disk $695.00.
System package. 3.5" disk $1795.00.
Data Acquisition; Laboratory Control.
IDAC, Inc.

MacOpener: For Windows. Nov. 1995. Items Included: Manual. Customer Support: Free 203-268-0030 9-6 Eastern time.
Windows 95, NT, 3.1. 386 (4Mb). disk $75.00 (Order no.: MO-WIN). Nonstandard peripherals required: ASPI for Windows compliant SCSI drives only, VGA.
Lets You Use Macintosh High Density Floppies, CD-ROMS & Removable Media - All on Your PC. It's Perfect for the User with Cross-Platform Software. Preview Macintosh Text & Graphics (PICT, EPS) Before Moving Files to PC & Vice Versa. Includes Support for Long File Names in Windows 95.
DataViz, Inc.

MacOrg.
Macintosh 512KE. 3.5" disk $109.00.
Organizational Chart Drawing Program That Lets User Draw Charts with up to Nine Boxes Across & Nine Boxes Down. Allows User To Export Charts to Microsoft Word, PageMaker, MacPaint, & Other Mac Applications.
The Claybrook Company.

MacPaint. Version: 2.0.
Macintosh 512KE or higher. 3.5" disk $125.00. upgrade to 2.0 $25.00,.
Free-Form Illustration.
Claris Corp.

MacPerspective. Version: 4.0. Feb. 1989. Items Included: Manual. Customer Support: Telephone questions answered.
Macintosh (512k). disk $295.00. Nonstandard peripherals required: Imagewriter or Laserwriter printer for printed drawings.
Allows Architects, Draftspeople, Artists & Engineers to Construct Accurate "Wire-Frame" Perspective Drawings of Houses, Buildings or Other Objects from Dimensioned Plan & Elevation Drawings or Sketches. Observer Viewpoint Can Be Changed at Any Time to See House or Building from a Different Angle Without Reconstructing Perspective. Program Permits Transfer of Perspective Drawings to Other Macintosh Applications Such As MacDraw & FullPaint via the Macintosh Clipboard, or As MacDraw Pict or Adobe Illustrator EPS Files.
Knick Drafting, Inc.

MacPhonebook. Version: 3.0. Compatible Hardware: Apple Macintosh 512KE or higher. General Requirements: ImageWriter, LaserWriter, SC, II, NTX, LQ. Items Included: Manual, disk, black covers, registration card. Customer Support: Yes (718) 369-2944.
3.5" disk $49.95 (ISBN 1-880773-01-5).
Creates Database of Names, Addresses & Phone Numbers. Prints Out Different Sizes of Directories, Little Black Book, Pocket Book Checkbook Format, In-House Directory, Prints on Plain Paper, Black Covers Included, up to 1600 Names, Dials Phone via Modem, Prints Calendar, Personal Data, Categories, Names. Prints All Popular Formats: FiloFax, Jr. & Sr. Organizer, Daytimer, etc.
Synex.

MacPhonetics. Version: 7.0. Mar. 1985. Compatible Hardware: Apple Macintosh.
3.5" disk $79.95.
Transliteration Program Featuring IPA, SIL & 130 Languages.
Linguist's Software, Inc.

McPic!; McPic!, Vol. 2. Compatible Hardware: Apple Macintosh.
3.5" disk $49.95.
Clip Art Library Containing 150 Professionally Drawn Pictures. Includes Flags of the World, World Maps, Occupations, Special Effects & People Maker, Which Allows User to Create Cartoon People from a Variety of Heads, Eyes, Noses, Mouths & Accessories.
Magnum Software Corp.

McPic!: Push Button Art, Vol. I. Compatible Hardware: Apple Macintosh. Memory Required: 128k. General Requirements: Paint program.
3.5" disk $49.95 (ISBN 0-944310-00-1, Order no.: MPI).
150 Pictures Ready to Use "As Is" or to Revise, Combine, Clone. For Newsletters, Stationery, Flyers, Ads, Brochures. Comes with Special Hint Manual Showing How to Make Picture Variations.
Magnum Software Corp.

McPic!: Push Button Art, Vol. II. Compatible Hardware: Apple Macintosh. Memory Required: 128k. General Requirements: Paint program.
3.5" disk $49.95 (ISBN 0-944310-01-X, Order no.: MP2).
150 New Pictures Covering Categories Like World Maps, World Flags, the Continents. Also Includes the Special "People Maker" with Dozens of Heads, Eyes, Noses, Mouths, Hats, etc. Users Can Create Their Own Cartoon People. Comes with Hint Manual Showing Tricks & Tips for Making Picture Variations.
Magnum Software Corp.

MacPlantManager. Version: 2.0. Compatible Hardware: Apple Macintosh Plus. General Requirements: Hard disk; ImageWriter II or LaserWriter.
3.5" disk $495.00.
Account Management Program for Interiorscapers.
Diamante Software.

MacPoint Shareware Collection. Compatible Hardware: Apple Macintosh.
postpaid on disk $10.00.
Includes Graphics, Productivity Aids & a Font.
MacPoint Pubns.

MacPoisson. Version: 1.1. Jan. 1987. Compatible Hardware: Apple Macintosh. Memory Required: 512k.
Student Version $99.95.
Professional Version $495.00.
Formulates & Solves Poisson's Equation for Electrostatics, Ideal Fluid Flow, Steady-State Heat Conduction, Seepage, etc. Intended for the First-Time User of This Method. Provides a Visual Interface for the Formulation, Solution & Presentation of Results.
Cooke Pubns.

MacProlog. Version: 2.5. Jan. 1989. Compatible Hardware: Apple Macintosh. Memory Required: 1000k. Items Included: License, disk, documentation. Customer Support: Comprehensive customer support.
3.5" disk $595.00.
Includes Fast Incremental & Powerful Optimizing Compilers, a Declarative Graphics System & Flexible C & Pascal Interfaces. A High Lever Tool Box Access Is Included.
Quintus Computer Systems, Inc.

MacPromo. General Requirements: 20Mb hard disk.
Macintosh or higher (512K). MacPromo II $95.00.
MacPromo II $169.00.
Public Relations & Advertising Information System.
Abacus, Inc.

MacProspect. Compatible Hardware: Apple Macintosh. Memory Required: 512k. General Requirements: Hard disk.
3.5" disk $195.00.
Prospect & Client Tracking.
Microserve, Inc.

MacQC. Compatible Hardware: Apple Macintosh. Memory Required: 1000k.
3.5" disk $999.95.
Clinical Laboratory Quality Control Manager for Engineers.
Data Management Assocs. of New York, Inc.

MacQwerty. Version: 3.1. Compatible Hardware: Apple Macintosh. Items Included: Disk, manual, overlay. Customer Support: Free telephone technical support.
3.5" disk $45.00.
Dvorak & Custom Keyboard Reconfiguration with Overlays.
Nisus Software, Inc.

MacRacquetball. 1987. Compatible Hardware: Apple Macintosh. Memory Required: 1024k. General Requirements: 800k disk drive.
3.5" disk $59.95.
Simulation Which Provides Full 3-D Display of Court, Players, & Ball. With a Mouse, Users Can Control Player Position, Ball Placement, Ball Speed, & Shots. Features 1000 Frames of High Speed Digitized Animation. Allows Two People to Play the Same Game over APPLETALK or Modem.
Practical Computer Applications, Inc.

MacRacquetball. May 1987.
Mac DOS (1Mb). Macintosh Plus, SE. 3.5" disk $59.95 (Order no.: 9016).
Full-Perspective Detailed in 3-D Graphic Simulation Which Pits a Player Against the Computer, or Against Another Human over Modem, Appletalk, or Printer Cable. Program Accurately Replicates Effects of Bounce, Gravity & Speed. Full Control of Numerous Player Characteristics, Positioning, Aiming, Power & Virtually Every Aspect of the Real Game. High-Speed Digitized Graphics & Sounds All Recorded from Live Action.
XOR Corp.

MacRepertory. Version: 3.41. Compatible Hardware: Apple Macintosh Plus; IBM. Items Included: 4Mb database, Manual. Customer Support: Telephone.
$1760.00.
Integrated Medical Program for Homeopathic Practitioners That Allows a User to Collect & Analyze Dozens of Symptoms, Check the Built-In Materia Medica to Confirm & Evaluate the Most Likely Remedies & Then Save the Case for Research or to Share with a Colleague. In Its

Deductive Mode, the Program Analyzes the Symptoms As They Are Entered & Suggests Questions to Confirm the Likely Remedies.
Kent Homeopathic Assocs.

MACRO. Ralph F. Lewis & Michael S. Magee. 1989. *Items Included:* User's Manual; Instructor's Supplement for instructor's Version. *Customer Support:* Warranty 90 days.
   MS-DOS 2.0 or higher. IBM PC, XT, AT, PS/2 or compatible (256k). disk $4.95 (ISBN 1-879995-14-X). *Optimal configuration:* 256k RAM.
   MS-DOS 2.0 or higher. IBM PC, XT, AT, PS/2 or compatible (256k). disk $7.95 (ISBN 1-879995-15-8). *Optimal configuration:* 256k RAM.
   MS-DOS 3.0 or higher. IBM PC, XT, AT, PS/2 or compatible (256k). disk $99.00 (ISBN 1-879995-15-8). *Optimal configuration:* 256k RAM. *Networks supported:* All Networks.
   MS-DOS. IBM PC, XT, AT, PS/2 or compatible (256k). disk $199.00 (ISBN 1-879995-16-6). *Optimal configuration:* 256k. *Networks supported:* All networks.
   A Computerized Simulation of the U. S. Economy. Students Enter Changes They Wish to Make in Government Expenditures, Marginal Tax Rates, & the Money Supply. The Effects of These Changes on the Macroeconomic Aggregates & the Economy are Displayed. Variables Can Be Plotted Against Each Other & Phillips Curves Plotted. Instructor's Version Provides for Utilities & Collection of Student Data for Monitoring Purposes & Reports. Ideal for Extra Credit.
Economics Research, Inc.

Macro Assembler. *Compatible Hardware:* Atari XL/XE. *Memory Required:* 32k.
   disk $24.95 (Order no.: CX8121).
Atari Corp.

Macro Library. *Version:* 1.2. Mar. 1993. *Items Included:* Instructions on disk. *Customer Support:* 90 days unlimited warranty.
   MS-DOS, Windows 3.1. IBM or compatibles (620k). disk $24.95 plus $3.50 S&H. *Addl. software required:* Lotus 1-2-3, Release for Windows 4.0 or higher. *Optimal configuration:* 620k RAM, Lotus 2, 3 or higher.
   A Library of 17 LOTUS Macros to Simplify Work on Most Spreadsheets.
Compiled Systems.

Macro Manager: For WordPerfect 5.0, 5.1. *Version:* 2.0. David G. Cohen. Sep. 1991. *Items Included:* Instructions. *Customer Support:* Free phone.
   PC-DOS, MS-DOS. IBM PC or compatible (640k). disk $19.95 (ISBN 0-8283-1985-5). *Addl. software required:* WordPerfect Release 5.0 or 5.1. *Optimal configuration:* WordPerfect 5.1 with 640k RAM, hard disk.
   Allows User of WordPerfect to Display Macros & Their Descriptions for Immediate Execution, or, to Copy, Rename, Delete, Point or Browse Through Contents of Any Macro. Displays Macro Names & Descriptions One Item Per Line, Selection Using a Scrollable Highlight Bar.
Popular Technology.

Macro*World Forecaster. *Compatible Hardware:* IBM PC & compatibles, PS/2. *Memory Required:* 512k. *General Requirements:* VGA or EGA card, dot-matrix or laser printer. *Items Included:* User manual. *Customer Support:* Telephone Support, On-Screen Help Menus.
   $699.95.
   monthly updates $29.00 ea., with 6 mos. update service.
   Includes a Database of Economic Indicators: Housing Starts, Gross National Product, Stock Prices, & Inflation, Interest, Exchange, & Unemployment Rates for the US, Japan, Germany, Canada & UK. Automatic Statistical-Analysis Techniques Allow User to Forecast Database Information, & Menu Selection Allows User to Load & Save Print Files from All Versions of LOTUS 1-2-3 & SYMPHONY.
Macro World Research Corp.

Macro*World Investor. *Items Included:* User manual, system & database diskettes. *Customer Support:* User manual, on-screen help, telephone support.
   MS-DOS (512k). IBM & compatibles. $899.95 for system, database, & 6 months of update service. *Nonstandard peripherals required:* EGA or VGA recommended.
   monthly updates $39.00 ea.
   Combines Investment Analysis & Economic Forecasting. Results Interpreted by System & Summarized into Reports. Makes Forecasts, Projects Rates of Return, Assesses Degree of Risk & Generates Buy/Sell Signals & Optimal Asset Allocation.
Macro World Research Corp.

MacroCircuits. *Customer Support:* 800-929-8117 (customer service).
   MS-DOS. Macintosh. disk $99.99 (ISBN 0-87007-722-8).
   Transforms a Macintosh into a Complete Engineering Workstation for Digital Circuit Design, Capable of Producing a Professional Quality Schematic & Providing Complete Fault & Logic Simulation of Design. Provides Nine Primitive Logic Functions That Can Be Selected from a Palette on the Screen. The Version for a 512K Macintosh Incorporates a Macro Library Capability that Allows a Designer to Define Custom or Standard Packages to Use Repetitively As New Primitive Functions.
SourceView Software International.

Macrolock. John B. Rose. Jan. 1986. *Compatible Hardware:* Data General. *Operating System(s) Required:* AOS, AOS/VS.
   l. $5000.00, lease avail.
   Prevents Unauthorized Coping & Use of Proprietary Software Programs. Used by Software Developers & Vendors Dealing with Data General Equipment.
Infodex, Inc.

Macromate. *Compatible Hardware:* Apple IIgs. *Memory Required:* 768k.
   3.5" disk $49.95 (ISBN 0-927796-29-5, Order no.: GRW-011).
   Features a Single Command Key That Can Be Set up to Automatically Run User's Word Processor, Load an Existing Document, & Type Letterhead. Defined by RECORD Mode or built-in MacroMate Editor. Also Features Auto-Macro Which Controls Computer During Boot Process & Performs All the Keypresses.
Roger Wagner Publishing, Inc.

MacroMedia Director. *Version:* MAC & Windows 4.0. *Customer Support:* First 90 days free. Priority access support available, phone, fax & online support.
   MAC w/680000 processor or higher. 3.5" disk $1195.00.
   486/33 or higher IBM-compatible computer processor. disk $1195.00.
   Powerful Authoring Tool for Multimedia Production Director Is Targeted at Design, Graphics, Animation & Video Professionals Who Need Precise Control over Their Interactive Productions.
Macromedia, Inc.

MacroModel. *Version:* 1.5. *Items Included:* Manuals. *Customer Support:* First 90 days free phone support for registered users; free online & fax support for registered users; contact Macromedia for Priority Access support information.
   System 6.0.7 or higher. Macintosh (8Mb). 3.5" disk $895.00. *Nonstandard peripherals required:* Math Co-Processor. *Optimal configuration:* MAC w/68030 Processor or higher, hard disk w/6Mb free disk space, System 6.0.7 or higher w/32-bit Quick Draw 8Mb RAM min.
   Windows 3.1. 486/33 Processor (IBM PC & compatibles) (8Mb). disk $895.00. *Nonstandard peripherals required:* 8 or 24 bit Video Math Co-Processor. *Optimal configuration:* 486/33 Processor or higher w/8- or 24-bit Video, 8Mb RAM min & Windows 3.1 w/6Mb free disk space.
   MacroModel's Spline-Based Tools Allow the Creation of 3D Models from 2D Reference Objects with a Click of the Mouse. Its Powerful Features & Intuitive Interface Simplify the Most Complex Model-Making with Familiar Tools That Deliver the High Performance Users Need.
Macromedia, Inc.

MacroModem. *Compatible Hardware:* Commodore Amiga.
   3.5" disk $69.95.
   Telecommunications with Macros.
Kent Engineering & Design.

MacroWorks. *Version:* 2.51. Randy Brandt. May 1986. *Compatible Hardware:* Apple IIe, IIc, IIgs. *Operating System(s) Required:* ProDOS. *Language(s):* Machine, BASIC. *Memory Required:* Apple IIe 128k. *General Requirements:* AppleWorks version 1.3 or earlier.
   $34.95.
   Adds a Number of New Features to the AppleWorks Word Processor. Enhancements Include Macro Capability, Mouse Support, the Ability to Replace the Original AppleWorks Help Screens with User-Created Messages. Compatible with Both the Applied Engineering & Checkmate Desktop Expanders. Not Copy Protected.
Beagle Brothers.

MacScan. *Version:* 1.7. Dec. 1989. *Items Included:* Comprehensive user's manual. *Customer Support:* Free telephone technical support for 90 days. 90 day limited warranty.
   6.0.2 or higher, System 7 supported. Macintosh (1Mb). 3.5" disk $199.00 (Order no.: M 2). *Networks supported:* Macintosh based networks.
   Strong Graphic Scanner Interface Software Which Scans, Edits, Prints & Saves Images in the Greatest Variety of Formats Used in Macintosh Applications. Offers Support for Black & White, Greyscale & Color Scanning (Depending on Hardware). Includes Complete Set of Editing Tools. OCR Software Friendly.
Prism Enterprises, Inc.

MacScripture (KJV). *Version:* 1.4. *Compatible Hardware:* Apple Macintosh. *General Requirements:* Hard disk or external disk drive; MacWrite, Microsoft Word or compatible. *Items Included:* Diskette(s) & manual. *Customer Support:* Complete telephone support, 90-day warranty.
   $29.95 entire Bible (KJV) (Order no.: 48842-545).
   $12.95 MacScripture I (New: KJV) (Order no.: 48842-550).
   $22.95 MacScripture II (Old: KJV) (Order no.: 48842-555).
   demo disk $5.00.
   Old & New Testament: KJV.
Medina Software, Inc.

MacScuba. *Compatible Hardware:* Apple Macintosh Plus, Macintosh SE, Macintosh II, Macintosh IIx, Macintosh SE/30. *General Requirements:* Two 800k floppy disk drives or hard disk.
3.5" disk $49.95.
Game, but Also a Scuba Diving Simulation Exercise That Incorporates Multilevel Decompression, Surface Time Intervals, & No-Compression Dives Using the U.S. Navy Dive Tables as Its Guide. The Program's Marine Database Contains Information About All Creatures Great & Small That You Encounter in the Ocean Wilderness. The Object of the Game is to Collect the Most Treasure, but Along the Way You'll Deal with How to Obtain Neutral Buoyancy with a Bouyancy Compensation Device & How to Use Tables to Do Multilevel No-Decompression Dives & Repetitive Decompression Dives. You'll Also Learn About Marine Plant & Animal Life While You're Down There.
Paradise Software Corp.

MacSection. *Compatible Hardware:* Apple Macintosh. *Memory Required:* 512k. *General Requirements:* 800k disk drive; ImageWriter or LaserWriter.
3.5" disk $399.00.
Strip-Log, Cross-Section & Fence Diagram Plotting Program.
RockWare, Inc.

MacSemitic Coptic. *Version:* 4.3. Dec. 1985. *Items Included:* User's manual, keyboard layout chart. *Customer Support:* Free telephone support; defective disks replaced free.
Macintosh. Macintosh (1Mb). 3.5" disk $79.95. *Addl. software required:* Any word processor. *Optimal configuration:* 4Mb RAM, hard drive.
20 English System Fonts. Automatic Non-Deleting Backspacing of Accents & Diacritical Marks Placeable over or under Any Letter & in Any Combination. Easy-to-Use Layout Corresponds As Closely As Possible to the English Keyboard. Select from the Font Menu of MACWRITE, MICROSOFT WORD, etc. Includes a Mini-Space Bar, Laminated Keyboard Layout Sheets, & User's Manual. Style Options: Plain, Bold, Italic, Underline, Outline, Shadow, Superscript, Subscript & Combinations. Includes Coptic, Syriac, Ethiopic, Ugaritic, Nestorian, Nag Hammadi, Sabean, Old Linear Phoenician, As Well As Several Proto-Semitic Scripts.
Linguist's Software, Inc.

MacServe. *Version:* 2.4. *Compatible Hardware:* Apple Macintosh. *Memory Required:* 512k.
$250.00 per server with no limit on user nodes.
File Sharing System Designed for Small APPLETALK Networks. Runs in the Background, Eliminating the Necessity for Dedicated Macintoshes. Users Can Add Macintoshes, PCs, Hard Disks, Servers, Printers, Modems, & E-Mail, As Needed. Features "Bulletproof" Automatic Crash Recovery to Prevent Loss of Data.
Infosphere.

MacShammes. *Compatible Hardware:* Apple Macintosh.
3.5" disk $1495.00.
Complete Synagogue Management System with Membership & Yahrtzeit Modules.
Davka Corp.

MacSimplex. *Compatible Hardware:* Apple Macintosh.
3.5" disk $12.00.
Tool for Linear Programming & Linear Algebra.
Kinko's.

MacSki. *Version:* 1.01. Oct. 1990. *Memory Required:* Black & White Monitor 1000k; Color Monitor 2000k.
Apple Macintosh. 3.5" disk $69.95 (ISBN 0-945749-28-7, Order no.: 501).
Choose Skis, Course & Course Conditions, up to 256 Different Configurations in This Action Game.
XOR Corp.

MacSLIP. Hydepark Software. May 1992. *Items Included:* Manual, NCSA Telnet. *Customer Support:* 30 day limited warranty, support free via telephone, FAX, & Internet E:mail.
System 6.0.7 or 7. Macintosh (4Mb). 3.5" disk $49.95 (Order no.: AA010). *Addl. software required:* MacTCP 1.1 or higher. *Networks supported:* All TCP/IP networks which support SLIP.
Communications Utility That Allows User to Extend the Network Connectivity of a Macintosh Computer to Remote Sites. Allows Many Simultaneous IP Connections to Run over a Single Serial Connection.
TriSoft.

MacSpeech Lab I. *Version:* 2.0. *Items Included:* Manuals, MacAdios 411 digitizer, microphone, speaker, record & play amplifiers, antialiasing filters, cables & documentation. *Customer Support:* Free technical support, upgrades.
Macintosh Plus, SE, SE 30. disk $3550.00 (Order no.: GWL-MSL-1).
Provides Waveform Analysis Used Extensively for Sound Research & Testing. System Records Waveforms (Words & Phrases When Used with Speech) Over Time & Stores Them in Memory, Where They Can Be Viewed, Analyzed, Edited, Printed & Played Back.
GW Instruments, Inc.

MacSpeech Lab II. *Version:* 1.4. *Items Included:* Manuals, MacAdios II Data Acquisition Board & Antialiasing Filter Daughterboard, microphone, speaker, record & play amplifiers, cables, documentation. *Customer Support:* Free technical support, upgrades.
Macintosh II, IIx, IIcx. disk $4990.00 (Order no.: GWL-MSL-1).
Speech/Sound Analysis System for Waveform Acquisition & Analysis. Used Extensively for Sound Research & Testing. System Records Waveforms (Words & Phrases When Used With Speech) over Time & Stores Them in Memory. They Then Can Be Viewed, Analyzed, Edited, Printed & Played Back.
GW Instruments, Inc.

MacSQZ! *Compatible Hardware:* Apple Macintosh. *General Requirements:* Microsoft Excel.
3.5" disk $79.95.
Combination Desk Accessory & Application Which Works with Microsoft EXCEL. Automatically Shrinks the Size of Spreadsheets by up to 95% to Provide Additional Disk Space. Also Provides Backup & File-Level Password Protection for EXCEL. Shows a History of Spreadsheet Changes & Shows Which Spreadsheets Are Linked Together.
Symantec Corp.

MacSRMS. *Compatible Hardware:* Apple Macintosh. *Memory Required:* 512k.
Single user version. 3.5" disk $195.00.
Three-user version. 3.5" disk $495.00.
Demo. 3.5" disk $5.00.
Revision Management; Source Code Control. It Is a Full-Featured Version Control System (Also Known As Source Code Control) That Can Be Used by Programmers & System Developers to Effectively Control the Proliferation of the Many Versions of Source Associated with Programming Projects.
Quilt Computing.

MCSS-Automated Search Software Containing Annually Updated CPT, ICD-9 & HCDC Codes. *Items Included:* Full manual. No other products required. *Customer Support:* Free telephone support - no time limit. 30 day warranty.
MS-DOS 3.2 or higher. IBM & compatibles (512k). disk $299.95. *Optimal configuration:* IBM, MS-DOS 3.2 or higher, 5Mb of hard disk space.
MCSS Simplifies the Coding of Procedures & Diagnoses So That Your Office Personnel Can Quickly & Easily Locate the Most Current, Specified Code. This Can Reduce the Search Time by As Much as 90%. Office Expenses Are Thereby Reduced by Improved Efficiency & by the Elimination of Coding Errors. You May Add MCSS to Your Current Software, or Use It As a Stand-Alone Application. MCSS Does More Than Just Find the Code Fast. It Extracts All CPT or ICD-9 Codes That Match Your Search Criteria.
Dynacomp, Inc.

MacStar II. *Compatible Hardware:* Apple Macintosh. *General Requirements:* Converter cable.
3.5" disk $99.95.
Star Micronics Printer Driver.
Star Micronics America, Inc.

MacStereo (R-S). *Compatible Hardware:* Apple Macintosh.
3.5" disk $17.00.
Illustrates the Cahn-Ingold-Prelog Stereochemical Designation System.
Kinko's.

MacStronomy. *Version:* 2.0. Jul. 1992. *Compatible Hardware:* Apple Macintosh. *Memory Required:* 2000k. *Items Included:* Manual with "Introduction to Astronomy". *Customer Support:* Telephone.
3.5" disk $60.00.
large database $25.00.
Displays Full-Screen Color Maps of the Stars & Planets in the Sky for Any Date, Time, Location, & Field of View. Planets Are Displayed As They Actually Appear Through a Telescope. Fly to Other Planets. Watch Eclipses of Moon & Sun. Time-Lapse Shows Movement of Solar System & Stars. Basic Control Window Makes Controlling MacStronomy Easy, While Expert Control Window Gives Precise Control for Advanced Users. Database Contains over 10,000 Objects Including All Stars to Magnitude 6.5. User Can Add Stars & Planets to Database. Optional Large Database Containing Stars to Magnitude 8.0 Is Available.
Etlon Software.

MacSurgery, Vols. 1 & 2. *Compatible Hardware:* Apple Macintosh Plus. *General Requirements:* Hard disk, HyperCard; 2Mb RAM recommended.
3.5" disk $95.00.
Self-Educational Interactive Program in General Surgery That Presents Users with Commonly Encountered Clinical Situations & Provides Answers & References. Format Is Multiple-Choice Questions & Answers.
MacMedic Pubns., Inc.

MacSurgery: Laparoscopic Cholecystectomy. Robert Davis. Apr. 1993. *Items Included:* User manual. *Customer Support:* Replacement or any defective CD-ROM.
Macintosh II or higher (5Mb). CD-ROM disk $159.00. *Nonstandard peripherals required:* Hard disk. *Addl. software required:* Quicktime 1.5 or higher, System 7.0 or higher, Hypercard 2.0 or higher. *Networks supported:* No.
This Program Was Designed to Bring This Surgical Procedure from the Operating Room into the Office. It Contains Anatomy, Physiology,

TITLE INDEX

Macsyma. Version: 417. Compatible Hardware: PC-DOS, 9 UNIX Workstations. Operating System(s) Required: DOS, UNIX, VMS. Items Included: Software, reference manual, user's guide, quick reference card. Customer Support: Service contracts available, 1 year term.
Starts at $349.00 Contact publisher.
Targeted at Those Working with Quantitative Models in Scientific or Engineering Disciplines. Its Capabilities for Symbolic Computation Can Be Applied in: Algebra - to Manipulate Large Expressions, Expand, Simplify & Factor Expressions, Handle Matrices & Arrays, & Solve Systems of Equations; or in Calculus - to Differentiate, Perform Definite & Indefinite Integration, Take Limits, Expand Functions in Taylor or Laurent Series, Solve Differential Equations, & Compute Laplace Transforms. Has the Capability to Generate FORTRAN Coding of Expressions for Numerical Analysis in Its Own (MACSYMA) Language. Can Plot in 2 or 3 Dimensions & Interface to Standard Mathematical Text Composers. Can Be Used in Applications Such As Structural Engineering, Fluid Mechanics, Acoustics, CAD, Electronic & VLSI Physics, Atomic Scattering Cross Sections, Control Theory, Maximum Likelihood Estimation, Genetic Studies, etc.
Macsyma, Inc.

MacTAE. 1988. Compatible Hardware: Apple Macintosh, DEC VAX/VMS. Memory Required: 512k.
$5000.00.
Consists of Two Communications Programs that Allow a Macintosh to Function as a VAX Front-End Workstation. Based on MacWorkStation, the Programs Enable Users to Access Data & Execute Programs on the VAX Using the Standard Macintosh Interface. Supports MultiFinder, Allowing Users to Transfer Data from VAX Applications into Macintosh Programs. The Program also Supports Desk Accessories. A Connection Command Language (CCL) Provides a Scripting Capability for Automatically Logging onto the VAX; Extended Code Segments (ECS) Enables Users to Integrate Programs in Custom Configurations.
Appaloosa Systems.

MacTamil. Version: 1.4. Jan. 1989. Items Included: User's manual, keyboard layout chart. Customer Support: Free telephone support; defective disks replaced free.
Any system. Macintosh (1Mb). 3.5" disk $79.95. Addl. software required: Any word processor. Optimal configuration: 4Mb RAM, hard drive.
12- & 24-Point Bit Map & Screen Sizes, High Quality Printing. Logical, Easy-to-Use Layout Based on the Standard English Typewriter. Not Copy Protected. User's Manual & Keyboard Layout Chart. Selected Directly from the Font Menu to Shift Instantly from English to Tamil in MACWRITE, MICROSOFT WORD & All Other Macintosh Word Processing Software. Full Style Option: Plain, Bold, Italic, Underline, Outline, Shadow, Superscript, Subscript & All Combinations.
Linguist's Software, Inc.

MacTides. Version: 3.0. General Requirements: ImageWriter or LaserWriter. Items Included: 3 spiral bound manuals, tables for tidal stations. Customer Support: 90 day unlimited warranty.
Help line: 1-800-999-5221.
Macintosh System 4.0 & Finder 5.4 or higher. Macintosh 512KE, Plus, SE, II, SE 30. 3.5" disk $99.00.
Computer Program That Produces Plots & Tables of Tide Height & Tidal Current. Multi-day Multi-station Output, Month Plots & Day Plots, 10,000 Stations in Continental U.S., Alaska, Hawaii & Canada Divided into 12 Regions.
Nautasoft, Inc.

MacToolkit. Compatible Hardware: Apple Macintosh. General Requirements: Hard disk; ImageWriter, LaserWriter.
Schedule. 3.5" disk $750.00.
Budget. 3.5" disk $695.00.
Entire package. 3.5" disk $1400.00.
Scheduling & Budgeting for Film & Television Production.
Max 3, Inc.

Mactools. Version: 2.0. Compatible Hardware: Apple Macintosh Plus, SE II. Items Included: Documentation, registration card, 3.5" diskettes. Customer Support: Toll-call telephone technical support; BBS; 60 day warranty.
3.5" disk $149.00.
Automatic & Complete Protection Which Offers Essential Data Recovery Utilities (MS Excel & Word File Repair, Deleted File Tracking, Disk Analysis & Optimization); Comprehensive Virus Protection Including Detection, Removal & Prevention; & Hard Disk Backup Including Tape Support & Scheduling Capabilities. System 7 Compatible.
Central Point Software, Inc.

MacTrac Fund Raising Software. Version: 3.0. Compatible Hardware: Any Macintosh with 2Mb or more of RAM. General Requirements: Hard disk & System 6.0.4 or higher. Items Included: Two diskettes with MacTrac & runtime Foxbase, user manual. Customer Support: Comes with 90 days of unlimited phone support, continued telephone support may be purchased for $250.00 per year, which includes all upgrades at cost. 3.5" disk $995.00.
The Premium Fund-Raising Program for Small to Mid-Sized Non-Profit Organizations. Multi-User Version Is Optional.
Technology Resource Assistance Ctr.

Mactran Plus. Version: 3.0. Compatible Hardware: Apple Macintosh. Memory Required: 512k.
3.5" disk $399.00.
Upgrade from Version 2.0. 3.5" disk $99.00.
Integrated FORTRAN 77 Development System.
DCM Data Products.

MacTree Plus. Compatible Hardware: Apple Macintosh 512KE. Memory Required: 512k.
3.5" disk $69.95.
Provides a Hard Disk Management System.
GO Technologies.

MacTunes. Version: 2.0. May 1991. Items Included: HyperCard 2.0 Runtime, User's Guide. Customer Support: Thirty days free telephone support, 9am-5pm mountain standard time, Monday-Friday.
Macintosh OS 6.0.5 or higher. MAC Plus (1Mb). $34.95; $29.95 for educators; lab pack $195.00 (Order no.: 602-951-3812). Nonstandard peripherals required: Hard Disk. Optimal configuration: MAC 12Mb RAM Hard disk, printer.
Allows Anyone to Write & Play Back Music Using 13 Fun "Instruments", Such As a Dog, & Bike Horn. Lyrics Are Displayed on the Screen. Includes 100 Complete Songs, an On-Line Music Tutorial, & Offers a "Toddler Mode" That Allows Young Children to Play Songs Without Modifying Them.
First Wave.

MacTut/ProGlyph: Wet Paint Volume 19.20. Version: 2.0.
Macintosh. 3.5" disk $89.95.
Ancient Egyptian Hieroglyphic Fonts & Artwork.
Dubl-Click Software.

Mactype. Customer Support: Telephone support (512) 854-8794.
Macintosh (128k). 3.5" disk $59.95.
A Touch Typing Tutorial Which Can Teach Either the DVORAK or Standard Keyboard. Includes a Utility to Change the MAC Keyboard to DVORAK.
Palsoft.

MacVision Color Video Digitizer with MacVision Image Processing Software 4.1. Version: 4.1. 1991. Items Included: 2 manuals, 3 disks (Program, Sample Scans, & plug-in modules for MacVision Image Processing Software 4.1, Digital Darkroom 2.0, & Photoshop 1.0.7). Customer Support: 90 day warranty; repair service, contact publisher for pricing.
6.0.4 or higher. Macintosh (4Mb). 3.5" disk $699.00. Addl. software required: 32-bit color QuickDraw, Color QuickDraw in ROM. Optimal configuration: Add 2Mb for use with System 7. Hard drive recommended.
Inexpensive Solutions for Image Capture & Enhancement on the Macintosh Plus - QUADRA 950. This Unique SCSI Device Captures Images in 24-Bit Color or Grayscale from a Variety of Video Sources. Images Can Be Edited, Merged with Text, or Enhanced to Produce High Quality Images.
Koala Acquisitions, Inc.

MacVision Image Processing Software. Version: 4.1. 1992. Items Included: 1 manual, 2 disks including Program, Sample Scans. Customer Support: 90 day warranty.
6.0.4 or higher. Macintosh (2Mb). 3.5" disk $99.00. Nonstandard peripherals required: MacVision Color Video Digitizer or MacVision Video Digitizer (Serial). Addl. software required: For color images 32-bit Color QuickDraw, Color QuickDraw in ROM. Optimal configuration: Recommended 4Mb, add 2Mb for use with System 7. Hard drive recommended.
An Inexpensive & Easy to Use Image Enhancement Application. Existing Images, or New Images Captured by MacVision Video Digitizers, Can Be Edited, Merged with Text, Enhanced or Manipulated to Produce High Quality Images. Supports RGB, Grayscale & Halftone Images.
Koala Acquisitions, Inc.

MacVision Video Digitizer with MacVision Image Processing Software 4.1. Version: 4.1. 1984. Compatible Hardware: Macintosh. Items Included: 2 manuals, 3 disks (Program Sample Scans & plug-in modules for MacVision Image Processing software 4.1, Digital Darkroom 2.0 & Photoshop 1.0.7). Customer Support: 90 day warranty; repair service, contact publisher for pricing.
6.0.4 or higher. Macintosh (2Mb). 3.5" disk $299.00.
Allows User to Enter a Digitized, Photographic Image of Any Picture or Object. After Image Has Been Entered It Becomes Very Simple to Modify & Manipulate.
Koala Acquisitions, Inc.

MacVoice. Compatible Hardware: Apple Macintosh.
3.5" disk $25.50.
Assists Music Theory Students in Writing Four-Part Music.
Kinko's.

Technique, Indications, Contraindications, & Instrumentation. Many Videoclips Are Available to Illustrate the Text & Can Be Shown Frame by Frame. It May Be Regarded As a "Lap Chole" Course That One Can Use at One's Own Leisure.
MacMedia Pubns., Inc.

MacWrite Pro. *Version:* 1.5. 1996.
System 6 (2.5 mb for System 7) System 6.05 or higher, System 7 or System 7 Pro required to use PowerTalk, QuickTime & Applescript features. Apple Macintosh Classic II/ SE/30, LC Powerbook, Centris, Performa or Quadra family of computers. 3.5" disk $249.00. *Nonstandard peripherals required:* Hard disk required.
MacWrite Pro 1.5 is the Macintosh word processor for creating documents with impact. MacWrite Pro 1.5 offers complete support for System 7 Pro operating system from Apple Computer Inc. that includes PowerTalk, AppleScript & QuickTime Video.
Claris Corporation.

MacYACC. *Version:* 6.0. *Compatible Hardware:* Apple Macintosh. *Memory Required:* 512k. *General Requirements:* MPW.
3.5" disk $495.00.
Automatically Generates C Source Code for Building Assemblers, Compilers, Calculators, Typesetting Languages Translators, Pattern Analyzers.
Abraxas Software, Inc.

Mac320. *Version:* 1.05. *Compatible Hardware:* Apple Macintosh. *Memory Required:* 512k. *Items Included:* Free Networking Software includes COMMTOOL BOX & TOOLS, MACTCP & TSSNET. *Customer Support:* 90-day unlimited technical support.
3.5" disk $149.00.
White Pine Software, Inc.

Mac330. *Version:* 1.0.5. *Compatible Hardware:* Apple Macintosh. *Items Included:* Free Networking Software includes COMMTOOL BOX & TOOLS, MACTCP & TSSNET. *Customer Support:* 90-day unlimited technical support.
$249.00.
upgrade $50.00.
VT330 Series Terminal Emulator.
White Pine Software, Inc.

Mac340. *Version:* 1.0.5. *Compatible Hardware:* Apple Macintosh. *Memory Required:* 512k. *Items Included:* Free Networking Software includes COMMTOOL BOX & TOOLS, MACTCP & TSSNET. *Customer Support:* 90-day unlimited technical support.
3.5" disk $349.00.
Terminal Emulation.
White Pine Software, Inc.

Mad Mines. *Compatible Hardware:* TRS-80.
disk $24.95 (ISBN 0-915149-15-X).
cassette $19.95 (ISBN 0-915149-10-9).
Destroy the Mad Mines Being Deployed by the Enemy in the Rapidly Diminishing Space Around Your Planet.
Blue Cat.

Mad Mines. *Compatible Hardware:* TRS-80 Model I, Model III. *Memory Required:* 16k.
contact publisher for price.
Funsoft, Inc.

The Madness of Roland. Jan. 1993. *Items Included:* Product registration card. *Customer Support:* (206) 451-7751.
System 6.07 or higher. Macintosh (4Mb). CD-ROM disk SRP $49.95 (ISBN 1-885835-00-0). *Nonstandard peripherals required:* CD-ROM drive. *Addl. software required:* QuickTime 1.5 or higher (included).
The World's First Interactive Multimedia Novel. The Original Story, Written by Greg Roach, Is Based on the Legend of the Paladin Roland, a Knight in the Service of Charlemagne. This Unique Story Is Told from Several Different Points of View, Which the Reader Can Move among at Will.
Hyperbole Studios.

MAG-Base1. MAG Software, Inc. *Operating System(s) Required:* MS-DOS, CP/M-86, Concurrent CP/M-86. *Memory Required:* 128k. *General Requirements:* Printer.
$295.00.
Personal Filing System.
Texas Instruments, Personal Productivit.

MAG/Base2. MAG Software, Inc. *Operating System(s) Required:* MS-DOS, CP/M-86, Concurrent CP/M-86. *Memory Required:* 128k. *General Requirements:* Printer.
$495.00.
Produces Reports & Forms for Business Applications.
Texas Instruments, Personal Productivit.

MAG/Base3. MAG Software, Inc. *Operating System(s) Required:* MS-DOS, CP/M-86, Concurrent CP/M-86. *Memory Required:* 128k. *General Requirements:* Printer.
$795.00.
Application Development System. MAG/base2 Plus Menu Definition, Password Protection, Screen Management Functions, Multi-Keyed File Management, etc.
Texas Instruments, Personal Productivit.

Magazine Article Filer. *Version:* 30.2. 1993. *Items Included:* Complete illustrated instructions. *Customer Support:* 1 year free replacement of damaged disks, free unlimited telephone customer support.
MS-DOS. IBM PC, PC XT, PC AT, PS/2 & compatibles (640k). disk $189.00 (ISBN 1-55812-095-5). *Addl. software required:* None.
$399.00 Network version.
$199.00 Windows version.
$419.00 Windows Network version.
No More Clipping Articles, Stuffing Them into a File Folder & Then Never Being Able to Find What You Want When You Want It. Give Each Article a Consecutive ID # & Place It in a File Folder. Enter Pertinent Information into the Computer. Search by the Following Fields: Title, Author, Magazine, Date, Subject (up to Ten), Blank User Field # 1 or # 2 (Enter Anything You Want), Comments (2 Lines). Another Program Produced at the Request of Librarians & Others.
Right On Programs.

Magellan. *Version:* 1.1.2. *Compatible Hardware:* Commodore Amiga. *Items Included:* 160 page manual & 24 page VI.I Addenda, Program disk & sample knowledge base disk.
3.5" disk $69.00.
Expert System Application Development Tool.
Emerald Intelligence.

Magellan. *Memory Required:* 512k.
PC-DOS 2.1 or higher (512k). IBM PC or compatible. disk $179.00.
Personal Information Manager/Disk Manager That Allows User To Find, View, & Use Any Information on PC. Every-Word Index Lets User Find Any Phrase in Less Than Three Seconds, See the Information Instantly Through Read-Only Viewers, Then Run Any Application Linked To the Information.
Lotus Development Corp.

Magellan Interface Toolkit. *Version:* 1.1. Jul. 1989. *Items Included:* 48 pp document, sample knowledgebases.
Amiga-DOS (1Mb). Commodore Amiga. $45.00, to registered users of Magellan VI.I. *Addl. software required:* Magellan VI.I.
$99.00, packaged with Magellan VI.I.
Provides Connections Between Magellan VI.I & Other Software & Hardware Utilities. The Five Interfaces Included Are: an Interface to Superbase Databases, Lotus 1-2-3 Format Spreadsheets, the Serial Port, ASCII Text & Macros for the AREXX Communications Language.
Emerald Intelligence.

Magic - Property Management Software. *Items Included:* Manuals. *Customer Support:* Software & hardware maintenance contracts available.
MS-DOS, Turbo-DOS, CP/M (256k). IBM & compatibles. Call for info. *Optimal configuration:* 640k RAM, DOS 3.3 or higher, IBM compatible, laser printer (HPLJT). *Networks supported:* Novell.
Maintains Complete, Detailed Records about All the Owners, Properties, Units, Tenants & Vendors. It Has Tenant Accounting, Vendor Accounting, Complete Financial Reporting, Checkbook Management, & a Database; Can Handle an Unlimited Number of Units.
Applied Business Software, Inc.

The Magic Applehouse. Nov. 1995. *Items Included:* School version contains CD & teacher's resource guide. Consumer version contains CD & parent's guide. *Customer Support:* 1-800-824-5179 product information; 1-800-543-0453 technical support.
Windows 3.1 or higher, DOS 3.3 or higher. 486 SX 25MHz (4Mb). CD-ROM disk $49.95 (ISBN 0-538-64674-8). *Nonstandard peripherals required:* Double speed CD-ROM, VGA 640x480, sound blaster or 100% compatible sound card.
System 7.0.1 or higher. Power Mac compatible, 68040 or higher (4Mb). *Nonstandard peripherals required:* Double speed CD-ROM, 13" monitor, 256 colors.
A Business & Computer Awareness Multimedia Program Aimed at Children Ages 5 to 10. Abigail Appleseed Runs a Very Successful Business with the Help of Her Computer. Abigail Teaches Children Basic Computer Skills While Helping Abigail Run Her business.
South-Western Publishing Co.

The Magic Death: MAC Jewel Case. Shannon Gilligan. Sep. 1993. *Items Included:* Registration card. *Customer Support:* Creative Multimedia Corporation warrants the CD-ROM disc & diskettes to be free from defects in materials & workmanship under normal use & service for a period of 90 days from date of purchase. Creative Multimedia Corporation offers Technical Support to customers as needed.
System Software 6.0.7 or higher, 8-bit color & color monitor, CD-Rom drive with 150k/sec transfer rate, 380 ms or less access rate & extension. Macintosh Plus or higher (3.5Mb). CD-ROM disk $49.99 (ISBN 1-880428-08-3, Order no.: 10353). *Optimal configuration:* Hard drive recommended.
The Second Multimedia Murder in the Award-Winning Virtual Murder Series. Multiple Endings Add to the Intrigue As You Play Detective in Solving the Murder of a Brilliant Doctoral Candidate in Anthropology Who Has Been Killed in a Bizarre Ritualistic Fashion.
Creative Multimedia Corp.

The Magic Death: MPC Jewel Case. Shannon Gilligan. *Items Included:* Registration card. *Customer Support:* Creative Multimedia Corporation warrants the CD-ROM disc & diskettes to be free from defects in materials & workmanship under normal use & service for a period of 90 days from date of purchase. Creative Multimedia Corporation offers Technical Support to customers as needed.
MS-DOS 3.1 or higher, MS-CDEX 2.0 or higher. 386SX or higher (4Mb). CD-ROM disk $49.99 (ISBN 1-880428-07-5, Order no.: 10360). *Nonstandard peripherals required:* Sound Blaster or Sound Blaster compatible board. CD-

TITLE INDEX

ROM drive with 150k/sec transfer rate, 380ms or less access rate. *Addl. software required:* Microsoft Windows 3.1. *Optimal configuration:* SuperVGA with 512k, video memory capable of 640x480x256 colors with Windows driver supported. *Networks supported:* All.
The Second Multimedia Murder in the Award-Winning Virtual Murder Series. Multiple Endings Add to the Intrigue As You Play Detective in Solving the Murder of a Brilliant Doctoral Candidate in Anthropology Who Has Been Killed in a Bizarre Ritualistic Fashion.
Creative Multimedia Corp.

Magic Gradebook. *Version:* DOS 2.1. Darice Angwin. 1991. *Items Included:* 1 manual. *Customer Support:* Self instruction.
DOS 2.1. IBM & compatibles (384k). disk $89.95. *Optimal configuration:* 384 RAM, DOS 2.1 or higher, hard drive 10Mb Plus.
A Computerized Database for Keeping Student Grades & Printing Records.
Info-Tec, Inc.

Magic Johnson's Basketball. *Customer Support:* 90 day warranty.
MS-DOS 2.1 or higher. IBM (512K). disk $14.99. *Nonstandard peripherals required:* CGA, EGA, Tandy, MCGA or VGA required.
Amiga (512K). 3.5" disk $49.99.
Commodore 64 (64K). disk $14.99.
Arcade Action Brings the Realism of the Big Time Game Home to You in This Direct Translation of the Popular Coin-Op Arcade Game, "Magic Johnson's Fastbreak Basketball". Make the "Jump Shot", the "Alley Oop", & the "Fast Break" with a "Slam Dunk" Finish.
Virgin Games.

Magic Mailer. *Version:* 2.0. 1980. *Compatible Hardware:* Apple II, II+, IIe, IIc; Franklin 1000, 2000, Series; Laser 128. *Operating System(s) Required:* Apple DOS 3.3. *Language(s):* Assembly. *Memory Required:* 48k.
disk $29.95, incl. sample data files & manual.
Mail Merge Word Processor with Database. Produces Customized Letters & Documents.
Artsci, Inc.

Magic Memory. *Version:* 1.31. 1983. *Compatible Hardware:* Apple II, II+, IIe, IIc, IIgs; Franklin 1000 & 2000 Series; Laser, 128. *Operating System(s) Required:* Apple DOS 3.3. *Language(s):* Assembly. *Memory Required:* 64k.
disk $29.95.
Personal Data Base That Simulates a Standard Address Book. A-Z Tabs Plus 24 Additional Tabs for Cross-Referencing.
Artsci, Inc.

Magic Mountain Memory. Andrew Gilbert. *Customer Support:* 90 day warranty against defective software.
DOS 3.3. Apple II (48k). $39.95 (Order no.: A-1237).
DOS 3.2 or higher. IBM (640k). disk $39.95 (Order no.: I-1237).
A Geography Game Designed to Teach Students the Heights of Well-Known Mountains in the World. Part One of the Program Features a Review of the Mountains Based upon Their Location by the Continent. The Second Part Is a Quiz Given by Displaying the Names of Two Mountains. The Students Must Then Recall & Compare the Heights of Both by Choosing the Highest Mountain.
Electronic Courseware Systems, Inc.

Magic Office System. *Version:* 2.0. Aug. 1984. *Compatible Hardware:* Apple IIc; Franklin Ace 1000 & 2000 Series; Laser 128. *Operating System(s) Required:* Apple DOS 3.3. *Language(s):* Assembly. *Memory Required:* 64k. *General Requirements:* 2 disk drives, 80-column card, printer.
disk $149.95 (ISBN 0-917963-00-8).
Integrated Word Processor, Spelling Checker, Spreadsheet, Graph, & Templates. Graphically Integrated Using Simulated File Drawers, File Folders & Stationery Pads. All Programs Can Exchange Information, Allowing User to Add Spreadsheets to Letters, or Transfer Data from Spreadsheet to Graph Tables.
Artsci, Inc.

Magic PC. *Version:* 3.00. Jul. 1989. *Compatible Hardware:* IBM PC, PC XT, PC AT, & compatibles. *Operating System(s) Required:* PC-DOS 3.1 & higher. *Memory Required:* 512k. *General Requirements:* Hard disk.
disk $299.00.
Magic LAN (multi-user version) Tutorial, Reference Manuals, Retrieve Runtime free 30 days, newsletter, hotline $699.00.
Database Applications Development Program Which Includes Built-In Screen Editor for Screen & Report Layouts, Window-Design Editor, Built-In Functions, Nested Tasks & Virtual Fields. Visual Design Language Eliminates Coding & Maintenance. Includes BTRIEVE File Manager from NOVELL.
Aker Corp.

The Magic School Bus Explores the Human Body. (Magic School Bus Ser.).
Windows. IBM & compatibles. CD-ROM disk $69.95 (Order no.: R1341). *Nonstandard peripherals required:* CD-ROM drive. *Optimal configuration:* 386 processor operating at 16Mhz or higher, MS-DOS 5.0 or higher, Windows 3.1 or higher, 30Mb hard drive, mouse, VGA graphic adapter & VGA color monitor (SVGA recommended), 4Mb RAM, external speakers or headphones (with sound card) that are Sound Blaster compatible.
Inspired by the "Magic School Bus" Books, Ms. Frizzle & Her Elementary Class Take Children on Unusual Field Trips, Exploring the Solar System, the Human Body, the Earth & More. Children Become Part of the Story in These Highly Interactive Adventures (Ages 6-10).
Library Video Co.

The Magic School Bus Explores the Solar System. (Magic School Bus Ser.).
Windows. IBM & compatibles. CD-ROM disk $69.95 (Order no.: R1342). *Nonstandard peripherals required:* CD-ROM drive. *Optimal configuration:* 386 processor operating at 16Mhz or higher, MS-DOS 5.0 or higher, Windows 3.1 or higher, 30Mb hard drive, mouse, VGA graphic adapter & VGA color monitor (SVGA recommended), 4Mb RAM, external speakers or headphones (with sound card) that are Sound Blaster compatible.
Inspired by the "Magic School Bus" Books, Ms. Frizzle & Her Elementary Class Take Children on Unusual Field Trips, Exploring the Solar System, the Human Body, the Earth & More. Children Become Part of the Story in These Highly Interactive Adventures (Ages 6-10).
Library Video Co.

Magic School Bus Series.
Windows. IBM & compatibles. CD-ROM disk $139.90, Set (Order no.: R1340). *Nonstandard peripherals required:* CD-ROM drive. *Optimal configuration:* 386 processor operating at 16Mhz or higher, MS-DOS 5.0 or higher, Windows 3.1 or higher, 30Mb hard drive, mouse, VGA graphic adapter & VGA color monitor (SVGA recommended), 4Mb RAM, external speakers or headphones (with sound card) that are Sound Blaster compatible.
Inspired by the "Magic School Bus" Books, Ms. Frizzle & Her Elementary Class Take Children on Unusual Field Trips, Exploring the Solar System, the Human Body, the Earth & More. Children Become Part of the Story in These Highly Interactive Adventures (Ages 6-10). 2 Volume Set.
Library Video Co.

Magic Typist. *Version:* 2.0. *Items Included:* Disks, manual & addendums. *Customer Support:* Free unlimited phone technical support, FAX & modem service. America Online, CompuServe, Applelink. Macintosh System 6.0.5 & higher. Mac Plus & higher (1Mb RAM). 3.5" disk $129.00.
Completes Long Frequently Used Words, As Well As User-Defined Words, Sentences & Entire Paragraphs. Employs an Auto-Learn Feature That Creates a Phrase Library of Each User. Works in Word Processors, Text Editors, Programming Languages, & Any Place Text Can Be Typed.
Olduvai Corp.

Magic Window IIe. *Version:* 2.e2. Sep. 1984. *Compatible Hardware:* Apple IIe, IIc, IIgs; Laser, 128. *Operating System(s) Required:* Apple DOS 3.3. *Language(s):* Assembly. *Memory Required:* 64k.
disk $479.98 (ISBN 0-917963-01-6).
upgrade from Magic Window II $40.00.
Word Processor That Supports Special Printer Functions. Works Like a Typewriter.
Artsci, Inc.

Magic Words. *Version:* 3.0. 1981. *Compatible Hardware:* Apple II, II+, IIe, IIgs; Franklin Ace 1000 & 2000 Series; Laser 128. *Operating System(s) Required:* Apple DOS 3.3. *Language(s):* Assembly. *Memory Required:* 48k.
disk $29.95.
Proofreading Program Designed to Eliminate Spelling or Typographical Errors in MAGIC WINDOW Word Processing Documents.
Artsci, Inc.

Magical Diary. Gerald J. Schueler. May 1984. *Compatible Hardware:* Commodore 64, 128; Atari XL/XE. *General Requirements:* Color display.
disk $24.95 ea.
Commodore. (ISBN 0-87542-982-3).
Atari. (ISBN 0-87542-984-X).
Structured File for Storage of Data from Magical Experiments & Experiences. Space for Technical & Time Data & Impressions.
Llewellyn Pubns.

MagiCalc. *Version:* 2.173. 1983. *Compatible Hardware:* Apple II, II+, IIe, IIc, II, IIgs; Franklin 1000 & 2000 Series; Laser 128. *Operating System(s) Required:* Apple DOS 3.3, ProDOS. *Language(s):* Assembly. *Memory Required:* 64k.
disk $39.95.
Electronic Spreadsheet.
Artsci, Inc.

MagicPrint. *Operating System(s) Required:* CP/M, SB-80. *Memory Required:* 64k.
disk $195.00.
Gives the User Proportional Printing from the Daisy Wheel Printer. Works in Conjunction with SB-80, WordStar, & Other CP/M-80 Compatible Text Editors. Produces Standard Word Processing Features, But Additionally Offers 4 Modes of Justification, Microcentering, Automatic Footnoting, Flush Right, Accents, Columns, Character Kerning, & More Than 50 Other Page Formatting Features.
Lifeboat Assocs.

MAGIS Plus. Management Accountability Group, Inc. *Operating System(s) Required:* MS-DOS. *Memory Required:* 128k. *General Requirements:* Printer.
$1995.00.

Automated Accounting System Designed to Be Used by Personnel Without Special Accounting or Computer Knowledge.
Texas Instruments, Personal Productivit.

Mahogany External Development Guide. Feb. 1990. *Items Included:* 2 60-page manuals, sample external functions.
MS-DOS/PC-DOS. IBM PC & compatibles (512k). disk $250.00. *Addl. software required:* Mahogany Professional v1.0.2 or higher.
Provides the Information Required by Software Developers to Create Their Own External Functions. External Functions Can Be Used to Interface Mahogany Professional with Other Software & Hardware. Several Prepackaged External Functions Are Also Available from Emerald.
Emerald Intelligence.

Mahogany Introductory. Aug. 1989. *Items Included:* 320 page manual, upgrade coupon to Mahogany Professional, sample knowledgebases. *Customer Support:* Corporate training packages from $1495.00.
MS/PC-DOS (512k). IBM PC &' compatibles. $149.00.
MAC-OS (1Mb). Macintosh. $149.00.
Windowed Environment Expert System Development Tool, Designed to Combine Ease of Use & Powerful Features. Mahogany Introductory Is Geared to the Novice Expert System Builder, Offering Full Tutorials & a Lengthy Description of the Technology & Its Applications.
Emerald Intelligence.

Mahogany Professional. Sep. 1989. *Items Included:* Manual, sample knowledgebases. *Customer Support:* Corporate training packages from $1495.00.
MS/PC-DOS (512k). IBM PC & compatibles. $495.00.
MAC-OS (1Mb). Macintosh. $495.00.
A Hybrid Rule Based & Object Oriented Expert System Development Tool Combining Ease of Use with Powerful Features Including Forward, Backward & Inference Modes, Multiple Object Inheritance, Certainty Factors & Threshold Values.
Emerald Intelligence.

MAI Integrated Accounting Software. 1985. *Compatible Hardware:* IBM PC, PC XT, PC AT. *Operating System(s) Required:* MS-DOS, Novell, UNIX, XENIX. *Language(s):* BB/M (source code included). *Memory Required:* 256k.
$195.00-$395.00 (Order no.: BBM 0100).
Comprised of 11 Application Modules Written to Conform to Accepted Accounting Principles & Provide Audit Trails for All Entries.
Promark, Ltd.

MAI-L-ET LIST. *Version:* 1.2. Peter C. Vonderhorst. 1982. *Compatible Hardware:* IBM PC & compatibles, PC XT, PC AT; TRS-80 Model II, Model IV. *Operating System(s) Required:* PC-DOS, MS-DOS, TRSDOS. *Language(s):* Compiled BASIC. *Memory Required:* 128k.
disk with WORD-SET $265.00.
Mailing List, Letter Writing, Sales, Customer, Prospect Control Program. Includes WORD-SET, a Mini Word Processing Program for Creating Form Letters, Individual Letters, Full Sort Capabilities.
Computx.

Mail. *Compatible Hardware:* TRS-80 Model I, Model III.
contact publisher for price.
Demi-Software.

Mail. *Version:* 2.0. Aug. 1988. *Items Included:* Comprehensive manual in 3 ring binder. *Customer Support:* 2 hours of no cost support to registered users during first 6 months of ownership. Service contracts available thereafter at a cost of $60.00 per hour with no minimum.
PC-DOS 2.1 or higher, MS-DOS 2.1 or higher (384k). IBM PC, XT, AT PS/2 or 100% compatible micro-computer. $17.50 (ISBN 1-877915-01-7). *Nonstandard peripherals required:* Dot matrix printer only. *Optimal configuration:* 640k RAM, hard disk for large files.
A General Purpose Address Manager That Produces 1, 2, 3 or 4 Across Labels, Address Books & Telephone Books. It Also Prints on Any Size Envelope, File Cards, Rolodex Cards & Postcards. It Will Print a Return Address & Automatically Eliminates Blank Lines When Printing. Other Automatic Features Include Capitalizing & Verifying States, Formatting Zip Codes, Repeating & Checking the First Three Digits of the Zip Code, Repeating Area Codes & Formatting Phone Numbers. Searching Is Done on Any, All or Some of Its 11 Fields Using These Conditions: Equal to, Greater Than, Less Than, Not Equal to, Less Than or Equal to, & Greater Than or Equal to. It Also Searches Phonetically & for Range of Values. It Sorts on Up to 2 Fields in Ascending or 1 Field in Descending Order. In Addition, It Can Sort to Zip+4 Requirements & Check for Duplicate Records. Imports from ASCII & dBASE, Exports to ASCII & Can Create WordStar Merge Files.
Phoenix Phive Software Corp.

Mail-Bulk-Rate II. *Version:* 2.00. Kailash Chandra. Apr. 1986. *Compatible Hardware:* IBM PC & compatibles. *Memory Required:* 256k.
5 1/4" or 3 1/2" disk $195.00 (ISBN 0-918689-06-6).
Presorts the Mail for Third Class & First Class Postal Discounts. Works with Mail-Track-II & Other Pure ASCII Data Files.
Sapana Micro Software.

Mail-Bulk-Rate-III. *Version:* 2.00. Kailash Chandra. Dec. 1986. *Compatible Hardware:* IBM PC, PC XT, PC AT. *Memory Required:* 256k. *General Requirements:* Printer.
3-1/2" or 5-1/4" disk $295.00 (ISBN 0-918689-08-2).
Presorts the Mail for Third Class & First Class Postal Discounts. Works with Mail-Track-III & Other ASCII Files. Can Handle up to 999,999 Addresses.
Sapana Micro Software.

Mail Business Manager (MBM). *Version:* 3.5. Sep. 1990. *Items Included:* Comprehensive manual & user's guide. *Customer Support:* Free telephone support.
MS-DOS, PC-DOS 2.1 or higher. PC, XT, AT, 386, 486, PS/2 (512k). 3.5" or 5.25" disk $495.00 (Order no.: MBM).
MBM demo $15.00.
A PC Computer Program Providing Support for All Aspects of Mail Order & Related Businesses: Fast Customer File Searching & Retrieval, Customer Tracking, Order Taking & Processing, Shipping, Personalized Invoices, Payment Processing, Response Tracking, Inventory, Backorders, Returns, Accounts Receivable, Mailing Lists with File Export, Management Reporting, & Marketing Analysis.
Metagroup Consultants.

Mail-Dex. *Compatible Hardware:* Apple Macintosh Plus. *Operating System(s) Required:* System 5.0 or higher. *General Requirements:* Printer.
3.5" disk $49.95.
Desk Accessory That Prints Envelopes & Labels.
Mission Accomplished Software Services, Inc.

Mail List of Computer Dealers & Retailers. *Compatible Hardware:* Apple II+. *Operating System(s) Required:* CP/M. *Language(s):* Machine. *Memory Required:* 48k.
contact publisher for price.
Provides Access to Computer Dealers & Retailers by Mail. List of Addresses Is an Aid to Prospective Hardware & Software Manufacturers Searching for Retail Outlets. After Booting up, a Menu Helps User Obtain a Printout of the List on Labels.
Connecticut Information Systems, Inc.

Mail List of Congressmen & Senators. *Compatible Hardware:* Apple II+. *Operating System(s) Required:* CP/M. *Language(s):* Machine. *Memory Required:* 48k.
contact publisher for price.
Disk Based Mailing List of 435 U.S. Congressmen & 100 Senators. Can Be Used Several Times to Print a Full Set of Labels. Any User with Political Interest Can Conduct Mail Campaigns for Any Purpose.
Connecticut Information Systems, Inc.

Mail Manager: Craft-Antique Mail Point of Sale & Accounts Payable. *Version:* 2.1. Feb. 1987. *Compatible Hardware:* IBM PC 286, 386, 486 or Fully Compatible. *Operating System(s) Required:* 3.1 or higher. *Memory Required:* 640k. *General Requirements:* 1 floppy, 10 MB free harddisk space. *Customer Support:* 90 Day Full Phone Support.
Single User. $1500.00 (ISBN 0-925961-04-3, Order no.: MMS).
Multiuser. $1800.00 (ISBN 0-925961-32-9, Order no.: MMM).
Provides Flexible Point of Sale for Mail Type Operation Extensive Daily & Period Sales Reporting, Automatic Posting to Dealer Accounts for Check Printing.
Organic Computing.

Mail Master. *Compatible Hardware:* IBM. *Language(s):* BASIC. *Memory Required:* 128k.
$39.95.
Dynacomp, Inc.

Mail-Merge with Formletters. *Version:* 1.1. 1990. *Items Included:* 36 page manual.
MS-DOS 2.X - 4.X. IBM PC/XT/AT or PS/2 or compatibles. disk $24.95.
This Software Package Consists of Two Major Parts: Text & Mailing List. Text Produced Using the Built-in Letter Writer Can Be Integrated with All or Selected Addresses of th Mailing Lists. The Concept of the Program Has Been Developed in a Way That Allows the User to Operate it with Very Few Commands.
Elcomp Publishing, Inc.

Mail Order Spreadsheet Kit. John Kremer. Sep. 1990. *Items Included:* Mail Order Selling Made Easier Book. *Customer Support:* Phone support.
MS-DOS. IBM PC or compatible (512k). disk $29.95 (ISBN 0-912411-35-X, Order no.: 490). *Addl. software required:* Lotus 1-2-3, Quatro Pro or compatible.
Macintosh. 3.5" disk $29.95 (Order no.: 491). *Addl. software required:* Any spreadsheet software that accepts Lotus 1-2-3 compatible templates.
Have You Ever Wondered What Effect a 10% Change in Response Would Have on the Profitability of a Mailing? Or How a Change in Your Selling Price Might Affect Your Profit Margin or Return on Investment? If So, Now You Can Easily Answer These Questions & Many Others. How? By Using This Mail Order Spreadsheet Kit. The Computer Disk In This Kit Includes Lotus 1-2-3 Spreadsheet Templates for Many of the Worksheets in Mail Order Selling Made Easier. With These Templates, You Can Easily Explore All the Possibilities of Your Promotions.
Open Horizons Publishing Co.

Mail-Outs. Alligator Software. Aug. 1987. *Operating System(s) Required:* PC-DOS/MS-DOS 2.1 or higher. *Memory Required:* 256k. *General Requirements:* Printer, hard disk recommended.
disk $89.95 (ISBN 1-55801-007-6, Order no.: MO1).
Mailing List Management System. It Maintains Names, Addresses, Telephone Numbers, etc. The Sort Capability Lets Users Sort on Any Field, While Data Search Features Allow Users to Find Cards. A Built-in Word Processor Is Included to Allow Users to Create Form Letters & Other Mail-Merge Documents.
Softdisk, Inc.

Mail-Phone List. 1982. *Compatible Hardware:* Apple II+, IIe. *Operating System(s) Required:* Apple DOS 3.3. *Language(s):* BASIC (source code included). *Memory Required:* 48k.
disk $34.95 (ISBN 0-917729-45-5).
back-up disk $10.00.
Designed for School, Home or Work. Allows User to Enter & Store Name, Address, & Phone Data for Friends or Businesses.
Compu-Tations, Inc.

MAIL-PLUS. *Version:* 2. Bill Etienne. May 1987. *Compatible Hardware:* IBM PC & compatibles. *Operating System(s) Required:* PC-DOS, MS-DOS. *Language(s):* Pascal. *Memory Required:* 128k.
disk $69.95.
Mail List Database Editor. Sorts & Selects 100 Records Based on Zip-Code, Last Name, & User-Defined Criteria. Provides Reports & Labels (up to 4 Across).
Generic Computer Products, Inc. (GCPI).

Mail-Second-Class-II. *Version:* 2.00. Kailash Chandra. Aug. 1987. *Compatible Hardware:* IBM PC, PC XT, PC AT. *Memory Required:* 256k. *General Requirements:* Printer.
3-1/2" or 5-1/4" disk $295.00 (ISBN 0-918689-11-2).
Presorts the Mail for Second Class Postal Discounts, Prints Summary Reports, Renewal/Form Letters. Works with Mail-Track-II & ASCII Files. Can Handle 32,766 Records.
Sapana Micro Software.

Mail-Second-Class-III. *Version:* 2.00. Kailash Chandra. Aug. 1986. *Compatible Hardware:* IBM PC, PC XT, PC AT. *Memory Required:* 256k. *General Requirements:* Printer.
3-1/2" or 5-1/4" disk $395.00 (ISBN 0-918689-12-0).
Presorts the Mail for Second Class Postal Discounts, Prints Summary Reports, Renewal/Form Letters. Works with Mail-Track-III & ASCII Files. Can Handle 999,999 Records.
Sapana Micro Software.

Mail-Star-One. Kailash Chandra. Jun. 1987. *Compatible Hardware:* IBM PC, PC XT, PC AT. *Memory Required:* 256k.
3-1/2" or 5-1/4" disk $695.00 (ISBN 0-918689-09-0).
Mail Management Program. Features Unlimited Number of Records, Auto City & State for More Than 40,000 ZIP Codes & Canadian Postal Codes, Duplicate Detection, Mail Merge, etc.
Sapana Micro Software.

Mail-Track-I with LetterMerge. *Version:* 2.00. Kailash Chandra. 1982. *Compatible Hardware:* AT&T PC; Columbia; Compaq; Corona; Data General One; Eagle PC; IBM PC, PCjr, PC XT, PC AT, & compatibles; Leading Edge PC; NCR PC; Sanyo 550; Sperry PC; Tandy 1000, Tandy 2000. *Operating System(s) Required:* PC-DOS 1.1, 2.0, 2.1, MS-DOS. *Language(s):* Compiled BASIC. *Memory Required:* 256k.
disk $49.95, incl. manual (ISBN 0-918689-00-7).
upgrade & manual $10.00.
disk restricted version $5.00.
Mailing List Management Program. Keeps Track of Foreign & Domestic Addresses & Prints Form Letters & Bills. LETTERMERGE Does Mail Merge to Print Form Letters. Merges the Selected Addresses in ZIP Code Order with a Text Created by WORDSTAR, VOLKSWRITER, EDLIN, or Any Other Word Processor or Text Editor Supporting PC-DOS ASCII Compatible Files.
Sapana Micro Software.

Mail-Track-II with LetterMerge II. *Version:* 2.00. Kailash Chandra. Jul. 1985. *Compatible Hardware:* IBM PC, PCjr, PC XT, PC AT, PC compatibles: AT&T PC, Data General One, Columbia PC, Compaq PC, Eagle PC, Corona PC, Leading Edge PC, Sperry PC, NCR PC, Sanyo 550, Zenith Z-150, Zenith Z-100. *Operating System(s) Required:* PC-DOS/MS-DOS 2.00 or higher. *Language(s):* Compiled BASIC. *Memory Required:* 256k.
disk $195.00, not copy-protected (ISBN 0-918689-05-8).
restricted version $5.00.
updates $10.00.
Advanced Version of the Mail-Track-I Program, Allows up to 24 Fields, & Can Handle up to 32,766 Addresses.
Sapana Micro Software.

Mail-Track-III. *Version:* 2.00. Kailash Chandra. May 1986. *Compatible Hardware:* IBM PC, PC XT, PC AT. *Memory Required:* 256k. *General Requirements:* Printer.
3-1/2" or 5-1/4" disk $295.00 (ISBN 0-918689-07-4).
Allows up to 24 Fields, 20 User-Defined Reports, Auto City & State for More Than 20,000 ZIP Codes, Duplicate Detection, Up to 999,999 Addresses, Mail Merge, etc.
Sapana Micro Software.

Mail-V. *Version:* 2.0. 1980. *Compatible Hardware:* TRS-80 Model I, Model III. *Operating System(s) Required:* TRSDOS. *Language(s):* BASIC (source code included). *Memory Required:* 32k.
disk $79.00.
manual $10.00.
Advanced Mailing List System Features Live Keyboard, Screen Input, Report Writer, etc.
Micro Architect, Inc.

Mail-X. *Compatible Hardware:* IBM PC. *Operating System(s) Required:* CP/M, TRSDOS, MS-DOS. *Language(s):* Compiled MBASIC. *Memory Required:* 64-128k.
disk $198.00.
manual $24.00.
Mailing List System with a Built-In Sort/Merge Package.
Micro Architect, Inc.

Mailbase. *Compatible Hardware:* Apple Macintosh. *Memory Required:* 1000k. *Customer Support:* Free phone support.
3.5" disk $149.00.
Mailing List Management.
Exceiver Corp.

Mailcall. *Version:* 1.2. Dennis Allen. 1986. *Compatible Hardware:* IBM PC & compatibles; TRS-80. *Operating System(s) Required:* TRSDOS 6.x, MS-DOS. *Memory Required:* 64k.
TRS-DOS. disk $79.95 (Order no.: D4MC).
MS-DOS. disk $79.95 (Order no.: DMMC).
Supports Names & Addresses from Around the World, Including Canadian & Most Foreign Postal Codes. Includes a Conversion Utility That Will Transfer Names from Current Format, Including Word Processing Files, Sequential Files & Many Other Mailing List Programs Formats, to the MAILCALL 1.2 Format. Enables User to Classify Each Name for up to 15 Unique, Qualified, Lists.
The Alternate Source.

Mailer. *Compatible Hardware:* Commodore 64.
disk $19.95.
Stores & Retrieves up to 800 Records. Each Record Contains Name, Address-1, Address-2, City, State, Zip Code, Telephone Fields. Prints a List of Records on File, Locates Records by Name Fields, Prints Labels on Most Common Forms of Computer Labels, Sorts File by Name or Record ID.
Raymond L. Reynolds.

Mailer PC. 1987. *Compatible Hardware:* IBM PC & compatibles. *Operating System(s) Required:* PC-DOS/MS-DOS. *Memory Required:* 128k. *General Requirements:* Printer recommended. *Items Included:* Disk, staple bound instructions.
disk $99.00 (ISBN 0-926152-61-0).
Complete Mailing List Management for Lists of up to 2000 Records. Particularly Adapted for Efficient Data Entry of Records with Repetitive Content. Wide Range of Features for Sorting, Selecting & Printing Mailing Label Data.
Persimmon Software.

MAILERMATE II. *Version:* 2.0. *Compatible Hardware:* IBM PC & compatibles. *Items Included:* Software & manual. *Customer Support:* Free.
$29.95 to $49.95.
Fills in & Prints Self-Mailers. Includes Math Calculations & Transaction Journal. Imports ASCII Files for Mass Mailings. Includes Interactive Database.
Transkrit Corp.

Mailer's GeoCode. Sep. 1993. *Items Included:* CD-ROM Program. *Customer Support:* Product information available over phone, toll free; technical support provided, unlimited over telephone; 30 day money back guarantee.
DOS 3.1 or higher. IBM & compatibles (640k). optical disk $1295.00. Optimal configuration: 386/486. Networks supported: All.
Will Add/Append Information to a User's Database/File. Adds/Appends Information Like Census Block Group/Census Track & Latitude Longitude to Each Record.
Mailer's Software.

Mailer's +4. Aug. 1993. *Items Included:* CD ROM Disc, manual. *Customer Support:* Product information available over phone, toll free technical support available, unlimited over phoneline; 30 day money back guarantee.
DOS 3.1 or higher. IBM & compatibles (640k). $340.00, updates ,195.00 individual, ,690.00 annual subscript. Optimal configuration: 386/486 hard drive. Networks supported: All.
Provides Mailers with the Correct Plus 4 Extension to All 5-Digit Zipcodes, Carrier Routes & Standardizes List to USPS Requirements. It Will Run Through a Whole List at Once or Allow for Individual Lookup in a Lookup Mode.
Mailer's Software.

Mailing List. *Compatible Hardware:* Apple II+. *Language(s):* Applesoft BASIC. *Memory Required:* 48k. *General Requirements:* Printer.
disk $29.95.
Handles up to 150 Names, Addresses, & Phone Numbers in Memory. Stores up to 450 Records on One Disk. Sorts a Data File by Last Name, Company Name, Alphabetically, or by Zip Code. Searches for Any Last Name or Company Name in a File. Prints Addresses on 2 Different Sized Envelopes. Built-In Safeguards Prevent Loss of Data Due to Operator Error.
Instant Software, Inc.

MAILING LIST

Mailing List. *Compatible Hardware:* Commodore 64, IBM PC, TI 99/4A. *Language(s):* Extended BASIC.
disk $14.95 (Order no.: 100XD).
IBM, Commodore. contact publisher for price.
River City Software, Inc.

Mailing List. *Compatible Hardware:* TI Home Computer.
contact publisher for price (Order no.: PHD 5001).
Stores, Alphabetizes, Sorts & Searches Information.
Texas Instruments, Personal Productivit.

Mailing List. *Version:* 8B. Sep. 1993. *Compatible Hardware:* PC-DOS, Xenix, Unix; 3COM, Novell. *Memory Required:* Multi-user 3Mb or higher, single user 1000k. *General Requirements:* Integrated accounting. *Customer Support:* Included with the support for the Integrated Accounting.
Single user. disk $200.00.
Multiuser. disk $495.00.
Module Expands the Mailing/Rolodex Features Found in Integrated Accounting. Maintains & Sorts Mailing Lists for Persons or Companies Not Recorded in the Customer File. Mailings Can Be Scheduled for Various Time Cycles, Marking Customers to Receive Pieces Daily, Monthly, Quarterly or Yearly. Maintains Independent Mailing Files. Has Full Add, Revise, Delete & Search Capability. Maintains Date of Last Mailing.
Trac Line Software, Inc.

Mailing List & Appointment Calendar. *Compatible Hardware:* Commodore 64, IBM PC, TI 99/4A. *Language(s):* Extended BASIC.
disk $19.95 (Order no.: 111XD).
IBM, Commodore. contact publisher for price.
River City Software, Inc.

Mailing List System, 2 disks. Andy Mau. Jul. 1984. *Compatible Hardware:* IBM PC. *Operating System(s) Required:* PC-DOS, MS-DOS. *Language(s):* COBOL (source code included). *Memory Required:* 256k. *General Requirements:* 2 disk drives.
disk $129.95 (Order no.: MM001).
Features Include Variable X-Up Labels, Print on Gum Label or Feed an Envelope for Printing. Corporate & Individual Name/Address Format.
Mau Corp.

Mailing List with Notepad. 1988. *Items Included:* 16 page manual.
MS-DOS 2.X - 4.X. IBM PC/XT/AT, PS/2 or compatibles (256K). disk $19.95 (Order no.: 9501).
Addresses Can Be Selected By Any Field. With the First Two Fields User May Even Select Any String or a Single Character. This Makes Searching Easy, Even if User Only Remembers Parts of a Name. Labels & Lists Can Be Printed Very Fast, Even with Large Amounts of Data. Functions Allows the Addition of Notes & Remarks to Each Address. User Select a Notepad Size of 120 or 896 Characters (per address). On a Floppy Disk User Can Store Approximately 1,000 Addresses with Notepads; on a Harddisk Store about 10,000 Addresses with Notepads. If Larger Notepad is Needed (896 Characters per Address) User Can Still Store about 260 Addresses on a Floppy Disk.
Elcomp Publishing, Inc.

MailList. *Compatible Hardware:* Apple Macintosh. *Customer Support:* 716-385-6120.
3.5" disk $24.95 (ISBN 1-55662-954-0).
Mailing List Data Management.
Artworx Software Co., Inc.

MAILLIST. *Version:* 3.8. *Operating System(s) Required:* CP/M, MS-DOS. *Language(s):* Quick Basic. *Items Included:* Manual, disk, warranty card. *Customer Support:* 18 month via telephone.
disk $89.00.
demo disk & manual $20.00.
source code $200.00.
Mailing List Program Which Maintains up to 900 Records per Disk. User Can Add or Delete Customer Records with New Files Inserted in Old Blank Spaces to Conserve Disk Space. Lists Are Sorted, Printed & Displayed by Customer Number, Last Name, City, State, Zip, or Customer Type.
Micro-Art Programmers.

MailMerge. Aug. 1989. *Items Included:* Instruction included on disk. *Customer Support:* 90 days unlimited warranty.
MS-DOS. IBM XT, AT or compatibles (512k). disk $34.95 plus $3.50 S&H (Order no.: 1072). *Addl. software required:* Lotus 1-2-3, Release 4.0 for Windows or higher. *Optimal configuration:* IBM AT, 640K RAM, Lotus 123 Rel. 2.2.
Allows Lotus Users to Merge Name & Address into a Letter. The Database & the Letter Are Both Contained in the Spreadsheet.
Compiled Systems.

MailMerge. MicroPro International. *Compatible Hardware:* HP 86/87 with CP/M System (HP 82900A).
3-1/2" or 5-1/4" disk $125.00 ea. (Order no.: 45587A).
Multi-Purpose Merging Program Which Can Be Used with WordStar to Produce a List of Names & Addresses, Form Letters, & Letters That Have Special Words or Phrases Unique to Each Addressee. Can Also Be Used to Print Mailing Labels & Envelopes.
Hewlett-Packard Co.

MailMinder. *Version:* 4.0. Apr. 1985. *Compatible Hardware:* IBM PC, PC XT; Compaq; NCR PC; Columbia MPC; Epson QX-10; Leading Edge; Sperry PC; Zenith 2100 or 2-150. *Operating System(s) Required:* MS-DOS. *Memory Required:* 256k.
contact publisher for price.
Automated Inquiry & Mailing List System. When Integrated with the SALESMINDER & STOCKMINDER Automatically Transfers Name & Address Information from Each Sales Transaction at the Close of the Day. In Addition to Standard Name & Address Information, up to 15 Other Facts Can Be Stored for Each of up to 32,000 Customers. Customer Entries Are Automatically Indexed Alphabetically by Name & Numerically by Zip Code. Numerous Combinations of Customer Information Such As Type of Purchase & Volume of Purchase Can Be Gathered. A Given Set of Customer Data Can Be Selected & Displayed Immediately or Queued for Later Printing.
Verifone, Inc.

MailSafe: Public Key Encryption Software. *Version:* 5.0. Jun. 1988. *Operating System(s) Required:* PC-DOS/MS-DOS 2.0 or higher. *Memory Required:* 384k.
disk $350.00.
Provides Secure Message Transfer in All PC Communications Network Environments. Verifies That Information Received Is the Same As Information Sent (Message Verification); Identifies Author (Using Digital Signatures); & Ensures Privacy of Information While in Transit. Uses the Patented RSA Public Key Cryptosystem.
Fischer International Systems Corp.

Mailtrak: List Management System. *Version:* 1.15. Mar. 1982. *Compatible Hardware:* IBM; Compaq; WYSE. *Operating System(s) Required:* PC-DOS, MS-DOS. *Language(s):* Compiled BASIC. *Memory Required:* 256k.
disk $65.00, incl. manual (ISBN 0-917099-01-X).
Mailing List Including Full Name & Address Information Plus 2 Phone Numbers, 5 Mail Profile Codes (User-Defined) & Four Activity Codes with Date, User Formatted Labels up to 4 Across.
TCI Software.

The Main Street Filer. Main Street Software. *Compatible Hardware:* TI Professional. *Operating System(s) Required:* MS-DOS. *Memory Required:* 128k. *General Requirements:* 2 disk drives, printer.
$295.00.
Texas Instruments, Personal Productivit.

Mainframe. *Compatible Hardware:* Commodore 64.
3.5" disk $24.95.
Arcade Game; Defeat the Super Computer. James Bond Style Adventure.
Microillusions, Inc.

MainPlan/EQ. *Version:* 1.4. Andre-Paul Pellet & Michael R. Pellet. Jun. 1990. *Items Included:* Tutorial, reference manual, tutorial disk, MainPlan/EQ 1.4. *Customer Support:* Direct on-line technical support ($60/hr); telephone support & free maintenance upgrade ($395/yr). System 6.0.5 or higher; finder 6.1, System 7.
Macintosh (2Mb). 3.5" disk $3995.00 (ISBN 1-877996-04-1, Order no.: MP0077). *Optimal configuration:* Macintosh LC, IIsi, Classic II, Powerbooks, QUADRAS. *Networks supported:* Localtalk, EtherNet.
Equipment Maintenance Management Program Designed for Use by Organizations Requiring Equipment Maintenance. MainPlan/EQ Provides Managers with All the Tools They Need to Plan, Organize, & Implement an Equipment Maintenance System. These Tools Include: Equipment History, Description, Task Description, Scheduling, Work Order Issuing & Reporting, Parts, Labor & Consumables.
M2, Ltd.

MAINSTAY. Aug. 1984. *Compatible Hardware:* IBM PC XT, PC AT & compatibles. *Operating System(s) Required:* MS-DOS, PC-DOS 2.1 or higher. *Memory Required:* 512k.
disk $1495.00.
reference manual $60.00.
user's guide $60.00.
computer-based training with guide $50.00.
Creates "Canned" Analysis & Reports & Delivers Data to Help Package & Deliver Information Products for the PC Market.
Mainstay Software Corp.

The Maintenance Authority-Facility Management. *General Requirements:* Omnis 3 Plus.
Macintosh Plus or higher. 3.5" disk $1995.00.
Facility Maintenance Management.
Better Business Solutions.

Maintenance Crib Simulator: MCS. Sep. 1993. *Items Included:* Manual. *Customer Support:* No customer support fee.
MS-DOS. IBM or compatible 386/486 (1Mb).
disk $295.00. *Optimal configuration:* 386/486 w/4Mb memory, one floppy, hard disk, printer.
Helps Companies Manage Their Maintenance/ Parts Crib Operation Efficiently. MCS Helps User Determine the Number of Crib Attendants You Need, Minimizes Wait Time, & Is Cost Effective. Is Also Very Simple to Use. Simply Input Data, (Like Average Service Time, Arrival Time, & Variance) Which Can Be Automated by the Use

of a Hand Held Data Collector Device, & Interfaced to MCS. Also Considers the Number of Shifts, & Divides Each Shift into Various Segments Depending on the Crib Activity. No Programming Experience Necessary.
Unik Assocs.

Maintenance Management. Oct. 1989. *Compatible Hardware:* IBM PC & compatibles. *Operating System(s) Required:* PC-DOS/MS-DOS. *Memory Required:* 640k. 3.5" or 5.25" disk $500.00.
Can Be Used to Handle Maintenance for a Single Piece of Equipment, a Factory Full of Machinery or a Maintenance Service Contract Covering the Whole City. Input for Each Maintenance Item Covers the What, When, by Who & with What. Reports Are Simple Reminders, Crew & Task Lists up to Full Detail on Each Maintenance Action, All by Day, Week or Month.
Rambow Enterprises.

Maintenance Management. *Version:* 7.0. *Customer Support:* Free telephone support: 90 days.
Macintosh 1Mb; IBM with Windows. $995.00.
A Complete Parts Inventory & Maintenance Management Program. Prepares Work Orders for Scheduled & Non-Scheduled Maintenance. Tracks Work Orders.
S & J Enterprises.

Maintenance Management System (MMS II). *Version:* 3.0. Jan. 1985. *Compatible Hardware:* IBM PC, PC XT. *Operating System(s) Required:* MS-DOS. *Language(s):* C. *Memory Required:* 512k. *General Requirements:* 2 disk drives, printer.
disk $5995.00.
demo disk & manual $50.00.
manual only $25.00.
Establishes a Maintenance Management System in a Shop or Improves an Existing System. Monitors Employee Productivity & Job Costs & Allows User to Maintain Records & Generate Reports on: Preventive Maintenance, Equipment History, Repair History, Work Orders, Productivity. Stores & Retrieves Part Numbers, Quantities, Dates Received, & Reorder Points, & Updates the Quantity On-Hand, Based on Transactions. When Inventory Goes Below a Reorder Point, a Warning Is Displayed. Not Copy Protected.
Unik Assocs.

Maintenance Manager. Jan. 1995. *Items Included:* Self-Documentation on Screen. *Customer Support:* 1 year free telephone support.
Compiled Basic. 286 (256k). 3.5" disk $275.00.
Addl. software required: PM Plus/1996, optional.
This Program Tracks All Maintenance Requests & Provides Lists of Requests in 4 Major Types. It Produces Request Lists, Priority Codes, User Codes & Complete Information Is Kept As Long As Desired. Work Orders Can Be Printed. Request Can Be Quickly Viewed & Edited on Screen. Mainman Is Designed to Interface with Property Management Plus & Enters All Tenant Information Automatically.
Realty Software.

Maintenance Package. *Memory Required:* 64k. $195.00 (Order no.: TI P/N 2223199-0001).
Diagnostic Tool That Aids in Identifying Hardware Problems with the TI Computer.
Texas Instruments, Personal Productivit.

Maintenance System.
contact publisher for price.
Designed to Handle Timely-Preventive Maintenance to Heavy Industrial Equipment.

Generate Multi-Line Maintenance Work Orders Which Are Posted to Maintenance. History File at End of Each Service.
Universal Data Research, Inc.

Major League Handicapper. *Items Included:* Bound manual. *Customer Support:* Free hotline - no time limit; 30 day limited warranty; updates are $5/disk plus S&H.
MS-DOS. IBM & compatibles (256k). disk $39.95.
Based on Multiple Linear Regression Technique. Record the Results of the Games As They Occur & MLH Does the Rest.
Dynacomp, Inc.

Major Motion. Philip MacKenzie & Jeff Sorenson. May 1986. *Compatible Hardware:* Atari ST, Sanyo MBC 555, Commodore Amiga. *Operating System(s) Required:* MS-DOS, TOS. *Memory Required:* 512k. *General Requirements:* Color display for Atari ST & Amiga.
Atari & Amiga. 3.5" disk $39.95 (ISBN 0-923213-06-6, Order no.: AT-MAJ).
Sanyo 5-1/4" disk. disk $29.95 (ISBN 0-923213-20-1, Order no.: SA-MAJ).
Race the Roadway in a Spy-Chase Arcade Game. Enemy Delivers Deadly Helicopters & Gaping Potholes Threaten to Destroy You. Defend Yourself with Smoke, Machine Guns, Oil Slicks & Missiles, or Escape down Branching Roads & Treacherous Rivers.
MichTron, Inc.

Make Path Flight Director. 1991. *Items Included:* 1 manual. *Customer Support:* 90 days unlimited warranty; free telephone support.
DOS. IBM 386 25 & higher (4Mb). disk $69.95 (ISBN 1-886082-11-1, Order no.: MP-130).
Addl. software required: Vista Pro. *Optimal configuration:* 8Mb.
Add on Program for Vista Pro Which Enables Animation of Any Landscape Designed.
Virtual Reality Laboratories, Inc.

Make-to-Order Net Requirements Planning: On-Target Job Shop Software. *Version:* 2.80. Aug. 1994. *Items Included:* User guide; flexible (SQL) report writer, menu & security management, 4th GL relational database, user modifiable. *Customer Support:* Consulting: pre-installation, startup & post installation. Training. On-line support & maintenance (including upgrades). Voice & modem one year renewable support contract.
MS-DOS. 486 (8Mb), PC-Networks, PC-LANs. $7500.00 to $40,000.00. *Networks supported:* Novell, Banyan, 3COM, Fox, Token Ring & More.
UNIX. 68000, based system, IBM RISC 6000. $12,000.00 to $60,000.00.
Used by Job Shops That Assemble or Remanufacture Machinery, Electronic Equipment, & Printed Circuit Assemblies to Order. Planning & Control Functions Meet All Types of Operating Needs for Manufacturing & Purchasing. Bills of Material Can Be up to Eleven Levels with up to 999 Items per Bill. Reports Include: Summarized Bill, Indented Bill, Costed Bill, Net Purchased Requirements & Net Manufacturing Requirements. Complete Costing Information Is Included in Displays & Reports with Security. Audit Trails Are Complete, On-Line & in Full Detail. Cost Changes Can Be Effected Globally.
Viehmann Corp.

Make Your Day's Multiuser Calendar & Appointment Scheduler. *Items Included:* Full manual. No other products required. *Customer Support:* Free telephone support - no time limit. 30 day warranty.
MS-DOS 3.2 or higher. IBM & compatibles (512k). disk $59.95. *Optimal configuration:*

IBM, MS-DOS 2.0 or higher, 256k RAM, CGA, EGA, VGA, Hercules, IBM 8514, PC 3270, ATT, or compatible graphics capability.
Flexible & Easy-to-Use Single or Multiuser Calendar System Which Can Accomodate up to 64 Individual Calendars. The Many Features Include: Daily or Weekly Calendar Display; Master Calendar for Company or Public Notices; Calendar Administrator Can Globally Set Appointments; Individuals Can Browse Through Other Calendars; Individuals Can Conceal Private Appointment Entries; Flexible Notes & Long Message Entry; Notes Are Easily Edited & Copied into Different Time Slots in Your Calendar, or Copies into Someone Else's or the Master Calendar & More.
Dynacomp, Inc.

Make Your Days: Multiuser Calendar & Appointment Scheduler. 1992. *Items Included:* Detailed manuals are included with all DYNACOMP products. *Customer Support:* Free telephone support to original customer - no time limit; 30 day limited warranty.
MS-DOS 3.2 or higher. IBM PC & compatibles (512k). $59.95 (Add $5.00 for 3 1/2" format; 5 1/4" format standard). *Optimal configuration:* IBM, 256k RAM, MS-DOS 2.0 or higher, CGA, EGA, VGA, Hercules, IBM 8514, PC 3270, ATT, or compatible graphics capability.
A Flexible & Easy-to-Use Single or Multiuser Calendar System Which Can Accomodate up to 64 Individual Calendars. The Many Features Include: Daily or Weekly Calendar Display. Master Calendar for Company or Public Notices. Calendar Administrator Can Globally Set Appointments. Individuals Can Browse Through Other Calendars. Appointments (Notes, etc.) May Be Entered up to Three Years into the Future, & 16 Months Back in the Past & More.
Dynacomp, Inc.

MAKER: Sheet Metal Shop Fabricating System. May 1991. *Items Included:* Microsoft Windows 3.0, various utilities, documentation. *Customer Support:* Free training & telephone support; service contracts available for hardware and/or software; free updates for the first year; if a service contract is maintained, all updates are included free of charge.
Microsoft Windows 3.0. IBM PC compatible 80286/80386 (4Mb). Contact Vendor.
Nonstandard peripherals required: VGA monitor with VGA graphics board, math coprocessor, hard disk, mouse.
Sheet Metal Shop Fabricating System That Contains: Specification Driven High Speed Input with Three-Dimensional, Rotational, & Exploded Fitting Views; Rectangular/Round/Oval Fittings Library; True Nest with Variable Gauge Nesting Capability; Interactive Nesting Options; Parts Creation; Automatic Label/Report Generation; Multiple Cutter Support; Multi-Tasking Environment with a Graphics-Oriented/Icon-Based Interface.
East Coast Sheet Metal Fabricating Corp.

Making the Modern: 19th Century Poetry in English. *Version:* 1.5. Feb. 1995. *Items Included:* BookWorm Student Reader (diskette). *Customer Support:* 30 day MBG. Technical support (toll call) - no charge.
System 7.0 or higher. Macintosh (5Mb). CD-ROM disk $79.95 (ISBN 1-57316-019-9, Order no.: 16154). *Nonstandard peripherals required:* CD-ROM drive, 12" color monitor. *Optimal configuration:* 13" color monitor recommended.
Windows 3.1 or higher. IBM compatible (MPC) 386 DX (4Mb). CD-ROM disk $79.95. *Nonstandard peripherals required:* Standard multimedia compatible CD-ROM. *Optimal*

configuration: 8Mb RAM recommended, 256 color monitor recommended.
A Generous Anthology That Explores the Great Flowering of Poetry in English During the 19th Century. The Great Romantics, the Best Victorians, & America's Greatest Masters of Verse Are All Represented in This Full-Scale Critical Edition. An Abundance of Illustrations & Spoken Recitations Are Also Included.
Communication & Information Technologies, Inc. (CIT).

Mammals: A Multimedia Encyclopedia.
(National Geographic Society CD-ROM Ser.). MS-DOS 3.1 or higher. 386 processor or higher (640k). CD-ROM disk $79.95 (Order no.: R1055). *Nonstandard peripherals required:* CD-ROM drive. *Optimal configuration:* 386 processor higher, MS-DOS 3.1 or higher, 20Mb hard drive, 640k RAM, external speakers or headphones (with sound card) that are Sound Blaster compatible, VGA graphics & adapter, VGA color monitor.
Macintosh (4Mb). (Order no.: R1055A). *Nonstandard peripherals required:* 14" color monitor or larger, CD-ROM drive.
This Fascinating Program Contains Pictures of Hundreds of Mammals, Videos, Essays, Vital Statistics, Animal Sounds, Range Maps & More (Grades 2 & Up).
Library Video Co.

Manage Stress. Crisp Publications. Oct. 1995. *Items Included:* Manual, registration card, one CD-ROM disk, product catalog, skills product brochure, America Online user card. *Customer Support:* Free technical support allows users to call support technicians anytime between 8:00am to 5:00pm Pacific Standard Time Monday through Friday.
Windows 3.1, Windows 95 or higher. 486 33MHz PC or higher (8Mb). CD-ROM disk $49.95 (ISBN 1-888226-00-5). *Nonstandard peripherals required:* Double speed CD-ROM drive, SVGA graphics, 8 bit sound card. *Optimal configuration:* 486 33MHz PC or higher, double speed CD-ROM drive, SVGA graphics, 16Mb RAM, 16 bit sound card.
A CD-ROM Based Software Product That Provides Users with Techniques for Diagnosing Stress, Mastering Key Coping Skills & Essential Steps for Building Mental Fitness.
Midisoft Corp.

Manage THAT! *Compatible Hardware:* Apple Macintosh Plus. *Memory Required:* 1000k. *General Requirements:* Hard disk; LaserWriter or ImageWriter for output. *Items Included:* Documentation & 4D runtime. *Customer Support:* Support & update service $135, update only $75.
3.5" disk $695.00.
Powerful & Easy-to-Use Project Scheduling System Designed to Meet Needs of the Experienced Project Manager. Output Includes Gantt, PERT, Work Breakdown Structure & Resource Charts as Well as Text Reports.
Varcon Systems.

Manage Time. Crisp Publications. Nov. 1995. *Items Included:* Manual, registration card, one CD-ROM disk, product catalog, skills product brochure, America Online user card. *Customer Support:* Free technical support allows users to call support technicians anytime between 8:00am to 5:00pm Pacific Standard Time Monday through Friday.
Windows 3.1, Windows 95 or higher. 486 33MHz PC or higher (8Mb). CD-ROM disk $49.95 (ISBN 1-888226-04-8). *Nonstandard peripherals required:* Double speed CD-ROM drive, SVGA graphics, 8 bit sound card. *Optimal configuration:* 486 33MHz PC or higher, double speed CD-ROM drive, SVGA graphics, 16Mb RAM, 16 bit sound card.
A CD-ROM Based Software Program That Gives People Strategies for Gaining Control of Their Time & Develop a Personal Time Management System.
Midisoft Corp.

Management Calendar Creator. Gary Sande. 1984. *Compatible Hardware:* Apple II series, IBM PC & compatibles. *Operating System(s) Required:* Apple DOS 3.3, PC-DOS 2.0 or higher. *Memory Required:* Apple 48k, IBM 256k. *General Requirements:* Printer.
disk $49.50 (ISBN 1-55797-172-2, Order no.: AP2-AG506).
disk $59.50 (ISBN 1-55797-239-7, Order no.: IBM-AG506).
Enables Users to Create Their Own Management Calendar. Users Provide the List of Jobs, the Starting Date, Days Between Jobs & the Program Calculates & Prints the List. Package Includes Program & Data Disk with Documentation Which Includes Sample Calendar & Worksheet. Applicable with Any Activity Requiring a Calendar Sequence Throughout the Year.
Hobar Pubns.

Management Diagnostic Series. *Compatible Hardware:* IBM PC, PC XT, PC AT, & 100% compatibles. *Operating System(s) Required:* PC-DOS 2.0 or higher. *Memory Required:* 128k. *General Requirements:* CGA card for IBM. Operates on "A" or "C" drives only.
$99.00 ea.
Thoughtware, Inc. (Florida).
 Assessing Personal Management Skills. *Version:* 4.0.
 Evaluating Organizational Effectiveness. *Version:* 2.0.
 Understanding Personal Interaction Styles. *Version:* 3.0.
 Understanding Decision Making Styles. *Version:* 1.0.
 Assessing Management Development Skills. *Version:* 1.0.

Management Expert. *Version:* 2.01. *Compatible Hardware:* IBM PC & compatibles. *Operating System(s) Required:* PC-DOS, MS-DOS. *Memory Required:* 256k. *General Requirements:* Hard disk recommended. *Items Included:* 32 pg. Thinking Software catalog.
3.5" or 5.25" disk $34.95.
Computer Aided Instructional Program Giving Interactive Instruction in Three Management Skills: Communication, Delegation, & Confrontation. At the End of Each Section Users Receive Tips & Techniques Based on Their Own Responses.
Thinking Software, Inc.

Management Simulator. *Compatible Hardware:* Apple II with Applesoft; IBM PC. *Memory Required:* 48k, IBM 128k.
disk $39.95.
Based on Games Played at MBA Schools.
Dynacomp, Inc.

The Management Tool Kit. Consulting Management Associates, Inc. *Compatible Hardware:* TI Professional. *Operating System(s) Required:* MS-DOS. *Language(s):* MSBASIC. *Memory Required:* 64k. *General Requirements:* Winchester hard disk, printer.
$425.00.
Texas Instruments, Personal Productivit.

Management Training Library. (Management Diagnostic Ser. - Management Training Ser.). 1983. *Compatible Hardware:* IBM PC, PC XT, PC AT, & 100% compatibles. *Operating System(s) Required:* PC-DOS/MS-DOS 2.0 or higher. *Language(s):* Compiled BASIC. *Memory Required:* 128k. *General Requirements:* CGA card for IBM. Operates on "A" or "C" drives only.
Diagnostic Series. disk $99.00 ea.
Training Series. disk $99.00 ea.
Diagnostic Programs Privately Assess Strengths & Weaknesses While the Training Programs Provide Interactive Learning to Improve Management Skills. Diagnostic Series Includes: ASSESSING PERSONAL MANAGEMENT SKILLS, EVALUATING ORGANIZATIONAL EFFECTIVENESS, & UNDERSTANDING. Understanding Personal Interaction Styles, Understanding Decision-making Styles; Assessing Management Skills. Training Series Includes: DEFINING GOALS & OBJECTIVES, IMPROVING EMPLOYEE PERFORMANCE, LEADING EFFECTIVELY, MANAGING TIME EFFECTIVELY, MOTIVATING TO ACHIEVE RESULTS, & PERFORMANCE APPRAISAL. Conducting Successful Meeting, Managing by Exception, Managing Stress, Life & Career Planning & Decision Making: Training & Applications.
Thoughtware, Inc. (Florida).

Management Training Series. *Compatible Hardware:* IBM PC, PC XT, PC AT, & 100% compatibles. *Operating System(s) Required:* PC-DOS 2.0 or higher. *Memory Required:* 128k. *General Requirements:* CGA card for IBM. Operates on "A" or "C" drives only.
$99.00 ea.
Thoughtware, Inc. (Florida).
 Leading Effectively. *Version:* 4.0.
 Motivating to Achieve Results. *Version:* 2.0.
 Defining Goals & Objectives. *Version:* 3.0.
 Improving Employee Performance. *Version:* 3.0.
 Performance Appraisal. *Version:* 3.0.
 Managing Time Effectively. *Version:* 3.0.
 Conducting Successful Meetings. *Version:* 3.0.
 Managing by Exception. *Version:* 2.0.
 Managing Stress. *Version:* 2.0.
 Life & Career Planning. *Version:* 2.0.
 Decision Making - Training & Applications. *Version:* 1.0.

Manager Series Acquisitions Module: Manager Series Library Automation System. *Version:* 7.0. 1994. *Compatible Hardware:* IBM PC & compatibles. *Memory Required:* 640k. *General Requirements:* 1 floppy & 1 hard drive; tape. *Items Included:* 3-ring bound reference & tutorial style manual; manual includes quick reference summary. *Customer Support:* Turn-key vendor: hardware, peripherals, hardware/software support contracts, toll-free phone & Internet access to product support, installations, training, user groups, quarterly technical newsletter.
PC-DOS/MS-DOS (640k). 3.5" or 5.25" disk Business/Professional $2450.00; multiple purchase discounts & GSA pricing available (ISBN 0-929795-03-2). *Networks supported:* Novell, IBM, Banyan, 3COM, LANtastic, PathWorks, Windows NT, NetWare.
Automate Journal, Report & Monograph Ordering. Ordering Statistics, Invoice Tracking & Processing, Generate Order & Claim Letters, Collection Maintenance, & Allocation of Costs Are All a Part of This Module. Also Provides Searching & Multi-User Options. Order Online with EBSCO, Majors, Dawson, the Information Store & Readmore & More. Entries Automatically Transfer Appropriate Data to the Cataloging & Serial Modules.
Data Trek, Inc.

Manager Series Cataloging Module: Manager Series Library Automation System. *Version:* 7.0. 1994. *Compatible Hardware:* IBM PC & compatibles. *Operating System(s) Required:*

PC-DOS/MS-DOS. *General Requirements:* 1 floppy & 1 hard disk, printer. *Items Included:* 3-ring bound reference & tutorial style manual; also includes quick reference summary. *Customer Support:* Turn-key vendor: hardware, peripherals, hardware/software support contracts, toll-free phone & Internet access to product support, installations, training, user groups, quarterly technical newsletter.
IBM (640k). 3.5" or 5.25" disk Business/Professional under 65k titles $2450.00; 65,000 plus titles $4995.00; multi-copy & GSA pricing available (ISBN 0-929795-00-8).
Provides for Printing Cross-Referenced Catalogs & New Book Lists by Author, Title & Subject Headings. Bibliographic Searching Through BOOLEAN Logic Statements Can Be Done on Most Elements in the Database. Generates New Book Lists, Shelf Lists & Catalog Cards and/or Spine & Book Labels, & Reports by Author, Title, Subject Headings. Integrates with Circulation & Acquisitions Modules.
Data Trek, Inc.

Manager Series Circulation Module: Manager Series Library Automation System. *Version:* 7.0. 1994. *Compatible Hardware:* IBM PC & compatibles. *Operating System(s) Required:* PC-DOS/MS-DOS. *General Requirements:* 1 floppy & 1 hard disk drive. *Items Included:* 3-ring reference & tutorial style manual; also includes quick reference summary. *Customer Support:* Turn-key vendor: hardware, peripherals, hardware/software support contracts, toll-free phone & Internet access to product support, installations, training, user groups, quarterly technical newsletter.
IBM (640k). 3.5" or 5.25" disk Business/Professional under 65k titles $2450.00; 65,000 plus titles $4995.00; multi-copy & GSA pricing available (ISBN 0-929795-01-6).
Facilitates Check in, Check Out, Hold & Renewal. Overdue Reports & Notices, & Fine Payments Are Generated along with Borrower Reports Listing Title, Cost, & Due Date for Holdings Out to Any Particular Borrower or Borrowers. A Full Complement of Management Reports, a Reserve Collection Management Option, & Inventory Options Provide Comprehensive Circulation Service, Reserve Collection Management Option & Inventory Options. Also Offers Full Bar Code Support. Integrates wtih Cataloging & Serials Modules.
Data Trek, Inc.

Manager Series Databridge Module: Manager Series Library Automation System. *Version:* 7.0. 1994. *Compatible Hardware:* IBM PC & compatibles. *Memory Required:* 640k. *General Requirements:* 1 floppy drive & 1 hard disk. *Items Included:* 3-ring reference & tutorial style manual, quick reference & disk. *Customer Support:* Turn-key vendor: hardware, peripherals, hardware/software support contracts, toll-free phone & Internet access to product support, installations, training, user groups, quarterly technical newsletter.
IBM. 3.5" or 5.25" disk, Business/Professional $995.00; multi-copy & GSA pricing available (ISBN 0-929795-04-0). *Networks supported:* Novell, Banyan, 3COM, IBM, LANtastic, PathWorks, Windows NT, NetWare.
Transfers Bibliographic Data Stored in MARC Formats from MARCIVE, OCLC & CD ROM to ACQUISITIONS, CATALOGING & CIRCULATION MODULES. Eliminates the Chores of Keyboard Entry into the Manager Series Library Automation System for Those Records Which Are Already Available in Machine-Readable Formats, Minimizes Initial Cataloging & the Export Functions Allow Users to Share Records with Other Sites or Institutions.
Data Trek, Inc.

Manager Series OPAC Module (Online Public Access Catalog): Manager Series Library Automation System. *Version:* 7.0. 1994. *Compatible Hardware:* IBM PC & compatibles. *Items Included:* Tutorial & reference style manual; quick reference summary & disk. *Customer Support:* Turn-key vendor: hardware, peripherals, hardware/software support contracts, toll-free phone & Internet access to product support, installations, training, user groups, quarterly technical newsletter.
PC-DOS (640k). disk 3.5" or 5.25" under 65k titles $995.00; over 65k titles $1995.00, multi-copy & GSA pricing available (ISBN 0-929795-07-5). *Addl. software required:* Data Trek's Manager Series Cataloging Module. *Networks supported:* Novell, LANtastic, 3COM, Banyan, IBM LAN Manager, PathWorks, Windows NT, NetWare.
Menu-Driven, Multi-User OPAC (Online Public Access Catalog) Search & Retrieval Software. Ten Search Options. Sort Capabilities: up to 10,000 Records per Second. On-Line Help Screens, Boolean Operators, Simultaneous Left & Right Truncation, Range/Keyword Searching, & Many Other Options Allow Patrons to Create Searches Closely Tailored to Their Needs. Integration with Other ASCII Files Optional with Customization.
Data Trek, Inc.

Manager Series Report Generator Module: Manager Series Library Automation System. *Version:* 7.0. 1994. *Items Included:* 3 ring bound reference style manual, including a quick reference summary & diskette. *Customer Support:* Data Trek Inc. is a turn-key vendor supplying software, hardware, peripherals, hardware/software support contracts, toll-free phone & Internet access to product support, installations, training, refresher training, user groups & a technical newsletter.
PC-DOS/MS-DOS. IBM PC & compatibles (640k). 3.5" or 5.25" disk $495.00 (multiple purchase discount & GSA pricing available (ISBN 0-929795-08-3, Order no.: 3-MAN-REP-1). *Nonstandard peripherals required:* 1 floppy & 1 hard disk drive, printer. *Optimal configuration:* IBM compatible 386; MS-DOS; 640k RAM; printer; modem with direct telephone line; Novell LAN for networking. *Networks supported:* Novell, IBM, 3COM, Banyan, LANtastic, PathWorks, Windows NT, NetWare.
Tailor More Than 150 Reports with Program's Creation Features. Fields in Existing Cataloging, Circulation, Acquisitions or Serials (Other Data Trek Modules) Reports Can Be Removed, Repositioned, Expanded or Contracted. New Fields Can Also Be Added to Make Manager Series Reports & Displays Conform to Your Library's Exact Specifications. Also Includes Pop-Up Menus, User Picklists, Field-Sensitive Help Screens, & Full-Screen Editing Report.
Data Trek, Inc.

Manager Series Serials Module: Manager Series Library Automation System. *Version:* 7.0. 1994. *Compatible Hardware:* IBM PC & compatibles. *Operating System(s) Required:* PC-DOS/MS-DOS. *Memory Required:* 640k. *General Requirements:* 1 floppy & hard disk drive, printer. *Items Included:* 3-ring tutorial & reference style manual; quick reference summary & disk. *Customer Support:* Data Trek Inc. is a turn-key vendor: hardware, peripherals, hardware/software support contracts, toll-free phone & Internet access to product support, installations, training, refresher training, user groups & a quarterly technical newsletter.
3.5" or 5.25" disk Business/Professional $2450.00; multi-copy & GSA pricing available (ISBN 0-929795-02-4). *Networks supported:* Novell, IBM, 3COM, Banyan, LANtastic, PathWorks, Windows NT, NetWare.
Provides for Check in, Routing Slip Maintenance & Production, Arrival Tracking, Issue Prediction, Claims Alert & Form Printing, & Renewal Alerts. Claims Online with EBSCO, Dawson Information Store & Majors. Reports Include Budget & Projection, Status of Missing Issues, & Serial's Catalog along with Claim Letter Printing. A History File Is Also Maintained. Integrates with Acquisitions & Circulation Modules.
Data Trek, Inc.

Manager's Assistant: Retail Point of Sale Inventory Control System. *Version:* 3.1. Jun. 1983. *Items Included:* (1) Annual update service, option $595.00 (2) Demo data base included for evaluation & training (3) 90 day "money back" (4) Spiral-bound user manual. *Customer Support:* (1) Telephone Hotline, hourly rate (2) Onsite installation & training, hourly rate (3) Online indexed manual, option $100.00 (4) First year product update included in the purchase price.
MS-DOS. IBM XT, AT & 386 compatible (512k). disk $2250.00. *Nonstandard peripherals required:* Receipt printers, cash drawers, bar code readers. *Networks supported:* Novell, Antisoft, Alloy.
Supports: Bar Codes, Price Label Printing, Purchase Order Entry & Tracking, Receiving, Open to Buy, Profitability Analysis & System Generated Suggested Orders. The Focus of the System Is Inventory Control; What to Order, When to Order, How Much to Order & What Not to Reorder. The System Provides Decision Oriented Reports to Make Better Inventory Control Decisions & to Maintain Better Managerial Control. It Is Not Unrealistic to Increase a StoreS Sales by 80% or More As a Result of This System.
Point of Sale Systems Corp.

Managers Toolbox. *Items Included:* Spiral bound manual. *Customer Support:* No charge.
MS-DOS 2.0 or higher (640k). IBM PC or compatibles. $195.00. *Addl. software required:* Lotus 1-2-3 Version 1A or higher.
A Series of Four Tactical Lotus 1-2-3 Applications That Allow User to Perform Individualized Analysis on Key Components of an Asset Liability Situation. Useful for Establishing & Reconciling Financial Goals, Pricing Deposit Services, Comparing Performance of Fixed Rate & Variable Rate Instruments, & Setting Meaningful Early Withdrawal Penalties.
Farin & Assocs.

Managing a Private Practice: Software for the Professional Therapists. Phyllis M. Cutcher & Harold Cutcher. Jul. 1990. *Items Included:* 3 ring loose-leaf bound documentation. *Customer Support:* 30 days free telephone support.
MS-DOS or IBM DOS 2.0 or higher. IBM PC/XT, AT, PS/2 & compatibles. 3.5" or 5.25" disk $325.00 (ISBN 0-9627313-0-7). *Optimal configuration:* IBM PC-XT, AT, PS/2 or compatibles with DOS 2.0 or later; 10Mb hard drive, 640k RAM (560K be must be available); graphics board. Dot matrix printer;with 132 characters per line on HP laserjet.
Initial Database Input of Clients, Therapists, Referral Sources. User Defined Time Changes. User Defined Treatment & Non-billable Modalities. Easy Entry for Daily Income & Expenses. Automatic Generation of Profit/Loss Statement, Individual Aged Receivable Statements, Records of Time. View Graphs of Profit & Variable Expenses Performance.
Info Systems.

Managing with Lotus 1-2-3. *Version:* 2.0. (Training Power Ser.). *Compatible Hardware:* IBM & compatibles. *Operating System(s) Required:* PC-DOS/MS-DOS 2.0 or higher.

Memory Required: 256k.
disk $75.00 (ISBN 0-922274-45-2, Order no.: MW01).
Provides Two-Part Interactive Training with a Case Study & Exercises Using the Actual 1-2-3 Software.
American Training International, Inc.

Mandelbrot/Julia Set. Sep. 1988. *Operating System(s) Required:* MS-DOS. *Memory Required:* 256k. *General Requirements:* CGA, EGA, or VGA; uses 80X87 if available. *Items Included:* Disk & instructions. *Customer Support:* Free.
disk $15.00.
Graphics Program That Plots the Mandelbrot or Julia Sets or Zooms in on Any Portion. Magnifies up to One Hundred Trillion Times.
Hinrichs Software.

Manson Evaluation-Revised (ME). Morse P. Manson & George J. Huba. *Customer Support:* Free unlimited phone support.
DOS 3.0 or higher. 286 (512k). disk $125.00 (Order no.: W-1044). Nonstandard peripherals required: Printer.
This Widely Used Test (More Than 300,000 Administered) Identifies Maladjusted Individuals: Alcoholics, Inadequates, & the Immature. It Measures Seven Characteristcs: Anxiety, Depressive Fluctuations, Emotional Sensitivity, Resentfulness, Incompleteness, Aloneness, & Interpersonal Relations.
Western Psychological Services.

Manufacturers Bill of Material Invoicing & Inventory Control Module. *Compatible Hardware:* DECmate II, DECmate III, PDP 11-23. *Operating System(s) Required:* COS-310, MICRO-RSX. *Language(s):* DIBOL-83.
$5000.00, incl. user's guide (Order no.: 85-6).
Combines Production Planning with Receivable Accounting to Serve the Special Needs of the Manufacturer Who Must Plan & Control Production According to Customer Demand. Production Reports Facilitate Planning by Organizing Production Requirements in Product, Scheduled Shipping Date, or Customer Order. New Production Reports Provide Prompt Information for Coordinating Current Schedules with New Needs, & Production Backlog Reports Help Insure That Orders Are Completely Filled on Time. Receivable Accounting Includes Customer Statements & Account Inquiry, Aged Trial Balance Reporting, & Cash Receipts Forecasting. Can Be Integrated with Corporate Consulting Company's General Ledger. Special Features for Order Processing & Invoicing Maintain a Customer's Order Until Shipped, Allow Adding, Editing, or Cancelling of Line Items at Any Time & Support Partial Shipments & Backordering.
Corporate Consulting Co.

Manufacturer's Inventory.
contact publisher for price.
Groups of Programs Allow Maintenance of Inventory.
Universal Data Research, Inc.

Manufacturer's Inventory Control System. *Compatible Hardware:* IBM PC & compatibles. *Operating System(s) Required:* MS-DOS. *Memory Required:* 512k. *General Requirements:* Printer; hard disk.
disk $495.00 (ISBN 0-923283-00-5).
User Can Define Manufactured Parts by Creating Bills-of-Materials, Including Labor & Overhead Costs, in Addition to Tracking Components. Features Parts Projections, Shortage Reports, Where-Used Reports, Four User-Defined Quantity Fields for Special Processing &/or Locations, Re-Order & Vendor Reports & Year-to-Date Sales Analysis. Also Includes an Integrated Purchase Order System Which Prints & Tracks Purchase Orders & a Sales Order Entry System Which Provides Customer Invoices, Automatic Decrement of Inventory & Autoposting to the Optional Accounts Receivable.
Computerware.

Manufacturers Job Cost-Inventory Control Module. *Compatible Hardware:* DECmate II, DECmate III, PDP 11-23. *Operating System(s) Required:* COS-310, MICRO-RSX. *Language(s):* DIBOL-83.
$2000.00, incl. user's guide (Order no.: 85-8).
Reports Materials Drawn for Jobs to Serve the Special Needs of Manufacturers & Suppliers Who Charge a Fixed Price for a Job. Materials Are Assigned to a Job When Drawn from Inventory, & the Month-End Movement Report Provides an Itemized Date-Ordered List of Materials Charged to Each Job. Includes Special Reports for Stock Status, Inventory Valuation, & Purchasing Advice, & Summarizes Draws & Receivings at Month-End to Show the Net Change to Inventory Value. Special Features Include Using a Bill of Material to Draw Items for a Job or Finished Good. All Quantities Specified in the Bill of Material List Are Drawn down from Inventory.
Corporate Consulting Co.

Manufacturer's 9-Pack. *Version:* 2.0. Feb. 1989. *Compatible Hardware:* IBM PC & compatibles; Macintosh. *Items Included:* Manual & software diskette. *Customer Support:* Free installation & technical support; limited warranty, call JIAN 415-941-9191.
$99.00. Nonstandard peripherals required: Hard drive recommended. Addl. software required: PC's: Any Lotus 1-2-3 version 2.01 compatible spreadsheet program. Macintosh: Any SYLK compatible spreadsheet including MS Excel, MS Works & others.
Consists of 9 Instant Worksheets for Controlling Daily Production Activities: Master Schedule, Costed Bill of Materials, Job Tracking, Inventory Modeling, Fiscal Calendar, Project Cost Tracking, QA Form, Supply Manager, & Labor Cost Report. Contains All the Software Reporting Tools That a Production Manager Would Need.
JIAN Tools for Sales.

Manufacturers Software. (Profit Ser.). *Compatible Hardware:* IBM 386 & compatibles, Novell & Unix. *Operating System(s) Required:* MS-DOS. (source code included). *Memory Required:* 512k. *General Requirements:* Hard disk 20Mb.
IBM 386 & compatibles. $2995.00 (Order no.: BOSS1).
System Novell & Unix. $3995.00.
Includes Accounts Receivable, Bill of Material Inventory, SalesTrak (Order Entry/Billing/Sales Analysis), May Be Purchased Separately. Other Modules Available Are Purchase Order, Accounts Payable, General Ledger, Payroll.
Crosstech Systems, Inc.

Manufacturing Accounting & Control System.
1981. *Compatible Hardware:* PC, PS/2 & compatibles, System 36, RS/6000. *Operating System(s) Required:* AIX, MS-DOS, SSP. *Language(s):* BASIC (source code included). *Memory Required:* IBM 512k, RS/6000 8Mb, S/36 256k. *General Requirements:* 120Mb hard disk, printer, RS/6000 320Mb.
disk $5000.00-$18,000.00.
Comprehensive Accounting & Control System. Provides Order Entry, Inventory, Bills of Materials, Work-in-Progress, Materials Requirements Planning, Payroll, Costing, A/P, A/R, & G/L.
Steppenwolff Corp.

Manufacturing Control System. Dec. 1979. *Compatible Hardware:* IBM PC, PC XT, PC AT & compatibles. *Operating System(s) Required:* PC-DOS/MS-DOS, UNIX, XENIX. *Language(s):* BASIC, Assembly (source code included). *Memory Required:* 512k. *Items Included:* Disks, manual. *Customer Support:* 90 days included, then 15% per year. On site installation & training available at $700.00 per day.
$2495.00 - $7990.00.
Inventory, Bill of Materials (BOM), Control & Materials Requirements Planning System (MRP). Purchase Orders & Numerous Reports Are Generated. User-Defined Fields Provide Flexibility for Firms Manufacturing Products as Diverse as Automotive Parts, Electrical Equipment, & Medical Products. Customization Available. Handles Real-World Situations Such as Variances Between Planned & Actual Consumption. Calculates Costs Based on Standard Costs, Average Costs, FIFO, or LIFO. Optional Order Processing Module Provides for Sales Order Entry, Generation of Pick Lists & Packing Lists, Sales Analysis, Invoices, & Back-Order Lists. Handles Various Price & Discount Structures. Interfaces to Accounting Packages.
Stolzberg Research, Inc.

Manufacturing Inventory Control. *Version:* 5.4. 1978. *Compatible Hardware:* IBM PC. *Operating System(s) Required:* MS-DOS, PC-DOS 1.1, 2.0. *Language(s):* MBASIC (source code included). *Memory Required:* 128k.
disk $1000.00.
Integrated Control of Finished Good, Sub-Assemblies & Component Inventories & Costs via a Bill-of-Material Processor, Cost Reports, Production Commitment Report. Interfaces with A/R & Billing & Order Entry, Purchase Order Systems.
CharterHouse Software Corp.

Manufacturing Inventory Control. Jan. 1985. *Compatible Hardware:* IBM PC, PC XT with 2 disk drives & printer. *Operating System(s) Required:* MS-DOS. *Language(s):* C. *Memory Required:* 512k.
disk $1995.00.
demo disk & manual $50.00.
manual only $25.00.
Contains the Following Features: Vendor File with Name, Code, Address, etc.; Inventory File That Stores Information Such As Part Name, Part Number, Re-Ordering Point, Preferred Inventory Level, Lead Time, Cost, etc.; Purchase Order File That Stores Information Including Date, Vendor Code, Purchase Order Number, Quantity Ordered, Quantity Received, Due Date, etc. Various Reports Are Generated.
Unik Assocs.

Manufacturing Inventory Control System. *Version:* 450.2. 1981. *Compatible Hardware:* IBM PC & compatibles. *Operating System(s) Required:* MS-DOS, PC-DOS. *Language(s):* QuickBASIC. *Memory Required:* 512k. *General Requirements:* Hard disk. *Items Included:* System diskettes, users guide, training tutorial. *Customer Support:* Telephone; annual contracts available.
$2995.00 to $3495.00.
Handles Multi-Level Bills of Material for Finished Goods & Subassemblies with Where-Used Lists. The MRP Module Calculates Part & Subassembly Requirements. System Creates Purchase Orders & Adjusts Inventory Balances & Costs When Merchandise Received. System Can Recall All Manufactured Products Based on Latest Part & Subassembly Costs. The System Uses a Production Work Order Concept to Initiate, Schedule, & Control Production. Compares Actual Production Costs to Standard Costs & Reports Cost Variances. Manufacturing May Be Interfaced to IMS Order Processing for Make-to-

TITLE INDEX

Order Manufacturers or with IMS Wholesale Distribution for Make-to-Stock Manufacturers. File Sizes Limited Only by Disk Capacity. Runs Single User or Multi-User on Many Networks.
International Micro Systems, Inc.

Manufacturing Inventory Control with MRP & BOMP. Charles F. Kerchner, Jr. 1980. *Compatible Hardware:* IBM PC XT; Apple II+ & IIe. *Operating System(s) Required:* MS-DOS, Apple DOS. *Language(s):* BASIC (source code included). *Memory Required:* 48k. *General Requirements:* 3 disk drives or hard disk, printer. *Items Included:* Software & 100 page manual. *Customer Support:* Free telephone support.
IBM, Apple. disk $299.95.
Inventory Control System with Bill of Material Processing & MRP for the Small Manufacturer of Standardized Products with Multi-Level Bill of Materials.
C. F. Kerchner & Assocs., Inc.

Manufacturing Job Cost Accounting. Richard A. Bilancia. *Compatible Hardware:* TRS-80 Model 16. *Operating System(s) Required:* UNIX, XENIX. *Language(s):* UNIFY (source code included). *Memory Required:* 512k.
8" disk $995.00.
manual $50.00.
Tailored for the Typical Manufacturing Operation. Written Using a Relational Database Management System. Includes Several Management Information Reports.
Computer Guidance & Support.

Manufacturing Job Cost II. *Compatible Hardware:* Apple Macintosh Plus. *General Requirements:* Hard disk.
3.5" disk $9500.00.
Designed for a Manufacturer Who Features Build-To-Order Products.
Advanced Data Systems, Inc.

Manufacturing Management: Manufacturing - Distribution. Version: 4.6.2. 1990. *Items Included:* Instruction manuals. *Customer Support:* First 90 days free, annually 15% of purchase price. Training customer site $800.00 per day plus expenses - training vendor office $500.00 per day.
MS-DOS, AIX, UNIX, VMS. Intel 486, IBM RS6000, DEC VAX (2MB), ALPHA. $1000.00 per module (1-5 user) plus Synergy. *Addl. software required:* Progress 4GL. *Optimal configuration:* 486-50mhz 16Mb RAM, 1.44 Mb diskette, 525Mb QIC tape, 1.0 GB hard disk, 8 port MUX & printer. *Networks supported:* Lantastic, Novell, Powerfusion.
MS-DOS, AIX, Novell, UNIX, VMS. 486-50mhz (4Mb). $1000.00 per module plus Synergy. *Addl. software required:* DBL-Synergy. *Optimal configuration:* 486-50mhz 16Mb RAM, 1.44 Mb diskette, 5.25Mb Qic tape, 1.0 GB hard disk, 16 port MUX & printer. *Networks supported:* Lantastic, Novell, Powerfusion.
Manufacturing Customer Order Processing, Bill of Materials, Shop Floor Control, Standard Product Costing & Routing, Materials Requirements Planning & Master Scheduling, with All the Accounting Modules, & Purchasing, Job Costing & Product Configuring.
Automation Resources Corp.

Manufacturing Management System. Fisher Business Systems, Inc. *Operating System(s) Required:* MS-DOS. *Memory Required:* 128k. *General Requirements:* Printer.
$2500.00.
Includes Sales Order Entry, Purchase Order Management, Inventory Control, Billing, Accounts Receivable, Sales Commission Processing, etc.
Texas Instruments, Personal Productivit.

Manufacturing Resource Planning - Decision Support System: MRP-DSS. *Version:* 4.07. Jul. 1991. *Items Included:* 1 manual, 296 pages; 5 diskettes: (1) Resource (2) Control (3) Planning (4) Data (5) Utilities. *Customer Support:* 30 days warranty, return if not satisfied; free telephone support.
DOS 2.1 or higher; OS/2. IBM PC, XT, AT, PS/2, 386, 486 (256k). tutorial version $119.95; industrial version $995.00 (ISBN 1-877928-00-3). *Networks supported:* Novell, LAN.
PC-Based Software Package Intended to Assist Small & Medium Sized Manufacturing Enterprises Through Automated Scheduling, Inventory Management & Production Control. It Combines Concepts of Materials Requirements Planning (MRPI) to Provide a Powerful Decision Support System for Manufacturing Managers & Engineers.
Orange Fortune.

Manufacturing II & Inventory Control. 1981. *Compatible Hardware:* IBM PC. *Operating System(s) Required:* MP/M, CP/M. *Language(s):* CBASIC. *Memory Required:* 64k.
demo disk $50.00.
Offers Management Assistance to Manufacturers in Two Key Functions. One Function Is Inventory Control of Parts, Subassemblies & Finished Items. Second Function Is That of Producing Work Orders to Establish & Maintain Manufacturing Schedules. Other Modules Allow Processing of Customer & Vendor Data, Issuing Shipping Orders, Adjusting Inventory, & Creating Bill-of-Materials Data for Analysis of Production Needs.
Intro-Logic, Inc.

Manx Aztec CII. *Compatible Hardware:* TRS-80 Model III, Model 4. *Operating System(s) Required:* CP/M.
Aztec CII-c (CP/M & ROM). disk $349.00.
Aztec CII-d (CP/M). disk $199.00.
C Compiler, 8080/Z80 Assembler, Linker, Librarian, UNIX Libraries, & Specialized Utilities.
Manx Software Systems.

Manx Aztec SDB for Amiga. *Compatible Hardware:* Commodore Amiga.
3.5" disk $125.00.
C Source Level Debugger for the Amiga. Has All the Standard Features, Including Line-by-Line Tracing; Conditional Breakpoints on Lines, Functions, or Variables; Examination, Modification, & Display of Global, Local, & Static Variables, Structure, or Expressions by Name. Other Features Include Reusable Command Macros & Procedures, Back Tracing, Active Frame Context Switching, etc.
Manx Software Systems.

The Many Faces of GO, 1992. David Fotland. Jul. 1992. *Items Included:* 5.25" & 3.5" diskettes, 44 page user guide with rules & strategies, game history. *Customer Support:* Telephone customer support at no charge available M-F 9:00-5:00 Pacific time. Upgrades from previous version & previous program "Cosmos" available at reduced price.
MS-DOS. IBM compatible (512k). $59.95 retail (upgrades from prev. versions $17.00; upgrades from "Cosmos" $27.00) (ISBN 0-923891-28-5, Order no.: GS19). *Optimal configuration:* Supports VGA, EGA, CGA Tandy & Hercules graphics. Mouse optional.
This Program Challenges Newcomers & Advanced Players Alike, Offering Playing & Game-Viewing Programs, On-Line Tutorial & Instruction, Pre-Recorded Problem Presenter Joseki Tutor & Modern Play Capability. Play at 20 Levels on 9x9 to 19x19 Line Boards with up to 29 Stones Handicap.
Ishi Press International.

MAPGRAFIX MAPPING SYSTEM

Manylink. *Operating System(s) Required:* PC-DOS/MS-DOS 3.0 or higher. *Memory Required:* 40k.
$695.00.
Local Disk File Transfer Package for NetWare Users. Operates in the Background & Lets Users Share Files & Printers. Users Can Send & Receive Files While Continuing to Work on Their Applications. Also Lets the User Network Local Printers & Increase NetWare's Five Printer Maximum.
Manylink.

MapArt: EPS Format. Jul. 1992. *Items Included:* 8 disks, manual for instruction, registration card. *Customer Support:* 30 day money back guarantee. Free technical support.
Macintosh or PC (2Mb). $179.00. *Addl. software required:* Adobe Illustrator or Aldus Freehand, or Corel Draw for PC.
A Collection of Clip Art Maps Which Can Be Manipulated with Either Adobe Illustrator or Aldus Freehand. Add Text, Symbols, Color, etc. Through Your Graphic Software to Create Presentation Quality Maps. Includes 4 World, 14 Regional, & 30 Countries by State or Province.
Cartesia Software.

MapArt: Paint (MAC) or.PCX (PC). Oct. 1990. *Items Included:* 1 800k disk for MAC, instructional manual, registration cards. *Customer Support:* 30 day money back guarantee. Free technical support.
Macintosh or PC. $79.00. *Addl. software required:* MAC-any paint, PC-Publisher's Paintbrush or PC Paintbrush Plus.
A Collection of Clip Art Maps Which Can Be Manipulated in Any Paint Program for the MAC & in PC Paintbrush Plus or Publisher's Paintbrush for the PC. Includes 4 world, 12 Regional, & 25 Countries with State & Province Outlines.
Cartesia Software.

MapArt: PICT (MacDraw II Format). Oct. 1990. *Items Included:* 5 disks, instruction manual, registration card. *Customer Support:* 30 day money back guarantee, Free Technical support.
Macintosh. $179.00. *Addl. software required:* MacDraw II, MacDraw Pro, or Canvas 2.1.1.
A Collection of Clip Art Maps Which Can Be Manipulated with MacDraw II or Pro, or the Current Version of Canvas. Add Text, Symbols, Color, etc. Through Your Graphic Software to Create Presentation Quality Maps. Includes 4 World Maps, 12 Regional, & 25 Countries by State or Province.
Cartesia Software.

MapArt: Volumes 1 - 4. 1994.
Macintosh. CD-ROM disk $199.00. *Nonstandard peripherals required:* CD-ROM drive. *Addl. software required:* Compatible Paint & Draw program.
MPC; 386 or higher (2Mb). CD-ROM disk $199.00. *Nonstandard peripherals required:* CD-ROM drive. *Addl. software required:* Compatible Paint & Draw program.
Collection of Maps Which Will Work with Many Popular Painting & Drawing Programs. Contains World, US States, & US Major Metropolitan Areas.
Cartesia Software.

MapBase. *Compatible Hardware:* Apple Macintosh Plus.
3.5" disk $595.00.
Computerized Mapping & RecordKeeping Database Program.
Komstock Co.

MapGrafix Mapping System. *Version:* 3.8. *Compatible Hardware:* All Mac II Series, Power Books, & Power Macintosh. *Memory Required:*

589

MAPINFO FOR WINDOWS: DESKTOP MAPPING

8000k. *General Requirements:* 40 - 80 Mb Hard disk; math coprocessor. *Customer Support:* $500.00 per year.
3.5" disk $2995.00.
Modules includes MapLink & MapView. disk $995.00.
Geographic Information Mapping System.
ComGrafix, Inc.

Mapinfo for Windows: Desktop Mapping - GIS. *Version:* 4.0. Mapinfo Corporation Staff. Dec. 1995. *Items Included:* 2 manuals, disks, CD-ROM & sample data sets. *Customer Support:* Basic - free 90 days, 1 yr at $225.00 maintenance - through Mapinfo.
IBM & compatibles (4Mb). CD-ROM disk $1295.00 (Order no.: DOS 3.1 OR HIGHER). *Addl. software required:* Windows 3.1 (Microsoft), Win95 or Windows NT. *Optimal configuration:* 1 floppy or CD-ROM & a hard disk with 12Mb free for install. Color printer (preferred).
Mac System 7.0 or higher. Macintosh with a 68020 processor or higher (4Mb). CD-ROM disk $1295.00. *Addl. software required:* Mac QuickDraw. *Optimal configuration:* 1 floppy or CD-ROM, hard disk with 12Mb free to install. Color printer (preferred).
Site Specific Precision Farming: Enables Users to Manage Farm Activities by Monitoring, Controlling & Navigation in the Field. Allows Users to Visualize Spatial Variations, & Analyze These Differences & How to Control for This Variation. Provides the Agriculturalist the Necessary Tools to Control for Spatial Variations.
Farmer's Software Assn.

MAPIT. *Items Included:* Bound manual. *Customer Support:* Free hotline - no time limit; 30 day limited warranty; updates are $5/disk plus S&H.
MS-DOS. IBM & compatibles (256k). disk $89.95. *Nonstandard peripherals required:* Works with monochrome systems. Screen graphics available with CGA, EGA, or Hercules. Works with almost any printer & also works with the HP 7400 series plotters.
A Program for the Creation of Maps. The Medium for MAPIT Is the Printer. In Particular, It Is Desirable to Have a Printer Which Has a Condensed Mode of about 17 Characters per Inch Across & 12 Lines per Inch Down. Included with MAPIT Are Outline Map Files of the United States, Canada, Europe, Asia, Africa, South America, & Australia. Besides These Base Maps You Can Easily Enter Your Own Maps.
Dynacomp, Inc.

Maple Five: Student Edition. *Version:* 3. 1994. *Items Included:* 3 paper bound manuals. *Customer Support:* Unlimited support for registered users.
DOS/Windows. IBM & compatibles (2Mb). disk $99.00 (ISBN 0-534-25560-4, Order no.: 800-354-9706). *Optimal configuration:* 2Mb of extended RAM, minimum 10-12Mb free hard disk space, & 1.2Mb or 1.44Mb floppy diskette drive. Coprocessor optional.
Macintosh. Macintosh (2Mb plus). 3.5" disk $99.00 (ISBN 0-534-25561-2, Order no.: 800-354-9706). *Optimal configuration:* 2.5Mb RAM & hard disk with minimum 7-9Mb free. Coprocessor optional.
Lab packs (DOS) $670.00 (ISBN 0-534-25564-7).
Lab packs (Macintosh) $670.00 (ISBN 0-534-25565-5).
Student Version Solves the Widest Range of Problems of Any Computer Algebra System Available. From Calculus Through Linear Algebra, Differential Equations, Real Analysis, Complex Variables & Beyond. More Than 2500 Built-In Math Functions That Can Be Modified or Extended, a Complete Online Help System, 3-D & 2-D Graphics Including Contour Plots & Implicit Plotting & New Animations Capabilities That Let User See How Model Changes As a Function of Time. Improved Worksheet Interface & New Formatted Input/Output Allows User to Read Data from Files Created by Other Applications.
Brooks/Cole Publishing Co.

Maple: Music Applications Programming Language Extension. John Miller. 1985. *Compatible Hardware:* Commodore 64, 128. *Language(s):* BASIC. *Memory Required:* 64k.
disk $99.95, incl. user's guide (ISBN 1-55603-014-2, Order no.: C-1166).
Utility Designed to Simplify the Programming of Sound & Music Notation. Can Be Used for Recreational & Compositional Purposes, As Well As for Creating Music Instruction & Tutorial Programs.
Electronic Courseware Systems, Inc.

MapLinx Try & Buy. MapLinx Corporation Staff. *Items Included:* The package includes a 3.5" diskette, a mini-manual & a Try & Buy Brochure.
DOS 3.3 or higher. IBM PC, AT PS/2 (2Mb). disk $79.99 (ISBN 1-57548-011-5).
Nonstandard peripherals required: Microsoft or compatible mouse.
An Interactive Mapping Tool Capable of Interfacing with Popular Database Management, Contact Management & Spreadsheet Packages.
IBM Software Manufacturing Solutions (ISMS).

Mapps: The Management & Project Planning System. *Compatible Hardware:* IBM PC. $16,000.00-$25,000.00.
Features a Mappin/Mappout Utility for Downloading of MAPPS Database Files into Other Database Systems Regardless of Hardware Platform. Supports Multi-Project Environments, Includes a Resource Utilization Utility, Resource Leveling, Cost Analysis & What-If Analysis Features.
Mitchell Management Systems.

MAP's Printer Tool Kit. *Operating System(s) Required:* PC-DOS/MS-DOS. *Memory Required:* 128k. *General Requirements:* PC-DOS/MS-DOS compatible printers.
IBM PC & compatibles. disk $79.95 (Order no.: MPTK).
M.A.P. Systems, Inc.

MapStar: Communications-Vehicle Training System. *Version:* 2.1. *Compatible Hardware:* PowerMac & Mac II Series. *General Requirements:* Hard disk, 20Mb; RAM 8Mb. *Customer Support:* $600.00 Annually.
$5000.00.
Terminal Package for Automatic Vehicle Location.
ComGrafix, Inc.

MAP3D. *Version:* 1.3. Sep. 1984. *Compatible Hardware:* IBM PC, PC XT, PC AT, & compatibles. *Operating System(s) Required:* MS-DOS, PC-DOS. *Memory Required:* 512k. *General Requirements:* Printer, plotter.
disk $2000.00 (Order no.: MAP3D).
Uses Two Cartesian Coordinates to Draw 3D Views of Data on a Plotter. Like ISOPOLY, the Program Uses the Gridded Output File of KRIGE3.
Geostat Systems International, Inc. (GSII).

MapVision. *Version:* 2.0. 1991.
IBM PC & compatibles. disk $295.00.
Desktop Geographic Information System. Features Include Reference Maps, Continuous Zoom in & Zoom out, Latitude & Longitude Position, Street Search, Intersection Search, & Address Search, Overlay & Icon Creation, Complete Control over the Display of Map Features & Overlays, Census Block Identification & Print Screen for All Common Printers.
Polestar, Inc.

SOFTWARE ENCYCLOPEDIA 1996

Marble Madness. Atari Games, Corp. *Compatible Hardware:* Apple II, II+, IIe, IIc; Commodore 64, 128, Amiga.
Apple. disk $14.95.
Commodore 64. disk $19.95.
Amiga. 3.5" disk $19.95.
There Are 6 Levels of 3-D Maze-Like Runways to Roll Through. Slip over Ice-Fields. Whip Through Perilous Pipes. Encounter the "Wave", the "Marble Munchers", & the "Humming Hoovers".
Electronic Arts.

MARC Record Reader. 1996.
disk $199.00.
Super circulation control expanded & on-line catalog expanded from RIGHT ON PROGRAMS now have the capacity to download from the MARC format.
Right on Programs.

MarcoPolo. *Version:* 3.5. Oct. 1992. *Items Included:* Comprehensive manual with tutorial. *Customer Support:* Free technical support for registered users.
System 7.0 or higher. Macintosh Plus or higher (2Mb). 3.5" disk $895.00. *Optimal configuration:* Macintosh 040 or higher, System 7.5, 8Mb RAM, scanner. *Networks supported:* Any Apple compatible network.
A Document Imaging, Archival & Retrieval System That Works in Conjunction with Imaging Hardware for the Macintosh. Can Search Documents at 100,000 Words/Second or the Equivalent of 10,000 Pages of Text per Second. When Documents Are Found, Visual Representations of Each Are Displayed on Screen Like Paper Documents on a Desk.
Mainstay.

MARGIN+. *Version:* 7.1. 1985. *Compatible Hardware:* IBM PC & compatibles, PC XT, PC AT. *Operating System(s) Required:* MS-DOS 5.0 or higher. *Language(s):* Compiled BASIC, Assembly. *Memory Required:* 2000k.
disk $3000.00.
disk $4500.00, Network.
Adds Adjustable Rate Mortgages & Graduated Payments to the LOANLEDGER+ Environment; 99 Indices, up to 360 Scheduled Rate Changes, Caps, & Negative Amortization. Features Include: Automatic Notification, Maturity Date/Rate Change Report, Loan-to-Value Compression, Automatically Updates New Amortization Schedule with Index Plus Margin Information.
Dynamic Interface Systems Corp.

The Marietta Libraries. May 1992. *Items Included:* Documentation. *Customer Support:* 12 months unlimited warranty & phone support.
DR-DOS. Symbol Technologies 3000 Series (256k). disk $1495.00. *Optimal configuration:* 640k memory.
Relational Database Development Product for the Symbol Technologies 3000 Series DOS Compatible Computers.
Marietta Systems, Inc.

The Marina Program. *Version:* 6. Nov. 1988. *Compatible Hardware:* IBM PC & compatibles. *Operating System(s) Required:* Windows 3.1. *Memory Required:* 16000k. *General Requirements:* Hard disk. *Customer Support:* On site or by phone, first 90 days free, travel extra.
Single-User. disk $1250.00.
Multi-User. disk $1750.00.
Accounts Receivable & Information System for Marinas. Prints Mailing Labels & Waiting Lists & Performs Automatic Boat Registration List Searches. The Receivables Section Performs Automatic Recurring Charges, Coded Miscellaneous Charges, Late Notices, Electric Meter Calculations, Security & Key Deposit Lists, Vacancy & Occupancy Lists, & Insurance Due Reports.
Computer Consultants.

TITLE INDEX

Mario Is Missing.
MS-DOS version 3.3 or higher. IBM PC-AT & compatibles (286 or higher) (640k). 3.5" or 5.25" disk $59.95 (Order no.: 111160; 111158). *Optimal configuration:* IBM PC-AT or compatible (286 or higher), 640k RAM, 12MHz or faster, hard disk, VGA Graphics Card, Microsoft Mouse or 100% compatible recommended, supports most popular sound cards & PC speaker.
In a Classic Mario Bros. Game Setting, Learn Geography While Helping Luigi Foil Bowser, & Rescue Mario! Visit Fascinating Cities Worldwide, As You Help Luigi Navigate Streets, Collect Clues, Return Artifacts, Outsmart Koopas, & Rescue Mario! Gather Clues & Information by Visiting Famous Landmarks & Interviewing People on the Street. An Intuitive Graphic User Interface Offers These Fun Tools: Globulator (for Exploring the Globe), Videophone, Pocket Computer, & Navigation Tools.
Software Toolworks.

Mario Is Missing! CD Deluxe. Mar. 1993.
IBM CD-ROM. CD-ROM disk $69.95 (Order no.: 111312).
Video Clips, Sound & Beautiful High-Resolution Graphics Make This Enhanced Version Twice As Fun for Playing & Learning. In a Dynamic Mario Bros. Game Setting, Players Learn Geography While Helping Luigi Foil Bowser. Bowser & His Gang of Koopas Have Kidnapped Mario & Looted Landmarks Around the Globe. This CD-ROM Version Offers Even More Than the Original Disk Product: More Cities to Explore, Additional Clues to Collect, New Artifacts to Return to Their Rightful Locations - All Enhanced by the Sights & Sounds of Multimedia Technology. An Enthralling Edutainment Experience for Kids & Adults.
Software Toolworks.

Mario Is Missing!: City Disk. Jun. 1993.
IBM PC & compatibles (640k). 3.5" or 5.25" disk $24.95 (Order no.: 111292; 111293). *Addl. software required:* Mario Is Missing! *Optimal configuration:* IBM AT or compatible (286 or higher, 12MHz or faster); 640k; MS-DOS 3.3 or higher; hard disk; VGA card; mouse recommended; supports most popular sound cards.
Just When You Thought Mario Was Safe & Sound, Bowser's Nasty Band Is at It Again. No Artifact Is Free from the Koopa's Clutches in These Ten Add-On Cities for Mario Is Missing! From the Icy North Seas to Continental Europe & North America, from the Searing Desert to Steamy Southeast Asia & South America, the Koopas Are Absconding with More Artifacts in New Cities Throughout the World. It's up to You to Return the Riches to Their Owners & Free Mario from Bowser's Grip! Mario Is Missing! Program Is Required.
Software Toolworks.

Mario's Time Machine. Nov. 1993.
DOS. 3.5" or 5.25" disk $59.95 (Order no.: 111390; 111389).
Join the Mario Bros. on a Wild Ride Through Time As They Relive Great Moments in History in This New Mario Discovery Series Title. Take a Romp with Dinosaurs During the Jurassic Period, Stop off in Ancient Egypt to Meet Cleopatra, & Arrive Just in Time to Witness the Discovery of the Theory of Relativity in the 20th Century - All in a Day's Work for the Popular Plumbers. This Exciting Game Scenario Incorporates 16 Different Historical Eras & the Important Events That Helped Shape Them. Entertaining & Educational for the Whole Family.
Software Toolworks.

Marital Satisfaction Inventory (MSI). *Version:* 2.011. Douglas K. Snyder. *Customer Support:* Free unlimited phone support.
IBM PC & compatibles. 3.5" or 5.25" disk $210.00 (Order no.: W-1011 (5.25"); W-1027 (3.5")). *Optimal configuration:* DOS 3.0 or higher (512k), & hard disk with one Mb of free disk space, printer.
Identifies the Nature & Extent of Conflict Within a Marriage or Relationship. Covers Nine Dimensions of Marital Interaction. Two Additional Scales Indicate Response Bias & Overall Dissatisfaction with the Marriage.
Western Psychological Services.

Market. *Compatible Hardware:* Apple II+, IIe, IIc; Franklin Ace; TRS-80 Model III, Model 4. *Memory Required:* 48k.
disk $24.95.
cassette $24.95.
Game Designed to Teach Production, Advertising, & Pricing of Products. Two People Compete Against Each Other to See Who Can Make the Most Money.
Compuware.

Market EAS-Alyzer. *Compatible Hardware:* Apple. *Operating System(s) Required:* Apple DOS 3.3. *Memory Required:* 48k.
contact publisher for price.
Features Oscillators, Moving Averages, Momentum, OBU, PUI, NUI, Intraday Intensity, Relative Strength, Filtered Waves, Member Trading, Put/Call Ratios, Auto-Chart & More.
Wall Street Graphics, Inc.

Market Edge. *Version:* 1.0. May 1991. *Items Included:* 100 page manual. Two years of stock market technical data. *Customer Support:* Free phone support.
MS-DOS. IBM or compatible (640k). disk $39.00. *Nonstandard peripherals required:* Graphics capability. *Optimal configuration:* 10MHz 286 with math coprocessor & 1meg RAM.
Stock Market Timing Software Package. The Package Focuses on Identifying Trend Changes Using New & Standard Techniques. The Technical Index, Sigma Limits & Other New Indicators Are Featured Along with Stockastics, RSI, & Bollinger Bands.
SASI Software Corp.

The Market Forecaster. *Items Included:* Bound manual. *Customer Support:* Free hotline - no time limit; 30 day limited warranty; updates are $5/disk plus S&H.
MS-DOS. IBM & compatibles (256k). disk $199.95.
Predicts the Magnitude & Direction of Stock Market Movements over the Next Two to Four Months. The Forecasts Are Based on the Statistically Weighted Factors That Have Been Out-Performing the Market for Years. Built-In Features Include: (1) the Ability to Play "What-If" Games; (2) an Audio Signal When It Is Time to Take Action; (3) Self-Checking to Assure the Right Forecast; & (4) an Encrypted Forecast & Other Recorded Information Available by Phone.
Dynacomp, Inc.

The Market Maker. *Compatible Hardware:* AT&T 6300, 6300 Plus; IBM PC & compatibles, PC XT, PC AT. *Operating System(s) Required:* MS-DOS. *Language(s):* C. *Memory Required:* 512k. *General Requirements:* Graphics card, 2 disk drives or hard disk.
disk $295.00.
demo disk $5.00.
Technical Analysis Software Able to Store & Recall Several Thousand Analysis Charts & Automatically Update Any Chart Upon Recall. Features Automatic Data Aquisition, Direct Comparison Windows That Enable User to View up to Four Horizontal Graphs On-Screen Simultaneously, Multiple Zooms & De-Zooms, Custom Formula Creation & Modification. Other Features Include: Multiple Charting Formats, Spread Charts & Comparisons, Trend Lines Can Be Tested & Fitted, Parallel Lines Define Trend Channels, Moving Averages, Time/Price Gann Support & Resistance Calculations, Speed Resistance Lines, Least Square Calculation with Linear Correlation Readout, RSI (Relative Strength Indicator), MSI (Master Strength Indicator), DMI (Directional Movement Indicator), Fast & Slow Stochastics, Multiple Volume Indicators, Master Oscillator with Flexible Formula, Momentum Indicator, Cycle Ruler & Cycle Remover.
Inmark Development Corp.

Market Master. *Customer Support:* 800-929-8117 (customer service).
MS-DOS. Apple II. disk $49.99 (ISBN 0-87007-809-7).
Uses Five Standard Measures to Predict Buy & Sell Points.
SourceView Software International.

Market Master for the Macintosh: Personal Version. *Version:* 3.6. *Compatible Hardware:* Apple Macintosh. *Memory Required:* 2000k. *General Requirements:* ImageWriter or LaserWriter, hard disk required. *Items Included:* Manual, tutorial, get acquainted demo, strategy samples, autodialer. *Customer Support:* 90 days free telephone support, unlimited tech support on America Online. Additional phone support $95.00/year.
3.5" disk $395.00.
Automated Sales & Marketing Follow-Up Software with Results Analysis.
Breakthrough Productions.

Market Master Manager. *Version:* 3.6. *General Requirements:* Hard disk. *Items Included:* Manual, tutorial, demo, strategy samples. *Customer Support:* 90 days free telephone support; unlimited support on America online. Additional support $95.00/year.
Macintosh (2Mb Minimum). Four salespeople, $595.00; up to ten, $895.00; up to twenty, $1295.00; unlimited, $1995.00.
Standardizes & Executes Automated Sales Follow-Up for an Entire Sales Force & Analyzes Results.
Breakthrough Productions.

Market Model. *Items Included:* Bound manual. *Customer Support:* Free hotline - no time limit; 30 day limited warranty; updates are $5/disk plus S&H.
MS-DOS. IBM & compatibles (128k). disk $249.95. *Nonstandard peripherals required:* One disk drive & an 80-column (or wider) printer.
Market Simulation Model for Organizing Information about a Brand/Product & Its Competition, & Then Estimating the Probable Effects of Various Marketing Strategies on Market Share & Volume.
Dynacomp, Inc.

Market Nicher. *Items Included:* Documentation in 3-ring binder with slip case; tutorial. *Customer Support:* 30 day free telephone support.
Macintosh Plus & higher (1Mb). 3.5" disk $695.00. *Optimal configuration:* Macintosh System 6.02 or higher; 1Mb RAM hard disk recommended.
Reveals & Evaluates Optimum Target Market Segments. It Includes Market Segment, Market Channel & Benefit Databases, & a Segment Generator Based on Standard Industrial Classification (S.I.C.) Codes. Program Is

MARKET SIMULATION

Designed by a Marketing Consultant; Runs Interactively on the Macintosh; Is Menu-Driven; & Produces Graphic Text & Output. It Includes User-Friendly Documentation, Tutorial & Online Help.
Good News Marketing, Inc.

Market Simulation. Compatible Hardware: TI Home Computer.
disk write for info. (Order no.: PHD 5018).
contact publisher for price (Order no.: PHT 6018).
Places 2 Contestants in Simulated Business Competition.
Texas Instruments, Personal Productivit.

Market Strategist. Version: 1.0. 1994. Items Included: 100 page bound manual. Customer Support: Free telephone hotline support 7 days a week.
MS-DOS 2.0 or higher. IBM PC, PS/2 & compatibles (512k). disk $99.00. Nonstandard peripherals required: Hard disk with 2Mb available & one 3.5" or 5.25" floppy drive.
Program & Database for Developing & Testing Strategies for Buying & Selling Stocks. Supplied with 8 Years of S&P 100 Historical Stock Market Data, the User Can Develop & Thoroughly Test under Actual Trading Conditions, a Set of Rules or "System" for Stock Investing. User Builds a Customized System Containing Technical, Fundamental, & Trading Account Criteria via Easy-to-Follow Menus. Rules Are Then Applied to the Historical Database, with Stocks Bought & Sold As Rules Are Met, & the Trading Accounting Updated Chronologically. Trading System Results Are Plotted Graphically along with the S&P 500 Index, & Several Reports Are Produced-Including Account Status, Industry Group Summary, Year by Year Summary, Stock by Stock Summary, & Trade by Trade Details. S&P 100 Stock Data Can Also Be Plotted Separately.
Hamilton Software, Inc.

Market Timer. Items Included: Bound manual. Customer Support: Free hotline - no time limit; 30 day limited warranty; updates are $5/disk plus S&H.
MS-DOS 2.0 or higher. IBM & compatibles (256k). disk $119.95. Nonstandard peripherals required: Color graphics card (for charts).
Designed to Provide the Necessary Signals As to When to Buy & Sell. The Signals Are Based on a Trend Analysis of the Value Line Composite Index Appearing in Your Newspaper. Features: Generates Buy & Sell Equity Market Switch Signals; Allows Performance Testing of Different Market Trend Sensitivities on Past Data; Includes a Daily 10-Year History of the Value Line Composite Index; Maintains a List of the Mutual Funds in Which You Are Invested; Easily Updated from Your Daily Newspaper; Displays Charts with Trend Lines for Any Selected Time Period.
Dynacomp, Inc.

Market Trend Charting. Compatible Hardware: TRS-80 Model I, Model III, Model 4.
disk $25.00.
Allows the Investor in Stocks or Commodities to Produce Daily or Weekly Charts of the High, Low, Close, & Volume.
Micro Learningware.

MarketForce Corporate: Telemarketing, Direct Marketing & Client Management Software. Version: 5.0. Aug. 1992. Items Included: System disks, reference manuals, getting started guide, helps. Customer Support: By contract. Approximately 18% annually of the cost of software.
PC-DOS/MS-DOS 3.3 or higher. IBM PC & compatibles, hard drive or LAN file servers (640k). Contact publisher for price. Nonstandard peripherals required: Hayes compatible modem for autodial function. GammaFAX FAX board for FAX server system, LAN file servers. Addl. software required: Network DOS (DOS LAN systems). Optimal configuration: 386 computer workstations, VGA color monitors, 9600 Baull modems 2Mb expanded, DOS 5.0 plus memory manager like QEMM or 386 to the Max. Networks supported: Novell NetWare & all DOS LANs.
Integrated Sales & Marketing Automation System Designed for Company Wide Implementation to Handle Field Sales, Telemarketing, Direct Marketing, Customer Service & Extensive Management Reporting. Includes Full Contact Management Functions Plus Advanced Marketing Features - Campaign Planning & Analysis, On-Line Graphic Monitoring of All Sales Activity, Automated Multi-Step Marketing, & FAX Direct from LAN Workstations. Priced by Bid According to Needed Configuration, $1000 to $1500 per Workstation.
Software of the Future, Inc.

MarketForce Plus: Telemarketing, Direct Marketing & Client Management Software. Version: 5.0. Jun. 1986. Compatible Hardware: IBM PC & compatibles, PC XT, PC AT. Memory Required: 640k. General Requirements: Hard disk. Items Included: System Disks, Reference manuals, Getting Started Guide, Helps. Customer Support: 30 days free support by phone.
Single-User. disk $695.00.
LAN. disk $2495.00.
Provides Comprehensive Client Information, Call Objectives, Results, Call History, Calendar, Expense Tacking, Sales Forecasting, Order Entry, Memo Pad, Scripting, Follow up Labels Letters, Sales Tracking & Complete Printed Reports. Full Mail Merge for Direct Marketing.
Software of the Future, Inc.

Marketing Decision Making Using Lotus 1-2-3. 1990.
IBM PC. write for info. (ISBN 0-538-80359-2, Order no.: 5580A81).
IBM PS/2. contact publisher for price (ISBN 0-538-80481-5, Order no.: 5580A88).
This Supplemental Package Consists of Lotus 1-2-3 Template Disks & a Student Book. It Integrates Realistic, Practical Application of Financial, Statistical, & Marketing Activities.
South-Western Publishing Co.

Marketing Edge Issue 4.0: The Market Planning Expert. Version: 4.0. May 1989. Items Included: User manual & software tutorials. Customer Support: 30 day money back guarantee, free phone support, on line tutorials & help in software.
DOS or O/S2 (256k). IBM PC, XT, AT, PS/2 or compatibles. $399.00 (US & Canada), $479.00 (International). Nonstandard peripherals required: CGA, EGA. VGA. or Hercules graphics board. Addl. software required: Lotus 1-2-3 release 2, 2.01, 2.2, or 3. Optimal configuration: IBM PCAT, DOS 2.1 or higher, 640k RAM, EGA board, 1-2-3 release 2 or higher. Networks supported: All that are supported by Lotus 1-2-3.
Assists Product/Marketing Managers, Entrepreneurs to Build Better & Faster Market Plans. Provides a Tool to Do a Fast "Market Audit" of a Product's Position or a Tool to Quickly "Screen" New Product Opportunities. Helps to Select Markets, Pinpoint Customer Needs, Evaluate Competitors, Price Products, Select Distribution Channels, & More.
Successware.

Marketing Management System. 1984.
Memory Required: 256k.
$795.00 (Order no.: MMS3.1).
Designed to Be Used by the Sales & Marketing Department of Companies Which Develop New Business from Leads & Prospects. Provides a Systematic Approach to Responding to Advertising & Telephone Leads Including Managing Literature Fulfillment, Telephone Qualifications & Lead Distribution to the Sales Force. Management Reports Show Activity by Product, Territory, Salesperson, Source & Buyer Profile.
Abacus, Inc.

Marketing Plan Pro. Tim Berry. Nov. 1994. Items Included: Manual. Customer Support: Free technical support (toll call) for 1 year via phone, fax, email.
Windows 3.1 or higher, including Windows 95 (4Mb). disk $149.95. Nonstandard peripherals required: 2Mb hard disk space.
System 7.0 or higher. Mac Plus or higher (6Mb). 3.5" disk $149.95. Nonstandard peripherals required: 2Mb disk space.
Combines the Tools & Know-How of a Professional Marketing Manager in an Easy-to-Use Program. It's Simple Enough for Novices Yet Powerful Enough for Pros. In Just a Few Simple Steps User Will Develop a Clear, Targeted Plan Complete with Text, Tables & Charts. Provides an Organized Action Schedule to Implement Your Plan with Total Confidence.
Palo Alto Software.

MARKETWATCH. Version: 3.0. 1993. Items Included: 100-page bound manual. Customer Support: Free telephone support.
DOS 2.0. IBM PC, PS/2 & compatibles (512k). $59.00.
Easy-to-Use Tool Simplifies Evaluation & Comparison of Multiple Types of Investments Including Mutual Funds, Stocks, Options, Commodities, Money Market, & Market Indexes. Allows Home Investors to Seriously Evaluate Such Investments Inexpensively, Allowing Either Manual or Imported Data Entry. Annualizes Returns (Including Proceeds from Dividends & Distributions), Evaluates Price Movement & Price-Volume Trends, Graphs Normalized Performances of Multiple Funds along with Moving Averages & Volumes, High-Low-Close & Candlesticks. Projects Total Returns on Individual Portfolios, & Provides Comprehensive Investment Comparisons. Accommodates an Unlimited Number of Securities for Which Share Prices (& Options Volumes) Are Updated According to Any Time Intervals, & Combined with Dividends, Distributions, & Transactions to Reveal Total Investment Performance.
Hamilton Software, Inc.

The Marks Adolescent Feedback & Treatment Report for the MMPI-A & MMPI. Version: 2.010. Phillip A. Marks & Richard W. Lewak. Customer Support: Free unlimited phone support with a toll free number.
DOS 3.0 or higher. IBM or 100% compatible (512k). 3.5" disk $99.50 (Order no.: W-1066). Optimal configuration: Hard disk with 1Mb free disk space, printer.
This Computer Program Helps Clinicians Provide Meaningful Feedback to Adolescents Who Have Taken the MMPI. Gives an Individualized Interpretation of MMPI Results, Based on Adolescent Norms & T-Scores Entered by the User. Especially Useful Because It Includes Interpretative Information for Both the Clinician & the Client.
Western Psychological Services.

TITLE INDEX

The Marks Adolescent Interpretive Report for the MMPI-A & MMPI. Version: 2.010. Phillip A. Marks & Richard W. Lewak. *Customer Support:* Free unlimited phone support.
MS-DOS 3.0 or higher (512k). IBM PC & 100% compatibles. 3.5" disk $130.00 (Order no.: W-1060). *Optimal configuration:* Hard disk with one Mb of free hard disk space, printer.
Designed for Use with 12-18 Year Olds Who Are Being Evaluated for Emotional or Behavioral Difficulties. The Report Is Based on MMPI Non-K-Corrected T-Scores & Adolescent Norms.
Western Psychological Services.

The Marks Adult Clinical Report for the MMPI-2 & MMPI. Version: 2.010. Phillip A. Marks et al. *Customer Support:* Free unlimited phone support.
MS-DOS 3.0 or higher (512k). IBM PC & 100% compatibles. 3.5" disk $140.00 (Order no.: W-1062). *Optimal configuration:* Hard disk with one Mb of free hard disk space, printer.
Intended for Use with Individuals 18 Years of Age & Older Who Are Being Evaluated for Mental, Behavioral, or Emotional Difficulty. The Report Is Based on MMPI or MMPI-2 K-Corrected T-Scores.
Western Psychological Services.

The Marks Adult Feedback & Treatment Report for the MMPI-2 & MMPI. Version: 2.010. Phillip A. Marks et al. *Customer Support:* Free unlimited phone support.
MS-DOS 3.0 or higher. IBM PC & 100% compatibles. 3.5" disk $140.00 (Order no.: W-1064). *Optimal configuration:* DOS 3.0 or higher (512k), & hard disk with one Mb of free disk space.
Computer Program Helps Clinicians Provide Meaningful Feedback to Clients Who Have Taken the MMPI or MMPI-2. User Enters the Clients T-Scores & the Program Gives an Individualized Interpretation of MMPI or MMPI-2 Results Based on K-Corrected Adult Norms.
Western Psychological Services.

MARKSTRAT: A Marketing Strategy Game. Jean-Claude Larreche. *Compatible Hardware:* DEC VAX, DEC-20; HP-3000. *General Requirements:* Mainframe.
tape $100.00 (ISBN 0-89426-066-9).
High-Level Simulation Game Designed for Teaching Marketing Strategy Concepts.
Boyd & Fraser Publishing Co.

MarkUp. Version: 2.0. Jul. 1992. *Items Included:* One manual with comprehensive tutorial. *Customer Support:* Free technical support to registered users.
System 6.0 or higher. Macintosh Plus or higher (1Mb). 3.5" disk $195.00. *Networks supported:* All Apple-compliant.
Now, One or More Reviewers Can Comment on a Document Simultaneously - Even If They Don't Have the Original Application. Images Documents from Any Macintosh Application, Creating a Version That Looks Exactly As the Original Would Look If Printed on Paper. Each Reviewer Makes Their Marks on a Named Overlay Atop the Image Document, Using the Two Full Palettes of Tools & Marks Provided. Marks Can Include VoiceNotes & QuickTime Movies. Can Merge Overlays & Has a Journal for Managing the Review Process.
Mainstay.

MarkUp. *General Requirements:* Two 800K disk drives.
Macintosh Plus or higher. Database/Two-user pack $495.00.
Database/five-user pack $995.00,.
Personal version of MarkUp $245.00,.
Workgroup Editing & Review. Permits Group Members to Edit Any Type of Macintosh Document, Without Having the Application That Created it. Members of a Group Can Edit the Same Document at the Same Time. It Provides Several Document Management Features, Including a Log of Editing Activity & the Ability for Reviewers to "Sign Off" Their Approval of Documents.
Mainstay Software Corp.

Marquis Who's Who Plus. 1995. *Items Included:* Annual Updates.
MS-DOS Compatibility. IBM 386 or higher. CD-ROM disk
82,000 record on living North American notables from "Who's Who in America, 1995." 6,000 profiles of leaders who have passed away since 1985 from "Who Was Who in America.".
R. R. Bowker.

Mars. *Compatible Hardware:* IBM PC. *Operating System(s) Required:* CP/M, CP/M-86, MP/M, PC-DOS, MS-DOS. *Memory Required:* 64k.
disk $595.00.
Procedural Language Used for Financial Modeling in Business Which Allows the User to Calculate Budgets, Project Current Data into the Future, Perform What If Analysis & Produce Formatted Reports of Detail or Summary Information.
Capital Systems Group, Inc.

Mars Explorer. 1992. *Items Included:* 1 manual. *Customer Support:* 90 days unlimited warranty; free telephone support.
DOS CD-ROM. IBM 386 25MHz & higher (4Mb). CD-ROM disk $69.95 (ISBN 1-886082-13-8, Order no.: ME-301). *Nonstandard peripherals required:* CD-ROM. *Optimal configuration:* 8Mb.
System 7. MAC (4Mb). CD-ROM disk $69.95 (ISBN 1-886082-14-6, Order no.: MEMCD-301). *Nonstandard peripherals required:* CD-ROM. *Optimal configuration:* 8Mb.
Explore Mars Through NASA's Viking Photo Mission. Allows You to Orbit & Survey the Red Planet.
Virtual Reality Laboratories, Inc.

MARS/2000: ACM Manufacturing Software. *Compatible Hardware:* IBM Systems 34/36. contact publisher for price.
Includes Master Production Scheduling, Material & Capacity Requirement Planning, Product Data Base, Purchase Orders, & Physical Inventory.
ACM Computer Services, Inc.

Martindale-Hubbell Law Directory on CD-ROM. 1995. *Items Included:* Quarterly Updates.
MS-DOS compatibility. IBM 386 or higher. CD-ROM disk $995.00 for 1 year (Order no.: MH110).
CD-ROM disk $2445.00 for 3 years.
Primary practice profiles on virtually every attorney in the U. S. & Canada. Professional biographies for leading attorneys, including education, memberships, languages spoken, & more. Firm profiles for over 50,000 American law firms covering areas of specialization, staff size & breakdown, representative clients, & more. Details on the in-house counsel of virtually every major corportion.
R. R. Bowker.

Marvels of Rome for Windows. (Historical Travel Guides Ser.). Edited by Ronald G. Musto & Eileen Gardiner. Apr. 1996.
Windows. IBM. disk $35.00 (ISBN 0-934977-55-0).
Twelfth-Century Guide to Rome on Diskette with Photographs, Plans, Maps, & Views That Supplement the Original Guide with an Electronic Guide to the Medieval & Ancient Sites. Includes Bibliography, Introduction, Notes, & Gazeteer.
Italica Pr.

Marvin the Ape: European, Dual. (Vroom Bks.).
IBM. CD-ROM disk Contact publisher for price (ISBN 0-918183-41-3).
T/Maker Co., Inc.

Marvin the Moose.
$29.95 Vol. I (Forest Friends, The Forest School Fun Fair) (Order no.: MMI100).
$29.95 Vol. II (The Forest Friends Go Camping, Marvin Meets a Special Friend) (Order no.: MMI200).
In Addition to the Educational Value, These Stories Also Emphasize Social Development Skills & Support Strong Moral & Family Values. Color Artwork, & Wonderfully Animated Characters with Real Human Voices. As They Read, Children May Also Enjoy Answering Random Questions about the Story, Where Correct Responses Are Rewarded with Sound Effects & Animations. Sound, Underlining, & Questions Are All Optional Features That You Can Set up Ahead of Time or Change at Any Point During the Story. Has Computerized Coloring Pages & Simple Word Processor That Allows Children to Create Their Own Storybook from Start to Finish. The Printed Copy of Their Storybook Even Includes a Custom Title Page with Their Name on It.
Milliken Publishing Co.

M.A.S. 90 EVOLUTION/2. Version: 1.3x. *Compatible Hardware:* IBM PC & compatibles. *Memory Required:* 640k. *General Requirements:* Hard disk.
$799.00 to $999.00 depending on application.
Comprehensive, Modular Series of Accounting & Manufacturing Control Programs. Series Includes 14 Modules: Library Master & Report Master, General Ledger, Accounts Receivable, Accounts Payable, Payroll, Inventory Management, Sales Order Processing, Purchase Order Processing, Bank Reconciliation, Time & Billing, Job Cost, Bill of Materials, Import Master, & PostMaster. Products Flexibility Allows It to Be Used by Companies of Any Size. In Addition to DOS Version, the Library Is Available on SCO XENIX/ UNIX & UNIX System V.
State Of The Art, Inc.

M.A.S. 90 EVOLUTION/2: Accounts Payable. Version: 1.3x. Dec. 1991. *Memory Required:* Single-user DOS 640k, Novell 640k, SCO/Altos Xenix & Unix 2000k, per additional users over two add (per user) 256k.
PC-DOS/MS-DOS. disk $799.00.
SCO XENIX 286 & 386 - Contact publisher for price.
Novell Networks. disk $799.00.
Enables Users to Manage Cash Flow, While Saving Time & Increasing Accuracy. Invoice Entry is Simplified by the Automatic Calculation of Discounts & Due Dates & the Distribution of Invoice Amounts to the Proper General Ledger Accounts. Checks, Which May Be Customized, Are Printed for Those Invoices Selected for Payment. Additional Accounts Payable Features Include: Manual Check Processing, 1099 Printing, Divisional Accounting, Multiple Bank Account Processing, & Automatic Payment Selection. You May Print Timely Management Reports, Such as the Cash Requirements Report & Aged Invoice Report. These Reports Provide the Cash Flow Projections & Aging Breakdowns Needed to Make Informed Financial Decisions & to Give You Control Over Your Costs.
State Of The Art, Inc.

M.A.S. 90 EVOLUTION/2: Accounts Receivable. Version: 1.3x. Sep. 1991. *Memory Required:* Single-user DOS 640k, Novell 640k, SCO/Altos Xenix & Unix 2000k, per additional users over two add (per user)256k.

PC-DOS/MS-DOS. disk $799.00.
SCO XENIX 286 & 386. disk $799.00.
Novell Networks. disk $799.00.
Provides a Solution to Managing Your Cash Flow & Collection. Accounts Receivable is Designed for Efficient Processing of Invoices. Sales Tax, Discount, & Commission Amounts are Automatically Calculated for Each Invoice. The Accounts Receivable System Features Include: Repetitive Invoice Processing, Divisional Accounting, Credit Limit Checking, Customized Designing of Invoices & Statements, Multiple Bank Account Processing, & Automatic Finance Charge Calculation. Additionally, the System Will Report on Salesperson Commissions & Sales Tax for the State, County, & Local Levels. Accounts Receivable Tracks Aging & Overall Sales History Information, & Produces Extensive Reports That Help you Analyze Customer Sales History & Forecast Future Cash Receipts.
State Of The Art, Inc.

M.A.S. 90 EVOLUTION/2: Bank Reconciliation. *Version:* 1.02. Jun. 1990. *Memory Required:* Single-user DOS 640k, Novell 640k, SCO/Altos Xenix & Unix 2000k, per additional users over two add (per user) 256k.
PC-DOS/MS-DOS. disk $199.00.
SCO XENIX 286 & 386. disk $199.00.
Novell Networks. disk $199.00.
Enables User to Take Full Advantage of Computerized Accounting by Quickly & Efficiently Completing the Bank Reconciliation Process. Reconcile Your Bank Statement by a "Check-off" Process to Indicate Whether the Checks Appearing On the Bank Statement Have Cleared & the Deposits & Charges Have Been Recorded Correctly. If your Bank Statement Does Not Agree With Your Cash Balance, a Register May Be Generated to Help You Find the Error by Detailing the Balance as Calculated by the Computer. When Used in Conjunction With the MAS 90 EVOLUTION/2 Accounts Payable, Accounts Receivable & Payroll Applications, Checks & Deposits Are Recorded Automatically for Each Bank Account. Bank Activity Detail May be Retained Indefinitely, or Cleared on a Monthly Basis.
State Of The Art, Inc.

M.A.S. 90 EVOLUTION/2: General Ledger. *Version:* 1.3x. Sep. 1991. *Memory Required:* Single-user DOS 640k, Novell 640k, SCO/Altos Xenix & Unix 2000k, per additional users over two add (per user) 256k.
PC-DOS/MS-DOS. disk $799.00.
SCO XENIX 286 & 386. disk $799.00.
Novell Networks. disk $799.00.
Provides User With Complete & Timely Financial Reports That Always Reflect "Up-To-Date" Information. Flexible Account Numbering Allows From 3 to 9 Alphanumeric Characters, Which Can Be Divided Into One, Two or Three Segments to Designate Sub-Accounts & Departments. Additional Features Include Recurring, Reversing, Standard & Transaction Journal Entries; a Flexible Chart of Account; Future Postings; the Calculation of 13 Standard Financial Ratios; Multiple Company Consolidations; Complete Audit Trails; & the Retention of Budget & History Information. Standard Financial Statements Include Departmental & Consolidated Income Statements.
State Of The Art, Inc.

M.A.S. 90 EVOLUTION/2: Inventory Management. *Version:* 1.14. Dec. 1991. *Memory Required:* Single-user DOS 512k, Novell 640k, SCO/Altos Xenix & Unix 2000k, per additional users over two add 256k.
PC-DOS/MS-DOS. disk $799.00.
SCO XENIX 286 & 386. disk $799.00.
Novell Networks. disk $799.00.
State of the Art, Inc.

M.A.S.90 EVOLUTION/2: Job Cost. *Version:* 1.3x. Dec. 1991. *Memory Required:* Single-user DOS 640k, Novell 640k, SCO Xenix & Unix 2000k, per additional users over two add (per user) 256k.
PC-DOS/MS-DOS. disk $999.00.
SCO XENIX 286 & 386. disk $999.00.
Novell Networks. disk $999.00.
State of the Art, Inc.

M.A.S. 90 EVOLUTION/2: Library Master & Report Master. *Version:* 1.3x. Sep. 1991. *Memory Required:* Single-user DOS 640k, Novell 640k, SCO, Xenix & Unix 2000k, per additional users over two add (per user) 256k.
PC-DOS/MS-DOS. disk $295.00.
SCO XENIX 286 & 386. Contact publisher for price.
Novell Networks. disk $795.00.
The Library Master May Be Thought of as the Engine Which Drives the Accounting Library. This Module Contains all the Necessary "System & Utility" Software Which Allows the Series To Be Installed & Function on Users Computer. Report Master Is a Full-Featured Report Writer That Allows User To Create Customized Financial & Management Reports According To the Specific Needs of the Business. While Each Individual M.A.S. 90 Application Already Produces Many Management Reports, the Report Master Allows User To Produce Custom Reports Using Data from any Data Field within an M.A.S. 90 Module. Reports May Be Printed or Displayed on the Screen. Additionally, Reports Can Be Placed in a File for Integration to Other Software Products Such as Word Processors or Spreadsheets.
State Of The Art, Inc.

M.A.S. 90 EVOLUTION/2: Payroll. *Version:* 1.3x. Dec. 1991. *Memory Required:* Single-user DOS 640k, Novell 640k, SCO, Xenix & Unix 2000k, per additional users over two add (per user) 256k.
PC-DOS/MS-DOS. disk $799.00.
SCO XENIX 286 & 386. Contact publisher for price.
Novell Networks. disk $799.00.
Provides a Solution to Payroll Paperwork Problems. The Payroll System Can Process City, State & Local Taxes, Apply Employee Earnings & Deductions, Process Tips, Calculate Both Employee & Employer Taxes, Process Multi-State Earnings, & Print Checks/Vouchers, Complete With Year-To-Date Earnings & Tax Information. Then, at the End of the Year, W-2 Forms Can be Printed Automatically. Quarterly & Annual Payroll Reports May be Produced to Provide Detailed Payroll Information. In Addition, Extensive Information Is Retained for Each Employee, Including Employee Emergency Contact, Review Date & Comments, Marital & Tax Status, Vacation & Sick Day Accruals, & QTD & YTD Earnings. All Current Federal & State Tax Calculation Tables are Included in the System. State Of The Art Offers an Annual Subscription Program for Updating the Tax Tables.
State Of The Art, Inc.

M.A.S. 90 EVOLUTION/2: Purchase Order Processing. *Version:* 1.3x. Dec. 1991. *Memory Required:* Single-user DOS 640k, Novell 640k, SCO Xenix & Unix 2000k, per additional users over two add (per user) 256k.
PC-DOS/MS-DOS. disk $799.00.
SCO XENIX 286 & 386. Contact publisher for price.
Novell Networks. disk $799.00.
State Of The Art, Inc.

M.A.S. 90 EVOLUTION/2: Sales Order Processing. *Version:* 1.14. Jul. 1991. *Memory Required:* Single-user DOS 640k, Novell 640k, SCO Xenix & Unix 2000k, per additional users over two add (per user) 256k.
PC-DOS/MS-DOS. disk $799.00.
SCO XENIX 286 & 386. Contact publisher for price.
Novell Networks. disk $799.00.
State Of The Art, Inc.

M.A.S. 90 EVOLUTION/2: Time & Billing. *Version:* 1.2x. May 1991. *Memory Required:* SCO XENIX/UNIX 2Mb, IBM 640k.
286, 386, 486-based IBM & compatibles. disk $999.00.
SCO XENIX/UNIX. Contact publisher for price.
Enter Time Sheet Information Online, Closely Emulating a Manual Billing Method. Time Worked Can Be Entered as Activities Are Completed. Program Offers Extensive Management Reporting Capabilities To Help Analyze the Profitibility of Client Engagements & the Productivity of Employees. Features Include Multiple Companies, Multiple Bank Accounts, Billing Rates, Client Memo Maintenance, & Sales Tax Reporting.
State Of The Art, Inc.

MASH. *Compatible Hardware:* TI 99/4A with PLATO interpreter solid state cartridge.
contact publisher for price (Order no.: PHM 3158).
*Airlift Soldiers Wounded on a Battlefield to the 4077th M*A*S*H Unit. Time Is Running Out & You Must Operate to Save Their Lives.*
Texas Instruments, Personal Productivit.

The Mask of the Sun. Ultrasoft, Inc. *Compatible Hardware:* Atari, Commodore.
disk $39.95 ea.
Broderbund Software, Inc.

MASM. *Version:* 5.1. *Compatible Hardware:* IBM PC AT. *Memory Required:* 320k.
disk $150.00.
Microsoft Pr.

Masque Blackjack. Jim Wisler. *Items Included:* 3.5" & 5.25" disks; 2 templates; manual. *Customer Support:* Free technical support, free sales support.
DOS. IBM; Tandy or compatibles (256k). $49.95 (ISBN 0-9624419-0-2).
Windows 3.0. IBM; Tandy or compatibles (640k). (ISBN 0-9624419-3-7). *Optimal configuration:* Windows 3.0, 640k RAM; VGA Video.
$49.95.
Covers the Full Range of Winning Blackjack Strategies from Beginner to Expert. Allows User to Set Rules, Play the Game of Blackjack, Practice Card Counting & Practice Strategy Skills. 86- Page Manual Explains Game, Strategies & Reason for Winning or Losing.
Masque Publishing.

Masque Video Poker. Nov. 1991. *Items Included:* 5.25" & 3.5" disks, manual, registration card. *Customer Support:* Free technical support, free sales support.
DOS 2.1 or higher. IBM; Tandy or compatible (256k). $49.95 (ISBN 0-9624419-1-0).
Windows 3.0. IBM; Tandy or compatible (640k). $49.95 (ISBN 0-9624419-4-5). *Optimal configuration:* 640k, Windows 3.0, VGA video.
Video Poker Tutorial. Features Expert Strategies for the Most Popular, Profitable Casino Video Poker Games Available. On-Line Strategy Tables & Expert Recommendation for Any Hand. Play Results are Evaluated & the Strategy Decision Errors Users Have Made are Recorded for Review. Computer Simulation Play Proves That the Average Payback Exceeds 100 Percent on Selected Casino Games When Expertly Played.
Masque Publishing.

TITLE INDEX

Masquerade. 1983. *Compatible Hardware:* Apple. *Memory Required:* 48k.
$34.95.
Clues Have Led to Dead Ends & No One Is Talking. Meanwhile, the Crime Boss Continues to Operate. Your Job Is to Find His Headquarters.
American Eagle Software, Inc.

Mass-11 CLASSIC Document Processor. *Version:* 8.6. *Compatible Hardware:* DEC, VAX/VMS. *Operating System(s) Required:* VMS 5.2 or higher. *Items Included:* Media, documentation & 6 months of support. *Customer Support:* Telephone, telex, FAX support & access to MEC's Electronic Bulletin Board. Updates as available. Training available.
Contact publisher for price.
Word Processor That Provides a Footnote Control Program, List Processing Feature, & Support for Printing Complex Mathematical Equations. Editing Feature Facilitates Proofreading by Marking Changes Made to Previously Entered Documents; New Entered Characters Are Displayed & Printed in Boldface. Supports Both Prompted & Global Replacement. Edit Screen Includes a Ruler Line Showing Line Spacing, Margin Settings, Tab Locations, & a Centering Point Other Than the Center of the Line. Assigns Documents to Directories from Which They Can Be Deleted, Renamed or Copied. Converts Documents to & from the ASCII Text File Format. VAX Product Includes a Communications Feature That Facilitates File Transfers Between VAX & PC Systems & Table Editor.
Microsystems Engineering Co.

Mass-11 Draw. *Version:* 7.0. *Compatible Hardware:* IBM PC & compatibles, VMS, DEC windows, VAX stations. *General Requirements:* Graphics card; PostScript, HP LaserJet or Digital LN03+ printer. *Items Included:* Media, documentation & PC support. *Customer Support:* Telephone, telex, & FAX support; MEC's Electronic Bulletin Board, training available.
$395.00.
Supports Free-Hand Drawing, Tracing, Print Resolution & Paragraph Text, Allowing Word Processing Within the Graphics, & Editing. Other Features Include Gray Scaling, Rotating & Scaling Combined Objects & a Zoom Range of 32 to 1.
Microsystems Engineering Co

Mass-11 Manager. *Version:* 9.03. *Compatible Hardware:* IBM PC & compatibles, DEC, VAX, VMS. *Items Included:* Media, documentation & PC support. *Customer Support:* Telephone, telex, FAX support & access to MEC's Electronic Bulletin Board. Training available.
disk $495.00.
Command & Menu-Driven Database-Management System Featuring Help Screen, On-Disk Tutorial, Automatic Indexing & Split/Merge Files. Offers a Maximum of 256 Fields per Record, 1000-8000 Characters per Field, 65,000 Records per File, 4000 Characters per Record, 50 Indexes per File, 1 Active Index & up to 10 Records Sorted. Allows User to Revise Field Descriptions at Will.
Microsystems Engineering Co.

MASS-11 SuperCom. *Version:* 8.2. *Compatible Hardware:* IBM PC, DEC, VAX VMS, DECmate. *Items Included:* Media, documentation & PC support. *Customer Support:* Telephone, telex, FAX support, access to MEC's Electronic Bulletin Board. Training available.
disk $195.00.
Programmable Communications Application. Integrates with Other MASS-11 Modules.
Microsystems Engineering Co.

Mass-11 CLASSIC Document Processor: Microsystems Administrative Support System for Personal Computers. *Version:* 8.6. 1994. *Compatible Hardware:* AT&T 6300; IBM PC, PC XT, PC AT. *Operating System(s) Required:* MS-DOS. *Language(s):* FORTRAN, Pascal & Macro. *Memory Required:* 480k. *Items Included:* Media & documentation & PC Support. *Customer Support:* Telephone, telex, FAX support & access to MEC's electronic bulletin board. Training available.
$495.00.
Word Processor That Provides a Footnote Control Program, List Processing Feature & Support for Printing Complex Mathematical Equations. Editing Feature Facilitates Proofreading by Marking Changes Made to Previously Entered Documents; Newly Entered Characters Are Displayed & Printed in Boldface. Supports Both Prompted & Global Replacement. The Edit Screen Includes a Ruler Line Showing Line Spacing, Margin Settings, Tab Locations, & a Centering Point Other Than the Center of the Line. Assigns Documents to Directories from Which They Can Be Deleted, Renamed or Copied. Converts Documents to & from the ASCII Text File Format. Also Includes a Communications Feature That Facilitates File Transfers Between VAX & Personal Computer Systems.
Microsystems Engineering Co.

Mass Storage ROM. *Compatible Hardware:* HP 85.
ROM cartridge $195.00 (Order no.: 00085-15001).
Allows Users to Interface the HP 85 with the HP 8290X-Series Flexible Disk Drive or the HP 0134A/9135A Winchester Disk Drive.
Hewlett-Packard Co.

Master CAD 3-D. I.N.D.I. Apr. 1988. *Compatible Hardware:* Atari ST. *Memory Required:* 1000k.
3.5" disk $199.95.
Features Unlimited Number of Viewing Angles. Two Projection or Limit Planes Can Be Defined in the Work Space, Move, Copy, Rotate & Flip Any Object Around a User-Defined Axis.
MichTron, Inc.

Master Chartist. *Version:* 2.67. *Compatible Hardware:* Apple Macintosh Plus; IBM PC & compatibles. *General Requirements:* Hard disk. *Customer Support:* Yes.
disk $1590.00.
Financial Planning Program Featuring Real-Time Charting & Technical Analysis.
Roberts-Slade, Inc.

Master Diagnostics. *Compatible Hardware:* Apple II, II+, IIe, IIc. *Operating System(s) Required:* Apple DOS 3.3. *Memory Required:* 48k.
disk Master Diagnostics $65.00.
disk $75.00, incl. head cleaning kit.
disk drive analyzer only $39.95.
Diagnostic Package Which Permits Examination of Computer Operations, Detects Hardware Problems, & Indicates When Periodic Maintenance Procedures Are Required, Such As Disk Speed Calibration, Drive Head Cleaning, & Monitor Alignment. Requires No Technical Knowledge.
Nikrom Technical Products, Inc.

Master Directory. *Compatible Hardware:* TRS-80 Model I, Model III. *Memory Required:* 32k.
disk $29.95.
Organizes Disks & Disk Files Alphabetically, by Data Category, or Extension.
Instant Software, Inc.

MASTER HARNESS HANDICAPPER ENHANCED

Master Disk Catalog. *Compatible Hardware:* TI 99/4A with Pascal Language card. *Operating System(s) Required:* DX-10. *Language(s):* Pascal. *Memory Required:* 16k.
disk or cassette $19.95.
Catalog of User's UCSD Pascal Disk Directories. The Directory Names Are Alphabetically Sorted & the Volume Name Is Added As a Prefix. All Occurrences of a Designated File Name Can Be Searched Out.
Eastbench Software Products.

Master Drill. 1992. *Items Included:* Detailed manuals included with all Dynacomp products. *Customer Support:* Free telephone support to original customer - no time limit; 30 day limited warranty.
MS-DOS 3.2 or higher. IBM PC & compatibles, Apple (512k). $29.95 (Add $5.00 for 3 1/2" format; 5 1/4" format standard).
A Utility Specifically Designed for the Educational Environment. With MASTER DRILL You Can Quickly & Easily Set up Multiple Choice Drills on Any Subject You Desire. All You Do As the Drill Creator Is Respond to the Prompts. The Program Will Ask You for the Question & Its Corresponding Answer. Later, When That Question Is Presented to the Student, Between Two & Nine (Your Choice) Multiple Choice Answers Will Be Presented, One of Which Is Correct. The Incorrect Answers Are Drawn at Random from the Answers to the Other Questions. For Those Who Have Written Multiple Choice Tests, You Know How Much Time This Feature Can Save.
Dynacomp, Inc.

Master Genealogist. *Items Included:* Bound manual. *Customer Support:* Free hotline - no time limit; 30 day limited warranty; updates are $5/disk plus S&H.
MS-DOS. IBM & compatibles (300k). disk $39.95. *Nonstandard peripherals required:* Two drives (or one drive & a hard disk; specify configuration when ordering); printer supported.
Designed to Fully Help the Genealogist Manage Family Data. It Provides Data-Base Management, Search, & Sort Features, a Variety of Ascending & Descending Tree Charts, & Other Useful Reports.
Dynacomp, Inc.

Master Graph III. *Version:* 3.0. Arthur Upton. 1985. *Compatible Hardware:* Sanyo MBC 555. *Memory Required:* 128k. *General Requirements:* Printer.
disk $89.95 (ISBN 0-923213-30-9).
Prints Bar, Line, Pie & 3-D Charts & Includes a Screen Dump Program.
MichTron, Inc.

Master Harness Handicapper Enhanced. Ronald D. Jones. 1984. *Compatible Hardware:* Apple II; Commodore 64; IBM PC; TRS-80 Model I, Model III, Color Computer. *Operating System(s) Required:* CP/M. *Memory Required:* 64k.
disk $199.95 ea.
Apple. (ISBN 1-55604-186-1, Order no.: T002).
CP/M. (ISBN 1-55604-187-X, Order no.: T002).
Commodore. (ISBN 1-55604-188-8, Order no.: T002).
Color Computer. (ISBN 1-55604-189-6, Order no.: T002).
IBM. (ISBN 1-55604-190-X, Order no.: T002).
Model I & Model III. (ISBN 1-55604-191-8, Order no.: T002).
Full-Featured Harness Analysis. Initialize System with Track Records, & Drivers' & Trainers' Records on Data Base System. Evaluates All Relevant Variables & Gives Accurate Prediction of the Finish. Eliminates False Favorites While Illustrating True Contenders. Features National

Tracks with Variance Table on Data Base. Master Bettor Evaluates Scores & Every Betting Combination Is Printed on Video or Printer.
Professor Jones Professional Handicapping Systems.

Master Harness Handicapper Limited. Compatible Hardware: Apple, Commodore 64, IBM, TRS-80, CP/M machines.
disk $159.95.
Designed to Provide an Analysis of All Trotter & Pacer Races of North America & Canada.
Professor Jones Professional Handicapping Systems.

The Master Menu. Richard J. McElhinney. Nov. 1984. Compatible Hardware: IBM PC & compatibles. Operating System(s) Required: PC-DOS 2.1. Memory Required: 192k.
disk $49.95, incl. manual.
Hard Disk Organizer Developed for Those Without Extensive Knowledge of DOS. Helps Users to Logically Store & Quickly Retrieve Programs. Includes Several Features Which Simplify the Operation of Personal Computers: SECURITY, BATCH FILE GENERATOR, TIME MANAGER (for Storing Daily & Weekly Reminders), FILE COMMANDER (Access to Most DOS Commands with Sufficient Priority Level), HELP MENU's, TIME-LOG RECORDER (Tracks Computer Usage).
Vector Systems, Inc.

Master Plot. Compatible Hardware: TRS-80 Model I with Epson MX-80(5) printer & Graptrax(2) modification.
disk $149.95, incl. manual (Order no.: 0435RD).
Enter Data from Keyboard, Equations, or BASIC Programs. Compose Your Own Symbols.
Instant Software, Inc.

Master Revival. Compatible Hardware: TRS-80.
contact publisher for price.
Instant Software, Inc.

Master Select Copy. Compatible Hardware: HP Series 200, 9816, 9826/9836, 9920. Language(s): BASIC 2.0.
disk $60.00, incl. instr's. guide.
Allows Copying of Files Created Using the Pascal Operating Systems Which Are Not Normally Accessible from the BASIC Operating System.
University Software Assocs., Inc.

Master String Editor. Compatible Hardware: HP 9845 C/T. Memory Required: 187k.
$495.00, incl. documentation.
extra documentation $20.00.
General-Purpose Full-Screen Editing Program for Creating & Modifying Serial & Random Access Files Whose Elements Are ASCII Strings.
University Software Assocs., Inc.

Master the Market. Customer Support: 800-929-8117 (customer service).
MS-DOS. IBM/PS2. disk $39.99 (ISBN 0-87007-713-9).
A Stimulation of the Actual Buying & Selling of Stock, with a Moving Tickertape, Important News Events That Affect the Price of Stock. Users Can Learn the Effects of Puts & Calls, Effects of Commissions on Earnings. Allows One to Ten Players to Buy & Sell from a Selection of Ten Blue Chip Stocks. No Two Games are Alike. Players Can Choose a Simple Case, Based Game or a More Sophisticated Short Selling & Margin Buying Game. User Have Full Control of Portfolio Through the Simple User Interface & Clear Reporting.
SourceView Software International.

Master Tracks Jr! Compatible Hardware: Apple IIgs. General Requirements: MIDI-equipped instruments. Passport or Apple MIDI interface or compatibles for Macintosh.
3.5" disk $129.95-249.95.
Allows Users to Compose & Record Their Own Songs. Designed for Musicians & Music Enthusiasts Who Want a Low-Cost, Entry-Level Music Sequencer. Can Change Tempos & Meters. On-Screen Play, Record, Pause, Fast-Forward & Rewind Controls Allow Users to Move Through a Song & Record or Play From Any Point. The MIDI-Compatible Sequencer Features 64 Tracks, Mute, Solo, & Looping. Tracks Are Displayed As Measures Over Time. Users Can See the Structure of Their Songs & Edit Measures Using Cut, Copy, & Paste Commands.
Passport Designs, Inc. (California).

Master Tracks Pro. Version: 3.5. Compatible Hardware: Apple Macintosh 512E, Macintosh Plus, Macintosh SE, Macintosh II; Atari 520ST, IBM, Amiga, Apple IIgs. General Requirements: MIDI-equipped instruments. Passport or Apple MIDI Interface or compatibles for Macintosh.
3.5" disk $395.00.
The Macintosh Version is Compatible With the Macintosh II & With Multifinder. A Dialog Window is Added for Automatic Setting of Punch-in & Out Points. Users Can Also Set the Punch In/Out Region by Highlighting the Area in the Song or Step Windows. A Conductor Track Data Window Has Been Added to the Windows Menu. This Window Graphically Reflects Changes Made to the Conductor Track from the Change Window, or With the Pencil & Eraser Tools. Improvements Have Been Made to Elapsed Time, Quantize Window & Measure Insertion.
Passport Designs, Inc. (California).

Master Word Processor. Compatible Hardware: HP 9816/9836, 9920. Language(s): BASIC. Memory Required: 500k.
$495.00, incl. documentation.
extra documentation $20.00.
Full-Screen, Cursor-Oriented Word Processor with Special Features for the Preparation of Scientific, Engineering, & Business Reports & Manuals As Well As Routine Correspondence.
University Software Assocs., Inc.

MasterClips 6000: The Art of Business.
Version: 2.0. Items Included: 1 manual - CD-ROM. Customer Support: Tech support.
Windows 3.1 or higher. IBM compatible PC 386 or higher (640k). disk $59.95 (ISBN 0-924677-26-0). Nonstandard peripherals required: EGA monitor recommended or higher. Addl. software required: Works in conjunction with any software application that imports .CGM or .WMF file formats.
Over 6000 Full Color Professionally Drawn Images Spanning More Than 60 Categories, Encompassing Every Business Need. Use MasterClips to Enhance Your Presentations, Proposals, Newsletters & Other Materials. Windows Browser Included.
IMSI (International Microcomputer Software, Inc.).

MasterClips 3000: The Art of Business.
Version: 2.0. Items Included: 1 manual - CD-ROM. Customer Support: Tech support.
Windows 3.1 or higher. IBM compatible PC 386 or higher. disk $29.95 (ISBN 0-924677-27-9). Nonstandard peripherals required: EGA monitor recommended. Addl. software required: Works with any software that imports CGM or WMF file formats.
Over 3000 Full Color Professionally Drawn Images Spanning More Than 100 Categories, Encompassing Every Business Need. Use MasterClips to Enhance Your Presentations, Proposals, Newsletters & Other Materials. Windows Browser Included.
IMSI (International Microcomputer Software, Inc.).

Masterfile. 1981. Compatible Hardware: IBM PC. Operating System(s) Required: PC-DOS, MS-DOS. Memory Required: 640k. Customer Support: License agreement. Maintenance fee $65.00 per month; additional rates are provided according to activity involved; includes: analysis & design, programming, data entry, training, telephone training & assistance, hardware installation & repair, & disaster recovery.
PC-DOS. disk write for info. (ISBN 0-918623-08-1, Order no.: PC849).
contact publisher for price (ISBN 0-918623-23-5, Order no.: MS849).
MS-DOS.
Data Base Management Program Which Uses 11 Commands to Run the Entire Program. Includes 26 Different Built-in Search Methods.
Evolution, Inc.

MasterFinder. Version: 1.2.1. Items Included: Disks, manual & addendums. Customer Support: Free unlimited phone technical support, FAX & modem service. America Online, CompuServe, Applelink.
Macintosh System 6.0.5 & higher. Mac Plus & higher (1Mb RAM). 3.5" disk $149.00.
Optimal configuration: Mac 6.05 1Mb, 7.0 2Mb. Networks supported: Yes & AUX 2.0.
Allows for the Complete Control & Manipulation of Files & Folders on Hard Drive or Floppy Disk. It Is a Total Replacement for the Macintosh Finder Using a Concept of Window Panes As Its Basic User Interface, Each Pane Displays File Names from a Directory of a Mounted Drive. MasterFinder's Startup View, the "Pane" View, Consists of Four Panes That Can Display Information on All Mounted Drives. MasterFinder Has a Sophisticated Find Command; It Is Compatible with Any Network Software to Show User Zones, Nodes & More; Allows for the Cataloging of On-Line & Off-Line Volumes for Fast Searches; Expanded Folder View for the Inspection of the Smallest of Details; Automatic Application & Document Launching; Application Not Found Override; File Aliasing AUX 2.0 Compatibility; & Much More.
Olduvai Corp.

Masterful Disassembler. Version: 2.XX. Jun. 1983. Operating System(s) Required: CP/M. Language(s): Pascal, Assembly. Memory Required: 48k.
$45.00, incl. manual.
Z-80 Disassembler That Provides an Automated Procedure for Disassembling, Labeling & Commenting 8080 or Z-80 Programs.
C.C. Software.

Mastering OS/2 Warp Book. Customer Support: All of our products are unconditionally guaranteed.
OS/2. CD-ROM disk $39.95 (Order no.: WARPBK). Nonstandard peripherals required: CD-ROM drive.
1250 Pages of Great Information & Tips for Mastering OS/2 Warp.
Walnut Creek CDRom.

Mastering Your Atari Through 8 Basic Projects. Micro Magazine Staff. Aug. 1984. Compatible Hardware: Atari 400, 800, XL series. Operating System(s) Required: Atari DOS. Language(s): Atari BASIC (source code included). Memory Required: 48k.
disk $19.95 (ISBN 0-13-559550-9).
Ready-to-Run Applications on Disk Including a Spreadsheet Program, Clock, Games, Sorting, Programmable Characters & Music.
Prentice Hall.

TITLE INDEX

Mastering Your Commodore 64 Through 8 Basic Projects. Micro Magazine Staff. Aug. 1984. *Compatible Hardware:* Commodore 64 or Portable 64. *Operating System(s) Required:* CBM DOS. *Language(s):* BASIC. *Memory Required:* 64k.
disk $19.95 (ISBN 0-13-559543-6).
Collection of BASIC Programs & Routines That Provide a BASIC Tutorial.
Prentice Hall.

MasterJuggler. *Items Included:* 92-page manual, 33-page utilities manual. *Customer Support:* Technical support 713-353-1510, 90-day repair or replacement of faulty manual or defective diskette.
Mac-DOS 5.0 or higher (512k). Macintosh 512KE. disk $89.95. *Networks supported:* Most LocalTalk including AppleShare, TOPS & MacServe.
Font/Desk Accessory (DA)/FKey/Sound/ & Application Utility. Greatly Extends Power of Macintosh by Giving User Access to Unlimited Numbers of Fonts, DAs, FKeys & Sounds. Up to 120 of These Resource Files Can Be Opened Up. Features 100% MultiFinder Compatibility, Font Compression, DA List, Sound List, User Definable Hot Keys, User Configurable Options & Much More.
ALSoft, Inc.

MasterKey. *Version:* 3.01. 1985. *Compatible Hardware:* IBM PC & compatibles, PC XT, PC AT. *Operating System(s) Required:* PC-DOS 2.0 or higher. *Memory Required:* 65k. *Items Included:* User documentation. *Customer Support:* Free telephone support.
contact publisher for price.
Provides Security Control for PRIVACYPLUS Files by Allowing Recovery of Lost or Forgotten Passwords.
United Software Security, Inc.

MasterMaker. *Version:* 5.02. Jan. 1996. *Customer Support:* Free one year phone support.
MS-DOS. CD-ROM disk $2000.00.
Graphical User Interface with Icons & Menu Bars Lets User See at a Glance the Current Assignments for Source & Destination Files; Plus a Feedback Windows Gives Instant System Status. Creates an Image of the Files You Have Collected & Keeps it in One DOS File. The CD-ROM Master Contains the Image Plus Information about the Location of Files & Subdirectories on the Final Disk. You Can Burn a Single CD-R Disk; Create a Virtual CD-ROM; Burn One or More Disks from a Virtual CD-ROM; or Create an ImageMaker CD-R Duplication System Master Image - All from One Collection of Files.
MicroTech Conversion Systems.

Mastermatch. *Compatible Hardware:* Atari 400, 800. *Memory Required:* 32k. *General Requirements:* Joystick.
disk $15.95.
cassette $14.95.
Match Patterns of Colors by Making Logical Choices Based on Clues Provided by the Computer.
Dynacomp, Inc.

MasterMenu. *Version:* 1.6. Feb. 1988. *Operating System(s) Required:* PC-DOS/MS-DOS. *Memory Required:* 60k. *General Requirements:* Hard disk.
disk $59.95.
Hard Drive Menu Which Allows Instant Creation & Deletion of Entire Menus & Menu-Driven Access to Any Software Products & DOS Commands That Can Be Placed on a Hard Drive. Features Include: Password Protection to Control Access to Modify Options, Individual Menu Items, & Root Directory, Ability to Install Batch Files, Operation from Any Directory, Single Function Key Operation, an Example Menu, Error Checking & Identification, Built-In Screen Saver, Help-Screens.
Applied Technologies, Inc.

MasterMenu Plus. *Version:* 2.0. May 1989. *Operating System(s) Required:* PC-DOS/MS-DOS. *Memory Required:* 90k. *General Requirements:* Hard disk. *Items Included:* Complete documentation in three ring binder with slipcase. *Customer Support:* Telephone.
disk $139.95 (Order no.: MM-PLUS).
Hard Disk Menu System with All Features of MASTERMENU, Plus 20 Level Password Protection Security, Data File Encryption/ Decryption, Reporting System Which Tracks Individuals Logging on, Which Files Were Used, & Duration of Time On-Line. Enhanced DOS Command Lines for Menu Generation. Ability to Manipulate File Attributes, Create/Execute Batch Files Within Menus, Menu to Menu with One Function Key, & More.
Applied Technologies, Inc.

MasterScript: Dedicated to the Flawless Scripting. *Items Included:* User manual. *Customer Support:* Phone, FAX, Apple Link, CompuServe, America On-Line.
System 6.0.5 or higher. Macintosh Plus or higher (2Mb). 3.5" disk $129.00. *Addl. software required:* HyperCard 2.0v2 or higher.
Script Editor & Source-Level Debugger Designed for Intermediate & Advanced HyperCard Developers. Sophisticated Features Such As the Externals Monitor & GREP Searching, Modular Design, Advanced Editing Facilities, Expanded Variables Monitoring, & Powerful Externals Monitor.
Heizer Software.

MasterTrend. *Version:* 1.83. 1989. *Operating System(s) Required:* PC-DOS/MS-DOS. *Memory Required:* 640k. *Items Included:* Manuals. *Customer Support:* On-site training, in-house training center, 1 yr. free maintenance includes hardware/software updates, phone support & is extendable for a fee.
3.5" or 5.25" disk $5995.00 (Order no.: 2002-S).
Vibration Analysis Diagnostics Program. Some of Its Capabilities Include Time, Waveform & Spectrum Analysis, History Compilation, Report Generations, Data Management, Route Creation, Frequency Calculations, etc.
Computational Systems, Inc.

Masterworks of Japanese Painting: The Etsuko & Joe Price Collection. Robb Lazarus et al. Jun. 1994. *Items Included:* Instruction manual, upgrade card (if available). *Customer Support:* Call-in, 1-800, fax back & on-line support are available at no charge for the lifetime of the disk.
Macintosh with 68030 processor or higher. Macintosh, double speed CD-ROM drive (8Mb). CD-ROM disk $79.95 (ISBN 1-886664-06-4). *Nonstandard peripherals required:* 24-bit graphics card strongly recommended, Quick Time Movie.
Windows 3.1 or higher. Windows System 3.1 or higher (8Mb). CD-ROM disk $79.95 (ISBN 1-886664-07-2). *Nonstandard peripherals required:* 24-bit graphics card strongly recommended.
A Fascinating Look into Japanese Culture, This CD-ROM Is Drawn from the Largest Private Collection of Edo Period Screens & Scrolls Outside Japan. During the Edo Period (1615-1868), Japan Closed Its Ports to the Outside World, Developing a Unique Artistic Vision. The Disk Features an Introductory Movie, over 1,100 Full-Color Images with Commentary on Each Work & More.
Digital Collections, Inc.

MATCH MAKER EXPRESS

Masterworks of Japanese Painting: The Exsuko & Joe Price Collection: Jewel Case. Robb Lazarus et al. Jun. 1994. *Items Included:* Instructional manual, upgrade card (if available). *Customer Support:* Call-in, 1-800, fax back & on-line support are available at no charge for the lifetime of the disk.
Macintosh with 68030 processor or higher (8Mb). CD-ROM disk $49.95 (ISBN 1-886664-37-4). *Nonstandard peripherals required:* Double speed CD-ROM drive, 24-bit graphics card strongly recommended.
Windows 3.1 or higher (8Mb). CD-ROM disk $49.95 (ISBN 1-886664-38-2). *Nonstandard peripherals required:* 24-bit graphics card strongly recommended.
Digital Collections, Inc.

Masticatory Muscles. Arto Demirjian. *Customer Support:* Toll-free technical support - no charge. In U.S. - 9AM-5PM EST 800-343-0064. In U.K. - 44(0)81-995-8242.
Microsoft Windows, Version 3.X. 386 IBM-compatible PC (3Mb). CD-ROM disk $249.00 Individual; $599.00 Institutional (ISBN 1-57276-008-7, Order no.: SE-008-001). *Nonstandard peripherals required:* MPC Standard CD-ROM drive, SVGA (640 x 480) 256 colors, MPC standard soundboard & speakers.
System 6.0.7 or higher. Apple Macintosh (3Mb). CD-ROM disk $249.00 Individual; $599.00 Institutional (Order no.: SE-008-001). *Nonstandard peripherals required:* CD-ROM drive.
Presents the Anatomy, Mechanics & Function of the Masticatory Muscle Group. The Content Includes High Quality Dissection Photographs & Medical Illustrations. The Tutorial Is Divided into Five Chapters: Introduction, Illustrations, Infrhyoid, Suprhyoid & Masticatory Muscle Groups.
SilverPlatter Education.

Masticatory Muscles. Arto Demirjian. Jan. 1994. *Customer Support:* Toll-free technical support - no charge. In U.S. 9AM - 5PM EST 800-343-0064; in U.K. 44(0)81-995-8242.
System 6.0.7 or higher. Apple Macintosh (3Mb). CD-ROM disk $249.00, Individual, ,599.00 Institutional (ISBN 1-57276-008-7, Order no.: SE-008-001). *Nonstandard peripherals required:* CD-ROM drive.
Microsoft Windows, Version 3.X. 386 IBM-Compatible PC (3Mb). CD-ROM disk $249.00, Individual, ,599.00 Institutional. *Nonstandard peripherals required:* MPC Standard CD-ROM drive, SVGA (640x480) 256 colors, MPC Standard Soundboard & Speakers.
Presents the Anatomy, Mechanics & Function of the Masticatory Muscle Group. The Content Includes High Quality Dissection Photographs & Medical Illustrations. The Tutorial Is Divided into Five Chapters: Introduction, Illustrations, Infrahyoid, Suprahyoid & Masticatory Muscle Groups.
SilverPlatter Education.

MAT One Interpreter. *Compatible Hardware:* Apple II, III.
contact publisher for price.
T & M Computing.

Match Maker Express. *Compatible Hardware:* Apple Macintosh 512KE. *Memory Required:* 512k. *General Requirements:* External disk drive or hard disk; Omnis 3 Plus.
3.5" disk $299.00.
Matches People Who Are Looking for Something with People Who Have That Something.
CP Software.

Match Point. DL Research. Jan. 1986. *Compatible Hardware:* Atari ST. *Memory Required:* 520k. *General Requirements:* Joystick optional.
3.5" disk $39.95 (ISBN 0-923213-53-8, Order no.: AT-MAT).
Simulates Tennis with Graphics, Scoring, & a 3-Dimensional Playing Screen.
MichTron, Inc.

Matching. *Compatible Hardware:* IBM PC, Tandy 2000, Kaypro. *Operating System(s) Required:* TRSDOS, CP/M, PC-DOS, DOS. *Language(s):* BASIC. *Memory Required:* 64k.
disk and update $1000.00.
Set of Programs Enters the Names of the Members of a Tennis or Golf Club, Assigns Them Their Ratings for Single & Doubles, or Other Criteria & Keeps Track of Expenses Chargeable to Their Accounts for Services Provided by the Club. Allows Periodic Preparation of Billings, at Any Given Interval. Also Permits Addressing Individual Communications to Each Member, & Routine Notifications, Like Dues Obligations. Keeps Track of the Increase & Decrease in the Number of Members. Contains Programs for Modifying, Eliminating, Changing & Updating the List of Members. Also Permits the Addressing of Communications to Former Members for Re-Recruiting Purposes.
Computer Technical Services of New Jersey.

MATCHNET. *Compatible Hardware:* TRS-80. *Language(s):* BASIC. *Memory Required:* 48k.
contact publisher for price.
Dynacomp, Inc.

MATCHNET: Microwave Matching Network Synthesis. Jan. 1991. *Items Included:* 44 page ring-bound user's manual.
IBM PC & compatibles. disk $150.00 (ISBN 0-89006-528-4).
Automates the Synthesis of Broadband Matching Networks with Arbitrary Gain-Shape Between Complex Sources & Loads. Also Suggests the Best Circuit Structure for a Given Set of Source & Load Requirements.
Artech Hse., Inc.

Material & Production Management. *Version:* 4.5. *Compatible Hardware:* IBM PC, PC XT, PC AT & compatibles. *Operating System(s) Required:* PC-DOS, MS-DOS, XENIX. *Language(s):* BASIC (source code included). *Memory Required:* 256k.
$895.00.
Manufacturing Control & Planning System, Including Bill of Material Processing. Designed for Any Business Involved in the Manufacturing of a Product. Tracks a Product from Production Scheduling to Inventory of Finished Goods, Prints Inventory & Work Center Where-Used Reports. Reports Generated As a Result of On-Line Interaction Include an Inventory Status/Alert, Price List, Inventory Evaluation, Detail List & Sales Analysis.
Open Systems Holdings Corp., Inc.

Material & Resource Requirements Planning System (MR2PS-II). *Operating System(s) Required:* MS/PC-DOS. *Language(s):* BASIC Compiled. *Memory Required:* 128k.
disk $500.00.
Creates & Edits Bills of Material & Other Job Costs; Provides for Inventory Management, Explode, Net & Set-Back Schedule Requirements; & Maintains & Updates the Status of Planned & Released Orders.
Bernard Giffler Assocs.

Material Planning. May 1983. *Compatible Hardware:* IBM PC, PC XT, PC AT. *Operating System(s) Required:* PC-DOS. *Language(s):* COBOL. *Memory Required:* 192k. *General Requirements:* 2 disk drives.
disk $6400.00-$8295.00.
Generates & Re-Schedules Planned Orders Based on Available Inventory, Purchase Orders, Work Orders, & Other Planning Requirements. Exception Reporting Is Produced for Each Material Planner. Single Level Pegging Traces the Material Requirement to the Item That Generated It. A Master Schedule Report Can Be Printed If the Master Schedule Module Is Installed. The BILL OF MATERIAL, WORK ORDER & PURCHASING Modules Are Required. The Material Planning Module Is Daily Net Change with the Option for Complete Regeneration. Supports a Three-Year, 1000 Day Dynamic Shop Calendar.
Twin Oaks, Inc.

Material Requirements Planning. 1996. *Customer Support:* Free telephone & BBS technical support; documentation; training from local dealers &/or vendor's CFPIM, C.P.M., CIRM, CQA Trainers. Customization available from vendor.
MS/PC DOS, Concurrent DOS, Xenix, Unix. IBM PC/XT/AT & compatibles; IBM PS/2 (512k).
single user $1095.00. *Networks supported:* Novell, Lantastic, BANTAN VINES; all NETBOIS compatible.
multi-user $1595.00.
This is a Regenerative MRP system. That is, the MRP report is created as a bath process after all Master Schedule transactions have been entered. Up to 100 variable length buckets can be defined with vertical or horizontal Bucket Reports.
INMASS/MRP.

Material Requirements Planning. *Version:* 3.3. (Integrated Manufacturing & Financial System Ser.). *Compatible Hardware:* Micro/VAX, UNIBUS/VAX, IBM PC. *Operating System(s) Required:* MS-DOS, Novell, Micro/VMS, VAS/VMS, UNIX. *Language(s):* DIBOL.
MS-DOS. single-user $500.00.
DEC PDP-11/VAX. multi-user $1500.00.
Uses Current & Projected Customer Order Gross Item Requirements on Master Schedule to Determine Net Material Requirements into Future Planning Periods. Item Requirement Is Netted to Expected Item Availability. Item Availability Is Based on Free Stock, Plus Open Purchase or Manufacturing Orders Becoming Due, Less Outstanding Reservations in That Period. Material Requirements Planning Report Shows Results of Planning, along with Suggested Action.
Primetrack.

Material Requirements Planning (a Part of ABECAS). *Customer Support:* On site training unlimited support services for first 90 days & through subscription thereafter.
PC/MS-DOS 3.x. IBM PC & compatibles.
Contact publisher for price. *Nonstandard peripherals required:* Hard disk (30Mb or higher); 132 column printer.
Allows Selected Master Schedule to Be Exploded into Material Requirements Plan. Plan Can Recognize Inventory on Hand & on Order As Well As Time Required to Plan Acquisition of Raw Materials for Production. Plan May Be Transferred to Purchase Order Module & Modified Manually. Alternate Vendors May Be Used for Some or All Requirements for Each Item. Numerous Analysis Reports Available. Requires Inventory Management, Bill of Materials & Master Scheduling Modules.
Argos Software.

Materials Inventory-Purchasing. *Version:* 3.3. (Integrated Manufacturing & Financial System Ser.). *Compatible Hardware:* Micro/VAX, UNIBUS/VAX; IBM PC. *Operating System(s) Required:* MS-DOS, Novell, Micro/VMS, VAX/VMS, UNIX. *Language(s):* DIBOL.
MS-DOS. $750.00 single-user.
DEC PDP-11/VAX. $1500.00 multi-user.
Provides Total Manufacturing Inventory Control. Keeps Track of Material Availability, Value, Usage, & Location. Produces Usage Analysis Reports, Shortage Reports, & Allocation Reports.
Primetrack.

Materials-Pro Analyzer. Jan. 1996. *Items Included:* 1 manual, copy protection key, Mat-Pro disks, Stage-Pro disks. *Customer Support:* 90 day unlimited warranty, maintenance applies if user has maintenance w/Image-Pro Plus.
Windows 3.1. 386, 256 colors (8Mb). disk $1499.00. *Addl. software required:* Image-Pro Plus.
A New Specialized Software Solution for the Analysis of Metals, Ceramics, Polymers, & Other Advanced Materials. A "Plug-In" Module for Image-Pro Plus, the Premier Image Analysis Software Package. Provides Materials Science Researchers with Cost-Effective & User Friendly Software Allowing Them to Automate the Analysis of Digitized Images of Specific Materials Products. Sophisticated Preprocessing Routines & Standard Materials Measurements Allow Users to Determine Grain Size, Measure Shape & Orientation, Gauge Porosity & Nodularity, & Perform Phase Analysis. Specifically Designed to Provide Solutions for the Materials Analysis Professional. Includes an Image Gallery Database Which Organizes & Stores the Images. Using This Database, Users Can Easily & Efficiently Capture, Store, & Retrieve Images in Any of the Industry Standard Formats.
Media Cybernetics, L. P.

Materials Requirements Planning. *Version:* 2.0. 1989. *Compatible Hardware:* Compupro; Compaq; Fujitsu; Heath-Zenith; HP; IBM PC, PC XT, PC AT; NEC; Tandy. *Operating System(s) Required:* MS-DOS, PC-DOS, Concurrent DOS, Unix, Xenix; Novell & Microsoft networks. *Language(s):* C. *Memory Required:* 640k. *General Requirements:* Hard disk, 132-column printer. *Items Included:* Disks & manuals. *Customer Support:* Through VARs, support.
single-user $995.00.
multi-user $1295.00.
Unix, Xenix $1495.00.
demo disk & manual $20.00.
Controls Inventory Balances, Purchase Orders & Production. Requires Inventory & BOM (Bill of Materials) Modules.
INMASS/MRP.

MATFOR: A System for Numerical Computations. *Version:* 1.15. 1990. *Items Included:* 400 page manual. *Customer Support:* Unlimited customer support; free updates for one year.
MS-DOS 3.1 or higher. IBM XT/AT/PS2 or compatibles (640k). disk $150.00. *Optimal configuration:* Math coprocessor.
IBM or compatibles with 1Mb of Extended Memory. disk $395.00. *Nonstandard peripherals required:* Intel 386 or 386 SX Processor.
Interpreter for Quick Solution of Problems in Applied Mathematics, Advanced Statistics, Signal Processing & Control Systems Analysis & Design. It Has Facilities for User-Defined Functions As Well As a Comprehensive Library of Built-In Functions.
Computational Engineering Assocs.

Math. *Compatible Hardware:* HP 85, 86/87.
HP 85. data cartridge, 3-1/2" or 5-1/4" disk $95.00 ea. (Order no.: 82811A).
HP 86/87. 3-1/2" or 5-1/4" disk $95.00 ea. (Order no.: 82841A).
Provides Access to Commonly Employed Mathematical Routines Used in Calculus,

Numerical Analysis, Linear Systems, Geometry, etc. Full Descriptions, Plus Relevant Equations & Other Data Are Included.
Hewlett-Packard Co.

Math - Reading - Writing K-8. Jan. 1994. *Items Included:* Program on CD-ROM, CD Booklet, & Registration Card. *Customer Support:* Free unlimited customer support via telephone.
Windows 3.1 or higher running under DOS 5.0 or higher. 386 SX (4Mb RAM; 500k low Dos Mem; 6Mb free disk space). CD-ROM disk $1499.00 (ISBN 1-57268-075-X, Order no.: 91002). *Nonstandard peripherals required:* Sound card (either: Sound Blaster - 8, 16, PRO; Media Vision ProAudio Spectrum; or Microsoft Sound System); MPC compatible CD-ROM drive; VGA monitor; & microphone. *Optimal configuration:* 25 MHz 386 SX.
These Programs Offer Comprehensive Instruction in Math, Reading, & Writing. Keyboarding Lessons Are Also Provided in the Writing Section. The Lessons Provide a Natural, Developmental Approach to Learning. Students Build New Skills As They Progress Through the Lessons.
Conter Software.

Math - Reading K-8. Jan. 1994. *Items Included:* Program on CD-ROM, CD Booklet, & Registration Card. *Customer Support:* Free unlimited customer support via telephone.
Macintosh System 7.0 or higher. Macintosh LC or higher (4Mb). CD-ROM disk $999.00 (ISBN 1-57268-076-8, Order no.: 92002). *Nonstandard peripherals required:* 12 inch monitor or larger; CD-ROM drive. *Optimal configuration:* 5Mb RAM.
CD-ROM Complements & Supplements Students' Classroom Experience. The Reading Lessons Teach Students to Become Proficient Readers. Students Build Vocabulary, Learn Word Meanings & Study Skills. Math Lessons Teach Essential Concepts & Skills. The Instruction Requires That Students Apply Basic Concepts & Think Critically As They Learn.
Conter Software.

Math - Reading Kindergarten. Jan. 1994. *Items Included:* Program on CD-ROM, CD Booklet, & Registration Card. *Customer Support:* Free unlimited support via telephone.
Windows 3.1 or higher running under DOS 5.0 or higher. 386 SX (4Mb RAM; 500k low Dos Mem; 6Mb free disk space). CD-ROM disk $49.00 (ISBN 1-57268-000-8, Order no.: 51000). *Nonstandard peripherals required:* Sound card (either: Sound Blaster - 8, 16, PRO; Media Vision ProAudio Spectrum; or Microsoft Sound System); MPC Compatible CD-ROM drive; VGA monitor; & microphone. *Optimal configuration:* 25MHz 386 SX.
Math for Windows: These Programs Offer Comprehensive, Individual Grade-Level Instruction in Math for Kindergarten Through High School. These Lessons Begin with Fundamental Math Skills & Concepts, & Build New Skills & Enthusiasm. These Programs Teach More Than the Memorization of Facts & Final Solutions. They Also Emphasize & Reinforce Logical Thinking Strategies to Improve Analysis & Problem-Solving Skills. Reading Grade-Level for Windows: These Programs Provide a Natural, Developmental Approach to Fundamental Reading Skills. Beginners Progress Through Reading-Readiness, Phonics, & Decoding. Imaginative Picture Stories & Sound Patterns Add New Dimensions & Excitement to the Learning Process.
Conter Software.

Math - Reading Kindergarten. Jan. 1994. *Items Included:* Program on CD-ROM, CD Booklet, & Registration Card. *Customer Support:* Free unlimited support via telephone.
Windows 3.1 or higher running under DOS 5.0 or higher. 386 SX (4Mb RAM; 500k low Dos Mem; 6Mb free disk space). CD-ROM disk $249.00 (ISBN 1-57268-043-1, Order no.: 11010). *Nonstandard peripherals required:* Sound card (either: Sound Blaster - 8, 16, PRO; Media Vision ProAudio Spectrum; or Microsoft Sound System); MCP Compatible CD-ROM drive; VGA monitor; & microphone. *Optimal configuration:* 25 MHz 386 SX.
Reading Grade-Level for Windows: These Programs Provide a Natural, Developmental Approach to Fundamental Reading Skills. Beginners Progress Through Reading-Readiness, Phonics, & Decoding. Imaginative Picture Stories & Sound Patterns Add New Dimensions & Excitement to the Learning Process. Math for Windows: These Programs Offer Comprehensive, Individual Grade-Level Instruction in Math for Kindergarten Through High School. These Lessons Begin with Fundamental Math Skills & Concepts, & Build New Skills & Enthusiasm. These Programs Teach More Than the Memorization of Facts & Final Solutions. They Also Emphasize & Reinforce Logical Thinking Strategies to Improve Analysis & Problem-Solving Skills.
Conter Software.

Math-Amation. *Compatible Hardware:* Commodore Amiga 500, 1000, 2000.
3.5" disk $99.95.
Provides a Scientific Calculator, Matrix Calculator, Graphics, & Statistics Functions. Supports the IFF Graphics Format, & Allows Users to Produce 3-Dimensional Bar Charts & Pie Charts. The Matrix Calculator Enables Users to Manipulate the A, B, & R Matrices. Can Solve Systems of Linear Equations, & Perform Invert, Transpose, Trace, Determinant, & Other Functions. Supports Matrices of Up to 1600 Elements. Can Have Up to 36 Global Variables in Any Expression & Keep Track of Previous Results. Can Also Perform Geometric Calculations on Triangles, Rectangles, Arcs, & 3-Dimensional Coordinates.
Progressive Peripherals & Software, Inc.

Math Baseball. 1984. *Customer Support:* Toll free customary service Hot Line 1-800-645-3739 (9a.m. - 5p.m. Eastern Time).
Apple II; IBM; Tandy (MS-DOS). disk $29.95, incl. 1 disk & documentaiton (Order no.: DB4000).
In This Program You Have the Fun of a Baseball Game Combined with Solving Math Problems. Players Control the Type of Math Problem to Be Solved & Its Level of Difficulty.
Educational Activities Inc.

Math Blaster Mystery: The Great Brain Robbery. (Math Blaster Ser.).
Windows. IBM & compatibles. CD-ROM disk $59.95 (Order no.: R1346). *Nonstandard peripherals required:* CD-ROM drive. *Optimal configuration:* 386 processor operating at 16Mhz or higher, MS-DOS 5.0 or higher, Windows 3.1 or higher, 30Mb hard drive, mouse, VGA graphic adapter & VGA color monitor (SVGA recommended), 4Mb RAM, external speakers or headphones (with sound card) that are Sound Blaster compatible.
Learn to Solve Word Problems, Use Whole Numbers, Fractions, Decimals, Integers, Create Mathematical Equations, Apply Order of Operations & Other Pre-Algebra Concepts (Ages 10-Adult).
Library Video Co.

Math Blaster Series.
Windows. IBM & compatibles. CD-ROM disk $179.85, Set (Order no.: R1344). *Nonstandard peripherals required:* CD-ROM drive. *Optimal configuration:* 386 processor operating at 16Mhz or higher, MS-DOS 5.0 or higher, Windows 3.1 or higher, 30Mb hard drive, mouse, VGA graphic adapter & VGA color monitor (SVGA recommended), 4Mb RAM, external speakers or headphones (with sound card) that are Sound Blaster compatible.
Three Volume Set.
Library Video Co.

Math Facts Lottery. Nan Watanabe. *Customer Support:* 90 day warranty against defective software.
DOS 3.3. Apple II (48k). disk $39.95 (Order no.: A-1165).
An Educational Computer Game Which Presents Drill-&-Practice of Addition, Subtraction, Multiplication & Division Equations in a Fun & Colorful Format. The Mathematical Operation & the Level of Difficulty May Be Selected with Addition & Subtraction Equations, of Either Two or Three Digit Numerals, Requiring the Carrying of Numbers.
Electronic Courseware Systems, Inc.

Math for Beginners. 1984. *Customer Support:* Toll free customary service Hot Line 1-800-645-3739 (9a.m. - 5p.m. Eastern Time).
Apple II; IBM; Tandy (MS-DOS). $39.95 ea., incl. 1 disk & documentation (Order no.: DB4030; DB4031; DB4032; DB4033; DB4034; DB4035).
$199.00 set incl. 6 disks & documentation (Order no.: DB4036).
These Outstanding Programs Offer Tutorial & Drill & Practice Activities to Develop Math Competency Skills to Be Relied on in Everyday Life.
Educational Activities Inc.

Math for Everyday Living. Ann Edson & Alan Schwartz. 1994. *Items Included:* Diskette, teachers guide & binders. *Customer Support:* Toll free customer service Hot Line 1-800-645-3739 (9a.m. - 5p.m. Eastern Time) software guaranteed for two years.
Mac 6.0 Plus. Macintosh (4Mb). 3.5" disk $237.00 (Order no.: DK158D1).
Teach Real Life Math & Business Skills with This Progressive Tutorial & Practice Program. Students Make Choices in Real-Life, Simulation-Type Activities. Individualized for Each Student.
Educational Activities Inc.

Math Grapher. Richard L. Anthony. 1984. *Customer Support:* ECS offers technical support to registered users. Call (217) 359-7099. Other than the telephone call - technical support is no charge.
DOS 3.3. Apple. disk $49.95 (Order no.: A-1117).
DOS 3.2 or higher. IBM. $49.95 single station/ $250.00 network (Order no.: I-1117).
Designed As an Aid to Mathematics Instructors Who Teach the Graphing of Functions. The Computer Will Plot Any of a Number of Prestored Functions, As Well As User-Defined Functions, on Both Rectangular & Polar Coordinates. The User Sets the Parameters. Graphs Can Be Displayed on the Screen, Saved on Disk, & Printed. The Function appears with the Graph, & Several Functions Can Be Displayed Together in the Same Picture.
Electronic Courseware Systems, Inc.

Math Gulper.
Apple II. disk $29.95.
MS-DOS. disk $29.95.
Though Still Educational, These Are Games That Make Learning Fun! Kids Must Answer Twenty Problems in Addition, Subtraction, Multiplication, or Division Before the Little Fish Are Caught by the Big Fish. If Successful, the Child Wins a Bonus

MATH LAB

Fishing Game. Programs Were Designed for Children in Grades 2 Through 6, However, Older Children Enjoy the Gamelike Format Presentation.
Milliken Publishing Co.

Math Lab. Dean M. Thompson. Sep. 1993. *Items Included:* Illustrated users manual. 5.25" & 3.5" HD diskettes. Practice/demonstration macro & puzzle examples. *Customer Support:* One year free curriculum assistance to teachers. One year free mail & Compuserve technical support.
IBM PC/MS-DOS 2.1 or higher. IBM-PC compatibles w/one disk drive (384k). disk $48.00 (ISBN 0-9627172-3-1, Order no.: 817-346-9116). *Nonstandard peripherals required:* VGA color graphics board. *Optimal configuration:* IBM-PC compatible with 384k RAM, VGA graphics. Hard disk, mouse & dot-matrix or HP Laser printer recommended, but not required.
Supplements High School & Early College Level Studies in Algebra, Geometry, & Trigonometry. Program Covers Points, Lines, Conic-Secitons, Trigonometrics, Parametrics, Composites, & Artistic Mathematics. Intuitive Menu Structure, Comprehensive Tutorial, & Context-Sensitive Help, Make It Suitable for Home Use Without Professional Supervision.
Insight Advantage.

Math Lib: Math Library. 1986. *Items Included:* Manual with theory, operating instructions. *Customer Support:* Free phone, on-site seminars.
MS-DOS. IBM (128k). disk $85.00. *Addl. software required:* BASIC.
Collection of Programs in BASIC That Solve Math Problems Commonly Encountered by Engineers & Scientists; Including Linear & Log Plots of X,Y Data, Least Squares Fit, Roots on Non-Linear Functions Using Half Interval Search, Cubic Spline Fit, Roots of a Polynomial Using Newton's Method, Gauss Jordan Inverse of a Matrix, Matrix Multiplication, Real & Complex Eigen Values, Runge-Kutta Solution of First Order Differential Equation.
Kern International, Inc.

Math Magic. 1986-1991. *Items Included:* Disk(s), user's guide, poster, coloring book, warranty card, swap coupon. *Customer Support:* 90 day unlimited warranty; 800 toll free number, 800-221-7911, 8:00 a.m.-5:00 p.m. Arizona time; Updates $10.
Macintosh System 6 or higher. Macintosh (1Mb monochrome, 2Mb color). 3.5" disk $69.99 (ISBN 1-55772-039-8, Order no.: 0102). *Optimal configuration:* 2Mb color monitor, Macintosh LC. *Networks supported:* Digicard.
MS-DOS. IBM, Tandy, MS-DOS compatible (128k). disk $49.99 (ISBN 0-918017-01-7, Order no.: 0101). *Nonstandard peripherals required:* VGA or CGA card. *Optimal configuration:* 128k, color monitor, VGA card. *Networks supported:* Velan, Novell, Digicard.
DOS. Apple II, Apple IIe, Apple IIGS, Apple II Plus (48k). disk $49.99 (ISBN 0-918017-00-9, Order no.: 0100). *Optimal configuration:* Apple II, printer, color monitor, 48k. *Networks supported:* Digicard.
In Award Winning Math Magic, Players Free the Captured Dragons Behind Colorful Brick Walls. This Game Combines Arcade Action with Counting, Addition & Subtraction. Beginners' Lessons Feature Counting Objects & Progress to Adding & Subtracting Numbers. Choose from Six Automatic Settings or Use Customize. Ages 3 to 10.
Mindplay.

Math Map Trip. *Items Included:* Manual in binder. *Customer Support:* Toll-free customer support: 1-800-645-3739.
Macintosh. Macintosh LC or higher (2Mb System 6.X, 4Mb System 7.X). $89.00 disks; $99.00 CD ROM Version (Order no.: DK-26110). *Networks supported:* Appleshare, Novell.
DOS. MS-DOS compatible. disk $89.00 (Order no.: DK-26110). *Networks supported:* Novell.
This Exciting Game Program Features Sound, Animation, Built-In Maps, Music & Fun in Addition to Teaching Vital Math & Geography Concepts. While You Take a Fascinating Tour of the Country by Land, Sea & Air, the Program's Extensive Branching Will Reinforce Important Concepts Many Students Find Difficult to Learn.
Educational Activities Inc.

Math Pack. *Compatible Hardware:* Apple II with Applesoft; IBM PC. *Operating System(s) Required:* Apple DOS 3.2, 3.3; PC-DOS. *Memory Required:* Apple 48k, IBM 128k. disk $49.95, incl. manual & demo disk.
Mathematical Analysis Routines. Programs Available: Statistical Analysis, Numerical Analysis, Matrix, 3D Surface Plotter.
Dynacomp, Inc.

Math Rabbit. 1986. *Compatible Hardware:* Apple II, II+, IIe, IIc, IIgs; IBM PC & compatibles; Tandy 1000. *Operating System(s) Required:* MS-DOS 2.0 or higher. *Language(s):* Machine. *Memory Required:* Apple 64k, IBM & Tandy 256k. *General Requirements:* IBM requires CGA card.
disk $39.95.
Builds Early Math Skills While Enriching a Child's Appreciation of Numbers. Children Explore Basic Number Concepts & Develop Skills in Counting, Adding, Subtracting & Recognizing Number Relationships & Patterns. Customizing Options Allow Child to Select Speed Settings, Math Operations, Target Numbers & Ranges.
The Learning Co.

Math Rabbit.
Windows. IBM & compatibles. CD-ROM disk $64.95 (Order no.: R1206). *Nonstandard peripherals required:* CD-ROM drive. *Optimal configuration:* 386 processor operating at 16Mhz or higher, MS-DOS 5.0 or higher, Windows 3.1 or higher, 30Mb hard drive, mouse, VGA graphic adapter & VGA color monitor (SVGA recommended), 4Mb RAM, external speakers or headphones (with sound card) that are Sound Blaster compatible.
Macintosh (4Mb). (Order no.: R1206). *Nonstandard peripherals required:* 14" color monitor or larger, CD-ROM drive.
Build Early Math & Thinking Skills with Math Rabbit at the Circus As He Introduces Key Math Concepts. Explore the Exciting World of Numbers While Sharpening Skills in Counting, Adding, Subtracting & Recognizing Number Relationships (Ages 4-7).
Library Video Co.

Math RCT Fun. Nov. 1993.
PC-DOS/MS-DOS. IBM & compatibles (256k). disk $53.99 (ISBN 0-9621501-5-0). *Nonstandard peripherals required:* VGA.
PC-DOS/MS-DOS. IBM & compatibles (256k). disk $199.99 (ISBN 0-9621501-7-7). *Nonstandard peripherals required:* VGA. *Networks supported:* Novell.
Review for the New York State Regents Competency Test in Mathematics Actual Exam Problems, a Management System, VGA Graphics & Animation.
Bellmore Software.

Math Routines Library. *Compatible Hardware:* TI 99/4A.
contact publisher for price.
Provides Users with Fourier Series Calculations, Function Analysis, Ordinary Differential Equations, Base Conversions, Prime Factorization, Hyperbolic Functions & Simultaneous Equation Calculation.
Texas Instruments, Personal Productivit.

Math SAT I. (Micro Learn Tutorial Ser.). *Customer Support:* Free telephone support.
MAC. IBM (128k), Macintosh (2Mb), Apple II series, (48k), Commodore 64. 5.25" disk, $39.95 (Lab pack/5) $99.00). 3.5" disk, $44.95 (Lab pack/5 $115.00). Apple, IBM or Macintosh $249.00 (ISBN 1-57265-042-7).
DOS. (ISBN 0-939153-79-3).
APP. (ISBN 0-939153-35-1).
Study Aid for the Math Portion of the SAT Test, Covering Fractions, Averages, Ratios, Rate, Linear Equations, Consecutive Integers, Algebra, Geometry, Quantitative Analysis. The tutorial modes gives explanations for every answer choice, correct & incorrect (plus help/practice on important ideas). The test mode gives no help; after the score appears, it presents missed questions in the tutorial mode.
Word Assocs., Inc.

Math Wizard Plus. Selena Studios Staff. Oct. 1995. *Customer Support:* Via online Selenaly-AOL.COM.
Windows 3.1 or 95. PC Multimedia (8Mb). CD-ROM disk $14.95 (ISBN 1-55727-032-5, Order no.: MWCDPC). *Optimal configuration:* PC Multimedia, Windows 3.1 or 95, 8Mb RAM, 1Mb SVGA card, CD-ROM.
Meet the Friendly Wizard in This Two Part Program That Lets Kids Practice Arithmetic or Play a Rescue Game. Zelda, the Hag, Has Played a Nasty Trick on Her Beautiful Sister. She Has Turned Her Niece, Princess Void, into Some Type of Object & Hidden Her in a Castle in the Sky. Prince Null & His Trusty Pet Fly, Buzz, Must Set Forth & Find the Missing Princess. The Game Is Different Each Time It Is Played - Making Learning Fun. Kids Will Enjoy Prince Null's Surfer-Type Personality & Find Humor in His Sister's Self-Centered persona.
Unicorn Educational Software.

Math 1. Jan. 1994. *Items Included:* Program on CD-ROM, CD Booklet, & Registration Card. *Customer Support:* Free unlimited support via telephone.
Windows 3.1 or higher running under DOS 5.0 or higher. 386 SX (4Mb RAM; 500k low Dos Mem; 6Mb free disk space). CD-ROM disk $49.00 (ISBN 1-57268-001-6, Order no.: 53001). *Nonstandard peripherals required:* Sound card (either: Sound Blaster - 8, 16, PRO; Media Vision ProAudio Spectrum; or Microsoft Sound System); MPC Compatible CD-ROM drive; VGA monitor; & microphone. *Optimal configuration:* 25MHz 386 SX.
Math for Windows: These Programs Offer Comprehensive, Individual Grade-Level Instruction in Math for Kindergarten Through High School. These Lessons Begin with Fundamental Math Skills & Concepts, & Build New Skills & Enthusiasm. These Programs Teach More Than the Memorization of Facts & Final Solutions. They Also Emphasize & Reinforce Logical Thinking Strategies to Improve Analysis & Problem-Solving Skills.
Conter Software.

Math 1. Jan. 1994. *Items Included:* Program on CD-ROM, CD Booklet, & Registration Card. *Customer Support:* Free unlimited support via telephone.
Macintosh System 7.0 or higher. Macintosh LC or higher (4Mb). CD-ROM disk $49.00 (ISBN 1-57268-026-1, Order no.: 63001). *Nonstandard peripherals required:* 12 inch monitor or larger; CD-ROM drive. *Optimal configuration:* 5Mb RAM.
Math for Macintosh. These Programs Complement & Supplement Students' Classroom Experiences. The Lessons Feature Essential Concepts & Skills, & Contain High-Interest Activities with Themes. The Instruction Provides

TITLE INDEX

MATH 4

Students with the Skills Needed to Move Through Each Level of Instruction. At the Same Time, the Instruction Requires Students to Think Critically & Apply the Concepts They Are Learning.
Conter Software.

Math 1-2. Jan. 1994. *Items Included:* Program on CD-ROM, CD Booklet, & Registration Card. *Customer Support:* Free unlimited support via telephone.
Windows 3.1 or higher running under DOS 5.0 or higher. 386 SX (4Mb RAM; 500k low Dos Mem; 6Mb free disk space). CD-ROM disk $249.00 (ISBN 1-57268-044-X, Order no.: 13120). *Nonstandard peripherals required:* Sound card (either: Sound Blaster - 8, 16, PRO; Media Vision ProAudio Spectrum; or Microsoft Sound System); MCP Compatible CD-ROM drive; VGA monitor; & microphone. *Optimal configuration:* 25 MHz 386 SX.
Math for Windows: These Programs Offer Comprehensive, Individual Grade-Level Instruction in Math for Kindergarten Through High School. These Lessons Begin with Fundamental Math Skills & Concepts, & Build New Skills & Enthusiasm. These Programs Teach More Than the Memorization of Facts & Final Solutions. They Also Emphasize & Reinforce Logical Thinking Strategies to Improve Analysis & Problem-Solving Skills.
Conter Software.

Math 1-2. Jan. 1994. *Items Included:* Program on CD-ROM, CD Booklet, & Registration Card. *Customer Support:* Free unlimited customer support via telephone.
Macintosh System 7.0 or higher. Macintosh LC or higher (4Mb). CD-ROM disk $249.00 (ISBN 1-57268-065-2, Order no.: 23120). *Nonstandard peripherals required:* 12 inch monitor or larger; CD-ROM drive. *Optimal configuration:* 5Mb RAM.
Math for Macintosh: These Programs Complement & Supplement Students' Classroom Experiences. The Lessons Feature Essential Concepts & Skills, & Contain High-Interest Activities with Themes. The Instruction Provides Students with the Skills Needed to Move Through Each Level of Instruction. At the Same Time, the Instruction Requires Students to Think, Critically & Apply the Concepts They Are Learning.
Conter Software.

Math 2. Jan. 1994. *Items Included:* Program on CD-ROM, CD Booklet, & Registration Card. *Customer Support:* Free unlimited support via telephone.
Windows 3.1 or higher running under DOS 5.0 or higher. 386 SX (4Mb RAM; 500k low Dos Mem; 6Mb free disk space). CD-ROM disk $49.00 (ISBN 1-57268-002-4, Order no.: 53002). *Nonstandard peripherals required:* Sound card (either: Sound Blaster - 8, 16, PRO; Media Vision ProAudio Spectrum; or Microsoft Sound System); MPC Compatible CD-ROM drive; VGA monitor; & microphone. *Optimal configuration:* 25MHz 386 SX.
Math for Windows: These Programs Offer Comprehensive, Individual Grade-Level Instruction in Math for Kindergarten Through High School. These Lessons Begin with Fundamental Math Skills & Concepts, & Build New Skills & Enthusiasm. These Programs Teach More Than the Memorization of Facts & Final Solutions. They Also Emphasize & Reinforce Logical Thinking Strategies to Improve Analysis & Problem-Solving Skills.
Conter Software.

Math 2. Jan. 1994. *Items Included:* Program on CD-ROM, CD Booklet, & Registration Card. *Customer Support:* Free unlimited support via telephone.
Macintosh System 7.0 or higher. Macintosh LC or higher (4Mb). CD-ROM disk $49.00 (ISBN 1-57268-027-X, Order no.: 63002). *Nonstandard peripherals required:* 12 inch monitor or larger; CD-ROM drive. *Optimal configuration:* 5Mb RAM.
Math for Macintosh. These Programs Complement & Supplement Students' Classroom Experiences. The Lessons Feature Essential Concepts & Skills, & Contain High-Interest Activities with Themes. The Instruction Provides Students with the Skills Needed to Move Through Each Level of Instruction. At the Same Time, the Instruction Requires Students to Think Critically & Apply the Concepts They Are Learning.
Conter Software.

Math 3. Jan. 1994. *Items Included:* Program on CD-ROM, CD Booklet, & Registration Card. *Customer Support:* Free unlimited support via telephone.
Windows 3.1 or higher running under DOS 5.0 or higher. 386 SX (4Mb RAM; 500k low Dos Mem; 6Mb free disk space). CD-ROM disk $49.00 (ISBN 1-57268-003-2, Order no.: 53003). *Nonstandard peripherals required:* Sound card (either: Sound Blaster - 8, 16, PRO; Media Vision ProAudio Spectrum; or Microsoft Sound System); MPC Compatible CD-ROM drive; VGA monitor; & microphone. *Optimal configuration:* 25MHz 386 SX.
Math for Windows: These Programs Offer Comprehensive, Individual Grade-Level Instruction in Math for Kindergarten Through High School. These Lessons Begin with Fundamental Math Skills & Concepts, & Build New Skills & Enthusiasm. These Programs Teach More Than the Memorization of Facts & Final Solutions. They Also Emphasize & Reinforce Logical Thinking Strategies to Improve Analysis & Problem-Solving Skills.
Conter Software.

Math 3. Jan. 1994. *Items Included:* Program on CD-ROM, CD Booklet, & Registration Card. *Customer Support:* Free unlimited support via telephone.
Macintosh System 7.0 or higher. Macintosh LC or higher (4Mb). CD-ROM disk $49.00 (ISBN 1-57268-028-8, Order no.: 63003). *Nonstandard peripherals required:* 12 inch monitor or larger; CD-ROM drive. *Optimal configuration:* 5Mb RAM.
Math for Macintosh. These Programs Complement & Supplement Students' Classroom Experiences. The Lessons Feature Essential Concepts & Skills, & Contain High-Interest Activities with Themes. The Instruction Provides Students with the Skills Needed to Move Through Each Level of Instruction. At the Same Time, the Instruction Requires Students to Think Critically & Apply the Concepts They Are Learning.
Conter Software.

Math 3-4. Jan. 1994. *Items Included:* Program on CD-ROM, CD Booklet, & Registration Card. *Customer Support:* Free unlimited support via telephone.
Windows 3.1 or higher running under DOS 5.0 or higher. 386 SX (4Mb RAM; 500k low Dos Mem; 6Mb free disk space). CD-ROM disk $249.00 (ISBN 1-57268-045-8, Order no.: 13340). *Nonstandard peripherals required:* Sound card (either: Sound Blaster - 8, 16, PRO; Media Vision ProAudio Spectrum; or Microsoft Sound System); MCP Compatible CD-ROM drive; VGA monitor; & microphone. *Optimal configuration:* 25 MHz 386 SX.
Math for Windows: These Programs Offer Comprehensive, Individual Grade-Level Instruction in Math for Kindergarten Through High School. These Lessons Begin with Fundamental Math Skills & Concepts, & Build New Skills & Enthusiasm. These Programs Teach More Than the Memorization of Facts & Final Solutions. They Also Emphasize & Reinforce Logical Thinking Strategies to Improve Analysis & Problem-Solving Skills.
Conter Software.

Math 3-4. Jan. 1994. *Items Included:* Program on CD-ROM, CD Booklet, & Registration Card. *Customer Support:* Free unlimited customer support via telephone.
Macintosh System 7.0 or higher. Macintosh LC or higher (4Mb). CD-ROM disk $249.00 (ISBN 1-57268-066-0, Order no.: 23340). *Nonstandard peripherals required:* 12 inch monitor or larger; CD-ROM drive. *Optimal configuration:* 5Mb RAM.
Math for Macintosh: These Programs Complement & Supplement Students' Classroom Experiences. The Lessons Feature Essential Concepts & Skills, & Contain High-Interest Activities with Themes. The Instruction Provides Students with the Skills Needed to Move Through Each Level of Instruction. At the Same Time, the Instruction Requires Students to Think, Critically & Apply the Concepts They Are Learning.
Conter Software.

Math 4. Jan. 1994. *Items Included:* Program on CD-ROM, CD Booklet, & Registration Card. *Customer Support:* Free unlimited support via telephone.
Windows 3.1 or higher running under DOS 5.0 or higher. 386 SX (4Mb RAM; 500k low Dos Mem; 6Mb free disk space). CD-ROM disk $49.00 (ISBN 1-57268-004-0, Order no.: 53004). *Nonstandard peripherals required:* Sound card (either: Sound Blaster - 8, 16, PRO; Media Vision ProAudio Spectrum; or Microsoft Sound System); MPC Compatible CD-ROM drive; VGA monitor; & microphone. *Optimal configuration:* 25MHz 386 SX.
Math for Windows: These Programs Offer Comprehensive, Individual Grade-Level Instruction in Math for Kindergarten Through High School. These Lessons Begin with Fundamental Math Skills & Concepts, & Build New Skills & Enthusiasm. These Programs Teach More Than the Memorization of Facts & Final Solutions. They Also Emphasize & Reinforce Logical Thinking Strategies to Improve Analysis & Problem-Solving Skills.
Conter Software.

Math 4. Jan. 1994. *Items Included:* Program on CD-ROM, CD Booklet, & Registration Card. *Customer Support:* Free unlimited support via telephone.
Macintosh System 7.0 or higher. Macintosh LC or higher (4Mb). CD-ROM disk $49.00 (ISBN 1-57268-029-6, Order no.: 63004). *Nonstandard peripherals required:* 12 inch monitor or larger; CD-ROM drive. *Optimal configuration:* 5Mb RAM.
Math for Macintosh. These Programs Complement & Supplement Students' Classroom Experiences. The Lessons Feature Essential Concepts & Skills, & Contain High-Interest Activities with Themes. The Instruction Provides Students with the Skills Needed to Move Through Each Level of Instruction. At the Same Time, the Instruction Requires Students to Think Critically & Apply the Concepts They Are Learning.
Conter Software.

Math 5. Jan. 1994. *Items Included:* Program on CD-ROM, CD Booklet, & Registration Card. *Customer Support:* Free unlimited support via telephone.
  Windows 3.1 or higher running under DOS 5.0 or higher. 386 SX (4Mb RAM; 500k low Dos Mem; 6Mb free disk space). CD-ROM disk $49.00 (ISBN 1-57268-005-9, Order no.: 53005). *Nonstandard peripherals required:* Sound card (either: Sound Blaster - 8, 16, PRO; Media Vision ProAudio Spectrum; or Microsoft Sound System); MPC Compatible CD-ROM drive; VGA monitor; & microphone. *Optimal configuration:* 25MHz 386 SX.
  Math for Windows: These Programs Offer Comprehensive, Individual Grade-Level Instruction in Math for Kindergarten Through High School. These Lessons Begin with Fundamental Math Skills & Concepts, & Build New Skills & Enthusiasm. These Programs Teach More Than the Memorization of Facts & Final Solutions. They Also Emphasize & Reinforce Logical Thinking Strategies to Improve Analysis & Problem-Solving Skills.
  Conter Software.

Math 5. Jan. 1994. *Items Included:* Program on CD-ROM, CD Booklet, & Registration Card. *Customer Support:* Free unlimited support via telephone.
  Macintosh System 7.0 or higher. Macintosh LC or higher (4Mb). CD-ROM disk $49.00 (ISBN 1-57268-030-X, Order no.: 63005). *Nonstandard peripherals required:* 12 inch monitor or larger; CD-ROM drive. *Optimal configuration:* 5Mb RAM.
  Math for Macintosh. These Programs Complement & Supplement Students' Classroom Experiences. The Lessons Feature Essential Concepts & Skills, & Contain High-Interest Activities with Themes. The Instruction Provides Students with the Skills Needed to Move Through Each Level of Instruction. At the Same Time, the Instruction Requires Students to Think Critically & Apply the Concepts They Are Learning.
  Conter Software.

Math 5-6. Jan. 1994. *Items Included:* Program on CD-ROM, CD Booklet, & Registration Card. *Customer Support:* Free unlimited support via telephone.
  Windows 3.1 or higher running under DOS 5.0 or higher. 386 SX (4Mb RAM; 500k low Dos Mem; 6Mb free disk space). CD-ROM disk $249.00 (ISBN 1-57268-046-6, Order no.: 13560). *Nonstandard peripherals required:* Sound card (either: Sound Blaster - 8. 16. PRO; Media Vision ProAudio Spectrum; or Microsoft Sound System); MCP Compatible CD-ROM drive; VGA monitor; & microphone. *Optimal configuration:* 25 MHz 386 SX.
  Math for Windows: These Programs Offer Comprehensive, Individual Grade-Level Instruction in Math for Kindergarten Through High School. These Lessons Begin with Fundamental Math Skills & Concepts, & Build New Skills & Enthusiasm. These Programs Teach More Than the Memorization of Facts & Final Solutions. They Also Emphasize & Reinforce Logical Thinking Strategies to Improve Analysis & Problem-Solving Skills.
  Conter Software.

Math 5-6. Jan. 1994. *Items Included:* Program on CD-ROM, CD Booklet, & Registration Card. *Customer Support:* Free unlimited customer support via telephone.
  Macintosh System 7.0 or higher. Macintosh LC or higher (4Mb). CD-ROM disk $249.00 (ISBN 1-57268-067-9, Order no.: 23560). *Nonstandard peripherals required:* 12 inch monitor or larger; CD-ROM drive. *Optimal configuration:* 5Mb RAM.
  Math for Macintosh: These Programs Complement & Supplement Students' Classroom Experiences. The Lessons Feature Essential Concepts & Skills, & Contain High-Interest Activities with Themes. The Instruction Provides Students with the Skills Needed to Move Through Each Level of Instruction. At the Same Time, the Instruction Requires Students to Think Critically & Apply the Concepts They Are Learning.
  Conter Software.

Math 6. Jan. 1994. *Items Included:* Program on CD-ROM, CD Booklet, & Registration Card. *Customer Support:* Free unlimited support via telephone.
  Windows 3.1 or higher running under DOS 5.0 or higher. 386 SX (4Mb RAM; 500k low Dos Mem; 6Mb free disk space). CD-ROM disk $49.00 (ISBN 1-57268-006-7, Order no.: 53006). *Nonstandard peripherals required:* Sound card (either: Sound Blaster - 8, 16, PRO; Media Vision ProAudio Spectrum; or Microsoft Sound System); MPC Compatible CD-ROM drive; VGA monitor; & microphone. *Optimal configuration:* 25MHz 386 SX.
  Math for Windows: These Programs Offer Comprehensive, Individual Grade-Level Instruction in Math for Kindergarten Through High School. These Lessons Begin with Fundamental Math Skills & Concepts, & Build New Skills & Enthusiasm. These Programs Teach More Than the Memorization of Facts & Final Solutions. They Also Emphasize & Reinforce Logical Thinking Strategies to Improve Analysis & Problem-Solving Skills.
  Conter Software.

Math 6. Jan. 1994. *Items Included:* Program on CD-ROM, CD Booklet, & Registration Card. *Customer Support:* Free unlimited support via telephone.
  Macintosh System 7.0 or higher. Macintosh LC or higher (4Mb). CD-ROM disk $49.00 (ISBN 1-57268-031-8, Order no.: 63006). *Nonstandard peripherals required:* 12 inch monitor or larger; CD-ROM drive. *Optimal configuration:* 5Mb RAM.
  Math for Macintosh. These Programs Complement & Supplement Students' Classroom Experiences. The Lessons Feature Essential Concepts & Skills, & Contain High-Interest Activities with Themes. The Instruction Provides Students with the Skills Needed to Move Through Each Level of Instruction. At the Same Time, the Instruction Requires Students to Think Critically & Apply the Concepts They Are Learning.
  Conter Software.

Math 7. Jan. 1994. *Items Included:* Program on CD-ROM, CD Booklet, & Registration Card. *Customer Support:* Free unlimited support via telephone.
  Windows 3.1 or higher running under DOS 5.0 or higher. 386 SX (4Mb RAM; 500k low Dos Mem; 6Mb free disk space). CD-ROM disk $49.00 (ISBN 1-57268-007-5, Order no.: 53007). *Nonstandard peripherals required:* Sound card (either: Sound Blaster - 8, 16, PRO; Media Vision ProAudio Spectrum; or Microsoft Sound System); MPC Compatible CD-ROM drive; VGA monitor; & microphone. *Optimal configuration:* 25MHz 386 SX.
  Math for Windows: These Programs Offer Comprehensive, Individual Grade-Level Instruction in Math for Kindergarten Through High School. These Lessons Begin with Fundamental Math Skills & Concepts, & Build New Skills & Enthusiasm. These Programs Teach More Than the Memorization of Facts & Final Solutions. They Also Emphasize & Reinforce Logical Thinking Strategies to Improve Analysis & Problem-Solving Skills.
  Conter Software.

Math 7. Jan. 1994. *Items Included:* Program on CD-ROM, CD Booklet, & Registration Card. *Customer Support:* Free unlimited support via telephone.
  Macintosh System 7.0 or higher. Macintosh LC or higher (4Mb). CD-ROM disk $49.00 (ISBN 1-57268-032-6, Order no.: 63007). *Nonstandard peripherals required:* 12 inch monitor or larger; CD-ROM drive. *Optimal configuration:* 5Mb RAM.
  Math for Macintosh. These Programs Complement & Supplement Students' Classroom Experiences. The Lessons Feature Essential Concepts & Skills, & Contain High-Interest Activities with Themes. The Instruction Provides Students with the Skills Needed to Move Through Each Level of Instruction. At the Same Time, the Instruction Requires Students to Think Critically & Apply the Concepts They Are Learning.
  Conter Software.

Math 7-8. Jan. 1994. *Items Included:* Program on CD-ROM, CD Booklet, & Registration Card. *Customer Support:* Free unlimited support via telephone.
  Windows 3.1 or higher running under DOS 5.0 or higher. 386 SX (4Mb RAM; 500k low Dos Mem; 6Mb free disk space). CD-ROM disk $249.00 (ISBN 1-57268-047-4, Order no.: 13780). *Nonstandard peripherals required:* Sound card (either: Sound Blaster - 8. 16. PRO; Media Vision ProAudio Spectrum; or Microsoft Sound System); MCP Compatible CD-ROM drive; VGA monitor; & microphone. *Optimal configuration:* 25 MHz 386 SX.
  Math for Windows: These Programs Offer Comprehensive, Individual Grade-Level Instruction in Math for Kindergarten Through High School. These Lessons Begin with Fundamental Math Skills & Concepts, & Build New Skills & Enthusiasm. These Programs Teach More Than the Memorization of Facts & Final Solutions. They Also Emphasize & Reinforce Logical Thinking Strategies to Improve Analysis & Problem-Solving Skills.
  Conter Software.

Math 7-8. Jan. 1994. *Items Included:* Program on CD-ROM, CD Booklet, & Registration Card. *Customer Support:* Free unlimited customer support via telephone.
  Macintosh System 7.0 or higher. Macintosh LC or higher (4Mb). CD-ROM disk $249.00 (ISBN 1-57268-068-7, Order no.: 23780). *Nonstandard peripherals required:* 12 inch monitor or larger; CD-ROM drive. *Optimal configuration:* 5Mb RAM.
  Math for Macintosh: These Programs Complement & Supplement Students' Classroom Experiences. The Lessons Feature Essential Concepts & Skills, & Contain High-Interest Activities with Themes. The Instruction Provides Students with the Skills Needed to Move Through Each Level of Instruction. At the Same Time, the Instruction Requires Students to Think, Critically & Apply the Concepts They Are Learning.
  Conter Software.

Math 8. Jan. 1994. *Items Included:* Program on CD-ROM, CD Booklet, & Registration Card. *Customer Support:* Free unlimited support via telephone.
  Windows 3.1 or higher running under DOS 5.0 or higher. 386 SX (4Mb RAM; 500k low Dos Mem; 6Mb free disk space). CD-ROM disk $49.00 (ISBN 1-57268-008-3, Order no.: 53008). *Nonstandard peripherals required:* Sound card (either: Sound Blaster - 8, 16, PRO; Media Vision ProAudio Spectrum; or Microsoft Sound System); MPC Compatible CD-ROM drive; VGA monitor; & microphone.

Optimal configuration: 25MHz 386 SX.
Math for Windows: These Programs Offer Comprehensive, Individual Grade-Level Instruction in Math for Kindergarten Through High School. These Lessons Begin with Fundamental Math Skills & Concepts, & Build New Skills & Enthusiasm. These Programs Teach More Than the Memorization of Facts & Final Solutions. They Also Emphasize & Reinforce Logical Thinking Strategies to Improve Analysis & Problem-Solving Skills.
Conter Software.

Math 8. Jan. 1994. *Items Included:* Program on CD-ROM, CD Booklet, & Registration Card. *Customer Support:* Free unlimited support via telephone.
  Macintosh System 7.0 or higher. Macintosh LC or higher (4Mb). CD-ROM disk $49.00 (ISBN 1-57268-033-4, Order no.: 63008). *Nonstandard peripherals required:* 12 inch monitor or larger; CD-ROM drive. *Optimal configuration:* 5Mb RAM.
Math for Macintosh. These Programs Complement & Supplement Students' Classroom Experiences. The Lessons Feature Essential Concepts & Skills, & Contain High-Interest Activities with Themes. The Instruction Provides Students with the Skills Needed to Move Through Each Level of Instruction. At the Same Time, the Instruction Requires Students to Think Critically & Apply the Concepts They Are Learning.
Conter Software.

MathCAD. *Version:* 2.5. *Compatible Hardware:* IBM PC. *Operating System(s) Required:* PC-DOS/MS-DOS 2.0 or higher. *Memory Required:* 512k. *General Requirements:* CGA, EGA, & Hercules mono/color graphics card or compatible supported. *Customer Support:* Free to registered user 9-5:30 EST M-F.
  disk $495.00.
Enables Users to Do Calculations on the Screen. After the Variables Are Defined, Formulas Can Be Entered Anywhere on the Screen. The Program Will Format the Equations As They Are Typed, Will Calculate the Results, & Display the Result in Real Math Notation. In Addition to the Usual Trigonometric & Exponential Functions, Program Provides Built-In Statistical Functions, Cubic Splines, Fourier Transforms, Bessel Functions, etc. Program Also Handles Complex Numbers & Unit Conversions in a Completely Transparent Way. Results Can Be Displayed As Numbers, Tables, or Graphs. Text Can Be Added Anywhere on the Screen. Not Copy Protected.
MathSoft, Inc.

Mathcad. *Version:* 4.0. Mar. 1993. *Items Included:* Manual, Quick Reference, Release Notes, registration card, disks. *Customer Support:* Free support to registered users M-F 9:00-5:30 EST.
  IBM & compatibles, 80386 or higher (4Mb). disk $495.00. *Addl. software required:* MS-DOS or PC-DOS version 3.X or higher, MicroSoft Windows version 3.1.
Award-Winning Technical Calculation Software That Allows Users to Easily Perform Complex Mathematical Calculations, & Then to Document & Graph the Results. Electronic Whiteboard That Allows You to Use Standard Math Notation & Perform Serious Numeric & Symbolic Math Calculations. "What If" Analyses Are Effortless Using Mathcad's Live Document Interface.
MathSoft, Inc.

Mathcad. *Version:* 3.1. Jan. 1993. *Items Included:* Manual, Quick Reference, Release Notes, registration card, disks. *Customer Support:* Free support to registered users M-F 9:00-5:30 EST.
  System 6, System 7. Macintosh Plus, SE, SE/30, Classic, LC, S1 Quadra Portable, Performa or II-Family personal computers (4Mb - System 6, 6Mb - System 7). 3.5" disk $495.00.
Award-Winning Technical Calculation Software That Allows Users to Easily Perform Complex Mathematical Calculations, & Then to Document & Graph the Results. Electronic Whiteboard That Allows You to Use Standard Math Notation & Perform Serious Numeric & Symbolic Math Calculations. "What If" Analyses Are Effortless Using Mathcad's Live Document Interface.
MathSoft, Inc.

The MathCorp Engine. May 1992. *Customer Support:* 1 yr. maintenance included in purchase. 15% of license fee per year thereafter.
  DOS, Windows NT, 95, UNIX, Solaris. 386 (256k). $15,000.00 for 50 seat license; $100.00/seat thereafter. *Addl. software required:* Development Environment (i.e. Visual Basic, C or C Plus Plus, Powerbuilder, other case tools, etc.).
A Customizable, Multi-Function Financial Calculation Engine Written in the C Programming Language. Calculations Cover the Securities Industry, Banking, Accounting, & General Finance. Clients Pick & Choose Those Calculations That Pertain to Their Particular Application. Therefore, Each Installation Is Unique to Each Client While All of the Calculations Are Pulled from Standard Libraries.
Math Corp.

MathEdit. *Compatible Hardware:* IBM PC, PC XT, PC AT & compatibles, PS/2. *Operating System(s) Required:* PC-DOS/MS-DOS 2.1 or higher. *Memory Required:* 256k. *General Requirements:* EGA or Hercules-compatible graphics card.
  $149.00.
Enables Users to Construct Math Equations for Insertions into Their Documents. Output Can Be in Either WordPerfect 5.0 for Printing with an Apple LaserWriter, or TEX for Typesetting Use. Provides a Display Window That Allows Users to See the Equations As They Are Created.
K-Talk Communications.

Mathematica. *Version:* 2. *Compatible Hardware:* Apple Macintosh SE, Macintosh II; 80386-based PCs, Windows, DOS, HP 9000 & Apollo Series, SunSPARC, IBM RISC; NeXT; Silicon Graphics Iris; Sun386i. *Language(s):* C. *Customer Support:* Tech support line, Mathematica Plus.
  Macintosh Enhanced. 3.5" disk $895.00.
  Macintosh Standard. $595.00.
Capable of Numeric, Symbolic, & Graphical Computations, as Well as Solving Equations & Performing Differentiation & Integrations.
Wolfram Research.

Mathematica for Students. *Version:* 2.2. 1994. *Items Included:* 2 perfect bound manuals, runtime version of Mathematica for Students, registration materials. *Customer Support:* Free installation support; MathSource: free publicly accessible collection of Mathematica-related materials; 30-day unlimited warranty for media.
  Macintosh. Macintosh (6Mb application memory). Starts at $199.00 (ISBN 1-880083-10-8). *Optimal configuration:* System 7 or higher, 10Mb RAM recommended. *Networks supported:* Apple Share, Ethertalk, Mac TCP.
  Microsoft Windows. IBM PC 386 & compatibles (4Mb). Starts at $199.00 (ISBN 1-880083-11-6). *Optimal configuration:* Microsoft Windows 3.1 or higher, 16Mb RAM recommended, 14Mb disk space to install, 16Mb swap space recommended. *Networks supported:* TCP/IP.
  MS-DOS. IBM PC 386 & compatibles (4Mb extended memory plus 640k required). Starts at $199.00 (ISBN 1-880083-12-4). *Optimal configuration:* MS-DOS 3.0 or higher, disk space: 10Mb to install, additional 16Mb swap space recommended.
This Powerful Computation & Visualization Software Is the Premier Tool Used by Engineers & Scientists Worldwide for Quick, Accurate Numeric & Symbolic Answers. Its Hundreds of Built-In Functions Can Also Be Easily Customized. Ideal for Creating Technical Reports & Presentations-Combining Text, Active Formulas, & Graphics-That Are Transferable among Different Platforms.
Wolfram Research, Inc.

Mathematician's Toolkit. *Compatible Hardware:* Apple Macintosh, IBM PC. *Memory Required:* 1000k. *General Requirements:* True BASIC 2.0 or higher.
  3.5" disk $79.95.
Extends the Power of the True BASIC Programming Language to Include Areas of Special Interest to Mathematicians.
True BASIC, Inc.

Mathematics Collection. 1995. *Items Included:* Full manual. *Customer Support:* Free telephone support - 90 days, 30-day warranty.
  MS-DOS 3.2 or higher. 286 (584k). disk $179.95. *Nonstandard peripherals required:* CGA/EGA/VGA.
Six-Diskette Series Includes Functions, Nonlinear Systems, Multiple Integration, Linear Ordinary Differential Equations, Regression Analysis II, & Linear Algebra.
Dynacomp, Inc.

MathLab. *Version:* 2.0. *Compatible Hardware:* Apple Macintosh. *Memory Required:* 512k.
  3.5" disk $49.95.
Algebra Calculus; Three-Dimensional Plotting.
E & M Software Co.

Mathology. Aug. 1993. *Items Included:* Program manual. *Customer Support:* Free technical support 800-421-4157, 90 day warranty.
  DOS 3.3 or higher. IBM (640k). 3.5" disk $49.95 (ISBN 1-882848-22-5). *Nonstandard peripherals required:* Hard drive, supports Ad Lib & Sound Blaster cards.
  DOS 3.3 or higher. IBM (640k). 3.5" disk $59.95 School Edition (ISBN 1-882848-23-3). *Nonstandard peripherals required:* Hard drive, supports Ad Lib & Sound Blaster cards.
  DOS 3.3 or higher. IBM (640k). 3.5" disk $149.95 School Edition, Lab Pack (ISBN 1-882848-24-1). *Nonstandard peripherals required:* Hard drive, supports Ad Lib & Sound Blaster cards.
Children Become Part of a Greek Legend in This Exciting, Arcade-Action Math Adventure. Users Solve Story Problems Involving U.S. Conventional & Metric Weight, Volume, Length, Math, & Area, As They attempt to Save Greece from the Evil God, Apathy, & His Minions. Ages 8 & Older.
Lawrence Productions, Inc.

Mathology II: Fractions. 1995. *Items Included:* Program manual. *Customer Support:* Free technical support; 90 day warranty.
  Consumer. MS-DOS or PC-DOS 3.1 or higher. IBM or 100% compatible (800k). disk $59.95 (ISBN 1-57204-086-6, Order no.: 18618). *Nonstandard peripherals required:* VGA monitor, graphics cards capable of displaying 256 colors in 360 x 200 resolution, sound card, keyboard & Microsoft compatible mouse.
  Lab pak. MS-DOS or PC-DOS 3.1 or higher. IBM or 100% compatible (800k). disk $149.95 (ISBN 1-57204-088-2, Order no.: 18618LPK). *Nonstandard peripherals required:* VGA monitor, graphics cards capable of displaying 256 colors in 360 x 200 resolution, sound card, keyboard & Microsoft compatible mouse.
  Lite license. MS-DOS or PC-DOS 3.1 or higher.

MATHOMATIC 2: ALGEBRAIC EQUATION

IBM or 100% compatible (800k). disk $699.00 (ISBN 1-57204-089-0, Order no.: 1B618SITE). *Nonstandard peripherals required:* VGA monitor, graphics cards capable of displaying 256 colors in 360 x 200 resolution, sound card, keyboard & Microsoft compatible mouse.
It is the year 2135 & the dastardly Dr. Ronan is threatening to take over the world. Only you can stop him! But, you find yourself more than 2000 years in the past. Can you battle through the land of Greecia, destroy the Green Dragon, & find the Time Portal to take you back to the future? A fun & exciting way to learn fractions, decimals, ratios, porportions & percents.
Lawrence Productions, Inc.

Mathomatic 2: Algebraic Equation Processor. *Items Included:* Bound manual. *Customer Support:* Free hotline - no time limit; 30 day limited warranty; updates are $5/disk plus S&H.
MS-DOS 2.0 or higher. IBM & compatibles (512k). disk $39.95.
Calculator That Can Solve Complicated Algebraic Equations. You Simply Enter Your Equation & MATHOMATIC Symbolically Solves for Any Chosen Variable. Also, Equations May Be Numerically Evaluated by Entering Values for the Variables.
Dynacomp, Inc.

Mathpack for Lotus 1-2-3. *Version:* 1.0M. Dan Heilman & Joe Applegate. Nov. 1990. *Items Included:* Educational manual. *Customer Support:* 30 day unlimited warranty; free telephone support; 800 number.
MS-DOS 2.11 or higher. IBM compatible (64k). disk $99.00. *Addl. software required:* Lotus 1-2-3 version 2.01, 2.2, 2.3. *Optimal configuration:* 286 or faster; 20Mb or higher hard disk, 640k RAM. *Networks supported:* All.
Adds Unit Conversion & Mathematical Functions to Lotus 1-2-3. Conversions Includes Metric, FT-Inches-Fraction (for Carpenters & Engineers), Fraction-Decimal (for Stocks & Bonds). Math Functions Includes Median, Factorial, & Taylor Series.
Workhorses, Inc.

Mathplot Numerical Data Analysis. *Items Included:* Full manual. No other products required. *Customer Support:* Free telephone support - no time limit. 30 day warranty.
MS-DOS 3.2 or higher. IBM & compatibles (512k). disk $49.95. *Optimal configuration:* IBM, MS-DOS 3.1 or higher, 640k RAM, & CGA/EGA/VGA (or compatible) graphics capability.
Can Analyze up to 200 Data Points & Calculate Simple Statistical Parameters, Fit Least-Squares Polynomials, Numerically Integrate under a Curve Defined by the Points, Calculate the Coefficients of a Fourier Series for a Periodic Function Described by the Points, Calculate & Plot Fourier Spectra & Bessel Functions, Plot & Compare a User-Specified Function with a Data Set, Solve up to 12 Simultaneous Equations, & Invert Matrices of Order up to 12. A User-Friendly Menu Allows You to Display the Results Both Numerically & Graphically.
Dynacomp, Inc.

Mathplot: Numerical Data Analysis. 1995. *Items Included:* Full manual. *Customer Support:* Free telephone support - 90 days, 30-day warranty.
MS-DOS 3.2 or higher. 286 (584k). disk $49.95. *Nonstandard peripherals required:* CGA/EGA/VGA.
MATHPLOT Can Analyze up to 200 Data Points & Calculate Simple Statistical Parameters, Fit Least-Squares Polynomials, Numerically Integrate under a Curve Defined by the Points, Calculate the Coefficients of a Fourier Series for a Period Function Described by the Points, Calculate & Plot Fourier Spectra & Bessel Functions, Plot & Compare a User-Specified Function with a Data Set, Solve up to 12 Simultaneous Equations, & Invert Matrices of Order up to 12. A User-Friendly Menu Allows You to Display the Results Both Numerically & Graphically.
Dynacomp, Inc.

Math77: Matehmatical Subprograms for FORTRAN 77. *Version:* 4.1. JPL Staff. May 1994. *Items Included:* 1 Math77 manual, 3 3.5" disks. *Customer Support:* Free unlimited phone support.
Macintosh. Mac (4Mb). 3.5" disk $249.00 (Order no.: P6000). *Nonstandard peripherals required:* hard drive. *Addl. software required:* FORTRAN compiler. *Networks supported:* Mac.
DOS. DOS or Windows (4Mb). disk $249.00 (Order no.: P6100). *Nonstandard peripherals required:* hard drive. *Addl. software required:* FORTRAN compiler. *Networks supported:* DOS.
Sun OS. SUN (4Mb). disk $249.00 (Order no.: P6200). *Nonstandard peripherals required:* hard drive. *Addl. software required:* FORTRAN compiler. *Networks supported:* Sun.
Portable Library of FORTRAN Subroutines for Use in Numerical Computation. Library Contains 454 User-Callable & 136 Lower-Level Subprograms. Supplies As Source Code, Which Has Been Tested with the Leading Mac, DOS & Sun Compilers. This Royalty-Free FORTRAN Source Code Comprises a Total of 4.5MB of Code.
Language Systems Corp.

MathStar. *Operating System(s) Required:* SB-80, CP/M with WordStar Program. *Memory Required:* 64k.
disk $125.00.
Allows WordStar Users to Perform Calculations While Editing. Supports Addition, Subtraction, Multiplication, & Division. Special Features Include: 19 Digit Number Entry, Automatic Rounding of Oversize Numbers, Entry of Equations Vertically or Horizontally, Specified Display Formatting, Commas, Decimals, Dollar Signs, Parentheses, & Negative Numbers.
Lifeboat Assocs.

MathStar PC. *Compatible Hardware:* IBM PC with WordStar Program. *Operating System(s) Required:* PC-DOS. *Memory Required:* 64k.
disk $125.00.
Allows WordStar Users to Perform Calculations While Editing. Supports Addition, Subtraction, Multiplication, & Division. Special Features Include: 19 Digit Number Entry, Automatic Rounding of Oversize Numbers, Entry of Equations Vertically or Horizontally, Specified Display Formatting, Commas, Decimals, Dollar Signs, Parentheses, & Negative Numbers.
Lifeboat Assocs.

MathType - the Equation Editor Upgrade: For Macintosh. *Version:* 3.1. Jul. 1992. *Items Included:* 1 manual, pgs. 218. *Customer Support:* 30-day money back guarantee; technical support.
Macintosh System 6.0 or higher (including System 7.5). Macintosh (1Mb). 3.5" disk $89.00 (ISBN 1-884799-03-5). *Optimal configuration:* Works with all printers.
The Intelligent Mathematical Equation Editor. Its Easy-to-Use WYSIWYG Interface Offers over 275 Mathematical Symbols & Templates, & It Automatically Formats Equations. Simply Point-&-Click on Symbols & Templates to Build Equations & Then Embed Them into Your Documents for Perfect Equations Every Time.
Design Science, Inc.

MathType - the Equation Editor Upgrade: For Windows. *Version:* 3.1. Dec. 1992. *Items Included:* 1 manual, pgs. 272. *Customer Support:* 30-day money back guarantee; technical support.
Microsoft Windows version 3.0 or higher, Windows NT, Windows 95 compatible. PC compatible (2Mb). disk $89.00 (ISBN 1-884799-01-9). *Nonstandard peripherals required:* Windows-supported printer & Windows-supported display (except CGA). *Addl. software required:* Microsoft WORD.
The Intelligent Mathematical Equation Editor. Its Easy-to-Use WYSIWYG Interface Offers over 275 Mathematical Symbols & Templates, & It Automatically Formats Equations. Simply Point-&-Click on Symbols & Templates to Build Equations & Then Embed Them into Your Documents for Perfect Equations Every Time.
Design Science, Inc.

MathType: For Macintosh. *Version:* 3.1. Jul. 1992. *Items Included:* 1 manual, pgs. 218. *Customer Support:* 30-day money back guarantee; technical support.
Macintosh System 6.0 or higher (including System 7.5). Macintosh (1Mb). List: $199.00; Education: $149.00 (ISBN 1-884799-02-7). *Optimal configuration:* Works with all printers (including LaserWriter, StyleWriter, ImageWriter, & HP DeskWriter models).
The Intelligent Mathematical Equation Editor. Its Easy-to-Use WYSIWYG Interface Offers over 275 Mathematical Symbols & Templates, & It Automatically Formats Equations. Simply Point-&-Click on Symbols & Templates to Build Equations & Then Embed Them into Your Documents for Perfect Equations Every Time.
Design Science, Inc.

MathType: For Windows. *Version:* 3.1. Dec. 1992. *Items Included:* 1 manual, pgs. 272. *Customer Support:* 30-day money back guarantee; technical support.
Microsoft Windows version 3.0 or higher, Windows NT, Windows 95 compatible. PC compatible (2Mb). List: $199.00; Education: $149.00 (ISBN 1-884799-00-0). *Nonstandard peripherals required:* Windows-supported printer & Windows-supported display (except CGA).
The Intelligent Mathematical Equation Editor. Its Easy-to-Use WYSIWYG Interface Offers over 275 Mathematical Symbols & Templates, & It Automatically Formats Equations. Simply Point-&-Click on Symbols & Templates to Build Equations & Then Embed Them into Your Documents for Perfect Equations Every Time.
Design Science, Inc.

MathVolley: For Apple II Computers. *Version:* 1.1. Robert Cummings. May 1993. *Items Included:* 1 - 10 page manual. *Customer Support:* Voice-Mail Technical support for "Registered Users".
PRODOS. AppleIIe, AppleIIc, AppleIIGS (64k). disk $69.00 (ISBN 0-9623926-4-2, Order no.: MVA3.5). *Optimal configuration:* Color monitor, Imagewriter or compatible printer, 3.5" disk drive format.
A Mathematics Drill & Practice Software in a Volleyball Game Format. Fashioned after the New York State Mathematics Regents Competency Test. MathVolley's Diagnostic Capability Tests 40 Different Mathematics Areas & Provides Results of Possible Areas Needing Remediation or Review. The Volleyball Game Format Makes This Software Enetertaining As Well As Educational.
Science Academy Software.

Matman: Robot Manipulator Design. *Items Included:* Manual with theory, sample runs. *Customer Support:* Free phone, on-site seminars.

TITLE INDEX

MS-DOS. IBM (128k). disk $120.00. *Addl. software required:* BASIC.
Designs a Robot Manipulator (Arm) with 6 Degrees of Freedom Such As the Stanford Arm. Motion of Each Link Described by a 6x6 Matrix, Complete Arm by a Chain of Matrices. Matman Solves Resulting System Using Symbolic Matrix Manipulation. Specify Control Parameters & Get Motion or Specify Desired Motion & Get Control Parameters.
Kern International, Inc.

Matrix Calculator. Leslie Hogben & I. R. Hentzel. 1987. *Compatible Hardware:* IBM PC, PCjr, PC XT. *Operating System(s) Required:* PC-DOS 2.10-3.10. *Language(s):* BASIC. *Memory Required:* 192k.
disk $60.00, incl. user's guide & backup (Order no.: MTH600I).
add'l. user's guide $5.00.
Allows Students to Manipulate Matrices the Same Way Numbers Are Manipulated on an Ordinary Calculator. Students Begin by Entering Matrices into the Program & Giving Them Specific Names. Then, When Prompted by the Program, Students Type in the Operation They Wish to Perform & the Names of the Matrices Involved. Allows Students to Perform the Following Operations: Addition, Multiplication, Row Operation, Reduction to Reduced Row Echelon Form, & Scalar Multiplication. They Can Also Find the Inverse, Determinant, Trace, Transpose, Rank, Adjoint, Characteristic Polynomial, Eigenvalues & Vectors, & Jordan Canonical Form Matrices. In Addition, Students Can Program the CALCULATOR to Perform a Sequence of Operations.
CONDUIT.

Matrix Calculator. *Version:* 4.00. Jan. 1989. *Operating System(s) Required:* PC-DOS/MS-DOS 2.X. *Memory Required:* 256k. *Items Included:* Diskette & manual.
disk $59.95 (ISBN 0-938087-00-2).
Programmable Scientific Calculator with 70+ Matrix Operations; Statistics; Solve System of Linear, Non-Linear, Differential Equations; Variety of Numerical Integration; User Programmable Functions. Stand Alone or RAM Resident.
Soft Tech, Inc.

Matrix Laboratory. *Items Included:* Bound manual. *Customer Support:* Free hotline - no time limit; 30 day limited warranty; updates are $5/disk plus S&H.
MS-DOS 2.0 or higher. IBM & compatibles (512k). disk $29.95.
Extensive Set of Stand-Alone Software for Matrix Operations. The Matrix Elements Can Be Either Real or Complex, & the Matrix Size Can Be up to 20 by 20. The Functions Provided Include the Determinant, Inverse, Condition, Eigenvalues, Eigenvectors, Characteristic Polynomial, Triangularization, Square Root, Trig Functions, Complex Conjugate, Diagonalization, Norm, Randomization, Inverse Hilbert, Base p Representation, Kronecker Tensor Product, & More.
Dynacomp, Inc.

Matrix Layout. *Compatible Hardware:* IBM PC, PC XT & compatibles, PS/2.
$149.95.
CASE Tool. Users Develop an Application by Creating an On-Screen Graphic Flowchart & Designing Programming Objects Such As Files, Graphics, & Variables. Will Generate Programs in Turbo Pascal, Microsoft C, Turbo C, Lattice C, Quick BASIC, or Will Directly Create an .EXE File. Package Includes MATRIX PAINT, MATRIX HELPMAKER, & MATRIX DESKTOP.
Matrix Software.

Matrix Madness. Henry L. Stuck. *Compatible Hardware:* IBM PC, PCjr with BASIC cartridge, PC XT, PC AT, Portable PC, 3270 PC. *Memory Required:* 128k. *General Requirements:* IBM Color Display.
disk $19.95 (Order no.: 6276512).
The Challenge Is to Fill in the One Missing Item in a Three-by-Three Grid. The Longer the Selection Takes, the Fewer Points Are Scored.
Personally Developed Software, Inc.

Matrix Magic: Matrix Manipulation Test Program. Jul. 1985. *Compatible Hardware:* AT&T 6300; DEC Rainbow, DEC VT 180; HP-125; IBM PC & compatibles, PCjr, PC XT, PC AT; Tandy 1000, 1200, 2000; TI Professional; Xerox 820, 820-II, 860. *Operating System(s) Required:* MS-DOS, PC-DOS. *Memory Required:* 256k.
disk $95.00.
Stand-Alone Matrix Manipulation & Test Program That Is Menu-Driven & Interactive. The Matrix Operations Program Performs Operations on a Matrix or Matrices Such As Inverse, Adjoint, or Eigenvalues. The Matrix Test Program Performs Tests on a Matrix or Matrices & Tells Whether a Matrix Is Skew-Hermitian, Tridiagonal, Jordan Canonical, etc. Operation on Matrices up to 20 Rows by 20 Columns Can Be Performed. An Optional Feature Is the Use of Reverse Polish Notation (RPN) & Stack Operations. The Stack Operations Allow Manipulation of Entire Matrices.
BV Engineering.

Matrix Master. *Items Included:* Bound manual. *Customer Support:* Free hotline - no time limit; 30 day limited warranty; updates are $5/disk plus S&H.
MS-DOS. IBM & compatibles (256k). disk $29.95 Single Precision; $37.95 Double Precision.
TRS-80. disk $29.95 Single Precision; $37.95 Double Precision.
Apple. disk $29.95 Single Precision (Double Precision not avail.).
Simplifies & Speeds up Matrix Operations Which Are Encountered. The Quotations Supported Are Addition, Subtraction, Multiplication, Transportation, Inversion, Scalar Operations, Identity Matrix Creation, & Fast Storage & Retrieval. Although Available in Single- & Double-Precision Versions, Double Precision Is Recommended for Matrix Inversion.
Dynacomp, Inc.

Matrix Operations. *Version:* 10.0. *Compatible Hardware:* Apple Macintosh, IBM PC & compatibles. *Items Included:* Disks, book, program instructions. *Customer Support:* Telephone.
disk $145.00 (ISBN 0-920387-88-8).
Includes Matrix Entry Routines, Addition, Multiplication, Transposition, & Inversion. Complex Routines Involve Finding the Eigenvalue of Symmetric & Non-Symmetric Matrices, & the Cholesky Decomposition of Matrices. The Solution of Sets of Similar Equations Is Provided. Also Provided Are Data Transfer Programs for the Moving of Files to & from Popular Spreadsheet Programs.
Lionheart Pr., Inc.

Matrix Processor. *Items Included:* Bound manual. *Customer Support:* Free hotline - no time limit; 30 day limited warranty; updates are $5/disk plus S&H.
MS-DOS 2.0 or higher. IBM & compatibles (128k). disk $39.95. *Nonstandard peripherals required:* Printer supported, but not necessary.
Menu-Driven, Stand-Alone Software Package for Manipulating Matrices up to 50 by 50. Emphasis Is Placed on Making Data Entry Easy. For Example, Matrices May Be Constructed from Parts of Other Matrices or the Results of Matrix Operations, Greatly Limiting the Amount of Data Entry Needed.
Dynacomp, Inc.

Matrix ROM. *Compatible Hardware:* HP 85, 86/87.
HP 85. ROM cartridge $195.00 (Order no.: 00085-15004).
HP 86/87. (Order no.: 00087-15004).
Provides a Set of Statements & Functions for Working with Arrays, Including Matrices (Two-Dimensional Arrays) & Vectors (One-Dimensional Arrays).
Hewlett-Packard Co.

Matrix Tutorial. 1992. *Items Included:* Detailed manuals included with all Dynacomp products. *Customer Support:* Free telephone support to original customer - no time limit; 30 day limited warranty.
MS-DOS 3.2 or higher. IBM PC & compatibles (512k). $29.95 (Add $5.00 for 3 1/2" format; 5 1/4" format standard). *Optimal configuration:* IBM, MS-DOS 2.0 or higher & 128K RAM.
Teaches Matrix Algebra & Techniques. It Is Applicable to High School & College Students, As Well As Professionals Needing a Refresher. Both Numeric & Symbolic Examples Abound, Giving the Student a "Feel" for What Is Going on, in Addition to a Technical Understanding. MATRIX TUTORIAL Is Menu-Driven, Making It Very Easy to Use. These Matrix Types Are Covered: Null, Unit, Diagonal, Banded, Symmetric, Sparse, Row, Column, & Triangular. These Operations Are Demonstrated: Addition, Subtraction, Multiplication, Transposition, Minors, Co-Factors, Inversion, Merging, Extraction, Eigenvalues, Eigenvectors, Triangularization, Escalation, etc.
Dynacomp, Inc.

Matrix Workshop. *Version:* 1.01. *Compatible Hardware:* Apple Macintosh 512KE, Plus, SE, Mac II. *Memory Required:* 512k. *Items Included:* 100 page manual with comprehensive examples. *Customer Support:* Free 6 mos. telephone support.
3.5" disk $295.00.
Programmable Environment for Numerical Calculations, Including Linear Algebra, Signal Processing, Polynomials, Graphic Display.
Puma Software, Inc.

Matrix 100. *Items Included:* Bound manual. *Customer Support:* Free hotline - no time limit; 30 day limited warranty; updates are $5/disk plus S&H.
MS-DOS. IBM & compatibles (128k). $79.95-$249.95. *Nonstandard peripherals required:* One drive. *Addl. software required:* BASICA.
Adds New Commands to BASIC. These Allow: Matrix Multiplication, Addition, Inversion, Determinant, etc.; Solving of Linear Equations; Multiple Regression; Obtaining LU, QR Factors, & Solving. In Addition, User Can Examine Regression Statistics, Numeric Stability, etc. The Package Includes Sample Code to Interactively Solve Linear Equations & Find Eigenvalues (for Real Symmetric Matrices).
Dynacomp, Inc.

A Matter of Fact Database. 1995. *Items Included:* Manual. *Customer Support:* One year of the CSAP is provided at n/c; 30 day no risk guarantee.
MS-DOS. IBM or compatibles (640k). disk $795.00 (ISBN 0-927875-65-9, Order no.: 1780). *Addl. software required:* Winnebago CIRC and/or CAT V 5.1 or higher. *Optimal configuration:* Same as Winnebago CIRC/CAT or Winnebago CAT, an additional 40Mb hard disk space per year. *Networks supported:* IPX or Netbios compatible.
3.5" disk $795.00 (ISBN 0-927875-64-0, Order no.: 1780).
A Compilation of More Than 10,000 Full-Text

Statistical Abastracts Added Yearly. It Includes Statistics on Health, Social Issues, Politics, Economics, the Environment, & More. The Database Also Includes Excerpted Transcripts of Congressional Hearings & Debates. The AMOF Database Represents More Than 1000 Different Sources.
Winnebago Software Co.

Matthew Henry Commentary. Aug. 1994. *Items Included:* Disks, marketing literature, order form. *Customer Support:* No fee for customer support: 30 day money back guarantee, limited replacement warranty on diskettes defective at time of purchase, free telephone technical support.
PC-DOS/MS-DOS 3.1 or higher & Windows 3.1 or higher. IBM XT/AT/286/386/486 or 100% compatibles (640k or 4Mb). 3.5" disk $79.95 (ISBN 1-56514-025-7). *Optimal configuration:* 3.5", 1.44Mb disk drive for installation, 16Mb hard drive space; mouse or pointer device recommended.
The Text of the Complete Six-Volume Set of Matthew Henry's Commentary. This Is an Add-On to Be Used with Biblesoft's PC Study Bible.
Biblesoft.

Mavis Accounting System.
contact publisher for price.
Includes General Ledger, Accounts Receivable, Accounts Payable, Order Entry, Inventory Control, Payroll, & Custom Business Subroutines.
Mavis Computer Systems.

Mavis Beacon Teaches Typing! *Version:* 2.0. MPC. IBM PC & compatibles. disk $79.95 (Order no.: 110526).
PC-DOS/MS-DOS Version 3.0 or higher. disk $49.95.
Windows 3.0 or higher. disk $59.95.
Macintosh. 3.5" disk $49.95.
This Critically Acclaimed Typing Tutor Is an Award-Winner in the Edutainment Field, Making Learning Fun & Effective. With a Master Teaching Mode That Tracks Multiple Student Records, Mavis Can Now Sense Frustration, Pace Progress, & Give More Personal Typing Analyses & Comments. Includes Typing Drills & Exciting Arcade-Style Games to Improve Word & 10-Key Skills. Students Can Also Build Custom Lessons, Using Mavis' or Their Own Text Files. The Program Supports Both Mouse & Keyboard. Students Can Enroll As Either Standard QWERTY or Dvorak Keyboard Users, & Can Change the Keyboard Layout Any Time.
Software Toolworks.

Mavis Pharmacy Computer System. *Version:* 9.N. *Memory Required:* 1000k. *Items Included:* Operators manual. *Customer Support:* Software maintenance contract available - drug price updates, drug interaction code updates.
contact publisher for price.
Contains All the Functions Necessary to Operate a Retail Pharmacy; Includes Telecommunications Billing Package.
Mavis Computer Systems.

MAX. *Version:* 2.0. *General Requirements:* Tandem computer. *Items Included:* User guide. *Customer Support:* Hotline.
Macintosh. contact publisher for price.
Tandem to Personal Computer File Transfers.
Menlo Business Systems, Inc.

Maxiledger. *Compatible Hardware:* Apple II+, IIe, III; IBM PC. *Operating System(s) Required:* CP/M, PC-DOS. *Language(s):* BASIC (source code included). *Memory Required:* 48k. *General Requirements:* 2 drives.
disk $98.50.
Menu-Driven General Ledger Program Offers Definable Detail & Subtotal Accounts & Divisional Reporting Capabilities. All Account Matching, Totaling, Balancing, & Report Generating Are Automatically Performed. Safeguards Prevent Data Loss Due to Incorrect Data Entry Procedures. Allows Conversion of Files from MICROLEDGER Format Using an Optional Convert Chart. Interactive with BILL OF MATERIALS, MICROPERS, MICROINV, MICROREC, & MICROPAY by Accepting Journal File Output of These Programs. Order Entry Information May Be Channeled Through MICROINV.
Compumax, Inc.

MAXIMO Series Five. *Version:* 2.0. Sep. 1994. IBM & compatibles (640k). $35,000.00 5 user LAN.
Organizations Are Able to Reduce Downtime, Control Maintenance Expenses, Cut Spare Parts Inventories & Costs, Improve Purchasing Efficiency, Shorten Product Development Cycles & More Effectively Deploy Productive Assets, Personnel & Other Resources. Also Supports the Progressive Implementation of Total Quality Management Principles & ISO 9000 Standards.
PSDI (Project Software & Development, Inc.).

The Maximum Six. Jun. 1995. *Items Included:* User manual. *Customer Support:* Free phone technical support via 1-800 number.
Windows; Macintosh. IBM 386DX 40, MPC 1 (4Mb); Macintosh LCIII, System 6.0.5 or higher (4Mb). CD-ROM disk $24.95 (ISBN 1-57600-014-1, Order no.: 33600).
A Multipack Containing Six Complete Titles. Includes over 6,000 Programs in All.
Digital Impact, Inc.

Maximum Six. Feb. 1995. *Customer Support:* Free phone technical support via 1-800 number.
Windows. CD-ROM disk Contact publisher for price (ISBN 1-57600-014-1).
Collection of Six Hot CDs Offers Users over 6,000 Games, Programs, & Resources. Offers Multimedia Users an Instant, Inexpensive & Diverse Library of Software.
Digital Impact, Inc.

Maximum Surge. *Items Included:* Instruction manual. *Customer Support:* Free Telephone support.
Saturn. Sega Saturn. Contact publisher for price.
DOS/Windows 95. IBM & compatibles (8Mb). Contact publisher for price. *Optimal configuration:* CD-ROM drive.
3DO. 3DO multiplayer. Contact publisher for price.
Digital Pictures, Inc.

MaxPage. *Version:* 1.2.
Macintosh Plus or higher. 3.5" disk $89.00.
Page Makeup Program.
Applied Systems & Technologies, Inc.

MaxRoute. *Version:* 5.0. MassTeck. *Items Included:* 1 manual; runtime version of windows. *Customer Support:* One year software support & maintenance, $525.00; 90 days warranty.
MS-DOS. IBM compatible (4Mb). write for info. *Addl. software required:* MS-DOS. *Optimal configuration:* 386/486 with MS-DOS, 8Mb RAM, mouse, VGA.
Push & Shove Autorouter. Intuitive & Interactive Routing Tool.
Team Visionics Corp.

MaxSPITBOL: The SNOBOL4 Language for the Mac User. *Version:* 1.3.2. Robert B. Dewar & Mark B. Emmer. Jan. 1989. *Compatible Hardware:* Apple Macintosh. *Memory Required:* 512k. *Items Included:* Software & documentation. *Customer Support:* Free.
3.5" disk $195.00 (ISBN 0-939793-05-9, Order no.: MAXSPIT).
Implementation of the SNOBOL4 Programming Language. Used for Complex Text Processing & Pattern Matching. Supports Windows, Binary & Direct-Access Files, Built-In Sort, & Numerous Language Extensions. Includes Text Editor, Compiler, Tutorial & Reference Manual, & over 50 Files of Example Programs & Functions.
Catspaw, Inc.

MaxThink. *Compatible Hardware:* Apple Macintosh, Atari ST, IBM PC. *Memory Required:* IBM 320k, Macintosh 512k.
$89.00.
Outliner with Features Such As Alarm & Report Generator.
MaxThink, Inc.

MaxThink 89.
IBM PC (300k); under MS-DOS. $89.00.
Integrated Application. Includes Word Processor, Database, Programmable Graphics Module, & Hypertext. Spreadsheet Sections & Graphics Can Be Pasted into Word Processing Files.
MaxThink, Inc.

Maxwell Electromagnetic Fields. 1995. *Items Included:* Full manual. *Customer Support:* Free telephone support - 90 days, 30-day warranty.
MS-DOS 3.2 or higher. 286 (584k). disk $59.95. *Nonstandard peripherals required:* CGA/EGA/VGA.
Enhances Understanding of Electrodynamic Phenomena by Displaying the Evolution of Electromagnetic Fields in Different Configurations & Devices. It Can Also Be Used As a Practical Engineering Design Tool for Quick, Low-Resolution Field Analysis. Applicable to a Wide Range of Educational Levels, from Undergraduate to Graduate. Included Are Simulations of Plane Waves, Solenoids, Capacitors, Magnetron Tubes, & Many Others.
Dynacomp, Inc.

Maxwell Manor. Jun. 1984. *Compatible Hardware:* Apple II+, IIe, IIc; Atari 800/XL/XE; Commodore 64/128. *Memory Required:* 64k.
disk $25.00 ea.
Apple. (Order no.: 48752).
Atari, Commodore. (Order no.: 48793).
Action Game Taking Place in a Haunted House Wrapped Around a Mystery. The Owner of the Manor Has Been Found... Minus His Head, & His House Is the Center of a Host of Horrors, from Bugs to Vampire Spiders. A Variety of Obstacles Must Be Overcome in Order for the Intrepid Explorer to Map the Maxwell Manor, Find the Head, & Determine How to End the Evil Infesting the House of 1313 Manor Road.
Avalon Hill Game Co., The Microcomputer Games Div.

May Clinic Family Pharmacist, 1996 Edition: Your Ultimate Guide to Medications, Early Detection & First Aid. Mayo Clinic Staff. 1995-96. *Customer Support:* Free 800 Number Technical Support.
Windows. PC with 386SX 33MHz or higher (8Mb). disk $59.95 (ISBN 1-884899-04-8). *Optimal configuration:* 486SX 25MHz or higher PC, 8Mb RAM, double-speed CD-ROM drive, VGA Plus 640x480 monitor displaying 256 colors, MS-DOS 5.0 or higher, Windows 3.1 MS-DOS CD-ROM Extensions (MSCDEX 2.2 or higher), stereo headphones or speakers, minimum 10Mb hard disk space for installation, mouse or compatible positioning device, minimum MPC-Level 1 compatible sound card.
Provides Information on More Than 8,100 Medications, First Aid Treatments & Early Disease Detection. Includes Updated Drug Information, Enhanced Drug Interaction &

TITLE INDEX

Precaution Information, New Drug Administration Videos, a Personal Profile Section for Recording Family Health Records & One Click Internet Access to a Unique Online Health Network for Additional Information.
IVI Publishing, Inc.

Mayo Clinic - the Total Heart: The Ultimate Interactive Guide to Heart Health. Mayo Clinic Staff. Nov. 1993. *Customer Support:* Free 800 Number Technical Support.
Windows. PC with 386SX 33MHz or higher (8Mb). disk $29.95 (ISBN 1-884899-02-1). *Optimal configuration:* 386SX 33MHz or higher PC, 8MB RAM, double-speed CD-ROM drive, VGA Plus 640x480 monitor displaying 256 colors, MS-DOS 5.0 or higher, Windows 3.1 MS-DOS CD-ROM Extensions (MSCDEX 2.2 or higher), stereo headphones or speakers, minimum 3Mb hard disk space for installation, mouse or compatible positioning device, minimum MPC-Level 1 compatible sound card.
Macintosh. Color Macintosh (LCIII, CI, VX, FX, Centris, Quadra, Performa 450 or higher) (68030 25MHz or higher) (5Mb). 3.5" disk $34.95 (ISBN 1-884899-03-X). *Optimal configuration:* Color Macintosh (LCIII, CI, VX, FX, Centris, Quadra, Performa 450) or higher (68030 25MHz or higher), Color monitor & video card supporting 256 colors at 640x480, 5Mb RAM, System 7.01 or higher, 1Mb free hard disk space for installation, double-speed CD-ROM drive, stereo headphones or speakers, mouse.
The Ultimate Combination of Technology, Medical Information & Art. Included Are Practical Strategies to Reduce Risk of Heart Disease, Up-to-Date Treatments & Explanations of the Cardiovascular System. Included Are over 60 Minutes of Sound & Narration, 48 Videos & Animations, & over 145 Color Illustrations.
IVI Publishing, Inc.

Mayo Clinic Family Health, 1996 Edition: The Ultimate Interactive Guide to Health. *Version:* 2.0. Mayo Clinic Staff. 1995-96. *Customer Support:* Free 800 Number Technical Support.
Windows. PC with 386SX 33MHz or higher (8Mb). CD-ROM disk $79.95 (ISBN 1-884899-95-1). *Optimal configuration:* 486 25MHz or higher PC, 8Mb RAM, double-speed CD-ROM drive, VGA Plus 640x480 monitor displaying 256 colors, MS-DOS 5.0 or higher, Windows 3.1 MS-DOS CD-ROM Extensions (MSCDEX 2.2 or higher), stereo headphones or speakers, minimum 10Mb hard disk space for installation, mouse or compatible positioning device, minimum MPC-Level 1 compatible sound card.
System 7.01 or higher. Color Macintosh (Centris, Quadra, Performa or higher) (68040 or higher) (8Mb). CD-ROM disk $79.95 (ISBN 1-884899-96-X). *Nonstandard peripherals required:* Double speed CD-ROM drive, 4Mb free hard disk space for installation. *Optimal configuration:* Color Macintosh (LCIII, CI, VX, FX, Centris, Quadra, Performa 450 or higher (68030 25MHz or higher), Color monitor & video card supporting 256 colors at 640x480, 5Mb RAM, System 7.01 or higher, 1Mb free hard disk space for installation, double-speed CD-ROM drive, stereo headphones or speakers, mouse.
Vital Health Information Is Provided on Hundreds of Topics on This CD-ROM. Top Quality Animated Illustrations, Photographs & Video Footage Depict Actual Medical Conditions & Procedures. The 1996 Edition Includes New Customer Requested Features Such As a Poison Reference, Common Symptoms Search, Personal Profile for Recording Family Health Records, & One Click Internet Access to a Unique Online Health Network for Additional Information.
IVI Publishing, Inc.

Mayo Clinic Health Encyclopedia 1996 Edition: Your 4 CD-ROM Health Library. Mayo Clinic. Nov. 1995. *Items Included:* Netscape Navigator personal edition. *Customer Support:* Free 800 number technical support.
Windows. 486SX 25MHz or higher (8Mb). CD-ROM disk $134.95 (ISBN 1-57602-015-0). *Nonstandard peripherals required:* Double speed CD-ROM drive, 10Mb free hard disk space. *Addl. software required:* MS-DOS 5.0 or higher, Microsoft Windows 3.1, 640x480 (VGA plus), MPC-level (8 bit).
A Four Disc Set Which Includes the 1996 Eiditons of Mayo Clinic Family Health, Mayo Clinic - The Total Heart, Mayo Clinic Family Pharmacist & Mayo Clinic Sports, Health & Fitness Together in One Comprehensive Health Resource.
IVI Publishing, Inc.

Mayo Clinic Sports Health & Fitness: Your Personal Guide to Physical Fitness. Mayo Clinic Staff & ESPN Staff. Oct. 1994. *Customer Support:* Free 800 Number Technical Support.
Windows. PC with 386SX 33MHz or higher (8Mb). CD-ROM disk $29.95 (ISBN 1-884899-02-1). *Optimal configuration:* 386SX 33MHz or higher PC, 8MB RAM, double-speed CD-ROM drive, VGA Plus 640x480 monitor displaying 256 colors, MS-DOS 5.0 or higher, Windows 3.1 MS-DOS CD-ROM Extensions (MSCDEX 2.2 or higher), stereo headphones or speakers, minimum 3Mb hard disk space for installation, mouse or compatible positioning device, minimum MPC-Level 1 compatible sound card.
Produced in Collaboration with ESPN, This Complete Fitness Guide Features Safe Workout Methods, Sports Psychology, & Sports Injury Prevention & Treatment, You'll See Exercise Techniques in 3-D Animation & Interviews Professional Athletes. Interactive Training Helps You Achieve Goals Safely & Effectively.
IVI Publishing, Inc.

Maze. Duane Bristow. *Compatible Hardware:* TRS-80 Model I, Model III. *Operating System(s) Required:* TRSDOS. *Language(s):* BASIC. *Memory Required:* 32k.
cassette $19.95.
Game in Which the Computer Designs a Maze of Whatever Size You Set & Populates the Maze with Treasures to Be Returned to Treasure Room & Hazards Which Will Have Varying Effects on Your Progress.
Duane Bristow Computers, Inc.

Maze Man. *Compatible Hardware:* Commodore 64.
contact publisher for price (Order no.: C-1504).
Arcade Game.
Creative Equipment.

The MBA Accountant. *Version:* 4.0. *Operating System(s) Required:* PC/MS-DOS. *Language(s):* Compiled MS-COBOL. *Memory Required:* 256k. *General Requirements:* Printer. *Customer Support:* Available.
Contact publisher for price.
Set of MBA Software Packages Which Includes the General Ledger, Accounts Payable & Accounts Receivable Modules. Also Includes ASCII File Interfaces for G/L, A/P & A/R, & General Ledger Spreadsheet Interface. Source Code Available.
MBA Business Accounting Software.

MBA Accounts Payable. *Version:* 4.0. *Operating System(s) Required:* MS-DOS, PC-DOS. *Language(s):* Compiled Microsoft COBOL. *Memory Required:* 256k. *Customer Support:* Available.
Contact publisher for price.
Provides File Payment Reports, Cash Requirements, Aged Details Payable, Writes Checks, Automatically Processes Credit Memos & Includes Provisions for Manually Operated Checks. Source Code Is Available.
MBA Business Accounting Software.

MBA Accounts Payable with Check Writing. *Version:* 4.0. *Operating System(s) Required:* MS-DOS, PC-DOS. *Language(s):* Compiled MS-COBOL. *Memory Required:* 256k.
Contact publisher for price.
Performs Accounts Payable Ledger Operations & Cash Requirements Management. Source Code Is Available.
MBA Business Accounting Software.

MBA Accounts Receivable with Invoicing. *Version:* 4.0. *Operating System(s) Required:* PC-DOS, MS-DOS. *Language(s):* Compiled MS-COBOL. *Memory Required:* 256k.
Contact publisher for price.
Performs Receivable Accounting & Credit Analysis. User Can Select Balance Forward or Open-Item Account Detailing on a Customer-by-Customer Basis. In Addition to Receivable Analysis Reports, Detailed & Summary Customer Reports Can Be Printed in Alphabetical, Name or Account Number Order, for All or Selected Billing Cycles, Sales Representatives, or Zip Codes. Also Generates Alphabetical Mail Labels & Rolodex Cards. Source Code Is Available.
MBA Business Accounting Software.

MBA Fixed Asset Accounting. *Version:* 3.30. *Operating System(s) Required:* MS-DOS, PC-DOS. *Language(s):* Compiled MS-DOS. *Memory Required:* 256k.
Contact publisher for price.
Compatible with FASB 96 Requirements Examines Tracking & Depreciation Methods for Businesses. Flexible Numbering System Allows Multiple Locations, Departments & Classes of Assets. Source Code Available.
MBA Business Accounting Software.

MBA General Ledger with Financial Report Writer. *Version:* 4.0. *Operating System(s) Required:* MS-DOS, PC-DOS. *Language(s):* Compiled Microsoft COBOL. *Memory Required:* 256k. *Customer Support:* Available.
Contact publisher for price.
Performs General Accounting & Financial Statement Operations. Provides a 10-Digit Alpha-Numeric Accounting Code, an On-Line Detail Inquiry, Multiple-Month Processing & User-Definable Reports. Source Code Is Available. Includes Spreadsheet Interface.
MBA Business Accounting Software.

MBA Inventory Control with Invoicing. *Version:* 4.0. *Operating System(s) Required:* PC-DOS, MS-DOS. *Language(s):* Compiled MS-COBOL. *Memory Required:* 256k.
Contact publisher for price.
Provides Accurate & Timely Multiple Warehouse Control by Tracking Product Usage & Costs. User Can Maintain Products at Optimum Levels, Eliminating over or under Stocking of Goods. Provides the Needed Flow of Information by Monitoring Inventory Issues, Receipts, Item Costs & Prices. By Interfacing with the MBA Sales Order Entry & Purchase Order Modules, Automatically Adjusts On-Hand, On-Order or Allocated Quantities. Produces a Detailed or Summary Subsidiary Ledger Which Can be Posted Automatically to the General Ledger System.
MBA Business Accounting Software.

MBA Job Cost. *Operating System(s) Required:* PC-DOS, MS-DOS. *Language(s):* Compiled MS-COBOL. *Memory Required:* 256k. *General Requirements:* Printer.
disk $495.00, incl. documentation.

MBA Multi-Company Option

Tracks Costs for Project-Oriented Businesses. Each Job Is Divided into Phases with User-Defined Cost Categories. Cost Can Be in Units or Dollars. Definitions Can Be Copied from a Previous Job or Library of Jobs & Modified. Overhead Can Be Allocated As a Percentage or a Fixed Amount. Billing Rates Can Be Defined for Each Phase. Monitors Job Status & Current Costs As Well As Projecting Costs & Profitability. Source Code Available.
MBA Business Accounting Software.

MBA Multi-Company Option. Version: 4.0. Operating System(s) Required: MS-DOS, PC-DOS. Language(s): Compiled MS-COBOL. Memory Required: 256k. General Requirements: Hard disk. Customer Support: Available.
Contact publisher for price.
Accounting Applications.
MBA Business Accounting Software.

MBA Payroll Multi-state, Local with Check Writing. Version: 4.0. Operating System(s) Required: PC-DOS, MS-DOS. Language(s): Compiled MS-COBOL. Memory Required: 256k.
Contact publisher for price.
Processes Payrolls for Salaried & Hourly Employees for Weekly, Bi-Weekly, Semi-Monthly & Monthly Pay Periods. Source Code Is Available.
MBA Business Accounting Software.

MBA PhD Data Utility. Version: 4.0. Operating System(s) Required: PC-DOS/MS-DOS. Memory Required: 256k.
Contact publisher for price.
Relational Data Base Management System That Will Integrate with MBA's Accounting Applications or Function As a Stand-Alone Product. Predefined "Views" of the Major MBA Accounting Files Are Included. Specific Reports & Queries Needed to Effectively Manage the User's Business Are Easily Produced. Capable of Calculating Totals, Subtotals & Averages from the Information in the Files. Utilizes the Concept of "Virtual Files" Which Allows Data from Multiple Files to Be Readily Available to the User Through the Views Without Taking up Additional Disk Space. Allows Both the Importation & the Exportation of ASCII Data to Facilitate Its Use by Productivity Tools Such As Word Processors, Spreadsheets & Other Data Base Products.
MBA Business Accounting Software.

MBA Professional Time Accounting. Operating System(s) Required: PC-DOS, MS-DOS. Language(s): Compiled MS-COBOL. Memory Required: 256k.
Contact publisher for price.
For Use in Any Professional Time-Billing Situation. Provides Reports for Bills or Un-Billed Items by Client or Partner, & Generates an Invoice. Source Code Available.
MBA Business Accounting Software.

MBA Professional Time Accounting with Billing. Operating System(s) Required: MS-DOS, PC-DOS. Language(s): 8-bit systems 64k, 16-bit systems 128. Memory Required: 256k.
disk $580.00, incl. documentation.
Recording & Billing Information for Professionals. Source Code Is Available.
MBA Business Accounting Software.

MBA Purchase Orders & Requisitions for Inventory. Version: 4.0. Operating System(s) Required: PC-DOS, MS-DOS. Language(s): Compiled Microsoft COBOL. Memory Required: 256k.
Contact publisher for price.
Optional Addition to the Inventory Control Package Provides Printing Methods & Purchase Ordering Methods. Generates an Automatic Requisition Form from User-Defined Order Points, & Automatically Generates Purchase Orders Using the A/P Vending File. Allows Input of Work, Sales & Internal Orders. Source Code Is Available.
MBA Business Accounting Software.

MBA Sales Order Entry. Version: 4.0. Operating System(s) Required: PC-DOS, MS-DOS. Language(s): Compiled MS-COBOL. Memory Required: 256k. General Requirements: Printer.
Contact publisher for price.
Allows Quick Access to Order Information. Produces a List of Tasks to Fill a Customer's Order & Prepares a Picking List or Invoices. 99 Shipping Addresses Are Available for Each Billing Address. Online Inquiry Allows User to Review Order Status. Integrates with the Inventory & Accounts Receivable, to Allow Automatic Posting to the General Ledger. Source Code Is Available.
MBA Business Accounting Software.

MBACOUNT. Version: 4.0. Compatible Hardware: CP/M based machines. Operating System(s) Required: CP/M, MS-DOS. Language(s): Quick Basic. General Requirements: 2 disk drives recommended. Items Included: Manual, disk, & warranty card. Customer Support: 18 month via telephone.
disk $89.00.
demo disk & manual $20.00.
source code $200.00.
Accounting Program for Small Business & Self-Employed Individuals.
Micro-Art Programmers.

MBADATA. Version: 2.4. Compatible Hardware: CP/M & MS-DOS based machines. Operating System(s) Required: MS-DOS, CP/M. Language(s): Quick Basic. Memory Required: 64k. Items Included: Manual, disk, warranty card. Customer Support: 18 month via telephone.
disk $89.00.
demo disk & manual $20.00.
Database Manager.
Micro-Art Programmers.

MBOS. Version: 6.1. Compatible Hardware: IBM PC, PC XT, AT, 386, PS/2, ALTOS. Language(s): BOS COBOL. Memory Required: 256k. General Requirements: Hard disk.
contact publisher for price.
Transportable Multi-Tasking, Multi-User Operating System for Hard Disk Business Computers. Supports 1-99 Terminals, Depending on Configuration. All Systems Developed under This Program Are Totally Transportable to Any Other BOS Supported Machine with No Modification. Multi-User Facilities Include File & Record Locking, Password Authorization, & Print Spooling. Supports a Development System, Including MicroCOBOL Compiler, Linkage Editor, Screen Mapping, Text Editor, Menu Generator, Symbolic Debugging, Multi-Key Sort, Multiple File Access Methods, Batch Job Management & Programmer Utilities.
BOS National, Inc.

MBP Visual COBOL 85. Version: 2.2. Jan. 1988. Compatible Hardware: CT N-GEN, IBM PC, PC XT, PC AT, 386 & 486 UNIX, 68xxx UNIX, IBM RS/6000 AIX, MIPS. Operating System(s) Required: MS-DOS, BTOS II, UNIX, PC Network, Novell Network, AIX, MIPS OS, ULTRIX. Language(s): COBOL. Memory Required: 640k. General Requirements: Hard disk. Customer Support: Basic support & 3 paid support levels.
IBM PC, MS-DOS - 4 disks, UNIX - 1 tape. $1195.00 MS-DOS / $1395.00 PC LANS, $2195.00 386 UNIX & XENIX, $3495.00 68xxx UNIX, $5995.00-$7995.00 RISC systems.
IBM PC AT, XENIX - 4 disks.
IBM PC, Novell Network - 1 disk.
IBM PC, Network - 1 disk.
CT N-GEN, CTOSVM BTOS I 5 disks, UNIX - 1 Tape.
manual $100.00.
Optimized Native Code COBOL Compiler Conforming to the ANSI-85 COBOL Standard. Its Full-Featured Production Environment Includes an Integrated Set of Programming Tools Designed to Aid the Development, Compilation, Debugging, & Testing of COBOL Applications. Includes a Screen Management System, a "Follow-the-Source" Debugger & a Menu-Driven Programmer Interface. Add-On Products Include a Syntax-Checking COBOL-Specific Source Code Editor & an Ad-Hoc Query SQL Report Writer. Code Is Portable Between All Supported Platforms, & Supports Most Popular Network Systems.
MBP Software & Systems Technology, Inc.

MBS Temp Package One. Version: A.02. Dec. 1993. Items Included: User guide, on-line training. Customer Support: 90 day warranty & service. DOS. PC (1Mb). disk $995.00. Nonstandard peripherals required: Wide carriage printer. Networks supported: Multi-User DOS (Concurrent DOS).
Job Order Based Payroll/Billing/Accounts Receivable System. Includes Customer/Temp/Job Order File Maintenance & Master Reporting. Single Entry Payroll System Automatically Transfers Detail to Billing System. Payroll & Billing Output Automatically Add to History Files. Job Order Also Contains Skill Code, for Workers Comp & Override for Bill Rate.
Micro Busines Systems (New York).

MC-Matrix Calculator. Donald Marsh. 1982. Compatible Hardware: Apple II, IBM PC compatibles. Memory Required: 48k. Items Included: Manual.
disk $27.50, incl. manual (Order no.: 00100-200).
Allows Addition, Multiplication, & Inversion of Matrices. Can Be Used to Solve Simultaneous Linear Equations. DC Circuit Example Included.
6502 Program Exchange.

MC Software General Ledger. Version: 2.0. 1989. Compatible Hardware: Compupro; Compaq; Fujitsu; Hewlett-Packard; IBM PC, PC XT, PC AT; Tandy; Texas Instuments. Operating System(s) Required: PC-DOS, MS-DOS, Concurrent DOS, Unix, Xenix; Novell & Microsoft networks. Language(s): C. Memory Required: 640k. General Requirements: Hard disk, 132-column printer. Items Included: Disks & manuals. Customer Support: Through VARs, support contracts available.
single-user $695.00.
multi-user $995.00.
Designed for Most Manufacturing, Wholesale, Retail, & Service Providing Businesses. Offers Flexibility in Financial Statement Formatting. Part of INCOME II, MC Software's Consultants' Integrated Company Management Accounting Series. Interfaces with the INCOME II, ACCOUNTS RECEIVABLE & ACCOUNTS PAYABLE Programs by Means of a Batch Update Usually Performed at Month-End.
INMASS/MRP.

MCBA Accounts Payable (A-P). Version: 5.2. 1992. Compatible Hardware: IBM RS/6000, Sun SPARC, HP UX Data General Aviion; Altos; IBM PC AT, XT; Intel 286/386, NCR Tower. Operating System(s) Required: PC-DOS/MS-DOS, UNIX, XENIX, AIX, Sun OS SCO UNIX. Language(s): RM/COBOL-85 (source code included). Memory Required: 1500k.

contact publisher for price.
Allows Entry & Editing of Vendor Invoices, Cash Requirements Reporting, Manual & Partial Payment of Vouchers, Printing Checks & 1099 Forms & Check Reconciliation. Interfaces to MCBA's General Ledger & Purchase Order & Receiving.
MCBA, Inc.

MCBA Accounts Receivable (A-R). *Version:* 5.2. 1992. *Compatible Hardware:* IBM RS/6000, Sun SPARC, HP UX Data General Aviion; Altos; IBM PC AT, XT; Intel 286/386, NCR Tower. *Operating System(s) Required:* PC-DOS/MS-DOS, UNIX, XENIX, AIX, Sun OS SCO UNIX. *Language(s):* RM/COBOL-85 (source code included). *Memory Required:* 1500k.
contact publisher for price.
Provides Tracking of Both Open Item & Balance Forward Customers. Generates Monthly Statements. Interface to MCBA's General Ledger.
MCBA, Inc.

MCBA Bill of Materials Processor (BOMP). *Version:* 5.2. 1992. *Compatible Hardware:* IBM RS/6000, Sun SPARC, HP UX Data General Aviion; Altos; IBM PC AT, XT; Intel 286/386, NCR Tower. *Operating System(s) Required:* PC-DOS/MS-DOS, UNIX, XENIX, AIX, Sun OS SCO UNIX. *Language(s):* RM/COBOL-85 (source code included). *Memory Required:* 512k. *Items Included:* Documentation, 1st year maintenance. *Customer Support:* Phone-in or write-in available; customization is available.
contact publisher for price.
Allows Full Product Structure Maintenance for Use in Engineering, Product Costing, Purchasing & Production. Provides Summarized Reports, & Creates Modular Bills for Products & Forecasted Bills.
MCBA, Inc.

MCBA Business Software. *Version:* 5.2. *Compatible Hardware:* IBM RS/6000, Sun SPARC, HP UX Data General Aviion; Altos; IBM PC AT, XT; Intel 286/386, NCR Tower. *Operating System(s) Required:* PC-DOS/MS-DOS, UNIX, XENIX, AIX, Sun OS SCO UNIX. *Memory Required:* 1500k. *General Requirements:* Hard disk.
contact publisher for price.
Multi-Company Financial/Accounting Software with Consolidated Financials. Posts Recurring Transactions, Report Format User Definable, Reports Comparative Statements, Links with External Software Programs, Password Access, Encryption, Audit Trail, Log off Out-of-Balance, Reject Erroneous Account Numbers, Source Code Available.
MCBA, Inc.

MCBA Capacity Requirements Planning (CRP). *Version:* 5.2. 1992. *Compatible Hardware:* IBM RS/6000, Sun SPARC, HP UX Data General Aviion; Altos; IBM PC AT, XT; Intel 286/386, NCR Tower. *Operating System(s) Required:* PC-DOS/MS-DOS, UNIX, XENIX, AIX, Sun OS SCO UNIX. *Language(s):* RM/COBOL-85 (source code included). *Memory Required:* 1500k. *Items Included:* Documentation, first year maintenance.
contact publisher for price.
Compares Each Work Center's Projected Load to Available Capacity, Providing Time-Phased Reports. Analysis Can Predict Results of Alternative Schedules. Facilitates Shop Planning by Reporting.
MCBA, Inc.

MCBA Classic Software. *Version:* 5.2. Feb. 1990. *Compatible Hardware:* ISA/EISA/McBus. *Operating System(s) Required:* DRDOS, PC-DOS/MS-DOS, Unix, Xenix. *Language(s):* COBOL-85. *Memory Required:* Unix 1Mb, ea. user 500k. *Customer Support:* Support contracts are available.
contact EMS for price.
Designed for Distributors & Medium to Large Manufacturers.
Executive Micro Systems, Inc.

MCBA Customer Order Processing (COP). *Version:* 5.2. 1992. *Compatible Hardware:* IBM RS/6000, Sun SPARC, HP UX Data General Aviion; Altos; IBM PC AT, XT; Intel 286/386, NCR Tower. *Operating System(s) Required:* PC-DOS/MS-DOS, UNIX, XENIX, AIX, Sun OS SCO UNIX. *Language(s):* RM/COBOL-85 (source code included). *Memory Required:* 1500k. *Items Included:* Documentation; first year maintenance. *Customer Support:* Phone-in or write-in; customization is available.
contact publisher for price.
Interactive Customer Order Processing with Separate Billing. Supports Multi-Level Pricing, On-Line Credit Checks, Order Status Reporting, Multiple Warehouse Locations, Back Order Control & Full & Selective Billing.
MCBA, Inc.

MCBA Fixed Assets & Depreciation (A-D). *Version:* 5.2. 1992. *Compatible Hardware:* IBM RS/6000, Sun SPARC, HP UX Data General Aviion; Altos; IBM PC AT, XT; Intel 286/386, NCR Tower. *Operating System(s) Required:* PC-DOS/MS-DOS, UNIX, XENIX, AIX, Sun OS SCO UNIX. *Language(s):* RM/COBOL-85 (source code included). *Memory Required:* 1500k. *Items Included:* Documentation; first year maintenance. *Customer Support:* Phone-in or write-in; customization is available.
contact publisher for price.
Tracks Depreciation Figures for Financial Reporting & Tax Purposes. Allows Depreciation by 9 Methods. Flexible Handling of Bonus Depreciation & Expense Accounts. Tracks Investment Tax Credits & Provides for Automatic Recapture on Early Disposition.
MCBA, Inc.

MCBA General Ledger (G-L). *Version:* 5.2. 1992. *Compatible Hardware:* IBM RS/6000, Sun SPARC, HP UX Data General Aviion; Altos; IBM PC AT, XT; Intel 286/386, NCR Tower. *Operating System(s) Required:* PC-DOS/MS-DOS, UNIX, XENIX, AIX, Sun OS SCO UNIX. *Language(s):* RM/COBOL-85 (source code included). *Memory Required:* 1500k.
contact publisher for price.
Supports User-Defined Accounting Periods & Adjustments to Prior & Future Periods. Financial Statements Can Be Generated for Any Period. Tracks Transactions by Source. 24-Character, 5 Level G/L Account Number Format.
MCBA, Inc.

MCBA Inventory Management (I-M). *Version:* 5.2. 1992. *Compatible Hardware:* IBM RS/6000, Sun SPARC, HP UX Data General Aviion; Altos; IBM PC AT, XT; Intel 286/386, NCR Tower. *Operating System(s) Required:* PC-DOS/MS-DOS, UNIX, XENIX, AIX, Sun OS SCO UNIX. *Language(s):* RM/COBOL-85 (source code included). *Memory Required:* 1500k. *Items Included:* Documentation; first year maintenance. *Customer Support:* Phone-in or write-in; customization is available.
contact publisher for price.
Programs for Distributors & Manufacturers Engaging in Inventory Control. Includes Multi-Warehouse Capabilities. Forecasts Future Needs Based on Past Usages & User-Defined Parameters.
MCBA, Inc.

MCBA Job Costing (J-C). *Version:* 5.2. 1992. *Compatible Hardware:* IBM RS/6000, Sun SPARC, HP UX Data General Aviion; Altos; IBM PC AT, XT; Intel 286/386, NCR Tower. *Operating System(s) Required:* PC-DOS/MS-DOS, UNIX, XENIX, AIX, Sun OS SCO UNIX. *Language(s):* RM/COBOL (source code included). *Memory Required:* 1500k.
contact publisher for price.
Provides Cost Reporting & Variance Analysis. Cost Analysis by Job Department & Work Center & Reports Variance Analysis for Labor, Material, & Sub-Contracting.
MCBA, Inc.

MCBA Labor Performance (L-P). *Version:* 5.2. 1992. *Compatible Hardware:* IBM RS/6000, Sun SPARC, HP UX Data General Aviion; Altos; IBM PC AT, XT; Intel 286/386, NCR Tower. *Operating System(s) Required:* PC-DOS/MS-DOS, UNIX, XENIX, AIX, Sun OS SCO UNIX. *Language(s):* RM/COBOL-85 (source code included). *Memory Required:* 1500k.
contact publisher for price.
Designed to Identify Productivity Problems & Improve Utilization of Labor Resources. Tracks Employee Production Statistics & Monitors Performance of Both Foreman & Crew. Barcode Interface.
MCBA, Inc.

MCBA Manufacturing Resource Planning: MRP II. *Version:* 5.2. *Compatible Hardware:* IBM RS/6000, Sun SPARC, HP UX Data General Aviion; Altos; IBM PC AT, XT; Intel 286/386, NCR Tower. *Operating System(s) Required:* PC-DOS/MS-DOS, UNIX, XENIX, AIX, Sun OS SCO UNIX. *Items Included:* Documentation; first year support. *Customer Support:* Phone-in or write-in; customization is available.
contact publisher for price.
Closed-Loop MRP II System with 19 Interactive Modules. Extensive Reporting Capability. Includes Accounting, Purchasing, Order Entry, Inventory, Costing, Shop Floor Controll & Payroll Functions.
MCBA, Inc.

MCBA Master Scheduling. *Version:* 5.2. *Compatible Hardware:* IBM RS/6000, Sun SPARC, HP UX Data General Aviion; Altos; IBM PC AT, XT; Intel 286/386, NCR Tower. *Operating System(s) Required:* PC-DOS/MS-DOS, UNIX, XENIX, AIX, Sun OS SCO UNIX.
$6,000.00-$9,000.00.
Provides Flexible Control of Overall Production Plans with a Detailed Master Schedule. Production Can Be Based on Predicted Demand. Allows "What If" Schedules, Optional Use of Customer Orders & Sales Forecasts & Rough Cut Capacity Planning.
MCBA, Inc.

MCBA Material Requirements Planning (MRP). *Version:* 5.2. 1992. *Compatible Hardware:* IBM RS/6000, Sun SPARC, HP UX Data General Aviion; Altos; IBM PC AT, XT; Intel 286/386, NCR Tower. *Operating System(s) Required:* PC-DOS/MS-DOS, UNIX, XENIX, AIX, Sun OS SCO UNIX. *Language(s):* RM/COBOL-85 (source code included). *Memory Required:* 1500k.
contact publisher for price.
Generates Material Requirements in Summary or Detail. Reports on Exceptions & Planned Orders, Recommends Purchases by Vendor or Items, Provides Cost Reports & Allows Multi-Level & End-Item "Pegging" for Tracing Items.
MCBA, Inc.

MCBA Payroll (PR). Version: 5.2. 1992. Compatible Hardware: IBM RS/6000, Sun SPARC, HP UX Data General Aviion; Altos; IBM PC AT, XT; Intel 286/386, NCR Tower. Operating System(s) Required: PC-DOS/MS-DOS, UNIX, XENIX, AIX, Sun OS SCO UNIX. Language(s): RM/COBOL-85 (source code included). Memory Required: 512k. contact publisher for price.
Handles Hourly & Salaried Employees. Calculates Payroll, Prints Checks, Allows Check Reconciliation & Permits Entry of Payroll Adjustments. Interactive Maintenance of Federal & State Payroll Tax Percents, Limits & Witholding Tax Tables. 401(k) Plans Supported.
MCBA, Inc.

MCBA Purchase Order & Receiving (P-O). Version: 5.2. 1992. Compatible Hardware: IBM RS/6000, Sun SPARC, HP UX Data General Aviion; Altos; IBM PC AT, XT; Intel 286/386, NCR Tower. Operating System(s) Required: PC-DOS/MS-DOS, UNIX, XENIX, AIX, Sun OS SCO UNIX. Language(s): RM/COBOL-85 (source code included). Memory Required: 1500k.
contact publisher for price.
Maintains Purchasing Records & Quality, Accuracy & Promptness of Purchased Materials. Supports Multiple Order Close Out, Vendor Performance Analysis & Commodity Coding.
MCBA, Inc.

MCBA Shop Floor Control (SFC). Version: 5.2. 1992. Compatible Hardware: IBM RS/6000, Sun SPARC, HP UX Data General Aviion; Altos; IBM PC AT, XT; Intel 286/386, NCR Tower. Operating System(s) Required: PC-DOS/MS-DOS, UNIX, XENIX, AIX, Sun OS SCO UNIX. Language(s): RM/COBOL-85 (source code included). Memory Required: 1500k.
contact publisher for price.
Creates Standard or Customized Shop Orders & Monitors Shop Floor Activity. Supports "Shop Bills" & "Shop Routings," Provides Operation Level Controls, Accommodates Shop Notes, Records Scrap, Material & Labor Extended, & Prints Dispatch List.
MCBA, Inc.

MCBA Standard Product Costing (SPC). Version: 5.2. 1992. Compatible Hardware: IBM RS/6000, Sun SPARC, HP UX Data General Aviion; Altos; IBM PC AT, XT; Intel 286/386, NCR Tower. Operating System(s) Required: PC-DOS/MS-DOS, UNIX, XENIX, AIX, Sun OS SCO UNIX. Language(s): RM/COBOL-85 (source code included).
contact publisher for price.
Maintains Standard or Estimated Cost for All Products, Parts & Services & Tracks Deviations from Planning Objectives. Facilitates "What-If" Cost Analyses & Reports Purchase Price Variance.
MCBA, Inc.

MCBA Standard Product Routing (SPR). Version: 5.2. 1992. Compatible Hardware: IBM RS/6000, Sun SPARC, HP UX Data General Aviion; Altos; IBM PC AT, XT; Intel 286/386, NCR Tower. Operating System(s) Required: PC-DOS/MS-DOS, UNIX, XENIX, AIX, Sun OS SCO UNIX. Language(s): RM/COBOL-85 (source code included). Memory Required: 1500k.
contact publisher for price.
Designed to Control the Sequence of Operations, Tools & Assembly Instructions Used in Product Manufacturing. Allows Interactive Entry & Editing of Routing Data, & Maintains Labor & Machine Hour Standards at Operation Level.
MCBA, Inc.

MCC Accounts Payable. Version: 4.50. 1977. Compatible Hardware: IBM PC & compatibles, PC XT, PC AT, PS/2. Operating System(s) Required: PC-DOS/MS-DOS 2.10 or higher. Language(s): FORTRAN. Memory Required: 640k. Items Included: Manual. Customer Support: 1 hour per package purchased.
5-1/4" or 8" or 3-1/2" disk $495.00.
Uses the Accrual Method of Accounting. Standard Features Include Maintenance of Vendor's Name & Address, Total Purchases to Date & Date of Last Purchase. All Vouchers, Vendors & Due Date Items Can Be Paid Selectively by the User. Discounts Are Managed to Insure They Are Not Lost. Vouchers Are Expensed As They Are Entered. All Journal Entries Are Automatically Created for Posting to the General Ledger.
MCC Software (Midwest Computer Ctr. Co.).

MCC Explosive Modeling Package. Jan. 1990. Customer Support: Free one-year technical support.
DOS or OS/2. IBM & compatibles. $10,000.00.
Addl. software required: C & FORTRAN compiler.
A Package of Codes for Computing Explosive & Propellant Performance & Behavior. Package Includes BKW, a Detonation Performance Code; SIN; a One-Dimensional Reactive Hydrodynamic Code; FIRE, a Reactive Code for Heterogeneous Explosives; TDF a Thermodynamic Function Code Used By BKW; SEQS a Solid Equation of State Code for Computing Shock Temperatures, ISPBKW a Propellant Performance Code; & TDL a Two-Dimensional Reactive Hydrodynamic Code.
Mader Consulting Co.

MCC Financial Analysis. Version: 3.50. 1977. Compatible Hardware: IBM PC & compatibles, PC AT, PC XT, PS/2. Operating System(s) Required: MS-DOS, PC-DOS. Language(s): FORTRAN. Memory Required: 320k. Items Included: Manual. Customer Support: 1 hour per package purchased.
5-1/4" or 8" or 3-1/2" disk $395.00.
Extension of General Ledger. Standard Features Include: Automatic Calculation & Posting of Depreciation Expenses, Automatic Generation of Fixed Monthly Journal Entries, Budget Comparison Reports & Financial Comparison Reports. Solves Financial Problems Such As Amortization Schedules, Analysis of Loan Costs, Savings Plans & Balances.
MCC Software (Midwest Computer Ctr. Co.).

MCC Job Costing/Job Budgeting. Version: 3.50. 1978. Compatible Hardware: IBM PC & compatibles, PC XT, PC AT, PS/2. Operating System(s) Required: MS-DOS, PC-DOS. Language(s): FORTRAN. Memory Required: 320k. Items Included: Manual. Customer Support: 1 hour per package purchased.
5-1/2" or 8" or 3-1/2" disk $495.00.
Cost Accounting Interface to General Ledger. Sets up a Job Ledger to Accumulate All Incomes, Materials & Labor Costs Against a Particular Job. Automatically (As a By-Product of Processing Users' Accounts Payable, Payroll, Accounts Receivable & Inventory) Program Will Accumulate All Expenses Associated with a Particular Job. Allows Users to Create Estimates Based on Operation Codes Which They Have Established. Provides Complete Management Reporting by Dollars & Units, Projecting Percent Complete & Profitability by Operation. Estimates Can be Built for Both Labor & Materials. Requires MCC's G/L.
MCC Software (Midwest Computer Ctr. Co.).

MCGRAPH: A Library of OS-2 & DOS Graphics & Print Screen Routines for FORTRAN & C Programs. Jan. 1990. Items Included: Manual. Customer Support: Free technical support.
DOS or OS/2. IBM & compatibles. $500.00 (ISBN 1-878936-01-8). Addl. software required: C Compiler for all programs; FORTRAN compiler for Fortran programs.
A Library of Graphics & Print Screen Routines Using FORTRAN or C Compilers on Personal Computers Operating under DOS or OS/2, or on VAX computers. Two or Three Dimensional Solid or Contour Plots with Control of Color, Viewing Angles, Markers, Text, Linestyle, Font Type, Windows, & Printing to HP Laserjet or Paintjet & Dot Matrix Printers.
Mader Consulting Co.

MCOGO. 1980. Compatible Hardware: Apple II+. Operating System(s) Required: Apple DOS. Language(s): Applesoft BASIC. Memory Required: 48k.
disk $95.00.
Coordinate Geometry Program, with 23 Routines. Includes: Recall Unknown Distance or Bearing, Printout for Field Stakeout by EDM Instruments, 5,000 Points Storage per Diskette, Moving an Array of Points from One Location to Another, Tangent to 2 Circles, etc.
M.P.S. Co.

MCS Appraisal System. Version: 6.07. Aug. 1989. Items Included: instruction manual, catalog/forms reference guide. Customer Support: 90 days free support, after that, $125.00 for annual customer maintenance policy.
PC-DOS/MS-DOS 3.1 & higher. IBM PC & compatibles (448k). Residential Forms Processor $995.00. Nonstandard peripherals required: Must have hard disk & laser printer (HP & compatible). Networks supported: Lantastic, Network O/S, Novell.
Commercial Forms Processor $695.00.
Farm/Ranch Forms Processor $695.00.
Apex Sketch System $199.00.
Argus Lease by Lease Cash Flow Analysis Module $995.00.
MCS Soft Font $95.00.
Provides Complete Office Automation for Real Estate Appraisers in the Form of Residential, Commercial & Farm/Ranch Forms Processing, Database Management, Invoicing, Accounts Receivable, Appraisal Tracking, Floor Plan Sketching & Lease by Lease Cash Flow Analysis.
Microcomputer Consulting Services.

MD-REBS. Version: 702. 1984. Compatible Hardware: Any micro having a hard disk & one of the listed operating systems. Operating System(s) Required: MP/M-86, MS-DOS, CP/M-86, Concurrent CP/M, Concurrent DOS. Language(s): CB-86. Memory Required: 512k. $6000.00-$8000.00.
manual & demo disk $165.00.
Medical Package Designed to Provide Family & Patient Medical History As Well As Offering Office & Hospital Scheduling & Insurance Billing. Heavy Emphasis on Remote Access to Medical Data for Emergency or Satellite Situations via Doctors' Use of Portable Terminals from Home or Hospital.
Dagar-Software Development Corp.

MDBS IV. Version: 4.42. Nov. 1995. Compatible Hardware: IBM PC, PC XT, PC AT, PS/2 & compatibles; RS/6000, SUN, UNIX. Operating System(s) Required: UNIX, PC-DOS/MS-DOS, OS/2, Windows 3.X, Novell NetWare, VLM, Win NT, Win 95. Language(s): C/C Plus Plus, Assembly, Vis BASIC, Cobol. Memory Required: 256k.
Contact publisher for price.
Mainframe-Style DBMS Which Allows Complex Data Relationships Without Resorting to Redundance. Allows Direct Representation of

TITLE INDEX

Many-to-Many & Recursive Relationships. Options Includes Transaction Logging, Query Language, Design Modification, Interactive Data Manipulation, Report Generator, & Data Base Restructuring System.
Micro Data Base Systems, Inc. (MDBS).

MD86, Masterful Disassembler 8086. *Version:* 2.4. Feb. 1990. *Items Included:* 2 indexed manuals, EXE file unpacker. *Customer Support:* Free technical support.
MS-DOS/PC-DOS 2.0 or higher. IBM PC/XT/AT, PS/2, compatibles (256K). disk $67.50. *Optimal configuration:* IBM PC/XT/AT, 512K RAM, hard disk.
An Interactive Macro Disassembler for the 8086/87-80386/387 Family of CPU's. Disassembles COM/EXE/SYS/Other Files or System Memory. Features Automatic Code/Data Separation (with Type Determination), Auto Commenting & Labeling, Plus on Screen Editing. User Defined Macros Allows Intelligent Disassemblies of Compiler Generated "Spaghetti" Code. Comprehensive, Indexed Manuals (100+ Pages) describe the Disassembly Process from Start to Finish.
C.C. Software.

MDX: Modular Medical Data-Management Software. *Version:* 7.9. 1982. *Compatible Hardware:* Altos, AT&T, Compaq, DEC, HP, IBM, NCR, NEC, Tandy, TI, UNISYS, Wyse or other compatibles. *Operating System(s) Required:* UNIX Version 7, UNIX System III, XENIX. *Language(s):* C. *Memory Required:* 4000k. *General Requirements:* 110Mb minimum disk storage, tractor feed printer with the ability to accept at least 2-part forms.
Multi-User, Multi-Tasking Modular Data Management Software Designed Specifically for Medical Practices Capable of Accommodating Any Speciality or Size. Users May Select Needed Modules & Add Others at Any Time. Offers a Simple Menu Format, Personal Defaulting, & HELP Screens. Can Interface with GLX General-Ledger Software. The Minimum System Configuration Is Any One of the Modules "F", "M", "A". Each Can Stand Alone, or Any Two or Any Three Combined. Each Patient Will Require at Least 4k of Additional Space. Two Technical Support Plans Are Available via a Toll-Free "800" Telephone Line.
Calyx Corp.
  F: Financial Accounting Module.
  $3195.00 base price.
    Maintains All Patient Data & Files. Enables Operator to Post Charges & Payments; Maintain Tables; Print Statements & Claim Forms; Generate a Variety of Reports. Includes Audit Trail, Backup & Restoration Utilities, Automatic Reprocessing After Hardware Problems.
  F.a: Route Slips.
  $695.00 base price; varies with number of workstations.
    Stores Patient Scheduling Data; Creates Daily Route Slips & Day Sheets for Each Physician (but Is Not a Full Appointment Scheduling Package).
  F.b.c: Cycle Billing.
  Incl. in financial module.
    Allows Clinic to Specify Its Own Billing Cycle; Offers Alphabetic Sorting. Ensures That Patients Are Always Billed on the First Cycle after They Are Seen.
  F.b.f: Family Billing.
  Incl. in financial module.
    Groups All Charges for All Family Members on a Single Patient Statement. Facilitates Allocation of a Single Payment among Several Family Members.
  F.b.i: Insurance-First Billing.
  Incl. in financial module.
    Prevents Patient Statements from Being Printed until after All Insurance Coverages for Those Patients Have Been Exhausted.
  F.c.# Each Additional Claim Form.
  $595.00 base price; varies with number of workstations.
    Necessary If an Insurer Requires a Form Other Than the Standard AMA-OP-503.
  F.c.m: Cash Management Module.
  Incl. in financial module.
    Facilitates Posting of Bulk Insurance Checks. Searches & Distributes Payments to the Oldest Date of Service, While Shipping Those Dates Which Have Insurance Pending Until Deemed Appropriate for Billing. Allows for the Distribution of Payments to a Family as a Unit or to an Individual Member of the Family. Quickly Apply a Patient Payment Across Several Family Members, Without Looking at Each Account Individually.
  F.e.# Electronic Claims.
  $1695.00 base price for one format.
    Submits Claim Data via Telephone Lines to a Cooperating Insurance Carrier. Each Such Format & Communication Protocol Is an Option. Clearing House Option Included in Financial Accounting Module. Direct E-Claim Formats Available Separately. Price Varies with Number of Workstations & Desired Formats.
  F.l: Letters.
  $695.00 base price; varies with number of workstations.
    Generates Letters with Operator-Specified Variables; Incorporates Messages on Patient Statements; Allows for Charging Interest on Patient Statements.
  F.o: Offline Data Entry System (Batch).
  $1295.00 base price; varies with number of workstations.
    Enables Large Clinics to Perform Batch Data Entry to Speed up the Process & Minimize System Loading.
  F.p: Demand Printing.
  $695.00 base price; varies with number of workstations.
    Allows Generation of "Walk-In" Route Slips & "Walk-Out" Patient Statements or Claim Forms (Queries May Be Written or Purchased in Order to Prepare Prescription or Other Custom Forms As Well).
  A: Appointment Scheduling Module.
  $1195.00 base price; varies with number of workstations.
    Maintains Appointment Calendars & Provides Searches for Available Time. Also Includes All Functions of F.a.
  E.d: Additional Data Base.
  $1495.00 base price; varies with number of workstations.
    Necessary If Two or More Separate Practices with Separate Files Will Be Using the Same Computer; Each Additional Practice Requires an Additional Data Base.
  M: Clinical History Module-Expanded.
  $1895.00 base price; varies with number of workstations.
    Offers Complete Freedom in Designing & Maintaining Patient Medical Histories. Allows Searches Oriented by Time or by Problem. Includes Several Forms of Summary Medical Record Printout & the Ability to Find Patients Based on the Content of Their Medical Record.
  R: Report Writer Module.
  $2295.00 base price; varies with number of workstations.
    Flexible Query Language Enables the User to Specify Special Reports Based on Any Data Contained Within MDX. Also Allows the System to Interface with Other Software Packages (e.g. Graphics Packages, Spreadsheets, etc.).

Me & My Body. Nov. 1990. *Items Included:* 16-page documentation. *Customer Support:* Backup disk $10.00 with original purchase or with return of damaged disk. Will replace defective materials free within 30 days of receipt or order. Toll-free software hotline.
Apple. Apple IIe, IIc, or IIGS, one disk drive (128k). disk $55.00 (ISBN 1-55942-001-4, Order no.: 5150). *Optimal configuration:* Color monitor is desirable.
Teaches Children About the Special Qualities of the Human Body - How the Body Parts Move, Its Special Parts, & How They Interact with Each Other. Also Teaches About Healthy Food & the Importance of Exercise & the Use of the Five Senses. Includes a Series of Colorful Puzzles to Be Assembled, Including The Skeleton, Breakfast Table, & Person Exercising.
Marsh Media.

Me & My Family. Nov. 1990. *Items Included:* 16-page documentation. *Customer Support:* Backup disk $10.00 with original purchase or with return of damaged disk. Will replace defective materials free within 30 days of receipt of order. Toll-free software hotline.
Apple. Apple IIe, IIc, or IIGS, one disk drive (128k). disk $55.00 (ISBN 1-55942-002-2, Order no.: 5151). *Optimal configuration:* Color monitor is desirable.
Teaches Children about Immediate & Extended Families, Stepparents, Adoption, & How Families Work & Play Together. The Importance of Communication Is Also Stressed. Includes a Game Allowing Users to Select from a Selection of Background Pictures & Arrange Their Family Members in the Picture.
Marsh Media.

Me, Myself & I. Jan. 1994. *Items Included:* Program on CD-ROM, CD Booklet, & Registration Card. *Customer Support:* Free unlimited customer support via telephone.
Macintosh System 7.0 or higher. Macintosh LC or higher (4Mb). CD-ROM disk $39.00 (ISBN 1-57268-091-1, Order no.: 20882). *Nonstandard peripherals required:* 12 inch monitor or larger; CD-ROM drive. *Optimal configuration:* 5Mb RAM.
Windows 3.1 or higher running under DOS 5.0 or higher. 386 SX (4Mb RAM; 500k low Dos Mem; 6Mb free disk space). CD-ROM disk $39.00 (Order no.: 20882). *Nonstandard peripherals required:* Sound card (either: Sound Blaster - 8, 16, PRO; Media Vision ProAudio Spectrum; or Microsoft Sound System; MPC compatible CD-ROM drive; VGA monitor; & microphone. *Optimal configuration:* 25 MHz 386 SX.
Students Meet a Little Girl Named Minh Who Is Making New Friends & Learning to Play Soccer. As Students Read along, Aided by Voiced Text, Colorful Graphics, & Animation, They Learn about Much More Than Soccer. Students Identify Different Body Parts, Such As Hands, Feet, Knees, & Elbows, & Learn about the Five Senses. Me, Myself, & I Is a Cross-Cultural, Language-Based Learning Experience.
Conter Software.

Me, Myself & I. Jan. 1994. *Items Included:* Program on CD-ROM, CD Booklet, & Registration Card. *Customer Support:* Free unlimited customer support via telephone.
Windows 3.1 or higher running under DOS 5.0 or higher. 386 SX (4Mb RAM; 500k low Dos Mem; 6Mb free disk space). CD-ROM disk $39.00 (ISBN 1-57268-092-X, Order no.: 21882). *Nonstandard peripherals required:* Sound card (either: Sound Blaster - 8, 16, PRO; Media Vision ProAudio Spectrum; or Microsoft Sound System; MPC compatible CD-ROM drive; VGA monitor; & microphone.

Optimal configuration: 25 MHz 386 SX.
Students Meet a Little Girl Named Minh Who Is Making New Friends & Learning to Play Soccer. As Students Read along, Aided by Voiced Text, Colorful Graphics, & Animation, They Learn about Much More Than Soccer. Students Identify Different Body Parts, Such As Hands, Feet, Knees, & Elbows, & Learn about the Five Senses. Me, Myself, & I Is a Cross-Cultural, Language-Based Learning Experience.
Conter Software.

Me, Myself & I. Jan. 1994. *Items Included:* Program on CD-ROM, CD Booklet, & Registration Card. *Customer Support:* Free unlimited customer support via telephone.
Macintosh System 7.0 or higher. Macintosh LC or higher (4Mb). CD-ROM disk $39.00 (ISBN 1-57268-093-8, Order no.: 22882). *Nonstandard peripherals required:* 12 inch monitor or larger; CD-ROM drive. *Optimal configuration:* 5Mb RAM.
Students Meet a Little Girl Named Minh Who Is Making New Friends & Learning to Play Soccer. As Students Read along, Aided by Voiced Text, Colorful Graphics, & Animation, They Learn about Much More Than Soccer. Students Identify Different Body Parts, Such As Hands, Feet, Knees, & Elbows, & Learn about the Five Senses. Me, Myself, & I Is a Cross-Cultural, Language-Based Learning Experience.
Conter Software.

Mean 18: Ultimate Golf. *Compatible Hardware:* Apple Macintosh IIgs; Commodore Amiga; IBM PC, PCjr, PC XT, PC AT. *Operating System(s) Required:* PC-DOS 2.1 or higher. *Memory Required:* 256k. *General Requirements:* CGA card.
IBM $19.95; Amiga & Mac $44.95.
One-to-Four Golf Simulation Game. Includes Four Courses, a Golf Course Architect Set, & Numerous Strategy & Play Options. Players Can Choose Among Practice Tee, Practice Green, Practice Hole, & Begin Game Options to Perfect Their Game Playing Abilities.
Accolade, Inc.

Mean Streets.
DOS 2.0 or higher. IBM PC & compatibles (512K). contact publisher for price.
It's the Year 2033, Your Name is Lex Murphy, Private Investigator in San Francisco. You've Been Hired by the Beautiful Daughter of a University Professor to Uncover the Facts about Her Father's Death. You Will Interact with More Than 27 Characters Which Animate & Respond to Questions, Bribes & Threats. Some Characters Actually Talk. This Spectacular Effect is Achieved by Synchronized Digitized Animation with Real Sound.
Access Software, Inc.

Means Data for Spreadsheets: Construction Costs for Spreadsheet Estimating. 1991. *Items Included:* Spiral bound manual with tutorials. *Customer Support:* Free 800 number available; no training necessary; annual database updates available at a cost.
MS-DOS & MS-DOS with Windows. IBM & compatibles (640k). $175.00 for annual license; $395.00 for outright purchase. *Addl. software required:* Must have either Lotus 1-2-3 Ver. 2.0-2.4, Lotus 1-2-3 for Windows, Quattro for Windows, Excel for Windows. *Networks supported:* If spreadsheet networks, Means Data for Spreadsheets will network.
Integrates R.S. Means Construction Cost Databases into Commonly Used Spreadsheet Programs. Allows User to Estimate Construction Projects with Means Data & Their Own Database Within a Spreadsheet.
R. S. Means Co., Inc.

Measurement & Display of Ecological Diversity. 1992. *Items Included:* Manual with theory & sample runs, program listings in BASIC. *Customer Support:* Free phone, on-site seminars.
MS-DOS. IBM (128k). disk $130.00.
Macintosh. Macintosh. 3.5" disk $130.00.
7 Programs to Model Species Abundance, Display Diversity Indices Graphically & Calculate Diversity Indices Including: Div-Lin, Which Plots Number of Species & Total Number of Individuals vs. Sample Size & Calculates Margalepi & Menhinick's Indices; Div-Log, Which Is Same As Div-Lin but Uses Log Scales; BStick, Which Sorts Species Abundance Data into Rank Order & Abundance Classes & Fits Broken Stock Model; LSeries, Same As BStick but Uses Log Axes; GSeries, Same but Fits Geometric Series Model; Rare, Which Carries Out Rarefaction Transformation, Indices, Which Calculates 7 Diversity Indices.
Kern International, Inc.

Meat Cutting. *Version:* 3.2. Aug. 1985. *Compatible Hardware:* TRS-80 Model I Level II, Model III, Model 4, Tandy 1000. *Operating System(s) Required:* TRSDOS. *Language(s):* BASIC. *Memory Required:* 32k.
disk $29.95.
Post-Secondary-Level Simulation Program of Meat Cutting & Pricing. User Must Face the Same Dilemmas As a Real Meat Cutter: How to Cut to Realize the Highest Dollar Yield from a Primal at Today's Market Price; How to Adjust Prices for Various Cuts When He Leaves the Price of One Cut, So That He Can Realize the Same Profit; How to Cut Most Efficiently; How to Figure Number Plus Dollars per 100.
Viking, Inc.

Mechanical Advantage 2. *Version:* 4.2. Feb. 1996. *Items Included:* Four manuals. *Customer Support:* Training, hotline, update support, maintenance, 90-day warranty.
Solaris 2.3, HPUX, IRIX, AIX. SUN4/SPARC, HP 9000/700, Silicon Graphics, IBM RS6000. disk $5000.00-$19,000.00 (Order no.: 384-021013). *Networks supported:* Ethernet.
MCAE (Mechanical Computer Aided Engineering) Tool Allowing Engineers to Model Performance of Part/Assembly During Design. Both Geometric Variables & Design Variables May Be Linked, Optimized, Iterated & Varied. External Programs May Be Linked to Design Variables. Applications Include Mechanisms, Tolerance Analysis & Performance Modeling, Variational Solid Modeling (ACIS Based) with Associative Drafting.
Cognition Corp.

Mechanical Design Failure Analysis. Sep. 1986. *Compatible Hardware:* IBM PC AT. *Memory Required:* 256k. *Items Included:* 184 page manual with diskette.
$109.25 (ISBN 0-8247-7534-1).
Provides the Tools That Enable the User to Evaluate the State of Stress or Strain in a Component for Static or Fatigue Failure. Allows Mechanical, Structural & Design Engineers & Students Predict the Structural Failure Potential of a Design.
Marcel Dekker, Inc.

Mechanical Engineering, No. 1. *Items Included:* Bound manual. *Customer Support:* Free hotline - no time limit; 30 day limited warranty; updates are $5/disk plus S&H.
MS-DOS. IBM & compatibles (128k). disk $99.95. *Addl. software required:* CALFEX.
Apple (48k). disk $99.95.
This Is a Collection of Mechanical Engineering Programs for Use with the General Purpose Analysis Program, CALFEX. All Allow the Powerful Exchange Variable Option, So User Can Interchange a Dependent Variable for an Independent Variable to Reverse Their Roles. Contents: Applied Math; Stress & Strain; Fluid Flow; Dynamics.
Dynacomp, Inc.

Mechanism Design. Hari. 1987. *Items Included:* Spiral manual contains theory, sample runs, programs in BASIC. *Customer Support:* Free phone, on-site seminars.
MS-DOS. IBM (128k). disk $110.00. *Addl. software required:* BASIC.
10 Programs for Simulation & Design of Mechanisms Including Slider Crank, Crank Rocker, Four Bar Linkage, Four Bar Crank Rocker.
Kern International, Inc.

Mechanisms. Jan. 1987. *Compatible Hardware:* IBM PC, PC XT & compatibles. *Operating System(s) Required:* PC-DOS/MS-DOS. *Memory Required:* 640k. *General Requirements:* CGA card plus.
disk $495.00, Basic System.
disk $695.00, CAD Interface available.
Designed to be Used for Analyzing Simple, Multi-Loop & Multiple Degrees of Freedom Mechanisms. Provides Three Different Types of Analyses to Cover a Wide Range of Applications: Kinematic Analysis, Dynamic Analysis & Force Analysis. The Number of Joints Is Unlimited.
Engineering Software Co.

MechWarrior 2. *Items Included:* Installation Guide.
IBM PC. Contact publisher for price (ISBN 0-87321-040-9, Order no.: CDD-3092-NFR).
Activision, Inc.

MechWarrior 2. *Items Included:* Installation Guide.
IBM PC. Contact publisher for price (ISBN 0-87321-039-5, Order no.: CDD-3115).
Activision, Inc.

MechWarrior 2: Australian Version. *Items Included:* Installation Guide.
IBM PC. Contact publisher for price (ISBN 0-87321-037-9, Order no.: CDD-3092-AU).
Activision, Inc.

MechWarrior 2 Ghost Bear Clan's Legacy. *Items Included:* Installation guide.
IBM. Contact publisher for price (ISBN 0-87321-111-1, Order no.: CDD-3194).
Activision, Inc.

MechWarrior 2: Singapore Version. *Items Included:* Installation Guide.
IBM PC. Contact publisher for price (ISBN 0-87321-038-7, Order no.: CDD-3092-SI).
Activision, Inc.

MechWarrior 2: U. S. Version. *Items Included:* Installation Guide.
IBM PC. Contact publisher for price (ISBN 0-87321-036-0, Order no.: CDD-3092).
Activision, Inc.

Med-Lab. *Version:* 5.1. Stephen R. Krause. Jun. 1983. *Compatible Hardware:* IBM PC & compatibles. *Operating System(s) Required:* MS-DOS, PC-DOS, Foxpro. *Language(s):* Foxbase, DBASE III Plus, & DBASE IV. *Memory Required:* 640k. *General Requirements:* 40Mb hard disk. *Customer Support:* 6 months free telephone support.
Single Users. disk $1995.00.
Multi-Users. disk $1995.95.
Provides Billing & Statistical Reports for Small Medical Laboratory. Keeps Records on Diagnosis of up to 65,000 Patients & Provides History Records for 2 or More Years.
Tele Vend, Inc.

TITLE INDEX

Med-Math: Test & Practice Problem Generator, 4 disks. Dec. 1985. *Compatible Hardware:* Apple II, IBM PC. *Memory Required:* 128k.
Apple. disk $300.00, incl. user's guide (Order no.: 64-71163).
IBM. disk $300.00, incl. user's guide (Order no.: 64-71143).
Used to Create Realistic, Randomly Generated Tests & Practice Problems in 9 Areas of Medication Administration.
J. B. Lippincott Co.

Med-Sheets: With Doctor's Orders. Robert H. Geeslin. Jul. 1987. *Operating System(s) Required:* PC-DOS, MS-DOS. *Memory Required:* 640k. *General Requirements:* Hard disk, printer. *Items Included:* Software & users guide. *Customer Support:* Telephone support for one year. Custom modification available.
disk $695.00.
Full-Screen Editor to Enter Patient Data, Doctor's Orders, Comments. Prints Doctor's Orders, Med Sheets, Patient List, etc.
Robert H. Geeslin (Educational Programming).

MedAccount. Software Products International. *Compatible Hardware:* IBM PC; Sage II, Sage IV.
disk $2500.00.
manual $50.00.
Medical Billing System Capable of Supporting Multiple Office, Each with an Unlimited Number of Providers & Patient Files. Print Bills or Insurance Form at Any Time.
Datamed Research, Inc.

MedAccount. Software Products International (S. P.I.). Jan. 1984. *Operating System(s) Required:* MS-DOS. *Memory Required:* 256k. *General Requirements:* Printer, color monitor, Winchester hard disk.
$2500.00.
Medical Billing & Patient Scheduling System.
Texas Instruments, Personal Productivit.

Medallion Accounts Payable. *Version:* 6.4. (Industry Ser.). Nov. 1983. *Compatible Hardware:* IBM PC, PC XT, PC AT, PS/2, or 100% compatibles. *Operating System(s) Required:* PC-DOS, MS-DOS. *Language(s):* C. *Memory Required:* 640k. *General Requirements:* Hard disk. *Customer Support:* 90 days free.
First station. disk $990.00, incl. documentation.
Builder Accounts Payable That Accelerates Check Writing. Helps Control Cash Disbursements & Assists in Forecasting Future Cash Requirements. Reports Include: Cash Requirements Forecast, Check Register, Aging Reports, Period End Analysis Reports, 1099's & Checks. Allows Posting of Manual Checks, On-Time Transactions & Voids & Partial Payments. Integrates with Other MEDALLION/Builder Modules.
Timberline Software Corp.

Medallion Accounts Receivable. *Version:* 4.2. (Industry Ser.). Dec. 1984. *Compatible Hardware:* IBM PC, PC XT, PC AT, PS/2 or 100% compatibles. *Operating System(s) Required:* PC-DOS/MS-DOS. *Language(s):* C. *Memory Required:* 640k. *General Requirements:* Hard disk. *Customer Support:* 90 days free.
First station. disk $490.00, incl. documentation.
Builder Accounts Receivable That Helps to Monitor Cash Flow & Streamline Billing Process. Generates Statements & Mailing Labels. Reports on Delinquency Exception on Past Due, Zero Balance & Credit Balance Customers Are Available. Provides Aged Trial Balance Report & Customer Listing.
Timberline Software Corp.

Medallion Equipment Management. *Version:* 4.5. Oct. 1991. *Items Included:* Full documentation included. *Customer Support:* 90 days free support.
DOS 3.1 or higher. IBM PC AT, XT, PS/2 & 100% compatibles (512k). disk $1290.00, first station. *Nonstandard peripherals required:* Hard disk required.
Helps Make Effective Decisions Concerning Your Equipment by Tracking Repair, Maintenance & Replacement. It Also Does a Brand Name & Equipment Analysis So You Can Decide Which Brand of Equipment, If Any, Will Be Most Cost Effective for Your Company to Purchase.
Timberline Software Corp.

Medallion General Ledger. *Version:* 4.2. Nov. 1983. *Compatible Hardware:* IBM PC, PC XT, PC AT, PS/2 or 100% compatible. *Operating System(s) Required:* PC-DOS/MS-DOS. *Language(s):* C. *Memory Required:* 640k. *General Requirements:* Hard disk. *Customer Support:* 90 days free.
First station. disk $990.00, incl. documentation.
General Ledger for Construction Industry. Includes: Trial Balance, Working Trial Balance, Current Ledger, Year-to-Date Ledger, Depreciation Schedule, Balance Sheet, Profit & Loss Statement & Changes in Financial Position. Shares Data Automatically with All Other MEDALLION/Builder Modules.
Timberline Software Corp.

Medallion General Ledger Plus. *Version:* 1.9. Oct. 1988. *Compatible Hardware:* IBM PC 386 or compatible. *Operating System(s) Required:* OS/2, Windows 3.1 or higher. *Customer Support:* 90 days free.
Single-User. disk Contact vendor for price.
Provides User with Information. Ability to Organize a Chart of Accounts by Owners, Properties or Any Combination of Three Groupings Desired. Also Features Custom Financial Statements Including Columnar Reports & Partnership Reporting, with Any Number of Consolidations. Capable of Pinpointing Next Year's Expected Budget Increases.
Timberline Software Corp.

Medallion Gold Accounts Payable. Oct. 1992. *Items Included:* Complete documentation. *Customer Support:* 1 yr. telephone support & software maintenance included; 5 day training class included with purchase; on-site consulting - fee negotiable.
Windows 3.1 or higher. 386 or 486 IBM compatible PC (4Mb). Contact publisher for price. *Networks supported:* Novell.
OS/2 1.3 or higher. 386 or 486 IBM compatible PC. *Networks supported:* IBM: LAN Server, Novell.
Construction Gold AP Is a Complete Accounts Payable System, with Above-Average Capabilities. User Can Track Invoices Being Routed for Approval. Control Exactly Who Gets Paid How Much & When, & Specify Exactly What Prints on Your Checks. Construction Gold AP Provides Efficient Methods to Address All Your Needs - from Lien Waiver Processing, to Tracking Subcontractor Insurance, to Giving You the Information You Need to Handle Payment Problems.
Timberline Software Corp.

Medallion Gold General Ledger. Oct. 1992. *Items Included:* Complete documentation. *Customer Support:* 1 year telephone support & software maintenance included with product; 5 day training class included with purchase; on-site consulting - fee negotiated.
Windows 3.1 or higher. 386 or 486 IBM compatible PC (4Mb). Contact publisher for price. *Networks supported:* Novell.

MEDALLION INVENTORY

OS/2 1.3 or higher. 386 or 486 IBM compatible PC (4Mb). *Networks supported:* IBM LAN Server, Novell.
Gives You the Ultimate Flexibility You've Probably Wished for Hundreds of Times. Although Construction Gold General Ledger Comes with a Complete Chart of Accounts & Set of Financial Reports, User Can Completely Redesign, & Inquiry & Reports to Meet Your Special Requirements.
Timberline Software Corp.

Medallion Gold, Job Cost. Oct. 1992. *Items Included:* Complete documentation. *Customer Support:* 1 yr. telephone support & software maintenance also; 5 day training class included with purchase; on-site consulting - fee negotiated.
Windows 3.1 or higher. 386 or 486 IBM compatible PC (6Mb). Contact publisher for price. *Networks supported:* Novell.
OS/2 1.3 or higher. 386 or 486 IBM compatible PC (4Mb). *Networks supported:* IBM LAN Server, Novell.
Job Cost Will Give You All the Flexibility You Need to Track Revenue, Costs, Commitments & Other Job-Related Information. Construction Gold Job Cost Also Allows Each Person to Individualize the Format & Content of Their Inquiry Screens & Reports To Give Them the Information They Need to Make Profitable Decisions.
Timberline Software Corp.

Medallion Gold Payroll. Oct. 1992. *Items Included:* Complete documentation. *Customer Support:* 1 yr. telephone support & software maintenance included; 5 day training class included with purchase; on-site consulting - fee negotiated.
Windows 3.1 or higher. 386 or 486 IBM compatible PC (6Mb). Contact publisher for price. *Networks supported:* Novell.
OS/2 1.3 or higher. 386 or 486 IBM compatible PC (4Mb). *Networks supported:* IBM LAN Server, Novell.
With Construction Gold Payroll, You'll Have the Ability to Set up As Many Different Pay Deductions & Fringe Benefits As Needed. And with a Formula System Similar to Spreadsheet Software, You'll Have the Flexibility to Calculate Any Type of Pay, Deductions or Fringe You Need. Construction Gold Payroll Also Lets User Design Time Entry Grid to Match Time Sheets for More Efficient Data Entry.
Timberline Software Corp.

Medallion Gold TS Report. Oct. 1992. *Items Included:* Complete documentation. *Customer Support:* 1 yr. telephone support & software maintenance included; 5 day training class included with purchase; on-site consulting - fee negotiated.
Windows 3.1 or higher. 386 or 486 IBM compatible PC (6Mb). Contact publisher for price. *Networks supported:* Novell.
OS/2 1.3 or higher. 386 or 486 IBM compatible PC (4Mb). *Networks supported:* IBM LAN Server, Novell.
Can Be Used to Design Custom Reports Accessing Data from Any Timberline Application. Designing Reports Is As Simple As Positioning Field Where You Want Them on the Screen, Often Referred to As WYSIWYG (What You See Is What You Get). TS-Report Contains a Variety of Options to Sort. Conditions & Total Your Data.
Timberline Software Corp.

Medallion Inventory. *Version:* 2.6. Apr. 1985. *Compatible Hardware:* IBM PC, PC XT, PC AT, PS/2 or 100% compatible. *Operating System(s) Required:* PC-DOS/MS-DOS. *Language(s):* C. *Memory Required:* 640k. *General Requirements:*

Hard disk. *Customer Support:* 90 days free. First station. disk $990.00, incl. documentation. *Builder Inventory System That Gives User Up-to-the-Minute Information on All Items in Stock & on Order. Capabilities Include: Reorder Report, On-Order Report, Backorder Report, Physical Count Worksheet, Stock Valuation, Stock Status, Product Price List, Sales Analysis & Transaction Recap. User Can Distribute Transaction Entries to Accounts Receivable & General Ledger of MEDALLION/Builder Package.*
Timberline Software Corp.

Medallion Job Cost. *Version:* 10.3. Oct. 1984. *Compatible Hardware:* IBM PC, PC XT, PC AT, PS/2 or 100% compatible. *Operating System(s) Required:* PC-DOS/MS-DOS. *Language(s):* C. *Memory Required:* 640k. *General Requirements:* Hard disk.
First station. disk $2790.00, incl. documentation. *Job Costing Package Designed for Medium to Large Home builders. Accommodates an Unlimited Number of Jobs & Sends Data to Payroll, Accounts Payable, & General Ledger. Calculates Variances Based on Percent Complete or Committed Dollars (PO's) & Tracks Fixed Lot & Soft (Indirect) Costs for Each Job. Handles Retainage & Certified Payroll. Standard Reports Include: Job Profits, Budget Variance, Detailed Transaction Listing, Cost Comparison by Category, & Phase Schedule Graph.*
Timberline Software Corp.

Medallion Payroll Plus. *Version:* 3.B. Nov. 1983. *Compatible Hardware:* IBM PC, PC XT, PC AT, PS/2 or 100% compatibles. *Operating System(s) Required:* PC-DOS/MS-DOS. *Language(s):* C. *Memory Required:* 640k. *Customer Support:* 90 days free.
1st Station. disk $990.00, incl. documentation. *Builder Payroll System That Handles Pay Functions, Accommodates Departments, Unions, Tip Credits, Draws & Advances, Sick & Vacation Pay, Bonuses, Commissions, Piece Work, & Other Payroll Data in All States. An Automatic State Tax Calculator Allows for All Deductions.*
Timberline Software Corp.

Medallion Property Management Gold. *Version:* 1.0. Oct. 1988. *Compatible Hardware:* IBM PC AT, PS/2 or 100% compatible. *Operating System(s) Required:* OS/2. *Memory Required:* 2000k. *General Requirements:* Hard disk; color or monochrome monitor. *Items Included:* Property management Gold, General Ledger Plus, Accounts Payable Gold, TS Report & Starter Set. *Customer Support:* 120 days free. Single-User. 3.5" or 5.25" disk $6990.00.
Multi-User. Contact publisher for price.
Provides Property Managers Who Handle Commercial, Residential, Retail & Mixed Use Properties with Automatic Lease Escalations; Retail Sales Tracking; & Access to Tenant, Unit & Vendor Information. Features Ability to Forecast Budgets, Control Details Involved with Tenant Move-Ins/Move-Outs & Project Future Available Space. Product Interfaces with On-Site Residential & On-Site Management. The On-Site Modules Provide On-Site Managers with Ability to Manage Tenants & Process Payments at the Property Site.
Timberline Software Corp.

Medallion Starter Set. *Version:* 2.A.0. Sep. 1991. *Compatible Hardware:* IBM PC, PC XT, PC AT, PS/2 or 100% compatibles. *Operating System(s) Required:* PC-DOS/MS-DOS. *Language(s):* C. *Memory Required:* 640k. *General Requirements:* Hard disk. *Customer Support:* 90 days free.
Contact publisher for info.
Includes Installation Guide, System Software Diskette, Keyboard Diagrams, & Operating Suggestions. Required Element of the MEDALLION/BUILDER Accounting Software.
Timberline Software Corp.

Medallion TenanTrac. *Version:* 1.5. May 1986. *Compatible Hardware:* IBM PC XT, PC AT, PS/2 or 100% compatibles. *Operating System(s) Required:* MS-DOS, PC-DOS. *Language(s):* C. *Memory Required:* 640k. *Customer Support:* 90 days free.
Contact vendor for price.
Designed to Provide the Owner of One or Several Residential Properties with the Information Essential to Determine the Profitability of the Enterprise. Program Tracks up to Five Deposit Amounts for Each Tenant with the Date Received & Refunded. Automatically Generates up to Five Recurring Charges for Each Tenant & Processes Transactions Using Open Item Accounting. Reports Generated Include: Rent Roll, Vacancy Listing, Delinquency Report, Tenant Ledger, Tenant/Unit/Property Profiles, Transaction Report & Tenant Late Notices. Prints Vendor Checks & 1099's, Produces Standard Financial Statements.
Timberline Software Corp.

Medallion TS-Bridge. *Version:* 7.2. Mar. 1992. *Compatible Hardware:* IBM PC XT, PS/2 or 100% compatibles. *Operating System(s) Required:* MS-DOS, PC-DOS, UNIX. *Language(s):* C. *Memory Required:* 640k. *Customer Support:* 90 days free.
First station. Contact publisher for price.
Transfers Information from Any Medallion Program to Many Other Popular Software Packages. Reads ASCII Files to Generate Medallion Data Files. Also Includes the Ability to Sort on Any Field from Any Medallion File & User-Defined Conditional Statements with up to Five Operands. Four Types of Files Can Be Created Including Text, DIF, SYLK & ASCII.
Timberline Software Corp.

Medallion/TS-Report I. *Version:* 3.4. Nov. 1991. *Compatible Hardware:* IBM PC XT, PC AT, PS/2 or 100% compatibles. *Operating System(s) Required:* PC-DOS/MS-DOS. *Language(s):* C. *Memory Required:* 640k. *Customer Support:* 90 days free.
First station. Contact publisher for price.
Creates Reports Containing Only the Information Requested. Reports Can Be Generated Using up to Three Medallion Files. Other Features Include User-Defined Calculations, the Ability to Run Sorts on up to Five Fields at Once, Saving Report Designs for Repetitive Use & Selecting Columnar Reports or Mailing Labels. Can Be Utilized with All Modules in the Medallion Collection.
Timberline Software Corp.

Medallion/TS-Report II. *Version:* 3.3. Nov. 1991. *Compatible Hardware:* IBM PC XT, PC AT, PS/2 or 100% compatibles. *Operating System(s) Required:* PC-DOS/MS-DOS. *Language(s):* C. *Memory Required:* 640k. *Customer Support:* 90 days free.
First station. Contact publisher for price.
Custom Report Writer Which Allows the User to Pull Information from up to 5 Files from Any Medallion Collection Module (or Combination Modules) & Design a Custom, Free Form Report to the User's Specifications. Designs Can Then Be Permanently Saved for Future, Repetitive Use. Changes to Existing Report Designs Can Be Easily Made to Such Items As Report Titles, Subtitles, Column Headings & Row Names. User Can Also Print Sample Report Designs for Review Before the Final Report Is Printed.
Timberline Software Corp.

MedBill. 1993. *Items Included:* User manuals. *Customer Support:* Three days of onsite training included in price - Continental U.S. Thirty day warranty included in price. Annual maintenance fee $1,500 includes enhancements & help line.
MS-DOS. IBM or compatible 386 or 486 class microcomputers (2Mb). $7500.00 per copy; volume discount; single site multi-user license. *Optimal configuration:* Laser-jet printer; 2Mb RAM, 486 class machine; one 9600 baud modem; DOS 5.0.
Patient Accounting Application for Outpatient Settings That Interfaces with MEDSYS. Maintains Histories of Patient Charges, Payments, Billings, & Receivables; Stores Insurance Carrier Information, Daily Transactions, Procedures & Diagnostic Codes; Reports on Daily, Month-to-Date & Year-to-Date Financial Information; & Produces Insurance Carrier Forms for Filings.
Medical Office Management Systems.

MEDCAPS Plus: Credential & Planning System. *Version:* 2.0. Aug. 1991. *Compatible Hardware:* IBM PC XT & compatibles. *Operating System(s) Required:* PC-DOS/MS-DOS. *Memory Required:* 640k. *General Requirements:* 5Mb on hard disk, printer.
$995.00.
Designed to Help a Hospital Identify Its Key Physicians, Analyze Physician Usage of a Hospital Inpatient Resources, & Project Future Needs. Tracks Physician Office Locations, Educational Data, Appointment Status/Credentials Review, Affiliations, Medical Practice(s), Insurance Status, & Medical Records Status. Can Generate User-Defined Queries & Reports.
Riverdale Systems Design, Inc.

MEDFormation. *Version:* 1.8.0. *General Requirements:* 40Mb hard disk drive - 5 Mb RAM. *Customer Support:* Toll free support link.
Macintosh IIci or Si or SE-30, Quadra, Powerbook. $555.00.
add'l. users $500.00 ea.
Physician Office Management, Billing & Collection. Functions Include Word Processing & Electronic Filing.
Medformatics.

Medi/Claims. Jeff Woolf. Apr. 1986. *Compatible Hardware:* IBM PC, PC XT, PC AT. *Operating System(s) Required:* PC-DOS, MS-DOS, Concurrent DOS. *Language(s):* CBASIC. *Memory Required:* 48k. *General Requirements:* Modem. disk $250.00.
Medical Transmission System for Medicare Claims. Allows Medical Practitioners to Electronically Submit Their Claims to TransAmerica-Occidental for Payment. Includes Such Features As the Ability to Enter & Modify Procedure & Diagnostic Codes, Display All Unprocessed Claims, Change & Reverse the Status of Claims, Automatically Add in Costs for Durable Medical Expenses, Print out All Claims for Record-Keeping, Move All Completed Claims to an Easily-Accessible Back-Up Disk, & Transmit Claims to TransAmerica with the Touch of a Key.
Woolf Software Systems, Inc.

Medi-Rx: Medical Office Management for Anesthesiology. *Version:* 4.4. Aug. 1994. *Items Included:* Ring bound manual. *Customer Support:* 90 day warranty, start up training, annual maintenance agreement available.
PC-DOS/MS-DOS 3.1 or higher. IBM PS/2, 386, 486, 586 or compatibles (450k). $4850.00 base price. *Networks supported:* Novell Netware, Lantastic, Alloy Multiware (multitasking).
Contains All of the Features Contained in the Standard Medi-Rx Medical Office Management System Plus Specialized Billing for Anesthesia Related Services. Calculates & Bills Time by Time Units, Hours & Mintues, or Minutes. Other Anesthesia Related Features Include Support for CRNA's, Risk Factors, & Narrative Records.
Prose Software.

TITLE INDEX

Medi-Rx: Medical Office Management System. Version: 4.4. Aug. 1994. Compatible Hardware: IBM PS/2, 486, 586 & compatibles. Operating System(s) Required: PC-DOS/MS-DOS 3.1 or higher. Language(s): MICROFOCUS COBOL/2. Memory Required: 450k. General Requirements: Floppy disk drive, hard disk 20Mb.
disk $4850.00. Networks supported: Novell, Multi-Ware 386 (multi-tasking), Lantastic.
Comprehensive Medical Accounts Receivable Software Package Which Incorporates True Cycle Billing & Insurance Filing with Follow-Ups, on Demand Reports on Practice Statistics & Analysis, Patient Recall, Aging, Labels, Automatic Daily-Monthly-Annual Audit. Special Versions Have Been Developed for Anesthesiology, Oral Surgery, Podiatry.
Prose Software.

Medi-RX: Office Management System for Podiatry. Version: 4.4. Aug. 1994. Items Included: User manual. Customer Support: On-site training (expenses not included), 90 day warranty, annual maintenance agreement available.
DOS 3.1 or higher. IBM PS/2, 486, 586 & compatibles (640k). disk $4850.00. Networks supported: Novell, Multiware 386 (multi-tasking).
Podiatry Specific Medical Package. Podiatric Diagnosis, Procedures, Views, Bones, Joints, & Tissues Already Pre-Loaded. System Incorporates True Cycle Billing, & Insurance Filing with Follow-ups, On Demand Reports on Practice Statistics & Analysis, Patient Recall, Ageing, Labels, Daily-Monthly-Annual Audit. Statistical Reports on Practice Performance, Referring Physicians, Diagnosis, Procedures, Service Locations, etc.
Prose Software.

Medi-Rx: Oral & Maxillo Facial Office Management System. Version: 4.1. Compatible Hardware: IBM PS/2, 386, 486 & compatibles. Operating System(s) Required: PC-DOS 2.0 & higher. Language(s): MICRO FOCUS COBOL 2. Memory Required: 384k. General Requirements: 20Mb hard disk.
disk $4850.00 (Order no.: 331). Networks supported: Novell, Multi-Ware 386 (multi-user/multi-tasking).
Designed to Separate File & Manage All AMA, ADA & Workers Compensation Claims. Incorporates True Cycle Billing on Demand Reports, Aging, Daily-Monthly-Annual Audit. Easy One Step Charge & Payment Posting.
Prose Software.

Media Flow Charts. Compatible Hardware: IBM PC & compatibles.
$69.50.
Helps Advertisers, Agencies & Media Design, Calculate, & Present Media Plans. Accepts Data on the Specific Publications (Dates, Circulation, Frequency, Size & Cost) & Computes Each Item's Total Cost & the Grand Total. Produces Media-Plan Flowcharts in 5-Week, 31-Day, & 12-Month Configurations. Each Configuration Is Available Separately.
Compu-Literate.

Media Master. Items Included: Bound manual. Customer Support: Free hotline - no time limit; 30 day limited warranty; updates are $5/disk plus S&H.
MS-DOS. IBM & compatibles (256k). disk $29.95.
Osborne; Kaypro; Z-100 series. disk $29.95.
For Osborne & Kaypro Users, Many Formats Can Be Formatted, Read, & Written. For IBM & Z-100 Machines, over 75 Double-Density Formats Are Handled. MEDIA MASTER Is Simple & Very Easy to Use. In Essence, User Can Set Each of Two Drives to a Different Format. For Example, You Can Set Drive A to KAYPRO II Format & Drive B to IBM MS-DOS. Then User Can Move Files Between Those Drives at Will. Here Is the Menu of Operations You Can Perform: Copy Files; Print Directory; Display Directory; Set Drive to Specified Format; Erase Files; Format.
Dynacomp, Inc.

Medicaid Patient Billing System (MPBS). Compatible Hardware: IBM PC & compatibles. Memory Required: 256k. General Requirements: Printer.
contact publisher for price.
Patient Tracking System Allows Electronic Transfer of Medicaid Forms to McAuto Systems Group via Diskettes (with Future Plans for Telecommunications Transfer). Features Patient Registration, Medicaid Form Entry, Print Claim Report, Patient Mailing, Claim Maintenance, Appointment Scheduling & Bookkeeping.
The International Computer Shop.

Medical. CYMA Corp. Operating System(s) Required: CP/M, MS-DOS. Memory Required: 64k.
$1695.00 (Order no.: SY P/N T039-115).
Provides Patient Billing, 3rd Party Billing, Practice Analysis & Patient Recall. Automatically Generates Multiple Insurance Forms.
Texas Instruments, Personal Productivit.

Medical Accounts Receivable. Compatible Hardware: Altos, IBM PC, Tandy. Operating System(s) Required: MS-DOS, XENIX. Language(s): RM/COBOL. Memory Required: 128k.
contact publisher for price.
Designed for Medical Clinics & Individual Practices. Automatically Handles Posting & Aging of Receivables Insurance & End of Month Processing. Features Include Immediate Account Number or Patient Name Inquiry, Doctor Production Reports Generation at End of Month. On-Line Historical Data Limited Only by Disk Capacity.
Edrington Data.

Medical Application ClipArt, Vol. 1. Version: 1.0. Jun. 1988. Items Included: Manual, registration card. Customer Support: Free telephone support.
Macintosh 512KE, Plus, SE, SE/30, II, IIx, IIcx, IIci, XL, Lisa, IIfx. 2 800k 3.5" disks $89.95 (Order no.: 1010). Addl. software required: Graphic editing software recommended.
Collection of Over 100 Medically Related BitMapped Images in MacPaint Format.
MacPDS.

Medical Appointment & Billing Software. 1985. Compatible Hardware: IBM PC, PC XT, PC AT & compatibles. Operating System(s) Required: MS-DOS. Language(s): BASIC (source code included). Memory Required: 640k. General Requirements: 2 disk drives & 20Mb hard disk.
IBM PC & compatibles. disk $499.00 (Order no.: LSC-2013).
Features Scheduling, Billing, Mailing Lists, Insurance Billing, Account Statements, Patient History, Procedure Codes & Diagnosis Codes List.
Lizcon Computer Systems.

Medical Billing Accounts Receivable. Version: 3.6. Lawrence Johnson. 1981. Compatible Hardware: Apple II, II+, IIe; IBM PC & compatibles. Operating System(s) Required: Apple DOS 3.3, MS-DOS. Language(s): Applesoft BASIC, QuickBASIC (source code included). Memory Required: 64k. General Requirements: Corvus 10Mb hard disk.
$1295.00.
Medical Office Management System for Any Medical Office. Includes Insurance Forms, Aged Patient & Insurance Billing, Recall, Payroll, Inventory, Payables, & Mailing List.
Johnson Assocs. (Arizona).

Medical Billing Package. Compatible Hardware: DEC Personal Computer.
contact publisher for price.
MEGAS Corp.

Medical Billing System. Compatible Hardware: TI Professional Computer.
contact publisher for price.
Provides Medical Billing for Group Practices & for the Individual Doctor. Provides a System for Patient & Third-Party Billing, Patient Scheduling, & Report Generation.
Texas Instruments, Personal Productivit.

Medical Electronic Desktop (MacM.E.D.). Compatible Hardware: Apple Macintosh Plus. Operating System(s) Required: System 4.1 or higher. General Requirements: Hard disk.
contact publisher for price.
Patient Clinical Records Management System That Supports a Physician in All Areas of Patient Care.
Jam Technologies.

Medical HouseCall. Jan. 1994. Items Included: User manual, Human anatomy poster. Customer Support: Free customer support; 30-day satisfaction guaranteed money back warranty.
Windows 3.1 or higher. IBM & compatibles (4Mb). $79.00 plus shipping/handling (ISBN 0-9639961-0-X). Optimal configuration: VGA monitor with 10Mb of free hard disk space.
Macintosh 6.1 or higher operating system. MAC (4Mb). $79.00 plus shipping/handling (ISBN 0-9639961-1-8). Optimal configuration: 10Mb of hard disk space.
Provides Medical Information & Diagnoses for 1,100 Diseases, Major Symptoms, Medical Tests, Surgery, Drugs, Drug Interactions, Nutrition, Poisons, & Injuries. Developed in Consultation with Physicians & Healthcare Professionals at the University of Utah School of Medicine & from Around the U.S., HouseCall Is Based on the Same Expert Knowledge Found in Iliad, the Parent Technology, Used in Training Students in More Than Half the Medical Schools in the U.S. & Utilized by Thousands of Medical Students, Residents & Practicing Physicians.
Applied Informatics, Inc.

Medical Housecall. Version: 1.1. Dec. 1994. Items Included: User manual. Customer Support: Free customer support, 30 day money back guarantee.
Windows 3.1 or higher. IBM & compatibles (4Mb). disk $89.95 (ISBN 0-9639961-4-2). Optimal configuration: VGA display with 8Mb available hard disk space; 4Mb RAM, 80386 CPU or higher.
Macintosh 6.1 or higher. Mactinosh. 3.5" disk $89.95 (ISBN 0-9639961-5-0). Optimal configuration: 11Mb available hard disk space; 4Mb RAM; 68030 CPU or higher.
An Easy-to-Use Symptom Analysis Tool & Reference Guide Designed to Help You Become a More Informed Consumer of Medical Care. This Easy-to-Understand Program Can Analyze Your Symptoms & List Possible Causes. It Lists Test Options & Their Cost. It Can Help Organize the Information You Take with You to Your Doctor. And, It Can Help You Confirm Your Doctor's Diagnosis. Developed in Consultation with 40 Practicing Physicians & 13 Healthcare Professionals in 23 Medical Specialties, Trained at Prominent Institutions Including Mayo Clinic, Johns Hopkins, Harvard, Duke, & Columbia School of Medicine. It Is Updated Regularly. User Can Build Medical Records for Family, Be

Informed about Many Drug Side-Effects & Their Interactions, & Have a Central Location for Immediate Access to Emergency Information.
Applied Informatics, Inc.

Medical Housecall. Version: 1.54. Oct. 1995. *Items Included:* User Manual. *Customer Support:* Free customer support, 30 day money back guarantee.
Windows 3.1 or higher; Macintosh 6.1 or higher. IBM (4Mb). disk $59.95 (ISBN 0-9639961-9-3).
Four Products in One. First, It Provides a Comprehensive Medical Encyclopedia; Second, You Can Enter Your Symptoms & Get a List of Possible Causes; Third You Can Educate Yourself about 300,000 Different Drugs & Learn about Multiple Drug Interactions & Side Effects.
Applied Informatics, Inc.

Medical Imaging Sciences: Additional Radiographic Procedures. Mark Hagy. 1994. *Items Included:* Operating instructions & a spiral bound cover for the programs is included. *Customer Support:* Customer/technical support is available at 800-748-7734 between 7:30am & 5:00pm Central Standard Time.
DOS 3.1 or higher. IBM & compatibles (512k). 3.5" disk $150.00 (Order no.: MIS9011).
Nonstandard peripherals required: VGA.
This Program Includes Additional Procedures Other Than Those Covered in Part I of This Module, BASIC RADIOGRAPHIC PROCEDURES. Procedures Covered Include the Spine, Skull, Facial Bones, & Selected Procedures Requiring the Use of Contrast Media. The Tutorial Is Designed to Enable the Learner to Efficiently Plan & Perform Radiologic Procedures. Essential Aspects of Radiographic Anatomy Are Incorporated. The Emphasis of the Program Is on Proper Positioning & Anatomic Landmarks.
Educational Software Concepts, Inc.

Medical Imaging Sciences: Advanced Concepts Exposure - Image Quality. Steven Dowd. 1994. *Items Included:* Operating instructions & a spiral bound cover for the programs is included. *Customer Support:* Customer/technical support is available at 800-748-7734 between 7:30am & 5:00pm Central Standard Time.
DOS 3.1 or higher. IBM & compatibles (512k). 3.5" disk $150.00 (Order no.: MIS9012).
Nonstandard peripherals required: VGA.
Radiographers Must Be Able to Evaluate the Effects of Various Factors on Entrance Skin Exposure & Image Quality to Achieve a Balance Between Risk & Benefit. This Program Defines Terms Related to Exposure & Image Quality & Describes the Ways in Which the Learner Can Produce a Radiograph of Sufficient Density, with the Desired Scale of Contrast, & with Good Representation of Geometric Factors, Lack of Distortion or Magnification.
Educational Software Concepts, Inc.

Medical Imaging Sciences: Alimentary Cancer: Pathology & Treatment. Larry Swafford. 1994. *Items Included:* Operating instructions & a spiral bound cover for the programs is included. *Customer Support:* Customer/technical support is available at 800-748-7734 between 7:30am & 5:00pm Central Standard Time.
DOS 3.1 or higher. IBM & compatibles (512k). 3.5" disk $150.00 (Order no.: MIS9027).
Nonstandard peripherals required: VGA.
This Set of Programs Provides an Overview of Pathology & Treatment Principles for the Major Malignancies. Each Disease Process Is Discussed in Detail to Include Anatomy, Etiology & Epidemiology, Pathology & Histopathology, Clincial Detection & Diagnostic Method, Staging & Classification Information, Current Treatment, Therapy Techniques, As Well As Morbidity & Prognosis.
Educational Software Concepts, Inc.

Medical Imaging Sciences: Basic Radiographic Physics. Donna Shehane. 1994. *Items Included:* Operating instructions & a spiral bound cover for the programs is included. *Customer Support:* Customer/technical support is available at 800-748-7734 between 7:30am & 5:00pm Central Standard Time.
DOS 3.1 or higher. IBM & compatibles (512k). 3.5" disk $150.00 (Order no.: MIS9003).
Nonstandard peripherals required: VGA.
This Program Provides a Review of the Basic Concepts & Principles of Physics Used in the Practice of Radiography. Lessons Focus on Physical Characteristics of Matter, Electrostatics & Electrodynamics, Electromagnetism, Generators, & Transformers. Graphics of Circuits & Presentation of Forumlas Allow the Student to Practice Necessary Calculations & Applications of the Laws Described Within the Lessons.
Educational Software Concepts, Inc.

Medical Imaging Sciences: Basic Radiographic Procedures. Mark Hagy. 1994. *Items Included:* Operating instructions & a spiral bound cover for the programs is included. *Customer Support:* Customer/technical support is available at 800-748-7734 between 7:30am & 5:00pm Central Standard Time.
DOS 3.1 or higher. IBM & compatibles (512k). 3.5" disk $150.00 (Order no.: MIS9004).
Nonstandard peripherals required: VGA.
This Program Is Designed to Enable the Learner to Efficiently Plan & Perform Radiologic Procedures. The Tutorial Describes Step by Step Performance of Basic Radiiographic Procedures Including Patient Position, Part Position, Central Ray, & Evaluation Aspects. Graphics of Essential Anatomy & Clinical Examples for Each Procedure Enhance the Program.
Educational Software Concepts, Inc.

Medical Imaging Sciences: Case Studies in Ethics. Steve Dowd. 1994. *Items Included:* Operating instructions & a spiral bound cover for the programs is included. *Customer Support:* Customer/technical support is available at 800-748-7734 between 7:30am & 5:00pm Central Standard Time.
DOS 3.1 or higher. IBM & compatibles (512k). 3.5" disk $150.00 (Order no.: MIS9014).
Nonstandard peripherals required: VGA.
Ten Case Studies Are Presented to Allow the Learner to Think about the Various Ethical Possibilities & Problems That Can Emerge When One Is Faced with a Real-Life Ethical Situation. The Learner Uses a Problem-Solving Approach to Make Decisions about the Situations Described. Included Is an In-Depth Discussion of the ASRT Code of Ethics & Its Effect on the Practice of Radiography.
Educational Software Concepts, Inc.

Medical Imaging Sciences: CT Registry Preparation. Deborah Durham. 1994. *Items Included:* Operating instructions & a spiral bound cover for the programs is included. *Customer Support:* Customer/technical support is available at 800-748-7734 between 7:30am & 5:00pm Central Standard Time.
DOS 3.1 or higher. IBM & compatibles (512k). 3.5" disk $300.00 (Order no.: MIS9017).
Nonstandard peripherals required: VGA.
This Program Provides Comprehensive Preparation for the CT Certification Exam. Students Elect Whether to Answer Practice Questions or a Diagnostic Test Designed from the Content Specifications on the Actual Exam. The Program Contains over 450 Questions from Which a Unique 150 Question Test Is Prepared. Each Question Is Multiple Choice with a Comprehensive Rationale for Correct & Incorrect Answers.
Educational Software Concepts, Inc.

Medical Imaging Sciences: Ethical Decision Making. Steve Dowd & Ben Miller. 1994. *Items Included:* Operating instructions & a spiral bound cover for the programs is included. *Customer Support:* Customer/technical support is available at 800-748-7734 between 7:30am & 5:00pm Central Standard Time.
DOS 3.1 or higher. IBM & compatibles (512k). 3.5" disk $150.00 (Order no.: MIS9007).
Nonstandard peripherals required: VGA.
This Program Enhances the Moral Reasoning of the Learner by Focusing on the Process & Foundations of Ethical Decision Making. The Tutorial Explains the Components of the Patient's Bill of Rights & the ASRT Code of Ethics As Guides for Ethical Practice. The Learner Has an Opportunity to Analyze Values Related to Current Ethical Issues.
Educational Software Concepts, Inc.

Medical Imaging Sciences: Integration of Radiographic Physics. Donna Shehane. 1994. *Items Included:* Operating instructions & a spiral bound cover for the programs is included. *Cusiomer Support:* Customer/technical support is available at 800-748-7734 between 7:30am & 5:00pm Central Standard Time.
DOS 3.1 or higher. IBM & compatibles (512k). 3.5" disk $150.00 (Order no.: MIS9010).
Nonstandard peripherals required: VGA.
This Tutorial Will Integrate the Physical Principles Reviewed in BASIC RADIOGRAPHIC PHYSICS & Provide the Student with the Application of Those Principles. The Program Discusses the Electrical Circuit, Component Parts, Production of X-Rays, & X-Ray Interaction.
Educational Software Concepts, Inc.

Medical Imaging Sciences: Introduction to Patient Care for Radiological Procedures. Audrey Perry. 1994. *Items Included:* Operating instructions & a spiral bound cover for the programs is included. *Customer Support:* Customer/technical support is available at 800-748-7734 between 7:30am & 5:00pm Central Standard Time.
DOS 3.1 or higher. IBM & compatibles (512k). 3.5" disk $150.00 (Order no.: MIS9001).
Nonstandard peripherals required: VGA.
This Program Introduces the Radiologist to Essential Patient Care Activities Including Communication, Basic Patient Assessment, Vital Signs, Treatment of Anaphylactic Shock, & Common Medical Equipment. The Tutorial Employs a Variety of Clinical Situations to Aid the Student in Learning the Concepts of Each Lesson.
Educational Software Concepts, Inc.

Medical Imaging Sciences: Introduction to Radiation Biology: Theoretical Considerations. Steve Forshier. 1994. *Items Included:* Operating instructions & a spiral bound cover for the programs is included. *Customer Support:* Customer/technical support is available at 800-748-7734 between 7:30am & 5:00pm Central Standard Time.
DOS 3.1 or higher. IBM & compatibles (512k). 3.5" disk $150.00 (Order no.: MIS9019).
Nonstandard peripherals required: VGA.
This Tutorial Discusses the History of Radiobiology. Cell Biology Is Reviewed. The Physical & Biological Factors Affecting Cell Radiosensitivity Are Analyzed. Direct & Indirect Effects of Radiation Are Examined. Radiolysis of Water Is Evaluated & Irradiation of Macromolecules Is Discussed. Dose-Response Relationships Are Inspected. The Target Theory of Radiation Is Explained. Cell Survival Curves Are Analyzed.
Educational Software Concepts, Inc.

TITLE INDEX

Medical Imaging Sciences: Introduction to Radiologic Technology, Pt. 1. Ted Vanderlaan. 1994. *Items Included:* Operating instructions & a spiral bound cover for the programs is included. *Customer Support:* Customer/technical support is available at 800-748-7734 between 7:30am & 5:00pm Central Standard Time.
DOS 3.1 or higher. IBM & compatibles (512k).
   3.5" disk $150.00 (Order no.: MIS9002).
   Nonstandard peripherals required: VGA.
This Program Is Designed for the Beginning Student in Radiologic Technology or As a Review of the Basics for Other Students. The Program Defines Terminology Used by the Radiology Profession, Describes the Titles & Duties of Imaging Personnel & Briefly Discusses Some of the Basic Principles Used in the Performance of Medical Imaging.
Educational Software Concepts, Inc.

Medical Imaging Sciences: Introduction to Radiologic Technology, Pt. 2. Ted Vanderlaan. 1994. *Items Included:* Operating instructions & a spiral bound cover for the programs is included. *Customer Support:* Customer/technical support is available at 800-748-7734 between 7:30am & 5:00pm Central Standard Time.
DOS 3.1 or higher. IBM & compatibles (512k).
   3.5" disk $150.00 (Order no.: MIS9009).
   Nonstandard peripherals required: VGA.
This Program Discusses the Technical Aspects of Radiologic Technology. The Student Will Learn the Terms & Definitions Related to Exposure, Radiographic Equipment, Protection Devices, & Monitoring Badges. This Program Is Designed to Complement the First Unit in the Module, INTRODUCTION TO RADIOLOGY TECHNOLOGY.
Educational Software Concepts, Inc.

Medical Imaging Sciences: MR Registry Preparation. Deborah Durham. 1994. *Items Included:* Operating instructions & a spiral bound cover for the programs is included. *Customer Support:* Customer/technical support is available at 800-748-7734 between 7:30am & 5:00pm Central Standard Time.
DOS 3.1 or higher. IBM & compatibles (512k).
   3.5" disk $300.00 (Order no.: MIS9018).
   Nonstandard peripherals required: VGA.
This Program Provides Comprehensive Preparation for the MR Certification Exam. Students Elect Whether to Answer Practice or a Diagnostic Test Created from the Content Specifications for the Actual Exam. The Program Contains over 525 Questions from Which a Unique 175 Question Test Is Prepared. Each Question Is Multiple Choice with a Comprehensive Rationale for Correct & Incorrect Answers.
Educational Software Concepts, Inc.

Medical Imaging Sciences: Patient Care During Procedures Using Contrast Media. Audrey Perry. 1994. *Items Included:* Operating instructions & a spiral bound cover for the programs is included. *Customer Support:* Customer/technical support is available at 800-748-7734 between 7:30am & 5:00pm Central Standard Time.
DOS 3.1 or higher. IBM & compatibles (512k).
   3.5" disk $150.00 (Order no.: MIS9008).
   Nonstandard peripherals required: VGA.
This Tutorial Discusses Essential Aspects of Caring for the Patient Undergoing Diagnostic Examinations Using Contrast Media. Specific Lessons Deal with Infection Control, Aseptic Techniques, Universal Precautions, & Disease Transmission. Selected Procedures Are Described Detailing Patient Preparation, Types of Contrast Media Used, & Other Activities Performed by the Technologist.
Educational Software Concepts, Inc.

Medical Imaging Sciences: Patient Protection During Diagnostic Radiography Procedures. Steve Forshier. 1994. *Items Included:* Operating instructions & a spiral bound cover for the programs is included. *Customer Support:* Customer/technical support is available at 800-748-7734 between 7:30am & 5:00pm Central Standard Time.
DOS 3.1 or higher. IBM & compatibles (512k).
   3.5" disk $150.00 (Order no.: MIS9006).
   Nonstandard peripherals required: VGA.
This Program Introduces the Radiologic Technologist to the Concept of Patient Safety During Diagnostic Radiological Procedures, & Focuses on Methods to Reduce Patient Dose from Unnecessary Repeat Exposures. Devices for Immobilization, Beam Limitation Devices Used to Decrease Absorbed & Scattered Radiation, Filters to Decrease the Intensity of Radiation, Shielding Devices to Protect Vital Organs, & Exposure Factors to Minimize Patient Dose Are Described.
Educational Software Concepts, Inc.

Medical Imaging Sciences: Personnel Protection During Diagnostic Radiography Procedures. Steve Forshier. 1994. *Items Included:* Operating instructions & a spiral bound cover for the programs is included. *Customer Support:* Customer/technical support is available at 800-748-7734 between 7:30am & 5:00pm Central Standard Time.
DOS 3.1 or higher. IBM & compatibles (512k).
   3.5" disk $150.00 (Order no.: MIS9013).
   Nonstandard peripherals required: VGA.
A Radiographer Will Be Subjected to Chronic Low Doses of Radiation & Can Be Affected by Its Damaging Effects If Protection Measures Are Not Applied. This Program Discusses the Methods & Means of Protecting Radiographers from Exposure to Ionizing Radiation.
Educational Software Concepts, Inc.

Medical Imaging Sciences: Radiation Biology: Theoretical Considerations & Clinical Applications. Steve Forshier. 1994. *Items Included:* Operating instructions & a spiral bound cover for the programs is included. *Customer Support:* Customer/technical support is available at 800-748-7734 between 7:30am & 5:00pm Central Standard Time.
DOS 3.1 or higher. IBM & compatibles (512k).
   3.5" disk $150.00 (Order no.: MIS9020).
   Nonstandard peripherals required: VGA.
This Tutorial Discusses the Genetic & Systemic Effects of Radiation. Irradiation of the Male & Reproductive Systems Is Analyzed. Carcinogensis Is Examined. Effects of Irradiation to the Fetus Are Explained. Radiation Dangers Are Identified. The Concept of Risk Versus Benefit Is Explained. Stochastic & Nonstochastic Radiation Effects Are Examined. Methods of Applying Radiation Biology in the Clinical Environment Are Discussed.
Educational Software Concepts, Inc.

Medical Imaging Sciences: Radiation Exposure - Image Quality. Steven Dowd. 1994. *Items Included:* Operating instructions & a spiral bound cover for the programs is included. *Customer Support:* Customer/technical support is available at 800-748-7734 between 7:30am & 5:00pm Central Standard Time.
DOS 3.1 or higher. IBM & compatibles (512k).
   3.5" disk $150.00 (Order no.: MIS9005).
   Nonstandard peripherals required: VGA.
This Program Teaches Radiographers How to Evaluate the Effects of Various Technical Factors on Entrance Skin Exposure & Image Quality to Achieve a Balance Between Risk & Benefit for the Patient. The Tutorial Contains Lessons on the Uses of Filtration & Grids & Their Effects on Image Quality & Exposure. Alternate Projections Are Discussed As a Method to Enhance Image Quality & Minimize Patient Exposure. Graphics Enhance the Text by Demonstrating the Effects of Technique Selection & Other Factors on the Patient & the Film.
Educational Software Concepts, Inc.

Medical Imaging Sciences: Radiologic Technology Registry Preparation. Steven Dowd. 1994. *Items Included:* Operating instructions & a spiral bound cover for the programs is included. *Customer Support:* Customer/technical support is available at 800-748-7734 between 7:30am & 5:00pm Central Standard Time.
DOS 3.1 or higher. IBM & compatibles (512k).
   3.5" disk $300.00 (Order no.: MIS9016).
   Nonstandard peripherals required: VGA.
This Program Provides Comprehensive Preparation for the ARRT Examination. Students Elect Whether to Answer Practice Questions or a Diagnostic Test from the Content Areas As Specified by the Actual Exam. The Program Contains over 650 Questions from Which a Unique 200 Question Test Is Prepared. Each Question Is Multiple Choice with a Comprehensive Annotated Rationale for Correct & Incorrect Answers.
Educational Software Concepts, Inc.

Medical Imaging Sciences: Radiologic Technology Test Bank & Test Generator. Donna Shehane & Ted Vanderlaan. 1994. *Items Included:* Operating instructions & a spiral bound cover for the programs is included. *Customer Support:* Customer/technical support is available at 800-748-7734 between 7:30am & 5:00pm Central Standard Time.
DOS 3.1 or higher. IBM & compatibles (512k).
   3.5" disk $350.00 (Order no.: MIS9015).
   Nonstandard peripherals required: VGA.
This Test Bank Contains a Pool of over 1000 Questions Keyed to the 5 Content Areas on the Certification Examination. The Test Generator Function Allows the Instructor to Select, Add to, or Edit Existing Questions Before Printing a Test. An Answer Key Is Printed to Correlate to the Selected Questions. Tests May Be Created, Named & Printed, or Saved on the Hard Drive for Future Use.
Educational Software Concepts, Inc.

Medical Insurance Form Writer. Version: 2. *Compatible Hardware:* Apple II+, IIc, IIe; Franklin Ace; IBM PC, PC XT, PC AT. *Operating System(s) Required:* Apple DOS 3.3, MS-DOS 3.1. *Language(s):* BASIC. *Memory Required:* Apple 48k, IBM 256k.
disk $100.00.
Word Processing Program for Universal/AMA 1500 Medical Forms. Does Billing, Prints Forms, Edits, Saves to Disk, & Speeds Forms Processing by 60%. Unlimited Number of Patients.
Andent, Inc.

Medical Laboratory Management Software. *Compatible Hardware:* IBM PC, PC XT, PC AT & compatibles. *Memory Required:* 640k. *General Requirements:* 20Mb hard disk, printer.
disk $499.00 (Order no.: LCS-2028).
Capable of Keeping Track of Patients, Carriers & Physician/Facilities Informations. Features Daily Report & Summary of Transactions of Providers. Generates Lists of Complete Blood Count (CBC) Test, Urinalysis, SMA, Procedure Codes, Patients, Providers, Carriers & Patients Admittance. Features Laboratory Results Printouts; Generates Receipts for Billing & Statement of Accounts. Provides Third Party/Insurance Billing.
Lizcon Computer Systems.

Medical Laboratory Sciences: Erythrocyte Morphology & Inclusions. Cindy Handley. 1994. *Items Included:* Operating instructions & a spiral bound cover for the programs is included.

MEDICAL LABORATORY SCIENCES:

Customer Support: Customer/technical support is available at 800-748-7734 between 7:30am & 5:00pm Central Standard Time.
DOS 3.1 or higher. IBM & compatibles (512k). 3.5" disk $175.00 (Order no.: MLS7006).
Nonstandard peripherals required: VGA.
This Tutorial Describes & Depicts Normal & Abnormal Erythrocyte Morphology. It Also Instructs the Learner to Match the Abnormal Morphology with Common Clinical Disorders Using a Case Study Approach. Erythrocyte Inclusions Are Discussed & Related to Their Associated Disease States.
Educational Software Concepts, Inc.

Medical Laboratory Sciences: Essential Concepts in Immunology. Abraham Furman. 1994. *Items Included:* Operating instructions & a spiral bound cover for the programs is included.
Customer Support: Customer/technical support is available at 800-748-7734 between 7:30am & 5:00pm Central Standard Time.
DOS 3.1 or higher. IBM & compatibles (512k). 3.5" disk $175.00 (Order no.: MLS7009).
Nonstandard peripherals required: VGA.
This Tutorial Describes the Mechanisms & Attributes of the Immune System. The Categories & Types of Immunity Are Discussed As Are Function of the Cells Involved, Including Phagocytosis. The Program Describes Characteristics of Humoral & Cellular Immunity.
Educational Software Concepts, Inc.

Medical Laboratory Sciences: Ethical Dilemmas: Approaches to Resolution. George Fritsma & Steven Dowd. 1994. *Items Included:* Operating instructions & a spiral bound cover for the programs is included. *Customer Support:* Customer/technical support is available at 800-748-7734 between 7:30am & 5:00pm Central Standard Time.
DOS 3.1 or higher. IBM & compatibles (512k). 3.5" disk $175.00 (Order no.: MLS7004).
Nonstandard peripherals required: VGA.
This Tutorial Enhances the Ethical Decision Making Capability of the Learner by Focusing on the Process & Foundations of Ethical Decision Making. The Program Explains the Components of the Patient's Bill of Rights & the ASCLS Code of Ethics As Guides for Professional & Ethical Practice.
Educational Software Concepts, Inc.

Medical Laboratory Sciences: Ethical Dilemmas: Case Studies. George Fritsma & Steven Dowd. 1994. *Items Included:* Operating instructions & a spiral bound cover for the programs is included. *Customer Support:* Customer/technical support is available at 800-748-7734 between 7:30am & 5:00pm Central Standard Time.
DOS 3.1 or higher. IBM & compatibles (512k). 3.5" disk $175.00 (Order no.: MLS7013).
Nonstandard peripherals required: VGA.
Twelve Case Studies Are Presented to Allow the Learner to Contemplate the Various Ethical Possibilities & Problems That Can Emerge in a Medical Laboratory Setting. The Learner Uses a Problem-Solving Approach to Make Decisions Concerning the Situations Described.
Educational Software Concepts, Inc.

Medical Laboratory Sciences: Guidelines for Laboratory Safety. Anne B. O'Neil. 1994. *Items Included:* Operating instructions & a spiral bound cover for the programs is included.
Customer Support: Customer/technical support is available at 800-748-7734 between 7:30am & 5:00pm Central Standard Time.
DOS 3.1 or higher. IBM & compatibles (512k). 3.5" disk $200.00 (Order no.: MLS7002).
Nonstandard peripherals required: VGA.
This Tutorial Focuses on Basic Safety Information & Procedures Essential for the Clinical Laboratory Scientist. Lessons Describe Electrical Safety, Biohazards, Chemical Safety, Contaminated Waste Disposal, & Outlines Guidelines for the Maintenance of a Safe Laboratory Area.
Educational Software Concepts, Inc.

Medical Laboratory Sciences: Laboratory Math: Solution Concentrations. Barb Feilmeier. 1994. *Items Included:* Operating instructions & a spiral bound cover for the programs is included.
Customer Support: Customer/technical support is available at 800-748-7734 between 7:30am & 5:00pm Central Standard Time.
DOS 3.1 or higher. IBM & compatibles (512k). 3.5" disk $175.00 (Order no.: MLS7001).
Nonstandard peripherals required: VGA.
This Tutorial Is Designed to Define Laboratory Solution Terminology & to Illustrate the Necessary Steps for Preparing a Percent, Molar, & Normal Solution. The Learner Will Be Able to Make a Solution from Solute & Solvents, & to Make a Solution from a More Concentrated Solution. Clinical Problems Are Used to Enhance Calculation Skills.
Educational Software Concepts, Inc.

Medical Laboratory Sciences: Leukemia: A Primer for Laboratory Scientists. Cheryl Goodwin. 1994. *Items Included:* Operating instructions & a spiral bound cover for the programs is included. *Customer Support:* Customer/technical support is available at 800-748-7734 between 7:30am & 5:00pm Central Standard Time.
DOS 3.1 or higher. IBM & compatibles (512k). 3.5" disk $175.00 (Order no.: MLS7005).
Nonstandard peripherals required: VGA.
This Unit Is Designed for the Clinical Laboratory Scientist with a Basic Knowledge of Normal White Cell Morphology & Who Is Now Ready to Begin a Basic Study of Leukemia. The Tutorial Defines Terminology Used in the Clinical Setting, Describes the Disease Process, Outlines Laboratory Procedures Utilized in the Diagnositc Process, & Correlates Data to Disease.
Educational Software Concepts, Inc.

Medical Laboratory Sciences: Principles of Therapeutic Drug Monitoring. Brenda Pinkerman. 1994. *Items Included:* Operating instructions & a spiral bound cover for the programs is included. *Customer Support:* Customer/technical support is available at 800-748-7734 between 7:30am & 5:00pm Central Standard Time.
DOS 3.1 or higher. IBM & compatibles (512k). 3.5" disk $175.00 (Order no.: MLS7008).
Nonstandard peripherals required: VGA.
This Tutorial Dicusses the Principles & Purposes of Therapeutic Drug Monitoring As a Diagnostic & Treatment Tool for Health Care Professionals. The Program Describes Criteria Used for the Selection of Drugs for Therapeutic Drug Monitoring & Emphasizes Its Importance in the Clinical Management of a Patient.
Educational Software Concepts, Inc.

Medical Laboratory Sciences: Renal Function & Routine Urinalysis. Phyllis Pacifico. 1994. *Items Included:* Operating instructions & a spiral bound cover for the programs is included.
Customer Support: Customer/technical support is available at 800-748-7734 between 7:30am & 5:00pm Central Standard Time.
DOS 3.1 or higher. IBM & compatibles (512k). 3.5" disk $175.00 (Order no.: MLS7003).
Nonstandard peripherals required: VGA.
This Tutorial Describes the Basic Anatomy & Physiology of the Urinary System & Discusses the Processes Involved in Urine Formation, Collection, & Evaluation. The Performance of the Urinalysis Is Described As Are the Normals & Abnormals Seen on the Examination.
Educational Software Concepts, Inc.

Medical Laboratory Sciences: The Plasma Coagulation System. George Fritsma. 1994. *Items Included:* Operating instructions & a spiral bound cover for the programs is included.
Customer Support: Customer/technical support is available at 800-748-7734 between 7:30am & 5:00pm Central Standard Time.
DOS 3.1 or higher. IBM & compatibles (512k). 3.5" disk $175.00 (Order no.: MLS7007).
Nonstandard peripherals required: VGA.
This Tutorial Depicts & Describes the Plasma Coagulation System, Its Components & Functions. Multiple Tables & Graphics of All Processes Are Included to Provide the Learner with a Thorough Understanding of the Steps Involved in the Pathway.
Educational Software Concepts, Inc.

Medical Laboratory-Third Party Billing & Accounts Receivable Package. *Compatible Hardware:* DECMate II, DECmate III, PDP 11-23. *Operating System(s) Required:* COS-310, MICRO-RSX. *Language(s):* DIBOL-83. $5000.00, incl. user's guide (Order no.: 85-10).
Designed for Any Medical Laboratory Which Must Keep a Medical Log Book & Invoice Private, Welfare, & Third Party Insurers. Records All Test Results by Patient & Physician & Keeps a Separate Log Book of Positive Tests. Print up to Ten Different Kinds of Invoices for Private Patients, Welfare Patients, Blue Cross & Other Common Insurers. Provides Receivable Accounting for Both Providers & Patients. Print Unpaid Patient Statements at Any Time. One Write Entry for Billing & Test Results.
Corporate Consulting Co.

The Medical Manager. *Version:* 8.0. Sep. 1993. *Compatible Hardware:* Altos, IBM PC & compatibles, 286 & 386 machines, UNIX. *Operating System(s) Required:* AIX, Novell, OS/2, PC-DOS/MS-DOS, PC-NET, UNIX, XENIX. *Language(s):* CB80, CB86, C. *Memory Required:* 640k. *General Requirements:* Hard disk, 132-column printer. *Customer Support:* Provided by reseller.
contact publisher for price.
Features Include Accounts Receivable, Insurance Billing, Appointment Scheduling, Nine User-Defined Files of Clinical History, First & Second Notices for Recalls, Referring Doctor Information, Hospital Rounds, & Diagnosis & Procedure History. Tracks Write Offs, Refunds, Unapplied Credits, & Settlements & Allows up to 40 User-Defined Adjustments. A Custom Forms Generator Provides Formatting of Insurance Forms, Encounter Forms, Superbills, Patient Statements, & Recall Notices to Doctors in a Practice. An Optional Electronic Claims Module Allows Paperless Report Generator That Can Provide the User with Virtually Any Report Desired. Program Also Includes a Data Merge Option Network, a Feature Which Allows User to Import & Export Data Between a Physician's Office & Hospitals, Laboratories & Insurance Carriers.
Systems Plus, Inc.

The Medical Manager. *Version:* 8.0.
IBM PCs & compatibles (386 & 486 machines). Contact publisher for price.
UNIX-based version runs on: Bull DPX-2, Motorola MultiPersonal Computer (88k), IBM RISC System/6000; PS/2 under Santa Cruz Operation operating systems, NCR Tower 32/400, 600, 650, 850, Data General AViiON, HP 900 Series 800 & others, Altos Series 1000, 2000, Unisys S/Series. Contact publisher for price.
Provides Complete Accounts Receivable, Insurance Billing, Office Management & Appointment Scheduling Capabilities. It Also Maintains Detailed Clinical, Procedure, Diagnosis & Financial Histories. Also Maintains Hospital

TITLE INDEX

Rounds & Referring Physician Information. Optional Features Include a Laboratory Interface; Electronic Data Interchange (EDI) Interface; Automated Collections; Managed Care Plan Management; Electronic Claims Billing; Electronic Remittance; UB Billing; HMO Tracking; & a Hospital-Physician Network. More Than 150 Reports Are Provided; Customized Reports Are Created with an Optional Custom Report Generator.
Systems Plus, Inc.

Medical Office Management. Compatible Hardware: IBM PC, TRS-80, Zenith.
contact publisher for price.
American Systems Development.

Medical Office Management I. Compatible Hardware: Apple II. Operating System(s) Required: Apple DOS 3.3. Memory Required: 48k. General Requirements: 2 to 4 disk drives.
disk $595.95.
demo disk $100.00.
manual $50.00.
source code avail.
Maintains Patient General Information Files, Appointment Schedules & a Daily Transaction Log, & Prints Private Patient Bills & Insurance Claim Forms. Provides for 10,000 Active Patients & Schedules up to 19,000 Appointments. Handles up to 190 Patients per Physician per Day with up to 250 Transactions. Maintains Past Due Accounts.
CMA Micro Computer.

Medical Office Management II. Compatible Hardware: Apple with Applesoft. Operating System(s) Required: Apple DOS 3.3. Memory Required: 48k. General Requirements: 2 to 4 disk drives, 132-column printer.
disk $795.95 (Order no.: D-074).
preview documentation $50.00.
source code avail.
demo disk $100.00.
Administrative Package with Such Features As Appointment Scheduling, Private Patient Accounts Receivable & AMA Universal Claim Form Preparation. Also Includes Patient Recall System to Improve Checkup Management in Appropriate Practices.
CMA Micro Computer.

Medical Office Management IIc. Compatible Hardware: Apple II, II+. Operating System(s) Required: Apple DOS 3.3. Language(s): Applesoft BASIC, Pascal. Memory Required: 48-64k. General Requirements: Corvus hard disk, 132-column printer.
disk $1995.95.
preview manual $50.00.
source code avail.
demo disk $100.00.
Management System Designed to Operate on the Corvus Systems Hard Disk. Features: Full Patient Registration, Appointment Management, Private Patient Billing, Medical Diagnostic Records Management & Third Party Claims Form Preparation Systems.
CMA Micro Computer.

Medical Office Management III H. Compatible Hardware: Apple III. Language(s): BASIC. Memory Required: 256k. General Requirements: Hard disk.
disk $1595.95 (Order no.: D-084).
disk preview documentation $50.00.
source code avail.
demo disk $100.00.
Designed to Handle Appointment Scheduling, Private Patient Billing, Superbill Preparation, General Patient Recall & Third Party Claims Form Preparation for the Medium-Sized Office.
CMA Micro Computer.

Medical Office Management PC. Compatible Hardware: IBM PC & compatibles. Operating System(s) Required: PC-DOS/MS-DOS. Memory Required: 128k. General Requirements: 2 disk drives.
disk $595.95.
manual $50.00.
demo disk $100.00.
source code avail.
Designed to Handle Medical Accounts Receivable, Claim Form Preparation & Appointment Scheduling for Medical Offices with up to Ten Practitioners or Specialists. Can Calculate Patient Billing on Either a Cash Only Basis or on a Partial Payment Basis As Well As Generate Patient Bills & Financial Reports. Also Features a Patient Recall Management System.
CMA Micro Computer.

Medical Office Management PCH. Compatible Hardware: IBM PC, PC XT. Operating System(s) Required: PC-DOS. Memory Required: 128k. General Requirements: Hard disk, 132-column printer.
disk $1595.95 (Order no.: D-107).
preview manual $50.00.
disk demo disk $100.00 (Order no.: D-113).
source code avail.
Private Billing Element That Allows the Time of Service Billing of Patients on Either a Cash Only or Partial Payment Basis. Extended Billing Includes Monthly Bill Printing, Account Review with Up-to-the-Moment Transaction Reporting, & Special Group Billing at Different Times During the Month. Daily Transactions Are Printed to a Daily Log along with Accounting & Fee Productivity Analyses Listed by Doctor. Designed to Meet the Operating Requirements of the General Practitioner & the Specialist.
CMA Micro Computer.

Medical Office Management PCHE. Compatible Hardware: IBM PC, PC XT & compatibles. Language(s): BASIC. Memory Required: 128k.
disk $1995.95.
demo disk $100.00.
manual $50.00.
source code avail.
Designed to Eliminate Disk Swapping & Expand Storage Capacity Through the Use of the Hard Disk System. Allows User to Manage up to 18,000 Patients. In Addition to the Billing Element, the Claim Form Preparation Element, & the Appointment Management Element, the Program Contains a Customized Backup Program to Help Protect Valuable Data. Can Also Be Operated in Conjunction with Any Other Applications the User May Currently Be Using on a Hard Disk System.
CMA Micro Computer.

Medical Office Management System. Version: 450.3. 1981. Compatible Hardware: IBM PC & compatibles. Operating System(s) Required: MS-DOS, PC-DOS. Language(s): QuickBASIC. Memory Required: 512k. General Requirements: Hard disk. Items Included: System diskettes, users guide, training tutorial. Customer Support: Telephone; annual contracts available.
$1995.00 to $2495.00.
Designed for Sole Practitioners or Small Clinics with Several Doctors. Productivity Reports Are Prepared for Each Doctor & Consolidated Reports for Practice. Systems Uses ICDA, CPT or RSV Codes to Itemize Patient Statements, Maintain Patient History, & Print Insurance Forms. Handles AMA, Blue Cross/Blue Shield, Medicare, CHAMPUS, & 1500 Forms. Custom Form Generator for Others. Accounts Receivable Module Uses Open Item & Balance Forward Methods. Prints Statements & Aged Trial Balance for Each Doctor. Uses Walk-Out Statements or Mail Statements to Head of Household. Office Scheduling Module Tracks Appointments & Open

MEDICAL ONE: MEDICAL OFFICE

Time for Each Doctor. Schedules up to Six Patients Per Time Slot. Appointment Times Variable from 5 to 30 Minutes. Supports up to 50 Doctors. Interfaces with IMS General Ledger. Runs Single User or Multi-User on Many Networks.
International Micro Systems, Inc.

Medical Office Scheduler. Version: 2.0a. 1993. Items Included: Complete instructions in 3-ring binder. Customer Support: Unlimited telephone support no charge; free replacement of damaged disks.
MS-DOS. IBM PC, XT, AT, PS/2 & compatibles (512k). disk $249.00; Network Version $899.00 (Order no.: MSCHED).
Forget about Appointment Books, Erasing, Rewriting, Whiting Out, & Filling In. Do it the Easy Way. "Preset" your Appointment Times (Change Them If Necessary) then just Type in the Name, Etc. of the Patient(s) to be Seen in that Time Slot. Time Slots may be Lengthened as Needed. Use Different Codes for Different Doctors. Highlight a Patient Name. Examine any Details that Might have been Entered for that Patient: Complaint, Tests to be Taken, Records to Have Available, Etc. Print the Day's SCHEDULE by Time or by Doctor. Print REMINDER Slips to Mail or Hand to Patients. SEARCH by Patient Name, Doctor, Date or Day. Print, REPORTS & Summaries. Print a List of Visits for a Specific Patient for a Specific Period of Time. Print a Weekly or Monthly List of Patients Seen by a Specific Doctor. At the End of a Time Period (Your Choice) Purge the Data Base of All Records from a Certain Period of Time. Enter the Days a Physician will be Away or Late.
p.r.n. medical software.

Medical Office System: MOS. Nov. 1985. Compatible Hardware: AT&T, DEC, IBM PC, Tandy, UNISYS, NCR, Hewlett Packard. Operating System(s) Required: MS-DOS, PC-DOS, UNIX, XENIX. Language(s): C & Assembly. Memory Required: MS-DOS 512k; UNIX & XENIX 768k.
contact publisher for price.
demo disk by modem avail.
Menu-Driven System for Collecting & Managing Accounts Receivable & the Patient Records of More Than 100,000 Patients. Provides Group Practices, As Well As Individual Practitioners, with the Ability to View, Add or Modify Patient Records, Billing Records, Diagnoses, Procedures, Physicians, Locations, Insurance Companies & Other Necessary Information. Other Options Include the Preparation of Insurance Forms & Monthly Statements Automatically.
Small Computer Co., Inc.

Medical One: Medical Office Management System. Items Included: Full manual. No other products required. Customer Support: Free telephone support - no time limit. 30 day warranty.
MS-DOS 3.2 or higher. IBM & compatibles (512k). $29.95 introductory version (100 patient limit); $379.95 full version (99,999 patient limit); $649.95 full version with Networking. Optimal configuration: IBM, MS-DOS 3.3 or higher, 640k RAM, hard disk & any 80-column (or wider) dot matrix printer.
Can Handle an Entire Practice Having up to 100 Physicians. Up to 99,999 Accounts Can Be Set up under a Variety of Conditions, Such As Taxable/Nontaxable, Budget Plan, Discount, No Statement, & Financing. There Can Be up to 100 Patients per Account. Includes 144-Page Bound Manual.
Dynacomp, Inc.

Medical One: Medical Office Management System. 1992. *Items Included:* Detailed manuals included with all Dynacomp products. *Customer Support:* Free telephone support to original customer - no time limit; 30 day limited warranty. MS-DOS 3.2 or higher. IBM PC & compatibles (512k). $29.95 Introductory Version (100 patient limit); $379.95 Full Version (99,999 patient limit); $649.95 Full Version with Networking (Add $5.00 for 3 1/2" format; 5 1/4" format standard). *Optimal configuration:* IBM, MS-DOS 3.3 or higher, 640k RAM, a hard disk, & any 80-column or wider dot matrix printer.
Up to 99,999 Accounts Can Be Set up under a Variety of Conditions, Such As Taxable/ Nontaxable, Budget Plan, Discount, No Statement, & Financing. There Can Be up to 100 Patients per Account. Reports Available Include Daily Charges, Daily Receipts, Month-to-Date Recap, General Ledger Detail & Summary, Aged Accounts, Statements, Patient Profiles, & Much More. Includes a 144-Page Bound Manual.
Dynacomp, Inc.

Medical Practice Management. Fisher Business Systems, Inc. *Operating System(s) Required:* MS-DOS. *Memory Required:* 128k. *General Requirements:* Printer.
$2500.00.
Facilitates the Processing of Insurance Forms, Schedules Patients, Collects Accounts Receivable & Analyzes the Nature of the Practice.
Texas Instruments, Personal Productivit.

Medical Practice Management System.
Compatible Hardware: IBM PC, PC XT. *Operating System(s) Required:* PC-DOS. *Language(s):* C. *Memory Required:* 128k. *General Requirements:* 2 disk drives, 5-10Mb on hard disk, printer.
$3500.00.
with Integrated Financials $5000.00.
Features Record Keeping, Billing, Accounts Receivable, Patient Scheduling, Insurance Form Preparation, Payroll, Accounts Payable, General Ledger, & Practice Analysis.
Fisher Business Systems, Inc.

Medical Practice Management System.
Professional Software Associates, Inc. *Operating System(s) Required:* UCSD p-System. *Memory Required:* 128k. *General Requirements:* Printer, Winchester hard disk.
$2995.00.
Generates Various Reports, Statements & Insurance Forms, & Recalls & Maintains Complete Detail As Long As Desired.
Texas Instruments, Personal Productivit.

Medical Record Release of Information Manager. *Version:* 2.0. Fred Levit. 1985. *Compatible Hardware:* IBM PC & compatibles, PC XT, PC AT. *Operating System(s) Required:* MS-DOS, PC-DOS. *Language(s):* C-BASIC. *Memory Required:* 256k. *Items Included:* Tutorial manual, program diskettes. *Customer Support:* Hotline.
$3595.00.
Manages the "Release of Information" Function for a Medical Record Department with or Without the Use of Outside Copying Services. Keeps Track of Records Copied & Copies Sent, Generates Bills, & Monitors Payments.
MIPS, Inc.

Medical Record Tracker. *Version:* 2. Fred Levit. 1985. *Compatible Hardware:* IBM PC & compatibles, PC XT, PC AT. *Language(s):* CBASIC. *Memory Required:* 256k. *Items Included:* Tutorial manual, program diskettes. *Customer Support:* Hotline.
disk $2495.00.
Keeps Track of Current Location of All Medical Records Checked Out from the Medical Record Department. Automatically Prints Deliquent Letters for Charts Not Returned Within a Specified Number of Days. Prints Lists of Records Currently Checked Out to Each Possible Location & Physician. Full Barcode Support & Deficiency Tracking Are Optionally Available.
MIPS, Inc.

Medical Terminology: General Terms. 1986. *Compatible Hardware:* Apple IIe, IIc. *Memory Required:* 64k. *General Requirements:* Printer.
disk $125.00 (Order no.: MT0000).
Designed for Students & Paraprofessionals in Any Health-Related Field That Requires Familiarity with General Medical Terminology. A Combination Tutorial & Drill System Provides Students with Repeated Exposure to Medical Terms in an Environment That Motivates by Assuring a High Degree of Success As They Proceed.
Educulture, Inc.

Medicard. *Compatible Hardware:* Apple II, II+, IIe, III; IBM PC & compatibles. *Operating System(s) Required:* Apple DOS 3.3, PC-DOS. (source code included). *Memory Required:* Apple 64k, IBM 96k. *General Requirements:* Printer.
Apple II. disk $199.95 (Order no.: D-102).
IBM PC. disk $199.95 (Order no.: D-103).
Apple III. disk $199.95 (Order no.: D-104).
demo disk $100.00.
manual $50.00.
Designed for Use in Small Medical Practice & Allows Users to Produce Professional Looking Private Patient Bills & Print the Universal AMA Claim Form.
CMA Micro Computer.

Medicine Monitor. Darwin Dennison. Sep. 1992. *Items Included:* User's manual. *Customer Support:* Free technical support, 10-day money-back guarantee, telephone support.
Macintosh (1Mb). Contact publisher for price.
Nonstandard peripherals required: Hard drive.
Optimal configuration: Macintosh with hard drive, 1Mb memory, 2Mb hard disk space.
Networks supported: Ethernet, AppleTalk.
Keep Track of the Prescription & Over-the-Counter Medicines You Are Taking & Become Aware of the Possible Health Problems Which May Be Caused by an Alcohol/Drug or Food/ Drug Interaction. Learn How Different Drugs Affect Your Nutritional Needs. Features Include a 620 Plus Drug Database, a Personalized Medicine-Taking Schedule & Food Frequency Analysis.
DINE Systems, Inc.

Medicolegal & Psychological Aspects of Patient Care. Ann M. Steves. 1996. *Customer Support:* Phone support by calling 1-800-748-7734 or 913-441-2881.
DOS 3.1 or higher. IBM or compatibles (512k).
disk $150.00 (Order no.: MIS9037).
Nonstandard peripherals required: VGA.
The special procedures technologist comes into contact with the very sickest patients under circumstances that are both frightening to the patient & allow no room for error by the health care team. Using legal cases to illustrate topics, this program guides the learner through the maze of concepts & terms asociated with tort law & medical malpractice.
Educational Software Concepts, Inc.

MediMac. *Version:* 3.9.3. Dec. 1995. *Compatible Hardware:* All Apple Macintosh. *Language(s):* Assembler, C & Pascal - combination. *Memory Required:* Minimum of 4000k. *General Requirements:* Minimum of 40Mb hard disk, Laser writer. *Items Included:* All software, standard insurance form files, fee files, all user manuals. *Customer Support:* 90 days free initial support; 1 year Technical Support/Enhancement Contract, $795.00 - single user; $995.00 - network user. Toll Free: 800-888-4344, Fax: 402-489-6411.
$2495.00 & up, single user.
network $5895.00.
Management System Designed for the Physician's Office.
HealthCare Communications.

Medina Spelling Dictionary. *Compatible Hardware:* Apple Macintosh. *General Requirements:* External disk drive, Microsoft Word. *Items Included:* Disk & manual in both English & Spanish. *Customer Support:* Complete telephone support, 90-day warranty.
3.5" disk $16.95.
demo disk $5.00.
Medical, Religious & Technical Spelling Dictionary.
Medina Software, Inc.

Mediplan Input Screens. *Compatible Hardware:* Altos Series 5-15D, Series 5-5D, 580-XX, ACS8000-XX; IBM PC with 2 disk drives, PC XT, IBM compatibles; Xerox 820 with 2 disk drives; ZILOG MCZ-250. *Operating System(s) Required:* CP/M, MP/M, PC-DOS, MS-DOS.
contact publisher for price (Order no.: MEDIPLAN INPUT SCREENS).
Simplifies Data Entry for Cost Reimbursement Reports. Front-End Package for MEDPLAN, Coopers' Time-Sharing Program on the GE Time-Sharing Network. Also Available As a Stand-Alone, In-House System That Runs on Any Large IBM Mainframe.
Coopers & Lybrand.

MEDLINE Core Journals CD-ROM Database. Oct. 1987.
MS Windows 3.1 or higher. IBM & compatibles (4Mb). CD-ROM disk $495.00-$1095.00; Networks $1995.00 & up. *Nonstandard peripherals required:* Magnetic or CD-ROM, using ISO 9660. *Optimal configuration:* IBM & compatibles, 80386 or higher, 4Mb RAM, 20Mb hard disk, mouse, MS Windows 3.1 or higher.
System 6.0.7 or higher. Apple Macintosh (3Mb). CD-ROM disk $495.00-$1095.00; Networks $1995.00 & up. *Optimal configuration:* Apple Macintosh Plus or higher, 3Mb RAM, System 6. 0.7 or higher.
Core Journals MEDLINE Is an Electronic Reference Database to the Primary Clinical Medical Journal Literature. Clinically-Oriented Excerpts (Including Abstracts) from More Than 360 Journals Indexed in the National Library of Medicine's MEDLINE Database Are Distributed on CD-ROM (Compact Disc, Read-Only Memory) Optical Disc. Knowledge Finder Search-&-Retrieval Software Makes Searching of the Core Journals MEDLINE Database Easy, Effective & Fast. After the User Types a Phrase or Sentence Describing the Information Needed, It selects the References in the Database That Appear to Best Match the Request, & Presents Them in Order of likely relevance. The Core Journals MEDLINE Database Covers the Most Recent Five or Ten Publication Years.
Aries Systems Corp.

Medline Knowledge Finder. *Compatible Hardware:* Apple Macintosh; IBM PC & compatibles. *General Requirements:* External disk drive or hard disk; Compatible CD-ROM drive; Compatible printer.
$325.00 to $3695.00.
Searches Subsets of the National Library of Medicine's MEDLINE Database (Distributed on CD-ROM Optical Disk).
Aries Systems Corp.

TITLE INDEX

Medline Knowledge Server. *Compatible Hardware:* Apple Macintosh; IBM PC & compatibles. *General Requirements:* Compatible CD-ROM player, Network support.
CD-ROM disk $1995.00 to $3695.00.
CD-ROM disk annual subscription.
Database of Citations to the Biomedical Literature Maintained by the National Library of Medicine, U.S. Department of Health & Human Sciences. Contains Citations to More Than 3,700 Medical Journals. Portions of the Database Are Selectively Extracted for Publication on CD-ROM. Provides Access to the Medline CD-ROM Databases Across Local-Area Networks. One or More Database Servers Can Be Accessed by Any Compatible Macintosh Workstation Connected to the Network. Up to Six CD-ROM Players May Be Connected to a Single Database Server, & a Virtually Unlimited Number of Servers May Be Configured on One or More Interconnected Networks.
Aries Systems Corp.

MEDLINE Unabridged CD-ROM Database. Mar. 1988.
MS Windows 3.1 or higher. IBM & compatibles (4Mb). CD-ROM disk $695.00-$2790.00; Networks $2195.00 & up. *Nonstandard peripherals required:* Magnetic or CD-ROM, using ISO 9660. *Optimal configuration:* IBM & compatibles, 80386 or higher, 4Mb RAM, 20Mb hard disk, mouse, MS Windows 3.1 or higher.
System 6.0.7 or higher. Apple Macintosh (3Mb). CD-ROM disk $695.00-$2790.00; Networks $2195.00 & up. *Optimal configuration:* Apple Macintosh Plus or higher, 3Mb RAM, System 6.0.7 or higher.
Unabridged MEDLINE Is an Electronic Reference Database to the World's Important Biomedical Journal Literature. Covering Approximately 3,700 Journals from Around the World, It Draws from the National Library of Medicine's MEDLINE Database. The Electronic Database Is Distributed on CD-ROM (Compact Disc, Read-Only Memory) Optical Disc. Knowledge Finder Search-&-Retrieval Software Makes Searching of the Unabridged MEDLINE Database Easy, Effective & Fast. After the User Types a Phrase or Sentence Describing the Information Needed, It selects the References in the Database That Appear to Best Match the Request, & Presents Them in Order of likely relevance. The Unabridge MEDLINE CD-ROM's Each Contain up to 1.5 Million References to Articles.
Aries Systems Corp.

MEDLOG. *Version:* 92.4. Jul. 1992. *Operating System(s) Required:* MS-DOS. *Language(s):* C. *Memory Required:* 640k. *Items Included:* Updated for first year; manual; tutorial. *Customer Support:* Included for first year.
disk $6500.00 (ISBN 0-924538-00-7).
Medical Data Base System That Stores, Organizes & Analyzes Large Amounts of Clinical Data. Extensive Facilities for Selecting Patient & Data Subgroups Are Provided, Including Selection According to Complex Time & Event-Related Criteria. Statistical Analysis, Reporting Procedures & Facilities for Remote Data Entry, Double Entry Verification & Audit Trails Are Included.
Information Analysis Corp.

MedQuest. *Version:* 5.21. *Compatible Hardware:* Apple Macintosh SE30 & above (preferably Mac II family) 5Mb RAM, 80Mb HD. *General Requirements:* Hard disk, ImageWriter II or LQ or LaserWriter. *Items Included:* OMNIS 5 Runtime. Full OMNIS available - call for pricing. *Customer Support:* $375.00 billed quarterly.
single user $3995.00.
$300.00 each added user.

demo $15.00.
Medical Office Computer System Developed by a Physician. It Is Designed to Handle Not Only the Routine Billing, Insurance & Appointment Functions of a Medical Office, But to Help with Patient Problem Management, Periodic Procedure Tracking for Recall, Gathering Data for Medical Research, & to Assist in the Financial Analysis of Your Practice. It Comes with all 14,000 ICD9 Codes & Will Do Electronic Billing.
The Program Workshop, Inc.

MEDSYS. *Version:* 1.41. 1993. *Items Included:* User manuals. *Customer Support:* Laboratory downloading included in price - setup, & testing. Three days of onsite training included in price - Continental U.S. Thirty day warranty included in price. Annual maintenance fee $2,500 includes enhancements & help line.
MS-DOS. IBM or compatible 386 or 486 class microcomputers (2Mb). $25,000.00 per copy; volume discount; single site multi-user license. *Optimal configuration:* One 9600 baud modem; Laser-jet printer; additional 8088 microcomputer for laboratory report capture; 2Mb RAM for all workstations; 486 class workstations; DOS 5.0. *Networks supported:* Novell NetWare; Arcnet; Ethernet; Token Ring.
Used for HIV & Oncology in Outpatient Settings to Collect, Review, & Respond to Large Volumes of Clinical Data. Flowsheets Available On-Line or Printed for: History of Current Illness; Past Medical History; Medication History; Physical Examination; Paraclinical Data; Plan. Laboratory Data Capture Is Automated. Appointments & "Rolodex" Features Included.
Medical Office Management Systems.

Meetings Catering System.
MS-DOS. IBM 386 & compatibles (640K). contact publisher for price. *Networks supported:* Novell.
Fully Automates All Aspects of a Hotel's Sales & Catering Operation. Menus, Banquet Event Orders, Group Room Control Book, Menu Costing, a Report Writer & More.
National Guest Systems Corp.

Mega-Farming.
DOS, UNIX (256k). PC/compatible. (02/1989) $99.00. *Optimal configuration:* Computer w/ 20Mb hard disk, 80 column printer, word processor (PFS-Write), Modem, PROCOMM.
Macintosh (256k). (10/1989) $99.00. *Optimal configuration:* Computer w/20 Mb hard disk, 80 column printer, word processor,modem.
System Provides Information for Marketing Service to Thousands of Homes. Basic Data Includes Name, Addess, & Telephone. Details Added from Public Records Include Size, Rooms, Zoning, Loans, etc. From Multiple Listing Activity, Information About Current & Completed Sales Is Included. The Fourth Data Set Is a "Tickle" File, Which Includes Information That Triggers Future Action, Or Can Be Used As a Log to Remember Past Action. There Is a Set of Codes That Can Be Used in a Myriad of Ways to Group Properties for Bulk Mailing, Telephone or Direct Contacts, or Very Precise Mail or Other Contacts, Such as Adjacent to Just Listed Or Just Sold, Families with Children, Families with Pets, etc. There Are Files of Form Letters That Can Be Merged with Property groups for Personal Mailing.
Pro Data Systems, Inc.

Mega Guide to LPs. Aug. 1994. *Customer Support:* One year free support via phone, mail, fax & BBS.
MS-DOS 3.3 or higher. Any IBM compatible (440k). CD-ROM disk $49.95. *Nonstandard peripherals required:* CD-ROM drive.
Windows 3.1. Any IBM compatible running Windows. CD-ROM disk $49.95.

MEGAFILE MANAGER

Computer-Based Catalog of Information about More Than 25,000 LPs- Including Song Titles, Artist & Label Information. Includes Every Charted LP up to 1990.
PSG-HomeCraft Software.

Mega Pack. *Customer Support:* 90 day warranty.
Commodore 64 (64K). disk $39.99. *Nonstandard peripherals required:* Joystick required.
A Colossal Compilation of Original Gameplays Brought Together in One Classic Collection of Action, Intrigue, Humor & Entertainment. Games Included Are: BULLDOG, REBOUNDER, JACK THE NIPPER II, NORTHSTAR, TRAIL BLAZER, COSMIC CAUSEWAY, KRACKOUT, THE THING BOUNCES BACK, MONTY ON THE RUN, FUTURE KNIGHT.
Virgin Games.

Mega Traveller 3: The Unknown Worlds. Dec. 1992. *Items Included:* Manual, technical supplement, game contest. *Customer Support:* Free contact support, 1-410-771-1151.
80286 minimum-hard disk required 16MHz. IBM PC & compatibles. disk $69.95. *Nonstandard peripherals required:* VGA/MCGA-256 Color. *Optimal configuration:* DOS 2.11 or higher; mouse recommended; Joystick, keyboard; Roland, Adlib, Sound Blaster.
The First Science Fiction Role-Playing Game That Offers Players Three Very Distinct Main Scenarios Instead of One Major Goal. Players Will Enjoy Exciting Cinematic Intros & Movie-Like Transition Scenes Which Expand the Plot, Heroic Finales in the Tradition of the Best Science Fiction Films.
MicroProse Software.

MegaAEC. *Version:* 8V1.01. *Compatible Hardware:* IBM PC & compatibles. *Memory Required:* 640k. *General Requirements:* Hard disk.
disk $895.00.
CAD Program for Architecture Featuring Wall Drawings with Mitred Corners & Door & Window Openings, Area Calculation, Ability to Add Attributes to Symbols, Text Editor & On-Line Help. Links Provided to dBASE III. Imports & Exports IGES & .DXF File Formats. Can Import ASCII Text Files into Drawing. Technical Phone Support Available.
Mega CADD, Inc.

MegaDots. Aug. 1992. *Items Included:* Manual in print, disk, reference card in braille. *Customer Support:* Technical phone line, 9-5 (M-F).
MS-DOS. AT Class 386 or higher. disk $540.00.
Braille Translator & Word Processing Program for the PC That Knows the Rules for Braille Translation & Braille Formatting Featuring a Style-Based System, Smart Importation System, Fast Translators, Virtually Perfect "Round-Trip" Translations Within the WYSIWYG Editing Environment.
Raised Dot Computing, Inc.

MegaDraft. *Compatible Hardware:* IBM PC & compatible.
disk $1595.00.
Used for Architectural Design. Includes 2-D Drafting.
Mega CADD, Inc.

Megafile Manager. *Version:* 3.1. May 1992. *Customer Support:* Technical support.
DOS/VSE. PC's AT & higher (640k). disk $295.00. *Optimal configuration:* DOS Version 5.0 or higher. *Networks supported:* All.
A Database Management Program Allowing Users to Maintain Large Archival Data Files of up to 32,000 Fields with Unlimited Numbers of Records. Comprehensive Facilities to Enter, Edit, Restructure, Report, Sort, Subset, Merge

(Including Relational Merge Options), Sort, Search/Replace, & Verify Data. Imports Many File Formats.
StatSoft, Inc.

Megaguide to CDs. Steve Hudgik & Todd Clark. Jan. 1996. *Items Included:* CD-ROM, Jewel Case, Installation Instructions. *Customer Support:* One year free support, 30 day unlimited warranty.
Windows 3.1, PC DOS/MS DOS 3.3 or higher. CD-ROM disk $49.95.
Computer-Based Catalog of Information about More Than 18,000 CDs - Including Song Titles, Artist & Label Information.
PSG-HomeCraft Software.

Megaguide to LPs. Steve Hudgik & Todd Clark. Feb. 1996. *Items Included:* CD-ROM, Jewel Case, Installation Instructions. *Customer Support:* One year free technical support, 30 day unlimited warranty.
CD-ROM disk $49.95.
Computer-Based Catalog of Information about More Than 23,000 Albums - Including Titles, Artist & Label Information.
PSG-HomeCraft Software.

Megaguide to Singles. Charlie Holz. Feb. 1996. *Items Included:* CD-ROM, Jewel Case, Installation Instructions. *Customer Support:* One year free technical support, 30 day unlimited warranty.
Windows 3.1, MS DOS/PC DOS 3.3 or higher. CD-ROM disk $49.95.
Computer-Based Catalog of Every 45 RPM Record Ever Made. Has Information on Approximately 400,000 45s - Including Song Titles, Artists & Label Information.
PSG-HomeCraft Software.

MegaMaze. Dec. 1994. *Items Included:* Jewel case, manual, warranty card, legal agreement. *Customer Support:* 90 limited warranty.
MS-DOS 5.0 or higher. 386-SX or higher (500k, DOS 2Mb XMS). Contact publisher for price (ISBN 1-57272-953-8). *Nonstandard peripherals required:* VGA, Sounblaster or compatible or Pro Audio spectrum, 1X CD-ROM. *Optimal configuration:* 486-SX or higher, 2X CD-ROM, 4Mb XMS.
A Unique Puzzle Strategy Game That Invites Players to Test Their Patience, Intelligence & Strategical Skills As They Attempt to Solve Mazes. The Mazes Range from Relatively Simple to Incredibly Complex & Are Enhanced by a Vast Variety of Obstacles That Make MegaMaze Challenging & Fun.
Capitol Multimedia, Inc.

MegaMed Medical Management System. Version: 63.201-6. Oct. 1988. *Compatible Hardware:* All Pick systems. *Operating System(s) Required:* PICK. *Language(s):* Pick DataBASIC (source code included). *Memory Required:* 512k. *General Requirements:* 40Mb hard disk.
$5,000.00 - $20,000.00 cartridge or tape.
Includes Patient Billing, Insurance Processing (Including Magnetic Tape Submission), Collections Management, Practice Analysis, Custom Report Generator, Patient Registration & Patient Scheduling, Surgery Scheduling, Hospital Census Tracking, Charge Slip Production & Tracking, Physician Encounter Forms, Word Processing, & Patient Medical Records. The Medical Records Programs Allow the Physician to Record Histories & Physicals, Immunizations, Problem Lists, Ongoing Progress Notes, Lab Results, Correspondence to Referring Physicians, & Drugs.
MegaWest Systems, Inc.

MegaModel. *Compatible Hardware:* IBM PC & compatible.
disk $995.00.
Architectural-Design Package Offering Perspective & Automatic Walk-Through.
Mega CADD, Inc.

Megatraveller: The Zhodani Conspiracy. Paragon Software. *Items Included:* Manual. *Customer Support:* Free customer service (412) 838-1173.
IBM PC & compatibles (512k). 3.5" or 5.25" disk $59.95. *Nonstandard peripherals required:* Supports CGA, EGA, VGA & Tandy 1000 graphic cards.
Based on the Popular Science Fiction Gaming System by Game Designers' Workshop, Megatraveller Puts You in Conntrol of Five Characters -- Each a Former Soldier with Different Abilities & Skills That User Can Select -- Trying to Unravel a Web of Political Treachery & Stop an Interstellar War.
MicroProse Software.

Melody Maker. Greg Susong. Oct. 1984. *Compatible Hardware:* NEC PC-8201A, Radio Shack Model 100, Tandy 200. *Language(s):* BASIC. *Memory Required:* 5k.
Radio Shack. cassette $19.95 (ISBN 0-932095-05-4).
NEC PC. cassette $19.95 (ISBN 0-932095-06-2).
Custom Software Engineering, Inc.

Member Services. Jan Jansen. *Compatible Hardware:* IBM PC, PC XT, PC AT, Portable PC, 3270 PC. *Operating System(s) Required:* PC-DOS 1.10, 2.00, 2.10, 3.00, 3.10. *Memory Required:* 192k. *General Requirements:* 2 double-sided disk drives, IBM Display, IBM Matrix printer.
disk $29.95 (Order no.: 6276566).
Designed to Help Improve an Organization's Control of Its Financial Objectives & to Produce Letters to Members & Status Reports. Some of Its Features Include: Prints Reports & Directories in Alphabetical Sequence, by Account Number, or by Unit Number; Make Inquiries by Entering Part of a Last Name, an Account Number, or the Unit Number; Maintain YTD Credit History Even After an Account Is Closed; Produce Form Letters & Mailing Labels; Maintain up to 600 Accounts per Program; Track Deposits, Late Charges, Individual Charges, & up to 10 Global Charges; Provide Separate Mailing Addresses for Absentee Owners or Members.
Personally Developed Software, Inc.

The Member Tender. *Items Included:* Bound manual. *Customer Support:* Free hotline - no time limit; 30 day limited warranty; updates are $5/disk plus S&H.
MS-DOS 2.0 or higher. IBM & compatibles (128k). disk $89.95. *Nonstandard peripherals required:* Printer.
Membership Management Package for Organizations. Category of Membership; Membership in Sub-Groups; Dues Tracking Categories; Geographical Categories; Dates of Membership; Form Letter Production. Keeps Track of Contributions, Membership in Other Organizations, & Maintains a "Privacy" Function Which Inhibits the Production of Mailing Labels for Specific Mailings. Reports & Labels May Be Produced to Include Any of the User-Defined Categories Above in Several Different Formats. Reports May Be Produced in Alphabetical Order or in Order by Category of Membership. Mailing Labels Are Produced in ZIP Code Order.
Dynacomp, Inc.

Member Tender II: Membership Management System. 1995. *Items Included:* Full manual. *Customer Support:* Free telephone support - 90 days, 30-day warranty.
MS-DOS 3.2 or higher. 286 (584k). disk $179.95. *Nonstandard peripherals required:* CGA/EGA/VGA.
Designed to Make Life Easier for Administrators of Associations, Foundations, Churches, Clubs, Societies, or Any Other Type of Membership Organization. Its Scope Includes Membership Rolls, Reporting, Mailing, Planning, Scheduling, Attendance, Billing, Contributions, & Pledges. It Encompasses All of the Powerful Features of DYNACOMP's MEMBER TENDER I in Addition to Having a Relational Database Structure Which Permits Unlimited Membership Lists along with an Unlimited Number of Associated Organizations & Profile Codes.
Dynacomp, Inc.

Member Tender 2 Membership Management System. *Items Included:* Full manual. No other products required. *Customer Support:* Free telephone support - no time limit. 30 day warranty.
MS-DOS 3.2 or higher. IBM & compatibles (512k). disk $179.95. *Optimal configuration:* IBM, MS-DOS 3.0 or higher, 640k RAM, & 132 column (or wider) printer.
Designed to Make Life Easier for Administrators of Associations, Foundations, Churches, Clubs, Societies, or Any Other Type of Membership Organization. Its Scope Includes Membership Rolls, Reporting, Mailing, Planning, Scheduling, Attendance, Billing, Contributions, & Pledges. Includes 1 20-Page Printed Manual & 75-Page On-Disk Manual.
Dynacomp, Inc.

Membermaster II. Version: 2.13. *Compatible Hardware:* MOTO680x0, IBM RS/6000, UNISYS, INTEL 80x86. *Items Included:* Documentation in 3-ring manual. *Customer Support:* On-site training, 800 number, 90 day warranty, user's group, documentation, updates.
Contact Publisher for price.
Designed to Support Membership Organizations Where Clubs, Status, & Renewal Dates Are Important to Track. Provides a Complete Record of a Profile's Membership History & Is Fully Integrated with the System's Word Processor. The Integration Allows for Timely & Tailored Renewal Notices & Sollicitation Letters. Multiple Memberships May Be Tracked, & Complete Statistical Reporting Is Provided.
Master Systems.

Membership. *Operating System(s) Required:* All CP/M based machines.
contact publisher for price.
Business Computers, Inc. (Florida).

Membership Accounts Receivable. Version: 3.2. 1995. *Operating System(s) Required:* MS-DOS, Xenix. *Language(s):* Compiled BASIC. *Memory Required:* 256k. *General Requirements:* Hard Drive, printer. *Items Included:* Manual, disk, demo. *Customer Support:* Free phone support for 90-days; $25.00 per call after.
disk $200.00 ea.
(ISBN 0-918185-58-0).
(ISBN 0-918185-59-9).
3.5" or 5.25" disk $200.00 (ISBN 0-918185-60-2).
Features Cash Accounting, Periodic Billing Facility, Recurring Transaction Facility for Individual Members, Aged Statement, Selective Mailing Label Facility, & Link to General Ledger System.
Taranto & Assocs., Inc.

Membership Management, Program Management, Auction Management, General Ledger, Accounts Receivable, Accounts Payable, Fixed Assets, Project Cost, Data Writer. 1979. *Compatible Hardware:* IBM PC, PC XT, PC AT & compatibles, PS/2 Model 50, 60, 70, 80. *Operating System(s) Required:* PC-DOS/MS-DOS. *Memory Required:* 512k. *General Requirements:* Hard disk.
contact publisher for price.
Designed for Non-Profit Orgnaizations, Alumni, Donor, Broadcast Management, Auction & Membership Tracking.
NCS/MEMTRAC.

TITLE INDEX

Membership Management System: MEMSYS.
Barbara H. Dotson. 1979. *Compatible Hardware:* DEC PDP-11/RSX, MICROVAX II, VAX. *Operating System(s) Required:* RSTS/E, RSX, VMS. *Language(s):* VAX BASIC. *Memory Required:* 32k.
$5000.00-$10,000.00.
Designed to Provide Associations with Accurate & Timely Information. Helps Associations Keep Track of Members, Legislators, & Convention Attendees. Keeps an Easily Retrievable Record & History of Transactions with Each Member. Also Functions As an Accounts Receivable & Billing System, Handles Mass Mailings, Keeps Track of Voting Records, & Generates Reports & Letters with Interface to Word Processing. Also Interfaces to General Ledger.
DWC Computer Solutions, Inc.

Membership Master. *Customer Support:* 800-929-8117 (customer service).
MS-DOS. IBM/PS2. disk $99.99 (ISBN 0-87007-422-9).
Start & Maintain an Accurate Alphabetic Order Membership List. Each Member File Can Include up to 15 Specialized 80 Column Text Fields That May Be Used for Keeping Track of Member Interest and Special SIG Memberships.
SourceView Software International.

Membership Plus Deluxe. *Version:* 2.0. Parsons Technology. Jun. 1994.
3.5" disk Contact publisher for price (ISBN 1-57264-006-5).
Includes MoneyCounts 8.0.
Parsons Technology.

Membership Plus Demo. *Version:* 2.0. Parsons Technology. Jun. 1994.
3.5" disk Contact publisher for price (ISBN 1-57264-044-8).
Parsons Technology.

Membership RV Park & Camp Reservations.
Mary James. Oct. 1985. *Language(s):* COBOL. *Items Included:* User manual & tutorial manual. *Customer Support:* Yearly maintenance: $200.00.
MS-DOS. MS-DOS. IBM PC or clone. disk $3250.00 (ISBN 0-928666-12-3, Order no.: CRIS01). *Nonstandard peripherals required:* 3.5" or 5.25" disk drive, printer, 90Mb hard disk. *Addl. software required:* WordPerfect or WordStar. *Networks supported:* Networks supported: Novell.
386/486. disk $3250.00.
Camp Ground Reservation & Member Usage Accounting. Maintains Member Reservations, Charges, Usage & Payments at the Resort. Prints Check In/Out List, "Who Is Here", Reservation Confirmation Letters, & Other Accounting Reports.
The James Gang.

Membership RV Park & Camp-Resort Marketing. Mary James. Jan. 1985.
Language(s): COBOL. *Customer Support:* Yearly maintenance contract: $200.00.
MS-DOS. IBM PC (640k). disk $3250.00 (ISBN 0-928666-02-6, Order no.: CMARK01). *Nonstandard peripherals required:* 3.5" or 5.25" disk drive, printer, 90Mb hard disk. *Networks supported:* Networks supported: Novell.
386/486. disk $3250.00.
Membership Sales Tracking, Prints Sales Contracts & Sales Reports. Maintains Sales Gift Inventories. Maintains Buyer Information, Salesperson Information, Sales Records & Non-Buyer Addresses. Merges Data with WordStar or WordPerfect Word Processing Package.
The James Gang.

Membership RV Park & Camp-Resort Receivables. Mary James. Jan. 1985.
Language(s): COBOL. *Items Included:* User manual & tutorial. *Customer Support:* Yearly maintenance contract: $200.00.
MS-DOS. IBM PC (640k). disk $3250.00 (ISBN 0-928666-08-5, Order no.: CMAN01). *Nonstandard peripherals required:* 3.5" or 5.25" disk drive, printer, 90Mb hard disk. *Networks supported:* Networks supported: Novell.
386/486. disk $3250.00.
Maintains Monies Received for Membership Loans & Maintenance Fees. Prints Aging, Monthly Statements & Investor Reports. Calculates Late Charges, Aging of Accounts, etc. Merges with WordStar or WordPerfect Word Processing to Prepare Late Notices, Receipts, & Other Correspondence.
The James Gang.

MemoMaker. *Compatible Hardware:* HP Series 200 HP-UX Models 217, 220, 236, the Integral PC; IBM PC.
HP single-user. 3.5" disk $195.00 (Order no.: 45420G).
Linus tape $315.00.
HP multi-user. 3.5" disk $395.00 (Order no.: 45420H).
Linus tape $515.00.
IBM. disk $160.00 (Order no.: 45420E).
Word Processor for Memos, Business Letters, or Reports. Creates WordStar Compatible Files. Also Provides Features Like Bold & Underline Print Enhancements.
Hewlett-Packard Co.

The Memory Disk Driver: NEW-DOS/80.
Compatible Hardware: TRS-80 Model I, Model III, Model 4. *Memory Required:* 64k.
disk $39.95 (Order no.: D8TMDD).
Enables the Model 4 Users to Utilize the Extra 64K As a RAM DISK When Using NEW-DOS/80 2.0.
The Alternate Source.

MemoryMate. *Version:* 3.01. *Compatible Hardware:* IBM PC or compatibles. *Operating System(s) Required:* PC-DOS/MS-DOS 2.0 or higher. *Memory Required:* 88k.
disk $69.95.
Free-Form Information & Database Manager. Offers Hypertext & Tickler File Features.
Broderbund Software, Inc.

Menstrual Distress Questionnaire-Form C.
Version: 1.010. Rudolf H. Moos. *Customer Support:* Free unlimited phone support with a toll free number.
DOS 3.0 or higher. IBM or 100% compatible (512k). disk $150.00 (Order no.: W-1022 5.25"; W-1045 3.5"). *Optimal configuration:* Hard disk with 1Mb free disk space, printer.
Well Established, Standardized Method for Measuring the Symptoms Associated with Premenstrual & Menstrual Distress. Allows You to Screen Your Patients & Identify Those Suffering from Menstrual Distress.
Western Psychological Services.

Mental Math Games. Sep. 1995. *Customer Support:* Telephone support - free (except phone charge).
Windows 3.1. IBM & compatibles (386 DX-20) (4Mb). CD-ROM disk $12.99 (ISBN 1-57594-004-3). *Nonstandard peripherals required:* 2x CD-ROM player, Sound Card, VGA monitor. *Optimal configuration:* 486 SX-33.
Interactive Math Lessons.
Kidsoft, Inc.

MENTOR NOTES

Mental Math Games. Sep. 1995. *Customer Support:* Telephone support - free (except phone charge).
Windows 3.1. IBM & compatibles (386 DX-20) (4Mb). CD-ROM disk $12.99 (ISBN 1-57594-043-4). *Nonstandard peripherals required:* 2x CD-ROM player, Sound Card, VGA monitor. *Optimal configuration:* 486 SX-33.
Interactive Math Lessons. Blister Pack Jewel Case.
Kidsoft, Inc.

Mentor Notes, Advanced Wordperfect.
Version: 1.0. Jul. 1991. *Items Included:* 1 spiral bound manual; 1 audio cassette tape; 1 5.25" disk; 1 3.5" disk. *Customer Support:* On-site training is available for a fee (fee varies); free telephone support.
MS-DOS. IBM compatible (640k). $69.95 (ISBN 1-56494-001-2). *Addl. software required:* Wordperfect.
OS/2. $69.95. *Addl. software required:* Wordperfect.
Self Study Courses Designed to Teach Software Skills. An Interactive Audio Tape Guides Students Through a Comprehensive Workbook Which Teaches Functional Tasks. The Course Explains Concepts & Procedures Through the Solution of "Real-World" Problems. The Workbook Also Serves As an Excellent Reference Tool.
Mentor Technologies, Inc.

Mentor Notes, Intermediate dBASE IV (Working Title). *Version:* 1.0. Jan. 1993. *Items Included:* 1 spiral bound manual; 1 audio cassette tape; 1 5.25" disk; 1 3.5" disk. *Customer Support:* On-site training is available for a fee (fee varies); free telephone support.
MS-DOS. IBM compatible (640k). $69.95. *Addl. software required:* dBASE.
XENIX. $69.95. *Addl. software required:* dBASE.
OS/2. IBM (2Mb). $69.95. *Addl. software required:* dBASE.
Self Study Courses Designed to Teach Software Skills. An Interactive Audio Tape Guides Students Through a Comprehensive Workbook Which Teaches Functional Tasks. The Courses Explain Concepts & Procedures Through the Solution of "Real-World" Problems. The Workbook Also Serves As an Excellent Reference Tool.
Mentor Technologies, Inc.

Mentor Notes, Intermediate DOS (Working Title). *Version:* 1.0. Jan. 1993. *Items Included:* 1 spiral bound manual; 1 audio cassette tape; 1 5.25" disk; 1 3.5" disk. *Customer Support:* On-site training is available for a fee (fee varies); free telephone support.
MS-DOS. IBM compatible (640k). $69.95.
Windows (1Mb). $69.95.
OS/2. IBM (2Mb). $69.95.
Self Study Courses Designed to Teach Software Skills. An Interactive Audio Tape Guides Students Through a Comprehensive Workbook Which Teaches Functional Tasks. The Courses Explain Concepts & Procedures Through the Solution of "Real-World" Problems. The Workbook Also Serves As an Excellent Reference Tool.
Mentor Technologies, Inc.

Mentor Notes, Intermediate Lotus. *Version:* 1.0. Jul. 1991. *Items Included:* 1 spiral bound manual; 1 audio cassette tape; 1 5.25" disk; 1 3.5" disk. *Customer Support:* On-site training is available for a fee (fee varies); free telephone support.
MS-DOS. IBM compatible (640k). $69.95 (ISBN 1-56494-003-9). *Addl. software required:* Lotus.
OS/2. $69.95. *Addl. software required:* Lotus. *Addl. software required:* Lotus.
Self Study Courses Designed to Teach Software Skills. An Interactive Audio Tape Guides Students Through a Comprehensive Workbook Which Teaches Functional Tasks. The Courses Explain

Concepts & Procedures Through the Solution of "Real-World" Problems. The Workbook Also Serves As an Excellent Reference Tool.
Mentor Technologies, Inc.

Mentor Notes, Introduction to dBASE IV (Working Title). *Version:* 1.0. Jan. 1993. *Items Included:* 1 spiral bound manual; 1 audio cassette tape; 1 5.25" disk; 1 3.5" disk. *Customer Support:* On-site training is available for a fee (fee varies); free telephone support.
MS-DOS. IBM compatible (640k). $69.95. *Addl. software required:* dBASE.
Windows (1Mb). $69.95. *Addl. software required:* dBASE.
OS/2. IBM (2Mb). $69.95. *Addl. software required:* dBASE.
Self Study Courses Designed to Teach Software Skills. An Interactive Audio Tape Guides Students Through a Comprehensive Workbook Which Teaches Functional Tasks. The Courses Explain Concepts & Procedures Through the Solution of "Real-World" Problems. The Workbook Also Serves As an Excellent Reference Tool.
Mentor Technologies, Inc.

Mentor Notes, Introduction to DOS (Working Title). *Version:* 1.0. Jan. 1992. *Items Included:* 1 spiral bound manual; 1 audio cassette tape; 1 5.25" disk; 1 3.5" disk. *Customer Support:* On-site training is available for a fee (fee varies); free telephone support.
MS-DOS. IBM compatible (640k). disk $69.95.
Windows (1Mb). disk $69.95.
OS/2. IBM (2Mb). 3.5" disk $69.95.
Self Study Courses Designed to Teach Software Skills. An Interactive Audio Tape Guides Students Through a Comprehensive Workbook Which Teaches Functional Tasks. The Courses Explain Concepts & Procedures Through the Solution of "Real-World" Problems. The Workbook Also Serves As an Excellent Reference Tool.
Mentor Technologies, Inc.

Mentor Notes: Introduction to Lotus. *Version:* 1.0. Jul. 1991. *Items Included:* 1 spiral bound manual; 1 audio cassette tape, 1 5.25" disk; 1 3.5" disk. *Customer Support:* On-site training is available for a fee (fee varies); free telephone support.
MS-DOS. IBM compatible (640k). $69.95 (ISBN 1-56494-002-0). *Addl. software required:* Lotus.
Windows (1Mb). $69.95. *Addl. software required:* Lotus.
OS/2. IBM (2Mb). $69.95. *Addl. software required:* Lotus.
Self Study Courses Designed to Teach Software Skills. An Interactive Audio Tape Guides Students Through a Comprehensive Workbook Which Teaches Functional Tasks. The Courses Explain Concepts & Procedures Through the Solution of "Real-World" Problems. The Workbook Also Serves As an Excellent Reference Tool.
Mentor Technologies, Inc.

Mentor Notes: Introduction to OS 2 2.0. Jun. 1992. *Items Included:* 1 spiral bound manual, 1 audio cassette tape, 1 3.5" diskette. *Customer Support:* On-site training is available for a fee (fee varies). Free telephone support.
OS/2 2.0. IBM PC & compatible. $69.95 (ISBN 1-56494-005-5).
Self Study Course Designed to Teach Software Skills. An Interactive Audio Tape Guides Students Through a Comprehensive Workbook Which Teaches Functional Tasks. Course Explains Concepts & Procedures Through the Solution of "Real-World" Problems. Workbook Also Serves as a Reference Tool.
Mentor Technologies, Inc.

Mentor Notes, Introduction to Windows. *Version:* 1.0. Jul. 1991. *Items Included:* 1 spiral bound; 1 audio cassette tape; 1 5.25" disk; 1 3.5" disk. *Customer Support:* On-site training is available for a fee (fee varies); free telephone support.
MS-DOS. IBM compatible (640k). $69.95 (ISBN 1-56494-004-7). *Addl. software required:* Windows.
Windows (1Mb). $69.95. *Addl. software required:* Windows.
OS/2. IBM (2Mb). $69.95. *Addl. software required:* Windows.
Self Study Courses Designed to Teach Software Skills. An Interactive Audio Tape Guides Students Through a Comprehensive Workbook Which Teaches Functional Tasks. The Courses Explain Concepts & Procedures Through the Solution of "Real-World" Problems. The Workbook Also Serves As an Excellent Reference Tool.
Mentor Technologies, Inc.

Mentor Notes, Introduction to Wordperfect. *Version:* 1.0. Jul. 1991. *Items Included:* 1 spiral bound manual; 1 audio cassette tape; 1 5.25" disk, 1 3.5 disk. *Customer Support:* On-site training is available for a fee (fee varies); free telephone support.
MS-DOS. IBM compatible (640k). $69.95 (ISBN 1-56494-000-4). *Addl. software required:* Wordperfect.
Windows (1Mb). $69.95. *Addl. software required:* Wordperfect.
OS/2. IBM (2Mb). $69.95. *Addl. software required:* Wordperfect.
Self Study Courses Designed to Teach Software Skills. An Interactive Audio Tape Guides Students Through a Comprehensive Workbook Which Teaches Functional Tasks. The Courses Explain Concepts & Procedures Through the Solution of "Real-World" Problems. The Workbook Also Serves As an Excellent Reference Tool.
Mentor Technologies, Inc.

Mentor Notes, Wordperfect Equations. *Version:* 1.0. Jul. 1991. *Items Included:* 1 spiral bound manual; 1 audio cassette tape; 1 5.25" disk; 1 3.5" disk. *Customer Support:* On-site training is available for a fee (fee varies); free telephone support.
MS-DOS. IBM compatible (640k). $69.95. *Addl. software required:* Wordperfect.
Windows (1Mb). $69.95. *Addl. software required:* Wordperfect.
OS/2. IBM (2Mb). $69.95. *Addl. software required:* Wordperfect.
Self Study Courses Designed to Teach Software Skills. An Interactive Audio Tape Guides Students Through a Comprehensive Workbook Which Teaches Functional Tasks. The Courses Explain Concepts & Procedures Through the Solution of "Real-World" Problems. The Workbook Also Serves As an Excellent Reference Tool.
Mentor Technologies, Inc.

Mentor Notes, Wordperfect Macros & Merge (Working Title). *Version:* 1.0. Dec. 1992. *Items Included:* 1 spiral bound manual; 1 audio cassette tape; 1 5.25" disk; 1 3.5" disk. *Customer Support:* On-site training is available for a fee (fee varies); free telephone support.
MS-DOS. IBM compatible (640k). $69.95. *Addl. software required:* Wordperfect.
Windows (1Mb). $69.95. *Addl. software required:* Wordperfect.
OS/2. IBM (2Mb). $69.95. *Addl. software required:* Wordperfect.
Self Study Courses Designed to Teach Software Skills. An Interactive Audio Tape Guides Students Through a Comprehensive Workbook Which Teaches Functional Tasks. The Courses Explain Concepts & Procedures Through the Solution of "Real-World" Problems. The Workbook Also Serves As an Excellent Reference Tool.
Mentor Technologies, Inc.

Mentor Notes, Wordperfect Manuscript & Report Writing. *Version:* 1.0. Jul. 1991. *Items Included:* 1 spiral bound manual; 1 audio cassette tape; 1 5.25" disk; 1 3.5" disk. *Customer Support:* On-site training is available for a fee (fee varies); free telephone support.
MS-DOS. IBM Compatible (640k). $69.95. *Addl. software required:* Wordperfect.
Windows (1Mb). $69.95. *Addl. software required:* Wordperfect.
OS/2. IBM (2Mb). $69.95. *Addl. software required:* Wordperfect.
Self Study Courses Designed to Teach Software Skills. An Interactive Audio Tape Guides Students Through a Comprehensive Workbook Which Teaches Functional Tasks. The Courses Explain Concepts & Procedures Through the Solution of "Real-World" Problems. The Workbook Also Serves As an Excellent Reference Tool.
Mentor Technologies, Inc.

Mentor Notes, Wordperfect Tables (Working Title). *Version:* 1.0. Dec. 1991. *Items Included:* 1 spiral bound manual; 1 audio cassette tape; 1 5.25" disk; 1 3.5" disk. *Customer Support:* On-site training is available for a fee (fee varies); free telephone support.
MS-DOS. IBM compatible (640k). $69.95. *Addl. software required:* Wordperfect.
Windows (1Mb). $69.95. *Addl. software required:* Wordperfect.
OS/2. IBM (2Mb). $69.95. *Addl. software required:* Wordperfect.
Self Study Courses Designed to Teach Software Skills. An Interactive Audio Tape Guides Students Through a Comprehensive Workbook Which Teaches Functional Tasks. The Courses Explain Concepts & Procedures Through the Solution of "Real-World" Problems. The Workbook Also Serves As an Excellent Reference Tool.
Mentor Technologies, Inc.

Mentor Notes, Wordperfect Word Publishing (Working Title). *Version:* 1.0. Dec. 1992. *Items Included:* 1 spiral bound manual; 1 Audio cassette tape; 1 5.25" disk; 1 3.5" disk. *Customer Support:* On-site training is available for a fee (fee varies); free telephone support.
MS-DOS. IBM compatible (640k). $69.95. *Addl. software required:* Wordperfect.
Windows (1Mb). $69.95. *Addl. software required:* Wordperfect.
OS/2. IBM (2Mb). $69.95. *Addl. software required:* Wordperfect.
Self Study Courses Designed to Teach Software Skills. An interactive Audio Tape Guides Students Through a Comprehensive Workbook Which Teaches Functional Tasks. The Courses Explain Concepts & Procedures Through the Solution of "Real-World" Problems. The Workbook Also Serves As an Excellent Reference Tool.
Mentor Technologies, Inc.

Menu. *Version:* 3.09. Pavel Breder. Mar. 1983. *Compatible Hardware:* IBM PC. *Operating System(s) Required:* MS-DOS, PC-DOS, CP/M, MP/M. *Language(s):* Assembly. *Memory Required:* 16k.
disk $149.00 ea.
(ISBN 0-913733-03-2).
(ISBN 0-913733-02-4).
File Management System That Allows Manipulation By-the-Numbers for One or a Series of Files for the Rename, Copy, Type-to-Screen or Printer. Creates an Automatic Menu of Runable Programs.
Computing!.

Menu Control System ("MCS"). *Version:* 2.0. Nov. 1989. *Items Included:* Users Guide; System information utility program. *Customer Support:* Free telephone support; 90-day media defect warranty.

MS/PC DOS 3.0 or higher. Any IBM PC/XT/AT or compatible with hard disk (512k). disk $35.00.
A Utility Which Allows End Users the Ability to Customize a Menu System for Their Computer. Runs Any DOS Program, Including Batch Files, & Takes NO Memory Away from the Application. Easily Configurable.
Software Engineering Technologies, Inc.

Menu Costing System. *Version:* 2. Jan. 1985. *Compatible Hardware:* IBM PC with 2 disk drives. *Operating System(s) Required:* MS-DOS. *Memory Required:* 256k.
IBM PC. disk $99.00 ea.
Designed to Assist Food Service Managers to Plan Menus & Control Food Costs. Keeps Track of Current Purchase Prices of Ingredients, Automatically Calculates Cost of Menu Items, Calculates the Gross Margin, & Recommends Selling Price Changes. Can Calculate Theoretical Food Costs & Print a Cross-Reference Report Showing All the Recipes That Use Each Ingredient.
Rapp Industries, Inc.

Menu Management. *Compatible Hardware:* IBM PC; TRS-80 Model I Level II, Model III, Model 4, Tandy 1000. *Operating System(s) Required:* TRSDOS. *Memory Required:* 16k.
disk or cassette $99.95.
Post-Secondary Level, Solving Program Relative to the Computerization of Restaurant Menus. User Can Computerize Any Menu, Figure Food Cost per Item & Determine Best Pricing per Item for a Return on Food Investment.
Viking, Inc.

Menu Master. *Version:* 1.6. Oct. 1991. *Items Included:* Manual & 3.5" disk (5.25" by request). *Customer Support:* 90 day limited warranty.
ProDOS 8 or 16. Apple II & Macintosh LC with IIe card (128k). single user version $49.00; network $169.00 (ISBN 0-9621393-3-5). *Networks supported:* AppleShare, Corvus, ELAN, VELAN, DIGICARD.
Complete Menu System for Launching ProDOS, GS/OS & DOS 3.3 Applications. Allows Creation of Customized Menus & Sub-Menus with Automatic Pathfinding for Each ProDOS Application. Operates on Any ProDOS Drive & All Apple II Networks. Provides All Features of Aristotle on AppleShare Networks. Password Protection for All Menus.
Electronic Learning Systems, Inc.

MenuFonts. *Version:* 4.5. Stuart Davidson. Aug. 1994. *Items Included:* The utilities Font Charter, fast formatter & sample fonts from our World Class Font library. *Customer Support:* Free phone support to registered users.
Macintosh. Mac plus or higher (1 meg). $69.95 (Order no.: 94627-00029). *Optimal configuration:* Mac plus or higher.
Replaces & Improves the Font Menu in Most Macintosh Applications. Displays the Fonts in Their Own Typeface, & Indicates If They Are a PostScript, TrueType or Bitmapped Font. Groups Font Families, & the KeyScroll Feature Allows Users to Quickly Select Their Desired Font Without Scrolling & Much More.
Dubl-Click Software.

Menumodifier. *Operating System(s) Required:* PC-DOS/MS-DOS, OS/2. *Memory Required:* 192k. *Items Included:* Includes 6-month warranty, user manual. *Customer Support:* Free updates, enhancements, & toll-free 800 lines for customers under warranty.
3.5" or 5.25" disk $500.00.
Provides Design of Regular & Modified Menus in a Production Sheet & a Meal Service Format. Prints a Weekly Cycle Menu.
Practorcare, Inc.

MenuPro. *Version:* 1.5. May 1992. *Items Included:* Spiral bound manual, 3.5" & 5.25" disks. *Customer Support:* 90 days unlimited warranty.
MS/PC-DOS 2.0 or higher. IBM PC & compatibles. disk $19.95 (ISBN 1-881432-27-0).
Menu Program Which Will Allow the User to Use DOS More Efficiently. Up to Ten Main Menu Choices with Ten Possible Sub-Menus. Optional Screen Saver. Comes with Several Disk Utilities.
BCS Publishing.

Menzoberranzan. DreamForge Internainment Staff. Nov. 1994. *Items Included:* 1 manual & 1 data card. *Customer Support:* 30 day limited warranty.
DOS 5.0 or higher. IBM PC compatible with CD-ROM, Hard drive & Mouse (4Mb & VGA card). CD-ROM disk $59.95 (ISBN 0-917059-21-2, Order no.: 062161). *Nonstandard peripherals required:* VGA card. *Optimal configuration:* 386/40 required, 486/33 recommended.
An Advanced Dungeons & Dragons Fantasy Role Playing Game That Takes Place in the Forgotten Realms World.
Strategic Simulations, Inc.

Mercenary: Escape from Targ. 1986. *Compatible Hardware:* Atari XL/XE, ST; Commodore 64, 128. *Memory Required:* Atari XL/XE, Commodore 64k; Atari ST 512k.
Atari XL/XE, Commodore. disk $19.95.
Atari ST. 3.5" disk $29.95.
Combines a Spaceship Flight Simulator with an Explore-the-Maze Graphic Adventure That Occurs on an Alien Planet. There Are Three Alternative Solutions for Extra Replays.
IntelliCreations, Inc.

Merchants Automated Business System (MABS). *Compatible Hardware:* IBM PC, PC XT, PC AT & compatibles.
contact publisher for price.
Includes Order Entry, Invoicing, Accounts Receivable, Inventory Control, Payroll, Bookkeeping, Sales Analysis & Mailing.
The International Computer Shop.

The Merck Manual TextStack: Professional Edition. Merck & Company Staff. Edited by Robert Berkow. Aug. 1994. *Items Included:* User manual, quick-start sheet, Keyboard Utilities, & Microsoft Multimedia Viewer (Windows version) or HyperCard (Macintosh version). *Customer Support:* Free, unlimited technical support via our toll-free number (1-800-945-4551).
Macintosh. Macintosh with a hard drive (2.5Mb). CD-ROM disk $199.00 (ISBN 1-57349-080-6). *Addl. software required:* System 7.0 or higher. *Networks supported:* All LANs.
Windows. IBM compatible with 80286 or higher processor, a hard drive & a mouse (2Mb). CD-ROM disk $199.00 (ISBN 1-57349-137-3). *Addl. software required:* MS-DOS 3.3 or higher, Windows 3.1 or higher. *Networks supported:* All LANs.
Macintosh. Macintosh with a hard drive (2.5Mb). CD-ROM version $199.00 (ISBN 1-57349-151-9). *Nonstandard peripherals required:* CD-ROM player required, 256-color monitor recommended. *Addl. software required:* System 7.0 or higher. *Networks supported:* All LANs.
Windows. IBM compatible with 80286 or higher processor, a hard drive & a mouse (2Mb). CD-ROM version $199.99 (ISBN 1-57349-141-1). *Nonstandard peripherals required:* CD-ROM player required, 256-color monitor recommended. *Addl. software required:* MS-DOS 3.3 or higher, Windows 3.1 or higher. *Networks supported:* All LANs.
The Complete Text with All Tables, Figures, Diagrams, & Illustrations from The Merck Manual, Sixteenth Edition. Includes a Collection of Tools for Searching, Capturing & Manipulating Data of Interest.
Keyboard Publishing, Inc.

The Merck Manual TextStack: Student Edition. Merck & Company Staff. Edited by Robert Berkow. Aug. 1994. *Items Included:* User manual, quick-start sheet, Keyboard Utilities, & Microsoft Multimedia Viewer (Windows version) or HyperCard (Macintosh version). *Customer Support:* Free, unlimited technical support via our toll-free number (1-800-945-4551).
Macintosh. Macintosh with a hard drive (2.5Mb). CD-ROM disk $99.00 (ISBN 1-57349-205-1). *Addl. software required:* System 7.0 or higher. *Networks supported:* All LANs.
Windows. IBM compatible with 80286 or higher processor, a hard drive & a mouse (2Mb). CD-ROM disk $99.00 (ISBN 1-57349-206-X). *Addl. software required:* MS-DOS 3.3 or higher, Windows 3.1 or higher. *Networks supported:* All LANs.
Macintosh. Macintosh with a hard drive (2.5Mb). CD-ROM disk $99.00 (ISBN 1-57349-207-8). *Nonstandard peripherals required:* CD-ROM player required, 256-color monitor recommended. *Addl. software required:* System 7.0 or higher. *Networks supported:* All LANs.
Windows. IBM compatible with 80286 or higher processor, a hard drive & a mouse (2Mb). CD-ROM disk CD-ROM version $99.00 (ISBN 1-57349-208-6). *Nonstandard peripherals required:* CD-ROM players required, 256-color monitor recommended. *Addl. software required:* MS-DOS 3.3 or higher, Windows 3.1 or higher. *Networks supported:* All LANs.
The Complete Text with All Tables, Figures, Diagrams, & Illustrations from The Merck Manual, Sixteenth Edition. Includes a Collection of Tools for Searching, Capturing & Manipulating Data of Interest.
Keyboard Publishing, Inc.

Merge 386. *Version:* 3.1. *Compatible Hardware:* 80386/80486/Pentium-based UNIX Systems. SCO Open Desktop, UnixWare, Dell Unix, SVR4. 2-at OEM prices. Add on for SCO UNIX - $395.00. Also available for UNISYS, SNI & IBM.
Will Run MS-DOS/Windows Applications under UNIX. Features Shared File System. Full Screen & Within X11 Window.
Locus Computing.

Merge 386. *Compatible Hardware:* PC 100, PC 200. *Operating System(s) Required:* CTIX 386, Convergent Unix Systm V Release 3.
$1150.00.
Emulates PC ROM BIOS Environment & Supports Standard DOS & DOS Applications.
Open Systems Holdings Corp., Inc.

Merge '386. *Operating System(s) Required:* Unix. Unlimited Users. $1800.00.
Runs Any DOS Program from Any Terminal or PC. Uses Compatibility of '386 Protected Mode.
Prime Computer, Inc.

MERGER. *Compatible Hardware:* Altos series 15-5D, Series 5-5D, 580-XX, ACS8000-XX; IBM PC with 2 disk drives, PC XT, IBM compatibles; Xerox 820 with 2 disk drives; ZILOG MCZ-250. *Operating System(s) Required:* CP/M, MP/M, CP/M-86/80, PC-DOS, MS-DOS.
contact publisher for price (Order no.: MERGER).
Determines the Impact of a Merger or Acquisition on the Financial Statements under the ABP16 Purchase Method. Adjusts Assets & Liabilities to Their Fair Market Value, Calculates Positive or

Negative Goodwill Arising from the Merger or Acquisition, Allocates Negative Goodwill Among Noncurrent Assets, Consolidates the Purchaser's & Target's Balance Sheets, Calculates the Impact over a Five-Year Period, on the Purchaser's Income Statement.
Coopers & Lybrand.

Mergers & Acquisitions. Barry Zelickson et al. *Items Included:* Spiral bound manual, spiral bound book on the product. *Customer Support:* 90-day warranty against defects, free assistance on prepaid phone calls.
DOS 2.0. IBM compatible. $595.00.
Provides User with Complete Narrative for a Business Plan As Well As Financial Data & Spreadsheets. Also Provides the Format for Presentation to Potential Funding Sources. The Financial Forms Utilize Lotus, Macro's & Prompt for Data Entry of Historical As Well As Predicted Company Performance.
American Institute of Small Business.

MergeWrite. *Version:* 1.1. *Compatible Hardware:* Apple Macintosh. *Memory Required:* 512k. *Items Included:* Manual. *Customer Support:* Free telephone support.
3.5" disk $49.95.
Designed to Be Used with MACWRITE As a Mail Merger. Can Also Be Used Alone to Produce Mailing Materials. Accepts Data from RECORDHOLDERPLUS or Other Popular Data Managers. Sorts by Alpha or ZIP.
Software Discoveries, Inc.

Merlin. Glen Bredon. 1984. *Compatible Hardware:* Apple II, II+, IIe, IIc, IIgs. *Operating System(s) Required:* Apple DOS 3.3. *Language(s):* Assembly. *Memory Required:* 64k.
disk $64.95, incl. manual (ISBN 0-927796-03-1).
Macro-Assembler Facilitating Assembly Language Programming. Includes 80 Column RAM Card Support, 28 Pseudo-Ops, Editor, Nested Macros, 16 Opcodes, & File Linking. An Additional Utility, SOURCEROR, Takes Raw Binary Data & Creates Labeled Source Listings.
Roger Wagner Publishing, Inc.

Merlin 8/16. *Compatible Hardware:* Apple II series. *Memory Required:* 64k.
3.5" or 5.25" disk $124.95 (ISBN 0-927796-28-7, Order no.: 155).
Assembler Features Macros, Macro Libraries, Nested Macros, Conditional Assembly, Assemble to Memory or Disk, Linked Files, Dummy Program Segments, & XREF Utilities. Includes Two Separate Assemblers, Also the SOURCEROR Which Converts Binary Files into Source Codes.
Roger Wagner Publishing, Inc.

Merlin Pro, 2 disks. *Version:* 2.54. Glen Bredon. *Compatible Hardware:* Apple IIe, IIc, IIgs, Laser 128. *Operating System(s) Required:* ProDOS 8, Apple DOS 3.3. *Language(s):* Assembly. *Memory Required:* 128k.
$99.95 (ISBN 0-927796-04-X).
Features All of the Standard Merlin Features (Macros, Macro Libraries, Nested Macros, Conditional Assembly, Assemble to Memory or Disk, Linked Files, Dummy Program Segments etc.), But Designed Specifically for the 128K IIe or IIc, & Comes with Both ProDOS & DOS 3.3 Versions. Enhancements Include a Full Screen Editor, a Relocating Linker to Generate Relocatable Object Code, the Use of Local Labels, & Entry & External Label Definitions. Merlin Pro Supports & Assembles All 6502, 65C02, & 65802 Opcodes. Also Includes SOURCEROR, an Easy to Use Disassembler That Creates Merlin Pro Source Files from Binary Programs, & SOURCEROR.FP Which Produces a Fully Labeled & Commented Source Listing of Applesoft BASIC.
Roger Wagner Publishing, Inc.

Merlin 64. Glen Bredon. 1984. *Compatible Hardware:* Commodore 64. *Operating System(s) Required:* 1541 disk drive or equivalent. *Language(s):* Assembly. *Memory Required:* 64k.
disk $49.95 (ISBN 0-927796-05-8).
6502 Macro Assembler for the Commodore 64 with 80-Column Support or Optional Soft-80 Display. Features Include Nestable Macros, Assemble to Disk, Use of Linked Source Files, & a Word Processor-Like Editor with Search & Replace. Also Features over 35 Pseudo-Opcodes, Conditional Assembly Within Macros, Cross Reference Utilities, & a Cycle Timer. Includes "Sourceror", a Disassembler That Creates MERLIN 64 Source Files out of Binary Programs, & a Monitor to Move, Compare, Disassemble & Dump Blocks of Memory.
Roger Wagner Publishing, Inc.

Merlin 128. *Compatible Hardware:* Commodore 128. *Memory Required:* 128k.
disk $69.95 (ISBN 0-927796-23-6, Order no.: 156).
Comprehensive Macro Assembler System with All Features Co-Resident, Including File Loading, Saving & Other Disk Management Operations. Full Screen Editor for Entering & Editing Programs Includes Advanced Assembler Features Such As Macros, Macro Libraries, Nested Macros, Conditional Assembly, Assemble to Disk, Dummy Program Segments & a Linker for Generating Relocatable Object Code Modules, Library Routines, Run-Time Packages etc. Includes SOURCERER, Disassembler That Creates MERLIN 128 Source Files from Binary Programs. Includes Over 15 Sample & Utility Programs Routines & Files Such As Disk Copy, Disk Zap, XREF, RAM Test, Keydefs & Printfiler.
Roger Wagner Publishing, Inc.

Merriam Webster's Dictionary for Kids.
MS-DOS 5.0 or higher, Windows 3.1 or higher. 386 processor or higher (4Mb). CD-ROM disk $59.95 (Order no.: R1347). *Nonstandard peripherals required:* CD-ROM drive. *Optimal configuration:* 386 processor operating at 16Mhz or higher, MS-DOS 5.0 or higher, Windows 3.1 or higher, 30Mb hard drive, mouse, VGA graphic adapter & VGA color monitor (SVGA recommended), 4Mb RAM, external speakers or headphones (with sound card) that are Sound Blaster compatible.
Based on the Popular "Merriam-Webster's Elementary Dictionary," This Program Contains 33,000 Entries, Usage, Synonyms & Word Histories. Animation, Color Illustrations & Spoken Pronunciations for over 20,000 Words Present Definitions & Phonetic Markings in a Fun & Playful Way (Ages 8-12).
Library Video Co.

Merriam-Webster's Word Crazy: Electronic Edition, Windows. SilverSun Editorial Staff. Oct. 1995.
Windows. IBM. 3.5" disk Contact publisher for price (ISBN 0-87779-456-1).
CD-ROM disk Contact publisher for price (ISBN 0-87779-457-X).
Integrates Four Innovative Word Games, Word Warp, Chain Reaction, Missing Link, & Letter Ball, Which Are Presented in a Tournament Format with 50 Computer Opponents Who Are Portrayed in Rich, Detailed Graphics. CD-ROM Version Also Includes Audio from All 50 Opponents.
Merriam-Webster, Inc.

Merrit Calc 2. *Version:* 2.0. 1986. *Items Included:* Documentation. *Customer Support:* Telephone support available at no cost.
MS-DOS. IBM XT, AT & compatibles (512k).
disk $300.00. *Addl. software required:* Lotus 1-2-3, Version 2.01 or prior. *Networks supported:* Any network which uses Lotus.
An Application Template for Lotus 1-2-3. It Is Designed to Calculate & Develop Merit Increase Guide Charts & Build Performance Differentiation into Salary Increases. The Product Combines with Lotus 1-2-3 to Calculate a Company's Merit Increase Budget Based upon: (1) Number of Employees and/or Payroll, & (2) Performance Ratings and/or Salary Position in Range. Graphics Illustrate Merit Increases Generated (Aggregate & Percent of Payroll) by Performance Rating Category.
Cammock & Cammock, Inc.

Mesa Graphics Plotter Utility. *Version:* 1.03. Nov. 1991. *Compatible Hardware:* Apple Macintosh System 6.0 or higher. *General Requirements:* Hewlett-Packard or Houston Instrument color plotter. *Items Included:* Manual & disk. *Customer Support:* Telephone.
3.5" disk $125.00.
$30.00 upgrade from older versions.
Will Plot MacDraw, MacDraft, MacProject, any PICT Document, or MacPaint. Users Are Able to Control Scale for MacDraw or MacDraft Plotter Output & Add Color to MacDraw, MacDraft, or MacPaint.
Mesa Graphics, Inc.

Mesa Graphics Terminal Utility: Text Term + Graphics. *Version:* 1.04. Dec. 1991. *Compatible Hardware:* Apple Macintosh System 6.0 or higher. *General Requirements:* LaserWriter, ImageWriter, or plotter. *Items Included:* Manual & disk. *Customer Support:* Telephone.
3.5" disk $195.00.
Enables the Macintosh to Act As a Graphics Terminal with Mainframe Applications from ISSCO GRAPHICS, MOLECULAR DESIGN, CHEMICAL ABSTRACTS SERVICE, PRECISION VISUALS, or SAS INSTITUTE. Users Can Save Mainframe Graphics for MACDRAW, MACPAINT, or PAGEMAKER. Emulates Tektronix 4014, 4010, 4105, 4107, 4115, 4205, 4207, 4215, 4006; VT100; VT640.
Mesa Graphics, Inc.

MessageNet: Advanced E-Mail System. *Items Included:* 1 spiral bound manual. *Customer Support:* $250.00 for telephone consultation, updates $20.00, documentation $20.00.
TSX-32. IBM PC AT, PS/2 or compatible, 386 or 486 processor (4Mb). disk $750.00.
Comprehensive E-Mail System for TSX-32 Which Allows Users to Send Messages to Each Other on the Local System, & Through Telecommunication Lines to Other TSX-3 Systems. Automated Access to AT&T Easylink Or MCI Mail Style & for Most E-Mail Systems. Includes Productivity Features Such as Calendar, Reminder.
S & H Computer Systems, Inc.

MetaDesign. *Version:* V.3.0 MAC; V.4.0 PC. 1986. *Compatible Hardware:* Apple Macintosh & Quadra, IBM PC. *Operating System(s) Required:* Macintosh OS, MS-DOS under MS Windows 3.1. *Memory Required:* IBM 2Mb, Macintosh 1000k. *General Requirements:* Microsoft Windows 3.1 for IBM. *Items Included:* Binder manuals. *Customer Support:* Telephone 800 number.
Macintosh $250.00.
IBM $350.00.
Graphics & Text Handling Program Which Lets Users Draw Flow Charts, Organizational Charts, Computer Programs, Communication Networks, Presentation Graphics, & Production Line Processes. Users Can Create Diagrams up to 999 Pages Long & Arrange Them in Hierarchical Structure. They Can Also Develop Successively Detailed Descriptions Within One Multi-Level Diagram. Text Inside Any Graphic Can Be Edited, Manipulated, & Styled. Hypertext Links Can Be Created to Organize Text Across Multiple Pages.
Meta Software.

METAFILE. Version: 10.0. Oct. 1990. Compatible Hardware: Compaq; IBM PC, PC XT, PS/2, PC AT & compatibles. Operating System(s) Required: PC-DOS. Language(s): Assembler. Memory Required: 128k. Items Included: Database language, documentation, 90 days free support. Customer Support: $100/year toll free phone support.
disk $695.00.
Information Management Tool Designed for Application Development. Provides Facilities for Managing Databases, Generating Reports, Writing Programs, Creating Menus, Preparing & Revising Text, Communicating Between Machines & Operating Within a Local Area Network. Also Provides Impromptu Access to Data & Commands to Meet Special Processing Needs. All METAFILE Facilities Contribute to a Single Environment for Flexible Interaction During All Phases of Development & Use.
Metafile Information Systems, Inc.

METAMORPH. Version: 3.5. Memory Required: 640k. Items Included: Program, associated utilities, hard copy & on-line documentation. Customer Support: Phone support to registered users.
PC/MS-DOS 2.1 or higher, Unix (AT&T or BSD), MVS (with TSO & ISPF). IBM PC & compatibles, Unix & MVS based machines. $1644.00 per copy (plus $1500.00 port chg on Unix where necessary), Quantity discounts available.
Natural Language Driven Text Analysis Application for Information Retrieval & Correlation. Used for Research & Strategic Information Analysis. Allows Users to Search Any Textbase for Concepts & Inference Patterns Relevant to a Particular Query with No Pre-Processing.
Thunderstone Software/Expansion Programs International, Inc.

Metamorphosis. Version: 3.0. 1988. Language(s): FORTRAN, BASIC, C, PL/I, Ada, CMS-2M, Etc.. General Requirements: 2 360k floppy disk drives.
MS-DOS/PC-DOS 2.0 or higher. IBM PC, XT, AT or compatibles (416k). disk $387.00.
Generic Computer Program Which Facilitates the Transformation of Any Syntactically Reducible Character Oriented File to Any Other Form While Preserving the Synonymy. When Configured with the Syntactical Definition of the Source & Target Languages, This Program Translates Any Source Program from One Language to Another.
J. H. Shannon Assocs., Inc.

Metamorphosis Professional. Version: 2.02. Macintosh Plus or higher (1Mb). 3.5" disk $149.00.
An Easy to Use Type Conversion Utility Which Creates Editable Outlines & Other Computer Font Formats from PostScript Language & TrueType Fonts.
Altsys Corp.

MetaStock. Version: 4.5. Feb. 1992. Compatible Hardware: IBM PC, PC XT, PC AT, PS/2, & compatibles. Operating System(s) Required: MS-DOS 3.0 or higher. Memory Required: 640k. General Requirements: 2 disk drives or hard disk; EGA or VGA card. Dot matrix, laser, or color print recommended. Items Included: User Manuals. Customer Support: Full technical support at (801) 265-9998.
$349.00.
demo disk $5.00.
Technical Analysis Software Which Includes More Than 75 Pre-Programmed Indicators, System Testing with Optimization, Desktop Publishing Compatibility, High Resolution Printing, Complete Mouse Support & an All New Graphical User Interface, Alphabetical Help System, Built-In Keyboard Macros & Page Layouts, Tile & Cascading Charts. Technical Studies Include Andrew's Pitch Fork, Demand Index, Fibonacci Arcs; Fans & Time Zones, Momentum, Performance, Expanded Use of Trendlines & Histogram Displays. Supports Manual Data Entry or Automatic Uploading with The Downlaoder Series. Converts Price to/from ASCII or LOTUS 1-2-3, or Imports CSI, CSL, & Dow Jones Data. Includes Japanese Candlestick, Option Analysis, Macro Editor & Debugger, Smart Charts, VGA Support & an Indicator Buffer, Explorer (Screening & Filtering), Option Worksheet, Tool Bar.
Equis International.

MetaStock RT: Real-Time Technical Analysis Charting Software. Version: 4.5. Jul. 1992. Items Included: Four paperback manuals: user's manual, utilities manual, resource guide, demo & tutorial manual. Customer Support: Free telephone assistance, free quarterly newsletter, product-specific user groups - both national & international, CompuServe BBS, extensive user manual.
DOS 3.0 or higher. IBM AT, PS/2 or true compatible (640k). disk $495.00. Nonstandard peripherals required: ADBC Signal receiver & password are required to collect real-time & delayed quotes. Optimal configuration: An 80386 or faster processor is strongly recommended. Microsoft compatible mouse is optional, but recommended. An 80x87 math coprocessor is also highly recommended.
Real-Time Technical Analysis Charting Software That Includes All the Features of MetaStock 4.5 Plus It Provides Instant Updates of Price Charts, Indicators & Studies. Using the Signal Datafeed from Data Broadcasting Corporation, MetaStock RT Offers Real-Time Access to over 55,000 Issues. Also Includes a Customizable Quote Screen to Track More Than 500 Different Securities. Price Alert Levels Can Be Selected, with Pop-Up Windows & Audio Alarms to Notify When Price and/or Volume Levels Are Reached.
EQUIS International.

Metaview. Version: 2.0. Compatible Hardware: IBM PC & compatibles, System 3x, AS/400, S/370, Btrieve. Customer Support: 800 number 365 days/yr..
$15,000.00 AS400 Model 60 Interface.
$495.00 PC Operating System.
A High-Level, Object-Driven Language for Easy Development of Document Imaging Solutions in a Cooperative Processing Environment. Applications Integrate Images from Optical Disk with Magnetically-Stored Information. The Two Are Combined on PCs with VGA Monitors (19", Ultra-High Resolution Monitors Are Also Available.) Most Processing Is Done at the PC Level. Images Enter the System Through High-Speed Scanners or FAX, are Stored on 5.25' or 12" Optical Disks & Are Read by Individual Drives or Jukeboxes. Up to 20 Jukeboxes Can Be Linked to a LAN, Making Millions of Images Available on Line with Minimal Space Requirements. Invokes & Runs Multiple AS/400 Sessions at the PC with No Hotkeying. It Brings Existing Mainframe Applications to the PC Through a Window & Adds Images at That Point. This Strengthens Existing Software Investments.
Metafile Information Systems, Inc.

Meteor Belt: Arcade Plus Series. Compatible Hardware: TI 99/4A with Milton Bradley's MBX System.
contact publisher for price (Order no.: PHM 3152).
Let Your Computer Co-Pilot Warn You of Enemy Ships in a Space Duel. Destroy Meteors & Rival Spaceships. Includes Speech Synthesis & Voice Recognition Features.
Texas Instruments, Personal Productivit.

METES & Bounds. Version: 86.01. Mark D. Floan. Jun. 1986. Compatible Hardware: IBM PC. Operating System(s) Required: MS-DOS 2.1 or higher. Language(s): Compiled BASIC. Memory Required: 256k. Items Included: Manual. Customer Support: 120 days free phone support; 90 day moneyback guarantee.
disk $199.00 incl. manual (ISBN 0-932071-03-1).
Checks and/or Writes Metes & Bounds Legal Descriptions for Closure & Area. Plots the Description on the Monitor & Dumps the Image to an Epson-Compatible Printer. Works Independently or with Data Generated by SURVEY!, SURVEY 3.0, SURVEY 4.0 or SURVEY LITE.
Simplicity Systems, Inc.

Metri-Pak. Samuel J. Levy. Jun. 1990. Items Included: Manual in 6x9, 3 ring binder, membership card. Customer Support: 90 day unlimited warranty. Our site training $25.00/hr. Hot line (free) to caller; none returned.
Apple MAC 6.2 or higher. Apple Macintosh. disk $55.00 (ISBN 1-883467-05-5, Order no.: IGTI 3 1/2). Addl. software required: Microsoft Excel 3.0 or higher. Optimal configuration: Color monitor, printer, 2Mb RAM (extended on IBM).
Macintosh OS. Apple Macintosh (1Mb). 3.5" disk $55.00 (Order no.: IGTI 2-3 1/2 800K). Addl. software required: Microsoft Excel 3.0 or higher. Optimal configuration: Color monitor, 2Mb RAM, printer. Networks supported: Appletalk.
Provides a Systems Solution to Metrication. Some of Its Main Features Include: Converts 400 Units, 6400 Counting Prefixes, to SI Metric (& Reverse); a Special Drawing Conversion Module (Every Type Dim./Tol. Converted); the Most Popular ANSI-DOD Approved Metric Fasteners; Precision Rounding per ASTM E-380, Methods A & B; Most Used Limits & Fits Is Automated (Enter Size & Fit Number Only); Converts Special Values Entered by Formula, Exponents, Prefixes, etc.; Metric Drills & Resulting Hole Sizes Are Looked up Automatically; Summary Conversion Sheets Cover an Entire Drawing/Document; & Full Drawing, Hard & Soft Conversion, Example with Summary Sheets. Not Protected.

Metri-Pak. Sam Levy. Sep. 1991. Items Included: 3 "D" ring binder manual. Customer Support: Hot line.
512k RAM DOS 4.2, Windows 3.0. IBM or compatible (512k). $50.00 (ISBN 1-883467-05-5, Order no.: IGTI2-720K, IGTI2-1.2M). Nonstandard peripherals required: Color Monitor. Addl. software required: Microsoft Excel 3.0.
Apple MAC. $50.00 (Order no.: IGTI2-800K). Addl. software required: Microsoft Excel 3.0.
Provides a System Solution to Metrication. Some of Its Main Features Are As Follows: SI Metric (and reverse) Units Conversion-400 Units; 6400 Counting Prefixes; A Special Drawing Conversion Module, Every Type Dim. & Tol. Converted; The Most Popular ANSI-DOD Approved Metric Fasteners Are Included; Precision Rounding per ASTM E-380, Methods A & B; The Most Used Limits & Fits Is Automated-Just Input Size & Fit Number; Converts Spec. Values Entered by Formula, Exponents, Prefixes, etc; Metric Drills & Resulting Hole Sizes-Looked up Automatically; Summary Conversion Sheets Cover the Entire Document; Full Drawing Hard & Soft Conversion Example with Summary Sheets.
International Geometric Tolerancing Institute, Inc.

Metric Unit Conversions Engineering Unit Conversions. Items Included: Full manual. No other products required. Customer Support: Free telephone support - no time limit. 30 day warranty.

METRICS

MS-DOS 3.2 or higher. IBM & compatibles (512k). $49.95 MS-DOS version; $69.95 Windows version. *Optimal configuration:* IBM, MS-DOS 3.2 or higher, 512k RAM.
MUC Converts a Unit of Measure to Any Other Unit of Measure Within the Same Category. It Can Convert English Units to Both Metric and/or Other English Units. Likewise, Metric Units Can Be Converted to Both English and/or Other Metric Units. Examples of Categories of Measurement Include: Length, Mass, Force, Area, Volume, Pressure, Temperature, Energy, Power Velocity, Acceleration, Wavelength, etc. 50-Page Manual Offers Step-by-Step Instructions, Sample Runs, & Background Information.
Dynacomp, Inc.

Metrics. *Version:* 2.0. Apr. 1993. *Items Included:* Comprehensive user's manual. *Customer Support:* 90 day free support, 30 day money back guarantee, telephone support only.
Any Macintosh 6.03 or higher, System 7 compatible. All Macintosh (340k). 3.5" disk $39.00 (ISBN 0-9636716-1-8, Order no.: 10024). *Optimal configuration:* Macintosh Operation System 6.08 or 7.1 1Mb RAM, 4Mb RAM respectively.
Handy Weights & Measures Conversion Calculator. Easy to Use Tool That Converts Numbers Between Various Systems & Units of Measurement Such As Feet to Meters, Pints to Liters, Sq. Kilometers to Sq. Feet. Data May Be Shared Between Metrics & Other Applications by Using the Copy & Paste Features of the Program. Solve These Conversions Quickly & Accurately: Liquid, Length, Speed, Temperature, Area, Troy Weight, Volume, Time, Recipe, & Weight (Avoirdupois). System 6/7 Compatible.
Expert Systems, Inc.

Metrics Manager. *Version:* Windows. Nov. 1995. *Items Included:* Documentation manuals, registration form, Client Support Program (CSP) guide. *Customer Support:* Client Support Program which includes: hotline support, newsletters, free upgrades, user groups, warranty extension. 90 day warranty - training & consulting available both public & onsite. Prices vary.
DOS 3.0 or higher. Any XT/AT/286 & machine. $14,950.00; Optional database $4000.00. *Addl. software required:* Microsoft Windows, Project Bridge Modeler.
A Robust Measurement Tool That Provides Project Data Collection, Analysis, Comparison Reporting of Project Metrics Data for Multiple Projects (or Products). It Provides Measurement of Definition, Construction & Operations Data & Delivers Quality, Performance & Value Metrics Information. Provides Measurement at the Enterprise Responsibility Center, Application & Project Levels. Metrics Database Is Also Available.
ABT Corp.

Metrics Manager. *Customer Support:* Client Support Program: unlimited technical support through ABT's hotline; extended assistance & support through FaxMail; ABT System Protection Plan; software upgrades; PROJECtions, ABT's quarterly newsletter. Price: 15% purchase with system, $1725 if purchased separately.
MS-DOS 3.0 or higher. IBM PC or compatible (486 (8Mb). 3.5" disk $7500.00 plus $750.00 per seat (users 2-10); $7500.00 (11th copy) plus $750.00 per seat (12-20). *Nonstandard peripherals required:* One floppy disk drive (3.5"), Monochrome (Hercules) or color monitor, hard disk drive with 5Mb free disk space.
A Windows-Based Measurement Tool That Provides Project Data Collection, Analysis & Comparison Reporting of Project Metrics Data for Multiple IS Projects. It Provides a Repository for Capturing Measurement Data Throughout the Project Life Cycle & Delivers Analysis of Quality, Performance, & Metrics Information. Provides Measurement at All Levels of the Organization & Helps to Build the Foundation for a Continuous Process Improvement Program.
ABT Corp.

Metrix: U. S. - Metric Conversion System. 1992. *Items Included:* Detailed manuals included with all Dynacomp products. *Customer Support:* Free telephone support to original customer - no time limit; 30 day limited warranty.
MS-DOS 3.2 or higher. IBM PC & compatibles (512k). $29.95 (Add $5.00 for 3 1/2" format; 5 1/4" format standard). *Optimal configuration:* IBM, MS-DOS 2.0, 56k RAM free memory (above running software).
Will Easily & Accurately Convert Virtually Any Measurement in the U.S. Standard (E.G., Lbs., Inches) to the International Standard (E.G., Newtons, Meters) & Vice Versa. Features Include: Menu-Driven; Integrated Pop-Up Calculator; Runs Standalone or As a TSR; User-Selectable Hotkey, Colors, Options; Supports over 100 Conversions & More.
Dynacomp, Inc.

Metrix U.S. - Metric Conversion System. *Items Included:* Full manual. No other products required. *Customer Support:* Free telephone support - no time limit. 30 day warranty.
MS-DOS 3.2 or higher. IBM & compatibles (512k). disk $29.95.
Will Easily & Accurately Convert Virtually Any Measurement in the U.S. Standard (e.g., Lbs., Inches) to the International Standard (e.g., Newtons, Meters) & Vice Versa. Features Include: Menu-Driver; On-Line Help Screens; Integrated Pop-Up Calculator; Integrated Screen Dump to Printer, Disk; Runs Standalone or As a TSR; Uses Only 56k RAM As a TSR; User-Selectable Hotkey, Colors, Option; Convenient Search Facilities; Supports over 100 Conversions & More.
Dynacomp, Inc.

Metro. *Compatible Hardware:* IBM PC, PC XT, PC AT; Compaq Portable, Plus, Deskpro; other Lotus-certified compatibles. *Operating System(s) Required:* PC-DOS 2.1 or higher. *Memory Required:* 640k. *General Requirements:* 2 double-sided disk drives (hard disk recommended), 80k for RAM portion.
disk $85.00.
Memory-Resident Time Management Program That Combines 12 Business Management Tools. Can Be Customized to User's Needs by Choosing Any of the Following Utilities: CLIPBOARD Lets User Move Data & Text Between 1-2-3 & Symphony or Other Software Products, As Well As Between METRO Utilities Themselves; APPOINTMENT BOOK; PHONE BOOK - Will Dial the Phone; CALCULATOR - Includes Financial Functions; NOTEPAD; EDITOR - Creates Business Letters & Spreadsheet Reports & Allows User to Edit Existing Files; WATCH - Records Time Spent on As Many as 100 Projects; DOS FILE MANAGER; KALEIDOSCOPE - Specifies Screen Colors; CONFIGURATION - Customize METRO; SPECIAL CHARACTERS - Includes Full 256 Character IBM Extended ASCII Table; & MACROS. Will Run with Symphony, Symphony Spelling Checker, Symphony Text Outliner, 1-2-3 Report Writer, & Signal.
Lotus Development Corp.

Metro ImageBase Electronic Art. *General Requirements:* Hard disk drive; laser printer, PageMaker, ReadySetGo! or QuarkXPress. Macintosh 512KE or higher. 3.5" disk $145.00.
High-Resolution Artwork.
Metro ImageBase, Inc.

SOFTWARE ENCYCLOPEDIA 1996

Metrowerks CodeWarrior. *Version:* CW4. Jan. 1994. *Customer Support:* 1 year.
Macintosh II (68020, 68030, 68040) or PowerMac 6100. CD-ROM disk $399.00 Gold; $99.00 Bronze (Order no.: MW-M2PSE). *Nonstandard peripherals required:* CD-ROM reader, hard disk recommended. *Networks supported:* Appletalk.
A Complete Development Solution for C/C Plus Plus & Pascal Programming on Both 68K Macintosh & the New PowerMacintosh from Apple Computer. Integrated Development Environments for C/C Plus Plus Run Native on Either Platform & Also Cross-Compile for Either Platform. You Can Therefore Build Power Macintosh Binaries on 68K or 68K Binaries on Power Macintosh -at Power Macintosh Speeds. The Compiler Technology Contained on This CD Is Based on an Advanced Architecture Where Multiple Language Front-Ends (C/C Plus Plus & Pascal) Share Multiple Back-Ends (680x0 & PowerPC 601) As Well As a Common Development Environment. This Ensures That As You Go Forward on Power Macintosh, You Also Conserve Your Investment in Your Installed Code Base on 68K Macintosh & Your Code Base Remains Backward-Compatible.
Metrowerks, Inc.

Metrowerks Modula-Two Startpak. *Version:* 1.2. Mar. 1990. *Items Included:* Tutorial documentation 180 pages; 1 800k diskette. *Customer Support:* 90 days.
Macintosh (1Mb). 3.5" disk $39.00 (ISBN 0-02-380810-1, Order no.: MW-M2SP). *Networks supported:* Appletalk.
Introductory-Level Programming Environment Published by the Macmillan Publishing Company Supported by Metrowerks. It Includes the Modula-2 Compiler for 680x0 Processors, the Multi-Window Text Editor & a Source-Level Debugger.
Metrowerks, Inc.

Metrowerks Modula-2 MPW Edition. *Version:* 3.0.1. *Items Included:* 100 pages MPW user's guide, 500 page Metrowerks Modula-2 reference manual, 2 800k diskettes (with MPW, & 5 diskettes & 2 copies of MPW manual). *Customer Support:* 90 days.
Macintosh (2.5Mb). 3.5" disk $150.00 (Order no.: MW-M2MPW). *Nonstandard peripherals required:* Hard disk. *Addl. software required:* MPW (Macintosh Programmer's Workshop). *Networks supported:* Appletalk.
with MPW $275.00.
For Macintosh Programmer's Workshop, Modula-2 MPW is a One-Pass MPW-Based Optimizing Compiler Generating MPW Linker Format Code for MC680x0 Processors & Offering Full Support for the Macintosh Toolbox & O/S Calls under MPW. The Compiler Generates Applications, MPW Tools & Drivers & Offers Support for XCMD Programming. This System Also Supports Both Macs Bug & SADE Symbol Generation & Is Source Compatible with SP & PSE Compilers.
Metrowerks, Inc.

Metrowerks Modula-2 Professional Standalone Edition. *Version:* 3.1. *Compatible Hardware:* Apple Macintosh Plus, Macintosh SE, SE/30, Macintosh II family. *Operating System(s) Required:* System 4.1 or higher. *General Requirements:* Two 800k disk drives; hard disk recommended. *Items Included:* 100 page user's guide, 550-page compiler reference manual, 3x800K disks. *Customer Support:* Telephone support for registered users..
3.5" disk $179.00.
Integrated Programming Environment for the Mac Includes a Multiwindow Text Editor, a One-Pass Compiler, & an Interactive Debugger. The

TITLE INDEX

Metrowerks Editor Uses Information from the Compiler to Show Various Positions in the Source Program Where Syntactic Errors Occur. The One-Pass Compiler Generates Native Code for the Motorola 680x0 Processors, & the Code Needs no Explicit Linking. Each Compilation Produces Two Files: an Object File Used by the Linker for Execution, & a Reference File Used by the Source-Level Debugger. Programmers Can View the Execution Environment at Runtime with the Runtime Examiner. If an Error Occurs, the Debugger is Called. A Variety of Libraries & Macintosh Interface Modules Are Included with the Program.
Metrowerks, Inc.

MEX-PC. *Version:* 1.65. *Compatible Hardware:* IBM PC & compatibles. *Operating System(s) Required:* PC-DOS/MS-DOS 2.1 or higher. *Memory Required:* 192k. *Items Included:* diskette & manual. *Customer Support:* (414) 563-04013.
disk $99.95.
Allows User to Create Phone Number Files for Automatic Dialing, Menu Screens, Log the Date & the Time As the First Line of a Captured File, Call on Subroutines, & Even Run Other Command Files from Within the Program.
NightOwl Software, Inc.

Mexinur Policy Writing Station. *Version:* 4.0. Mike Flynn. Sep. 1984. *Compatible Hardware:* IBM PC, PC XT, PC AT. *Operating System(s) Required:* PC-DOS, MS-DOS. *Language(s):* PL/1, Assembly. *Memory Required:* 256k.
contact publisher for price.
Enables the Writing of Vehicle Insurance Policies for 1 to 365 Days, Supporting Collision, Fire & Theft, Bodily Injury, Medical & Property Coverage.
Personal Systems Consulting.

Meyer Multimedia: Das Flaggschiff des Konigs.
80386 (4Mb). CD-ROM disk $105.95 (ISBN 3-411-06741-1, Order no.: 067411). *Addl. software required:* Microsoft Windows 3.1 or higher (mouse recommended). *Networks supported:* IBM 2Mb.
Adventures Aboard an 18th Century British Flagship with 500 Illustrations, 200 Animations & over 2 Hours of Sound: 110 Windows Define Seaman's Specific Vocabulary.
Langenscheidt Pubs., Inc.

Meyers Lexikon: Das Wissen A-Z. *Version:* 1.1. IBM compatible PC (2Mb). 7 disks $99.95 (ISBN 3-411-06835-3, Order no.: 06835-3). *Addl. software required:* Microsoft Windows Version 3.1 or higher (mouse recommended).
100,000 Entries & Numerous Charts.
Langenscheidt Pubs., Inc.

Meyers Lexikon: Die Okologie.
IBM compatible PC (2Mb). 2 disks $39.95 (ISBN 3-411-06821-3, Order no.: 068213). *Addl. software required:* Microsoft Windows Version 3.1 or higher (mouse recommended).
2800 Entries from the Field of Ecology & Environment.
Langenscheidt Pubs., Inc.

Meyers Lexikon: Informatik.
80386 (4Mb). CD-ROM disk $70.00 (ISBN 3-411-06891-4, Order no.: 068914). *Addl. software required:* Microsoft Windows 3.1 or higher (mouse recommended). *Networks supported:* IBM 2Mb.
Numerous Charts Defining Terms from the Computer & Related Fields.
Langenscheidt Pubs., Inc.

Meyers Lexikon: Politik und Gesellschaft.
IBM compatible PC (2Mb). 2 disks $39.95 (ISBN 3-411-06801-9, Order no.: 068019). *Addl. software required:* Microsoft Windows Version 3.1 or higher (mouse recommended).
2,300 Entries.
Langenscheidt Pubs., Inc.

Meyers Multimedia: Das Wunder un Seres Korpers. Jun. 1996.
80386 (4Mb). CD-ROM disk $141.95 (ISBN 3-411-06721-7, Order no.: 067217). *Addl. software required:* Microsoft Windows 3.1 or higher (mouse recommended). *Networks supported:* IBM 2Mb.
A Discovery Journey Through the Body with over 1,000 Illustrations & over 600 Views of the Human Body.
Langenscheidt Pubs., Inc.

Meyers Multimedia: Wie Funktioniert Das?
80386 (4Mb). CD-ROM disk $141.95 (ISBN 3-411-06751-9, Order no.: 067519). *Addl. software required:* Microsoft Windows 3.1 or higher (mouse recommended). *Networks supported:* IBM 2Mb.
1,000 Colorful Illustrations, over 300 Animations, 22 Film Clips, 60 Min. of Sound, a Time Line with Famous Inventions, 160 Biographies of Famous Inventors, an Anachronistic Mammoth Travels Through the Ages Discovering New Inventions, Highly Entertaining & Educational.
Langenscheidt Pubs., Inc.

MFGCON: Manufacturing Control Training System. *Version:* 3.11. Keith R. Plossl. Jul. 1988. *Operating System(s) Required:* CP/M 2.1, PC-DOS/MS-DOS 2.1 or higher. *Language(s):* CBASIC. *Memory Required:* 64k.
PC/MS-DOS. disk $1100.00 (ISBN 0-926219-05-7).
PC/MS-DOS. disk $1100.00 (ISBN 0-926219-06-5).
Designed to Be Used by an Instructor with a Thorough Knowledge of Manufacturing Control in a Classroom Environment. Specifically Designed to Show the Use of a Complete MPP II System in a Manufacturing Plant. Contains a Database Which Cannot Be Changed by Programs. Not Designed As a Working System.
George Plossl Educational Services, Inc.

MFM/Medical Financial Management.
Compatible Hardware: DEC.
contact publisher for price.
Professional Data Corp.

MGA Paperless Office Policywriting: MGA Policywriting. *Version:* 1.6. Oct. 1995. *Items Included:* Manuals, NT Windows run time, custom changes. *Customer Support:* Train on site $520.00 per day plus expenses. Warranty 90 days free, after that 15% purchase price per year.
NT, Novell, VMS, AIX. Pentium (48Mb). CD-ROM disk Contact publisher for price.
Nonstandard peripherals required: 1.44Mb diskette, 1.06Mb hard disk, 1.06B tape, CD-ROM, all SCSI Scanner, Laser, SVGA 1029-768. *Addl. software required:* Progress 4GL Ver. 7.3B GUI. *Networks supported:* Novell, NT, Unix Progress platforms 300 Plus.
Florida PIP/PD Policywriting Scan Application, Underwrite, Rate Issue under Class, No Paper in the Office. Automatic Agent Communications, Cash Central, Premium Finance Company Interface.
Automation Resources Corp.

MGM - MacMUMPS 2. *Version:* 5.11. *Compatible Hardware:* Macintosh II series, LC, Classic II, QUADRA, Macintosh SE30. *Customer Support:* BBS 409-883-8537.
$495.00.
Mumps Programming Language.
MGlobal International, Inc.

MICA ACCOUNTING SERIES

MGM PC MUMPS: 386-486 Window 3.1 Required. *Version:* 5.10. Sep. 1991. *Items Included:* MUMPS diskette; 575 page manual in 2 binder boxes. *Customer Support:* 90 days unlimited warranty; Annual support; $125.00 MGM-PC single user multi tasking; $125.00 MGM-Mac.
MS-DOS 3.1 or higher. PC 80386 (2Mb). $295.00 (Order no.: MGM-PC SINGLE USER MULTI TASKING). *Addl. software required:* Microsoft Windows 3.1 or higher. *Networks supported:* Novell, SPXIIPX, NETBIOS, Ethernet, Token Ring, TCP/IP, DEC LAT, DEC DDP (All MGM Networks can use the Novell B-TRIEVE FILESERVER).
MAC OS 7.0 or higher. MacMUMPS II (LC, SE 30, Mac II Series), Classic II, QUADRA (2Mb). $495.00 (Order no.: MGM-MAC). *Networks supported:* Appletalk, Ethernet, TCP/IP, DEC LAT, DEC DDP, Novell SPX/IPX.
An Implementation for PC's, MACS, & UNIX Systems. It Is Completely 1990 ANSI MUMPS Standard. Includes Advanced Debugging Facilities. 2Mb Character Support (for Chinese, Japanese, Thai) Languages & a GRAPHICAL USER INTERFACE (GUI) with Image Processing Capabilities.
MGlobal International, Inc.

MGM-Station: Micro Graphic Manufacturing Station. Dec. 1985. *Compatible Hardware:* Apple Macintosh Plus, Macintosh XL, Lisa.
disk $8000.00 (Order no.: 46194).
Machinery Alternative.

MI-KEY. Dean Brown. 1985. *Compatible Hardware:* Sanyo MBC 555.
disk $34.95 (ISBN 0-923213-33-3, Order no.: SA-MIK).
Defines Standard ASCII Keys Plus 50 Control Keys.
MichTron, Inc.

MI-Print. Robert Ficher. Nov. 1986. *Compatible Hardware:* Atari ST. *Memory Required:* 520k.
3.5" disk $29.95 (ISBN 0-923213-49-X, Order no.: AT-MIP).
Can Take Almost Any Text File & Dump It Out to a Printer with the Specifications Defined by the User.
MichTron, Inc.

MI-Term. *Version:* 4.0. *Compatible Hardware:* Atari ST; IBM PC with GEM; Sanyo MBC 555. *Operating System(s) Required:* MS-DOS, TOS. *General Requirements:* Modem.
Atari. 3.5" disk $29.95.
Sanyo & IBM. disk $29.95 (ISBN 0-923213-31-7, Order no.: SA-MIT).
Terminal Communications Program. Features 26 User-Definable Preset Keys for Automated Log-Ons & Commands; DFT, XMODEM, & ASCII File Transfers; 300/1200/9600 Baud Support; Online Parameter Changes; Printer Echo; Automatic Capture Buffer; Connect-Time Clock; etc. A Built-In Preset Language Enables Users to Design Their Own Custom Communication System.
MichTron, Inc.

MICA. 1982. *Compatible Hardware:* IBM PC & compatibles. *Operating System(s) Required:* MS-DOS. *Language(s):* BASIC. *Memory Required:* 128k.
$125.00.
Used to Calculate Moment of Inertia & Section Properties of Supports & Beams.
Technical Research Services, Inc.

MICA Accounting Series. *Version:* 3.2. *Compatible Hardware:* IBM PC & compatibles. *Memory Required:* 384k. *General Requirements:* Hard disk. *Customer Support:* Annual Support $100.00 per module. Per call $1.50 per minute.

MICA-ACCOUNTS PAYABLE

$189.00 to $295.00.
Financial/Accounting Package. Posts Recurring Transactions, Automatic Posting from Other Modules, Reports Comparative Statements, Links with External Software Programs, Password Access, Audit Trail, Error Recovery, Reject Erroneous Account Numbers & On-Line Help.
Mica Accounting Software.

MICA-Accounts Payable. *Version:* 3.2. Nov. 1985. *Compatible Hardware:* PC XT, PC AT, PS/2 & compatibles. *Operating System(s) Required:* MS-DOS, PC-DOS. *Language(s):* Compiled Microsoft BASIC using QB3. *Memory Required:* 384k.
disk $189.00 ea.
IBM. (ISBN 0-918641-16-0).
AT&T. (ISBN 0-918641-17-9).
Reports: Unposted Transaction Proof; Transaction Posting Record & Summary; Vendor & Invoice Aging; Vendor Analysis; Master Vendor List; Cash Requirements; Check Preview; A/P Checks; G/L Posting; Current A/P Distribution & Vendor Mailing Labels.
Mica Accounting Software.

MICA-Accounts Payable. Micro Associates, Inc. *Operating System(s) Required:* MS-DOS. *Memory Required:* 128k.
$395.00.
Maintains Records for up to 500 Vendors & 1200 Open Invoices. Vendors May Be Referred Either by ID Number or Name.
Texas Instruments, Personal Productivit.

MICA-Accounts Receivable. *Version:* 3.2. Nov. 1985. *Compatible Hardware:* PC XT, PC AT, PS/2 & compatibles. *Operating System(s) Required:* MS-DOS, PC-DOS. *Language(s):* Compiled Microsoft BASIC using QB3. *Memory Required:* 384k.
disk $189.00 ea.
IBM. (ISBN 0-918641-10-1).
AT&T. (ISBN 0-918641-11-X).
Reports: Summarized & Detailed Aging; Transaction Posting; Customer Listing, Statements & Activity Tickler; Mailing Labels; Reminders; General Ledger Posting; Sales Report for Period & Trend; Salesperson Commission.
Mica Accounting Software.

MICA-Accounts Receivable. Micro Associates, Inc. *Operating System(s) Required:* MS-DOS. *Memory Required:* 128k.
$395.00.
Maintain Records for up to 400 Customers & 1600 Open Invoices. Customers May Be Individually Specified As Either "Balance Forward" or "Open Item".
Texas Instruments, Personal Productivit.

MICA-Applications Manager. *Version:* 3.2. Nov. 1985. *Compatible Hardware:* IBM PC XT, PC AT, PS/2 & compatibles. *Operating System(s) Required:* MS-DOS, PC-DOS. *Language(s):* Compiled Microsoft BASIC using QB3. *Memory Required:* 384k.
disk $49.00 ea.
IBM. (ISBN 0-918641-42-X).
IBM. (ISBN 0-918641-46-2).
AT&T. (ISBN 0-918641-47-0).
Designed to Set up a Master Menu of All MICA Programs on a Hard Disk System. Provides Security for All MICA Programs down to the Activity Level, & Provides for Multi-Company Accounting As Well.
Mica Accounting Software.

MICA-General Ledger. *Version:* 3.2. Nov. 1985. *Compatible Hardware:* IBM PC XT, PC AT, PS/2 & compatibles. *Operating System(s) Required:* PC-DOS, MS-DOS. *Language(s):* Compiled Microsoft BASIC using QB3. *Memory Required:* 384k.
disk $189.00 ea.
IBM. (ISBN 0-918641-04-7).
Designed for the First Time Computer User Running a Small to Medium-Sized Business. Can Be Used Stand-Alone or Can Be Integrated with MICA Accounts Receivable, Accounts Payable, Inventory Control, Payroll, Sales/Invoicing, Job Cost, Order Entry & Point of Sale.
Mica Accounting Software.

MICA-General Ledger. Micro Associates, Inc. *Operating System(s) Required:* MS-DOS. *Memory Required:* 128k.
$395.00.
Small/Medium Sized Business Accounting Ledger. 500 Accounts May Be Specified, Using up to 6-Digit Account Number.
Texas Instruments, Personal Productivit.

MICA-Inventory Control. *Version:* 3.2. Nov. 1985. *Compatible Hardware:* PC XT, PC AT, PS/2 & compatibles. *Operating System(s) Required:* MS-DOS, PC-DOS. *Language(s):* Compiled Microsoft BASIC using QB3. *Memory Required:* 384k.
disk $189.00 ea.
IBM. (ISBN 0-918641-22-5).
AT&T. (ISBN 0-918641-23-3).
Reports: Transaction Posting; Inventory List-Abbreviated, Detailed & Price; Physical Work Sheets; Stock Labels; Vendor Listing; Inventory-Status, Activity; Purchase; Inventory-Re-Order, Back-Order & Order Status; End-of-Period Close-Out. Handles Bill of Materials & Serialization.
Mica Accounting Software.

MICA-Inventory Control. Micro Associates, Inc. *Operating System(s) Required:* MS-DOS. *Memory Required:* 128k.
$395.00.
Maintain Records for up to 1000 Stock Items. Costing Methods Include LIFO, FIFO, Weighted Average or Average & May Be Individually Specified for Each Stock Item.
Texas Instruments, Personal Productivit.

MICA-Job Cost. *Version:* 3.2. Nov. 1985. *Compatible Hardware:* IBM PC XT, PC AT, PS/2 & compatibles. *Operating System(s) Required:* MS-DOS, PC-DOS. *Language(s):* Compiled Microsoft BASIC using QB3. *Memory Required:* 384k.
disk $295.00 ea.
IBM. (ISBN 0-918641-40-3).
AT&T. (ISBN 0-918641-41-1).
Designed to Track Project Related Job Cost Covering Labor, Materials & Equipment. Forecasts Cost to Completion, Generates Invoices & Provides Reports Based on Management by Exception Principles.
Mica Accounting Software.

MICA/Network Manager. *Version:* 3.2. Dec. 1985. *Compatible Hardware:* IBM PC XT, PC AT, PS/2 & compatibles. *Operating System(s) Required:* PC-DOS. *Language(s):* Compiled Microsoft BASIC using QB3. *Memory Required:* 384k.
disk $295.00 (ISBN 0-918641-48-9).
Provides the Interface Between All of the MICA Products & Networking Environments. Permits the Software to Work in All Networks Which Fully Support DOS 3.0 or Higher.
Mica Accounting Software.

MICA-Order Entry. *Version:* 3.2. Sep. 1987. *Compatible Hardware:* IBM PC, PC XT, PC AT & compatible, PS/2. *Language(s):* BASIC. *Memory Required:* 384k.
disk $189.00.
Operates in Conjunction with Accounts Receivable, & May Be Integrated with Inventory Control & General Ledger. Integration with MICA/AR Allows Retrieval of Customer Billing Information While Updating Sales Information in the Customer's File. Integration with MICA/IC Allows User to Retrieve Stock Descriptions & Pricing While Updating Stock Records for Sales. Integration with MICA/GL Permits Posting of Sales Revenue.
Mica Accounting Software.

MICA-Payroll. *Version:* 3.2. Nov. 1985. *Compatible Hardware:* PC XT, PC AT, PS/2 & compatibles. *Operating System(s) Required:* MS-DOS, PC-DOS, CP/M. *Language(s):* Compiled Microsoft BASIC using QB-3. *Memory Required:* 384k.
disk $189.00 ea.
IBM. (ISBN 0-918641-28-4).
AT&T. (ISBN 0-918641-29-2).
Payroll System That Can Be Performed for up to 2500 Employees (Active & Inactive), with Provisions for Departmentalization. Maintains All Payroll Information for Tax Reporting, & Several Types of Payroll Compensation, Including Commissions & Non-Taxable Wages. Multiple Payroll Cycles May Be Specified for Various Employee Categories (Weekly, Monthly, etc.). Automatic & Manual Posting to General Ledger Accounts. Reports Include: Payroll Transaction Proof, Payroll Register (Separates Full Time & Contract Employees), Payroll Earnings Summary, Quarterly & Year-to-Date Tax Reports, Employee Data Report, Employee Wage Schedule, Worker's Compensation Report, Employee Roster, General Ledger Posting Report, Check Printout, W-2/1099 Statements, Vacation & Sick Leave.
Mica Accounting Software.

MICA-Payroll. Micro Associates, Inc. *Operating System(s) Required:* MS-DOS. *Memory Required:* 128k.
$395.00.
Features: 300 Employee Payroll, Maintain Payroll Tax Information, Several Types of Payroll Compensation Allowed, Withholding Tax Schedule, Records of Employee Vacation/Sick Leave & More.
Texas Instruments, Personal Productivit.

MICA-Productivity Interface. *Version:* 3.2. Sep. 1986. *Compatible Hardware:* PC XT, PC AT, PS/2 & compatibles. *Operating System(s) Required:* PC-DOS/MS-DOS. *Language(s):* Compiled Microsoft BASIC Using QB-3. *Memory Required:* 384k.
disk $189.00.
Improves User Productivity by Allowing the Output of Information from MICA Files into a New File Which May Be Accessed by Popular Productivity Packages, Including Databases, Word Processors, & Spreadsheets. Can Transfer Information in SDF, DIF, & ASCII, or Users Can Define Their Own Formats.
Mica Accounting Software.

MICA/PS-Point of Sale. *Version:* 3.2. Feb. 1988. *Compatible Hardware:* IBM PC, PC XT, PC AT & compatibles, PS/2. *Language(s):* BASIC. *Memory Required:* 384k.
disk $189.00.
Processes Sales, Returns, Layaways, Adjustments, Quotes, Credit Memos, Paid-Ins, Paid-Outs, & Received on Account Entries. Analyzes Sales by Register, Salesperson, Department, Date, Customer, & Inventory Items. Supports Cash Drawers & Bar Code Readers. Accepts up to 10 Payment Types Tracking Cash, Credit Purchases, Company Checks, Gift Certificates, etc.
Mica Accounting Software.

TITLE INDEX

MICA-Sales Invoicing. *Version:* 3.2. Nov. 1985. *Compatible Hardware:* PC XT, PC AT, PS/2 & compatibles. *Operating System(s) Required:* MS-DOS, PC-DOS. *Language(s):* Compiled Microsoft BASIC using QB-3. *Memory Required:* 384k.
disk $189.00 ea.
IBM. (ISBN 0-918641-34-9).
AT&T. (ISBN 0-918641-35-7).
Reports: Sales Invoices, Credit Memos, Daily Sales Journal, Sales Summary, Salesperson Commission, Daily G/L Distribution, Period to Date G/L Distribution, General Ledger Posting.
Mica Accounting Software.

MICA-Sales Invoicing. Micro Associates, Inc. *Operating System(s) Required:* MS-DOS. *Memory Required:* 128k.
$395.00.
Allows Automatic Retrieval of Customer Information from MICA/AR Accounts Receivable & Stock Data from MICA/IC Inventory Control.
Texas Instruments, Personal Productivit.

Mica 4 Accounting Series. *Version:* 2.0. Aug. 1992. *Items Included:* Spiral bound manual. *Customer Support:* 30 day free support; 1 yr. support contract $100.00; pay per call support $1.50/minute, 15 minute minimum.
PC-DOS/MS-DOS. 286, 386, 486 (640k). $795.00 per module. *Addl. software required:* Mica Systems Manager. *Optimal configuration:* 386 CPU of 640k RAM & 80Mb hard drive. *Networks supported:* Novell 2.X & higher, LANtastic.
High End Multi-User Accounting Application for Medium to Large Sized Businesses. BTRIEVE File Structure, Pop-Up Windows for Inquiries, Cut & Paste Functions, On-Line Help, Data Import/Export, Multi-Level Security, Total Integration, Unlimited Notes per Record, Interface with Report Writer. Extremely Powerful yet Very Easy to Learn & Use.
Mica Accounting Software.

Mica 4 Accounts Payable. *Version:* 2.0. Aug. 1992. *Items Included:* Spiral bound manual. *Customer Support:* 30 day free support; 1 yr. support contract $100.00; pay per call support $1.50/minute, 15 minute minimum.
PC-DOS/MS-DOS. 286, 386, 486 (640k). disk $795.00. *Addl. software required:* Mica Systems Manager. *Optimal configuration:* 386 CPU of 640k RAM & 80Mb hard drive. *Networks supported:* Novell 2.X & higher, LANtastic.
High End Multi-User Accounting Application for Medium to Large Sized Businesses. BTRIEVE File Structure, Pop-Up Windows for Inquiries, Cut & Paste Functions, On-Line Help, Data Import/Export, Multi-Level Security, Total Integration, Unlimited Notes per Record, Interface with Report Writer. Extremely Powerful yet Very Easy to Learn & Use.
Mica Accounting Software.

Mica 4 Accounts Receivable. *Version:* 2.0. Aug. 1992. *Items Included:* Spiral bound manual. *Customer Support:* 30 day free support; 1 yr. support contract $100.00; pay per call support $1.50/minute, 15 minute minimum.
PC-DOS/MS-DOS. 286, 386, 486 (640k). disk $795.00. *Addl. software required:* Mica Systems Manager. *Optimal configuration:* 386 CPU of 640k RAM & 80Mb hard drive. *Networks supported:* Novell 2.X & higher, LANtastic.
High End Multi-User Accounting Application for Medium to Large Sized Businesses. BTRIEVE File Structure, Pop-Up Windows for Inquiries, Cut & Paste Functions, On-Line Help, Data Import/Export, Multi-Level Security, Total Integration, Unlimited Notes per Record, Interface with Report Writer. Extremely Powerful yet Very Easy to Learn & Use.
Mica Accounting Software.

Mica 4 Bank Reconciliation. *Version:* 2.0. Aug. 1992. *Items Included:* Spiral bound manual. *Customer Support:* 30 day free support; 1 yr. support contract $100.00; pay per call support $1.50/minute, 15 minute minimum.
PC-DOS/MS-DOS. 286, 386, 486 (640k). disk $295.00. *Addl. software required:* Mica Systems Manager. *Optimal configuration:* 386 CPU of 640k RAM & 80Mb hard drive. *Networks supported:* Novell 2.X & higher, LANtastic.
High End Multi-User Accounting Application for Medium to Large Sized Businesses. BTRIEVE File Structure, Pop-Up Windows for Inquiries, Cut & Paste Functions, On-Line Help, Data Import/Export, Multi-Level Security, Total Integration, Unlimited Notes per Record, Interface with Report Writer. Extremely Powerful yet Very Easy to Learn & Use.
Mica Accounting Software.

Mica 4 General Ledger. *Version:* 2.0. Aug. 1992. *Items Included:* Spiral bound manual. *Customer Support:* 30 day free support; 1 yr. support contract $100.00; pay per call support $1.50/minute, 15 minute minimum.
PC-DOS/MS-DOS. 286, 386, 486 (640k). disk $795.00. *Addl. software required:* Mica Systems Manager. *Optimal configuration:* 386 CPU of 640k RAM & 80Mb hard drive. *Networks supported:* Novell 2.X & higher, LANtastic.
High End Multi-User Accounting Application for Medium to Large Sized Businesses. BTRIEVE File Structure, Pop-Up Windows for Inquiries, Cut & Paste Functions, On-Line Help, Data Import/Export, Multi-Level Security, Total Integration, Unlimited Notes per Record, Interface with Report Writer. Extremely Powerful yet Very Easy to Learn & Use.
Mica Accounting Software.

Mica 4 Inventory Control. *Version:* 2.0. Aug. 1992. *Items Included:* Spiral bound manual. *Customer Support:* 30 day free support; 1 yr. support contract $100.00; pay per call support $1.50/minute, 15 minute minimum.
PC-DOS/MS-DOS. 286, 386, 486 (640k). disk $795.00. *Addl. software required:* Mica Systems Manager. *Optimal configuration:* 386 CPU of 640k RAM & 80Mb hard drive. *Networks supported:* Novell 2.X & higher, LANtastic.
High End Multi-User Accounting Application for Medium to Large Sized Businesses. BTRIEVE File Structure, Pop-Up Windows for Inquiries, Cut & Paste Functions, On-Line Help, Data Import/Export, Multi-Level Security, Total Integration, Unlimited Notes per Record, Interface with Report Writer. Extremely Powerful yet Very Easy to Learn & Use.
Mica Accounting Software.

Mica 4 Job Cost. *Version:* 2.0. Aug. 1992. *Items Included:* Spiral bound manual. *Customer Support:* 30 day free support; 1 yr. support contract $100.00; pay per call support $1.50/minute, 15 minute minimum.
PC-DOS/MS-DOS. 286, 386, 486 (640k). disk $795.00. *Addl. software required:* Mica Systems Manager. *Optimal configuration:* 386 CPU of 640k RAM & 80Mb hard drive. *Networks supported:* Novell 2.X & higher, LANtastic.
High End Multi-User Accounting Application for Medium to Large Sized Businesses. BTRIEVE File Structure, Pop-Up Windows for Inquiries, Cut & Paste Functions, On-Line Help, Data Import/Export, Multi-Level Security, Total Integration, Unlimited Notes per Record, Interface with Report Writer. Extremely Powerful yet Very Easy to Learn & Use.
Mica Accounting Software.

Mica 4 Payroll. *Version:* 2.0. Aug. 1992. *Items Included:* Spiral bound manual. *Customer Support:* 30 day free support; 1 yr. support contract $100.00; pay per call support $1.50/minute, 15 minute minimum.
PC-DOS/MS-DOS. 286, 386, 486 (640k). disk $795.00. *Addl. software required:* Mica Systems Manager. *Optimal configuration:* 386 CPU of 640k RAM & 80Mb hard drive. *Networks supported:* Novell 2.X & higher, LANtastic.
High End Multi-User Accounting Application for Medium to Large Sized Businesses. BTRIEVE File Structure, Pop-Up Windows for Inquiries, Cut & Paste Functions, On-Line Help, Data Import/Export, Multi-Level Security, Total Integration, Unlimited Notes per Record, Interface with Report Writer. Extremely Powerful yet Very Easy to Learn & Use.
Mica Accounting Software.

Mica 4 Purchase Order Processing. *Version:* 2.0. Aug. 1992. *Items Included:* Spiral bound manual. *Customer Support:* 30 day free support; 1 yr. support contract $100.00; pay per call support $1.50/minute, 15 minute minimum.
PC-DOS/MS-DOS. 286, 386, 486 (640k). disk $795.00. *Addl. software required:* Mica Systems Manager. *Optimal configuration:* 386 CPU of 640k RAM & 80Mb hard drive. *Networks supported:* Novell 2.X & higher, LANtastic.
High End Multi-User Accounting Application for Medium to Large Sized Businesses. BTRIEVE File Structure, Pop-Up Windows for Inquiries, Cut & Paste Functions, On-Line Help, Data Import/Export, Multi-Level Security, Total Integration, Unlimited Notes per Record, Interface with Report Writer. Extremely Powerful yet Very Easy to Learn & Use.
Mica Accounting Software.

Mica 4 Sales Order Processing. *Version:* 2.0. Aug. 1992. *Items Included:* Spiral bound manual. *Customer Support:* 30 day free support; 1 yr. support contract $100.00; pay per call support $1.50/minute, 15 minute minimum.
PC-DOS/MS-DOS. 286, 386, 486 (640k). disk $795.00. *Addl. software required:* Mica Systems Manager. *Optimal configuration:* 386 CPU of 640k RAM & 80Mb hard drive. *Networks supported:* Novell 2.X & higher, LANtastic.
High End Multi-User Accounting Application for Medium to Large Sized Businesses. BTRIEVE File Structure, Pop-Up Windows for Inquiries, Cut & Paste Functions, On-Line Help, Data Import/Export, Multi-Level Security, Total Integration, Unlimited Notes per Record, Interface with Report Writer. Extremely Powerful yet Very Easy to Learn & Use.
Mica Accounting Software.

Michtron BBS. *Version:* 3.0. Timothy Purves. Dec. 1985. *Compatible Hardware:* Atari ST, Sanyo, IBM PC with GEM. *Operating System(s) Required:* MS-DOS, TOS. *Memory Required:* 512k. *General Requirements:* Modem.
Atari. 3.5" disk $79.95 (ISBN 0-923213-16-3, Order no.: AT-BBS).
IBM. disk $79.95 (ISBN 0-923213-22-8, Order no.: SA-BBS).
Complete Bulletin Board System. The Message Base Can Be Set to Any Size, Limited by Disk Space, with Messages up to 99 Lines Long, Public or Private. Supports up to 16 SIG's, Each with Its Own Uploading Area, or Shared with the Others. The Operator & One Caller Can Both Use the BBS at the Same Time, Independently. Supports XMODEM, DFT, & ASCII Protocols for File Transfer. Automatically Adapts to Most Users' Modem & Terminal Set-Ups. Multi-Line Capability.
MichTron, Inc.

Micro Bridge Companion. *Items Included:* Bound manual. *Customer Support:* Free hotline - no time limit; 30 day limited warranty; updates are $5/disk plus S&H.
MS-DOS 2.0 or higher. IBM & compatibles (512k). disk $49.95. *Nonstandard peripherals required:* CGA, VGA, or EGA (or compatible) graphics; printer is supported.
Offers Three Complete Programs for Bridge Players: BRIDGE BARON III, BRIDGE WORLD CHALLENGES, & PERSONAL PLAY LIBRARY. Enhanced Graphics; Choice of Who Gets the Best Hand, Bid/Play Review Displayed on Screen or Printer, & Saved to Disk; & Automatic Play.
Dynacomp, Inc.

Micro Bridge Companion. *Version:* Windows. Oct. 1993. *Customer Support:* 800 number.
DOS Windows, MAC. IBM, MAC (640k). disk $59.95. *Optimal configuration:* Minimal is fine. IBM or MAC, DOS or MAC, 640k total more than enough.
Computer Bridge Program Judged by the American Contract Bridge League & Bridge Writers Such As Alfred Sheinwold to Be the Strongest & Most User Friendly Program on the Market. It Has Captured the World Championships. Over 2 Billion Random Deals. Program Provides Advice with Hints upon Request & Bidding Flow Charts. DOS Version Supports Mouse. MAC Version Also Exists.

Micro Bridge Companion. *Customer Support:* 90-day warranty against defects.
MS-DOS. IBM PC & compatibles (256k), DOS & Windows, MAC. disk $59.95.
Consists of 3 Computer Programs: Bridge Baron V, Winner of Two World Championships (1990 & 1991), Allowing User to Bid, Play, or Bid & Play More Than 2 Billion Deals; Sheinwold Bridge Challenges, Offering 24 Deals Designed by Bridge Expert Alfred Sheinwold Which the User Is Challenged to Play Correctly; & Personal Play Library, Enabling the User to Build a Collection of Bridge Deals for Later Recall & Replay.
Great Game Products.

Micro Business Applications Accounting Software. *Version:* 4.0. *Compatible Hardware:* IBM PC & compatibles. *Memory Required:* 256k. *General Requirements:* Hard disk recommended. *Items Included:* Software & documentation.
Contact publisher for price.
Financial/Accounting Package. Posts Recurring Transactions, Automatic Posting from Other Modules, Report Format User Definable, Reports Comparative Statements, Links with External Software Program, Password Access, Encryption, Audit Trail, Error Recovery, Log off Out-of-Balance, Reject Erroneous Account Numbers & Source Code Available.
MBA Business Accounting Software.

Micro-Cap IV. *Version:* 2.00. Andy Thompson & Tim O'Brien. Jun. 1993. *Items Included:* 2 spiral bound - 150 page tutorial, 300 page reference. *Customer Support:* Free, unlimited.
DOS 3.3 & higher. IBM PC & compatibles (640k). disk $2495.00. *Optimal configuration:* 486 with 4Mb RAM, Super VGA graphics, Microsoft mouse, HP7475 plotter, HP LaserJet.
System 6 & 7. Macintosh (640k). 3.5" disk $2495.00.
Graphic Based Window Oriented SPICE Analog Circuit Simulator. It Provides Schematic Capture Capability with Additional SPICE Netlist Simulation Capability. Allows User to Interactively Simulate & Alter Circuit Designs in One Environment. A SPICE Model Optimization Program Is Also Included.
Spectrum Software (California).

Micro Cap Microcomputer Analysis Program. *Items Included:* Full manual. No other products required. *Customer Support:* Free telephone support - no time limit. 30 day warranty.
MS-DOS 3.2 or higher. IBM & compatibles (512k). $2495.00 full system; $250.00 evaluation version; $10.00 10 demo disks. *Optimal configuration:* IBM, MS-DOS 3.3 or higher, 80286 or higher, math coprocessor, 640k RAM, hard disk, 720k minifloppy or 1.2Mb floppy drive, Microsoft (or compatible mouse), Hercule/EGA/VGA/SVGA/MCGA graphics capability.
Macintosh. $2495.00 full system; $250.00 evaluation version.
Professional Windows-Based Design Tool Created to Enhance the Productivity of Electronics Design by Providing an Interactive Drawing & Analysis System. It Allows the Engineer to Quickly Design & Predict the Performance of a Circuit Without Actually Having to Build It. Includes Advanced Simulation Features Which Take It Beyond Circuit Simulation.
Dynacomp, Inc.

Micro CAP: Microcomputer Circuit Analysis Program Advanced Version. 1995. *Items Included:* Full manual. *Customer Support:* Free telephone support - 90 days, 30-day warranty.
MS-DOS 3.2 or higher. 286 (584k). $250.00-$2495.00. *Nonstandard peripherals required:* CGA/EGA/VGA.
A Professional Windows-Based Design Tool Created to Enhance the Productivity of Electronics Design by Providing an Interactive Drawing & Analysis System. It Allows the Engineer to Quickly Design & Predict the Performance of a Circuit Without Actually Having to Build It. Further, It Includes Advanced Simulation Features Which Take It Beyond Circuit Simulation.
Dynacomp, Inc.

MICRO CAP 2: Microcomputer Circuit Analysis Program, Advanced Version. *Items Included:* Bound manual. *Customer Support:* Free hotline - no time limit; 30 day limited warranty; updates are $5/disk plus S&H.
MS-DOS 2.0 or higher. IBM & compatibles (256k). $100.00-$749.95. *Nonstandard peripherals required:* CGA board.
Macintosh (512k). $100.00-$749.95. *Nonstandard peripherals required:* Two disk drives.
A Professional Design Tool Created to Enhance the Productivity of Electronics Design by Providing an Interactive Drawing & Analysis System. It Allows an Engineer to Quickly Design & Predict the Performance of a Circuit Without Having to Actually Build It. Allows User to: Draw an Electronic Circuit Diagram Directly on the CRT Screen; Run a Time-Domain Simulation of the Circuit Responding to User-Defined Input Sources; Perform an AC (Bode) Analysis Showing Gain & Phase Shift vs. Frequency; Perform a DC Transfer Characteristic Analysis Showing Output Voltage vs. Input Voltage.
Dynacomp, Inc.

Micro-Cap 3. *Items Included:* Bound manual. *Customer Support:* Free hotline - no time limit; 30 day limited warranty; updates are $5/disk plus S&H.
MS-DOS. IBM & compatibles (640k). disk $1295.00. *Nonstandard peripherals required:* Requires a Microsoft compatible mouse, 640k of RAM, & a hard disk or two 720k or 1.2k disk drives. 1Mb of expanded memory & an 80x87 coprocessor are recommended.
Window-Based Interactive Design & Analysis System for Analog Electronics. It Features an Integrated Schematic Editor & SPICE-Like Analysis Routines That Can Perform AC, DC, Fourier, or Transient Analysis Directly from the Schematic. Simulation Results Are Displayed in Graphic Form Similar to Instrument Displays.
Dynacomp, Inc.

Micro Control. *Version:* 3.5. 1982. *Items Included:* Administrator manual, user manual, reporting manual. *Customer Support:* Free hotline, consulting-varied pricing, training-varied pricing.
MS-DOS/PC-DOS 3.0 or higher (640k). IBM PC/XT/AT, 386, 486 & compatibles. headquarter site fee $95.000.00, reporting site fee $3500.00 ea., annual license renewal fee 15%. *Networks supported:* 3Com, Banyan Vines, IBM PC LAN, IBM Token Ring, Novell Netware.
Market Leading Software for Financial Reporting & Consolidation. Based on Corporate Chart of Accounts It Gives Corporations Business Benefits of Increased Control & Access to Financial Data. Fully LAN-Ready, System Enables Financial Staff to Independently Manage Collection, Consolidation, Analysis & Flexible Reporting of Financial Data.
IMRS, Inc.

Micro CookBook. *Version:* 3.2. 1987. *Compatible Hardware:* IBM PC. *Operating System(s) Required:* MS-DOS. *Memory Required:* 256k. *Customer Support:* 707/523-0400.
$49.95.
receipe disks $19.95 ea.
Cookbook & Recipe Systems. Features Automatic Adjustment of Ingredients According to the Number of Servings; Printing of Complete Shopping Lists, On-Line Reference Guides, & Calorie Guide; Selection of Recipes by Name, Category or Ingredient. Allows Input of Personal Recipes.
Pinpoint Publishing.

Micro Decision Support System Analysis. *Compatible Hardware:* Apple II, III; IBM PC. *Operating System(s) Required:* UCSD p-System. *Memory Required:* 128-256k.
disk $495.00.
instr's. manual $10.00.
user reference manual $35.00.
Designed to Help Executives Analyze Available Information.
Addison-Wesley Publishing Co., Inc. (School Division).

Micro-Decision Support System Finance. *Compatible Hardware:* Apple II, III; IBM PC. *Operating System(s) Required:* UCSD p-System. *Language(s):* Pascal. *Memory Required:* 64-256k. *General Requirements:* 2 disk drives.
disk $1500.00.
instr's manual $10.00.
user reference manual $35.00.
Enables User to Manipulate, Cross-Reference, & Rearrange Financial Information.
Addison-Wesley Publishing Co., Inc. (School Division).

Micro Dynamics MARS. *Compatible Hardware:* Apple Macintosh. *Memory Required:* 2000k. *General Requirements:* 20Mb on hard disk, 2 dedicated Macintoshes for servers, WORM drive(s), scanner(s), printer(s), LocalTalk or Ethernet network.
server license $15,000.00.
Optional Access Management Module $3000.00.
Optional FreeForm Module $3000.00.
Turnkey Network-Based Solution Providing On-Line Access to an Organization's Vital Information. Handles Scanned Paper Documents As Well As Files from Most Computers. Supports WORM Drives & Jukeboxes. Takes Advantage of High Speed Scanners, CCITT Group IV Data Compression Boards, Text Recognition (OCR) Devices, LANs, & Laser Printers. Uses Either Standard Keyword Searching ot Optional FreeForm Full Text Searching. Retrieved Documents Can Be Viewed, Printed, Revised, or Distributed Electronically. An Optional Access Management Module Controls Access to the

TITLE INDEX

System As a Whole & Selectively to Each Electronic "File Drawer." Currently Used by Law Firms for Litigation Support, & in Large Corporations, the Military, & Government for Archiving Contracts, Proposals, Technical Reports, Documentation, Marketing Information, Image Libraries, etc.
Micro Dynamics, Ltd.

Micro-Dynamo: System Dynamics Modeling Language. Compatible Hardware: Apple II, II+, IIe; Compaq; IBM PC, PC XT. Operating System(s) Required: UCSD p-System. Language(s): Pascal. Memory Required: Apple 64k, IBM 128k. General Requirements: 2 disk drives.
Apple II. XSch Div. disk $248.00.
IBM. disk $245.00.
user reference manual $12.00.
optional textbk. $19.95.
Compiles & Simulates Complex Models of Cause & Effect Relationships over Time.
Addison-Wesley Publishing Co., Inc. (School Division).

Micro Focus COBOL/2. Version: 1.1. Compatible Hardware: IBM PC & compatibles. Operating System(s) Required: PC-DOS 3.X, OS/2. Memory Required: 384k. General Requirements: Hard disk.
disk $900.00.
COBOL Compiler Meeting Level 1 Requirements in Sort/Merge Category & Level 2 Requirements in Nucleus, Table Handling, Sequential I/O, Relative I/O, Indexed I/O, Library & Debug for a High Federal Standard Level. Compilation Is an Added-Step Process. Features Assembler Access, Integrated Linker & Math Coprocessor. Supports Technical Hot Line.
Micro Focus, Inc. (California).

Micro Focus COBOL/2 Workbench. Version: 2.1. Compatible Hardware: IBM PC, PC XT, PC AT & compatibles, PS/2. Operating System(s) Required: MS-DOS, OS/2.
$3290.00 & up.
Supports the Development of Multi-User, Multitasking Applications. Enhancements Include ANSI 85 COBOL Certification, IBM SAA Conformance, 16Mb Capacity, Transparent EBCDIC Data Support, a Flow Chart Animation Option in the Debugger, a New File Editor, & an Intelligent Source File Comparision Utility.
Micro Focus, Inc. (California).

Micro Focus COBOL/2. Items Included: Manuals. Customer Support: 30-day warranty, hotline, newsletter, electronic bulletin board.
An 80386-based system under SCO Xenix 386 System V. $3500.00.
Xenix Implementation of Micro Focus COBOL/2. Includes COBOL/2 & Forms/2 Runtime System.
Santa Cruz Operation, Inc.

Micro Focus COBOL/2 for UNIX. Jul. 1988. Compatible Hardware: 80386-based PCs, Unix-based systems. Operating System(s) Required: Unix, Xenix, AIX.
contact publisher for price.
COBOL Compiler & Debugging Environment That Allows Applications to Take Advantage of Large Amounts of Memory & Is Compatible with Many COBOL Dialects. Includes ANIMATOR, a Visual Debugger & Profiler, a Performance Analysis Tool.
Micro Focus, Inc. (California).

Micro Focus COBOL/2 Toolset. Version: 07/1987. Compatible Hardware: IBM PC, PC XT, PC AT, PS/2, 3270 PC. Operating System(s) Required: PC-DOS, OS/2. Language(s): Micro Focus COBOL, C. Memory Required: 512k. General Requirements: 10Mb on hard disk.

contact publisher for price.
Package of Four Micro Focus Software Tools Which Complement the Micro Focus COBOL/2 Compiler. These Tools Are the Micro Focus COBOL/2 Editor & Forms Facility for Source/Text Editing & Screen Design; the Micro Focus Run Time Environment for Window Support & Dynamic Loading & Execution of Large Programs; the Micro Focus Xilerator Debugging Tool, Which Allows Debugging of COBOL Source & Machine Code; & the Micro Focus XM DOS Memory Extender Product, Which Allows the Creation of COBOL Applications That Can Address the Full 16Mb Memory Capacity of an 80286-Based System.
Micro Focus, Inc. (California).

Micro for OMCARE Microbiology System. Customer Support: 24 hour/day, 7 day/week customer support; 90 day warranty; yearly maintenance fee approx. 15% of software purchase price.
DOS, Novell, Windows. IBM compatible 486 or Pentium PCs. Contact publisher for price.
Networks supported: Novell.
Features Capabilities Vital to the Operation of the Microbiology Laboratory Whether You Are in the Clinical or Industrial Environment. New Features Include a Paperless Workcard Designed to Use Data Entry via Barcodes, Lightpen, & Touchscreen Essentially Eliminating the Need for a Workstation Keyboard at the Working Bench. It Also Includes User-Designed Specimen Tracking & Alerts Allowing for Support of Sophisticated Protocols & Procedures Plus Real Time Quality Assurance. Uses PC Workstations on a NOVELL Network. Provides You with Capability to Develop & Maintain Your Databases, Screens, Reports, & Logic Which in Turn Allows You to Gain the Full Benefits of the New Features.
LCI.

Micro-Formatting Software. S. E. Warner Software. May 1989.
IBM. 3.5" disk $449.00 (ISBN 1-57094-028-2).
5.25" disk $449.00 (ISBN 1-57094-029-0).
Software-Business Education.
S. E. Warner Software, Inc.

Micro Graphic Kernal System: MGKS. 1984. Operating System(s) Required: MS-DOS. Memory Required: 64k.
contact publisher for price.
Frontier Technologies Corp.

Micro Hardy Cross. Jim VanWinkle. Compatible Hardware: IBM PC. Operating System(s) Required: DOS. Language(s): Pascal. Memory Required: 256k. General Requirements: Printer, graphics card.
disk $450.00.
The Hardy Cross Technique Is a Method of Solving Looped Liquid Flow Systems. Use of Menus Makes It Easy for a User to Input & Edit Data. Large Systems Can Be Handled -- up to 3000 Nodes, 4000 Pipes, 200 Pump Curves, 200 Valve Configurations. Pressure Control Valves, Back Pressure Relief, & Check Valves Are Supported.
Techdata.

Micro-Host Payroll Program. Pay-Fone Systems, Inc. Operating System(s) Required: MS-DOS. Memory Required: 128k. General Requirements: Winchester hard disk, printer.
$150.00.
Transmits Data Entered by User to Host Computer for Payroll Processing.
Texas Instruments, Personal Productivit.

Micro, Inc: Computerized Audit Practice Case. Version: IBM. L. H. Lambert. Feb. 1986. Compatible Hardware: IBM PC, PC XT. Memory Required: 256k. General Requirements: Lotus 1-2-3.
disk $19.32 (ISBN 0-07-831048-2).
Computerized Audit Case of One Company, Micro, Inc. Using LOTUS 1-2-3.
McGraw-Hill, Inc.

The Micro Integrated Planner. Version: 3.20. Mar. 1990. Customer Support: Free 1 day on-site training, free simulation of benefits, unlimited telephone support.
MS-DOS 3.0 or higher. IBM Micro computer or compatible (640k). contact publisher for price.
Expert Decision Support System to Consistently Make Better Decisions to Replenish Inventories. Its Goal Is to Minimize Investment in Inventories While Limiting the Probability of Stockout. It Uses Advanced Time Series Analysis & Linear Optimization Techniques. MIP Automatically Selects the Best of Several Statistical Forecasting Techniques. It Automatically Selects the Best Method to Compute Optimal Order Quantities. It Suggests When & How Many to Actually Order After Solving a Set of Minimization Formulas. It Dynamically Adjusts Reorder Points to Reflect the Changing Patterns of Demand. It Copes with Uncertainties of Demand & Variabilities of Lead Times. It Does All this for Each Planning Period, Item by Time. MIP Comes As a Turnkey Hardware/Software System Ready for Immediate Use with Minimal Implementation Hassle.
Headway Solutions.

Micro Kitchen Companion. May 1984. Compatible Hardware: Apple II+, IIe, IIc, Macintosh; Atari ST; Commodore 64; IBM PC & compatibles. Operating System(s) Required: PC-DOS/MS-DOS 1.1, Apple DOS 3.3. Memory Required: Apple 48k, IBM 128k.
disk $49.95 ea.
IBM. (ISBN 0-935745-00-9, Order no.: MKP).
Apple. (ISBN 0-935745-01-7, Order no.: AKP).
Commodore. (ISBN 0-935745-02-5, Order no.: CKP).
Allows Users to Keep Track of Their Own Recipes or Use BOOK-ON-DISK (Also Published by CDA, Inc.). Users Can Search for Recipes Based on Any Combination of 21 Search Fields & Full Ingredient Lists. Provides Meal Planning & Shopping List Capabilities.
Concept Development Assocs., Inc.

Micro Kitchen Companion. Items Included: Bound manual. Customer Support: Free hotline - no time limit; 30 day limited warranty; updates are $5/disk plus S&H.
MS-DOS. IBM & compatibles (128k). disk $34.95.
Apple II series (64k). disk $34.95.
Atari ST; C-64. disk $34.95.
Macintosh (512k). 3.5" disk $34.95.
Lets User Build a "Bookshelf" of Recipes - an Integrated Data Base - Using Clippings & Books. It Helps You Plan Meals Using an Index System Called "Exceptionally Good" by COOKS MAGAZINE, While Suggesting New Ideas to Spice up Your Style. It Prints Custom Cookbooks, Organizes Shopping Lists, & Even Resizes Recipes for up to 999 Guests! The Complete Package Includes MICRO KITCHEN Software, Plus A TASTE FOR ALL SEASONS Recipe Disk, & a Coupon Good for Another Free Cooking Disk.
Dynacomp, Inc.

Micro Logic II. 1995. Items Included: Full manual. Customer Support: Free telephone support - 90 days, 30-day warranty.
MS-DOS 3.2 or higher. 286 (584k). $100.00-$799.95. Nonstandard peripherals required: CGA/EGA/VGA.
Created to Enhance the Productivity of Electronic Digital Design by Providing an Interactive

Drawing & Simulation System, Allowing You to Quickly Design & Predict the Performance of a Circuit Without You Having to Actually Build It. This Software Product Will Help You to: Draw a Logic Diagram Directly on the CRT Screen; Run a Timing Simulation of the Network Responding to User-Defined Input Sources.
Dynacomp, Inc.

Micro Logic 2. *Items Included:* Bound manual. *Customer Support:* Free hotline - no time limit; 30 day limited warranty; updates are $5/disk plus S&H.
MS-DOS. IBM & compatibles (128k). $100.00-$799.95. *Nonstandard peripherals required:* Requires a hard disk or two 1.2Mb drives; supports 8087/80287/80387 math coprocessors; works with CGA, EGA, Hercules graphics cards.
Created to Enhance the Productivity of Electronic Digital Design by Providing an Interactive Drawing & Simulation System, Allowing User to Quickly Design & Predict the Performance of a Circuit Without Your Having to Actually Build It. This Software Product Will Help You to: Draw a Logic Diagram Directly on the CRT Screen; Run a Timing Simulation of the Network Responding to User-Defined Input Sources.
Dynacomp, Inc.

Micro Logic 2. *Items Included:* Full manual. No other products required. *Customer Support:* Free telephone support - no time limit, 30 day warranty.
MS-DOS 3.2 or higher. IBM & compatibles (512k). $100.00-$799.95. *Optimal configuration:* IBM & compatibles, hard disk or two 1.2 Mb drives.
Created to Enhance the Productivity of Electronic Digital Design by Providing an Interactive Drawing & Simulation System, Allowing You to Quickly Design & Predict the Performance of a Circuit Wihtout Your Having to Actually Build It. Product Will Help You to: Draw a Logic Diagram Directly on the CRT Screen & Run a Timing Simulation of the Network Responding to User-Defined Input Sources.
Dynacomp, Inc.

Micro-Logic II. *Version:* 2.12. Jan. 1987. *Compatible Hardware:* IBM PC & compatibles. *General Requirements:* Mouse. *Items Included:* Manual, 175p. *Customer Support:* Free, unlimited.
disk $895.00.
Interactive Design & Analysis System for Digital Electronics. Includes: Schematic Editor, Component Library Editor, Shape Editor, Data Channel & Clock Waveform Pattern Editors, & a High-Speed Logic & Timing Simulator. Can Handle up to 1,000 Components on a Circuit. The Included Library Has More Than 200 Standard TTL/COMS Logic Packages. The Timing Simulator Will Handle up to 10,000 Equivalent 2-Input Gates.
Spectrum Software (California).

Micro Manufacturer. Jan. 1990. *Compatible Hardware:* IBM PC AT. *Memory Required:* 640k. *General Requirements:* Hard disk.
disk $2500.00 (Order no.: MAR-X10).
Contains Most Functions Needed by the Small to Medium-Sized Manufacturing Concern. Can Be Integrated with a Leading Accounting System. All Modules Are Supportable & Can Be Enhanced & Customized to Meet Customer Needs.
Howard W. Myers & Assocs.

Micro-Map. *Compatible Hardware:* Atari.
disk $24.95 (ISBN 0-936200-55-3).
Creates Custom Arcade-Type Characters & Screens, or Modifies Characters from Existing Game Software.
Blue Cat.

Micro MAST-MT. *Version:* 3.0. Nov. 1988. *Compatible Hardware:* IBM PC. *Operating System(s) Required:* DOS. *Language(s):* C. *Memory Required:* 1000k. *Items Included:* Real Time Data Base/Graphics. *Customer Support:* Phone.
disk $7500.00.
Multi-Tasking Supervisory Control System. Other Programs Can Be Run While This Software Is in Operation.
Baker CAC.

Micro-MAX MRP. *Customer Support:* Telephone technical support, training, TIPs, 24 hour bulletin board.
MS-DOS 3.1 & above. IBM PC & compatibles. $495.00 for starter kit to $25,000.00 for unlimited users.
Manufacturing & Financial Control Software for IBM & Compatible Computers & Networks. Closed-Loop System Primarily for Small-to-Medium Make-to-Stock (Repetitive) Manufacturers. Features 18 Available Modules Including: Master Production Scheduling, Shop Floor Control, Management Performance, Report Writer & More. Interfaces with Three Separate Microcomputer Based Accounting Systems: Solomon Accounting, Great Plains & TCS. The Modules That Are Interfaced with the Manufacturing System Are Accounts Payable, General Ledger, & Accounts Receivable.
Micro-MRP, Inc.

Micro-Mech: Planar Mechanism Analysis.
Items Included: Bound manual. *Customer Support:* Free hotline - no time limit; 30 day limited warranty; updates are $5/disk plus S&H.
MS-DOS. IBM & compatibles (256k). disk $595.00. *Nonstandard peripherals required:* CGA compatible graphics card (EGA, etc.); printer recommended, but not required; 8087 math coprocessor is supported, but is optional.
manual only $29.95.
Engineering Package for Analyzing the Behavior of Planar Mechanisms Consisting of Rigid Links Connected by Combinations of Revolute & Sliding Joints. Analyses Available Include: Kinematic; Force; Dynamic Time Response; Equilibrium Analysis.
Dynacomp, Inc.

Micro Memo. Dennis Allen. 1985. *Compatible Hardware:* TRS-80. *Operating System(s) Required:* CP/M, MS-DOS, TRSDOS 6.x. *Memory Required:* 64k.
disk $49.95 ea.
TRS-DOS. (Order no.: D4MEMO).
CP/M. (Order no.: DCMEMO).
MS-DOS. (Order no.: DMMEMO).
The Alternate Source.

Micro Modeler. *Version:* 2. Dec. 1988. *Compatible Hardware:* IBM PC XT, PC AT. *Memory Required:* 640k. *General Requirements:* Math coprocessor.
disk $1995.00 to $4995.00.
Provides Graphic Link Between Various CAD Packages & the Roland DG CAMM-3 3-Access Milling Machine. 2 Axis & 3 Axis Versions Now Available.
Roland Digital Group.

MICRO PLANNER Manager. *Version:* 1.2. *Items Included:* Reference manual. *Customer Support:* Hotline telephone support, disk updates, disk replacement service.
Macintosh System 6.01 or higher. Apple Macintosh Plus, SE, SE/30 or II (2Mb). 3.5" disk Version 1.2 (11/1989) $695.00. *Networks supported:* Tops, Ethernet, Apple.
Full-Featured Project Management Tool Allowing for Projects of up to 1500 Tasks & 5 Subprojects. Custom Symbols, Custom Reports & Presentation Quality Graphics.
Micro Planning International.

Micro Planner Manager. *Version:* 1.1. 1994. *Items Included:* 4 manuals. *Customer Support:* Free lifetime phone support, training & consulting available for a charge.
MS-DOS. PC (4Mb). disk $695.00 (Order no.: WMGR). *Addl. software required:* Windows 3.0 or higher. *Optimal configuration:* 486PC, 33Mhz, 8Mb RAM, 20Mb hard disk. *Networks supported:* Novell, Banyan, Lantastic, & more.
SUN OS 4.1X/UNIX. SUN SPARC (16Mb). disk $695.00 (Order no.: UMGR). *Optimal configuration:* SUN SPARC, SUN OS 4.1X, 32Mb Ram, 20Mb hard disk.
Mid-Range Project Management Software Able to Handle 1,500 Activities. Program Is Ideal for Managing Projects at the Project Level. Works Best As an Integrator with MPI's High-End Planner, Micro Planner X-Pert.
Micro Planning International.

Micro Planner Professional. *Version:* 7.3G. 1989. *Items Included:* Full set of documentation. *Customer Support:* 6 months free technical phone support.
DOS. IBM XT & compatibles (512k). disk $1995.00 (Order no.: MTP). *Nonstandard peripherals required:* 10Mb hard disk. *Optimal configuration:* IBM AT or 80386-based compatible, 30Mb hard disk, 640k RAM, EGA/VGA monitor, mouse.
High-End Project Management Software for DOS. Precendence & Activity-on-Arrow PERT Model for up to 13,000 Operations & 27 Subprojects. Menu-Driven Structure for Constructing Logical Planning Models Through Graphical or Form-Based Input. Includes Comprehensive Work Breakdown Structure (WBS) for Cost & Date Summaries. WYSIWYG Screen Preview of Standard & Custom Reports.
Micro Planning International.

MICRO PLANNER X-Pert. *Version:* 2.2. *Customer Support:* 30 days free support included in purchase price. Annual contract available thereafter for a small fee.
Mac SE, II (2Mb). disk $1995.00.
High-End Project Management Software Can Handle up to 15,000 Activities & Events, Multiple Projects & Subprojects. Includes Earned Value Analysis Costing & Ability to Break down Work Structures to Eight Levels. User Can Enter up to Four Different Cost Rates per Resource & Compare Actual Cost Information with Budgeted Cost. Can Handle up to 500 Calendars per Project, 100 Zone, Responsibility & Cost Labels & 100 Subprojects with 1364 Records in Each. Roll-Up Multiple Projects from MICRO PLANNER MANAGER for Comprehensive Resource & Cost Analyses.
Micro Planning International.

Micro Radiology Manager. Nov. 1983. *Compatible Hardware:* IBM PC Nestar based LAN, PS/2, token ring network. *Operating System(s) Required:* PC-DOS, MS-DOS. *Language(s):* C. *Memory Required:* 640k. *General Requirements:* Nestar Network on token ring network.
contact publisher for price.
Provides Access to Patient Records & Establishes Controls for Film Transfer & Loans Also Available; Patient Registration, Scheduling, Patient Tracking, Accounting & Billing, Teaching & Research, & Quality Control.
Trinity Computing Systems, Inc.

Micro-Remote 2780-3780 Emulator. *Operating System(s) Required:* CP/M. *Language(s):* C. *Memory Required:* 8k.
contact publisher for price.
IBM 2780 & 3780 Remote Batch Terminals Are Used to Interchange Large Volumes of Batched Data with IBM 360/370/30XX Type Mainframes

TITLE INDEX

Computers. User Can Transfer Data Files Between Local Disk or Printer & the Mainframes, & Perform Local Processing. Emulates IBM 2780 Model 2 with Card Reader/Punch & Printer or IBM 3780 with IBM 3781 Card Punch; Includes Protocol for Single or Multi-Point, Non-Switch Communication Line; Operator Controls System Parameters; Normal & Transparent (Binary) Modes of Operation Are Available; ASCII or EBCDIC Transmission Supported; Line Monitor Routines Allow Operator to Display Communication Line Sequences. Protocol Features Conversational Mode, Inquiry Mode, Switched Line Control, Processor Interrupt, & Space Compression & Expansion.
Aton International, Inc.

Micro-Remote 3270 Emulator. *Operating System(s) Required:* CP/M. *Language(s):* C. *Memory Required:* 6k.
contact publisher for price.
Allows Application Programs to Access a Mainframe Database Using the Micro/Remote "Virtual Screen" Capability, a Buffer Containing 3270 Data Translated into ASCII. Attribute Character Remain in Untranslated EBCDIC Form. Local Program Can Examine Virtual Screen Buffer after a Screen Image Is Received, Modify It, & Cause It to Be Transmitted to the Mainframe on the Next Poll. Program Emulates IBM 3275 Model 2 with IBM 3284 Model 3 Printer; Includes Protocol for Single or Multi-Point, Non-Switched Communications Line; Line Monitor Routines Displays Communication Line Sequences on Screen; Print Key Allows Operator to Dump Screen Contents to a List Device; Printer Output May Go to Disk File.
Aton International, Inc.

Micro SAINT 3.1. May 1988. *Compatible Hardware:* IBM PC & compatibles. *Operating System(s) Required:* MS-DOS. *Memory Required:* 640k. *Items Included:* Manual. *Customer Support:* 1 Year of free telephone support & software updates.
disk $1495.00 (ISBN 0-937197-00-9).
Educational Institutions. $250.00.
Menu-Driven Simulation System. Users Can Design & Test Their Operations by Experimenting with a Simulation Model Rather Than by Trial-&-Error. Models Are Created Using the Task Network Modeling Technique, Which Is Similar to Flowcharting. Graphics are Generated Automatically with Animation.
Micro Analysis & Design, Inc.

Micro-Set. *Version:* 2.1. Dec. 1987. *Compatible Hardware:* IBM PC & compatibles. *Operating System(s) Required:* MS-DOS. *Memory Required:* 384k.
disk $595.00.
Reads & Writes Comugraphic MCS Compatible Disks in a PC. Use Any Word Processor to Prepare Files for the Typesetter.
Mumford Micro Systems.

Micro Share Thrift-401(k): MST. *Version:* 1.18. Feb. 1992. *Compatible Hardware:* IBM PC XT, PC AT. *Operating System(s) Required:* MS-DOS, PC-DOS. *Memory Required:* 256k. *General Requirements:* Hard disk. *Items Included:* Manual, diskettes, training. *Customer Support:* Yes.
$12,500.00, one-time base price.
monthly license fee $200.00.
Provides Professional Participant Recordkeeping for Defined Contribution Plans. Performs All Required Government Tests for 401k Discrimination. Top Heavy & 415 Tests. Maintains Separate Accounting for Pre- & Post-Tax Plus Employer Contributions. All Tax Calculations Automatically Performed on Distribution & 1099R or W2P Printed. Prints 5498's on Request. Provides Recordkeeping for 401k, Thrift, Profit Sharing & Stock Bonus Plans, Multiple Investment Options, Variable Vesting Schedules, Taxable/Pre-Taxed Contributions, Full Tax Tables. Automatic Posting of Salaries & Contributions from Other Systems & Automatic Conversion of Data from Other Computers.
Trilog, Inc.

Micro-SPF. Phaser Systems. May 1984. *Compatible Hardware:* Texas Instruments. *Operating System(s) Required:* MS-DOS, CP/M-86, Concurrent CP/M-86. *Memory Required:* 320k. *General Requirements:* 2 disk drives.
$450.00.
Structured Programming Facility That Emulates Mainframe Software on the TI Computer.
Texas Instruments, Personal Productivit.

Micro-Typewriter Software. *Version:* 4.03. S. E. Warner Software. Jul. 1991.
IBM. 3.5" disk $795.00 (ISBN 1-57094-000-2).
5.25" disk $795.00 (ISBN 1-57094-001-0).
Software-Business Education.
S. E. Warner Software, Inc.

Micro-VTLS. *Version:* 3.1. Jan. 1986. *Compatible Hardware:* IBM PC & compatibles. *Operating System(s) Required:* MS-DOS. *Language(s):* CLIPPER, compiled dBase. *Memory Required:* 2Mb, recommended 4000k. *Customer Support:* On-site training available, toll-free support & updates $1145.00 yr.
disk $4975.00 (Order no.: MICRO-VTLS).
Includes the Following Modules: Circulation, Cataloging with Authority Control, On-Line Catalog, Community Information, & Statistical Management. The System Can Be Searched Using Authors, Titles, Subjects, Series, Call Number, Keyword, ISBN, ISSN, LCCN, & Many More Indexes. Complete Right Truncation Is Permitted on All Searches. Micro-VTLS Can Be Combined with VTLS Libraries via Modem or Direct Connect Cable to Allow On-Line Downloading of MARC Records. The System Can Be Networked Within a Library to Provide All Users with Access to a Single Database. Keyword & Boolean Searching Is Available. Multi-Media Support Is Available.
VTLS, Inc.

Micro Wine Companion. May 1984. *Compatible Hardware:* Apple II+, IIc, IIe; Commodore 64; IBM PC & compatibles; Macintosh. *Operating System(s) Required:* PC-DOS/MS-DOS 1.1, Apple DOS 3.3. *Memory Required:* Apple 48k, IBM 128k.
disk $49.95 ea.
IBM. (ISBN 0-935745-03-3, Order no.: MWP).
Apple. (ISBN 0-935745-04-1, Order no.: AWP).
Commodore. (ISBN 0-935745-05-X, Order no.: CWP).
Cellar Log Which Enables Users to Keep Track of & Search for Wines. Based on 19 Different Search Fields. Features Full Cellar Statistics. Includes over 300 reviews.
Concept Development Assocs., Inc.

Microbe Base. John Magee & Philip Wheat. *Compatible Hardware:* Apple IIe, Commodore 64.
Apple II Package. $974.00 (ISBN 0-12-465014-7).
Apple II manual. $24.00 (ISBN 0-12-465012-0).
Commodore 64 Package. $594.00 (ISBN 0-12-465010-4).
Commodore 64 manual.
Designed to Facilitate Routine Cross-Infection, Epidemiological, & Susceptibility Investigations by Microbiological Laboratories. Can Be Tailored to Suit Individual Laboratories.
Academic Pr., Inc.

MICROBIOLOGY QUIZBANK

Microbes Savant: Antimicrobial Treatment Advisor. *Version:* 2.0. G. B. Cook. May 1987. *Compatible Hardware:* IBM PC. *Operating System(s) Required:* PC-DOS. *Memory Required:* 640k. *Customer Support:* Toll free telephone support.
disk $195.00.
From Lightbar Menu, Clinician Selects Class of Microbe for Treatment. Next Menu Shows All Organisms in This Category. Offending Agent Is Selected. First, a Screen of All Primary-Choice & Secondary Antimicrobials Is Shown; Next, a Screen of All Agents Effective for Organism Against Urinary Tract Involvement; Last, a Screen of Additional Information Where Special Noteworthy Data Is Important.
SRC Systems, Inc.

Microbiology QuizBank, Vol. 1. David Hentges & James Booth. Jan. 1993. *Items Included:* User manual, quick-start sheet, Keyboard Utilities, & Microsoft Multimedia Viewer (Windows version) or HyperCard (Macintosh version). *Customer Support:* Free, unlimited technical support via our toll-free number (1-800-945-4551).
Macintosh. Macintosh with a hard drive (2.5Mb). 3.5" disk $220.00 (ISBN 1-57349-084-9). *Addl. software required:* System 7.0 or higher. *Networks supported:* All LANs.
Windows. IBM compatible with 80286 or higher processor, a hard drive & a mouse (2Mb). disk $220.00 (ISBN 1-57349-180-2). *Addl. software required:* MS-DOS 3.3 or higher, Windows 3.1 or higher. *Networks supported:* All LANs.
Over 400 Multiple-Choice Questions Covering All Areas of Microbiology, with Detailed Feedback & Direct Links to Related Materials Appearing in the Microbiology TextStack.
Keyboard Publishing, Inc.

Microbiology QuizBank, Vol. 2. Joseph Gotts. Oct. 1994. *Items Included:* User manual, quick-start sheet, Keyboard Utilities, & Microsoft Multimedia Viewer (Windows version) or HyperCard (Macintosh version). *Customer Support:* Free, unlimited technical support via our toll-free number (1-800-945-4551).
Macintosh. Macintosh with a hard drive (2.5Mb). 3.5" disk $199.00 (ISBN 1-57349-087-3). *Addl. software required:* System 7.0 or higher. *Networks supported:* All LANs.
Windows. IBM compatible with 80286 or higher processor, a hard drive & a mouse (2Mb). disk $199.00 (ISBN 1-57349-147-0). *Addl. software required:* MS-DOS 3.3 or higher, Windows 3.1 or higher. *Networks supported:* All LANs.
Over 400 Multiple-Choice Questions Covering All Areas of Microbiology, with Detailed Feedback & Direct Links to Related Materials Appearing in the Microbiology TextStack.
Keyboard Publishing, Inc.

Microbiology QuizBank, Vol. 3. James Booth. Oct. 1994. *Items Included:* User manual, quick-start sheet, Keyboard Utilities, & Microsoft Multimedia Viewer (Windows version) or HyperCard (Macintosh version). *Customer Support:* Free, unlimited technical support via our toll-free number (1-800-945-4551).
Macintosh. Macintosh with a hard drive (2.5Mb). 3.5" disk $199.00 (ISBN 1-57349-221-3). *Addl. software required:* System 7.0 or higher. *Networks supported:* All LANs.
Windows. IBM compatible with 80286 or higher processor, a hard drive & a mouse (2Mb). disk $199.00 (ISBN 1-57349-224-8). *Addl. software required:* MS-DOS 3.3 or higher, Windows 3.1 or higher. *Networks supported:* All LANs.
Over 400 Multiple-Choice Questions Covering All Areas of Microbiology, with Detailed Feedback & Direct Links to Related Materials Appearing in the Microbiology TextStack.
Keyboard Publishing, Inc.

Microbiology TextStack. Edited by John Sherris. Oct. 1994. *Items Included:* User manual, quick-start sheet, Keyboard Utilities, & Microsoft Multimedia Viewer (Windows version) or HyperCard (Macintosh version). *Customer Support:* Free, unlimited technical support via our toll-free number (1-800-945-4551).
Macintosh. Macintosh with a hard drive (2.5Mb). CD-ROM disk $280.00 (ISBN 1-57349-091-1). *Nonstandard peripherals required:* CD-ROM player required, 256-color monitor recommended. *Addl. software required:* System 7.0 or higher. *Networks supported:* All LANs.
Windows. IBM compatible with 80286 or higher processor, a hard drive & a mouse (2Mb). CD-ROM disk $280.00 (ISBN 1-57349-155-1). *Nonstandard peripherals required:* CD-ROM player required, 256-color monitor recommended. *Addl. software required:* MS-DOS 3.3 or higher, Windows 3.1 or higher. *Networks supported:* All LANs.
The Complete Text with All Tables, Figures, Diagrams, & Color Illustrations from Appleton & Lange's Medical Microbiology, 3rd Edition, John Sherris, Editor. Includes a Collection of Tools for Searching, Capturing & Manipulating Data of Interest.
Keyboard Publishing, Inc.

Microbiology VideoIndex. Kenneth Ryan. Oct. 1994. *Items Included:* User manual, quick-start sheet, Keyboard Utilities, & Microsoft Multimedia Viewer (Windows version) or HyperCard (Macintosh version). *Customer Support:* Free, unlimited technical support via our toll-free number (1-800-945-4551).
Macintosh. Macintosh with a hard drive (2.5Mb). 3.5" disk $195.00 (ISBN 1-57349-095-4). *Nonstandard peripherals required:* Level 3 NTSC videodisc player with RS-232 interface & connecting cables, video monitor. *Addl. software required:* System 7.0 or higher, Slice of Life VI videodisc. *Networks supported:* All LANs.
Windows. IBM compatible with 80286 or higher processor, a hard drive & a mouse (2Mb). disk $195.00 (ISBN 1-57349-158-6). *Nonstandard peripherals required:* Level 3 NTSC videodisc player with RS-232 interface & connecting cables, video monitor. *Addl. software required:* MS-DOS 3.3 or higher, Windows 3.1 or higher, Slice of Life VI videodisc. *Networks supported:* All LANs.
Descriptive Captions for Hundreds of Microbiology-Related Images from the University of Utah's Slice of Life VI Videodisc (Available Separately), with Direct Links into Related Materials Appearing in the Microbiology TextStack.
Keyboard Publishing, Inc.

Microbiz 6-Pak. *Compatible Hardware:* IBM PC, PC XT, PC AT & compatibles; Apple II with 2.80 SoftCard.
6-Pak $148.50; single module $48.50.
Consists of Six Modules. MICROLEDGER General Ledger, MICROPAY Accounts Payable with Check Printing, MICROREC Accounts Receivable with Aging, Customer Statement & Short Summary Invoice, MICROINV Inventory Control, MICROPERS Payroll/Personnel Control for Weekly/Biweekly Payments with California Witholdings (Can Be Customized to Other States/Countries), ORDER ENTRY Producing Sales Orders/Purchase Orders.
Compumax, Inc.

MICROBJ: Box Jenkins Forecasting, Arima Modeling. *Items Included:* Bound manual. *Customer Support:* Free hotline - no time limit; 30 day limited warranty; updates are $5/disk plus S&H.
MS-DOS. IBM PC & compatibles (256k). disk $99.95. *Nonstandard peripherals required:* One or two disk drives; printer supported, but not required.
Apple II series (64k). disk $149.95.
Multipurpose Time Series Forecasting System Based on the BOX-JENKINS Methodology. MICROBJ Does Not Require Programming Experience. By Using Simple Commands, User Easily Proceeds Through the Data Manipulation, Analysis, Graphics, & Forecasting Modules. Not Only Do You Have Mainframe Analysis Capability at Your Fingertips, but the Cost Is Less & the Ease of Use Is Much Greater. Also, MICROBJ Is Fast (Because It's Compiled).
Dynacomp, Inc.

microBOCS. 1985.
MS-DOS (512k). disk $800.00 (Order no.: 811000). *Addl. software required:* Lotus 1-2-3 Ver. 2 or higher.
Estimates Cost of Barge Transportation Using Transportation Date & Characteristics of User Shipments. Lotus 1-2-3 Template Allows Full User Access & Ability to Modify, As Well As Compatibility with Other Applications.
DNS Assocs., Inc.

Microbol Accounts Payable. *Compatible Hardware:* IBM PC & compatibles, PC XT, PC AT. *Operating System(s) Required:* MOS. (source code included). *Memory Required:* 4 users 256k, 9 users 512k.
$995.00, incl. basic system.
Includes Accrual System, Vendor File Maintenance, Interactive Inquiry by Vendor, Entry & Editing, G/L Account, Automatic Verification, Checks, Check SR & PS, Reports - Cash Requirement Report.
Hurricane Systems, Inc.

Microbol Accounts Receivable. *Compatible Hardware:* IBM PC & compatibles, PC XT, PC AT. *Operating System(s) Required:* MOS. (source code included). *Memory Required:* 4 users 256k, 9 users 512k.
$995.00, incl. basic system.
Includes Balance Forward or Open Item System, Customer Master File, Complete File Maintenance, Interactive Inquiry by Customer, Mailing Labels, Sales Analysis, Transaction Types & Reports. True Multi-User - Using VT-100 Type Dumb Terminals (up to 8 on AT Type Computers) & Standard RS232 Serial Ports.
Hurricane Systems, Inc.

Microbol General Ledger. *Compatible Hardware:* IBM PC & compatibles, PC XT, PC AT. *Operating System(s) Required:* MOS. (source code included). *Memory Required:* 4 users 256k, 9 users 512k.
$995.00, incl. basic system.
Up to 6000 Entries in Ledger per Reporting Period. Includes Complete File Maintenance, Interactive Inquiry, Automatic Verification, Balancing of Journal or Ledger, Journal & Ledger Listing, Trial Balance, Budget & Reports. Financial Statements Can Be Run at Any Time During Accounting Period.
Hurricane Systems, Inc.

MicroBOMP Bill of Materials Processor. *Compatible Hardware:* Apple, IBM PC XT. *Operating System(s) Required:* CP/M, MS-DOS, Apple CP/M. *Language(s):* BASIC. *Memory Required:* 64k. *General Requirements:* 2 disk drives, 80-column printer.
disk $148.50.
demo disk $30.00.
Bill of Materials Processor That Can Be Stand Alone or Used in Conjunction with MICROINV & MICROPERS. Designed to Handle Inventory Control & Materials Requirement Planning. Sets up & Maintains a Stock File, a Bill of Materials File, & a Scheduling File That Contains Production Schedule Data. Inventory Information Is Automatically Updated by Entry of Issue & Receive Transactions &/or by Processing an Inventory Net-Out after Bill of Materials Program Is Run. A Journal File Is Automatically Written & Can Be Posted to MAXILEDGER or MICROLEDGER. Reports Include Standard Stock Status Showing Inventory Valuation at Cost, Retail, & Discounted Retail; ABC Analysis; Materials Requirement Planning; Bill of Materials Explosion; & Maximum/Minimum Report.
Compumax, Inc.

MicroCase Analysis System. Version: 3.0. *Items Included:* Perfect bound manual, tutorial data sets. *Customer Support:* Free phone technical support; application workshops for a fee.
DOS 3.2 or higher. IBM PC, XT & AT & PS/2 series & compatibles (640k). disk $495.00. *Nonstandard peripherals required:* Color graphics card (or Hercules Monochrome Graphics Card).
A Screen-Oriented Statistical Analysis & Data Management Program for the Micro Computer. With a Capacity to Quickly Handle 32,000 Variables & 9,999,999 Cases, This Program Provides Traditional Social Science Statistics Plus Advanced Factor Analysis, Regression Modelling & Curve-Fitting Functions. Includes a C.A.T.I System, Internal Codebooks, Mapping & Recode Functions etc.
MicroCase Corp.

Microcomputer Assisted Heat Transfer Analysis - Professional COM 4403B. Venkata Josyula & Harris Greenberg. 1987. *Compatible Hardware:* IBM PC & compatibles. *Operating System(s) Required:* MS-DOS 2.1-3.1. *Memory Required:* 256k. *General Requirements:* CGA card.
disk $95.00 (ISBN 0-88720-520-8, Order no.: COM4403B).
Collection of 15 Programs & Workbook Which Cover the Basics of Steady State & Transient Heat Conduction, Forced & Free Convection, Radiation Heat Transfer, & Heat Exchangers. The Program Provides a Graphical Output Which Helps the Student Visualize Effects of Varying Parameters, & Makes the Program Suited for Classroom Display on a Large Screen for Demonstration Purposes.
COMPress.

Microcomputer Bond Program (MBP). *Compatible Hardware:* Apple II with Applesoft; Macintosh, IBM. *Operating System(s) Required:* MS-DOS. *Memory Required:* 48k, except IBM 128k, Macintosh 512k.
disk $49.95.
Evaluates Bonds by Providing a Way to Estimate the Prices & Yields of Fixed Income Securities, under a Broad Range of Assumptions & Estimations about the Future. Factors Taken into Account Include: Risk, Interest, Date of Maturity, & Market Expectation. Provides for Complete Bond Data Entry, Flexible Analysis Environment, Bond Prices Estimated over Time, Bond Valuations, etc.
Dynacomp, Inc.

Microcomputer Chart Program. *Items Included:* Bound manual. *Customer Support:* Free hotline - no time limit; 30 day limited warranty; updates are $5/disk plus S&H.
MS-DOS. IBM & compatibles (256k). disk $59.95.
Software to Create Charts to Follow the Stock Market. MCP Uses Either Daily or Weekly Stock High, Low & Close Prices & Trading Volume. The Data Files It Creates Are Completely Compatible with Those Created by MICROCOMPUTER STOCK PROGRAM (MSP). MCP Has Features

TITLE INDEX

Which Make It Unique among the Investment Software Available Today. These Features Include: the Same Data Editing, Maintenance, Printing & Price Adjustments As MSP; Stock Price Charts; Volume Bar Chart; Smoothed Volume Line; up to 3 Stock Price or Volume Charts Overlaid on a Chart; Smoothed Velocity (Price Change) Line; on Balance Volume, Using Percent Price Change; Support for Printers from 31 to 223 Columns per Line.
Dynacomp, Inc.

Microcomputer Circuit Analysis Program II.
Compatible Hardware: Apple II with Applesoft, Apple II+, IIe with DOS 3.3 Macintosh; IBM PC with color graphics adapter & DOS 2.1. Memory Required: Apple 64k, IBM 512k. General Requirements: 2 disk drives.
disk $799.95.
evaluation kit $100.00.
Design Tool Created to Enhance the Productivity of Electronic Design by Providing an Interactive Drawing & Analysis System.
Dynacomp, Inc.

Microcomputer Graphics. Roy E. Myers. Aug. 1984. Compatible Hardware: Apple II, II+, IIe; IBM PC. Operating System(s) Required: MS-DOS 1.1 for IBM. Memory Required: 48k.
Apple. disk $29.95, incl. bk. (ISBN 0-201-05312-8).
IBM. disk $29.95, incl. bk. (ISBN 0-201-05158-3).
bk. alone $12.95 (ISBN 0-201-05092-7).
Provides Essential Mathematics & Programming Techniques for Creating a Variety of Graphics. Contains over 70 BASIC Programs (Knowledge of BASIC Is Assumed).
Addison-Wesley Publishing Co., Inc.

Microcomputer Logic Design Program II.
Compatible Hardware: Apple II, IIplus, IIe Macintosh; IBM PC. Memory Required: Apple 64k, IBM 256k, Macintosh 512k. General Requirements: 2 disk drives; CGA card for IBM.
disk $799.95.
evaluation kit $100.00.
Created to Enhance the Productivity of Electronic Digital Design by Providing an Interactive Drawing & Simulation System.
Dynacomp, Inc.

Microcomputer Stock Program (MSP).
Compatible Hardware: Apple II with Applesoft; Macintosh; IBM PC. Memory Required: 48k, except IBM 128k, Macintosh 512k.
disk $59.95.
Designed to Help Analyze Stock Prices. Provides Timing Signals for Stock Purchases & Sales. Buy & Sell Indicators Are Generated by Means of an Auto-Regressive Price Trend Analysis. Requires Weekly High, Low & Close Prices & the Volume of Shares to Aid Investment Decisions.
Dynacomp, Inc.

Microcomputer Use. Version: 2.0. Teresa Alberte-Hallam et al. Mar. 1989. Compatible Hardware: IBM PC & compatibles. Operating System(s) Required: MS-DOS 2.0 or higher. Language(s): C. Memory Required: 128k. Items Included: Disk & manual (3.5" & 5.25" disk available).
Customer Support: 619-699-6227; will accept collect calls.
disk $29.00, incl. manual (ISBN 0-15-558390-5).
Teaches the Fundamental Concepts of the Three Most Frequently Used Types of Software Programs; Word Processing, Spreadsheets, Data Bases. Each Lesson Includes a Step-by-Step Tutorial That Lets the User Apply New Concepts As They Are Learned. Complete Package Is Available for Examination by Faculty Who Are to Planning to Adopt the Program for Their Classes.
Harcourt Brace Jovanovich, Inc. (College Div.).

MicroConcepts Digitizer Overlay. Richard J. McElhinney. Jun. 1985. Compatible Hardware: Apple Macintosh II; IBM PC & compatibles. Operating System(s) Required: MS-DOS. (source code included). Memory Required: 512k. General Requirements: Hard disk, AutoCAD software.
disk $235.00, incl. manual.
Simplifies & Speeds Up Drafting & Editing of Drawings on AutoCad Systems. The Program Has Been Written & Tested by Practicing Engineering Personnel with the Aim of Increasing Productivity & Operator Discipline. Comes Complete with a Laminated Overlay, Diskettes, LISP Routines, Installation Manual, & a Customizable Screen Symbol Library Which Includes Over 1000 Symbols.
Vector Systems, Inc.

MicroCTS: Corporate Treasurer's System. Jan. 1984. Operating System(s) Required: MS-DOS, PC-DOS 2.0. Memory Required: 192k. General Requirements: 2 disk drives, printer, modem.
disk $5995.00 (ISBN 0-928406-00-8, Order no.: CTS1).
Capital Systems Group, Inc.

MicroExpert. B. Thompson & W. Thompson. 1985. Compatible Hardware: Apple II, IBM. Items Included: 2 disks & documentation.
Apple Set. $54.95, incl. 2 disks & manual (ISBN 0-07-852110-6).
IBM Set. $69.95, incl. disk & manual (ISBN 0-07-852109-2).
Allows User to Design a Knowledge Base Without Having Programming Skills. Explains Why a Question Is Being Asked, Shows How a Fact Has Been or Can Be Proved, Permits User to Ask What Conclusions Have Been Drawn from Facts So Far. Includes a Step-by-Step Tutorial for Design & Entry of Knowledge Base.
McGraw-Hill, Inc.

Microfiche Filer Plus. Compatible Hardware: Commodore Amiga.
3.5" disk $179.00.
Microfiche Style Professional Database with ARexx Support.
Software Visions, Inc.

Microfiche Filer: The Graphic Database.
Compatible Hardware: Commodore Amiga.
3.5" disk $99.00.
Database Where Data Is Organized As on Microfiche - As a Condensed Two-Dimensional Sheet of Text & Pictures Over Which the Users Drags a "Magnifying Glass" to Locate the Information. Can Store Pictures of Any Size. Several Pictures Can Be Displayed Simultaneously & Pictures Can Be Mixed with Text. Features Include: Sorting, Selecting & Printing; Fields May Be Added or Deleted at Any Time; Adaptable Forms with Which to Display Data. Not Copy Protected.
Software Visions, Inc.

Microgammon II. 1981. Compatible Hardware: Apple II+, IIe, IIc; Franklin Ace; Laser 128. Operating System(s) Required: Apple DOS 3.3. Language(s): Assembly. Memory Required: 48k.
disk $8.95.
Microgammon Board Game Helps to Develop a Better Concept of Backgammon & Automatically Adjusts to Skill Level of Its Opponent.
Artsci, Inc.

MicroGANTT. Earth Data Corp. Operating System(s) Required: MS-DOS. Memory Required: 128k. General Requirements: 2 disk drives, printer.
$399.00.
Project Scheduling Package.
Texas Instruments, Personal Productivit.

MICROLINX CHECK-IN

Microgolf. Compatible Hardware: Apple II, II+, IIe; Franklin Ace. Operating System(s) Required: Apple DOS 3.3. Language(s): BASIC, Machine. Memory Required: 48k.
disk $24.95.
Miniature Golf Simulation Which Can Be Played by 1-4 Players. User Can Play on the Three Courses Included or on User-Designed Courses. Realistic Ball Movement. Use Keyboard or Optional Game Paddles.
Compuware.

Microinv. Compatible Hardware: Apple II+, IIe, III; IBM PC XT. Operating System(s) Required: CP/M, CP/M-86, MS-DOS. Language(s): BASIC. Memory Required: CP/M, CP/M-86, CP/M-68000 & Apple 48k, MS-DOS & IBM 64k. General Requirements: 2 disk drives, printer.
disk $48.50.
Series of Programs That Carry Out the Inventory Control Functions of a Small Business. Master File Maintains Information on Inventory Stock. Transaction File Monitors Data on Items Received into Inventory or Issued to Jobs or Locations. Stock Status Report Supplies Status & Valuation of Each Item & Cumulative Value for All Items On-Hand; ABC Analysis Categorizes Inventory According to Frequency of Usage; & Job Cost Report/Materials Shows Total Cost of Materials Allocated to Each Job of Issue. When Used in Conjunction with MICROPERS, Total Job Costing Can Be Obtained. When Used in Conjunction with MICROLEDGER, a Journal File Is Created.
Compumax, Inc.

Microlawyer. Compatible Hardware: Apple II series, Macintosh; Atari ST; Commodore 64/128, Amiga; IBM PC & compatibles. General Requirements: Word processor.
disk $59.95.
Library of Over 100 Common Legal Documents. The Documents are ASCII Text Files Divided Into Personal, Business, & Corporate Categories. Documents Include Power of Attorney, Pre-Marital Agreements, Affidavits, Leases, Loans & Mortgage Forms, Real Estate Contracts, Wills, Notary Public Forms, Generic Contracts for Services, & Articles of Incorporation.
Progressive Peripherals & Software, Inc.

Microledger. Compatible Hardware: Apple II+, IIe, III; Atari; IBM PC. Operating System(s) Required: CP/M, MS-DOS. Language(s): BASIC (source code included). Memory Required: 48k. General Requirements: 2 disk drives, printer.
disk $48.50.
Apple II. demo disk $30.00.
General Ledger System That Performs Double Entry Bookkeeping. User Can Generate Trial Balance, Financial Reports, Profit & Loss Statement, & Balance Sheet. Assets, Liabilities, & Owner Equities Are Shown by Account & by Totals on Balance Sheet. Interactive with Accounts Payable, Accounts Receivable, Inventory, & Payroll.
Compumax, Inc.

MicroLinx Check-In. Jan. 1986. Compatible Hardware: IBM PC with hard disk. Operating System(s) Required: DOS 3.0 or higher. Language(s): C. Memory Required: 6-9 megabytes per 1000 titles plus 640k.
$3500.00, incl. reference manual & tutorial.
initial license & installation $300.00.
annual license $800.00.
DataLinx access (optional-annually) $900.00.
Serials Management System Offering Local Control with Network Access. Automatically Predicts & Records Check-In Information on Each Title Received. Alerts User to Missing Issues. Facilitates Transmission of Claims to Faxon for Handling-Placed Titles. Stores & Retrieves Information about the User's Journal Collection,

& Sorts & Prints Reports According to User Specifications. Built-In Route Feature Automatically Prints Routing Slips. Prints Available Binding Data. Users Have Access to Faxon's DataLinx Database, Infoserv's Databases for Collection Development, & LINX Courier Electronic Mail Service.
The Faxon Co.

MicroLinx Route. Jun. 1986. *Operating System(s) Required:* PC-DOS 3.0 or higher. *Language(s):* C.
initial license $600.00.
installation $250.00.
annual license $90.00.
Routing Module for Locally Controlled Serials.
The Faxon Co.

MicroMain.DB. *Customer Support:* 800-929-8117 (customer service).
MS-DOS. Commodore 128; CP/M. disk $99.99 (ISBN 0-87007-019-3).
A Menu-Driven Data Management System Enabling the User to Easily Perform Complex File Handling Procedures. Sets no Limit on the Number of Fields per Record; 99 Fields May Be Fit into a Standard 80x24 Screen. Fields can Accommodate 79 Characters; Although Sugested Record Length Is 512 Bytes, User can Opt for Longer Lengths. The Maximum Number of Records Allowed Is Over 32,000 per Data File. All Data & Program Files Can Reside on Either A or B Drives or a Hard Disk, & May Be Redefined As Desired.
SourceView Software International.

MicroMan Esti-Mate. Jun. 1992. *Items Included:* Tutorial & User Guide. *Customer Support:* 24 hour bulletin board; hot-line; training in Santa Monica, CA or on-site. Cost: annual fee of 15% of purchase price.
MS-DOS 3.3 or OS/2 2.0. IBM PC & compatible (480k). $5000.00; 2000.00 for limited function version. *Networks supported:* Netbios.
PC-Based Estimating & Planning Tool for Information Services Projects Used To Calculate Overall Project Effort & Create Project Plans Which Include Estimated Hours for all Project Events. Supports Function Point Analysis, Supports Re-Estimates of Project Effort after a Project Has Begun, Provides Project Templates Which Can Be Modified, Has an "Expert" Feedback Mechanism for Improving Project Estimates.Integrated with Micro-Man II Project & Staff Management System.
POC-IT Management Services, Inc.

MicroMan II Project & Staff Management System. *Version:* 1.3. Oct. 1990. *Compatible Hardware:* IBM PC, PC XT. *Operating System(s) Required:* PC-DOS, MS-DOS. *Memory Required:* 640k. *General Requirements:* Color monitor, printer, hard disk. *Items Included:* Software, reference manual, reports manual, introductory tutorial. *Customer Support:* Training in Santa Monica or on-site, hot line, bulletin board. $2895.00 ea.
Designed for information Services. Provides Project Management to Schedule & Track Projects; Staff Management to Monitor Resource Use & Do Staff Planning; Executive Information for Overall Management of MIS. The System Handles an Unlimited Number of Projects & Resources. The Scheduler Considers Resource Availability, Event Dependencies, Corporate & Resource Calendars, & Other Projects (Multiproject Scheduling). Staff Timesheets Are Produced to Be Used for Tracking Project Progress. There Are 50 Standard Reports & a Flexible Report Writer. Can Run Both Stand Alone or on a LAN.
POC-IT Management Services, Inc.

MicroManager Editor.
Hard drive; 640k RAM; & DOS 3.1 or higher; DOS 5.0 or some other memory manager may be required if you run any TSRs. IBM (640k). Contact publisher for price. *Addl. software required:* APBA Baseball Classic Deluxe.
User-Programmable, Rule-Base Expert System That Lets You Define Baseball Concepts & Strategies in Baseball & Strategies in Baseball Talk(TM). Allows You to Create Managers with Your Own Rational.
Miller Assocs.

MicroMind Knowledge Engineering Tool.
Customer Support: 800-929-8117 (customer service).
MS-DOS. IBM/PS2. disk $99.99 (ISBN 0-87007-175-0).
Enables Designers to Create Knowledge-Based Expert Systems. Enables the Formation of Prototype Expert Systems to Evaluate the Correctness of the Rule Base & to Determine How Well the System Achieves the Objectives. Has the Facilities to Create a Stand-Alone Expert System for End Users. The Format of the Rules is an IF-THEN-DO Construction.
SourceView Software International.

MiniNEIL Time/Cost Billing System. *Version:* 6.1. Feb. 1989. *Items Included:* Operations manual - NEIL Guide to Operations. *Customer Support:* Telephone support - free, upgrades - $450/yr. subscription.
IBM PC or compatible (640k). $1495.00 (single) $1695.00 (multi-user) (Order no.: N-50). *Addl. software required:* None with single user. Network: Novell Module. *Optimal configuration:* IBM PC 150Mb hard drive, 2Mb, MS-DOS, H.P. Laser Jet printer. *Networks supported:* Novell.
Time/Cost Billing with Accounts Receivable Detail & Aging, Full Trust Management, 2000 Characters of Description Available for Each Time Slip, Pop-Up Screen, 90 Billing Cycles, All Files Updated Immediately, Multiple Matters for Same Client Can Print on Bill, No File Sorting Required, Unlimited Number of Timekeepers.
Law Firm Management, Inc.

Micronics Accounts Payable. *Customer Support:* 800-929-8117 (customer service).
MS-DOS. Commodore 128; CP/M. disk $99.99 (ISBN 0-87007-048-7).
Allows Simple Selection of Procedures from a Menu. Interactive Data Entry & Error Correction Routines Are Provided, along with Extensive Operator Error Detection & Prevention. Discounts on Vendor Balances When Allowed Are Automatically Calculated. Accounts Payable for a Company May be Created & Maintained in Accordance with Generally Accepted Accounting Procedures.
SourceView Software International.

Micronics Balance Forward. *Customer Support:* 800-929-8117 (customer service).
MS-DOS. Commodore 128; CP/M. disk $99.99 (ISBN 0-87007-046-0).
Simple Selection of Procedures from an Options Menu; Interactive Data Entry & Error Correction Routines; Automatic Calcuations of Finance Charges on Past Due Customer Balances; Printed Monthly Statements Ready for Mailing; Month-end Account Aging; the Ability to Quickly Reference a Customer by Name or Account Number; & the Ability to Change any Item in any Account While Preventing Unauthorized Entries. Number of Customers per Diskette Is Limited Only by Available Disk Space, with up to 36 Different Companies' Files Coexisting on the Same Diskette or Hard Disk. Mailing Labels & Automatic Letter Generation are Included. A Company's Accounts Receivable Records May be Created & Maintained in Accordance with Generally Accepted Accounting Standards.
SourceView Software International.

Micronics General Ledger. *Customer Support:* 800-929-8117 (customer service).
MS-DOS. Commodore 128; CP/M. disk $99.99 (ISBN 0-87007-009-6).
An Integrated Hard Disk System. Includes all Accounts Receivable Modules. Complete Set of Management Reports Are Easily Generated. Integrated General Ledger Is Designed So That Company's General Ledger Accounting Records Are Set up & Maintained in Accordance with Generally Accepted Accounting Standards. All Operations Are Menu-Driven, & No Pre-Purchased Programming Language Is Required.
SourceView Software International.

Micronics Integrated. *Customer Support:* 800-929-8117 (customer service).
MS-DOS. Commodore 128; CP/M. disk $399.99 (ISBN 0-87007-254-4).
A Menu Driven, Integrated Package. Includes Password Protection, Monthly, Quarterly & Annual Aging of Accounts & Personalization for Different Terminal Types.
SourceView Software International.

Micronics Inventory. *Customer Support:* 800-929-8117 (customer service).
MS-DOS. Commodore 128; CP/M. disk $99.99 (ISBN 0-87007-049-5).
Provides All of the Features for Other Micronics Accounting System Modules. Inventory Files Are Limited by the Amount of Space on the Diskette or Disk. An Inventory Parts Status Report May Be Obtained Interactively, As Can All Inventory Functions. Management Reports May Be Generated on Demand. Work Orders & Back Orders May Be Edited & Listed. A Bill of Materials Explosion Is Produced & May Be Listed or Edited at Any Time. Invoices May Be Printed from Work Orders to Minimize Paperwork. Inventory Records May Be Created & Maintained in Accordance with Generally Accepted Accounting Procedures.
SourceView Software International.

Micronics Open Account. *Customer Support:* 800-929-8117 (customer service).
MS-DOS. Commodore 128; CP/M. disk $99.99 (ISBN 0-87007-047-9).
Simple Selection of Procedures from an Options Menu; Interactive Data Entry & Error Correction Routines; Automic Calculations of Finance Charges on Past Due Customer Balances, Printed Monthly Statements Ready for Mailing; Month-end Account Aging; the Ability to Quickly Reference a Customer by Name or Account Number; & the Ability to Change Any Item in Any Account While Preventing Unauthorized entries. The Number of Customers per Diskette Is Limited only by Available Disk Space, with up to 36 Different Companies' Files Coexisting on the Same Diskette or Hard Diskisk. Mailing Labels & Automatic Letter Generation are Included. A Company's Accounts Receivable Records May Be Created & Maintained in Accordance with Generally Accepted Accounting Standards.
SourceView Software International.

Micronics Payroll. *Customer Support:* 800-929-8117 (customer service).
MS-DOS. Commodore 128; CP/M. disk $99.99 (ISBN 0-87007-010-X).
Used to Handle Payrolls for Several Companies on the Same Disk or Diskette. System Processes Hourly and/or Salaried Payrolls Together or Separately. It Will Print on Several Reports. A Complete Employee Record Is Kept. Several Management Reports Are Produced. Historic Reports May Be Printed upon Request.
SourceView Software International.

TITLE INDEX

MicroOHMTADS (Oil & Hazardous Materials Technical Assistance Database). Environmental Protection Agency-PSI International. *Compatible Hardware:* IBM PC, PC XT, PC AT & compatibles. *Operating System(s) Required:* PC-DOS/MS-DOS 3.0. *General Requirements:* 10Mb hard disk space. *Customer Support:* 30 day money-back guarantee.
3.5" or 5.25" disk $1200.00.
Provides Information on 1400 Compounds Selected for Spill History, Production Volume, & Toxicity, Including 15,000 Material, Brand, & Trade Names, with Standard Codes to Aid in Identification. Information Includes Personal Safety Precautions; Hazard Levels; Fire Protection; Explosiveness; Handling & Storage Procedures; Disposal Information; Effects on Humans, Animals, Plants, Air, Soil & Water; Procedures for Notification of Proper Authorities; Protective Clothing; Reactivity; Detection; Physical & Chemical Properties; Environmental Chemistry & Fate. Runs on Portables for Use in Emergency Response Vehicles. Allows Retrieval by Name or Identification Code; by Word or Combination of Words (e.g., "Brown Liquid & Monsanto" As the Only Input Would Retrieve All Compounds with Those Three Phrases in Their Descriptions); by "Late", Regardless of the Words in Between Such As Ethyl Acrylate, Ethyl Phthalate, etc.
Gulf Publishing Co.

Micropay. *Compatible Hardware:* Apple II+, IIe, III; Atari; IBM PC. *Operating System(s) Required:* CP/M, CP/M-86, CP/M-68000, MS-DOS. *Language(s):* BASIC (source code included). *Memory Required:* 48k. *General Requirements:* 2 disk drives, printer.
disk $48.50.
Handles Operations of Accounts Payable Required by Most Small Businesses. Contains Transaction & Master File. Activity on Accounts Is Entered into Transaction File. Master File Contains Permanent Records of All Due & Paid Accounts Payable. Handles Data Entry; Prints Actual Checks for User-Defined Dates; Generates Reports by Vendor or Date; Calculates Cash Requirements for Individual Vendors & Single Due Dates or a Range of Dates. Creates & Maintains a Journal File When Used in Conjunction with MICROLEDGER. All Listings & Reports Can Be Printed.
Compumax, Inc.

Micropers. *Compatible Hardware:* Apple II+, IIe, III; IBM PC XT. *Operating System(s) Required:* CP/M, MS-DOS. *Language(s):* BASIC. *Memory Required:* CP/M & Apple 48k, MS-DOS & IBM 64K. *General Requirements:* 2 disk drives, printer.
disk $48.50.
California Payroll & Personnel Management System. Handles Hourly Employees Paid on a Weekly Basis & Salaried Employees Paid Biweekly. Figures Federal & State Withholdings, Social Security Tax, Disability Insurance, Miscellaneous Deductions, & Gross & Net Pay. Prints Paychecks & Debits & Credits Net Pay & Various Deductions to Proper Accounts in Chart of Accounts (When Using MICROLEDGER). Provides Values for the Quarterly 941 Report & Fills Out W-2 Forms. Calculates Amount Spent on Labor for Each Job Coded in Data Entry. Provides Total Job Costing When Used with MICROINV. Complete Employment History for Each Employee Is Provided & Vital Statistics, Status, Position, & Earnings, Current & Previous for Each Employee in Master File Are Displayed. Can Be Customized for Other States & Countries.
Compumax, Inc.

MicroPhone II. *Version:* 5.0.2. David Rowland et al. Dec. 1993. *Items Included:* Two perfect bound manuals - User's guide, Scripting manual, disks. *Customer Support:* 30 day money back warranty; free telephone technical support (not toll free); support available through on-line services including AppleLink, Compuserve, GEnie, MCI, Internet.
System 6.0.5 or higher. Macintosh Plus or higher. 3.5" disk $195.00 (ISBN 0-924169-02-8). *Nonstandard peripherals required:* Modem or direct connect to another computer.
Telecommunications Program That Automates Many Operations Generally Performed Manually. Allows the User to Create Macros of Any Complexity. "Watch Me" Feature Automatically Records Scripts Typed in by the User. Modem Drivers for Control of Nonstandard Modems & Corporate PBX's Supports XMODEM, YMODEM, ZMODEM, Kermit & ASCII Protocols. Emulates TTY, VT52, VT100, VT102, VT220 & VT320. System 7 Savvy.
Software Ventures Corp.

MicroPhone LT for Macintosh. *Version:* 2.0.2. *Compatible Hardware:* Macintosh Plus or higher. *Memory Required:* 512k. *General Requirements:* Modem or direct connect to mother computer. *Items Included:* 1 bound manual; disk. *Customer Support:* 30-Day money back warranty; free telephone technical support (not toll free); support available through on-line services including Applelink, Compuserve, Genie, MCI, Internet.
disk $49.95 (ISBN 0-924169-00-1).
Telecommunications Program That Automates Many Operations Generally Performed Manually. Supports XMODEM, YMODEM, Kermit, ZMODEM & ASCII Protocols. Emulates TTY, VT52, VT100, VT102, VT220 & VT320. System 7 Savvy.
Software Ventures Corp.

MicroPhone Pro for Macintosh. *Version:* 2.0.2. *Items Included:* 5 bound manuals, send & receive fax software, MP Telnet Tool for TCP/IP connectivity. *Customer Support:* 30-day moneyback guarantee, free technical support.
System 6.0.5 or higher. Macintosh Plus or higher (512K). 3.5" disk $295.00 (ISBN 0-924169-16-8). *Addl. software required:* Modem, network, or direct connection to a remote computer.
Communications Made Simple! Connect Easily to Online Services Like CompuServe, GEnie & MCI Mail at the Touch of a Button. Or Build Your Own Time-Saving Scripts to Other Services & Remote Computers. Also Comes with Send & Receive Fax Software & TCP/IP Connectivity. Supports XMODEM, YMODEM, ZMODEM, Kermit & CompuServe Quick B Protocols. Supports TTY, VT102, VT100, VT220, VT320, IBM PC ANSI Terminal Emulations. System 7 Savvy.
Software Ventures Corp.

MicroPhone Pro for Windows. *Version:* 1.0.1. John Sellers. Nov. 1992. *Items Included:* Two bound manuals - User's Guide, Reference Manual, disks, Fax software. *Customer Support:* 30 day money back warranty; free technical telephone support (not toll free); support available through on-line services including GEnie, Compuserve, Internet, etc.
Microsoft Windows 3.1 or higher. IBM PC/AT/286 or compatible. disk $195.00 (ISBN 0-924169-03-6). *Nonstandard peripherals required:* Modem or direct connection to another computer. *Addl. software required:* Microsoft Windows.
Telecommunications Software for Microsoft Windows Which Automates the Entire Telecommunications Process Using Macros. User Can Automate Activities Such As Log-On, File Transfer, & Unattended Operations. Integrated Send & Receive Fax Makes Faxing As Easy As Dragging & Dropping. File Transfer Protocols Include XMODEM, YMODEM, Kermit & ZMODEM. Emulates VT52, VT100, VT102 & TTY Type Terminals. Multimedia Support.
Software Ventures Corp.

MICROPHYS PHYSICS LABORATORY

Microphys Computer-Generated Physics Exams & Homework Assignments. 1995. *Items Included:* Full manual. *Customer Support:* Free telephone support - 90 days, 30-day warranty.
MS-DOS 3.2 or higher. 286 (584k). $29.95 ea.; $395.00 complete set. *Nonstandard peripherals required:* CGA/EGA/VGA.
A Series of Computer Products Which Generate Individualized Exams and/or Homework Assignments for Each Unit in a Traditional Introductory Physics Course. The Software Is Completely Menu-Driven, & All Needed Instructions Are Clearly Displayed on the Screen. Each of the 18 Packages Consists of Three Modules That Permit the Creation, Generation, & Grading of the Unique Sets of Problems Which Are Given to Each Student.
Dynacomp, Inc.

Microphys Geometrical Optics: Optics Simulations. 1995. *Items Included:* Full manual. *Customer Support:* Free telephone support - 90 days, 30-day warranty.
MS-DOS 3.2 or higher. 286 (584k). disk $29.95. *Nonstandard peripherals required:* CGA/EGA/VGA.
Permits the Student to Study the Optical Properties of Concave & Convex Mirrors & Lenses. The Computer Clearly Illustrates, in a Step-Wise Fashion, the Rays of Light Which Come from the Object, Strike the Mirror or Lens, & Then Form the Image. The Cases of Object Position Yielding Both Real & Virtual Images Are Treated.
Dynacomp, Inc.

Microphys Inorganic Equation Balancer: Computer-Aided Chemistry. 1995. *Items Included:* Full manual. *Customer Support:* Free telephone support - 90 days, 30-day warranty.
MS-DOS 3.2 or higher. 286 (584k). disk $49.95. *Nonstandard peripherals required:* CGA/EGA/VGA.
A Must for Any Inorganic Chemistry Class. It Is Designed to Balance Virtually Any Inorganic Chemical Equation. You Simply Enter the Word or Skeletal Equation. IEB Then Develops a System of Simultaneous Equations in Which the Integer Coefficients of the Chemical Reactants & Products Are Determined by Gaussian Elimination. IEB Is Generally Successful in Balancing Complicated Types of Oxidation-Reduction Reactions.
Dynacomp, Inc.

Microphys Physic-AI: Computer-Aided Physics Experiments. 1995. *Items Included:* Full manual. *Customer Support:* Free telephone support - 90 days, 30-day warranty.
MS-DOS 3.2 or higher. 286 (584k). disk $99.95. *Nonstandard peripherals required:* CGA/EGA/VGA.
A Coordinated Collection of Simulation/Instructional Software Modules Which Assist Students in Performing Physics Experiments. By Varying the Experimental Parameters, the Student May Investigate How They Influence the Results. The Software Displays These Results in a Revealing Fashion Using High Resolution Graphics, Concise Comments, & On-Screen Instructions. Menu-Driven & All Necessary Instructions Appear on the Screen.
Dynacomp, Inc.

Microphys Physics Laboratory Experiments. 1995. *Items Included:* Full manual. *Customer Support:* Free telephone support - 90 days, 30-

day warranty.
MS-DOS 3.2 or higher. 286 (584k). $29.95 per unit; $995.00 complete set. *Nonstandard peripherals required:* CGA/EGA/VGA.
Using Conventional Laboratory Apparatus, the Student Makes Measurements & Enters the Data into the Computer. The Software Then Generates an Evaluation of the Student's Work & Assigns a Suggested Lab Grade. The Student Submits This Report along with the Lab Write-Up to the Instructor for Final Evaluation. Each of the 40 Labortory Modules Is Accompanied by Student Experiment Sheets Which May Be Duplicated & Handed Out.
Dynacomp, Inc.

Microphys Waves & Superposition: Physics Simulations. 1995. *Items Included:* Full manual. *Customer Support:* Free telephone support - 90 days, 30-day warranty.
MS-DOS 3.2 or higher. 286 (584k). disk $29.95. *Nonstandard peripherals required:* CGA/EGA/VGA.
Permits the Student to Examine Each of the Following Concepts: 1. Pulses & Reflection. 2. Waves & the Principle of Superposition. 3. Creation of Standing Waves. 4. Production of Beats. The Computer Simulates the Interference Between Two Waves.
Dynacomp, Inc.

Micropix. Microsimulations Research. *Operating System(s) Required:* MS-DOS. *Memory Required:* 128k. *General Requirements:* Printer, color monitor.
$200.00.
Allows the Creation of Free-Form Computer Graphics. Users Can Create New Symbols & Store Them for Later Use.
Texas Instruments, Personal Productivit.

MicroPlan. Chang Laboratories, Inc. *Compatible Hardware:* HP 86/87 with CP/M System (HP 82900A), HP 150 Touchscreen.
HP 86/87. disk $525.00 (Order no.: 45502A). 3.5" disk $500.00.
HP 150. 3.5" disk $400.00.
Financial Planning Package for the Business User. Formulas Are Built-In & No Replication Is Required. On-Screen Commands Are Referenced by Numbers, So Typing Screens Are Not Needed. As the Spreadsheet Is Developed, the Commands Used Are Automatically Documented. The Report Generator Includes Features Such As Variable Column Width, "$" & "%" Signs for Rows & Columns, Automatic Pagination, & "<>" for Negative Numbers. Financial Commands Include Depreciation, Loan Amortization, Discounted Cash Flow, Internal Rate of Return, & Tax Scheduling. Statistical Commands Include Variance, Delta, Sigma, & Mean.
Hewlett-Packard Co.

MicroPlan Consolidation Module. Chang Laboratories, Inc. *Compatible Hardware:* HP 86/87 with CP/M System (HP 82900A), HP 150 Touchscreen.
HP 86/87. disk $325.00 (Order no.: 45503A). 3.5" disk $300.00.
HP 150. 3.5" disk $200.00 (Order no.: 45466A).
Add-On to MICROPLAN for Consolidation of Different Reports, & for Drawing Data into MICROPLAN from Outside Sources Such As Spreadsheets, General Ledgers, & Databases. Reports from Different Departments, Individuals, Services, Regions, or Time Periods Can Be Consolidated for Variance Analysis or Other Management Summaries.
Hewlett-Packard Co.

Microplate Manager. *Compatible Hardware:* Apple Macintosh. *Memory Required:* 512k. *General Requirements:* ImageWriter; Bio-Rad's Model 2550 & 3550 Microplate Readers; Microsoft BASIC.
3.5" disk $750.00.
Microtitration ELISA Data Analysis.
Bio-Rad Laboratories.

Microport System V/4. *Compatible Hardware:* 286 or 486 EISA or ISA bus or VL or PCI or Pentium. *Items Included:* Complete system. *Customer Support:* 30 day installation warranty.
3.5" disk $1740.00.
Complete & Enhanced Distribution of Unix System V Release 4 Including Graphics, Networking, & Development Utilities & Sun OS, BSO & XENIX Compatibility. Suited for Any Platform Application.
Microport, Inc.

Microrec. *Compatible Hardware:* Apple II+, IIe, III; Atari; IBM PC XT. *Operating System(s) Required:* CP/M, CP/M-86, CP/M-68000, MS-DOS, PC-DOS. *Language(s):* BASIC (source code included). *Memory Required:* CP/M, CP/M-86, CP/M-68000 & Apple 48k, MS-DOS & IBM 64k. *General Requirements:* 2 disk drives, printer.
disk $48.50.
Manages & Documents Accounts Receivable Functions. Contains Transaction & Master File. Transaction File Holds Accounts Receivable Transactions Until Period Is Ended. Master File Is a Permanent Record of All Accounts Receivable Entries & Customer Payment Receipts. User Can Print Customer Invoices & Handle Data Entry & Update & Receipt of Customer Payments. Additional Features Include: File Listings; Accumulation of Transaction Records into Master File; Customer Statements Showing Invoice Numbers, Aging, Amounts Invoiced, Payments Received & Final Balance Due Figure; Aging Reports; Accounts Receivable Reports by Customer & Date; Creates & Maintains Journal File When Used with MICROLEDGER; Reports & Listings Can Be Printed.
Compumax, Inc.

Microsoft BASIC Interpreter. *Compatible Hardware:* CP/M-80 based machines; MS-DOS based machines. *Memory Required:* 64k.
disk $350.00.
Interprets BASIC for General-Purpose Computer Programming.
Microsoft Pr.

Microsoft BASIC Interpreter. *Items Included:* Documentation. *Customer Support:* 30-day warranty, hotline, newsletter, electronic bulletin board.
An 80386-based system under SCO Xenix 386 System V. $395.00.
Xenix Implementation of Microsoft BASIC.
Santa Cruz Operation, Inc.

Microsoft Bookshelf. *Compatible Hardware:* IBM PC & compatibles. *Operating System(s) Required:* PC-DOS/MS-DOS 3.0 or higher. *Memory Required:* 640k, with hard disk 512k. *General Requirements:* CD-ROM disk drive. Hard disk recommended, MS-DOS CD-ROM extensions.
CD-ROM disk $295.00.
Includes a Dictionary with Definitions & a Biographical/Geographical Appendix, an Almanac, a Spelling Checker, a ZIP Code Guide, & Roget's Thesaurus.
Microsoft Pr.

Microsoft C Cross Compiler, Assembler, Linker Package. *Customer Support:* Maintenance available, call for pricing.
Ultrix. DEC VAXstation, DECstation. $4000.00 & up.
UNIX. Sun-3, Sun-4 SPARC, IBM RS/6000. $4000.00 & up.
Allows Mini- & Workstation-based Developers to Write Code for MS-DOS Environments Using the Same Microsoft Tools That Are Available on the PC. This Is Ideal for Large Work Groups of VAX or Workstation Users Who Can Use the Sophisticated UNIX or VMS Development Tools While Developing for MS-DOS Machines Compatible with Microsoft Cv 5.1.
Oasys, Inc.

Microsoft C Optimizing Compiler. *Version:* 5.1. *Compatible Hardware:* Commodore Amiga. *Memory Required:* recommended 512k.
3.5" or 5.25" disk $450.00.
Development Package for the Professional.
Microsoft Pr.

Microsoft Chart (IBM). *Version:* 3.0. *Compatible Hardware:* IBM PC & compatibles. *Operating System(s) Required:* PC-DOS 3.1 or higher. *Memory Required:* 320k. *General Requirements:* Graphics adapter card.
disk $395.00.
$195.00 workstation pack.
Business Graphics Package with Non-Windows Mouse Control & Extensive Data Analysis Tools. Not Copy Protected.
Microsoft Pr.

Microsoft Chart (Mac). *Version:* 3.0. *Compatible Hardware:* Apple Macintosh. *Memory Required:* 128k.
disk $95.00.
Enables the User to Turn Complex Data & Ideas into Presentation-Quality Charts. Up to 16 Charts Can Be Viewed at One Time. Text Can Be Added to Clarify Data, Charts Can Be Overlayed to Compare Data, etc. Information Can Be Read from LOTUS 1-2-3, VISICALC, DBASE III, or from Any Other Software That Supports DIF, ASCII, or SYLK Files.
Microsoft Pr.

Microsoft COBOL Compiler. *Compatible Hardware:* Apple II, IIe; CP/M-80 based machines; MS-DOS based machines. *Operating System(s) Required:* MS-DOS. *Memory Required:* recommended 512k. *General Requirements:* 2 disk drives.
disk $900.00.
Provides the Following Features: Compiles & Executes Large Programs, Including Those That Are Many Times Larger Than Memory; Allows Data to Be Entered in Program; Aids in Quick Debugging of Programs; Uses Four Types of Files to Retrieve Data Quickly; Lets User Connect & Execute COBOL Programs with Programs Written with Macro Assembler; Accepts Numbers of up to 18 Digits & Performs Accurate Calculations Internally with Numbers of up to 30 Digits. Produces Object Programs That Can Be Linked to Microsoft COBOL Compiler Run-Time Library. Includes a Linking Loader That Allows the User to Combine COBOL with One or More Subprograms from Library. The User Can Enter Information While the Program Is Running. Also Provides a High Level of Screen Formatting Options & Dynamic Debugging for Faster Program Development.
Microsoft Pr.

Microsoft Excel. *Version:* 3.0. 1991.
System 6.0.2 & Finder 6.1 or higher. Macintosh Plus or higher (1Mb). 3.5" disk $495.00. *Nonstandard peripherals required:* Hard disk drive or SuperDrive.
Spreadsheet Integrated with a Graphics Program & a Data Filing Application. Provides Macro Capabilities. Can Handle 256 Columns by 16,384 Rows. Offers over 130 Financial, Math & Logical

Functions. Icon-Based On-Screen Toolbar to Automate Common Operations; Autosum Automatically Totals a Row or Column. Mix Text, Charts, & Cells Freely on One Page; All New Charts & Graphs, Many in 3D. Full Color Support. Outliner Shows Big Picture, or Expands to Display Details. Goal Seeking Function Automates Analysis & Problem Solving. Supports DAL & System 7.0.
Microsoft.

Microsoft Excel Business Sourcebook, 5. Version: 2.0 or higher. Charles W. Kyd. Oct. 1988. Compatible Hardware: Apple Macintosh, IBM PC & compatibles. Memory Required: 640k. General Requirements: Microsoft Excel PC & MAC.
disk $20.00 ea. (ISBN 1-55615-133-0).
book $24.95.
Include All of the Spreadsheets & Models Discussed in Kyd's Book, Microsoft Excel Business Sourcebook.
Cashmaster Business Systems, Inc.

Microsoft File. Version: 2.0. Jan. 1985. Compatible Hardware: Apple Macintosh. Memory Required: enhanced 512k.
3.5" disk $195.00.
Electronic Filing System That Helps the User Record, Organize, Manage, Sort, & Report Information of Almost Any Kind. Files Can Contain Dates, Numbers, & Text, As Well As Pictures Created with MACPAINT & MACDRAW & Graphs from MICROSOFT CHART. Reporting Capability Is Included.
Microsoft Pr.

Microsoft Flight Simulator (Mac). Compatible Hardware: Apple Macintosh.
3.5" disk $49.95.
The Player Is Piloting a Cessna 182 & Can Control Everything from Flaps & Ailerons to the Magneto Switch. The Player Navigates Using Radio Signals, or If Bad Weather Occurs, Can Fly Totally by Instruments. Features a Full-Color, Out-of-the-Window Flight Display with Detailed Graphics That Closely Simulate a Pilot's Actual Perspective. The Player Can Take off & Land at over 20 Airports, Each with Its Own Particular Set of Challenges. An "Easy" Mode for the Beginner Pilot Is Available. The "British Ace" Scenario Allows the Player to Fly in a World War II Air Battle.
Microsoft Pr.

Microsoft Flight Simulator 3.0. Compatible Hardware: IBM PC, PC XT, PC AT, PS/2 & true compatibles. Operating System(s) Required: PC-DOS/MS-DOS 2.0 or higher. Memory Required: 256k. General Requirements: Hercules, CGA, EGA, or VGA card.
$49.95.
This Version's New Features Include the Ability to Run on High-Speed AT-Compatibles, 16-Color, 640X350 EGA Display, More Aircraft Models, a Learning Mode, & Flight Analysis. Allows Two Players to Fly Together by Linking Two Computers Through a Null Modem Cable or Telephone Lines.
Microsoft Pr.

Microsoft FORTRAN Compiler. Compatible Hardware: MS-DOS based machines. Language(s): Assembly. Memory Required: recommended 512k. General Requirements: 2 disk drives.
disk $450.00.
Provides an Implementation of FORTRAN-77 for the 16-Bit Microprocessor Environment.
Microsoft Pr.

Microsoft FORTRAN Compiler. Items Included: Documentation. Customer Support: 30-day warranty, hotline, newsletter, electronic bulletin board.
An 80386-based system under SCO Xenix 386 System V. $695.00.
Xenix Implementation of Microsoft FORTRAN.
Santa Cruz Operation, Inc.

Microsoft 4.0 (Macintosh). Version: 4.0. Jul. 1989. Customer Support: Hotline support. Macintosh 512KE & up. starter pack $900.00 (Order no.: 40-363-PK). Addl. software required: Microsoft Word 4.0 Macintosh. Instructor-Led Courseware. Starter Kit Includes Instructor's Guide & 12 Student Manuals with Practice Activities & Data Disks. Also, Instructor's Guide Includes Overhead Transparencies & Two-Year Free Upgrade Service. Additional Student Manuals Available Separately for $28.00 each. Also Available in Advanced Level 1 & Advanced Level 2.
Logical Operations.

Microsoft II. Compatible Hardware: Atari XL/XE. Memory Required: 16k.
disk or cartridge $29.95 (Order no.: AX2025).
Atari Corp.

Microsoft Macro Assembler 5.1. Compatible Hardware: IBM PC & compatibles. Memory Required: 320k.
disk $150.00.
Enables Users to Create Subroutines That Can Be Easily Integrated into Microsoft QUICKBASIC or QUICKC Programs. Package Includes the CODEVIEW Debugger.
Microsoft Pr.

Microsoft Mail. Version: 2.0. Compatible Hardware: Apple Macintosh. Memory Required: 512k.
Up to 4 users. 3.5" disk $299.95.
Up to 10 users. 3.5" disk $499.95.
Up to 20 users. 3.5" disk $749.95.
21 to 32 users. 3.5" disk $949.95.
AppleTalk Electronic Mail System.
Microsoft Pr.

Microsoft Multiplan. Version: 1.11. Compatible Hardware: Apple Macintosh. Memory Required: 128k.
3.5" disk $395.00.
Spreadsheet Package Includes Financial Analysis.
Microsoft Pr.

Microsoft Pascal Compiler. Version: 4.0. Compatible Hardware: MS-DOS based machines. Operating System(s) Required: MS-DOS. Memory Required: recommended 512k. General Requirements: 2 disk drives.
disk $300.00.
Offers Systems Programmers a Clean, Structured Language Especially Suited to Handle Complex Problems Quickly. Specifically Designed for the 16-Bit Microprocessor Environment. Interfaces with Microsoft FORTRAN & Micro Assembler. Gives User Several Options for Floating-Point Operations Including Support for the Generating Intel 8087 Coprocessor In-Line Instructions for Fast Numeric Processing. An Additional Math Library Emulates the 8087 in Software. The Decimal Math Package Has a 14-Bit BCD Format That Ensures More Accurate Dollars-&-Cents Calculations. Provides Many Extensions to Standard Pascal to Aid Programmers. Separate Compilation Is Supported. Super Arrays Permit Dynamic Allocation of Arrays at Runtime.
Microsoft Pr.

Microsoft Pascal Compiler. Items Included: Manuals. Customer Support: 30-day warranty, hotline, newsletter, electronic bulletin board.
An 80286 or 80386-based system under SCO Xenix 386 System V. $695.00.
Unix Implementation of Microsoft Pascal.
Santa Cruz Operation, Inc.

Microsoft PowerPoint. Version: 2.01. Compatible Hardware: Apple Macintosh Plus, SE, II. Operating System(s) Required: System 4.1 or higher. Memory Required: 1000k.
3.5" disk $395.00.
Desktop Presentation Program Which Includes a Built-In Word Processor & Drawing Tools Enabling Users to Prepare Overheads or 35mm Slides. Can Integrate Graphics, Charts, or Illustrations from Other Macintosh Programs, Such As Microsoft EXCEL. "Slide Sorter" Lets Users Rearrange Presentations Slide-by-Slide. "Slide Show" Feature Allows Users to Rehearse Their Presentations by Viewing Them One Slide at a Time.
Microsoft Pr.

Microsoft Project. Version: 4.0. Compatible Hardware: IBM PC & compatibles. Operating System(s) Required: DOS 2.0 or higher. Memory Required: 256k. General Requirements: 2 disk drives.
disk $495.00.
Project-Management Package That Offers Resource Calendars & Resource Leveling Within the Confines of Float. Allows User to Customize Reports in a Tabular Format. Its Main Project View Is the Gantt Chart. Not Copy Protected.
Microsoft Pr.

Microsoft QuickBASIC for the Macintosh. Version: 1.11. Compatible Hardware: Apple Macintosh, Macintosh Plus. General Requirements: Hard disk.
3.5" disk $99.00.
Basic Development Environment.
Microsoft Pr.

Microsoft QuickBASIC 4.5. Compatible Hardware: IBM PC & compatibles. Operating System(s) Required: PC-DOS/MS-DOS 2.1 or higher. Memory Required: 320k.
disk $99.00.
BASIC Implementation That Eliminates the Compiling Step Without a Trade-Off in Execution Speed. This Version Adds Source-Level Debugging, Large Arrays, & Unlimited String Space. Other Features Include: User-Definable Variable Types & Record Structures Enabling Programmers to Combine Different Types of Data into a Single Entity. The Incremental Compiler That Converts Each Line of Source Code As It Is Entered. Programs Can Call Routines Written in Any of the Other Microsoft's Languages. Not Copy Protected.
Microsoft Pr.

Microsoft QuickC. Version: 2.0. Compatible Hardware: IBM PC & compatibles. Memory Required: 512k.
disk $99.00.
library source code $150.00.
Compiler's Features Include: Debugger - Integrated Debugger & Editor, Source-Level Debugging, Watch Local & Global Variables, Set Breakpoints, Stack Tracing; Editor & Environment - WORDSTAR Compatible, Context-Sensitive Help for Language & Functions, Brace, Bracket & Parenthesis Matching, Mouse Support, Support for EGA 43-Line Mode; Compiler - Completely Microsoft CODEVIEW Compatible, Automatic Registering; Integrated MAKE - Automatically Generates .MAK File, In Memory MAKE Compatible with Stand-Alone MAKE; Libraries - Graphics Library Included, CGA, EGA, & VGA Support, MICROSOFT C OPTIMIZING COMPILER 5.0 Compatible.
Microsoft Pr.

Microsoft Windows. *Version:* 3.1. *Compatible Hardware:* IBM PC & compatibles. *Operating System(s) Required:* MS-DOS, PC-DOS. *Memory Required:* 256k. *General Requirements:* Graphics adapter.
disk $99.00.
Graphical Extension of MS-DOS. Allows Users to Work with Multiple Applications & Switch from Program to Program. Supports More Than 640k. Users with Hard Disks, the Intel AboveBoard, or Expanded Memory Will Be Able to Work with More Programs Than Memory Can Hold at One Time. Also Accelerates the Movement of Information from One Program to Another. The Windows Interface Establishes a Common Set of Command Conventions, Drop-Down Menus, Dialog Boxes, & Icons for Standardized Operations for All Forthcoming Windows Applications. The Package Includes a Collection of Window Desktop Applications: Calendar, Cardfile, Notepad, Calculator, & Telecommunications Software.
Microsoft Pr.

Microsoft Windows Excel. *Version:* 2.11. *Compatible Hardware:* IBM PC AT, PS/2. *Operating System(s) Required:* PC-DOS, OS/2. *Memory Required:* 640k. *General Requirements:* Microsoft Windows. Mouse recommended.
$495.00.
Spreadsheet Application Designed to Take Advantage of MICROSOFT WINDOWS Graphics Interface & 80286/80386 Microprocessors' Capabilities. Features Compatibility with LOTUS 1-2-3 Commands & Macro Language, Presentation-Quality Graphics with 44 Chart Styles, Spreadsheet Linking Capabilities, & Network Support. Other Features Include Sideways Printing, Cell Annotation, Auditing, an UNDO Key, & Prompts Reminding Users to Save the Spreadsheet Before Leaving the Program. For Those Familiar with the LOTUS 1-2-3 Command Language, There Is a Special Help Facility Which Shows Users How to Convert Certain 1-2-3 Commands to Their EXCEL Equivalents.
Microsoft Pr.

Microsoft Windows in Your Classroom: A Student Introduction. Steve Corder et al. 1994. *Items Included:* Package includes disk & reproducible teacher book. Accompanying student activity text is $9.95, or $8.95 for 10 or more copies. *Customer Support:* Returnable if not satisfied. Call 1-800-341-6094 for technical support. 30-day preview available.
MS-DOS Windows. IBM & compatibles. disk $68.95 (ISBN 0-8251-2491-3, Order no.: 0-24913). *Addl. software required:* Windows.
Guided Self-Paced Instruction in Using the Windows Program Manager, File Manager, & Accessories Programs Is Provided in the Activity Text. Students Manipulate the Files on the Disk in Order to Practice Integrating Accessories into a Simulated Home-Office Operation.
J. Weston Walch Pub.

Microsoft Windows 386. *Version:* 2.11. *Compatible Hardware:* 80386-based systems including AT&T, Compaq Deskpro 386, Hewlett-Packard, IBM PS/2 Model 80, & Tandy 4000. *Memory Required:* 2048k. *General Requirements:* Hard disk; EGA or VGA card.
disk $195.00.
Enables 80386 Personal Computer Users to Do Multitasking. Allows Users to Run Applications Simultaneously, Each Application Being Made to "Think" That It Has Its Own 8086 Computer with 640k of RAM. Data Can Be Cut & Pasted Between Applications.
Microsoft Pr.

Microsoft Word. Microsoft, Inc. *Compatible Hardware:* HP 150 Touchscreen, HP 110 Portable.
3.5" disk $375.00 (Order no.: 45474D).
User Can See on Screen What the Document Will Look Like. Features: Automatic Page Numbering & Footnoting, Subscript & Superscript, Windowing, Multi-Columnar Text, Glossary, Support of Documents of up to 255 Characters Wide, Automatic Printer Configuration, & up to 64 Fonts to Choose From. Works with the HP Laserjet PC Printer. Includes a Context-Sensitive, On-Line HELP Facility.
Hewlett-Packard Co.

Microsoft Word. *Version:* 5.0. *Operating System(s) Required:* PC-DOS/MS-DOS 2.0 or higher. *Memory Required:* 512k.
disk $450.00.
Features Mail Merge, Also Allows the User to Request Information from the Keyboard. Can Also Calculate New Field at Print Time, Skip Records or Print Individualized Letters Based on Conditional Fields or Insert One Document with Another. The Master Document Lets the User Use Variable Names That Are Self Explanatory Such As City, State & Zip Code. The Data File Uses Comma-Delimited or Tab-Delimited Format. Also Includes a Style Sheet Feature That Lets the User Customize Styles Such As Print Enhancements, Line Spacing, Margins & Other Formats & Then Change Them Item by Item with a Two Letter Code.
Microsoft Pr.

Microsoft Word. *Version:* 5.0. *Items Included:* Manuals. *Customer Support:* 30-day warranty, hotline, newsletter, electronic bulletin board.
An 80386 or 80286-based system under SCO Xenix 386 System V. $695.00.
Multiuser Xenix Version of Microsoft Word.
Santa Cruz Operation, Inc.

Microsoft Word for Everyone: Basics. 1993. *Items Included:* Includes data diskette. *Customer Support:* 30 day free phone support.
Windows. $29.95 (ISBN 0-935987-46-0). *Addl. software required:* Microsoft Word for Windows.
Self-Study Guide Provides Step by Step Instructions. Teaches How to Create a Document, Edit Text, Save & Print, Search & Replace, Move & Copy, Set Margins & Tabs, Spell Checker & Thesaurus, Must Be in Conjunction with Microsoft Word for Windows Software.
Edutrends, Inc.

Microsoft Word for the Macintosh. *Version:* 5.0. *Compatible Hardware:* Macintosh (1Mb) Grammar Checker requires 2Mb. *General Requirements:* Hard disk.
3.5" disk $495.00.
Word Processing Program with New Features That Include the "Ribbon" Which Gives the User Easy Access To Frequently Used Features Such As Columns, Fonts, Format Changes, & a New Drawing Tool. User Can Move Text with a Drag & Drop. The Print Merge Process Has Been Simplified. This Version Also Includes a Built-In Grammar Checker, a File Find Feature That Can Locate Documents Based on Dates, Keywords, or the Author, & an Auto-Save Reminder. Full System 7.0 Support.
Microsoft Pr.

Microsoft Word for Xenix. *Compatible Hardware:* IBM PC & compatibles. *Operating System(s) Required:* Xenix 2.0, Xenix V/286. *Memory Required:* 1000k. *General Requirements:* Hard disk.
$595.00.
Features MS-DOS Compatible Files & Provides the Capabilities of Word 3.0 for MS-DOS.
Among These Are Automatic Generation of Form Letters, Indexes, Tables of Contents, & Footnotes. The Program also Includes Style Sheets, an Outline Processor, & Numerical Sorting & Basic Mathematics Operations. Users Can View Multiple Windows & Documents Simultaneously.
Microsoft Pr.

Microsoft Works. *Version:* 2.00. *Compatible Hardware:* Apple Macintosh, IBM PC. *Memory Required:* IBM 384k, Macintosh 768k.
3.5" disk $295.00.
Integrated Word Processor, Database, Spreadsheet, Graphics, Communications.
Microsoft Pr.

Microsoft WRITE. *Compatible Hardware:* Apple Macintosh.
3.5" disk $175.00.
Word Processor Which Provides the Following Features: Pull-Down Menus; Point-&-Click Operation; On-Line Context-Sensitive HELP; 80,000-Word, Customizable Dictionary; Built-In Spelling Corrector; Page Preview Command, Which Displays an Entire Page On-Screen So That Users Can Review & Revise Such Aspects As Margins & Page Breaks; Automatic Footnotes; Newsletter-Column Formatting; & the Capability to Mix Text & Graphics on the Same Line. Uses the Same Commands As MICROSOFT WORD, Version 3.
Microsoft Pr.

Microsolve - Network Flow Programming. Paul A. Jensen. Nov. 1987. *Compatible Hardware:* Apple II, II+, IIe, IIc; IBM PC. *Operating System(s) Required:* MS-DOS 2.0 or higher. (source code included). *Memory Required:* Apple 48k, IBM 128k.
disk $39.95, incl. manual.
IBM.
Apple.
Programs Allow the Creation, Solution & Analysis of Single Commodity Network Flow Programming Models.
Holden-Day, Inc.

Microsolve Operations Research. *Version:* 2.0. Paul A. Jensen. 1985. *Compatible Hardware:* Apple II, II+, IIe, IIc; IBM PC. *Operating System(s) Required:* MS-DOS 2.0, Apple DOS 3.3. (source code included). *Memory Required:* Apple 48k, IBM 128k.
$29.95 ea., incl. manual.
Operations Research for Both Business & Industrial Engineering.
Holden-Day, Inc.

MicroSPEED. *Compatible Hardware:* Apple II, II+; Commodore Amiga.
contact publisher for price.
Language System Capable of Running Programs 1000-2500% Faster.
Applied Informatics, Inc.

MicroSpell. Lifeboat Associates. *Operating System(s) Required:* MS-DOS, CP/M-86, Concurrent CP/M-86. *Memory Required:* 64k.
$249.00.
25,000 Word Dictionary May Be Increased by Over 8,000 Additional Words to Suit User's Application. Displays List of Guesses As to What a Misspelled Word May Be.
Texas Instruments, Personal Productivit.

Microspell. *Version:* 8.1. 1991. *Compatible Hardware:* IBM PC, PC XT & compatibles, PC AT, PCjr, 3740. *Operating System(s) Required:* PC-DOS, MS-DOS. *Language(s):* C. *Memory Required:* 128k.
$79.95, incl. manual.
manual only $20.00.
Interactive Spelling Correction Program Intended

TITLE INDEX

for Professionals & Other Word Processing Users. Features a "True" Dictionary of Approximately 80,000 Words, & Provides Automctic Context Display, & In-File Correction Ability. Automatically Suggests Alternate Spellings for Suspect Words, & Makes the Replacements in the Text with a Single Keystroke. Dictionary Contains Many Proper Nouns, Such As Cities, States, Countries, & English Names, & User Can Add or Remove Entries.
Trigram Systems.

Microstat-II. Version: 2.5. 1978-88. Compatible Hardware: IBM PC, PC XT, PC AT, OS/2 & compatibles. Operating System(s) Required: PC-DOS/MS-DOS 2.1 or higher. Memory Required: 512k.
3.5" or 5.25" disk $395.00.
Full-Featured Statistics Package; General Areas of Coverage Are Stepwise Multiple Regression, Correlation Analysis, ANOVA, Crosstabs, Hypothesis Testing, Probabilities, Descriptive Statistics, Time Series, Nonparametric Statistics, Data Entry, Data Transformation, Data Import/Export & File Manipulation.
Ecosoft, Inc.

MicroStation PC. Version: 3.0. Compatible Hardware: IBM PC & compatibles. Memory Required: 640k. General Requirements: Hard disk.
disk $3300.00.
CAD Program for Architecture Featuring Autodimensioning, Patterning, Hidden Line Removal, Rendering, Reference Files, Multiple Views, User-Definable Menus, 3-D Capabilities, Macro Facilities & On-Line Help. Links Provided to dBASE III Plus. Exports .DXF & .CSV File Formats. Imports .DXF File Formats & ASCII Text Files into Drawing. Technical Phone Support Available.
Intergraph Corp.

Microstats: Sports Statistics Programs.
Compatible Hardware: Apple. Memory Required: 48k. General Requirements: Printer.
All 4 programs. $325.00 (Order no.: 3014).
module $99.00 ea.
Microstats Baseball. (Order no.: 3011).
Microstats Football. (Order no.: 3010).
Microstats Basketball. (Order no.: 3012).
Microstats Volleyball. (Order no.: 3013).
Computes Averages, Percentages, & Totals. All of the Team's Statistics (up to 99 Players & 50 Games) Are Stored on the Team's Data Disk. Each Program Generates Seven Different Printouts. The Informational Printouts Include: Input Sheet for Taking Stats at the Game, Player List with Names & Positions, Team Information Sheet Listing All Coaching & Support Staff. The Statistical Printouts Include: Single Game Statistics Including Each Player's Performance, Cumulative Game Statistics, Plus Game Totals, Cumulative Team Statistics, Player Sheet Report Card.
K-12 MicroMedia Publishing, Inc.

Microtec ASM68K.
contact publisher for price.
Implementation of the Assembly Language Specified by Motorola Corporation for the 68000 Microprocessor Family. Package Includes Macro Assembler, Linking Loader, Tektronix Conversion Utility, & Download Utility. An Optional Object Module Librarian Is Also Available.
Microtec Research.

Microtec MCC68K C Cross Compiler.
Compatible Hardware: DEC VAX, DG MV-Series; Apollo; IBM PC & compatibles.
contact publisher for price.
Package Includes the Compiler, Relocatable Macro Assembler, Linking Loader, Run-Time Library, & User's Guide. Features: Full Standard C, Compiler Option, Global Code Optimization, Optional Register Allocation Via Coloring, ROMable & Reentrant Code, Royalty-Free Run-Time Library, Floating Point Routines Library, Intermix with ASM68K ASSEMBLY or PAS68K PASCAL, Symbolic Debug Capability. Emits Code for the MICROTEC ASM68K Motorola Compatible Assembler.
Microtec Research.

Microtec 68020 Cross Assembler.
contact publisher for price.
Features: Instruction Set Fully Compatible with Motorola (Including 68000/08/10, & 68020 Instructions); User-Defined Symbols Unique to 31 Characters; Addressing Supporting All Motorola Addressing Modes; Macro Facility; Structured Directives; Linking Loader; Motorola Standard Hexadecimal S-Record Format Object Module Output; Librarian; Conversion & Download Utilities Supporting Tektronix & Hewlett-Packard.
Microtec Research.

Microtemp Financial Calculators. Compatible Hardware: Apple Macintosh Plus. General Requirements: Microsoft Excel or Works.
3.5" disk $79.95.
Allows User to Customize Financial Formulas.
Microtemp.

Microterm. Version: 1.4. Compatible Hardware: IBM PC.
disk $79.95.
Smart Terminal Program That Includes a Print Spooler & Special Screen Print Functions. Translation Tables with Default Values Are Included.
Blue Cat.

MicroTEX. Version: 1.5. Compatible Hardware: IBM PC, PC XT, PC AT & compatibles; Supports dot matrix printer, laser printers, & phototypesetters, including Epson & IBM dot matrix printers, QMS & Imagen laser printers, Apple LaserWriter & other Postscript machines, & the APS5 phototypesetter. Operating System(s) Required: MS-DOS. Memory Required: 512k.
disk $295.00.
printer or display drivers $100.00-$300.00.
Full Implementation of TEX, the Document Preparation Language. Enables Writers & Publishers to Typeset Technical Documents: Articles, Reports, or Books. Especially Suitable for Documents Containing Extensive Mathematics. Users Have Complete Control over Justification, Hyphenation, & Pagination. Supports Kerning & Ligature of Characters, Automatic Placement of Footnotes, Window Control, Automatic Insertion of Running Heads, & User-Defined Macros.
Addison-Wesley Publishing Co., Inc.

microTOCS. 1984.
MS-DOS (512k). disk $800.00 (Order no.: 812000). Addl. software required: Lotus 1-2-3 Ver. 2 or higher.
Estimate Cost of Truck Transportation Using Transportation DTA & Characteristics of User Shipments. Lotus 1-2-3 Templates Allow Full User Accessibility & Changeability, As Well As Compatibility With Other Applications.
DNS Assocs., Inc.

MicroTrak. SofTrak Systems. Compatible Hardware: HP Series 200 HP-UX Models 217, 220, 236, the Integral PC.
Single-user. 3.5" disk $775.00 (Order no.: 45524G).
Linus tape $900.00.
Multi-user. 3.5" disk $1550.00 (Order no.: 45524H).
Linus tape $1675.00.
Professional Project Management System. Users Can Plan Projects, Coordinate Resources, Track Costs, Compare "What-If" Scenarios, Generate Up-to-Date Reports, & Print Time-Scaled Schedules.
Hewlett-Packard Co.

MicroTrak. Compatible Hardware: DEC; IBM PC, PX XT, PC AT, PS/2, & compatible; Unix-based systems. Operating System(s) Required: PC-DOS/MS-DOS 2.0 or higher, Unix, Xenix, VMS.
DOS. disk $595.00.
Unix/Xenix. $895.00 & up.
VMS. $1995.00.
Project-Management Program. Includes the Overuse/Underuse Report, which Enables Users to Specify a Maximum Daily Limit for Each Resource. The Program Calculates Daily, Weekly, & Monthly Resource Usage Based on the Way User Allocates Resources to Individual Activities in a Schedule. Can Produce Reports that Are Cut Off Before, After, or Between Specified Dates. Supports Up to 5000 Tasks per Project with an Unlimited Number of Resources per Schedule & Activity. Can Display Up to 18 Tasks Simultaneously. Can Transfer Data to dBASE II & III, Lotus 1-2-3, & Supercalc, & in ASCII Format.
SofTrak Systems.

MicroTSP: For Macintosh. Version: 6.6. Jan. 1991. Items Included: User's manual, sample data.
Macintosh (1Mb). $595.00 single copy (multiple copy & academic discounts, network pricing available) (ISBN 1-880411-06-7). Networks supported: All.
Econometric Software Package with Emphasis on Time Series Analysis & Forecasting, but Encompassing a Wide Range of Statistical & Graphical Tools. Its Primary Market Is in the Research & Finance Departments of Fortune 500 Firms, Government Agencies & in Economics Departments & Business Schools at Major Universities. In Addition, We Have a Student Edition That Is Widely Used in Econometrics & Forecasting Courses in Economics & Business Programs.
Quantitative Micro Software.

MicroTSP: For PC Compatibles. Version: 7.0. Dec. 1990. Items Included: User's manual, sample data.
MS-DOS. IBM PC compatible (640k). $595.00 single copy (multiple copy & academic discounts, network pricing available) (ISBN 1-880411-03-2). Networks supported: All.
Econometric Software Package with Emphasis on Time Series Analysis & Forecasting, but Encompassing a Wide Range of Statistical & Graphical Tools. Its Primary Market Is in the Research & Finance Departments of Fortune 500 Firms, Government Agencies & in Economics Departments & Business Schools at Major Universities. In Addition, We Have a Student Edition That Is Widely Used in Econometrics & Forecasting Courses in Economics & Business Programs.
Quantitative Micro Software.

MicroType Pro. Truman Jackson. Mar. 1996.
Customer Support: 1-800-824-5179 product information; 1-800-543-0453 technical support.
Windows 3.1 or higher, DOS 3.3 or higher. 386 DX/16 (4Mb). 3.5" disk Contact publisher for price (ISBN 0-538-65380-9). Nonstandard peripherals required: 256 colors, sound card optional. Addl. software required: 40Mb hard drive.
Macintosh 68030/16 LCII or higher (4Mb). Contact publisher for price (ISBN 0-538-65381-7). Nonstandard peripherals required: 256 colors, sound card optional. Addl. software

required: 40Mb hard drive.
A Multifunctional Software Program Containing Alphabetic, Numerical, Skill Development, & Keypad Modules "All in One." Includes a Timing Component for Testing Understanding of Concepts & a Game Option for Motivation. Provides Enhanced Graphics, Color, On-Screen Photos, Animation & a Built-In Word Processor.
South-Western Publishing Co.

microURCS. 1983.
MS-DOS (512k). disk $1000.00 (Order no.: 813000). *Nonstandard peripherals required:* Hard disk.
Estimates Cost of Moving Shipments by Rail Using Uniform Rail Costing System. Spreadsheet Approach to Entry of Shipment Size, Commodity & Mileage, As Well As Optimal Modification for All Variables & Unit Costs, Allows Immediate Estimates of Railroad Cost for Negotiation, Sensitivity Studies & Decision Analysis.
DNS Assocs., Inc.

MicroVet: Veterinary Management. *Version:* 2.0. Michael Forrester. Jan. 1992. *Compatible Hardware:* IBM PC XT & compatibles, PC AT. *Operating System(s) Required:* PC-DOS, MS-DOS, Novell, NTNX, Netbios compatible Networks. *Language(s):* Assembler, CB 86. *Memory Required:* 256k. *General Requirements:* Hard disk with at least 20Mb capacity, 132-column printer.
disk $995.00.
full demo disk $100.00.
Client Accounting System for the Veterinary Office Consisting of Separate Modules That Run As an Integrated System. Includes Billing, Accounts Receivable, a Complete Recall Tracking & Notification System, Comprehensive Reports Generator with a Custom Reports Writer, Spay/Neuter & Vaccination Certificates, After-Care Instructions, Walk-Out Bill/Receipt, Mail List Manager, & Inventory Tracking.
Artificial Intelligence, Inc.

Microworx Courseware for Lotus, Level I. Aug. 1987. *Memory Required:* 256k.
$725.00.
additional student manuals may be purchased separately.
Instructor-Led Courseware Introduces Spreadsheet Design & Covers Release 2 Features. Includes Instructor's Manual, Student Manual & Disk, & Transparencies.
Entex Information Services.

Microworx Courseware for Lotus, Level II. Aug. 1987. *Compatible Hardware:* IBM PC & compatibles. *Memory Required:* 256k.
$725.00.
additional student manuals may be purchased separately.
Instructor-Led Courseware Includes Release 2 Features & Covers Advanced Spreadsheet Design & Database Functions. Includes Instructor's Manual, Student Manual & Disk, & Transparencies.
Entex Information Services.

Microworx Courseware for Lotus, Level III. Aug. 1987. *Memory Required:* 256k.
$725.00.
additional student manuals may be purchased separately.
Instructor-Led Courseware Includes Release 2 Features & Covers Graphics, Macros, & the Integration of all 1-2-3 Functions. Includes Instructor's Manual, Student Manual & Disk, & Transparencies.
Entex Information Services.

Midas Software. *Compatible Hardware:* TI. *Operating System(s) Required:* DX10, MS-DOS. *Language(s):* BASIC (source code included). *Memory Required:* 512k.
contact publisher for price.
Features Detailed Sales Analysis, & Management Control Features for Multi-Shop Owners As Well As a Computerized Midas Catalog for P.O.S Applications.
Pac Corp.

MIDI & Sound Book for the Atari ST. Bernd Enders & Wolfgang Klemme. May 1989. *Compatible Hardware:* Atari ST.
book & disk $34.95 (ISBN 1-55851-043-5).
book only $17.95 (ISBN 1-55851-042-7).
Provides an Introduction to the Acoustics & Musical Basics of Sound Synthesis & Sound Chip Programming. Along with a Discussion of Commercially Marketed Samplers, the Package Includes an Assembler Routine Plus Hardware Description of a Do-It-Yourself 8-Bit Converter. A GFA BASIC Program on the Disk Provides a Short Introduction to Music Theory. Other Example Programs Are Also Included on Disk.
M & T Bks.

MIDI Bass Works. Vincent Oddo. 1994. *Customer Support:* ECS offers technical support to registered users. Call (217) 359-7099. Other than the telephone call - technical support is no charge.
DOS 3.3 or higher. IBM. $39.95 single station/$200.00 netowrk (Order no.: MI-1482).
This Exciting New Program Is a Terrific Tool That Lets Users Create Bass Lines & Practice along with Them. Different Tuning Standards May Be Selected to Offer Versatility & Basslines May Be Printed. A Great Program for All Musicians.
Electronic Courseware Systems, Inc.

MIDI Jazz Improvisaton Series. Tom Rudolph & Roger Morgan. *Items Included:* This two-volume series includes 2 3-ring binder manuals. *Customer Support:* 90 day warranty against defective software.
DOS 3.3 or higher. IBM (640k). $79.95 each volume (Order no.: MI-1252/1253). *Nonstandard peripherals required:* MIDI keyboard, MIDI interface.
System 6.0.7 - 7. MAC (1Mb). $79.95 each volume (Order no.: MAC-1252/1253). *Nonstandard peripherals required:* MIDI interface, MIDI keyboard. *Addl. software required:* Sequencer that reads standard MIDI files.
This Series Provides Instrumental & Vocal Students Play-Along Materials to Learn Jazz Improvisation Using Original Tunes Based on Traditional Chord Progressions. Volume I Exercises Introduce II-V-I Progressions, Slow Blues in B Flat, Medium Blues in F, Fast Blues in C, Minor Blues & a Sample Tune. Volume II Exercises Introduce More Advanced Concepts Including; "Samba", Ballads with II-V Progressions, 12-Bar Blues with Substitutions, Blues with a Bridge, Funk/Rock Improvisation & Complex II-V-I Progressions.
Electronic Courseware Systems, Inc.

Midi Music Gallery. Feb. 1996. *Items Included:* 4 page instructional booklet, "Audition" software. *Customer Support:* Free customer support available Mon-Fri, 9-6pm via telephone, fax, mail, BBS, e-m ail.
Windows 3.1x or Windows 95. IBM PC or compatible. disk $39.95 (ISBN 1-888743-02-6). *Nonstandard peripherals required:* Sound card & or midi instrument with PC interface, VGA monitor headphones & speakers. *Optimal configuration:* IBM PC or compatible, Windows 3.1x or 95, 8 Mb RAM, sound board & or midi instrument w/PC interface, midi sequencing software.
"Midi Music Gallery" is a collection of music in midi format.
Voyetra Technologies.

MIDI Programming for the Macintosh. Steve De Furia & Joe Scacciaferro. Jan. 1989. *Compatible Hardware:* Apple Macintosh.
book & disk $37.95 (ISBN 1-55851-022-2).
book only $22.95 (ISBN 1-55851-021-4).
Provides the Musician & Programmer with the Background Necessary to Program Music Applications. Includes an Overview of the MIDI Programming Language, Paying Special Attention to the Macintosh Interface with Example Programs That Show How to Use Pull-Down Menus, Dialog Windows, & a Mouse. In Addition, the Users Will Learn How to Program the Various Peripherals Associated with MIDI. Specific Example Programs Are Presented & All the Source Code Is Available on Disk. Requires MIDIBASIC & MINIPASCAL.
M & T Bks.

MIDI Sample Wrench. *Version:* 1.3. Jun. 1989. *Items Included:* Hard cover manual, 2nd data disk. *Customer Support:* 1 yr. limited warranty, phone tech support.
Amiga DOS 1.2 or higher (512k). Commodore Amiga 500/1000/2000. $279.00. *Nonstandard peripherals required:* MIDI interface, one or more supported samplers. *Optimal configuration:* 1Mb RAM or more, 2 floppies and/or hard drive.
Sound Sample Editor for MIDI Samplers. Cut/Paste Editing with Digital EQ, Cross-Fade Looping, Free Hand Drawing, etc. Able to Cross Load Sounds Between Different Samplers.
Dissidents.

MIDI Screen Saver. David Willcoxen. 1990. *Customer Support:* ECS offers technical support to registered users. Call (217) 359-7099. Other than the telephone call - technical support is no charge.
DOS 3.2 or higher. IBM. disk $39.95 (Order no.: MI-1414). *Nonstandard peripherals required:* Roland MPU-401, MIDI interface or compatible, MIDI keyboard.
System 6.0.4 or higher. Macintosh. 3.5" disk $39.95 (Order no.: MAC-1414). *Nonstandard peripherals required:* MIDI interface, MIDI keyboard.
This Exciting & Innovative Screen Saver Not Only Will Protect Your Computer from Having Images "Burned-In" to Your Screen but Will Play Music Through Your MIDI Keyboard Choreographed Perfectly with the Images Displayed. The MIDI "TUNES" Can Be Selected from a List of Many, & New Tunes Can Be Added.
Electronic Courseware Systems, Inc.

MIDI Sequencing in C. Jim Conger. Apr. 1989. *Operating System(s) Required:* MS-DOS. *General Requirements:* Roland MPU 401 MIDI interface or equivalent; CGA, EGA or VGA card. Microsoft or Turbo C compiler.
book & disk $39.95 (ISBN 1-55851-046-X).
book only $24.95 (ISBN 1-55851-045-1).
Approaches the Recording & Playback of MIDI Data from the Perspective of both Users & Programmers. For Users, the Optional Source Code Disk Provides a Ready-to-Run 8-Track MIDI Sequencer/Editor, along with Full Documentation of Each Function.
M & T Bks.

MIDI Stack. *Compatible Hardware:* Apple Macintosh. *Memory Required:* 1000k. *General Requirements:* Hard disk, HyperCard.
3.5" disk $15.00.
Allows MIDIPAINT Segments or ONE-STEP Files to Be Played As a Background Task under HYPERCARD.
Southwest Music Systems, Inc.

TITLE INDEX

MidiFile Reader. *Version:* 1.2. Feb. 1991. *Items Included:* User's manual; Demo program available for $5.00. *Customer Support:* Telephone support, cost of call; Electronic Computer Bulletin Board, cost of call.
MS-DOS. IBM PC, XT, AT, PS/2 or compatible (256k). disk $25.00. *Networks supported:* All.
Provides Users with New Approach to Editing & Understanding Standard MIDI Files. Program Converts MIDI Files into Readable Text File That Can Be Viewed or Edited with Any Text Editor. Text File Provides Translation of Every Musical Event in the MIDI File Such As Note on/off, Tempo, Key Signature etc. Text Files Can Be Edited & Then Converted Back into Standard MIDI Files. User's Own Text Editor Can Be Integrated into Program. Also Provides Extensive Profile Feature Which Allows User to Customize Many Aspects of the Program.
Spartan Software Systems.

MidiPaint. *Version:* 2.0. *Compatible Hardware:* Apple Macintosh 512KE. *Memory Required:* 512k.
3.5" disk $295.00.
Professional MIDI Sequencer Program.
Southwest Music Systems, Inc.

MidiShare. *Compatible Hardware:* Apple Macintosh. *Memory Required:* 512k.
3.5" disk $49.00.
Utility Program for MultiFinder.
Southwest Music Systems, Inc.

Midisoft Studio: Advanced Edition. 1990. *Items Included:* Full GEM operating system, box, manual, disk(s). *Customer Support:* Free to all registered users.
IBM PC & compatibles. Version 2.02 $339.95 with Interface Card, $219.95 software only. *Nonstandard peripherals required:* Midisoft or Roland Compatible MIDI Interface Card, a MIDI equipped instrument.
Atari ST. 3.5" disk $159.95. *Nonstandard peripherals required:* MIDI equipped instrument.
Includes the Same Features of the Standard Edition Plus Added Editing, Programming & Other Capabilities. Allows Users to Record in Real-Time, Playback, Overdub, Rewind, etc., on 64 Polyphonic Independently Controlled Tracks. Product Offers MIDI Event Editing, Which Gives Users Control over Entering, Changing & Removing All Aspects of the Music. Lets User Program Tempo Changes, Supports up to 16 MIDI Channels per Track, Offers Real-Time MIDI Volume Control & Real-Time Octave Transpose for Each Track, & Displays MIDI Thru Controls on the Main Screen.
Midisoft Corp.

Midisoft Studio: Standard Edition. 1990. *Items Included:* Full GEM operating system, box, manual, disk(s). *Customer Support:* Free to all registered users.
IBM PC & compatibles. Version 2.02 $249.00 with Interface Card, $139.95 Software only. *Nonstandard peripherals required:* Midisoft or Roland Compatible MIDI Interface Card, Midi equipped instrument.
Atari ST. Version 2.18 $99.95. *Nonstandard peripherals required:* MIDI equipped instrument.
Menu or Mouse Driven 32 Track MIDI "Recording Studio". Features Editing Capabilities (Insert, Delete, Erase, Paste), Selectable Time Signature, Use of All MIDI Signals Including Pitch Bend & Keystroke Velocity, Full Disk Storage File System, Step Record for Note-by-Note Entry, Real Time Tempo Changing & Track Mixing, Optional Metronome or Pulse Set by Drum Machine.
Midisoft Corp.

Midisoft Windows DLL. *Customer Support:* Free to all owners of Midisoft Studio.
IBM PC & compatibles. $100.00 or free to owners of Midisoft Studio. *Nonstandard peripherals required:* Asymetrix Toolbook or Windows development environment, MIDI equipped instrument. *Addl. software required:* Windows 3.
Music Design Tool Which Interfaces the Midisoft Studio Sequencer with Asymetrix Toolbook & Windows 3 to Add Sound & Music to Computer Presentations.
Midisoft Corp.

A Midsummer Night's Dream. *Version:* 1.5. Feb. 1995. *Items Included:* BookWorm Student Reader (diskette). *Customer Support:* 30 day MBG. Technical support (toll call) - no charge.
System 7.0 or higher. Macintosh (5Mb). CD-ROM disk $29.95 (ISBN 1-57316-023-7, Order no.: 16158). *Nonstandard peripherals required:* CD-ROM drive, 12" color monitor. *Optimal configuration:* 13" color monitor recommended.
Windows 3.1 or higher. IBM compatible (MPC) 386 DX (4Mb). CD-ROM disk $29.95. *Nonstandard peripherals required:* Standard multimedia compatible CD-ROM. *Optimal configuration:* 8Mb RAM recommended, 256 color monitor recommended.
Whether Seen As an Innocent Fantasy, a Mythic Romance, or a Sinister Nightmare, A Midsummer Night's Dream Has Long Been One of Shakespeare's Most Popular Works. Beautifully Illustrated with Pictures from Stage Performance & Art Masterpieces from Shakespeare's Day.
Communication & Information Technologies, Inc. (CIT).

Midway. *Compatible Hardware:* Atari 400, 800. *Language(s):* Atari BASIC (source code included). *Memory Required:* 32k.
disk $18.95.
Naval Battle Simulation.
Dynacomp, Inc.

Mighty Draw. *Version:* Windows 1.01, DOS 1.0, Macintosh 1.1.
Windows, 3.1 or higher. disk $59.95 (Order no.: 744734 30160 8). *Optimal configuration:* Windows, 3.1 or higher, 2Mb RAM.
DOS 3.0 or higher. disk $49.95 (Order no.: 744734 30130 8). *Optimal configuration:* DOS, 640k, DOS 3.0 or higher, mouse & hard drive recommended.
Macintosh (1Mb). 3.5" disk $49.95 (Order no.: 744734 30150 6). *Optimal configuration:* Macintosh, 1Mb RAM, hard drive recommended.
An Object-Oriented, General-Purpose Drawing Program Which Includes the Ability to Create Pie Charts, Exploding Pie Charts, Column Charts, Bar Charts & Flowcharts. It Will Draw Graphs, Electrical Schematics, & Diagrams & Help the User Create Newsletters, Greeting Cards, Logos, Clip Art, etc. This Product Includes Hundreds of Pre-Drawn Symbols, Including: Maps, Flags, Trees & Shrubs, Furniture, Children's Clip Art, People, Business Symbols, Buildings, Vehicles, Sports, Military, & Users Can Import Symbols from Other Programs. Images Can Be Exported to Other Programs As Well.
Abracadata, Ltd.

Mighty Mail. Tim Purves. 1985. *Compatible Hardware:* Atari ST, IBM PC, Sanyo MBC 555. *Memory Required:* 128k. *General Requirements:* Printer.
IBM. disk $99.95 (ISBN 0-923213-36-8, Order no.: SA-MIG).
Atari. 3.5" disk $49.95.
Sanyo & IBM. disk $49.95.
Mailing-List Manager with Multi-Level Sorts & Conditional "Flags" for Specialized Reports.
MichTron, Inc.

Mighty Morphin Power Rangers Coloring Screens Box. *Items Included:* Installation guide.
IBM. Contact publisher for price (ISBN 0-87321-101-4, Order no.: CDD-3124).
Activision, Inc.

Mighty Morphin Power Rangers Coloring Screens Book. *Items Included:* Installation guide.
IBM. Contact publisher for price (ISBN 0-87321-100-6, Order no.: CDD3123).
Activision, Inc.

Mighty Morphin Power Rangers Jigsaw Puzzle Book. *Items Included:* Installation guide.
IBM. Contact publisher for price (ISBN 0-87321-106-5, Order no.: CDD-3129).
Activision, Inc.

Mighty Morphin Power Rangers Jigsaw Puzzle Box. *Items Included:* Installation guide.
IBM. Contact publisher for price (ISBN 0-87321-107-3, Order no.: CDD-3130).
Activision, Inc.

Mighty Morphin Power Rangers Print Kit Book. *Items Included:* Installation guide.
IBM. Contact publisher for price (ISBN 0-87321-104-9, Order no.: CDD-3127).
Activision, Inc.

Mighty Morphin Power Rangers Print Kit Box. *Items Included:* Installation guide.
IBM. Contact publisher for price (ISBN 0-87321-105-7, Order no.: CDD-3128).
Activision, Inc.

Mighty Morphin Power Rangers Screen Scenes Box. *Items Included:* Installation guide.
IBM. Contact publisher for price (ISBN 0-87321-103-0, Order no.: CDD-3126).
Activision, Inc.

Mighty Morphin Power Rangers Screen Scenes Book. *Items Included:* Installation guide.
IBM. Contact publisher for price (ISBN 0-87321-102-2, Order no.: CDD-3125).
Activision, Inc.

Mighty Morphy Power Rangers T. B. D. Book. *Items Included:* Installation Guide.
IBM. Contact publisher for price (ISBN 0-87321-108-1, Order no.: CDD-3131).
Activision, Inc.

Mighty Morphy Power Rangers T. B. D. Box. *Items Included:* Installation Guide.
IBM. Contact publisher for price (ISBN 0-87321-109-X, Order no.: CDD-3132).
Activision, Inc.

Mike Dipka Ultimate Football. Aug. 1991. *Items Included:* Catalog, copy protection device, manual, proof of purchase card. *Customer Support:* Technical support 408-296-8400, 90 day limited warranty, Bulletin Board (modem) 408-296-8800 (settings: 300, 1200, 2400 baud; 8 data; no parity; 1 stop bit).
IBM DOS 2.1 or higher, Tandy-DOS (640k - recommended: 10MHz or faster AT class machines). IBM PC, XT, AT, & compatibles, Tandy 1000 series, 3000, 4000. $54.95. *Optimal configuration:* Hard drive installable, keyboard, mouse or joystick, graphics, & sound board.
Football Simulation with Graphics, Animation, Sounds, & More. Delivers Big Hits, Fast Action, NFL-Style Strategy, & Total Control.
Accolade, Inc.

MIKSAM ROM. *Compatible Hardware:* HP 86/87 with one disk drive. *Memory Required:* 4k.
ROM cartridge $195.00 (Order no.: 00087-

15011).
Software Development Tool for Application Programmers. Serves As a Core Around Which Custom File Management Can Be Designed. Also Allows Search for More Than One Category of Data at a Time.
Hewlett-Packard Co.

Milano Quinella Analysis. Ronald D. Jones. 1985. *Compatible Hardware:* Apple; Commodore; IBM; TRS-80 Model I, Model III, Color Computer. *Operating System(s) Required:* CP/M. *Memory Required:* 64k.
disk $149.95 ea.
Apple. (ISBN 1-55604-096-2, Order no.: D005).
CP/M. (ISBN 1-55604-097-0, Order no.: D005).
Commodore. (ISBN 1-55604-098-9, Order no.: D005).
Color Computer. (ISBN 1-55604-099-7, Order no.: D005).
IBM. (ISBN 1-55604-100-4, Order no.: D005).
Model I & Model III. (ISBN 1-55604-101-2, Order no.: D002).
Stores Last 25 Races of Each Dog at the Track & Does an Analysis on Their Running Patterns.
Professor Jones Professional Handicapping Systems.

Milestone. *Compatible Hardware:* Apple II+, IIe; Franklin Ace. *Memory Required:* 48k.
disk $24.95.
Complete a 700 Mile Autotrip Before the Computer Opponent. The User Must Deal with Hazards of the Roads, Stop Lights, Flat Tires, Speed Limits, Accidents, & Gas Shortages. High-Resolution Graphics Are Featured.
Compuware.

Milestone. Organic Software, Inc. *Compatible Hardware:* HP 86/87 with CP/M System (HP 82900A).
3-1/2" or 5-1/4" disk $295.00 ea. (Order no.: 45580A).
Project Management & Time Scheduling Product Using PERT/CPM Techniques to Increase Productivity & Management of Small Projects. Helps Project Leaders & Small Business Owners Clarify the Tasks at Hand & Communicate Schedules & Priorities. Stresses Interactivity & Comprehensive Reporting. The List of Associated Activities Provides a Thread Used to Link All Jobs Together into an Overall Project Schedule. Adding or Changing Activities Are Re-Computed into the Schedule & the Results Are Immediately Displayed on the Screen.
Hewlett-Packard Co.

MILESTONES, ETC. *Version:* 3.0. Aug. 1991. *Items Included:* 1 spiral bound manual, 1 5.25" disk, & 1 3.5" disk. *Customer Support:* Free technical hot-line.
MS-DOS. DOS compatible (1Mb). $189.00 (Order no.: A-01). *Addl. software required:* Windows 3.0 or higher. *Optimal configuration:* IBM 386 or compatible 2Mb or more of RAM. *Networks supported:* Any network compatible with Windows.
Designed to Simplify the Job of Preparing Project Status Charts. Anything from a Gantt Chart to a Detailed Milestone Chart Can Be Prepared Easily with This Program. Runs in the Microsoft Windows Environment & Supports Windows, Printers & Plotters.
KIDASA Software.

Milkpay. *Version:* 3.1. Jan. 1989. *Customer Support:* On site training unlimited support services for first 90 days & through subscription thereafter.
MS-DOS, PC-DOS. Contact publisher for price. *Nonstandard peripherals required:* Hard disk (30Mb); 132-column printer. *Networks supported:* Novell, NTNX, 10-Net, Unix, Xenix, Turbo DOS (Multi-User version for all). Module Specialized to Needs of Milk Receivers. Allows Milk Received by a Dairy Plant to Be Entered with Butter Fat & Solids Content of Milk. Argos Software.

MILKPRO. *Version:* 1.0. 1993. *Items Included:* User's Guide. *Customer Support:* Free technical support.
PC-DOS/MS-DOS. IBM PC & compatibles (384k). disk $195.00. *Addl. software required:* MIXIT-2+. *Optimal configuration:* IBM PC compatible computer with MS-DOS, minimum 384k, 80-column printer. *Networks supported:* Novell.
MS Windows 3.0 or higher. IBM PC & compatibles (384k). disk $195.00. *Addl. software required:* MIXIT-2+. *Optimal configuration:* IBM PC compatible computer with MS Windows 3.0 or higher, 80-column printer. *Networks supported:* Novell.
Calculates Required Amounts of Two Grains to Be Added to a Feed Base Mix for Protein & Energy Balance in Dairy Rations. Concise Reports Show the Complete Rations, Grain Values, Cost & Profit per Cow for a Range of Milk Production, & More. Used with MIXIT-2plus, It Has Windows, Menus, Mouse Support, & Context Sensitive Help Screens.
Agricultural Software Consultants, Inc.

Milky Way Merchant. *Compatible Hardware:* HP 150 Touchscreen.
3.5" disk $39.95 (Order no.: 92243BA).
Become a Galactic Merchant! Sharpen Your Skills As You Try to Beat Your Opponents to the Best Deals. The Game Provides You with the Opportunities & the Barriers in a Strategy Game That Spans the Galaxy. Up to Four Merchants Can Play at One Time.
Hewlett-Packard Co.

Milky Way Merchant. *Customer Support:* 800-929-8117 (customer service).
MS-DOS. IBM/PS2. disk $39.99 (ISBN 0-87007-479-2).
A Trading Strategy Game in Which Users Make Deals for Profit, Identify Markets & Their Needs, & Plan Trading Route. Beginning Players May Use the Automatic Set-up Feature of the Game, While Varying the Number of Players & Random Number Seed to Obtain Different Star Maps. More Advanced Player May Completely Set up His Own Game. Sample Modules Are Included. Every Game Requires Different Strategies to Win.
SourceView Software International.

Millennia Hotel Management System. *Compatible Hardware:* IBM 486, 586, RS 6000. *Operating System(s) Required:* Unix. *Language(s):* C, 4GL. *Customer Support:* 24 hours, 7 days a week.
IBM (8Mb). disk Contact publisher for price.
Designed for Resorts & Luxury Hotels. Provides Management for: Reservations, Front Desk, Telephone, Housekeeping, Building Maintenance Control, Night Audit, Restaurant Cashier, Restaurant Pre-Check, Back Office Accounting, Sales, Catering & Marketing Departments.
National Guest Systems Corp.

Millie's Math House. Oct. 1992. *Items Included:* Manual. *Customer Support:* 30-day satisfaction guarantee, 90-day warranty, technical support.
Macintosh, System 6.0.7 or higher. Mac Plus or higher (1Mb for System 6.0.X, 2Mb for System 7.0). 3.5" disk $49.95. *Optimal configuration:* Macintosh with color monitor System 7, 4Mb RAM, equipped with microphone for sound input.
MS-DOS. IBM, Tandy or compatible (640k). disk $49.95. *Nonstandard peripherals required:* VGA or EGA graphics. *Optimal configuration:* IBM, Tandy or compatible with color monitor, Sound Blaster with microphone for sound input.
Windows (4Mb). IBM or compatible. disk $49.95. *Nonstandard peripherals required:* VGA or EGA. *Optimal configuration:* IBM or compatible with color monitor, 4Mb RAM, VGA or EGA, Sound Blaster with microphone.
Designed by Early Childhood Experts for Children Ages Two to Six, the Six Activities in Millie's Math House Are Interactive, Open-Ended, Multi-Sensory, Animated & Full of Captivating Characters - a Combination That Makes Children's Math Education a Rich & Fun Experience.
Edmark Corp.

Millie's Math House.
Windows. IBM & compatibles. CD-ROM disk $49.95 (Order no.: R1349). *Nonstandard peripherals required:* CD-ROM drive. *Optimal configuration:* 386 processor operating at 16Mhz or higher, MS-DOS 5.0 or higher, Windows 3.1 or higher, 30Mb hard drive, mouse, VGA graphic adapter & VGA color monitor (SVGA recommended), 4Mb RAM, external speakers or headphones (with sound card) that are Sound Blaster compatible.
Macintosh (4Mb). (Order no.: R1349). *Nonstandard peripherals required:* 14" color monitor or larger, CD-ROM drive.
Children Are Given the Building Blocks They Need to Develop a Solid Foundation in Math. Six Activities Are Packed with Learning Concepts Such As Problem Solving, Exploring Shapes, Playing with Patterns & More.
Library Video Co.

The Milliken Storyteller Children's Classics.
Apple IIGS. $29.95 Vol. I (Henny Penny, Little Red Riding Hood, & The Ugly Duckling). $29.95 Vol. II (Jack & Beanstalk, Aladdin & the Magic Lamp & Peter Rabbit).
MS-DOS. $29.95 ea. (Vol. I & Vol. II).
Macintosh. $29.95 ea. (Vol. I & Vol. II).
Traditional Children's Classics. Color Artwork, & Wonderfully Animated Characters with Real Human Voices. As They Read, Children May Also Enjoy Answering Random Questions about the Story, Where Correct Responses Are Rewarded with Sound Effects & Animations. Sound, Underlining, & Questions Are All Optional Features That You Can Set up Ahead of Time or Change at Any Point During the Story. Has Computerized Coloring Pages & Simple Word Processor That Allows Children to Create Their Own Storybook from Start to Finish. The Printed Copy of Their Storybook Even Includes a Custom Title Page with Their Name on It.
Milliken Publishing Co.

Millionaire II. Britannica Software, Pubs. *Compatible Hardware:* TRS-80.
disk $49.95.
Stock Market Simulation Where, in a Period of 90 Simulated Days, the User Tries to Earn $1,000,000 by Studying the Investment Environment & Trading Stocks or Options.
Compton's NewMedia, Inc.

Millionaire: The Stock Market Simulation. Blue Chip Software, Inc. *Compatible Hardware:* HP 150 Touchscreen, IBM PC.
3.5" disk $59.95 (Order no.: 92243JA).
You Begin with $10,000 & Invest in Stocks from Five Different Industry Groups. As Stock Prices Respond to Dynamic Market Forces You'll Become Involved in Sophisticated Trading Like Buying-on-Margin, Call Options, & Put Options. The Market Trends of the Game Are Based on Actual Stock Market Trends. Headlines from Major Financial Publications Yield Clues About Price Trends. You'll Have Access to Information

TITLE INDEX

About the Profitability of the Corporations, the Number of Shares Traded on the Exchange, Stock Price Trends, Industry Trends, & Daily Price Changes.
Hewlett-Packard Co.

Millionwaire. Jan. 1984. *Customer Support:* 90-Day limited warranty.
  Apple-DOS 3.3. Apple II Family (48k). disk $35.00 (ISBN 0-917277-00-7).
  Commodore 64/128 (64k). disk $35.00 (ISBN 0-917277-60-0).
  PC/MS-DOS 2.0 or higher. IBM & compatibles (64k). disk $35.00 (ISBN 0-917277-01-5).
Tests User's Trivia Capability with a Series of Rounds Randomly Selected from More Than 40 Graphically Illustrated Categories (Cartoons, World Cities, Ethnic Foods, Sports Characters, etc.) & More than 1200 Questions. The Harder the Question, the Higher the Odds. Ages 14 & up.
BrainBank/Generation Ahead of Maryland.

Millipede. *Compatible Hardware:* Atari XL/XE.
  ROM cartridge $19.95 (Order no.: RX8048).
Atari Corp.

Milon Plus. *Version:* 1.2. *Items Included:* Manual. Macintosh Plus or higher. 3.5" disk $49.95.
  Nonstandard peripherals required: Hard drive.
Desk Accessory That Contains a 250,000 Word Dictionary. Can Translate Individual Words from Hebrew to English & from English to Hebrew. It Can Be Used to Spell-Check Hebrew & English & to Suggest Synonyms in Either Language.
Davka Corp.

Milton Berle's Private Joke File.
  MS/PC-DOS. IBM PC & compatibles. disk $29.95, plus ,3.00 S&H.
Comedian Milton Berle Has Put a Data Base of More Than Ten Thousand of His Favorite Jokes on One 5.25" or 3.5" Disk. Data Base Utilizes the Clipper Application & Development System from Nantucket Corporation. Search Any Category, Tag Single or Multiple Jokes for Printing or Saving to Disk, & Once Written to Disk, They Can Be Integrated into User's Word Processor for Use in Speeches or Scripts or Any other Document. Product Has a Graphical User Interface with Movable Windows & Mouse-Driven Menus. Users Can Add Their Own Jokes to it by Category. MAC & Windows Version Available Mid-1993.
Comedy Software Limited.

MIM-CD: Mendelian Inheritance in Man. Oct. 1993.
  MS Windows 3.1 or higher. IBM & compatibles (4Mb). CD-ROM disk $395.00 & up. *Nonstandard peripherals required:* Magnetic or CD-ROM, using ISO 9660. *Optimal configuration:* IBM & compatibles, 80386 or higher, 4Mb RAM, 20Mb hard disk, mouse, MS Windows 3.1 or higher.
  System 6.0.7 or higher. Apple Macintosh (3Mb). CD-ROM disk $395.00 & up. *Optimal configuration:* Apple Macintosh Plus or higher, 3Mb RAM, System 6.0.7 or higher.
MIM-CD Is the Electronic Version of Victor A. McKusick, M.D.'s Publication Mendelian Inheritance in Man: Catalogs of Autosomal Dominant, Autosomal Recessive, & X-Linked Phenotypes (MIM). It Contains over 6,000 Defect & Disorder Entries, As Well As the MIM Gene Map Descriptions & Defect/Disorder Lists. Many Bibliographic References in the Text Are Hot-Linked to Their Corresponding Abstracts from the National Library of Medicine's MEDLINE Database. Knowledge Finder Search-&-Retrieval Software Makes Searching of the MIM-CD Database Easy, Effective & Fast. After the User Types a Phrase or Sentence Describing the Information Needed, It selects the References in the Database That Appear to Best Match the Request, & Presents Them in Order of likely relevance. The CD-ROM Covers All Materials Published in MIM since 1966.
Aries Systems Corp.

Mimic. *Version:* 2.3. *Items Included:* Manual. *Customer Support:* 90 days free support; Annual support contract - $150.00; Free 24-hour BBS.
  IBM & compatibles (640K). disk $129.00.
Provides Remote Control of Main Console on a Multiuser DOS or REAL/32 System. Allows for Execution of DOS Programs from Remote Location. Performs File Transfers Simultaneously with Program Execution. Both Local & Remote Keyboard & Screen Remain Active, Allowing for Remote Support, Configuration, & Training.
Logan Industries, Inc.

Mince. *Compatible Hardware:* IBM PC & compatibles. *Operating System(s) Required:* CP/M, PC-DOS, MS-DOS. *Language(s):* C. *Memory Required:* 64-128k.
  disk $175.00.
Screen-Oriented Text Editor Featuring Global Search & Replace, Word Wrap, & Block Move & Delete. An Automatic Virtual Memory Page Swapping Scheme Allows Editing of a Document That Is Larger Than the Main Memory. Multiple Buffers Allow Displaying & Editing of Several Files at the Same Time.
Mark of the Unicorn.

Mind Castle: The Spell of the Word Wizard.
Aug. 1993. *Items Included:* Program manual. *Customer Support:* Free technical support 800-421-4157, 90 day warranty.
  System 6.0.5 or higher. Macintosh (1Mb). 3.5" disk $59.95 (ISBN 1-882848-13-6).
  System 6.0.5 or higher. Macintosh (1Mb). $69.95 School Edition (ISBN 1-882848-14-4).
  System 6.0.5 or higher. Macintosh (1Mb). $149.95 School Edition, Lab Pack (ISBN 1-882848-15-2).
  PC-DOS/MS-DOS 3.0 or higher. IBM (640k). $59.95 3 1/2" disks (ISBN 1-882848-16-0).
  PC-DOS/MS-DOS 3.0 or higher. IBM (640k). $59.95 5 1/4" disks (ISBN 1-882848-17-9). *Nonstandard peripherals required:* Microsoft mouse recommended, supports Ad Lib & Sound Blaster cards, hard drive.
  PC-DOS/MS-DOS 3.0 or higher. IBM (640k). $69.95 School Edition, 3 1/2" disks (ISBN 1-882848-18-7). *Nonstandard peripherals required:* Microsoft mouse recommended, supports Ad Lib & Sound Blaster cards, hard drive.
  PC-DOS/MS-DOS 3.0 or higher. IBM (640k). $69.95 School Edition, 5 1/4" disks (ISBN 1-882848-19-5). *Nonstandard peripherals required:* Microsoft mouse recommended, supports Ad Lib & Sound Blaster cards, hard drive.
  PC-DOS/MS-DOS 3.0 or higher. IBM (640k). $149.95 School Edition, Lab Pack, 3 1/2" disks (ISBN 1-882848-20-9). *Nonstandard peripherals required:* Microsoft mouse recommended, supports Ad Lib & Sound Blaster cards, hard drive.
  PC-DOS/MS-DOS 3.0 or higher. IBM (640k). $149.95 School Edition, Lab Pack, 5 1/4" disks (ISBN 1-882848-21-7). *Nonstandard peripherals required:* Microsoft mouse recommended, supports Ad Lib & Sound Blaster cards, hard drive.
An Evil Wizard Has Zapped You into a Frog & Tossed You Inside the Dungeon Tower of His Creepy Castle. You Must Make Your Escape Through Five Frightening Floors Before Morning or Forever Remain a Lowly Amphibian. Solving Word Puzzles & Decodiing Passwords Will Help You Uncover Hidden Portals in the Armory, the Study, & the Alchemy Room. Word Wizard Is a Vocabulary Building Adventure for Ages 8 & Up.
Lawrence Productions, Inc.

Mind Challengers. *Compatible Hardware:* TI-99/4A with PLATO interpreter solid state cartridge.
  contact publisher for price (Order no.: PHM 3025).
Game I Challenges the Player to Echo a Sequence of Notes; Game II Involves Code Breaking Using Shapes & Colors.
Texas Instruments, Personal Productivit.

A Mind Forever Voyaging. Steve Meretzky.
Aug. 1985. *Compatible Hardware:* Apple II, II+, IIe, IIc, Macintosh; Atari 400, 800, 1200, ST; Commodore 64, 128, Amiga; IBM PC & compatibles; Kaypro. *Operating System(s) Required:* CP/M, MS-DOS. *Memory Required:* IBM 128k, Macintosh 512k.
  $44.95.
Text Adventure Game in Which the Player "Sees" the Future & Learns the Consequences of a Government Plan for "Renewed National Purpose".
Activision, Inc.

Mind Master Introductory Software.
  Commodore 64, 128; IBM PC & compatibles. disk $124.95. *Nonstandard peripherals required:* Mind Master biofeedback device, similar to mouse.
  Apple II series. contact publisher for price.
Consists of Four Programs: Icarus, Thought Waves, Magic Mirror & Slalom Skier. These Are Designed to Help User Become Familiar with the Galvanic Skin Response & Bring it Under Control. IBM Version Does Not Include Some of the Programs.
Behavioral Engineering.

Mind over Mac. *Version:* 1.8. May 1989. *Compatible Hardware:* Macintosh Plus, SE, II, Classic. *Memory Required:* 128k.
  3.5" disk $49.95 (Order no.: T-010).
Contains 5 Entertainment Games: DESTROYER, TRIVIAL INTRIGUE, ON-THE-CONTRARY, MASTERCODE & THIRD DIMENSION. Mac O/S Included on Disk.
Think Educational Software, Inc.

Mind Pursuit. Jun. 1986. *Compatible Hardware:* Apple; Commodore 64, 128. *Memory Required:* 64k.
  disk $19.95 ea.
  Commodore. (ISBN 0-88717-133-8, Order no.: 1500CDO).
  Apple. (ISBN 0-88717-134-6, Order no.: 1500APO).
  disk clue library $12.95.
Test Your Level of Intelligence & Knowledge of Trivia on 32 Different Skill Levels - True/False, Multiple Choice, or Fill-in-the-Blanks, for Children.
IntelliCreations, Inc.

MindLab. *Compatible Hardware:* Apple Macintosh. *Memory Required:* 512k.
  3.5" disk $8.00.
Creates, Edits & Runs Cognitive Psychology Experiments with Visual Stimuli.
Kinko's.

MindReader. *Version:* 2.0. *Compatible Hardware:* IBM PC & compatibles. *Operating System(s) Required:* PC-DOS/MS-DOS 2.0 or higher. *Memory Required:* 256k. *Customer Support:* Free unlimited tech support for 1 year.
  disk $89.95, incl. manual.
Allows Users to Have Complete Word-Processing Function but Also the Ability to Use Artificial Intelligence Mail Merge & Assign Text to a Single Keystroke. Includes Spelling Checker.
Brown Bag Software.

Mindwheel. Robert Pinsky et al. *Compatible Hardware:* Apple II+, IIe, IIc, Macintosh; Atari 400, 800, XL, XE Series, 520 ST (all Atari's require 2 hard disks); Commodore 64, IBM PC & compatibles, PC XT, PCjr. *Operating System(s) Required:* PC-DOS, MS-DOS.
disk $44.95 ea.
Atari 520 ST. (Order no.: ATDSK-2292).
Apple II+, IIe & IIc. (Order no.: APDSK-1228).
IBM. (Order no.: IBMDSK-4228).
Macintosh. 3.5" disk $44.95 (Order no.: MACDSK-5228).
Commodore. disk $39.95 (Order no.: COMDSK-3228).
Atari 400, 800, XL & XE Series. disk $39.95 (Order no.: ATDSK-2228).
Electronic Novel Featuring a Parser with More Than a 1200-Word Vocabulary & a Continuosly Changing Real-Time Universe. The Only Way to Save the Earth from Self-Destruction Is to Take a Telepathic Trip Back to the Beginning of Human Civilization to Retrieve the Wheel of Wisdom. You Must Successfully Negotiate a Labyrinth of Four Minds of Unusual Power: the Peace Activist/Rock Star, the Monstrous Dictator, the Heroic Poet, & the Gifted Scientist; All Linked to a Common Neuro-Electronic Matrix That Leads to the Cave Master & the Wheel.
Broderbund Software, Inc.

MineORE. *Version:* 2.0. Oct. 1985. *Compatible Hardware:* IBM PC, PC XT, PC AT & compatibles. *Operating System(s) Required:* MS-DOS, PC-DOS. *Language(s):* FORTRAN. *Memory Required:* 512k. *General Requirements:* Printer.
disk $5000.00, incl. PREPIT, PITKOR, PSTPIT, & RESIT (Order no.: MINEORE).
Complete Mine Planning from Pit Optimization to Production Scheduling Is Available. Calculates the Economic Value of a Deposit Block Model Based Mineral Concentrations & Spatial Position.
Geostat Systems International, Inc. (GSII).

Miner 2049er. (Series B).
IBM. disk $15.00. *Optimal configuration:* IBM, joystick.
Electronic Games Hall of Fame! 11 Wild, Challenging Screens! Saddle up with Bounty Bob - & Follow the Notorious Yukon Yohan into an Abandoned Uranium Mine! You're in for a Wild Chase Through 10 Levels of Traps, Tricks & Lethal Challenges! You Have to Climb up Ladders, Make Death-Defying Leaps, Jump from Moving Platforms, Neutralize Deadly Mutants, Avoid Crushing Stompers. And at the End, Load up Bounty Bob with Dynamite & Shoot Him Out of a Cannon. It's a Blast! You Need Skill, Endurance & Guts to Conquer All 10 Levels. If You've Got Them, Then Mount up & Move Out Right Now.
Word Assocs., Inc.

Miner 2049er II. (Series A).
All Apple IIs. disk $5.00. *Optimal configuration:* Apple II, joystick.
Bounty Bob Rides Again in a Hot Action Adventure! Just When You Thought It Was Safe to Go Back into the Mine...Safe? This Smashing Sequel to the Original Miner 2049er Is More Dangerous Than Ever! You Have to Deal with Ricocheting Ore Humps, Time Warp Transporters, Radioactive Stalactites. An Ounce of Skill Is Worth a Pound of Uranium in This Explosive Test of Your Joystick Handling. You're in Control of Gigantic Girder Cranes, High-Speed Conveyor Belts & Hyperspace Pads. You May Not Make It Through All 10 Screens (Each in Two Levels of Difficulty), Because Yukon Yohan Has a Whole New Bag of Dirty Tricks to Throw You & Bounty Bob off his Trail.
Word Assocs., Inc.

Mineral Data Bases for the Macintosh. *Compatible Hardware:* Apple Macintosh. *Memory Required:* 512k. *General Requirements:* 2 disk drives; FileMaker Plus.
Thin Section Data File. 3.5" disk $75.00.
Hand Specimen Data File. 3.5" disk $50.00.
Mineral Databases.
RockWare, Inc.

Mines of Morell. *Customer Support:* 800-929-8117 (customer service).
MS-DOS. Apple II. disk $59.99 (ISBN 0-87007-075-4).
A Fantasy Adventure Designed for the Serious Game Player. Users Need More Than Luck & a Good Shot to Play This One.
SourceView Software International.

Mines of Moria II. *Version:* 1.0.1. Apr. 1989. *Compatible Hardware:* Apple II series, IIgs. *Memory Required:* Apple II series 64k, Apple IIgs 256k.
Apple II series. 3.5" disk $19.95 (ISBN 1-55616-058-5).
Apple II series.
Apple IIgs. 3.5" disk $19.95 (ISBN 1-55616-060-7).
Adventure Game.
DAR Systems International.

The Mines of Moria. *Version:* 6.1.2. Mar. 1988. *Compatible Hardware:* Apple II series, IIgs, Macintosh; IBM PC & compatibles. *Memory Required:* Apple II series 64k; Apple IIgs & IBM 256k; Macintosh 512k.
Apple II series. 3.5" disk $19.95 (ISBN 0-916163-87-3).
Apple II series.
Apple IIgs. 3.5" disk $19.95 (ISBN 1-55616-047-X).
Apple Macintosh. 3.5" disk $19.95 (ISBN 1-55616-054-2).
IBM. disk $19.95 (ISBN 0-916163-69-5).
IBM. 3.5" disk $19.95 (ISBN 1-55616-031-3).
Adventure Game.
DAR Systems International.

The Mini-Encyclopedia of Public Domain Songs. Oct. 1993. *Items Included:* Printed materials: 1) introduction to the material; 2) caution section about the use of public domain material.
DOS (Windows, ASCII). IBM. disk $299.00 (ISBN 1-884286-01-1).
DOS (Windows, ASCII). IBM. 3.5" disk $299.00 (ISBN 1-884286-02-X).
Macintosh. Macintosh. 3.5" disk $299.00 (ISBN 1-884286-03-8).
A Listing of over 600 Famous Songs That Are Guaranteed to Be in the Public Domain in the United States. Arranged in Two Parts; an Alphabetical List of Song Titles with a Notation of Previous Usage in a Musical, Play, or Film; & a List of Song Categories Such As Songs by Irving Berlin, Christmas Music, Children's Songs, Popular Songs, etc. Compiled by Copyright Expert Barbara Zimmerman Who Heads BZ/Rights & Permissions Inc. & Is Published by a Subsidiary Called The BZ/Rights Stuff Inc.
BZ-Rights Stuff, Inc.

MINI-MAX. *Version:* 1.5. Aug. 1982. *Compatible Hardware:* IBM PC & compatibles. *Operating System(s) Required:* MS-DOS. *Language(s):* MS BASIC. *Memory Required:* 64k. *Items Included:* Manual & Beginners' Guide. *Customer Support:* Free technical support.
disk $145.00.
Solves Linear Programming Problems by the SIMPLEX Algorithm. Problems Are Saved on Disk, May Be Printed, Solved, Changed. Sensitivity Analysis Includes Price Ranges, Slack Variables, Shadow Prices, & Range Resources. Solves Problems from 30x100 to 300x39. User's Guide Contains Practical Examples from Business & Industry.
Agricultural Software Consultants, Inc.

MINI-MAX for Windows. *Version:* 1.0. 1991. *Items Included:* Reference manual with tutorial section. *Customer Support:* Free technical support.
MS-DOS or PC-DOS 3.1 or higher with Microsoft Windows 3.0 or higher. IBM PC or compatible (640k). disk $295.00. *Addl. software required:* Microsoft Windows 3.0 or higher. *Optimal configuration:* MS-DOS 5.0; 4Mb RAM; Windows 3.1 or higher. *Networks supported:* All that support MS Windows 3.0.
A Professional, User Friendly Linear Programming Program That Offers a Great Deal of Power & Clarity. LP Problems are Solved by the Simplex Algorithm. This Program Solves Problems with 140 Variables & 140 Constraints (Windows 3.0) & Twice That Size with Windows 3.1. Double Precision; Full Screen Data Entry & Edit; Instant Problem Solving; Displays Problem, Solution, Sensitivity Analysis Simultaneously in Five Windows; Prints Optimal Solution, Basic Variables & Their Price Ranges, Non Basic Variables & Their Entering Prices, Slack & Surplus Variables, Dual Variables & Their Shadow Prices, Range of Feasibility of Resources, & More. German Version Available.
Agricultural Software Consultants, Inc.

Mini-Memory. *Compatible Hardware:* TI 99/4A.
contact publisher for price (Order no.: PHM 3058).
Provides Additional Memory & Tools for Program Development.
Texas Instruments, Personal Productivit.

Mini-Pace. 1985. *Compatible Hardware:* IBM PC. *Language(s):* BASIC (source code included). *Memory Required:* 3k.
disk or cassette $24.95.
Handicapping Program.
COM-CAP.

Mini-Pro Analysis Professional Series Thoroughbred Version. 1986. *Compatible Hardware:* Apple II; Commodore 64/128; IBM PC & compatibles. *Memory Required:* IBM 256k, Apple 64k, Commodore 64k.
IBM. 3.5" or 5.25" disk $149.95 (Order no.: MH01).
Apple. disk $149.95 (Order no.: MH01).
Commodore. disk $149.95 (Order no.: MH01).
Designed to Help Evaluate All Relevant Variables Related to Horse Racing. Displays Can Be Made by Printer, On-Screen or Both. Predicts the Finish Using Both Charts & Graphs.
Professor Jones Professional Handicapping Systems.

Miniature Math. *Compatible Hardware:* Commodore Amiga.
3.5" disk $39.95.
Miniature Golf Game Teaches Math.
Learners Image.

MiniCad. *Version:* 6. Oct. 1995. *Compatible Hardware:* Apple Macintosh Plus or higher, Native Power Macintosh. *Memory Required:* 2000k. *General Requirements:* Hard drive. *Items Included:* 2D, 3D, spreadsheet, DXF translator, programming language, relational database. *Customer Support:* Free, Monday through Friday, 9:00 - 5:30 EST.
3.5" disk $795.00.
Professional Level CAD & Analysis Application That Includes 2D & 3D in the Same Window. A Hot Linked Database/Spreadsheet, Also Included in the Same Window, Allows the User to Track & Automatically Calculate the Cost of Supplies &

Scheduling, Perform Flow Analysis, Analyze Power Needs, etc. A Programming Language Allows Users to Write Their Own Routines. CAD & Analysis Can Be Performed Together, Within the Same Window. Features Associative Auto-Dimensioning & Filleting, a Smart Cursor Which Provides Verbal & Graphical Cues As You Draw, Wall, Floor, & Roof Tools, 3d Walkthrough, Tolerancing, Auto Section Generation, Layering, Zoom, Multiple Line Types & Arrowheads. 2D-Specific Features Include Complex Duplication with Arrays, Cubic & Bezier Splines, Symbol Editing, Hierarchical Symbol Library, the Ability to Move Objects by Precise Intervals, & the Color Capability to Paint on Any Layer with a Full Color Palette. New Features: customizable menus & Palettes.
Graphsoft, Inc.

Minicomputer Chart Program. *Compatible Hardware:* IBM; Macintosh. *Memory Required:* IBM 128k, Macintosh 512k.
disk $63.95.
Dynacomp, Inc.

Minimal Contrast Therapy. Fred Weiner. *Compatible Hardware:* Apple II+, IIe, IIc, IIgs; IBM PC. *Memory Required:* 48k.
disk $99.95 (ISBN 0-942763-26-2).
Articulation Treatment Program for Children with Unintelligible Speech.
Parrot Software.

miniMast. *Version:* 5.0. Jul. 1988. *Compatible Hardware:* Concurrent Computer. *Operating System(s) Required:* OS/32. *Language(s):* FORTRAN. *Memory Required:* 2000k.
$10,000.00-$100,000.00 disk or cartridge.
Supervisory Control & Data Acquisition System That Supports Multiple Color Graphic Displays for Control Operations.
Baker CAC.

MININEC for Radio amateurs. R P Haviland. Jun. 1990.
Amiga, any size (256k). 3.5" disk $49.95 (ISBN 0-9621208-8-X). *Addl. software required:* BASIC.
MS-DOS. IBM-PC & compatibles (256k). disk $49.95 (ISBN 0-9621208-9-8). *Addl. software required:* BASIC.
Extended Versions of MININEC 3.09 Antenna Analysis Programs. Includes Data Files for Common Antenna Types, Generating Programs for Dipoles, Verticals, Yagis, Quads, Plot Programs & Variable Load & Frequency Versions. Problem Size Limited by Available Memory.
MiniLab Books.

Minipix, 3 disks. Fred Crane & Sara Crane. *Compatible Hardware:* Apple II, II+, IIe, IIc, IIgs; IBM PC. *Operating System(s) Required:* Apple DOS 3.3, ProDOS, MS-DOS. *Language(s):* Machine, BASIC. *Memory Required:* DOS 3.3 48k, ProDOS 64k. *General Requirements:* Broderbund's Print Shop software.
Apple. disk $29.95 ea.
IBM. disk $34.95 ea.
Each MINIPIX Disk Contains 200 Original "Graphics" That Can Be Used on Cards, Banners, & Signs Made with the PRINT SHOP. Each Package Also Contains a Special Picture Editor That Lets Users Make Mirror Images of MINIPIX Pictures, Turn Them Upside Down, etc.
Beagle Brothers.

MINISIMULATOR IIc. Amnon Katz. *Compatible Hardware:* IBM PC, PC XT, PC AT; COMPAQ 386. *Operating System(s) Required:* MS-DOS. *Memory Required:* 256k. *General Requirements:* RGB color graphics.
disk $1445.00, incl. control console, connecting hardware program disk, & manual (ISBN 0-938245-51-1, Order no.: A02).
demo disk $99.00.
manual $15.00.
Instrument Flight Simulation. Requires Use of Special Control Console (Included). Accepted by the FAA for Currency & Training Credits.
Inverted-A, Inc.

Minitab Statistical Software. *Version:* 8. 1991. *Compatible Hardware:* Apple Macintosh; Control Data; Data General; DEC; Evans & Sutherland; Groupe Bull; HCL; H-P; IBM Mainframe, PC, RS/6000, & compatibles; ICL; Kubota; Nixdorf; Point 4; Prime; Pyramid; Siemens; Silicon Graphics; Sumitomo; Sun; Wang. *Operating System(s) Required:* AOS/VS, HP-UX, MPE, MPE-XL, Music, PC-DOS/MS-DOS, PRIMOS, Risc/OS, ULTRIX, Unix, VMS. *Language(s):* FORTRAN. *Memory Required:* PC 1000k. *General Requirements:* Hard disk, co-processor recommended.
IBM PC & compatibles; mainframes. 695.00 single copy; $1,900.00-$8,000.00 mainframe license.
$495.00 multiple copies.
avail. 30 days evaluation.
Statistical Software for Organizing, Analyzing, & Presenting Statistical Data. The Package Features Intuitive Commands for Interactive Data Analysis. Capabilities Include Descriptive Statistics, Regression, ANOVA, Time Series, Non-Parametrics, EDA, Plots, Histograms, Statistical Process Control, Design of Experiments, etc.
Minitab, Inc.

MiniWareHouse Manager: Rentals Management for the MAC & DOS Platforms. *Version:* 7.53. Jan. 1993. *Items Included:* 3 ring binder documentation, run time interpreter. *Customer Support:* Yearly support & upgrades - $90.00 per year. On-site install & training if desired - all expenses.
Macintosh OS. Macintosh (2.5Mb System 6.X, 4.0Mb System 7.X). $499.95 single user; $699.95. *Optimal configuration:* Macintosh with 030 or 040 processor, 4Mb RAM, fast hard drive, accelerated video, System 7.X, laser or dot matrix printer. *Networks supported:* 100% network interoperable.
Microsoft Windows & DOS 5.X or higher. MS-DOS PC 386 or higher (4Mb). $499.95 single user; $699.95. *Addl. software required:* Windows. *Optimal configuration:* 386 or 486, DOS 5.X or higher, 4Mb RAM, fast hard drive, accelerated video, laser or dot matrix printer. *Networks supported:* 100% network interoperable.
Manages the Leasing of Storage Facilities. Multi-User & Cross Platform. Tracks Units Leased, Availabilities, Receivables, Deposits & More. Allows Automatic Billing & Assesses Late Fees. Complete Line Item Control During Invoicing. Export Data to Other Programs Supporting: DIF, SYLK, dBASE, LOTUS, ASCII. Multi-User & Cross Platform. 100% Network Interoperable.

MINIX Operating System. *Version:* 1.5. Andrew Tanenbaum et al. Oct. 1990. *Items Included:* Diskettes, 1 documentation manual in binder, 688 pg. *Customer Support:* (800) 624-0023 phone support, commercial licensing available.
IBM PC, XT, AT, 386, PS/2 & compatibles. 3.5" or 5.25" disk $169.00 (ISBN 0-13-585076-2). *Optimal configuration:* 512k, & at least a 10Mb hard disk.
Macintosh Plus or higher. 3.5" disk $169.00. *Optimal configuration:* 1Mb of memory, 800k floppy disk drive.
Amiga 500 or Amiga 2000 (1Mb). 3.5" disk $169.00. *Optimal configuration:* 1Mb of RAM & 1 disk drive, hard disk not required or supported.
Atari ST 1Mb of RAM. *Optimal configuration:* 1 720k diskette drive, hard disk optional 1MB of RAM.
UNIX-Like Operating System for Learning Operating Systems.
Prentice Hall.

Minnesota SNOBOL4.2. *Version:* 2.01. Jan. 1984. *Compatible Hardware:* IBM PC. *Operating System(s) Required:* PC-DOS/MS-DOS 2.0. *Memory Required:* 192k.
disk $59.95, incl. guide.
"green" book $28.95 (ISBN 0-13-815373-6).
Programming Language That Supports over 512K, Pattern Matching, Random File I/O Strings up to 64K Characters. Features Compatibility with Mainframe SNOBOL4, 32-bit Integer, & 8087 Support.
Berstis International.

Minor Planet Ephemeris. *Compatible Hardware:* TI 99/4A. *Operating System(s) Required:* DX-10. *Language(s):* Extended BASIC. *Memory Required:* 48k.
cassette $16.95.
Application Program Used with the Astronomical Ephemeris to Derive Information on the Minor Planets.
Eastbench Software Products.

Minorities in Science: Women & Minority Scientists Database CD-ROM Program. James Perkins. Aug. 1995. *Items Included:* Runtime version of Windows/MAC. *Customer Support:* 30 days unlimited warranty; Toll free customer support (800-352-0477).
Windows 3.1 or higher; Macintosh. 386/486/586 (Pentium) compatible PC (4Mb); Macintosh IIfx or higher (1Mb). CD-ROM disk $300.00 (ISBN 1-57585-004-4, Order no.: P105-1). *Nonstandard peripherals required:* CD-ROM drive.
Approximately 500 Women & Minority Scientists, Engineers, Mathematicians, Science Teachers Are Presented in the MIS Database. Provides a Powerful Tool for Career Exploration, Counseling, & a Source of Mentors for Students. All of Them Have Agreed to Be Mentors to Young Students. A Profile of Each of Them Provides the Following: A Statement of Their Interest; Family Background; Answers to Some Commonly Asked Questions; A Picture (in Most Cases); Ethnicity; & More.
CSY, Inc.

MINSQ Chemical Kinetic Library. *Items Included:* Bound manual. *Customer Support:* Free hotline - no time limit; 30 day limited warranty; updates are $5/disk plus S&H.
MS-DOS. IBM & compatibles (256k). disk $89.95.
This Package Includes 14 Models (on Disk) for Several Types of Reactions. You May Use These Models Directly, or Modify (Edit) Them to Suit Your Needs. Included Are Zero-First-Second Order Irreversible Reactions, & Parallel First Order Irreversible Reactions with up to Three Products. Other Models May Be Used to Fit pH Profiles, the Arrhenius Equation, or the Eyring Equation. Sample Data Files Are Included, & the 75-Page Manual Thoroughly Describes Each Model & Example.
Dynacomp, Inc.

MINSQ Nonlinear Curve Fitting & Model Development. *Items Included:* Bound manual. *Customer Support:* Free hotline - no time limit; 30 day limited warranty; updates are $5/disk plus S&H.
MS-DOS 3.1 or higher. IBM & compatibles (640k). disk $239.95. *Nonstandard peripherals required:* Two floppy disk drives (or one floppy & a hard disk), & graphics capability. Almost all dot matrix printers are supported.

MINSQ PHARMOKINETIC LIBRARY

Package for Modeling Nonlinear Processes & Fitting Data. It Also Provides Publication-Quality X-Y Plots for Reporting Results. Data May Be Entered from the Keyboard or from a Data File, Plotted on the Screen, Edited, Annotated, Archived, & Reproduced in High Resolution on Almost Any Dot Matrix Printer (Including PostScript Printers & HPGL Plotters). Similarly, Models May Be Easily Constructed, Edited, Saved, Fitted to Data, & Fitted Curves Plotted with or Without the Associated Data.
Dynacomp, Inc.

MINSQ Pharmokinetic Library. *Items Included:* Bound manual. *Customer Support:* Free hotline - no time limit; 30 day limited warranty; updates are $5/disk plus S&H.
MS-DOS. IBM & compatibles (256k). disk $89.95.
This Library Includes One- & Two-Compartment Models, As Well As Exponential-Biexponential-Triexponential Models. The One- & Two-Compartment Models Have Bolus, Constant Rate I.V., or First-Order Input. The One-Compartment Models Have Either First-Order or Michaelis-Menten Output. The Two-Compartment Models Have First-Order Output. The Exponential Models Include Both Single Dose & Multiple Dose. Other Features Available in Some Models Include Length of Infusion & a Time Lag Before Dosing Begins.
Dynacomp, Inc.

Miracle Regional Sales Lead System.
MS-DOS. IBM 386/486 & compatibles (640k). contact publisher for price. *Networks supported:* Novell.
Fully Automates All Aspects of a Hotel's Sales & Catering Operation. Menus, Banquet Event Orders, Group Room Control Book, Menu Costing, a Report Writer & More.
National Guest Systems Corp.

Miracle Sales & Catering System.
MS-DOS. IBM 386/486 & compatibles (640k). contact publisher for price. *Networks supported:* Novell.
Fully Automates All Aspects of a Hotel's Sales & Catering Operation. Menus, Banquet Event Orders, Group Room Control Book, Menu Costing, a Report Writer & More.
National Guest Systems Corp.

Mirror-Fax with Voice. *Version:* 2.0. Oct. 1993. *Items Included:* 1 3.5" disk (HD), 1 178 pg. Mirror-Fax User's Guide, 1 booklet - Voice/Fax messaging system.
MS-DOS 2.0 or higher. IBM PC & 100% compatibles (640k). disk $99.00. *Nonstandard peripherals required:* Data/fax/voice modem using Cirrus Logic, Rockwell or Sierra or ZyXel chip sets. *Optimal configuration:* Minimum requirement is a 12-15MHz 286.
Integrates Data, Fax, & Voice Allowing You to Set up a Structured Set of Messages, Mailboxes, & Faxes That Provide You with Answering Machine, Voice Mailbox & Fax-Back Capabilities on Your PC. Designed for IBM or IBM Compatible PCs Running MS-DOS 2.0 or Higher.
Softklone Distributing Corp.

MIRROR for Windows. *Version:* 1.2. Aug. 1992. *Items Included:* Dual media (3.5" & 5.25" disk set) & one user's guide. *Customer Support:* Telephonic technical support 9:00-5:00 Eastern M-F - no charge - 904-878-8564. BBS-SoftKlone's Bulletin Board - open 24 hrs. 904-878-9884. Internet - address - softklon freenet.tlh.fl.us.
MicroSoft Windows version 3.0 or higher. IBM or 100% compatible. $195.00 single user - volume discount & site licensing available (Order no.: MIRROR FOR WINDOWS). *Addl.*

software required: Not unless running in network-then need an asynchronous communication server for managing communications. *Optimal configuration:* 1.4Mb on hard drive. *Networks supported:* Any network which supports NASI, NCSI, NETCI or INT-14 and/or any network supporting Telnet, LAT or TES protocols.
A LAN & Modem-Based Asynchronous Terminal Emulation & File Transfer Package Supporting Direct Serial Connections & INT14, NASI, NCSI, NETCI, Telnet, LAT & TES Protocols. Features a Powerful Macro Language, DDE Support, DLL Manipulation, Numerous File Transfer Protocols, Automatic Learn Mode, Cut/Paste, Multiple Capture Features, 100% Keyboard Mapping.
SoftKlone Distributing Corp.

MIRROR III. *Version:* 2.5. *Compatible Hardware:* IBM PC, PC XT, PC AT & compatibles. *Items Included:* 5.25" & 3.5" disk & two manuals. *Customer Support:* Free; (904) 878-8564. disk $149.00.
Provides Background Operation Capability & a Built-In WORDSTAR-Like Text Editor. File Transfer Protocols Supported Include XMODEM, XMODEM MULTI-FILE, ZMODEM, KERMIT, HAYES, & CROSSTALK-FILE. Not Copy-Protected. Dialing Directed Features Pull-Down Menus with Keyboard or Mouse Support.
SoftKlone Distributing Corp.

MIRROR III LAN. *Version:* 2.5. *Compatible Hardware:* IBM PC & true compatibles, PC XT, PC AT. *Operating System(s) Required:* PC-DOS/MS-DOS 2.0 or higher. *General Requirements:* Modem.
$595.00 for 8 workstations; $195.00 for single workstation.
An Asynchronous Communications Software Package Designed for Local Area Networks (LANs). Lets User Share Network Modems, Ports, & Data Lines When Used with an ACS (Asynchronous Communications Server). Includes all the features of MIRROR III.
SoftKlone Distributing Corp.

MIRROR 3-FAX. *Version:* 2.5. Aug. 1991. *Items Included:* Dual media (3.5" & 5.25" disk sets) & 3 manuals. *Customer Support:* Telephonic technical support 9:00-5:00 Eastern M-F - no charge - 904-878-8564. BBS-SoftKlone's Bulletin Board - open 24 hrs. 904-878-9884. Internet - address - softklon freenet.tlh.fl.us.
MS-DOS 2.0 or higher. IBM PC or 100% compatibles (260k-full program or 73k fax driver only). $179.00 - volume discount & site license available (Order no.: MIRROR III-FAX). *Nonstandard peripherals required:* DATA/FAX Modem. *Optimal configuration:* If using fax only, can load fax-driver takes 73k, if running complete MIRROR III-FAX 500k is optional.
Includes a Complete Set of Send, Receive & Conversion Features for Faxing As Well As the Data Communications Features of MIRROR III. SENDAFAX, A Utility, Allows You to Send a Fax(es) to a Fax Number(s) from the DOS Command Line. With Print Capture, Send Faxes Directly Within Another Application.
SoftKlone Distributing Corp.

MIRROR-VFMS (Voice - Fax - Messaging System). *Version:* 3.1. Feb. 1993. *Items Included:* 3.5" media w/two (2) user's guides. *Customer Support:* Telephonic technical support 9:00-5:00 Eastern M-F - no charge - 904-878-8564. BBS-SoftKlone's Bulletin Board - open 24 hrs. 904-878-9884. Internet - address - softklon freenet.tlh.fl.us.
MS-DOS 2.0 or higher. 386 16Mhz PC (540k). disk $149.00 (Order no.: MIRROR-VFMS). *Nonstandard peripherals required:* Voice class modem using Rockwell, Cirrus Logic or Sierra

data/fax/voice chip sets. *Optimal configuration:* 640k - 386/16Mhz PC.
Set Your PC up As an Interactive Information Center. People Can Call into Your System via Telephone to Listen to Pre-Recorded Voice Messages, Leave Voice Messages, Retrieve Faxes from, & Send Faxes into Your PC. Turn Your PC into an Answering Machine, Voice Mailbox, Fax Machine & Fax-Back System. Includes Subset of MIRROR III-FAX.
SoftKlone Distributing Corp.

Mischievous Marvin. Jan. 1994. *Items Included:* Program on CD-ROM, CD Booklet, & Registration Card. *Customer Support:* Free unlimited support via telephone.
Macintosh System 7.0 or higher. Macintosh LC or higher (4Mb). CD-ROM disk $49.00 (ISBN 1-57268-040-7, Order no.: 49001). *Nonstandard peripherals required:* 12 inch monitor or larger; CD-ROM drive. *Optimal configuration:* 5Mb RAM.
In This Program a Mischievous & Elusive Monkey Named Marvin Causes a Multitude of Mix-Ups in the Classroom. Students Interacting with the Story Enjoy the Challenges of Fixing the Problems Marvin Creates. Undoing Marvin's Mischief Brings Many Fun Skills & Acitivites into Play, Such As Vocabulary, Puzzles, Riddles, Songs, Alphabet Games, & More.
Conter Software.

Mi6-29: Deadly Adversary of Falcon. *Version:* 3.0. Jul. 1993.
IBM MS-DOS. IBM 12Mhz AT & compatibles w/ DOS 5.0 (1Mb). disk $59.95. *Nonstandard peripherals required:* VGA for 256-colors.

Missile Command. *Compatible Hardware:* Atari XL/XE.
ROM cartridge $16.95 (Order no.: CXL4012).
Atari Corp.

Mission Critical. Michael A. Verdu. 1995. *Items Included:* CD disc, game manual, warranty card, product catalog. *Customer Support:* Toll free technical assistance (1-800-658-8891). Computer operated pre-recorded hint line (1-900-933-CLUE). Hint book $9.95 plus s/h.
DOS 5.0 or higher. IBM PC 386/33 or higher (4Mb). CD-ROM disk $59.95 (ISBN 1-880520-19-2, Order no.: MC-CD). *Nonstandard peripherals required:* VESA compatible Super VGA, CD-ROM, Microsoft compatible mouse. *Optimal configuration:* 486/33 w/8Mb RAM, Sound Blaster compatible audio card, double-speed CD-ROM.
An Adventure Game with Combat Sequences Where the Player Must Investigate an Alien Presence on an Unexplored World 68 Light Years from Earth.
Legend Entertainment.

Mission Impossible. *Compatible Hardware:* TI-99/4A.
disk or casette - contact publisher for price.
Texas Instruments, Personal Productivit.

Mission: Intergalactic Diplomacy. *Items Included:* Bound manual. *Customer Support:* Free hotline - no time limit; 30 day limited warranty; updates are $5/disk plus S&H.
MS-DOS. IBM & compatibles (256k). disk $19.95.
Your Mission, Should You Choose to Accept It, Is to Bring Peace to a War-Torn Region of the Universe. Region W-4, Though Remote, Is Close Enough to Galactic Trade Lanes That Wars Between Planets in This Region Are Beginning to Disrupt Intergalactic Shipping. Are You a Risk Taker? Bold Strategies Might Mean Quick Success - or Might Mean Ignominious Defeat. Each Time You Play the Game, a New Universe, with New Planets, Will Challenge You to Try Different Strategies.
Dynacomp, Inc.

Mission: Mud. *Compatible Hardware:* TRS-80. contact publisher for price.
Instant Software, Inc.

Mission on Thunderhead. *Compatible Hardware:* Apple II, II+, IIe, IIc; Atari 800/XL/XE; Commodore 64/128. *Memory Required:* 64k. disk $25.00 ea.
Apple. (Order no.: 49352).
Commodore, Atari. (Order no.: 49993).
Adventure Game with Two Scenarios: OPERATION TEMPEST - Find the Device Needed to Destroy the Complex & Free the Human Race; THE FINAL APPEAL - a Planet-Wide Scavenger Hunt, Find the Objects Necessary to Open the Freedom Gate & Escape. Provides over 50 Rooms & Four Mazes; 100 Variations Combined with Nine Skill Levels.
Avalon Hill Game Co., The Microcomputer Games Div.

Mission Starlight. *Version:* 1.1. 1989. *Items Included:* Instructions & reg. card. *Customer Support:* Free phone support.
6.02 & higher. Macintosh. 3.5" disk $31.95 (Order no.: M101).
Explosive, Realistic, Flying Action & a Mission to Save the Solar System from Dreaded, Invading Aliens.
Casady & Greene, Inc.

MIST (Microcomputer Information Support Tools) Plus. *Version:* 1.3. Peter Johnson-Lenz & Trudy Johnson-Lenz. Nov. 1989. *Compatible Hardware:* Compaq; IBM PC, PC XT, PC AT, PS/2 & compatibles. *Operating System(s) Required:* PC-DOS/MS-DOS 2.1 or higher. *Language(s):* FORTRAN. *Memory Required:* 256k. *General Requirements:* Hayes Smartmodem. *Customer Support:* Unlimited. $50.00 incl. Conexus.
Application Language with Advanced Scripting Capabilities That Turns PC into Intelligent Terminal & Remotely Accessible Host. Allows Routines to Be Written for Variety of Applications, Including Computer Conferencing, Bulletin Boards, In-House Message Systems, Remotely Accessible Databases, & Transferring Files. Integrates Telecommunications, Remote Use, Text Editor, & Text Information Retrieval into One Package Included.
OMM Corp.

MISTER. *Version:* 7.0. Oct. 1988. *Compatible Hardware:* DEC VAX; IBM PC XT, PC AT; Prime. *Operating System(s) Required:* MS-DOS, VMS, UNIX, PRIMOS. *Language(s):* FORTRAN. *Memory Required:* 640k.
MS-DOS. disk $1000.00-$5000.00.
Prime Primos. cassette $2000.00-$42000.00.
DEC VAX, VMS; & UNIX. $2,000.00-$42,000.00.
Utilizes Both Activity on Arrow & Activity on Node Networks to Calculate Project Schedules. Schedule Reports Can Be Expressed As Listings, Time Scaled Bar Charts, & Time Scaled Network Plots. Analyzes Projects During Planning & Performance Phases. Identifies Potential Time, Resource, & Cash Flow Problems Before Their Occurrence & While Corrective Action Can Be Taken. Monitors Progress & Shows Impact of Changes in Plan or Irregular Events Which Might Upset the Plan. 3 Model Sizes Available with Each Having the Same Scheduling Logic. Project Size, Resources, & Other Variables Differ by Model.
Shirley Software Systems.

Mr. Boston Official Bartenders' Guide. *Items Included:* Bound manual. *Customer Support:* Free hotline - no time limit; 30 day limited warranty; updates are $5/disk plus S&H.
MS-DOS. IBM & compatibles (128k). disk $29.95.
Apple II series (64k). disk $29.95.
Atari ST; C-64. disk $29.95.
Macintosh (512k). 3.5" disk $29.95.
Features: Instantly Select Any Drink Using 21 Combinations of Ingredients, Mood, Personal Taste, Season, & More; Resize Recipes for up to 999 Guests, Instantly; Plan Your Parties Using VIP DRINK REMINDERS That Can Print Recipes & a Shopping List Based on the Preferences of Your Guests; Change Recipes to Suit Your Tastes or Add Your Own with Our Exclusive FASTRAC Data Entry; Print Pocket Recipe Books or Index Cards to Share with Friends.
Dynacomp, Inc.

Mr. Potato Head Saves Veggie Valley. Nov. 1995. *Items Included:* Registration card, manual, brochure. *Customer Support:* Free 1-800 number, 10:00 a.m. to 10:00 p.m. (EST) Monday-Saturday.
Mac System 7.0.1 or higher. Mac 68030 25MHz (8Mb). Contact publisher for price (ISBN 1-888208-00-7). *Nonstandard peripherals required:* CD-ROM drive (double speed). *Optimal configuration:* Mac 68030 25MHz, CD-ROM drive (double speed), System 7.0 or higher, color monitor (640x480, 256 colors), 8Mb RAM.
Windows 3.1, Windows 95 compatible. IBM compatible 486DX 33 MHz (8Mb). *Nonstandard peripherals required:* CD-ROM drive (double speed). *Optimal configuration:* IBM compatible 486DX 33MHz, CD-ROM drive (double speed), Windows 3.1 or Windows 95, Super VGA (640x480, 256 colors), sound card, 8Mb RAM.
Mr. Potato Head, One of Children's Best Loved Toy Characters, Extends into Children's Educational Software in This Early Learning Story Adventure (Quest) That Helps Children 3-6 Build Investigative, Problem Solving & Creative Design Skills. There Is a Drought in Veggie Valley & It's up to the Child to Help Mr. Potato Head, & His Fun-Loving Daughter Sweet Potato, Bring Rain to the Valley. They Must Traverse the Valley & Move on to the Country Fair Where a Big Rain Cloud Looms Overhead.
Hasbro, Inc.

Mr. QuarterMaster. *Version:* 2.5. 1983. *Compatible Hardware:* IBM PC. *Operating System(s) Required:* PC-DOS. *Language(s):* BASIC. *Memory Required:* 256k.
disk $140.00, incl. manual.
demo disk & manual $30.00.
Inventory Control System for Consumable Stock Items. Features Include: Receipts & Issues Updating, File Maintenance, Label Printing & Automatically Adjusted Reorder Points.
RJL Systems.

Mr. QuarterMaster Jr. 1984. *Compatible Hardware:* IBM PC, PC XT, PCjr. *Operating System(s) Required:* PC-DOS. *Language(s):* BASIC. *Memory Required:* IBM PC & PC XT 64k; PCjr 128k.
disk $55.00.
Inventory Control System That Can Be Used by Any Business, Institution, or Individual Who Wants to Maintain & Monitor Non-Consumable Inventory Items. A Receipts & Issues Feature Is Provided for Those Locations Where Merchandise Is Being Continually Issued & Returned Such As Tool & Clothing Supply Rooms. Contains a File Maintenance That Allows the User to Add, Change, & Delete Stock Items. An Inventory File of 32,766 Stock Items Can Be Maintained.
RJL Systems.

Mr. Tester. *Compatible Hardware:* Commodore VIC-20.
contact publisher for price.
Micro-W Distributing, Inc.

MIT: Menu Integrity Tool. *Version:* 3.1. Jun. 1990. *Customer Support:* 30 day limited warranty & customer support.
DOS 2.1 or higher. IBM PC & compatibles; PS/2 (256K). $35.00 (free with site license of ASP 3.1 or Pat Mat). *Addl. software required:* ASP 3.1 or Pat Mat.
Menu Based Tool for ASP 3.1 & Pat Mat.
ASP.

MITINET/Marc. *Version:* Apple II 2.0, Macintosh 1.0, PC 3.0. Jun. 1991. *Items Included:* User manual, tutorial & cataloger's reference guide (O Ring Manuals) (MAC only); PC & Apple: User manuals cataloger's reference included in manual. *Customer Support:* First six months of customer support & software upgrades is free, user may call collect for support. After six months user may extend their support/upgrade package for $150.00 per year.
System 6.0.4 or higher. Any Macintosh (1Mb). $399.00. *Nonstandard peripherals required:* Hard disk. *Optimal configuration:* Macintosh, Hard disk, printer.
MS-DOS 2.01 or higher. IBM PC, XT, AT, PS/2 or compatible with 2 floppy drives or 1 floppy drive & a hard disk (256k). $399.00. *Optimal configuration:* IBM PC or compatible with 1 floppy drive, hard disk, & a printer.
Apple Pro DOS. Apple IIe with an "Extended 80 column card or Apple IIc, Apple IIgs with 2 3.5" floppy drives or 1 floppy drive (3.5") & a hard disk (128k). *Optimal configuration:* Apple II, hard disk, printer, excellarator board.
A Unique Cataloging Software That Allows the User to Create Full USMARC Records Without Having to Learn Anything about MARC. Used for Original Cataloging Needs for Any "Unmatched Titles: or Ongoing New Material MITINET Records". Can Be Imported into over 60 Different Vendor Systems. Free IBM PC & Macintosh Demos Are Available. Please Indicate Disk Size or PC Version (3.5" or 5.25").
Information Transform, Inc.

MIX C Compiler. *Compatible Hardware:* IBM PC; Tandy 2000; Kaypro II, Kaypro 4; Apple CP/M; Osborne; Morrow MD II; other compatibles. *Operating System(s) Required:* PC-DOS/MS-DOS 2.0 or higher, CP/M-80 2.2 or higher. (source code included).
Editor. $19.95.
C. $19.95.
C & Editor. $39.90.
ASM Utility. $10.00.
Full Feature Standard K&R C Compiler with the UNIX V7 Extensions. Includes a 450 Page Tutorial. The UNIX Compatible Function Library Contains More Than 150 Functions (C Source Code Included). Includes a Programmable Full/Split Screen Text Processor Which Lets the User Split the Screen Horizontally or Vertically & Edit Two Files at Once. The ASM Utility Allows the Linkage of Object Files Created by MICROSOFT's MASM or M80 Assemblers.
MIX Software.

MIX Split Screen Editor. *Operating System(s) Required:* MS-DOS, PC-DOS, CP/M-80.
disk $19.95.
General Purpose, Programmable, Full/Split Text Processor with Auto Indent for Structured Languages, Auto Line Numbering for BASIC, & Fill & Justify for English. Other Features Include: Split Screen (Horizontally or Vertically), Custom Key Layouts, Macro Commands, Custom Setup Files. Can Execute Any DOS Command or Run Another Program from Inside the Editor.
MIX Software.

MIXIT Student Version. 1991. *Items Included:* Student manuals, flowcharts, instructor's change disk. *Customer Support:* Free technical support.

PC-DOS/MS-DOS. IBM PC or compatible (256k). $495.00 per dept. license. *Optimal configuration:* IBM PC or compatible with a minimum of 256k RAM & an 80-column printer. Hard disk is desirable.
University Undergraduate Version of the Popular Feed Formulation Program MIXIT-2 Plus. The Student Version Is Fast & Extremely Easy to Use; Yet It Has Most of the Features of Computerized Single-Mix Feed Formulation Programs. Teaches the Principles of Ration Formulation to Beginning Feed & Feeding Classes & Includes Such Features As Ratios, Factoring, Optimal Density, & the "Costs" of Constraints. The Program Was Developed in Cooperation with Texas A&M University & Is Now in Use in Many US & Canadian Universities & Colleges.
Agricultural Software Consultants, Inc.

MIXIT-2. *Version:* 2.5. Nov. 1989. *Compatible Hardware:* IBM PC & compatibles. *Operating System(s) Required:* MS-DOS. *Language(s):* MS BASIC. *Memory Required:* 256k. *Items Included:* Comprehensive Reference Guide & Tutorial. *Customer Support:* Free technical support.
disk $595.00.
Calculates Least Cost Blends, Nutritional Content, Mixing Instruction for Animal Feeds Based on 50 Ingredients, 50 Restrictions; Stores Hundreds of Ingredient Names, 57 Nutrient Names. Names & Units Can Be Selected & Altered by User. Ingredient/Nutrient Information Available on Data Disk. American, Metric, or Any System. Also Available in Spanish.
Agricultural Software Consultants, Inc.

MIXIT-2+. *Version:* 3.3. 1994. *Compatible Hardware:* IBM PC & compatibles. *Operating System(s) Required:* MS-DOS. *Language(s):* Microsoft BASIC. *Memory Required:* 384k. *General Requirements:* 2 disk drives, printer. *Items Included:* Comprehensive Reference Guide with Training Guide in 3-ring binder. *Customer Support:* Free technical support.
disk $995.00.
An Expanded Version of MIXIT-2 in Which Feed Mixes Are Stored As Formulas & Edited by the User. Formulas Are Shared with the Program PRICE-IT. Prints Feedmill Production Reports. Batch Weights Include Animal Units As Well As Weights. The Least Cost Blends Use Ingredient & Nutrient Ratios, & Optimal Density. Always Gets a Ration. Shows, in Addition to the Nutritional Content, Nutrient Ratios & Nutrients on a Per-Day Basis. Formulates Feed, Food, Chemical Mixes. Also in Spanish.
Agricultural Software Consultants, Inc.

MIXIT-3. *Version:* 3.1. Jul. 1983. *Compatible Hardware:* IBM PC & compatibles. *Operating System(s) Required:* MS-DOS. *Language(s):* MS BASIC. *Memory Required:* 256k. *Items Included:* Comprehensive Reference Guide. *Customer Support:* Free technical support.
disk $795.00.
Calculates & Prints Dozens of Rations Automatically with One Keyboard Entry. Calculates New Rations Without Changing Current Ones. Rations Are Stored on Disk, Summarized on One-Page Reports. Special Report Gives Price/Composition Comparison Between Old & New Rations. User Has the Option of Replacing Old Ration with New. Also Available in Spanish.
Agricultural Software Consultants, Inc.

MIXIT-3 plus. *Version:* 3.3. 1994. *Compatible Hardware:* IBM PC & compatibles. *Operating System(s) Required:* MS-DOS. *Language(s):* Microsoft BASIC. *Memory Required:* 256k. *General Requirements:* 2 disk drives, printer. *Items Included:* Comprehensive Reference Guide with Training Guide in 3-ring binder. *Customer Support:* Free technical support.
disk $1395.00.
Consists of MIXIT-2 plus & AUTOMIXIT Which Can Be Preset to Calculate up to 1000 Least Cost Ratios Automatically & Save Them As Formulas Which Can Be Shared with PRICE-IT. Prints On-Page Summaries, Batch & Scale 6eight Reports. Also in Spanish.
Agricultural Software Consultants, Inc.

MIXIT-4. *Version:* 3.3. 1994. *Compatible Hardware:* IBM PC & compatibles. *Operating System(s) Required:* MS-DOS. *Language(s):* Microsoft BASIC. *Memory Required:* 384k. *General Requirements:* 2 disk drives; hard disk recommended. *Items Included:* Comprehensive Reference Guides & Training Guides in 3-ring binder. *Customer Support:* Free technical support.
disk $1895.00.
Designed for Feed Mills. Completely Integrated Least Cost Formulation, Pricing, & Inventory Package Consisting of MIXIT-2+, AUTOMIXT, & PRICE-IT. Has All the features of These Programs Such as Calculating Hundreds of Rations Automatically, Saving & Editing Formulas, Saving Formulas As Ingredients, etc. Also available in Spanish.
Agricultural Software Consultants, Inc.

MIXTURE-DESIGN. *Version:* 2.1. Sridhar Seshadri & Stanley N. Deming. 1990. *Items Included:* Manual, 3.5" diskette. *Customer Support:* Free telephone support to registered users.
MS-DOS. IBM PC/XT/AC & compatibles (384k). disk $295.00 (ISBN 0-932651-20-8). *Optimal configuration:* Suggested 512k.
Uses Mixture Experimental Designs to Investigate 3- & 4- Component Formulations. Mixture-Design Helps Researchers Determine What Formulation Will Best Produce the Desired Result.
Statistical Programs.

MJA Accounting. Sep. 1979. *Memory Required:* 128k. *General Requirements:* 2 disk drives, printer.
General Ledger, Payroll, Accounts Receivable, Accounts Payroll, Inventory. disk $600.00 ea.
Prodata, Inc. (New Mexico).

MktSim: Marketing Simulation Model. *Version:* 2.4. Apr. 1990. *Items Included:* Hard copy manual, manual on disk in Hg PCV text mode, 2-D & 3-D mapping, trial disk available for $20.00. *Customer Support:* Phone free to get started; after that, $1 per minute, minimum of 10 minutes. IBM DOS 2.1 or higher (250k), Windows 3.X. PC/XT/AT/PS2 or compatibles. $250.00 for system; $20.00 for trial disk; $40.00 for Windows trial disk. *Optimal configuration:* Hard disk, color monitor, any printer, Graphics Board (CGA, EGA, VGA, HGA).
A Marketing Simulation Model for Organizing Information About a Brand/Product & Its Competition, Fitting Parameters to This Information & Then Simulating/Forecasting the Probable Outcomes of Various Marketing Strategies. Includes Spreadsheet-Like Data Entry/Editing; on Disk Help/Documentation in Hyper Text Format; 2-D & 3-D Perceptual Maps.
Spring Systems, Inc.

MM-ENTR: Mail Merge Entry Program. Jun. 1985. *Operating System(s) Required:* CP/M, MS-DOS, PC-DOS. *Memory Required:* 48k.
5-1/4" or 8" $19.95.
Data Entry Program for Creating WordStar Mail Merge Files. Takes Care of Commas & Double Quotes Automatically. Can Backup & Correct Previously Entered Data Before Writing the Record.
Elliam Assocs.

MMED 3780. *Version:* 2.10. Oct. 1981. *Compatible Hardware:* IBM PC & compatibles; PC AT & compatibles recommended. *Operating System(s) Required:* MS-DOS, PC-DOS, PC-MOS. *Language(s):* Microsoft Quick Basic 4.0. *Memory Required:* 640k.
disk $2500.00.
3.5" or 5.25" disk $2500.00.
Single/Multi-User Menu-Driven, Balance Forward Receivables System That Handles up to 13 Doctors/Dentists at up to 99 Locations with Patient or Family Billing & All Access to Records by Patient Name. Also Provides Complete Medicare Claims Transmission at Extra Cost.
Adapt, Inc.

MMS-II (Materials Management System). *Version:* 9.0. 1983. *Compatible Hardware:* IBM PC & compatibles. *Operating System(s) Required:* PC-DOS, MS-DOS 2.1 & higher. *Language(s):* CB-86. *Memory Required:* 512k. *General Requirements:* Hard disk, 132-column printer.
$695.00.
Material Management System Providing a Project Manager Control of Bid Items. Up to 1000 Purchase Orders Can Be Entered into the Purchase Order Data Base for up to 500 Different Vendors. Up to 32,000 Line Items of Material Can Be Allocated to "n" Activities in the "n" Projects. Works in Conjunction with PMS-II. Entries to MMS-II Automatically Update Material Budget & Actual Values in PMS-II, & Are Shown on the Activity Report, Funding Schedule, & Earned Value Analysis. Subsystem to PMS-II.
North America MICA, Inc.

MMSFORTH. *Version:* 2.4. 1985. *Compatible Hardware:* IBM PC, PC XT, PC AT, PS/2; TRS-80 Model I, Model III, Model 4. *Operating System(s) Required:* MS-DOS. *Language(s):* MMSFORTH (source code included). *Memory Required:* 24k.
disk for personal (one person one-computer) license, corporate site licensing from $179.95,1,180.00.
Full 79-Standard Forth Wordset Plus Advanced Editor, Assembler, Arrays, Strings, Double-Length Numbers, Low-Res Graphics (Monochrome & 16-color), Quans, Temp-Heads, Demo Programs, 400-Page Manual & Many Advanced Features. Supports Many Other MMSFORTH Applications Such As DATAHANDLER, DATAHANDLER-PLUS, FORTHCOM, etc. Additional Utilities Are Available.
Miller Microcomputer Services.

MMSFORTH GAMES. *Compatible Hardware:* IBM PC, PC XT, PC AT, PS/2; TRS-80 Model I, Model III, Model 4. *Language(s):* MMSFORTH (source code included). *Memory Required:* 32k.
disk $39.95.
Includes Arcade Games (Breakforth, Crashforth & Freeway), Board Games (Othello & Tic-Tac-FORTH) & Cryptoquote Puzzle Solver.
Miller Microcomputer Services.

MMSFORTH General Ledger. *Compatible Hardware:* IBM PC, PC XT, PC AT, PS/2; TRS-80 Model I, Model III, Model 4. *Language(s):* MMSFORTH (source code included). *Memory Required:* 48k. *General Requirements:* 2 disk drives.
disk $250.00.
In-House Accounting Support Including Subsidiary Ledgers & Journals. Large Capacity Built-In Information Safeguards, & an Optimized User Interface Which Can Double Per-Person Productivity.
Miller Microcomputer Services.

TITLE INDEX

MMSFORTH Utilities. *Compatible Hardware:* IBM PC, PC XT, PC AT, PS/2; TRS-80 Model I, Model III, Model 4. *Language(s):* MMSFORTH (source code included). *Memory Required:* 32k. disk $49.95 ea.
Disk 1.
Disk 2 for IBM PC with 8087.
Utilities-1 Includes ROM-Based Floating Point Math Utility with Complex Numbers, Radian & Degree Trigonometry, Rectangular & Polar Coordinate Conversion, a Program Cross-Referencing Utility & a (Forth Blocks-FORTHWRITE/DH Files-DOS Files) Transfer Utility. Utilities-1 for TRS-80 Also Includes a Full Z80 Assembler (to Supplement MMSFORTH's 8080 Assembler). Utilities-1 for IBM PC Also Includes Very Fast & Accurate TGRAPH Vector Graphics Support (for CGA, with Many Demo Routines, Screen Dump Routines for Popular 9-Pin & 24-Pin Printers, & Vectored Output to Popular X-Y Plotters), Plus an Unusual & Very Accurate N-Length Number Mathematics Utility. Utilities-2 (for IBM PC with 8087 Math Co-Processor Chip) Offers 8087 Support Which Can Speed Number-Crunching Operations by Better Than 100x.
Miller Microcomputer Services.

Mocha Image Analysis Software. Feb. 1993. *Items Included:* 2 bound manuals, tutorial w/ sample files. *Customer Support:* 90 day money back guarantee, free technical support.
Windows (3.1 in enhanced mode). 386 or higher w/at least 10Mb free space (4Mb). disk $1495.00 (Order no.: SMOWR103).
Nonstandard peripherals required: MS compatible mouse, 256 Color VGA, 640 x 480 or higher monitor. *Addl. software required:* Windows 3.1 in enhanced mode. *Optimal configuration:* 386 or higher, 3 1/2" floppy w/at least 20Mb free disk space & 256 VGA monitor.
Brings Automated Color & Monochrome Image Analysis Capabilities to the PC. Integrates Powerful Image Processing & Measurement, a Scientific Data Worksheet, Transform Language, Object Classification, Plotting, & Annotation Tools in One Easy-to-Use Windows package.
Jandel Scientific.

ModaCAD. *Compatible Hardware:* Apple Macintosh, MS-Windows. *Customer Support:* Full service.
$2000.00-$12,500.00.
Fashion Design & Manufacturing System for Apparel Industry.
ModaCAD, Inc.

ModaCAD Design System.
Macintosh Quadra or higher / MS-DOS windows. $12,500.00.
Design System for Fashion Design Including Full Design, Surface Design, & Fabric Draping Capabilities.
ModaCAD, Inc.

MODBIL. *Version:* 8. Jan. 1991. *Customer Support:* 1 year free telephone support & 1 year free Fax support.
MS-DOS, PS-DOS (256k). 8080 - 386 IBM & compatibles. disk $20.00 (Order no.: MB75).
Nonstandard peripherals required: HD recommended.
Billing System for Professionals. 3-Digit Transaction Codes Produce Description on Bill/Invoice. Does Automatic Repeat Billing & Regular Billing. Clients Can Be Billed in Any of Thirteen Cycles. Produces Many Reports. Tracks Money by Transaction Codes. Balance Forward. Produces Labels. Blank Paper, Letterhead, Pre-Printed Forms or Return Mailers for Bills.
Modern Microcomputers.

MODEL: Financial Modeling. *Version:* 6.0. Jan. 1983. *Compatible Hardware:* DEC VAX. *Operating System(s) Required:* VMS. *Language(s):* BASIC, Pascal. *Memory Required:* 512k. *Items Included:* User Guide, Reference Guide. *Customer Support:* Training included, Hotline, dail-in access with maintenance.
$19,000.00 & up.
Used in Areas Such As: Budget & Performance Reporting, Performance Tracking, Financial Statement Preparation, Consolidations, Cash Flow Forecasting, Production Modeling, Capital Budgeting, Resource Allocation, & Marketing Analysis.
Ross Systems, Inc.

Model Neuron. *Compatible Hardware:* Apple Macintosh. *Memory Required:* 512k.
3.5" disk $14.00.
Interactive Simulation of Neuron Activity by Means of User-Designed Experiments.
Kinko's.

Model Railroaders. *Customer Support:* 800-929-8117 (customer service).
MS-DOS. IBM/PS2. disk $99.99 (ISBN 0-87007-292-7).
This Program Converts Prototype Linear Measures to Scale Linear Measures in Any Gauge & Vice Versa. Converts Prototype Miles per Hour to Feet per Minute, Converts Real Time in Hours & Minutes to Scale Time in Minutes & Seconds & More. Can Be Used with Any of the Seven Popular Gauges (O, S, OO, HO, TT, N & Z).
SourceView Software International.

Model Rocket Analyzer & Preflight Check. *Compatible Hardware:* TRS-80 Model I, Model III. *Memory Required:* 16k.
disk $24.95 (Order no.: 0024R).
Compute Flight Characteristics for Almost Any Model Rocket. Predict Launch & Flight Conditions Before Lift-Off.
Instant Software, Inc.

ModelCAD. *Version:* 3.0. *Items Included:* Manual. *Customer Support:* 90 days free phone support.
DOS 3.0 or higher. IBM & compatibles (640k). disk $99.00 (Order no.: 712-3003-3 (3.5"); 712-3003-5 (5.25")). *Nonstandard peripherals required:* EGA or higher. *Optimal configuration:* Math coprocessor & hard drive.
First & Only CAD Program Designed Specifically for the Model-Building Industry & Hobbyists. Includes ModelCALC, the Model Airplane Model Analysis Program Which Produces Three-View Drawings Automatically. Comes with Pre-Drawn Symbols for Airfoils, Model Train Switches & Track, & Others. Includes 17 Fonts; Center of Gravity; Much More.
American Small Business Computers, Inc.

ModelMate Plus +. *Version:* 4.3. Aug. 1990. *Items Included:* Reference manuals. *Customer Support:* Free telephone support. All major upgrades cost $249.00.
IBM PC & compatibles (640k). disk $375.00. *Nonstandard peripherals required:* Math coprocessor, mouse.
An MS-DOS Based Solid Modeler Which Utilizes Both Boundary Defined & CSA Capabilities. Modeler Requires 640K & an Intel Based Math Coprocessor.
Control Automation, Inc.

ModelShop II: 3D Spatial Design & Presentation. *Version:* 1.2. Jul. 1991. *Items Included:* Tutorials, libraries. *Customer Support:* Free 90-day telephone support; 30 day money back guarantee.
6.0.5 or better - 7.0 compatible. Macintosh Plus or better with 32-bit QuickDraw (2Mb). 3.5" disk $495.00. *Optimal configuration:* Macintosh II FX with 8Mb RAM.
Mouse-Controlled, Animated Walk-Throughs & Fly-Bys. Claris CAD & AutoCAD DXF In & Out for Extrusion of 2D Plans into 3D Models & Taking 3D Perspectives into 2D As Basis for Working Drawings. Shadows Cast According to Sun Position. 24-Bit Color Rendering. Easily Build Bezier (Curved) Surfaces. Quick Contour Terrain Modeling.
Macromedia, Inc.

Modem 80. *Compatible Hardware:* TRS-80 Model I Level I, Model III, Model 4. *Operating System(s) Required:* TRSDOS. *Memory Required:* 32k. *General Requirements:* RS-232 modem.
disk $39.95.
Telecommunications Package Designed for Users with Disk-Based Systems. In Standard Form, the Program Communicates with a Wide Variety of Computer Systems, Including "The Source", "Micronet" & Other Bulletin Board Systems. Can Also Be Adapted to Communicate with Other Computers Using EBCDIC Code.
The Alternate Source.

Modern Artist. *Compatible Hardware:* Apple Macintosh II.
3.5" disk $395.00.
Color Painting Software.
Computer Friends.

Modern Drafting Practices & Standards Manual on CD-ROM. Nov. 1995. *Items Included:* Adobe Acrobat Reader 2.1, instruction manual. *Customer Support:* Free telephone support, 30 day return guarantee.
Microsoft Windows 3.1 or higher. 386 (4Mb). CD-ROM disk $250.00 plus $129.00 yr. updating service. *Nonstandard peripherals required:* CD-ROM.
Macintosh System 7.0 or higher. 68020 (3Mb). 2-5 workstations $739.00 plus $387.00 yr. updating service; 6-10 workstations $1108.00 plus $581.00 yr. updating service. *Nonstandard peripherals required:* CD-ROM drive.
Unix. HP Unix, Sun OS. *Nonstandard peripherals required:* CD-ROM drive.
A Comprehensive Reference of Drafting Standards & Techniques. Follows the Guidelines of ANSI & Other National Standards Organizations. First Publishing in 1901, the Manual Provides an Efficient & Proven System for Establishing Authoritative, Uniform Graphic Communication among Engineers, Draftsmen, Designers, Vendors, & Customers. Over 1300 pages.
Genium Publishing Corp.

Modern Greek for System 7. *Version:* 1.2. May 1994. *Items Included:* User manual, Keyboard Layout Chart. *Customer Support:* Free telephone support, defective disks replaced.
Macintosh. Macintosh (1Mb). 3.5" disk $99.95. *Addl. software required:* Any Word Processor. *Optimal configuration:* 4Mb RAM & a hard drive.
Includes Type-1 & TrueType Times-Style Olympus & Helvetica-Style Philippi Fonts in Plain, Bold, Italic & Bold-Italic. The Greek System 6.0.7 Times & Helvetica Style, Type-3 Fonts (Plain & Bold) Are Also Included. All Fonts Have Matching English Characters in Same Font. The Product Comes with a Modern Greek Keyboard Layout for Switching Between English & Greek Just by Pressing the Caps Lock Key.
Linguist's Software, Inc.

The Modern IC-Databook: A Key Aid for Every Electronics Amateur & Professional. Edited by Dramos Kalapodas et al.
disk $59.95, incl. text (ISBN 0-929321-04-9).
Electronic Reference. Includes 1200 Page Text & 176 Pages of Supplements.
WEKA Publishing, Inc.

Modern Jazz. *Compatible Hardware:* Apple Macintosh Plus, Macintosh SE, Macintosh II. $395.00.
Integrated Business Package Which Combines Worksheet, Graphics, Database, Forms, Word Processing & Communications Functions. Features Include HotView, Which Provides Dynamic Data Integration Between Functions; the Command Language, a Library of English Language Macro Commands; & Advanced Memory Management. Directly Imports & Exports Lotus 1-2-3 & Symphony, Microsoft Sylk & Text Files.
Lotus Development Corp.

ModernGreek for Windows. *Version:* 1.3. Feb. 1995. *Items Included:* User's manual; keyboard layout chart; keycap sticker sheet. *Customer Support:* Free telephone support, defective disks replaced free.
Windows. IBM or compatibles (4Mb). disk $99.95. *Addl. software required:* MS Windows 3.1X or ATM.
Professional-Quality, Hinted, Scalable Fonts in Both TrueType & Type 1 Formats: Olympus (Times-Style), & Philippi (Helvetica-Style), Both in Plain, Bold, Italic, & Bold-Italic Styles. Contains All Modern Greek Characters & Accents, Matching English Characters, & Both Modern Greek & Greek Transliterated Keyboard Layouts. These Fonts Follow the Microsoft Greek Windows Standard, & Files May Be Exchanged Between Greek & U.S. Windows Systems with No Conversion Necessary. TrueType Requires Microsoft Windows 3.1; Also Works with Word 6 for DOS, WordPerfect 6.0b for DOS & AutoCAD R.13. Type 1 Works with ATM & Windows; Also Works with OS/2 & AutoCAD R.12 & 13. WordPerfect for Windows Users Must Upgrade to Version 6.0a or Newer. Includes Keyboard Switcher, a Utility Providing Four Characters per Key in Windows.
Linguist's Software, Inc.

MODFIN. *Version:* 93. Nov. 1991. *Customer Support:* Free telephone support.
MS-DOS, PC-DOS (256k). 8080 - 386 IBM. disk $29.00 (Order no.: MF91). *Nonstandard peripherals required:* Dual drive or HD.
Twenty Assorted Money Manipulation Programs. Does Various Mortgage & Depreciation Schedules. Does Mortgage Comparisons. Various Interest & Loan Programs. Includes Lease/Rental Comparison. Break-Even Analysis. Produces W-2's & Various 1099 Forms.
Modern Microcomputers.

Modler Blue: Advanced Regression Package. *Version:* 5.51. C. G. Renfro & Assoc. Oct. 1995. *Items Included:* Users manual, complete documentation, installation assistance, re-installation if accidentally destroyed. *Customer Support:* 1st year Alpha Plus support is free, subsequent years are optional & cost about 20% of the software price, includes telephone technical assistance, free updates with new releases, conferences, training & user seminars.
MS-DOS 3.0 or higher (640k); Windows 3.X; OS/2. IBM compatible XT & up. $750.00. *Nonstandard peripherals required:* Math coprocessor chip. *Networks supported:* Ethernet or Token Ring coaxil cable or twisted pair, Novell, 3 Com, IBM.
Regression Package Offering Techniques Not Ordinarily Available on a Microcomputer - Restricted, Weighted, Two & Three Stage Least Squares; Ridge & Seemingly Unrelated Regression; Cross Equation Restrictions; Autoregressive Corrections. Open Architecture Allows Researchers to Write Their Own Routines.
Alphametrics Corp.

Modler MBA: Business Analysis Package Package. *Version:* 5.51. Oct. 1995. *Items Included:* Users manual, complete documentation, installation assistance, re-installation if accidentally destroyed. *Customer Support:* 1st year Alpha Plus support is free, subsequent years are optional & cost about 20% of the software price, includes telephone technical assistance, free updates with new releases, conferences, training & user seminars.
MS-DOS 3.0 or higher (640k); Windows 3.X; OS/2. IBM compatible XT & up. $1250.00. *Nonstandard peripherals required:* Math coprocessor chip. *Networks supported:* Ethernet or Token Ring coaxil cable or twisted pair, Novell, 3 Com, IBM.
Provides a Wide Range of Facilities for Analyzing, Interpreting, Modelling, & Forecasting the Behavior of Business Variables. Includes Complete Time-Series Data Management, Regression, High Quality Graphics & Reporting Capabilities. Allows for Simultaneity in Product Line Forecasts & Industry Analyses.
Alphametrics Corp.

Modler 100: Economic Finanical Analyses Package. *Version:* 5.51. C. G. Renfro Assoc. Oct. 1995. *Items Included:* Users manual, complete documentation, installation assistance, re-installation if accidentally destroyed. *Customer Support:* 1st year Alpha Plus support is free, subsequent years are optional & cost about 20% of the software price, includes telephone technical assistance, free updates with new releases, conferences, training & user seminars.
MS-DOS 3.0 or higher (640k); Windows 3.X; OS/2. IBM compatible XT & up. $2000.00. *Nonstandard peripherals required:* Math coprocessor chip. *Networks supported:* Ethernet or Token Ring coaxil cable or twisted pair, Novel, 3 Com, IBM.
Integrated Data Management, Modelling, Estimation, Model Management & Forecasting Software. Includes High Quality Presentation Graphics & a Complete Linear Regression Facility. Supports the Construction & Simulation of Models Containing Economic & Financial Relations. Financial Databases Available As Add-on Package.
Alphametrics Corp.

Modler: Statistical Information & Modelling System System. *Version:* 5.51. C. G. Renfro & Assoc. Oct. 1995. *Items Included:* Users manual, complete documentation, installation assistance, re-installation if accidentally destroyed. *Customer Support:* 1st year Alpha Plus support is free, subsequent years are optional & cost about 20% of the software price, includes telephone technical assistance, free updates with new releases, conferences, training & user seminars.
MS-DOS 3.0 or higher (640k); Windows 3.X; OS/2. IBM compatible XT & up. $4000.00. *Nonstandard peripherals required:* Math coprocessor chip. *Networks supported:* Ethernet or Token Ring coaxil cable or twisted pair, Novell, 3 Com, IBM— 6.
Integrated Economic Information & Modelling System. Includes Complete Time-Series, Data Management, Regression, Model Building, & Model Solution Facilities. Advanced Productivity Improving Features Across All Facilities (Estimation, Construction, Testing, Maintenance & Solution). A Thoroughly Tested & Highly Driven Modelling Package.
Alphametrics Corp.

MODMAIL 3. *Version:* 3.1. Feb. 1991. *Customer Support:* 1 year free telephone or FAX support.
MS-DOS, PC-DOS (256k). 8080 - 386 IBM. 3.5" disk $20.00 (Order no.: MM3). *Nonstandard peripherals required:* Dual drive or HD.
Complete Mailing List Generator That Remembers Zip Codes. List Can Be Sorted by Zip, Area Code or Any of 999 ID Codes. All or Parts of the List Can Be Printed. Produces Labels & Continuous Run Post Cards. Allows for Text on Reverse Side of Post Cards.
Modern Microcomputers.

MODSTAT. *Version:* 8. Jan. 1991. *Items Included:* Manual & bibliography on disk. *Customer Support:* 1 year free telephone support & 1 year free Fax support.
MS-DOS, PC-DOS (256k). 8080 - 386 IBM. disk $30.00 (Order no.: MS3). *Nonstandard peripherals required:* Dual drive or HD.
Over Fifty Statistical Tests Including a Routine to Help Determine the Best Test to Apply to Collected Research Data. Various ANOVA, Co-Variance, Correlation, Regression (Linear, Curvilinear, Power, Exponential & Log), Chi Square, Fischers' Exact Probability, & Other Parametric & Non-Parametric Tests. Group Comparisons, Matched & Unmatched. Between & Within Tests.
Modern Microcomputers.

MODULA-2 for CP/M. Hochstrasser Computing. 1985. *Operating System(s) Required:* CP/M. disk $165.00, incl. instrs. (Order no.: DCML2).
Takes the Concept of "Local" & "Global" Variables to New Dimensions. Includes 2-6 Disks of Support Routines (Depending on CP/M Disk Format Ordered), the Compiler, a Linker, Reference Lister, Converter & System Configuration Package.
The Alternate Source.

Modula-2PC, 2 disks. *Compatible Hardware:* IBM PC, PCjr, PC XT, PC AT, PC compatibles. *Memory Required:* 512k.
$59.95, incl. manual.
Provides: Native Code Support; Full Language Support, Including Long Integers; One-Pass Compilation; Automatic Generation of "EXE" Files; Program Overlays; Range/Pointer Checking. System Programming Facilities Include: Access to I/O Ports/Interrupt Vectors; Absolute Addresses for Variables; In-Line Instruction Generation. Library Modules Included Cover: All Standard I/O, Conversion & String Modules, Plus PC Screen/Keyboard Control, DOS/BIOS Interfaces, Concurrent Processes, Advanced Memory Allocation, etc. Not Copy Protected.
PCollier Systems.

Modules. Duane Bristow. *Compatible Hardware:* TRS-80 Model III. *Operating System(s) Required:* TRSDOS. *Language(s):* BASIC. *Memory Required:* 48k.
disk $69.95.
Contains Subroutines & Comments for Most Commonly Needed Functions in BASIC for the TRS-80 Disk System. Can Also Be Used As a Game, Simple Database Manager, & Screen Sketch Pad.
Duane Bristow Computers, Inc.

Moebius. Greg Malone. *Compatible Hardware:* Apple II, II+, IIe, IIc, Macintosh; Atari XL/XE, ST; Commodore 64, 128, Amiga; IBM PC. *Memory Required:* 64k. *Items Included:* Play book, reference card, Moebius headband. $39.95.
Danger-Filled Adventure Through a Complex & Colorful Oriental World of Magic, Mysticism, & Intrigue. The Player Has Been Chosen by Moebius, the Fabled Deity of the Island Kingdom of Khantun, to Recover the Stolen Orb of Celestial Harmony from the Renegade Warlord & Prevent the Destruction of the Universe, & He Will Have to Journey Through the Ascending Planes of Earth, Water, Air, & Fire. At Each Level the Challenges Increase in Difficulty, Demanding Greater Courage & Cunning.
Origin Systems, Inc.

Molarbyte Manager. *Version:* 4.6. *Compatible Hardware:* Apple Macintosh Plus, SE, MAC II. *General Requirements:* 20Mb hard disk. *Items Included:* User manual. *Customer Support:* 1 year free telephone support.
3.5" disk $850.00.
sample disk $35.00.
Dental Office Management System.
Molarbyte Data Systems.

Molecular Cloning. William Sofer. Jan. 1992. *Items Included:* User manual & HyperCard (black-&-white version) or SuperCard (full-color version). *Customer Support:* Free, unlimited technical support via our toll-free number (1-800-945-4551).
   Macintosh. Macintosh with a hard drive (2Mb). HyperCard version $65.00 (ISBN 1-57349-098-9). *Addl. software required:* System 6.0.7 or higher. *Networks supported:* All LANs.
   Macintosh. Macintosh with a hard drive (2Mb). SuperCard version $75.00 (ISBN 1-57349-105-5). *Addl. software required:* System 6.0.7 or higher. *Networks supported:* All LANs.
An Easy-to-Use & Highly Interactive Tutorial That Uses Integrated Text, Lessons, Animated Demonstrations, & Sound to Illustrate the Basic Concepts & Techniques in Molecular Cloning, Available in Black-&-White HyperCard Version or Full-Color SuperCard Version.
Keyboard Publishing, Inc.

Molecular Editor. *Compatible Hardware:* Apple Macintosh.
3.5" disk $30.50.
Construction Kit for Building & Displaying Molecules, Crystals & Other Structures.
Kinko's.

Molecular Graphics on the IBM PC Microcomputer. *Version:* 2.0. James G. Henkel & Frank H. Clarke. Feb. 1986. *Compatible Hardware:* IBM PC with 1 double-sided disk drive, color graphics adaptor & monitor. *Operating System(s) Required:* DOS 1.1, 2.0, 2.1, 3.0. *Language(s):* BASIC. *Memory Required:* DOS 1.1 192k; DOS 2.0, 2.1, 3.0 256k.
disk $199.00, incl. user's manual (ISBN 0-12-340822-9).
Applications Include the Study of Conformation of Organic Molecules & the Organization of Organic & Inorganic Crystal Lattices. Can Also Be Used for the Researcher Who Is Studying How a Substrate Fits in the Binding Site of an Enzyme or Who Is Comparing the Structures of a Series of Potential Ligands.
Academic Pr., Inc.

Molecular Modeling. *Items Included:* Bound manual. *Customer Support:* Free hotline - no time limit; 30 day limited warranty; updates are $5/disk plus S&H.
MS-DOS. IBM & compatibles (640k). disk $29.95. Nonstandard peripherals required: EGA (or equivalent).
A Chemical Modeling System Which Provides 3-D Representations of Chemical Structures.
Dynacomp, Inc.

Molecular Modeling 2: Molecular Graphics. *Items Included:* Bound manual. *Customer Support:* Free hotline - no time limit; 30 day limited warranty; updates are $5/disk plus S&H.
MS-DOS 2.0 or higher. IBM & compatibles (384k). disk $19.95. Nonstandard peripherals required: CGA/EGA (or compatible) graphics, & two drives (two floppies or one floppy & a hard disk).
Uses Cartesian or X-Ray Coordinates to Graphically Describe Molecules of Almost Any Size, with Much Data Already on Disk. Multiple Models May Be Displayed, Translated, & Overlayed for Comparison & Measurement. Molecules May Be Rotated about Any Axis or Bond. Reduction & Enlargement Is Also Available.
Dynacomp, Inc.

Molecular Presentation Graphics (MPG). *Version:* 4.2. Nov. 1988. *Compatible Hardware:* IBM PC & compatibles; PC XT, PC AT, Wang. *Operating System(s) Required:* MS-DOS 2.0 or higher. *Memory Required:* 384k.
MPG $275.00.
Drawing Software for Chemists. Creates Chemical Structure Diagrams for Use in Reports.
Hawk Scientific Systems, Inc.

Molecular Weight Calculator. *Compatible Hardware:* Apple Macintosh.
3.5" disk $13.00.
Desk Accessory for Computing the Molecular Weight of an Entered Formula.
Kinko's.

MOLECULES. *Version:* 6.2. *Items Included:* Diskette & manual. *Customer Support:* Telephone Inquiries.
   MAC-DOS (1Mb). Macintosh, Mac Plus & higher. disk $249.00.
Generate 3-Dimensional Perspective Views of Molecules Starting with Cartesian Coordinates or Angles & Distances. Magnify & Rotate Views, Compute Nonbonded Interaction Energy, Illustrate Principles of Stereochemistry. Create, Edit & Save Coordinate Data Files for Future Use or Export to Other Programs. Use As Graphical Display for Coordinates Generated on a Mainframe (Color Mac-II).
Atlantic SoftWare.

MOM: Medical Office Manager. B. R. Bortz. Apr. 1980. *Operating System(s) Required:* THEOS, Oasis. *Memory Required:* 64k.
disk or tape $6000.00 (Order no.: MOM3).
Multi-User Accounting System for the Doctor's Office.
BRB Software Systems.

MOMS: Medical Office Management System. *Version:* 2.1. 1984. *Compatible Hardware:* IBM PC & compatibles. *Operating System(s) Required:* OS-9, MS-DOS, PC-DOS. *Language(s):* Compiled BASIC. *Memory Required:* 256k. *Items Included:* Manual. *Customer Support:* Yes.
contact publisher for price.
Accounts Receivable & Billing System Designed for Medical Office Management.
Trend Computer Systems.

Monarch. *Compatible Hardware:* Apple II with Applesoft; Macintosh; IBM PC. *Memory Required:* IBM 128k, Macintosh 512k.
$19.95.
Rule a Nation. In Order to Stay in Power, You Must Balance the Budget While Keeping the People Happy.
Dynacomp, Inc.

Monarch. Jun. 1990. *Customer Support:* Unlimited telephone support, 30 day money-back guaranty.
DOS 2.01 or higher. IBM PC XT, AT, PS-2 or compatible (512k). $495.00.
A PC Program That Turns Any Report File into a Database or Spreadsheet. It Lets User Select Data & Export It As a Lotus 1-2-3 Worksheet, dBase Dbf File, Delimited Ascii or Text File. Eliminates the Need to Rekey Information Because It Reads Data Directly from Report Files. A Special Analysis Module Generates Summary Reports About the Data As Well.
Personics Corp.

Monarch Digital Signal. *Items Included:* Full manual. No other products required. *Customer Support:* Free telephone support - no time limit. 30 day warranty.
MS-DOS 3.2 or higher. IBM & compatibles (512k). $189.95 full system; $89.95 Digital Filters; $89.95 Siglab.
$39.95 student version.
demo disks $10.00.
Complete Menu-Driven Digital Signal Processing Package Which Includes a Wide Array of Filter Design, Signal Analysis, & Graphical Capabilities. Desired Filter Specifications Are Easily Transformed into a Realizable & Tested Architecture. Using Monarch's Fixed- or Floating-Point SIGLAB Analysis Features, You Can Be Sure That Your Design Performs Properly under a Variety of Conditions Before Implementing It.
Dynacomp, Inc.

Monarch: Digital Signal Processing. 1992. *Items Included:* Detailed manuals included with all Dynacomp products. *Customer Support:* Free telephone support to original customer - no time limit; 30 day limited warranty.
MS-DOS 3.2 or higher. IBM PC & compatibles (512k). $549.95 Full System (Add $5.00 for 3 1/2" format; 5 1/4" format standard). Optimal configuration: IBM, MS-DOS 3.0 or higher, 640k RAM, a hard disk (or a 2Mb floppy). Math coprocessor & mouse are supported, but not necessary. Rquires CGA, MCGA, EGA, VGA, Hercules, IBM 8514, AT&T 440, PC 3270 or compatible graphics capability.
demo disks $10.00.
A Complete Menu-Driven Digital Signal Processing Package Which Includes a Wide Array of Filter Design, Signal Analysis, & Graphical Capabilities. Desired Filter Specifications Are Easily Transformed into a Realizable & Tested Architecture. Using Monarch's Fixed- or Floating-Point SIGLAB Analysis Features, You Can Be Sure That Your Design Performs Properly under a Variety of Conditions Before Implementing It.
Dynacomp, Inc.

M1 Tank Platoon. 1989. *Items Included:* manual, Keyboard template, map. *Customer Support:* Free customer service (410) 771-1151, ext. 350.
MS-DOS. IBM PC/Tandy; Amiga. $69.95. Optimal configuration: 384k, CGA, EGA, Hercules mono, VGA/MCGA, or Tandy 1000 joystick optional but recommended.
Amiga. 3.5" disk $59.95.
Puts Player In Charge of a Four-tank Platoon for Battles Against the Warsaw Pact in Germany. The Player Not Only Has Control Over Four Tanks, but Also Over Four Positions in Each Tank. The Game Features MicroProses Super 3-D Graphics & Usual Attention to Realism & Detail.
MicroProse Software.

Monetary Unit Sampling. *Compatible Hardware:* Altos Series 5-15D, Series 5-5D, 580-XX, ACS8000-XX; DEC Rainbow 100 with 2 disk drives, Rainbow 100+ with 10Mb hard disk; IBM PC with 2 disk drives, IBM PC XT, & compatibles; Kaypro 11/IV with 2 disk drives, Kaypro 10; Xerox 820 with 2 disk drives; ZILOG MCZ-250. *Operating System(s) Required:* CP/M, MP/M, CP/M-80, CP/M-86, PC-DOS, MS-DOS.
contact publisher for price (Order no.: MUS).
Handles Several Individual Monetary Unit Sampling Results, with a Combined Maximum of 100 Errors, to Be Combined to Produce a Single Overall Evaluation. Produces Both One-Sided & Two-Sided Reliability Statements at Selected Reliability Levels. Also Provides Either a One-Sided or Two-Sided Evaluation of a Single Sample.
Coopers & Lybrand.

Money. *Items Included:* Bound manual. *Customer Support:* Free hotline - no time limit; 30 day limited warranty; updates are $5/disk plus S&H.
MS-DOS. IBM & compatibles (256k). disk $39.95.
Financial Analysis Computer Program Which Can Provide Valuable Assistance in Managing Your

MONEY DECISIONS

Money Wisely & Making the Most of Your Investments. It Can Be Used to Compute Compound Interest, Analyze Periodic Savings or Direct-Reduction Loans, Determine an Amortization Schedule, or Analyze Depreciation for Income Tax Purposes.
Dynacomp, Inc.

Money Decisions. *Items Included:* Bound manual. *Customer Support:* Free hotline - no time limit; 30 day limited warranty; updates are $5/disk plus S&H.
MS-DOS. IBM & compatibles (128k). disk $79.95-$99.95. *Nonstandard peripherals required:* 80-column (or wider) printer is supported, but not necessary.
Financial System Consisting of 70 Interactive Problem-Solving Programs for Investments, Loans, Business Management, & Forecasting & Graphics. Areas Covered: Investments; Loans; Business Management; Forecasting Graphics. A Communications Interface Is Provided (You Must Have a Modem for This), along with One Free Hour of Connect Time to CompuServe, Which Allows User Access to the Following: Up-to-the-Minute Stock Quotations; Ticker Retrieval; Standard & Poor's; Historical Market Information; Evans Economics; Issue Examination; Electronic Mail; Prices & Dividends.
Dynacomp, Inc.

Money Market Dealer Support System: FXAT. *Version:* 6.1. Dec. 1995. *Items Included:* Users manual, complete documentation, installation assistance, re-installation if accidentally destroyed. *Customer Support:* 1st year Alpha Plus support is free, subsequent years are optional & cost about 20% of the software price, includes telephone technical assistance, free updates with new releases, conferences, training & user seminars.
MS-DOS 3.0 & up (640k); Novell Netware; Windows 3.X & up. 386 IBM compatibles & up. $16,000.00 with multi-user discounts. *Networks supported:* Novell Token Ring-Advanced Network.
Automates the Management of All Information Flows Associated with Money Market Trading Including Front Office Information Flow & Input into Back Office Accounting. Installation on Individual Micros Or Novell Networks. Integrated Money Market & Foreign Exchange Trading Systems Are Available.
Alphametrics Corp.

Money Plans. Sep. 1990. *Items Included:* Spiral-bound, illustrated, step-by-step manual. *Customer Support:* Free, unlimited technical support.
DOS 2.0 or higher. IBM or compatible (384k). disk $49.00.
Helps User Plan for Retirement, College, Life & Disability Expenses. Includes Mortgage Analysis, Lease vs. Loan vs. Buy Options, Certificate of Deposit, Comparisons. Helps Organize Information on Household Inventory, Insurance Policies & Financial Advisors. Includes Questionnaire to Help User Pinpoint Financial Strengths & Weaknesses.
Parsons Technology.

Money Smart. Jan. 1988. *Items Included:* Operators manual. *Customer Support:* Onsite training, telephone support, 1st year maintenance free, annual maintenance $900.00 plus $400.00 per additional instrument.
PC-DOS. IBM's & compatibles (640k). Initial customization, monthly lease varies with modules used & number of nodes on network. *Networks supported:* Novell, Banyan.
A Complete Liability Accounting System for a Money Desk. Handles Accounting & Customer Management for Repurchase Agreements, Jumbo Certificates of Deposit, Commercial Paper & Master Notes. Cost Center, Client, 1099, Cash, Accrual, GL, Collateral Accounting. Client Tickets, Confirms, Prematurity Notices, GL Transmit Sheets. Over 150 Standard Reports Including a User Report Writer.
Wall Street Consulting Group.

Money Tools. *Version:* 2.3. Apr. 1991. *Items Included:* User Manual. *Customer Support:* Telephone support.
MS-DOS. IBM or compatible (640k). disk $295.00. *Optimal configuration:* 386 or higher with hard drive.
Database Program for Tracking Client of a Financial Planner or Insurance Representative. Collect & Manage Comprehensive Personal & Financial Data. Print Portfolio Reports, Maturity Dates, Tickler File, Net Worth Statement & More.
Money Tree Software.

MoneyCalc IV. *Version:* 4.6. Dec. 1981. *Compatible Hardware:* IBM PC & compatibles, PC XT, PC AT. *Operating System(s) Required:* MS-DOS. *Language(s):* Lotus 1-2-3 (source code included). *Memory Required:* 640k. *General Requirements:* Lotus 1-2-3 or Quattro Pro. *Customer Support:* User manual & telephone support.
$700.00.
Financial Planning Program for Individuals. For Use by Insurance Agents, Financial Planners, Stock Brokers, & CPA's. 50 Lotus 1-2-3 Templates.
Money Tree Software.

MoneyCounts. *Version:* 6.5. Mar. 1990. *Items Included:* Printed manual. *Customer Support:* Free technical support.
DOS 2.0 or higher (384k). IBM/Tandy/Compaq or compatible. $35.00. *Optimal configuration:* IBM or compatible, 384K or more RAM, 2 disk drive (or a hard disk). Works with all printers & monitors.
Can Handle Up to 999 Accounts & 100,000 Transactions, Estimates Income Tax, Analyzes Financing Options, Manages Mailing Lists, Prints Labels, Displays Three-Dimensional Graphics. Provides Password Protection, Fiscal Year Support, Pop-up Note Pad, Interfaces with Checkfree.
Parsons Technology.

MoneyMaster. *Version:* 2.1. *General Requirements:* Hard disk recommended.
MS/PC-DOS. IBM PC & compatibles, 8086, 286, 386, 486 (256k). $295.00 per package. *Networks supported:* Novell (Files Nonsharable).
Financial/Accounting Package. Posts Recurring Transactions, Automatic Posting from Other Modules, Report Format User Definable, Reports Comparative Statements, Links with External Software Programs, Password Access, Audit Trail, Error Recovery, Reject Erroneous Account Numbers & On-Line Help.
Pacific Data Systems, Inc.

MONEYMAX: Investment Management System. Jan. 1975. *Memory Required:* 512k. contact publisher for price.
Designed for Public Sector Investors with Short-Term Investment Portfolios. Provides Investment Position Reporting, Transaction Journals, Income Projection, Maturity Distribution Reports, Cash & Accrual Based Earnings, Risk Monitoring, Yield Calculations, Income Summary, Bank Summary, & Daily Market Pricing Reports. Handles Government Treasury & Agency Issues, Time Deposits, Bankers Acceptances, Repurchase Agreements, Reverse Repurchase Agreements, GNMAs, Variable Rates, Corporate Bonds, & Commercial Paper. Produces Reports on Demand for All or Selected Funds over User-Specified Time Periods. Modules Include Investment Accounting & Reporting, Cash Flow Forecasting & Tracking, Cash Management Strategy, Investment Trading Selection & Analysis, Fund Accounting & Interest Apportionment.
Wismer Assocs., Inc.

MONITOR-IBM PC. *Compatible Hardware:* IBM PC. *Operating System(s) Required:* PC-DOS 2.0 or higher. *Memory Required:* 128k.
disk $95.00 (Order no.: 45439A).
File Transfer Monitor for the IBM PC Designed to Work with ADVANCELINK on the Touchscreen PC. They Enable Error-Free Transfer of ASCII or Binary Files Between the Two Systems. Both Programs & Data Files May Be Transferred, but Compatibility of Data Formats or Program Instructions Is Not Guaranteed. Files May Be Transferred Either Using Full-Duplex Modems & Telephone Lines or Using an HP 13242H Cable to Connect the HP System & the IBM PC.
Hewlett-Packard Co.

Monkey Business Typing Tutor. *Items Included:* Bound manual. *Customer Support:* Free hotline - no time limit; 30 day limited warranty; updates are $5/disk plus S&H.
MS-DOS. IBM & compatibles (128k). disk $17.95. *Nonstandard peripherals required:* One disk drive.
Apple, C-64 (48k). disk $17.95.
Written with the Objective of Providing the New Typist with the Keyboard Skills Needed for Effectively Using a Typewriter or Word Processor. It Allows Practice at 20 Distinct Levels. User May Practice the Home Row, Home & Top Rows, Home & Bottom Rows, or All Three Rows. The Computer (Patiently) Provides the Exercises, Testing, & Rewards. The Game Aspect Takes Much of the Tedium Out of Learning Touch Typing. It Is a Race. Your Monkey Is Picking Coconuts in Competition with a Computer Robot Coconut Picker. These Coconuts Turn into Gold As They Are Picked.
Dynacomp, Inc.

Monologue for Windows 32. *Version:* 2.0. Feb. 1996. *Customer Support:* 90 days-toll free - 800-556-6141.
Windows 95 or Windows NT. 486 (8Mb). disk $69.95 (ISBN 0-7849-0861-3, Order no.: 2731). *Nonstandard peripherals required:* Sound card.
A Software Porgram That Reads Text from the Clipboard in Windows 32 Bit Applications. Can Add the Element of Speech to Virtually Any Text Oriented Application. Any Pronounceable Combination of Letters & Numbers Will Be Spoken Clearly. It Can Be Applied to Tasks Such As Eyes-Free Proofreading, Data Verification (e.g. Spreadsheets), Reading E-Mail & More. User-Changeable Parameters Provide Control over the Sound Quality by Allowing for Changes in Pitch, & the Speed of Speech. An Exception Dictionary Saves Preferred Pronunciation of Words & Abbreviations. Works with Sound Devices That Comply with the Windows Sound API. Male "SpeechFonts" Are Available for U.S. English, British English, German, French, Latin American Spanish, Italian. A U.S. English Female SpeechFont Is Also Available. Also Microsoft Speech API (SAPI) Compliant.
First Byte.

Monster Fonts.
Macintosh. 3.5" disk $49.95.
8Mb of Fonts.
Showker Graphic Arts & Design.

TITLE INDEX

Monster Lab. Dec. 1995. *Customer Support:* Telephone support - free (except phone charge). Windows 3.1. IBM & compatibles (386 DX-20) (4Mb). CD-ROM disk $12.99, Jewel (ISBN 1-57594-086-8). *Nonstandard peripherals required:* 2X CD ROM player, sound card, VGA monitor. *Optimal configuration:* 486 SX-33.
CD-ROM disk $12.99, Blister.
Build Your Child's Memory Skills & Have Fun Testing Their Wits Against 12 Different Monsters. Test Their Memory Skills in Matchum & Practice Pattern Recognition Skills in Morfum. Hours of Fun Learning Experiences.
Kidsoft, Inc.

Monster Lab. Jan. 1996. *Customer Support:* Telephone support - free (except phone charge). System 7.0 or higher. 256 color capable Mac with a 68030 processor (5Mb). CD-ROM disk $12.99 (ISBN 1-57594-110-4). *Nonstandard peripherals required:* 2X CD ROM drive, 640/480 resolution monitor.
Build Your Child's Memory Skills & Have Fun Testing His or Her Wit Against 12 Different Monsters. Test Their Memory Skills in Matchum & Practice Pattern Recognition Skills in Morfum. Hours of Fun Learning Experiences.
Kidsoft, Inc.

Monster Lab. Feb. 1996. *Customer Support:* Telephone support - free (except phone charge). Windows 3.1. IBM compatible 386 DX-20 (4Mb). CD-ROM disk $12.99 (ISBN 1-57594-099-X). *Nonstandard peripherals required:* 2x CD-ROM, sound card, VGA monitor. *Optimal configuration:* 486, SX-33.
Develop Memory Skills, Pattern Recognition. Blister Pack.
Kidsoft, Inc.

Monster Lab. Dec. 1995. *Customer Support:* Telephone support - free (except phone charge). Windows 3.1. IBM & compatibles (386 DX-20) (4Mb). CD-ROM disk $12.99 (ISBN 1-57594-086-8). *Nonstandard peripherals required:* 2X CD-ROM player, sound card, VGA monitor. *Optimal configuration:* 486 SX-33.
Build Your Child's Memory Skills & Have Fun Testing Their Wits Against 12 Different Monsters. Test Their Memory Skills in Matchum & Practice Pattern Recognition Skills in Morfum. Hours of Fun Learning Experiences. Jewel Case.
Kidsoft, Inc.

MONTAGE for the Video Toaster. Version: 1.02. Aug. 1993. *Items Included:* Manual, quick reference guide, keyboard template. *Customer Support:* Free telephone support to registered users, 24 hr. Fax line.
WB 1.3 or higher. Amiga (8Mb, 1Mb Chip). disk $499.95 (Order no.: MT-VT). *Nonstandard peripherals required:* Video Toaster 2.0, 3.0 or Toaster 4000. *Optimal configuration:* Amiga 2000, 3000 or 4000, WB 2.0 & Accelerator strongly recommended.
Broadcast Quality Character Generator, 24-Bit Graphics & Automated Transition Program for the Video Toaster. Realtime Font Scaling at 1 Nanosecond Resolution, 24-Bit Image Compositing & Processing, Smooth Interactive Credit Roll in 4,096 Colors. Enhanced Video Output Signal & NTSC Filter. PostScript Module & Font Pack Also Available.
InnoVision Technology.

MONTAGE 24 for the Amiga. Sep. 1993. *Items Included:* Manual, keyboard template, quick reference guide. *Customer Support:* Free telephone technical support to registered users. 24 hr. Fax line.
Amiga WB 1.3 or higher. Amiga (8Mb). disk $399.98 (Order no.: MT24). *Nonstandard peripherals required:* AGA 1200/4000 Amiga, or Amiga with OpalVision or ImpactVision Board. *Optimal configuration:* Amiga AGA 1200 or 4000 with hard disk.
Broadcast Quality CB & 24-Bit Graphics Program for Amiga AGA, OpalVision & ImpactVision 24 Platforms. Realtime Font Scaling at 1 Nanosecond Resolution. 24-Bit Image Creation & Processing. Sequencing of 24-Bit Images. 4,096 Color Credit Roll. PostScript Module & Font Pack Also Available. Available in NTSC or PAL Formats.
InnoVision Technology.

Monte Carlo. May 1988. *Compatible Hardware:* Apple IIgs. *Operating System(s) Required:* ProDOS. *Memory Required:* 512k.
3.5" disk $39.95.
Casino Games. Includes Blackjack, Roulette, Craps, Baccarat, Poker, Trente-et-Quarante.
PBI Software, Inc.

Monte Carlo Analysis Toolbox: Monte Carlo BSC Throughput. Jan. 1996. *Items Included:* Sample input & output files & users manuals on disk. *Customer Support:* Assistance in formulative inputs & understanding outputs, price free or variable.
MS-DOS. IBM PC (8Mb). disk $799.00 (Order no.: 706). *Nonstandard peripherals required:* Math coprocessor. *Addl. software required:* FORTRAN Compiler & Linker. *Optimal configuration:* Source code can be compiled & linked for execution on any Machine with a FORTRAN compiler & linker.
Performs a Monte Carlo Cumulative Probability Analysis of Throughput, of a Channel Employing the IBM Binary Synchronous Communications(BSC) Protocol, Where Throughput Is a Measure of the Amount of user Information That Can Be Transmitted over a Channel, Expressed As a Percent of Channel Capacity. This Product Is Supported by Product 408.
Cane Systems.

Monte Carlo Analysis Toolbox: Monte Carlo HDLC Throughput. Jan. 1996. *Items Included:* Sample input & output files & users manuals on disk. *Customer Support:* Assistance in formulative inputs & understanding outputs, price free or variable.
MS-DOS. IBM PC (8Mb). disk $799.00 (Order no.: 707). *Nonstandard peripherals required:* Math coprocessor. *Addl. software required:* FORTRAN Compiler & Linker. *Optimal configuration:* Source code can be compiled & linked for execution on any Machine with a FORTRAN compiler & linker.
Performs a Monte Carlo Cumulative Probability Analysis of the Throughput of a Channel Employing the High Level Data Link Control(HDLC) Protocol, Where Throughput Is a Measure of the Amount of User Information That Can Be Transmitted over a Channel, Expressed As a Percent of Channel Capacity. Considers Both the Non-Selective Reject Option, EREJ & the Selective Reject Option, ESREJ. This Product Is Supported by Product 408.
Cane Systems.

Monte Carlo Analysis Toolbox: Monte Carlo Intranodal Response Time. Jan. 1996. *Items Included:* Sample input & output files & users manuals on disk. *Customer Support:* Assistance in formulative inputs & understanding outputs, price free or variable.
MS-DOS. IBM PC (8Mb). disk $999.00 (Order no.: 704). *Nonstandard peripherals required:* Math coprocessor. *Addl. software required:* FORTRAN Compiler & Linker. *Optimal configuration:* Source code can be compiled & linked for execution on any Machine with a FORTRAN compiler & linker.
Performs a Monte Carlo Cumulative Probability Analysis of Intranodal Response Times, Where Response Time Is Defined As the Elapsed Time from the Time That a Request Message Is Ready to Be Sent to the Time That the Last Bit of a Response Message Is Received. This Product Is Supported by Product 408.
Cane Systems.

Monte Carlo Analysis Toolbox: Monte Carlo Internodal Response Time. Jan. 1996. *Items Included:* Sample input & output files & users manuals on disk. *Customer Support:* Assistance in formulative inputs & understanding outputs, price free or variable.
MS-DOS. IBM PC (8Mb). disk $1099.00 (Order no.: 705). *Nonstandard peripherals required:* Math coprocessor. *Addl. software required:* FORTRAN Compiler & Linker. *Optimal configuration:* Source code can be compiled & linked for execution on any Machine with a FORTRAN compiler & linker.
Performs a Monte Carlo Cumulative Probability Analysis of Internodal Response Times, Where Response Time Is Defined As the Elapsed Time from the Time That a Request Message Is Ready to be Sent to the Time That the Last Bit of a Response Message Is Received. This Product Is Supported by Product 408.
Cane Systems.

Monte Carlo Analysis Toolbox: Monte Carlo One Way Link Delay. Jan. 1996. *Items Included:* Sample input & output files & users manuals on disk. *Customer Support:* Assistance in formulative inputs & understanding outputs, price free or variable.
MS-DOS. IBM PC (8Mb). disk $399.00 (Order no.: 702). *Nonstandard peripherals required:* Math coprocessor. *Addl. software required:* FORTRAN Compiler & Linker. *Optimal configuration:* Source code can be compiled & linked for execution on any Machine with a FORTRAN compiler & linker.
Performs a Monte Carlo Cumulative Probability Analysis of One Way Link Delay, Which Is Defined As the Total Elapsed Time from the Time a Message Is Ready for Transmission to the Time the Last Message Bit Is Received. One Way Link Delay Is Fundamentally the Sum of the Time a Message Spends in the Queue & Transmission Delay. This Product Is Supported by Product 408.
Cane Systems.

Monte Carlo Analysis Toolbox: Monte Carlo One Way Path Delay. Jan. 1996. *Items Included:* Sample input & output files & users manuals on disk. *Customer Support:* Assistance in formulative inputs & understanding outputs, price free or variable.
MS-DOS. IBM PC (8Mb). disk $465.00 (Order no.: 703). *Nonstandard peripherals required:* Math coprocessor. *Addl. software required:* FORTRAN Compiler & Linker. *Optimal configuration:* Source code can be compiled & linked for execution on any Machine with a FORTRAN compiler & linker.
Performs a Monte Carlo Cumulative Probability Analysis of the Mean One Way Multi-Link Path Delay, Which Is Defined As the Total Elapsed Time from the Time a Message Is Ready for Transmission to the Time the Last Message Bit Is Received. One Way Multi-Link Path Delay Is Fundamentally the Sum of the Time a Message Spends in Each Nodal Queue & the Transmission Delay on Each Link on the Path. This Product Is Supported by Product 408.
Cane Systems.

Monte Carlo Analysis Toolbox: Monte Carlo Transmission Delay. Jan. 1996. *Items Included:* Sample input & output files & users manuals on disk. *Customer Support:* Assistance in formulative inputs & understanding outputs, price free or variable.
  MS-DOS. IBM PC (8Mb). disk $335.00 (Order no.: 701). *Nonstandard peripherals required:* Math coprocessor. *Addl. software required:* FORTRAN Compiler & Linker. *Optimal configuration:* Source code can be compiled & linked for execution on any Machine with a FORTRAN compiler & linker.
Performs a Monte Carlo Cumulative Probability Analysis of Link Transmission Delays of a Message Transmitted on a Link, Where Transmission Delay Is Defined As the Elapsed Time from the Transmission of the First Message Bit to the Receipt of the Last Message Bit. Takes into Consideration Link Capacity, Protocol Bit Size, Bit Error Rate, Length, & DCE Pair Delay & Mean Message Size. This Product Is Supported by Product 408.
Cane Systems.

Monte Carlo Plus. *Version:* 2. Oct. 1987.
  MS-DOS (512k). IBM PC & compatibles. disk $89.00. *Addl. software required:* Lotus 1-2-3, 2, 2.01, 2.2, 2.3, & 3, Lotus Symphony 1.0, 1.1, 1.2, 2.0.
Menu-Driven Program Attaches to Existing 1-2-3 or Symphony Spreadsheet Model to Assess Downside & Upside Potential by Monte Carlo Statistical Risk Analysis. User's Model is Computed Many Times. Each Scenario Draws Variable Values from Normal Probability Distributions Set by Accuracy of Input Information (e.g. Sales, Expenses). Probabilities of Dependent Items (e.g. Profit) Exceeding Various Levels Are Presented as Tables & Graphs. Also Does Sensitivity Analysis, in Which Model's Result (e.g. Profit) is Shown as One Variable (e.g. Sales) Changes from a Low Value to a High Value. Sensitivity Analysis Indicate Variables Which Have Least & Greatest Effect on Model's Outcome.
Suntex National Corp.

Monte Carlo Simulation. *Version:* 1.1. *Compatible Hardware:* IBM PC & compatibles, PS/2. *Memory Required:* 160k. *General Requirements:* Lotus 1-2-3. *Items Included:* On disk, Hypertext Tutorial & Lotus models. *Customer Support:* Yes.
  disk $45.00.
Risk-Forecasting Tool. User Can Learn to Run Simulations & Sensitivity Analyses with Multiple Variables. Includes an Engineering & Financial Forcasting Model.
Entropy Assocs., Inc.

Monte Carlo Simulations (Advanced Version). *Version:* 2.1. Sep. 1986. *Compatible Hardware:* Apple Macintosh; IBM PC. *Memory Required:* 512k. *General Requirements:* 2 disk drives. disk $495.00 ea.
  IBM PC. (ISBN 0-922109-10-9).
  Macintosh. (ISBN 0-922109-12-5).
Consists of Three Fully-Integrated Modeling Tools: Statistical Analysis; Simulation; Long Term Projection. Completely Menu-Driven. Features On-Line Documentation, Windows & the Ability to Interface with Other Applications Such As Spreadsheet Programs. Up to 100 Variables Allowed. Thirteen Probability Distributions Available. Detailed Reports & Graphics Are Produced.
Actuarial Micro Software.

MonteCarloSMITH. Robert Abernethy & Wes Fulton. Jul. 1994. *Customer Support:* 30-day limited warranty.
  MS-DOS. IBM (512k). disk $320.00 (Order no.: S105). *Optimal configuration:* 5Mb hard disk storage required.
Program Accurately Estimates Confidence Limits for Data with Random Suspensions. Will Generate Lists of Random Sample Data, Data Set Parameters Such As Weibull Shape Factor, & Characteristic Life, One or Two - B Values & Correlation Coefficients & Coefficients of Determination.
Gulf Publishing Co.

MonteCarloSMITH: Monte Carlo Probability Analysis. 1995. *Items Included:* Full manual. *Customer Support:* Free telephone support - 90 days, 30-day warranty.
  MS-DOS 3.2 or higher. 286 (584k). disk $319.95. *Nonstandard peripherals required:* CGA/EGA/VGA.
Handles Probability Analysis Problems Which Are Difficult or Near-Impossible by Other Means. It Allows the Accurate Estimation of Confidence Limits for Data with Random Suspensions, a Previously Impossible Task. It Also Provides a Reference for Checking the Validity of Other Confidence Calculation Methods.
Dynacomp, Inc.

Monthly Astro-Report. Arthur Blackwell & John Kahila. 1983. *Compatible Hardware:* Apple Macintosh; CP/M-based machines with 2 148-200k disk drives or 1 241k disk drive; IBM PC. *Operating System(s) Required:* CP/M-80, MacFinder, MS-DOS, PC-DOS. *Language(s):* BASIC. *Memory Required:* CP/M 64k, PC-DOS 256k, MS-DOS 128k or 256k, Macintosh 512k. *General Requirements:* Printer, Dot-Matrix or Hewlett Packard Laser. *Items Included:* Manual. *Customer Support:* Free phone support.
  CP/M. disk $195.00 (ISBN 0-913637-53-X).
  IBM PC. disk $195.00 (ISBN 0-913637-54-8).
  MS-DOS. disk $195.00 (ISBN 0-913637-66-1).
Forecasts for One-Month or Other Periods Using Natal Horoscope Compared with Lunar Return Horoscope. Includes License to Sell Printed Output.
Astrolabe, Inc.

Monthly Feed Consumed. *Version:* 1.7. Jan. 1981. *Compatible Hardware:* IBM PC & compatibles. *Operating System(s) Required:* MS-DOS 3.0 or higher. *Language(s):* BASIC (source code included). *Memory Required:* 256k. *Customer Support:* Telephone.
  disk $20.00.
Figures Out Amount of Feed Actually Consumed During the Month, Based on Deliveries & On-Hand Figures.
Locus Systems.

MONTY Plays Monopoly. Robert J. Walls. *Items Included:* Directions, general information. *Customer Support:* We will answer any questions.
  ProDOS (64k); DOS 3.3 (48k). Apple II family. 5.25" disk $34.95 (Order no.: 34).
Take a Ride on the Reading & Buy & Sell Properties Against MONTY "He'll" Entertain You with Music & Graphics & Lead You Through the Game. Plays 1-7 People; Use with Your Monopoly Board.
Ritam Corp.

MONTY Plays Scrabble. *Version:* 3.0. Sep. 1984. *Compatible Hardware:* Apple II, II+ with Applesoft, IIgs; IBM PC, PCjr; TRS-80 Model III. *Memory Required:* TRS-80 32k, Apple 48k, IBM 64k.
  $39.95.
Opponent for the Scrabble Game. Plays up to Three Opponents.
Ritam Corp.

Monty Python's Complete Waste of Time. Oct. 1994. *Customer Support:* Technical support is available free of charge through our technical support phone line by calling 214-437-5531 Monday through Saturday 8:00am-5:00pm, online via CompuServe by typing Go Seventh at any! prompt, or via Internet mail at Support-7thlevel.com.
  Windows 3.1 or higher. IBM compatible 486 25MHz (4Mb). CD-ROM disk $54.95 (ISBN 0-9641098-3-2, Order no.: 10014). *Nonstandard peripherals required:* 256-color display or higher, mouse; CD-ROM drive, MPC-compatible sound card; amplified speakers. *Optimal configuration:* IBM-compatible 486 33MHz with 8Mb RAM.
Monty Python's Complete Waste of Time Gives You a Chance to Solve the Secret to Intergalactic Success. Interact with More Than 30 of Your Favorite Skits, Brand New Dialog & Graphics, Songs & Arcade-Like Games. Customize Your Computer with Screen Savers, Wallpaper, Audio Clips, Desktop Icons, Phone Messages, & More.
Seventh Level, Inc.

Monty Python's Flying Circus Desktop Pythonizer. Oct. 1994. *Customer Support:* Technical support is available free of charge through our technical support phone line by calling 214-437-5531 Monday through Saturday 8:00am-5:00pm, online via CompuServe by typing Go Seventh at any! prompt, or via Internet mail at Support 7thlevel.com.
  Windows 3.1 or higher. IBM-compatible 386 25MHz (4Mb). disk $29.99 (ISBN 0-9641098-4-0, Order no.: 10015). *Nonstandard peripherals required:* 256-color display or higher; mouse. *Optimal configuration:* MPC compatible sound card with amplified speakers.
Customizes Your Computer Adding Anarchy Everywhere. Choose from More Than 20 Interactive Screen Savers & Living Wallpaper, Create New Wallpaper & Replace Your Icons with Monty Python Images. Use Audio Clips Including Prerecorded Phone Messages. Invade Your Other Windows Applications with OLE-Compatible Animation.
Seventh Level, Inc.

MoonMine. *Compatible Hardware:* TI 99/4A with PLATO interpreter solid state cartridge.
  contact publisher for price (Order no.: PHM 3131).
You Are the Captain of the U.S.S. MoonMine & Your Mission Is to Capture Treasures Stolen from Earth.
Texas Instruments, Personal Productivit.

Moonmist. Stu Galley & Jim Lawrence. Oct. 1986. *Compatible Hardware:* Apple II, II+, IIe, IIc, IIgs, Macintosh; Atari XL/XE, ST; Commodore 64, 128, Amiga; DEC Rainbow; IBM PC & compatibles; TI Professional. *Memory Required:* 48k.
  Apple II, Macintosh, Atari ST, Amiga, DEC, IBM. disk $39.95.
  Atari XL/XE, Commodore 64/128. $34.95.
More Ghosts Haunt the Coast of Cornwall, England, Than Any Place Else on Earth. One Such Soul Roams Tresyllian Castle: a Pale Phantom in a Luminous Gown. It Seems Like a Fanciful Legend...Until the Spectral "White Lady" Threatens the Life of Your Friend Tamara. Arriving at the Fog-Shrouded Castle, You Find a Cast of Odd, Eccentric Characters & a Very Real Mystery to Be Solved. Put Your Detecting Skills to Use As You Hunt the Phantom & Search for Hidden Treasure in the Lavish Rooms & Secret Passageways of the Castle. The Story Has Four Variations, Each with a Different Hidden Treasure & Solution to the Mystery.
Activision, Inc.

TITLE INDEX

Moonprobe. *Compatible Hardware:* Apple II with Applesoft; IBM PC. (source code included). *Memory Required:* Apple II 48, IBM PC 128k.
disk $19.95.
Space Arcade Game.
Dynacomp, Inc.

More About Lotus 1-2-3 Commands. Jan. 1986.
$245.00 each for 1 to 4 packages.
$220.00 each for 5 to 20.
$196.00 each for more than 20.
extra workbook sets also available, as well as a reproduction license for $295.00 per course.
Videotape Tutorial Includes Workbook, Practice Disk, Quick-Reference Guide, & Command Chart. Also Provides a Course-Management Guide for Instructor. Covers Release 2 Features.
Alcatel Servcom.

More After Dark: For Macintosh. Aug. 1991. *Customer Support:* 415-540-5535, available 8am-5pm PST weekdays.
Macintosh 4.x & up. Mac Plus & up (1Mb). $39.95. *Networks supported:* All.
Over 25 New Displays for After Dark. Features Contest Winners Mowin' Man, Tunnel, GraphStat, & Beautiful New Fish! Boris the Cat & Lunatic Fringe Game Module Help Save Your Screen from Phosphor Burn-In. Virex-D Virus Detector Module from Microcom Scans for Viruses While After Dark Sleeps. (Requires After Dark Software).
Berkeley Systems, Inc.

More Loveplay. *Version:* 2.0. Rob Reinish. Aug. 1995. *Items Included:* CD or 3 1/2" diskettes, instruction booklet. *Customer Support:* 801-253-2252.
Windows 3.1 or Windows 95. PC (4Mb). CD-ROM disk $29.95 (ISBN 1-887867-00-7). *Nonstandard peripherals required:* CD-ROM drive. *Optimal configuration:* 8 Mb, Sound card, True Color monitor.
Windows 3.1 or Windows 95. PC (4Mb). 3.5" disk $29.95 (ISBN 1-887867-02-3). *Nonstandard peripherals required:* 3 1/2" drive. *Optimal configuration:* 8Mb, Sound card, True Color monitor.
A Computer Game Developed to Enhance Romance & Breathe New Excitement & Fun into a Couple's Love Life, & Sets the Standard for How Computers Can Be Used to Enliven Intimacy in Relationships.
Relationship Software, LLC.

More LovePlay. Sep. 1995.
3.5" disk $29.95 (ISBN 1-887867-02-3, Order no.: ML20S3).
CD-ROM disk $29.95 (ISBN 1-887867-00-7, Order no.: ML20SC).
Relationship Software, LLC.

More Myths, Magic & Monsters. (Micro Learn Tutorial Ser.). *Items Included:* Teacher's manual.
MAC. IBM (128k), Macintosh (2Mb), Apple II series, (48k). 5.25" disk $39.95 (Lab pack/5 $99.00); 3.5" disk, $44.95 (Lab pack/5 $115.00). Apple, IBM or Macintosh, $249.00 (ISBN 1-57265-045-1).
IBM. (ISBN 0-939153-80-7).
APP. (ISBN 0-939153-40-8).
A Sequel to Our Popular Reading Skills Program, Emphasis on Greek Myths, Develops the Skills of Recall, Sequencing, Defining the Main Idea, Identifying the Speaker, Recognizing Cause & Effect, Developing Vocabulary Through Context Clues, Analyzing Figurative Language, Drawing Conclusions, & Recognizing Mood. The tutorial mode gives explanations & help for every answer choice, correct & incorrect. The test mode gives no help for the test, but then presents missed questions & tutorial mode.
Word Assocs., Inc.

More Powers to You!: Exponents & Scientific Notation. (Micro Learn Tutorial Ser.). *Items Included:* Manual including tests, worksheets, quizzes, puzzles. *Customer Support:* Free telephone support.
MAC. IBM (128k), Macintosh (2Mb), Apple II Series, (48k), Commodore 64. 5.25" disk, $39.95 (Lab pack/5 $99.99), 3.5" disk, $44.95 (Lab pack/5 $115.00). Apple, IBM or Macintosh, $249.00 (ISBN 1-57265-064-8).
DOS. (ISBN 0-939153-47-5).
APP. (ISBN 0-939153-98-X).
Leads Learner Through the World of Exponents & Scientific Notation. Topics Include Exponents, Powers of 10, Multiplying & Dividing in Scientific Notation, Problem Solving. The tutorial mode gives explanations for every answer choice, correct & incorrect (plus help/practice on important ideas). The test mode gives no help; after the score appears, it presents missed questions in the tutorial mode.
Word Assocs., Inc.

More $ales. *Version:* 7.1. Nov. 1991. *Items Included:* Complete manual. *Customer Support:* 1 year maintenance available. Training available on site.
MS-DOS 5.0 or higher. IBM PC XT, PC AT, PS/2 (640k). Contact publisher for price. *Optimal configuration:* IBM PS/2, hard disk 30Mb, 2Mb. *Networks supported:* Novell, 3COM, PC NET.
Allows User to Increase Revenues, Reduce Expenses, Improve Customer Relations by Having All Your Calls & Contacts on the System. Appointment Calendar, Unlimited Notepad. Can Scroll Back to See Prior Calls. Competition Analysis, Report Writer. Mailmerge Letters. Pre-Planning Questions Built In.
Dynamic Interface Systems Corp.

More II. *Version:* 3.0. *Compatible Hardware:* Apple Macintosh. *Memory Required:* 1000k. *General Requirements:* 800k disk drive or hard disk. *Items Included:* 3 disks, 3 manuals. *Customer Support:* (408) 372-8100.
3.5" disk $197.50.
Planning, Writing & Desktop Presentations Program.
Symantec Corp.

Morgan's Trivia Machine. Oct. 1994. *Customer Support:* Technical support phone line.
PC - Windows. 486 or higher, double speed CD-ROM drive (4Mb). disk $19.95 (ISBN 1-887423-00-1). *Optimal configuration:* VGA/SVGA w/256 colors, MPC compliant sound card & mouse required.
MAC. System 7.1 or higher, double CD-ROM drive (4Mb). 3.5" disk $19.95 (ISBN 1-887423-01-X). *Nonstandard peripherals required:* 256 colors. *Optimal configuration:* VGA/SVGA w/256 colors, MPC compliant sound card & mouse required.
Children Learn Interesting Facts about Geography, Science & the World While Having Fun with Their Family & Friends. Players Can Identify Their Appropriate Skill Level So Adults & Children, or Children of Different Ages & Abilities, Can Play Together. Hilarious Gags, Quicktime Video, Film Quality Animation, & over 1,000 Questions Make This Program an Entertaining & Educational Experience.
Morgan Interactive.

Morgan's Trivia Machine, Jr. Sep. 1995.
Customer Support: Telephone support - free (except phone charge).
Windows 3.1. IBM & compatibles (386 DX-20) (4Mb). CD-ROM disk $12.99 (ISBN 1-57594-027-2). *Nonstandard peripherals required:* 2x CD-ROM player, Sound Card, VGA monitor. *Optimal configuration:* 486 XS-33.
Hijinks & Hilarity When the Gang Meets Hamgood, Morgan's Homemade Trivia Machine.
Kidsoft, Inc.

Morgan's Trivia Machine, Jr. Sep. 1995.
Customer Support: Telephone support - free (except phone charge).
Windows 3.1. IBM & compatibles (386 DX-20) (4Mb). CD-ROM disk $12.99 (ISBN 1-57594-066-3). *Nonstandard peripherals required:* 2x CD-ROM player, Sound Card, VGA monitor. *Optimal configuration:* 486 SX-33.
Hijinks & Hilarity When the Gang Meets Hamgood, Morgan's Homemade Trivia Machine. Blister Pack Jewel Case.
Kidsoft, Inc.

Morgan's Trivia Machine, Jr. Jan. 1996.
Customer Support: Telephone support - free (except phone charge).
System 6.0.7 or higher. 256 color capable Macintosh (4Mb). CD-ROM disk $12.99 (ISBN 1-57594-103-1). *Nonstandard peripherals required:* 2X CD ROM drive, 640/480 resolution monitor.
Choose from Six Skill Levels & Three Awesome Activities Such As Mountain Climbing (on Mars!) to Learn Essential Facts about the World, Including Science, History, & Geography. Morgan's Trivia Machine, Jr. Includes More Than 700 Questions Accompanied by Spectacular Video, Stunning Animation & Hilarious Gags. Experience Fun-Filled Facts with HAM Gooo. Morgan's Home-Made Trivia Machine Jr. Is Full of Questions & Mischief.
Kidsoft, Inc.

Morgan's Trivia Machine, Jr. Jan. 1996.
Customer Support: Telephone support - free (except phone charge).
7.1. 256 color capable Mac with a 68030 processor (4Mb). CD-ROM disk $12.99 (ISBN 1-57594-103-1). *Addl. software required:* 2X CD-ROM drive, 640x480 monitor.
Choose from Six Skill Levels & Three Awesome Activities Such As Mountain Climbing (on Mars!) to Learn Essential Facts about the World, Including Science, History, & Geography. Includes More Than 700 Questions Accompanied by Spectacular Video, Stunning Animation & Hilarious Gags. Experience Fun-Filled Facts with HAMgooo. Full of Questions & Mischief.
Kidsoft, Inc.

Morningstar General Ledger: MGLS. *Version:* 3.0.8. 1992. *Compatible Hardware:* IBM PC & compatibles. *Operating System(s) Required:* PC-DOS. *Language(s):* COBOL. *Memory Required:* 526k. *General Requirements:* Hard disk, printer. *Items Included:* Disks, manuals, 90 days of support. *Customer Support:* Direct from Morningstar.
disk $295.00 single-user; $395.00 multi-user.
demo disk $50.00.
Designed to Improve Processing of Accounting Data via a Double Entry System Which Allows for Rapid Transmission of Information among Different Areas Within a Firm, May Run in a Stand-Alone Mode or Entries Can Be Automatically Fed from Other Systems. Includes Features Such As Control File Maintenance, Chart of Accounts, Trial Balance Report, Balance Sheet & Statement of Operations Including Standard, Budgetary & Comparatives, Year End Closing, & User-Definable Source Journals Such As Cash Disbursements, Cash Receipts & Payroll. Provides for Multi-Company Processing.
Morningstar Technology Corp.

Morningstar Payroll. *Version:* 1.1. 1984. *Compatible Hardware:* IBM PC & compatibles. *Operating System(s) Required:* PC-DOS. *Language(s):* COBOL. *Memory Required:* 512k. *General Requirements:* Hard disk, printer. *Items Included:* Disks, manuals, 90 days of support. *Customer Support:* Direct from Morningstar.
$295.00 single-user; $395.00 multi-user.

demo disk $50.00.
Allows for Multi-Firm Processing & May Be Used in Stand-Alone Mode or Integrated Directly into the General Ledger System. Provides for Writing Multiple Checks, State & Federal Reporting, Processing of Manual Checks, Overrides of Any Data Item for a Single Pay Period, & up to 8 Voluntary Deductions.
Morningstar Technology Corp.

Morse Code Drills. Ronald Pedowitz. *Compatible Hardware:* IBM PC, PCjr, PC XT, PC AT, Portable PC with IBM Display. *Operating System(s) Required:* DOS 1.10, 2.00, 2.10, 3.00, 3.10. *Memory Required:* IBM PCjr 256k, all others 128k.
disk $14.95 (Order no.: 6276525).
User Can Vary the Speed at Which the Code Is Sent, Vary the Pitch of the Signal, Use a Designated Key to Pause at Any Time, Observe Audio & Visual Indicators.
Personally Developed Software, Inc.

Mortgage. Dec. 1989. *Items Included:* Instruction included on disk. *Customer Support:* 90 days unlimited warranty.
MS-DOS, Windows 3.1. IBM XT, AT or compatible (512K). disk $24.95 plus $3.50 S&H (Order no.: 1077). *Addl. software required:* Lotus 1-2-3, Release 4.0 or higher. *Optimal configuration:* IBM AT, 640k RAM.
Produces Mortgage Amortization Table with Total Interest, Total Principal & Loan Balance for Each Year.
Compiled Systems.

The Mortgage Analyzer. *Version:* 1.04. Michael D. Jones. Mar. 1993. *Items Included:* 1 manual. *Customer Support:* 90 day warranty, notification of major updates.
MS-DOS. IBM PC, XT, AT & compatibles (512k). disk $25.00. *Optimal configuration:* 386 or higher, printer capable of condensed print - 15CPI or higher, hard drive.
Contains Options for Amortizaiton Schedules, Loan Qualification, Refinancing, Mortgage Acceleration, Side by Side Mortgage Comparisons, & Mortgage Related Calculators. Schedule Detail Is Monthly or Annual, Calendar or Fiscal, Cumulative or Non-Cumulative, Whole Dollars or Cents. Tax Analysis, Daily Interest, Points, etc. Save & Retrieve Multiple Clients. Fixed, Stepped, ARM.
Insight Software Solutions.

Mortgage Banking. *Version:* 1230D. *Compatible Hardware:* Sharp ZL-6100 System, ZL-6500 System. *Language(s):* Sharp Microcode. $550.00.
Computes & Discloses Standard & Balloon Mortgages with Prepaid Finance Charges & Odd Days. Both Types of Mortgages Can Be Written with a Construction Option at the Beginning; the Mortgage Is Disclosed As a Single Transaction. Computes Single-Payment Construction Loans. 4 Different Amortization Schedule Routines Provided. Finds Payment & Blended Interest Rate for Wraparound Mortgages.
P-ROM Software, Inc.

Mortgage Loan Calculator. *Version:* IBM 7.17, Macintosh 3.5. *Memory Required:* 640k. *Items Included:* Operator manual. *Customer Support:* Unlimited telephone support.
Macintosh. 3.5" disk $129.00.
IBM PC, XT, AT, PS/2 & compatibles. disk $149.00.
Qualifies Home Buyers by Loan Type, Calculation Max Loan or Minimum Income.
HMS Computer Co.

Mortgage Loans -- to Refinance or Not. *Version:* 92.6. Lawrence R. Rosen. *Items Included:* Extensive on-disk documentation. *Customer Support:* Telephone support, free.
MS-DOS. IBM PCs & PS/2 (64k). disk $89.00. *Addl. software required:* Lotus 1-2-3.
Macintosh (128k). 3.5" disk $89.00. *Addl. software required:* Excel, Claris Works or MicroSoft Works.
PRODOS, DOS 3.3. Apple II Series (64k). disk $89.00. *Addl. software required:* Appleworks.
Analysis & Decision Making Program Regarding Mortgage Loans & Refinancing.
Larry Rosen Co.

Mortgage Maker. 1982. *Compatible Hardware:* Apple II, Commodore 64, IBM PC. *Memory Required:* 64k. *General Requirements:* Printer. disk $29.00.
For Accountants, Attorneys, Brokers & Others Who Are in the Business of Arranging Financing on Monthly Payment Plans. Two Routines Calculate Amount of Monthly Payment Required for a Loan of Any Value, Term & Interest Rate, & Print Complete Amortization Schedules.
Navic Software.

The Mortgage Office. *Version:* 2.0. Aug. 1989. *Customer Support:* Free telephone support, detailed user manual.
Macintosh Plus, SE, SE30, II, IIx, IIcx (1Mb). Loan Processing module $1495.00; Loan Processing, Agent Prospecting, Management Reporting modules (single-user) $2495.00; Loan Processing, Agent Prospecting, Management Reporting modules (multi-user) $3995.00.
Complete Loan Processing & Office Automation System for Originating FNMA/FHLMC Loans. Three Functional Modules Are Fully Integrated. Only Available Through Specialized Reseller, Concept 2001, at (408) 263-2122.
Metropolis Software, Inc.

Mortgage Switch Calculator. Apr. 1985. *Compatible Hardware:* Macintosh; IBM PC, PC XT. *Memory Required:* Macintosh 128k, IBM with 1-2-3 256k, IBM with Symphony 384k. *General Requirements:* Lotus 1-2-3, or Symphony. $65.00.
Spreadsheet Template Compares the True Cost of Keeping a Current First (& Second) Mortgage Versus Refinancing with a New Mortgage. Special Features Deal with Both Fixed & Variable Interest Rate Mortgage Terms. Includes an Audio Cassette Which Provides an Introduction to the Use of the Program.
AIS Microsystems.

Moses #1. Three Rivers Software Co. *Compatible Hardware:* IBM PC, Commodore 64/128.
IBM PC. disk $29.95 (Order no.: 01006).
Commodore 64/128. disk $29.95 (Order no.: 05006).
The Greatest Part of History of All Time Is Portrayed in a Fast-Paced, Action-Packed Adventure. See the Old Testament Come Alive, Experience the Many Pitfalls & Puzzles to Make Your Mission Challenging, Like Leading the Children of Israel to the Promised Land. Designed for the Novice Adventurer, but with Enough Puzzles to Keep Even the Veterans on Their Toes.
First Row Software Publishing.

Motion Commotion. Feb. 1995. *Items Included:* CD-ROM booklet. *Customer Support:* Free technical support via phone as of release date.
MPC Windows/DOS. 386SX/25MHz or higher processor (640k). CD-ROM disk $29.95 (ISBN 1-885784-21-X, Order no.: 1037). *Optimal configuration:* 386XS/25MHz or higher processor, 1Mb of free hard drive space for sound installation, dual spin CD-ROM, 4Mb or more of RAM, DOS 3.3 or higher.
Dazzle Your Senses with More Than 100 Puzzles of Whirling Video Motion! Challenge Your Solving Skills with over 500 Video, Image Morph & Still Shot Puzzles. Mix It up with Music, On-the-Screen Help, Border Position Hints & Three Choices of Puzzle Speed. Get Scrambling with Motion Commotion, an Entertaining Twist to Traditional Puzzle Play.
Technology Dynamics Corp.

Motion Commotion: Jewel. *Items Included:* CD-ROM booklet. *Customer Support:* Free technical support via phone as of release date.
MPC/Windows/DOS. 386MHz or higher (4Mb). CD-ROM disk $29.95 (ISBN 1-885784-66-X, Order no.: 1030). *Optimal configuration:* MPC CD-ROM player, S-VGA graphics card (640x480x256 colors) with compatible monitor, MPC compliant sound card, mouse, Windows 3.1 or higher, Windows 95 compatible.
Dazzle Your Senses with More Than 100 Puzzles of Whirling Video Motion! Challenge Your Solving Skills with over 500 Video, Image Morph & Still Shot Puzzles. Mix It up with Music, On-Screen Help, Border Position Hints & Three Choices of Puzzle Speed.
Technology Dynamics Corp.

Motive Power for Mitchell. Oct. 1994. *Customer Support:* 90 days support included with purchase. After the free period support is free by Fax & $/min by phone or modem.
Windows. IBM & compatibles (8Mb). CD-ROM disk $750.00 first year, $600.00 a year after that, data updated quarterly with new CD-ROM (Order no.: MP301). *Nonstandard peripherals required:* CD-ROM Reader. *Optimal configuration:* 486-66, Windows 3.1, 2X CD Reader, laser printer. *Networks supported:* Novell Netware if CD Reader is on the server, Windows.
Uses a CD-ROM Database from Mitchell International to Provide a Quick & Easy Way to Look up Job Descriptions & Times, Recommended Service Intervals, Parts Numbers & Prices, & Display Graphics.
Computer Assistance, Inc.

Mount Everest: Quest for the Summit of Dreams. *Version:* 1.0. 1995. *Items Included:* Quest for the Summit of Dreams Documentary on VHS tape. A compelling story of the experiences of the U.S. expedition to the North side of Mt. Everest in 1994. Introduces the team, region, & risks. *Customer Support:* Toll free support line.
MS-DOS/Windows 3.1 (8Mb). Multimedia PC, Level 2. CD-ROM disk $69.95 (ISBN 0-9645603-0-5, Order no.: 95100). *Nonstandard peripherals required:* 1 Mb Video card supporting 16 bit color (64k colors). *Optimal configuration:* 486X-33 PC, 8 Mb RAM, 24 bit color.
Adventure & Travel CD-ROM. Dramatic Video Shot from Base Camp to the Summit of Mt. Everest. Stunning 24 Bit Photographs. A Wonderful & Dramatic Story Backed up by Information About Nepal & Tibet. Sections on Culture, History, Technology, Mountaineering & Suppliers of Travel Services, Equipment & Even Expedition Planning. Targeted at the Adventurer in All of Us.
Peak Media, Inc.

Mountain Pilot. *Compatible Hardware:* TRS-80. contact publisher for price.
Instant Software, Inc.

Mountain Pilot-Precision Approach Radar. *Compatible Hardware:* Apple.
contact publisher for price.
Instant Software, Inc.

TITLE INDEX

Mouse Bowling. *Compatible Hardware:* Commodore Amiga. *Items Included:* Source code. *Customer Support:* Telephone support.
3.5" disk $19.95.
Arcade Game.
Silver Software.

MouseWrite. *Version:* 2.6.8b. Steve Cochard. 1986. *Compatible Hardware:* Apple IIe with extended 80-column card, IIc, IIgs, Mouse recommended. *Operating System(s) Required:* ProDOS 8. *Language(s):* Assembly. *Memory Required:* 128k. *General Requirements:* Printer, modem.
disk $149.95 (ISBN 0-927796-22-8).
Designed Specifically for the 128K Enhanced IIe, IIc, or IIGS, & Facilitates the Writing of Anything from Memos to Manuscripts. Includes a Built-in Spell Checker, Communications, Mail Merge, Glossary Macros & More. Macintosh-Like Interface Includes a Desktop, Pull Down Menus, Multiple Open Documents, Clipboard, Ruler, Dialog Boxes, Scroll Bars, Grow Boxes, a Built-in Clock, & Even a Puzzle for Fun. Adjustable Margins & Page Sizes, Plus Full Cursor Control. All Commands Are Available at All Times with Both Mouse & Keyboard.
Roger Wagner Publishing, Inc.

Mouthpiece. Jan. 1985. *Compatible Hardware:* Commodore 64. *Language(s):* Machine.
disk $39.95 (ISBN 0-13-604257-0).
Transforms the Computer into a Smart Terminal. Features Include On-Line HELP Screen, Down- & Uploading, etc.
Prentice Hall.

Move-It. *Version:* 4.02. Nov. 1985. *Compatible Hardware:* IBM PC & compatibles. *Operating System(s) Required:* MS-DOS. *Language(s):* Assembly. *Memory Required:* 32k. *General Requirements:* Modem or cable.
disk $150.00, incl. manual.
Allows User's Computer to Communicate with Any Other Computer Regardless of Operating System As Well As Dial up Bulletin Board Systems & Information Utilities. Also Includes File Compression, Scripting System, Macro Keys, Xmodem Protocol & Compatibility with Windowing Software.
Woolf Software Systems, Inc.

Movie Magic. *Compatible Hardware:* Apple Macintosh. *Memory Required:* 512k. *General Requirements:* 2 disk drives or hard disk.
3.5" disk $595.00.
Film & Television Budgeting Program.
Screenplay Systems, Inc.

Movie Magic Scheduling/Breakdown. *General Requirements:* Two disk drives or hard disk drive. Macintosh Plus or higher (1Mb). 3.5" disk $695.00.
Movie Scheduling & Breakdown Program.
Screenplay Systems, Inc.

Movie Maker. (Creative Pastimes Ser.). Interactive Picture Systems. 1983. *Compatible Hardware:* Apple II, II+, IIe; Atari 800, 1200, 1400XL; Commodore 64; IBM PC. *Memory Required:* 16-48k.
disk $49.95 ea.
Atari. (ISBN 0-8359-4675-4).
Apple. (ISBN 0-8359-4678-9).
Commodore. (ISBN 0-8359-4679-7).
IBM. (ISBN 0-8359-4681-9).
The User Devises the Action, Sets the Scene, Creates the Actors, Directs the Action, Adds the Movement, Overlays the Sound, & Plays Back the Finished Film.
Prentice Hall.

Movie Match. *Version:* 1.1. Jan. 1989. *Customer Support:* 90 days unlimited warranty.
MS-DOS 2.0 or higher (512k). IBM PC & compatibles. disk $29.95. *Optimal configuration:* Color (EGA, CGA or VGA), printer.
Data Base of Video Tapes Cross-Indexed by Star, Date Made, Rating & Category. Data Base Has Over 5000 Tapes & 2000 Stars & Is Updated Quarterly.
Maasta Software.

The Movie Stack. *Compatible Hardware:* Apple Macintosh. *Memory Required:* 1000k. *General Requirements:* HyperCard.
Each disk. 3.5" disk $39.95.
Both disks. 3.5" disk $70.00.
Ready-Made Database Containing More Than 2,000 Movies per Disk.
Southeastern Software.

Movies. *Items Included:* Installation Guide.
IBM PC. Contact publisher for price (ISBN 0-87321-080-8, Order no.: MS2-3019).
Activision, Inc.

Movies Pack. *Items Included:* Installation Guide.
IBM PC. Contact publisher for price (ISBN 0-87321-081-6, Order no.: CDD-3019).
Activision, Inc.

Mowgli's Brother. Feb. 1995. *Items Included:* CD-ROM booklet. *Customer Support:* Free technical support via phone as of release date.
MPC/Windows. 386.25 or higher IBM compatible (4Mb). CD-ROM disk $29.95 (ISBN 1-885784-14-7, Order no.: 1202). *Optimal configuration:* MPC CD-ROM player, S-VGA graphics card (640x480x256 colors) with compatible monitor, MPC compliant sound card, mouse, Windows 3.1.
This First Story of The Jungle Book Series by English Author Rudyard Kipling Tells the Story of Mowgli, a Young Boy Raised by Wolves in the Jungle. See How Mowgli Gains Wisdom & Honor from the Great Bear Baloo. Learn about His Painful Lesson of Betrayal. Experience the Magic & Mystery of the 19th Century Indian Jungle.
Technology Dynamics Corp.

Mozart. Feb. 1995. *Items Included:* CD-ROM booklet. *Customer Support:* Free technical support via phone as of release date.
MPC/Windows. 386.25 or higher IBM compatible (4Mb). CD-ROM disk $24.95 (ISBN 1-885784-17-1, Order no.: 1233). *Optimal configuration:* MPC CD-ROM player, S-VGA graphics card (640x480x256 colors) with compatible monitor, MPC compliant sound card, mouse, Windows 3.1.
Revel in the Genius of Wolfgang Amadeus Mozart, the "Prince of Harmony." Meet the Precocious Child Whose Music Became His Life until His Early Death at 35. Explore His Biography, the Influences on His Work, & of Course, His Magnificent Musical Compositions Performed by World Class Orchestras.
Technology Dynamics Corp.

Mozart: Jewel. *Items Included:* CD-ROM booklet. *Customer Support:* Free technical support via phone as of release date.
MPC/Windows. 386MHz or higher (4Mb). CD-ROM disk $24.95 (ISBN 1-885784-68-6, Order no.: 1236). *Optimal configuration:* MPC CD-ROM player, S-VGA graphics card (640x480x256 colors) with compatible monitor, MPC compliant sound card, mouse, Windows 3.1 or higher, Windows 95 compatible.
Revel in the Genius of Wolfgang Amadeus Mozart, the "Prince of Harmony." Meet the Precocious Child Whose Music Became His Life until His Early Death at 35. Explore His Biography, the Influences on His Work, & of Course, His Magnificent Musical Compositions Performed by World Class Orchestras.
Technology Dynamics Corp.

MP System. *Version:* 3.1. 1990. *Compatible Hardware:* DEC, IBM PC & compatible. *Operating System(s) Required:* CTS 300, RSTS/E, MS-DOS. *Language(s):* DIBOL. *Memory Required:* 128k.
contact publisher for price.
Hartley Data Systems, Ltd.

MPAC: Manufacturing Planning & Control. *Version:* 1.4. W. R. McCullough. Apr. 1993. *Compatible Hardware:* UNIX compatibles. *Operating System(s) Required:* AIX, Opus, UNIX, XENIX. *Language(s):* C.
contact publisher for price.
Integrated Group of Software Modules for the Application of Automated Production & Inventory Control Techniques in the Modern Manufacturing Facility. Modules Include: Inventory Control, Order Entry, Bill of Materials, Production Control, Purchasing & Receiving, Master Scheduling, Requirements Planning, & Capacity Planning & Financials, E.D.I., Image Processing, Document Imaging, Data Collection, Database, Office Automation.
Solid State Software, Inc. (Missouri).

MPO: Managing Participation in Organizations. *Version:* 1.1. Apr. 1990. *Operating System(s) Required:* PC-DOS/MS-DOS 2.0 or higher. *Memory Required:* 256k. *Items Included:* Disk & manual; reference text optional.
Copy protected. disk $59.00 (ISBN 0-944222-01-3, Order no.: 002).
Not copy protected. disk $79.00 (ISBN 0-944222-00-5, Order no.: 001).
Diagnoses a Decision-Making or Problem-Solving Situation Encountered by a Manager & Suggests an Appropriate Method of Dealing with the Circumstance. Recommends Autocratic vs. Participative Mechanisms Depending upon the Situation. Based upon the Research of Dr. Victor H. Vroom (Yale University) & Dr. Arthur G. Jago (University of Houston).
Leadership Software, Inc.

MPS Station Management. Oct. 1985. *Operating System(s) Required:* MS-DOS, PC-DOS. *Memory Required:* 400k.
single user $12,000.00.
multi-user $15,000.00.
Includes: Attendance, Vehicle & Officer Assignments, Dispatching, Notes, Records Check & Name File, Vehicle Control & Maintenance. Dispatch Log Is Electronically Archived. Booking, Offense, IBR Reporting, Accidents, Citations & Much More.
Information Management Corp.

MRBARS. *Version:* 7.0. Jul. 1988. *Compatible Hardware:* DEC VAX; IBM PC & compatibles; Prime; Unix-based systems. *Operating System(s) Required:* PC-DOS/MS-DOS, PRIMOS, Unix, VMS. *Memory Required:* IBM 640k.
contact publisher for price.
Produces Color Bar Charts of Any Schedule Created from Any External Source. Some of the Options Include: Plans Shown - Current or Current vs. Original; Schedules - Early, Late, or Both for Each Plan or Resources; Activities - All or Selected by WBS, OBS, Date Window, Float, Completion Status, etc.; Information - Selected Description, Scheduled Dates, Duration, Float, Cost, etc.; Activities - Color Coded by WBS, OBS & Other or Critical vs. Non-Critical; Time Scales - at Top, Bottom or Both with Selected Dates & Counter Times (Work or Calendar) to Completion or into Project at User Specified Intervals.
Shirley Software Systems.

MRCS. Sep. 1985. *Compatible Hardware:* IBM PC, PC AT, PC XT & compatibles. *Operating System(s) Required:* PC-DOS, MS-DOS. *Language(s):* FORTRAN. *Memory Required:* 512k. *General Requirements:* Printer, plotter. disk $2500.00 (Order no.: MCRS).
Computes Ore Reserves & the Associated Precision of a Deposit at Any Specified Cut-Off. The Deposit Is Divided into Annual Production Volumes, Which Are Calculated from the Block Estimations of Sample Data. The Variance Correction Factor from VARCUT & the Sample Data File Are Input to Produce Global Precisions of the APV.
Geostat Systems International, Inc. (GSII).

MRP-II Manufacturing Resource Planning. *Compatible Hardware:* Apple II, IBM PC XT. *Operating System(s) Required:* CP/M, MS-DOS PC-DOS. *Language(s):* BASICA, MBASIC 5.xx (source code included). *Memory Required:* 64k. *General Requirements:* 2 disk drives, printer. disk $295.00.
Menu-Driven Program Designed for Small to Medium-Sized Manufacturers. Can Be Used for Any Job That Puts Together a Final Product from Subassemblies & Components. Includes MICROBOMP BILL OF MATERIALS Program. Computes All Assembled Costs, Projected Requirements & Scheduled Receipts, & Provides a Balanced Set up for Each Item over the Entire Planning Horizon. Route File Sequence Is Generated for Each Product Manufactured. Generates 3 Sets of Reports in 1 of 4 Options: in Quantities, at Retail Price, at Discounted Retail, or at Standard Cost. Prints Invoices & Permits User to Automatically Create Corresponding Debitor & Creditor Entries. Shipping Orders for All Ready Products & Purchase Orders for All Scheduled Purchases Are Also Printed.
Compumax, Inc.

MRPLOTA. *Version:* 7.0. Jul. 1988. *Compatible Hardware:* DEC VAX, IBM PC & compatibles, Prime, Unix-based systems. *Operating System(s) Required:* PC-DOS/MS-DOS, PRIMOS, Unix, VMS. *Memory Required:* IBM 640k.
contact publisher for price.
Produces Time Scaled, Color Coded Network Plots of Schedules Externally Created from Arrow Activity Networks. Some of the Options Include: Schedules - Early, Late, or Resources Can Be Shown; Activities - All or Selected by WBS, OBS, Date Window, Float, Completion Status & Others; Information - Selected Description, Duration, Float, & Cost; Zoning - Can Be Done with WBS, OBS, & Others; Time Scales - at Top, Bottom, or Both with Selected Dates & Counter Times (Work or Calendar) to Completion or into Project at User Specified Intervals.
Shirley Software Systems.

MRPLOTP. *Version:* 7.0. Jul. 1988. *Compatible Hardware:* DEC VAX, IBM PC & compatibles, Prime, Unix-based systems. *Operating System(s) Required:* PC-DOS/MS-DOS, PRIMOS, Unix, VMS. *Memory Required:* IBM 640k.
contact publisher for price.
Produces Time Scaled, Color Coded Network Plots of Schedules Externally Created from Precedence or Arrow Activity Networks. Some of the Options Include: Schedules - Either Early or Late Can Be Shown; Activities - All or Selected by WBS, OBS, Date Window, Float, Completion Status, & Others; Information - Selected Description, Duration, Float, & Cost; Headings - up to 18 Lines in Title Block; Time Scales - at Top, Bottom, or Both with Selected Dates.
Shirley Software Systems.

Mrs. Frisby & the Rats of NIHM. Intentional Education Staff & Robert O'Brien. *Items Included:* Program manual. *Customer Support:* Free technical support, 90 day warranty.
School ver.. Mac System 7.1 or higher. Macintosh (4Mb). 3.5" disk contact publisher for price (ISBN 1-57204-335-0). *Nonstandard peripherals required:* 256 color monitor, hard drive, printer.
Lab pack. Mac System 7.1 or higher. Macintosh (4Mb). 3.5" disk contact publisher for price (ISBN 1-57204-311-3). *Nonstandard peripherals required:* 256 color monitor, hard drive, printer.
Site license. Mac System 7.1 or higher. Macintosh (4Mb). 3.5" disk contact publisher for price (ISBN 1-57204-336-9). *Nonstandard peripherals required:* 256 color monitor, hard drive, printer.
School ver.. Windows 3.1 or higher. IBM/Tandy & 100% compatibles (4Mb). disk contact publisher for price (ISBN 1-57204-312-1). *Nonstandard peripherals required:* VGA or SVGA 640x480 resolution (256), mouse, hard drive, sound device.
Lab pack. Windows 3.1 or higher. IBM/Tandy & 100% compatibles (4Mb). disk contact publisher for price (ISBN 1-57204-337-7). *Nonstandard peripherals required:* VGA or SVGA 640x480 resolution (256), mouse, hard drive, sound device.
Site license. Windows 3.1 or higher. IBM/Tandy & 100% compatibles (4Mb). disk contact publisher for price (ISBN 1-57204-313-X). *Nonstandard peripherals required:* VGA or SVGA 640x480 resolution (256), mouse, hard drive, sound device.
This companion for young adult literature is ideal for students who don't know how to start that book report, or give that needed summary. Gentle prompts throughout the guide section of the program include Warm-up Connections, Thinking about Plot, Quoting & Noting, Keeping a Journal, If I Were ———' Responding to Questions, Using Quotations, Taking a Personal View, Write to Others, & Write a Sequel.
Lawrence Productions, Inc.

MS-BASIC. Microsoft Corp. Feb. 1984. *Operating System(s) Required:* MS-DOS. *Memory Required:* 128k. *General Requirements:* Color monitor.
$40.00 (Order no.: TI P/N 2223153-0001).
BASIC Program Features: Full Screen Editor, Keyboard Input of Keywords, RS-232C Asynchronous Communication Support, Joystick & Light Pen Support, Event Trapping, Advanced Music Capabilities & Advanced Graphics Capabilities.
Texas Instruments, Personal Productivit.

MS-BASIC Compiler. Microsoft, Inc. Feb. 1984. *Compatible Hardware:* color monitor optional. *Operating System(s) Required:* MS-DOS. *Memory Required:* 128k.
$250.00 (Order no.: TI P/N 2237362-0001).
Improves the Performance of a BASIC Program, As Much As 130 Times, with Little or No Modification.
Texas Instruments, Personal Productivit.

MS-COBOL. Microsoft, Inc. *Operating System(s) Required:* MS-DOS. *Memory Required:* 64k. *General Requirements:* 2 disk drives, printer.
$750.00 (Order no.: TI P/N 2223165-0001).
ANSI Standard & GSA Validated.
Texas Instruments, Personal Productivit.

MS DOS Graphics Screen Printing Utilities. *Items Included:* Full manual. No other products required. *Customer Support:* Free telephone support - no time limit. 30 day warranty.
MS-DOS 3.2 or higher. IBM & compatibles (512k). disk $9.95.
The Programs in This Collection Are Terminate-&-Stay-Ready Routines Which, Once Loaded, Stay Resident in Memory. They Allow You to "Dump" Your Screen to the Printer at a Press of a Key.
Dynacomp, Inc.

MS DOS Graphics: Screen Printing Utilities. 1995. *Items Included:* Full manual. *Customer Support:* Free telephone support - 90 days, 30-day warranty.
MS-DOS 3.2 or higher. 286 (584k). disk $9.95. *Nonstandard peripherals required:* CGA/EGA/VGA.
The Programs in This Collection Are Terminate-&-Stay-Ready Routines Which, Once Loaded, Stay Resident in Memory. They Allow You to "Dump" Your Screen to the Printer at a Press of a Key. The Graphics Cards Handled Are CGA, EGA, & Hercules. The Graphic Printing Devices Supported Are HP Laserjet, HP Thinkjet, Epson, Okidata 92, Okidata 192, & C. Itoh.
Dynacomp, Inc.

MS-DOS 2.1. Microsoft, Inc. *Memory Required:* 128k. *General Requirements:* 2 disk drives, printer.
$75.00 (Order no.: TI P/N 2239873-0001).
Contains a Disk Directory Structure, a Background Print Capability, Program Input & Output Redirection, Piping & User-Installable Device Drivers.
Texas Instruments, Personal Productivit.

MS-DOS 1.25. Microsoft, Inc. *Memory Required:* 64k. *General Requirements:* 2 disk drives, printer.
$40.00 (Order no.: TI P/N 2223129-0001).
Single-User Operating System That Runs on 8086/8088-Based 16-Bit Microprocessors.
Texas Instruments, Personal Productivit.

MS-FORTRAN. *Operating System(s) Required:* MS-DOS. *Language(s):* Assembly. *Memory Required:* 128k. *General Requirements:* 2 disk drives, printer.
disk $450.00 (Order no.: TI P/N 2223159-0001).
Compiler That Implements FORTRAN-77 in Microprocessor & Saves Space & Execution Time, Particularly with Mathematical Expressions. An 8087-Emulator Is Included.
Microsoft Pr.

MS-FORTRAN Compiler. Microsoft, Inc. *Operating System(s) Required:* MS-DOS. *Memory Required:* 128k. *General Requirements:* 2 disk drives, printer.
$350.00 (Order no.: SS P/N 516-620).
16-Bit Microcomputer Implementation of Science & Engineering Programming Language.
Texas Instruments, Personal Productivit.

Ms. Pac Man. *Compatible Hardware:* Atari XL/XE.
ROM cartridge $19.95 (Order no.: RX8043).
Atari Corp.

MS-Pascal. Microsoft Corp. *Operating System(s) Required:* MS-DOS with 2 disk drives & printer. *Memory Required:* 128k.
$300.00 (Order no.: TI P/N 2223171-0001 MD P/N 273373).
Texas Instruments, Personal Productivit.

MS-Pascal Compiler. Microsoft, Inc. *Operating System(s) Required:* MS-DOS. *Memory Required:* 128k. *General Requirements:* 2 disk drives, printer.
$350.00 (Order no.: SS P/N 516-639).
Generate Compact System Software.
Texas Instruments, Personal Productivit.

MSC - NASTRAN. *Version:* 68. Nov. 1993. *Customer Support:* Technical support, training class & thorough documentation. Client support available throughout the world at MSC offices.
UNIX, IBM, DEC, ULTRIX, HP, CDC, Cray, Sun, SGI, UNICOS, Convex. UNIX, IBM, DEC, ULTRIX, HP, CDC, Cray, Sun, SGI, UNICOS, Convex (8Mb). Contact publisher for price;

TITLE INDEX

leasing varies. *Addl. software required: DEC Windows. Optimal configuration: MSC/XL Plus.*
Powerful, General Purpose Finite Element Analysis Program Used by Engineers & Designers Around the World to Analyze the Stress, Vibration, & Heat Transfer Characteristics of Structures & Mechanical Components. Used in a Broad Range of Industries Including Automotive, Aerospace, & Heavy Machinery.
MacNeal-Schwendler Corp.

MSDS Form. *Version:* 2.0. Oct. 1994. *Customer Support:* 30 day satisfaction guarantee.
MS-DOS, MS-Windows. IBM PC & compatibles. disk $99.00 (Order no.: (518) 377-8854). *Addl. software required:* Word Perfect 5.1, or Word Perfect 6.1 for Windows, Word 6.0 for Windows.
Macintosh. Macintosh. 3.5" disk $99.00 (Order no.: (518) 377-8854). *Addl. software required:* Microsoft Word Version 5.0 or Microsoft Word Version 6.0 for Macintosh.
Helps User Produce 9-Section & 16-Section Material Safety Data Sheets. Provides a Template to Assist in MSDS Layout & Make Certain Necessary/Required Information Is Not Omitted. Prints Out a Professional-Looking MSDS.
Genium Publishing Corp.

MSI Access. *Version:* 1.5. Dec. 1991. *Items Included:* Manual, diskette. *Customer Support:* First 60 days free support; 1 yr. support contract available for $150. Support available via FAX, mail, on-line services.
Mac System 6 or 7. Mac Plus or higher. $95.00 Development Version; $495.00 Production Version. *Addl. software required:* 4th Dimension; Allows client applications in HyperCard, ProGraph, MPW Pascal, MPW C, Think Pascal, & Think C.
Client-Server Development Tool That Allows You to Build Client Applications That Access 4th Dimension Databases. Enables the Development of Extremely Fast Multi-User Applications with Clients Written in 4th Dimension, HyperCard, ProGraph, or C.
Metropolis Software, Inc.

MSI BASIC. *Compatible Hardware:* Apple, Commodore, IBM PC XT. *Memory Required:* 48-128k.
contact publisher for price.
Programming Language for MSI Portable Data Collection Terminals.
MSI Data Corp.

MSI Print. *Customer Support:* 800-929-8117 (customer service).
MS-DOS. Commodore 128; CP/M. disk $49.99 (ISBN 0-87007-411-3).
Full Control of Printer Characteristics for MSI Printers from Any ASCII File & Any Text Editor or Word Processor.
SourceView Software International.

MSI TMS-PC. *Compatible Hardware:* IBM PC, PC XT, PC AT. *Operating System(s) Required:* PC-DOS 2.0. *Language(s):* Pascal. *Memory Required:* 128-256k.
contact publisher for price.
Manages Communication with MSI Terminals over Ordinary Phone Lines.
MSI Data Corp.

MSI TMS-1, TME. *Compatible Hardware:* IBM PC & compatibles. *Operating System(s) Required:* PC-DOS 2.0, EDX. *Language(s):* EDL, Pascal & IBM Macro Assembly. *Memory Required:* TMS-1 186k, TME 256k. *General Requirements:* MSI Handheld Computer.
contact publisher for price.
Manages Communications with MSI HandHeld Computers over Ordinary Phone Lines in Conjunction with MSI 2741 Protocol Converter.
MSI Data Corp.

MSI UBASIC. *Compatible Hardware:* DEC VAX, M VAX, C7000. *Memory Required:* 512k.
contact publisher for price.
Programming Language for MSI Terminals.
MSI Data Corp.

M65 Astrological Chart Service. *Compatible Hardware:* Apple II, Commodore 64. *Memory Required:* Apple 48k, Commodore 64k. *General Requirements:* 2 disk drives.
disk $300.00.
Functions As a Complete Chart & Research Data Base. Suited for Professional Astrologers.
Matrix Software.

M65 Home Chart Service. *Compatible Hardware:* IBM PC.
disk $300.00.
Power Menu That Runs the Complete M65 System. Includes Many Features of Interest to Both Professional & Amateur Astrologers. (Ascendent, MC, Vertex, etc.).
Matrix Software.

The M65 Screen Module: M65C. 1984.
Compatible Hardware: Apple II+, IIe, IIc; Commodore 64, PET. *Memory Required:* 48k.
Apple II. disk $100.00 (ISBN 0-925182-33-8, Order no.: M65C).
Commodore 64. disk $100.00 (ISBN 0-925182-34-6, Order no.: M65C).
On Screen Chart Study.
Matrix Software.

MSS Payroll System. *Items Included:* On line documentation & help.
MS-DOS (640k). PC compatible. disk $495.00.
Networks supported: Mainlan.
Xenix (640k). disk $495.00.
A Multi-State &/or Multi-Company Payroll System with Multiple Departments. Stand Alone or General Ledger Integrated.
Rowlette Enterprises, Inc.

MSX Software Sampler, Vol. 1: Entertainment & Home Applications. Nicholas P. Kiefer & Kenneth Chan. Jun. 1985. *Operating System(s) Required:* MSX.
3.5" disk $29.95, incl. bk. (ISBN 0-201-15265-7).
25 Ready-to-Run BASIC Programs, Including Star Trek, Backgammon, a Paint/Draw Program, & a Music Editor. Book Contains Information about Using the Programs & Instructions on Programming MSX-Based Computers in BASIC.
Addison-Wesley Publishing Co., Inc.

MSX Software Sampler, Vol. 2: Business & Scientific Applications. Nicholas P. Kiefer & Kenneth Chan. Jun. 1985. *Operating System(s) Required:* MSX.
3.5" disk $29.95, incl. bk. (ISBN 0-201-15272-X).
25 Ready-to-Run BASIC Programs, Including a Checkbook Manager, Home Budgeting Program, Typing Tutor, Auto Maintenance Log, & Database Manager. Book Contains Information about Using the Programs & Instructions on Programming MSX-Based Computers in BASIC.
Addison-Wesley Publishing Co., Inc.

MTBASIC. *Items Included:* Bound manual. *Customer Support:* Free hotline - no time limit; 30 day limited warranty; updates are $5/disk plus S&H.
MS-DOS. IBM & compatibles (256k). disk $79.95.
You Can Write MTBASIC Code Using the Built-In Editor. As User Enters the Program, the Syntax Is Checked Line by Line. The Dialect of BASIC Used Is Similar to Microsoft BASIC, but with Some Differences (No Double Precision Mode, For Example). The Differences Usually Relate to Maximizing Speed; You Can Expect a Twenty to Fifty Fold Speed Increase over the Microsoft Interpreters. Compiling MTBASIC Is Extremely Easy. You Do Not Have to Load, Link, etc. MTBASIC Does It All for You, & Quickly (Roughly 100 Lines/Second). You Can Break Out of a Run Easily, Make a Change, & Re-Compile/Run in a Fraction of a Minute.
Dynacomp, Inc.

MT983 Emulator. *Compatible Hardware:* B-20 series, B-22. *Operating System(s) Required:* BTOS. *Language(s):* PL/M. *Memory Required:* 256k.
disk $750.00.
Allows the B20 to Emulate an MT983 Terminal, Permitting B20 Users to Interact with Applications Available to an MT983 User. These Include Electronic Mail, Calendar, Scheduler, Personal Filing System, Command & Edit Language for Burroughs Systems, Online Data Entry & Verification System, Business Planning System, etc.
Burroughs Corp.

MTOS-UX/68k, MTOS-UX/386, MTOS-UX/88k, MTOS-UX/AT 386, MTOS-UX/860, MTOS-UX/R3k. Jun. 1985. *Operating System(s) Required:* Host OS UNIX, DOS, VMS. (source code included). *Memory Required:* 16k - 35k. *Items Included:* Manuals, tech support for 3 months. *Customer Support:* Training available, telephone support, update service.
Development Kit, $5000.00 & up (Order no.: 68UX-SUXX).
Real-Time, Multi-Tasking, Multi-Processor Operating System for Industrial Control, Communications, Medical Instruments, Etc. Has Links to UNIX. Fully Configured Versions for PC.
Industrial Programming, Inc.

MTplus Tools for Pascal MTplus-86. Mel Tainiter. *Compatible Hardware:* IBM PC & compatibles, PC XT. *Operating System(s) Required:* PC-DOS 2.0 or higher. *Language(s):* Assembly (source code included). *Memory Required:* 64k.
disk $65.00 (ISBN 0-934577-01-3).
Helps Programmers Access Resources of the IBM PC & XT Directly from Pascal MTplus-86 in PC-DOS 2.0.
Softext Publishing Corp.

MTS. *Compatible Hardware:* IBM PC & compatibles. *Operating System(s) Required:* PC-DOS, MS-DOS. *Memory Required:* 320k. *General Requirements:* 2 disk drives.
disk $995.00.
Provides Complete Vector ARIMA Modeling. Includes Both Automatic & Non-Automatic Modeling. Some of the Advanced Modeling Features Offered Are: Exogonous Time Series Variables May Be Included, Automatic Model Stepdown, & Extended Matrix Method Estimation.
Automatic Forecasting Systems, Inc.

Mud Pies: Mario's Early Years, Card Shop, It's a Bird's Life. Nintendo Staff et al. Sep. 1995. *Items Included:* Set up instruction sheet, registration card. *Customer Support:* Customer support helpline 503 639-6863.
DOS. IBM PC 386 or higher (640k w/550 avail.). CD-ROM disk $34.95 Mario's Early Years (ISBN 1-887783-12-1, Order no.: 5400-8004).
Win 3.13. IBM PC (4Mb). $39.95 Card Shop.
Win 3.1. IBM PC. $39.95 It's a Bird's Life.
Self-Teaching, Entertaining, Educational Package for Children to Familiarize Them with Colors, Numbers & Reading.
Entertainment Technology.

muLISP-90. *Version:* 7.2. Albert D. Rich. Jun. 1993. *Compatible Hardware:* IBM PC & compatibles. *Operating System(s) Required:* PC-DOS/MS-DOS, OS/2. *Memory Required:* 256k. *Items Included:* Diskette(s) & Manual. *Customer Support:* Limited 90-day warranty; technical support by mail.
  Interpreter & compiler. $150.00 suggested retail price, available through dealers.
  Interpreter & compiler muLISPX M (Extended Memory Version). $300.00 suggested retail price, available through dealers.
A High Performance LISP Programming Environment for MS-DOS. Includes over 450 Common LISP Functions & Special Forms, a Multi-Window Based Editing & Debugging System, Medium & High Resolution Graphics, On-Line Tutorial & Help System, Demonstration Game Programs, Flavors Package, & Detailed Reference Manual. An Optional Native Code Compiler Can Increase the Speed of Application up to 3 Times.
Soft Warehouse, Inc. (Hawaii).

MULTI. *Version:* 1.8.6. Green Hills Software. Oct. 1992. *Items Included:* Complete documentation included. *Customer Support:* Telephone support, electronic mail support; 6 months support included with product; 1 yr. maintenance available - contact vendor for pricing.
  UNIX, SunOS. Sun-4 SPARC (4Mb). Starts at $1400.00 (Order no.: MUSPN). *Addl. software required:* X-Windows based GUI (i.e. Open Windows, Motif). *Networks supported:* RS-232, Ethernet.
  MIPS Ultrix. DECstation (4Mb). Starts at $1400.00 (Order no.: MUMPN). *Addl. software required:* Motif. *Networks supported:* RS-232, Ethernet.
  Sys V. Motorola UNIX Sys V (4Mb). Starts at $1400.00 (Order no.: MU68N). *Addl. software required:* X-Windows based GUI. *Networks supported:* RS-232, Motif.
Multi-Target, Multi-Language, Multi-Window, Multi-Process, Source Level Debugger. Can Be Used for Native or Cross Development. MULTI's Customizable X Window User Interface (OPEN LOOK) Is Easy to Use, Easy to Learn, Consistent Across Platforms & Versatile. Enables Software Developers to Simultaneously Debug Software Applications Written in Four Languages (C Plus Plus, C, Pascal, FORTRAN) As Well As Assembly Code.
Oasys, Inc.

Multi-Ad Creator. *Version:* 3.8. *Items Included:* Extensive manuals, tutorial. *Customer Support:* Technical support free for current version.
  6.0.5 or higher, recommend System 7.5. All Apple Macintosh computers with 68020 & higher processor w/at least 5Mb of dedicated RAM. 3.5" disk $995.00. *Networks supported:* Appletalk compatible.
Special Software Designed for Display Advertisement Layout in the Macintosh Production Environment. Current Version Features over 100 PICT Borders, Multiple Special Text Effects, Color-to-Color Gradient Fills, automatic Drop Shadow, & the Ability to Create & Manipulate Starbursts. Style Models & Paragraph Styles Can Be Saved So Users Can Efficiently Apply Often-Used Text Formats. Creator's Auto-Masking Capabilities Provide for Immediate Masking & Editing to White Backgrounds of Scanned Gray-Scale & 4-Color Images. Creator Performs Spot & Process Separations & Has the Ability to Save a File As EPS for Exploration. Creator Supports the Industry Standard OPI (Open Prepress Interface) Plus Improved Printer Support via PPD Printing Files.
Multi-Ad Services, Inc.

Multi-Ad Search. *Version:* 3.1. Oct. 1995. *Items Included:* Manual & tutorial. *Customer Support:* Technical support free with most current version.
  Version 6.03 or higher system software; System 7.5 recommended. All Macintosh computers (2Mb). 3.5" disk $249.00.
Graphic Cataloging & Retrieval Application for Macintosh. Search 3.1 Supports "Drag & Drop" Cataloging for EPS, TIFF, RIFF, MacPaint, JPEG, & Multi-Ad Creator Formats. Users Can Open & Search up to Ten Catalogs at once by a Variety of Criteria. Searches Can Be Performed with Several Options: and/or, Not & Searches Within Searches. Catalog Size Is Virtually Unlimited at 160,000 Plus Images per Catalog. The Multi-User Version of Search Features Monitoring & Password Protection Capabilities. In Addition, Images Can Be Edited by Launching the Application Which Created an Image from Within Search.
Multi-Ad Services, Inc.

Multi-Basic. *Compatible Hardware:* Apple II; Osborne 1; TRS-80 Model I, Model II, Model III, Model 4, Model 12, Model 16. *Operating System(s) Required:* CP/M, TRSDOS & compatibles. *Language(s):* CBASIC. *Memory Required:* TRS-80 Model I & Model III 48k; Model 4, Model 12; CP/M 52k.
  $139.00.
Designed to Provide the Speed & Power of a Compiled Language Without Sacrificing the Advantages of Interactive Debugging.
Alcor Systems.

Multi-Company. *Version:* 7.2. *Compatible Hardware:* IBM PC & compatibles. *Memory Required:* 512k. *General Requirements:* Hard disk. *Items Included:* Ring binder documentation. *Customer Support:* 1 hour telephone support included, on-site training at $75 per hour.
  $495.00 per module.
Financial/Accounting Package. Posts Recurring Transactions. Automatic Posting from Other Modules, Report Format User Definable. Wild Card. Links with External Software Programs. Password Access. Audit Trail. Error Recovery, Automatic Back-Up for Each Module. Reject Erroneous Account Numbers, On-Line Help & Source Code Available.
Lake Avenue Software.

Multi-Currency. *Version:* 5.2. 1992. *Items Included:* User Manual & reference manual. *Customer Support:* 90 day warranty.
  UNIX, VMS, DOS. All UNIX, Digital VAX, IBM compatible (512k). Contact vendor for price. *Networks supported:* Novell.
Allows Users to Issue Purchase Orders & Received Invoices in an Unlimited Number of Foreign Currencies. The Package Will Convert Foreign to Local Currency & Provides for Freight Handling.
MCBA, Inc.

Multi-Currency General Ledger. (International Finance Ser.). Spot Systems, Inc. Staff. Jun. 1983. *Compatible Hardware:* IBM PC, PC XT, PC AT, PS/2, 386, 486 & compatibles. *Operating System(s) Required:* MS-DOS 3.0 & higher, Windows. *Language(s):* Compiled BASIC. *Memory Required:* 640k. *General Requirements:* Hard disk.
  Base system. Contact publisher for price. *Networks supported:* LAN-Novell, Token Ring.
The Spot System's Multi-Currency General Ledger System Captures Transactions in Their Original Currency, Revalues Account Balances to Whatever Currency Is Specified, Consolidates Information for Position & Financial Reports, & Produces Detailed Statements of Due to, Due from, & Customer Reporting. Program Is Menu-Driven, with Fill-in-the-Blanks Data Entry Forms. All Foreign Currency Transactions Are Captured in Original Currency & Stored in Individual Accounts by Currency Type. Revaluation of Current Foreign Exchange Rates Can Be Performed As Often As Needed. Both Stand-Alone & Network Versions Are Available. Produces Swift 950 Messages & Customer Statements.
Spot Systems, Inc.

Multi-Layer Dielectric Optical Filter Design. *Compatible Hardware:* HP 9000 Series 200, 300, 520, 9845. *Language(s):* BASIC (source code included).
  $295.00.
Series of Programs Which Calculate the Transmission & Reflection of Multi-Layer Dielectric Filters.
James Assocs.

Multi-Level Financing Calculations. *Compatible Hardware:* Altos Series 5-15D, Series 5-5D, 580-XX, ACS8000-XX; IBM PC with 2 disk drives, PC XT, & compatibles; Xerox 820 with 2 disk drives, Zilog MCZ-250. *Operating System(s) Required:* CP/M, MP/M, PC-DOS, MS-DOS.
  contact publisher for price (Order no.: MORTGAGE).
Automates the Calculations of Interest & Principal Payments for Complex Loan Situations. Calculations Can Be Made Using Such Methods As Level Payment Amortization, Interest Only Loans, Level Principal Payments, Construction Loan Draw-Downs, or a Combination of All of These. Determines Interest, Principal, & Remaining Loan Balance.
Coopers & Lybrand.

Multi-Lingual Scholar. *Version:* 4.0. Jan. 1992. *Items Included:* Font editor, 1 spiral bound manual. *Customer Support:* Free telephone support.
  DOS 5.0 Plus. IBM PC & compatibles (1Mb). disk $695.00. *Nonstandard peripherals required:* Graphics.
Word Processing for DOS Based PC Users That Need to Write in Non-Latin Alphabets or Multiple Alphabets. Supports Arabic, Greek, Hebrew, Russian & Most Other Languages.
Gamma Productions, Inc.

Multi-Lingual Word Processor: The Math & Science Disk. 1984. *Compatible Hardware:* Apple II, II+, IIe, IIc; Franklin Ace. *Operating System(s) Required:* Apple DOS 3.3. *Language(s):* BASIC, Machine. *Memory Required:* 64k. *Customer Support:* Help at (305) 977-0686.
  disk $29.95, incl. manual (ISBN 0-87284-006-9).
Provides a Variety of Math & Science Symbols for the Keyboard.
The Professor Corp.

Multi Media Bulletin Board System: MMBBS. *Version:* 1.2. Jan. 1996. *Items Included:* Multi Media Terminal software for remote PC, Amiga, freely distributable, manual. *Customer Support:* Free upgrades 1st yr.; custom modifications $10 min..
  Workbench 1.3 or higher. Any Amiga (1Mb). 3.5" 880k disk $25.00 (Order no.: AMB). *Nonstandard peripherals required:* Hayes-compatible modem, telephone line. *Optimal configuration:* 2nd floppy or hard drive, fast modem.
  MS-DOS 5.0 or higher. PC-286 or higher (1Mb). 3.5" 720k or 5.25" 1.2M disk $30.00 (Order no.: PMB). *Nonstandard peripherals required:* Hayes-compatible modem, telephone line. *Optimal configuration:* 2nd floppy or hard drive, fast modem.
Plain Text BBS. Graphics, Animation, Audio. Optional Modules Available Separately: File

TITLE INDEX

Transfers, News Items, Home Pages, EMAIL. Go On-Line to Our BBS: 1-612-825-5628, Noon-Midnight CST, 300/14400,N,8,1 for Details.
United ProCom Systems.

Multi Media Terminal: MMTERM. Version: 1.2. Jan. 1996. Items Included: List of current Multi Media Bulletin Board Systems, manual. Customer Support: Free upgrades 1st yr.; custom modifications $5 min..
MS-DOS 5.0 or higher. Any PC-286 or higher (1Mb). 3.5" 720k or 5.25" 1.2M disk $10.00 (Order no.: PMT). Nonstandard peripherals required: Hayes-compatible modem, telephone line. Optimal configuration: Fast modem, VGA graphics video.
Workbench 1.3Plus. Any Amiga (512k). 3.5" 880k disk $10.00 (Order no.: AMT). Nonstandard peripherals required: Hayes-compatible modem, telephone line. Optimal configuration: Fast modem, 1Mb Plus RAM.
Standalone Non-Distributable Version of Terminal Software Included in Our Amiga & PC Multi Media Bulletin Board System. Does Automated File Transfers, etc. to/from a PC or Amiga Multi Media BBS. Call Our BBS: 1-612-825-5628, Noon-Midnight CST, 300/14400,N,8,1 for Details.
United ProCom Systems.

Multi-Pro: Accounts Payable. Version: 4.0. John K. Quick. Feb. 1993. Items Included: Executable code & supporting documentation. Customer Support: 90 day warranty; onsite/inhouse training; user groups; optional Annual Maintenance Agreement at 15% of current list; toll free support line included in Annual Maintenance; consulting, systems integration, research & product customization 75/hr.
DOS & Novell, Token Ring. IBM PC, LAN or PC compatibles (1Mb). Contact publisher for price. Optimal configuration: PC 386/33 w/ 120Mb 1Mb. If using LAN environment 486/66 & 4+ Mb memory. Disk based on transaction history & addition of other applications. Networks supported: Novell & Token Ring.
IBM SSP. System 36 (256k). Contact publisher for price. Addl. software required: Query & Display Write optional, PC Support optional. Optimal configuration: 1Mb memory w/ minimum 105Mb disk. (Dependent on history & transaction base) (2) terminals & 200+ 1pm printer.
IBM OS400. AS400 (8Mb). Contact publisher for price. Addl. software required: Office Vision & PC Support optional. Optimal configuration: Memory dependent on # users. 200+ 1pm printer, disk sufficient to support transaction history base, PC Support, Office Vision.
Accounts Payable System That Supports Multiable Companies, Handles Standard Payables Check Writing & Reconciliation. Supports up to 5 Checking Accounts per Company. Handles Imprest/Trust Accounts/Allocation Tables & Inter-Company Relationships (Parent, Subsidizing). Great for Home-Owners Associations, Property Management, Country Clubs & Resorts.
Information Systems Design of Stuart, Inc.

Multi-Pro: Club Management & Accounts Receivable. Version: 3.4. John K. Quick. Jun. 1993. Items Included: Executable code & supporting documentation. Customer Support: 90 day warranty; onsite/inhouse training; user groups; optional Annual Maintenance Agreement at 15% of current list; toll free support line included in Annual Maintenance; consulting, systems integration, research & product customization 75/hr.
DOS & Novell; Token Ring. IBM PC, LAN or PC compatible (1Mb). Contact publisher for price. Optimal configuration: PC 386/33 w/ 120Mb 1Mb. If using LAN environment 486/66 & 4+ Mb memory. Disk based on transaction history & addition of other applications. Networks supported: Novell, Token Ring.
IBM SSP. System 36 (256k). Contact publisher for price. Addl. software required: Query & Display Write optional, PC Support optional. Optimal configuration: 1Mb memory w/ minimum 105Mb disk. (dependent on history & transaction base) (2) terminals & 200+ 1pm printer.
IBM OS400. AS400 (8Mb). Contact publisher for price. Addl. software required: Office Vision & PC Support optional. Optimal configuration: Memory dependent on # users. 200+ 1pm printer, disk sufficient to support transaction history base, PC Support, Office Vision.
Private Membership Data Base, Billing & Receivable System That Tracks Member Charges, Special Assessments, Dues Assessments, Spending Habits & Guest Tracking (Visits). Supports Food Minimums, Late Fees, Member Discounts, Statements Generation & up to Four Alternate Billing/Contact Addresses.
Information Systems Design of Stuart, Inc.

Multi-Pro: General Ledger. Version: 5.0. John Quick. Nov. 1992. Items Included: Executable code & supporting documentation. Customer Support: 90 day warranty; onsite/inhouse training; user groups; optional Annual Maintenance Agreement at 15% of current list; toll free support line included in Annual Maintenance; consulting, systems integration, research & product customization 75/hr.
DOS & Novell, Token Ring. IBM PC, LAN or PC compatibles (1Mb). Contact publisher for price. Optimal configuration: PC 386/33 w/ 120Mb 1Mb. If using LAN environment 486/66 & 4+ Mb memory. Disk based on transaction history & addition of other applications. Networks supported: Novell & Token Ring.
IBM SSP. System 36 (256k). Contact publisher for price. Addl. software required: Query & Display Write optional, PC Support optional. Optimal configuration: 1 Mb memory w/ minimum 105Mb disk. (dependent on history & transaction base) (2) terminals & 200+ 1pm printer.
IBM OS400. AS400 (8Mb). Contact publisher for price. Addl. software required: Office Vision & PC Support optional. Optimal configuration: Memory dependent on # users. 200+ 1pm printer, disk sufficient to support transaction history base, PC Support, Office Vision.
General Ledger System That Fully Supports Multiable Companies. Highest Productivity in Real Estate Fee Management Companies. Supports Unlimited Years of General Ledger History & Budget for Accounting. Handles Consolidations, Partnership Financials & Has Complete Financial Report Writer. Job Cost Reports Can Be Separated for Project Level Developers. Currently Used in Property Management, Resorts & Country Clubs.
Information Systems Design of Stuart, Inc.

Multi-Pro: Payroll. Aug. 1993. Items Included: Executable code & supporting documentation. Customer Support: 90 day warranty; onsite/inhouse training; user groups; optional Annual Maintenance Agreement at 15% of current list; toll free support line included in Annual Maintenance; consulting, systems integration, research & product customization 75/hr.
DOS & Novell, Token Ring. IBM PC, LAN or PC compatibles (1Mb). Contact publisher for price. Optimal configuration: PC 386/33 w/ 120Mb 1Mb. If using LAN environment 486/66 & 4 Mb memory. Disk based on transaction history & addition of other applications. Networks supported: Novell & Token Ring.
IBM SSP. System 36 (256k). Contact publisher for price. Addl. software required: Query & Display Write optional, PC Support optional. Optimal configuration: 1Mb memory w/ minimum 105Mb disk. (Dependent on history & transaction base) (2) terminals & 200 1pm printer.
IBM OS400. AS400 (8Mb). Contact publisher for price. Addl. software required: Office Vision & PC Support optional. Optimal configuration: Memory dependent on # users. 200+ 1pm printer, disk sufficient to support transaction history base, PC Support, Office Vision.
Services Multi-Companies Within One Entity. Handles All Mandatory Deductions, Plus Ninety-Nine User Defined Other Pay & Voluntary Deductions. Deductions Can Be Tax Exempt. Any Employee Can Be Tax Exempt. Earnings & Deductions History Kept in Detail & Summary Format for M.T.D., 1st, 2nd, 3rd, & 4th Quarters & Y.T.D. User Maintained Tax Tables. Capable of Running Weekly, Bi-Weekly, Semi-Monthly or Monthly Payroll by Any or All Categories. Simple Retrieval of History Information.
Information Systems Design of Stuart, Inc.

Multi-Pro: Point-of-Sale. Version: 2.0. John Quick. Jun. 1993. Items Included: Executable code & supporting documentation. Customer Support: 90 day warranty; onsite/inhouse training; user groups; optional Annual Maintenance Agreement at 15% of current list; toll free support line included in Annual Maintenance; consulting, systems integration, research & product customization 75/hr.
DOS & Novell, Token Ring. IBM PC, LAN or PC compatibles (1Mb). Contact publisher for price. Optimal configuration: PC 386/33 w/ 120Mb 1Mb. If using LAN environment 486/66 & 4 Mb memory. Disk based on transaction history & addition of other applications. Networks supported: Novell & Token Ring.
IBM SSP. System 36 (256k). Contact publisher for price. Addl. software required: Query & Display Write optional, PC Support optional. Optimal configuration: 1Mb memory w/ minimum 105Mb disk. (Depen6ent on history & transaction base) (2) terminals & 200 1pm printer.
IBM OS400. AS400 (8Mb). Contact publisher for price. Addl. software required: Office Vision & PC Support optional. Optimal configuration: Memory dependent on # users. 200 1pm printer, disk sufficient to support transaction history base, PC Support, Office Vision.
Retail/Inventory Management Systems That Handles Interface to a Member or Customer Systems. Handles Cash/Charge Account/Credit Card Gift Certificates/Automatic Discounts/Line Item Discounts. Interface to Electronic Cash Drawers & Receipt Printers. Has Price & Inventory.
Information Systems Design of Stuart, Inc.

Multi-Pro: Resort Management. 1982. Compatible Hardware: IBM S/36 /AS400. Operating System(s) Required: SSP/OS400. Language(s): RPG. Memory Required: 256k. Customer Support: Annual Maintenance & Support Agreement available which includes training/installation support; toll-free software support line & more.
$12500.00.
Provides Centralized Control for Management Resorts. Provides an On-Line Reservation Board for Viewing Unit Availability. Flexible Unit Rate Determination. Efficient Front Desk Operations & Reservations Process. Owner Accounting/Check Disbursement. Bookings for Groups/Conventions.
Information Systems Design of Stuart, Inc. (ISD).

Multi-Pro: Tee Time Reservations. Items Included: Operator manual. Customer Support: Annual maintenance & support agreement

available.
DOS. IBM PC & compatible (640k). $2995.00 for 18 holes; $3995.00 for 36 holes; $500.00 each additional 18 holes.
SSP. IBM System 36 (256k). $4000.00 for 18 holes; $2000.00 for next 36 holes; $1000.00 each additional 18.
OS400. AS400 (4Mb). $5000.00 for 18 holes; $2500.00 for next 36 holes; $1000.00 each additional 18.
Supports Unlimited Advance Tee-Time Scheduling, Allows Three Time Frames per Day, Customizes Intervals on Daily, Weekly, or Monthly Basis. Schedules First & Tenth Tees, Supports Nine Hole Play, Generates Confirmation. Allows Special Event Reservations. Supports Rebate Tracking for Hotel Accounts & Tracks Travel Agent Discounts.
Information Systems Design of Stuart, Inc. (ISD).

Multi-State-Local Payroll. *Version:* 4.0. *Operating System(s) Required:* MS-DOS, PC-DOS. *Language(s):* Compiled Microsoft COBOL. *Memory Required:* 128k. *Customer Support:* Available.
Contact publisher for price.
Allows Concurrent Processing of Payrolls for Multiple States & Localities with Employer Liability Reports & Check Writing. Source Code Is Included.
MBA Business Accounting Software.

Multi-Variable Regression Analysis. Jun. 1985. *Compatible Hardware:* TRS-80 Model I Level II, Model III, Model 4; IBM PC & compatibles. *Operating System(s) Required:* TRSDOS, MS-DOS. *Language(s):* BASIC, Compiled BASIC (source code included). *Memory Required:* TRS-80 disk 32k, MS-DOS 128k. *Items Included:* Disk & 46-page manual. *Customer Support:* Free.
TRS-80 or MS-DOS. disk $25.00.
Statistical Package That Does Multi-Variable Regression. Data Can Be Edited & Added. Handles up to 90 Variables & 9999 Observations. Variables Can Be Changed & Named. Has Precise Algorithms, Double Precision, Transformations, & Graphics.
Hinrichs Software.

MultiClip. *Version:* 3.1. *Items Included:* Disks, manual & addendums. *Customer Support:* Free unlimited phone technical support, FAX & modem service. America Online, CompuServe, Applelink.
Macintosh System 6.0.5 & higher. Mac Plus & higher (1Mb). 3.5" disk $149.00. *Optimal configuration:* Mac Plus 6.0.5 1Mb, 7.0x 2Mb RAM with hard drive. *Networks supported:* Yes.
Clipboard & Scrapbook Enhancement Utility. It Allows a User to Have Multiple Clipboards "ClipFrames" & Scrapbooks, Access Them Instantly, Cut/Copy, & Paste, Edit or Select Parts of Elements Cut or Copied to the Clipboard, View Clipboard Contents at Different Enlargement Settings & Transfer Multiple Clipboard Contents to the Scrapbook at Any Time. MultiClip Is Easy to Use & Works Transparently with All Popular Applications. It Is Not Copy Protected, & On-Line Help Is Always Available. System 7 Compatible, Including Balloon Help & Support for Sound.
Olduvai Corp.

Multicomponent Separations Process. *Items Included:* Full manual. No other products required. *Customer Support:* Free telephone support - no time limit, 30 day warranty.
MS-DOS 3.2 or higher. IBM & compatibles (512k). disk $979.95. *Optimal configuration:* IBM, MS-DOS 3.1 or higher, 640k RAM, hard disk, & CGA/EGA/VGA (or compatible) graphics capability, & a math coprocessor.
Simulate the Separation of Feeds of up to 50 Components in Columns of up to 100 Stages with This Powerful Analysis Tool. You May Choose the VLE Method Most Appropriate (SRK, Peng-Robinson, Grayson-Streed, Chao-Seader, UNI-QUAC, Wilson, Van Lear, NRTL, & UNIFAC), & MSP Will Select the Most Appropriate Algorithm. The Inside-Out or Boston Method Is Used for Petrochemical, Refining, & Natural Gas Applications.
Dynacomp, Inc.

Multicomponent Separations Process. 1995. *Items Included:* Full manual. *Customer Support:* Free telephone support - 90 days, 30-day warranty.
MS-DOS 3.2 or higher. 286 (584k). disk $979.95. *Nonstandard peripherals required:* CGA/EGA/VGA.
demo disk $5.00.
Simulate the Separation of Feeds of up to 50 Components in Columns of up to 100 Stages with This Powerful Analysis Tool. You May Choose the VLE Method Most Appropriate (SRK, Peng-Robinson, Grayson-Streed, Chao-Seader, UNIQUAC, Wilson, Van Laar, NRTL, & (UNIFAC), & MSP Will Select the Most Appropriate Algorithm. The Inside-Out or Boston Method Is Used for Petrochemical, Refining, & Natural Gas Applications.
Dynacomp, Inc.

MultiCurrency Aware. *Version:* 2.32. *General Requirements:* Hard disk drive.
Macintosh Plus or higher. 3.5" disk $1995.00.
General Ledger.
Database International, Inc.

MultiDisk. *Items Included:* 24-page manual. *Customer Support:* Technical support 713-353-1510, 90-day repair or replacement of faulty manual or defective diskette.
MacODOS 5.0 or higher (512k). Macintosh 512KE or higher. disk $69.95. *Networks supported:* Most AppleTalk including AppleShare, TOPS & MacServe.
Ultimate Macintosh Disk Partitioning Program. User Can Partition Any Disk into Multiple Disks. Each Partition Is Just Like Original Disk. Partitions Can Be Created As Resizable, Password Protected & Encrypted. Grouping Files into Partitions Increases Overall Disk Performance & Locking Partitions Adds Security Against Viruses. Features Addition or Deletion of Partitions Without Disk Reinitialization, Convenient Access to Partitions Through Desk Accessory, Password Protection & More.
ALSoft, Inc.

MULTIDOS. Vernon Hester. 1981. *Compatible Hardware:* TRS-80 Model Model I, Model III, Model 4. *Memory Required:* 32k.
disk $89.95.
Disk-Operating System Designed As an Alternate to TRS-DOS. Comes with Utilities for Copying & Purging Files, a Complete ZAP Program, 40 Library Commands, & Enhancements to Microsoft BASIC. Compatible with Other TRS-80 DOS's, & (in Model 4 Version) with MULTIDOS 80/64.
Alpha Bit Communications, Inc.

MultiDOS. *Version:* 1.7. *Compatible Hardware:* TRS-80 Model I, Model III, Model 4.
Model 4. disk $99.95 (Order no.: D4MD).
Model I. disk $89.95 (Order no.: D1MD).
Model III. disk $89.95 (Order no.: M3MD).
Will Read Most Diskettes Created by Popular TRS-DOS-Like Operating Systems.
The Alternate Source.

MultiExpress for DOS: Data Communications Software. *Version:* 2.20. Apr. 1992. *Items Included:* Softback reference manual. *Customer Support:* Toll free technical support, 2 year limited warranty.
DOS. PC, PC XT, PC AT, 386, 486 (640k). disk $199.00 (Order no.: ME-DOS). *Optimal configuration:* 386, DOS 5.0, 1M, Multi-Tech ISI board (ISI552M), Multi-Tech MultiModemII MT2834BA or MultiModem U (MultiModem MU) or MultiModem MT2834BC, MultiExpress. *Networks supported:* Novell IPX, NetBIOS on all others.
A Combined Asynchronous Dial-In/Dial-Out Data Communications Software & Remote-Control Software. The Remote-Control Portion Consists of Two Programs MEREMOTE & MEHOST. They Operate over a Variety of Communications Interfaces (e.g., Serial Ports (COM1-COM4), Multi-Tech ISI Boards, Asynchronous Communications Servers with INT-6B (MCSI) Support, & Peer-to-Peer over IPX or NetBIOS LANs.
Multi-Tech Systems, Inc.

MultiExpress for Windows: Communications Software. *Version:* 3.00. Sep. 1992. *Items Included:* Softback reference manual. *Customer Support:* Toll-free technical support, two year limited warranty.
Windows 3.1x. PC AT, 386, 486. disk $149.00 (Order no.: MEW). *Addl. software required:* Windows 3.1. *Optimal configuration:* 386, DOS & Windows, Multi-Tech MultiModemII MT2834BA or MultiModem U (MultiModem MU) or MultiModem MT2834BC, MultiExpress for Windows, 600k disk space.
Designed for the Windows Environment, Provides Standard File Transfer Protocol Support & Standard Terminal Emulation Support, under a User-Friendly Interface. Also Offers Programmable Function Keys; Supports CTS/RTS & XON/XOFF Flow Control; Tool Bar; Scroll Mode; & Extensive Script Language.
Multi-Tech Systems, Inc.

MultiExpressFAX for DOS: Facsimile Software. *Version:* 3.30. Jul. 1992. *Items Included:* FAX command reference manual, FAX reference manual. *Customer Support:* Toll free technical support, 2 year limited warranty.
DOS. PC, PC XT, PC AT, 386, 486 (640k). disk $99.00 (Order no.: MEFAX). *Nonstandard peripherals required:* Multi-Tech Class 2 FAX/data modem. *Optimal configuration:* 386, DOS 5.0, 1M, Multi-Tech MultiModemII 2834BA or MultiModem U (MultiModem MU) or MultiModem MT2834BC or MultiExpress FAX.
Send/Receive FAX Software. It Operates with All Multi-Tech FAX/Data Modems & Some Class 2 FAX Cards & Modems. It Provides Time Scheduling of FAXES, Send by Individual or Group, FAX Activity Log & Status Reporting, View FAX Utility & FAX from Application.
Multi-Tech Systems, Inc.

MultiExpressFAX for Windows: Facsimile Software. *Version:* 3.00. Jun. 1993. *Items Included:* Reference manual in 3-ring binder. *Customer Support:* Toll-free technical support, two year limited warranty.
Windows 3.1x. PC AT, 386, 486 or higher & compatibles. disk $99.00 (Order no.: MEWFAX). *Addl. software required:* Windows 3.1x. *Optimal configuration:* 386, DOS & Windows, Multi-Tech MultiModemII, MT2834BA, MultiModem MU (Pocket Modem), MultiModem MT2834BC or MultiExpress FAX for Windows.
Communications Package Designed for the Windows Environment, Providing Complete Facsimile Operation under a User-Friendly Interface. MEWFAX Can Be Installed As a Stand-Alone. Users Are Able to Send & Receive Faxes; Log, Review & Schedule Faxes. Users Create Phone Books of Individuals & of Groups.
Multi-Tech Systems, Inc.

MultiGantt. *Version:* 2.0. 1989. *Items Included:* 300-page user manual. *Customer Support:* Onsite training available $750.00/day plus expenses.
MS-DOS. IBM PC, PC XT, PC AT, PS/2 & compatibles. disk $295.00. *Nonstandard peripherals required:* Dot matrix printer, laser printer or pen printer required.
Graphics Package That Creates Time-Scaled Network Diagrams & Gantt Charts From Data Created by Microsoft Project 4.0 or SuperProject Expert. Graphics May Be Plotted on Transparency Film for Group Presentations, or Plotted or Printed to Be Included in Reports.
SofTrak Systems.

Multilayer Interference. *Items Included:* Bound manual. *Customer Support:* Free hotline - no time limit; 30 day limited warranty; updates are $5/disk plus S&H.
MS-DOS 2.0 or higher. IBM & compatibles (128k). disk $49.95.
Designing & Evaluating the Optical Properties of Multilayer Films. For Each Layer (up to 50), You Supply the Parameters of Layer Thickness & Real & Imaginary Refractive Index. Also, You Specify the Angle of Incidence, Substrate Refractive Index (Real & Imaginary), Input Medium Index, Polarization, & Vacuum Wavelength. User May Choose to Have Any One of These Parameters Automatically Vary (i.e., Stepped from Low to High in Chosen Increments). The Results Calculated Are the Power Reflected, Transmitted, & Absorbed; the Reflection or Transmission Amplitude & Phase; & Principal Azimuth & Principal Angle of Incidence (for Ellipsometry).
Dynacomp, Inc.

Multilayer Thin Film Interference Program: (MIP). *Version:* 2.23. Oct. 1985. *Items Included:* Documentation in the form of a users guide. *Customer Support:* 90 days unlimited warranty, telephone support.
PC-DOS, MS-DOS 2.0 or higher (256k). IBM PC, PC XT, PC AT, PS/2, or compatible. $179.00. *Optimal configuration:* PC with 256k RAM.
Easy-to-Use Design Tool for the Study of Dielectric Mirrors & A/R Coatings, Reflection Characteristics of Thin Evaporated or Sputtered Films, & Ellipsometric Evaluation of Layered Structures. The Program Provides a Convenient Menu-Drive, Data Entry Format.
Sound Decisions.

Multilinear Regression. *Compatible Hardware:* Apple II Applesoft; Macintosh; IBM PC. *Memory Required:* 48k, IBM 128k, Macintosh 512k.
disk $29.95, include manual.
Capable of Treating Multi-Variate Situations with No Limit on the Number of Dimensions.
Dynacomp, Inc.

Multilingual CAT. Apr. 1994. *Items Included:* Included in the IBM CIRC/CAT manual 428 pg. 3 ring binder. *Customer Support:* Guaranteed 2 hr call-back; 1st year of support included with program purchase; toll-free 1-800 number; modem support; program updates & manual revisions; replacement program disks if necessary; subscription to the WUG Letter, 30 day money back guarantee.
MS-DOS. IBM or compatible PC-Based computer, DOS 3.0 or higher (640k). 3.5" disk $995.00 ea. (Spanish or French) (ISBN 0-927875-37-3, Order no.: 1240 SPANISH; 1260 FRENCH). *Nonstandard peripherals required:* Epson or compatible printer with tractor feed, barwand, & keyboard. 2Mb hard drive space. *Optimal configuration:* 486 or higher processor, MS-DOS 5.0 or higher, 1Mb RAM, 2Mb hard disk space for every 1,000 MARC records in database. *Networks supported:* Winnebago LAN, Novell, ICLAS, & LANtastic.
5.25" disk $995.00 ea. (Spanish or French) (ISBN 0-927875-38-1, Order no.: 1250 SPANISH; 1270 FRENCH).
Allows Patrons to View the On-Line Catalog Search Screen Prompts in up to Three Languages: Spanish, French, or English. Spanish & French Language Modules Are Purchased Separately & English Is Included with Any CAT Purchase. The Module Interfaces with Winnebago CAT 5.1 for IBM or Compatibles. Multilingual CAT Supports Referenced Words.
Winnebago Software Company.

Multilingual On-Line Catalog - French. *Version:* 5.1. 1994. *Items Included:* Manual. *Customer Support:* One year of CSAP is provided at N/C; 30 day no risk guarantee.
MS-DOS. IBM & compatibles (640k). 5.25" disk $995.00 (ISBN 0-927875-38-1, Order no.: 1260). *Addl. software required:* Winn CAT. *Optimal configuration:* Same as Winn CAT. *Networks supported:* Netbios or IPX compatible.
3.5" disk $995.00 (ISBN 0-927875-37-3, Order no.: 1260).
An Optional Add-On Feature That Interfaces with Winnebago CAT. Search Screens & Command Key Displays Are Provided in Other Languages for Patrons to Use in Addition to English. A Function Key Allows User the Option to Display Search Results in Language They Are Familiar With.
Winnebago Software Co.

Multilingual On-Line Catalog - Spanish. *Version:* 5.1. 1994. *Items Included:* Manual. *Customer Support:* One year of CSAP is provided at N/C; 30 day no risk guarantee.
MS-DOS. IBM & compatibles (640k). 5.25" disk $995.00 (ISBN 0-927875-44-6, Order no.: 1240). *Addl. software required:* Winn CAT. *Optimal configuration:* Same as Winn CAT. *Networks supported:* Netbios or IPX compatible.
3.5" disk $995.00 (ISBN 0-927875-43-8, Order no.: 1240).
An Optional Add-On Feature That Interfaces with Winnebago CAT. Search Screens & Command Key Displays Are Provided in Spanish for Patrons to Use As a Second Language. A Function Key Allows User the Option to Display Search Results in Language They Are Familiar With.
Winnebago Software Co.

Multilingual Online Catalog. 1994. *Items Included:* Manual. *Customer Support:* 1 year free customer support including 800 support & our 2 hour call-back guarantee.
MS-DOS. IBM PC & compatibles (640k). French $995.00; Spanish $995.00.
Lets Patrons View the Online Catalog Search Screen in English, French or Spanish (French & Spanish Are Sold Separately). Integrates with Winnebago CAT. Patrons May Enter Key Words or Phrases in Other Languages, No Matter Which Language Is Selected for Display.
Winnebago Software Co.

Multilingual Word Processor. *Items Included:* Bound manual. *Customer Support:* Free hotline - no time limit; 30 day limited warranty; updates are $5/disk plus S&H.
MS-DOS 2.0 or higher. IBM & compatibles (256k). disk $99.95. *Nonstandard peripherals required:* Color graphics adapter (CGA, EGA, or equivalent), & an Epson or Epson-compatible graphics printer (e.g, IBM Prowriter).
Produce Text in Spanish, French, Italian, Portuguese, Rumanian, Russian, Modern Greek, German, Arabic, & Hebrew, Including Accents. All of These Can Be Included in Any Line of Text at the Same Time. Keytops Are Provided Which Contain All of the Letters Corresponding to All of the Above Languages. Keytop Placement Is Kept Close to English (e.g., "Alpha" Is Located at the "A" Key), to Make It Easy to Find the Keys. The Basic Word Processing Features Include: Underlining, Paragraph Reformatting, Search-&-Replace, Block Delete & Move, Variable Justification, Page up & Page down, Home, Page Length, etc.
Dynacomp, Inc.

MULTILOG. *Version:* 6. David Thissen. 1993. *Items Included:* Manual. *Customer Support:* Free technical support, 90 day limited warranty.
MS-DOS. IBM & compatibles. disk $200.00 (ISBN 1-56321-058-4).
3.5" disk $200.00 (ISBN 1-56321-059-2).
3.5" disk $270.00 386 DOS Extender Version (ISBN 1-56321-109-2).
158p. manual $30.00 (ISBN 1-56321-121-1).
Employs Item Response Theory (IRT) to Perform Analysis & Test Scoring for Multiple Category Items. Provides Item Parameter Estimation & Subject Scoring under Four Different Multiple Category Logistic Models.
Lawrence Erlbaum Assocs., Software & Alternate Media, Inc.

MultiMagic. *Compatible Hardware:* Apple Macintosh. *Memory Required:* 512k.
3.5" disk $99.95.
Multifinder Enhancement That Allows Users to Configurate Multiple Sets of Application Programs & Desk Accessories.
Magnus Corp.

MultiMate. Multimate International. *Compatible Hardware:* HP 150 Touchscreen. *Memory Required:* 384k.
3.5" disk $495.00 (Order no.: 45424A).
Full Function Word Processing with Training Lessons, a Spelling Checker, & Merge Printing Capabilities. Reformats Text As You Edit, Provides In-Document Math Capability, etc.
Hewlett-Packard Co.

The MultiMate Advantage. Graham. 1987. *Compatible Hardware:* IBM PC & compatibles. *General Requirements:* Printer, MultiMate.
disk $29.50 (Order no.: W188-1).
Text/Workbook & Template Diskette Tutorial to Be Used with MultiMate Word Processing Software.
South-Western Publishing Co.

MultiMate Local Area Network Versions. Aug. 1985. *Compatible Hardware:* IBM PC & true compatibles, PC XT, PC AT. *Operating System(s) Required:* PC-DOS 2.0 or higher, PC-DOS 3.1 for PC Net. (source code included). *Memory Required:* Professional 256k, Advantage 320k. *General Requirements:* 2 double-sided disk drives.
contact publisher for price.
Versions of MultiMate Advantage Word Processor & MultiMate Professional Word Processor (3.3 Series), Designed to Work with 3 Popular LAN Systems. Offers Access to MultiMate Word Processing to All Users in a Local Area Network Environment. Permits Standardization of Office Document Handling, File Sharing & Electronic File Transfer Between Work Stations in the LAN. Includes All Advantage Text Exiting Functions Found in the Stand-Alone Version of MultiMate. User Can Share a Single Printer. A Printer Spooler Allows Documents to Be Queued & Printed in the Order They Come into the Network Server. Supports 3Com Ethernet, Novell Netware/86 (Version 4.6 or Higher) & the IBM PC Network.
Borland International, Inc.

MultiMate Professional Word Processor.
Version: 4.0. *Compatible Hardware:* IBM PC, PC XT, PC AT & compatibles. *Operating System(s) Required:* PC-DOS 1.1 or higher. *Memory Required:* 256k. *General Requirements:* 2 disk drives.
disk $565.00.
Access over 100 Features & Functions with 1 or 2 Keystrokes; Prompts in Plain English; Create, Copy, Move & Delete Text; Supports over 50 Printers. Page & Text Features Include: Right Justify, Center, Header, Footer, Multiline Headers, Multiline Footers, Page Numbering & Alter Margins. Also Available in French, Spanish, Swedish, Norwegian, Danish, & an English Version Specially Revised for Users in the United Kingdom & Former Commonwealth Nations.
Borland International, Inc.

Multimedia Animals Encyclopedia.
MS-DOS 5.0 or higher, Windows 3.1 or higher. 386 processor or higher (4Mb). CD-ROM disk $59.95 (Order no.: R1052). *Nonstandard peripherals required:* CD-ROM drive. *Optimal configuration:* 386 processor operating at 16Mhz or higher, MS-DOS 5.0 or higher, Windows 3.1 or higher, 30Mb hard drive, mouse, VGA graphic adapter & VGA color monitor (SVGA recommended), 4Mb RAM, external speakers or headphones (with sound card) that are Sound Blaster compatible.
Macintosh (4Mb). (Order no.: R1052A). *Nonstandard peripherals required:* 14" color monitor or larger, CD-ROM drive.
2,000 Animals Are Depicted with High Quality Photos, Summary Descriptions, Facts, Statistics, Animal Sounds & More.
Library Video Co.

Multimedia Audubon's Birds: DOS-MAC Jewel Case. *Items Included:* Registration card. *Customer Support:* Creative Multimedia Corporation warrants the CD-ROM disc & diskettes to be free from defects in materials & workmanship under normal use & service for a period of 90 days from date of purchase. Creative Multimedia Corporation offers Technical Support to customers as needed.
MS-DOS 3.1 or higher. IBM PC & compatibles with VGA Monitor (640k). CD-ROM disk $49.99 (ISBN 1-880428-01-6, Order no.: 10131). *Optimal configuration:* SuperVGA with 512k video memory. *Networks supported:* All LAN.
System Software 6.0.5 or higher. Macintosh Plus or higher (2Mb). 3.5" disk $49.99 (Order no.: 10131). *Nonstandard peripherals required:* Images display on all systems. *Optimal configuration:* Color image display requires 8-bit color, 32-bit QuickDraw & Color monitor. *Networks supported:* All.
Audubon's Complete 1840 First Edition Plates in Full Color & Text, Plus Superb Quality Bird Calls from Cornell Laboratory of Ornithology. Each Bird Has a Fascinating Story Told by Audubon, Including Its Habitat & Range, Plus Details of the Bird's Life.
Creative Multimedia Corp.

Multimedia Audubon's Mammals: DOS-MAC Jewel Case. *Items Included:* Registration card. *Customer Support:* Creative Multimedia Corporation warrants the CD-ROM disc & diskettes to be free from defects in materials & workmanship under normal use & service for a period of 90 days from date of purchase. Creative Multimedia Corporation offers Technical Support to customers as needed.
MS-DOS 3.1 or higher. IBM PC & compatibles with VGA Monitor (640k). CD-ROM disk $49.99 (ISBN 1-880428-00-8, Order no.: 10148). *Optimal configuration:* SuperVGA with 512k+ video memory. *Networks supported:* All LAN.
System Software 6.0.5 or higher. Macintosh Plus or higher (2Mb). 3.5" disk $49.99 (Order no.: 10148). *Nonstandard peripherals required:* Images display on all systems. *Optimal configuration:* Color image display requires 8-bit color, 32-bit QuickDraw & Color monitor. *Networks supported:* All.
Rare & Complete 1840 Edition of "Quadrupeds of North America". Includes Color Plates & CD Quality Mammal Sounds.
Creative Multimedia Corp.

The Multimedia Bird Book. *Items Included:* Installation instructions, registration cards. *Customer Support:* Phone support by calling 302-234-1750, no charge. Fax support by faxing to 302-234-1760, no charge. E-Mail support at Compuserve ID 76004,3520 or MCI Mail/560-7116, no charge.
CD-ROM disk $39.95 (ISBN 1-887468-00-5). Windows 3.1. 386SX or higher (4Mb). *Nonstandard peripherals required:* Mouse-Microsoft compatible, SoundBlaster or compatible sound card. *Optimal configuration:* 8Mb RAM.
Macintosh. Macintosh running System 7 or higher (4Mb). *Nonstandard peripherals required:* 13" monitor or higher. *Optimal configuration:* 2.5Mb of free RAM.
Interactive Multimedia Software Product Which Presents Children with Exercises in Classifying, Comparing & Identifying Birds. The Software Features Bird Illustrations, Photos, Video & Sounds.
SWFTE International, Ltd.

The Multimedia Bird Book. *Items Included:* Installation instructions, registration cards. *Customer Support:* Phone support by calling 302-234-1750, no charge. Fax support by faxing to 302-234-1760, no charge. E-mail support at Compuserve ID 76004,3520 or MCI mail 560-7116, no charge.
Windows 3.1. 386SX or higher (4Mb). CD-ROM disk $39.95 (ISBN 1-887468-00-5). *Nonstandard peripherals required:* Mouse-Microsoft compatible, soundblaster or compatible sound card. *Optimal configuration:* 486 processor, 8Mb of RAM.
Macintosh. Macintosh running System 7 or higher (4Mb, 2.5Mb of free RAM). *Nonstandard peripherals required:* 13" monitor or higher.
Interactive Multimedia Software Product Which Presents Children with Exercises in Classifying, Comparing & Identifying Birds. The Software Features Bird Illustrations, Photos, Video & Sounds.
Swfte International, Ltd.

The Multimedia Bug Book. *Items Included:* Installation instructions, registration cards. *Customer Support:* Phone support by calling 302-234-1750, no charge. Fax support by faxing to 302-234-1760, no charge. E-Mail support at Compuserve ID 76004,3520 or MCI Mail/560-7116, no charge.
CD-ROM disk $39.95 (ISBN 1-887468-01-3). Windows 3.1. 386SX or higher (4Mb). *Nonstandard peripherals required:* Mouse-Microsoft compatible, SoundBlaster or compatible sound card. *Optimal configuration:* 8Mb RAM.
Macintosh. Macintosh running System 7 or higher (4Mb). *Nonstandard peripherals required:* 13" monitor or higher. *Optimal configuration:* 2.5Mb of free RAM.
Interactive Multimedia Software Product Which Presents Children with the Tools Needed to Locate & Identify Bugs. The Software Features Bug Illustrations, Animations, Video & Sounds.
SWFTE International, Ltd.

The Multimedia Bug Book. *Items Included:* Installation instructions, registration cards. *Customer Support:* Phone support by calling 302-234-1750, no charge. Fax support by faxing to 302-234-1760, no charge. E-Mail support at Compuserve ID 76004,3520 or MCI mail 560-7116, no charge.
Windows 3.1. 386SX or higher (4Mb). CD-ROM disk $39.95 (ISBN 1-887468-01-3). *Nonstandard peripherals required:* Mouse-Microsoft compatible, soundblaster or compatible sound card. *Optimal configuration:* 486 processor, 8Mb of RAM.
Macintosh. Macintosh running System 7 or higher (4Mb, 2.5Mb of free RAM). *Nonstandard peripherals required:* 13" monitor or higher.
Interactive Multimedia Software Product Which Presents Children with the Tools Needed to Locate & Identify Bugs. The Software Features Bug Illustrations, Animations, Video & Sounds.
Swfte International, Ltd.

MultiMedia Cookbook for Hyper Studio. Mo Cooling. Mar. 1995. *Items Included:* Hands-on tutorial of Hyper Studio, an authoring program.
Macintosh 7 or higher. Macintosh (color) (8Mb). CD-ROM disk $19.95 (ISBN 1-887107-00-2, Order no.: 00-2). *Optimal configuration:* Double-speed CD-ROM drive.
An Interactive Teacher Guide That Shows How Students Can Create Exciting Multimedia Projects. It Outlines the Process & the Hardware & Software Needed; Includes a Student-Produced Magazine Template & Other K-12 Projects; & a Tutorial of the Authoring Program HyperStudio.
Opportune Pr.

Multimedia Creation Collection Images CD. Feb. 1995. *Items Included:* Image catalog.
386. CD-ROM disk $49.00. *Addl. software required:* Any image application supporting TIFF files.
Comprehensive Collection of High Quality Photographic Images, Textures & Artist Designed Clip-Art for Royalty Free Use. All Images/Backgrounds Are Full 24-Bit & Can Be Used with Any Application Supporting TIFF Files. User Can Create Thousands of Combinations to Be Used in Presentation, Layout & Even Full Multimedia Productions.
AT&T Multimedia Software Solutions.

Multimedia Music Clips. *Items Included:* Browser/copier front end software. *Customer Support:* 90 day warranty, free call back technical support.
System 6. Mac Plus. CD-ROM disk $20.00. *Nonstandard peripherals required:* CD-ROM drive. *Networks supported:* Apple File Sharing.
Windows 3.1. IBM 386 (4Mb). CD-ROM disk $20.00. *Nonstandard peripherals required:* CD-ROM drive, sound card.
BeachWare.

Multimedia Nursery Rhymes. *Customer Support:* Free, unlimited.
System 6 Mac. 030 Mac, 256 colors (4Mb). CD-ROM disk $24.95. *Nonstandard peripherals required:* Sound card, CD-ROM drive.
Windows 3.1 PC. 486 PC (4Mb). *Nonstandard peripherals required:* Any Windows supported sound card, CD-ROM drive.
Contains Forty Nursery Rhymes, Ten of Which Include On-Screen Fingerplays! Each Rhyme Has Its Own Screen with Original Artwork, Wonderful Animations, Fun Sound Effects, & Great Songs.
BeachWare.

Multimedia Presentation Aid. Donald L. Raimondi. *Compatible Hardware:* IBM PC, PCjr, PC XT, PC AT, Portable PC, 3270 PC. *Operating*

System(s) Required: DOS 2.00, 2.10, 3.00, 3.10. Memory Required: 128k. General Requirements: Optional hardware: IBM Graphics Printer, Matrix Printer, or Color Printer; IBM 7371, 7372, 749, or 750 plotter (with IBM asynchronous communications adapter).
disk $24.95 (Order no.: 6276611).
Can Be Used with a Text Editor to Create Presentations for Viewing on a PC, to Prepare Multicolored Transparencies Using a Plotter, or to Produce Transparency-Quality Presentations on a Printer.
Personally Developed Software, Inc.

Multimedia Reference for Writers. Clifford House & Kathie Sigler. Mar. 1996. *Items Included:* CD-ROM. *Customer Support:* 1-800-824-5179 product information; 1-800-543-0453 technical support.
Windows 3.1 or higher. 486SX 25MHz (8Mb). CD-ROM disk Contact publisher for price (ISBN 0-538-65372-8). *Nonstandard peripherals required:* Double speed CD-ROM, 256 color display, sound card. *Addl. software required:* 10Mb free hard drive space.
Mac System 6.0.5 or higher. 68030 16MHz (8Mb). *Nonstandard peripherals required:* Double speed CD-ROM, 256 color display, sound card. *Addl. software required:* 10Mb free hard drive space.
This Interactive Multimedia Program Is a Comprehensive Tool for Writers in Business or Academics As Well As for Personal Use. It Includes Mastery Exercises for Grammar, Punctuation & Style. Works in Windows & Macintosh Environments with Graphics, Sound, Photos & Videos.
South-Western Publishing Co.

Multimedia Typing Instructor. 1994.
MPC; 386 or higher (2Mb). CD-ROM disk $29.95. *Nonstandard peripherals required:* CD-ROM with CD-DA outputs, DAC, ADC, music synthesizer, VGA.
Using Sound, Video, Graphics, & Animation This Interactive Program Teaches Typing.
Individual Software.

Multimedia Typing Instructor. *Items Included:* 1 CD-ROM, user's guide. *Customer Support:* Toll free: 800-822-3522.
Microsoft Windows 3.1 or higher, 8Mb RAM. 386 based 33Mhz PC or higher. disk $28.95. *Nonstandard peripherals required:* CD-ROM drive, 256 color VGA or higher, sound card, speakers or headphones, mouse.
Get out of the classroom & improve your Keyboarding skills with "Multimedia Typing Instructor!" Travel the world & take a typing adventure that begins with an "in-flight" movie demonstrating effective typing techniques.
Individual Software.

MULTIMIXIT. *Version:* 1.3. 1989. *Compatible Hardware:* IBM PC & compatibles. *Language(s):* Microsoft BASIC. *Memory Required:* 384k. *General Requirements:* Hard disk, MIXIT-3plus program. *Items Included:* Spiral bound Reference Guide. *Customer Support:* Free technical support.
disk $1895.00.
A MIXIT-3 plus Option Consisting of a Multi Blend Feed Formulation System for Feed Mills That Will Least Cost up to 75 Formulas at Once. Will Make the Most Economical Use of Inventory, Save Formulas & Print Usage & Summary Reports. Reduces the Problems of Substitutions, Saves Feed Ingredient Purchase, & Anticipates Shortages. Ideal for Optimal Inventory Management. Also Available in Spanish.
Agricultural Software Consultants, Inc.

MultiNode. Jun. 1992. *Items Included:* Bound manuals. *Customer Support:* 30 day unlimited warranty on software, 90 day warranty on hardware. Free technical support for resellers, pay-for-support for end users.
MS-DOS. 386-SX or higher. Contact vendor for price. *Nonstandard peripherals required:* Proprietary IMP boards for larger than 3 on a network system. *Optimal configuration:* 386 SX or higher PC with MultiNode (MN Server requires minimum of 2Mb RAM, workstations 256k) printers & modems & resources shared. *Networks supported:* Proprietary & can be linked to Novell NetWare.
MS-DOS Based LAN Which Provides Peer-to-Peer Flexibility & Multi-User DOS Cost Effectiveness in One High-Performance, Integrated System. It Allows Both PCs & Terminals to Reside on the Same Network. Both Can Share Each Others' Resources. MultiNode Can Support up to 254 PCs.
Alloy Computer Products, Inc.

Multiphase Flow in Pipeline Networks & Wells. *Items Included:* Full manual. No other products required. *Customer Support:* Free telephone support - no time limit, 30 day warranty.
MS-DOS 3.2 or higher. IBM & compatibles (512k). disk $2899.95. *Optimal configuration:* IBM, MS-DOS 3.3 or higher, 512k RAM, hard disk, graphics capability & printer.
demo disk $5.00.
If You Have Multiple Wells on One Platform, or a Gathering System (with or Without Loops), or Pipelines with Lateral Feeders, Then MFPNET Will Calculate the Flowing Temperatures, Pressures, Liquid Holdup, Velocities, & Flow Patterns. Up to 1000 Pipes & Well Tubing Segments with Different Properties & Ambient Conditions Are Allowed. Both U.S. & S.I. Units Are Supported.
Dynacomp, Inc.

Multiphase Flow in Pipelines & Oil Wells. *Items Included:* Full manual. No other products required. *Customer Support:* Free telephone support - no time limit, 30 day warranty.
MS-DOS 3.2 or higher. IBM & compatibles (512k). disk $1069.95. *Optimal configuration:* IBM & compatibles 512k RAM, hard disk, & color graphics capability.
Models Pipes Which Carry Oil, Gas, & Water Through a Variety of Environments (e.g., from the Bottom of a Well to the Surface, Through a River, Then Underground, etc.). It Calculates Pressures, Temperatures, Liquid Holdup, Velocities, & Flow Patterns. Flowstring May Have up to 40 Pipe & Well Tubing Elements, Each Having Different Properties & Conditions.
Dynacomp, Inc.

Multiplan. *Compatible Hardware:* B-20 series, B-22. *Operating System(s) Required:* BTOS. *Language(s):* PL/M. *Memory Required:* 256k. *General Requirements:* Printer.
disk $200.00.
Designed to Be Used As a Management Tool in Forecasting, Planning, Modeling & Tracking of Information. Allows Keyboard Creation & Screen Display of Worksheets, Descriptions & Formulas. Once Created, Worksheets May Be Saved on Disk & Re-Used with New Data or Data from Other Saved Worksheets, & Printed.
Burroughs Corp.

Multiplan. Microsoft, Inc. *Compatible Hardware:* HP 86/87 with CP/M System (HP 82900A), HP 150 Touchscreen, HP 110 Portable, HP Series 200 HP-UX Models 217, 220, 236, the Integral PC.
HP 86/87. 3-1/2" or 5-1/4" disk $295.00 ea. (Order no.: 82855A).
HP 150, HP 110. 3.5" disk $195.00 (Order no.: 45473D).
HP 217, 220, 236, the Integral PC; single-user. 3.5" disk $345.00 (Order no.: 45473G).
Linus tape $470.00.
HP 217, 220, 236, the Integral PC; multi-user. 3.5" disk $595.00 (Order no.: 45473H).
Linus tape $720.00.
Electronic Worksheet Which Features the Ability to Build Formulas by Highlighting Cells, As Well As Command Prompting, Full English Words for Commands, On-Line Reference Guide, & up to Eight Display Windows. Cell Referencing Methods Include Naming, Relative Reference, & Absolute Reference. Includes Built-In Functions Such As Arithmetic, Trigonometric, Conditional (IF-THEN, AND, OR), Table (Lookup, Index), Net Present Value, & Standard Deviation. Also Offers Variable Column Width, User-Assignable Decimal Point, Text Calculation, & Alphabetical & Numerical Sorting. Report Options Include Variable Margins, Automatic Pagination, & Print Formulas.
Hewlett-Packard Co.

Multiplan: Electric Spreadsheet. Microsoft. Nov. 1981. *Compatible Hardware:* AT&T 6300+ & compatibles; IBM PC, PC XT, PC AT. *Operating System(s) Required:* XENIX, UNIX. *Memory Required:* 128k. *Items Included:* Manuals. *Customer Support:* 30-day warranty, hotline, newsletter, electronic bulletin board.
disk $495.00.
Multiuser Version of MicroSoft's MULTIPLAN.
Santa Cruz Operation, Inc.

Multiplan for TI. Microsoft Corp. *Compatible Hardware:* TI 99/4A. *Memory Required:* 32k. *General Requirements:* TI impact printer, RS-232C interface.
contact publisher for price (Order no.: PHM 3113).
Modeling & Planning Using Spreadsheets.
Texas Instruments, Personal Productivit.

The Multiplan Teach Program. (Micro Learning System Ser.). Bill Judis. *Compatible Hardware:* Compaq, IBM PC. *Memory Required:* 64k. *General Requirements:* Double-sided disk drive, MULTIPLAN program, blank disk.
disk $59.95 (ISBN 0-8359-4740-8).
Teaches the First Time User How to Use MULTIPLAN & How to Create Applications.
Prentice Hall.

Multiple Bank Account Reconciliation. $250.00.
Automatically Accumulates Check Information in a Bank Transaction File.
Advanced Concepts, Inc.

Multiple Checkbook System. *Compatible Hardware:* Apple Macintosh. *Memory Required:* 512k.
3.5" disk $29.95.
Financial Management Program.
Disk-Count Software, Inc.

Multiple Factor Analysis. *Version:* 4.0. Allen Easton. Oct. 1983. *Compatible Hardware:* IBM PC & compatibles, Macintosh 68030. *Operating System(s) Required:* PC-DOS 2.0, 2.1, 3.2. *Language(s):* Compiled BASIC. *Memory Required:* 256k. *General Requirements:* Hard disk drive printer optional.
Rev 4.0. $150.00.
manual $15.00.
source code avail.
Enter Primary Data by Case or Variables, Intercorrelation Matrix or a Matrix of Factor Loading. Tutorials Included.
Mathematical Software Co.

MULTIPLE FACTOR ANALYSIS:

Multiple Factor Analysis: Multidimensional Statistics. *Items Included:* Bound manual. *Customer Support:* Free hotline - no time limit; 30 day limited warranty; updates are $5/disk plus S&H.
MS-DOS 2.0 or higher. IBM & compatibles (256k). disk $99.95. *Nonstandard peripherals required:* CGA (or equivalent) graphics, & two floppy disk drives (or one floppy & a hard disk); math coprocessor is supported (though not necessary), as well as a printer.
Macintosh (1Mb). 3.5" disk $99.95. *Nonstandard peripherals required:* Hard disk.
Useful for Analyzing Questionnaire Responses or Complex Test Data, & for Identifying the Attributes of Members of a Test Population. Can Analyze Three Types of Data: Primary Data (up to 125 Variables x 1000 Cases); Intercorrelation Matrices (up to 125 x 125 Variables); & Matrices of Factor-Loadings (up to 20 Factors x 125 Variables). User Can Factor Analyze New Primary Data or Intercorrelation Matrices, or Try Different Rotational Schemes. For the Computation of Factor Scores the Analysis Must Start with Primary Data.
Dynacomp, Inc.

Multiple Integration. *Items Included:* Bound manual. *Customer Support:* Free hotline - no time limit; 30 day limited warranty; updates are $5/disk plus S&H.
MS-DOS. IBM & compatibles (256k). disk $49.95. *Nonstandard peripherals required:* Color graphics card. *Addl. software required:* BASICA.
Commodore 64. disk $49.95.
Computes Integrals of Any Order, That Is, Single, Double, Triple, ...n-Tuple Integrals, to an Accuracy Specified by the User. This Is Accomplished by Employing an Adaptable Integration Scheme. The Integration is Performed Using Fourth Degree Approximating Polynomials, Hence Yielding More Accurate Results Than Using Simpson's Rule. User May Select the Names of the Variables to Be Used & Predefine Any Recurrent Constants.
Dynacomp, Inc.

Multiple Organizational Management. *Version:* 1.0. Jan. 1992.
MS-DOS. IBM & compatibles (512k). $1995.00 (with accounting features) (ISBN 1-56756-008-3, Order no.: OD300I).
$995.00 (without accounting features) (ISBN 1-56756-009-1, Order no.: OD310I).
Full Fledge, Full Featured Membership Database Application with or without Full Accounting Features.
Advantage International.

Multiple Precision Math Subroutines for BASIC & FORTRAN. *Items Included:* Full manual. No other products required. *Customer Support:* Free telephone support - no time limit, 30 day warranty.
MS-DOS 3.2 or higher. IBM & compatibles (512k). $49.95 BASIC version; $59.95 FORTRAN version.
Designed to Support the Need for High Precision Calculations in BASIC & FORTRAN Programs. This Is Provided in the Form of Subroutines (Source Code) Which Can Be Merged with the User's Application Programs. You Can Choose the Level of Precision (up to 140 Digits, in Steps of 14). Manual Includes Specific Operating Instructions & Several Examples.
Dynacomp, Inc.

Multiple Regression & Multiple-Partial Correlation. *Compatible Hardware:* Apple II with Applesoft, IBM PC. *Operating System(s) Required:* Apple DOS 3.2 or 3.3.
disk $49.95.
Designed for the Statistician in Mind & Is Reminiscent of the Statistical Routines Provided on the Large Mainframes.
Dynacomp, Inc.

Multiple Statement Program Generator. *Compatible Hardware:* TI 99/4A. *Operating System(s) Required:* DX-10. *Language(s):* Extended BASIC. *Memory Required:* 48k.
disk $18.95.
Conversion Utility Program Which Converts TI Console BASIC Programs to Extended BASIC. Some Features Include: REM Statement Removal, Multiple Statements per Line & Insertion of a ":" for Multiple PRINT Statements.
Eastbench Software Products.

Multipurpose Lab Interface. 1989. *Items Included:* 12-bit A-to-D Converter board, connection box; 60-page manual. *Customer Support:* Telephone support; newsletter.
MS-DOS. IBM compatible, XT, AT, PS/2 Models 25, 30 (512k). $310.00 (Includes Hardware) (ISBN 0-918731-36-4, Order no.: MPLI-IBM). *Nonstandard peripherals required:* MPLI Hardware, CGA, EGA or Hercules Graphics. *Optimal configuration:* 512k RAM.
Apple II (ProDOS). Apple II (64k). $290.00- Includes Hardware - $49.95-Software alone) (ISBN 0-918731-37-2, Order no.: MPLI-APPLE II). *Nonstandard peripherals required:* MPLI Hardware. *Optimal configuration:* 128k RAM is optimal.
Turns Your Computer into a Powerful Laboratory Instrument by Allowing You to Use a Wide Variety of Sensors to Make Measurements & to analyze & Graph the Results. Three Input Signals Can Be Monitored Simultaneously. Data Can Be Collected at a Rate of Thousands of Samples Per Second (Fast Enough to Allow You to Display Sound Wave Patterns) or Slowly over Periods As Long As Several Months.
Vernier Software.

Multiscore Depression Inventory for Adolescents & Adults. *Version:* 2.011. David J. Berndt. *Customer Support:* Free unlimited phone support with a toll free number.
DOS 3.0 or higher. IBM or 100% compatible (512k). disk $295.00 (Order no.: W-1010 5.25"; W-1034 3.5"). *Optimal configuration:* Hard disk with 1Mb free disk space, printer.
Measures Not Only the Severity but Also the Specific Aspects of Depression. In Addition, This Highly Sensitive Measure Detects Subtle Variations in Milder Forms of Depression. With These Two Features, the MDI Overcomes the Principal Limitations of Other Depression Inventories.
Western Psychological Services.

The MULTITRAK Enterprise-Wide Work Management System. *Version:* 2.9. *Compatible Hardware:* IBM mainframes with MVS/CICS. *Customer Support:* Phone & on-site, hotline/technical support.
Starting at $40,000 for mainframe version.
Provides the Automated Infrastructure for Enterprise-Wide Planning, Budgeting, Management & Evaluation of All Projects & People in the IS Organization. Specifically Designed to Control Hundreds, Even Thousands, of Software Development & Maintenance Activities. Provides Integrated Time Reporting, Project Accounting, Resource Management, Maintenance Management & Methodology Automation. Helps IS Deliver & Support High-Quality Software with Greater Cost & Schedule Predictability & Improved Quality. Bi-Directional Interface Available to Microsoft Project & Project Workbench for Windows.
Multitrak Software Development Corp.

SOFTWARE ENCYCLOPEDIA 1996

MULTITRAK Work Request System. *Items Included:* Full documentation. *Customer Support:* On-site training & maintenance & phone support.
MVS/CICS. IBM Mainframes. $40,000.00.
Dramatically Simplifies the Effort of Initiating, Tracking & Managing All Work Including Maintenance Activities. Streamlines & Automates a Range of Management Functions: Request Initiation; Request Tracking; Request Status Reporting; Request Authorization & Backlog management. Integrates with MULTITRAK's Project Planning & Scheduling; Resource Scheduling; Time Reporting; Schedule & Status Tracking; Project Accounting & Chargeback.
Multitrak Software Development Corp.

Multivariance. *Version:* 7.32. Jeremy Finn & R. Darrell Bock. 1993. *Customer Support:* Free technical support, 90 day limited warranty.
MS-DOS, OS/2. IBM & compatibles. disk $300.00.
3.5" disk $300.00 (ISBN 1-56321-061-4). 366p. manual $35.00 (ISBN 1-56321-119-X).
Precedent-Setting Multivariance Program Is Now Available in a Convenient, Fast, & Economical PC Version for IBM-Compatible Machines Running under DOS or OS/2. Offers Versatile Commands & Easily Interpreted Output for Analysis of Variance, Regression, Covariance, & Multivariate Statistical Techniques.
Lawrence Erlbaum Assocs., Software & Alternate Media, Inc.

Multivariate Analysis. *Version:* 10.0. *Compatible Hardware:* Apple Macintosh, IBM PC & compatibles. *Items Included:* Disks, book, program instructions. *Customer Support:* Telephone.
disk $145.00 (ISBN 0-920387-20-9).
Cover the Major Topics of the Discipline, Including Multilinear Regression, Correlation Analysis (Including Part & Partial Correlation Between Data Sets), Factor Analysis (with Varimax & Quartimax Rotations), Principal Component Analysis, Discriminant Analysis, Canonical Component Analysis, & Residual Analysis. Multiple Population Topics Include MANOVA with & Without a Covariate. A Full Cross-Tabulation Program Is Included, As Well As Probit Analysis Programs.
Lionheart Pr., Inc.

Multivariate Non-Linear Regression & Optimization. *Items Included:* Bound manual. *Customer Support:* Free hotline - no time limit; 30 day limited warranty; updates are $5/disk plus S&H.
MS-DOS. IBM & compatibles (256k). disk $99.95.
Allows User to Easily Apply Regression & Optimization to Multidimensional Non-Linear Problems. The Mathematical Expression Is Entered Using BASIC Syntax. All of the Functions in BASIC (e.g., SIN, COS, LOG, etc.) Are Available. Multi-Line Functions Are Permitted, As Well As Logical Statements. The Multi-Line Expression Can Also Be Saved to Disk & Recalled for Later Editing.
Dynacomp, Inc.

Multivariate Non-Linear Regression & Optimization. *Items Included:* Full manual. No other products required. *Customer Support:* Free telephone support - no time limit, 30 day warranty.
MS-DOS 3.2 or higher. IBM & compatibles (512k). disk $99.95.
Allows You to Easily Apply Regression & Optimization to Multidimensional Non-Linear Problems. For Example, You Might Wish to Fit a Three-Dimensional Function Like F(X,Y,Z) equals aX3Y Plus b cos(cYZ) plus exp(dX)/(YZ) to a Set of Data to Find (a,b,c,d), or Find the Maximum

TITLE INDEX

or Minimum of Such a Function, Given (a,b,c,d), Either with or Without Constraints. Mathematical Expression Is Entered Using BASIC Syntax. All of the Functions in BASIC (e.g., SIN, COS, LOG, etc.) Are Available. For Regression, Data Entry Is Simple & Painless. Data May Also Be Loaded from Existing ASCII Data Files, Added to, & Generally Edited. MNLRO Can Regress up to 10 Unknown Coefficients for a Data Set of up to 10 Dimensions by 500 Data Points.
Dynacomp, Inc.

Multivariate Non-Linear Regression & Optimization. 1992. *Items Included:* Detailed manuals included with all Dynacomp products. *Customer Support:* Free telephone support to original customer - no time limit; 30 day limited warranty.
MS-DOS 3.2 or higher. IBM PC & compatibles (512k). $99.95 (Add $5.00 for 3 1/2" format; 5 1/4" format standard).
Allows You to Easily Apply Regression & Optimization to Multidimensional Non-Linear Problems. Also Permits Non-Linear Programming with a Non-Linear Objective Function. Non-Linear Constraint Equations Can Be Entered Using the Constraint Editor. These Constraints Can Include Functions, As Well As Multiline Statements. Fitting Functions, Objective Functions, & Constraints Are All Created Using the MNLRO Editor. Can Regress up to 10 Unknown Coefficients for a Data Set of up to 10 Dimensions by 300 Data Points. Includes a 186-Page Manual.
Dynacomp, Inc.

Multivariate Regression Analysis. *Items Included:* Full manual. No other products required. *Customer Support:* Free telephone support - no time limit, 30 day warranty.
MS-DOS 3.2 or higher. IBM & compatibles (512k). disk $59.95.
Statistics Package Which Compliments MULTILINEAR REGRESSION (MLR). In Essence, MRA Approaches Multivariate Regression from a Different Computational Perspective. This Approach Is a Little Slower & Does Not Include Standard Errors of the Estimates for the Calculated Coefficients. However, It Does Handle Much Larger Data Sets, & Has a Few Different Features. Besides the Standard Data Editing, Variable Removal, etc., Capabilities, MRA Also Includes the Following: Reverse Stepwise Regression, up to 54 Named Variables (9,999 Observations for Six Variables).
Dynacomp, Inc.

Multiware Multimedia Collection. *Items Included:* Browser/installer/launcher front-end program. *Customer Support:* 90 day warranty, free call back technical support.
System 6. Color Mac (4Mb). CD-ROM disk $20.00. *Nonstandard peripherals required:* CD-ROM drive. *Addl. software required:* Whatever uses the media clips. *Optimal configuration:* 8Mb RAM. *Networks supported:* Apple File Sharing.
BeachWare.

Munch Mobile. *Compatible Hardware:* TI-99/4A with PLATO interpreter solid state cartridge.
contact publisher for price (Order no.: PHM 3146).
Car Has Arms to Grab at Goodies along the Highway, But Don't Forget to Watch Your Fuel Level.
Texas Instruments, Personal Productivit.

MunchMan. *Compatible Hardware:* TI-99/4A with PLATO interpreter solid state cartridge.
contact publisher for price (Order no.: PHM 3057).
Move Quickly to Out-Maneuver "Hoonos" While Connecting Maze Passages with a Chain.
Texas Instruments, Personal Productivit.

MUNI Water Billing. *Customer Support:* 800-929-8117 (customer service).
MS-DOS. IBM/PS2. disk $499.99 (ISBN 0-87007-155-6).
A Detailed Billing System for Municipal Water Districts. Designed for Use Primarily on Hard Disk Drives, but Smaller Districts Are Able to Use Floppies. There are Four Different Charge Usage Levels as Well as a Flat Billing Rate. Includes Online Tutorials, and a Detailed Manual.
SourceView Software International.

Municipal. 1992. *Compatible Hardware:* IBM AS 400. *Customer Support:* On or off site training, toll free HOT-LINE support & training, user manuals, Online Help text.
Price varies according to system configuration, customization, training, installation & maintenance.
Fully Integrated Software package Catering to State & Local Governments. Includes General Ledger, Accounts Receivable, Accounts Payable, Inventory, Budgeting, Payroll/Personnel, Purchase Order Tracking/Encumbrance, Utility Billing, Real Estate/Personal Tax Billing, Work Management, Job Cost & Much More.
Automation Counselors, Inc.

Municipal Accounting Package: General Ledger, Accounts Payable, Budget. Jan. 1986. *Compatible Hardware:* Tandy 6000 with 2 disk drives, M-BASIC interpreter & XENIX Development System. *Memory Required:* 500k. disk $495.00.
Has the Ability to Keep up & Maintain Multiple Fiscal Years at Once. Accounts Payable Maintains Files for up to 10,000 Vendors. Chart of Accounts Is Unlimited (Limited Only by Available Disk Storage).
Raymond L. Reynolds.

Municipal Management System. Jan. 1980. *Compatible Hardware:* Data General Aviion, Hewlett Packard 9000/800, NCR 3000, Unisys 6000, IBM RS/6000. *Operating System(s) Required:* PC-DOS, MS-DOS, XENIX, UNIX, HP-UX, DG-UX. *General Requirements:* Hard disk, printer.
contact publisher for price.
Designed for Local Government. Consists of the Following Integrated Modules: Budgetary Accounting, Purchasing, Payroll, Utility Billing, General Ledger, Asset Management, Miscellaneous, Billing, Inventory, & Building Permits.
Software Solutions, Inc.

MUNIS. *Version:* 7.0. *Compatible Hardware:* Altos, AT&T, Bull, IBM, NCR Tower, UNISYS. *Operating System(s):* AIX, PC-DOS, SCO, UNIX, XENIX. *Language(s):* RM/COBOL. *Memory Required:* 512k. *Items Included:* Documentation. *Customer Support:* Available/contract.
contact publisher for price.
Multi-Fund Budgetary System Used in Government, Cities, Towns, & Schools.
Computer Center.

The Muppet CD-ROM: Muppets Inside. Mar. 1996. *Customer Support:* Toll-free technical support, on0line, fax back.
Windows 95. 8Mb, 16 bit color, 16 bit + speakers. CD-ROM disk $50.00 (ISBN 1-888104-02-3). *Nonstandard peripherals required:* 2x CD-ROM drive or faster, 16 Mb recommended.
A Hilarious "Misadventure" That Combines Challenging Gameplay with the Muppets' Unique Brand of Humor. Play by Yourself Or with Your Kids. Muppets Inside Is for Ages 99 & Under.
Starwave Corp.

MUSEUM COLLECTOR

Muppet Treasure Island. *Items Included:* Installation Guide.
IBM PC. Contact publisher for price (ISBN 0-87321-041-7, Order no.: CDD-3113).
Activision, Inc.

The Muppets CD-ROM: Muppets Inside. Jan. 1996. *Customer Support:* Toll-free technical support by phone, fax-back & online.
Windows 95. 486/66 or higher (8Mb). CD-ROM disk $50.00 (ISBN 1-888104-02-3, Order no.: 7-14120-70903-2). *Nonstandard peripherals required:* 2X CD-ROM drive. *Optimal configuration:* 486/66 w/16Mb RAM, 4X CD-drive, 16-bit color.
Muppets Inside Is an Adventure Game for All Ages on CD-ROM.
Starwave.

Mural Maker. John Rader. 1990. *Items Included:* 1 manual & overlay. *Customer Support:* 1-800 Help Line.
DOS 3.3, DOS 5.0. IBM PS/2 & compatibles (640k). disk $54.95 (ISBN 1-878842-07-2). *Nonstandard peripherals required:* VGA graphics board & monitor, IBM speech adapter card, external speaker, mouse, PowerPad. *Addl. software required:* DOS 3.3, DOS 5.0 & software associated with mouse. *Optimal configuration:* One IBM PS/2 Model 25 or Model 30 with 640k RAM, color display (MCGA or VGA), one 720k 3.5" disk drive, IBM speech adapter, one IBM proprinter & one external speaker, PowerPad, keyboard, IBM mouse, DOS 3.3 & DOS 5.0. *Networks supported:* Novell, ICLAS.
Works with Groups of Children Who Select & Printout Different Objects That Can Be Made into a Mural. Objects Organized into Seven Categories in 3 Sizes.
Mobius Corp.

Muscial Words Game. *Version:* 2.0. Sara R. Nussel. *Compatible Hardware:* Macintosh. *Memory Required:* 1000k. *General Requirements:* Hard disk; Hypercard. *Customer Support:* Free by prepaid phone (904) 528-0371. Updates $3.50 with your disk.
3.5" disk $7.50, both staves.
Visual/Audio Note Placement Training Program.
A. H. Nussel.

The Muscle Cars: The Duel - Test Drive II Car Disk. Feb. 1990. *Items Included:* Catalog, copy protection device, manual, proof of purchase card. *Customer Support:* Technical support 408-296-8400, 90 day limited warranty.
Apple IIGS - Pro DOS 16 (512k). Apple IIGS. $43.90. *Addl. software required:* The Duel: Test Drive II. *Optimal configuration:* Hard drive, keyboard, joystick, & graphics card.
IBM DOS 2.1 or higher, Tandy-DOS (512k). IBM PC, XT, AT, PS/2 models 25, 30, 50, 60, Tandy 1000, 3000, 4000. $43.90. *Addl. software required:* The Duel: Test Drive II. *Optimal configuration:* Hard drive, keyboard, joystick, & graphics card.
Macintosh (800k drive, 1Mb). Macintosh Plus, 512K, SE, II, 512ke. $43.90. *Addl. software required:* The Duel: Test Drive II. *Optimal configuration:* Hard drive, keyboard, joystick, & graphics card.
Car Driving Simulation. Five All-American, Street-Scorching Muscle Cars.
Accolade, Inc.

Museum Collector. 1980. *Compatible Hardware:* Apple II+, IIc, IIe; Basis; Franklin Ace; IBM PC, PC XT, PC AT. *Operating Systems Required:* Apple DOS 3.3, MS-DOS 3.1. *Language(s):* BASIC (source code included). *Memory Required:* Apple 48k, IBM 256k.
disk $150.00.

Package for a Small Museum or an Individual Collector. Allows Both Collection & Research & Includes Schedules, Literature Files, Subscriptions, a Text Editor, & Mail List Capabilities, As Well As Acquisitions Information.
Andent, Inc.

Museum Collector Catalog. 1982. *Compatible Hardware:* Apple II+, IIc, IIe; Franklin Ace; IBM PC, PC XT, PC AT. *Operating System(s) Required:* Apple DOS 3.3, MS-DOS 3.1. *Language(s):* BASIC (source code included). *Memory Required:* Apple 48k, IBM 256k. *General Requirements:* Printer.
disk $150.00.
Data Base System for Museums, Professional & Amateur Anthropologists, Naturalists, & Collectors. Consists of 11 Programs in Which Collection, Staff & Administration Information Can Be Entered, Deleted, Changed, Sorted, Searched & Printed in Multiple Formats.
Andent, Inc.

Music Achievement Series. Sandy Feldstein. 1985. *Compatible Hardware:* Atari, Apple II, Commodore 64, IBM PC & compatibles, Macintosh. *Memory Required:* 48k. *General Requirements:* CGA card & color monitor for IBM.
IBM. 3.5" disk $199.95 (ISBN 0-88284-451-2, Order no.: 7235).
IBM. disk $199.95 (ISBN 0-88284-452-0, Order no.: 7234).
Apple, Commodore. disk $199.95 (ISBN 0-88284-453-9, Order no.: 7225).
Atari. 3.5" disk $199.95 (ISBN 0-88284-454-7, Order no.: 3511).
Macintosh. disk $249.95 (ISBN 0-88284-455-5, Order no.: 3485).
Yamaha C1. disk $199.95 (ISBN 0-88284-456-3, Order no.: 3484).
Apple 3.5. disk $199.95 (ISBN 0-88284-479-2, Order no.: 3459).
Text Book That Correlates with Alfred's "Practical Music Theory Method". Tests All Aspects of Music Theory. MIDI Compatible.
Alfred Publishing Co., Inc.

Music Analyzer-Synthesis. *Compatible Hardware:* TI 99/4A. *Operating System(s) Required:* DX-10. *Language(s):* Console BASIC. *Memory Required:* 16k.
cassette $20.00.
Using Fourier's Analysis, User Can Analyze or Modify Melodies. The Pitch & Duration of the Notes Can Be Analyzed. Using This Technique, New Melodies Can Be Created & Analyzed.
Eastbench Software Products.

Music & Sound for the Commodore 64. Bill Behrendt. Jun. 1984. *Compatible Hardware:* Commodore 64. *Operating System(s) Required:* Commodore 64 DOS. *Language(s):* BASIC (source code included). *Memory Required:* 64k.
disk $29.95, incl. bk. (ISBN 0-13-607102-3).
disk $21.95 (ISBN 0-13-607151-1).
Use the Computer to Write Music.
Prentice Hall.

Music & Sound for the PCjr. Bill L. Behrendt. Jul. 1984. *Compatible Hardware:* IBM PCjr. *Operating System(s) Required:* PC-DOS 2.1. *Language(s):* Cartridge BASIC (source code included). *Memory Required:* 64k.
disk $29.95 (ISBN 0-13-607128-7).
bk. $14.95 (ISBN 0-13-607110-4).
Use the Computer to Write Music.
Prentice Hall.

Music & Speech Programs for the IBM PC. Robert J. Traister. Jul. 1983. *Compatible Hardware:* IBM PC. *Operating System(s) Required:* PC-DOS. *Memory Required:* 64k.
disk $40.50, incl. bk. (ISBN 0-8306-5034-2, Order no.: 5034C).
More Than 125 Ready-to-Run Programs Including Sound Effects, Christmas Songs, Country Songs, Country Music, & Bach.
TAB Bks.

Music Appreciation. *Compatible Hardware:* Apple II, II+, IIc. *Memory Required:* 48k.
disk $39.95 (Order no.: INT 2001A).
disk $49.95, incl. management (Order no.: INT2001AM).
Tutorial Which Begins with an Overview of the 4 Instrument Families. A Survey of Music History Follows, Concentrating on Major Composers, Major Works, & Characteristic Musical Forms of the Middle Ages, the Renaissance, the Baroque, Classical, Romantic, & Impressionistic Periods, & the Twentieth Century. Each Wrong Answer Branches to an Explanation.
Intellectual Software.

Music Appreciation - A Study Guide: The Musical Language/Music History, 2 disks. Joseph E. Koob, II. 1986. *Compatible Hardware:* Apple II+, IIe, IIgs; IBM PC. *Language(s):* QuickBasic. *Memory Required:* Apple 48k, IBM 640k. *General Requirements:* CGA card.
$79.95 ea.
Apple. (ISBN 1-55603-039-8, Order no.: A-1195).
IBM. (ISBN 1-55603-038-X, Order no.: I-1195).
Facilitates the Study of Music Terminology & History Emphasized in Music Appreciation Courses Using the Book & Exploring Music Through Experience. THE MUSICAL LANGUAGE Is a Review & Short-Answer Quiz on Music Terminology. MUSIC HISTORY is a Review of Western Music History from Greek Times to Contemporary Music Followed by a Short-Answer Quiz.
Electronic Courseware Systems, Inc.

Music Boosters: An Entrepreneurial Adventure. 1989. *General Requirements:* VHS videocassette player.
IBM/Tandy. contact publisher for price (ISBN 0-538-07037-4, Order no.: G03P).
IBM/PS-2. contact publisher for price (ISBN 0-538-07039-0, Order no.: G03P1).
Instructor's Package for Music Boosters. Contains Manual, Software, & VHS Videocassette. This Package is an Interactive Business Simulation Which Depicts the Start-up of a Business & Allows Students to Make Decisions Required During the First 8 Quarters of the Life of the Company.
South-Western Publishing Co.

Music Composer Quiz. Joe Brownlee. 1987. *Customer Support:* ECS offers technical support to registered users. Call (217) 359-7099. Other than the telephone call - technical support is no charge.
Apple. disk $39.95 (Order no.: A-1173).
DOS 3.2 or higher. IBM. $39.95 single station/ $200.00 network (Order no.: I-1173). *Networks supported:* Novell.
System 6.0.4 or higher. Macintosh. $39.95 single station/$200.00 network (Order no.: MAC-1173).
Consists of 20 Questions Randomly Selected from a Pool Created by the Author. Users Are Given Three Chances to Answer a Question Correctly Before the Answer Is Displayed. The Instructor May Edit or Print Any of the 100 Quiz Questions. Feedback Is Given at the End of Each Quiz Session; Student Records Are Retained.
Electronic Courseware Systems, Inc.

Music Concepts. 1986. *Items Included:* 3 ring binder with program disk(s), teacher's guide & reproducible student worksheets. *Customer Support:* Phone support (805) 473-7383.
Apple II. (128k). $59.95 single, $109.95 5-user, $159.95 10-user, $359.95 30-user (SL/Ntwk). *Networks supported:* All.
This Program Introduces Basic Concepts of Music Pertaining to Music Theory, Music History, & the Science of Sound. Topics Include Music Symbols & Notation, Types of Instruments, Composers, the Orchestra, the Physics & Physiology of Sound. Also Includes a Melody Match Which Challenges the Student to Listen to a Simple Melody & Then Match What Was Heard to What Is Represented on the Screen in Musical Notation. Rhythm Match Plays a Pattern of Notes & Then Challenges the Student to Select the Correct Musical Notation for What Was Heard. Allows Students to Enter Simple Melodies by Placing Notes on a Staff That Is Represented on the Screen & Then to Play Back the Melodies.
Ventura Educational Systems.

Music Designer II. *Compatible Hardware:* Apple II+, IIe. *Memory Required:* 64k. *General Requirements:* 3-voice ALF music synthesizer, game paddles.
contact publisher for price.
Compositional Program That Allows Creation of Complex Musical Textures with 3 Voices. As the Computer Generates the Musical Environment, the User Can Make All Changes Desired, Including: Volume, Envelope (Attack, Sustain, or Decay) Ranges, 9 Different Scales, Silence, Tone, Clusters, Voice Arrangement. No Format Serves As an Aural Trainer for Music Students of All Levels.
CAPS Software.

Music Flash Cards. Vincent Oado. *Compatible Hardware:* Apple II (48k), IBM (640k), Macintosh (512k).
$99.95 (ISBN 0-942132-42-4).
Important Music Material Is Presented in Nine Lessons. The Lessons Include: Note Naming, Rhythm Values & Equivalents, Major & Minor Scales, Modal Scales, Key Signatures, Intervals, & Basic Chords.
Electronic Courseware Systems, Inc.

Music Fundamentals, 9 disks. Marc Apfelstadt & Bruce Benward. May 1986. *Compatible Hardware:* Apple II, II+, IIe. *Language(s):* Applesoft. *Memory Required:* 64k. *General Requirements:* Applesoft Language Card, DAC board & headphones or speaker.
disk $300.00 (ISBN 0-697-00294-2).
Package of Tutorial & Drill Programs Designed to Provide Students with the Aural Component Needed to Complement Knowledge Gained from Any Beginning Music Theory Text. Each Program Contains Multiple Musical Examples, & the Materials on Each Disk Are Organized in Order of Relative Difficulty for the Task or Specific Musical Element Involved. The Materials Are Grouped by Musical Function.
Wm. C. Brown Pubs.

Music History Review: Composers. William Higgins & Ronald L. Miller. 1991.
MS-DOS. IBM PC (512k). disk $39.95 (ISBN 1-55603-325-7, Order no.: I-1308). *Nonstandard peripherals required:* CGA monitor & board minimum. *Optimal configuration:* DOS 3.3 or higher. *Networks supported:* Novell.
MAC System 6.0.3 - System 7.0. Macintosh Plus or higher (512k). 3.5" disk $59.95 (ISBN 1-55603-324-9, Order no.: MAC-1308).
Tests Users Knowledge of Composers, from Renaissance to Twentieth Century. The User Can Select a Quiz from Ten Categories. Questions Are Presented in a Multiple-Choice Format; Feedback Is Given at the End of Each Quiz. Coordinates with "A History of Western Music," 4th Edition by Grout & Palisca (published by W. W. Norton). Student Records Are Retained.
Electronic Courseware Systems, Inc.

TITLE INDEX

Music Index. Version: 4.0. Compatible Hardware: IBM PC & compatibles, PC XT, PC AT, PS/2. Operating System(s) Required: MS-DOS, 3.0 or higher recommended. Language(s): PL/1. Memory Required: 64k. General Requirements: 2 disk drives, DOT Matrix Printer. Items Included: User manual. Customer Support: 1 year telephone support.
contact publisher for price.
Maintains a Rotary Index of an Unlimited Number of Music Titles, Allowing a Station to Define Its Music Program Formats. Allows Full Customized Reporting from Music Library Data Base Plus Basic Inventory Reporting by Catalogue Number, Title, Artist, etc., & Play History Reporting.
Computer Broadcasting International.

Music Made Easy. Sandy Feldstein. 1985.
Apple DOS 3.3. Apple II Plus, IIe, IIc, (48k). disk $29.95, incl. bk. (ISBN 0-88284-480-6, Order no.: 8281). *Nonstandard peripherals required:* Disk drive.
Commodore 64. disk $29.95, incl. bk. (ISBN 0-88284-481-4, Order no.: 8282). *Nonstandard peripherals required:* Disk drive.
Book & Software Package Which Contains Definitions & Musical Examples of Basic Music Theory.
Alfred Publishing Co., Inc.

Music Maker. John Rader. Items Included: 1 manual & 1 overlay. Customer Support: 1-800 Help Line.
DOS 3.3 or DOS 5.0. IBM PS/2 Models or compatibles (640k). Contact publisher for price; part of KIDWARE 2 PLUS package. *Nonstandard peripherals required:* VGA graphics board & monitor, IBM speech adapter card or Digispeech, M-Audio, or Soundblaster, external speaker, mouse; Powerpad optional. *Addl. software required:* DOS 3.3, DOS 5.0 & software associated with mouse. *Optimal configuration:* One IBM PS/2 Model 25 or Model 30 with 640k RAM, color display (MCGA or VGA), one 720k 3.5" disk drive, IBM Speech Adapter, one IBM Proprinter or Star Micronics color printer & one external, keyboard, IBM mouse, DOS 3.3 & DOS 5.0. *Networks supported:* Novell, ICLAS.
Compose Your Own Music Tunes. The Color-Coded System Makes It Easy to Discriminate Different Notes. Record & Play Your Own Music As Well As Listen to Old Favorites. Print Out Your Tunes along with Words or Stories.
Mobius Corp.

Music Maker. Compatible Hardware: TI Home Computer, cassette or disk data storage system.
contact publisher for price (Order no.: PHM 3020).
Music Composition Package.
Texas Instruments, Personal Productivit.

Music Master. Customer Support: 800-929-8117 (customer service).
MS-DOS. Apple II. disk $49.99 (ISBN 0-87007-770-8).
A Complete Music Writer System, along with a Variety of Music Already Written, & Several Music Routines That May be Used Inside Other Programs.
SourceView Software International.

Music Room. Ray E. Zubler. 1984. Compatible Hardware: Commodore 64, 128. Language(s): BASIC. Memory Required: 64k.
disk $39.95 (ISBN 0-942132-24-6, Order no.: C-1119).
Simulates the Problem a Musician Has in Tuning Diverse Musical Instruments. Six Instruments Must Be Tuned to a Tuning Pitch. The Instruments Include a Piccolo, a Violin, a Trumpet, a Saxophone, a Cello, & a Tuba. The Instruments Must Be Tuned Individually, Each in Its Own Register. Tuning Instructions Such As "Lengthening" or "Shortening" Are Used to Match the Pitches of Each Instrument.
Electronic Courseware Systems, Inc.

The Music Shop. Don Williams. Compatible Hardware: Commodore 64.
disk $44.95 (Order no.: COMDSK-259).
Allows Users to Compose, Edit, Save, Print & Play Music Using Standard Music Notation. Features Include: Whole to 32nd Notes, Dotted Notes, Rests, 8 Time Signatures, Triplets, Ties, Octave-Up, First & Second Endings, Double- & Single-Staff Modes, Treble or Bass Clefs, Options to Change Key/Time Signatures & Sound/Tempo in Mid-Composition, Selection of Pre-Set Instrument Sounds, Printing of Standard Format Sheet Music, & an Assortment of Finished Music Which Can Be Played As Is or Customized.
Broderbund Software, Inc.

The Music Studio. Compatible Hardware: Commodore Amiga.
3.5" disk $49.95.
Music Editor.
Activision, Inc.

Music Terminology. Vincent Oddo. 1984. Compatible Hardware: Apple II+, IIc, IIe, IIgs; IBM PC; Commodore 64, 128, Macintosh. Operating System(s) Required: Apple DOS 3.3, MAC System 6.0.3-7.1, PC-DOS 3.3. Language(s): QuickBasic. Memory Required: Apple 48k, Commodore 64k, IBM 640k, MAC 512k. General Requirements: CGA card for IBM.
disk $39.95 ea.
Apple. (ISBN 0-942132-13-0, Order no.: A-1115).
IBM PC. (ISBN 0-942132-14-9, Order no.: I-1115).
Commodore 64. (ISBN 0-942132-15-7, Order no.: C-1115).
MAC. disk $59.95.
Designed to Improve the User's Knowledge of Music Terminology. It Is a Set of Five Independent Programs: Glossary of Terms, Categories of Terms, True/False Test, Multiple-Choice Test, & Fill-In Questions. Each Program Randomly Selects Questions from a Pool of over 100 Music Terms. A Summary of Terms to Be Reviewed Is Displayed at the End of Each Program.
Electronic Courseware Systems, Inc.

Music Terminology for Bands, Orchestras & Choirs. Joseph Koob & Jerome Letcher. 1990. Customer Support: ECS offers technical support to registered users. Call (217) 359-7099. Other than the telephone call - technical support is no charge.
DOS 3.2 or higher. IBM. $39.99 single station/$200.00 network (Order no.: I-1382). *Networks supported:* Novell.
System 6.0.4 or higher. Macintosh. $39.95 single station/$200.00 network (Order no.: MAC-1382).
Designed to Facilitate Learning of Fundamental Musical Terminology. Topics Include Dynamics, Tempo Markings, Stylistic Expression Markings, Music Symbols, Key Signatures, Scales & String Terminology. A Final 50-Question Test & Recordkeeping Included.
Electronic Courseware Systems, Inc.

Music Workshop. Customer Support: All of our products are unconditionally guaranteed.
Windows. CD-ROM disk $39.95 (Order no.: MUSICWS). *Nonstandard peripherals required:* CD-ROM drive.
Over 500 MB of Music Shareware, Prof Demos, Wavs, Mids, Educ, More.
Walnut Creek CDRom.

THE MUSICIAN'S TOOLBOX

Music-X. Version: 1.2. Compatible Hardware: Commodore Amiga.
$299.95.
MIDI-Based Music System. Includes Features Such As: Librarian, Patch Editors, Sequence Editor, MIDI Filtering, up to 250 Sequences, High Resolution Clock, Key Mapping, Realtime/Steptime, Record & Playback, etc.
Microillusions, Inc.

Music II: Rhythm & Pitch. Compatible Hardware: Atari XL/XE.
disk $6.95 (Order no.: AED80049).
Atari Corp.

Musical Instrument Rental. 1985. Compatible Hardware: DECmate I, DECmate II, DECmate III, PDP 11-23. Operating System(s) Required: COS-310, MICRO-RSX. General Requirements: Hard disk.
disk $5000.00.
Combines Inventory Control with a Complete Rental Accounting System to Serve the Special Needs of Instrument Rental Companies Supplying Schools & Professionals. The Inventory System Keeps Detailed Records of Unassigned & Assigned Instruments. Rented Instruments Record the Borrower & Remain in Inventory. The Accounting System Prepares Rental Payment Ticket Books for Each Borrower, Processes Receipts, & Keeps Monthly Sales Tax Records. Special Features Include Rental Contract Renewal Letters, Delinquency Statements, & Automatic Rent Control.
Corporate Consulting Co.

Musician Royal. Version: 3.0. Sep. 1990. Compatible Hardware: IBM PC & compatibles. Operating System(s) Required: PC-DOS 2.0 or higher. Memory Required: 192k. General Requirements: 2 disk drives, printer. Items Included: 4 5.25" diskettes or 2 3.5" diskettes & 78-page manual.
disk $35.00 (ISBN 0-917406-07-9).
demo disk $5.00.
Integrated System of Four Multifunction Programs for Transcribing, Editing, Playing, Saving, & Printing Music. A Graphics Program Capable of Handling .BMP, .PCX, or TIF Files is Needed for Printing Sheet Music. Note Capacity: 2500 Notes; Note Values: Unrestricted; Range: over 7 Octaves; Tempo: Unrestricted; Number of Tempo Changes Within a Composition: 9; Key Signatures: Automatic from 7 Flats to 7 Sharps; Set of Options in All Modes.
Electret Scientific Co.

The Musician's Toolbox. Paul Daley et al. Mar. 1987. Compatible Hardware: Apple II, II+, IIe. Memory Required: 64k. General Requirements: Either the Temporal Activity DAC board, Tronix Software Automatic Mouth, Mockingboard, or any MIDI keyboard instrument using the Passport Designs or Roland MIDI hardware.
disk $39.95 (ISBN 0-697-01511-4).
Designed for the Computer Generalist Who May Not Know How, or Who May Not Have the Time, to Program Music Graphics & Sound. Provides Commands Which Enable the User to Perform the Following Functions: Plot a Musical Staff on the Screen, Draw a Score on a Musical Staff, Play a Musical Score, Draw Key Signatures, Clear All or a Portion of the Graphics Screen, Print a String Literal or String Variable Anywhere on the Graphics Screen, Print an Entire Screen of Text Scored in a Text Table, Store & Retrieve up to Four Windows, & Draw a Single Line Border Anywhere on the Graphics Screen. Can Also Be Used by Programmers Outside the Music Discipline. The Routines Allow the Development of New Graphic Shapes for Mathematical Studies, & Greek. European Languages Are Supported in the Existing Character Set.
Wm. C. Brown Pubs.

MusicROM Perspectives: Blues. Aug. 1994. *Customer Support:* Free technical support 810-477-1205.
Windows 3.1 or higher. IBM 386 or higher, or compatible (4Mb). CD-ROM disk $29.95 (ISBN 1-57037-008-7). *Optimal configuration:* CD-ROM drive, 3Mb free hard disk space, 256 color SVGA graphics card & monitor, Mouse (required); MPC compatible sound card (recommended).
This Enhanced Audio Sizzles with Powerhouse Blues. From the Scorching Guitar Licks of Buddy Guy, Albert Collins, & A.C. Reed (with Stevie Ray Vaughan) to the Legendary Sounds of Sonny Boy Williamson, James Cotton, & John Lee Hooker, MusicROM Really Cooks! You Can Also Check Out Rare Photographs, Biographies, the Unique MusicROM Segment Called "Refelctions" (Featuring an Audio Interview with A.C. Reed), & Much More! You Can Also Browse Through Data from the All-Music Guide, Packed with the Most Complete Blues Information Ever.
SelectWare Technologies, Inc.

MusicROM Perspectives: Jazz. Dec. 1994. *Customer Support:* Free technical support 810-477-1205.
Windows 3.1 or higher. IBM 386 or higher, or compatible (4Mb). CD-ROM disk $29.95 (ISBN 1-57037-009-5). *Optimal configuration:* CD-ROM drive, 4Mb free hard disk space, 256 color SVGA graphics card & monitor, Mouse (required); MPC compatible sound card (recommended).
Echoing in Your Ears, & Happening Right Before Your Eyes...Journey Through Jazz & Beyond. This Enhanced Audio CD Features Some of the Most Influential Jazz Artists of the 20th Century. Join Us for a Jazz Odyssey with Art Hodes, Donald Byrd, Coleman Hawkins, Jimmy Forrest, & Others. Check Out Rare Photographs, Biographies, the Unique MusicROM Segment "Reflections" (Featuring an Audio Interview with Bob Koester, President of Delmark Records), & Much More! You Can Also Browse Through the All-Music Guide, Packed with the Most Complete Jazz Information Ever.
SelectWare Technologies, Inc.

MusicROM Perspectives: R & B. Dec. 1994. *Customer Support:* Free technical support 810-477-1205.
Windows 3.1 or higher. IBM 386 or higher, or compatible (4Mb). CD-ROM disk $24.95 (ISBN 1-57037-011-7). *Optimal configuration:* CD-ROM drive, 5Mb free hard disk space, 256 color SVGA graphics card & monitor, Mouse (required); MPC compatible sound card (recommended).
This Enhanced Audio CD Overflows with All the Emotions of the Magical Era of Rhythm & Blues. From the Sultry Tones of "The Duke" Gene Chandler, Jimmy Reed & Little Richard, to the Smooth Harmonies of The Dells, & Jerry Butler & The Impressions, MusicROM Recaptures the Magic! Check Out Rare Photographs, Biographies, the Unique MusicROM Segment "Reflections" (Featuring an Audio Interview with The Impressions' Jerry Butler), & Much More! You Can Also Browse Through the All-Music Guide, Packed with the Most Complete R&B Information Ever.
SelectWare Technologies, Inc.

MusicROM Perspectives: Reggae. Sep. 1995. *Customer Support:* Free technical support 810-477-1205.
Windows 3.1 or higher. IBM 386 or higher, or compatible (4Mb). CD-ROM disk $29.95 (ISBN 1-57037-022-2). *Nonstandard peripherals required:* CD-ROM drive, 7Mb free hard disk space, 256 color SVGA card & monitor, mouse (required), MPC compatible sound card (required for audio), extra video requirements: IBM 486 33 MHz or higher or compatible, double-speed CD-ROM drive, accelerated 256 color SVGA graphics, Microsoft Video for Windows included for digital audio.
Echoing in Your Ears, & Happening Right Before Your Eyes...Journey to the Island As You Embrace This Unique Cultural Explosion with the MusicROM Perspectives Series, Featuring the Sensational Rhythms of Reggae. Experience Reggae Like Never Before! This Enhanced Audio CD Smokes with Rastafarian Sounds of Legendary Reggae Players Such As Black Uhuru, Freddie McGregor, Culture, & Yellowman, to Name a Few! Check Out Yellowman's Red Hot Music Video, Rare Photographs, Biographies, the Unique MusicROM Segment "Reflections" (Featuring an Audio Interview with Doctor Dread), & Much More! You Can Also Browse Through the All-Music Guide, Packed with the Most Complete Reggae Information Ever.
SelectWare Technologies, Inc.

MusicROM Perspectives: Special Edition. May 1995. *Customer Support:* Free technical support 810-477-1205.
Windows 3.1 or higher. IBM 386 or higher, or compatible (4Mb). CD-ROM disk $14.95 (ISBN 1-57037-021-4). *Nonstandard peripherals required:* CD-ROM drive, 6Mb free hard disk space, 256 color SVGA card & monitor, mouse (required), MPC compatible sound card (required for audio), extra video requirements: IBM 486 33 MHz or higher or compatible, double-speed CD-ROM drive, accelerated 256 color SVGA graphics, Microsoft Video for Windows included for digital video.
Echoing in Your Ears, & Happening Right Before Your Eyes...Join Us As We Survey the Best of the MusicROM Perspectives Series, Featuring Spotlighted Performances & Artists from Blues, R&B, Jazz, Latin & Reggae. This Enhanced Audio CD Taps the Nation's Vintage Sounds for Its Series. Check Out Music Videos, Rare Photographs, Biographies, the Unique MusicROM Segment "Reflections" (Featuring an Audio Interview with Ron Wynn, Editor of the "All-Music Guide to Jazz"), & Much More! You Can Also Browse Through the MusicROM Database with Data from the All-Music Guide.
SelectWare Technologies, Inc.

MusicShapes. Sep. 1988. *Compatible Hardware:* Apple IIgs. *Memory Required:* 512k. *Items Included:* Disk, user's guide.
3.5" disk $79.95 (ISBN 0-941849-04-X, Order no.: B0611).
Provides User with Intuitive Musical Graphics & Allows User to Manipulate the Sounds of the Instruments Used by the ENSONIQ Chip of the IIgs or Any Electronic Sound Source Through MIDI. User Travels Back & Forth Between Screens Making & Arranging Graphic Patterns to Make Rhythmic, Melodic & Sound Patterns & Build These into Complex Musical Structures.
Music Systems for Learning, Inc.

MusicType. *Compatible Hardware:* Apple Macintosh.
3.5" disk $59.95.
Music Notation.
Shaherazam.

Musicus. Joseph Koob. 1990.
DOS 3.3, Windows 3.1. IBM PC, PC XT, PC AT, PS/2 (640k) 386, 486. disk $29.95 (Order no.: I-1343). *Nonstandard peripherals required:* Minimum CGA board & color monitor. Macintosh Plus or higher. 3.5" disk $29.95. Atari St. 3.5" disk $29.95.
Falling Note Blocks of Different Point Values Must Strategically Be Maneuvered into Position in Measures of Music of Specific Rhythmic Meter. Each Game Is Timed & Difficulty Level May Be Adjusted at the Beginning of Each Session.
Electronic Courseware Systems, Inc.

Mutrax Monitor. Jan. 1988. *Compatible Hardware:* IBM PC & compatibles. *Memory Required:* recommended 512k. *General Requirements:* Lotus 1-2-3 releases 2 and 2.01. $79.95.
Worksheet Application for Monitoring Mutual Funds. Stores Net-Asset Values, Computes Relative & Absolute Changes, Prepares Data for Graphing, & Produces Transactional-Activity Statements That Include Complete Balance & Dividend Information.
Mutrax.

Mutual. Dec. 1989. *Items Included:* Instruction Included on disk. *Customer Support:* 90 days unlimited warranty.
MS-DOS, Windows 3.1. IBM XT, AT or compatibles (512k). disk $39.95 plus $3.50 S&H (Order no.: 1078). *Addl. software required:* Lotus 1-2-3, Release 4.0 or higher. *Optimal configuration:* IBM AT, 640k RAM.
Mutual Fund Performance Analyzer Showing Tax Cost, Market Value, Gain/Loss, Annualized Rate of Return & Periodic Rate of Return on an Investment.
Compiled Systems.

Mutual Fund Decision Aide. *Version:* 1.1. Apr. 1990. *Items Included:* Complete detailed instruction manual. *Customer Support:* Free unlimited telephone support.
PC-DOS/MS-DOS (IBM). IBM compatible (240k). $49.00. *Addl. software required:* Lotus 1-2-3 V.2.0 or higher.
From Readily Available NAV & Distribution Data, Calculates Total Compounded Returns from Each of up to 12 Past Years to the Present Date, & Returns & Yields Each Year - All after Taxes (0%, 15% & 28%) & after Your Applicable Load Fee. Funds Can Be Compared for the Same Current Date & Market Conditions. See Trends in Performance. Includes Comparison with DJIA & S&P500 Performance, & Calculation of the Annualized Return on One's Personal Investments in a Fund.
V. A. Denslow & Assocs.

MVP-FORTH Cross Compiler. *Version:* 1.xx. Glen Haydon. Mar. 1983. *Compatible Hardware:* CP/M based machines. *Operating System(s) Required:* CP/M. *Language(s):* FORTH (source code included). *Memory Required:* 48k. *Items Included:* Disks & manual. *Customer Support:* Telephone.
8" disk $300.00 (ISBN 0-914699-40-7).
Generates Headerless Code for ROM or Target CPU.
Mountain View Pr., Inc.

MVP-FORTH Expert-2 System. *Version:* 1.xx. Jack Park. Mar. 1984. *Compatible Hardware:* Apple II, II+, IIe, IIc; CP/M-based machines, IBM PC, PC XT, PC AT; Amiga. *Operating System(s) Required:* PC-DOS, Apple DOS, or CP/M. *Language(s):* FORTH (source code included). *Memory Required:* 48k. *Items Included:* Disk & two manuals. *Customer Support:* Telephone.
IBM. disk $175.00 (ISBN 0-914699-48-2). CP/M. 8" disk $175.00 (ISBN 0-914699-49-0). Apple. disk $175.00 (ISBN 0-914699-50-4).
For Development of Knowledge-Based Programs.
Mountain View Pr., Inc.

MVP-FORTH Meta Compiler. *Version:* 1.xx. Glen Haydon. Mar. 1983. *Compatible Hardware:* CP/M based computers with 8" drive. *Operating System(s) Required:* CP/M. *Language(s):* FORTH

TITLE INDEX

(source code included). *Memory Required:* 48k. *Items Included:* Disks & manuals. *Customer Support:* Telephone.
contact publisher for price (ISBN 0-914699-41-5).
Use for Applications on CP/M Based Computers. Includes Public Domain Source.
Mountain View Pr., Inc.

MVP-FORTH PADS. *Version:* 1.xx. T. Wempe. Mar. 1982. *Compatible Hardware:* IBM PC, PC AT. *Language(s):* FORTH (source code included). *Memory Required:* 48k. *Items Included:* Disks & 300+ page manual. *Customer Support:* Telephone.
IBM. disk $500.00 (ISBN 0-914699-46-6).
A FORTH Professional Application Development System.
Mountain View Pr., Inc.

MVP-FORTH Programmer's Kit. *Version:* 1.xxxx.03. Glen Haydon. Mar. 1985. *Compatible Hardware:* Adam; Apple II+, IIe, Macintosh; Atari ST, 600, 800, 1200; Commodore Amiga; Compupro; Cromemco; DEC PDP-11; HP 150; IBM PC, PC XT, PC AT. *Language(s):* FORTH (source code included). *Memory Required:* 48k. *Items Included:* Disks, books, tutorial & manuals. *Customer Support:* Telephone.
$225.00 ea., incl. user's manual.
Apple II. (ISBN 0-914699-07-5).
IBM. (ISBN 0-914699-05-9).
Atari 600, 800 & 1200. (ISBN 0-914699-37-7).
HP 150. (ISBN 0-914699-39-3).
DEC (ISBN 0-914699-33-4); Apple II & 8080 (ISBN 0-914699-14-8); Z-80 (ISBN 0-914699-15-6); & Apple II 8086 (ISBN 0-914699-16-4). 8" disk $225.00 ea., incl. user's manual.
Apple II & 8088 (ISBN 0-914699-17-2); Compupro (ISBN 0-914699-18-0); & Cromemco (ISBN 0-914699-19-9). 8" disk
Amiga (ISBN 0-914699-34-2); Atari ST (ISBN 0-914699-35-0); & Macintosh (ISBN 0-914699-38-5). 3.5" disk $225.00 ea., incl. user's manual.
Adam. cassette $225.00, incl. user's manual (ISBN 0-914699-36-9).
Used for Learning & Developing FORTH Computer Language Programs.
Mountain View Pr., Inc.

MVP-FORTH Programmer's Kit. *Version:* 1.XXXX.03. Glen Haydon. Mar. 1982. *Compatible Hardware:* DEC Rainbow, NEC 8201, TRS-80 Model 100, TI PC. *Operating System(s) Required:* CP/M-86, MS-DOS, CP/M Plus. *Language(s):* FORTH (source code included). *Memory Required:* 48k. *Items Included:* Disks, books, tutorial & manuals. *Customer Support:* Telephone.
DEC Rainbow. disk $195.00 (ISBN 0-914699-21-0).
CP/M+, Z-80. 8" disk $195.00 (ISBN 0-914699-22-9).
TI PC. disk $195.00 (ISBN 0-914699-23-7).
NEC 8201. cassette $195.00 (ISBN 0-914699-24-5).
TRS-80 Model 100. cassette $195.00 (ISBN 0-914699-25-3).
Complete FORTH Computer Language Package Including Disks, User's Manual, Glossary, Source Code & Tutorial.
Mountain View Pr., Inc.

MVP-FORTH Programmer's Kit (HP). *Version:* 1.xxxx.03. Glen Haydon. Mar. 1982. *Compatible Hardware:* HP 89, Kaypro, MicroDecision, North Star, Osborne. *Language(s):* FORTH (source code included). *Memory Required:* 48k. *Items Included:* Disks, books, tutorial & manuals. *Customer Support:* Telephone.
Osborne. disk $225.00 (ISBN 0-914699-08-3).
Kaypro. disk $225.00 (ISBN 0-914699-09-1).
HP 89. disk $225.00 (ISBN 0-914699-10-5).
Z89. disk $225.00 (ISBN 0-914699-11-3).
MicroDecisions. disk $225.00 (ISBN 0-914699-12-1).
North Star. disk $225.00 (ISBN 0-914699-13-X).
Complete FORTH Computer Language Package Including Disks, User's Manual, Glossary, Source Code & Tutorial.
Mountain View Pr., Inc.

MVP-FORTH Programming Aids. *Version:* 1.xx. Wempe. Mar. 1982. *Compatible Hardware:* IBM PC, PC XT, PC AT. *Items Included:* disk & manual. *Customer Support:* telephone.
disk $200.00 (ISBN 0-914699-43-1).
FORTH Tools for Decompiling, Callfinding, Translating & Debugging.
Mountain View Pr., Inc.

MWS Baseball Stats. *Compatible Hardware:* Commodore 64, 128; IBM PC. *Memory Required:* 64k. *General Requirements:* Printer.
disk $50.00 (Order no.: D976F (C64)).
disk $50.00 (Order no.: D9761 (IBM)).
Up to 90 Games per Data Disk. Provides All Advanced Stats. Reports Include: Season Record, Single Game Summaries, Stat Summaries, Run Production by Inning. Uses One Data Disk per Team Being Tracked. Allows Corrections.
Briley Software.

MWS Basketball Stats. *Compatible Hardware:* Commodore 64, 128; IBM PC. *Memory Required:* 64k. *General Requirements:* Printer.
disk $50.00 (Order no.: D972F (C64)).
disk $50.00 (Order no.: D9721 (IBM)).
Custom TEAM Worksheet, up to 15 Stats Printed, 11 Stats Built-In, Roster of 18 Players, up to 30 Games per Season on Same Data Disk. Allows Corrections.
Briley Software.

MWS Bible Concordance: New Testament (KJV), 3 disks. Mark Haney. *Compatible Hardware:* Commodore 64, 128. *General Requirements:* Printer recommended.
disk $50.00 (Order no.: D970F).
Provides the Entire New Testament. Enables Users to Locate Verses Containing Any Word (or Word Combination). May Be Used for Classes, Home Study, or Sermons.
Briley Software.

MWS Gymnastics. *Compatible Hardware:* Commodore 64, 128. *Memory Required:* 64k. *General Requirements:* Printer.
disk $35.00 (Order no.: D978F).
Provides a Summary of the Men's/Women's Record for Every Event During Season. Features up to 24 Team Members in a 32-Team Tournament, Automatic Team Totals, & Instant Corrections.
Briley Software.

MWS Volleyball Stats. *Compatible Hardware:* Commodore 64, 128. *Memory Required:* 64k. *General Requirements:* Printer.
disk $50.00 (Order no.: D974F).
Over 21 Stats Built-In. Reports Include: Team & Individual Summary per Match, Seasons Totals Summary, Season Record of Matches, League Game Summary. Uses One Data Disk per Team Being Tracked. Allows Corrections.
Briley Software.

My First Incredible Amazing Dictionary.
Windows. IBM & compatibles. CD-ROM disk $59.95 (Order no.: R1196). Nonstandard peripherals required: CD-ROM drive. Optimal configuration: 386 processor operating at 16Mhz or higher, MS-DOS 5.0 or higher, Windows 3.1 or higher, 30Mb hard drive, mouse, VGA graphic adapter & VGA color monitor (SVGA recommended), 4Mb RAM, external speakers or headphones (with sound card) that are Sound Blaster compatible.
This Program Introduces Children to 1,000 Words & Meanings Through Text-Accompanied Speech, Pictures, Sounds & Animation. Geared to Allow Children to Learn at Their Own Pace. Perfect for Children Who Cannot Read or Have Never Used a Computer (Ages 4-7).
Library Video Co.

My Very First CD, Hybrid. (VroomBooks Ser.).
Contact publisher for price (ISBN 0-918183-33-2).
T/Maker Co., Inc.

My Word! *Version:* 2.4. *Compatible Hardware:* IBM PC & compatibles. *Operating System(s) Required:* MS-DOS 3.0 or higher. *Memory Required:* 640k. *Customer Support:* 30-day money-back guarantee, free phone support.
disk $29.00, incl. documentation.
source code $29.00.
Features Merge Print, Calculator, Sort, Macros, Color, Word Wrap, Search/Replace, Block Ops, All 256 Characters. Commands Are Similar to WORDSTAR's.
TNT Software.

MYDIET Nutrition & Diet Helper, 2 diskettes.
Items Included: Bound manual. *Customer Support:* Free hotline - no time limit; 30 day limited warranty; updates are $5/disk plus S&H.
MS-DOS. IBM & compatibles (256k). $49.95.
Creates Your Personal Nutritional Profile, Based on Your Height, Weight, Age, Sex, Daily Activity, & the Food You Eat. This Profile Lets You Compare What You Eat to the Recommended Daily Allowances (RDA) Which Are Published by the US Food & Nutrition Board. Clearly Shows Your Nutrition Excesses & Deficiencies & Shows a Bar Chart Comparing What You Eat to Your RDA. In Addition, It Breaks down Your Food Energy to Show the Percentage of Calories You Are Getting from Fat, Protein, & Carbohydrate. Create a Diet Plan to Gain or Lose Weight over a Specified Period of Time. Your Diet Plan Is Displayed in a Table Which Tells What Your Daily Calorie Intake Should Be to Lose or Gain Weight.
Dynacomp, Inc.

MYM (Media Yield Management for Spot TV). *Version:* 2.0. May 1991. *Items Included:* Spiral-bound manuals & on-line help; source code. *Customer Support:* 30 days unlimited warranty; maintenance 1 1/2% per month of license fee; training packages available; customization of software; hotline included.
MS-DOS, MS-Windows. IBM compatible (4Mb). $50,000.00-$100,000.00 (Order no.: MYM20). *Optimal configuration:* 4Mb of RAM; 300Mb disk storage; 386 microprocessor/33 MHz. Networks supported: Novell.
Maximizes the Revenue Potential of Time Periods & Typically Increases Average Rates 2-4%. Establishes the "True" Market Value of Spots Relative to Current Demand. Stations Can Evaluate Every Potential Deal & Objectively Determine How a Specific Transaction Impacts & Effects Business Objectives.
MIT Group, Inc.

MYSTERY AT LASER-AGE HARDWARE:

Mystery at Laser-Age Hardware: Exploring Microsoft Works for MS-DOS. Patricia McKelvey & Philip Thorpe. 1994. *Items Included:* Starter package includes data disks, teacher guide (91pp) & student activity text. Additional copies of activity text are $8.95, or $7.95 for 10 or more copies. *Customer Support:* Returnable if not satisfied. Call 1-800-341-6094 for technical support. 30-day preview available.
MS-DOS. IBM & compatibles. disk $99.95 (ISBN

675

0-8251-2502-2, Order no.: 0-25022). *Addl. software required:* Microsoft Works. Students Investigate Suspects in the Murder of the President of Laser Age Hardware by Analyzing Documents, Databases & Spreadsheets in Microsoft Works, & Organize Information Using the MS-Works Applications. Choose from Three Possible Solutions.
J. Weston Walch Pub.

Mystery Fun House. *Compatible Hardware:* TI-99/4A.
disk or cassette - contact publisher for price.
Texas Instruments, Personal Productivit.

Mystery Games. 1988. *Customer Support:* Toll free customery service Hot Line 1-800-645-3739 (9a.m. - 5p.m. Eastern Time).
Apple II; IBM; Tandy (MS-DOS). $29.95 ea., incl. 1 disk & documentation (Order no.: DB7000; DB7001).
Children Develop Reading & Reasoning Skills While They Play Private Detective in These High-Tech Adventures.
Educational Activities Inc.

Mystery Math Island. 1995. *Items Included:* Program manual. *Customer Support:* Free technical support (800-421-4157), 90 day warranty.
Consumer. Windows; Mac system 7.0.1 or higher. IBM PC or compatible, (4Mb); Macintosh LC 550 or later (2500kb). CD-ROM disk $59.95 (ISBN 1-57204-051-3, Order no.: CD951). *Nonstandard peripherals required:* 256 color monitor; sound card, mouse, double speed CD-ROM drive.
School ver.. Windows; Mac system 7.0.1 or higher. IBM or 100% compatible (4Mb); Macintosh LC 550 or later (2500kb). CD-ROM disk $69.95 (ISBN 1-57204-052-1, Order no.: CD95TT). *Nonstandard peripherals required:* 256 color monitor, sound card, mouse, double speed CD-ROM drive.
Lab pak. Windows; Mac system 7.0.1 or higher. IBM or 100% compatible (4Mb):Macintosh LC 550 or later (2500kb). CD-ROM disk $145.95 (ISBN 1-57204-054-8, Order no.: CD951LPK). *Nonstandard peripherals required:* 256 color monitor, sound card, mouse, double speed CD-ROM drive.
Site license. Windows; Mac system 7.0.1 or higher. IBM or 100% compatible (4Mb); Macintosh LC 550 or later (2500kb). CD-ROM disk $699.00 (ISBN 1-57204-053-X, Order no.: CD951SITE). *Nonstandard peripherals required:* 256 color monitor, sound card, mouse, double speed CD-ROM drive.
Search for the lost pirate treasure on this nutty tropical island. Meet the island shop keeper & buy the tools you need to secure the treasure. Three levels of math equations & story problems stand in your way. Follows national standards & curriculum guidelines for ages 7 to 13.
Lawrence Productions, Inc.

Mystery Mazes: High Tech Detective Adventures Through Reading, 2 disks. Donna Paltrowitz & Stuart Paltrowitz. 1985. *Compatible Hardware:* Apple IIe, IIc, Macintosh. *Language(s):* BASIC, HyperCard. *Memory Required:* 2 Mb RAM, 48k.
The Carnival Caper. disk $49.95, incl. back-up disk, management & documentation (ISBN 0-89525-622-3, Order no.: DK-21120).
Houseboat Hideway. disk $49.95, incl. back-up disk, management & documentation (ISBN 0-89525-623-1, Order no.: DK-21130).
Castle Clues. $49.95, incl. back-up, management & documentation.
Disk Set. $129.00, incl. 3 back-up disks, management & documentation (Order no.: DK-21160).
Graphic Traps, Sound Tricks & False Clues Are Features of This Adventure Game of Interlocking Puzzles. Reading Through the Mysteries, Players Face Surprises & Pesky Obstacles & Must Use Their Reasoning Skills to Unravel the Secrets.
Educational Activities, Inc.

Mystery Melody. *Compatible Hardware:* TI 99/4A.
disk or cassette - contact publisher for price.
Musical Game for 1 or 2 Players. Object Is to Recognize the Title of a Song As Quickly As Possible.
Texas Instruments, Personal Productivit.

Mystical Tarot PC. Jan. 1996. *Items Included:* Instruction Handbook.
DOS. PC (640k). disk $29.95 (ISBN 1-56087-127-X). *Optimal configuration:* Min. 286, DOS, 2k RAM.
PC Computer Software to Easily Learn to Read the Mystical Tarot for Yourself & Others. Unlike Other Programs, You Will Learn the True, Mystic Card Layouts Including the Classic Grand Cross, Plus the Gypsy 5, the Hexagon & the Mystic Clock (Also Called the Medicine Wheel Layout).
Top of the Mountain Publishing.

Myte Myke Business & Manufacturing Software. *Compatible Hardware:* IBM PC & compatibles, HP 9000, NCR Tower, AT&T, RISC 6000. *Operating System(s) Required:* PC-DOS, MS-DOS, Novell Netware, Xenix, UNIX, Unix. *Language(s):* Acu COBOL 85. *Memory Required:* 256k. *General Requirements:* Hard disk. *Items Included:* Manuals. *Customer Support:* Available. call for info.
A Closed Loop System for Manufacturing Resource Planning (MRPII). All Aspects of Production; i.e., Scheduling, MRP, Work-in-Process Tracking, Inventory Control, Shop Floor Control & Standard Costing Are Considered. Accounting & Distribution Modules Handle Receivables, Payables, Financials, Sales & Purchasing for Full Control of All Business Functions.
M & D Systems, Inc.

Myte Myke Business Sys. *Operating System(s) Required:* PC-DOS, MS-DOS, Novell Networks, XENIX, UNIX, AIX. *Items Included:* Manuals.
$7200.00 & up depend on hardware/operating systems & number of users.
Integrated Business Application Software. Includes Order Entry, Inventory Control, Sales Analysis, Accounts Receivable, Accounts Payable, General Ledger, Purchase Orders.
M & D Systems, Inc.

Myte Myke Comparative Sales Report Writer. (Myte Myke Business Software Ser.). *Compatible Hardware:* AT&T; IBM PC, PC XT, PC AT, PS/2 & compatibles, Novell Networks; NCR Tower, HP 9000; RISC 6000. *Operating System(s) Required:* PC-DOS/MS-DOS, XENIX, UNIX Novell Netware, AIX. *Language(s):* Acu COBOL 85. *Items Included:* Manuals. *Customer Support:* Available.
$800.00 & up depending on hardware/operating systems & number of users.
Maintains 2-yr Comparative Sales Information in Accessible, Retrievable Format. Writes Sales Reports by Product, Customer, Territory & Compares Year-Year, Month-Month, Year-to-Date.
M & D Systems, Inc.

Myte Myke Manpower Planning. (Myte Myke Manufacturing Control System). Sep. 1984. *Compatible Hardware:* AT&T 382; IBM PC, PC XT, PC AT, PS/2 & compatibles, Novell Networks; NCR Tower, HP 9000; RISC 6000. *Operating System(s) Required:* PC-DOS, MS-DOS, UNIX, XENIX Novell Netware, AIX. *Language(s):* Acu COBOL 85. *Items Included:* Manuals. *Customer Support:* Available.
$1250.00 & up depending on hardware/operating systems & number of users.
Provides Labor Requirements by Time Period. Shows Man Hours for Scheduling or Dollars for Budgeting Purposes.
M & D Systems, Inc.

Myte Myke Material Requirements Planning. (Myte Myke Manufacturing Control System). Sep. 1984. *Compatible Hardware:* AT&T; IBM PC, PC XT, PC AT, PS/2 & compatibles, Novell Networks; NCR Tower, HP 9000; RISC 6000. *Operating System(s) Required:* PC-DOS/MS-DOS, XENIX, UNIX Novell Netware, AIX. *Language(s):* Acu COBOL 85. *Items Included:* Manuals. *Customer Support:* Available.
$1250.00 & up depending on hardware/operating systems & number of users.
Provides Raw Material Requirements by Time Period. Considers Both Manufacturing & Acquistion Lead Times. Shows Quantity for Buying or Dollars for Budgeting Purposes.
M & D Systems, Inc.

Myte Myke Production Costing. (Myte Myke Manufacturing Control System). Oct. 1985. *Compatible Hardware:* AT&T; IBM PC, PC XT, PC AT, PS/2 & compatibles, Novell Networks; NCR Tower, HP 9000; RISC 6000. *Operating System(s) Required:* PC-DOS, MS-DOS, UNIX, XENIX Novell Netware, AIX. *Language(s):* Acu COBOL 85. *Items Included:* Manuals. *Customer Support:* Available.
$1250.00 & up depending on hardware/operating systems & number of users.
Reports Work in Process Based on Level to Relieve Manufacturing Costs at Standard. Automatically Creates General Ledger Entries. Updates Production Order Status.
M & D Systems, Inc.

Myte Myke Production Forecasting-Sched. (Myte Myke Manufacturing Control System). Sep. 1984. *Compatible Hardware:* AT&T; IBM PC, PC XT, PC AT, PS/2 & compatibles, Novell Networks; NCR Tower, HP 9000; RISC 6000. *Operating System(s) Required:* PC-DOS, MS-DOS, UNIX, XENIX Novell Netware, AIX. *Language(s):* Acu COBOL 85. *Items Included:* Manuals. *Customer Support:* Available.
$1700.00 & up depending on hardware/operating systems & number of users.
Capacity Planning Based on Customer Backlog or Salesman's Forecast. Calculates Latest Start Date Based on Time Frame to Produce Product.
M & D Systems, Inc.

Myte Myke Production Order Processing. (Myte Myke Manufacturing Control Software). 1984. *Compatible Hardware:* AT&T; IBM PC, PC XT, PC AT, PS/2 & compatibles, Novell Networks; NCR Tower, HP 9000; RISC 6000. *Operating System(s) Required:* XENIX, UNIX, MS-DOS, PC-DOS Novell Netware, AIX. *Language(s):* Acu COBOL 85. *Items Included:* Manuals. *Customer Support:* Available.
$1700.00 & up depending on hardware/operating systems & number of users.
Backlog Based on Promise Date. Production Based on Completion Date. Inquiry by Shop Order or Product. Prints Material Requisition Ticket & Make Sheets. Updates Finished Inventory upon Completion.
M & D Systems, Inc.

Myte Myke Shop Floor Control. (Myte Myke Manufacturing Control System). Sep. 1983. *Compatible Hardware:* AT&T; IBM PC, PC XT, PC AT, PS/2 & compatibles, Novell Networks;

NCR Tower, HP 9000; RISC 6000. *Operating System(s) Required:* PC-DOS, MS-DOS, UNIX, XENIX Novell Netware, AIX. *Language(s):* Acu COBOL 85. *Items Included:* Manuals. *Customer Support:* Available.
$1250.00 up depending on hardware/operating systems & number of users.
Collects Actual Material Used & Man Hours by Operator from the Shop Floor. Production Reporting Based on Actuals Rather Than Standards. Reports Variances in Method & Deficiencies in Standards. Updates Raw & Finished Inventories.
M & D Systems, Inc.

Myte Myke Standard Cost Module. (Myte Myke Manufacturing Control System). Sep. 1984. *Compatible Hardware:* AT&T; IBM PC, PC XT, PC AT, PS/2 & compatibles, Novell Networks; NCR Tower, HP 9000; RISC 6000. *Operating System(s) Required:* PC-DOS, MS-DOS, UNIX, XENIX Novell Netware, AIX. *Language(s):* Acu COBOL 85. *Items Included:* Manuals. *Customer Support:* Available.
$1700.00 & up depending on hardware/operating systems & number of users.
Combination Bill of Material & Operation Routing for Each Product Produced or Job Quoted, Based on Materials Used, Operations Performed, Packaging Consumed, Overhead Applied & Scrap Projected at Any Level. Recost Single/All Products Based on the Same Parameters.
M & D Systems, Inc.

Myte Myke Wholesale Distribution System: Accounts Payable. Jan. 1984. *Compatible Hardware:* AT&T; IBM PC, PC XT, PC AT, PS/2 & compatibles, Novell Networks; NCR Tower, HP 9000; RISC 6000. *Operating System(s) Required:* PC-DOS, MS-DOS, UNIX, XENIX Novell Netware, AIX. *Language(s):* Acu COBOL 85. *General Requirements:* Printer. *Items Included:* Manuals. *Customer Support:* Available.
$800.00 & up depending on hardware/operating systems & number of users.
Unlimited Expense Allocation & Alternative Automatic Distributions Based on Journal Source & Vendor Coding Coupled with User Definable Terms Coding Create Flexible Open Payables System. Generates Cash Requirements Reports, Payables Agings, Voucher Checks, Disbursement Registers & Month End Distribution Audit Report.
M & D Systems, Inc.

Myte Myke Wholesale Distribution System: Accounts Receivable. Jan. 1984. *Compatible Hardware:* AT&T; IBM PC, PC XT, PC AT, PS/2 & compatibles, Novell Networks; NCR Tower, HP 9000; RISC 6000. *Operating System(s) Required:* PC-DOS, MS-DOS, UNIX, XENIX Novell Netware, AIX. *Language(s):* Acu COBOL 85. *General Requirements:* Printer. *Items Included:* Manuals. *Customer Support:* Available.
$800.00 & up depending on hardware/operating systems & number of users.
Open Item & Balance Forward Methods Are Supported & May Be Intermixed. Customer Inquiry Reflects Most Current Status Including Last Payment Date, Check Number & Amount. Aging Reports in Detail Reflect Phone Number & Payment History.
M & D Systems, Inc.

Myte Myke Wholesale Distribution System: General Ledger. Jan. 1984. *Compatible Hardware:* AT&T; IBM PC, PC XT, PC AT, PS/2 & compatibles, Novell Networks; NCR Tower, HP 9000; RISC 6000. *Operating System(s) Required:* PC-DOS, MS-DOS, UNIX, XENIX Novell Netware, AIX. *Language(s):* Acu COBOL 85. *General Requirements:* Printer. *Items Included:* Manuals.
$800.00 & up depending on hardware/operating

systems & number of users.
Provides Departmental or Divisional Schedules & 10-Digit Accounts. Defines Sub-Users, & Charts Budgets & Previous Year Comparisons.
M & D Systems, Inc.

Myte Myke Wholesale Distribution System: Inventory Control. Jan. 1984. *Compatible Hardware:* AT&T 382; IBM PC, PC XT, PC AT, PS/2 & compatibles, Novell Networks; NCR Tower, HP 9000; RISC 6000. *Operating System(s) Required:* PC-DOS, MS-DOS, UNIX, XENIX Novell Netware, AIX. *Language(s):* Acu COBOL 85. *General Requirements:* Printer. *Items Included:* Manuals. *Customer Support:* Available.
$1500.00 & up depending on hardware/operating systems & number of users.
Over 80 Data Elements per Item Record Are Provided, 30 User Defined. Numerous Pricing Methods Are Available Including Matrix Pricing, Add-Ons, Subtractions & Quantity Break or Customer Type Pricing. Item Lisings Are Printed in Item, Price List or Description Sequence.
M & D Systems, Inc.

Myte Myke Wholesale Distribution System: Order Entry-Billing. Jan. 1984. *Compatible Hardware:* AT&T 382; IBM PC, PC XT, PC AT, PS/2 & compatibles, Novell Networks; NCR Tower, HP 9000; RISC 6000. *Operating System(s) Required:* PC-DOS, MS-DOS, UNIX, XENIX Novell Netware, AIX. *Language(s):* Acu COBOL 85. *General Requirements:* Printer. *Items Included:* Manuals. *Customer Support:* Available.
$1500.00 & up depending on hardware/operating systems & number of users.
Keeps Track of Overrides on a Day to Day Basis. Custom Selection of the Sequence of Picking Documents, Invoices & Backlog Listing Is Provided. Specify Picking Lists to Be Run in Entry, Catalog or Warehouse Location Sequence.
M & D Systems, Inc.

Myte Myke Wholesale Distribution System: Purchase Order Processing. Jan. 1984. *Compatible Hardware:* AT&T 382; IBM PC, PC XT, PC AT, PS/2 & compatibles, Novell Networks; NCR Tower, HP 9000; RISC 6000. *Operating System(s) Required:* PC-DOS, MS-DOS, UNIX, XENIX Novell Netware, AIX. *Language(s):* Acu COBOL 85. *General Requirements:* Printer. *Items Included:* Manuals. *Customer Support:* Available.
$1500.00 & up depending on hardware/operating systems & number of users.
Purchase Order Entry, Inquiry, Change & Update. Multiple Vendors per Item, Creates PO's Receivers, Open Order Reports by Vendor & Item. Customizable Entry Screens.
M & D Systems, Inc.

Myte Myke Wholesale Distribution System: Sales Analysis. *Compatible Hardware:* AT&T 382; IBM PC, PC XT, PC AT, PS/2 & compatibles, Novell Networks; NCR Tower, HP 9000; RISC 6000. *Operating System(s) Required:* PC-DOS, MS-DOS, UNIX, XENIX Novell Netware AIX. *Language(s):* Acu COBOL 85. *Items Included:* Manuals. *Customer Support:* Available.
$800.00 & up depending on hardware/operating systems & number of users.
M & D Systems, Inc.

Myths, Magic & Monsters: Comprehensive Reading Skills. (Micro Learn Tutorial Ser.). *Items Included:* Teacher-learner materials. *Customer Support:* Free telephone support.
MAC. IBM (125k), Macintosh (2Mb), Apple II series, (48k), Commodore 64. 5.25" disk, $39.95 (Lab pack/5 $99.00), 3.5" disk, $44.95 (Lab pack/5 $115.00). Apple, IBM or Macintosh, $249.00 (ISBN 0-939153-09-2).

DOS. Macintosh. Single copy, $44.95; Lab pack/5, $115.00; Network v., $249.00 (ISBN 0-939153-57-2).
APP. (ISBN 0-939153-70-X).
Systematic Development of Reading Comprehensive Skills While Reading Entertaining Stories of Monsters, Superstitions & Magical Happenings. Skills Practiced Are Recall, Sequencing, Defining the Main Idea, Identifying the Speaker, Recognizing Cause & Effect, Vocabulary Development Through Context Clues, Analyzing Figurative Language, Drawing Conclusions, Recognizing Mood, Tone & Setting. The tutorial mode gives explanations & help for every answer choice, correct & incorrect. The test mode gives no help for the test, but then presents missed questions in tutorial mode.
Word Assocs., Inc.

N-See: NC Verification Software. *Version:* 3.0. Jan. 1996. *Items Included:* User manual. *Customer Support:* Annual support 10% system price.
MS-Windows. 386 (16Mb). disk $1795.00. *Nonstandard peripherals required:* 640x480x256.
Windows NT. 486 (32Mb). disk $1795.00. *Nonstandard peripherals required:* 640x480x256.
Windows 95. 386 (12Mb). disk $1795.00. *Addl. software required:* 640x480x256.
Solid Model NC Verification System. Modules Include: Verify: True Solid Model Image of Part. Rotate, Cross-Section, Zoom at Any Angle. Preview: See Tool Animation. Turbo: High Speed Verification of 500 Blocks of G-Code per Second. Advanced Inspection: Compare Part with CAD STL Data. Advanced Milling: 4th Axis Indexing. Advanced Tools: Add Taper, Taper with Ballend, Dove Tail, Chamfer, Radius/Corner Rounding etc. Complex Stack & Fixture; G-Code Library.
MicroCompatibles, Inc.

NAG FORTRAN Workstation Library. *Compatible Hardware:* IBM PC. *General Requirements:* IBM Professional FORTRAN, Ryan-McFarland FORTRAN.
disk $295.00.
Contains 254 Routines Designed to Give Broad Coverage to the Principal Areas of Mathematics & Statistics for Implementation on Workstations & Personal Computers. It Is a Significant Subset of the Renowned NAG FORTRAN LIBRARY, Which Is Widely Available on Mainframes & Supercomputers.
Numerical Algorithms Group, Inc.

NAGWare f90 Compiler. *Version:* 2.1. Sep. 1991. *Items Included:* Users guide, F90 Explained; users notes & installers notes. *Customer Support:* 90 days free maintenance; additional maintenance available, includes free telephone support & updates.
DOS 3.3 or higher (DOS 5 & 4.1 compatible). 486 processor upwards, 386SX processors. disk $495.00. *Addl. software required:* DBOS included.
World's First Fortran90 Compiler to Support the Full ISO Standard for Fortran 90. The f90 User Can Enjoy All the Features of f90 Including Automatic & Allocatable Arrays, Derived Data Types, Pointers, 'Stream' Based Operations & Much More.
Numerical Algorithms Group, Inc.

Name-Address Program. *Version:* 14.0. (Accounting Software Ser.). Aug. 1993. *Compatible Hardware:* IBM PC & compatibles. *Operating System(s) Required:* MS-DOS, PC-DOS 3.X & up. *Language(s):* MegaBASIC. *Memory Required:* 640k. *General Requirements:* Hard disk, wide-carriage printer. *Customer*

Support: (203) 790-9756.
disk $195.00, Network Option ,200.00 more. manual $50.00.
Allows Entry & Maintenance of Names & Addresses, & Prints Labels. User Defined Data Tag, Entry of Contact & Title, Sort by Name, Zip Code, Area Code, Phone Number, Street, City, State & Contact. Two Sort Criteria Available per List. Prints Mailing Lables, Envelopes Code List or Full Format List.
Applications Systems Group (CT), Inc.

NamePro. Version: 1.01. Jan. 1995. *Items Included:* Complete "Perfect Binding" user's guide. *Customer Support:* 90-day free telephone support, free support via FAX or CompuServe.
MS-Windows 3.1 or higher. IBM PC & compatibles - 386 or higher (4Mb). disk $495.00. *Optimal configuration:* 8Mb RAM, 15Mb plus of free hard disk space. *Networks supported:* NamePro is a single user license product which will support a networked printer and/or networked hard drives.
NamePro Is a Windows Name Development System. It Comes with 9 Databases, Including a Namebase of 30,000 Plus Names Coded by Connotation, Category, & Trademark Status. Its Search Engine Helps You Find Names You Like. Its Name Building Tools Help You Construct Names from Its Wordbase (100,000 Plus Words) & NamePart Databases.
The Namestormers.

Namer. Version: 2.2. 1988. *Items Included:* Spiral bound user's guide. *Customer Support:* Free telephone support.
PC-DOS/MS-DOS 2.1 or higher. IBM PC & compatibles (256k). disk $195.00. *Optimal configuration:* 800k of free hard disk space.
Namer Is a DOS Name Generator for Unique Product, Service, or Company Names. It Consists of 11 Naming Methods Such As Connotation Synthesizer, Phrase Maker, Dodging Profanities, & Original Name Generator. It Includes Databases of Existing Names, 10,000 Plus Name Parts & Roots.
The Namestormers.

NANOS. Version: 2.60. Ira Ellenbogen. Aug. 1989. *Compatible Hardware:* Data General, Strobe Data Hawk, PC compatible. *Operating System(s) Required:* RDOS. *Language(s):* Assembly. *Memory Required:* 256k. *General Requirements:* Data General 16 bit CPU.
$350.00 (Order no.: NANOS/MODEL).
Fully Mapped DG/RDOS Compatible Replacement Operating System. Manages up to 16 Simultaneous Program Grounds Including the Ability to Run the CLI & All Standard Languages & Applications Programs. Each Ground May Use Extended Memory, Multi-Tasking, User Devices, User Clocks, etc. Enhancements Include Synchronized Interprogram Communication, Assignable Printer, Direct Access to DOS & Network Files, & More.
Nanosecond Systems, Inc.

NanoVision: Molecular Presentation Graphics. Version: 1.2. William R. Light. Jan. 1992. *Items Included:* One spiral-bound manual. *Customer Support:* Free customer support, 800 number.
Macintosh (2Mb). disk List $295.00; Academic $265.00 (ISBN 0-8412-1920-6).
Makes Top-Quality Molecular Images. Can Visualize Molecules Containing up to 32,000 Atoms, Create Publication-Quality Images & Slides, & Produce Smooth-Motion Animation. Reads Popular File Formats Such As Cartesian, Chem3D Cartesian, Alchemy II, Moldat, Brookhaven PDB, etc. Offers Speed & Special Clipping & Color Capabilities to Selectively Hide or View Parts of a Model the Obstruct Investigation. Converts Screen Images into Hard Copy, Saving the Image As a PICT File, & Copying It into a Word Processor Document.
American Chemical Society.

Napoleon in Russia-Borodeno 1812. *Compatible Hardware:* Atari; Commodore 64/128; IBM PC & compatibles. *Memory Required:* Atari 64k, Commodore 64k, IBM 512k. *General Requirements:* Joystick optional.
Atari. disk $24.95 (ISBN 0-88717-225-3, Order no.: 16308-43499).
Commodore. disk $24.95 (ISBN 0-88717-226-1, Order no.: 16301-43499).
IBM. 3.5" or 5.25" disk $34.95 (ISBN 0-88717-227-X, Order no.: 1630443499).
Game Features Include Command over Infantry, Cavalry & Artillery Divisions & Scrolling Battle Map with Prominent Terrain. Also Includes Several Options Covering Fatigue, Morale Levels, Battle Speed, Difficulty Modes & Player Selctions.
IntelliCreations, Inc.

NAS2: Nutrient Analysis System 2. Version: 4.0. Jun. 1990. *Compatible Hardware:* Apple II, IIc, IIe, IIgs, Macintosh; IBM PC, PC XT, PC AT & compatibles, PS/2. *Operating System(s) Required:* Apple DOS 3.3, ProDOS; PC-DOS/MS-DOS 3.0 or higher. *Memory Required:* 1Mb Mac, Apple & IBM 128k. *General Requirements:* 2 disk drives or hard disk, printer. *Items Included:* Disks (5 IBM, 6 Apple, 1 Mac). *Customer Support:* Telephone support - one hour free.
disk $289.00.
Provides an Analysis of Food Intake Data for over 2700 Foods Including Name Brands & Fast Foods. Includes 24 Nutrients (Expandable to 32), & Costing Information. Printouts for Clients & Professionals Are Automatically Created. Users Can Sequence Foods Analyzed in Descending Order by Amount of Nutrient. Search for Foods with Specific Characteristics; & Compare a Diet, Menu, Meal or Recipe to the USRDA, RDA, FAO/WHO, Canadian RNI or Any Other Standard.
DDA Software.

Natal Horoscope. (Star Track Ser.). Robert S. Hand. 1980. *Compatible Hardware:* Apple II with Applesoft, Apple II+, IIe, IIc, III. *Operating System(s) Required:* Apple DOS. *Language(s):* Applesoft BASIC (source code included). *Memory Required:* 48k. *General Requirements:* Printer. *Items Included:* Manual. *Customer Support:* Free phone support.
disk $75.00 (ISBN 0-913637-05-X).
Computes Natal Horoscopes with Wheel, Aspectarian & Other Features.
Astrolabe, Inc.

Natal Horoscope Interpreter: M90J. Charles Jayne & Vivia Jayne. *Compatible Hardware:* Apple II+; Commodore 64, PET; TRS-80; IBM PC. *Language(s):* BASIC. *General Requirements:* 2 disk drives, printer.
disk $300.00 (Order no.: M90).
Provides 12 Page Natal Interpretation Divided into Chapter Format.
Matrix Software.

Natal Starter Package: M-0. *Compatible Hardware:* Atari 400, 800; Commodore CBM, VIC-20; IBM PC; TI 99/4; Timex Sinclair ZX-81; TRS-80 Model I, Model III, Model 100, Color Computer, Pocket Computer 1 & 2.
contact publisher for price.
Introduction to the Use of the Home Computer for Astrology.
Matrix Software.

The National Directory of Addresses & Telephone Numbers. Version: 1989.
Macintosh Plus or higher (1Mb). $130.00 retail; $110.00 with educational discount.
Nonstandard peripherals required: Apple CD SC, Toshiba or NEC ROM drive. *Addl. software required:* Hypercard 1.2.2 or 1.2.5;

Xearch version 1.0.1.
Designed for Macintosh Users to Help Them Optimize Their Voice, Data & Facsimile Communications. Includes over 120,000 Listings of the Most Useful & Important Addresses, Telephone Numbers & Fax Numbers Throughout the U.S. & World.
Xiphias.

The National Gallery of Art Laserguide. *Items Included:* 2 floppy disks, user's guide. *Customer Support:* M-F 9 AM-5 PM Pacific Time (213) 451-1383.
Macintosh Plus, SE, II or Portable (1 Mb). 3.5" disk $59.95. *Nonstandard peripherals required:* Videodisc player, monitor & cables; The National Gallery of Art videodisc. *Addl. software required:* HyperCard 1.2.2 or higher.
Lets User Organize & View Works of Art by Artist, Nationality, Period, Style, Date, Medium or Subject. The Subject Index Contains over 1000 Key Words for Handling Rapid Searches, & Users Can Add Their Own Impressions or Notes to Personalize the Database, or Create Slide Lists for Lectures or Presentations.
The Voyager Co.

National Lampoon's Blind Date. Three Vision Staff. Nov. 1994.
DOS, Windows 3.1. PC 386 or higher (4Mb). CD-ROM disk Contact publisher for price (ISBN 1-885932-03-0). *Nonstandard peripherals required:* CD-ROM drive, SoundBlaster. *Addl. software required:* 8Mb RAM, Double Spin CD-ROM, 386 15MHz SoundBlaster.
System 7. MAC LC3 or higher (4Mb), 4Mb hard drive, 256 color. CD-ROM disk Contact publisher for price (ISBN 1-885932-04-9). *Nonstandard peripherals required:* CD-ROM. *Optimal configuration:* 8Mb RAM.
A Humorous Interactive CD-Romance Adventure in Which the Player Is Experiencing the Angst of a First Date. His Task Is to Say All the Right Things in Order to "Further" the Date.
Trimark Interactive.

National Lampoon's Chess Maniac 5 Billion & 1. Apr. 1993.
MS-DOS. IBM & compatibles. disk $69.95 floppy; $59.95 CD-ROM.

National Parks of America. Jun. 1993. *Items Included:* Manual. *Customer Support:* Free telephone technical support.
DOS & Microsoft Windows 3.1. 12 Mhz 80386SX (2Mb). CD-ROM disk Contact publisher for price (ISBN 1-884014-22-4). *Nonstandard peripherals required:* MPC-compatible CD-ROM drive (680Mb); SVGA display; audio board; mouse, 486DX processor. *Addl. software required:* Microsoft CD-ROM extensions v.2.2. *Optimal configuration:* 4Mb RAM; double-speed CD-ROM drive.
Macintosh System 6.05. Color Macintosh (256 colors) (3.5Mb free RAM). CD-ROM disk Contact publisher for price (ISBN 1-884014-34-8). *Nonstandard peripherals required:* CD-ROM drive. *Optimal configuration:* Double speed CD-ROM; 13" color monitor; 8Mb RAM; fast processor.
Expands upon the Book of the Same Name by Photographer David Muench (ISBN 1-55868-124-8). This Multimedia Tour of National Parks Features over 970 Full Color Photographs by David Muench, Combined with Narration, Video, & Animation. Electronic Indexing & Sorting Allows Travel Planning Based upon Park Amenities & Location.
Multicom Publishing, Inc.

TITLE INDEX

National Semiconductor Series 32000 C Cross Compiler. Version: 2.2.4. Jul. 1986. *Compatible Hardware:* DEC; IBM PC, 370; Motorola 68000. *Operating System(s) Required:* Idris, PC-DOS, VAX/VMS, RSX-11M. *Language(s):* C. *Memory Required:* 64k.
$1,500.00-$5,000.00.
manual only $25.00.
Provides for Downloading Programs to the DB16000 Development Board. Comprised of Both a Native Code Generator for the Host Development Machine & a Code Generator for the 32000. Also Included Is a Cross Assembler Which Optionally Produces Complete Assembler Listings with Addresses, Object Code, & Assembler Source Code. Additional Programming Utilities, Including a Linker & Librarian Are Provided. Portable C Library with Formatted I/O & String Handling Routines Is Provided for Both the Host Development Machine & the 32000.
JMI Software Consultants, Inc.

The Native Americans. Nov. 1995. *Items Included:* Soft cover, stapled manual & registration card. *Customer Support:* Free customer service via our 800 number, unlimited warranty on disk replacement.
Mac System 7.1 or higher, Windows 3.1 or higher, 486 or higher. 256 color capable Macintosh (8Mb). CD-ROM disk $39.95 (Order no.: ISNA1004). *Nonstandard peripherals required:* 13" or higher monitor, 2Mb hard disk space, mouse, CD-ROM player, Super VGA, sound card (100% sound blaster compatible).
Windows 3.1 or higher, 486 or higher (8Mb).
Turner Publishing's Book Put into a CD-ROM Format. Includes Full Narration, Video Interactivity, & Music.
Image Smith, Inc.

Natural. Version: 1.4. *Operating System(s) Required:* VAX/VMS.
$6250.00 to $50,000.00.
Features Online Digital Command Language Support. Stores & Executes Programs from Director & Can Call Programs from a Third-Generation Language.
Software AG.

Natural-Connection. *Compatible Hardware:* IBM PC Compatibles. *Operating System(s) Required:* PC-DOS, MS-DOS. *Memory Required:* 128k.
contact publisher for price.
Allows PC to Run with Mainframe That Uses NATURAL Information Processing System.
Software AG.

Natural Construct. *Compatible Hardware:* DEC's 32-bit VAX computers.
$3,130.00 to $25,000.00.
Set of Automated Tools That Work with the Natural Application Developer Product to Design & Implement Systems Written in the Natural Forth-Generation Language. Four Additional Software Tools include Adabas SQL, Natural Graphics, Natural Elite & Workbench. Features a Program Generator, an On-Line Help Facility, & a Library of Customizable Model Programs & Program Functions.
Software AG.

Natural Language. Version: 5.1. *Compatible Hardware:* Sun 3,4 & Sparc; II; DEC VAX; Apollo; HP9000; Sun; Compaq 386; IBM RT, PS/2-70,80. *Operating System(s) Required:* A/UX, Unix, Ultrix, VMS, AIX, Hp/Ux, Xenix, Sun, SCO Unix; Dynix; Dynix/ptx; OSX. *Memory Required:* 8000k. *General Requirements:* Hard disk & RDBMS. *Items Included:* Documentation, 90-day warranty, upgrades. *Customer Support:* Consulting/training class available for fee; upgrades & hotline supported under maintenance.

Natural Language. $4950.00 & up.
Connector. $10,000.00.
English-Based Data-Access Tool for Managers & Professionals. Translates User's Typed Conversational English into Native SQL Which Is Run Against the Database. Resulting Information Is Displayed As Graph, in Tabular Format or As English Sentence. Additional Features Include Spelling Checker, Context-Sensitive Help & Support for User-Defined Synonyms & Concepts. Product Is Sold Bundled with the NLI Connector (ICon), Which Is a Tool To Help the Developer Customize Natural Language for the Database Application.
Natural Language, Inc.

Natural Sound "Sound Effects". *Compatible Hardware:* Apple Macintosh. *Memory Required:* 512k.
3.5" disk $39.95 (ISBN 0-944310-05-2, Order no.: NSSFX).
Library of Sound Effects to Be Used with SLIDE SHOW MAGICIAN Presentations or with BASIC or Pascal Programs.
Magnum Software Corp.

NaturaLink Access to Dow Jones News-Retrieval. *Operating System(s) Required:* MS-DOS. *Memory Required:* 256k. *General Requirements:* 2 disk drives.
$150.00 (Order no.: TI P/N 2234230-0001).
Texas Instruments, Personal Productivit.

Nature Meditations from the Essays of John Burroughs. (Nature Meditations from...Ser.). Pref. by Walt Carroll. 1994.
IBM & compatibles. 3.5" or 5.25" disk $35.00 (ISBN 0-88367-507-2).
Electronic Book.
Olympic Media Information.

The Nature of Genes. Haig H. Kazazian, Jr. et al. *Customer Support:* Toll-free technical support - no charge. In U.S. - 9AM-5PM EST 800-343-0064. In U.K. - 44(0)81-995-8242.
System 6.07 or higher. Apple Macintosh (4Mb). CD-ROM disk $175.00 Individual, $495.00 Institutional (ISBN 1-57276-001-X, Order no.: SE-001-001). *Nonstandard peripherals required:* CD-ROM drive.
This Is a Genetic Education & Reference Tool Which Is User-Interactive, Presents High Definition Color Pictures with Rapid Data Access. Tutorial Covers the Following Subjects: DNA, DNA Replication, Genetic Message, Genetic Code, Genes, Transcription, Translation, Proteins, Inheritance, Human Genome.
SilverPlatter Education.

The Nature of Genes. Haig H. Kazazian, Jr. et al. Jan. 1993. *Customer Support:* Toll-free technical support - no charge. In U.S. 9AM - 5PM EST 800-343-0064; in U.K. 44(0)81-995-8242.
System 6.07 or higher. Apple Macintosh (4Mb). CD-ROM disk $175.00, Individual, ,495.00 Institutional (ISBN 1-57276-001-X, Order no.: SE-001-001). *Nonstandard peripherals required:* CD-ROM drive.
This Is a Genetic Education & Reference Tool Which Is User-Interactive, Presents High Definition Color Pictures with Rapid Data Access. This Tutorial Covers the Following Subjects: DNA, DNA Replication, the Genetic Message, the Genetic Code, Genes, Transcription, Translation, Proteins, Inheritance, the Human Genome.
SilverPlatter Education.

Nature Photo Collection. *Items Included:* Browser/installer front end software. *Customer Support:* 90 day warranty, free call back technical support.
System 6. Color Mac (4Mb). CD-ROM disk

$9.95. *Nonstandard peripherals required:* CD-ROM drive. *Optimal configuration:* 8Mb RAM. *Networks supported:* Apple File Sharing.
Windows 3.1. IBM 386 (4Mb). CD-ROM disk $9.95. *Nonstandard peripherals required:* CD-ROM drive. *Optimal configuration:* IBM 486, 8Mb RAM.
BeachWare.

Nave's Topical Bible. Parsons Technology. Nov. 1992.
3.5" disk Contact publisher for price (ISBN 1-57264-035-9).
Parsons Technology.

Naves Topical Bible & Cross Reference System. Aug. 1990. *Customer Support:* No fee is charged for our customer support: 30 day money back return guarantee; lifetime warranty on defective disk replacement; free telephone technical support.
PC or MS-DOS 2.0 or higher. IBM PC/XT/AT or compatible. 3.5" or 5.25" disk $39.95. *Addl. software required:* PC Study Bible. *Optimal configuration:* Hard disk with 2Mb available will be required for this add-on.
Add-On Module to Be Used with PC STUDY BIBLE. More Than 100,000 Bible Verses Are Cross-Referenced under Nearly 20,000 Topic Headings. User Can Display Detailed Outlines with Verse References on the Topic of Choice. Naves Is Included As Part of PC STUDY BIBLE's Complete Package.
Biblesoft.

Navigate! Version: 3.2. *Compatible Hardware:* Apple Macintosh Plus or better, IBM compatibles 386 or better. *Items Included:* Manual, OPS Loran connection cable, chart file of your choice.
3.5" disk $295.00 monochrome or color.
3.5" disk upgrade $99.00.
additional digital charts $95.00.
Digital Chart Navigation System.
Fair Tide Technologies, Inc.

Navigational Star Identification. *Compatible Hardware:* TI 99/4A with Extended BASIC module. *Operating System(s) Required:* DX-10. *Language(s):* Extended BASIC. *Memory Required:* 48k.
cassette $18.95.
User Provides the Coordinates of an Unknown Star. If One of the 57 Navigational Stars Is Within 3 Degrees of the Stated Coordinates, the Declination, Hour Angle & Name of the Navigational Star Are Displayed. A Modification of the Navigational Star Program.
Eastbench Software Products.

The Navigational Star Program. *Compatible Hardware:* TI 99/4A with Extended BASIC module. *Operating System(s) Required:* DX-10. *Language(s):* Extended BASIC. *Memory Required:* 48k.
cassette $18.95.
User Provides Date, Greenwich Mean Time & Geographical Coordinates. Calculates the Altitude & Horizontal Coordinates of Azimuth for Each of the 57 Primary Navigational Stars. Then Picks Only Those Stars Which Are Above the Horizon at the Input Date & Time, & Sorts, Then Lists Them in Order of Increasing Azimuth.
Eastbench Software Products.

NBA. *Compatible Hardware:* Apple II, II+, IIe, IIc; Commodore 64/128; IBM PC & compatibles; Tandy 1000. *Operating System(s) Required:* Apple DOS, MS-DOS.
disk $39.95.
1986-1987 Season Disk $20.00.
Statistical Basketball Game Licensed by the National Basketball Association. Puts You on the Court with the Best of Professional Basketball.

Play Begins with 20 Teams, Including the Champions from the Last Five Years. Your Play Calling Is Re-Enacted by All 10 Players Animated on Screen. Comes with an Accelerated "AutoPlay" Mode & Stat-Keeping Programs So That Aspiring League Commissioners Can Run Their Own Leagues.
Avalon Hill Game Co., The Microcomputer Games Div.

NBA Basketball Addition. Ronald D. Jones. 1985. *Compatible Hardware:* Apple; Commodore; IBM; TRS-80 Model I, Model III, Color Computer. *Operating System(s) Required:* CP/M. *Memory Required:* 64k.
disk $149.95 ea.
Apple. (ISBN 1-55604-144-6, Order no.: B003).
CP/M. (ISBN 1-55604-145-4, Order no.: B003).
Commodore. (ISBN 1-55604-146-2, Order no.: B003).
Color Computer. (ISBN 1-55604-147-0, Order no.: B003).
IBM. (ISBN 1-55604-148-9, Order no.: B003).
Model I & Model III. (ISBN 1-55604-149-7, Order no.: B003).
Win/Loss Power Designed to Isolate "Ripe" Opportunities & Provide a Second Opinion, Based on Wins & Losses, Consecutive Losses & Home Team Advantages. Road Games & Conceaptive Road Game Strengths Are Also Taken into Account with a Strength Analysis. Gives Out Complete Statistical Results & Features Better Bets Playing upon Consecutive Losses When at Home.
Professor Jones Professional Handicapping Systems.

NBA Basketball Analysis. Ronald D. Jones. 1985. *Compatible Hardware:* Apple; Commodore; IBM; TRS-80 Model I, Model III, Color Computer. *Operating System(s) Required:* CP/M. *Memory Required:* 64k.
disk $99.95 ea.
Apple. (ISBN 1-55604-132-2, Order no.: B001).
CP/M. (ISBN 1-55604-133-0, Order no.: B001).
Commodore. (ISBN 1-55604-134-9, Order no.: B001).
Color Computer. (ISBN 1-55604-135-7, Order no.: B001).
IBM. (ISBN 1-55604-136-5, Order no.: B001).
Model I & Model III. (ISBN 1-55604-137-3, Order no.: B001).
Complete Data Base Program Designed to Evaluate NBA Games & Predict the Outcome. All Teams Are Stored on Disk for Update & Game Evaluation.
Professor Jones Professional Handicapping Systems.

NBA Basketball Analysis with College Version. Ronald D. Jones. 1985. *Compatible Hardware:* Apple; Commodore; IBM; TRS-80 Model I, Model III, Color Computer. *Operating System(s) Required:* CP/M. *Memory Required:* 64k.
disk $129.95 ea.
Apple. (ISBN 1-55604-138-1, Order no.: B002).
CP/M. (ISBN 1-55604-139-X, Order no.: B002).
Commodore. (ISBN 1-55604-140-3, Order no.: B002).
Color Computer. (ISBN 1-55604-141-1, Order no.: B002).
IBM. (ISBN 1-55604-142-X, Order no.: B002).
Model I & Model III. (ISBN 1-55604-143-8, Order no.: B002).
Evaluates Average Points Scored, Wins, Losses, Average Points Given up Home, Away Games & Wild Card Games. Results Include "Too Close to Call" Games, Regular Play Games & Super Play Games, All in Accordance with Win Percentages. All Teams Are Stored on Disk & Available for Update & Evaluation.
Professor Jones Professional Handicapping Systems.

NBA Wager Analyzer. *Items Included:* Bound manual. *Customer Support:* Free hotline - no time limit; 30 day limited warranty; updates are $5/disk plus S&H.
MS-DOS. IBM & compatibles (128k). disk $39.95.
Uses 17 Different Wagering Systems (Recommended by Expert Handicappers) to Predict Point Spread Winners in the MBA. It Maintains Information on Past Performances for Use in Analyzing Future Games.
Dynacomp, Inc.

NCAP: Intersection Capacity Analysis. *Version:* 2.1. 1987. *Compatible Hardware:* IBM PC, PC XT, PC AT & compatibles. *Operating System(s) Required:* PC-DOS/MS-DOS. *Language(s):* Compiled BASIC. *Memory Required:* 256k. *General Requirements:* 2 disk drives or hard disk. *Customer Support:* Unlimited telephone, BBS. disk $295.00 (Order no.: NCAP).
Provides Transportation Engineers & Planners with the Ability to Evaluate Current & Future Adequacy Level of Intersections. The Latest Adopted Transportation Research Board Highway Capacity Manual Techniques Are Employed to Provide a Quantitative Analysis of the Travel Conditions. The Utility of This Package Is Further Enhanced by the Ability to Directly Read Output from TMODEL2, Transportation Modeling System. Output Is In Standard HCM Format.
TModel Corp.

NCR PC2PC. *Compatible Hardware:* Compaq; IBM PC, PC XT & compatibles; NCR PC. *Memory Required:* 256k.
contact publisher for price; Interface, cable, tap box, user guide, tool kit, & Network Diagnostic tool.
Office Communications Program That Can Put up to 64 IBM-Compatibles Online to Each Other. Features File-Sharing, Electronic Mail & Transfer of Documents. Every Connected PC Has Access to Printers, Plotters, & Storage Devices.
NCR Corp., Personal Computer Div.

NCSS-PC. *Compatible Hardware:* IBM PC & compatibles. *Memory Required:* 512k.
disk $125.00.
Menu-Driven Statistical Package Features Multiple & Stepwise Regression, up to 10 Way ANOVA, Time Series, Scatter Plots, T-Tests, Cross Tabs, Nonparametrics, Spreadsheet Input, Sort, Join, & Merge. Also Reads ASCII Files & Features 3D Graphics, Add-Ons Available.
NCSS-PC.

NCTALK. Feb. 1987. *Items Included:* 1 manual, 1 diskette. *Customer Support:* 90 day warranty.
DOS 3.3. Any PC with 1 or more serial/parallel ports (256k). disk $695.00 (ISBN 1-887777-07-5).
A Data Communication Utility for the Metalworking Industry. It Transfers NC Programs Between a Computer & Paper Tape Punch/Reader, down & Uploads with a CNC Control, Provides Parallel/Serial Communications to Devices Including Floppy Disks, Store/Forward Devices, Modems, etc. Also Included Are ASCII Terminal Emulation, a Text Editor & Block Number Resequencer for Creating, Modifying an NC Program.
Datacut, Inc.

NDP C-C Plus Plus 386. *Version:* 4.21. 1988. *Memory Required:* 3000k. *General Requirements:* Hard disk, math coprocessor (80387, 80287, 83D87, MW1167, or 3167). *Items Included:* NDPTools: NDPLIB, NDPLINK, & NDPRUN (in the DOS version). *Customer Support:* 1 year free technical support; $300.00 maintenance fee after initial one year warranty.
DOS, UNIX V.3 or V.4, OS/2, NT, Coherent, Solaris. $695.00.
A Full AT&T 2.1 Compliant C plus plus Compiler. A True Compiler That Also Translates the ANSI & K&R Dialects of C As Validated by Plum Hall. In Addition to Making It Possible to Build Mixed Applications Which Call Fortran or Pascal from C or C plus plus, This Product Provides Numeric Optimizations Not Usually Found in C Compilers, Such As Loop Unrolling & Register Caching. Like All NDP Compilers, C/C plus plus Includes a Built-In Intelligent Assembler. Validation Suites for C/C plus plus Include Plum Hall, C Front, & Rogue Wave. QuickView Source Level Debugger Is Included.
Microway, Inc.

NDP C/C++ 486. *Version:* 4.21. 1990. *Items Included:* The DOS version of the compiler includes the NDPTools, NDPLIB, NDPLINK, & NDPRUN, ClearView source level debugger. *Customer Support:* One year of free technical support; $400.00 maintenance fee after initial warranty.
DOS, or UNIX 386 V.3 or V.4, Solaris, OS/2, NT, Coherent. 80486-based system (can also be run on an 80386-based system without taking advantage of all of the 80486 features). $995.00. *Nonstandard peripherals required:* Hard disk. *Addl. software required:* NDP Tools (included in the compiler).
A Full AT&T 2.1 Compliant C++ Compiler. It Is a True Compiler That Also Translates the ANSI & K&R Dialects of C As Validated by Plum Hall. In Addition to Making It Possible to Build Mixed Applications Which Call Fortran or Pascal from C or C++, This Product Provides Numeric Optimizations Not Usually Found in C Compilers, Such As Loop Unrolling & Register Caching. It Incorporates All of the Features of NDP 386 Version with Several New Enhancements Designed to Take Advantage of the 486. Like All NDP Compilers, C/C++ Includes a Built-In Intelligent Assembler. Validation Suites for C/C++ Include Plum Hall, C Front, & Rogue Wave. ClearView Source Level Debugger Is Included.
Microway, Inc.

NDPFFT. *Version:* 1.0f. Jun. 1988. *Compatible Hardware:* 386/486. *Customer Support:* One year free technical support.
disk $250.00.
Library of Optimized 1- & 1-Dimensional FFT & Related Functions That Is Cellable from the DOS Version of Microway's NDP FORTRAN-386 Protected Mode Compiler. It Runs on 80386-Based Systems Equipped with an Intel 80387 or 80287, CYMX 83087, or WEITEK 3167 or MW1167. At Runtime, NDPFFT Automatically Detects Which Coprocessors Is Present & Makes the Best Use of the Available Coprocessor Instructions & Features. Each Function Is Highly Optimized. It Can Access the Entire Four Gigabyte Protected Mode Address Space of the 80386 to Support Super-Huge Arrays. The Practical Limit on Array Sizes, It is Determined by the Amount of Physical Memory in the System. Includes DISK FFT, a Utility That Performs Off-Disk 2D Transforms Directly on Disk Files.
Microway, Inc.

NDP FORTRAN-486. *Version:* 4.21. 1990. *Items Included:* The DOS version of the compiler includes the NDPTools: NDPLIB, NDPLINK, & NDPRUN. *Customer Support:* One year of free technical support; $400.00 maintenance fee after initial warranty.
DOS, or UNIX Sys V.3 or V.4, Solaris, OS/2, NT, Coherent. 80486-based system (3Mb) (can also be run on an 80368-based system without taking advantage of all of the 80486 features). $995.00. *Nonstandard peripherals required:* Hard disk.

TITLE INDEX

A Full 32 Bit, Highly Optimized Implementation of Fortran 77 with VMS, BSD 4.2, Fortran-66, DOD, & MS Fortran Extensions. Fortran 90 Version Is Also Available. Incorporates All of the Features of NDP 386 Version with Several New Enhancements Designed to Take Advantage of the 486. Support for Weitek, Intel & Cyrix Coprocessors Is Also Included. Validation Codes Include the Dept. of Commerce Test Suite & NAG, IMSL, & LAPACK Libraries, All of Which Are Available from Microway. NDP Fortran Can Be Interfaced with NDP C/C++, NDP Pascal, & UNIX C Compilers. ClearView Source Level Debugger Is Included.
Microway, Inc.

NDP Fortran-386. *Version:* 4.21. Oct. 1987. *Compatible Hardware:* 80386-based system. *Memory Required:* 3000k. *General Requirements:* Hard disk, math coprocessor (MW1167, 3167, 83D87, 80387 or 80287). *Items Included:* NDPTools: NDPLIB, NDPLINK, & NDPRUN (in the DOS version). *Customer Support:* One year of free technical support; $300.00 maintenance fee after initial warranty.
DOS, UNIX V.3, V.4, Solaris, Coherent, NT, OS/2. $695.00.
A Full 32 Bit, Highly Optimized Implementation of Fortran 77 with VMS, BSD 4.2, Fortran-66, DOD, & MS Fortran Extensions. Fortran 90 Version Is Also Available. Optimization Features Include Special Optimizations for the Intel 387/487 Relating to Storage Allocation & Inline Execution of Intrinsic Functions. Support for Weitek, Intel & Cyrix Coprocessors Is Also Included. Validation Codes Include the Dept. of Commerce Test Suite & NAG, IMSL, & LAPACK Libraries, All of Which Are Available for UNIX from Microway. NDP Fortran Can Be Interfaced with NDP C/C++, NDP Pascal, & UNIX C Compilers. QuickView Source Level Debugger Is Included.
Microway, Inc.

NDP Fortran 90. *Version:* 4.4. Sep. 1993. *Items Included:* 3 notebook manuals, NDPTools (includes linker, library manager, DOS extender) DOS version. Royalty free binder. *Customer Support:* Includes 1 year of technical support. For renewal: $300.
DOS, UNIX V.3 or V.4, Coherent, Solaris, OS/2 or NT. 386/486. disk $295.00, plus NDP compiler on selected platform. *Optimal configuration:* 3Mb RAM.
Incorporates All of the Features of the NDP Fortran 386/486 with the New ANSI X3J3 Fortran 90 Standard. Some of These Additions to the Standard Are: Vastly Improved Array Syntax & Operations for the Generations of Highly Optimized Code, Dynamic Storage Mechanisms, Improved I/O, New Control Constructs, Pointers, Expanded Intrinsics, User Defined Types, Module Definitions & More.
Microway, Inc.

NDP Pascal-386. *Version:* 4.21. 1989. *Items Included:* NDPTools, NDPLIB, NDPLINK, & NDPRUN (in the DOS version). *Customer Support:* Free support for one year. $300.00 maintenance fee after initial warranty period.
UNIX V.3, V.4, DOS, OS/2, Solaris, Coherent, NT. 386/486. $695.00 all versions.
Nonstandard peripherals required: Hard disk, math coprocessor (80287, 80287, 83D87, 3167, or MW1167).
A Fully Optimized Implementation of Standard Pascal with Several Extensions. Implements the ANSI/IEEE Standard 770X3,97-1983, a Superset of Niklaus Wirth's Pascal. Includes Several Extensions from Berkeley 4.2 BSD Pascal & the British Standards Institute (BSI) Level O, a Preprocessor. Weitek, Intel & Cyrix Coprocessor Support Is Included. Can Be Interfaced with NDP C/C++, NDP Fortran, & UNIX C Compilers. QuickView Source Level Debugger Is Included.
Microway, Inc.

NDP Pascal 486. *Version:* 4.21. 1989. *Items Included:* NDPTools, NDPLIB, NDPLINK, & NDPRUN (in the DOS version). *Customer Support:* Free support for one year. $400.00 maintenance fee after initial warranty period.
UNIX V.3, V.4, DOS, OS/2, Solaris, Coherent, NT. 386/486. all versions $995.00.
Nonstandard peripherals required: Hard disk, math coprocessor (80287, 80287, 83087, 3167, or MW1167).
A Fully Optimized Implementation of Standard Pascal with Several Extensions. Implements the ANSI/IEEE Standard 770X3,97-1983, a Superset of Niklaus Wirth's Pascal. Includes Several Extensions from Berkeley 4.2 BSD Pascal & the British Standards Institute (BSI) Level O, a Preprocessor. Weitek, Intel & Cyrix Coprocessor Support Is Included. Incorporates All of the Features of NDP 386 Version with Several New Enhancements Designed to Take Advantage of the 486. Can Be Interfaced with NDP C/C plus plus, NDP Fortran, & UNIX C Compilers. ClearView Source Level Debugger Is Included.
Microway, Inc.

NDP Plot. *Version:* 2.0. Sep. 1988. *Compatible Hardware:* 80386-based system. *Operating System(s) Required:* DOS. *General Requirements:* Math coprocessor, NDP FORTRAN-386. *Customer Support:* One year free technical support.
disk $195.00.
Library of Calcomp & Versatec Compatible FORTRAN Routines That Provides Minicomputer & Mainframe Type Graphics on 386/486 Systems Running the DOS Version of NDP FORTRAN-386. Generates Plots in Two or Three Dimensions & Provides 3D Graphics Functions. Plots Functions to the Screen in Black/White or Color. Produces Publication Quality, High Resolution Graphics on a Dot Matrix Printer, Laser Printer or Plotter. Supports 640 x 480 16-Color Mode for VGA Boards & 640 x 350 16-Color & Monochrome Modes for EGA & CGA Boards. It Also Supports INTEL, CYMX & WEITEK Math Coprocessors.
Microway, Inc.

Near Drowning. *Version:* 2. 1990. *Compatible Hardware:* IBM PC & compatibles. *Operating System(s) Required:* MS-DOS. *Language(s):* BASIC. *Memory Required:* 512k.
disk $200.00 (Order no.: CCS-8115).
Care of a Drowning Victim Provides the Content for This Simulation. Oxygen Therapy & Knowledge of Fluid & Electrolyte Balance Are Tested.
Educational Software Concepts, Inc.

Nebs. *Compatible Hardware:* Atari 400, 800. *Language(s):* Atari BASIC (source code included). *Memory Required:* 48k. *General Requirements:* Joystick.
disk $19.95.
Space Arcade Game.
Dynacomp, Inc.

Nebula NeXTSTEP. *Customer Support:* All of our products are unconditionally guaranteed.
NeXTSTEP. CD-ROM disk $59.95 (Order no.: NEBULA). *Nonstandard peripherals required:* CD-ROM drive.
500 MB of NeXSTEP Programs for Intel NeXTSTEP.
Walnut Creek CDRom.

The Neil Legal System for Microcomputers. *Compatible Hardware:* IBM PC & compatibles. *Operating System(s) Required:* PC-DOS, MS-DOS; Novell 2.0A or compatible networks. *Language(s):* C & COBOL. *Memory Required:* 2000k. *General Requirements:* 150Mb on hard disk, 300Mb recommended.

NEIL LEGAL TIME/COST BILLING WITH

$450.00 yearly software maintenance (Order no.: M-100).
telephone support free (Order no.: S-100).
training $75.00/hr (Order no.: TR-01).
Can Be Used by Any Size Law firm in Both Single- & Multi-User Modes. Features: Total Integration of All Modules, No Monthly Closings, 99 Rates per Timekeeper, Billings for Contingencies, Fixed Fees, Fixed Rates & Non-Chargeable, up to 100 Addresses per Client, 75 Management Reports, Numerous Billing Formats, Menu-Driven, Reprint Bills, Complete Screen Inquiry, Client/Matter Number Either Numeric or Alpha-Numeric (13 Characters), Interfaced with Telephone & Photocopy Control Systems, Branch Office Accounting, Budgets.
Law Firm Management, Inc.
 Neil Legal Time/Cost Billing System with Accounts Receivable, Trust Management, General Ledger, Accounts Payable & Checkwriting.
 $3995.00 (Order no.: N-300).
 Neil Legal Time/Cost Billing System with Accounts Receivable, Trust Management & General Ledger.
 $3495.00 (Order no.: N-200).
 Neil Legal Time/Cost Billing System with Accounts Receivable & Trust Management.
 $2995.00 (Order no.: N-100).
 Conflict of Interest (optional).
 $450.00 (Order no.: CI-01).
 Photocopy Interface (optional).
 $450.00 (Order no.: PI-01).
 Telephone Interface (optional).
 $450.00 (Order no.: TI-02).
 Novell Netware Runtime License (optional).
 $450.00 (Order no.: NW-10).
 For Multiuser Installations Per Terminal.
 Remote Time Entry Module (optional).
 $450.00.

Neil Legal Time/Cost Billing System. *Version:* 6.1. 1988. *Items Included:* Operations manual - Neil Guide to Operations. *Customer Support:* Telephone support - free, software maintenance - $450/yr, on site training - $75/hr daily rates available.
IBM PC or compatible (640k). $2985.00 (single) $3435.00 (multi-user) (Order no.: N-300). *Addl. software required:* With Netware: Novell Netware Runtime Module. *Optimal configuration:* IBM PC 300Mb hard drive, 2Mb MS-DOS, H.P. Laser Jet printer, Matrix Printer. *Networks supported:* Novell.
Totally Interfaced System with Billing, General Ledger, Receivables, Accounts Payable & Checkwriting. No Monthly Closings. Reports, Financial Statements, etc., Can Be Printed Anytime. Interfaces with Major Cost Recovery Systems. System Runs Any Size Firm.
Law Firm Management, Inc.

Neil Legal Time/Cost Billing with General Ledger, Accounts Payable with Check Writing. *Version:* 6.1. 1981. *Compatible Hardware:* IBM PC & compatibles. *Operating System(s) Required:* MS-DOS, PC-DOS. *Language(s):* COBOL. *Memory Required:* 2000k.
Neil Legal Time/Cost Billing, G/L & A/P. disk $3995.00 (Order no.: N-300).
Neil General Ledger. disk $495.00.
Neil Legal Time/Cost Billing. disk $2995.00 (Order no.: N-100).
Handles the Following Functions: Time Slips, Cost Charges, Cash Receipts, Cash Disbursements, Client Billings, Trust Management, Statistical Reports, Master File Listings, Screen Inquiry, File Maintenance, Financial Statements, Trial Balance, Budget Entry, Comparative Budget Reports, Monthly Cash Receipts Report. Provides Total Interface Between Time/Cost Billing System & General Ledger & Accounts Payable with Check Writing.
Law Firm Management, Inc.

NEKTON. Version: 3.0. Nektonics & M.I.T. *Items Included:* 2 volume user reference manual, unlimited telephone consultation. *Customer Support:* linclued on lease: Maintenance, documentation, training, help-line (unlimited). UNIX or VMS (8Mb). contact publisher for price. *Nonstandard peripherals required:* Mouse. *Addl. software required:* X Windows. *Optimal configuration:* UNIX or VMS machine running X windows with 16Mb RAM.
Spectral Elements Based Code for the Simulation of 3D Unsteady, Incompressible Fluid Flow & Heat Transfer. It Provides High-Order Accuracy While Retaining Geometric Flexibility. The System Solves General Moving Boundary Problems with Conjugate Heat Transfer, Heat Generation, &/or Forced & Natural Convection, in Newtonian & New-Newtonian Fluids. Its Pre- & Post-Processors Allow Problem Geometries & Parameters to Be Specified Interactively.
Fluent, Inc.

Nelson's Bible Dictionary. Mar. 1991. *Items Included:* Disks, marketing literature, order form. *Customer Support:* No fee for customer support: 30 day money back guarantee, limited replacement warranty on diskettes defective at time of purchase, free telephone technical support.
PC-DOS/MS-DOS 3.1 or higher or Windows 3.1 or higher. IBM 386/486 or 100% compatible (Windows); Also AT/XT/286 (DOS) (640k DOS or 4Mb Windows). 3.5" disk $49.95 (ISBN 1-56514-503-8). *Addl. software required:* Biblesoft's PC Study Bible. *Optimal configuration:* 3.5" 1.44Mb disk drive for installation & 3Mb of hard drive space, mouse or pointer device recommended.
Informative Encyclopedia-Like Articles On-Line, Authoritative In-Depth Background Information on Bible Persons, Places, Topics or Events - an Add-On to Biblesoft's PC Study Bible.
Biblesoft.

Nelson's Bible Dictionary. Thomas Nelson. Mar. 1994. *Items Included:* Disks, marketing literature, order form. *Customer Support:* No fee for customer support: 30 day money back guarantee, limited replacement warranty on diskettes defective at time of purchase, free telephone technical support.
PC-DOS/MS-DOS 3.1 or higher or Windows 3.1 or higher. IBM 386/486 or 100% compatible (640k or 4Mb). disk $79.95 (ISBN 1-56514-525-9). *Addl. software required:* Biblesoft's PC Study Bible. *Optimal configuration:* 5.25" 1.2Mb disk drive for installation & 3Mb of hard drive space, mouse or pointer device recommended.
Informative Encyclopedia-Like Articles On-Line, Authoritative In-Depth Background Information on Bible Persons, Places, Topics or Events - an Add-On to Biblesoft's PC Study Bible.
Biblesoft.

Nelson's Bible Dictionary. Herbert Lockyer, Sr. & Thomas Nelson Publishers. May 1993. *Customer Support:* No fee for customer support: (1) 30 day money back guarantee (2) Lifetime warranty replacement on defective disks (3) Free telephone technical support.
PC-DOS/MS-DOS 2.0 or higher. IBM PC, XT/AT/286/386/486 or 100% compatibles (640k). disk $69.95 (ISBN 1-56514-525-9). *Addl. software required:* PC Study Bible. *Optimal configuration:* Requires 5 1/4" 1.2Mb disk drive for installation & 3Mb of hard drive space. Mouse or pointer device recommended.
Computerized Text of NELSON'S ILLUSTRATED BIBLE DICTIONARY. Quick Access from Within PC Study Bible to over 5,500 Informative Articles on Bible Topics, People, Places & Events. Add-On Module to Be Used with BIBLESOFT'S PC Study Bible.

Nelson's Illustrated Bible Dictionary. Feb. 1991. *Customer Support:* No fee is charged for our customer support: 30 day money back return guarantee; lifetime warranty on defective disk replacement; free telephone technical support.
PC or MS-DOS 2.0 or higher. IBM PC/XT/AT or compatible. 3.5" or 5.25" disk $69.95. *Addl. software required:* PC STUDY BIBLE. *Optimal configuration:* Hard disk with 3Mb of the hard drive will be required for this dictionary.
Add-On Module for PC STUDY BIBLE. It Gives Quick Access from Within Any of PC STUDY BIBLE's Bible Versions of over 5,500 Informative Articles on Bible Topics, People, Places & Events. Contains Full Text of Nelson's Illustrated Bible Dictionary.
Biblesoft.

Nemesis: A Wizardry Adventure. Sep. 1996. *Customer Support:* Free hint line service available 4:00-8:00p.m. (EST) weekdays, 12:00-4:00p.m. (EST) weekends & holidays. Technical support on weekdays 9:00a.m.-5:00p.m. (EST), 30-day warranty with dated proof of purchase. After 30-day warranty expires, $12.50 replacement fee applied.
MS-DOS. IBM 100% compatible 486/66 MHz (8Mb). CD-ROM disk Contact publisher for price (ISBN 0-926846-87-6). *Nonstandard peripherals required:* Mouse, double speed CD-ROM, SVGA, sound blaster.
Breathtaking Adventure & Inviting Role-Playing Meet in This Intriguing World of Fantasy & Imagination. Rich Detail & a Mesmerizing Epic Story Are Combined with an Intuitive Interface to Create a Gaming Experience Accessible to All Types of Players. Fascinating Puzzles, Steamlined Interaction, Uncomplicated Magic & Modified Role-Playing Elements Make for a Lighter Approach to Gaming Without Sacrificing Depth of Game Play. A True Blend of Adventure & Role-Playing. Nemesis Upholds the Essence of Quality Entertainment Made Famous by the Wizardry Series.
Sir-Tech Software, Inc.

NEOchrome. *Compatible Hardware:* Atari ST. 3.5" disk $49.95 (Order no.: DS5027).
Atari Corp.

Neonatal Distress. 1985. *Compatible Hardware:* Apple II+, IIe, IIc; IBM PC & compatibles. *Operating System(s) Required:* Apple DOS 3.3, MS-DOS. *Language(s):* BASIC. *Memory Required:* Apple 48k, IBM 512k.
disk $200.00 (Order no.: CCS-8231).
Deals with the Post-Term Neonate Who Aspirates Meconium & Has Persistent Fetal Circulation (PFC). Management Immediately after Birth, Identification of PFC, & Appropriate Medical & Ventilator Treatments Are Stressed.
Educational Software Concepts, Inc.

NET/MASTER. Version: 2.2. *Items Included:* Manuals. *Customer Support:* Annual renewal fee 20% of purchase price/yr..
MVS/ESA, MVS/XA, MVS/SP; VM/XA, VM/SP, VM/HPO; DOS/VSE, DOS/VSE/SP; FUJITSU MSP, FUJITSU FSP. IBM system/370 & system/390 (and compatibles). $20,000.00-$66,500.00. *Addl. software required:* VTAM. *Networks supported:* IBM SNA.
This Program Is Part of the ASM Product Line Which Provides Management & Automation of SNA Networks. The System Has Both Hardware & Session Monitors. Extensive Error Warning, Network Monitoring, Land Network Control in Single or Multi-Domain Environments. Optional Components Provide Rule-Based Status Monitoring, Added Security, Multiple Session Management, & Interface to AT&T's Accumaster Integrator.
Sterling Software.

NET-MASTER: Advanced System Management (ASM). Version: 2.2. *Items Included:* Documentation included. *Customer Support:* Annual renewal fee 20% of purchase price/yr..
MVS/ESA, MVS/XA, MVS/SP; VM/SP, VM/XA, VM/HPO; DOS/VSE, DOS/VSE SP; FUJITSU MSP, FUJITSU FSP. IBM system/370 & system/390 (and compatibles). one-time fee $15,500.00-$160,000.00. *Addl. software required:* VTAM.
Fully Integrated Software Solution for End-to-End Management & Automation of SNA/VTAM Networks & Systems. Offers Integrated Network Management, Systems Automation & Information Management, Featuring a Built-In 4GL Designed Specifically for Network/Systems Management.
Sterling Software.

Net Mech Eight-Player Pack PCCD. *Items Included:* Installation Guide.
IBM. Contact publisher for price (ISBN 0-87321-110-3, Order no.: CDD-3137).
Activision, Inc.

Net Present Value. *Compatible Hardware:* Altos Series 15-5D, Series 5-5D, 580-XX, ACS8000-XX; DEC Rainbow 100 with 2 disk drives, Rainbow 100+ with 10 MB hard disk; IBM PC with 2 disk drives, PC XT, & compatibles; Kaypro 11/IV, with 2 disk drives, Kaypro 10; Xerox 820 with 2 disk drives; Zilog MCZ-250. *Operating System(s) Required:* CP/M, MP/M, CP/M-86/80, PC-DOS, MS-DOS.
contact publisher for price (Order no.: NETPV).
Deals with the Value of Money over Time. Specifically Calculates the Net Present Value or Compound Future Value for a Series of Cash Flows.
Coopers & Lybrand.

NetCounter. Version: 2.03. Jul. 1990. *Items Included:* User manual. *Customer Support:* Telephone technical support. Free telephone support for 90 days. Limited 90 day warranty. 6.0.2 or higher, System 7 supported. Macintosh (1Mb). 3.5" disk $75.00 (Order no.: NC 2). *Networks supported:* Macintoshed based networks.
Provides Accurate Audit of Pages Printed Per Workstation Networked Printers. Ability to Restrict Access to the Printer. Provides Ability to Turn Off Apple LaserWriter's Automatic "Test Page." Allows User to Turn Printer on & off via Software. Includes a Variety of Use Accounting Information & Printer Resources.
Prism Enterprises, Inc.

NetMaster. Version: 2.2. Oct. 1983. *Compatible Hardware:* Apple II+, IIe, IIe. *Operating System(s) Required:* Apple DOS 3.3. *Memory Required:* 64k.
$49.00 (Order no.: NM).
Zoom Telephonics, Inc.

The NETMASTER System. 1983.
contact publisher for price.
PC Based Retail In-Store Processing (ISP) System That Interfaces POS to an IBM SNA Mainframe Applications Program. The Netmaster ISP System Combines PC Based (UNIX or DOS) In-Store Hardware & Software with Host Application Software. Each Retail Store is Linked to the IBM Mainframe in the Data Center Via 3270 SNA Emulation, Enabling the Retailer to Utilize the Network for POS as Well as General Merchandising.
Innovative Electronics, Inc.

NetMech Eight-Player Pack. *Items Included:* Installation Guide.
IBM. Contact publisher for price (ISBN 0-87321-043-3, Order no.: MS2-3092).
Activision, Inc.

TITLE INDEX

NetMech Eight-Player Pack. *Items Included:* Installation Guide.
IBM PC. Contact publisher for price (ISBN 0-87321-042-5, Order no.: CDD-3092A).
Activision, Inc.

NetPAC. 1996. *Items Included:* Spiral bound reference & tutorial style manual. Quick reference summary. *Customer Support:* Turn-key vendor: hardware, peripherals, hardware/software support contracts, toll free Internet Access to customer support, & training.
Windows 3.1X, TCP/IP stack compliance with Windows Sockets, Library Version 1.1 or higher. 386/33MHz (4Mb). 3.5" disk $95.00 (ISBN 0-929795-47-4). *Nonstandard peripherals required:* Established connection to the Internet.
Graphical Access Z39.50 Compliant Databases on the Internet with NetPAC. Search a Library Catalog or other Z39.50 Information Database. Search, Retrieve & View Data - On-Line or Off-Line. Search Results Can Be Bibliogrphic Records As Well As Actual Abstract Publications. Support of Both MARC & Labeled Record Display Formats; Support for Off-Line Viewing of MARC Records; Support for a Single Connection; Saving of Current, All, or a Range of Retrieve Records to Disks & Much More.
Data Trek, Inc.

NetPoint. *Customer Support:* 800-929-8117 (customer service).
MS-DOS. IBM/PS2. disk $399.99 (ISBN 0-87007-281-1).
A Complete Order Entry, Point of Sale, Inventory Control & Aged Billing System That Gives the User Control. NOVELL Network Compatible. Handle 99 Work Stations at 99 Store Locations. Price Listed is for Single User Version. Networked Version is $999.99 Plus $400 per Workstation.
SourceView Software International.

NetUtils 2. *Version:* 2.10. Dec. 1991. *Compatible Hardware:* IBM PC & compatibles, PC XT, PC AT. *Memory Required:* 128k. *General Requirements:* Novell Netware. *Customer Support:* Technical support via telephone, Internet & BBS.
disk $124.95.
A Collection of Expert Hard Drive Utilities Providing the Most Complete Preventative Maintenance & Data Recovery Software Available for Your Novell 2.x File Server. You Can Prevent Data Loss Situations Using the Most Powerful Diagnostic, Maintenance, & Recovery Tools Available for NetWare.
Ontrack Computer Systems, Inc.

NetUtils 3. *Version:* 3.0. May 1992. *Items Included:* Manual. *Customer Support:* Technical support via telephone.
NetWare 386 V3.x - Program Runs under DOS on a downed server. 386 or 486, NetWare 386 server. disk $395.00. *Addl. software required:* DOS V3.1 or higher. *Networks supported:* Novell NetWare 386 V3.x.
Collection of Expert Hard Drive Utilities Providing the Most Complete Preventative Maintenance & Data Recovery Software Available for Your NetWare 3.x File Server. You Can Prevent Data Loss Situations Using the Most Powerful Diagnostic, Maintenance, & Recovery Tools Available for NetWare.
Ontrack Computer Systems, Inc.

NetWare-ACS: Gateway Software.
Network-Products. 1986. *Compatible Hardware:* IBM PC & compatibles. *Operating System(s) Required:* MS-DOS, PC-DOS. *Memory Required:* 256k.
disk $1490.00.
Allows Multiple Users an Asynchronous In/Out Capability from the LAN. Capable of Connecting Local Area Network to As Many As 12 Remote Workstations or Asychronous Host Systems.
Novell, Inc.

NetWare-ARCNET: Starter Kit. *Version:* 2.0a. Jun. 1986. *Compatible Hardware:* IBM PC & compatibles, PC AT, PC XT with hard disk. *Operating System(s) Required:* PC-DOS/MS-DOS 2.0, 2.1, 3.0, 3.1, 3.2. *Memory Required:* per workstation 192k, per file server 512k.
disk $2595.00, incl. manuals, cards, cables & keycard (Order no.: 850-41-001).
Starter Kit Combines Advanced NetWare Operating System Software with Enough Hardware to (Boards, Cabling, etc.) for One Non-Dedicated File Server & One Workstation Using Standard Microsystems Corp. ARCNET-PC Network Controller Module.
Novell, Inc.

NetWare-BI-286. 1984. *Operating System(s) Required:* MS-DOS, CP/M, CP/M-86, UCSD p-System. *Language(s):* BASIC. *Memory Required:* 128k.
1-6 users $595.00.
1-12 users $795.00.
Business BASIC II Interpreter.
Novell, Inc.

NetWare for the Macintosh. *Compatible Hardware:* Apple Macintosh. *Operating System(s) Required:* NetWare 2.15 or higher.
3.5" disk $200.00.
Allows Macintosh, IBM PC & PS/2 Users to Share Files & Data in a Network. Allows the Use of a Lower-Cost IBM-Compatible File Server, While Macintosh Computers Can Continue to Use the Standard AppleShare Client Software to Access the NetWare File Server.
Novell, Inc.

NetWare-G-Net: Starter Kit. *Version:* 2.0a. Jun. 1986. *Compatible Hardware:* IBM PC & compatibles, PC AT, PC XT with hard disk. *Operating System(s) Required:* PC-DOS/MS-DOS 2.0, 2.1, 3.0, 3.1. *Memory Required:* per workstation 192k, per file server 512k.
disk $1995.00, incl. manuals, cards, cables & keycard (Order no.: 850-39-001).
Starter Kit Combines Advanced NetWare Operating System Software with Enough LAN Hardware (Boards, Cables, etc.) for One Non-Dedicated File Server & One Workstation Using Gateway Communication's Network Interface Module.
Novell, Inc.

NetWare-ProNET: Starter Kit. Jun. 1985. *Compatible Hardware:* IBM PC & compatibles, PC AT, PC XT with hard disk. *Operating System(s) Required:* PC-DOS/MS-DOS 2.0, 2.1, 3.0, 3.1, 3.2. *Memory Required:* per workstation 192k, per file Server 512k.
disk $3395.00, incl. manuals, cards, cables & keycard (Order no.: 850-43-001).
Combines Advanced NetWare Operating System Software with Enough Hardware (Boards, Cables, etc.) for Non-Dedicated File Server & One Workstation Using the Protcon p1300 Network Interface Card.
Novell, Inc.

NetWare-RM: Runtime. 1976. *Compatible Hardware:* IBM PC, NCR, TRS-80. *Operating System(s) Required:* PC-DOS, MS-DOS, CP/M, CP/M-86, UNIX. *Memory Required:* 256k.
disk $495.00.
Allows Applications That Use the Record-Locking Features of RM/COBOL to Operate Without Changes to the Source Code, in an MS-DOS or PC-DOS Environment. Makes over 200 Existing Business Applications & Development Tools Immediately Available to NETWARE Users.
Novell, Inc.

NETWORK ANALYSIS TOOLBOX: HDLC

NetWare-S-Net: Basic System. *Version:* 2.0a. Feb. 1983. *Compatible Hardware:* IBM PC & compatibles, PC XT, PC AT; TI Business Pro; Victor 9000. *Operating System(s) Required:* PC-DOS/MS-DOS 2.0, 2.1, 3.0, 3.1. *Memory Required:* 192k.
disk $12,295.00 incl. manuals, cards, cables, keycard & file server 23 mb hard disk storage (Order no.: 440-20020-001).
Complete LAN System Based on the Motorola 68000 for Four Workstations Using Advanced NetWare Operating System Software.
Novell, Inc.

NetWare-SNA: Gateway Software. NAS. Nov. 1985. *Compatible Hardware:* IBM PC & compatibles, PC XT, PC AT. *Operating System(s) Required:* MS-DOS, PC-DOS. *Memory Required:* 256k.
disk $6095.00.
Allows Multiple Users on a LAN to Access 3270-SNA Host.
Novell, Inc.

Netware User's Guide. Edward Liebing. Sep. 1989.
MS-DOS. IBM PC & compatibles. disk $22.95 (ISBN 1-55851-071-0). *Addl. software required:* Netware Version 2.1 through 2.15.
Complete Guide to Services & Utilities Available Through Netware. Introduces Users to Netware & Guides Them Through Basics of Netware Menu & Command Line Utilities. For Advanced Users Includes Workstation Troubleshooting Section & Appendices That Provide Quick Reference to Services Available in Each Menu or Command Line Utility. Edited by Novell, Inc.
M & T Bks.

NetWare VMS. *Compatible Hardware:* DEC VAX. *General Requirements:* DEC Ethernet controller to link the PCs & VAXs.
$5500.00 to $26,500.00 per server-based package.
Allows Personal Computers on a NetWare Network to Share Data, Print Services & Applications with DEC VAX Computers. Supports 30 Network Topologies, Including Token-Ring, StarLAN & Arcnet.
Novell, Inc.

Network Analysis Toolbox: BSC Throughput. Jan. 1996. *Items Included:* Sample input & output files & users manuals on disk. *Customer Support:* Assistance in formulative inputs & understanding outputs, price free or variable.
MS-DOS. IBM PC (8Mb). disk $399.00 (Order no.: 606). *Nonstandard peripherals required:* Math coprocessor. *Addl. software required:* FORTRAN Compiler & Linker. *Optimal configuration:* Source code can be compiled & linked for execution on any Machine with a FORTRAN compiler & linker.
Determines the Throughput of a Channel Employing the IBM Binary Synchronous Communications(BSC) Protocol, Where Throughput Is a Measure of the Amount of User Information That Can Be Transmitted over a Channel, Expressed As a Percent of Channel Capacity. This Product Is Supported by Product 408.
Cane Systems.

Network Analysis Toolbox: HDLC Throughput. Jan. 1996. *Items Included:* Sample input & output files & users manuals on disk. *Customer Support:* Assistance in formulative inputs & understanding outputs, price free or variable.
MS-DOS. IBM PC (8Mb). disk $399.00 (Order no.: 607). *Nonstandard peripherals required:* Math coprocessor. *Addl. software required:* FORTRAN Compiler & Linker. *Optimal configuration:* Source code can be compiled &

linked for execution on any Machine with a FORTRAN compiler & linker.
Determines the Throughput of a Channel Employing the High Level Data Link Control(HDLC) Protocol, Where Throughput Is a Measure of the Amount of User Information That Can Be Transmitted over a Channel, Expressed As a Percent of Channel Capacity. Considers Both the Non-Selective Reject Option, EREJ & the Selective Reject Option, ESREJ. This Product Is Supported by Product 408.
Cane Systems.

Network Analysis Toolbox: Internodal Response Time Analysis. Jan. 1996. *Items Included:* Sample input & output files & users manuals on disk. *Customer Support:* Assistance in formulative inputs & understanding outputs, price free or variable.
MS-DOS. IBM PC (8Mb). disk $599.00 (Order no.: 605). *Nonstandard peripherals required:* Math coprocessor. *Addl. software required:* FORTRAN Compiler & Linker. *Optimal configuration:* Source code can be compiled & linked for execution on any Machine with a FORTRAN compiler & linker.
Determines the Internodal Response Times for Full & Half Duplex Circuits, with & Without Polling, Where Response Time Is Defined As Elapsed Time from the Time a Request Message Is Ready to Be Sent to the Time That the Last Bit of a Response Message Is Received. This Product Is Supported by Product 408.
Cane Systems.

Network Analysis Toolbox: Intranodal Response Time. Jan. 1996. *Items Included:* Sample input & output files & users manuals on disk. *Customer Support:* Assistance in formulative inputs & understanding outputs, price free or variable.
MS-DOS. IBM PC (8Mb). disk $530.00 (Order no.: 604). *Nonstandard peripherals required:* Math coprocessor. *Addl. software required:* FORTRAN Compiler & Linker. *Optimal configuration:* Source code can be compiled & linked for execution on any Machine with a FORTRAN compiler & linker.
Determines the Intranodal Response Times for Full & Half Duplex Links, with & Without Polling, Where Response Time Is Defined As Elapsed Time from the Time a Request Message Is Ready to Be Sent to the Time That the Last Bit of a Response Message Is Received. This Product Is Supported by Product 408.
Cane Systems.

Network Analysis Toolbox: One Way Link Delay. Jan. 1996. *Items Included:* Sample input & output files & users manuals on disk. *Customer Support:* Assistance in formulative inputs & understanding outputs, price free or variable.
MS-DOS. IBM PC (8Mb). disk $199.00 (Order no.: 602). *Nonstandard peripherals required:* Math coprocessor. *Addl. software required:* FORTRAN Compiler & Linker. *Optimal configuration:* Source code can be compiled & linked for execution on any Machine with a FORTRAN compiler & linker.
Determines the Mean One Way Link Delay, Which Is Defined As the Total Elapsed Time from the Time a Message Is Ready for Transmission to the Time the Last Message Bit Is Received. One Way Link Delay Is Fundamentally the Sum of the Time a Message Spends in the Queue & Transmission Delay. This Product Is Supported by Product 408.
Cane Systems.

Network Analysis Toolbox: One Way Path Delay. Jan. 1996. *Items Included:* Sample input & output files & users manuals on disk. *Customer Support:* Assistance in formulative inputs & understanding outputs, price free or variable.
MS-DOS. IBM PC (8Mb). disk $225.00 (Order no.: 603). *Nonstandard peripherals required:* Math coprocessor. *Addl. software required:* FORTRAN Compiler & Linker. *Optimal configuration:* Source code can be compiled & linked for execution on any Machine with a FORTRAN compiler & linker.
Determines the Mean One Way Multi-Link Path Delay, Which Is Defined As the Total Elapsed Time from the Time a Message Is Ready for Transmission to the Time the Last Message Bit Is Received. One Way Multi-Link Path Delay Is Fundamentally the Sum of the Time a Message Spends in the in Each Nodal Queue & the Transmission Delay on Each Link on the Path. This Product Is Supported by Product 408.
Cane Systems.

Network Analysis Toolbox: Transmission Delays. Jan. 1996. *Items Included:* Sample input & output files & users manuals on disk. *Customer Support:* Assistance in formulative inputs & understanding outputs, price free or variable.
MS-DOS. IBM PC (8Mb). disk $135.00 (Order no.: 601). *Nonstandard peripherals required:* Math coprocessor. *Addl. software required:* FORTRAN Compiler & Linker. *Optimal configuration:* Source code can be compiled & linked for execution on any Machine with a FORTRAN compiler & linker.
Determines the Mean Transmission Delay of a Message Transmitted on a Link, Where Transmission Delay Is Defined As the Elapsed Time from the Transmission of the First Message Bit to the Receipt of the Last Message Bit. Takes into Consideration Link Capacity, Protocol Bit Size, Bit Error Rate, Length, & DCE Pair Delay & Mean Message Size. This Product Is Supported by Product 408.
Cane Systems.

Network Analyzer for Piping Systems: NAPS. *Version:* 3.0. Dec. 1986. *Compatible Hardware:* IBM PC, PC XT. *Operating System(s) Required:* MS-DOS. *Language(s):* FORTRAN. *Memory Required:* 256k. *General Requirements:* 2 disk drives.
disk $149.00, incl. instr. manual.
Designed for Analyzing Steady Incompressible Flow in Single & Multiple Branch Piping Networks. Suited for Solving Municipal Water Systems, Fire Sprinkler Systems, Irrigation Systems, & Chilled Water Systems. Will Calculate Pressure at All Nodes, Flow in All Branches, Head Loss in Each Component & the Flow in or Out of the System at All Ports. User Is Allowed Maximums of 150 Branches, 100 Nodes & up to 600 Components in Any Model. Includes a Built-In Library of over 35 Common Piping System Components, Including Pumps & Regulating Valves with User-Specified Characteristics.
J. P. Axe.

Network Bundle for DOS. *Version:* 3.0.
IBM PC & compatibles (512k). disk $249.00. *Nonstandard peripherals required:* TOPS FlashCard, FlashCard Micro Channel, FlashCard Toshiba or compatible AppleTalk cards or Ethernet cards; Ethernet, LocalTalk or other twisted-pair cabling. *Networks supported:* AppleTalk LAN.
Provides Software for One PC to Share Files, Print Spool Documents, & Send Electronic Mail on a TOPS Network.
Sitka Corp.

Network Docket. *Compatible Hardware:* IBM PC, PC XT, PC AT. *Operating System(s) Required:* PC-DOS, MS-DOS; Novell, 3Com or other compatible network. *Customer Support:* 60 days toll-free.
$1495.00-$4995.00.
Calendaring & Reporting System for Law Firms of up to 100 Attorneys or More. The Program Maintains a Law Firm's Caledar. Has the Ability to Search for Words or Fragments of Words Within the Text Fields of Entries. Another Special Feature Is CalcuDator, a Pop-Up Date Calculator Used to Determine the Number of Workdays, Calendar Days, Work Weeks & Calendar Weeks Within a Range of Dates. Also Includes a Report Writer Option for Design of Custom Reports. Reports Can Be Sorted by Virtually All Fields Simultaneously Including by Department.
CompuLaw, Ltd.

The Network Illustrator. *Version:* 8.20. 1995. *Items Included:* Thousands of pre-drawn exact replica hardware device images used to document computer networks & telecommunication systems, relational database integration, full drawing tool & the capability to draw multiple network levels & link them together. *Customer Support:* Telephone, telex, Fax support, access to MEC's Electronic Bulletin Board, training available.
DOS/VMS & Windows. PC/VAX. disk $395.00-$995.00. *Optimal configuration:* Graphics card, Postscript, HP LaserJet or Digital LN03+ printer. *Networks supported:* Most.
Network Design & Documentation Package That Allows You to Create Detailed Representations of Computer Networks & Telecommunication Systems. Provides over 4000 Images of Hardware & Networking Symbols to Document the Essential Components of Local & Wide Area Networks - Drag & Drop Images - Relational Database Integration, Technical Drawing Tool & the Capability to Draw Multiple Network Levels & Link Them Together.
Microsystems Engineering Co.

Network Mathematics Toolbox: All Internodal Distances. Jan. 1996. *Items Included:* Sample input & output files & users manuals on disk. *Customer Support:* Assistance in formulative inputs & understanding outputs, price free or variable.
MS-DOS. IBM PC (8Mb). disk $25.00 (Order no.: 405). *Nonstandard peripherals required:* Math coprocessor. *Addl. software required:* FORTRAN Compiler & Linker. *Optimal configuration:* Source code can be compiled & linked for execution on any Machine with a FORTRAN compiler & linker.
This Tool Determines the Distances Between Each Nodal Pair for All Nodes Specified in the Input on the Basis of Vertical & Horizontal Coordinates.
Cane Systems.

Network Mathematics Toolbox: Communications Traffic Profiles Generator. Jan. 1996. *Items Included:* Sample input & output files & users manuals on disk. *Customer Support:* Assistance in formulative inputs & understanding outputs, price free or variable.
MS-DOS. IBM PC (8Mb). disk $499.00 (Order no.: 401). *Nonstandard peripherals required:* Math coprocessor. *Addl. software required:* FORTRAN Compiler & Linker. *Optimal configuration:* Source code can be compiled & linked for execution on any Machine with a FORTRAN compiler & linker.
Designers Need to Know the Peak & Average Size Distribution of Traffic in Each Traffic Stream Passing Through a Network, Taking into Consideration Variations Caused by Season, Month, Week, Day, & Hour, So They Can Accurately Predict Performance & Optimize Topology. The Traffic Profile Tool Can Be of Immeasurable Value to the User in Making Traffic Estimates for His Network. It Generates 5 Types of Peak & Average Traffic by Traffic Stream & Traffic Substream, & by Season, Month, Week, Day, & Hour.
Cane Systems.

TITLE INDEX

Network Mathematics Toolbox: Erlang Analysis. Jan. 1996. *Items Included:* Sample input & output files & users manuals on disk. *Customer Support:* Assistance in formulative inputs & understanding outputs, price free or variable.
MS-DOS. IBM PC (8Mb). disk $99.00 (Order no.: 402). *Nonstandard peripherals required:* Math coprocessor. *Addl. software required:* FORTRAN Compiler & Linker. *Optimal configuration:* Source code can be compiled & linked for execution on any Machine with a FORTRAN compiler & linker.
This Tool Allows the User to Evaluate Link Capacity Requirements by Determining the Probability That a Call Will Be Lost for a Given Link, Taking into Consideration the Mean Number of Transactions per Second, Mean Transaction Size, Number of Channels, & Channel Capacity.
Cane Systems.

Network Mathematics Toolbox: Link Message Requirements. Jan. 1996. *Items Included:* Sample input & output files & users manuals on disk. *Customer Support:* Assistance in formulative inputs & understanding outputs, price free or variable.
MS-DOS. IBM PC (8Mb). disk $999.00 (Order no.: 408). *Nonstandard peripherals required:* Math coprocessor. *Addl. software required:* FORTRAN Compiler & Linker. *Optimal configuration:* Source code can be compiled & linked for execution on any Machine with a FORTRAN compiler & linker.
Determines the Messages That Must Be Carried by Each Link in a Network. Under User Control, This Analysis Can Be Performed for: Each Link, All Links for a Given Source Node, All Links for a Given Sink Node, Specific Links, All Links on a Path for Each Path, All Links on All Paths with a Given Source Node, All Links on All Paths with a Given Sink Node, All Links on Specific Paths, & All Nodes. Generates Message Rate & Size Inputs Required by Many of the 600 & 700 Tools.
Cane Systems.

Network Mathematics Toolbox: Message Arrival Time & Size Generator. Jan. 1996. *Items Included:* Sample input & output files & users manuals on disk. *Customer Support:* Assistance in formulative inputs & understanding outputs, price free or variable.
MS-DOS. IBM PC (8Mb). disk $199.00 (Order no.: 407). *Nonstandard peripherals required:* Math coprocessor. *Addl. software required:* FORTRAN Compiler & Linker. *Optimal configuration:* Source code can be compiled & linked for execution on any Machine with a FORTRAN compiler & linker.
This Tool Generates Message Arrival Times & Sizes for Messages Whose Interarrival Times & Sizes Are Either Constant, Exponential, Gamma, Normal, Lognormal, or Uniformly Distributed.
Cane Systems.

Network Mathematics Toolbox: Monte Carlo Cumulative Probability Analysis. Jan. 1996. *Items Included:* Sample input & output files & users manuals on disk. *Customer Support:* Assistance in formulative inputs & understanding outputs, price free or variable.
MS-DOS. IBM PC (8Mb). disk $180.00 (Order no.: 406). *Nonstandard peripherals required:* Math coprocessor. *Addl. software required:* FORTRAN Compiler & Linker. *Optimal configuration:* Source code can be compiled & linked for execution on any Machine with a FORTRAN compiler & linker.
This Tool Performs a Monte Carlo Analysis for Exponential, Gamma, Normal, Log Normal, Uniform, & Poisson Distributed Data. The User Can Generate Random Values Either by Use of the Machine Timer or by a Machine-Independent Technique. There Are Three Sets of Outputs Generated: 1. Statistics: Generated Mean, Generated Standard Deviation, Variance, Median, Mode, 90, 95, 99 Percentiles, Minimum Value of the Random Variable, Maximum Value of the Random Variable, Probability of Exceeding the Mean, Probability of Random Value Being Less Than the Mean; 2. Cumulative Probability Table of All Values Generated for the Random Variable; & 3. Sorted Table of All Values Generated for the Random Variable.
Cane Systems.

Network Mathematics Toolbox: Probability of Queueing. Jan. 1996. *Items Included:* Sample input & output files & users manuals on disk. *Customer Support:* Assistance in formulative inputs & understanding outputs, price free or variable.
MS-DOS. IBM PC (8Mb). disk $199.00 (Order no.: 403). *Nonstandard peripherals required:* Math coprocessor. *Addl. software required:* FORTRAN Compiler & Linker. *Optimal configuration:* Source code can be compiled & linked for execution on any Machine with a FORTRAN compiler & linker.
This Tool Allows the User to Evaluate Channel Capacity Requirements by Determining the Probability that a Message Will Be Queued Before Transmission, Taking into Consideration the Number of Channels on a Link & Channel Utilization.
Cane Systems.

Network Mathematics Toolbox: Specific Internodal Distances. Jan. 1996. *Items Included:* Sample input & output files & users manuals on disk. *Customer Support:* Assistance in formulative inputs & understanding outputs, price free or variable.
MS-DOS. IBM PC (8Mb). disk $20.00 (Order no.: 404). *Nonstandard peripherals required:* Math coprocessor. *Addl. software required:* FORTRAN Compiler & Linker. *Optimal configuration:* Source code can be compiled & linked for execution on any Machine with a FORTRAN compiler & linker.
This Tool Determines the Distances Between Specific Nodal Pairs on the Basis of Vertical & Horizontal Coordinates.
Cane Systems.

Network Multiphase Flow with Total Energy Balance. *Items Included:* Full manual. No other products required. *Customer Support:* Free telephone support - no time limit. 30 day warranty.
MS-DOS 3.2 or higher. IBM & compatibles (512k). disk $2899.95.
demo disk $5.00.
Top-of-the-Line Liquid & Gas Network Flow Analysis Tool. Includes All of the Capabilities of PIPELINE MULTIPHASE FLOW, but Extended to Networks Having up to 1000 Pipes, Each Having Different Properties & Ambient Conditions. NMF Can Treat Problems Such As Multiple Wells on One Platform, a Gathering System with (or Without) Loops, Pipelines with Lateral Feeders, & So On. At Any Point in the System You May Determine the Temperature, Pressure, Liquid Holdup, Velocity, Flow Pattern, etc.
Dynacomp, Inc.

Network Multiphase Flow with Total Energy Balance. 1992. *Items Included:* Detailed manuals included with all Dynacomp products. *Customer Support:* Free telephone support to original customer - no time limit; 30 day limited warranty.
MS-DOS 3.2 or higher. IBM PC & compatibles (512k). $2395.00 (Add $5.00 for 3 1/2" format; 5 1/4" format standard). *Optimal configuration:* IBM, MS-DOS 3.0 or higher, 512k RAM, a hard disk, & CGA or compatible graphics capability.
demo disk $5.00.
NMF Is a Top-of-the-Line Liquid & Gas Network Flow Analysis Tool. Includes All of the Capabilities of PIPELINE MULTIPHASE FLOW, but Extended to Networks Having up to 1000 Pipes, Each Having Different Properties & Ambient Conditions. Both U.S. & Metric Units.
Dynacomp, Inc.

NETWORK-OS. Version: 7.27. Nov. 1990. *Compatible Hardware:* IBM PC, PC XT, PC AT & compatibles, 286, 386 & 486-based PCs, PS/2. *Operating System(s) Required:* DR-DOS 6.0, PC-DOS/MS-DOS 3.X or higher, Windows 3.0. *Memory Required:* As low as 0k with memory boards, Workstations 31k, server 56k, Printsrver 69k & IBM 640k. *Customer Support:* Free technical support; 404-446-3337..
disk $190.00, per node.
prices vary on interface boards.
avail. 30 days money back guarantee.
80 & 255 licenses avail.
PC-to-PC, Multi-Tasking, LAN Operating System for PS/2s, IBM PC XTs, ATs & Compatible Microcomputers. Supports over 50 Micro Channel Cards, & Other Major LAN Interface Boards. Network Security Features Include Passworded Network Access, Administrator Access to Encrypted Passwords, & Access to Network Resources Controlled by User Passwords. PSP Enables Users to Get On-Line with Familiar & Identical Operating Environment from Any Workstation on Their Network & Supports ODI, Enables Sharing of up to 4 CD-ROM Drives Across the Network; RADAR (Advanced Network Monitoring); SNOOP (Instructional Interactive Monitoring); Multiple Printer Selection from Within an Application & Direct Printing Capability; Modem Sharing Capability; Bridging Software Included for Network-OS Plus LANs Using Different Topologies.
CBIS, Inc.

Network Topology Evaluation & Management Science Toolboxes: Acyclic Shortest Paths. Jan. 1996. *Items Included:* Sample input & output files & users manuals on disk. *Customer Support:* Assistance in formulating inputs & understanding outputs, price free or variable.
MS-DOS. IBM PC (8Mb). disk $1135.00 (Order no.: 107). *Nonstandard peripherals required:* Math coprocessor. *Addl. software required:* FORTRAN Compiler & Linker. *Optimal configuration:* Source code can be compiled & linked for execution on any machine with a FORTRAN compiler & linker.
A Path from One Node to Another Is Shortest, If the Sum of the Path Link Weights, e.g., Cost, Distance, etc., Is Minimum. An Acyclic Path Is One in Which None of the Nodes Are Repeated. Using Fast Polynomial Time Algorithms, This Tool Generates the Acyclic Shortest Paths of a Network.
Cane Systems.

Network Topology Evaluation & Management Science Toolboxes: Cyclic Shortest Paths. Jan. 1996. *Items Included:* Sample input & output files & users manuals on disk. *Customer Support:* Assistance in formulating inputs & understanding outputs, price free or variable.
MS-DOS. IBM PC (8Mb). disk $599.00 (Order no.: 108). *Nonstandard peripherals required:* Math coprocessor. *Addl. software required:* FORTRAN Compiler & Linker. *Optimal configuration:* Source code can be compiled & linked for execution on any machine with a FORTRAN compiler & linker.
A Path from One Node to Another Is Shortest, If the Sum of the Path Link Weights, e.g., Cost,

Distance, etc., Is Minimum. A Cyclic Path Is One in Which Some of the Nodes Are Repeated. Using Fast Polynomial Time Algorithms, This Tool Generates Possibly Cyclic Shortest Paths of a Network.
Cane Systems.

Network Topology Evaluation & Management Science Toolboxes: Euler Circuits in a Network. Jan. 1996. *Items Included:* Sample input & output files & users manuals on disk. *Customer Support:* Assistance in formulating inputs & understanding outputs, price free or variable.
MS-DOS. IBM PC (8Mb). disk $190.00 (Order no.: 117). *Nonstandard peripherals required:* Math coprocessor. *Addl. software required:* FORTRAN Compiler & Linker. *Optimal configuration:* Source code can be compiled & linked for execution on any machine with a FORTRAN compiler & linker.
Using Fast Polynomial Time Algorithms, This Tool Determines If an Undirected & Connected Network Has a Euler Circuit & If It Does, It Determines the Nodes & Links of the Euler Circuit, Where a Euler Circuit Is a Circuit That Begins & Ends on the Same Node & No Link Is Traversed More Than Once.
Cane Systems.

Network Topology Evaluation & Management Science Toolboxes: Fundamental Circuits of a Network. Jan. 1996. *Items Included:* Sample input & output files & users manuals on disk. *Customer Support:* Assistance in formulating inputs & understanding outputs, price free or variable.
MS-DOS. IBM PC (8Mb). disk $360.00 (Order no.: 118). *Nonstandard peripherals required:* Math coprocessor. *Addl. software required:* FORTRAN Compiler & Linker. *Optimal configuration:* Source code can be compiled & linked for execution on any machine with a FORTRAN compiler & linker.
Using Fast Polynomial Time Algorithms, This Tool Determines the Links & Nodes of All the Fundamental Circuits in an Undirected Network, Where a Fundamental Circuit Is Created by the Addition of a Single Link to a Spanning Tree. Given That the Network Contains N Nodes & M Links, & Its Spanning Tree Contains N-1 Links, There Are M-(N-1) Non-Spanning Tree Links, & Therefore, M-(N-1) Fundamental Circuits.
Cane Systems.

Network Topology Evaluation & Management Science Toolboxes: Hamilton Circuits of a Network. Jan. 1996. *Items Included:* Sample input & output files & users manuals on disk. *Customer Support:* Assistance in formulating inputs & understanding outputs, price free or variable.
MS-DOS. IBM PC (8Mb). disk $450.00 (Order no.: 119). *Nonstandard peripherals required:* Math coprocessor. *Addl. software required:* FORTRAN Compiler & Linker. *Optimal configuration:* Source code can be compiled & linked for execution on any machine with a FORTRAN compiler & linker.
Using Fast Polynomial Time Algorithms, This Tool Determines If a Network Has a Hamilton Circuit & If It Does, It Determines the Nodes & Links of the Hamilton Circuit, Where a Hamilton Circuit Is a Circuit Containing All the Nodes.
Cane Systems.

Network Topology Evaluation & Management Science Toolboxes: Maximum Cardinality Matching. Jan. 1996. *Items Included:* Sample input & output files & users manuals on disk. *Customer Support:* Assistance in formulating inputs & understanding outputs, price free or variable.
MS-DOS. IBM PC (8Mb). disk $250.00 (Order no.: 101). *Nonstandard peripherals required:* Math coprocessor. *Addl. software required:* FORTRAN Compiler & Linker. *Optimal configuration:* Source code can be compiled & linked for execution on any machine with a FORTRAN compiler & linker.
A Matching Is the Pairing of One Node with Another Node in the Same or Another Nodal Set to Obtain Same Goal. Using Fast Polynomial Time Algorithms, This Tool Maximizes the Number of Matchings. It Is Possible That Not All Nodes Will Be Matched.
Cane Systems.

Network Topology Evaluation & Management Science Toolboxes: Maximum Independent Sets of a Network. Jan. 1996. *Items Included:* Sample input & output files & users manuals on disk. *Customer Support:* Assistance in formulating inputs & understanding outputs, price free or variable.
MS-DOS. IBM PC (8Mb). disk $350.00 (Order no.: 114). *Nonstandard peripherals required:* Math coprocessor. *Addl. software required:* FORTRAN Compiler & Linker. *Optimal configuration:* Source code can be compiled & linked for execution on any machine with a FORTRAN compiler & linker.
Using Fast Polynomial Time Algorithms, This Tool Determines the Maximum Independent Sets of a Network, Where an Independent Set of Nodes Is a Subset of Nodes in a Network Such That No Two Nodes Are Adjacent & an Independent Set of Nodes Is Maximum If No Other Independent Set Contains It.
Cane Systems.

Network Topology Evaluation & Management Science Toolboxes: Minimum Link Equivalent of a Network. Jan. 1996. *Items Included:* Sample input & output files & users manuals on disk. *Customer Support:* Assistance in formulating inputs & understanding outputs, price free or variable.
MS-DOS. IBM PC (8Mb). disk $195.00 (Order no.: 116). *Nonstandard peripherals required:* Math coprocessor. *Addl. software required:* FORTRAN Compiler & Linker. *Optimal configuration:* Source code can be compiled & linked for execution on any machine with a FORTRAN compiler & linker.
Using Fast Polynomial Time Algorithms, This Tool Generates a Network That Is Directed & Strongly Connected Using a Minimum Number of Links from a Given Directed & Strongly Connected Network.
Cane Systems.

Network Topology Evaluation & Management Science Toolboxes: Min-Max Spanning Tree. Jan. 1996. *Items Included:* Sample input & output files & users manuals on disk. *Customer Support:* Assistance in formulating inputs & understanding outputs, price free or variable.
MS-DOS. IBM PC (8Mb). disk $825.00 (Order no.: 105). *Nonstandard peripherals required:* Math coprocessor. *Addl. software required:* FORTRAN Compiler & Linker. *Optimal configuration:* Source code can be compiled & linked for execution on any machine with a FORTRAN compiler & linker.
A Spanning Tree of a Network Is a Subnetwork Containing All the Network Nodes & A Subset of Links Such That There Is Exactly One Path Between Each Pair of Nodes. A Min/Max Spanning Tree Is a Spanning Tree in Which the Maximum Link Weight Is Minimum. Using Fast Polynomial Time Algorithms, This Tool Generates a Min/Max Spanning Tree.
Cane Systems.

Network Topology Evaluation & Management Science Toolboxes: Minimum Weight Bipartite Matching. Jan. 1996. *Items Included:* Sample input & output files & users manuals on disk. *Customer Support:* Assistance in formulating inputs & understanding outputs, price free or variable.
MS-DOS. IBM PC (8Mb). disk $260.00 (Order no.: 102). *Nonstandard peripherals required:* Math coprocessor. *Addl. software required:* FORTRAN Compiler & Linker. *Optimal configuration:* Source code can be compiled & linked for execution on any machine with a FORTRAN compiler & linker.
A Matching Is the Pairing of One Node with Another Node in the Same or Another Nodal Set to Obtain Same Goal. If the Nodes to Be Matched Are in Different Nodal Sets, the Matching Is Said to Be Bipartite. Using Fast Polynomial Time Algorithms, This Tool Minimizes the Sum of All Link Weights Between Matched Nodes. It Is Possible That Not All Nodes Will Be Matched.
Cane Systems.

Network Topology Evaluation & Management Science Toolboxes: Minimum Weight Non-Bipartite Matching. Jan. 1996. *Items Included:* Sample input & output files & users manuals on disk. *Customer Support:* Assistance in formulating inputs & understanding outputs, price free or variable.
MS-DOS. IBM PC (8Mb). disk $775.00 (Order no.: 103). *Nonstandard peripherals required:* Math coprocessor. *Addl. software required:* FORTRAN Compiler & Linker. *Optimal configuration:* Source code can be compiled & linked for execution on any machine with a FORTRAN compiler & linker.
A Matching Is the Pairing of One Node with Another Node in the Same or Another Nodal Set to Obtain Same Goal. If the Nodes to Be Matched Are in the Same Nodal Set, the Matching Is Said to Be Non-Bipartite. Using Fast Polynomial Time Algorithms, This Tool Minimizes the Sum of All Link Weights Between Matched Nodes. It Is Possible That Not All Nodes Will Be Matched.
Cane Systems.

Network Topology Evaluation & Management Science Toolboxes: Minimum Weight Spanning Tree. Jan. 1996. *Items Included:* Sample input & output files & users manuals on disk. *Customer Support:* Assistance in formulating inputs & understanding outputs, price free or variable.
MS-DOS. IBM PC (8Mb). disk $140.00 (Order no.: 104). *Nonstandard peripherals required:* Math coprocessor. *Addl. software required:* FORTRAN Compiler & Linker. *Optimal configuration:* Source code can be compiled & linked for execution on any machine with a FORTRAN compiler & linker.
A Spanning Tree of a Network Is a Subnetwork Containing All the Network Nodes & a Subset of Links Such That There Is Exactly One Path Between Each Pair of Nodes. A Minimum Weight Spanning Tree Is a Spanning Tree in Which the Sum of the Link Weights Is a Minimum. Using Fast Polynomial Time Algorithms, This Tool Generates a Minimum Weight Spanning Tree.
Cane Systems.

Network Topology Evaluation & Management Science Toolboxes: Network Bridges. Jan. 1996. *Items Included:* Sample input & output files & users manuals on disk. *Customer Support:* Assistance in formulating inputs & understanding outputs, price free or variable.
MS-DOS. IBM PC (8Mb). disk $350.00 (Order no.: 112). *Nonstandard peripherals required:* Math coprocessor. *Addl. software required:*

FORTRAN Compiler & Linker. *Optimal configuration:* Source code can be compiled & linked for execution on any machine with a FORTRAN compiler & linker.
Using Fast Polynomial Time Algorithms, This Tool Determines the Cut Nodes & Bridges for Undirected Networks, Where a Cut Node Is a Node Whose Removal from the Network Will Disconnect the Network & Create at Least One More Network & a Bridge Is a Link, Whose Removal from the Network Will Disconnect the Network & Create at Least One More Network.
Cane Systems.

Network Topology Evaluation & Management Science Toolboxes: Network Cliques. Jan. 1996. *Items Included:* Sample input & output files & users manuals on disk. *Customer Support:* Assistance in formulating inputs & understanding outputs, price free or variable.
MS-DOS. IBM PC (8Mb). disk $195.00 (Order no.: 113). *Nonstandard peripherals required:* Math coprocessor. *Addl. software required:* FORTRAN Compiler & Linker. *Optimal configuration:* Source code can be compiled & linked for execution on any machine with a FORTRAN compiler & linker.
Using Fast Polynomial Time Algorithms, This Tool Determines Cliques for Undirected Networks, Where a Clique Is a Subset of Nodes in Which Every Pair of Nodes Are Adjacent, i.e. They Share a Common Link.
Cane Systems.

Network Topology Evaluation & Management Science Toolboxes: Network Link Connectivity Analysis. Jan. 1996. *Items Included:* Sample input & output files & users manuals on disk. *Customer Support:* Assistance in formulating inputs & understanding outputs, price free or variable.
MS-DOS. IBM PC (8Mb). disk $320.00 (Order no.: 111). *Nonstandard peripherals required:* Math coprocessor. *Addl. software required:* FORTRAN Compiler & Linker. *Optimal configuration:* Source code can be compiled & linked for execution on any machine with a FORTRAN compiler & linker.
Using Fast Polynomial Time Algorithms, This Tool Determines Link Connectivity of a Network, Where Link Connectivity Is the Minimum Number of Links That Must Be Removed in Order to Disconnect a Network into 2 or More Networks.
Cane Systems.

Network Topology Evaluation & Management Science Toolboxes: Optimal Acyclic Routing. Jan. 1996. *Items Included:* Sample input & output files & users manuals on disk. *Customer Support:* Assistance in formulating inputs & understanding outputs, price free or variable.
MS-DOS. IBM PC (8Mb). disk $1250.00 (Order no.: 109). *Nonstandard peripherals required:* Math coprocessor. *Addl. software required:* FORTRAN Compiler & Linker. *Optimal configuration:* Source code can be compiled & linked for execution on any machine with a FORTRAN compiler & linker.
Using Fast Polynomial Time Algorithms, This Tool Determines Alternative Acyclic Routes, e.i. No Nodes Are Repeated, on the Basis of Shortest Paths & Route Capacity.
Cane Systems.

Network Topology Evaluation & Management Science Toolboxes: Optimal Cyclic Routing. Jan. 1996. *Items Included:* Sample input & output files & users manuals on disk. *Customer Support:* Assistance in formulating inputs & understanding outputs, price free or variable.
MS-DOS. IBM PC (8Mb). disk $625.00 (Order no.: 110). *Nonstandard peripherals required:* Math coprocessor. *Addl. software required:* FORTRAN Compiler & Linker. *Optimal configuration:* Source code can be compiled & linked for execution on any machine with a FORTRAN compiler & linker.
Using Fast Polynomial Time Algorithms, This Tool Determines Alternative Routes, Which May Be Cyclic - e.i. They May Have Repeated Nodes - on the Basis of Shortest Paths & Route Capacity.
Cane Systems.

Network Topology Evaluation & Management Science Toolboxes: Strongly Connected Components of a Network. Jan. 1996. *Items Included:* Sample input & output files & users manuals on disk. *Customer Support:* Assistance in formulating inputs & understanding outputs, price free or variable.
MS-DOS. IBM PC (8Mb). disk $150.00 (Order no.: 115). *Nonstandard peripherals required:* Math coprocessor. *Addl. software required:* FORTRAN Compiler & Linker. *Optimal configuration:* Source code can be compiled & linked for execution on any machine with a FORTRAN compiler & linker.
Using Fast Polynomial Time Algorithms, This Tool Determines the Strongly Connected Components of a Network, Where a Strongly Connected Component of a Network Is a Maximum Set of Nodes with a Directed Path from Each Node to Every Other Node.
Cane Systems.

Network Topology Evaluation & Management Science Toolboxes: Shortest Path Trees. Jan. 1996. *Items Included:* Sample input & output files & users manuals on disk. *Customer Support:* Assistance in formulating inputs & understanding outputs, price free or variable.
MS-DOS. IBM PC (8Mb). disk $200.00 (Order no.: 106). *Nonstandard peripherals required:* Math coprocessor. *Addl. software required:* FORTRAN Compiler & Linker. *Optimal configuration:* Source code can be compiled & linked for execution on any machine with a FORTRAN compiler & linker.
A Tree Has a Root at Node N If There Is a Path from N to Every Other Node. A Shortest Path Tree Is an Array of Links Rooted at a Node, Such That the Path from the Root to Any Other Node in the Array Is Shortest. Using Fast Polynomial Time Algorithms, This Tool Generates Shortest Path Trees.
Cane Systems.

Neural Networks. Version: 1.1. *Compatible Hardware:* IBM PC & compatibles. *Operating System(s) Required:* PC-DOS/MS-DOS. *Memory Required:* 256k. *General Requirements:* Hard disk recommended. *Items Included:* 32 pg. Thinking Software catalog.
5.25" or 3.5" disk $99.95.
Introduces Neural Nets at the Tutorial Level. Performs Closest Word Match.
Thinking Software, Inc.

NEURAL/QUERY. *Customer Support:* Free on-line technical support for all registered users.
IBM PC/AT/XT, PS/2 & compatibles (640K). $490.00 3.5" or 5.25" disk. *Networks supported:* Supports database files in Ascii, Lotus, dBASE, Oracle, XDB, Interbase, Teradata, etc.
Uses Neuralnetwork Technology to Find Partial Matches in Databases. Operating Similar to the Human Mind, Makes Educated Guesses, Deals with Partial Matches & Searches for Information Based on Concepts Such As Short & Long, Weak & Strong. Its Results Provide "Best Guess" Answers & Degree of Confidence for How Well a Record Matches a Query.
IntelligenceWare, Inc.

Neuralog. 1989. *Items Included:* Program disk, 1 manual, source code included. *Customer Support:* Free telephone support 1 year.
MS-DOS. IBM PC & compatibles (256k). disk $149.00.
Tool for the Development of Neural Networks That Has Been Implemented in Turbo Prolog (TM Borland International). It Can Be Used for Education & Training, for Research & Exploration or for the Actual Development of Neural Network Applications. Employs the Well Known Propagation Algorithm. Product is Comprised of the Following Components: An Executable Module for Performing Pattern Recognition. An Executable Module Implementing the Back Propagation Neural Network Solution to the Famous XOR Problem Posed by Minsky & Papert in Their "Book Perceptrons." Complete Source Code Implemented in Turbo Prolog. The Source Code Also Includes a Separate Module Containing All Predicates Required to Implement a Generic Back Propagation Neural Network.
Berkshire Software Co.

Neuranotomy Foundations. *Compatible Hardware:* Apple Macintosh. *Memory Required:* 512k. *General Requirements:* HyperCard or Atlas.
contact publisher for price.
Introductory Brain Anatomy Program.
Kinko's.

NeuroLine CD-ROM Database for Neurology. Aug. 1992.
MS Windows 3.1 or higher. IBM & compatibles (4Mb). CD-ROM disk $325.00-$995.00; Networks $1895.00 & up. *Nonstandard peripherals required:* Magnetic or CD-ROM, using ISO 9660. *Optimal configuration:* IBM & compatibles, 80386 or higher, 4Mb RAM, 20Mb hard disk, mouse, MS Windows 3.1 or higher.
System 6.0.7 or higher. Apple Macintosh (3Mb). CD-ROM disk $325.00-$995.00; Networks $1895.00 & up. *Optimal configuration:* Apple Macintosh Plus or higher, 3Mb RAM, System 6.0.7 or higher.
NeuroLine Is an Electronic Reference Database to the Neurology & Neuroscience Journal Literature. Neuroscience-Specific Excerpts (Including Abstracts) from the National Library of Medicine's MEDLINE Database Are Distributed on CD-ROM (Compact Disc, Read-Only Memory) Optical Disc. Knowledge Finder Search-&-Retrieval Software Makes Searching of the NeuroLine Database Easy, Effective & Fast. After the User Types a Phrase or Sentence Describing the Information Needed, It selects the References in the Database That Appear to Best Match the Request, & Presents Them in Order of likely relevance. The NeuroLine Archive CD-ROM Contains over 430,000 References to Articles Published in 235 Neurology & Neuroscience Journals over the Most Recent 10 Full Years.
Aries Systems Corp.

Neuromuscular Concepts. 1988. *Compatible Hardware:* Apple II+, IIe, IIc, IIgs. *Operating System(s) Required:* Apple DOS 3.3. *Language(s):* BASIC. *Memory Required:* 48k.
disk $49.95.
Set of Tutorials Examine Muscle Action Potentials, Skeletal Muscle Contraction, Muscles in Action & Disorders of Movement Using the Electromyogram. Contains a Self-Test Which Gives the Students a Presentation of Questions (Manual, Rapid, Intermediate or Slow Advance), a Ten Question Test over One Tutorial or 25 to 50 Question Comprehensive Exam over All Tutorials. After Taking the 25 or 50 Question Comprehensive Exam, the Student Receives a Breakdown of Performance on All Five Tutorials.
Biosource Software.

Neuron Data Open Interface. *Version:* 2.0. *Items Included:* 8 binder-bound manuals. *Customer Support:* 1 yr. maintenance, 20% of development licence list price, 90 days free installation support.
Mac, Windows, PM, Motif, Open Look. Mac, PC, OS/2, UNIX 386, UNIX & VAX workstation. $7000.00-$15,000.00. *Addl. software required:* Standard platform specific "C" compiler.
A Powerful Development Environment for Building Portable GUIs That Are Portable Across Macintosh, Presentation Manager, Windows, Motif & Open Look, Without Changing a Line of Code.
Neuron Data, Inc.

Neuron Expert. *Version:* 2.1. *Compatible Hardware:* IBM PC & compatibles. *Operating System(s) Required:* PC-DOS/MS-DOS. *Memory Required:* 256k. *General Requirements:* Hard disk recommended. *Items Included:* 32 pg. Thinking Software catalog.
$59.95.
Neural Network Environment Where Users Enter the Questions They Want the Network to Ask & All the Possible Solutions the Network Can Select from at the Conclusion of the Consultation. Then, Users 'Train' the Network by Answering All the Questions & Choosing the Correct Solution. Only One Training Session Is Required for Each Solution. Menu Options Include: Demo Consultation, Quick Reference, Enter Queries, Enter Solutions, Train the Network, Expert Consultation, Tutorial. Up to Ten Queries & Three Solutions Are Supported.
Thinking Software, Inc.

Neuron Expert Professional II. *Version:* 3.1. *Compatible Hardware:* IBM PC & compatibles. *Operating System(s) Required:* PC-DOS/MS-DOS. *Memory Required:* 256k. *General Requirements:* Hard disk recommended. *Items Included:* 32 pg. Thinking Software catalog.
5.25" or 3.5" disk $99.95.
The Professional Version of NEURON EXPERT. Increases the Maximum Number of Queries up to 100, & the Maximum Number of Solutions to Ten. Can Be Included As Part of Users' Own Programs, Written in Any MICROSOFT Compiler Language Which Produces Standard Linkable Object Modules.
Thinking Software, Inc.

NeuroShell. *Compatible Hardware:* IBM PC & compatibles. *Operating System(s) Required:* PC-DOS/MS-DOS. *Memory Required:* 256k. *General Requirements:* Hard disk recommended. *Items Included:* 32 pg. Thinking Software catalog.
5.25" or 3.5" disk $195.00.
Expert System Shell That Mimics the Biological Learning & Decision Making Process, Learning from Examples.
Thinking Software, Inc.

The Never-Ending Story. Ocean Software. Jun. 1986. *Compatible Hardware:* Apple; Atari; Commodore 64, 128. *Memory Required:* 64k. Commodore, Atari. disk $19.95 (ISBN 0-88717-135-4, Order no.: 1505WCF).
Apple. disk $19.95 (ISBN 0-88717-136-2, Order no.: 1505ADO).
Graphics-Text Adventure Game Set in the Land of Fantasia, a World Fighting Extinction by the "All Consuming Nothing". Your Quest Is to Save the Kingdom & Rescue the Empress.
IntelliCreations, Inc.

The New England Journal of Medicine on CD-ROM: DOS-MAC. Feb. 1994. *Items Included:* Registration Card. *Customer Support:* Creative Multimedia Corporation warrants the CD-ROM disc & diskettes to be free from defects in materials & workmanship under normal use & service for a period of 90 days from date of purchase. Creative Multimedia Corporation offers Technical Support to customers as needed.
MS-DOS 3.1 or higher. IBM PC & compatibles with VGA monitor (350k). CD-ROM disk $295.00 Suggested Retail Price (ISBN 1-880428-32-6, Order no.: 10531). *Optimal configuration:* Super VGA with 512k video memory capable of 640x480x256 colors.
Networks supported: All.
System Software 6.0.5 or higher. Macintosh Plus, SE, Classic, SE/30, LC & any Model II (2Mb). CD-ROM disk $295.00 Suggested Retail Price. *Optimal configuration:* Color display requires 8-bit color, 32-bit QuickDraw & color monitor.
Networks supported: All.
The "Journal", First Established in 1812, Is the Oldest Continuously Published Medical Journal in the World. NEJM Publishes the Most Important, Previously Unpublished, Research Results, & Is Now Available with Complete Text & Images. In Addition, the Special Articles & Opinion Pieces Express Original Viewpoints & Ideas. The Most Important Criteria Determining the Acceptance of Articles for Publication Are Originality, Scientific Soundness, & Interest to Both Practitioners & Researcher.
Creative Multimedia Corp.

The New Grolier Multimedia Encyclopedia. *Version:* 1993.
MS-DOS Version 3.1 or higher. IBM PC, XT, AT, PS/2 or higher & compatibles (640k). CD-ROM disk $395.00 (Order no.: 111188). *Optimal configuration:* Hard disk with at least 1Mb free, VGA card & color monitor, CD-ROM drive, Microsoft Extensions, Version 2.1 or higher.
DOS 3.1 or higher, Windows 3.0 or higher. IBM PC & compatibles with 80386sx processor or higher (4Mb). CD-ROM disk $395.00 (Order no.: 111190). *Optimal configuration:* MPC-compatible sound card, MPC-compatible CD-ROM drive, Super VGA Graphics adapter & monitor, DOS 3.1 or higher, Microsoft compatible mouse recommended, Windows 3.0 or higher.
System 6.0.5 or higher. Macintosh Plus, Classic, SE or any color Macintosh (4Mb). CD-ROM disk $395.00 (Order no.: 111189). *Optimal configuration:* Hard disk, CD-ROM drive.
For Serious Research or Just Curious Exploration, This 21-Volume Encyclopedia Sets a New Standard in Information Tools. One Single CD-ROM Disc Puts Incredible Volumes of Knowledge at Your Fingertips with 3,000 Photographs & Illustrations, over 250 High-Resolution Color Maps, & 7,000 New or Updated Articles. Pull-Down Menus & On-Line Help Make It Easy to Delve into It All with Awesome CD-ROM Speed & Power. Multiple Window Display Lets You Compare & Correlate Facts Fast. This Is the Resource of the Future.
Software Toolworks.

New International Version. Jun. 1988. *Customer Support:* No fee is charged for our customer support: 30 day money back return guarantee; lifetime warranty on defective disk replacement; free telephone technical support.
PC or MS-DOS 2.0 or higher. IBM PC/XT/AT or compatible. 3.5" or 5.25" disk $49.95. *Addl. software required:* PC Study Bible. *Optimal configuration:* Hard disk with 1.5Mb hard disk space for each Bible version.
The Text of the New International Version of the Bible. Add-On Bible Version to Be Used with BIBLESOFT'S PC STUDY BIBLE.
Biblesoft.

New International Version. Kenneth Taylor. May 1993. *Items Included:* Disks, marketing literature, order form. *Customer Support:* No fee for customer support: 30 day money back guarantee, limited replacement warranty on diskettes defective at time of purchase, free telephone technical support.
PC-DOS/MS-DOS 3.1 or higher or Windows 3.1 or higher. IBM 386/486 or 100% compatible (Windows); Also AT/XT/286 (DOS) (640k DOS or 4Mb Windows). 3.5" disk $39.95 (ISBN 1-56514-253-5). *Addl. software required:* Biblesoft's PC Study Bible. *Optimal configuration:* 3.5" disk drive for installation & 1.5Mb of hard drive space, mouse or pointer device recommended.
The Text of the New International Version of the Bible - an Add-On Version to be Used with Biblesoft's PC Study Bible.
Biblesoft.

New International Version. Kenneth Taylor. May 1993. *Items Included:* Disks, marketing literature, order form. *Customer Support:* No fee for customer support: 30 day money back guarantee, limited replacement warranty on diskettes defective at time of purchase, free telephone technical support.
PC-DOS/MS-DOS 3.1 or higher or MS Windows 3.1 or higher. 386/486 or 100% IBM PC compatible (Windows); Also AT/XT/286 (DOS) (640k DOS or 4Mb Windows). disk $39.95 (ISBN 1-56514-555-0). *Addl. software required:* Biblesoft's PC Study Bible. *Optimal configuration:* 5.25" 1.2Mb disk drive for installation & 1.5Mb of hard drive space, mouse or pointer device recommended.
The Text of the New International Version of the Bible - an Add-On Bible Version to be Used with Biblesoft's PC Study Bible.
Biblesoft.

New International Version. Kenneth N. Taylor. May 1993. *Customer Support:* No fee for customer support: (1) 30 day money back guarantee (2) Lifetime warranty replacement on defective disks (3) Free telephone technical support.
PC-DOS/MS-DOS 2.0 or higher. IBM PC, XT/AT/286/386/486 or 100% compatibles (640k). disk $49.95 (ISBN 1-56514-555-0). *Addl. software required:* PC Study Bible. *Optimal configuration:* Requires 5 1/4" 1.2Mb disk drive for installation & 3Mb of hard drive space. Mouse or pointer device recommended.
Text of the NEW INTERNATIONAL VERSION of the Bible. Add-On Bible Version to Be Used with BIBLESOFT'S PC Study Bible.

The New Kid on the Block. (Living Book Ser.). Jack Prelutsky.
MS-DOS 5.0 or higher, Windows 3.1 or higher. 386 processor or higher (4Mb). CD-ROM disk $49.95 (Order no.: R1045). *Nonstandard peripherals required:* CD-ROM drive. *Optimal configuration:* 386 processor operating at 16MHz or higher, MS-DOS 5.0 or higher, Windows 3.1 or higher, 30Mb hard drive, mouse, VGA graphic adapter & VGA color monitor (SVGA recommended), 4Mb RAM, external speakers or headphones (with sound card) that are Sound Blaster compatible.
Macintosh (4Mb). (Order no.: R1045). *Nonstandard peripherals required:* 14" color monitor or larger, CD-ROM drive.
Highly Interactive Animated Stories for Children That Have Hundreds of Beautiful Animations & Have Received Countless Awards. In English only (Ages 6-12).
Library Video Co.

TITLE INDEX

New King James Version. Aug. 1990. *Customer Support:* No fee is charged for our customer support: 30 day money back return guarantee; lifetime warranty on defective disk replacement; free telephone technical support.
PC or MS-DOS 2.0 or higher. IBM PC/XT/AT or compatible. 3.5" or 5.25" disk $49.95. *Addl. software required:* PC STUDY BIBLE. *Optimal configuration:* Hard disk with 1.5Mb hard disk space.
The Text of the New King James Version of the Bible. Add-On Bible Version to Be Used with BIBLESOFT'S PC STUDY BIBLE.
Biblesoft.

New King James Version. Thomas Nelson Publishers Staff. May 1993. *Items Included:* Disks, marketing literature, order form. *Customer Support:* No fee for customer support: 30 day money back guarantee, limited replacement warranty on diskettes defective at time of purchase, free telephone technical support.
PC-DOS/MS-DOS 2.0 or higher or Windows 3.0 or higher. 386/486 or 100% compatible (Windows); Also AT/XT/286 (DOS) (640k DOS or 4Mb Windows). disk $39.95 (ISBN 1-56514-585-2). *Addl. software required:* Biblesoft's PC Study Bible. *Optimal configuration:* Requires 5.25" 1.2Mb disk drive for installation & 1.5Mb of hard drive space, mouse or pointer device recommended.
The Text of the New King James Version of the Bible Is an Add-On Version to Be Used with Biblesoft's PC Study Bible.
Biblesoft.

New King James Version. Thomas Nelson Publishers. May 1993. *Customer Support:* No fee for customer support: (1) 30 day money back guarantee (2) Lifetime warranty replacement on defective disks (3) Free telephone technical support.
PC-DOS/MS-DOS 2.0 or higher. IBM PC, XT/AT/286/386/486 or 100% compatibles (640k). disk $49.95 (ISBN 1-56514-585-2). *Addl. software required:* PC Study Bible. *Optimal configuration:* Requires 5 1/4" 1.2Mb disk drive for installation & 3Mb of hard drive space. Mouse or pointer device recommended.
Text of the NEW KING JAMES VERSION of the Bible. Add-On Bible Version to Be Used with BIBLESOFT'S PC Study Bible.

New King James Version Add-On Text. May 1993. *Items Included:* Disks, marketing literature, order form. *Customer Support:* No fee for customer support: 30 day money back guarantee, limited replacement warranty on diskettes defective at time of purchase, free telephone technical support.
PC-DOS/MS-DOS 3.1 or higher or MS Windows 3.1 or higher. IBM 386/486 or 100% compatible (Windows); Also AT/XT/286 (DOS) (640k DOS or 4Mb Windows). 3.5" disk $39.95 (ISBN 1-56514-203-9). *Addl. software required:* Biblesoft's PC Study Bible. *Optimal configuration:* 3.5" 1.44Mb disk drive for installation & 1.5Mb of hard drive space, mouse or pointer device recommended.
The Text of the New King James Version of the Bible Is an Add-On Version to Be Used with Biblesoft's PC Study Bible.
Biblesoft.

New Scofield Study Bible. Parsons Technology. Jan. 1993.
3.5" disk Contact publisher for price (ISBN 1-57264-034-0).
Parsons Technology.

New Unger's Bible Dictionary for Windows. Feb. 1996. *Items Included:* Disks, marketing literature, order form, registration card. *Customer Support:* 30 day money back guarantee; limited replacement warranty on diskettes defective at time of purchase; free telephone technical support.
Windows 3.1 or higher. IBM 386/486 or 100% compatible (4Mb, 8Mb recommended). 3.5" disk $49.95 (ISBN 1-56514-119-9). *Addl. software required:* Biblesoft's PC Study Bible. *Optimal configuration:* 3.5, 1.44Mb disk drive for installation, mouse or pointer device recommended.
A Thorough Dictionary of Bible Words & Concepts with Encyclopedia-Like Articles on People, Places & Events to Be Used with the PC Study Bible. Includes over 6,000 Separate Entries.
Biblesoft.

New Word 3. *Compatible Hardware:* IBM PC, PC XT, PC AT, PCjr & compatibles. *Operating System(s) Required:* PC-DOS/MS-DOS 2.0 or higher, TurboDOS, CP/M-86, Concurrent CP/M. *Memory Required:* 128k.
$349.00.
Word Processing Program That Works Just Like Wordstar. Includes Adding Macros, Indexing, a Spelling Checker & Networking Capabilities.
Newstar Software.

New York City - Air Support. (Double-Play Ser.). Greg Nelson & Rich Carr. *Compatible Hardware:* Commodore 64 with joystick.
disk $24.95 (Order no.: COMDSK-3341).
NEW YORK CITY - Visit New York & Encounter Big City Adventures. AIR SUPPORT - Choose Between Arcade & Strategy Play, Select the Difficulty, Terrain, Enemy Strength & Weapons, & Then Assume Command of an Arsenal of Choppers & Robots.
Broderbund Software, Inc.

New York City - Electrician. (Double-Play Ser.). Russ Segal & David Bunch. *Compatible Hardware:* Atari 400, 800, XL series. *General Requirements:* Joystick.
disk $24.95 (Order no.: ATDSK-2341).
NEW YORK CITY - Visit New York & Encounter Big City Adventures. ELECTRICIAN - Wire Eight Buildings Before Going Home, While Avoiding Wire-Eating Bats, Worms, Mice, Spiders & Alligators.
Broderbund Software, Inc.

New York Net Worth. *Version:* 6.0. Steven R. Kursh. May 1993. *Items Included:* 1 manual. *Customer Support:* Toll free phone support.
DOS 3.1 or higher. IBM PC & compatibles (640k). Contact publisher for price. *Networks supported:* Novell 3.11.
Allows User to Open a Case & Retrieve the Submenu, Then Information Can Be Entered Regarding the Plaintiff or Defendant. This Includes Family Data, Expenses & Gross Income, Assets, Liabilities, Assets Transferred, Requirements & Net Worth Summary.
Shepard's/McGraw-Hill, Inc.

New York Times Crosswords. *Items Included:* Installation instructions, registration card. *Customer Support:* Phone support by calling 302-234-1750, no charge. Fax support by faxing to 302-234-1760, no charge. E-Mail support at Compuserve ID 76004,3520 or MCI Mail/560-7116, no charge.
Windows 3.0 or higher. 286 (1Mb). disk $29.95 (ISBN 1-887468-24-2). *Nonstandard peripherals required:* EGA, VGA, 8514/A or higher resolution monitor, Microsoft mouse or compatible.
Test Crossword Skills with 200 Daily Puzzles & 50 Brainteasing Sunday Puzzles form The New York Times.
SWFTE International, Ltd.

NEWTECH EXPERT CHOICE

Newsdex. Theodore Hines. 1982. *Compatible Hardware:* IBM PC & Compatibles. *Operating System(s) Required:* MS-DOS. *Language(s):* BASIC. *Memory Required:* 64k.
disk $450.00.
Capital Systems Group, Inc.

Newsflow. *Version:* 4.0. Nov. 1988. *Compatible Hardware:* Apple Macintosh, IBM PC & compatibles.
$150.00.
Customized PostScript Template Which, When Downloaded to a PostScript Output Device, Translates a Text File into Hyphenated, Customized Galleys That Can Be Printed in Multiple Columns.
Random Access.

Newsletter Art: ClickArt. *Items Included:* Visual index, user's guide. *Customer Support:* Free & unlimited technical support to registered users; 60 day money-back guarantee.
Macintosh. Macintosh, System 6.0.7 or higher (1Mb). 3.5" disk $49.95. *Addl. software required:* Any word-processing, desktop publishing or works program that accepts graphics.
Windows MS-DOS. IBM PC & compatibles. 3.5" disk $49.95. *Addl. software required:* Any word processing, desktop publishing or works program that accepts graphics.
Over 220 Images! Full-Color Images; Ready-to-Use, or Changed in Appropriate Drawing Program; Designed in Full-Color (CMYK); Produced to Print in Detailed Greyscale on Black & White Printers; Includes the ClickArt Trade Secret - Images Traded to Every Popular Graphics Format, Guaranteed to Work with All Popular Applications.
T/Maker Co., Inc.

NewsMaster II. *Operating System(s) Required:* PC-DOS/MS-DOS 2.1 or higher. *Memory Required:* 512k. *General Requirements:* 2 disk drives. *Customer Support:* 510-748-6938.
disk $79.95.
Page Layout Package Designed to Work with Most Dot Matrix Printers. Also Supports HP's Laser Jet Printer. Users Can Create Multiple Column Layouts, Import ASCII Text Files, & Choose Graphics from Libraries Available from Unison World Software. Extremely Easy to Use.
Unison World.

Newsweek Interactive, Vol. 1. Jun. 1993. IBM CD-ROM. CD-ROM disk $49.95 (Order no.: 111313).
In a Quarterly CD-ROM, Examine up to Four Topics on Current Events, Using Motion Video, Audio, Animations, Photo Essays, & Selected Text from the Previous 3 Months...Includes Highlighted Text from the Last 3 Months of Newsweek, Relevant Daily Material from The Washington Post, & over 100 Pages of Text in Every Edition. More Than Just a Periodical on Disc, This Is an Almanac with Reference Value on News Topics of Enduring Interest.
Software Toolworks.

Newtech Expert Choice. *Version:* 7.1. Aug. 1989. *Customer Support:* Telephone support. DOS 3.2 or higher. IBM PC, PS/2 & compatibles (340k). disk $150.00. *Optimal configuration:* Graphics card, CGA & VGA, 640k RAM, printer. *Networks supported:* Novell.
Decision Support System for the Adoption of New Technology. The Integration of Computer-Aided Techniques into Manufacturing Process. It Contains the Expert Choice Decision Support Software System & Has More Than 110 Variables That Allow Users to Organize Their Thoughts Concerning NT Adoption. It Takes a Systems Approach to the Inital Cost Analysis,

Purchase, & Implementation of New Technology That Integrates the Operational Components into the Strategic & Tactical Decision-Making Process of the Firm.
Expert Choice, Inc.

NewWord. *Version:* 3.01. Feb. 1986. *Compatible Hardware:* IBM PC with double-sided disk drive, printer, & 80-column screen. *Operating System(s) Required:* PC-DOS, MS-DOS 2.0 or higher, CP/M-86, TurboDOS. *Language(s):* Assembly. *Memory Required:* 128k.
disk $349.00.
Menu-Driven Command & File Word Processing System. Offers "Living" Ruler Lines the Ability to Store Margins & Tabs & Have Them Automatically Change As User Moves Through a File. Unerase Command Recovers Deleted Text.
Newstar Software.

Nexpert Object. *Version:* 2.0B. *Compatible Hardware:* OS/2; Macintosh, PC; UNIX 386, UNIX & VAX workstations. *Items Included:* 1 runtime version, 5 spiral bound manuals. *Customer Support:* 1 yr. support & upgrade, 20% dev. license price, 90 day free installation support.
Contact publisher for price.
Features Expert Development Tool; Rule & Object-Based System; Access to External Programs & Databases.
Neuron Data, Inc.

Next Step: Mars?: An Exciting Learning Adventure about Space. Qed New Media Staff. Dec. 1994. *Customer Support:* Free 800 Number Technical Support.
Windows. PC with 486SX 25MHz or higher (8Mb). disk $39.95 (ISBN 1-884899-14-5). *Optimal configuration:* 486SX 25MHz or higher PC, 8Mb RAM, double-speed CD-ROM drive, VGA plus 640x480 monitor displaying 256 colors, MS-DOS 5.0 or higher, Windows 3.1, MS-DOS CD-ROM Extensions (MSCDEX) 2.2 or higher, stereo headphones or speakers, 2Mb free hard disk space for installation, mouse or compatible positioning device, 16-bit sound card (100% Sound Blaster compatible), VL bus or PCI VGA video card recommended.
Macintosh. Color capable Macintosh (8Mb). disk $39.95 (ISBN 1-884899-16-1). *Optimal configuration:* Color Macintosh computer (LCIII, CI, FX, Quadra, Performa 400/600 Power Macintosh or Powerbook with color video out), 8Mb RAM, System 7.1 or higher, 13" color monitor, 2Mb free hard disk space for installation, double-speed CD-ROM drive, stereo headphones or speakers, mouse.
Based on the Public Television Series "Space Age," Hosted by Patrick Stewart, This Is a Learning Adventure about Space. It Teaches about the Past, Present & Future of Space Exploration Through Video Footage, Learning Activities, Colorful Animations & Comprehensive Text. An Excellent Learning Tool for Ages 12-Adult.
IVI Publishing, Inc.

Nextra.
Macintosh II (2Mb). 3.5" disk $4000.00.
Knowledge Acquisition Transfer Tool for Expert Systems Development.
Neuron Data, Inc.

NFC: Non-Flashing Cursor. Jan. 1979. *Compatible Hardware:* Apple II, II+. *Operating System(s) Required:* Apple DOS 3.2, 3.3. (source code included). *Memory Required:* 16k.
disk $9.95 (ISBN 0-926567-00-4, Order no.: NFC).
Self Installing Modification Which Eliminates the Flashing Cursor.
Rettke Resources.

NFL Challenge. *Version:* 1.03. *Compatible Hardware:* Apple Macintosh, Plus, SE, SE/30, Mac II, IIx, IIcx; IBM PC, PC XT, PC AT, & compatibles. *Memory Required:* 1000k.
IBM PC, PC XT, PC AT & compatibles (320k). Version 2.01 (08/1989) $99.95.
Apple Macintosh (1Mb). Version 1.03 (03/1989) $99.95.
Football Simulation. Features Updatable Rosters of All 28 NFL Teams, Offensive & Defensive Playbooks, & Real Game Factors Such As Penalties, Injuries, & Substitutions.
XOR Corp.

NFL Football Trivia Challenge. Sep. 1994. *Items Included:* QuickTime 2.0 for MAC.
MS-DOS. PC 486sz 25mhz (4Mb). CD-ROM disk $54.95 (ISBN 1-57272-951-1). *Nonstandard peripherals required:* Sound card, VGA display-256 colors, MS-DOS CD-ROM. *Optimal configuration:* 486/33 8Mb double speed CD-ROM/speakers.
MAC System 6.07 or higher. Color MAC IICI or higher (4Mb). CD-ROM disk $54.95 (ISBN 1-57272-952-X). *Nonstandard peripherals required:* CD-ROM drive/speakers. *Addl. software required:* Quick Time 2.0. *Optimal configuration:* 68040/33mhz w/double CD-ROM drive, speakers.
Ultimate Game for the Armchair Quarterback! This Unique Trivia Title Will Put Your Knowledge of the Game of Football to the Test. Choose Your Team from Either the AFC or the NFC, & Decide If Your Skill Level Is Rookie, Pro, or Veteran. Then Try to Gain Yardage by Correctly Answering Multiple Choice Questions Hall-of-Famers, Official Signals, Games of the Past, etc. Game Contains over 1,500 Questions, Approved by the NFL, Pertaining to Super Bowls, MVP's, Rules & Many Aspects of Football. Nearly 1200 Still Photographs & 1 Hour of Video from the Archives of NFL Films & NFL Photo Services. Pat Summerall & Tom Brookshier Provide Commentary.
Capitol Multimedia, Inc.

NFL Forecaster. *Compatible Hardware:* Apple II+, IIe, IIc, IIgs; CP/M systems; IBM PC & compatibles. *Memory Required:* CP/M 64k, IBM 128k, Apple 140k.
disk $39.95.
Helps Fans Predict the Winners & Point Spreads of NFL Games. Ranks the League's 28 Teams by Offense, Defense, Total Points for & Against, & Conference Rankings. Also Allows Users to View or Print the Complete NFL Schedule.
Cotton Software, Inc.

NFL Forecaster. *Items Included:* Bound manual. *Customer Support:* Free hotline - no time limit; 30 day limited warranty; updates are $5/disk plus S&H.
MS-DOS. IBM & compatibles (256k). disk $49.95.
Predicts Winners & Spreads of NFL Games Using Only Game Scores; There Is No Need to Type in Pages of Statistics. Usually Picks More Winners Correctly Than Las Vegas Odds-Makers. Maintains a Number of Statistics & Ranks Teams by Offense & Defense Ranking, Total Points Scored by & Against Each Team, & by Win/Loss/Tie Record.
Dynacomp, Inc.

NFL Handicapper. *Items Included:* Bound manual. *Customer Support:* Free hotline - no time limit; 30 day limited warranty; updates are $5/disk plus S&H.
All computers (except C-64). disk $59.95.
Uses Multiple Linear Regression to Statistically Handicap the National Football League. All You Need to Do Is Enter the Results of Past Games. After 30 or More Sets of Scores Have Been Entered, You Can Start to Handicap.
Dynacomp, Inc.

NFL Prognosticator. *Compatible Hardware:* Apple. *Language(s):* Applesoft. *Memory Required:* 32k.
disk $24.95 (Order no.: 0145AD).
Keeps Updated Records of Each Team's Season, Gives Accurate Predictions & Point Spreads Each Week.
Instant Software, Inc.

NI-DAQ. Mar. 1989. *Customer Support:* Toll-free technical support.
PC-DOS, Microsoft Windows 3.0, Macintosh Operating System, Solaris. IBM PC, PC XT, PC AT, PS/2; MicroChannel, EISA, Macintosh, Sun SPARCstations. disk # no charge with purchase of data acquisition board (Order no.: 776250-01FD5). *Nonstandard peripherals required:* PC, AT Series or MC Series data acquisition board (A/O, D/A, digital I/O, timing I/O, waveform generation), NB Series Boards, or plug-in data acquisition boards for Sun SPARCstations.
3.5" disk # no charge with purchase of data acquisition board (Order no.: 776250-11FD3).
Provides High-Level Software Modules for Developing Data Acquisition Applications with the Company's PC, AT, MC, NB, & SB Series Boards for A/D & D/A Conversion, DI/O, Timing I/O, Wave Form Generation, DMA & RSTI Bus for Precising Timing Between Boards. The Library of Functions Are Available for Microsoft C, QuickBASIC, Borland Turbo C Plus Plus & Turbo Pascal, Turbo C, Turbo C Plus Plus, Quick C, Professional BASIC, ThinkC, MPWC, ThinkPascal.
National Instruments Corp.

NI-488.2 Software. *Items Included:* 5.25" or 3.5" floppies, or 9-track mag tape of Sun Cartridge when applicable, documentation. Macintosh version provided with GPIB board purchase. *Customer Support:* Toll-free technical support.
MS-DOS (32k). IBM PC/XT/AT, PS/2, PC convertible. $50.00, each. BASIC A, C, & Quick BASIC provided w/interface purchase (Order no.: N1-488 MS-DOS). *Nonstandard peripherals required:* IEEE-488 interface. *Addl. software required:* Language interfaces for several versions of C, BASIC, Pascal, Fortran, & 8086 Assembler-Version for IEEE-488.2-compatible interfaces.
Macintosh (111k). MacSE or II series. no cost w/purchase of GPIB interface for Macintosh. *Nonstandard peripherals required:* NB-GPIB, NB-DMA-8-G, NB-DMA2800, GPIB-SE. *Addl. software required:* (Optional) HyperCard.
UNIX, XENIX, SunDOS, 386ix (multitasking) (601k). PC/AT bus, VMEbus, & MULTIBUS. $200.00 upgrade price for current users. $495.00 stand alone price for XENIX & 386ix versions. $500.00 - $600.00 for sunOS & UNIX versions. (Order no.: N1-488M). *Nonstandard peripherals required:* IEEE-488 interface.
Software Package Has a High-speed Driver That Installs As Part of the Operating System & has Several Utilites That Help Users Develop & Debug Application Programs. The Handler Controls the Company's GPIB Interfaces on IBM, Macintosh, Sun, AT&T 3B2, & Pro-log STD-DOS Computers Running Under DOS, OS/2, UNIX, SunDS, XENIX, & 386/ix Operating Systems.
National Instruments Corp.

NI-VXI. *Items Included:* Software, documentation. *Customer Support:* Toll-free technical support, training, field seminar, user group meetings.
DOS, Windows, OS/2, Macintosh, Unix, Real-Time. VXIpc-486 series, VXIcpu-030, PC AT, EISA, PS/2, Macintosh, IBM RS/6000, DECstation 5000, Sun SPARCstation. disk $795.00. *Nonstandard peripherals required:* Embedded VXI bus computer or MXI bus interface.
A Comprehensive Software Package for

TITLE INDEX

Configuring, Programming, & Troubleshooting a VXI System. Features Intuitive Tools for Interacting with & Learning about VXI, Comprehensive High-Performance Routines for Programming VXI Using Industry-Standard Programming Languages, Multiple-Mainframe Configuration Capability, & Software Compatibility Across a Variety of Operating Systems & Works with Both Embedded & MXI-Equipped VXI Controller Platforms.
National Instruments.

NicBase3. *Version:* 3. 1991. *Items Included:* Utilities, 5000 master-level games & latest classification key. *Customer Support:* Free telephone support by appointment.
MS-DOS 2.0 or higher. 80086 (512k). disk $158.00. *Nonstandard peripherals required: ouse, any graphics.*
Atari ST. 520. *Nonstandard peripherals required: Monochrome monitor.*
Designed to Compile, Classify, & Annotate Chess Games, NicBase3 Is the Same Program Used by the Editors of the New in Chess Yearbooks.
Chess Combination, Inc.

Nicpublish. *Customer Support:* Free telephone support by appointment.
MS-DOS 2.0 or higher. 80386 (512k). disk $250.00. *Nonstandard peripherals required: Mouse, any graphics. Addl. software required: NicBase3 & Ventura Publisher.*
For Production of Chess-Related Publications Including Figurine Notation & Chess Programs. Requires NicBase3 & Ventura Publisher.
Chess Combination, Inc.

Nifty Note Handler. *Compatible Hardware:* IBM PC; TRS-80 Model I Level I, Model III, Model 4, Color Computer, Tandy 1000. *Operating System(s) Required:* TRSDOS. *Language(s):* Extended Color BASIC. *Memory Required:* 16k. cassette $19.95.
Assists in the Administration of a 'Personal' Correspondence System. Keeps Track of 26 Names & Addresses. Other Features Include Support for Producing a Single Page Letter with Corrections, Retyped Lines & the Ability to Provide Typing for Labels & Envelopes.
Viking, Inc.

Nigel's World Adventure in World Geography. Dec. 1995. *Customer Support:* Telephone support - free (except phone charge).
Windows 3.1. IBM & compatibles (386 DX-20) (4Mb). CD-ROM disk $12.99, Jewel (ISBN 1-57594-084-1). *Nonstandard peripherals required:* 2X CD ROM player, sound card, VGA monitor. *Optimal configuration:* 486 SX-33.
CD-ROM disk $12.99, Blister.
Kids Help Their Scottish Friend in His Cameraman's Quest to Snap Shots from Around the World & Wins the Coveted Diamond Tripod Award. Kids Encounter Legions of Facts, Folk Songs & Fun.
Kidsoft, Inc.

Nigel's World Adventure in World Geography. Jan. 1996. *Customer Support:* Telephone support - free (except phone charge).
System 6.0.7 or higher. 256 color capable Mac with a 68030 processor (4Mb). CD-ROM disk $12.99 (ISBN 1-57594-108-2). *Nonstandard peripherals required:* 2X CD ROM drive, 640/480 resolution monitor.
Kids Help Their Scottish Friend in His Cameraman's Quest to Snap Shots from Around the World & Win the Coveted Diamond Tripod Award. Kids Encounter Legions of Facts, Folk Songs, & Fun.
Kidsoft, Inc.

Nigel's World Adventure in World Geography. Feb. 1996. *Customer Support:* Telephone support - free (except phone charge).
Windows 3.1. IBM compatible 386 DX-20 (4Mb). CD-ROM disk $12.99 (ISBN 1-57594-097-3). *Nonstandard peripherals required:* 2x CD-ROM, sound card, VGA monitor. *Optimal configuration:* 486, SX-33.
Travel Around the World with Nigel While Encountering Legions of Facts, Folk Songs & Fun. Blister Pack.
Kidsoft, Inc.

Nigel's World Adventure in World Geography. Dec. 1995. *Customer Support:* Telephone support - free (except phone charge).
Windows 3.1. IBM & compatibles (386 DX-20) (4Mb). CD-ROM disk $12.99 (ISBN 1-57594-084-1). *Nonstandard peripherals required:* 2X CD-ROM player, sound card, VGA monitor. *Optimal configuration:* 486 SX-33.
Kids Help Their Scottish Friend in His Cameraman's Quest to Snap Shots from Around the World & Win the Coveted Diamond Tripod Award. Kids Encounter Legions of Facts, Folk Songs & Fun. Jewel Case.
Kidsoft, Inc.

Nigel's World: Adventures in World Geography. Aug. 1991. *Items Included:* Program manual. *Customer Support:* Free technical support 800-421-4157, 90 day warranty.
PC-DOS/MS-DOS 3.0 or higher. IBM (640k). disk $39.95 (ISBN 0-917999-84-3). *Nonstandard peripherals required:* Microsoft mouse recommended, supports Ad Lib & Sound Blaster sound cards, hard drive. *Networks supported:* I-Class, Novel.
System 6.0.5 or higher. Macintosh (1Mb). 3.5" disk $49.95 (ISBN 1-882848-63-2).
PC-DOS/MS-DOS 3.0 or higher. IBM (640k). $49.95 School Edition, 3 1/2" disks (ISBN 0-917999-89-4). *Nonstandard peripherals required:* Microsoft mouse recommended, supports Ad Lib & Sound Blaster sound cards, hard drive. *Networks supported:* I-Class, Novel 599.00.
PC-DOS/MS-DOS or higher. IBM (640k). $49.95 School Edition, 5 1/4" disks (ISBN 0-917999-90-8). *Nonstandard peripherals required:* Microsoft mouse recommended, supports Ad Lib & Sound Blaster cards, hard drive. *Networks supported:* I-Class, Novel 599.00.
PC-DOS/MS-DOS 3.0 or higher. IBM (640k). $99.00 School Edition, Lab Pack, 3 1/2" disks (ISBN 0-917999-91-6). *Nonstandard peripherals required:* Microsoft mouse recommended, supports Ad Lib & Sound Blaster cards, hard drive. *Networks supported:* I-Class, Novel 599.00.
PC-DOS/MS-DOS 3.0 or higher. IBM (640k). $99.00 School Edition, Lab Pack, 5 1/4" disks (ISBN 0-917999-92-4). *Nonstandard peripherals required:* Microsoft mouse recommended, supports Ad Lib & Sound Blaster cards, hard drive. *Networks supported:* I-Class, Novel 599.00.
System 6.0.5 or higher. Macintosh (1Mb). $59.95 School Edition (ISBN 0-917999-93-2).
System 6.0.5 or higher. Macintosh (1Mb). $129.00 School Edition, Lab Pack (ISBN 0-917999-94-0).
Nigel's World Takes Kids Ages 7-12 Around the World "on Assignment" with Nigel, a Scottish Photogrpaher. Users Learn Map Geography & Cultural Information As They Trot the Globe, Taking Amazing Photographs of People, Animals, & Monuments. The Game Includes 40 Maps, 90 Photos, 100 Animated Scenes, 30 Folk Songs & 1,000 Facts.
Lawrence Productions, Inc.

NIGHT SKY INTERACTIVE

Nighlight. Jan. 1996. *Customer Support:* Telephone support - free (except phone charge).
System 7.0 or higher. 256 color capable Mac with 68030 processor (5Mb). CD-ROM disk $12.99 (ISBN 1-57594-116-3). *Nonstandard peripherals required:* 2X CD ROM drive, mouse, 640/480 resolution monitor.
With Helpful Tools, Nightlight Encourages Children to Learn How to Identify Shapes & Objects by Exploring 8 Areas of a Dark House with Screen Companions, Pixel & Pandora.
Kidsoft, Inc.

Night Light. Feb. 1996. *Customer Support:* Telephone support - free (except phone charge).
Windows 3.1. IBM compatible 386 DX-20 (4Mb). CD-ROM disk $12.99 (ISBN 1-57594-098-1). *Nonstandard peripherals required:* 2x CD-ROM, sound card, VGA monitor. *Optimal configuration:* 486, SX-33.
Encourages Children to Learn How to Identify Shapes & Objects by Exploring 8 Areas of a Dark House with Screen Companions, Pixel & Pandora. Blister Pack.
Kidsoft, Inc.

A Night Out on the Internet: Entertainment, Fun, & Excitement on the World Wide Web. Julie Charles. Apr. 1996. *Items Included:* A 64-page companion booklet that reviews web sites & includes instructions on how to use the software. *Customer Support:* Access to the Go!Guides web site & FAQ, customer support by email at help goguides.com.
Macintosh System 7.0 or higher. Macintosh (4Mb). 3.5" disk $12.99 (ISBN 1-57712-006-X). *Nonstandard peripherals required:* Modem 14.4 or faster. *Addl. software required:* Internet account & connection. *Optimal configuration:* Macintosh System 7.0 or higher, at least 4Mb of RAM, at least 2Mb of free disk space, color monitor, 14.4 or 28.8 modem, Internet account.
Windows 3.1 or Windows 95. IBM or compatible (4Mb). disk $12.99. *Nonstandard peripherals required:* 14.4 or 28.8 modem. *Addl. software required:* Internet account. *Optimal configuration:* IBM-compatible running Windows 3.1 or Windows 95, at least 2Mb free space on hard drive, at least 4Mb RAM, color monitor, 14.4 or 28.8 modem, Internet account.
From Live Concerts & Real-Time Chats with Celebrities to Fast-As-Lightning Scoops on Your Favorite Entertainers, It's All There on the Internet, Waiting to Be Accessed.
Motion Works Publishing.

Night Rider: Pinball Simulation Game. *Compatible Hardware:* IBM PC. *Operating System(s) Required:* PC-DOS, MS-DOS. $29.95.
Transforms the Computer into a Pinball Machine. Provides 1- or 2-Player Options & Maintains High-Ball & High Game Scores on Disk. Multiple Skill Levels Can Be Selected to Challenge Both Novice & Experienced Players.
Generic Computer Products, Inc. (GCPI).

Night Sky Interactive. *Customer Support:* Free, unlimited.
System 6 Mac. 030 Mac, 256 colors (4Mb). CD-ROM disk $24.95. *Nonstandard peripherals required:* Sound card, CD-ROM drive.
Windows 3.1 PC. 486 PC (4Mb). *Nonstandard peripherals required:* Any Windows supported sound card, CD-ROM drive.
Constellations, Comets, Stars, Planets, Meteors, Galaxies, the Moon & More Are Yours to Explore in This CD. Watch Animations & Hear Narratives about How the Moon Orbits the Earth & Many Other Topics. Fabulous Introduction to Astronomy for Young & Old.
BeachWare.

Night Trap. *Items Included:* Instruction manual. *Customer Support:* Free Telephone support. DOS/Windows 95. IBM & compatibles (8Mb). Contact publisher for price. *Nonstandard peripherals required:* CD-ROM drive.
Digital Pictures, Inc.

Nightlight. Feb. 1996. *Customer Support:* Telephone support - free (except phone charge). System 6.0.7 or higher. 256 color Mac with 68030 processor (5Mb). CD-ROM disk $12.99 (ISBN 1-57594-116-3). *Nonstandard peripherals required:* 2x CD-ROM drive, mouse, 640/480 resolution monitor.
With Helpful Tools, NightLight Encourages Children to Learn How to Identify Shapes & Objects by Exploring 8 Areas of a Dark House with Screen Companions, Pixel & Pandora. Jewel case.
Kidsoft, Inc.

Nightlite. Dec. 1995. *Customer Support:* Telephone support - free (except phone charge). Windows 3.1. IBM & compatibles (386 DX-20) (4Mb). CD-ROM disk $12.99, Jewel (ISBN 1-57594-085-X). *Nonstandard peripherals required:* 2X CD ROM player, sound card, VGA monitor. *Optimal configuration:* 486 SX-33.
CD-ROM disk $12.99, Blister.
With Helpful Tools, Night Light Encourages Children to Learn How to Identify Shapes & Objects by Exploring 8 Areas of a Dark House with Screen Companions, Pixel & Pandora.
Kidsoft, Inc.

Nightlite. Dec. 1995. *Customer Support:* Telephone support - free (except phone charge). Windows 3.1. IBM & compatibles (386 DX-20) (4Mb). CD-ROM disk $12.99 (ISBN 1-57594-085-X). *Nonstandard peripherals required:* 2X CD-ROM player, sound card, VGA monitor. *Optimal configuration:* 486 SX-33.
With Helpful Tools, Night Light Encourages Children to Learn How to Identify Shapes & Objects by Exploring 8 Areas of a Dark House with Screen Companions, Pixel & Pandora. Jewel Case.
Kidsoft, Inc.

NightWatch 2. *Version:* 2.01. *Compatible Hardware:* Apple Macintosh. *Memory Required:* 512k. *General Requirements:* Hard disk. *Customer Support:* For registered owners.
3.5" disk $159.95 site licensing available.
Shuts Down a Hard Disk by Preventing Unauthorized Access, Erasure, or the Introduction of a Virus. Authorized User Enters Name & Password to Unlock the Hard Disk, & System Records Every Attempt to Unlock. Application Includes Override Function in Case User Has Forgotten Password or Lost User Disk. Has Dynamic Update Capacity When Encountering New Systems/Hardware.
Kent Marsh Ltd.

Nimbus. *Version:* 1.4. *Compatible Hardware:* Commodore Amiga. *Language(s):* C.
3.5" disk $149.00.
Cash Management Accounting System for Small Businesses Which Allows Access to the General Ledger by Accounts Payable & Accounts Receivable. Automatically Updates the General Ledger When Data Is Entered into Either the Accounts Payable or Accounts Receivable Files. Customers & Vendors Are Tracked by Name Rather Than by Number.
Oxxi, Inc.

Nimrod. Duane Bristow. *Compatible Hardware:* TRS-80 Model I, Model III. *Operating System(s) Required:* TRSDOS. *Language(s):* BASIC. *Memory Required:* 32k.

cassette $19.95.
Combination of Maze, Adventure, & Dungeon Type Games.
Duane Bristow Computers, Inc.

The 940/941 Solution. *Version:* Updated Annually. Jan. 1987. *Items Included:* Manual. *Customer Support:* Free telephone support during tax year; 30-day money-back guarantee.
PC-DOS/MS-DOS. IBM PC compatibles (512k). (Annual) Site: $125.00, 4-user: $165.00, unlimited user: $195.00. *Addl. software required:* The Write-Up Solution II. *Optimal configuration:* IBM PC - AT class or faster; DOS 3.1 or higher, 640k, HP LaserJet + or later. *Networks supported:* Novell, LANtastic.
Works with CSi's Write-Up Solution II (WS2) to Prepare 940/941s Without Rekeying Any Data. Information from WS2 Transfers Directly for Printing on 940/941 Forms - Reducing the Time Spent Completing 940/941 Forms. Also Produces Laser Facimiles of Forms.
Creative Solutions, Inc. (Michigan).

931 Emulator. *Compatible Hardware:* TI Professional with modem. *Operating System(s) Required:* MS-DOS, DX10 3.6, DNOS 1.2. *Memory Required:* 128k.
$150.00 (Order no.: TI P/N 2237368-0001).
Gives Computer the Functionality of a TI 931 Terminal.
Texas Instruments, Personal Productivit.

1996 California Manufacturers Register: Database Prospect System. Jan. 1996. *Customer Support:* Free telephone hotline support.
MS-DOS, PC-DOS 3.3 or higher. IBM PC compatible (640k). disk $795.00. *Nonstandard peripherals required:* None. *Addl. software required:* None. *Optimal configuration:* IBM or compatible, with 640k RAM, 3.3 DOS or higher, 15.0Mb of hard disk space, printer. Also available on CD-ROM.
This "Desktop Database" Contains the Contents of the 1996 Edition of the California Manufacturers Register Together with Retrieval Software. Approximately 28,500 Manufacturers & Selected Wholesalers Are Profiled, Software Enables User to Select, Retrieve, Sort & Output Information. Output Includes Complete Record, Telemarketing Prospect Cards, Mailing Labels & ASCII Files. Information Includes Company Name, Address, Parent, Telephone, FAX, & WATS Numbers; Year Established, Number of Employees, Annual Revenues, Plant Size, Business Description, up to Six SIC Codes, Import/Export Designators, Bank, Names & Title of Key Executives, Type of Ownership, etc.
Database Publishing Co.

1996 California Wholesalers, Distributors & Services Companies: Database Prospect System. Jan. 1996. *Items Included:* 9 diskettes & user manual. *Customer Support:* Free customer hotline support.
DOS, Windows. IBM PC & compatibles (512k). disk $795.00. *Optimal configuration:* 386 or 486 PC with 640k RAM, 17Mb hard disk space, DOS 3.3 or higher, printer. Also available on CD-ROM.
This Is a Database of the Contents of the California Services Register Together with Retrieval Software (DOS Only). 34,000 Wholesalers, Distributors & Selected Services Businesses Throughout California Are Listed. Software Enables the User to Select, Retrieve, Sort, & Output Data. Output Includes Complete Record, Selected Fields, Mailing Locales & ASCII Files. Information Includes Company Name, Address, Parent, Telephone, Fax, & WATS Numbers; Year Established, Number of Employees, Annual Revenue, Plant Size, Business

Description, up to Six SIC Codes, Import/Export Designations, Names & Titles of Key Executives, Legal Structure, etc.
Database Publishing Co.

97 Golf Courses CD-ROM. Jan. 1996. *Items Included:* Instruction booklet.
DOS & Windows 3.1. PC (4k). CD-ROM disk $29.90 (ISBN 1-56087-133-4). *Addl. software required:* Mean 18, Signature or Links 386. *Optimal configuration:* 386, Windows 3.1 4k RAM.
Play 97 of the World's Greatest Golf Courses on Your Computer. You Can Also Figure Golf Handicaps for Yourself or for Your Whole League. There Are Scoring Managers for Tournaments, Fun & Instructional Interactive Games & Lessons, Even a Golf Almanac.
Top of the Mountain Publishing.

Ninvoice. *Compatible Hardware:* TRS-80 Model I, Model III, Model 4. *Operating System(s) Required:* TRSDOS. *Language(s):* BASIC (source code included). *Memory Required:* 32k. *General Requirements:* 2 disk drives, Radio Shack Inventory Control System.
disk $50.00.
Produces Invoices on NEBS Pre-Printed Form #9040 from Radio Shack's ICS Inventory Files. Extends Amounts & Allows Manual Entries.
Computer/Business Services.

Nisus. *Version:* 3.4. *Compatible Hardware:* Apple Macintosh. *Memory Required:* 1000k, with MultiFinder 2000k. *General Requirements:* LaserWriter & ImageWriter supported. *Items Included:* Disks, manual. *Customer Support:* Free telephone technical support.
3.5" disk $395.00.
Includes Menu Keys, Spelling Check, Mail Merge, Glossary & Macros. Unlimited Undos, Drag-and-Drop, Multiple Clipboards & Noncontiguous Selection. Precision Find & Replace Lets User Search Unopened Files & Format Downloaded Mainframe Files in an Instant. User Can Create, Scale, Rotate Graphics & Have Text Wrap Automatically. Writes in over 18 Languages Including Arabic, Czech, Hebrew (Right to Left), Hungarian, Japanese, Korean, Polish, Russian, & Many More. Foreign Menus & Dictionaries. Available in Two Versions, Limited Flag & Complete Flag. The Two Versions Are Identical in Interface & Feature Set, but Differ in Foreign Languages (Script) Capability.
Nisus Software, Inc.

Nisus Compact. *Version:* 3.31. Jan. 1992. *Items Included:* Spiral bound users manual. *Customer Support:* Unlimited free telephone technical support for registered owners.
Mac 6.07 or higher (System 7 required for networking). Macintosh. 3.5" disk $150.00. *Addl. software required:* Optional: menu reqs/ mail merge module; spellcheck/thesaurus module.
A Streamlined Version of the Basic Nisus Word Processor for the Macintosh. Designed with Macintosh PowerBooks in Mind. Special PowerBook Features Include Optional Thick I-Beam, Battery Level & Clock Display, Sleep Command Within the Program. New Feature: FileClerk, Which Allows Intuitive File Organization, Categorization & Retrieval.
Nisus Software, Inc.

The Nite Owl Journal #1. *Version:* 1.4. *Compatible Hardware:* Apple IIe, IIc, IIgs. *Memory Required:* 64k. *General Requirements:* Printer.
disk $29.95.
Features the HOME FILING SYSTEM, a General Purpose Filing Program for the Home User. Also Includes FAST DISK COPY II for Non-Copy-

TITLE INDEX

Protected 5-1/4" Floppies & a MAIL LABEL WRITER Program for Making Mailing & Return Address Labels.
Nite Owl Productions.

NLP "Anchoring" Software Package.
Apple II series. disk $100.00.
Leads User Through Techniques Developed for Practitioners of NLP (Neuro-Linguistic Programming). Helps User Learn New Habitual Reactions & Change Limiting Conditioned Reactions. Consists of Two Primary Programs: Calibration Incorporates Principles of Artificial Intelligence to Help Computer Analyze GSR (Galvanic Skin Response) Features of User; Anchoring Uses Computer Sound & Graphics to Create Associations to Positive & Resourceful Psychological States. These States Are Used to Reprogram Limiting Feelings & Habits.
Behavioral Engineering.

NLP Tools Volume 1.
Macintosh. disk $250.00.
Package Includes: Eyepilot, Which Uses Computer Graphics to Help User Observe & Interpret Eye Movements; Eyeskating, Game Using Computer Animation to Teach User to Observe & Remember Eye Movements; Predicates, Teaches User to Identify Language Patterns in Order to Understand Others' View of the World; Predicate Analyzer, Identifies Important Language Patterns in Response to User-Typed Sentences; Utilization, Combines Computer Animated Eye Movements & Sensory Based Statements into an Easily Identifiable & Memorable Strategy Sequence; Installation, Leads User Through Behavior Generator Strategy Using Directions & Flashing Arrows with Any Outcome Desired Available to User.
Behavioral Engineering.

N.N. Charge. Jul. 1990. *Items Included:* Diskette & manual. *Customer Support:* Telephone Inquiries.
Macintosh (1Mb), all models. 3.5" disk $199.00.
Neural Network-Based Program for Computing Estimated Atomic Partial Charges in Neutral, Covalent Molecules. Calculate Charges Using One of the Parameter Sets Supplied with the Program, or with New Parameters Generated Using Data Bases of Charges from Model Compounds. Parameters May Be Learned & Refined by the Program, Then Saved for Future Use.
Atlantic Software.

No Blink-Accelerator. *Version:* 5.3. *Items Included:* Disk; Manual. *Customer Support:* Available 8-5 MST.
MS-DOS. IBM compatible (6k). disk $49.00. *Networks supported:* LAN, Novell.
A Cursor Control Software Package. It Provides the Ability to Select Non-Blinking, High Intensity Non-Blinking, Conditional Blinking, or Standard Blinking. Cursor Speed Selection Is Provided. On a Standard Color Monitor, NoBlink Provides a Choice of 26 Color Options. Each Cursor Has Two Colors. the Character Inside, & the Surrounding Color Block. As the Character Moves Across the Screen, the Character Within the Cursor Takes on the Selected Color. Also Includes a Zoom Control Feature for Eliminating Beeps & Overruns. Requires 6k of RAM.
Instant Replay Corp.

No More #*!$ Viruses. Oct. 1995. *Items Included:* User manual. *Customer Support:* Free support, 90 day warranty.
Win 95/Windows/DOS (120k). 3.5" disk $89.95. *Nonstandard peripherals required:* Hard drive. *Networks supported:* Workstations.
Virus Technology That Automatically Detects & Destroys Any Known or Unknown Boot Virus, Included Multi-Partite Viruses & Many of the Fast File Infector Viruses. It Is an "Install & Forget" Utility. It's Not a TSR, & Once Installed, It Never Needs Updating.
RG Software Systems, Inc.

No Mouse for Windows: Run Windows Without a Mouse! *Version:* 4.0. Paul Symanski. Jan. 1993. *Items Included:* 1 saddle-stitched manual, registration card. *Customer Support:* 60 day money back guarantee, free technical support.
Windows. IBM PC & compatibles (2Mb). disk $49.95 (ISBN 1-55755-169-3, Order no.: S169). *Optimal configuration:* 2Mb RAM, 286 or higher.
Software Replacement for the Hardware Mouse. The Cursor Keys Duplicate Mouse Actions with No Delay. Single Key Performs Most Mouse Functions. Cursor Speed & Some Key Settings Are User Definable. Includes Easy Find, Enlarged Cursor for Less Eye Strain on Smaller Monitor Screens. Uses Only 30K of Hard Disk Space.
Abacus.

No Trust? No Sale!: Build Lasting Customer Relationships. Jun. 1994. *Customer Support:* Toll-free telephone number for technical support. 90 days warranty for defects in materials & workmanship.
Macintosh System 7.0. Macintosh with 68040 processor (5Mb). CD-ROM disk $49.95 (ISBN 1-886806-05-5). *Nonstandard peripherals required:* Double speed CD-ROM drive. *Addl. software required:* QuickTime (included on CD-ROM disc).
Microsoft Windows 3.1. PC compatibles; 486/33 MHz (runs slow on 386/25MHz) (8Mb). CD-ROM disk $49.95. *Nonstandard peripherals required:* 256 color display card (640x480); double speed CD-ROM drive. *Addl. software required:* QuickTime for Windows (included on CD-ROM disc).
Shows You the Steps to Establishing Credibility & Gaining Customer Trust. It Helps You Build Stronger Customer Relations That Can Lead to Increased Sales, Valuable Customer Referrals, & Repeat Sales. Highly Interactive Video Exercises & Simulations Help You Learn by Doing.
Wilson Learning Corp.

Nolo's Living Trust. *Items Included:* Disk & 384-page manual. *Customer Support:* Free technical support Monday-Friday 9-5 PST; unconditional money-back guarantee at any time.
Macintosh System 6.01 or higher. Macintosh (1Mb). 3.5" disk $79.95 (ISBN 0-87337-163-1).
Easy-to-Use Software Package That Lets Users Create Their Own Living Trust Documents Without a Lawyer. People Can Avoid the Time & Cost of Probate, Transfer Property to Heirs - Quickly & Safely, Keep Financial Affairs Confidential & Avoid Excessive Lawyer's Fees.
Nolo Pr.

Nolo's Personal Recordkeeper. *Version:* 3.0. Carol Pladsen & Ralph Warner. *Operating System(s) Required:* System 4.1 or higher. *Items Included:* Disk & a 320-page manual. *Customer Support:* Free technical support Monday-Friday, 9-5 PST; unlimited money back guarantee.
Macintosh Plus or higher. 3.5" disk $49.95 (ISBN 0-87337-186-0).
IBM PC or compatible (384k), DOS 3.1 or higher. 3.5" & 5.25" disks included $49.95 (ISBN 0-87337-187-9). *Optimal configuration:* One 720k drive, two 36k drives or hard disk.
Organizes Personal Financial & Legal Records, Keeps Track of Emergency Information, Sources of Income, Real Estate, Business Interests, Collectibles, Tax Records, Medical Info & More.
Nolo Pr.

NONLINEAR SYSTEMS

Nomination. *Compatible Hardware:* IBM PC. *Memory Required:* 128k. *General Requirements:* Color display.
disk $29.95.
A Political Party Game Where One to Five Players Run Against the Actual Candidates for 1984 Democratic Nomination in Six Primaries. Each Player Must Take a Stand & Go for As Many Votes As Needed to Win the Election.
Brady Computer Bks.

Non-Linear Parameter Regression (Parafit II).
Items Included: Bound manual. *Customer Support:* Free hotline - no time limit; 30 day limited warranty; updates are $5/disk plus S&H.
Apple II (256k). disk $49.95. *Nonstandard peripherals required:* One drive.
The Apple Version of PARAFIT II Is Very Similar to the IBM Version. The Differences Are That Intermediate Results, the Partial Derivative Matrix, & the Parameter Correlation Matrix Are Not Displayed. Also, Only the Least-Squares Matrix Method Is Used.
Dynacomp, Inc.

Non-Prismatic Concrete Beams Analysis. 1995. *Items Included:* Full manual. *Customer Support:* Free telephone support - 90 days, 30-day warranty.
MS-DOS 3.2 or higher. 286 (584k). disk $99.95. *Nonstandard peripherals required:* CGA/EGA/VGA.
NONPCB Analyzes Concrete Beams in Slabs with Non-Uniform Section Properties. It Calculates Beam Stiffness Factors, & Fixed End Moment Coefficients for Uniform, Point, Partial Distributed, & Self-Weight Loads. It Makes Effective Use of Screen Graphics.
Dynacomp, Inc.

Non-Profit & Membership. *Compatible Hardware:* IBM PC, PC XT. *Operating System(s) Required:* MS-DOS. *Language(s):* BASIC. *Memory Required:* 256k. *General Requirements:* 2 disk drives, hard disk, printer. *Customer Support:* Mon-Fri EST 9:00AM-5:00PM, Modem support & on-site.
contact publisher for price.
Enters & Updates Membership, Shows Membership Payment History for Previous 52 Donations, Has Relations Files of Members, & Title Files. Membership Is Sorted by Number, Alphabet, Zip Code & Active Membership Type. Includes Fund Accounting for Budgeting & Full Financials Such As Accounts Receivable, Accounts Payable, & General Ledger.
M&C Systems, Inc.

Nonlinear Parametric Regression (Parafit II).
Items Included: Bound manual. *Customer Support:* Free hotline - no time limit; 30 day limited warranty; updates are $5/disk plus S&H.
MS-DOS. IBM & compatibles (256k). disk $79.95; math coprocessor version $99.95.
Apple. disk $79.95.
Nonlinear Regression Program to Fit Complicated Equations to Experimental Data to Determine the Unknown Parameters. Generalized So That It Will Fit to Any Function That User May Wish to Define Within the Syntax Constraints of the Program.
Dynacomp, Inc.

Nonlinear Systems. *Items Included:* Bound manual. *Customer Support:* Free hotline - no time limit; 30 day limited warranty; updates are $5/disk plus S&H.
MS-DOS. IBM & compatibles (256k). disk $49.95. *Nonstandard peripherals required:* Color graphics card; printer supported. *Addl. software required:* BASICA.
Commodore 64. disk $49.95.
Solves Systems of Simultaneous Linear &

Nonlinear Equations to User-Specified Error Limits. User May Select the Names of the Variables to Be Used & Predefine Any Recurrent Constants. Can Also Fully Explore Defined Intervals to Search for Multiple Solutions. It Also Can Quickly Find Single Solutions Starting with an Initial Guess. Equation Entry Is Identical to FUNCTIONS, with the Same Flexibility & Capability. This Is True for Each Equation.
Dynacomp, Inc.

Nord & Bert Couldn't Make Head or Tail of It: Eight Tales of Cliches, Spoonerisms, & Other Verbal Trickery. Jeff O'Neil. *Compatible Hardware:* Apple II+, IIe, IIc, IIgs, Macintosh; Atari ST; Commodore 64/128, Amiga; IBM PC & compatibles.
Apple II, Macintosh, Atari ST, Amiga, IBM. disk $39.95.
Commodore 64/128. $34.95.
Takes You to the Mixed-Up Town of Punster, Where Nothing Is Quite As It Seems. It's a Place Where You Really Can Make a Mountain out of a Molehill, Where 'the Fur Is Flying' Is Taken Literally, & Where a Happy Sam Is Transformed into a Sappy Ham. Each of the Short Stories Involves a Different Type of Wordplay. Challenge Your Wits & Memory to Come up with the Idioms, Homonyms, & Other Verbal Trickeries Needed to Complete the Puzzles. There Are Built-In Hints to Help You Out, & an Easy Method of Moving from Place to Place.
Activision, Inc.

norgen. *Version:* 2.01. *Compatible Hardware:* Commodore Amiga. *Items Included:* 2 disks & manual. *Customer Support:* By phone or letter.
3.5" disk $99.95.
Genealogical Database.
Norris Software, Inc.

Normal-Aid. *Customer Support:* 800-929-8117 (customer service).
MS-DOS. IBM/PS2. disk $99.99 (ISBN 0-87007-750-3).
A Productivity Tool Used to Assist in the Normalization & Logical Record Development Phases of Database Design. Provides the Ability to Create Fully Attributed Data Elements.
SourceView Software International.

Norman London for Mac & Windows. (Historical Travel Guides Ser.). William F. Stephen et al. Jun. 1996.
Windows. IBM. disk $20.00 (ISBN 0-934977-57-7).
Macintosh. 3.5" disk $20.00 (ISBN 0-934977-54-2).
Twelfth-Century Description of London on Diskette with Essays & Maps, & an Electronic Guide to the City. Includes Bibliography & Notes.
Italica Pr.

North Star BASIC, Utlity Set, North Star Sort Statement. *Compatible Hardware:* North Star Advantage, Horizon.
contact publisher for price.
SZ Software Systems.

North Star Utilities Package. *Compatible Hardware:* North Star with North Star BASIC or CP/M with MBASIC. *Operating System(s) Required:* CP/M, MS-DOS. (source code included). *Memory Required:* 48k.
disk $29.95.
Consists of 4 General Functions: Compression, Comparisons, Expansion & Formatted Program Displays (e.g. FOR/NEXT Indentations).
Dynacomp, Inc.

The Norton Commander. *Compatible Hardware:* IBM PC, PC AT, PC compatibles; mouse optional. *Operating System(s) Required:* PC-DOS, MS-DOS.
disk $75.00.
Hard Disk Manager. Enables Users to Speed Through Listings, Update Files, Delete, or Copy. Supports User-Defined Menus for One-Key Operation.
Peter Norton Computing, Inc.

The Norton Commander 2.0. *Compatible Hardware:* IBM PC & compatibles.
disk $89.00 (Order no.: RNC20006).
DOS Shell Application Providing a User Interface Programmed to Automate Most Common Tasks. Lets Users View, Edit, Copy, Rename, Move, & Delete Files by Scrolling Through a Directory & Pressing a Function Key. Also Allows Users to Create, Delete, or Rename Directories. Features a Graphic Tree Directory Display, Allowing Users to Move to a Particular Subdirectory by Highliting It & Pressing the ENTER Key.
Peter Norton Computing, Inc.

The Norton Editor. May 1986. *Compatible Hardware:* IBM PC & compatibles. *Operating System(s) Required:* PC-DOS, MS-DOS 2.0 & higher. *Language(s):* Assembly. *Memory Required:* 90k.
disk $75.00 (Order no.: RNE20006).
Program Editor Featuring Split Screen Editing, Condensed/Outline Display. Structured Programming Features Include: Auto-Indenting for Pascal & C, "Find Matching Punctuation" Feature. Word Features Include: Paragraph Reformat, Word Wrap. Supports Mouse.
Peter Norton Computing, Inc.

The Norton Guides: BASIC. *Compatible Hardware:* IBM PC & compatibles. *Operating System(s) Required:* MS-DOS 2.0 or higher.
disk $100.00 (Order no.: RGB10005).
Provides Programmers with Instant Access to Information While Running Any Other Application. Cross Referencing Is Supported & a Reference Database Compiler Allows Users to Create Their Own Reference Databases.
Peter Norton Computing, Inc.

The Norton, Guides: BIOS/DOS/Assembly. *Compatible Hardware:* IBM PC & compatibles. *Operating System(s) Required:* MS-DOS 2.0 or higher.
disk $100.00 (Order no.: RGA10005).
Provides Programmers with Instant Access to Information While Running Any Other Application. Cross Referencing Is Supported & a Reference Database Compiler Allows Users to Create Their Own Reference Databases.
Peter Norton Computing, Inc.

The Norton Guides: C. *Compatible Hardware:* IBM PC & compatibles. *Operating System(s) Required:* MS-DOS 2.0 or higher.
disk $100.00 (Order no.: RGC10005).
Provides Programmers with Instant Access to Information While Running Any Other Application. Cross Referencing Is Supported & a Reference Database Compiler Allows Users to Create Their Own Reference Databases.
Peter Norton Computing, Inc.

The Norton Guides: OS/2. *Compatible Hardware:* IBM PC & compatibles, PS/2. *Operating System(s) Required:* MS-DOS 2.0 or higher, OS/2.
$150.00 (Order no.: RGS10006).
Provides Programmers with Instant Access to Information While Running Any Other Application. Cross Referencing Is Supported & a Reference Database Compiler Allows Users to Create Their Own Reference Databases.
Peter Norton Computing, Inc.

The Norton Guides: Pascal. *Compatible Hardware:* IBM PC & compatibles. *Operating System(s) Required:* MS-DOS 2.0 or higher.
disk $100.00 (Order no.: RGP10005).
Provides Programmers with Instant Access to Information While Running Any Other Application. Cross Referencing Is Supported & a Database Compiler Allows Users to Create Their Own Reference Databases.
Peter Norton Computing, Inc.

Norton Utilities. *Version:* 3.1. Nov. 1985. *Compatible Hardware:* IBM PC, PC XT, PCjr, & PC compatibles. *Operating System(s) Required:* MS-DOS, PC-DOS. *Language(s):* Pascal. *Memory Required:* IBM PC, PC XT, & PC compatibles (MS-DOS) 64k, IBM PCjr 128k.
disk $99.95.
Includes Two File Recovery Programs: UnErase, for Files Lost from Erasure, Which Recovers Data That Can Be Saved from Bad Disk. Also Includes Programs to Control Hidden Files, to Display & Modify Disks, Arrange Disk Directory, & Control Display Screen.
Peter Norton Computing, Inc.
Disklook. *Version:* 2.0.
  disk $20.00.
  Display Program That Will Show Hidden or Erased Files, Provide Full Sector Displays, Map Storage, File Location, etc.
FileFix. *Version:* 2.0.
  disk $80.00.
Filehide. *Version:* 2.0.
  disk $10.00.
  Hides & Unhides Files, Allowing the User to Protect Files from Erasure.
Secmod. *Version:* 2.0.
  disk $20.00.
  Reads & Modifies Diskette Sectors in ASCII & Hex.
UnErase. *Version:* 2.0.
  disk $80.00.

Norton Utilities Advanced Edition 4.5. *Compatible Hardware:* IBM PC & compatibles.
disk $150.00 (Order no.: RAE20006).
Includes the NORTON DISK DOCTOR, a Disk Diagnostic Program That Can Repair Damaged Boot Records, Media Descriptor Bytes, & File Allocation Tables. Also Includes Is the NORTON CONTROL CENTER Which Lets Users Set Screen & Color Attributes, Adjust the Keyboard Rate, & Set Other System Parameters.
Peter Norton Computing, Inc.

Norton Utilities Standard Edition 4.5. *Compatible Hardware:* IBM PC & compatibles.
disk $100.00 (Order no.: RSE10006).
Lets Users Recover Erased Files, Modify & View Files, Optimize Hard Disks, etc. Also Included Is the NORTON CONTROL CENTER That Allows Users to Set Screen & Color Attributes, Adjust Keyboard Rate, & Set Other System Parameters.
Peter Norton Computing, Inc.

The Not-So-Fancy Menu System. Alan J. Chwick. Mar. 1987. *Compatible Hardware:* IBM PC & compatibles. *Operating System(s) Required:* DR DOS, PC-DOS/MS-DOS 3.0 or higher, PC-MOS. *Memory Required:* 2k. *Customer Support:* Telephone Support.
disk $25.95 (ISBN 0-928407-03-9, Order no.: MENUINST).
Menu Generator That Works from Either Hard or Floppy Disk. Can Be Used to Create Menu Systems for Technical or Non-Technical PC End-Users. A Created Menu Can Drive a Program (.exe or .com), Batch Files, or Another Menu. System Paths Are Fully Supported. Program Is Not Copy Protected. There Are No Royalties or Licenses for Distributed Menus.
The COMPLETE Machine.

TITLE INDEX

Nota Bene. *Version:* 4.0. *Compatible Hardware:* IBM PC & compatibles. *Operating System(s) Required:* PC-DOS/MS-DOS 2.0 or higher. *Memory Required:* 512k, recommended 640k. *General Requirements:* 2 disk drives or hard disk (recommended). EGA, Hercules Graphics Plus, or Hercules InColor card for special-language supplements.
disk $495.00.
special-language supplements $125.00.
Word Processing Application Built Around a Customized Version of XYWRITE III PLUS. Enhancements Include the Ability to Easily Manipulate Footnotes, Indexes, Bibliographies, & to Automatically Update Cross References. Uses a 1-2-3 Style Menu Interface or an Optional Command Mode. The Special-Language Supplements Enable Users to Display & Print Different Alphabets in the Same Document. Not Copy Protected.
N.B. Informatics, Inc.

Note Detective. Reid Alexander & JoEllen DeVilbiss. 1989.
 DOS 3.3. Apple II (48k). $100.00 (ISBN 1-55603-122-X, Order no.: MA-1323). *Nonstandard peripherals required:* Internal MIDI interface, MIDI compatible music keyboard, MIDI cables.
 DOS 3.3. IBM (640k). $100.00 (ISBN 1-55603-120-3, Order no.: MI-1323). *Nonstandard peripherals required:* MIDI interface, MIDI compatible music keyboard, MIDI cables.
 Macintosh Plus or higher (512k). 3.5" disk $100.00. *Nonstandard peripherals required:* External MIDI device & MIDI keyboard.
Introduces Basic Musical Concepts Such As High & Low Sounds, Musical Alphabet, & Staff Note Reading As Well As Develop Fluent Music Reading Skills. Practice in Note Reading, Ledger Line Recognition, Interval Recognition, & Reading Sharps & Flats Are Included.
Electronic Courseware Systems, Inc.

Note-It Plus: One Two Three Documentation Utility. David R. Whitney. Jun. 1987. *Compatible Hardware:* IBM PC & compatibles. *Operating System(s) Required:* DOS 2.x, 3.x. *Language(s):* Assembly. *Memory Required:* 70k. *General Requirements:* Lotus 1-2-3 Release 1.1A or 2.
disk $79.95.
Lets LOTUS 1-2-3 Users Electronically Annotate New or Existing Spreadsheets. A Note Can Be Attached to a File Name or Any Cell - Labels, Numbers, or Formulas. Not Copy Protected.
Turner Hall Publishing.

Note Pad. Aug. 1986. *Compatible Hardware:* IBM PC, PC XT, PC AT. *Memory Required:* 128k. *General Requirements:* Printer. Color monitor & CGA card recommended.
disk $25.00.
Full-Featured Word Processor That Generates up to 10 Pages of Text at 63 Lines per Page.
Robert L. Nicolai.

NoteBuilder: The Cornerstone of Your Data. *Version:* 1.12. Apr. 1993. *Items Included:* 1 perfect bound manual, quick reference card, 3.5" & 5.25" disks. *Customer Support:* 30 day unlimited warranty, telephone/fax technical support.
 MS-DOS 3.0 or higher. IBM & compatibles (640k). disk $99.00 if upgrading from Notebook II, $199.00 new users. *Optimal configuration:* 2Mb hard disk space available, 640k RAM, color monitor (not required).
Lets User Store & Retrieve Collections of Unlimited Text. Features Changeable/Expandable Fields, Word Wrap, Can Export As MSWORD, WPS.1 or ASCII. Creates Automated Bibliographies, Prints Labels & Reports. Analyze Feature Gives Instantaneous Qualitative Analysis Results. Automatically Imports Down-Loaded Databases & Text Files.
Pro/Tem Software.

Noteworthy. *Version:* 1.01. *Compatible Hardware:* IBM PC. *General Requirements:* Lotus 1-2-3 Release 2.x or Symphony.
disk $79.95.
Annotation & Documentation Software for 1-2-3. Allows Users to Attach a Note, up to 8,000 Characters Long for Each Spreadsheet Cell. Allows Copying Text from the Note to the Spreadsheet or from the Spreadsheet to the Note.
Funk Software.

Nova. *Version:* 2.X. Robert S. Hand. Nov. 1986. *Compatible Hardware:* IBM PC & compatibles. *Operating System(s) Required:* MS-DOS, PC-DOS. *Memory Required:* 256k. *General Requirements:* 2 disk drives or hard disk, printer. *Items Included:* Manual. *Customer Support:* Free phone support.
$225.00 ea.
 IBM PC. (ISBN 0-87199-061-X).
 IBM PC, 8087 version. (ISBN 0-87199-072-5).
Encyclopedically Copmplete Astrological Calculation System. Includes Natal, Progressed, Synastry, & Other Usual Calculations Plus Fixed Stars; Complete Arabic Parts; Ephemeris Printer; Transit, Progression, & Direction Listings; etc., All over a 3,000-Year Timespan. Outputs Chart Files Compatible with Chartwheels Timegraphs, the Blackwell & Mackey-Saunders Data Collections Printwheels, the Astrologer's Companion, the CCRS Horoscope Program, & Solar Fire.
Astrolabe, Inc.

Nova. *Customer Support:* All of our products are unconditionally guaranteed.
 NeXT. CD-ROM disk $59.95 (Order no.: NOVA). *Nonstandard peripherals required:* CD-ROM drive.
600 MB of Current Black NeXT Source, Aps, & Docs.
Walnut Creek CDRom.

Nova, Core Version. Jan. 1985. *Compatible Hardware:* CP/M-based machines. *Operating System(s) Required:* CP/M-80. *Language(s):* BASIC. *Memory Required:* 64k. *General Requirements:* Printer. *Items Included:* Manual. *Customer Support:* Free phone support.
disk $150.00 ea.
 CP/M (Kaypro 2). (ISBN 0-87199-003-2).
Calculates, Stores & Prints Many Types of Astrological Charts; Suited to Many Styles & Schools of Doing Astrology.
Astrolabe, Inc.

Novell Netware Power Tools. Mike Edelhart. *Items Included:* One 1.4Mb 3.5" high-density disk. *Customer Support:* Phone number available for technical support, 212-492-9832; free disk replacement within 90 days of purchase.
 IBM PC & compatibles. disk $49.95 (ISBN 0-553-35224-5). *Addl. software required:* Novell Netware.
Use This Book/Software Package As a Guide & a Toolkit to Get the Most Out of This Powerful Network. Includes Disk with Many Utilities/Batch Files to: Speed Log-In Procedure, Automate E-Mail Operation, Facilitate Printer Sharing/ Mainframe Access. Mike Edelhart Is Publisher & Editor-in-Chief of PC Computing & a Leading Networking Expert. He Has Authored More Than 10 Books on Personal Computing.
Bantam Bks., Inc.

Now! PC/Host Autoware. *Version:* 1.12. Feb. 1992. *Items Included:* Documentation. *Customer Support:* Toll-free technical support hotline.
 PC-DOS, MS-DOS 3.0. IBM PC's & compatibles, PS/2 (40k). disk Author's version $565.00. *Networks supported:* NetBois.
 disk User's version $195.00.
A 3270 Emulation Product That Speeds, Simplifies, Automates PC-to-Mainframe Operation Including Logon/Logoff & Unattended Data Transfers. Reduces Lengthy, Complex Time-Consuming PC-Mainframe Jobs to Quick, Single-Keystroke Tasks. 2 Versions: Author's Version for HLLAPI Programmers to Develop Simple, Customized NOW! Applications; User's Version for PC Users - Allows Non-Technical Users to Access Sophisticated Mainframe Information.
Attachmate Corp.

NOZZLE. *Compatible Hardware:* IBM PC & compatibles. *Operating System(s) Required:* MS-DOS. *Language(s):* BASIC. *Memory Required:* 128k.
$110.00.
Calculates Velocities Through Nozzles or Pipes from 1/2" Through 12". User Inputs Flow in #/HR., & Either Specific Gravity or Specific Volume. Output Is Velocity Through Each Size Nozzle. Handles Liquids or Vapors.
Technical Research Services, Inc.

NPAQ: Nursing Productivity & Quality. *Compatible Hardware:* IBM PC, PC XT, PC AT or compatibles. *Operating System(s) Required:* UCSD p-System. *Memory Required:* 640k. *General Requirements:* 2 disk drives, printer.
contact publisher for price.
Provides the Key to Success in Optimizing Nursing Productivity & Quality. Also Provides Methodologies & Software for: Scheduling, Quality Management, Costing, Patient Classification/Staffing, Budgeting, Personnel Management & National Database Reporting. Connectivity Is Maximized Through Its NPAQ Capabilities.
Medicus Systems Corp.

NR: An Implementation of the UNIX NROFF Word Processor. Allen Holub. *Operating System(s) Required:* MS-DOS. *Language(s):* C.
disk $29.95, incl. manual (ISBN 0-934375-33-X).
Text Formatter Compatible with UNIX's NROFF. Source Code Is Included, So That the Program Can Be Customized to Fit User's Needs. Does Hyphenation & Simple Proportional Spacing. Supports Automatic Table of Contents & Index Generation, Automatic Footnotes & Endnotes, Italics, Boldface, etc. Configurable for Most Printers.
M & T Bks.

NS Connection. *Version:* 4.1. Oct. 1994. *Items Included:* User guide, reference manual, technical reference (server versions only), online reference material, WRQ newsletter, Reflection mousepad, keyboard template. *Customer Support:* Free technical support & 90-day materials & workmanship warranty.
 System 6.0.5 or higher, System 7.x, Power Macintosh. Macintosh Plus or higher. 3.5" disk $299.00. *Addl. software required:* Multifinder: required for multitasking. *Networks supported:* Ethernet, token-ring, or gateway-equipped Localtalk networks.
Delivers Quick, Smooth Access to Host Applications with Concurrent Access to LocalTalk, Ethernet, or Token Ring Networks, Making It Easy to Use LAN- & Host-Based Services Simultaneously.
Walker, Richer & Quinn, Inc.

NSL Diet Analyzer. Oct. 1986. *Compatible Hardware:* IBM PC & compatibles. *Operating System(s) Required:* MS-DOS. *Language(s):* Assembler. *Memory Required:* 256k.
disk $49.95 ea., incl. manual, tutorial disk, &

automatic installation.
Analyzes Calories & 23 Nutrients, Including Sodium & Cholesterol for Individual Foods, Complete Meals, or Entire Days. Computes Multi-Day Averages of All Nutrients Compared with an Ideal Diet. Also Includes Expandable USDA Food Dictionary, with 1,000 Foods & 100 Exercises.
Natural Software Ltd.

NSNA NCLEX EXCEL! Computerized Nursing Q & A. Jan. 1994. *Items Included:* User's Manual, Quick Tips Card.
DOS 3.0 or higher. IBM PC & compatibles (512k). 5.25" disk $79.95 (ISBN 1-884901-04-2). *Nonstandard peripherals required:* Graphics adapter: CGA, VGA or EGA non-Hercules; monitor that works with adapter; floppy disk drive for 3.5" disks. *Optimal configuration:* All of the above & a monitor & printer that work with computer.
3.5" disk $79.95 (ISBN 1-884901-05-0).
A Question & Answer Learning Program Designed to Help Nursing Students Practice for the Boards. Nursing Q&A Features 1,200 Questions on Pediatrics, Obstetrics, Psychiatric & Medical/Surgical Nursing. Features Include Practice Tests, Test Scores & Feedback.
Medical College of Pennsylvania.

NSNA NCLEX EXCEL! Computerized Nursing Q & A: Nursing & Pharmacology Combined. Jan. 1994. *Items Included:* User's Manual, Quick Tips Card.
DOS 3.0 or higher. IBM PC & compatibles (512k). 5.25" disk $79.95 (ISBN 1-884901-00-X). *Nonstandard peripherals required:* Graphics adapter: CGA, VGA or EGA non-Hercules; monitor that works with adapter; floppy disk drive for 3.5" disks. *Optimal configuration:* All of the above & a monitor & printer that work with computer.
3.5" disk $79.95 (ISBN 1-884901-01-8).
A Question & Answer Learning Program Designed to Help Nursing Students Practice for the Computerized Version of the Boards. Nursing Q&A Features 1,200 Questions on Pediatrics, Obstetrics, Psychiatric & Medical/Surgical Nursing. Features Include 200 Pharmacology Questions Free, Practice Tests, Test Scores & Feedback.
Medical College of Pennsylvania.

NSNA NCLEX-RN EXCEL! Computerized Pharmacology Q & A. Jan. 1994. *Items Included:* User's Manual, Quick Tips Card.
DOS 3.0 or higher. IBM PC & compatibles (512k). 5.25" disk $19.95 (ISBN 1-884901-02-6). *Nonstandard peripherals required:* Graphics adapter: CGA, VGA or EGA non-Hercules; monitor that works with adapter; floppy disk drive for 3.5" disks. *Optimal configuration:* All of the above & a monitor & printer that work with computer.
3.5" disk $19.95 (ISBN 1-884901-03-4).
A Question & Answer Learning Program Designed to Help Nursing Students Practice for the Computerized Version of the Boards. Pharmacology Q&A Features 200 Questions on Drug Classifications, Nursing Implications, Drug Administration, Side Effects & Commonly Questioned Drugs. Features Include Practice Tests, Feedback & Suggested Areas of Study.
Medical College of Pennsylvania.

NTSYS-pc: Numerical Taxonomy system.
Version: 1.7. F. James Rohlf. Mar. 1992. *Items Included:* User manual in 3-ring notebook. *Customer Support:* Technical support by phone.
MS-DOS 3.0. IBM PC & compatibles (512K). disk $195.00 (ISBN 0-925031-11-9).
ten user site license $780.00.
Statistical Analysis Program Used to Discover Pattern & Structure in Multivariate Data. The Data Can Be Descriptive Information about Collections of Objects or Directly Measured Similarity Between Pairs of Objects. The Kinds of Descriptors & Objects Used Depend upon the Application: Morphological Characters, Abundances of Species, Presence & Absence of Properites, etc. NTSYS-PC Can Transform Data, Estimate Dissimilarities among Objects, & Prepare Summaries of the Relationships. It Can Cluster Similar Objects Together & Make Ordination Plots of the Objects & of the Variables.
Exeter software.

nu/TPU. *Version:* 3.0. Feb. 1992. *Compatible Hardware:* IBM PC & compatible, Unix-based systems. *Operating System(s) Required:* PC-DOS/MS-DOS 3.0 & up. *Memory Required:* 560k. *Items Included:* Media, manual, installation guide, lesson guide. *Customer Support:* Free hotline telephone support, optional maintenance.
DOS. $325.00.
Unix. $499.00 & up.
Modeled after DIGITAL's Text Processing Utility. Compatible with VMS 5.4 TPU. Integrated with MS Windows, Motif, & Open Windows. Includes EVE, EDT, WPS & VI Editing Interfaces, Unlimited Windows & Buffers, Learn Sequences, Dynamically Built Help Screens, Rectangular Box Operations, Color Support, 108 Built-In Subroutines, Its Own Programming Language, Unlimited Extensions & Automated Error Recovery. User Can Import User's Customized VAX TPU Programs to UNIX or DOS System Without Change. Supports over 50 Platforms Including MS-DOS, OS/2 & UNIX Systems from DEC, SUN, HP, IBM, CONVEX, SCO & Many Others.
a/Soft Development, Inc.

Nuametrics Econometric Analysis. *Items Included:* Bound manual. *Customer Support:* Free hotline - no time limit; 30 day limited warranty; updates are $5/disk plus S&H.
MS-DOS. IBM PC & compatibles (128k). disk $99.95. *Nonstandard peripherals required:* One or two disk drives; printer supported, but not necessary.
Apple (48k). disk $99.95.
Menu-Driven Program for Professionals Interested in Serious Econometric Analysis. It Incorporates Widely Used Statistical Methods with Simple Operational Instructions. By Controlling the Computer's Arrow Keys & the Return Key, a User Can Move from Menu to Menu Developing Data Files or Selecting Procedural Methods.
Dynacomp, Inc.

Nuclear Power Plant. *Compatible Hardware:* Apple II, II+, IIe, IIc. (source code included). *Memory Required:* 48k.
disk $9.95 (ISBN 0-918547-23-7).
illustration files on disk avail.
Simulation of the Operation of a Nuclear Power Plant with a Graphic Representation of the System, Its Components, Structure & Function. Designed to Reveal the Economics of the Nuclear Power Industry.
AV Systems, Inc.

Nude Private Works, Vol. 1. Shohei Takahashi. Jun. 1995.
CD-ROM disk $44.95 (ISBN 4-89621-018-2).
65 International Photographers Present over 700 Fascinating Photo Images.
Books Nippan.

Number Kruncher I. *Version:* 2.0, 2.1. *Compatible Hardware:* TRS-80 Model I, III, 4 with Level II BASIC. *Memory Required:* 32k.
disk $73.95, incl. documentation.
Data Processing Package.
Dynacomp, Inc.

Number Kruncher II. *Compatible Hardware:* TRS-80 Model I, Model III, Model 4. *Language(s):* Level II BASIC. *Memory Required:* 32k.
disk $73.95, incl. instr. manual.
Revised Version of NUMBERKRUNCHER I.
Dynacomp, Inc.

Number the Stars. Intentional Education Staff & Lois Loury. Apr. 1996. *Customer Support:* Free technical support, 90 day warranty.
School ver.. System 7.1 or higher. Macintosh (4Mb). 3.5" disk contact publisher for price (ISBN 1-57204-298-2). *Nonstandard peripherals required:* 256 color monitor, hard drive, printer.
Lab pack. System 7.1 or higher. Macintosh (4Mb). 3.5" disk contact publisher for price (ISBN 1-57204-274-5). *Nonstandard peripherals required:* 256 color monitor, hard drive, printer.
Site license. System 7.1 or higher. Macintosh (4Mb). 3.5" disk contact publisher for price (ISBN 1-57204-299-0).
Schol ver.. Windows 3.1 or higher. IBM/Tandy & 100% compatibles (4Mb). disk contact publisher for price (ISBN 1-57204-300-8). *Nonstandard peripherals required:* VGA or SVGA 640 x 480 resolution (256), mouse, hard drive, sound device.
Lab pack. Windows 3.1 or higher. IBM/Tandy & 100% compatibles (4Mb). disk contact publisher for price (ISBN 1-57204-301-6). *Nonstandard peripherals required:* VGA or SVGA 640 x 480 resolution (256), mouse, hard drive, sound device.
Site license. Windows 3.1 or higher. IBM/Tandy & 100% compatibles (4Mb). disk contact publisher for price (ISBN 1-57204-301-6). *Nonstandard peripherals required:* VGA or SVGA 640 x 480 resolution (256), mouse, hard drive, sound device.
This Companion for young adult literature is ideal for students who don't know how to start that book report, or give that needed summary. Gentle prompts throughout the guide section of the program include Warm-up Connections, Thinking about Plot, Quoting & Noting, Keeping a Journal, If I Were ———' Responding to Questions, Using Quotations, Taking a Personal View, Write to Others, & Write a Sequel.
Lawrence Productions, Inc.

NumberCruncher. *Version:* 11.0. Stephan R. Leimberg & Robert T. LeClair. Mar. 1995. *Items Included:* 300-page reference manual. *Customer Support:* 30-day money-back guarantee, 1-year service contract for $89, telephone support, facsimile service.
PC-DOS (256k). IBM PC, PC XT, PC AT & compatibles. disk $299.00.
disk $299.00.
Financial & Estate Planning Computations Covering More Than 45 Business Valuation, Charitable Giving, Estate Planning Techniques, Income, Estate & Gift Taxes, Present & Future Value Calculations.
Leimberg & Leclair, Inc.

Numberscope Plus. Jun. 1987. *Compatible Hardware:* IBM PC, PC XT, PC AT. *Operating System(s) Required:* Apple DOS 3.3, PC-DOS 2.1. *Memory Required:* 256k.
disk $29.95 ea.
IBM. (ISBN 0-918219-45-0).
Provides Traditional Numerological Analysis & Readings for Name & Date of Birth.
Zephyr Services.

Numeric Keyboarding. *Version:* 3. 1994. *Memory Required:* Apple IIe & IIc, Apple IIgs 54-512k, IBM/Tandy 128-512, PS/2, Macintosh 512k.

Apple II series; IIgs. 5.25" disk Contact publisher for price (ISBN 0-538-61183-9, Order no.: Z377-3C).
Apple II series; IIgs. 3.5" disk Contact publisher for price (ISBN 0-538-62085-4, Order no.: Z378-1C).
DOS. 5.25" disk Contact publisher for price (ISBN 0-538-61184-7, Order no.: Z378-8C).
DOS. 3.5" disk Contact publisher for price (ISBN 0-538-61185-5).
MAC. 3.5" disk Contact publisher for price (ISBN 0-538-62047-1).
Combination Diskette that Provides Instruction for Developing Basic "Touch" Keyboarding Skill on Top-row Number & Symbol Keys. Can Be Used with any Keyboarding Program.
South-Western Publishing Co.

Numeric Keypad Operation. Version: 3. 1994. *Memory Required:* Apple IIe & IIc 512k, IBM/Tandy 128-512, PS/2, Macintosh 512k.
DOS. 5.25" disk Contact publisher for price (ISBN 0-538-61190-1, Order no.: Z397-3C).
DOS. 3.5" disk Contact publisher for price (ISBN 0-538-61191-X, Order no.: Z398-1C).
MAC. 3.5" disk Contact publisher for price (ISBN 0-538-62049-8, Order no.: Z398-8C).
7 Lessons Teaching "Touch" Operation of the Numeric Keypad Found on Most Computer Keyboards. Can be Used with any Keyboarding Program.
South-Western Publishing Co.

Numerical Analysis Library. *Compatible Hardware:* HP Series 200 Models 216/220, 226/236, 217/237 Personal Technical Computers with BASIC 3.0. *Memory Required:* 100k.
HP 216/220, 217/237. 3-1/2" or 5-1/4" disk $500.00 ea. (Order no.: 98821A).
HP 226/236. 5-1/4" disk $500.00 ea.
Contains Seven Main Sections: Root-Finders, Numerical Integration, ODE Solvers, Eigen Analysis, Interpolation, General Functions, & Fourier Analysis.
Hewlett-Packard Co.

Numerical Control. *Compatible Hardware:* Unix, Sun; Aegis; HP Apollo; Ultrix; DEC VMS. *Items Included:* Documentation. *Customer Support:* Maintenance plan, training; 800 number.
contact publisher for price. *Addl. software required:* Series 7000. *Networks supported:* ETHERNET LAN.
Combines 7 NC Modules; Punching, Lathe, Pocket/Profile, Surface Milling, Electrical Discharge Machining (EDM), Flam Cutting, & Multi-Surface Milling. It Also Provides General NC Utilities: Point-to-Point, Macros, Tooling, CLFile Output & Powerful Tool Path Verification & Editing Functions.
Auto-Trol Technology Corp.

Numerical Data Analysis. 1995. *Items Included:* Full manual. *Customer Support:* Free telephone support - 90 days, 30-day warranty.
MS-DOS 3.2 or higher. 286 (584k). disk $49.95. *Nonstandard peripherals required:* CGA/EGA/VGA.
Now Students Have an Easy-to-Use & Precise Method for Analyzing Numerical Data. MATHPLOT Can Analyze up to 200 Data Points & Calculate Simple Statistical Parameters, Fit Least-Squares Polynomials, Numerically Integrate under a Curve Defined by the Points, Calculate the Coefficients of a Fourier Series for a Periodic Function Described by the Points, Calculate & Plot Fourier Spectra & Bessel Functions, Plot & Compare a User-Specified Function with a Data Set, Solve up to 12 Simultaneous Equations, & Invert Matrices of Order up to 12. A User-Friendly Menu Allows You to Display the Results Both Numerically & Graphically.
Dynacomp, Inc.

Numerical Integration. *Compatible Hardware:* TI 99/4A. *Operating System(s) Required:* DX-10. *Language(s):* Console BASIC. *Memory Required:* 16k.
disk or cassette $19.00.
Performs Trapezoidal, Simpson or Gaussian Integration on Functions Which Are Tabulated or Explicitly Known. For Integrating over an Unevenly Spaced Number of Points, a Quartic Routine Is Performed.
Eastbench Software Products.

Numerical Methods Software: Computational Software Library (CSL). Shoichiro Makamura. *Compatible Hardware:* Macintosh, IBM, VAX. *Memory Required:* 1000k. *General Requirements:* Basic, QuickBasic or Fortran. *Items Included:* Paperback manual (170 pages). *Customer Support:* 90 days warranty.
3.5" or 5.25" disk $43.00 (ISBN 0-9626943-8-X).
Includes Approximately 50 Programs to Show Implementation of Fundamental Numerical Methods, Including Interpolation, Integration, Difference Approximation, Nonlinear Equations, Linear Algebra, Eigenvalue Problems, Curve Fitting, OPEs & PDEs.
Computational Methods, Inc.

The Numerologist. Version: 3.0. 1993. *Compatible Hardware:* IBM PC XT, AT, PS/1, PS/2 & compatibles. *Operating System(s) Required:* PC-DOS/MS-DOS. *Memory Required:* 320k. *Items Included:* 69 page comprehensive user's manual. *Customer Support:* Full phone support.
disk $99.95 ea.
IBM. (ISBN 0-933281-00-5).
Generates a Complete & Detailed 3-Page Numerology Chart Including the Progressed Chart from Ages 0-91 with Over 1000 Important Numbers User Would Have Had to Calculate by Hand. Program Can Be Customized by User to Match His System of Numerology.
Widening Horizons, Inc.

Numerologist Report Writer. Version: 3.0. 1993. *Compatible Hardware:* IBM PC, XT, AT, PS/1, PS/2 & compatibles. *Operating System(s) Required:* PC-DOS/MS-DOS. *Memory Required:* 320k. *General Requirements:* 2 disk drives or hard disk, printer. *Items Included:* 61 page comprehensive user's manual. *Customer Support:* Full phone support.
disk $295.00 ea.
IBM PC, MS-DOS. (ISBN 0-933281-04-8). (ISBN 0-933281-05-6).
Produces Fully Integrated Personality Reports Which Reveal a Person's Destiny Through Text Averaging 9 to 17 Pages. The Program Looks at the Numerology Chart As a Whole, Then Delineates Complexes of Numbers in Complete Paragraphs. The Current Name Is Compared with the Original Name at Birth. Supports Batch Operations, How the Letter 'Y' & 'W' Are Treated, & Allows Reports to Be Edited with a Word Processor.
Widening Horizons, Inc.

Numerology. *Items Included:* Bound manual. *Customer Support:* Free hotline - no time limit; 30 day limited warranty; updates are $5/disk plus S&H.
MS-DOS. IBM & compatibles (128k). disk $19.95. *Nonstandard peripherals required:* Monochrome or graphics.
Uses the Most Common Method for Describing Aspects of Your Inner Self from Your Name, Either Common or Birth, & Your Birth Date. It Gives You a Basic Makeup Analysis & Allows You to Look into Your Future to Find Compatibilities Involving People, Places, & Lucky Numbers.
Dynacomp, Inc.

Numerology Pro PC. *Items Included:* Bonus: 256-page Numerologoy Course (book) by Jackie Suggs.
DOS. PC (640k). disk $29.95 (ISBN 1-56087-128-8). *Optimal configuration:* Min. 286, DOS, 2k RAM.
PC Computer Software to Learn & Use Numerology to Better Help Yourself & Others on a Daily Basis. Prints Out Individual Charts Which Discloses the Various Aspects of a Person, Their Challenges, Characteristics & Their Life's Purpose.
Top of the Mountain Publishing.

Numerology Report Writer: M93. 1983. *Compatible Hardware:* Apple II+, IIe, IIc; Commodore 64, PET; IBM PC with 2 disk drives. *Language(s):* BASIC. *Memory Required:* PET 32k, Apple 48k, Commodore 64k, IBM 256k. *General Requirements:* Printer.
disk $300.00 ea. (Order no.: M93).
Commodore 64. (ISBN 0-925182-20-6).
IBM. (ISBN 0-925182-21-4).
Apple. (ISBN 0-925182-22-2).
Writes Personal Numerology Interpretations for Resale. Analyzes a Name & Birthdate Through Traditional Pythagorean Numerology & Produces a 7 Page Report. Cover Page, Instructions, Charts & the Familiar 'Diamond' of Life Pinnacles & Challenges Are All Built-In. Performs 'Life Progression' to Age 87.
Matrix Software.

Nursery Inventory Control System (N*I*C*S). Version: 6.0. Jun. 1992. *Items Included:* Manual. *Customer Support:* 90-day warranty - yearly maintenance $480.00 + (updates included), on-site training $350.00 per day plus expenses.
MS-DOS, Novell, OS/2 (512k). IBM compatibles. $3800.00-$7600.00 (Order no.: NICS). *Networks supported:* Novell.
Tracking Inventory, Acknowledging Order, Shipping Schedules, Sales Analysis, Accounts Receivable, Invoicing & Credit Memos, Mailing List as Well as Prospect Mailing List, Production Schedule & Routing, & Production Costing.
Condor Computing, Inc.

NurseWorks. Version: 3.0. Mar. 1993. *Customer Support:* Replacement of defective media free within 30 days, unlimited user support.
MS-DOS. IBM PC & compatibles (256k). disk $99.00 (ISBN 1-883441-36-6). *Optimal configuration:* IBM or compatible PC with 256k or higher RAM & one floppy disk drive, color monitor is not required, but is desirable.
3.5" disk $99.00 (ISBN 1-883441-35-8).
demo disk $5.95.
Point-of-Care Clinical Nursing Support System. Enables Nurses to Quickly & Accurately Calculate Virtually All Medication Dosage & I.V. Flow Rate Problems. Does Unit Conversions, Tallies Intake-and-Output Sheets, Interprets Arterial Blood Gases, Assists with Nutritional Assessment (Body Mass Index, Caloric Requirements). Specific Modules for Morphine PCA & Body Surface Area Calculations.

NURSIMS. 1986. *Compatible Hardware:* Apple II, IBM PC. *Memory Required:* 64k.
Apple set. $800.00, incl. instr's. guide (Order no.: 64-71569, 64-71577, 64-71593, 64-71601, 64-71585).
IBM set. $800.00, incl. instr's. guide (Order no.: 64-70911, 64-71007, 64-71023, 64-71031, 64-71015).
Designed to Evaluate a Learner's Decision-Making Abilities in Realistic Nurse-Client Interactions.
J. B. Lippincott Co.

Nursing Diagnosis: Basic Concepts. Version: Apple. California State University. Jul. 1986. *Compatible Hardware:* Apple II, II+, IIe, IIc.

Memory Required: 64k.
disk $65.45 (ISBN 0-07-831026-1).
With the Help of a Nurse & Hospital Staff, Students Achieve an Understanding of the Definition & Components of a Nursing Diagnosis.
McGraw-Hill, Inc.

The Nutcracker: An Interactive Holiday Fantasy (Jewel). *Items Included:* CD-ROM booklet. *Customer Support:* Free technical support via phone as of release date.
MPC/Windows. 386 or higher (4Mb). CD-ROM disk $39.95 (ISBN 1-885784-44-9, Order no.: 1448). *Optimal configuration:* MPC CD-ROM player, S-VGA graphics card (640x480x256 colors) with compatible monitor, MPC compliant sound card, mouse, Windows 3.1 or higher, Windows 95 compatible.
System 7.0 or higher. Macintosh (4Mb). *Optimal configuration:* CD-ROM drive, color monitor (256 plus colors), mouse.
A Favorite Holiday Story, Unfolds with the Magic of Tchaikovsky's Music, Video from Its Ballet Performances & Colorful Illustration & Graphics. With Ballet Performances, Music, Games, Interactive Audio/Video Puzzles & Story Narration, the Timeless "Nutcracker" Story Is Now an Interactive Masterpiece. One Disc Offers French, German, Spanish & English.
Technology Dynamics Corp.

The Nutcracker: An Interactive Holiday Fantasy. *Items Included:* CD-ROM booklet. *Customer Support:* Free technical support via phone as of release date.
MPC/Windows. 386MHz or higher (4Mb). CD-ROM disk $39.95 (ISBN 1-885784-44-9, Order no.: 1445). *Optimal configuration:* MPC CD-ROM player, S-VGA graphics card (640x480x256 colors) with compatible monitor, MPC compliant sound card, mouse, Windows 3.1 or higher, Windows 95 compatible.
System 7.0 or higher. Macintosh (4Mb). CD-ROM disk $39.95 (ISBN 1-885784-57-0, Order no.: 1575). *Optimal configuration:* CD-ROM drive, color monitor, mouse.
A Favorite Holiday Story, Unfolds with the Magic of Tchaikovsky's Music, Video from Its Ballet Performances & Colorful Illustration & Graphics. With Ballet Performances, Music, Games, Interactive Audio/Video Puzzles & Story Narration, the Timeless "Nutcracker" Story Is Now an Interactive Masterpiece. One Disc Offers French, German, Spanish & English.
Technology Dynamics Corp.

Nutri-Calc: Diet-Recipe Analysis Software. *Version:* 2.1. Aug. 1994. *Items Included:* 55 page user manual, on-line user help. *Customer Support:* Telephone support provided during office hours (8:30am- 4:30pm MST).
DOS 2.0 or higher. IBM PC's & compatibles (512k). disk $39.95. *Optimal configuration:* IBM PC or compatible with 512k RAM, DOS 2.0 or higher & hard disk (printer & hard disk not required but recommended).
Analyzes Diets, Foods & Recipes for Their Nutrient Content. It Analyzes for 30 Nutrients & Has a Database with over 1600 Foods. Features Include: Multiple Users, Meals Analysis, Recipe & Menu Analysis, Comparisons to RDA's & Activity Analysis. Foods Include Handbook Number 8 Series, Fast Prepared, Frozen & Health Foods.
CAMDE Corp.

Nutri-Calc HD. *Version:* System 1.11, Database Version 4.5. Jun. 1994. *Items Included:* 91 page manual, on-line user help. *Customer Support:* Telephone support provided during hours of 8:30 am - 4:30 pm (MST).
DOS 2.0 or higher. IBM PC or compatibles (512k). disk $225.00. *Nonstandard peripherals required:* Hard disk. *Optimal configuration:* IBM PC or compatible with a hard disk, 640K RAM.
Analyzes Diets, Foods & Recipes for Nutrient Content. It Analyzes for 30 Nutrients & Has 3400 Foods. Features Include: Multiple Users, Meals Analysis, Recipe/Menu Analysis, Patient Notes, Comparison to RDA, History Plotting & Activity Analysis. Foods Include Handbook #8 Series Foods, Fast, Prepared, Frozen & Health Foods.
CAMDE Corp.

NUTRI-CALC PLUS: Diet-Recipe Analysis Software. *Version:* 1.2.1. Oct. 1993.
Compatible Hardware: Apple Macintosh.
Memory Required: 640k. *Items Included:* 62 page user manual, on-line user help. *Customer Support:* Telephone Support: (8:30-4:30 MST).
3.5" disk $159.00.
Dietary Analysis Program Which Computes the Nutritional Content of Menus & Diets. Includes 3600 Foods, Expandable, with 23 Nutrients per Food, Plus 10 Amino Acids. Other Features Include Comparison to U.S.A. RDA Values, Protein Analysis, Energy Sources Analysis, User Nutritional History Data, & User Help.
CAMDE Corp.

Nutrilabel. *Operating System(s) Required:* PC-DOS/MS-DOS, OS/2. *Memory Required:* 192k. *Items Included:* Includes 6-month warranty, user manual. *Customer Support:* Free updates, enhancements, & toll-free 800 lines for customers under warranty.
3.5" or 5.25" disk $1000.00.
Provides Database for 1,000 Patients. Prints Nourishment & Menu Labels, Automates Manual Nourishment Writing & Menu Heading in a Diet Center.
Practorcare, Inc.

Nutriplan. *Compatible Hardware:* Apple II; IBM & compatibles. *Memory Required:* 512k.
3.5" disk $75.00.
Diet-Nutrition Analysis.
NutriPlan.

Nutriplanner. *Operating System(s) Required:* PC-DOS/MS-DOS, OS/2. *Memory Required:* 6000 version 5 MG, 4000 version 256k. *Items Included:* Includes 6-month warranty, user manual. *Customer Support:* Free updates, enhancements, & toll-free 800 lines for customers under warranty.
Version 4000. disk $1500.00.
Version 6000. 3.5" disk $2000.00.
Nutrient Analysis on User Intake for 24 Hour & Multiple Day Periods, Recipes & Menus. Analysis for up to 100 Nutrients. Database Expandable. Cost Recipes, Menus & Scale Recipes for Different Production Numbers. User Determined Printouts.
Practorcare, Inc.

Nutripractor. *Operating System(s) Required:* PC-DOS/MS-DOS, OS/2. *Memory Required:* 6000 version 5MG, 4000 version 256k. *Items Included:* Includes 6-month warranty, user manual. *Customer Support:* Free updates, enhancements & toll-free 800 lines for customers under warranty.
Version 4000. disk $800.00.
Version 6000. 3.5" disk $1100.00.
Features 24 Hour & Multiple Day Periods. Calorie Intake Based on Age, Sex, Weight, Activity, & Injury Level. User Specific RDA's Determined. Expandable Database. Analysis of 100 Nutrients. User Determined Printouts. Educational Printouts.
Practorcare, Inc.

Nutristatus. *Operating System(s) Required:* PC-DOS/MS-DOS, OS/2. *Memory Required:* 256k. *General Requirements:* 5Mb on hard disk. *Items Included:* Includes 6-month warranty, user manual. *Customer Support:* Free updates, enhancements, & toll-free 800 lines for customers under warranty.
3.5" or 5.25" disk $1000.00.
Provides Evaluation of Adult & Pediatric Nutritional Assessment. Features Five Areas of Evaluation Which Include Demographic Information, Clinical Assessment, Laboratory Evaluation, Anthropometrics & Caloric Assessment. Parameters Can Be Graphed to Show Trends over Time Duration.
Practorcare, Inc.

Nutrition-A Balanced Diet. *Version:* 1.2. 1985.
Compatible Hardware: Apple II series, IIgs.
Memory Required: 48k.
disk $43.00 (Order no.: NB-A324).
Covers the Basics of Good Nutrition, Analyzes the Quality of User's Diet Compared to the RDA & Makes Recommendations for Improvements.
EME Corp.

Nutrition Pro!: Exercise, Nutrient Analysis Software. Elizabeth S. Hands & Robert B. Geltz. Aug. 1991. *Items Included:* Manual; discount coupons. *Customer Support:* Free demo; telephone assistance; menu/intake analysis service available - quote per job.
PC-DOS, MS-DOS. IBM compatibles (384k). disk $79.00 (Order no.: 60044).
Nutrient Analysis for the Individual. 2000 Foods, 18 Nutrients Analyzed & Compared to Personalized Recommendations. Ratios Shown in Numeric/Graphic Form. Easy to Use. Choose from 100 Exercises. Exchanges. Expandable Database. Search for Foods by Name, Group, Exchanges. Hi/Low Search for 2 Nutrients.
ESHA Research.

The Nutrition Stack. *Version:* 2.1. Richard D. Lasky. Jan. 1991. *Items Included:* One 800k diskette, 26 page user's manual. *Customer Support:* Free support for all registered owners by phone & on-line services.
Macintosh Plus, SE, SE/30 or Mac II family (1Mb). 3.5" disk $79.00 (ISBN 1-878081-01-2). *Nonstandard peripherals required:* Hard disk drive with 1Mb free space. *Addl. software required:* Hypercard 1.2 or higher.
Keeps Daily Records of Nutritional Value of Meals. Provides a Detailed Analysis of Each Meal, Displayed in Tables & Graphs. Database of over 2700 Foods May Be Expanded by the User. Tracks Protein, Carbohydrate, Fat, Fiber, Sodium, Cholesterol, Calories, Vitamin & Mineral Content of Meals. RDA Values Customized for Each User. Writes Reports to Disk & Tracks Nutrients over Time. Includes On-Screen Help. Now Includes Fast Foods.
Big Byte Software.

Nutritionist IV: Diet Analysis. *Version:* 4.0. Jun. 1995. *Items Included:* User's manual. *Customer Support:* Included with purchase.
Windows 3.1 or Windows for Workgroups 3.11. 386 (4Mb). disk $495.00. *Addl. software required:* DOS 5.0 with Windows 3.1 or WG 3.11.
Analyzes Diets, Recipes & Menus for 74 Nutrients Plus Cost & Weight. Includes 13,000 Plus Foods/Ingredients & 300 Plus Recipes. Evaluate Caloric Expenditure & Track Weight over Time. Purchase Includes a One Year Subscription.
First DataBank.

Nutritionist IV: Diet Analysis. *Version:* 4.1. Jun. 1996. *Items Included:* User's manual. *Customer Support:* Included with purchase.
Windows 3.1 or Windows for Workgroups 3.11 or Windows 95. 386 (4Mb). disk $495.00. *Addl. software required:* DOS 5.0 with

Windows 3.1 or WG 3.11.
Analyzes Diets, Recipes & Menus for 74 Nutrients Plus Cost & Weight. Includes 13,000 Plus Foods/Ingredients & 300 Plus Recipes. Evaluate Caloric Expenditure & Track Weight over Time. Purchase Includes a One Year Subscription.
First DataBank.

Nutritionist IV: Food Labeling. *Version:* 4.1. Jun. 1996. *Items Included:* User's manual. *Customer Support:* Included with purchase. Windows 3.1 or Windows for Workgroups 3.11 or Windows 95. 386 (4Mb). disk $495.00. *Addl. software required:* DOS 5.0 with Windows 3.1 or WG 3.11.
Performs Nutrient Analysis of Formulations & Generates Camera-Ready Nutrition Facts Labels That Comply with FDA Regulations. Use Database Foods & Ingredients for Analysis, or Generate Labels Using Laboratory Values. Add More Specialty & Proprietary Ingredients to the Database, & Retain Formulations for Future Reference & Revision.
First DataBank.

Nutritionist IV: Food Labeling. *Version:* 4.0. Jun. 1995. *Items Included:* User's manual. *Customer Support:* Included with purchase. Windows 3.1 or Windows for Workgroups 3.11. 386 (4Mb). disk $495.00. *Addl. software required:* DOS 5.0 with Windows 3.1 or WG 3.11.
Performs Nutrient Analysis of Formulations & Generates Camera-Ready Nutrition Facts Labels That Comply with FDA Regulations. Use Database Foods & Ingredients for Analysis, or Generate Labels Using Laboratory Values. Add More Specialty & Proprietary Ingredients to the Dadtabase, & Retain Formulations for Future Reference & Revision.
First DataBank.

NWA Quality Analyst. *Version:* 4.3. Feb. 1995. *Compatible Hardware:* IBM PC & compatibles. *Operating System(s) Required:* PC-DOS/MS-DOS, Windows 3.1, Windows for Workgroups 3.11, Windows 95. *Language(s):* C Plus Plus, Visual BASIC. *Memory Required:* 4000k. *Items Included:* User manual, tutorial, & product disks. *Customer Support:* Free technical support to registered users of product, via phone during normal business hours.
disk $795.00 single user; $2895.00 5 user LAN.
User Friendly Statistical Quality Control Charting & Analysis Program. Combines Data Management & Manipulation with Control Charting Techniques & Statistical Analysis. Turns the Microcomputer into a Tool for Process Control. Includes Batch Processing Capability, Graphics & the Ability to Interface with Most of the Database & Spreadsheet Software Products. Work Flows Are Straight Forward.
Northwest Analytical, Inc.

NWA Quality Monitor: Real-Time SPC Workstation Software. *Version:* 1.2. Feb. 1996. *Items Included:* Configuration kit - documentation, diskettes. *Customer Support:* Unlimited telephone/fax support, training seminars (fee based) as announced.
MS-DOS. IBM & compatibles (640k). $895.00 configuration kit, $495.00 ea. run-time modules. *Networks supported:* Novell, Banyan, Windows NT, Windows 95, Windows/Workgroups.
Three Primary Functions - 1) Configure PC Serial Port to Collect Data from Plant Floor Measurement (Weight, Dimensional, etc.), 2) User Configurable Operator Interface, 3) SPC Charting Engine (Same As NWA Quality Analyst). Consists of Configuration Kit Which Sets up Serial Port(s) for Data Capture from Measurement Devices & Multiplexers, Configures Operator Interface & Selects Control Charts. Individual Runtime Modules Are Used at Each Plant Floor Workstations.
Northwest Analytical, Inc.

NY Warriors. *Customer Support:* 90 day warranty.
MS-DOS 2.1X. IBM (512K). disk $14.99. *Nonstandard peripherals required:* CGA, EGA or Tandy Graphics required.
Amiga (512K). 3.5" disk $39.99.
As the Commander of an Elite Strike Force, You Are the Only One Who Can Keep Terrorists from Blowing up the World Trade Center. Fight Your Way Through Ramboids, Rasts, Killer Klowns, & Others. Blow Them Away with Your Powerful Arsenal of Bazookas, Guided Missiles, Flames Throwers, & Other Weapons of Destructions.
Virgin Games.

NYINDEX. *Compatible Hardware:* Atari 400, 800. *Language(s):* BASIC (source code included). *Memory Required:* 48k. *General Requirements:* Atari BASIC.
disk $29.95.
Store, Retrieve & Plot New York Stock Exchange Information.
Dynacomp, Inc.

O C Compiler. *Operating System(s) Required:* CP/M. *Memory Required:* 56k.
contact publisher for price.
Jeffries Research.

O. M. S. Optical Mark System. *Version:* 6.0. Sep. 1993. *Customer Support:* On-site, classroom & phone training; 800 line, 900 line & modem support; monthly or per call options.
Novell, SCO UNIX, AIX. 486 or RISC (8Mb). $40,000.00. *Optimal configuration:* IBM RISC AIX, 3 laser printing & 1 dot matrix scanner.
SCO UNIX. IBM. $30,000.00. *Optimal configuration:* 8Mb RAM 1 laser, 1 dot & scanner.
Rovak's Optical Mark System Utilizes Optical Mark Reading to Reduce Keyboard Entry by 75%. A User Definable Scan Form Is Completed by the Provider & Then Scanned. DMS Will Then Generate Medical Histories Operative Reports, Post to Patient Ledgers, Prescriptions, Insurance Forms, Patient Receipts, Referral Letters, 3rd Party Billing & More. The Result Is Reduced Overhead, Cost Savings, Increased Accuracy & Higher Patient Satisfaction.
Rovak, Inc.

O. R. Suite Management & Scheduling System. *Customer Support:* 24 hour/day, 7 day/week customer support; 90 day warranty; yearly maintenance fee approx. 15% of software purchase price.
DOS, Novell, Windows. IBM PCs & compatibles. Contact publisher for price. *Networks supported:* Novell.
The O.R. Scheduling Option Is One of the Few Scheduling Systems That Manages Surgical Scheduling Information & Integrates That Information with the Rest of Patient Care. From Within the Surgical Appointment Screen, You Can Access Any Non-Surgical Information going on Behind the Appointment to Prevent Any Unanticipated Conflicts with Surgery. Further, O.R. Keeps an Eye on Material Management, Helping Track All Surgical Inventory Before, During, & after Surgery.
LCI.

OAG Travel Planner. Dec. 1989. *Items Included:* User documentation. *Customer Support:* Free customer support, 1 year warranty for parts & labor.
MS-DOS (256k). IBM PC or compatible. disk $22.95 (Order no.: FI-240). *Addl. software required:* Casio FA-120 PC-Link.
Software Package Designed For Use with the Casio-FA-120 & Casio B.O.S.S., Business Organizer Scheduling System Product. Allows User To Select Travel Information For 25 Cities, & Download That Information into the Casio B.O.S.S. For Portability.
Casio, Inc.

OakWord. Daniel LaSpesa. 1980. *Compatible Hardware:* IBM System-34, System-36, System-38, S/36 PC. *Language(s):* RPG II. *Memory Required:* S-34 96k.
IBM System-34, 36. 8" disk $1500.00 ea.
IBM System-38. 8" disk $2500.00.
S/36 PC. $795.00.
Maintains 4 File Types: Return Addresses, Customer Names, Documents, & a Spelling Dictionary. Includes Spreadsheet, Data Base Interface, Readability Index.
Oak Software.

Oasis. *Version:* 2.02. *Compatible Hardware:* Apple Macintosh.
3.5" disk $22.95.
Finder Replacement & Utility Program.
Jan Eugenides.

OASYS 88000 C, C++ Pascal & FORTRAN Cross Compilers. *Customer Support:* Maintenance available, call for pricing.
UNIX, VMS. Apple MAC II A/UX, IBM RT, Motorola, DG AVIION, Apollo, DEC VAX, DEC station, Sun. $3000.00 & up.
VMS. DEC Vax, VAX station, MicroVAX. $3000.00 & up.
VMS. DEC Vax, VAX station, MicroVAX.
Based upon Green Hills Software's Integrated Family of Compilers. They Are Constructed As a Combination of Language Specific "Front Ends" (C++ Pascal, FORTRAN) & Target Specific "Code Emitters" (88000). The Compilers Emit 88000 Assembly Code & Are Compatible with the 88 open Binary Compatibility Standard.
Oasys, Inc.

OASYS 88000 Cross Assembler/Linker. *Customer Support:* Maintenance available, call for pricing.
UNIX. Apple MAC II A/UX, IBM RT, Motorola, DG AViiON, Apollo, DECstation. $2800.00 & up.
Sun OS. Sun-3, Sun-4 (SPARC). $2800.00 & up.
VMS. DEC Vax, VAXstation, MicroVAX. $2800.00 & up.
Consists of a Macro Assembler, Linker, Librarian, Cross Reference Utility & Symbol File Format Utility. Provides Software Developers with Feature-rich, Motorola Compatible Tools for Generating 88000 COFF Object Modules & Binary Compatibility Standard Compliant Binaries. The Assembler Supports Macros & Conditional Assembly.
Oasys, Inc.

OASYS 680x0 C, C++, Pascal & FORTRAN Cross Compilers. *Customer Support:* Maintenance available, call for pricing.
UNIX, VMS. DG AViiON 3xx, 5xxx/6xxx; Pyramid, HP 9000/3xx, Motorola, IBM RT, Apollo, Gould, DEC VAX, UNISYS CT, DECstation, NEC Astra, Sun, IBM RS/6000. $2000.00 & up.
Sun OS. Sun-3, Sun-4 (SPARC). contact publisher for price.
VMS. DEC VAX, VAXstation, MicroVAX. contact publisher for price.
Based on the Green Hills Software Integrated Family of Compilers, They Produce the Most Optimized 68000/10/20/30/40 or 683xx Assembly Code Available. The Compilers Are Constructed As a Combination of Language Specific "Front-Ends" (C, C++ Pascal,

FORTRAN) & Target Specific "Code-Emitters" (88000, 68k 80x86, i860) That Are Inter Language Callable.
Oasys, Inc.

OASYS 680x0 Cross Assembler/Linker. *Customer Support:* Maintenance available, call for pricing.
UNIX. DECstation, DG AViiON, Pyramid, HP9000/3xx, Motorola, IBM RT, Apollo, Gould, DEC VAX, UNISYS CT, NEC Astra, Sun, IBM RS/6000. $1600.00.
SUN OS. Sun-3, Sun-4 (SPARC). contact publisher for price.
VMS. DEC VAX, VAXstation, MicroVAX. contact publisher for price.
Consists of a Macro Assembler, Linker, Librarian, Cross Reference Utility, & Symbol File Format Utility. Provides Software Developers with Feature-rich, Motorola Compatible Tools for Generating 680x0 Modules with Full 68881 Floating Point Support. The Assembler Supports Macros, Conditional Assembly & Can Be Used As a "Hands-on" Assembler.
Oasys, Inc.

The Oberon System. Eidgenossische Technische Hochschule-ETH Staff. Sep. 1994. *Items Included:* 12-page booklet. *Customer Support:* Tech support: interest group E-mail. Bug reports: ETH E-mail or mail, fax.
Unix, MS-DOS, Nextstep, Linux, Amiga, Macintosh, MS-Windows. DEC-Station, IBM RS-6000, HP-700, Silicon Graphics. CD-ROM disk $39.95 (ISBN 0-9642953-0-X). *Nonstandard peripherals required:* SunSPARC, Amiga, Apple Macintosh II. *Addl. software required:* Native operating systems. *Optimal configuration:* Intel 80386 min. Motorola 68020 min.
Anthra Norell, Inc.

Obesity Savant: Obesity Diagnostic Screening. *Version:* 2.0. G. B. Cook. Apr. 1987. *Compatible Hardware:* IBM PC. *Operating System(s) Required:* PC-DOS. *Language(s):* Quicksilver. *Memory Required:* 640k. *Customer Support:* Toll free telephone support.
disk $595.00.
Patient Interactive Program That Interviews (with or Without Nursing Assistance) to Ascertain Which of the 18 Recognized Causes Is Present to Account for Patient's Obesity. Provides Significant Liability Protection from Overlooked, Rarely Encountered Syndromes Which May Be Present but Obscured.
SRC Systems, Inc.

OBGLine CD-ROM Database for Obstetrics-Gynecology. Sep. 1990.
MS Windows 3.1 or higher. IBM & compatibles (4Mb). CD-ROM disk $325.00-$995.00; Networks $1895.00 & up. *Nonstandard peripherals required:* Magnetic or CD-ROM, using ISO 9660. *Optimal configuration:* IBM & compatibles, 80386 or higher, 4Mb RAM, 20Mb hard disk, mouse, MS Windows 3.1 or higher.
System 6.0.7 or higher. Apple Macintosh (3Mb). CD-ROM disk $325.00-$995.00; Networks $1895.00 & up. *Optimal configuration:* Apple Macintosh Plus or higher, 3Mb RAM, System 6.0.7 or higher.
OBGLine Is an Electronic Reference Database to the Obstetrics & Gynecology Journal Literature. Obstetrics/Gynecology-Specific Excerpts (Including Abstracts) from the National Library of Medicine's MEDLINE Database Are Distributed on CD-ROM (Compact Disc, Read-Only Memory) Optical Disc. Knowledge Finder Search-&-Retrieval Software Makes Searching of the OBGLine Database Easy, Effective & Fast. After the User Types a Phrase or Sentence Describing the Information Needed, It selects the References in the Database That Appear to Best Match the Request, & Presents Them in Order of Likely Relevance. The OBGLine Archive CD-ROM Contains More Than 390,000 References to Articles Published in 100 Obstetrics/Gynecology Journals over the Most Recent 10 Full Years. Obstetrics/Gynecology Articles from More Than 2,500 Other Journals Are Also Included.
Aries Systems Corp.

Object Library Maintenance. Daniel R. Hicks. *Compatible Hardware:* IBM PC, PCjr, PC XT, PC AT, Portable PC, 3270 PC with IBM Display & IBM Matrix printer (optional). *Operating System(s) Required:* DOS 2.00, 2.10, 3.00, 3.10. *Memory Required:* 128k.
disk $19.95 (Order no.: 6276543).
Provides a Group of Programs That Can Help User Create, Modify, or Take Apart PC-DOS Object Module Library (LIB) Files. Library Files Permit Individual Object (OBJ) Files to Be Combined into One LIB File So That the DOS Linker Program Can Process Them As a Single File Rather Than Individually.
Personally Developed Software, Inc.

Object-Oriented FORTRAN 77 for NeXT. *Version:* 3.2. Jun. 1989. *Items Included:* Complete documentation. *Customer Support:* Free unlimited telephone support, maintenance agreement available.
NeXT System Release 2.0 or higher. NeXTStation or Cube (4Mb). $995.00 (Order no.: FUV3NEX2). *Addl. software required:* NeXt System Release 2.0 extended.
ANSI X3.9-1978/ISO 1539-1980 Compiler That Supports All DoD MIL-STD 1753 Extensions. V3.1 Includes Most VAX/VMS Extensions Including STRUCTURE, UNION, MAP, & BYTE, All VAX Intrinsic Functions, & CRAY/Sun-Style POINTER. Threaded Math Library is Included Which Increases Execution Speed up to 2X Over Standard 68040 Kernal Math.
Absoft Corp.

Object Professional. *Version:* 1.3. Apr. 1994. *Items Included:* 3 lay-flat perfect bound manuals, pop-up online reference guide. *Customer Support:* Free technical support, 60 day money-back guarantee, free electronic maintenance upgrades.
MS-DOS 2.0 or higher (360k). IBM PC, AT, PS/2, compatibles. $249.00. *Addl. software required:* Turbo Pascal 5.5, 6.0, 7.0. *Optimal configuration:* Hard disk, 640k RAM.
Provides More Than 30 High-Level Object Types with Over 1000 Methods & Routines in Several Categories: User- Interface Design, Data Manipulation, & Low-Level System Access. Includes Objects for Windows, Data Entry Fields, Full-Screen Forms, Pulldown & Horizontal-Bar Menu Systems, Pick Lists, File Selection Boxes, Context-Sensitive Help Systems, Text Editing, File Browsing, & More. Data Manipulation Objects Include Stacks, Linked Lists, & Virtual Arrays. System-Oriented Routines Provide a TSR Manager That Swaps to Disk or EMS, Squeezing Complex Pop-up Programs into as Little as 6K of Normal RAM Space.
TurboPower Software.

Object Professional for C Plus Plus. *Version:* 1.0. Feb. 1994. *Items Included:* 2 volumes lay-flat perfect bound manuals, pop-up help reference. *Customer Support:* 60 day money back guarantee, free technical support, CompuServe technical support, free electronic maintenance updates.
MS-DOS 3.3 or higher. Any PC compatible, 286 or higher (3Mb). $279.00. *Addl. software required:* Borland C Plus Plus 3.1 or higher, Microsoft C/C Plus Plus 7.0 or higher.
A Class Library for Writing Sophisticated DOS Text Mode User Interfaces. Includes Design Programs for Menus & Data Entry Screens. Includes Classes for General Purpose Windows, Menu Systems, Entry Screens, Hypertext Help Systems, Text Editors, File Browsers, CUA-Style Dialog Boxes, List Boxes, File Dialogs, & More. Includes Complete Source Code & Numerous Example Programs.
TurboPower Software.

Object/1. *Version:* 3.0. *Items Included:* 2 spiral bound manuals.
OS/2, Presentation Manager (4Mb), Windows 3.X. disk $4000.00. *Nonstandard peripherals required:* Mouse. *Optimal configuration:* 386 PS/2, 6Mb. *Networks supported:* OS/2 or Windows supported LANs.
Application Tool That Allows Rapid Development of Presentation Manager Applications. Includes Interactive Forms/Window Painter That Allows User to Design Data Entry & Retrieval Forms. Includes Relational Database. Interfaces to MDBS IV & Other SQL DBMS's Available.
Micro Data Base Systems, Inc. (MDBS).

ObjectGraphics.
Windows 3.0 or higher. IBM PC/XT/AT, PS/2, 80386 & compatibles (1Mb). disk $195.00. *Nonstandard peripherals required:* Hard disk, mouse or other pointing device. *Addl. software required:* Turbo Pascal for Windows.
Source Code - $195.00.
High-Level Object-Oriented Graphics Library That Extends the Power of TURBO PASCAL FOR WINDOWS to Create Platform-Independent Support for Graphics. Product Masks the Graphics Engine in WINDOWS, & Allows Users to Develop Graphical Applications Using a Set of Graphic Objects Rather Than Multiple Procedure Calls. Users Can Create & Use Tools Such As "Pens", "Brushes" & "Textpens" to Control the Look of Graphic Images.
The Whitewater Group.

Objective-C Compiler. *Version:* 4.3. Nov. 1988. *Compatible Hardware:* HP 9000, 300; Sun 3, 4 SPARC system; DEC VAX; IBM PC, PC AT & compatibles, PS/2; DG AViiON; HP 9000, 400, 700, 800; IBM RISC System/6000; DECstations; MIPS Magnum; Macintosh. *Operating System(s) Required:* PC-DOS/MS-DOS; HP-UX, SunOS, DEC Ultrix, VAX Ultrix; OS/2, OG/UX; AIX; SCO UNIX; RISC/OS, Mac OS. *Language(s):* C. *Memory Required:* 2000k. *General Requirements:* 1.5Mb disk space. *Items Included:* Manual, operator guide, tutorial. *Customer Support:* Call toll free number.
$249.00 DOS; $500.00 SCO/UNIX, OS/2; $1000.00-$2500.00 workstation.
Macintosh. 3.5" disk $149.00.
Object Oriented Superset of ANSI C. Supplements C with Strong Type Checking, under Programmer Control, & Gives the Programmer Fine-Grained Control of Run-Time Optimization with Binding Options Available. Packaged with the ICpak 101 Foundation Class Library, Designed for Professional Software Development.
The Stepstone Corp.

Objects in Motion: Physics Simulation. 1995. *Items Included:* Full manual. *Customer Support:* Free telephone support - 90 days, 30-day warranty.
MS-DOS 3.2 or higher. 286 (584k). disk $84.95. *Nonstandard peripherals required:* CGA/EGA/VGA.
A Collection of Six Simulations - CARS, CANNON, RIVER, PLANET, CIRCLE, & COLLIDER - That Focus on the Physics of Moving Objects to Teach Students about Kinematics, Rotational Motion, Projectiles, Collisions, Relative Motion, Kepler's Laws, Scattering, & Galilean Relativity.
Dynacomp, Inc.

TITLE INDEX

ObjectVision. Version: 2.0. Feb. 1991. *Items Included:* Reference manual, step-by-step tutorial, quick reference guide, custom applications disk, & free runtime.
  Windows 3.0 or higher. IBM 286, 386, 486 & compatibles (1Mb). disk $495.00 (ISBN 0-87524-229-4).
  Program to Create Custom-Tailored Interactive Windows Applications. Includes Direct Links to Multiple Databases Including One-to-Many Data Structures; Application Protection; Free Runtime for Distributing Applications; Incremental Development; Full Support of DDE, DLL, & OLE; SQL Link Option. A Separate OS/2 Version is Available.
  Borland International, Inc.

Objectworks For Smalltalk-80. *General Requirements:* 10 MB hard disk drive.
  Macintosh Plus or higher (4MB). 3.5" disk $595.00.
  Object-Oriented Programming.
  ParcPlace Systems.

OBRIEF (Hebrew Brief). 1988.
  MS-DOS (256k). IBM PC, PC XT, PC AT & compatibles. disk $99.00 (ISBN 0-938245-54-6). *Addl. software required:* BRIEF by Underware, Inc., MXK by Inverted-A.
  laser printer support pkg. $99.00.
  Hebrew English Word Processor That Supports Pointing. Add-On to BRIEF Editor. Edits Extended ASCII Files in Two Hebrew Modes in Addition to English. Hebrew Is Entered Right to Left; Pointing Marks Are Placed Above or Below Cursor As Appropriate. Features Hebrew Wraparound & Paragraph Formatting. Uses Standard Keyboard Interpreted by Historic Identification of Letters.
  Inverted-A, Inc.

OBRIT: Hebrew Printing. Amnon Katz. 1987. *Compatible Hardware:* IBM PC, PC XT, PC AT. *General Requirements:* IBM PC with graphics capability or Brother HR-15, HR-25, or HR-35 with "Galil" Hebrew printwheel.
  disk $25.00 (ISBN 0-938245-52-X, Order no.: A80).
  Prints Hebrew Text with No Special Equipment (Dot Matrix) or Only a Special Printwheel (Daisy Wheel). Text Is Prepared in ASCII Characters by Standard Word Processors, & Is Printed in Traditional Square Characters from Right to Left. Word-End Forms Automatically Supplied.
  Inverted-A, Inc.

OCC-Accounts Receivable, Billing & Inventory Control. Version: 5.5. 1978. *Compatible Hardware:* IBM PC. *Operating System(s) Required:* MS-DOS, PC-DOS, TRSDOS. *Language(s):* Microsoft BASIC (source code included). *Memory Required:* 128k. *General Requirements:* 2 disk drives or hard disk, monitor, printer.
  $1200.00-$1500.00.
  Prints Invoice, Reduces Inventory & Posts to Customer Ledger & General Ledger, Accumulates Sales Analysis Information, On-Line Invoicing, Sales Journals, Aging, Commissions, Credit Checks. Interfaces with Order Entry, Manufacturing & General Ledger.
  CharterHouse Software Corp.

OCC-General Ledger: Client Write-Up. Version: 5.7. 1978. *Compatible Hardware:* IBM PC. *Operating System(s) Required:* PC-DOS, MS-DOS. *Language(s):* Microsoft BASIC (source code included). *Memory Required:* 128k. *General Requirements:* 2 disk drives, hard disk, printer.
  GL Standard. $500.00.
  GL Advanced. $1000.00.
  Allows Customized Chart of Accounts for Individual Clients. User Defined Journals, Detailed G/L. Optional: Departmental Financial Statements, Budgeting, Automatic Adjustments. Interfaces to Payroll, A/R, A/P, Fixed Assets.
  CharterHouse Software Corp.

Occasions & Celebrations: ClickArt. *Items Included:* Visual index, user's guide. *Customer Support:* Free & unlimited technical support to registered users; 60 day money-back guarantee.
  Macintosh. Macintosh, System 6.0.7 or higher (1Mb). 3.5" disk $49.95. *Addl. software required:* Any word-processing, desktop publishing or works program that accepts graphics.
  Windows MS-DOS. IBM PC & compatibles. 3.5" disk $49.95. *Addl. software required:* Any word processing, desktop publishing or works program that accepts graphics.
  Over 200 Images! Full-Color Images; Ready-to-Use, or Changed in Appropriate Drawing Program; Designed in Full-Color (CMYK); Produced to Print in Detailed Greyscale on Black & White Printers; Includes the ClickArt Trade Secret - Images Traded to Every Popular Graphics Format, Guaranteed to Work with All Popular Applications.
  T/Maker Co., Inc.

Occupational Computing Accounts Payable. Version: 5.4. 1978. *Compatible Hardware:* IBM PC. *Operating System(s) Required:* PC-DOS 1.1, 2.0, MS-DOS. *Language(s):* MBASIC (source code included). *Memory Required:* 128k.
  disk $500.00.
  Allows Processing of Vendor Invoices Including Automatic Expense Distribution to G/L & Job Costing. Cash or Accrual Methods of Accounting, Aged Trial Balance, Cash Requirement Reports, Automatic Vouchering, & Check Writing.
  CharterHouse Software Corp.

Occupational Computing General Ledger. Version: 5.7. 1978. *Compatible Hardware:* IBM PC with 2 320k disk drives or hard disk, & printer. *Operating System(s) Required:* PC-DOS 1.1, 2.0, UNIX, XENIX. *Language(s):* MBASIC (source code included). *Memory Required:* 128k.
  Standard. disk $499.00.
  Advanced XENIX. disk $1000.00.
  Allows User-Controlled Formatting of the Financial Statements, Through the Chart of Accounts. Features: User-Defined Journals, Detailed General Ledger (Monthly & a History/Yearly Option). Interfaces with A/P, P/R, A/R & Fixed Assets.
  CharterHouse Software Corp.

Occupational Skills Analysis System: Job Match-Job Placement. Oct. 1987. *Compatible Hardware:* IBM-PC & compatibles. *Operating System(s) Required:* PC-DOS. *Memory Required:* 256k. *General Requirements:* Hard disk, printer.
  disk $2995.00.
  Skills Management Software That Permits the User to Create & Manipulate a Database of Task Based Job Skills for Each Employee's Position. Helps Determine What Areas to Train People. Enables User to Objectively Measure an Employee's or Student's Proficiency. Analyzes Jobs & Develops Training Forecasts.
  Educational Data Systems, Inc.

Ocean Escape. Holly Oliver. Oct. 1994. (source code included). *Items Included:* Bound parent activity guide & user manual. *Customer Support:* Free 800 # support for registered users. 90 days limited warranty.
  System 7.0 or above. Macintosh LC II or above. disk $49.95 (ISBN 1-57026-035-4).
    Nonstandard peripherals required: CD-ROM Crive, microphone (optional). *Optimal configuration:* MAC LC II, System 7, 4 mb RAM, color monitor, CD-ROM drive, hard drive, microphone (optional).
  MPC Windows 3.1.1, 4 mb RAM. PC or compatible, 386 or above. *Nonstandard peripherals required:* CD-ROM drive, soundblaster or 100% compatible, audio card, speakers, microphone (optional). *Optimal configuration:* 386 PC or compatible, Windows 3.1.1, 4 mb RAM, CD-ROM drive, hard drive, soundblaster or 100% compatible, basic audio card, VGA graphics & color monitor, mouse & speakers, microphone (optional).
  Ocean Escape is a children's multimedia product that features a story about a little boy's adventures in the ocean, context based activities & a multi-media glossary. This product helps young children build pre-reading & beginning reading skills.
  Computer Curriculum Corporation.

OceanLife, Vol. 2: Micronesia. Oct. 1993.
  Mac: System 7.X, 13-inch monitor (256 or better colors) (6Mb). CD-ROM disk $49.95 (ISBN 1-57047-004-9, Order no.: OL 2). *Nonstandard peripherals required:* CD-ROM drive with a sustained transfer rate of 150 Kbps or higher.
  CPU with 486/33 MHz or higher processor (6Mb). CD-ROM disk $49.95. *Nonstandard peripherals required:* CD-ROM drive with a sustained transfer rate of 150 Kbps or higher.
  The Second in an Interactive Series of CD-ROM Based Books on Marine Life. This Two-CD Set Includes Original Narrated Underwater Video by Jerry Borrell & Photography by Robert F. Myers, Author of the Definitive Guide to Tropical Fishes of Micronesia. With More Than 150 Species, in Territories Ranging from Pohnpei to Belau, This CD Fetures Video of Heretofore Undocumented Fish Behavior on Subjects Like Mating, Predation, Camouflage, Brooding, & Nesting. Learn More about Micronesia by Exploring the Full Color Topographical, Relief, & Political Maps of the Region.
  Sumeria, Inc.

OceanLife, Vol. 3: Hawaii. Apr. 1994.
  Mac: System 7.0, 13-inch monitor (256 or better colors) (6Mb). CD-ROM disk $49.95 (ISBN 1-57047-005-7, Order no.: OL 3). *Nonstandard peripherals required:* CD-ROM drive with a sustained transfer rate of 150 Kbps or higher.
  CPU with 486/33 MHz or higher processor (8Mb). CD-ROM disk $49.95. *Nonstandard peripherals required:* CD-ROM drive with a sustained transfer rate of 150 Kbps or higher.
  The Third in a Series of Interactive CD-ROM Based Books on Marine Life from Hawaii. This CD Features Comprehensive Text, Range Maps, Photographs, & Full Color Video for over 90 Species & Multi-Mode Access That Lets You Browse by Photo, Name, or Keyword. Unique Interactive Maps of the Hawaiian Archipelago Provide Bathymetric & Topographical Information for the Reefs of Hawaii. An Expanded Interactive Morphology Section Details Anatomical Variations That Help Aquarists & Divers Identify Species. New in This Volume Is an Easy-to-Use Visual Index of Families & Phyla of Hawaiian Marine Life.
  Sumeria, Inc.

OceanLife, Vol. 4: The Great Barrier Reef. Oct. 1994.
  Mac: System 7.0, 13-inch monitor (256 or better colors) (6Mb). CD-ROM disk $49.95 (ISBN 1-57047-006-5, Order no.: OL 4). *Nonstandard peripherals required:* CD-ROM drive (double speed recommended).
  CPU with 486/33 MHz or higher processor (8Mb). CD-ROM disk $49.95. *Nonstandard peripherals required:* CD-ROM drive (double speed recommended).
  This Fourth Issue in the Series Features Extensive Text, Range Maps, Photographs, & Movies for over 200 Species of Fishes. This 2-CD Set Includes Approximately Three Hours of Original, Narrated Underwater Video, Music, Photography & Information on the Great Barrier Reef. Comprehensive Charts & Unique Interactive Maps

of the Region Allow the User to Explore with Great Detail the Largest Coral Reef in the World. A New Section on the Ecology of the Great Barrier Reef Allows Readers to Explore the Formation & Development of the Reef. Other Features Include Text Search & Movie & Text Export.
Sumeria, Inc.

OCTACOMM - LINK. Version: 1.3.2. Compatible Hardware: IBM PC; TI 990. Operating System(s) Required: DX10 3.5, 3.6, 3.7, DNOS 1.2, 1.3. Memory Required: 256k.
$195.00.
Allows Texas Instruments Business System Computer to Exchange Data Files with Other Computer Systems Using a Proprietary "ARQ" Error-Detecting Protocol.
Houston Computer Services, Inc.

OCTACOMM-PC. Version: 2.59. 1987. Compatible Hardware: IBM PC, PC XT, PC AT; TI PC, Busness Professional. Memory Required: 256k.
disk $125.00 ea.
 TIPC - TI940. (Order no.: OCBSTS).
 TIPC - VT100. (Order no.: OCVT1S).
 TIPC - TI931. (Order no.: OCT313).
 IBM - TI931. (Order no.: PCT31S).
 IBM - TI 940. (Order no.: PCBSTS).
Allows IBM PC's & TI PC's to Connect to Host Computers As Interactive Workstations. The PC's Retain Their Ability to Run Local Programs (Such As Spreadsheets & Word Processing) & Gain the Ability to Execute Programs on the Larger Computer. The PC's & the Larger Computer Function As an Integrated Network, Cooperating to Improve the Productivity of the Entire Organization.
Houston Computer Services, Inc.

ODBS - The O'Hanlon Database Solution. Version: 3.6. Items Included: Manual, screen generator, report/inquiry program. Customer Support: 90 days free. After the first 90 days, 3-hour support blocks are available for $180.00. MS/PC-DOS 3.0 or higher. IBM PC XT, AT, PS/2 & compatibles (384k). Single user $650.00; Multi-user $995.00. Networks supported: Novell, Alloy, etc.
Complete Multi-User Application Development System, Incorporating the Tools Users Need with the Power, Depth, & Flexibility You Want in Development Software. Designed to Create Error-Free, Sophisticated Multi-File Data Management Applications, This System Removes Virtually All Limitations Typical of Other Database Development Tools.
EKD Computer Sales & Supplies Corp.

Odds Calculator for Draw Poker. Sep. 1985. Compatible Hardware: IBM PCjr, PC XT, PC AT. Operating System(s) Required: MS-DOS. Language(s): Compiled BASIC. Memory Required: 64k. General Requirements: Printer.
disk $30.00 (ISBN 0-925825-04-2).
Computes the Exact Odds of Holding Any Poker Hand at the End of the Second Draw.
Robert L. Nicolai.

The Oddsmaker. Version: 3.0. Dec. 1983.
disk $29.95.
A Betting System. Handles 14 Betting Events.
CZ Software.

Odesta ODMS.
 UNIX, NetWare, VMS, NT & OS/2, MS-Windows, Macintosh & Motif. Sun Sparc, HP, IBM RISC System/6000, DEC VAXs Intel & Power PC-based machines. Contact publisher for price.
 A Family of Workflow & Document Management Products Proving Client/Server Application Solutions to Fortune 1000 Companies. Key Components Are: the ODMS Toolkit - a Graphical, Object-Based Toolset for Rapid Development of Cross-Platform Work Management Applications; the ODMS Workgroup Systems - Full Tailorable Horizontal & Vertical Work Management Applications; & Odesta Workflow - Client/Server Workflow Engines & a Graphical Workflow Painter for Workflow-Enabling Any Application.
Odesta Corp.

The Odyssey. John Kallas.
 IBM. disk $29.99 (Order no.: 6091).
 disk $39.99, incl. backup disk (Order no.: 6091B).
 Apple II. 3.5" disk $29.99 (Order no.: 6083).
 3.5" disk $39.99, incl. backup disk (Order no.: 6083B).
Software Games on the History, Art, & Culture of Ancient Greece. Contains Four or Five Different Games. The Games Are Designed for One, Two, or Three Players. Players Are Given a Question & Challenged to Spell the Correct Answer Letter by Letter. Points Are Assigned by Letter & for Answering the Entire Word Correctly. The Answer Is Reinforced with Information. This Is Sophisticated Material in an Enjoyable Format.
Trillium Pr.

Odyssey in Time. Compatible Hardware: Apple II Plus, IIe, IIc; Franklin 100, 1000 & 2000 series.
$49.95 (ISBN 0-918349-30-3, Order no.: OIT).
Advanced Form of TIME TRAVELER with More Treasure, More Adventure & More Danger. Includes All the Intellectual Challenges of TIME TRAVELER Plus You Must Contend with Adversary, an Opponent Who Also Moves Through Time & Space Hunting for the Ring to Increase His Power.
Krell Software Corp.

OFE3: Offset File Editor. Version: 3.3. Aug. 1988. Compatible Hardware: IBM PC, PC XT, PC AT, PS/2. Operating System(s) Required: CP/M, MS-DOS, TRSDOS 1.3. Language(s): QuickBASIC. Memory Required: 640k. General Requirements: EGA, VGA, or Hercules card.
$249.00.
Offset File Editor for Entering, Editing & Disk Storage of an Offset Table in Standard Format Needed for Input to Hydrostatics & Hydrodynamics Programs, in Particular, HYDRO/1 & HYDRO/2.
AeroHydro, Inc.

Off Shore Warrior. Aug. 1988.
 MS-DOS (256k). $39.95.
 Amiga 500, 1000, 2000 (512k). 3.5" disk $39.95. Nonstandard peripherals required: Joy stick.
 Atari ST 520, 1040, ST2, ST4 (512k). 3.5" disk $39.95. Nonstandard peripherals required: Color monitor.
Shooting Speed Boats Race.
Titus Software Corp.

Off-the-Wall. Compatible Hardware: Apple II with paddle. Operating System(s) Required: Apple DOS 3.2, 3.3. Language(s): Applesoft. Memory Required: 48k.
disk $14.95.
Arcade Game.
Dynacomp, Inc.

Offer Self-Image Questionnaire for Adolescents-Revised (OSIQ-R). Version: 3.010. D. Offer et al. Mar. 1996. Customer Support: Free unlimited phone support.
 Windows 3.X, Windows 95. 286 (4Mb). disk $195.00 (Order no.: W-1070). Nonstandard peripherals required: Printer.
This Widely Used Self-Report Inventory Measures Adjustment & Self Image in Adolescents from 13 to 19 Years of Age.
Western Psychological Services.

Office Building Load Estimator: Heating, Cooling, Electrical. W. C. Dries. 1984. Compatible Hardware: IBM PC. Operating System(s) Required: MS-DOS. Language(s): FORTRAN. Memory Required: 128k. General Requirements: Printer.
disk $150.00 (ISBN 0-9606344-2-8).
Interactive Program That Estimates the Cooling, Heating & Electrical Loads in an Office Building.
Blitz Publishing Co.

Office Manager. Version: 2.0. 1980. Operating System(s) Required: THEOS, UNIX. Language(s): THEOS BASIC, UX-BASIC.
contact publisher for price.
Integrated Retail/Wholesale Accounting/Sales Information System.
Comcepts Systems.

Office of the General Manager. Compatible Hardware: Apple II, II+, IIe, IIc; Commodore 64. General Requirements: Super Sunday program (Avalon Hill).
disk $30.00.
Allows You to "Own" a Professional Football Team. You Name & Run Your Team, & Can Acquire Any Player from Any of the Existing SUPER SUNDAY Disks. You Can Keep Track of Statistics Generated by the SUPER SUNDAY Game, Including Those of Your Punter, Place Kicker, & Special Teams, & You Can Print out Everything from Team Rosters to the Latest Standings.
Avalon Hill Game Co., The Microcomputer Games Div.

Office Services Inventory System. Version: 2.0. Jul. 1992. Items Included: Reference manual. Customer Support: 60-days free phone support; annual phone support - $250/yr.
 Mac OS - System 6 or 7. Macintosh (2Mb). 3.5" disk $3995.00. Optimal configuration: Mac Si or Ci, 13" monitor, 2Mb RAM, 20Mb HD. Networks supported: AppleTalk.
System Designed to Manage Office Installations & Reconfigurations. It Will Track Work Requests, Manage Inventory, & Provide for the Allocation & Tracking of Inventory to Work Requests. Tracks Inventory from Most of the Major Brand Name Office Furnishings Vendors. Also Manages Information about Purchase Orders, Shipments & Employees.
AD/C Solutions.

Office Spirometry Program. Compatible Hardware: Apple II+.
contact publisher for price.
Vitalograph.

Office-Star Secretarial-Office Management System. 1983. Operating System(s) Required: CP/M. Memory Required: 128k.
disk $295.00.
Combination of Univair's UNI-FILE & UNI-DATE. Database Management & Appointment/Project Scheduler. UNI-FILE Allows the Operator to Define a Database or Mailing List Containing up to 20 Fields of Information per Record. Report Generator Program Is Included with the Ability to Store up to 30 Standard Reports or Forms. Records Can Be Sorted & Used by Other Database Management & Word Processing Systems. UNI-DATE Allows Operator to Maintain Scheduling for up to 99 Staff Members & Major Resource Units.
Univair, Inc.

TITLE INDEX

OfficeWorks. Sue V. Stacy. 1988. *Items Included:* 1 disk & 42 page manual. *Customer Support:* Telephone support to purchasers, 90 day warranty.
  DOS, Windows, Apple ProDos. Apple II series, IBM & compatibles, Macintosh. disk $49.95 (ISBN 0-943646-54-5). *Addl. software required:* AppleWorks 3.0 Microsoft Works DOS or Macintosh any version. *Optimal configuration:* Any, so long as Works or AppleWorks is in use. *Networks supported:* Those that run Works.
  Includes Predesigned Forms for Ledgers, Journals, Registers, Statements, & Financial Reports. Program Helps Any Bookkeeper Use the Power of MICROSOFT WORKS, or APPLEWORKS on the Desktop Computer. Takes the Hassle Out of Designing & Layout of Your Own Applications. Also an Excellent Training Tool for Integrated Applications.
  K-12 Micromedia Publishing, Inc.

The Official Arts & Letters Handbook: Covers Versions 3.0 & 3.1. *Version:* Arts & Letters - 3.0 & 3.1. Michael Utvich. *Items Included:* One 5.25" disk. *Customer Support:* Phone number available for technical support, 212-492-9832; free disk replacement within 90 days of purchase.
  IBM PC & compatibles. disk $49.95 (ISBN 0-553-35243-1). *Addl. software required:* Arts & Letters.
  This Is the Official Book/Disk Guide to Arts & Letters Versions 3.0 & 3.1 for the PC. Includes: Step-by-Step Tutorials, Troubleshooting Reference, Explanations of Advanced Techniques. Disk Contains: Arts & Letters Clip Art Library (Worth over $125) & Valuable Ready-to-Use Templates. Michael Utvich Authored Bantam's "The Ventura Publisher Solutions Book".
  Bantam Bks., Inc.

Official Mr. Boston - New Edition. Nov. 1985. *Compatible Hardware:* Apple II, Macintosh; Atari ST; Commodore 64; IBM PC & compatibles. *Operating System(s) Required:* PC/MS-DOS 1.1. *Memory Required:* 128k.
  disk $29.95 (ISBN 0-935745-87-4, Order no.: ISB0).
  This Program Contains More Than 1200 Drink Recipes. Resize Any Recipe up to 999. Search for Recipes Using over 21 Fields, Plan Party Needs...a Collector's Classic.
  Concept Development Assocs., Inc.

The Official Software for GMAT Review. *Version:* 4.0. Jul. 1992. *Items Included:* Two sets of disks: 4 - 5.25" & 2 - 3.5"; user's manual.
  DOS 2.0 through 5.0. IBM PC, PC XT, PC AT, PS/2 or 100% compatibles (512k). disk $59.95 (ISBN 0-446-39443-2, Order no.: 299654). *Nonstandard peripherals required:* Hard disk with 3.6Mb of free space; CGA, EGA, VGA, Hercules Graphics or 100% compatible; graphics card & monitor.
  Includes Interactive Tutorials with Examples of Each Question Type, Plus Step-by-Step Explanations; One Actual Test (Different from Those in the GMAT Review Book), with On-Screen Timer & Automatic Scoring; Individualized Feedback on Your Test Performance Including: How Scores Are Calculated & What They Mean, an Analysis of Your Math & Verbal Scores, & How You Compare with Others Who Took This Test; & Two (2) Sets of Disks (Four 5.25" & Two 3.5") Plus User's Manual.
  Educational Testing Service.

Offline. *Version:* 4.0. Oct. 1994. *Items Included:* User's manual. Registration card. *Customer Support:* Unlimited support to registered users. Requires Mac Plus or higher, System 6.05 or higher. Macintosh. 3.5" disk $99.95.
  The Complete Disk Management System Isn't Just for Floppies Anymore! Catalogs Hard Drives, Suggest Cartridges, Even CD ROMS. Quick & Flexible Search Engine Lets You Find Any File on Any Disk, Even If It's not Mounted. Prints Disk Labels & Exports to Other Applications.
  SNA, Inc.

OGI Development System Linker. *Version:* 1.0. Aug. 1991. *Items Included:* Users manual. *Customer Support:* 30 day media replacement, 1 year maintenance.
  ProDos (128k). Apple IIe, IIc, IIgs, MAC LC with IIe Emulator, Laser 128. disk $35.00 (ISBN 0-918667-09-7). *Addl. software required:* OGI Pascal Development System V2. *Optimal configuration:* Additional disk drives.
  This Program Takes the Output from the OGI Pascal Development System & Creates ProDOS System Programs. These Programs May Be Run on Any Computer Running ProDOS Without the Need for OGI Pascal Development System. Unlimited Distribution of Programs Created with the System.
  On-Going Ideas.

OGI Fig-FORTH. *Version:* 1.2. Hal Clark. 1980. *Compatible Hardware:* Apple II+, IIe. *Operating System(s) Required:* Apple DOS 3.3. *Language(s):* Machine, FORTH. *Memory Required:* 48k. *Items Included:* Manual, installation guide & Fig-FORTH glossary. *Customer Support:* 30 day media replacement. $40.00 (ISBN 0-918667-03-8).
  Implementation of Fig-FORTH Includes Screens Disk with Many Utilities Including an 80 Column Full Screen Editor.
  On-Going Ideas.

OGI FORTH-79. *Version:* 1.1. Hal Clark. 1982. *Compatible Hardware:* Apple II+, IIe. *Operating System(s) Required:* Apple DOS 3.3. *Language(s):* Machine, FORTH. *Memory Required:* 48k. *Items Included:* Manual installation guide & FORTH-79 glossary. *Customer Support:* 30 day media replacement.
  disk $50.00 (ISBN 0-918667-05-4).
  Implementation of FORTH/79 Includes Screens Disk with Many Utilities Including 80-Column Full Screen Editor with Apple IIe, IIc Support.
  On-Going Ideas.

OGI Pascal Development System VI: Pascal Level 1. *Version:* 1.8. Hal Clark. 1984. *Compatible Hardware:* Apple II+, IIe, IIc, IIgs. *Operating System(s) Required:* Apple DOS 3.3. *Language(s):* Applesoft, Machine. *Memory Required:* 48k. *Items Included:* users manual. *Customer Support:* 30 day free media replacement. Upgradable to OGI Pascal Development System V2.
  single user $45.00 (ISBN 0-918667-01-1). classroom $175.00.
  Pascal Subset Includes Editor, Compiler, Debugger & Linker. Generates BRUN-able Programs.
  On-Going Ideas.

OGI Pascal Development System V2: OGI Pascal2. *Version:* 2.2. Jul. 1990. *Items Included:* ProDOS included on disk. Also includes users guide & language reference manual. *Customer Support:* 30 free media replacement. 1 year maintenance, new version upgrade for price difference.
  ProDOS (128K). Apple IIc, IIc Plus, enhanced IIe, IIgs MAC LC with 2E emulation or LASER 128 with 2 5.25" disk drives or 1 3.5 disk. single user $65.00 (ISBN 0-918667-08-9). *Networks supported:* AppleShare, Aristotle.
  classroom $275.00.
  network $375.00.
  Complete Package That Allows User to Create, Compile & Execute Programs Written in Pascal. Supports Boolean, Char & Integer Variable Types, Constants, Pascal Standard File I/O & Printing. Also Support Calls to ROM Routines & Memory Peeks & Pokes Allowing Access to Graphics & Other Features Not Directly Supported by This Compiler.
  On-Going Ideas.

OGI ProFORTH. *Version:* 1.1. Hal Clark. Mar. 1985. *Compatible Hardware:* Apple II+, IIe, IIc, IIgs, LASER 128. *Operating System(s) Required:* Apple ProDOS. *Language(s):* Machine, FORTH. *Memory Required:* 64k. *Items Included:* users manual. *Customer Support:* 30 day free media replacement.
  disk $60.00 (ISBN 0-918667-06-2).
  Implementation of FORTH-79 Interfaced to the Apple Pro-DOS Operating System. Includes Screens Disk with Many Utilities Including 80-Column Screen Editor & Apple Mouse Support.
  On-Going Ideas.

O'Hanlon Development Solution: Professional Programming Language. *Version:* 3.6C. Sep. 1991. *Items Included:* Hardcover manual, 3-ring, looseleaf. *Customer Support:* 90 day limited warranty; telephone support per fixed fee schedule.
  MS-DOS; CDOS; DR-DOS. IBM compatible (256k). $650.00 single user; $995.00 multiuser. *Networks supported:* Novell, Alloy, Banyan Vines, LANtastic, Network OS, PC-MOS, 3COM3 Plus, 10Net, Webnet.
  Complete Multi-User Application Development System to Create Error-Free, Sophisticated Multi-File Data Management Applications in 1/10th the Time. Features: Data Dictionary Control; Interactive Screen & Report Format Painting; Self-Prompting, English, Source Code Editor; Debugger; High-Speed; Non-Syntax Compiler; External Calls; Utility Toolkits; Multi-File Report Generator.
  O'Hanlon Computer Systems, Inc.

Ohio Jury Instructions on CD-ROM. *Items Included:* Spiral-bound documentation & quick reference card. *Customer Support:* Free on-site training, 30 day money-back guarantee, toll-free technical support, 1 yrs. free upkeep service (biannual updates).
  MS-DOS 3.3 or higher & Windows 3.1 or higher. 386 or higher (4Mb). CD-ROM disk $600.00 single user; Network: $300.00 each additional user. *Nonstandard peripherals required:* CD-ROM reader.
  Standard, Approved, & New Instructions, with Jury Instructions Committee Comments, General Instructions, Civil Instructions, Criminal Instructions. Full Text of Relevant Statutes. Full Text of Relevant Ohio Case Law. Edit, Save, Copy or Print All Information to Word Processing Applications. Save Time When Compiling & Evaluating Jury Instructions. Toll-Free Technical Support. Updated Biannually.
  Anderson Publishing Co.

Oids. *Items Included:* Manual, registration card Logo sticker. *Customer Support:* 90-day unlimited warranty.
  Atari ST (512k). 3.5" disk $34.95.
  Arcade/Adventure Game. Tasked with Saving an Exploited Race of Mechanical Beings, You Have to Pilot Your Fighter Craft Through a Gauntlet of Biocrete Defenses. Should You Deftly Avoid Those Deadly Subterranean Bases or Blow Them up, Flip on the Shields & Use Valuable Fuel or Try for a Pick-Up Later. When the Levels on the Disk Become Routine, You Can Switch on the Oids Editor & Design Your Own Levels & Problems. Your Custom Levels Can Then Be Traded with Your Friends.
  FTL Games.

Oil Accounting Package. *Compatible Hardware:* TRS-80 Model III, Model 4, Model 12, Model 16. *Operating System(s) Required:* TRSDOS II, LDOS. *Language(s):* Microsoft BASIC. $2485.00.
instructions $10.00.
Multiple Profit Center Accounting System Including General Ledger, Accounts Payable & Accounts Receivable Functions. Designed Especially for Small Independent Oil Companies. Keeps Information on up to 300 Wells with up to 50 Participants per Well.
Duane Bristow Computers, Inc.

Oil & Gas Accounting System Depletions Reporting. *Items Included:* Software, documentation. *Customer Support:* Telephone, modem, on-site.
PC-DOS, MS-DOS, Xenix (256k-512k). IBM, Compaq, Altos, NCR, AT&T, IBM-RT, others. $995.00-$1900.00.
Directly Interfaces to Enertech Oil & Gas Property Reporting Modules to Extract Depletion Information. Provides for Hand Working & Royalty Interest & Cost & Percentage Depletion Computations. Provides for Overhand Allocation by Five Different Methods.
Enertech Information Systems.

OIL/PACK: Bulk Oil & Gas Billing & Inventory. *Version:* 3.85. Ken Youngstrom. 1982. *Compatible Hardware:* IBM PC or compatibles. *Operating System(s) Required:* MS-DOS, Novell, PC-DOS, NETBIOS. *Language(s):* DBXL & Quicksilver. *Memory Required:* 640k. *General Requirements:* Hard disk, Epson-compatible printer. *Items Included:* Software, documentation. *Customer Support:* Toll free technical support.
$3995.00.
Real-Time Interactive Inventory & AR. Month-End, Quarterly, & Annual Reports. Prices to One Thousandth of a Cent & Changes Amounts While Processing Invoice. Scans by Account Number, Part Number or Description, or Company Name. Tracks Inventory Transactions, MSDS Issues, etc. & Reports Costs. Novell Compatible.
Alpine Data, Inc.

Oil Purchasing, Oil Accounting & Oil Well Reports to Interest Holders. Duane Bristow. *Compatible Hardware:* TRS-80 Model II, Model III. *Operating System(s) Required:* TRSDOS. *Language(s):* BASIC.
contact publisher for price.
Helps Small Oil Companies to Keep Accounts & to Write Financial Reports to Interest Holders.
Duane Bristow Computers, Inc.

Oil Tycoon. *Compatible Hardware:* Apple, TRS-80.
contact publisher for price.
Instant Software, Inc.

Oil Well Blowout. *Compatible Hardware:* Apple Macintosh. *Memory Required:* 512k.
3.5" disk $4500.00.
Relief Well Proposal Program.
Houston Directional Software.

Oil Well Database. Duane Bristow. *Compatible Hardware:* TRS-80 Model III with hard disk system. *Operating System(s) Required:* TRSDOS. *Language(s):* BASIC. *Memory Required:* 48k.
disk $995.00.
Keeps Data From Well Logs in a Database. Sorts by Location, Initial Production, Producing Formation, etc.
Duane Bristow Computers, Inc.

Oil Well Directional Package. *Compatible Hardware:* Apple Macintosh.
Survey Calculation Program. 3.5" disk $2500.00.
Proposal Program. 3.5" disk $4500.00.
Complete Directional Well Package. 3.5" disk $18,000.00.
Oil Well Planning & Drilling.
Houston Directional Software.

Oil Well Screen Plot. *Compatible Hardware:* Apple Macintosh.
3.5" disk $2000.00.
Scaled Plan & Section Views of Well Paths.
Houston Directional Software.

Oil's Well. *Compatible Hardware:* Apple; Atari; Commodore 64; IBM PC, PCjr. *Memory Required:* 48k.
disk $14.95.
Arcade Game in Which Player Drills Underground to Find Oil Deposits While Avoiding Nasty Creatures.
Sierra On-Line, Inc.

OKARA: CP/M Shell Programs. Kiai Systems. Jan. 1982. *Operating System(s) Required:* CP/M-80. *Memory Required:* 48k.
disk $39.95, 40 TPI (ISBN 0-923875-44-1).
disk $39.95, 80 TPI (ISBN 0-923875-45-X).
8" disk $39.95 (ISBN 0-923875-43-3).
Suite of Small Programs That Jointly & Modularly Constitute a Programmable User Interface for CP/M. Also a Tool for Creating Many Shells.
Elliam Assocs.

OKyto. *Version:* 1.02. *Customer Support:* Customer support available for registered users.
Macintosh Plus or higher. $39.95.
Mac-to-Mac File Transfer Program.
The FreeSoft Co.

Old Yeller. Apr. 1996.
School ver.. System 7.1 or higher. Macintosh (4Mb). 3.5" disk contact publisher for price (ISBN 1-57204-240-0). *Nonstandard peripherals required:* 256 color monitor, hard drive, printer.
Lab pack. System 7.1 or higher. Macintosh (4Mb). 3.5" disk Contact publisher for price (ISBN 1-57204-216-8). *Nonstandard peripherals required:* 256 color monitor, hard drive, printer.
Site license. System 7.1 or higher. Macintosh (4Mb). 3.5" disk contact publisher for price (ISBN 1-57204-241-9). *Nonstandard peripherals required:* 256 color monitor, hard drive, printer.
School ver.. Windows 3.1 or higher. IBM/Tandy & 100% compatibles (4Mb). disk contact publisher for price (ISBN 1-57204-217-6). *Nonstandard peripherals required:* VGA or SVGA 640 x 480 resolution (256), mouse, hard drive, sound device.
Lab pack. Windows 3.1 or higher. IBM/Tandy & 100% compatibles (4Mb). disk contact publisher for price (ISBN 1-57204-242-7). *Nonstandard peripherals required:* VGA or SVGA 640 x 480 resolution (256), mouse, hard drive, sound device.
Site license. Windows 3.1 or higher. IBM/Tandy & 100% compatibles (4Mb). disk contact publisher for price (ISBN 1-57204-218-4). *Nonstandard peripherals required:* VGA or SVGA 640 x 480 resolution, (256), mouse, hard drive, sound device.
This companion for young adult literature is ideal for students who don't know how to start that book report, or give that needed summary. Gentle prompts thoughout the guide section of the program include Warm-up Connections, Thinking about Plot, Quoting & Noting, Keeping a Journal, If I Were _____' Responding to Questions, Using Quotations, Taking a Personal View, Write to Others, & Write a Sequel.
Lawrence Productions, Inc.

The Olde Gin Parlour (Gin Rummy). *Compatible Hardware:* Apple II+ with Applesoft BASIC, Commodore 64, IBM. *Memory Required:* Apple & Commodore 48k, IBM 128k.
disk $19.95.
One Player Against the Computer.
Dynacomp, Inc.

Oldies but Goodies Games I. *Compatible Hardware:* TI-99/4A.
disk or cassette - contact publisher for price.
Contains 5 Games: Word Scrabble, Number Scrabble, Tic-Tac-Toe, Biorhythm & FactorFoe. For 1 or 2 Players.
Texas Instruments, Personal Productivit.

Oldies but Goodies Games II. *Compatible Hardware:* TI-99/4A.
disk or cassette - contact publisher for price.
Second in a Series of Game Collections. Includes Hammurabi, Hidden Pairs, Peg Tump, 3D Tic-Tac-Toe & Word Safari.
Texas Instruments, Personal Productivit.

OldSlavonic. *Version:* 4.0. Dec. 1994. *Items Included:* User's manual; keyboard layout chart; keycap sticker sheet. *Customer Support:* Free telephone support, defective disks replaced free.
Macintosh. Macintosh (1Mb). 3.5" disk $99.95. *Addl. software required:* Any word processor.
5 Professional-Quality, Hinted, Type-1 & TrueType Slavonic Fonts - Old SlavonicLS, SlavonicLS, BookSlavonic, ChurchSlavonicLS, & SlavonicExtras - Each with Polished Bitmaps in 10, 12, 14, 18, & 24-Point Sizes. Each Font Contains Abbreviation Characters. The Fonts Can Be Used with the Regular U.S., System-7, Transliterated Keyboard. Also Includes a Remapped Transliterated Keyboard for Even Greater Ease of Use. Prints All Sizes. Specify If for System 6.
Linguist's Software, Inc.

OldSlavonic for Windows. *Version:* 2.0. Jan. 1995. *Items Included:* User's manual; keyboard layout chart; keycap sticker sheet. *Customer Support:* Free telephone support, defective disks replaced free.
Windows. IBM or compatibles (4Mb). disk $99.95. *Addl. software required:* MS Windows 3.1X or ATM.
Professional-Quality, Hinted, Scalable, Times-Style Fonts in Both TrueType & Type 1 Formats: OldSlavonicLS, SlavonicLS, BookSlavonic, ChurchSlavonicLS, & SlavonicExtras. For All Windows 3.1-Compatible Applications. Type 1 Works with ATM & Windows 3.X; Also Works with OS/2 & AutoCAD R.13. Includes Keyboard Switcher Utility Providing Four Characters per Key in Windows Applications. Fonts Alone Work in Word 6 for DOS, WordPerfect 6.0b for DOS or Newer, AutoCAD R.12 & 13; OS/2; NeXT (Available by Request). WordPerfect for Windows 6.0 Users Must Upgrade to 6.0a or Newer to Type Overstrikes. These Fonts Contain All Characters for Typing Old & Church Slavonic. Each Font Also Contains Characters for Abbreviations & Contractions.
Linguist's Software, Inc.

Ole' BASIC: On-Line Encyclopedia. May 1985. *Compatible Hardware:* IBM PC & true compatibles. *Operating System(s) Required:* PC-DOS/MS-DOS 2.X, 3.0. *Language(s):* C. *Memory Required:* 256k. *General Requirements:* 2 disk drives, CGA card.
disk $69.95.
Includes All Commands & Functions for Programming in Microsoft BASIC. The BASIC Programmer Can Toggle from Program to the OLE' Reference Set to Get Immediate Answers on Syntax, Sub-Routines, & Other Programming Rules. The Escape Key Returns the Programmer

to the Same Line of Code. Allows the Programmer to Code in BASIC Without Constant Reference to Their Manual.
HyperGraphics Corp.

Ole' DOS: On-Line Encyclopedia. Mar. 1985. *Compatible Hardware:* IBM PC & true compatibles. *Operating System(s) Required:* PC-DOS/MS-DOS 2.X, 3.0. *Language(s):* C. *Memory Required:* 256k. *General Requirements:* 2 disk drives, CGA card.
disk $69.95.
Covers PC-DOS/MS-DOS Commands & Functions, Allowing the Novice & Experienced PC User Alike to Operate in DOS Without a Manual.
HyperGraphics Corp.

OMD Management Information System. *Compatible Hardware:* IBM PC, Unisys, AT&T, Texas Instruments. *Operating System(s) Required:* DNOS, UNIX, ZENIX. *Memory Required:* 2000k. *Items Included:* Classroom education, implementation plan. *Customer Support:* Telephone & on-site assistance, software update service.
contact publisher for price.
Distribution System; Includes Capability for Serialized Inventory Control, Service Dispatch & Management, & Sales Prospect Management.
OMD.

Omni Accounts Receivable-Plus. Version: 4.7. Sep. 1995. *Compatible Hardware:* IBM PC. *Operating System(s) Required:* DOS 2.1. *Language(s):* C (source code included). *Memory Required:* 128k. *General Requirements:* 2 disk drives.
disk $300.00.
manual $25.00.
Stand-Alone System Designed to Provide for over 700 Active Customers & up to 700 Transactions on Double Density Disk. Reports Generated Include: Current Transactions Listing &/or Summary, Updated Accounts Receivable, Billing Statements, Client Name & Number in Numerical or Alphabetical Order, Client Name & Address Listing, & Inactive Name Records Listing. Transactions Can Be Transferred to Archive File of up to 3100 Records. Inactive Client Records Can Be Transferred to Inactive & Name & Address File of 1000 Records. Billing Systems Is Normally Balance-Forward, but with Combination of Archive Files, Transactions Can Be Recalled for Audit Purposes & Item Billing. Statements Are Printed on Forms That Can Be Purchased in One to Five Parts with No Carbon Paper Required.
Omni Software Systems, Inc. (Indiana).

Omni-Fit. *Items Included:* Bound manual. *Customer Support:* Free hotline - no time limit; 30 day limited warranty; updates are $5/disk plus S&H. MS-DOS. IBM & compatibles (256k). disk $49.95.
Provides the Most Common Curve Forms As Menu-Selectable Options (Linear Regression, Polynomial Exact Fit, Polynomial Least Squares Fit to Order 8, Exponential, Power Curve, Cubic Spline Between Neighboring Points). Can Also Fit Data to Forms Defined by the User.
Dynacomp, Inc.

Omni-Med. *Compatible Hardware:* Apple Macintosh Plus. *General Requirements:* Hard disk; ImageWriter or LaserWriter, Omni 3 Plus.
single user $2495.00.
multiuser $3495.00 & up.
limited working demo $100.00.
Medical Management.
Broderbund Software, Inc.

OMNI-PLAY Basketball. Ed Ringler. May 1989. *Items Included:* manual, catalog, registration card, reference card. *Customer Support:* Always free over the phone; disks replaced free for first 30 days & for $15.00 after 30 days.
Commodore 64/128. disk $19.95.
Commodore Amiga 500, 1000, 2000. 3.5" disk $29.95.
IBM PC & compatibles. 3.5" or 5.25" disk $29.95.
Fast-Paced Hoops Action with Full 5-On-5 Game Play. Games Provide Challenging Play Combined with First-Rate Graphics & Sound. Full League Stats Included.
SportTime Computer Software.

OMNI-PLAY Horse Racing. Ed Ringler. May 1989. *Items Included:* manual, catalog, registration card, reference card. *Customer Support:* Always free over the phone; disks replaced free for first 30 days & for $15.00 after 30 days.
Commodore 64, 128. disk $19.95.
Commodore Amiga 500, 1000, 2000. 3.5" disk $29.95.
IBM PC & compatibles. 3.5" or 5.25" disk $29.95.
Fast-Paced Version of the Sport of Kings with Plenty of Stats. Up to 4 Players Can Try to Beat the Computer & Predict the Winners in a Series of Races.
SportTime Computer Software.

Omnibase. *Customer Support:* 800-929-8117 (customer service).
MS-DOS. Apple II. disk $79.99 (ISBN 0-87007-078-9).
Relational Database Management System with all the Features of More Expensive Programs.
SourceView Software International.

OmniBooks. *Compatible Hardware:* Apple Macintosh 512KE. *Memory Required:* 512k. *General Requirements:* 2 800k disk drives or hard disk; Omnis 3 Plus or Runtime. *Customer Support:* Free 60 day phone support from receipt of registration card.
3.5" disk $139.95.
With runtime disk. 3.5" disk $169.95.
Accounts Receivable, Accounts Payable, General Ledger.
Janac Enterprises.

OmniCalc. *Customer Support:* 800-929-8117 (customer service).
MS-DOS. Apple II. disk $79.99 (ISBN 0-87007-859-3).
Uses All of the Same Commands as VisiCalc & Most of Lotus 1-2-3. Special Disk Based Memory Usage Allows Expansion of Spreadsheets Larger Than Available RAM.
SourceView Software International.

OmniCat. Version: 3.0.2. Mar. 1990. *Items Included:* Manual, DOS. *Customer Support:* 24-hour unlimited software support included for first 12 months. $490.00 per year after 12 months. 2 days training at one of 6 training centers - $500.00.
MS-DOS or IBM PC-DOS 3.2 or higher. IBM or compatible (640k). disk full software $6494.00. *Nonstandard peripherals required:* 20Mb fixed disk, 1 floppy drive, C.A.T. shorthand writer.
disk edit software $3495.00.
Computer-Assisted-Transcription Software for Court/Convention Reporters Translates into English Text Stenographic Notes of Court, Convention, Deposition Verbatim Proceedings. Notes Are Written on a Computerized C.A.T. Shorthand Machine to a 3.5" Floppy Disk, Then Translated by Matching Steno Notes to Personalized English Dictionary Via C.A.T. Software for Editing/Printing Via Built-In Word Processor.
Stenograph Corp.

Omnicoder: ICD-9-CM code finder. Version: 3.0. G. B. Cook. Apr. 1992. *Compatible Hardware:* IBM PC. *Operating System(s) Required:* PC-DOS. *Language(s):* Quicksilver. *Memory Required:* 640k. *Customer Support:* Toll free telephone support.
disk $295.00.
Assists Medical Clerical Staff in Finding ICD-9-CM Codes & Non Surgical CPT Codes for over 5000 Frequently Encountered Disease As Required for Payment Information from All Health Insurance Carriers. Permits Entry of Additional Diagnoses & Codes Should the Need Arise.
SRC Systems, Inc.

OmniFiler. *Customer Support:* 800-929-8117 (customer service).
MS-DOS. Apple II. disk $49.99 (ISBN 0-87007-826-7).
A Simple Menu Oriented Filing System. Allows 50 Files of 9 Fields with up to 75 Characters. File Can Be Searched for Category Matches, Sorted & Information Printed.
SourceView Software International.

Omnilaw: Series 500 to 2000. *Compatible Hardware:* IBM PC, PS/2, System/36, System/36 PC; AS/400.
contact publisher for price.
Ties the Automation of the Law Firm Together. Provides Linkages & Instructions to Use Report Writers & Spreadsheets with Manac Data. Time & Disbursements Can Be Entered on a Remote PC & Later Transferred to Client Files.
Manac-Prentice Hall Software, Inc.

OmniMailer. *Compatible Hardware:* Apple Macintosh. *Memory Required:* 512k. *General Requirements:* External disk drive; ImageWriter; Omnis 3 Plus or Runtime. *Customer Support:* Free 60 day phone support.
3.5" disk $54.95.
Runtime disk. 3.5" disk $84.95.
Mailing List Manager.
Janac Enterprises.

OmniPage. *Compatible Hardware:* Apple Macintosh II or SE. *Memory Required:* 4000k. *General Requirements:* Scanner.
3.5" disk $795.00.
Allows Scanners to Recognize a Variety of Pages with a Mixture of Images & Text on a Page. Allows the User to Save Text from Scanned Pages in MacWrite or ASCII Formats, & to Search Text, Insert/Delete Text Blocks & Crop, Copy & Paste Images. Automates Form Processing.
Caere Corp.

OmniPATH Gateway. Version: 2.0a. Aug. 1985. *Compatible Hardware:* IBM PC & compatibles. *Operating System(s) Required:* MS-DOS, PC-DOS. *Memory Required:* 256k. *General Requirements:* SNA/3270 or SNA 3770.
SNA/3270. disk 8 sessions $2595.00.
SNA/3270. disk 16 sessions $3595.00.
SNA/3270. disk 32 sessions $4595.00.
SNA/3770. disk 8 sessions $2290.00.
Allows Networked IBM PCs & Compatibles to Communicate with a Remote IBM Host Using a Single Modem & Communications Line. Supports SNA & BSC Communications over Leased, Dial-Up or Dedicated Lines. Includes FtPATH, a Bidirectional File Transfer Package for Text & Binary Data.
ICOT Corp.

OmniPATH PC. Version: 3.1b for SNA/3270, 1.6d for SNA/3770, 2.2b for BSC/3270, 1.7a for BSC/3780/2780. 1983. *Compatible Hardware:* IBM PC & compatibles. *Operating System(s) Required:* MS-DOS, PC-DOS. *Memory Required:* 256k. *General Requirements:*

SNA/3270, SNA 3770, BSC/3270, or BSC/3780/2780.
disk $890.00.
Communications Product That Allows IBM & Compatible Personal Computers to Communicate with a Remote IBM Host over Leased, Dial-Up or Dedicated Lines Using SNA/SDLC & BSC Protocols. Includes FtPATH, a Bidirectional File Transfer Package for Text & Binary Data.
ICOT Corp.

OmniPay. *Compatible Hardware:* Apple Macintosh. *Memory Required:* 512k. *General Requirements:* External disk drive; ImageWriter; Omnis 3 Plus or Runtime.
3.5" disk $79.95.
With runtime disk. 3.5" disk $109.95.
Payroll Program.
Janac Enterprises.

Omnis II. *Compatible Hardware:* Apple IIe, Macintosh, Macintosh XL, Macintosh Plus. *Memory Required:* Apple IIe 128k, Macintosh 512k.
3.5" disk Macintosh single-user $275.00.
disk Apple IIe single-user $295.00.
$590.00-$1180.00 5 to 10 users with Corvus Omninet.
File Manager Incorporating Many of the Features of OMNIS 3, Without the Complexity of Relational Capability or Programmability. OMINS 2 Databases Can Be Directly Read & Enhanced with OMNIS 3. Can Be Upgraded to OMNIS 3 for the Difference in Retail Price.
Blyth Software, Inc.

Omnis III. *Compatible Hardware:* Apple IIe, Macintosh, Macintosh XL, Macintosh Plus; IBM PC. *Memory Required:* Apple IIe 128k, IBM 256k, Macintosh 512k. *General Requirements:* 3 disk drives or hard disk & Apple Pascal for Apple; hard disk recommended.
3.5" disk Macintosh single-user $275.00.
$990.00-$2995.00 Macintosh multi-user from 5 to 64 users using Corvus Omninet.
disk Apple IIe single user $445.00.
$890.00-$1780.00 Apple IIe multi-user from 5 to 20 users using Corvus Omninet.
disk IBM single-user $495.00.
runtime disks avail.
Relational Data Base That Can Be Used to Create Business Data Base & Accounting Applications. The Data Base Can Be up to 64Mb in Size with No Limit in the Number of Records. Provides 9 Levels Password Protection. Information Can Be Changed with Other Applications Using DIF, SILK, & Text File Formats. The Multi-User Version Will Operate with Corvus OmniDrive, OmniNet, the 3Com Fileserver with EtherMac or the Hyperdrive with HyperNet. Not Copy-Protected.
Blyth Software, Inc.

Omnis III Plus. *Version:* 3.3. *Compatible Hardware:* Apple II, II+, III, Macintosh; Apricot; IBM PC, PC XT, PC AT & compatibles. *Operating System(s) Required:* MAC, MAC LAN. *Memory Required:* Apple 64k; IBM, Apricot 128k; Macintosh 512k.
Single User. 3.5" disk $575.00.
Database Management System Provides Structured File Definition, Automatic Indexing, Built-In Editor, & Run-Time Version Available. Features 120 Fields per Record; 79 Characters in Field; 9,480 Characters in Record; 12 Indexes per File, & 12 Active Indexes. Includes 84 Commands; 21 Functions; 12,000 Lines Per Command File; & up to 7,274 Variables. Data-Import Capabilities Consist of Comma-Delimited ASCII, DIF, DBF, SYLK, Tab-Delimited ASCII, One Field per Line; Data-Export Capabilities Consist of Comma-Delimited ASCII, DIF, SYLK, Tab-Delimited ASCII, One Field per Line, & Chart Graphics. Supports BASIC, Pascal, C, COBOL, FORTRAN & Assembler Languages.
Blyth Software, Inc.

Omnis Quartz. *Compatible Hardware:* IBM PC & compatibles.
$575.00 & up.
Free-Form, Command or Menu-Driven Database-Management System Featuring Automatic Indexing & Split/Merge Files. Offers a Maximum of 120 Fields per Record, 2400 Characters per Field, Unlimited Records per File, 30,000 Characters per Record, 12 Indexes per File, 144 Active Indexes & up to 9 Records Sorted. Allows User to Revise Field Descriptions at Will.
Blyth Software, Inc.

Omnis Quartz: Windows Version. *Operating System(s) Required:* Windows, PC LAN.
Single User. disk $795.00.
Database Management System Provides Structured File Definition, Automatic Indexing, Built-In Editor, & Run-Time Version Available. Features 120 Fields per Record; 2,400 Characters in Field; 24,000 Characters in Record; 12 Indexes per File, & 12 Active Indexes. Offers 184 Commands; 27 Functions; 12,000 Lines per Command File & up to 7,274 Variables. Includes Comma-Delimited ASCII, DIF, DBF, SYLK, WKS, Tab-Delimited ASCII, One Field per Line in Data-Import/Export Capabilities.
Blyth Software, Inc.

Omnis V.
Macintosh Plus or higher (1Mb). $695.00.
additional mulit-user pack $145.00.
Relational &/or Hierarchical Database Program Designed to Utilize the Graphical Interface, Enhance Memory & Storage & Color Capabilities of Both Macintosh & IBM PS/2 Hardware. A Comprehensive Program for Developing Business Data-Management Applications. Program Also Includes Omnis Express to Allow User to Produce Outline Requirements of an Application & with a Click of the Start Button, It Automatically Builds the Omnis 5 Application.
Blyth Software, Inc.

Omnitrax. *Compatible Hardware:* Apple Macintosh. *Memory Required:* 512k, recommended 1000k. *General Requirements:* External disk drive or hard disk; printer.
Single user runtime system (includes bar-code reader equipment, bar-code printing program, updates & modem support service). 3.5" disk $2795.00.
Video Store Business Management, Development, Accounting.
Essex Systems.

OmniTrend's Universe. *Version:* 1.4. Dec. 1983. *Compatible Hardware:* Apple, Atari, IBM. *Operating System(s) Required:* MS-DOS 2.X. *Memory Required:* Atari & Apple 48k; IBM 192k.
Atari. disk $49.95 (ISBN 0-932549-00-4, Order no.: OU-AT-1).
IBM. disk $49.95 ea. (ISBN 0-932549-02-0, Order no.: OU-MS-1).
Apple. (ISBN 0-932549-03-9, Order no.: OU-AP-1).
product guide accessory $14.95 (ISBN 0-932549-01-2, Order no.: OU-AA-1).
Adventure/Strategy Game for 1 Player.
Omnitrend Software, Inc.

OmniTrend's Universe II. *Version:* 1.0-1.3. Oct. 1985. *Compatible Hardware:* Apple II with 2 disk drives, Macintosh; Atari; IBM. *Operating System(s) Required:* MS-DOS 2.X. *Memory Required:* Apple 128k, Atari & IBM 256k, Macintosh 512k.
disk $49.95 ea., incl. manual.
Atari. (ISBN 0-932549-07-1, Order no.: U2-AT-1).
IBM. (ISBN 0-932549-05-5, Order no.: U2-MS-1).
Macintosh. (ISBN 0-932549-04-7, Order no.: U2-MA-1).
Apple II. (ISBN 0-932549-06-3, Order no.: U2-AP-1).
Adventure/Strategy Game for One Player.
Omnitrend Software, Inc.

OmniTrend's Universe III. Jul. 1989. *Customer Support:* 90 day media warranty.
MS-DOS 3.0 or higher (512k). IBM PC. $49.95 (ISBN 0-932549-16-0, Order no.: U3-MS-1). *Nonstandard peripherals required:* CGA or EGA. *Optimal configuration:* Mouse optional.
AmigaDos (512k). $49.95 (ISBN 0-932549-17-9, Order no.: UC-AM-1).
TOS (512k). Atari ST. $49.95 (ISBN 0-932549-18-7, Order no.: U3-ST-1).
Graphics Adventure Game. 3rd in the Universe Series.
OmniTrend Software, Inc.

OmniVet. *Compatible Hardware:* Apple Macintosh 512KE. *General Requirements:* Hard disk; ImageWriter or LaserWriter.
$795.00 includes Runtime Omnis 3 Plus.
demo disk $20.00.
Veterinary Management System.
Commonwealth Veterinary Consultants.

Omniview. *Compatible Hardware:* IBM PC & compatibles, PS/2, HP 3000. *Memory Required:* 640k. *General Requirements:* Lotus 1-2-3 release 2/2.01; hard disk, Image database for HP computer.
contact publisher for price.
Provides a Direct Link from an HP Database to Lotus 1-2-3. Gives Users the Ability to Instantly Select Subsets of Data, Summarize That Data, & Download the Result into a Spreadsheet Cell for Lotus 1-2-3 Manipulation. Program Is Written As a Lotus Add-In Using the Lotus Syntax & Functions, & Is Compatible with the Cognos, Rapid, QDD & QDDR Dictionaries So That Users from Both the PC & HP Environments Can Be Immediately Productive.
Dynamic Information Systems Corp. (DISC).

OmniWriter & OmniSpeller. *Customer Support:* 800-929-8117 (customer service).
MS-DOS. Commodore 64. disk $59.99 (ISBN 0-87007-847-X).
The Premier Word Processing Packages for the Commodore 64 Computer. Easily Create, Edit, & Polish Any Written Document. Reduces the Tedium of Rewriting. Contains a 30,000 Word Dictionary. The Program Will Examine for Spelling Accuracy. All Misspelled Words Are Highlighted & Can Be Easily Identified & Corrected. Users Can Add Words to the Dictionary, or Even Create Your Own Dictionary. A Program for Writers of All Ages. Formats Text on the Screen As It Will Print, & Will Merge with Multiplan Documents.
SourceView Software International.

On Balance. David Eisler. *Compatible Hardware:* Apple IIe, IIc, IIgs. *Memory Required:* 128k. *General Requirements:* Apple IIe requires extended 80-column card.
disk $99.95 (Order no.: APDSK-72).
Enables Users to Record & Reconcile Bank & Credit Card Transactions, As Well As to Create & Track Budgets, Print Custom Reports, or Print Checks. May Record up to 800 Transactions per Month with the Ability to "Flag" Certain Items Such As Tax-Deductible Expenses. Exports to AppleWorks, Providing Spreadsheet Capability. Offers Pop-Up Calculator & Note Pad. Supports 5-1/4" & 3-1/2" Disks. Not Copy Protected.
Broderbund Software, Inc.

TITLE INDEX

On Command: Writing a UNIX-Like Shell for MS-DOS. Allen Holub. *Operating System(s) Required:* MS-DOS.
book & disk $39.95 (ISBN 0-934375-29-1).
Shows How to Write a UNIX-Like Shell for MS-DOS, with Techniques Applicable to Most Other Programming Projects. The Book & Disk Include a Description & Working Version of the Shell, Complete C Source Code, a Discussion of Low-Level MS-DOS Interfacing, & Examples of C Programming at the System Level. The Program & All C Source Code Are on Disk.
M & T Bks.

On Cue II. *Version:* 2.0. *Compatible Hardware:* Apple Macintosh. *Customer Support:* Warranty for replacement of defective product, free technical support & upgrade information for registered users.
3.5" disk $99.95.
An Easy-to-Use File Launching Utility That Allows the User to Select Applications & Documents with a Single Click of the Mouse Without Accessing the Finder. Drag the Mouse on the On Cue Icon, Pull Down the Menu & Immediately Select the Application or Document Needed. This Process Eliminates "Window Build-Up" & Increases Efficiency.
ICOM Simulations, Inc.

On Family Life. GNC. Sep. 1992. *Items Included:* User manual.
DOS 3.0 or higher. IBM PC & compatibles (640k). disk $300.00. *Optimal configuration:* DOS PC with 640k RAM - 20Mb hard disk & printer.
Personal Development Software Package Designed to Interest Students in Understanding Importance of Personal Goals & to Enhance Their Abilities in the Subject. Consisting of Five Themes (Family, Life, Jobs, Kids & Friends) & Written at the Sixth Grade Level, "On Family Life" Utilizes a Writing-to-Learn Approach to Focus on the Subject Matter. The Approach Also Allows Students to Adjust Their Pace for Maximum Benefit.
Motivational Developers.

On-Hand Inventory. Charles E. Aylworth. Nov. 1984. *Compatible Hardware:* IBM PC & compatibles. *Operating System(s) Required:* PC-DOS/MS-DOS 2.0 or higher. *Language(s):* Pascal. *Memory Required:* 256k. *General Requirements:* 2 disk drives or hard disk, printer; Kitchen Help program.
disk $300.00 (ISBN 0-937973-03-3).
Prepares Worksheets & Hand Inventory Price Extentions.
Bottom Line Software.

On-Line Catalog Expanded. *Version:* 2.0a. 1995. *Items Included:* Complete illustrated instructions. *Customer Support:* Unlimited telephone support no charge; free replacement of damaged disks.
MS-DOS. IBM PC, XT, AT, PS/2 & compatibles (512k). disk $459.00. *Networks supported:* Novell etc. & 869.
Network version $899.00.
$479.00 Windows version.
$899.00 Windows Network version.
This Newest Version of ON-LINE CATALOG PLUS Does Not Print Catalog Cards. By Eliminating the Constraints Caused by Printing 3 x 5 Catalog Cards We Have Been Able to Provide Many More Valuable Features for Library Patrons. The Following Is a List of the Features That Have Been Added to ON-LINE CATALOG to Produce ON-LINE CATALOG EXPANDED: Searches by up to Three Joint Authors, & up to 10 Subjects; Searches by Title & Call Number; Greatly Expanded Length of Subject Fields; Expanded Title & Annotation Fields; Prints to Laser Printer.
Right On Programs.

On-Line Catalog with Carder. 1995. *Items Included:* Complete illustrated instructions. *Customer Support:* 1 year free replacement of damaged disks, free unlimited telephone customer support.
MS-DOS. IBM-PC, XT, AT, PS-2 or compatible (512k). disk $459.00 (ISBN 1-55812-082-3). *Addl. software required:* None.
Network version $899.00.
$479.00 Windows version.
$899.00 Windows Network version.
Outstanding On-Line Catalog. Easy to Learn & Use, Affordable & Friendly. Follow the On-Screen Prompts & Enter Books. Computer Will Format. Search & Bring a Perfect Catalog Card to the Screen. Print Catlaog Cards (AACR II Format) to the Screen or Printer. Print a Complete Set, Just Shelf List Cards or No Cards at All. Easy for Patrons to Use & Librarians to Manage.
Right On Programs.

On-Line Help Utility. *Version:* 2.1. PC Consulting. 1984. *Compatible Hardware:* IBM PC, PC XT, PC AT, PCjr & compatibles. *Operating System(s) Required:* PC-DOS 2.0, 2.1. *Memory Required:* 64k.
disk $39.00.
disk with 5 add'l. utilities $59.95.
Display Instructions on How to Use PC-DOS 2.00/2.1 Commands & Features along with Examples. Also Available Bundled with 5 Additional Practical Utilities As Time Savers.
DataSource Publishing Co.

On Schedule. *Version:* 2.0. Irwin Nestler. 1984-88. *Compatible Hardware:* Apple Macintosh; IBM PC & compatibles. *Operating System(s) Required:* MS-DOS Windows, Macintosh. *Language(s):* Template (source code included). *Memory Required:* IBM & Macintosh 4000k. *General Requirements:* Spreadsheet program, printer, IBM Lotus 1-2-3 or MS-Excel; MAC: MS-Excel. *Items Included:* Manual. *Customer Support:* (203) 838-2670, free.
disk $195.00.
Real Estate & Construction Analysis Program Designed Specifically for Developers & Lenders. To Forecast Cash Flow, Construction, & Sales Progress of Condominium or Subdivision Projects. Prepares Schedules That Demonstrate the Monthly Progress of Units Through Construction, Sale, & Settlement; Shows How Development Loan Will Be Drawn down, Utilized, & Repaid.
RealData, Inc.

On-Side. Apr. 1986. *Items Included:* Disk, printed manual. *Customer Support:* One year free technical support.
IBM & compatibles (256k). disk $19.95.
  Nonstandard peripherals required: IBM or Epson graphics printer.
Sideways Printing Program. Any ASCII Text File May Be Printed Sideways on an IBM or Epson Graphics Printer. Includes Seven Fonts Which May Be Stretched to Over 25 Sizes Each. Custom Fonts May Also Be Created.
Expressware Corp.

On-Site Management. *Customer Support:* 90 days free.
IBM 386 & compatibles, PS/2, OS/2. Contact vendor for price.
Handles Commercial, Residential, & Mixed-Use Properties, with a Five-Property Limit. The System Gives Managers Control over Their Property's Accounting & Overall Tenant Management. Tenant Receivables Can Be Processed Right at the Property Site, Enabling the Home Office to Focus on Financial Operations. The Modules Allow Site Personnel to Process All Functions of Tenant Receivables, Including Commercial Escalations & Reconciliations. Tenant Move-In & Move-Outs Can Be Done Quickly & Efficiently, Including Deposit Management & Proration of Last Month's Charges. SiteLink Will Transfer Information from the Site to Timberline's Property Management Gold Files Located at the Home Office.
Timberline Software Corp.

On-Site Residential. *Items Included:* Manual. *Customer Support:* 90 days free.
IBM 386 & compatibles, PS/2. Contact vendor for price.
Developed for Residential Managers with over 100 Units. The System Provides Control over Property's Accounting & Overall Tenant Management. Tenant Receivables Can Be Processed Right at the Property Site, Enabling the Home Office to Focus on Financial Operations. The Module Lets Site Personnel Process All Functions of Tenant Receivables. Tenant Move-In & Move-Outs Can Be Done Quickly & Efficiently, Including Deposit Management & Proration of First & Last Months' Charges. SiteLink Will Transfer Information from the Site to Timberline's Property Management Gold Files Located at the Home Office.
Timberline Software Corp.

ON-TARGET Job Shop Management. *Version:* 2.60. Mar. 1993. *Compatible Hardware:* IBM PC & compatibles; UNIX based minis, Bull, H-P, NEC, Prime, UNISYS, DEC VAX, IBM RISC 6000. *Operating System(s) Required:* DOS/MS-DOS, UNIX, VMS or IBM AIX. *Language(s):* DataFlex. *Memory Required:* 512k. *Items Included:* SQL Report Generator, Menu & Security Management, 4GL Relational Database Management. Interfaces to Lotus, WordPerfect, dBASE, etc. *Customer Support:* Includes updates & telephone support; annual contract 12-14%.
$4850.00-$49,000.00.
Used by Contract Machine Shops. Provides Estimating Bidding, Order Entry, Job Scheduling, Work Center Loading & Scheduling, Finite & Infinite Machine Loading, Capacity Planning, Job Status, Job Costing, Resource Management & Performance Analysis, Purchasing, Multi-Level Bills of Material/Requirements Planning, Inventory Management, Tooling Management & General Accounting. These Integrated Application Modules Are Available Independently. Barcode, EDI & Foreign Language Options.
Viehmann Corp.

On the Dotted Line: Legal Forms. *Items Included:* Bound manual. *Customer Support:* Free hotline - no time limit; 30 day limited warranty; updates are $5/disk plus S&H.
MS-DOS. IBM & compatibles (256k). $39.95-$129.95.
Apple. $39.95-$129.95.
Collection of Pre-Written, Ready-to-Use Contracts, Agreements, & Letters. The Forms Are in Standard ASCII Format, & Can Be Read & Modified by Any of the Popular Word Processors. "Fill in the Blanks" & Create Customized, Professional, & Legally-Binding Documents for Every Situation.
Dynacomp, Inc.

On the Job: ClickArt Cartoons. *Customer Support:* Free & unlimited technical support to registered users; 60 day money-back guarantee.
Macintosh. Macintosh, System 6.0.7 or higher (1Mb). 3.5" disk $49.95. *Addl. software required:* Any word-processing, desktop publishing or works program that accepts graphics.
Windows MS-DOS. IBM PC & compatibles. 3.5" disk $49.95. *Addl. software required:* Any word processing, desktop publishing or works program that accepts graphics.
Over 100 Images! Black & White Cartoons;

Ready-to-Use, or Changed in Appropriate Drawing Program; Contains 12 Bonus Images Pre-Colored for Use in Presentations; Includes the ClickArt Trade Secret - Images Traded to Every Popular Graphics Format, Guaranteed to Work with All Popular Applications.
T/Maker Co., Inc.

On the Road. Version: 1.0. Jan. 1993. Customer Support: Unlimited telephone support at caller's expense.
System 7.0.1 or higher. Macintosh PowerBook (2Mb). 3.5" disk $99.00.
Foe Mac PowerBook Users. Automates Tedious Routine Connectivity Tasks Such as Print & Volume Selection without Going Through the Chooser. Deters Printing or Faxing When Not Connected To a Printer or Phone Line, & Later, When Connected, Automatically Prints or Faxes the Files.
Palomar Software, Inc.

On Time! Business Calendar. Items Included: Bound manual. Customer Support: Free hotline - no time limit; 30 day limited warranty; updates are $5/disk plus S&H.
MS-DOS 2.0 or higher. IBM & compatibles (256k). $59.95-$599.95. Nonstandard peripherals required: Printer supported, but not necessary.
Graphics-Based, Well-Organized Appointment Calendar System Designed for the Person Who Does Not Have Much Time to Spare & Needs to Make the Most of It. Features Include: A Day-Planner Screen Which Displays Timeslots in 15, 30, & 60 Minute Increments; Automatic Projection of Recurring Events (e.g., Weekly, Bi-Weekly, Monthly, Yearly). Automatically Remind Yourself of Birthdays, etc.; Powerful Keyword or Name Search (When Is That Meeting with Joe What's-His-Name?); Automatic Date Calendar with Entries Through 2079; Graphic Display of Starting Times, Ending Times, & Scheduled Durations of Appointments & Meetings, Including Scheduled Conflicts & More.
Dynacomp, Inc.

Oncolib. Mar. 1995.
Windows Floppy. disk Contact publisher for price.
A Data Base Reference of Chemotherapy Protocols for the Practicing Physicians.
ISM, Inc.

1dir+ (Wonder Plus). Version: 3.0. Jun. 1985. Compatible Hardware: IBM PC, PC XT, PC AT, PC compatibles. Operating System(s) Required: PC-DOS 2.00 or higher. Language(s): Assembly, C. Memory Required: 256k.
disk $95.00.
Menus, Commands & Directories Can Be Customized with Easy to Use Point & Shoot Commands. The Tree Structured Display Can Be Used to Make, Change, & Remove Directories. There Is a View/Editor for Any Type of File, & Global File Operations Across Multiple Directories. Version 3.0 Includes Dedicated Mouse Support & an Optional Logon Utility That Prompts for a Password at Boot Up, or with Any Command or Menu. Features Nine Optional "Faces" (Screen Displays) & the Ability to Be Customized to Suit Individual Needs & Applications.
Bourbaki, Inc.

100 Best Computer Games CD-ROM. Jan. 1996. Items Included: Instruction booklet.
DOS & Windows 3.1. PC (4k). CD-ROM disk $29.95 (ISBN 1-56087-113-X). Optimal configuration: 386, Windows 3.1 4k RAM, joy stick.
Over 200 of the Most Popular Ready-to-Run Arcade-Quality Game Programs. Includes: Doom, Wolfstein 3D, Raptor, Night Raid, Plus 146 Other Top Action/Adventure Games. Bonus: 100 Las Vegas Card & Casino Games.
Top of the Mountain Publishing.

100 Cards. Duane Bristow. Compatible Hardware: TRS-80 Model I, Model III. Operating System(s) Required: TRSDOS. Language(s): BASIC.
cassette $19.95.
Play Against Another Person or Any of Ten Computer-Generated Personalities in Guessing If Next Card Will Be Higher or Lower Than the One Before.
Duane Bristow Computers, Inc.

100 Japanese Photographers. (Photopaedia Ser.: Vol. 1). Feb. 1995. Items Included: Warranty/registration card, game manual. Customer Support: Technical Support Number: 1-800-734-9466, 90 days limited warranty.
Windows 3.1; Macintosh System 7 or higher. IBM 33MHz i80486DX (8Mb); Macintosh 15MHz 68030 or higher, 25MHz 68LC040 or higher (8Mb). CD-ROM disk $59.99 (ISBN 1-888158-05-0). Nonstandard peripherals required: Double-speed CD-ROM drive. Addl. software required: MS-DOS 5.0 or higher.
The First-Ever "Encyclopedic Directory of Photographers," This Digital Collection Contains the Work of a Hundred Photographers Active in Japan. Photographs Representing a Variety of Artistic Approaches & Styles Have Been Selected, Ranging from Fashion & Advertising to Documentary & Art.
Synergy Interactive Corp.

101 ArcView/Avenue Scripts: The Disk. John Alexander & Valerie Warwick.
DOS/Windows, Windows NT, UNIX, Mac, Open VMS. disk $101.00 (ISBN 1-56690-086-7, Order no.: 4205).
Includes All Scripts from the ArcView/Avenue Programmer's Reference with Installation Notes.
High Mountain Pr., Inc.

One Hundred One Financial Spreadsheet Templates: Excel for Macintoosh. John R. Taylor.
Macintosh. 3.5" disk $39.95 (ISBN 1-883671-02-7).

101 MDL Commands Disks. Version: 5.X. Bill Steinbock.
DOS/Windows, Windows NT. disk $101.00 (ISBN 1-56690-076-X, Order no.: 1440).
The Source Disks Were Designed for Users Who Are Looking to Master MicroStation Development Language. The MDL Commands Covered Include MATCH, Creation, Multi-Line, Preview, Text, Fence, 3D Surfaces, Dialog Boxes, Search Criteria, & More.
High Mountain Pr., Inc.

101 MDL Commands Disks. Version: 5.0. Bill Steinbock.
DOS/Windows, Windows NT. disk $259.95 (ISBN 1-56690-075-1, Order no.: 1447).
The Source Disks Were Designed for Users Who Are Looking to Master MicroStation Development Language. The MDL Commands Covered Include MATCH, Creation, Multi-Line, Preview, Text, Fence, 3D Surfaces, Dialog Boxes, Search Criteria, & More. 6 Source Disks on One Diskette.
High Mountain Pr., Inc.

101 More of the World's Golf Courses to Play on Your Computer. Jan. 1996. Items Included: Directions sheet.
DOS & Windows 3.1. PC (4k). CD-ROM disk $29.90 (ISBN 1-56087-134-2). Addl. software required: Signature, Links 386 or Mean 18. Optimal configuration: 386, Windows 3.1 4k.
107 New Famous Courses to Expand Your Computer Golf Games Like Links 386, Jack Nicklauss Signature & Mean 18. Enjoy the Challenge of St. Andrews, Crooked Stick, Mauna Lani & 98 More Exciting Courses. Free Bonus: Design Your Own Golf Course Program.
Top of the Mountain Publishing.

101 Programming Surprises & Tricks for Your Apple II or IIe Computer. David L. Heiserman. May 1984. Compatible Hardware: Apple II, IIe. Operating System(s) Required: Apple DOS. Memory Required: 48k.
disk $25.50, incl. bk. (ISBN 0-8306-5061-X, Order no.: 5061C).
Programs Designed to Entertain. Includes Music & Sound, Animated Graphics, Games & Novelties.
TAB Bks.

101 Programming Surprises & Tricks for Your TRS-80 Computer. David L. Heiserman. 1984. Compatible Hardware: TRS-80 Model I, Model III, Model 4. Operating System(s) Required: TRSDOS. Memory Required: 32k.
disk $25.50, incl. bk. (ISBN 0-8306-5063-6, Order no.: 5063C).
Programs Designed to Entertain. Includes Music & Sound, Animated Graphics, Games & Novelties.
TAB Bks.

101 Ready-to-Run Programs & Subroutines for the IBM PCjr. Jeff Bretz & John C. Craig. 1984. Compatible Hardware: IBM PCjr. Operating System(s) Required: PC-DOS. Language(s): BASIC. Memory Required: 128k.
disk $28.50, incl. bk. (ISBN 0-8306-5114-4, Order no.: 5114C).
Designed to Take Advantage of PCjr's Capabilities.
TAB Bks.

170-C & 184-C. Compatible Hardware: Commodore 64, 64C, 128, 5X64. General Requirements: Commodore 1541 Disk Drive, or equivalent for use with demo disk.
One Seventy-C. 3.5" disk $99.95.
One Eighty-Four-C. 3.5" disk $59.95.
Both Inkwell Systems' Light Pens Can Be Used Immediately As Data Entry Devices for Many Popular Software Programs or for Programs Written by You, Using the Demonstration Software & Technical Information in This Package.
Inkwell Systems.

The One-Minute Bible for Windows.
Windows 3.1, DOS 3.0. 386, 486, or Pentium (2Mb). disk $39.95 (Order no.: SW925-2G). Optimal configuration: 386, 486, or Pentium, 2Mb RAM, Windows 3.1, DOS 3.0, Sound card optional. Allow approximately 3.5Mb disk space.
3.5" disk $39.95 (Order no.: SW911-2G).
A Complete Daily Devotional & Learning Tool for Self-Directed Bible Study. An Easy-to-Use Software Package As Well As an Educational Tool. Brings State-of-the-Art Computer Efficiency to the Age-Old Wisdom of God's Word. In Addition to the Carefully Edited & Organized Readings from the NIV Text the One Minute Bible Has over 25 In-Depth Learning Aids.
Gospel Films Inc.

1-Minute Convection. Jan. 1988. Operating System(s) Required: PC-DOS/MS-DOS. Memory Required: 512k. Items Included: Manual with Example Problems. Customer Support: 90 day warranty.
disk $288.00 (ISBN 0-931690-29-3).
Fast Calculation of Convective Heat Transfer Problems for Various Common Geometries. Results Include Surface Temperature, Heat Flux, on Heat Transfer Coefficient. Includes over 500

TITLE INDEX

Built-In Correlations, over 20 Temperature Dependent Fluid Properties for Liquids, Gases, or Liquid Metals, or User May Input Correlations & Fluid Properties.
Genium Publishing Corp.

One-Minute Convection: Convective Heat Transfer. *Items Included:* Full manual. No other products required. *Customer Support:* Free telephone support - no time limit. 30 day warranty.
MS-DOS 3.2 or higher. IBM & compatibles (512k). disk $259.95.
Menu-Driven Software Package Which Calculates the Surface Temperature, Heat Flux, or Heat Transfer Coefficient for Various Common Convective Heat Transfer Geometries. Employs a Database of over 500 Correlations, As Well As General Expressions for Which You Supply the Coefficients.
Dynacomp, Inc.

1-Minute Convection: Convective Heat Transfer. 1995. *Items Included:* Full manual. *Customer Support:* Free telephone support - 90 days, 30-day warranty.
MS-DOS 3.2 or higher. 286 (584k). disk $259.95. *Nonstandard peripherals required:* CGA/EGA/VGA.
A Menu-Driven Software Package Which Calculates the Surface Temperature, Heat Flux, or Heat Transfer Coefficient for Various Common Convective Heat Transfer Geometries. It Employs a Database of over 500 correlations, As Well As General Expressions for Which You Supply the Coefficients. MKS, CGS, & British Units Are Supported. The Temperature-Dependent Properties for over 20 Liquids & Gases are Calculated Internally, & You May Define Your Own Fluids in Terms of Density, Specific Heat, Thermal Conductivity, Volume Expansivity, & Dynamic Viscosity.
Dynacomp, Inc.

One Page Printer: M-310 Printing Package 2. 1982. *Compatible Hardware:* Commodore 64, PET. *Memory Required:* 64k. *General Requirements:* Printer.
disk $100.00 (ISBN 0-925182-40-0).
Combines Chart Wheel & Planet Listing, Traditional Aspect Grid, & Sorted Table.
Matrix Software.

One-Step. *Compatible Hardware:* Apple Macintosh. *Memory Required:* 512k.
3.5" disk $69.00.
MIDI Sequencer Program.
Southwest Music Systems, Inc.

1000 Games for Macintosh. *Customer Support:* Free, unlimited.
System 6 Mac. 030 Mac, 256 colors (4Mb). CD-ROM disk $17.95. *Nonstandard peripherals required:* Sound card, CD-ROM drive.
Contains over One Thousand Great Shareware & Public Domain Programs. Battle Ugly Aliens, Blast Apart Run-Away Asteroids, Deal Yourself That Royal Flush or Solve That 3-D Puzzle.
BeachWare.

1000 Games for Windows & DOS. *Customer Support:* Free, unlimited.
Windows 3.1 or higher (4Mb). CD-ROM disk $17.95. *Nonstandard peripherals required:* Sound board, CD-ROM drive. *Networks supported:* Yes.
This Disc Has over 1000 Windows & DOS Games for Everyone! Go Duck Hunting, Travel Through Space, Play a Hand of Cards, Coach a Football Team, Hit Some Golf Balls, Become a Knight, Solve Brain Tweaking Puzzles, or Even Fight in the Dreaded Icon Wars.
BeachWare.

1001 Things to Do with Your Commodore 128. Mark R. Sawusch & Dave Prochnow. Jul. 1986. *Compatible Hardware:* Commodore 128. *Operating System(s) Required:* CP/M.
disk $32.95, incl. bk. (ISBN 0-8306-5228-0, Order no.: 5228C).
Provides a Wide Range of Commercial Programs for Financial, Business, Educational, & High-Tech Applications Plus Games & Puzzles. Also Includes a Library of Computer-Specific Utilities & Subroutines. Printouts, Flowcharts, Diagrams, Step-by-Step Instructions & Illustrations Are All Featured.
TAB Bks.

1001 Things to Do with Your Amiga. Mark R. Sawusch & Dave Prochnow. Sep. 1986. *Compatible Hardware:* Commodore Amiga.
disk $32.95, incl. bk. (ISBN 0-8306-5229-9, Order no.: 5229C).
Provides a Wide Range of Commercial Programs for Financial, Business, Educational, & High-Tech Applications Plus Games & Puzzles, Also a Library of Computer-Specific Utilities & Subroutines. Printouts, Flowcharts, Diagrams, Step-by-Step Instructions, & Illustrations Are All Featured.
TAB Bks.

1001 Things to Do with Your Atari ST. Mark R. Sawusch & Linda M. Schreiber. Nov. 1986. *Compatible Hardware:* Atari ST.
disk $32.95, incl. bk. (ISBN 0-8306-5230-2, Order no.: 5230C).
Provides a Wide Range of Commercial Programs for Financial, Business, Educational, & High-Tech Applications, Plus Games & Puzzles. Also Includes a Library of Computer-Specific Utilities & Subroutines. Printouts, Flowcharts, Diagrams, Step-by-Step Instructions & Illustrations Are All Included.
TAB Bks.

1001 Things to Do with Your TRS-80, Apple II, IIe, IBM PC, Commodore 64 & Macintosh. Mark Sawusch & Tan Summers. Aug. 1984. *Compatible Hardware:* Apple II, II+, IIe, Macintosh; Commodore 64; IBM PC; TRS-80 Model III, Model 4. *Operating System(s) Required:* PC-DOS, Apple DOS, TRSDOS, CBM. *Language(s):* BASIC, MS BASIC for Macintosh. *Memory Required:* TRS-80 32k; Apple 48k; IBM PC & Commodore 64k; Macintosh 128k.
disk $31.50 ea.
IBM. (ISBN 0-8306-5110-1, Order no.: 5110C).
TRS-80. (ISBN 0-8306-5104-7, Order no.: 5104C).
Macintosh. (ISBN 0-8306-0220-8, Order no.: 5120C).
Commodore. disk $30.95, incl. bk. (ISBN 0-8306-5098-9, Order no.: 5098C).
Apple. disk $30.95, incl. bk. (ISBN 0-8306-5101-2, Order no.: 5101C).
Covers from Household Record-Keeping to Game Playing & Hobby Use. Includes Actual Programs, Flowcharts, Diagrams, & Step-by-Step Instructions.
TAB Bks.

1065 Solutions. *Version:* 99.2. *Customer Support:* Unlimited free.
PC-DOS 3.0 (256k). $895.00; $495.00 renewal. *Networks supported:* Novell.
Facilitates In-House Preparation & Printing of 1065 Partnership Tax Returns & Related Transmittal Letters.
Creative Solutions, Inc. (Michigan).

1000 Years of Russian Art: The State Russian Museum, St. Petersburg. Robb Lazarus et al. Nov. 1995. *Items Included:* Instruction manual, upgrade card (if available). *Customer Support:* Call-in, 1-800, fax back & on-line support are available at no charge for the lifetime of the disk.
Macintosh with 68030 processor or higher. Macintosh, double speed CD-ROM drive (8Mb). CD-ROM disk $79.95 (ISBN 1-886664-12-9). *Nonstandard peripherals required:* 24-bit graphics card strongly recommended, Quick Time Movie.
Windows 3.1 or higher. Windows System 3.1 or higher (8Mb). CD-ROM disk $79.95 (ISBN 1-886664-13-7). *Nonstandard peripherals required:* 24-bit graphics card strongly recommended.
The Distinguished Collection of the State Russian Museum, St. Petersburg Introduces a Broad Spectrum of Russian Art to the Western World. Enjoy Canvases by Recognized Russian Artists Including Karl Briullov, Vasily Kandinsky, Kazimir Malevich, Vladimir Tatlin & Marc Chagall. Delve into the Works of Controversial Artists, Relatively Unknown Before the Fall of Communism. The Collection, Which Spans 1,000 Years of Russian Art History, Features an Array of Works from Ancient Icons to Avant-Garde Canvases, All Displayed in Full Color.
Digital Collections, Inc.

1000 Years of Russian Art: The State Russian Museum, St. Petersburg: Jewel Case. Robb Lazarus et al. May 1996. *Items Included:* Instructional manual, upgrade card (if available). *Customer Support:* Call-in, 1-800, fax back & on-line support are available at no charge for the lifetime of the disk.
Macintosh with 68030 processor or higher (8Mb). CD-ROM disk $49.95 (ISBN 1-886664-43-9). *Nonstandard peripherals required:* Double speed CD-ROM drive, 24-bit graphics card strongly recommended.
Windows 3.1 or higher (8Mb). CD-ROM disk $49.95 (ISBN 1-886664-44-7). *Nonstandard peripherals required:* 24-bit graphics card strongly recommended.
Digital Collections, Inc.

1-2-3: Database Graphics. *Version:* 3.1. Jul. 1991. *Compatible Hardware:* IBM PC & compatibles. *Memory Required:* 1000k. *General Requirements:* Lotus 1-2-3 release 3.1. *Customer Support:* Hot line support.
disk $900.00.
Instructor-Led Courseware. Starter Kit Includes an Instructor's Manual & 12 Student Manuals with Practice Activities & Data Disks. Two Year Free Upgrade for Instructor Guide.
Logical Operations.

1,2,3 Lead Prioritizer. Jan. 1989. *Items Included:* User manual & software tutorials. *Customer Support:* 30 day money back guarantee, free phone support, on line tutorials & help in software.
DOS or O/S2 (256k). IBM PC, XT, AT, PS/2 or compatibles. $109.00 (US & Canada), $149.00 (International). *Nonstandard peripherals required:* CGA, EGA, VGA, or Hercules graphics board. *Addl. software required:* Lotus 1-2-3 release 2, 2.01, 2.2, or 3. *Optimal configuration:* IBM PCAT, DOS 2.1 or higher, 640k RAM, EGA board, 1-2-3 release 2 or higher. *Networks supported:* All that are supported by Lotus 1-2-3.
Quickly Selects & Prioritizes Leads That Are Most Likely to Convert into Substantial Sales/Orders, Reinforces or Changes Their Decisions as to Which Leads to Target First, Eliminates Leads that Should Not Be Pursued at All & Helps to Quickly Get Newer Sales Personnel up to a High Sales Performance Level.
Successware.

1-2-3 Macro Library, 3rd Edition. Que Corporation. *Compatible Hardware:* IBM PC & compatibles with 2 disk drives. *Operating*

1-2-3: MACRO PROGRAMMING

System(s) Required: PC-DOS/MS-DOS 2.0 or higher. (source code included). *Memory Required:* 256k. *Items Included:* Book & disk. book & disk $39.95 (ISBN 0-88022-418-5, Order no: 962).
Includes Companion Disk from Simple Key Stroke Macros to Complex Macro Programs, This Book Helps Users Automate Spreadsheet Applications.
Que.

1-2-3: Macro Programming. *Version:* 2.2. Jun. 1987. *Compatible Hardware:* IBM PC & compatibles. *Memory Required:* 1000k. *General Requirements:* Lotus 1-2-3 Release 2.2 & 3.0. *Customer Support:* Hot line support.
disk $900.00.
Instructor-Led Courseware. Starter Kit Includes an Instructor's Guide & 12 Student Manuals with Practice Activities & Data Disks. Additional Student Manuals Available Separately. Two Year Free Upgrade on Instructor Guide.
Logical Operations.

One-Two-Three Power Tools. *Version:* 3.1 & 2.3. E. Michael Lunsford & H. Scott Tucker. *Items Included:* Two 5.25" disks. *Customer Support:* Phone number available for technical support, 212-492-9832; free disk replacement within 90 days of purchase.
IBM PC & compatibles. disk $49.95 (ISBN 0-553-34966-X). *Addl. software required:* Lotus 1-2-3.
Provides User Tips & over 100 Ready-to-Use Utilities to: Automate Spreadsheets, Extend Productivity, Provide Macro Libraries. Lunsford Is a Well-Known 1-2-3 Developer/Author, & Has Written for PC World & Lotus Magazine. Tucker Is Lotus' Senior Product Design Manager & the Bestselling Author of "Inside Lotus 1-2-3 Macros". He Is Also a Frequent Contributor to Lotus Magazine.
Bantam Bks., Inc.

1-2-3 Release 3 Business Applications. Edward M. Donie. *Compatible Hardware:* IBM PC. *Operating System(s) Required:* PC-DOS/MS-DOS 2.0 or higher. (source code included). *Memory Required:* 1-2-3 R1A 256k; 1-2-3 R2 320k. *Items Included:* Book & disk. book & disk $39.95 (ISBN 0-88022-439-8, Order no.: 972).
Ready-to-Run Business Models are the Focus of This Book & Disk Set. Highlights the New Features of 1-2-3 Release 3 & Comes Complete with Directions for Building & Customizing Each Model.
Que.

1-2-3 Release 2.2; Advanced; 1-2-3 Release 3.1; Advanced. Jul. 1991. *Compatible Hardware:* IBM PC & compatibles. *Memory Required:* 1000k. *General Requirements:* Lotus 1-2-3 Release 2.2 & 3.1. *Customer Support:* Hot line support.
$900.00.
Instructor-Led Courseware. Starter Kit Includes an Instructor's Guide & 12 Student Manuals with Practice Activities & Data Disks. Additional Student Manuals Available Separately at $28.00 each, 2 Year Free Upgrade on Instructor Guide.
Logical Operations.

1-2-3: Spreadsheets. *Version:* 3.1. Jul. 1991. *Compatible Hardware:* IBM PC & compatibles. *Memory Required:* 1000k. *General Requirements:* Lotus 1-2-3 Release 3.1. *Customer Support:* Hot line support.
disk $900.00.
Instructor-Led Courseware. Starter Kit Includes Instructor's Manual & 12 Student Manuals with Practice Activities, Data Disks & Overhead Transparencies. Two Year Free Upgrade on Instructor Guide.
Logical Operations.

1-2-3 Support Library. Dec. 1987. *Compatible Hardware:* IBM PC & compatibles. *Memory Required:* 256k. *General Requirements:* Lotus 1-2-3.
$179.95.
Self-Paced, Interactive, Disk-Based Tutorial Includes Teach Yourself Lotus (Introductory & Advanced), Teach Yourself 1-2-3 Macros, & 1-2-3 QuickRef for Instant Help.
American Training International, Inc.

One-Up. *Items Included:* Reference manual, summary of information, "What's New", service bulletin, run-time guide, communications guide. *Customer Support:* Optional training & maintenance package. Training available through headquarters or locally. Unlimited helpline (8-8 EST) with maintenance agreement.
DOS 3.1 or higher. IBM AT, PS/2 series, MS-DOS based hardware. Contact publisher for price. *Networks supported:* Novell, Banyan, IBM, PathWorks.
Standalone Five-Dimensional Modeling & Analysis for PC-Based Decision Support Systems. Full Screen Model Definition. Users Can Process Models Locally, Transfer Models to Host Mainframe, or Download Host Models, All Using Simple Menu-Pick. Full Screen Report Writer Allows What-You-See-Is-What-You-Get (WYSIWYG) Screen Creation of Reports Right from a Spreadsheet. With Execu-View, Explore & Chart Model Data in Detail from Many Perspectives. Optional Application Builder & Runtime Version for Packaged End-User Applications.
Comshare, Inc.

One-Way Two-Way Concrete Slab Design - ST19M. *Version:* 03/1993. 1982. *Compatible Hardware:* IBM PC & compatibles. *Operating System(s) Required:* MS-DOS, PC-DOS. *Language(s):* Compiled. *Memory Required:* 256k. *Customer Support:* Technical hotline, "Lifetime" support at no charge.
$395.00.
One-Way, Two-Way Concrete Slab Design - ST19M Uses the Winter & Nilson & ACI 318-77 Direct Design Method to Design Concrete Slabs Under Uniform Applied Loads. Outputs Are Minimum Slab Thickness Required, Flexural Bar Sizes, Design Moments, Actual & Allowable Shear Stresses, & Reinforcing Steel Requirements. Prompted, Interactive. Fully Compiled. SI Metric or English Units.
MC2 Engineering Software.

OnGuard. *Version:* 4.10. 1987. *Compatible Hardware:* IBM PC, PC XT, PC AT. *Operating System(s) Required:* PC-DOS 2.0, 3.3 & 4.01. *Memory Required:* 128k. *General Requirements:* Hard disk. *Items Included:* User documentation. *Customer Support:* Free telephone support.
disk $295.00.
avail. site & corporate licensing.
Hard Disk Security, Includes Access Control, Encryption, & Encryption Password Recovery Modules. Supports Independent Read, Write, Execute, Delete Access Privileges for Files & Directories for up to 24 Users or Groups.
United Software Security, Inc.

Online Catalog. *Version:* 2.15. Oct. 1995. *Customer Support:* Free, unlimited telephone support.
MS-DOS or Windows. IBM PC, XT, AT, PS/2. disk $1200.00.
Fully MARC Compatible Catalog. Supports Searching by Author, Title, Subject, or Keyword. Allows Importing & Exporting of MARC Records. Enables Librarian to Create MARC records Via Keyboard Input Without Having to Know Details of MARC Record Specification.
Professional Software.

OnLines: Chronicles of Electronic Days. Paul Levinson. 1990.
DOS. Any type of IBM (64k). $9.95 (ISBN 1-56178-010-3).
MAC. Any type of Macintosh (64k). $9.95 (ISBN 1-56178-029-4).
Collection of Commentaries on Popular Culture, Rock Music, Movies, Political Events, New Technologies, Computer Telecommunications, Media Theory.
Connected Editions, Inc.

OnTime Enterprise. *Version:* 3.0. Jan. 1996. *Customer Support:* Free technical support for Network products. Maintenance agreement available.
MS Windows 3.X or higher. IBM PC & compatibles (340k). disk $64.95 single user, Network versions available. *Networks supported:* NetWare, Vines, Windows NT, TCP/IP.
Macintosh. disk $64.95 single user, Network versions available.
Lifetime Calendar, To-Do List Manager. Features Include: Immediate Communication of Time Availability & Conflicts, Alarm, Date Entry Through 2079, Attractive Calendar Printouts for up to 9 Weeks, Keywordsearch, One Entry for Recurring Events. Network Version Adds Group Scheduling Capabilities, RSVP Functions, Workgroup Support, & E-Mail Notification.
Campbell Services, Inc.

OnTime for Windows. *Version:* 1.5. Jun. 1993. *Customer Support:* Limited free support for Network products. Maintenance agreements available.
MS-DOS 3.1 or higher. IBM PC or compatible (380k). disk $64.95 single user, Network versions available. *Optimal configuration:* IBM PC or compatible, MS-DOS 3.1 or higher & Windows 3.1 or higher.
Lifetime Calendar & To-Do List Manager. Features Include Attractive Calendar Printouts, Alarm, One Entry for Recurring Events, Automatic Roll over of Non-Completed Items, Week & Month at a Glance Graphic Displays, & Notepad. The Network Version Adds Group Scheduling Capabilities, RSVP Functions, Workgroup Support, & E-Mail Notification.
Campbell Services, Inc.

Ontrack Data Recovery for NetWare. *Version:* 4.1. Dec. 1994. *Items Included:* 1 spiral bound manual. *Customer Support:* Technical support via telephone. (Only cost involved would be the phone call - paid by caller).
Supports NetWare Versions 3.11, 3.12, 4.0, 4.01, 4.02 & 4.1. Any IBM 386/486 or compatible (128k). disk $395.95. *Networks supported:* Supports Name Spacing for DOS, Macintosh, OS/2, & NFS (Unix) files & subdirectories.
Formerly NetUtils, Contains the Most Advanced Data Recovery Tools Commercially Available for NetWare. Offers the Ability to Perform File Recovery & File System Repairs Without Bringing the File Server Off-Line. You May Also Copy Files from a Downed Server Volume to Other Servers or Volumes on the Network, or Repair File System Structures. In Addition, You Can Prevent Possible Data Loss Situations with a Complete Array of Diagnostic, Maintenance, & Data Recovery Routines. Supports NetWare Versions 3.11, 3.12, 4.0, 4.01, 4.02, & 4.1.
Ontrack Computer Systems, Inc.

Ontrack Netshield: VLM Protection for Novell Netware File Savers. *Version:* 2.0. Jan. 1995. *Items Included:* Extensive manual, virus alerts. *Customer Support:* Technical support via telephone, Internet & BBS. long distant calls free.
any Novell file server running netware 3.11, 3.12,

4.01, 4.02, 4.1. 3.5" disk for 1st copy $99.95.
Ontrack Netshield provides uninterrupted virusprotection, consistently detecting over 95% of all known viruses. Through the most sophisticated signature checking technology, Ontrack Netshield is 100% server-based, password protected & supports mixed computing environments including DOS, Windows, OS/2 & Macintosh.
Ontrack Computer Systems, Inc.

Opel Hershiser's Strike Zone. *Customer Support:* 90 day warranty.
MS-DOS. IBM (512K). disk $17.99.
Nonstandard peripherals required: CGA, EGA, Tandy, Hercules MCGA or VGA Graphics required.
The Major League's Most Valuable Pitcher & Virgin Mastertronic Have Joined Forces to Bring You the #1 Coin-Operated Baseball Arcade Game. All the Exciting Features That Made the Arcade Game Great Are Included in the Home Computer Version.
Virgin Games.

Open Access. Jun. 1984. *Compatible Hardware:* Columbia; Compaq; Corona; DEC Rainbow; Fujitsu M516; HP-150 Touchscreen; IBM PC, PC XT; NCR; Protege; Tandy 2000; TI Professional; Toshiba T-300; Wang. *Operating System(s) Required:* PC-DOS/MS-DOS 2.0 or higher. *Language(s):* Assembly. *Memory Required:* 256k. *General Requirements:* 2 disk drives, printer; modem optional.
$395.00 (ISBN 0-927048-00-0).
Integrated Package Consisting of 6 Modules. Virtual Memory Program Based on a Relational Database Management System. Includes Capabilities for Information Management, Graphics, Spreadsheet, Word Processing, Communications, & Time Management. Modules Operate Completely Independent of Each Other, but All May Share Data Either by Exporting/Importing Data Files or by Virtually "Contexting" Data Directly from One Program to Another.
Software Products International.

Open Access II. *Version:* 2.05. *Compatible Hardware:* IBM PC & compatibles, PS/2.
contact publisher for price.
demo tutorial $19.95.
Relational Database & Spreadsheet with 3-D Graphics That Also Features a Word Processor, Communications & Desk Accessories.
Software Products International.

Open Access II Plus. *Compatible Hardware:* IBM PC & compatibles. *Operating System(s) Required:* MS-DOS, NetBIOS, Novell Advanced NetWare. *Memory Required:* 384k, network 448k. *General Requirements:* Hard disk for network version.
$695.00 all modules.
$295.00 database/programmer.
$180.00 word processor/communications.
$295.00 spreadsheet/statistics/graphics.
$895.00 4 users.
$2295.00 10 users.
$3495.00 20 users.
$4995.00 unlimited users.
$195.00 network installation pack.
Integrated Software Package Featuring Word Processing, Spreadsheet, Database, Graphics, Communications & Statistics Modules. Includes Mail/Merge Database Link, Built-In Language in Spreadsheet & Database Modules, 216 by 3000 Spreadsheet Matrix Size & Context-Sensitive On-Screen Help. Links 4 Spreadsheets & 8 Database Tables in One Query. Pastes Spreadsheet Sections & Graphics into Word Processing Files. Imports & Exports ASCII, DIF, DCA, WKS & WordStar File Formats.
Software Products International.

Open Channel Flow: Network Irrigation & Water Drainage. *Items Included:* Bound manual. *Customer Support:* Free hotline - no time limit; 30 day limited warranty; updates are $5/disk plus S&H.
MS-DOS 2.0 or higher. IBM & compatibles (640k). disk $249.95. *Nonstandard peripherals required:* Two-button mouse supported, but not necessary.
Analyzes the Flow of Water in Open Channel Networks, Such As Storm & Sewer Systems, Process Gravity Lines, Floor & Roof Drains, Irrigation Systems, & the Like. It Can Treat Individual Elements, or Networks Having up to 250 Elements. Element Sections May Be Circular, Rectangular, Triangular, Parabolic, or Trapezoidal. The User May Define & Re-Define Units at Will. Friction Factors May Be Chosen from a Pop-Up Reference Table, or Specified.
Dynacomp, Inc.

Open It. Nov. 1988.
Macintosh Plus, SE or II (2k). disk $89.95 (Order no.: ID-187).
User Can Share Files & Information with Other Macintosh Users, Even Those with Different Applications. Can Save Documents from Any Mac Application in a Common Format for Use in Any Other Mac Program. Can View It, Clip It, Scale It & Paste It in Another File or Print It. Works As a Desk Accessory As Well. Also Can Be Replacement for Mac Scrapbook. Create Multiple Scrapbook Files of Full-Size Pages, Then Select Image & Scale It from 1 to 1000 Percent.
10.0.

Accounts Receivable. *Version:* 450.2. 1978. *Compatible Hardware:* IBM PC & compatibles. *Operating System(s) Required:* MS-DOS, PC-DOS. *Language(s):* QuickBASIC. *Memory Required:* 512k. *General Requirements:* Hard disk. *Items Included:* System diskettes, users guide, training tutorial. *Customer Support:* Telephone; annual contracts available.
$395.00 to $495.00.
Combines Balance Forward Method for Service-Oriented Businesses & Non-Profit Organizations Who Bill by Statement & Open Item Method for Product-Oriented Companies Who Bill Primarily by Invoice. Enter, Print & Post Invoices. Post-Only Capability for Invoices Created Outside System. Automatic Posting of Recurring Charges. Automatic Cash Application to Specific Invoices of Account Balance. System Identifies Past Due Accounts the Day They Become Delinquent & Provides Extensive On-Line Collection Assistance. Primary Reports Include Aged Trial Balance (User May Specify Aging Periods), Cash & JE Register, Projection of Cash Income, Detailed Account Inquires, Statements, & Series of Past Due Notices. Interfaces with the IMS General Ledger & Order Processing Systems. Number of Accounts & Transactions Limited Only by Capacity of Hard Disk. Runs Single User or Multi-User on Many Networks.
International Micro Systems, Inc.

OPEN$LINE. *Version:* 7.1. 1985. *Compatible Hardware:* IBM PC & compatibles, PC XT, PC AT. *Operating System(s) Required:* MS-DOS 5.0 or higher. *Language(s):* Compiled BASIC, Assembly. *Memory Required:* 2000k.
disk $3000.00.
disk Network $4500.00.
Adds Revolving Credit/Credit Cards to the LOANLEDGER+ Environment; Fully Accounts for & Controls Advances for Customers (or Purchases from Vendors by Customers) & Repayment by the Customer. Features Include: Detailed Billing Statements, Average Daily Balance, Individual Cut-Offs, Renewal Fees, & Credit Limits.
Dynamic Interface Systems Corp.

Open Link Extender: (OLE'). Jun. 1990. *Items Included:* One manual & one diskette. *Customer Support:* Customer support is offered via telephone form 9:00 AM to 5:30 PM EST 603-644-5555. No charge for service other than the phone call.
PC-DOS & MS-DOS V 3.10 or higher. IBM PC, XT, AT, PS/2 & compatibles (512K). disk $69.95. *Addl. software required:* Must have the NETBOIS Interface or the 802.2 connections loaded & Software Carousel.
Network Extension to the Program Software Carousel.
Softlogic Solutions.

Open PL/I.
Sun SPARC SunOS 4.x, & Solaris 2.x; HP 9000 HP-UX; IBM RS/6000 AIX; IntelX86 & Pentium UNIX SVR3 & SVR4; Microsoft NT. Contact publisher for price.
Flexible Migration System That Allows PL/I Mainframe Users to Rehost Existing PL/I Applications to Open Systems Environments. Supports an Extensive List of Full IBM PL/I Extensions, Many DEC VAX Extensions, & Is Compatible with DG, Wang, & Prime PL/I. Provides Supprot for VSAM & Integration for Leading RDBMS's, OLTP/CICS Monitors & Numerous Third Party Client/Server Products. Includes CodeWatch, an X/Motif Debugger for Fast, Easy Debugging of Software Programs. CodeWatch Allows Testing & Debugging of Programs Using the Conventions & Symbols of the PL/I Language. It Supports Standard PL/I Expression & Evaluation Including Built-Ins, Arrays, & PL/I Data Types. Also Includes a Powerful Macro Preprocessor to Ease the Conversion of Mainframe PL/I Code to Open Systems; Enabling the PL/I Programmer to Have Control of the Source Program During Compile Time.
Liant Software Corp.

Open Plan. *Version:* 4.0. Jul. 1991. *Compatible Hardware:* IBM PC, 286 & 386 compatibles, IBM PS/2 Model 150 or above, DEC VAX, Macintosh or Macintosh II, SCO UNIX Sys V/386. *Items Included:* Disks, documentation. *Customer Support:* Free telephone support 8AM-6PM CST, training & consulting available.
disk $4200.00. *Addl. software required:* dBase III, IV, Foxbase Plus or FoxPro.
Offers an Integrated Solution to Planning & Scheduling. User Interface, Project Executive, Allows Users to Switch Between Three Alternate Project Views: Barchart, Network, or WBS Views. Resource Scheduling Capabilities, Along with the Flexible WRL Reporting Language & a Total Integration with a Relational Database Produce a Powerful Yet Versatile Means of Managing Projects. Provides the Same User Interface Across Hardware Platforms; Operating on PCs, Macintosh, LANs, VAX/VMS & UNIX.
Welcom Software Technology.

Open System Interconnection: An Overview. Dec. 1994. *Items Included:* User manual. *Customer Support:* Free technical support & a 30-day warranty (1-800-521-CORE).
MS-DOS. IBM & compatibles (512K). 3.5" disk $199.00 (ISBN 1-57305-013-X). *Nonstandard peripherals required:* High-density 3.5" disk drive; VGA color monitor. *Addl. software required:* MS-DOS version 3.3 or higher. *Optimal configuration:* IBM (512K), MS-DOS version 3.3 or higher, VGA color monitor, keyboard, Microsoft compatible mouse (optional).
This Tutorial Begins by Exploring the Need for Standards in General & for Standards in Data Communications in Particular. The Concept of a Layered Data Communications Architecture Is Presented & Its Operation Is Explored. The Seven

OPEN SYSTEMS GENERAL LEDGER

Layers of the Open System Interconnection Reference Model Are Considered & the Interaction Between Layers Is Examined. The Training Will Take Approximately 2 Hours to Complete.
Bellcore.

Open Systems General Ledger. Open Systems, Inc. *Compatible Hardware:* TI Professional. *Operating System(s) Required:* MS-DOS, CP/M-86, Business BASIC Interpreter from Open Systems. *Memory Required:* 128k. *General Requirements:* Winchester hard disk.
$375.00.
Texas Instruments, Personal Productivit.

Open Systems Payroll. Open Systems, Inc. *Operating System(s) Required:* MS-DOS, CP/M-86, Business Interpreter from Open Systems. *Memory Required:* 64k.
$650.00.
Texas Instruments, Personal Productivit.

OpenPerformance. *Items Included:* Documentation. *Customer Support:* Dial-in hot line, maintenance, extended hours, in-person, service.
IBM. Contact publisher for price.
DST Belvedere.

Opera. *Version:* 1.1. *Compatible Hardware:* IBM PC & compatibles; Dec Vax IBM PS/2 model or above, 286 & 386. *Items Included:* Disks, documentation. *Customer Support:* Telephone support 8AM-5PM CST, training & consulting available.
$2200.00.
An Extension to OPEN PLAN Includes Four Added Options for Target Dates, an Increased Number of Calendars, & Uses dBASE III Plus, FoxBASE Plus, or dBASE IV As a User Interface & Data Storage, & Monte Carlo Simulation Techniques to Provide Estimates of Project Completion Dates.
Welcom Software Technology.

Operation Combat; Magnuflux Runner. Merit Software & Three DI. Jan. 1996. *Items Included:* Set-up instruction sheet. *Customer Support:* 310-403-0043.
Operation Combat: DOS 5.0; Magnuflux: Win 3.1, DOS 5.0. IBM PC. disk $12.95 (ISBN 1-887783-16-4, Order no.: 5100-2004). *Optimal configuration:* Operation Combat: IBM PC 386 or higher, DOS 5.0 or higher, VGA. Supports Adlib, Soundblaster & compatibles; Magnuflux: Win 3.1, DOS 5.0, 3Mb HD, joystick, keyboard or mouse, VGA or higher, Soundblaster or Windows compatible soundcard.
Magnuflux Is a Space Game. The Game Player Battles Against Aliens from Other Planets. Operation Combat Is a Battle Game. The Game Player Plays Against Enemy Aircraft, Ground Forces & Inter-Planetary Enemies.
Entertainment Technology.

Operation: Frog. *Customer Support:* Customer service 800-541-5513.
Apple. Apple II plus, IIe, IIc, IIc plus, IIgs (64k). $79.95 (Order no.: 95283-85459). *Optimal configuration:* Joystick or mouse optional.
MS-DOS. IBM & compatibles (384k). $89.95 (Order no.: 85455-85457). *Nonstandard peripherals required:* Color graphics card required; fully supports VGA, MCGA, EGA & TGA. *Optimal configuration:* Joystick or mouse optional.
Macintosh. Mac Plus, SE, SE3, OLC, Classic, Model II line. $99.95 (Order no.: 85453). *Optimal configuration:* Mouse optional.
Lifelike Simulation of the Dissection of a Bullfrog. Select the Proper Instruments - Surgical Scissors, Probe, Forceps, Tweezers & Magnifying Glass. Probe & Snip Body Organs, Remove Them to the Examination Tray, & Investigate Frog Body Parts & Systems. Animation Shows How These Parts & Systems Function in a Living Frog. MS-DOS & Mac Versions Will Even Compare Frog & Human Body Parts. Once the Dissection Is Completed, User Can then Reconstruct the Frog. When Finished the Frog Will Jump Off the Table.
Scholastic Software.

Operation Whirlwind. Roger Damon. *Compatible Hardware:* Atari 400, 800, XL, XE Series; Commodore 64. *Memory Required:* Atari 48k, Commodore 64k. *General Requirements:* Joystick.
Commodore. disk $39.95 (Order no.: COMDSK-248).
Atari. disk $39.95 (Order no.: ATDSK-127).
Commodore. (Order no.: COMDSK-248).
Strategy Game of War Tactics. Player Becomes the Batallion Commander of an Armored Tank Force & Tries to Cross 2 Rivers & 15 Kilometers to Reach the City.
Broderbund Software, Inc.

Operations - Integrator. *Items Included:* Manual & software (single 360k 5.25" & 720k 3.5" diskette, or 800k 3.5" for Macintosh). *Customer Support:* Provided by JIAN at (415) 941-9191.
IBM PC & compatibles (640K), Macintosh. $149.00. *Nonstandard peripherals required:* Math co-processor & hard disk recommended. *Addl. software required:* PC's: spreadsheet processor compatible with Lotus 1-2-3 version 2.01 or higher. Macintosh: SYLK compatible spreadsheet including MS Excel, MS Works & others.
Spreadsheet Model to Structure, Modify, Evaluate & Balance the Financial Impact of Sales Forecasts with a Variety of Manufacturing & Service Opportunities. User Enters Components, Services, Pricing & Usage on a Master Table. Spreadsheet Calculates Inventory Requirements, Manpower Loading & Costs Plus Financial Figures (Gross/Net & Cash Flow) & Ratios (Return on Investment & Assets).
JIAN Tools for Sales.

Operations Research Tutorial. *Compatible Hardware:* Apple II+, IIe; IBM PC. *Memory Required:* Apple 48k, IBM 128k.
disk $99.95.
Collection of 17 Menu-Selected Programs Which Provide Data File Creation, Manipulation, & Calculation Capabilities in Support of the Analysis of Payoff Tables, Simplex Linear Programming, Distribution/Transportation Methods, & CPM/PERT Analysis.
Dynacomp, Inc.

OphthaLine CD-ROM Database for Ophthalmology. Aug. 1992.
MS Windows 3.1 or higher. IBM & compatibles (4Mb). CD-ROM disk $325.00-$995.00; Networks $1895.00 & up. *Nonstandard peripherals required:* Magnetic or CD-ROM, using ISO 9660. *Optimal configuration:* IBM & compatibles, 80386 or higher, 4Mb RAM, 20Mb hard disk, mouse, MS Windows 3.1 or higher.
System 6.0.7 or higher. Apple Macintosh (3Mb). CD-ROM disk $325.00-$995.00; Networks $1895.00 & up. *Optimal configuration:* Apple Macintosh Plus or higher, 3Mb RAM, System 6.0.7 or higher.
OphthaLine Is an Electronic Reference Database to the Ophthalmology Journal Literature. Ophthalmology-Specific Excerpts (Including Abstracts) from the National Library of Medicine's MEDLINE Database Are Distributed on CD-ROM (Compact Disc, Read-Only Memory) Optical Disc. Knowledge Finder Search-&-Retrieval Software Makes Searching of the OphthaLine Database Easy, Effective & Fast. After the User Types a Phrase or Sentence Describing the Information Needed, It selects the References in the Database That Appear to Best Match the Request, & Presents Them in Order of likely relevance. The OphthaLine Archive CD-ROM Contains over 300,000 References to Articles Published in 100 Ophthalmology-Related Journals over the Most Recent 10 Full Years. Ophthalmology Articles from More Than 2,500 Other Journals Are Also Included.
Aries Systems Corp.

OPS/83. *Version:* 2.2. Nov. 1984. *Compatible Hardware:* IBM PC & compatibles; VAX Series; Apollo; Sun; HP 9000/300; Tektronix 4400 Workstations. *Operating System(s) Required:* MS-DOS, VMS, Ultrix, Unix System V. *Language(s):* C. *Memory Required:* 512k.
from $1950.00 for MS-DOS to $20,000.00 for VAX 8500 or larger.
Rule-Based Programming Language Designed for the Solution of Real-World Problems. Used for Commercial Applications Involving Diagnosis, Configuration, Realtime Command & Control, & Other Problem Domains in Aerospace, Telecommunications, Industrial Process Control, Electronics, & Other Industries.
Production Systems Technologies, Inc.

OPS/83 for OS/2. *Compatible Hardware:* IBM PS/2 & compatibles. *Operating System(s) Required:* OS/2. *General Requirements:* Microsoft C Compiler.
3.5" disk $2950.00.
Allows User to Develop Artificial-Intelligence Applications in Protected Mode. Features Pascal-Like Syntax & Supports Separate Compilation for Program Development Efficiency & Standard Subroutine Linkages That Allow Interface with Other Languages. The Development Environment Is Coded in C & Assembly Language.
Production Systems Technologies, Inc.

Opt-Tech Sort. *Version:* 5.0. Sep. 1982. *Compatible Hardware:* IBM PC, PC XT, PC AT & compatibles. *Operating System(s) Required:* PC-DOS, MS-DOS, OS/2, Unix, Xenix, Windows. *Language(s):* Assembly & C. *Memory Required:* 64k. *Items Included:* Disks & Manual. *Customer Support:* Telephone - no charge.
disk $149.00.
Sort/Merge/Record Selection Utility That Can Be Used As a Stand-Alone Program or Called As a Subroutine to Most Languages. Supports Unlimited File Sizes, Multiple Input Files, & Fixed or Variable Length Records. Up to Twenty Sort Fields, All Common Data Types Supported. Output File Can Be Full Records, Keys, or Pointers.
Opt-Tech Data Processing.

OPTI-NET Lite. Jan. 1994. *Items Included:* 1 user's guide. *Customer Support:* A toll-free customer support line is available, as well as access to technical documents via a FlashFAX system & an electronic bulletin board.
MS-DOS V3.3 or higher. 80286 IBM & compatibles (1Mb or higher). CD-ROM disk $179.00 (ISBN 1-56953-002-5). *Nonstandard peripherals required:* CD-ROM drive(s) & controller. *Addl. software required:* Peer-to-Peer Network software, XMS memory manager. *Networks supported:* Peer-to-Peer Networks such as LANtastic, Netware Lite, Windows for Workgroups, IONET, PowerLAN.
A Software Program That Allows You to Increase the CD-ROM Sharing Performance of a Peer-to-Peer Network Server by Providing Data Caching Using XMS Memory & Through the Use of Prefetching Technology.
Online Computer Systems, Inc.

TITLE INDEX

Optical Concentrator of Solar Energy.
Compatible Hardware: HP 9000 Series 200, 300, 520, 9845. *Language(s):* HP BASIC.
$1975.00.
Solar Optics Utilities $400.00.
James Assocs.

Optical RayTracing Software: Ray Trace. Terry Anderson. Jan. 1986. *Compatible Hardware:* IBM PC with graphics card & 2 disk drives. *Operating System(s) Required:* PC-DOS 2.0. *Memory Required:* 64k.
disk $120.00.
Traces Rays Through a Lens System Having Circular Surfaces with Any Configuration & Spacing. Graphical Output Shows the Lens with Rays.
Kern International, Inc.

Optics One. *Compatible Hardware:* IBM PC & compatibles. *Operating System(s) Required:* PC-DOS/MS-DOS 2.0 or higher. *Memory Required:* 256k.
disk $199.95, incl. manual.
Menu-Driven Optical Ray Tracing Application Which Can Be Used for Optical System Design or Educational Instruction. The Manual Includes Tutorials & Examples.
Dynacomp, Inc.

OPTIMA. *Version:* MARK XVI. 1991. *Compatible Hardware:* IBM PC. *Operating System(s) Required:* MS-DOS. *Language(s):* MEGABASIC. *Memory Required:* 512k. *General Requirements:* Hard disk recommended. *Items Included:* On-disk manual. *Customer Support:* By telephone to registered users.
disk $100.00.
Shareware Designed for Managing Work of Billable Professionals. Provides Tools to Plan & Schedule Work, Analyze Costs, Track Performance & Control Results. Includes: Projects Sharing Resources; Scheduling by Resource Allocation; Planning Aids; Fixed & Variable Overhead Costs at Project & Activity Level; Resource Costs for Each Activity; Work Group Structuring; Narrative Text for Each Activity. Produces over 21 Reports. No Graphics or Plotters Needed. May Be Downloaded from Compuserve.
Azimuth Group, Ltd.

Optima Accounting. *Customer Support:* 800-929-8117 (customer service).
MS-DOS. IBM/PS2. disk $1999.99 (ISBN 0-87007-371-0).
A High-Level Integrated Accounting System, Which May Be Modified In-House for Specialized Business Applications.
SourceView Software International.

Optima Accounts Payable. *Customer Support:* 800-929-8117 (customer service).
MS-DOS. IBM/PS2. disk $599.99 (ISBN 0-87007-357-5).
Establishes & Maintains Vendor Information for Automating Vendor Accounting for Trade & Non-Trade Vendors.
SourceView Software International.

Optima Accounts Receivable. *Customer Support:* 800-929-8117 (customer service).
MS-DOS. IBM/PS2. disk $599.99 (ISBN 0-87007-358-3).
Utilizes Customer Records, Provides Processing of Customer Payments, Processes Credit & Debit Memos. When Processing Credit Memos for Returned Merchandise, the Items Returned Automatically Increase the Inventory for Those Products. Provides for Automatic Interest Calculation on Past-Due Invoices, & for Producing Debit Memos for Those Interest Charges. It Produces Delinquent Account Reminders & A New Delinquency Report for Immediate Follow-up, As Well As a Delinquent Indicator Which Is Set During Printing of the Customer Statements Reflecting the Current Delinquency Status. Produces a Monthly Check Register, Customer Statements, an Open Item List. All Financial Information Is Posted to the General Ledger System.
SourceView Software International.

Optima General Ledger. *Customer Support:* 800-929-8117 (customer service).
MS-DOS. IBM/PS2. disk $599.99 (ISBN 0-87007-355-9).
Automates Record Keeping, Produces a Financial Statement. User Defines & Establishes a Chart of Accounts, Which Is Divided into Assets, Liabilities, Capital, Income & Expenses, & for Manufacturing Companies, Manufacturing Expenses. Within Each of These Groups, Major Accounts May Be Defined & Each Individual Account Provides up to 99 Subaccounts. The Information Contained in Each Account & Subaccount Is Retained by the System for 26 Accounting Periods. The General Ledger & Fixed Asset System Contains Temporary Posting Files to Which the Other Systems (AR, AP, etc.) Post Financial Information. This Provides the Flexibility of Processing Data for a New Accounting Period, While Balancing the Transactions of the Previous Period. The Following Fixed Asset Groups Are Provided for Buildings, Building Improvements, Machinery & Equipment, Office Equipment, Automobiles, Computer, & Miscellaneous Equipment.
SourceView Software International.

Optima Inventory. *Customer Support:* 800-929-8117 (customer service).
MS-DOS. IBM/PS2. disk $599.99 (ISBN 0-87007-359-1).
Automates Inventory Control & Open Order Status Reporting. Inventory Control Features Finished Products, Multi-Level, Sub-Assemblies, Raw Material, & Parts & Supplies.
SourceView Software International.

Optima Load Scheduling. *Customer Support:* 800-929-8117 (customer service).
MS-DOS. IBM/PS2. disk $399.99 (ISBN 0-87007-363-X).
Records Workload Scheduling Information, & Produces Work Center Loading Reports.
SourceView Software International.

Optima Order Processing & Sales Analysis. *Customer Support:* 800-929-8117 (customer service).
MS-DOS. IBM/PS2. disk $399.99 (ISBN 0-87007-361-3).
Establishes & Maintains Customer Information, Produces Customer Order Reports, Customer Billings, Updates Inventories with Billing Information, Updates Sales Statistics & Salespersons' Commissions, Produces Daily Sales Summary Report, Salesperson Commission Report, Does Sales Projections, Produces Sales Analysis by Customer, Line of Business, & Territory. Produces Sales Analysis by Salesperson, by Product & Product Group. Produces a Taxable Invoice Register, Posts Sales Information Automatically to the General Ledger System, Reflects Customer Deposits on Invoices.
SourceView Software International.

Optima Payroll. *Customer Support:* 800-929-8117 (customer service).
MS-DOS. IBM/PS2. disk $599.99 (ISBN 0-87007-356-7).
Automates Payroll Earning Calculation & Recordkeeping. Provides up to 15 Types of Payments & 15 Types of Deductions. Processes Hourly & Salaried Pay Calculations in One Payroll Run, Provides for Commissions, Vacations, & Bonus Payments. Accrues Sick, Vacation, & Bonus Pay by Week & Posts Them to the GL. Provides for Check & Cash Payments, Allows Pay Calculation to be Interrupted & Restarted Without Duplicating Earnings, Produces Payroll Register for Verification Prior to Printing Checks, Posts All Payroll Information to the Appropriate GL Accounts, Employee Information May Be Queried Online, Produces Tax Balance & Government Reports, Year-End Earnings Statements, Christmas Bonus Report, Protects Records with Passwords for Confidentiality, Provides for State & City Taxes.
SourceView Software International.

Optima Production & Cost Control System. *Customer Support:* 800-929-8117 (customer service).
MS-DOS. IBM/PS2. disk $399.99 (ISBN 0-87007-364-8).
Provides for Daily Production Reporting by Work Center & by Job. If Desired, the Productivity of Each Employee Can Be Measured & Controlled. The System Produces Daily & Weekly Machine Utilization Reports, Specifying the Reason for Downtime. The Production & Cost Control Report Lists by Job, the Components Used with Their Costs As Well As the Production Quantities Per Work Center, or Employee & Unit Cost Information Per Work Center or Employee. For Finished Jobs, It Produces Total Material & Production Cost Per Finished Product.
SourceView Software International.

Optima Project Cost Control System. *Customer Support:* 800-929-8117 (customer service).
MS-DOS. IBM/PS2. disk $399.99 (ISBN 0-87007-360-5).
Provides for Budget Entry of Labor Hours & Amounts, Overhead, Materials, Equipment, Subcontractors, & Other Costs by Project & Phase. Provides for Budget & Cost Control at Every Level of a Project. Reports Actual to Budgeted Costs, Controls Materials at the Warehouse & at Projects. Provides for an Extension to the Payroll System Permitting Entry of Time Card Information, Pays Car & Meal Allowances & Is Fully Integrated into the General Ledger System.
SourceView Software International.

Optima Requirements Generation System. *Customer Support:* 800-929-8117 (customer service).
MS-DOS. IBM/PS2. disk $399.99 (ISBN 0-87007-362-1).
Requirements Are Generated for Products Not yet Available. Bill of Material Cost Report Lists All the Parts or Components Costs Contained in Each Product & in Each Subassembly with Total Cost per Product &/or Subassembly.
SourceView Software International.

Optimac. *Compatible Hardware:* Apple II with Applesoft. *Memory Required:* 48k.
disk $43.95.
Work-Day Simulation for Machines.
Dynacomp, Inc.

Optimal Engineer. *Version:* 1.0. 1991. *Items Included:* 215 page manual with tutorial, bibliography, glossary index, 75 solved problems. *Customer Support:* 30 day money back guarantee; free support by phone, mail or fax.
MS-DOS 2.X & higher. IBM PC, XT, AT, PS/2 & compatibles (640k). disk $495.00. *Optimal configuration:* IBM compatible 386, 16MHZ or higher, 640k, math coprocessor (recommended, not required). *Networks supported:* All.
General Purpose Engineering Optimization Package Based on Sequential Quadratic Programming. Handles Linear & Nonlinear

Objective Functions & Constraints, & Real, Integer, & Mixed Problems. Can Optimize External Programs As Well As Internal Functions. Includes 75 Solved Problems.
Transpower Corp.

Optimal Manager. Version: 2.0. 1984. *Items Included:* 212 page manual with tutorial, bibliography, glossary index, & numerous solved problems. *Customer Support:* 30 day money back guarantee; free support by phone, mail, or fax.
MS-DOS 2.X & higher. IBM PC, XT, AT, PS/2 compatibles (256k). disk $495.00, for all four. *Optimal configuration:* IBM compatible 386, 16MHZ or higher, 640k.
A Comprehensive Business Optimization & Decision-Support Software Package of 47 Program Units Covering All Essential Applications of Operations Research & Management Science. It's Organized into 4 Modules: Optimal Product Investment, Manufacture, Distributions & Pricing & Advertising.
Transpower Corp.

Optimal Scientist: Designs & Analyzes Optimal Experiments. 1993. *Items Included:* 458 page manual with tutorial, bibliography, glossary/index, & numerous solved problems. *Customer Support:* 30 day money back guarantee; free support by phone, mail, or fax.
MS-DOS 3.X & higher. IBM PC, XT, AT, PS/2 compatibles (640k). disk $595.00. *Optimal configuration:* 386, 16MHz or higher (extended memory can be used, but not required).
Experiment Design & Analysis Program, Able to Determine the Optimal Value of Predictor Variables & the Resultant Optimal Regression Equation. Contains Built-In Data Base System & General Purpose Graph Program.
Transpower Corp.

Optimal Solutions. Version: 2.30. May 1987. *Compatible Hardware:* IBM PC & compatibles. *Memory Required:* 64k. *General Requirements:* Lotus 1-2-3 Releases 2 & 2.01, Symphony Releases 1, 1.01, 1.1, & 1.2.
$99.95.
Finds Optimal Solutions for Achieving Designated Objectives under Limited Resources, Calculating Maximal or Minimal Values with As Many As 300 Variables & 80 Constraints. Also Calculates Slack, Shadow Prices, & Reduced Costs. Works with Macros. Provides Indexed Help Screens.
Enfin Software Corp.

Optimal Solutions-Plus. Version: 1.20. Aug. 1987. *Compatible Hardware:* IBM PC & compatibles. *Memory Required:* 320k. *General Requirements:* Lotus 1-2-3 Releases 2 & 2.01, Symphony Releases 1, 1.01, 1.1, & 1.2.
$295.00.
Finds Optimal Solutions for Achieving Designated Objectives under Limited Resources by Calculating Maximal or Minimal Values with As Many As 8,000 Variables & 8,000 Constraints. Performs Impact & Sensitivity Analyses, Allowing As Many As 25 Variables. Provides Indexed Help Screens & Works with Macros. Supports the 8087 Math Coprocessor & Extended Memory Specification.
Enfin Software Corp.

Optimization, Risk, Simulations. Version: 10.0. (Professional Ser.). 1989. *Compatible Hardware:* Apple Macintosh, IBM PC & compatibles. *Memory Required:* 512k. *Items Included:* Disks, book. program instructions. *Customer Support:* Telephone.
disk $145.00 (ISBN 0-920387-12-8).
Topics Covered Are: Optimization by Sampling & Inference; Optimization by Experiment, Including the Use of Response-Surface Experiments & the Use of Orthogonal Arrays; Optimization by Mathematical Programming, Including Linear Programming & Goal Programming for Multi-Criteria Optimization; Optimization by Simulation. Special Topics Include the Study of Queues & Simulated Queuing Systems; Inventory Problems; the Optimization of Financial Portfolios. A General Purpose Optimization Program OPTIMIZE Allows the Optimization of a User-Defined Function; Similarly, SIMULATE Provides the Response of a User-Defined Function to Random Inputs.
Lionheart Pr., Inc.

Optimizer. Version: 7.0. Medical Informatics, Inc. Staff. Jan. 1993. *Compatible Hardware:* IBM PC & compatibles, UNIX, XENIX. *Language(s):* FoxPro. *Memory Required:* 4000k. *General Requirements:* Multi-user Novell. *Items Included:* Tutorial, reference, implementation, installation bks. *Customer Support:* 90 days toll free with purchase, yearly contract $879.00.
disk $3349.00 & up.
IBM. (ISBN 0-925222-00-3).
UNIX. (ISBN 0-925222-01-1).
Accounts Receivable, Billing & Insurance Program Designed for Use in Medical Offices. Allows Multiple Doctors, Multiple Locations, User Defined Charge & Credit Codes, & User Defined Billing Cycles, Keeps Audit Information & Has Safeguards to Protect Patient Balances from Alteration. Basic Reports Such As Account Aging, Delinquent Accounts, Patient & Guarantor Lists, Bills & Invoices Are Included. Practice Activity Report Generator Allows User to Specify Reports Broken down by Provider, Location, Procedure Code & Time Period. Measured Care Module Calculates Cost & Quality That Individuals Physicians Provide.
Pacific Medsoft, Inc.

The Optimizer Linear Programmer. *Items Included:* Bound manual. *Customer Support:* Free hotline - no time limit; 30 day limited warranty; updates are $5/disk plus S&H.
MS-DOS. IBM & compatibles (256k). disk $149.95.
Disk-Based Linear Programming System for Solving Business Problems. Also Provides Sensitivity Analysis Including the Shadow Price (Dual Variable), Range of Resources over Which the Shadow Prices Are Valid, Slack Quantities (Helpful in Further Improving Efficiency or Costs), & Stability (How Sensitive Is the Solution to the Objective Function Coefficients).
Dynacomp, Inc.

Optimum Data Management System. UVEON. *Operating System(s) Required:* MS-DOS. *Memory Required:* 128k. *General Requirements:* 2 disk drives, printer.
$595.00.
Texas Instruments, Personal Productivit.

Optimum Tax Shelter Determination.
Compatible Hardware: Altos Series 15-5D, Series 5-5D, 580-XX, ACS8000-XX; DEC Rainbow 100 with 2 disk drives, Rainbow 100+ with 10MB hard disk; IBM PC with 2 disk drives, PC XT, IBM compatibles; Kaypro 11/IV with 2 disk drives, Kaypro 10; Xerox 820 with 2 disk drives, ZILOG MCZ-250. *Operating System(s) Required:* CP/M, MP/M, CP/M-86/80, PC-DOS, MS-DOS.
contact publisher for price (Order no.: SHELTER).
Template That Calculates the Tax on the Original Regular Taxable Income & the Original Alternative Minimum Taxable Income. Goes Through Several Iterations, Reducing the Original Regular Taxable Income Each Time, Until the Regular Tax Equals the Revised Alternative Minimum Tax.
Coopers & Lybrand.

Optina Slavonic for Windows. Apr. 1995. *Items Included:* User's manual; keyboard layout chart; keycap sticker sheet. *Customer Support:* Free telephone support, defective disks replaced free. Windows. IBM or compatibles (4Mb). disk $99.95. *Addl. software required:* MS Windows 3.1X or ATM.
Contains Professional, Hinted, Scalable TrueType & Type-1 Fonts. TrueType Requires Microsoft Windows 3.1; Also Works with Word 6 for DOS, WordPerfect 6.0b for DOS & AutoCAD R. 13. Type 1 Works with ATM & Windows; Also Works with OS/2 & AutoCAD R.12 & 13. WordPerfect for Windows Users Must Upgrade to Version 6.0a or Newer. A NeXT Version Is Available.
Linguist's Software, Inc.

OptinaSlavonic. Version: 1.1. Mar. 1995. *Items Included:* User's manual; keyboard layout chart; keycap sticker sheet. *Customer Support:* Free telephone support, defective disks replaced free. Macintosh. Macintosh (1Mb). 3.5" disk $99.95. *Addl. software required:* Any word processor.
Cyrillic Font Used for Labeling Icons. Professional-Quality, Hinted, Type-1 & TrueType Font.
Linguist's Software, Inc.

Option Arbitrage Software. Albert Bookbinder. Aug. 1993. *Compatible Hardware:* IBM PC. *Operating System(s) Required:* MS-DOS. *Language(s):* BASIC. *Memory Required:* 32k. *Items Included:* Handbook. *Customer Support:* Telephone support.
disk $144.00 (ISBN 0-916106-09-8).
Includes 8 Interactive Programs for Options on Stocks or Futures to Be Used to Evaluate Price, Return, & Risk in Option Investment or Speculation. Programs Include: Range Coefficient (Range Divided by Highest & Lowest Values), Which Is Useful in Measuring Variance in Option Valuation; Arbitrage-Conversion, Which Calculates Potential Profit & Investment Return on Arbitrage, Using Options & Stock; Arbitrage-Reverse Conversion, Which Calculates Potential Profit & Annualized Return on Arbitrage by Reverse Conversion, Using Options to Hedge Against Short Sales of Stock; Merton-Black-Scholes Call Value, Which Computes Fair Conversion Value of Put; Bookbinder Put Value Model, Which Calculates Actuarial Value of Put, Using Bookbinder Option Valuation Model; & Stock Index Future Value, Which Computes Value of Stock Index Future Contracts.
Programmed Pr.

Option Valuation & Implied Volatility. Version: 1.01. Mar. 1990. *Items Included:* Diskette of any desired size plus manual & book bound together. *Customer Support:* Limited support available.
MS-DOS. IBM PC/AT & compatibles (512k). contact publisher for price. *Nonstandard peripherals required:* Math Co-processor. *Addl. software required:* Lotus 1-2-3 release 2.01 or 2.2.
Valuation & Analysis of Financial Options Using Lotus 1-2-3.
Sah Research, Inc.

Options Analysis. *Compatible Hardware:* Apple II with Applesoft; Macintosh; IBM PC. *Memory Required:* 48k, IBM 128k, Macintosh 512k. disk $99.95.
Provides Analysis for Put & Call Prices As a Function of Both Stock Price & Time-to-Expiration Based on the Principal Investment Strategies Which One Might Employ.
Dynacomp, Inc.

Options-80A: Advanced Stock Option Analyzer. Version: 3.0. Patrick N. Everett. *Items Included:* Spiral bound manual, runtime version of Microsoft Basic for Mac version. *Customer*

TITLE INDEX

Support: 30 day money-back guarantee, free telephone support.
Macintosh Series (256K). 3.5" disk $150.00 (Order no.: 80A-MAC).
PC-DOS/MS-DOS. IBM PC/XT/AT & compatibles (256K). disk $150.00 (Order no.: 80A-PC).
Analyzes Calls, Puts & Spreads. Does Black-Scholes Modeling & Calculates Market-Implied Volatility. Plots Annualized Return on Real Investment Against Expiration Price of Underlying Stock, Guiding User to Optimum Investment. Unique Algorithms Include Buying & Selling Costs & Time Value of Money. Prints Tables & Charts, Comprehensive Indexed Manual.
Options-80.

Options Valuation. Version: 92.6. Lawrence R. Rosen. Mar. 1992. Items Included: Full documentation in word processor format. Customer Support: Free telephone support.
Macintosh (128k). 3.5" disk $89.00. Optimal configuration: Bare bones system - one drive.
MS-DOS. IBM PC's (64k). disk $89.00. Optimal configuration: One drive.
ProDOS or DOS 3.3. Apple II series (64k). disk $89.00. Optimal configuration: One 140k drive.
Computes Option Values for Stocks, Including Dividend-Paying Stocks & European & American Options, As Well As Option Values for Futures. Additionally Programs Are Included Which Calculate: (a) Time Spread or Elapsed Time; (b) Average Weighted Life; (c) Macaulay Duration; (d) Modified Duration, (e) Spot Rates & Forward Rates, As Well As (f) Historic or Future Volatility (of the Security Underlying the Option), & (g) Implied Volatility (of the Security Underlying).
Larry Rosen Co.

OptionVue IV. Version: 1.24. Leonard Yates. Oct. 1989. Compatible Hardware: IBM PC & compatibles. Operating System(s) Required: PC-DOS 2.0 or higher, MS-DOS 2.00 or higher. Language(s): Modula-2. Memory Required: 640k. General Requirements: hard disk. Customer Support: By phone.
disk $895.00.
$44.00 trial pack.
Strategy Maintenance & Analysis System for the Serious Private Investor. Handles Stock Options, Index Options, Currency Options, Bond Options, Commodity Options, Convertible Securities & Warrants. Provides for Testing Strategies Through Simulation on Computer Prior to Committing Real Money. Will Retrieve Data Automatically from Dow Jones, FNN Signal, & Comstock. A Market Maker Version is Available.
OptionVue Systems International, Inc.

OPTune. Version: 1.4. Apr. 1993. Items Included: Manual. Customer Support: 30-day money back guarantee, technical support (toll), maintenance agreement available.
MS-DOS/PC-DOS 2.0 or higher (256k). IBM PC, PC XT, PC AT & compatibles, PS/2. disk $79.00. Optimal configuration: 640k RAM.
First All-in-One hard-disk Repair, Survival, & Maintenance Utility. Will Defragment Files, Verify Disk Media Using In-Depth "Bit Pattern" Tests, Nondestructively Test & Adjust Disk's Interleave, & Much More. Run Automatically from Your AUTOEXEC.BAT File to Keep Hard Disks Spinning Faster & Longer.
GTM Software.

OR-D Dental System. 1981. Compatible Hardware: IBM PC & compatibles. Operating System(s) Required: UCSD Pascal, MS-DOS. Language(s): Pascal. Memory Required: 256-512k.
$3500.00.
Designed Especially for the Dental Profession. Includes Diagnostic & Treatment, Billing & Aging Reports, Insurance Co-Payment, Patient History, Provider Analysis, Practice Building & Integrated Letter Writing. Monitors a Patient from the Patient's Entry into the Practice Throughout His Treatment History. System Is Equipped to Monitor up to 60,000 Patients, 999 Codes, 500 Insurance Companies & 35 Providers. Insurance (Outstanding Balance), Patient History of Transactions, Referral List, Management & Insurance Statistics Reports, etc. Also Included Is Word Processing & Office Accounting.
OR-D Systems.

OR-D Medical System. 1981. Compatible Hardware: IBM PC & compatibles. Operating System(s) Required: UCSD p-System, MS-DOS. Language(s): Pascal. Memory Required: 256-512k.
disk $3500.00.
Designed to Assist Physicians in All Aspects of the Medical Profession. Includes Diagnostic & Treatment, Billing & Aging Reports, Insurance Co-Payment, Patient History, Provider Analysis, Practice Building & Integrated Letter Writing, Prescription & Patient Chart. Monitors Patient from Patient's Entry into the Practice Throughout His Treatment History, for up to 10,000 Patients, 1000 Codes, 1000 Insurance Companies & 35 Providers. System Is Available for Single-User or Multi-User System for up to 64 Stations.
OR-D Systems.

OR-D Tutorial System. Jan. 1987. General Requirements: Hard disk, printer.
contact publisher for price.
Teaches Medical & Dental Students the Use of Computer Systems in a Practice Environment.
OR-D Systems.

ORACLE. Oracle Corp. Apr. 1984. Operating System(s) Required: MS-DOS 2.1. Memory Required: 512k. General Requirements: Printer, Winchester.
contact publisher for price (Order no.: TI P/N 2240338-0001).
Texas Instruments, Personal Productivit.

Oracle for Macintosh. Compatible Hardware: Apple Macintosh, Macintosh Plus. Memory Required: 2000k.
Developer version. 3.5" disk $199.00.
Networking version. 3.5" disk $999.00.
Transforms HyperCard into a Full-Function SQL.
Oracle Corp.

Oracle Quicksilver. Compatible Hardware: IBM PC & compatibles (80286/80386 PC recommended). Operating System(s) Required: PC-DOS 3.0 or higher. Memory Required: At least 640k, recommended 1640k. General Requirements: Hard disk.
$699.00, incl. Oracle SQL*Tutor.
Compiler That Adds SQL & Connectivity Features to dBASE Applications. Builds Multi-User Applications That Can Access Both Distributed ORACLE & dBASE Data. Delivers All Capabilities of dBASE Plus Windowing, Graphics, & User-Defined Functions.
Oracle Corp.

Oracle SQL*Tutor. Compatible Hardware: IBM PC & compatibles. Memory Required: 256k. General Requirements: Hard disk.
$199.00.
Tutorial for ORACLE QUICKSILVER.
Oracle Corp.

ORACLE Tools & Database. Version: 6.0. 1991. MS-DOS 3.1 or higher or OS/2 V1.1 or higher. IBM or COMPAQ PCs (286 or greater) & compatibles. Contact publisher for price.
Nonstandard peripherals required: Hard disk.
User Can Develop Powerful Multi-User Database Applications on the PC & Port Them, without Modification to Run on All Major Microcomputers, Workstations, Minicomputers & Mainframes.
Oracle Corp.

Oral & Cutaneous Manifestations of HIV. Richard Johnson. Feb. 1995. Customer Support: Toll-free technical support - no charge. 9AM - 5PM EST 800-343-0064.
System 7.0 or higher. Apple Macintosh (8Mb). CD-ROM disk $175.00, Individual, ,495.00 Institutional (ISBN 1-57276-012-5, Order no.: SE-012-001). Nonstandard peripherals required: CD-ROM drive.
Microsoft Windows, Version 3.1. 386 IBM-Compatible PC (8Mb). CD-ROM disk $175.00, Individual, ,495.00 Institutional. Nonstandard peripherals required: MPC Standard CD-ROM player, 640x480 display w/256 colors, MPC Standard Soundboard & Speakers.
This CD-ROM Contains about 300 Original Photographic Images with Accompanying Text Describing the Clinical Lesions, Treatment Options, & Some Histo-Pathological Comparisons. Case Vignettes for Diagnosis & Management, Differential Diagnosis of Various Types of Clinical Lesions, Including Papules, Nodules & Vesicles, & Discussions of Universal Precautions Are All Covered.
SilverPlatter Education.

Oral Surgery PC. Compatible Hardware: IBM PC & compatibles. Operating System(s) Required: PC-DOS/MS-DOS. (source code included). Memory Required: 128k. General Requirements: 2 disk drives, 132-column printer.
disk $3595.95 (Order no.: D-126).
demo disk $100.00.
manual $50.00.
Office Management System That Prepares Bills, Claim Forms, Attending Dentist's Statement, Account Reviews, Daily Journals, Monthly Aged Accounts Receivable Reports As Well As Numerous Practice Productivity Reports.
CMA Micro Computer.

Orbiter: Space Shuttle Simulation. Version: 1.02. Mar. 1986. Compatible Hardware: Atari 520/1040 ST, Mega 2/4.
Atari ST. disk $14.95.
A Space Shuttle Simulation, Which Allows You to Command a Shuttle Launch, Travel in Earth Orbit, Rescue Damaged Satellites, Build a Space Station, Take a Space Walk in the MMU, & Land the Shuttle with Such a High Degree of Realism It Can Be Classified As Educational As Well As Entertaining. Voice Synthesis Incorporated into the Program Enables You to Hear NASA Control During Flight.
Spectrum HoloByte.

Orbits: Orbital Motion Simulation. 1995. Items Included: Full manual. Customer Support: Free telephone support - 90 days, 30-day warranty.
MS-DOS 3.2 or higher. 286 (584k). disk $59.95. Nonstandard peripherals required: CGA/EGA/VGA.
Simulate the Orbital Motion of Planets, Rockets, & Stars. Calculate & Plot Their Motions under the Gravitational Influence of Two Heavy Bodies, & up to Five Light Bodies. Versatile & Interactive, ORBITS Is Not Limited to Only Introductory Physics Students. It Also Provides a Valuable Tool for Advanced Students in Numerical Analysis & Orbital Mechanics As Well.
Dynacomp, Inc.

OrCAD Capture for Windows. Version: 6.11. Jan. 1996. Items Included: 8 product disks, 2 Win 32s disks, Capture manual & user's guide. Customer Support: 90 days free technical support & version changes.

Microsoft Windows 3.1 or higher' DOS 5.0 or later. 486 Pentium PC or better. disk $995.00.
OrCAD Capture seamlessly integrates with all Microsoft Windows applications. OrCAD Capture runs with optimal performance on all Windows-based platforms & was specifically designed to leverage all emerging Windows-based technology.
OrCAD.

OrCAD Layout for Windows. *Version:* 6.41. Jan. 1996. *Items Included:* 10 product disks, Layout manual & user's guide, Autorouter user's guide, Footprint library. *Customer Support:* 90 days free technical support & version changes.
Windows 3.1 or higher; DOS 6.0 or later. 486 Pentium PC or better. disk $4995.00.
Speeds the design of general purpose PCB's & includes a translator for OrCAD PCB 386 files. Translators for five additional PCB software packages are also available for use with Layout.
OrCAD.

OrCAD Layout Ltd. for Windows. *Version:* 6.41. Jan. 1996. *Items Included:* 10 product disks, layout manual & users guide, OrCAD footprint library. *Customer Support:* 90 days free technical support & version changes.
Microsoft Windows 3.1 & Windows for Workgroups 3.11, DOS 6.0 or later. 486 Pentium PC or better. disk $1995.00.
OrCAD Layout Ltd. is a robust productivity tool, giving you the same output & reporting capabilities as OrCAD Layout & OrCAD Layout Plus.
OrCAD.

OrCAD Layout Plus for Windows. *Version:* 6.41. *Items Included:* 10 product disks, manual & users guide, Autorouter & autoplacement user's guide, OrCAD Footprint Library. *Customer Support:* 90 free technical support & version changes.
Microsoft Windows 3.1, Windows for workgroups 3.11, Windows 95, Windows NT 351, or later, Windows 3.1 & Windows for Workgroups 3.11 require DOS 6.0 or later. 486 Pentium PC or better. disk $9995.00.
Delivers all the capabilities of OrCAD Layout, plus advanced features that accelerate the design of high speed, high density, or analog printed circuit boards. To handle the most difficult routes in complex designs, Layout Plus includes automatic component placement & a push-&-shove autorouter with manual-assist & auto-path-completion modes.
OrCAD.

OrCAD PCB: OrCAD Printed Circuit Board Layout Tools 386. *Version:* 2.20. Aug. 1995. *Items Included:* 6 product disks, Installing PCB 386 instructions, user's guide, reference guide, update guide, PLD device list, PCBView 386, 916 design modules product. *Customer Support:* 1 yr free technical support & version changes.
MS-DOS 5.0 or higher. 386/486 or Pentium PC-compatible. disk $2995.00.
OrCAD PCB 386 is a complete layout solution for boards ranging from the simple to the complex. It delivers superior functionality, with over 1,000 footprints, automatic footprint generation, & on-line all object editing. Includes an embetted, 100% completion autorouter that provides functionality needed for all but a small percentage of the most dense boards.
OrCAD.

OrCAD PCB 386Plus: Printed Circuit Board Tools 386Plus. *Version:* 2.0. Oct. 1994. *Items Included:* ESP Design Environment, all manuals, disks. *Customer Support:* 30 day money back guarantee, 1 year free telephone technical support, free program updates while support agreement is current.
MS-DOS 3.3 or higher. 386/486 or Pentium IBM-compatible (4Mb). disk $2495.00 (Order no.: PRPCB3-(3/5)(N/H)).
A Fast, Powerful, Full-Featured, DOS Based Design Tool for Creating Electronic Printed Circuit Boards of up to 32 Layers. It Includes Versatile Component Placement & Manual & Automatic Routing of Traces & Planes. It Reads EDIF Netlist Files & Outputs Data to Graphics Formats, Printers, Plotters, & Photoplotters.
OrCAD.

OrCAD PCR 386Plus: Placement & Critical Route 386Plus. *Version:* 1.10. Feb. 1994. *Items Included:* ESP Design Environment, all manuals, disks. *Customer Support:* 30 day money back guarantee, 1 year free product support, low cost product support agreement annually, thereafter, free updates while product support agreement is current, low cost upgrade policy.
MS-DOS 3.3 or higher. 386/486 or Pentium IBM-compatible (4Mb). disk $595.00 (Order no.: PRPCR3-(3/5)(N/H)).
A Full-Featured, Yet Low Cost DOS Based Design Tool That Allows Designers to Create a "First-Pass" PC Board Layout. It Includes an Easy to Use Manual Router, a Large Footprint Library & Component Generation Capabilities. It Reads EDIF Netlists & Outputs Data for Printers, Plotters & Photoplotters.
OrCAD.

OrCAD/PLD. *Version:* Release IV. *Items Included:* Manual, disk of part libraries, printer drivers. *Customer Support:* Free telephone support for 1 year - $125.00 each additional year. 30 day return policy, free access to BBS, product updates free for one year.
disk $795.00.
Programmable Logic Device Design Software that Allows Input in Forms of: Boolean Equations, Procedural State Machines, Truth Tables, Indexed Equations & Numerical Mapping (a Form of Logic Synthesis). Also Takes Schematic Input. Output is Jedec File, Hex, Netlist.
OrCAD.

OrCAD PLD 386: OrCAD Programmable Logic Design Tools 386. *Version:* 2.01. 1988. *Items Included:* Ten product disks (8-PLD, 1-install, 1 ESP), Installation instructions, User's guide, Language guide, ESP user guide, PLD device list. *Customer Support:* 1 year free technical support & version changes.
MS-DOS 3.3 or higher. 386/486 or Pentium PC-compatible. disk $1995.00.
With OrCAD PLD 386 the engineer can create designs using OrCADs Powerful hardware description language (OHDL), Or-CAD schematics or both. The compiler accepts seven forms of input, including; Boolean equations, indexed equations, streams, numerical maps, truth tables, state machines, & schematics. Includes software fitters for most popular devices at no extra charge.
OrCAD.

OrCAD PLD386Plus: Programmable Logic Design 386Plus. *Version:* 2.0. Mar. 1994. *Items Included:* ESP Design Environment, all manuals, disks. *Customer Support:* 30 day money back guarantee, 1 year free product support, low cost product support agreement annually, thereafter, free updates while product support agreement is current, low cost upgrade policy.
MS-DOS 3.3 or higher. 386/486 or Pentium IBM-compatible (4Mb). disk $1895.00 (Order no.: PRPLD3-(3/5)(N/H)).
A Fast, Powerful, Full-Featured, DOS Based Design Tool for Creating Programmable Logic Designs. It Includes OrCAD's Hardware Description Language (OHDL), a Logic Compiler & Fitters for Most Major Programmable Devices. It Reads SDT386Plus Schematic Files, OHDL or Both, & Produces All Necessary Files for the Selected Device.
OrCAD.

OrCAD/SDT. *Version:* Release IV. *Compatible Hardware:* IBM PC & compatibles. *Customer Support:* Free telephone support for 1 year - $125.00 each additional year. 30 day return policy, free access to BBS, product updates for one year-free.
disk $795.00.
Schematic-Capture Program That Offers over Six Thousand Library Parts.
OrCAD.

OrCAD SDT386Plus: Schematic Design Tools 386Plus. *Version:* 1.2. Sep. 1994. *Items Included:* ESP Design Environment, all manuals, disks. *Customer Support:* 30 day money back guarantee, 1 year free product support, $175 per year thereafter, free updates with valid product support agreement.
MS-DOS 3.3 or higher. 386/486 or Pentium IBM-compatible (4Mb). disk $895.00 (Order no.: PRSDT3-(3/5)(N/H)).
A Fast, Powerful, Full-Featured, DOS Based Design Tool for Schematic Entry, Editing & Creating Standard & Custom Library Parts, & Extracting Part List & Net List Data. It Interfaces Directly to PCB386Plus for Circuit Board Design, VST386Plus for Digital Circuit Simulation, & PLD386Plus for Programmable Logic Design.
OrCAD.

OrCAD Simulate for Windows. *Version:* 6.0. *Items Included:* 4 product disks, 2 Win 32s disks, Simulate manual & user's guide. *Customer Support:* 90 day free technical support & version changes.
Windows 3.1 or higher; DOS 5.0 or later. 486, Pentium PC or better. disk $3495.00.
Simulate provides a powerful debugging environment for AMD, Actel, Altera, Lattice, Or Xilinx schematic designs.
OrCAD.

OrCAD STD 386: OrCAD Schematic Design Tools 386. *Version:* 1.21. Apr. 1995. *Items Included:* 7 product disks, Installing SDT instructions, SDT user's guide, ESP users guide, SDT reference guide, M-2 Edit user's guide. *Customer Support:* 1 year free technical support & version changes.
MS-DOS or higher. 386/486 or Pentium PC-compatible. disk $995.00.
OrCAD.

OrCAD Verification & Simualtion Tools 386. *Version:* 1.2. *Items Included:* 4 product disks (3-VST, 1-install), Installing VST 386 instructions, VST 386 reference guide, PLD Modeling Tools Reference Guide, VGEN-ATO. *Customer Support:* 1 year free technical support & version changes.
MS-DOS 3.3 or higher. 386/486 or Pentium PC-compatible. disk $1995.00.
Or-CAD VST 386 allows the simulation of digital designs of up to 200,000 gates. The PLD modeling capability enables simulation of multiple PLDs in a single deisgn. This Product includes thousands of device models, & allows the user to create models in support of new technologies. The newest version of VST 386 supports timing simulation of boards with multiple Xilinx & Actel FPGAs mixed with TTL & other parts from the extensive VSG 386 simulation parts library.
OrCAd.

OrCAD/VST. *Version:* Release IV. *Compatible Hardware:* IBM PC & compatibles. *Customer Support:* Free telephone support for 1 year -

TITLE INDEX

$225.00 each additional year. 30 day return policy, free access to BBS, free product updates for one year.
disk $1495.00.
Digital Simulator.
OrCAD.

OrCAD VST386Plus: Verification & Simulation Tools 386Plus. *Version:* 1.2. *Items Included:* ESP Design Environment, all manuals, disks. *Customer Support:* 30 day money back guarantee, 1 year free product support, low cost product support agreement annually, thereafter, free updates while product support agreement is current, low cost upgrade policy.
MS-DOS 3.3 or higher. 386/486 or Pentium IBM-compatible (4Mb). disk $1995.00 (Order no.: PRVST3-(3/5)(N/H)). *Optimal configuration:* Add 1Mb memory for each additional 15000 gates.
A Fast, Powerful, Full-Featured, DOS Based Design Tool for Simulating & Verifying a Digital Electronic Circuit Design. It Includes Thousands of Simulation Models & Model Creation Capabilities. It Reads OrCAD SDT386Plus Generated Netlist Files of Mixed FPGA, PLD, & TTL Devices & Provides Logic Analyzer-Like Circuit Timing Displays.
OrCAD.

Orchard & Grove Management.
Agri-Management Services, Inc. *Operating System(s) Required:* MS-DOS. *Memory Required:* 64k. *General Requirements:* Printer.
$495.00.
Texas Instruments, Personal Productivit.

Orchestrator.
one-time software license $3000.00.
monthly maintenance fee $35.00.
Micro-to-Mainframe Link. Includes a Telecommunications Program; Four Data Entry Modules; Printer Support Software; & Report Backup, Restoration & Deletion; & File Transfer.
Control Data Business Management Services.

Orchestrator Premier. *Compatible Hardware:* IBM PC.
$3000.00.
Additional charges for processing & program maintenance.
Data Entry & Communications Program Which Links PCs to CDBC's Mainframe Payroll, Human Resources & Accounting Services. Includes Reporting, Linking & File Translation Modules.
Control Data Business Management Services.

Order Distibution. *Compatible Hardware:* Apple Macintosh. *General Requirements:* Macintosh Plus.
3.5" disk $6000.00.
Designed for Distributors of Discrete Ready-Made Products.
Advanced Data Systems, Inc.

Order Entry. *Version:* 5.7. 1978. *Compatible Hardware:* IBM PC, TRS-80. *Operating System(s) Required:* PC-DOS 1.1, 2.0, MS-DOS. *Language(s):* MBASIC (source code included). *Memory Required:* 128k. *General Requirements:* Hard disk recommended.
disk $500.00.
Prints Customer Workorder, Commits Finished Goods Ordered, Updates Customer Order & Backorders. Shipping Labels, Open & Back-Order Reports by Customer & Item, Selective Partial Billing. Interfaces with A/R & Manufacturing Inventory.
CharterHouse Software Corp.

Order Entry. *Compatible Hardware:* Apple II+, IIe, III; Atari; IBM PC XT. *Operating System(s) Required:* CP/M, CP/M-86, CP/M-68000, MS-DOS. *Language(s):* BASIC (source code included). *Memory Required:* 48k. *General Requirements:* 2 disk drives, printer.
disk $69.50.
Handles Documentation & Control of Purchase Orders & Sales Orders. Generates & Prints Orders & Statements in Mailable Form at up to 9 Line Items per Order. Manages Changes in Description, Price, & Quantity. When Orders Are Shipped or Delivered, Computes Tax & Monitors Backorders. Interacts with Accounts Payable, Accounts Receivable, & Inventory to Update Records. Lists Vendors & Customers, & Reports on Order Histories for Individual Vendors/Customers. When Partial Delivery or Shipment Is Made on an Order, a New Order for the Backordered Portion Can Be Generated. Purchase Order/Sales Order History Programs Provide Printouts That Document All Activity on Original Orders. All Reports & Listings Can Be Printed.
Compumax, Inc.

Order Entry. *Version:* 2.0. 1989. *Compatible Hardware:* Altos; Compupro; Compaq; Fujitsu; Heath-Zenith; HP; IBM PC, PC XT, PC AT; NEC; Tandy. *Operating System(s) Required:* PC-DOS, MS-DOS, Concurrent DOS, Unix, Xenix; Novell & Microsoft networks. *Language(s):* C. *Memory Required:* 640k. *General Requirements:* Hard disk & 132-column printer. *Items Included:* Disks & manuals. *Customer Support:* Through VARs, support contracts available.
single-user $995.00.
multi-user $1295.00.
Unix, Xenix $1495.00.
demo disk & manual $20.00.
Order Entry & Tracking System That Provides the Management Information for Keeping Response Time at Acceptable Levels & Identifying Bottlenecks. As Orders Are Entered, the Available Balance of Each Part Ordered Is Displayed. Order Quantity Can Be Adjusted to Match the Balance Available or Held until All Parts Are Available. Released Orders Can Be Billed When Shipped, with Multiple Billings Possible. Tracks All Backordered Items, Providing a Variety of Reports That Assist in Monitoring Backorders. Contains a Backordered Items Report Which Lists Items That Are Backordered in Data Sequence. Interacts with the MC Software's Accounts Receivable & Inventory Packages. Part of the Integrated Manufacturing Software Series & the Integrated Company Management Accounting Series.
INMASS/MRP.

Order Entry. *Version:* 4.5. 1985. *Compatible Hardware:* IBM PC & compatibles, PC XT, PC AT, 386, 486, Pentium, PS/2. *Operating System(s) Required:* PC-DOS/MS-DOS 3.X, 4X, 5X, 6X, Windows 3.1, Windows 95. *Language(s):* BASIC, C, Assembler. *Memory Required:* 640k. *General Requirements:* Stand-alone or 2Mb Network file server. *Customer Support:* 90 day warranty, onsite training, telephone support.
Contact publisher for price.
Allows User to Enter Order & Immediately Allocate Inventory. This On-Line Capability Insures That Inventory Is Kept Current. Creates User-Defined Invoices Immediately to Allow an Invoice to Accompany All Merchandise That Goes Out the Door. Selects Which Orders Are to Be Released at Any Given Time. After Orders Have Been Entered, They May Be Individually Released for Shipment & Invoiced. Automatically Updates LIBRA ACCOUNTS RECEIVABLE, INVENTORY CONTROL, JOB COSTING, SALES ANALYSIS & GENERAL LEDGER DATA VOLUMES. This Interface Will Keep Information Current & Accurate among All Systems.
LIBRA Corp.

ORDER ENTRY-INVOICING

Order Entry. *Version:* 5.9. 1995. *Operating System(s) Required:* MS-DOS. *Language(s):* Compiled BASIC. *Memory Required:* 256k. *General Requirements:* Printer, monitor. *Items Included:* Manual, demo, disk. *Customer Support:* Free phone support for 90-days; $25.00 per call after.
disk $200.00 (ISBN 0-918185-66-1).
Records Orders, Produces Invoices & Transmits the Information to the Accounts Receivable System. A Standard Invoice Form Is Included. Links to Inventory Control for Sales Analysis by Seller & Product Category. Creates General Ledger Transactions If Sales by Invoice Line Items Is Selected.
Taranto & Assocs., Inc.

Order Entry. Information Unlimited Software, Inc. (IUS). *Operating System(s) Required:* MS-DOS. *Memory Required:* 64k. *General Requirements:* 2 disk drives, printer.
$595.00 (Order no.: TI P/N 2311480-0001).
Texas Instruments, Personal Productivit.

Order Entry - Invoicing.
DOS Network. IBM & compatibles (4Mb). Contact publisher for price. *Addl. software required:* RM COBOL Runtime. *Networks supported:* Novell.
Allows Entry of Customer Orders & Invoicing of Those Orders. Line Items Can Be Applied to Cc :tracts, Applied to a Promotion, or Applied to a Custom Formula. Allows for Different "Bill to" - "Ship to", 9999 Price Schedules, & Many Other Features. Integrates to Grossman Inventory Control, Which Ties to All Other Grossman Modules.
Grossman & Assocs., Inc.

Order Entry & Inventory Control. *Compatible Hardware:* IBM PC, PC XT, PC AT. *Operating System(s) Required:* MS-DOS, PC-DOS. *General Requirements:* Hard disk, printer.
disk $195.00 (Order no.: D/A).
All Transactions Are On-Line, Allowing Instant Access. Prints Daily Order Log by Crder or Product, Open Order Analysis Repoits by Customer or Product, Separate Ship to Addresses Maintained, Orders Changed or Deleted, Automatically Adjusts Inventory. Billing Done in This Module.
Theta Business Systems.

Order Entry & Invoicing. *Version:* 14.0. (Accounting Software Ser.). Aug. 1993. *Compatible Hardware:* IBM & compatibles. *Operating System(s) Required:* MS-DOS, PC-DOS 3.X & up. *Language(s):* MegaBASIC. *Memory Required:* 640k. *General Requirements:* Hard disk, wide carriage printer. *Customer Support:* (203) 790-9756.
$395.00, Network Option ,400.00 more.
$50.00.
Features Automatic Posting of Invoices, Printing of Packing Slips, Credit Memos, Orders, & Invoices. Computes Salesman Commissions & Updates Inventory for Sales, Returns, etc. Allows Invoicing for Special Parts (Not in Inventory). Automatic Lookup of Customer, & Inventory Items. Allows Default Information (eg. Salesman, Tax %), & Special Charges. Calculates Discounts. Choice of 3 Sales Commission Methods. Users Can Print As They Go or Delay Printing by Spooling Data.
Applications Systems Group (CT), Inc.

Order Entry-Invoicing. *Version:* 3.3. (Integrated Manufacturing & Financial System Ser.). *Compatible Hardware:* Micro/VAX, UNIBUS/VAX; IBM PC. *Operating System(s) Required:* MS-DOS, Novell, Micro/VAX, VAX/VMS, UNIX. *Language(s):* DIBOL.
MS-DOS. $750.00 single-user.

ORDER ENTRY: MODULE 7

DEC PDP-11/VAX. $1500.00 multi-user. *Produces a Number of Reports to Aid in Managing Manufacturing Activity. Reports Include: Master Schedule, Open or Backorder, Order Status, Promise Date, & Aged Open Order. Maintains Order Backlog & Provides Picking Tickets, Acknowledgements, Shipping Papers, & Invoices.*
Primetrack.

Order Entry: Module 7. *Version:* 7.11. Sep. 1991. *Items Included:* Perfect-bound manual. *Customer Support:* 90 days toll-free technical phone support, each additional year $150.. MS-DOS 3.1 or higher. IBM PS/2, PC, PC XT, PC AT & compatibles (384k). disk $295.00. *Addl. software required:* System Manager, Inventory Control, Accounts Receivable. *Networks supported:* PC-Lan, 3COM, Novell, LANtastic.
Automates the Process of Issuing Quotes, Taking Sales Orders, Credit Approval; Packing List Generation & Issuing Invoices. Allows for Backorders, Automatic Reduction of Inventory, Invoice History & Multiple Ship-To Addresses. Tracks Sales by Customer, Sales Representative, Part & Product Line.
Manzanita Software Systems.

Order Entry: OE. *Version:* 5.8. May 1993. *Language(s):* DIBOL & C, COBOL. *General Requirements:* Depends on specific configuration. *Customer Support:* Full service, update service; by quotation.
VMS, Open VMS. DEC VAX Series, DEC Alpha AXP. $3500.00-$15,000.00.
source code by quotation.
Operates With the RE RECEIVABLES MANAGEMENT SYSTEM to Provide an Interactive Method of Entering & Processing Orders, Generating Invoices, & Analyzing Sales. Features User-Designed Forms for Order Processing Using User-Defined Parameter Files. Inventory Levels for Multiple Warehouses Shown on Order Screen. Ideal for Phone Orders with Pertinent Account Information Retrieved Automatically.
Compu-Share, Inc.

Order Express. *Compatible Hardware:* Apple Macintosh 512KE. *Memory Required:* 512k. *General Requirements:* External disk drive or hard disk; Omnis 3 Plus.
3.5" disk $399.00.
Order Entry System.
CP Software.

Order House. *Version:* 3.6. *Compatible Hardware:* Apple Macintosh SE 30, II series, Centris, Quadra. *Items Included:* Manual, runtime Helix Express. *Customer Support:* 3 hrs. customization included, free phone support. Order House. $2995.00-$4995.00. *Nonstandard peripherals required:* High performance hard drive.
Integrated Multiuser Program Designed to Completely Manage Wholesale, Mailorder & Distribution Businesses. Designed to Handle All Business Data Tasks with a Minimum of Keystrokes. Full Sales, Inventory, Purchasing, Accounting, Inventory, UPS Shipping, Mailmerge & More Are On-Line at All Times.
Elefunt Software.

Order Processing. *Version:* 450.2. 1979. *Compatible Hardware:* IBM PC & compatibles. *Operating System(s) Required:* PC-DOS, MS-DOS. *Language(s):* QuickBASIC. *Memory Required:* 512k. *General Requirements:* Hard disk. *Items Included:* System diskettes, users guide, training tutorial. *Customer Support:* Telephone; annual contracts available.
$395.00 to $495.00.

Designed to Enter Customer Orders & Print Shipping Orders (If Required) & Invoices Including Any Discounts, Sales Tax, & Freight Charges Applicable. Customers May Be Assigned to One of Three Pre-Set Pricing Columns for Quick Order Extension & Totalling. Checks Stock Status As Order is Being Entered to Determine Ship or Backorder Status. Operator May Override Customer & Inventory Parameters When Order is Being Entered. System Automatically Reduces Inventory, Increases Sales, & Posts to Receivables If Interfaced to Those IMS Systems. Order Status Inquiries Let User Answer Customer Questions. Interfaces with IMS Inventory Control & Accounts Receivable Systems. Runs Single User or Multi-User on Many Networks.
International Micro Systems, Inc.

Ordinary Income Acceleration. *Compatible Hardware:* Altos Series 5-15D, Series 5-5D, 580-XX, ACS8000-XX; DEC Rainbow 100 with 2 disk drives, Rainbow 100+ with 10mb hard disk; IBM PC with 2 disk drives, PC XT, IBM compatibles; Kaypro II/4 with 2 disk drives, Kaypro 10; Xerox 820 with 2 disk drives, ZILOG MCZ-250. *Operating System(s) Required:* CP/M, MP/M, CP/M-86, CP/M-80, PC-DOS, MS-DOS.
contact publisher for price (Order no.: ALTROD). *Template Helps Determine the Amount of Ordinary Income Which Must Be Accelerated into the Current Period to Equalize the Regular Tax & the Alternative Minimum Tax. For Each Alternative, the Template Uses the Following Assumptions: Regular Taxable Income, Alternative Minimum Taxable Income, & Marital Status.*
Coopers & Lybrand.

Oregon Trail.
Windows. IBM & compatibles. CD-ROM disk $69.95 (Order no.: R1377). *Nonstandard peripherals required:* CD-ROM drive. *Optimal configuration:* 386 processor higher, MS-DOS 3.1 or higher, 20Mb hard drive, 640k RAM, external speakers or headphones (with sound card) that are Sound Blaster compatible, VGA graphics & adapter, VGA color monitor.
Macintosh (4Mb). (Order no.: R1377A). *Nonstandard peripherals required:* 14" color monitor or larger, CD-ROM drive.
This Learning Simulation Adventure Enables Students to Learn about the Westward Movement. Explore American History & Geography While Improving Reading Comprehension & Writing Skills (Ages 10-Adult).
Library Video Co.

OREntry. Jun. 1985. *Compatible Hardware:* IBM PC, PC AT, PC XT & compatibles. *Operating System(s) Required:* PC-DOS, MS-DOS. *Language(s):* BASIC. *Memory Required:* 512k. disk $100.00.
Drill Log Data Can Be Input into a Geostat Drill Hole File Using ORENTRY. The Program Is Interactive, Permitting the User to Edit the Data after Input.
Geostat Systems International, Inc. (GSII).

The OREO Manager. *Items Included:* Manuals & 2 days of on-site training. *Customer Support:* Annual maintenance agreement. 15% of license fees includes: unlimited technical telephone support & modem support, free new versions, free update documentation, free updates, future enhancement input & special offers on new products.
MS Microsoft DOS. IBM & compatibles (386sx) (640k). $9995.00-$30,000.00 based on number of properties. *Optimal configuration:* 486SX25, DOS 6.0 or higher, min. 640k RAM, color monitor, laser printer, 300Mb HD. *Networks supported:* Novell, Lantastic, or similar product with dedicated server.

Designed for Management & Expenditure Tracking of Other Real Estate Owned. The System, Modular in Design (General Ledger, Commercial & Residential Accounts Receivable, Accounts Payable, Brokers Register, & Real Asset Management), Is Fully Integrated. A Custom Report Writer & Customization of the Software Are Available.
Classic Real Estate Systems, L.L.C.

Org Plus Advanced. *Version:* 3.1. *Compatible Hardware:* IBM PC & compatibles, PS/2. *Operating System(s) Required:* PC-DOS/MS-DOS 2.0 or higher. *Memory Required:* 320k. *General Requirements:* Printer or HP plotter. *Items Included:* Users guide. *Customer Support:* M-F 8AM to 5PM Pacific Standard Time.
disk $79.95.
Enables Users to Create Organization Charts after the User Types Names, Titles, & Comments, the Program Automatically Draws & Spaces the Boxes, Centers the Text, & Lays Out the Connecting Lines. Users May Choose from Seven Chart Styles & Eight Box Styles. Boxes Can Have Eight Fields of Text. Creates a Mini-Spreadsheet for Each Employee So That Numerical Information Such As Salaries, Commissions, Budgets, Office Space, & Project Hours Can Be Tracked. Has Report Generation. Not Copy Protected.
Banner Blue.

Organization Master. *Customer Support:* 800-929-8117 (customer service).
MS-DOS. IBM/PS2. disk $199.99 (ISBN 0-87007-600-0).
Construct & Print Out Master Tables of Organization for Complex Organizatins. Subtables & Components of Organizations are Identified Through the Use of Numerical Identifiers. Table of Organization is Projected on the Screen, & Both Vertical & Horizontal Scrolling are Available.
SourceView Software International.

Organize for Success. Crisp Publications. Nov. 1995. *Items Included:* Manual, registration card, one CD-ROM disk, product catalog, skills product brochure, America Online user card. *Customer Support:* Free technical support allows users to call support technicians anytime between 8:00am to 5:00pm Pacific Standard Time Monday through Friday.
Windows 3.1, Windows 95 or higher. 486 33MHz PC or higher (8Mb). CD-ROM disk $49.95 (ISBN 1-888226-01-3). *Nonstandard peripherals required:* Double speed CD-ROM drive, SVGA graphics, 8 bit sound card. *Optimal configuration:* 486 33MHz PC or higher, double speed CD-ROM drive, SVGA graphics, 16Mb RAM, 16 bit sound card.
A CD-ROM Based Software Program That Gives People a Proven Process on How to Become More Organized & Stay in Control of Their Workspace.
Midisoft Corp.

Organize! Your Art Collection. *Version:* 7.0. Aug. 1994. *Items Included:* 200 plus page perfect bound manual, quick reference card, newsletter, program disks. *Customer Support:* 1 year free support, 30 day unlimited warranty.
IBM DOS Version 3.20 or higher (400k). IBM & compatibles (400k). disk $39.95. *Optimal configuration:* Hard disk is recommended.
A Specialized Database Designed Specifically for Cataloging Art Collections. User Can Catalog All Forms of Art, Including Sculpture, Paintings, Weavings, Castings, etc. Includes Fast Index Based Searches, a Complete Cross Reference Capability, User Definable Reports & a 10,000, 000 Entry Capacity.
PSG-Homecraft Software.

TITLE INDEX

ORGANIZE

Organize! Your Books & Magazines. *Version:* 7.0. Aug. 1994. *Operating System(s) Required:* PC-DOS/MS-DOS 3.20 or higher. *Memory Required:* 400k. *General Requirements:* 80-column printer & hard disk. *Items Included:* Disk, manual, free support, quick reference card. *Customer Support:* 1 year free with purchase (via telephone).
3.5" or 5.25" disk $39.95.
Database Manager Specifically Designed for Cataloging Books, Short Stories, Articles, & Technical Papers. The Data Base Can Be Searched by Any Criteria or Cross Referenced by Any Combination of Criteria (Title, Author, Subject, Subtopic, Notes, Publisher, etc.). Can Produce Printed Reports. A Hard Disk Menu System Is Included.
PSG-Homecraft Software.

Organize! Your Books & Magazines in Windows. *Version:* 3.x. Sep. 1995. *Items Included:* Manual, 1 3.5" diskette. *Customer Support:* One year free technical support, 30 day unlimited warranty.
Windows 3.1. 80286(AT), (512k). 3.5" disk $59.95.
The Complete Windows Cataloging System for Books. Any Type of Printed Material Can Be Cataloged In As Much (or As Little) Detail As You Want. Catalog Each Chapter In a Book, or Individual Articles In Magazines, If You Want & Everything You Enter In Your Catalog Is Fully Searchable & Can Be Sorted, Alphabetized & Cross-Referenced Automatically By the Software.
PSG-HomeCraft Software.

Organize! Your Business. *Version:* 7.0. Jul. 1994. *Items Included:* 200 plus page perfect bound manual, quick reference card, newsletter, program disks. *Customer Support:* 1 year free support, 30 day unlimited warranty.
IBM DOS Version 3.20 or higher. IBM & compatibles (400k). disk $59.95. *Optimal configuration:* Hard disk is recommended.
A Specialized Database Designed Specifically for Cataloging & Inventorying the Contents of Your Building, Suite or Office. Includes Fast Index Based Searches, a Complete Cross Reference Capability, User Definable Reports & a 10,000,000 Entry Capacity. Great for Insurance Purposes.
PSG-HomeCraft Software.

ORGANIZE! Your Business - Industrial Version. *Version:* 7.0. Jun. 1993. *Items Included:* Disk (high density only), manual, newsletter. *Customer Support:* 1 year free support, 30 day unlimited warranty.
DOS Version 3.2 or higher. IBM & compatibles (400k). disk $59.95. *Optimal configuration:* EGA/VGA/SVGA color, hard drive, & printer. *Networks supported:* All.
Software Designed for Organizing a Small Manufacturing or Service Business. Includes Cataloging Systems for: Tool Inventory, Warehouse Inventory, Bill of Materials, Spare Parts Lists, Engineering Drawing Files, Maintenance Records, Motor/Drive Inventory & More. Provides Fast Cross Referencing & Reporting Capabilities.
PSG-Homecraft Software.

Organize! Your CDs & Albums in Windows. *Version:* 3.x. Sep. 1995. *Items Included:* Manual, 1 3.5" diskette. *Customer Support:* One year free technical support, 30 day unlimited warranty.
Windows 3.1. 80286(AT), (512k). 3.5" disk $59.95.
Windows Multimedia Software for Cataloging All Types of Music Collections--Rock, Classical, Jazz, Country, etc. Works with PSG-HomeCrafts Megaguide for Single Key Data Entry.
PSG-HomeCraft Software.

Organize! Your Classical Music. *Version:* 7.0. Aug. 1994. *Operating System(s) Required:* PC-DOS/MS-DOS 3.20 or higher. *Memory Required:* 400k. *General Requirements:* 80-column printer & a hard disk. *Items Included:* Disk, manual, free support, quick reference card. *Customer Support:* 1 year telephone support, 1 year warranty.
3.5" or 5.25" disk $39.95.
Database Manager Specifically Designed for Classical Music Collectors. Users Enter Information About Each Composition. The Data Base Can Be Searched by Any Criteria or Combination of Criteria (Composer, Title, Label, Soloists, Conductor, Orchestra, etc.). Can Produce Reports on Printer or in Disk File. A Hard Disk Menu System Is Included.
PSG-HomeCraft Software.

Organize! Your Coin Collection. *Version:* 7.0. Aug. 1994. *Items Included:* Disk, manual, free support, quick reference card. *Customer Support:* 1 year free with purchase (via telephone).
PC-DOS/MS-DOS 3.20 or higher. IBM or compatibles (410k). disk $39.95.
Database Manager Specifically Designed for Cataloging Coin Collections. The Database Can Be Searched by Any Criteria or Cross Referenced by Any Combination of Criteria. Automatic B-Triere Indexing, 10,000,000 Entry Capacity & Including Easy Menu Driven Interfaces.
PSG-HomeCraft Software.

Organize! Your Coin Collection in Windows. *Version:* 3.x. Sep. 1995. *Items Included:* Manual, 1 3.5" diskette. *Customer Support:* One year free technical support, 30 day unlimited warranty.
Windows 3.1. 80286(AT), (512k). 3.5" disk $59.95.
A Complete Cataloging System for Both Investors & Collectors. Each Coin Can Be Cataloged, in Detail If You Wish Using up to 20 Criteria, Plus a Free Form Text Memo. An Image of Each Coin Can Also Be Included & Not Only Is This Software Powerful, It Is Fast & Flexible! You Can Catalog Your Collection the Way You Want & Get the Reports You Want.
PSG-HomeCraft Software.

Organize! Your Comic Books. *Version:* 7.0. Aug. 1994. *Operating System(s) Required:* PC-DOS/MS-DOS 3.20 or higher. *Memory Required:* 410k. *General Requirements:* 80-column printer & a hard disk. *Items Included:* Disk, manual, free support, quick reference card. *Customer Support:* 1 year telephone support, 1 year warranty.
3.5" or 5.25" disk $39.95.
Database Manager Specifically Designed for Cataloging Comic Books. The Data Base Can Be Searched by Any Criteria or Cross Referenced by Any Combination of Criteria (Title, Writer, Artist, Publisher, Appearances, Hero(s), etc.) Can Produce Printed Reports. 10,000,000 Entry Capacity. A Hard Disk Menu System Is Included.
PSG-HomeCraft Software.

Organize! Your Fabrics (for Sewing). *Version:* 7.0. Jul. 1993. *Items Included:* 150 plus page perfect bound manual, quick reference card, newsletter, program disks. *Customer Support:* 1 year free support, 30 day unlimited warranty.
IBM DOS Version 3.20 or higher. IBM & compatibles (400k). disk $39.95. *Optimal configuration:* Hard disk is recommended.
A Specialized Database Designed Specifically for Cataloging Fabrics & Notions. Includes Fast Index Based Searches, a Complete Cross Reference Capability, User Definable Reports & a 10,000,000 Entry Capacity.
PSG-HomeCraft Software.

Organize! Your Guns. *Version:* 7.0. Aug. 1994. *Items Included:* Disk, manual, free support, quick reference card. *Customer Support:* 1 year free with purchase (via telephone).
PC-DOS/MS-DOS 3.20 or higher. IBM & compatibles (410k). disk $39.95. *Optimal configuration:* IBM PC (XT, AT or PS/2) with 640k, 20Mb hard disk & 80 column printer.
Database Manager Specifically Designed for Cataloging All Types of Guns Suitable for Licensed & Casual Collectors. The Database Can Be Searched by Any Criteria or Cross Referenced by Any Combination of Criteria. Automatic B-Triere Indexing, 10,000,000 Entry Capacity & Includes Easy Menu Driven Interfaces.
PSG-HomeCraft Software.

Organize! Your Home (Home Inventory). *Version:* 7.0. Aug. 1994. *Operating System(s) Required:* PC-DOS/MS-DOS 3.20 or higher. *Memory Required:* 400k. *General Requirements:* 80-colum printer. *Items Included:* Disk, manual, free support, quick reference card. *Customer Support:* 1 year telephone support, 1 year warranty.
3.5" or 5.25" disk $39.95.
Data Base Manager Specifically Designed for Maintaining a Home Inventory. Searches Can Be Based on Any Criteria or Cross-Referenced by Any Combination of Criteria. Also Includes Life Insurance Planning & an Insurance Policy Record Keeping System. Can Produce Printed Reports. Can Handle 10,000,000 Entries. A Hard Disk Menu Is Included.
PSG-HomeCraft Software.

Organize! Your Home in Windows. *Version:* 3.x. *Items Included:* Manual, 1 3.5" diskette. *Customer Support:* One year free technical support, 30 day unlimited warranty.
Windows 3.1. 80286(AT), (512k). 3.5" disk $59.95.
The Complete Home Inventory System. Great for Insurance Purposes--Tracks Everything of Value in Your Home & Even in a Second Home. Photographs of Each Item Can Be Included. You Can Also Find Out the Replacement Value (Or Original Cost) of Any Group of Items In Your Home, Everything Owned By a Specific Person, In a Specific Location, Or of Everything.
PSG-HomeCraft Software.

Organize! Your Jazz Collection. *Version:* 7.0. Jul. 1993. *Operating System(s) Required:* PC-DOS/MS-DOS 3.20 or higher. *Memory Required:* 410k. *General Requirements:* 80-column printer. *Items Included:* Disk, manual, free support, quick reference card. *Customer Support:* 1 year free telephone support, 1 year warranty.
3.5" or 5.25" disk $39.95.
Database Manager Specifically Designed for Cataloging Jazz Records. Instantly Alphabetize a Collection or Search the Data Base by any Criteria or Cross Reference. 10,000,000 Entry Capability, Can Produce Printed Reports. Includes a Hard Disk Menu System.
PSG-HomeCraft Software.

Organize! Your Memorabilia. *Version:* 7.0. Aug. 1994. *Items Included:* Manual, quick reference card, newsletter, disks. *Customer Support:* 1-yr warranty, 30-day money back guarantee, 1 yt telephone support.
MS-DOS 3.20 or higher (400k). IBM PC, PC XT, PC AT & compatibles, PS/2. $39.95. *Optimal configuration:* Hard disk, 80-column printer.
Specifically Designed for Cataloging Elvis Presley Memorabilia from Betty Boop to Elvis. Catalog Bells, Plates, Pillows & Pens. Data Base Can Be Searched by Any Criterion or Cross-Referenced by Any Combination of Criteria (Item Type, Description, Value, Condition, etc.) Can Produce Printed Reports.
PSG-HomeCraft Software.

Organize! Your Model Railroad. *Version:* 7.0. Jun. 1994. *Items Included:* 200 plus page perfect bound manual, quick reference card, newsletter, program disks. *Customer Support:* 1 year free support, 30 day unlimited warranty.
IBM DOS Version 3.20 or higher. IBM & compatibles (400k). disk $39.95. *Optimal configuration:* Hard disk is recommended.
A Specialized Database Designed Specifically for Cataloging Model Railroads. Includes Fast Index Based Searches, a Complete Cross Reference Capability, User Definable Reports & a 10,000,000 Entry Capacity. Provides Two Systems - One for the Collector & Another for Investors.
PSG-HomeCraft Software.

Organize! Your Music. *Version:* 7.0. Aug. 1994. *Compatible Hardware:* IBM PC & compatibles. *Operating System(s) Required:* PC-DOS 3.20 or higher. *Language(s):* QuickBASIC, Assembly. *Memory Required:* 400k. *General Requirements:* 80-column printer & hard disk. *Items Included:* Disk, manual, free support, quick reference card, newsletter. *Customer Support:* 1 Year telephone support, 1 year warranty.
3.5" or 5.25" disk $39.95.
Database Manager Especially Designed for Collectors of LPs, Tapes, CDs & 45s. Users Enter Information about Each Song in the Collection. The Data Base Can Be Searched by Any Criterion or Combination of Criteria (Title, Artist, Value, Year of Release, Type of Song, Catalog Number, etc.). Can Produce Printed Reports. Capacity Is 10,000,000 Songs per Filename. A FREE Hard Disk Menu System Is Also Included.
PSG-HomeCraft Software.

Organize! Your Phone Cards in Windows. *Version:* Manual, 1 3.5" diskette. Sep. 1995. *Customer Support:* One year free technical support, 30 day unlimited warranty.
Windows 3.1. 80286(AT), (512k). 3.5" disk $59.95.
For Cataloging Prepaid Telephone Credit Cards. Each Card Can Be Tracked Using up to 20 Criteria, Plus an Image of the Card Can Be Included. You'll Know What Cards You Have, Which Ones You Are Looking for, What They Are Worth & Why They Were Issued. It's a Fast & Easy Way to Keep Track of Your Collection.
PSG-HomeCraft Software.

Organize! Your Photographs & Slides. *Version:* 7.0. Aug. 1994. *Operating System(s) Required:* PC-DOS/MS-DOS 3.20 or higher. *Memory Required:* 400k. *General Requirements:* 80-column printer. *Items Included:* Disk, manual, free support, quick reference card, newsletter. *Customer Support:* 1 year telephone support, 1 year warranty.
3.5" or 5.25" disk $39.95.
Database Manager Specifically Designed for Cataloging Negatives, Slides & Prints. The Data Base Can Be Searched by Any Criteria or Cross Referenced by Any Combination of Criteria (Subject, Description, Equipment/Film Used, Subtopic, Client, Fee, etc.). Can Produce Printed Reports. 10,000,000 Entry Capacity. A Hard Disk Menu System Is Included.
PSG-HomeCraft Software.

Organize! Your Plants & Garden. *Version:* 7.0. May 1994. *Items Included:* 200 plus page perfect bound manual, quick reference card, newsletter, program disks. *Customer Support:* 1 year free support, 30 day unlimited warranty.
IBM DOS Version 3.20 or higher. IBM & compatibles (400k). disk $39.95. *Optimal configuration:* Hard disk is recommended.
A Specialized Database Designed Specifically for Cataloging Plants. User Can Keep Track of Feeding Requirements, Growth Rate, Watering Schedules & Flowering. Includes Fast Index Based Searches, a Complete Cross Reference Capability, User Definable Reports & a 10,000,000 Entry Capacity.
PSG-HomeCraft Software.

Organize! Your Professional Books. *Version:* 7.0. Aug. 1994. *Items Included:* Disk, manual, free support, quick reference card, newsletter. *Customer Support:* 1 year free with purchase (via telephone).
PC-DOS/MS-DOS 3.20 or higher. IBM & compatibles (310k). disk $39.95.
Database Manager Specifically Designed for Cataloging Technical Books, Magazones & Papers. The Database Can Be Searched by Any Combination of Criteria. Automatic B-Triere Indexing, 10,000,000 Entry Capacity & Includes Easy Menu Driven Interfaces.
PSG-HomeCraft Software.

Organize! Your Sports Cards - Windows Version. *Version:* 3.x. Sep. 1995. *Items Included:* Manual, 1 3.5" diskette. *Customer Support:* One year free technical support, 30 day unlimited warranty.
Windows 3.1. 80286(AT), (512k). 3.5" disk $59.95.
A Complete Cataloging System for All Types of Sports Cards--Including Pictures of Cards. You'll Know What You Have, What You Want, & What Your Collection--or Any Part of It--Is Worth. Use up to 20 Criteria to Catalog Each Card & the Cataloging Format Is Fully User Definable, So You Can Set up Your Catalog to Do Exactly What You Want to Do.
PSG-HomeCraft Software.

Organize! Your Stamp Collection. *Version:* 7.0. Aug. 1994. *Items Included:* Disk, manual, free support, quick reference card, newsletter. *Customer Support:* 1 year free with purchase (via telephone).
PC-DOS/MS-DOS 3.20 or higher. IBM & Compatibles (400k). disk $39.95. *Optimal configuration:* IBM PC, PC-XT, PC-AT or PS/2 with 640k, 40Mb hard disk & 80 column printer.
Database Manager Specifically Designed for Cataloging Stamp Collectors. The Database Can Be searched by Any Criteria. Automatic B-Triere Indexing, 10,000,000 Entry Capacity & Includes Easy Menu Driven Interfaces.
PSG-HomeCraft Software.

Organize! Your Stamps in Windows. *Version:* 3.x. Sep. 1995. *Items Included:* Manual, 1 3.5" diskette. *Customer Support:* One year free technical support, 30 day unlimited warranty.
Windows 3.1. 80286(AT), (512k). 3.5" disk $59.95.
Windows Multimedia Version. Catalogs All Types of Stamps from Any Country. Use up to 20 Criteria to Catalog Each Stamp, & Be Able to Search for Any Information You've Entered. Starting a Search Is As Easy As Filling In the Blanks--the Software Even Automatically Performs Cross-References. Get a Total Value for Your Collection, or Any Part of It. This Software Does It All.
PSG-HomeCraft Software.

Organize! Your Token Collection. *Version:* 7.0. Aug. 1994. *Items Included:* 200 page perfect bound manual, quick reference card, newsletter, program disks. *Customer Support:* 1 year free support, 30 day unlimited warranty.
IBM DOS Version 3.20 or higher. IBM & compatibles (400k). disk $39.95. *Optimal configuration:* Hard disk is recommended.
A Specialized Database Designed Specifically for Cataloging All Types of Tokens. Includes Fast Index Based Searches, a Complete Cross Reference Capability, User Definable Reports & a 10,000,000 Entry Capacity. Allows All of the Information on a Token to Be Recorded & Cataloged.
PSG-HomeCraft Software.

Organize! Your Video Games in Windows. Sep. 1995. *Items Included:* Manual, 1 3.5" diskette. *Customer Support:* One year free technical support, 30 day unlimited warranty.
Windows 3.1. 80286(AT), (512k). 3.5" disk $59.95.
A Complete System for Tracking Video Games, Game Hints, Passwords, Strategies & More. Searches Are Fast & Easily Accessible. It's Great Software That Helps You Know What You Have, What You Think about Each Game (a Personal Review), & Whatever Other Information You Need to Keep Track Of.
PSG-HomeCraft Software.

Organize! Your Video Tapes. *Version:* 7.0. Aug. 1994. *Operating System(s) Required:* PC-DOS/MS-DOS 3.20 or higher. *Memory Required:* 400k. *General Requirements:* 80-column printer. *Items Included:* Disk, manual, free support, quick reference card. *Customer Support:* 1 year telephone support, 1 year warranty.
3.5" or 5.25" disk $39.95.
Database Manager Specifically Designed for Cataloging Films & Video Tapes. The Data Base Can Be Searched by Any Criteria or Cross Referenced by Any Combination of Criteria (Title, Description, Star(s), Director, Screenplay, Type, etc.) Can Produce Printed Reports. 10,000,000 Entry Capacity. A Hard Disk Menu System Is Included.
PSG-HomeCraft Software.

Organize! Your Video Tapes in Windows. *Version:* 3.x. Sep. 1995. *Items Included:* Manual, 1 3.5" diskette. *Customer Support:* One year free technical support, 30 day unlimited warranty.
Windows 3.1. 80286(AT), (512k). 3.5" disk $59.95.
A Complete Movie, TV Show, Home Video Cataloging System. An Unlimited Number of Video Segments, Per Tape, Can Be Cataloged. You'll Know What You Have & Where It Is. Each Video Segment Can Be Cataloged Using up to 20 Criteria--All of Which Are Fully Searchable & Can Be Alphabetized, Sorted & Cross-Referenced. You Get a Catalog Set up the Way You Want.
PSG-HomeCraft Software.

Organize! Your Wines. *Version:* 7.0. Aug. 1995. *Items Included:* 200 plus page perfect bound manual, quick reference card, newsletter, program disks. *Customer Support:* 1 year free support, 30 day unlimited warranty.
IBM DOS Version 3.20 or higher. IBM & compatibles (400k). disk $39.95. *Optimal configuration:* Hard disk is recommended.
A Specialized Database Designed Specifically for Cataloging Wine & Wine Cellars. User Can Catalog Wine & Track When It Will Be Ready to Drink. Includes Fast Index Based Searches, a Complete Cross Reference Capability, User Definable Reports & a 10,000,000 Entry Capacity.
PSG-HomeCraft Software.

ORIFICE. Kyle Engineering. 1984. *Compatible Hardware:* IBM PC. *Operating System(s) Required:* DOS. *Memory Required:* 256k.
disk $150.00.
Sizes Orifice Plates for Measurement of Gas or Liquid Flow Using Either the Spink or Miller Method. Finds Orifice Diameter for Specified Flow or Pressure Drop for a Given Orifice Plate. Contains a Help Section to Find Density (Using the Soave Redlich-Kwong Equation) for Gas Mixtures.
Techdata.

TITLE INDEX

ORIFICE: Flow Element Sizing. Version: 20D. Sep. 1978. Compatible Hardware: IBM PC & compatibles, PC XT, PC AT. Operating System(s) Required: PC-DOS/MS-DOS 2.X, 3.0. Memory Required: 256k. General Requirements: Printer. disk $499.95 (ISBN 0-935509-01-1, Order no.: 5000).
Flow Element Sizing Program for Liquid, Gas, or Steam Service Using Flange, Pipe, Corner, Radius or Vena Contracta Taps for Concentric Orifices. Will Size Flow Nozzle Venturi's, Low Loss Tubes, & Restriction Orifices. Will Solve for Beta Ratio, Flow Rate, or Differential Pressure. Built-In Tables for Water, Steam & over 260 Different Sizes of Pipes. Allows the User to Input the Data in Various Units. Menu-Driven & Not Copy-Protected.
FlowSoft, Inc.

ORIFLO: Orifice Meter Calculation. Version: 4.0. 1994. Items Included: User manual with sample problems. Customer Support: Free telephone support.
PC-DOS/MS-DOS. IBM PC, XT, AT, PS/2 & compatibles. disk $495.00 (ISBN 0-932507-65-4, Order no.: 765). Optimal configuration: IBM compatible with DOS 5.0 or higher with 2Mb RAM, floppy disk, hard disk, color monitor, printer, Windows 3.1.
Calculates Discharge Coefficient, Expansion Factor, Differential Pressure for Orifice Meters for Liquids, Steam & Gases. Flange, Pipe & Radius Taps Are Options Available. Built-In Steam Tables for Steam Flow Calculations. Uses Spink or Miller Methods.
Systek (California).

Original Adventure. Compatible Hardware: Atari 800, 1200XL. Language(s): BASIC. Memory Required: 24k.
disk $24.95.
cassette $24.95.
Somewhere Nearby Is a Colossal Cave Where Some Have Found Fortunes in Treasures & Gold, but Others Have Entered & Have Never Been Seen Again. Try to Find Your Way into the Underground Caverns, Where You Meet a Glan Clam, Nasty Little Dwarves, etc.
Compuware.

The Original Adventure. Compatible Hardware: IBM. Memory Required: 128k.
disk $9.95.
Adventure Game.
Dynacomp, Inc.

The Original Complete Carnegie Hall Concert. Eddie Cantor. 1990.
IBM. CD-ROM disk Contact publisher for price (ISBN 1-887958-00-2).
Gari Brian.

Original Issue Discount. Compatible Hardware: Altos Series 15-5D, Series 5-5D, 580-XX, ACS8000-XX; IBM PC with 2 disk drives, PC XT, IBM compatible; Xerox 820 with 2 disk drives, ZILOG MCZ-250. Operating System(s) Required: CP/M, MP/M, PC-DOS, MS-DOS.
contact publisher for price (Order no.: OID).
In Compliance with the TEFRA (the Tax Equity & Fiscal Responsibility Act of 1982), the Program Calculates Bond Interest Deduction & Interest Income Inclusion.
Coopers & Lybrand.

Orion Chiropractic. Version: 3.71. Items Included: Microsoft Word version 4.0, front desk, appointment scheduler, accounts payable/checkwriter. Customer Support: Six months free support with training; continued support - single user $50.00, multi-user $80.00.
Macintosh OS. Apple Macintosh (1Mb). single user $3495.00; multiuser $5995.00. Optimal configuration: Macintosh SE/30 or IIcx, 4 Mb RAM, Imagewriter II printer, hard disk according to size of practice. Networks supported: AppleShare & TOPS.
A Macintosh based System, Providing Claims Processing, Billing, Accounts Receivable, Word Processing, Payables/Checkprinting, & Appointment Scheduling. It Also Provides a Wide Range of Management Reports. Available Options: Electronic Claims Submission, Payroll, Inventory Control, General Ledger, & Drug Interaction.
Orion Computer Systems, Inc.

Orion Dental. Version: 3.71. Compatible Hardware: Apple Macintosh Plus. General Requirements: Hard disk; ImageWriter II or LQ. Items Included: Patient Module, Billing, Accounts Receivable, Accounts Payable, Word Processing, Scheduling. Customer Support: 24-hour 800 hotline.
single user $3495.00.
multiuser $5995.00.
Dental Management.
Orion Computer Systems, Inc.

Orion Family Practice. Version: 3.71. Compatible Hardware: Apple Macintosh Plus. General Requirements: Hard disk drive, ImageWriter II or LQ. Items Included: Patient Module, Billing, Accounts Receivable, Accounts Payable, Word Processing, Scheduling. Customer Support: 24-hour 800 hotline.
single user $3495.00.
multiuser $5995.00.
Pediatrician/General & Family Practitioner.
Orion Computer Systems, Inc.

Orion Optometric. Version: 3.71. Compatible Hardware: Apple Macintosh Plus. General Requirements: Hard disk; ImageWriter II or LQ. Items Included: Patient Module, Billing, Dispensing, Accounts Receivable, Accounts Payable, Word Processing, Scheduling. Customer Support: 24-hour 800 hotline.
single user $3495.00.
multiuser $5995.00.
Optometry Management.
Orion Computer Systems, Inc.

Orion Psychiatric. Items Included: Microsoft Word version 4.0, front desk, appointment scheduler, accounts payable/checkwriter. Customer Support: Six months free support with training; continued support - single user $50.00, Multi-user $80.00.
Macintosh OS. Apple Macintosh (1Mb). single user $3495.00, multi-user $5995.00. Optimal configuration: Macintosh SE/30 or IIcx, 4 Mb RAM, Imagewriter II printer, hard disk according to size of practice. Networks supported: AppleShare & TOPS.
A Macintosh Based System, Providing Claims Processing, Billing, Accounts Receivable, Word Processing, Payable/Checkprinting, & Appointment Scheduling. It Also Provides a Wide Range of Management Reports. Available Options: Electronic Claims Submission, Payroll, Inventory Control, General Ledger, & Drug Interaction.
Orion Computer Systems, Inc.

Orion Radiology Information Management. General Requirements: Hard disk drive; ImageWriter II.
Macintosh Plus or higher. $3995.00 single user. $5995.00 multiuser.
Radiology Management.
Orion Computer Systems, Inc.

Orion Surgical. Version: 3.71. Compatible Hardware: Apple Macintosh Plus. General Requirements: Hard disk; ImageWriter II or LQ. Items Included: Patient Module, Billing, Accounts Receivable, Accounts Payable, Word Processing, Scheduling. Customer Support: 24-hour 800 hotline.
single user $3495.00.
multiuser $5995.00.
Office Management for Surgeons, Opthalmologists, Otolaryngologists, Podiatrists, Obstetricians & Urologists.
Orion Computer Systems, Inc.

Orpheus. Dec. 1995. Items Included: Manual, online help, example programs. Customer Support: Free technical support, 60 day money-back guarantee, free electronic maintenance updates, E-mail technical support.
Windows 3.1 or higher. 386 IBM PC (4Mb). disk $199.00. Addl. software required: Borland Delphi 1.0.
A Collection of Native VCL Components That Extend the Data Entry Capabilities of Delphi. You Get Validated String, Number, & Date/Time Fields; Form Controller for Calculated & Required Fields; Virtual List Box; Win95-Style Top & Side Tabs; Text Editor with Word Wrap & 16Mb Capacity; Flexible 2D Table That Holds Fields, Check Boxes, Bitmaps, Combo Boxes; Virtual File Viewer; Two-Way, Four-Way, & Five-Way Spinners; & More. Full Source Code Included.
TurboPower Software.

Orthodontic. CYMA Corp. Operating System(s) Required: CP/M, MS-DOS. Memory Required: 64k. General Requirements: Printer.
$1695.00 (Order no.: SY P/N T039-135).
Texas Instruments, Personal Productivit.

Orthodontic Practice Management System. Professional Software Associates, Inc. Operating System(s) Required: UCSD p-System. Memory Required: 128k. General Requirements: Printer, Winchester hard disk.
$3495.00.
Texas Instruments, Personal Productivit.

OrthoLine CD-ROM Database for Orthopaedics. Jun. 1990.
MS Windows 3.1 or higher. IBM & compatibles (4Mb). CD-ROM disk $325.00-$995.00; Networks $1895.00 & up. Nonstandard peripherals required: Magnetic or CD-ROM, using ISO 9660. Optimal configuration: IBM & compatibles, 80386 or higher, 4Mb RAM, 20Mb hard disk, mouse, MS Windows 3.1 or higher.
System 6.0.7 or higher. Apple Macintosh (3Mb). CD-ROM disk $325.00-$995.00; Networks $1895.00 & up. Optimal configuration: Apple Macintosh Plus or higher, 3Mb RAM, System 6.0.7 or higher.
OrthoLine Is an Electronic Reference Database to the Orthopaedics Journal Literature. Orthopaedics-Specific Excerpts (Including Abstracts) from the National Library of Medicine's MEDLINE Database Are Distributed on CD-ROM (Compact Disc, Read-Only Memory) Optical Disc. Knowledge Finder Search-&-Retrieval Software Makes Searching of the OrthoLine Database Easy, Effective & Fast. After the User Types a Phrase or Sentence Describing the Information Needed, It selects the References in the Database That Appear to Best Match the Request, & Presents Them in Order of Likely Relevance. The OrthoLine Archive CD-ROM Contains More Than 240,000 References to Articles Published in 100 Orthopaedics-Related Journals over the Most Recent 10 Full Years. Orthopaedics Articles from More Than 2,500 Other Journals Are Also Included.
Aries Systems Corp.

OS/2. *Compatible Hardware:* IBM PC AT & compatibles, PS/2. *Memory Required:* 2000k. contact publisher for price.
Operating System Designed for 80286-Based Computers. Features Multi-Tasking, 16Mb Addressability, Grahpical User Interface (Presentation Manager), Database Engine, Networking Support, & Communications.
Microsoft Pr.

OS/2 Ada Compilation System & Toolset. *Version:* 4.2. Dec. 1988. *Compatible Hardware:* Compaq Deskpro 386; IBM PC, PC AT, PS/Z Model 60, PS/2 Model 80; Zenith Z-248. *Operating System(s) Required:* OS/2 V1.0. *Memory Required:* 512k.
disk 286-based machines (includes 4Mb RAM board) $3595.00.
disk 386-based machines $3095.00.
Includes All Required Software & Complete Documentation. 286-Based Version Comes with an Additional 4 Mb of Memory. System Includes Compiler, Multi-Library Environment, Binder & Run-Time Executive. Options Available Are Developer's Toolset Including AdaProbe, a Symbolic Source Level Debugger & Program Viewer; AdaXref, a Cross-Reference Generator; AdaMake, a Recompilation Aid; & AdaReformat, a Source Reformatter.
Alsys, Inc.

OS-9000.
disk $1000.00.
Real-Time Operating System & Development Environment Upwardly Compatible with OS-9. Supports 68020/70/40 & Intel's 80386. Can Be Used for Developing Everything from Stand-Alone ROMable Kernels to Complete Multiuser Developing System. System Kernel Is 95 Percent C, with 5 Percent Written in Assembler. Will Support Resident Processors, Allowing User to Edit, Compile & Debug Code Directly on Target Hardware. Also Supports Unix & DOS Cross-Development. Time-Sliced Multitasking Scheduling Module & Priority-Based Pre-Emptive Scheduling Mode Are Available. Industrial Version Includes Real-Time Kernel with Interprocess Communication & Console I/O Managers. Professional Version Includes Industrial Version with 70 Utility Commands, C Compiler, & Disk & Tape Support.
Microware Systems Corp.

Oscar: Reading Software for the Blind. *Version:* 4.0A. Mar. 1995.
MS-DOS. 386-25 (8Mb). disk $995.00 (Order no.: NA4A). *Nonstandard peripherals required:* Requires compatible speech synthesizer & scanner.
A Reading System Which, When Used with a Compatible Speech Synthesizer & Scanner, Scans a Document & Provides Audio Output of the Scanned Document. The System Can Also Be Used with a Braille Display for Braille Output.
TeleSensory Corp.

OSHALOG Four PC Pro. *Version:* 2.0. Jul. 1993. *Items Included:* Guideline manual. *Customer Support:* Telephone support - no charge.
DOS 2.0 or higher. PC XT AT with hard drive (640k). disk $99.95 (ISBN 1-880147-11-4). *Networks supported:* Novell, Novell compatible.
Database to Maintain OSHA Recordable Injuries & Illnesses. Printout Approved by US DOL/OSHA.
Safety Software, Inc.

OSHALOG.200. *Version:* 1.1. Jan. 1993. *Items Included:* Guidelines manual. *Customer Support:* Free telephone technical support, notice of bug fixes, upgrades.
DOS 2.0 or higher. PC XT, AT or compatible with hard drive (640k). disk $125.00 (ISBN 1-880147-07-6). *Networks supported:* Novell or compatible.
Database to Maintain OSHA 200 Injury & Illness LOG & Summary. Printout Approved by U. S. DOL/OSHA. Includes Additional Fields for SSN, Employee #, Date of Birth, Sex & Supervisors Nane. Can Be Sorted in Various Fields for Management Reports. Paradox RunTime Application.
Safety Software, Inc.

OSHALOG.200 Manager. *Version:* 1.1. Feb. 1993. *Items Included:* Guidelines manual. *Customer Support:* Free telephone technical support, notice of bug fixes & upgrades.
DOS 2.0 or higher. PC XT, AT or compatible with hard drive (640k). disk $375.00 (ISBN 1-880147-09-2). *Networks supported:* Novell or compatible.
Database to Maintain OSHA Form 200, LOG of Occupational Injuries & Illnesses with Extensive Safety Management & Worker's Compensation Claims Management Tools, Reports & Graphs. Can Associate Accident Factors by Cost. Paradox Runtime Application. LOG & Summary Printout Approved by U. S. DOL/OSHA.
Safety Software, Inc.

OSHALOG.200 Manager Plus. *Version:* 1.1. Apr. 1993. *Items Included:* Guidelines manual. *Customer Support:* Free telephone technical support. Notice of upgrades, bug fixes, etc.
DOS 2.0 or higher. PC XT, AT or compatible with hard drive (640k). disk $750.00 (ISBN 1-880147-10-6). *Networks supported:* Novell & compatible.
Database to Maintain OSHA Form 200, LOG of Occupational Injuries/Illnesses with Extensive Multiple Location Safety & Worker's Compensation Claims Management. Generates Reports, Graphs & U. S. DOL/OSHA Approved Printout of LOG & Summary. Paradox RunTime Application.
Safety Software, Inc.

OSHALOG.200 Plus. *Version:* 1.1. Jan. 1993. *Items Included:* Guidelines manual. *Customer Support:* Free telephone technical support. Notice of bug fixes, upgrades.
DOS 2.0 & higher. PC XT, AT or compatible (640k). disk $250.00 (ISBN 1-880147-08-4). *Networks supported:* Novell or compatible.
Relational Safety Management Database Which Maintains the OSHA Form 200. In Addition to Printing a U. S. DOL/OSHA Approved LOG & Summary, Numerous Analytical Reports & Graphs Such As Injuries by Department, Supervisor & Number of Lost Days for Those Categories. Accepts Queries to Identify Problem Areas. Paradox Runtime Application.
Safety Software, Inc.

OSHALOG.4PC. *Version:* 2.0. Sep. 1993. *Items Included:* Documentation upon registration. *Customer Support:* One year free telephone technical support.
DOS 2.0 or higher. PC, XT, 286, 386 (IBM compatible) with hard drive (640k). disk $50.00 (ISBN 1-880147-05-X).
Tests for OSHA "Recordability" Factors for Injury & Illness & Maintains OSHA Form 200 Injury & Illness LOG & Summary, User Friendly & Menu Driven. Two Function Keys to Operate. Only Accepts "Recordable" Cases. Print-Out Approved by U. S. DOL/OSHA. Shareware.
Safety Software, Inc.

The OTC Software Products: (Option Tracking Capability), 3 disks. *Version:* 6.0. Dec. 1983. *Compatible Hardware:* IBM PC & compatibles. *Operating System(s) Required:* MS-DOS 3.1 or higher. *Language(s):* Turbo Pascal. *Memory Required:* 512k. *General Requirements:* Hard disk. *Customer Support:* Application & Technical telephone support; system training, updates & enhancements.
$3,500.00 to $15,000.00 license. *Networks supported:* LANs.
$595.00-2000.00, Annual Service Fee.
These Products (OTC Basic, OTC Plus, & OTC LTI) Automate Employee Stock Plan Administration for Public & Private Companies. OTC Basic & OTC Plus Software Account for Incentive, Non-Qualified, & Discounted Stock Options, Stock Appreciation Rights, & Restricted Stock Purchase. Systems Automatically Calculate Vesting & Expiration Dates, Taxes Due Upon Exercise, & the ISO Vesting Limitations for Post-1986 Incentive Stock Option Grants. Systems Process Cash Exercises, Stock Swaps, Trading Shares for Taxes, & More. OTC LTI Has Features of OTC Plus with the Additional Capacity To Support Restricted Stock Awards, Performance Units, Performance Shares & Performance Returns with the Ability To Process Dividends for All Award Types. All Reports Satisfy SEC, IRS, & Internal Reporting Requirements.
ShareData (California).

The Other Side: A Global Conflict Resolution Kit. *Version:* 2.0. Apr. 1985. *Compatible Hardware:* Apple II Plus, IIe, IIc. *Memory Required:* 64k. *Customer Support:* Customer support line 1-800-342-0236.
$69.95, incl. tchr's. guide, 2 student guides & back-up disk (ISBN 0-926891-00-6).
Game in Which Two Teams (or Individuals) Compete to Build a Bridge Between Their Territories. Designed to Teach Conflict Resolution, Program Can Also Be Used in a Classroom. Duplicate Disks, Maps & Player Guides Included.
Tom Snyder Productions, Inc.

Otzar Plus. *Compatible Hardware:* Mac Plus or higher.
$39.95.
Treasury of Judaic Wit & Wisdom in a HyperCard Stack. Numerous Subjects Are Represented with Classic Jewish Tales, Parables, & Sayings. Users Can Search for Citations by Key Words, by Source, or by Any Word or Phrase.
Davka Corp.

Oubliette. *Customer Support:* 800-929-8117 (customer service).
MS-DOS. Commodore 128; CP/M; IBM PC, PS/2. disk $49.99 (ISBN 0-87007-484-9).
Roughly Translates from French As 'Dungeon', Subterranean Bastian of Traps, Monsters, Gold, Magic & Witchcraft. A Random Number Generator Takes the Place of the Dice & Determines the Trails & Wealth of Each Player. This Is a Tough Dungeon, Requiring High Levels of Skill & Planning. Each Session is Recorded for the Next Round of Play. The User Chooses His/Her Party from Among Several Races, with Various Strengths & Weaknesses. Each Session Is Recorded, & May Be Resumed at a Later Time. Apple-CP/M Also Available.
SourceView Software International.

Our Times Multimedia Encyclopedia of the 20th Century.
Macintosh, MPC. CD-ROM disk $69.95 (ISBN 1-884906-07-9).
Narrated Journey Through the 20th Century. 65,000 Hypertext Links with the Columbia Ency. 52,000 Articles, 8 Million Words, 2500 Charts & Graphs.
Vicarious Entertainment, Inc.

Outage Plus. *Version:* 1.4. Kip Wright. Jan. 1990. *Memory Required:* 640k. *Items Included:* Outage Plus Reference Manual. *Customer Support:* As a registered user, you will receive free technical telephone support for 90 days from

the date of purchase. After such period, advisory service will be continuously available at PSE's standard hourly rate.
DOS Version 3.0 or higher (512k). IBM PC/XT, PC/AT, PS/2 or compatible. $3500.00. *Nonstandard peripherals required:* Draft printer - Epson compatible. *Optimal configuration:* IBM PC/AT, 640k Internal memory, Color Monitor w/EGA Graphics Card, High Density Diskette Drive, a Hard Drive, Math Coprocessor, Draft printer.
A Comprehensive Database Application to Record Service Interruptions (Outages) Quickly & Efficiently. Will Aid in: Providing Information Required by Power Suppliers & Public Service Commissions. Producing Historical Outage Data for Maintenance & Planning System Improvements. Informing Consumers in Response to Complaints.
Power System Engineering, Inc.

outSPOKEN: The Talking Macintosh Interface.
Version: 1.7. *Items Included:* Braille manual available upon request. *Customer Support:* 30 days unlimited warranty, free technical assistance via telephone, 510-540-5535.
6.0.2 or higher. Macintosh Plus or higher. 3.5" disk $495.00.
Complete Screen Navigation & Screen Reading Package. The Blind User Can Browse & Edit Text Based Displays in Applications Like Word Processors, Spreadsheets, or Databases. Using Macintalk, Product Reads Just about Anything on the Screen: Windows Titles, Menu Selections, Document Names, Folder Titles & Icons.
Berkeley Systems, Inc.

Outward Bound: Book Delivery Manager for the Housebound.
DOS (640K). disk $259.00.
This is a program for all the schools, libraries, & book mobiles that loan material to people who are housebound & can't come to the library or school.
Right on Programs.

Outward Bound for Shut Ins. 1993. *Items Included:* Disks, Complete illustrated instructions. *Customer Support:* Technical 8:30 am - 4:00 pm telephone-No Charge.
DOS. IBM & compatibles (512k). disk $259.00.
Complete Program to Maintain Records & Choices of Library Patrons Who Cannot Get to a Library. Maintains Data on Patrons, Prints Out Various Reports.
Right On Programs.

Overdrive 2 for WordPerfect. *Version:* 2.0. *Items Included:* Manual. *Customer Support:* Unlimited free support.
DOS 2.0 or higher. IBM XT, AT, PS/2 or compatible. disk $149.00. *Nonstandard peripherals required:* Hard disk. *Addl. software required:* WordPerfect.
Productivity Tool That Automatically Organizes, Assembles & Merges WordPerfect Documents. MergeLink Imports ASCII & dBASE Data Directly into Form Letters & Mail Merge Forms. Multiple Document Assembly Allows Selection, Assembly (Merge) & Printing of Retailed Groups of WordPerfect Documents, All at the Same Time from a Single Merge of Data.
OverDrive Systems, Inc.

Overdue Books Manager. *Version:* II. 1995. *Compatible Hardware:* Apple; IBM PC, PC XT, & compatibles. *Memory Required:* Apple 128k, PC 512k. *General Requirements:* 2 disk drives or hard disk, printer. *Items Included:* Disks, Complete illustrated instructions. *Customer Support:* Technical 8:30-4pm M-F telephone no charge.
disk $179.00 (ISBN 0-87132-969-7, Order no.: ODCON).
Windows version $199.00.
Allows User to Keep Track of Overdue Books. Package Includes Starter Pack of Preprinted, Non-Carbon Overdue Notices. Two Versions - Public Library, School Library Included.
Right On Programs.

Overdue Books Manager.
DOS 5 or Win 3.01 (640k). IBM PC. DOS 179.00; Windows 199.00.
New for 1996, this program makes it sensible, simple, & effective to manage overdue material on the computer. No more searching & picking through cards. Enter patron information one time & call it back each time that patron has overdue material. Perfect for every type of library that needs a top performance package to manage overdues.
Right on Programs.

Overload. 1990. *Customer Support:* 90 day warranty.
MS-DOS 2.1 or higher. IBM (512K). disk $49.99. *Nonstandard peripherals required:* EGA, Tandy or VGA Graphics required.
Amiga (512K). 3.5" disk $49.99.
Commodore 64 (64K). disk $39.99. *Nonstandard peripherals required:* Joystick required.
An Epic Plot with Intricately Detailed Graphics Creates an Atmospheric, Addictive Simulation Like None Before. Terraforming of Lower Worlds - Establishing Planetatary Outposts Are Just a Few of the Components You Will Need to Master to Take by Force an Enemy Planet at the Far Side of the Galaxy.
Virgin Games.

Overrun! Gary Grigsby. *Customer Support:* Technical assistance line: (408) 737-6800 (9am-5pm, PST); 14 day money back guarantee/30 day exchange policy.
Apple II (64k). disk $49.95.
Commodore 64/128 (64k). disk $49.95.
An Improved Version of the Game System PANZER STRIKE! & TYPHOON OF STEEL. The Action Is So Detailed That the Computer Keeps Track of the Ammunition Fired By an Infantryman Down to the Last Round! Each Unit Symbol Represents Either One Tank, Gun, or Squad of Infantry Where Each Square of the 40 x 90 Map Equals 50 Yards. Powerful Tools Are Provided So You Can Easily Create Your Own Maps, Troops, & Missions -- Making the Game System a Full-Fledged Construction Set As Well. Europe & the Middle East Serve As the Near-Future Battlefields, Where Russia & Soviet Allies Battle the Forces of the U.S. & Her Allies.
Strategic Simulations, Inc.

Overture. *Compatible Hardware:* Apple Macintosh.
3.5" disk $150.00.
Financial Planning & Analysis Program.
Brainstorm Development, Inc.

An Overview of Object-Oriented Analysis & Design Methods. Jun. 1994. *Customer Support:* Telephone.
System 6.07 or higher. Macintosh (5Mb). CD-ROM disk $995.00. *Nonstandard peripherals required:* Single speed CD-ROM drive. *Optimal configuration:* Macintosh IIci or higher, single speed CD-ROM drive, 13" color monitor (bit color), 5Mb RAM, System 6.07 or greater.
A Fully-Interactive Training Course in Object-Oriented Analysis & Design Methods.
ICONIX Software Engineering, Inc.

OverVUE. *Version:* 2.0. *Compatible Hardware:* Apple Macintosh. *Memory Required:* 128-512k. 3.5" disk $295.00.
Upgrade for current OverVUE owners. $22.95.
Free-Form Relational DBMS Which Can Sort 1000 Records in Less Than 2 Seconds. Also Features Charting & Macros. New Data Bases Can Be Created & Existing Ones Modified. File Capacity Examples 8,000 Names & Addresses on a 512k Macintosh, or 20,000 Names & Addresses on a Macintosh Plus. Will Import DIF, SYLK, DBASE II, & Text Files into OverVUE from Other Databases.
Provue Development Corp.

OverVue Mail Manager Template. *Compatible Hardware:* Apple Macintosh.
3.5" disk $39.95.
Mailing List Manager.
Provue Development Corp.

Ozzie's Fun Time Garden. Sep. 1995. *Customer Support:* Telephone support - free (except phone charge).
Windows 3.1. IBM & compatibles (386 DX-20) (4Mb). CD-ROM disk $12.99 (ISBN 1-57594-028-0). *Nonstandard peripherals required:* 2x CD-ROM player, Sound Card, VGA monitor. *Optimal configuration:* 486 SX-33.
Learn about Science & Ecology Through Games, Stories & Fun Activities.
Kidsoft, Inc.

Ozzie's Fun Time Garden. Sep. 1995. *Customer Support:* Telephone support - free (except phone charge).
Windows 3.1. IBM & compatibles (386 DX-20) (4Mb). CD-ROM disk $12.99 (ISBN 1-57594-067-1). *Nonstandard peripherals required:* 2x CD-ROM player, Sound Card, VGA monitor. *Optimal configuration:* 486 SX-33.
Learn about Science & Ecology Through Games, Stories & Fun Activities. Blister Pack Jewel Case.
Kidsoft, Inc.

Ozzie's Funtime Garden. Jan. 1996. *Customer Support:* Telephone support - free (except phone charge).
System 6.0.5 or higher. 256 color capable Mac with a 68030 processor (4Mb). CD-ROM disk $12.99 (ISBN 1-57594-106-6). *Nonstandard peripherals required:* 2X CD ROM drive, 640/480 resolution monitor.
Develop Memory, Critical Thinking, Problem Solving & Basic Science Skills with Engaging Animations, Sound Effects, Stories, Games & Music. Ozzie's Funtime Garden Multimedia Is a Wonderland for Parents, Educators & Kids.
Kidsoft, Inc.

Ozzie's Travels Destination Japan. *Customer Support:* Free phone technical support via 1-800 number.
Macintosh (4Mb). Contact publisher for price (ISBN 1-57600-020-6).
Windows.
Educational Games & Activities for Children Which Teach Social Studies & Appreciation for World Cultures, Specifically the Japanses Culture.
Digital Impact, Inc.

Ozzie's Travels Destination: Japan Lab Pack.
Customer Support: Free phone technical support via 1-800 number.
Macintosh (4Mb). Contact publisher for price (ISBN 1-57600-022-2).
Windows.
Educational Games & Activities for Children Which Teach Social Studies & Appreciation for World Cultures, Specifically the Japanese Culture. To Be Used by Teachers or Home Schoolers of Social Studies, Language, etc.
Digital Impact, Inc.

Ozzie's Travels Destination Mexico. *Customer Support:* Free phone technical support via 1-800 number.

Macintosh (4Mb). Contact publisher for price (ISBN 1-57600-015-X).
Windows.
Educational Games & Activities for Children Which Teach Social Studies & Appreciation for World Cultures, Specifically the Mexican Culture.
Digital Impact, Inc.

Ozzie's Travels Destination: Mexico Lab Pack.
Customer Support: Free phone technical support via 1-800 number.
Macintosh (4Mb). Contact publisher for price (ISBN 1-57600-019-2).
Windows.
Educational Games & Activities for Children Which Teach Social Studies & Appreciation for World Cultures, Specifically the Mexican Culture. To Be Used by Teachers or Home Schoolers of Social Studies, Language, etc.
Digital Impact, Inc.

Ozzie's Travels: First Grand Tour. *Customer Support:* Free phone technical support via 1-800 number.
Macintosh (4Mb). Contact publisher for price (ISBN 1-57600-050-8).
Windows.
Educational Games & Activities for Children Which Teach Social Studies & Appreciation for World Cultures. Contains 3 Full Destinations: Mexico, Japan, India.
Digital Impact, Inc.

Ozzie's Travels: Mexico. Sep. 1995. *Items Included:* User manual - parent/teacher guide. *Customer Support:* Free phone technical support via 1-800 number.
Windows; Macintosh. IBM 386DX 40, MPC 1 (4Mb); Macintosh LCIII, System 6.0.5 or higher (4Mb). CD-ROM disk Contact publisher for price (ISBN 1-57600-015-X, Order no.: 70102).
Interactive Educational Game Which Teaches Social Studies & Appreciation for World Cultures Through Stories & Activities.
Digital Impact, Inc.

Ozzie's World. Sep. 1994. *Items Included:* User manual - parent/teacher guide. *Customer Support:* Free phone technical support via 1-800 number.
Windows; Macintosh. IBM 386DX 40, MPC 1 (4Mb); Macintosh LCIII, System 6.0.5 or higher (4Mb). CD-ROM disk $39.95 (ISBN 0-933031-99-8, Order no.: 70101).
Interactive Educational Game Which Teaches Science Skills & Ecology Through Stories & Activities.
Digital Impact, Inc.

Ozzie's World.
Windows. IBM & compatibles. CD-ROM disk $59.95 (Order no.: R1354). *Nonstandard peripherals required:* CD-ROM drive. *Optimal configuration:* 386 processor higher, MS-DOS 3.1 or higher, 20Mb hard drive, 640k RAM, external speakers or headphones (with sound card) that are Sound Blaster compatible, VGA graphics & adapter, VGA color monitor.
Macintosh (4Mb). (Order no.: R1354). *Nonstandard peripherals required:* 14" color monitor or larger, CD-ROM drive.
Children Will Develop Deductive Reasoning, Critical Thinking & Memorization Skills As They Join Ozzy S. Otter on a Magical, Animated, Earth-Friendly Exploration. Animals Share Their Stories & Puzzles, While Games & Fun Scientific Activities Are Hidden Around Every Corner. Based on the Best-Selling Book "Earth Child" (Ages 3-8).
Library Video Co.

P & ID Clip Symbols. Oct. 1994.
DOS and/or Windows. PC compatible. disk $50.00 (ISBN 1-55617-530-2, Order no.: 530-2). *Addl. software required:* CAD/Drawing software.
A Collection of 150 Symbols Used in the Development of Process Instrument Diagrams. The Symbols Are Provided in Four Formats - .DWG, .DXF, .DGN, .PCX. to Work with Nearly All CAD & Drawing Software.
Instrument Society of America (ISA).

P-Lisp. *Customer Support:* 800-929-8117 (customer service).
MS-DOS. Apple II. disk $99.99 (ISBN 0-87007-198-X).
An True Interpreter Subset of the Golden Common Lisp & Set of Basic Tools for Writing Profession Quality Programs in P-Lisp, Such as Function Editor, a Printer, Disk File I/O Functions, Mathematical & Trigonometry Functions, an Apple IIe Conversion Program, & Several Sample Programs, Including Towers of Hanoi & Eliza. Operates in a READ-EVAL-PRINT Loop: It Reads Some Input, Evaluates it. Prints a Result & Waits for More Input. No Restrictions on the Lengths of Atom Print Names; There is no Limit to the Nesting Levels of Lists; all DOS Commands can be Entered from P-Lisp.
SourceView Software International.

P S Graph. *Operating System(s) Required:* MS-DOS, PC-DOS, CP/M, Concurrent DOS, Novell. *Memory Required:* 256k. *General Requirements:* Hard disk.
disk $495.00.
Integrated Program That Produces Statistical Graphs on the Screen or Printer. User Can Define Time Period, Range, Minimum/Maximum, & Increments. User May Graph the Entire Clinic or an Individual Doctor's Statistics. Special Feature Allows the User to Set up Criteria for Daily, Weekly, & Monthly Graphs Which Can Be Accessed Automatically.
ProGroup.

P-tral: BASIC to Pascal Translation Software.
Operating System(s) Required: Apple DOS 3.3; PC-DOS/MS-DOS. *Items Included:* Tutorial, 100 page manual. *Customer Support:* To registered users.
Apple II, IIe, IIc. disk $179.00.
IBM PC/XT (256k).
Converts Applesoft BASIC Programs to Apple Pascal. Translates Any Business, Scientific, Graphics & Game Software from Source, Converts MS BASIC to MS PASCAL Also.
Woodchuck Industries, Inc.

PA-ROLL. *Version:* 1.1. Peter C. Vonderhorst. Mar. 1983. *Compatible Hardware:* IBM PC, PC XT, PC AT & compatibles; TRS-80 Model III, Model 4. *Operating System(s) Required:* TRSDOS, PC-DOS, MS-DOS, CP/M. *Language(s):* Compiled BASIC. *Memory Required:* 64k. *General Requirements:* Printer. disk $350.00.
Prints Formatted Hard Copy Weekly, Monthly, Quarterly & Annually. Prints Checks, & Analyzes Payroll by Category, Employee or Quarter.
Computx.

Pac Man. *Compatible Hardware:* Atari XL/XE. ROM cartridge $19.95 (Order no.: CXL4022).
Atari Corp.

The Pacemaker Followup System. *Compatible Hardware:* IBM PC AT, PC XT, PS/2 Model 30. *Operating System(s) Required:* MS-DOS. *Language(s):* C. *Memory Required:* 640k.
contact publisher for price.
Designed to Provide Continuity of Patient Care & Pacemaker Maintenance from the Time the Pulse Generator & Lead Is Purchased, until It Is Implanted into the Patient, & Through Subsequent Followup Activity.
Trinity Computing Systems, Inc.

PacerConnect. *Items Included:* Documentation. *Customer Support:* Maintenance available, customer support, warranty, training available.
Macintosh. Free with 25 copies of PacerTerm; $2000.00 for any VAX/VMS host. *Addl. software required:* PacerTerm, or other terminal emulator package. *Optimal configuration:* Macintosh-to-VMS host. *Networks supported:* AppleTalk, LocalTalk bridged to Ethernet.
File Transfer & Terminal Emulation That Takes Advantage of the ADSP (Apple Data Stream Protocol) for Fast, Reliable MAC-to-VMS Connection Services.
Pacer Software, Inc.

PacerForum. *Items Included:* Documentation; product registration card included. *Customer Support:* Maintenance available; customer support; warranty.
System 6.0.4 or higher; System 7 compatible. Macintosh Plus, Classic, LC, SE, SE/30, any II or higher, 1Mb (2Mb recommended). 5 user pack $549.00; 25 users $1995.00 (educational, volume & special discounts). *Optimal configuration:* Hard drive required for server, dedicated or non-dedicated. *Networks supported:* Compatible with LocalTalk & Ethernet networks, ARAP support.
Collaborative Computing Product That Provides Bulletin Board, Broadcast & Conferencing Functionality to Apple Macintosh Clients on an AppleTalk Network. It Employs an Icon Based Graphical User Interface to Support the Distribution of Text, Pictures, Sounds & Files.
Pacer Software, Inc.

PacerLink. *Compatible Hardware:* Apple Macintosh. *Memory Required:* 512k. *General Requirements:* Hard disk recommended. *Items Included:* Software, documentation. *Customer Support:* By telephone & on-line via support at Pacer Soft. Com.
3.5" disk $2000.00, per VAX & up.
Classic Terminal Emulation & Desktop Communications Software That Connects Macintosh Users to Many Host Computers, Solving Communication & Resource-Sharing Problems. Allows Simultaneous Terminal Emulation Sessions by Connecting to One or More Hosts, Each in Its Own Window. It Offers Network Independence by Supporting Host Connections via RS-232, Ethernet or LocalTalk. For Ethernet Connections to UNIX Systems, PacerLink Supports the TCP/IP & Telnet Protocols. The PacerLink Server Runs on a Host VMS or UNIX System & Provides Terminal Emulation, File Transfer, Virtual Disk & Print Services to Client Macintosh Computers. Carries Out Requests to Copy Files, Access Local or Remote Printers & Performs Other Host Functions Such As Virtual Disk Storage. Special Client Features Include Programmable On-Screen SoftKeys, MiniWindows, & Automated Scripting. A Flexible Command Language Makes It Easy to Automate Repetitive Functions.
Pacer Software, Inc.

PacerPrint. *Compatible Hardware:* Apple Macintosh. *Items Included:* Software, documentation & registration cards. *Customer Support:* By telephone & on-line via support at Pacer Soft. Com.
Micro VAX. 3.5" disk $1000.00.
VAX. 3.5" disk $2000.00.
VAX Cluster. 3.5" disk $4000.00.
Software That Resides on a Host UNIX or VMS System & Drives Postscript-Compatible Printers. It Allows Host & Macintosh Users to Share Access

TITLE INDEX

to LocalTalk-Based Printers (Such As Apple's LaserWriter Family) from Anywhere on the Network. With PacerPrint, Sites with Macintosh, VMS & UNIX Users Can Design Flexible Network Topologies That Make LaserWriter Printers Simultaneously Accessible for Host & Macintosh Print Jobs. Printers Can Be Centralized in One Location or Distributed Throughout a Large Network. Printers Can Reside Either on a LocalTalk LAN Bridged to the Network Through an Ethernet Gateway or at Any Point on the Network That Supports RS-232 Communication - Directly Connected or Through a Terminal Server. Converts ASCII Files to PostScript, Automatically Manages Downloading of Fonts & LaserPrep Files, & Provides Full Page Accounting.
Pacer Software, Inc.

PacerShare. *Compatible Hardware:* Apple Macintosh. *General Requirements:* PacerLink. *Items Included:* Software, documentation & registration cards. *Customer Support:* By telephone & on-line via support at Pacer Soft. Com. On-site as required.
3.5" disk per VAX $400.00.
An AppleShare File Server Implementation That Lets a UNIX or VMS Host Act Like a Large Macintosh File Server. With PacerShare, Macintosh Computers Connect to Host Computers via Either a Direct Ethernet Connection or a LocalTalk LAN Bridged to Ethernet. Using PacerShare, the Host File System Is Viewed from the Macintosh As a Series of Volumes with the Host Directories & Files Represented As Folders & Files. No Translation Is Required to Move Between Host & Macintosh Files. The Macintosh User Can Easily Peruse the Host File System, Create Directories, or Move Directory Trees. In Addition, the Macintosh Users Can Store Macintosh Files on the Host, Increasing Backup Efficiency & Eliminating the Need for Separate Macintosh Backups. Conforms Fully to Host System Security. Users Cannot View or Modify Directories That They Could Not Otherwise Access Through a Normal Terminal Session.
Pacer Software, Inc.

PacerTerm. *Items Included:* Documentation; product registration card included. *Customer Support:* Maintenance available; customer support; warranty.
System 6.0.4 or higher; System 7 compatible. Macintosh Plus, Classic, LC, SE, SE/30, any II or higher, 1Mb (2Mb recommended). $249.00 (educational, quantity & special discounts avail.). *Networks supported:* RS-232C, LocalTalk, Ethernet.
Emulation & File Transfer. Scripting Functions & Multiple Simultaneous Sessions Capability.
Pacer Software, Inc.

Pacesetter. *Compatible Hardware:* 80386/based PCs, DG Aviion, HP 9000, Risc 6000, TI 1500. *Language(s):* Progress, Unix. *Customer Support:* Full Hardware & Software Support.
contact publisher for price.
Point of Sale, Inventory Control, Purchasing/Receiving, Accounts Receivable, Service Shop, Sales Analysis Software for Retail & Wholesale Businesses.
Icas Systems, Inc.

Pacific War: Jewel Case CD. Gary Grigsby. Nov. 1995. *Customer Support:* 30 day limited warranty.
DOS 5.0 or higher. 386 CD-ROM with hard drive (2Mb). CD-ROM disk $9.95 (ISBN 0-917059-42-5, Order no.: 062631).
As the Supreme Commander of Allied or Japanese Forces on All Fronts - Land, Air & Sea - Yours Is Definitely the Biggest Battlefield Ever. WWII Strategy Wargame.
Strategic Simulations, Inc.

PACK-ER II. *Version:* 4.0. Jan. 1990. *Items Included:* One spiral bound manual, two 3.5" disks. *Customer Support:* Free phone support.
6.0.2 or higher. Macintosh (1Mb). 3.5" disk $450.00.
Comes with Five Programs. The Curves Program Generates Cushion Curves. These Curves Can Be Edited & Stored As Files. The Park Acceleration Program Shows Peak G vs Static Load Charts. Total Encapsulation, Corner Pads, & Face Pads Are Programs That Find the Least Amount of Cushion Needed for a Product. Included Are MIL Spec 304-B, & Dow Ethafoam Curves.
Flight Engineering.

Pack Master. Tom Sherer. 1985. *Compatible Hardware:* IBM PC compatible, THEOS compatible. *Operating System(s) Required:* THEOS.
disk $5000.00.
Integrated Accounting/Sales System from Field/Grove to Retailer for Produce Packing Houses.
Comcepts Systems.

The P.A.C.K (Programmer's Assembly-Language Construction Kit). Bob Bishop & Lucia Grossberger. *Operating System(s) Required:* Apple DOS 3.3, ProDOS.
$49.95.
Programming Construction Kit That Gives User Building Blocks (Subroutine Modules) & the Utilities (Editor, Assembler & Linking Loader) to Put These Blocks Together to Build or Add Programs.
Interactive Arts.

Packet/PC for Windows. *Version:* 3.21. 1992. *Customer Support:* One-year free maintenance, toll-free technical support, free upgrades.
DOS, Windows or OS/2. 16 user system $6995.00.
Allows Remote Windows Users to Connect to Their Mainframe or Midrange (3270 or 5250) via Asynchronous Direct-Dial, X.25 Packet Networks, or Wireless Networks. Using the Windows Applications the User Is Familiar with, PACKET/PC Provides the Capability to Access Corporate Databases & Upload or Download Data, All with the Click of a Mouse. Easy to Use & Comes with Many Standard Features. Includes Inbound Like Character Compression & DYNAFLASH!, an Advanced, Dynamic Compression Technique. Provides up to 80% Compression of All Outbound Data, Significantly Saving Time & Network Charges.
Telepartner International.

Packet/Main. *Items Included:* Documentation. *Customer Support:* Toll-free technical support; 1st year maintenance free, thereafter 20% current list price; training offered-contact vendor.
MVS, VM. IBM Mainframe required. Contact publisher for price. *Addl. software required:* Packet/3270 at PC.
The Mainframe Software Component of the Packet/3270 SNA/ASYNC Micro-to-Mainframe Communications Link. Features Include Full Duplex Blocked Transmission, 8-Bit Data Stream, Error Detection (CRC Algorithm), Selective Retransmission, Multiple Session Support, Flexible User Exits, & Extended Diagnostic Tests. Dynamic Compression Reducing the Data Stream Up to 90%
Telepartner International.

Packet/PC for Windows. *Version:* 3.21. 1992. *Customer Support:* One year free maintenance, toll-free technical support, free upgrades.
Windows (4Mb). disk $295.00.
Allows Remote Windows Users to Connect to Their Mainframe or Midrange (3270 or 5250) via Asynchronous Direct-Dial, X.25 Packet Networks, or Wireless Networks. Using the Windows Applications the User Is Familiar with, Packet/PC for Windows Provides the Capability to Access Corporate Databases & Upload or Download Data, All with the Click of a Mouse. Easy to Use & Comes with Many Standard Features, Including: WinMENU - an Automatic Scripting Facility That Allows Easy Network Access, Customization, & Optimal Performance; a Multiple Document Interface (MDI) - Which Allows Each User to Run up to 32 Simultaneous Host Sessions; Dynamic Data Exchange (DDE) - Which Provides Real-Time Data Transfer Between Your Host & Windows Applications; & a Simple Function-Based Interface to Visual Basic & C Language Programming.
Telepartner International.

Packet Switching Fundamentals. Jul. 1995. *Items Included:* User manual. *Customer Support:* Free technical support & a 30-day money back guarantee.
MS-DOS. IBM & compatibles (640k). 3.5" disk $395.00 (ISBN 1-57305-019-9). *Nonstandard peripherals required:* High-density 3.5" disk drive; VGA color monitor. *Addl. software required:* MS-DOS version 3.3 or higher.
Optimal configuration: IBM (640k), MS-DOS version 3.3 or higher, VGA color monitor, keyboard, Microsoft compatible mouse.
This Is a 3-Hour Computer-Based Training Program That Explores the Characteristics of a Packet Switch Network & the Typical Hardware Components & Their Interactions.
Bellcore.

PACKET/3270. *Items Included:* documentation. *Customer Support:* Toll free technical support; 1st year of maintenance free, thereafter 20% current list price; training offered-contact vendor.
DOS 2.0 or higher for extended memory DOS 3.0 or higher. IBM PC, XT, AT, PS/2 & compatibles (360k). disk $295.00. *Nonstandard peripherals required:* TeleServer or Packet/Main Software at the mainframe site; connection to packet network, local PAD or IBM 3708.
$295.00 based on number of users.
An Asynchronous SNA Link for Micro-to-Mainframe Communications. Combines the Functionality of the SNA/ASYNC Protocol with the Economics of Packet Network Access for Interactive 3270 Application Support, Printer Support, File Transfer, & Three Application Program Interfaces, Including HLLAPI. LAN, MAC & Windows Versions Are Available.
Telepartner International.

PACorp: PA Corp. Tax Returns. Dec. 1991. *Items Included:* Manual. *Customer Support:* Free 90 day maintenance.
PC-DOS/MS-DOS 2.0 or higher. IBM PC-AT or compatible (512k). $189.00, 2nd year renewal ,89.00.
Pennsylvania Corporate Income Tax Forms for a Regular & Sub Chapter "S" Election Corporation.
Profitime, Inc.

PACS PLUS. *Compatible Hardware:* DEC VAX/VMS.
contact publisher for price.
Allocates & Reports Costs, Bills Users, & Monitors System Utilization. Capabilities Include Chargeback, Session & Image Accounting, Multi-Level Reporting, Capacity Planning, Screen-Oriented Data Management, & General-Purpose Report Writing.
Signal Technology, Inc.

Padlock. Dick Rettke. Oct. 1982. *Compatible Hardware:* Apple II, II+, IIe. *Operating System(s) Required:* Apple DOS 3.3, Pascal 1.1. *Language(s):* Pascal, Assembly. *Memory Required:* 48k.

Set. disk $100.00 (ISBN 0-926567-04-7, Order no.: PADLOCK).
per key $20.00.
Software Developers Install Their Own Software & Disks Will only Run When a Padlock Key Is Inserted in the Game Port.
Rettke Resources.

Padlock II. *Version:* 4.58. Jan. 1984. *Operating System(s) Required:* MS-DOS, PC-DOS. *Memory Required:* 64k.
$150.00 (Order no.: 412028).
Provides High Level Copy Protection with a Special Analog Magnetic Fingerprint. This Fingerprint - Placed on the Floppy with Equipment Designed & Used Exclusively at GLENCO - Contains a Unique Company Assigned ID No. & Sequentially Assigned S/Ns. The Serial Numbers Can Be Used to Set up a Tracking System, Version Control, or May Simply Be Displayed by the Program. The Analog Signal Cannot Be Written to a Disk Using the Read/Write Head on a Disk Drive. Copy Protection System Includes a Master Disk along with the Appropriate Number of Preformatted or Duplicated Disks. The Master Disk Contains the Necessary Subroutines along with Example Programs in the Language Specified. An Option, Called HDCOPY, Frees the Need to Have a PADLOCK I Key Disk Drive A in Order for the Program to Run.
Glenco Engineering, Inc.

PADS-Logic. *Version:* 4.01. Jul. 1994. *Items Included:* User Manuals, Training Manual, extensive parts library. *Customer Support:* 30 Day Money Back Guarantee, 30 Day Warranty, 1 year maintenance $200.00.
MS-DOS, MS-Windows, Windows NT. IBM 286/386 & compatibles (2 Mb). disk $450.00 (Order no.: P-1). *Nonstandard peripherals required:* no. *Addl. software required:* recommend PADS-Perform. *Networks supported:* Novell.
Unix. Unix workstations. disk $750.00.
PADS-Logic, with Its Multi-Sheet Database, Is Unmatched As a General Purpose Schematic & Logic Capture Tool for the Electronic Engineer & the PCB Designer. Through the Use of Expanded Memory, User Can Design Very Large Circuits of up to 100 D-Size Sheets & 1,000 IC's. These Sheets Can All Reside Simultaneously in Memory.
PADS Software, Inc.

PADS-Perform. *Version:* 6.0. *Items Included:* Training Manuals, User Manuals, Extensive Parts library. *Customer Support:* 1 year maintenance $500.00, 30 Day Warranty, Hot Line Support.
MS-DOS, MS-Windows, MS-Windows NT, Unix. IBM PC 80386/80486 & compatibles (4Mb) & Unix workstations. disk $3495.00 & up (Order no.: H-1). *Nonstandard peripherals required:* large variety of high-end graphics cards available. *Optimal configuration:* 486 pc 30 mgz 20 megabyte RAM, laser printer, PADS-Logic Schematic Capture. *Networks supported:* Novell.
Sun Sparc 1, 2 System 4, HP700 series, SGI. $3495.00 & up. *Optimal configuration:* Sun Sparc 2 operating on Unix RAM 16 mhgz, laser printer. *Networks supported:* PCNFS.
High-End State-of-the-Art Printed Circuit Board Design Software Operating in DOS on 386 or 486 Personal Computers & UNIX Workstations. PADS Software's PCB Software Has Many Workstation Features Such As 1 Micron Grid, Copper Fill, 1 Degree Component Rotation, Tear Drop Pads, On-Line & Batched Design Rules Checkin & Much More with Unlimited Design Capacity. Many Available Options.
PADS Software, Inc.

PADS: Productivity Analysis Database System. *Version:* 2.3. Jun. 1989. *Compatible Hardware:* IBM PC, PC XT, PC AT, & true compatibles. *Operating System(s) Required:* PC-DOS 2.1 or higher. *Memory Required:* 256k. *General Requirements:* Hard disk, printer, color graphics adapter.
$15,000.00 per yr.
Quantitative Software Management, Inc.

PADS-WORK. *Version:* 7.0. *Compatible Hardware:* IBM PC AT; 80386/80486-based PCs, Unix workstations. *Operating System(s) Required:* MS-DOS, MS-Windows, Windows NT, Unix. *Language(s):* C. *General Requirements:* 20Mb hard disk. *Customer Support:* 30 days no charge, $350 includes free hotline resolution of questions, free update for software.
$995.00.
Evaluation Package on 3 disks with manual on DOS or Windows avail.
Printed Circuit Board CAD Application with the Following Features: Inputs from FutureNet, ORCAD, SCHEMA, & Others; Design on CRT Without Schematic Input; up to 30 Layers & 500 IC's; Automatic & Interactive Placement Aids; True Width Tracks & Pads at the CRT; Rip-Up & Retry Auto Routing; 2-D Documentation Capability; Air Gap Chekcing; TTL/CMOS Library Included; Full SMD & ANALOG Board Design Supported; Plotting on Matrix Printer & Ink Plotter, User Printer. Additional Options Are Available.
PADS Software, Inc.

Page-A-Ranger. *Version:* 2.1. Sep. 1994. *Items Included:* (40 page) user manual. *Customer Support:* 90 day limited warranty, 6 mos. limited tech support.
DOS 2.1 or higher. PC/XT/AT or compatible (256k). $39.95 plus $5.00 S&H (ISBN 1-886019-01-0, Order no.: PAGE-A-RANGER 2.1). *Nonstandard peripherals required:* LaserJet I & II or compatible. *Addl. software required:* WordPerfect 5.1. *Optimal configuration:* Hard drive or RAM disk.
A Program to Make Books, Booklets or Pamphlets Easily. Create Your Document Using WordPerfect 5.1. Will Place 2 or 4 Pages on Each Sheet Retaining All Document Attributes & Will Re-Order Those Pages in Book Order. You Can Then Print for a Fold/Staple or Cut/Bind Without Having to Collate.
Waltech.

Page-A-Ranger: Book Making Software. *Version:* 2.1. Walter L. Smith. Nov. 1994. *Items Included:* User manual, floppy disk with software & examples, customer service card. *Customer Support:* Satisfaction guaranteed for 90 days, limited free customer support, custom versions available.
PC-DOS/MS-DOS 2.1 or higher. PC/XT/AT 8088, 8086, 80286, 80386, 80486 (256k). disk $39.95 (ISBN 1-886019-01-0, Order no.: PAGE-A-RANGER 2.1). *Nonstandard peripherals required:* LaserJet 1, Plus, Series II or upward compatible (III or IV). *Addl. software required:* WordPerfect 5.1 recommended with bitmapped fonts. *Optimal configuration:* DOS, 256k RAM, WordPerfect 5.1, hard disk recommended for speed, can be used with 2 floppy drives for production printing.
Book Making Program for DOS WordPerfect 5.1 Files Retaining ALL ATTRIBUTES Including Headers, Footers, Page Numbers, Graphics & Fonts. Also Works with ASCII Files. This Program Is Executable Code & Is Not a MACRO. Your Original Document is UNALTERED. Use with Your LaserJet or Upward Compatible Printer to Do 1 Book or Short Production Runs of 10 or 20 Books. Your Book Is Printed with 1 or 2 Pages Per Side per Sheet, Pages Re-Ordered So, No Page Collation Is Needed. Print Forward or Backward.
Waltech.

Page Designs Quick! *Version:* 1.0. *Compatible Hardware:* Apple Macintosh; IBM PC & compatibles. *General Requirements:* Aldus Pagemaker 4.0-6.0 Mac & PC versions. *Items Included:* Manuals & disks. *Customer Support:* Call company or E-mail.
3.5" disk $69.95.
Template Which Contains 120 Newsletter Page Layout Templates; Half Are Three-Column Layouts, Half Four-Column. Users Can Adjust the Layouts for Page Size & Modify Them to Meet Specific Needs; Divide or Combine Stories; Expand or Reduce Pictures in Width or Depth; & Change Headline Configurations. Includes Hard Copy Template Booklet.
PAR Publishing Co.

Page Designs Quick! 5. *Version:* 1.0. *Compatible Hardware:* Apple Macintosh; IBM PC & compatibles. *General Requirements:* Aldus Pagemaker 4.0-5.0, Mac & PC versions. *Items Included:* Manuals & disks. *Customer Support:* Call company or E-mail.
3.5" disk $139.95.
Template Program Which Includes 225 Page-Layout Templates for Five-Column Tabloid Newspapers. The Program Is Designed for High School & College Papers, Trade Papers, & Government Publications. Allows the User Line Art & Other Graphic Techniques. Package Includes a Template Booklet.
PAR Publishing Co.

Pagemaker in Your Classroom for Macintosh & Windows: Starter Package. *Version:* 5.0. Steve Corder et al. 1996. *Items Included:* Disk; reproducible teacher book, 195 pp.; 1 student activity text, 150 pp. Additional copies of activity text available for $12.95; 10 or more copies, each $11.95. *Customer Support:* Call 1-800-341-6094 for free technical assistance, 30 day approval policy, money back guarantee.
Macintosh. 3.5" disk $79.95 (ISBN 0-8251-2722-X, Order no.: 0-2722X). *Addl. software required:* Pagemaker 5.0.
Windows. IBM & compatibles. disk $79.95 (ISBN 0-8251-2723-8, Order no.: 0-27238). *Addl. software required:* Pagemaker 5.0.
Students Gain Hands-On, Real-Life Practice in Using Page Layout, Graphics, Typefaces, & Formatting to Create Professional Looking Documents. Self-Paced Lessons in the Activity Text Provide Directions for Manipulating Files on the Data Disk.
J. Weston Walch Pub.

Pagemaker: Introduction Level 1 & Level 2. *Version:* 4.0. Jul. 1991. *Customer Support:* Hotline support.
Macintosh. starter pack $900.00 (Order no.: 41-391-PK, 41-392-PK9). *Addl. software required:* PageMaker.
Instructor-Led Courseware. Starter Kit Includes Instructor's Guide & 12 Student Manuals with Practice Activities & Data Disks. Also Instructor Guide Includes Overhead Transparencies & Two-Year Free Upgrade Service. Additional Student Manuals Available Separately.
Logical Operations.

Pagemaker-Japanese. *Version:* 5.0. Jul. 1992. *Compatible Hardware:* Apple Macintosh. *Memory Required:* 4000k.
3.5" disk $1095.00.
Japanese Language Version of Pagemaker.
Qualitas Trading Co.

TITLE INDEX

PageMaker: Korean. *Version:* 3.0. Feb. 1993. *Customer Support:* For customer service, product registration, upgrades, technical support, & CustomerFirst service plans, customers may call Aldus Customer Services at (206) 628-2320. Macintosh. Contact publisher for price (ISBN 1-56026-141-2).
Aldus Corp.

PageMaker 3 by Example. *Version:* PC. David Webster & Tony Webster. Jul. 1989.
MS-DOS. IBM PC & compatibles. $22.95 (ISBN 1-55851-050-8).
Apple II series, Macintosh. $22.95 (ISBN 1-55851-049-4).
Hands-On Tutorial to Learning Pagemaker. Broken Down into Modules with Each Progressive Module Covering More Detailed Operations of PageMaker. Topics Include Loading Files, Manipulating Text Blocks, Page Printing & More. Extensive Use of Exercises & Illustrations Reinforce the Learning Process.
M & T Bks.

PageMill: Training on CD. Quay2 Multimedia. Feb. 1996.
IBM. CD-ROM disk $49.95 (ISBN 0-201-88616-2).
Peachpit Pr.

Pages & Windows. *Items Included:* 1 disk, 1 manual. *Customer Support:* Telephone.
PC-DOS, MS-DOS. disk $19.95 (ISBN 0-8283-1990-1). *Nonstandard peripherals required:* Laser Printer, Dot Matrix with graphics.
Using WordPerfect 5.1 This Package Allows Virtual Desktop Publishing on the Fly, with a Minimum Number of Key Strokes (No Mouse Necessary). Files-Copy or Graphics Can Be Imported & Transformed; They Can Also Be Generated. Graphics, of Any Size, Can Be Created or Imported on the Fly. Creates Camera Ready Copy for Newspapers, the Book Industry, or Magazine Trade.
Popular Technology.

Page's CONCEPTUAL COST ESTIMATOR. John S. Page. Sep. 1987. *Compatible Hardware:* IBM PC, PC XT, PC AT & compatibles. *Operating System(s) Required:* PC-DOS/MS-DOS 3.1. *Language(s):* Compiled BASIC. *Memory Required:* 64k. *Customer Support:* 30 day money-back guarantee.
3.5" or 5.25" disk $695.00, incl. 48-page manual.
Using the Data from Page's Conceptual Cost Estimating Manual & Inputting Project Type, Estimated Major Process Equipment Cost, & Plant Location, This Program Will Calculate a Six-Page Comprehensive Conceptual Estimate of Total Cost (Labor, Materials, & Subcontracts) to Give Engineers, Contractors, & Managers a Way to Evaluate the Feasibility of Refinery & Chemical/Petrochemical/Petrochemical Plant Construction Projects. Includes Project Cash Flow Analysis.
Gulf Publishing Co.

Pages Plus with VoiceDrive. SuperSoft. Jun. 1984. *Operating System(s) Required:* MS-DOS. *Memory Required:* 128k. *General Requirements:* Printer, speech command system, Winchester hard disk.
$495.00.
Texas Instruments, Personal Productivit.

PAGEWORK. *Version:* 3.10. Nov. 1988. *Compatible Hardware:* IBM PC, PC XT, PC AT, & compatibles. *Operating System(s) Required:* PC-DOS/MS-DOS. *Language(s):* C. *Memory Required:* 512k. *General Requirements:* Graphics card.
Targa 16. included in StudioWorks System.

Page-Layout Program Which Allows for the Integration of High Quality Text & Graphics Which Can Be Viewed & Manipulated on the Screen, & Then Printed on Any Printer Equipped with POSTSCRIPT, Such As the Apple Laserwriter. Charts Can Be Imported Through CHARTWORK from 1-2-3 Data As Well As Graphics from the ARTWORK Package, & Scanned Images from the BRUSHWORK Package.
West End Film, Inc.

PAIGE. *Version:* 1.5. Gary Crandall. Jan. 1994. *Items Included:* 300 Plus Programmer's Guide. *Customer Support:* One year unlimited warranty. After first year customers can subscribe to one of our Extended Service Plans.
Macintosh System 6 or higher. Macintosh (1Mb). Object Code: $3500.00; Source Code: $25,000.00 (Order no.: 700). *Addl. software required:* Think C, MPW or Metrowerks Codearrior 4D. *Networks supported:* All.
Windows 3.X, Windows NT, Windows 95. 486 (1Mb). Object Code: $3500.00; Source Code: $25,000.00 (Order no.: 701). *Addl. software required:* Standard compilers.
Windows NT. 486 (1Mb). Object Code: $3500.00; Source Code: $25,000.00 (Order no.: 702).
Cross-Platform Library for Developers Who Want to Incorporate Textediting, Word Processing, Page Layout, or Multi-Media Features into Their Application. Since PAIGE Makes No Assumptions about a Document's Data Type, Anything Can Be Embedded into a Text Stream, Such As, Pictures, Arbitrary Objects, Buttons or Hypertext Links.
DataPak Software, Inc.

Paint It! *Items Included:* Manual. *Customer Support:* Unlimited technical support; 60 day moneyback guarantee.
MAC. Macintosh (2Mb). 3.5" disk $59.95. *Addl. software required:* System 6.05 or higher, 32-bit QuickDraw. *Optimal configuration:* MAC Quadra, Classic II, SE/30, LC, Si or II family, hard drive, mouse.
Easy-to-Use 32-Bit Color Paint Program. Includes a Graphical Interface & Space-Saving Color/Pattern Palette; Customizable Tools with Anti-Aliasing to Smooth Rough Edges & Built-In Virtual Memory for Working with Multiple or Large Images. Supports Color Postscript, TIFF, PICT, GIF & QuickTime PICT File Formats.
Timeworks, Inc.

PAL-DOC. *Version:* 4.0. Sep. 1988. *Compatible Hardware:* HP Series 200. *Operating System(s) Required:* BASIC. *Memory Required:* 768k. *General Requirements:* Printer, digital plotter.
contact publisher for price.
Documents PAL Program Configurations. Designed Specifically to Draw & Print Allen-Bradley Tape Configurations Produced by 8200 CNC Machine Controllers. Suited for Machine Tool Builders, Industrial Robot Builders & Certain Users Whose Machines Are Controlled with an A-B 8200 Controller. Uses PAL Binary Tape to Produce Printed Report Documents Including: Ladder Diagram, Display Pages, Tables, I/O Assignments, & Both Line & Rung Cross Reference.
Howard W. Myers & Assocs.

Paladin. *Compatible Hardware:* Commodore Amiga, IBM PC, Apple Macintosh, Atari ST. 3.5" disk $39.95 ea.
IBM. (ISBN 0-932549-14-4, Order no.: PL-MS-1).
MAC. (ISBN 0-932549-15-2, Order no.: PL-MA-1).
Atari ST. (ISBN 0-932549-13-6, Order no.: PL-ST-1).
Amiga. (ISBN 0-932549-12-8, Order no.: PL-AM-1).
Animated Fantasy Combat Game.
Omnitrend Software, Inc.

Palantir Filer for Windows. *Version:* 3.01. Aug. 1990. *Customer Support:* Telephone support (512) 854-8794.
MS-DOS. IBM-AT & compatibles (512k). disk $195.00. *Addl. software required:* MS Windows.
A Flat Database Which Reads dBase II/III Files & Can Display Graphics.
Palsoft.

Palantir Spell for Windows. *Version:* 3.1. Jun. 1990. *Compatible Hardware:* Compaq; HP Vectra; IBM PC, PC XT, PC AT. *Operating System(s) Required:* MS-DOS 2.0 or higher. *Memory Required:* 512k. *General Requirements:* Graphics card, Microsoft Windows environment. *Customer Support:* Telephone support: 512-854-8794.
disk $95.00. *Addl. software required:* MS-Windows.
Speller for MICROSOFT WINDOWS That Comes with a 130,000-Word Dictionary & Multiple User Dictionaries. Works Well with Other MS-WINDOWS-Based Application Files. Not Copy Protected.
Palsoft.

Palantir Word Processor. *Version:* 3.1. Jul. 1986. *Compatible Hardware:* IBM PC & compatibles. *Operating System(s) Required:* MS-DOS. (source code included). *Memory Required:* 256k. *Customer Support:* Telephone support, (512)854-8794.
disk $295.00.
Full-Featured & Menu-Driven Executive Word Processor Suitable for All Types of Writing. Utilizes Dedicated Function Keys, Logical Keystrokes & Screen Attributes & Supplies As Standard Features. Spell Checking & Mail Merge Included.
Palsoft.

PAMS: Political Activist Monitoring System. *Version:* 3.90. Aug. 1986. *Items Included:* Manual. *Customer Support:* 90 days unlimited support after training, ongoing support $300/yr..
PC-DOS 3.30 (512k). PC AT & compatibles. disk $2000.00 (ISBN 0-928246-01-9, Order no.: PAMS). *Nonstandard peripherals required:* Modem for remote support. *Addl. software required:* "PC Anywhere" for remote support. *Optimal configuration:* Hard disk, 690k RAM. *Networks supported:* Novell.
Tracks Political Issues & People or Organizations Concerned with Social and/or Political Issues of the Day. Multi-User System Allows User to Track 20 Key Issues per Year & an Unlimited Number of Key Votes per Political Personage.
HEL Custom Software, Inc.

Pandemonium. *Compatible Hardware:* Apple II+, IIe; Atari 400, 800; TRS-80. *Memory Required:* Atari 40k, TRS-80, Apple 48k.
disk $39.95.
Played on a 5" x 5" Grid. User Chooses the Time Limit & Mode of Play. After This Has Been Decided, the Letters Are Randomly Selected. The Frequency of Any Letter Is Listed in the Game Book, the Point Value Being the Exact Inverse of the Frequency. Word Values Will Be Determined by the Letter Value on the Placement. There Are Two Available Options: One Is to Bypass Letters That Are Too Difficult & the Other Is to Rearrange the Letters Once the Grid Is Filled In.
Soft Images.

P&L. Frazier, Peper, & Assocs. Jun. 1987. *Compatible Hardware:* IBM PC, PC XT, PC AT. *Operating System(s) Required:* PC-DOS 2.0 or higher. *Memory Required:* 256k. *General Requirements:* Printer.
disk $199.95.
RAM-Resident Software Tool for Structuring &

Analyzing Financial Models. Designed for Corporate Executives & Managers Who Need "Quick & Dirty" Analyses of Financial Decisions.
Brady Computer Bks.

P&RC: Performance & Resource Chart. *Version:* 11.0. Aug. 1985. *Compatible Hardware:* IBM PC & compatibles, 286, 386, 486 etc.. *Operating System(s) Required:* MS-DOS 2.00 or higher. *Memory Required:* 256k. *General Requirements:* Epson MX, FX, LQ or compatible printers. $295.00.
Handles Computerized Data Analysis of Dozens or Hundreds of Daily, Weekly or Monthly Statistics. The Output Is Balanced Alpha-Numeric, Graphic Hardcopy. It Applies to Single & Multi-Level Operations & Adapts to Any Organizational Chart. Whether Economic Operations, Personnel or Financial Statistics Are Reported, It Is an Early Warning System & Provides An Overview With Demand Detail Zoom. It Is Not the Computerization of a Former Manual System, But Is Specifically Developed to Evaluate Large Volumes of Periodic Numeric Data for Quick & Easy Comprehension.
Stansfield & Assocs.

PANEL- Panel Design & Component Sizing. Jul. 1989. *Items Included:* Bound user manual. *Customer Support:* Unlimited telephone support. MS-DOS (384k). IBM PC, PC XT, PC AT, AT 286 & 386. disk $695.00 (Order no.: 800-648-9523). *Optimal configuration:* Hard disk (20Mb); color monitor; floppy drive. *Networks supported:* All networks supported.
Automatically Sizes All Components in an Electric Power Distribution System. Also, Panel Schedules, Motor Control Centers & Switchboards Are Printed. Allows Designer to Define Radial One-Line Diagram with Loads & Associated Power Factors. Components Are Sized According to NEC Handbook. Project Data Can Then Be Analyzed, & Schedules Can Be Created & Viewed. Optional AutoCAD DXF File Can Be Created As Well.
Elite Software Development, Inc.

Panel-86. Lifeboat Associates. *Operating System(s) Required:* MS-DOS. *Language(s):* MSPascal. *Memory Required:* 64k. *General Requirements:* Printer. $380.00.
Texas Instruments, Personal Productivit.

PANEL: Panel Design & Component Sizing. *Items Included:* Manual. *Customer Support:* Toll free telephone support. IBM PC compatible (256k). disk $695.00.
Automatically & Optimally Sizes All Components (Cables, Bus Ducts, Transformers, etc.) in an Electric Power Distribution System. In Addition, Panel Schedules for General Purpose Panels, Motor Control Centers, & Switchboards are Printed.
Elite Software Development, Inc.

PANEL Plus. (ADVANTAGE Library Ser.). *Compatible Hardware:* IBM PC. *General Requirements:* Compatible compiler. contact publisher for price.
Screen Management Library for Data Display, Entry, & Editing. Supports Pop-Up Fields & Windows, Multi-Line Fields, Horizontal & Vertical Field Scrolling, Menus, Help Boxes, & Custom Field Validation. Full Library Source Code Is Included with Variant Fields for All Supported Environments. This Allows for Applications to Be Ported, Virtually Unchanged, to Almost Any Environment Supporting a C Compiler. There Are No Royalties for the Use of Libraries When Linked into User's Own Applications. The Library Includes over 150 Functions & Is Organized So That Most Programmers Only Need a Maximum

Subset of about Two Dozen Calls, Which Are Defined in Logical Groupings for Ease of Use. A Screen Painter/Field Attribute Editor & a C Source Code Generator Are Included to Create Screens for Use with the Screen Function Library. Multiple Screen & Keyboard Low-Level Files Are Included Which Can Be Built-In at Link Time.
Lifeboat Assocs.

Panorama. *Version:* 3.15. *Compatible Hardware:* IBM PC AT. *Memory Required:* 6000k. *General Requirements:* ATVista board. 40Mb hard disk recommended. *Items Included:* Panorama Software, user guide, installation guide, security block. *Customer Support:* Free customer support - only cost of phone charges. $795.00, TARGA.
Presentation-Graphics Package for On-Screen Slide Shows Featuring Dissolves & Wipes. Output Options Include to Screen or to Videotape via Encoder. Imports TGA & VST File Formats. Other Features Include On-Screen Help, Fades, Louver Effects, Fade to Black, Implode & Vacuum.
AT&T Multimedia Software Solutions.

Panorama.
MS-DOS 5.0 or higher. 386 or higher (6Mb). Contact publisher for price. *Nonstandard peripherals required:* 40Mb available on hard drive (additional space required for image & audio storage), color monitor, graphics display cards: TARGA/TARGA Plus or compatible, audio board, CD-ROM player for audio input, video camera or VCR (optional), touch screen (optional), mouse or digitizing table (optional).
Combines State-of-the-Art Transition Effects with 2D Animation & Live Video to Create Dynamic Desktop Presentations, Speaker Support Programs & Video Productions.
AT&T Multimedia Software Solutions.

Panorama. *Version:* 1.5. Nov. 1989. *Customer Support:* 60 day money back guarantee. Macintosh Plus or higher. 3.5" disk Panorama $245.00.
3.5" disk Mail manager template $35.00.
3.5" disk Personal Finance template $25.00.
Visual Flat-File Manager. Uses a Spreadsheet-Like Screen for Easy Data Entry. Work with Form & Spreadsheet Views Simultaneously. Open up to 25 Windows/Databases at Once & with Entire Databases in Memory. It Can Record Macros & Has Great Built-In Charting & Graphics.
Provue Development Corp.

Panzer General. Nov. 1994. *Items Included:* 96 page rulebook & data card. *Customer Support:* 30 day limited warranty.
DOS 5.0 or higher. IBM PC based with CD drive 386 or higher (4Mb). CD-ROM disk $69.85 (ISBN 0-917059-18-2, Order no.: 062141). *Nonstandard peripherals required:* Hard drive, CD-ROM & mouse. *Optimal configuration:* Optimal config 486, uncompressed hard drive.
The Year Is 1939 & You Are a German General with a Fresh Command in Poland. Win & Advance to the Next Front of Your Choice. A WWII Campaign Simulation Covering Battles in Norway, Belgium, France, North Africa & the Eastern Front. 35 Progressive Scenarios Which You May Play Either the Allied of Axis Side.
Strategic Simulations, Inc.

Panzer General for Sony Playstation. Dec. 1995. *Items Included:* 48 page rulebook. *Customer Support:* 30 day limited warranty. Sony Playstation. CD-ROM disk $59.95 (ISBN 0-917059-10-7, Order no.: 082141).
Player Assumes the Role of a German General Starting in Poland in 1939. It's an Innovative Approach to Strategy Gaming Set in World War II.
Strategic Simulations, Inc.

Panzer General 3DO. May 1995. *Items Included:* 1 saddle stitched rulebook. *Customer Support:* 30 day limited warranty.
3DO compatible systems. Panasonic, Goldstar, & Creative Labs. disk $59.95 (ISBN 0-917059-01-8, Order no.: 032141). *Optimal configuration:* Basic unit.
World War II Strategy Game. Play As a Promising German General Where Victories Increase "Prestige" & Allow the Upgrading of Your Troops & Equipment. Historical Campaign Begins in 1939 Poland. Successive Campaigning Will Lead Your Troops Through Norway, Belgium, France, North Africa, the Eastern Front & Possibly the Shores of America! Features WWII Film Footage, over 35 Scenarios, over 350 Unit Types of Infantry & Equipment. One or Two Players. Playing Time: 30 Minutes to 2 Hour Scenarios, 60 Hour Campaign Game.
Strategic Simulations, Inc.

Panzer-Jagd. Richard W. Scorupski. *Compatible Hardware:* Atari 800/XL/XE, Commodore 64/128.
disk $30.00 (Order no.: 46655).
Armored Combat on the Eastern Front of WWII. The Year Is 1943, the Setting Is the Russian Front. Your Panzer Units Have Been Ordered to Secure the Left Flank for a Planned Offensive Laced with Ambush Points. You Are to Seek Out & Eliminate All Enemy Units in the Sector Commanding an Assault Force of 25 Armored & Invading Units with Artillery Support. Units Surviving the Initial Encounter Are Available for the Next Battle (a New Map Is Created).
Avalon Hill Game Co., The Microcomputer Games Div.

Panzer's East! *Compatible Hardware:* Commodore 64/128.
disk $30.00 (Order no.: 45455).
Strategic Level Simulation of the 1941 Invasion of the Soviet Union. Command Your Army & Air Force & Capture Enough of the Country to End the War. Attacking Involves Careful Management of Your Armed Forces. Too Few Troops in Any One Area & Partisans Will Recapture It. Break the Line in the Right Places & You Can Recreate the Encirclements That Devastated the Soviet Army.
Avalon Hill Game Co., The Microcomputer Games Div.

Paparazzi. *Items Included:* Installation Guide. IBM PC. Contact publisher for price (ISBN 0-87321-044-1, Order no.: CDD-3100).
Activision, Inc.

Paparazzi. *Items Included:* Installation Guide. MAC. Contact publisher for price (ISBN 0-87321-045-X, Order no.: CDM-3100).
Activision, Inc.

Paparazzi Tales of Tinseltown. *Items Included:* Installation Guide.
Mac. Contact publisher for price (ISBN 0-87321-047-6, Order no.: CDM-3100S).
Activision, Inc.

Paparazzi Tales of Tinseltown: 7 Pack. *Items Included:* Installation Guide.
IBM PC. Contact publisher for price (ISBN 0-87321-046-8, Order no.: CDD-3100S).
Activision, Inc.

Paper Boy. *Compatible Hardware:* Apple II; Atari 400, 800. *Language(s):* Applesoft, Atari BASIC (source code included). *Memory Required:* Atari cassette 24k, Atari disk 32k, Apple 48k. disk $18.95.
Deliver Papers While Being Chased by Rabid Bulldogs.
Dynacomp, Inc.

TITLE INDEX

Paperboy Two.
IBM. disk $24.95.
Hop on Your Bike for a Brand New, Free-Wheeling Ride up & down the Avenues of Suburbia. You'll Have to Move Quickly, As You Move Around Tricycles, Lawnmowers, Not-So-Domesticated Animals & Other Hazards in Your Efforts to Flawlessly Deliver to Subscribers (& Break Windows of Non-Subscribers). More Enemies, More Obstacles, More Houses, Different Challenges, & Twice the Fun.
Software Toolworks.

Paperchaser Computer System. Gene Kadish. Jan. 1985. *Memory Required:* 768k.
contact publisher for price.
Legal Technologies, Inc.

PaperClip Publisher (Commodore Version).
Compatible Hardware: Commodore 64/128. *Memory Required:* 64k. *General Requirements:* 1541 or 1571 floppy drive; mouse or joystick.
disk $49.95.
Users Can Create Documents of up to 50 Pages in Length; Manipulate Text & Graphics with Ruler, Margin, & Column Guides; Enlarge Pages with the Magnify Mode; & Resize Boxes & Text Flows Between Them. A Text Editor Is Included, & the Font Converter Utility Lets User Convert Fonts from Popular Word Processors. Can Also Import Text Files from PaperClip II & Other Word Processors. The Built-In Graphics Editor Allows Users to Import & Edit Graphics from Other Programs. Users Can Choose from a Variety of Box Backgrounds & Outlines, Work on Pages from 3 by 3 Inches or 8 by 14 Inches with As Many Columns As Desired. Supports a Wide Variety of Printers Including Epsons, the Panasonic 1091, & the Star NP-10.
Electronic Arts.

Paperscreen Plus. *Version:* 1.1. Sep. 1985. *Operating System(s) Required:* PC-DOS. *Memory Required:* 128k.
disk $59.95 (Order no.: PSP).
Screen Print Program for Toshiba Printers Which Allows Users to Dump Screen Images in Text and/or Graphics Mode. Includes Epson Emulator Program Which Permits Using Standard Epson Driver Routines to Drive Toshiba Printers Without Modification. Includes: Screen Cropping, Number Aspect Ratios, Graphics Text Prints, Rotation, & Variable Output Placement.
M.A.P. Systems, Inc.

Parables Plus. *Compatible Hardware:* Apple IIe, IIc, IIgs.
$100.00.
Designed to Retrain Memory & Logical Reasoning Skills in Brain Injured Patients. Consists of 3 Programs: "Fill in the Blank", "Multiple Choice", & "Meanings". May Be Used As a Companion Program with WHAT BELONGS? to Build Memory, Logic, & Recognition Skills.
Greentree Group, Inc.

Parade. *Version:* 3.0. May 1993. *Operating System(s) Required:* PC-DOS/MS-DOS. *Memory Required:* 640k. *Customer Support:* First year free telephone support & upgrades. Additional years at 20% purchase price.
disk $3000.00.
Provides Measuring Project Performance Using Earned Value Techniques. Structures the Work & Establishes Measurement & Exception Criteria. Provides Graphic Display of Project Status & Variance Trends.
Primavera Systems, Inc.

Paradox. Sep. 1985. *Compatible Hardware:* Compaq, Compaq+; Deskpro; IBM PC & compatibles. *Operating System(s) Required:* PC-DOS 2.0 or higher, PC-DOS 3.1 or higher on a network. *Memory Required:* 512k, on a network 640k. *General Requirements:* 2 disk drives.
Paradox 1.1. disk $495.00.
Paradox 2.0. $725.00.
Paradox Network Pack. $995.00.
Relational Database Program for All Levels of Users from Novice to the Applications Developer. The Lotus-Like Menu Structure Provides Access to the Majority of Functions in the Program. Querying Is Done By Checking off Columns That the User Is Interested In. Not Copy Protected.
Ansa Software.

Paradox. *Version:* 3.5. Jan. 1989. *Compatible Hardware:* IBM PC & compatibles. *Memory Required:* 512k. *Customer Support:* 60 day money back guarantee.
disk $795.00 (ISBN 0-87524-206-5).
Menu-Driven Database-Management System Featuring Help Screen, On-Disk Tutorial, Automatic Indexing & Split/Merge Files. Offers a Maximum of 255 Fields per Record, 255 Characters per Field, 2 Billion Records per File, 4000 Characters per Record, 2 Indexes per File, 2 Active Indexes & up to 255 Records Sorted. Allows User to Revise Field Descriptions at Will. Presentation Quality Graphics. Turns Tables Into Graphs with One Keystroke. Features Record Locking & Automatic Updating.
Borland International, Inc.

Paradox OS/2. *Compatible Hardware:* IBM PS/2 & compatibles. *Operating System(s) Required:* OS/2. *Memory Required:* 3000k. *General Requirements:* Hard disk, Paradox 386.
$725.00.
Provides the Same Features As PARADOX 2.0 for DOS & Takes Advandage of OS/2's Protected Mode Operating Environment, Allowing Users to Run More Than One Program Simultaneously, Including Multiple Copies of PARADOX. Different PARADOX Sessions Can Pass Data to One Another, Creating Distributed Applications.
Borland International, Inc.

Paradox 386. *Compatible Hardware:* 80386-based PCs; IBM PC & compatibles. *Memory Required:* 1500k. *General Requirements:* Hard disk.
$895.00.
upgrade from Paradox 2.0 $125.00.
Provides the Same Features As PARADOX for DOS & Takes Advantage of the 32-Bit Data Path, Being Able to Address All Machine's Memory.
Borland International, Inc.

Paragon. *Version:* 4.3. *Compatible Hardware:* IBM PC & compatibles. *Memory Required:* 384k. *General Requirements:* Hard disk. *Items Included:* GL, AR, AP, Invoicing, Financials, Payroll, Job Cost, Inventory. *Customer Support:* $90.00 per hour prepaid (telephone).
$850.00 per package.
Automatic Posting from Other Modules, Reports Comparative Statements, Ability to Jump Modules, Wild Card, Password Access, Encryption, Audit Trail, Error Recovery, Automatic Back-Up for Each Module, Log off Out-of-Balance, Reject Erroneous Account Numbers & On-Line Help.
P&L Associates.

Paragon ASM186 Cross Assembler System. *Version:* 4. *Compatible Hardware:* IBM PC & compatibles. *Operating System(s) Required:* PC-DOS/MS-DOS 2.1 or higher. *Memory Required:* 223k. *General Requirements:* 1Mb of disk storage; Paragon MT100 Terminal Emulator/File Transfer Utility & Microtek INT186 Interactive Simulator for minicomputer hosts are optional.
contact publisher for price.
Implementation for the Structured Assembly Language Specified by Intel for the 8086/8088 & 80186/80188 Microprocessors. Floating Point Instructions & Directives Required to Support the 8087/80287 Numeric Data Processors Are Also Included. It Is Used to Assemble & Link/Load Programs on an IBM PC or Compatible Host Computer, Then Download Those Programs for Execution on One of the Above Microprocessors, Optionally in Combination with the 8087 or 80287 Co-Processor. The Assembler Translates the Assembly Language Code Into Relocatable Object Code in Intel's OMF Format, or ASCII Hex Format. Thus, Output Modules Can Be Used As Input into Intel's LINK86 by Using the OMF Option.
Microtec Research.

Paragon HC86 Cross Compiler System. *Version:* 1.2. *Compatible Hardware:* IBM PC & compatibles. *Memory Required:* 229k. *General Requirements:* 2Mb of disk storage (3.1Mb required for permanent installation with additional disk storage required for temporary files).
contact publisher for price.
Full Implementation of the C Programming Language As Described by Keringhan & Ritchie in Their Book "C Programming Language". In Addition, It Supports the Extensions Contained in the UNIX Version 7 C Compiler. Extensions Facilitate Program Development for Dedicated or Stand ALone Processors. Generates Optimized, ROMable Code That Takes Full Advantage of the Target Hardware Instruction Set & Memory Capabilities. The Language Contains a Variety of Control Statements, Data Types, & Predeclared Procedures & Functions That Promote the Development of Well Structured Programs. It Emits Intel Object Module Format (OMF) Code Which Can Be Combined with Other Relocatable Object Modules by Using the Paragon LOD186 Linking Loader or Any Other Industry Standard MS-DOS Linker. The Resulting Absolute Object Module May Be Downloaded to a Microcomputer Environment, Debugged on the Host Computer by Uploading to a Minicomputer Environment, or Placed into PROM.
Microtec Research.

Parameter Design & Tolerance Design. *Version:* 10.0. Richard Stevenson. 1989. *Compatible Hardware:* Apple Macintosh, IBM PC & compatibles. *Items Included:* Disks, book, program instructions. *Customer Support:* Unlimited telephone support.
3.5" or 5.25" disk $145.00.
Application of Statistical Techniques to the Problem of Parameter & Tolerance Design. In Particular, the Use of Techniques Developed by G. Taguchi Such As Orthogonal Arrays.
Lionheart Pr., Inc.

Parameter Manager Plus. *Version:* 3.5. *Compatible Hardware:* Apple Macintosh. *Items Included:* Software & documentation. *Customer Support:* Via Morgan Hill phone number.
3.5" disk $795.00.
For Gathering, Analyzing, & Displaying Specific Quality Cahracteristics Such as Dimensions, Temperature, Hardness, or Strength. Changes & Trends in Data are Immediately Revealed Using Built-in Analysis Commands. Features the Following Control Charts: Variables; X Bar & R Chart, X Bar & s Chart, Charts of Individuals & Moving Range, Charts of Moving Average & Moving Range. Attributes; np Charts, p Charts with Variable Control Limits, c Charts, u Charts with Variable Control Limits. Additional Analysis Features; Pareto Analysis, Cp & Cpk Calculations, CuSum Calculation, Forecasting, Strip Charting & Data Compression.
BlackHawk Technology.

PARAMETRICS. Version: 1.1. 1989. *Customer Support:* Free technical support.
MS-DOS or PC-DOS. IBM compatible (256k). disk $595.00. *Addl. software required:* MIXIT-2+. *Optimal configuration:* Hard Disk Recommended; 80 Column Printer. *Networks supported:* Novell.
Produces Five Parametric Reports That Show How a Least Cost Ration & Its Cost Will Change When Some Important Quantity in the Ration Is Changed. These Reports Shows the Least Cost Ration That Results from Varying the Prices of Three Ingredients, the Percentage by Which an Ingredient Is Included in the Ration, the Amount of Any Nutrient in a Single Ingredient, & the Minimum or Maximum Value of a Single Nutrient or Nutrient Ratio. Also Available in Spanish.
Agricultural Software Consultants, Inc.

Pararena 2.0. Version: 2.0. John Calhoun. Sep. 1992. *Customer Support:* Free phone support.
6.02 or greater. Macintosh (2Mb). 3.5" disk $31.95.
New Futuristic Sports Adventure Game by the Author of Best Selling Game, Glider. Picture Rollerball, Picture Graphics, Sounds Crowds, Cheers, Speed & Skill. Network with One Other Player or Play Against the Computer. A Fast, High Pitched Game for All Ages.
Casady & Greene, Inc.

Paratest: Non-Parametric Statistics. 1992.
Items Included: Detailed manuals included with all Dynacomp products. *Customer Support:* Free telephone support to original customer - no time limit; 30 day limited warranty.
MS-DOS 3.2 or higher. IBM PC & compatibles (512k). $69.95 (Add $5.00 for 3 1/2" format; 5 1/4" format standard).
A Compendium of Non-Parametric Statistical Tests Based on the Book "Non-Parametric Statistics for the Behavioral Sciences", Written by Sidney Siegal, & Published by McGraw-Hill. A 100-Page Manual Is included. The Tests Covered Include: Binomial Test; Kolmogorov-Smirnov One Sample, McNermar Test; Sign Test; Randomization Test for Matched Pairs; Fisher-Tocher Test; Yates 2x2 Chi; Mann-Whitney U Test & More.
Dynacomp, Inc.

Paratest Two Non-Parametric Statistics. *Items Included:* Full manual. No other products required. *Customer Support:* Free telephone support - no time limit. 30 day warranty.
MS-DOS 3.2 or higher. IBM & compatibles (512k). disk $69.95.
Compendium of Non-Parametric Statistical Tests Based on the Book "Non-Parametric Statistics for the Behavioral Sciences", Written by Sidney Siegal, & Published by McGraw-Hill. PARATEST Is Menu-Driven & Can Read or Create Standard ASCII Data Files. The Data File Structure for Each Procedure Is Carefully Described in the Manual So That You May Import Data from External Sources. A 100-Page Manual Is Included Which Describes Each Procedure.
Dynacomp, Inc.

Parcel Manifest System. Version: 6. 1985. *Compatible Hardware:* IBM PC. *Operating System(s) Required:* MS-DOS. *Memory Required:* 640k.
turnkey $2995.00-$12,995.00.
Computerized Parcel Processing System. Weighs, Zones, Rates & Prints Approved Manifests, & Other Reports. Comes with Personal Computer, Weighing Scale & Manifest Printer & Label Printer.
TanData Corp.

Parent-Child Relationship Inventory (PCRI). Version: 2.010. Anthony B. Gerard. *Customer Support:* Free unlimited phone support with a toll free number.
Windows 3.X, Windows 95. Recommend 486 or higher processor. 3.5" disk, 1 at $250.00, 2 at $225.00 each (Order no.: W-1081-474 (5. 25"); W-1080-474 (3.5")). *Optimal configuration:* One Mb of free hard disk space, printer.
A Self-Report Inventory Telling You How Parents View the Task of Parenting & How They Feel about Their Children. It Gives a Clear, Quantified Description of the Parent-Child Relationship & Identifies Specific Areas in Which Problems May Occur.
Western Psychological Services.

Parenting: Prenatal to Preschool: DOS-MAC Jewel Case. Robert A. Mendelson & Lottie Mendelson. Sep. 1993. *Items Included:* Registration card. *Customer Support:* Creative Multimedia Corporation warrants the CD-ROM disc & diskettes to be free from defects in materials & workmanship under normal use & service for a period of 90 days from date of purchase. Creative Multimedia Corporation offers Technical Support to customers as needed.
MS-DOS 3.1 or higher, MS-CDEX 2.0 or higher. IBM PC & compatibles with VGA Monitor (500k). CD-ROM disk $79.99 (ISBN 1-880428-06-7, Order no.: 10352). *Optimal configuration:* SuperVGA with 512k+ video memory capable of 640x480x256 colors. *Networks supported:* All LAN.
System Software 6.0.5 or higher. Macintosh Plus or higher (2Mb). CD-ROM disk $79.99 (Order no.: 10352). *Nonstandard peripherals required:* Images display on all systems. *Optimal configuration:* Color display requires 8-bit color, 32-bit QuickDraw & color monitor. *Networks supported:* All.
This Multimedia Resource Will Prove Invaluable to All Who Are Just Starting Their Families, or Already Have Small Children. Information Covers Everything from Fertility, Problem Pregnancies, Adoption, Childbirth, Baby Naming, & the Milestones of Child Development Through Age Five. Includes over 400 Images, Plus Audio Clips Demonstrating Language Development.
Creative Multimedia Corp.

Parenting: Prenatal to Preschool: DOS-MAC Retail Box. Robert A. Mendelson & Lottie M. Mendelson. Sep. 1993. *Items Included:* Registration card. *Customer Support:* Creative Multimedia Corporation warrants the CD-ROM disc & diskettes to be free from defects in materials & workmanship under normal use & service for a period of 90 days from date of purchase. Creative Multimedia Corporation offers Technical Support to customers as needed.
MS-DOS 3.1 or higher, MS-CDEX 2.0 or higher. IBM PC & compatibles with VGA Monitor (500k). CD-ROM disk $79.99 (ISBN 1-880428-14-8, Order no.: 10385). *Optimal configuration:* SuperVGA with 512k+ video memory capable of 640x480x256 colors. *Networks supported:* All LAN.
System Software 6.0.5 or higher. Macintosh Plus or higher (2Mb). CD-ROM disk $79.99 (Order no.: 10385). *Nonstandard peripherals required:* Images display on all systems. *Optimal configuration:* Color display requires 8-bit color, 32-bit QuickDraw & Color monitor. *Networks supported:* All.
This Multimedia Resource Will Prove Invaluable to All Who Are Just Starting Their Families, or Already Have Small Children. Information Covers Everything from Fertility, Problem Pregnancies, Adoption, Childbirth, Baby Naming, & the Milestones of Child Development Through Age Five. Includes over 400 Images, Plus Audio Clips Demonstrating Language Development.
Creative Multimedia Corp.

Parenting Three to Six, 8 disks. Control Data Corporation. Sep. 1986. *Operating System(s) Required:* Apple DOS 3.3. *Memory Required:* 48k.
Set. $295.00, incl. audio cassette, standard manual, tchr's. guide (ISBN 0-8219-0261-X, Order no.: 95460F).
Designed for Young Parents of Children Between the Ages of 3 and 6. Helps Parents Understand Developmental Stages That Children Go Through.
EMC Publishing.

Parents Magazine's Simply Kids. 1994. *Customer Support:* Support Agreement Available.
Windows. IBM PC & compatibles. disk $29.99.
Windows-Based Recording Tool Which Allows Parents to Journal Their Children's Childhood Events from Birth Through Adulthood. Records Birth Statistics, Special Moments, the Child's Favorites, Family Medical History, Dental Records, Allergies, Illnesses, or Special Conditions, & Emergency Information for Baby-Sitters. Lists Common Immunizations Required & Lets User Record When Shots Are Administered. Scrapbook Includes Ability to Scan Photos. Features Health & Development Advice from Parents Magazine.
FourHome Productions.

ParGRADE. Version: 4.0. John R. Lucas & Ralph F. Lewis. 1992. *Items Included:* Sample Data: Class roster & test data; User's Manual; Testing Manual: A Guide to Classroom Testing & Evaluation. *Customer Support:* Initial warranty 90 days, maintenance & upgrade 10% per year of original purchase price (minimum $195.00), workshop for additional fee.
MS-DOS 3.1 or higher. IBM PC, XT, AT, PS/2 or compatible (640k). disk $195.00 (ISBN 1-879995-05-0). *Optimal configuration:* 640k RAM, LaserJet printer, hard disk required.
MS-DOS 3.1 or higher. IBM PC, XT, AT, PS/2 or compatible (640k). disk $995.00 (ISBN 1-879995-06-9). *Optimal configuration:* 640k RAM, LaserJet printer, hard disk required. *Networks supported:* All networks.
An Electronic Gradebook. Also Designed As a Companion & Complement to ParSCORE. Compatible with ParSCORE's Data Files. In Effect, It Is Gradebook Portion of ParSCORE. In Addition, Once a Test Is Scanned & Scored by ParSCORE, ParGrade Can Record Tests & Provide Revised Item Analysis As Well As Full Gradebook & Reporting Functions.
Economics Research, Inc.

Parimutuel Betting Bet Management for Golf & Other Events. *Items Included:* Full manual. No other products required. *Customer Support:* Free telephone support - no time limit. 30 day warranty.
MS-DOS 3.2 or higher. IBM & compatibles (512k). disk $49.95. *Optimal configuration:* IBM, MS-DOS 3.2 or higher, 256k RAM. Printer is supported, but optional.
Supplies the Computing Muscle Needed for Running Your Own Pari-Mutuel Betting Pool. Although Originally Designed for Golf Tournaments, DERBY Is Applicable to Any Competition Where Betting Is Based on the Order of Finish. Computes the Board Odds; Determines the Payoffs for Win, Place & Show Bets; & Produces a List of Winning Bettors along with Their Winnings. Is Limited to 999 Bets on 80 Different Terms.
Dynacomp, Inc.

Parish Data System Census-Contribution Program. Version: 16.1. 1989. *Compatible Hardware:* IBM PC & compatibles. *Operating System(s) Required:* MS-DOS 2.0 or higher. *Language(s):* Pascal. *Memory Required:* 256k. *Items Included:* 2 manuals. *Customer Support:*

TITLE INDEX

Free support & user newsletters.
disk $1100.00.
Includes Census Information on Each Family & Member in That Family; User Defined Fields, Special Operator Features; Family Reports, Member Reports & Financial Reports; User Has the Ability to Create Own Letters & Reports Inserting Census or Financial Data; Menu Driven. Multi-User Version Available.
Parish Data Systems, Inc.

Paroll Master. Version: 2.6. Jun. 1988.
Atari ST (512k). 3.5" disk $99.95.
Payroll Program.
Royal Software.

PARSCALE. Eiji Muraki & R. Darrell Bock. 1993. Items Included: Manual. Customer Support: Free technical support, 90 day limited warranty.
MS-DOS. IBM & compatibles. 3.5" disk $440.00 386 DOS Extender (ISBN 1-56321-127-0). 180p. manual $30.00 (ISBN 1-56321-118-1).
Extends Item Response (IRT) Measurement Methods to Multiple-Category Rating Scale Items in Order to Provide Efficient Scaling of the Data Obtained.
Lawrence Erlbaum Assocs., Software & Alternate Media, Inc.

ParSCORE. Version: 3.70. John R Lucas & Ralph F. Lewis. 1992. Items Included: Sample Data: Class roster & test data; User's Manual; Testing Manual: A Guide to Classroom Testing & Evaluation; Sample Scannable Forms. Customer Support: Initial warranty 90 days, maintenance & upgrade 10% per year of original purchase price (minimum $195.00), workshop for additional fee.
MS-DOS 3.1 or higher. IBM PC, XT, AT, PS/2 or compatible (640k). disk $995.00 (ISBN 1-879995-03-4). Nonstandard peripherals required: SCANTRON, NCS, or HEI omr, hard disk. Optimal configuration: 640k RAM, HP LaserJet printer, optical mark scanner, hard disk required.
MS-DOS 3.1 or higher. IBM PC, XT, AT, PS/2 or compatible (640k). disk $1495.00 (ISBN 1-879995-04-2). Nonstandard peripherals required: SCANTRON, NCS, or HEI omr, hard disk. Optimal configuration: 640k RAM, HP LaserJet printer, optical mark scanner, hard disk required.
Computerized Test Scoring, Test Analysis, Gradebook, a Reporting System. Response Data Scanned & Analyzed to Insure the Reliable & Accurate Scoring of Tests. Weighting & Recording Options. Student Records Updated. Sophisticated Item Analysis. Copies Item Analysis Data to Item Banks of ParTEST. Full Range of Gradebook Options & Feedback Reports. Compatible with SCANTRON, NCS, or HEI Optical Mark Scanners.
Economics Research, Inc.

Parsec: Speech Synthesizer. Compatible Hardware: TI 99/4A with PLATO interpreter solid state cartridge.
contact publisher for price (Order no.: PHM3112).
Player Battles Alien Ships on a Planet in Outer Space. A Voice Tells You Current Conditions.
Texas Instruments, Personal Productivit.

ParSURVEY-GST: General Survey Tool. Version: 3.5. John R. Lucas & Ralph F. Lewis. 1991. Items Included: Sample Data; User's Manual; Sample Scannable Forms. Customer Support: Initial warranty 90 days, maintenance & upgrade 10% per year of original purchase price (minimum $75.00), workshop for additional fee.
MS-DOS 2.0 or higher. IBM PC, XT, AT, PS/2 or compatible (256k). disk $495.00 (ISBN 1-879995-09-3). Nonstandard peripherals required: SCANTRON, NCS, or HEI omr. Optimal configuration: 256 RAM, laser printer, optical mark scanner.
Tabulates, Analyzes, & Reports on Surveys for Attitudinal, Psychological, Opinion, or Any Other Informational Purpose. Provides Likert Scale Response Analysis Capabilities, Unlimited Subsample & Cross-Tabulation Capabilities. Will Record, Analyze & Print Statistical Reports. Can Further Analyze Data Generated by the SEI Program.
Economics Research, Inc.

ParSURVEY-SEI: Student Evaluation of Instruction. Version: 3.5. John R. Lucas & Ralph F. Lewis. 1991. Items Included: Sample Data; User's Manual; Sample Scannable Forms. Customer Support: Initial warranty 90 days, maintenance & upgrade 10% per year of original purchase price (minimum $75.00), workshop for additional fee.
MS-DOS 2.0 or higher. IBM PC, XT, AT, PS/2 or compatible (256k). disk $495.00 (ISBN 1-879995-10-7). Nonstandard peripherals required: SCANTRON, NCS, or HEI omr. Optimal configuration: 256 RAM, laser printer, optical mark scanner.
Tabulates, Analyzes, & Reports Student Evaluation of Instruction Surveys. Instructor & Class Identifying Information Can Be Entered & Is Included on Reports. Provides Automatic Printing of Reports for All Classes Comparing Each Item to Overall School Statistics. Reports Can Be Generated for Each Class, Department, or Other Subsamples.
Economics Research, Inc.

ParSURVEY SITE License. Version: 3.50. John R. Lucas & Ralph F. Lewis. 1991. Items Included: Sample Date: for all products; User's Manuals: three copies for each product; Sample Scannable Forms. Customer Support: Comprehensive warranty, free updates & upgrades, on-site workshops for additional fee.
MS-DOS 3.0 or higher. IBM PC, XT, AT, PS/2 or compatible (256k). $1995.00 initial fee & $195.00 per year annual fee (ISBN 1-879995-13-1). Nonstandard peripherals required: SCANTRON, NCS, or HEI omr. Optimal configuration: 640k RAM, LaserJet printer, scanner.
Includes Unrestricted On-Site Use of Three Survey Products That Form a Powerful, Comprehensive Computerized Survey System. See ParSURVEY-TABulator, ParSURVEY-SEI, & ParSURVEY-GST for Detail Descriptions. Customer Pays a One-Time Initial Site License Fee & a Maintenance Fee Annually.
Economics Research, Inc.

ParSURVEY-TABulator. John R. Lucas & Ralph F. Lewis. 1988. Items Included: User's Manual; Sample SCANTRON Scannable Form Number 20788-ERI. Customer Support: Initial warranty 90 days, maintenance & upgrade 10% per year of original purchase price (minimum $195.00), workshop for additional fee.
MS-DOS 2.0 or higher. IBM PC, XT, AT, PS/2 or compatible (256k). disk $99.00 (ISBN 1-879995-11-5). Nonstandard peripherals required: SCANTRON scanner (OMR). Optimal configuration: 256k RAM, laser printer, SCANTRON omr.
TAB & Your Scanner Work Together to Tabulate Survey Responses. Generates Frequency, Mean, & Standard Deviation for Each Item. Handles up to 50 Items in a Batch. Data Files Can Be Appended.
Economics Research, Inc.

ParSYSTEM SITE License. Version: 4.00. John R. Lucas & Ralph E. Lewis. 1991. Items Included: Sample Data: for all products; User's Manuals: three copies for each product; Testing Manuals: A Guide to Classroom Testing & Evaluation; Sample Scannable Forms. Customer Support: Comprehensive warranty, free updates & upgrades, on-site workshops for additional fee.
MS-DOS 3.1 or higher. IBM PC, XT, AT, PS/2 or compatible (640k). disk $1595.00 (ISBN 1-879995-12-3). Nonstandard peripherals required: SCANTRON, NCS, or HEI scanner, hard disk. Optimal configuration: 640k RAM, VGA monitor, LaserJet printer, scanner, hard disk. Networks supported: All networks.
Includes Unrestricted On-Site Use of Four Testing Products That integrate to Form a Powerful, Comprehensive Computerized Testing System. See ParTEST, ParTEST On-Line, ParSCORE, & ParGRADE for Detail Descriptions. Customer Pays a One-Time Initial Site License Fee & a 10 Percent Maintenance Fee Annually.
Economics Research, Inc.

ParTEST. Version: IBM 4.00, Apple 1.0. John R. Lucas & Ralph F. Lewis. 1991. Items Included: Sample Data: Test items including text & graphics files; User's Manual; Testing Manual: A Guide to Classroom Testing & Evaluation. Customer Support: Initial warranty 90 days, maintenance & upgrade 10% per year of original purchase price (minimum $195.00), workshop for additional fee.
MS-DOS 3.1 or higher. IBM PC, XT, AT, PS/2 or compatible (640k). disk $299.00 (ISBN 1-879995-00-X). Optimal configuration: 640k RAM, VGA Monitor, Laserjet Printer.
MS-DOS 3.1 or higher. IBM PC, XT, AT, PS/2 or compatible (640k). disk $995.00 (ISBN 1-879995-01-8). Optimal configuration: 640k RAM, VGA monitor, LaserJet printer, hard disk. Networks supported: All networks.
ProDOS. Apple IIe, IIc, IIgs or compatible (128k). 5.25" disk $99.00 (ISBN 1-879995-02-6). Optimal configuration: 128k RAM & Imagewriter II.
Item Banking & Test Generation. Any Question Type Can Be Categorized, Stored, & Retrieved for Generating Tests. Items Can Be Selected by Number, by Limiting Criteria, or At Random. Banks Graphics & Automatically Prints on Tests for Student Reference. Will Scramble Questions &/or Answers to Create up to Four Versions. Imports & Tracks Item Analysis Data. Built-In Spell Checking Features.
Economics Research, Inc.

ParTEST On-Line. Version: 4.00. John R. Lucas & Ralph F. Lewis. 1991. Items Included: User's Manual. Customer Support: Initial warranty 90 days, maintenance & upgrade 10% per year of original purchase price (minimum $195.00), workshop for additional fee.
MS-DOS 3.1 or higher. IBM PC, XT, AT, PS/2 or compatible (640k). disk $99.00 (ISBN 1-879995-07-7). Addl. software required: ParTEST. Optimal configuration: 640k RAM, VGA Monitor, LaserJet printer.
MS-DOS 3.0 or higher. IBM PC, XT, AT, PS/2 or compatible (384k). disk $995.00 (ISBN 1-879995-08-5). Optimal configuration: 640k RAM, VGA Monitor, LaserJet printer. Networks supported: All networks.
Students Take Tests at the Computer's Keyboard. Uses Data Files of ParTEST. Questions & Graphics Displayed for Students to Read & Analyze. Student Enters Choice(s) by Keyboard. Students Can Review Items Previously Answered & Change Answers. Prints Feedback Report & Class Score Report. Scores & Response Data Can Be Automatically Imported to Gradebook of ParScore or ParGrade.
Economics Research, Inc.

Parthian Kings. Compatible Hardware: Apple II+, IIe, IIc; Commodore 64/128. Memory Required: 48k.
disk $25.00 ea.

Apple. (Order no.: 46532).
Commodore. (Order no.: 46555).
Game Which Places User in World of Conquest & Pageantry. Involves Upcoming Feudal Civil War Where Many Nobles Are Declaring Themselves King of Parthia. Entire Situation Is Open for Outstanding Commander, Great Strategist, & Leader of Men. User Can Create, Buy & Command Army, & Use Great Wizard to Cast Terrible Spells on Enemies. One to Four May Play.
Avalon Hill Game Co., The Microcomputer Games Div.

Parties & Events: ClickArt Cartoons. *Customer Support:* Free & unlimited technical support to registered users; 60 day money-back guarantee.
Macintosh. Macintosh, System 6.0.7 or higher (1Mb). 3.5" disk $49.95. *Addl. software required:* Any word-processing, desktop publishing or works program that accepts graphics.
Windows MS-DOS. IBM PC & compatibles. 3.5" disk $49.95. *Addl. software required:* Any word processing, desktop publishing or works Program that accepts graphics.
Over 100 Images! Black & White Cartoons; Ready-to-Use, or Changed in Appropriate Drawing Program; Contains 12 Bonus Images Pre-Colored for Use in Presentations; Includes the ClickArt Trade Secret - Images Traded to Every Popular Graphics Format, Guaranteed to Work with All Popular Applications.
T/Maker Co., Inc.

Partnership.
IBM PC & compatibles (640k). contact publisher for price.
Eliminates the Manual Preparation & Transfer of Documents, Saving As Much As 90% in Administrative Expenses & Ensuring Rapid Pay-Back; Reduces Errors from Illegible Handwriting Manual Data Entry; Receives, Stores, Displays, & Prints Shipment Status Messages & More; Integrated with a Parcel Manifest System, It Automatically Transmits Shipment Documents to Customers & Carriers; in Industry-Standard Formats.
TanData Corp.

PartnersLTD. *Version:* 3.0. *Items Included:* Manual (110 pages including hard copy of the documents on the disk) & software (single 360k 5.25" & 720k 3.5" diskette, or 800k 3.5" for Macintosh - offering Circular, subscription application, purchaser questionnaire, power of attorney, purchaser representative questionnaire, corporate buy/sell agreement, capitalization spreadsheet. *Customer Support:* Provided by JIAN at (415) 941-9191.
IBM PC & compatibles (512K), Macintosh. $149.00. *Nonstandard peripherals required:* Hard disk recommended. *Addl. software required:* PC: word processor compatible with MS Word, PCWrite, Q&A, 1st Choice, WordPerfect & most others.'PC's spreadsheet: Lotus 1-2-3 & 2.01 compatible. Macintosh: word processor: MacWrite 4.5 MS Word 3.01 compatible. Macintosh spreadsheet: SYLK compatible (includes MS Excel, MS Works & others).
Template with Nomenclature for a Limited Partnership Legal Agreement (Including Requirements of California, Pennsylvania, & Washington). Annotated for Easy Interpretation. Designed to Be Edited &/or Customized to Suit Specific Situations.
JIAN Tools for Sales.

PARTS: Electronic Catalog. May 1990. *Items Included:* Complete manual. *Customer Support:* Free toll-free telephone support.
MS-DOS. IBM PC compatible (256k). disk $149.00.
Computerizes the Lookup & Pricing of Component Parts Used in the HVAC Industry Speeding & Facilitating Parts Selection. The Program Eliminates Awkward, Time-Consuming Searching Through Bulky Catalogs. Designed to Work with Many Different Parts Lists Including Ones from HVAC Manufacturers & Supply Houses.
Elite Software Development, Inc.

Parts Inventory. *Version:* 2.3. Jul. 1982. *Compatible Hardware:* IBM PC. *Operating System(s) Required:* MS-DOS. *Language(s):* Compiled BASIC. *Memory Required:* 384k.
disk $300.00.
demo disk $50.00.
Originally Designed to Track Auto Parts Based on Manufacturer's Number, Part Title or Entry Number. Can Be Used by Anyone Needing Inventory Control That Relies on Parts Numbers As a Primary Listing. 3 Price Levels Can Be Supported, Reorder Points Are Flagged Based on Quantities on Hand, Purchases & Sales Can Be Tracked & Several Reports Printed. Point-of-Sale Entries Are Supported with the Printing of a Sales Invoice & Automatic Update of Inventory on Hand. Capacity of Inventory Is Nearly 10,000 Parts for 2 Double-Sided Disks or 99,000 Parts on a Hard Disk.
Rambow Enterprises.

Parts Inventory (Warehouse Version). *Version:* 2.0. Feb. 1988. *Items Included:* Manual & program disk. *Customer Support:* Phone support.
PC/MS-DOS 3.0 (640k). PC/XT/AT/386 & PS 2. disk $400.00. *Optimal configuration:* DOS 3.3 286 computer with 640k RAM, 20Mb hard disk, any monitor (but color is best), & standard printer, (will use EMS memory).
A Warehouse Inventory Management System That Provides Instant Access to Parts by Manufacturer's Code, Description, Location, & Comments. Also Tracks Orders & Back Orders. Provide Simple to Use Menu System & Detailed Transaction Reporting.
Rambow Enterprises.

Party Program. *Compatible Hardware:* TRS-80 Model I Level II, Model III, Model 4. *Operating System(s) Required:* TRSDOS. *Language(s):* BASIC. *Memory Required:* 16k.
disk or cassette $19.95.
Identify Party Supplies on Hand & the Program Displays a List of All Possible Drinks Which Can Be Made with Those Supplies. Also Displays Recipes for Specific Drinks. Party Program Also Tells Fortunes or Jokes.
Viking, Inc.

PAS. *Compatible Hardware:* Cromemco Systems. *Operating System(s) Required:* UNIX. $1995.00.
Introduces Pascal Languages Contained in the Proposed ISO Standard.
Cromemco, Inc.

PAS: Personal Accounting System. Sep. 1983. *Memory Required:* Lotus 1-2-3 192k, Symphony 384k. *General Requirements:* Lotus 1-2-3 or Symphony.
disk $35.00 ea.
Lotus 1-2-3. (Order no.: PAS-I).
Symphony. (Order no.: PAS-S).
Complete System for Organizing & Retaining Financial Information. Used to Simplify Budgeting & Obtaining Information Required for Tax Preparation.
Easy-As, Inc.

PAS-3 PLUS Chiropractic. *Version:* 3.0. May 1992. *Compatible Hardware:* IBM PC & compatibles. *Operating System(s) Required:* PC-DOS/MS-DOS; Novell, NTNX, Netbios or compatible networks. *Memory Required:* 256k. *General Requirements:* 132-column printer, 20 Mb hard disk.
PC-DOS/MS-DOS. disk $3495.00.
Novell, NTNX, Netbios. disk $4495.00.
Features 4 Permanent Diagnosis Codes per Patient, Degree of Subluxation, Treatment Plans, Last X-Ray Date, Doctor's Initial & Progress Report, Lawyer's Monthly & Final Reports, Billing Controls, Accounts Receivable, Billing, Password Security for System, Insurance Billing, Complete Recall System, Data Merge Files, Custom Report Generator, Workman's Compensation Billing. Supports New Medicare Requirements (5/92).
Artificial Intelligence, Inc.

PAS-3 PLUS System II Medical Practice Management. *Version:* 4.01. Michael Forrester. May 1992. *Compatible Hardware:* IBM PC & compatibles, PC AT. *Operating System(s) Required:* MS-DOS, PC-DOS, Novell, NTNX, Netbios compatible Networks. *Language(s):* Assemblor, CB 86. *Memory Required:* 256k. *General Requirements:* 80 hard disk, printer.
disk $3995.00.
Includes Billing & Insurance Billing (Electronic Claims Submission in Some Areas), Accounts Receivable, a Complete Reports System Including Custom Reports Generator, a Complete Recall System, & a Mail List Manager. Password Protection Provides System Security. Helps Collections & Reduces Accounts Receivable. Helps Standardize Front Office Procedures. Analyzes All Services Provided by Each Provider in the Practice & for the Practice As a Whole, Supports New Medicare Requirements (5/92).
Artificial Intelligence, Inc.

PAS-3 System II: Anesthesiology Practice Management. *Version:* 4.0. May 1992. *Compatible Hardware:* IBM PC & compatibles. *Operating System(s) Required:* PC-DOS/MS-DOS; Novell, NTNX, Netbios compatible networks. *Memory Required:* 256k. *General Requirements:* 132-column printer, 20Mb hard disk.
MS-DOS/PC-DOS. disk $3495.00.
Novell, NTNX, Netbios. disk $4495.00.
Includes Software Multiplexer Liability to Work with Two Functions Concurrently, Units Billing, Certification Messages, Billing, Accounts Receivable, Reports System Including Custom Reports Generator, Complete Recall System, Mail List Manager. Features Password Protection System, Analysis of Services by Provider & Practice, Supports New Medicare Requirements (5/92).
Artificial Intelligence, Inc.

PAS-3 PLUS Dental Practice Management. *Version:* 2.01. Dec. 1990. *Compatible Hardware:* IBM PC & compatibles. *Operating System(s) Required:* MS-DOS, PC-DOS, Novell, NTNX, Netbios compatible Networks. *Language(s):* Assemblor, CB 86. *Memory Required:* 256k. *General Requirements:* 20Mb hard disk, 132-column printer.
disk $995.00 ea.
Includes Billing & Insurance Billing (Either Preauthorization or Actual Treatment), Accounts Receivable, a Complete Reports System Including Custom Reports Generator, a Complete Recall System & Mail List Manager. Password Protection Provides System Security. Helps Collections & Reduces Accounts Receivable. Analyzes All Services Performed by Each Provider in the Practice. Helps Standardize Front Office Procedures, Plain Paper Insurance Forms.
Artificial Intelligence, Inc.

TITLE INDEX

PASCAL. *Items Included:* Software, manuals. *Customer Support:* 1 full year of support is included with each product purchased. Support includes hotline phone support, technical mailings, & free upgrades.
  PDOS+ Motorola 680 x 0 based systems. $1200.00 (Order no.: 3530). *Networks supported:* Ethernet, MAP.
  Modem, Multiple-Pass, Optimizing Compiler That Generates Assembler Text for the MC68000 Micrprocessor Instruction Sets. The PDOS Pascal Language Defined by Jensen & Wirth That Includes Extensions for Writing Multiple Task Programs for Concurrent Programming. This Capability Makes PDOS Pascal Ideal for Process Control, Instrumentation, Automation, Robotics, CAD/CAM, & Numerous Other Applications Requiring Real-Time Response & Interrupt Handling.
  Eyring Corp.

PASCAL. Microsoft, Inc. *Compatible Hardware:* HP 150 Touchscreen, HP 110 Portable.
  3.5" disk $350.00 (Order no.: 45447D).
  Optimizing 2-Pass Compiler with an Optional Third Pass to Produce Object Listings. Accepts & Compiles Programs Written According to the ISO Standard, As Well As the Full Microsoft Syntax Extensions. Generates Native Machine Code Instead of Intermediate P-Code in Order to Provide the Advantage of Faster Execution While Maintaining the ISO Standard of High Level Code Transportability.
  Hewlett-Packard Co.

Pascal Development System. *Compatible Hardware:* TI 99/4A.
  contact publisher for price (Order no.: PHP 1280).
  Includes P-Code Card & UCSD Pascal Compiler, UCSD p-System Assembler/Linker, & Editor/Filer/Utilties.
  Texas Instruments, Personal Productivit.

Pascal 86. *Compatible Hardware:* IBM PC & compatibles. *Memory Required:* 192k.
  disk $1295.00.
  Pascal Compiler Featuring Intel Object-Code Format. Compilation Is an Added-Step Process. Supports Overlays, Math Coprocessor & Technical Hot Line.
  Real-Time Computer Science Corp.

Pascal for the Apple. Iain MacCallum. 1983. *Compatible Hardware:* Apple II, II+. *Memory Required:* 48k. *General Requirements:* 2 disk drives, TV, MACC disk.
  disk incl. bk. $35.00 (ISBN 0-13-652909-7).
  Provides Hands-On Exercises to Assist User in Mastering Features of Pascal. Teaches Advanced Skills Such As Creation of Pointers & Files.
  Prentice Hall.

Pascal-MT Plus. *Compatible Hardware:* Apple II, 3740 Format, IBM PC, Displaywriter. *Operating System(s) Required:* CP/M, MP/M-II, CP/NET, CP/NOS. *Memory Required:* 56k.
  Apple II. disk single density with documentation $350.00.
  documentation $30.00.
  Format 3740, 8-bit. 8" disk $350.00.
  Format 3740, 8066 CPU. 8" disk $600.00.
  IBM PC. disk $400.00.
  IBM Display Writer. $600.00.
  Integrated Set of Programs That Allows the User to Develop Production Software. The Language Is a Superset of the ISO Standard Pascal & Provides Additional Facilities for Developing Applications & Systems Level Programs. Includes a Native Code Compiler, Linker, & a Range of Run-Time Routines. The Compiler Generates Relocatable Object Code for Use with the Linker. The Linker Generates Output that Can Execute under the Associated Operating System or Can Be Placed in the PROM's. The Run-Time Library Supports Transcendental Operations, Data Transfer, Input/Output, String Manipulation, & Includes a Host of Other Procedures & Functions. Supports Extended Features Such As Modular Compilation, Variable Length Strings, Linkage to Assembly Language & Random Access File I/O. Also Provides Debugging Capabilities Designed to Aid the Development of Complex Programs & a Disassembler to Assist the Programmer in Understanding the Program's Final Form.
  Digital Research, Inc.

Pascal Pointers. *Version:* 4.1. *Compatible Hardware:* Apple Macintosh.
  3.5" disk $17.00.
  Pictorially Interprets & Displays the Results of Pascal Commands That Use Pointers & Dynamic Variables.
  Kinko's.

Pascal Programming for IBM PC. *Compatible Hardware:* IBM PC.
  disk $50.00.
  Allows the User to Transform the Confines of BASIC. The Emphasis Is on Graphic & Sound Applications.
  Prentice Hall.

Pascal-68k. *Compatible Hardware:* TRS-80 Model 16, Tandy 6000. *Operating System(s) Required:* CP/M. *Memory Required:* CP/M 68k, TRS-80 & Tandy 256k.
  disk $25.00.
  Enhanced Version of the USCD Pascal Language. Includes a Program Compiler, 68000 Code Generator, Module Linker, & Full Run-Time Library.
  TriSoft.

A Pascal Tutorial with PMS. *Version:* IBM. Tomek-Muldner. Aug. 1985. *Compatible Hardware:* IBM PC with 2 disk drives. *Memory Required:* 128k. *General Requirements:* CGA card, color monitor. *Items Included:* 4 disks & manual.
  $115.45 (ISBN 0-07-831133-0).
  Step-by-Step Tutorial Teaches the Pascal Programming Language. Ten Modules, Each Designed to Teach a Specific Feature of the Language, Let Users Write & Execute Pascal Programs. Demonstrates What Is Actually Happening Inside the Computer. Can Be Used in Conjunction with a Standard Lecture or As a Stand-Alone Course.
  McGraw-Hill, Inc.

A Passion for Art: Renoir, Cezanne, Matisse, & Dr. Barnes. Corbis Productions Staff. Jan. 1995. *Customer Support:* Toll-call phone support.
  Microsoft Windows 3.1. 486/25 or higher IBM-compatible PC (8Mb). CD-ROM disk $40.00-$50.00 (ISBN 1-886802-00-9). *Nonstandard peripherals required:* 256-color SVGA display, double-speed CD-ROM drive, 8-bit sound card, speaker.
  Macintosh System 7. 68040-based Macintosh or Power Macintosh (8Mb). CD-ROM disk $40.00-$50.00 (ISBN 1-886802-01-7). *Nonstandard peripherals required:* Double-speed CD-ROM drive.
  Continuum Productions.

PassKey Source Level Cross Debugger. *Version:* 5.0. 1989. *Compatible Hardware:* IBM PC, PC XT, PC AT & compatibles, 80386; Sun; Apollo; HP; DEC; VMS, Ultrix, Unix, MS-DOS. *Memory Required:* 250k. *Customer Support:* Phone tech support, training programs, user documentation.
  $1975.00-$2500.00 one copy, IBM PC. Microsoft Windows & Sun OpenWindows

PATHLINE CD-ROM DATABASE FOR

Source-Code Debugger Integrated with C Cross Compiler, Cross Assembler Linker, Locator, Toolkit for Writing ROMable Code & Formatter. Supports 68000, 8086, 80186, 80286, 80386, 68000 Series, NEC V Series & AMD 29000 & DSP 960002. Features Multi-Windowing, Interface, Code & Command Windows Displays & Machine or Source Instruction Breakpoint Types. Also Includes Single-Step Execution, Assembly Stepping, Source Stepping, Step into & Around Procedure Calls, Script Capabilities, Split Screen, Extensive Record/Playback Capabilities, Emulator & ROM Monitor Versions All from the Familiar Windows Interface.
Intermetrics Microsystems Software, Inc.

PassMaster: CPA Review. *Version:* 1.1. Scott Kramer et al. Jul. 1991. *Items Included:* 4 bound textbooks - optional; 1 bound manual. *Customer Support:* Toll free technical support line-unlimited use.
  MS-DOS. IBM & compatibles (384k). $590.00 with University & corporate discounts available.
  Macintosh. All Macintosh (512k). $590.00 with University & corporate discounts available. *Optimal configuration:* 1Mb RAM, 1 hard drive, 1 floppy drive.
  Test Preparation Package for Students Taking CPA Exam. Contains over 3900 Questions & Essays from Previous Exams with Detailed Explanations Cross-Referenced with On-Line Conviser & Duffy Textbooks. Tracks Performances of Students & Diagnoses Weaknesses Enabling Students to Structure Study Sessions As Well As Take Actual Exams under Test Conditions.
  Logicat, Inc.

The Password Security System. *Version:* 9409. Sep. 1994. *Compatible Hardware:* IBM PC & compatibles. *Operating System(s) Required:* MS-DOS. *Language(s):* Clipper. *Memory Required:* 640k. *General Requirements:* Hard disk recommended.
  disk $99.00.
  Gives Managers the Opportunity to Select the "Champion" Menu Option That Each Individual Employee Can Access. Up to 10,000 Security Codes Can Be Generated.
  Champion Business Systems, Inc.

Pat Mat: Pattern Matcher. Jun. 1990. *Items Included:* User help card. *Customer Support:* Free 30 day warranty & customer support; 1 year maintenance & upgrades & support, $100.
  PC-DOS 2.1 or higher. IBM PC & compatibles; PS/2 (256K). disk $36.00.
  Scans Disks for Known Computer Viruses.
  ASP.

Patch Com. *Customer Support:* 800-929-8117 (customer service).
  MS-DOS. Commodore 128; CP/M. disk $59.99 (ISBN 0-87007-250-1).
  A Terminal Installation Program for Turbo Pascal Programs. This Program Allows Any User to Customize Any Program Written & Compiled in Turbo Pascal for Their Particular Terminal Characteristics.
  SourceView Software International.

PathLine CD-ROM Database for Pathology. Jun. 1988.
  MS Windows 3.1 or higher. IBM & compatibles (4Mb). CD-ROM disk $235.00-$1295.00; Networks $1895.00 & up. *Nonstandard peripherals required:* Magnetic or CD-ROM, using ISO 9660. *Optimal configuration:* IBM & compatibles, 80386 or higher, 4Mb RAM, 20Mb hard disk, mouse, MS Windows 3.1 or higher.
  System 6.0.7 or higher. Apple Macintosh (3Mb). CD-ROM disk $235.00-$1295.00; Networks

733

$1895.00 & up. *Optimal configuration:* Apple Macintosh Plus or higher, 3Mb RAM, System 6.0.7 or higher.
PathLine Is an Electronic Reference Database to the Pathology Journal Literature. Pathology-Specific Excerpts (Including Abstracts) from the National Library of Medicine's MEDLINE Database Are Distributed on CD-ROM (Compact Disc, Read-Only Memory) Optical Disc. Knowledge Finder Search-&-Retrieval Software Makes Searching of the PathLine Database Easy, Effective & Fast. After the User Types a Phrase or Sentence Describing the Information Needed, It Selects the References in the Database That Appear to Best Match the Request & Presents Them in Order of Likely Relevance. The PathLine Archive CD-ROM Contains More Than 435,000 References to Articles Published in 370 Pathology-Related Journals over the MostRecent 4 or 8 Full Years. Pathology Articles from More Than 2,500 Other Journals Are Also Included.
Aries Systems Corp.

Pathology QuizBank, Vol. 1. Robert Trelstad. Nov. 1990. *Items Included:* User manual, quick-start sheet, Keyboard Utilities, & Microsoft Multimedia Viewer (Windows version) or HyperCard (Macintosh version). *Customer Support:* Free, unlimited technical support via our toll-free number (1-800-945-4551).
Macintosh. Macintosh with a hard drive (2.5Mb). 3.5" disk $220.00 (ISBN 1-57349-107-1). *Addl. software required:* System 7.0 or higher. *Networks supported:* All LANs.
Windows. IBM compatible with 80286 or higher processor, a hard drive & a mouse (2Mb). disk $220.00 (ISBN 1-57349-161-6). *Addl. software required:* MS-DOS 3.3 or higher, Windows 3.1 or higher. *Networks supported:* All LANs.
Over 2,500 Multiple-Choice Questions Covering All Areas of Pathology, with Feedback.
Keyboard Publishing, Inc.

Pathology QuizBank, Vol. 2. Robert D. Cardiff et al. Oct. 1994. *Items Included:* User manual, quick-start sheet, Keyboard Utilities, & Microsoft Multimedia Viewer (Windows versions) or HyperCard (Macintosh version). *Customer Support:* Free, unlimited technical support via our toll-free number (1-800-945-4551).
Macintosh. Macintosh with a hard drive (2.5Mb). 3.5" disk $280.00 (ISBN 1-57349-110-1). *Addl. software required:* System 7.0 or higher. *Networks supported:* All LANs.
Windows. IBM compatible with 80286 or higher processor, a hard drive & a mouse (2Mb). disk $280.00 (ISBN 1-57349-164-0). *Addl. software required:* MS-DOS 3.3 or higher, Windows 3.1 or higher. *Networks supported:* All LANs.
Over 1,300 Multiple-Choice Questions Covering All Areas of Pathology, with Detailed Feedback & Direct Links to Related Materials Appearing in the Pathology TextStack.
Keyboard Publishing, Inc.

Pathology TextStack. Cotran, Kumar & Robbins Staff. Oct. 1994. *Items Included:* User manual, Quick-start sheet, Keyboard Utilities, & Microsoft Multimedia Viewer (windows version) or HyperCard (Macintosh version). *Customer Support:* Free, unlimited technical support via our toll-free number (1-800-945-4551).
Macintosh. Macintosh with a hard drive (2.5Mb). CD-ROM disk $280.00 (ISBN 1-57349-114-4). *Nonstandard peripherals required:* CD-ROM player required, 256-color monitor recommended. *Addl. software required:* System 7.0 or higher. *Networks supported:* All LANs.
Windows. IBM compatible with 80286 or higher processor, a hard drive & a mouse (2Mb). CD-ROM disk $280.00 (ISBN 1-57349-168-3).
Nonstandard peripherals required: CD-ROM player required, 256-color monitor recommended. *Addl. software required:* MS-DOS 3.3 or higher, Windows 3.1 or higher. *Networks supported:* All LANs.
The Complete Text with All Tables, Figures, Diagrams, & Color Illustrations from W.B. Saunders' Robbins Pathologic Basis of Disease, 5th Edition. Includes a Collection of Tools for Searching, Capturing & Manipulating Data of Interest.
Keyboard Publishing, Inc.

Pathology VideoIndex, Vol. 1. Robert Trelstad. Nov. 1990. *Items Included:* User manual, quick-start sheet, Keyboard Utilities, & Microsoft Multimedia Viewer (Windows version) or HyperCard (Macintosh version). *Customer Support:* Free, unlimited technical support via our toll-free number (1-800-945-4551).
Macintosh. Macintosh with a hard drive (2.5Mb). 3.5" disk $180.00 (ISBN 1-57349-118-7). *Nonstandard peripherals required:* Level 3 NTSC videodisc player with RS-232 interface & connecting cables, video monitor. *Addl. software required:* System 7.0 or higher, Slice of Life VI videodisc. *Networks supported:* All LANs.
Windows. IBM compatible with 80286 or higher processor, a hard drive & a mouse (2Mb). disk $180.00 (ISBN 1-57349-172-1). *Nonstandard peripherals required:* Level 3 NTSC videodisc player with RS-232 interface & connecting cables, video monitor. *Addl. software required:* MS-DOS 3.3 or higher, Windows 3.1 or higher, Slice of Life VI videodisc. *Networks supported:* All LANs.
Descriptive Captions for Hundreds of Pathology-Related Images from the University of Utah's Slice of Life VI Videodisc (Available separately), with Direct Links into Related Materials Appearing in the Pathology TextStack.
Keyboard Publishing, Inc.

Pathology VideoIndex, Vol. 2. Robert Trelstad. Oct. 1994. *Items Included:* User manual, quick-start sheet, Keyboard Utilities, & Microsoft Multimedia Viewer (Windows version) or HyperCard (Macintosh version). *Customer Support:* Free, unlimited technical support via our toll-free number (1-800-945-4551).
Macintosh. Macintosh with a hard drive (2.5Mb). 3.5" disk $180.00 (ISBN 1-57349-215-9). *Nonstandard peripherals required:* Level 3 NTSC videodisc player with RS-232 interface & connecting cables, video monitor. *Addl. software required:* System 7.0 or higher, Slice of Life VI videodisc. *Networks supported:* All LANs.
Windows. IBM compatible with 80286 or higher processor, a hard drive & a mouse (2Mb). disk $180.00 (ISBN 1-57349-218-3). *Nonstandard peripherals required:* Level 3 NTSC videodisc player with RS-232 interface & connecting cables, video monitor. *Addl. software required:* MS-DOS 3.3 or higher, Windows 3.1 or higher, Slice of Life VI videodisc. *Networks supported:* All LANs.
Descriptive Captions for Hundreds of Pathology-Related Images from the University of Utah's Slice of Life VI Videodisc (available separately), with Direct Links into Related Materials Appearing in the Pathology TextStack.
Keyboard Publishing, Inc.

Patient Assessment. *Items Included:* Manuals, training exercises, quick reference.
IBM PC, XT, AT, & compatibles; PS/2. contact publisher for price.
Unlimited Flexibility To Create the Elements of Assessment That the Facility Is Interested in Using.
Beechwood Software.

Patient Spending Account Package.
contact publisher for price.
Monitors Individual Patient Spending Allowances on Individual Ledgers in One Account.
Beechwood Software.

Patients Statistics & Accounts Receivable Package.
contact publisher for price.
Handles Long-Term Care Facility Management.
Beechwood Software.

Patrick & Emma Lou. Nan Holcomb & Jane Steelman. Oct. 1993. *Items Included:* Directions on use of the program, registration card. *Customer Support:* 90 days limited warranty, replacement disks for fee of $10.00 & proof of purchase.
6.07. MAC LC (2Mb). 3.5" disk $29.95 (ISBN 0-944727-24-7). *Optimal configuration:* MAC LC, System 7.1, 4Mb RAM.
Story about a Child with CP Who Learns to Use a Walker. User Can Click on a Button on the Screen or Use a Switch to Hear the Story Read Word by Word or Sentence by Sentence, As the Text Is Highlighted in Color of Choice.
Jason & Nordic Pubs.

Patrol Deployment Planning System. 1988. *Memory Required:* 256k.
PC-DOS/MS-DOS. disk $295.00.
Used by Police Departments to Determine How Many Patrol Cars Are Needed, & Where & When They Should Be Deployed. Estimates Field Operation Performance Characteristics, Determines the Minimum Number of Units Needed to Simultaneously Satisfy Performance Standards. Allocates Units Among Time Periods or Geographic Areas.
Computing Power Applied.

Patterns in Pitch: Level 1, Level II, Level III, 3 disks. Vincent Oddo. 1985-1986. *Compatible Hardware:* Apple II+, IIe, IIc, IIgs; Commodore 64, 128; IBM PC. *Operating System(s) Required:* Apple DOS 3.3, PC-DOS 3.3. *Language(s):* QuickBasic. *Memory Required:* Apple 48k, Commodore 64k, IBM 640k.
Set. disk $99.95 ea.
Apple. (ISBN 0-942132-95-5, Order no.: A-1190).
Commodore. (ISBN 1-55603-008-8, Order no.: C-1190).
IBM. (ISBN 1-55603-007-X, Order no.: I-1190).
Aural-Visual Program Comprised of 2 Parts. Part 1, the COMPOSER, Allows user to Create Pitch Patterns in Treble or Bass Clef. Part 2, the DICTATOR, Plays Pitch Patterns Based on the Key and Number of Pitches Selected by the User, Which Must Be Notated on the Computer. Level 1 Uses the Keys C, G, & F with up to 8 Notes in the Series. Level II Adds D, A, B-Flat, & E-Flat & Plays up to 12 Pitches. In Level III the User May Choose Any Major or Minor Key & up to 12 Pitches to Be Played.
Electronic Courseware Systems, Inc.

Patton Versus Rommel. Chris Crawford. *Compatible Hardware:* Apple Macintosh, Commodore 64, IBM PC.
Macintosh. 3.5" disk $19.95.
Commodore, IBM. disk $14.95.
Become Either Lt. General George Patton, Commander of the American Forces or Field Mashall Erwin Rommel, Commander of the German Seventh Army. As a Commander You Have Numerous Divisions (Infantry & Armor) at Your Disposal on a Map of 150,000 Locations. Simulates the Effects of Unpredictable Terrain, Losing Air Support During Bad Weather, Incomplete Reconnaissance, etc. For 1-2 Players at 3 Levels of Play.
Electronic Arts.

TITLE INDEX

PAYROLL

Paul Cezanne: Portrait of My World. Mar. 1996. *Items Included:* Manual, registration card. *Customer Support:* Phone technical & customer support Mon-Fri 9:00-5:00 PST. Email & Web-site support.
Microsoft Windows 3.1, Windows 95.
  Multimedia PC with 486/33 or higher (8Mb). CD-ROM disk $45.00-$55.00 (ISBN 1-886802-08-4).
  Nonstandard peripherals required: 256-color Super VGA display, double-speed CD-ROM drive, 8-bit Windows-compatible sound card & speakers, mouse.
System 7.1. Macintosh 25MHz 68030 or higher (LCIII, IIVX, Centris, Quadra, performa, or higher) (8Mb, 12Mb for Power Mac).
  Nonstandard peripherals required: Double-speed CD-ROM drive, 13" monitor or higher, 256 colors.
Journey into the Fascinating World of One of the Greatest Originators of Modern Art. As He Guides You Through His World, Paul Cezanne Reveals the Profound Influences on His Creativity & Life's Work. Magnificent Artwork by Cezanne & Other Masters Such As Picasso, Rembrandt, & Van Gogh Can Be Explored in Exquisite Detail.
Continuum Productions.

Paul Whitehead Teaches Chess. *Items Included:* Bound manual. *Customer Support:* Free hotline - no time limit; 30 day limited warranty; updates are $5/disk plus S&H.
MS-DOS. IBM & compatibles (256k), IBM PCjr (128k). disk $29.95.
Apple II; Commodore 64. disk $29.95.
Chess-Teaching Program for Group or Individual Study. It Contains the COFFEEHOUSE CHESS MONSTER, the First Place Winner in the 1987 U.S. Computer Chess Open (PC Division), & Best PC-Based Program at the 1986 World Micro Open. 40 Hours of Chess Instruction, Complete with On-Screen Explanations, Text, Graphics, & Animations, Covering More Than 600 Chess-Playing Techniques.
Dynacomp, Inc.

PAULA: Pipeline Algorithm for Unsteady Liquid Analysis.
DOS. IBM compatibles. disk $995.00.
  Nonstandard peripherals required: Math coprocessor.
Calculates Pressures & Flow Rates in a Liquid Pipeline System Under These Unsteady State Conditions. Pipes, Pumps, Valves, Surge Tanks, Variable Supply/Delivery Pressures or Flow Rates Can Be Modeled in Any Combination & Configuration. Pressures & Flow Rates in Various Pipe Sections & at Every Time Step of the Simulation Are Calculated in Response to a Pressure or Flow Upset Anywhere in the Line. Combinations of Pressure & Flow Variations May Be Used. Various Flow Regimes Are Considered. Maximum Pressure, PRV & Surge Tank Summaries Are Reported.
Techdata.

Paws in Typing Town. Mar. 1996. *Customer Support:* 1-800-824-5179 product information; 1-800-543-0453 technical support.
Windows 3.1 or higher. 486 SX 25MHz (4Mb). CD-ROM disk $49.50 (ISBN 0-538-65150-4).
  Nonstandard peripherals required: Double speed CD-ROM, VGA 640x480, sound blaster or 100% compatible sound card.
Macintosh, 68030 (5Mb). *Nonstandard peripherals required:* Double speed CD-ROM, 256 colors.
A Multimedia Version of an Award Winning Keyboarding Program. Features Dazzling Animation, Wonderful Characters, an Arcade with Awesome Typing Games & a Journal for Practicing Skills. Paws, the Cat, & His Pals Teach Basic Keyboarding Skills While Giving Hints & Positive Reinforcement along the Way.
South-Western Publishing Co.

PayBreeze. Version: 1992. *Customer Support:* One year - $44, $79, $94.
DOS. IBM PC & compatibles (320k). disk $169.00, $254.00, $359.00.
Calculates Payroll Handchecks & Gross-Ups for 51 States, & Produces a Report Answering Employee W-4 Inquiries by Listing All Possible Federal & State Withholding Permutations for a Paycheck. Does Not Print Checks, but Does Print an Employee Earnings Statement. Sold Only by 12 Month Subscription. All Tax Tables & User Instructions Embedded in Programs; No Manuals.
General Programming, Inc.

PayCalc: How to Create Customized Payroll Spreadsheets. Thomas E. Towle. Feb. 1984. *Compatible Hardware:* IBM PC with & VisiCalc & SuperCalc; Osborne I with SuperCalc. *Operating System(s) Required:* PC-DOS, CP/M. *Language(s):* Assembly. *Memory Required:* 64k.
IBM PC. disk $35.50, incl. bk. (ISBN 0-8306-5073-3, Order no.: 5073C).
Osborne. disk $35.50, incl. bk. (ISBN 0-8306-5071-7, Order no.: 5071C).
IBM PC. disk $35.50, incl. bk. (ISBN 0-8306-5072-5, Order no.: 5072C).
Explains How to Use Electronic Spreadsheets to Create Customized Payrolls.
TAB Bks.

Payfive. *Compatible Hardware:* Apple II. (source code included). *Memory Required:* 48k.
disk $149.95.
Dynacomp, Inc.

Paylode. Version: 3.3. *Customer Support:* Free telephone support.
DOS 2.0 or higher. IBM PC, XT, AT & compatibles (512k). single company $295.00.
  Nonstandard peripherals required: Hayes compatible modem at 300 to 19,200 baud.
multi-company $595.00.
Electronic Funds Transfer Software Program That Enables Organizations to Utilize Direct Deposit & Direct Debit Banking Transactions for Payroll & Fee Collection Operations.
Gaskins, Stern & Assocs., Ltd.

Paymaster Payroll. 1996.
MS-DOS; requires 1 MEG of RAM with hard disk space dependent on number of employees. 386 & higher. disk *Networks supported:* Available in single user or multi-user network version.
Computer Aid.

PayMaster Plus: Automated Time & Attendance. Version: 2.1. Jul. 1994. *Items Included:* 2 spiral-bound manuals, time clock terminal, software on 3.5 diskette, 10 magnetic stripe cards. *Customer Support:* 90 days - money back guarantee, hardware maintenance with loaner - $200 per year/per clock; annual toll-free phone support - $100/year.
Windows under DOS. IBM & compatibles (8Mb). disk $2000.00. *Nonstandard peripherals required:* Modem, laser printer. *Addl. software required:* Windows 3.1 or higher. *Optimal configuration:* 12Mb RAM, laser printer, large hard drive. *Networks supported:* Novell.
Electronic Time Clock & Software That: Automatically Computes Hours & Overtime; Allows Export into PayMaster, an In-House Payroll System & Eliminates All Keying of Hours. Windows-Based for Easy Setup & Learning - Available in Single or Network - Battery Back-Up to Prevent Data Loss in a Power Outage.
Computer Aid Corp.

PayMaster Plus Time Clock. 1996. *Items Included:* No-Risk, 90-day money-back guarantee. *Customer Support:* 208.
disk *Networks supported:* Available in single-user or multi-user network verion.
Installs with regular telephone wires & standard RS232 connection to your computer, or over existing telephone wires via modem.
Computer Aid.

PayMaster's Direct Deposit. Version: .7.
disk contact publisher for price.
Includes tax law changes, state child support, state new hire report, state withholding, state unemployment.
Computer Aid.

Payroll. *Compatible Hardware:* Apple Macintosh. *General Requirements:* Macintosh Plus.
3.5" disk $995.00.
Calculates Payroll Deductions.
Advanced Data Systems, Inc.

Payroll. Version: 12.0. (Accounting Software Ser.). Oct. 1985. *Compatible Hardware:* IBM PC & compatibles. *Operating System(s) Required:* MS-DOS, PC-DOS 3.X & up. *Language(s):* MegaBASIC. *Memory Required:* 640k. *General Requirements:* Hard disk, wide carriage printer. *Customer Support:* (203) 790-9756.
disk $295.00, Network Option ,300.00 more.
manual $50.00.
Handles Payroll for Hourly, Salaried & Commissioned Employees & Allows for Pay & Special Deductions. General Ledger Tie-In, Multiple Tax Tables for Federal, State, Local, & Special Tax. Tracks Sick Leave & Vacation. Operator Defined Deductions. Prints Paychecks. Optional Bargaining Unit Feature Tracks Multiple Union. Reports Include W-2 Forms, 1099 Forms, 941 Forms, State & Federal Unemployment Reports, & Payroll Worksheets. Features, Automatic Check Printing, Automatic Update of Employee Records, Calculates/Reports Employer Payroll Costs, Posts Handwritten Checks, Checkbook Balancing, Handles Inactive (Terminated) Employees for Year End Reports.
Applications Systems Group (CT), Inc.

Payroll. Version: 5.6. 1978. *Compatible Hardware:* IBM PC. *Operating System(s) Required:* MS-DOS, PC-DOS 1.1, 2.0. *Language(s):* MBASIC (source code included). *Memory Required:* 128k.
disk $500.00.
Calculates Tax Withholding & Deductions, All States User-Specified Deductions, Check Writer, Check Requirements & User Specified Deductions, Check Register, Employee Journal, Processes Handwritten Checks. Interfaces to G/L & Job Costing.
CharterHouse Software Corp.

Payroll. Version: 5.3. *Items Included:* Diskette & manual. *Customer Support:* 60 days free support, starting with the first call. $79/year extended support plan.
Apple Macintosh (1Mb). 3.5" disk $295.00.
Complete Payroll System for Organizations with 1 to 1000 Employees. All Federal & State Tax Tables Are Included, & All Can Be Modified by the User. Prints Checks & W-2's. Numerous Reports Including Posting Summary, Check Register, & Monthly/Quarterly Tax Summaries.
CheckMark Software, Inc.

Payroll. Version: 5.8. May 1993. *Language(s):* DIBOL & C, COBOL. *General Requirements:* Depends on the specific configuration. *Customer Support:* Full service, update service; by quotation.
VMS, Open VMS. DEC VAX Series, DEC Alpha AXP. disk $2500.00-$15,000.00.
source code by quotation.
Direct Deposit, Utilizing ACH Standards, Accommodates Multiple Pay Rates, Tips, Extra Withholdings, W-2 Forms, Form 941, State

PAYROLL

Unemployment Withholding, etc. Immediate On-Line Calculation of All Pays & Deductions Including the Net Check Amount.
Compu-Share, Inc.

Payroll. May 1989. *Memory Required:* 640k. *Items Included:* Disks & manuals. *Customer Support:* Through VARs, support contracts available.
MS/PC DPS, Concurrent DOS. Xenix. Unix. IBM PC/Xt/AT & compatibles, IBM PS/2. disk single-user $995.00. *Nonstandard peripherals required:* Hard disk, 132-column printer.
multi-user $1295.00.
Unix, Xenix $1495.00.
General Purpose Payroll Program for Single- & Multi-User Micros & Can Be Used As a Stand-Alone Module or Integrated with MC Software's INMASS II (Manufacturing) or INCOME II (Accounting) Software. Handles Hourly & Salaried Employees & Commissioned & Permits up to 20 Allowances & Deductions. Multi-Level Verification Options Prior to Check Printing. Maintains Records for up to 100 Companies.
INMASS/MRP.

Payroll. *Customer Support:* free telephone & BBS technical support; documentation; training from local dealers & or vendor's CFPIM, C.P.M., CIRM, CQA Trainers. Customization available from vendor.
Ms/PC DOS; Concurrent DOS, Xenix, Unix. IBM PC/XT/AT & compatibles; IBM PS/2 (512k). single user $995.00. *Networks supported:* Novell, Lantastic, Banyan VINES; all NETBIOS compatible.
multi-user or network $1295.00.
"Payroll" is an online, interactive payroll system. Major modules are employee file, history file, tax file, general ledger code file, & deduction/allowances file.
INMASS/MRP.

Payroll. *Version:* 450.3. 1978. *Compatible Hardware:* IBM PC & compatibles. *Operating System(s) Required:* PC-DOS, MS-DOS. *Language(s):* QuickBASIC. *Memory Required:* 512k. *General Requirements:* Hard disk. *Items Included:* System diskettes, users guide, training tutorial. *Customer Support:* Telephone; support contracts available.
$395.00 to $495.00.
Supports Three Payroll Methods: Regular, Labor Distribution, & After-the-Fact. The System Simultaneously Processes Payroll for up to Four States with Deductions for FIT, FICA, State & Local Taxes, & up to Eight Additional User-Defined Deductions. Tax Tables Are Included for All 50 States. Processes Payroll for Hourly & Salaried Employees. Checks May Be Printed Weekly, Bi-Weekly, Semi-Monthly, & Monthly. Reports Include Employee Master List & Check Register. Handles 401(k) Tax Sheltered Annuities & Prints W-2s & 941 Forms. Payroll Interfaces with IMS General Ledger System. The System May Be Run Single User or Multi-User on Many Networks.
International Micro Systems, Inc.

Payroll. *Version:* 4.00. 1978. *Compatible Hardware:* IBM PC & compatibles, PC XT, PC AT, PS/2. *Operating System(s) Required:* MS-DOS, PC-DOS. *Language(s):* FORTRAN. *Memory Required:* 640k. *General Requirements:* Hard Disk. *Items Included:* Manual. *Customer Support:* 1 hour per package purchased.
5-1/4" or 8" or 3-1/2" disk $495.00.
Standard Features Include Support of up to 8 Deductions per Employee, Automatic Calculation of Withholding Deductions (Including Medicare) & Net Pay, Calculation of Union Fringe Benefits, Quarterly Reports, W2's, Distribution of Payroll Expense to Multiple Jobs or Account Numbers, & Automatic Generation of All Journal Entries. Supports 401k & Cafeteria Plans.
MCC Software (Midwest Computer Ctr. Co.).

Payroll. *Version:* 3.96. Dec. 1991. *Items Included:* Comprehensive manual in cloth covered 3 ring binder with slipcase. Optional forms creation software available. *Customer Support:* 2 hours of no cost support to registered users during first 6 months of ownership. Thereafter, $60.00 per hour with 1 hour minimum contract. Optional Tax Table update service available for $45.00 covering a tax year. Optional program maintenance service available for $45.00 for a tax year.
MS-DOS 2.1 or higher, PC-DOS 2.1 or higher (384k). IBM PC, XT, AT, PS/2 or 100% compatible micro-computer. $95.00 (ISBN 1-877915-05-X). *Nonstandard peripherals required:* Printer must be capable of printing 132 characters in condensed or normal mode or Hewlett-Packard LaserJet Series II or 100% compatible laser. *Optimal configuration:* 384k, Hard Disk.
Designed to Automate a Weekly, Bi-Weekly, Semi-Monthly or Monthly Payroll for Up to 200 Employees. Accommodates Hourly & Salaried Personnel; Provides 8 Earnings Categories Plus Tips & Up to 7 Deductions, 6 of Which Are Automatic; Records After-the-Fact Payroll; Calculates Federal, State, FICA, Disability Insurance, & City Withhold; Maintains Personnel History Data & Prints W-2 Forms & Quarterly Reports Including FUTA & SUTA Information; Prints Paychecks with Y-T-D As Well As Current Payroll Information on the Stubs; Handles 401(k) Deferred Compensation. Can Accept Time Entered As Hours & Minutes, As Well As Hours & Fractions of Hours. Comes Complete with User-Modifiable Tax Tables for All 50 States, the District of Columbia, & New York City.
Phoenix Phive Software Corp.

Payroll. *Version:* 3.3. (Integrated Manufacturing & Financial System Ser.). *Compatible Hardware:* Micro/VAX, UNIBUS/VAX; IBM PC. *Operating System(s) Required:* MS-DOS, Novell, Micro/VMS, VAX/VMS, UNIX. *Language(s):* DIBOL.
MS-DOS. single-user $750.00.
DEC PDP-11/VAX. $1500.00 multi-user.
Uses Employee Hours to Calculate Earnings, to Pay Employee, & to Distribute Labor Expenses to GENERAL LEDGER by Type of Labor Expense Account Number. Payroll Can Be Hourly or Salary, & Hours Worked Can Optionally Be Fed from SHOP FLOOR CONTROL Module. Calculates Federal & State Withholding Tax Deductions for Multiple States. Prints Payroll Register, Deduction Register, Checks & Stubs, Distribution Report, & Tax Forms & Reports.
Primetrack.

Payroll. *Version:* 4.3. 1995. *Operating System(s) Required:* MS-DOS, XENIX. *Language(s):* Compiled BASIC. *Memory Required:* 256k. *Items Included:* Manual, disk, demo. *Customer Support:* Free phone support for 90-days; $25.00 per call after.
disk $200.00 (ISBN 0-918185-18-1).
Computes Regular, Overtime, & Piece Work Pay. Employee File Maintenance. Figures Tax & Deductions, Prints Checks, Journal, 941-A & W-2 Forms - 1991 Federal Tax Changes.
Taranto & Assocs., Inc.

Payroll (a Part of ABECAS). *Version:* 3.3. *Operating System(s) Required:* MS-DOS. *Customer Support:* On site training unlimited support services for first 90 days & through subscription thereafter.
Contact publisher for price.
Agricultural Payroll System That Can Handle Hourly, Piece-Rate & Salaried Employees. Supports Multiple States As Well As 941 & 943 Type Employees. Numerous Reports Available. Options: Personnel, Equipment Charge-Out, Deferred Tax Programs, Magnetic Reporting of W2's, Work Crew, Time & History.
Argos Software.

Payroll Accounting. *Compatible Hardware:* IBM PC & compatibles, PC XT, PC AT. *Operating System(s) Required:* MOS. (source code included). *Memory Required:* 4 users 256k, 9 users 512k.
$995.00, incl. basic system.
Includes File Maintenance, Interactive Inquiry, Balancing, Automatic Verification, Corrections to Payroll, Manual or Automatic Entry of Payroll Data, Tax Tables & Reports.
Hurricane Systems, Inc.

Payroll Accounting. *Version:* 7.2. *Items Included:* Disks, manual, sample data. *Customer Support:* 90 days free telephone support.
IBM PC, PC/XT, PC/AT, PS/2 & compatibles (512k). disk $495.00.
Menu Driven Comprehensive Payroll Program, Designed to Interface Directly with Yardi Programs Such As Construction Accounting, General Accounting, Deluxe Property Management & Real Estate Office Management. Program Also Functions As a Stand-Alone System. Provides Automated Check Writing for any Type of Pay Period (Including Weekly, Bi-Weekly, Semi-Monthly, Monthly).
Yardi Systems.

Payroll Accounting for Microcomputers. 1986. *Memory Required:* IBM/Tandy 128-256k, Apple 48-256k. *General Requirements:* Driver disks.
IBM/Tandy. contact publisher for price (ISBN 0-538-52633-5, Order no.: Q80633).
Apple II Series/IIgs. contact publisher for price (ISBN 0-538-52634-3, Order no.: Q80634).
IBM PS/2. contact publisher for price (ISBN 0-538-51080-3, Order no.: Q30081).
Text-Workbook & Individual Diskette Package Emphasizing Methods of Computing Wages & Salaries, Keeping Records, & Preparing Government Reports. Disks Can be Updated Annually with Instructions Contained in the Instructor's Manual.
South-Western Publishing Co.

Payroll Ease: Reco, Inc. Payroll System. *Version:* 2.0. Jul. 1991. *Items Included:* User & system documentation; runtime version of DataEase. *Customer Support:* Free customization for individual purchaser; free telephone support.
DOS 3.1 or higher. IBM or compatible (640k). disk $500.00. *Addl. software required:* DataEase 4.2 or higher - or DataEase RunTime (included).
Maintains Employee & Payroll Records - Automates Payroll & Withholding Calculations - Produces Payroll Report for Any Selected Date - Produces Withholding Report for Any Selected Period - Prints W-2's - Application Is Designed to Be Perpetual & Will Not Become Obsolete. It Will Allow Future Changes to Withholding Percentages As Necessary.
Reco, Inc.

Payroll-Labor Costing. Richard T. Scott. Sep. 1981. *Compatible Hardware:* IBM PC XT, PC AT, PS/2 & compatibles. *Operating System(s) Required:* MS-DOS. *Language(s):* BASIC. *Memory Required:* 128k. *General Requirements:* 10Mb hard disk, printer.
MB Version. disk $1775.00 (ISBN 0-923933-23-9).
video tape demo available.
source code available.
Interacts with Accounting/Job Costing Package in Order to Incorporate Union & Merit Shops. Calculates State & Local Taxes, with Simplest Possible Input Procedure for Data. Prints Weekly Certified Payroll Report, Job-by-Job Cost Report & Report Which Totals All Items on Weekly Checks, EEO, & W-2 Reports.
Esccomate.

Payroll Management Program. *Version:* 2.2. 1990. *Items Included:* 2 manuals. *Customer Support:* Free support.
MS-DOS 2.0 or above. IBM & compatibles. disk $300.00. *Addl. software required:* PDS Ledger/Payables Program.
Allows User to Prepare Payroll for Salaried, Hourly, Exempt, Contract & Clergy Personnel; to Calculate All Taxes & Deductions; Print Paychecks & Accumulate Necessary Totals for Monthly, Quarterly & Annual Government & Office Management Reports. Accommodates an Unlimited Number of Employees. Prints W-2's & 1099's. Integrated with PDS Ledger/Payables Program.
Parish Data Systems, Inc.

Payroll Manager. *Version:* 1.12. May 1991. *Items Included:* 1 hard bound manual. *Customer Support:* Free phone technical support.
DOS 3.1 or higher. IBM PC XT, AT, 386 or higher compatible (512k). disk $95.00. *Addl. software required:* Quicken version 6 or 7 for DOS. Optimal configuration: IBM compatible with 640k, 20Mb hard disk & printer. *Networks supported:* Net BIOS.
A Comprehensive, Accurate & Easy-to-Use Payroll System Designed for Any Small Business. Payroll Manager Automatically & Accurately Calculates Federal, State, Local, Social Security Medicare, FUTA, SUTA & Many Other Withholdings & Deductions. In Addition Payroll Manager Offers a Quicken Interface in Which Automatically Updates Quicken Accounts While Giving You Professional Check Printing Capabilities.
Ghost Software.

Payroll: Module 5. *Version:* 7.11. Jeff Gold. Jul. 1991. *Items Included:* Perfect-bound manual. *Customer Support:* 90 days toll-free technical support; each additional year $150.
MS-DOS 3.1 or higher (384k). IBM PS/2, PC, PC XT, PC AT & compatibles. disk $295.00. *Addl. software required:* System Manager. *Networks supported:* PC-LAN, 3COM, Novell, Lantastic.
Automatically Produces Checks with Detailed Stubs for Weekly, Biweekly, Monthly or Semimonthly Pay Periods. Also Produces Government Reports Such As 940 & 941 & W-2 Forms. System Can Prepare Payroll for Hourly, Salaried, Commissioned & Piece Rate Employees. Number of Deductions & Job Codes Are Only Limited By Available Disk Space. System Can Record Handwritten Payroll Checks.
Manzanita Software Systems.

Payroll Partner. *Compatible Hardware:* Apple Macintosh; IBM PC & compatible. *Memory Required:* 512k. *General Requirements:* Microsoft Excel.
disk $99.00.
Payroll.
Heizer Software.

Payroll Program. *Compatible Hardware:* IBM PC, PC XT, PC AT. *Operating System(s) Required:* MS-DOS. *Memory Required:* 256k. *Customer Support:* Toll free telephone.
disk $995.00.
Payroll Processing & Post Facto Functions.
Ernest A. Jonson & Co.

PayrollTax Calculation System. *Version:* 2.0. 1989. *Compatible Hardware:* IBM, DEC, HP, & PC. *Operating System(s) Required:* Any system supporting a COBOL RPG III computer, including MUS, OS, AS400, DOS, MS-DOS, UNIX, VMS. *Memory Required:* 250k. *Items Included:* Documentation, Installation & Geo-Code manuals. *Customer Support:* First year support included; renewal year support is based on orginal purchase price.
contact publisher for price.
Tax Calculation & Reporting System. Maintains File of U.S. Federal, State & Local Payroll Taxes & Reciprocals. Interfaces with User's Payroll System & Calculates Employee & Employer Tax. Features 401k, 125 Plan, Gross up & Retroactive Calculations. Canadian Version Available. Updates Handled by Vertex.
Vertex, Inc.

PBAR-PC: Patient Billing & Accounts Receivable. *Version:* 6.1. 1984. *Operating System(s) Required:* MS-DOS, UNIX, XENIX, Amos. *Memory Required:* 256k. *General Requirements:* Hard disk. *Customer Support:* 90 days free, $600 yearly thereafter.
disk $4000.00.
Billing & Receivables Management System. Includes: Insurance Billing by Form or Electronic Transmission, Full Appointment Scheduling, Chance Ticket Generation, Recalls, Letter Writer, & Analysis Reports by Procedures, Doctor & Practice.
Far West Systems, Inc.

PBG 100. *Compatible Hardware:* IBM PC with 2 disk drives, graphics peripheral, RS232 serial ports. *Operating System(s) Required:* CP/M, CP/M, CP/M-86. *Language(s):* FORTRAN, C. *Memory Required:* CP/M, MP/M 64k; CP/M-86, IBM PC 128k.
disk $295.00.
Graphics System That Produces Graphics from a Variety of Data Sources. Features Include: Full Range of Business Graphics Including Line Graphs, Stacked Bar Charts, Clustered Bar Charts, Three-Dimensional Bar Charts with Pieces Called Out; Charts & Graphs Automatically Saved on Disk; Supports a Host of Output Devices Including the C.Itoh CX-4800 Multi-Pen Plotter & Epson Printer; Graphs Can Be Printed with One Command; Data Can Be Taken Directly from SuperCalc Spreadsheets, dBASE II Files, or Microsoft's MicroPlan Without Any Manipulation.
Pacific Basin Graphics.

PBG 300: Business Graphics Package. John E. Blackburn. May 1986. *Operating System(s) Required:* UNIX. *Memory Required:* 256k.
disk, cassette or cartridge $995.00.
Menu-Driven Program Which Produces Presentation Business Graphics on a Wide Variety of Monochrome & Color Terminals, Plotters, Dot-Matrix & Laser Printers. Stores Resulting Charts on Disk So That User Can Print Them Later at His Convenience & Takes Complete Advantage of All the Individual Characteristics of Each Output Device.
Pacific Basin Graphics.

PBI Goldilocks & the Three Bears. Jan. 1996. *Items Included:* 1 manual, 1 registration card, 1 product catalog. *Customer Support:* 30 day return warranty, free technical support via telephone.
Win 95. Pentium P60 or higher (8Mb). CD-ROM disk $24.00-$29.00 (ISBN 1-888646-01-2). *Nonstandard peripherals required:* CD-ROM.
Win 3.1. PC 486 or higher (8Mb). *Nonstandard peripherals required:* Speakers, sound card, CD-ROM.
Mac. Mac 68040 or higher (8Mb).
The Traditional Adventures of Goldilocks Take a New & Enticing Turn into the World of Multimedia. Bring the Characters to Life While Learning Reading & Other Skills. Sing-Along, Coloring & Other Activities Featured.
Packard Bell Interactive.

PBI Little Red Riding Hood. Jacob Grimm & Wilhelm K. Grimm. Jan. 1996. *Items Included:* 1 manual, 1 registration card, 1 product catalog. *Customer Support:* 30 day return warranty, free technical support via telephone.
Win 95. Pentium P60 or higher (8Mb). CD-ROM disk $24.00-$29.00 (ISBN 1-888646-02-0). *Nonstandard peripherals required:* CD-ROM.
Win 3.1. PC 486 or higher (8Mb). *Nonstandard peripherals required:* Speakers, sound card, CD-ROM.
Mac. Mac 68040 or higher (8Mb).
This Traditional Tale Takes a New, Exciting Turn into the World of Multimedia. Learn Reading & Other Skills, Sing-Along with the Original Soundtrack, & Color the Characters & More in Little Red Riding Hood's Interactive World.
Packard Bell Interactive.

PBI Milly Fitzwilly's Mousecatcher. Mracia Vaughn. Jan. 1996. *Items Included:* 1 manual, 1 registration card, 1 product catalog. *Customer Support:* 30 day return warranty, free technical support via telephone.
Win 95. Pentium P60 or higher (8Mb). CD-ROM disk $24.00-$29.00 (ISBN 1-888646-03-9). *Nonstandard peripherals required:* CD-ROM.
Win 3.1. PC 486 or higher (8Mb). *Nonstandard peripherals required:* Speakers, sound card, CD-ROM.
Mac. Mac 68040 or higher (8Mb).
Welcome to the Great Mouse Chase. As Milly Tries to Outsmart the Mice That Have Overrun Her Home She Manages to Amuse Them Instead with Her Crafty Contraptions. Learn to Spell, Read & Sound Out Words. Skillbuilding Activities Accompany This Delightful Tale. Winner of the National Parenting Center Seal of Approval.
Packard Bell Interactive.

PBI Storybook Library: Bundle Trio of The Pirate Who Wouldn't Wash, Wrong Way-Around the World & The Friends of Emily Culpepper. Michael Salmon et al. Jan. 1996. *Items Included:* 1 manual, 1 registration card, 1 product catalog. *Customer Support:* 30 day return warranty, free technical support via telephone.
Win 95. Pentium P60 or higher (8Mb). CD-ROM disk $24.00-$29.00 (ISBN 1-888646-05-5). *Nonstandard peripherals required:* CD-ROM.
Win 3.1. PC 486 or higher (8Mb). *Nonstandard peripherals required:* Speakers, sound card, CD-ROM.
Mac. Mac 68040 or higher (8Mb).
This Trio of Fun-Filled Adventures Will Entertain Children While Teaching Them about Cleanliness, Order & Other Important Concepts. Spelling, Phonetics & Reading Lessons Are Built In.
Packard Bell Interactive.

PBI The Little Engine. Julie Holland. Jan. 1996. *Items Included:* 1 manual, 1 registration card, 1 product catalog. *Customer Support:* 30 day return warranty, free technical support via telephone.
Win 95. Pentium P60 or higher (8Mb). CD-ROM disk $24.00-$29.00 (ISBN 1-888646-04-7). *Nonstandard peripherals required:* CD-ROM.
Win 3.1. PC 486 or higher (8Mb). *Nonstandard peripherals required:* Speakers, sound card, CD-ROM.
Mac. Mac 68040 or higher (8Mb).
The Little Engine Is a Charming Tale of a Community Coming Together for a Friend in Need. Children Will Improve Important Skills Such As Reading, Spelling, Phonetics, & Active Reasoning & More with This Engaging Story & Its Built-In Activities.
Packard Bell Interactive.

PBI There's a Dinosaur in the Garden. Jan. 1996. *Items Included:* 1 manual, 1 registration card, 1 product catalog. *Customer Support:* 30 day return warranty.
Win 95. Pentium P60 or higher (8Mb). CD-ROM

disk $24.00-$29.00 (ISBN 1-888646-00-4). *Nonstandard peripherals required:* CD-ROM. Win 3.1. PC 486 or higher (8Mb). *Nonstandard peripherals required:* Speakers, sound card, CD-ROM.
Mac. Mac 68040 or higher (8Mb).
What If Those Enormous Creatures - the Dinosaurs - Came Back to Life & Visited Your House. Get Some Ideas & a Wealth of Dinosaur Education in This Exciting Interactive Book. Skillbuilding Abounds with Reading, Spelling & Phonetics Lessons on Every Page Including Various Activities, Such As Coloring & Puzzle Solving.
Packard Bell Interactive.

PC Accountant. *Customer Support:* 800-929-8117 (customer service).
MS-DOS. IBM/PS2. disk $99.99 (ISBN 0-87007-268-4).
Accounting for Non-Accountants. PC Accountant Comes with Predefined Account Files for a Household & Small Business. It Keeps Track of Income & Expenses, Categorized by Accounts Defined. User Can Review Total Income & Expenses to Date & for Any Given Month. Enter Income & Expenses Under the Guidance of Deposit & Check Forms. A Calculator Is Available Online to Help Make Calculations. Checks Can Be Printed As They Are Entered. Addresses Are Printed on the Checks Allowing Them to Be Placed in Window Envelopes. Includes Budgets with Graphs, Will Handle 200 Accounts with Balances, 200 Names & Addresses, Unlimited Journals, Figures to $99,999,999.99.
SourceView Software International.

PC Accounting Solutions.
MS-DOS. IBM PC & compatibles. disk $22.95 (ISBN 1-55851-009-5).
MS-DOS. IBM PC & compatibles. disk $37.95, incl. book (ISBN 1-55851-008-7).
Articles Written by Accounting Experts for Users Who Want to Implement a PC-Based Accounting System or Gain Better Control of Their Current System. Topics Include Choosing & Maximizing a Microcomputer-Based Accounting System, Taking Charge of Accounts Receivables, Implementing Projects, Job Costing & Building Better Spreadsheets.
M & T Bks.

PC-Advantage. *Version:* 4.0. *Operating System(s) Required:* PC-DOS/MS-DOS, SuperDOS. *Memory Required:* 512k.
disk $895.00-$5500.00.
Provides Employment Agency with Retrievals, Applicant Information & Job Order Search.
QAX International Systems Corp.

PC-Aid. *Items Included:* User manual. Interactive tutorial. *Customer Support:* 1 year updates & telephone support included, additional support available.
PC-DOS (512k). IBM compatible with hard disk. $7500.00. *Nonstandard peripherals required:* 8" floppy drive from Flagstaff Engineering. *Addl. software required:* 8" floppy driver form Flagstaff Engineering.
Collects Data from Foxboro Videospec Disks & from FOX-1/A Reports. It Performs Loop Analysis & Provides Reports & Drawings Maintenance. Free Demonstration Version Is Available.
Paracomp, Inc.

PC Album. *Items Included:* 3 ring spiral-bound manual, tutorial program. *Customer Support:* Technical support line (no fee), co-op marketing program.
PC-DOS 2.1 & higher. IBM PC/XT/AT (512K). contact publisher for price. *Nonstandard peripherals required:* Image capture board, hardware compression board (optional). *Networks supported:* Novell, ethernet, 3Com, IBM Networks, AT&T Starlan.
Fully Integrated Text & Image Database That Comes Complete with Its Own Programmer's Application Language (PAL). Images Can Be Input From Video Cameras, Optical Discs, or Scanners, & Then Stored & Output to Printing Devices. Allows User to Create & Design Integrated Image Database Applications or Integrate Powerful Imaging Routines into Existing Applications.
PCM, Inc.

PC Album Network. *Compatible Hardware:* IBM PC AT & compatibles. *Operating System(s) Required:* MS-DOS 3.0 or higher, LANs. *Memory Required:* 512k. *Items Included:* Documentation manual, tutorial. *Customer Support:* Technical phone support.
$2495.00.
Image Database that Allows Users to Store Images with Text. The Database Program, Which Includes a Programmer's Application Language, Allows Users to Capture Images Through VCR, Laser Disk, Video Camera, & any Source that Creates National Television Standards Committee Compliant Signals & Combine Them with Text. The Program also Works with the Panasonic FXRS-506 Scanner. Applications of the Image Database Include Personnel, Security, Banking, Law Enforcement, & Even Theatrical Casting. The Network Version Includes File Locking & Runs on any PC Network.
PCM, Inc.

PC ANOVA: Analysis of Variance. *Items Included:* Bound manual. *Customer Support:* Free hotline - no time limit; 30 day limited warranty; updates are $5/disk plus S&H.
MS-DOS 2.0 or higher. IBM PC & compatibles (128k). disk $99.95. *Nonstandard peripherals required:* Two disk drives (or a hard disk), & a CGA (or equivalent); printer supported.
Allows Sophisticated Statistical Analysis Without Prior Computer Experience. It Treats All Standard ANOVA Research Designs with Both Speed & Accuracy; Accepts DIF Files Created by, for Example, Lotus & VisiCalc; & Provides Full Data Entry, Storage, Retrieval, & Editing Capability.
Dynacomp, Inc.

PC Anywhere III. *Version:* 3.11a. Nov. 1985. *Memory Required:* 48k RAM, 256k. *General Requirements:* IBM PC, XT, AT, PS/2 & compatible, 1 commport or internal modem. *Items Included:* Host & remote software, documentation. *Customer Support:* (516) 462-6961.
PC-DOS 2.1 or higher. disk $145.00.
IBM PC, XT, AT, PS/2 & compatibles. 3.5" or 5.25" disk $145.00.
Allows Any Terminal Computer with a Modem to Remotely Access an IBM PC, XT, AT, or Compatible & Run All Programs. Features Include File Transfer, Remote Printing Conversational Mode & Crash Proof Operation.
DMA, Inc.

PC Assembly Screens. *Items Included:* Bound manual. *Customer Support:* Free hotline - no time limit; 30 day limited warranty; updates are $5/disk plus S&H.
MS-DOS 2.0 or higher. IBM PC & compatibles (128k). disk $49.95. *Nonstandard peripherals required:* 86 family macroassembler; monochrome/color graphics compatible; printer supported, but not necessary.
Collection of Screen-Development Programs for the Assembly-Language Software Writer. Design & Incorporate Professional-Quality Screen Displays into Your Programs & Manipulate Them As Desired. Create Full-Color Screens, Including Attributes & the Extended Graphic Character Set. The Software Automatically Generates an ASCII Source File Which Can Be Assembled As-Is, or Merged with a Word Processor into Another Program File. Link As Many Screens As Desired, & Call on Them at Will. Any 80-Column Screen Can Be Created, Modified, & Retrieved.
Dynacomp, Inc.

PC-Bartender for Windows. *Version:* 1.3. Aug. 1994. *Items Included:* GBC bound users manual. Includes over 200 drink recipes. *Customer Support:* One year free support via phone, mail, fax & BBS.
Windows 3.1. IBM compatible running Windows. disk $29.95.
More Than Just a Drink Recipe Database, PC-Bartender for Windows Can Link Recipes; Adjust Their Size for Groups of up to 999 People; Maintain a Bar Inventory; & More. Includes the Ability to Handle Non-Alcohol Drinks & Appetizers.
PSG-HomeCraft Software.

PC Bible Atlas. *Version:* 1.04. Parsons Technology. May 1992.
3.5" disk Contact publisher for price (ISBN 1-57264-007-3).
Parsons Technology.

PC Bible Atlas for Windows. *Version:* 1.02. Parsons Technology. Aug. 1993.
3.5" disk Contact publisher for price (ISBN 1-57264-008-1).
Parsons Technology.

PC Braille. Peter Duran. Apr. 1987. *Compatible Hardware:* IBM PC & compatibles, RT PC. *Operating System(s) Required:* PC-DOS, MS-DOS, UNIX System 5, UNIX Berkeley 4.2. *Memory Required:* 128k. *General Requirements:* Braille embosser.
PC-DOS, MS-DOS. disk $495.00.
UNIX System 5, UNIX Berkeley 4.2, IBM RT PC. $1495.00.
braille printer avail.
Translates ASCII Text Files to Braille Ready for Embossing. Totally Automated.
Arts Computer Products, Inc.

PC-Browse. *Version:* 1.01. *Items Included:* disk set, 96 pg. coil-bound manual, technical support & quarterly newsletter for one year. *Customer Support:* One year telephone support with registration; renewal $29/yr.
IBM PC & compatibles (60k RAM; with EMS, takes 3k from DOS 640k limit). $39.00 for the registered package.
Pop-Up File Scan & Hypertext Tool for the IBM PC That Lets User View Files, Find Lost Files & Search in Multiple Files or Multiple Drives for a Given Word or Phrase. Can Find Files with Sorted Records Within 1.1 Seconds in a 2-Megabyte File. User Can Search Any File with One Marked Lookup Word per Page & with Lookup Words Sorted in ASCII Order. Hypertext Linking Can Cross-Reference Pieces of Information by Word Flagging. Can Also Set up Cross References for Reference Manuals, Telemarketing Scripts, On-Line Help & Decision Trees. Product in Non-Resident Mode Provides DOS Menu Shell that Executes Programs that User Selects. Like PC-Write, Program Is Shareware.
Starlite Software Corp.

PC-Buddy. *Compatible Hardware:* IBM PC, PC XT, PC AT, & compatibles. *Operating System(s) Required:* PC-DOS/MS-DOS 2.0 or higher. *Memory Required:* 256k. *General Requirements:* Hard disk.
disk $49.95.
Enables Users to Access Any File on Their System by Choosing File's Name from a Menu. Users

TITLE INDEX

Can Also Password-Protect Individual Programs or Submenus. It Is Possible to Change the DOS Command-Based Set System into a Menu-Driven System Where All Functions Can Be Performed by Selecting Menu Options Without Exiting to DOS.
Automated Ideas, Inc.

PC Calculator Plus. *Items Included:* Bound manual. *Customer Support:* Free hotline - no time limit; 30 day limited warranty; updates are $5/disk plus S&H.
MS-DOS. IBM PC & compatibles (128k). disk $39.95. *Nonstandard peripherals required:* Printer optional.
Features Include: 15-Digit Precision; Roots, Squares, Powers, Logs, Factorials, Exponentials; Sine, Cosine, Tangent, & Inverses; Average, Standard Deviation, Variance, Max./Min.; Compounding, Discounting, Future/Present Value of Annuities, Loan Analysis, Amortization Schedules, Internal Rate of Return; Transaction Printing; Spreadsheet.
Dynacomp, Inc.

PC Canary. *Version:* 91g. 1991. *Items Included:* Disk & manual. *Customer Support:* 90 days included in purchase price; support agreement available.
PC-MS/DOS 2.1 or higher. IBM PC & compatibles (100k). disk $19.95. *Nonstandard peripherals required:* 200k disk.
Site license available.
Virus Alarm Which Detects Modifications to .EXE, .DAT & Command.COM Files. Installs Easily & Does Not Modify Files, Allowing Its' Use with Other Security Programs. Allows DOS Upgrades. Named for Miner's Canary Whose Death Signalled Invisible Toxic Fumes. Demo Available.
Compass New England.

PC Cardmaker. *Version:* 3.2. *Items Included:* Manual. *Customer Support:* 1 year free with purchase price.
MS-DOS (640k). IBM AT, PS/2, or compatible. disk $279.00 (ISBN 0-927875-11-X, Order no.: 454). *Optimal configuration:* 1 or 2 floppy disk drive, hard disk (optional) Epson or compatible printer.
Produces Catalog Cards According to AACR2 Rules. Allows Records to Be Entered in MARC Format. Interfaces with Winnebago CIRC/CAT or with Any Other USMARC MicroLIF Compatible Circulation & Card Catalog Systems.
Winnebago Software Co.

PC Chart Plus: Technical Analysis Software. 1995. *Items Included:* Well-written 150-page manual with detailed operating instructions & examples. *Customer Support:* Free telephone support - 90 days, 30-day warranty.
MS-DOS 3.2 or higher. 286 (584k). disk $149.95. *Nonstandard peripherals required:* CGA/EGA/VGA.
Combines Powerful Technical Indicators with Superior Charting, Database, & Communications into One Easy-to-Use Package. All in All, PC CHART PLUS Provides You with Many Paths for Obtaining Data, As Well As Many Ways to Analyze It.
Dynacomp, Inc.

PC Checkbook. Jack Cameron. *Compatible Hardware:* IBM PC, PCjr, PC XT, PC AT, Portable PC, 3270 PC. *Memory Required:* 128k. *General Requirements:* IBM Display & IBM Matrix Printer recommended.
disk $19.95 (Order no.: 6276617).
Helps User to Manage His/Her Checkbook. User Can Create & Manage Several Accounts with up to 350 Checks Each, Use the Browse/Edit/Print Options to Review Various Checkbook Tasks, & Keep Track of Checks, Cash Withdrawals, Service Charges, & Deposits.
Personally Developed Software, Inc.

PC Chord Primer. *Items Included:* Bound manual. *Customer Support:* Free hotline - no time limit; 30 day limited warranty; updates are $5/disk plus S&H.
MS-DOS 2.0 or higher. IBM PC & compatibles (128k). disk $49.95. *Nonstandard peripherals required:* CGA or equivalent graphics capability; printer supported, but not necessary.
Package of Software Programs for the IBM Personal Computer That Are Designed to Provide Interactive Assistance to the Serious Guitarist. The Program Capabilities Range from a Built-In Library of over 600 Chords to a Set of Automated Lessons on Music Theory for Guitar. The Program Is Divided into Two Major Components. One Consists of Educational Programs That Include Lessons on General Chord Structure & Chord Progression Patterns. The Other Serves As a Computerized Reference Manual or Handbook. It Provides a Chord Encyclopedia That Automatically Searches for Chords by Name or Musical Key, Programs to Assist Music Composition & Transposition, & a Guitar Tuner.
Dynacomp, Inc.

PC*Claim Link. 1986. *Compatible Hardware:* IBM PC & compatibles. *Memory Required:* 320k. *General Requirements:* Hard disk, modem.
disk $649.00 (Order no.: 1).
Features a Software Bridge to the CLAIM*NET Electronic Insurance Claims Network for A/R Packages That Do Not Have Electronic Claims Capabilities.
Physicians Practice Management, Inc.

PC-Claim, PC-Claim Plus. *Version:* 2.0. Aug. 1984. *Compatible Hardware:* Compaq, Compaq Plus; IBM PC, PC XT, PC Portable. *Operating System(s) Required:* MS-DOS, PC-DOS 2.0, 2.1. *Language(s):* COBOL. *Memory Required:* 320k. *General Requirements:* 2 disk drives.
PC-Claim. $89.95.
PC-Claim Plus. $459.00.
Eliminates Typing of Doctor Names, Addresses, Billing Numbers, Procedure & Diagnosis Narratives & Other Repetitive Information. Translates Office Procedure & Diagnosis Codes to Accepted Insurance Company Codes. Prints Separate Claims for Multiple Policies from One Entry. Prints Mailing Labels for Insurance Company, Patient or Guarantor. Allows up to Six Procedures on a Single Entry. Sends Electronic Claims at Night, Unattended, with Full Retransmission on Error, & Automatic Restart Capabilities & More.
Physicians Practice Management, Inc.

PC Classic Art, Vol. 2: Domestic. Dec. 1992. *Customer Support:* For customer service, product registration, upgrades, technical support, & CustomerFirst service plans, customers may call Aldus Customer Services at (206) 628-2320.
Macintosh. Contact publisher for price (ISBN 1-56026-157-9).
Aldus Corp.

PC Client Accounting. *Version:* 4.5. 1995. *Items Included:* Complete operating manual. *Customer Support:* Unlimited telephone support.
MS-DOS. IBM PC or compatible (256k). $300.00. *Optimal configuration:* IBM PC or compatible, 256k RAM, printer. *Networks supported:* Novel, Unex.
Designed for the Professional Accountant Who Does Client Write-Up Work for Several Small to Medium Sized Businesses on a Monthly or Quarterly Basis. Produces a Statement of Income with Current Period & Year to Date Columns, with Percentages Based on Total Income, As Well As a Balance Sheet & General Ledger with Detail Showing Date, Check Number, Description & Amount of Each Entry. Data Entry Is Easy & Fast.
Up to 200 Ledger Accounts Are Permitted & All Titles Are Designated by the Accountant. Special Preview Function Allows User to View the Financial Statements Before They Are Printed. If Changes Are Required, They Can Be Made Before the Financial Statements Are Generated. All Reports Are Printed on 8 1/2" x 11" Paper. A Complete Audit Trail Is Generated by All Input Routines & an Automatic Back-Up Feature Preserves the Integrity of the Entries Before Posting to the Ledger. Comes with Samples of All Reports Generated by the System.
Omni Software Systems, Inc. (Indiana).

PC Complete. *Version:* 4.00. *Compatible Hardware:* IBM PC. *Operating System(s) Required:* MS-DOS 2.0 or higher. *Language(s):* Pascal. *Memory Required:* 320k.
$229.95.
Electronic Mail Package Featuring Fully Unattended Operation Including Electronic Mail Transfer Between PCs & Information Services Including Transmission of Binary Files with XMODEM Error Checking Protocol, Text Editor & Terminal Emulation.
Transend Corp.

PC Connection. *Compatible Hardware:* IBM PC & compatibles. *Operating System(s) Required:* MS-DOS.
$550.00, incl. WS100 Terminal Emulator (Order no.: PC01).
manual $10.00 (Order no.: A-0025).
Enables Personal Computer to Operate As an Interactive Workstation of Any Multi-User Computer Which Employs POINT 4's IRIS Operating System. Provides Transmission of Data Files & Large-Capacity, Mass-Storage Facilities.
Point 4 Data Corp.

PC CYACCT. *Compatible Hardware:* IBM PC & compatibles, PC XT; DEC Rainbow 100+; Altos 586 & 8600; Hyperion; Compaq. *Operating System(s) Required:* PC-DOS, MS-DOS. *Language(s):* BASIC. *Memory Required:* 128k.
contact publisher for price.
Manages a CPA Practice. Features Complete Job Accounting, Client Billing with User-Designed Invoice Formatting, Custom Report Printing & Client Write-Up Capabilities.
Cybernetics Technology Corp.

PC CYLAW. *Compatible Hardware:* IBM PC & compatibles, PC XT, PC AT; DEC Rainbow 100+; Altos 586 & 8600; Hyperion; Compaq. *Operating System(s) Required:* PC-DOS, MS-DOS. *Language(s):* BASIC (source code included). *Memory Required:* 128k.
disk basic system $1495.00, write for specifics.
CYLAW for Personal Computers.
Cybernetics Technology Corp.

PC CYPRO. *Compatible Hardware:* IBM PC & compatibles, PC XT, PC AT; DEC Rainbow 100+; Altos 586 & 8600; Hyperion; Compaq. *Operating System(s) Required:* PC-DOS, MS-DOS. *Language(s):* BASIC. *Memory Required:* 128k.
$1495.00.
Manages a Professional Practice. Features Complete Accounting Capabilities, Client Billing with User-Designed Invoice Formatting.
Cybernetics Technology Corp.

PC Data Master. *Version:* 2.0. *Compatible Hardware:* IBM PC & compatibles. *Operating System(s) Required:* PC-DOS/MS-DOS 2.0 or higher. *Memory Required:* 256k. *General Requirements:* Hard disk & math co-processor recommended; CGA, Hercules, AT&T, EGA, & VGA graphics supported.
disk $135.00.
DOS Environment for Signal Processing &

Display Enhanced with Separately Compiled Modules for Systems with & Without a Math Coprocessor, a Multisignal Plot Utility, & an Enhanced DOS Shell. The Program Combines Graphics Routines, Real & Complex Data File Math Routines, DSP Utilities, Test Data Generation Routines, Data Sampling Routines, & Binary Data Pipes to Create a DOS-Based DSP System. Most Graphics Boards Are Supported. The Shell Lets Users Implement Independent DOS Console & Graphics Screen Windows. A Waveform Module is Also Included. Users Can Display Individual or Multiple Data Files Using the Plot System's Autoconfiguration Capabilities. Version 2.0 Comes with an Augmented Set of DSP Utility Modules. Operations Include Forward & Inverse FFT & Fast Hartley Transform Routines, Convolution, Correlation, Window Generation, FIR Filter Design, & Test Data Generation. Users Can Implement Many Multistage Transformations by Combining These Basic Operations with Data File Math.
Durham Technical Images.

PC-Date. *Version:* 2.0. *Compatible Hardware:* IBM PC & compatibles. *Operating System(s) Required:* PC-DOS/MS-DOS. *Memory Required:* 64k. *General Requirements:* Two floppy disks drives or a hard disk, modem.
disk $79.00.
Computerized Matchmaking System. Users Are Asked a Series of Questions & Then the System Compares & Answers with Others to Find Users with Similar Personalities. Questionnaire Can Be Customized. Public & Private Message Areas, Demographic Analysis & Other Features.
Protosoft.

PC-Elastic. *Version:* 1.5. J. Robert Cooke et al. Jul. 1987. *Operating System(s) Required:* PC-DOS/MS-DOS. *Memory Required:* 512k. *General Requirements:* 2 disk drives.
disk student $99.95 (ISBN 0-940119-08-0).
disk professional $495.00.
Solves Problems in Elasticity Theory.
Cooke Pubns.

PC-ELITE. *Version:* Release E3.0. Dec. 1991. *Items Included:* Documentation. *Customer Support:* Performance Plus Service/Support Subscriber Maintenance Program; 90-day limited warranty (on-site for hardware).
PC/UNIX-based INTEL, Wang or IBM compatible PC's (128k). Contact publisher for price.
Designed to Meet the Needs of a Wide Variety of Insurance Agencies, from Small to Large, from Those Automating for the First Time to Those Replacing a System. Offers Expanded RISKFILE Information Capabilities, Access to Additional Detail Functions, Enhanced Branch Office Support & Multiple Producer Commission Splits. Release E3, Features an Array of 45 System Enhancements, Including Support for Nine Additional ACORD Applications in Laser Plain Paper Format.
Delphi Redshaw.

PC EmuLink. *Version:* 2.11. Rod Roark. *Items Included:* A user guide for installation & technical information. *Customer Support:* Three day on-site training program & three day workshop, contact TSL for pricing information.
PC/MS-DOS 2.0 or higher (64k). IBM PC & compatibles, AT, XT, PS/2. disk $199.00.
A Terminal Emulation Software That Lets an IBM-Compatible Computer Emulate a Dumb Terminal to Gain Full Access to a PC-MOS Host Computer's Resources. In Terminal Emulation Mode, the Computer Appears as a Dumb Terminal Sharing the Resources of a PC-MOS Host. Can Support Functions Such as Color, Graphics, a 25-Line Display, Standard IBM Scan Codes & Function Keys. Also Can Be Used to Allow PCs at Multiple Remote Sites to Communicate with a Netware Server Through a Single PC-MOS Node on a Novell Network.
The Software Link, Inc.

PC Estimator Construction Cost Estimation. *Items Included:* Full manual. No other products required. *Customer Support:* Free telephone support - no time limit. 30 day warranty.
MS-DOS 3.2 or higher. IBM & compatibles (512k). disk $189.95. *Optimal configuration:* IBM, MS-DOS 3.2 or higher, 448k RAM, hard disk, & printer.
Designed in Collaboration with Professional Estimators for Both Residential & Commercial Construction Cost Estimation. Built-In Cost Code Library Contains Unit Prices & Unit Labor Rates. It Is Accessed by Look-Up Windows. Selections May Be Made Individually or in a Batch Mode from Within the Estimate Worksheet. You Can Preview Bottom-Line Estimates at Any Time, & Apply Different Markups to Each Estimate. Also Prepares a Materials Order Report for Each Cost Item, or Gives Phase & Job Totals.
Dynacomp, Inc.

PC Estimator: Construction Cost Estimation. 1995. *Items Included:* Full manual. *Customer Support:* Free telephone support - 90 days, 30-day warranty.
MS-DOS 3.2 or higher. 286 (584k). disk $189.95. *Nonstandard peripherals required:* CGA/EGA/VGA.
Designed in Collaboration with Professional Estimators for Both Residential & Commercial Construction Cost Estimation. It Is Fully Menu-Driven with Pull-Down Menus, Look-Up Windows, Dialog Boxes, & On-Screen Instructions. Also Includes a CSI-Standard Cost Code Library (Which May Be Expanded), Provides Comprehensive Reports, Is dBASEIII File-Compatible, & Is Digitizer-Compatible.
Dynacomp, Inc.

PC Expert. *Compatible Hardware:* IBM PC & compatibles. *Operating System(s) Required:* PC-DOS, MS-DOS. *Memory Required:* 256k. *General Requirements:* Hard disk recommended. *Items Included:* 32 pg. Thinking Software catalog.
5.25" or 3.5" disk $129.00.
Turbo Pascal version $99.00.
C version $99.00.
Expert System Development Environment. Can Be Used As a Stand-Alone Expert System Shell, or Integrated As a Unit into User's Own Program for Creation of a Customized Expert System.
Thinking Software, Inc.

PC-File. *Version:* 7.0. Feb. 1993. *General Requirements:* 2 720k floppy disk drives or hard disk. *Items Included:* 2 bound manuals for LANS, 1 for PC. *Customer Support:* 800-809-0027: $15/call or 900-555-8800: $2/min.
MS-DOS or PC-DOS 3.0 or higher. IBM PC, XT, AT, PS/2 & compatibles (450k). $129.95 single user (ISBN 0-922692-21-1). *Networks supported:* Microsoft LAN manager, Novell Netware, Artisoft Lantastic or Banyan Vines. $395.95 LAN version.
Database with a GUI Interface with Flexible Reporting Capabilities. DBASE Compatible, Importing & Exporting, Prints Labels, Cards, Tags, Easily. Spelling Checker, Phonetic Retrieve, Bar & Pie Charts, Scatter Graphs, Relational Retrieval & Posting, Global Operations, Password Protection, Keystroke Macros, Auto-Dial Phone Numbers, Full Mouse Support, Context-Sensitive Help Screens, User-Defined Formula Indexes, Bar-Code Printing, Mail Merge Functions.
Outlook Software.

PC File 'N' Report Integrated Database. *Items Included:* Full manual. No other products required. *Customer Support:* Free telephone support - no time limit. 30 day warranty.
MS-DOS 3.2 or higher. IBM & compatibles (512k). disk $79.95.
manual $12.95.
demo disk $5.00.
General Purpose Program Which Allows You to Easily Create Custom Screen Formats & Enter Data via the Newly Created Screen, All Within a Few Minutes. Up to 99 Fields Can Be Specified. The Records' Length Can Be up to 1771 Characters. Number of Data Records Is Only Limited by the Disk Capacity. You Can Print Mailing Labels, Filing Cards, Invoices, & Statements on Either Blank or Printed Forms, with the Data Fields Extracted from the Data File.
Dynacomp, Inc.

PC Flight Guide. *Version:* 2.0.
IBM PC & compatibles (640k). disk & up $131.50. *Nonstandard peripherals required:* 2 floppy disk drives.
Shows Every Flight Option Available Between 200 North American Cities. User Receives Monthly Floppy Disk with Updated Schedules. No Modem Necessary. Features Saving of User Travel Intineraries & Flight Schedules for 100 Foreign Cities (Outside U.S. & Canada). Database of 3000 Restaurants Has Been Added to List of 2500 Hotels & Meeting Places. Includes Hotel Fax Numbers, Major Airport Layouts & Seating Charts of 85 Airplanes.
PC Flight Guide.

PC/FOCCALC. Jul. 1986. *Operating System(s) Required:* PC-DOS, MS-DOS. *Memory Required:* 640k.
disk $495.00, with quantity discounts avail.
Combines Enhanced Spreadsheet Capabilities with Modeling & Graphics Features.
Information Builders, Inc.

PC/Focus. *Version:* 2.0. Jul. 1986. *Compatible Hardware:* Compaq; IBM PC & compatibles, PC XT, PC AT; NCR; TI Professional; Wang. *Operating System(s) Required:* PC-DOS 2.0 or higher. *Language(s):* Assembly, FORTRAN. *Memory Required:* 640k.
disk $1295.00, with quantity discounts avail.
Free-Form Relational DBMS. Features a Window-Driven Front End Called Table Talk Which Leads the User Through Report Generation; Micro-Mainframe Link; Ability to Export Data to Lotus Software, & to Word Processing Files in DIF or ASCII Formats. Supports an Unlimited Number of Records per File with up to 255 Fields per Record. Up to 16 Files Can Be Open at One Time.
Information Builders, Inc.

PC Focus. Information Builders, Inc. Feb. 1984. *Compatible Hardware:* Texas Instruments. *Operating System(s) Required:* MS-DOS. *Memory Required:* 512k. *General Requirements:* 8087 co-processor, printer, 768k RAM, Winchester hard disk.
$1595.00.
Texas Instruments, Personal Productivit.

PC/Focus Multi-User. *Version:* 1.5. *Compatible Hardware:* IBM PC, PC XT, PC AT, 3270 PC; Texas Instruments; Wang Professional; HP 150 Touchscreen; AT&T 6300; Convergent Technologies NGEN. *Operating System(s) Required:* PC-DOS/MS-DOS 2.0 or higher. *Memory Required:* 640k. *General Requirements:* IBM, NESTAR, Novell, Token Ring, or StarLAN Network for Network versions; 20Mb hard disk recommended.
$1595.00.
Multi-User versions.

TITLE INDEX

4-User version $1995.00.
8-User version $4000.00.
16-User version $6000.00.
8- to 16-User upgrade $2000.00.
Network Version of Relational Data Base & Forth Generation Language That Contains Facilities for Data Base Management, Forms Management, Transaction Processing, Graphics, Statistics, & Micro/Mainframe Communications. Components Included with the Release 1.5 Are: Report Generator (FOCUS & Non-FOCUS Files), Dialogue Manager, File Scanner (SCAN), Full-Screen Editor (TED), Micro-to-Mainframe Communication Program (LINK), Data Management Language (MODIFY & Compiled MODIFY), Dull-Screen Data Entry (FIDEL), Graphics (High & Low Resolution), Financial Modeling (FML), Statistics (ANALYSE), TableTalk/FileTalk/AutoMod, Plotter Support (HP 7475A).
Information Builders, Inc.

PC/Focus Multiuser. *Version:* 3.0. *Compatible Hardware:* IBM PC & compatibles. *Operating System(s) Required:* DOS 3.0 or higher. *Memory Required:* 640k. *General Requirements:* Hard disk.
$1995.00 1-4 users.
$4000.00 5-8 users.
$6000.00 9-16 users.
$9000.00 17-24 users.
Hierarchical, Networked Database-Management System with a Mix of PC & Mainframe Interfaces. Documentation Is Geared Toward the Corporate MIS Department. Also Features Screen Painting, Forms Design & Report Generator Capabilities. Dedicated Database Server Computer Required for Network Operation; No Record Locking Necessary.
Information Builders, Inc.

PC Forms. *Customer Support:* 800-929-8117 (customer service).
MS-DOS. IBM/PS2. disk $149.99 (ISBN 0-87007-017-7).
Fills out Any Number of Forms, Edits Numeric, Amount, Date & State Fields for Correct Format & Data Content, Saves or Rewrites Data That User Entered on the Form to Disk or Diskette So That It Can be Retrieved or Modified, & Allows the User to Export Selective Form Data Fields to an ASCII File So That User Can Import It to a Spreadsheet or Send It to a Mainframe Application to Update the Mainframe Data Bases. Uses Function Keys.
SourceView Software International.

PC Gallery Effects User Manual. *Version:* 1.5. Apr. 1993. *Customer Support:* For customer service, product registration, upgrades, technical support, & CustomerFirst service plans, customers may call Aldus Customer Services at (206) 628-2320.
Macintosh. Contact publisher for price (ISBN 1-56026-185-4).
Aldus Corp.

PC Graphics. *Items Included:* Bound manual. *Customer Support:* Free hotline - no time limit; 30 day limited warranty; updates are $5/disk plus S&H.
MS-DOS. IBM PC & compatibles (128k). disk $49.95. *Nonstandard peripherals required:* Color graphics; printer is supported.
Integrated Graphics Package Designed for Both Engineering & Educational Applications. Graph XY & XYZ Coordinate Equations, As Well As Parametric & Polar Equations. Experiment with Data While Maintaining Control over Scaling, Position of the Origin, Interval, & Increment for the Dependent Variable(s), etc. User May Even Determine Relative Maxima & Minima, Solutions to Polynomial Equations, Intersection Points, etc.
Dynacomp, Inc.

PC Graphics. *Items Included:* Full manual. No other products required. *Customer Support:* Free telephone support - no time limit. 30 day warranty.
MS-DOS 3.2 or higher. IBM & compatibles (512k). disk $49.95.
User May Graph XY & XYZ Coordinate Equations, As Well As Parametric & Polar Equations. Experiment with Data While Maintaining Control over Scaling, Position of the Origin, Interval, & Increment for the Dependent Variable(s), etc. You May Even Determine Relative Maxima & Minima, Solutions to Polynomial Equations, Intersection Points, etc. Easy to Set up Multi-Line Functions Using a BASIC-Like Syntax. The 50 Page Manual Also Includes Information on Advanced Applications, Such As How To Graph Discrete Sequences, Recursively Defined Functions, Functions in the Complete Plane, etc. Program Is Both Powerful & Versatile, & Can Be Used in a Mathematical Class As Well As In Engineering Applications Requiring Visual Representations of Functions.
Dynacomp, Inc.

PC Gypsy. *Version:* 2.5. Carol Jean Logue. Dec. 1989. *Items Included:* Manual, velvet drawstring pouch. *Customer Support:* Yes.
IBM & compatibles (192k). disk $69.00 (ISBN 1-879490-57-5).
Enables Users to Have a "Reading" of the Tarot Cards in the Privacy of Their Personal Keyboards. Program Includes History of the Cards, Prose, & Poetic Insights About Each of the 78 Cards in a Traditional Tarot Deck. Available on 5.25" & 3 5" Floppy Disks Shipped in Hand Made Velvet Pouch.
Rosehips Ink.

PC Hebrew Writer. *Items Included:* Manual.
MS-DOS. IBM. disk $99.00.
A Hebrew-English Word Processor with Pull-Down Menus in Hebrew & English. Compatible with Dot Matrix & Laser Printers.
Davka Corp.

PC-HIBOL. *Version:* 4.1. David Johnson. Jan. 1990. *Compatible Hardware:* IBM PC & compatibles, PC XT, PC AT. *Operating System(s) Required:* PC-DOS/MS-DOS 2.0 or higher. *Language(s):* COBOL. *Memory Required:* 512kk. disk $995.00.
Has the Capability to Develop & Test IBM Mainframe CICS/VS COBOL Applications on the PC. Generates CICS/VS COBOL & BMS Maps for IBM Mainframe Operation & Microcomputer COBOL Maps for IBM PC Operation for the Same Program Specification. It Thus Allows the Testing of Mainframe Programs on the PC. The PC Application Appears the Same As the Mainframe to the Operator Due to the Product's 3270-Like Screen Management System.
PLE, Inc.

PC Home Bartender: Ultimate Guide to Expertly Prepared Cocktails. Oct. 1994. *Items Included:* Registration card, instruction sheet. *Customer Support:* 900 support number $2.00 per minute; limited 60 day warranty.
Windows. IBM PC & compatibles (2Mb). disk $9.95 (ISBN 1-57269-006-2, Order no.: 3202 42215). *Addl. software required:* Windows 3.1 or higher. *Optimal configuration:* VGA or higher monitor, Hard disk required. Use with any mouse.
Become a Mixologist Like the Professional Barkeepers in the Finest Establishments. Its Easy & Fun.
Memorex Products, Inc., Memorex Software Division.

PC Home Checkbook. *Customer Support:* 800-929-8117 (customer service).
MS-DOS. Commodore 64. disk $49.99 (ISBN 0-87007-624-8).
Enables Users to Organize Checkbook Without Having to Learn Lists of Accounting Terms. This Program Lets Users Record Four Kinds of Transactions: Checks Written, Automated Teller Activity, & Bank Fees. Allows Space for Recording the Transaction or Check Number, Date, Amount, Tax-Deductible Status, Recipient ("Made to") Purpose, & Category. User May Create up to 20 Categories. Displays Balance on Its Main Menu for User Convenience; the Program Allows User to List All Categories. User May Print an Individual Transaction Record via the Edit Mode or the Entire File via the Searches & Statements Menu.
SourceView Software International.

PC-Hypertext. *Compatible Hardware:* IBM PC & compatibles. *Operating System(s) Required:* PC-DOS/MS-DOS 2.0 or higher. *Memory Required:* 256k. *General Requirements:* Hard disk, monochrome or CGA monitor.
PC-Hypertext. $5.95.
Houdini. $89.00.
MaxThink. $89.00.
HyperLink. $89.00.
Separate Collections of Programs & Utilities. Turns Files of ASCU Text Information into Outlines, Knowledge Networks, & Hypertext Systems.
MaxThink, Inc.

PC InfoPublisher Database Edition. *Version:* 2.0. Aug. 1993. *Customer Support:* For customer service, product registration, upgrades, technical support, & CustomerFirst service plans, customers may call Aldus Customer Services at (206) 628-2320.
Macintosh. Contact publisher for price (ISBN 1-56026-250-8).
Aldus Corp.

PC Instructor. *Compatible Hardware:* IBM & compatibles. *Operating System(s) Required:* DOS 2.0 or higher. *Items Included:* 2 Diskettes, reference manual. *Customer Support:* Call Individual Software (90 days).
disk $49.95.
Introduction to Computer Keyboard, Teaches Use of Menus & Colors. Features Animated Graphics.
Individual Software.

PC IntelliDraw: Domestic. *Version:* 2.0. Feb. 1994. *Customer Support:* For customer service, product registration, upgrades, technical support, & CustomerFirst service plans, customers may call Aldus Customer Services at (206) 628-2320.
Macintosh. Contact publisher for price (ISBN 1-56026-256-7).
Aldus Corp.

PC-Intercomm. *Compatible Hardware:* IBM PC & compatibles with asynchronous serial port, monochrome display adapter. *Operating System(s) Required:* PC-DOS, MS-DOS. *Language(s):* C. *Memory Required:* 64-128k.
disk $99.00.
Communications Package That Allows the PC to Emulate a DEC VT-100. All of the Documented VT-100 Features That Are Electronically Possible on the IBM PC Are Supported. Allows User to Talk to Any Manufacturer's Computer & Transfer Information & Files Back & Forth. As a "Smart Terminal" System Allows Users to Run Applications on Remote Computers with Video Feedback. Improves the IBM PC from Its "Teletype-Line-at-a-Time" Capabilities to Full Video Communications.
Mark of the Unicorn.

PC-Interface for DOS - Windows. *Customer Support:* 30 days free telephone support; Extended services available $30.00 per user additional for one year.
An 80386-based system. $255.00 (host), $235.00 (PC).
Networks DOS or Windows PCs to a Unix System V/386 Host Providing File & Application Sharing. PCs Can Re-Direct Print Jobs to Unix Printers. Emulate VT100 Terminal Connected to Unix Host.
Locus Computing.

PC-Interface for Macintosh. *Items Included:* User manuals; PC-Interface for DOS server. *Customer Support:* 30 days free telephone support; Extended services available for one year at 18% of list price additional.
Macintosh System 6.0-7.1. Macinstosh SE, II, Classic, LC, PowerBook, Centris, Performa (1Mb). 3.5" disk $720.00 2 users; $1200.00 5 users; $2100.00 10 users. *Optimal configuration:* 1Mb RAM, 1Mb hard disk space (2Mb with System 7). *Networks supported:* LocalTalk, EtherTalk.
Networks Macintosh to UNIX. Files & Applications Can Be Shared by Using UNIX System As Non-Dedicated File Server. Uses Standard Macintosh Interfaces; No New Interfaces to Learn. Any User with PC-Interface Installed Can Use AppleTalk Connected Laser Printers. Conduct Terminal Sessions on UNIX Host.
Locus Computing.

PC-Interface Plus. *Customer Support:* 30 days free telephone support; Extended services available at $30 per copy additional for one year.
DOS 3.X-6.0, Windows 3.0-3.1. PC, PC/AT, PC/XT, or 100% compatibles (512k). disk $369.00; multi-user packages avail. *Optimal configuration:* 1Mb hard drive space. *Networks supported:* Ethernet, Token Ring, RS-232 Dial-out modem.
Networks DOS & Windows PCs with UNIX Systems. Files & Applications Can Be Shared by Using UNIX System As Non-Dedicated File Server. Printers Anywhere on the Network Can Be Used by Any PC for Print Jobs. Includes TCP/IP Stack, 8 Terminal Types in Emulating UNIX-Attached Terminal. Novell NetWare Simultaneous Connections.
Locus Computing.

PC-Key-Draw. *Version:* 3.76. *Compatible Hardware:* IBM PC & compatibles. *Items Included:* Manual, clip out library, font libraries, support. *Customer Support:* Free.
disk $100.00.
General Purpose 2-D CAD Program Combines Graphical Database Hyperdraw Features with CAD Capabilities.
Oedware.

PC-Kwik Power Disk. *Version:* 1.1. Feb. 1990. *Items Included:* Manual, Diskette. *Customer Support:* Toll-Free, unlimited support.
PC/MS-DOS 2.0 or higher. IBM, XT, AT, 286, 386, 486, PS/2 & compatibles (384k). disk $79.95.
A High Performace File Reorganizer, Data Reliability Test & Repair Utility, & a Tool for Viewing File Structures on a Disk.
PC-Kwik.

PC-Kwik Power Pak. *Version:* 2.1. Oct. 1988. *Operating System(s) Required:* PC-DOS/MS-DOS 2.0 or higher. *Memory Required:* 128k. *Items Included:* Dual diskettes (5.25" & 3.5"), Manual, Quick reference sheet. *Customer Support:* Toll-free, unlimited support.
disk $129.95.

Performance Enhancement Programs for Any Personal Computer Running DOS. It Centers Around the Super PC-Kwik Disk Accelerator, Which Provides Advanced Disk Reading & Writing Technology with RAM-Based Disk Caches up to 16 Megabytes. Also Includes RAM Disks, Print Spoolers, Screen Accelerator, & Keyboard Accelrator.
PC-Kwik.

PC Lens. *Version:* 1.14. Mar. 1987. *Compatible Hardware:* IBM PC & compatibles. *Operating System(s) Required:* PC-DOS, MS-DOS. *Memory Required:* 128k, recommended 192k. *General Requirements:* MDA & CGA cards, color or B&W monitor.
disk $180.00, incl. manual.
Allows IBM & compatible computers to Display Large Print. Will Run with Virtually Any Software Which Supports the Monochrome Display Adaptor Card. Users Can Adjust Character Size, Intercharacter & Interline Spacing, Foreground Color, & Other Features.
Arts Computer Products, Inc.

PC-Letter. 1988. *Items Included:* Manual.
MS-DOS 2.X -4.X. IBM PC/XT/AT, PS/2 or compatibles. disk $24.95 (Order no.: 9502).
PC-Letter Combines An Address List with a Letter Writer Program with Heading & Ending Options. The Mailing List Consists of an Address-Mask for Entering or Editing Multiple Addresses. The Program Also Permits a Form Letter & a Heading/Ending Section Which Can Be Merged with All or Selected Addresses. A Text Editor is Used for Writing the Short Form Letter & Supplemental Section. The Note-Pad Window is Very Convenient to Make Notes about the Information in the Letter or about the Addressee. The Program Functions on a PC/XT/AT with MDA, EGA, Herc. or CGA on One or Two Disks &, As Well, on RAM Disks & Hard Disks.
Elcomp Publishing, Inc.

PC Librarian. *Version:* 2.0. Sep. 1990. *Compatible Hardware:* IBM PC & compatibles. *Operating System(s) Required:* MS-DOS 2.1 or higher; Novell, 3Com, MS-Net. *Memory Required:* 512k. *Items Included:* User documentation, 50 pre-printed archive labels. *Customer Support:* Free telephone support.
Single User $69.00, LAN version $299.00. avail. site & corporate licensing.
Archiving Product that Removes Inactive Files from Users Hard Disk Drive while Retaining a Catalog of Information on the Archived Files. Users Specify Which Files Users Want to Archive, to Which Medium, & Whether Users Want to Delete the File or Leave It on the Hard Disk Drive; the Program Will Then Automatically Archive & Catalog the File. The Catalog, Which Remains on the Hard Drive, Lists the Contents of the Files, Where They Reside, Date the Files Reside, When They Were Removed, & File Size. Can also Tell Users Which Files Users Haven't Used in a Specified Time Period. Through an Optional 59-Character Note Function, Users Can also Recall the Contents of a File Without Actually Accessing It. Users Can also Pre-Examine the First Screen of the File Before Archival to Ensure It is the Exact One that Users Wish to Archive.
United Software Security, Inc.

PC Line Monitor. *Customer Support:* 800-929-8117 (customer service).
MS-DOS. IBM/PS2. disk $199.99 (ISBN 0-87007-613-2).
Designed to Allow a PC, or Compatible Computer, to Replace an $8000 & up Communications Line Monitor. The Program Displays All Data Sent by Either End of a Communications Link in Either ASCII or HEXAdecimal, Enabling the Operator to Analyze Protocol Information on a Communications Link. PC Line Monitor Supports All Parity Modes & Baud Rates from 50 to 9600. Combined with a Portable Computer, the Program Will Allow Complete Mobilty in Analyzing Communications Hardware & Software.
SourceView Software International.

PC-lint for C/C Plus Plus. *Version:* 7.0. Oct. 1996. *Compatible Hardware:* IBM PC & compatibles, any MS-DOS machine. *Operating System(s) Required:* PC-DOS/MS-DOS, OS/2, Windows NT, Windows 95. *Language(s):* C & C Plus Plus. *Memory Required:* 640k. *Items Included:* Software & user manual. *Customer Support:* Fax, mail & telephone tech support included.
disk $239.00.
quantity & educational discounts & site license avail.
Diagnostic Facility for C & C Plus Plus. Analyzes C & C Plus Plus Programs & Reports on Bugs, Glitches & Inconsistencies. Features Full K&R & ANSI Support, One-Pass, Use of Large Memory Model Internally with All Tables Expandable. Fully Customizable; All Error Messages Can Be Selectively Inhibited, Size of Scalers Can Be Altered, Format of Error Messages Can Be Adjusted. Provides for Strong Type Checking Based on Typedefs.
Gimpel Software.

PC-LISP. *Compatible Hardware:* IBM PC & compatibles. *Operating System(s) Required:* PC-DOS/MS-DOS. *Memory Required:* 256k. *General Requirements:* Hard disk recommended. *Items Included:* 32 pg. Thinking Software catalog.
3.5" or 5.25" disk $29.95, incl. manual.
LISP Implementation for IBM PC.
Thinking Software, Inc.

PC MacTerm. *Compatible Hardware:* Apple Macintosh 512KE. *Operating System(s) Required:* System 4.1 or higher.
3.5" disk $99.00.
Controls a Distant PC from User's Macintosh. Can Access Host PC's Peripherals, Transfer Files Between Host & Remote Computers, Print on Either Computer, Run DOS Programs in a Window, Copy & Paste Between Mac & DOS Applications.
Data Management Assocs. of New York, Inc.

PC Mailer. *Customer Support:* 800-929-8117 (customer service).
MS-DOS. IBM/PS2. disk $49.99 (ISBN 0-87007-346-X).
A Permanent Place for all Names, Addresses, Phone Numbers of Users Associates, Friends & Relatives. Will Print out a Tiny Black Book in Alphabetical or Zipcode Order.
SourceView SoftWare International.

PC Master for Windows. 1983. *Compatible Hardware:* IBM PC & compatibles. *Language(s):* COBOL. *Memory Required:* 4000k. *Items Included:* Manuals included. *Customer Support:* Telephone support, country law updates & training.
contact publisher for price.
An Intellectual Property Record Management System Used by over 400 Organizations. Principal Features Include: the Most Automatically Calculated Worldwide Action Due Dates, Custom Report/Letter Generation & Runs in a Client/Server Environment.
Master Data Center, Inc.

PC MASTER Lite. Jun. 1991. *Items Included:* User manual. *Customer Support:* Telephone support & country law updates.

TITLE INDEX

MS-DOS 3.3. IBM PC or 100% compatible (640k). $4000.00-$7000.00 License fee. Patterned after MDC's Popular PC MASTER, a Patent & Trademark Docketing System Developed for Use by Firms with Less Comprehensive Docketing & Reporting Requirements. Affordable & Easy to Use, but Powerful Enough to Manage Your Information Efficiently.
Master Data Center, Inc.

PC-Mathematics: Mathematical Software Library. *Items Included:* Full manual. No other products required. *Customer Support:* Free telephone support - no time limit. 30 day warranty.
MS-DOS 3.2 or higher. IBM & compatibles (512k). disk $149.95.
Giving a Detailed Description of PC MATHEMATICIAN Is Difficult. After over 10,000 Hours of Designing & Programming, Quite a Bit Has Been Crammed into This Product (Which Comes on 8 Full Disks). A Partial List of the Procedures Includes: Functions & Equations, Differential Equations, Regression Analysis, Approximation & Interpolation, Fourier Transforms, Simultaneous Linear Equations, Matrix Operations, Series, File Manipulation, Stereoscopic Graphs, & Miscellaneous Procedures.
Dynacomp, Inc.

PC-Mathematics: Mathematical Software Library. 1992. *Items Included:* Detailed manuals included with all Dynacomp products. *Customer Support:* Free telephone support to original customer - no time limit; 30 day limited warranty.
MS-DOS 3.2 or higher. IBM PC & compatibles (512k). $149.95 Text & 8-diskette set (Add $5.00 for 3 1/2" format; 5 1/4" format standard). *Optimal configuration:* IBM, 256k RAM, MS-DOS 2.0 or higher, & CGA/EGA/VGA or compatible graphics capability.
$39.95 Text only.
A Powerhouse Full of Efficient, Up-to-Date, & Well-Tested Mathematical Procedures Designed for Engineers, Scientists, & College Students. It Is Fully Menu-Driven & Covers Several Areas of Interest, Including: Functions & Equations; Differential Equations (Including Boundary-Value Problems & Nonlinear Equations); Regression; Approximation & Interpolation (up to Four Variables); Linear Algebra; Multi-Variable Power Series; Fourier Transforms; Partial Differentiation; Multiple Integration with Constant & Variable Limits; Maxima & Minima; Stereographic Plotting; & More. Includes 206-Page Manual.
Dynacomp, Inc.

PC Mathematics: Mathematical Software Library. 1995. *Items Included:* Full manual. *Customer Support:* Free telephone support - 90 days, 30-day warranty.
MS-DOS 3.2 or higher. 286 (584k). disk $149.95. Nonstandard peripherals required: CGA/EGA/VGA.
Text only $39.95.
A Powerhouse Full of Efficient, Up-to-Date, & Well-Tested Mathematical Procedures Designed for Engineers, Scientists, & College Students. Besides Being an On-the-Job Toolbox of Mathematical Software, PC MATHEMATICS May Also Be Used As an Educational Tool in College & Beyond. It Is Fully Menu-Driven & Covers Several Areas of Interest, Including: Functions & Equations; Differential Equations (Including Boundary-Value Problems & Nonlinear Equations); Regression; Approximation & Interpolation (up to Four Variables); Linear Algebra; Multi-Variable Power Series; Fourier Transforms; Partial Differentiation; Multiple Integration with Constant & Variable Limits; Maxima & Minima; Stereographic Plotting; & More.
Dynacomp, Inc.

PC Menu. *Version:* 3.0. Dec. 1984. *Compatible Hardware:* IBM PC. *Operating System(s) Required:* PC-DOS 2.0-3.1. *Language(s):* PASCAL, Assembler. *Memory Required:* 128k. *Items Included:* Media & documentation. *Customer Support:* 90 days included. Toll-free hotline.
disk $139.95.
Allows Users to Develop Custom Menu Systems. Any Programs Resident on the Fixed Disk Drive Can Be Put under Menu Control to Avoid Dealing with DOS Commands. Menu Manager Creates a Master Menu Test File Using a Word Processor (Provided). This Text File Is Processed by PC MENU Resulting in Another Program File That Interfaces with Casual Users in an Interactive Menu Mode. Menu Manager Can Control Access, Provide Special Help Screens for Every Item or Every Menu, & Build up to 15 Layers of Sub-Menus.
Touch Technologies, Inc.

PC Morse Code. Alden B. Johnson. *Compatible Hardware:* IBM PC, PCjr, PC XT, PC AT, Portable PC with IBM Display. *Operating System(s) Required:* DOS 2.00, 2.10, 3.00, 3.10. *Memory Required:* 128k.
disk $19.95 (Order no.: 6276612).
Breaks down the Alphabet, Numbers, & Special Symbols into "Byte-Sized" Groups That Can Be Learned & Practiced Individually. The User Can Adjust the Tone of the Signal, Set the Transmission Speed from 5 to 60 Words per Minute, & Practice with an Online Dictionary Containing More Than 6000 Words.
Personally Developed Software, Inc.

PC-MOS 3.0. May 1987. *Memory Required:* 128k. *Items Included:* Quick start guide, user guide. *Customer Support:* Three-day on-site training program & three-day workshop; contact company for pricing.
Single, five-, & 25-user versions. single user $195.00, five-user $595.00, 25-user $995.00. *Networks supported:* Multi-user terminal interface to Novell.
Multi-User, Multi-Tasking, DOS-Compatible Operating System. Designed for Compatibility with Applications Such As Lotus 1-2-3, DBASE IV & Some Windows Applications, Including Excel As Well As Sun River Graphics Workstations & Color Graphic Workstations.
The Software Link, Inc.

PC-MOS 4.0. *Memory Required:* 128k.
single user $195.00; five users $595.00; 25-users $995.00.
Operating System That Supplants DOS to Run Most DOS Applications in a MultiUser, Multitasking Environment. A Single User Can Reboot a Task Without Interrupting Other Users. Other Additions Include New Driver Software That Lets PC-MOS Support Full-Color, Bit-Mapped Graphics with VGA Resolutions, Allowing up to 16 Workstations with Graphics to Tag onto a Single CPU. New Print Spooler Allows Single Print Processor to Control Output to Multiple Printers Simultaneously. Monitor Program Utility Lets System Administrator Control Various Aspects of Task, Including Priority & Time Allocation.
The Software Link, Inc.

PC Networks Fundamentals, Communications & LANS. *Version:* 2.1. 1990. *Operating System(s) Required:* PC-DOS/MS-DOS. *Memory Required:* 640k. *General Requirements:* Color monitor; CGA, EGA, or VGA graphics board, monochrome monitor with Hercules graphics.
3.5" or 5.25" disk $495.00 (ISBN 0-935987-16-9).
Computer-Based Training Course Which Teaches PC-to-PC Communications. Topics Covered Include PCs in Communications, PC to PC Communications, PC Communication Concepts, Network Components, Error Detection/Correction, Public Domain & Proprietary Protocols, Communications Adapters, Software Products. Color, Animated Graphics Simulate Communications Concepts Help Make Learning Fun. Review Quizzes Evaluate Learning & Progress.
Edutrends, Inc.

PC/NOS. *Version:* 2.0. Nov. 1988. *Operating System(s) Required:* PC-DOS/MS-DOS. *Memory Required:* Workstation 66k, Server 184k. *General Requirements:* Network hardware: Omninet, Arcnet, Ethernet, Token Ring, NetBIOS Networks.
disk $1395.00.
Distributed Network OS for Omninet, ARCNET, Ethernet, Token Ring, & NetBIOS Networks. Includes Asynchronous Gateway, NetBIOS Support, Print Spool Manager, & Virtual Console Network Management System. Also Features EMS Support & Full Security for Multiple Servers. Provides Support for Unlimited Network Nodes, Users, & Servers for One Network Site Fee.
Corvus Systems, Inc.

PC-Outline. *Version:* 3.35. *Compatible Hardware:* IBM PC & compatibles. *Operating System(s) Required:* PC-DOS/MS-DOS 2.0 or higher. *Memory Required:* 128k. *Customer Support:* Free unlimited tech support for 1 year.
manual & technical support $89.95.
Allows Users to Write down Their Thoughts, Plans, & Ideas; Then Organize Them by Moving Text & Selectively Hiding & Unveiling Information. Support for a Number of Printers & Plotters.
Brown Bag Software.

PC Padlock. *Version:* 2.1. Jan. 1983. *Compatible Hardware:* IBM compatibles. *Operating System(s) Required:* MS-DOS, PC-DOS. *Memory Required:* 64k.
disk $99.00 (Order no.: 411001).
Protection Device. Includes: Hard Disk Compatibility, Object Module for Interfacing, Low Overhead Required on Diskette, User Installable Finger Print & Demonstration Applications.
Glenco Engineering, Inc.

PC PageMaker: Danish. *Version:* 5.0. Sep. 1993. *Customer Support:* For customer service, product registration, upgrades, technical support, & CustomerFirst service plans, customers may call Aldus Customer Services at (206) 628-2320. Macintosh. Contact publisher for price (ISBN 1-56026-171-4).
Aldus Corp.

PC PageMaker: Domestic. *Version:* 5.0. Jun. 1993. *Customer Support:* For customer service, product registration, upgrades, technical support, & CustomerFirst service plans, customers may call Aldus Customer Services at (206) 628-2320. Macintosh. Contact publisher for price (ISBN 1-56026-161-7).
Aldus Corp.

PC PageMaker: Dutch. *Version:* 5.0. Jul. 1993. *Customer Support:* For customer service, product registration, upgrades, technical support, & CustomerFirst service plans, customers may call Aldus Customer Services at (206) 628-2320. Macintosh. Contact publisher for price (ISBN 1-56026-168-4).
Aldus Corp.

PC PageMaker: Finnish. *Version:* 5.0. Mar. 1994. *Customer Support:* For customer service, product registration, upgrades, technical support,

& CustomerFirst service plans, customers may call Aldus Customer Services at (206) 628-2320.
Macintosh. Contact publisher for price (ISBN 1-56026-170-6).
Aldus Corp.

PC PageMaker: French. *Version:* 5.0. Jul. 1993. *Customer Support:* For customer service, product registration, upgrades, technical support, & CustomerFirst service plans, customers may call Aldus Customer Services at (206) 628-2320.
Macintosh. Contact publisher for price (ISBN 1-56026-163-3).
Aldus Corp.

PC PageMaker: German. *Version:* 5.0. Jul. 1993. *Customer Support:* For customer service, product registration, upgrades, technical support, & CustomerFirst service plans, customers may call Aldus Customer Services at (206) 628-2320.
Macintosh. Contact publisher for price (ISBN 1-56026-164-1).
Aldus Corp.

PC PageMaker: International English. *Version:* 5.0. Jun. 1993. *Customer Support:* For customer service, product registration, upgrades, technical support, & CustomerFirst service plans, customers may call Aldus Customer Services at (206) 628-2320.
Macintosh. Contact publisher for price (ISBN 1-56026-162-5).
Aldus Corp.

PC PageMaker: Italian. *Version:* 5.0. Sep. 1993. *Customer Support:* For customer service, product registration, upgrades, technical support, & CustomerFirst service plans, customers may call Aldus Customer Services at (206) 628-2320.
Macintosh. Contact publisher for price (ISBN 1-56026-166-8).
Aldus Corp.

PC PageMaker: Japanese. *Version:* 4.0. Mar. 1993. *Customer Support:* For customer service, product registration, upgrades, technical support, & CustomerFirst service plans, customers may call Aldus Customer Services at (206) 628-2320.
Macintosh. Contact publisher for price (ISBN 1-56026-187-0).
Aldus Corp.

PC PageMaker: Norwegian. *Version:* 5.0. Oct. 1993. *Customer Support:* For customer service, product registration, upgrades, technical support, & CustomerFirst service plans, customers may call Aldus Customer Services at (206) 628-2320.
Macintosh. Contact publisher for price (ISBN 1-56026-169-2).
Aldus Corp.

PC PageMaker: Spanish. *Version:* 5.0. Jul. 1993. *Customer Support:* For customer service, product registration, upgrades, technical support, & CustomerFirst service plans, customers may call Aldus Customer Services at (206) 628-2320.
Macintosh. Contact publisher for price (ISBN 1-56026-167-6).
Aldus Corp.

PC PageMaker: Swedish. *Version:* 5.0. Aug. 1993. *Customer Support:* For customer service, product registration, upgrades, technical support, & CustomerFirst service plans, customers may call Aldus Customer Services at (206) 628-2320.
Macintosh. Contact publisher for price (ISBN 1-56026-165-X).
Aldus Corp.

PC Paint Plus. Oct. 1985. *Compatible Hardware:* IBM PC & compatibles, PC XT, PC AT. *Operating System(s) Required:* PC-DOS 2.0, 2.1, 3.0, 3.1. disk $99.00.
with PC Mouse $220.00.
Allows the User to Adapt Graphics from Other Programs, Take Advantage of Its Own Ready-to-Use 'Clip Art', or Other Clip-Art Files, or Create Original Artwork with a Complete Graphics Library of Drawing Tools. Text Can Be Created or Brought in from Another Program to Fill Designated Areas. Images Can Exceed the Screen Size Allowing Creation of Full-Page Art or Full-Size Overhead Projections. Works with All Popular Printers, a Wide Variety of Plotters, & the POLAROID PALETTE.
MSC Technologies, Inc.

PC Paintbrush IV. Aug. 1989. *Compatible Hardware:* IBM PC, AT, PS/2 & compatibles. *Operating System(s) Required:* MS-DOS 3.0 or higher. *Memory Required:* 640k. *Items Included:* Desks, documentation, binder, slipcase. *Customer Support:* Free, 10AM-6PM (EST) M-F.
$99.95 (ISBN 1-877728-01-2).
Delivers Everything Needed to Create, Refine, & Retouch Images. Includes Automatic Text Effects, Gray Scale Image Editing, 256 On-Screen Colors, Blend, Smudge, Gradient, & Repeating Designs. Capture Screens, Graduate Colors, Make 3-D Shadowed Letters, Edit Text & Enhance Any Part of Your Image.
ZSoft Corp.

PC Paintbrush IV+. Nov. 1989. *Compatible Hardware:* IBM PC, AT, PS/2 or compatible. *Operating System(s) Required:* MS-DOS 3.0 or higher. *Memory Required:* 640k. *General Requirements:* Drawing device required. *Items Included:* Disks, documentation, binder, slipcase. *Customer Support:* Free support 10AM-6PM (EST) M-F.
disk $199.00 (ISBN 1-877728-00-4).
Designed to Scan, Create, Edit & Dramatically Enhance Images. Includes All the Image Processing Features, As Well As Complete Scanner Control, Large-Scale Image Editing, EMS Support, Pre-Scan Feature & More.
ZSoft Corp.

PC Palette. Kai-ching Chu. *Compatible Hardware:* IBM PC, PCjr, PC XT, PC AT, Portable PC, 3270 PC. *Operating System(s) Required:* DOS 2.00, 2.10, 3.00, 3.10. *Memory Required:* IBM PCjr 256k, all others 128k. *General Requirements:* Double-sided disk drive, IBM Color Display; IBM Graphics Printer or IBM Color Printer recommended; joystick, touch tablet, mouse, or graphics tablet optional.
disk $39.95 (Order no.: 6276537).
Graphics Program Which Allows Users to: Select from 4 Line Widths & 12 Drawing Styles; Create Animation & Other Special Effects; Include Sections of One Drawing in Another; Make Graphics Presentations Using Their Graphics Files; Illustrate Numerical Data with Pie Charts, Bar Charts, Line Graphs, & Scatter Plots; Choose from 4 Palettes; & Add Text to Drawings in Any of 12 Fonts.
Personally Developed Software, Inc.

PC Palette Utility. Kai-ching Chu. *Compatible Hardware:* IBM PC, PC XT, PC AT, Portable PC, 3270 PC. *Operating System(s) Required:* PC-DOS 2.00, 2.10, 3.00, 3.10. *Memory Required:* 128k. *General Requirements:* IBM 7371, 7372, or 7374 plotter, IBM PC Pallette program.
disk $19.95 (Order no.: 6276640).
Lets Users Plot PC PALETTE Stroke Files (Vector Files). Offers Additional Text Fonts for PC PALETTE in Nine New Type Styles, Each Available in Four Colors or Textures. Ready-Made Graphic Pictures Are Also Available & Can Be Included in PC PALETTE File & Modified in PC PALETTE.
Personally Developed Software, Inc.

PC-PAROT: Production Analysis Reports on Time. *Version:* 1.1. Jan. 1992. *Items Included:* One manual in 3-ring binder. *Customer Support:* Unlimited telephone support free for 1 year; unlimited telephone support $995 for each year thereafter.
DOS 3.0. IBM PC & compatibles, 8086-80486 CPU (500k). disk $4295.00; multiple copy discounts. *Nonstandard peripherals required:* Hewlett-Packard Laser Jet printer or compatible. *Addl. software required:* AutoSketch & Ventura Publisher recommended. *Optimal configuration:* 80486 PC w/4Mb RAM, Windows 3.1, AutoSketch, Ventura Publisher, HP Laser Jet III.
Performs Line of Balance (LOB) Analysis for Improved Visibility of Complex Manufacturing Programs. LOB Analysis Is a Production Analysis Technique That Provides Top Management an Overview of Production Progress in a Concise Graphic Format. Produces Delivery Charts, Progress Charts, & Past Due Reports Directly from Production Data.
P/Soft Consulting.

PC Payroll. *Version:* 7.2. 1995. *Items Included:* Complete operating manual. *Customer Support:* Unlimited telephone support.
MS-DOS. IBM PC or compatible (256k). $200.00. *Optimal configuration:* IBM PC or compatible, 256k RAM, printer. *Networks supported:* Novel, Unex.
Full Capability Payroll Program That Handles the Processing & Reporting Needs of Most Small Business & Professional Offices. Handles Weekly, Bi-Weekly or Semi-Monthly Pay Periods for Hourly, Salaried or Commissioned Employees. All Quarterly & Yearly Reports & W-2 Forms Are Prepared by the System. Updated Yearly.
Omni Software Systems, Inc. (Indiana).

PC Photo Styler: Domestic. *Version:* 2.0. Jul. 1993. *Customer Support:* For customer service, product registration, upgrades, technical support, & CustomerFirst service plans, customers may call Aldus Customer Services at (206) 628-2320.
Macintosh. Contact publisher for price (ISBN 1-56026-209-5).
Aldus Corp.

PC PhotoStyler: French. *Version:* 1.1. Feb. 1993. *Customer Support:* For customer service, product registration, upgrades, technical support, & CustomerFirst service plans, customers may call Aldus Customer Services at (206) 628-2320.
Macintosh. Contact publisher for price (ISBN 1-56026-153-6).
Aldus Corp.

PC PhotoStyler: International English. *Version:* 2.0. Dec. 1993. *Customer Support:* For customer service, product registration, upgrades, technical support, & CustomerFirst service plans, customers may call Aldus Customer Services at (206) 628-2320.
Macintosh. Contact publisher for price (ISBN 1-56026-210-9).
Aldus Corp.

PC PhotoStyler Special Edition: Domestic. *Version:* 2.0. Aug. 1993. *Customer Support:* For customer service, product registration, upgrades, technical support, & CustomerFirst service plans, customers may call Aldus Customer Services at (206) 628-2320.
Macintosh. Contact publisher for price (ISBN 1-56026-246-X).
Aldus Corp.

PC PhotoStyler Special Edition: French. *Version:* 2.0. Dec. 1993. *Customer Support:* For customer service, product registration, upgrades, technical support, & CustomerFirst service plans, customers may call Aldus Customer Services at (206) 628-

TITLE INDEX

2320.
Macintosh. Contact publisher for price (ISBN 1-56026-248-6).
Aldus Corp.

PC PhotoStyler Special Edition: German.
Version: 2.0. Dec. 1993. *Customer Support:* For customer service, product registration, upgrades, technical support, & CustomerFirst service plans, customers may call Aldus Customer Services at (206) 628-2320.
Macintosh. Contact publisher for price (ISBN 1-56026-249-4).
Aldus Corp.

PC PhotoStyler Special Edition: International English. *Version:* 2.0. Dec. 1993. *Customer Support:* For customer service, product registration, upgrades, technical support, & CustomerFirst service plans, customers may call Aldus Customer Services at (206) 628-2320.
Macintosh. Contact publisher for price (ISBN 1-56026-247-8).
Aldus Corp.

PC PhotoStyler Special Edition: Italian. *Version:* 2.0. Jan. 1994. *Customer Support:* For customer service, product registration, upgrades, technical support, & CustomerFirst service plans, customers may call Aldus Customer Services at (206) 628-2320.
Macintosh. Contact publisher for price (ISBN 1-56026-270-2).
Aldus Corp.

PC PhotoStyler Special Edition: Spanish.
Version: 2.0. Jan. 1994. *Customer Support:* For customer service, product registration, upgrades, technical support, & CustomerFirst service plans, customers may call Aldus Customer Services at (206) 628-2320.
Macintosh. Contact publisher for price (ISBN 1-56026-268-0).
Aldus Corp.

PC PhotoStyler Trial Version: Domestic.
Version: 2.0. Jan. 1994. *Customer Support:* For customer service, product registration, upgrades, technical support, & CustomerFirst service plans, customers may call Aldus Customer Services at (206) 628-2320.
Macintosh. Contact publisher for price (ISBN 1-56026-262-1).
Aldus Corp.

PC Planetarium. *Language(s):* BASIC. *Items Included:* Bound manual. *Customer Support:* Free hotline - no time limit; 30 day limited warranty; updates are $5/disk plus S&H.
MS-DOS 2.0 or higher. IBM PC & compatibles (128k). disk $39.95. *Nonstandard peripherals required:* CGA (or equivalent) card.
demo disk & manual $9.95.
Draws a Map of the Sky (926 Stars, the Sun, Moon, & Planets Out to Saturn) from Any Point on Earth, & for Any Time, Past or Future. For the Few Hundred Years Around the Present, the Calculated Coordinates Are Accurate to 4 or 5 Significant Figures.
Dynacomp, Inc.

PC-Poisson. *Version:* 1.5. Jul. 1987. *Operating System(s) Required:* PC-DOS/MS-DOS. *Memory Required:* 512k. *General Requirements:* Math coprocessor.
disk student $99.95 (ISBN 0-940119-07-2).
disk professional $495.00.
Formulates & Solves Poisson's Equation for Electrostatics, Ideal Fluid Flow, Steady-State Heat Conduction, Seepage, etc.
Cooke Pubns.

PC-POS. *Version:* 3.0. Sep. 1994. *Items Included:* 1 - 8 1/2" x 11" 3-ring binder, 300 pages.
Customer Support: 1 year maintenance $250.00 single user, $350.00 network version. Note: 1st year support free with purchase of software.
MS-DOS. IBM PC XT or compatible. $695.00 single user; $995.00 network version. *Optimal configuration:* IBM AT, 640k 40 meg hard disk drive, bar code reader, bar code label printer, cash drawer, 40 col. receipt printer, 80 col. Matrix printer. *Networks supported:* Novell Netware or Lantastic.
A Complete Point-of-Sale Solution for the Retailer Who Needs to Track Inventory & Sales. Ease of Use Makes Employee Training Possible in Just Minutes. Features Include: Modern User Interface, UPC Bar Code Support, Up to 100 Depts., Sales Commission Tracking, Sales Quota Tracking, Purchase Order Tracking, Soft Goods Support, Parts Explosion, Batch Or Real-time Invoice, GL, AR, AP, & Payroll.
MicroSpec.

PC Print. Gary Dix. *Compatible Hardware:* IBM PC, PCjr, PC XT, PC AT, Portable PC with IBM Display, IBM Graphics printer or IBM Color Printer. *Operating System(s) Required:* DOS 2.00, 2.10, 3.00, 3.10. *Memory Required:* 128k.
disk $24.95 (Order no.: 6276613).
Enables User to Print 10, 12, 15, or 17 Characters per Inch, As Well As to Use Large Type Styles, Design Customized Fonts, Print Documents with Titles & Page Numbers, Specify Indentation, Reflow Text to Desired Width, Right-Justify Text, & Print Sideways.
Personally Developed Software, Inc.

PC-PROLOG. *Version:* 1.01. *Compatible Hardware:* IBM PC & compatibles. *Operating System(s) Required:* PC-DOS/MS-DOS. *Memory Required:* 256k. *General Requirements:* Hard disk recommended. *Items Included:* 32 pg. Thinking Software catalog.
3.5" or 5.25" disk $29.95, incl. manual.
PROLOG Implementation for IBM PC.
Thinking Software, Inc.

PC Proofreader. *Compatible Hardware:* Compaq; Corona; Colombia; IBM PC, PCjr, PC XT & compatibles. *Operating System(s) Required:* MS-DOS, PC-DOS 1.0, 1.1, 2.0, 2.1. *Memory Required:* 128k.
disk $129.95 (ISBN 0-936200-43-X).
For Use with the ELECTRIC PENCIL PC. Checks, Corrects & Hyphenates ELECTRIC PENCIL Documents.
Blue Cat.

PC Purchase Advisor. *Version:* 2.01. Apr. 1989.
Customer Support: 90 day warranty against defects in disk manufacture, immediate replacement of defective media.
MS-DOS/PC-DOS 3.1 or higher (256k). IBM PC/XT/AT/PS2 compatible. disk $59.95. *Optimal configuration:* PC/AT or PS/2, hard disk, EGA or VGA graphics, 640k, one floppy drive. *Networks supported:* Novell.
PC Purchase Advisor is an Expert System to Help User Purchase the Exact Computer System Right for Your Needs. Includes 9 Chained Knowledgebases to Assist in Choosing a PC, AT or 386, & the Right Monitor, Hard Drive, Floppy Drives, Memory, Operating System & Printer. Includes 30 Page User Manual.
Thinking Software, Inc.

PC Register. *Version:* 8B. Sep. 1993. *Operating System(s) Required:* PC-DOS 3.0 or higher. *Memory Required:* 640k. *General Requirements:* Color monitor, 40-column point-of-sale printer. *Customer Support:* $400.00 per year.
disk $350.00.
Includes: Inventory Control, Online Price & Quantity Searches, Automatic Item Description, Automatic Item Price, Processes Non-Inventory Items, Can Set Decimal Quantity from 0-4 Places, Can Set Decimal List Price from 2-4 Places, Price Lookup, Quantity Lookup, Permits Manual Ring-Ups, Trade Discount, Batch Discount, Line Item & Mark-Down, Line Item & Mark-Down, Price Changes, Complete Revision for Line Items & Payments.
Trac Line Software, Inc.

PC Register Interface. *Version:* 8B. Sep. 1993. *Compatible Hardware:* PC-DOS, Xenix, Unix; 3 COM, Novell. *Language(s):* COBOL 85. *General Requirements:* Integrated Accounting Retailing & Distributing modules. *Customer Support:* Included with the Support for the Integrated Accounting.
disk $995.00.
Provides the Capability to Merge Transaction Data Created by the PC Register Package. The Transaction File Produced on a Daily Basis Is Transmitted (Communication Package Required) to the Master Site & Then Updated into the Accounting System. Merges into the Accounting System: RECEIPT RECORD, LINE ITEM RECORD, DEPOSIT RECORD.
Trac Line Software, Inc.

PC Regression: Multiple Regression & Correlation. *Items Included:* Bound manual.
Customer Support: Free hotline - no time limit; 30 day limited warranty; updates are $5/disk plus S&H.
MS-DOS 2.0 or higher. IBM PC & compatibles (256k). disk $99.95. *Nonstandard peripherals required:* Two floppy drives (or one floppy & a hard disk), a CGA (or equivalent). For printed graphs an Epson, IBM, or C. Itoh or compatible dot matrix printer is required.
Statistical Analysis Tool Which Includes Extensive Data File Handling, Transformation, & Selection Capabilities. It Can Read Data Files Created by PC STATISTICIAN & PC ANOVA, As Well As Standard DIF (e.g., from LOTUS) & ASCII.
Dynacomp, Inc.

PC-RTX. *Version:* 5.0. Jan. 1983. *Compatible Hardware:* IBM PC, PC XT. *Operating System(s) Required:* IRMX86. *Language(s):* C86, PL/M86, FORTRAN 86, Pascal 86. *Memory Required:* 512k. *General Requirements:* 2 disk drives.
disk $995.00.
Implementation of Intel's IRMX86 Real-Time Operating System Specially Configured to IBM PC & XT Device Driver Specifications. Includes Intel Family Utilities & Disk Conversion Utilities. Supports IBM's Enhanced Graphics Adapter.
Real-Time Computer Science Corp.

PC Scheme. *Compatible Hardware:* IBM PC & compatibles; TI Professional, Business-Pro.
disk $95.00.
LISP Implementation Featuring: an Optimizing Incremental Compiler; an EMACS-Like Editor; Extensions for Debugging, Graphing, & Windowing; DOS-CALL Capability; & a Programming System for the Development of Object-Oriented Applications.
Texas Instruments, Personal Productivit.

PC Scope. Scott Vanderlip. Sep. 1988.
Compatible Hardware: IBM PC & compatibles with LAB 40 hardware interface & printer.
Operating System(s) Required: MS-DOS. (source code included). *Memory Required:* 192k.
disk $100.00 (Order no.: PC-SCOPE).
With LAB 40 Analog to Digital Interface, a Complete Turn Key Digital Oscilloscope is Generated with Setable Timebase, Trigger Level, & Voltage Slides.
Computer Continuum.

PC SCREEN

PC Screen. *Customer Support:* 800-929-8117 (customer service).
MS-DOS. IBM/PS2. disk $49.99 (ISBN 0-87007-312-5).
Paints User's Screen with Any Type of Menu or Data Input Format. Makes It into a Ready-to-Run BASIC Subprogram Segment, Which Is Linked to Another Program with Gosubs. Standardizes All Screen Generation Code.
SourceView Software International.

PC Secretary, 2 diskettes. *Items Included:* Bound manual. *Customer Support:* Free hotline - no time limit; 30 day limited warranty; updates are $5/disk plus S&H.
MS-DOS 2.0. IBM PC & compatibles (128k). $49.95. *Nonstandard peripherals required:* Two disk drives (or one hard disk), a printer, & a Hayes-compatible MODEM (if autodialing is desired).
Correspondence System Containing a Built-In Text Editor. Features Include: Letter Writing; Envelope or Label Addressing; Auto Dialing. User May Store an Unlimited Number of Name-&-Address Records, with up to 1450 per Disk. Sorts Both Alphabetically by Name, or by Zip Code.
Dynacomp, Inc.

PC Secure. *Customer Support:* 800-929-8117 (customer service).
MS-DOS. IBM/PS2. disk $99.99 (ISBN 0-87007-018-5).
A Datafile Encryption Program That is Written in Machine Language & Features Key Driven Codes & Password Protection. Multi-key Version Using U.S. Bureau of Standards Encryption Protocols Will Not Allow Partial Decoding. Easy to Use with Spreadsheets & Words Processors.
SourceView Software International.

PC SHARE/VM. *Items Included:* PC SHARE/vm Board, 50' Cable, Server Interface Box, Workstation Box, MultiUser Software & Documentation. *Customer Support:* Call-in tech support & 90 days unlimited warranty.
MS-DOS or PC-DOS. Compaq 386 & compatibles. $362.00, per user.
By Multi Tasking PC SHARE/VM Converts a 386SX, 386 or 486 Based System into a Host for up to 16 Users. Each User Can Execute One or More Off-the-Shelf Single User or Multi User DOS Based Programs. Users Can Be in the Same Program or in Completely Different Programs. All of the Users Get to Share Programs, Date, All of the System Resources & Peripherals.
Zaki Corp.

PC SHARE/VM-2. *Items Included:* PC SHARE/vm-2 Board, Multiuser Software & Documentation. *Customer Support:* Call-in tech support & 90 days unlimited warranty.
MS-DOS or PC-DOS (640k). Compaq 386 & compatibles. disk $169.00.
Based on Dynamic Time Sharing Technology PC SHARE/VM-2 Allows One PC to Be Used by Two Users at the Same Time. Each of Them Running One or More Off-the-Shelf Single or Multi User DOS Based Program. Both Users Can Be in the Same Program or in Two Completely Different Programs. Both Users Get to Share Programs, Data, All of the System Resources & Peripherals.
Zaki Corp.

PC SHAREplus. *Items Included:* PC SHAREplus Card, 50' Cable, Workstation Interface Box, Multiuser Software & Documentation. *Customer Support:* Call-in tech support & 90 days unlimited warranty.
MS-DOS or PC-DOS. PC XT, PC AT, Compaq 386, PS/2 or compatibles. disk $645.00.
Using Multi Processing Technology PC SHAREplus Makes It Possible to Add up to 8 Additional Users to a Single PC. Each User Can Execute Any Off-the-Shelf Single User or Multi User DOS Based Program. Users Can Be in the Same Program or in Completely Different Programs. All of the Users Get to Share Programs, Data & Printers.
Zaki Corp.

PC Sift. *Compatible Hardware:* IBM PC & compatibles. *Operating System(s) Required:* PC-DOS/MS-DOS. *General Requirements:* PC Braille word processor.
disk $180.00.
Helps PC BRAILLE Users Translate Files Created by Other Word Processors by Sifting Out the Embedded Control Codes.
Arts Computer Products, Inc.

PC-Softsource: Directory of Software Information. Sep. 1989.
IBM PC/XT/AT or compatible (512k). 3.5" disk $22.95 (ISBN 0-924264-01-2, Order no.: PCS02).
disk $21.95 (ISBN 0-924264-00-4, Order no.: PCS01).
Directory of Commercial & Public Domain Packages for IBM PC's & Compatibles, Available in Major Categories of: Business, Home, Education, Computer, Publishing, Accounting, Word Processing, Spreadsheets, Database Management, etc. A Major Category, "Sources of Software Information" Lists Sources of Software by Topics. Most Item Listings Have One Line Descriptions. Over 1500 Items Listed in Fall 1989 Version.
Megacom.

PC/SQL-link for Windows. *Version:* 1.04.01. *Memory Required:* 320k. *General Requirements:* Hard disk. *Items Included:* Hotline, maintenance, minor enhancements, documentation updates. *Customer Support:* Telephone support, on-site support, education.
Host software. Contact publisher for price.
PC software. disk $595.00.
Annual maintenance. 15% of purchase price.
SQL Generator. Uses Menus to Develop SQL Statement. Accesses Corporate Information Stored in IBM's, DB2 & SQL/DS, or OS/2 Database Manager, Microsoft SQL Server, Tandem Nonstop SQL, Teradata DBC 1012, Britton Lee Data Base Machines, & Honeywell's PDQ. Returns Data to PC & Reformats for Use in Many PC Programs. Provides Data Extract, Update, & Unload Functions.
Micro Decisionware, Inc.

PC Statistician (by HSD). *Items Included:* Bound manual. *Customer Support:* Free hotline - no time limit; 30 day limited warranty; updates are $5/disk plus S&H.
MS-DOS 2.0 or higher. IBM PC & compatibles (128k). disk $99.95. *Nonstandard peripherals required:* Two disk drives. For screen graphics, a color-graphics card is required; printer supported.
Statistics Package Aimed at the User with No Previous Computer Experience. Accepts DIF Files Created by LOTUS 1-2-3 & VISICALC, or You Can Easily Create & Edit Your Own Data Files. PC STATISTICIAN Performs: Data Ranking; File Ranking; File Restructuring; File & Subfile Creation; Record or Case Selection; 1- to 5-Way Cross-Tabulation; 1- to 4-Way Data-File Search.
Dynacomp, Inc.

PC Study Bible for DOS: New American Standard Version. *Version:* 1.7. Dec. 1993. *Items Included:* Disks, marketing literature, order form, registration card, manual, free American Standard Version offer. *Customer Support:* No fee for customer support; 30 day money back guarantee, limited replacement warranty on diskettes defective at time of purchase, free telephone technical support.
PC-DOS/MS-DOS 3.1 or higher. IBM 386/486 or 100% compatible (640k). disk $69.95 (ISBN 1-56514-090-7). *Optimal configuration:* 5.25 1.2Mb disk drive for installation; 4Mb hard drive space; mouse or pointer device recommended.
A Computerized Cross-Reference Bible with Concordance, Nave's Topical Bible, & the New American Standard Version Text. Upon Return of Registration Card, Receive the American Standard Version Text of the Bible Free.
Biblesoft.

PC Study Bible for DOS: New American Standard Version. *Version:* 3.1. Dec. 1993. *Items Included:* Disks, marketing literature, order form, registration card, manual, free American Standard Version offer. *Customer Support:* No fee for customer support; 30 day money back guarantee, limited replacement warranty on diskettes defective at time of purchase, free telephone technical support.
PC-DOS/MS-DOS 3.1 or higher. IBM XT/AT/286/386/486 or 100% compatible (640k). 3.5" disk $69.95 (ISBN 1-56514-089-3). *Optimal configuration:* 3.5" 4Mb disk drive for installation; 4Mb hard drive space; mouse or pointer device recommended.
A Computerized Cross-Reference Bible with Concordance, Notepad, Nave's Topical Bible, & the New American Standard Version Text. Upon Return of Registration Card, Receive the American Standard Version Text of the Bible Free.
Biblesoft.

PC Study Bible for Windows. *Version:* 1.7. Sep. 1994. *Items Included:* Disks, marketing literature, order form, registration card, manual, free American Standard Version offer. *Customer Support:* No fee for customer support; 30 day money back guarantee, limited replacement warranty on diskettes defective at time of purchase, free telephone technical support.
PC-DOS/MS-DOS 3.1 or higher & Windows 3.1 or higher. IBM 386/486 or 100% compatibles (4Mb). 3.5" disk $129.95 (ISBN 1-56514-023-0). *Optimal configuration:* 3.5" disk drive for installation, 17Mb hard drive space; mouse or pointer device recommended.
PC Study Bible Program with King James Version Text, New International Version Text, Nave's Topical Bible, Nelson's Bible Dictionary, Bible Maps & Bible Book Outlines.
Biblesoft.

PC Study Bible for Windows: Discovery Plus Edition on CD-ROM. *Version:* 2.0. Sep. 1995. *Items Included:* Disks, marketing literature, order form, registration card, manual. *Customer Support:* No fee for customer support; 30 day money back guarantee, limited replacement warranty on diskettes defective at time of purchase, free telephone technical support.
PC-DOS/MS-DOS 3.1 or higher & Windows 3.1 or higher. IBM 386/486 or 100% compatibles (8Mb). CD-ROM disk $99.95 (ISBN 1-56514-134-2). *Addl. software required:* Biblesoft's PC Study Bible. *Optimal configuration:* CD-ROM drive for installation, 6.5Mb hard drive space; mouse or pointer device recommended.
PC Study Bible Program with King James Version Text, New International Version Text, American Standard Version 1901 Text, Concordances to Each Version, Personal Study Notes, Daily Bible Reading Plan, Nelson's Bible Outlines, Maps, Nave's Topical Bible, Nelson's Bible Dictionary, Treasury of Scripture Knowledge & Photo Collection.
Biblesoft.

TITLE INDEX

PC STUDY BIBLE FOR WINDOWS: NEW

PC Study Bible for Windows: King James Version Edition. *Version:* 2.0. Sep. 1995. *Items Included:* Disks, marketing literature, order form, registration card, manual, free American Standard Version offer. *Customer Support:* No fee for customer support: 30 day money back guarantee, limited replacement warranty on diskettes defective at time of purchase, free telephone technical support.
PC-DOS/MS-DOS 3.1 or higher or Windows 3.1 or higher. IBM 386/486 or 100% compatible (4Mb). 3.5" disk Contact publisher for price (ISBN 1-56514-128-8). *Addl. software required:* Biblesoft's PC Study Bible. *Optimal configuration:* 3.5 1.44Mb disk drive for installation; 6.5Mb hard drive space; mouse or pointer device recommended.
A Computerized Cross-Reference Bible with King James Version Bible Text, Maps, Outlines, Concordance, Nave's Topical Bible, Nelson's Bible Dictionary Text.
Biblesoft.

PC Study Bible for Windows: King James Version Edition. *Version:* 1.7. Sep. 1992. *Items Included:* Disks, marketing literature, order form, registration card, manual, free American Standard Version offer. *Customer Support:* No fee for customer support: 30 day money back guarantee, limited replacement warranty on diskettes defective at time of purchase, free telephone technical support.
PC-DOS/MS-DOS 3.1 or higher & Windows 3.1 or higher. IBM 386/486 or 100% compatibles (4Mb). disk $69.95 (ISBN 1-56514-175-X). *Optimal configuration:* Requires 5.25" 1.2Mb disk drive for installation & 5Mb of hard drive space, mouse or pointer device recommended.
A Computerized Cross-Reference Bible with Concordance, the Nave's Topical Bible & the King James Version Text. Upon Return of Registration Card - Receive the American Standard Version Text of the Bible Free.
Biblesoft.

PC Study Bible for Windows: King James Version Edition. *Version:* 1.7. *Items Included:* Disks, marketing literature, order form, registration card, manual, free American Standard Version text offer. *Customer Support:* No fee for customer support: 30 day money back guarantee, limited replacement warranty on diskettes defective at time of purchase, free telephone technical support.
PC-DOS/MS-DOS 3.1 or higher & Windows 3.1 or higher. IBM 386/486 or 100% compatibles (4Mb). 3.5" disk $69.95 (ISBN 1-56514-173-3). *Optimal configuration:* 3.5" 1.44Mb disk drive for installation & 3Mb of hard drive space, mouse or pointer device recommended.
A Computerized Cross-Reference Bible with Concordance, the Nave's Topical Bible & the King James Version Text. Upon Return of Registration Card - Receive the American Standard Version Text of the Bible Free.
Biblesoft.

PC Study Bible for Windows: King James Version Edition CD-ROM. *Version:* 1.7B. Apr. 1995. *Items Included:* CD, marketing literature, order form, jewel case, manual, registration card. *Customer Support:* No fee for customer support: 30 day money back guarantee, limited replacement warranty on diskettes defective at time of purchase, free telephone technical support.
PC-DOS/MS-DOS 3.1 or higher & Windows 3.1 or higher. IBM 386/486 or 100% compatibles (4Mb). CD-ROM disk Contact publisher for price (ISBN 1-56514-056-7). *Optimal configuration:* CD-ROM drive for installation, 2Mb hard drive space; mouse or pointer device recommended.
A Computerized Cross-Reference Bible with the Text of the King James Version of the Bible, Concordance, Nave's Topical Bible, Bible Maps & Bible Book Outlines on Compact Disk. The Text of the American Standard 1901 Version of the Bible Is Also Included.
Biblesoft.

PC Study Bible for Windows: King James Version on CD ROM. *Version:* 2.0. Sep. 1995. *Items Included:* Disks, marketing literature, order form, registration card, manual. *Customer Support:* No fee for customer support: 30 day money back guarantee, limited replacement warranty on diskettes defective at time of purchase; free telephone technical support.
PC-DOS/MS-DOS 3.1 or higher or Windows 3.1 or higher. IBM 386/486 or 100% compatible (8Mb). CD-ROM disk $49.95 (ISBN 1-56514-139-3). *Addl. software required:* Biblesoft's PC Study Bible. *Optimal configuration:* CD ROM drive for installation; 6.5Mb hard drive space; mouse or pointer device recommended.
PC Study Bible Program with King James Version Text, American Standard Version 1901 Text, Concordances to Each Version, Personal Study Notes, Daily Bible Reading Plan, Maps, Nave's Topical Bible, Nelson's Bible Dictionary & Photo Collection.
Biblesoft.

PC Study Bible for Windows: KJV Discovery Edition on CD ROM. *Version:* 2.0. Sep. 1995. *Items Included:* Disks, marketing literature, order form, registration card, manual. *Customer Support:* No fee for customer support: 30 day money back guarantee, limited replacement warranty on diskettes defective at time of purchase; free telephone technical support.
PC-DOS/MS-DOS 3.1 or higher or Windows 3.1 or higher. IBM 386/486 or 100% compatible (8Mb). CD-ROM disk $79.95 (ISBN 1-56514-135-0). *Addl. software required:* Biblesoft's PC Study Bible. *Optimal configuration:* CD ROM drive for installation; 6.5Mb hard drive space; mouse or pointer device recommended.
PC Study Bible Program with King James Version Text, American Standard Version 1901 Text, Concordances to Each Version, Personal Study Notes, Daily Bible Reading Plan, Maps, Nave's Topical Bible, Nelson's Bible Dictionary & Photo Collection.
Biblesoft.

PC Study Bible for WINDOWS KJV Edition. *Version:* 3.0. Sep. 1993. *Items Included:* One manual - perfect bound. *Customer Support:* No fee for customer support: (1) 30 day money back guarantee (2) Lifetime warranty replacement on defective disks (3) Free telephone technical support.
PC-DOS/MS-DOS 3.1 or higher & MS WINDOWS 3.1. IBM PC, XT/AT/286/386/486 or 100% compatibles (640k). disk $69.95 (ISBN 1-56514-175-X). *Optimal configuration:* Requires 5 1/4" 1.2Mb disk drive for installation & 5Mb of hard drive space. Mouse or pointer device recommended.
PC-DOS/MS-DOS 3.1 or higher & MS WINDOWS 3.1. IBM PC, XT/AT/286/386/486 or 100% compatibles (640k). 3.5" disk $69.95 (ISBN 1-56514-173-3). *Optimal configuration:* Requires 3 1/2" disk drive for installation & 5Mb of hard drive space. Mouse or pointer device recommended.
Computerized Cross-Reference Bible with Concordance, Notepad, Nave's Topical Bible, & the King James Version Text. Upon Return of Registration Card - Receive the American Standard Version Text of the Bible (Free of for a Minimal Charge).

PC Study Bible for WINDOWS MASTER Edition. *Version:* 3.0. Sep. 1993. *Items Included:* One manual - perfect bound. *Customer Support:* No fee for customer support: (1) 30 day money back guarantee (2) Lifetime warranty replacement on defective disks (3) Free telephone technical support.
PC-DOS/MS-DOS 3.1 or higher & MS WINDOWS 3.1. IBM PC, XT/AT/286/386/486 or 100% compatibles (640k). disk $149.95 (ISBN 1-56514-075-3). *Optimal configuration:* Requires 3 1/2" disk drive for installation & 10Mb of hard drive space. Mouse or pointer device recommended.
Computerized Cross-Reference Bible with Concordance, Notepad, Nave's Topical Bible, Nelson's Bible Dictionary Text, King James Version Text & the New International Version Text. Upon Return of Registration Card - Receive the American Standard Version Text of the Bible (Free of for a Minimal Charge).

PC Study Bible for WINDOWS MASTER Edition. *Version:* 3.0. Sep. 1993. *Items Included:* One manual - perfect bound. *Customer Support:* No fee for customer support: (1) 30 day money back guarantee (2) Lifetime warranty replacement on defective disks (3) Free telephone technical support.
PC-DOS/MS-DOS 3.1 or higher & MS WINDOWS 3.1. IBM PC, XT/AT/286/386/486 or 100% compatibles (640k). disk $149.95 (ISBN 1-56514-077-X). *Optimal configuration:* Requires 5 1/4" 1.2Mb disk drive for installation & 10Mb of hard drive space. Mouse or pointer device recommended.
Computerized Cross-Reference Bible with Concordance, Notepad, Nave's Topical Bible, Nelson's Bible Dictionary Text, King James Version Text & the New International Version Text. Upon Return of Registration Card - Receive the American Standard Version Text of the Bible (Free of for a Minimal Charge).

PC Study Bible for Windows: New American Standard Bible Discovery Edition on CD ROM. *Version:* 2.0. Sep. 1995. *Items Included:* Disks, marketing literature, order form, registration card, manual. *Customer Support:* No fee for customer support: 30 day money back guarantee; limited replacement warranty on diskettes defective at time of purchase; free telephone technical support.
PC-DOS/MS-DOS 3.1 or higher or Windows 3.1 or higher. IBM 386/486 or 100% compatible (8Mb). CD-ROM disk $79.95 (ISBN 1-56514-138-5). *Addl. software required:* Biblesoft's PC Study Bible. *Optimal configuration:* CD ROM drive for installation; 6.5Mb hard drive space; mouse or pointer device recommended.
PC Study Bible Program with King James Version Text, American Standard Version 1901 Text, Concordances to Each Version, Personal Study Notes, Daily Bible Reading Plan, Maps, Nave's Topical Bible, Nelson's Bible Dictionary & Photo Collection.
Biblesoft.

PC Study Bible for Windows: New American Standard Bible Edition. *Version:* 2.0. Sep. 1995. *Items Included:* Disks, marketing literature, order form, registration card, manual, free American Standard Version offer. *Customer Support:* No fee for customer support: 30 day money back guarantee, limited replacement warranty on diskettes defective at time of purchase, free telephone technical support.
PC-DOS/MS-DOS 3.1 or higher or Windows 3.1 or higher. IBM 386/486 or 100% compatible (4Mb). 3.5" disk Contact publisher for price (ISBN 1-56514-131-8). *Addl. software required:* Biblesoft's PC Study Bible.

PC STUDY BIBLE FOR WINDOWS: NEW

Optimal configuration: 3.5 1.44Mb disk drive for installation; 6.5Mb hard drive space; mouse or pointer device recommended.
A Computerized Cross-Reference Bible with Concordance, Notepad, the Nave's Topical Bible, & the New American Standard Bible Text. Upon Return of Registration Card - Receive the American Standard Version Text of the Bible Free.
Biblesoft.

PC Study Bible for Windows: New American Standard Version. *Version:* 1.7. Dec. 1993. *Items Included:* Disks, marketing literature, order form, registration card, manual, free American Standard Version offer. *Customer Support:* No fee for customer support: 30 day money back guarantee, limited replacement warranty on diskettes defective at time of purchase, free telephone technical support.
PC-DOS/MS-DOS 3.1 or higher or Windows 3.1 or higher. IBM 386/486 or 100% compatible (4Mb). disk $69.95 (ISBN 1-56514-092-3). *Optimal configuration:* 5.25 1.2Mb disk drive for installation; 11Mb hard drive space; mouse or pointer device recommended.
A Computerized Cross-Reference Bible with Concordance, Nave's Topical Bible, & the New American Standard Version Text. Upon Return of Registration Card - Receive the American Standard Version Text of the Bible Free.
Biblesoft.

PC Study Bible for Windows: New American Standard Version. *Version:* 1.7. Dec. 1993. *Items Included:* Disks, marketing literature, order form, registration card, manual, free American Standard Version offer. *Customer Support:* No fee for customer support: 30 day money back guarantee, limited replacement warranty on diskettes defective at time of purchase, free telephone technical support.
PC-DOS/MS-DOS 3.1 or higher or Windows 3.1 or higher. IBM 386/486 or 100% compatible (4Mb). 3.5" disk $69.95 (ISBN 1-56514-091-5).
PC Study Bible Program with the Text of the New American Standard Version of the Bible, a Concordance, Nave's Topical Bible, Bible Maps & Bible Book Outlines.
Biblesoft.

PC Study Bible for Windows: New International Version Edition. *Version:* 2.0. Sep. 1995. *Items Included:* Disks, marketing literature, order form, registration card, manual, free American Standard Version offer. *Customer Support:* No fee for customer support: 30 day money back guarantee, limited replacement warranty on diskettes defective at time of purchase, free telephone technical support.
PC-DOS/MS-DOS 3.1 or higher or Windows 3.1 or higher. IBM 386/486 or 100% compatible (4Mb). 3.5" disk Contact publisher for price (ISBN 1-56514-129-6). *Addl. software required:* Biblesoft's PC Study Bible. *Optimal configuration:* 3.5 1.44Mb disk drive for installation; 6.5Mb hard drive space; mouse or pointer device recommended.
A Computerized Cross-Reference Bible with New International Version Bible Text, Maps, Outlines, Concordance, Nave's Topical Bible, Nelson's Bible Dictionary Text.
Biblesoft.

PC Study Bible for Windows: New International Version Edition. *Version:* 1.7. Sep. 1992. *Items Included:* Disks, marketing literature, order form, registration card, manual, free American Standard Version text offer. *Customer Support:* No fee for customer support: 30 day money back guarantee, limited replacement warranty on diskettes defective at time of purchase, free telephone technical support.
PC-DOS/MS-DOS 3.1 or higher & Windows 3.1 or higher. 386/486 or 100% IBM PC compatible (4Mb). disk $69.95 (ISBN 1-56514-435-X). *Optimal configuration:* Requires 5.25" 1.2Mb disk drive for installation & 11Mb of hard drive space, mouse or pointer device recommended.
A Computerized Cross-Reference Bible with Concordance, the Nave's Topical Bible & the New International Version Text. Upon Return of Registration Card - Receive the American Standard Version Text of the Bible Free.
Biblesoft.

PC Study Bible for Windows: New International Version Edition. *Version:* 1.7. Sep. 1992. *Items Included:* Disks, marketing literature, order form, registration card, manual, free American Standard Version text offer. *Customer Support:* No fee for customer support: 30 day money back guarantee, limited replacement warranty on diskettes defective at time of purchase, free telephone technical support.
PC-DOS/MS-DOS 3.1 or higher & Windows 3.1 or higher. 386/486 or 100% IBM PC compatible (4Mb). 3.5" disk $69.95 (ISBN 1-56514-433-3). *Optimal configuration:* 3.5" 1.44Mb disk drive for installation; 11Mb of hard drive space, mouse or pointer device recommended.
A Computerized Cross-Reference Bible with Concordance, the Nave's Topical Bible & the New International Version Text. Upon Return of Registration Card - Receive the American Standard Version Text of the Bible Free.
Biblesoft.

PC Study Bible for Windows: New Internatinoal Version Edition CD-ROM. *Version:* 1.7B. Apr. 1995. *Items Included:* CD, marketing literature, order form, jewel case, manual, registration card. *Customer Support:* No fee for customer support: 30 day money back guarantee, limited replacement warranty on diskettes defective at time of purchase, free telephone technical support.
PC-DOS/MS-DOS 3.1 or higher & Windows 3.1 or higher. IBM 386/486 or 100% compatibles (4Mb). CD-ROM disk Contact publisher for price (ISBN 1-56514-058-3). *Optimal configuration:* CD-ROM drive for installation, 2Mb hard drive space; mouse or pointer device recommended.
A Computerized Cross-Reference Bible with the Text of the New International Version of the Bible, a Concordance, Nave's Topical Bible, Bible Maps, & Bible Book Outlines. American Standard Version 1901 Text Also Included.
Biblesoft.

PC Study Bible for Windows: New King James Version. *Version:* 1.7. Oct. 1993. *Items Included:* Disks, marketing literature, order form, registration card, manual, free American Standard Version text offer. *Customer Support:* No fee for customer support: 30 day money back guarantee, limited replacement warranty on diskettes defective at time of purchase, free telephone technical support.
PC-DOS/MS-DOS 3.1 or higher & Windows 3.1 or higher. IBM 386/486 or 100% compatible (4Mb). 3.5" disk $69.95 (ISBN 1-56514-084-2). *Optimal configuration:* 3.5" 1.44Mb disk drive for installation; 16Mb of hard drive space, mouse or pointer device recommended.
A Computerized Cross-Reference Bible with Concordance, Nave's Topical Bible & the New King James Version Text. Upon Return of the Registration Card - Receive the American Standard Version Text of the Bible Free.
Biblesoft.

PC Study Bible for Windows: New King James Version. *Version:* 1.7. Oct. 1993. *Items Included:* Disks, marketing literature, order form, registration card, manual, free American Standard Version text offer. *Customer Support:* No fee for customer support: 30 day money back guarantee, limited replacement warranty on diskettes defective at time of purchase, free telephone technical support.
PC-DOS/MS-DOS 3.1 or higher & Windows 3.1 or higher. IBM 386/486 or 100% compatible (4Mb). 3.5" disk $69.95 (ISBN 1-56514-083-4). *Optimal configuration:* 3.5" 1.44Mb disk drive for installation; 17Mb of hard drive space, mouse or pointer device recommended.
A Computerized Cross-Reference Bible with Concordance, Nave's Topical Bible & the New King James Version Text. Upon Return of the Registration Card - Receive the American Standard Version Text of the Bible Free.
Biblesoft.

PC Study Bible for Windows: New King James Version Edition. *Version:* 2.0. Sep. 1995. *Items Included:* Disks, marketing literature, order form, registration card, manual, free American Standard Version offer. *Customer Support:* No fee for customer support: 30 day money back guarantee, limited replacement warranty on diskettes defective at time of purchase, free telephone technical support.
PC-DOS/MS-DOS 3.1 or higher or Windows 3.1 or higher. IBM 386/486 or 100% compatible (4Mb). 3.5" disk Contact publisher for price (ISBN 1-56514-130-X). *Addl. software required:* Biblesoft's PC Study Bible. *Optimal configuration:* 3.5 1.44Mb disk drive for installation; 6.5Mb hard drive space; mouse or pointer device recommended.
A Computerized Cross-Reference Bible with Concordance, Notepad, the Nave's Topical Bible, & the New King James Version Text. Upon Return of Registration Card - Receive the American Standard Version Text of the Bible Free.
Biblesoft.

PC Study Bible for Windows: New Master Edition CD-ROM. *Version:* 1.7B. Apr. 1995. *Items Included:* CD, marketing literature, order form, jewel case, manual, registration card. *Customer Support:* No fee for customer support: 30 day money back guarantee, limited replacement warranty on diskettes defective at time of purchase, free telephone technical support.
PC-DOS/MS-DOS 3.1 or higher & Windows 3.1 or higher. IBM 386/486 or 100% compatibles (4Mb). CD-ROM disk CD-ROM disk Contact publisher for price (ISBN 1-56514-054-0). *Optimal configuration:* CD-ROM drive for installation, 2Mb hard drive space; mouse or pointer device recommended.
A Computerized Cross-Reference Bible with Concordance, Nave's Topical Bible, Nelson's Bible Dictionary Text, King James Version of the Bible Text, New International Version of the Bible Text, American Standard Version 1901 Bible Text.
Biblesoft.

PC Study Bible for Windows: New Master Edition. *Version:* 2.0. Sep. 1995. *Items Included:* Disks, marketing literature, order form, registration card, manual, free American Standard Version text offer. *Customer Support:* No fee for customer support: 30 day money back guarantee, limited replacement warranty on diskettes defective at time of purchase; free telephone technical support.
PC-DOS/MS-DOS 3.1 or higher or Windows 3.1 or higher. IBM 386/486 or 100% compatible (4Mb). 3.5" disk $129.95 (ISBN 1-56514-127-X). *Addl. software required:*

TITLE INDEX

PC STUDY BIBLE FOR WINDOWS: REFERENCE

Biblesoft's PC Study Bible. *Optimal configuration:* 3.5" 1.44Mb disk drive for installation; 6.5Mb hard drive space; mouse or pointer device recommended.
PC Study Bible Program with King James Version Text, New International Version Text, Concordances to Each Version, Annotations, Maps, Nave's Topical Bible, Nelson's Bible Dictionary, Treasury of Scripture Knowledge.
Biblesoft.

PC Study Bible for Windows: New Reference Library. *Version:* 2.0. Sep. 1995. *Items Included:* Disks, marketing literature, order form, registration card, manual, free American Standard Version text offer. *Customer Support:* No fee for customer support: 30 day money back guarantee; limited replacement warranty on diskettes defective at time of purchase; free telephone technical support.
PC-DOS/MS-DOS 3.1 or higher or Windows 3.1 or higher. IBM 386/486 or 100% compatible (4Mb). 3.5" disk $179.95 (ISBN 1-56514-126-1). *Addl. software required:* Biblesoft's PC Study Bible. *Optimal configuration:* 3.5" 1.44Mb disk drive for installation; 6.5Mb hard drive space; mouse or pointer device recommended.
PC Study Bible Program with King James Version Text, New International Version Text, New American Standard Version Text, Concordances to Each Version, Annotations, Daily Bible Reading Plan, Maps, Nave's Topical Bible, Nelson's Bible Dictionary, Treasury of Scripture Knowledge, Strong's Vines, Interlinear Bible, Thayers Brown-Driver-Briggs, 6-Volume Set of Matthew Henry's Commentary, 100 Photos & Life Application Notes.
Biblesoft.

PC Study Bible for Windows: New Reference Library CD-ROM. *Version:* 1.7B. Apr. 1995. *Items Included:* CD, marketing literature, order form, jewel case, manual, registration card. *Customer Support:* No fee for customer support: 30 day money back guarantee; limited replacement warranty on diskettes defective at time of purchase, free telephone technical support.
PC-DOS/MS-DOS 3.1 or higher & Windows 3.1 or higher. IBM 386/486 or 100% compatibles (4Mb). CD-ROM disk $179.95 (ISBN 1-56514-052-4). *Optimal configuration:* CD-ROM drive for installation, 2Mb hard drive space; mouse or pointer device recommended.
A Computerized Cross-Reference Bible with King James Version Text, New International Version Text, Concordances, Nave's Topical Bible, Nelson's Bible Dictionary, Treasury of Scripture Knowledge, Strong's Greek-Hebrew Dictionary, Englishman's Greek Hebrew Concordance, Bible Maps, & Bible Outlines.
Biblesoft.

PC Study Bible for Windows: New Reference Library Edition. *Version:* 1.7. Oct. 1992. *Items Included:* Disks, marketing literature, order form, registration card, manual, free American Standard Version offer. *Customer Support:* No fee for customer support: 30 day money back guarantee, limited replacement warranty on diskettes defective at time of purchase, free telephone technical support.
PC-DOS/MS-DOS 3.1 or higher & Windows 3.1 or higher. IBM 386/486 or 100% compatible (4Mb). 3.5" disk $179.95 (ISBN 1-56514-018-4).
PC Study Bible Program with the Text of the New American Standard Version of the Bible, a Concordance, Nave's Topical Bible, Bible Maps & Bible Book Outlines.
Biblesoft.

PC Study Bible for Windows: New Reference Library on CD-ROM. *Version:* 2.0. Sep. 1995. *Items Included:* Disks, marketing literature, order form, registration card, manual. *Customer Support:* No fee for customer support: 30 day money back guarantee, limited replacement warranty on diskettes defective at time of purchase, free telephone technical support.
PC-DOS/MS-DOS 3.1 or higher & Windows 3.1 or higher. IBM 386/486 or 100% compatibles (8Mb). CD-ROM disk $149.95 (ISBN 1-56514-133-4). *Addl. software required:* Biblesoft's PC Study Bible. *Optimal configuration:* CD-ROM drive for installation, 6.5Mb hard drive space; mouse or pointer device recommended.
PC Study Bible Program with King James Version Text, New International Version Text, New King James Text, New American Standard Version Text, Concordances to Each Version, Annotations, Daily Bible Reading Plan, Nelson's Bible Outlines, Nave's Topical Bible, Nelson's Bible Dictionary, Treasury of Scripture Knowledge, Strong's Englishman's Vines, Thayers, Brown-Driver-Briggs, 6-Volume Set of Matthew Henry's Commentary & Photo Collection.
Biblesoft.

PC Study Bible for Windows: NIV Discovery Edition on CD-ROM. *Version:* 2.0. Sep. 1995. *Items Included:* Disks, marketing literature, order form, registration card, manual. *Customer Support:* No fee for customer support: 30 day money back guarantee, limited replacement warranty on diskettes defective at time of purchase, free telephone technical support.
PC-DOS/MS-DOS 3.1 or higher & Windows 3.1 or higher. IBM 386/486 or 100% compatibles (8Mb). CD-ROM disk $79.95 (ISBN 1-56514-136-9). *Addl. software required:* Biblesoft's PC Study Bible. *Optimal configuration:* CD-ROM drive for installation, 6.5Mb hard drive space; mouse or pointer device recommended.
PC Study Bible Program with New International Version Text, American Standard Version Text, Concordances to Each Version, Personal Study Notes, Daily Bible Reading Plan, Nelson's Bible Outlines, Maps, Nave's Topical Bible, Nelson's Bible Dictionary & Photo Collection.
Biblesoft.

PC Study Bible for WINDOWS NIV Edition. *Version:* 3.0. Sep. 1993. *Items Included:* One manual - perfect bound. *Customer Support:* No fee for customer support: (1) 30 day money back guarantee (2) Lifetime warranty replacement on defective disks (3) Free telephone technical support.
PC-DOS/MS-DOS 3.1 or higher & MS WINDOWS 3.1. IBM PC, XT/AT/286/386/486 or 100% compatibles (640k). disk $69.95 (ISBN 1-56514-435-X). *Optimal configuration:* Requires 5 1/4" 1.2Mb disk drive for installation & 5Mb of hard drive space. Mouse or pointer device recommended.
Computerized Cross-Reference Bible with Concordance, Notepad, Nave's Topical Bible, & the New International Version Text. Upon Return of Registration Card - Receive the American Standard Version Text of the Bible (Free of for a Minimal Charge).

PC Study Bible for WINDOWS NIV Edition. *Version:* 3.0. Sep. 1993. *Items Included:* One manual - perfect bound. *Customer Support:* No fee for customer support: (1) 30 day money back guarantee (2) Lifetime warranty replacement on defective disks (3) Free telephone technical support.
PC-DOS/MS-DOS 3.1 or higher & MS WINDOWS 3.1. IBM PC, XT/AT/286/386/486 or 100% compatibles (640k). disk $69.95 (ISBN 1-56514-433-3). *Optimal configuration:* Requires 3 1/2" disk drive for installation & 5Mb of hard drive space. Mouse or pointer device recommended.
Computerized Cross-Reference Bible with Concordance, Notepad, Nave's Topical Bible, & the New International Version Text. Upon Return of Registration Card - Receive the American Standard Version Text of the Bible (Free of for a Minimal Charge).

PC Study Bible for Windows: NKJ Discovery Edition on CD ROM. *Version:* 2.0. Sep. 1995. *Items Included:* Disks, marketing literature, order form, registration card, manual. *Customer Support:* No fee for customer support: 30 day money back guarantee; limited replacement warranty on diskettes defective at time of purchase; free telephone technical support.
PC-DOS/MS-DOS 3.1 or higher or Windows 3.1 or higher. IBM 386/486 or 100% compatible (8Mb). CD-ROM disk $79.95 (ISBN 1-56514-137-7). *Addl. software required:* Biblesoft's PC Study Bible. *Optimal configuration:* CD ROM drive for installation; 6.5Mb hard drive space; mouse or pointer device recommended.
PC Study Bible Program with King James Version Text, American Standard Version 1901 Text, Concordances to Each Version, Personal Study Notes, Daily Bible Reading Plan, Maps, Nave's Topical Bible, Nelson's Bible Dictionary & Photo Collection.
Biblesoft.

PC Study Bible for Windows: Reference Library Plus. *Version:* 2.0. Sep. 1995. *Items Included:* Disks, marketing literature, order form, registration card, manual, free American Standard Version text offer. *Customer Support:* No fee for customer support: 30 day money back guarantee; limited replacement warranty on diskettes defective at time of purchase; free telephone technical support.
PC-DOS/MS-DOS 3.1 or higher or Windows 3.1 or higher. IBM 386/486 or 100% compatible (4Mb). 3.5" disk $249.95 (ISBN 1-56514-125-3). *Optimal configuration:* 3.5" 1.44Mb disk drive for installation; 6.5Mb hard drive space; mouse or pointer device recommended.
PC Study Bible Program with King James Version Text, New International Version Text, New American Standard Version Text, Concordances to Each Version, Annotations, Daily Bible Reading Plan, Maps, Nave's Topical Bible, Nelson's Bible Dictionary, Treasury of Scripture Knowledge, Strong's Vines, Interlinear Bible, Thayers Brown-Driver-Briggs, 6-Volume Set of Matthew Henry's Commentary, ISBE, Unger's Bible Dictionary, Photo Collection & Life Application Notes.
Biblesoft.

PC Study Bible for Windows: Reference Library Plus. *Version:* 1.7. Nov. 1994. *Items Included:* Disks, marketing literature, order form, registration card, manual, free American Standard Version offer. *Customer Support:* No fee for customer support: 30 day money back guarantee, limited replacement warranty on diskettes defective at time of purchase, free telephone technical support.
PC-DOS/MS-DOS 3.1 or higher & Windows 3.1 or higher. IBM 386/486 or 100% compatible (4Mb). 3.5" disk $249.95 (ISBN 1-56514-021-4). *Optimal configuration:* 3.5", 1.44Mb disk drive for installation, mouse or pointer device recommended.
PC Study Bible Program with King James Version Text, New International Version Text, New American Standard Version Text, Concordances to Each Version. Also, Nave's Topical Bible, Nelson's Bible Dictionary, Treasury of Scripture Knowledge, Strong's Greek Hebrew Dictionary, Englishman's Concordance, Vine's Expository Dictionary, Interlinear Bible, Bible Maps & Bible Book Outlines.
Biblesoft.

PC STUDY BIBLE FOR WINDOWS REFERENCE

PC Study Bible for WINDOWS Reference Library Edition. *Version:* 3.0. Sep. 1993. *Items Included:* One manual - perfect bound. *Customer Support:* No fee for customer support: (1) 30 day money back guarantee (2) Lifetime warranty replacement on defective disks (3) Free telephone technical support.
PC-DOS/MS-DOS 3.1 or higher & MS WINDOWS 3.1. IBM PC, XT/AT/286/386/486 or 100% compatibles (640k). disk $239.95 (ISBN 1-56514-015-X). *Optimal configuration:* Requires 5 1/4" 1.2Mb disk drive for installation & 17Mb of hard drive space. Mouse or pointer device recommended.
PC-DOS/MS-DOS 3.1 or higher & MS WINDOWS 3.1. IBM PC, XT/AT/286/386/486 or 100% compatibles (640k). 3.5" disk $239.95 (ISBN 1-56514-013-3). *Optimal configuration:* Requires 3 1/2" disk drive for installation & 17Mb of hard drive space. Mouse or pointer device recommended.
Computerized Cross-Reference Bible with Concordance, Notepad, Nave's Topical Bible, Nelson's Bible Dictionary Text, Strong's Greek-Hebrew Dictionary, Englishman's Concordance, Vine's Expository Dictionary of Biblical Words, King James Version Text & the New International Version Text. Upon Return of Registration Card - Receive the American Standard Version Text of the Bible (Free or for a Minimal Charge).

PC Study Bible for Windows: Reference Library Plus with Matthew Henry CD-ROM. *Version:* 1.7B. Dec. 1994. *Items Included:* CD, marketing literature, order form, jewel case, manual, registration card. *Customer Support:* No fee for customer support: 30 day money back guarantee, limited replacement warranty on diskettes defective at time of purchase, free telephone technical support.
PC-DOS/MS-DOS 3.1 or higher & Windows 3.1 or higher. IBM 386/486 or 100% compatibles (4Mb). CD-ROM disk $279.95 (ISBN 1-56514-050-8). *Optimal configuration:* CD-ROM drive for installation, 2Mb hard drive space; mouse or pointer device recommended.
A Computerized Cross-Reference Bible with King James Version Text, New International Version Text, New American Standard Text, Nave's Topical Bible, Nelson's Bible Dictionary, Concordances for Each Bible Version Text, the Treasury of Scripture Knowledge, Strong's Greek-Hebrew Dictionary, Englishman's Greek Hebrew Concordance, Vine's Expository Dictionary, Interlinear Bible, Bible Maps, Bible Book Outlines & the Entire Six-Volume Matthew Henry Commentary.
Biblesoft.

PC Study Bible for Windows: Reference Library Plus with Matthew Henry on CD-ROM. *Version:* 2.0. Sep. 1995. *Items Included:* Disks, marketing literature, order form, registration card, manual, free American Standard Version text offer. *Customer Support:* No fee for customer support: 30 day money back guarantee, limited replacement warranty on diskettes defective at time of purchase, free telephone technical support.
PC-DOS/MS-DOS 3.1 or higher & Windows 3.1 or higher. IBM 386/486 or 100% compatibles (8Mb). CD-ROM disk $249.95 (ISBN 1-56514-132-6). *Optimal configuration:* CD-ROM drive for installation, 6.5Mb hard drive space; mouse or pointer device recommended.
PC Study Bible Program with King James Version Text, New International Version Text, New King James Version Text, New American Standard Version Text, American Standard 1901 Version Text, Concordances to Each Version, Personal Study Notes, Daily Bible Reading Plan, Maps, Nave's Topical Bible, Nelson's Bible Dictionary, Treasury of Scripture Knowledge, Strong's Englishman's Vines, Interlinear Bible, Thayers, Brown-Driver-Briggs, 6-Volume Set of Matthew Henry's Commentary, ISBE, Unger's Bible Dictionary & Photo Collection.
Biblesoft.

PC Study Bible: King James Version. *Version:* 3.0. Sep. 1992. *Items Included:* Disks, marketing literature, order form, registration card, manual, free American Standard Version text offer. *Customer Support:* No fee for customer support: 30 day money back guarantee, limited replacement warranty on diskettes defective at time of purchase, free telephone technical support.
PC-DOS/MS-DOS 3.1 or higher. IBM 386/486 or 100% compatibles (640k). 3.5" disk $69.95 (ISBN 1-56514-603-4). *Optimal configuration:* 3.5" 1.44Mb disk drive for installation; 4Mb of hard drive space, mouse or pointer device recommended.
A Computerized Cross-Reference Bible with Concordance, Notepad, Nave's Topical Bible & the King James Version Text. Upon Return of Registration Card - Receive the American Standard Version Text of the Bible Free.
Biblesoft.

PC Study Bible: KJV Edition. *Version:* 3.0. Sep. 1992. *Items Included:* Disks, marketing literature, order form, registration card, manual, free American Standard Version text offer. *Customer Support:* No fee for customer support: 30 day money back guarantee, limited replacement warranty on diskettes defective at time of purchase, free telephone technical support.
PC-DOS/MS-DOS 3.1 or higher. XT/AT/286/386/486 or 100% IBM PC compatible (640k). disk $69.95 (ISBN 1-56514-605-0). *Optimal configuration:* 5.25" 1.2Mb disk drive for installation & 5Mb of hard drive space, mouse or pointer device recommended.
A Computerized Cross-Reference Bible with Concordance, Notepad, the Nave's Topical Bible & the King James Version Text. Upon Return of Registration Card - Receive the American Standard Version Text of the Bible Free.
Biblesoft.

PC Study Bible KJV Edition. *Version:* 3.0. Sep. 1992. *Items Included:* One manual - perfect bound. *Customer Support:* No fee for customer support: (1) 30 day money back guarantee (2) Lifetime warranty replacement on defective disks (3) Free telephone technical support.
PC-DOS/MS-DOS 3.1 or higher. IBM PC, XT/AT/286/386/486 or 100% compatibles (640k). disk $69.95 (ISBN 1-56514-605-0). *Optimal configuration:* Requires 5 1/4" 1.2Mb disk drive for installation & 5Mb of hard drive space. Mouse or pointer device recommended.
PC-DOS/MS-DOS 3.1 or higher. IBM PC, XT/AT/286/386/486 or 100% compatibles (640k). 3.5" disk $69.95 (ISBN 1-56514-603-4). *Optimal configuration:* Requires 3 1/2" disk drive for installation & 5Mb of hard drive space. Mouse or pointer device recommended.
Computerized Cross-Reference Bible with Concordance, Notepad, Nave's Topical Bible, & the King James Version Text. Upon Return of Registration Card - Receive the American Standard Version Text of the Bible (Free of for a Minimal Charge).

PC Study Bible: Master Edition. *Version:* 3.0. Sep. 1992. *Items Included:* One manual. *Customer Support:* No fee is charged for our customer support: 30 day money back return guarantee; lifetime warranty on defective disk replacement; free telephone technical support.
PC or MS-DOS 2.0 or higher. IBM PC/XT/AT or compatible. 3.5" or 5.25" disk $149.00. *Optimal configuration:* Hard disk with 8Mb hard disk space.
Computerized Parallel Cross-Reference Bible, Concordance, & Word Processor with the Text of the King James Version, the New International Version, Nave's Topical Bible, Nelson's Illustrated Bible Dictionary & upon Return of Registration Card & $5.00, the Text of the American Standard Version of the Bible.
Biblesoft.

PC Study Bible: Master Edition. *Version:* 3.0. Sep. 1992. *Items Included:* Disks, marketing literature, order form, registration card, manual, free American Standard Version text offer. *Customer Support:* No fee for customer support: 30 day money back guarantee, limited replacement warranty on diskettes defective at time of purchase, free telephone technical support.
PC-DOS/MS-DOS 3.1 or higher. XT/AT/286/386/486 or 100% IBM PC compatible (640k). disk $99.95 (ISBN 1-56514-705-7). *Optimal configuration:* Requires 5.25 1.2Mb disk drive for installation; 10Mb of hard drive space, mouse or pointer device recommended.
A Computerized Cross-Reference Bible with Concordance, Notepad, the Nave's Topical Bible, Nelson's Bible Dictionary Text, King James Version Text & the New International Version Text. Upon Return of Registration Card Receive the American Standard Version Text of the Bible Free.
Biblesoft.

PC Study Bible: Master Edition. *Version:* 3.0. Sep. 1992. *Items Included:* Disks, marketing literature, order form, registration card, manual, free American Standard Version text offer. *Customer Support:* No fee for customer support: 30 day money back guarantee, limited replacement warranty on diskettes defective at time of purchase, free telephone technical support.
PC-DOS/MS-DOS 3.1 or higher. IBM 386/486 or 100% compatible (640k). 3.5" disk $99.95 (ISBN 1-56514-703-0). *Optimal configuration:* 3.5" 1.44Mb disk drive for installation; 10Mb of hard drive space, mouse or pointer device recommended.
A Computerized Cross-Reference Bible with Notepad, Concordance, Nave's Topical Bible, Nelson's Bible Dictionary Text, King James Version Text & the New International Version Text. Free American Standard Version upon Return of Registration Card.
Biblesoft.

PC Study Bible MASTER Edition. *Version:* 3.0. Sep. 1992. *Items Included:* One manual - perfect bound. *Customer Support:* No fee for customer support: (1) 30 day money back guarantee (2) Lifetime warranty replacement on defective disks (3) Free telephone technical support.
PC-DOS/MS-DOS 3.1 or higher. IBM PC, XT/AT/286/386/486 or 100% compatibles (640k). disk $149.95 (ISBN 1-56514-705-7). *Optimal configuration:* Requires 5 1/4" 1.2Mb disk drive for installation & 10Mb of hard drive space. Mouse or pointer device recommended.
PC-DOS/MS-DOS 3.1 or higher. IBM PC, XT/AT/286/386/486 & 100% compatibles (640k). 3.5" disk $149.95 (ISBN 1-56514-703-0). *Optimal configuration:* Requires 3 1/2" disk drive for installation & 10Mb of hard drive space. Mouse or pointer device recommended.
Computerized Cross-Reference Bible with Concordance, Notepad, Nave's Topical Bible, Nelson's Bible Dictionary Text, King James Version Text & the New International Version Text. Upon Return of Registration Card - Receive the American Standard Version Text of the Bible (Free of for a Minimal Charge).

TITLE INDEX

PC Study Bible New International Edition: PC Study Bible with Nave's - NIV. Sep. 1992. *Items Included:* One manual. *Customer Support:* No fee is charged for our customer support: 30 day money back return guarantee; lifetime warrenty on defective disk replacement; free telephone technical support.
PC or MS-DOS 2.0 or higher. IBM PC/XT/AT or compatible. 3.5" or 5.25" disk $69.95. *Optimal configuration:* Hard disk with 3.5Mb hard disk space.
Computerized Bible (with the Text of the New International Version of the Bible), Concordance, Word Processor & Nave's Topical Bible. The Text of the American Standard Version of the Bible Will Be Added for $5.00 Once the Registration Card Is Received.
Biblesoft.

PC Study Bible: New International Version Edition. *Version:* 3.1. Sep. 1992. *Items Included:* Disks, marketing literature, order form, registration card, manual, free American Standard Version text offer. *Customer Support:* No fee for customer support: 30 day money back guarantee, limited replacement warranty on diskettes defective at time of purchase, free telephone technical support.
PC-DOS/MS-DOS 3.1 or higher. XT/AT/286/386/486 or 100% IBM PC compatible (640k). disk $69.95 (ISBN 1-56514-615-8). *Optimal configuration:* 5.25" disk drive for installation & 5Mb of hard drive space, mouse or pointer device recommended.
A Computerized Cross-Reference Bible with Concordance, Notepad, the Nave's Topical Bible & New International Version Text. Upon Return of Registration Card - Receive the American Standard Version Text of the Bible Free.
Biblesoft.

PC Study Bible: New International Version Edition. *Version:* 3.0. Sep. 1992. *Items Included:* Disks, marketing literature, order form, registration card, manual, free American Standard Version text offer. *Customer Support:* No fee for customer support: 30 day money back guarantee, limited replacement warranty on diskettes defective at time of purchase, free telephone technical support.
PC-DOS/MS-DOS 3.1 or higher. IBM 386/486 or 100% compatible (640k). 3.5" disk $69.95 (ISBN 1-56514-613-1). *Optimal configuration:* 3.5" 1.44Mb disk drive for installation; 4Mb of hard drive space, mouse or pointer device recommended.
A Computerized Cross-Reference Bible with Notepad, Concordance, Nave's Topical Bible & the New International Version Text. Free American Standard Version upon Return of Registration Card.
Biblesoft.

PC Study Bible: New King James Version. *Version:* 3.1. Oct. 1993. *Items Included:* Disks, marketing literature, order form, registration card, manual, free American Standard Version text offer. *Customer Support:* No fee for customer support: 30 day money back guarantee, limited replacement warranty on diskettes defective at time of purchase, free telephone technical support.
PC-DOS/MS-DOS 3.1 or higher. IBM 386/486 or 100% compatible (640k). disk $69.95 (ISBN 1-56514-082-6). *Optimal configuration:* 5.25" 1.2Mb disk drive for installation; 4Mb of hard drive space, mouse or pointer device recommended.
A Computerized Cross-Reference Bible with Concordance, Notepad, Nave's Topical Bible & the New King James Version Text. Upon Return of the Registration Card - Receive the American Standard Version Text of the Bible Free.
Biblesoft.

PC Study Bible: New King James Version. *Version:* 3.1. Oct. 1993. *Items Included:* Disks, marketing literature, order form, registration card, manual, free American Standard Version text offer. *Customer Support:* No fee for customer support: 30 day money back guarantee, limited replacement warranty on diskettes defective at time of purchase, free telephone technical support.
PC-DOS/MS-DOS 3.1 or higher. IBM 386/486 or 100% compatible (640k). 3.5" disk $69.95 (ISBN 1-56514-081-8). *Optimal configuration:* 3.5" 1.44Mb disk drive for installation; 4Mb of hard drive space, mouse or pointer device recommended.
A Computerized Cross-Reference Bible with Concordance, Notepad, Nave's Topical Bible & the New King James Version Text. Upon Return of the Registration Card - Receive the American Standard Version Text of the Bible Free.
Biblesoft.

PC Study Bible NIV Edition. *Version:* 3.0. Sep. 1992. *Items Included:* One manual - perfect bound. *Customer Support:* No fee for customer support: (1) 30 day money back guarantee (2) Lifetime warranty replacement on defective disks (3) Free telephone technical support.
PC-DOS/MS-DOS 3.1 or higher. IBM PC, XT/AT/286/386/486 or 100% compatibles (640k). disk $69.95 (ISBN 1-56514-615-8). *Optimal configuration:* Requires 5 1/4" 1.2Mb disk drive for installation & 5Mb of hard drive space. Mouse or pointer device recommended.
PC-DOS/MS-DOS 3.1 or higher. IBM PC, XT/AT/286/386/486 or 100% compatibles (640k). 3.5" disk $69.95 (ISBN 1-56514-613-1). *Optimal configuration:* Requires 3 1/2" disk drive for installation & 5Mb of hard drive space. Mouse or pointer device recommended.
Computerized Cross-Reference Bible with Concordance, Notepad, Nave's Topical Bible, & the New International Version Text. Upon Return of Registration Card - Receive the American Standard Version Text of the Bible (Free of for a Minimal Charge).

PC Study Bible Reference Libary Edition. *Version:* 3.0. Sep. 1992. *Items Included:* One manual - perfect bound. *Customer Support:* No fee for customer support: (1) 30 day money back guarantee (2) Lifetime warranty replacement on defective disks (3) Free telephone technical support.
PC-DOS/MS-DOS 3.1 or higher. IBM PC, XT/AT/286/386/486 or 100% compatibles (640k). disk $239.95 (ISBN 1-56514-805-3). *Optimal configuration:* Requires 5 1/4" 1.2Mb disk drive for installation & 17Mb of hard drive space. Mouse or pointer device recommended.
Computerized Cross-Reference Bible with Concordance, Notepad, Nave's Topical Bible, Nelson's Bible Dictionary Text, Strong's Greek-Hebrew Dictionary, Englishman's Concordance, Vine's Expository Dictionary of Biblical Words, King James Version Text & the New International Version Text. Upon Return of Registration Card - Receive the American Standard Version Text of the Bible (Free of for a Minimal Charge).

PC Study Bible: Reference Library Edition. *Version:* 3.0. Sep. 1992. *Items Included:* One manual. *Customer Support:* No fee is charged for customer support; 30 day money back guarantee; lifetime warranty on defective disk replacement; free telephone technical support.
DOS 2 & higher. IBM (512k). 5.25" diskettes, contact publisher for price (ISBN 1-56514-805-3). *Optimal configuration:* Requires 15.5Mb of hard disk storage.
3.5" diskettes, contact publisher for price (ISBN 1-56514-803-7).
Computer-Based Parallel Cross-Reference Bible, Concordance, & Word Processor with the Text of the King James & New International Translations of the Bible. Includes Nave's Topical Bible, Nelson's Illustrated Bible Dictionary, Strong's Greek-Hebrew Dictionary, Englishman's Greek-Hebrew Concordance, Vine's Expository Dictionary of New Testament Word Combined with Nelson's Expository Dictionary of the Old Testament. Upon Return of Registration Card & $5.00, the American Standard Version of the Bible Will Be Sent to the Purchaser.
Biblesoft.

PC Study Bible: Reference Library Edition. *Version:* 3.0. Sep. 1992. *Items Included:* Disks, marketing literature, order form, registration card, manual, free American Standard Version text offer. *Customer Support:* No fee for customer support: 30 day money back guarantee, limited replacement warranty on diskettes defective at time of purchase, free telephone technical support.
PC-DOS/MS-DOS 3.1 or higher. XT/AT/286/386/486 or 100% IBM compatible (640k). disk $179.95 (ISBN 1-56514-805-3). *Optimal configuration:* Requires 5.25" 1.44Mb disk drive for installation & 17Mb of hard drive space, mouse or pointer device recommended.
A Computerized Cross-Reference Bible with Concordance, Notepad, Nave's Topical Bible, Nelson's Bible Dictionary Text, Strong's Greek-Hebrew Dictionary, Englishman's Concordance, Vine's Expository Dictionary of Biblical Words, King James Version Text & the New International Version Text. Upon Return of the Registration Card - Receive the American Standard Version Text of the Bible Free.
Biblesoft.

PC Study Bible Reference Library Edition. *Version:* 3.0. Sep. 1992. *Items Included:* One manual - perfect bound. *Customer Support:* No fee for customer support: (1) 30 day money back guarantee (2) Lifetime warranty replacement on defective disks (3) Free telephone technical support.
PC-DOS/MS-DOS 3.1 or higher. IBM PC, XT/AT/286/386/486 or 100% compatibles (640k). 3.5" disk $239.95 (ISBN 1-56514-803-7). *Optimal configuration:* Requires 3 1/2" disk drive for installation & 17Mb of hard drive space. Mouse or pointer device recommended.
Computerized Cross-Reference Bible with Concordance, Notepad, Nave's Topical Bible, Nelson's Bible Dictionary Text, Strong's Greek-Hebrew Dictionary, Englishman's Concordance, Vine's Expository Dictionary of Biblical Words, King James Version Text & the New International Version Text. Upon Return of Registration Card - Receive the American Standard Version Text of the Bible (Free of for a Minimal Charge).

PC-Sweep. William H. Zaggle. Oct. 1984. *Operating System(s) Required:* CP/M, MS-DOS. *Memory Required:* CP/M 56k, MS-DOS 128k. $49.00.
Utility Program That Allows User to Perform File Operations. Single Keystroke Commands Will Copy, Rename, Delete, Sort, View, Print & "Tag" Files. Also Displays the Directory of Any Given Drive, Protects the User from Invalid Drive Designators, Displays Disk Parameter Information, & Shows All Tagged & Untagged Files.
Elite Software Development, Inc.

PC-Talk III. Apr. 1983. *Compatible Hardware:* IBM PC & compatibles. *Operating System(s) Required:* PC-DOS, MS-DOS. *Language(s):* BASIC (source code included). *Memory Required:* 64k.
$35.00, incl. guide.
Communications Program That Uploads & Downloads Files & Has a 60 Entry Auto-Dial

Directory. *Optional Parameters in the Dialing Directory Allow Selective Character Stripping/ Converting & Storing of Pacing Instructions for Each Entry. Transmit Option Allows for Transmitting Binary Files, Line Pacing Files & Transmitting Files Using XModem Error-Checking Protocol at 300 to 1200 Baud. There Are 40 Programmable Permanent Logon/Input Strings.*
Jerome Headlands Pr.

PC-TAX. *Compatible Hardware:* Tandy. *Operating System(s) Required:* MS-DOS. *Language(s):* Basic.
contact publisher for price.
manual $7.50, incl. demo disk - *Computerizing the Professional Tax Office.*
Supplies Telephone Support Through the Tax Season. Ships Systems to Users Order in Advance of the Tax Season. Computes All Tax Amounts, All Fixed & Income-Related Limitations. Automatically Totals W-2's, Income Averages, Computes Depreciation, etc.
Contract Services Assocs.

PC TEX. *Version:* 3.14. 1992. *Compatible Hardware:* IBM PC & compatibles, PC XT, PC AT. *Operating System(s) Required:* PC-DOS/MS-DOS 2.0 or higher. *Language(s):* Pascal, C. *Memory Required:* 512k. *General Requirements:* Hard disk for printer drivers & fonts; any dot matrix, deskjet or laser printer. *Customer Support:* Free technical support.
disk $199.00.
Personal Computer Typesetting Software.
Personal Tex, Inc.

PC Tex: Personal Computer Typesetting Software. *Version:* 3.14. 1992. *Items Included:* Two tutorial books, installation guides, typesetting ruler. *Customer Support:* Free technical support to registered users.
PC-DOS/MS-DOS. IBM 286, 386, 486 or compatible (512k). disk $199.00. *Addl. software required:* Text editor or word processor. *Networks supported:* Most networks are supported.
Typesetting Software for Desktop Publishing.
Personal Tex, Inc.

PC to Host Networks & Applications. *Version:* 2.0. Edutrends, Inc. & Delphi, Inc. 1990. *Customer Support:* 30 day free phone support.
MS-DOS, PC-DOS. IBM PC, PS/2 & compatibles (640K). disk $495.00 (ISBN 0-935987-50-9). *Nonstandard peripherals required:* CGA, EGA or VGA graphics board with color monitor. Monochrome monitor with hercules graphics board.
Interactive Computer Based Training Course Which Teaches PC to Mainframe Communications. Topics Include PC to Host Applications, Equipment & Software, Mainframe Protocols, File Formats & Mainframe Transfer, On-Line Services, Compatibility & Connectivity. Includes Colorful, Animated Graphics Which Simulate Concepts. Review Quizzes Evaluate Learning. Electronic Bookmark & Progress Reports. On-Line Glossary with over 1,000 Terms.
Edutrends, Inc.

PC Tools. *Version:* 8.0. 1991. *Compatible Hardware:* IBM PC, XT, AT, PS/2 & 100% compatibles. *Memory Required:* 640k. *Items Included:* Documentation, registration card, 5.25" diskettes or 3.5" diskettes. *Customer Support:* Toll-call telephone technical support; BBS; 60 day warranty.
disk $179.95.
Includes More Than 30 Easy-to-Use Utilities That Can Be Accessed Through an Integrated Desktop Environment. In Addition to Hard Disk Backup, Data Recovery, Disk Diagnostics & Remote Computing Utilities, Now Provides Complete Anti-Virus Protection, a Powerful Memory Optimizer, Integrated File & Program Management, a Disk Editor & Remote Device Mapping.
Central Point Software, Inc.

PC Tools for Windows. Mar. 1993. *Items Included:* Documentation; registration card; 3 1/2" or 5 1/4" diskettes. *Customer Support:* Toll-call telephone technical support; BBS; 60-day warranty.
Contact Publisher for price.
An Essential Companion for Windows Users That Saves Time, Reduces Visual Clutter, & Provides Easier Access to the Functions & Files They Use Most Often. Product Features a Complete, Integrated Suite of Utilities That Enhance User Productivity, Boost System Performance & Protects the Computing Investment. The MultiDisk Desktop, an Intuitive Extenstion to Windows, Gives Users a More Natural Way to Organize Their Work. Also Provides Comprehensive WinShield Protection Against Data Loss & Disk Failure, Including a Wide-Ranging Network Support & Compatibility with Novell NetWare & Windows for Workgroups.
Central Point Software, Inc.

PC TouchBase: Domestic. Dec. 1993. *Customer Support:* For customer service, product registration, upgrades, technical support, & CustomerFirst service plans, customers may call Aldus Customer Services at (206) 628-2320. Macintosh. Contact publisher for price (ISBN 1-56026-264-8).
Aldus Corp.

PC-Translator. *Version:* 3.4. George Mallard & Ralph Dessau. *Items Included:* 6 diskettes (3.5 or 5.25); manual, binder, & box; copy protect key. *Customer Support:* Telephone/FAX support - No charge, No time limit.
MS-DOS 5.0 or higher. IBM PC & compatibles, 386SX or higher (1MB). $985.00 per language pair.
Dealers - Request discount price sheet.
Technology for Translating Documents between English & 9 European Languages. Processes the Input Text Sentence by Sentence, Preserving All Formatting Codes, Tables, Graphics, & Fonts from Documents in WordPerfect, MS-Word, & WordStar. Also Accepts Documents in ASCII Format. Open Dictionary Design Allows Importation of User Terms from Existing Databases. Pull-Down Menus. Edit Directly with any Text Editor or Word Processor. Up to 10 Word Dictionaries & 10 Phrase Dictionaries Can Be On-Line at any Time. Language Pairs Available: English-to-Spanish; Spanish-to-English; English-to-French; French-to-English; English-to-Italian; Italian-to-English; English-to-Swedish; Swedish-to-English; English-to-Danish; Danish-to-English; English-to-German; German-to-English; English-to-Norwegian; Norwegian-to-English; English-to-Dutch; English-to-Portuguese.
Linguistic Products.

PC TrapWise Trial Version. Mar. 1993. *Customer Support:* For customer service, product registration, upgrades, technical support, & CustomerFirst service plans, customers may call Aldus Customer Services at (206) 628-2320. Macintosh. Contact publisher for price (ISBN 1-56026-186-2).
Aldus Corp.

PC-Trend. *Items Included:* User manual. Interactive tutorial. *Customer Support:* 1 year updates & telephone support included, additional support available.
PC-DOS (512k). IBM compatible with hard disk. $1000.00. *Nonstandard peripherals required:* 8" floppy drive from Flagstaff Engineering. *Addl. software required:* 8" floppy driver form Flagstaff Engineering.
Analyzes Foxboro Videospec Trend Disks. Data from Either Product May Be Imported into 1-2-3, dBase, etc.
Paracomp, Inc.

PC-Trust. *Version:* 6.0. Aug. 1985. *Compatible Hardware:* IBM PC & compatibles. *Memory Required:* 512k. *General Requirements:* Lotus 1-2-3 Releases 1A & 2. *Items Included:* Disk & manual. *Customer Support:* Telephone support. $595.00.
Three Worksheets Balance Pension Assets for Annual Reporting to IRS. Calculates Realized & Unrealized Investment Gains & Losses & Handles Pooled-Asset Division for Multiple Trusts. Prints Worksheets & Reports Including Page 3 of the 5500-C, a Three-Page Financial Report, & Summary Annual Report.
PDC Pension Templates.

PC TypeTwister: Domestic. Mar. 1994. *Customer Support:* For customer service, product registration, upgrades, technical support, & CustomerFirst service plans, customers may call Aldus Customer Services at (206) 628-2320. Macintosh. Contact publisher for price (ISBN 1-56026-258-3).
Aldus Corp.

The PC User's Survival Guide. Jim Aspinwall et al. Nov. 1989.
MS-DOS. IBM PC & compatibles. disk $22.95 (ISBN 1-55851-053-2).
Includes How-To Instructions on Everything from Disks to Technical Support, Including the Best in Utilities, PC Management & Expert Techniques.
M & T Bks.

PC Word. *Customer Support:* 800-929-8117 (customer service).
MS-DOS. IBM/PS2. disk $79.99 (ISBN 0-87007-016-9).
A Full Screen Text Editor & Formatter Which Runs under MS-DOS Within 64 Kbytes of Memory. Several Functions Including: Global Search Ahead & Back, Replace, Automatically Saving Files, Paging up & Down, Construction of Macros 10 Deep & Full Commands with Functions Keys. A Text Formatter Module Runs under DOS & Disk BASIC with at Least 32K Bytes of Memory. The Five Main Functions are: Setting Text Characteristics, Text Formatting, Page Control, Printer Control & Macros.
SourceView Software International.

PC World Interactive. Sep. 1995. *Items Included:* Free Internet Browser, free copy of Media Magazine (with one-year subscription).
Windows 3.1. 486 or higher (4Mb). CD-ROM disk $17.95 one issue; $49.95 four issues (ISBN 1-888022-00-0). *Nonstandard peripherals required:* CD ROM drive, Sound Board (Windows compatible).
This Quarterly CD-ROM Includes a Year's Worth of Back Issues (Browsable & Searchable) & an "Interactive Top 20," Which Allows Users to Create Custom Reports & Charts. The CD ROM Also Includes Shareware, Utilities, a Database of Animated Tips, an Internet Browser, & Links to World Wide Web Home Pages.
PC World New Media.

PC-Write Advanced Level. *Version:* 4.16. Bob Wallace. Jun. 1992. *Items Included:* Diskettes, Getting Started booklet, reference manual, technical support for one year, & license to use. *Customer Support:* One year technical support with registration.
PC-DOS/MS-DOS 3.0 or higher. IBM PC & compatibles (512k). disk $69.00; upgrades; additional user pkg. *Networks supported:*

LANs, most networks.
Word Processor. The Successor to PC-Write 3.0, It Has Pull-Down Menus, Mouse Support, a Customizable Button Bar, Improved Column Support, Advanced Mail Merge Capabilities, Roget's Thesaurus, Multiple Windows (up to 10), Graphic Importation, CGM PCX, PIX Plus Formats & Much More.
Starlite Software Corp.

PC-Write Standard Level. *Version:* 2.02. Bob Wallace. Sep. 1991. *Items Included:* Diskettes, Getting Started booklet, reference manual, technical support for one year, & license to use. *Customer Support:* One year technical support with registration; 90-day full warranty.
PC-DOS/MS-DOS 2.0 or higher. IBM PC & compatibles (448k). $49.00; upgrades; additional user pkg. *Networks supported:* LANs, most networks.
Adaptable Word Processor. Pull-Down Menus, Roget's Thesaurus, Integrated Mouse Support, Context-Sensitive Help, Multiple Windows (up to 10), & a Conversion Tool That Translates Files Between PC-Write Standard Level & WordPerfect, DCA-RFT, & ASCII Top the List of Program Features. It Offers Hundreds of Customization Options.
Starlite Software Corp.

PC-Xview. *Version:* 2.21. May 1991. *Items Included:* User's Guide in 3-ring binder, Release Notes. *Customer Support:* Free telephone support, 90 day unlimited warrenty on disks.
DOS 3.2. AT286 or PS/2 (1.5Mb). disk $445.00. *Nonstandard peripherals required:* 2 or 3 button mouse, network adapter. *Addl. software required:* TCP/IP network software. *Optimal configuration:* 386/486 PC, DOS 5.0, 3Mb Ram, Hi-Res graphics adapter. *Networks supported:* TCP/IP from many vendors.
Convert IBM-Compatible 286, 386 or 486 PC into an X Terminal Emulator. Full X11R4 Based Server with Extensions. A Wide Range of Graphics & Network Adapters Are Supported. Access to Local DOS Applications, File Transfer Between Host & PC, & Local Printing of Remote Files Supported.
Graphic Software Systems, Inc.

The PCAid Utilities. *Version:* 2. Apr. 1990. *Items Included:* Spiral bound manual, 3.5" & 5.25" disks. *Customer Support:* 90 days unlimited warranty. $100 annual maintenance agreement or $50/hour telephone support.
MS/PC-DOS 2.1 or higher. IBM PC & compatibles (256k). disk $59.95 (ISBN 1-881432-26-2).
Collection of Computer Utility Programs Including a Calculator, Number Converter, File Undeleter, ASCII & Keyboard Scan Code Tables, System Info, Directory Tree, Directory Sorter, File & Text Finders, File Mover, File Encryptor, & Other Miscellaneous File & Directory Utility Programs.
BCS Publishing.

PCAP: Accounts Payable. *Version:* 3.2. Jan. 1986. *Compatible Hardware:* IBM PC & compatibles. *Operating System(s) Required:* PC-DOS 2.0 or higher. *Language(s):* COBOL. *Memory Required:* 256k.
disk $695.00, incl. user's guide (Order no.: PCAP).
demo disk free (Order no.: PRI.AP).
Designed to Maintain All of a Company's A/P, Whether Checks Are Written by the Computer, or by Hand. Entries Are Made into the System for All Invoices Received from Vendors with Whom the User Does Business. Based on This Information, the System Can Project Future Cash Requirements, Calculate Discounts, Write Checks, Produce Journal Transactions for the CRS PCGL System, & Maintain Historical Data for Each Vendor Paid.
Computer Related Services, Inc.

PCAR: Accounts Receivable. *Version:* 3.2. May 1985. *Compatible Hardware:* IBM PC. *Operating System(s) Required:* PC-DOS 2.0 or higher. *Language(s):* COBOL. *Memory Required:* 256k. *General Requirements:* Printer. *Customer Support:* Hourly & yearly fees.
disk $695.00, incl. user's guide (Order no.: PCAR).
demo disk free (Order no.: PRI.AR).
Comprehensive Program for Tracking Company Receivables. Offers Features to Handle Specific Requirements. Invoices and/or Monthly Statements Can Be Produced. Reports Can Be Produced at Any Time During the Month.
Computer Related Services, Inc.

PCAS: Personal Computer Accounting System. *Version:* 5.1. *Compatible Hardware:* IBM PC & compatibles. *Operating System(s) Required:* PC-DOS/MS-DOS 2.1 or higher. *Memory Required:* 512k. *Customer Support:* $1.00/minute.
disk $129.95.
Designed for the Computer User with Little or No Accounting Experience. Some of Its Features Include: Menu-Driven, Optional Password Protection, Standardized Formatted Reports, Simple to Follow Formatted Input Screens. Individual Modules Can Be Used Independently or As an Integrated Accounting System. All Modules Contain User Inquiry Screens which Allow Search of Account, Vendor, Customer or Employee Numbers.
D & L Software (Texas).
  General Ledger.
    Double Entry Accounting System, Multi-Level Accounts, Screen Transaction Inquiry, Transaction Reports, Balance Sheet, Income Statement & Cash Journal.
  Accounts Payable.
    Check Printing with Multiple Invoices, Mailing Labels, Unlimited Allocations per Invoice, Vendor Number Verification During Input, Screen Inquiry of Vendor Activity, Printed Vendor History at Any Time.
  Accounts Receivable.
    Open Item or Balance Forward, Aging Report with 30-, 60-, 90-, & over 90-Day Columns, Mailing Labels, Supports Partial Payments, Statements, Screen Inquiry of Customer Activity, Printed Customer History.
  Payroll.
    Manages Employee Records, Automatic Payroll Calculations, 5 User-Defined Deductions, Prints Checks with Check Stub Information, Provides Quarterly & Year End Information, Screen Inquiry of Employee Payroll Records Including YTD Information, Built-In Federal Tax Tables, Four Payroll Periods to Choose From.

PCAT Professional Contact & Tracking System. *Version:* 5.2. Oct. 1988. *Compatible Hardware:* IBM PC & compatibles. *Operating System(s) Required:* PC-DOS/MS-DOS. *Memory Required:* 384k. *Items Included:* Free demo disk. *Customer Support:* 60 days free.
disk $195.00.
For Use in Sales, Customer Service & Telemarketing, Schedules & Dials Calls. Displays Complete Account Information. Prepares Customized Letters & Other Mailings Without Retyping Information Already in Database.
Arlington Software & Systems Corp.

PCAT System 6: Personal Computer Automated Telemarketing. *Version:* 6.0. (Office Information Ser.). Gary R. Pannone. Apr. 1990. *Compatible Hardware:* IBM PC, PC XT, PC AT & compatibles. *Operating System(s) Required:* PC-DOS/MS-DOS 2.1 or higher. *Language(s):* BASIC & Assembly. *Memory Required:* 512k. *Items Included:* Free demo disk. *Customer Support:* 60 days free.
disk $595.00.
demo disk $5.00.
Telemarketing & Sales Management Tool Includes Script, Customer Data File, Autodialer, Word Processing, Mailing List, Report-Generator & Other Features.
Arlington Software & Systems Corp.

PCBanner. *Customer Support:* 800-929-8117 (customer service).
MS-DOS. IBM/PS2. disk $49.99 (ISBN 0-87007-077-0).
Prints Large 6 1/2 Inch High Characters Ideally Suited for Business Signs & Personal Posters. Works with Both Letter Quality & Matrix Printers. Prints Letters, Numbers & over Thirty Special Symbols. Prints in Regular or Full Reverse.
SourceView Software International.

pcCOMMANDER. *Items Included:* High-speed file transfer system. *Customer Support:* Free, unlimited.
MS/PC-DOS 3.0 or higher. Any IBM PC XT, AT, PS/2 & compatibles (384k). disk $149.00. *Optimal configuration:* Any IBM PC XT, AT, PS/2 & compatibles.
PC Task Scheduling System. Allows User to Record "Tasks" As the User Performs Them. Can Then Perform That Task Again, At Any Scheduled Time. Includes a File Transfer Module That Includes a Sophisticated Error-Detection & Recovery Protocol, File Compressions, Auto-Restart, & Much More.
EKD Computer Sales & Supplies Corp.

PCDI Profit Source Computes Data Integration System. *Version:* 2.0. Aug. 1993. *Items Included:* Manual, reference sheet. *Customer Support:* 90 day limited warranty, annual maintenance for normal business hours available, extended support available, training included.
DOS. IBM Compatible 80386/80486 (2Mb). Contact publisher for price. *Optimal configuration:* IBM compatible 80486 PC, DOS, 4Mb. *Networks supported:* Novell, Banyan.
Has the Ability to Accept Data from Multiple Sources, Combine & Organize It, & Report the Consolidated Information. Profitability Module Reports Customer Status, Service Usage, Profitability Goals, How the Goals Are Met, & Identifies Trends. Merger Control Module Reports on the Status of Customers Transferring to the New Bank by Date & Service Milestones. Typically Delivers Data Through Local & Wide Area Networks, or Other Advanced Communication Links.
Automated Financial Systems, Inc.

PcEXPRESS. *Version:* 3.0. *Compatible Hardware:* IBM PC & compatibles, MS-DOS based LANs, Ethernet, Novell, etc. *Operating System(s) Required:* MS-DOS Version 2.0 or higher. *Memory Required:* 640k. *Items Included:* Documentation & reference guide. *Customer Support:* training at nominal rates.
disk $2000.00. *Networks supported:* Asynchronous, synchronous.
Decision Support System (DSS). A 4GL Key Features Include Powerful Multi-Dimensional/Relational Database & Integrated Capabilities for Reporting, Modeling, Statistical Analysis & Graphics. Family of Turnkey Application Products Written in EXPRESS Complement the Product. Included are: DataServer, (Marketing Management System), Sales Management System, Financial Management System & Executive Information System.
Information Resources, Inc.

PCGL: General Ledger. *Version:* 3.2. Apr. 1986. *Compatible Hardware:* IBM PC. *Operating System(s) Required:* PC-DOS 2.0 or higher.

Language(s): COBOL. *Memory Required:* 256k. *Customer Support:* Hourly & yearly support fees.
disk $695.00, incl. user's guide (Order no.: PCGL).
demo disk free (Order no.: PRIGL).
Double Entry Ledger System Which Provides the User with Financial Information. Transactions Can Be Entered Individually by the Operator or Automatically Generated from other CRS Accounting Systems As Standard Recurring Journal Entries.
Computer Related Services, Inc.

PCHunter RMS. *Version:* 4.0. *Items Included:* Omnis 7, ROBMS Runtime. *Customer Support:* Help desk - hotline telephone support, 24 hour bulletin board system (BBS), authorized consultants nationwide. Support contract annual fee: 1st year 15% of price of RMS.
Windows 3.1. IBM PC/AT & compatibles (4Mb). $2600.00 first workstation, (includes Run Time Omnis 7.0), $1100.00 ea. additional workstation. *Nonstandard peripherals required:* VGA or Hi Res monochrome monitor required. *Addl. software required:* MS Windows 3.1. *Optimal configuration:* 386/25Mhz, 4Mb RAM, FAST (<22ms) hard disk, VGA monitor, mouse, Microsoft Word for Windows. *Networks supported:* 3Com, Novell, LAN Manager, TOPS, Apple-SHARE.
Comprehensive Recruitment-Management Information System Designed Specifically for Search firms, Employment Agencies & In-House Employment Departments. Provides Candidate, Client & Requisition Search & Retrieval, Activity Tracking & Reporting. Also Included Are Integrated Productivity Tools: a Daily Planner & Time Management System, On-Line Rolodex with Automatic Phone Dialing Capability. Word Processing Features Include Text Processor, Mail Merge for Fast Production of Form Letters & Labels Plus an Individual Envelope Printing Utility.
MacHunter.

PCINV: Inventory Control. *Version:* 3.2. May 1985. *Compatible Hardware:* IBM PC. *Operating System(s) Required:* PC-DOS 2.0 or higher. *Language(s):* COBOL. *Memory Required:* 256k. *Customer Support:* Hourly & yearly fees.
incl. user's guide $695.00 (Order no.: PCINV).
demo disk free (Order no.: PRI.INV).
Designed to Handle the Inventory Requirements for Many Types of Businesses. Maintains Up-to-Date Information for Each Item Such As Sales & Cost Dollars, Units Sold, Quantity on Hand, How Many Times Sold, etc. An Inventory Manager Needs Only Display (or Print) an Item to Determine What's on Hand, on Order, How Much to Order, How Much It Costs, & What It Sells For.
Computer Related Services, Inc.

PCM: Project Cost Monitor. Micro Computations, Inc. Apr. 1987. *Compatible Hardware:* IBM PC & compatibles. *Operating System(s) Required:* MS-DOS. *Language(s):* BASIC. *Memory Required:* 256k. *General Requirements:* 2 disk drives, printer.
disk $695.00.
Maintains Data Base of Information about Projects (Project Manager, Owner, Description), Contractors (Name, Address, Telephone Number), Contracts (Date, Contractor, Retainage, Status), & Contracted Line Items (Contract Amount, Subcontractor, Status). Tracks Requests for Payment, Payments, & the Receipt of Lien Waivers by Contract, Line Item, & Subcontractor. Displays/Prints Project Summary Report Showing Contractor/Subcontractor, Contract Amount, Total Previous Payments, Amount Due, Amount Retained, & Balance to Complete by Contracted Line Item. Displays/Prints Detailed Report Showing All Project Activity Including Dates & Amounts of All Payment Requests, Payments, & Lien Waivers.
Computing Power Applied.

PCNC. *Compatible Hardware:* IBM PC with 320k disk drive, graphics monitor, color/graphics card, RS-232 tape punch reader. *Memory Required:* 128k.
disk $1495.00.
Manual Programming Package Developed for Numerican Control (NC) Machine Tools. Contains a Text Editor & an Adaptive Backplotting System. Predicts Cutting Times by a Machine Specific Cycle Time Analysis. The User Can Perform DNC Operations Using an Automatic Disk File Management System with RS-232 I/O.
Suburban Machinery, Software Div.

PCOE: Order Entry-Invoicing. *Version:* 3.2. May 1985. *Compatible Hardware:* IBM PC. *Operating System(s) Required:* PC-DOS 2.0 or higher. *Language(s):* COBOL. *Memory Required:* 256k. *General Requirements:* Printer. *Customer Support:* Hourly & yearly fees.
disk $695.00, incl. user's guide (Order no.: PCOE).
demo disk free (Order no.: PRI.OE).
Ordering & Billing System Designed to Meet the Needs of Different Companies. Orders Are Processed with the Ability to Produce Picking Documents, Invoices, or Just for Historical Data. System Is Integrated with the CRS PCAR & PCINV Modules. A Full Complement of Reports Are Provided to Give the User MTD, YTD, & Prior YTD Sales Analysis by Customer, Product, & Salesperson.
Computer Related Services, Inc.

PCPLOT: High Resolution Graphics Program. *Version:* 3. Sep. 1984. *Compatible Hardware:* Apple Macintosh; AT&T 6300; DEC Rainbow, DEC VT 180; HP-125; IBM PC & compatibles, PCjr, PC XT, PC AT; Tandy 1000, 1200, 2000; TI Professional; Xerox 820, 820-II, 860. *Operating System(s) Required:* MS-DOS, PC-DOS. *Language(s):* Compiled BASIC. *Memory Required:* Apple Macintosh 512k, others 256k. *General Requirements:* CGA card for IBM PC & compatibles.
disk $125.00.
Creates Pixel-Resolution Screen & Printer Graphs for Scientific & Financial Purposes. Creates Linear, Semi-Logarithmic & Full Logarithmic Plots in Any Combination of x & Two y Axes. Up to Five Plots Can Be Made on the Same Graph with Optional Legends Superimposed on the Data Points to Separate Plots. Data Points May Be Connected If Desired. Forced Scaling & Auto-Scaling Are Supported. Grid Lines May Be Specified for Linear, Semi-Logarithmic, Logarithmic & Financial Data. Plots May Be Made of Time History, Frequency Response, etc. Also Creates Templates of the Physical Appearance of Any Graph & May Be Saved to Disk.
BV Engineering.

PCPR: Payroll. *Version:* 3.1. Dec. 1984. *Compatible Hardware:* IBM. *Operating System(s) Required:* PC-DOS 2.0 or higher. *Language(s):* COBOL. *Memory Required:* 256k. *Customer Support:* Hourly & yearly fees.
disk $695.00, incl. user's guide (Order no.: PCPR).
demo disk free (Order no.: PRI.PR).
Designed to Handle the Payroll Requirements of Various Types of Businesses with Weekly, Bi-Weekly, Semi-Monthly, & Monthly Pay Schedules. The System Calculates Net Pay, Produces Pay Checks, Automatically Calculates the Deductions for Federal, FICA, State & Local Taxes. Up to 9 Additional User Defined Deductions Can Also Be Handled for Insurance, Savings, Hospitalization, etc.
Computer Related Services, Inc.

PCPro Light Pen System. *Items Included:* Light Pen, internal interface card, light pen holder, users manual & software driver. *Customer Support:* One-year warranty. Customer support by telephone.
DOS/Windows 3.1. PC 286 (1Mb). disk $299.00. *Nonstandard peripherals required:* VGA.
Enables Users to Make Menu Selections, Draw, Paint, & Perform Other Input Functions Directly on the Computer Screen. Works with DOS & Windows Applications. Interfaces with Inkwell Systems' EasyKey Visual Keyboard to Create Typed Input Without an External Keyboard in Windows Applications.
Inkwell Systems.

pcSECRETARY: The Ultimate Information Utility. *Version:* 1.0. *Customer Support:* Free, unlimited.
PC/MS-DOS 3.0 or higher. Any IBM PC XT, AT, PS/2 & compatibles (384k). disk $99.00.
Personal Information Manager for Home & Office That Lets Users Organize Their Schedule, Thoughts, Contacts & Communications Effortlessly. Auto-Dials Phone Numbers (Using a Hayes-Compatible Modem), Maintains Multiple Address Books, Area Code Reference (U. S. 7 Foreign), & Much More.
EKD Computer Sales & Supplies Corp.

PCTex for Windows. *Version:* 2.1. Sep. 1995. *Items Included:* 3 manuals; True Type math & symbol fonts, Latex & Amstex (popular Tex macros). *Customer Support:* Free technical support - unlimited.
MS-DOS, Windows. 386 (4Mb). disk $299.00. *Nonstandard peripherals required:* Printer, VGA.
Provides a Complete TEX, LATEX, & AMSTEX System for Professionally Typesetting Books of Any Size, Complex Technical Journals, Scientific Notation, High-Quality Mathematical Equations, Tables, & Other Documents. Excels at Typesetting: Short Papers, or Books with Hundreds of Pages; Scientific Notation & Mathematical Formulas; Documents with Perfect Word & Letter Spacing; Text with Complex Hyphenation; Foreign Languages.
Personal Tex, Inc.

PC220: VT220 Terminal Emulator. Nov. 1986. *Operating System(s) Required:* PC-DOS/MS-DOS. *Memory Required:* 128k. *General Requirements:* Hard disk, printer, modem COM1-COM4 async. card.
3-1/2" or 5-1/4" disk $169.00 (Order no.: PC220).
Allows Full Keyboard & Screen Emulations of DEC VT220, 200, 102, 101, 100 & VT52 Terminals. Provides: All DEC VT220 Features Including Slow Scroll, 132-Column Support & Status Line; Thirty Softkeys to Allow Repetitious Tasks to Be Performed with a Single Keystroke; User May Program Scripts for Login & Other Functions; DOS Commands/Programs, Macros, & Other Script Files May Be Executed As Commands Within a Script; Debug Display (Line Monitor) Aids in Perfecting Newly Written Scripts; DOS Key to Suspend PC220 & Hop out to DOS & Back; KERMIT Binary File Transfer Protocol with Wildcard Support; Baud Rates Selectable from 110-38.4k Baud.
General Micro Systems.

PCYACC: Professional Language Development Toolkit. *Version:* 6.0. *Compatible Hardware:* IBM PC & compatibles, PS/2, Macintosh. *Operating System(s) Required:* OS/2, VMS, IBM AIX, Sun UNIX, Apple DOS. *Memory Required:* 2000k. *Customer Support:* Free.
DOS, $495.00; OS/2 NT, $995.00; MAC, $495.00; UNIX, $1995.00 single seat server

TITLE INDEX

license.
Language Development Environment Can Generate ANSI C Source Code from Grammar Inputs. Users Can Use the Code to Build Assemblers, Compilers, Interpreters, Browsers, Page Description Languages, Language Translators, Syntax Directed Editors, & Query Languages for OS/2 & Presentation Manager. The Code Is Optimized for Microsoft & Lattice OS/2 Optimizers. Grammar for C++, ANSI C, K&R C, ISO Pascal, YACC, LEX, Apple HyperTalk, SmallTalk-80, Prolog, PostScript, dBASE III/Plus/IV, & SQL Is Included with the Package. Can Generate Code for Large Grammars on PS/2s & Generate Syntax Trees at Run Time to a Target Product to Expedite Debugging. Other Features Include a Quick Syntax Feature Analysis for Fast Grammar Implementation & Error Recovery Support for Target Products.
Abraxas Software, Inc.

PC102: Terminal Emulator. *Version:* 6.3. *Compatible Hardware:* IBM PC, PC XT, PC AT, PS/2 & compatibles. *Operating System(s) Required:* UNIX, MS-DOS. *Language(s):* Assembly, C. *Memory Required:* 96k.
PC102-AT. $149.00.
Provides Full Keyboard & Screen Emulation of DEC VT102, VT101, & VT52 Terminals. The Setup Screens Are Accessed with a Single Keystroke & Selected Options Can Be Stored on Disk. Multiple Setups Can Be Saved Under Different Names for Various Host Computers & Users. The Keyboard Layout Allows Accessing of Each VT Terminal Key Equivalent with a Single Keystroke, & 10 Soft Keys Can Be Assigned a User-Defined 40-Character Message. Features Include: File Transfer, XON/XOFF & Pause/Kick Protocols for Full & Half Duplex Operations, etc. Baud Rate Is 110 to 9600 & a 2k Buffer Is Included.
General Micro Systems.

PC4010: Graphics Terminal Emulator. *Version:* 2.3. *Compatible Hardware:* IBM PC, AT, PS/2 & compatibles. *Operating System(s) Required:* PC-DOS 2.0, 3.XX or higher. *Language(s):* ASM, C. *Memory Required:* 96k.
disk $199.00.
Provides Full Tektronix 4010 Graphics Terminal Emulation with IBM, Hercules, & Other Graphic Boards. Displayed Graphics Can Be Saved to Disk or Printed. All PC102 Features Are Included. Terminal Modes (4010, VT102, VT52) Are Operator or Host Computer Selectable. Full GIN (Graphics Input) Support Included.
General Micro Systems.

P.D. Queue. Jul. 1990. *Items Included:* 1 spiral-bound manual with outer hard cover, 1 5.25" program disk, 1 3.5" program disk. *Customer Support:* Unlimited telephone support.
DOS 2.0 or higher. IBM PC & compatibles (512k). disk $89.95. *Nonstandard peripherals required:* Hard disk. *Addl. software required:* Lotus 1-2-3 2.0, 2.01 or 2.2; Symphony 1.1 or higher.
Add-In Print Spooler for Lotus 1-2-3 & Symphony. The Program Eliminates Long, Unproductive Delays Waiting for the Keyboard to Free up While the Printer Finishes Printing. Automatically Intercepts Data & Sends It Directly to the Hard Disk, Freeing up Machine So User Can Continue Working While Product Sends the Print Data to Printer.
Funk Software.

PDIR. *Operating System(s) Required:* CP/M. *Language(s):* Assembly. *Memory Required:* 24k.
disk $15.00.
Dictionary Display Program That Lists the Directory File Names in Alphabetical Order & Stops When the Screen Is Full.
Elliam Assocs.

PDOS Full Spectrum Development Kit. *Items Included:* Software, Documentation. *Customer Support:* 1 Year toll-free support & free upgrades - renewable at 20% annually.
PDOS. Motorola 680 x 0 based system, PC, HP & SUN Sparc Hosts. $3000 - $5000.
Applications Can Be Developed for the System on a PC, (under MS-DOS or Windows) AT HP9000, SUN, VAX, & Others with VMEPROM Cross Development Package. This Package Includes an ANSI C Cross Compiler, PDOS C Libraries, Over One Hundred PDOS Primitive Calls, & a Number of Development Utilities. Features Include: Support for Subset of the ANSI I/O Library; Direct Access to 100 PDOS/VMEPROM System Caller.
Eyring Corp.

PDOS InSpector. 1995. *Customer Support:* 1 Year phone support & free upgrades. Annual maintenance fee is 20% of product price.
PDOS. Motorola 680X0 & 683xx-based systems; PC-MS-DOS & Windows. disk $2800.00.
Networks supported: Ethernet.
Full-Featured Windows-Based Tool for Source & System Level Debugging of PDOS Real-Time Applications Running on 68K Targets. Allows User to Test & Debug Optimized C or Assembly Language Programs Using Interactive Windows. It is Designed to Support Non-Intrusive Debugging of Optimized Code & Can Be Used to Debug Single or Multiple Task Target Applications over Serial & Ethernet Links Originating from the Host.
Eyring Corp.

PDOS-MRI ANSI C & Cplus plus Compiler. *Version:* 4.3k. 1990. *Items Included:* Software, manuals. *Customer Support:* One full year of support is included with each product pubchased. Additional support may be purchased yearly at 20% of the end-user price. Support includes hotline phone support, technical mailings, & free upgrades.
PDOS. Motorola 680X0-based Systems. $2400.00 & up (Order no.: 3755). *Networks supported:* Ethernet, Mup.
Implements ANSI C Standard, Supporting Function Prototypes, Preprocessor Extensions & Extended Data Types. Based on Microtec Research's ANSI C Compiler. Available for PC, Sun, & HP Host Computers.
Eyring Corp.

PDP2: Scientific/Financial Graph Plotting Program. *Version:* 2. Apr. 1986. *Compatible Hardware:* Apple Macintosh, IBM PC. *Operating System(s) Required:* MS-DOS. *Language(s):* Compiled BASIC. *Memory Required:* IBM 256K, Macintosh 512k. *General Requirements:* 2 disk drives or hard disk, plotter.
$125.00.
Stand-Alone Program Which Makes Multi-Color Scientific & Financial Graphs on Pen Plotters. Data May Be Entered Manually or Come From Previously Generated Data Files. Data Files Can Originate from BASIC, Fortran, or Pascal Programs, Word Processors, Text Editors, LOTUS 1-2-3, LabTech Notebook, or Other B.V. Engineering Software Such as ACNAP or SPP. Plots Line Graphs, Bar Charts, Stacked Bar Charts, & Line Plots with Error Bars. Graphs May Be Specified by Dotted, Dashed, or Solid Lines, with Linear or Log Scaling.
BV Engineering.

P.D.Q. *Version:* 3.0. (source code included). Microsoft QuickBASIC 4.0 or higher (256k) BASIC 7. disk $149.00.
Allows User to Create BASIC Programs That Are Smaller & Faster. Includes a DOS "Filter" Program That Takes 1400 Bytes of Memory, a TSR Printer Set-Up Utility in 3k. TSR & Interrupt Handling Are Built Directly into the PDQ Library.

PDS RELIGIOUS EDUCATION MANAGEMENT

The Program Is a Complete Replacement for the BCOM Libraries Included with QuickBASIC, BASIC 6.0 & BASIC 7, Ideal for Writing Small Applications & TSR Utilities, Where Program Size & Execution Speed Is Critical. Alternate Libraries Are Provided for Creating 80386-Specific Applications. All Source Codes Included.
Crescent Software.

PDQComm. *Version:* 2.50. Dec. 1990. *Items Included:* spiral bound Manual. *Customer Support:* Free telephone support.
DOS. IBM PC or compatible (320k). disk $99.00. *Addl. software required:* Microsoft Quickbasic or Basic 7 PDS.
Adds Serial Communications to Basic Programs, Supports COM Ports 1-4, & Hardware & Software Handshaking. Uses Syntax Nearly Identical to Basic for Fast Integration & Minimal Learning Curve. Features XMODEM Plus ASCII File Transfers, Many Terminal Emulations.
Crescent Software.

PDS-ADEPT. *Operating System(s) Required:* BTOS, CTOS, MS-DOS, SCO UNIX, SCO XENIX. *Memory Required:* 2000k. *Items Included:* Documentation. *Customer Support:* $300.00 per year.
BTOS & CTOS. $1675.00 & Run-Time $325.00.
MS-DOS. $595.00 & Run-Time $200.00-$600.00.
Unix/Xenix. $1000.00 & Run-Time $200.00 Plus.
A 4GL Application Generator-Database Manager. Programs Can Be Created to: Enter Data in Real-Time or Batch Mode; Format & Generate Reports or Pre-Printed Forms; Link Programs via Menus; Inquire into Data Files; Perform Batch Updates; Create Files for Data Storage.
PDS, Inc.

PDS-C Source Generator. *Version:* 1.000. Mar. 1990. *Items Included:* Documentation. *Customer Support:* $300.00 per year. Training available - please contact PDS for prices.
SCO UNIX/SCO XENIX; MS-DOS; BTOS/CTOS. DEC 433, NCR Tower 32/400-800, NCR3000, Unisys U6000; IBM compatible PCs. $595.00-$4500.00; PDS Development Kit $595.00-$2000.00. *Addl. software required:* C compiler, Language Development Kit, PDS Development Kit.
Translates PDS-ADEPT Programs into Standard "C" Source Code. The Result Is a Combination of the Best of Both Worlds: 4GL Development Ease & 3GL Speed. An Added Benefit Is the Standardized "C" Code Generated by the PDS-C Source Generator, Which Can Be Ported Across Hardware Platforms.
PDS, Inc.

PDS Ledger/Payable Program. *Version:* 2.2. Oct. 1986. *Compatible Hardware:* IBM PC & compatibles. *Operating System(s) Required:* MS-DOS. *Language(s):* Pascal. *Memory Required:* 256k. *General Requirements:* Hard disk, printer. *Items Included:* 1 manual. *Customer Support:* Free support & user newsletters.
disk $400.00.
Fully Integrated General Ledger & Accounts Payable Program. Holds an Unlimited Number of Transactions, Vendors, & Invoices. Each Account Stores 3 Years Comparatives & 2 Years Budgets & Future Budgets; Vendor Record Contains Current Balance & Year-to-Date Payments. Checks & Check Register, Balance Sheet & Income Statement, & Monthly & Yearly Comparatives or Budget Figures.
Parish Data Systems, Inc.

PDS Religious Education Management Program. 1991. *Items Included:* 2 manuals. *Customer Support:* Free support.

MS-DOS 2.0 or above. IBM & compatibles. $800.00. *Networks supported:* Any NetBIOS compatible network.
Keeps Thorough Records on Everyone Involved in Religious Education Programs. Handles Student, Family, Teacher & Financial Information. Names of Many Fields Displayed on Screen Are Defined by Users to Provide a More "Customized" Program. Information Can Be Quickly & Easily Entered & Is Available for Instant Retrieval.
Parish Data Systems, Inc.

PD2 POWERPak. *Version:* 4.0. George Kwascha. Dec. 1994. *Compatible Hardware:* IBM PC. *Operating System(s) Required:* PC-DOS/MS-DOS. *Language(s):* Pascal. *Memory Required:* 640k. *Items Included:* User's manual.
disk $165.00 (ISBN 0-917825-03-9).
Designed for Electric Utility Power Distribution Engineers & Consultants. Tabulates Transformer, Wire & Cable Specification into Disk Files. These Files Are Utilized to Calculate Transformer Voltage Drops, Secondary Cable Voltage Drops, Secondary Fault Currents, & to Perform Complete Three Phase Distribution Feeder Analysis. Not Copy Protected.
Information Management Solutions, Inc.

Peace of Mind. *Compatible Hardware:* Commodore 64, 128. *General Requirements:* Biofeedback Temperature sensor & Sensor Adapter Cable.
ROM cartridge $49.95 (Order no.: SOFC64-08-011/C).
Helps User Recognize & Control Indicators of Stress. Using Visual &/or Auditory Feedback User Can: (a) Directly Observe Their Body Signals, (b) Play a Game Using Their Body Signals to Control Progress, or (c) Plot the Previous 3 or 30 Minutes of Changes.
Bodylog.

Peachtree Accounting for Macintosh. *Version:* 2.0. Nov. 1992. *Customer Support:* 30 days free telephone support, support plans available.
System 6.0 or higher. Macintosh Plus or higher. 3.5" disk $169.00. *Nonstandard peripherals required:* Hard disk, ImageWriter or LaserWriter printer. *Networks supported:* Appleshare.
Fully Integrated Accounting System Providing: General Ledger, Accounts Receivable, Accounts Payable, Payroll, Inventory, Job Cost, & Bank Reconciliation. Interacative Hypercard Tutorial Provides Hands-On Practice. Program Allows up to 26 General Ledger Periods (2 Years) Open at Any One Time & up to $99,999,999.99 Transactions. Allows Immediate On-Line Posting to Any Open Period, 20 User Defined Journals, an On-Line Help Feature, & Accomodates Recurring Invoices, Bills, & Journal Entries. Allows User to Customize Invoices, Statements, Vendor & Payroll Checks As Well As W-2 Forms.
Peachtree Software, Inc.

Peachtree Accounting for Windows. *Version:* Release 3. *Items Included:* One manual called "User Manual". Additional materials: Peachtree Toolkit, Installation, Accounting Primer & Import Export Pamphlets. *Customer Support:* 30 days free support from the date of first call. Free automated support, Peach fax support, & Bulletin Board services (Compuserve, Prodigy, American Online). Peach CARE support offers 75 minutes for $129. Pay per call support - $3 per minute. MS-DOS. IBM & compatibles (4Mb). disk $169.00. *Optimal configuration:* 486 66MHz, 8Mb RAM, 10Mb of disk space above size of company. Any Windows compatible peripherals. *Networks supported:* Anything supported by Windows.
Built from the Ground-Up for Business. Offers Business People All the Accounting Functionality They Need. Offers Growing Businesses the Flexibility of Network Compatibility & Password Protection. And Its Custom Forms Designer & Customized Reporting Tools Make It the Clear Choice for Growing Buisnesses.
Peachtree Software, Inc.

Peachtree Accounts Payable. Peachtree Software, Inc. *Compatible Hardware:* TI Professional. *Operating System(s) Required:* MS-DOS. *Memory Required:* 128k. *General Requirements:* 2 disk drives, printer.
$750.00 (Order no.: SS P/N PTT-103 MD P/N 400912).
Features Vendor File List, Control Reports of All Invoices & Credits Entered, Transaction Register, Vendor Status, Aging Report, Check Register, etc.
Texas Instruments, Personal Productivit.

Peachtree Accounts Receivable. Peachtree Software, Inc. *Compatible Hardware:* TI Professional. *Operating System(s) Required:* MS-DOS. *Memory Required:* 128k. *General Requirements:* 2 disk drives, printer.
$750.00 (Order no.: SS P/N PTT-102 MD P/N 400917).
Texas Instruments, Personal Productivit.

Peachtree Complete Accounting: Easy to Use Accounting for Small Businesses. *Version:* 8.0. Sep. 1994. *Compatible Hardware:* IBM & compatibles. *Operating System(s) Required:* PC-DOS/MS-DOS 3.1 or higher. *Language(s):* BASIC. *Memory Required:* 640k. *General Requirements:* 12Mb hard disk. *Customer Support:* Installation support available on toll-free number. Other support via contract or pay-per call. Support also available from over 85 independent & locally owned authorized support centers. Charges vary.
1 pkg.. $249.00, incl. QuickStart guide, accounting & DOS primer, ten volume reference library & tutorials.
Complete Accounting System Which May Be Integrated or Installed Individually. Contains the Following Functionality: General Ledger, Budgeting, Order Entry, Accounts Receivable, Invoicing, Accounts Payable, Inventory, Fixed Assets, Job Cost, Payroll, Purchase Order & Custom Report Writing. Features Pop-Up Menus, Short-Cut Keys, Error Handling, & Range Printing. A Multi-User Version Is Also Available.
Peachtree Software, Inc.

Peachtree Insight Accounting for Macintosh. *Version:* 4.0. Jan. 1986. *General Requirements:* Hard disk & one 800k floppy drive. *Customer Support:* 30 days free support starting with the first call; support plans available via contract or pay per call.
Macintosh (1Mb). 3.5" disk $395.00.
Includes General Ledger, Accounts Receivable/ Billing, Accounts Payable, Payroll & Inventory.
Peachtree Software, Inc.

PeakFit: Chromatography-Spectroscopy Analysis. *Version:* 3.1. Mar. 1992. *Items Included:* 3 spiral-bound manuals (reference manual, tutorial, technical guide). *Customer Support:* 90 day money-back guarantee; free technical support.
DOS. IBM PC & compatibles (640k). disk $595.00 (Order no.: SPFDR318). *Optimal configuration:* Math coprocessor strongly recommended.
Offers Sophisticated Non-Linear Curve Fitting Techniques to Resolve & Analyze Overlapping Peak Data (Typical to Chromatography & Spectroscopy Applications). Results Include Peak Characterization Data (Amplitudes, Areas, Centers, Widths), System Suitability Information (Column Efficiency, Peak Asymmetry, Resolution) & All Parameter Values & Fit Statistics. Offers 30 Built-In Equations (Gaussian, Lorenztian, Voigt, etc.) & Accepts User-Defined Equations up to 68 Adjustable Parameters.
Jandel Scientific.

Peanuts Math Matcher. Jul. 1985. *Compatible Hardware:* Apple II series. *Memory Required:* 64k.
disk $29.95 (ISBN 0-676-32334-0).
back-up disk $4.95.
Build Knowledge of Arithmetic in a Matching Memory Game.
Random House Schl. Div.

Peanuts Maze Marathon. *Compatible Hardware:* Apple II series, Commodore 64. *Memory Required:* 48k.
Apple. disk $29.95 (ISBN 0-676-32112-7).
Commodore 64. disk $9.98 (ISBN 0-676-32236-0).
back-up disk $10.00 ea.
A Maze Program with Animated Graphics.
Random House Schl. Div.

Peanuts Picture Puzzlers. *Compatible Hardware:* Apple II+, IIe, IIc, with Applesoft; Commodore 64, IBM PCjr. *Memory Required:* Apple 48k, Commodore & IBM 64k.
Apple. disk $39.95 (ISBN 0-676-32127-5).
Commodore. disk $19.95 (ISBN 0-676-32237-9).
IBM. disk $29.95 (ISBN 0-676-32242-5).
back-up disk $5.00.
Animated Puzzle Program.
Random Hse., Inc.

PEARLMASTER. *Version:* 2.0. Apr. 1991. *Customer Support:* Toll free telephone support.
MS-DOS 3.1. IBM-PC. disk $595.00.
Contains 1260 Diseases Labeled According to Their ICD-9-CM Titles & Displayed on Screen in a Scroll. Jump Quickly to Any System-Specific Section in the List or Add More Diseases If Desired. Each Disease with at Least One Pearl is Marked. When the Sought-After Disease is Highlighted, a Single Keystroke Displays Every Pearl Stored for That Entity. Shipped with over 1000 Pearls Containing Thousands of Links to the Diseases in the System. Additional Pearls Can Be Written to Make an Ideal Storehouse for Treasured Clinical Facts over the Physician's Lifetime. Any Pearl May May Have As Many As Six Lines & Be Linked to Every Relevant Disease That You Choose.
SRC Systems, Inc.

Pediatric Airway Obstruction. Donna Santer. *Customer Support:* Toll-free technical support - no charge. In U.S. - 9AM-5PM EST 800-343-0064. In U.K. - 44(0)81-995-8242.
System 7.0 or higher. Apple Macintosh (4Mb). CD-ROM disk $175.00 Individual, $495.00 Institutional (ISBN 1-57276-004-4, Order no.: SE-004-001). *Nonstandard peripherals required:* CD-ROM drive.
Provides Instruction in the Identification of Respiratory Distress in the Pediatric Population. The Instruction Uses Digital Video, Audio, Radiographic Images, Pathology Images, Diagrams, & Supplementary Text Throughout the Main Chapters, Which Are: Introduction & Anatomy, Croup Syndromes, Acute Epiglottitis, Subglottic Stenosis, & Tracheomalacia & Laryngomalacia.
SilverPlatter Education.

Pediatric Airway Obstruction. Donna Santer. Sep. 1993. *Customer Support:* Toll-free technical support - no charge. In U.S. 9AM - 5PM EST 800-343-0064; in U.K. 44(0)81-995-8242.
System 7.0 or higher. Apple Macintosh (4Mb). CD-ROM disk $175.00, Individual, ,495.00 Institutional (ISBN 1-57276-004-4, Order no.:

SE-004-001). *Nonstandard peripherals required:* CD-ROM Drive.
Provides Instruction in the Identification of Respiratory Distress in the Pediatric Population. The Instruction Uses Digital Video, Audio, Radiographic Images, Pathology Images, Diagrams, & Supplementary Text Throughout the Main Chapters, Which Are: Introduction & Anatomy, the Croup Syndromes, Acute Epiglottitis, Subglottic Stenosis, & Tracheomalacia & Laryngomalacia.
SilverPlatter Education.

The Pediatric Infectious Disease Journal on CD-ROM: DOS-MAC. Feb. 1994. *Items Included:* Registration Card. *Customer Support:* Creative Multimedia Corporation warrants the CD-ROM disc & diskettes to be free from defects in materials & workmanship under normal use & service for a period of 90 days from date of purchase. Creative Multimedia Corporation offers Technical Support to customers as needed.
  MS-DOS 3.1 or higher. IBM PC & compatibles with VGA monitor (350k). CD-ROM disk $295.00 Suggested Retail Price (ISBN 1-880428-35-0, Order no.: 10541). *Optimal configuration:* Super VGA with 512k video memory capable of 640x480x256 colors. *Networks supported:* All.
  System Software 6.0.5 or higher. Macintosh Plus, SE, Classic, SE/30, LC & any Model II (2Mb). CD-ROM disk $295.00 Suggested Retail Price. *Optimal configuration:* Color display requires 8-bit color, 32-bit QuickDraw & color monitor. *Networks supported:* All.
Nine Years of The Pediatric Infectious Disease Journal Provides Clinically Useful Material for the Front Line Practitioner, & Is Available on a Single Disc with Full Text Articles, Images, & References. The Journal Features Review Articles & Original Studies on Viral & Bacterial Illness in Children Plus Late Breaking News on Diseases, Techniques & Drugs. Edited by John D. Nelson, MD & George H. McCracken, Jr., MD, University of Texas, Southwestern Medical Center.
Creative Multimedia Corp.

Pediatrics on CD-ROM: DOS-MAC. Feb. 1994. *Items Included:* Registration Card. *Customer Support:* Creative Multimedia Corporation warrants the CD-ROM disc & diskettes to be free from defects in materials & workmanship under normal use & service for a period of 90 days from date of purchase. Creative Multimedia Corporation offers Technical Support to customers as needed.
  MS-DOS 3.1 or higher. IBM PC & compatibles with VGA monitor (350k). CD-ROM disk $295.00 Suggested Retail Price (ISBN 1-880428-33-4, Order no.: 10535). *Optimal configuration:* Super VGA with 512k video memory capable of 640x480x256 colors. *Networks supported:* All.
  System Software 6.0.5 or higher. Macintosh Plus, SE, Classic, SE/30, LC & any Model II (2Mb). CD-ROM disk $295.00 Suggested Retail Price. *Optimal configuration:* Color display requires 8-bit color, 32-bit QuickDraw & color monitor. *Networks supported:* All.
Eight Years of the Journal Pediatrics on a Single Disc. Contains Full Text Articles, Images (in Black & White & Color), Line Art, References Cited & Captions. An Excellent Tool for the Clinician, Educator, Researcher & Student Making Access to This Literature Available in Seconds. Pediatrics Is the Official Clinical Journal of the American Academy of Pediatrics. Edited by Jerold F. Lucey.
Creative Multimedia Corp.

Pediatrics Review & Education Program (PREP) on CD-ROM: DOS-MPC. Feb. 1994. *Items Included:* Registration Card. *Customer Support:* Creative Multimedia Corporation warrants the CD-ROM disc & diskettes to be free from defects in materials & workmanship under normal use & service for a period of 90 days from date of purchase. Creative Multimedia Corporation offers Technical Support to customers as needed.
  MS-DOS 3.1 or higher. IBM PC & compatibles with VGA monitor (350k). CD-ROM disk $295.00 Suggested Retail Price (ISBN 1-880428-34-2, Order no.: 10546). *Optimal configuration:* Super VGA with 512k video memory capable of 640x480x256 colors. *Networks supported:* All.
  System Software 6.0.5 or higher. Macintosh Plus, SE, Classic, SE/30, LC & any Model II (2Mb). CD-ROM disk $295.00 Suggested Retail Price. *Optimal configuration:* Color display requires 8-bit color, 32-bit QuickDraw & color monitor. *Networks supported:* All.
Pediatrics in Review & the Self-Assessment Exercise Includes The Pediatrics Review & Education Program (PREP). Each Issue of the Journal Contains Comprehensive Review Articles Related to Important Pediatric Topics, As Well As Commentaries, Editorials, Abstracts & References to the Current Literature. The Self-Assessment Exercise (1992, 1993) Contains over 300 Multiple Choice Questions, Critiques & Verified References Covering Pediatric Medicine.
Creative Multimedia Corp.

Pedigree. Jul. 1987. *Compatible Hardware:* IBM PC & compatibles. *Operating System(s) Required:* MS-DOS. *Language(s):* BASIC. *Memory Required:* 256k. *General Requirements:* 2 disk drives, printer.
  disk $95.00, incl. manual.
Maintains Data Base of Information about Cat Owners (Name, Address), Breeders (Name, Address, Cattery Name), & Cats (Name, Registration Numbers, Owner, Birth Date, Sex, Breed, Color, Eye Color, Ancestry, Shows Entered, Ribbons Awarded, Championship Status). Prints Pedigree Certificates on Standard Forms Available from Associations Such As CFA & ACFA. Prints Lists of All Owners, Breeders, & Cats on File.
Computing Power Applied.

Pedigree. Version: 4.0. 1990. *Compatible Hardware:* IBM PC, PC XT. *Operating System(s) Required:* CP/M, MP/M, CP/M-86, PC-DOS, MS-DOS. *Language(s):* CB-80, CB-86. *Memory Required:* 48k. *General Requirements:* 2 disk drives or hard disk. *Customer Support:* Unlimited telephone support.
  $100.00, incl. manual.
  demo disk $10.00.
  manual $25.00.
Maintains & Constructs up to 5 Generation Pedigrees on Any, All, or Selected Groups of Animals in the Data File. Can Work with Any Kind of Livestock. Can Also Be Used to Prepare Matings and/or Refresh Memory As to the Ancestry of Any Animal in the Herd.
St. Benedict's Farm.

PediLine CD-ROM Database for Neurology. Aug. 1992.
  MS Windows 3.1 or higher. IBM & compatibles (4Mb). CD-ROM disk $325.00-$995.00; Networks $1895.00 & up. *Nonstandard peripherals required:* Magnetic or CD-ROM, using ISO 9660. *Optimal configuration:* IBM & compatibles, 80386 or higher, 4Mb RAM, 20Mb hard disk, mouse, MS Windows 3.1 or higher.
  System 6.0.7 or higher. Apple Macintosh (3Mb). CD-ROM disk $325.00-$995.00; Networks $1895.00 & up. *Optimal configuration:* Apple Macintosh Plus or higher, 3Mb RAM, System 6.0.7 or higher.
PediLine Is an Electronic Reference Database to the Pediatric Journal Literature. Pediatrics-Specific Excerpts (Including Abstracts) from the National Library of Medicine's MEDLINE Database Are Distributed on CD-ROM (Compact Disc, Read-Only Memory) Optical Disc. Knowledge Finder Search-&-Retrieval Software Makes Searching of the PediLine Database Easy, Effective & Fast. After the User Types a Phrase or Sentence Describing the Information Needed, It selects the References in the Database That Appear to Best Match the Request, & Presents Them in Order of likely relevance. The PediLine Archive CD-ROM Contains over 270,000 References to Articles Published in 170 Pediatrics-Related Journals over the Most Recent 10 Full Years.
Aries Systems Corp.

Peer Planner for Windows. Version: 2.01. Sep. 1994. *Items Included:* 100 page manual, on-line help. *Customer Support:* 180 days free telephone support & upgrades. Annual maintenance 15% of system cost. Training available (5 days free with purchase of system).
  Windows 3.1 or higher. I486 (8Mb). $9600.00-$80,000.00. *Optimal configuration:* I486 (8Mb) hard disk. *Networks supported:* Novell.
Integrated Forecasting System for Item Level to Product Level Planning. Expert, Batch Forecasting, Management Overrides Both Manually & Graphical. Forecast Error Tracking & Analysis. Low Level Proration of Forecasts for Customer & Product Components. Product Rollups to Regional & Organizational Entities. LAN Supported, Multiuser Database.
Delphus, Inc.

PEGASUS. Version: 4.0. Sep. 1985. *Compatible Hardware:* IBM PC XT, PC AT, PS/2. *Operating System(s) Required:* Concurrent PC-DOS. *Language(s):* Pascal. *Memory Required:* 1152k. *General Requirements:* Hard disk, 2 printers.
  disk $6500.00 (ISBN 0-922866-00-7, Order no.: V4.0).
Multi-Task Environmental Management System Featuring Color Graphics, Command Sequencing, Set Point Controls, Duty Cycling, Time Scheduling & Event Driven Controls.
Centaurus Systems, Inc.

Pegman Space Management Software. Version: 5.0. Sep. 1991. *Items Included:* Comprehensive manual; template; mouse. *Customer Support:* Free program updates; on-line technical help; free shapes library; free re-training; data backup protection; discount on planogram service.
  MS-DOS (640k). IBM PC or compatible. Contact publisher for price. *Nonstandard peripherals required:* Graphics board. *Networks supported:* Net BIOS.
Computerized Planogramming for Section or Whole Store Planning, to Increase Profitability/Productivity of Retail Space.
MarketWare Corp.

PEH (Positive Expection Handicapper). Version: 2. Dick Mitchell. Jun. 1985. *General Requirements:* Hard disk recommended. *Items Included:* Complete manual. *Customer Support:* Telephone support handicapping & technical; 60 day limited money back guarantee.
  MS-DOS. IBM & compatibles (384k). disk $199.00 (ISBN 0-9614168-1-5).
A Well-Tested Handicapping Program Which Performs a Sophisticated Class & Pace Analysis on Information Entered into It from the Daily Racing Form. It Lists the Horses in Order of Their Probability of Winning, & Also Creates a "Betting Line" for Each Race. The User Is Also Given a Betting Strategy for Each Race Which Helps to Optimize Racetrack Profits.
Cynthia Publishing Co.

P8CDA. David Lyons. *Compatible Hardware:* Apple IIgs. *Operating System(s) Required:* ProDOS 8. *Memory Required:* 512k.
3.5" disk $29.95 (ISBN 0-927796-31-7, Order no.: 143).
Accessory Lets Users Put CLASSIC DESK ACCESSORIES on Their ProDos 8 Startup Disks, Thus Avoiding the Long Startup Time of ProDOS 16.
Roger Wagner Publishing, Inc.

Pencil ACE. *Compatible Hardware:* IBM PC. disk $89.95 (ISBN 0-936200-45-6).
Provides Enhanced Editing Commands. For Use with ELECTRIC PENCIL PC.
Blue Cat.

Pengo. *Compatible Hardware:* Atari XL/XE. ROM cartridge $19.95 (Order no.: RX8045).
Atari Corp.

Penn Dragon Fonts: Graphic Astrology. Feb. 1996. *Items Included:* Documentation. *Customer Support:* Free unlimited phone support.
System 6.0.2 or higher, System 7 Savvy. Macintosh (1Mb). Contact publisher for price.
Windows. IBM PC. Contact publisher for price.
Unique Collection of Distinctive, High-Quality Astrological Symbol Fonts in TrueType & PostScript Formats. For Use with Io Series Programs, Desktop Publishing Applications, Word Processors, Graphics Tools, & Other Popular Software.

Penny Pincher II. Jun. 1984. *Items Included:* Communications disk, instruction manual, screwdriver, pencil, questionnaire master. *Customer Support:* Training available (free if in Atlanta), 90-day warranty, toll-free 800 number, maintenance available after 90 days at $369/yr, upgrade to more powerful software, monthly newsletter.
MS-DOS 2.1 or higher (256k). IBM PC, PC XT, PC AT, PS/2 & 100% compatibles. disk $550.00. *Optimal configuration:* 640k RAM; 10Mb hard disk.
Produces Basic Financial Plan Including Balance Sheet, Net Worth Analysis, Federal Income Tax Estimate, Cash Flow Analysis, Retirement Planning, Education Planning & Life Insurance Needs Analysis.
IFDS, Inc.

PenPlot. Nov. 1987. *Compatible Hardware:* IBM PC. *Memory Required:* 384k. *General Requirements:* 2 disk drives, plotter, Generic CADD. *Customer Support:* 60 day money back guarantee, unlimited technical support to registered users.
IBM. disk $49.95 (ISBN 1-55814-139-1, Order no.: F0900).
IBM. (ISBN 1-55814-140-5, Order no.: T0900). 3.5" disk $49.99.
Takes Generic CADD Drawing Files in Vector Format & Converts It to a Format That Plotters Work With. Imitates & Optimizes the Plot of the Drawing File.
Autodesk, Inc.

PENPLOT. *Version:* 2.2. Nov. 1985. *Compatible Hardware:* IBM PC, PC AT, PC XT & compatibles. *Operating System(s) Required:* PC-DOS, MS-DOS. *Language(s):* FORTRAN. *Memory Required:* 512k. *General Requirements:* Plotter.
disk $250.00 (Order no.: PENPLOT).
Plotter Driver That Translates a Geostat Plot File to One a Pen Plotter Can Understand. The Program Can Currently Translate to Houston Instruments or Ioline DM/PL, Hewlett Packard HP-GL & Calcomp 907 Formats.
Geostat Systems International, Inc. (GSII).

Pension & Excise Tax Planner. *Version:* 2.05. Alex Brucker & Paul G. Hoffman. Apr. 1991. *Items Included:* User manual, 12 months of maintenance coverage. *Customer Support:* Free telephone support: 1-800-367-1040, Annual maintenance contract: $99.00.
PC-DOS/MS-DOS 2.0 & higher. IBM PC & compatibles (512k). disk $249.00 (Order no.: 1693).
Computes 15% Excise Tax on Excess Pension Distributions & Accumulations. Distribution Options Include Minimum Distribution, Lump Sum, Grandfathered Amount & Threshold Amount. Minimum Distribution Rules Are Automatically Applied. Print Graphs & Customizable Reports Comparing Alternatives to Make Planning Easy.
CCH Access Software.

Pension Profile. *Version:* 1992-1993. Jan. 1995. *Items Included:* 1 - '92-'93, CD-ROM containing 800,000 pension plans. 1 - 3 1/2" Pension Profile program diskette. 1 - operational manual. *Customer Support:* Telephone technical support.
IBM. CD-ROM disk Contact publisher for price.
A Reference for Marketing Professionals. Its 800,000 Pension & Welfare Benefit Plans Are Easily Accessed to Create the Most Comprehensive Resource Tool Available. Marketing Efforts Become More Efficient Cross Reference Indexes, Identify Competitor's, Their Clients & Fees. The Software Program Prints Reports, Lists, Labels, Envelopes, & Generates TXT or DBF Files.
G. E. Matthews & Assocs., Inc.

Pension Resource. *Version:* 3.96. 1996. *Compatible Hardware:* IBM PC with 1 floppy disk drive & hard disk. *Operating System(s) Required:* PC-DOS 3.1 & higher. *Memory Required:* 250k. disk $795.00, incl. manual.
Financial Modelling of Qualified Plans. Features Grid Style Presentation of Alternative Plan Designs to Calculate & Compare More Than 19 Plan Types Including 401(K) Profit Sharing, Money Purchase, Defined Benefit with & Without Integration/Split Finding. Has Unique "Shelter Analysis" to Determine If a Selected Plan Is a Good Tax Shelter for the Employer. Also Includes Several Supporting Programs Such As Pension Distribution & Pension Maximization. Benefit Analysis.

PENSIONMAX: Investment Management System. 1977. *Compatible Hardware:* IBM PC, PC XT, PC AT & compatibles; Prime. *Operating System(s) Required:* PC-DOS/MS-DOS, PRIMOS. *Language:* C, ANSI FORTRAN 77. *Memory Required:* 512k.
contact publisher for price.
Designed for Institutional Investors with Long-Term Investment Portfolios. Provides Securities Accounting & Reporting for Bonds, Stocks, Mortgage-Backed Securities, Treasuries, Governmental Agencies, Collateral-Backed & Money Market Securities. Also Provides Investment Inventory, Transaction & Income Reporting, Cash Accounting, Bond Swapping, Performance Measurements, Deferred Gains & Losses, & a Complete, Continuous Record of All Investment Activity in Each Issue Owned or Previously Owned. Reports, Which are Produced on Demand, Include: the Current Position on a Trade or Settlement Date Basis; the Details of Purchase & Sale Transactions; Projections of Interest & Principal Cash Flow; & All Amortization or Accretion Changes to Book Value.
Wismer Assocs., Inc.

PentaxPlus. Jan. 1996.
DOS. Contact publisher for price.
Government Forms System for the DOS Platform. The Combination of the Best Features of Corbel's Pentabs Government Forms System with the Former EBG & Associates, Inc. Pentax System. Updates Include the Ability to Filter Plans Using a Number of Parameters, Menus & Screens Designed for Better Readability, Much Faster Printing of Government Forms, & the Ability to Print up to Three Blank Attachments. All of the Necessary Forms for Basic Plan Administration Are Included.
Corbel & Co.

Penthouse: CD-ROM Virtual Photo Shoot 2. Oct. 1994.
IBM. CD-ROM disk $69.95 (ISBN 1-56832-244-5, Order no.: 50642-2).
WarnerVision Entertainment, Inc.

People. *Version:* 6.1. Kent Ochel & Bert Brown. Oct. 1989. *Items Included:* Tutorial disk; 3-ring binder with manual. *Customer Support:* Unlimited free technical support at (512) 251-7541.
Any DOS or Windows. IBM PC; XT; AT or compatibles (512k). 3.5" disk $49.95.
Any Macintosh. 3.5" disk $49.95.
Set of Indexes Created Using LIBRARIAN. These Indexes Cross Reference the Bible by More Than 140 of the Most Frequently Referenced Personalities, Allowing the User to Study the Lives of the Most Significant People in the Scriptures.
Bible Research Systems.

PEOPLE-PLANNER Labor Forecaster. *Version:* 6.0. Jan. 1996. *Items Included:* Documentation; 60 days support. *Customer Support:* 60 day free support with purchase. Afterward, support can be purchased as an annual contract or hourly. Training is additional (per day fee plus expenses).
MS-DOS 5.0 or higher, Unix System V, AIX, HP-UX, SUN-OS, SCO UNIX, SCO XENIX, OS/2 2.1. HP 9000, IBM PC & compatibles, PS/2 (590k)), RS6000; ICL DRS 3000; NCR 3000 & Towers; SUNSPARC, Siemens Nixdorf PCD Series, other V.4 platforms. $1500.00-$2500.00 per module/list. *Optimal configuration:* 486 Processor (or Pentium) 1Mb RAM or more, 60Mb plus hard disk. *Networks supported:* Novell & Similar.
DOS 5.0 or higher, Unix V.4, AIX, HP-UX, SUN-OS, OS/2, SCO UNIX, SCO XENIX. HP 9000, ICL DRS 3000, IBM RS6000, NCR Tower Line/NCR 3000 Series, SUNSPARC, Siemens Nixdorf PCD Series, other V.4 platforms. $1500.00-$2500.00 per module/list. *Optimal configuration:* 1Mb RAM or more, 60Mb plus hard drive.
Creates a Historical Database from POS Data & Projects Both Sales & Labor, Based on Items, Customers, Transactions or Unit Criteria. Other Factors, Such As Min/Max Coverage, Store Hours, Productivity & Special Events Are Considered As Well. Accommodates Non-Revenue Departments Such As Stock & Maintenance. Volume Discount & Licenses Available.
Information Marketing Businesses, Inc.

People-Planner Schedule Manager. Feb. 1996. *Items Included:* Documentation; Quick Start Guide; on-line help; interactive coaches. *Customer Support:* Available.
Windows 3.1, Windows NT, Win 95. 486 (4Mb). disk $495.00. *Nonstandard peripherals required:* Mouse, color monitor, printer (suggested). *Addl. software required:* Form & Report Writer if desired.
A Windows-Based Software Tool That Simplifies the Scheduling Process. Within Minutes, Managers Point, Click, Drag & Drop Their Way to Producing the Best Schedule for Any Department or Store. Featuring On-Line Help & Interactive Coaches, SmartLists, Scheduled Time Away, Real-Time Schedule Costing & Other Features.
Information Marketing Businesses, Inc.

TITLE INDEX

PEOPLE-PLANNER Scheduler & Time & Attendance System. Version: 6.0. Jan. 1996. Compatible Hardware: HP 9000; ICL DRS 3000; IBM PC & compatibles, PS/2, RS6000; NCR Tower, NCR 3000 Series; SUNSPARC, Siemens Nixdorf PCD Series & other V.4 platforms. Operating System(s) Required: MS-DOS 5.0 or higher, Unix V.4, AIX, UP-UX, SUN-OS, SCO UNIX, SCO XENIX, OS/2 2.1. Language(s): C & Informix. Memory Required: Unix 16Mb plus, PCs 1000k. Items Included: Documentation. Customer Support: 60 day free support with purchase. Available as an annual contract or hourly afterward. Training is additional (per day fee plus expenses).
$1500.00-$2500.00 per module/list.
Manages Information Concerning Personnel & Work Requirements, Producing Weekly Work Schedules. Time & Attendance Monitors Employee Work Time Using Electronic Timeclocks to Produce Timecards & Management Reports. Produces ASCII Payroll File. Volume discounts & licenses available.
Information Marketing Businesses, Inc.

A People with One Heart: Stories from Around the World for the Child Within Us All CD. Mike Pinder. Nov. 1995.
IBM. CD-ROM disk Contact publisher for price (ISBN 1-888057-05-X).
Mike Pinder, Singer, Songwriter of The Moody Blues, Narrates Seven Uplifting & Imaginative Stories or Myths for Children over a Musical Atmosphere Created by Mike Pinder. The Second of a Series of Three Spoken Word Albums for Children. Also "A Planet with One Mind" & "An Earth with One Spirit".
One Step Records.

peopleBASE. Version: 4.2. Jul. 1993. Compatible Hardware: IBM PC & compatibles. Operating System(s) Required: PC-DOS, MS-DOS. Language(s): DBASE/Clipper. Memory Required: 2000k. General Requirements: Hard disk, 80386 CPU. Items Included: 400 page manual. Customer Support: 1 year free phone. Site or headquarters training available.
disk $199.00 (Order no.: SE3).
3.5" disk $199.00 (Order no.: SE3/M).
test disks (4) $5.00.
LAN version $699.00.
Integrated System That Combines Database Management, Word Processing, "Mail Merge", Appointment Scheduling, Phone Dialing, & Analytic Reporting Capabilities. The Goal: to Make Users More Effective in Day-to-Day Telephone/Mail Correspondence. Using Simple Pull-Down Menus, Users Can Select a Person to Be Called, Review That Person's Correspondence History, Auto-Dial the Phone, Update the History, & Print a Personalized "Thank-You" Letter; Manage Mailing Lists, Print Labels &/or Form Letters, Print Call Reports & Custom Lists, & Analyze Information Stored in the Database.
High Caliber Systems, Inc.

Pepper: Examine Phonetic & Program to Phonologic Evaluation Records. Lawrence D. Shriberg. 1990. Customer Support: Free technical support, 90-day limited warranty.
DOS. 3.5" disk $495.00 (ISBN 1-56321-047-9).
Provides Comprehensive Phonetic & Phonological Analyses of Spontaneous Speech Samples.
Lawrence Erlbaum Assocs. Software & Alternate Media, Inc.

Percentage Hold'em. Version: 1.1. Steven R. Jacobs. May 1994. Items Included: Manual, 3.5" disk (free exchange). Customer Support: Limited phone support.
MS-DOS 3.2 or higher. IBM PC & compatibles (640k). $30.00 plus shipping (ISBN 1-886070-03-2, Order no.: 9405).
Simulate the Performance of Hold'em Pocket Cards Against Any Number of Players. Compare Starting Hands Against Each Other Using Simulation or Exact Analysis.
ConJelCo.

Perception: A Computerized Approach. Version: 3.0. Theodore T. Hirota. Items Included: Quick Reference. Customer Support: Free telephone support.
MS-DOS, PC-DOS 2.1 or higher. IBM & AT & compatible (128k). disk $395.00 (Order no.: 820). Optimal configuration: IBM-AT, Hard drive, EGA or VGA required, 8Mb hard drive space required. Networks supported: Novell.
A Landmark in the Teaching of Perception. Using High-Resolution EGA/VGA Graphics, Sound, Movement & Text, the Programs Cover Theory Methodology, & Experiments. Students May Work Independently or in Groups Using the Programs & the Lab Manuals That May Be Printed from Text Files. Major Topics Include: Energy, Light & Color, the Visual System, Demonstration of Visual Phenomena.
Life Science Assocs.

Perfect-Assistant. May 1991. Items Included: 3 bound manuals. Customer Support: Free support for current version, 90-day money back guarantee.
DOS 3.1 or higher. 286, 386 recommended (640k). $269.00 single user, $1495.00 multi-user with unlimited license on a single server. Addl. software required: WordPerfect 5.0 or 5.1. Optimal configuration: 386 with 1Mb RAM, hard disk, & WordPerfect 5.1. Networks supported: Any that are NetBios compatible.
Tracks WordPerfect Documents by Simply Typing in a Name. Its Online Guidebook Gives Contact Sensitive Help. The Program Searches, Copies & Archives by Many Categories So You Don't Have to Remember File Names. Also Includes: E-Mail; a Scheduler with Calendars; an Address File for Mail Merges; a System Which Bills for Documents by the Word, Page, Typist, or Hour; & a Report Writer.
Unlimited Processing, Inc.

Perfect Balance. Version: 1.1. Jan. 1987. Compatible Hardware: IBM PC & compatibles, PC XT, PC AT, DisplayWriter. Operating System(s) Required: MS-DOS, UCSD p-System. Language(s): Pascal. Memory Required: 256k. General Requirements: Hard disk, printer.
IBM PC & compatibles, PC XT, PC AT. disk $99.00.
DisplayWriter. 8" disk $99.00.
Maintains "Perfect Balance" of Checkbook by Posting All Deposits & Disbursements. Prints Checks on Users Pre-Printed Check Forms. Makes Bank Reconciliation Easy. Use of RAM Makes Processing Very Rapid. Easy-to-Follow Screen Menus & Instructions.
Helu Software Corp.

Perfect Match. Mark C. Nelson. Mar. 1987. Compatible Hardware: Atari ST. Memory Required: 512k.
3.5" disk $39.95 (ISBN 0-923213-63-5, Order no.: AT-PMAT).
Educational "Concentration" Type Program Which Allows Users to Enter Their Own Questions & Answers.
MichTron, Inc.

Perfect Merge. Apr. 1989. Items Included: 1 program disk, 1 manual. Customer Support: Telephone support free 1 yr.
MS-DOS (256k). IBM PC & compatibles. $149.00.
Converts ASCII Records Containing Upper Case Name Address Information to Clean Personalized Mixed Case Output. Salutation Can Be Generated Based on Gender of Name. Input File Can Be Any Size from Large Mainframe Database Extracts to Small PC File Output File Generated in WordPerfect Secondary Merge Format with Control Characters.
Berkshire Software Co.

Perfect Sound: Digital Sound Sampler. Compatible Hardware: Commodore Amiga. Language(s): C.
$89.95.
Stereo Digitizer. Allows Users to Record Any Sound in Mono or Stereo, & Then Use the PERFECT SOUND Editor to Modify the Sound: Delete, Insert, Graph, or Flip Recorded Sounds. Features Include: Records Both Channels Simultaneously, 8-Bit Sample Length, up to 23,283 per Second Sample Rate, 11.6 KHz Frequency Response. Source Code Is Included.
MicroSearch.

The Perfect Word. Compatible Hardware: Apple Macintosh 512KE. General Requirements: Hard disk.
3.5" disk $170.00.
$60.00 each text module.
Bible Study & Research Program with Word & Phrase Search, Verse Text Display & Word Count Statistics. Available in Different Text Modules, Including King James, the New International & the Revised Standard Versions.
Star Software, Inc.

Perfect Writer/Speller. Perfect Software. Operating System(s) Required: MS-DOS. Memory Required: 128k.
$399.00.
Texas Instruments, Personal Productivit.

Perfect Writer/Speller/Calc. Perfect Software. Operating System(s) Required: MS-DOS. Memory Required: 128k.
$549.00.
Texas Instruments, Personal Productivit.

PerfectCache: File Caching & Virtual Disk. Version: 2.0. 1991. Items Included: Manual, quarterly newsletter. Customer Support: Customer support included in price.
VMS. VAX. $217.00-$850.00.
Maximizes I/O Throughput by Placing Files or Applications in Main Memory. Accesses to These Files or Applications Occur at Memory Speed Versus Disk Speed. The Resulting Improvements in I/O Performance Can Be Significant, Especially for I/O Intensive Applications.
Raxco, Inc.

PerfectDisk: Disk Defragmentation & Optimization. Version: 5.0. 1991. Items Included: Manuals, quarterly newsletter. Customer Support: Customer support included in price.
VMS. VAX (2Mb main memory). $199.00-$1232.00.
Technically Advanced Disk Defragmentation & Optimization System Designed to Reduce File Fragmentation & to Consolidate Free Space. File Optimization Positions Files on the Disk to Minimize Average Seek Time, Which Is a Major Component of I/O Performance. By Using "Watch Mode", System Triggers a Pass Based on File Fragmentation Activity. Defragments/Optimizes & Positions Files in a Single Pass. Supports Users of INGRES, ORACLE, RDB, ALL-IN-1, & More.
Raxco, Inc.

PerfectTune: Dynamic Online System Tuning. Version: 3.1. 1990. Items Included: Manual, quarterly newsletter. Customer Support: Customer support included in price.
VMS. VAX (300 blocks, disk space). $217.00-$850.00.

Monitors System Workload & Adjusts System Parameters in Response to Workload Changes. Results in More Efficient Use of Available CPU & Memory Resources & Improved End-User Terminal Response Time.
Raxco, Inc.

Perform II. *Version:* 1.1 or higher. *Compatible Hardware:* IBM PC, PC XT, PC AT & compatibles. *Operating System(s) Required:* MS-DOS. *Memory Required:* 128k.
$495.00.
Sort Utility $395.00.
Performance Measurement Program to Monitor Productivity. Assigns Situations Such As Employees Working with Multiple Machines & Many Part Numbers. Compares Employee's Actual Hours for Each Operation Part Number Combination to Its Associated Time Standard & Calculates Earned Hours & Percentage of Performance.
Indiana Digital Corp.

Performance Analysis of Passive Solar Heated Buildings. *Compatible Hardware:* IBM PC. *Operating System(s) Required:* PC-DOS. *Language(s):* Microsoft BASIC. *Memory Required:* 64k. *General Requirements:* Lotus 1-2-3.
disk $60.00.
Calculates Energy Provided by Solar Heat, Heating Load, Alternate Energy Sources Required per Month, & Yearly Totals. Based on the Solar Load Ratio Method Developed by Los Alamos Scientific Laboratory. Sample Input & Output Printouts Are Available.
Caldwell Software.

Performance Measurement: PMS. Oct. 1985. *Compatible Hardware:* IBM PC XT, PC AT, all Intel. *General Requirements:* Hard disk, printer.
disk $1495.00.
Based on Management-by-Objective, This System Encourages Thorough Planning Which Establishes Objectives & Goals. Provides Management Reports & Documentation of the Activities of Sales Staff. Provides Salesman with Daily Planning Tools, Long Range Forecasting by Probability, Initial Problem Areas & Day-to-Day Administration Which Provides Updates, Communication, Documentation & Prioritizes Calls Efficiently.
Datamatics Management.

Performance Monitor. *Version:* 2.0. Sep. 1994. *Items Included:* 100 page manual. *Customer Support:* After the first year, $150.00 per year, includes upgrades & toll-free support.
DOS 2.0. IBM or compatible (640k). disk $595.00. *Addl. software required:* CENTERPIECE 3.2.
Provides Comprehensive Performance Measurement & Reporting by Total Portfolio, Asset Class, or Individual Security Using BAI Prescribed Methods. The System Is Compatible with the AIMR Performance Presentation Guidelines. It Allows Comparisons with Multiple Market Indices & Allows the Construction of Properly Weighted Composite Returns.
Performance Technologies, Inc.

Performance Now! *Version:* 2.02. Aug. 1995. *Items Included:* User manual, online tutorial. *Customer Support:* Unlimited free phone support for registered users.
Windows 3.1 or higher. 386 or higher (4Mb). disk $129.00, Multi-user pricing avail. *Optimal configuration:* Windows 3.1 compatible graphics card & monitor, mouse, 8Mb space on hard disk, floppy disk drive. *Networks supported:* Most Local Area Networks.
A Knowledge-Based Interactive Software Program That Coaches Users Through the Process of Writing Clear & Effective Performance Reviews. Based on the User's Answers, KnowledgePoint's Exclusive Intelli-Text Technology Writes a Fully-Formatted Review Using the Standard Ratings/Essay Appraisal Format. Includes Employee Log & Form Design Too.
KnowledgePoint.

Performance Now!: Computer Aided Performance Review. 1995. *Items Included:* Full manual. *Customer Support:* Free telephone support - 90 days, 30-day warranty.
MS-DOS 3.2 or higher. 286 (584k). $119.95-$199.95. *Nonstandard peripherals required:* CGA/EGA/VGA.
This Remarkable Product Actually Writes the Reviews for You - in Just Minutes. Simply Choose from Dozens of Performance Factors & Rate Your Employee. PERFORMANCE NOW! Does the Rest. Coaches You Through Each Step of the Review, Providing Expert Advice, & Even Checking Your Work.
Dynacomp, Inc.

Performer. *Version:* 3.3.
Macintosh Plus or higher. 3.5" disk $495.00.
MIDI Sequencer. Provides Synthesizer Control for Recording, Editing, & Playing Back Musical Compositions.
Mark of the Unicorn.

Periodical Indexing Manager. *Version:* I. 1991. *Compatible Hardware:* Apple IIe, IIc; IBM PC, PC XT, PS/2 & compatibles. *Memory Required:* Apple 64k, IBM 512k. *General Requirements:* 2 disk drives or hard disk, printer. *Items Included:* Disks, Complete illustrated instructions binder. *Customer Support:* Technical 8:30-4pm M-F telephone no charge.
Apple $99.00, IBM $149.00 (Order no.: PUBIND).
Apple. (ISBN 0-87132-957-3).
IBM. (ISBN 0-87132-956-5).
Allows Periodicals to Be Indexed When They Arrive, Eliminating the Need to Wait for Publication's Index Which Arrives at the End of the Year.
Right On Programs.

Periodical Manager. *Version:* 4.0. 1995. *Items Included:* Complete instructions. *Customer Support:* 1 year free replacement of damaged disks, free unlimited telephone customer support.
MS-DOS. IBM PC, PC XT, PC AT, PS/2 & compatibles (640k). disk $369.00 (ISBN 1-55812-084-X). *Addl. software required:* None. Network version $499.00.
$379.00 Windows version.
Windows Network version $499.00.
Combines Subscription Manager & Routing Manager (See Complete Descriptions). Enter Data in One Portion & It Is Read in Both. Interact to Produce an Outstanding Serial Control Program. Prints on Horizontally Perforated Paper for Economy. Paper Supplied with Program.
Right On Programs.

Periscope-EM. *Version:* 5.4. Brett Salter. Jun. 1993. *Compatible Hardware:* 8088 or higher PC. *Operating System(s) Required:* PC-DOS/MS-DOS 3.1 or higher. *Language(s):* Assembly. *Items Included:* Software, manual, & break-out switch. *Customer Support:* 1PM-5PM EST, M-F.
$295.00 (ISBN 0-923537-04-X).
Full-Featured, Memory-Resident, Symbolic Debugger Which Supports Popular PC Programming Languages Like Microsoft & Borland Compilers & Linkers, & Others. Does Not Use Conventional DOS Memory If You Use Supporting 386 Memory Manager on 386 or Higher Machine.
Periscope Co.

Periscope I. *Version:* 5.4. Brett Salter. Jun. 1993. *Compatible Hardware:* 8088 or higher PC. *Operating System(s) Required:* PC-DOS/MS-DOS 3.1 or higher. *Language(s):* Assembly. *Memory Required:* 32k in high DOS memory; 0k in lower 640k. *Items Included:* Manual, 512k memory board, software & break-out switch. *Customer Support:* 1PM-5PM EST, Mon.-Fri..
$495.00 (ISBN 0-923537-00-7).
Full-Featured, Symbolic Debugging System with Crash Recovery Capability. Includes Both Protection for Debugger Software & Symbols via Write-Protected RAM Board & Ability to Interrupt System Anytime via Break-Out Switch. Supports the Most Popular Languages, Microsoft & Borland Compilers & Linkers, & Others.
Periscope Co.

Periscope IV. *Version:* 5.4. Sep. 1991. *Items Included:* Manual, software, breakout switch, pod (pod must be ordered separately but is required). *Customer Support:* M-F, 1-5 PM East Coast time.
PC-DOS/MS-DOS 3.1 or higher. 286, 386, 386SX, 486DX, & 486DX2. $1295.00-$2695.00 (ISBN 0-923537-06-6, Order no.: PERISCOPEIV).
Full-Featured Symbolic & Source Level Debugging System That Also Provides Hardware Trace Buffer & Hardware Breakpoint Capabilities Like an In-Circuit Emulator (ICE).
Periscope Co.

Perl. *Customer Support:* All of our products are unconditionally guaranteed.
DOS, Unix. CD-ROM disk $39.95 (Order no.: PERL). *Nonstandard peripherals required:* CD-ROM drive.
7000 Files for the Perl Lang. from over a Dozen Perl Archives.
Walnut Creek CDRom.

Perpetual Calendar. *Customer Support:* 800-929-8117 (customer service).
MS-DOS. IBM PC, PS/2. disk $59.99 (ISBN 0-87007-628-0).
Apple II. disk $39.99 (ISBN 0-87007-630-2).
Print Calendars for Any Year Using a Choice of Five Heading Pictures. Calculate Julian Date, Gregorian Date, Days Between Dates, & Day of the Week of a Given Date.
SourceView Software International.

Perquackey. *Compatible Hardware:* Apple II+. *Language(s):* Applesoft BASIC. *Memory Required:* 16k.
disk $14.95.
Vocabulary Game That Is Played Against the Clock. Form Words from Ten Computer Generated Letters Before the Time Runs out.
Powersoft, Inc.

Personal Architect. *Version:* 2.1. *Compatible Hardware:* IBM PC & compatibles. *Memory Required:* 640k. *General Requirements:* Hard disk.
disk $4500.00.
CAD Program for Architecture Featuring 3-D Building Modeling, Automatic Drawing Generation, Plans, Sections, Elevations, Perspectives, Automatic Bill-of-Materials Take-Off, 3-D Capabilities, Macro Facilities, Text Editor, On-Line Help & User-Customizable, Integrated Non-Graphic Database. Imports & Exports IGES & .DXF File Formats. Technical Phone Support Available.
Computervision Corp.

Personal Balance Sheet. *Operating System(s) Required:* Apple Macintosh, IBM PC. *Language(s):* MBASIC (source code included). *Memory Required:* IBM 128k, Macintosh 512k. *General Requirements:* Printer.

disk $29.95.
Provides a Way to Create a Statement of Users Financial Position.
Dynacomp, Inc.

Personal BASIC. Digital Research, Inc. *Operating System(s) Required:* CP/M-86, Concurrent CP/M-86. *Memory Required:* 128k. *General Requirements:* Winchester hard disk.
$150.00.
Texas Instruments, Personal Productivit.

Personal Best: The Mental Breakfast of Champions. *Version:* 3.1. R. Steve Walker. Mar. 1993. *Items Included:* 25 page user guide, Quick Reference guide. *Customer Support:* Free phone support.
MS-DOS 2.1 & higher or Windows. IBM & compatibles (128k). $20.00 Basic Edition; $50.00 Pro Edition; $25.00 Kid's Edition; $5.00 extra databases; $15.00 upgrades (Order no.: (404) 351-1055). *Optimal configuration:* Works on all systems with 720k drive & higher. *Networks supported:* Will work with all networks.
System 6.0 & higher. Macintosh (512k). $20.00 Basic Edition; $50.00 Pro Edition; $25.00 Kid's Edition; $5.00 extra databases; $15.00 upgrades (Order no.: (404) 351-1055). *Optimal configuration:* Works on all systems. *Networks supported:* Will work with all networks.
Unique Application Provides Daily 'Food for Thought' to Motivate You with Jokes, Quotes, Wisdom, Words, Reviews, & Insights. Maintains a Diary Entry, a to Do List, a Phone List, Reminds You of Birthdays & Important Dates. Time Management Features Are Designed for People, Not Superhumans, & Are Kept Simple. Variety of Quotes & Quips Is Both Extensive & Fascinating. Can Help You Improve Your Productivity, Creativity, Energy, Positive Attitude, Reading Skills, Writing Skills, & Time Management. Speed Modes Make It a Breeze to Automate: QuickView (Displays All Screens for N Seconds), QuickEntry (Loads Editor Each Day for Daily Data), QuickFax (Faxes Screens Each Day to Mailing List), QuickPrint (Prints Screens Each Day), & Archive (Archives Daily Data to .XXX Each Day). Pro Edition Includes Greeting Cards & Envelope Printing.
Protronics Computer Systems.

Personal Bill Paying. *Compatible Hardware:* TRS-80 Model I, Model III. *Memory Required:* 16k.
cassette $14.95 (Order no.: 0103R).
List Household Accounts Month-by-Month (Current Debts, Bills Paid & Any Other Info.).
Instant Software, Inc.

Personal Budget System. *Customer Support:* 800-929-8117 (customer service).
MS-DOS. IBM/PS2. disk $99.99 (ISBN 0-87007-195-5).
A Flexible System Because User Can Structure Information in Whatever Way Chosen. Allows for As Many As 200 Categories of Income and/or Expense. User Will Provide a Description for Each Category to Be Used, & Will Assign Each One a Category Code Number. Each Category Must Also Be Assigned to a Group of Budget Class. Thereafter User May Enter Transactions, Maintain Files, Balance Accounts, Look up Items in the Budget History, Create Current, Next Year & Year-End Budget Estimates, Report Variances, & Year-End Reorganization. System Is Menu Driven.
SourceView Software International.

Personal Card File. *Compatible Hardware:* HP 150 Touchscreen, IBM PC.
HP. 3.5" disk $160.00 (Order no.: 45422A).
IBM. disk $160.00 (Order no.: 45422E).
Works & Looks Like a Rolodex Card File. To Create a New Card File the User Designs the Card for the Desired Specifications by Painting the Fields on the Screen.
Hewlett-Packard Co.

Personal Commentary. *Version:* 6.1. Kent Ochel & Bert Brown. Oct. 1989. *Items Included:* Tutorial disk; 3-ring binder with manual. *Customer Support:* Unlimited free technical support at (512) 251-7541.
Any DOS or Windows. IBM PC; XT; AT or compatibles (512k). disk $49.95.
Any Macintosh. 3.5" disk $49.95.
Provides the User with a Full-Featured Text Editor for Entering, Editing, Saving, Retrieving & Printing Commentary for Any Verse in the Bible. Up to 2 Type-Written Pages May Be Entered for Each Verse. VERSE SEARCH is required.
Bible Research Systems.

Personal Computer Automatic Investment Management. *Items Included:* Bound manual. *Customer Support:* Free hotline - no time limit; 30 day limited warranty; updates are $5/disk plus S&H.
MS-DOS. IBM PC & compatibles (128k). disk $149.95. *Nonstandard peripherals required:* Two floppy-disk drives (minimum of 360k each), or one floppy & one hard-disk drive; 80-column printer (dot matrix or daisy wheel).
CP/M (64k). disk $79.95. *Nonstandard peripherals required:* Two floppy-disk drives (minimum of 160k each), or one floppy & one hard-disk drive; 80-column printer (dot matrix or daisy wheel).
Enables the Investor to Easily Create & Maintain Data Files Containing Company/Corporation Name, Number of Shares, Cash, & Interest Earned. It Calculates Stock Price, Portfolio Value, Buy/Sell Advice, & Market Orders, As Well As Return on Investment (ROI). In Addition, It Maintains Current & Historical Records of All Transactions for Evaluation of Investment Performance. Provides the Following Capabilities/Functions: Inputting/Maintaining Stock & Cash Information; Adjusting Stock Price(s); Calculating Buy/Sell Advice & Market Orders; Maintaining a SAFE (Braking Factor) Dollar Amount; Maintaining Historical Records of All Transactions; Computing Return on Investment.
Dynacomp, Inc.

Personal Computer Picture Graphics. Eugene M. Ying. *Compatible Hardware:* IBM PC, PCjr, PC XT, PC AT, Portable PC, 3270 PC. *Operating System(s) Required:* DOS 2.00, 2.10, 3.00, 3.10. *Memory Required:* IBM PCjr 256k, all others 128k. *General Requirements:* Double-sided disk drive, IBM Color Display, IBM Graphics Printer recommended; joystick, lightpen, & plotter optional.
disk $29.95 (Order no.: 6276508).
Allows User to Mix & Match over 300 Existing Images to Create New Graphics. 6 Typefaces Are Available for Text, & Text & Images Can Be Combined to Create Document Covers, Signs, & Graphic Presentations. User Can Produce Graphs, & Can Digitize Photographs & Illustrations for Output to a Plotter.
Personally Developed Software, Inc.

Personal Consultant Easy (PC Easy). *Compatible Hardware:* IBM PC & compatibles; TI Professional.
disk $495.00.
Expert System Development Tool for Prototyping & Development of Expert Systems Applications on Personal Computers. Designed for Those Just Getting Started in Expert System Development. Features a Rule Entry Language with Integrated Window-Oriented Editor; Comprehensive User Explanation Facilities Such As WHY, HOW, HELP, & REVIEW; Support for IBM & TI EGA Graphics; & Access to External Information Through DOS Files or dBASE Inquiries. The Knowledge Bases Are 100% Upwardly Compatible with PC PLUS Products. Optional Run-Time Diskette Is Available.
Texas Instruments, Personal Productivit.

Personal Consultant Plus (PC Plus). *Compatible Hardware:* IBM PC AT & compatibles, TI Professional.
$2950.00.
Expert System Development Tool. Provides Extended Knowledge Representation Features; Increased Rule Capacity; & Access to the LISP Language. Features a Rule Entry Language with Comprehensive User Explanation Facilities Such As WHY, HOW, HELP, & REVIEW; Support for TI & IBM EGA Graphics Cards; & Access to External Information Through DOS Files or dBASE Inquiries. An Optional Run-Time Diskette Is Available.
Texas Instruments, Personal Productivit.

Personal Correspondence Manager. E. D. Gough. *Compatible Hardware:* IBM PC, PC XT, PC AT, Portable PC, 3270 PC. *Operating System(s) Required:* PC-DOS 2.00, 2.10, 3.00, 3.10. *Memory Required:* 256k. *General Requirements:* IBM Display, 2 double-sided disk drives or one hard disk, IBM Matrix printer.
disk $39.95 (Order no.: 6276615).
Allows User to Start IBM SCRIPT/PC, IBM PERSONAL EDITOR, or IBM WORD PROOF with a Single Keystroke; Select the Mail Log Function to Log the Filename to the Item, Author, Addressee, & Subject; Add Documents Not Created with the PERSONAL CORRESPONDENCE MANAGER to the Mail Log; Create Formatted Text.
Personally Developed Software, Inc.

Personal Datebook. Organic Software, Inc. *Compatible Hardware:* HP 86/87 with CP/M System (HP 82900A).
3-1/2" or 5-1/4" disk $150.00 ea. (Order no.: 45582A).
Includes Some of the Features of DATEBOOK II, but Is Designed for the Individual Who Keeps a Personal Calendar. Maintains Appointment for up to Nine People. The Group Feature Is Not Included.
Hewlett-Packard Co.

Personal Designer. *Compatible Hardware:* IBM PC & compatibles.
Version 2-D. disk $2400.00.
3-D Mechanical Design & Drafting Program.
Computervision Corp.

Personal Editor III. *Version:* 5.0. Oct. 1995. *Items Included:* Spiral-bound manual. *Customer Support:* Technical support.
IBM PC & compatible (256k). disk $89.95.
Text Editor. Includes Word Wrapping, Text Reformatting, Paragraph, Line, Word & Character Markings For Moving, Copying, Deleting, or Overlaying Text & Tab & Margin Adjusting. Allows User to Customize Keyboard Designations to Reflect Editing Preferences & Can Redefine Up-Key Combinations for Executing User-Defined Commands.
Personally Developed Software, Inc.

Personal Estimator: Computer Aided Estimating. *Version:* 0.22. C. W. Kanavle. Jan. 1992. *Operating System(s) Required:* MS-DOS. *Memory Required:* 512k. *Customer Support:* Unlimited telephone assistance.
disk $195.00.
Electrical Job Estimating System Which Is Complete with 7 Megabyte Data File of Labor Units & Component Costs Covering over 33,000 Electric Assemblies.
Litek, Inc.

Personal Experience Inventory for Adults (PEI-A). *Version:* 1.010. Mar. 1996. *Customer Support:* Free unlimited phone support.
Windows 3.X, Windows 95. 286 (4Mb). disk $275.00 (Order no.: W-1089).
This Self-Report Inventory Provides Comprehensive Information about Substance Abuse Patterns in Adults. It Can Be Used to Identify Alcohol & Drug Problems, Make Referrals, & Plan Treatment.
Western Psychological Services.

Personal Experience Inventory (PEI). *Version:* 2.012. Ken C. Winters & George A. Henly. *Customer Support:* Free unlimited phone support.
IBM PC & 100% compatibles. 3.5" or 5.25" disk $285.00 (Order no.: W-1035 (5.25"); W-1036 (3.5")). *Optimal configuration:* DOS 3.0 or higher (512k), & hard disk with one Mb of free hard disk space, printer.
Documents the Onset, Nature, Degree, & Duration of Chemical Involvement in 12- to 18-Year-Olds. And Identifies Personal Risk Factors That May Precipitate or Sustain Substance Abuse. The PEI Is Particularly Useful Because It Covers All Forms of Substance Abuse, Assesses Both Chemical Involvement & Related Psychosocial Problems, Is Designed Specifically for Adolescents, & Documents the Need for Treatment.
Western Psychological Services.

Personal Fansim. *Version:* 2.4. Jan. 1992. *Items Included:* Disk & manual. *Customer Support:* Free telephone support.
MS-DOS. IBM PC/AT/XT/286/386 (512k). disk $119.00 (Order no.: FSP-PF). *Optimal configuration:* Math coprocessor.
Frequency Analysis & Synthesis on up to 2k Records. Allows FFT Operations, Windowing, Transfer Functions, Time & Special Function Generation, Curve Fitting, Bode Plots. Limited License Version.
Tutsim Products.

Personal Finance. 1989. *General Requirements:* Lotus 1-2-3.
IBM PC. contact publisher for price (ISBN 0-538-80058-5, Order no.: FH60BD).
Study Guide & Student Template Disk for Use with Lotus 1-2-3 & the Text - Personal Finance by Mathur. Contains Set-ups for Problems from the Text, Study Guide Problems & Solutions, & Selected Tables from the Text.
South-Western Publishing Co.

Personal Finance Aids. *Compatible Hardware:* TI Home Computer.
contact publisher for price.
Home Finance Aid.
Texas Instruments, Personal Productivit Products.

Personal Finance Manager. *Compatible Hardware:* IBM PC; Apple. *Memory Required:* Apple 48k, IBM 128k. *General Requirements:* Printer.
disk $49.95.
Updated Version of PERSONAL FINANCE SYSTEM.
Dynacomp, Inc.

Personal Finance Planner. *Items Included:* Bound manual. *Customer Support:* Free hotline - no time limit; 30 day limited warranty; updates are $5/disk plus S&H.
MS-DOS. IBM & compatibles (128k). disk $29.95. *Nonstandard peripherals required:* 80-column printer is suggested, but is optional. *Addl. software required:* BASICA/GWBASIC.
Apple (48k). disk $29.95.
Financial Management Tool. Prepares Personal Balance Sheets, Income Statements, & Detailed Financial Analyses. Insurance, Real Estate, Stocks, Bonds, Mutual Funds, & IRA Analyses & Projections Are Provided.
Dynacomp, Inc.

Personal Finance System. *Compatible Hardware:* Apple; IBM PC. *Memory Required:* 48k, IBM 128k.
contact publisher for price.
Dynacomp, Inc.

Personal Finances with Lotus. *Version:* 3.0. 1990. *Items Included:* 300 page user's guide, 46 page quick start manual, two 5.25" disks, one 3.5" disk. *Customer Support:* Toll free phone support.
MS-DOS, PC-DOS (256k). IBM or compatible. $99.00 (ISBN 0-936667-11-7). *Addl. software required:* Lotus 1-2-3.
Menu Driven Program Covering Stock Investment, Bonds, Options, Planning for Retirement, Budgeting Family Finances, Determining Borrowing Costs & More. Available for All Versions of Lotus 1-2-3.
Automated Reasoning Technologies, Inc.

Personal Financial Forecaster. *Compatible Hardware:* IBM PC & compatibles. *Memory Required:* 256k.
$69.95.
Lets User See the Detailed Accounting of Their Portfolio & See the Impact of a Change in the Portfolio. Program's Worksheet Format Creates Accountings of Financial Products Including Investments, Savings Accounts, Credit Accounts, Loans, Income & Expenses.
LTD Software.

The Personal Financial Manager. *Compatible Hardware:* IBM PC. *Memory Required:* 128k. $200.00 (ISBN 0-13-658386-5).
Financial Management Package for High-Income Individuals. Keeps Track of Credit Card Accounts, Checking Accounts, Assets/Liabilities, Budgets. Also Does Check Printing, Budget Tracking, Double Entry Bookkeeping; Keeps Tax Records, & Has an Account Status Report Feature for 170 Pre-Defined Accounts.
Prentice Hall.

Personal Financial Plan (PFP): A Guide. *Version:* 1.1. William T. Streeter. Nov. 1994. *Items Included:* Instruction booklet w/exercises.
MS-DOS 3.3 or higher. IBM or compatible PC (4Mb). Contact publisher for price (ISBN 1-886572-07-0). *Optimal configuration:* PC compatible MS-DOS 3.3 or higher, 4Mb RAM, 300k expandable (EMS) memory, Buffer-35, Files-60 min.
Automated Financial Spreadsheet Tracks & Compiles Personal Spending (Expenses) & Income to Provide Detailed Monthly Journals Income Statements, Balance Sheets, Income Tax Projections & Much More. Analyze Charge Card Debt, Installment Loans & Mortgages Using the Debt & Loan Amortization File. PFP Automatically Posts Data on All Other Files (Reports). Ideal for Beginning Money Management.
Baypointe Publishing.

Personal Financial Planner. *Items Included:* Spiral-bound manual. *Customer Support:* Free telephone Support.
MS/PC-DOS (640k). IBM PC, PC XT, PC AT & compatibles. disk $295.00. *Addl. software required:* Lotus 1-2-3.
Includes Personal Financial Statements (Statement of Financial Condition, Net Worth, Current Period, 12-Month & 5-Year Cash Flow Statements), Estate Tax Planner, Insurance Needs Planner, Disability Needs Planner, Real Estate Planner, Retirement Needs Planner, Education Fund Planner, Investment Analysis & Amortization Schedules.
Accounting Professionals Software, Inc.

Personal Financial Planner. Stephan R. Leimberg & Joseph Coluzzi. Mar. 1994. *Customer Support:* 30-day money-back guarantee, telephone support, facsimile service.
DOS. 386 or higher speed personal computer. disk $549.00. *Addl. software required:* Lotus 2.3 or higher. *Optimal configuration:* IBM PC or compatible system, 2Mb RAM, expanded memory driver DOS version 3.0 or higher, Lotus 123 version 2.3 or higher.
Windows. 386 or higher speed personal computer. disk $549.00. *Addl. software required:* Lotus or Excel for Windows. *Optimal configuration:* IBM PC or compatible system, 4Mb RAM, expanded memory driver, Windows version 3.0 or higher, Excel or Lotus 123 for Windows.
Full Blown Gift & Estate, Life Insurance, Education & Retirement Planning. Powerful Color or Black & White Results. Modular So You Don't Have to Spend a Lot of Time to Get the Answers You Want. Incredicble Graphs/Flowcharts!
Dynamic Financial Logic Corp.

The Personal Financial Planner. *Compatible Hardware:* IBM PC. *Memory Required:* 128k. disk $200.00 (ISBN 0-13-658402-0).
Designed to Help the High-Income Individual Making $35,000 or More Chart His Financial Future Considering Such Financial Goals As a Child's College Education, Additions to the Home, Vacations, Retirement, etc.
Prentice Hall.

The Personal Financial Planner: Professional Edition. *Compatible Hardware:* IBM PC. *Memory Required:* 128k.
disk $695.00 (ISBN 0-13-658477-2).
Financial Planning Tool Assists Lawyers, CPA's, Financial Planners, & Other Professionals in Analyzing & Generating Reports (up to 50 Pages) on Their Clients' Financial Status.
Prentice Hall.

Personal Financial Planning Made Easy. *Version:* 3.0. May 1991. *Compatible Hardware:* IBM PC, PC XT, PC AT & compatibles. *Memory Required:* 256k. *General Requirements:* Hard disk. *Items Included:* 4 5-1/4" disks of 2 3-1/2" disks, plus 169 page manual. *Customer Support:* Provided, limited.
disk $89.95 (ISBN 0-929416-00-7, Order no.: 11).
Provides Personal Financial Planning, Financial Problems Solutions, & Financial Information Systems Methods. Runs with Lotus 1-2-3. Planning Topics Include: Cash Flow, Balance Sheet, Income Tax, Portfolio Management, Financial Simulation, Real Estate, Life Insurance, College Education & Retirement.
Advanced Financial Planning Group, Inc.

Personal Income & Expense Report. *Compatible Hardware:* TI 99/4A. *Operating System(s) Required:* DX-10. *Language(s):* Extended BASIC. *Memory Required:* 48k.
cassette $27.95.
Month-to-Date & Year-to-Date Record of Personal Income, Expenses, Bank Accounts & Credit Accounts. Up to 10 Bank Accounts, 50 Credit Cards or Accounts & 100 Expense Categories Can Be Handled. Up to 10 Master Categories Are Provided for Expenses.
Eastbench Software Products.

Personal Injury Case Evaluation Program. *Customer Support:* 1 year.
IBM PC & compatibles (256k). disk $29.95.
Assists in the Evaluation of Personal Injury Claims.
Lawyers Software Publishing Co.

TITLE INDEX

Personal Investment Package, 3 disks.
Compatible Hardware: Commodore 64, IBM PC, TI 99/4A Home Computer. *Language(s):* Extended BASIC.
Set. $99.95 (Order no.: 233XD).
IBM, Commodore. write for info.
River City Software, Inc.
Call & Put Option Analysis.
   disk $34.95 (Order no.: 230XD).
Investment Aids I.
   disk $29.95 (Order no.: 211XD).
Portfolio Analysis.
   disk $59.95 (Order no.: 220XD).

Personal Lawyer-Power of Attorney & Statement of Guardianship. (Personal Lawyer Ser.). 1983. *Compatible Hardware:* IBM PC & compatibles, PC XT, PC AT. *Operating System(s) Required:* DOS 2.x, 3.x. *Memory Required:* 128k.
$69.95.
Creates Legal Documents Based on User's Responses to Questions Asked by Program. Documents Include: GENERAL POWER OF ATTORNEY Which Gives General Powers to a Person of Author's Choice; SPECIAL POWER OF ATTORNEY, Like General Power, but Limited to Things That User Specifies; REVOCATION OF POWER OF ATTORNEY, Revokes a Power Previously Given; & STATEMENT OF GUARDIANSHIP, Which Allows User to Give Control of Children to a Friend When Necessary.
Lassen Software, Inc.

Personal Lawyer-Promissory Notes. (Personal Lawyer Ser.). Sep. 1983. *Compatible Hardware:* IBM PC & compatibles, PC XT, PC AT. *Operating System(s) Required:* PC-DOS 2.x, 3.x. *Memory Required:* 12k.
$69.95.
Produces Promissory Notes That Are Legally Enforceable & Can Be Specifically Designed by User for Maximum Flexibility. Creates Notes That Are Paid Back with or Without Interest, with Installments, with Balloon Payments, or Even Simple Notes Payable Only on Demand. User Can Also Write a Note That Is Secured or Unsecured & Specify Type of Security Given.
Lassen Software, Inc.

Personal Lawyer-Residential Real Estate Lease. (Personal Lawyer Ser.), *Compatible Hardware:* IBM PC & compatibles, PC XT, PC AT. *Operating System(s) Required:* PC-DOS 2.x, 3.x. *Memory Required:* 128k.
disk $99.95.
Interactive Program That Helps User Write a Properly Structured & Legally Binding Lease for Residential Property.
Lassen Software, Inc.

Personal Lawyer-Wills. Version: 2.0. 1984. *Compatible Hardware:* Apple II+, IIe, IIc; IBM PC & compatibles. *Operating System(s) Required:* MS-DOS, PC-DOS, ProDOS. *Memory Required:* Apple 64k, IBM 128k.
disk $79.95.
Interactively Creates a Last Will & Testament by Asking User a Series of Questions As an Attorney Would. Each Response Is Analyzed, Then the Next Appropriate Question Is Selected. Upon Completion of This Phase, a Will That Is Unique to the Needs of the Individual User Is Printed. Wills May Be Updated. Legal in Every State Except Louisiana.
Lassen Software, Inc.

Personal Lawyer-Wills Professional Version. Version: 2.0. (Professional Lawyer Ser.). Sep. 1984. *Compatible Hardware:* IBM PC. *Operating System(s) Required:* PC-DOS 1.1, 2.0, 2.1, 3.x. *Memory Required:* 128k.
$149.95.
By Asking a Series of Questions & Incorporating the Answers with Correct Language to Insure Legality, Program Generates a User-Specific Will Which May Be Updated. Wills May Be Written to Disk & Amended with a Word Processor. Designed for Law Offices & Legal Clinics.
Lassen Software, Inc.

Personal Mailing List. Oct. 1986. *Compatible Hardware:* IBM PC, PC XT, PC AT. *Operating System(s) Required:* PC-DOS/MS-DOS. *Language(s):* Compiled BASIC. *Memory Required:* 128k. *General Requirements:* Printer (including letter quality).
disk $35.00.
Allows User to Create & Update a Mailing List of up to 500 Entries & Then Type Address Labels from That List on Any One Across Label.
Robert L. Nicolai.

Personal Money Manager. Version: 2.0. Jonathan King. *Compatible Hardware:* Atari ST, IBM PC with GEM, Sanyo 550.
3.5" disk $49.95.
Data Base Keeps Track of All User's Personal Finances from Yearly Budget to Checking Records in up to 999 Accounts. Supplies a Variety of Preformatted Reports.
MichTron, Inc.

Personal Numerologist. Version: 2.6. 1993. *Items Included:* 43 page comprehensive users manual. *Customer Support:* Free phone support.
PC-DOS, MS-DOS. IBM PC, XT, AT, PS/1, PS/2 & compatibles. disk $69.95 (ISBN 0-933281-07-2). *Optimal configuration:* 1 floppy drive, 80 column printer.
Provides Personalized Reports That Reveal the Most Intimate Characteristics & Motivations of User's Personality. Printed Reports Are Ideal to Better Understand Friends, Lovers & Co-Workers. Uses a Fully Integrated Approach to Delineate Complete Complexes of Numbers into Flowing, Well-Written Paragraphs. Reports Average 6 to 8 Pages & Includes a Yearly Forecast.
Widening Horizons, Inc.

Personal Numerology Report: Printing Version. Mike Quillman et al. 1983. *Compatible Hardware:* Apple II with Applesoft, II plus, IIc, IIe, III, Macintosh with 2 disk drives; Commodore 64; CP/M-based machines. *Operating System(s) Required:* Apple DOS, CP/M-80, MacFinder, MS-DOS. *Language(s):* MBASIC. *Memory Required:* Apple 48k; CP/M 64k; Macintosh 512k. *General Requirements:* Printer, dot-matrix or laser. *Items Included:* Manual. *Customer Support:* Free phone support.
disk $195.00 ea.
CP/M (Kaypro 2). (ISBN 0-913637-57-2).
MS-DOS. (ISBN 0-913637-85-8).
Apple. (ISBN 0-913637-55-6).
Macintosh. (ISBN 0-87199-055-5).
Commodore. (ISBN 0-87199-059-8).
Prints 7-Page Numerological Analysis Based on Name & Birth Date. Includes License to Sell Printed Output.
Astrolabe, Inc.

Personal Numerology Report 3. Version: 3. Feb. 1993. *Items Included:* Manual. *Customer Support:* Free phone support.
MS-DOS. 286 (640k). disk $250.00 (ISBN 0-87199-131-4). Nonstandard peripherals required: Hercules, EGA.
Prints or Displays Numerology Interpretations of 9 or More Pages. Includes Delineations for Motivation, Expression, Karma, Subconscious-Response, Destiny, Life-Cycle, Turning-Point & Challenge Numbers; Career, Gem & Color Advice; & Lucky Numbers for Each Day of Current Year. Fully Editable Text; Choice of Fonts for Printout. Can Also Be Used for Basic Numerology Calculations Alone.
Astrolabe, Inc.

PERSONAL PUBLISHING

Personal Numerology: Screen Version. (Ancient Arts Ser.). Apr. 1986. *Compatible Hardware:* Apple II, II+, IIe, IIc, IIgs with 5-1/4" disk drive, Macintosh with 2 disk drives; CP/M-based Machines; IBM PC. *Operating System(s) Required:* CP/M-80, MacFinder, MS-DOS, PC-DOS. *Language(s):* BASIC. *Memory Required:* Apple 32k, CP/M 64k, PC-DOS & MS-DOS 128k, Macintosh 512k. *Items Included:* Manual. *Customer Support:* Free phone support.
disk $39.95 ea., incl. manual.
CP/M (Kaypro 2). (ISBN 0-87199-025-3).
PC/MS-DOS. (ISBN 0-87199-023-7).
Macintosh. (ISBN 0-87199-056-3).
Apple II. (ISBN 0-87199-021-0).
Numerological Analysis Based on Name & Birth Date.
Astrolabe, Inc.

Personal Pediatrician. Version: 1.2. Joyce G. Wolf et al. *Items Included:* 25 page, easy to use user guide. *Customer Support:* Toll-free technical support hotline (800) 426-8426, free updates, unconditional 30-day money back guarantee.
DOS 3.3 or higher. IBM or compatibles (640k). disk $69.95 (Order no.: 1-800-426-8426). *Optimal configuration:* Requires IBM or compatible, operates on DOS 3.3 or higher & requires at least 640k memory.
Macintosh 4.1-6.08. Macintosh (512k). Contact publisher for price (Order no.: 1-800-426-8426). *Optimal configuration:* Macintosh System 4.1-6.08, at least 512k of memory.
Medical Diagnostic Software Will Assure Peace of Mind for Caring Parents by Giving Them Access to Instant Medical Advice. Asks Series of Questions, Quickly Zeros in on the Most Probable Diagnosis for a Child's Condition, & Then Recommends the Best Treatment, Medication & Course of Action.
Family Care Software.

Personal Physician. Version: 1.4. Isadore Rosenfeld. *Items Included:* 25 page, easy to use user guide. *Customer Support:* Toll-free technical support hotline (800) 426-8426, free updates, unconditional 30-day money back guarantee.
DOS 3.3 or higher. IBM or compatibles (640k). disk $69.95 (Order no.: 1-800-426-8426).
Optimal configuration: Requires IBM or compatible, operates on DOS 2.0 or higher & requires at least 640k memory.
Contact publisher for price (Order no.: 1-800-426-8426).
Medical Diagnostic Software That Gives Consumers Access to Instant Medical Advice on Their Home Computer. Asks a Series of Questions, Quickly Zeros in on the Most Probable Diagnosis for the User's Specific Condition & Then Recommends the Best Treatment, Medication & Course of Action.
Family Care Software.

Personal Property Inventory. *Compatible Hardware:* IBM PC & compatibles. *Operating System(s) Required:* MS-DOS, UNIX, ZENIX. *Language(s):* Compiled BASIC, C. *Memory Required:* 256k. *General Requirements:* 132-column printer (may be compressed).
disk $25.00.
telephone support ea. yr. $10.00.
Maintains Inventory of Personal Property for Insurance, Inheritance, etc.
Pro Data Systems, Inc.

Personal Publishing. *Compatible Hardware:* IBM PC. *Operating System(s) Required:* DOS. *Language(s):* Assembly. *Memory Required:* 512k. *General Requirements:* 2 disk drives.
disk $50.00.
Exclusively for Intergraphics Inc. Typesetting Service Customers. Aids in Preparation & Formatting of Texts Prior to Typesetting. For Use by Those Already Using Intergraphics Inc. for Their Typesetting.
Intergraphics, Inc.

PERSONAL REAL ESTATE

Personal Real Estate. *Compatible Hardware:* TI Home Computer, cassette or disk data storage system. *Memory Required:* 32k.
contact publisher for price (Order no.: PHM 3022).
Evaluates Personal Real Estate Investments.
Texas Instruments, Personal Productivity Products.

Personal Real Estate Manager. *Items Included:* Bound manual. *Customer Support:* Free hotline - no time limit; 30 day limited warranty; updates are $5/disk plus S&H.
MS-DOS 2.0 or higher. IBM & compatibles (128k). disk $49.95. *Nonstandard peripherals required:* Printer supported, but not required.
Record-Keeping System for the Part-Time Investor Having up to 10 Properties. Organizes & Automates the Accounting Tasks of the Part-Time Landlord, Keeping Track of All Expenses by Category, Rent, Security Deposits, & Basic Tenant Information. Year-to-Date Summaries Are Readily Available, along with Status Reports on Profitability, Cash Flow, & Asset/Liability/Net Worth.
Dynacomp, Inc.

Personal Record Keeping. *Compatible Hardware:* TI Home Computer, cassette or disk data storage system. *Memory Required:* 32k.
cassette write for info. (Order no.: PHM 3013).
Filing System.
Texas Instruments, Personal Productivity Products.

Personal Report Generator. *Compatible Hardware:* TI Home Computer, controller or cassette recorder & cable, TI impact printer, RS 232 interface & personal record keeping cartridge. *Memory Required:* 32k.
contact publisher for price (Order no.: PHM 3044).
Produces Reports According to User's Design Specifications.
Texas Instruments, Personal Productivity Products.

Personal Scientific Calculator. Donald L. Raimondi & Jerome D. Swalen. *Compatible Hardware:* IBM PC, PCjr, PC XT, PC AT, Portable PC, 3270 PC with IBM Display & one double-sided disk drive. *Operating System(s) Required:* DOS 1.10, 2.00, 2.10, 3.00, 3.10. *Memory Required:* IBM PCjr 256, all others 128k.
disk $24.95—6276513.
Allows User to Perform Scientific Calculations; Displays a Full Screen of Active Stack & Memory Areas for Variables; Access Standard Constants for Commonly Used Conversion Factors; Designate Fixed Decimal or Scientific Notation; Program Standard Calculations Once; Display Degrees or Radians, Real & Complex Numbers, Cartesian or Polar Coordinates; Compute SIN, COS, TAN, ARCSIN, ARCCOS, ARCTAN, SINH, COSH, TANH, ARCTANH, Factorials, Inverse Log to Base 10, Log to Base e, e Raised to a Power.
Personally Developed Software, Inc.

Personal STORM. *Version:* 3.0. 1992. *Items Included:* User's Manual.
MS-DOS 2.0 or higher. IBM PC & compatibles. Contact publisher for price.
Educational Version of Professional STORM, a Commercial Software Package Used in over 100 Corporations. Designed for Courses in Production & Operations Management Science, & Quantitative Methods &/or Research. Consists of a Set of Quantitative Modeling Techniques Which Can Be Used with any Textbook.
Allyn & Bacon, Inc.

Personal Task Manager. *Items Included:* Bound manual. *Customer Support:* Free hotline - no time limit; 30 day limited warranty; updates are $5/ disk plus S&H.

MS-DOS. IBM & compatibles (128k). disk $49.95. *Nonstandard peripherals required:* At least one disk drive & a printer.
Personal Task Organizer & Time-Management Tool. Allows You to Enter Your Most Important "Things to Do Today"; to Rank in Order of Priority; to Sort According to Ranks; to Save in a File; & to Display the List on a Printer. User May (Optionally) List the Estimated Time That Each Task Should Take & the Projected Starting Time; the Finishing Time Will Be Automatically Calculated & Displayed.
Dynacomp, Inc.

Personal Tax Plan. *Compatible Hardware:* TI Home Computer, controller & P-Code.
contact publisher for price (Order no.: PHD5077).
Analyzes Income & Expense Items for Tax Purposes.
Texas Instruments, Personal Productivit.

Personal Training for Adobe Illustrator 5.0. *Version:* 3.2. *Items Included:* Private tutor on audio cassette, diskette of lesson files, command summary card, extra practice card. *Customer Support:* Unlimited free technical support offered, 800-832-2499.
Apple Macintosh. 3.5" disk $99.95. *Addl. software required:* Appropriate software application.
Interactive Audio Training for the Macintosh & Macintosh Business Application.
Personal Training Systems.

Personal Training for Adobe Photoshop. *Version:* 2.5. *Customer Support:* Unlimited free technical support offered, 800-832-2499.
Macintosh. Contact publisher for price.
Personal Training Systems.

Personal Training for Excel. *Version:* 4.0. *Items Included:* Private tutor on audio cassette, diskette of lesson files, command summary card, extra practice card. *Customer Support:* Unlimited free technical support offered, 800-832-2499.
Apple Macintosh. 3.5" disk $99.95. *Addl. software required:* Appropriate software application.
Interactive Audio Training for the Macintosh & Macintosh Business Application.
Personal Training Systems.

Personal Training for FileMake Pro. *Version:* 2.0. *Items Included:* Private tutor on audio cassette, diskette of lesson files, command summary card, extra practice card. *Customer Support:* Unlimited free technical support offered, 800-832-2499.
Apple Macintosh. 3.5" disk $99.95. *Addl. software required:* Appropriate software application.
Interactive Audio Training for the Macintosh & Macintosh Business Applications.
Personal Training Systems.

Personal Training for Fonts. *Customer Support:* Unlimited free technical support offered, 800-832-2499.
Macintosh. 3.5" disk $59.95.
Page Layout & Presentations.
Personal Training Systems.

Personal Training for FreeHand. *Version:* 3.1. *Items Included:* Private tutor on audio cassette, diskette of lesson files, command summary card, extra practice card. *Customer Support:* Unlimited free technical support offered, 800-832-2499.
Apple Macintosh. 3.5" disk $99.95. *Addl. software required:* Appropriate software application.
Interactive audio training for the Macintosh & Macintosh Business Applications.
Personal Training Systems.

Personal Training for HyperCard. *Version:* 2.1. *Items Included:* Private tutor on audio cassette, diskette of lesson flies, command summary card, extra practice card. *Customer Support:* Unlimited free technical support offered, 800-832-2499.
Apple Macintosh. 3.5" disk $99.95. *Addl. software required:* Appropriate software application.
Interactive Audio Training for the Macintosh & Macintosh Business Aplications.
Personal Training Systems.

Personal Training for Intuit Quicken. *Customer Support:* Unlimited free technical support offered, 800-832-2499.
Macintosh. disk $59.95.
Personal Training Systems.

Personal Training for Lotus 1-2-3. *Version:* 1.1. *Customer Support:* Unlimited free technical support offered, 800-832-2499.
Macintosh. Contact publisher for price.
Personal Training Systems.

Personal Training for Macintosh Performa. *Version:* 7.01. *Customer Support:* Unlimited free technical support offered, 800-832-2499.
7.01. Macintosh Performa. 3.5" disk $99.95.
Personal Training Systems.

Personal Training for Microsoft Office. *Customer Support:* Unlimited free technical support offered, 800-832-2499.
Macintosh. 3.5" disk $399.00.
Personal Training Systems.

Personal Training for Microsoft PowerPoint. *Version:* 3.0. *Customer Support:* Unlimited free technical support offered, 800-832-2499.
Macintosh. Contact publisher for price.
Personal Training Systems.

Personal Training for Microsoft Works. *Version:* 3.0. *Items Included:* Private tutor on audio cassette, diskette of lesson files, command summary card, extra practice card. *Customer Support:* Unlimited free technical support offered, 800-832-2499.
Apple Macintosh. 3.5" disk $99.95. *Addl. software required:* Appropriate software application.
Interactive Audio Training for the Macintosh & Macintosh Business Applications.
Personal Training Systems.

Personal Training for PageMaker. *Version:* 5.0. *Items Included:* Private tutor on audio cassette, diskette of lesson files, command summary card, extra practice card. *Customer Support:* Unlimited free technical support offered, 800-832-2499.
Apple Macintosh. 3.5" disk $99.95. *Addl. software required:* Appropriate software application.
Interactive Audio Training for the Macintosh & Macintosh Business Applications.
Personal Training Systems.

Personal Training for Persuasion. *Version:* 2.1. *Items Included:* Private tutor on audio cassette, diskette of lesson files, command summary card, extra practice card. *Customer Support:* Unlimited free technical support offered, 800-832-2499.
Apple Macintosh. 3.5" disk $99.95. *Addl. software required:* Appropriate software application.
Interactive Audio Training for the Macintosh & Macintosh Business Applications.
Personal Training Systems.

Personal Training for QuarkXPress. *Version:* 3.1. Oct. 1990. *Items Included:* Private tutor on audio cassette, diskett of lesson files, command

TITLE INDEX

PERSONAL TRAINING SYSTEMS SOFTWARE

summary card, extra practice card. *Customer Support:* Unlimited free technical support offered; 800-832-2499.
Apple Macintosh. 3.5" disk $99.95. *Addl. software required:* Appropriate software application.
Interactive Audio Training for the Macintosh & Macintosh Business Application.
Personal Training Systems.

Personal Training for the Macintosh System 7.
Version: 7.0 & 7.1. *Items Included:* Private tutor on audio cassette, diskette of lesson files, command summary card, extra practice card. *Customer Support:* Unlimited free technical support offered, 800-832-2499.
System 7.0 & 7.1. Apple Macintosh. 3.5" disk $99.95. *Addl. software required:* Appropriate software application.
Interactive Audio Training for the Macintosh & Macintosh Business Applications.
Personal Training Systems.

Personal Training for Word. *Version:* 5.1. *Items Included:* Private tutor on audio cassette, diskette of lesson files, command summary card, extra practice card. *Customer Support:* Unlimited free technical support offered, 800-832-2499.
Apple Macintosh. 3.5" disk $99.95. *Addl. software required:* Appropriate software application.
Interactive Audio Training for the Macintosh & Macintosh Business Applications.
Personal Training Systems.

Personal Training for WordPerfect. *Version:* 2.1. *Customer Support:* Unlimited free technical support offered, 800-832-2499.
Macintosh. Contact publisher for price.
Personal Training Systems.

Personal Training Systems Claris Works.
Version: 2.0. *Customer Support:* Unlimited free technical support offered, 800-832-2499.
Macintosh. Contact publisher for price.
Personal Training Systems.

Personal Training Systems Software Made Easy: Advanced Adobe Illustrator. *Version:* 5.50. *Items Included:* Private tutor on audio cassette, diskette of lesson files, command summary card, extra practice card. *Customer Support:* Free Technical Support 800-832-2499.
Apple Macintosh. 3.5" disk $99.95 (ISBN 1-57217-005-0). *Addl. software required:* Appropriate software application for Title.
Interactive Audio Training for the Macintosh & Macintosh Business Applications.
Personal Training Systems.

Personal Training Systems Software Made Easy: Advanced Adobe Photoshop. *Version:* 2.50. *Items Included:* Private tutor on audio cassette, diskette of lesson files, command summary card, extra practice card. *Customer Support:* Free Technical Support 800-832-2499.
Apple Macintosh. 3.5" disk $99.95 (ISBN 0-944124-49-6). *Addl. software required:* Appropriate software application for Title.
Interactive Audio Training for the Macintosh & Macintosh Business Applications.
Personal Training Systems.

Personal Training Systems Software Made Easy: Advanced Adobe Photoshop. *Version:* 2.50. *Items Included:* Private tutor on audio cassette, diskette of lesson files, command summary card, extra practice card. *Customer Support:* Free Technical Support 800-832-2499.
Windows. Apple Macintosh. 3.5" disk $59.95 (ISBN 1-57217-010-7). *Addl. software required:* Appropriate software application for Title.
Interactive Audio Training for the Windows & Windows Business Applications.
Personal Training Systems.

Personal Training Systems Software Made Easy: Advanced Adobe Photoshop. *Version:* 3.00. *Items Included:* Private tutor on audio cassette, diskette of lesson files, command summary card, extra practice card. *Customer Support:* Free Technical Support 800-832-2499.
Apple Macintosh. 3.5" disk $99.95 (ISBN 1-57217-013-1). *Addl. software required:* Appropriate software application for Title.
Interactive Audio Training for the Macintosh & Macintosh Business Applications.
Personal Training Systems.

Personal Training Systems Software Made Easy: Advanced Aldus PageMaker. *Version:* 5.00. *Items Included:* Private tutor on audio cassette, diskette of lesson files, command summary card, extra practice card. *Customer Support:* Free Technical Support 800-832-2499.
Apple Macintosh. 3.5" disk $99.95 (ISBN 0-944124-46-1). *Addl. software required:* Appropriate software application for Title.
Interactive Audio Training for the Macintosh & Macintosh Business Applications.
Personal Training Systems.

Personal Training Systems Software Made Easy: Advanced Aldus PageMaker. *Version:* 5.00. *Items Included:* Private tutor on audio cassette, diskette of lesson files, command summary card, extra practice card. *Customer Support:* Free Technical Support 800-832-2499.
Windows. Apple Macintosh. 3.5" disk $59.95 (ISBN 1-57217-022-0). *Addl. software required:* Appropriate software application for Title.
Interactive Audio Training for the Windows & Windows Business Applications.
Personal Training Systems.

Personal Training Systems Software Made Easy: Advanced Claris Filemaker Pro.
Version: 2.00. *Items Included:* Private tutor on audio cassette, diskette of lesson files, command summary card, extra practice card. *Customer Support:* Free Technical Support 800-832-2499.
Apple Macintosh. 3.5" disk $99.95 (ISBN 1-57217-048-4). *Addl. software required:* Appropriate software application for Title.
Interactive Audio Training for the Macintosh & Macintosh Business Applications.
Personal Training Systems.

Personal Training Systems Software Made Easy: Advanced Claris Filemaker Pro.
Version: 2.00. *Items Included:* Private tutor on audio cassette, diskette of lesson files, command summary card, extra practice card. *Customer Support:* Free Technical Support 800-832-2499.
Windows. Apple Macintosh. 3.5" disk $59.95 (ISBN 1-57217-051-4). *Addl. software required:* Appropriate software application for Title.
Interactive Audio Training for the Windows & Windows Business Applications.
Personal Training Systems.

Personal Training Systems Software Made Easy: Advanced Excel Spreadsheets. *Version:* 4.00. *Items Included:* Private tutor on audio cassette, diskette of lesson files, command summary card, extra practice card. *Customer Support:* Free Technical Support 800-832-2499.
Apple Macintosh. 3.5" disk $99.95 (ISBN 0-944124-04-6). *Addl. software required:* Appropriate software application for Title.
Interactive Audio Training for Macintosh & Macintosh Business Applications.
Personal Training Systems.

Personal Training Systems Software Made Easy: Advanced Excel Spreadsheets. *Version:* 5.00. *Items Included:* Private tutor on audio cassette, diskette of lesson files, command summary card, extra practice card. *Customer Support:* Free Technical Support 800-832-2499.
Windows. Apple Macintosh. 3.5" disk $59.95 (ISBN 1-57217-094-8). *Addl. software required:* Appropriate software application for Title.
Interactive Audio Training for Windows & Windows Business Applications.
Personal Training Systems.

Personal Training Systems Software Made Easy: Advanced Excel 5.0. *Version:* 5.00. *Items Included:* Private tutor on audio cassette, diskette of lesson files, command summary card, extra practice card. *Customer Support:* Free Technical Support 800-832-2499.
Apple Macintosh. 3.5" disk $99.95 (ISBN 1-57217-091-3). *Addl. software required:* Appropriate software application for Title.
Interactive Audio Training for Macintosh & Macintosh Business Applications.
Personal Training Systems.

Personal Training Systems Software Made Easy: Additional Features Word. *Version:* 5.10. *Items Included:* Private tutor on audio cassette, diskette of lesson files, command summary card, extra practice card. *Customer Support:* Free Technical Support 800-832-2499.
Apple Macintosh. 3.5" disk $99.95 (ISBN 1-57217-124-3). *Addl. software required:* Appropriate software application for Title.
Interactive Audio Training for Macintosh & Macintosh Business Applications.
Personal Training Systems.

Personal Training Systems Software Made Easy: Advanced Lotus Spreadsheets. *Version:* 4.00. *Items Included:* Private tutor on audio cassette, diskette of lesson files, command summary card, extra practice card. *Customer Support:* Free Technical Support 800-832-2499.
Windows. Apple Macintosh. 3.5" disk $59.95 (ISBN 1-57217-073-5). *Addl. software required:* Appropriate software application for Title.
Interactive Audio Training for Windows & Windows Business Applications.
Personal Training Systems.

Personal Training Systems Software Made Easy: Adobe Photoshop. *Version:* 3.00. *Items Included:* Private tutor on audio cassette, diskette of lesson files, command summary card, extra practice card. *Customer Support:* Free Technical Support 800-832-2499.
Apple Macintosh. 3.5" disk $99.95 (ISBN 1-57217-159-6). *Addl. software required:* Appropriate software application for Title.
Interactive Audio Training for the Macintosh & Macintosh Business Applications.
Personal Training Systems.

Personal Training Systems Software Made Easy: Aldus PageMaker 5.0 Mac. *Version:* 5.00. *Items Included:* Private tutor on audio cassette, diskette of lesson files, command summary card, extra practice card. *Customer Support:* Free Technical Support 800-832-2499.
Apple Macintosh. 3.5" disk $99.95 (ISBN 1-57217-021-2). *Addl. software required:* Appropriate software application for Title.
Interactive Audio Training for the Macintosh & Macintosh Business Applications.
Personal Training Systems.

Personal Training Systems Software Made Easy: Aldus PageMaker 5.0 Windows.
Version: 5.00. *Items Included:* Private tutor on audio cassette, diskette of lesson files, command summary card, extra practice card. *Customer Support:* Free Technical Support 800-832-2499.

Windows. Apple Macintosh. 3.5" disk $59.95 (ISBN 1-57217-023-9). *Addl. software required:* Appropriate software application for Title.
Interactive Audio Training for the Windows & Windows Business Applications.
Personal Training Systems.

Personal Training Systems Software Made Easy: Advanced Quattro Pro Features. *Version:* 1.00. *Items Included:* Private tutor on audio cassette, diskette of lesson files, command summary card, extra practice card. *Customer Support:* Free Technical Support 800-832-2499.
Windows. Apple Macintosh. 3.5" disk $59.95 (ISBN 1-57217-043-3). *Addl. software required:* Appropriate software application for Title.
Interactive Audio Training for the Windows & Windows Business Applications.
Personal Training Systems.

Personal Training Systems Software Made Easy: Advanced System Features. *Version:* 7.10. *Items Included:* Private tutor on audio cassette, diskette of lesson files, command summary card, extra practice card. *Customer Support:* Free Technical Support 800-832-2499.
Apple Macintosh. 3.5" disk $99.95 (ISBN 1-57217-028-X). *Addl. software required:* Appropriate software application for Title.
Interactive Audio Training for the Macintosh & Macintosh Business Applications.
Personal Training Systems.

Personal Training Systems Software Made Easy: Advanced System Features. *Version:* 7.50. *Items Included:* Private tutor on audio cassette, diskette of lesson files, command summary card, extra practice card. *Customer Support:* Free Technical Support 800-832-2499.
Apple Macintosh. 3.5" disk $99.95 (ISBN 1-57217-034-4). *Addl. software required:* Appropriate software application for Title.
Interactive Audio Training for the Macintosh & Macintosh Business Applications.
Personal Training Systems.

Personal Training Systems Software Made Easy: Advanced Word. *Version:* 5.10. *Items Included:* Private tutor on audio cassette, diskette of lesson files, command summary card, extra practice card. *Customer Support:* Free Technical Support 800-832-2499.
Apple Macintosh. 3.5" disk $99.95 (ISBN 1-57217-123-5). *Addl. software required:* Appropriate software application for Title.
Interactive Audio Training for Macintosh & Macintosh Business Applications.
Personal Training Systems.

Personal Training Systems Software Made Easy: Advanced Word. *Version:* 6.00. *Items Included:* Private tutor on audio cassette, diskette of lesson files, command summary card, extra practice card. *Customer Support:* Free Technical Support 800-832-2499.
Windows. Apple Macintosh. 3.5" disk $59.95 (ISBN 1-57217-129-4). *Addl. software required:* Appropriate software application for Title.
Interactive Audio Training for Windows & Windows Business Applications.
Personal Training Systems.

Personal Training Systems Software Made Easy: Advanced Wordperfect. *Version:* 6.00. *Items Included:* Private tutor on audio cassette, diskette of lesson files, command summary card, extra practice card. *Customer Support:* Free Technical Support 800-832-2499.
Windows. Apple Macintosh. 3.5" disk $59.95.
Addl. software required: Appropriate software application for Title.
Interactive Audio Training for Windows & Windows Business Applications.
Personal Training Systems.

Personal Training Systems Software Made Easy: Advanced Word 6.0. *Version:* 6.0. *Items Included:* Private tutor on audio cassette, diskette of lesson files, command summary card, extra practice card. *Customer Support:* Free Technical Support 800-832-2499.
Apple Macintosh. 3.5" disk $99.95 (ISBN 1-57217-127-8). *Addl. software required:* Appropriate software application for Title.
Interactive Audio Training for Macintosh & Macintosh Business Applications.
Personal Training Systems.

Personal Training Systems Software Made Easy: Beginning Access. *Version:* 2.00. *Items Included:* Private tutor on audio cassette, diskette of lesson files, command summary card, extra practice card. *Customer Support:* Free Technical Support 800-832-2499.
Windows. Apple Macintosh. 3.5" disk $59.95 (ISBN 1-57217-081-6). *Addl. software required:* Appropriate software application for Title.
Interactive Audio Training for Windows & Windows Business Applications.
Personal Training Systems.

Personal Training Systems Software Made Easy: Beginning Aldus Freehand. *Version:* 3.10. *Items Included:* Private tutor on audio cassette, diskette of lesson files, command summary card, extra practice card. *Customer Support:* Free Technical Support 800-832-2499.
Apple Macintosh. 3.5" disk $99.95 (ISBN 0-944124-26-7). *Addl. software required:* Appropriate software application for Title.
Interactive Audio Training for the Macintosh & Macintosh Business Applications.
Personal Training Systems.

Personal Training Systems Software Made Easy: Beginning Aldus Freehand. *Version:* 3.10. *Items Included:* Private tutor on audio cassette, diskette of lesson files, command summary card, extra practice card. *Customer Support:* Free Technical Support 800-832-2499.
Windows. Apple Macintosh. 3.5" disk $59.95 (ISBN 0-944124-73-9). *Addl. software required:* Appropriate software application for Title.
Interactive Audio Training for the Windows & Windows Business Applications.
Personal Training Systems.

Personal Training Systems Software Made Easy: Beginning Adobe Illustrator. *Version:* 5.50. *Items Included:* Private tutor on audio cassette, diskette of lesson files, command summary card, extra practice card. *Customer Support:* Free Technical Support 800-832-2499.
Apple Macintosh. 3.5" disk $99.95 (ISBN 1-57217-003-4). *Addl. software required:* Appropriate software application for Title.
Interactive Audio Training for the Macintosh & Macintosh Business Applications.
Personal Training Systems.

Personal Training Systems Software Made Easy: Beginning Adobe Photoshop. *Version:* 2.50. *Items Included:* Private tutor on audio cassette, diskette of lesson files, command summary card, extra practice card. *Customer Support:* Free Technical Support 800-832-2499.
Apple Macintosh. 3.5" disk $99.95 (ISBN 0-944124-47-X). *Addl. software required:* Appropriate software application for Title.
Interactive Audio Training for the Macintosh & Macintosh Business Applications.
Personal Training Systems.

Personal Training Systems Software Made Easy: Beginning Adobe Photoshop. *Version:* 2.50. *Items Included:* Private tutor on audio cassette, diskette of lesson files, command summary card, extra practice card. *Customer Support:* Free Technical Support 800-832-2499.
Windows. Apple Macintosh. 3.5" disk $59.95 (ISBN 1-57217-008-5). *Addl. software required:* Appropriate software application for Title.
Interactive Audio Training for the Windows & Windows Business Applications.
Personal Training Systems.

Personal Training Systems Software Made Easy: Beginning Adobe Photoshop. *Version:* 3.00. *Items Included:* Private tutor on audio cassette, diskette of lesson files, command summary card, extra practice card. *Customer Support:* Free Technical Support 800-832-2499.
Apple Macintosh. 3.5" disk $99.95 (ISBN 1-57217-011-5). *Addl. software required:* Appropriate software application for Title.
Interactive Audio Training for the Macintosh & Macintosh Business Applications.
Personal Training Systems.

Personal Training Systems Software Made Easy: Beginning Aldus PageMaker. *Version:* 5.00. *Items Included:* Private tutor on audio cassette, diskette of lesson files, command summary card, extra practice card. *Customer Support:* Free Technical Support 800-832-2499.
Apple Macintosh. 3.5" disk $99.95 (ISBN 0-944124-42-9). *Addl. software required:* Appropriate software application for Title.
Interactive Audio Training for the Macintosh & Macintosh Business Applications.
Personal Training Systems.

Personal Training Systems Software Made Easy: Beginning Aldus PageMaker. *Version:* 5.00. *Items Included:* Private tutor on audio cassette, diskette of lesson files, command summary card, extra practice card. *Customer Support:* Free Technical Support 800-832-2499.
Windows. Apple Macintosh. 3.5" disk $59.95 (ISBN 0-944124-98-4). *Addl. software required:* Appropriate software application for Title.
Interactive Audio Training for the Windows & Windows Business Applications.
Personal Training Systems.

Personal Training Systems Software Made Easy: Beginning Claris Filemaker Pro. *Version:* 2.00. *Items Included:* Private tutor on audio cassette, diskette of lesson files, command summary card, extra practice card. *Customer Support:* Free Technical Support 800-832-2499.
Apple Macintosh. 3.5" disk $99.95 (ISBN 1-57217-046-8). *Addl. software required:* Appropriate software application for Title.
Interactive Audio Training for the Macintosh & Macintosh Business Applications.
Personal Training Systems.

Personal Training Systems Software Made Easy: Beginning Claris Filemaker Pro. *Version:* 2.00. *Items Included:* Private tutor on audio cassette, diskette of lesson files, command summary card, extra practice card. *Customer Support:* Free Technical Support 800-832-2499.
Windows. Apple Macintosh. 3.5" disk $59.95 (ISBN 1-57217-049-2). *Addl. software required:* Appropriate software application for Title.
Interactive Audio Training for the Windows & Windows Business Applications.
Personal Training Systems.

TITLE INDEX

PERSONAL TRAINING SYSTEMS SOFTWARE

Personal Training Systems Software Made Easy: Beginning Excel Spreadsheets. *Version:* 4.00. *Items Included:* Private tutor on audio cassette, diskette of lesson files, command summary card, extra practice card. *Customer Support:* Free Technical Support 800-832-2499. Apple Macintosh. 3.5" disk $99.95 (ISBN 0-944124-02-X). *Addl. software required:* Appropriate software application for Title.
Interactive Audio Training for Macintosh & Macintosh Business Applications.
Personal Training Systems.

Personal Training Systems Software Made Easy: Beginning Excel Spreadsheets. *Version:* 5.00. *Items Included:* Private tutor on audio cassette, diskette of lesson files, command summary card, extra practice card. *Customer Support:* Free Technical Support 800-832-2499. Windows. Apple Macintosh. 3.5" disk $59.95 (ISBN 0-944124-87-9). *Addl. software required:* Appropriate software application for Title.
Interactive Audio Training for Windows & Windows Business Applications.
Personal Training Systems.

Personal Training Systems Software Made Easy: Beginning Excel 5.0. *Version:* 5.00. *Items Included:* Private tutor on audio cassette, diskette of lesson files, command summary card, extra practice card. *Customer Support:* Free Technical Support 800-832-2499. Apple Macintosh. 3.5" disk $99.95 (ISBN 1-57217-089-1). *Addl. software required:* Appropriate software application for Title.
Interactive Audio Training for Macintosh & Macintosh Business Applications.
Personal Training Systems.

Personal Training Systems Software Made Easy: BEGINNING Lotus AMIPRO. *Version:* 2.00. *Items Included:* Private tutor on audio cassette, diskette of lesson files, command summary card, extra practice card. *Customer Support:* Free Technical Support 800-832-2499. Windows. Apple Macintosh. 3.5" disk $59.95 (ISBN 0-944124-66-6). *Addl. software required:* Appropriate software application for Title.
Interactive Audio Training for the Windows & Windows Business Applications.
Personal Training Systems.

Personal Training Systems Software Made Easy: Beginning Lotus Notes. *Version:* 3.00. *Items Included:* Private tutor on audio cassette, diskette of lesson files, command summary card, extra practice card. *Customer Support:* Free Technical Support 800-832-2499. Windows. Apple Macintosh. 3.5" disk $59.95 (ISBN 1-57217-074-3). *Addl. software required:* Appropriate software application for Title.
Interactive Audio Training for Windows & Windows Business Applications.
Personal Training Systems.

Personal Training Systems Software Made Easy: Beginning Lotus Spreadsheets. *Version:* 1.00. *Items Included:* Private tutor on audio cassette, diskette of lesson files, command summary card, extra practice card. *Customer Support:* Free Technical Support 800-832-2499. Apple Macintosh. 3.5" disk $99.95 (ISBN 0-944124-15-1). *Addl. software required:* Appropriate software application for Title.
Interactive Audio Training for the Macintosh & Macintosh Business Applications.
Personal Training Systems.

Personal Training Systems Software Made Easy: Beginning Lotus Spreadsheets. *Version:* 4.00. *Items Included:* Private tutor on audio cassette, diskette of lesson files, command summary card, extra practice card. *Customer Support:* Free Technical Support 800-832-2499. Windows. Apple Macintosh. 3.5" disk $59.95 (ISBN 1-57217-071-9). *Addl. software required:* Appropriate software application for Title.
Interactive Audio Training for the Windows & Windows Business Applications.
Personal Training Systems.

Personal Training Systems Software Made Easy: BeginningQuattro Pro. *Version:* 1.00. *Items Included:* Private tutor on audio cassette, diskette of lesson files, command summary card, extra practice card. *Customer Support:* Free Technical Support 800-832-2499. Windows. Apple Macintosh. 3.5" disk $59.95 (ISBN 1-57217-040-9). *Addl. software required:* Appropriate software application for Title.
Interactive Audio Training for the Windows & Windows Business Applications.
Personal Training Systems.

Personal Training Systems Software Made Easy: Beginning Power Point. *Version:* 4.00. *Items Included:* Private tutor on audio cassette, diskette of lesson files, command summary card, extra practice card. *Customer Support:* Free Technical Support 800-832-2499. Windows. Apple Macintosh. 3.5" disk $59.95 (ISBN 1-57217-111-1). *Addl. software required:* Appropriate software application for Title.
Interactive Audio Training for Windows & Windows Business Applications.
Personal Training Systems.

Personal Training Systems Software Made Easy: Beyond the Basics. *Version:* 6.0X. *Items Included:* Private tutor on audio cassette, diskette of lesson files, command summary card, extra practice card. *Customer Support:* Free Technical Support 800-832-2499. Apple Macintosh. 3.5" disk $99.95 (ISBN 1-57217-027-1). *Addl. software required:* Appropriate software application for Title.
Interactive Audio Training for the Macintosh & Macintosh Business Applications.
Personal Training Systems.

Personal Training Systems Software Made Easy: Beginning Word. *Version:* 5.10. *Items Included:* Private tutor on audio cassette, diskette of lesson files, command summary card, extra practice card. *Customer Support:* Free Technical Support 800-832-2499. Apple Macintosh. 3.5" disk $99.95 (ISBN 0-944124-44-5). *Addl. software required:* Appropriate software application for Title.
Interactive Audio Training for Macintosh & Macintosh Business Applications.
Personal Training Systems.

Personal Training Systems Software Made Easy: Beginning Word. *Version:* 6.00. *Items Included:* Private tutor on audio cassette, diskette of lesson files, command summary card, extra practice card. *Customer Support:* Free Technical Support 800-832-2499. Windows. Apple Macintosh. 3.5" disk $59.95 (ISBN 0-944124-85-2). *Addl. software required:* Appropriate software application for Title.
Interactive Audio Training for Windows & Windows Business Applications.
Personal Training Systems.

Personal Training Systems Software Made Easy: Beginning Wordperfect. *Version:* 2.10. *Items Included:* Private tutor on audio cassette, diskette of lesson files, command summary card, extra practice card. *Customer Support:* Free Technical Support 800-832-2499. Apple Macintosh. 3.5" disk $99.95 (ISBN 1-57217-151-0). *Addl. software required:* Appropriate software application for Title.
Interactive Audio Training for Macintosh & Macintosh Business Applications.
Personal Training Systems.

Personal Training Systems Software Made Easy: Beginning Word Perfect. *Version:* 6.00. *Items Included:* Private tutor on audio cassette, diskette of lesson files, command summary card, extra practice card. *Customer Support:* Free Technical Support 800-832-2499. Windows. Apple Macintosh. 3.5" disk $59.95 (ISBN 1-57217-154-5). *Addl. software required:* Appropriate software application for Title.
Interactive Audio Training for Windows & Windows Business Applications.
Personal Training Systems.

Personal Training Systems Software Made Easy: Beginning Word 6.0. *Version:* 6.00. *Items Included:* Private tutor on audio cassette, diskette of lesson files, command summary card, extra practice card. *Customer Support:* Free Technical Support 800-832-2499. Apple Macintosh. 3.5" disk $99.95 (ISBN 1-57217-125-1). *Addl. software required:* Appropriate software application for Title.
Interactive Audio Training for Macintosh & Macintosh Business Applications.
Personal Training Systems.

Personal Training Systems Software Made Easy: Beginning XPress Quark. *Version:* 3.20. *Items Included:* Private tutor on audio cassette, diskette of lesson files, command summary card, extra practice card. *Customer Support:* Free Technical Support 800-832-2499. Apple Macintosh. 3.5" disk $99.95 (ISBN 0-944124-90-9). *Addl. software required:* Appropriate software application for Title.
Interactive Audio Training for Macintosh & Macintosh Business Applications.
Personal Training Systems.

Personal Training Systems Software Made Easy: Charts & Databases Excel 5.0. *Version:* 5.00. *Items Included:* Private tutor on audio cassette, diskette of lesson files, command summary card, extra practice card. *Customer Support:* Free Technical Support 800-832-2499. Apple Macintosh. 3.5" disk $99.95 (ISBN 1-57217-092-1). *Addl. software required:* Appropriate software application for Title.
Interactive Audio Training for Macintosh & Macintosh Business Applications.
Personal Training Systems.

Personal Training Systems Software Made Easy: Cards & Stacks. *Version:* 2.10. *Items Included:* Private tutor on audio cassette, diskette of lesson files, command summary card, extra practice card. *Customer Support:* Free Technical Support 800-832-2499. Apple Macintosh. 3.5" disk $99.95 (ISBN 1-57217-053-0). *Addl. software required:* Appropriate software application for Title.
Interactive Audio Training for the Macintosh & Macintosh Business Applications.
Personal Training Systems.

Personal Training Systems Software Made Easy: Color & Type Quark. *Version:* 3.20. *Items Included:* Private tutor on audio cassette, diskette of lesson files, command summary card,

extra practice card. *Customer Support:* Free Technical Support 800-832-2499.
Apple Macintosh. 3.5" disk $99.95 (ISBN 0-944124-93-3). *Addl. software required:* Appropriate software application for Title.
Interactive Audio Training for Macintosh & Macintosh Business Applications.
Personal Training Systems.

Personal Training Systems Software Made Easy: Creating Excel Business Graphs. *Version:* 4.00. *Items Included:* Private tutor on audio cassette, diskette of lesson files, command summary card, extra practice card. *Customer Support:* Free Technical Support 800-832-2499.
Apple Macintosh. 3.5" disk $99.95 (ISBN 0-944124-05-4). *Addl. software required:* Appropriate software application for Title.
Interactive Audio Training for Macintosh & Macintosh Business Applications.
Personal Training Systems.

Personal Training Systems Software Made Easy: Creating Special Affects. *Version:* 3.10. *Items Included:* Private tutor on audio cassette, diskette of lesson files, command summary card, extra practice card. *Customer Support:* Free Technical Support 800-832-2499.
Windows. Apple Macintosh. 3.5" disk $59.95 (ISBN 0-944124-75-5). *Addl. software required:* Appropriate software application for Title.
Interactive Audio Training for the Windows & Windows Business Applications.
Personal Training Systems.

Personal Training Systems Software Made Easy: Creating Special Effects. *Version:* 3.10. *Items Included:* Private tutor on audio cassette, diskette of lesson files, command summary card, extra practice card. *Customer Support:* Free Technical Support 800-832-2499.
Apple Macintosh. 3.5" disk $99.95 (ISBN 0-944124-28-3). *Addl. software required:* Appropriate software application for Title.
Interactive Audio Training for the Macintosh & Macintosh Business Applications.
Personal Training Systems.

Personal Training Systems Software Made Easy: Converting to System 7-P1. *Version:* 7.10. *Items Included:* Private tutor on audio cassette, diskette of lesson files, command summary card, extra practice card. *Customer Support:* Free Technical Support 800-832-2499.
Apple Macintosh. 3.5" disk $99.95 (ISBN 1-57217-029-8). *Addl. software required:* Appropriate software application for Title.
Interactive Audio Training for the Macintosh & Macintosh Business Applications.
Personal Training Systems.

Personal Training Systems Software Made Easy: Converting to System 7-P2. *Version:* 7.10. *Items Included:* Private tutor on audio cassette, diskette of lesson files, command summary card, extra practice card. *Customer Support:* Free Technical Support 800-832-2499.
Apple Macintosh. 3.5" disk $99.95 (ISBN 1-57217-030-1). *Addl. software required:* Appropriate software application for Title.
Interactive Audio Training for the Macintosh & Macintosh Business Applications.
Personal Training Systems.

Personal Training Systems Software Made Easy: Excel Graphs & Business. *Version:* 5.00. *Items Included:* Private tutor on audio cassette, diskette of lesson files, command summary card, extra practice card. *Customer Support:* Free Technical Support 800-832-2499.
Windows. Apple Macintosh. 3.5" disk $59.95 (ISBN 1-57217-095-6). *Addl. software required:* Appropriate software application for Title.
Interactive Audio Training for Windows & Windows Business Applications.
Personal Training Systems.

Personal Training Systems Software Made Easy: Excel Macros. *Version:* 4.00. *Items Included:* Private tutor on audio cassette, diskette of lesson files, command summary card, extra practice card. *Customer Support:* Free Technical Support 800-832-2499.
Apple Macintosh. 3.5" disk $99.95 (ISBN 0-944124-07-0). *Addl. software required:* Appropriate software application for Title.
Interactive Audio Training for Macintosh & Macintosh Business Applications.
Personal Training Systems.

Personal Training Systems Software Made Easy: Excel Powerful Spreadsheets. *Version:* 4.00. *Items Included:* Private tutor on audio cassette, diskette of lesson files, command summary card, extra practice card. *Customer Support:* Free Technical Support 800-832-2499.
Apple Macintosh. 3.5" disk $99.95 (ISBN 0-944124-06-2). *Addl. software required:* Appropriate software application for Title.
Interactive Audio Training for Macintosh & Macintosh Business Applications.
Personal Training Systems.

Personal Training Systems Software Made Easy: Excel 5.0 Mac CD-ROM. *Version:* 5.00. *Items Included:* Private tutor on audio cassette, diskette of lesson files, command summary card, extra practice card. *Customer Support:* Free Technical Support 800-832-2499.
Apple Macintosh. CD-ROM disk $99.95 (ISBN 1-57217-093-X). *Addl. software required:* Appropriate software application for Title.
Interactive Audio Training for Macintosh & Macintosh Business Applications.
Personal Training Systems.

Personal Training Systems Software Made Easy: Excel 5.0 Windows CD-ROM. *Version:* 5.00. *Items Included:* Private tutor on audio cassette, diskette of lesson files, command summary card, extra practice card. *Customer Support:* Free Technical Support 800-832-2499.
Windows. Apple Macintosh. CD-ROM disk $59.95 (ISBN 1-57217-096-4). *Addl. software required:* Appropriate software application for Title.
Interactive Audio Training for Windows & Windows Business Applications.
Personal Training Systems.

Personal Training Systems Software Made Easy: Getting Started. *Version:* 7.10. *Items Included:* Private tutor on audio cassette, diskette of lesson files, command summary card, extra practice card. *Customer Support:* Free Technical Support 800-832-2499.
Apple Macintosh. 3.5" disk $99.95 (ISBN 0-944124-00-3). *Addl. software required:* Appropriate software application for Title.
Interactive Audio Training for the Macintosh & Macintosh Business Applications.
Personal Training Systems.

Personal Training Systems Software Made Easy: Getting Started with Windows. *Version:* 3.10. *Items Included:* Private tutor on audio cassette, diskette of lesson files, command summary card, extra practice card. *Customer Support:* Free Technical Support 800-832-2499.
Windows. Apple Macintosh. 3.5" disk $59.95 (ISBN 1-57217-112-X). *Addl. software required:* Appropriate software application for Title.
Interactive Audio Training for Windows & Windows Business Applications.
Personal Training Systems.

Personal Training Systems Software Made Easy: Getting Started with Windows. *Version:* 4.00. *Items Included:* Private tutor on audio cassette, diskette of lesson files, command summary card, extra practice card. *Customer Support:* Free Technical Support 800-832-2499.
Windows. Apple Macintosh. 3.5" disk $59.95 (ISBN 1-57217-113-8). *Addl. software required:* Appropriate software application for Title.
Interactive Audio Training for Windows & Windows Business Applications.
Personal Training Systems.

Personal Training Systems Software Made Easy: Getting Started with Windows V4.0. *Version:* 4.00. *Items Included:* Private tutor on audio cassette, diskette of lesson files, command summary card, extra practice card. *Customer Support:* Free Technical Support 800-832-2499.
Windows. Apple Macintosh. 3.5" disk $59.95 (ISBN 1-57217-115-4). *Addl. software required:* Appropriate software application for Title.
Interactive Audio Training for Windows & Windows Business Applications.
Personal Training Systems.

Personal Training Systems Software Made Easy: GETTING STARTED 3.1. *Version:* 3.10. *Items Included:* Private tutor on audio cassette, diskette of lesson files, command summary card, extra practice card. *Customer Support:* Free Technical Support 800-832-2499.
Windows. Apple Macintosh. 3.5" disk $59.95 (ISBN 0-944124-50-X). *Addl. software required:* Appropriate software application for Title.
Interactive Audio Training for Windows & Windows Business Applications.
Personal Training Systems.

Personal Training Systems Software Made Easy: Intermediate Access. *Version:* 2.00. *Items Included:* Private tutor on audio cassette, diskette of lesson files, command summary card, extra practice card. *Customer Support:* Free Technical Support 800-832-2499.
Windows. Apple Macintosh. 3.5" disk $59.95 (ISBN 1-57217-082-4). *Addl. software required:* Appropriate software application for Title.
Interactive Audio Training for Windows & Windows Business Applications.
Personal Training Systems.

Personal Training Systems Software Made Easy: Intermediate Aldus Freehand. *Version:* 3.10. *Items Included:* Private tutor on audio cassette, diskette of lesson files, command summary card, extra practice card. *Customer Support:* Free Technical Support 800-832-2499.
Apple Macintosh. 3.5" disk $99.95 (ISBN 0-944124-27-5). *Addl. software required:* Appropriate software application for Title.
Interactive Audio Training for the Macintosh & Macintosh Business Applications.
Personal Training Systems.

Personal Training Systems Software Made Easy: Intermediate Aldus Freehand. *Version:* 3.10. *Items Included:* Private tutor on audio cassette, diskette of lesson files, command summary card, extra practice card. *Customer Support:* Free Technical Support 800-832-2499.
Windows. Apple Macintosh. 3.5" disk $59.95 (ISBN 0-944124-74-7). *Addl. software required:* Appropriate software application for Title.
Interactive Audio Training for the Windows & Windows Business Applications.
Personal Training Systems.

TITLE INDEX

PERSONAL TRAINING SYSTEMS SOFTWARE

Personal Training Systems Software Made Easy: Intermediate Adobe Illustrator. *Version:* 5.50. *Items Included:* Private tutor on audio cassette, diskette of lesson files, command summary card, extra practice card. *Customer Support:* Free Technical Support 800-832-2499. Apple Macintosh. 3.5" disk $99.95 (ISBN 1-57217-004-2). *Addl. software required:* Appropriate software application for Title. *Interactive Audio Training for the Macintosh & Macintosh Business Applications.* Personal Training Systems.

Personal Training Systems Software Made Easy: Intermediate Adobe Photoshop. *Version:* 2.50. *Items Included:* Private tutor on audio cassette, diskette of lesson files, command summary card, extra practice card. *Customer Support:* Free Technical Support 800-832-2499. Apple Macintosh. 3.5" disk $99.95 (ISBN 0-944124-48-8). *Addl. software required:* Appropriate software application for Title. *Interactive Audio Training for the Macintosh & Macintosh Business Applications.* Personal Training Systems.

Personal Training Systems Software Made Easy: Intermediate Adobe Photoshop. *Version:* 2.50. *Items Included:* Private tutor on audio cassette, diskette of lesson files, command summary card, extra practice card. *Customer Support:* Free Technical Support 800-832-2499. Windows. Apple Macintosh. 3.5" disk $59.95 (ISBN 1-57217-009-3). *Addl. software required:* Appropriate software application for Title. *Interactive Audio Training for the Windows & Windows Business Applications.* Personal Training Systems.

Personal Training Systems Software Made Easy: Intermediate Adobe Photoshop. *Version:* 3.00. *Items Included:* Private tutor on audio cassette, diskette of lesson files, command summary card, extra practice card. *Customer Support:* Free Technical Support 800-832-2499. Apple Macintosh. 3.5" disk $99.95 (ISBN 1-57217-012-3). *Addl. software required:* Appropriate software application for Title. *Interactive Audio Training for the Macintosh & Macintosh Business Applications.* Personal Training Systems.

Personal Training Systems Software Made Easy: Intermediate Aldus PageMaker. *Version:* 5.00. *Items Included:* Private tutor on audio cassette, diskette of lesson files, command summary card, extra practice card. *Customer Support:* Free Technical Support 800-832-2499. Apple Macintosh. 3.5" disk $99.95 (ISBN 0-944124-43-7). *Addl. software required:* Appropriate software application for Title. *Interactive Audio Training for the Macintosh & Macintosh Business Applications.* Personal Training Systems.

Personal Training Systems Software Made Easy: Intermediate Aldus PageMaker. *Version:* 5.00. *Items Included:* Private tutor on audio cassette, diskette of lesson files, command summary card, extra practice card. *Customer Support:* Free Technical Support 800-832-2499. Windows. Apple Macintosh. 3.5" disk $59.95 (ISBN 0-944124-99-2). *Addl. software required:* Appropriate software application for Title. *Interactive Audio Training for the Windows & Windows Business Applications.* Personal Training Systems.

Personal Training Systems Software Made Easy: Intermediate Claris Filemaker. *Version:* 2.00. *Items Included:* Private tutor on audio cassette, diskette of lesson files, command summary card, extra practice card. *Customer Support:* Free Technical Support 800-832-2499. Apple Macintosh. 3.5" disk $99.95 (ISBN 1-57217-047-6). *Addl. software required:* Appropriate software application for Title. *Interactive Audio Training for the Macintosh & Macintosh Business Applications.* Personal Training Systems.

Personal Training Systems Software Made Easy: Intermediate Claris Filemaker. *Version:* 2.00. *Items Included:* Private tutor on audio cassette, diskette of lesson files, command summary card, extra practice card. *Customer Support:* Free Technical Support 800-832-2499. Windows. Apple Macintosh. 3.5" disk $59.95 (ISBN 1-57217-050-6). *Addl. software required:* Appropriate software application for Title. *Interactive Audio Training for the Windows & Windows Business Applications.* Personal Training Systems.

Personal Training Systems Software Made Easy: Intermediate Excel. *Version:* 4.00. *Items Included:* Private tutor on audio cassette, diskette of lesson files, command summary card, extra practice card. *Customer Support:* Free Technical Support 800-832-2499. Apple Macintosh. 3.5" disk $99.95 (ISBN 0-944124-03-8). *Addl. software required:* Appropriate software application for Title. *Interactive Audio Training for Macintosh & Macintosh Business Applications.* Personal Training Systems.

Personal Training Systems Software Made Easy: Intermediate Excel. *Version:* 5.00. *Items Included:* Private tutor on audio cassette, diskette of lesson files, command summary card, extra practice card. *Customer Support:* Free Technical Support 800-832-2499. Windows. Apple Macintosh. 3.5" disk $59.95 (ISBN 0-944124-88-7). *Addl. software required:* Appropriate software application for Title. *Interactive Audio Training for Windows & Windows Business Applications.* Personal Training Systems.

Personal Training Systems Software Made Easy: Intermediate Excel 5.0. *Version:* 5.00. *Items Included:* Private tutor on audio cassette, diskette of lesson files, command summary card, extra practice card. *Customer Support:* Free Technical Support 800-832-2499. Apple Macintosh. 3.5" disk $99.95 (ISBN 1-57217-090-5). *Addl. software required:* Appropriate software application for Title. *Interactive Audio Training for Macintosh & Macintosh Business Applications.* Personal Training Systems.

Personal Training Systems Software Made Easy: Intermediate Lotus. *Version:* 4.00. *Items Included:* Private tutor on audio cassette, diskette of lesson files, command summary card, extra practice card. *Customer Support:* Free Technical Support 800-832-2499. Windows. Apple Macintosh. 3.5" disk $59.95 (ISBN 1-57217-072-7). *Addl. software required:* Appropriate software application for Title. *Interactive Audio Training for the Windows & Windows Business Applications.* Personal Training Systems.

Personal Training Systems Software Made Easy: Intermediate Lotus Notes. *Version:* 3.00. *Items Included:* Private tutor on audio cassette, diskette of lesson files, command summary card, extra practice card. *Customer Support:* Free Technical Support 800-832-2499. Windows. Apple Macintosh. 3.5" disk $59.95 (ISBN 1-57217-075-1). *Addl. software required:* Appropriate software application for Title. *Interactive Audio Training for Windows & Windows Business Applications.* Personal Training Systems.

Personal Training Systems Software Made Easy: Integrating MS Office 4.20. *Version:* 4.20. *Items Included:* Private tutor on audio cassette, diskette of lesson files, command summary card, extra practice card. *Customer Support:* Free Technical Support 800-832-2499. Windows. Apple Macintosh. 3.5" disk $59.95 (ISBN 1-57217-106-5). *Addl. software required:* Appropriate software application for Title. *Interactive Audio kTraining for Windows & Windows Business Applications.* Personal Training Systems.

Personal Training Systems Software Made Easy: Integrating Office PRO 4.0 MAC. *Version:* 4.00. *Items Included:* Private tutor on audio cassette, diskette of lesson files, command summary card, extra practice card. *Customer Support:* Free Technical Support 800-832-2499. Apple Macintosh. 3.5" disk $99.95 (ISBN 1-57217-102-2). *Addl. software required:* Appropriate software application for Title. *Interactive Audio Training for Macintosh & Macintosh Business Applications.* Personal Training Systems.

Personal Training Systems Software Made Easy: Introduction to Claris Works. *Version:* 2.00. *Items Included:* Private tutor on audio cassette, diskette of lesson files, command summary card, extra practice card. *Customer Support:* Free Technical Support 800-832-2499. Apple Macintosh. 3.5" disk $99.95 (ISBN 1-57217-045-X). *Addl. software required:* Appropriate software application for Title. *Interactive Audio Training for the Macintosh & Macintosh Business Applications.* Personal Training Systems.

Personal Training Systems Software Made Easy: Introduction to DOS 6.2. *Version:* 6.20. *Items Included:* Private tutor on audio cassette, diskette of lesson files, command summary card, extra practice card. *Customer Support:* Free Technical Support 800-832-2499. Windows. Apple Macintosh. 3.5" disk $59.95 (ISBN 0-944124-89-5). *Addl. software required:* Appropriate software application for Title. *Interactive Audio Training for Windows & Windows Business Applications.* Personal Training Systems.

Personal Training Systems Software Made Easy: Integrating the Microsoft Office. *Version:* 4.20. *Items Included:* Private tutor on audio cassette, diskette of lesson files, command summary card, extra practice card. *Customer Support:* Free Technical Support 800-832-2499. Apple Macintosh. 3.5" disk $99.95 (ISBN 1-57217-158-8). *Addl. software required:* Appropriate software application for Title. *Interactive Audio Training for Macintosh & Macintosh Business Applications.* Personal Training Systems.

Personal Training Systems Software Made Easy: Introduction to Microsoft Works. *Version:* 3.00. *Items Included:* Private tutor on audio cassette, diskette of lesson files, command summary card, extra practice card. *Customer Support:* Free Technical Support 800-832-2499. Windows. Apple Macintosh. 3.5" disk $59.95

(ISBN 1-57217-121-9). *Addl. software required:* Appropriate software application for Title.
Interactive Audio Training for Windows & Windows Business Applications.
Personal Training Systems.

Personal Training Systems Software Made Easy: Introduction to Persuasion. *Version:* 3.00. *Items Included:* Private tutor on audio cassette, diskette of lesson files, command summary card, extra practice card. *Customer Support:* Free Technical Support 800-832-2499.
Apple Macintosh. 3.5" disk $99.95 (ISBN 1-57217-015-8). *Addl. software required:* Appropriate software application for Title.
Interactive Audio Training for the Macintosh & Macintosh Business Applications.
Personal Training Systems.

Personal Training Systems Software Made Easy: Introduction to Power Point. *Version:* 3.00. *Items Included:* Private tutor on audio cassette, diskette of lesson files, command summary card, extra practice card. *Customer Support:* Free Technical Support 800-832-2499.
Apple Macintosh. 3.5" disk $99.95 (ISBN 1-57217-108-1). *Addl. software required:* Appropriate software application for Title.
Interactive Audio Training for Macintosh & Macintosh Business Applications.
Personal Training Systems.

Personal Training Systems Software Made Easy: Introduction to Power Point 4.0. *Version:* 4.00. *Items Included:* Private tutor on audio cassette, diskette of lesson files, command summary card, extra practice card. *Customer Support:* Free Technical Support 800-832-2499.
Apple Macintosh. 3.5" disk $99.95 (ISBN 1-57217-110-3). *Addl. software required:* Appropriate software application for Title.
Interactive Audio Training for Macintosh & Macintosh Business Applications.
Personal Training Systems.

Personal Training Systems Software Made Easy: Introduction to Quicken. *Version:* 4.00. *Items Included:* Private tutor on audio cassette, diskette of lesson files, command summary card, extra practice card. *Customer Support:* Free Technical Support 800-832-2499.
Apple Macintosh. 3.5" disk $99.95 (ISBN 1-57217-067-0). *Addl. software required:* Appropriate software application for Title.
Interactive Audio Training for the Macintosh & Macintosh Business Applications.
Personal Training Systems.

Personal Training Systems Software Made Easy: Introduction to Works. *Version:* 3.00. *Items Included:* Private tutor on audio cassette, diskette of lesson files, command summary card, extra practice card. *Customer Support:* Free Technical Support 800-832-2499.
Apple Macintosh. 3.5" disk $99.95 (ISBN 1-57217-120-0). *Addl. software required:* Appropriate software application for Title.
Interactive Audio Training for Macintosh & Macintosh Business Applications.
Personal Training Systems.

Personal Training Systems Software Made Easy: Introduction to Works. *Version:* 4.00. *Items Included:* Private tutor on audio cassette, diskette of lesson files, command summary card, extra practice card. *Customer Support:* Free Technical Support 800-832-2499.
Apple Macintosh. 3.5" disk $99.95 (ISBN 1-57217-122-7). *Addl. software required:* Appropriate software application for Title.
Interactive Audio Training for Macintosh & Macintosh Business Applications.
Personal Training Systems.

Personal Training Systems Software Made Easy: Introduction to Windows. *Version:* 3.11. *Items Included:* Private tutor on audio cassette, diskette of lesson files, command summary card, extra practice card. *Customer Support:* Free Technical Support 800-832-2499.
Windows. Apple Macintosh. 3.5" disk $59.95 (ISBN 1-57217-132-4). *Addl. software required:* Appropriate software application for Title.
Interactive Audio Training for Windows & Windows Business Applications.
Personal Training Systems.

Personal Training Systems Software Made Easy: Intermediate Windows. *Version:* 4.00. *Items Included:* Private tutor on audio cassette, diskette of lesson files, command summary card, extra practice card. *Customer Support:* Free Technical Support 800-832-2499.
Windows. Apple Macintosh. 3.5" disk $59.95 (ISBN 1-57217-114-6). *Addl. software required:* Appropriate software application for Title.
Interactive Audio Training for Windows & Windows Business Applications.
Personal Training Systems.

Personal Training Systems Software Made Easy: Intermediate Word. *Version:* 5.10. *Items Included:* Private tutor on audio cassette, diskette of lesson files, command summary card, extra practice card. *Customer Support:* Free Technical Support 800-832-2499.
Apple Macintosh. 3.5" disk $99.95 (ISBN 0-944124-45-3). *Addl. software required:* Appropriate software application for Title.
Interactive Audio Training for Macintosh & Macintosh Business Applications.
Personal Training Systems.

Personal Training Systems Software Made Easy: Intermediate Word. *Version:* 6.00. *Items Included:* Private tutor on audio cassette, diskette of lesson files, command summary card, extra practice card. *Customer Support:* Free Technical Support 800-832-2499.
Windows. Apple Macintosh. 3.5" disk $59.95 (ISBN 0-944124-86-0). *Addl. software required:* Appropriate software application for Title.
Interactive Audio Training for Windows & Windows Business Applications.
Personal Training Systems.

Personal Training Systems Software Made Easy: Intermediate Word Perfect. *Version:* 6.00. *Items Included:* Private tutor on audio cassette, diskette of lesson files, command summary card, extra practice card. *Customer Support:* Free Technical Support 800-832-2499.
Windows. Apple Macintosh. 3.5" disk $59.95 (ISBN 1-57217-155-3). *Addl. software required:* Appropriate software application for Title.
Interactive Audio Training for Windows & Windows Business Applications.
Personal Training Systems.

Personal Training Systems Software Made Easy: Intermediate Word 6.0. *Version:* 6.00. *Items Included:* Private tutor on audio cassette, diskette of lesson files, command summary card, extra practice card. *Customer Support:* Free Technical Support 800-832-2499.
Apple Macintosh. 3.5" disk $99.95 (ISBN 1-57217-126-X). *Addl. software required:* Appropriate software application for Title.
Interactive Audio Training for Macintosh & Macintosh Business Applications.
Personal Training Systems.

Personal Training Systems Software Made Easy: Microsoft Office Pro (Windows). *Version:* 4.30. *Items Included:* Private tutor on audio cassette, diskette of lesson files, command summary card, extra practice card. *Customer Support:* Free Technical Support 800-832-2499.
Windows. Apple Macintosh. 3.5" disk $59.95 (ISBN 1-57217-099-9). *Addl. software required:* Appropriate software application for Title.
Interactive Audio Training for Windows & Windows Business Applications.
Personal Training Systems.

Personal Training Systems Software Made Easy: Microsoft Office Pro on CD-ROM. *Version:* 4.30. *Items Included:* Private tutor on audio cassette, diskette of lesson files, command summary card, extra practice card. *Customer Support:* Free Technical Support 800-832-2499.
Windows. Apple Macintosh. CD-ROM disk $59.95 (ISBN 1-57217-100-6). *Addl. software required:* Appropriate software application for Title.
Interactive Audio Training for Windows & Windows Business Applications.
Personal Training Systems.

Personal Training Systems Software Made Easy: Microsoft Office Standard. *Version:* 4.00. *Items Included:* Private tutor on audio cassette, diskette of lesson files, command summary card, extra practice card. *Customer Support:* Free Technical Support 800-832-2499.
Windows. Apple Macintosh. 3.5" disk $59.95 (ISBN 1-57217-104-9). *Addl. software required:* Appropriate software application for Title.
Interactive Audio Training for Windows & Windows Business Applications.
Personal Training Systems.

Personal Training Systems Software Made Easy: MS Office 4.2 Mac CD-ROM. *Version:* 4.20. *Items Included:* Private tutor on audio cassette, diskette of lesson files, command summary card, extra practice card. *Customer Support:* Free Technical Support 800-832-2499.
Apple Macintosh. CD-ROM disk $99.95 (ISBN 1-57217-103-0). *Addl. software required:* Appropriate software application for Title.
Interactive Audio Training for Macintosh & Macintosh Business Applications.
Personal Training Systems.

Personal Training Systems Software Made Easy: MS Office 4.20. *Version:* 4.20. *Items Included:* Private tutor on audio cassette, diskette of lesson files, command summary card, extra practice card. *Customer Support:* Free Technical Support 800-832-2499.
Windows. Apple Macintosh. 3.5" disk $59.95 (ISBN 1-57217-105-7). *Addl. software required:* Appropriate software application for Title.
Interactive Audio Training for Windows & Windows Business Applications.
Personal Training Systems.

Personal Training Systems Software Made Easy: MS Office 4.2 CD-ROM. *Version:* 4.20. *Items Included:* Private tutor on audio cassette, diskette of lesson files, command summary card, extra practice card. *Customer Support:* Free Technical Support 800-832-2499.
Windows. Apple Macintosh. CD-ROM disk $59.95 (ISBN 1-57217-107-3). *Addl. software required:* Appropriate software application for Title.
Interactive Audio Training for Windows & Windows Business Applications.
Personal Training Systems.

TITLE INDEX

PERSONAL TRAINING SYSTEMS SOFTWARE

Personal Training Systems Software Made Easy: Master Pages Quark. Version: 3.20. Items Included: Private tutor on audio cassette, diskette of lesson files, command summary card, extra practice card. Customer Support: Free Technical Support 800-832-2499.
Apple Macintosh. 3.5" disk $99.95 (ISBN 0-944124-91-7). Addl. software required: Appropriate software application for Title.
Interactive Audio Training for Macintosh & Macintosh Business Applications.
Personal Training Systems.

Personal Training Systems Software Made Easy: Office 4.0 Mac. Version: 4.00. Items Included: Private tutor on audio cassette, diskette of lesson files, command summary card, extra practice card. Customer Support: Free Technical Support 800-832-2499.
Apple Macintosh. 3.5" disk $99.95 (ISBN 1-57217-101-4). Addl. software required: Appropriate software application for Title.
Interactive Audio Training for Macintosh & Macintosh Business Applications.
Personal Training Systems.

Personal Training Systems Software Made Easy: Precision Drawing Tech. Version: 3.10. Items Included: Private tutor on audio cassette, diskette of lesson files, command summary card, extra practice card. Customer Support: Free Technical Support 800-832-2499.
Apple Macintosh. 3.5" disk $99.95 (ISBN 0-944124-29-1). Addl. software required: Appropriate software application for Title.
Interactive Audio Training for the Macintosh & Macintosh Business Applications.
Personal Training Systems.

Personal Training Systems Software Made Easy: Precision Drawing Techniques. Version: 3.10. Items Included: Private tutor on audio cassette, diskette of lesson files, command summary card, extra practice card. Customer Support: Free Technical Support 800-832-2499.
Windows. Apple Macintosh. 3.5" disk $59.95 (ISBN 0-944124-76-3). Addl. software required: Appropriate software application for Title.
Interactive Audio Training for the Windows & Windows Business Applications.
Personal Training Systems.

Personal Training Systems Software Made Easy: PTS MacPAK. Version: 1.00. Items Included: Private tutor on audio cassette, diskette of lesson files, command summary card, extra practice card. Customer Support: Free Technical Support 800-832-2499.
Apple Macintosh. 3.5" disk $99.95 (ISBN 1-57217-157-X). Addl. software required: Appropriate software application for Title.
Interactive Audio Training for Macintosh & Macintosh Business Applications.
Personal Training Systems.

Personal Training Systems Software Made Easy: PTS Productivity Pack. Version: 1.00. Items Included: Private tutor on audio cassette, diskette of lesson files, command summary card, extra practice card. Customer Support: Free Technical Support 800-832-2499.
Windows. Apple Macintosh. 3.5" disk $59.95 (ISBN 1-57217-136-7). Addl. software required: Appropriate software application for Title.
Interactive Audio Training for Windows & Windows Business Applications.
Personal Train Systs.

Personal Training Systems Software Made Easy: Quattro Pro Presentation. Version: 1.00. Items Included: Private tutor on audio cassette, diskette of lesson files, command summary card, extra practice card. Customer Support: Free Technical Support 800-832-2499.
Windows. Apple Macintosh. 3.5" disk $59.95 (ISBN 1-57217-042-5). Addl. software required: Appropriate software application for Title.
Interactive Audio Training for the Windows & Windows Business Applications.
Personal Training Systems.

Personal Training Systems Software Made Easy: System 7.5 - Macintosh Basics. Version: 7.50. Items Included: Private tutor on audio cassette, diskette of lesson files, command summary card, extra practice card. Customer Support: Free Technical Support 800-832-2499.
Apple Macintosh. 3.5" disk $99.95 (ISBN 1-57217-032-8). Addl. software required: Appropriate software application for Title.
Interactive Audio Training for the Macintosh & Macintosh Business Applications.
Personal Training Systems.

Personal Training Systems Software Made Easy: System 7.5 - Beyond the Basics. Version: 7.50. Items Included: Private tutor on audio cassette, diskette of lesson files, command summary card, extra practice card. Customer Support: Free Technical Support 800-832-2499.
Apple Macintosh. 3.5" disk $99.95 (ISBN 1-57217-033-6). Addl. software required: Appropriate software application for Title.
Interactive Audio Training for the Macintosh & Macintosh Business Applications.
Personal Training Systems.

Personal Training Systems Software Made Easy: System 7 Mac CD-ROM. Version: 7.10. Items Included: Private tutor on audio cassette, diskette of lesson files, command summary card, extra practice card. Customer Support: Free Technical Support 800-832-2499.
Apple Macintosh. CD-ROM disk $99.95 (ISBN 1-57217-031-X). Addl. software required: Appropriate software application for Title.
Interactive Audio Training for the Macintosh & Macintosh Business Applications.
Personal Training Systems.

Personal Training Systems Software Made Easy: System 7.5 Mac CD-ROM. Version: 7.50. Items Included: Private tutor on audio cassette, diskette of lesson files, command summary card, extra practice card. Customer Support: Free Technical Support 800-832-2499.
Apple Macintosh. CD-ROM disk $99.95 (ISBN 1-57217-035-2). Addl. software required: Appropriate software application for Title.
Interactive Audio Training for the Macintosh & Macintosh Business Applications.
Personal Training Systems.

Personal Training Systems Software Made Easy: Tips & Techniques Quark. Version: 3.20. Items Included: Private tutor on audio cassette, diskette of lesson files, command summary card, extra practice card. Customer Support: Free Technical Support 800-832-2499.
Apple Macintosh. 3.5" disk $99.95 (ISBN 0-944124-94-1). Addl. software required: Appropriate software application for Title.
Interactive Audio Training for Macintosh & Macintosh Business Applications.
Personal Training Systems.

Personal Training Systems Software Made Easy: "The Basics-Classic, SE, Plus". Version: 6.0X. Items Included: Private tutor on audio cassette, diskette of lesson files, command summary card, extra practice card. Customer Support: Free Technical Support 800-832-2499.
Apple Macintosh. 3.5" disk $99.95 (ISBN 1-57217-025-5). Addl. software required: Appropriate software application for Title.
Interactive Audio Training for the Macintosh & Macintosh Business Applications.
Personal Training Systems.

Personal Training Systems Software Made Easy: The Basics-Mac II. Version: 6.0X. Items Included: Private tutor on audio cassette, diskette of lesson files, command summary card, extra practice card. Customer Support: Free Technical Support 800-832-2499.
Apple Macintosh. 3.5" disk $99.95 (ISBN 1-57217-026-3). Addl. software required: Appropriate software application for Title.
Interactive Audio Training for the Macintosh & Macintosh Business Applications.
Personal Training Systems.

Personal Training Systems Software Made Easy: The Basics-2 Floppy Drives. Version: 6.0X. Items Included: Private tutor on audio cassette, diskette of lesson files, command summary card, extra practice card. Customer Support: Free Technical Support 800-832-2499.
Apple Macintosh. 3.5" disk $99.95 (ISBN 1-57217-024-7). Addl. software required: Appropriate software application for Title.
Interactive Audio Training for the Macintosh & Macintosh Business Applications.
Personal Training Systems.

Personal Training Systems Software Made Easy: Text Formats Quark. Version: 3.20. Items Included: Private tutor on audio cassette, diskette of lesson files, command summary card, extra practice card. Customer Support: Free Technical Support 800-832-2499.
Apple Macintosh. 3.5" disk $99.95 (ISBN 0-944124-92-5). Addl. software required: Appropriate software application for Title.
Interactive Audio Training for Macintosh & Macintosh Business Applications.
Personal Training Systems.

Personal Training Systems Software Made Easy: Using HyperCard. Version: 2.10. Items Included: Private tutor on audio cassette, diskette of lesson files, command summary card, extra practice card. Customer Support: Free Technical Support 800-832-2499.
Apple Macintosh. 3.5" disk $99.95 (ISBN 1-57217-052-2). Addl. software required: Appropriate software application for Title.
Interactive Audio Training for the Macintosh & Macintosh Business Applications.
Personal Training Systems.

Personal Training Systems Software Made Easy: Using Macintosh ATM Fonts. Version: 1.00. Items Included: Private tutor on audio cassette, diskette of lesson files, command summary card, extra practice card. Customer Support: Free Technical Support 800-832-2499.
Apple Macintosh. 3.5" disk $99.95 (ISBN 1-57217-058-1). Addl. software required: Appropriate software application for Title.
Interactive Audio Training for the Macintosh & Macintosh Business Applications.
Personal Training Systems.

Personal Training Systems Software Made Easy: Using Macintosh Fonts. Version: 1.00. Items Included: Private tutor on audio cassette, diskette of lesson files, command summary card, extra practice card. Customer Support: Free Technical Support 800-832-2499.
Apple Macintosh. 3.5" disk $99.95 (ISBN 1-57217-055-7). Addl. software required: Appropriate software application for Title.
Interactive Audio Training for the Macintosh & Macintosh Business Applications.
Personal Training Systems.

PERSONAL TRAINING SYSTEMS SOFTWARE

Personal Training Systems Software Made Easy: Using Macintosh TrueType. Version: 1.00. *Items Included:* Private tutor on audio cassette, diskette of lesson files, command summary card, extra practice card. *Customer Support:* Free Technical Support 800-832-2499. Apple Macintosh. 3.5" disk $99.95 (ISBN 1-57217-056-5). *Addl. software required:* Appropriate software application for Title. *Interactive Audio Training for the Macintosh & Macintosh Business Applications.*
Personal Training Systems.

Personal Training Systems Software Made Easy: Using Macintosh TrueType. Version: 1.00. *Items Included:* Private tutor on audio cassette, diskette of lesson files, command summary card, extra practice card. *Customer Support:* Free Technical Support 800-832-2499. Apple Macintosh. 3.5" disk $99.95 (ISBN 1-57217-057-3). *Addl. software required:* Appropriate software application for Title. *Interactive Audio Training for the Macintosh & Macintosh Business Applications.*
Personal Training Systems.

Personal Training Systems Software Made Easy: Using Quattro Pro For Windows. Version: 1.00. *Items Included:* Private tutor on audio cassette, diskette of lesson files, command summary card, extra practice card. *Customer Support:* Free Technical Support 800-832-2499. Windows. Apple Macintosh. 3.5" disk $59.95 (ISBN 1-57217-041-7). *Addl. software required:* Appropriate software application for Title. *Interactive Audio Training for the Windows & Windows Business Applications.*
Personal Training Systems.

Personal Training Systems Software Made Easy: Using Quicken 3.0 Windows. Version: 3.00. *Items Included:* Private tutor on audio cassette, diskette of lesson files, command summary card, extra practice card. *Customer Support:* Free Technical Support 800-832-2499. Windows. Apple Macintosh. 3.5" disk $59.95 (ISBN 1-57217-066-2). *Addl. software required:* Appropriate software application for Title. *Interactive Audio Training for the Windows & Windows Business Applications.*
Personal Training Systems.

Personal Training Systems Software Made Easy: Using the Mac Interface. Version: 7.10. *Items Included:* Private tutor on audio cassette, diskette of lesson files, command summary card, extra practice card. *Customer Support:* Free Technical Support 800-832-2499. Apple Macintosh. 3.5" disk $99.95 (ISBN 0-944124-01-1). *Addl. software required:* Appropriate software application for Title. *Interactive Audio Training for the Macintosh & Macintosh Business Applications.*
Personal Training Systems.

Personal Training Systems Software Made Easy: Using Windows ATM Fonts. Version: 1.00. *Items Included:* Private tutor on audio cassette, diskette of lesson files, command summary card, extra practice card. *Customer Support:* Free Technical Support 800-832-2499. Windows. Apple Macintosh. 3.5" disk $59.95 (ISBN 1-57217-061-1). *Addl. software required:* Appropriate software application for Title. *Interactive Audio Training for the Windows & Windows Business Applications.*
Personal Training Systems.

Personal Training Systems Software Made Easy: Using Windows Fonts. Version: 1.00. *Items Included:* Private tutor on audio cassette, diskette of lesson files, command summary card, extra practice card. *Customer Support:* Free Technical Support 800-832-2499. Windows. Apple Macintosh. 3.5" disk $59.95 (ISBN 1-57217-059-X). *Addl. software required:* Appropriate software application for Title. *Interactive Audio Training for the Windows & Windows Business Applications.*
Personal Training Systems.

Personal Training Systems Software Made Easy: Using Windows TrueType. Version: 1.00. *Items Included:* Private tutor on audio cassette, diskette of lesson files, command summary card, extra practice card. *Customer Support:* Free Technical Support 800-832-2499. Windows. Apple Macintosh. 3.5" disk $59.95 (ISBN 1-57217-060-3). *Addl. software required:* Appropriate software application for Title. *Interactive Audio Training for the Windows & Windows Business Applications.*
Personal Training Systems.

Personal Training Systems Software Made Easy: Word 6.0 Mac CD-ROM. Version: 6.00. *Items Included:* Private tutor on audio cassette, diskette of lesson files, command summary card, extra practice card. *Customer Support:* Free Technical Support 800-832-2499. Apple Macintosh. CD-ROM disk $99.95 (ISBN 1-57217-128-6). *Addl. software required:* Appropriate software application for Title. *Interactive Audio Training for Macintosh & Macintosh Business Applications.*
Personal Training Systems.

Personal Training Systems Software Made Easy: Word 6.0 Windows CD-ROM. Version: 6.00. *Items Included:* Private tutor on audio cassette, diskette of lesson files, command summary card, extra practice card. *Customer Support:* Free Technical Support 800-832-2499. Windows. Apple Macintosh. CD-ROM disk $59.95 (ISBN 1-57217-130-8). *Addl. software required:* Appropriate software application for Title. *Interactive Audio Training for Windows & Windows Business Applications.*
Personal Training Systems.

Personal Tutsim. Version: 7.12. Feb. 1992. *Items Included:* Program disk, utilities disk, manual/text. *Customer Support:* Free telephone support. MS-DOS. IBM PC/AT/286/386 (256k). disk $149.00 (Order no.: FI-PT). *Optimal configuration:* IBM, 640k, EGA/VGA, Math Coprocessor. *Simulation for Designing & Optimizing Continuous Systems. Permits Graphic, Numeric & Plotted Representation of Linear & Piecewise-Linear Systems. Lets user Solve Engineering Design Problems by Constructing a Block Diagram Simulation Model, Operating the Simulation & Evaluating Results. User Can Vary Model Design, Add or Delete Blocks, Change Parameters, Alter Interconnections, Change Timing, or Vary Method of Output Anytime During Simulation. Limited License Version.*
Tutsim Products.

Personal Video Studio. Jul. 1994. *Items Included:* Board, 2 software disks (3.5"), S Video to Composite Adapter Cable, manual, installation video. *Customer Support:* 90 day unlimited warranty; installation & training video; 800 technical support; Fax Back & BBS. Windows. IBM PC 386 25MHz (4Mb). disk $499.95. *Nonstandard peripherals required:* VCR, TV. *Optimal configuration:* PC, 386 25MHz or higher, 4Mb RAM, VCR, TV, Sound Board, CD ROM, VGA Card & monitor, H.D. *A Videotape Production Studio in a Box. It Lets You Connect Two Video Sources As Input, Create Titles & Special Effects & Add Computer Graphics, Images, Sound & Music for Final Output to Your Video Tape and/or TV. For Home, Education & Business.*
Studio Magic Corp.

Personality Inventory for Children (PIC). Version: 3.012. Robert D. Wirt et al. *Customer Support:* Free unlimited phone support. IBM PC & 100% compatibles. 3.5" or 5.25" disk $295.00 (Order no.: W-1007 (5.25"); W-1026 (3.5")). *Optimal configuration:* DOS 3.0 or higher (512k), & hard disk with one Mb of free hard disk space, printer. Apple. 5.25" disk $250.00 (Order no.: W-1001). *The PIC Is One of the Most Widely Used Diagnostic Instruments for Children. It Assesses Behavior, Affect, & Cognitive Status in Children 3 Through 16 Years of Age. Unlike Many Other Personality Inventories for Children, It Can Be Used to Screen for Developmental Problems, to Assess Psychopathology, & to Assist in Educational Placement.*
Western Pyschological Services.

Personality Prober. Version: 3.1. Apr. 1989. *Customer Support:* 90 day warranty against defects in disk manufacture, immediate replacement of defective media. MS-DOS/PC-DOS 3.1 or higher (256k). IBM PC/XT/AT/PS2 compatible. disk $34.95. *Optimal configuration:* PC/AT or PS/2, hard disk, EGA or VGA graphics, 640k, one floppy drive. *Networks supported:* Novell. *Analyze Your Personality-or Anyone Elses on Ten Personality, Scales: Masculine/Feminine, Aggressive/Passive, Dominant/Submissive, etc. View Results on Screen or Print Definitive Analysis.*
Thinking Software, Inc.

Personnel Agency Management System. Fisher Business Systems, Inc. *Operating System(s) Required:* MS-DOS. *Memory Required:* 128k. *General Requirements:* Printer. $1500.00.
Texas Instruments, Personal Productivit.

Personnel Management II. Version: 2.11. *Items Included:* 8 1/2" X 11" hard-cover manual. *Customer Support:* 90-day free telephone support; optional annual maintenance, $300; On-site training, & other services available; 30-day limited guarantee. MS-DOS 2.00 or higher. IBM PC/XT, AT, PS/2 & compatibles (640K). disk $795.00 - $2295.00. *Networks supported:* Novell, 3-COM, token ring, etc. *A Complete Personnel Tracking Systems. Includes Employee Benefits, Sick/Vacation Accrual & Applicant Tracking.*
Weston & Muir.

Personnel Management Software. MS-DOS (640k). disk $5000.00 (ISBN 0-929490-03-7). *Nonstandard peripherals required:* Hard disk, printer. *Tracks All Personnel, Their Demographics, Positions, Seniority, Leaves, Certifications, Inservice Credits, Salaries, Salary Deductions, Benefits. Generates Reports by Department, Area, Employee Status, Position, etc. Features Include: Easy To Use Menus, Point & Shoot Capabilities, & the Ability To Design Your Own Custom Reports, As Well As User Defined Codes To Personalize the Application. Can Be Linked To Mainframe or Used As Stand Alone Program.*
Diamond Chip Technologies, Inc.

TITLE INDEX

Personnel Master III. *Version:* 3.3. Dec. 1992. *Memory Required:* 640k. *General Requirements:* Hard disk, 80 column printer or laser printer. *Items Included:* Indexed manual. *Customer Support:* Six months free phone/FAX support plus updates; E-mail; Compuserve 72137,3266; Internet: 72137.3266@compuserve.com. PC-DOS/MS-DOS 3.3 plus. UBM AT or compatibles. disk 479.00, multiple user version $795.00; maintenance; $75.00/yr. single user, $125.00/yr. multi user.
Personnel Management for All Size Companies. Includes EEOC, OSHA & ADA Reporting, FMLA I-9 citizenship Tracking, EMployee Benefits Tracking, Employee Profiles, Salary Budgeting, Attendance Control. COBRA Billing, Review Histories, skills & training inventory, Emergency Contact Lists, Professional Licenses Expirations, & Prints Review Forms. Over 100 reports Selectable by Employee, Department, Division or Whole Company. Pop-up Calculator, Appointment Scheduler, & Context-Sensitive HELP. Fully Indexed Manual. Six months Free Phone Support & Program Updates.
MST Software.

Personnel Master Lite. *Items Included:* Fully indexed manual. *Customer Support:* First six months free phone;fax/e-mail support plus minor updates. Subsequent annual maintenance $75.00. DOS 3.3. 286 plus. disk $179.00.
"Personnel Management" for organizations with up to 50 employees. Includes EEOC, OSHA & ADA Reporting, I-9 Citizenship Tracking, Employee Benefits Tracking, Tracking, Employee Profiles, Salary Budgeting, Attendance Control, Cobra billing, Review Histories, Skills & Training Inventory, Over 75 reports selectable by Employee, Department, of Whole Company. Pop-up Calculator, Appoint Scheduler, & Context-Sensitive Help. Fully Indexed Manual. Shipping cost not included.
MST Software.

Personnel Scheduler. *Version:* II. 1992. *Items Included:* Complete illustrated instructions. *Customer Support:* 1 year free replacement of damaged disks, free unlimited telephone customer support.
MS-DOS. IBM-PC, XT, AT, PS-2 or compatible (512k). disk $249.00 (ISBN 1-55812-092-0). *Addl. software required:* None.
*Schedule All Employees in All Departments Doing All Jobs. Program Will Take Care of People, Holidays, Sick Time, Vacations & More. Print Out Schedules by Person or Department by Week, Month or Year. When an Employee Leaves, Delete That Name & It Is Instantly Deleted from the Schedule Leaving an * for Replacement. Leave All Data, Delete As Desired, Print It out ... do Whatever You Want. An Outstanding Program That Is Affordable, Friendly & Efficient.*
Right On Programs.

Personnel Supervisor. *Version:* 1.9. Aug. 1988. *Compatible Hardware:* IBM PC/AT or compatible. *Operating System(s) Required:* PC-DOS/MS-DOS 3.1. *Memory Required:* 512k. *General Requirements:* Hard disk, 80 column printer. *Items Included:* Six months free phone/FAX support plus updates. disk $149.00. demo disk $20.00.
Personnel Management for Companies with Less Than Thirty Employees. Includes Employee Profiles, Compensation Histories, Review Histories, Attendance Control, Emergency Contact Lists, I-9 Citizenship Tracking, Salary Budgeting, Reviews Pending List, etc. Fully Indexed Manual. Six Months Free Phone Support & Updates. Price Does Not Include Shipping Costs.
MST Software.

The Personnel System - TPS. *Version:* 4.2. Jan. 1989. *Operating System(s) Required:* DOS. *Language(s):* FoxPro. *Memory Required:* 640k. *Items Included:* Customization, training, support. *Customer Support:* Hotline.
write for info.
Provides the Personnel Department with Complete Control over Its Human Resource Management Tasks by Providing Storage for All Pertinent Employee Information, Including Job & Salary History, Performance Reviews, Benefit Administration & Dependent, Whom to Notify in Case of an Emergency, & All of the Basic Information Such As Dates of Hire, Termination, Birthdate, Service Anniversary, Active or Inactive Status, Leave, Absenteeism & Vacation Entitlement.
SPS, Inc.

Perspectives by Libra: P2. *Version:* 2.0. Jun. 1995. *Customer Support:* Account Manager purchased as part of the Total Solution. Installation, training, consulting & support negotiated as line item costs. Dependent on customer requirements & needs.
Independent. 486/Pentium (16Mb). Contact publisher for price. *Nonstandard peripherals required:* 256 Cache.
Object Oriented, Accounting Applications for Medium to Large Size Enterprises. Applications Are Client Platform Independent, Network & Operation System Independent. A Rapid Application Tool Is Available to Customize the Applications or to Develop New Mission Critical Accounting Applications. The Tool Comprises Accounting Objects. The Applications Are Completely Open & for Client Server Environments.
LIBRA Corp.

Perspectives in Music History. Vincent Oddo. 1990.
MS-DOS. IBM PC (640k). disk $39.95 (ISBN 1-55603-113-0, Order no.: I-1285). *Nonstandard peripherals required:* CGA board & CGA monitor minimum. *Optimal configuration:* DOS 3.3 or higher. *Networks supported:* Novell.
Designed to Help Users Discover Important Interrelationships Between & among Composers, Countries, Dates, Style Periods, & Compositions. The User Can Examine Events, Dates, & Connections Which Have Occurred Between 1400 & 1987. The Program Also Includes a Graph of Style Periods & Four Quizzes.
Electronic Courseware Systems, Inc.

Perspectives in Music History. Vince Oddo. *Customer Support:* 90 day warranty against defective software.
DOS 3.2 or higher. IBM (640k). disk $39.95 (Order no.: I-1285).
DOS 3.3. Apple II (48k). disk $39.95 (Order no.: A-1285).
Designed to Help the User Discover Important Interrelationships Between & among Composers, Countries, Dates, Style Periods, & Compositions. The User Can Examine Events, Dates, & Connections Which Have Occurred Between 1400 & 1987. The Program Also Includes a Graph of Style Periods & Four Quizzes.
Electronic Courseware Systems, Inc.

Peter & Santa: Enchanting Fun in Santa's Interactive Wonderland of Toys, Games & Crafts. *Items Included:* Instructions. *Customer Support:* Tech support, 60 day money-back guarantee.
Windows; Macintosh. IBM compatible 386SX or higher (4Mb); Mac LC or higher (2.5Mb). CD-ROM disk $49.95 (ISBN 0-924677-04-X). *Nonstandard peripherals required:* Audio board, mouse, CD-ROM drive. *Addl. software required:* Video card 640x480 with 256 colors; Quicktime 2.0.
Experience the Magic of Christmas As You & Peter Step into a Wonderland Full of Surprises. Explore, Play & Learn As You Help Santa Prepare for That Special Night. Help Build Toys, Create & Color Your Own Holiday Cards, or Play Christmas Songs. Early Learning Fun for Ages 4-8 MAC & Windows-Compatible. Will Run in English, Spanish, French & German.
IMSI (International Microcomputer Software, Inc.).

Peter & the Wolf.
MS-DOS 5.0 or higher, Windows 3.1 or higher. 386 processor or higher (4Mb). CD-ROM disk $74.95 (Order no.: R1355). *Nonstandard peripherals required:* CD-ROM drive. *Optimal configuration:* 386 processor operating at 16Mhz or higher, MS-DOS 5.0 or higher, Windows 3.1 or higher, 30Mb hard drive, mouse, VGA graphic adapter & VGA color monitor (SVGA recommended), 4Mb RAM, external speakers or headphones (with sound card) that are Sound Blaster compatible.
Macintosh (4Mb). (Order no.: R1355). *Nonstandard peripherals required:* 14" color monitor or larger, CD-ROM drive.
Children Enjoy Hours of Fun & Discovery Through This Colorful Interpretation of Prokofiev's Classic Tale. View the Fully Animated Tale of "Peter & the Wolf," Explore Various Instruments of the Orchestra Through Live-Action Video Clips & Play a Fun-Filled Game with Peter & His Friends.
Library Video Co.

Peter & the Wolf. Feb. 1995. *Items Included:* CD-ROM booklet. *Customer Support:* Free technical support via phone as of release date.
MPC/Windows. 386.25 or higher IBM compatible (4Mb). CD-ROM disk $34.95 (ISBN 1-885784-09-0, Order no.: 1141). *Optimal configuration:* MPC CD-ROM player, S-VGA graphics card (640x480x256 colors) with compatible monitor, MPC compliant sound card, mouse, Windows 3.1.
Macintosh. Macintosh (4Mb). CD-ROM disk $34.95 (ISBN 1-885784-29-5, Order no.: 1288). *Optimal configuration:* CD-ROM drive, color monitor with 256 plus colors, system version 6.07 or higher.
Academy Award Winner Jack Lemmon & the Music of the Prague Festival Orchestra Bring the Tale of Peter & the Wolf to Life. Explore the Interactive Story of a Young Boy Who Overcomes His Fears to Outsmart a Hungry Wolf. Discover the Magic of the Symphony. Learn an Important Moral While Enjoying This Timeless Classic.
Technology Dynamics Corp.

Peter & the Wolf. *Items Included:* CD-ROM booklet. *Customer Support:* Free technical support via phone as of release date.
MPC/Windows. 386MHz or higher (4Mb). CD-ROM disk $34.95 (ISBN 1-885784-65-1, Order no.: 1144). *Optimal configuration:* MPC CD-ROM player, S-VGA graphics card (640x480x256 colors) with compatible monitor, MPC compliant sound card, mouse, Windows 3.1 or higher, Windows 95 compatible. System 6.07 or higher. Macintosh (4Mb). *Optimal configuration:* Color monitor (256 plus colors), mouse, CD-ROM drive.
Academy Award Winner Jack Lemmon & the Music of the Prague Festival Orchestra Brings the Tale of Peter & the Wolf to Life. Explore the Interactive Story of a Young Boy Who Overcomes His Fears to Outsmart a Hungry Wolf. Discover the Magic of the Symphony. Learn an Important Moral While Enjoying This Timeless Classic.
Technology Dynamics Corp.

Peter Pan: Kids Creative Reader.
MS-DOS 3.1 or higher. 386 processor or higher (640k). CD-ROM disk $49.95 (Order no.: R1140). *Nonstandard peripherals required:* CD-ROM drive. *Optimal configuration:* 386 processor or higher, MS-DOS 3.1 or higher, 20Mb hard drive, 640k RAM, external speakers or headphones (with sound card) that are Sound Blaster compatible, VGA graphics & adapter, VGA color monitor.
Macintosh (4Mb). (Order no.: R1140). *Nonstandard peripherals required:* 14" color monitor or larger, CD-ROM drive.
Children Become the Animator to Help Peter Defeat the Evil Captain Hook. With the Aid of Animated Paint Tools, Children Actually Affect Events in the Story While Expanding Reading, Decision Making & Story Telling Skills.
Library Video Co.

Peter's Alphabet Adventure: Learn the ABCs in over 60 Interactive Games, Rhymes & Activities. *Items Included:* Pamphlet of instructions. *Customer Support:* Tech support, 60 day money-back guarantee.
Windows. IBM compatible 386SX or higher (4Mb). disk $49.95 (ISBN 0-924677-01-5). *Nonstandard peripherals required:* Audio board, mouse. *Addl. software required:* Video card 640x480 with 256 colors. *Optimal configuration:* Multimedia PC 386SX or higher, 4-8Mb RAM, CD-ROM drive.
Macintosh. Mac LC or higher (2.5Mb). 3.5" disk $49.95. *Nonstandard peripherals required:* Mouse, CD-ROM drive. *Addl. software required:* Quicktime 2.0 or higher. *Optimal configuration:* 4Mb RAM, CD-ROM drive, 13" color monitor.
Explore, Play & Learn with Your New Pal, Peter. Step into a Wild Animals Kingdom Where You Meet Magnificent New Friends with Each Letter. Learning the ABC's Is Lots of Fun in This Multimedia Adventure with over 60 Interactive Games, Rhymes & Activities. English Only in This Version.
IMSI (International Microcomputer Software, Inc.).

Peter's Colors Adventure: Explore & Discover the Wonder of Colors in an Interactive Journey to Faraway Lands. *Items Included:* Pamphlet of instructions. *Customer Support:* Tech support, 60 day money-back guarantee.
Windows; Macintosh. IBM compatible 386SX or higher (4Mb); Mac LC or higher (2.5Mb). CD-ROM disk $49.95 (ISBN 0-924677-02-3). *Nonstandard peripherals required:* Audio board, mouse, CD-ROM drive. *Addl. software required:* Video card 640x480 with 256 colors; Quicktime 2.0.
Explore, Play & Learn with Your New Pal, Peter. Discover the Wonder of Colors As You Visit Faraway Lands That Come Alive with Magical Games & Activities in This Fun-Filled Multimedia Adventure. Over 10 Games & Activities. Will Run English, French & German.
IMSI (International Microcomputer Software, Inc.).

Peter's Magic Adventure: Explore the Wonders of the World in an Interactive Journey of Learning & Fun. *Items Included:* Pamphlet of instructions. *Customer Support:* Tech support, 60 day money-back guarantee.
Windows; Macintosh. IBM compatible (4Mb); Mac LC or higher (2.5Mb). CD-ROM disk $49.95 (ISBN 0-924677-00-7). *Nonstandard peripherals required:* Audio board, mouse, CD-ROM drive. *Addl. software required:* Video card capable of displaying 640x480 & 256 colors; Quicktime 2.0.
Explore, Play & Learn with Your New Pal, Peter. From the Breakfast Table to Outer Space, Kids Have Fun Discovering Animals, People, Geography, the Planets, & Much More in This Exciting Multimedia Adventure. Early Learning Fun for Ages 4 to 8; 14 Games & Activities; Mac & Microsoft Windows Compatible. Will Run in English, Spanish, French, or German.
IMSI (International Microcomputer Software, Inc.).

Peter's Numbers Adventure: Explore 10 Enchanted Islands on an Interactive Voyage of Learning & Fun. *Items Included:* Pamphlet of instructions. *Customer Support:* Tech support, 60 day money-back guarantee.
Windows; Macintosh. IBM compatible 386SX or higher (4Mb); Mac LC or higher (2.5Mb). CD-ROM disk $49.95 (ISBN 0-924677-03-1). *Nonstandard peripherals required:* Audio board, mouse, CD-ROM drive. *Addl. software required:* Video card 640x480 with 256 colors; Quicktime 2.0.
Explore, Play & Learn with Your New Pal, Peter. Travel to Ten Enchanted Islands That Come Alive & Teach Numbers with Magical Games & Adventure. Will Run in English, Spanish, French & German.
IMSI (International Microcomputer Software, Inc.).

Peterson's Career Options. Sep. 1991. *Items Included:* Manual, Sample Interest Assessment booklets for high school & middle school. *Customer Support:* Toll free customer service 1-800-338-3282.
DOS 3.1 or higher. IBM (512k). $295.00 (Order no.: C2094 (5.25); C2108 (3.5)). *Optimal configuration:* Hard drive.
This Package Guides Users Through Personal Assessment Exercises That Helps Them Recognize Their Interests & Abilities. Provides Personalized Career Suggestions. Defines Occupations, Related Jobs, & Training Requirements. Helps Users Plan Concrete Strategies for Achieving Career Goals.
Peterson's Guides, Inc.

Peterson's College Selection Service, Peterson's College Selection Service 2 (with Financial Aid File). *Version:* 1995. Oct. 1994. *Items Included:* User's manual. *Customer Support:* 800-338-3282 no charge.
Macintosh. MAC Plus or higher (1Mb). 3.5" disk $425.00 College Selection Service; $395.00 College Selection Service 2 with Financial Aid File (Order no.: C4135). *Optimal configuration:* MAC Plus or higher, hard drive, System 6.05 or higher.
Has Information on over 3,400 Two- & Four-Year Colleges. Search Program to Help Students Identify Colleges That Meet Their Criteria. Students Can Sort Their College Pool, Print Application Checklists, Personal Inquiry Letters, & Comparison Charts. A Quick Find Feature Goes Directly to Specific Majors & Categories. Two-Page Profiles Are Given for Each College. Why-Not Feature Tells Why a College Was Excluded. Extensive Management System Allows Counselors to Access Student Searches. College Selection Service 2 Includes a Scholarship & Loan Search for Sources of Private, State, & Corporate Financial Aid with a Local Award Entry System.
Peterson's Guides, Inc.

Peterson's College Selection Service: 1995 Four-Year Colleges. Aug. 1995. *Items Included:* Manual with complete instructions & sample screens from each step with descriptions. *Customer Support:* (800) 338-3282, no charge.
Apple IIc, IIe, IIgs (128k). disk $165.00 (Order no.: C4097 (5.25); C4100 (3.5)).
XT, PS/2 or compatible (256k). 3.5" disk $165.00 (Order no.: C4119 (5.25); C4127 (3.5)).
DOS 2.1 or higher. disk $165.00 (Order no.: 1942).
Contains Over 1800 College Selection Possiblities in Both the U.S. & Canada. Peterson's CSS is a Search Program to Help College-Bound Students Identify the Colleges That Meet Their Needs. The Program Is Fully Interactive, Easy to Use, & Comprehensive with Nearly 600 Different Search Characteristics to Choose from, in Such Categories As Location, Size, Majors, Sports, Entrance Difficulty Level, & Admission Requirements. With Printer Availability, a Unique Personal Inquiry Letter Can Be Created by the User for a Personal Profile to Generate a Personalized Letter to Admissions Officers at the College of Their Choice. Program Updated Annually.
Peterson's Guides, Inc.

Peterson's College Selection Service: 1995 Two-Year Colleges. Sep. 1994. *Items Included:* Manual with complete listing of institutions on software. Manual has complete instructions & sample screens. *Customer Support:* (800) 338-3282; no charge.
IBM PC, XT, PS/2 & compatibles (256k). disk $125.00 (Order no.: C4186 (5.25); C4194 (3.5)).
Has Information on Nearly 1400 Schools of Higher Learning in the U.S. The Program Will Search Out & Identify Automatically or by Menu Two Year Institutions That Meet Their Needs. The Program Is Fully Interactive & Comprehensive with Nearly 600 Different Search Characteristics to Choose from, in Such Categories As Location, Size, Majors, Sports, Including Intermural, Entrance Difficulty Level, & Admission Requirements. With a Printer, the Student Can Create a Personal Profile to Generate Personalized Letters to Admission Officers at the Colleges of Their Choice. Program Updated Annually.
Peterson's Guides, Inc.

Peterson's Financial Aid Service 1995. Oct. 1994. *Items Included:* Manual plus a copy of "Peterson's Paying Less for College 1995". Manual contains complete instructions with sample screen for each menu. *Customer Support:* (800) 338-3282; no charge.
Apple IIc, IIe, IIgs (128k). disk $235.00 (Order no.: C4208 (5.25); C4216 (3.5)).
IBM PC, XT, PS/2 & compatibles (256k). disk $235.00 (Order no.: C4224 (5.25); C4232 (3.5)).
Program That Takes College-Bound Students or Their Parents Through the Financial Aid Process. It Specifically Lets Students Calculate Their Expected Family Contribution Toward College Costs Using the Federal Need Analysis Methodology. It Estimates the Amount of Aid Students May Need at Each of Their Selected Colleges, Gives Federal & State Aid Program Descriptions, Searches Through the File of over 500 Private Awards Programs to Find Private Sources of Aid They May Be Eligible for, & Directs Students with Special Talents & Abilities to Colleges That Offer Incentives to Them. Contains Both Need & Non-Need Sources.
Peterson's Guides, Inc.

Petrocalc 14: Horizontal & Vertical Borehole Modeling. Wilson Chin. Oct. 1991. *Customer Support:* 30-day money back guarantee.
MS-DOS. IBM (512k). disk $695.00 (Order no.: S042). *Nonstandard peripherals required:* 1Mb hard disk space.
This Program Solves "Real-World" Hole Cleaning, Stuck Pipe, Coiled Tubing, & Cementing Problems by Annular Flow Simulation. It Uses State-of-the-Art Modeling Techniques Including Boundary Conforming Grids & Relaxation Methods to Produce an Accurate Model of the Annular Flow.
Gulf Publishing Co.

TITLE INDEX

Petrocalc 2: Drilling Engineering. Martin Chenevert. Jan. 1984. *Compatible Hardware:* IBM PC, PC XT, PC AT & compatibles. *Operating System(s) Required:* PC-DOS/MS-DOS 2.1. *Language(s):* Compiled BASIC. *Memory Required:* 64k. *Customer Support:* 30 day money-back guarantee.
3.5" or 5.25" disk $95.00, incl. 110-page manual (ISBN 0-87201-728-1).
Program Useful for Determining Optimum Circulation Rates of Drilling Fluids. Features a Program on Casing Design. Operates in U.S. & SI Units. Contains 6 Sections; Basic Drilling Engineering, Drilling Fluid Evaluation, Drilling Fluids Clrculation, Cementing, Well Control, & Casing Design.
Gulf Publishing Co.

Petrocalc 3: Reservoir Economics & Evaluation. R. L. McCoy. Jan. 1984. *Compatible Hardware:* IBM PC, PC XT, PC AT & compatibles. *Operating System(s) Required:* PC-DOS/MS-DOS 2.1. *Language(s):* Compiled BASIC. *Memory Required:* 128k. *Customer Support:* 30 day money-back guarantee.
3.5" or 5.25" disk $95.00, incl. 132-page manual (ISBN 0-87201-729-X).
Provides the Means for Petroleum Engineers to Perform Oil & Gas Related Forecasts for up to 20 Years & Compute Internal Rates of Return, Profit/Investment Ratios, & Other Economic Yardsticks. Predicts Single-Well Deliverability into a Gathering System with Constant or Varying Pressure; Generates an Exponential-Type Decline Schedule for Oil & Gas Wells Based Upon Known Input Data; Computes Volumes for Gas & Oil Reservoirs & Calculates Risk-Adjusted Return-on-Investment Ratios.
Gulf Publishing Co.

Petrocalc 6: Wellbore Stimulation. Richard Sinclair. Jul. 1985. *Compatible Hardware:* IBM PC, PC XT, PC AT & compatibles. *Operating System(s) Required:* PC-DOS/MS-DOS 2.1. *Language(s):* Compiled BASIC. *Memory Required:* 128k. *Customer Support:* 30 day money-back guarantee.
3.5" or 5.25" disk $95.00, incl. 76-page manual (ISBN 0-87201-732-X).
Solves Fracturing & Acidizing Design Problems Using the Standard Design Methods Available. Helps Evaluate the Effectiveness & Size of Treatment along with the Choice of Different Fluids & Proppant. Calculates the Effects of Damage, Flowback, Proppant Concentration & Scheduling.
Gulf Publishing Co.

Petrocalc 7: Applied Well Log Analysis. R. L. McCoy. Jan. 1985. *Compatible Hardware:* IBM PC, PC XT, PC AT & compatibles. *Operating System(s) Required:* PC-DOS/MS-DOS 2.1. *Language(s):* Compiled BASIC. *Memory Required:* 128k. *Customer Support:* 30 day money-back guarantee.
3.5" or 5.25" disk $95.00, incl. 154-page manual (ISBN 0-87201-734-6).
Designed to Facilitate the Usual Analysis of Wireline Well Log Data. Emphasis on Open-Hole Applications Although Several of the Programs Are Equally Applicable to Cased Hole Interpretation. Designed to Allow the Well Log Analyst to Assess the Effects of Various RW, Cutoffs, & Other Parameters. User Can Create & Edit Log Data Files Through the Keyboard or with a Digitizing Device. Using the Data from the Files or Input By the User, the Program Produces Comprehensive Log Analyses & Summary Reports.
Gulf Publishing Co.

Petrocalc 12: Joint Interest Billing with dBASE III+. Sigma Energy Consultants. Jan. 1987. *Compatible Hardware:* IBM PC, PC XT, PC AT & compatibles. *Operating System(s) Required:* PC-DOS/MS-DOS 3.0. *Language(s):* C. *Memory Required:* 640k. *General Requirements:* 10Mb hard disk space. *Customer Support:* 30 day money-back guarantee.
3.5" or 5.25" disk $550.00, incl. 54-page manual (ISBN 0-87201-840-7).
Applying All of the Database Management Capabilities of dBASE III+, the Program Is Used for Joint Interest Billing & for Production History Record Keeping. The Program Does Not Require dBASE Itself, Nor Any Knowledge of How to Use dBASE. Contains the Following Features: Menu-Driven, Data Entry Including Well, Owner, Revenue, Expense & Production Information (Oil & Gas & 8-User Defined Phases). Report Generator -- Revenue Statements, Invoices, Production Statements, Monthly Joint Interest Billing, Monthly Owner Summaries, 1099 Tax Forms, etc. Database Indexing, Sorting, Deleting, etc. Check Writing; Mailing Labels. Import/Export ASCII Files to or from Lotus 1-2-3, PETEC1 & Petrocalc 5.
Gulf Publishing Co.

Petrocalc 13: Quik-Flo Gas Volume & Flow Calculation. R. C. Miner. Jun. 1989. *Compatible Hardware:* IBM PC, PC XT, PC AT & compatibles. *Operating System(s) Required:* PC-DOS/MS-DOS 3.0. *Language(s):* Compiled BASIC. *Memory Required:* 256k. *Customer Support:* 30 day money-back guarantee.
3.5" or 5.25" disk $295.00 (ISBN 0-87201-557-2).
Calculates to Full AGA-3 Precision, Gas Volume & Flow for Standard Orifice Meters. Production Monitoring Tool for Well Operators, Engineers, Gaugers, Owners, & Government Agencies. Can Be Used to Calculate Daily, Weekly, or Monthly Statements; Audit Pipeline Charts for Correct Volume & Payment; Monitor Gas Lift Systems Daily; & Balance Gas Plant or Field Systems. Eliminates the Need for Field Estimates or Time-Consuming Hand Calculations, & Helps Avoid Lost Production While Speeding up Correct Volume Reports. Features; Audits Previously Integrated Charts Without Re-Integrating; Maintains a Database of Technical Specs on Each Field Meter for Instant Retrieval & Calculations; Figures Gas Flow from Average Differential, Pressure, & Temperature, or from Integrator Counts from Previously Integrated Charts; Evaluates Beta Ratio; Calculates Volumes for Square Root Charts, & Performs Meter Sizings.
Gulf Publishing Co.

Petroleum Transportation Marketing Emissions Analysis. *Items Included:* Full manual. No other products required. *Customer Support:* Free telephone support - no time limit. 30 day warranty.
MS-DOS 3.2 or higher. IBM & compatibles (512k). disk $679.95.
demo disk $5.00.
Efficient Tool for Performing the Required EPA Emissions Estimates for Underground Storage Tanks & Loading Transit Losses (EPA AP-42, Section 4.4). Vapors Can Be Lost As Liquids Are Moved from Tanks to Transportation Equipment Such As Rail Cars, Trucks, & Ships, or from Transportation Equipment to Storage Tanks. Also, As Liquids Are Loaded into Tanks, They Displace the Vapors Already in Those Tanks. Includes a Complete & Detailed Manual Which Describes All Procedures.
Dynacomp, Inc.

PFP Partner. Jul. 1993. *Items Included:* 1 wiro bound manual. *Customer Support:* Free for the first 3 months; $195 annual fee after that.
DOS 3.1 or higher. IBM w/ 800k configured under EMS (2Mb, 520k free). disk $495.00 nonmembers; $445.50 AICPA members (Order no.: 800-862-4272). *Optimal configuration:* 4Mb RAM configured to 2Mb of EMS & 1Mb of disk cache; use of a memory manager (eg. HIMEM, 386MAX, QEMM) & a disk cache. *Networks supported:* Novell, Lantastic, 3Com. *Features Include: Preparation of Workpapers for Assets, Liabilities or Income & Expense Line Items; Education Funding, Simultaneously Calculating Lumpsum, Fixed Annual, Serial Annual Funding Amounts; Retirement Funding; 5-Year Projects Statement of Net/Worth; 5-Year Cash Flow Projection; Insurance Needs Analysis for Life Insurance & Disability Insurance.*
American Institute of Certified Public Accountants.

PFS:ACCESS with Zoom Disk. Oct. 1985. *Compatible Hardware:* IBM PC & compatibles. *Operating System(s) Required:* PC-DOS. *Memory Required:* 128k.
contact publisher for price.
Zoom Telephonics, Inc.

PFS:FILE & PFS:REPORT. Software Publishing Co. *Compatible Hardware:* HP 150 Touchscreen.
3.5" disk $265.00 (Order no.: 45488A).
File Management & Reporting System.
Hewlett-Packard Co.

PFS:GRAPH. Software Publishing Co. *Compatible Hardware:* HP 150 Touchscreen.
3.5" disk $140.00 (Order no.: 45490A).
Graphics Package That Works Alone or Directly with PFS:FILE, DIF, & Multiplan SYLK Files. Accepts Data Directly from the Keyboard, or It Can Retreive Data from PFS, Multiplan, or VisiCalc Files. GRAPH Charts Can Be Used in PFS:WRITE Documents As Well.
Hewlett-Packard Co.

PFS:WRITE. Software Publishing Co. *Compatible Hardware:* HP 150 Touchscreen.
3.5" disk $140.00 (Order no.: 45489A).
Allows User to Create Personalized Form Letters with PFS:FILE, Include Data Tables in Documents with PFS:REPORT, & Include Graphs with PFS:GRAPH. Documents Can Also Include Output from Other Software Programs.
Hewlett-Packard Co.

Phantom Stormers: Alien Logic, Arc of Doom, Command Adventures Starship. Ceridus Software Staff et al. Sep. 1995. *Items Included:* Set up instruction sheet, registration card. *Customer Support:* Customer support helpline 503 639-6863.
DOS. IBM PC (8Mb). CD-ROM disk $34.95 Alien Logic (ISBN 1-887783-11-3, Order no.: 5400-8003). *Optimal configuration:* IBM PC, 486 DX or higher, MS DOS 5.0 or higher, Uncompressed HD w/10Mb free, SVGA, Mouse w/driver 8.0, CD-ROM drive.
IBM PC (2Mb). CD-ROM disk $39.95 Arc of Doom. *Optimal configuration:* IBM PC 386SX or higher, 2Mb RAM with 575k free low RAM, mouse, HD, CD-ROM drive.
Plot Your Survival As You Take off to the Future in Space.
Entertainment Technology.

The Phantom Tollbooth. Intentional Education Staff & Norton Juster.
School ver.. System 7.1 or higher. Macintosh (4Mb). 3.5" disk contact publisher for price (ISBN 1-57204-280-X). *Nonstandard peripherals required:* 256 color monitor, hard drive, printer.
Lab pack. System 7.1 or higher. Macintosh

(4Mb). 3.5" disk contact publisher for price (ISBN 1-57204-256-7). *Nonstandard peripherals required:* 256 color monitor, hard drive, printer.
Site license. System 7.1 or higher. Macintosh (4Mb). 3.5" disk contact publisher for price (ISBN 1-57204-281-8). *Nonstandard peripherals required:* 256 color monitor, hard drive, printer.
School ver.. Windows 3.1 or higher. IBM/Tandy & 100% compatibles (4mb). disk contact publisher for price (ISBN 1-57204-257-5). *Nonstandard peripherals required:* VGA or SVGA 640 x 480 resolution (256), mouse, hard drive, sound device.
Lab pack. Windows 3.1 or higher. IBM/Tandy & 100% compatibles (4mb). disk contact publisher for price (ISBN 1-57204-282-6). *Nonstandard peripherals required:* VGA or SVGA 640 x 480 resolution (256), mouse, hard drive, sound device.
Site license. Windows 3.1 or higher. IBM/Tandy & 100% compatibles (4mb). disk contact publisher for price (ISBN 1-57204-258-3). *Nonstandard peripherals required:* VGA or SVGA 640 x 480 resolution (256), mouse, hard drive, sound device.
This companion for young adult literature is ideal for students who don't know how to start that book report, or give that needed summary. Gentle prompts throughout the guide section of the program include Warm-up Connections, Thinking about Plot, Quoting & Noting, Keeping a Journal, If I Were——'Responding to Questions, Using Quotations, Taking a Personal View, Write to Others & Write a Sequel.
Lawrence Productions, Inc.

Pharmaceutical Manufacturing Control System. *Items Included:* Manuals. *Customer Support:* 90 days included, then 15% per year of the current price. On-site installation & training available at $700.00/day & expenses.
MS-DOS, Xenix. IBM PC, XT, AT (512k). $4495.00 to $12,990.00. *Networks supported:* Novell, Lantastic, 3COM.
Inventory, Formulations Blending, Bill of Materials (BOM) Control & Materials Requirements Planning System (MRP) Featuring Multi-Level Traceability by Lot. Purchase Orders & Numerous Reports Are Generated. User-Defined Fields Provide Flexibility for Diverse Pharmaceutical Manufacturing Firms. Customization Available. Assists in Complying with the FDA Good Manufacturing Practices, EPA, & Other Governmental Record-Keeping Requirements. Inventory Records Are Kept at Both the Item & the Lot Level. Handles Real-World Situations Such as Variances between Planned & Actual Consumption. Calculates Costs Based on Lot Costs, Standard Costs, Average Costs, FIFO, or LIFO.
Stolzberg Research, Inc.

Pharmacological Calculations-Research. *Version:* 3.3. R. J. Tallarida & R. B. Murray. 1987. *Compatible Hardware:* IBM PC. *Operating System(s) Required:* PC-DOS 2.0 or higher. *Language(s):* BASIC (source code included). *Memory Required:* 128k.
disk $275.00, incl. documentation.
manual $52.00.
Scientific Drug Testing Which Includes 33 of the Most Often Used Computational & Statistical Procedures. Examples Are: Regression, t-Test, ANOVA, Litchfield & Wilcoxin Test, etc.
Life Science Assocs.

Pharmacology TextStack: Professional Edition. Theoharis C. Theoharides. Aug. 1994. *Items Included:* User manual, quick-start sheet, Keyboard Utilities, & Microsoft Multimedia Viewer (Windows version) or HyperCard (Macintosh version). *Customer Support:* Free, unlimited technical support via our toll-free number (1-800-945-4551).
Macintosh. Macintosh with a hard drive (2.5Mb). 3.5" disk $200.00 (ISBN 1-57349-121-7). *Addl. software required:* System 7.0 or higher. *Networks supported:* All LANs.
Windows. IBM compatible with 80286 or higher processor, a hard drive & a mouse (2Mb). disk $200.00 (ISBN 1-57349-175-6). *Addl. software required:* MS-DOS 3.3 or higher, Windows 3.1 or higher. *Networks supported:* All LANs.
An Electronic Teaching System Built Around Little, Brown & Co.'s Pharmacology by Theoharis C. Theoharides. Includes the Complete Text & All Figures, Diagrams & Tables, Plus Review & Self-Testing Materials with Complete Feedback for All Questions & Direct Access to Related Sections in the Text for Additional Review. Also Features Easy-to-Use Lesson-Building Tools to Customize the Program.
Keyboard Publishing, Inc.

Pharmacology TextStack: Student Edition. Theoharis C. Theoharides. Aug. 1994. *Items Included:* User manual, quick-start sheet, Keyboard Utilities, & Microsoft Multimedia Viewer (Windows version) or HyperCard (Macintosh version). *Customer Support:* Free, unlimited technical support via our toll-free number (1-800-945-4551).
Macintosh. Macintosh with a hard drive (2.5Mb). 3.5" disk $135.00 (ISBN 1-57349-213-2). *Addl. software required:* System 7.0 or higher. *Networks supported:* All LANs.
Windows. IBM compatible with 80286 or higher processor, a hard drive & a mouse (2Mb). disk $135.00 (ISBN 1-57349-214-0). *Addl. software required:* MS-DOS 3.3 or higher, Windows 3.1 or higher. *Networks supported:* All LANs.
An Electronic Teaching System Built Around Little, Brown & Co.'s Pharmacology by Theoharis C. Theoharides. Includes the Complete Text & All Figures, Diagrams & Tables, Plus Review & Self-Testing Materials with Complete Feedback for All Questions & Direct Access to Related Sections in the Text for Additional Review. Also Features Easy-to-Use Lesson-Building Tools to Customize the Program.
Keyboard Publishing, Inc.

Pharmacy. *Compatible Hardware:* Apple Macintosh 512KE. *General Requirements:* 20Mb hard disk, ImageWriter.
3.5" disk $995.00.
Pharmacy Management.
Pharmacy Management Systems, Inc.

PharmaSim: A Brand Management Simulation. Stuart James et al. 1994.
MS-DOS. disk $25.00 (ISBN 1-885837-03-8).
Windows. disk $25.00 (ISBN 1-885837-04-6).
Macintosh. 3.5" disk $25.00 (ISBN 1-885837-05-4).
Administrator's Guide $10.00 (ISBN 1-885837-08-9).
$25.00 MBA; $95.00 Consulting (ISBN 1-885837-07-0).
Marketing Software.
Interpretive Software Inc.

PHARMIS: Pharmacy Information System. *Version:* 2.0. Jun. 1986. *Compatible Hardware:* IBM PC & compatibles. *Operating System(s) Required:* PC-DOS, Novell, UNIX, Windows NT. (source code included). *Memory Required:* 4000k. *General Requirements:* Hard disk, printer, modem.
IBM PC version. $5000.00.
Pharmacy Operation, Billing, Statistics, Reporting: Labels, Medicaid, Private Insurance, Daily/Monthly/Special Reports, Patient Profile, Interaction, Interaction, Auto Pricing, Generics, & A/R.
Southern Software Systems, Inc.

Phase Locked Loop Tutorial. (Electrical Engineering Ser.). *Operating System(s) Required:* Apple DOS 3.2, 3.3, MS-DOS. *Memory Required:* Apple 48k, IBM 128k.
disk $49.95.
Includes Discussion of Synchronized Multivibrators, VCO's, the NE55, MC1648, Phase Detectors, AFC, Hold-In Range, etc.
Dynacomp, Inc.

PhasePlane: The Dynamical System Too! *Version:* 3.0. Bard Ermentrout. *Items Included:* One 5 1/4" & one 3 1/2" disk, a 144-page "Guide to PhasePlane" paperback book. *Customer Support:* Unlimited technical support for registered users.
DOS. IBM PC, XT, AT, or similar clone (360k). $50.00 (Single User package) (ISBN 0-534-12894-7). *Optimal configuration:* IBM PC, XT, AT, or similar clone; 360k RAM, (640k desirable); floppy or hard disk drive; graphics card & monitor supporting CGA, EGA, VGA, Hercules, or AT & T graphics. Optional: math coprocessor, EPSON or IBM graphics printer, Hewlett-Packard Laserjet; HP pen-plotter, LIM Expanded memory.
(Site License) $400.00 (ISBN 0-534-12895-5).
Interactive Program for Solving up to 20 Differential Equations, Difference Equations, & Differential-Delay Equations. With PhasePlane, Users Can: Choose from Seven Different Numerical Methods, Including Gear's Method for "Stiff" Equations, Create Self-Running & Interactive Demos or Movies for Later Playback; Compute Energy, Poincare Maps, Fourier Transforms, Successive Maxima/Minima, & More; Find Equilibria, Stability, & Trace Bifucations for Arbitrary N-Dimensional Systems; Draw nullclines, Direction Fields, & Global Flows for Two-Dimensional Models; Access up to Four Plotting Windows for Simultaneous Viewing of Phase-Space Projections and/or Time Courses; Take Advantage of Many Other Features Such As: a Built-In Scientific Calculator, Plotter Support, Laserjet Support, & the Ability to View up to Four Windows.
Brooks/Cole Publishing Co.

Phasor Belt. *Compatible Hardware:* TRS-80. contact publisher for price.
Instant Software, Inc.

PHD+: Portable Handheld Device. *Customer Support:* Price includes one-year manufacturer's maintenance warranty. An annual extended maintenance agreement is available after the first year for $125.00 per site, per year.
IBM PC-MS/DOS, Apple. disk $950.00 (Order no.: BM067). *Addl. software required:* Circulation Plus.
Is Our Innovative Handheld Scanner Having Many Practical Uses. With the Power of Follett's PHD Plus Scanning Unit & Portable Scan Plus Software (Included with Your Circulation Plus Package), You Have the Capability of a Full-Sized Computer in the Palm of Your Hand. The PHD Plus Is a High-Quality, High-Performance, Multi-Use Scanner. The Handheld Computer is Designed for Sophisticated or Novice Operators. Its Versatility Enables You to Be More Efficient While Reducing Your Work Load & to Manage Your Library in an Innovative Manner. It Has an LCD Display & a Reversible Scanning Head for Right or Left Handed Operators. Information Is Scanned into the PHD Plus by Simply Wanding Barcode Labels or Manually Keying Information Using the Alpha-Numeric Keypad. The Information Is Then Uploaded to Your Computer Using a Cable Included in the Package.
Follett Software Co.

TITLE INDEX

Philip Hal Likes E, I Reckon Maybe. Intentional Education Staff & Bette Green. Apr. 1996. *Items Included:* Program manual. *Customer Support:* Free technical support, 90 day warranty.
School ver.. System 7.1 or higher. Macintosh (4Mb). 3.5" disk contact publisher for price (ISBN 1-57204-243-5). *Nonstandard peripherals required:* 256 color monitor, hard drive, printer.
Lab pack. System 7.1 or higher. Macintosh (4Mb). 3.5" disk contact publisher for price (ISBN 1-57204-219-2). *Nonstandard peripherals required:* 256 color monitor, hard drive, printer.
Site license. System 7.1 or higher. Macintosh (4Mb). (ISBN 1-57204-244-3). *Nonstandard peripherals required:* 256 color monitor, hard drive, printer.
School ver.. Windows 3.1 or higher. IBM/Tandy & 100% compatibles (4Mb). disk contact publisher for price (ISBN 1-57204-220-6). *Nonstandard peripherals required:* VGA or SVGA 640 x 480 resolution (256), mouse, hard drive, sound device.
Lab pack. Windows 3.1 or higher. IBM/Tandy & 100% compatibles (4Mb). disk contact publisher for price (ISBN 1-57204-245-1). *Nonstandard peripherals required:* VGA or SVGA 640 x 480 resolution (256), mouse, hard drive, sound device.
Site license. Windows 3.1 or higher. IBM/Tandy & 100% compatibles (4Mb). disk contact publisher for price (ISBN 1-57204-221-4). *Nonstandard peripherals required:* VGA or SVGA 640 x 480 resolution (256), mouse, hard drive, sound device.
This companion for young adult literature is ideal for students who don't know how to start that book report, or give that needed summary. Gentle prompts throughout the guide section of the program include Warm-up Connections, Thinking about Plot, Quoting & Noting, Keeping a Journal, If I Were ——' Responding to Questions, Using Quotations, Taking a Personal View, Write to Others, & Write a Sequel.
Lawrence Productions, Inc.

The Philistine Ploy. *Compatible Hardware:* Apple II+, IIe, IIc. *Memory Required:* 48k.
disk $14.95.
Player Seeks a Long-Lost Hoard of Untold Wealth. On the Player's Trail Is a Philistine Warrior Who Wants It for Himself. Using Clues, the Player Must Traverse Four Episodes. Travel Through Stables, Palaces, Tunnels, Tool Houses, Barley Fields & Tent Camps of Hostile Troops. Along the Way, Meet Deborah, Samson & Delilah, Gideon & Other Biblical Figures.
Davka Corp.

PHIPS-Professional Hi-Resolution Image Processing System. *Version:* 1.4. Dec. 1989. *Items Included:* 1 manual & 2 disks with sample images. *Customer Support:* Product support is available 11:00 am to 4:30 pm EST Monday thru Thursday.
DOS 2.0 or higher. IBM-PC (512K). disk $349.00.
Reduces TARGA 16, 24 or 32 Type Files to SVGA, VGA, EGA, or CGA, Analog or Digital Modes. Contains Color-Reduction Options, Dither Options & Supports a Wide Range of Video Adapters.
TerraVision, Inc.

Phone Directory. *Compatible Hardware:* Atari 400, 800. *Language(s):* Atari BASIC. *Memory Required:* 48k.
disk $19.95.
Stores over 300 Names Indexed by Last Name. Includes Auto Dial Capability.
Dynacomp, Inc.

Phone Directory On-Line. Tony Drumm & Clifford Spinac. *Compatible Hardware:* IBM PC, PC XT, PC AT, Portable PC with IBM Display, Communications Adapter & modem (optional for automatic dialing), IBM Matrix printer (optional). *Operating System(s) Required:* DOS 1.10, 2.00, 2.10, 3.00, 3.10. *Memory Required:* 128k.
disk $24.95 (Order no.: 6276522).
Enables User to Maintain Approximately 1000 Listings for Immediate Access. Each Listing Can Include Last Name, Initial, Phone & Extension Numbers, & Other Information (Spouse's Name, Hobbies, Associations, etc.). Listings Can Be Called by Entering Only Part of Last Name or Comment. The Program Is Resident in Memory & Can Be Called up at Any Time. If Connected to a Modem It Also Provides Auto-Dialing Capability.
Personally Developed Software, Inc.

PhoneNET CheckNET. *Version:* 2.0. *Compatible Hardware:* Apple Macintosh. *Items Included:* Multi user license for up to 10 workstations. *Customer Support:* Free phone support, 90 day warranty.
3.5" disk $95.00.
Network Management Tool & Desk Accessory for Network Users & Managers. Displays Name, Address, & Type of Every Device on the Network & Across Multiple Bridges & Zones, & Sorts by Same.
W O S Data Systems, Inc.

Photo Textures. *Items Included:* Browser/installer/launcher front end software. *Customer Support:* 90 day warranty, free call back technical support.
System 6. Color Mac (4Mb). CD-ROM disk $20.00. *Nonstandard peripherals required:* CD-ROM drive. *Optimal configuration:* 8Mb RAM. *Networks supported:* Apple File Sharing.
BeachWare.

PhotoAlbum the ScreenSaver: For Windows. Ronald C. Nagel. Sep. 1995. *Items Included:* Operating manual, several sample images, instructions on how to get your image scanned for use in PhotoAlbum the ScreenSaver. *Customer Support:* 90 day unlimited warranty. Satisfaction guaranteed. On-line support available via Compuserve or the Internet.
Microsoft Windows 3.1; Workgroups for Windows 3.11, Windows 95. 386 SX microprocessor or higher (4Mb). disk $29.95 (ISBN 0-9648917-0-0). *Nonstandard peripherals required:* Use of sound requires a sound card capable of playing *.wav files. *Optimal configuration:* 486DX w/8Mb RAM, 2Mb video RAM. *Networks supported:* Workgroups for Windows; Novell Netware w/ Windows as active interface.
A Multimedia Product That Allows You to Run Your Photographs As the Active ScreenSaver for Windows. Your Family, Friends or Favorite Place Fill Your Screen. Can Also Be Used to Display Company Logos or Messages to Workers. At Last, You Control Your Screensaver!
Computer Management Technologies.

Photojournalism: An Ethical Approach. Paul Lester. 1991. *Customer Support:* Free technical support, 90-day limited warranty.
DOS. disk $17.95, incl. wkbk. (ISBN 1-56321-081-9).
DOS. 3.5" disk $17.95, incl. wkbk. (ISBN 1-56321-082-7).
Mac. 3.5" disk $17.95, incl. wkbk. (ISBN 1-56321-084-3).
This Volume Is Designed to Put Newspaper Photojournalism Assignment Techniques into an Ethical Context.
Lawrence Erlbaum Assocs. Software & Alternate Media, Inc.

PhotoMagic.
MS-DOS 5.0 or higher. IBM 386 or 486 PC (4Mb). disk $149.00 (Order no.: PH3L10ENG). *Addl. software required:* Windows 3.1. *Optimal configuration:* 8Mb RAM, scanner.
First-Image-Editing Program to Break the Dependency on Scanners. Provides All of the Tools & Special Effects You'll Need to Edit Photos on Your PC - Whether You're Manipulating One of the More Than 250 Images Included with the Program, or from CompuServe, a CD-ROM, or Your Photo Album.
Micrografx, Inc.

PhotoMetric SlideMaker - PrintMaker. Jan. 1985. *Memory Required:* 256k.
Spectra Star PhotoMetric SlideMaker. disk $4999.00.
Printmaker. disk $99.00.
Spectra Star SlideMaker Enables Owners of PICTUREIT & VIDEOSHOW to Produce Professional, High Resolution Color Slides in Minutes. PRINTMAKER Permits the User to Produce Professional Quality, Full Color Overhead Transparencies & Handouts.
General Parametrics Corp.

Photon Paint. *Version:* 2.0. *Compatible Hardware:* Apple Macintosh; Commodore Amiga. *Memory Required:* Recommended 2000k. *General Requirements:* Color QuickDraw.
3.5" disk $149.95.
Third-Generation Graphics Program Featuring 256-Color Palette, File Compatibility with Other Paint Programs, Brush Manipulation, Tilt, Rotate, Resize, Mapping on 3-D Objects & Luminance. User Can Also Execute Blending, Add & Subtract Colors & Have Full Control of Dithering in the X & Y Directions.
MicroIllusions, Inc.

Photon Paint Expansion Disks. *Compatible Hardware:* Commodore Amiga.
3.5" disk $19.95.
A Variety of Wood & Marble Surfaces.
Microillusions, Inc.

Photon Video: CellAnimator. *Compatible Hardware:* Commodore Amiga.
3.5" disk $49.95.
Professional CellAnimation, Sync Sound.
Microillusions, Inc.

Photon Video: Transport Controller. *Compatible Hardware:* Commodore Amiga.
3.5" disk $299.95.
Drives Single-Frame Video Controller.
Microillusions, Inc.

PhotoOffice II. *Compatible Hardware:* Apple Macintosh Plus. *Memory Required:* 1000k. *General Requirements:* Hard disk; ImageWriter or LaserWriter.
Single user. 3.5" disk $995.00.
Multiuser. 3.5" disk $1390.00.
Demo & Tutorial. 3.5" disk $49.95.
Studio Management System.
Gene Howell.

PhotoPaq. WEKA Publishing.
CD-ROM. CD-ROM disk $249.00 (ISBN 0-929321-08-1).
Photo Collection on CD-ROM. Computer Images; Basework 200 Images, Supplements 60 Images.
WEKA Publishing, Inc.

PhotoRobot. *Version:* 1.20. Dec. 1995. *Items Included:* 1 3.5" diskette, 1 Jewel Case, Installation Instructions. *Customer Support:* One year free technical support, 30 day unlimited warranty.
Windows 3.1. 80286(AT), (512k). 3.5" disk

$19.95.
Kids Can Create Faces & Characters to Illustrate Stories, School Projects, Make Halloween Masks, Make Posters & More. No Art Experience Or Skill Needed to Make Quality Imnages! Anyone Can Create Characters That Reflect Any Type of Personality from Happy to Sinister.
PSG-HomeCraft Software.

Phraze Maze: Grammar Through Phrases.
(Micro Learn Tutorial Ser.). *Items Included:* Teacher-learner materials. *Customer Support:* Free telephone support.
MAC. IBM (125k), Macintosh (2Mb), Apple II series, (48k), Commodore 64. 5.25" disk, $39.95 (Lab pack/5 $99.00), 3.5" disk, $44.95 (Lab pack/5 $115.00). Apple, IBM or Macintosh network, $249.00 (ISBN 1-57265-048-6).
DOS. (ISBN 0-939153-59-9).
APP. (ISBN 0-939153-27-0).
Tutorial Teaches Grammar, While Covering Various Types of Phrases & Their Application in Sentences. Topics Include Verb, Prepositions, Adjective, Adverb, Participial, Gerund & Infinitive Phrases, & Appositives. The tutorial mode gives explanations for every answer choice, correct & incorrect (plus help/practice on important ideas). The test mode gives no help; after the score appears, it presents missed questions in the tutorial.
Word Assocs., Inc.

Phyla. Jan. 1995. *Items Included:* Comprehensive manual. *Customer Support:* Free technical support.
Mac System 7.0. Mac 030 (8Mb). disk $295.00. *Networks supported:* Yes.
Finally There's a Database That Gives You the Power to Handle Complex Situations, Simply. Phyla Is the First Object-Oriented Database That Anyone Can Use & You Don't Need to Be a Programmer, or Even Think Like One. In Fact It's So Easy, You'll Produce Real Results Within an Hour of Opening the Box.
Mainstay.

PHYSCHED: Physician Scheduling System. Jan. 1986. *Compatible Hardware:* IBM PC & compatibles. *Operating System(s) Required:* MS-DOS. *Language(s):* BASIC. *Memory Required:* 256k.
disk $350.00, incl. user manual.
Assigns On-Call Responsibilities to Physicians in Medical Clinics, Emergency Rooms, etc. Accommodates Regular Days off, Requested Days of, Preferences for Days of the Week On-Call & Off-Duty. Fairly Distributes Weekend Assignments among Physicians. Eliminates Subjectivity in Designing Schedules. Reports Schedule Inequities Which Are Automatically Corrected in Next Schedule Period. Last-Minute Requests for Time off Can Be Incorporated in Schedule. Prepares Calendars for Each Physician.
Computing Power Applied.

Physical Exam for 1571, 1541, 8050, 4040 Disk Drives. Version: 4.0. May 1989. *Compatible Hardware:* Commodore 64, 128; PLUS 4; 8032. *Memory Required:* 32k. *Items Included:* Instructions, test disk. *Customer Support:* Free call 703-491-6502.
disk $39.95.
Tests Alignment, Speed & Stop Position for All Commodore Disk Drives. Includes Instructions for Correcting Alignment, Speed & Mechanical Stops.
Cardinal Software (Virginia).

Physical Fitness. *Compatible Hardware:* TI Home Computer.
contact publisher for price (Order no.: PHM 3010).
Helps in Planning a Personal Exercise Program.
Texas Instruments, Personal Productivit.

Physical Properties of Hydrocarbon Liquids.
Items Included: Bound manual. *Customer Support:* Free hotline - no time limit; 30 day limited warranty; updates are $5/disk plus S&H.
MS-DOS. IBM & compatibles (128k). disk $89.95.
Apple (48k). disk $89.95.
Calculate the Physical Properties of Liquid Hydrocarbons, Including Viscosity, Gravity, & Thermal Conductivity. Charts, Graphs, Tables, Log-Log Plots, & Tedious Hand Calculations Are Now Replaced by a Few Simple Keystrokes on the Computer Keyboard.
Dynacomp, Inc.

Physician Fee Analyzer Plus. *Items Included:* Full manual. No other products required. *Customer Support:* Free telephone support - no time limit. 30 day warranty.
MS-DOS 3.2 or higher. IBM & compatibles (512k). $349.95-$699.95.
Macintosh. $349.95-$699.95.
Supplies the Fee Information You Need to Develop a Rational Fee Schedule for Your Medical Practice. Based on Data Compiled from More Than 235 Million Billings. Included Are Your Geographic Area's Average Fees, As Well As the 40th & 80th Percentiles. Additional Features Include: Average Follow-Up Days for Surgical Services, Assist Surgeon Designated Services, Allowable Anesthesia Units, Your Medicare Locality Unblended Fee.
Dynacomp, Inc.

Physician Orders. *Items Included:* Manuals, training exercises, quick reference guide.
IBM PC, AT, XT, & compatibles; PS/2. contact publisher for price.
Medications, Treatments, & Other Orders. Med Sheets, Treatment Sheets & Reports.
Beechwood Software.

Physicians' Desk Reference on CD-ROM.
Version: 3.0. *Items Included:* User guide. *Customer Support:* Free customer support. Dial 1-800-232-7379.
DOS. IBM compatibles (450k). CD-ROM disk $595.00, $895.00 incl. Merck Manual. *Nonstandard peripherals required:* CD-ROM drive. *Optimal configuration:* DOS 3.1 or higher, 640k, CD-ROM drive. *Networks supported:* Novell - most DOS related systems.
The Complete Text of Physicians' Desk Reference, PDR for NonPrescription Drugs, PDRs Drug Interaction & Side Effects Index, PDRs Indication Index & PDR for Ophthalmology - All on One Compact Disc. All Information Is Fully Searchable. Optional Merck Manual May Be Included.
Medical Economics Data.

Physician's Office Computer. Version: 3.4-4. Jeff Balsam et al. Oct. 1977. *Items Included:* End user manual. *Customer Support:* Local on-site training through dealers; 90 day warranty; one year maintenance-$1200, covers unlimited phone support plus updates & mandatory changes..
IBM PC & compatibles (640K). $495.00 to $5750.00. *Networks supported:* Novell, NTNX, CDOS.
Complete In-Office Medical Software System for Patient Financial & Clinical Data Management As Well As Appointment Scheduling. Currently in Use by More Than 2000 Physicians Throughout the Country. Will Operate on Most Micro Computers in Either Single or Multi-Terminal Environments & Handles from One to Ninety-Nine Physicians, Seeing from Ten to Three Hundred Patients per Day. An Optional Electronic Claim Submission Program is Also Available in Some Areas for Payless Insurance Processing.
Physicians Office Computer.

Physics Simulation. 1995. *Items Included:* Full manual. *Customer Support:* Free telephone support - 90 days, 30-day warranty.
MS-DOS 3.2 or higher. 286 (584k). disk $49.95. *Nonstandard peripherals required:* CGA/EGA/VGA.
A Set of Eight Independent Modules Which Provides Introductory Physics Students with a Leading-Edge Tool for Studying Physical Processes Involving Motion. Quantitatively Accurate Algorithms & Graphics Make the Software Well-Suited to Interactive, Exploration-Oriented Lecture Demonstrations. The Simulations Cover Wave Motion, Chain Reactions, Maxwell's Demon, Moving Charges, Radiating Dipoles, & the Movement of Light Through a Thin Lens.
Dynacomp, Inc.

Physics, Vol. 1: Motion. 1995. *Items Included:* Full manual. *Customer Support:* Free telephone support - 90 days, 30-day warranty.
MS-DOS 3.2 or higher. 286 (584k). disk $44.95. *Nonstandard peripherals required:* CGA/EGA/VGA.
Learn Relative Motion, Speed, Velocity, Gravitational Acceleration, Newton's Laws, & Much More.
Dynacomp, Inc.

Physics, Vol. 2: Heat & Light. 1995. *Items Included:* Full manual. *Customer Support:* Free telephone support - 90 days, 30-day warranty.
MS-DOS 3.2 or higher. 286 (584k). disk $44.95. *Nonstandard peripherals required:* CGA/EGA/VGA.
Discover Characteristics & Theories of Light Including Particles Theory, Wave Theory, Speed of Light, Interference, Diffraction, & More.
Dynacomp, Inc.

Piano Partners Music Learning System, 4 levels. *Items Included:* Instructional booklet, order blank, registration card. *Customer Support:* 90 day warranty.
MS-DOS (640k). $99.00 each level (3.5" or 5.25" disks). *Nonstandard peripherals required:* MIDI card; Roland, MPU-401, Voyetra or MUSIC QUEST PC MIDI card. *Optimal configuration:* Color monitor, CGA/EGA/VGA card, graphics card (not Hercules), MIDI card, MIDI keyboard.
instructional manual avail. (ISBN 1-878391-05-4).
Interactive Computerized Music Instruction System with Color & Cartoon-Style Graphics, Animated by the Student Learning Basic Concepts & Skills.
Piano Partners, Inc.
Level I.
 (ISBN 1-878391-01-1).
 High/Low Pitches, Basic Note Values, Black Key Groupings, Names of White Piano Keys & Basic Melodic Patterns.
Level II.
 (ISBN 1-878391-02-X).
 Naming All Piano Keys, Finger Numbers, Transposing Finger Exercises, Making Variations, Music Notation & Terminology, Conducting 4/4 & 3/4, Improvising Musical Questions & Answers (3 Tones).
Level III.
 (ISBN 1-878391-03-8).
 Improvising Musical Questions & Answers (3-32 Tones), Improvising to a Waltz Bass, Playing 12-Bar Blues, Primary Tones, Grand Staff, Learning Note Names, Exercising 10 Fingers in 12 Keys, Dotted Rhythm.
Level IV.
 (ISBN 1-878391-04-6).
 Playing in a Minor Mode, Playing Chaconne Bass, Sharp/Flat Key Signatures, Half/Whole Steps, All Major Scales, Major/Minor Triads, I, IV, V Chords, Inversions, Chord Tones in All Keys.

TITLE INDEX

Picaresque: The Graphic Novel Publisher.
1995. *Items Included:* Full manual. *Customer Support:* Free telephone support - 90 days, 30-day warranty.
MS-DOS 3.2 or higher. 286 (584k). disk $49.95. *Nonstandard peripherals required:* CGA/EGA/VGA.
Now Students Can Easily Combine Words & Pictures to Print Out Their Own Graphic Novels in a Variety of Print Sizes, from Minibooks to Posters. Features: Large Library of Awesome, Easy-to-Use Graphics; Word Processor with an Assortment of Type Styles; Variety of Printout Sizes from Minibooks to Posters.
Dynacomp, Inc.

Pick PC System. *Version:* 3.0. *Compatible Hardware:* IBM PC XT, 286, 386. *Operating System(s) Required:* Pick. *Memory Required:* 512k. *General Requirements:* Hard disk.
from 1-user $495.00 to 33-users $3995.00 (Order no.: PC386).
Virtual Memory Manager, Multi-User, Multi-Tasking, Database Management O/S. Features Include Support Up to 33 Users, Print Spooler, 3-Dimensional File Structure, Systems Monitor, Dictionary System, High-Level Programming Language (Pick BASIC), Stored Procedure Language (PROC), Text Formatting (Editor), Page Formatting/Document Processor (RUNOFF), Terminal Control Language (TCL), & 4-Level Security.
Pick Systems.

Picnic. *Compatible Hardware:* Commodore PET with Commodore BASIC. (source code included). *Memory Required:* 16k.
disk $16.95.
Protect Your Food from Ants & Crabs.
Dynacomp, Inc.

PICT Detective. *Version:* 2.0. Sep. 1988. *Compatible Hardware:* Apple Macintosh. *Memory Required:* 1000k. *Items Included:* PICT detective application, MPW tools. *Customer Support:* Technical support 619-721-7000, sample documents, illustrated manual & limited manual.
3.5" disk $125.00.
Analyzes & Modifies QuickDraw Pictures. Given a PICT Document, Resource File, or the Scrapbook, It Gives Programmers a Complete Description of Each Element of a Picture: Shape, Location, Font, Color, & Other Properties.
Palomar Software, Inc.

Picture Atlas of the World. (National Geographic Society CD-ROM Ser.).
Windows. IBM & compatibles. CD-ROM disk $99.95 (Order no.: R1054A). *Nonstandard peripherals required:* CD-ROM drive. *Optimal configuration:* 386 processor operating at 16Mhz or higher, MS-DOS 5.0 or higher, Windows 3.1 or higher, 30Mb hard drive, mouse, VGA graphic adapter & VGA color monitor (SVGA recommended), 4Mb RAM, external speakers or headphones (with sound card) that are Sound Blaster compatible.
Macintosh (4Mb). (Order no.: R1054A). *Nonstandard peripherals required:* 14" color monitor or larger, CD-ROM drive.
Browse among Maps, Video Clips, Photographs & Animations. Hear Languages & Music of the World. Read Entertaining Captions & Informative Essays (Grade 4 & Up).
Library Video Co.

Picture Draw. Doug Olufsen. *Compatible Hardware:* IBM PC, PCjr, PC XT, PC AT, Portable PC, 3270 PC; joystick, Mouse Systems mouse, & IBM Graphics Printer are optional. *Operating System(s) Required:* PC-DOS 2.00, 2.10, 3.00, 3.10. *Memory Required:* 256k.
disk $24.95 (Order no.: 6276628).
Enables Users to Create Diagrams, Graphs, Scaled Drawings, & Freehand Artwork. Drawing Options Allow Users to Define Points to Create Lines, Squares, Rectangles, Circles, & Ellipses; Pictures Can Be Created Using the Cursor Movement Keys, a Joystick or a Mouse; Screen Images Are Manipulated Using the Sizing, Rotating, Mirroring, Outlining, Overlaying, & Multiple Centering Options; Nine Proportionally Spaced Lettering Fonts Are Available in a Variety of Styles, Sizes, & Colors; Images Can Be Zoomed or Filled.
Personally Developed Software, Inc.

Picture Factory Set 1. Oct. 1993. *Items Included:* 20 page booklet (manual), Photodex Search software. *Customer Support:* Free technical support & upgrades.
MS-DOS. IBM AT w/386 or higher including compatibles (2Mb). CD-ROM disk Contact publisher for price (ISBN 1-884379-01-X). *Nonstandard peripherals required:* SuperVGA w/640x480x256 colors. *Addl. software required:* Himen.Sys. *Networks supported:* All.
Microsoft Windows. IBM AT w/386 or higher including compatibles (4Mb). CD-ROM disk Contact publisher for price. *Optimal configuration:* 8Mb RAM, 800X600 or higher display w/256 colors or better. *Networks supported:* All.
Macintosh OS. 68020 or higher processor (4Mb). CD-ROM disk Contact publisher for price (ISBN 1-884379-00-1). *Optimal configuration:* 8Mb RAM, 8 bit display, Quadra or higher. *Networks supported:* All.
CD-ROM Software Program with over 1,500 Photographs for Desktop Publishing & Graphical Design. All Photographs Are Royalty Free. Catagories Represented Are: Backgrounds, Business & People, Sunsets, Clouds, Animals, Signs, Objects, Space Food, Industrial, & Many Subcatagories. Available on MPC, MS-DOS, Windows & Macintosh.
Raxsoft, Inc.

Picture It with Words. Yvonne Richardson. 1986. *Compatible Hardware:* Apple II+, IIe, IIc. *Memory Required:* 48k.
disk $35.00 (ISBN 1-55763-074-7, Order no.: ML101D-A).
Designed to Help Children Learn 100 Words by Using Pictures, Graphics, Letter & Music. Includes Three Games: Rhyming, Beginning Letter & Words.
Micro Learningware.

Picture Perfect. *Version:* 4.1. Sep. 1988. *Compatible Hardware:* AT&T 6300, AT&T 6300 Plus; Compaq; HP 150 Touchscreen, HP 200/16, HP 200/17, HP 200/36, HP Vectra; IBM PC, PC XT, PC AT, PS/2. *Operating System(s) Required:* MS-DOS, HP-UX. *Language(s):* Pascal, Assembly. *Memory Required:* 512k. *General Requirements:* Hercules, Tecmar, CGA, EGA, or VGA card; hard disk.
$295.00, incl. manual (Order no.: 35004).
Menu-Driven, Interactive Graphics Software Package That Can Transform Data into Pie, Vertical Bar, Horizontal Bar, or Line Charts. Data Values May Be Windowed or on Top of Bars. Bars May Be Simple, Stacked, Comparative, or Overlapping with up to 24 Bars. Legends May Be Windowed or Placed at Any Location. Blocks of Annotations May Be Placed As Desired. Two Independent Y Axes Allow Comparison of Different Data Sets in the Same Chart. Pie Charts May Have up to 16 Segments. 58 Shading Patterns Allow User to Control the Final Appearance of the Charts. Users Are Then Able to Export a .PIC File, Enabling Them to Read a Chart into Another Software Program for Desktop Publishing Purposes.
Computer Support Corp.

Picture Publisher. *Version:* 4.0. Jun. 1993.
MS-DOS 5.0 or higher. IBM 386 or 486 & compatibles (4Mb). CD-ROM disk $595.00 (Order no.: PP2L40ENG). *Addl. software required:* Windows 3.1. *Optimal configuration:* 16Mb RAM, CD-ROM drive, scanner.
Features Improved Speed & Productivity Capabilities Unmatched by Its Competition. Its New Object Layers, FastBits, & Low Res Image Open Option Ensure Quick Edits of Layered Objects & Large Files. For Even More Speed, Use the Macro Recording & Playback Feature, Which Automates Any Function. Provides Thumbnail Sketches That Show Color Balance, Contrast, & Brightness, & an ImageBrowser That Stores Thumbnail Images in Albums.
Micrografx, Inc.

PICTure This. *Version:* 2.0.
Macintosh. disk $149.00.
Converts Graphics Files from More Than 24 Formats into Macintosh PICT Files. Graphics Can Be Used As They Are after Conversion or Edited Like Any Other PICT File. Converts TARGA, CGM, PCX, Sun Raster, Lotus PIC, Lotus BIT, Dr. Halo CUT, GEMIMG, Amiga IFF, GIF, TIFF, RIFF, X.11 Bitmaps, OS/2 BMP, Windows BMP, Silicon Graphics RGB, Apollo GPR, RIX, XII XWD, Photoshop, PCPaint PIC, Pixelpaint & MacPaint Formatted Files. Features Support for Color, Batch Processing, Automatic File Sensor.
FGM.

PictureEze. Apr. 1991. *Items Included:* Complete manual & both 3.25 & 5.25 Media. *Customer Support:* 30 day money back guarantee, 90 day unlimited technical support.
MicroSoft Windows 3.0 or higher. IBM 100% compatible (2Mb). disk $149.00.
File Conversion & Viewing Software for More Than Sixty Distinct File Types. Rotate, Mirror, or Flip the Image. Adjust Color, Brightness, & Contrast. Crop or Change Image Size. Reverse Color to Produce a Negative, or Transform a Color Image into a High Quality Gray-Scaled Image. Makes Enhancements & Conversions Easy.
Application Techniques, Inc.

PictureIt. Jan. 1984. *Operating System(s) Required:* PC-DOS. *Memory Required:* 256k.
disk $495.00.
Presentation Software Package with a Wide Variety of Animated, Bar, Pie, Line & Word Charts. With the Simple Fill-in-the-Blank Format.
General Parametrics Corp.

PicturePower. *Version:* 3.0. *Compatible Hardware:* IBM PC, PS/2 & compatibles. *Items Included:* Software, documentation. *Customer Support:* Phone support.
disk $1995.00.
Free-Form, Menu-Driven Photographic-Quality Database-Management System Featuring Help Screen & Automatic Indexing. Offers a Maximum of 128 Fields per Record, 254 Characters per Field, Unlimited Records per File, 4000 Characters per Record, 7 Indexes per File, 1 Active Index & up to 7 Records Sorted. Allows User to Revise Field Descriptions at Will.
PictureWare, Inc.

PicturePower HC. *Version:* 3.0. *Compatible Hardware:* IBM PC & compatibles. *Items Included:* Software, documentation, compression board. *Customer Support:* Telephone support.
$3900.00, incl. hardware-compression capabilities.
Free-Form, Menu-Driven Photographic-Quality Database-Management System Featuring Help Screen & Automatic Indexing. Offers a Maximum of 128 Fields per Record, 254 Characters per Field, Unlimited Records per File, 4000 Characters per Record, 7 Indexes per File, 1 Active Index & up to 7 Records Sorted. Allows User to Revise Field Descriptions at Will.
PictureWare, Inc.

Piers-Harris Children's Self-Concept Scale. Version: 2.011. Ellen V. Peirs & Dale B. Harris. Customer Support: Free unlimited phone support. IBM PC & 100% compatibles. 3.5" or 5.25" disk $225.00 (Order no.: W-1014 (5.25"); W-1029 (3.5")). Optimal configuration: DOS 3.0 or higher (512k), & hard disk with one Mb of free hard disk space, printer.
Helps User Evaluate the Psychological Health of Children & Adolescents, Quickly Identifying Those Who Need Further Testing or Treatment. Unlike Many Other Measures of Self-Concept, It Is Based on the Child's Own Perceptions Rather Than the Observation of Parents or Teachers. Assesses Self-Concept in Individuals 8 to 18 Years of Age.
Western Psychological Services.

PIG. John Migliavacca. 1985. Compatible Hardware: IBM PC & compatibles. Operating System(s) Required: DOS. Memory Required: 256k. General Requirements: Dot matrix printer. $500.00 per module.
Simulates the Process of "Pigging" & Estimates the Quantities of Gas & Pressure Required. Specific Pipeline Data Such As Distance, Elevation at Various Points, & Other Properties Can Be Stored in a File So That Repeated Calculations Can Be Made. Seperate Modules Are Available for Constant Velocity, Constant Pressure, & Constant Injection Rate.
Techdata.

Pigmented Lesions of the Skin. Arto Demirjian et al. Customer Support: Toll-free technical support - no charge. In U.S. - 9AM-5PM EST 800-343-0064. In U.K. - 44(0)81-995-8242.
386 IBM-compatible PC (3Mb). CD-ROM disk $249.00 Individual; $599.00 Institutional (ISBN 1-57276-013-3, Order no.: SE-013-001). Nonstandard peripherals required: MPC Standard CD-ROM drive, SVGA (640 x 480) 256 colors, MPC standard soundboard & speakers.
System 6.0.7 or higher. Apple Macintosh (3Mb). CD-ROM disk $249.00 Individual; $599.00 Institutional (Order no.: SE-013-001). Nonstandard peripherals required: CD-ROM drive.
With over 100 Color Images, This CD-ROM Provides Quick & Easy Access to Important Clinical Data on Twenty-Five Different Pigmented Cutaneous Lesions, As Well As Relevant Histopathological Information. Both Benign & Malignant Lesions Are Represented.
SilverPlatter Education.

Pigmented Lesions of the Skin. Ari Demirjian et al. Jun. 1994. Customer Support: Toll-free technical support - no charge. In U.S. 9AM - 5PM EST 800-343-0064; in U.K. 44(0)81-995-8242.
System 6.0.7 or higher. Apple Macintosh (3Mb). CD-ROM disk $249.00, Individual, ,599.00 Institutional (ISBN 1-57276-013-3, Order no.: SE-013-001). Nonstandard peripherals required: CD-ROM drive.
Microsoft Windows, Version 3.X. 386 IBM-Compatible PC (3Mb). CD-ROM disk $249.00, Individual, ,599.00 Institutional. Nonstandard peripherals required: MPC Standard CD-ROM drive, SVGA (640x480) 256 colors, MPC Standard Soundboard & Speakers.
With over 100 Color Images, This CD-ROM Provides Quick & Easy Access to Important Clinical Data on Twenty-Five Different Pigmented Cutaneous Lesions, As Well As Relevant Histopathological Information. Both Benign & Malignant Lesions Are Represented.
SilverPlatter Education.

PIIGS: Publishers' Invoice & Information Generating System. Version: 1.08. Jun. 1990. Items Included: Program comes on 5.25" or 3.5" diskettes, with ring bound manual. Customer Support: 24-Hour, Toll-free user support for all licensed users; customizing & mail list conversion available.
IBM PC & compatibles (640k); Macintosh (pre-release version). Program $500.00 - Price increase anticipated for version 2.0 (ISBN 0-942679-12-1, Order no.: 1.0L). Nonstandard peripherals required: 20Mb hard disk or higher suggested.
Demo version $15.00 (ISBN 0-942679-13-X).
Handles & Tracks Invoices, Inventory, Back Orders, Royalties, Sales Tax, Sales Reps, Marketing Codes, Customer Codes, Mailing Lists, Purchase Orders, Consignment in, Consignment out, Accounts Receivable, Sales Reports, & Other Business Information for Small Book Publishers.
Upper Access, Inc.

PILAW: Personal Injury Legal Care Management System. Version: 4.11. Jul. 1987. Items Included: Manual. Customer Support: 90 days unlimited support after installation & training, ongoing support $1350/yr.
PC-DOS (640k). IBM PC & compatibles as workstations. disk $9000.00 (ISBN 0-928246-07-8, Order no.: PILAW). Nonstandard peripherals required: Modem for remote support. Addl. software required: "PC Anywhere". Networks supported: Novell, 3-Com, PC-LAN.
Comprehensive Law Office Management System for the Attorney Who Specializes in Personal Injury Practice. Handles Total Case Management, Automatic Letter Writing & Critical Data Management. Written in a 4th Generation Language.
HEL Custom Software, Inc.

PILOT. Compatible Hardware: Atari XL/XE. Operating System(s) Required: AOS. Language(s): BASIC. Memory Required: 16k. ROM cartridge $39.95 (Order no.: CXL4018). Programming Language with Turtle Graphics. Textual & Syntactical in Orientation, Rather Than Mathematical. The User Can Draw Geometric Shapes. Commands Such As GOTO, DRAWTO, TURNTO & FILLTO Are Used. Offers Full Screen Editing Capabilities, As Well As Full Sound & Color Features. Both Home & Educational Packages Are Available.
Atari Corp.

Pilot. Compatible Hardware: Commodore Amiga. 3.5" disk $39.95.
Authoring Language for Instructional Programs.
Flight Training Devices.

Pilot Interpreter. Compatible Hardware: Prime 50, Prime 250, Prime 450, Prime 750. Language(s): Info-BASIC.
manual & source listing in Info-BASIC $19.95.
manual with sample programs $5.00.
Raymond L. Reynolds.

Pilot Master. Customer Support: 800-929-8117 (customer service).
MS-DOS. Apple II. disk $49.99 (ISBN 0-87007-808-9).
A Pilot to BASIC Convertor, Based on 7 Public Domain Version, but Significantly Enhanced & Includes Conversion Direct to Microsoft Compiler Source Code.
SourceView Software International.

Pinball Construction Set. Compatible Hardware: Apple II, II+, IIe, Macintosh, Macintosh 512k; Atari 400, 800, 1200XL; Commodore 64, Amiga; IBM PC. Memory Required: 48k.
Apple, Atari, Commodore 64, IBM. disk $14.95.
Amiga, Macintosh. 3.5" disk $19.95.
Allows Players to Create Their Own Pinball Games. Features MACPAINT Backgrounds & Realistic Sounds.
Electronic Arts.

Pinball Factory. Kary McFadden. Aug. 1986. Compatible Hardware: Atari ST. Operating System(s) Required: TOS. Memory Required: 512k. General Requirements: Color monitor.
3.5" disk $39.95 (ISBN 0-923213-40-6, Order no.: AT-PIN).
Users Can Design Their Own Screens. Place Tabs, Bumpers & Ball Traps. The Drawing System Will Help to Put on the Walls. Other Parameters Under User's Control Are Speed, Gravity, Scoring, & Elasticity.
MichTron, Inc.

Pinball Math. Steve Walker. 1984. Compatible Hardware: Apple II+, IIe, IIc, IIgs; Commodore 64, 128; IBM PC; NEC APC III. Operating System(s) Required: DOS 3.3, PC-DOS. Language(s): BASIC. Memory Required: Apple 48k, Commodore 64k, IBM 640k. General Requirements: CGA card for IBM.
disk $39.95 ea.
Apple. (ISBN 0-942132-96-3, Order no.: A-1162).
Commodore 64. (ISBN 1-55603-010-X, Order no.: C-1162).
IBM PC. (ISBN 1-55603-009-6, Order no.: I-1162).
NEC. (ISBN 1-55603-018-5, Order no.: N-1162).
Educational Computer Game for Math Students Learning the Basic Operations of Addition, Subtraction, Multiplication, & Division. The Mathematical Operations & the Level of Difficulty Can Be Selected by the User. Equations, Using Either 1 or 2 Digit Numbers, Are Then Presented in a Pinball Game Format. High Scores Are Displayed in a Hall of Fame.
Electronic Courseware Systems, Inc.

PINS: Personal Injury Negligence System. Chesapeake Interlink, Ltd. Compatible Hardware: IBM PC. Operating System(s) Required: PC-DOS 3.1 or higher. Memory Required: 256k. General Requirements: Hard disk, printer.
price varies with no. of stations & no. of cases.
Provides Plaintiff Attorneys with Case Management System That Will Assist Them in Controlling Their Law Practice. Special Features Include Instant Client ID, Diary Control System, Case Accounting.
Cybernetics Technology Corp.

Pinstripe Presenter. Version: 1.0. Compatible Hardware: IBM PC XT AT, PS/2, Tandy 1000/3000. Memory Required: 512k. General Requirements: Hard disk. Customer Support: (617)925-1220, 925-1221.
disk $199.95.
Presentation-Graphics Package for On-Screen Slide Shows. Graphics & Chart-Making Features Include Object Rotation, Image Reduction & Enlargement, Zoom & Undo Commands & Picture/Symbol Library; Bar, Line, Pie & Text Charts; & Multiple Charts on One Screen. Provides 64 User-Selectable Colors, Color Schemes, 3 Typefaces & 9 Font Sizes. Outputs to PostScript Printer, HP LaserJet, Dot-Matrix Printer & Film Recorder, with Optional Support for Plotter, Color Ink-Jet Printer & Thermal Printer. Imports PIC File Formats. Also Features On-Screen Help, Integrated Transmission of 35mm Slides to Service Bureaus & 20 Preformatted Styles.
Spinnaker Software Corp.

TITLE INDEX

Pipe Stress II: Piping Through Stress Analysis Single Plane, Two Anchor. 1995. *Items Included:* Full manual. *Customer Support:* Free telephone support - 90 days, 30-day warranty. MS-DOS 3.2 or higher. 286 (584k). disk $569.95. *Nonstandard peripherals required:* CGA/EGA/VGA.
Calculates the Anchor Forces & Stresses Generated by Thermal Expansion in a Single Plane, Single Size, Two Anchor, Un-Restrained Piping System. Stress Intensification Caused by Junction with a Stiff Fitting Is Applied, with the Flexibility of the Fittings Ignored. This Makes the Results Slightly Conservative for Small Pipes, & Moderately Conservative for Large Ones.
Dynacomp, Inc.

Pipecalc. *Items Included:* Full manual. No other products required. *Customer Support:* Free telephone support - no time limit. 30 day warranty.
MS-DOS 3.2 or higher. IBM & compatibles (512k). disk $695.00.
Package Contains Programs for Solving Flow-Rate & Pressure Problems & Calculates Pressure Needs, Pipe Sizes, & Line Lengths. Also Performs Water System Pipe Network Analysis, Surge Control & Analysis, & Leak Detection. The Hazen-Williams Fluid Flow Model Handles Both Water Systems & Petroleum Product Systems. The Beggs-Brill Multiphase Flow Model Calculates Mixture Velocity, Liquid Holdup, & Two-Phase Density in Addition to Pressures & Reynolds Numbers.
Dynacomp, Inc.

Pipecalc 1: Practical Pipeline Hydraulics.
Version: 3.0. J. E. Roye & Martin Chenevert. Jan. 1988. *Compatible Hardware:* IBM PC, PC XT, PC AT & compatibles. *Operating System(s) Required:* PC-DOS/MS-DOS 3.1. *Language(s):* Compiled BASIC. *Memory Required:* 384k. *General Requirements:* 2Mb hard disk space. *Customer Support:* 30 day money-back guarantee.
3.5" or 5.25" disk $695.00, 80-page manual (Order no.: 716).
Version 3.0 Contains the Following Improvements: Color Support, Pop-Up Menus, Full-Screen Editing, Context-Sensitive Help, Data Validation, & Selected File Support. Several New Programs Have Also Been Added, Including Fluid Gathering System Network Analysis, Gas Gathering System Network Analysis, Gas Injection System Network Analysis, & Design & Analysis for Both Centrifugal & Reciprocating Compressors. The Package Contains Programs for Solving Flowrate & Pressure Problems & Calculates Pressure Needs, Pipe Sizes, & Line Lengths & Includes the Beggs-Brill Multiphase Flow Model, Which Calculates Mixture Velocity, Liquid Holdup, & Two-Phase Density in Addition to Pressures & Reynolds Number. It Also Performs Network Analysis for Gas & Liquid Pipeline Systems. Each Option of the Program Is Illustrated in the Manual with an Example Run. Operates in U.S. & SI Units.
Gulf Publishing Co.

PIPECON: Liquid Pipeline Economics. *Version:* 3.5. E. S. Menon. 1993. *Compatible Hardware:* IBM PC, XT, AT, & compatibles, PS/2. *Language(s):* Compiled BASIC, Pascal, C. *Memory Required:* 640k. *Customer Support:* Free phone support.
disk $395.00, incl. manual.
Determines the Economical Diameter for a Pipeline System Transporting a Liquid Petroleum Product under Steady State Isothermal Conditions. For Given Pipeline Profile (Data File), Liquid Properties, Flow Rate, Pipe Cost, Installation Cost & Cost per Installed HP, the Program Calculates the Number of Pump Stations Required, HP, Total Capital Investment Required & Yearly Operating Costs for Selected Pipe Sizes.
Systek (California).

PIPEDP. John Migliavacca. Dec. 1983. *Compatible Hardware:* IBM PC & compatibles. *Operating System(s) Required:* DOS. *Language(s):* BASIC. *Memory Required:* 256k.
disk $80.00 (ISBN 0-917405-03-X).
Calculates Pressure Drop of Liquids or Gases Through Pipes & Ducts Using Darcy's Formula with Colebrook Equation for Friction Factor. Finds Pressure Drop & Computes Yearly Cost of Liquid Flow. Equivalent Lengths of Valves & Fitting is Calculated. Has Default Properties for Water & Help Features to Find Pipe Inside Diameter, Units Convertor for Flowrate & Density. Fully Menu Driven.
Techdata.

Pipeflow. *Items Included:* Bound manual. *Customer Support:* Free hotline - no time limit; 30 day limited warranty; updates are $5/disk plus S&H.
MS-DOS 2.1 or higher. IBM & compatibles (128k). disk $129.95.
Uses the Darcy Equation to Calculate Liquid & Gas Flow Pressure Drops in Pipes. It Treats Pipe Size, Fittings, Valves, Elevation Changes, & Other Commonly Encountered Situations. Pipe-Fitting Types Include Tees, Elbows, Contractions, Expansions, Mitered Fittings, Exits, & Entrances. Valving Types Include Gate, Ball, Globe, Plug, Butterfly, Swing Check, Lift Check, & Foot Valves. In Most Cases, There Are Also Subclassifications (e.g., Amount of Bend in Elbow, etc.).
Dynacomp, Inc.

Pipeline Multiphase Flow with Total Energy Balance. 1992. *Items Included:* Detailed manuals included with all Dynacomp products. *Customer Support:* Free telephone support to original customer - no time limit; 30 day limited warranty.
MS-DOS 3.2 or higher. IBM PC & compatibles (512k). $1089.95 Full System (Add $5.00 for 3 1/2" format; 5 1/4" format standard). *Optimal configuration:* IBM, MS-DOS 2.0 or higher, 384k RAM, a hard disk, & CGA or compatible graphics capability.
demo disk $5.00.
PMF Is a Menu-Driven & Easy-to-Use Analysis Package Which Calculates Pressures, Temperatures, Liquid Holdup, Velocities, & Flow Patterns in Pipes. The Pipe May Have up to 40 Segments (with Different Properties & Conditions). PMF Dynamically Determines PVT & Mass Transfer Between Phases, & Does a Total Energy Balance for All Temperatures & Pressures. Both U.S. & Metric Units.
Dynacomp, Inc.

Pipeline Pressure Loss. *Compatible Hardware:* IBM PC. *Language(s):* BASIC (source code included). *Memory Required:* 128k.
disk $59.95.
Calculates the Pressure Head Loss in Simple Piping Systems.
Dynacomp, Inc.

Pipemate. Jan. 1993. *Customer Support:* 30-day money-back guarantee.
DOS 3.X (640k), 15Mb hard disk space required. disk $2495.00 (Order no.: S089). *Optimal configuration:* 132-column printer, color monitor.
Based on John Pages Estimator's Piping Man-Hour Manual. Automatically Calculate the Man-Hours Based Only on Input from a Bill of Materials & It Will Calculate Mass & Surface Areas Using Its Extensive Built-In Database of Piping Components. Produce Detailed Piping Bills of Materials, Detailed Piping Material Costs, & Detailed Estimates. Maintain Separate Tender, Contract Award, & Construction Details That Allow for Easy Comparison. Keep Track of Purchase Orders & Actual Deliveries.
Gulf Publishing Co.

Pipemate Piping Project Cost Estimation. *Items Included:* Full manual. No other products required. *Customer Support:* Free telephone support - no time limit. 30 day warranty.
MS-DOS 3.2 or higher. IBM & compatibles (512k). disk $2399.95. *Optimal configuration:* IBM, MS-DOS 3.1 or higher, 286 or higher PC, 640k RAM, hard disk (uses 15Mb), 132-column (or wider) printer, & CGA/EGA/VGA (or compatible) graphics capability.
Powerful & Easy-to-Use Piping Man-Hours & Material Package That Uses the Most Respected Man-Hour Information in the World (from John S. Page's Estimator's Piping Man-Hour Manual). Can Automatically Calculate Man-Hours Based Only on Input from a Bill of Materials. It Will Calculate Mass & Surface Areas Using Its Extensive Built-In Database of Piping Components. Produces Detailed Piping Bills of Materials, Detailed Piping Material Costs, & Detailed Estimates. Will Maintain Separate Tender, Contract Award, & Will Keep Track of Purchase Orders & Actual Deliveries. You Can Even Save Time by Reusing Already-Completed Bids for New Projects. Includes a Complete & Detailed Manual & Three Copies of Page's Book.
Dynacomp, Inc.

PIPEQ. John Migliavacca. Dec. 1983. *Compatible Hardware:* IBM PC with printer. *Operating System(s) Required:* DOS 2.0. *Language(s):* BASIC. *Memory Required:* 256k.
disk $60.00 (ISBN 0-917405-05-6).
Calculates the Heat Loss to Atmosphere from Insulated Pipes Carrying Hot Fluids. Effect of Winds Can Be Considered, Any Surface Emissivity Can Be Specified.
Techdata.

Piper: A VideoActive Adventure for Children of All Ages. Oct. 1995. *Items Included:* Newspaper style manual. *Customer Support:* Free telephone & e-mail support.
Windows 3.1 or Windows 95. IBM PC compatible 486/50 MHz (8Mb). CD-ROM disk $39.95-$44.95 (ISBN 1-888102-00-4, Order no.: 1-800-70-SPASH). *Nonstandard peripherals required:* CD-ROM drive - doublespeed. *Optimal configuration:* Pentium, Windows 95, 8Mb RAM, doublespeed CD-ROM, local bus VGA.
An InterActive Adventure for Children Ages 4 to 12. Includes Live Action Actors & Animated Rates in an Adaptation of the Story of the Pied Piper. Discovery, Challenge & Action Are Used to Create an Engaging & Exciting Experience.
Splash Studios.

Piper-Stiff. *Version:* 2.0. *Compatible Hardware:* Apple Macintosh. *Memory Required:* 512k. *General Requirements:* ImageWriter or LaserWriter.
3.5" disk $275.00.
Diagram Plotter That Enables User to Enter Chemical Assay Values, Calculate the Ion Balance & Then Plot Piper-Trilinear or Stiff Diagrams from the Data Set.
RockWare, Inc.

Pipestress 1: Pipe Wall Thickness Specification. 1995. *Items Included:* Full manual. *Customer Support:* Free telephone support - 90 days, 30-day warranty.
MS-DOS 3.2 or higher. 286 (584k). disk $379.95. *Nonstandard peripherals required:* CGA/EGA/VGA.
Calculates the Required Pipe Wall Thickness to

Comply with ASME/ANSI B31.1. If the Piping Material Used Is ASTM A53 Grade B Seamless, ASTM A53 Grade B ERW, ASTM A106 Grade B Seamless, API-5L Grade B Seamless, API-5L Grade B ERW, or ASTM A335 Grade P11 Seamless, PIPESTRESS 1 Will Retrieve the Allowable Stress upon Giving the Design Temperature.
Dynacomp, Inc.

Piping-Plumbing Estimating. Richard T. Scott. Dec. 1978. *Compatible Hardware:* IBM PC XT, PC AT, PS/2 & compatibles. *Operating System(s) Required:* MS-DOS, PC-DOS. *Language(s):* BASIC. *Memory Required:* 256k, with Lotus interface 512k. *General Requirements:* 10Mb hard disk, printer.
   MB Version MS-DOS. disk $2870.00 (ISBN 0-923933-03-4).
   MCAA Labor Units Fee. $300.00 (ISBN 0-923933-04-2).
   NAPHCC Labor Units Fee. $300.00 (ISBN 0-923933-05-0).
   video tape demo avail.
   source code avail.
   demo disk is available only to selected dealers.
Designed for Mechanical Contractors. Has a Patented, Single-Key Parts Description to Input Data Without Having to Key in Parts Numbers or Select from a Series of Menus. Master Parts File Is Preloaded with 6300 Items & Has Capacity of Approximately 100,000 Items. File Addition, Deletion & Correction Programs Are Also Included.
Esccomate.

Pirates. *Compatible Hardware:* Apple II+, IIe, IIc IIgs, Macintosh; Commodore 64, 128; IBM PC & compatibles, PCjr; Amiga; Atari ST.
   Apple, Commodore, IBM. disk $44.95.
   Amiga. 3.5" disk $54.95.
   Atari. 3.5" disk $44.95.
Adventure-Simulation Game Where the Player Is Cast in the Leading Role As Pirateer Captain, Criss-Crossing the Spanish Main, Slipping into Ports As Needs or Opportunities Require, but Always Eager to Return to the Freedom of the Open Seas.
MicroProse Software.

Pitfall. *Items Included:* CD Manual.
   Win '95. IBM. Contact publisher for price (ISBN 0-87321-002-6, Order no.: CDD-3117).
Activision, Inc.

Pitfall, Mayan Adventure with Hintbook. *Items Included:* Installation Guide.
   IBM PC. Contact publisher for price (ISBN 0-87321-048-4, Order no.: CDD-3119).
Activision, Inc.

Pitfall Strategy Guide. *Items Included:* Installation Guide.
   IBM. Contact publisher for price (ISBN 0-87321-092-1, Order no.: HBK-4016).
Activision, Inc.

PITKOR. *Version:* 2.2. Jul. 1985. *Compatible Hardware:* IBM PC, PC XT, PC AT & compatibles. *Operating System(s) Required:* MS-DOS, PC-DOS. *Language(s):* FORTRAN. *Memory Required:* 512k. *General Requirements:* Printer.
   disk $5000.00, incl. PSTPIT, RESPIT, & PREPIT (Order no.: PITKOR).
Pit Optimization Program Based on the Korobov Algorithm, a Modified Floating Cone Miner. When Using It, Pit Slope Constraints Are Not Given by a Graph, but by the Parameters of a Cone of Material Which Must Be Removed to Mine a Particular Block. The Advantage of Mining Blocks Via Cone Parameters Is That the Algorithm Allow Pit Slope Constraints to Change with Direction. As the Program Is Running, the Algorithm Modifies the Model & Always Conveges to a Solution.
Geostat Systems International, Inc. (GSII).

The Pits of Doom! *Version:* 2.4.3. Sep. 1988. *Compatible Hardware:* Apple II series, IIgs, Macintosh; IBM PC & compatibles. *Memory Required:* Apple II series 64k; Apple IIgs & IBM 256k; Macintosh 512k.
   Apple II series. 3.5" disk $19.95 (ISBN 0-916163-90-3).
   Apple IIgs. 3.5" disk $19.95 (ISBN 1-55616-048-8).
   Apple Macintosh. 3.5" disk $19.95 (ISBN 1-55616-055-0).
   IBM. disk $19.95 (ISBN 1-55616-004-6).
   IBM. 3.5" disk $19.95 (ISBN 1-55616-034-8).
IBM.
Adventure Game.
DAR Systems International.

Pixie. *Version:* 2.31. Mar. 1988. *Compatible Hardware:* IBM PC/AT & compatibles, PS/2. *Operating System(s) Required:* Microsoft Windows 3.0 or higher, PC-DOS 3.0 or higher. *Memory Required:* 1000k. *Items Included:* Manual. *Customer Support:* Technical support operators, 7 AM to 4 PM PST, Mon-Fri.
   disk $149.00.
Presentation Graphics Package Features Direct Manipulation of Graphics Figures On-Screen, a 325-Element Symbol Library & User-Definable. Italics, Underline & Density of Bold. Interfaces with Microsoft Windows, Including Dynamic Data Exchange (DDE). Uses Any Windows-Compatible Graphics Card & Mouse.
Zenographics.

Pixmate. *Version:* 1.1. Jan. 1988. *Compatible Hardware:* Commodore Amiga 500, 1000, 2000. *Memory Required:* 512k.
   3.5" disk $69.95.
Image Enhancement Program that Enables Users to Perform Up to 3000 Special Effects on Any Image, with Full-Range Variable Control Over Each Special Effect. The Program Utilizes Hyper-Slice Technology to Accelerate the Graphics Processing Speed of the Amiga's Blitter Chip by a Factor of 10. Can Convert Graphics Within All Graphics Modes & Resolutions. Its Color Functions Allow Users to Modify All Colors Simultaneously; Modify Hue, Saturation, & Luminance; Modify Balance Between Colors; Extract & Merge Color Information; Force an Image to Use Fewer Colors; & Match Colors.
Progressive Peripherals & Software, Inc.

PixTex/EFS: Electronic Filing Software. *Version:* 3.0.3. Aug. 1992. *Items Included:* For each platform, unique sets of manuals, guides, quick reference cards, release notes, proof of license, warranty card, schedule of training classes & systems managers guides are included. *Customer Support:* Hot line technical support, training (1 day, $550), maintenance (15% of list price of the product), installation ($1250), customization services ($1250), third party hardware installation ($1250), system admin training for Unix ($1100-2 days), utilities & integration techniques training ($1100-2 days).
Contact publisher for price.
Allows Users to Store Documents in Electronic Format. Multi-Platform Software for Document Imaging That Allows the User to Scan in Paper Documents, Automatically Indexes Them for Fast, Efficient Retrieval Utilizing Fuzzy Search Technology. The User Can Type in a Key Word to Search Through the Document & PixTex/EFS Will Find the Match. The Indices Are Small, Usually One-Third the Size of the Original Data, So You Can Maximize the Productivity & Minimize the Cost of Computer Resources.
Excalibur Technologies Corp.

PIXymbols Special Purpose Pictorial Symbol Fonts & EPS Packages: 60 Specific Titles. 1986-94. *Items Included:* Instructions for installation & use. *Customer Support:* Tech support - free over phone. Fax info - full character set of specific font, on request.
   Macintosh Apple OS. Macintosh (1Mb). from $29.00 to $275.00. *Addl. software required:* Application Software: Minimum - Word Processing, Better - page layout, drawing. *Optimal configuration:* Any Macintosh using System 6.0.7 or higher, 4 to 8Mb RAM, hard drive.
   MS-Windows. IBM & compatibles (1Mb). from $29.00 to $275.00. *Addl. software required:* Applications Software: Minimum - Word Processing, Better - page layout, drawing. Adobe Type Manager for PostScript. *Optimal configuration:* 386 DX or higher, with MS-Windows 3.1, 4Mb RAM, hard drive.
Sixty Packages of Fonts, or Combined Font & EPS Files, Totaling Well over 100 Fonts, Designed As Tools for Use in a Variety of Applications: Computer Training Documentation & Manuals; City & State D.O.T. Signs; Mechanical Engineering Tolerancing Documentation; Lodging & Travel Industry Signs & Publications; Braille Architectural Signs; Hospital & Safety Signs; American Sign Languages; Cross-Stitch; Musical Instruments; Recycling; Crossword Puzzles; Chess Reviews; Apothecary; Astrology; Moon Phases; Preschoolers' Handwriting; Phone Buttons & Symbols; FAR Aircraft Markings; & Many More.
Page Studio Graphics.

Pizazz Plus. *Version:* 4.0. May 1993. *Items Included:* Complete manual & both 3.25 & 5.25 media. *Customer Support:* 30 day money back guarantee, 90 day unlimited technical support.
   PC-DOS/MS-DOS & Windows. IBM 100% compatible (34k). disk $149.00.
Screen-Capture & Print Software. Supports VGA, CGA, EGA, MCGA, & Extended VGA from a Variety of Manufacturers. Image Capture Board Support Includes: AT&T ICB, TrueVision TARGA, ATronics PIB/PIB.
Application Techniques, Inc.

PL/D. *Version:* 2.01. *Compatible Hardware:* IBM PC & compatibles. *Operating System(s) Required:* PC-DOS/MS-DOS. *Memory Required:* 256k. *General Requirements:* Hard disk recommended. *Items Included:* 32 pg. Thinking Software catalog.
   5.25" or 3.5" disk $124.95.
PC Computer Language that Can Be Used to Write Neural Networks, AI Applications, Utilities, Systems Software & Operating Systems. Package Includes User's Manual, Internals Manual, & Source Code for the PL/D Compiler.
Thinking Software, Inc.

PL/1. *Compatible Hardware:* Apple. *Operating System(s) Required:* CP/M, CP/M-86, MP/M, MP/M-86. *Memory Required:* CP/M, MP/M & Apple 64k; CP/M-86 & MP/M-86 128k.
   CP/M, MP/M & Apple. disk $550.00.
   CP/M-86 & MP/M-86. disk $750.00.
Software Development Package Designed for Zilog Z-80 or the Intel 8080 & 8086 Family of Microprocessors, Running under the CP/M Family of Operating Systems. System Includes an Optimizing, Native Code Compiler, an Assembler, a Relocating Linker, a Librarian, & a Cross-Reference Generator. Together They Form a Complete Program Development Tool. PL/1 Language Includes the Advantages of the Block Structuring of ALGOL, the String Handling & Decimal Arithmetic of COBOL, & the Numeric Functions & Standardized Input-Output of FORTRAN. Commercial, Scientific, & System Level Programs Can Be Written in PL/1.
Digital Research, Inc.

TITLE INDEX

PL/1. Digital Research. *Operating System(s) Required:* CP/M-86, Concurrent CP/M-86. *Memory Required:* 128k.
$750.00 (Order no.: DRT-012 (SS)).
Texas Instruments, Personal Productivit.

Placement Power. *Version:* 3.0. Dec. 1985. *Compatible Hardware:* IBM PC, PC AT, PC XT; Altos; AT&T 3B2, 6300. *Operating System(s) Required:* PC-DOS, MS-DOS, XENIX, UNIX. *Language(s):* C. *Memory Required:* 25k.
contact publisher for price.
Stores, Updates, Searches & Retrieves Data Used by Employment Recruiters. Offers Features Such As Automatic Search & Retrieval, Automatic Tracking, Online Storage, Updating & Client Profiles. Can Be Integrated with Word Processing & LOTUS 1-2-3.
Resource Control Systems Corp.

Plague Fighters. *Compatible Hardware:* Apple, Franklin.
disk $49.95 (ISBN 0-918349-55-9).
Demonstrates the Problems of Epidemic Control & Illustrates the Choices Required of Health Professionals. Players Must Battle the Plague Without Spreading It Themselves. Poses Ethical Questions & Considers the Economic & Social Issues Involved.
Krell Software Corp.

Plain-Payroll. *Compatible Hardware:* Apple Macintosh 512KE. *Memory Required:* 512k. *General Requirements:* External disk drive; ImageWriter; Omnis 3 Plus.
3.5" disk $395.00.
Payroll.
Technology with Ease, Inc.

Plains & Simple One-Write Accounting. Nov. 1985. *Compatible Hardware:* Apple Macintosh II, Macintosh Plus, Macintosh SE. *Language(s):* Pascal. *Memory Required:* 512k.
$395.00.
Easy to Learn Accounting Package That Includes General Ledger, Accounts Payable & Accounts Receivable Functions.
Great Plains Software.

Plan-a-Year. David Newman. *Compatible Hardware:* IBM PC, PCjr, PC XT, PC AT, Portable PC. *Operating System(s) Required:* PC-DOS 2.00, 2.10, 3.00, 3.10. *Memory Required:* IBM PCjr with DOS 3.00 or 3.10 256k, all others 128k. *General Requirements:* Double-sided disk drive; IBM Graphics printer optional.
disk $19.95 (Order no.: 6276588).
Helps Users Plan Their Finances on a Monthly Basis for the Coming Year. Users Enter Income & Expenses for Item by Item. Tabulates the Totals & Shows How Much Can Be Spent While Still Reaching the Desired Financial Goal. Users Can Enter & Display up to 75 Expense Items, 15 Income Items, & 20 Special Accounts; Add, Rename, & Delete, & Move Items or Accounts; Use the Graph Option to Display the Plan for an Entire Year; Print Data & Graphs.
Personally Developed Software, Inc.

Plan & Track. *Version:* 3.5. *Items Included:* Manual. *Customer Support:* Free tech support to registered users.
Macintosh Plus or higher. 3.5" disk $249.00.
Visual Schedule Design & Presentation. System 7.5 Savvy. Power Mac Native.
Mainstay.

Plan & Track. *Version:* 3.5. Nov. 1994. *Items Included:* Comprehensive manual. *Customer Support:* Free technical support.
Windows 3.1 or Windows 95. 386 (2Mb). disk $249.00.
Mac System 7.0. Mac 030 (2Mb). 3.5" disk $249.00.
Helps You Plan & Manage Any Project. With Plan & Track, You Can Create a Project Plan Minutes after Opening the Package. There's No Faster or Easier Way to Keep Things on Track & Within Budget Than with Plan & Track.
Mainstay.

Plan Project Management. 1982. *Compatible Hardware:* IBM PC, PC XT; TRS-80 Model I, Model III, Model 4. *Operating System(s) Required:* TRSDOS 1.3, PC-DOS. *Language(s):* BASIC. *Memory Required:* 48k.
disk $49.95 (Order no.: UT 010).
manual $5.00.
Project Management Tools That Allow User to Define & Maintain a File of Project Tasks & Resources. This Information Is Used to Print Various Forms of Gantt Charts, Resource Histograms & Task/Resource Reports.
Demi-Software.

PLAN Strategist: Strategic Planning for Competitive Advantage. *Version:* 2.2. Eben G. Fetters. Feb. 1996. *Items Included:* Manual & strategic planning book. *Customer Support:* Free phone support.
Windows. IBM PC & compatibles, 386 or higher. $129.00 (ISBN 0-923680-03-9, Order no.: 4104).
Includes Spreadsheets & Processes That Assist in the Strategic Planning Process. Features Programs That Measure & Track Relevant Market Data, Calculate Financial Results & Track Performance.
American ComVision, Inc.

PLAN Tactician: Business Planning for Healthcare Organizations. *Version:* 3.2. Jeff Rogers. *Items Included:* Manual & business planning book. *Customer Support:* Free phone support.
Windows. IBM PC or compatible. disk $129.00 (ISBN 0-923680-01-2, Order no.: BPS-1).
Provides Useful Healthcare Business Planning Worksheets. Included Are Programs That Value Projects, Assist in Project Planning, Forecast Staffing, Calculate Salary Expense, Track Results, Assure Due Diligence, Perform Competitor Analysis, Measure Financial Performance, Conduct Trend Analysis, Cash Flow, Pro Formas, etc.
American ComVision, Inc.

Plan 1040. *Version:* 13.01. Sep. 1993. *Compatible Hardware:* IBM PC, PC XT; PS/2. *Operating System(s) Required:* PC-DOS, MS-DOS. *Memory Required:* 256k. *General Requirements:* Disk drives, printer. *Items Included:* Manual. worksheets, sample reports. *Customer Support:* Unlimited telephone support.
disk $425.00.
Designed for Planning Use by Accountants to Figure a Person's Tax Liability According to Several Different, Allowable Methods. Prints a Table That Displays the Various Alternatives.
Prentice Hall Professional Software.

Plan Write for Marketing. *Version:* 3.0. Oct. 1994. *Items Included:* Sample Plan. *Customer Support:* Unlimited free technical support at 512-251-7541.
PC-DOS/MS-DOS; Windows 3.1 or higher. 80386 (2Mb). disk $129.95 (Order no.: 800-423-1228). *Nonstandard peripherals required:* Hard disk. *Networks supported:* LAN.
Employs Proven Marketing Plan Formats along with a Powerful Integrated Outliner, Interactive Word Processor W/ Spell Checker & Spreadsheet W/ Pre-Defined Financial Templates. It Provides a Step-by-Step Guide for Creating Your Marketing Plan Making It Possible for Almost Anyone to Create an Impressive Document for Presentation.
Business Resource Software.

PLANEASE GRAPHICS EXTENSION

planEASe/Windows. *Customer Support:* Update Subscription Program ($95/year covers all products purchased) which includes unlimited 800 number telephone support, all new versions issued during the year, & discount price offers on any new products.
Windows 3.1, Windows 95. IBM & compatibles (4Mb). disk $995.00. *Optimal configuration:* Windows 3.1, 4Mb memory, mouse.
Enables the Financial Analysis & Cash Flow Projection of Any Income-Producing Property. No Limit on the Number of Leases, Expenses, Loans, or Depreciation Schedules for a Property. User Specifies the Holding Period. Handles Calendaring, So User Can Project Buying in April & Selling in September & Get a True Calendar Year Forecast for Tax Purposes. Internal Rates of Return, Financial Management Rates of Return, & Net Present Values Are Computed Before & after Taxes. Features Sensitivity Analysis, with a Printed Graph of Results, & Monte Carlo Risk Analysis with a Printed Histogram of Results. All Reports & Graphs May Be Directed to the Windows Clipboard & Pasted into Your Favorite Windows Word Processor and/or Spreadsheet for Further Processing. Revised for All Current Tax Provisions, & Provides Many Choices for Handling Depreciation & Passive Losses.
Analytic Assocs.

planEASe Financial Utilities. *Customer Support:* Update Subscription Program ($95/year covers all products purchased) which includes unlimited 800 number telephone support, all new versions issued during the year, & discount price offers on any new products.
Windows 3.1. IBM & compatibles (4Mb). disk $395.00. *Addl. software required:* planEASe Windows. *Optimal configuration:* Windows 3.1, 4Mb memory, mouse.
Adds Major Client-Oriented Reporting Capabilities to PlanEASe, As Well As Providing Loan Amortization, Discounted Cash Flow Analysis, & Depreciation Modules. Added Client Reports Include Proforma Income Statements in Dollars, % of Gross Income & $/SqFt, a Broker's Setup (or APOD), Acquisition & Sales Reports & an Analysis Assumptions Report. Writes a Loan Amortization Report & a Separate Depreciation Report. Discounted Cash Flow Analysis Module Produces IRR, NPV, FMRR & Accumulation of Wealth Verification Reports Showing the Actual Discounting Calculations Leading to These Measures, Both for the Cash Flows from the PlanEASe Analyses & for Cash Flows You Enter Yourself.
Analytic Assocs.

planEASe Graphics Extension. *Customer Support:* Update Subscription Program ($95/year covers all products purchased) which includes unlimited 800 number telephone support, all new versions issued during the year, & discount price offers on any new products.
Windows 3.1. IBM & compatibles (4Mb). disk $395.00. *Addl. software required:* planEASe Windows. *Optimal configuration:* Windows 3.1, 4Mb memory, mouse.
Adds Screen & Printed Graphics Capability to All the Analytical Functions of PlanEASe. Graphs Are Automatically Formatted with Titles, Customizable Defaults, etc. for Almost Instant Production. Formatted Graphs May Be Quickly & Conveniently Edited If Desired. Our Graphs May Be Placed on the Windows Clipboard As Bitmaps, Metafiles, or Data, Which Then May Be Pasted into Virtually All Windows Word Processing, Spreadsheet & Desktop Publishing Programs. Graphs Feature Professional Effects Such As Font Control, 3-D Effects, Color Control, Many Chart Types, & Other Enhancements. One Mouse Click Brings a Fully Formatted Graph of Your Analysis to the Screen. Another Click Changes the Graph Specification You Choose.
Analytic Assocs.

planEASe Monthly Extension. *Customer Support:* Update Subscription Program ($95/year covers all products purchased) which includes unlimited 800 number telephone support, all new versions issued during the year, & discount price offers on any new products. Windows 3.1. IBM & compatibles (4Mb). disk $595.00. *Addl. software required:* planEASe Windows. *Optimal configuration:* Windows 3.1, 4Mb memory, mouse.
Expands PlanEASe to Produce Monthly Cash Flow Reports in Addition to the Standard Annual Reports. This Is Most Useful for Commercial Property Analysis, Development Feasibility Studies, & Complex Partnership Forecasts. The Monthly Extension Works with the Partnership Models As Well As the Basic PlanEASe, & Monthly Forecasts Are Made from the Same Assumptions As the Yearly Forecasts, So That No Additional Data Entry Is Required to Produce the Monthly Reports. Internal Rates of Return, etc., Are Computed Monthly with This Extension, Increasing Their Accuracy in Certain Situations.
Analytic Assocs.

PlanEASe Partnership Models. *Version:* 3.33. 1992. *Compatible Hardware:* IBM PC, PC XT, PC AT. *Operating System(s) Required:* MS-DOS, PC-DOS 2.0, 2.1. *Memory Required:* 256k. disk $495.00.
documentation & demo disk $50.00.
Addition to PlanEASe Enabling the User to Take Any Property That Has Been Projected with PlanEASe & Convert the Analysis into a Limited Partnership Forecast with Reports Suitable for Discussions with Potential Investors. These Models Contain All of the Capabilities of PlanEASe & Also Offers the Following Features: Separate Allocation for Tax & Cash Benefits, Working Capital Fund, Handles Preferred Returns, Handles Staged Investments, Comprehensive Reporting, Sensitivity & Risk Analysis.
Analytic Assocs.

planEASe Partnership Models. *Customer Support:* Update Subscription Program ($95/year covers all products purchased) which includes unlimited 800 number telephone support, all new versions issued during the year, & discount price offers on any new products. Windows 3.1. IBM & compatibles (4Mb). disk $495.00. *Addl. software required:* planEASe Windows. *Optimal configuration:* Windows 3.1, 4Mb memory, mouse.
Adds Partnership Analysis Capability to PlanEASe, Enabling You to Take Any Property Projected with PlanEASe & Easily Convert the Analysis into a Limited Partnership Forecast wiht Final Reports & Graphs Suitable for Investor Presentation. These Models Allow As Many Partnership Fees As You Want, Allow for Separate Allocation of Tax & Cash Benefits, & Handle Working Capital, Preferred Returns & Staged Investments.
Analytic Assocs.

Plan80. *Operating System(s) Required:* CP/M, CP/M-86, MS-DOS.
contact publisher for price.
Business Planning Systems, Inc.

Planet Earth: Explore the Worlds Within. Oct. 1995. *Customer Support:* 800 number (free), online support forums.
Windows 486SX, 25MHz; Macintosh. IBM & compatibles (8Mb); LCIII/Performa 475 (8Mb). CD-ROM disk $49.95 (ISBN 1-57595-002-2). *Nonstandard peripherals required:* Double-speed CD-ROM drive, Super VGA color card-256 color display, "SoundBlaster" compatible sound card; Mac 256 color/14" display, CD-ROM drive (double-speed). *Addl. software required:* QuickTime for Windows; System 7.0, Quicktime 2.0.
A Dazzling Multimedia Guide to the Lands, Habitats, Peoples, & Cultures of Our World. 1, 500 Photographs; over an Hour Each of Audio & Video; Dozens of Fly-Through Animations; Satellite Photos, Political Maps, Physical Maps; Geographic Data; & Encyclopedic Information for More Than 200 Countries.
Macmillan Digital U. S. A.

Planet Invasion. *Language(s):* Color BASIC. *Memory Required:* 16k.
contact publisher for price.
Spectral Assocs.

Planet of Lust. Jul. 1989. *Customer Support:* Free technical support at 215-683-5699.
Amiga DOS (512k). 3.5" disk $39.95.
MS-DOS (376k). disk $39.95. *Nonstandard peripherals required:* Color monitor; graphics card.
Adult Graphic Adventure Game.
Free Spirit Software, Inc.

Planet of the Robots: Adventure Game for Fido-Opus Systems. *Version:* 1.01. 1986. *Compatible Hardware:* IBM PC & compatibles. *Memory Required:* 256k. *General Requirements:* Hard disk, modem; Fido, Opus, or other compatible BBS software with provision for an outside section with on-line games.
$5.00 (ISBN 0-943871-54-9, Order no.: PLANET).
Daniel Tobias.

A Planet with One Mind; A People with One Heart; An Earth with One Spirit: Stories from Around the World for the Child Within Us All CD. Mike Pinder. Jan. 1995.
IBM. CD-ROM disk Contact publisher for price (ISBN 1-888057-07-6).
Mike Pinder, Singer, Songwriter of The Moody Blues, Narrates Seven Uplifting & Imaginative Stories or Myths for Children over a Musical Atmosphere Created by Mike Pinder. This Is a Three CD Box Set.
One Step Records.

A Planet with One Mind: Stories from Around the World for the Child Within Us All CD. Mike Pinder. Oct. 1995.
IBM. CD-ROM disk Contact publisher for price (ISBN 1-888057-04-1).
Mike Pinder, Singer, Songwriter of The Moody Blues, Narrates Seven Uplifting & Imaginative Stories or Myths for Children over a Musical Atmosphere Created by Mike Pinder. The First of a series of Three Spoken Word Albums for Children. Also "A People with One Heart" & "An Earth with One Spirit".
One Step Records.

Planetary Ephemerides. *Compatible Hardware:* TI 99/4A with Extended BASIC. *Operating System(s) Required:* DX-10. *Language(s):* Extended BASIC. *Memory Required:* 48k.
cassette $18.95.
Includes: Ephemeris for Any Planet in the Solar System, Geocentric Ecliptic Longitude & Latitude & the Planets' Distance from Earth. Comes in 2 Versions: Superior Planets (Mars, Jupiter, Neptune, Uranus & Saturn) & Inferior Planets (Venus & Mercury).
Eastbench Software Products.

Planetary Orbital Elements. *Compatible Hardware:* TI 99/4A with Extended BASIC. *Operating System(s) Required:* DX-10. *Language(s):* Extended BASIC. *Memory Required:* 48k.
disk or cassette $18.95.
Similar to PLANETARY EPHEMERIDES. Lists Orbital Elements As They Are Computed at One Instant of Ephemeris Time. Comes in 2 Versions: Superior Planets (Jupiter, Mars, Neptune, Saturn, Uranus) & Inferior Planets (Venus & Mercury).
Eastbench Software Products.

Planetary Taxi. (Visual Almanac Ser.). Macintosh (4Mb). CD-ROM disk $39.95 (Order no.: R1108). *Nonstandard peripherals required:* 14" color monitor or larger, CD-ROM drive.
As Children Zoom Through a Scale Model of the Solar System at the Wheel of a Cosmic Taxi Cab, Facts about Our Solar System Come to Life in This Entertaining Game of Discovery (Ages 8-14).
Library Video Co.

Planetfall. Steve Meretzky. 1983. *Compatible Hardware:* Apple Series, Macintosh; Atari XL/XE, ST; Commodore 64, Amiga; IBM PC; TI 99/4A; TRS-80 Model I, Model III. *Operating System(s) Required:* CP/M, MS-DOS. *Memory Required:* IBM 48k.
$39.95.
Teleports You Forward Roughly One Hundred Centuries to a Stellar Patrol Ship. Starting at the Bottom As an Ensign 7th Class, You Are Confined to Swabbing Decks Aboard the Feinstein. Suddenly, Your Ship Explodes, & You Are Jettisoned Away to a Mysterious Deserted World. The Planet Is Plagued by Floods, Pestilence, & a Mutant Wild Kingdom. But There's Also Floyd, a Mischievous Multi-Purpose Robot & the Ideal Companion with Whom to Brave Your New World. Explore Its Secrets, Dare Its Dangers, & Find a Means of Saving It.
Activision, Inc.

Planetfall. Infocom. *Compatible Hardware:* HP 150 Touchscreen, HP 110 Portable.
3.5" disk $39.95 (Order no.: 92243PA).
Science Fiction Adventure Which Takes Place in the Future on a Deserted World.
Hewlett-Packard Co.

Planfin. Business Software Pty., Ltd. *Operating System(s) Required:* CP/M-86. *Memory Required:* 64k.
$195.00.
Requires Printer.
Texas Instruments, Personal Productivit.

PlanFlow. *Version:* PC6.0. Oct. 1985. *Compatible Hardware:* IBM PC, PC XT, PC AT. *Operating System(s) Required:* MS-DOS, PC-DOS 2.0. *Language(s):* Pascal. *Memory Required:* 256k. *General Requirements:* 132-column printer.
disk $85.00, incl. manual.
Designed for Projecting Capital Cash Flow & Manpower. Can Be Used by Planners, Estimators, or Cost Engineers Involved in Budgeting, Forecasting, or Proposals. The Projected Cash Flow Is Based on User-Defined Standardized Distributions; 40 of Them Can Be Defined & Saved for Future Use. Uses Screen Graphics to Display Distributions That Can Be Sent to the Printer. Functional Reports Detail the Distributions (Monthly & Annually) for up to 600 Accounts & 10 Years.
Project Control Systems.

Planit. Icads. 1987. *Items Included:* Hard bound ring with sleeve cover. *Customer Support:* 1 year free technical support then $400.00 per year maintenance fee for tech support & updates (504) 648-0484.
Macintosh OS. Mac Plus or higher. 3.5" disk $3995.00. *Addl. software required:* Macintosh IIcx, 2Mb hard drive.
Will Design a Kitchen Automatically & Produce Architectural Quality Plans & Elevations, Dimensional & Drawn to Scale of Choice. It Will Print a Detailed Costed Quotation, Manufacturer's Order & Customer's Invoice. Perspective Views from Any Angle Can Be Viewed, Printed or Plotted in Full Color.
CompServCo.

TITLE INDEX

Planix Home Architect. Aug. 1994. *Items Included:* CD, users guide. *Customer Support:* Free & unlimited technical support.
Windows 3.1. 386 or 486 IBM PC & compatibles (2Mb). disk $99.00, SRO. *Nonstandard peripherals required:* Mouse or pointing device. *Optimal configuration:* 486DX50 or higher, 4Mb RAM.
Everything in One Package to Design a House, Room Addition, Pool, Deck or Landscaping. Includes CD with 500 Professional Home Plans from Home Planners Inc. That Can Be Modified. 800 Home & Landscape Symbols Included. 26 Different Reports Are Generated Automatically Including Insurance Inventory, Electrical Cabling, or Create Your Own.
Foresight Resources Corp.

Planix Office. Aug. 1993. *Customer Support:* Free & unlimited technical support (816) 8891-8418.
Microsoft Windows 3.1 or higher. 386 or 486 (2Mb). disk SRP: $249.00. *Nonstandard peripherals required:* Mouse or pointer device. *Optimal configuration:* 4Mb RAM, Math coprocessor recommended for 386 computers, 1,2Mb or 1.44 floppy & hard disk drives. *Networks supported:* Any Microsoft Windows support.
Quickly Create an Accurate Drawing of an Office & Its Contents. AutoLayout Speeds up Space Planning for Office Systems, Furniture & Panels. Draft-and-Drop Furniture, Equipment & People & Generate Any of Twenty Built-In Reports Including Office Equipment Inventory, Network Report, Personnel Directory, Furniture Bill of Materials, Cabling Lengths or User Defined.
Foresight Resources Corp.

Planned Maintenance System. Version: 1.02. Jan. 1984. *Operating System(s) Required:* CP/M, CP/M-86, MS-DOS, PC-DOS. (source code included). *Memory Required:* 64k.
disk $49.95.
Masters Software Co.

The Planner. *Compatible Hardware:* HP 150 Touchscreen, HP 110 Portable.
3.5" disk $49.95 (Order no.: 35155D).
Spreadsheet with 16,384 Cells Arranged As 64 Columns by 256 Rows. Features Include Naming & Protecting Cells or Blocks, Copying Blocks, Joined Spreadsheets, Windows, Extensive Formatting Capability, Variable Column Widths, Titles, & Numerous Math & Trig Functions. Offers "Help" Screens to Assist the Occasional User.
Hewlett-Packard Co.

PlanPerfect: Spreadsheet. Version: 5.1. 1991. *Compatible Hardware:* Data General, DEC VAX, IBM PC & compatibles. *Operating System(s) Required:* MS-DOS 2.0 or higher; Novell, Netware, AST-PCnet, 3Com Ether Series, 3COM 3Plus, IBM PC Network. *Language(s):* Assembly. *Memory Required:* 384k. *General Requirements:* 2 disk drives (hard disk required for the file server), printer.
5.25" or 3.5" disks $395.00.
network version (first station) $495.00.
$79.00 ea. network version (additional network stations).
Spreadsheet Supporting the Following Features: 8192 Rows by 256 Columns, Virtual Memory Design with Support of up to 8Mb of Expanded Memory; Integrated Word Processing with WordPerfect File Compatibility; Individual Cells Can Be Boldfaced, Underlined, Double-Underlined, Printed in a Different Font, or Hidden; User-Selected Fonts, Margins, Headers, Footers, Borders, Page Numbering, etc.; Automatic Linking; Dual Worksheet Editing; Fully Integrated Graphics for Bar, Stacked Bar, Pie, Line, Hi-Lo, & Scatter Charts; Special Functions Such As Single & Multiple Linear Regression, What-If Tables, Matrix Inversion/Multiplication, & User-Defined Function Capability for Customized Worksheets. Also Features Undelete, Automatic Back-up & Optimal Recalc. Support for over 600 Printers.
WordPerfect Corp.

Plans & Elevations. Version: 5.3. May 1989. *Items Included:* 1 spiral bound manual. *Customer Support:* Free telephone support.
MS-DOS. IBM PC & compatibles (640k). contact publisher for price. *Nonstandard peripherals required:* Hard disk, digitizer, plotter. *Addl. software required:* AutoCAD software (Autodesk, Inc.).
Eases the Process of Creating Structural Steel Framing Plans. Scaling Functions Are Automatic, Including the Ability to Have Several Different Scales on the Same Drawing. Sizes of Rolled Shapes Can Be Set to Plot at a Preset Size Regardless of the Scale. Shapes Can Be Drawn to Exact Scale for Layout Purposes & Precise Dimensions Can Be Determined, Eliminating Calculations. Railing, Ladders & Stairs along with Other Structural Items Can Be Automatically Drawn in Elevation. System Can Be Used to Create Detail Drawings for Trusses, Girders & Other Complex Frames.
Computer Detailing Corp.

Plant Management Package. *Operating System(s) Required:* CP/M.
contact publisher for price.
Masters Software Co.

Plant Nursery Management. Agri-Management Services, Inc. *Operating System(s) Required:* MS-DOS. *Memory Required:* 64k. *General Requirements:* Printer.
$495.00.
Texas Instruments, Personal Productivit.

Plantrax 3. Version: 3.0. May 1985. *Compatible Hardware:* IBM PC. *Operating System(s) Required:* PC-DOS. *Language(s):* BASIC, Machine, C. *Memory Required:* 320k. *General Requirements:* Color Graphics Monitor.
disk $995.00, incl. manual.
General Project Management Package Which Uses Both Gantt & CPM Scheduling. Designed to Support up to 750 Tasks & 10 Resource Categories. Features Two Example Projects Which Are Described in the Manual to Facilitate Understanding of the Package.
Engineering Science, Inc.

PlanView. Version: 2.0F. Jun. 1994. *Items Included:* Complete documentation. *Customer Support:* Hotline/Technical support, implementation services, consulting & training fees are based upon initial license fee.
MS Windows Version 3.1 or higher, OS/2 Version 2.0 or higher. IBM-compatible 80386, or higher (Client); (Server): Oracle-Sybase-, DB/2, SQLBase, & ODBC-compatible databases running on most popular operating systems & hardware platforms (4Mb extended). Contact publisher for price. *Optimal configuration:* Client -IBM 486 w/6-8Mb RAM; Server running Oracle. *Networks supported:* Novell, NetWare, IBM LANManager, Microsoft LANManager, Banyan VINES, All NetBIOS compatible, Named Pipes, LV 6.2, TCP/IP Networks.
An Advanced Windows Based System That Allows Multiple Users to Access/Share Any SQL Database. Addresses the Full Scope of Work Management Processes: from Work Authorization, Scoping, Planning & Reporting Progress to Closing Out Work. Productivity Gains Result from Improved Resource Usage, Work-Scheduling & Cost Goals.
Work Management Solutions, Inc.

PLAY 'N' LEARN IN WINDOWS

PlanWrite for Business. Version: 3.0. Apr. 1994. *Items Included:* Pre-defined outlines, spreadsheet templates & business plan examples. *Customer Support:* Unlimited free technical support at 512-251-7541.
MS/PC-DOS Windows 3.1 or higher. IBM PC, XT, AT or compatible (640k). disk $129.95 (Order no.: 800-423-1228). *Nonstandard peripherals required:* Hard disk. *Networks supported:* LAN.
Employs Proven Business Plan Formats Along with a Powerful Integrated Outliner, Interactive Word Processor, & Spreadsheet Processor Specifically Oriented to Documenting Your Business Plan. It Provides a Step-by-Step Guide for Creating Your Business Plan Making It Possible for Almost Anyone to Create an Impressive Document for Presentation.
Business Resource Software.

PLATE, Orifice PLATE. Version: .05. P. L. Mariam. Sep. 1978. *Compatible Hardware:* IBM PC & compatibles, PC XT, PC AT. *Operating System(s) Required:* PC-DOS/MS-DOS 2.X, 3.0. *Memory Required:* 256k. *General Requirements:* Printer.
disk $99.95 (ISBN 0-935509-04-6, Order no.: 5250).
Computes the Physical Dimensions of a Concentric, Segmental, or Eccentric Orifice Plate for Manufacture. Conforms to ISA RP3.2 & Will Generate All Necessary Dimensions & Printout All Data. Also Computes the Equivalent Segmental Orifice Plate Dimensions Based upon a Concentric Orifice Size. Checks If the Selected Dimensions Conform to AGA, ASME, Spink, or Miller's "Flow Engineering Handbook".
FlowSoft, Inc.

Play Bridge with Dorothy Truscott. *Compatible Hardware:* Apple IIplus, IIe, IIc, IIgs, Macintosh; Atari ST; Commodore 64, 128; IBM PC, MAC.
disk $29.95.
Teaches Advanced Bridge-Hands the Secrets of World-Famous Bridge Player Dorothy Truscott.
Great Game Products.

Play Bridge with Sheinwold. *Items Included:* Bound manual. *Customer Support:* Free hotline - no time limit; 30 day limited warranty; updates are $5/disk plus S&H.
MS-DOS. IBM & compatibles (256k). disk $34.95.
Apple, Atari ST, C-64. disk $29.95.
Macintosh. 3.5" disk $29.95.
Test Your Declarer Play at the Bridge Table with Deals Designed by Alfred Sheinwold, World Famous Author & Teacher.
Dynacomp, Inc.

Play Bridge with Sheinwold. Tom Throop & Alfred Sheinwold. Nov. 1985. *Compatible Hardware:* Apple, Macintosh; Atari ST; Commodore; IBM.
disk $29.95 ea., incl. bk.
Apple & IBM. (ISBN 0-935307-51-6).
Commodore. (ISBN 0-935307-52-4).
Macintosh. (ISBN 0-935307-53-2).
Atari ST. (ISBN 0-935307-54-0).
Improve Your Declarer Play As You Are Guided along Correct Play in 91 Challenging Deals.
Great Game Products.

Play 'n' Learn in Windows. *Operating System(s) Required:* Windows 3.1.
3.5" disk $19.95.
Eight Educational Games (with an Additional 12 Variations) That Teach Very Young Children about Using a Computer, the Alphabet, Numbers, Shapes & Colors. Includes Color Matching. Amanda's Letter Lotto, Zach-A-Doodle (Drawing Game), Word Wheel, Black Board Shapes & Others.
PSG-HomeCraft Software.

Play...Childrens Bible.
CD-ROM disk $39.99 (ISBN 7-90088-291-X, Order no.: 3-0010).
Scripture Pr. Pubs., Inc.

Player Maker. *Compatible Hardware:* Atari XL/XE.
disk $6.95 (Order no.: AED80034).
Atari Corp.

Player-Missile Graphics Tool Kit. *Compatible Hardware:* Atari 400, 800. *Language(s):* Atari BASIC. *Memory Required:* 24k.
disk $29.95.
Teaches the Basics of Player Missile Graphics & Provides Tools for Graphics Development.
Dynacomp, Inc.

Player-Missile Player Editor. *Compatible Hardware:* Atari 400, 800. *Memory Required:* 24k. *General Requirements:* Joystick.
disk $19.95.
Generates Characters That Move about on the Screen.
Dynacomp, Inc.

Player Piano. *Compatible Hardware:* Atari. (source code included). *Memory Required:* 48k.
$19.95.
Dynacomp, Inc.

Playskool Puzzles. Nov. 1995. *Items Included:* Registration card, manual, brochure. *Customer Support:* Free 1-800 number, 10:00 a.m. to 10:00 p.m. (EST) Monday-Saturday.
Mac System 7.0.1 or higher. Mac 68030 25MHz (8Mb). Contact publisher for price (ISBN 1-888208-01-5). *Nonstandard peripherals required:* CD-ROM drive (double speed). *Optimal configuration:* Mac 68030 25MHz, CD-ROM drive (double speed), System 7.0 or higher, color monitor (640x480, 256 colors), 8Mb RAM.
Windows 3.1, Windows 95 compatible. IBM compatible 486 DX 33 MHz (8Mb). *Nonstandard peripherals required:* CD-ROM drive (double speed). *Optimal configuration:* IBM compatible 486DX 33MHz, CD-ROM drive (double speed), Windows 3.1 or Windows 95, Super VGA (640x480, 256 colors), sound card, 8Mb RAM.
A Digital Collection of over 100 Animated Puzzles & 5 Fun Puzzle Activities That Help Children 3-6 Develop Spatial Reasoning, Pattern Matching, Creative Design Skills. Children Can Solve Paint, or Make Their Own Puzzle Creations. There Are 5 Modules, Jigsaw, Puzzle Maker, Explore It, Mix 'N Match & Connect the Dots Puzzles.
Hasbro, Inc.

PLEAS - Personal Injury Litigation Evaluation & Accounting System. *Version:* 2.90. *Items Included:* Guided tour disk. *Customer Support:* 1 year.
disk $995.00.
manual $59.50.
demo disk avail.
Record, Control & Report Information on Personal Injury Cases.
Lawyers Software Publishing Co.

Plenary Express: Checkwriting Payroll. *Compatible Hardware:* Compaq; IBM PC, PC AT, PC XT. *Operating System(s) Required:* PC-DOS, MS-DOS, Netware. *Language(s):* COBOL. *Memory Required:* 640k. *General Requirements:* Hard disk.
$995.00.
Offers Payroll Functions, Quarterly Records, Multiple Deductions & Checkwriting Features Including Tips & 401k Plans.
Plenary Systems, Inc.

Plenary Express: Client Write-Up. *Compatible Hardware:* Compaq; IBM PC, PC AT, PC XT. *Operating System(s) Required:* PC-DOS, MS-DOS, Netware. *Language(s):* COBOL. *Memory Required:* 640k. *General Requirements:* Hard disk.
$1495.00.
Financial Reporting Package Including a General Ledger Application Permitting the Creation of Customized Reports for Each Client, After-the-Fact Payroll & Depreciation.
Plenary Systems, Inc.

PLINK. *Operating System(s) Required:* CP/M, SB-80. *Memory Required:* 64k.
disk $129.00.
2-Pass Disk-to-Disk Linkage Editor/Loader. Supports Re-Entrant, ROMable Code, Links Programs Larger Than Available Memory for Execution Targeted on Another Machine, & Has Full Library Capabilities. Input Can Be PSA Relocatable Binary Module, TDL Object Module, or Microsoft REL Files; Output Can Be a COM File, Intel Hex File, TDL Object Module or PSA Relocatable File.
Lifeboat Assocs.

PLINK II. *Compatible Hardware:* IBM PC. *Operating System(s) Required:* PC-DOS. *Memory Required:* 64k.
disk $350.00.
2-Pass Linkage Editor That Supports Arbitrarily Complex Overlay Schemes. Faster Than PLINK, It Links Full 64k Resident Segment on Smaller Machines. Construct Programs up to 8Mb, Using Overlays Which Can Be Used Only with Languages Having Subroutine Capability. No Source Code Modifications or Special Compilation Is Necessary to Link with Overlays.
Lifeboat Assocs.

PLINK-86. *Operating System(s) Required:* CP/M-86. *Memory Required:* 64k.
disk $395.00.
Disk-to-Disk Linkage Editor/Loader. Supports Re-Entrant, ROMable Code, Links Programs Larger Than Available Memory for Execution Targeted on Another Machine, & Has Full Library Capabilities. Input Can Be PSA Relocatable Binary Module, TDL Object Module, or Microsoft REL Files; Output Can Be COM File, Intel HEX File, TDL Object Module or PSA Relocatable File.
Lifeboat Assocs.

PLINK-86. Phoenix Software Associates. *Operating System(s) Required:* MS-DOS, CP/M-86. *Memory Required:* 128k.
$395.00.
Requires 2 Disk Drives.
Texas Instruments, Personal Productivit.

Plot! *Items Included:* Bound manual. *Customer Support:* Free hotline - no time limit; 30 day limited warranty; updates are $5/disk plus S&H.
MS-DOS 2.0 or higher. IBM & compatibles (128k). disk $39.95. *Nonstandard peripherals required:* CGA graphics (or equivalent), & an IBM Prowriter or Epson MX-80 (or compatible) dot matrix printer (for screen dumps).
Plot & Process Data or Curves (or Both) Described by Mathematical Functions. The Processing Features Allow User to Switch Back & Forth Between Linear, Semi-Log, & Double-Log Scales, to Calculate & Plot the Inverse, Power, & Linear Functions of the Data Points. User Can Calculate Slopes, Add Data Stored on a Diskette to the Data Entered from the Keyboard, & Find & Plot the Least-Squares Fit to the Data Points.
Dynacomp, Inc.

PLOT-D: Plotter Interface. *Version:* 1.20. Apr. 1987. *Operating System(s) Required:* MS-DOS. *Items Included:* disk, user's manual. *Customer Support:* 30 day unlimited warranty.
disk $75.00 (ISBN 0-927449-24-2, Order no.: IPPM).
Provides Plotter Support for ECA-2 & EC-ACE. Configurable for Any Plotter.
Tatum Labs, Inc.

PLOT80.
disk $59.95 (Order no.: D8P80).
Designed to Take Advantage of the High Resolution Graphics Mode of Both Prowriter & Epson Compatible Printers. Tool for Producing Pictures, Drawings Lines, Dots, Windowing, Positioning, Rotating & Scaling. Also Provides a Convenient Linkage to the Application Programs.
The Alternate Source.

Plotrax. *Version:* 2.0. 1984. *Compatible Hardware:* IBM PC with color board/adapter. *Operating System(s) Required:* PC-DOS. *Language(s):* BASIC, Machine. *Memory Required:* 256k.
disk $450.00, incl. manual.
Business & Scientific Graphics with Statistical Functions. Trend Analysis Capabilities Allow Plotting of Predictive Trend Lines to Assist with Business Decisions. Percentages Can Be Automatically Calculated & Included on Circular or Elliptical Pie Charts. Includes 2 & 3-Dimensional Multi-Color Bar Charts. Allows Plotting of Data Transferred from Other Applications Such As dBASE & Lotus 1-2-3. User Can Select a Best Fit from a Variety of Statistical Models. Data Normalization & Double Precision Arithmetic Insure Accuracy in Computations. Provides Regression Coefficients, Analysis of Variance (ANOVA), & Ability to Plot Residuals.
Engineering Science, Inc.

Plots Unlimited. *Version:* 1.0. Tom Sawyer & Arthur David Weingarten. Jul. 1990. *Items Included:* Diskettes & manual. *Customer Support:* Free technical support at 800-833-PLOT.
MS-DOS 3.0 or later. IBM or compatible (640k). $399.00 (plus $8.00 S & H). *Nonstandard peripherals required:* Hard drive - 3.3Mb to install.
All Macintoshes with hard drive (1Mb - 2Mb recommended). $399.00 (plus $8.00 S&H). *Nonstandard peripherals required:* Hard drive.
Reference & Educational Tool for Both Student & Professional Writers Consisting of Several Thousand Interlinked Plot Fragments, Character & Thematic Combinations from Which the Writer Can Generate Plots and/or Outlines. Can Also Be Used to Add Plot Twists & Character Relationships to Works-in-Progress.
Ashleywilde, Inc.

PlotSmith. *Compatible Hardware:* IBM PC & compatibles. *Operating System(s) Required:* PC-DOS/MS-DOS 2.0 or higher. *Memory Required:* 256k.
disk $29.95.
Menu-Driven Data Plotting Application Which Allows Least Square Line Fitting, Linear & Logarithmic Scales, Zoom, & Data Transformation. Other Features Include Grid Removal, Parametric Plots, & One-Dimensional Input.
Dynacomp, Inc.

Plotter-Printer ROM. *Compatible Hardware:* HP 85.
ROM cartridge $195.00 (Order no.: 00085-15002).
Allows Users to Interface the HP 85 with HP's High-Resolution Graphics Plotters & Full-Width Line Printers.
Hewlett-Packard Co.

TITLE INDEX

Plotter ROM. *Compatible Hardware:* HP 86/87. ROM cartridge $195.00 (Order no.: 00087-15002).
Allows Data to Be Transferred from an HP 86/87 to an HP Plotter. Also Provides Single Commands to Dump CRT Graphics & Alpha Screens to Any HP Dot Matrix Printer.
Hewlett-Packard Co.

PLOTTERgeist. *Version:* 2.0. Jun. 1991. *Items Included:* Manual, RS-232 cable. *Customer Support:* Free telephone technical support, 30 day money back guarantee.
System 6. Macintosh 2Mb. 3.5" disk $395.00.
Optimal configuration: Adobe Type Manager or TrueType fonts, when installed, allow perfect outline font output.
A Chooser Level Plotter-Vinyl Cutter Driver for the Macintosh. It Features Background Plotting (Allowing the User to Work While Plotting), Full System 7 Compatibility, Direct Support for Many Different Plotter & Vinyl Cutter Models & a Plot to Disk Option for Sending Work to a Service Bureau or Different Machine.
Palomar Software, Inc.

PlotTrak. *Compatible Hardware:* DEC VAX; IBM PC, PC XT, PC AT, PS/2, & compatible. *Operating System(s) Required:* PC-DOS/MS-DOS 2.0 or higher, Unix, Xenix, VAX. *Memory Required:* PC-DOS/MS-DOS 384k.
DOS. disk $295.00.
Unix/Xenix. $495.00 & up.
VAX. $1495.00 & up.
Companion to SofTrak's MicroTrak Project-Management Program. Enables Users to Create Gantt Charts & Time-Scaled Network Diagrams Using MicroTrak Data. Added in this New Version Is a Linked Gantt Chart which Enables Users to See Links Between Project Activities. Also Added Is Support for Ioline & Western Graphtec Plotters.
SofTrak Systems.

PLOT2D. *Version:* 5.0. Mar. 1986. *Compatible Hardware:* IBM PC, PC XT, PC AT, & compatibles. *Operating System(s) Required:* MS-DOS, PC-DOS. *Language(s):* FORTRAN. *Memory Required:* 512k. *General Requirements:* Printer, plotter.
disk $1500.00 (Order no.: PLOT2D).
Draws Sample or Drill Hole Locations on the Plotter. The User Can Plot a Label and/or the Numeric Value with the Location of Any Variable. The User Has Complete Control over Map Scale, Axis Graduation, & Drill Hole Projection. The Analyst Can Screen the Data File According to the Limits Coordinated (along 3 Axes) & Limit Values for Any Given Variable.
Geostat Systems International, Inc. (GSII).

PlotView. *Version:* 2.5. Mar. 1989. *Compatible Hardware:* IBM PC, PC XT, PC AT, PS/2 & compatibles. *Operating System(s) Required:* PC-DOS/MS-DOS 3.0 or higher; Microsoft Windows 2.0 or higher, 286, 386. *Memory Required:* 512k. *General Requirements:* Hard disk, mouse, graphics monitor, CGA, EGA, VGA, Hercules or Compaq graphics adapter. *Items Included:* Manual, disk. *Customer Support:* Telephone.
(without Windows) $99.00.
Utility for Viewing, Printing, & Cutting & Pasting Hewlett-Packard Graphics Language (HPGL) Format Plot Files. Users Can Create Graphics in Drawing, Paint, or CAD/CAM Programs & Then Examine & Manipulate Them. Plots Can Be Displayed on the Screen, Output to Graphics Printer, or Pasted into Documents & Reports. Features Include: Scaling, Rotating, & Scrolling; Plot Size Selection (A-E & A0-A4); Cutting & Pasting (Bitmaps & Metafiles); Emulation of 5 Plotter Models; Selectable Pen Colors & Widths; Zooming in & Out; Unlimited Input File Size; Output to Laser, Inkjet, & Other Printers. Images Can Be Copied into the Clipboard &, from There, Pasted into Other Applications Such As Word Processors, Spreadsheets, & Desktop Publishers.
Ajida Technologies, Inc.

PlotView. *Version:* 3.4. *Compatible Hardware:* Apple Macintosh 512k & higher. *Memory Required:* 512k. *Items Included:* Manual. *Customer Support:* Free by phone, fax & e-mail.
3.5" disk $119.95.
HP Plotter Emulation - Converts HP-GL Input from TEXT file or Modem Port into Macintosh Screen (PICT) drawing.
Stevens Creek Software.

PLSyn: Programmable Logic Synthesis. *Version:* 6.1. Jul. 1994. *Items Included:* Programmable Logic Synthesis User's Guide, Schematic Capture User's Guide, Circuit Analysis Reference Manual, Circuit Analysis User's Guide. *Customer Support:* Free technical support w/purchase of product.
IBM-PC - Windows 3.1 or higher, MS-DOS 5.0 or higher. IBM- PC & compatibles (640k; 4-8Mb extended memory). $495.00-$5500.00.
Nonstandard peripherals required: 80387 floating-pt. coprocessor. *Addl. software required:* Design Center with Schematic Capture & Digital Simulation. *Networks supported:* Novell, IPX, or Net Bios Protocol.
Combines Device-Independent, Mixed-Level Design Capture, Efficient Min-Max Timing Simulation, Optimized Logic Synthesis, & Automated Goal-&-Constraint Directed Device Selection. An Automatic Logic Partitioning Algorithm Is Available Which Can Split the Design into Several Parts to Accomplish the Physical Design Goals or Implement Large Designs. Choose from Three Design Modules Consisting of over 4,000 Devices from 20 Manufacturers Containing Speed, Price, Power, Packaging, & Logic Architecture Information. The AMD MACH Design Module Supports Even the Large New Complex PLDs.
MicroSim Corp.

The Plumber's Helper: Job Cost Estimation. *Items Included:* Bound manual. *Customer Support:* Free hotline - no time limit; 30 day limited warranty; updates are $5/disk plus S&H.
MS-DOS 2.0 or higher. IBM & compatibles (384k). disk $149.95. *Nonstandard peripherals required:* 80-column (or wider) printer.
demo disk $10.00.
Aimed at the Contractor Who Has Little Knowledge of Computers. Maintain a Master Parts List Which Contains the Descriptions & Costs of the Common Parts & Other Items That You Use on Most of Your Jobs. Create a Job Estimate Which Includes the Parts, Labor, Fees, Taxes, & Other Cost Items. Print a Job Summary Which Shows the Total Costs, the Prices Charged to the Customer, & the Profit Margins. Parts May Be Added/Deleted & Costs Changed at Will. Print a Professional-Looking Customer Estimate/ Invoice to Be Presented to Your Customer. The Estimate or Invoice May Be Easily Modified to Reflect Changes Which Occur As the Work Progresses or Is Finished. Print a Parts Order List Which Can Be Given to Your Supplier.
Dynacomp, Inc.

Plundered Hearts. Amy Briggs. *Compatible Hardware:* Apple II+, IIe, IIc, IIgs, Macintosh; Atari XL/XE, ST; Commodore 64/128, Amiga; DEC Rainbow; IBM PC & compatibles; TI Professional.
Apple II, Macintosh, Atari ST, Amiga, DEC, IBM. disk $39.95.
Atari XL/XE, Commodore 64/128. $34.95.
In the 17th Century, the Seas Are As Wild As the Untamed Heart of a Young Woman. But When You Set Out on the Schooner Lafont Deux, Bound for the West Indies, Your Thoughts Are Only of Your Ailing Father Awaiting Your Care. Little Do You Know That Your Innocent Journey Will Soon Turn to Dangerous Adventure. You Barely Survive an Encounter with Pirates, Whose Plans for You Include a Fate Worse Than Death. The Explosives, the Rocky Reefs, the Vicious Crocodile - All These Are Obstacles You Must Overcome with Cunning & Agility. True, It's Not Easy; But at Least You Can Control Your Fate. What You Can't Control Is Much More Dangerous: Your Passion for Nicholas Jamison, the Handsome Pirate Captain.
Activision, Inc.

Mailer's Look-Up. Sep. 1993. *Items Included:* CD-ROM with manual on disk. *Customer Support:* Customer support over telephone; technical support over telephone no charge; 30-day money back.
DOS 3.0 or higher. IBM & compatibles (640k). CD-ROM disk $59.00. *Networks supported:* Lantastic.
Can Provide 5-Digit Plus 4-Digit Extra Zip Code, City, State, Country & Area Code Information for Posting into Programs.
Mailer's Software.

Pluto: Business BASIC & Interpreter. Jan. 1984. *Compatible Hardware:* IBM PC & compatibles; XENIX minicomputers. *Operating System(s) Required:* MS-DOS, XENIX. *Memory Required:* 256k.
MS-DOS, IBM PC & compatibles. disk $595.00.
XENIX. disk $795.00.
Business Basic Environment & Interpreter That Interprets MAI/BASIC FOUR & Science Management Corp. (SMC) Basic Programs to Run on MS-DOS & XENIX Based Systems. Multiple User; Easy File Access; Keyed or Direct Files; Host System Text Serial Files. Math Functions with Pluto; Terminal Emulation Included; Business Basic Programs Can Be Run, Customized or Created on the PC.
Southwest Data Systems.

PM-100 Professional Microsoftware for Physicians, 4. 1978. *Customer Support:* Fax Documented Transmissions.
contact publisher for price.
Self-Contained Medical Management Package Consisting of over 50 Programs for Doctors. Designed to Efficiently Manage Any Size Professional Office with Emphasis on Speed of Operation & Precise Data Control. Features Include: Patient Management, Patient Accounting, Insurance Claims, Clinical Programs, Built-In Word Processing, & System Maintenance. Uses the Latest Operating Systems, & is Compatible with a Variety of Manufacturer's Equipment.
Ashwin Systems International, Inc.

PM-Status 111: Preventive Maintenance Scheduling. *Version:* 1.6. David G. Johnson. Feb. 1990. *Operating System(s) Required:* PC-DOS, MS-DOS. *Language(s):* Compiled BASIC. *Memory Required:* 256k. *Items Included:* 1 Disk & Manual. *Customer Support:* Free for life of program.
disk $395.00.
Designed to Monitor Equipment Preventative Maintenance Schedules, an Alternative to Full Featured Maintenance Management Systems.
Anawan Computer Services.

PM-Turbo. May 1985. *Compatible Hardware:* IBM PC, Network, Novell. *Operating System(s) Required:* MS-DOS, PC-DOS, Xenix. *Language(s):* DataFlex. *Memory Required:* 640k.
Single-User. $1750.00-$3500.00.
Multi-User. disk $5000.00.

Property Management Accounting Program. Uses Names Instead of Numbers. Prints Checks, Late Rent Notices & 1099 Forms. Handles Recurring Payables, Tracks Loan Balances, etc. Additional Features Include Deposit Slips, Rent Increase Processing, & Tracking Expenses by Unit, Tenant or Property. Handles Both Commercial & Residential Properties.
Caldwell Software Solutions.

PMACS - Physicians Management & Control System. Version: 4.2. Jan. 1992. *Operating System(s) Required:* DOS, DOS-LAN, UNIX, XENIX, OS/2. *Language(s):* Microfocus COBOL. *Memory Required:* 256k. *Items Included:* Appointment scheduling. User defined claim forms, online documentation. *Customer Support:* Telephone support, manual.
single user $499.00.
multi-user, from $799.00.
Offers Complete Tracking of Unlimited Patient Service, Medications & Diagnosis, Billing, Insurance Form Generation.
Verite Corp.

Pmap: Professional Map Analysis Package. Spatial Information Systems Inc. Staff. 1993. *Items Included:* Includes supporting utilities, user manual, brief text & tutorials.
MS-DOS 3.1 or higher. IBM & compatibles (2Mb). disk $495.00. *Nonstandard peripherals required:* EGA/VGA Graphics, math coprocessor. *Optimal configuration:* 1 floppy, hard drive with 8Mb free space.
User Can Create, Store, Analyze, & Display Maps. Provides a Low Cost Software System for Analyzing Spatial Data. Provides a Level of Analytic & Modeling Capabilities Unavailable in the Most Costly GIS Systems.
Farmer's Software Assn.

PMATE. *Operating System(s) Required:* CP/M, SB-80, CP/M-86, MS-DOS. *Memory Required:* 64k.
disk $195.00.
Text Editor with Special Features Including Full Side Scrolling & 2 Visible Cursors Manipulatable from the Command Mode: One in the Video Area, the Other on the Command Line. Uses Disk Buffering to Manipulate Files Larger Than Memory. 11 General Purpose Buffer Registers Are Available for Text or Macro Storage.
Lifeboat Assocs.

PMATE PC. *Compatible Hardware:* IBM PC. *Operating System(s) Required:* PC-DOS. *Memory Required:* 64k.
disk $225.00.
Text Editor with Special Features Including Full Side Scrolling & 2 Visible Cursors Manipulatable from the Command Mode: One in the Video Area, the Other on the Command Line. Uses Disk Buffering to Manipulate Files Larger Than Memory. 11 General Purpose Buffer Registers Are Available for Text or Macro Storage.
Lifeboat Assocs.

PMATE 86. *Compatible Hardware:* Victor 9000, TI Professional. *Operating System(s) Required:* CP/M-86, MS-DOS. *Memory Required:* 64k.
disk $225.00.
Text Editor with Special Features Including Full Side Scrolling & 2 Visible Cursors Manipulatable from the Command Mode: One in the Video Area, the Other on the Command Line. Uses Disk Buffering to Manipulate Files Larger Than Memory. 11 General Purpose Buffer Registers Are Available for Text or Macro Storage.
Lifeboat Assocs.

PMATE 86. Agri-Management Services, Inc. *Operating System(s) Required:* MS-DOS, CP/M-86, Concurrent CP/M-86. *Memory Required:* 64k.
$995.00.
Texas Instruments, Personal Productivit.

PMS: Personal Mailing System. Feb. 1984. *Compatible Hardware:* IBM PC & compatibles. *Memory Required:* Lotus 1-2-3 192k, Symphony 384k. *General Requirements:* Lotus 1-2-3 or Symphony.
disk $35.00 ea.
Lotus 1-2-3. (Order no.: PMS-I).
Symphony. (Order no.: PMS-S).
Provides a Means of Easily Maintaining Name & Address Information & Preparing Mailings.
Easy-As, Inc.

PMS-II (Project Management System). Version: 9.0. 1980. *Compatible Hardware:* IBM PC & compatibles. *Operating System(s) Required:* MS-DOS, PC-DOS 2.1 & higher. *Language(s):* CB-86. *Memory Required:* 512k. *General Requirements:* Hard disk drive, 132-column printer.
disk $1295.00, incl. manual.
Critical Path Project Management System Which Calculates Early & Late Start & Finish, Float, & Critical Path(s) for Networks of up to 3000 Activities. Super & Sub-Networking Features Permit Unlimited Size. Prints Activity Reports & Gantt Charts with Sort & Select Capabilities, Activity Diagram, Funding Schedule & Graph, & Three Part Earned Value Analysis Reports. On-Screen Bar Chart & On-Screen Logic Display. Tracks Budget & Actual Material, Labor, & Overhead Dollars, Interfaces to Any Job Cost System, dBASE III, Lotus 1-2-3. Program Is Not Copy-Protected.
North America MICA, Inc.

PMS80 Project Management Application Software. Version: 6.30. Jan. 1981. *Operating System(s) Required:* MS-DOS 2.0 or higher, UNIX. *Memory Required:* 640k. *General Requirements:* 40 Mb hard disk space. *Items Included:* Reference manual, users guide.
BASIC. disk $995.00.
ADVANCED. disk $2500.00.
DATA BASE MANAGER. disk $500.00.
GRAPHICS. disk $1500.00.
Manages Costs, Resources, Scheduling of Projects/Multi-Projects. Generates Reports & Allows User Design of Report Data & Screen Forms. Uses Critical Path Method for Scheduling for Projects up to $100 Million & 10 Years in Duration. Contains Data Base Management, Mailing Management & Advanced Graphics Time Scale Arrow Diagram.
Pinnell/Busch, Inc.

Pocket APL System. Oct. 1984. *Compatible Hardware:* IBM. *Operating System(s) Required:* MS-DOS. *Memory Required:* 128k.
disk $95.00, incl. reference guide & textbk.
 (ISBN 0-926683-00-4).
 (Order no.: P120).
Includes On-Line Calculator, Help Facility, Report Formatting & Error Trapping.
Manugistics, Inc.

Poems of the Place. James McCrary. Dec. 1994. *Items Included:* Descriptive instructions. *Customer Support:* Free by phone.
Apple/MAC. MAC. 3.5" disk $9.00 (ISBN 1-887638-06-7). *Optimal configuration:* Hypertext Viewer supplied.
Windows. PC compatible. disk $9.00 (ISBN 1-887638-07-5). *Optimal configuration:* Hypertext Viewer supplied.
MS-DOS - ASCII. All platforms. disk $9.00 (ISBN 1-887638-12-1). *Addl. software required:* Any Word processor.
A Hypertext Collection of Poetry by an Important Contemporary Poet.
GRIST On-Line.

Point & Shoot. *Items Included:* Bound manual. *Customer Support:* Free hotline - no time limit; 30 day limited warranty; updates are $5/disk plus S&H.
MS-DOS. IBM & compatibles (256k). $39.95-$399.95.
User Interface for Computer Users Who Are Not Programmers or Who Are Not Familiar with the Intricacies of DOS Software. Users Who Merely Want to Access Their Application Programs Can Do So Without Any Knowledge of DOS. Provides a Very Easy-to-Modify Menu Interface Which Lets User Select an Application in Only One or Two Keystrokes. Invoke a Program by Its Name, Run a Batch File, & Return to the Menu; or User Can Execute a "Script" File When Invocation Involves a Series of Keystrokes. Provides Password Protection on Menu Selections So That Outsiders Will Not Be Able to Sneak a Peek at Proprietary Data.
Dynacomp, Inc.

Point & Shoot. 1992. *Items Included:* Detailed manuals included with all Dynacomp products. *Customer Support:* Free telephone support to original customer - no time limit; 30 day limited warranty.
MS-DOS 3.2 or higher. IBM PC & compatibles (512k). $39.95 (Add $5.00 for 3 1/2" format; 5 1/4" format standard).
A Friendly User Interface for Computer Users Who Are Not Programmers or Who Are Not Familiar with the Intricacies of DOS Software. Users Who Merely Want to Access Their Application Programs Can Do So Without Any Knowledge of DOS. Provides a Very Easy-to-Modify Menu Interface Which Lets You Select an Application in Only One or Two Keystrokes.
Dynacomp, Inc.

Point of Sale. *Compatible Hardware:* Apple Macintosh Plus, SE, II. *General Requirements:* Hard disk; FileMaker 4; ImageWriter I or II; LaserWriter optional (required for printing bar codes). *Items Included:* Software for bar code reader communications & user's manual, some customizing included. *Customer Support:* Free telephone support.
Includes Bar code software & documentation; includes some customizing. Bar code printing software. 3.5" disk $1195.00.
Bar-Code System Which Turns a Macintosh into a Cash Register Without the Cash Drawer. With a FileMaker Sales Receipt Template Open on a User's Macintosh Screen, a User Scans Bar Codes Affixed to Products Being Sold to a Customer. The Descriptions & Prices of the Products Are Automatically Entered into the FileMaker Receipt Form When the Bar-Code Data Is Transferred to the Computer. Customer Names & Addresses Are Automatically Entered When a Customer Number Is Typed into the FileMaker Receipt Template.
Computext.

Point of Sale. *Compatible Hardware:* IBM PC & compatibles, PC XT, PC AT. *Operating System(s) Required:* MOS. (source code included). *Memory Required:* 4 users 256k, 9 users 512k.
$995.00, incl. basic system.
POS module $500.00.
Includes Daily Sales Entry, Scroll Selecting, Write-In, Invoice Printing, Cash Drawer, Inventory Examination, Void Sale & Return Item, Unlimited Credit Card & End of Sale Prompting. Real Time Inventory Updating. Automatic Real Time Credit Checking on A/R Customers.
Hurricane Systems, Inc.

Point of Sale. 1996. *Customer Support:* Free telephone & BBS technical support; documentation; training from local dealers & or vendor's CFPIM, C.P.M., CIRM, CQA Trainers.

TITLE INDEX

MS-DOS. IBM PC/XT/AT & compatibles (512k). $995.00-$1295.00 Basic; $2195.00 Enhanced; $3395.00 Professional. *Networks supported:* Novell, Lantastic, Banyan VINES; all NETBOIS compatible.
This is a comprehensive "Point-of-Sale" program for microcomputers. The system is interactive with single or multiple cash registers & the most respected names in "Point-of-Sale" hardware driven by INMASS/MRP inventory, purchasing, & accounting software. "Point of Sale" can be effectively utilized with a barcode system. Up to 20 price-levels are available. Prints sales receipts & reports to track cash sales totals useful for daily readings & shift change totals.
INMASS/MRP.

Point of Sale. *Compatible Hardware:* IBM PC. contact publisher for price.
Inventory Control Program Designed for Part-Number Oriented Industries. Prints Invoices, Statements, & Management Reports.
Intelligent Business Systems (West Virginia).

Point-of-Sale. *Version:* 4.6. 1995. *Operating System(s) Required:* MS-DOS, XENIX. *Language(s):* Compiled BASIC. *Memory Required:* 640k. *General Requirements:* 10Mb hard disk, printer, cash drawer. *Items Included:* Manual, disk, demo. *Customer Support:* Free phone support for 90-days; $25.00 per phone call after.
disk $500.00 (ISBN 0-918185-65-3).
Point-of-Sale System Which Provides Complete Inventory Control, Mailing List, & All Accounting Functions from a Single Entry. Available for Automobile Machine Shops, Pet Stores, Softgoods (Apparel) & General Merchandise. Can Be Modified to Suit Other Needs. Does Bar Code Label Printing, Balance Forward Receivable 8,000 Customers & Handles 31,000 Inventory Items.
Taranto & Assocs., Inc.

Point of Sale Inventory System. *Compatible Hardware:* IBM PC & compatibles. *Operating System(s) Required:* MS-DOS. *Memory Required:* 512k. *General Requirements:* Printer; hard disk.
disk $250.00 (ISBN 0-923283-04-8).
Designed for Retailers & Distributors. Features Sales Analysis Reports, Re-Order Reports, Three Cost Levels, Four User-Definable Quantity Fields (for Different Locations If Needed) & Multiple Vendors for Alternate Sourcing. Also Includes an Integrated Invoicing System Which Prints Invoices, Automatically Decrements Inventory, & Also Collects Information for Sales Tax Reporting & In-Depth Profitability Analysis. Customer Invoices Can Be Autoposted to the Optional Accounts Receivable.
Computerware.

Point of Sale Management System. *Version:* 4.0. Jun. 1994. *Items Included:* Sample data, full manual. *Customer Support:* Free installation support (via phone) first 30 days; FAX & Bulletin Board: free, with response within 1-3 days; Phone support: 1 year, unlimited calls, 1-5pm M-F $150/year; Training is available from 3rd party.
DOS 3.3 or higher. PC compatibles/clones (2Mb). disk $299.00 (Order no.: POS 4.0). *Addl. software required:* Recommend an expanded memory manager; must have Advanced Accounting 4.03. *Optimal configuration:* Intel 486 or clone, DOS 5.0, 4Mb RAM, 386 MAX memory manager, Novell 3.12 network (for multiuser). *Networks supported:* Any NetBIOS compatible network; recommend Novell or LANtastic.
Add-On to Advanced Accounting 4.03 That Handles All Aspects of Face-to-Face Sales, Including Customer & Product Look-Ups, Choice of Terms, Tax Computation, Subtotals, Discounts, & Promotional Pricing. Built-In Security System & Audit Trail. Handles Cash-Outs, Layaways, & Refunds. Multiuser Ready. Source Code Is Available.
Business Tools Software.

Point of Sale Register. *Version:* 14.0. (Accounting Software Ser.). Aug. 1993. *Compatible Hardware:* IBM & compatibles. *Operating System(s) Required:* PC-DOS, MS-DOS 3.X & up. *Language(s):* MegaBASIC. *Memory Required:* 640k. *General Requirements:* Hard disk, wide carriage printer. *Customer Support:* (203) 790-9756.
disk $395.00, Network Option ,400.00 more. manual $50.00.
Prints Register Slips, Credit Memos & Invoices. Computes Salesmen Commissions & Updates Inventory Automatically. Handles Cash Sales, Checks, Credit Cards, Housecharge, & Layaway. Allows Sale of Special Items (Not in Inventory). Daily Report to Balance Cash Draw & Calculates Deposit. Posts Daily Figures to Monthly File. Automatic Lookup of Customer, Inventory Data. Calculates Discount Tax, Commission.
Applications Systems Group (CT), Inc.

Point of Sale System. *Version:* 7.2. 1989. *Compatible Hardware:* IBM PC & compatibles. *Memory Required:* 512k. *General Requirements:* Hard disk. *Items Included:* Ring binder documentation. *Customer Support:* 1 hour phone support included, on-site training at $75 per hour.
$295.00 Single user; $495.00 multi user.
Designed Specifically for Retailers. Allows Users to Record Retail Sales Transactions in an Online/Real-Time Environment; Dynamically Add Customers & Edit Transactions; Check Inventory for Stock & Prices; Handle the Return & Echange of Items; Discount All or Selected Items; Provide for Backorders & Layaways; & the Printing of Various Reports. Interfaces with The Assistant Controller Series Inventory & Accounts Receivable, Systems or Can Operate as a Stand-Alone Product.
Lake Avenue Software.

Pok the Little "Artiste": Explore the World of Art & Colors with Your New Friend Pok. *Items Included:* Pamphlet of instructions. *Customer Support:* Tech support, 60-day money-back guarantee.
Windows; Macintosh. IBM compatible 386SX or higher (4Mb); Mac LC or higher (2.5Mb). CD-ROM disk $39.95 (ISBN 0-924677-08-2). *Nonstandard peripherals required:* Audio Board, mouse, CD-ROM drive. *Addl. software required:* video card; Quicktime 2.0.
Discover the Magical World of Colors & Crafts in Twelve Games & Activities Introduced by Pok, the Little "Artiste".
IMSI (International Microcomputer Software, Inc.).

Poker Machine. *Compatible Hardware:* Apple II with Applesoft. *Operating System(s) Required:* Apple DOS 3.2, 3.3. *Memory Required:* 48k. disk $19.95.
Simulates Card-Playing Slot Machines.
Dynacomp, Inc.

Poker Party. *Compatible Hardware:* Apple II with Applesoft; IBM PC. *Memory Required:* 48k, IBM 128k.
disk $19.95.
7-Handed Poker. The User Plays Against 6 Computer Players That Each Have Different Playing Strategies.
Dynacomp, Inc.

POLITICALLY CORRECT BEDTIME STORIES:

Pole Position. *Compatible Hardware:* Apple II, II+, IIc, IIe; Atari 400, 800, 600XL, 800XL, 1200, 1600; Commodore 64, VIC-20; IBM PC. contact publisher for price.
Car Racing Game.
Atari Corp.

Police Records System. *Version:* 2.0. Jan. 1984. *Compatible Hardware:* IBM PC & compatibles. *Operating System(s) Required:* PC-DOS, MS-DOS. *Language(s):* Compiled dBASE III. *Memory Required:* 512k. *Items Included:* Documentation on diskette. *Customer Support:* Toll number provided, no charge for support.
disk $125.00.
(Order no.: PRS).
Maintains Records for Dispatched Calls, Residents, Firearms, Arrests, Criminal Records, Warrants & Stolen/Missing Property, Field Interviews, Parking & Traffic Tickets, Traffic Accidents & Abuse Protection Orders. A Variety of Reports Can Be Generated, Including the Uniform Crime Report.
MicroServices, Inc.

Policies Now! *Version:* 1.6. Jun. 1995. *Items Included:* User manual. *Customer Support:* Unlimited free phone support for registered users.
MS-DOS 2.11 or higher. PC, XT, AT, PS/2 or compatible (512k). Stnadard Edition $79.00; Update Service: 1 year $79.00, 3 years $159.00. *Optimal configuration:* Color or Monochrome monitor, hard disk required.
MS-DOS 2.11 or higher. PC, XT, AT, PS/2 or compatible (512k). HR Pro Edition $395.00; Update Service: 1 year $145.00, 3 years $245.00. *Optimal configuration:* Color or Monochrome monitor, hard disk required. *Networks supported:* Most Local Area Networks.
A Knowledge-Based Interactive Software Program That Custom Writes a Complete Employee Handbook. The Software Provides Concise Human Resources & Labor Law Information on 75 Policy Subjects. Then It Asks Key Questions on the Chosen Policy & Uses the Answers to Write a Custom Policy.
KnowledgePoint.

Policy/Goal Percentaging: A Decision-Aiding Program. *Version:* 8.7. Stuart S. Nagel & John Long. Feb. 1986. *Compatible Hardware:* IBM PC & compatibles. *Operating System(s) Required:* DOS. *Language(s):* Plato, TenCore, BASIC. *Memory Required:* 256k.
disk $90.00.
Can Process a Set of Goals to Be Achieved, Alternatives for Achieving Them, & Relations Between Goals & Alternatives in Order to Choose the Best Alternative, Combination, or Allocation. Deals with Problems Such As Multiple Dimensions on Multiple Goals, Multiple Missing Information, Multiple Alternatives, of Which There Are Too Many to Determine the Effects of Each One, Multiple & Possibly Conflicting Constraints, & the Need for Simplicity in View of All That Multiplicity.
Decision Aids, Inc.

Politically Correct Bedtime Stories: Cyber Sensitivity for Our Life. Nov. 1995. *Customer Support:* 800 number (free), online support forums.
Windows 486SX, 25MHz; Macintosh. IBM & compatibles (4Mb); Performa 550 (33MHz 68030) (5Mb). CD-ROM disk $34.95 (ISBN 1-57595-001-4). *Nonstandard peripherals required:* Double-speed CD-ROM drive, Super VGA color card-256 color display, "SoundBlaster" compatible sound card; Double-speed CD-ROM drive.
Based on the Number 1 Bestselling Books by James Finn Garner - over 3 Million Copies Sold.

Interactive, Animated, Stories Free from the Patriarchal Influences of Hegemonic Linear Structure & Purged of All Cultural Bias. Contains Four Politically Correct Applications, Including a PC Phrase Generator, Screen Savers, Printable PC Stationery, & a Game to Test User's Politically Correct Quotient (PCQ).
Macmillan Digital U. S. A.

Poly-COM/320. Version: 2.0. Customer Support: 90 days free support.
PC-DOS 2.0 or higher. IBM PS/2, AT, PC/XT, PC or compatibles (256k). disk $199.00.
Networks supported: Novell, 3Com, Banyan, AT&T Stargroup, Digital PCSA, ExeceLAN LAN Workplace & more.
Terminal Emulation & File Transfer for PC to DEC Communications. VT100, VT220 & VT320 Emulation. Hot-Keys, Remappable Keyboard & Multi-National Character Sets Are Featured.
Polygon, Inc.

Poly-LINK. Version: 2.2. Jun. 1990. Customer Support: 90 days free support.
PC-DOS or MS-DOS 3.0 or Higher; VMS 4.4 or Higher. IBM PS/2, AT, PC/XT, PC & compatibles (15k). disk $299.00 per user.
Networks supported: Novell, Banyan, 3COM, AT&T Stargroup & most Ethernet based networks, LAN Manager.
Allows PC Users to Share VAX/VMS Services over Ethernet Based Networks. Disk, Mail, Print, & File Services Are Shared & Treated As Virtual Extensions to the PC User. The Program Is Compatible with the Following Polygon Emulators: Poly-Star/G 2.31 or Higher, Poly-Star/T 2.31 or Higher, & Poly-Com/320 2.0 or Higher.
Polygon, Inc.

Poly-Net. Jan. 1990. Customer Support: 90 days free support.
3Com 3Station, 3Station 2E; IBM PS/2, AT, PC/XT, PC & compatibles. disk $149.00.
Nonstandard peripherals required: Call for Ethernet boards supported. Addl. software required: Poly-Com, or Poly-Start/T or /G Terminal Emulator; & appropriate Network software, ie., Novell, 3Com. Networks supported: Novell, 3COM, Banyan/Vines, AT&T Stargroup, LAN Manager.
Allows Users of 3Com, Banyan, Novell, or AT&T Stargroup Networks to Stack LAT & the Network Communication Protocol Simultaneously Without Rebooting to Change from a VT Terminal to the Network & Back. Simultaneous User Licenses for Multiple PC's Available.
Polygon, Inc.

Poly-STAR/G: PC-to-VAX Communication Software. Version: 2.31. Compatible Hardware: IBM PC, PC XT, PC AT. Operating System(s) Required: PC-DOS/MS-DOS 2.0 or higher. Memory Required: 512k.
from $299.00.
Will Emulate DEC's Text Terminals. Features File Transfer Capabilities, Pop-Up Window Menus, Hot-Key Switching, International Keyboard Support, & Enhanced Remote Control. Includes a User-Programmable Communication Language. The Phone Book Feature Will Enable User to Automatically Dial, Connect, & Log On. Supports Modems. Supports Graphs VT340.
Polygon, Inc.

Poly-XFR Plus. Customer Support: 90 days free support.
VAX/VMS. DEC. disk $495.00.
Second Generation Async. File Transfer Program That Automatically Matches the Protocol at the Other End. Error-Free Transfer of ASCII or Binary Files. Protocols Supported: KERMIT, Poly-XFR, & Poly-XFR Plus.
Polygon, Inc.

PolyFORTH. Jun. 1989. Compatible Hardware: IBM PC & compatibles. Operating System(s) Required: MS-DOS. Language(s): FORTH (source code included). Memory Required: 64k. Items Included: Editor, compiler, assembler, utilities, polyFORTH manual, CPU manual. Customer Support: 1 year customer support & updates; programming classes available at additional cost. contact publisher for price.
Real-Time Operating System; Multiuser, Multitasking, Integrated Software Development Package; Custom System & Application Programming Services; Courses in FORTH Programming & Application Design.
FORTH, Inc.

Polyglott Stadtefuhrer Berlin.
80386 (4Mb). CD-ROM disk $59.95 (ISBN 3-493-61205-2, Order no.: 612052). Addl. software required: Microsoft Windows 3.1 or higher (mouse recommended). Networks supported: IBM 6Mb.
Maps, Annotated Walking Tours & Appropriate Cultural Information (Art History, Architecture, Culinary Delights, Points of Interest, etc.), Videos Narrated Slide Shows, & Pictures Which Illuminate Tourist Attractions. The Ultimate Trip Planner. Print What Is Useful & Leave the Rest Home.
Langenscheidt Pubs., Inc.

Polyglott Stadtefuhrer London.
80386 (4Mb). CD-ROM disk $59.95 (ISBN 3-493-61206-0, Order no.: 612060). Addl. software required: Microsoft Windows 3.1 or higher (mouse recommended). Networks supported: IBM 6Mb.
Maps, Annotated Walking Tours & Appropriate Cultural Information (Art History, Architecture, Culinary Delights, Points of Interest, etc.), Videos Narrated Slide Shows, & Pictures Which Illuminate Tourist Attractions. The Ultimate Trip Planner. Print What Is Useful & Leave the Rest Home.
Langenscheidt Pubs., Inc.

Polyglott Stadtefuhrer New York.
80386 (4Mb). CD-ROM disk $59.95 (ISBN 3-493-61207-9, Order no.: 612079). Addl. software required: Microsoft Windows 3.1 or higher (mouse recommended). Networks supported: IBM 6Mb.
Maps, Annotated Walking Tours & Appropriate Cultural Information (Art History, Architecture, Culinary Delights, Points of Interest, etc.), Videos Narrated Slide Shows, & Pictures Which Illuminate Tourist Attractions. The Ultimate Trip Planner. Print What Is Useful & Leave the Rest Home.
Langenscheidt Pubs., Inc.

Polyglott Stadtefuhrer Paris.
80386 (4Mb). CD-ROM disk $59.95 (ISBN 3-493-61208-7, Order no.: 612087). Addl. software required: Microsoft Windows 3.1 or higher (mouse recommended). Networks supported: IBM 6Mb.
Maps, Annotated Walking Tours & Appropriate Cultural Information (Art History, Architecture, Culinary Delights, Points of Interest, etc.), Videos Narrated Slide Shows, & Pictures Which Illuminate Tourist Attractions. The Ultimate Trip Planner. Print What Is Useful & Leave the Rest Home <end>
Langenscheidt Pubs., Inc.

POLYGON. Version: 2.2. Jun. 1985. Compatible Hardware: IBM PC, PC XT, PC AT & compatibles. Operating System(s) Required: MS-DOS, PC-DOS. Language(s): FORTRAN. Memory Required: 512k. General Requirements: Printer, plotter.
disk $1500.00 (Order no.: POLYGON).
Computes & Plots Polygons of Influence Around Sample Locations.
Geostat Systems International, Inc. (GSII).

PolyMath. Compatible Hardware: Apple Macintosh. Memory Required: 512k.
3.5" disk $19.95.
Symbolic Algebra Program for Uni-Variate Polynomials.
E & M Software Co.

Polyps from Pluto. Compatible Hardware: Commodore 64 with joystick.
disk $19.95.
Space Game in Which You Must Defend Solar Refueling Stations.
Dynacomp, Inc.

POLYSIM. Version: 1.2. Jun. 1983. Compatible Hardware: IBM PC, PC XT, PC AT & compatibles. Operating System(s) Required: PC-DOS, MS-DOS. Language(s): FORTRAN. Memory Required: 512k. General Requirements: Printer.
disk incl. ITGAUSS, TGAUSS, SIM3, SIM3C $5600.00 (Order no.: POLYSIM).
Geostatistical Simulation Package. The Programs Reproduce the Variability, Continuity & Distribution of Any Given Parameters. For a Situation Where Sample Values Change Very Rapidly over Short Distances, Simulation Shows the Highs & Lows Realistically. The Variance, Variogram & Histogram of the Simulated Values Are the Same as Those of Real Measured Values.
Geostat Systems International, Inc. (GSII).

PolyTape. Version: 4.25. Jan. 1992. Items Included: Manuals. Customer Support: Phone support free.
MS-DOS. 286, 486 (512k). disk $695.00.
Optimal configuration: DOS 5.0. Networks supported: Yes.
Allows Users to Convert Data Between Different Platforms UNIX, DOS, OS/2 & Between Different Media, 4mm, 8mm, QIC, 9 Track IBM 3480, CD-ROM.
MicroTech Conversion Systems.

Pony Express. Compatible Hardware: Apple Macintosh, Macintosh XL.
3.5" disk $169.00.
Pony Express XL. 8" disk $238.00.
Prints Names, Addresses, Phone Numbers, etc. Features: Sort by Name, Zip Code, Zip & Name, Zip & Address. Records Can Be Printed in Single Line Format for Master List Printouts, or Label Format for Mailing Purposes. Specific Zips or Zip Code Ranges Can Be Printed & More.
Computech.

Pool & Billiards. Items Included: Bound manual. Customer Support: Free hotline - no time limit; 30 day limited warranty; updates are $5/disk plus S&H.
MS-DOS. IBM & compatibles (256k). disk $19.95.
Programs: CAROM BILLIARDS, THREE-CUSHION BILLIARDS, & POCKET BILLIARDS (POOL). Instructive As Well As Entertaining. Each Game Is An Example of a Two-Dimensional Many-Body Problem in Classical Mechanics. All Collisions Are Treated As Perfectly Elastic Collisions Between Hard Spheres, or Between a Hard Sphere & a Rigid Wall. The Trajectories of the Balls Also Resemble the Motions of Molecules in a Gas As Described by Molecular Dynamics Calculations.
Dynacomp, Inc.

Pool Of Radiance, 4 disks.
PC-DOS/MS-DOS 2.11 or higher. IBM PC & compatibles (384k-CGA, 512k-EGA). disk $39.95. Nonstandard peripherals required: color monitor & a graphic card.
Apple II (128k). disk $44.95. Nonstandard peripherals required: 80 column expanded

TITLE INDEX

memory card.
DOS 6.0.2 or higher. Macintosh (1Mb). 3.5" disk $39.95.
Commodore 64/128 (64k). disk $39.95.
Located on the Northern Shore of the Moonsea in the Forgotten Realms, the Fabled City of Phlan Had Been Overrun by Monsters Led by a Mysterious Leader. Your Quest: Discover the Identity of This Evil Force & Rid Phlan of Its Scourge. POOL OF RADIANCE Represents the First in a Line of Software Created by SSI in Collaboration with TSR - the Producer of the Legendary ADVANCED DUNGEONS & DRAGONS. It Adheres Faithfully to AD&D Game Standards. The Monsters, Items & Spells Used are From the Famous AD&D Monster Manuals, Dungeon Masters Guide & Players Handbook. Roll Up Your Characters From Four Classes, Six Races & Nine Alignments in Classic AD&D Game Fashion; Or Use the Party Already Provided.
Strategic Simulations, Inc.

Pop-Up Alarm Clock. *Version:* 3.0. *Compatible Hardware:* IBM PC, PC XT, PCjr, AT, 386 or compatibles. *Operating System(s) Required:* MS-DOS/PC-DOS. *Memory Required:* 64k.
disk $39.95 (ISBN 0-916435-08-3).
Popular Programs, Inc.

Pop-Up Calculator & Financial Calculator. *Version:* 3.0. *Compatible Hardware:* IBM PC, PC XT, PCjr, AT, 386 or compatibles. *Operating System(s) Required:* MS-DOS/PC-DOS. *Memory Required:* 64k.
disk $39.95 (ISBN 0-916435-04-0).
Popular Programs, Inc.

Pop-Up DeskSet & DeskSet PLUS. *Version:* 3.0. *Compatible Hardware:* IBM PC, PC AT, PC XT, 3270 PC, PCjr & compatibles. *Operating System(s) Required:* MS-DOS/PC-DOS. *Memory Required:* 128k.
DeskSet. disk $69.95 (ISBN 0-916435-11-3).
DeskSet PLUS. disk $129.95 (ISBN 0-916435-12-1).
Popular Programs, Inc.

Pop-Up DeskSet Plus. *Version:* 3.0. *Compatible Hardware:* IBM PC, XT, 386 & compatibles. *Operating System(s) Required:* DOS 1.0 or higher. *Memory Required:* 128k.
disk $129.95.
Features Pop-Up Word, a File & Text Editor with a Built-In Scheduler, Address Book, & Cut-&-Paste Facility. Also Features Pop-Up Calendar, Pop-Up Alarm Clock, Two Pop-Up Calculators (10-Memory Standard & Advanced Financial/Statistical), Pop-DOS (Disk & File Utilities), Pop-Up Anything (a RAM Partition), Pop-Up Voice (an Auto-Dialer), & Pop-Up Modem Data Communications Support with VT-52/VT-100 Terminal Emulation, XMODEM Support, Automatic Log-On Scripts, & 300-9600 Baud Rates. Pop-Up Word Plus & Pop-Up Scheduler Now Included.
Popular Programs, Inc.

Pop-Up PopDOS & Pop-Up Anything. *Version:* 3.0. *Compatible Hardware:* IBM PC, PC XT, PCjr. *Operating System(s) Required:* MS-DOS. *Memory Required:* 64k.
disk $39.95 (ISBN 0-916435-07-5).
Popular Programs, Inc.

Pop-Up TeleComm. *Version:* 3.0. *Compatible Hardware:* IBM PC, PC XT, PCjr. *Operating System(s) Required:* MS-DOS. *Memory Required:* 128k.
disk $49.95 (ISBN 0-916435-06-7).
Popular Programs, Inc.

Population Simulation. Duane Bristow. *Compatible Hardware:* TRS-80 Model I, Model III. *Operating System(s) Required:* TRSDOS. *Language(s):* BASIC.
cassette $19.95.
Two Players Govern Two Planets: One Technologically Advanced & the Other Primitive. Use Your Resources to Best Advantage to Coexist or to Compete.
Duane Bristow Computers, Inc.

Portable Troll. *Items Included:* TROLL Primer, user's guide, six volume reference manual. *Customer Support:* Telephone technical support 9AM-5PM, M-F, EST.
PC, Sun Workstation, HP9000, IBM RS/6000, Cray. contact publisher for price.
Interactive Decision Support System (DSS) for DB Management, Econometric Modeling, Forecasting, & Statistical Analysis.
Intex Solutions, Inc.

PORTAL. Micro Computations, Inc. Jan. 1986. *Compatible Hardware:* IBM PC & compatibles. *Operating System(s) Required:* MS-DOS. *Language(s):* BASIC. *Memory Required:* 256k.
disk $495.00, incl. demo & user's manual.
Calculates Approximate Shears & Moments in Girders/Columns of Multi-Story/Multi-Bay Structures Due to Lateral & Vertical Loads Using Portal, Cantilever, or Factor Method. Approximate 'I' Values of Columns & Girders May Be Calculated or Specified by User. Calculates Approximate Lateral Loads on Vertical Surfaces per B.O.C.A., National, Uniform, or Southern Building Codes. Accounts for Braced Portals, Girder & Joint Loads, & Fixed, Pinned, or Partial Pinned Ground End Conditions. Calculates Approximate Overturning & Stabilizing Moments. Tunes Portals to User-Specified Drift Index. Output Can Be Displayed or Printed.
Computing Power Applied.

Portal. *Version:* 3.5. M. E. Glover & J. R. Haley. 1981-96. *Compatible Hardware:* ITT, AT&T, DEC VAX, Alpha, IBM PC & compatibles, Bull, DG, IBM RS 6000, Sun, 386 UNIX, HP. *Operating System(s) Required:* VMS, PC-DOS/MS-DOS, UNIX, AIX, HP/UX. *Language(s):* C. *Memory Required:* 512k. *Customer Support:* Hotline, newsletter, 90-day warranty.
disk $700.00.
Programmers Slash Application Development Time with Portal 4GL Tools: a ChUI, Interactive Access to Standard Data Files & File Manipulation Capabilities.
Viking Software Services, Inc.

Portfolio Analyzer. *Version:* 3.0. 1995. *Operating System(s) Required:* PC-DOS/MS-DOS, OS/2. *Memory Required:* 320k. *Items Included:* 100-page bound manual. *Customer Support:* Hotline.
3.5" or 5.25" disk $79.00.
Integrated Menu-Driven System for Maintenance & Analysis of Diverse Investment Portfolios Containing Stocks, Bonds, Options, Savings Accounts, Annuities, Collectibles, Mortgages & Others - Ideal for Home or Business. Accommodates Many Separate Portfolios & Produces Numerous Financial Reports for Any Combination. Tracks Performance of Investments Individually & in Groups Including Proceeds from Dividends & Option Writing, & Tax Treatment of Capital Gains. Prints IRS Form 1040 Schedules B & D. Allows Both Manual & Automatic (Modem) Price Updating, Retains All Transactions for As Long As Desired, & Holds Descriptive Information for Each Account.
Hamilton Software, Inc.

THE PORTFOLIO MANAGEMENT SYSTEM

Portfolio Data Manager. *Items Included:* Bound manual. *Customer Support:* Free hotline - no time limit; 30 day limited warranty; updates are $5/disk plus S&H.
MS-DOS. IBM & compatibles (256k). disk $99.95. *Nonstandard peripherals required:* Two drives (e.g., two floppies, one floppy & a hard disk, etc.), & CGA (or equivalent) graphics capability; Epson, IBM Prowriter, or equivalent printer is supported.
manual only $19.95.
Record & Monitor the Performance of Your Portfolio (Which May Consist of Stocks, Bonds, Mutual Funds, CD's, Cash, etc.). It Maintains & Reports Important Information Which Is Usually Not Available in Monthly Broker Statements. Features Include: Record Keeping; Monitoring; Technical Analysis; User's Manual; Special Data Fields; Date Entry.
Dynacomp, Inc.

Portfolio Decisions. *Items Included:* Bound manual. *Customer Support:* Free hotline - no time limit; 30 day limited warranty; updates are $5/disk plus S&H.
MS-DOS 2.0 or higher. IBM & compatibles (128k). $99.95. *Nonstandard peripherals required:* Two floppy disk drives (or one floppy & a hard disk), & an 80-column (or wider) printer; modem required if you wish to download data over the telephone line.
Comprehensive Analysis Package Designed to Help User Organize, Record, & Evaluate Investments. Avoid Financial Confusion & Keep Track of All Profits & Losses (a Must for Income Tax Purposes). Ability to Communicate (If You Have a Modem) with the Dow Jones or CompuServe Services. (One Hour of 300-Baud CompuServe Connect Time Is Included). This Allows Immediate Updates of Market Prices As Well As Access to Other CompuServe Facilities, & Automatic Daily Updating of Your Portfolio.
Dynacomp, Inc.

Portfolio Management. *Version:* 4.5. *Compatible Hardware:* IBM PC & compatibles. *Operating System(s) Required:* PC-DOS, MS-DOS. *Language(s):* Compiled BASIC. *Memory Required:* 128k. *General Requirements:* Printer.
$49.95, incl. documentation.
Manages up to 2 Portfolios with up to 35 Stocks in Each.
Dogwood Software.

Portfolio Management. *Compatible Hardware:* HP 85 with 16k memory module (HP 82903A), HP 86/87 with 96k RAM.
3-1/2" or 5-1/4" disk $250.00 ea.
HP 85. (Order no.: 82814A).
HP 86/87. (Order no.: 82844A).
Helps Individual Investors & Professional Investment Managers Monitor Their Portfolios. Softkey & Prompt-Driven Commands Enter Investments for Net Worth Valuation & Tax Planning. A Connection with the Dow Jones News/Retrieval Service Allows Automatic Updates of the Current Value of the Portfolio. Handles up to 100 Investment Items with an Unlimited Number of Portfolios (35 Portfolios Stored on Each Data Cartridge or Disk).
Hewlett-Packard Co.

The Portfolio Management System. *Version:* 5.2. 1995. *Items Included:* Complete operating manual. *Customer Support:* Unlimited telephone support.
MS-DOS. IBM PC or compatible (256k). $150.00. *Optimal configuration:* IBM PC or compatible, 256k RAM, printer. *Networks supported:* Novel, Unex.
Designed Specifically for the Small Investor Who Had Need for a Sophisticated Portfolio System but Cannot Justify the Investment for Just a Few

Stocks. System Will Manage a 100 Stock Portfolio & Give User Several Management Reports Plus Schedules for Reporting Dividend & Gains/Losses.
Omni Software Systems, Inc. (Indiana).

Portfolio Management System. William F. Barber. *Compatible Hardware:* IBM PC, PC XT, PC AT, Portable PC, 3270 PC with IBM Display, 2 double-sided disk drives, Autodial Modem (optional for Dow Jones News/Retrieval service), IBM Matrix printer. *Operating System(s) Required:* DOS 2.00, 2.10, 3.00, 3.10. *Memory Required:* 128k.
disk $99.95 (Order no.: 6276538).
Allows Users to Create & Maintain Their Own Portfolio and/or Customers' Portfolios, Compute Current Market Values of Portfolios, Calculate Long- & Short-Term Gains & Losses, Generate Reports, & Produce Labels for Customer Mailings.
Personally Developed Software, Inc.

Portfolio Manager. *Compatible Hardware:* Apple Macintosh. *Memory Required:* 512k. *General Requirements:* 400k disk drive. Hayes-compatible modem optional.
3.5" disk $34.95.
Portfolio Management Program Allowing Users to Update & Manage Securities. With Optional Modem Feature, Update of Portfolio Prices Is Accomplished Through Dow Jones News Retrieval Service or Warner Financial Access.
Disk-Count Software, Inc.

Portfolio Manager. *Compatible Hardware:* Apple; IBM PC. *Operating System(s) Required:* CP/M, MS-DOS. *Memory Required:* Apple 48k, IBM 128k.
disk $69.95.
Allows Data Files to Be Created & Kept up to Date. Tailored to the Individual Investor, Who May Design His Own Investment Categories. File Sorting & Plotting Capabilities Are Included.
Dynacomp, Inc.

Portfolio Manager. *Compatible Hardware:* IBM PC & compatibles. *Operating System(s) Required:* MS-DOS, CP/M-80. *Memory Required:* CP/M 48k; IBM 128k.
contact publisher for price.
Produces 5 Reports: Inventory, Security Performance, Portfolio Performance, Tax & Transaction.
The Walton Group.

Portfolio Master. *Customer Support:* 800-929-8117 (customer service).
MS-DOS. IBM/PS2. disk $199.99 (ISBN 0-87007-653-1).
A Complete Portfolio Management System That Employs all of the New IRS Rules & Regulations, & Allows for the Analysis of Existing Stocks by Several Methods. A Special IRS Schedule D Report is Provided.
SourceView Software International.

Portfolio Status. *Items Included:* Bound manual. *Customer Support:* Free hotline - no time limit; 30 day limited warranty; updates are $5/disk plus S&H.
MS-DOS. IBM & compatibles (128k). disk $29.95.
Provides a Convenient Means for Generating Timely Analyses of Security Portfolios for the Individual Investor or the Investment Advisor. The User Enters the Name of Each Security, the Ticker Symbol (If Desired), the Number of Shares, the Purchase Date, & the Cost. To Generate an Analysis of the Portfolio, the User Enters the Price of Each Security & the Program Proceeds to Compute the Current Market Value, Profit or Loss, Percent Profit, & Days since Purchase for Each Security, & Then to Compute Totals.
Dynacomp, Inc.

Portfolio Watcher. Aug. 1992. *Items Included:* 1 manual. *Customer Support:* Free phone support & newsletter.
Macintosh System 6.0. Apple Macintosh (2Mb). 3.5" disk $149.95. *Networks supported:* AppleTalk.
Portfolio Management Software for Macintosh Computers. Generates a Variety of Reports for Investment Planning & Tax Accounting. Retrieves Prices from CompuServe & Dow Jones.
Micro Trading Software, Inc.

Portfolio II. 1981. *Compatible Hardware:* Apple II, IBM PC. *Memory Required:* 64k. *General Requirements:* Printer.
disk $35.00.
Analyzes Stock Market Investments. Price Information Entered on a Daily or Weekly Basis Is Compared with Purchase Price to Establish Gains & Losses for up to 40 Individual Securities & for Entire Portfolio. History of Each Security's Price Fluctuations Is Accumulated. Trends Are Then Presented As Line Graphs, with Stop-Loss & Profit-Taking Limits.
Navic Software.

Portfol1. *Compatible Hardware:* IBM PC, PCjr, PC XT; TRS-80. *Operating System(s) Required:* MS-DOS. *Language(s):* BASIC. *Memory Required:* 64k. *General Requirements:* 2 disk drives.
contact publisher for price.
Designed to Generate a Periodic Updated Status Report of a Given Portfolio. Carries a Limited Amount of Detail in the Stock Category Including the Following Information: Dates of Purchase, Average Cost per Share, Annualized Income, Market Value, Performance Versus DJ Averages, Yields at Cost & Market, & Indicated Capital Gains or Losses.
R & M Assocs.

PORTIA. *Memory Required:* at least 3-4Mb extended memory; 640k. *Customer Support:* Installation support; training & documentation consulting; telephone hotline assistance; ongoing enhancement & support included in maintenance agreement.
3.1 or greater. Also runs as a DOS application under Microsoft Windows 3.0. 386 or 486 based IBM PS/2, Compaq, or any fully compatible 386 or 486 based PC. $7500.00-$750000.00 based on number of users & features. *Networks supported:* Most DOS networks.
The Portia Family of Portfolio Reporting, Trading & Investment Analysis Systems Offers Comprehensive Support for the Entire Portfolio Management Process; Applications Range from What-If Analysis & Portfolio Modeling to Order Tracking, Performance Measurement & Multicurrency Reporting. Portia supports the Full Range of Equity & Fixed Income Security Types, Including Specialized Securities Such As International Issues, Mortgage-Backeds, & Option & Futures. The Local Area Network Environment Lets Traders, Portfolio Managers & Operations Staff Simultaneously Enter, Access & Analyze Up-to-the-Minute Portfolio Information.
Thomson Financial Services.

Portrait U. S. A. CD-ROM. Joint Education Initiative, University of Maryland with American Geological Institute Staff. Aug. 1995. *Items Included:* User's Manual, Registration Postcard, Portrait USA shaded-relief map Poster offer. Optional: Portrait USA Shaded-Relief Map Poster.
DOS 3.3 or higher. 80386DX or higher (4Mb). $93.95 or $103.90 with Portrait USA shaded-relief map poster; for members, teachers, students: $63.95, or $73.90 with poster (ISBN 0-922152-29-2). *Nonstandard peripherals required:* 6Mb free hard disk space, SVGA graphics card & monitor, CD-ROM drive, MS compatible mouse, MSCDEX 2.2 or higher.
Geologic & Geographic Data Sets Include: Digital Shaded Relief Image; Topography & Bathymetry; 10 Landsat 5 Thematic Mapper Scenes; 150,000 Place Names; Geology, Earthquakes (1534-1994), Faults & Rivers; Gravity, Magnetics, Geothermal & More. Lets You Zoom into Your State or Region to View Landforms, Earthquake Sites, & Waterways.
American Geological Institute.

Portraits in History: The Best of Our Century, Encyclopedia of the JFK Assassination, Encyclopedia of West, Lawmen & Outlaws. ZCI Library Staff et al. Sep. 1995. *Items Included:* Set up instruction sheet, registration card. *Customer Support:* Customer support helpline 503 639-6863.
Win. IBM PC (4Mb). CD-ROM disk $34.95 Ency. JFK Assassination (ISBN 1-887783-10-5, Order no.: 5400-8001). *Optimal configuration:* IBM PC 386/20 or higher, Win 3.1, 4Mb RAM, VGA, SVGA, CD-ROM.
Win. IBM PC (4Mb, 8Mb recommended). CD-ROM disk $34.95 Ency. West, Lawmen & Outlaws (Order no.: 5400-8001). *Optimal configuration:* 386/33 or higher, Win 3.1 or higher, 4Mb RAM (8Mb recommended), VGA, SVGA, CD-ROM, Soundcard, mouse.
DOS 3.3. IBM PC (1Mb). CD-ROM disk $34.95 Best of Our Century (Order no.: 5400-8001). *Optimal configuration:* IBM PC 386/16 or higher, MS-DOS 3.3 or higher, MSCDEX 2.2 or higher, 1Mb RAM, VGA, CD-ROM drive, mouse, Sound Blaster, or compatible.
A Multi-Media Time Machine of People, Places & Events.
Entertainment Technology.

Portview 2020. *Items Included:* Full manual. No other products required. *Customer Support:* Free telephone support - no time limit. 30 day warranty.
MS-DOS 3.2 or higher. IBM & compatibles (512k). disk $79.95.
Record Keeper, Investment Analyzer, & Tax Planner All in One. Will Easily Compute Your Return on Investment (ROI) for Any Investment & Will, Optionally, Adjust All Figures for Inflation. Handles Any Investment: Stocks, Bonds, Mutual Funds, Real Estate, Commodities, Partnerships, Options, etc. Well Organized 64-Page Manual with Many Examples.
Dynacomp, Inc.

POS. Jan. 1987. *Compatible Hardware:* IBM PC. *Operating System(s) Required:* PC-DOS 3.3 or higher. *Memory Required:* 640k. *General Requirements:* 20Meg internal drive, printer.
contact publisher for price (ISBN 0-924638-03-6).
Used to Simulate Functions of Cash Register. Provides for Price Lookup, Bar Code Scanning, Cash Drawer Interface, Descriptive Receipt. Full Alphabetic Entry for Customer Profile Analysis, & Commission Accounting. Sales Audit & Flash Sales Available, Inventory Control, Transfers.
Interactive Business Systems, Ltd.

P.O.S.-Auto & Truck Parts Dealers/Retailers. MS-DOS, Unix, Xenix (512k). IBM PC, PC XT, PC AT & compatible mini/micros. contact publisher for price.
Integrated On-Screen Point of Sale Invoicing, Accounts Payable Purchasing & On-Line Inventory Control. Includes Customer Discount Price Matrix, Lost Sales Reporting & Back Order Tracking. General Ledger, Payroll Optional.
Universal Data Research, Inc.

TITLE INDEX

POS-IM. Version: 2.0. Jul. 1989. *Compatible Hardware:* Apple Macintosh Plus, SE, II, IIcX. *General Requirements:* 1Mb RAM, hard disk storage, printer. *Items Included:* Tutorial; setup & reference manuals including a setup checklist, technical appendix & peripheral suppliers. *Customer Support:* Dealer-supported training, 60 days free telephone support; additional support as needed or under contract. Corporate & retail consulting in inventory management.
single user $1795.00, multi-user $2495.00.
Provides an Integrated Approach to Managing Inventory Levels, Analyzing Sales & Tracking Accounts Receivable.
Ensign Systems, Inc.

POS Record Package I. *Compatible Hardware:* Apple, IBM PC, TRS-80.
contact publisher for price.
Educational Programming, Inc.

P.O.S. Supplement. Version: 8B. Sep. 1993. *Compatible Hardware:* PC-DOS, Xenix, Unix; 3COM, Novell, IBM RT, PS/2. *Memory Required:* Multi-user 3Mb or higher, single user 1000k. *General Requirements:* Integrated Accounting & the Point-of-Sale module. *Customer Support:* Included with the support for the Integrated Accounting.
Single user. disk $1120.00.
Multiuser. disk $1245.00.
Used by Companies Who Run Large Retail Outlets & Often Ship Merchandise from Other Stores or Warehouses. Can Break up Receipts into Those Items That Have Been Taken & Those to Be Shipped from Any Location, Including Directly from the Vendor. Other Features Speed up Entering Sales by Turning a Single Key into a "Function Key" to Record or Call up Needed Information. User Can Set up to 25 Keys.
Trac Line Software, Inc.

Position of the Comet Halley. *Compatible Hardware:* TI 99/4A. *Operating System(s) Required:* DX-10. *Language(s):* Extended BASIC. *Memory Required:* 48k.
cassette $16.95.
Derives the Declination, Right Ascension, Radius Vector, Elongation from the Sun & the Visual Magnitude of the Comet for Any Instant of Ephemeris Time.
Eastbench Software Products.

The Post-Soviet Industrial Geolocator: SSS Industrial Atlas. Jul. 1995. *Items Included:* 3 page introduction & how to, help for Windows. *Customer Support:* CD-ROM single with 150 ready-to-use layers, import capability/ compatibility to ARCINFO-MAPINFO, SPANS, IDRISI, AUTOCAD. Requires Windows environment.
Windows. IBM & compatibles (8Mb). CD-ROM disk $1195.00 (ISBN 1-887486-10-0, Order no.: SSS-GEOLOCATOR). *Optimal configuration:* DOS-OS, Windows, 8Mb.
Complete & Accurate Geo Locator of the Post-Soviet Industry & Industrial Data-Sets. Contains 40,500 Industrial Enterprise Data-Sets, 150 Digital Maps & Layers.
C I S M A P/Industrial Information Resources, Inc.

The Post-Soviet Industrial GeoLocator: SSS Industrial Atlas. Jul. 1995. *Items Included:* 3 page introduction & How to, help for Windows. *Customer Support:* CD-ROM single with 150 ready-to-use layers import capability/ compatibility to ARCINFO-MAPINFO, Spans IDRISI, AUTOCAD. Requires Windows Environment.
Windows - MS-DOS, OS/2. IBM & compatibles (8Mb). CD-ROM disk $1195.00 (ISBN 1-887486-10-0, Order no.: SSS-GEOLOCATOR). *Optimal configuration:* DOS-OS Windows 8Mb.
Complete & Accurate GeoLocator of the Post-Soviet Industry & Industrial Data-Sets. Contains 40,500 Industrial Enterprise Data-Sets, 150 Digital Maps & Layers.
CISMAP/Industrial Information Resources, Inc.

Postall. Version: 1.0. Jun. 1992. *Items Included:* Instruction manual. *Customer Support:* Customer support available.
MS-DOS 2.0 or higher. IBM compatibles (640k). disk $39.95. *Optimal configuration:* IBM compatible, all CPUs, MS-DOS or Windows, 640k RAM, VGA, EGA, OR CGA, printer.
Post & Distribute Documents to Accounting Categories Using Simple, Easily Understood Menu & Screen Format. Will Handle Sales, Cash Receipts, Checks, Payables, & Vouchers. Prints Comprehensive Reports. Provides for on Screen Corrections, Lookups of Previous Postings or Chart of Accounts. Also Monitors Document Numbers.
D W N.

PostCard/Tape Vault.
Macintosh Plus or higher. 3.5" disk $2999.00. $549.00 Tape Vault only.
Postproduction Facility Management System; Videotape Tracking & Management System.
Max 3, Inc.

PostCode. Version: 2.0. Nov. 1988. *Compatible Hardware:* Apple Macintosh. *Memory Required:* 512k. *Items Included:* 5.25" disk drive, cables. *Customer Support:* Free telephone support.
3.5" disk $1695.00.
Translates the Output from Most Macintosh Programs into Coding for a Compugraphic MCS Typesetter.
Mumford Micro Systems.

Postermaker Plus, 2 disks. Apr. 1988. *Compatible Hardware:* Apple Macintosh. *Memory Required:* 512k. *General Requirements:* Hard disk, printer.
3.5" disk $59.95 (Order no.: 33155).
Broderbund Software, Inc.

PosterMaker Plus Graphic. *Compatible Hardware:* Apple Macintosh.
3.5" disk write for info.
Broderbund Software, Inc.

Postermaker Plus Graphics Library, Vol. 1. Apr. 1988. *Compatible Hardware:* Apple Macintosh. *Memory Required:* 512k. *General Requirements:* Hard disk.
3.5" disk $29.95 (Order no.: 33455).
Broderbund Software, Inc.

PostHaste. *Compatible Hardware:* Apple Macintosh.
3.5" disk $59.95.
PostScript Programming for the Macintosh. Includes an Integrated Window Editor; Uploads & Captures Error Messages Without Leaving the Editor; Provides an Interactive Environment over AppleTalk. There Is No 32k File Limit. Numerous "Cookbook" Examples Are Included.
Micro Dynamics, Ltd.

PostScript Type: Volumes 1-17. *Customer Support:* Telephone support.
Macintosh Plus (1Mb). 3.5" disk $79.00-$129.00.
17 Volumes of PostScript for the Macintosh. Type Styles Include Script, Display & Body Text.
Publishing Solutions/MacTography.

PostScript UPC Version A Bar Code Font. Version: 1.0. Joel R. Postman. Feb. 1989. *Items Included:* Spiral bound manual, Hypercard stack. *Customer Support:* 90-day warranty, telephone support.
Macintosh (any). Apple Macintosh. contact publisher for price. *Optimal configuration:* Any Macintosh with a true PostScript- compatible printer.
This Font Enables the Macintosh User to Print PostScript UPC Version A Bar Codes Using Any Application Program Which Supports Fonts of Sixty Points or More, Including Most Popular Word Processors, Page Layout Programs & Label Printing Programs. An Included HyperCard Application, UPCMaker, Automatically Calculates the UPC Check Character Digit.
TPS Electronics.

Poultry Layer Management System.
Agri-Management Services, Inc. *Operating System(s) Required:* MS-DOS. *Memory Required:* 64k.
$995.00.
Texas Instruments, Personal Productivit.

POV-Ray. *Customer Support:* All of our products are unconditionally guaranteed.
DOS, Windows, Unix. CD-ROM disk $39.95 (Order no.: POVRAY). *Nonstandard peripherals required:* CD-ROM drive.
Compilation of Images, Source, Utilities & Tips on POV-Ray & 3D.
Walnut Creek CDRom.

Power! Version: 3.09. Pavel Breder. 1983-1985. *Compatible Hardware:* IBM PC & compatibles. *Operating System(s) Required:* CP/M, MS-DOS. *Language(s):* Assembly. *Memory Required:* 24k. *General Requirements:* 2 disk drives.
disk $169.00 ea., incl. manual.
MS-DOS. (ISBN 0-913733-01-6).
CP/M. (ISBN 0-913733-00-8).
Master Utility for Copying, Renaming, Deleting, Sizing, & Performing Other Operations on Any Disk Files. Ends Mistyping of Filenames by Allowing User to Select Files by Number. Also Tests Disks & Performs Other Disk Management Functions.
Computing!.

Power Amplifier Design Tutorial. (Electrical Engineering Tutorial Ser.: No. 6). *Compatible Hardware:* Apple II with Applesoft. *Operating System(s) Required:* Apple DOS 3.2, 3.3. (source code included). *Memory Required:* Apple 48k.
disk $39.95.
Deals with Vacuum Tube RF Power Amplifiers.
Dynacomp, Inc.

Power BASIC. Version: 2.0. Bob Zale. Feb. 1990. *Items Included:* 2 manuals, user's guide & reference guide 5.25" & 3.5" disks. *Customer Support:* Phone, fax, Vendor Forum B or Compuserve.
PC-DOS. IBM PC, XT, AT, 386 (512k). disk $129.00.
Accurate BASIC Language Compiler. Formerly Known as Turbo BASIC by Borland.
Spectra Publishing.

Power Bytes Action & Arcade. Oct. 1995. *Customer Support:* Free phone technical support via 1-800 number.
Windows. Contact publisher for price (ISBN 1-57600-025-7).
Top 10 Action & Arcade Games Available.
Digital Impact, Inc.

Power Bytes Board & Strategy. Oct. 1995. *Customer Support:* Free phone technical support via 1-800 number.
Windows. Contact publisher for price (ISBN 1-57600-026-5).
Top 10 Board & Strategy Games Available.
Digital Impact, Inc.

793

POWER BYTES BUSINESS & OFFICE

Power Bytes Business & Office Utilities. Oct. 1995. *Customer Support:* Free phone technical support via 1-800 number.
Windows. Contact publisher for price (ISBN 1-57600-027-3).
Top Ten Tools Used Most Frequenetly for Businesses & Offices.
Digital Impact, Inc.

Power Bytes Card & Casino Games. Oct. 1995. *Customer Support:* Free phone technical support via 1-800 number.
Windows. Contact publisher for price (ISBN 1-57600-028-1).
Top 10 Card & Casino Games Available.
Digital Impact, Inc.

Power Bytes Crossword Challenge. Oct. 1995. *Customer Support:* Free phone technical support via 1-800 number.
Windows. Contact publisher for price (ISBN 1-57600-036-2).
Top 10 Crossword Programs Available.
Digital Impact, Inc.

Power Bytes Desktop Tools & Personal Organizers. Oct. 1995. *Customer Support:* Free phone technical support via 1-800 number.
Windows. Contact publisher for price (ISBN 1-57600-029-X).
Top Desk Top Publishing Programs & Organizers.
Digital Impact, Inc.

Power Bytes Drawing & Publishing. Oct. 1995. *Customer Support:* Free phone technical support via 1-800 number.
Windows. Contact publisher for price (ISBN 1-57600-030-3).
Top Ten Drawing & Publishing Programs Available.
Digital Impact, Inc.

Power Bytes Education for All Ages. Oct. 1995. *Customer Support:* Free phone technical support via 1-800 number.
Windows. Contact publisher for price (ISBN 1-57600-031-1).
Top 10 Education Programs for Fun Learning Available.
Digital Impact, Inc.

Power Bytes Money & Finance. Oct. 1995. *Customer Support:* Free phone technical support via 1-800 number.
Windows. Contact publisher for price (ISBN 1-57600-032-X).
Top 10 Programs Available for Money & Finance.
Digital Impact, Inc.

Power Bytes Multimedia Tools. Oct. 1995. *Customer Support:* Free phone technical support via 1-800 number.
Windows. Contact publisher for price (ISBN 1-57600-033-8).
Top 10 Multimedia Tools Available.
Digital Impact, Inc.

Power Bytes Pro Football Guru. Oct. 1995. *Customer Support:* Free phone technical support via 1-800 number.
Windows. Contact publisher for price (ISBN 1-57600-035-4).
Top 10 Football Programs Available.
Digital Impact, Inc.

Power Bytes Utilities for Windows. Oct. 1995. *Customer Support:* Free phone technical support via 1-800 number.
Windows. Contact publisher for price (ISBN 1-57600-034-6).
Top 10 Utility Programs Available for Windows.
Digital Impact, Inc.

Power C. *Compatible Hardware:* IBM PC, PC XT, PC AT; IBM PS/2 Models 25/30/50/60/80. *Operating System(s) Required:* PC-DOS/MS-DOS 2.0 or higher. *Memory Required:* 256k. *General Requirements:* 2 disk drives or hard disk.
5-1/4" or 3-1/2" disk $19.95.
Library Source Code $10.00.
BCD Business Math $10.00.
C Compiler Including a 400-Function Library with Graphics Functions for Drawing Lines, Boxes, Circles, Pie Charts, etc. Supports the Latest Features of the Proposed ANSI C Standard & Is Compatible with Both MICROSOFT C & TURBO C. Includes Step-by-Step Tutorial & Sample Programs for Each Function.
MIX Software.

Power Ctrace. *Version:* 1.2. Nov. 1988. *Compatible Hardware:* IBM PC & compatibles. *Operating System(s) Required:* MS-DOS 2.0 or higher. *Memory Required:* 265k.
disk $19.95.
Stand-Alone Source-Code & Symbolic Debugger. Compatible with Mix Software Power C Compiler Language. Supports 8088, 8086, 80186, 80286 & 80386 Instruction Sets. Features Full Screen Interface; Code, Data, Stack Values, Register Values & Program Output Windows Display; & Instructions, Conditional Breakpoints on Values or Predefined Conditions Breakpoint Types. Also Includes Single Step by C Statement or Assembly Instruction, Continuous Stepping at Trace Speed, On-Line Help & Automatically Displays Variables.
MIX Software.

Power Disk. *Version:* 2.0. *Compatible Hardware:* Apple Macintosh.
3.5" disk $79.95.
Disk Cache.
Software Power Co.

Power Japanese. *Version:* 2.0. Nov. 1993. *Items Included:* Exercise book, pocket dictionary, installation guide, registration card, promotional material(s), flash cards. *Customer Support:* Free technical support; one year subscription to bi-weekly supplements, on line dictionary sent upon registration.
Microsoft Windows 3.1. IBM PC & compatibles (4Mb). CD-ROM disk $278.00 (ISBN 1-883653-02-9). *Nonstandard peripherals required:* Any MultiMedia (MPC) compatible soundcards. *Optimal configuration:* CD-ROM version requires a CD-ROM drive. *Networks supported:* Any (LAN) software such as Novell.
MultiMedia Windows Based for the PC in CD-ROM Format Which Integrates Approach to Speaking, Reading, & Writing Japanese & Uses Sound, Graphics, & Animation.
Bayware, Inc.

Power Japanese. *Version:* 2.0. Oct. 1995. *Items Included:* One registration card, one dictionary, one set of flashcards, one writing exercise book, one installation guide, one "Learning Strategy" book, Nikke weekly sample issue card, & Mangajm sample issue card. *Customer Support:* 30 day money-back guarantee & free technical support.
Microsoft Windows 3.1 or higher. IBM/PC compatible (8Mb). CD-ROM disk $278.00 (ISBN 1-883653-10-X). *Nonstandard peripherals required:* Multimedia PC with double-speed CD-ROM drive & Soundcard with microphone. *Networks supported:* Any Local Area Network (LAN) software such as Novell Lite or Personal Netware.
Multimedia Windows Based Program for the PC on CD-ROM for Learning Japanese. Consists of Sounds, Colorful Graphics & Animation.
BayWare, Inc.

Power Japanese. *Version:* 2.0. Dec. 1995. *Items Included:* 1 exercise book (spiral wrap bound), installation guide, reg. card. *Customer Support:* Free technical support.
Microsoft Windows 3.1. PC 386 or higher (4Mb, 8Mb recommended). CD-ROM disk $278.00. *Nonstandard peripherals required:* 7Mb HD space, VGA/SVGA, MPC. *Networks supported:* Novell or any LAN software.
This Is Arguably the Most Widely-Acclaimed Learning Program & Method for the Japanese Language. Power Japanese Enables You to Speak, Read, & Write Japanese in As Little As Ten Weeks. Colorful Graphics, Animation, Sound, & Innovative Drills & Games Are Combined to Provide a Rich & Exciting Learning Environment. Includes a 10,000 Word On-Line Dictionary, Option to Record & Compare Your Voice Against Native Speakers, Ability to Group & Play Different Phrases to Meet Your Specific Needs, & a Kana Word Processor. Also Comes with Flashcards, Romaji Chart, Comprehensive Learner's Dictionary, & an Exercise Book.
Bayware, Inc.

Power Macros for the Lotus 1-2-3 User. *Compatible Hardware:* IBM PC & compatibles. *General Requirements:* Lotus 1-2-3. *Items Included:* 2 diskettes, reference manual. *Customer Support:* Call individual software (90 days).
disk $49.95.
Eliminate Frustration & Increase User's Productivity with This Collection of Utility & Time-Saving Macros. Provides Users with an Instant Macro Locator, a Facility for Modifying Current Macros & Adding Additional Macros to the Library. A Point-&-Shoot Method of Accessing Macros Through a Pop-Up List of "Short Names".
Individual Software.

The Power of: Construction Management Using Multiplan. Jay C. Compton. Oct. 1984. *Operating System(s) Required:* MS-DOS.
disk $44.95 (ISBN 0-13-688094-0).
Supplies Worksheet Model for Analyzing Construction Information for MULTIPLAN. Readers Will Learn How to Use This Software to Determine Hourly Ownership & Operations Rates; Required Haul Units for Specific Jobs; Unit & Lump Sum Cost Estimates; Unit & Lump Sum Bidding; Labor, Equipment, & Other Costs; Subcontractor Payment Schedules; Cash Flow Management.
Prentice Hall.

The Power of: Construction Management Using 1-2-3. Jay C. Compton. Oct. 1984. *Operating System(s) Required:* MS-DOS.
disk $44.95 (ISBN 0-13-688243-9).
Supplies Worksheet Models for Analyzing Construction Information for 1-2-3. Readers Will Learn How to Use This Software to Determine Hourly Ownership & Operations Rates; Required Haul Units for Specific Jobs; Unit & Lump Sum Cost Estimates; Unit & Lump Sum Bidding; Labor, Equipment, & Other Costs; Subcontractor Payment Schedules; Cash Flow Management.
Prentice Hall.

The Power of: Financial Calculations for Lotus 1-2-3. Robert Williams. Mar. 1984. *Operating System(s) Required:* MS-DOS.
disk $28.95 (ISBN 0-13-687732-X).
Guide for Doing Financial Calculations with 1-2-3. Covers Interest & Annuity, Status, & Marketing.
Prentice Hall.

The Power of: Financial Calculations for Multiplan. Robert Williams. Mar. 1984. *Operating System(s) Required:* MS-DOS.
disk $28.95 (ISBN 0-13-687724-9).
Offers Guide to Financial Calculations, Including Interest & Annuities, Status, & Marketing.
Prentice Hall.

TITLE INDEX

The Power of: Multiplan. Robert Williams. Mar. 1984. *Operating System(s) Required:* MS-DOS. disk $28.95 (ISBN 0-13-687765-6).
Covers Accounts Receivable, Invoicing, Cost Recovery, Production Scheduling, Estimating, Checkbook, Accounts Payable, Payroll, Monthly Sales Report, Daily Inventory & Financial Forecasting.
Prentice Hall.

The Power of: 1-2-3. Robert Williams. Apr. 1984. *Operating System(s) Required:* MS-DOS. disk $28.95 (ISBN 0-13-687757-5).
Introduces & Teaches How to Use Lotus 1-2-3.
Prentice Hall.

The Power of: Professional Tax Planning Using Multiplan. Mitchell H. Jacobs. Oct. 1984. *Operating System(s) Required:* MS-DOS. disk $44.95 (ISBN 0-13-688268-4).
Attorney Shows How to Enlist the Help of MULTIPLAN to Calculate & Plan Both Individual & Corporate Federal Income Taxes. Topics Include: Using Joint & Unmarried Rates; Net Capital Gains; Fiduciary Income Taxes; Corporate Taxes; Lump Sum Distributions; Tax Shelters; & More.
Prentice Hall.

The Power of: Professional Tax Planning Using 1-2-3. Mitchell H. Jacobs. Oct. 1984. *Operating System(s) Required:* MS-DOS. disk $44.95 (ISBN 0-13-688264-6).
In This Guide, an Attorney Shows How to Enlist the Help of 1-2-3 to Calculate & Plan Both Individual & Corporate Federal Income Taxes. Topics Include: Using Joint & Unmarried Rates; Net Capital Gains; Fiduciary Income Taxes; Corporate Taxes; Lump Sum Distributions; Tax Shelters; & More.
Prentice Hall.

The Power of: Word by Microsoft. Robert Williams. Jul. 1984. *Operating System(s) Required:* MS-DOS. disk $29.95 (ISBN 0-13-688037-1).
Step-by-Step Exercises Show User How to Expand the Use of MICROSOFT WORD, No Matter What the Application.
Prentice Hall.

Power Print. *Version:* 1.1. Rob Renstrom. Nov. 1986. *Compatible Hardware:* Apple II, II+, IIe, IIc, IIgs. *Operating System(s) Required:* Apple DOS 3.3, ProDOS. *Language(s):* Machine, BASIC. *Memory Required:* 64k. *General Requirements:* Apple DMP, Apple ImageWriter I & II, Brother M-1509, Citizen 20 & 25, Epson (FX, JX, & EX Series), Okidata (92, 93, 192, & 193), Panasonic 1092 & 1093, or Star (Delta, Radix, SG, SD, & SR) printer.
disk $39.95.
Enables Users to "Download" a Second Typestyle into the Printer's Memory, So They Can Alternate Between the Standard Printer Font & a Custom Font with Special Characters & Symbols. Ten Custom Fonts Are Included on the Disk. a Font Editor Allows Users to Design Their Own Custom Fonts. AppleWorks Compatible. Allows Mixing of Graphics & Text.
Beagle Brothers.

Power Screen. *Compatible Hardware:* Atari. *Language(s):* BASIC.
disk $24.95 (ISBN 0-936200-54-5).
cassette $24.95 (ISBN 0-936200-54-5).
Menu-Driven Display List Generator.
Blue Cat.

Power-Sort. *Operating System(s) Required:* CP/M 80, MS-DOS, PC-DOS.
contact publisher for price.
Disk File Select/Sort/Merge Package Including Several Advanced Capabilities. Select Keys May Be Combined with Logical AND or OR Operations, May Contain Wild Card Characters, & May Each Compare on Less, Equal to, or Greater. Select & Sort Keys May Be Single or Double Integer, Alphanumeric, or HEX Strings. The Parameter String to Control the Select/Sort/Merge Operations May Be Interactively Provided, or May Be Supplied from a Parameter File.
Inner Access Corp.

Power Spanish. Jul. 1994. *Items Included:* 1 user manual (saddle-stitched). *Customer Support:* Free technical support, online grammar reference sent in registration.
Microsoft Windows 3.1. IBM PC & compatibles (4Mb). CD-ROM disk $189.00 (ISBN 1-883653-04-5). *Nonstandard peripherals required:* Any Multimedia (MPC) compatible soundcards, CD-ROM drive. *Optimal configuration:* Double speed CD-ROM drive. *Networks supported:* Any LAN (Local Area Network) such as Novell Netware Lite.
MultiMedia Windows Based for the PC on CD-ROM Format Which Integrates Approach to Speaking, Reading, & Grammatical Structure in Spanish. It Uses Sound, Colorful Graphics, Animation & Video Clips.
Bayware, Inc.

Power Spanish. Nov. 1995. *Items Included:* One registration card, one saddle-stitched installation guide, & one "Learning Strategy" manual, video for Windows. *Customer Support:* 30 day money-back guarantee & free technical support.
Microsoft Windows 3.1 or higher. IBM/PC compatible (8Mb). CD-ROM disk $189.00 (ISBN 1-883653-11-8). *Nonstandard peripherals required:* Multimedia PC with double-speed CD-ROM drive & Sound Blaster compatible soundcard with microphone.
Networks supported: Any Local Area Network (LAN) software such as Novell Netware Life or Personal Netware.
Multimedia Windows Based Program for the PC on CD-ROM for Learning Spanish. Consist of Sounds, Videos, Colorful Graphics & Animation.
BayWare, Inc.

Power Spanish. Sep. 1995. *Items Included:* Registration card, installation guide, Learning Strategy Book, video for Windows. *Customer Support:* 30 day money-back guarantee & free technical support.
Microsoft Windows 3.1 or higher. IBM PC or compatibles (8Mb). CD-ROM disk $189.00 (ISBN 1-883653-08-8). *Nonstandard peripherals required:* Multimedia PC with CD-ROM drive (double-speed or higher) & soundcard with microphone. *Networks supported:* Any Local Area Network (LAN) software such as Novell Netware Lite or Personal Netware.
Multimedia Windows Based Program for the PC on CD-ROM for Learning Spanish. Consist of Sounds, Videos, Colorful Graphics & Animation.
BayWare, Inc.

Power Spanish. Dec. 1995. *Items Included:* 1 exercise book (spiral wrap bound), installation guide, reg. card. *Customer Support:* Free technical support.
Microsoft Windows 3.1. PC 386 or higher (4Mb, 8Mb recommended). CD-ROM disk $189.00. *Nonstandard peripherals required:* 7Mb HD space, VGA/SVGA, MPC. *Networks supported:* Novell or any LAN software.
A Quick & Painless Approach to Learning the Basics of Spanish Without Being Bogged down in a Lot of Unnecessary Grammatical Details. Uses Animation, Color Graphics, Sound, Games, Drills & Videos to Provide You with Enough Confidence to Start Communicating in Spanish As Soon As Possible. Includes Option to Record & Compare Your Voice Against Native Speakers, Instantaneous Translation of Every Word & Phrase in the Program, & the Ability to Set the Playback Speed of Words & Phrases in the Program Dynamically. Ideal for the Busy Student & Professional.
Bayware, Inc.

Power Transmission I. Apr. 1985. *Compatible Hardware:* Apple II+, IIe; IBM PC. *Operating System(s) Required:* PC-DOS, Apple DOS 3.3. *Language(s):* BASIC (source code included). *Memory Required:* Apple 48k, IBM 128k. *Customer Support:* Telephone.
$125.00.
Contains 5 Sub-programs Including Rotating Moment of Inertia, Drive Calculations, Shaft Properties, Shaft Stresses & Belt & Chain Center Distance/Length Calculations. Includes Graphics.
PEAS (Practical Engineering Applications Software).

PowerBase. *Version:* 2.3. Dec. 1986. *Compatible Hardware:* IBM PC & compatibles, PC XT, PC AT, PS/2. *Operating System(s) Required:* PC-DOS, MS-DOS 2.0 or higher. *Memory Required:* 384k. *General Requirements:* 2 disk drives.
$349.00 (ISBN 0-924138-00-9, Order no.: P230CU5).
Dealer Starter Kit. $235.00 (ISBN 0-924138-02-5, Order no.: P23DSK).
Dealer Starter Kit for Wang.
Relational Data Base Management System Enabling User to Store up to 64,00 Records per File with 5,200 Bytes per Record, 64 Fields per Record, & 80 Bytes per Field. All Files Are Randomly Accessed Using a B-Tree for Indexing. ZOOM Features Allow Instant Access to Other Levels Within the Data Base. Includes Password Protection & TopView Compatibility. Operations Are Both Menu & Command Driven, & up to 10 Files Can Be Opened at Once. Links to Popular Software Packages.
PowerBase Systems, Inc.

POWERBASE APPLICATION TEMPLATES

PowerBase Application Templates, 8 disks. Apr. 1985. *Compatible Hardware:* IBM PC & compatibles. *Operating System(s) Required:* MS-DOS, PC-DOS. *Memory Required:* 384k. *General Requirements:* 2 disk drives, PowerBase 2.10 to 2.3 software.
Set. $239.60 (ISBN 0-924138-17-3, Order no.: A8).
disk $29.95 ea.
Contains 8 Application Templates for Use in Conjunction with POWER-BASE 2.10 or 2.2. Designed for Dealers Only.
PowerBase Systems, Inc.
Business T&E Analysis System.
(ISBN 0-924138-10-6, Order no.: ABTEA).
Tracks Travel & Entertainment Expenses by Department & Employee. Reports on Expenses by Employee, by Department, etc.
Fixed Asset Management System.
(ISBN 0-924138-11-4, Order no.: AFAM).
Maintains Records of Fixed Assets, Both Owned & Leased, Their Worth (During Depreciation), Employees Who Use Them, Leasors & Leasing Terms. Reports on Leased & Owned Assets, Employees Who Use the Assets & Current Value of Each Asset.
Human Resource Management System.
(ISBN 0-924138-12-2, Order no.: AHRM).
Maintains Detailed Employee Records, Including General Personnel Data, Salaries/Wage Rates & History, Education & Skills, Benefits, Attendance & Vacation Time, etc. Reports on Employees in Each EEO Classification & Department, Current Salary Expenses, & Employee/Personnel Detail Listings.

Inventory Control Management System.
(ISBN 0-924138-13-0, Order no.: AIC). *Tracks Invoices, Parts Suppliers, Shipping, Warehousing, Receiving & Purchase Orders. Reports on Inventory Status & Valuation, Reorder Points, Suppliers, etc.*
Job Costing System.
(ISBN 0-924138-14-9, Order no.: AJC). *Maintains Records on Current, Past & Prospective Projects, Tasks Involved in Each Project, & Fee Structures & Time Frames; Lets User Track Current Status of Each Project, Costs Incurred to Date Variance Between Budgeted & Actual Costs & Project Prioritizing; Labels Definitions to Send Correspondence & Current Clients; Reports for Analyzing Project Statuses & Costs.*
Membership Association Management System.
(ISBN 0-924138-09-2, Order no.: AAMT). *Maintains Detailed Records of Current, Past & Prospective Members, As Well As Registrants at Meetings or Special Events. Has Prepared Form Letters, Label Definitions & Reports for Various Member Statuses, & Creates Invoices & Statements for Sign-Ups & Renewals.*
Order Processing-Invoicing System.
(ISBN 0-924138-15-7, Order no.: AOPI).
Sales Prospect Tracking System.
(ISBN 0-924138-16-5, Order no.: ASPT).

PowerBuilder 3 Application Development for Windows. James Pujals, Jr. Oct. 1994. *Items Included:* 624 page book with diskette. *Customer Support:* Free telephone support 8am to 5pm CST; 30 day unlimited warranty.
PC-DOS/MS-DIS operating system, Version 3.3 or higher. Microsoft Windows 3.1. 386SX personal computer or higher. A 3.5" high density disk drive (8Mb or higher). disk $60.00 (ISBN 0-9644117-0-9, Order no.: BK9401). *Nonstandard peripherals required:* VGA display, a mouse that is supported by your Windows system. *Addl. software required:* PowerBuilder 3 Enterprise or Desktop. *Optimal configuration:* 1Mb hard disk space plus the space required for Windows & PowerBuilder & your database & applications.
Learn Powersoft's PowerBuilder & How to Develop PowerBuilder Applications Using Corporate PowerBuilder Application Development Methodology. Learn the Technology & Usage of the Included PBADTOOL Toolset. The Book Contains Cross Reference Tables & Undocumented Information. Learn Client-Server Concepts, Object-Oriented Programming, Event-Driven Programming, Relational Databases, SQL, & the Use of PowerBuilder Painters.
Client-Server Campaigns, Inc.

PowerCADD: Power Macintosh Version of PowerDraw. *Version:* 2.0. Apr. 1994. *Items Included:* User manual, Applicaiton diskettes, Samples of libraries available. *Customer Support:* Free with registration, Newsletter.
Macintosh. PowerMacintosh (4Mb). 3.5" disk $795.00, International Version ,895.00.
A Full-Featured ComputerAided Design Application Designed to Take Advantage of the PowerPC Technology in the Power Macintosh. Modular, PowerCADD Can Be Customized for Even Greater Efficiency. Externals for Trade Specific Functions Are Included. Addresses the Design & Drafting Needs of Architects, Mechanical & Electrical Engineering, As Well As Facilities Management, Graphic Designers & More.
Engineered Software.

PowerChurch Plus. *Version:* 4.3. Aug. 1989. *Items Included:* Manual. *Customer Support:* Available by telephone.
MS-DOS (640k). IBM PC compatible. disk $795.00. *Networks supported:* Novell, any NetBios.
Church Administration Package. Integrated System Includes Membership Contributions, & Other Functions. Demo Package.
F1 Software.

PowerDot II. *Compatible Hardware:* TRS-80 Model I Level I, Model III, Model 4. *Operating System(s) Required:* TRSDOS. *Language(s):* Machine. *Memory Required:* 48k. *General Requirements:* Printer.
disk $59.95.
Graphics Program Which Allows the User to Make Low-Resolution Graphics (Using the Computer's Memory As a "Drawing Board") & Turn Them into High-Resolution Dot Graphics on a Printer. Designed for Use by Designers, Architects, Engineers, & Other Graphics Users. AUTODRAW Routines Draw Lines or Circles Between Any 2 Points, Even If 1 Point Is Not Visible on Screen. Makes Block Graphics, Hi-Res Mode & an Ultra-Res Mode Possible, Depending upon Printer Capabilities.
Powersoft, Inc.

PowerDraw. *Compatible Hardware:* TRS-80 Model I Level I, Model III, Model 12. *Operating System(s) Required:* TRSDOS. *Language(s):* Assembly. *Memory Required:* 32k.
disk $39.95.
Screen Graphics Editor That Assists in Designing, Printing or Using Graphics Screens in Other Programs. Controlled by Joystick or Cursor Controls; Has Both Graphics & Text Modes; Merges Graphics & Text; Saves Graphics on Disk or Tape in 6 Possible Formats; Allows Manipulation of Whole Screen Position; Sequences Screen in Movie-Like Fashion.
Powersoft, Inc.

PowerDraw: Advanced CAD Drafting Design System. *Version:* 6.0. *Items Included:* User manual, 5 diskettes. *Customer Support:* free with registration.
Macintosh Plus or higher. disk $795.00, International Version ,895.00 (ISBN 1-878250-00-0). *Nonstandard peripherals required:* Hard disk drive, ImageWriter, LaserWriter or plotter.
A CAD Standard in 36 Countries & 5 Languages. One of the Fastest 2-D Drafting & Design Programs on the Market. Provides Mainframe Features with Macintosh Ease. A Built In Plotter Driver, Macro Programming Language, Full Color Printing/Plotting, Multiple Scale, Unlimited Layers, Isometric Shear & Perspective, Array Duplication, User Definable Line Attributes, Fill/Hatch Patterns, Editable Text, Bit Map/Object Fractional-Degree Rotation, Auto Dimensioning, Symbol Libraries, Read/Write PICT Files & Advanced Dynamic Snapping are Just a Few of PowerDraw's Hundreds of Reliable Features.
Engineered Software.

Powerdraw Translator. *Version:* 2.0. *Items Included:* 1 user's manual, 1 diskette. *Customer Support:* Free with registration.
Macintosh (1Mb). 3.5" disk $275.00.
System Reliability, Flexibly & Accurately Converts Drawings Between PoverDraw, Illustrates/EPS & PICT File Formats. It Also Gives User the Ability to Read PowerDraw 2.0, Clipboard/Scrapbook, MacDraw, MacDraw II, Claris CAD, Library & HPGL File Formats.
Engineered Software.

PowerForms. Sep. 1995. *Items Included:* Users manual. *Customer Support:* Technical support.
Newton can build forms on Macintosh, Windows or Newton (2Mb). disk $119.00.
Lets You Design Custom Data-Entry Forms on the Macintosh, PC-Compatible Computer or Directly on the Newton PDA. Provides a Variety of Creation Tools Such As Text Fields, Radio Buttons, Check Boxes, Pop Lists, Ink & Paragraph Fields, Formulas & Currency Fields, & Graphical Borders & Text.
HealthCare Communications.

Powerful Business Software. *Version:* 4.1. 1982. *Compatible Hardware:* IBM PC & compatibles. *Operating System(s) Required:* MS-DOS. *Language(s):* Compiled QUICKBASIC. *Memory Required:* 128k. *Customer Support:* Unlimited telephone support for life of originally installed software.
disk $995.00.
demo disk $56.00.
Order Entry, Invoicing, Inventory Control, Accounts Receivable & Sales Analysis with Mailing Lists, Call Planning & History/Forecasting. Options Include Accounts Payable, Payroll, General Ledger, Job Costing, Bill-of-Materials.
Media Computing Corp.

Powerful Presentations Using Your IBM-PC for the Classroom of the Future. Annette Lamb. 1992. *Items Included:* Handbook/workbook with 3 1/2" work diskette that contains exercises, graphics, sample files. Instructor's guide with instructor's diskette. *Customer Support:* Technical support from editorial staff.
MS-DOS 2.1 or higher. IBM PS/2, PC/XT, AT & compatibles (512k). $39.95 handbook/wkbk. (ISBN 0-89262-394-2). *Optimal configuration:* Mouse recommended.
$50.00 instr's. guide (ISBN 0-89262-406-X).
Learn to Create Printed, Projected, & Desktop Presentations As Well As Professional Display Materials Using Your IBM or Compatible, LINKWAY, & EXPRESS PUBLISHER Software. Project or Print Your Creations.
Career Publishing, Inc.

Powerful Presentations Using Your Macintosh for the Classroom of the Future: With Publish It! Easy. Annette Lamb. 1992. *Items Included:* Handbook/workbook; 3 1/2" diskette (contains exercises, graphics, sample files). Instructor's guide: $50.00 includes instructor's diskette, schedules, lesson plans & objectives, test items, outlines, project ideas, checklists, transparency masters. *Customer Support:* Technical support from editorial staff.
Macintosh Plus, MAC Classic, SE, II, IIcx, LC, IIsi. $39.95 handbook/wkbk. (ISBN 0-89262-393-4). *Optimal configuration:* Two 3 1/2" disk drives. Hard drive strongly recommended.
$50.00 instr's. guide (ISBN 0-89262-401-9).
Create Printed, Projected, & Desktop Presentations. Provides Step-by-Step Instructions to Help You Create Effective Presentation & Display Materials on the Computer. Project Those Items for Classroom Use. Print on Printer.
Career Publishing, Inc.

Powergames III. *Items Included:* Installation Guide.
IBM PC. Contact publisher for price (ISBN 0-87321-090-5, Order no.: CDD-3051).
Activision, Inc.

PowerLedger. *Compatible Hardware:* Atari ST. 3.5" disk $79.95 (ISBN 0-916439-82-8, Order no.: 510).
Analysis Package Featuring 65536 x 65536 Spreadsheet Cells, Built-In Calculator, Notepad, & Integrated Graphics. Other Features Include 37 Math Functions, 14-Digit Precission, & Seven Windows to Show One of Seven Types of Charts or Another Section of the Spreadsheet.
Abacus.

Powerload. *Version:* 1.0. Apr. 1987. *Compatible Hardware:* Commodore 64, IBM PC, PS/2 & MS-DOS & compatibles. (source code included).

TITLE INDEX

Memory Required: 64k. General Requirements: X-10, Inc. Powerhouse Programmable Controller-power line carrier for home/industrial control.
disk $20.00.
Software Package to Load X-10 Inc. POWERHOUSE Computer Interface Model CP290 for Power Line Carrier Home Control. Features: (1) Read or Enter Day & Time; (2) Enter or Delete Exciting Events; (3) Display All Programmed Events to Screen; (4) Print out to Printer All Programmed Events; (5) Powerload 128 Events in Less Than 3 Minutes; (6) Use Computer As a Direct Controller.
Jance Assocs.

PowerMacros for the Excel User. *General Requirements:* Microsoft Excel. *Items Included:* 2 Diskettes, reference manual. *Customer Support:* Call Individual Software (90 days).
Macintosh. 3.5" disk $49.95.
IBM & compatibles. disk $49.95.
Collection of Shortcuts, Utilites & Keystroke & Time Savers for Excel. Provides for Additional Macros to Be Added to the Current Library.
Individual Software.

PowerMail. *Compatible Hardware:* TRS-80 Model I Level I, Model III. *Operating System(s) Required:* TRSDOS. *Language(s):* Machine. *Memory Required:* 32k. *General Requirements:* 2 disk drives.
disk $99.95.
Mass Mailing System with Enhanced Operating Speed. 24 User-Defined "Flags" Allow User to Track Mailings. User Decides on Category Separations & the Ways in Which They Are to Be Accomplished. Manipulates Files up to 65,535 Names; Allows 2-Level Sorts; Prints File Subsets with the Use of Flag Settings; Binary Search Mode for Item Location; Converts Files from Some Other Mailing List Systems Without Re-Entering the Information.
Powersoft, Inc.

PowerMail Plus. *Compatible Hardware:* TRS-80 Model I, Model II, Model III, Model 4, Model 12, Model 16.
contact publisher for price.
Powersoft, Inc.

PowerMenu. *Version:* 5.0. *Compatible Hardware:* IBM PC, PCjr, PC XT, PC AT, PC compatibles. *Operating System(s) Required:* PC-DOS/MS-DOS 2.0 or higher. *Memory Required:* 256k. *Customer Support:* Free unlimited tech support for 1 year.
disk $89.95, incl. manual.
Menu-Driven Software Which Enables Users to Use Their PC in a Menu Mode. Provides On-Line Help. Includes Menu-Driven Tools That Enable Users to Change File Attributes, Change Disk Labels, Modify Screen Colors, or Locate a Lost File. Works with Either Floppy or Hard Disks.
Brown Bag Software.

Powerpak Electrical Distribution. *Items Included:* Bound manual. *Customer Support:* Free hotline - no time limit; 30 day limited warranty; updates are $5/disk plus S&H.
MS-DOS 2.0 or higher. IBM & compatibles (128k). disk $169.95. *Nonstandard peripherals required:* Color graphics card; printer optional.
Simplifies the Calculations Associated with Electric Utility Service. Facilitates Secondary-Voltage & Primary-Distribution Radial-Feeder Analyses. Menu-Driven & Data-File Oriented. Establish Your Own Parameter Files for Primary & Secondary Conductors & Distribution Transformers. This Eliminates the Need to Repeatedly Look up Specifications When Analyzing Circuits.
Dynacomp, Inc.

Powersheet. Sep. 1989. *Items Included:* Spiral bound manual, 3 free worksheet business applications for Lotus 1-2-3. *Customer Support:* 90 day free, phone support.
MS-DOS (512k). IBM XT/AT or PS/2 & compatibles. $45.00. *Addl. software required:* Lotus 1-2-3 2.0/2.01. *Optimal configuration:* 640k RAM, hard disk.
Serves as Control Center for One-Touch Access to User Worksheets. Fully Menu Driven Macro Library for Essential Worksheet Functions Including Data & Range Manipulation, File Handling, String Manipulation, Printing & Printer Control. Macros Can Be Transferred to User Worksheets Via Transfer Menus.
Compusense.

Powerstation: Data Analysis Package. *Version:* 5.51. Oct. 1995. *Items Included:* Users manual, complete documentation, installation assistance, re-installation if accidentally destroyed. *Customer Support:* 1st year Alpha Plus support is free, subsequent years are optional & cost about 20% of the software price, includes telephone technical assistance, free updates with new releases, conferences, training & user seminars.
MS-DOS 3.0 or higher (640k); Windows 3.X; OS/2. IBM compatible XT & up. $1250.00. *Nonstandard peripherals required:* Math coprocessor chip. *Networks supported:* Ethernet or Token Ring coaxil cable or twisted pair, Novell, 3 Com, IBM.
Provides Statistical Analysis, Word Processing, Communications, Graphics, Data Base Management, & Spreadsheet Operations. Designed for Accountants, Economists, Financial Analysts, Market Analysts, Planners & Others Who Use Time Series Data. Menu or Command Driven Options for Ease of Use.
Alphametrics Corp.

Powerstation: Integrated Research Publishing System. *Version:* 5.51. Oct. 1995. *Items Included:* Users manual, complete documentation, installation assistance, re-installastion if accidentally destroyed. *Customer Support:* 1st year Alpha Plus support is free, subsequent years are optional & cost about 20% of the software price, includes telephone technical assistance, free updates with new releases, conferences, training & user seminars.
MS-DOS 3.0 or higher; Windows 3.X; OS/2. IBM compatible XT & up. $1500.00. *Nonstandard peripherals required:* Math Coprocessor chip. *Addl. software required:* Image management/DTP package. *Networks supported:* Ethernet or Token Ring coaxil cable or twisted pair Novell, 3 Com, IBM.
Turnkey System Reduces Turnaround Time for Preparation of Research Publications. Prepares Presentation-Quality Graphs for Incorporation into Publications Without Pasteup. Spreadsheets Are Seamlessly Imported/Exported. Complete Analysis Capabilities Are Included.
Alphametrics Corp.

Powerstyx. *Customer Support:* Back up disks available.
Amiga (512k). $14.95.
Battle Your Way Through Chomping Skulls, Perilous Scissors, Deadly Crosses & Heart Pounding Time Restrictions in This Action Packed Game. You, As the Artist, Must Uncover 15 Different Art Masterpieces, Hidden Beneath Each Treacherous Screen.
DigiTek Software.

PowerText BookMaker. *Version:* 3.2. Apr. 1988. *Compatible Hardware:* IBM PC & compatibles; Tandy 1000 or compatibles. *Operating System(s) Required:* PC-DOS/MS-DOS, OS/2. *Memory Required:* 512k. *General Requirements:* Laser printer; PowerText Formatter V-3.2 & any word processor. *Items Included:* Manual & disks. *Customer Support:* By telephone or mail.
3.5" or 5.25" disk (Includes PowerText) Formatter $395.00.
In Conjunction with Word Processing Software, Automatically Lays Out & Prints a Wide Variety of Book & Booklet Formats Ready for Binding (Center Stitching, Perfect Binding, or Looseleaf). Supports Two Varieties of Calendar Layouts, & Two Types of Mailer/Flyers, Addressed from a List of Names & Addresses (Typed or Extracted from a Database), Ready for Folding, Stapling & Mailing. Typesets Letters, Memos, & Reports.
Beaman Porter, Inc.

PowerText Formatter. *Version:* 3.2. Mar. 1989. *Compatible Hardware:* Compaq 386; IBM PC, PS/2; Tandy 1000. *Operating System(s) Required:* PC-DOS, MS-DOS. *Language(s):* Turbo Pascal. *Memory Required:* 512k. *General Requirements:* Laser or any other printer. *Items Included:* Manual & disks. *Customer Support:* By mail or telephone.
disk $199.00, incl. Font Manager.
Allows Users to Produce Documents with Justified, True Proportional Text; Footnotes on the Same Page; Multiple Columns of Text and/or Numbers; Outlines with Automatically Numbered & Indented Entries; & Wide Documents. The Program Is an Adaptation of the PowerText Word Processing System, & Can Be Used with Any Editor or Word Processor Which Produces Standard ASCII Files. Supports All LaserJet's Cartridges & Soft Fonts. Not Copy Protected. Supports Any Dot Matrix or Letter Quality Printer. Includes a Font Manager.
Beaman Porter, Inc.

PowerText Professional & BookMaker. *Version:* 4.0. David P. Guest. Apr. 1992. *Items Included:* Speller, 300 page manual, fonts, pre-defined styles. *Customer Support:* Telephone & mail - no charge, on site training $35 an hr., 5 yr. warranty.
MS-DOS. IBM & compatibles. disk $250.00 ea., $495.00 for both PowerPro & BookMaker. *Optimal configuration:* IBM or compatible MS-DOS, any printer, laserjet for the BookMaker. *Networks supported:* All.
State of the Art Product, Featuring Pull down Menus, Multiple Resizable Windows, Context Sensitive Help, Mouse Support, Clock, Calendar & Calculator. The PowerText BookMaker Is an Imposition & Printing Product Which Takes PowerText Professional Output & Transforms It into Books, Booklets, Flyers, Calendars & Invitations - Ready for Mailing, Binding, or Folding & Stapling.
Beaman Porter, Inc.

P.P. Memo. *Version:* 3.0. *Items Included:* Manual (with 90+ page hard copy of document contents on disk) & software (single 360K 5.25" or 720K 3.5" diskette, or 800K 3.5" for Macintosh)-- annotated offering circular, glossary of terms, sample introduction letter to potential investors, subscription agreement, subscription administration & tracking spreadsheet, list of agencies to contact for more information. *Customer Support:* Provided by JIAN at (415) 941-9191.
IBM PC & compatibles (512K), Macintosh. $149.00. *Nonstandard peripherals required:* Hard disk recommended. *Addl. software required:* PC: word processor compatible with MS Word, PCWrite, Q&A, 1st Choice, WordPerfect & most others. PC's spreadsheet: Lotus 1-2-3 & 2.01 compatible. Macintosh: word processor: MacWrite 4.5 MS Word 3.01 compatible. Macintosh spreadsheet: SYLK compatible (includes MS Excel, MS Works & others).
Template with Nomenclature for a Private

PR*Plus (Payroll). Version: 6.35. Oct. 1990. Compatible Hardware: IBM PC & compatibles. Operating System(s) Required: PC-DOS/MS-DOS 3.1. Memory Required: 640k. Items Included: Documentation manual; Quick Start Users Guide. Customer Support: 6 months toll free support & updates; 90 day unlimited warranty; annual maintenance (support & updates) $200.00.
$795.00.
Includes: Check Writing or After-the-Fact, Multiple Rate Tables, 941, W-2's, etc. & Handles Tip Income.
UniLink.

Practica Musica. Version: 2.2. Feb. 1989. Compatible Hardware: Apple Macintosh. Memory Required: 512k. Items Included: disk operating manual, textbook. Customer Support: 206-889-0927.
3.5" disk $125.00 (ISBN 0-929444-01-9, Order no.: PM01).
Music Training Program Featuring Sampled Sound, MIDI Compatibility, Interactive Staff Notation, & a Wide Range of Activities. The User Can Practice Ear Training for Intervals, Melody, Rhythm, & Chords. Learn Pitch Reading, Spelling of Intervals & Chords, & Write Custom Ear Training Melodies. Can Also Invent Its Own Melodies & Rhythms with the User's Choice of Scale, Meter, & Keep Personal Scores.
Ars Nova Software.

Practical Antenna Design & Analysis: Volume 1. R P Haviland. Jun. 1988. General Requirements: BASIC.
Amiga, any series (256k). 3.5" disk $39.95 (ISBN 0-9621208-2-0).
Apple & compatibles (64k). disk $39.95 (ISBN 0-9621208-3-9).
Commodore C-64/C-128 (64k). disk $39.95 (ISBN 0-9621208-4-7).
IBM-PC (256k). disk $39.95 (ISBN 0-9621208-5-5).
Thirty-Two Computer Programs for the Design & Analysis of Practical Antennas: Dipole, Vertical, Loop, Helix, Horn, Dish, Diskcone, Quad, Yagi, Arrays. Mast & Tower Design, Plus Wire & Element Selection. A Copy of the Original Mininec is Included.
MiniLab Books.

Practical Antenna Design & Analysis, Volume 2. Jun. 1991.
Amiga. disk $39.95. Addl. software required: Basic.
PC-DOS. IBM (256k). disk $39.95. Addl. software required: Basic.
Extends Computer Programs from Volume 1 with an Additional 33 Programs: Broad-Band Dipoles, Arrays, Beverage Antenna, Rhombics Loops, Waveguide Types. Includes Programs for Waveguide & Transmission Lines, Others.
MiniLab Books.

Practical Pipeline Hydraulics Gas & Liquid Networks. Items Included: Full manual. No other products required. Customer Support: Free telephone support - no time limit. 30 day warranty.
MS-DOS 3.2 or higher. IBM & compatibles (512k). disk $689.95.
Menu-Driven Collection of Routines for Solving Standard Pipeline Engineering Problems. With PPH You May Calculate Pressure Needs, Required Pipe Sizes, & Pipe Lengths, As Well As Steady-State Network Analysis for Gas & Liquid Pipeline Systems. The Steady-State Flow Models Used Include: Hazen-Williams, Oliphant, Panhandle A & B, A.G.A. Fluid Flow, Beggs-Brill Multiphase Flow, Weymouth, & Colebrook-White. Handles Both U.S. & Metric Units.
Dynacomp, Inc.

Practical Pipeline Hydraulics: Gas & Liquid Networks. 1992. Items Included: Detailed manuals included with all Dynacomp products. Customer Support: Free telephone support to original customer - no time limit; 30 day limited warranty.
MS-DOS 3.2 or higher. IBM PC & compatibles (512k). $649.95 (Add $5.00 for 3 1/2" format; 5 1/4" format standard). Optimal configuration: IBM, MS-DOS 2.0 or higher, 384k RAM, CGA or compatible graphics capabilities, & a hard disk.
A Menu-Driven Collection of Routines for Solving Standard Pipeline Engineering Problems. With PPH You May Calculate Pressure Needs, Required Pipe Sizes, & Pipe Lengths, As Well As Steady-State Network Analysis for Gas & Liquid Pipeline Systems. The Steady-State Flow Models Used Include: Hazen-Williams, Oliphant, Panhandle A & B, A.G.A. Fluid Flow, Beggs-Brill Multiphase Flow, Weymouth, & Colebrook-White. U.S. & Metric Units.
Dynacomp, Inc.

Practical Theory. Sandy Feldstein. 1984-85. Compatible Hardware: Atari, Apple II, Commodore 64, IBM PC & compatibles, Macintosh. Memory Required: 64k. General Requirements: CGA card & color monitor for IBM.
IBM. 3.5" disk $299.95 (ISBN 0-88284-457-1, Order no.: 3535).
IBM. disk $299.95 (ISBN 0-88284-458-X, Order no.: 3500).
Apple, Commodore. disk $299.95 (ISBN 0-88284-459-8, Order no.: 2404).
Atari. 3.5" disk $299.95 (ISBN 0-88284-460-1, Order no.: 3510).
Macintosh. 3.5" disk $399.95 (ISBN 0-88284-461-X, Order no.: 3483).
Yamaha C1. disk $299.95 (ISBN 0-88284-462-8, Order no.: 3482).
Apple 3.5. disk $299.95 (ISBN 0-88284-482-2, Order no.: 3460).
Complete Sequential Course in Music Theory Correlated with a Text/Workbook. Reinforces All Music Theory Learning. MIDI Compatible. 3-Volume Set.
Alfred Publishing Co., Inc.

Practice Advantage. Version: 2.02. Items Included: Complete documentation. Customer Support: Toll-free support (prices vary); hands-on seminars & on-site instruction (price varies).
MS-DOS. IBM or 100% compatible (384k). disk $595.00. Optimal configuration: 80286, 80386, or 80486-based PC, 640k RAM. Networks supported: Novell.
Features Batch or On-Line Transaction Entry, Quick Billing, Complete Accounts Receivable, & Flexible Management Reports. Staff or Operators Can Enter Time & Expenses Daily, Weekly, or Monthly. Can Bill by Service & Retainer. Plain Paper & Form Invoices & Statements Available. Can Add Free-Form Text to Each Description on an Invoice.
Prentice Hall Professional Software.

Practice Partner Appointment Scheduler. Version: 4.3. 1993. Compatible Hardware: IBM PC & compatibles. Operating System(s) Required: MS-DOS, SCO UNIX. Memory Required: 512k. General Requirements: Hard disk, printer. Items Included: Manual, diskettes. Customer Support: Through local resellers or by telephone to main office.
disk $595.00 (ISBN 0-926202-01-4, Order no.: 200).
Coordinates Appointments with Physicians' Schedules & Office Resources. Users May Define an Unlimited Number of Different Daily Schedules. Includes Unlimited Double Bookings, Hold Slots for Drop-Ins, Patient Registration, & Patient Inquiry. Reports Include Encounter Forms, Hospital Rounds List, Charts to Pull, Reminders, & Productivity Analysis.
Physician Micro Systems, Inc.

Practice Partner Medical Billing III. Version: 4.1. Jul. 1994. Compatible Hardware: IBM PC & compatibles. Operating System(s) Required: MS-DOS or SCO UNIX. Language(s): C. Memory Required: 640k. Items Included: Manuals, diskettes. Customer Support: Through local resellers or by telephone to main office. $3200.00 - $4500.00.
Medical Billing & Posting Is Done from a Single Screen, Comprehensive Reports, Aged Accounts Receivables, & Relational Query for Custom Reports; Forms Generator for Customizing Insurance, Billing & Encounter Statements; Built-In Letters; Unlimited Fee Schedules; Electronic Claims Submission.
Physician Micro Systems, Inc.

Practice Partner Medical Writer. Version: 3.0. Oct. 1985. Compatible Hardware: IBM PC & compatibles. Operating System(s) Required: MS-DOS. Language(s): C. Memory Required: 384k. General Requirements: 2 disk drives or hard disk, printer. Items Included: Manual, diskettes. Customer Support: Through local resellers or by telephone to main office.
disk $295.00 (Order no.: 700).
Word Processor for Physicians. Features Fill-in-the-Blank Boilerplate and 157,000 Word English-Medical Spelling Checker.
Physician Micro Systems, Inc.

Practice Partner: Patient Records. Version: 4.0. 1993. Compatible Hardware: IBM PC & compatibles. Memory Required: 640k. General Requirements: Hard disk, printer. Items Included: Manuals, diskettes. Customer Support: Through local resellers or by telephone to main office.
disk $1995.00-$3995.00 (Order no.: 300).
Allows the Physician to Store a Complete Chart Electronically. Progress Notes Can Be Retrieved by Problem or by Special Criteria. Problem Lists, Vital Signs, Medications List & Health Maintenance Status Are Maintained Automatically. Flow Charts of Vital Signs & Lab Data May Be Retrieved Remotely.
Physician Micro Systems, Inc.

Practice Star. Robert Van Denburgh. 1980. Compatible Hardware: Altos, IBM, Kaypro, Morrow Designs. Operating System(s) Required: CP/M, MS-DOS, Concurrent DOS, Novell. Memory Required: 64k.
Accounts Manager. disk $1495.00.
Practice Manager. disk $1495.00.
disk $495.00 ea.
Insurance Adjustor.
Written Reports.
Narrative Reports.
Finance Manager. disk $1495.00.
Written by Chiropractors for Control of Practice, to Increase Staff Performance & Monitor Cash Flow.
ProGroup.

The Practitioner. Cheyenne Software, Inc. Apr. 1986. Operating System(s) Required: PC-DOS/MS-DOS 2.0 or higher. Memory Required: 512k. General Requirements: Hard disk, printer, modem.
disk $3500.00 (Order no.: FPS-001).

TITLE INDEX

Includes Record Keeping, Billing, Accounts Receivable, Patient Scheduling, Insurance Billing, Payroll, & Other Applicators.
Fisher Business Systems, Inc.

PRA's Experience Modification System.
Version: 8.3. Jun. 1985. Compatible Hardware: IBM PC, PC XT, PCjr, PS/2. Operating System(s) Required: MS-DOS 2.0 or higher, PC-DOS. Language(s): Microsoft C. Memory Required: 256k. General Requirements: Printer. Customer Support: Telephone support, 603-888-9361.
disk $395.00-$2000.00, include. Documentation.
Permits Employers to Calculate, Verify, or Project Their Workers Compensation Experience Modification. Computes an Experience Modification in All States That Have Adopted the "NCCI" Experience Rating Plan. Will Accept up to 1800 Claims, 40 Classification Codes, & 15 Different States at a Time. Permits an Employer to Project a Future Modifier, Verify a Current One, & See the Effect of Large Claims. Can Also Weigh the Feasibility of Self Insurance Mechanisms.
Premium Review Assocs.

PRD+: (Productivity Plus). Compatible Hardware: Compaq; IBM PC, PC XT, PC AT & compatibles. Operating System(s) Required: MS-DOS, PC-DOS. Memory Required: 52k. Items Included: Manual & 1 disk. Customer Support: Phone in (hotline), bulletin board.
Contact publisher for price.
Decreases the Number of Keystrokes Needed to Enter Text by Allowing User to Define Abbreviations (Words or Phrases). As the Abbreviation Is Keyed It Is Replaced on the Screen by Its Word or Phrase.
Productivity Software International, Inc.

Pre-Algebra. Jan. 1994. Items Included: Program on CD-ROM, CD Booklet, & Registration Card. Customer Support: Free unlimited support via telephone.
Windows 3.1 or higher running under DOS 5.0 or higher. 386 SX (4Mb RAM; 500k low Dos Mem; 6Mb free disk space). CD-ROM disk $49.00 (ISBN 1-57268-021-0, Order no.: 53101). Nonstandard peripherals required: Sound card (either: Sound Blaster - 8, 16, PRO; Media Vision ProAudio Spectrum; or Microsoft Sound System); MPC Compatible CD-ROM drive; VGA monitor; & microphone. Optimal configuration: 25MHz 386 SX.
High School Math for Windows. These Programs Offer Interactive Instruction for High-School-Aged Students. These CD-ROMs Contain Interactive Lessons Which Parallel the Pre-Algebra Concepts Taught in Eighth & Ninth Grades. Algebra 1 Reinforces Major Algebraic Concepts Your Child Must Master in School. Individual CD-ROMs for Geometry, Algebra 2, & Trigonometry Complement Programs for Grades Nine Through Twelve.
Conter Software.

Pre-Audit. Version: 2.01. Compatible Hardware: Altos Series 5-15D, Series 5-5D, 580-XX, ACS8000-XX; Burroughs B20-3 with 2 disk drives, DEC Rainbow 100 with 2 disk drives, DEC Rainbow 100+ with 10Mb hard disk; IBM PC with 2 disk drives, PC XT, PC AT, IBM compatibles; Kaypro 11/IV with 2 disk drives, Kaypro 10; TeleVideo TS 806/20, TS 803 with 2 disk drives, TS 803H; Xerox 820 with 2 disk drives; Zenith-H89 with 2 disk drives; ZILOG MCZ-250. Operating System(s) Required: CP/M, MP/M, CP/M-86/80, PC-DOS, MS-DOS.
License fee unit. $1800.00 (Order no.: PRE-AUDIT).
License fee site. $2700.00.
Maintenance unit. $360.00.
Maintenance site. $540.00.

Designed to Speed up the Processes of Auditing, Compilation, & Review by Preparing the Trial Balance Worksheet, Adjusting Journal Entries, Fluctuation & Ratio Analysis, & Financial Statements Including the Statement of Changes in Financial Position in Working Capital & Cash Formats. Interfaces with a Number of Other Microcomputer Products.
Coopers & Lybrand.

Precious Metals Evaluator. 1980. Compatible Hardware: Apple IIe, TRS-80 Model I Level II, Model III. Language(s): BASIC (source code included). Memory Required: 4k.
program listing $15.00 (ISBN 0-918737-00-1).
Determines the Intrinsic & Premium Values of a Piece of Precious Metal at Today's Spot Price.
Peter Wolmut.

Precision BASIC. Operating System(s) Required: SB-80, CP/M. Memory Required: 64k.
disk $150.00.
Interpreter Which Can Accurately Crunch Numbers & Can Hold up to 122 Decimal Digits for Applications Requiring Exactness. All Number Computations Are Faster Than with Compiled BASIC. Employs a System of Error Monitoring Enabling All Results to Be Tested Prior to Print Out.
Lifeboat Assocs.

Precision Bid Analysis. Version: 5.1. Apr. 1989. Items Included: Manuals. Customer Support: 90 days free phone support, additional support & maintenance available.
PC-DOS/MS-DOS (640k). IBM PC, PC XT, PS/2 100% & compatibles. Contact publisher for price.
Program That Helps Contractors Accumulate Optimun Mix of Subcontractors & Vendors & Calculate Total Bid Price. Operates in Real-Time Mode, Allowing User to Perform "What-If" Type Simulations. Interfaces with Medallion Job Cost & Precision Estimating Modules.
Timberline Software Corp.

Precision Buyout. Version: 5.2. Oct. 1991. Items Included: Full documentation. Customer Support: 90 days free support.
DOS 3.1 or higher. IBM PC AT, XT, PS/2 & 100% compatibles (640k). Contact publisher for price. Nonstandard peripherals required: Hard disk required. Addl. software required: Precision Estimating.
Turns a Complex Estimate into a Set of Purchase Orders & Subcontracts. Also Converts International Currencies to a User-Defined Base Currency Using Current Exchange Rates.
Timberline Software Corp.

Precision CAD Integrator. Version: 5.1. Compatible Hardware: IBM PC & compatibles. Operating System(s) Required: MS-DOS 3.1 or higher; NETBIOS-compatible LANs. Memory Required: 640k. General Requirements: AutoCAD Release 10 with 640k of extended memory. Items Included: Full documentation. Customer Support: 90 days free.
Contact publisher for price.
Allows Building Estimators to Take off Dimensions & Building Specs Electronically from an AutoCAD Drawing File for Use in Precision Estimating Plus Software from Timberline Links Similar Information Needs of Design/Build Phases.
Timberline Software Corp.

Precision Digitizer. Version: 5.0. Jun. 1988. Items Included: Manuals. Customer Support: 90 days free phone support, additional support & maintenance available.
PC-DOS/MS-DOS (640k). IBM PC, PC XT, PS/2 & 100% compatibles. Contact publisher for price. Nonstandard peripherals required:

PRECISION EXTENDED

Digitizer.
Software That Allows Estimate Takeoff Through Digitizing & Graphic Display Technology. Displays All Areas, Lengths & Counted Points Graphically on the Screen for Instantaneous Identification of Errors & Omissions Without Retracing or Counting. Interfaces with Precision Estimating & Precision Estimating Plus.
Timberline Software Corp.

Precision Estimating. Version: 5.4. Jun. 1987. Compatible Hardware: IBM PC AT, XT, PS/2 or 100% compatibles. Memory Required: 640k. General Requirements: 1 high density floppy drive & a hard disk (10Mb recommended). Items Included: Full documentation. Customer Support: 90 days free phone support, additional support & maintenance available.
Contact publisher for price.
Offers an Easy-to-Use Spreadsheet Format, Powerful Takeoff Capabilities & Pre-Built Databases. Allows Estimator to Control & Use Formulas; Create and/or Select Items, Phases; & Show Item Details & Totals.
Timberline Software Corp.

Precision Estimating Extended: Student Workbook. May 1993.
MS-DOS. IBM & compatibles. disk $125.00 (ISBN 0-927550-02-4, Order no.: 772405).
Optimal configuration: 486 with 8Mb RAM.
Student Workbook for Teaching the Advanced Level of Precision Estimating Including Workpackages.
Timberline Software Corp.

Precision Estimating Plus. Version: 5.3. Jul. 1989. Items Included: Manuals. Customer Support: 90 days free phone support, additional support & maintenance available.
PC-DOS/MS-DOS (640k). IBM PC, PC XT, PS/2 & 100% compatibles. Contact publisher for price.
Uses Point & Press Windowing to Allow the Estimator to Create & Use Formulas; Create & Select Items, Phases & Crews; Show Item Detail & Totals & Perform Work Package Takeoff. Interfaces with Medallion Accounting & Project Management Software.
Timberline Software Corp.

Precision Estimating Plus: Student Workbook. May 1993.
MS-DOS. IBM & compatibles. disk $100.00 (ISBN 0-927550-01-6, Order no.: 772404).
Optimal configuration: 486 with 8Mb RAM.
Student Workbook for Teaching the Advanced Level of Precision Estimating.
Timberline Software Corp.

Precision Estimating: Student Workbook.
MS-DOS. IBM & compatibles. disk $50.00 (ISBN 0-927550-00-8, Order no.: 772403). Optimal configuration: 486 with 8Mb RAM.
Student Workbook for Teaching the Basic Level of Precision Estimating.
Timberline Software Corp.

Precision Extended. Version: 5.3. Dec. 1991. Items Included: Manuals. Customer Support: 90 day free telephone support, additional support & maintenance available.
MS-DOS. IBM & compatibles (640k). Contact publisher for price. Nonstandard peripherals required: Hard disk. Networks supported: 3.1 DOS compatible LANs such as IBM PC Network, Novell Advanced Netware & Microsoft LanManager.
Allows User to Assign WBS Codes Allowing Them to Resort Their Estimates. Allows Use of Alternates. Easily Adjust Workpackage (Assembly) Productivity. Adjust Square Foot Cost & Easily Spread Cost Through Estimate.
Timberline Software Corp.

Precision Inventory Control & Order Entry.
Compatible Hardware: Apple Macintosh Plus.
General Requirements: Hard Disk; ImageWriter; LaserWriter.
3.5" disk $995.00.
Inventory Control-Order Entry System for Mail Order Businesses.
Precision Computer Systems.

Precision Time & Cost Billing System. Version: 1.2.0. Apr. 1991. Items Included: 2 program disks & comprehensive user's guide. Customer Support: Free telephone for 90 days; $350.00 annual fee after 90 days.
Macintosh Plus with external hard disk.
  Macintosh (2Mb). $795.00. Optimal configuration: Macintosh Classic, 2Mb RAM & 40Mb hard disk. Networks supported: AppleShare, Easyshare, tops up to 3 users in original package.
Provides for a Comprehensive Organized Database for Maintaining & Managing Insurance Claims. A 3 User Version Provided. Can Be Configured for Additional Users.
Precision Computer Systems.

Precision Timer III. David L. Vernier. 1988. Compatible Hardware: Apple II+, IIe, IIc, IIgs; IBM PC, PC XT, PC AT, PS/2. Operating System(s) Required: Apple ProDOS, MS-DOS. Language(s): Applesoft BASIC, Machine (source code included). Memory Required: Apple 64k, IBM 256k. General Requirements: PASCO or homemade photogates; CGA card & game port (IBM only).
Apple. disk $39.95, incl. manual (ISBN 0-918731-28-3).
IBM. disk $39.95 (ISBN 0-918731-21-6).
Turns the Apple into a Laboratory Timer. Measures Times to 0.1 Milliseconds in 14 Different Timing Modes. Time Data Is Collected & the Computer Can Help User Analyze It. Times May Be Displayed in Large Block Digits, Graphed, or Saved on Disk.
Vernier Software.

Precision Unit Price. Version: 5.0. Mar. 1993. Items Included: Full documentation. Customer Support: 90 days free telephone support, additional support & maintenance available.
DOS 3.1 or higher. IBM PC/XT, PC/AT, PS/2 (640k). Contact publisher for price. Addl. software required: Precision Estimating Plus. Optimal configuration: 386 or higher, 2Mb RAM, DOS 3.1 or higher. Networks supported: 3.1 DOS compatible LAN.
Allows User to Easily Set up a Bid, Analyze & Adjust Unit Prices, & Print the Final Bid Form. User Can Pro-Rate Indirect Costs Any Way You Need to, Mark up Risky Items & Mark down Sub-Contracted Ones. Last Minute Cuts & Adds Can Be Done on the Fly.
Timberline Software Corp.

PreCursor: Menu Program. Version: 4.1. Apr. 1992. Compatible Hardware: IBM PC & compatibles. Operating System(s) Required: PC-DOS/MS-DOS 2.0 & higher. Language(s): BASIC & Assembly. General Requirements: Hard disk. Items Included: Manual, diskette. Customer Support: Technical support, 8-5 Mon-Fri CST, 30 day moneyback guarantee.
disk $96.00.
Sophisticated Menu Interface System That Makes Access to Any Program on the Hard Disk As Easy As Pressing a Key. Unlimited Menu Selections, Utilities, Mouse Support, Menu Cloning, Built-In Password Security. Network Compatible, Includes API Support, Computer Usage Reports, User Help Files & Screen Blanking.
The Aldridge Co.

Preferred Series Accounts Payable. Version: 5.00. Jun. 1993. Items Included: Documentation. Customer Support: $300.00 per year. Training available - please contact PDS for prices.
SCO UNIX/SCO XENIX, MS-DOS, AIX. DEC 433, RS6000, NCR Tower 32/400-800, NCR3000, Unisys U6000, IBM compatible PCs. 1-2 users $495.00.
Features Include: Vendor Analysis Information, New Vendor Setup While Posting, Automatic Recurring Monthly Payments, On-Line Inquiries, Previous/Future Period Posting & Reporting, Age Analysis Reports, Manual, Automatic Check Writing, & 1099 Forms Prepared & Printed.
PDS, Inc.

Preferred Series Accounts Receivable. Version: 5.00. Jul. 1993. Items Included: Documentation. Customer Support: $300.00 per year. Training available - please contact PDS for prices.
SCO UNIX/SCO XENIX, MS-DOS, AIX. DEC 433, RS6000, NCR Tower 32/400-800, NCR3000, Unisys U6000, IBM compatible PCs. $1200.00 Plus, 1-2 users.
Features Include: Open Item, Balance Forward Statements, Summary/Detailed Age, Cash Flow Analysis Reports, Credit Limit Reports, New Customer Setup While Posting, On-Line Inquiries, Previous/Future Period Posting, Reporting & Automatic Hold for Disputed Invoices.
PDS, Inc.

Preferred Series General Ledger. Version: 5.0. Jun. 1993. Items Included: Documentation. Customer Support: $300.00 per year. Training available - please contact PDS for prices.
SCO UNIX/SCO XENIX, MS-DOS, AIX. DEC 433, RS6000, NCR Tower 32/400-800, NCR3000, Unisys U6000, IBM compatible PCs. $1200.00 Plus, 1-2 users.
Features of the Preferred Series General Ledger Module Includes: Financial Statements Include Comparative, Summarized, Budgetary, Departmentalized; Flexible Financial Statement Formatting; Multi-Line Input That Enforces Zero Proof; Multiple Period Posting & Reporting; Recurring Entries Posting; Statement of Change in Cash Flow; On-Line Inquires; Real-Time Hash Totals; Chart of Accounts Transfer.
PDS, Inc.

Preferred Series Inventory Control. Version: 5.00. Jun. 1993. Items Included: Documentation. Customer Support: $300.00 per year. Training available - please contact PDS for prices.
SCO UNIX/SCO XENIX, MS-DOS, AIX. DEC 433, RS6000, NCR Tower 32/400-800, NCR3000, Unisys U6000, IBM compatible PCs. $1200.00 Plus, 1-2 users.
Features Include: Supports 8 Pricing Levels for Every Item; Unit Price Conversions; Item Pricing by Customer W/Effective Date; Item Substitution File; Item Cross Reference File; Tracking of Lot, Serialized Items; Multiple Warehouses.
PDS, Inc.

Preferred Series Order Entry. Version: 5.00. Jun. 1993. Items Included: Documentation. Customer Support: $300.00 per year. Training available - please contact PDS for prices.
SCO UNIX/SCO XENIX, MS-DOS, AIX. DEC 433, RS6000, NCR Tower 32/400-800, NCR3000, Unisys U6000, IBM compatible PCs. $1200.00 Plus, 1-2 users.
Features Include: Replacements/Substitutions on Picking Ticket & Invoice, Prices Optionally Printed on Picking Ticket, Backorders Not Created If Not Accepted by Customer, Customer Sales Ranking by Sales & Margin, Multiple Ship-To Addresses, Automatic Start Date/End Date for Sale Prices, LIFO/FIFO Costing.
PDS, Inc.

Preferred Series Payroll. Version: 4.2. May 1992. Items Included: Documentation. Customer Support: $300.00 per year. Training available - please contact PDS for prices.
SCO UNIX/SCO XENIX, MS-DOS, AIX. DEC 433, RS6000, NCR Tower 32/400-800, NCR3000, Unisys U6000, IBM compatible PCs. $1200.00 1-2 users.
Features Include: 12-Character Employee Number; Automatic Hourly/Salary Processing; Multiple Check Printing; Tracks Vacation, Holiday, Sick Pay; Maintains 401K Government Plans; Recurring Time Posting; & W-2 Magnetic Media Reporting.
PDS, Inc.

Preferred Series Purhcase Order. Version: 5.00. Jul. 1993. Items Included: Documentation (2 volumes). Customer Support: $300.00 per year.
SCO UNIX. DEC 433, NCR Tower 32/400-800, NCR3000, Unisys U6000 (4Mb). $1200.00 & up.
MS-DOS. IBM PC & compatibles (4Mb). $1200.00 & up. Networks supported: Novell.
AIX. RS6000. $1200.00 & up.
4GL-Based State-of-the-Art Distribution Module Which Is Equipped with a List of Features Designed to Accommodate Virtually Any Distribution Function. The Option to Print the Vendor's Stock Number on Forms Is Available. The Module Also Has an Automated Interface to Inventory Control & Accounts Payable.
PDS, Inc.

Prefixes One & Two. Jun. 1983. Items Included: Teacher's guide. Customer Support: 90-day limited warranty.
Apple-DOS 3.3. Apple II Family (48k). disk $59.00, Prefixes 1 (ISBN 0-917277-40-6).
disk $59.00, Prefixes 2 (ISBN 0-917277-41-4).
Five Computer Programs Teaching the Usage & Meaning of the Prefixes Sub-, Uni-, Bi-, Tri-, Semi-, Hemi-, Inter-, Trans- & Intra-. (Prefixes 1). Prefixes 2 Includes Mal-, Mis-, Dis- & Dys-. Both Complete with a Review Test. Ages 9 & Up.
BrainBank/Generation Ahead of Maryland.

Premiere Video Rental Management System.
Compatible Hardware: Apple Macintosh.
Memory Required: 512k. General Requirements: Hard disk; ImageWriter.
Single user (includes Runtime Omnis 3). 3.5" disk $995.00.
Multiuser (requires Multiuser Omnis 3). 3.5" disk $1795.00.
Demo. 3.5" disk $15.00.
Manages Video Rental Store Operations.
Graftech.

Premium Finance. Version: 9. Compatible Hardware: IBM PC & compatibles. Operating System(s) Required: MS-DOS. Memory Required: 640k. General Requirements: Hard disk. Customer Support: License agreement. Maintenance fee $65.00 per month; additional rates are provided according to activity involved; includes: analysis & design, programming, data entry, training, telephone training & assistance, hardware installation & repair, & disaster recovery.
contact publisher for price.
Loan Processing from Quotation to Maturity with Complete Audit Trail. Provides Printing of Any Form Required from Payment Vouchers to Cancelation Notices. Features Include: Day the Money Runs Out, Credit Limits, Guaranteed Loans, Loan Table Printing, Track Companies, MGA's, Producers, Automatic Aging, Endorsements, & Multistate.
Evolution, Inc.

TITLE INDEX

Premium Mouse Black: Three-Button. *Items Included:* Mouse & Cursorama Plus Software. *Customer Support:* Tech support.
Windows 3.1 or higher. IBM PC & compatibles. disk $29.95 (ISBN 0-924677-34-1).
A Fully Microsoft & Windows Compatible Pointing Device. Dynamic Resolution of 3-30,000 DPI, a Full Two-Year Warranty, & Free Bonus Software Make It the Ideal Windows Mouse.
IMSI (International Microcomputer Software, Inc.).

Premium Mouse White: Three-Button. *Items Included:* Mouse & Cursorama Plus Software. *Customer Support:* Tech support.
Windows 3.1 or higher. IBM PC & compatibles. disk $29.95 (ISBN 0-924677-33-3).
A Fully Microsoft & Windows Compatible Pointing Device. Dynamic Resolution of 3-30,000 DPI, a Full Two-Year Warranty, & Free Bonus Software Make It the Ideal Windows Mouse.
IMSI (International Microcomputer Software, Inc.).

PremiumMaster. *Version:* 1.13. *Items Included:* Documentation in 3 ring manual. *Customer Support:* On-site or school training, 800 number, 90 day warranty, user's group.
DOS, Unix, Xenix (640k), Novell, AIX, Sun OS. Contact Publisher for price. *Addl. software required:* DonorMaster II. *Networks supported:* Most LAN environments.
Premium Fulfillment System for Fund Raising & Membership Support, Complete Inventory Management, Vendoe Information, Previous Premium History, & the Like Maintained.
Master Systems.

The Prentice Hall Tax Advantage System - 1120, 11205, 1065. *Version:* 93.01. Jan. 1994. *Items Included:* Software, documentation, cross reference guide to Federal & State forms. *Customer Support:* Unlimited telephone support via Watts line included.
DOS/Novell 286/386. IBM compatibles (520k). $595.00 per module-Bundled pricing available. *Optimal configuration:* IBM 386. *Networks supported:* Novell & 3COM.
Can Transfer Data Directly From Your General Ledger or Spreadsheet to Prepare Both Federal & Most State Tax Returns. Including Preparation of Book-to-Tax Workpapers, Depreciation Calculations, & Special Allocations for K-1s.
Prentice Hall Professional Software.

Preparation of Technetium-99m Labeled Radiopharmaceuticals. Ann M. Steves. 1996.
DOS 3.1 or higher. IBM or compatible (512k). disk $150.00 (Order no.: MIS9024).
Nonstandard peripherals required: VGA.
Educational Software Concepts, Inc.

Preparation of Technetium-99m Labeled Radiopharmaceuticals. Ann M. Steves. 1996.
DOS 3.1 or higher. IBM or compatibles (512k). disk $150.00 (Order no.: MIS9024).
Nonstandard peripherals required: VGA.
This program reviews the contents of commerically prepared kits used for labeling radiopharmaceuticals with Tc-99m & identifies the purpose of each component.
Educational Software Concepts, Inc.

Prepare Your Own Will: The National Will Kit.
(The/Legal Self-Help Ser.). Daniel Sitarz. Oct. 1995.
IBM. 3.5" disk $12.95 (ISBN 0-935755-22-5).
Contains All of the Legal Forms & Documents Necessary to Prepare Your Own Will.
Nova Publishing Co.

Prepare Your Own Will: The National Will Kit.
(Legal Self-Help Ser.). Daniel Sitarz. Apr. 1996.
IBM. 3.5" disk $12.95 (ISBN 0-935755-22-5).
Forms-On-Disk - Containing All of the Legal Forms Necessary to Prepare Your Own Will.
Nova Publishing Company.

Preparing Your Business Budget with Framework. Dennis P. Curtin & William R. Osgood. Jan. 1985. *Compatible Hardware:* IBM PC & compatibles. *Operating System(s) Required:* MS-DOS, PC-DOS. *Memory Required:* 320k. *General Requirements:* 2 disk drives, dot matrix printer for graphics.
disk $29.95 (ISBN 0-13-698796-6).
bk. $18.95 (ISBN 0-13-698770-2).
Contains a Gross Margin Worksheet, a Fixed Cost Worksheet, a Break-Even Worksheet, a Monthly Sales Forecast, & a Proforma Income Statement & Cash Budget. Automatic Features Have Been Added to Take Advantage of FRAMEWORK's Versatility & Power.
Prentice Hall.

Preparing Your Business Budget with Symphony. Dennis P. Curtin. Jan. 1985. *Compatible Hardware:* IBM PC & compatibles. *Operating System(s) Required:* MS-DOS, PC-DOS. *Memory Required:* 320k. *General Requirements:* 2 disk drives, dot matrix printer for graphics.
disk $29.95 (ISBN 0-13-698820-2).
bk. $18.95 (ISBN 0-13-698804-0).
Contains a Gross Margin Worksheet, a Fixed Cost Worksheet, a Break-Even Worksheet, a Monthly Sales Forecast, & a Proforma Income Statement & Cash Budget. Automatic Features Have Been Added to Take Advantage of SYMPHONY's Capabilities.
Prentice Hall.

Preparing Your Business Plan with Lotus 1-2-3. William R. Osgood & Dennis P. Curtin.
disk $38.95, incl. bk. (Order no.: 69843-1).
Prentice Hall.

Preparing Your Business Plan with Multiplan. William R. Osgood & Dennis P. Curtin.
disk $38.95, incl. bk. (Order no.: 69896-9).
Prentice Hall.

PREPIT. *Version:* 2.0. Mar. 1985. *Compatible Hardware:* IBM PC, PC XT, PC AT & compatibles. *Operating System(s) Required:* PC-DOS, MS-DOS. *Language(s):* FORTRAN. *Memory Required:* 512k. *General Requirements:* Printer.
disk $5000.00, incl. PSTPIT, RESPIT, & PITKOR (Order no.: PREPIT).
Economic Valuation Program for Block Models of Ore Deposits. The Program Will Assign a Value to Each Block Based on the Concentrations of Its Mineral Components & Position in Space. The Analyst Can Impose Ore/Waste Cut-Off Grades for Commodities & PREPIT Will Value Each Block Considering the Mining & Processing Cost, the Mining Milling & Smelting Recoveries, & the Commodity Price of the Ore.
Geostat Systems International, Inc. (GSII).

PREPLOT. *Version:* 2.0. Mar. 1985. *Compatible Hardware:* IBM PC, PC AT, PC XT & compatibles. *Operating System(s) Required:* PC-DOS, MS-DOS. *Language(s):* FORTRAN. *Memory Required:* 512k. *General Requirements:* Graphic screen.
disk $250.00 (Order no.: PREPLOT).
Gives User the Ability to Preview a Plot File. Displays a Geostat Plot File on a Graphics Screen & Permits the Analyst to Look at Plot Files Before Investing Time Using a Plotter.
Geostat Systems International, Inc. (GSII).

PrePrint Japanese. *Version:* 1.5. Nov. 1992. *Customer Support:* For customer service, product registration, upgrades, technical support, & CustomerFirst service plans, customers may call Aldus Customer Services at (206) 628-2320.
Macintosh. Contact publisher for price (ISBN 1-56026-133-1).
Aldus Corp.

Preschool Parade. Aug. 1994. *Items Included:* Manual & diskettes.
6.07 or higher. Color Macintosh with hard drive (1Mb). 3.5" disk $49.95 (ISBN 0-940081-79-2). *Nonstandard peripherals required:* For CD-ROM version CD drive required.
Windows 3.1 or higher. 386SX or higher (4Mb). 3.5" disk $49.95 (ISBN 0-940081-71-7). *Nonstandard peripherals required:* Mouse, SVGA, sound card recommended.
Macintosh & Windows. CD-ROM disk $49.95 (ISBN 0-940081-80-6).
Have Children Join the Preschool Parade & the Parade Full of Activities. Learn the Alphabet & Counting, Play Dot-to-Dot & Concentration, Have Fun with Music. There Is Even a Coloring Book. Your Child Will Enjoy the Variety of Activities Available in One Program.
Nordic Software, Inc.

Prescription Form Writer. *Version:* 2.0. 1981. *Compatible Hardware:* Apple II, IIe; Basis 6502; Franklin Ace; IBM PC, PC XT; PC AT. *Operating System(s) Required:* Apple DOS 3.3, MS-DOS 2.1. *Language(s):* BASIC (source code included). *Memory Required:* Apple 48k, IBM PC 256k.
disk $20.00 (ISBN 0-914555-15-4).
Prepares Multiple Pre-Printed Prescription Blanks for the Busy Doctor. Enter Any Drug, Dosage, Quantity & Instructions.
Andent, Inc.

Prescription Writer: Current Clinical Strategies. *Version:* 5.0. Paul D. Chan. Sep. 1992.
MS-DOS. IBM PC & compatibles. Contact publisher for price (ISBN 1-881528-03-0).
This Program Produces Drug Prescriptions & Maintains Patient Drug Records.
Current Clinical Strategies Publishing.

Prescriptions for Type II Diabetes. (Health Care Professional Ser.).
MS-DOS 2.1 or higher. IBM PC & compatibles. disk $49.95 (Order no.: 4HCP).
Discusses Monitoring Feature for Blood Glucose, & Examines Situations Involving Treatment of Type II Diabetes with Oral Agents & Insulin. Provides Three Components That: Assist in Prescription of Oral Agents for Persons with Type II Diabetes; Summarizes Clinical Information About Individual Oral Agents; Provides Tables That Summarize Insulin Information for Rapid-Acting, Intermediate-Acting & Long-Acting Insulins.
Cardinal Health Systems, Inc.

Presentation Express 2. *Version:* 3.03. *Items Included:* 1 user manual. *Customer Support:* Free technical support on 800 Number. Priority support - $250/yr..
DOS. XT, AT or higher (512k). disk $495.00. *Networks supported:* Novell.
Easy-to-Use Presentation Package Designed to Produce Charts & Graphs for Output to a Variety of Film Recorders, Printers, etc. Output Media Includes Slides, Overhead Transparencies, Paper Handouts, & On-Screen Electronic Presentations. Product Can Import Scanned Images & Has Basic Charting Capabilities As Well As An Emphasis on Scientific Chart Types, & Drawing Tools. Also Available - Medical Clip Art in CGM Format.
Business & Professional Software, Inc.

Presenter Professional. Version: 3.0. Jul. 1991. Customer Support: 30 days free phone support, $500 training per day.
Macintosh with a math coprocessor installed or a Power Macintosh. Macintosh IIfx or Quadra (5Mb). 3.5" disk $1995.00.
Macintosh IIFX or Quadra with 16Mb RAM & a 160Mb hard disk. Macintosh II or higher (5Mb). Contact publisher for price.
A Powerful, Intuitive, 3D, Spline-Based, Conceptual Design & Visualization Package for the Macintosh. It Provides Detailed Modeling & Free-Form Sculpting, Photorealistic Imaging Combining Phong & Ray Traced Rendering, Path/Object Animation & the Best Render/Man Interface Available. Advanced Features Include Volumetric Analysis, Hierarchical Grouping, & Extensive File Import/Export Options.
VIDI.

Presenter Series: Access Fundamentals.
Version: 2.0. Items Included: Participant workbook, instructor guide, Powerpoint presentation, Powerpoint viewer, camera-ready copy of slide show & participant workbook, master diskette of participant workbook. Customer Support: Toll-free, fee free technical support on product & the subject software application.
disk $595.00. Nonstandard peripherals required: Access.
Presentation Tools for Instructor to Conduct Lecture Based, Minds-On Training Sessions. Includes Student Manuals for Class & Hands-On Training.
Infosource, Inc.

The Presidents: A Picture History. (National Geographic Society CD-ROM Ser.).
MS-DOS 3.1 or higher. 386 processor or higher (640k). CD-ROM disk $69.95 (Order no.: R1056). Nonstandard peripherals required: CD-ROM drive. Optimal configuration: 386 processor higher, MS-DOS 3.1 or higher, 20Mb hard drive, 640k RAM, external speakers or headphones (with sound card) that are Sound Blaster compatible, VGA graphics & adapter, VGA color monitor.
Hear Rousing Stump Speeches, Inaugural Addresses & Radio Talks. Watch Video Clips of the Presidents. Flip Through Snapshots & Read Hundreds of Pages of Text (Grades 6 & Up).
Library Video Co.

Pressure Sewer. 1989. Compatible Hardware: IBM PC & compatibles. Operating System(s) Required: PC-DOS/MS-DOS. Language(s): QBASIC. Customer Support: Telephone assistance.
disk $47.00, incl. user guide.
disk $127.00, incl. source code.
Handles up to 200 Lines on a Tree-Structured System. No Loops Are Allowed. Output Is Similar to Water Distribution with Discharge Time Also Provided. Lines May Be Sized on Velocity & Head Loss Criteria. Input Is Free-Format, Menu Driven.
Systek, Inc. (Mississippi).

Prestige PC. Version: 3.1. Compatible Hardware: IBM PC XT, PC AT, PS/2, DEC VAX, UNIX Mini computers. Memory Required: 640k.
per single user $2995.00.
Project-Management Package Featuring Automatic Resource Leveling, On-Disk Tutorial, Context-Sensitive On-Screen Help, Task-by-Task Data-Entry Style, Plotter Support, LAN-Specific Version, Multi-User File Reading, Backward Calculation, 4000 Activities per Level & Disk Data Storage. The Number of Resources Leveled Simultaneously, Simultaneous Select Criteria & Simultaneous Sort Fields Is Limited by Memory. Automatically Draws PERT Charts. Interfaces with Premis & Cue Software Without Additonal Programming.
K&H Professional Management Services, Inc.

Pretty Printer. Compatible Hardware: TI 99/4A. Operating System(s) Required: DX-10. Language(s): Extended BASIC. Memory Required: 48k.
DX-10. disk $17.95.
Utility Program to Format & Paginate BASIC & Extended BASIC Program Listings. Prints Title, Program Name & Page Number at the Top of Each Page.
Eastbench Software Products.

Preventive Methods in Coronary Artery Disease: Diet Analysis Tool. (Wellness Ser.).
MS-DOS 2.1 or higher. IBM PC & compatibles. $99.95 ea. or $249.95 for all four Preventive Tools (Diet Analysis, Smoking Cessation, Exercise Prescription & Life Style Change) (Order no.: 6W).
Prevention of Coronary Heart Disease Includes Regulating the Intake of Calories & Limiting the Intake of Cholesterol, Total Fat, Saturated Fat & Sodium. Allows User to See Content of Calories, Sodium, Fat (Polyunsaturated, Monounsaturated & Unsaturated) & Cholesterol in 850 Individual Food Items, Including Popular Fast Food Items. Printouts Available.
Cardinal Health Systems, Inc.

Preventive Methods in Coronary Heart Disease: Exercise Prescription Tool. (Wellness Ser.).
MS-DOS 2.1 or higher. IBM PC & compatibles. $99.95 ea. or $249.95 for all four Preventive Tools (Exercise Prescription, Diet Analysis, Smoking Cessation, Life-Style Change) (Order no.: 8W).
Purpose Is to Aid in Development of a Regular Exercise Program. Information Is Obtained Regarding Age, Activity Level, Evidence of Previous Cardiac, Orthopedic, or Neuromuscular Disease, Exercise Tolerance & Goals of an Exercise Program. After Date Is Entered, Program Will Calculate User's Maximum Heart Rate in Beats per Minute, Intensity of Exercise in Beats per Minute, Target Rate Heart Zone & Duration & Frequency of Aerobic Exercise. Printout Is Available for Each User Outlining Above Data & Duration, Frequency & Specifics of Chosen Exercise Training Program (Walking/Jogging, Swimming or Bicycling).
Cardinal Health Systems, Inc.

Preventive Methods in Coronary Heart Disease: Life-Style Change Tool. (Wellness Ser.).
MS-DOS 2.1 or higher. IBM PC & compatibles. $99.95 ea. or $249.95 for all four Preventive tools (Life-Style Change, Diet Analysis, Smoking Cessation, Exercise Prescription) (Order no.: 9W).
Assists in Application of Systematic & Comprehensive Approach to Identification & Modification of Risk Factors for Coronary Heart Disease As Affected by Life-Style Components, Namely: Diet, Exercise, Smoking, Use of Oral Contraceptives, High Blood Pressure & Stress. This Tool May Be Used Individually or in Conjunction with the Other Tools. Individual Printouts Available.
Cardinal Health Systems, Inc.

Preventive Methods in Coronary Heart Disease: Smoking Cessation Tool. (Wellness Ser.).
MS-DOS 2.1 or higher. IBM PC & compatibles. $99.95 ea. or $249.95 for all four Preventive Tools (Smoking Cessation, Diet Analysis, Exercise Prescription, Life-Style Change) (Order no.: 7W).
Physicians & Other Members in the Health Care Field Can Have a Definite Impact on Smokers by Providing Clear & Simple Messages About the Risk of Smoking & Smoking Cessation. This Tool Helps User Decide What Type of Questions to Ask the Participant & What Type of Advice to Give. Also Discusses Counseling & Use of Nicotine Gum As an Aid in the Smoking Cessation Effort (As Directed by a Physician). A Database Provides Information on Levels of Tar, Nicotine & Carbon Monoxide in 207 Domestic Brands of Cigarettes. Printout of This Information Available.
Cardinal Health Systems, Inc.

Price Deflator Worksheet: For Lotus 1-2-3.
James E. Kristy. Feb. 1993. Compatible Hardware: IBM PC & compatibles; PC XT, PC AT. Memory Required: 256k. General Requirements: Lotus 1-2-3 or Symphony. Customer Support: Phone support: (714) 523-0357.
disk $29.00 (ISBN 0-932355-16-1, Order no.: 651).
Enables the User to Calculate Sales, Prices, Salaries, Profits, or Any Other Dollar History in Real-Dollar Terms. As the Historic Data Is Entered, This Spreadsheet Template Automatically Calculates Annual, 5-Year Average, & Compound Growth Rates. Includes CPIs Back to 1913.
Books On Business.

PRICE-IT. Version: 3.0. 1994. Compatible Hardware: IBM PC & compatibles. Operating System(s) Required: MS-DOS. Language(s): MS BASIC. Memory Required: 384k. Items Included: Reference Manual & Training Guide in 3-ring binder. Customer Support: Free technical support.
disk $595.00.
Feed Pricing & Inventory Program Which Shares Prices & Formulas with the MIXIT Programs. Will Print Price Sheets with Markups, Price & Inventory Data, up to Nine Usage Levels & Reordering Information. All the Words in the Printed Reports May Be Changed (Can Be Customized by Non-English Speaking Users). Version. 2.5 Has Many New Features Including Point-of-Sale Invoicing. Also Available in Spanish.
Agricultural Software Consultants, Inc.

The PriceBook. 1984. Compatible Hardware: IBM PC, PC XT; with printer. Operating System(s) Required: PC-DOS. Language(s): COBOL. Memory Required: 128k.
disk $99.95.
Maintains a Price Book on the PC. Generates Itemized Price & Purchase/Service Listings to Disk &/or Printer As Well As Performing an Assortment of Other Tasks. Generates Invoices, Quotations, Purchase Orders, Acknowledgments, or Any Other Business Application That Requires an Itemized Listing with Price Extension & Totals Calculated.
RJL Systems.

Pricing Edge. May 1989. Items Included: User manual & software tutorials. Customer Support: 30 day money back guarantee, free phone support, on line tutorials & help in software.
DOS or O/S2 (256k). IBM PC, XT, AT, PS/2 or compatibles. $199.00 (US & Canada), $249.00 (International). Nonstandard peripherals required: CGA, EGA, VGA, or Hercules graphics board. Addl. software required: Lotus 1-2-3 release 2, 2.01, 2.2, or 3. Optimal configuration: IBM PCAT, DOS 2.1 or higher, 640k RAM, EGA board, 1-2-3 release 2 or higher. Networks supported: All that are supported by Lotus 1-2-3.
Helps to Set Optimum Competitive Prices for New Products, Assists with a Competitive Re-Positioning (Raising or Lowering) of Existing Product Prices, Ensures Price/Performance Consistency of Your Product Line. It Can Even Be Used to Price a One-Time Competitive Bid & Automatically Builds a Price Vs. Performance Positioning Map/Graph of Your Competitors' Products as Compared to Yours.
Successware.

TITLE INDEX

Primary Cancers of the Skin. Arto Demirjian et al. *Customer Support:* Toll-free technical support - no charge. In U.S. - 9AM-5PM EST 800-343-0064. In U.K. - 44(0)81-995-8242.
Microsoft Windows, Version 3.X. 386 IBM-compatible PC (3Mb). CD-ROM disk $249.00 Individual; $599.00 Institutional (ISBN 1-57276-014-1, Order no.: SE-014-001). *Nonstandard peripherals required:* MPC Standard CD-ROM drive, SVGA (640 x 480) 256 colors, MPC standard soundboard & speakers.
System 6.0.7 or higher. Apple Macintosh (3Mb). CD-ROM disk $249.00 Individual; $599.00 Institutional (Order no.: SE-014-001). *Nonstandard peripherals required:* CD-ROM drive.
This Is a Dermatology Education & Reference Tool Which Is User Interactive, Presents High Definition Color Pictures with Rapid Data Access. Based on Malignant Cutaneous Tumors, the Course Covers the Following Skin Cancers: Malignant Malanoma, Basal Cell Carcinoma, & Squamous Cell Carcinoma.
SilverPlatter Education.

Primary Cancers of the Skin. Ari Demirjian et al. Jun. 1994. *Customer Support:* Toll-free technical support - no charge. In U.S. 9AM - 5PM EST 800-343-0064; in U.K. 44(0)81-995-8242.
System 6.0.7 or higher. Apple Macintosh (3Mb). CD-ROM disk $249.00, Individual, ,599.00 Institutional (ISBN 1-57276-014-1, Order no.: SE-014-001). *Nonstandard peripherals required:* CD-ROM drive.
Microsoft Windows, Version 3.X. 386 IBM-Compatible PC (3Mb). CD-ROM disk $249.00, Individual, ,599.00 Institutional. *Nonstandard peripherals required:* MPC Standard CD-ROM drive, SVGA (640x480) 256 colors, MPC Standard Soundboard & Speakers.
This Is a Dermatology Education & Reference Tool Which Is User Interactive, Presents High Definition Color Pictures with Rapid Data Access. Based on Malignant Cutaneous Tumors, the Course Covers the Following Skin Cancers: Malignant Malanoma, Basal Cell Carcinoma, & Squamous Cell Carcinoma.
SilverPlatter Education.

Primavera Project Planner: Project Management & Control Software. Version: 5.1. Mar. 1993. *Compatible Hardware:* IBM PC, PS/2 & compatibles. *Operating System(s) Required:* PC-DOS/MS-DOS 3.1 or higher. *Language(s):* FORTRAN, Assembly. *Memory Required:* 640k. *General Requirements:* 10Mb hard disk. *Customer Support:* First year free telephone support & upgrades. Additional years at 20% purchase price.
disk $4000.00.
Manages Projects with Unlimited Activities; Performs Resource Leveling & Cost Management; Compares Current Schedules to Targets; Performs "What-If" Analysis. Provides Standard & Custom Reports in Virtually Any Format. Produces Bar Charts & Network Logic Diagrams.
Primavera Systems, Inc.

Prime Factor FFT for DOS. Version: 3.0. Jun. 1993. *Items Included:* Manual. *Customer Support:* Free customer telephone support, risk free 30-day trial period.
PC-DOS/MS-DOS, Pentium. IBM PC XT, AT, 386, 486, OS/2 & compatibles (64K). $295.00 (Order no.: AT11). *Nonstandard peripherals required:* Math coprocessor for 386 & 486SX computers only.
Fast Fourier Transform Assembly Language Subroutine Library. It Is Callable from Any High Level Language. Choose from over 800 Data Set Sizes; from 2 to 64350 Datapoints. Not limited to a Power of 2 Data Set Sizes. Integer, Single, & Double Precision IEEE Floating Points Numbers Are Supported. For 1 & 2 Dimensional Analysis.
Alligator Technologies.

Prime Factor FFT for Windows. Version: 3.0. May 1993. *Items Included:* Comprehensive user manual that lists all the program's functions & their usage. Also includes DOS version of program. Example application programs written for most popular programming languages. *Customer Support:* Free technical phone support, unlimited lifetime warranty, & 30-day money-back guarantee. Registered users also qualify for reduced product upgrades.
PC, DOS & Windows. PC AT, 386, 486 or Pentium (4Mb). disk $395.00. *Nonstandard peripherals required:* Math coprocessor for 386 & 486SX-based machines. *Addl. software required:* DOS 3.0 or higher, Windows 3.0 or higher.
Fast Fourier Transform (FFT) Analysis Software for Determining Frequency Content of Signal. Complex Forward & Inverse FFTs in 1 & 2 Dimensions. Hamming & Hanning Windowing Functions, Analysis on Any Date Set Size. Callable from Any Language.
Alligator Technologies.

Prime Numbers: Generating Prime Numbers, Testing & Factoring Numbers. George Peninger. 1993.
IBM PC & compatibles. disk $38.50 (ISBN 1-882873-10-6).
IBM PC & compatibles. 3.5" disk $38.50 (ISBN 1-882873-05-X).

Prime Time. Michael Bregger. *Compatible Hardware:* IBM PC, Atari ST, Commodore Amiga.
IBM PC. disk $39.95 (Order no.: 01001).
Atari ST. 3.5" disk $39.95 (Order no.: 08001).
Amiga. 3.5" disk $39.95 (Order no.: 06001).
Gives Players the Chance to Run a TV Network, Cancel Shows, Buy Shows, Do Lunch, etc. With Graphics & Animation, Digitized Speech & Sound Effects.
First Row Software Publishing.

PrimeTime. *Items Included:* Manual, keyboard template, hot-key reference card. *Customer Support:* Free telephone support with registration.
MS-DOS 3.1 or higher. IBM AT or compatible (2Mb EMS). disk $898.00. *Nonstandard peripherals required:* Graphics board: TARGA 16, any TARGA Plus model, any TARGA register-compatible board. *Optimal configuration:* AT computer with 486 processor, DOS 5.0, 4Mb EMS expanded memory, TARGA Plus 64.
MS-DOS 3.1 or higher. IBM AT or compatible (2Mb EMS). disk $398.00. *Nonstandard peripherals required:* Graphics board: any Super VGA card with a minimum of 512k video RAM & a TSENG Lab ET-4000 control chip recommended. *Optimal configuration:* AT computer with 486 processor, DOS 5.0, 4Mb EMS expanded memory, Super VGA card with 1Mb video RAM.
Broadcast Quality Tilting & Effects Package for the IBM AT & Compatibles. It Features High-Quality Anti-Aliased Typestyles, Real-Time Transition Effects, Extensive Graphics Capabilities & a User-Friendly Menu Driven Interface. Optional Modules Allow for Interactive Font Scaling & High Performance Sprite Animation. Available in NTSC or PAC.
InnoVision Technology.

PrimeTime with Animation. Apr. 1992. *Items Included:* Manual, template, quick reference guide, demo disk. *Customer Support:* 24 hr. Fax line, free telephone support for registered users.
286 or 386 IBM compatible PC, MS-DOS 3.0 or higher. IBM AT & compatibles (4Mb). disk SVGA $598.00; TARGA $1198.00 (Order no.: PTWA). *Nonstandard peripherals required:* TrueVision TARGA Board or SVGA Board with TSEVG Lab Chip ET-4000. *Optimal configuration:* 2Mb EMS expanded memory, 530-550k free base memory.
Network Quality CG & Graphics Program for the IBM: Realtime Transitions, Anti-Aliased Fonts, Frame Grabbing, Translucency & More. Animation Option Allows 10 Objects Moving on the Screen at 1 Time. SuperVGA or TARGA Available with or Without Animation Option. Call for Free Guide. NTSC or PAL.
InnoVision Technology.

Principal Component & Factor Analysis. *Compatible Hardware:* Apple II with Applesoft; IBM PC. *Memory Required:* Apple 48k, IBM 128k.
disk $89.95.
Menu-Driven Collection of Subprograms with Which User May Enter & Edit Data & Perform Various Calculations.
Dynacomp, Inc.

Principles of Cost Accounting - Computerized Practice Set. 1988. *Memory Required:* Apple 64-256k, IBM/Tandy 128-256k.
Apple II Series/IIgs. contact publisher for price (ISBN 0-538-51037-4, Order no.: Q30038).
IBM/Tandy. contact publisher for price (ISBN 0-538-51038-2, Order no.: 30039).
Practice Set with Individual Diskette: "Liberty Electronics Inc.: A Computerized Job Order Simulation".
South-Western Publishing Co.

Principles of Environmental Sampling. Mar. 1991. *Customer Support:* Free customer support, 800 number.
MS-DOS. IBM PC, PC XT, PC AT, PS/2, or compatibles. disk List $59.95; Academic $59.95 (ISBN 0-8412-1943-5).
Explains the Many Variables & Special Techniques Needed to Plan & Execute Reliable Sampling Activities. With the Program's Easy-to-Read & Easy-to-Learn Format, Users Will Quickly Pick up the Principles & Important Matrix Requirements of Sampling Covered in the Book's Six Sections: Planning & Sample Design; Quality Assurance & Quality Control; Sampling Waters; Sampling Air & Stacks; Sampling Biota; Sampling Solids, Sludges, & Liquid Wastes. The Menu-Driven Electronic Version Allows Users to Search Quickly & Easily for Multiple Keyword Combinations That Are Impossible to Locate in a Printed Text.
American Chemical Society.

Principles of Pharmacology. 1986. *Compatible Hardware:* Apple II, II+, IIe, IIc, IIgs. *Language(s):* BASIC. *Memory Required:* 64k.
$49.95.
The Origins of Pharmacology, Drug Absorption & Distribution, Drug Biotransformation & Elimination, Mechanisms of Drug Action, & Drug Safety & Efficacy Are Studied.
Biosource Software.

Print Artist Try & Buy. Pixellite Group Staff. *Items Included:* 3.5" diskettes, 10 page document, 1 colorful Try & Buy Brochure.
Windows 3.1 or higher. IBM 386 or higher or 100% PC compatibles (2Mb). disk $34.99 (ISBN 1-57548-004-2).
Will Introduce Users to Some of the Powerful Design & Publishing Tools Contained in the Print Artist Program. It Contains Library of Customizable Graphics & Many Document Layouts That Can Be Freely Edited. The Users Will Be Able to Import & Export Graphics in a Variety of File Formats.
IBM Software Manufacturing Solutions (ISMS).

PRINT-CHARACTERS

Print-Characters. *Compatible Hardware:* IBM PC. *Language(s):* Assembly. *Memory Required:* 64k.
disk $35.00.
User Transparent, Assembly Language Program That Remains Resident As an Addition to DOS. When Loaded, Will Allow the User to Print a Majority of the IBM PC Character Set.
Soft & Friendly.

Print*File. *Version:* 3.43 & 4.0. Daniel D. Stuhlman. Aug. 1985. *Compatible Hardware:* IBM PC & compatibles. *Operating System(s) Required:* MS-DOS. *Language(s):* Turbo Pascal. *Memory Required:* 128k. *General Requirements:* Ver. 3.43 requires MS-DOS 2.01 or higher; Ver. 4.0 requires MS-DOS 3.1 or higher.
MS-DOS. disk $19.95-$29.95 (ISBN 0-934402-16-7).
Provides Additional Printer Functions. Supports Italics, Elite, Bold, Enlarged, etc.
BLYS Pr.

Print File. *Items Included:* Bound manual. *Customer Support:* Free hotline - no time limit; 30 day limited warranty; updates are $5/disk plus S&H.
MS-DOS. IBM & compatibles (128k). disk $19.95. *Nonstandard peripherals required:* Epson (or compatible) printer.
Lister Utility for ASCII Text Files. Print Any Word in Italic, Bold, Superscript, Subscript, Expanded, Condensed, Pica, Elite, Underline, Vertically Enlarged, etc., Formats. Have the Printout Paginated, & "Stamped" with the Time & Date. You Can Also Toggle (Turn on & off at Will) Proportional Spacing, Correspondence Quality, Reverse, & Similar Printer Features.
Dynacomp, Inc.

Print-It. *Memory Required:* 128k.
IBM PC & compatibles. disk $44.95.
M.A.P. Systems, Inc.

Print Man Spooler System. Data Base Administrators, Inc. *Operating System(s) Required:* CP/M-86, Concurrent CP/M-86. *Memory Required:* 64k.
$195.00.
Texas Instruments, Personal Productivit.

Print Screen. *Compatible Hardware:* IBM PC with color graphics adapter. *Operating System(s) Required:* MS-DOS. *Language(s):* Assembly (source code included). *Memory Required:* 96k.
disk $35.00.
Transparent, Assembly Language Program That Becomes a Part of DOS When Loaded. Enables User to Make a Hard Copy of Screen Displays, Either Text or Graphics.
Soft & Friendly.

The Print Shop. David Balsam & Martin Kahn. *Compatible Hardware:* Apple II+, IIe, IIc, IIgs, Macintosh; Atari 400, 800, XL, XE Series; Commodore 64, 128; IBM PC, PCjr, PC XT, PC AT; Tandy. *Memory Required:* Atari 48k, Apple & Commodore 64/128 64k, IBM & Tandy 128k, Macintosh 512k. *General Requirements:* Compatible printer. Apple II, Commodore, & Atari versions support KoalaPad & joystick; Macintosh version supports mouse.
Apple. disk $49.95 (Order no.: APDSK-86).
Atari. disk $44.95 (Order no.: ATDSK-100).
Commodore. disk $44.95 (Order no.: COMDSK-95).
IBM, Tandy. disk $59.95 (Order no.: IBMDSK-210).
Macintosh. 3.5" disk $59.95 (Order no.: MACDSK-53).
Apple IIgs. 3.5" disk $59.95 (ISBN 0-922614-89-X, Order no.: 20052).
Paper Pack (120 sheets of pinfeed paper in assorted colors plus 42 matching envelopes).

$19.95 (Order no.: SUP-860).
Beginning Printing Package Including an Illustrated Reference Manual with Examples, Plus a Starter Supply of Pinfeed Paper & Matching Envelopes. Features 8 Typestyles in Multiple Sizes & Formats, Dozens of Pictures & Symbols with a Graphic Editor for Creating Designs, Text & Editing Features, Border Designs & Abstract Patterns. Supports Most Popular Printers.
Broderbund Software, Inc.

The Print Shop Companion. Roland Gustafsson. *Compatible Hardware:* Apple II+, IIe, IIc, IIgs; Atari 400, 800, XL, XE; Commodore 64, 128; IBM PC & compatibles; Tandy. *Memory Required:* IBM & Tandy 128k, all others 64k. *General Requirements:* The Print Shop software; CGA, EGA, or Hercules monochrome card for IBM. Apple, Atari, & Commodore versions support KoalaPad & joystick; IBM & Tandy versions support mouse.
Apple. disk $39.95 (Order no.: APDSK-69).
Atari & Commodore. disk $34.95 ea.
Atari. (Order no.: ATDSK-109).
Commodore. (Order no.: COMDSK-93).
IBM & Tandy. disk $49.95 (Order no.: IBMDSK-201).
Includes New Typestyles, Dozens of Creative New Borders, a Custom Calendar Feature, & New Type & Border Editors. Also Incorporates a Specially-Enhanced Graphic Editor Which Lets User "Grab" Graphics from Other Programs. Some Graphics Features Are Flood Fill Patterns, Mirror Imaging, Inverting & Flipping of Graphics. Has Optional Mouse Control & Requires THE PRINT SHOP for Use.
Broderbund Software, Inc.

The Print Shop Graphics Library, Disk 1. David Balsam & Martin Kahn. *Compatible Hardware:* Apple II+, IIe, IIc, IIgs; Atari 400, 800, XL, XE Series; Commodore 64, 128; IBM PC, PCjr, PC XT, PC AT; Tandy. *Memory Required:* Apple II & Atari 48k, Commodore 64k, IBM & Tandy 128k. *General Requirements:* The Print Shop program; CGA, EGA, or Hercules monochrome card for IBM & compatibles.
disk $24.95 ea.
Atari. (Order no.: ATDSK-99).
Commodore. (Order no.: COMDSK-97).
Apple. (Order no.: APDSK-71).
IBM, Tandy. disk $34.95 (Order no.: IBMDSK-213).
Expands the Capabilities of THE PRINT SHOP with Additional Ready-to-Use Graphic Designs. Includes Holidays, Special Occasions, Sports, School, Astrological Signs, Animals, etc. Apple, Atari & Commodore Versions Include 120 Graphics; IBM Version Includes 175 Graphics.
Broderbund Software, Inc.

The Print Shop Graphics Library, Disk 2. David Balsam & Martin Kahn. *Compatible Hardware:* Apple II+, IIe, IIc, IIgs; Atari 400, 800, XL, XE Series; Commodore 64, 128; IBM PC, PCjr, PC XT, PC AT; Tandy. *Memory Required:* Apple II & Atari 48k, Commodore 64k, IBM & Tandy 128k. *General Requirements:* The Print Shop program; CGA, EGA, or Hercules monochrome card for IBM & compatibles.
disk $24.95 ea.
Apple. (Order no.: APDSK-70).
Commodore. (Order no.: COMDSK-94).
Atari. (Order no.: ATDSK-98).
IBM, Tandy. disk $34.95 (Order no.: IBMDSK-202).
Expands the Capabilities of THE PRINT SHOP with Additional Ready-to-Use Graphic Designs. Includes Graphics Dealing with Jobs, Hobbies & People, with a Special Selection of Graphics Covering Health, Travel, Sports & Music.
Broderbund Software, Inc.

SOFTWARE ENCYCLOPEDIA 1996

The Print Shop Graphics Library, Disk 3. David Balsam & Martin Kahn. *Compatible Hardware:* Apple II+, IIe, IIc, IIgs; Atari 400, 800, XL, XE Series; Commodore 64, 128. *Memory Required:* Apple & Atari 48k, Commodore 64k. *General Requirements:* The Print Shop program.
disk $24.95 ea.
Apple. (Order no.: APDSK-73).
Atari. (Order no.: ATDSK-90).
Commodore. (Order no.: COMDSK-290).
Provides 120 Designs, Symbols & Pictures for 6 Categories: Christmas, Business, International Symbols, Myths & Fantasy, Seasons, & Animals.
Broderbund Software, Inc.

The Print Shop Graphics Library: Holiday Edition. David Balsam & Martin Kahn. *Compatible Hardware:* Apple II+, IIe, IIc, IIgs; Commodore 64, 128; IBM PC & compatibles; Tandy. *Operating System(s) Required:* PC-DOS/MS-DOS 2.0 or higher. *Memory Required:* Apple & Commodore 64k, IBM & Tandy 128k. *General Requirements:* The Print Shop program; Apple & Commodore versions support KoalaPad & joystick.
Apple. disk $24.95 (Order no.: APDSK-68).
IBM. disk $34.95 (Order no.: IBMDSK-468).
Commodore. disk $24.95 (Order no.: COMDSK-275).
Includes Graphics for 26 Holidays, Including Easter, Christmas, Hanukkah, New Years, etc. Also Included Are New Type Fonts, Borders, & Full-Panel Designs.
Broderbund Software, Inc.

PRINT to LPRINT & LPRINT to PRINT Utilities. 1981. *Compatible Hardware:* TRS-80 Model I. *Language(s):* Z-80 Assembly, BASIC. *Memory Required:* 4k.
cassette $4.95.
listing $2.00.
Changes Either Print & Print Statements to LPrint or LPrint Statements to Print.
Raymond L. Reynolds.

PrintAPlot Pro. *Version:* 4.0. Oct. 1994. *Items Included:* Printer handbook, 1 staple-stitched manual, disk, 2 3.5" disks. *Customer Support:* Free with registered serial number.
DOS. IBM AT, XT (256k). disk $199.00. *Optimal configuration:* 286 or higher, optional math coprocessor, 1Mb memory, hard disk. *Networks supported:* Novell Aware.
Software That Runs Inside AutoCAD & Turns Virtually Any Printer into a Plotter. Includes ADI Drivers, 255 Pens/Colors, HPGL/2 & HPGL at Resolutions to 600 DPI & Plot Preview. Features A to E Size Tiling, Continuous Plots, Scaling/ Rotation, Batch Printing (Standalone or Novell). Change Pen/Line Widths, Shading, & Colors.
Insight Development Corp.

PrintDW. David Bishop. *Compatible Hardware:* IBM PC, PCjr, PC XT, PC AT, Portable PC with IBM Display. *Operating System(s) Required:* DOS 2.00, 2.10, 3.00, 3.10. *Memory Required:* 128k.
disk $19.95 (Order no.: 6276604).
Converts IBM DisplayWrite Print Files to Standard ASCII Files Without Embedded Printer Controls. Enables User to: Prepare IBM DisplayWrite Files for Use on Printers Capable of Printing Files with Only Graphics Characters; Convert DisplayWrite Files to Files That Can Be Uploaded to a Host Computer; Copy or Move a Range of Lines from an ASCII File to a New File or Device; Remove Nulls from a File; Delete or Change up to Eight Characters or Eight Two-Byte Escape Sequences; Add or Delete Line Feeds & Carrier Returns or Reverse Their Positions; & Customize Print to Recognize & Strip Out Escape Sequences for Specific Printers.
Personally Developed Software, Inc.

804

TITLE INDEX

Printer Drivers. *Compatible Hardware:* Commodore Amiga.
contact publisher for price.
Printer Drivers for Mitsubishi Printers.
ACDA Corp.

Printer Genius. *Version:* 3.0. *Items Included:* 105 page manual. *Customer Support:* Free phone support.
MS-DOS/PC-DOS 2.0 or higher. IBM PC, XT, AT, PS/1, PS/2 & compatibles. disk $49.00.
Printer Management Utility. Offers Printer Fonts, Spacing & Other Controls From Pop-Up Menus or From Inside Documents Using Command Macros. Also Provides Print Spooling, Background Printing & File Brousing. Works with All Printers. Uses 32k Resident Memory.
Highland Software, Inc.

Printer Genius: Printer Driver. *Version:* 3.0. *Items Included:* Manual & other documentation. *Customer Support:* Free phone support.
MS-DOS/PC-DOS 2.0 or higher. PC, XT, AT, PS/1, PS/2 & compatibles. disk $49.00.
Printer Add-On to Other Software. Provides Printer Functions: Fonts, Spacing & Other Controls to Calling Program. Also Provides Background Priority & Print Queing. Calling Program's Language Is Irrelevant. Supports Most Printers.
Highland Software, Inc.

Printer Plotter. *Compatible Hardware:* TI 99/4A with Automatic Filer Program. *Operating System(s) Required:* DX-10. *Language(s):* Extended BASIC. *Memory Required:* 48k.
cassette $19.95.
Prints Plot of up to 100 Data Values. User Has Option of Logarithmic or Linear Scales & Automatic or User-Selected Scales. Categories & Number of Dependent Variables Are Prompted. Regression Equation Is Derived & the Coefficients Are Displayed on the Printer.
Eastbench Software Products.

Printers Bid System. DBi Software Products. *Operating System(s) Required:* MS-DOS, CP/M-86. *Memory Required:* 64k. *General Requirements:* Printer.
$600.00.
Texas Instruments, Personal Productivit.

Printers Inc. Oct. 1988. *Compatible Hardware:* Apple Macintosh II, SE or Plus; IBM PC & 100% compatibles. *Memory Required:* 1024k. *General Requirements:* 20Mb hard disk, compatible printer (impact printer required for multi-part forms).
disk $1495.00.
Designed to Help Small Commercial & Quick Printers Estimate, Schedule & Track the Progress of Print Jobs. Uses the Variable Factors Users Enter, Such As Labor & Waste Costs, to Calculate Estimates. Prints a Work in Process Report & Keeps Track of Sales. Can Also Be Used on a Network with Several Workstations when Used with GREAT PLAINS NETWORK MANAGER. Can Be Used Alone or As Part of the GREAT PLAINS ACCOUNTING SERIES. When Integrated with Other Modules Provides a Business Management Solution for Commercial & Quick Printers.
Great Plains Software.

PrintMaster Plus. *Memory Required:* 256k. *General Requirements:* Printer; hard disk recommended. *Customer Support:* 510-748-6938.
IBM PC & compatibles. 5.25" or 3.5" disk $39.95 (ISBN 0-928475-00-X, Order no.: IBMPMP).
Printing Program Which Helps Users to Create Calendars, Cards, Posters, Banners, & Stationery. Provides 11 Borders, over 100 Graphics (& Hundreds More with ART GALLERY), & Nine Typefaces in Upper & Lower Case. Permits Users to Preview & Make Changes Without Starting Over. Not Copy Protected.
Unison World.

Printographer. *Version:* 8.9. Stephen Billard. 1984. *Compatible Hardware:* Apple II, II+, IIe, IIc, IIgs. *Operating System(s) Required:* Apple ProDOS 8. *Language(s):* Assembly. *Memory Required:* 64k. *General Requirements:* Printer.
disk $39.95 (ISBN 0-927796-01-5).
Menu-Driven Printing Utility for Printing Hi-Res Screens on Any Graphics Printer. Includes Picture Cropping (Horizontal, Vertical, Diamond or Oval), Normal or Inverse Inking, Horizontal or Vertical Printouts, Indentation & Justification. Supports Color Printing.
Roger Wagner Publishing, Inc.

Printrix. *Version:* Apple 1.15, IBM 3.1. Steve Boker. Feb. 1986. *Compatible Hardware:* Apple IIe, IIc, IIgs; IBM PC & compatibles, PC XT, PC AT. *Operating System(s) Required:* MS-DOS/PC-DOS 2.0 or higher, ProDOS. *Language(s):* Assembly. *Memory Required:* Apple 128k, IBM 512k. *General Requirements:* Supports dot-matrix & laser printers.
Apple. disk $65.00.
IBM. disk $165.00.
limited warranty avail.
Post-Processor of Word Processor Files, Typesetting in Any Combination of 23 Included Fonts. Page Layout, Headers & Footers, Mixed Graphics & Text, Mail Merge, etc.
Data Transforms, Inc.

Prints Charming. Mary Lou East & Federick B. East. Jan. 1985. *Compatible Hardware:* Apple II, II+, IIe. *Operating System(s) Required:* Apple DOS 3.3, ProDOS. *Memory Required:* 32k. *General Requirements:* Printer (Apple Imagewriter, DMP, Epson FX-80, RX-80, MX-80, Panasonic).
disk $24.95 ea.
Allows the Apple Computer User with an Epson Printer, Panasonic Printer, or Apple Printer to Configure the Printer Without Having to Look-Up & Input the Proper Function Commands.
Cardinal Point, Inc.
  ProDOS/Apple Imagewriter. (ISBN 0-932065-17-1, Order no.: PC2IM).
  DOS 3.3/Apple Imagewriter. (ISBN 0-932065-18-X, Order no.: PC1IM).
  ProDOS/Apple DMP. (ISBN 0-932065-19-8, Order no.: PC2DMP).
  DOS 3.3/Apple DMP. (ISBN 0-932065-20-1, Order no.: PC1DMP).
  DOS 3.3/Epson FX-80. (ISBN 0-932065-01-5, Order no.: PC1FX).
  ProDOS/Epson FX-80. (ISBN 0-932065-02-3, Order no.: PC2FX).
  DOS 3.3/Epson RX-80. (ISBN 0-932065-03-1, Order no.: PC1RX).
  ProDOS/Epson RX-80. (ISBN 0-932065-04-X, Order no.: PC2RX).
  DOS 3.3/Epson MX-80 Type 3 or MX-80 with GraphTrax Plus. (ISBN 0-932065-05-8, Order no.: PC1MX-3).
  ProDOS/Epson MX-80 Type 3 or MX-80 with GraphTrax Plus. (ISBN 0-932065-06-6, Order no.: PC2MX-3).
  DOS 3.3/Epson MX-80 with GraphTrax. (ISBN 0-932065-07-4, Order no.: PC1MX-2).
  ProDOS/Epson MX-80 with GraphTrax. (ISBN 0-932065-08-2, Order no.: PC2MX-2).
  ProDOS/Epson MX-80. (ISBN 0-932065-09-0, Order no.: PC2MX-1).
  DOS 3.3/Epson MX-80. (ISBN 0-932065-10-4, Order no.: PC1MX-1).
  ProDOS/Panasonic KX-P1092. (ISBN 0-932065-11-2, Order no.: PC292).
  DOS 3.3/Panasonic KX-P1092. (ISBN 0-932065-12-0, Order no.: PC192).
  ProDOS/Panasonic KX-P1091. (ISBN 0-932065-13-9, Order no.: PC291).
  DOS 3.3/Panasonic KX-P1091. (ISBN 0-932065-14-7, Order no.: PC191).
  ProDOS/Panasonic KX-P1090. (ISBN 0-932065-15-5, Order no.: PC290).
  DOS 3.3/Panasonic KX-P1090. (ISBN 0-932065-16-3, Order no.: PC190).

Prints-Pro. Jul. 1995. *Items Included:* Manual, Prints-Pro disks. *Customer Support:* 90 day unlimited warranty.
Windows 3.1. 386, 256 colors (8Mb). disk $999.00. *Addl. software required:* Image-Pro Plus.
A New Specialized Software Solution for Latent Fingerprint & Other Print & Impression Analyses. A "Plug-In" Module for Image-Pro Plus, the Company's Premier Image Analysis Software Package. Provides Forensic Criminalists with User Friendly Software Allowing Them to Input, Enhance, & Output Fingerprints into an Automated Fingerprint Identification System (AFIS). It Can Also Be Used for Other Prints & Impression Analyses. Side-by-Side Display of Prints Makes Comparing, Tracing, Charting, Panning, & Zooming Easy & Accurate. Using Standard File Formats, Images Can Be Transferred Freely to Other State & Federal Agencies for Matching. Localized Histogram Equalization Provides Multiple Area of Interest (AOI) Processing & Interactive Manual Object Tagging & Classifying.
Media Cybernetics, L. P.

Printwheels. Robert S. Hand. Aug. 1992. *Items Included:* Manual. *Customer Support:* Free phone support.
PC-DOS/MS-DOS. IBM PC & MS-DOS & compatibles, 286 or higher (640k). disk $75.00 (ISBN 0-87199-119-5). *Nonstandard peripherals required:* Hard disk; IBM- or Epson-compatible Dot-matrix printer, or Hewlett Packard laser or inkjet printer. *Addl. software required:* Nova-compatible Horoscope Calculation Program (Nova Chartwheels, Professional Natal Report, CCRS Horoscope Program 92, Solar Fire Blackwell & Mackey-Saunders' Data Collections). *Optimal configuration:* 1 or more Mb RAM; Math co-processor with 286 or 386 systems; VGA, ETA or Hercules monitor.
Allows User to Print Out High-Resolution Horoscope Wheels, Aspectarians & Other Tables Using Birth Data Calculated by Any Nova-Compatible Horoscope Calculation or Chart Database Program. Includes 101 Pre-Formatted Chart Pages, & the User Can Customize Each of These Through Menu Choices or Changes in the Program's Graphics Language. Includes American, European, Traditional, Decorative & Dial-Type Chart Styles, & Also a Selection of Uranian & Cosmobiology Dials to Fit over Charts.
Astrolabe, Inc.

Printwheels DTP. Robert S. Hand. Aug. 1992. *Items Included:* Spiral-bound manual. *Customer Support:* Free phone support.
PC-DOS/MS-DOS. IBM PC & MS-DOS & compatibles, 286 or higher (640k). disk $200.00 (ISBN 0-87199-120-9). *Nonstandard peripherals required:* Hard disk; IBM- or Epson-compatible Dot-matrix printer, or Hewlett Packard laser or inkjet printer, or any Postscript device. *Addl. software required:* Nova-compatible Horoscope Calculation Program. DTP functions require a word processing, Desktop Publishing or Graphics Program. *Optimal configuration:* 1 or more Mb

RAM; Math co-processor; VGA, EGA or Hercules monitor.
High-Resolution Horoscope Printing Program for Authors, Editors & Artists. Includes Everything That Is in the Regular Version of Printwheels, Plus 90 Additional Chart Forms & the Ability to Output Any Chart As a Vector or Bitmapped Graphics File That Can Be Used in a Painting, Drawing or Desktop Publishing Program. Outputs Graphic Files in TIFF, PCX, BMP, IMG, CGM, HPGL, WPG, EPS & Other Graphics Formats.
Astrolabe, Inc.

PRISE: Plume Rise & Dispersion Model. *Version:* 2.1. B. Henderson-Sellers. Jan. 1988. *Items Included:* Manual, binder, description of code. *Customer Support:* Fax support.
MS-DOS 2.0 or higher. IBM PC & compatibles (256k). software pkg. $690.00 (ISBN 0-931215-84-6).
An Advanced Software Package to Calculate Air- or Water-Borne Effluent Dispersion. Calculates All Phases of the Plume in One Continuous Formulation, Taking the Ambient Meteorological Conditions Fully into Account. Data May Be Input from Files or Keyboard.
Computational Mechanics, Inc.

PRISM. Vincente Lozada. *Operating System(s) Required:* MS-DOS. *Memory Required:* 128k. *General Requirements:* Printer, Winchester hard disk.
$500.00.
Texas Instruments, Personal Productivit.

PRISM Business Planning & Control Systems. *Version:* 2.0. *Compatible Hardware:* IBM, AS/400 series. *Items Included:* 1 set documentation, object code, source code. *Customer Support:* 6 month warranty. Options available for different levels of support. Contact vendor.
contact publisher for price.
Business Planning & Control System Exclusively for Process Manufacturers. Based on Resource Management Concepts That Enable Users to Manage Labor Grades, Utilities & Other Cost & Revenue Elements of Production. Co-Product & By-Product Management, Yield Planning, Process Casting & Schedule Control Are Fully Supported by the Software. Also Available Are Formula Management, Regulatory Compliance, Quality Management, Warehouse Management & Full Financials Including Activity Costing & Currency.
Marcam Corporation.

Privacode. *Compatible Hardware:* IBM PC XT & compatibles. *Operating System(s) Required:* PC-DOS, MS-DOS.
disk $395.00, incl. manual.
add'l. network copies $295.00.
special order fee $25.00.
Designed to Protect Sensitive Information. Formats User's Private Files into Unreadable Blocks of Letters That Only the Owner of the Privacode Disk Can Read. Translates Files Made by Word Processors, Data Bases, & Spreadsheet Application Programs. Also Functions Through Modems in Dialup Links & Links with ASCII Electronic Mail Networks.
Eden Pr. (California).

Privacy Plus. *Version:* 3.01. 1980. *Compatible Hardware:* IBM PC & compatibles, PC XT, PC AT. *Operating System(s) Required:* PC-DOS 2.0 or higher. *Memory Required:* 65k. *Items Included:* User documentation. *Customer Support:* Free telephone support.
Single User $195.00, LAN version $495.00.
site & corporate licensing avail.
File by File Encryption Module for Data on Both Hard & Floppy Disks.
United Software Security, Inc.

Private Membership Club. ADS Software, Inc. *Operating System(s) Required:* MS-DOS. *Memory Required:* 128k. *General Requirements:* 2 disk drives, printer.
$895.00.
Texas Instruments, Personal Productivit.

Private Pilot Written Test Simulator. *Items Included:* Bound manual. *Customer Support:* Free hotline - no time limit; 30 day limited warranty; updates are $5/disk plus S&H.
MS-DOS 2.1 or higher. IBM & compatibles (256k), not available for PCjr. disk $49.95.
Nonstandard peripherals required: Two 360k disk drives (or one 360k drive & one hard disk); works on both color & monochrome monitors & with all types of video-display cards.
Educational Tutorial for Student Pilots & Those Wishing to Take up Flying. It Prepares You for the FAA Official Private-Pilot Written Test. This Easy-to-Use Menu-Driven Software Was Designed by Licensed Pilots & Requires No Formal Computer Training.
Dynacomp, Inc.

Prize Fighter. *Items Included:* Instruction manual. *Customer Support:* Free Telephone support.
Saturn. Sega Saturn. Contact publisher for price.
Digital Pictures, Inc.

PRNSPOOL. F. Andy Seidl. Jun. 1985. *Compatible Hardware:* IBM PC & compatibles, Zenith Z-100. *Operating System(s) Required:* PC-DOS/MS-DOS 2.0 or higher. *Language(s):* Assembly. *Memory Required:* 128k. *General Requirements:* Printer.
disk $54.95.
Allows User to Use His Computer While the Output from His Word Processor, Spreadsheet or Other Application, Is Printing. Works with Any Printer & Can Be Used with Multiple Printers/Plotters. Uses the DOS PRINT Command.
Generic Computer Products, Inc. (GCPI).

Pro-Accountant: Integrated Business System. *Version:* 2.6. Jul. 1985. *Compatible Hardware:* DEC Pro-350, DEC VAX 8600. *Operating System(s) Required:* P/OS, VMS. *Memory Required:* 500k. *General Requirements:* 2 disk drives, printer.
Pro-350 DEC. disk $895.00 (Order no.: MODULE).
VAX 8600 DEC. disk $90,000.00 (Order no.: SYSTEM).
Modular Multi-User System Which Is Fully Integrated to Perform in Any DEC (Micro, SuperMicro, PDP, VAX) System. Functions As a Self-Guided, Menu-Driven Code Generator in Batch or Interactive Environments.
DecComp, Inc.

Pro-Board. *Version:* 2.0B. *Compatible Hardware:* Commodore Amiga. *Items Included:* Diskette & manual. *Customer Support:* Direct; indirect through distributors; new version update, nominal fee.
3.5" disk $299.00.
PCB CAD Program.
Prolific, Inc.

Pro-Bookie Combo. 1986. *Compatible Hardware:* Apple II, III; Commodore 64/128; IBM PC & compatibles. *Memory Required:* IBM 256k, Apple 64k, Commodore 64k.
3.5" or 5.25" disk $299.95.
Features a Combination of Both the Professional Series Football & the Bookie Buster I. Single Input Will Give Results for Both Programs.
Professor Jones Professional Handicapping Systems.

Pro Bookkeeper. Chuck Atkinson Programs. *Operating System(s) Required:* CP/M-86. *Memory Required:* 320k.
$95.00 (Order no.: QC).
Texas Instruments, Personal Productivit.

Pro-Byter. Bert Kersey & Jack Cassidy. Apr. 1986. *Compatible Hardware:* Apple II, II+, IIe, IIc, IIgs. *Operating System(s) Required:* ProDOS. *Language(s):* Machine, BASIC. *Memory Required:* 64k.
disk $34.95.
Disk Inspector/ProDOS Utility. The BYTEZAP PRO Program Lets User Inspect & Change ProDOS & DOS 3.3 Disks at the Byte Level: Users Can Find Any Word or Phrase on a Disk or Search a Specific File, & Change It on the Spot. Also Included Is an Easy-to-Use Memory Inspector That Lets Users Not Only View & Change Apple's Memory, But Insert & Delete Bytes As Well. Other Included Utilities Are: Machine Language Sorter, AppleSoft Converter, Text Typer, etc.
Beagle Brothers.

PRO Challenge. *Compatible Hardware:* Apple Macintosh; IBM PC, PC XT, PC AT, & compatibles.
IBM. Version 2.00 (10/1987) $49.95.
Macintosh SE, Plus, SE/30, II, IIx, IIcx. Version 1.02 (03/1989) $49.95.
Football Simulation. Starting with Two All-NFL Teams of Equal Strength, You Choose from 27 Offensive & 14 Defensive Plays to Outwit Your Opponent or the Computer. Incorporates Such Real-Life Game Events As Fumbles, Interceptions, & Penalties.
XOR Corp.

Pro-Cite. *Version:* 2.1. Aug. 1991. *Compatible Hardware:* Macintosh. *Language(s):* C. *Memory Required:* 1000k. *Items Included:* Disk, manual, binder, basic guide, quick reference card. *Customer Support:* Free phone support, Mon-Fri 9-5 EST, 30 day money back guarantee, free newsletter.
CD-ROM disk Contact publisher for price.
Full Featured Reference Management Database Program That Produces Formatted Bibliographies. Stores Bibliographic Data, Notes, & Keywords. You Can Search, Sort, & Print Your Citations Within Seconds. Generates Any Type of Bibliography in Any Style. Works with the Word Processor for Bibliography Creation from References Cited in the Manuscript. With ProCite, You Can Create Your Own Electronic Catalog, Efficiently Update References, Print Formatted Bibliographies, & Even Provide Current Awareness Service to Others. Records Can Be Downloaded from Online Services, Automated Library Systems & CD-ROM Services (an Optional Biblio Link Program May Be Necessary). The Network Version Enables Multiple Users to Simultaneously Search, Sort, Index, Print, & Output Records to Disk All Without Altering the Original Database.
Personal Bibliographic Software, Inc.

Pro-Cite (IBM). *Version:* 2.2. Jul. 1993. *Items Included:* Disks, manuals, binder, basic guide, quick reference card. *Customer Support:* Free phone support Mon-Friday 9-5, 30 day-money back guarantee, free newsletter.
PC-DOS or MD-DOS. IBM PC or compatible (256k). CD-ROM disk Contact publisher for price. *Nonstandard peripherals required:* hard disk or two DS disk drives.
Full Featured Reference Management Database Program That Produces Formatted Bibliographies. Stores Bibliographic Data, Notes, & Keywords. You Can Search, Sort, & Print Your Citations Within Seconds. Generates Any Type of Bibliography in Any Style. Works with the Word

TITLE INDEX

Processor for Bibliography Creation from References Cited in the Manuscript. With ProCite, You Can Create Your Own Electronic Catalog, Efficiently Update References, Print Formatted Bibliographies, & Even Provide Current Awareness Service to Others. Records Can Be Downloaded from Online Services, Automated Library Systems & CD-ROM Services (an Optional Biblio Line Program May Be Necessary). The Network Version Enables Multiple Users to Simultaneously Search, Sort, Index, Print, & Output Records to Disk All Without Altering the Original Database.
Personal Bibliographic Software, Inc.

Pro-Desk. *Compatible Hardware:* Apple Macintosh Plus. *Operating System(s) Required:* System 5.0 or higher. *General Requirements:* Printer.
3.5" disk $499.00.
Office Automation Workstation.
Mission Accomplished Software Services, Inc.

PRO DGI Word Search. *Version:* 1.11. Charles D. Blish. Mar. 1986. *Compatible Hardware:* Apple II+, IIe, IIc; IBM PC, PC XT, PC AT. *Operating System(s) Required:* Apple DOS 3.3, PC-DOS 2.0 or higher. *Memory Required:* Apple 48k, IBM 128k.
disk $24.95 ea.
Apple. (ISBN 0-932779-05-0, Order no.: AP-WORD).
IBM. (ISBN 0-932779-06-9, Order no.: IBM-WORD).
Allows User to Create Word Search Puzzles That Are from 10 x 10 to 25 x 50 Characters in Size. User Can Control the Difficulty Level of Puzzles by Dictating in Which Combinations of Six Directions Words Can Appear. Up to 100 Words Can Be Input for Each Puzzle.
Decision Graphics, Inc. (Colorado).

Pro-IV Accountant. *Version:* 2.5. *Compatible Hardware:* IBM PC & compatibles, DOS, XENIX, VMS, UNIX. *Memory Required:* 160k. *General Requirements:* Hard disk. *Customer Support:* Maintenance -1yr. $1000-1500.
$350.00 to $10,000.00 per module.
Posts Recurring Transactions, Automatic Posting from Other Modules, Report Format User Definable, Reports Comparative Statements, Ability to Jump Modules, Wild Card, Links with External Software Programs, Password Access, Encryption, Audit Trail, Reject Erroneous Account Numbers, On-Line Help & Source Code Available.
Applications Systems Corp.

Pro League Option Module. *Items Included:* Manual, catalog, update card. *Customer Support:* Always free over the phone, disks replaced free for first 30 days, disks replaced for $10.00 after 30 days.
Commodore 64/128. $14.95.
Choose Any of 27 Professional Teams & Try to Lead Them into the Finals. Use Actual Player Names or Add Your Own. Includes a Mid-Season All-Star Game Where You Select the Rosters for Both Teams.
SportTime Computer Software.

The Pro-Mation Advantage: Accounts Payable. *Version:* 4.0. *Compatible Hardware:* Altos; AT&T; IBM PC, PC XT, PC AT, PC RT; 386, 486, IBM RS6000. *Operating System(s) Required:* PC-DOS/MS-DOS, XENIX, UNIX V, AIX, Windows, Networks. *Language(s):* ACUCOBOL. *Memory Required:* 640k. *Customer Support:* Available with 800 number, regional & onsite training.
contact publisher for price.
Subcontractor Control, Invoice Distribution to Multiple Jobs, Flexible Selection for Payment, Partial Payment, Manual Checks, Automatic Void, On Screen Inquiry, Indepth or Summary Reporting, Recurring Invoices.
Pro-Mation, Inc.

The Pro-Mation Advantage: Accounts Receivable. *Version:* 4.0. *Compatible Hardware:* Altos; AT&T; IBM PC XT, PC AT, PC RT; 386, 486, RS6000. *Operating System(s) Required:* PC-DOS/MS-DOS, UNIX V, XENIX, AIX, Windows, Networks. *Language(s):* ACUCOBOL. *Memory Required:* 640k. *Customer Support:* Available w/800 #, regional & onsite training.
contact publisher for price.
Pro-Mation, Inc.

The Pro-Mation Advantage: Equipment Control. *Version:* 4.0. *Compatible Hardware:* Altos; AT&T; IBM PC, PC XT, PC AT, PC RT; 386, 486, IBM RS6000. *Operating System(s) Required:* PC-DOS/MS-DOS, XENIX, UNIX V, AIX, Windows Network. *Language(s):* ACUCOBOL. *Memory Required:* 640k. *General Requirements:* 40Mb. *Customer Support:* Available with 800 number, regional & onsite training.
contact publisher for price.
Revenue/Expense by Equipment, Idle Time, Location, Ownership Costs (Depreciation, Taxes, Insurance, etc.), Flexible Internal Billing Rates, External Billing for T&M Jobs.
Pro-Mation, Inc.

The Pro-Mation Advantage: General Ledger. *Version:* 4.0. *Compatible Hardware:* Altos; Compaq; IBM PC XT, PC AT, PC RT. *Operating System(s) Required:* PC-DOS/MS-DOS, XENIX, UNIX V, AIX, Windows Network. *Language(s):* ACUCOBOL. *Memory Required:* 640k. *Customer Support:* Available w/800 #, regional & onsite training.
contact publisher for price.
Flexible Format for Financials, Departmentalization, Auto Interface to All Accounting Modules, On Screen Inquiry, Work in Multiple Accounting Periods, Option to Retain Detailed Journal Entries.
Pro-Mation, Inc.

The Pro-Mation Advantage: Inventory Control-Purchase Orders. *Version:* 4.0. *Compatible Hardware:* Altos; Compaq; IBM PC XT, PC AT, PC RT; 386, 486, RS6000. *Operating System(s) Required:* PC-DOS/MS-DOS, XENIX, UNIX V, AIX, Windows Network. *Language(s):* ACUCOBOL. *Memory Required:* 640k. *General Requirements:* Hard disk, printer. *Customer Support:* Available w/800 #, regional & onsite training.
contact publisher for price.
Multiple Locations, Inventory Used on Jobs/Equipment, Tracks Average/Last Cost, Tracks Cost by Vendor, PO Interface W/ Accounts Payable & Inventory, PO Committed Costs Tracked in Job Cost.
Pro-Mation, Inc.

The Pro-Mation Advantage: Job Costing. *Version:* 4.0. *Compatible Hardware:* Altos; AT&T; Compaq; IBM PC XT, PC AT, PC RT; 386, 486, RS6000. *Operating System(s) Required:* PC-DOS/MS-DOS, XENIX, UNIX V, AIX, Windows, Networks. *Language(s):* ACUCOBOL. *Memory Required:* 640k. *Customer Support:* Available w/800 #, regional & onsite training.
contact publisher for price.
Flexible Job Setup, Auto Interface to All Accounting Modules, Interactive Inquiry, Comprehensive Reporting, Contract Change Detail, %/Quantity Complete, Unit/Hourly Cost Analysis, Detail Retained.
Pro-Mation, Inc.

The Pro-Mation Advantage: Payroll. *Version:* 4.0. *Compatible Hardware:* Altos; AT&T; Compaq; IBM PC XT, PC AT, PC RT; 386, 486, RS6000. *Operating System(s) Required:* PC-DOS/MS-DOS, XENIX, UNIX V, AIX, Windows, Networks. *Language(s):* ACUCOBOL. *Memory Required:* 640k. *Customer Support:* Available w/800 #, regional & onsite training.
contact publisher for price.
Multiple State, Union, Certified, Comprehensive Workers Comp & Liability Tracking & Reporting, 401(K)/125 Options.
Pro-Mation, Inc.

Pro-Net. *Version:* 2.0B. *Compatible Hardware:* Commodore Amiga. *Items Included:* Diskettes, manual. *Customer Support:* Direct; indirect through distributors; new version update, nominal fee.
3.5" disk $249.00.
Schematic Capture CAD System.
Prolific, Inc.

Pro Plus Accounting. *General Requirements:* Hard disk drive.
Macintosh Plus or higher. $350.00 per module; $995.00 complete system.
General Ledger, Accounts Receivable, Accounts Payable, Inventory Control.
Pro Plus Software, Inc.

Pro Predictions. *Items Included:* Bound manual. *Customer Support:* Free hotline - no time limit; 30 day limited warranty; updates are $5/disk plus S&H.
MS-DOS. IBM & compatibles (128k). disk $69.95.
Apple (48k); Commodore 64. disk $69.95.
Capabilities for Analyzing, Forecasting, & Producing a Wide Range of Statistics on Professional Football in the National & U.S. Football Leagues.
Dynacomp, Inc.

Pro Tools. Aug. 1991. *Items Included:* 3 manuals, 5 disks. *Customer Support:* Free telephone technical support.
Macintosh II, IIx, IIcx, IIci, IIfx. 3.5" disk $5995.00.
New Technology Integrating Multitrack Digital Audio Recording & Editing, DSP, MIDI Sequencing & Automated Digital Mixing into a Single Digital Audio Workstation Based on the Macintosh II Platform. Consists of ProDECK Software for Recording & Mixing & ProEDIT Software for Graphic Editing of Both Digital Audio & MID! & Two Hardware Components, the Audio Interface for Analog & Digital I/O & the Audio Card Installed in the Macintosh. With add Aimalcards, Can Record & Edit 16 Tracks of Audio Simultaneously.
Digidesign, Inc.

Pro Tutor Accounting. *Compatible Hardware:* IBM PC & compatibles. *Memory Required:* 128k. $99.00.
Basic Accounting Principles. Designed for Use by Accounting Students, New Employees, Self Learners, etc. Contains over Three Thousand Questions about Debits & Credits, Journalizing & Balance Sheets. Tutor Keeps Track of Correct & Incorrect Answers, Shows Where Mistakes Were Made & Identifies Strengths & Weaknesses. Teachers's Version Includes Utilities for Tabulating Student's Scores.
Professional Software, Inc.

Pro-Vision. *Compatible Hardware:* IBM PC & compatibles.
disk $2400.00 to $9600.00.
Includes a Family of CAD Products: ProCADD; Pro-Solid; Pro-Fem; & Pro-CAM.
Infinite Graphics, Inc.

PROART PROFESSIONAL ART LIBRARY

ProArt Professional Art Library. *General Requirements:* Layout or draw program that supports encapsulated postscript illustrations. *Items Included:* Pictorial index, user guide. *Customer Support:* Technical support.
Macintosh. 3.5" disk $64.00.
IBM PC & compatibles. 3.5" or 5.25" disk $64.00.
A Comprehensive, Easy-to-Use Art Collection Designed to Meet Electronic Art Needs. Available As Collections, Trilogies, or the Portfolio. Thirteen Different Collections, Comprised of 100 Images per Collection, Are Available on Macintosh or PC Floppy Disks. Four Trilogies, Made of 300 Images per Trilogy, Are Available on a Macintosh/PC Hybrid Compact Disc. The Comprehensive Portfolio Macintosh-Format Compact Disc Contains over 3,000 Images Covering More Than Fifty Different Topics. All Images Are Created in Adobe Illustrator & Saved in High-Quality EPS Format.
Multi-Ad Services, Inc.

ProAssist. Oct. 1989. *Items Included:* Complete reference manual. *Customer Support:* 90 days limited warranty.
MS-DOS/PC-DOS 2.0 or higher (512k). IBM PC, PC XT, PC AT, PS/2 model 30 & compatibles. disk $199.00. *Nonstandard peripherals required:* TrueSOUND Card. *Addl. software required:* TrueSOUND Card Drivers. *Networks supported:* All Netbios LANS (Novell, 3Com, etc.).
Software Package Which Is Used with TrueSOUND Card to Offer Interactive, Context Sensitive Audio Help. Can Also Be Used with Various Presentation Graphics Software Packages to Create Television Quality Audio/Visual Presentations.
Webco Computers.

ProAUCTIONEER. Version: 2.81. 1995. *Items Included:* Manual included. *Customer Support:* 90-days free phone support; $25.00 per call after.
MS-DOS. IBM & compatibles. disk $299.00.
Greatly Simplifies the Process of Clerking an Auction. Controls the Auction Items & Provides for Their Cataloging. Keeps Track of Bidders Names & Addresses, with an Account Record of Their Purchases. Records Who Bought What & for How Much. Provides Bills for Bidders & Accepts Payment. Tracks Results of the Auction Including Items Sold & Unsold. Maintains a List of Bidders & Other Attendees for Advising of Future Auctions. Provides for Consignors.
Taranto & Assocs., Inc.

Probability & Statistics. *Items Included:* Bound manual. *Customer Support:* Free hotline - no time limit; 30 day limited warranty; updates are $5/disk plus S&H.
MS-DOS. IBM & compatibles (256k). disk $179.95.
Factorials/Counting; Permutations - Pts. 1 & 2; Combinations; Permutations & Combinations; Probability - Pts. 1-4; Mean, Mode, & Median; Range, Variance, & Deviation; Z-Scores & Std. Scores.
Dynacomp, Inc.

Probability Toolkit. 1994. *Items Included:* Book & software (teacher's manual). *Customer Support:* Technical support available - no charge; free upgrading.
System 7.0 or higher. Mac LC or higher (1Mb). $79.95 school; $129.95 5-user; $179.95 10-user; $379.95 30-user (ISBN 1-57116-007-8). *Networks supported:* Yes.
Imagine Having a Powerful Tool for Exploring Probability Instantly at Your Fingertips. According to NCTM, the Role of Data & Chance in School Mathematics Is Rapidly Changing Both in Increased Emphasis & in Methods of Instruction. Provides Teachers & Students with an Easy to Use Computer-Based Environment for Simulating & Analyzing Chance Events. Simulations Include Tossing Chips, Selecting Colored Marbles from a Set, Choosing a Color on a Spinner, Rolling a Pair of Dice, Picking a Random Number, Dropping a Marble Through a Peg Board, & Guessing a Card from a Set of 5 Cards. Grade Levels K-8.
Ventura Educational Systems.

Probaloto. *Items Included:* Bound manual. *Customer Support:* Free hotline - no time limit; 30 day limited warranty; updates are $5/disk plus S&H.
MS-DOS. IBM & compatibles (256k). disk $39.95.
Menu-Driven System That Incorporates a Sophisticated Mathematical Formula to Analyze & Weigh the Numbers Previously Chosen Using a Data File That Is Automatically Updated As You Use PROBALOTO. Data Files Are Created by Just Typing in How Many Times a Number Has Been Chosen.
Dynacomp, Inc.

Probit. *Compatible Hardware:* Apple Macintosh Plus or higher.
3.5" disk $110.00.
Provides a Method for Estimating a Multiple Regression Model or Analysis of Covariance When the Dependent Variable Is Catergorical & Can Take Only One of Two Values.
Systat, Inc.

Problem Analysis. Version: 3.0. Aug. 1987. *Compatible Hardware:* IBM PC & compatibles. *Operating System(s) Required:* PC-DOS 2.1 or higher. *Language(s):* Pascal. *Memory Required:* 256k.
5-1/4" or 3-1/2" disk $49.95.
Helps Training. Human Factors-Professionals Collect Performance Data. Worksheets Are Included for Task Analysis, Time & Motion Studies, Process Analysis, Focus Groups, Critical Incident Techniques, & Others.
Park Row Software.

ProCalc. Software Products International (S.P.I.). Jan. 1984. *Operating System(s) Required:* MS-DOS. *Memory Required:* 192k. *General Requirements:* Printer, Winchester hard disk. $275.00 (Order no.: TI P/N 2311415-0001). Texas Instruments, Personal Productivit.

Process BASIC Software Interpreter. *Compatible Hardware:* Z-80 based microcomputer systems.
contact publisher for price.
Extended Implementation of Microsoft BASIC-80, Version 5.0.
Thomson Semi Conductors-Mostek Corp.

Process Breakthrough. H. James Harrington. Jan. 1994. *Customer Support:* Unlimited support.
Contact publisher for price.
This Interactive Software Provides a Road Map That Helps Your Organization Improve Your Critical Processes As Much As 1500%. It Streamlines Your Critical Business Processes with Tools Like Process Redesign, New Process Design, & Benchmarking. It Maintains an Extensive Database & Produces Reports.
LearnerFirst.

Process Control Chart Tool Kit. Version: 6.0. *Compatible Hardware:* Apple Macintosh; Windows. *Memory Required:* 1000k. *Items Included:* Spiral bound manual. *Customer Support:* Free telephone support.
3.5" disk $399.00.
Statistical Graphing, Charting, Quality Control Analysis & Graphs.
Sof-Ware Tools.

Process Engineering Software Package, 3 disks/3 notebooks. Version: 2.11. Jan. 1990. *Compatible Hardware:* IBM PC & compatibles, PC XT, PC AT. *Operating System(s) Required:* DOS. *Language(s):* BASIC, ASSEMBLER (source code included). *Memory Required:* 96k.
Equipment Evaluation (set of 6 programs) $195.00.
Fluid Flow (set of 7 programs) $195.00.
Heat Transfer (set of 6 programs) $195.00.
Consists of a Selection Menu & Individual Modules for Solving Specific Engineering Problem Sets.
Engineering Software, Inc.
  EE1 Compressor Sizing-Multistage.
    Find Power, Pressures, Temperatures, for 1 to 3 Stages, Including Losses.
  EE2 Compressor Sizing-Single Stage.
    Find Power, Head, ACFM, Temperatures, Adiabatic or Polytropic Efficiency.
  EE3 Compressor Evaluation-Reciprocating.
    Find Volumetric Efficiency, Flow, Temperatures, Horsepower, Rod Load.
  EE4 Pump Sizing.
    Find Power, NPSHA, Estimate Efficiencies, Includes Viscosity Correction.
  EE5 Pump Evaluation.
    Find Either Efficiency or Temperature Rise; Only for High Head Pumps.
  EE6-Separator Sizing.
    Find Particle Diameter or Vessel ID Using Stokes, Intermed, Newton Law.
  FF1 Incompressible Pressure Loss.
    Find Piping Loss & Velocity, Including Fittings, Valves, Evaluation Inputs.
  FF2 Two Phase Pressure Loss.
    Find Horizontal Loss & Baker Coefficient with Lockhart-Martinelli, Including Fittings.
  FF3 Compressible Pressure Loss.
    Find Upstream or Downstream Pressure, MACH Numbers for Isothermal Gas Flow.
  FF4 Weymouth Flow Calculation.
    Find Flow, Pipe ID, Upstream or Downstream Pressure for Gas Pipelines.
  FF5 Packed Bed Pressure Loss.
    Find Loss Across a Vessel Containing Pellets Using Ergun Correlation.
  FF6 Manning Flow Calculation.
    Find Flow or Slope for Gravity Water Flow in Open or Closed Channels.
  FF7 Gas Orifice Pressure Loss-Sizing.
    Find Flow, Pressure Loss, or Orifice ID Using AGA or SPINK Methods.
  HT1 Pipe Insulation Heat Loss.
    Find TEMPERATURES, Heat Flow for 0-3 Layers; Input for Film Coefficient.
  HT2 Pipe Inside Heat Tranfer Coefficient.
    Find Inside Film Coefficient for Laminar Through Turbulent Pipe Flow.
  HT3 Shell & Tube Evaluation (1 Pass).
    Find LMTD & Either Overall U, Exit TEMPERATURES, or Fouling Factor.
  HT4 Shell & Tube Evaluation (2,4,6,. . pass).
    Find LMTD & Either Overall U, Exit Temperatures, or Fouling Factor.
  HT5 Heat Emission & Surface Temperature.
    Find Convective & Radiant Heat Flow, or Temperatures for Hot Pipes.
  HT6 Composite Wall Heat Tranfer.
    Find Temperatures, Heat Flow for 0 to 4 Layers; Input for Film Coefficient.
  UCI Engineering Units Conversion.
    Over 200 Conversion Factors for English & Metric Units in 19 Categories, Included with All Sets.

Process Engineer's Conversion Kit. *Items Included:* Bound manual. *Customer Support:* Free hotline - no time limit; 30 day limited warranty; updates are $5/disk plus S&H.
MS-DOS. IBM & compatibles (256k). disk $29.95.
Apple. disk $29.95.

TITLE INDEX

Convert Between Units Commonly Used in the Process Industries. Measurements of Temperature, Pressure, Mass, Density, & Other Process Parameters Are Easily Converted Between Standards.
Dynacomp, Inc.

Process Management. Tennessee Associates International Staff. Dec. 1993. *Items Included:* Flowcharting Tools. *Customer Support:* Unlimited support.
Contact publisher for price.
This Interactive Software Application Provides a Road Map to Help You Understand & Apply Methods to Enhance Customer Satisfaction. It Gives You a Jump-Start for Improving Your Buisness Performance on a Timely Basis by Systematically Focusing on Defining, Analyzing, Re-Engineering, & Improving Processes. It Maintains an Extensive Database & Produces Reports.
LearnerFirst.

Process Server. *Version:* 3.1. Jan. 1989. *Customer Support:* On site training unlimited support services for first 90 days & through subscription thereafter.
MS-DOS, PS-DOS. Contact publisher for price. *Nonstandard peripherals required:* Hard disk (30Mb); 132-column printer. *Networks supported:* Novell, NTNX, 10-Net, Unix, Xenix, Turbo DOS (Multi-User version for all).
Specialized to Businesses Serving Legal & Other Documents. Manages Serving of Papers & Associated Court Reporting.
Argos Software.

ProcessTerm. *Version:* 2.4. Alexander Perlis Inc. Oct. 1988. *Items Included:* Comprehensive user & technical manual. *Customer Support:* 7 day-a-week telephone, BBS, & mail support free for 1 year; on-site training & installation available; one year free upgrades..
Macintosh (1 Mb). 3.5" disk $595.00.
Turns Macintosh into an ISC-8000 & ISC-8820 Graphics Terminal.
Software Development Group.

ProCite: For Windows. *Version:* 3.1. Nov. 1995. *Items Included:* Disk, reference manual, user guide. *Customer Support:* Free phone support, Monday-Friday 9am-5pm, 30-day money back guarantee, free newsletter.
DOS, Microsoft Windows. IBM & compatibles (4Mb). CD-ROM disk Contact publisher for price. *Optimal configuration:* 4Mb RAM, hard disk.
Reference Management Database & Bibliography Maker. Stores Bibliographic Data, Notes, & Keywords. Search, Sort, & Print Citations Within Seconds. Generates Bibliographies in Any Style. Works with Wordprocessor to Produce Bibliography Automatically. Accepts Records from Online, Automated Library, & CD-ROM Services.
Personal Bibliographic Software, Inc.

ProClass. *Version:* 1.7. *Items Included:* Installation guide, operator handbook. *Customer Support:* Unlimited telephone support. On-site training for daily fee.
IBM PC & compatibles. 3.5" disk $295.00.
IBM PC, XT, AT, PS/2 & compatibles (640k). disk $295.00.
Prepares Home Purchase Price & Proposal for Buyers.
HMS Computer Co.

ProComm. *Version:* 2.4.3. Jan. 1989. *Items Included:* manual, dual media. *Customer Support:* Unlimited voice-line tech support, CompuServe forum ("GO DATASTORM").
PC/MS-DOS 2.0 or higher. IBM (192k). disk $50.00.
Communications Package for the IBM PC & Compatible Family of Microcomputers. Powerful, Yet Easy to Use for the Novice. Features Include 7 Popular File Transfer Protocols, An Automated Dialing Directory, a Full Script Command Language, Host Mode for Remote Access, & 10 Terminal Emulations.
Datastorm Technologies, Inc.

ProComm Plus. *Version:* 2.01. *Compatible Hardware:* IBM PC & compatibles. *Operating System(s) Required:* PC-DOS/MS-DOS 2.0 or higher. *Memory Required:* 192k. *Items Included:* Program & supplemental diskettes, printed manuals, quick-start guide. *Customer Support:* Unlimited voice line tech support.
disk $119.00.
Communications Program That Supports 33 Popular Terminal Emulations & 15 File-Transfer Protocols. The Program Works With Most Internal & External Modems, Supports up to Eight User- Defined COM Ports, & Includes a Fully Automated Dialing Directory That Allows 200+ entries.
Datastorm Technologies, Inc.

ProComm Plus Network Version. *Version:* 1.0. Jul. 1989. *Items Included:* Dual media, licenses & documentation for 5 concurrent users. *Customer Support:* Unlimited voice-line tech support, CompuServe forum ("GO DATASTORM").
PC-DOS/MS-DOS 2.0 or higher. IBM (192k). LAN 5-PAR: $595.00; additional workstation licenses: $119.00. *Addl. software required:* Any product that supports NCSI/NASI, ACSI, BAPI, INT 14h & NETCI (int 6Bh).
Works in Conjunction with Third-Party Asynchronous Communications Servers (ACS). The ACS Usually Functions As a Modem "Pool" on the LAN. Supports Any ACS That Uses One of These Five Application Program Interfaces (API): NCSI/NASI, ACSI, BAPI, INT 14h & NETCI (int 6Bh).
Datastorm Technologies, Inc.

ProCrypt. *Compatible Hardware:* IBM PC & compatibles. *Operating System(s) Required:* PC-DOS/MS-DOS 2.0 or higher. *Memory Required:* 40k.
disk $149.95.
Personal Security System that Reminds Users to Enter a Password Even from Within Application Programs. The Program Offers DES & Proprietary Encryption Methods. An Audit Trail Lets Users Monitor Unauthorized Attempts to Access Data. Users Can Change Their Password & Delete Sensitive Information or Close Protected Volumes Automatically After a Designated Time Period of No Activity.
Maverick Software, Inc.

PRODAS DATABASE. *Version:* 3.2. *Compatible Hardware:* IBM PC & compatibles.
disk $720.00.
Command-Driven Database-Management System Featuring On-Disk Tutorial & Split/Merge Files. Offers a Maximum of 200 Characters per Field, Unlimited Fields per Record, Unlimited Records per File, Unlimited Characters per Record, Unlimited Indexes per File, Unlimited Active Indexes & Unlimited Number of Records Sorted. Allows User to Revise Field Descriptions at Will.
Conceptual Software, Inc.

PRODAS Evaluation System. *Version:* 3.2. Aug. 1986. *Compatible Hardware:* IBM PC & compatibles. *Operating System(s) Required:* PC-DOS/MS-DOS, UNIX. *Memory Required:* 320k. *Customer Support:* 1 year free telephone support.
disk $1505.00.
PRODAS evaluation system. disk $40.00.
manual $35.00.
Programmable Database Manager, Statistics Package & Graphics. File Formats, Record Length, & Other Details Are Handled by the Program Allowing the User to Concentrate on Data Analysis. Can Be Utilized by the Financier or Engineer or Anyone Who Needs a Data Management System. A Set of Trigonometric & Logarithmic Functions Are Featured. Stores Values to 16 Digits & Minimizes Round off Errors. Allows the User to Print Numbers in Free Format, Fixed Format, or Scientific Notation. Includes Procedures to Calculate Means, Min, Max, Sum, Range, Standard Deviation, Skewness.
Conceptual Software, Inc.

Code Visualizer re/Nu Sys Workbench. *Version:* 96.1. Mar. 1996. *Items Included:* Technical & user manuals (spiral). *Customer Support:* Updates & telephone support 15%; training/consulting from $1200 for 1 day to $900 per day for 2 or more days; customization (by project).
Windows 3X, Windows 95, NT, Unix. IBM & compatible, 386 & higher (8Mb). $6000.00 first; discounts on multiples starting with 2nd system. *Optimal configuration:* IBM, Windows 95 or NT, 8Mb, VGA, Laser Printer, LAN, Pascal, C, Ada, COBOL, Fortran, and/or C Plus Plus compilers. *Networks supported:* all.
UNIX 5.4. Sun SPARC Station Workstation (2Mb). $12,000.00 first; discounts on multiples starting with 2nd system. *Optimal configuration:* Sun SPARC Station Workstation, UNIX 5.4 or higher, VGA, Laser Printer, Network, Pascal, C, Ada, COBOL, Fortran, and/or C Plus Plus compilers. *Networks supported:* Ethernet.
UNIX 5.4 or higher. IBM RS 6000 (2Mb). $6000.00 first; discounts on multiples starting with 2nd system. *Optimal configuration:* IBM RS 6000, UNIX 5.4, VGA, Laser Printer, Network, Pascal, C, Ada, C OBOL, Fortran, and/or C++ compilers. *Networks supported:* IBM compatible.
Integrated Workbench for Development & Maintenance of Systems. Provides a Uniform Visual Representation Based on a Cognitive Methodology Combining Data & Process. FLOWforms Provide Visual Representation of System at Any Level of Detail with Retinaes Always Positioned in Proper Context. Other Visual Test Coverage Executable Specificating, Prototyping Pseudo Code Support, Automatic Generation of Source Code & a Modular Data Repository. Supports Pascal COBOL, Fortran, C, Ada & C Plus Plus Development, Reverse Engineering, Call Hierarchies with Report Card & Code Generation.
IMS-Scandura.

Product Controller. *Version:* 2.0. Open Door Software Division. Oct. 1993. *Items Included:* Spiral manual, video (when available). *Customer Support:* 30 day free customer support; 900 line $2.00/min.; 1 yr. maintenance $400/mo. Includes: toll free line & fax back priority service.
DOS. IBM compatible 386, 25Mhz, 5Mb free space on hard disk, VGA monitor, 3.5" floppy, keyboard, mouse (1Mb). disk $99.00 $11.00, Network version ,299.00 (ISBN 1-56756-043-1, Order no.: OD500I). *Addl. software required:* Operating system. *Optimal configuration:* IBM or compatible 486, 66Mhz, 5Mb free space on hard disk, 4Mb RAM-3Mb expanded usable, VGA monitor, 3.5" high density floppy, keyboard, mouse, tape backup, & uninterruptable power supply. *Networks supported:* Novell Netware Lite.
Windows. IBM compatible 386, 25Mhz, 5Mb free space on hard disk, VGA monitor, 3.5" floppy, keyboard, mouse (1Mb). disk $99.00 (ISBN 1-56756-065-2, Order no.: OD505W). *Addl. software required:* Windows 3.1 or

higher. *Optimal configuration:* IBM or compatible 486, 66Mhz, 5Mb free space on hard disk, 4Mb RAM-3Mb expanded usable, VGA monitor, 3.5" high density floppy, keyboard, mouse, tape backup, & uninterruptable power supply. *Networks supported:* Novell Netware Lite.
MAC. 3.5" disk $99.00 (ISBN 1-56756-044-X, Order no.: OD510M). *Addl. software required:* System 7.
Sales Automation Tool That Provides Cosmetic Consultants the Flexibility & Control over Their Everyday Tasks Such As Quoting Inventory, Pricing, Invoicing, & Reordering from Their Suppliers. Stores Information about Individual Customers, What They Have Bought, Single or Multiple Vendors, As Well As Complete Product Descriptions. If Changes in Pricing Occurs, Repetitive Orders & Quotes to Customers Can Be Updated with the Touch of a Button. Great Product for Beginner with It's Windowed Interface.
Advantage International.

Product Costing (Quotation) System.
Operating System(s) Required: MS/PC-DOS. *Language(s):* BASIC Compiled. *Memory Required:* 128k.
disk $500.00.
Engineered Via Explode & Set-Back Schedule to Figure End Variable Costs for Producing Any Specified End-Product Mix. Designed to Be Cost Efficient & to Save Users' Time. Totals Costs by Products &/or Cost Categories.
Bernard Giffler Assocs.

Product Idea Evaluator - Questionnaires. *Items Included:* Bound manual. *Customer Support:* Free hotline - no time limit; 30 day limited warranty; updates are $5/disk plus S&H.
MS-DOS 2.0 or higher. IBM & compatibles (256k). disk $99.95. *Nonstandard peripherals required:* 80-column (or wider) printer.
manual only $19.95.
Specifically Directed at the Individual or Company That Wishes to Use Questionnaires to Determine the Viability of a Particular Product or Service. However, It Is Also Applicable to General Questionnaire Creation & Analysis.
Dynacomp, Inc.

Product Management System for Architects/ Engineers. *Compatible Hardware:* IBM PC, PC XT, PC AT & compatibles. *Operating System(s) Required:* MS-DOS, UNIX. *Memory Required:* 640k. *General Requirements:* Hard disk, printer, modem.
contact publisher for price.
Administers Funding for Each Project by Manager & Provides Management with Reports on Project Profitability & Status. Job Cost Module Is Interactive with the Custom Designed General Ledger, Accounts Payable & Accounts Receivable Modules.
Simmons Computing Service, Inc.

Product Planner 10. *Version:* 1.6. Apr. 1991. *Items Included:* One three ring binder containing tutorial. *Customer Support:* All products are warranted for 60 days; Customer support available at additional cost; On-Site training available at additional cost.
PC-DOS. IBM 386 or higher. $2500.00.
A Parametric Bill of Material System That Is Unique yet Especially Designed for Manufacturers of Standard Cabinets & Furniture. It Allows the Batching of Any Combination of Product Mix into Organized Lists for All Kind of Parts. Makes It Easy for the User to Set up His Own Product Catalog with Parts Hardware & Subassemblies. Once Entered, a Parts List for Cutting Can Be Printed Out in Minutes. Reports for a Production Run Include Total Costs, Hardware & the Master Cutlist. The Master Cutlist Is Transferred Automatically to Cut Planner for Optimization.
Pattern Systems International, Inc.

Product Planner 20. *Version:* 1.6. Aug. 1986. *Compatible Hardware:* IBM 386 or higher. *Operating System(s) Required:* MS-DOS. *Language(s):* C. *Memory Required:* 1000k. *General Requirements:* Hard disk, printer, CGA or EGA graphics card. *Items Included:* Binder with tutorial, installation product catalogs. *Customer Support:* Yes.
$4500.00 3.5" or 5.25" disk.
Special Parametric Bill of Material System That Contains Graphics of the Unit to Be Built. Computes the Part Sizes of All Components Based on the Outside Dimension of the Unit. System Reports Sub-Assemblies, Costing, Parts & Hardware Buy Outs.
Pattern Systems International, Inc.

Production Management (a Part of ABECAS). *Version:* 3.3. Jan. 1989. *Customer Support:* On site training unlimited support services for first 90 days & through subscription thereafter.
PC/MS-DOS 3.x. IBM PC & compatibles. Contact publisher for price. *Nonstandard peripherals required:* Hard disk (30Mb or higher); 132 column printer.
Production Unit Activities Generate Future Ones Based on Their Completion or a Specific Projected Date. In Turn, Work Orders Are Created. Unit Activity Data Can Be Entered & Update Future Generated Activities. Selected Data Updates Production Unit Master File & Count Summary File. Projections Can Be Posted to Inventory & Exploded by Lot/Size Detail. Numerous Reports Available. Multi-User Version for Novell, NTNX, 10-Net, Unix/Xenix, Turbo DOS & Others.
Argos Software.

Production Planning. *Version:* 3.3. (Integrated Manufacturing & Financial System Ser.). *Compatible Hardware:* Micro/VAX, UNIBUS/ VAX, IBM PC. *Operating System(s) Required:* MS-DOS, Novell, Micro/VMS, VAX/VMS, UNIX. *Language(s):* DIBOL.
MS-DOS. $750.00 single-user.
DEC PDP-11/VAX. $1500.00 multi-user.
Schedules Jobs Interactively to Perform Capacity & Process Planning. Uses Production Information to Compile a Time-Phased Schedule of Work Through Plant.
Primetrack.

Productivity Analysis: Piecework/Payroll Reporting. *Compatible Hardware:* IBM PC, PC XT, PC AT & compatibles. *Operating System(s) Required:* MS-DOS, UNIX. *Memory Required:* 512k. *General Requirements:* Hard disk, printer.
contact publisher for price.
Automates the Piecework Reporting Process of a Bedding Manufacturer. Also Provides a Daily & Weekly Piecework Summary, a Production History by Department & Individual, & an Overall Labor Analysis by Week, Quarter & Year.
Simmons Computing Service, Inc.

Productivity Pack. Software Publishing Corp. *Operating System(s) Required:* MS-DOS. *Memory Required:* 128k. *General Requirements:* 2 disk drives, printer.
$345.00 (Order no.: TI P/N 2311494-0001).
Texas Instruments, Personal Productivit.

Productivity Series. *Version:* 2.0.
disk $995.00.
Combines Word Prcessor, Painting, & Drawing Programs Under One Package for Desktop Publishing under SCO Open Desktop. WYSIWYG System Lets User Create Multiple Column Newsletters & Specification Sheets, Illustrated Memos, & Other Types of Documents.
Island Graphics.

Productivity Tools for the Microcomputer. 1990.
IBM PC (WordPerfect, dBASE III+ & Lotus). contact publisher for price (ISBN 0-538-80750-4, Order no.: DF60A8H81).
IBM PS/2 (WordPerfect, dBASE III+ & Lotus). contact publisher for price (ISBN 0-538-80751-2, Order no.: DF60A8H88).
IBM PC (WordStar). contact publisher for price (ISBN 0-538-80752-0, Order no.: DF60A8H811).
IBM PS/2 (WordStar). contact publisher for price (ISBN 0-538-80753-9, Order no.: DF60A8H881).
IBM PC (WordPerfect). contact publisher for price (ISBN 0-538-80754-7, Order no.: DF60A8H12).
IBM PS/2 (WordPerfect). contact publisher for price (ISBN 0-538-80755-5, Order no.: DF60A8H822).
IBM PC (dBASE III+ & Lotus). contact publisher for price (ISBN 0-538-80756-3, Order no.: DF60A8H813).
IBM PS/2 (dBASE III+ & Lotus). contact publisher for price (ISBN 0-538-80757-1, Order no.: DF60A8H883).
IBM PC (Lotus) contact publisher for price (ISBN 0-538-80758-X, Order No.: DF60A8H814);
IBM PS/2 (Lotus) contact publisher for price (ISBN 0-538-80759-8, Order No.: DF60A8H884).
Text-workbook & Tutorial Software Packages Designed to Help Students Learn Various Software Packages. Includes Realistic Business Applications & Cases & an Introduction to Computers & MS-DOS. Available Spring 1989.
South-Western Publishing Co.

ProEST. *Version:* 7.0. Feb. 1993. *Compatible Hardware:* IBM PC & compatibles. *Operating System(s) Required:* PC-DOS/MS-DOS, Windows 3.1, Windows 95. *Language(s):* FoxPro Microsoft. *Memory Required:* 490k. *General Requirements:* Hard disk. *Items Included:* User's manual, on-line help - support policy. *Customer Support:* Telephone $15.00/15 minutes.
disk $395.00-$995.00.
Windows Construction Cost Estimating Program That Generates a Job Estimate for Materials & Labor, Subcontractors, & Equipment. Can Automatically Convert Takeoff Units to Order Units & Cuts Estimating Time 50 to 80 Percent While Maintaining Accuracy of Estimate. Used in General Construction, Building, Electrical & Mechanical Contracting.
Computerized Micro Solutions.

PROFBILL/PC. *Version:* 4.0. *Operating System(s) Required:* MS-DOS. *Language(s):* Quick Basic. *Memory Required:* 512k. *Items Included:* Manual, disk, warranty card. *Customer Support:* 18 month via telephone.
disk $199.00.
source code $200.00.
demo disk & manual $20.00.
Designed for Lawyers, CPA's, & Other Professionals Who Invoice at Various Hourly Rates. User May Insert up to 80 Different Tasks, 40 Out of Pocket Descriptions. Up to 20 Different Partners/Employees/Lab Fees Can Be Listed per Task with Various Hourly Rates/Costs Assigned & Billed to That Task.
Micro-Art Programmers.

Professional Accounting Series. *Compatible Hardware:* IBM PC & compatibles. *Memory Required:* 128k. *General Requirements:* Hard disk.
$695.00 to $995.00 per package.
Financial/Accounting Package. Posts Recurring Transactions, Automatic Posting from Other Modules, Report Format User Definable, Reports Comparative Statements, Wild Card, Links with

TITLE INDEX

External Software Programs, Password Access, Audit Trail, Error Recovery, Log off Out-of-Balance, Reject Erroneous Account Numbers & On-Line Help.
CYMA/McGraw-Hill.

The Professional Bailbondman. Version: 1.0. Beverly B. McDonald. Jun. 1986. Compatible Hardware: IBM PC & compatibles. Operating System(s) Required: PC-DOS. Memory Required: 256k. General Requirements: Hard disk, printer.
disk $695.00 (ISBN 0-938793-00-4, Order no.: BB-0010).
Covers All Aspects of Bailbonding. Will Generate Required Reports, Notify Clients of Upcoming Courtdates, etc. Password Protection Included.
DataCompatible.

Professional Billing System. Version: 4.2. Items Included: Complete operating manual. Customer Support: Unlimited telephone support.
MS-DOS. IBM PC or compatible (256k). $300.00. Optimal configuration: IBM PC or compatible, 256k RAM, printer. Networks supported: Novel, Unex.
Billing System Designed for Self Employed Professionals Who Cannot Use Standard Phrases to Bill Their Clients Since Each Billing Takes a Different Description. Each Item on the Statement May Be up to Four Lines Long & Contain a Descriptive Phrase That Is User Generated. This Phrase Could Be a Description of the Work Done, Travel Expense, Out of Pocket Expenses, etc. System Is Unique in That It Performs Most of the Functions of an Accounts Receivable System, Yet Is Easy to Learn & Use & Is Flexible Enough to Fit the Needs of a Wide Range of Businesses or Professions.
Omni Software Systems, Inc. (Indiana).

Professional Business Barometers. Dec. 1989. IBM PC & compatibles. disk $99.00.
Allows Ratio, Z-Score & Growth Analysis of a Business.
Stafford Financial Services Corp.

Professional CAD for Mac. Jan. 1986. Compatible Hardware: Apple Macintosh. Memory Required: 512k. General Requirements: 2 disk drives.
3.5" disk $799.00 (Order no.: 03056).
Supports 2 Axis Parts Drafting & 3-D. Symbols Libraries Are Available.
Machinery Alternative.

Professional-Class Golf. 1992. Items Included: Detailed manuals included with all Dynacomp products. Customer Support: Free telephone support to original customer - no time limit; 30 day limited warranty.
MS-DOS 3.2 or higher. IBM PC & compatibles (512k). $29.95 (Add $5.00 for 3 1/2" format; 5 1/4" format standard). Optimal configuration: IBM, 128k, color graphics card, MS-DOS 2.0 or higher.
Apple (64k). $29.95 (add $5.00 for 3 1/2" format; 5 1/4" format standard).
An Accurate Simulation of the Game of Golf at the Firestone Country Club. Each of the 18 Holes in PCG Is Patterned after the Corresponding Holes at That Famous Course, Including the Greens, Sand Traps, & Trees. You May Play the Course, or Just Practice at a Particular Hole. You May Even Practice at the Driving Range or Putting Green. Your Caddy Carries a Complete Set of Clubs, Including a Wedge, Nine Irons, & Four Woods. You May Adjust Your Swing According to Strength, Stance, & Timing; a Very Realistic Simulation.
Dynacomp, Inc.

Professional COBOL. Compatible Hardware: IBM PC, PC XT, PC AT. Memory Required: 256k. General Requirements: 2 floppy disk drives or hard disk.
contact publisher for price.
Fully Integrated Workstation for the COBOL Programmer Tailored to the IBM Personal Computer. All the Programming Tools Needed to Develop, Test, Run, & Maintain Business Applications on a Workstation Are in One Integrated Package. Takes Full Advantage of the Features of the IBM Personal Computer & Allows User to Switch Context from Tool to Tool with a Single Keystroke & Get Subsecond Response Time.
Micro Focus, Inc. (California).

Professional College Planner. Dec. 1989. IBM PC & compatibles. disk $99.00.
Assists in Planning College Funding & Income Shifting Strategies.
Stafford Financial Services Corp.

Professional Communications. Compatible Hardware: HP 85 with Plotter/Printer ROM (HP 00085-15002), serial interface (HP 82939A); HP 86/87 with ROM Drawer (HP 82936A), HP-IB interface (HP 82937A), Advanced Programming ROM (00085-45005). General Requirements: I/O ROM (HP 00087-15003).
3-1/2" or 5-1/4" disk $200.00 ea. (Order no.: 82850A).
Allows User to Create, Edit, & Merge Text Files. Allows Users to Perform the Following Functions: Transfer Files/Keystrokes to Another Personal Computer; Receive & Store Text from Another Personal Computer; Set up the Series 80 Computer As a "Bulletin Board" System; Audit All Communications Activity; & Secure or Encrypt Files & Communications. All of the Above Can Be Done Within a Single Software Environment.
Hewlett-Packard Co.

Professional Composer. Compatible Hardware: Apple Macintosh.
3.5" disk $495.00.
Provides Performance-Ready Sheet-Music for Music Professionals.
Mark of the Unicorn.

Professional Corporate Financial Planning Models. Version: 1.0. Oct. 1986. Compatible Hardware: IBM PC & compatibles. Memory Required: 384k of expanded memory for the MFPM & 640k. General Requirements: Lotus 1-2-3 Release 1A, printer with 16.6 compressed-print capability. Items Included: 6 speadsheet templates. Customer Support: Free telephone support.
$195.00.
Prepares Profit & Loss & Cash-Flow Statements & Balance Sheets, Along with Supporting Marketing, Manufacturing, & Financial Schedules. Designed for Managers of Manufacturing, Marketing & Service Companies, As Well As Venture Capitalists, Entrepreneurs, Financial Consultants, & CPAs. The Applications Include: THE STRATEGIC FINANCIAL PLANNING MODEL Evaluates Factors Determining Corporate-Earnings Growth, Profitability, & Cash Flow. Has an Eight-Year Planning Horizon. THE ANNUAL FINANCIAL PLANNING MODEL Performs Strategic Business Planning & Acquisition Analysis. Has a Five-Year Planning Horizon. THE QUARTERLY/ANNUAL FINANCIAL PLANNING MODEL Performs Strategic Business Planning, Acquisition Analysis, & Loan Presentations. Has a Four-Year Planning Horizon with the First Two Years Planned Quarterly. THE MONTHLY FINANCIAL PLANNING MODEL Creates the Annual Budget & Performs Monthly Forecasting. Has a 12-Month Planning Horizon. THE PRODUCTION PLANNING MODEL, Used with THE MONTHLY FINANCIA.
Stephen Archer Assocs.

PROFESSIONAL IMAGE II

Professional Data Center Curriculum. Items Included: Bound manuals, video tape training. Customer Support: On-site training, customer telephone hotline for terminal support.
MS-DOS 2.0 or higher. PS2, PC & compatibles (256k). contact publisher for price.
Approximately 200 Titles of Computer Education Courseware Covering IBM Enterprize System Operation, MVS, JES2, JES3, Data Communications & Data Center Management. Courses Are Video Tape & Computer Based Instruction.
CSR Macmillan/McGraw-Hill.

Professional DYNAMO Plus. 1986. Compatible Hardware: IBM PC, AT, PS/2 & compatibles. Operating System(s) Required: MS-DOS 2.0 or higher. Memory Required: 256k. Customer Support: Phone, mail, disk.
disk $1995.00.
Designed for Individuals to Create Models & Perform Simulation Analyses of Continuous Systems with Dynamic Feedback. Facilities for Advanced Computational & Analytical Tasks. Access Via Menu or Operating System Command Line Mode (Allows Batch Mode Operation & Embedding Dynamo with Other Program Interfaces). 2000+ Active Equation Capacity. Built-In Functions & Macros, User-Defined Macros, Array Variables (Subscript up to 8 Dimensions), Fast Simulation & Reiteration with Parameter Experiments, Import/Export Parameter Values with Spreadsheets, Table Values Represented & Changed Graphically, Optional Integration Methods, Create Custom Plots & Reports (Compare Runs on One Graph Grid), Create Gaming Framework to Compare Results.
Pugh-Roberts Assocs., Inc.

Professional Energy Analyst Deluxe. Version: 3.2. Raymond W. Merry. May 1987. Compatible Hardware: IBM PC. Operating System(s) Required: MS-DOS. (source code included). Memory Required: 256k.
IBM. disk $490.00 (ISBN 0-936561-17-3, Order no.: PEAV3/MSDOS).
disk $2000.00, incl. set-up & 5 days of training.
Energy Accounting System for Small or Large Businesses. Multiple Linear Regression Analyzes Effects of Weather, Occupancy, Humidity or Any 5 Variables on Energy Usage & Cost. Predicts Savings from Energy Conservation HVAC & Insulation, Analyzes Results, Economic Analysis, Handles Weather Data, etc.
Rays Computers & Energy.

Professional Font Library, 5. Version: 4.3. Compatible Hardware: Commodore Amiga 500, 1000, 2000+. Items Included: Reference charts, 90 page manual, Font Utilities, Icon Interface. Customer Support: Technical assistance provided by phone: (206)733-8342.
Commodore Amiga 500, 1000, 2000, 3000. $74.95.
60 Professional, Bitmap Fonts (200 Styles). Monochrome & Multicolor Fonts (Gold, Chrome, Pipeline) from 7-88 Lines (23 Typefaces with European Characters). For Word Processing, Paint Programs, Headlines, Newsletters, & Video Titling.
CLASSIC CONCEPTS Futureware.

Professional Image II. Compatible Hardware: Apple Macintosh. Items Included: Template, 30-day guarantee, $50 worth of free slides. Customer Support: Free technical support.
3.5" disk $149.00.
Business Graphics & Business Presentations Package.
Stokes Imaging Services.

PROFESSIONAL LAYOUT TEMPLATES

Professional Layout Templates Collection I for Pagemaker 2.0. *Compatible Hardware:* Apple Macintosh.
3.5" disk $69.95.
Contains Page Layout Templates for Use on the Macintosh.
Solutions, Inc.

Professional Lottery/Lotto. 1986. *Compatible Hardware:* Apple II, III; Commodore 64/128; IBM PC & compatibles; Macintosh. *Memory Required:* IBM 256k, Apple 64k, Commodore 64k.
3.5" or 5.25" disk $149.95.
Can Be Used to Analyze up to Twenty-Five Two Digit Numbers Ranging from One to Ninety-Nine. Dimitrov Systems & Dr. Rodney T. Hard's Positional Analyses Are Also Incorporated. Other Analysis Included Are Central Tendency, Linear Regression, Bell Curve, Cluster Analysis, Column Charts & Trend Lines.
Professor Jones Professional Handicapping Systems.

Professional Lottery-Lotto with ACS. 1986. *Compatible Hardware:* Apple I, II; Commodore 64/128; IBM PC & compatibles. *Memory Required:* IBM 256k, Apple 64k, Commodore 64k.
3.5" or 5.25" disk $179.95.
Contains All the Features of the Professional Lottery-Lotto Product, But Is Expanded & Has Ten More Dimitrov Systems for Predicting Numbers.
Professor Jones Professional Handicapping Systems.

Professional Manager. *Version:* 3.1. Jun. 1983. *Compatible Hardware:* IBM PC XT, Pc AT, PS/2; Apple Macintosh. *Operating System(s) Required:* MS-DOS, Xenix, PC-MOS, Apple Macintosh, Novell, Windows 3.0. *Language(s):* DBASE III. *Memory Required:* 640k. *General Requirements:* Modem, printer. *Customer Support:* 90 days telephone support, annual maintenance available.
IBM PC XT, MS-DOS. disk $1495.00 (Order no.: PM-IBM-1).
IBM PC AT. disk $1495.00 (Order no.: PM-IBM-2).
Apple Macintosh. disk $1495.00 (Order no.: PM-AM-1).
Fully Integrated Financial Accounting System for Architectural & Engineering Firms. Provides Job Cost/Billing with Integrated Payroll, General Ledger, Accounts Payable, & Accounts Receivable. Complete Canadian Payroll is Available.
Automate Computer Software.

Professional Marketing System: Prospect Ranking. *Version:* 2. 1982. *Compatible Hardware:* IBM; Intel & compatibles. *Language(s):* Microsoft BASIC.
$995.00 5 1/4" or 3.5" disk (Order no.: 264).
Ranks New Customers According to Their Returns on Investment Values by Systematically Analyzing Relative & Subjective Estimates Forcing Them to Be Quantitative.
Resource Software International, Inc.

Professional Natal Report. *Version:* 1.1. Steven Blake et al. Nov. 1987. *Items Included:* Manual. *Customer Support:* Free phone support.
MS-DOS. IBM PC compatible (512k). 3.5" disk $350.00 (05/1990) (ISBN 0-87199-077-6). *Nonstandard peripherals required:* Hard disk, DOT-Matrix or HP-compatible inkjet or laser printer.
Macintosh (1Mb). 3.5" disk $395.00 (05/1990) (ISBN 0-87199-097-0). *Nonstandard peripherals required:* Hard disk, 800k floppy, MacIntosh compatible DOT-Matrix, Laser or Inkjet printer.
Produces Natal Horoscope Interpretations of up to 25 Pages, in Flowing, Natural Paragraphs. Includes a Selection of Graphics Chart Wheels, Aspect List, Explanation of Astrological Terms. Can Be Configured to Produce Short or Long Reports, & Both the Text Database & Individual Reports Can Be Edited by the User. German-Language Version Available for Macintosh.
Astrolabe, Inc.

Professional Oracle. *Compatible Hardware:* IBM PC & compatibles.
disk $1295.00.
Free-Form, Command-Driven Database-Management System Featuring Help Screen, On-Disk Tutorial, Automatic Indexing & Split/Merge Files. Offers a Maximum of 254 Fields per Record, 240 Characters per Field, 64,000 Characters per Record, Unlimited Indexes per File, Unlimited Active Indexes & up to 15 Records Sorted. (The Number of Record's per File Is Limited to Disk Space.) Allows User to Revise Field Descriptions at Will.
Oracle Corp.

Professional Patient Scheduling. *Customer Support:* 800-929-8117 (customer service).
MS-DOS. IBM PC, PS/2. disk $199.99 (ISBN 0-87007-279-X).
Commodore 128, CP/M. disk $299.99 (ISBN 0-87007-251-X).
Handles up to Sixteen Practitioners or Professionals in the Scheduling of Their Patients or Clients. Allows for Double Booking and a Variety of Time Periods.
SourceView Software International.

Professional Property Manager. *Version:* 1.51. Apr. 1991. *Items Included:* Complete manual, tutorial & problem disks (3). *Customer Support:* Toll-free voice support "800" number.
MS-DOS (512k). IBM compatible. disk $995.00 (ISBN 0-929770-20-X). *Optimal configuration:* MS-DOS, 512k memory, hard disk, printer.
Integrated Accounting (G/L, A/R, A/P) Including Databases for the Properties, Tenants, Vendors & Past Tenants. Designed for Commercial Property That Has Double/Triple Net Leases as Well as Industrial or Top-Level Residential Properties. Produces Financial Reports & Exports Data to Other Spreadsheets, Databases or Word Processor. Does Both Cash & Accrual Accounting. Multiple Properties Can Be Used with Mixed Fixed & Variable Rents. Handles Shopping Centers, Office Buildings, Apartment Complexes or Condominiums as Well as Industrial Projects.
!Solutions! Publishing Co.

Professional Ration Package: For Beef, Swine, Dairy, Rabbits, Fish, Fertilizer, Poultry Load Sheet Calculator, Formula Pricing. May 1984. *Compatible Hardware:* Altos; Compupro; Cromemco; DEC Rainbow; Digital Microsystems; Eagle I, Eagle III, Eagle 4, Eagle PC; Epson QX-10; HP 87, 125; IBM PC; IMS; Kaypro; Micromation; Molecular; Morrow; North Star; Osborne; TeleVideo; TRS-80 Model II, Model 12, Model 16; Xerox; Zenith. *Operating System(s) Required:* CP/M 2.2, MS-DOS. *Memory Required:* transient program area 48k, capacity 170k.
$750.00.
demo package $30.00.
Designed for Professional Cattle Nutritionists, Used in Private Practice or Mill Feed Situations. Can Be Customized for Any Species, Using a Menu-Driven Customizing Program.
Loren Bennett.

The Professional Recipe Manager, 2 disks. *Version:* 6.5. Jul. 1987. *Compatible Hardware:* IBM PC & compatibles. *Operating System(s) Required:* PC-DOS/MS-DOS 2.1 or higher. *Memory Required:* 384k. *General Requirements:* Hard disk, printer. *Customer Support:* Free. $295.95.
Combines Recipe Costing, Nutrition, & Serving Size Adjustment in a Single Software Package. Ingredient Costs & Nutritional Information Are Entered Once for Each Ingredient & Referenced by All Recipes Using the Ingredient. Displays & Prints Total Cost & Cost per Serving for Entire Recipe & Cost, Cost per Serving & Percentage of Total Cost for Each Ingredient. Displays & Prints Common Nutrition Items per Serving for Entire Recipe & for Each Ingredient. Generates Consolidated Shopping List of Multiple Recipes Including Summary Totals. Serving Size Is Adjustable from 1 to 9999. Includes Manual with Tutorial & Sample Database.
Gem Island Software.

Professional Relationship Report. Joan Negus & Josh Prokop. Mar. 1996. *Items Included:* Manual. *Customer Support:* Free phone support.
MS-DOS. 8088 (640k). disk $350.00 (ISBN 0-87199-136-5). *Nonstandard peripherals required:* High-density floppy, Hercules Mono.
Prints Detailed Astrological Reports on Compatibility Between Two People; Analyzes Each Person's Relationship Potential & Then Compares the Two Charts. Very Customizable; Includes Synastry Aspectarian, Choice of Wheel Styles, Ability to Print Long & Short Reports, Fully Editable Text, Seamless Interface with ACS PC Atlas.
Astrolabe, Inc.

Professional Retirement Planner. Stafford H. Krause. Oct. 1987.
IBM PC. disk $99.00.
Compares Client Retirement Needs & Provisions, & Allows What-If Analysis of Action Alternatives.
Stafford Financial Services Corp.

Professional Retirement Toolbox. Dec. 1989.
IBM PC & compatibles. disk $99.00.
Provides Lump-Sum Vs. Rollover Comparison & Several Other Post-Retirement Tools.
Stafford Financial Services Corp.

Professional ScanLab. *Version:* 1.1. *Items Included:* Amiga expansion slot board.
AmigaDOS 1.2 or higher (2Mb). Amiga 2000 or 2500. disk $995.00. *Nonstandard peripherals required:* Sharp JX-300 & JX-450 24-bit scanners.
24-Bit Color Separation Package Makes Allowances for Impurities in Printer Ink, So That Final Print Is Not Different from Original Scanned Image. Lets User Scan 16 Million Color Images at 300 DPI. After Document Color Separation Conversion, Output Can Be Sent to Service Bureau for Offset Printing.
Elastic Reality, Inc.

Professional Series Acquisitions Module: Professional Series Library Automation System. *Version:* 2.1. 1994. *Items Included:* 3 ring bound reference style manual; manual includes quick reference summary. *Customer Support:* Data Trek Inc. is a turn-key vendor supplying: software, hardware, peripherals, hardware/software support contracts, toll-free phone & Internet access to product support, installations, training, refresher training, user groups, technical bi-monthly newsletter.
PC-DOS/MS-DOS. IBM 386, 486 or compatible (640k). 3.5" or 5.25" disk $3950.00 (multiple purchase discount & GSA pricing available) (ISBN 0-929795-15-6). *Nonstandard peripherals required:* 1 floppy & 1 hard disk drive, printer. *Optimal configuration:* IBM compatible 386; MS-DOS; 640k RAM; printer; modem with direct telephone line; Novell LAN if want to network. *Networks supported:* Novell LAN, 3COM, Banyan, IBM LAN Manager,

TITLE INDEX

PathWorks, Windows NT, NetWare.
Automates Ordering of Library Materials. Checks New Orders Against Current & Historical Order Files & Professional Cataloging & Serials Modules. Prepaying, Invoicing, Tracking & Receiving Orders, & Allocating Costs to Fund Accounts Further Standardize & Simplify Ordering. Boolean Searching, Online Vendor Interfaces, & Management Reports Are Standard Features; Adheres to Latest Standards Including Z39.49 Computerized Book Ordering, Z39.55 Computerized Serials Orders, Claims & Cancellations, & X1Z EDI.
Data Trek, Inc.

Professional Series Cataloging Module: Professional Series Library Automation System. Version: 2.1. 1994. *Items Included:* 3 ring bound reference style manual; manual includes quick reference summary. *Customer Support:* Data Trek Inc. is a turn-key vendor supplying: software, hardware, peripherals, hardware/software support contracts, toll-free phone & Internet access to product support, installations, training, refresher training, user groups, technical bi-monthly newsletter.
PC-DOS/MS-DOS. IBM 386, 486 or compatible (640k). 3.5" or 5.25" disk, $3950.00 under 65k titles; $6500.00 65k-130k titles; $7500.00 over 130k titles, (multiple purchase discount & GSA pricing available) (ISBN 0-929795-12-1). *Nonstandard peripherals required:* 1 floppy & 1 hard disk drive, printer. *Optimal configuration:* IBM compatible 386; MS-DOS; 640k RAM; printer; modem with direct telephone line; Novell LAN if want to network. *Networks supported:* Novell, LAN, 3COM, Banyan Vines, IBM LAN Manager, PathWorks, Windows NT, NetWare.
Completely Supports Full MARC Records. Provides Variable Field Lengths & User Friendly Pop-Up Menus & Pick-Lists for Easy & Accurate Data Entry. Powerful Bibliographic Searching Can Be Done Using Simple Keyword Searches or Sophisticated Boolean Logic Statements. Integrates with Professional Circulation, Serials, Acquisitions, Databridge, OPAC & GOPAC (Graphical OPAC) Modules.
Data Trek, Inc.

Professional Series Circulation Module: Professional Series Library Automation System. Version: 2.1. 1994. *Items Included:* 3 ring bound reference style manual; manual includes quick reference summary. *Customer Support:* Data Trek Inc. is a turn-key vendor supplying: software, hardware peripherals, hardware/software support contracts, toll-free phone & Internet access to product support, installations, training, refresher training, user groups, technical bi-monthly newsletter.
PC-DOS/MS-DOS. IBM 386, 486 or compatible (640k). 3.5" or 5.25" disk, $3950.00 under 65k titles; $6500.00 68k-130k titles; $7500.00 over 130k titles (multiple purchase discount & GSA pricing available) (ISBN 0-929795-13-X). *Nonstandard peripherals required:* 1 floppy & 1 hard disk drive, printer. *Optimal configuration:* IBM compatible 386; MS-DOS; 640k RAM; printer; modem with direct telephone line; Novell LAN if want to network. *Networks supported:* Novell, LAN, 3COM, Banyan Vines, IBM LAN Manager, PathWorks, Windows NT, NetWare.
Facilitates Fast & Simple Check-In, Check-Out, Hold, & Renewal Using Barcode & Laser Scanning Technology. System Also Provides: Unlimited Due Date Setting; Patron "Trap" Setting; Overdue, Hold, Reserve, & Recall Notice Generation; & Numerous Reports. Integrates with Professional Cataloging, Serials, Acquisitions, Databridge, OPAC & GOPAC (Graphical OPAC) Modules.
Data Trek, Inc.

Professional Series Databridge Module: Professional Series Library Automation System. Version: 2.1. 1994. *Items Included:* 3 ring bound reference style manual; manual includes quick reference summary. *Customer Support:* Data Trek Inc. is a turn-key vendor supplying: software, hardware, peripherals, hardware/software support contracts, toll-free phone & Internet access to product support, installations, training, refresher training, user groups, technical bi-monthly newsletter.
PC-DOS/MS-DOS. IBM 286, 386, 486 or compatible (640k). 3.5" or 5.25" disks $1500.00 (multiple purchase discount & GSA pricing available) (ISBN 0-929795-16-4). *Nonstandard peripherals required:* 1 floppy & 1 hard disk drive, printer. *Optimal configuration:* IBM compatible 386; MS-DOS; 640k RAM; printer; modem with direct telephone line; Novell LAN if want to network. *Networks supported:* Novell, LAN, 3COM, Banyan Vines, IBM LAN Manager, PathWorks, Windows NT, NetWare.
Provides Easy Downloading of MARC Records to All Other Professional Series Modules. Supports Importing & Exporting of All 7 MARC Material Formats. Provides Validity Checking of Downloaded Data Using the MARC Rules Set Selected. Compares Incoming Records to Existing Records & Only Updates Existing Records with More Current Information.
Data Trek, Inc.

Professional Series Drafting Symbols. Version: 3.0. Jan. 1991. *Items Included:* All symbols are printed in 3-ring "lay-flat" type. Manual includes set-up procedure, productivity hints, etc. *Customer Support:* Free telephone support.
Macintosh; IBM & compatibles. all 4 modules $199.00.
A Collection of the Most Commonly Used Architechtural Drafting Symbols, Includes Plan Symbols, Plumbing, Electrical, Furniture, "Style Sheets", Schedules, People, Cars, Etc.
Williams AG Products.

Professional Series Football. 1986. *Compatible Hardware:* Apple II; Commodore 64/128; IBM PC & compatibles. *Memory Required:* IBM 256k, Apple 64k, Commodore 64k.
3.5" or 5.25" disk $199.95.
Designed to Predict Team Scores, Over-Under, Non-Bets, Regular Bets & Super Bets. Contains Complete Built-In Schedule, Single Input for Two Teams, Third Set of Results Based on Score Capability, Expanded File Capacity, Increased Performance & Greater Accuracy, Yardage Separated into Passing-Rushing & Flexibility. Regression Analysis Can Be Adjusted to Give Prediction Based on Any Desired Number of Previous Week's Performance.
Professor Jones Professional Handicapping Systems.

Professional Series OPAC Module (Online Public Access Catalog): Professional Series Library Automation System. Version: 2.1. 1994. *Items Included:* 3 ring bound reference style manual; manual includes quick reference summary. *Customer Support:* Data Trek Inc. is a turn-key vendor supplying: software, hardware, peripherals, hardware/software support contracts, toll-free phone & Internet access to product support, installations, training, refresher training, user groups, technical bi-monthly newsletter.
PC-DOS/MS-DOS. IBM 386, 486 or compatible (640k). 3.5" or 5.25" disks, under 65k titles $1500.00; 65-130k titles $2500.00; above 130k titles $3500.00; (multiple purchase discount & GSA pricing available) (ISBN 0-929795-17-2). *Nonstandard peripherals required:* 1 floppy & 1 hard disk drive, printer. *Addl. software required:* Data Trek's Professional Series Cataloging Module. *Optimal configuration:* IBM compatible 386; MS-DOS; 640k RAM; printer; modem with direct telephone line; Novell LAN if want to network. *Networks supported:* Novell LAN, IBM LAN Manager, 3COM, Banyan Vines, PathWorks.
Provides Rapid & Powerful Online Public Access to Catalog Data. It Allows Searches on Any Keyword or Combination of Words in Virtually Any Field. Truncated Searches or Searches Utilizing Boolean Logic Can Be Completed in Seconds Even in Large Bibliographic Databases. Multiple User-Selectable Display Styles Shows Real Time Circulation, Cataloging & Order Status. Shows Status Changes of Checked In/Out Materials Immediately. Online Help Available. Integrates with Professional Cataloging, Circulation, Serials, Acquisitions, & Databridge Modules.
Data Trek, Inc.

Professional Series Serials Module: Professional Series Library Automation System. Version: 2.1. 1994. *Items Included:* 3 ring bound reference style manual; manual includes quick reference summary. *Customer Support:* Data Trek Inc. is a turn-key vendor supplying: software, hardware, peripherals, hardware/software support contracts, toll-free phone & Internet access to product support, installations, training, refresher training, user groups, technical bi-monthly newsletter.
PC-DOS/MS-DOS. IBM 386, 486 or compatible (640k). $3950.00 (multiple purchase discount & GSA pricing available) (ISBN 0-929795-14-8). *Nonstandard peripherals required:* 1 floppy & 1 hard disk drive, printer. *Optimal configuration:* IBM compatible 386; MS-DOS; 640k RAM; printer; modem with direct telephone line; Novell LAN if want to network. *Networks supported:* Novell LAN, IBM LAN Manager, 3COM, Banyan Vines, PathWorks, Windows NT, NetWare.
Designed to Maintain Periodicals Collection. Check-In & Claiming Are Single-Keystroke Operations. Routing Slips & Claim Letters Are Generated Automatically. Maintaining Current Routing Slips & Patron Information Is Easy. Boolean Searching, Renewal Alerts, Budget Reports, File Management, Online Vendor Interfaces, & Overdue Reports Are Also Included. Adheres to Most Standards Including ANSI Z39.44, X1Z EDI, & Z39.56; These Standards Allow Users to Take Advantage of New Automation Standards Such As SICI Barcode Check-In. Compatible with All Other Professional Series Software.
Data Trek, Inc.

Professional Service Manager I. Jul. 1985. *Memory Required:* 256k.
disk Single user $299.95.
disk Multi user $699.95.
Time & Billing Package for Lawyers, Engineers, Accountants, Advertising Agencies, & Consultants. Includes: Client Services Rendered, Variable Invoice Formats, Hourly/Fixed/Contingency Billing Methods, Accounts Receivable, Client Statements, Diary/Docket/Calendaring, Escrow Accounting, Mortgage Amortization, & Operating & History Reports.
Information Management Corp.

Professional Social Security Planner. Dec. 1989.
IBM PC & compatibles. disk $99.00.
Develops Retirement, Disability & Survivor Benefits from Current Income or Complete Wage History.
Stafford Financial Services Corp.

Professional STORM. Version: 2.0. Hamilton Emmons et al. *Items Included:* 500 pg manual w/ sample problems in 3-ring binder & slipcase. *Customer Support:* Free tech support to all registered users.
MS-DOS 2.0 or higher. IBM PC, XT, AT, PS/2 or compatible (256k). disk $895.00. *Nonstandard peripherals required:* Will take advantage of math co-processor if available; but not required. *Optimal configuration:* Hard disk installation requires 850k. *Networks supported:* Single user product.
Consists of the Most Frequently Used Quantitative Modeling Techniques for Business & Engineering Problems. While STORM Is Powerful Enough to Be Applied to Complex & Sophisticated Situations, It Is Easy to Use, Providing an Interactive, Menu Driven User Interface, Spreadsheet Format Data Editor, Error Checking, & Help Prompts with Each Entry.
Storm Software, Inc.

Professional Symbol Libraries. *Compatible Hardware:* IBM PC, PC XT, PC AT. *General Requirements:* Drafix CAD Ultra or Windows CAD.
disk $150.00.
Architectural, Electrical, Mechanical & Landscape Symbol Libraries to Be Used with DRAFIX CAD Software.
Foresight Resources Corp.

Professional Timekeeping System. Version: 3.1-C. William D. Castagna. Jun. 1983. *Compatible Hardware:* Apple II, II+, IIe. *Operating System(s) Required:* Apple DOS 3.3. *Language(s):* Applesoft BASIC (source code included). *Memory Required:* 48k.
floppy version $595.00.
Corvus hard disk version $995.00.
demo disk & manual $100.00.
Handles Time Accounting, Client Tracking, Combined Aged Accounts Receivable & Client Bills. Generates Productivity Analysis Reports for Each Professional or Entire Firm. Allows up to 100 Professionals, 40 Fee Codes, 10 Expense Codes, 7000 Clients & up to 64 Workstations.
Better Business Solutions.

Professional Transit Report. Bruce Scofield & Josh Prokop. Mar. 1996. *Items Included:* Manual. *Customer Support:* Free phone support.
MS-DOS. 386 33MHz (640k). disk $350.00 (ISBN 0-87199-135-7). *Nonstandard peripherals required:* Math coprocessor, hard drive with minimum 20Mb, Hercules Mono.
Prints Detailed Astrological Forecasts Based on Transiting Aspects to the Birth Chart. Very Customizable; Includes 9 Wheel Styles & 2 Proportional Fonts; Graphic Transit Calendars for a Year, Month or Week; Ultra-Precision Planetary Routines; Fully Editable Text; Extra Interpretations for Planetary Stations, Void-of-Course Moon & Other Non-Personal Phenomena.
Astrolabe, Inc.

Professional Warranty System. *Items Included:* Installation guide, operator handbook. *Customer Support:* Free telephone support, on-site training for daily fee.
MS/PC-DOS 2.0 or higher (640k). IBM PC, PC XT, PC AT & compatibles, PS/2. disk $695.00 (Order no.: PROWARRANTY). *Nonstandard peripherals required:* Hard disk. *Optimal configuration:* Compatible 80 column or larger printer.
Comprehensive Warranty Tracking System for New Home Builders. Provides Required Documentation Including: Work Orders, Customer Acknowledgment & Property ID History. Monitors Subcontractor Performance. Provides Fast Access to Property Unit & History & Includes Valuable Management Reporting Options. Word Processing Interface Permits Selective Mailings to Owners & Subs.
HMS Computer Co.

Professional-YAM. Version: 17.01. *Compatible Hardware:* IBM PC & compatibles, UNIX, XENIX. *Operating System(s) Required:* PC-DOS/MS-DOS 2.0 or higher. *Memory Required:* 96k.
disk $139.00.
Offers Multiple Types of Security & Encryption, Host Mode for Remote Access, Automatic Logging of Incoming & Outgoing Transactions, Nine or More Different Transfer Protocols, & the Ability to Work with Nearly Any Modem. Creates a Script That Presents Menus & Specifies ASCII Character to Be Sent Using the Put Command. Allows Two Number Bases Only (Hexadecimal & Octal).
Omen Technology.

Professor C. D. Smart. Sep. 1994. *Items Included:* User manual. *Customer Support:* Free phone technical support via 1-800 number.
Windows. 386DX 40, MPC 1 (4Mb). CD-ROM disk $24.95 (ISBN 1-57600-013-3, Order no.: 62101). *Optimal configuration:* 386DX 40, CD-ROM drive, 4Mb.
Program Which Teaches the Basics of Using Windows 3.1.
Digital Impact, Inc.

Professor DOS with SmartGuide for DOS. Version: 4.0. *Compatible Hardware:* IBM & compatibles. *Operating System(s) Required:* DOS 1.0 or higher. *Memory Required:* 128k. *Items Included:* Diskettes & reference manuals. *Customer Support:* Call Individual Software (90 days).
$49.95 on 3.5" or 5.25" diskettes.
Provides Self-Paced, Interactive Lessons That Teach Both Novice & Experienced Computer Users How to Utilize & Manage Their IBM PC. Teaches DOS Applications, Command & Editing Keys. Includes Smart-Guide for DOS Which is an On-Line Reference Guide.
Individual Software.

Professor Iris Fun Field Trip: Animal Safari.
MS-DOS 5.0 or higher, Windows 3.1 or higher. 386 processor or higher (4Mb). CD-ROM disk $49.95 (Order no.: R1252A). *Nonstandard peripherals required:* CD-ROM drive. *Optimal configuration:* 386 processor operating at 16Mhz or higher, MS-DOS 5.0 or higher, Windows 3.1 or higher, 30Mb hard drive, mouse, VGA graphic adapter & VGA color monitor (SVGA recommended), 4Mb RAM, external speakers or headphones (with sound card) that are Sound Blaster compatible.
Macintosh (4Mb). (Order no.: R1252A). *Nonstandard peripherals required:* 14" color monitor or larger, CD-ROM drive.
Professor Iris Leads Children on a Wild Safari to Africa. Promotes Creative Exploration As Children Learn about Animal Habits, Habitats Camouflage & More. Includes Point-&-Click Navigation, Music Videos in Four Languages: English, French, Spanish & Japanese, & an Interactive Coloring Book (Ages 3 & Up).
Library Video Co.

Professor Multimedia. Version: 2. 1996. *Customer Support:* Hours: 8:00 am to 5:30 pm, pst, call toll free: 800-822-3522.
Mocrosoft Windows 3.1 or higher. IBM (8Mb). disk $24.95. *Nonstandard peripherals required:* Hard drive, CD-ROM drive, 256 color, VGA or higher, sound card, speakers or headphones, mouse.
Enter the world of multimedia with "Professor Multimedia", today's most comprehensive & interactive learning program. You will Learn about multimedia & experience it first hand.
Individual Software.

Professor Office (Excel 5.0, Word 6.0, Learn Mac): PRF OM2. Version: 3.0. *Items Included:* Manual. *Customer Support:* Free telephone support.
Mac & compatibles. Contact publisher for price (ISBN 0-918617-00-6).
Computer Based Training for Word 6.0, Excel 5.0 for the Macintosh with an Extra Bonus Package Called Learn to Use Mac. The Tutorials Are Designed to Help Anyone Get the Most Out of Their Mac.
Individual Software.

Professor Pix Football. *Compatible Hardware:* Apple, Commodore, IBM, TRS-80, CP/M machines.
disk Statistical Series $99.95.
disk w/Win-Loss Power Ratings $149.95.
Complete Statistical Analysis on Database Allowing "Designated" Previous Games to Be Evaluated.
Professor Jones Professional Handicapping Systems.

Professor Windows Multimedia. *Items Included:* 1 CD-ROM; user's guide. *Customer Support:* Hours: 8:00 am to 5:30 pm, pst; call toll free: 800-822-3522.
Microsoft Windows 3.1. 386-Based 33MHz PC or higher. disk $19.95
Nonstandard peripherals required: Double speed CD-ROM drive; 256 color VGA or higher; sound card; speakers or headphones; mouse.
Forget lengthy manuals, classes & video tape tutorials! Professor Windows Multimedia with Windows for Dummies takes interactive learning to a new level. Hear clear digital sound, see color video, stunning animation 7 graphics - all from a CD-ROM designed to help you learn Microsoft Windows quickly & effectively.
Individual Software.

Professor Windows Multimedia with Windows for Dummies: PRF 31C. Jun. 1995. *Items Included:* User's guide. *Customer Support:* Toll-free customer service, 30 day satisfaction guarantee.
IBM & compatibles. Contact publisher for price (ISBN 0-918617-01-4).
Combines Three Key Learning Components to Make Using Windows 3.11 Easier: a Multimedia Version of the Professor Windows Tutorial; an Electronic Version of the Windows 3.11 for Dummies Book, & a Library of Windows How-To Tips.
Individual Software.

Professor Windows 95 Deluxe CD: PRF 95C. Aug. 1995. *Items Included:* User's guide. *Customer Support:* Toll-free customer service, 30 day satisfaction guarantee.
IBM & compatibles. Contact publisher for price (ISBN 0-918617-03-0).
An Interactive, Multimedia-Based Tutorial That Teaches Users about the Major Elements of Windows '95 Using Sound, Video, Graphics & Animations. The Program Offers Two "Learning Tracks" - One for Beginner-Intermediate Users & the Other for Experienced-Enthusiast Users.
Individual Software.

Professor Windows 95 Deluxe CD. 1996. *Items Included:* 1 CD-ROM; users guide. *Customer Support:* Hours 8:00 am to 5:30 pm pst, call toll

free; 800-822-3522.
Micosoft Windows 95; 8 mb RAM. 486SX 25 Mhz PC or higher. disk $29.95. *Nonstandard peripherals required:* Double speed CD-ROM drive.
Nonstandard peripherals required: 256 color VGA or higher; sound card; speakers or microphones, mouse.
Explore the professor's neighborhood & experience three interactive learning tracks. Choose the Learning Track, Information Track or Review Track. Over 50 Comprehensive lessons teach you aeverything about Microsoft Windows 95!
Individual Software.

Professor Wise & His X-Ray Eyes. Jan. 1996.
Customer Support: Telephone support - free (except phone charge).
System 7.0 or higher. 256 color capable Mac with a 68030 processor (5Mb). CD-ROM disk $12.99 (ISBN 1-57594-111-2). *Nonstandard peripherals required:* 2X CD ROM drive, 640/480 resolution monitor.
Enhance Your Child's Deductive Reasoning, Vocabulary Development, & Comprehension Skills with Professor Wise on His Explorations to Various Places in Search of Hidden Objects. Take a Peek Inside Various Buildings & Artifacts As They Have Fun in This Learning Adventure.
Kidsoft, Inc.

Professor Wise & His X-Ray Eyes. Feb. 1996.
Customer Support: Telephone support - free (except phone charge).
Windows 3.1. IBM compatible 386 DX-20 (4Mb). CD-ROM disk $12.99 (ISBN 1-57594-100-7). *Nonstandard peripherals required:* 2x CD-ROM, sound card, VGA monitor. *Optimal configuration:* 486.
Enhance Deductive Reasoning, Vocabulary Development, & Comprehension Skills.
Kidsoft, Inc.

Professor Wise X-Ray Eyes. Dec. 1995.
Customer Support: Telephone support - free (except phone charge).
Windows 3.1. IBM & compatibles (386 DX-20) (4Mb). CD-ROM disk $12.99, Jewel (ISBN 1-57594-087-6). *Nonstandard peripherals required:* 2X CD ROM player, sound card, VGA monitor. *Optimal configuration:* 486 SX-33.
CD-ROM disk $12.99, Blister.
Enhance Your Child's Deductive Reasoning, Vocabulary Development, & Comprehension Skills with Professor Wise on His Explorations to Various Places in Search of Hidden Objects. Take a Peek Inside Various Buildings & Artifacts As They Have Fun in This Learning Adventure.
Kidsoft, Inc.

Professor Wise X-Ray Eyes. Dec. 1995.
Customer Support: Telephone support - free (except phone charge).
Windows 3.1. IBM & compatibles (386 DX-20) (4Mb). CD-ROM disk $12.99 (ISBN 1-57594-087-6). *Nonstandard peripherals required:* 2X CD-ROM player, sound card, VGA monitor. *Optimal configuration:* 486 SX-33.
Enhance Your Child's Deductive Reasoning, Vocabulary Development, & Comprehension Skills with Professor Wise on His Explorations to Various Places in Search of Hidden Objects. Take a Peek Inside Various Buildings & Artifacts As They Have Fun in This Learning Adventure. Jewel Case.
Kidsoft, Inc.

Professors for Microsoft Office. *Items Included:* Powerpoint 4, word 6, excel 5, ms-mail 3.2, access 2. *Customer Support:* Toll free: 800-822-3522.
Microsoft Windows 3.1 or higher. IBM (480k) RAM. disk $29.95. *Nonstandard peripherals required:* Hard disk with 6mb space, 250 color VGA or higher, sound card, speakers of Headphones, microsoft compatible mouse.
Getting the most out of Microsoft Office is easy with step-by-step instructions. The professors will turn your computer into a friendly tutor & show you how to use each Microsoft Office Product effectively. One easy step makes all five Professors available for on-demand learning covering every product in Microsoft Office.
Indivual Software.

Profile. *Compatible Hardware:* IBM PC; TRS-80 Model II, Model III, Model 4, Model 12, Model 16; Tandy 2000.
contact publisher for price.
Uses up to 112 Yes & No Questions to Develop Personal Profiles for Individuals in Church Donations Data Base.
Custom Data (New Mexico).

The Profile. *Version:* 6.0. *Operating System(s) Required:* MS-DOS 2.11 or higher. *Memory Required:* 384k. *General Requirements:* Printer.
disk $650.00-$3900.00.
Evaluates Individual in Six Mental Aptitude Areas & Ten Personality Areas in Reaction to Specific Jobs, i.e., Sales, Management, etc. Provides Methods to Improve Areas of Weakness.
Profile Technologies, Inc.

Profile Grade, Street, Sewer & Water Line Profiler. *Items Included:* Full manual. No other products required. *Customer Support:* Free telephone support - no time limit. 30 day warranty.
MS-DOS 3.2 or higher. IBM & compatibles (512k). disk $395.33. *Optimal configuration:* IBM, MS-DOS 3.2 or higher, 640k RAM, hard drive. Printer is optional.
Provides All of the Analyses Needed for Normal Street Grade Computations, Storm Drainage Design, & Profile Preparation. Also Creates DXF Data Files with User-Defined Horizontal & Vertical Scales for Transfer to AUTOcad. Features Include: Generation of Street Profiles, Screen Preview of Profile Prior to Generating DXF File, Pipe Sizes May Be Computed Using Mannings Formula, Tops of Frames for Inlets Are Computed to Match Street Grade with Given Grade Differential, Tangent & Vertical Curve Grade Calculations, Easy-to-Use Menus, Clear Prompts.
Dynacomp, Inc.

The Profiler. *Version:* 1.2. Jeff Erwin. Feb. 1984. *Compatible Hardware:* IBM PC, PC XT. *Operating System(s) Required:* MS-DOS. *Memory Required:* 64k.
disk $179.95 (Order no.: PRO012).
manual $7.50.
Allows Users to Determine Where Their Program Is Consuming the Most CPU Time.
DWB Assocs.

Profiles of America: An Informational, Statistical, & Relocation Encyclopedia of All U. S. Cities, Towns, Counties. Nov. 1995.
CD-ROM disk $735.00 (ISBN 1-884925-04-9).
Toucan Valley Publications.

PROFIN. Business Software Pty., Ltd. *Operating System(s) Required:* CP/M-86. *Memory Required:* 64k. *General Requirements:* Printer.
$295.00.
Texas Instruments, Personal Productivit.

PROFIT. *Version:* SFP 110. 1990. *Operating System(s) Required:* T/OS, UNIX, XENIX, AIX, IDOL IV. *Language(s):* Business BASIC (source code included). *Memory Required:* 512k. *Items Included:* Application software & ReportWriter & Mail. *Customer Support:* On-site and/or modem.
$15,000.00-$75,000.00.
Online, Interactive, Business & Manufacturing Control System with Optional Modules That Make It Usable in Manufacturing Environments from Assemble-for-Distribution to Job Shops, to Make-to-Order, to Make-to-Stock/Plan.
MIS Technology.

Profit Builder. *Version:* 6.9. Dec. 1989. *Compatible Hardware:* IBM PC & compatible, PC XT, PC AT, 386. *Operating System(s) Required:* PC-DOS, MS-DOS. *Memory Required:* 640k.
(sold by module) $6000.00.
Designed to Assist Small & Medium-Sized Construction Firms in Managing Their Business. Composed of 9 Major Modules. Includes IC, AP, AR, GL, Payroll, Purchase Order, Subcontract Control, Draw Request, Billing & Report Writer.
Construction Data Control, Inc. (CDCI).

The Profit Center Accounts Payable.
Compatible Hardware: IBM, Wang, Texas Instruments.
disk $695.00.
IBM. (ISBN 0-13-002288-8).
Wang. (ISBN 0-13-003245-X).
Texas Instruments. (ISBN 0-13-003229-8).
demo disk $25.00.
Learning Kit. $64.00.
Learning Kit demo. $25.00.
Payment Processing & Cash Forecasting System, Supplementing GENERAL ACCOUNTING for Improving a Company's Continued Control over Cash Outlays to Vendors & Employees.
Prentice Hall.

The Profit Center Accounts Receivable.
Compatible Hardware: IBM, Wang, Texas Instruments.
disk $695.00.
IBM. (ISBN 0-13-002346-9).
Wang. (ISBN 0-13-003286-7).
Texas Instruments. (ISBN 0-13-003260-3).
Demo Disk. $25.00.
Learning Kit. $64.95.
Learning Kit Demo. $25.00.
Invoicing & Credit Management System, Supplementing GENERAL ACCOUNTING for Tracking Monies Due from Customers.
Prentice Hall.

The Profit Center Business Word Processor.
Compatible Hardware: IBM, Wang, Texas Instruments.
disk $250.00.
IBM. (ISBN 0-13-108317-1).
Wang. (ISBN 0-13-108366-X).
Texas Instruments. (ISBN 0-13-108341-4).
Demo. $25.00.
Learning Kit. $59.95.
Learning Kit Demo. $25.00.
Text Processing System for Revising Most Types of Written Documents. Used in Conjunction with Other PROFIT CENTER Software, It Can Produce Customized Accounting Reports & Letters.
Prentice Hall.

The Profit Center General Accounting.
Compatible Hardware: IBM, Wang, Texas Instruments.
disk $595.00.
IBM. (ISBN 0-13-347682-0).
Wang. (ISBN 0-13-347592-1).
Texas Instruments. (ISBN 0-13-347576-X).
Demo Disk. $25.00.
Learning Kit. $74.95.
Learning Kit Demo. $25.00.
Cornerstone of the Profit Center Series. Provides Companies with an Accounting System for Improving Cash-Flow Planning & Profitability. Also Improves Clerical Productivity by Reducing Time-Consuming & Error-Prone Bookkeeping.
Prentice Hall.

The Profit Center Information Query for General Accounting. *Compatible Hardware:* IBM, Wang, Texas Instruments.
disk $150.00.
Learning Kit. $25.00.
Provides the Capability to Generate Almost Any Accounting Report the User May Require. Permits the Use of the Entire Data Base As a Pool for Information; IDF Capability Also Allows Interface with Data Base Management.
Prentice Hall.

The Profit Center Job Costs. *Compatible Hardware:* IBM, Wang, Texas Instruments.
disk $695.00.
IBM. (ISBN 0-13-509498-4).
Wang. (ISBN 0-13-509092-X).
Texas Instruments. (ISBN 0-13-509076-8).
Demo. $25.00.
Learning Kit. contact publisher for price.
Learning Kit Demo. $25.00.
Full-Featured Job Tracking & Control System for Monitoring Job Profitability from the Time of Initial Estimate to the Job's Final Completion.
Prentice Hall.

The Profit Center Job Estimator. *Compatible Hardware:* IBM, Wang, Texas Instruments.
disk $395.00.
(ISBN 0-13-510280-4).
IBM. (ISBN 0-13-510405-X).
Texas Instruments. (ISBN 0-13-510322-3).
Demo. $25.00.
Learning Kit. contact publisher for price.
Learning Kit Demo. $25.00.
Designed to Be Used Independently or with JOB COSTS for Formulating Job Estimates.
Prentice Hall.

The Profit Center Master Menu. *Compatible Hardware:* IBM, Wang, Texas Instruments.
disk $25.00.
IBM. (ISBN 0-13-559592-4).
Wang. (ISBN 0-13-559485-5).
Texas Instruments. (ISBN 0-13-559469-3).
Demo. $25.00.
Learning Kit. $24.95.
Learning Kit Demo. $25.00.
Makes It Possible to Run One or More of the Profit Center Programs.
Prentice Hall.

The Profit Center NEAT: The Time & Information Managers. *Compatible Hardware:* IBM, Wang, Texas Instruments.
disk $150.00.
IBM. (ISBN 0-13-610676-5).
Wang. (ISBN 0-13-611195-5).
Texas Instruments. (ISBN 0-13-611179-3).
Demo. $25.00.
Learning Kit. $39.95.
Learning Kit Demo. $25.00.
Desktop Information Manager for Organizing Short Notes, Expenses, Addresses, & Time.
Prentice Hall.

The Profit Center Spellproof. *Compatible Hardware:* IBM, Wang, Texas Instruments.
disk $75.00.
IBM. (ISBN 0-13-834151-6).
Wang. (ISBN 0-13-834177-X).
(ISBN 0-13-834136-2).
Demo. $25.00.
Learning Kit. contact publisher for price.
Learning Kit Demo. $25.00.
50,000 Word Dictionary for Verifying Spelling Accuracy in Documents Created with BUSINESS WORD PROCESSING.
Prentice Hall.

Profit Planner. *Version:* 2.5. *Items Included:* Inc. Magazine's "How to Really Create a Successful Business Plan" by David Gumpert.
DOS. IBM or compatible (300k). disk $139.00.
Addl. software required: Lotus 1-2-3, Versions 2, 2.01, 2.2, 2.3, 3, 3.1; Quattro Pro 1, 2, & 3; 1-2-3 for Windows or Mac, Microsoft Excel for Windows & Stand Alone.
Does Business Financial Analysis & Planning. Enter Titles & Amounts on Pop-up Data Sheets. The Program Automatically Builds Earnings Statement, Cash Flow Statement, & Balance Sheet in Detailed, Summary & Percentage Format. Covers up to 12 Prior & 25 Future Periods. Over 70 Ratios. Accepts & Displays Industry Averages by Dun & Bradstreet & Robert Morris Associates. Graphs Any Line Items by Point & Shoot Technique. Drives WYSIWYG, Impress, & Allways Desktop Publishing.
Suntex National Corp.

Profit Projection Analysis. *Customer Support:* 800-929-8117 (customer service).
MS-DOS. Apple II. disk $49.99 (ISBN 0-87007-835-6).
Graphically Displays Monthly Sales, Expenses, Overhead, & Profit for a One Year Period.
SourceView Software International.

Profit Series Accounts Payable. *Compatible Hardware:* IBM 386 & compatibles, Novell, Unix. *Language(s):* BASIC (source code included). *Memory Required:* 512k. *General Requirements:* Hard disk 20Mb, printer.
IBM 386 & compatibles. disk $695.00.
System Novell & Unix. disk $995.00.
Allows Partial or Full Payment. Generates Payables Check Register, Check & Cash Required Forecasts. Includes Cash Disbursements. Interfaces with PROFIT SERIES FINANCIAL ACCOUNTING Package (G/L).
Crosstech Systems, Inc.

Profit Series Accounts Receivable. *Compatible Hardware:* IBM 386 & compatibles, System Novell & Unix. *Operating System(s) Required:* PC-DOS/MS-DOS. (source code included). *Memory Required:* 512k. *General Requirements:* Hard disk 20Mb, printer.
IBM 386 & compatibles. disk $695.00.
System Novell & Unix. disk $995.00.
Includes Two Data Entry Phases for Initial Entry & Regular Invoices, Performs Setting up of AR Master File & Posting of Payments Received. Provides Back End with PROFIT SERIES SalesTrak, INVENTORY CONTROL & Front End into FINANCIAL ACCOUNTING PACKAGE III (G/L) Generates Interface Area Reports on Request for Variable Parameters.
Crosstech Systems, Inc.

Profit Series for Accountants. *Compatible Hardware:* IBM 386 & compatibles, System Novell & Unix. *Operating System(s) Required:* PC-DOS/MS-DOS. *Language(s):* BASIC (source code included). *Memory Required:* 512k. *General Requirements:* Hard disk 20Mb, printer.
IBM 386 & compatibles. disk $2995.00.
Syystem Novell & Unix. disk $3995.00.
Includes FINANCIAL ACCOUNTING PACKAGE III (Client-Write-up, 1099, After-the-Fact Payroll) & Time Management & Billing. May Be Purchased Separately. TM&B Includes Full Accounts Receivable. Other Modules Available Include Payroll, Accounts Payable, Amortization, Random Number Generator.
Crosstech Systems, Inc.

Profit Series for General Business Accounting. *Compatible Hardware:* IBM 386 & compatibles, System Novell & Unix. *Operating System(s) Required:* PC-DOS/MS-DOS. *Language(s):* BASIC (source code included). *Memory Required:* 512k. *General Requirements:* Hard disk 20Mb, printer.
disk $1995.00.
Includes Accounts Receivable, SalesTrak (Order Entry/Billing/Sales Analysis), Inventory with Bill of Materials, Accounts Payable. May Be Purchased Separately. Other Modules Available Are: Payroll, Purchase Order, General Ledger, Job Estimating & Tracking Contract Billing.
Crosstech Systems, Inc.

Profit Series for Wholesalers/Distributors. *Compatible Hardware:* IBM 366 & compatibles, System Novell & Unix. *Operating System(s) Required:* PC-DOS/MS-DOS. *Language(s):* BASIC (source code included). *Memory Required:* 512k. *General Requirements:* Hard disk 20Mb.
IBM 386 & compatibles. disk $2995.00.
System Novell & Unix. disk $3995.00.
Includes SalesTrak (Order Entry/Billing/Sales Analysis), INVENTORY WITH BILL OF MATERIALS & ACCOUNTS RECEIVABLE. May Be Purchased Separately. Other Modules Available Are: PURCHASE ORDER, ACCOUNTS PAYABLE, GENERAL LEDGER, PAYROLL & JOB ESTIMATING AND TRACKING.
Crosstech Systems, Inc.

Profit Series Inventory-Bill of Materials. *Compatible Hardware:* IBM 386 & compatibles, System Novell & Unix. *Operating System(s) Required:* PC-DOS/MS-DOS. *Language(s):* BASIC (source code included). *Memory Required:* 512k. *General Requirements:* Hard disk 20Mb, printer.
IBM 386 & compatibles. disk $695.00.
System Novell & Unix. disk $995.00.
Builds Finished Part in Inventory from Existing Subcomponents. Provides Costing Runs for Price Changes. Allows Increased/Decreased Cost of Finished Goods, Minimum/Maximum Level Tracking. Parts Explosion & 12 Character Part Number. Interfaces with PROFIT SERIES SalesTrak & AR.
Crosstech Systems, Inc.

Profit Series Job Estimating & Tracking. *Compatible Hardware:* IBM 386 & compatibles, System Novell & Unix. *Operating System(s) Required:* PC-DOS/MS-DOS. *Language(s):* BASIC (source code included). *Memory Required:* 512k. *General Requirements:* Hard disk 20Mb, printer.
IBM 386 & compatibles. disk $695.00.
Novell & Unix. disk $995.00.
Compares Estimated & Actual Figures. Tracks Time, Materials & Labor for Each Job. Shows Job Profitability. Stores Customer Job Listing, Job Estimate Report, Shop Report & Transaction Report. Interfaces with PROFIT SERIES AR & Inventory.
Crosstech Systems, Inc.

Profit Series Payroll. *Compatible Hardware:* IBM 386 & compatibles, System Novell & Unix. *Operating System(s) Required:* PC-DOS/MS-DOS. *Language(s):* BASIC (source code included). *Memory Required:* 512k. *General Requirements:* Hard disk 20Mb, printer.
IBM 386 & compatibles. disk $695.00.
Novell & Unix. disk $995.00.
Produces Normal & After-the-Fact Payroll. Supports up to 500 Employees, Nine Earnings Categories & Sixteen Deductions Categories. Prints Quarterly Reports & W2 & WRS2 Forms. Supports Tips, Meals & Unions. Human Resource Module Also Available. Interfaces with PROFIT SERIES FAPIII (G/L).
Crosstech Systems, Inc.

Profit Series Purchase Order. *Compatible Hardware:* IBM 386 & compatibles, System Novell & Unix. *Operating System(s) Required:* PC-DOS/MS-DOS. *Language(s):* BASIC (source code included). *Memory Required:* 512k. *General Requirements:* Hard disk 20Mb, printer.

TITLE INDEX

IBM 386 & compatibles. disk $695.00.
Novell & Unix. disk $995.00.
Tracks Order Quantity by Job & Inventory. Interfaces with PROFIT SERIES AP, Inventory & Job Estimating & Tracking. When Account Created in AP, Tracks Unit Cost & Purchase History.
Crosstech Systems, Inc.

Profit Series SalesTrak: Order Entry/Billing/Sales Analysis. *Compatible Hardware:* IBM 386 & compatibles, System Novell & Unix. *Operating System(s) Required:* PC-DOS/MS-DOS. *Language(s):* BASIC (source code included). *Memory Required:* 512k. *General Requirements:* Hard disk 20Mb, printer.
IBM 386 & compatibles. disk $695.00.
Novell & Unix. disk $995.00.
Provides Billing. Generates Packing Slips, Reports, Invoices & Back Orders. Sales Analysis, Gross Profit Report. Interfaces with Inventory & AR.
Crosstech Systems, Inc.

Profit Series Time Management & Billing With AR. *Compatible Hardware:* IBM 386 & compatibles, System Novell & Unix. *Operating System(s) Required:* PC-DOS/MS-DOS. *Language(s):* BASIC. *Memory Required:* 512k. *General Requirements:* Hard disk 20Mb, printer.
IBM 386 & compatibles. disk $695.00.
Novell & Unix. disk $995.00.
Defines Time Parameters & Billing Structures. Creates Work-in-Progress Reports, Billing, Aging of AR & Cash Receipts. Provides Analysis Studies to Determine Profitable/Non-Profitable Activities, Employees & Clients.
Crosstech Systems, Inc.

ProfitCAD. *Version:* 2.2. Feb. 1990. *Items Included:* Reference guide, quick start booklet, getting started tutorial. *Customer Support:* Training class (4 days) cost $595.00, 90 days telephone support, on-site training available at cost, 1 yr. telephone support available at cost.
80386 based computers (Intel chip) (2Mb). $5995.00. *Nonstandard peripherals required:* Math co-processor, high resolution graphics card, mouse.
CAD System with Complete Estimating System for Construction Projects. Draw & Revise Plans While System Simultaneously Tracks Quantities & Costs Required to Build Plan, Including Labor Costs & Mark-Ups. Produces Detailed Estimates & Accurately Scaled Drawings. Includes Symbol Library. Data Base Available.
Construction Data Control, Inc. (CDCI).

Profitime/Plus: Professional Time & Billing. *Items Included:* Manual. *Customer Support:* Free 90 day maintenance.
PC-DOS, MS-DOS 2.0 or higher. IBM PC-XT, IBM PC-AT or compatible (512k). disk $389.00.
Complete Time & Billing Program Designed for Professionals Who Bill for Time.
Profitime, Inc.

ProfitManager I. *Compatible Hardware:* IBM PC, PC XT. *Memory Required:* 256k. *General Requirements:* Hard disk.
contact publisher for price.
Provides the Ability to Define Client Relationships & Evaluate Profitability. Also Provides a Flexible Method of Repricing.
Distributed Planning System Corp.

ProfitShare. *Customer Support:* 800-929-8117 (customer service).
MS-DOS. IBM/PS2. disk $99.99 (ISBN 0-87007-179-3).
A Profit-Sharing DBMS Which Allows Individual & Batch Updating. Prints Disbursement Checks, Profit-Sharing Statistics & Activities Reports, Quarter & Year-End Statements of Account 1099R & W2P Forms. Keeps Track of Activity Status, Prerequisites for Profit Sharing, Agreed upon Benefit Levels, Company Number, Fund Type, Annual Compensation, Fund Adjust Balances, Earnings, Contributions, Forfeitures & Ending Balances. Successfully Allocates Earnings, Contributions & Forfeitures for Participants of a Profit Sharing Fund, Which Is Often the Case for Professionals in Private Practice.
SourceView Software International.

Profit$ource. *Version:* 2. Jul. 1987. *Compatible Hardware:* IBM PC, PC XT, PC AT & compatibles. *Operating System(s) Required:* DOS Ver. 3.1 or higher. *Memory Required:* 256k. *General Requirements:* Hard disk. *Items Included:* Binder with documentation. *Customer Support:* 1 yr. maintenance, $75.00, entitles users to phone support, quarterly newsletters & enhancements made available for their computer during the year at no charge.
disk $295.00.
maintenance fee (optional) $75.00.
demo disk $45.00.
Time & Billing System for Producing Client Billing Statements, Keeping Track of Accounts Receivable, & Work in Progress for the 1 to 9 Timekeeper Firm. A Finance Charge Can Be Assessed for Selected Clients. Allows 25 Billing Cycles Including Billing on Demand. Features a Built-In Trust Accounting System & Pop-Up Timer. Upgradeable to TABS III Jr., TABS III-M Jr., TABS III or TABS III-M. 30 Day Money Back Guarantee.
Software Technology, Inc.

ProfitTime Plus: Time & Billing. *Compatible Hardware:* IBM PC & compatibles. *General Requirements:* Lotus 1-2-3 Release 2.0 or 2.01. *Items Included:* Manual. *Customer Support:* Free 90 day maintenance.
disk $329.00.
demo disk $10.00.
Menu-Driven Template Designed for Those Who Charge a Fee for Their Services. Manages Variable Rate Schedules, Timekeeper Worksheets, & Accounts Receivable Records. Produces Computer-Generated Statements. Prepares a Cash-Receipts Journal, Productivity Reports, & Client Activity Reports.
Profitime, Inc.

ProFont: Editing for Laser Printers. Jim Boemler. Mar. 1985. *Compatible Hardware:* IBM PC, PC XT, PC AT. *Operating System(s) Required:* PC-DOS, MS-DOS, Concurrent DOS. *Language(s):* C, Assembler. *Memory Required:* 128k. *General Requirements:* IBM graphics card, laser printer.
disk $400.00.
Designed to Create New Fonts from Scratch or to Modify Existing Ones for a Variety of Laser Printers. Editing Can Be Done Either by Way of a Microsoft Mouse or, If a Mouse Is Not Available or Desired, Directly with the PC's Cursor Keys. Requires No Technical Knowledge - the Program Works in a Manner Similar to That of the Familiar "Etch-a-Sketch".
Woolf Software Systems, Inc.

ProFonts: Decorative, Vol. 2. *Compatible Hardware:* Commodore Amiga. *Memory Required:* 512k. *Items Included:* Disk & manual. *Customer Support:* Phone-in support available free of charge.
$34.95.
Contains Several High Quality Creative Fonts for Non-PostScript Printers.
New Horizons Software.

PROGRAM FOR THE CBCL/4-18 PROFILE

ProFonts: Professional, Vol. 1. *Compatible Hardware:* Commodore Amiga. *Memory Required:* 512k. *Items Included:* Disk & manual. *Customer Support:* phone-in support available free of charge.
$34.95.
Contains Several Professional High Quality Fonts for Dot Matrix Printers.
New Horizons Software.

Progeny. Aug. 1991. *Items Included:* Software documentation/owners manual. *Customer Support:* Customer service is provided to all customers free of charge for 30 days after the purchase date. After that time, maintenance may be purchased at $125 per year.
IBM DOS. IBM compatible (640k). disk $595.00 stand alone version (ISBN 0-943293-01-4).
Networks supported: Novell, Lantastic & Banyon.
Simplifies the Topic of Generation Skipping, Allowing Clients to Understand the Savings Available Through This Additional Area of Estate Tax Law. Creates Flowchart Presentations & Includes Text Explanations. Compares the Client's Estate with & Without the Use of Generation Skipping.
ViewPlan, Inc.

Progistics. *Version:* 2.0. 1992. *Items Included:* User manuals, on line help, tutorials. *Customer Support:* Yearly maintenance; online support via remote electronic communications.
OS/2. IBM PC or compatible 486 (12Mb). Contact publisher for price (dependent upon configuration). *Addl. software required:* OS/2; database manager. *Optimal configuration:* 486-33Mhz, 16Mb RAM. *Networks supported:* NetBIOS compatible.
Client/Server Based Logistics Management Software Product Line for Flexible Adaptation to Any Distribution Environment. Customers Can Purchase Pre-Packaged or Customized Applications. Functionality Includes Shipment Planning, Carrier Rating/Selection, Document Production, Shipment Confirmation, Warehouse/Inventory Control Interfaces, Barcode Scanning, EDI, Customer Service Interface. Host System Communication Options Available. Progistics Can Be Seamlessly Linked to a Wide Range of Host System Configurations. User Friendly Software with Graphic User Interface (GUI); Easy to Learn & Train On. All Progistics Products Can Be Operated As Standalone Systems or As an Integrated Solution with Other Systems. Two-Way Communications of Pre-Shipment & Post Shipment Information Is Available.
TanData Corp.

Program Animator for BASIC. *Items Included:* Bound manual. *Customer Support:* Free hotline - no time limit; 30 day limited warranty; updates are $5/disk plus S&H.
MS-DOS 2.0 or higher. IBM & compatibles (256k). disk $29.95. *Addl. software required:* BASIC or BASICA (IBM); or GWBASIC (compatibles).
Interactive Educational Tool. It Can Also Be Used to Help Develop BASIC Programs. When Running a BASIC Program in the Animation Mode, PAB Displays the Program Portion Currently Being Executed. As Each Statement Is Executed, the Cursor Moves along the Statement. The Values of Variables Used Are Shown Both Before & After Execution of the Statement. Loop Counts & Nesting Levels Are Displayed, As Well As Condition Results.
Dynacomp, Inc.

Program for the CBCL/4-18 Profile, 1991 - Apple II Version. *Version:* 3.0. Thomas M. Achenbach. Oct. 1991. *Items Included:* Documentation. *Customer Support:* Free

telephone support with no time limit. ProDOS. Apple II (64k). disk $175.00 (ISBN 0-938565-17-6). *Optimal configuration:* Apple II with 64k & printer capable of 132-character lines if user wishes to print out profiles.
Provides for Entry & Scoring of Data from the Child Behavior Checklist/4-18. Options Include Storing Scores for Analysis & Printing of Profiles.
Univ. of Vermont, Dept. of Psychiatry.

Program for the 1992 CBCL/2-3 Profile - IBM PC Version. *Version:* 3.0. Thomas M. Achenbach. Jun. 1992. *Items Included:* Detailed manual. *Customer Support:* Free telephone support with no time limit.
MS-DOS. IBM PC & compatibles (512k). disk $135.00 (ISBN 0-938565-21-4). *Optimal configuration:* IBM PC compatible with 512k, & printer capable of 132-character lines if user wishes to print profiles.
For Entering & Scoring Data from the Child Behavior Checklist for Ages 2-3. Options Include Storing Scores for Analysis & Printing of Profiles. Also Displays Item & Scale Scores Side-by-Side from up to 5 Completed Copies of the CBCL/2-3 & Computes Q Correlations Between Item Scores from Each Pair of Copies.
Univ. of Vermont, Dept. of Psychiatry.

Program for the 1992 CBCL/2-3 Profile - Apple II Version. *Version:* 3.0. Thomas M. Achenbach. Jul. 1992. *Items Included:* Detailed manual. *Customer Support:* Free telephone support with no time limit.
ProDOS. Apple II series (512k). disk $135.00 (ISBN 0-938565-22-2). *Optimal configuration:* Apple II with 64k & printer capable of 132-character lines if user wishes to print profiles.
For Entering & Scoring Data from the Child Behavior Checklist for Ages 2-3. Options Include Storing Scores for Analysis & Printing of Profiles. Also Displays Item & Scale Scores Side-by-Side from up to 5 Completed Copies of the CBCL/2-3 & Computes Q Correlations Between Item Scores from Each Pair of Copies.
Univ. of Vermont, Dept. of Psychiatry.

Program for the 1993 CBCL/4-18 Profile - IBM Version. *Version:* 4.0. Thomas M. Achenbach. Jun. 1993. *Items Included:* Detailed manual. *Customer Support:* Free telephone support with no time limit.
MS-DOS. IBM-PC compatible (512k). disk $175.00 (ISBN 0-938565-28-1). *Optimal configuration:* IBM-PC compatible with 512k, & printer capable of 132-character lines if user wishes to print profiles.
For Entering & Scoring Data from the Child Behavior Checklist for Ages 4-18. Options Include Storing Scores for Analysis & Printing Profiles. 1993 Version Compares up to 5 CBCLs & Computes Intraclass Correlations with Profile Types.
Univ. of Vermont, Dept. of Psychiatry.

Program for the 1993 Teacher's Report Form Profile - IBM Version. *Version:* 4.0. Thomas M. Achenbach. Jun. 1993. *Items Included:* Detailed manual. *Customer Support:* Free telephone support with no time limit.
MS-DOS. IBM-PC compatible (512k). disk $175.00 (ISBN 0-938565-30-3). *Optimal configuration:* IBM-PC compatible with 512k, & printer capable of 132-character lines if user wishes to print profiles.
For Entering & Scoring Data from the Teacher's Report Form. Options Include Storing Scores for Analysis & Printing Profiles. 1993 Version Compares up to 5 TRFs & Computes Intraclass Correlations with Profile Types.
Univ. of Vermont, Dept. of Psychiatry.

Program for the 1993 YSR Profile - IBM Version. *Version:* 4.0. Thomas M. Achenbach. Jun. 1993. *Items Included:* Detailed manual. *Customer Support:* Free telephone support with no time limit.
MS-DOS. IBM-PC compatible (512k). disk $175.00 (ISBN 0-938565-29-X). *Optimal configuration:* IBM-PC compatible with 512k, & printer capable of 132-character lines if user wishes to print profiles.
For Entering & Scoring Data from the Youth Self-Report. Options Include Storing Scores for Analysis & Printing Profiles. 1993 Version Compares up to 5 YSRs & Computes Intraclass Correlations with Profile Types.
Univ. of Vermont, Dept. of Psychiatry.

Program for the Teacher's Report Form, 1991 - Apple II Version. *Version:* 3.0. Thomas M. Achenbach. Oct. 1991. *Items Included:* Documentation. *Customer Support:* Free telephone support with no time limit.
ProDOS. Apple II (64k). disk $175.00 (ISBN 0-938565-18-4). *Optimal configuration:* Apple II with 64k & printer capable of 132-character lines if user wishes to print out profiles.
Provides for Entry & Scoring of Data from the Teacher's Report Form. Options Include Storing Scores for Analysis & Printing of Profiles.
Univ. of Vermont, Dept. of Psychiatry.

Program for the Youth Self-Report, 1991 - Apple II Version. *Version:* 3.0. Thomas M. Achenbach. Nov. 1991. *Items Included:* Documentation. *Customer Support:* Free telephone support with no time limit.
ProDOS. Apple II (64k). disk $175.00 (ISBN 0-938565-19-2). *Optimal configuration:* Apple II with 64k & printer capable of 132-character lines if user wishes to print out profiles.
Provides for Entry & Scoring of Data from the Youth Self-Report. Options Include Storing of Scores for Analysis & Printing of Profiles.
Univ. of Vermont, Dept. of Psychiatry.

Program Interfacing for MS-DOS. William G. Wong. *Operating System(s) Required:* MS-DOS.
disk $29.95, incl. manual (ISBN 0-934375-34-8).
Orients Experienced Programmers to the MS-DOS Environments. Topics Include Program Construction, Character Base Input & Output Functions, & File Access. The Manual Also Contains Sample Program Files & a Description of How to Build Device Drivers. The Disk Includes Macro Assembly Source Code.
M & T Bks.

Program Manager Plus. *Items Included:* 140 page manual. *Customer Support:* Free telephone support to registered users.
PC-DOS/MS-DOS 2.1 or higher. IBM PC, PC XT, PC AT, PS/2 & compatibles. contact publisher for price.
Powerful Menu Shell Designed Specifically for Corporate "PC Coordinator" & System Integrator. Single Keystroke or Mouse Click Can Call Any Program on System. Programs Can Be in Memory, on Floppy Disk, Local Hard Disk or on Network.
Lassen Software, Inc.

Program Solving in Apple Pascal. 1984. *Compatible Hardware:* Apple II+, IIe. *Language(s):* Pascal. *Memory Required:* 64k.
disk $20.00 (ISBN 0-88175-023-9).
txbk. $19.95.
Instructor's Disk Includes a Guide with Suggestions & Solutions to Programs in Text Format. Student's Disk Reproduces the Programs in the Book but Does Not Provide the Solutions.
W. H. Freeman & Co. (Computer Science Press).

Programmer Aptitude. *Compatible Hardware:* Atari.
contact publisher for price.
Tridata Corp.

Programmer's Apprentice MailMerge Option. *Compatible Hardware:* IBM PC with 2 disk drives. *Operating System(s) Required:* MS-DOS, CP/M-86, PC-DOS, SB-86. *Memory Required:* 64k.
disk $100.00.
Enables the User to Generate a Program Which Will Automatically Extract Data from Previously Created Files. Creates Files Compatible with WordStar MailMerge Software.
Lifeboat Assocs.

Programmers Converter. *Compatible Hardware:* TRS-80 Model I, Model III. *Memory Required:* 16k.
cassette $14.95 (Order no.: 0058R).
Convert Decimal Number to Binary, Octal, or Hexadecimal & Back Again.
Instant Software, Inc.

The Programmer's Essential OS/2 Handbook. David E. Cortesi. *Operating System(s) Required:* OS/2.
book & disk $39.95 (ISBN 0-934375-89-5).
book only $24.95 (ISBN 0-934375-82-8).
Reference Guide That Organizes the Features of OS/2 into Related Topics, While Highlighting Their Uses. All Sample Programs Are Available on Disk with Full Source Code.
M & T Bks.

Programmer's Line Editor. Aug. 1986. *Compatible Hardware:* TI Pro, Business Pro. *Operating System(s) Required:* MS-DOS. *Memory Required:* 256k. *General Requirements:* Hard disk recommended.
disk $39.95 (ISBN 0-9615084-2-6).
Allows User to Create & Edit Source Code for Assembly, C, Pascal, Modula 2, Compiler BASIC, Prolog, dBASE, COBOL, LOGO, & LISP.
J. B. Dawson.

The Programmer's Online Companion. *Version:* 2.0. *Compatible Hardware:* Apple Macintosh. *Memory Required:* 512k.
3.5" disk $49.95.
Utility Program That Allows Access to Text Material from Inside Macintosh Volumes I-V & the Apple Numerics Manual.
Addison-Wesley Publishing Co., Inc.

Programmers' PAC 1 Z80 Assembler. *Version:* 1.1. 1983. *Compatible Hardware:* CP/M based machines. *Operating System(s) Required:* CP/M 2.2. *Language(s):* Assembly (source code included). *Memory Required:* 48k.
disk $99.00.
The Hawkeye Grafix "Fast" 8080/Z80 Assembler Uses DRI (& TDL) Extended 8080 Pneumonics for Z-80 OP Codes.
Hawkeye Grafix.

Programmer's Tool Kit. May 1988. *Operating System(s) Required:* PC-DOS/MS-DOS 2.0 or higher. *Memory Required:* 128k.
3.5" or 5.25" disk $95.00 (Order no.: PTK-1).
Tool Box of Utilities Consisting of 7 Programs: Bed - a Binary File Editor; Hex2Bin - Convert Intel Hex to Binary; Stohex - Convert Motorola to Intel Hex; GHEX2 - Convert Binary to Intel Hex; Split - Split 16 or 32 Bit Binary Files to 8 Bit Binary File for Programming 8 or 16 Bit Eproms; Strip - Convert ASCII Source Code Files Made with WS in Document Mode to Non-Document; Uncase - Convert All Lower Case to Upper Case in an ASCII File.
GTEK Development Hardware/Software.

TITLE INDEX

Programmer's Tools. *Compatible Hardware:* HP 110 Portable.
3.5" disk $325.00 (Order no.: 45419C).
Includes MASM, DEBUG, LINK, CREF, EDLIN, EXE2BIN, etc.
Hewlett-Packard Co.

Programming Aids I. *Compatible Hardware:* TI 99/4A.
disk or cassette - contact publisher for price.
Provides Knowledgable Programmmers with More Powerful Tools for Enhancing TI BASIC.
Texas Instruments, Personal Productivit.

Programming Aids II. *Compatible Hardware:* TI 99/4A.
contact publisher for price (Order no.: PHD 5005).
Provides the Experienced User with the Ability to Sort Information into Alphabetical or Numerical Order for Reporting or Processing Purposes.
Texas Instruments, Personal Productivit.

Programming Aids III. *Compatible Hardware:* TI 99/4A.
contact publisher for price (Order no.: PHD 5012).
Permits Experienced Programmers to Cross Reference a List of All Variables, Arrays, Keywords, Functions & Line Number References.
Texas Instruments, Personal Productivit.

Programming the IBM Personal Computer: BASIC. Neill Graham. Edited by Paul Becker. Nov. 1983. *Compatible Hardware:* IBM PC.
disk $39.95, incl. bk. (ISBN 0-03-069631-3).
Introduction to Programming in the BASIC Language.
Dryden Pr.

Programming the IBM Personal Computer: COBOL. Neill Graham. Edited by Paul Becker. Jul. 1984. *Compatible Hardware:* IBM PC.
disk $39.95, incl. bk. (ISBN 0-03-071773-6).
Covers the Basic Features of COBOL & Facilitates Interactive Programming after the Program Has Been Compiled.
Dryden Pr.

Programming the IBM Personal Computer: FORTRAN 77. Robert Rouse et al. Edited by Paul Becker. Mar. 1984. *General Requirements:* IBM PC.
disk $39.95, incl. bk.
Development of Computing Skills: Computer Capabilities, Algorithm Definition & Expression, Programming.
Dryden Pr.

Programming the IBM Personal Computer: Pascal. Neill Graham. Edited by Paul Becker. 1984. *Compatible Hardware:* IBM PC.
disk $39.95, incl. bk (ISBN 0-03-071777-9).
Structured Presentation of Pascal & Programming.
Dryden Pr.

Programming Tools for Quickbasic. *Items Included:* Full manual. No other products required. *Customer Support:* Free telephone support - no time limit. 30 day warranty.
MS-DOS 3.2 or higher. IBM & compatibles (512k). disk $29.95.
Collection of over 60 Linkable Routines (.OBJ Files) for Use with QuickBASIC. These Routines Include Very Useful Functions, Such As Saving Screens to Disk Files, Restoring Them, Printing a Screen, Checking on the Remaining Disk Space, etc. Resulting Compiled Code Is Smaller & Faster Than If You Included the Routines Within Your Main BASIC Program. Also Gives You More Space for Your Program to Run in (You Can Dimension Larger Arrays, Avoid Overlays, etc.). Includes an 80-Page Manual Which Describes Each Routine & the Calling Structure.
Dynacomp, Inc.

Programming with dBASE III Plus. Cary N. Prague & James E. Hammitt. Jul. 1986. *Compatible Hardware:* IBM PC. *Operating System(s) Required:* PC-DOS, MS-DOS.
disk $41.95, incl. bk. (ISBN 0-8306-5234-5, Order no.: 5234C).
Advanced Programming Techniques & Shortcuts. Includes Use-it-Now Advice & Guidance for Beginning PC Users. Also Includes Programming Techniques That Allow More Advanced Users to Increase Productivity, Reducing Application Development Time. Highlights of the New Generation Enhancements.
TAB Bks.

Progress. *Compatible Hardware:* IBM PC & compatibles.
$1000.00 to $125,000.00.
Command & Menu-Driven Database-Management System Featuring Help Screen, On-Disk Tutorial, Automatic Indexing & Split/Merge Files. Offers a Maximum of 2000 Fields per Records, 2000 Characters per Field, Unlimited Records per File, 2000 Records per File, Unlimited Indexes per File & 10 Records Sorted. Allows User to Revise Field Descriptions at Will.
Progress Software Corp.

Progress Billing. *Version:* 3.3. Apr. 1985. *Compatible Hardware:* IBM PC AT, PC XT, PS/2 or 100% compatibles. *Operating System(s) Required:* MS-DOS, PC-DOS. *Language(s):* C. *Memory Required:* 640k. *Customer Support:* 90 days free telephone support, additional support & maintenance available.
First station. Contact publisher for price.
Enables the User to Prepare & Print Project Billing Documents. User Can Produce Facsimiles of AIA-Specified Reports G702 & G703. User Can Also Print Information Directly on to AIA Form G703. Allows the User to Determine Billing Amounts Based on Total Work Figures or on the Work in Place for a Particular Billing Item. The User Can Also Modify & Submit Statements for Multiple Items Prior to Final Billing.
Timberline Software Corp.

Progress D. *Operating System(s) Required:* MS-DOS, Xenix.
contact publisher for price.
Provides User with the Capability to Configure a Network in Which the Database Resides on Xenix-Based Server Machine, & the Client Processes Can Reside on Xenix, Unix or DOS Platforms.
Progress Software Corp.

Progress: Database & 4GL Application Development System. *Version:* 4.0. Aug. 1986. *Compatible Hardware:* Altos, Apple Macintosh II, Apollo, Arix, AT&T, Bull, CCI, CT, DDE, Fortune, Hewlett Packard, Harris, Honeywell Bull, IBM PC & compatibles, ICL, Intel, Motorola, NCR, NEC, Nixdorf, Plexus, Prime, Pyramid, Sequent, Sun, UNISYS. *Operating System(s) Required:* A/UX, PC-DOS/MS-DOS, ULTRIX, UNIX, VMS, XENIX. *Language(s):* C. *Memory Required:* 512k. *General Requirements:* Hard disk.
Integrates Three Primary Components: DBMS Providing Full Relational Capabilities & the Ability to Handle More Complex Application Requirements; a High Level Application Language That Uses Natural Syntax; & a User Interface That Automatically Provides Structured Screens & Reports.
Progress Software Corp.
  Database-Application Development System.
  IBM PC & compatibles. disk $695.00.
  Altos 1086, 2086, 3086, Fortune, NCR Mini Tower, Plexus P-15, Unisys 5000/20, Microport. disk $2450.00.
  AT&T-3B2/300, 3B2/310, CT Miniframe, Motorola 6300, 2000, NCR Tower 1632, Sun 2, DEC VAX Station 2000, Honeywell X10, General Robotics Python Jr.. disk $3450.00.
  AT&T-3B2/400; CT Mini 20, CT S/120, S/220; Motorola 8000/20; Plexus P-35, Plexus P-20; NCR Tower XP, 32/400; Unisys 5000/30, 5000/40. cassette $3950.00.
  AT&T-3B5, CT Megaframe, Motorola 6600, Plexus P-60, P-55, DEC MICRO VAX 2000, General Robotics/32, IBM RT/PC, Sanyo/Icon MPS020-2, Unisys 5000/70. cassette $4450.00.
  Pyramid, VAX 750, AT&T 3B15, Unisys 5000/90. cassette $14,500.00.
  Introductory System. $50.00.
  manual $95.00.
  AT&T 7300, IBM PC, XENIX, Altos 686, 886, CT S/50, Intel 286/310. disk $1450.00.
  Developer's Toolkit.
  IBM. disk $350.00.
  Fortune. disk $1250.00.
  AT&T, CT Miniframe, Motorola 6300, NCR Tower 1632. disk $1750.00.
  Plexus P-35, NCR Tower XP. disk $1950.00.
  AT&T-3B5, CT Megaframe, Burroughs, Motorola 6600, Plexus P-60. cassette $2250.00.
  Pyramid, VAX 750. cassette $7250.00.
  manual $95.00.
  Query-Run-Time System.
  IBM. disk $200.00.
  Fortune. disk $700.00.
  AT&T, CT MiniframeMotorola 6300, NCR Tower 163. disk $1050.00.
  Plexus P-35, NCR Tower XP. disk $1200.00.
  CT Megaframe, Burroughs, Motorola 6600, Plexus P-60. disk $1350.00.
  Pyramid. disk $4300.00.
  manual $95.00.
  Run-Time System.
  IBM. disk $100.00.
  Fortune. disk $350.00.
  AT&T, CT Miniframe, Motorola 6300, NCR Tower 1632. disk $525.00.
  Plexus P-35, NCR Tower XP. disk $600.00.
  CT Megaframe, Burroughs, Motorola 6600, Plexus P-60. disk $675.00.
  Pyramid. disk $2150.00.

Progress Fast Track.
An 80386-based system under SCO Xenix 386 System V or 386/ix. $1300.00.
Menu-Driven Database Application Builder.
Progress Software Corp.

Progressed Astro-Report. Nancy Hastings & John Kahila. 1984. *Compatible Hardware:* MS-DOS based machines; IBM PC. *Operating System(s) Required:* PC-DOS, MS-DOS. *Language(s):* Pascal. *Memory Required:* 256k. *General Requirements:* 2 disk drives, printer. *Items Included:* Manual. *Customer Support:* Free phone support.
disk $195.00 ea.
IBM PC. (ISBN 0-913637-92-0).
MS-DOS. (ISBN 0-913637-93-9).
Produces Printed Forecasts Using the Progressed & Natal Horoscopes. Includes License to Sell Printed Output.
Astrolabe, Inc.

PROJCON: Project Management & Control System. *Version:* 1.96. WJJ Computer System. Sep. 1988. *Compatible Hardware:* IBM PC, PC XT, PC AT & compatibles. *Operating System(s) Required:* PC-DOS/MS-DOS 3.1. *Language(s):* COBOL. *Memory Required:* 640k. *General Requirements:* 10 Mb on hard disk. *Customer Support:* 30 day money-back guarantee.
3.5" or 5.25" disk $995.00, incl. 75-page manual (Order no.: 853).
Computer Tool for Planning, Controlling, &

Reporting Related to Projects Executed by Engineering & Drafting Offices. Utilizes Manhour Control Via Time Sheets Dealing with Estimated, Currently Spent, Total-Spent, Estimated-to-Complete, & Estimated-Total Manhours. Calculates Project Progress and Manhours to Complete, & Forecasts Projects Overruns If Any Program Screens (On-Line) & Reports (Displayed or Printed) Show the Status of Every Project & Each of the Activities/Documents. Weekly Bar-Charts (with Monday's Date & S-Curves) Are Generated Automatically.
Gulf Publishing Co.

Project Billing. *Version:* 1.58. Chris LeCroy. *Compatible Hardware:* Apple Macintosh, IBM PC & compatibles. *Memory Required:* Macintosh 512k. *Items Included:* Manual, disk. *Customer Support:* Free phone support.
IBM. disk $595.00.
Macintosh. 3.5" disk $595.00.
Time Billing Package Designed for Ad Agencies, Graphic Designers, & Print Shops. Tracks All Aspects of Project Billing, Including Budgets for Time & Expense, Actual Costs & Billed Out Amounts for Both Employee & Expenses, & Project Profitability. Automatically Marks up Expenses & Prints Productivity Reports & Client Bills.
Satori Software.

Project Bridge Modeler (for Windows). *Version:* 3.02. Dec. 1995. *Items Included:* Documentation manuals, registration form, Client Support Program (CSP) guide. *Customer Support:* Client Support Program which includes: hotline support, newsletters, free upgrades, user groups, warranty extension. 90 day warranty - training & consulting available both public & onsite. Prices vary.
DOS 3.0 or higher. Any XT/AT/286 & machine. $1950.00. *Addl. software required:* Microsoft Windows. *Networks supported:* IBM PC Network Control Program (DOS server), IBM LAN Server (OS/2 server), Microsoft MS-NET (DOS server), Microsoft LAN Manager (OS/2 server), Novell NetWare, Banyan Vines, DEC Pathworks, AT&T STARLAN, any 100% NetBIOS/LAN Manager compatible LAN.
Amplifies & Extends the Powers of Methods-Based Estimating & Project Modeling by Taking Advantage of the Graphics Capabilities of the Microsoft Windows Platform. Its Functions Include: Estimating, Profiling, User-Defined Windows of Project Data; Fully Customizable View Definition Similar to Project Workbench 1.0W for Windows Interface; Resource Assignment to Tasks or Project Teams with a Single Click; Expanded Resource Capability.
ABT Corp.

Project Control One. *Compatible Hardware:* IBM PC. *Memory Required:* 128k.
disk $49.95.
Basic Project Control & Scheduling Program Designed for Engineers, Managers, Builders & Other Supervisory Personnel.
Dynacomp, Inc.

Project Cost Accounting System. *Compatible Hardware:* DECMate, PDP 11-23. *Operating System(s) Required:* COS-310, MICRO-RSX. *Language(s):* DIBOL-83.
$15,000.00, incl. user's guide (Order no.: 85-2).
Combines Project Cost Reporting for Management with an Accounting System to Serve the Special Needs of Engineering, Contracting, Consulting, & Aerospace Companies. Reporting System Prints Detailed Labor & Purchase Distribution Reports & Shows Project & Task Activity on the Project Status Reports. P.S. R.'s Include Labor, Expense, & Line Item Budgets & Variances for Each Task, & Contain

Information for the Current Week, Month, Year-to-Date, & Project Life. Accounting System Records Labor, Billing, & Purchase Transactions, & Prints Payroll & Vendor Checks. Month-End Accounting Figures Collect to the General Ledger & Report on Financial Statements & Supporting Schedules. Special Features Include Project Budgeting, Labor Forecasting & Time Planning, Cash Use, Automatic Adjustments for Unbilled Work in Process, & User-Controlled Overhead Rate Application.
Corporate Consulting Co.

Project D. *Version:* 2.0. *Compatible Hardware:* Commodore Amiga. *Items Included:* Editor, catalog system, & disk copiers (including copy-protected). *Customer Support:* 602-497-6070.
3.5" disk $49.95.
Integrated Disk Utility.
Fuller Computer Systems, Inc.

Project Gutenberg. *Customer Support:* All of our products are unconditionally guaranteed.
All Systems. CD-ROM disk $39.95 (Order no.: GUTENBERG). *Nonstandard peripherals required:* CD-ROM drive.
150 Plus Works of Literature & U.S. Historical Documents.
Walnut Creek CDRom.

Project KickStart. *Version:* 1.00E. May 1992. *Items Included:* Manual. *Customer Support:* Telephone hot line.
DOS 2.0 or higher. IBM PC or compatibles (256k). disk $79.95 (ISBN 0-928615-03-0, Order no.: 700).
First 30-Minute Project Organizer. Develops Task Lists, Resource Lists & Assignments in 30 Minutes. Automatically Downloads This Information to Project Management & Scheduling Programs, or Can Be Used As a Stand-Alone Package.
Experience in Software, Inc.

Project KickStart for Windows. *Version:* 1.03. Aug. 1995. *Items Included:* User's guide. *Customer Support:* 60 day money back guarantee. Telephone hot line.
Windows 3.1. 386 PC (4Mb). disk $99.95 (Order no.: 710). *Nonstandard peripherals required:* VGA.
30-Minute Project Organizer. This User Friendly Program Asks Key Questions Which Help You Conceptualize a Project from Scratch. You'll Be Able to Develop Task Lists, Resource Lists, & Assignments. It Also Has Built in Links with Popular Project Management Programs, Such As Microsoft Project.
Experience in Software, Inc.

Project Management. *Compatible Hardware:* HP Series 200: Models 216/220, 226/236, 217/237 Personal Technical Computers with BASIC 3.0. *Memory Required:* 130k.
3-1/2" or 5-1/4" disk $500.00 ea. (Order no.: 98817A).
Analyzes Project Networks Using CP/M, PERT & MP/M Techniques. Outputs in Gantt Chart Form.
Hewlett-Packard Co.

Project Management Advantage. *Version:* 1.1. Jan. 1989. *Items Included:* Users guide; audio tape. *Customer Support:* Free, brief phone consultation, on-site consultation available.
MS-DOS (256k). IBM PC (or compatible). $199.00. *Addl. software required:* Lotus 1-2-3 2.0 for Lotus template. *Optimal configuration:* MS-DOS (512k).
PC-Based Artificial Intelligence/Expert System That Addresses Each of the 55 Issues That Commonly Arise in the Life Cycle of the Typical Major Project. By Posing a Series of Questions to the User, Customized Advice Is Delivered to Assure Timely & Appropriate Action. It Is Also a Superior, Personalized Training Medium.
All-Tech Project Management Services.

Project Management Systems I. *Compatible Hardware:* IBM PC. *Operating System(s) Required:* CP/M.
contact publisher for price.
Produces Time, Manpower, & Cost Reports. Maintains Projects & Subprojects That Can Be Updated.
Softpoint Co.

Project Master. *Customer Support:* 800-929-8117 (customer service).
MS-DOS. IBM/PS2. disk $199.99 (ISBN 0-87007-352-4).
Project Management System, Employing PERT, GANTT, & the Critical Path Method, Along with Arbitrary Prioritization of Tasks.
SourceView Software International.

Project Outlook. *Version:* 3.0. *Compatible Hardware:* IBM PS/2, PC AT & compatibles. *General Requirements:* Microsoft Windows, mouse. *Customer Support:* 90 day unlimited warranty, yearly maintenance plans available. $295.00.
Microsoft Windows-Based Project Planning & Scheduling Tool.
Cambridge Management Systems, Inc.

Project Planner (PERT & CPM). *Version:* 10.0. *Compatible Hardware:* Apple Macintosh, IBM PC & compatibles. *Memory Required:* 512k. *Items Included:* Disks, book, program instructions. *Customer Support:* Telephone.
disk $145.00 (ISBN 0-920387-14-4).
Analyze the Network & Provide Various Results Useful for Scheduling Purposes. PERT Produces the Critical Path & the Probability of Finishing on Time; It Is Possible to Go Back & Adjust Individual Times to See the Effect on the Overall Probability of Finishing on Time. CRITIPATH Produces the Critical Path, Then Provides a Report on All Non-Critical Activities, Giving the Latest Starting Times, the Earliest Finishing Times, & So Forth. Allows Full & Selective Crashing to See Whether or Not Extra Expenditure of Money Will Speed up Completion of the project. PLANNER Is a Full-Featured Project Management Program, Allowing the Inclusion of Holidays in the Schedule, Continual Updates of Activities, the Preparation of Cash Flow Reports, the Printing of Gannt Charts, & So Forth.
Lionheart Pr., Inc.

Project Planning & Scheduling. L. Chip Getter. *Compatible Hardware:* IBM PC, PC XT, PC AT, Portable PC, 3270 PC. *Operating System(s) Required:* DOS 1.10, 2.00, 2.10, 3.00, 3.10. *Memory Required:* DOS 1.10 128k, DOS 2.00 & higher 160k. *General Requirements:* IBM Display, IBM Matrix printer; DOS 2.00 & higher requires 2 double-sided floppy disk drives or hard disk.
disk $149.95 (Order no.: 6276500).
Project Planning Program with Applications Ranging from Building a House to Manufacturing a Product. Features "What-If" Time Cost Analyses, & Prints-Out Tables, Charts, & Schedules for Personal Use or for Presentations.
Personally Developed Software, Inc.

Project Reporter. *Version:* MS-DOS 4.0, CP/M 3.0. *Operating System(s) Required:* CP/M-80, CP/M-86, Turbo DOS, MS-DOS. *Language(s):* BASIC. *Memory Required:* 64k. *General Requirements:* Micro Mode, Inc. Integrated Accounting & Financial Management General Accounting system.
contact publisher for price.
Series of Project Management Reports. Programs Track & Report on Actual Hours & Dollars & Budgeted Hours & Dollars for Individual Projects Being Used om the System. Reports Are Based on Phase & Phase-Task Information. Some of the Items Tracked or Calculated Are Budgeted Hours

TITLE INDEX

Original & Revised Hours to Date Reported Completed to Date Hours, Reported Completed to Date Percentage; Reported Hours to Complete; Variance in Hours Based upon Reported & Budgeted Variance Percentage; Accumulated Levels for a Total Project; or Original Hours, Revised Hours, Experienced Hours, Reported Hours, Percent Hours Completed, Variance Hours, Variance Percentage, Original & Revised Budgeted Dollars, Experience-to-Date Dollars, & Percent Complete Hours. The System Is Designed to Flag Projects That Are in Trouble Based upon Their Original Dollars & Hours Budgeted. Designed to Aid Controllers for Multiple Project Tracking at the Consulting Engineering & General Engineering Type Companies.
Management Systems, Inc.

Project Scheduler Five. *Items Included:* Spiral-bound reference manual, spiral-bound tutorial manual, import/export utility program. *Customer Support:* Free technical support by phone; 2-day training classes, either on customer's site or Scitor's corporate headquarters in Sunnyvale, CA (call for current pricing); 90-day warranty on diskettes.
MS-DOS 3.0 or higher V. IBM XT, AT, or PS/2 (512k). Version 1.5 (04/1992) $695.00. *Nonstandard peripherals required:* Graphics board (either CGA, MCGA, EGA, VGA, Super VGA, Hercules Graphics Card, 3270 APA monochrome, or AT&T 640x400 black & white), hard disk, graphical printer/plotter. *Optimal configuration:* 386-based computer with math coprocessor, DOS 3.0 or higher, 640k RAM, 8Mb expanded memory, Microsoft-compatible mouse, Super VGA (VESA-compatible), PostScript printer. *Networks supported:* Project Scheduler 5 Version 1.5 for the IBM PC is the network version, providing file locking & password protection. PS5 v.1.5 supports Novell, Banyan Vines, 3COm, & LANmanager LANs. Concurrent use license.
Mac DOS 6.0 or higher, System 7 compatible. Mac Plus or higher. Version 1.0 (10/1990) $695.00.
Interactive CPM Project Management System That Provides Scheduling, Resource, & Cost Planning Capabilities, Through a High-Resolution Graphical User Interface with Mouse Support. Features Include Gantt, Network, & Tree Charts; Graphs; WBS & OBS; Multiple Projects; Subprojects; External Links; Resource Leveling; Filtering; & Sorting.
Scitor Corp.

Project Task Control & Scheduling. *Items Included:* Full manual. No other products required. *Customer Support:* Free telephone support - no time limit. 30 day warranty.
MS-DOS 3.2 or higher. IBM & compatibles (512k). disk $1899.95.
demo disk $5.00.
Allows User to Efficiently Track & Control the Work Progress of Thousands of Engineering Activities Such As Developing Drawings & Documents, Procurement, Purchasing, & Expediting. Generates DCI Reports & Statistics, Progress Curves, & Barcharts, with up to 12 Milestones for Progress Control. Can Also Be Used As a Scheduling Tool, Using Barcharts Ranging from 30 Days to Six Years per Page.
Dynacomp, Inc.

Project Time Reporting System. *Items Included:* Bound manual. *Customer Support:* Free hotline - no time limit; 30 day limited warranty; updates are $5/disk plus S&H.
MS-DOS. IBM & compatibles (256k). disk $69.95.
Data-Base System Designed Specifically for Accumulating, Distributing, & Reporting Hours Spent by Employees on Individual Projects. Set up Data Files Containing Time-Distribution Data for up to Ten Projects. An Unlimited Number of Individual Files, Each with up to Ten Projects, Can Be Created & Maintained.
Dynacomp, Inc.

Project Workbench PMW. *Version:* 3.02. Sep. 1992. *Customer Support:* Client Support Program which includes: hotline support, newsletters, free upgrades, user groups, warranty extension. 90 day warranty - training & consulting available both public & onsite. Prices vary.
DOS 3.0 or higher. Any XT/AT/286 & machine. $1275.00 incl. manuals. *Nonstandard peripherals required:* PC standalone and/or LAN. *Addl. software required:* Microsoft Windows (for PW1.0W). *Networks supported:* IBM PC Network Control Program (DOS server), IBM LAN Server (OS/2 server), Microsoft MS-NET (DOS server), Microsoft LAN Manager (OS/2 server), Novell NetWare, Banyan Vines, DEC Pathworks, AT&T STARLAN, any 100% NetBIOS/LAN Manager compatible LAN.
A Powerful Project Planning, Control & Decision-Support System for the Project Manager Integrating Gantt Charts, Resource Spreadsheets & CPM Networks. System Features Include the Unique Query & Report Systems, Variable Resource Assignment to Projects & Loading to Tasks, Variable Task Duration, Resource Leveling, Multiple Tracking Levels, an Electronic Timesheet, "What-If" Capabilities, Multiproject, & Subproject Management & Reporting, Import/Export with Other Systems & Expanded Memory Support. A Comprehensive, On-Line, Context Sensitive Help Facility Is Available Throughout the Program.
ABT Corp.

ProKey. *Version:* 3.0. RoseSoft, Inc. Mar. 1984. *Operating System(s) Required:* MS-DOS. *Memory Required:* 64k.
$129.95.
Texas Instruments, Personal Productivit.

ProKey for DOS. *Version:* 5.1. Jun. 1991. *Compatible Hardware:* IBM PC, PC XT, PC AT, PS/2 & compatibles. *Operating System(s) Required:* MS-DOS, PC-DOS. *Language(s):* Assembly. *Memory Required:* 128k. *Items Included:* disk & manual. *Customer Support:* Complete support for registered users; no charge.
disk $99.00.
Allows User to Customize Software. Memorize Command Sequences or Text & Play Them Back at the Touch of a Key. Use to Load & Operate Other Programs, or Perform Routine Typing. Create Menus & User Messages, Cut & Paste to Move Text, Unload from Memory, View History of Last 300 Keystrokes, Event Scheduler to Automate Task Execution, Compatible with DOS 5.0.
CE Software, Inc.

ProKey for Windows. *Version:* 1.0. Aug. 1991. *Items Included:* Disk, manual. *Customer Support:* Free for registered users.
Windows 3.0 & 3.1. IBM PC AT, PS/2 & compatibles. disk $99.00.
Intuitive Script Processor (Macros) for WINDOWS. Automates Keystrokes & Commands in Windows Applications, As Well As Between Applications. Easy to Edit Scripts; Convenient Script Palette for Mouse Playback or Keystroke Execution; Script Playback Independent of Window Position or Size; Fill-in-the-Blank Input; User Defined Screen Messages.
CE Software, Inc.

ProLink. *Compatible Hardware:* Apple Macintosh 512k, Macintosh 512e, Macintosh Plus.
3.5" disk $39.95.
Allows the Use of APPLEWORKS & Other Apple II Files on the Macintosh or Vice Versa. Users Can Insert a 3.5" ProDOS Disk Directly into a Macintosh 800k Disk Drive & Select the Files to Be Copied to & from Any Directory on the ProDOS Disk. Accepts Data from APPLEWORKS, PFS, MACWRITE, WORD, EXCEL, MICROSOFT WORKS, & Other Programs on Either the Apple II or Macintosh. Supports Any Macintosh Floppy or Hard Disk in Either MFS or HFS Formats. Supports 3.5" ProDOS 8 & ProDOS 16 Disks from the Apple IIe, IIc, & IIgs. Eliminates the Need for Transfer Files Using Communications Programs, Protocols, Cables, etc.
ALSoft, Inc.

PROLISP. *Version:* 3.01. *Compatible Hardware:* IBM PC & compatibles. *Operating System(s) Required:* PC-DOS/MS-DOS. *Memory Required:* 256k. *General Requirements:* Hard disk recommended. *Items Included:* 32 pg. Thinking Software catalog.
3.5" or 5.25" disk $39.95.
LISP Implementation for IBM PC. Includes Example Programs & Documentation.
Thinking Software, Inc.

Prolook QuickBASIC Subroutine Library. *Items Included:* Bound manual. *Customer Support:* Free hotline - no time limit; 30 day limited warranty; updates are $5/disk plus S&H.
MS-DOS. IBM & compatibles (256k). disk $29.95. *Addl. software required:* QuickBASIC Version 4.00 (or higher).
QuickBASIC Library of over 50 Frequently-Used Statements/Functions Which the Programmer May Add to His Own Applications. Typical Routines Include: Mouse Input; Attractive Screen Displays (e.g., Windows); Input Routines (1-2 Dimensional Menus, Formatted Input Fields); Advanced Disk Access Features (Free Space on Disk, Load Directory to a String Array, Change Default Drive, etc.); Screen Dump to Printer; Data Manipulation (Such As Sorting).
Dynacomp, Inc.

PROMAC. 1985. *Compatible Hardware:* Burroughs B20, IBM RS 6000. *Operating System(s) Required:* AIX, BTOS, CTOS, UNIX, XENIX. *Language(s):* COBOL (source code included). *Memory Required:* 1000k.
contact publisher for price.
General Accounting Software Includes Accounts Receivable, Inventory Control, Order Entry, Fixed Assets, Purchasing, & Sales Analysis. Special Features Include Special Pricing, Bill of Materials, & Extended Description. Designed for Distributors, Manufacturing, & Most Small Businesses.
CMV Software Specialists, Inc.

Promal: Mechanics of Composites. 1990. *Items Included:* Spiral manual contains theory, sample runs. *Customer Support:* Free phone, on-site seminars.
MS-DOS. IBM (640k). disk $120.00.
Macro & Micromechanical Analysis of a Composite Laminate or Lamina. Four Programs Included for Matrix Algebra Manipulations Commonly Required in Analysis of Composites, Develop, Update & Correct a Database of Composites, Macromechanical Analysis of a Lamina, Macromechanical Analysis of a Laminate.
Kern International, Inc.

ProMaster. *Customer Support:* 800-929-8117 (customer service).
MS-DOS. IBM/PS2. disk $79.99 (ISBN 0-87007-225-0).
Designed to Provide the Programmer with the Structure That Is Available in Many Other Languages. Tools Provide a Structured, Organized Method for Management & Usage of

This Valuable Collection of "Burned in" Routines Provide a Highly Structured Language with Macro Programming, Macro & Subroutine Libraries. Provides the Programmer with Tools That Can Make Them More Productive.
SourceView Software International.

PromKit. Foster & Choisser. *Items Included:* Three-ring binder, 5.25" diskette. *Customer Support:* By telephone or fax, normally no charge, 30-day money back guarantee.
IBM PC (640k). disk $179.00 (ISBN 0-929392-05-1). *Nonstandard peripherals required:* Hard disk; EPROM programmer.
Allows User to Put Any DOS Program (or DOS Itself) into EPROM or Static RAM. One-Line Command Turns Application or DOS into PROM-Loadable Binary Image for Placement into PC Motherboard or Adapter Cards. User Can Choose Which Specific Drives Are to Be Emulated. Paged EPROM's Emulate Full 360k Drive by Using Three 27011 Chips for Data & Single 27128 for Driver Module.
Annabooks.

PROMOT. *Version:* 6.1. 1980. *Compatible Hardware:* IBM PC & compatibles, PC XT, PC AT, PS/2. *Operating System(s) Required:* MS-DOS. *Language(s):* CBASIC. *Memory Required:* 256k. *Customer Support:* Yearly support contract $500.00.
disk $1595.00.
Designed for CPA's, Architects & Other Time Keeping & Billing Professionals. Prepares Invoices, Ages Receivables & Provides Complete Management Reports.
KIS Computer Corp.

Prompt! 1.2. Aug. 1988. *Items Included:* 60 pg. manual included. *Customer Support:* Free unlimited phone tech. support; 30 day unlimited warranty.
MS-DOS (640k). IBM 286 & above. $129.00. *Addl. software required:* MS windows.
Hard-Disk File Manager That Runs under MS Windows, Shows Entire Hard Disk as Directory Tree in Window. Allows User to Copy/Move/Rename/Delete An Entire File List or Directory in a Single Step. Finds Files by Name, Extension or Date Created. Stores Lists of Files by File name Without Using Extra Disk Space. Supports a Direct Link with Dragnet 2.0, Which Finds Hard Disk Files by Keyword, Phrase, or Boolean Expression & Sends Those Files to Prompt 1.2.
Access Softek.

Proneat. Chris Feuchter. Apr. 1985. *Operating System(s) Required:* MS-DOS. *Language(s):* FORTRAN. *Memory Required:* 128k.
disk $39.95.
Renumbers FORTRAN Source Code & Otherwise Improves Source Code Readability by Standardizing Source Statement Appearance. Indents IF, THEN, ELSE Statements. Deletes Unused Statement Numbers & CONTINUE Statements. Collects FORMAT Statements at End of Program Unit. Designed to Reduce Programmer Errors Caused by Difficult to Read Source Code.
Suresoft.

Pronto DOS. Tom Weishaar. Aug. 1984. *Compatible Hardware:* Apple II, II+, IIe, IIc, IIgs. *Operating System(s) Required:* Apple DOS 3.3. *Language(s):* Machine, BASIC. *Memory Required:* 48k.
disk $29.50.
Triples the Speed of Apple's DOS. Allows User to Place DOS into Auxiliary Memory, Giving an Extra 10k of Programmable Memory As Well As 15 Extra Sectors of Disk Space.
Beagle Brothers.

Proofreader for AtariWriter. *Compatible Hardware:* Atari XL/XE. *Memory Required:* 32k. disk $16.95 (Order no.: AX2033).
Atari Corp.

ProofWriter Color Graphics. *Version:* 2.33. Apr. 1985. *Compatible Hardware:* Columbia; Compaq; Corona; Eagle; Hyperion; IBM PC & compatibles, PC XT; Leading Edge; TI PC; Zenith 150. *Operating System(s) Required:* PC-DOS, MS-DOS. *Language(s):* Pascal, Assembly. *Memory Required:* 256k. *General Requirements:* 2 disk drives or hard disk.
$425.00.
demo disk & tutorial $5.00.
Possesses All the Features of PROOFWRITER INTERNATIONAL Plus an Additional Feature Which Allows User to Design the Character Set Displayed on the Screen.
Image Processing Software, Inc.

ProofWriter Enhanced Color Version. *Version:* 2.33. Jun. 1985. *Compatible Hardware:* IBM PC & compatibles, PC XT, PC AT. *Operating System(s) Required:* PC-DOS, MS-DOS. *Language(s):* Pascal, Assembly. *Memory Required:* 256k. *General Requirements:* 2 disk drives or hard disk, IBM enhanced color board.
$475.00.
Provides All the Features of ProofWriter International/Scientific As Well As an Additional Feature Which Allows Users to Design Their Own Characters & See Them on the Screen.
Image Processing Software, Inc.

ProofWriter Hercules Graphics. *Version:* 2.33. *Compatible Hardware:* IBM PC & compatibles, PC XT, PC AT. *Operating System(s) Required:* PC-DOS, MS-DOS. *Language(s):* Pascal, Assembly. *Memory Required:* 256k. *General Requirements:* 2 disk drives or hard disk, Hercules monochrome graphics board.
disk $425.00.
Provides All the Features of ProofWriter International/Scientific As Well As an Additional Feature Which Allows Users to Design Their Own Characters & See Them on the Screen.
Image Processing Software, Inc.

ProofWriter International-Scientific. *Version:* 2.33. Feb. 1984. *Compatible Hardware:* Columbia; Compaq; Corona; Eagle; Hyperion; IBM PC & compatibles, PC XT; Leading Edge; TI PC; Zenith 150. *Operating System(s) Required:* PC-DOS, MS-DOS. *Language(s):* Pascal, Assembly. *Memory Required:* 256k. *General Requirements:* 2 disk drives or hard disk.
$300.00.
demo disk & tutorial $5.00.
Character PROM (Optional). $125.00.
Word Processing & Program Editing Package Similar to PROOFWRITER STANDARD with Additional Features for Applications Involving Scientific Word Processing or for Word Processing in Languages Other Than English.
Image Processing Software, Inc.

ProofWriter Standard. *Version:* 2.33. Jan. 1983. *Compatible Hardware:* Columbia; Compaq; Corona; Eagle; Hyperion; IBM PC & compatibles, PC XT; Leading Edge; TI PC; Zenith 150. *Operating System(s) Required:* MS-DOS, PC-DOS. *Language(s):* Pascal, Assembly. *Memory Required:* 256k. *General Requirements:* 2 disk drives or hard disk.
$250.00.
demo disk & tutorial $5.00.
Character PROM (Optional). $125.00.
Word Processing & Program Editing Package Composed of 3 Integrated Subprograms: an Editor, a Formatter, & a Proofreader. Included Are Programs to Customize Supplied Dictionary with Additional Words, & to Configure Formatter for Any Printer.
Image Processing Software, Inc.

PROP: Project Planning & Reporting. A. K. Nagrani. Mar. 1984. *Compatible Hardware:* IBM PC & compatibles. *Operating System(s) Required:* MS-DOS. *Language(s):* BASIC. *Memory Required:* 128k.
disk $295.00.
User Can Input Desired Calendar End Date & Program Converts All Schedules to Match That Condition.
Antech, Inc.

PROPAK. *Compatible Hardware:* IBM PC. disk $499.85 (ISBN 0-936200-51-0).
Complete System Which Includes ELECTRIC PENCIL, PENCIL ACE & the ELECTRIC PENCIL TUTOR.
Blue Cat.

Property Listings Comparables. *Compatible Hardware:* Apple, IBM PC & compatibles. *Operating System(s) Required:* MS-DOS, Apple DOS. *Language(s):* BASIC. *Memory Required:* 48k.
disk $425.00.
System for Maintaining Real Estate Listings & Comparable Sold Properties, Including a Screening Capability for Selecting Properties.
Realty Software.

Property Management. *Version:* 4.0. (DOMIPRO Ser.). 1985. *Compatible Hardware:* PC compatibles. *Operating System(s) Required:* PC-DOS. *Language(s):* Microsoft BASIC 7.0/C. *Memory Required:* 640k. *Customer Support:* Training.
$695.00-$4995.00.
Property Management/Financial Account System for Property Management. Multi-Site, Multi-User. Full GAAP Accounting.
DOMICO.

Property Management. *Version:* 7.0. Wallace L. Rankin. Jan. 1987. *Compatible Hardware:* IBM Displaywriter, IBM PC, PC XT, PC AT & compatibles; NEC APC. *Operating System(s) Required:* MS-DOS, UCSD p-System. *Language(s):* Pascal. *Memory Required:* 256k.
disk $499.00.
Accounting Program for Small Business Designed to Produce Rapid Data Manipulation & Sorting. Complete Tenant File Maintenance & Preparation of Aged Rentals Due, Summary & Monthly Statements Are Provided. Capable of Updating Income & Expense Records for Each Unit & Printing Disbursement Checks to Owners & Vendors on Pre-Printed Forms. Custom Modifications Are Available.
Helu Software Corp.

Property Management. *Version:* 4.5. 1981. *Compatible Hardware:* IBM PC & compatibles, PC XT, PC AT, 386, 486, Pentium, PS/2. *Operating System(s) Required:* PC-DOS/MS-DOS 3.X, 4X, 5X, 6X, Windows 3.1, Windows 95. *Language(s):* BASIC, C, Assembler. *Memory Required:* 640k. *General Requirements:* Stand-alone or 2Mb Network file server. *Customer Support:* 90 day warranty, onsite training, telephone support.
disk $1295.00.
Designed to Meet the Tracking Needs of Managers of Apartments, Condominiums, Office Buildings, Shopping Centers, Mobile Home Parks & Mini-Warehouses. System Deals with Multiple Tenants in Same Unit; Sets up an Unlimited Number of Accounts for Each Tenant; Activates Tenant Charges for Any Number of Months; & Prints Reports for Individual or for all Properties. Automatically Updates General Ledger.
LIBRA Corp.

Property Management. 1978. *Compatible Hardware:* Apple II, IIc, III. *Operating System(s) Required:* Apple DOS. *Language(s):* BASIC. *Memory Required:* 48-128k.
$350.00.
Contains Detailed Tenant History Capabilities. Allows Complete Tracking of Income & Expenses of Real Property. Produces Operating Statements, Late Rent Reports, Vacancy Reports, Expired Leases. Prints Checks, & Rent Receipts.
Realty Software.

Property Management for Commercial Real Estate. Real Estate Computer Systems.
Operating System(s) Required: MS-DOS 2.1. *Language(s):* MSBASIC. *Memory Required:* 256k. *General Requirements:* 2 disk drives, printer.
$4000.00.
Texas Instruments, Personal Productivit.

Property Management Gold. *Version:* 1.9. Oct. 1988. *Compatible Hardware:* IBM PC, 386 or 100% compatible. *Operating System(s) Required:* OS/2. *General Requirements:* Hard disk, VGA monitor. *Customer Support:* 90 days free, additional support & maintenance available.
disk Contact vendor for price.
Functions Include Future Available Space & Projected Revenues, Also Handles Lease Escalations, Charge-Backs & Pass-Throughs, & Has Built-In Tickler System for Date Reminders, Pinpointing Retail Sales Trends, Multi-Tasking Also Can Be Done.
Timberline Software Corp.

Property Management III. *Version:* IBM 1.25, MAC 1.25. Aug. 1994. *Memory Required:* MS-DOS/1Mb on Macintosh (minimum) 2000k. *Items Included:* manual, user's guide. *Customer Support:* Toll telephone unlimited free support.
50 unit capability. IBM & compatibles; Macintosh Plus or higher. $395.00.
200 unit capability. $695.00.
500 unit capability. $995.00.
Unlimited version. $1495.00.
Maintains Property Profiles, Accounts Payable, Accounts Receivable, General Ledger, Repair & Maintenance Orders, Lease Abstracts, Open Item Accrual Based Accounting with Detail Retained Beyond Year End. Produces Detailed Tenant Statements, Aging & Automated Collection Letters, & 32 Other Reports. Each Property Can Have a Different Fiscal Year, Chart of Accounts. All Financial Statements Are Available to Print at Any Time. Automatic Posting & Payment of Recurring Monthly Expenses, Check Printing. Also Includes On-Line Help & Pop up Lists for GL Accounts, Property ID Lease Numbers Without Losing Screen.
RealData, Inc.

Property Management Plus. *Version:* 1996. Jan. 1996. *Compatible Hardware:* IBM PC & compatibles. *Operating System(s) Required:* MS-DOS. *General Requirements:* Printer. *Customer Support:* 1 year free telephone support.
MS-DOS. disk $575.00.
Accounting & Management System for Any Type of Rental Properties, Including Single Family, Multi-Family, Commercial & Condo Management, Airports, Marinas, etc., Owned by One or Many Owners. Features Include: Tenant Information, Late Rent, Vacancy & Expired Lease Reporting, Rent Receipts, 2-Way Rent Statements/Late Notices, Bank Deposit Slips, & an Automatic Checkwriter for Repeating Expenses. Can Work with the MANAGEMENT OPTION Which Is Designed for Managers of Other Peoples Property.
Realty Software.

Property Management System. *Version:* 7. Jun. 1991. *Items Included:* Complete operator instructions available on-line. *Customer Support:* On site training, software support program available.
DOS, Networking (Novell). IBM PC & compatibles, PS/2 (640k). Contact publisher for prices. *Optimal configuration:* IBM PC, DOS, 1Mb, 40Mb disk. *Networks supported:* Novell, Concurrent DOS.
OS/400. All models of IBM AS/400 (8Mb). Contact publisher for prices. *Optimal configuration:* AS/400 12Mb, 600Mb Disk.
Comprehensive Information Management Accounting Package Designed to Handle the Control & Reporting Needs of the Commercial, Residential, Industrial, & Retail Property Managers. When Combined with PAC Accounting Packages (General Ledger, Accounts Payable, Payroll, Costing, etc.) Provides a Fully Integrated Accounting-Management Reporting System.
Pac Corp.

Property Management System III (PMS III). *Version:* 4. Jan. 1992. *Compatible Hardware:* IBM PC & compatibles. *Operating System(s) Required:* PC-DOS/MS-DOS 3.1 or higher. *Language(s):* Compiled Microsoft Business BASIC. *Memory Required:* 256k. *General Requirements:* Hard disk. *Customer Support:* 7 days a week, 8 a.m. to 6 p.m. PST.
disk $549.00.
Eval. Sys. (disks & manual) $50.00.
Automates Most Accounting Required to Manage & Control Income Property. Consists of a Complete General Ledger, Accounts Payable, & Accounts Receivable Accounting System Optimized for Property Management, & a Database Management System for Tenant, Vendor, & Property Information & Maintenance. Produces Fully Formatted Financial Statements, Receipts, Disbursements Reports, Tenant & Vendor Reports, Mailing Labels, 1099's & Check Writer (Dot Matrix, Laser & MICR). Also Contains a Series of Utility Programs Which Allow the User to Sort Files, Swap Data Disks, etc. Although the System Keeps Track of Each Property Individually, It Will Accommodate Either One Checkbook per Property or One Checkbook for Multi-Property Complexes. Also Provides a Common Set of Financial Statements (Balance Sheet, Operating Statement, Transaction Ledgers (MTD & YTD), Chart of Accounts & Budget Analysis) by Combining the Statements from Any Number of User-Specified Properties.
Matrix Systems.

Property Manager. *Items Included:* Bound manual. *Customer Support:* Free hotline - no time limit; 30 day limited warranty; updates are $5/disk plus S&H.
MS-DOS 2.0 or higher. IBM & compatibles (256k). disk $299.95. *Nonstandard peripherals required:* Two double-sided disk drives - or a fixed-disk drive - & a printer.
Apple II Plus (requires 64k RAM, lower case adapter), IIe, or IIc. disk $299.95. *Nonstandard peripherals required:* 1 or 2 floppy disk drives or fixed drive; printer.
Integrated System That Covers All Facets of Rental Property Management. It Exceeds the Recommended Minimum Standards for Computerized Property Management Systems As Established by the Institute of Real Estate Management. The Tenant Record for Each Unit Includes the Current & Past Occupant along with Related Information, Such As Monthly Rent, Amount Due, Security Deposits Being Held in Escrow, Move-In Date, Lease Expiration Date, Mailing Address, & So Forth. Cash Receipts Are Entered Directly from Your Bank Deposit Slip with All Updating of the Tenant's Accounts & General Ledger Taken Care of Automatically.
Dynacomp, Inc.

The Property Manager. *Compatible Hardware:* Apple Macintosh Plus. *General Requirements:* Hard disk; Omnis 3 Plus.
Tenant Control Module. 3.5" disk $495.00.
Professional System (single user). 3.5" disk $995.00.
Professional System (multiuser). 3.5" disk $1795.00.
Residential Property Management.
MPM Computing.

Property Manager: Instant Relief from Landlord's Headaches. *Version:* 1.2. 1989. *Items Included:* 78 page manual.
MS-DOS 2.X - 4.X. IBM PC/XT/AT, PS/2 or compatible (256K). disk $49.00 (Order no.: 9510).
A System for Single or Multi-Family Properties As Well As for Commercial, Residential Office Buildings, & Condominiums. It Keeps Track of All Tenant & Property Data, Rent Statements, Income/Expense & Operating Statements. Includes Accounts Receivable & Accounts Payable. Includes a Full Mail Merge System to Write Formletters, Labels & Automatic Late Rent Letters to Tenants. Automatic Check Writing.
Elcomp Publishing, Inc.

Property Managers Option. *Version:* 1996. Jan. 1996. *Compatible Hardware:* IBM PC & compatibles. *Operating System(s) Required:* MS-DOS. *Language(s):* BASIC. *Memory Required:* 128k.
MS-DOS 2.1 or higher. disk $475.00.
Calculates & Posts Management Fees; Writes Checks to Owners; Prints 1099 IRS Forms; Reports Owner Balances; Prints Balance Sheets; & Maintains Information on Owners & Buildings - a Real Time Saver. Also Calculates Interest on Tenant Deposits.
Realty Software.

Property Sale. *Compatible Hardware:* IBM PC; Apple. *Operating System(s) Required:* MS-DOS. *Language(s):* BASIC. *Memory Required:* 48k.
disk $50.00.
Shows the Sellers the Net Financial Result of a Property Sale. Calculates the Total Taxable Gain, Total Gain Realized, a Return on Investment, & the Total Cash to Seller.
Realty Software.

Prophet-East. Jun. 1987. *Compatible Hardware:* IBM PC, PC XT, PC AT. *Operating System(s) Required:* Apple DOS 3.3, PC-DOS 2.1. *Memory Required:* 256k.
disk $24.95 ea.
IBM. (ISBN 0-918219-44-2).
Computerized Version of the I Ching, the Ancient Chinese Method of Divination. Generates Hexagrams & Gives Readings.
Zephyr Services.

PROplanner: Business Planning for Growing Companies. *Version:* 3.1. Jeff Rogers. Feb. 1996. *Items Included:* Complete business planning manual - "Business Planning for Growing Companies". *Customer Support:* Free phone support.
MS-DOS, Windows. IBM PC & compatibles. disk $129.00 (ISBN 0-923680-05-5). *Optimal configuration:* Any Windows system.
A Complete Planning & Financial Analysis Package. It Provides the How-To & Tools to Analyze Your Market, Your Competition, & Your Product or Service. Includes Financial Statements, Data Base, Project Planner, Break-Even Analysis, Ratio Analysis, Business Valuations, Trend Analysis & More.
American ComVision, Inc.

Proportional Spacing. *Compatible Hardware:* TRS-80 Model I, Model III, Model 4. *Operating System(s) Required:* TRSDOS. *Language(s):* Z80 Assembly. *Memory Required:* 32k. *General Requirements:* LazyWriter program.
 disk $29.95.
Extention Program to LAZYWRITER Word Processor Which Allows Each Character to Take up a Different Space, Depending upon the Size of the Character.
Alpha Bit Communications, Inc.

Proportional Spacing for C. Itoh F10. *Compatible Hardware:* TRS-80 Model I, Model III, Model 4. *Operating System(s) Required:* TRSDOS. *Language(s):* Z80 Assembly. *Memory Required:* 32k. *General Requirements:* LazyWriter printer.
 disk $49.95.
Features Similar to PROPORTIONAL SPACING, but Specially Designed for the F10 Printer.
Alpha Bit Communications, Inc.

ProScale. *Version:* 2.1. Jul. 1987. *Items Included:* Manual. *Customer Support:* Phone support, $15/15 min; Training available; Free 30 day phone support.
 DOS only. IBM AT, XT, 386, 486 (45k). disk $495.00. *Optimal configuration:* IBM AT, 640k RAM, Digitizer.
Digitizer Interface. Allows the Electronic Transfers of Lengths, Areas & Counts Into a Spreadsheet or Estimative System. It Is Memory Resident Allowing It to Be Utilized with Any Computer Software.
Computerized Micro Solutions.

ProScript. *Version:* 1.0. *Compatible Hardware:* Commodore Amiga. *Items Included:* disk & manual. *Customer Support:* phone-in support available free of charge.
 $49.95.
Can Translate Files Created with PROWRITE into ProScript. Files Can Then Be Printed on a PostScript-Compatible Printer or Saved As a File to Be Printed Later. Other Features Allow User to Reduce or Enlarge the Printout, Choose the Paper Size, Mailweight Documents, & Control the Number of Gray Shades Used for Graphics.
New Horizons Software.

ProServe CX: Automated, Server-Based NLM Backup for Novell NetWare. *Version:* 1.2. Mar. 1994. *Customer Support:* Tech support via BBS, & Fax.
 DOS, Windows, Workstations (3Mb-Tape Server, 2Mb-Admin. workstation). $295.00 (10 client); $595.00 (25 client); $995.00 (50 client); $1495.00 (100 client); $1895.00 (unlimited client). *Optimal configuration:* DOS, Windows, Workstations (3Mb-Tape Server, 2Mb-Admin. workstation); disk space: 3Mb-Tape Server, 3Mb-Admin. workstation, mouse. *Networks supported:* Novell NetWare 3.1x & 4.x.
Sophisticated Data Storage Management Solution Offering Network-Wide Backup & Restore for All Workstations & Servers in a Local Area Network. Under Novell NetWare 3.11 Operating System, It Runs As a NetWare Loadable Module (NLM) & Reliably Backs up All NetWare 2.x & 3.x Server Files Including NetWare Bindery Files, Security Information, & DOS, OS/2, NFS, FTAM & Macintosh Name Spaces. Supporting a Client Server Architecture, It Is Administered from a Single Workstation, & Will Automatically Protect all DOS, Windows & OS/2 Workstations in the Network. Provides Users with Tremendous Functionality & Flexibility by Offering a Windows-Based Interface, Centralized Administration, Automated Operations, Server-Based Performance, Hardware Independence, & Scalability for Networks of All Sizes. Available in English, French & German.
Sytron Corp.

ProServe CX Lite: Automated, Server-Based NLM Backup for Novell NetWare. *Version:* 1.2. Jun. 1994. *Customer Support:* Tech support via BBS, & Fax.
 DOS, Windows, Workstations (3Mb-Tape Server, 2Mb-Admin. workstation). disk $145.00. *Optimal configuration:* DOS, Windows, Workstations (3Mb-Tape Server, 2Mb-Admin. workstation), disk space: 3Mb-Tape Server, 3Mb-Admin. workstation, mouse. *Networks supported:* Novell NetWare 3.1x & 4.x.
Single Server Backup & Restore Application for Novell NetWare 3.1x & 4.x Servers with an Attached Tape Drive. Backup & Restore Operations Can Be Administered from Either a Windows Workstation, or from the NetWare Server. Running As a NetWare Loadable Module (NLM), It Provides Reliable Backup & Restore of All Server Files Including NetWare Bindery Files, NetWare Directory Services, Security Information, & DOS, Windows, OS/2, NFS, FTAM, UNIX & Macintosh Name Spaces. Available in English, French & German.
Sytron Corp.

Proshop Retail. *Version:* 1.95. *Compatible Hardware:* PS/2; 486, Pentium, RISC. *Operating System(s) Required:* MS-DOS, XENIX, UNIX, Windows, NT. *Language(s):* Visual BASIC. *Memory Required:* 4000k. *General Requirements:* Hard disk. *Customer Support:* Toll free hotline. Contact publisher for price.
MultiNational, Multi-Lingual & MultiCurrency Retail Inventory & Point-of-Sale System. Perfect for the Small Retail Store, Golf Proshop & Tennis Proshop. Easy to Use. Maintains Extensive Membership Profiles, Including Two Addresses, Spouse, Dependents, Birthdays, Anniversaries, User-Definable Apparel Sizes, Lockers, Club Storage & Certificate History. Reports Include Member Statements, Aging Reports, Selected Purchase Amounts, Price Tickets, Slow-Moving Inventory, Critical Items & Inventory Worksheets. Sales Reports Include Point-of-Sale Option, Salesperson Tracking, Cash Receipts & Historical Comparison.
Cosmos International, Inc.

Prospect - Contact Manager. 1996.
 DOS, Unix. IBM PC. disk contact publisher for price.
This module allows you to see all general information about each company on one screen, as well as the last four contacts. Your prospects will be very impressed when you tell them you had previously talked to them 2 years ago & exactly what that conversation was regarding. Some features are, Multi Salesperson Support, Lookup by Company Name or Phone Number, Next contact list by sales person, etc.
Core Software, Inc.

Prospect Tracking: Sales Control. Jan. 1992. *Items Included:* Manual on software, run-time version of Superbase 4. *Customer Support:* Training - $55.00/hour; phone support - $55.00/hour; 1 yr. maintenance - free of charge.
 Microsoft (PC) MS-DOS. IBM & compatibles (640k). disk $200.00 (Order no.: PROSTRK). *Nonstandard peripherals required:* Mouse. *Addl. software required:* Windows 3.0 & higher. *Optimal configuration:* IBM compatible 386, 4Mb RAM, Windows 3.1, MS-DOS 5.0, at least 1Mb disk space for programs. *Networks supported:* Novell, LANtastic.
Sales Force Can Track Their Contacts with Prospective & Existing Customers. Sales Manager Can Monitor the Productivity of the Sales Team. Next Contact Notification. Allowed 400 Character Note per Contact. Unlimited Contacts per Customer.
Software Design, Inc.

Prospect Tracking System. *Compatible Hardware:* Apple Macintosh. *Memory Required:* 640k. *General Requirements:* External disk drive, hard drive recommended. *Items Included:* Installation guide, operator manual. *Customer Support:* Unlimited telephone support, on-site training for daily fee.
 Apple Macintosh (1Mb). 3.5" disk $195.00.
 IBM PC, XT, AT, PS/2 & compatibles (640k). disk $295.00.
Interactive Sales Tool. Tracks Prospects Through Buying Cycle, Provides Reports on Prospect Profiles, Sales Activity & Performance. Complete Follow-up with Mailings to All or Selected Prospects.
HMS Computer Co.

PRO$PER. Oct. 1991. *Customer Support:* Telephone support 8AM-7PM EST, Endusen Training; 5 days in Atlanta $500.00.
 AIX. IBM RS 6000 (512k). Contact publisher for price. *Optimal configuration:* 4mb or higher memory, 300mb disc, 2 printers.
Automated Inventory Control & Complete General Accounting System for Wholesale/Distributors. Fully Integrated System Featuring Inventory Control, Purchase Order Processing, Sales Order Processing, General Ledger, Sales Analysis, Fixed Assets, Reportwriter & Query, Office Automation, Freight Manifest Subsystem, Industry Feature Rich Yet Easy to Install & Operate.
Software Solutions, Inc.

Prosper in the '90s on the Job & at Home: Wilson Learning CD-ROM Sampler. Oct. 1995. *Customer Support:* Toll-free telephone number for technical support, 90 days warranty for defects in materials & workmanship.
 Macintosh System 7.0. Macintosh with 68040 processor (5Mb). CD-ROM disk $7.95 (ISBN 1-886806-11-X). *Nonstandard peripherals required:* Double speed CD-ROM drive. *Addl. software required:* QuickTime (included on CD-ROM disc).
 Microsoft Windows 3.1. PC compatible; 486/33MHz (runs slow on 386/25MHz) (8Mb). *Nonstandard peripherals required:* 256 color display card (640x480); double speed CD-ROM drive. *Addl. software required:* QuickTime for Windows (included on CD-ROM disc).
Lets User Try 10 Different CD-ROMs That Include Personal Effectiveness, Selling, Career & Life Planning, & Management Skills. Wilson Learning Has Put the Wisdom of 30 Years Experience Improving People's Performance into a Series of Interactive CD-ROMs So You Can Learn at Home or at Work.
Wilson Learning Corp.

Prostat. Charles Ward & James Reeves. 1986. *Compatible Hardware:* IBM PC & compatibles. *Operating System(s) Required:* MS-DOS 2.1-3.1. *Memory Required:* 256k. *General Requirements:* CGA card.
 disk $75.00 (ISBN 0-88720-287-X, Order no.: COM3100B).
Set of Statistical Programs & File Utilities Intended for Analysis of Laboratory Data. May Be Used As a Supplement for Courses in Statistics, or Where the Analysis of Data Is an Integral Part of the Study. Graphics Are Used Throughout to Aid in the Interpretation of Data, & the Routines Allow Students to Experiment & Develop Statistical Concepts.
COMPress.

The Protector. *Version:* 2.01. Feb. 1989. *Customer Support:* 90 day warranty against defects in disk manufacture, immediate replacement of defective media.
 MS-DOS/PC-DOS 3.1 or higher (256k). IBM PC/XT/AT/PS2 compatible. disk $34.95.

TITLE INDEX

Optimal configuration: PC/AT or PS/2, hard disk, EGA or VGA graphics, 640k, one floppy drive. Networks supported: Novell.
Protect Original Programs from Unauthorized Duplication by DISKCOPY. Works with Any Language & Even Protects Compiled COM & EXE Programs.
Thinking Software, Inc.

Protein Music. Version: 2.0. Compatible Hardware: Commodore Amiga. Items Included: Source code. Customer Support: Telephone support.
3.5" disk $19.95.
Music Based upon 20 Amino Acids.
Silver Software.

Protein Predictor. Version: 2.0. Items Included: Diskette & manual. Customer Support: Telephone inquiries.
MAC-DOS (1Mb). Macintosh, MacPlus & higher. disk $399.00.
Secondary Structure Prediction Program. Input Simple 1-Letter Polypeptide Sequence up to 1000 Residues. Predict Alpha Helix, Beta Sheet Hydropathy & Turns Using Neural Net Methods or Standard Literature Parameters. Also, Latest Coiled Coil Algorithim. User Can Use Own Parameters (Color Mac-II).
Atlantic Software.

ProTex. Customer Support: 800-929-8117 (customer service).
MS-DOS. Commodore 128; CP/M. disk $49.99 (ISBN 0-87007-414-8).
A Text Formatter & Repetitive Letter Mailer. Supports Proportional Spacing on Printers That Support It. Long Documents May Be Partitioned into Several Files & Then Chained at Print Time. Boilerplate Paragraphs Can Be Automatically Inserted into a Document. Up to 99 Variables Can Be Used to Store Information That Is Used in Several Documents. A Variety of Special Print Effects Are Supported.
SourceView Software International.

Protext. Version: 4.4. Arnor. Aug. 1989.
MS-DOS, TOS, Amiga DOS (512k). IBM PC, Atari ST, Amiga DOS. disk $199.95. Optimal configuration: 1Mb RAM.
Fully Integrated Word Processing Package Which Combines Features of Word Processor, Text Editor, & Command Line Interpreter in One Package.
Michtron, Inc.

PROTRACS PROFESSIONAL. Version: 2.0. 1983. Compatible Hardware: IBM PC, PC XT, PC AT. Operating System(s) Required: PC-DOS 2.0, 2.1, 3.0. Language(s): Assembly. Memory Required: 384k. Customer Support: Free telephone support, free BBS.
$89.95.
Full-Feature Project Scheduling & Action-Item Tracking System. Handles 100 Separate Projects Containing up to 2000 Tasks Each. Produces Four Gantt Charts (in Either Monthly or Annual Formats) & Seven Business-Quality Reports. Ad Hoc Report Generator Included. Operates in Both English & French. Spanish Version Available Separately.
Applied MicroSystems, Inc. (Georgia).

Protracs Project Tracking - Reporting. Items Included: Full manual. No other products required. Customer Support: Free telephone support - no time limit. 30 day warranty.
MS-DOS 3.2 or higher. IBM & compatibles (512k). $79.95 single user version; $239.95 network version.
User Can Define over 2000 Activities per Project & Track Them over Time Based on Responsibility & Priority. User Can Even Follow Project-Related Activities Belonging to Others As Well As Your Own. Holidays & Work Schedules Are Automatically Handled. Four Separate Gantt Charts Graphically Display Your Porject in a Variety of Formats. Can Scroll Vertically & Horizontally; Charts Are Not Limited by Screen Size. Charts May Display on Screen, Print or Save to Disk. Six Standard Reports Are Available.
Dynacomp, Inc.

Protracs Project Tracking/Reporting. Items Included: Bound manual. Customer Support: Free hotline - no time limit; 30 day limited warranty; updates are $5/disk plus S&H.
MS-DOS 2.0 or higher. IBM & compatibles (256k RAM, 200 tasks - 512k, 2000 tasks). $79.95-$239.95.
Define over 2000 Activities per Project & Track Them over Time Based on Responsibility & Priority. Follow Project-Related Activities Belonging to Others As Well As Your Own. Holidays & Work Schedules Are Automatically Handled. Four Separate Gantt Charts Graphically Display Project in a Variety of Formats. Scroll Vertically & Horizontally; Charts Are Not Limited by Screen Size. Charts May Be Displayed on Screen, Printed, or Saved to Disk.
Dynacomp, Inc.

Protrip. Version: 2.0. J. E. Mitchell. 1984. Compatible Hardware: Burroughs, Convergent Technology, IBM PC & compatibles, IBM RS6000. Operating System(s) Required: AIX, BTOS, CTOS, MS-DOS, UNIX, XENIX. Language(s): Adept, C (source code included). Memory Required: 1000k.
$4995.00 to $25000.00.
Designed for the Operation of a Trucking Firm Which Includes Billing, Accounts Receivable, Dispatch, Routing, Fuel Tax Reporting, Owner-Operation Settlements, Payroll, General Ledger, Accounts Payable, Logs Shop Maintenance, EDI, Satellite Tracking Safety & Various Analysis Reports.
CMV Software Specialists, Inc.

The Provider. Compatible Hardware: Apple Macintosh SE; IBM PC AT. General Requirements: Hard disk, printer. Customer Support: 6 months free.
single user $950.00.
demo $25.00.
Medical Billing System.
Mark Kalish.

ProWrite. Version: 3.1. Jul. 1990. Compatible Hardware: Commodore Amiga. Operating System(s) Required: Kickstart 1.2. Memory Required: 1000k. Items Included: disks & manual. Customer Support: phone-in support available free of charge.
$175.00.
Word-Processing Program Which Supports Smoothing During High-Resolution Printing, Sideways Printing, & Wide-Carriage Printers. Includes a 100,000-Word Spelling Checker & Large Thesaurus. Users Can Insert Graphics in Documents & Resize Them. HAM Files Are Supported as are Multiple Columns. Includes Arexx Support, Paragraph-Sorting Capabilities, Default Start Up Parameters, & User-Settable Colors & Document Information Such as Character, Word, Line, Paragraph, Picture, & Page Counts.
New Horizons Software.

ProWriter Utilities. Compatible Hardware: IBM PC, PCjr, PC XT. Language(s): Assembly. Memory Required: IBM PC 64k, IBM PCjr & PC XT 128k. General Requirements: Color board adapter, ProWriter Series.
contact publisher for price.
Consists of 3 Separate Software Procedures That May Be Used Independently or in a Combination. Designed for Use with the ProWriter I & II Dot Matrix Printers.
Soft & Friendly.

PRS Legal Billing System. Mar. 1984. Compatible Hardware: IBM PC & compatibles. Operating System(s) Required: MS-DOS, PC-DOS, CP/M. Language(s): BI-280, 286 (source code included). Memory Required: 128k.
BI 286. disk $950.00.
manual $50.00.
trial package (refundable) $100.00.
Records Time, Costs & Payments. Uses Office Defined Case Codes, Transaction Codes & Descriptor Codes. Generates Pre-Billing Ledgers for Review.
PRS-Software.

Psion Chess. Version: 2.13. Dec. 1985. Compatible Hardware: Apple Macintosh Plus; Atari ST; IBM PC & compatibles. Memory Required: Apple 128k, IBM 256k. General Requirements: CGA or Hercules card for IBM. Customer Support: Yes.
$59.95.
Allows Players to Choose from 28 Levels of Difficulty, from Novice to Infinite. On the Novice Level the Computer Senses the Opponent's Strength, Playing More Gently Against Weaker Opponents. On the Infinite Level the Computer Keeps Thinking until It Is Stopped, at Which Point It Displays the Best Move It Has Found. On the Equal Level the Computer Takes the Same Amount of Time to Think As Its Opponent. The Chessboard & Pieces Can Be Displayed Either in Two- or Three-Dimensional Representation.
Psion, Inc.

PSP - The Parcel Shipping Program for UPS Shipments. Version: 7.0. Apr. 1989. Items Included: Operators manual included with software. Customer Support: 1-800-645-1188.
PC-DOS 2.0 (640k). IBM & most compatibles. $99.00 (ISBN 0-934556-21-0, Order no.: 550).
A Software Program That Produces UPS Shipper Manifests, Shipping Labels & Maintains a Shipper Address List & All UPS Rates. Approved by UPS. Eliminates the Need to Use a UPS Log Book.
East Hampton Industries, Inc.

PStext-plus: PostScript Print Utility for Unix Systems. Items Included: Installation/administration instructions, user manual. Customer Support: On-Site training, service upgrade available as extra cost options; additional user manual $75.
Unix System V or Equivalent. contact publisher for price (Order no.: PSTP). Nonstandard peripherals required: PostScript printer.
PostScript Support Package Which Provides Interface Between Unix Applications & Spoolers. Formats Text Files with Intelligent Professional Quality Forms into PostScript Format. Options Include Exact Fit Capability to Scale Text to Fit Within Margins of a Page, As for Spreadsheets. Users Can Create Intelligent Forms for Merging As Underlays or Overlays with Text. Forms Are Included to Create Pie & Bar Charts.
J&KH Software.

PSTPIT. Sep. 1984. Compatible Hardware: IBM PC, PC AT, PC XT & compatibles. Operating System(s) Required: PC-DOS, MS-DOS. Language(s): FORTRAN. Memory Required: 512k. General Requirements: Printer.
disk $5000.00, incl. PITKOR, RESPIT, & PREPIT (Order no.: PSTPIT).
Converts the Ultimate Pit Limit File Generated by PITKOR into a Topographic Grid File Containing True Elevations. This Ultimate Pit Limit Represents

the Post-Mining Surface As Discrete Blocks. The Level Numbers of the Model Must Be Converted to True Elevations to Map the Pit & Complete Further Design Work.
Geostat Systems International, Inc. (GSII).

Psych-Log. *Compatible Hardware:* Apple Macintosh Plus. *Operating System(s) Required:* System 5.0 or higher. *General Requirements:* Printer.
entry level version $995.00.
single-provider version $2395.00.
multiprovider version $3495.00.
Office Management for Mental Health Care.
Mission Accomplished Software Services, Inc.

PSYCHART: Psychometric Analysis. *Items Included:* Manuel. *Customer Support:* Free toll free telephone support.
IBM PC & compatibles (256k). disk $295.00.
Displays the Psychrometric Chart on the Computer Screen & Allows the Designer to Carry Out All Operations & Analysis Normally Done Using a Conventional Psychrometric Chart. Program Uses Equations from the 1985 ASHRAE Handbook.
Elite Software Development, Inc.

Psychiatric Diagnostic Interview-Revised.
Version: 2.010. Ekkehard Othmer et al. *Customer Support:* Free unlimited phone support with a toll free number.
WIndows 3.X. IBM or 100% compatible. 3.5" disk $195.00 (Order no.: W-1048). *Addl. software required:* Windows 3.1 or higher. *Optimal configuration:* 486 or higher, hard disk with one Mb of free disk space, printer.
Helps User Determine Whether An Individual Is Suffering, or Has Ever Suffered, from a Major Psychiatric Disorder. Designed for Use with Individuals 18 Years of Age or Older, the PDI-R Evaluates 17 Basic Psychiatric Syndromes.
Western Psychological Services.

The Psychiatry Expert. *Version:* 2.1. *Compatible Hardware:* IBM PC & compatibles. *Operating System(s) Required:* PC-DOS, MS-DOS. *Memory Required:* 256k. *General Requirements:* Hard disk recommended. *Items Included:* 32 pg. Thinking Software catalog.
3.5" or 5.25" disk $34.95.
Helps Users Understand the Details of Actual Psychiatric Diagnoses. The Nine Knowledge Bases Included in the Package Are: Personality Disorders, Neurosis, Sexual Deviation, Drug Dependence, Manic/Depressive Syndrome, Mental Retardation, Psychosis, Psychosomatic Illness, & Psychiatric Emergency.
Thinking Software, Inc.

Psychological Experiments & Research.
Version: 2.0. Thomas B. Perera. Edited by Dirk Houben. 1981. *Compatible Hardware:* Apple II plus, IIe; IBM PC & compatibles. *Operating System(s) Required:* Apple DOS 3.3; PC-DOS/MS-DOS 2.1 or higher. *Language(s):* BASIC (source code included). *Memory Required:* 48k.
series $495.00.
$40.00 ea.
21 Programs Simulate College Level Psychology Laboratory Experiments. Examples Include Reaction Time, Verbal Learning, & Signal Detection.
Life Science Assocs.

The Psychology Experimenter. Ben R. Lowery & M. David Merrill. Jan. 1987. *Items Included:* Disk & manual. *Customer Support:* 619-699-6227.
IBM PC. disk $200.00 (ISBN 0-15-572674-9).
Harcourt Brace Jovanovich, Inc. (College Div.).

The Psychology Expert. *Version:* 4.2. *Compatible Hardware:* IBM PC & compatibles. *Operating System(s) Required:* PC-DOS, MS-DOS. *Memory Required:* 256k. *General Requirements:* Hard disk recommended. *Items Included:* 32 pg. Thinking Software catalog.
3.5" or 5.25" disk $34.95.
Helps Users Deal with Mild Everyday Psychological Problems. The Main Menu Includes Topics Such As Anxiety, Depression, Insomnia, Men's Sexual Problems, Women's Sexual Problems, Disturbing Thoughts & Feelings, & Children's Problems.
Thinking Software, Inc.

Psychrometric Analysis: PSYCHART. Ed Sowell. Jan. 1985. *Operating System(s) Required:* MS-DOS. *Memory Required:* 256k.
3-1/2", 5-1/4", or 8" disk $295.00.
Graphically Oriented Program That Displays a Complete Psychrometric Chart on the Computer's Screen. User Can Move the Cursor Around the Psych Chart & Define As Many State Points (Only Two Psychometric Parameters Are Necessary to Define a State Point) As Desired. Once State Points Are Defined User Can Then Select from Seven Different Processes: Heating Coil, Cooling/Dehumidification Coil, Humidifier (3 Types), Mixing, Collecting & General Linear Processes. Since Processes May Be Defined in Combination, PSYCH Can Perform Any Psychrometric Calculation Right on the Screen. Also Allows Elevations from -1000 to 24,000 Feet & Dry Bulb Temperatures Between -40 & 140 F. Five Reports Are Available. The Output Can Be Printed with Either Metric or English Units.
Elite Software Development, Inc.

PsychStat MAX 2.11: Psychometric - Statistical Programs. *Version:* 2.11. Jan. 1992. *Items Included:* 57,500 word technical manual. *Customer Support:* 30 day money back return policy, author support.
PC or MS-DOS 3.0 or higher, hard disk with at least 2Mb. IBM PC or compatible (256k). $59.95 software & manual (not sold separately) (ISBN 0-9631763-0-7). *Optimal configuration:* IBM or compatible with 80486 cpu or 80386 with 80387 math coprocessor.
Statistical Applications: Frequency, Chi-Square, T-Test, Correlated T-Test, ONEWAY, ANOVA, Analysis of Covariance, Repeated Measures ANOVA, Pearson Correlation, Multiple Regression. Psychometric Applications: Item Analysis, Point-Biserial, Corrected Item-Total Correlation, Cronbach's Alpha for Both Right-Wrong & Likert Type Scales. Percent Agreement Program. Transformation Program, Merge Program, Reverse Scale Program, Data Entry Program, Roster or Codebook Creation Program.
PsychStat.

PSYCOM: Psychology on Computer: Simulations, Experiments & Projects. Duane M. Belcher & Stephen D. Smith. Sep. 1986. *Compatible Hardware:* Apple IIe, IIc; IBM PC. *Memory Required:* Apple 64k, IBM 128k. *General Requirements:* 2 disk drives; DOS 2.1 or lower.
disk $395.00 ea.
Apple. (ISBN 0-697-01195-X).
IBM. (ISBN 0-697-01194-1).
Teaches Students to Collect Data, & to Analyze & Discuss the Results Within the Context of Scientific Study. Programs Include: Precognition, Labels & Prejudice, Human Factors, Training a Rat with Reinforcements, Sensory Register, Love Test, Western Electric Study, a Teaching Machine/Mnemonic Learning, Poll on 55, Locus of Control & Activities, IQ/Learn a Novel Task, & Type a Behavior.
Wm. C. Brown Pubs.

PT-109: WWII Patrol Torpedo Simulation.
Version: IBM CGA 1.10; Mac 1.2; IBM EGA 1.20. Jul. 1987. *Compatible Hardware:* Apple Macintosh Plus, SE, Mac II; IBM PC, PC XT, PC AT & compatibles. *Operating System(s) Required:* PC-DOS/MS-DOS 2.0 or higher. *Memory Required:* IBM CGA 384k, IBM EGA 512k, Macintosh 1000k. *General Requirements:* Color monitor.
Apple Macintosh. 3.5" disk $49.95 (ISBN 0-928784-50-9).
IBM. disk $14.95 (ISBN 0-928784-50-9).
WWII Patrol Torpedo Boat Simulation with Real-Time Graphics, Varying Levels of Difficulty & Several Different Mission Types.
Spectrum HoloByte.

PTERM. *Version:* 4.7. *Customer Support:* 90 days free support, then $150.00 per year. 24 hour bulletin board system.
Multiuser DOS, PC-DOS/MS-DOS, REAL/32. $139.00.
Provides PC Term Emulation, Allowing Existing PC's To Be Used as Intelligent Terminals on Concurrent DOS 386 Host. Includes Background File Transfer, Modem Support, Host Console & Keyboard Mimicking.
Logan Industries, Inc.

Public Domain Software on File Collection, 20 disks. Public Domain Research. Nov. 1985. *Compatible Hardware:* Apple II, II+, IIe, IIc. *Memory Required:* 64k.
Set. $195.00 (ISBN 0-8160-1251-2).
Includes Over 250 Programs Which Users Can Copy & Modify with No Restrictions. Targeted Specifically to Librarians.
Facts on File, Inc.

Public Opinion Survey. Mark E. Stolzberg & Hubert S. Howe. Dec. 1979. *Compatible Hardware:* Apple; CP/M or MS-DOS based systems; IBM PC; TRS-80. *Operating System(s) Required:* MS-DOS. *Language(s):* BASIC (source code included). *Memory Required:* 256k. *Items Included:* Disks, manual. *Customer Support:* Telephone.
disk $180.00.
Public Opinion Poll Data Analysis for Market Research, Political Polls & Social Science Research. Summarizes Responces Using Frequencies & Percentages. Handles Demographic Categories & Sub-Categories.
Stolzberg Research, Inc.

Public Works Management. *Compatible Hardware:* IBM PC. *Operating System(s) Required:* MS-DOS.
contact publisher for price.
Service & Recording Package Constructed As an Aid for Local Government Public Works Offices. Optional Features Include: Work Reporting, Problem Recording & a Streets Inventory Capacity.
Automation Counselors, Inc.

PubliCalc. Jan. 1986. *Operating System(s) Required:* XENIX 5, UNIX. (source code included).
disk binary $10.00 (ISBN 0-916151-16-6).
disk source $50.00.
Spreadsheet Designed for UNIX/XENIX.
Specialized Systems Consultants, Inc.

Publicity & Promotional Events Data File.
Version: 3.0. John Kremer. Sep. 1992. *Items Included:* Calendar. *Customer Support:* Telephone support.
MS-DOS. IBM PC or compatible. disk $29.95 (Order no.: 494). *Addl. software required:* Any database program.
Macintosh. 3.5" disk $29.95 (Order no.: 495). *Addl. software required:* Any database

program.
6,650 Special Days, Weeks, Months, Anniversaries, Trade Shows, & Other Annual Events Are Featured in This Data File. Besides Events & Dates, P&P Also Lists the Sponsoring Organization (with Address & Phone Number) & Indicates Which Special Topics Are Related to Each Event - Whether Business, Food, Travel, Families, Science, Politics, Entertainment, or Any of 50 Other Subject Areas. By Using This P&P, User Can Quickly Target All Dates Related to Food, Children's Interests, Recreation, Computers, or Whatever.
Open Horizons Publishing Co.

Publish It! Version: 3.0. Sep. 1992. Items Included: Manual. Customer Support: Unlimited technical support; 60 day moneyback guarantee. IBM-DOS. IBM or compatibles (1Mb). disk $149.95. Addl. software required: DOS 3.0 or higher (DOS 3.0 or 4.0 requires an Extended Memory Manager. Optimal configuration: IBM PC, XT, AT, PS/1, PS/2 or compatible, hard drive, mouse.
Includes Complete Page Layout, Word Processing & Graphics Tools. Version 3.0 Also Features an Improved Graphical User Interface with a Toolbar; On-The-Fly Font Scaling with 20 Scalable Fonts; over 100 Templates & 150 Clip Art Illustrations; an 80,000-Word Spell Checker & PowerText for Creating Special Text Effects.
Timeworks, Inc.

Publish It! Easy. Version: 3.0. Jul. 1992. Items Included: Manual. Customer Support: Unlimited technical support; 60 day moneyback guarantee. MAC. Macintosh (1074k). 3.5" disk $199.95. Addl. software required: System Version 4.2, Finder Version 5.0 (System 6.0 or higher is recommended). Optimal configuration: Hard drive, all MACs except 128, 512k, mouse.
Includes Page Layout, Word Processing & Graphics Tools, a Database/Mail-Merge Program & Slide Show Feature. Version 3.0 Supports Paragraph Tags; Multiple Ruler Guides; Changeable Specifications on Grouped Objects; Expanded Drawing Tools; Graduated Fills for Rectangles; Color TIFF Images & Image Control for Grayscale & Color PICT2 & TIFF Images.
Timeworks, Inc.

Publish It! for Windows. Version: 3.1. Oct. 1992. Items Included: Manual. Customer Support: Unlimited technical support; 60 day moneyback guarantee. Windows. IBM (2Mb). disk $149.95. Addl. software required: DOS 3.1 or higher; Windows 3.0 or higher. Optimal configuration: 286/386/486 DOS based computer, hard disk drive, Windows-compatible video adapter & monitor.
Full-Featured, Easy-to-Learn Desktop Publisher with Page Layout, Word Processing, Typesetting & Graphics Tools. Features a 96,000-Word Spell Checker, over 100 Templates, over 150 Clip Art Illustrations & Adobe Type Manager with 25 Scalable Fonts; & PowerText, a Feature for Creating Special Text Effects.
Timeworks, Inc.

Publish It! Lite. Version: 2.0. Jun. 1993. Items Included: Manual. Customer Support: Unlimited technical support; 60 day moneyback guarantee. IBM-DOS. IBM or compatibles (640k). disk $59.95. Addl. software required: DOS 3.0 or higher. Optimal configuration: IBM PC or compatible 640k computer, hard drive.
The Only True Desktop Publisher for the PC Designed for the Beginning User. Easy-to-Learn & Use, Lite Is Powerful Enough to Create Exiting Brochures, Ads, Newsletters & More. Features Include Built-In Word Processing & Drawing Tools; 9 Sample Layouts, 40 Clip Art Images & over 140 Possible Font Combinations; Text & Graphic Importing; Precision Object Placement; Paragraph Tags; Automatic Column-to-Column or Page-to-Page Text Flow; Page Numbering, Hyphenation & Bulleting; & Much More. The Quick Start Mini Manual Will Help Users Produce Their First Document in Less Than One Hour.
Timeworks, Inc.

Publish or Perish: Macintosh Version. Version: 5.0. Compatible Hardware: Apple Macintosh. Memory Required: 512k.
3.5" disk $74.95.
Bibliographic Database That Allows Search & Formatting of References. Refereneces Can Be Printed or Output As Text Files As Well. Features Include Field Lengths up to 240 Characters; Notes Unlimited, Select References to Be Included in Bibliography & a Choice of Font & Formatting Options for Printing.
Park Row Software.

Publisher's Paintbrush. Version: 2.0. 1991. Compatible Hardware: IBM PC & compatibles. Operating System(s) Required: MS-DOS 3.0 or higher & Windows 3.0 or higher. Language(s): Assembly, C. Memory Required: 640k. General Requirements: hard disk, graphics display, drawing device; full-page, 300 dpi images require up to 2Mb of RAM. Supports major-brand image scanners, & most printers & video display boards.
disk $495.00.
Publisher's Paintbrush Version 2.0 Is an Image Processing & Paint Program That Features Scanner Control from Within the Program & Advanced Image Enhancement Tools & Filters. Other Features Include: Virtual Memory Support, Which Allows Users to Edit Images Regardless of Their System's RAM Capacity; an Array of Tools for Retouching Images, Gradient Fills, "Tiling" Features; Text Capabilities That Include Outlining, Resizing, Underlining, Italics, Shadows, & 3-D Shadows; 256 Gray Scale Editing; 24-Bit Color (16.7 Million Colors) Editing; Compensation for Display & Output Devices; Automatic Scanner Calibration; Program Supports PCX, TIF, BMP, GIF, MSP, & ESP (Write Only) Formats.
ZSoft Corp.

Publisher's Type Foundry. Version: 1.5. Compatible Hardware: IBM PC. Operating System(s) Required: MS-DOS 3.0 or higher & MS Windows 3.0 or higher. Memory Required: 640k. Items Included: Disks, documentation, binder, slipcase. Customer Support: Free, 10AM-6PM (EST) M-F.
disk $545.00 (ISBN 1-877728-00-4). Addl. software required: Microsoft Windows, version 2.1 or higher.
Creates or Captures Type Fonts, Logos, & Special Symbols. Consists of a Bitmap & Outline Editors. Resolution up to 3000 DPI. Support Windows.
ZSoft Corp.

Publishing Contracts, Sample Agreements for Book Publishers on Disk. Version: 1.1. Dan Poynter. Jul. 1987. Compatible Hardware: IBM PC & compatibles, Apple Macintosh. Operating System(s) Required: MS-DOS, Apple DOS, Windows. Memory Required: 640k. General Requirements: Word processing program. Items Included: Manual. Customer Support: Yes.
disk $29.95 (ISBN 0-915516-46-2).
Contains 22 Different Contracts for Book Publishing from Author-Publisher Trade Book Agreements to Foreign Rights Contracts to Special Sales Agreements. Formatted on Disk for IBM & Available in 12 Different Word Processing or Macintosh & MS-Word or Macwrite (Specify) Programs. Saves the User the Time Involved in Retyping & Facilitates Customized Editing.
Para Publishing.

Publishing Market Place Reference Plus. 1995. Customer Support: Information & Assistance Hotline; Electronic Bulletin Board.
DOS 3.1 or higher. IBM 286 or higher & compatibles (535k). CD-ROM disk $795 for 1 year. Nonstandard peripherals required: Hard disk (minimum 10 Mb free space); CD-ROM player running under MS-DOS extensions 2.2 or later.
CD-ROM disk $2266.00 for 3 years.
Features 83,000 Unabridged Profiles from the AMERICAN LIBRARY DIRECTORY & the WORLD GUIDE TO LIBRARIES. Also Includes 32,000 Listings for Bookstores & Antiquarian Book Dealers Found in the AMERICAN BOOK TRADE DIRECTORY; 79,000 Companies Cited in PUBLISHERS, DISTRIBUTORS & WHOLESALERS; 103,000 SANs (Standard Address Numbers) for Schools & Service Organizations, 16,000 Records for Publishers, Printers, Sales, & Media Services, Distribution & Editorial Support Services, Literary Agents, Trade Associations & More from LITERARY MARKET PLACE & INTERNATIONAL LITERARY MARKET PLACE, Facts & Statistics About the Publishing Industry from the BOWKER ANNUAL LIBRARY & BOOK TRADE ALMANAC.
R.R. Bowker.

Publishing Packs. Compatible Hardware: Apple Macintosh Plus. General Requirements: 800K disk drive, PostScript printer.
Newsletters. 3.5" disk $395.00.
Forms & Schedules. 3.5" disk $475.00.
Displays & Presentations. 3.5" disk $475.00.
Group of Typefaces; Each Package Consists of Typefaces Selected by Experts in Typography & Graphic Design. Includes a How-To Booklet from Each Expert with Tips on How to Use a Type for Maximum Effect.
Adobe Systems, Inc.

Publishing Production Design. Customer Support: 800-929-8117 (customer service).
MS-DOS. Apple II. disk $99.99 (ISBN 0-87007-532-2).
A Tutorial on All Aspects of Designing & Producing Publications Such as School Yearbooks, Newspapers, Church or Corporate Newsletters & House Organs. There are Several Lessons on Proper Page Design, Planning for Photos, Using the Mondrian Theory of Page Composition. For Students Who Want to Excel in Journalism, & Get Positions on Their Newspaper Staff. Also for Anyone Who Wants to Learn the Principles of Journalism Design.
SourceView Software International.

Pulsar Cuisitech. Version: 3.74. Pulsar Software Canada Staff. Jun. 1994. Items Included: Spiral bound manuals. Customer Support: Tech support hot line $50/hr.
Windows. 486/66 or higher (8Mb). disk $950.00. Optimal configuration: 256 color graphic card, 12Mb RAM.
Low Cost Powerful Room Design System Operating in WINDOWS. User May Create His Own Shapes of Cabinets, Furniture & Appliances Quickly & Easily. User Can Maintain His Own Catalog of Shapes & Prices. Design in the Floor Plan Display Accurate Detail in 3D Perspective. User Can Also Create Products from Part & Create His Own Styles & Other Motifs. Connects to Product Planner for Cutlisting.
Pattern Systems International, Inc.

Pulse Portfolio Management System. Version: 1.1. Aug. 1991. Items Included: Manual with discussion of portfolio theory. Customer Support: Free technical support at (800) 265-9998.
DOS 2.0 or higher. IBM PC, XT, AT, PS/2 & compatibles (640k). disk full version $349.00. 60 day trial version $49.00.

Full-Featured Portfolio Program That Manages a Broad Range of Investments. System Allows the User to Track Stocks, Options, Bonds, Mutual Funds, Money Market Accounts, CDs, MOrtgages, Collectibles, Treasury Bills, Futures, Real Estate, Zeros & Precious Metals. It Can Manage up to 75 Real & Hypothetical Portfolios with an Unlimited Number of Transactions. Also Offers a Variety of Pre-Defined Reports, & Allows Reports to Be Customized into Hundreds of Different Combinations.
Equis International.

PUMP. John Migliavacca. Mar. 1986. *Operating System(s) Required:* PC-DOS. *Memory Required:* 192k. *General Requirements:* Printer, Lotus 1-2-3. disk $100.00.
Compiled Lotus 1-2-3 Spreadsheet for Sizing Piping in a Pumped Liquid System. Calculates Equivalent Lengths of Bends & Fittings, Fluid Velocities, & Pressure Loss Due to Friction for Both Suction & Discharge Piping. Considers Evaluation Differences, Source & Destination Pressures, & Variable Liquid Properties, Calculates Required Control Valve Presure Drop for Operation at a Rated Point, & Finds the Valve Cv. A Graph is Produced Showing the Pump Curve & the System Head Curve. Aids in Designing a Controllable System.
Techdata.

PUMPCURV. *Version:* 3.5. 1993. *Compatible Hardware:* IBM PC; IBM PC, PC XT, PC AT & compatibles, PS/2. *Operating System(s) Required:* PC-DOS/MS-DOS. *Language(s):* BASIC. *Memory Required:* 640k. *General Requirements:* Printer. *Customer Support:* Free phone support.
IBM & compatibles. disk $395.00, incl. manual (ISBN 0-932507-40-9, Order no.: IBM-109). demo disk $5.00.
Predicts the Performance of a Centrifugal Pump at Different Speeds. Impeller Diameters & Stages. Calculates Performance for Several Pumps in Series or Parallel Configuration. Uses the Affinity Laws for Centrifugal Pumps. Screen & Printer Graphics.
Systek (California).

PUMPERF. *Version:* 4.3. E. Shashi Menon. Jun. 1995. *Compatible Hardware:* IBM PC, PC XT, PC AT, PS/2. *Operating System(s) Required:* PC-DOS/MS-DOS, Windows 3.1. *Language(s):* C. *Memory Required:* 4000k. *General Requirements:* Printer optional for plots. *Customer Support:* Free phone support.
IBM PC, XT, AT, PS/2. disk $495.00 (ISBN 0-932507-45-X, Order no.: IBM-110).
5.00 demo disk.
Predicts the Performance of a Centrifugal Pump Used on a Liquid Pipeline System. Calculates Flow Rate, Pressure, Horsepower & Efficiency at the Operating Point of Intersection Between the Pipeline System Head Curve & the Pump Head-Capacity Curve. Handles Several Pumps in Series & Parallel Configurations. Considers Throttling to Limit Pipe Pressure. Screen & Printer Graphics.
Systek (California).

Puppy Love. *Compatible Hardware:* Apple Macintosh.
3.5" disk $29.95.
Entertainment & Educational Product. As Students Teach the Puppy Tricks, They Learn Basic Programming Logic.
Addison-Wesley Publishing Co., Inc.

Puppy to Dogs.
Windows. CD-ROM disk $49.95 (ISBN 1-882949-92-7, Order no.: 91618107ND).
You Love Your Pet, & You've Made an Emotional & Financial Commitment to Seeing That It Grows up As Healthy & Happy. With This Interactive CD-ROM, You'll Learn the Techniques the Experts Use to Make Their Pets the Best They Can Be! An Easy-to-Use, VCR-Like Interface Guides You Through Each Important Stage of Your Pet's Life. Includes Free Video!
Paragon Media.

Purchase Order. *Version:* 9.05. May 1986. (source code included). *Memory Required:* 512k. *General Requirements:* Hard disk, printer. *Items Included:* Reference manual. *Customer Support:* Phone/modem support included first year, nominal fee thereafter.
$800.00.
Interfaces with the STOCKROOM Inventory Program. Prepares, Tracks, & Maintains a History of Purchase Orders Issued.
Fogle Computing Corp.

Purchase Order. *Version:* 2.0. *Operating System(s) Required:* VAX/VMS. *Items Included:* User Guide, Technical Documentation. *Customer Support:* Training included, hot-line, dial-in access w/maintenance.
$29,000.00 & up.
Interactive Administrative Purchase Order System. Features Include Purchase Order Processing, Receipt Processing, Requisition Processing, etc.
Ross Systems, Inc.

Purchase Order Management System. *Version:* 2.00. 1978. *Compatible Hardware:* IBM PC & compatibles, PC XT, PC AT, PS/2, XT, PS/2. *Operating System(s) Required:* MS-DOS, PC-DOS. *Language(s):* FORTRAN. *Memory Required:* 512k. *Items Included:* Manual. *Customer Support:* 1 hour per package purchased.
5-1/4" or 8" disk, 3-1/2" disk $495.00.
Designed to Provide Maximum Output & Management Information from Minimal Entries. Whenever Purchase Orders Are Entered & Posted, the System Automatically Updates Inventory On-Hand & On-Order Quantities, Prints a Receiving Report for Received Items, Generates Purchase History Information, & Manages Outstanding Purchase Orders.
MCC Software (Midwest Computer Ctr. Co.).

Purchase Order Module. *Version:* 8B. Sep. 1993. *Compatible Hardware:* Altos; AT&T; IBM PC, RT & compatibles; NCR; UNISYS. *Operating System(s) Required:* PC-DOS/MS-DOS, UNIX, XENIX, 3COM, NOVELL, AIX. *Language(s):* COBOL 85. *Memory Required:* Multi-user 3Mb or higher, single-user 1000k. *General Requirements:* Integrated Accounting Software. *Customer Support:* Included with the support for the Integrated Accounting.
UNIX/XENIX, 3COM, NOVELL. disk $620.00. MS-DOS. disk $745.00.
Can Be Added to Integrated Accounting to Automatically Print & Track Purchase Orders, Maintain & Report on the Status of Each Order, & Present Statistics on Vendor's Delivery Schedules. Item Number Is Different from That of Vendor, Users Can Enter Number into the Purchase Order Module & It Automatically Prints User's Existing Purchase Orders. Releases Purchase Orders by Date, Automatically Costs Items by the method Chosen by Date, Automatically Costs Items by the Method Chosen by User & Calculates Vendor's Payment Terms. It Also Gives Statistics on Vendor Performance.
Trac Line Software, Inc.

Purchase Order: PO. *Version:* 5.8. May 1993. *Compatible Hardware:* DEC VAX Series, DEC Alpha AXP. *Operating System(s) Required:* VMS, Open VMS. *Language(s):* DIBOL, C, COBOL. *Memory Required:* Depends on the specific configurationk. *General Requirements:* Depends on the specific configuration. *Customer Support:* Full service, update service; by quotation.
$3500.00-$15,000.00.
Interactive Screen Allows Unlimited Lines on PO's. Products Are Accessed by Entering Partial Code or Description. Scheduled Arrival Is Shown on Customer Order Entry Screen. PO's Create "Commitments" in AP to Track Cash Requirements Before Receiving Invoices. Other Interfaces Include GL, JC, & IC.
Compu-Share, Inc.

Purchase Order Processing. (Service Management Ser.). 1996.
DOS, Unix. IBM PC. disk contact publisher for price.
The FAsTrak "Purchase Order" module will track inventory from initial entry to receipt of goods.
Core Software, Inc.

Purchase Order Processor: Add-On Option. 1982. *Compatible Hardware:* IBM PC. *Language(s):* BASIC (source code included).
disk $69.00 (Order no.: 612).
Purchase Order Processor for Accounts Payable Module of Accounting System.
Micro Architect, Inc.

Purchase Order System. *Version:* 7.2. 1988. *Compatible Hardware:* IBM PC & compatibles. *Memory Required:* 512k. *General Requirements:* Hard disk. *Items Included:* 3-ring binder documentation. *Customer Support:* 1 hour phone support included, on-site training at $75 per hour.
$295.00.
Produces Custom Generated Purchase Orders & Maintains Detailed Information on the Status of Orders Such As Receipt & Return of Merchandise. Integrates with the Accounts Payable & Inventory Systems. Includes an On-Line Help Feature.
Lake Avenue Software.

Purchase Order System. Mar. 1988.
PC-DOS/MS-DOS (128k). disk $95.00.
Theta Business Systems.

Purchase Orders. May 1984. *Compatible Hardware:* Intel 80286, 80386, 80486, etc.. *Operating System(s) Required:* MS-DOS, Novell, THEOS, UNIX, Win 95, Win/NT. *Language(s):* BASIC. *Memory Required:* 44k. *General Requirements:* Compass INVENTORY CONTROL Package.
disk $1995.00.
Provides Flexible Ordering Formulas & Base Flexible Formatting.
COMPASS.

Purchase Orders Processing. *Version:* 4.1. *Customer Support:* On site training unlimited support services for first 90 days & through subscription thereafter.
Contact publisher for price.
Allows the Purchase of Inventory Items in the IM Module & of Non-Inventory Items to Be Managed Through the Issuance of Purchase Order. Purchase Information May Be Entered Prior to the Creation of Purhcase Order. Performance Dates Are Summarized by Vendor. Numerous Analysis Reports Are Available.
Argos Software.

Purchasing. *Version:* 14.0. (Accounting Software Ser.). Aug. 1993. *Compatible Hardware:* IBM & compatibles. *Operating System(s) Required:* MS-DOS, PC-DOS 3.X & up. *Language(s):* MegaBASIC. *Memory Required:* 640k. *General Requirements:* Hard disk, wide carriage printer. *Customer Support:* (203) 790-9756.
disk $395.00, Network Option ,400.00 more. manual $50.00.
Features Print Receivers, Debit Memos, Inventory

TITLE INDEX

Labels, Special Parts Purchase Orders & Updates Inventory Automatically. Tie-in to Accounts Payable (Automatic Posting). Allows Entry & Maintenance of Vendor Address, Alternate Vendor. Auto Purchasing Available, Tracks Special Parts, Discounts, & Shipping Charges. Allows Drop Shipping Address. Analyzes Purchase Orders/Incoming Inventory vs. Outstanding Orders to Be Filled.
Applications Systems Group (CT), Inc.

Purchasing. Version: 2.0. 1989. Language(s): C. Customer Support: Free telephone & BBS technical support; documentation; training from local dealers &/or vendors CFPIM, C.P.M., CIRM, CQA Trainers. Customization available from vendor.
MS/PC DOS; Concurrent DOX, Xenix, Unix. IBM PC/XT/AT & compatibles; IBM PS/2 (512k).
single-user $995.00. Nonstandard peripherals required: Hard disk, 132-column printer.
multi-user $1295.00.
Unix, Xenix $1495.00.
demo disk & manual $20.00.
Creates Orders & Monitors Goods Received.
INMASS/MRP.

Purchasing. May 1983. Compatible Hardware: IBM PC, PC XT, PC AT. Operating System(s) Required: PC-DOS. Language(s): COBOL. Memory Required: 192k. General Requirements: 2 disk drives.
disk $1550.00-$2335.00.
Tracks the On-Order Information for an Item. Reports Are Produced by Item Number, Order Number, Vendor & Due Dates. Balance Information Includes On-Order, Received, On-Hand, Inspected & Rejected. Automatic Posting of Inventory Is Provided. The Advanced Purchasing Module Prints the Purchase Order, Tracks Buyer & Vendor Performance & Creates Financial Variance Information. The Historical Transactions from Both Modules Can Be Used to Post an Accounts Payable System.
Twin Oaks, Inc.

Purchasing Management. Version: 2.1. Jul. 1990. Items Included: Manual. Customer Support: 90 days free, additional support & maintenance available.
DOS 3.1 or higher. IBM PC AT, PS/2 & compatibles (640k). Contact publisher for price.
Tracks Expected Subcontractor & Material Costs Before the Job Starts. Produces Purchase Orders, Either Original or Confirming, That Tie Down Costs Up-Front, Reserve Necessary Material Quantities & Notify Vendors in Advance of Desired Delivery Schedules & Special Instructions.
Timberline Software Corp.

Purimaze. Compatible Hardware: Apple II+, IIe, IIc. Language(s): BASIC, Machine. Memory Required: 48k.
disk $14.95.
A Game for Purim. Tricky & Mysterious Maze & a Special Version of Hang Haman Are Included. Features Include: a Race Against Time to Figure Out the Hidden Words of Haman, a Mysterious Labyrinth Full of Surprises & More.
Davka Corp.

Purposeful Patterns. 1983. Compatible Hardware: Apple IIe, IIc, IIgs. Operating System(s) Required: Apple DOS 3.3. Language(s): Applesoft BASIC. Memory Required: 48k.
disk $250.00.
Multi-Level Program Originally Designed for the Purpose of Retraining Visual Perception & Memory Skills in Brain Injured Patients at a Rehabilitation Hospital in Reading, Pennsylvania.
Greentree Group, Inc.

Purposeful Symbols. Compatible Hardware: Apple IIe, IIc, IIgs.
$75.00.
Companion Program to PURPOSEFUL PATTERNS. The 3 Tasks Making up This Program Are: Letter Match, Number Match I, & Number Match II. These Tasks Allow for a Sequential Building of Cognitive Skills Specifically in the Areas of Recognition, Comparison, & Recall of Letters & Numbers. In Addition, Spatial Relations May Be Introduced as the Therapist Pre-Selects Various Positionings of Letters & Numbers Seen on the Monitor Screen.
Greentree Group, Inc.

The Pushcart War. Intentional Education Staff & John Merrill. Apr. 1996. Items Included: Program manual. Customer Support: Free technical support, 89 day warranty.
School ver.. System 7.1 or higher. Macintosh (4Mb). 3.5" disk contact publisher for price (ISBN 1-57204-329-6). Nonstandard peripherals required: 256 color monitor, hard drive, printer.
Lab pack. System 7.1 or higher. Macintosh (4Mb). 3.5" disk contact publisher for price (ISBN 1-57204-305-9). Nonstandard peripherals required: 256 color monitor, hard drive, printer.
Site license. System 7.1 or higher. Macintosh (4Mb). 3.5" disk contact publisher for price (ISBN 1-57204-330-X). Nonstandard peripherals required: 256 color monitor, hard drive, printer.
School ver.. Windows 3.1 or higher. IBM/Tandy & 100% compatibles (4Mb). disk contact publisher for price (ISBN 1-57204-306-7). Nonstandard peripherals required: VGA or SVGA 640 x 480 resolution (256), mouse, hard disk, sound device.
Lab pack. Windows 3.1 or higher. IBM/Tandy & 100% compatibles (4Mb). disk contact publisher for price (ISBN 1-57204-331-8). Nonstandard peripherals required: VGA or SVGA 640 x 480 resolution (256), mouse, hard disk, sound device.
Site license. Windows 3.1 or higher. IBM/Tandy & 100% compatibles. disk contact publisher for price (ISBN 1-57204-307-5). Nonstandard peripherals required: VGA or SVGA 640 x 480 resolution (256), mouse, hard disk, sound device.
This companion for young adult literature is ideal for students who don't know how to start that book report, or give that needed summary. Gentle prompts throughout the guide section of the program include Warm-up Connections, Thinking about Plot, Quoting & Noting, Keeping a Journal, If I Were ———' Responding to Questions, Using Quotations, Taking a Personal View, Write to Others, & Write a Sequel.
Lawrence Productions, Inc.

Putt-Putt Goes to the Moon.
MS-DOS 3.1 or higher. 386 processor or higher (640k). CD-ROM disk $59.95 (Order no.: R1141). Nonstandard peripherals required: CD-ROM drive. Optimal configuration: 386 processor or higher, MS-DOS 3.1 or higher, 20Mb hard drive, 640k RAM, external speakers or headphones (with sound card) that are Sound Blaster compatible, VGA graphics & adapter, VGA color monitor.
Macintosh (4Mb). (Order no.: R1141). Nonstandard peripherals required: 14" color monitor or larger, CD-ROM drive.
An Adventure Game Designed Especially for Children That Bursts with State-of-the-Art Animation, Dazzling Sound, Hundreds of Clicks-Points & Talking Characters. Logic Puzzles Enhance Problem-Solving Skills, Critical Thinking Skills & Teach Valuable Lessons (Ages 3-8).
Library Video Co.

Putting Pascal to Work. Don Etling. Jul. 1986. Compatible Hardware: IBM PC. Operating System(s) Required: PC-DOS, MS-DOS.
disk $36.95, incl. bk. (ISBN 0-8306-5232-9, Order no.: 5232C).
Intermediate Level Instructional Package Which Deals with the Use of Pascal in the Business World. Highlights Practical Routines, Programs & Procedures That Will Help Eliminate Trial-&-Error Efforts.
TAB Bks.

Puzzle Antics. ZH Computer Corporation Staff et al. Aug. 1995. Items Included: Set up instruction sheet. Customer Support: (503) 639-6863.
Windows 3.0, DOS. IBM PC. $14.95 Klotski (ISBN 1-887783-05-9, Order no.: 5300-4001). Optimal configuration: IBM PC, Windows 3.0 or higher, mouse.
DOS 3.0 or higher. IBM PC (256k). $14.95 Gemstorm (Order no.: 5300-4001). Optimal configuration: IBM PC, 256k RAM, CGA, keyboard.
DOS 3.0 or higher. IBM PC. $14.95 Puzzle Master (Order no.: 5300-4001). Optimal configuration: IBM PC, DOS 3.0 or higher, mouse.
A Compilation of Gem Storm, Puzzle Master & Klotski Which Are All Logic & Skill Games. The Player Completes Crossword Puzzles or Maneuvers Blocks Around a Screen to Increase Problem Solving Ability.
Entertainment Technology.

Puzzle Antics: Gemstorm, Puzzle Master, Klotski. ZH Computer Corp. et al. Jan. 1996. Items Included: Set-up instruction sheet. Customer Support: 310-403-0043.
Klotski: Windows 3.0, DOS; Gemstorm & Puzzle Master: DOS 3.0 or higher. IBM PC. disk $14.95 (ISBN 1-887783-19-9, Order no.: 5200-3001). Optimal configuration: Klotski: IBM PC, Windows 3.0 or higher, mouse; Gemstorm: IBM PC, 256k RAM, CGA, keyboard; Puzzle Master: IBM PC, DOS 3.0 or higher, mouse.
Puzzle Antics Is a Compilation of Gemstorm, Puzzle Master & Klotzki Which Are All Logic & Skill Games. The Player Completes Crossword Puzzles or Maneuvers Around a Screen to Increase Problem Solving Ability.
Entertainment Technology.

Puzzle Master, 8 modules. Version: 1.3. Michael Stoloff. Oct. 1984. Compatible Hardware: TRS-80 Model III, Model 4. Operating System(s) Required: TRSDOS. Language(s): BASIC. Memory Required: 48k. General Requirements: 2 disk drives.
Set. $89.00, incl. manual (ISBN 0-918693-04-7, Order no.: A1021C).
word list disk $19.00 ea., incl. documentation.
Set. $74.00 (Order no.: A1021D).
manual only $15.00 (Order no.: A1021M).
Creates Word Games That Can Be Line Printed or Played at the Keyboard.
Shenandoah Software.

Puzzle Master; Crosswords. Centron Software & Caribbean Software. Jan. 1996. Items Included: Set-up instruction sheet. Customer Support: 310-403-0043.
DOS 3.0 or higher for Puzzle Master; DOS for Crosswords. IBM PC. disk $12.95 (ISBN 1-887783-14-8, Order no.: 5100-2002). Optimal configuration: IBM PC, DOS 3.0 or higher, mouse for Puzzle Master; IBM PC 286 or higher, DOS 3.3 or higher, EGA/VGA/SVGA, mouse for Crosswords.
Crossword Puzzle Program.
Entertainment Technology.

Puzzle Series: Jumblezzz; Crozzzwords; Wordzzzearch. 1987-1991. *Items Included:* Disk(s), user's guide, poster, coloring book, warranty card, swap coupon. *Customer Support:* 90 day unlimited warranty; 800 toll free number, 800-221-7911, 8:00 a.m.-5:00 p.m. Arizona time; Updates $10.
3.5" disk $49.95.
MS-DOS. IBM, Tandy, MS-DOS compatible (128k). disk $49.99 (ISBN 1-55772-089-4, Order no.: 6411). *Nonstandard peripherals required:* VGA or CGA card. *Optimal configuration:* 128k, color monitor, VGA card. *Networks supported:* Velan, Novell, Digicard.
DOS. Apple II, Apple IIe, Apple IIGS, Apple II Plus (48k). disk $49.99 (ISBN 1-55772-274-9, Order no.: 6410). *Optimal configuration:* Apple II, printer, color monitor, 48k. *Networks supported:* Digicard.
Brings Together the Word Attack Skills of Jumblezzz, the Crossword Puzzles of Crozzzwords & the Vocabulary Skill Building Techniques Found in Wordzzzearch. With CHALLENGE UPGRADE, Each Puzzle in This Series Can Be Customized to Fit the Particular Needs & Levels of Individual Players. Ages 9 to Adult.
Mindplay.

PxRay & XRAY/MTD: Source Level Debugger. 1990. *Items Included:* Software, manuals. *Customer Support:* One full year of support is included with each product purchased. Additional support may be purchased yearly at 20% of the end-user price. Support includes hotline phone support, technical mailings & full upgrades.
PDOS. PC, HP, & Sun Hosts, Motorola 680X0-based systems. $2,800.00 to $7,485.00.
Networks supported: Ethernet, Map.
Debugger That Is Based on Microtec Research's X-Ray Debugger. Debugs Fully Optimized C Programs. Supports Non-Intrusive Debugging of Optimized Code Without Adding Bytes to User's Executable Program. XRAY/MTD Available for Debugging Multiple Tasks.
Eyring Corp.

Pyotr Ilyich Tchaikovsky: A Multimedia Music Production. *Items Included:* CD-ROM booklet. *Customer Support:* Free technical support via phone as of release date.
MPC/Windows. 386MHz or higher (4Mb). CD-ROM disk $39.95 (ISBN 1-885784-64-3, Order no.: 1438). *Optimal configuration:* MPC CD-ROM player, S-VGA graphics card (640x480x256 colors) with compatible monitor, MPC compliant sound card, mouse, Windows 3.1 or higher, Windows 95 compatible.
System 7.0 or higher. Macintosh (4Mb). CD-ROM disk $39.95 (ISBN 1-885784-56-2, Order no.: 1568). *Optimal configuration:* CD-ROM drive, color monitor, mouse.
The Great Romantic Composer Pyotr Ilyich Tchaikovsky Is Known for His Moving Musical Creations: "The Nutcracker," "Swan Lake" & the "1812 Overture." Explore Full Orchestral Scores of This Fantastic Composer, Video Clips of His Most Famous Ballets & Fascinating Facts about the Man & His Music.
Technology Dynamics Corp.

Pyotr Ilyich Tchaikovsky: A Multimedia Music Production (Jewel). *Items Included:* CD-ROM booklet. *Customer Support:* Free technical support via phone as of release date.
MPC/Windows. 386 or higher (4Mb). CD-ROM disk $39.95 (ISBN 1-885784-43-0, Order no.: 1431). *Optimal configuration:* MPC CD-ROM player, S-VGA graphics card (640x480x256 colors) with compatible monitor, MPC compliant sound card, mouse, Windows 3.1 or higher, Windows 95 compatible.
System 7.0 or higher. Macintosh (4Mb). *Optimal configuration:* CD-ROM drive, color monitor (256 plus colors), mouse.
The Great Composer Pyotr Ilyich Tchaikovsky Is Known for His Moving Musical Creations: "The Nutcracker," "Swan Lake" & "1812 Overture." Explore Full Orchestral Scores of This Fantastic Composer, Video Clips of His Most Famous Ballets & Fascinating Facts about the Man & His Music...All in Exciting Interactive Detail.
Technology Dynamics Corp.

Pyramid of Doom. *Compatible Hardware:* TI-99/4A.
disk or cassette - contact publisher for price.
Texas Instruments, Personal Productivit.

Pyramids of Gar. *Compatible Hardware:* TRS-80 Model I, Model III, Model 4 with Level II BASIC. *Memory Required:* 48k.
disk $15.95.
Treasure-Maze Game.
Dynacomp, Inc.

Pyro! Steve Brecker & Bill Steinberg. Apr. 1990. *Items Included:* Manual. *Customer Support:* Free, toll call.
System 4.1. Macintosh 512k. 3.5" disk $39.95.
Screen Saver for the Macintosh Version 4.0 Sports Not Only the Traditional "Fireworks" & "Dream of Clocks" But Also Many New Modules & the Ability to Create Personal Screen Saver.
Fifth Generation Systems, Inc.

DataDirect MultiLink/VB. *Version:* 2. 1993. *Items Included:* Single bound manual & help text. *Customer Support:* Free 30-day technical support w/paid programs available, on-site & off-site training.
Microsoft Windows 3.1 or higher, Microsoft Visual Basic. IBM PC/AT, PS/2 & compatibles (4Mb). disk $399.00. *Addl. software required:* Visual Basic. *Optimal configuration:* 386 PC 25 mhz, Windows 3.1, 4Mb.
Client/Server Development Tool That Links Microsoft Visual Basic to over (30) Thirty, PC & SQL Database System. Custom Controls Enable User to Develop Client/Server Applications Without Writing Code. Application Can Be Distributed Royalty Free.
Intersolv.

Q-Art. *Compatible Hardware:* Apple Macintosh. 3.5" disk $34.95.
Clip Art Library with More Than 200 Pictures, Including Animals & Children.
Queue, Inc.

Q-C Compiler. *Compatible Hardware:* IBM PC. *Operating System(s) Required:* CP/M. *Language(s):* C (source code included). *Memory Required:* 56k.
disk $95.00, incl. user's manual.
manual only $20.00.
Compiler for the C Programming Language.
Jeffries Research.

Q-CALC RealTime Spreadsheet. *Items Included:* 1 spiral bound manual. *Customer Support:* Installation support free up to 60 days. Maintenance after 60 days is 25% of product price.
UNIX, XENIX, ULTZIX. Priced from $1,995.00 per CPU.
IBM PC AT & compatibles. Priced from $1,995.00 per CPU.
Realtime Spreadsheet That Can Be Linked to Financial, Process Control & Other On-Line Datafeeds. Data Is Posted Instantly & Automatically, with Automatic Analysis & Alert Messages. Supports Queries to Sybase & Other SQL Databases As Well As Data Export to Other Programs. Contains All Feature of Q-CALC Standard.
Unipress Software, Inc.

Q-Calc Standard. *Compatible Hardware:* IBM PC AT & compatibles; Unix, Xenix, or Ultrix based systems.
IBM PC AT. $450.00.
Unix, Xenix, Ultrix. $750.00 to $4000.00.
Spreadsheet That Supports Lotus 1-2-3 Compatible Files. Includes Macros & 100 Statistical, Financial, & Mathematical Functions. Provides Unix File Permissions & Password Protection. An Optional Graphics Module Enables Users to Create Bar, Pie, Line, X/Y, & Commodity Graphs. Can Produce up to Four Graphs on One Page.
UniPress Software, Inc.

Q-DOS 3. *Version:* 1.4. May 1994. *Compatible Hardware:* IBM. *Operating System(s) Required:* PC-DOS/MS-DOS 2.0 or higher. *Memory Required:* 720k. *General Requirements:* Hard disk highly recommended. *Items Included:* Manual. *Customer Support:* 30-day money back guarantee, maintenance agreement available.
disk $79.00.
Performs DOS Functions (Copy, Erase, Rename & Others) Faster Than DOS. Provides Features Such As: View & Edit Files; Sort Files by Name, Date, Size, Extension or Unsorted Display; Make or Remove Directories from a Pictorial Directory "Map;" View & Alter File Attributes. Finds Files on Hard Disk & Executes Them. Will Work on a Single File or "Tagged" Groups.
GTM Software.

Q-M Secure/Net. *Version:* 1.2. *Items Included:* Example source code; routines for C, Clipper & FoxPro. *Customer Support:* 90 days unlimited warranty, free phone support & optional training seminar (1/2 day). You pay travel expenses.
MS-DOS, Novell Netware 2.15 or higher. IBM 286 or higher (512k). $1500.00. *Addl. software required:* Application which uses QM Secure/Net written by developer. *Optimal configuration:* Netware 3.11. *Networks supported:* Novell Netware.
Allows Developers to Create Applications That Dynamically Allocate Access Rights to Files and/or Directories So That Users Cannot Access Files When Not in the Application.
Q-M Consulting Group, Inc.

Q-Sheet A-V. *Compatible Hardware:* Apple Macintosh Plus, SE, SE/30, II, IIx, IIcx. *Memory Required:* 1000k.
3.5" disk $995.00.
Audio Post-Production Software.
Digidesign, Inc.

Q-Track Corrective Action & Inspection Software. *Version:* 3.002. Apr. 1992. *Items Included:* User's manual. *Customer Support:* Free telephone support, FAX, BBS.
DOS 3.3, Microsoft Windows 3.0 or higher. IBM compatible PC (1Mb). disk $495.00. *Optimal configuration:* 386 PC, 3Mb RAM, 40Mb hard disk. *Networks supported:* All PC's.
Provides a Computerized Method of Internal Corrective Action Reporting. Follows up Customer (or Internal) Complaints by Tracking Defects to the Root Cause. Report Defects by Department, Machine, Customer, or Defect Type. Also Provides Checklists for Internal Audits, As Well As Audit History Reports.
Hertzler Systems, Inc.

QA/S Net Statistical Process Control Software: Full System: Network Version. *Version:* 3.602. Jun. 1993. *Items Included:* Operations manual, installation & customization manual, system tutorial. *Customer Support:* Telephone support, BBS support, FAX support.
DOS 3.1 or higher. IBM PC & compatibles (640K). $4950.00 & up (Order no.: QIBM-309). *Networks supported:* All PC Networks.

Enter, Retrieve, & Analyze SPC Data Simultanously at Workstations Throughout Plant. Contains Unique Security Rights, Passwords, & Configurations Settings for Each User. A Single Database Eliminates the Time Lag Between Data Entry & Analysis, Reducing Response Time to Problem Areas.
Hertzler Systems, Inc.

QA/S Statistical Process Control Software: Defect Management System. Version: 3.602. Jun. 1993. Items Included: Free training operations manual, installation & customization manual, system tutorial. Customer Support: Telephone support, BBS support, FAX support.
DOS 3.1 or higher, Windows 3.0 or higher. IBM compatibles (640K). disk $1295.00 (Order no.: QIBM-001). Networks supported: All PC Networks.
Statistical Process Control System. Features Complete Attribute Data Analysis in an Easy to Use Menu Driven Style. Enter Data Manually Through the Keyboard, or Automatically with Bar Codes Readers. Incorporates a New Defect Management System (DMS), Developed Jointly with Motorola, Inc. System Meets Motorola System Standards.
Hertzler Systems, Inc.

QA/S Statistical Process Control Software: Full System. Version: 3.602. Jun. 1993. Items Included: Free training, operations manual, installation & customization manual, system tutorial. Customer Support: Telephone support, BBS support, FAX support.
DOS 3.1 or higher. IBM PC & compatibles (640K). disk $2295.00 (Order no.: QIBM-009). Networks supported: All PC Networks.
Statistical Process Control System. Features Complete Variable, Short Run & Attribute Data Analysis in an Easy to Use Menu Driven Style. Models & Manipulates Normal As Well As Non-Normal. Data Enter Manually Through the Keyboard, or Automatically with Digital Gages, RS-232 Devices, or Bar Code Readers.
Hertzler Systems, Inc.

QA-S Variable Process Capability System: Short Run & Variable SPC. Version: 3.602. Jun. 1993. Items Included: Operators manual, installation & customization manual, system tutorial, free training. Customer Support: Free telephone support, FAX, BBS.
DOS 3.1 or higher. IBM compatible PC (640k). disk $1295.00 (Order no.: QIBM-008). Networks supported: All PC Networks.
Lets You Track Process Control by Parameters Like Machine, or Lot Number. For Example, See One Control Chart for One CNC with Data from Many Different Parts, with Different Specs. This Chart Tracks Trend, Run Sum, Spec, etc, Across Part Numbers.
Hertzler Systems, Inc.

Q&A. Version: 3.0. Oct. 1986. Compatible Hardware: IBM PC & compatibles, PS/2. Operating System(s) Required: PC-DOS/MS-DOS 2.0 or higher. Memory Required: 512k. General Requirements: 2 disk drives or hard drive. Items Included: 6 disks, 2 manuals. Customer Support: (408) 372-8100.
disk $174.50.
Data Base Manager/Word Processor with Natural Language Processing. Features a Standard Menu-Driven User Interface Combined with a Natural-Language Capability Called the Intelligent Assistant (IA). The IA Understands Requests & Commands in English, Follow-Up Questions, & Multi-Level Queries. Integrates with the Data Base, Permitting Data Changes & Updates to Be Made Directly Through the Natural-Language Interface. The IA Also Features a "Teach" Capability Which Allows User to Expand & Personalize Its Vocabulary. Automatically Transfers in & Uses Data from 1-2-3, dBASE II & III, PFS:FILE; & IBM FILING ASSISTANT.
Symantec Corp.

Q&A Write. Version: 2.0. Compatible Hardware: IBM PC, PS/2. Memory Required: 512k. Items Included: 2 disks & 1 manual. Customer Support: (408) 372-8100.
disk $99.95.
Enhanced Version of Q&A's Word Processor. Includes a Built-In Card File for Customized Mailings Creation (Addresses May Be Imported from dBASE, 1-2-3, Q&A, or Most Other Databases. Also Included Are Column/Row Math, Spelling Checker, & Multi-Column Printing. Enables Users to Import 1-2-3 Spreadsheets & Graphs. Supports Most Printers, Including POSTSCRIPT Compatibles, AboveBoard, & Networks.
Symantec Corp.

Q&A 386. Version: 3.0. May 1987. Compatible Hardware: IBM PC & compatibles, PS/2. Operating System(s) Required: PC-DOS/MS-DOS 2.1 or higher. Memory Required: 640k. General Requirements: 2 disk drives. Items Included: 6 disks & 3 manuals. Customer Support: (408) 372-8100.
5-1/4 or 3-1/2" disks $349.00.
Specially Optimized Version of Q&A for 386 Computers. Takes Advantage of the 80386 Microprocessor Features. Includes Improved Performance (up to 35% Faster), Aboveboard Support & Smaller Code Size.
Symantec Corp.

QB Plus. Version: 1.0. Aug. 1991. Items Included: spiral bound manual. Customer Support: Free telephone support.
DOS. IBM PC or compatible (320k). disk $79.00. Addl. software required: Microsoft Quickbasic or Basic 7 PDS.
Unique Add-In Expands Capabilities of QB & QBX Environment. Allows Any Compile & Link Options to be Specified. Features Super B Memory Viewer, Execution Profiling (Timing), Keyboard Macros. Shell from QB to Other Programs with Full DOS Memory Available.
Crescent Software.

QC Plot Statistical Process Control. Items Included: Bound manual. Customer Support: Free hotline - no time limit; 30 day limited warranty; updates are $5/disk plus S&H.
MS-DOS 2.0 or higher. IBM & compatibles (128k). disk $169.95. Nonstandard peripherals required: CGA (or equivalent).
Apple (48k). disk $169.95.
Provides a Comprehensive Statistical Quality Control System for Overseeing Production & Fabrication. Menu-Driven. Automatically Produces the Tables of Critical Values & Charts, with Titles & Axis Labelling. There Is Complete Data Entry & Editing. User Can Print, Merge, Transform, & Search (with Select) Data Files. Trial, Revised Control Charts, & Parameters Are Set Easily & Quickly. Plot Control Charts, Frequency Distributions, Bar Graphs, Polygons, & Distribution Curve Overlays.
Dynacomp, Inc.

QC Validator. Version: 1.1. James O. Westgard. Mar. 1993. Items Included: Spiral-bound manual, tutorial. Customer Support: 90 day warranty, free telephone customer support.
Windows 3.1 or higher. IBM (2Mb). $500.00 single user; $1500.00 network (ISBN 1-886958-02-5). Nonstandard peripherals required: VGA interface card, printer supported by Windows. Addl. software required: Windows. Optimal configuration: TrueType fonts activated; approx. 500k hard disk memory. Networks supported: Novell.
Helps Medical Laboratories & Device Manufacturers Select QC Procedures to Assure the Quality Required by CLIA PT Criteria. Users Can Improve Their Cost-Effectiveness by Using Unique Graphic Tools: Power Functions, OPSpecs Charts, & Critical-Error Graphs. This PC Program Allows Users to Select Control Rules in Minutes, Not Hours.
Westgard Quality Corp.

QCal. 1984. Compatible Hardware: IBM PC & compatibles, NEC-APC with a graphics device (plotter or CRT). Operating System(s) Required: CP/M, CP/M-86, MS-DOS, PC-DOS. Language(s): FORTRAN. Memory Required: 32k. Items Included: Disk, manual. Customer Support: One year warranty.
disk $295.00.
Device-Independent Graphics Support Package for Engineering or Scientific Application Programmers or Consultants Requiring Drawing, Maps, Graphs, etc. on an Arbitrary Graphic Device. Emulates the Industry-Standard CALCOMP-Compatible FORTRAN Calls.
Diacad Assocs.

QCARS: Quick Computer Assisted Repair System. Items Included: Manual. Customer Support: 4 months phone support.
DOS 3.1 or higher. IBM PC or compatible (640k). disk $495.00, single store, ,795.00, multi-store.
3, 5 & 6 Month Personalized Postcards; Annual State Safety Inspection Reminder Postcards; Vehicle Service History; Customer Lists (Retail & Fleet); Uses Generic Postcards or Those Provided by Franchise Operations (i.e. Jiffy Lube); Bulk Mail Stamp Can Be Printed on Postcards; Next Oil Change Date Is Computed & Available for Review; Supports Individually Owned & Fleet Vehicles; Fleet Service Reminder Reports. 1 Hour Training Required.
Miramar, Ltd.

QCPAC Statistical Quality Control on the IBM PC. Zimmerman. Jul. 1985. Compatible Hardware: IBM PC. Memory Required: 64k. General Requirements: 2 disk drives. Items Included: 168 page manual & diskettes.
disk $210.00 (ISBN 0-8247-7430-2).
Collection of Applied Quality Control Programs Which Are Designed for Quality Control Managers & Technicians Resolving Such On-the-Job Issues As Acceptance Sampling of Lots of Materials, Process Control for Both Attribute & Variable Type Measurements, Identifying Differences Due to Controllable Variables. Features Step-by-Step Guidelines to Using the IBM PC, Reducing the Time Required to Perform Quality Analysis; Easy-to-Use Quality Control Programs, Requiring Minimal Skill of the User; & Menu-Driven Programs, Eliminating Costly Calculating Errors. Covers Control Charts for Variables; Xbar, Sigma, & Range, Control Charts for Attributes; Percent Defective Charts with Variable Subgroup Sample Size & Average Defects per Unit of Output, & U Charts.
Marcel Dekker, Inc.

QCRYPT: CP/M File Decipher & Encipher Program. Operating System(s) Required: CP/M, CP/M-86. Language(s): MACRO-80. Memory Required: 32k. Items Included: Disk, documentation. Customer Support: One year warranty.
disk $65.00.
Can Be Used As a Command in Any CP/M System to Encipher/Decipher Any Specified File. User Can Protect Sensitive Business Data & Records, Development Work, etc. Allows User to Choose from over Seven Trillion Unique Keys.

Files May Always Be Deciphered by Any Other CP/M System Running QCRYPT Provided the Key Is Known.
Diacad Assocs.

QEMM 7. *Version:* 7.01. *Compatible Hardware:* 80386-based PCs & higher; includes Pentium support. *Operating System(s) Required:* PC-DOS/MS-DOS 2.0 or higher. *Memory Required:* 1024k. *Customer Support:* 3-mo. from date of first call to technical support.
$99.95.
update $19.95.
Memory Manager Capable of Maximizing the System's Use of Memory. Loads Memory-Resident Applications into Expanded Memory. Also, Will Transform Extended Memory into LIM 4.0 Expanded Memory, Speeding up BIOS Operations & Graphics Cards by Copying Slow ROM into Fast RAM. Occupies Only 1.5k of Standard DOS Memory.
Quarterdeck Office Systems.

QHVAC: Quick Commercial HVAC Loads. *Items Included:* Manual. *Customer Support:* Free toll free telephone support.
IBM PC & compatibles (256k). disk $395.00.
Calculates the Maximum Heating & Cooling Loads for Commercial Buildings. QHVAC Is the Quick Version od Elite Software's Full Fledged Commercial HVAC Loads Program.
Elite Software Development, Inc.

QI Analyst: Statistical Process Control Software.
386-based computer or higher (2Mb). Contact publisher for price. *Optimal configuration:* 386-based computer or higher, 2Mb RAM minimum, 4Mb recommended, hard disk space, Microsoft Windows 3.1 or higher, VGA monitor or higher.
Combines Windows' Ease of Use with Data Management, Statistics, Reporting & SPC Charts to Give You an Integrated, Easy-to-Use Quality Improvement Software Package. Helps You Improve Processes, Cut Waste, Reduce Non-Conformance & Meet Customers' & Management's Requirements.
SPSS, Inc.

Qix. *Compatible Hardware:* Atari XL/XE. ROM cartridge $6.95 (Order no.: CXL4027).
Atari Corp.

QM Filer for FoxPro: FoxPro File Manager. *Version:* 2.0. Jun. 1992. *Items Included:* Sample data files, API function to open/index data files. *Customer Support:* 90 day unlimited warranty. MS-DOS. IBM 286 or higher (640k). disk $99.00. *Addl. software required:* FoxPro 2.0. *Optimal configuration:* 486, 8Mb RAM.
Allows Developers to Easily Track Database Files & Their Indices. The API Allows the Developer to Open a File Knowing Only Its Module & Alian. Full Path Independence Allows Files to Be Moved to New Driver or Dirs Without Re-Coding. Full Data Dictionary Also Included with Field Level Comments & Prescriptions.
Q-M Consulting Group, Inc.

The QM Library for FoxPro. *Version:* 3.0. Jun. 1992. *Items Included:* Sample source code, documentation, training seminars available. *Customer Support:* 90 day unlimited warranty. MS-DOS. IBM 286 or higher (640k). disk $359.00. *Addl. software required:* FoxPro 2.0. *Optimal configuration:* 486 with 8Mb.
A FoxPro 2.0 Library. Routines Include: Progress Thermometer, Memory Boxes, List Boxes, Error Tracking, Multi-User Routines, Temp File Management, Printing Routines, Browse Baud Search Utility Using a PLB. Other PLB Routines Include: Is Menu Pulled down?, Buffered Low Level File Read from Bottom up, Use Arrow Keys to Scroll & Browse or Memo Windows.
Q-M Consulting Group, Inc.

QMAPS: Premium Memory Management for 386-486. *Version:* 2.01. Scott Daniel et al. Sep. 1991. *Items Included:* 3.5" & 5.25" media; User Guide; Registration card; Network license registration card. *Customer Support:* Free customer support 9-6, M-F, 714-754-4017.
DOS. 386-486 (1Mb). $129.95. *Optimal configuration:* hard disk is preferred.
A Complete Memory Management System for 386-486 Computers. Recovers Shadow RAM on 22 Different "Chipsets" for Highest Overall Memory. Supports EMS Standards, XMS Specifications & Upper Memory. Easy, "Smart" Installation Program. Includes QUADTOOLS-RAMDisk, Disk Cache, Spooler. Windows 3.0 & DOS 5.0 compatible.
Quadtel Corp.

QRS Music Rolls. *Compatible Hardware:* Commodore Amiga.
3.5" disk $19.95.
Demo Disk of Sample Songs.
Micro W Distributing, Inc.

QRZ! Ham Radio. *Customer Support:* All of our products are unconditionally guaranteed.
Windows, Unix. CD-ROM disk $29.95 (Order no.: HAM). *Nonstandard peripherals required:* CD-ROM drive.
U.S. & Canadian Call Signs Plus Related Programs.
Walnut Creek CDRom.

QSL Manager. *Compatible Hardware:* TRS-80 Model I, Model III. *Memory Required:* 32k.
disk $24.95 (Order no.: 0151RD).
Ham Radio Operators Can Make & Review Log Entries, Search Files & Print Summary Reports.
Instant Software, Inc.

Quadralien & Stargoose. May 1989. *Compatible Hardware:* IBM PC, PC XT, PX AT, PS/2 & true compatibles. *Memory Required:* 384k. *General Requirements:* Quadrilien - CGA, MCGA or CGA; Stargoose - CGA, EGA. *Customer Support:* Unlimited free support: (617) 494-1220, (617) 494-1221.
disk $39.95.
In Quadralien, Find & Destroy the Evil Quadralien Who've Infested ASTRA & Bring the Reactor Back Under Control. But You Must Hurry, the Temperature Is Rising Toward a Meltdown. In Stargoose, As the New Top Secret Fighter Codename Stargoose, You Must Steal the Power Crystals from the Eight Cities on the Planet Nom Through a Maze of Danger & Adventure.
Spinnaker Software Corp.

Quality Assurance Reports. *Items Included:* Manuals, training exercises, quick reference guide.
IBM PC, XT, AT, & compatibles; PS/2. contact publisher for price.
Program To Determine How Well Care Plans Have Been Working.
Beechwood Software.

Quality Clip Art Collection. WEKA Publishing. disk $149.00, incl. text (ISBN 0-929321-08-1).
Collection of Pictures on Disk & Text. Basework 68/92 Page Supplements.
WEKA Publishing, Inc.

Quality Control & Industrial Experiments. *Version:* 10.0. (Professional Ser.). 1989. *Compatible Hardware:* Apple Macintosh, IBM PC & compatibles. *Memory Required:* 512k. *Items Included:* Disks, book, program instructions. *Customer Support:* Telephone.
disk $145.00 (ISBN 0-920387-22-5).
All Popular Types of Quality Control Charts Have Been Implemented (with Constant & Variable Sample Sizes), & the Chart Presentations Conform to the ASQC Standards. The Statistical Background of Statistical Quality Control Is Discussed in Detail, & All Information Relevant to the Preparation of the Charts Is Provided. The Book & the Programs Go Much Farther Than the Usual Quality Control Description & Treat the Use of Experiments for Quality Control Sampling, in General & Particular. A Large Section on the Analysis of Variance & the Design of Experiments Is Included; in Particular, the Taguchi Methods Applying Orthogonal Arrays Are Described, As Is the Use of Experiments in Parameter Design & Tolerance Design. Cover All the Traditional Methods of Quality Control As Well As the Latest Techniques.
Lionheart Pr., Inc.

Quality Control Charts: QC Charts. Wan-Lee Cheng & Kin Chung Siv. Jan. 1986. *Compatible Hardware:* Apple II, IBM PC with graphics card. *Operating System(s) Required:* Apple DOS 3.3, PC-DOS 2.0. *Memory Required:* 48k. *General Requirements:* 2 disk drives, printer.
disk $120.00.
Data Management System That Gives User Complete Control over Process Data. Package Includes a Manual with Full Discussion of Control Charts, Central Limit Theorem, & Control Limits.
Kern International, Inc.

Quality Control of Molybdenum-99 Technetium-99m Generator Eluate. Ann M. Steves. 1996. *Customer Support:* Phone support by calling 1-800-748-7734 or 916-441-2881.
DOX 3.1 or higher. IBM or compatibles (512k). disk $150.00 (Order no.: MIS9023). *Nonstandard peripherals required:* VGA.
Tutorial defines radionuclidic & chemical purity, describes the methods used to determine Mo-99 & aluminum contamination in Tc-99 eluate, defines the regulatory limits for these contaminants & describes the effect of these contaminants onpatient radiation exposure & the biodistribution of radiopharmaceuticals.
Educational Software Concepts, Inc.

Quality Control of Technetium-99m Labeled Radiopharmaceuticals. Ann M. Steves. 1996. *Customer Support:* Phone support by calling 1-800-748-7734 or 913-441-2881.
DOS 3.1 or higher. IBM or compatibles (512K). disk $150.00 (Order no.: MIS9025).
Defines Radiochemical purity & describes chromatography as a method to determine the radiochemical purity of a radiopharmaceutical.
Educational Software Concepts, Inc.

Quality Plus: Customer Service Management & Warranty Control. *Version:* 2.0. 1988. *Items Included:* Documentation & training included in price. *Customer Support:* Annual support agreements are available & include product enhancements & telephone support. Price varies depending on modules.
DOS 3.x or higher or Novell Netware 2.1 or higher. IBM or compatibles (640k). Single user $3000.00; Multi-user $4000.00. *Optimal configuration:* IBM or compatible; 640k; 40Mb or higher; color monitor; wide carriage printer/parallel port. *Networks supported:* Novell Netware.
Provides Complete Control of Walk-Through & Customer Service Requests, Subcontractor Work Orders & Homeowner Communications. Detailed Tracking of Customer Service Requests; Automatic Selection & Creation of Work Order; Summary & Detail Aging Reports; Detailed Homeowner History; Standard and/or Customized Letters to Homeowners & Subcontractors; Defect Analysis by Model, Tract, Subcontractor, etc.
Execudata.

TITLE INDEX

QUANT IX Portfolio Evaluator. Version: 4.5. Nov. 1992. Compatible Hardware: IBM PC XT, PC AT, true PC compatibles, PS/2. Operating System(s) Required: MS-DOS 2.1 or higher. Memory Required: 640k. Customer Support: Free unlimited support.
disk $129.00.
Offers: Six Security Valuation Models for Stock Selection; Ratio-Analysis Mode; a Diversification Risk Index; the Ability to Ask "What If" Questions; Security Cross Referencing; Total Portfolio Accounting; 13 Client Presentable Reports; Single or Multiple Portfolio Management; Pull down Menu of Operation. Built-In Communications Program Allows Data Retrieval from Warner Computer System's Database; Also Able to Download from CompuServe.
QUANT IX Software.

Quantech. Version: 2.1. Jan. 1996.
Windows. Contact publisher for price.
CD-ROM disk Contact publisher for price.
Windows-Based Retirement Plan Administration Software. A Number of New Features & Enhancements Have Been Added to the System, Including Insurance Subsystem, Data Collection Module, Further Enhancements to the Client Management System (CMS), Improved Handling of Loans, 70-1/2 Calculations/Minimum Distributions, Forfeiture Suspense Accounts, Hardship Calculations & Distributions, Sole Proprietary Partnership Calculations, & Improved Performance in Report Generation.
Corbel & Co.

Quantity Estimation. 1989. Compatible Hardware: IBM PC & compatibles. Operating System(s) Required: PC-DOS/MS-DOS. Language(s): QBASIC. Customer Support: Telephone assistance.
disk $47.00, incl. user guide.
disk $127.00, incl. source code.
Allows the User to Determine the Volume of Material (+ Cut or - Fill) Between a Set of Original Cross-Sections & an Overlaid Final Set of Cross-Sections. Outputs End Areas at Each Station & Volumes (Cut, Fill & Cumulative) Between Stations. A Second Program Is Also Provided to Check Cross-Section Data Files for User-Input Errors. The Check Program Can Also Be Used for Data Files Being Prepared for the EARTHWORK Program.
Systek, Inc. (Mississippi).

QuarkXPress. Version: 3.2. 1993.
Mac DOS 6.0, Windows 3.0, 386 or higher. Macintosh SE, Plus, II (2Mb). 3.5" disk $895.00. Nonstandard peripherals required: Hard disk, LaserWriter 5.2 or 6.0 printer.
Page Makeup Program with Word Processing Features & an 80,000-Word Check Spelling Dictionary. Features Precise Placement of Frames of Text & Graphics, Automatic Wraparound Frames, & Reflowing of Text When the Layout Changes. Supports Automatic Hyphenation, Kerning, Tracking Control, & Horizontal Scaling of Characters. Support for Phantom Colors, & Color Separation for Both Spot & Process Color.
Quark, Inc.

QuarterBack. Jan. 1988. Compatible Hardware: Commodore Amiga.
3.5" disk $69.95.
Backs up to or Restores from Floppy Disks, Streaming Tape, the Konica 10.7Mb, High-Density Floppy Drive, the Bernoulli Drive or Any Amiga DOS-Compatible Device. The System Can Back up or Restore a Whole Hard Disk, Selected Sub-Directories & Individual Files, by Date or by Archive. If Two Floppy Devices Are Available, It Will Automatically Switch Between the Two.
Central Coast Software.

Quarterback Attack. Items Included: Instruction manual. Customer Support: Free Telephone support.
DOS/Windows 95. IBM & compatibles (8Mb). Contact publisher for price. Nonstandard peripherals required: CD-ROM drive.
MAC. Macintosh (4Mb). Contact publisher for price. Nonstandard peripherals required: CD-ROM drive.
Saturn. Sega Saturn. Contact publisher for price.
3DO. 3DO Multiplayer. Contact publisher for price.
Digital Pictures, Inc.

Quarterback Tools. George Chamberlain. Aug. 1990. Items Included: User's guide & a product registration business reply card. Customer Support: 90 day unlimited warranty.
Amiga DOS 1.2 or higher. Amiga (any model) (512k). 3.5" disk $89.95.
Maximizes the Speed & Reliability of Amiga Hard Disks & Floppy Disks by Repositioning Files to Optimum Locations of the Disk. It Eliminates File Fragmentation, Consolidates Disk Free Space, Recovers Deleted Files Easily & Safely, & "Unformats" Disks Formatted by Mistake.
Central Coast Software.

Quarterhorse Gold Edition. Ronald D. Jones. 1983. Compatible Hardware: Apple; Commodore; IBM; TRS-80 Model I, Model III, Color Computer. Operating System(s) Required: CP/M. Memory Required: 64k.
disk $129.95 ea.
Apple. (ISBN 1-55604-042-3, Order no.: Q001).
CP/M. (ISBN 1-55604-043-1, Order no.: Q001).
IBM. (ISBN 1-55604-046-6, Order no.: Q001).
disk or cassette $129.95 ea.
Commodore. (ISBN 1-55604-044-X, Order no.: Q001).
Color Computer. (ISBN 1-55604-045-8, Order no.: Q001).
Model I & Model III. (ISBN 1-55604-047-4, Order no.: Q001).
Designed for the "Close" Finishes Involved in This Type of Race. Designed Around Intricate "Speed" Ratings, but Includes All Handicapping Variables. Can Be Fine Tuned to Area & Track.
Professor Jones Professional Handicapping Systems.

Quasimodo - Air Support. (Double-Play Ser.). Jon Atack & Rich Carr. Compatible Hardware: Atari 400, 800, XL series.
disk $24.95 (Order no.: ATDSK-2421).
Help QUASIMODO Recover the Stolen Jewels While He Stones Soldiers & Dodges Deadly Bats. In AIR SUPPORT You Choose Between Arcade or Strategy Play, Select the Difficulty, Terrain, Enemy Strength & Weapons, & Then Assume Command of an Arsenal of Choppers & Robots.
Broderbund Software, Inc.

Quasimodo - Warriors of Zypar. (Double-Play Ser.). Mark Bigelow & Joe Vierra. Compatible Hardware: Commodore 64 with joystick.
disk $24.95 (Order no.: COMDSK-3461).
Help QUASIMODO Recover the Stolen Jewels As He Stones Soldiers & Dodges Deadly Bats. WARRIORS OF ZYPAR Is a Two-Player 3-D Action Game Set in a Futuristic Arena.
Broderbund Software, Inc.

Quattro. Compatible Hardware: Compaq; IBM PC & compatibles, PS/2. General Requirements: Hard disk recommended.
disk $247.50.
Spreadsheet Featuring File & Macro Language Compatibility with LOTUS 1-2-3. Provides a Variety of Graphs Which Can Be Printed Directly from the Spreadsheet, Without Leaving the Program; Also Provides POSTSCRIPT Support. Features Fast Recalc by Recalculating Only the Cells Affected by Modified Formulas or Data. In Addition to 1-2-3 Files, It Can Also Load/Save ASCII, PARADOX, & dBASE Files. Not Copy Protected.
Borland International, Inc.

QUATTRO PRO. Version: 3.0. Mar. 1991. MS-DOS/PC-DOS 3.3 or higher. IBM PC/XT/AT/PS2 & compatibles. disk $495.00 (ISBN 0-87524-230-8).
Fully Integrated WYSIWYG Displays Documents as They'll Print. WYSIWYG Zoom Command Reduces or Enlarges Screen Display. Adjustable Row Heights. Snap-To Grid & Object Alignment Tools for Easier Graphic Layout. 24 Slide Show Transition Effects for Professional Presentations. Sound F/X Technology Adds Sound to Slide Shows Without Special Equipment. Print-To-Fit Automatically Prints Large Spreadsheets on One Page.
Borland International, Inc.

QuattroPro in Your Classroom: A Student Introduction. Version: 5.0. Steve Corder et al. 1996. Items Included: MS-DOS data disk; reproducible book, 145 pp.; 1 student activity text, 120 pp. Additional copies of activity text available for $10.95; 10 or more copies, each $9.95. Customer Support: Call 1-800-341-6094 for free technical assistance, 30 day approval policy, money back guarantee.
MS-DOS. disk $79.95 (ISBN 0-8251-2783-1, Order no.: 0-27831). Addl. software required: QuattroPro 5.0.
Students Manipulate Files on the Data Disk According to Guided Self-Paced Instruction the Activity Text. Students Learn How to Move Within the Program, Make Notebooks, & Create Budget Spreadsheets. They Progress to Advanced Spreadsheet Techniques & Graphing, Sorting, & Functions, & to Creating & Using Databases.
J. Weston Walch Pub.

Qued-M. Version: 2.5. Compatible Hardware: Apple Macintosh. Memory Required: 512k. Items Included: Manual & disk. Customer Support: Free telephone technical support.
3.5" disk $149.00.
Text Editor of Choice for Programmers & Writers, the Newest Version Offers a Powerful Macro Language, File Comparison Feature, Code Modules & Extended Keyboard Support.
Nisus Software, Inc.

Queers in History Classic. Version: 1.1. Keith Stern. Feb. 1993. Items Included: Manual. Customer Support: Free telephone support.
DOS. IBM XT or higher (384k). disk $14.95 (ISBN 0-9642091-0-1, Order no.: 1). Optimal configuration: DOS 3.1 or higher.
Macintosh 6.0.5. Apple (1Mb). 3.5" disk $14.95 (ISBN 0-9642091-1-X, Order no.: 2). Addl. software required: Hypercard or Stack Runner. Optimal configuration: 1Mb RAM, 2Mb hard disk, System 6.0.5 or higher.
A Database of Historical Gay, Lesbian, & Bisexual People & a Program to Display Them.
Quistory, Inc.

Queers in History Deluxe. Version: 2.0. Keith Stern. Dec. 1993. Items Included: Manual. Customer Support: Free telephone support.
Windows 3.1. IBM 386 or higher (2048k). disk $34.95 (ISBN 0-9642091-2-8, Order no.: 3). Optimal configuration: DOS 3.1, SVGA color monitor, Windows 3.1, 2Mb RAM, 2Mb hard disk.
MAC 6.0.5. Apple (2Mb). 3.5" disk $34.95 (ISBN 0-9642091-3-6, Order no.: 4). Addl. software required: Hypercard 2.1 or Stack Runner. Optimal configuration: 1Mb RAM, 2Mb hard disk.

A Database of Historical Gay, Lesbian, & Bisexual People & a Program to Access Them. The Deluxe Edition Also Includes Queeries, the Gay/Lesbian Trivia Game.
Quistory, Inc.

Query Condex 10x1 - D Ramdrive. May 1990. *Items Included:* Diskettes, instruction book. PC-DOS/MS-DOS 2.0 or higher (1Mb Ram Drive). IBM & compatibles (540k). disk $19.95 (ISBN 0-945541-08-2, Order no.: 082).
Enhancement Condex (Concept Index) Reader For Ram Drives. 10 Line Answers - D Drive.
CSY Publishing, Inc.

Query Condex 10x1-C. May 1990. *Items Included:* Diskettes, instruction book. PC-DOS/MS-DOS 2.0 or higher. IBM & compatibles (540k). disk $19.95 (ISBN 0-945541-04-X, Order no.: 04X).
Structured Body of Data on Diskette (or Other Storage Medium) Along with a Query Algorithm So That the Data May Be Interrogated in Plain Language & Elicit the Best Possible Answer from the Data, Also in Plain Language - on Any Subject - on a Computer. Replacement Condex (Concept Index) Reader with 10 Line Answers C Drive Normally Packaged with Each Condex.
CSY Publishing, Inc.

Query Condex 20x-D. May 1990. *Items Included:* Diskettes, instruction book. PC-DOS/MS-DOS 2.0 or higher. IBM & compatibles (540k). disk $19.95 (ISBN 0-945541-05-8, Order no.: 058).
Replacement Condex (Concept Index) Reader - 20 Line Answers C Drive (Normally Packaged with Each Condex).
CSY Publishing, Inc.

Query Condex 20x1 - D Ram Drive. May 1990. *Items Included:* Diskettes, instruction book. PC-DOS/MS-DOS 2.0 or higher (1Mb Ram Drive). IBM & compatibles (540k). disk $19.95 (ISBN 0-945541-09-0, Order no.: 090).
Enhancement Condex (Concept Index) Reader For Ram Drives. 20 Line Answers. D Drive.
CSY Publishing, Inc.

Query: Opinion Surveys & Questionnaires. *Items Included:* Bound manual. *Customer Support:* Free hotline - no time limit; 30 day limited warranty; updates are $5/disk plus S&H. MS-DOS 3.3 or higher. IBM & compatibles (512k). disk $99.95. *Nonstandard peripherals required:* Monochrome or color graphics; IBM Prowriter- or Epson-compatible printer.
Interactive System for Designing & Administering Multiple Choice Opinion Surveys, Questionnaires, & Other Probes Involving Questions & Answers. Master Question/Answer Data Sets May Be Designed, & Specific Questionnaires Built from That Data. The Questionnaire May Then Be Presented on Disk (or Printed) for Testing. If the Disk Approach Is Used, the Results May Also Be Returned on Disk & Automatically Tabulated/Summarized in Report & Bar Graph Formats. Includes Extensive Assembling & Editing Features to Speed the Preparation of Your Questionnaire.
Dynacomp, Inc.

Quest. *Version:* 1.0. Aug. 1991. *Items Included:* Complete documentation.
DOS 3.0 or higher, Window 3.0 or higher, OS/2. 386 (2Mb). $495.00. *Networks supported:* Novell Netware, IBM OS/2 LAN Server, MS LAN Manager, Banyan Vines, 3 Com, any NetBios LAN.
A Graphical Data Access, Query & Reporting Tool for Use from Microsoft Windows Desktops. It Allows End Users, with no Knowledge of SQL, to Access Data from Corporate Databases. It Works Against Gupta's Own SQLBase Server, DBZ, Oracle, SQL Server & OS/2 EE Database Manager. It Comes with a Powerful Report Writer & Allows Users to Put Corporate SQL Data into Popular Programs Such As Excel, Microsoft Word & Aldus PageMaker. Is a Companion Product to SQLWindows, But Can Also Be Used As a Stand-Alone Product Since It Comes with Single User SQLBase Engine.
Gupta Technologies, Inc.

The Quest. *Operating System(s) Required:* CP/M. contact publisher for price.
Infoquest.

The Quest for Varsar. *Version:* 1.3.1. Sep. 1988. *Compatible Hardware:* Apple II series, IIgs. *Memory Required:* Apple II series 64k, Apple IIgs 256k.
Apple II series. 3.5" disk $24.95 (ISBN 1-55616-017-8).
Apple II series.
Apple IIgs. 3.5" disk $24.95 (ISBN 1-55616-015-1).
Adventure Game.
DAR Systems International.

Quest of the Space Beagle, 2 disks. *Compatible Hardware:* Atari 800/XL/XE, Commodore 64/128. *Memory Required:* 48k. *General Requirements:* Joystick; Jupiter Mission 1999 recommended.
$35.00 (Order no.: 47493).
Sequel to JUPITER MISSION 1999. You Are the Sole Survivor of That Mission & Before You Can Get Back Home You Must Help the Faunians Defend Themselves Against the Barbaric Gentuzians. If You Defeat Them, Then You Become Emperor & the Faunians Dump You into the Labyrinths of Kamera. If You Find Your Way Out, You Not Only Prove Your Emperorship, but You Are Also Free to Get Back Home. Then, If You Can Overcome Those Pesky Temporal Perturbations That Get in the Way Any Time You Try to Make a Hyperspace Jump, You Might Live to See Your Old Friends.
Avalon Hill Game Co., The Microcomputer Games Div.

Quick-Art Borders & Vignettes. *Version:* 1.1. *Compatible Hardware:* Commodore Amiga, 500, 1000, 2000. *Items Included:* Two resolutions of illustrations, coil bound manual with samples. *Customer Support:* Technical assistance provided by telephone: (206)733-8342.
3.5" disk $39.95.
Over 160 Monochrome Bitmap "Brush" Illustrations (Borders & Vignettes) Easy to Insert into Popular Paint, Desktop Publishing & Word Processing Applications. Especially Suitable for Newsletters, Memos, Cards, Worksheets, Name Tags, Invitations & Small Signs. Manual Includes Sample Printouts.
CLASSIC CONCEPTS Futureware.

Quick Base. *Version:* 3.0. Jan. 1987. *Compatible Hardware:* IBM PC, PC XT, PC AT, PS/2 & compatibles. *Operating System(s) Required:* PC-DOS 2.X-3.X. *Language(s):* BASIC, Assembler. *Memory Required:* 256k. *General Requirements:* Printer.
disk $99.00 (Order no.: HG11).
Filing & Reporting System. Uses Are Client Files, Inventory, Mail Lists, Customer Prospects, Bill of Materials, etc. Report Select & Sort to 15 Levels.
Hawkeye Grafix.

Quick C Compiler. *Compatible Hardware:* IBM PC & compatibles. *Memory Required:* 440k. disk $99.00.
C Compiler Featuring Assembler Access, Integrated Linker, MAKE, Source Debugger, Integrated Editor, Compiler Wildcards & Subdirectories, Screen/Cursor Control, DOS Service Functions & Low Level Keyboard Input. Compilation Is an Added-Step Process. Supports Math Coprocessor & Technical Hot Line & Is MASM & LINK-Compatible.
Microsoft Pr.

Quick Card (Apple). *Version:* Apple. 1987. Apple; Pascal. Apple (64k). $234.95 (Order no.: B92488A). *Nonstandard peripherals required:* 80-column display, two floppy disk drives, printer.
A Program for Printing Catalog Cards, Spine Labels, Book Card Labels, & Book Pocket Labels. The Information for the Main Entry Card Is Typed, & the Program Automatically Prints the Shelflist Card. Author Card, Title Card, All Subject Cards, Additional Cards As Appropriate, & Labels. Apple Quick Data Can Be Used by Apple Circulation Plus; Therefore, Rekeying of Information Is not Required.
Follett Software Co.

Quick Card MS-DOS. *Version:* MS-DOS. 1987. Pascal. MS-DOS compatibles (256k). disk $234.95 (Order no.: B92488B). *Nonstandard peripherals required:* One floppy disk drive with a hard disk drive, or 2 floppy disk drives, printer.
A Program for Printing Catalog Cards, Spine Labels, Book Card Labels, & Book Pocket Labels. The Information for the Main Entry Card Is Typed, & the Program Automatically Prints the Shelflist Card, Author Card, Title Card, All Subject Cards, Additional Cards As Appropriate, & Labels. Quick Card MS-DOS Data Is not Formatted for Use with Circulation Plus MS-DOS Version 7.
Follett Software Co.

Quick Ceph. *Version:* 9.0. *Compatible Hardware:* Apple Macintosh SE, Macintosh II, SE/30. *General Requirements:* Mac compatible printer.
Quick Ceph I - Apple Macintosh SE,. 3.5" disk $1500.00.
Quick Ceph II - Macintosh II, SE/30. 3.5" disk $2500.00.
Digitizer $1100.00.
Cephalometric Analysis.
Orthodontic Processing.

Quick Check with Accounts Payable & Receivable. *Version:* 96.1. (Money Management Ser.). Chuck Atkinson. 1995. *Compatible Hardware:* IBM PC & compatibles. *Operating System(s) Required:* PC-DOS/MS-DOS. *Language(s):* CB-86, Btrieve File Manager. *Memory Required:* 128k.
$49.95 (ISBN 0-917081-02-1).
Bookkeeping, Checking, & Accounts Payable System That Prints Checks & Sends Them in Window Envelopes, & Keeps Track of Income & Expenses. Sends Statements & Prints Reports on Accounts Receivable. Fast & Easy.
CAP Automation.

Quick-Copy. Nicholas A. Romanc. 1984. *Compatible Hardware:* Apple II, II+, IIe, IIc. *Operating System(s) Required:* ProDOS, Apple DOS 3.3. *Memory Required:* 48k.
disk $29.95 (Order no.: 920).
Nikrom Technical Products, Inc.

Quick CSS. *Version:* 3.1. May 1992. *Customer Support:* Technical support.
DOS/VSE. PC's AT & higher (640k). disk $295.00. *Optimal configuration:* DOS Version 5.0 or higher. *Networks supported:* All.
Includes Basic Statistics, Nonparametrics, Crosstabulation, Multiple Regression, General ANOVA/ANCOVA/MANOVA & More. Over 50 Types of Graphs Integrated Within all Analyses. Data Management Features Include Fast Spreadsheet Editor, Relational Joining of

TITLE INDEX

Files, Nested Sorting, Powerful Transformations, & Comprehensive Reporting Options. Import/Export of Many File Formats.
StatSoft, Inc.

Quick DIRT. *Version:* 2.07. Jun. 1986. *Compatible Hardware:* IBM PC & compatibles. *Operating System(s) Required:* MS-DOS 3.1 or higher. *Language(s):* Basic. *Memory Required:* 640k. *General Requirements:* 2 disk drives, CGA or EGA card. *Customer Support:* Mail, in-house support, telephone support, training classes.
disk $2495.00 (Order no.: QD).
Cut/Fill Estimating Package. Options Include 3-D Graphics. Integrates to QuickEST Products.
Constructive Computing.

Quick Docket. Dec. 1987. *Operating System(s) Required:* PC-DOS/MS-DOS. *Memory Required:* 256k. *General Requirements:* Hard disk, printer.
disk $39.95 (ISBN 0-938793-01-2).
Docket & Meeting Scheduler with Conflict Resolution. Includes a Rolodex Type Module to Record & Recall Phone Numbers & Addresses. Menu Driven.
DataCompatible.

Quick*Locate. Aug. 1993. *Items Included:* Disks, manual. *Customer Support:* Product information available over phone, toll free; technical support provided, unlimited over telephone; 30 day money back guarantte.
DOS 3.1 or higher. IBM & compatibles (640k). $340.00; updates $95.00; auto updates $55.00 ea.; updates every 6 mos. *Optimal configuration:* 386/486 - 4Mb space free on hard drive. *Networks supported:* Lantastic.
Program That Allows for the Look up of the Closest Location to a Zip Code or Area Code/Prefix. Unlimited Amount of Records in Each Location File Is Allowed & User Defines the Number of Locations Searched for (1-20). Also Looks up Zip Code Information & Area/Code-Prefix Information.
Mailer's Software.

Quick-Plan: Executive Project Planning System. *Version:* 4.0. Sep. 1984. *Compatible Hardware:* Data General Desktop; DEC Rainbow; HP 9807A the Integral PC; IBM PC, PC AT, PC XT, PCjr; Wang PC. *Operating System(s) Required:* MS-DOS. *Language(s):* Pascal. *Memory Required:* 384k. *General Requirements:* 2 disk drives, printer.
disk $995.00.
Provides the Decision Support Means via a Personal Computer for Control of the Planning Process. Uses the Network-Based, Critical Path Method (CPM) of Modeling to Control Project Time, Costs & Resource Expenditures So As to Produce an Optimum Plan.
Mitchell Management Systems.

Quick Quant Plus. *Version:* 3.0. 1991. *Items Included:* Operating manual.
IBM PC & compatibles (256k). 3.5" or 5.25" disk $495.00.
Macintosh Plus or higher (256k). 3.5" disk $495.00.
Series of Programs That Solve a Variety of Problems Using Quantitative Methods. Included Are Linear Programming, Forecasting, Simulation & Decision Trees. Student Versions Are Also Available.
Alamo Publishing.

QUICK QUOTE: HVAC Sales Tool. *Version:* 2.0. May 1990. *Items Included:* Complete manual. *Customer Support:* Free toll-free telephone support; optional updates available at nominal charge.
MS-DOS. IBM PC & compatible (256k). disk $395.00.

Professional, Exceptionally Accurate Quotes & Complete Sales Agreements for the Sale of HVAC Systems & Related Items. It Virtually Eliminates Pricing Errors & Expensive, Time-Consuming Manually Prepared Proposals. Because Product Greatly Speeds the Quoting Process, Contractors Can Quote on More Projects & Thus Create More Sales Opportunities.
Elite Software Development, Inc.

Quick Reference Guide: Marc Coding & Tagging Booklet. 1994. *Customer Support:* 30 day no risk guarantee.
IBM. disk $4.95 (ISBN 0-927875-58-6, Order no.: 7460).
A Quick Reference Guide When Using Marc Records. Common Tags & Subfields Are Listed along with the Correct Punctuation Which Follows the AACR 2 Cataloging Rules. A List of All Valid Marc Tags Is Also Included.
Winnebago Software Co.

Quick Register. Chuck Atkinson Programs. *Operating System(s) Required:* CP/M-86. *Memory Required:* 320k. *General Requirements:* Printer.
$250.00 (Order no.: QR).
Texas Instruments, Personal Productivit.

Quick Ship. *Version:* 6.0. Jan. 1993. *Items Included:* 1 manual. *Customer Support:* 90 days free, $39.00 yearly - rate update.
6.03 & higher. Macintosh (1Mb). 3.5" disk $99.00 (ISBN 1-879815-04-4, Order no.: SS/). *Optimal configuration:* Macintosh, 6.03 & higher, 1Mb, printer.
Quick Calc Shipping Charges Calculator: Minimum, Maximum, Percentage Handling Charge; Fixed Amount Handling Charge; Finds UPS USA Rate & Zone from the Zip Code Entered. Full UPS Manifest Systems: UPS Ground & Air USA; UPS Ground & Air Canada; UPS International Air, Fast "C-Tree" Filing System, Prints C.O.D. Tags (Dot Matrix Printer), Prints UPS Manifest & Summary (DM or Laser Printers), Keeps Client Shipping History, Prints Shipping Labels (DM or Laser Printers), Tracks C.O.D. Collections, Customer/Client Data Base, Imports Manifest Information from Other Programs, Creates International Waybills. Multiuser, Cross Platform Versions of Program & Related Modules (Invoicing, Inventory, Accounts Receivable, etc.) Are Available.
Shopkeeper Software International, Inc.

Quick STATISTICA/Mac. *Version:* 3. Aug. 1992. *Customer Support:* Technical support.
Macintosh System 6.X, 7.X. All Macintosh (1Mb). 3.5" disk $295.00. *Networks supported:* All.
Fully Integrated Statistics, Graphics, & Data Management System with Many Graphs Integrated with All Analyses. Full 2D & 3D Graphing Abilities, Including On-Screen Customization via MACDRAW-Like Tools. Data Management Features Include Fast Spreadsheet Editor, Merging/Splitting Files, Nested Sorting, Transformations.
StatSoft, Inc.

Quick STATISTICA/w. *Version:* 4.1. Mar. 1993. *Customer Support:* Technical support.
Windows 3.X. Microcomputer, PC's 286 & higher (2Mb). disk $495.00. *Optimal configuration:* 4Mb RAM, Windows 3.1. *Networks supported:* Novell, Banyan-Vines, Lantastic.
Fully Integrated Statistics, Graphics, & Data Management System Which Completely Supports the Conventions of the Windows Environment (TT-Fonts, DDE, Clipboard Support, etc.). Offers Hundreds of 2D & 3D Graphs. On-Screen Customization Options Give the User Complete Control over Graph Specifications.
StatSoft, Inc.

QUICK STATISTICA

Quick STATISTICA for D... *Items Included:* 1 loose-... Quick Start manual. C... technical support by p... money back guarantee; se... available.
MS-DOS (Version 3.1 or higher), DR DOS. ... XT & compatibles with hard drive & 3 1/2" or 5 1/4" floppy drive (640k). Contact publisher for price (ISBN 1-884233-03-1). *Optimal configuration:* 386 SX/DX-25Mhz; MS-DOS 5.0 or higher; 640k RAM (expanded memory recommended); EGA or higher. *Networks supported:* Novell, Lantastic, Banyan Vines, & Others.
Includes Basic Statistics, Nonparametrics, Crosstabulation, Multiple Regression, General ANOVA/ANCOVA/MANOVA & More. Over 50 Types of Graphs Integrated Within All Analyses. Data Management Features Include Fast Spreadsheet Editor, Relational Joining of Files, Nested Sorting, Powerful Transformations, & Comprehensive Reporting Options. Import/Export of Many File Formats.
StatSoft, Inc.

Quick STATISTICA for the Macintosh. *Version:* 4.0. 1993. *Items Included:* 1 bound manual, Quick Start Manual. *Customer Support:* Free technical support by phone, Fax, or mail; 14 day money back guarantee; service contract available.
System 6.05. MAC Plus or higher (1Mb). Contact publisher for price (ISBN 1-884233-09-0). *Optimal configuration:* System 7, 4Mb RAM, color monitor, (co-processor not required). *Networks supported:* Yes.
System 6.05. Any Macintosh with a math coprocessor & hard drive (1Mb). Contact publisher for price. *Optimal configuration:* Macintosh with FPU; System 7; hard drive; 4Mb RAM; color monitor. *Networks supported:* Yes.
Fully Integrated Statistics, Graphics, & Data Management System with Many Graphs Integrated with All Analyses. Along with Full 2D & 3D Graphing Abilities (Including On-Screen Customization via MACDRAW-Like Tools), a Selection of Statistical Analyses Is Offered. Other Features Include Spreadsheet Editor, Merging/Splitting Files, Nested Sorting, Transformations.
StatSoft, Inc.

Quick STATISTICA for the Macintosh. *Version:* 4.1. 1994. *Items Included:* 1 bound manual, Quick Start Manual. *Customer Support:* Free technical support by phone, Fax, or mail; 14 day money back guarantee; service contract available.
System 6.0.5. Mac Plus or higher (1Mb). 3.5" disk $395.00 (ISBN 1-884233-31-7). *Optimal configuration:* Mac IIs; System 7; 4Mb RAM; color monitor; (co-processor not required). *Networks supported:* Yes.
A Fully Integrated Statistics, Graphics, & Data Management System with Many Graphs Integrated with All Analyses. Along with Full 2D & 3D Graphing Abilities, (Including On-Screen Customization via MacDraw-Like Tools) a Selection of Statistical Analyses Is Offered. Other Features Include Spreadsheet Editor, Merging/Splitting Files, Nested Sorting, Transformations.
StatSoft, Inc.

Quick STATISTICA for Windows. *Version:* 4.5. 1993. *Items Included:* 2 bound manuals, Quick Reference manual. *Customer Support:* Free technical support by phone, Fax, or mail; 14 day money back guarantee; service contract available.
MS-Windows 3.0 or higher (version 3.1 recommended). 386DX with hard drive, 3 1/2" or 5 1/4" high density floppy drive (2Mb).

...ntact publisher for price (ISBN 1-884233-
...6-6). *Optimal configuration:* 386DX-25Mhz;
MS-Windows 3.1 (or higher); 4Mb RAM;
VGA; mouse. *Networks supported:* Novell,
Lantastic, Banyan Vines, Windows for
Workgroups, & Others.
*Fully Integrated Statistics, Graphics, & Data
Management System Which Completely Supports
MS Windows Conventions (TT-Font, DDE,
Clipboard, etc.). Offers a Selection of Statistical
Analyses, Database Management & Hundreds of
2D & 3D Graphs. On-Screen Customization
Options Allow Complete Control over Graph
Specifications.*
StatSoft, Inc.

Quick STATISTICA for Windows. *Version:* 5.0.
1994. *Items Included:* 2 bound manuals,
Addendum, Quick Reference. *Customer Support:*
Free technical support by phone, Fax, or mail; 14
day money back guarantee; service contract
available.
MS Windows 3.1. 386 DX with hard drive, 3
1/2" or 5 1/4" high density floppy drive
(4Mb). disk $495.00 (ISBN 1-884233-34-1).
Optimal configuration: 386 DX-25MHz;
MSWindows 3.1 (or higher); 4Mb RAM; VGA;
mouse. *Networks supported:* Novell, Lantastic,
Banyan Vines, Windows for Workgroups; &
others.
*A Fully Integrated Statistics, Graphics, & Data
Management System Which Completely Supports
MS Windows Conventions (TT-Font, DDE, OLE,
Clipboard, etc.). Offers a Selection of Statistical
Analyses, Database Management & Hundreds of
2D & 3D Graphs. On-Screen Customization
Options Allow Complete Control over Graph
Specifications.*
StatSoft, Inc.

QuickAccount. *Version:* 2.61. Jun. 1985.
Compatible Hardware: AT&T; Compaq; IBM PC,
PC XT, PC AT; IT&T; Sperry; Zenith. *Operating
System(s) Required:* PC-DOS/MS-DOS.
Language(s): BASIC. *Memory Required:* 640k.
General Requirements: 10Mb. *Items Included:*
Free demo disk. *Customer Support:* Mail, in-
house, telephone support, training classes.
disk $1000.00 to $7500.00.
*Construction Accounting System with Fully
Integrated Documentation, Training, Operator
Help, & Backup/Restore Functions. Includes
Payroll, Billing/Accounts Receivable, Job Costing,
General Ledger, Accounts Payable, & Inventory.
T&M Billing Programs Can Be Run As Stand-
Alone Systems or They Can Be Integrated with
Each Other.*
Constructive Computing.

**QuickBASIC: Programming Techniques &
Library Development.** Namir C. Shammas.
Operating System(s) Required: MS-DOS.
book & disk $34.95 (ISBN 1-55851-004-4).
book only $19.95 (ISBN 1-55851-003-6).
*Introduces Programmers to the New & Enhanced
Programming Features of QuickBASIC 4.0 &
Provides the Tools Needed to Exploit This
Environment. Included Are an Orientation to the
Features of QuickBASIC & a Discussion on
Creating Subroutines, Functions, & Libraries to
Permit More Structured Programming. Programs
& Subroutines Are Available on Disk with Full
Source Code.*
M & T Bks.

QuickBeam: Finite Analysis of Beams.
Compatible Hardware: IBM PC & compatibles.
Operating System(s) Required: MS-DOS, PC-
DOS. *Language(s):* BASIC & FORTRAN.
Memory Required: 512k. *Items Included:*
Complete documentation & example problems.
Customer Support: Extended Support Program
(12 mos.) 100.00.
$495.00.
*Finite Analysis of almost any beam configuration.
Includes Deflection & Stresses & Structure Screen
Graphic Plots. Most Solutions in 5 Seconds.*
Engineering Software Co.

QuickCalc Loan Analyzer. Simple Soft.
Operating System(s) Required: MS-DOS, CP/M,
SuperCalc, VisiCalc or PeachCalc. *Memory
Required:* 64k.
$99.95.
Texas Instruments, Personal Productivit.

QuickColumn. *Items Included:* Full documentation
- 3 ring binder.
MS-DOS 2.0 or higher. IBM PC, XT, AT or
compatible (512k). $295.00. *Optimal
configuration:* Color monitor/graphics card,
Epson Dot Matrix printer. *Networks supported:*
BASIC source code not available.
*Column Design & Analysis of Columns with
Uniaxial or Biaxial Bending & Loads. It Can Be
Integrated with a Materials Library Data Base
(Shape) So That the Desired Section Properties
Can Be Immediately Accessed & Transferred into
the Analysis. A Design Library Saves Column
Specifications for Later Recall & Use. Graphics of
Your Design Are Available to Simplify Problem
Analysis.*
Engineering Software Co.

Quicken. *Version:* 2. *Compatible Hardware:* Apple
IIe with extended 80-column text card, IIc, IIgs,
Macintosh; IBM PC, PC AT, PS/2. *Operating
System(s) Required:* PC-DOS 2.0 or higher.
Memory Required: Apple 128k, IBM 256,
Macintosh 512k. *General Requirements:* 2 disk
drives recommended.
3-1/2" or 5-1/4" disk $49.95, incl. manual &
free technical support.
*Enables Users to Write Checks, Keep Financial
Records, Track Income & Expenses, Budget, &
Manage the Cash Flow. Features Macros & On-
Line Help. For Business Users, It Provides Special
Sections Covering Payables, Receivables, Cash
Flow Forecasting, Payroll, Petty Cash Control, &
Job, Client, & Property Bookkeeping. Exports
Data & Reports in ASCII; Also Exports in LOTUS
Format with Optional Transfer Utility. Not Copy
Protected.*
Intuit.

Quicken CheckArt. Jun. 1988. *Compatible
Hardware:* Apple Macintosh. *Memory Required:*
512k. *General Requirements:* Printer.
3.5" disk $19.95.
*Graphics Library for Quicken Software Which
Contains over One Hundred Check Graphics to
Be Used with QUICKEN CHECKS.*
Intuit.

Quicken for the Macintosh. *Version:* 1.5.
Compatible Hardware: Apple Macintosh.
Memory Required: 512k.
3.5" disk $59.95.
*Single-Entry Bookkeeping Program Which Writes
& Prints Checks Automatically on Either Laser or
Dot Matrix Printers. When Amount of Check Is
Entered, 14 Automatic Bookkeeping Steps Are
Performed, Producing the Check. Automatically
Writes Recurring Checks While Simultaneously
Updating Financial Records. Manages Unlimited
Number of Bank Accounts, Transactions, &
Income/Expense Categories for Amounts up to
$10 Million. Generates Financial Reports Which
Include Income & Expenses, P&L, Budget vs.
Actual, Taxable Income/Deductions, Rental
Property/Job Cost, Accounts Payable, Cash
Flow/Cash Flow/Cash Needs & Payroll Taxes.*
Intuit.

Quicken Tax Reform Analyzer. 1987.
Compatible Hardware: Apple IIe, IIc, IIgs; IBM
PC, PC XT, PC AT & compatibles, PS/2.
Operating System(s) Required:
PC-DOS/MS-DOS 2.0 or higher. *Memory
Required:* 125k. *General Requirements:* Printer.
IBM. 3.5" or 5.25" disk $29.95.
Apple. disk $29.95.
*Calculates Taxes & Allows Tax Planning for
Quicken Software Users. Calculates Taxes for
1987, 1988, & 1989. Handles the 1040 &
Schedules A, B, D, E, Plus Both New W-4 Forms.*
Intuit.

Quicken Transfer Utility. 1987. *Compatible
Hardware:* IBM PC, PC XT, PC AT &
compatibles, PS/2. *Operating System(s)
Required:* PC-DOS/MS-DOS 2.0 or higher.
Memory Required: 256k. *General Requirements:*
Printer.
3.5" or 5.25" disk $19.95.
*Utility Disk for Quicken Software Which Transfers
Data from Quicken's Check Register to
Spreadsheets in Lotus 1-2-3, Symphony, or
Compatible Programs. Consolidates Data from
Different Quicken Accounts into a Single Lotus
Spreadsheet.*
Intuit.

QuickEST. *Version:* 3.5. Mar. 1983. *Compatible
Hardware:* AT&T; Compaq; IBM PC, PC XT, PC
AT; Sperry. *Operating System(s) Required:*
MS-DOS. *Language(s):* BASIC & Assembler.
Memory Required: 640k. *General Requirements:*
10Mb hard disk recommended. *Customer
Support:* Mail, in-house, telephone support,
training classes.
disk $995.00 to $5495.00.
write for info.
*Application Software System Developed by
Contractors for Contractors, Subcontractors &
Professional Estimators. Allows the Estimator to
Assemble the Elements of Labor, Material,
Equipment, Suppliers, Subcontractors, Overhead
& Profit to Produce an Estimated Price.*
Constructive Computing.

QuickEST. *Version:* 2.3. Nov. 1985. *Compatible
Hardware:* IBM PC, PC AT, PC XT &
compatibles. *Operating System(s) Required:*
PC-DOS, MS-DOS. *Language(s):* FORTRAN.
Memory Required: 512k. *General Requirements:*
Printer, plotter.
disk $1500.00 (Order no.: QUICKEST).
*Self-Contained Estimation Program Which Can
Rapidly Give Average Grade & Reserve
Estimates. The Program Works in 3-D Space &
Can Be Run in Plan View or Section. It Limits the
Extent of Estimation by User-Defined Blocks,
Search Ellipses & Grade Cut-Offs. For Each
Layer & the Total Deposit, the Program Will
Report Average Grade, Total Volume, Average
Vertical Continuity Factor, & Sampling Factor.*
Geostat Systems International, Inc. (GSII).

QuickEST/CAD. Jun. 1987. *Compatible
Hardware:* IBM PC & compatibles. *Operating
System(s) Required:* MS-DOS 3.1 or higher.
Language(s): BASIC. *Memory Required:* 640k.
General Requirements: 2 disk drives or hard disk,
printer, CGA or EGA card. *Customer Support:*
Mail, in-house, telephone, training classes.
disk $1495.00 (Order no.: QEC).
*Interfaces to Automatically Extract Quantity,
Length, & Area from AutoCAD Drawings to
QuickEST System. Provides Estimates While
Design Is in Progress.*
Constructive Computing.

QUICKEY: CTC Data Entry-Micro. *Version:* 2.0.
Mar. 1986. *Compatible Hardware:* IBM PC, PC
XT, PC AT. *Operating System(s) Required:*
PC-DOS 2.1-3.1, MS-DOS 2.1. *Memory*

TITLE INDEX

Required: 256k. General Requirements: 2 disk drives.
disk $295.00.
Production Data Entry System. Data Can Be Collected, Stored, & Verified on a Microcomputer Disk for Transmission to a Host Computer & Batch Update. Interfaces with All Popular Mainframes, Including Burroughs, DEC, Hewlett-Packard, Honeywell, IBM, & Prime. Designed to Replace Keypunch or "Key-to-Disk" Systems Such As the IBM 3741-2. The Micro Keyboard May Be Set Like a 3741 Keyboard or the Standard Micro Keyboard. Program Allows 15 Accumulations for Totals, Range Checking, Verifications, & Check Digit Verify along with Production Statistics.
Core Technology Corp.

QuicKeys. Version: 3.0. Donald Brown. Compatible Hardware: Macintosh Plus or higher. Items Included: QK install disks, extras disk, full set of manuals. Customer Support: Free to registered users.
3.5" disk $169.00.
Macro Program. Allows Users to Assign Keys for Repetitive Text, Programs, Commands, Desk Accessories, etc. Also Works Within Programs; Users Can Assign Command Keys for Such Operations As Save, Print, & Typeface Selection.
CE Software, Inc.

QuickFrame Design Package. Jan. 1988. Compatible Hardware: IBM PC, PC XT & compatibles. Operating System(s) Required: PC-DOS/MS-DOS. Memory Required: 640k. General Requirements: CGA Card. Items Included: Complete documentation & tutorial. Customer Support: Extended Support Program (12 mos.).
disk Basic QuickFrame Analysis $495.00.
disk QuickFrame Design Package (3D) $1995.00.
disk QuickFrame Design Package (2D) $1295.00.
Designed to Provide Complete Solutions - 2D or 3D Structures, up to 1000 Joints & 1200 Members, up to 20 Different Types of Beams/Trusses, Plates Concentrated Forces & Moments at Any Joint. Includes Materials Library with All AISC Steel Specifications. Any Other Materials May Be Added As Well. Unknown Section Properties Are Also Calculated. CAD Interface available.
Engineering Software Co.

QuickHelp. Version: 1.2. Compatible Hardware: IBM PC & compatibles. Memory Required: 22k.
disk $59.00.
Features a Complete Help Message System That Lets the User Add Instant Pop-Up Help to Any Application. Also Includes Indexed File Access for Fast Retrieval, User-Defined Hot Key & Customized Colors.
Crescent Software.

QuickLetter. Version: 2.0 (System 7 compatible). Compatible Hardware: Apple Macintosh.
$49.95.
Word Processor with Special Features for Writing Letters. Can Be Used As an Application or As a Desk Accessory. Writing Features Include: Spelling Checker, Address Book, Automatic Envelope Addressing, Page Preview with Automatic Vertical Centering of the Letter on the Page. Ability to Mix Different Fonts, Styles, & Sizes.
Working Software, Inc.

QuickLink Gold. Version: 1.1. Jan. 1993. Items Included: 1 spiral bound manual. Customer Support: 60 day free phone; BBS.
Microsoft Windows 3.0 or higher (running in Standard or Enhanced mode). IBM. disk $99.95. Nonstandard peripherals required: Class 1 or Class 2 Fax/Modem.
Integrated Data Communication/Fax Application with Optical Character Recognition for Windows. Acts As a Print Device for Windows, Making It Easy to Send True WYSIWYG Faxes from Within Any Windows Application. Additional Features Like the QuickLink GOLD ToolBar Provide Easy Access to Commonly Used Features, & the ModemMonitor Emulates the Status LED's Normally Seen on External Modems.
Smith Micro Software, Inc.

QuickLock. Sep. 1989. Customer Support: Available for registered owners.
MAC-DOS (512k). disk $59.95 volume purchase discounts available.
Password Protects User Screen & Network Connections with Touch of Key or Mouse Stroke. Prevents Others from Viewing or Altering User's Work, but Allows Background Processing. Darkens Screen, Protecting It from Phosphor "Burn-In". Remains Active Even if System Is Restarted. Automatic Lockout Feature Can Be Invoked After Preselected Period of Inactivity.
Kent Marsh Ltd.

QuickLookups. Version: 6.0. Mike Nudd. Customer Support: 90 days free, yearly rate about $39.00.
System 7. Macintosh Plus or higher. 3.5" disk $49.00.
UPS Shipping Program. Designed for the Business That Does UPS Shipping but Averages Less Than the 20 or So Packages a Day Needed to Justify Using a Fully UPS Manifest System. Works As a Fast Shipping Charges Calculator That Can Work As a Desk Accessory under System 7. Handles Both Domestic & International UPS Shipping.
Shopkeeper Software.

QuickMail. Version: 2.6. Compatible Hardware: Apple Macintosh, DOS, Windows. General Requirements: Hard disk. Items Included: Getting started manual, 11 disks, user manuals & quick reference guides. Customer Support: Free to registered users.
Per Ten Users. $599.00, 10-Pak; $399.00, 5-Pak; $199.00, single user pak; $99.00, single user add-on.
Electronic Mail.
CE Software, Inc.

QuickMap. General Requirements: HyperCard. Macintosh Plus or higher. 3.5" disk $99.00.
Geographic Analysis & Mapping Program.
Cartesia Software.

QuickMenu. Version: 3.0. Compatible Hardware: IBM PC & compatibles. Memory Required: 256k.
disk $59.00.
Features up to Nine Commands per Menu; an Unlimited Number of Menus; a Full Screen Command Editor & Context-Sensitive Help. File Import & Export Capability Lets the User Bring in Existing Batch Files or Create New Ones. Also Allows-User Defined Color Schemes & Background Patterns for Each Menu.
Crescent Software.

QuickPak Professional. Version: 4.0. Compatible Hardware: IBM PC & compatibles. Language(s): Assembly, BASIC. Memory Required: 256k. Items Included: Slipcase/binder/assembly tutor.
disk $199.00.
Comprehensive Set of Extensions & Tools for Use with Compiled BASIC. Includes All the Routines for QuickPak Plus a Complete Collection of Financial & Mathematical Functions & Video Services That Automatically Accommodate Any of the Text Screen Modes & Display Sizes. Also Included Are a Pop-Up Calculator, Calendar, ASCII Chart, & Dialog Box. Version also Available for use with Visual Basic.
Crescent Software.

QUICKSCREEN

QuickPak Scientific. Version: 3.0. Compatible Hardware: IBM PC & compatibles. Language(s): BASIC. Memory Required: 256k.
disk $149.00.
Functions & Subprograms Written for Scientists & Engineers. Routines Utilize Algorithms Organized into Seven Major Categories: Linear Algebraic, Ordinary Differential, Numerical Integration, Numerical Differentiation, Root Finding, Minimization & Maximization & Curve Fitting, Complex Numbers, Statistics & Fast Fourier Transforms.
Crescent Software.

QuickPie 2.1. Version: 2.1. Kendall J. Redburn. Aug. 1989. Items Included: Manual, clip art (custom) collection on disk for making custom pie charts. Customer Support: Unlimited warranty.
Macintosh 512KE & higher (512k). disk $55.00.
Creates Pie Charts with Many Controls Over Appearance & Style as a Desk Accessory. Allows Graphics to Be Used to Make the Pies.
BugByte, Inc,.

Quickplot/Quickstudy. Version: 4.06. 1994. Compatible Hardware: IBM PC & compatibles. Operating System(s) Required: PC-DOS/MS-DOS. Language(s): Compiled BASIC. Memory Required: 640k. General Requirements: IBM-CGA, EGA, Hercules or VGA card. Customer Support: Monday-Friday 8:00 a.m. to 11:30 p.m. EST; Saturday: 9:00 a.m. to 1:00 p.m. EST.
$89.00 Requires purchase of QuickTrieve.
Aids the Stock or Commodity Trader to Graphically Review & Analyze Market Information. 23 Technical Indicators Include: RSI; Moving Averages; Stochastics; CCI; Directional Movement Index; Probable-Direction Index (PDI); CSI-Trend; CSI-Stop; On-Balance-Volume; Call-Put Ratio; MACD; Detrend; Spread-Ratio of Two Fields & More. QuickPlot, QuickStudy & QuickTrieve Are Registered Trademarks of Commodity Systems, Inc.
Commodity Systems, Inc. (CSI).

QuickREPORT. Jun. 1986. Customer Support: Mail, in-house, telephone support, training classes.
PC-DOS/MS-DOS. AT&T: COMPAQ: IBM PC, PC XT, PC AT; IT&T SPERRY: ZENITH (640K-10Mb). disk $995.00.
General Purpose Report Writing System for the Construction Industry. Create & Output Custom Reports & Exchange Files from Data Stored in Other Systems. Operates As a Stand-Alone System, or Interfaces with Constructive Computing's Advanced Accounting System, & Estimating System.
Constructive Computing.

QuickScreen. Version: 4.0. Compatible Hardware: IBM PC & compatibles. Language(s): Assembly, BASIC. Memory Required: 256k. General Requirements: recommended 512.
disk $149.00.
Screen Builder. Includes All the Routines to Display Screens & Enter & Edit Input Fields.
Crescent Software.

QuickScreen. (ADVANTAGE Library Ser.). Compatible Hardware: IBM PC, PC XT, PC AT, 3270 PC. Memory Required: 256k. General Requirements: Hard disk.
contact publisher for price.
Productivity Tool for Application Developers. Supports Full 3270 Keyboard Emulation, Allowing Users to Easily Migrate from 3270 Terminal Applications to PCs. Supports Both Transaction Processing and/or Conventional Programming. The Editor Allows Screens to Be Painted & Tested in Real Time & Then Compiled into Object Modules by the Built-In Screen

Compiler. The Editor Can Directly Execute Screen Objects, Without Linking, in Order to Test or Modify Any Pre-Compiled Screen. In Addition, Screen Colors Are End-User Selectable. Package Contains a 45-Minute Tutorial Disk Covering All the Screen Painter's Features & a Reference Manual. Supports LATTICE & MICROSOFT C COMPILERS.
Lifeboat Assocs.

Quicksearch. Customer Support: 800-929-8117 (customer service).
MS-DOS. IBM/PS2. disk $99.99 (ISBN 0-87007-085-1).
Designed for Real Estate Offices That Are Not Able to Computerize Their Property Offerings or Are Not Subscribing to a Computerized Multiple Listing Service. Allows Noncomputer Personnel to Update Real Estate Files & Search for Residential or Commercial Properties. It Is Not Designed to Take the Place of Listings Sheets, but to Help Them be Used More Effectively. Designed to Create a Customer File. An Amortization Table is Provided.
SourceView Software International.

Quicksilver. Version: 1.3R. Memory Required: 512k. Customer Support: 1 hour free technical support, extended support available; private & public bulletin board.
disk $599.00.
Quicksilver/SQL $795.00.
Quicksilver/UNIX $995.00.
EXE Compiler for dBXL & dBASE III Plus, Creating Independently Executable Program in Three Steps. It Includes the R & R Code Generator for Integrating Report Capability. Automatically Finds All Files in an Application That Need to be Compiled. A Special Linker Links Object-Code Files Into Directly Executable Code. After Debugging & Compilation, Program Performance is Enhanced with Quicksilver's Optimizer, Converting the Compiled Application to 8086 Assembly Code. Fully Compatible with the Language Extensions Offered by dBXL. Specify Disk Size.
WordTech Systems, Inc.

Quicksilver Diamond Release. Operating System(s) Required: PC-DOS 3.1.
disk $599.00.
dBASE Compiler Which Features Windowing, User-Defined Functions, Native Code Compiling, Graph & Chart Capabilities, Ability to Export Graphs & Data to a Format That Works Directly with Many Desktop Publishing Packages, Multidimensional Arrays, & Multitasking.
WordTech Systems, Inc.

QuickTime: The CD 1992. Aug. 1992.
Macintosh System 6.0.8, 13" monitor (256 or higher colors) (4Mb). CD-ROM disk $29.95 (ISBN 1-57047-008-1, Order no.: QT92-MAC). Nonstandard peripherals required: CD-ROM drive with a sustained transfer rate of 150Kbps or higher.
Winners of the 1992 QuickTime Film Festival in San Francisco, California. Nearly 500 Megabytes of Digital Movies Selected As the Best of the Year by a Distinguished Panel of Computer Scientists & Film Industry Computer Experts. Categories Include: Animation, Commercial, Documentary, Education, Experimental, Micromovies, Narrative, Apple Entries, & More.
Sumeria, Inc.

QuickTime: The CD 1992-1993. Jun. 1993.
Windows 3.1. PC Compatible CPU with 386/33MHz or higher processor (4Mb). CD-ROM disk $64.95 (ISBN 1-57047-010-3, Order no.: QT92/93-WIN). Nonstandard peripherals required: VGA plus display (256 or higher colors at 640x480 resolution); CD-ROM drive with a sustained transfer rate of 150 Kbps or higher.
Winners of the 1992 & 1993 International QuickTime Film Festival in San Francisco, California. This Two-CD ROM Set of Digital Movies Was Selected As the Best of the Year, by a Distinguished Panel of Computer Scientists & Film Industry Computer Experts, Including for the First Time, Entries from Japan. Categories Include: Animation, Commercial, Documentary, Education, Experimental, Interactive, Micro-Movies, Narrative, & Others. See What the Best in the World Are up to Now.
Sumeria, Inc.

QuickTime: The CD 1993. May 1993.
Macintosh System 6.0.8, 13" monitor (256 or higher colors) (4Mb). CD-ROM disk $49.95 (ISBN 1-57047-009-X, Order no.: QT93-MAC). Nonstandard peripherals required: CD-ROM drive with a sustained transfer rate of 150Kbps or higher.
Winners of the 1993 International QuickTime Film Festival in San Francisco, California. This Two-CD ROM Set of Digital Movies Was Selected by a Distinguished Panel of Computer Scientists & Film Industry Computer Experts As the Best of the Year, Including for the First Time, Entries from Japan. Categories Include: Animation, Commercial, Documentary, Education, Experimental, Interactive, Micro-Movies, Narrative, & Others. See What the Best in the World Are up to Now.
Sumeria, Inc.

QuickTime: The CD 1994. Jun. 1993.
Mac: System 7.0, 13-inch monitor (256 or better colors) (4Mb). CD-ROM disk $49.95 (ISBN 1-57047-012-X, Order no.: QT94). Nonstandard peripherals required: CD-ROM drive (double-speed recommended) with sustained transfer rate of 150 Kbps or higher.
CPU with 486/33 MHz or higher processor (6Mb). CD-ROM disk $49.95. Nonstandard peripherals required: CD-ROM drive (double-speed recommended) with sustained transfer rate of 150 Kbps or higher.
This Edition Contains the Winners of the Annual International QuickTime Film Festival Held in Tokyo & San Francisco. This CD-ROM Ships with All Software Necessary to Run the CD-ROM on Your Macintosh, Power PC, or Windows Computers. Categories Include: Humor, Narrative, Animation, Education, Interactive, Music Video, Commercial, Micromovies, Experimental & Documentaries. The Latest Addition to Your Collection of Digital Video from the World's Best QuickTime Movie Producers.
Sumeria, Inc.

QuickTrieve/QuickManager. Version: 4.06. 1994. Compatible Hardware: IBM PC & compatibles. Language(s): Compiled BASIC. Memory Required: 640k. General Requirements: IBM-Hayes Smart modem or compatible; one hard disk & one floppy disk drive; DOS 2.0 or higher. Items Included: Three program disks, manual, data bank information. Customer Support: Monday-Friday: 8:00 a.m. to 11:30 p.m. EST; Saturday: 9:00 a.m. to 1:00 p.m..
$39.00 with the CSI Data Retrieval or $99.00 for Unrestricted use.
Data Retrieval Module of QUICKTRIEVE. Retrieves Daily Updates & Historical Data on Commodity Options, Mutual Funds, Stock & Stock Index Options, Commodity Price, Volume, & Open Interest. Data Acquired by Phone or Disk. Builds a Database. Date Manipulation Module of QUICKMANAGER Gives CSI Subscribers the Ability to Manipulate, List, Print, Move, Create, Initialize, Condense, Delete, & Edit Own Private Data Bank. QUICKPLOT Offers the Capability of Producing Charts along with a Few Technical Indicators. QuickTrieve & QuickManager Are Registered Trademarks of Commodity Systems, Inc.
Commodity Systems, Inc. (CSI).

QuickVerse Bible Concordance. Version: 2.0. Items Included: Printed manual. Customer Support: Free technical support.
DOS 2.0 or higher (512k). IBM or compatible. $49.00. Optimal configuration: IBM or compatible with 512k RAM, 2 floppy disk drives (or a hard disk) & any printer.
$69.00. Optimal configuration: MacIntosh with a minimum of 512k & any disk drive configuration.
Tool for General Bible Study & In-Depth Bible Research. Puts the Complete Text of the King James, New King James, New International, or Revised Standard Version New Revised Standard, Hebrew & Greek Transliteration & the Living Bible of the Bible at Users Fingertips.
Parsons Technology.

QuickVerse Bible Reference Collection. Parsons Technology. Jun. 1994.
3.5" disk Contact publisher for price (ISBN 1-57264-036-7).
Parsons Technology.

QuickVerse Bible Reference Collection. Parsons Technology. Jul. 1994.
CD-ROM Contact publisher for price (ISBN 1-57264-037-5).
Parsons Technology.

QuickVerse Bible Text: King James Translation. Parsons Technology. Jan. 1989.
3.5" disk Contact publisher for price (ISBN 1-57264-025-1).
Parsons Technology.

QuickVerse Bible Text: New American Standard Bible Translation. Parsons Technology. Nov. 1993.
3.5" disk Contact publisher for price (ISBN 1-57264-032-4).
Parsons Technology.

QuickVerse Bible Text: New Century Version Translation. Parsons Technology. Sep. 1992.
3.5" disk Contact publisher for price (ISBN 1-57264-029-4).
Parsons Technology.

QuickVerse Bible Text: New International Version Translation. Parsons Technology. Jan. 1989.
3.5" disk Contact publisher for price (ISBN 1-57264-031-6).
Parsons Technology.

QuickVerse Bible Text: New King James Translation. Parsons Technology. May 1990.
3.5" disk Contact publisher for price (ISBN 1-57264-026-X).
Parsons Technology.

QuickVerse Bible Text: New Revised Stanard Version Translation. Parsons Technology. Oct. 1990.
3.5" disk Contact publisher for price (ISBN 1-57264-028-6).
Parsons Technology.

QuickVerse Bible Text: Revised Standard Version Translation. Parsons Technology. Jan. 1989.
3.5" disk Contact publisher for price (ISBN 1-57264-027-8).
Parsons Technology.

QuickVerse Bible Text: The Living Bible Translation. Parsons Technology. Jun. 1992.
3.5" disk Contact publisher for price (ISBN 1-57264-030-8).
Parsons Technology.

QuickVerse for DOS: King James Translation with Naves. Version: 3.0. Parsons Technology. May 1994.
3.5" disk Contact publisher for price (ISBN 1-57264-009-X).
Parsons Technology.

QuickVerse for DOS: Living Bible Translation with Naves. Version: 3.0. Parsons Technology. May 1994.
3.5" disk Contact publisher for price (ISBN 1-57264-014-6).
Parsons Technology.

QuickVerse for DOS: New American Standard Translation with Naves. Version: 3.0. Parsons Technology. May 1994.
3.5" disk Contact publisher for price (ISBN 1-57264-016-2).
Parsons Technology.

QuickVerse for DOS: New Century Translation with Naves. Version: 3.0. Parsons Technology. May 1994.
3.5" disk Contact publisher for price (ISBN 1-57264-013-8).
Parsons Technology.

QuickVerse for DOS: New International Translation with Naves. Version: 3.0. Parsons Technology. May 1994.
3.5" disk Contact publisher for price (ISBN 1-57264-015-4).
Parsons Technology.

QuickVerse for DOS: New King James Translation with Naves. Version: 3.0. Parsons Technology. May 1994.
3.5" disk Contact publisher for price (ISBN 1-57264-010-3).
Parsons Technology.

QuickVerse for DOS: New Revised Standard Translation with Naves. Version: 3.0. Parsons Technology. May 1994.
3.5" disk Contact publisher for price (ISBN 1-57264-012-X).
Parsons Technology.

QuickVerse for DOS: Revised Standard Translation with Naves. Version: 3.0. Parsons Technology. May 1994.
3.5" disk Contact publisher for price (ISBN 1-57264-011-1).
Parsons Technology.

QuickVerse for Windows Demo. Parsons Technology. Jan. 1994.
3.5" disk Contact publisher for price (ISBN 1-57264-045-6).
Parsons Technology.

QuickVerse for Windows: King James Translation with Naves. Version: 3.0. Parsons Technology. Jun. 1994.
3.5" disk Contact publisher for price (ISBN 1-57264-017-0).
Parsons Technology.

QuickVerse for Windows: Living Bible Translation with Naves. Version: 3.0. Parsons Technology. Jun. 1994.
3.5" disk Contact publisher for price (ISBN 1-57264-022-7).
Parsons Technology.

QuickVerse for Windows: New American Standard Translation with Naves. Version: 3.0. Parsons Technology. Jun. 1994.
3.5" disk Contact publisher for price (ISBN 1-57264-024-3).
Parsons Technology.

QuickVerse for Windows: New Century Translation with Naves. Version: 3.0. Parsons Technology. Jun. 1994.
3.5" disk Contact publisher for price (ISBN 1-57264-021-9).
Parsons Technology.

QuickVerse for Windows: New International Translation with Naves. Version: 3.0. Parsons Technology. Jun. 1994.
3.5" disk Contact publisher for price (ISBN 1-57264-023-5).
Parsons Technology.

QuickVerse for Windows: New King James Translation with Naves. Version: 3.0. Parsons Technology. Jun. 1994.
3.5" disk Contact publisher for price (ISBN 1-57264-018-9).
Parsons Technology.

QuickVerse for Windows: New Revised Standard Translation with Naves. Version: 3.0. Parsons Technology. Jun. 1994.
3.5" disk Contact publisher for price (ISBN 1-57264-020-0).
Parsons Technology.

QuickVerse for Windows: Revised Standard Translation with Naves. Version: 3.0. Parsons Technology. Jun. 1994.
3.5" disk Contact publisher for price (ISBN 1-57264-019-7).
Parsons Technology.

QuickVerse Home Bible Study Collection. Parsons Technology. Jul. 1994.
3.5" disk Contact publisher for price (ISBN 1-57264-038-3).
Parsons Technology.

QuickVerse Home Bible Study Collection. Parsons Technology. Jul. 1994.
CD-ROM Contact publisher for price (ISBN 1-57264-039-1).
Parsons Technology.

QuickVerse Strong's Concordance: With Transliterated Hebrew-Greek Dictionary. Parsons Technology. Jun. 1994.
3.5" disk Contact publisher for price (ISBN 1-57264-033-2).
Parsons Technology.

QUID: The QUIck Depreciation Template. Version: 4. William H. Downs. Jul. 1989. Items Included: 8 1/2 x 11 manual, 26 pages. Customer Support: 30-days full money-back guarantee, free telephone support.
MS-DOS or PC-DOS (512k). disk $99.00. Addl. software required: Lotus 1-2-3, ver 2X or 3X. Optimal configuration: 640k.
This Template Creates Depreciation Schedules for Accountants. Methods of Depreciation Include: SL, DB, ACRS, MACRS & Alternative Minimum Tax MACRS. Separate Computations Are Done Simultaneously for Federal Tax, Federal AMT, & State. Federal Automobile Limits Are Included in the "Listed Property" Schedule. A Form 4562 is Also Created.
WD Templates.

Quik BOM: Bill of Materials Processor in dBASE.
disk $119.95.
Helps a Design Engineer, Manufacturing Planner or Inventory Control Manager to Organize Materials & Identify Components Hierarchy, Relationships & Quantities.
Orange Fortune.

Quik-Lab Three for Digital Electronics. Albert P. Malvino. Jun. 1993.
MS-DOS. IBM PC. disk $18.45 (ISBN 1-56048-996-0, Order no.: 995.5). Optimal configuration: IBM PC, VGA-EGA Graphics.
3.5" disk $18.45 (ISBN 1-56048-995-2, Order no.: 995).
Used As a Tutorial System in Digital Electronics Courses. Software Includes Animations of Key Concepts. Simulated Labs, Testing Modules & a "Global Glossary". Mouse Supported. Topics Include: Number Systems, Gates, Boolean Algebra, Logic Circuits, Simplifying Logic Circuits, Flip-Flops, Registers, Counters, Memories & Computer Operation.
Malvino, Inc.

Quik MAN: Manufacturing Management System in dBASE.
disk $300.00.
A System for Planning & Control of Inventory, Cost & Transactions.
Orange Fortune.

QuikCost. Aug. 1988. Operating System(s) Required: MS-DOS. Memory Required: 256k, 360k.
disk $99.00.
Utility System for Filing, Costing, Re-Costing & Re-Sizing Recipe Files. The Program Includes Space for Recipe Preparation Methods.
Advanced Analytical/CharterHouse.

Quikey. PC Consulting. 1984. Compatible Hardware: IBM PC, PCjr, PC XT, PC AT & compatibles. Operating System(s) Required: DOS 1.0 or higher.
disk $39.00.
Redefines up to 485 Keys & Keystroke Combinations. Customizes the Keyboard & Allows User to Type Commonly Used Text on Command Sequences by Pressing a Single Key. Has Few Restrictions & Exceptions. Allows User to Define Macros. Once Installed, It Runs with Any Application Software & Can Be Invoked at Any Time. Can Also Be Turned off at Any Time.
DataSource Publishing Co.

Quintominoes. Compatible Hardware: Atari 400, 800. Language(s): Atari BASIC (source code included). Memory Required: 16k.
disk $16.95.
Easier to Play Version of NOMINOES JIGSAW. Correctly Connect Shapes That You Lay down on a Grid.
Dynacomp, Inc.

Quintus Prolog for IBM PS/2.
IBM PS/2. AIX. $2000.00.
Optimized for PS/2 AIX Systems.
Quintus Computer Systems, Inc.

Quintus Prolog For 80386. Mar. 1989.
80386-based computers. Unix Version 3. $2000.00.
High-Performance Prolog for PC-Compatible Workstations.
Quintus Computer Systems, Inc.

Quirin. Compatible Hardware: IBM PC. Language(s): BASIC (source code included). Memory Required: 7k.
disk or cassette $49.95.
Handicapping Program.
COM-CAP.

QuiteWrite. *Items Included:* Printed manual. *Customer Support:* Free technical support. DOS 2.0 or higher (256k). IBM or compatible. $49.00. *Optimal configuration:* IBM or compatible, 256k, & any printer. *Word Processing Package that Includes Graphics, Spell Checker, Autosave, Pop-up Menus, On-line Help, Macros, Mail Merge & Much More.* Parsons Technology.

Quotation. Jan. 1985. *Operating System(s) Required:* MS-DOS, UNIX, Novell. *Memory Required:* 30k.
MS-DOS. disk $500.00.
UNIX. disk $500.00.
Helps the Manufacturer to Create, Calculate, & Maintain Customer Quotations. Specifications & Historical Pricing Information Can Be Maintained to Aid in the Quoting Process. This Information Can Be Retrieved by Material Specification, Customer, Item or Quote Number. The User Can Use This Information &/or Calculate New Material, Labor, Burden, & Outside Service Cost. The System Prints a Completed Quotation Worksheet. Quotations Are Maintained, Used to Create Manufacturing Orders in the System, & When the Job Is Completed Receive Actual Cost Information.
Primetrack.

Quote Builder. *Version:* 2.0. Open Door Software Division. Oct. 1993. *Items Included:* Spiral manuals, video (when available). *Customer Support:* 30 day free customer support; 900 line $2.00/min.; 1 yr. maintenance $400/mo. Includes: toll free line & fax back priority service.
DOS. IBM compatible 386, 25Mhz, 5Mb free space on hard disk, VGA monitor, 3.5" floppy, keyboard, mouse (1Mb). disk $99.00; Network version $299.00 (ISBN 1-56756-039-3, Order no.: OD400I). *Addl. software required:* Operating system. *Optimal configuration:* IBM or compatible 486, 66Mhz, 5Mb free space on hard disk, 4Mb RAM-3Mb expanded usable, VGA monitor, 3.5" high density floppy, keyboard, mouse, tape backup, & uninterruptable power supply. *Networks supported:* Novell Netware Lite.
Windows. IBM compatible 386, 25Mhz, 5Mb free space on hard disk, VGA monitor, 3.5" floppy, keyboard, mouse (1Mb). $99.00; Network versino $199.00 (ISBN 1-56756-064-4, Order no.: OD405W). *Addl. software required:* Windows 3.1 or higher. *Optimal configuration:* IBM or compatible 486, 66Mhz, 5Mb free space on hard disk, 4Mb RAM-3Mb expanded usable, VGA monitor, 3.5" high density floppy, keyboard, mouse, tape backup, & uninterruptable power supply. *Networks supported:* Novell Netware Lite.
MAC Jan '94. 3.5" disk $99.00 (ISBN 1-56756-040-7, Order no.: OD420M). *Addl. software required:* System 7.
Sales Automation Tool Designed for Any Industry. Has the Flexibility & Control over Quoting Inventory, with a Unique Category Function That Can Make a New Salesperson an Expert Overnight. Pricing, Invoicing, & Reordering from Suppliers Is Easy. Stores Information about Individual Customers, What You Have Quoted & What They Have Bought, from Single or Multiple Vendors, As Well As Complete Product Descriptions. If Changes in Pricing Occurs, Repetitive Orders & Quote to Customers Can Be Updated with the Touch of a Button. Great Product for Beginner with It's Windowed Interface. Purchase Orders for "Just in Time Inventory" Is As Easy As Finding the Quote or Invoice & Pressing a Button. Client & Vendor Tracking Is Also Made Easy with Pop-Ups. Organizes Product & Service Options & Saves Them for Easy Retrieval So Sales Representatives Can Create Quotes That Sell.
Advantage International.

Quote Capture, 2 disks. Jul. 1987. *Compatible Hardware:* IBM PC XT, PC AT & compatibles. *Operating System(s) Required:* PC-DOS/MS-DOS 2.0 or higher. *Memory Required:* 320k. *General Requirements:* CompuTrac/PC software, supported live quote machine.
disk $300.00 (ISBN 0-944173-02-0).
Database Management System Used for Data Collection.
CompuTrac, A Telerate Co.

Quote Master. *Version:* 1.51. *General Requirements:* Hard disk drive.
Macintosh with 2 meg. of memory (20Mb). 3.5" disk $395.00.
Real-Time Stock Monitoring System.
Strategic Planning Systems.

The Quote-r. *Version:* Fall, 1994. Sep. 1985. *Compatible Hardware:* 486 PC. *Operating System(s) Required:* DOS 6.0 or higher. *Language(s):* Clipper. *Memory Required:* 4000-8000k. *General Requirements:* 15Mb hard disk, 132 column printer, multi- or single-user. *Items Included:* Documentation, updates - two a year. *Customer Support:* User manuals, conference, workshop, telephone support, training.
disk $1500.00 single user; $2500.00 multi-user.
Salesmen's Tool - Track Prospects, Present a Thorough Lease vs. Purchase Comparison from a Financial Perspective, Quote Payments, Take Credit Applications, Print Documents, Produce Management Reports, Over 175 Installations Nationwide.
LeaseTek, Inc.

The QWERTY Text Merge. Jun. 1983. *Compatible Hardware:* IBM PC & compatibles. *Operating System(s) Required:* PC-DOS/MS-DOS. *Language(s):* Assembly. *Memory Required:* 128k.
disk $59.00 (ISBN 0-918813-48-4).
Tool for Producing Custom Copies of a Template Document. Works with Standard ASCII Files.
HFK Software.

QWERTY Word Processor. *Version:* 7.3. Jun. 1985. *Compatible Hardware:* IBM PC & compatibles. *Operating System(s) Required:* PC-DOS/MS-DOS. *Language(s):* Assembly. *Memory Required:* 256k.
disk $20.00 (ISBN 0-918813-25-5).
Provides a Range of Features Such As Automatic Continuous Screen Formatting, Single Keystroke Character/Word/Line Operations, Tabs & Centering, Unlimited Margin & Tab Stop Changes, Cut & Paste, Use of ASCII Files, & Keysaver Macro Function. Special Support for LaserJet Printers.
HFK Software.

QwikBid Residential Estimating System. 1991. PC-DOS. IBM PC & compatible. disk Single User $745.00.
disk Multi-User $1295.00.
Estimating & Proposal Generating Program Designed Specifically for Use by Specialty Contractors & Others Who Perform Repetitive Bidding & Proposal Writing. Detailed Estimate Listing All Job Costs, Labor, & Pricing Is Calculated & a Custom Proposal Is Printed, Ready for the Customer's Signature.
Personalized Business Resources.

R. A. M. *Version:* 1.14. *Items Included:* Complete bound instruction guide. *Customer Support:* Free support for first 60 days; 1 year toll-free support, $295.00.
DOS. IBM & compatibles. $595.00-$1495.00.
Optimal configuration: 486, 4Mb memory, fast hard disk. *Networks supported:* LANtastic, Novell.
Rental Software for Appliance, Furniture, or Similar Stores with Long Term or Short Term Rentals. Keeps Track of Rentals down to the Minute, Perfect for Tool Rental Stores. Has Graphical Calendar Showing When an Item Is Available. A Shipping Computer & Memo Function Are Included - All Work Right from the Invoice Screen. Complete Accounting with Accounts Receivable. User Can Even Configure the Terms/Conditions, & Print & Invoice on Plain Paper or Custom Receipt.
Aphelion, Inc.

R & R Code Generator. *Version:* 6. Sep. 1994. *Items Included:* Manuals. *Customer Support:* 60 day return policy, technical support.
MS-DOS. IBM (640k). disk $199.00.
Converts XBASE Reports Designed with R & R Report Writer into dBASE IV, Clipper or Fox Code. Reduces Memory Overload.
Concentric Data Systems, Inc.

R&R Report Writer. *Version:* 7. Feb. 1996. *Customer Support:* 60-days telephone technical support, annual support-1 yr. $150 per contact; Upgrade Express - all upgrades for single product - 1 yr. $150 per contract; Support Plus - 1 yr. annual support plus Upgrade Express - $250 per contract, one copy per contract.
Windows 95, Windows NT 32-bit. 386 or higher (2Mb). CD-ROM disk $249.00 (Order no.: 0418). *Addl. software required:* Any dbf compatible database including dBASE, FoxPro, Clipper, & Alpha 4.
Concentric Data Systems, Inc.

R & R Report Writer for Paradox. *Version:* 4. *Items Included:* Full documentation, royalty-free runtime. *Customer Support:* 60 day telephone technical support.
DOS 3.0. IBM PC (2Mb). disk $249.00; multi-user packs available. *Addl. software required:* Paradox Ver. 3.5, 4.0, 4.5, & Paradox for Windows. *Optimal configuration:* 2Mb hard disk space & high-density disk drive. *Networks supported:* Net-BIOS compatible.
Fully-Featured, Relational Report Writer for Paradox Tables & Databases. End Users or Developers Can Create Reports Quickly & Easily, Without Programming.
Concentric Data Systems, Inc.

R&R Report Writer: SQL Edition. *Version:* 6.5. Aug. 1995. *Customer Support:* 60-days telephone technical support, annual support-1 yr. $150 per contact; Upgrade Express - all upgrades for single product - 1 yr. $150 per contract; Support Plus - 1 yr. annual support plus Upgrade Express - $250 per contact, one copy per contract.
Windows 3.X, Windows NT, Windows 95 16-bit. 386 or higher (2Mb). 3.5" disk $395.00 (Order no.: 0328). *Addl. software required:* Any data source.
Concentric Data Systems, Inc.

R&R Report Writer: XBase Edition. *Version:* 6.5. Aug. 1995. *Customer Support:* 60-days telephone technical support, annual support-1 yr. $150 per contact; Upgrade Express - all upgrades for single product - 1 yr. $150 per contract; Support Plus - 1 yr. annual support plus Upgrade Express - $250 per contact, one copy per contract.
Windows 3.X, Windows NT 16-bit. 386 or higher (2Mb). 3.5" disk $249.00 (Order no.: 0318). *Addl. software required:* Any dbf compatible database including dBASE, FoxPro, Clipper, & Alpha 4.
Concentric Data Systems, Inc.

TITLE INDEX

R:BASE: For DOS. Version: 5.5. Feb. 1996. Customer Support: Free Basic support - (206) 649-9551; R:BASE Premium support 800 Line ($225.00 per year); 900 support ($2.00 per minute).
DOS. 386 or higher (4Mb). disk $795.00.
One of the Most Powerful Database Management Systems Available. Provides 32-Bit Processing & Data Integrity. While the Programming Language Makes It Possible to Create a Wide Variety of Custom Applications, Basic Database Application Development Requires No Programming.
Microrim, Inc.

R:BASE: For OS-2 PM. Version: 5.5. Feb. 1996. Customer Support: Free Basic support - (206) 649-9551; R:BASE Premium support 800 Line ($225.00 per year); 900 support ($2.00 per minute).
OS/2 PM. 386 or higher (8Mb). disk $495.00. Nonstandard peripherals required: 15Mb hard disk space. Addl. software required: OS/2 2.0 or higher.
Features Include Programming-Free Application Development, Automatic Multi-User Mode, & 4GL with Embedded ANSI SQL. Takes Full Advantage of the Multi-Tasking Environment of OS/2 As Well As the 32-Bit Architecture of OS/2. Adds a New Graphical User Interface & Design Tool Set.
Microrim, Inc.

R:BASE: For Windows. Version: 5.5. Feb. 1996. Customer Support: Free Basic support - (206) 649-9551; R:BASE Premium support 800 Line ($225.00 per year); 900 support ($2.00 per minute).
Windows. 386 or higher (8Mb). disk $495.00. Nonstandard peripherals required: 15Mb hard disk space. Addl. software required: Microsoft Windows 3.1, Windows 95 or Windows NT.
Features Include Programming-Free Application Development, Automatic Multi-User Mode, & 4GL with Embedded ANSI SQL. Fully 32-Bit & Was Developed to the Win32s Specifications to Be Windows 95 & OS/2 Warp V3 Compatible. Version 5.5 Adds a New Graphical User Interface & Design Tool Set for Creating Truly Powerful Database Applications.
Microrim, Inc.

R/C RaceTrak. Version: 4.25. Jan. 1993. Items Included: User's manual, signup forms.
PC-DOS/MS-DOS. disk $169.00 (ISBN 0-917825-04-7).
Complete Race Track Management System for Radio-Controlled Car Racing. Maintains Lap Counts, Lap Times, Car & Driver Information. Menu Driven with Complete Context Sensitive Help Screens & Full Screen Data Entry & Edit. Not Copy Protected.
Information Management Solutions, Inc.

R-Doc/X. Version: 5.1. Jun. 1986. Compatible Hardware: IBM PC & compatibles. Operating System(s) Required: MS-DOS, PC-DOS, OS/2. Language(s): Assembly, PL/I, C. Memory Required: MS-DOS 128k.
5-1/4" or 3-1/2" disk $149.00.
Converts Documents (Including Formatting & Control Codes) Between Different Word Processing Software Formats. Program Is Not Copy Protected, & Works with Other Memory-Resident Programs & in Networked Environments. Supports Most of the Popular Word Processing Programs (Including WORDPERFECT, MULTIMATE, DISPLAY WRITE, WORDSTAR, OFFICEWRITER, XYWRITE, PALANTIR, SPELLBINDER, VOLKSWRITER, MICROSOFT WORD, LEADING EDGE, LOTUS MANAGEMENT, WORDMARC COMPOSER, ENABLE (WP), WORDSTAR-2000, PEACHTEXT-5000, DCA/RFT, FREESTYLE, Standard ASCII, PFS:PROFESSIONAL, PFS:FIRST CHOICE, WRITING ASSISTANT & PC-WRITE) & Is Regularly Updated to Include More Formats.
Advanced Computer Innovations, Inc.

R-Maker. Compatible Hardware: IBM PC, PC XT. Memory Required: 320k, recommended 512k. General Requirements: Revelation database.
single user $195.00.
multi user $295.00.
Organizes REVELATION Database into Menus & Screens. Users Can Define All Files, & Get All Screens & Menus Working & Interfaced with R/LIST REPORT WRITER.
Eight Hundred Software, Inc.

R. S. Football. Compatible Hardware: Atari XL/XE.
ROM cartridge $16.95 (Order no.: RX8029).
Atari Corp.

R-Tree Report Generator. Version: 1.5B. Compatible Hardware: DOS, Windows 3.X, NT, OS/2, Unix, QNX 4.X, Coherent, Xenix or Macintosh. Items Included: Manual. Customer Support: 3 months free unlimited technical support; maintenance plan thereafter.
3.5" disk from $445.00.
Produces Complex, Multi-Line Reports from Multiple C-Tree Plus Data Files, Both Fixed & Variable Length. Handles Virtually Every Aspect of Report Generation. Only Programming Requirement Is to Call the Report Function Which Reads C-Tree Plus Data Files; Perfomrs Necessary Calculations; Monitors Control Breaks & Accumulators; & Produces a Formatted Report. It Allows You to Distribute Report Scripts in Either Their Original Form, or in a Special Compiled Form. Report Scripts in Text Form Can Be Modified by Your Customers. Report Scripts in Compiled Form Cannot Be Modified by Customers. Other Features: Define Any Number of Virtual Fields; Sort by Any Number of Criteria; Any Number of Nested Control Breaks; Accumulators Automatically Track Each Control Break Level; Complete Layout Control with Conditional Breaks, Page Headers/Footers, Report Headers/Footers, & Control Headers/Footers.
FairCom Corp.

R:WEB. Items Included: R:BASE 5.5 for Windows is included for free. Customer Support: Free Basic support - (206) 649-9551; R:BASE Premium support 800 Line ($225.00 per year); 900 support ($2.00 per minute).
Windows. 386 or higher (8Mb). disk $995.00.
Addl. software required: Runs with R:BASE 5.5 for Windows, included for free with R:WEB as a development tool.
The First Real Internet Database. Provides Companies with an Affordable, Powerful & Programming-Free Internet Database Solution. Allows a WWW Site Owner to Design a Dynamic Database Application That Posts Live Data to Customers over the Internet, Allowing Real-Time Solutions to Product Orders & Inquiries.
Microrim, Inc.

R. Zork. Items Included: Installation Guide.
MAC. Contact publisher for price (ISBN 0-87321-059-X, Order no.: CDM-3034).
Activision, Inc.

R. Zork. Items Included: Installation Guide.
IBM PC. Contact publisher for price (ISBN 0-87321-049-2, Order no.: MS2-3034).
Activision, Inc.

RABBIT-8 REPORT ARCHITECT: (R-8)

R. Zork Anthology. Items Included: Installation Guide.
IBM PC. Contact publisher for price (ISBN 0-87321-051-4, Order no.: CDD-3047).
Activision, Inc.

R. Zork CD. Items Included: Installation Guide.
IBM PC. Contact publisher for price (ISBN 0-87321-052-2, Order no.: CDD-3034).
Activision, Inc.

R. Zork CD Mac OEM. Items Included: Installation Guide.
MAC. Contact publisher for price (ISBN 0-87321-053-0, Order no.: CDM-3034B).
Activision, Inc.

R. Zork CD Mac with Anthology & Hintbook. Items Included: Installation Guide.
MAC. Contact publisher for price (ISBN 0-87321-054-9, Order no.: CDM-3049).
Activision, Inc.

R. Zork CD OEM. Items Included: Installation Guide.
IBM PC. Contact publisher for price (ISBN 0-87321-056-5, Order no.: CDD-3034B).
Activision, Inc.

R. Zork MPEG CD OEM. Items Included: Installation Guide.
IBM PC. Contact publisher for price (ISBN 0-87321-060-3, Order no.: CDD-3034R).
Activision, Inc.

R. Zork Nemesis. Items Included: Installation Guide.
IBM PC. Contact publisher for price (ISBN 0-87321-063-8, Order no.: CDD-3112).
Activision, Inc.

R. Zork with Anthology. Items Included: Installation Guide.
MAC. Contact publisher for price (ISBN 0-87321-055-7, Order no.: CDM-3048).
Activision, Inc.

R. Zork with Anthology. Items Included: Installation Guide.
IBM. Contact publisher for price (ISBN 0-87321-062-X, Order no.: MS2-3048).
Activision, Inc.

R. Zork with Anthology. Items Included: Installation Guide.
IBM PC. Contact publisher for price (ISBN 0-87321-058-1, Order no.: CDD-3048).
Activision, Inc.

R. Zork with Anthology & Hintbook. Items Included: Installation Guide.
IBM PC. Contact publisher for price (ISBN 0-87321-057-3, Order no.: CDD-3049).
Activision, Inc.

R. Zork with Anthology & Hintbook. Items Included: Installation Guide.
IBM PC. Contact publisher for price (ISBN 0-87321-050-6, Order no.: MS2-3049).
Activision, Inc.

R. Zork with Hintbook. Items Included: Installation Guide.
IBM PC. Contact publisher for price (ISBN 0-87321-061-1, Order no.: 3034H).
Activision, Inc.

Rabbit-8 Report Architect: (R-8). Operating System(s) Required: VAX/VMS.
$1,995.00 to $4,995.00.
Produces Optimized FORTRAN, COBOL or BASIC Source Code While Directly Accessing the

Common Data Dictionary (CDD). Produces Hard-Copy Programs & Designs Documentations & Can Use a Split-Screen Character Editor to Perform Complex Logic Operations.
Raxco, Inc.

Rabbit Hill. Intentional Education Staff & Robert Lawson. Apr. 1996. *Items Included:* Program manual. *Customer Support:* Free technical support, 90 day warranty.
School ver.. System 7.1 or higher. Macintosh (4Mb). 3.5" disk contact publisher for price (ISBN 1-57204-289-3). *Nonstandard peripherals required:* 256 color monitor, hard drive, printer.
Lab pack. System 7.1 or higher. Macintosh (4Mb). 3.5" disk contact publisher for price (ISBN 1-57204-265-6). *Nonstandard peripherals required:* 256 color monitor, hard drive, printer.
Site license. System 7.1 or higher. Macintosh (4Mb). 3.5" disk contact publisher for price (ISBN 1-57204-290-7). *Nonstandard peripherals required:* 256 color monitor, hard drive, printer.
School ver.. Windows 3.1 or higher. IBM/Tandy & 100% compatibles (4Mb). disk contact publisher for price (ISBN 1-57204-263-X). *Nonstandard peripherals required:* VGA or SVGA 640 x 480 resolution (256), mouse, hard drive, sound device.
Lab pack. Windows 3.1 or higher. IBM/Tandy & 100% compatibles (4Mb). disk contact publisher for price (ISBN 1-57204-291-5). *Nonstandard peripherals required:* VGA or SVGA 640 x 480 resolution (256), mouse, hard drive, sound device.
Site license. Windows 3.1 or higher. IBM/Tandy & 100% compatibles (4Mb). disk contact publisher for price (ISBN 1-57204-267-2). *Nonstandard peripherals required:* VGA or SVGA 640 x 480 resolution (256), mouse, hard drive, sound device.
This companion for young adult literature is ideal for students who don't know how to start that book report, or give that needed summary. Gentle prompts throughout the guide sections of the program include Warm-up Connections, Thinking about Plot, Quoting & Noting, Keeping a Journal If I Were——'Responding to Questions, Using Quotations, Taking a Personal View, Write to Others, & Write a Sequel.
Lawrence Productions, Inc.

Rabbit-9 VAX Acceleration Software Technology. *Compatible Hardware:* DEC VAX.
MicroVAX II, VAX 11/725 or 730 licenses $995.00.
MicroVAX 3000 to VAX 8300 licenses $1795.00.
VAX 8500 & higher performing CPUs $2495.00. *Incorporates Heuristic Programming, Artificial Intelligence & Classic Feedback Loops Techniques to Speed Program Response Time. Continuously Adjusts Key Dynamic System & Process Parameters for Optimum Response Time Efficiency.*
Raxco, Inc.

RABBIT-1: Resource Accounting, Auditory & Billing System. 1980. *Compatible Hardware:* DEC. *Operating System(s) Required:* VMS. *Memory Required:* 500k.
1600 bpi or TK50 tape $995.00-$12,995.00. *Menu-Driven System That Supports Charge Assessments on All VMS Resources. Features Include "Session-Level" Accounting for Audit Purposes & Four Different Charge Environments. Operates on a Single CPU or in a Cluster Environment.*
Raxco, Inc.

RABBIT-2: System Performance-Capacity Planning. 1980. *Compatible Hardware:* DEC. *Operating System(s) Required:* VMS. *Memory Required:* 100-250k.
1600 bpi or TK50 tape $995.00 $12,995.00. *Provides Detailed, Graphic Analysis of VMS Resource Consumption. It Identifies Who Is on the System, When They Are on, & What They Are Doing. Provides Resource Usage Analysis by Account, Username, Terminal, Queue, CPU, or Image.*
Raxco, Inc.

Rabbit-2 VMS Know-It-All. *Operating System(s) Required:* VAX/VMS.
$1995.00-$4995.00. *Analysis-Planning Tool. Includes Synthetic Entity Capabilities Which Allows Users to Construct Virtual Entities from Real Data Entities.*
Raxco, Inc.

RABBIT-5: High Speed VMS Archiving Backup. 1980. *Compatible Hardware:* DEC. *Operating System(s) Required:* VMS. *Memory Required:* 25-50k.
1600bpi or TK50 tape $995.00-$9995.00. *Performs Disk to Tape Backup 3 to 5 Times Faster Than VMS Backup in Elapsed Time & 90% Faster in CPU Time. A Tape Librarian Minimizes the Potential for Operator Mistake While Enhanced Error Checking Capabilities Insure Reliability.*
Raxco, Inc.

RABBIT-7: Disk Optimizer. Nov. 1986. *Compatible Hardware:* DEC. *Operating System(s) Required:* VMS. *Memory Required:* 700k.
1600bpi or TK50 tape $995.00-$2495.00. *Eliminates File Fragmentation & Optimizes a Disk's Free Space. Designed to Run On-Line, It Offers Flexibility in File Positioning & Full Recovery from Any Crash or Abort. Also Draws a Map of the Disk Showing Before & after Formats.*
Raxco, Inc.

The Rabbitry System. *Compatible Hardware:* Commodore 64, 128; IBM PC & compatibles. *Operating System(s) Required:* PC-DOS or MS-DOS. *Language(s):* BASICA.
disk $45.00.
IN-TEC Equipment Co.

Rabbits. Duane Bristow. *Compatible Hardware:* TRS-80 Model I, Model III. *Operating System(s) Required:* TRSDOS. *Language(s):* BASIC.
cassette $14.95. *Wildlife Population Simulation. User Can Practice Wildlife Management by Fertilizing or Destroying Soil & by Releasing or Hunting Rabbits or Foxes.*
Duane Bristow Computers, Inc.

Race-Trac. *Version:* 2.0. Charles Bello. *Items Included:* 1 Spiral-bound user guide, 1 50' cable with push button. *Customer Support:* (716) 377-3570 for support.
PC-MS DOS 2.0 or higher. IBM PC & compatibles (256k). disk $195.00. *Provides Timing & Scoring for up to 8000 Entrants in Marathons & 10K Races. A Cable with Push-Button Is Included. Printed & On-Screen Results Are Provided for up to 20 Age Groups in Each of the Men's & Women's Divisions with 10 Winners in Each Age Group.*
CEL Development.

RacePro for Windows. Frederick Mensch. Sep. 1995. *Customer Support:* Unlimited telephone support.
Windows 3.1 & Windows 95. 386 (4Mb). Contact publisher for price (ISBN 0-934777-20-9). *Allows Handicappers to Access an Expanded 14-Line Racing Program Downloaded from Racing Greyhounds BBS.*
Pico Publishing.

Racial Attitude Survey. Thomas J. Rundquist et al. May 1995. *Items Included:* Paper version of Survey. *Customer Support:* By Fax, Phone, Mail for free.
PC Windows (3.11) or higher, DOS 5 or higher, 386 PC or higher. IBM PC & compatibles (2Mb). disk $39.95 (ISBN 1-884239-03-X). *A Survey Meant to Test & Evaluate Attitudes of Individuals Toward Any Ethnic Grouping. Test Results Can Be Sent to Nova Media for Comparison to Our Database.*
Nova Media, Inc.

Racial Attitude Survey. Thomas J. Rundquist. Dec. 1994. *Items Included:* Results of test taken can be compared to our data base anonymously at no extra charge. Unless the sample is extremely large, in that case contact us for a price. *Customer Support:* Fax support 1-616-796-7539, Phone support 10-5 EST 616-796-7539, By letter.
DOS 6.0, Windows 3.0 or higher. PC IBM & compatibles (2Mb). disk $39.95 (ISBN 1-884239-03-X). *Optimal configuration:* DOS 6.2, Windows 3.1 4Mb RAM. *Networks supported:* All. *Original Version Reviewed in Mental Measurements Yearbook. Update Survey Allows Test Result Comparason to Data Base Anonymously. Has Been Used Previously by Universities & Industry to Evaluate Prejudice & Attitudes Toward Any Ethnic Group, but Especially AfroAmericans. Also Can Be Used to Evaluate Compliance with Civil Rights Acts State & Federal. Mr. Rundquist Has a Masters in Counseling & Has Been in the Field over 20 Years.*
Nova Media, Inc.

Racing Greyhounds Combo. Jun. 1989. *Items Included:* Documentation is on disk. *Customer Support:* 30-day guarantee, free telephone support.
MS-DOS/PC-DOS (512k). IBM PC or compatibles. $10.00. *Optimal configuration:* Printer. *Includes Programs to Do the Following: ANALYST-Enter Race Data & See Graphic Comparisons, BETS-Calculate Bet Costs, BREAKER-Simulate Break, WAGERS-Track Wagers & Profits, WPS-Analyze Win, Place & Show Data, for Greyhound Racing.*
Pico Publishing.

Radiological Safety Analysis. Sep. 1987. *Compatible Hardware:* IBM PC & compatibles. *Memory Required:* Menu-driven worksheet application 25k.
$800.00.
site license $8,000.00. *Helps Identify Internal Hazards, Controlled Primarily Through Containment, & External Hazards, Requiring Shielding & Time & Distance Factors. Analysis Determines Appropriate Types of Radionuclide Workplaces & Operating Limits to Be Used. Maintains Permanent Analysis Records.*
Orval D. Simpson Scientific Consultant.

Radionuclide Generators. (Nuclear Medicine -- Radiopharmacy Ser.). Ann M. Steves. 1996.
DOS 3.1 or higher. IBM or compatible (512k). disk $150.00 (Order no.: MIS9022). *Nonstandard peripherals required:* VGA. *This tutorial describes the parent-daughter decay & its application in radionuclide generators; describes the construction & operation of radionuclide generators with emphasis on the Molybdenum-99/Technetium generator.*
Educational Software Concepts, Inc.

TITLE INDEX

RadioView. Version: 2.1.1. 1986. *Compatible Hardware:* Macintosh. *Operating System(s) Required:* Apple DOS 3.3. *Language(s):* Turbo PASCAL. *Memory Required:* 1Mbk. *General Requirements:* 20Mb printer.
contact publisher for price.
Log & Billing System for AM & FM Radio Stations. Computerizes Logs & Traffic Scheduling, Tracks Sales & Traffic, & Provides Detailed Reports for Analyzing Revenue. Schedules Availabilities, Affidavits, Sales Projections, Log Generation, Billing, Sales Recap, Traffic Order, & Client Lists. Produces Up-to-Date Reports Which Include Details on Sales Personnel, Agencies, & Clients. Client Master Forms Central Database, & Records All Current Information on Each Client Including Name & Address for Billing & Affidavits, Contact & Phone Number, Clients Agency or Co-Op, Sales Executive Handling Account, & Transactions (Payments, Balances Due, Write-Offs) That Have Occurred. Optional Features Such as General Ledger, Accounts Payable, & Payroll Can Be Purchased Separately.
Nordic Software, Inc.

RadLine CD-ROM Database for Radiology. Nov. 1989.
MS Windows 3.1 or higher. IBM & compatibles (4Mb). CD-ROM disk $325.00-$995.00; Networks $1895.00 & up. *Nonstandard peripherals required:* Magnetic or CD-ROM, using ISO 9660. *Optimal configuration:* IBM & compatibles, 80386 or higher, 4Mb RAM, 20Mb hard disk, mouse, MS Windows 3.1 or higher.
System 6.0.7 or higher. Apple Macintosh (3Mb). CD-ROM disk $325.00-$995.00; Networks $1895.00 & up. *Optimal configuration:* Apple Macintosh Plus or higher, 3Mb RAM, System 6. 0.7 or higher.
RadLine Is an Electronic Reference Database to the Radiology Journal Literature. Radiology-Specific Excerpts (Including Abstracts) from the National Library of Medicine's MEDLINE Database Are Distributed on CD-ROM (Compact Disc, Read-Only Memory) Optical Disc. Knowledge Finder Search-&-Retrieval Software Makes Searching of the RadLine Database Easy, Effective & Fast. After the User Types a Phrase or Sentence Describing the Information Needed, It selects the References in the Database That Appear to Best Match the Request, & Presents Them in Order of Likely Relevance. The RadLine Archive CD-ROM Contains More Than 440,000 References to Articles Published in 160 Radiology-Related Journals over the Most Recent 10 Full Years. Radiology Articles from More Than 2,500 Other Journals Are Also Included.
Aries Systems Corp.

Raffle Do. Philip Rodgers, Jr. Dec. 1992. *Items Included:* Instruction manual (perfect bound), Visual Basic 1.0 Runtime Module - VBRUN100. DLL. *Customer Support:* 90 day free support, free updates to correct bugs.
MS-Windows 3.0 or 3.1. IBM 80386 or compatible PC (1Mb). $60.00; on-site licensing & volume discounts available (Order no.: 1100101). *Nonstandard peripherals required:* Laser jet printer. *Addl. software required:* MS-DOS 3.1 or higher. *Optimal configuration:* IBM 80386 or compatible PC, 2Mb RAM, VGA monitor, 80Mb hard drive, MS-Windows 3.0 or 3.1, DOS 5.0, mouse, laser jet printer.
Automates Design of Templates for Raffle Tickets. Start & End Printing at Any Number Between 0 & 999999. Customize & Print Replacement Tickets. Includes NUMSET, a Numbering System That Emulates Numbering Machines. Number Documents, Self Adhesive Labels, Pictures, Tickets, Forms.
Resolutions Now.

Rags to Riches Ledger. Chang Laboratories. *Compatible Hardware:* HP 110 Portable.
3.5" disk $99.00 (Order no.: 45520C).
General Ledger Program for Small Businesses. Constantly Displays Income, Expenses, Assets, Liabilities, Estimated Profits, & Net Worth. The Screen Is Updated Each Time a Transaction Is Posted. The Ledger Can Integrate with RAGS TO RICHES SALES, PAYROLL & RECEIVABLE Modules.
Hewlett-Packard Co.

Rags to Riches Payables. Chang Laboratories. *Compatible Hardware:* HP 110 Portable.
3.5" disk $99.00 (Order no.: 45523C).
Keeps Track of Purchases, Credit/Debit Memos, & Payments to Vendors. As Invoices & Payments Are Recorded, the Totals Immediately Accumulate on the Screen. Integrates with RAGS TO RICHES LEDGER.
Hewlett-Packard Co.

Rags to Riches Receivables. Chang Laboratories. *Compatible Hardware:* HP 110 Portable.
3.5" disk $99.00 (Order no.: 45522C).
Keeps Track of Purchases, Payments, & Credit/Debit Memos by Customer. Shows the Exact Status of Any Customer Account at the Touch of a Key. Order History, Payment History, & Aging Reports Are Available on Screen or in Printed Reports. Integrates with RAGS TO RICHES LEDGER.
Hewlett-Packard Co.

Rags to Riches Sales. Chang Laboratories. *Compatible Hardware:* HP 110 Portable.
3.5" disk $99.00 (Order no.: 45521C).
Provides Record Keeping, Sales Analysis, & Point-of-Sales Applications for Small Retail Businesses, & Automatically Calculates Tax & Change. Individual Keys Can Be Assigned to Record the Sales of a Specific Item or to Identify a Type of Payment. Receipts & Invoices Can Be Customized to the Individual Retailer. Integrates with RAGS TO RICHES LEDGER.
Hewlett-Packard Co.

R.A.I.D. Version: 1.1. Larry Bank & Adam Sherer. Jan. 1987. *Compatible Hardware:* Atari ST. *Memory Required:* 512k.
3.5" disk $39.95 (ISBN 0-923213-52-X, Order no.: AT-RAI).
Program Debugger with the Following Features: Mini Assembler/Disassembler; Full Screen Editing; Tracer Options; Copy, Fill, & Move Block Commands; Breakpoints That Can Be Reset; & Two Separate Screen Displays to Keep Program & Debugging Activity Isolated.
MichTron, Inc.

Raid on Bungeling Bay. Will Wright. *Compatible Hardware:* Commodore 64.
disk $29.95 (Order no.: COMDSK-235).
Control a Lone Helicopter Flying a Mission of Heroism over a Vast Scrolling Landscape of Heavily-Defended Islands. Your Mission: Destroy the Bungeling Empire's Munitions Factories Before They Complete the Ultimate Weapon of Destruction.
Broderbund Software, Inc.

Raima Database Manager. Version: 3.21a. Randall Merilatt & Wayne Warren. Sep. 1984. *Compatible Hardware:* C compilers running under MS-DOS (including Microsoft, Turbo C) UNIX & XENIX 286/386 systems, VMS, OS/2. *Operating System(s) Required:* PC-DOS/MS-DOS 3.1 or higher, UNIX, XENIX, SCO XENIX, ULTRIX, VMS, OS/2; Windows. *Language(s):* C. *Memory Required:* 256k. *Customer Support:* 60 days free.
$395.00 & up, depending upon configuration.

RAIMA OBJECT MANAGER

DBMS Aimed at the Technical C Programmer. The Package Uses the Network Model DBMS Consisting of a Data Definition Language Processor & a Library of C Functions. Multi-User Capability, Transaction Processing & B-Tree Indexing. Includes Interactive Database Access Utility & dBASE II/III, R:base & ASCII File Transfer Capabilities.
Raima Corp.

Raima Database Manager Plus Plus. Version: 4.0. Jan. 1996. *Items Included:* Complete manuals. *Customer Support:* Support is provided by a team of engineers based at Raima, & cost 20 percent of software's list price. Support is provided via phone, fax, Internet e-mail, World Wide Web page (for upgrades, beta copies & patches) & BBS. Users also gain information on Raima products through an independent Listserv Internet mail group.
Windows 3.1. 386 (on Intel-based PC) (2Mb). $995.00 & up, depending on platform & number of users.
A High Performance Database Engine for C & C Plus Plus Application Development. It Provides a Proven C-API Library with over 200 Functions for Database Manipulation & Control, As Well As a Class Library That Encapsulates Database Storage & Manipulation in C Plus Plus Class Libraries, Providing an Object-Oriented Interface for Raima Database Manager. This Database Supports Database Architecture Using the Network, Relational & Combined Database Models.
Raima Corp.

Raima Database Manager System. Version: 3.21a. *Operating System(s) Required:* MS-DOS, UNIX, VAX/VMS, OS/2; Windows. *Language(s):* C. *Customer Support:* 60 days free.
695.00 & up depending upon configuration.
Database Management System Allowing Users to Build Applications for Single-User Microcomputers to Multi-User LAN's, up to Minis & Mainframes. The Three Modules Are: Raima Database Manager, Including Multiple Database Access; File & Record Locking; Automatic Database Recovery; Transaction Processing & Logging; Timestamping; Database Consistency Check Utility; Fast Access Methods Based on the Network Database Model & B-Tree Indexing (Uses Both Direct "Set" Relations & B-Tree Indexing Independently for Design Flexibility & Performance); an Interactive Database Access Utility; File Transfer Utilities for Importing/Exporting ASCII Text Files; a Database Definition Language Patterned after C; Virtual Memory Disk Côching for Fast Database óccess, db-QUERY, an SQL Based Query & Report Writer, & db-REVISE, a Database Restructure Program.
Raima Corp.

Raima Database Server: Client-Server Database Engine. Jul. 1993. *Items Included:* 7 manuals (perfect bound). *Customer Support:* 60 days of free phone support with purchase. Extended support - call for quote. Consulting services - call for quote. Training classes - $350 per day (basics, advanced, internals).
Netware 386, OS/2, Windows NT, UNIX. Hardware independent. disk $1995.00 (1-8 users); $8995.00 (unlimited). *Networks supported:* Names Pipes, SPX IX, TCP IP.
Offers a Client-Server Database for High-Performance Applications. Supports Multiple APIS, & Complies with Industry Standards, Including ANSI SQL & ODBL. Now Available for WINDOWS NT & NETWARE 386.
Raima Corp.

Raima Object Manager. Version: 1.3.1. Aug. 1995. *Items Included:* Complete manuals. *Customer Support:* Support is provided by a

team of engineers based at Raima, & cost 20 percent of software's list price. Support is provided via phone, fax, Internet e-mail, World Wide Web page (for upgrades, beta copies & patches) & BBS. Users also gain information on Raima products through an independent Listserv Internet mail group.
Windows 3.1. 386 (on Intel-based PC) (2Mb). $595.00 & up, depending on platform & number of users.
A C Plus Plus Class Library That Allows Use of Velocis Database Server & Raima Database Manager As an Object-Oriented Database Management System. ROM Encapsulates Object Storage & Database Navigation into C Plus Plus Class Definitions to Provide a Consistent Object-Oriented Interface to Raima Databases.
Raima Corp.

Rainbow Bar Code Data Collection Kits: Inspection-Scan, SCBA-Scan. *Version:* 1.1. 1987. *Items Included:* One year of free telephone technical support, an operations manual in a 3-ring binder, the Runtime Version of Revelations, one hand held bar code scanner & cabling, a bar code writing package for generating paper bar codes, & set-up forms. *Customer Support:* After the first year of free telephone technical support, additional tech support can be purchased if needed.
MS-DOS. IBM compatible PC's (320k). disk $1830.00. *Networks supported:* Novell, IBM PC-Net, Banyan Vines, LAN Manager for MS-DOS, & most other DOS compatible networks.
Pathworks or Digital Equipment Corp.'s VMS. VAX (320k). disk $1830.00. *Networks supported:* DECnet.
UNIX or SunOS. SPARC Station. Contact publisher for price.
Cost Effective Data Collection Utilizing Bar Code Technology for Regular Inspections of SCBA Units & Various Types of Equipment. Inventory, Safety Contacts, & Custom Written Bar Code Packages Are Also Available.
Pro-Am Software.

Rainbow Bar Code Data Collection Kits: SCBA-Scan, Inspection-Scan. *Version:* 1.1. 1987. *Items Included:* One hand held bar code scanner & cabling, a bar code writing package for generation of paper bar codes, one year of free telephone technical support, an operations manual in a 3-ring binder, the "Inspection-Scan" or "SCBA-Scan" software, & the Revelations Runtime. *Customer Support:* After the first year, additional technical support can be purchased if needed.
MS-DOS. IBM compatible PC's (320k). disk $1830.00. *Networks supported:* Novell, IBM PC-Net, Banyan Vines, LAN Manager for MS-DOS, & most other DOS compatible networks.
Pathworks or Digital Equipment Corp.'s VMS. VAX (320k). disk $1830.00. *Networks supported:* DECnet.
UNIX or SunOS. SPARC Station. Contact publisher for price.
Cost Effective Data Collection Utilizing Bar Code Technology for Regular Inspections of SCBA Units & Fire Extinguishers. Inventory, Safety Contacts, & Custom Written Bar Code Packages Are Also Available.
Pro-Am Software.

Rainbow MSDS Module. *Version:* 3.0. 1986. *Items Included:* One year of free telephone technical support, an operations manual in a 3-ring binder, the runtime version of Revelations. *Customer Support:* After the first year, additional technical support can be purchased if needed.
MS-DOS. IBM compatible PC's (320k). $1995.00 single user; $4595.00 5 user network version. *Networks supported:* Novell, IBM PC-Net, Banyan Vines, LAN Manager for MS-DOS, & most other DOS compatible networks.
Pathworks or Digital Equipment Corp.'s VMS. VAX (320k). $4595.00 5 user; $6795.00 10 user. *Networks supported:* DECnet.
UNIX or SunOS. SPARC Station. Contact publisher for price.
This Easy to Use Program Enables Every Piece of Information from a Material Safety Data Sheet to Be Entered Verbatim for Creating a Consistent & Standardized Database. Extensive Reporting, Tracking, & Updating of MSDSs Is Provided by the Program. Can Be Used with "RAINBOW SARA" Module.
Pro-Am Software.

Rainbow MSDS Module. *Version:* 3.0. 1986. *Items Included:* One year of free telephone technical support, an operations manual in a 3-ring binder, the Runtime Version of Revelations. *Customer Support:* After the first year of free telephone technical support, additional tech support can be purchased if needed.
MS-DOS. IBM compatible PC's (320k). $1995.00 single user; $4595.00 5 user network version. *Networks supported:* Novell, IBM PC-Net, Banyan Vines, LAN Manager for MS-DOS, & most other DOS compatible networks.
Pathworks or Digital Equipment Corp.'s VMS. VAX (320k). $4595.00 5 user; $6795.00 10 user. *Networks supported:* DECnet.
UNIX or SunOS. SPARC Station. Contact publisher for price.
This Easy to Use Program Enables Every Piece of Information from a Material Safety Data Sheet to Be Entered Verbatim for Creating a Consistent & Standardized Database. Extensive Reporting, Tracking, & Updating of MSDSs Is Provided by the Program. Can Be Used with "RAINBOW SARA" Module.
Pro-Am Software.

Rainbow Safety. *Version:* 2.0. 1986. *Items Included:* One year of free telephone technical support, an operations manual in a 3-ring binder, the runtime version of Revelations. *Customer Support:* After the first year, additional technical support can be purchased if needed.
MS-DOS. IBM compatible PC's (320k). $1995.00 single user; $4595.00 5 user network version. *Networks supported:* Novell, IBM PC-Net, Banyan Vines, LAN Manager for MS-DOS, & most other DOS compatible networks.
Pathworks or Digital Equipment Corp.'s VMS. VAX (320k). $4595.00 5 user; $6795.00 10 user. *Networks supported:* DECnet.
UNIX or SunOS. SPARC Station. Contact publisher for price.
Designed for Compliance with OSHA Regulations, the Program Is for Recording, Tracking, & Analyzing All Employee Accidents & Illnesses. The Extensive Reporting Includes Incidence & Frequency Reports & Also the Compiling & Printing of the OSHA 200 Log.
Pro-Am Software.

Rainbow Safety. *Items Included:* One year of free telephone technical support, an operations manual in a 3-ring binder, the Runtime Version of Revelations. *Customer Support:* After the first year of free telephone technical support, additional tech support can be purchased if needed.
MS-DOS. IBM compatible PC's (320k). $1995.00 single user; $4595.00 5 user network version. *Networks supported:* Novell, IBM PC-Net, Banyan Vines, LAN Manager for MS-DOS, & most other DOS compatible networks.
Pathworks or Digital Equipment Corp.'s VMS. VAX (320k). $4595.00 5 user; $6795.00 10 user. *Networks supported:* DECnet.
UNIX or SunOS. SPARC Station. Contact publisher for price.
Designed for Compliance with OSHA Regulations, the Program Is for Recording, Tracking, & Analyzing All Employee Accidents & Illnesses. The Extensive Reporting Includes Incidence, Frequency, & Severity Reports, & Also the Compiling & Printing of the OSHA 200 Log.
Pro-Am Software.

Rainbow SARA Module. *Version:* 2.0. 1987. *Items Included:* One year of free telephone technical support, an operations manual in a 3-ring binder, the runtime version of Revelations. *Customer Support:* After the first year, additional technical support can be purchased if needed.
MS-DOS. IBM compatible PC's (320k). $1495.00 single user stand-alone; $2790.00 single user with Rainbow MSDS. *Networks supported:* Novell, IBM PC-Net, Banyan Vines, LAN Manager for MS-DOS, & most other DOS compatible networks.
Pathworks or Digital Equipment Corp.'s VMS. VAX (320k). $3445.00 5 user stand-alone; $6385.00 5 user with Rainbow MSDS. *Networks supported:* DECnet.
UNIX or SunOS. SPARC Station. Contact publisher for price.
For Compliance with Titles 311 & 312 of the Superfund Amendments & Reauthorization Act. The Program Compares Inventory with the EPA's Extremely Hazardous Substance List & Reports on Those Exceeding TPQ. It Generates the Extremely Hazardous Substance Release Form & Tier II Reports. Can Be Used with "RAINBOW MSDS".
Pro-Am Software.

Rainbow SARA Module. *Version:* 2.0. 1987. *Items Included:* One year of free telephone technical support, an operations manual in a 3-ring binder, the Runtime Version of Revelations. *Customer Support:* After the first year of free telephone technical support, additional tech support can be purchased if needed.
MS-DOS. IBM compatible PC's (320k). $1495.00 single user stand alone; $2790.00 single user combined with Rainbow MSDS. *Networks supported:* Novell, IBM PC-Net, Banyan Vines, LAN Manager for MS-DOS, & most other DOS compatible networks.
Pathworks or Digital Equipment Corp.'s VMS. VAX (320k). $3445.00 5 user stand alone; $6385.00 5 user combined with Rainbow MSDS. *Networks supported:* DECnet.
UNIX or SunOS. SPARC Station. Contact publisher for price.
For Compliance with Titles 311 & 312 of the Superfund Amendments & Reauthorization Act. The Program Compares Inventory Against the EPA's Extremely Hazardous Substance List & Reports on Those Exceeding TPQ. It Generates the Extremely Hazardous Substance Release Form & the Tier II Reports. Can Be Used with "RAINBOW MSDS".
Pro-Am Software.

Rainbow Walker - Countdown. (Double Play Ser.). Steve Coleman & Ken Rose. *Compatible Hardware:* Atari 400, 800, XL series. *General Requirements:* Joystick.
disk $24.95 (Order no.: ATDSK-2501).
RAINBOW WALKER - Try to Outsmart the Devil & Avoid Lightning Bolts & Tornadoes As You Create a Rainbow to Reach the Pot of Gold. COUNTDOWN - Infiltrate an Enemy Missile Base & Fight Through Heavily-Guarded Rooms, Picking up Security Passwords As You Go.
Broderbund Software, Inc.

Rainbow Walker - Doughboy. (Double Play Ser.). Steve Coleman & Ken Coates. *Compatible Hardware:* Commodore 64 with joystick.
disk $24.95 (Order no.: COMDSK-3501).
RAINBOW WALKER - Try to Outsmart the Devil & Avoid Lightning Bolts & Tornadoes As You

Create a Rainbow to Reach the Pot of Gold. DOUGHBOY Puts You in Command of a Heavily Armed Squad on a Mission to Rescue the President (1 or 2 Players).
Broderbund Software, Inc.

RainMaker: Legal Data's Client Accounting Software. Version: 5.2. Apr. 1987. *Compatible Hardware:* IBM PC AT, PC XT; DEC VAX. *Operating System(s) Required:* MS-DOS 3.1, VMS 4.3. *Language(s):* Mumps (source code included). *Memory Required:* 512k. *General Requirements:* Hard disk, printer, modem.
RainMaker Client Accounting & Financial Management for Dec VAX, DG Aviion. $10,000.00-$75,000.00.
RainMaker Plus, for PC. disk $3995.00.
General Ledger, for PC. disk $500.00.
Accounts Payable, for PC. disk $500.00.
Legal Data Systems, Inc.

RAM Driver 2.0. PC Consulting. 1983. *Compatible Hardware:* IBM PC, PC XT, PC AT, PCjr & compatibles. *Operating System(s) Required:* PC-DOS 2.0 or higher. *Memory Required:* 64k.
disk $39.00.
disk with 5 add'l. utilities $59.95.
Consists of 2 Programs That Permit Extra Memory to Be Used As an Ultra Fast Electronic Disk Drive. User Can Configure As Many RAM Drivers As Desired. Drivers Can Be Set up to Emulate Any of IBM's 4 Supported Formats. Package Is Also Available Bundled with 5 Additional Utilities As Time Savers.
DataSource Publishing Co.

RAMAS/age: Modeling Fluctuations in Age-structured Populations. Version: 2.0. Mar. 1990. *Items Included:* User manual in three-ring notebook. *Customer Support:* Technical support by phone.
MS-DOS 2.0 or higher. IBM PC XT, AT, PS/2. disk $265.00 (ISBN 0-925031-07-0, Order no.: RA).
Macintosh Plus System 6.0.2. Macintosh Plus. 3.5" disk $265.00.
Used to Produce & Analyze Models of the Population Dynamics of a (Biological) Species. Allows Users to Define Simple or Age-Structured Models That Include Density Dependence & Variance Due to Environmental Fluctuations or Demographic Stochasticity. Computes the Expected Growth or Decline & Estimates the Risks of Extinction & the Chances of Population Explosion.
Exeter Software.

RamCam. *Compatible Hardware:* IBM PC & compatibles.
disk $5000.00.
Designed for Use in Manufacturing Applications.
Ram/Tek.

RAMD: Memory Disk. Pickles & Trout. Jul. 1984. *Compatible Hardware:* TRS-80 Model 11, Model 12, Model 16; Tandy 6000. *Memory Required:* 64k.
8" disk $10.00.
Enhancements to Any PICKLES & TROUT CP/M-2.2M System Allowing All or Part of Any 68000 Memory to Be Used As a Very High Speed Disk Drive.
TriSoft.

RAMDISK PC. Dale Buscaino & Scott Daniel. Sep. 1984.
disk $29.95, incl. manual (ISBN 0-932679-07-2).
Package Includes Documentation & Software for Creation of a RAMdisk (a Virtual Disk Drive in Computer Memory).
Blue Cat.

RAMFAS: Route Accounting & Manufacturing Financial Accounting System. *Compatible Hardware:* IBM PC, PC XT. *Operating System(s) Required:* MS-DOS. *Language(s):* BASIC. *Memory Required:* 256k. *General Requirements:* Hard disk, printer. *Customer Support:* Mon-Fri EST 9:00AM-5:00PM, Modem support & on-site. contact publisher for price.
Includes an Automatic Payroll Update of Commissions. Provides Management Control over Settlements, Invoicing, Sales, Delinquencies, & Financial Areas. Costing on Batch & Continuous Manufacturing Processes Is Included. Capable of Handling Small & Large Bakeries, Beverage & Food Distributors, & Vending Machine Companies. Includes Driver Settlements, Printing of Route Books, Product Master & Prices, Daily Sales, Reporting, Automatic Call of Payroll, Commission Maintenance, General Ledger & Payroll Updating, Preprinted Delivery Tickets, Sales Tax Analysis, Inventory Control, Sales Analysis, Vending Machine Inventory, & Financials.
M&C Systems, Inc.

CA-Ramis/PC. 1986. *Customer Support:* Available.
PC-MS/DOS. IBM PC & compatibles. Contact vendor for price. *Networks supported:* Novell, Banyan, Token Ring.
Information Management System with Integrated Relational Database Manager, Report Wirter, Micro-to-Mainframe Link & Workstation Manager. Develops & Maintains Standalone PC Applications & Prototypes & Distributes Applications in Conjunction with Mainframe CA-Ramis.
Computer Assocs. International, Inc.

RAMPANT. Version: 2.0. Aug. 1993. *Items Included:* Maintenance, documentation, training. *Customer Support:* Unlimited telephone support.
UNIX, AIX, OS/2. HP 9000, 700 Series, SPARCstation, IBM RS/6000, 561, IRIS, ConVex, Cray. Contact publisher for price. *Optimal configuration:* 16Mb RAM.
Computer Program for Modeling Compressible & Incompressible Flow & Heat Transfer in Complex Geometries Using Triangular Elements in 2D & Tetrahedral Elements in 3D. Spatial Discretization Is Accomplished Using a Finite Volume Method & Temporal Discretization Is Accomplished with a Multi-Stage Time Stepping Scheme. Inviscid & Viscous (Both Laminar & Turbulent) Forms of the Governing Equations Are Solved for Modeling Compressible & Incompressible Flows. Has Solution Adaptive Mesh Refinement Capabilities & Employs a Novel Multigrid Scheme to Accelerate Convergence to Steady Solutions.
Fluent, Inc.

Rampant. Version: 4.0.
AIX 3.2.5. IBM RS6000 UNIX workstations. Contact publisher for price.
A Computational Fluid Dynamics Package Ideally Suited for Modeling Turbulent Fluid Flow & Heat Transfer Problems in & Around Complex Geometries Encountered in Aerospace & Turbomachinery Applications. Provides Unparalleled Mesh Flexibility since Triangular, Quadrilateral, Tetrahedral, Hexahedral, Prismatic & Other Element Shapes Can All Be Utilized. Includes a True CAD Preprocessor for Geometry Modeling & Mesh Generation & Import/Modification of Models from Other CAD/CAE Software. State-of-the-Art Numerical Methods & Physical Models for High Speed Compressible Flows Are Provided Within the Framework of a Solver Capable of Utilizing Fully Unstructured & On-the-Fly Solution Adaptive Meshes. A Modern Graphical User Interface, Convenient Model Definition Toolkits & Powerful 3D Graphics Make Possible Easy Model Building, Solution & Postprocessing.
Fluent, Inc.

Ramping Up: Becoming Agile by 2000: 1996 Agility Conference Proceedings. Mar. 1996. *Items Included:* Adobe Acrobat Reader.
Windows 3.11, Apple DOS, Unix. 486 XS 25 (8Mb). CD-ROM disk $19.95 (ISBN 1-885166-09-5, Order no.: CP96-03). *Optimal configuration:* Windows 95', 16Mb RAM, Pentium.
This CD-ROM includes the complete text of the approximately 130 papers delivered at the agility forum's fifth annual conference. These papers focus on a rich array of practical experiences, tools, resources, issues, & ideas relating to the implementation of agility by U. S. industry.
Agile Manufacturing Enterprise Forum.

R&D Partnership Analysis. *Compatible Hardware:* Altos Series 5-15D, Series 5-5D, 580-XX, ACS8000-XX; DEC Rainbow 100 with 2 disk drives, Rainbow 100+ with 10MB hard disk; IBM PC with 2 disk drives, PC XT, IBM compatibles; Kaypro 11/IV with 2 disk drives, Kaypro 10; Xerox 820 with 2 disk drives; ZILOG MCZ-250. *Operating System(s) Required:* CP/M, MP/M, CP/M-86/80, PC-DOS, MS-DOS.
contact publisher for price (Order no.: R&D).
Template for Research & Development Partnerships That Analyzes the Internal Rate of Return & the Present Value of Cash Flows from Investments in R&D Partnerships. R&D Partnerships with Lives As Long As Ten Years. Useful Both to Investors Who Are Considering Making Commitments to R&D Partnerships, & to Their Professional Advisors.
Coopers & Lybrand.

Random House Electronic Thesaurus. *Compatible Hardware:* Apple, IBM. *Operating System(s) Required:* CP/M.
disk $150.00.
disk $50.00, purchased with Peachtree's 'Peachtext'.
Stops at Any of 5,000 Words & at Your Command & Provides 5 to 10 Synonyms on the Screen. Can Be Combined with PEACHTEXT & WORDSTAR.
Wang Laboratories, Inc.

Random House Kid's Encyclopedia.
MS-DOS 3.1 or higher, Windows. 386 processor or higher (640k). CD-ROM disk $69.95 (Order no.: R1356). *Nonstandard peripherals required:* CD-ROM drive. *Optimal configuration:* 386 processor or higher, MS-DOS 3.1 or higher, 20Mb hard drive, 640k RAM, external speakers or headphones (with sound card) that are Sound Blaster compatible, VGA graphics & adapter, VGA color monitor.
This Program Includes Everything Children Need for Topical Research, Including Text Entries & Video Clips. Challenging Puzzles, Simulations & 3-D Exploratory Games Are Used to Help Children Learn How to Research Facts for Homework & Reports (Ages 7-12).
Library Video Co.

Random House Webster's Electronic Dictionary & Thesaurus: College Edition. Reference Software International Staff. 1992. *Items Included:* License, user's guide, system admin. guide. *Customer Support:* Free support at toll number: DOS 801-228-9918, Windows 801-228-9919, Macintosh 801-228-9917.
DOS 3.0 or higher. IBM PC & compatibles (640k). $99.00 SRP. *Optimal configuration:* 9Mb for full package installation.
Windows 3.0 or higher & DOS 3.1. IBM PC & compatibles (2Mb). $99.00 SRP. *Optimal configuration:* 9Mb required for full installation.
Macintosh System 6.0.3 or higher. Mac Plus or higher (1Mb). $99.00 SRP. *Optimal configuration:* Hard disk space of 9Mb required for full installation. *Networks supported:*

Network ready.
Based on the Random House Webster's College Dictionary, Published in 1991. The Dictionary Contains 180,000 Words, While the Thesaurus Contains 275,000 Synonyms & Antonyms. In Addition, the Disk-Based Dictionary Includes Both Biographical & Geographical Information.
WordPerfect Corp.

R&R Report Writer for 1-2-3, Symphony, & Quattro Pro. *Version:* 4.0. Feb. 1992. *Operating System(s) Required:* PC-DOS/MS-DOS. *Memory Required:* as stand-alone 320k, as add-in 20k. *General Requirements:* Lotus 1-2-3 or Symphony, Quattro Pro. *Customer Support:* 60 day telephone technical support.
$249.00.
Allows the Freeform Layout of Text & Fields Within All Areas of a Database Report Including Page Headers & Footers, Group Headers & Footers, Body & Report Summary. Includes Information from Several Database Ranges or Worksheets in a Single Report. Also Features 8 Levels of Subtotals & Calculations.
Concentric Data Systems, Inc.

R&R Report Writer Xbase. *Version:* 6. Sep. 1994. *Compatible Hardware:* IBM PC & compatibles. *Operating System(s) Required:* PC-DOS. *Language(s):* C, Assembler. *Memory Required:* 384k. *General Requirements:* Any .dbf file. *Items Included:* Full documentation. *Customer Support:* For registered users.
disk $249.00.
Allows the Free Form Layout of Text & Fields Within All Areas of dBASE Reports: Page Headers & Footers, Group Headers & Footers, Record Body, & Report Summaries. Allows Information from Several Databases to Be Stored in One Report.
Concentric Data Systems, Inc.

Randt Memory Test. *Version:* 2.0. C. T. Randt et al. 1983. *Compatible Hardware:* Apple. *Operating System(s) Required:* Apple DOS 3.3. *Language(s):* BASIC (source code included).
$115.00, incl. manuals, documentation & picture cards.
$85.00, paper & pencil test only, with picture cards.
Test Is a Combination of Paper & Pencil Items, Picture Recognition Cards & Software for Guiding Test Administration & Scoring. Designed for Evaluation of Mild to Moderate Memory Loss in Elderly & Neurologically Involved Populations.
Life Science Assocs.

RAPID: File Manager for Windows. *Version:* 2.0. Nov. 1994. *Items Included:* Diskettes & manual, registration card. *Customer Support:* No fees charged - tech. support.
Windows 3.1 or higher. $79.00 MSRP.
Simplifies File & Directory Management in Windows. Functions Like Copy, Move, Edit, Rename, View, Erase, Launch, Find, Zip & Unzip Are Accessible from a Button Bar. Unique Interface Allows You to Work with As Many Drives As You Want.
GTM Software.

Rapid Recall II. Marvin Shapiro. 1987. *Compatible Hardware:* IBM PC. *Operating System(s) Required:* MS-DOS. *Memory Required:* 256k. *General Requirements:* 1 disk drive or hard ddisk, printer, color or mono monitor. *Customer Support:* 800-654-8715, full lifetime guarantee.
single site license disk $69.95 (ISBN 0-940503-16-6).
site license disk $139.95 (ISBN 0-940503-26-3).
Free-Form Database "Electronic Notebook." Allows Entry of Data & Retrieved by Entering Matchcode. Can Collate, Index & Print. Contains Word Processor.
Research Design Assocs., Inc.

Rapid Response Manufacturing System. *Version:* 5.6.1. 1993. *Operating System(s) Required:* XENIX, UNIX, AIX, Oracle, Novell. *Language(s):* RM Cobol, Cobol 400, 4GL. *Memory Required:* 128k. *General Requirements:* Hard disk. *Customer Support:* Includes regional classroom & on-site training, 12-hour customer service with modem, complete documentation, local & national user group, free during warranty period, 15% thereafter.
OS/400. Contact publisher for price.
UNIX, Novell. Contact publisher for price.
Enables Custom Manufacturers to Manage Capacity & Track & Cost Jobs Throughout the Manufacturing Process. RRM Can Also Handle Both Make-to-Order & Make-to-Stock Manufacturing Environments Easily. RRM Is Comprised of a Core Software Module Plus Other Optional Manufacturing, Financial, & Utility Software Modules. The System Offers a Wide Range of Easy-to-Use Tools, Including: a Complete Work-Bench Framework; Extensive On-Screen Inquiry Displays; Flexible Browse Features; Pop-Up Windows; Graphs; Screen Customization; Color Availability; Numerous Printed Reports; & VisionWorks, a Graphic Tool for Discrete Manufacturers. Core Software Module Is Comprised of: Order Entry; BOM/Routing; Job Control/History; Costing; Loading & Scheduling; Inventory Management/Control; Estimating; Purchasing; Sales Analysis; VisionWorks; & Report Writer (with RW Plus).
ProfitKey International, Inc.

Rapid Transfer. Great Plains Software. Jan. 1984. *Operating System(s) Required:* MS-DOS. *Memory Required:* 256k. *General Requirements:* Printer, Winchester hard disk.
$295.00, incl. module (Order no.: TI VERSION).
Texas Instruments, Personal Productivit.

RapidFile. *Version:* 1.2. Diamond Software. Jan. 1987. *Compatible Hardware:* IBM PC & compatibles, PC XT, PC AT, PS/2. *Memory Required:* 384k.
disk $395.00.
demo disk $9.95.
Filer That Provides the Following Capabilities: File Management Which Stores Inventory Data, Names, Addresses, or Mailing Labels; Word Processing Including Form Letter Functions That Allow User to Create Memos or Mailmerge Mailing Lists Without Programming; Report Writing That Makes It Easy to Print Standard Forms, Checks, or Mailing Labels. Directly Reads dBASE Files, Imports 1-2-3, Framework, PFS, & ASCII Files & Shares Data with the Above Mentioned Programs. Menu or Command Driven.
Borland International, Inc.

Rapunzel: A Retelling of the Brothers Grimm Fairy Tale. Oct. 1994. *Items Included:* One 8 page booklet.
MAC System 7 or higher/Windows 3.1. Macintosh (4Mb, 8 recommended). CD-ROM disk $19.95 (ISBN 1-883586-01-1). *Optimal configuration:* 8Mb RAM, 13" monitor.
CD-ROM for Macintosh & Windows with the "Rapunzel" Story from the Brothers Grimm Retold Interactively Through Animations. For Kids from 3 to 8. Combines Reading with Narration, Vocabulary Words with Animated Objects.
Boraventures Publishing.

Rat Maze. Warren Allen. 1980. *Compatible Hardware:* TRS-80 Model III, Model 4, Color Computer. *Memory Required:* 16-32k.
disk $20.00 ea.
TRS-80 Color Computer. (ISBN 1-55763-146-8, Order no.: ML065D-CC).
TRS-80 Model III, Model 4. (ISBN 1-55763-145-X, Order no.: ML065D-T).
Direct a Rat Through the Maze.
Micro Learningware.

RATE: Risk Analysis Template Evaluation System. Jul. 1987. *Compatible Hardware:* IBM PC & compatibles. *Memory Required:* 192k. *General Requirements:* Lotus 1-2-3 releases 1A thru 3.1. *Items Included:* Full documentation. *Customer Support:* Yes.
$195.00.
Advanced Financial-Analysis Program Manages Risk in Capital-Investment Projects. Evaluates 11 Major Sources of Uncertainty, Showing the Potential Impact of Each on Investment Performance. Includes a Cash-Flow Model with 32 Line Items & Unlimited Time Periods. Graphical & Tabular Results Show Escalated & Deflated Cash Flows, Key-Investment Indexes, Detailed Analysis of the Impact from Uncertainties, & the Probability for Project Success. Uses Lotus 1-2-3 Templates & Menu-Driven Programs.
Productivity Computing Services.

RateChart. Richard A. Olin. Mar. 1984. *Compatible Hardware:* IBM PC. *Operating System(s) Required:* MS-DOS. *Language(s):* MBASIC. *Memory Required:* 64k.
disk $970.00.
Rate Chart for Consumer Credit Lenders. Calculates All Loan Disclosures with up to 7 Insurance Products & Split Interest Rates. Prints Custom Rate Charts.
Commercial Investment Assocs.

RateFinder. *Version:* 1.8. Oct. 1992. *Items Included:* Manual, tipsheet, 6 month subscription to the RateFinder update "Datazine", to insure up to the minute rates. *Customer Support:* Free phone support.
DOS 3.3 or higher. IBM & compatibles (520k). disk $139.00 (Order no.: RFPL). *Optimal configuration:* 640k RAM.
Macintosh 6.0.5 or higher. Mac Plus or higher (4Mb). 3.5" disk $139.00 (Order no.: RRMAC). *Optimal configuration:* 16mhz Mac or higher, RAM disk. *Networks supported:* Appletalk, Ethernet.
Elefunt Software.

Rational Apex. 1993. *Items Included:* All documentation included. *Customer Support:* Toll-free phone support, customer support newsletter, contact vendor for pricing.
IBM AIX, Sun OS. RS/6000, SPARC (32Mb). $21,000.00 for one license, discounts start at 2 licenses. *Addl. software required:* Motif Windows Manager. *Optimal configuration:* 64Mb RAM. *Networks supported:* TCP/IP, NFS.
An Integrated, Interactive Software-Engineering Environment for Total Lifecycle Control of Ada Projects. It Supports Design, Development, Unit Test, Maintenance, Verification, Documentation Generation, Configuration Management & Version Control, Subsystems Tools, Optimal Recompilation, Integration with External Front-End CASE Tools & External Target Compilers.
Rational.

The Rational Environment. *Version:* 3. 1983-1992. *Items Included:* All documentation included. *Customer Support:* Toll-free phone support, customer support newsletter, contact vendor for pricing.
UNIX. IBM RS/6000, SunSPARC. Starts at $25,000 per user. *Nonstandard peripherals required:* R1000 processor. *Networks supported:* TCP/IP.
An Integrated, Interactive Software-Engineering Environment for Total Lifecycle Control of Ada Projects. It Supports Design, Development, Unit Test, Maintenance, Verification, Documentation Generation, Configuration Management & Version Control, Subsystem Tools, Incremental Compilation, Integration with External Front-End CASE Tools & External Target Compilers.
Rational.

Ratios. *Items Included:* Bound manual. *Customer Support:* Free hotline - no time limit; 30 day limited warranty; updates are $5/disk plus S&H. MS-DOS. IBM & compatibles (256k). disk $29.95.
Designed for the Sole Purpose of Computing Various Financial Ratios Given Certain Standard Financial Data. It Computes the Ratios Calculable Given the Data Present. Included Are the More Popular Ratios Such As Net Operating Margin, ROA, ROE, Current Ratio, Quick Ratio, Debt Ratio, & Inventory Turnover. Also Computed Are Ratios Such As Times Interest Earned, Fixed Charges, Coverage, Funded Debt to Working Capital, Net Working Capital Turnover, Earnings per Share, Price Earnings Ratio, & Numerous Others. In All, 34 Different Ratios Are Evaluated.
Dynacomp, Inc.

Rats. *Compatible Hardware:* Apple II+, IIe, IIc; Commodore; Franklin Ace; TRS-80 Model III; Model 4. *Language(s):* Applesoft BASIC. *Memory Required:* 48k.
disk $24.95.
cassette $24.95.
Students Play the Role of a Health Department Official Who Has to Come up with a Practical Plan for Control of the Rat Population. The Plan Can Combine the Use of a Slow Kill/Quick Kill Poison & Sanitation. Students Can Change the Population Size & Growth Rate. The User Has the Option of Selecting an Apartment Building or an Entire City As the Simulation.
Compuware.

RATS: Rapid Assessment & Treatment Strategies. Oct. 1988. *Compatible Hardware:* Apple II series, IBM PC & compatibles. *Memory Required:* 64k.
disk $19.95 (ISBN 0-931821-97-5).
Provides Help & Assistance to Human Resource Personnel Management. Matches Counseling Approaches/Models to Employee Behavioral Problems. Formal Diagnostic Testing Is By-Passed. Pinpoints Responsibility for Employee's Behavioral Problems & Matches the Appropriate Treatment.
Information Resource Consultants.

RAVE.
OS-9 or OS-9000 real-time operating system. *Real-Time Audio/Video Environment Used to Design User Interfaces & Control Panels with Real-World Sounds & Images. Incorporates Friendly User Interface for a Nontechnical User. Creates Intuitive Interfaces Without Requiring Any Coding. Indicators, Controls & Menus Are Available As Library Components That Can Be Accessed Through Presentation Editor. Components Can Be Added by Combining Primitives in Graphics Support Library. Consists of Three Packages: Presentation Editor, Graphics Support Library & Graphics File Manager.*
Microware Systems Corp.

Ravenloft: Stone Prophet. DreamForge Intertainment Staff. Mar. 1995. *Items Included:* 1 96 page perfect bound manual & 1 data card. *Customer Support:* 30 day limited warranty.
DOS 5.0 or higher. IBM PC compatible with CD-ROM, Hard drive & Mouse (4Mb & VGA card). CD-ROM disk $69.95 (ISBN 0-917059-23-9, Order no.: 062271). *Nonstandard peripherals required:* Uncompressed hard drive recommended. *Optimal configuration:* 386/33 required, 486/33 recommended.
Advanced Dungeons & Dragons Fantasy Role Playing That Takes Place in the Ravenloft Game World.
Strategic Simulations, Inc.

Ravenloft Stone Prophet Cluebook. May 1995. *Customer Support:* 30 day limited warranty.
IBM & compatibles. CD-ROM disk $14.95 (ISBN 0-917059-02-6, Order no.: 190341). *Addl. software required:* Ravenloft Stone Prophet CD game product.
Hints & Clues for the Successful Completion of the Ravenloft Stone Prophet CD Software Game.
Strategic Simulations, Inc.

RaxManager: Resource Management System. *Version:* 3.0. 1990. *Items Included:* Manual, quarterly newsletter. *Customer Support:* Customer support included in price.
VMS. VAX. $650.00-$14,800.00.
Comprehensive VAX/VMS Resource Management Tool. Effectively Provides Performance Analysis Information in Graphic & Tabular Reports on Resource Utilization & System Performance to Support Resource Allocation, System Management & Capacity Planning Decisions.
Raxco, Inc.

RaxMaster: Comprehensive Performance Enhancement Solution. *Version:* 3.0. 1991. *Items Included:* Installation manual, how-to manual, PerfectDisk - technically advanced disk defragmentation & optimization system, PerfectTune - monitors system workload & dynamically adjusts system parameters, PerfectCache - maximizes I/O throughput by placing files in main memory. *Customer Support:* Customer support included in price.
VMS. VAX. $550.00-$7550.00.
Complete, System-Wide Performance Management Solution for VAX/VMS. Optimizes the Performance of Entire VAX/VMS System by Balancing Resources (Memory, I/O & CPU) According to System Demands. These Capabilities Enable the System Manager to Maintain Consistent, Optimal System Performance. Provides Disk Defragmentation & Optimization, Dynamic System Tuning, Caching & Virtual Disk Capabilities.
Raxco, Inc.

RBCA Tool Kit: RBCA Spreadsheet System. Jan. 1996. *Items Included:* Complete 3-volume set of manuals (ISBN 1-882713-03-6); summary report forms in bound (paperback) volume; electronic copies of summary report forms in Microsoft Word format. *Customer Support:* Toll-call, fee-based technical support for registered users only.
MS-DOS, with MS Windows 3.1 or higher. IBM-PC & compatibles; Intel i486 or higher processor (8Mb). disk $495.00 (ISBN 1-882713-04-4). *Addl. software required:* Microsoft Excel Spreadsheet Version 5.0 or higher. *Optimal configuration:* IBM-PC or compatible w/Pentium processor, 16Mb RAM.
MacOS System 7 or higher. Apple Macintosh w/ 68040 or higher processor (16Mb). 3.5" disk $495.00. *Addl. software required:* Microsoft Excel 5.0. *Optimal configuration:* Mac or compatible with PowerPC processor, System 7.5, & 16Mb RAM.
The Risk-Based Corrective Action (RBCA) Tool Kit Is a Comprehensive Software/Book Package to Complete Tier 1 & Tier 2 RBCA Analysis in Accordance with ASTM E-1739 "Standard Guide for Risk-Based Corrective Action Applied at Petroleum Release Sites" & Applicable U.S. EPA Guidelines. The Tool Kit Includes a Detailed RBCA Guidance Manual & a Comprehensive RBCA Spreadsheet System.
Groundwater Services, Inc.

RBUG86: Symbolic Software Debugger. *Version:* 2.51. Jun. 1985. *Compatible Hardware:* IBM PC, PC XT, PC AT or BIOS-level compatibles. *Operating System(s) Required:* DOS 2.0 or higher. *Memory Required:* 256k. *Items Included:* manual & diskette.
disk $395.00 (Order no.: 09500).
Symbolic Debugger for the IBM Family of Personal Computers & Compatible Machines. Provides Support for Both the Assembly Language & High-Level Language Programmer, with a Full Screen Display of Registers, Variables & Code. Supports Dual Display Adapters & an External Terminal or Uses a Screen-Swapping Technique to Preserve the Application Display. Other Features Include Symbolic Assembler & Disassembler, Macros, IEEE Floating Point Supports, etc.
Answer Software Corp.

RDS System Seven. *Items Included:* Extensive manuals, operational hints, sample data for practice. *Customer Support:* 1 year free support; after that, $500 per year. All support includes updates, revisions, enhancements, 24-hour toll-free 800 support, free on-site set-up & training.
MS-DOS 3.3 or higher. IBM PC & compatible (640k). Contact publisher for price. *Nonstandard peripherals required:* Hard disk. *Networks supported:* 386/MultiWare, Lantastic.
Fully Integrated System for Sales, Sales Management, Traffic, Logging, Billing with Affidavits & Co-Op Copy, Open Items Accounts Receivable, Accounts Payable, Multi-State Payroll & General Ledger. Fully Compatible with Satellite Formats & Automated Stations. Includes Thousands of Sales & Management Reports.
Register Data Systems.

RDS System Six. *Items Included:* Extensive reference manuals, operational suggestions, newsletter, sample data. *Customer Support:* Price includes installation & on-site training, 1-year support with all new releases, & 24-hour telephone assistance.
MS-DOS 3.3 or higher (640k). contact publisher for price. *Nonstandard peripherals required:* Hard disk. *Networks supported:* 386/MultiWare, Lantastic.
Fully Integrated System for Sales, Traffic, Logging, Billing with Affidavits & Co-Op Copy, Open Items Accounts Receivable. Fully Compatible with Satellite Formats & Automated Stations. Includes Numerous Sales, Accounting & Management Reports.
Register Data Systems.

RDS Traffic Master I. *Items Included:* 200+ page manual, installation instructions, newsletter, sample practice data. *Customer Support:* 1 year free support; after that, $500.00 per year; includes updates, revisions, enhancements, toll-free 1-800 support.
MS-DOS 2.1 or higher (256k). Any MS-DOS compatible. contact publisher for price. *Nonstandard peripherals required:* Hard disk.
Integrated System Handles Sales of Advertising, Logging, Invoicing, Affidavits of Performance & Complete Accounts Receivable. Includes Numerous Sales, Traffic & Management Reports.
Register Data Systems.

RDS Traffic Master II. *Items Included:* Extensive reference manual, newsletter, sample practice data. *Customer Support:* Free on-site training, 1 yr. free support with 800 phone support 24 hrs.; after 1st year, $500.00 per year.
MS-DOS 2.1 or higher (256k). contact publisher for price. *Nonstandard peripherals required:* Hard disk.
Integrated System Handles Sales of Advertising, Traffic, Logging, Invoicing, Affidavits, Co-Op Copy & Complete Open-Items Accounts Receivable. Fully Compatible with Satellite & Automated Stations. Includes Numerous Sales, Traffic, Accounting & Management Reports.
Register Data Systems.

RDS Traffic Master III. *Items Included:* Extensive reference manuals, operational pointers, newsletter, sample practice data. *Customer Support:* Price includes installation & on-site training, 1-year support with all new releases & 24-hour 800 telephone support; after 1st year, continuing support is $500.00 per year.
MS-DOS 2.1 or higher (256k). contact publisher for price. *Nonstandard peripherals required:* Hard disk. *Networks supported:* NTNX, PC-MOS.
Integrated System for Sales, Traffic, Logging, Invoicing, Affidavits, Co-Op Copy, Open Items Accounts Receivable, Accounts Payable, Payroll & General Ledger. Fully Compatible with Satellite Formats & Automated Stations. Includes Numerous Sales, Traffic, Billing, Accounting & Management Reports.
Register Data Systems.

R.E. List: Real Estate Brokerage Program.
Thomas Philip Degnon. May 1986. *Compatible Hardware:* IBM PC & compatibles. *Operating System(s) Required:* MS-DOS. *Memory Required:* 384k.
disk $695.00.
Stores & Retrieves Listings of Condominiums for Sale, Apartments for Rent & Buildings for Sale.
Boston Educational Computing, Inc.

Re: Members. *Version:* 1.4. Jul. 1989. *Items Included:* Manual with binder. *Customer Support:* 12 mo. maintenance $110.00, full year installation support.
PC-DOS/MS-DOS v. 2.11 or better (640k). IBM compatible. $269.00. *Optimal configuration:* 286 machine, VGA monitor, 1 Mb RAM, hard disk.
Tracks Families & Members with Member Involvement in Activities As Well As Giving Financial Records. Records Contributions by Name, Envelope, or Accounts for Families or Individuals. Extensive Report Writer Allows for Lists of All Types, Labels, Envelopes, File Folder Labels, As Well As Individually Tailored Letters to All or Selected Members. Finance System Allows Entry of Checks & Receipts, Journal Entries, & Transfer of Contribution Postings. Helps Bank Reconciliation, Check Writing, & a Variety of Reports.
EZ Systems, Inc.

REA/L Estate Analysis. 1990. *Items Included:* Manual. *Customer Support:* Free support with developer.
MS-DOS. IBM PC & compatibles (640k). disk $325.00. *Addl. software required:* Lotus 1-2-3, Version 1A or higher, Quattro, VPPlanner, Excel 2.0, New DOS Version (no-host). Macintosh (640k). 3.5" disk $325.00.
30 Plus Complete Worksheets for Investment Real Estate Analysis. Templates Take User from Lease Analysis to Rental Projection to Operating Statement & Finally a Cashflow Projection Including Current Tax Laws. Rates of Return As If Sold Each Year, Multiple Loans, Participation, Depreciation, etc. Amortization Schedules, Exchange Structuring, Loan Evaluations & More Included.
Roger Martin Co.

Reaching Out with Sign: A Basic Sign Language Phrase Manual. Anita Piskula. Jan. 1994.
Contact publisher for price.
The Manual Provides 1,300 Black & White Photographs of Signed ASL Phrases. Illustrates the Expressive Qualities of the Face & Visual Cues of Body Language. Enhances the Perceptual Skills of the Developmentally Disabled Deaf Population. Repetitive Vocabulary Is Used Throughout Manual for Increased Retention of Words. English/American Sign Language.
Elwyn, Inc.

Reaction Time. 1981. *Compatible Hardware:* Apple II+, IIc, IIe; Franklin Ace. *Operating System(s) Required:* Apple DOS 3.3. *Language(s):* Applesoft BASIC (source code included). *General Requirements:* Printer. disk $20.00.
Helps the User Determine His/Her Reaction Time to a Visual Stimulus. Recommended to Those Involved in Scientific & Medical Experiments.
Andent, Inc.

Reactions.
Apple Macintosh (512k). 3.5" disk $28.00.
Chemical Reaction Rate Program That Runs on the Apple Macintosh Computers. Written in Microsoft Basic 2.0, Reactions Calculates the Time-Varying Species Contrations for up to 18 Species Involved in up to 18 Reaction Equations. It Also Calculates the Reaction Temperature & the Heat of Reaction (Enthalpy). The Final Product of the Calculations Is a Semi-Log of Concentration vs. Time.
E & M Software Co.

Read-a-Logo: Concentration. *Version:* Home. Shelley B. Wepner. 1992. *Customer Support:* Free - 800-228-2871.
MS-DOS. IBM Tandy & compatibles (640k). disk $29.95. *Nonstandard peripherals required:* Optional: For speech add Echo PC, Soundblaster or Covox. *Optimal configuration:* MCGA.
Improves Visual Memory! This All-Time Favorite Game Will Keep Children Entertained for Hours Matching Logos & Their Associated Words. The Animated Graphic at the End Is Their Reward for a Job Well Done. Start Children Reading Today.
Teacher Support Software, Inc.

Read-a-Logo: Group-a-Logo. *Version:* Home. Shelley B. Wepner. 1992. *Customer Support:* Free - 800-228-2871.
MS-DOS. IBM Tandy & compatibles (640k). disk $29.95. *Nonstandard peripherals required:* Optional: For speech add Echo PC, Soundblaster or Covox. *Optimal configuration:* MCGA.
Every First-Grade Teacher Knows the Importance of Categorization for Reading Readiness. In This Fun Activity, Children Will Decide If a Logo Fits in the Category & Select Words Related to That Logo. Give Children a Head Start in First Grade.
Teacher Support Software, Inc.

Read-a-Logo: Rebus Stories. *Version:* Home. Shelley B. Wepner. 1992. *Customer Support:* Free - 800-228-2871.
MS-DOS. IBM Tandy & compatibles (640k). disk $29.95. *Nonstandard peripherals required:* Optional: For speech add Echo PC, Soundblaster or Covox. *Optimal configuration:* MCGA.
A Beginning Reading Strategy! Now Youngsters Can Begin to Read Simple Sentences with the Help of Colorful Logos & Signs. Twenty Personal, Theme-Related Stories Are Included & Can Be Printed When Completed. It's Fun & Children Will Love Learning to Read.
Teacher Support Software, Inc.

Read-a-Logo: Write-about-Logos. *Version:* Home. Shelley B. Wepner. 1992. *Customer Support:* Free - 800-228-2871.
MS-DOS. IBM Tandy & compatibles (640k). disk $29.95. *Nonstandard peripherals required:* Optional: For speech add Echo PC, Soundblaster or Covox. *Optimal configuration:* MCGA.
Begin Building Essential Writing Skills with This Simple Word Processor. A Variety of Logos, Graphics, Font Options & Color Choices Will Delight Budding Writers & Keep the Stories Coming. Each Story Can Be Printed to Share with Family & Friends. It's Never Too Early to Start Children Writing.
Teacher Support Software, Inc.

Read-A-Rama. Selena Studios Staff. Oct. 1995. *Customer Support:* Free onliIne tech support Selenaly-AOL.COM.
Windows 3.1 or 95. PC Multimedia (8Mb). CD-ROM disk $14.95 (ISBN 1-55727-034-1, Order no.: RDEC01). *Nonstandard peripherals required:* 1Mb video card.
Joey, the Genie, Has a Problem. His Great-Looking Lamp Has Been Taken to Demetri, the Giant's Den. Joey Is Stuck Living in a Perfume Bottle Which Is Unfitting for a Genie of His Stature. Venture into the Sky on Joey's Magic Carpet & Clear Away the Bad Weather by Pacifying the Rain Babies, Thunder Drummer, Lightning Man, & Rainbow Girl. Kids Learn How to Read & Spell the Names of Colors, Shapes, Vegetable, & over 100 Everyday Words. They'll Love Flying Around with Joey on This Amusing Quest.
Unicorn Educational Software.

Read-It! Personal OCR. *Items Included:* Disks, manual & addendums. *Customer Support:* Free unlimited phone technical support, FAX & modem service. America Online, CompuServe, Applelink.
Macintosh System 6.0.5 & higher. Mac Plus & higher (1Mb RAM). 3.5" disk $295.00. *Nonstandard peripherals required:* Scanner 300dpi (hand). *Optimal configuration:* 68030 or accelerator with 4Mb RAM 300dpi scanner.
Allows Users to Convert Any Macintosh-Compatible Scanner into a Sophisticated OCR System. The Program Is Capable of Automatically Recognizing Proportionally-Spaced Characters & Standard Monospaced Characters, Predefined "Type Tables" for Most Popular LaserWriter, Typewriter & ImageWriter Typefaces, As Well As OmniFont Capabilities, Allow Read-It! to Recognize Characters Automatically Without Training. The Program Has the Ability to Learn from New Typefaces, Including Foreign & Special Characters. Uses Pattern-Recognition Algorithms That Recognize Serif & Sans Serif Typefaces in Varied Sizes from 7 Point; to More Than 48 Points. The Program Can Also Recognize Bold, Underline & Italic Text (with Proper Training). A Built-In Intelligent Dictionary Is Included.
Olduvai Corp.

Read-It! Personal OCR for Windows 3.X (IBM). *Version:* 2.1c. *Items Included:* Disks, manual & addendums. *Customer Support:* Free unlimited phone technical support, FAX & modem service. America Online, CompuServe, Applelink.
Windows 3.X. IBM PC & compatibles (640k). disk $295.00. *Optimal configuration:* 386-486, 4Mb RAM.
Allows Users to Convert Any Macintosh-Compatible Scanner into a Sophisticated OCR System. The Program Is Capable of Automatically Recognizing Proportionally-Spaced Characters & Standard Monospaced Characters, Predefined "Type Tables" for Most Popular LaserWriter, Typewriter & ImageWriter Typefaces, As Well As OmniFont Capabilities, Allow Read-It! to Recognize Characters Automatically Without Training. The Program Has the Ability to Learn from New Typefaces, Including Foreign & Special Characters. Uses Pattern-Recognition Algorithms That Recognize Serif & Sans Serif Typefaces in Varied Sizes from 7 Point; to More Than 48 Points. The Program Can Also Recognize Bold, Underline & Italic Text (with Proper Training). A Built-In Intelligent Dictionary Is Included.
Olduvai Corp.

Read-It! Pro: Macintosh Version. *Version:* 4.02.
Macintosh Plus (2Mb). 3.5" disk $595.00. *Nonstandard peripherals required:* Mac-compatible scanner.
Optical Character Scanning Program. Includes Universal Omnifont Recognition for Typical Business Documents & Page Recognition

Capabilities for Distinguishing among Graphics & Text. Program Can Read Most Standard Fonts & Styles Without a Specific Recognition Library. Program Will Also Handle Multiple Page Documents & Support Scanner Document Sheet Feeders. An Expert Mode Now Combines Trainable & Automatic Modes.
Olduvai Corp.

Read-It! Pro OCR for Windows 3.X (IBM).
Version: 2.1c. *Items Included:* Disks, manual & addendums. *Customer Support:* Free unlimited phone technical support, FAX & modem service. America Online, CompuServe, Applelink. Windows 3.0 or higher. IBM PC & compatibles (640k). disk $595.00. *Nonstandard peripherals required:* 300dpi scanner. *Optimal configuration:* 386-486 with Windows 3.1 4Mb RAM.
Allows Users to Convert Any Macintosh-Compatible Scanner into a Sophisticated OCR System. The Program Is Capable of Automatically Recognizing Proportionally-Spaced Characters & Standard Monospaced Characters, Predefined "Type Tables" for Most Popular LaserWriter, Typewriter & ImageWriter Typefaces, As Well As OmniFont Capabilities, Allow Read-It! to Recognize Characters Automatically Without Training. The Program Has the Ability to Learn from New Typefaces, Including Foreign & Special Characters. Uses Pattern-Recognition Algorithms That Recognize Serif & Sans Serif Typefaces in Varied Sizes from 7 Point; to More Than 48 Points. The Program Can Also Recognize Bold, Underline & Italic Text (with Proper Training). A Built-In Intelligent Dictionary Is Included.
Olduvai Corp.

Read-It!: Windows Version. *Version:* 2.1c. Apr. 1989. *Compatible Hardware:* IBM PC AT & compatibles. *Operating System(s) Required:* Microsoft Windows. *Memory Required:* 640k. *General Requirements:* Hard disk.
$495.00.
OCR Software. Works with Most Scanners, Can Recognize Typeset, Proportionally-Spaced Characters & Mixed Serif & Sans-Serif Typefaces from Seven to 48 Points. It Can also Handle Bold & Italic Text. Includes Scanner Drivers for Canon/Princeton, Microtek, Hewlett-Packard, & DEST Scanners. It also Reads Files from any Scanner or Fax Modem that Supports the TIFF or PCX File Format, Converting Them into Standard Text Files.
Olduvai Corp.

Readability Formulas, 2nd ed. Jan. 1989. *Items Included:* user's manual, diskette. *Customer Support:* telephone.
Apple IIe, IIc, IIgs (64k). disk $69.00 (ISBN 1-877666-00-9, Order no.: 490AP).
IBM PC & compatibles (128k). disk $69.00 (ISBN 1-877666-01-7, Order no.: 490IP).
Determines Reading Level of Portion of Text (100 Words). Samples May Be Entered, Edited & Saved with the Word Processor or Entered As Text File from Other Word Processors. Samples may Be Grouped Together to Obtain An Average Reading Level.
Looking Glass Learning Products, Inc.

Reader Rabbit.
Windows. IBM & compatibles. CD-ROM disk $64.95 (Order no.: R1207). *Nonstandard peripherals required:* CD-ROM drive. *Optimal configuration:* 386 processor or higher, MS-DOS 3.1 or higher, 20Mb hard drive, 640k RAM, external speakers or headphones (with sound card) that are Sound Blaster compatible, VGA graphics & adapter, VGA color monitor.
Macintosh (4Mb). (Order no.: R1207).
Nonstandard peripherals required: 14" color monitor or larger, CD-ROM drive.
Young Minds Will Delight in This Animated Word Factory That Helps Children Build Early Reading, Spelling & Vocabulary Skills. Four Carefully Sequenced Games Develop Skills in Word & Spelling Pattern Recognition, Concentration, Memory & Thinking (Ages 3-6).
Library Video Co.

Reading Blaster.
Windows. IBM & compatibles. CD-ROM disk $59.95 (Order no.: R1357). *Nonstandard peripherals required:* CD-ROM drive. *Optimal configuration:* 386 processor or higher, MS-DOS 3.1 or higher, 20Mb hard drive, 640k RAM, external speakers or headphones (with sound card) that are Sound Blaster compatible, VGA graphics & adapter, VGA color monitor.
Children Can Learn to Read & Understand over 1,000 Words As They Join Blasternaut & His Crew. Through Five Exciting Games Children Will Be Able to Distinguish Between Antonyms & Synonyms, Understand Connector Words, & Apply Logic & Critical Thinking Skills (Ages 7-10).
Library Video Co.

Reading for Beginners. 1988. *Customer Support:* Toll free customary service Hot Line 1-800-645-3739 (9a.m. - 5p.m. Eastern Time).
Apple II; IBM; Tandy (MS-DOS). $39.95 ea., incl. 1 disk & documentation (Order no.: DB7020; DB7021; DB7022; DB7023; DB7024; DB7025).
$199.00 set incl. 6 disks & documentation (Order no.: DB7026).
A Highly Interactive Program Which Helps Beginners Develop the Core Vocabularies Needed to Function in Our Society.
Educational Activities Inc.

Reading for Facts, Information, & Details: The Cloze Reading Tutor Starter Package. Frances H. Dickinson & Intentional Educations Staff. 1994. *Items Included:* Package contains disk, software guide, perfect bound student book, & a teacher guide. Additional copies of the student book may be purchased for $7.95 ($6.95 each for 10 or more copies). *Customer Support:* Returnable if not satisfied. Call 1-800-341-6094 for technical support. 30-day preview available.
MS-DOS. IBM & compatibles (128k). disk $61.95 (ISBN 0-8251-2300-3, Order no.: 0-23003).
Apple. Apple IIE (128k). disk $61.95 (ISBN 0-8251-2301-1, Order no.: 0-23011).
Helps Students Develop Reading Skills Necessary for Obtaining Information & Following Directions Using These Selections about Interesting Topics. Students Can Take a Pretest, Complete Exercises about the Selection, & Take a Post-Test, While Gaining Skills in Evaluating Data, Drawing Inferences, etc.
J. Weston Walch Pub.

Reading in the Workplace. Beverly Davis et al. 1995. *Items Included:* CD-ROM, documentations, binders & activities masters. *Customer Support:* Toll free customer service Hot Line 1-800-645-3739 (9a.m. - 5p.m. Eastern Time) software guaranteed for two years.
System 6.07 or higher (2Mb); System 7.0 or higher (4Mb). Macintosh. CD-ROM disk $295.00 (Order no.: DK21051).
Each Program Has Three Progressive Levels of Difficulty & a Built-In Dictionary to Identify the Meaning of Unfamiliar Words in Context. The Motivating Lessons Provide Immediate Feedback & Reinforcement. Errors Are Automatically Flagged & the Student Is Branched to Hints that Explain How to Find the Correct Answer.
Educational Activities Inc.

Reading Magic Library: Fizz & Martina in "Tough Krudd".
Mac 3 (2Mb) color, QuickTime capable. 3.5" disk $59.95 (Order no.: FIZ-K). *Networks supported:* AppleShare.
3.5" disk $119.95 5 Disk Lab Pack (Order no.: FIZ-LAB-K).
3.5" disk $179.95 Network (Order no.: FIZ-NET-K).
Remember the Meanest Kid in Your School? Well, Meet Krudd. He's New in Blue Falls & Quickly Makes Life Miserable for Fizz. That Is, until a Hair-Raising Adventure Forces Krudd to Rethink His Nasty Attitude.
Tom Snyder Productions, Inc.

Reading Magic Library: Flodd, the Bad Guy.
Version: 2.0. 1988. *Items Included:* Manual & teacher guide. *Customer Support:* 90 day warranty.
Apple IIgs. Apple IIgs (512k). $59.95 (ISBN 0-926891-44-8, Order no.: FL3-A).
MS-DOS. IBM PC/Tandy 1000 & compatibles (256k). $59.95 (ISBN 0-926891-41-3, Order no.: FL-I).
Apple II Series. Apple IIe, IIc, IIgs (64k). $59.95 (ISBN 0-926891-40-5, Order no.: FL-A).
Macintosh. $59.95.
Animated Interactive Storybook That Lets You Choose What Happens Next. You'll Put Yourselves in the Shoes of Heroes & Heroines, Making Exciting Choices for Them. Each Choice Is Illustrated with Colorful Pictures, Letters & Words. The Perfect Way for Your Child to Learn Reading Skills While the Two of You Share Unforgettable Adventures.
Tom Snyder Productions, Inc.

Reading Magic Library: Hansel & Gretel.
Mac 3 (2Mb) color, QuickTime capable. 3.5" disk $59.95 (Order no.: GIN-K). *Networks supported:* AppleShare.
3.5" disk $119.95 5 Disk Lab Pack (Order no.: GIN-LAB-K).
3.5" disk $179.95 Network (Order no.: GIN-NET-K).
A Modern Twist on a Classic Tale! Hansel & Gretel Wander into the Endless Forest Because Their Parents Are Busy Watching TV. Instead of Discovering a Gingerbread House, They Come upon a House Made of Television Sets! What Does the Misguided Robot, Switch, Have in Store for Her Guests.
Tom Snyder Productions, Inc.

Reading Magic Library: Hilary & the Beast.
Mac 3 (2Mb) color, QuickTime capable. 3.5" disk $59.95 (Order no.: HIL-K). *Networks supported:* AppleShare.
3.5" disk $119.95 5 Disk Lab Pack (Order no.: HIL-LAB-K).
3.5" disk $179.95 Network (Order no.: HIL-NET-K).
Meet Hilary LuvHeart, a Brave & Smart Seven Year Old. Follow Hilary on Her Adventures As She Rescues & Befriends a Lovable Beast from a Travelling Circus. As the Star of Several of Our Monthly Stories on the Prodigy Service, Hilary Has Received over 10,000 Pieces of Fan Mail from Kids Across the Country. Discover Her for Yourself in This Delightful Tale.
Tom Snyder Productions, Inc.

Reading Magic Library: Jack & the Beanstalk.
Version: 2.0. 1988. *Items Included:* Manual & teacher guide. *Customer Support:* 90 day warranty.
Apple IIgs. Apple IIgs (512k). $59.95 (ISBN 0-926891-42-1, Order no.: JA3-A).
MS-DOS. IBM PC/Tandy 1000 & compatibles (256k). $59.95 (ISBN 0-926891-39-1, Order no.: JA-I).
Apple II series. Apple IIe, IIc, IIgs (64k). $59.95

READING ONE-FIVE: FOUR SKILLS

(ISBN 0-926891-38-3, Order no.: JA-A).
Macintosh. $59.95.
Animated Interactive Storybooks That Let You Choose What Happens Next. You'll Put Yourselves in the Shoes of Heroes & Heroines, Making Exciting Choices for Them. Each Choice Is Illustrated with Colorful Pictures, Letters & Words. The Perfect Way for Your Child to Learn Reading Skills While the Two of You Share Unforgettable Adventures.
Tom Snyder Productions, Inc.

Reading One-Five: Four Skills, Practice A-D.
Dec. 1981. *Items Included:* Teacher's guide. *Customer Support:* 90-day limited warranty.
Apple-DOS 3.3. Apple II Family (48k). disk $59.00 ea. (Set) (ISBN 0-917277-25-2).
Commodore 64/128 (64k). disk $59.00 ea. (Reading 1) (ISBN 0-917277-38-4).
TRS-DOS. TRS-80 (34k). disk $59.00 ea. (Set) (ISBN 0-917277-37-6).
Teaches & Reinforces the Main Idea, Drawing Conclusions & Putting Things in Order Using Reading Lessons. Also Practices Recalling Details & Reading in the Content Area. Each of the Series Presents 10 Reading Passages, Followed by 5 or More Questions about the Reading Skill Being Taught. Ages 10 Up.
BrainBank/Generation Ahead of Maryland.

The Reading Professor: Faster Reading with Comprehension. *Items Included:* Bound manual. *Customer Support:* Free hotline - no time limit; 30 day limited warranty; updates are $5/disk plus S&H.
MS-DOS 2.0 or higher. IBM & compatibles (128k). $14.95-$59.95.
Designed to Increase Reading Speed While Maintaining Comprehension. Consists of Two Parts; the Lessons & the Exercises. The Lessons Have Ten Parts, Each of Which Takes 15-20 Minutes to Complete. There Are Seven Types of Exercises with 50 Different Passages. There Are Eight Variables to Select, Including Character Size, Line Width, & Speed. In Addition, Scan Highlights May Be Used for Pacing. Comes with a General Interest Reading Library. Extra Libraries Are Available.
Dynacomp, Inc.

Reading Programs: Diascriptive Reading in the Content Area Social Studies. Carol Buchter & Ron Buchter. *Items Included:* Diskettes, guides, documentation & binder. *Customer Support:* Toll free customer service Hot Line 1-800-645-3739 (9a.m. - 5 p.m. Eastern Time) software guaranteed for two years.
System 6.07 or higher (2Mb); System 7.0 or higher (4Mb). Macintosh. 3.5" disk $335.00 (Order no.: DK21114).
Each Comprehensive Program Has Five Diagnostic Tests (One for Each Skill Area) & 25 Developmental Reading Programs. Main Idea, Details, Vocabulary, Sequence & Inference. The Specific Reading Skills Developed Help Students Interpret Content Materials for Any Type.
Educational Activities Inc.

Reading 1. Jan. 1994. *Items Included:* Program on CD-ROM, CD Booklet, & Registration Card. *Customer Support:* Free unlimited support via telephone.
Windows 3.1 or higher running under DOS 5.0 or higher. 386 SX (4Mb RAM; 500k low Dos Mem; 6Mb free disk space). CD-ROM disk $49.00 (ISBN 1-57268-009-1, Order no.: 55001). *Nonstandard peripherals required:* Sound card (either: Sound Blaster - 8, 16, PRO; Media Vision ProAudio Spectrum; or Microsoft Sound System); MPC Compatible CD-ROM drive; VGA monitor; & microphone. *Optimal configuration:* 25MHz 386 SX.
Reading Grade-Level for Windows: These Programs Provide a Natural, Developmental Approach to Fundamental Reading Skills. Beginners Progress Through Reading-Readiness, Phonics, & Decoding. Imaginative Picture Stories & Sound Patterns Add New Dimensions & Excitement to the Learning Process.
Conter Software.

Reading 1. Jan. 1994. *Items Included:* Program on CD-ROM, CD Booklet, & Registration Card. *Customer Support:* Free unlimited support via telephone.
Macintosh System 7.0 or higher. Macintosh LC or higher (4Mb). CD-ROM disk $49.00 (ISBN 1-57268-034-2, Order no.: 65001). *Nonstandard peripherals required:* 12 inch monitor or larger; CD-ROM drive. *Optimal configuration:* 5Mb RAM.
Reading Grade-Level for Macintosh. The Reading Grade-Level CD-ROMs Were Designed to Help Students Become Proficient Readers by Providing Them with a Balance of Strategy & Application Lessons. Students Build Vocabulary, Learn Word Meanings, & Practice Study Skills in a Variety of Interesting Lessons.
Conter Software.

Reading 1-2. Jan. 1994. *Items Included:* Program on CD-ROM, CD Booklet, & Registration Card. *Customer Support:* Free unlimited customer support via telephone.
Windows 3.1 or higher running under DOS 5.0 or higher. 386 SX (4Mb RAM; 500k low Dos Mem; 6Mb free disk space). CD-ROM disk $249.00 (ISBN 1-57268-048-2, Order no.: 15120). *Nonstandard peripherals required:* Sound card (either: Sound Blaster - 8, 16, PRO; Media Vision ProAudio Spectrum; or Microsoft Sound System); MPC compatible CD-ROM drive; VGA monitor; & microphone. *Optimal configuration:* 25 MHz 386 SX.
Reading Grade-Level for Windows: These Programs Provide a Natural, Developmental Approach to Fundamental Reading Skills. Beginners Progress Through Reading-Readiness, Phonics, & Decoding. Imaginative Picture Stories & Sound Patterns Add New Dimensions & Excitement to the Learning Process.
Conter Software.

Reading 1-2. Jan. 1994. *Items Included:* Program on CD-ROM, CD Booklet, & Registration Card. *Customer Support:* Free unlimited customer support via telephone.
Macintosh System 7.0 or higher. Macintosh LC or higher (4Mb). CD-ROM disk $249.00 (ISBN 1-57268-069-5, Order no.: 25120). *Nonstandard peripherals required:* 12 inch monitor or larger; CD-ROM drive. *Optimal configuration:* 5Mb RAM.
Reading Grade-Level for Macintosh: The Reading Grade-Level CD-ROMs Were Designed to Help Students Become Proficient Readers by Providing Them with a Balance of Strategy & Application Lessons. Students Build Vocabulary, Learn Word Meanings, & Practice Study Skills in a Variety of Interesting Lessons.
Conter Software.

Reading 2. Jan. 1994. *Items Included:* Program on CD-ROM, CD Booklet, & Registration Card. *Customer Support:* Free unlimited support via telephone.
Windows 3.1 or higher running under DOS 5.0 or higher. 386 SX (4Mb RAM; 500k low Dos Mem; 6Mb free disk space). CD-ROM disk $49.00 (ISBN 1-57268-010-5, Order no.: 55002). *Nonstandard peripherals required:* Sound card (either: Sound Blaster - 8, 16, PRO; Media Vision ProAudio Spectrum; or Microsoft Sound System); MPC Compatible CD-ROM drive; VGA monitor; & microphone. *Optimal configuration:* 25MHz 386 SX.
Reading Grade-Level for Windows: These Programs Provide a Natural, Developmental Approach to Fundamental Reading Skills. Beginners Progress Through Reading-Readiness, Phonics, & Decoding. Imaginative Picture Stories & Sound Patterns Add New Dimensions & Excitement to the Learning Process.
Conter Software.

Reading 2. Jan. 1994. *Items Included:* Program on CD-ROM, CD Booklet, & Registration Card. *Customer Support:* Free unlimited support via telephone.
Macintosh System 7.0 or higher. Macintosh LC or higher (4Mb). CD-ROM disk $49.00 (ISBN 1-57268-035-0, Order no.: 65002). *Nonstandard peripherals required:* 12 inch monitor or larger; CD-ROM drive. *Optimal configuration:* 5Mb RAM.
Reading Grade-Level for Macintosh. The Reading Grade-Level CD-ROMs Were Designed to Help Students Become Proficient Readers by Providing Them with a Balance of Strategy & Application Lessons. Students Build Vocabulary, Learn Word Meanings, & Practice Study Skills in a Variety of Interesting Lessons.
Conter Software.

Reading 3. Jan. 1994. *Items Included:* Program on CD-ROM, CD Booklet, & Registration Card. *Customer Support:* Free unlimited support via telephone.
Windows 3.1 or higher running under DOS 5.0 or higher. 386 SX (4Mb RAM; 500k low Dos Mem; 6Mb free disk space). CD-ROM disk $49.00 (ISBN 1-57268-011-3, Order no.: 55003). *Nonstandard peripherals required:* Sound card (either: Sound Blaster - 8, 16, PRO; Media Vision ProAudio Spectrum; or Microsoft Sound System); MPC Compatible CD-ROM drive; VGA monitor; & microphone. *Optimal configuration:* 25MHz 386 SX.
Reading Grade-Level for Windows: These Programs Provide a Natural, Developmental Approach to Fundamental Reading Skills. Beginners Progress Through Reading-Readiness, Phonics, & Decoding. Imaginative Picture Stories & Sound Patterns Add New Dimensions & Excitement to the Learning Process.
Conter Software.

Reading 3. Jan. 1994. *Items Included:* Program on CD-ROM, CD Booklet, & Registration Card. *Customer Support:* Free unlimited support via telephone.
Macintosh System 7.0 or higher. Macintosh LC or higher (4Mb). CD-ROM disk $49.00 (ISBN 1-57268-036-9, Order no.: 65003). *Nonstandard peripherals required:* 12 inch monitor or larger; CD-ROM drive. *Optimal configuration:* 5Mb RAM.
Reading Grade-Level for Macintosh. The Reading Grade-Level CD-ROMs Were Designed to Help Students Become Proficient Readers by Providing Them with a Balance of Strategy & Application Lessons. Students Build Vocabulary, Learn Word Meanings, & Practice Study Skills in a Variety of Interesting Lessons.
Conter Software.

Reading 3-4. Jan. 1994. *Items Included:* Program on CD-ROM, CD Booklet, & Registration Card. *Customer Support:* Free unlimited customer support via telephone.
Windows 3.1 or higher running under DOS 5.0 or higher. 386 SX (4Mb RAM; 500k low Dos Mem; 6Mb free disk space). CD-ROM disk $249.00 (ISBN 1-57268-049-0, Order no.: 15340). *Nonstandard peripherals required:* Sound card (either: Sound Blaster - 8, 16, PRO; Media Vision ProAudio Spectrum; or Microsoft Sound System); MPC compatible CD-ROM drive; VGA monitor; & microphone.

TITLE INDEX

Optimal configuration: 25 MHz 386 SX.
Reading Grade-Level for Windows: These Programs Provide a Natural, Developmental Approach to Fundamental Reading Skills. Beginners Progress Through Reading-Readiness, Phonics, & Decoding. Imaginative Picture Stories & Sound Patterns Add New Dimensions & Excitement to the Learning Process.
Conter Software.

Reading 3-4. Jan. 1994. *Items Included:* Program on CD-ROM, CD Booklet, & Registration Card. *Customer Support:* Free unlimited customer support via telephone.
Macintosh System 7.0 or higher. Macintosh LC or higher (4Mb). CD-ROM disk $249.00 (ISBN 1-57268-070-9, Order no.: 25340). *Nonstandard peripherals required:* 12 inch monitor or larger; CD-ROM drive. *Optimal configuration:* 5Mb RAM.
Reading Grade-Level for Macintosh: The Reading Grade-Level CD-ROMs Were Designed to Help Students Become Proficient Readers by Providing Them with a Balance of Strategy & Application Lessons. Students Build Vocabulary, Learn Word Meanings, & Practice Study Skills in a Variety of Interesting Lessons.
Conter Software.

Reading 4. Jan. 1994. *Items Included:* Program on CD-ROM, CD Booklet, & Registration Card. *Customer Support:* Free unlimited support via telephone.
Windows 3.1 or higher running under DOS 5.0 or higher. 386 SX (4Mb RAM; 500k low Dos Mem; 6Mb free disk space). CD-ROM disk $49.00 (ISBN 1-57268-012-1, Order no.: 55004). *Nonstandard peripherals required:* Sound card (either: Sound Blaster - 8, 16, PRO; Media Vision ProAudio Spectrum; or Microsoft Sound System); MPC Compatible CD-ROM drive; VGA monitor; & microphone. *Optimal configuration:* 25MHz 386 SX.
Reading Grade-Level for Windows: These Programs Provide a Natural, Developmental Approach to Fundamental Reading Skills. Beginners Progress Through Reading-Readiness, Phonics, & Decoding. Imaginative Picture Stories & Sound Patterns Add New Dimensions & Excitement to the Learning Process.
Conter Software.

Reading 4. Jan. 1994. *Items Included:* Program on CD-ROM, CD Booklet, & Registration Card. *Customer Support:* Free unlimited support via telephone.
Macintosh System 7.0 or higher. Macintosh LC or higher (4Mb). CD-ROM disk $49.00 (ISBN 1-57268-037-7, Order no.: 65004). *Nonstandard peripherals required:* 12 inch monitor or larger; CD-ROM drive. *Optimal configuration:* 5Mb RAM.
Reading Grade-Level for Macintosh. The Reading Grade-Level CD-ROMs Were Designed to Help Students Become Proficient Readers by Providing Them with a Balance of Strategy & Application Lessons. Students Build Vocabulary, Learn Word Meanings, & Practice Study Skills in a Variety of Interesting Lessons.
Conter Software.

Reading 5. Jan. 1994. *Items Included:* Program on CD-ROM, CD Booklet, & Registration Card. *Customer Support:* Free unlimited support via telephone.
Windows 3.1 or higher running under DOS 5.0 or higher. 386 SX (4Mb RAM; 500k low Dos Mem; 6Mb free disk space). CD-ROM disk $49.00 (ISBN 1-57268-013-X, Order no.: 55005). *Nonstandard peripherals required:* Sound card (either: Sound Blaster - 8, 16, PRO; Media Vision ProAudio Spectrum; or Microsoft Sound System); MPC Compatible CD-ROM drive; VGA monitor; & microphone. *Optimal configuration:* 25MHz 386 SX.
Reading Grade-Level for Windows: These Programs Provide a Natural, Developmental Approach to Fundamental Reading Skills. Beginners Progress Through Reading-Readiness, Phonics, & Decoding. Imaginative Picture Stories & Sound Patterns Add New Dimensions & Excitement to the Learning Process.
Conter Software.

Reading 5. Jan. 1994. *Items Included:* Program on CD-ROM, CD Booklet, & Registration Card. *Customer Support:* Free unlimited support via telephone.
Macintosh System 7.0 or higher. Macintosh LC or higher (4Mb). CD-ROM disk $49.00 (ISBN 1-57268-038-5, Order no.: 65005). *Nonstandard peripherals required:* 12 inch monitor or larger; CD-ROM drive. *Optimal configuration:* 5Mb RAM.
Reading Grade-Level for Macintosh. The Reading Grade-Level CD-ROMs Were Designed to Help Students Become Proficient Readers by Providing Them with a Balance of Strategy & Application Lessons. Students Build Vocabulary, Learn Word Meanings, & Practice Study Skills in a Variety of Interesting Lessons.
Conter Software.

Reading 5-6. Jan. 1994. *Items Included:* Program on CD-ROM, CD Booklet, & Registration Card. *Customer Support:* Free unlimited customer support via telephone.
Windows 3.1 or higher running under DOS 5.0 or higher. 386 SX (4Mb RAM; 500k low Dos Mem; 6Mb free disk space). CD-ROM disk $249.00 (ISBN 1-57268-050-4, Order no.: 15560). *Nonstandard peripherals required:* Sound card (either: Sound Blaster - 8, 16, PRO; Media Vision ProAudio Spectrum; or Microsoft Sound System); MPC compatible CD-ROM drive; VGA monitor; & microphone. *Optimal configuration:* 25 MHz 386 SX.
Reading Grade-Level for Windows: These Programs Provide a Natural, Developmental Approach to Fundamental Reading Skills. Beginners Progress Through Reading-Readiness, Phonics, & Decoding. Imaginative Picture Stories & Sound Patterns Add New Dimensions & Excitement to the Learning Process.
Conter Software.

Reading 5-6. Jan. 1994. *Items Included:* Program on CD-ROM, CD Booklet, & Registration Card. *Customer Support:* Free unlimited support via telephone.
Macintosh System 7.0 or higher. Macintosh LC or higher (4Mb). CD-ROM disk $249.00 (ISBN 1-57268-071-7, Order no.: 25560). *Nonstandard peripherals required:* 12 inch monitor or larger; CD-ROM drive. *Optimal configuration:* 5Mb RAM.
Reading Grade-Level for Macintosh: The Reading Grade-Level CD-ROMs Were Designed to Help Students Become Proficient Readers by Providing Them with a Balance of Strategy & Application Lessons. Students Build Vocabulary, Learn Word Meanings, & Practice Study Skills in a Variety of Interesting Lessons.
Conter Software.

Reading 6. Jan. 1994. *Items Included:* Program on CD-ROM, CD Booklet, & Registration Card. *Customer Support:* Free unlimited support via telephone.
Windows 3.1 or higher running under DOS 5.0 or higher. 386 SX (4Mb RAM; 500k low Dos Mem; 6Mb free disk space). CD-ROM disk $49.00 (ISBN 1-57268-014-8, Order no.: 55006). *Nonstandard peripherals required:* Sound card (either: Sound Blaster - 8, 16, PRO; Media Vision ProAudio Spectrum; or Microsoft Sound System); MPC Compatible CD-ROM drive; VGA monitor; & microphone. *Optimal configuration:* 25MHz 386 SX.
Reading Grade-Level for Windows: These Programs Provide a Natural, Developmental Approach to Fundamental Reading Skills. Beginners Progress Through Reading-Readiness, Phonics, & Decoding. Imaginative Picture Stories & Sound Patterns Add New Dimensions & Excitement to the Learning Process.
Conter Software.

Reading 6. Jan. 1994. *Items Included:* Program on CD-ROM, CD Booklet, & Registration Card. *Customer Support:* Free unlimited support via telephone.
Macintosh System 7.0 or higher. Macintosh LC or higher (4Mb). CD-ROM disk $49.00 (ISBN 1-57268-039-3, Order no.: 65006). *Nonstandard peripherals required:* 12 inch monitor or larger; CD-ROM drive. *Optimal configuration:* 5Mb RAM.
Reading Grade-Level for Macintosh. The Reading Grade-Level CD-ROMs Were Designed to Help Students Become Proficient Readers by Providing Them with a Balance of Strategy & Application Lessons. Students Build Vocabulary, Learn Word Meanings, & Practice Study Skills in a Variety of Interesting Lessons.
Conter Software.

Reading 7. Jan. 1994. *Items Included:* Program on CD-ROM, CD Booklet, & Registration Card. *Customer Support:* Free unlimited support via telephone.
Windows 3.1 or higher running under DOS 5.0 or higher. 386 SX (4Mb RAM; 500k low Dos Mem; 6Mb free disk space). CD-ROM disk $49.00 (ISBN 1-57268-015-6, Order no.: 55007). *Nonstandard peripherals required:* Sound card (either: Sound Blaster - 8, 16, PRO; Media Vision ProAudio Spectrum; or Microsoft Sound System); MPC Compatible CD-ROM drive; VGA monitor; & microphone. *Optimal configuration:* 25MHz 386 SX.
Reading Grade-Level for Windows: These Programs Provide a Natural, Developmental Approach to Fundamental Reading Skills. Beginners Progress Through Reading-Readiness, Phonics, & Decoding. Imaginative Picture Stories & Sound Patterns Add New Dimensions & Excitement to the Learning Process.
Conter Software.

Reading 7-8. Jan. 1994. *Items Included:* Program on CD-ROM, CD Booklet, & Registration Card. *Customer Support:* Free unlimited customer support via telephone.
Windows 3.1 or higher running under DOS 5.0 or higher. 386 SX (4Mb RAM; 500k low Dos Mem; 6Mb free disk space). CD-ROM disk $249.00 (ISBN 1-57268-051-2, Order no.: 15780). *Nonstandard peripherals required:* Sound card (either: Sound Blaster - 8, 16, PRO; Media Vision ProAudio Spectrum; or Microsoft Sound System); MPC compatible CD-ROM drive; VGA monitor; & microphone. *Optimal configuration:* 25 MHz 386 SX.
Reading Grade-Level for Windows: These Programs Provide a Natural, Developmental Approach to Fundamental Reading Skills. Beginners Progress Through Reading-Readiness, Phonics, & Decoding. Imaginative Picture Stories & Sound Patterns Add New Dimensions & Excitement to the Learning Process.
Conter Software.

Reading 8. Jan. 1994. *Items Included:* Program on CD-ROM, CD Booklet, & Registration Card. *Customer Support:* Free unlimited support via telephone.
Windows 3.1 or higher running under DOS 5.0 or higher. 386 SX (4Mb RAM; 500k low Dos

Mem; 6Mb free disk space). CD-ROM disk $49.00 (ISBN 1-57268-016-4, Order no.: 55008). *Nonstandard peripherals required:* Sound card (either: Sound Blaster - 8, 16, PRO; Media Vision ProAudio Spectrum; or Microsoft Sound System); MPC Compatible CD-ROM drive; VGA monitor; & microphone. *Optimal configuration:* 25MHz 386 SX.
Reading Grade-Level for Windows: These Programs Provide a Natural, Developmental Approach to Fundamental Reading Skills. Beginners Progress Through Reading-Readiness, Phonics, & Decoding. Imaginative Picture Stories & Sound Patterns Add New Dimensions & Excitement to the Learning Process.
Conter Software.

ReadingEdge: O. C. R. Software. *Version:* 1.0. Jun. 1991. *Items Included:* Comprehensive instructions manual & 90 days of unlimited telephone technical support.
6.0 through 7.0. MAC (1Mb). 3.5" disk $99.00 (Order no.: 301-604-6611). *Networks supported:* All MAC networks.
O. C. R. Software for Handheld Scanners Including SCAN-MAN, Thunderware, & the Complete PC. Reads Proportionally Spaced, Typeset, Dot-Matrix, & Kerned Characters. Includes Built-In 40,000 Plus Word Dictionary.
Prism Enterprises, Inc.

ReadiWriter. *Version:* 2.0. Jan. 1983. *Compatible Hardware:* IBM PC & compatibles. *Operating System(s) Required:* MS-DOS, PC-DOS. *Language(s):* C. *Memory Required:* 256k. *General Requirements:* 2 disk drives. *Items Included:* Program disks, user manual.
disk $395.00.
Word Formatter Based on IBM's Generalized Markup Language & Script Formatters Found on IBM Mainframes. Macro Facility Allows User-Created Formats with No File Size Limitations. Uses REdit (Included) or User's Own Editor. Compatible with GML. Supports Italics, Boldface, & Underlining, Scripts, Subscripts & Superscripts, & Places Footnotes & Footnote Numbers Automatically. Automatically Centers & Right Aligns & Permits Proportional Spacing. Creates Table of Contents & Index. Supports Most Printers.
ReadiWare Systems, Inc.

Ready, Set, Go! 3.0. Manhattan Graphics Corp. Nov. 1986. *Compatible Hardware:* Apple Macintosh, Macintosh II. *Memory Required:* 512k.
3.5" disk $395.00 (ISBN 0-925118-00-1).
PostScript-Based Desktop Publishing System Supporting the Standard Apple LaserWriter Driver. Text-Handling Features Include: Fully-Functional Word Processor; Automatic or Manual Kerning; Real-Time Justification & Hyphenation; 72,000 Word Spelling Checker; Imports of ASCII, Macwrite, & Word Text Files; Global Font, Style, & Size Changes; etc. Page-Handling Features Include: Grid-Design System for Page Layout; "Master Pages" to Handle Repetitive Elements; Automatic Text Runarounds; "Specification Sheets" for Placement in Inches, Centimeters, Picas, or Points. User Features Include: Multi-Document Windows; Five-Page Viewing Sizes; Direct PostScript Programming Capabilities; Graphic Primitives Such As Rules, Borders, Fill Patterns, etc. Ability to Open MacPaint & PICT Files Directly. Not Copy-Protected. Free Technical Support from Manufacturer.
Letraset USA.

Ready, Set, Go! 4.0. Manhattan Graphics Corp. *General Requirements:* External disk drive. Macintosh plus or higher. 3.5" disk $495.00.
Page Layout Software. New Design Tools Supported by This Version Include a Grabber Hand for Easier Scrolling & a Diagonal-Line Drawing Tool. Automatic Runarounds Allow Users to Drop Objects of Any Size into the Text & Set the Specified Distance Between Text & Image. The "Lock & Don't Print" Feature Allows Creating Multiple Pages for Color Overlays. Offers Full Support for Encapsulated PostScript Files (EPFS) & Can Reproduce High-Resolution Graphics from Scanners That Support Gray-Scale Tag Image File Format (TIFF). Enables Users to Create Style Sheets with Type, Styles, & Formats. Includes a Word Processor with 100,000-Word Spelling Checker Including a "Suggest Correct Spelling" Feature. Can Import Word Processing Files from MICROSOFT WORD 3.0, MACWRITE, & WRITENOW While Retaining Formatting Properties. Other Product Features Include a Linker Tool That Moves Text Throughout the Document While Changes Are Made, Global Search & Replace, up to 99" x 99" Pages, etc. Not Copy Protected.
Letraset USA.

Ready Set Grow!: A Fun, Interactive & Informative Guide for Expecting & New Parents. *Items Included:* 1 user manual. *Customer Support:* Tech support, 60-day money-back guarantee.
Macintosh. Macintosh with System 6.04 or higher (2Mb). 3.5" disk $39.95 (ISBN 0-924677-12-0). *Optimal configuration:* Macintosh Sytem 6.04 or higher, 4Mb RAM, hard disk drive.
Mac with 6.04, 1Mb RAM, hard disk drive. Macintosh (1Mb). 3.5" disk $39.95 (ISBN 0-924677-14-7). *Optimal configuration:* 386 16MHz or higher PC, 5Mb free hard disk space, 2Mb RAM, Windows 3.0 or higher, Super VGA graphics w/256 colors, Soundcard, CD-ROM drive for CD-ROM users, & a mouse.
A Fun, Interactive & Informative Guide to Pregnancy, Childbirth, & the First Five Years of Parenthood. Created by a Successful Physician & Mother of Five. What to Expect When Pregnant, What to Expect from Your Child, & How to Manage a Growing Family. Includes Graphics, Sound, & a Wealth of Information.
IMSI (International Microcomputer Software, Inc.).

Readynet. *Version:* 1.2. Jul. 1989. *Items Included:* All hardware & software for local area network. *Customer Support:* 30-days free phone support, extended support subscription service available.
MS-DOS or PC-DOS 3.x to 4.x (664k workstation). Any IBM or compatible. Starter kit $499.00. *Networks supported:* OMNINET. Add-on kit $249.00.
Complete Off-the-Shelf Network Kit That Includes All Necessary Hardware & Software for Two Nodes Add-on Package Provides Expandability for Additional Nodes. Provides Print Sharing & Print Spooling, File & Record Locking, Full Security, EMS Support, Messaging & Remote Control Features. Installs with Pre-Set Connections in Five Minutes Per Computer. No Training Required. Can Be Loaded into Upper Memory.
Corvus Systems, Inc.

Real/32: Multiuser DOS-Windows Operating System. *Version:* 7.51. Intelligent Micro Software. Nov. 1995. *Items Included:* Installation & user's guide, release notes, running applications guide. *Customer Support:* 2-hours included with product, additions support packages available.
Real/32. 486-33 (4Mb), VGA. disk $649.00 (Order no.: 2261). *Networks supported:* Novell Netware, Real/32 NET.
Real-Time DOS & Windows Compatible Operating System. Supports up to 64 Users on a Single CPU via Multiport VGA Stations from Maxpeed or Serial Terminals.
Logan Industries, Inc.

Real Analyzer. *Version:* 2.1. Ed Lichtman. Sep. 1983. *Compatible Hardware:* Apple II+, IIe, III; IBM PC, PCjr, PC XT & compatibles, PS/2. *Operating System(s) Required:* PC-DOS/MS-DOS 2.0. *Language(s):* Compiled BASIC. *Memory Required:* Apple 48k; IBM 128k. *Items Included:* Manual, demo, 30 day-money back guarantee. *Customer Support:* Telephone support free.
IBM & Apple. disk $95.00 ea.
Contains Five Menu-Driven Programs Which Analyze Income Property & Residence, & Help User to Decide When to Buy, Sell, Exchange, or Refinance Any Property by Projecting Cash Flow & Profitability Before & after Taxes for Infinite Number of Years. First Year of Analysis Can Begin in Any Month. Programs Can Also Be Used for Year-End Income Tax Projection. Covers Five Types of Loans, & Includes Two Depreciation Schedules. Allows User to Change Assumptions & Formulas As Tax Laws Change.
Real-Comp, Inc.

Real Estate. *Version:* Series V. *Operating System(s) Required:* DOS, Novell & Lantastic Networks. *Items Included:* Software & manuals. *Customer Support:* 800 number telephone support, Bulletin Board service, remote support, product enhancements available.
Prices start at $995.00.
Programs Include: Forms Generation, Settlement/Disclosure, Regulation Z, Tracking, Indexing, Escrow/Trust Accounting, Amortization, IRS Reporting to Automate Small to Multioffice Title Companies or Law Offices Doing Real Estate Closings.
Sulcus Law Management Services, Inc.

Real Estate - Mortgage Analyzer: Loan Amortization. Oct. 1986. *Compatible Hardware:* IBM PC. *Operating System(s) Required:* PC-DOS 3.1. *Memory Required:* 256k. contact publisher for price.
Provides Estimated Projections of Accumulated Appreciation, Equity, Tax Savings, Interest, & Principal for a Given Investment Based on the Rates & Amounts Entered. Additional Information Based on These Results Consists of the Total Investment, Capital Gain, Realized Gain, & Gain per Payments. Online Displays Include: Multiple Screens Showing the Projected Accumulation of Appreciation, Equity, Tax Savings, Interest, & Principal As of Each Payment for the Entire Duration of the Mortgage. Also Includes the Projected Accumulated Appreciation, Equity, Tax Savings, Interest, Principal, & a Standard Amortization Schedule Showing the Interest & Principal Portion of Each Payment along with the Outstanding Balance.
Automatronics.

Real Estate Aids. *Customer Support:* 800-929-8117 (customer service).
MS-DOS. Apple II. disk $49.99 (ISBN 0-87007-813-5).
Variety of Real Estate Aids, Including Listing Database.
SourceView Software International.

Real Estate Analysis. *Compatible Hardware:* IBM PC, PC XT. *Operating System(s) Required:* PC-DOS. *Language(s):* BASIC. *Memory Required:* 32-48k.
disk $99.95.
Real Estate Investment Analysis Program. Provides User with a Complete Amortization Schedule As well As a Depreciation Schedule for Numerous Properties. Incorporates Financial Routines for Property & Investment.
Powersoft, Inc.

TITLE INDEX

Real Estate Analysis Program. *Compatible Hardware:* Apple II, II+. *Language(s):* Applesoft II. *Memory Required:* 24k.
disk $29.95 (Order no.: 10027).
Provides Real Estate Investment Analysis for Buy/Sell Decisions.
Powersoft, Inc.

Real Estate Analyzer. *Version:* 3rd Edition. 1985. *Compatible Hardware:* Apple II series, IBM PC & compatibles. *Operating System(s) Required:* MS-DOS for IBM Version. *Language(s):* Machine language & BASIC. *Memory Required:* Apple 128k, IBM 128k, MS-DOS 256k. *General Requirements:* GW-BASIC for MS-DOS computers. *Items Included:* Financial reports. *Customer Support:* Available free.
IBM. disk $395.00.
Apple. $350.00.
Reveals Investment Opportunities. The Professional Report Lets You Compare Properties, Creative Financing, Tax Consequences, Depreciation, Cash Flow & More! With Built-In Tax Laws & Measures of Profitability, Real Estate Analyzer Gives You the Investment Edge. Project Investment Results with 30-Year Tables of Pre-Tax & After-Tax Cash Flow & 7 Measures of Return on Investment. It Features 10 Loans & 50 Leases, Built-In Tax Laws, Menu Driven Control, Monthly Precision, Flexible Inflation Modeling & "What If" Planning. HowardSoft Provides an Investment Guide & Examples, On-Screen Help Keys, & Free Phone Support.
HowardSoft.

Real Estate Asset Management Software System. *Version:* 3.31/R2. Nov. 1987. *Compatible Hardware:* IBM PC, PC XT, PC AT, PS/2 & compatibles. *Operating System(s) Required:* MS-DOS, PC-DOS. *Language(s):* CBASIC, C. *Memory Required:* 128k. *General Requirements:* 2 disk drives, hard drive. *Items Included:* Six individual modules including: Investment Analysis; Acquisition & Disposition Analysis; Land & Lease Analysis; Commercial Finance; Residential Finance; Property Income Analysis. *Customer Support:* Free.
disk $395.00.
Comprehensive System of Programs Designed to Perform In-Depth Analysis of the Aquisition, Financing, Holding, & Disposition of Properties, & to Perform Rapid Evaluation of Real Estate Investment Opportunities & Alternatives.
Berge Software.

The Real Estate Closing System. *Operating System(s) Required:* PC-DOS, MS-DOS. *Memory Required:* 128k. *General Requirements:* 2 floppy disk drives, hard disk, printer.
$3500.00.
Provides Control for Real Estate Closings. System Can Produce Settlement Statements, T-I-L, & Most Other Documents Required for Closings. User Defines Data Base & Forms Design.
Cybernetics Technology Corp.

Real Estate Collection. *Customer Support:* 800-929-8117 (customer service).
MS-DOS. IBM/PS2. disk $99.99 (ISBN 0-87007-288-9).
For Persons Involved in the Business of Selling or Buying Real Estate. One Program Shows Clients Rent vs. Properties Analysis Data. Other Programs Store & Recall Appointments, Analyze Advertising Costs vs. Returns, Keep a Name & Address List That Includes an Option to Print Envelopes & Labels.
SourceView Software International.

Real Estate Investment Analysis. Feb. 1985. *Compatible Hardware:* TRS-80 Model I, Model III, Model 4. *Operating System(s) Required:* MS-DOS, CP/M.
$99.00.
Allows a Real Estate Salesperson or Investor to Evaluate a Property's Return on Investment. Salesperson Can Use It As a Tool for Establishing Price & Terms to Expedite a Sale for the Seller. Generates a Personalized Report to Investors That Bases the Return on Investment on Cash Flow & Tax Benefits. Investment Property Buyer Can Screen Properties by Entering Price & Net Operating Income. The Program Allows the User to Play a "What If" Game. Compares Several Properties, Allowing the Investor to Select the One That Best Meets His or Her Criterion for Cash Flow, Tax Shelter Benefits, or Both.
The Alternate Source.

Real Estate Investment Analysis. *Version:* 9.0. 1982-95. *Compatible Hardware:* Apple Macintosh; IBM PC & compatibles. *Operating System(s) Required:* Macintosh, Windows 3.1, Windows 95. (source code included). *Memory Required:* Macintosh 4Mb, Windows 4000k. *General Requirements:* Lotus 1-2-3, Excel 5.0 or higher. *Items Included:* User's manual. *Customer Support:* Telephone support (free).
3.5" disk $395.00.
Designed to Analyze Income-Producing Real Estate Investments. CASH FLOW/SENSITIVITY ANALYSIS Generates 10-Year Cash & Tax Projections for User's Planned Real Estate Investment, & Produces a Detailed Year-by-Year Report As Well As a Presentation-Style Report. Also Includes: ANNUAL OPERATING STATEMENT Computes Income, Expenses, & Expense Ratios; LEASE-BY-LEASE ANALYSIS - All Applications for Tax Reform Act, Updated Consistently When Tax Laws Change. Version 9 Includes Partnership Analysis & Lease U.S. Buy.
RealData, Inc.

Real Estate Investment Analysis Customizing Kit. *Version:* 4.5. Jul. 1991. *Operating System(s) Required:* PC-DOS/MS-DOS 2.0 or higher, Windows. *Language(s):* Compiled BASIC. *Memory Required:* 340k. *Customer Support:* Telephone support with no fees.
$220.00 (ISBN 0-928463-00-1).
Buy/Hold/Sell/Refinancing/Exchange Decisions Analyzed. Variables Include: Loans, Depreciation, Taxes, Holding Periods, Inflation Rates, etc. Stand-Alone, Completely Menu-Driven with 30 Minute Learning Time. Includes Cash Flow Analysis & Investment Analysis. Investment Analysis Can Be Customized to Include a More Detailed Analysis for Any Specific Year & to Select Different Measures of Investment Performance. Complete Loan Amortization & Depreciation Schedules (Screen or Printout) Can Be Generated. Add Ons Include Lease Analysis & Buy Versus Lease Analysis.
Soft Estate.

Real Estate Investment Comparisons. *Compatible Hardware:* Apple II, II+, IIe; Atari 400, 800; Columbia; Compaq; Commodore CBM 8096; Franklin Ace; Fujitsu; HP 150 Touchscreen; IBM PC, PCjr, PC XT; LNW 80; Sharp PC 5000; Sperry; Tandy 2000; TI Professional; TRS-80 Model I, Model II, Model III, Model 4, Model 12, Model 16; Wang. *Operating System(s) Required:* CP/M, CP/M-86, MS-DOS. (source code included). *Memory Required:* 48k. *General Requirements:* 2 disk drives, printer, VisiCalc, SuperCalc, Multiplan, or Lotus 1-2-3.
disk $59.95.
Collection of Spreadsheet Templates Designed for Real Estate Personnel Selling Investments & Commercial Property. Analyzes Single Income Properties, Allowing "What-If" Calculations to Be Made on the Effect of Various Financing Arrangements upon Owner Income. Summarizes Financial Data of Various Alternative Investments in Terms of Net Spendable on an Annual Basis, Allowing Comparisons of One Type of Investment Versus Another. Computes Taxable Income from Real Estate Investments, & Reports the Gain on Sales Subject to Income Tax.
Software Models.

The Real Estate Investor. *Version:* 1.2. Sep. 1987. *Compatible Hardware:* Commodore 64, 128, Plus 4; IBM PC, PCjr, PC XT, PC AT & compatibles PS/2 & Compatibles. *Language(s):* Microsoft BASIC (source code included). *Memory Required:* 64k.
IBM. disk $25.00.
Commodore 64 & Plus 4. disk or cassette $25.00.
Real Estate Financial Analysis. Calculates Conventional, ARM, Balloon Mortgage Payments; Mortgage Amortization; Depreciation for 15, 18, 19 Year Life & Low Income Housing (IRS Publication 534 Revised 12/85); Cash Flow Forecasts; Income Tax Consequences; Appreciation.
Jance Assocs.

Real Estate Lawyer. *Version:* 1.5. Oct. 1993. *Items Included:* One 312 page spiral bound manual, both 3.5" & 5.25" disks included. *Customer Support:* Unlimited free technical support.
MS-DOS. IBM & compatibles (256k). List: $129.95, $90.00 is avg. street price. *Optimal configuration:* 286 or higher, PC-DOS/MS-DOS, 256k RAM, 700k hard disk space, mouse recommended.
Prepares 22 Binding Real Estate Documents Without an Attorney. Includes Sales Agreements, Residential & Commercial Leases, Deeds, Mortgages, Notes, Assignments, Lien Releases, & Landlord Letters. Valid in All States Except Louisiana. Documents May Be Exported to Any Word Processor. Features Pull-Down Menus, Context-Sensitive Help, Mouse Support. Windows Compatible.
Z-Law Software, Inc.

Real Estate Lawyer. *Version:* 1.5. Oct. 1993. *Items Included:* One 312 page spiral bound manual, both 3.5" & 5.25" disks included. *Customer Support:* Unlimited free technical support.
MS-DOS. IBM & compatibles (256k). disk $129.95. *Optimal configuration:* 286 or higher, PC MS-DOS, 256k RAM, 700k hard disk space, mouse recommended.
Prepares 22 Binding Real Estate Documents Without an Attorney. Includes Sales Agreements, Residential & Commercial Leases, Deeds, Mortgages, Notes, Assignments, Lien Releases, & Landlord Letters. Valid in All States Except Louisiana. Documents May Be Exported to Any Word Processor. Features Pull-Down Menus, Context-Sensitive Help, Mouse Support. Windows Compatible.
Z-Law Software, Inc.

Real Estate Lawyer. *Version:* 1.5. Oct. 1993. *Items Included:* One 312 page spiral bound manual, both 3.5" & 5.25" disks included. *Customer Support:* Unlimited free technical support.
MS-DOS. IBM & comaptibles (256k). $90.00-$129.95. *Optimal configuration:* 286 or higher, PC MS-DOS, 256k RAM, 700k hard disk space, mouse recommended.
Prepares 22 Binding Real Estate Documents Without an Attorney. Includes Sales Agreements, Residential & Commercial Leases, Deeds, Mortgages, Notes, Assignments, Lien Releases, & Landlord Letters. Valid in All States Except Louisiana. Documents May Be Exported to Any Word Processor. Features Pull-Down Menus, Context-Sensitive Help, Mouse Support. Windows Compatible.

Real Estate Management. Version: 13.0. Aug. 1993. Items Included: Manual on disk & hard copy. Customer Support: 90 day unlimited warranty, 1 yr. maintenance $200.00/yr. PC-DOS/MS-DOS V3.X & higher. IBM & compatibles (640k). disk $595.00 stand alone; $1195.00 network (Order no.: ASG-REM). Optimal configuration: Hard disk, wide carriage printer. Networks supported: Novell 2X, 3X & 4X.
Designed Specifically for Use by Real Estate Managers. Handles Industrial, Retail, Commercial & Apartment Properties. Extensive Accounting & Management Reporting Is Provided. Entry & Maintenance of Rental Properties, Tenant Information & Charges. Provides Credit/Debt Memos & Open Balances. Automatic Tie in to General Ledger & Built-In Audit Trail.
Applications Systems Group (CT), Inc.

Real Estate Models for the Eighties. Version: 2.61. Gregory F. Glazner & Jan Glazner. 1982. Compatible Hardware: IBM PC & compatibles. Operating System(s) Required: PC-DOS, MS-DOS. (source code included). Memory Required: 256k. General Requirements: Lotus 1-2-3 Releases 1A or 2.
disk $89.00 (ISBN 0-917717-02-3).
Collection of 16 Templates for Real Estate Analysis. Geared to Users Familiar with Amortization, Depreciation, Interest, & Other Computations Relating to the Real-Estate Field. Users Must Provide Their Own Spreadsheet Program.
Commercial Software Systems, Inc.

Real Estate Office Management. Version: 9.0. Items Included: Manual, sample data disk. Customer Support: 90 days of free telephone support.
IBM PC/XT, AT, PS/2 & compatibles (640k). disk $1195.00. Nonstandard peripherals required: 20 Mb hard disk.
Tracks Information About Agents, Sales, Listings, Receivables, & Payables in One Package. Features Include Commission Tracking, Agent Billing, Bank Reconciliation, Check Writing, Vendor Ledger Help Window & More. Multi-User Version is Also Available.
Yardi Systems.

Real Estate Partners. Version: 1.03. Jun. 1988. Compatible Hardware: Apple Macintosh. Memory Required: 512k. General Requirements: External disk drive; ImageWriter. Customer Support: Free telephone support. Program. 3.5" disk $295.00.
Demo. 3.5" disk $10.00.
Business Development; Syndication Analysis; Real Estate Analysis.
Meta Venture Technology.

Real Estate Planner. Harry S. Chud. Feb. 1984. Compatible Hardware: Apple Macintosh; IBM PC & compatibles, PC XT, PC AT. Operating System(s) Required: MS-DOS. (source code included). Memory Required: 64k. Customer Support: Free telephone Support.
disk $150.00.
Evaluates the Economics of a Real Estate Investment over a Period of One to Ten Years. Shows the Taxable Income on Loss, Tax Payable on Benefit, Net Cash Flow for Each Period & Cumulative Cash Flow Through the Latest Period & Net Present Value of Cash Flowed at Both 8% & 12% Discount Rates. Assumptions Input Allows for Changing of Facts So As to Evaluate a Real Estate Investment from Various Perspectives.
Accounting Professionals Software, Inc.

Real Estate Resident Expert. Items Included: Bound manual. Customer Support: Free hotline - no time limit; 30 day limited warranty; updates are $5/disk plus S&H.
MS-DOS 2.0 or higher. IBM & compatibles (256k). disk $99.95. Nonstandard peripherals required: Printer.
Real Estate Analysis Package for Analyzing Single Family Houses & Fully Estimating the Soft Factors Which Affect Their Value.
Dynacomp, Inc.

Real Estate 64. Compatible Hardware: Commodore 64.
disk $5.00.
Board Game Where You Travel Around the City, Buying up Pieces of Property & Developing Them. The Winner Is the Player Who Bankrupts All His Opponents, or the One Who Has Most Cash & Property When Everyone Decides to End the Game. A Solitaire Option with up to Three Computer Opponents Is Available. Players Are Allowed to Choose One of Five Languages & Seven Cities to Play the Game.
ScanAm Enterprises, Inc.

Real Estate System. Version: 2.0. Apr. 1984. Compatible Hardware: IBM PC & compatibles. Operating System(s) Required: PC-DOS, MS-DOS. Language(s): Compiled dBASE III. Memory Required: 256k. Items Included: Documentation on diskette. Customer Support: Toll number provided, no charge for support.
disk $50.00.
(Order no.: OFCMGR).
Online, Interactive Real Estate Office System. Tracks the Status of New Property Listings, Their Pending & Final Sale, As Well As Details About Commissions & Sales Agents. Provides a Variety of Reports & the Ability to Match Available Properties to Customer Profiles.
MicroServices, Inc.

Real Estate Tool Kit: Financial Analysis Software. Version: 8.0. Items Included: Disks, manual. Customer Support: 90 days free telephone support.
IBM PC/XT, PC/AT, PS/2 & compatibles (512k). disk $495.00.
Provides Investors, Developers & Real Estate Practitioners with a Variety of Financial Analysis Functions, Including Investment Analysis, Loan Amortizations, Development Analysis, Depreciation Schedules, Buy vs Rent Analysis, Buyer Qualification & Closing Costs, Net Proceeds to Seller, & More. Interfaces with Other Programs from Yardi Systems Including Deluxe Property Management & General Accounting Packages.
Yardi Systems.

Real Monsters - Ickis. Sep. 1995. Items Included: Installation instructions, registration card. Customer Support: Phone support by calling 302-234-1750, no charge. Fax support by faxing to 302-234-1760, no charge. E-Mail support at Compuserve ID 76004,3520 or MCI Mail/560-7116, no charge.
Windows 3.1 or higher. 386 or higher (4Mb). disk $4.99 (ISBN 1-887468-54-4).
Nonstandard peripherals required: Video for Windows, color VGA, mouse. Optimal configuration: SVGA, sound card.
Multimedia Collector's Disk Filled with Popular Cartoon Character Images & Sounds. Packaged in a Blister Pack & Features Nickelodean's Characters.
SWFTE International, Ltd.

Real Monsters - Krumm. Sep. 1995. Items Included: Installation instructions, registration card. Customer Support: Phone support by calling 302-234-1750, no charge. Fax support by faxing to 302-234-1760, no charge. E-Mail support at Compuserve ID 76004,3520 or MCI Mail/560-7116, no charge.
Windows 3.1 or higher. 386 or higher (4Mb). disk $4.99 (ISBN 1-887468-55-2).
Nonstandard peripherals required: Video for Windows, color VGA, mouse. Optimal configuration: SVGA, sound card.
Multimedia Collector's Disk Filled with Popular Cartoon Character Images & Sounds. Packaged in a Blister Pack & Features Nickelodean's Characters.
SWFTE International, Ltd.

Real Monsters - Oblina. Sep. 1995. Items Included: Installation instructions, registration card. Customer Support: Phone support by calling 302-234-1750, no charge. Fax support by faxing to 302-234-1760, no charge. E-Mail support at Compuserve ID 76004,3520 or MCI Mail/560-7116, no charge.
Windows 3.1 or higher. 386 or higher (4Mb). disk $4.99 (ISBN 1-887468-56-0).
Nonstandard peripherals required: Video for Windows, color VGA, mouse. Optimal configuration: SVGA, sound card.
Multimedia Collector's Disk Filled with Popular Cartoon Character Images & Sounds. Packaged in a Blister Pack & Features Nickelodean's Characters.
SWFTE International, Ltd.

Real Net Cost Ownership - Depreciation. Items Included: Full manual. No other products required. Customer Support: Free telephone support - no time limit. 30 day warranty.
MS-DOS 3.2 or higher. IBM & compatibles (512k). disk $29.95.
RNC Calculates the Actual Cost of Owning Depreciating Items, Such As Boats, Automobiles, RV's, Machinery, & Other Durable Goods. Using RNC, User Will Be Better Equipped for Making Wise Financial Decisions, Such As Determining Whether or Not an Item Has Any Real Useful Economic Life Left. Fully Menu-Driven & Easy-to-Use. 30-Page Manual Offers Step-by-Step Instructions, Sample Runs, & Background Discussion.
Dynacomp, Inc.

Real Net Cost: Ownership - Depreciation. 1992. Items Included: Detailed manuals included with all Dynacomp products. Customer Support: Free telephone support to original customer - no time limit; 30 day limited warranty.
MS-DOS 3.2 or higher. IBM PC & compatibles (512k). $29.95 (Add $5.00 for 3 1/2" format; 5 1/4" format standard). Optimal configuration: IBM, MS-DOS 2.0 or higher, 256k RAM. A printer is supported, but not necessary.
Calculates the Actual Cost of Owning Depreciating Items, Such As Boats, Automobiles, RV's, Machinery, & Other Durable Goods. The 30-Page Manual Offers Step-by-Step Instructions, Sample Runs, & Background Discussions.
Dynacomp, Inc.

Real Property Management II. Version: 1.7. Ed Lichtman. Jun. 1984. Compatible Hardware: IBM PC, PC XT, PC AT & compatibles, PS/2. Operating System(s) Required: PC-DOS/MS-DOS 2.0 or higher. Language(s): Compiled BASIC. Memory Required: 192k. General Requirements: 2 disk drives or hard disk. Items Included: Manual, demo disk, 30-day money back guarantee. Customer Support: Telephone support free.
$145.00-$920.00.
Menu-Driven Program Which Records & Budgets Monthly Income & Expenses of Properties Such As Apartments, Offices, Mini-Storage Units, & Single Family Houses. Compares Actuals to Budget by Account, by Unit, & by Month, & Covers 12 Months of Income & Expense,

Including Profit, Cash Flow, & Bank Balance. Maintains Tenant Files, Reports Vacancies, Delinquencies & Records Lost Revenue. Provides up to 33 Different Printed Reports. Also Performs Personal Accounting. Tenant Invoicing, 1099 Form Cost & Allocation, Sort Disbursements. Macro Reporting & Export Modules Are Available.
Real-Comp, Inc.

Real Prospects. Version: 1.2. Memory Required: 512k. General Requirements: Hard disk. Items Included: 3 ring binder containing manual. Customer Support: 90 days free phone support; 1 yr. extended phone support at $200.00 single-user, $400.00 multi-user, or $60.00/hr.; training $400.00/day to $800.00/day plus expenses. Macintosh Plus, SE, SE/30, II, IIx, IIcx (1Mb). $20.00 demo, $595.00 single-user; $1495.00 multi-user (1 to 3 users, plus $100.00/user for each multi-user over three users). Networks supported: AppleShare, TOPS, Novell.
For Commercial Real Estate Brokers Tracking Persons, Properties, Agents, Contact Histories, Expenses, & ToDos. Prints Productivity & Commission Reports for Managers. Matches Buyers & Sellers. Unique, Flexible Searching Provides 54 Searchable, User-Definable Data Fields. Cross References Information for Easy Recall. Does Mailings. Allows Agents to Share Information in Networks.
Data Workshop.

Real-t-PRO. Version: 5.X. May 1991. Operating System(s) Required: MS-DOS 2.1 or higher. Language(s): C, Assembly & QuickBASIC. Memory Required: 512k.
$150.00-$1000.00.
Office Management Program for Residential Real Estate Brokers. Does Accounting, Agent Billing, Inventory Control, Production Reporting, Escrow Management, Prospect/Property Matching & Client Follow-Up, Advertising, Referral Tracking, Video Presentations, Call Tracking, etc.
Real-E-Data, Inc.

Real World Math Adventures in Flight. Feb. 1996. Customer Support: Telephone support - free (except phone charge).
System 6.0.7 or higher. 256 color Mac with 68030 processor (4Mb). CD-ROM disk $12.99 (ISBN 1-57594-123-6). Nonstandard peripherals required: 2x CD-ROM drive, mouse, 640/480 resolution monitor.
Featuring Addison-Wesley's Revolutionary Program That Teaches Math by Taking Children on a Trip to the Airport where They Explore & Apply Math in True-Life Situations. Kids Learn Six Key Mathematical Concepts - Problem Solving, Measurement, Operations, Graphing, Geometry & Numeracy.
Kidsoft, Inc.

Real World Sales Analysis. Version: 7. 1995. Compatible Hardware: Altos, IBM PC, XT, AT & compatibles; Tandy. Operating System(s) Required: DOS, Xenix, Unix; Novell network. Language(s): MicroFocus & RM Cobol. Memory Required: 640k. General Requirements: Hard disk, 132-column printer. Customer Support: Support subcription available for fee.
IBM, Networks. $400.00-$500.00 incl. manuals. UNIX,XENIX. $400.00-$500.00.
source code avail.
Helps Analyze Sales, Product Usage, & Customer Purchases. User Can Consolidate & Tabulate Information from Accounts Receivable, Inventory Control, Professional Invoicing & Order Entry/ Billing; & Print Numerous Reports Such As Sales Analysis by Customer/Item Item Sales Volume/ Responsible Sales Rep.
RealWorld Corp.

Realms of Arkania: Blade of Destiny. Attic Entertainment & Fantasy Productions GmbH. Jun. 1993. Items Included: Three (3) 3.5" diskettes, four-color map, 8-page System Reference Card, 112-page player's guide. Customer Support: Hint line available 4:00-8:00 p.m. EST Monday-Friday; 12:00-4:00 p.m. EST weekends & holidays. 30-day warranty - free replacement with dated proof of purchase. After 30 days, please provide $12.50 replacement fee.
PC-DOS/MS-DOS. IBM PC & 100% compatibles (640k). disk $39.95 (ISBN 0-926846-68-X). Optimal configuration: Hard disk drive, 640k RAM, 80286 processor or higher, PC-DOS/MS-DOS 3.X, 5.0 or 6.0, 16Mhz or faster.
Commodore Amiga. disk $39.95.
The Proud Thorwalians of Arkania's Northern Reaches Face a Dismal Future. Rumors Abound of a Waiting Army, Banded Together under One Powerfull Orc Chieftain, Standing Ready to Lay Waste to Arkania's Town & Villages. All Hope of Survival Rests on Your Ability to Discover the Whereabouts of a Legendary Artifact Thought Lost with Its Wielder in the Midst of Orcish Territory. Can This Renowned Sword, the Blade of Destiny, Stop the Siege.
Sir-Tech Software, Inc.

Realms of Arkania: Shadows over Riva. Attic Entertainment. Apr. 1996. Customer Support: Free hint line service available 4:00-8:00p.m. (EST) weekdays, 12:00-4:00p.m. (EST) weekends & holidays. Technical support on weekdays 9:00a.m.-5:00p.m. (EST). 30-day warranty with dated proof of purchase. After 30-day warranty expires, $12.50 replacement fee applied.
MS-DOS. IBM PC 486/33 MHz (5Mb). CD-ROM disk Contact publisher for price (ISBN 0-926846-83-3). Nonstandard peripherals required: Mouse, CD-ROM drive, 265 Comp SVGA, sound blaster.
Something Sinister Is Happening in the Seaside City of Riva. Outside Its Protective Walls, Thousands of Orcs Threaten the People's Existence. Within City Center, Brave & Honored Warriors Lay down Their Swords & Refuse to Fight for the City's Good. What Preys upon Them Will Consume the City Mind, Body, & Soul. Unless You Find the Answer That Looms in the Shadows over Riva.
Sir-Tech Software, Inc.

Realms of Arkania: Star Trail. Attic Entertainment Staff & Fantasy Productions GmbH Staff. Customer Support: Free hint line service available 4:00-8:00 p.m. (EST) weekdays, 12:00-4:00 p.m. (EST) weekends & holidays. Technical support - weekdays 9:00 a.m. to 5:00 p.m. (EST) 30-day warranty with dated proof of purchase. After 30-day warranty expires, $12.50 replacement fee applied.
PC-DOS/MS-DOS. IBM PC/100% compatible (4Mb). CD-ROM disk $59.95 (ISBN 0-926846-78-7). Optimal configuration: 4Mb RAM, CD-ROM drive, 5Mb free hard disk space, 80386 processor or higher, PC/MS-DOS 5.0 or 6.X, Recommend 80486/33 or higher, sound card or PC speaker.
PC-DOS/MS-DOS. IBM PC/100% compatibles (2Mb). CD-ROM disk $59.95 (ISBN 0-926846-77-9). Optimal configuration: 2Mb RAM, 25Mb free hard disk space, 80386 processor (recommend 80486/33 or higher & 4Mb RAM), PC/MS-DOS 5.0 or 6.X, hard disk drive.
Part II in the Internaitonal Realms of Arkania Series. East of Thorwal & Deep into the Orclands, an Old Rivalry Comes to a Head As Feuding Between Elves & Dwarves Begins to Overshadow the Ageless Orc Terror. In an Epic Continuation of Its Predecessor, Blade of Destiny, Star Trail Features a Riveting Storyline, State-of-the-Art Graphics, Animated, Isometric Combat, Revamped Automaps, Print Option for Character Generation & Diary Information, Digitized Speech & a Full Musical Score.
Sir-Tech Software, Inc.

REALPLAN. Compatible Hardware: Altos Series 15-5D, Series 5-5D, 580-XX, ACS8000-XX; DEC Rainbow 100 with 2 disk drives, Rainbow 100+ with 10Mb hard disk; IBM PC with 2 disk drives, PC XT, IBM compatibles; Kaypro 11/IV with 2 disk drives, Kaypro 10; Xerox 820 with 2 disk drives, ZILOG MCZ-250. Operating System(s) Required: CP/M, MP/M, CP/M-86/80, PC-DOS, MS-DOS.
contact publisher for price (Order no.: REALPLAN).
Designed for Planning Joint Real Estate Ventures. Calculates the Internal Rate of Return & the Present Value for up to Twenty Years of a Real Estate Investment. Computes Even Payment Schedules for Loans, But Allows for Manual Input of Uneven Loan Payment Schedules.
Coopers & Lybrand.

RealShar. Version: 91f. 1991. Items Included: Disk & manual. Customer Support: 90 days included in purchase price; support agreement available.
PC-MS/DOS 2.1 or higher. IBM PC & compatibles (200k). disk $399.00. Nonstandard peripherals required: 350k disk.
Market Share/Segmentation Analysis Program for Real Estate Brokers. Uses MLS Data to Report List, Sold & Direct Sides, Average Price, Days on Market & Price Ratio by Date, Town, Property Type, Price Range, Agent or Office, Two Optional Fields. Demo Available.
Compass New England.

RealSoft Integrated Appraisal System. Version: 5. Brian G. Goodheim. Compatible Hardware: Altos; IBC; IBM. Operating System(s) Required: Theos, MS-DOS. Language(s): Assembly, Oasis BASIC. Memory Required: 512k. Items Included: Integrated appraisal system software. Customer Support: Support contract.
single-user $995.00 (Order no.: 5600).
multi-user $1995.00.
Handles Office Accounting, Assignment Scheduling, Database of Comparable Sales, Word Processing, Form Generation & Other Aspects of Appraisal Office Automation.
Real Soft Systems, Inc.

Realtime Information Management System (RIMS): Point of Sale Tire Software. Version: 94.1. May 1990. Compatible Hardware: Alpha Micro, UNIX, DOS, Novell. Operating System(s) Required: AMOS, UNIX, DOS, Novell. Language(s): BASIC. Memory Required: 200k. General Requirements: Hard disk.
$1200.00-$30,000.00 disk, VCR, streamer (based on number of users).
Fully Integrated Accounting Software - Accounts Payable, Accounts Receivable, Check Reconciliation, Fixed Assets, General Ledger, Order Entry/Inventory Control, Payroll, Purchase Order, Report Writer, Screen Writer, File Manager, System Manager, User Manager. Other modules available - Manufacturers & Contractors Job Costing, Dealer Support, Property Management, Prospect Tracking, Serial Number Tracking, EDI.
Christensen Computer Company, Inc.

Realtime Vision: Operator Interface. Version: 2.0. Jul. 1994. Items Included: 1 manual, 3 1/2" disks only. Customer Support: Free 90 days, 30-day money back guarantee.
Windows 3.1. 386 or 486 (4Mb). Vision $195.00; Visionpro $495.00 (Order no.: 800-879-5228). Optimal configuration: 486, Win 3.1,

4Mb RAM, 2Mb disk space. *Networks supported:* All, Windows for Workgroups. *Provides Real-Time Graphics under Windows. Link Charts & Graphs to Data Sources to Create Dynamic Graphics. The Link Between VISION's Graphics & a Data Service Is Made with Windows DDE. Includes Control Objects Such As Knobs, Sliders, Buttons & Switches That Can Be Linked to Other Objects & Software for Windows, Including LABTECH NOTEBOOK & CONTROL. Used With These Products, It Is a Cost Effective Menu for Companies to View & Control Processes from Many Locations.*
Laboratory Technologies Corp.

RealWorld Accounting & Business System. *Version:* 6.5. *Compatible Hardware:* IBM PC, PC XT, PC AT & compatibles; Altos, Tandy. *Operating System(s) Required:* DOS, UNIX, XENIX. *Memory Required:* 640k. *General Requirements:* Hard disk. *Items Included:* User manual. *Customer Support:* Support subscription available for fee, 900 number.
 $795.00 single user & network.
 $995.00 XENIX/UNIX version.
Consists of a Fully Integrated Line of 19 Accounting & Business Software Packages Designed to Meet the Needs of a Wide Range of Businesses.
RealWorld Corp.

RealWorld Accounts Payable. *Version:* 7. 1995. *Compatible Hardware:* Altos; IBM PC, XT, AT & compatibles; Tandy. *Operating System(s) Required:* MS-DOS, Novell Network, Xenix, Unix. *Language(s):* MicroFocus & RM Cobol. *Memory Required:* 640k. *General Requirements:* Hard disk, 132-column printer. *Customer Support:* Support subscription available for fee.
 IBM, Networks. $795.00, incl. manuals.
 UNIX. $795.00-$995.00.
 source code avail.
Provides the Tools Necessary to Track & Control Expenditures. A/P Provides Users with Information for Tracking Vendors; Access to Details of All Entry & Payment Activity from a Separate Vendor History File; On-Line Vendor Account Inquiry; & Reports Such As Cash Requirements, 1099 Forms, & Cash Disbursements Projections.
RealWorld Corp.

RealWorld Accounts Receivable. *Version:* 7. 1995. *Compatible Hardware:* Altos; IBM PC, PC XT, PC AT & compatibles; Tandy. *Operating System(s) Required:* DOS, UNIX, Novell Network. *Language(s):* MicroFocus & RM Cobol. *Memory Required:* 640k. *General Requirements:* Hard disk, 132-column printer.
 DOS, Networks. $795.00, incl. manual.
 UNIX. $795.00-$995.00.
 source code avail.
Provides Tools Needed to Handle Everyday Problems of Tracking & Collecting Monies Owed by Customers. Some of Its Many Features Allow Users to Track Customers; Age Receivables by Invoice or Due Date; Access Detailed On-Line Customer Inquiry; & Print Statements & Reports Such As Aging, Commissions Due, & Cash Receipts History.
RealWorld Corp.

RealWorld Check Reconciliation. *Version:* 7. 1995. *Compatible Hardware:* Altos, IBM PC, PC XT, PC AT & compatibles, Tandy. *Operating System(s) Required:* DOS, Networks, UNIX. *Memory Required:* 512, recommended 640k. *General Requirements:* Hard disk, 132-column printer. *Customer Support:* Support subscription available for fee.
 PC-DOS/MS-DOS. 3.5" or 5.25" disk $265.00.
 UNIX. $895.00.
Helps Maintain Checkbooks & Reconcile Checking Accounts with Bank Statements. The Features of This Package Include Unlimited Checking Accounts; Automatic Transfers of Deposits & Check Information from Accounts Receivable, Accounts Payable & Payroll Packages; Two Reconciliation Methods; & Reports Such As Reconciliation, Checkbook & Account Activity.
RealWorld Corp.

RealWorld General Ledger. *Version:* 6.5. 1991. *Compatible Hardware:* Altos, IBM PC, PC XT, PC AT & compatibles; Tandy. *Operating System(s) Required:* PC-DOS/MS-DOS, UNIX; Novell network. *Language(s):* MicroFocus & RM Cobol. *Memory Required:* 640k. *General Requirements:* Hard disk, 132-column printer. *Customer Support:* Support subscription available for fee.
 IBM, Network. $795.00.
 UNIX, XENIX. $995.00.
 source code avail.
Categorizes & Summarizes Your Accounting Information. Custom Designed Financial Statements Clearly Show the Company's Profit (or Loss) As Well As Its Assets, Liabilities & Equity Position. General Ledger Allows for up to Thirteen Accounting Periods; Complete Audit Trails; Loan Calculations & Amortization Schedules For Fixed Rate Loans; Custom-Designed Financial Statements; & Numerous Reports Such As Consolidation Register & Changes in Financial Position.
RealWorld Corp.

RealWorld Inventory Control. *Version:* 7. 1996. *Compatible Hardware:* Altos, IBM PC, XT, AT & compatibles; Tandy. *Operating System(s) Required:* PC-DOS/MS-DOS, UNIX; Novell network. *Language(s):* MicroFocus & RM Cobol. *Memory Required:* 640k. *General Requirements:* Hard disk, 132-column printer. *Customer Support:* Support subscription available for fee.
 IBM, Networks. $795.00-$995.00 incl. user manual.
 UNIX, XENIX. $995.00.
 source code avail.
Tracks Product Usage & Costs, & Maintains Inventory at Optimum Levels. Includes Features for Multiple Warehouse Usage; Tracking Inventory Usage for up to Twelve Prior Periods; & Reports Such As Purchasing Advice, Stock Status, Inventory Valuation, Inventory Usage, & Physical Count Worksheet.
RealWorld Corp.

RealWorld Order Entry-Billing. *Version:* 7. 1995. *Compatible Hardware:* Altos; IBM PC, XT, AT & compatibles. *Operating System(s) Required:* PC-DOS/MS-DOS, UNIX, Novell network. *Language(s):* MicroFocus & RM Cobol. *Memory Required:* 640k. *General Requirements:* Hard disk, 132-column printer.
 IBM, Networks. disk $795.00-$995.00 incl. manual.
 UNIX, XENIX. $995.00.
 source code avail.
Helps Process Customer Orders & Issue Invoices. Offers Many Features Such As One Order Can Include Items from Several Warehouses; Full Invoice History Can Be Kept; & Many Reports Such As Cash Receipts Journal, Back Orders by Customer; & Invoice History by Invoice Can Be Printed.
RealWorld Corp.

RealWorld Payroll. *Version:* 7. 1995. *Compatible Hardware:* Altos, IBM PC, XT, AT & Tandy compatibles. *Operating System(s) Required:* DOS, UNIX, Novell Network, Altos, Tandy. *Language(s):* MicroFocus & RM Cobol. *Memory Required:* 640k. *General Requirements:* Hard disk, 132-column printer. *Customer Support:* Support subscription available for fee.
 IBM, Network. $795.00-$995.00 incl. user manual.
 UNIX, XENIX. $995.00.
 source code avail.
Helps Maintain Employee Payroll Information, Handle Voluntary Deductions, Calculate Taxes, & Print Payroll Checks, Forms, & Reports. Some of Its Features Include Hourly & Salary Employees, Plus a Variety of Pay Frequencies; Automatic Calculation of Payroll; Printing of Payroll Checks; Workers' Compensation; & Printing of Numerous Reports Such As Direct Deposit Register, Time Worked Register, & a Customized Quarterly Report.
RealWorld Corp.

RealWorld Professional Invoicing. *Version:* 6.5. 1990. *Compatible Hardware:* IBM PC, XT, Tandy, Altos, AT & compatibles. *Operating System(s) Required:* PC-DOS/MS-DOS, Networks, UNIX. *Memory Required:* 640k. *General Requirements:* Hard disk; 132-column printer. *Customer Support:* Support subscription available for fee.
 PC-DOS/MS-DOS, Networks. $795.00-$995.00.
 XENIX/UNIX. disk $995.00.
Provides User with the Tools Needed to Bill & Print Invoices for Professional Services. Features Include Custom Designed Invoices; a Full Invoice History; & Reports Such As Recurring Bills List, Sales Journal, Cash Receipts Journal & Invoice History.
RealWorld Corp.

RealWorld Professional Time & Billing. *Version:* 6.5. *Customer Support:* Support subscription, 900 number.
 DOS, Network. $1095.00 incl. accounts receivable.
 UNIX. $1295.00 incl. accounts receivable.
Designed for Firms That Bill for Services on the Basis of Time. Some of the Many Features of Professional Time & Billing Include Tracking How Valuable Staff Time Is Spent; Monitoring Client Expenses; Printing Invoices & Statements; Collecting Receivables; & Printing Vital Aging, Profitability, & Productivity Reports.
RealWorld Corp.

RealWorld Purchase Order. *Version:* 7. 1996. *Operating System(s) Required:* PC-DOS/MS-DOS, networks, UNIX. *Memory Required:* 640k. *General Requirements:* Hard disk, 132-column printer. *Customer Support:* Support subscription available for fee.
 PC-DOS/MS-DOS, Networks. 3.5" or 5.25" disk $795.00-$995.00.
 XENIX, UNIX. 3.5" or 5.25" disk $795.00-$995.00.
 3.5" or 5.25" disk $795.00.
Assists User in Ordering Goods & Services from Vendors. Allows User to Maintain Separate Remittance & Purchasing Addresses; Quickly Enter Receivings; Enter & Print Purchase Orders; Handle Blanket Purchase Orders; & Print Reports Such As Expedite Shipment, Follow-Up Past-Due Shipment, Cash Disbursements Projection, Receivings History & Purchasing Advice.
RealWorld Corp.

RealWorld Sales Management Solutions. *Version:* 6.5. American Information Systems. 1992. *Items Included:* Manuals, registration card, license. *Customer Support:* Support & training available from dealers or from vendor for a fee. Telephone support & training (on site or at our facilities) to users for a fee.
 MS-DOS 3.3 or higher. IBM XT/AT PS/2, Tandy & compatibles (640k). disk $695.00. *Addl. software required:* System kit (one per installation). *Optimal configuration:* Hard disk, 132 column printer.
 Network/UNIX. IBM XT/AT & compatibles (640k). disk $895.00. *Addl. software required:*

TITLE INDEX

System kit (one per installation). *Optimal configuration:* Hard disk, 132 column printer. *Provides Sales Professionals with the Tools for Increasing Sales & Profits. Both Sales Managers & Sales Reps Can Benefit from the Many Features of Sales Management Solutions Which Include Tracking Income Due & Received; Defining up to 999 Statistics & Five Levels of Territories; Tracking Lead Sources; Tracking Call-Backs by Date; & Printing Numerous Reports Such As Sales Activity, Income Variance, Statistic History, Revenue Variance & Hot Leads.*
RealWorld Corp.

REAP Plus: Real Estate Analysis Program. 1985. *Compatible Hardware:* IBM & compatibles. *Operating System(s) Required:* MS-DOS. *Language(s):* BASIC. *Memory Required:* 64k.
disk $200.00.
Real Estate Investment 5 Year Forecasting/ Planning Model. Allows Forecasting of Rents, Expenses, Vacancy Factor, Taxes, & Before & after Taxes, Cash Flows & Internal Rate of Return.
Realty Software.

Rear Guard. 1988.
MS-DOS, PC-DOS (256k). disk $29.00.
Software Utility That Establishes Password Protection on Each FORMAT.COM & FORMAT.EXE Program on a Local or LAN Drive Across Volumes. Helps Prevent Accidental Hard Disk Formatting.
Microbridge Computers.

Recall List. B. Neiburger. 1983. *Compatible Hardware:* Apple II, IIc, IIe; Basis 6502; Franklin Ace; IBM PC, PC XT, PC AT. *Operating System(s) Required:* Apple DOS 3.3, MS-DOS 3.1. *Language(s):* BASIC (source code included). *Memory Required:* Apple 48k, IBM PC 256k.
disk $39.00 (ISBN 0-914555-17-0).
Keeps Track of Thousands of Patient/Client Records. Each Record Lists: Name, Address, City/State/Zip, Telephone Number, Last Visit, Next Visit, Remarks.
Andent, Inc.

RECAPBOWL. *Version:* K1. Ron Gunn. 1993. *Compatible Hardware:* IBM PC & compatibles; Commodore 64, 128. *Operating System(s) Required:* CBM DOS, DOS 2.1 or higher. *Language(s):* BASIC for C64, Compiled .EXE for IBM. *Memory Required:* C64 64k, IBM 512k. *General Requirements:* Printer, 3-part recap paper. *Items Included:* A sample of 3-part recap paper.
disk $25.00 ea. *Addl. software required:* LeagueBowl.
IBM. (Order no.: D051I).
Commodore. (Order no.: D025F).
Prints Statistics Using Data Files from LEAGUEBOWL. Its LISTIT Feature Produces Thirty-One Different Bowler & Five Team Lists in Rank Order under User Control. Requires LEAGUEBOWL Data.
Briley Software.

Receivables. *Version:* 1.1. Oct. 1989. *Items Included:* Instruction included on disk. *Customer Support:* 90 days unlimted warranty.
MS-DOS, Windows 3.1. IBM XT, AT or compatibles (512k). disk $34.95 plus $3.50 S&H (Order no.: 1073). *Addl. software required:* Lotus 1-2-3, Release 4.0 or higher. *Optimal configuration:* IBM AT, 640k RAM. *Maintain Receivables Database & Produce Aged Receivables Report with Removal of Paid Items.*
Compiled Systems.

Recess in Greece.
MS-DOS 5.0 or higher, Windows 3.1 or higher. 386 processor or higher (4Mb). CD-ROM disk $49.95 (Order no.: R1358). *Nonstandard peripherals required:* CD-ROM drive. *Optimal configuration:* 386 processor operating at 16Mhz or higher, MS-DOS 5.0 or higher, Windows 3.1 or higher, 30Mb hard drive, mouse, VGA graphic adapter & VGA color monitor (SVGA recommended), 4Mb RAM, external speakers or headphones (with sound card) that are Sound Blaster compatible.
Macintosh (4Mb). (Order no.: R1358A).
Nonstandard peripherals required: 14" color monitor or larger, CD-ROM drive.
Children Can Explore Ancient Greece As They Take Part in This Exciting Story. Educational Games & Puzzles Show the Influence of Ancient Greece on Our Modern World. Explore Further to Learn More about Greek History, Geography, Mythology, Math, Music & More (Ages 7-12).
Library Video Co.

Recess in Greece. Nov. 1994. *Customer Support:* Technical support phone line.
PC. Windows 3.1, 486 or higher, double speed CD-ROM drive (4Mb). disk $24.95 (ISBN 1-887423-02-8). *Optimal configuration:* VGA/SVGA w/256 colors, MPC compliant sound card & mouse required.
MAC. System 7.1 or higher, double CD-ROM drive (4Mb). 3.5" disk $24.95 (ISBN 1-887423-03-6). *Nonstandard peripherals required:* 256 colors. *Optimal configuration:* VGA/SVGA w/256 colors, MPC compliant sound card & mouse requried.
Morgan Interactive.

Recipe-Fax. *Version:* 2.0. *Compatible Hardware:* Commodore Amiga.
$44.95.
Complete Recipe Creation/Editing Environment. Individual Editing/Rearrangement (Cut, Copy, Paste) for Ingredients/Procedures. Intelligent Unit Amount Adjuster Works Automatically. Handles Fractional & Decimal Amounts. Powerful Multiple Recipe Processor. Convert Units to/from Metric/ US Standards. Adjust Serving Size up or down. Create/Edit Shopping Lists.
Meggido Enterprises.

Recipe-FAX Plus. *Version:* 2.0. *Compatible Hardware:* Commodore Amiga.
3.5" disk write for info.
Includes All the Benefits of Recipe-Fax U2, Plus Nutritional Analysis of Recipes. Set/Save Personalized Nutrient Allowance Goals. Compare Recipe(s) Nutrients to RDA & Personalized Values. User Expandable Ingredient Database. Costing Analysis/Reporting Support.
Meggido Enterprises.

The Recipe Manager, 2 disks. *Version:* 5.2. May 1987. *Compatible Hardware:* IBM PC & compatibles. *Operating System(s) Required:* PC-DOS, MS-DOS. *Language(s):* Turbo Pascal. *Memory Required:* 128k. *Customer Support:* Free demo disk & support.
Set. $59.95, incl. manual.
Handles a Maximum of 65,000 Recipes per Database (Disk Space Permitting), & an Unlimited Number of Databases Can Be Created. Recipes Can Be Listed Alphabetically by Title, by Recipe Number, or by Category. Generates Shopping Lists & a Hard-Copy Paged Cookbook of the Database. The Number of Servings in Each Recipe Is Adjustable from 1 to 999, & the Units of Measure Will Automatically Convert to the Most Appropriate Measure (Such As Tablespoons to Cups). Includes a Database of 115 Gourmet Entree Recipes.
Gem Island Software.

Recipe Master. *Version:* 1.1. Richard D. Lasky. Apr. 1993. *Items Included:* 19 page manual. *Customer Support:* No charge for support, over regular phone lines.
Macintosh. Mac Plus, Classic, SE, II series, etc. (1Mb). 3.5" disk $59.00 (ISBN 1-878081-02-0, Order no.: RM1). *Addl. software required:* HyperCard version 1.2 or higher.
Full-Featured Nutritional Analysis Program, Specifically Designed for Writing & Storing Recipes, Complete with Nutritional Informaton. Recipes Are Composed from Menus of over 2,000 Foods. The Nutrient Content of the Recipe Is Given in a Table, & a Text Report May Be Generated. The Nutrient Content of Each Ingredient May Be Examined Before Its Addition to the Recipe. Recipes May Be Stored in Special Files, along with Cooking Instructions. Reports on These Stored Recipes May Be Generated at Any Time. Recipes May Be Scaled up or down. Prints Shopping Lists.
Big Byte Software.

Recipe Profit Analyzer. Harry Skolnik. Oct. 1985. *Compatible Hardware:* Apple Macintosh, IBM PC & compatibles. *Language(s):* Compiled dBASE III Plus. *Memory Required:* 512k. *General Requirements:* Hard disk.
RPA I. disk $495.00.
RPA II. disk $695.00.
Reports Food & Beverage Recipe Costs & Profits Based on the Latest Ingredient Costs. Changes Can Be Made in Recipes, Ingredient Costs, & Menu Prices to See the Effect These Changes Will Have on Recipe Costs & Profits. One Version of the Program Links to Any of RestaurantComp's Inventory Programs, & a Second Version Operates Stand-Alone.
RestaurantComp.

The Recipe Writer. *Version:* 3.0. Jun. 1984. *Compatible Hardware:* IBM PC & compatibles. *Operating System(s) Required:* MS-DOS. *Language(s):* Turbo Pascal. *Memory Required:* 264k. *Customer Support:* Free unlimited.
disk or $49.95,69.95 for program plus merge utility & professional receipe collection.
Recipe Management Program Featuring User Defined Categories for Customized Cross Referencing, Bibliography for Referencing Favorite Cookbooks & Recipe Magazines, Intelligent Conversions, a To-Taste Option for Ingredients that Don't Convert Exactly, Menu Planning by Dynamically Linking Recipes Together, Unlimited Capacity, an Automated Shopping List, Alphabetized & Printable, a Notepad Manager to Organize Tips, Reactions, Reminders, etc., Space Allocated for Large Recipes, Including Instructions. Available Recipe Merge Feature for Sharing Recipes with Friends or Buying Recipes on Disk at Your Service Software.
At Your Service Software, Inc.

The Recipe Writer Pro - Plus. *Version:* 5.11. Mar. 1986. *Compatible Hardware:* IBM PC & compatibles, Net Workable, Net BIOS. *Operating System(s) Required:* PC-DOS/MS-DOS 3.X or higher. *Language(s):* C, Clarion. *Memory Required:* 640k. *General Requirements:* Hard disk. *Items Included:* Disk & full documentation with tutorial. *Customer Support:* 90 days free unlimited telephone support. Extended support plans are available that include upgrades.
disk $295.00 Pro; $395.00 Plus.
$395.00 Pro network; $595.00 Plus network.
Professional Recipe Management/Pricing System. Features What-If Capabilities, Flexible Pricing, Instant Order Forms/Production Sheets, Intelligent Conversions, Dynamic Recipe Linking, Text Editing for Recipe Method, Customized Categories, Unlimited Capacity, Bulk Recipe Reprise Utility, & Multiple Reports. Documentation Includes a Complete Tutorial, Table of Contents & Index. Additional Modules

RECLAIM

Include: Inventory Pro & Sales Analysis Pro. ASCII Files Allow Data Transfer to Word Processors, Spreadsheets, Accounting Packages, & POS/Register Systems. New Plus Module Allows Theoretical Inventory Depletion by Catering Jobs & Standard Requisitions. Interface to Catered Event Management Software available.
At Your Service Software, Inc.

Reclaim. *Operating System(s) Required:* CP/M, SB-80. *Memory Required:* 64k.
disk $80.00.
Tests the Surface of All Disks, Floppy or Hard & Assigns Defective Portions to Special Hidden Files. Further Writing on Defective Blocks Is Not Permitted. Users Can Perform Full Read/Write Testing on Disks with Files Without Logging Them. Not Designed for the Recovery of Erased Files.
Lifeboat Assocs.

RecordHolderPlus. *Version:* 3.1. Jun. 1990. *Compatible Hardware:* Apple Macintosh. *Memory Required:* 512k. *Items Included:* Manual. *Customer Support:* Free telephone support.
3.5" disk $85.95.
Database Management Software That Accepts up to 32,000 Characters per Field, Without Requiring the User to Specify Field Length. Users Can Put Text, Graphics, Clickable Checkboxes, & Buttons in Their Window Formats Anywhere They Are Needed. Stores Both Text & Pictures. Supports Color Printing of Reports with an ImageWriter II.
Software Discoveries, Inc.

Records Management Control. 1992. *Items Included:* Complete illustrated instructions. *Customer Support:* Unlimited telephone support no charge; free replacement of damaged disks. MS-DOS. IBM PC, XT, AT, PS/2 & compatibles (512k). disk $189.00 (Order no.: RECO).
The Purpose of This Program Is to Properly Manage All Records That Are Vital (in Different Ways & for Different Reasons) to a Company. All Companies, Regardless of Size or Purpose, Must Retain Certain Records for Historical, Tax, Archival or Other Reasons. This Program Is Designed to Maintain, Manage &, When Appropriate, Flag the Disposal of Such Records.
Right On Programs.

Records Retention. *Version:* 3.0. Jan. 1988. *Compatible Hardware:* IBM PC, PC AT, PS/2. *Memory Required:* 512k. *General Requirements:* Hard disk, parallel printer. *Items Included:* Reference manual. *Customer Support:* Phone/modem support included first year, nominal fee thereafter.
disk $250.00 (Order no.: RR1).
Keeps Track of Old Files Which Must Be Legally Maintained for a Certain Number of Years. Allows Files to Be Checked Out, & Reminds the User When It Is Time to Erase a File.
Fogle Computing Corp.

RECOS. *Compatible Hardware:* IBM PC. *Operating System(s) Required:* PC-DOS 3.3 or higher. *Language(s):* COBOL. *Memory Required:* 640k. contact publisher for price (ISBN 0-924638-51-6).
Designed for Shoe & Apparel Importer/Distributor/Retailer. Provides for: Customer Orders Consolidating into Factory Orders; Tracking of Onhand, Onorder, Committed by Size-Color-Width-Length; Backorder Allocations; Online Inquiry; Sales Analysis; Commission Reporting; Departmental Planning; Customer Analysis; Bar Coding; Portable Device for On-Site Inventory or Order Entry.
Interactive Business Systems, Ltd.

RecoverEase: Data Recovery & Protection Utilities for UNIX Systems. *Version:* 1.1. May 1992. *Items Included:* 90 page manual. *Customer Support:* Technical support via telephone <h>. SCO UNIX 3.2 & higher; SCO XENIX 286 2.3 & above; SCO XENIX 386 2.3 & higher; SCO ODT V1.0 & higher; Interactive System V/386 Rel. 3.2.X. disk $395.00. *Addl. software required:* DOS Boot Diskette 3.X or higher. *Optimal configuration:* 2Mb RAM for two of four modules; 512/640k for remaining two modules.
Collection of Expert Hard Drive Utilities Providing the Most Complete Preventative Maintenance & Data Recovery Software Available for Unix Systems. Prevent Data Loss Situations Using the Most Powerful Diagnostic, Maintenance, & Recovery Tools Available for Unix.
Ontrack Computer Systems, Inc.

Rectangular Combined Footings. 1995. *Items Included:* Full manual. *Customer Support:* Free telephone support - 90 days, 30-day warranty. MS-DOS 3.2 or higher. 286 (584k). disk $99.95. *Nonstandard peripherals required:* CGA/EGA/VGA.
RCF Is a Versatile, Interactive System for Analyzing & Designing a Rectangular Combined Footing Supporting Two Columns. It Is Able to Handle Problems Where the Footing Slab Is in Partial Contact with the Soil.
Dynacomp, Inc.

Red Lighting. Norman Koger, Jr. *Customer Support:* Technical support line: (408) 737-6800 (9am-5pm, PST); 14 day money back guarantee/30 day exchange policy.
DOS 2.11 or higher. IBM PC & compatibles (512k). disk $59.95. *Nonstandard peripherals required:* Requires a color monitor & a graphic adaptor (i.e., CGA, EGA).
Workbench. Amiga (512k). disk $59.95.
TOS. Atari ST (512k). disk $59.95.
An Explosive Depiction of the Potential War in Central Europe Between NATO & the Warsaw Pact. This Simulation Is As Advanced As the Weapon Systems Used in Modern Land & Air Combat, Such As the Soviet T-80 Tank & the U.S. F-117 Stealth Bomber. It Accounts for Every Vehicle & Aircraft! Three Scenarios, Five Difficulty Levels, & Multiple Options Challenge the Avid Wargamer to Explore the Myriad Possible Outcomes Should World War III Erupt!
Strategic Simulations, Inc.

Red Pencil. *Compatible Hardware:* TRS-80. disk $59.95 (ISBN 0-936200-13-8).
Program Is Accessed Directly Within the ELECTRIC PENCIL Version 2.0 Word Processing System. Corrects Spelling & Typographical Errors, & Maintains the BLUE PENCIL 50,000 Word Dictionary.
Blue Cat.

Red River Crop & Livestock Accounting. *Version:* 2.2. Red River Software. *Items Included:* 3 ring notebook manual. *Customer Support:* Available.
MS-DOS 3.1 or higher. IBM or compatible (512k). contact publisher for price. *Optimal configuration:* 1 floppy or 1 hard drive, 80 column printer.
Comprehensive Crop & Livestock Accounting. Income Statement, Balance Sheet, Cash Flow Report, Schedule F Report, detail & Activity Report. Feed/Lot Analysis Report & Enterprise Analysis Report.
Farmer's Software Assn.

Red Storm Rising. 1987. *Compatible Hardware:* Commodore 64/128; IBM PC; Tandy, Amiga; Atari. *Items Included:* Manual, keyboard overlay, map. *Customer Support:* Free customer service, (410) 771-1151, Ext. 350.
Commodore, Tandy. disk $44.95.
IBM. disk $54.95.
Amiga. 3.5" disk $54.95.
Atari. disk $44.95.
Based on Tom Clancy's Best-Selling Book of Modern Warfare Between the Superpowers. Many Scenarios from the Book "Red Storm Rising" Have Been Recreated.
MicroProse Software.

Red Wing Accounts Payable. *Version:* 5.0.1. Sep. 1991. *Compatible Hardware:* IBM PC & compatibles. *Operating System(s) Required:* PC-DOS, MS-DOS. *Language(s):* Compiled BASIC. *Memory Required:* 640k. *General Requirements:* Hard disk. *Customer Support:* 3 different technical support plans available.
disk $495.00.
Produces 1099 Reports. Monitors Unpaid Invoices, Gives Instant Retrieval of Purchases from Specific Suppliers, & Can Select Payment of Invoices by Discounts or Due Dates. Produces Reports That Show Future Cash Requirements, Cash Flow, & Prints Checks & Performs Checking Account Reconciliation. Allows Partial Payment of Invoices. Integrates with Red Wing PAYROLL, Red Wing BUSINESS INVENTORY, & Red Wing GENERAL LEDGER.
Red Wing Business Systems, Inc.

Red Wing Accounts Receivable. *Version:* 5.5.1. Feb. 1990. *Compatible Hardware:* IBM PC & compatibles. *Operating System(s) Required:* PC-DOS, MS-DOS. *Language(s):* Compiled BASIC. *Memory Required:* 640k. *General Requirements:* 2 disk drives or hard disk. *Customer Support:* 3 different technical support plans available.
$495.00.
Available Management Information: Sales by Date, Product, Salesman, Customer, State/Province; Payments by Customer by Month; Accounts Receivable by Due Date or Age, Complete Customer Transactions by Month or Year-to-Date, Sales Tax Reports by State, Finance Charges by Customer, Open Credit Report, Customer Statements, Invoices, Quotes, Receipts Report, Yearly Transaction Report & Customer Mailing Labels. Helps the User Determine Who Is Selling What & Where, Who Is Buying What, & Who Is Paying. Invoices & Statements Can Be Completely Customized by the Customer.
Red Wing Business Systems, Inc.

Red Wing Business Inventory System. *Version:* 5.5. Mar. 1990. *Compatible Hardware:* IBM PC & compatibles. *Operating System(s) Required:* MS-DOS, PC-DOS. *Language(s):* Compiled BASIC. *Memory Required:* 640k. *General Requirements:* Hard disk. *Customer Support:* 3 different technical support plans available.
$495.00.
Available Management Information: Sales Analysis by Quantity, Sales Analysis by Dollars, Inventory Item Labels, General Ledger Journal Entries, Excess/Obsolete Inventory Report, Inventory Transactions, Inventory Item Price Report, Open Purchase Order, Detail Inquiry Report, Reorder Report, & Inventory Item Status Report.
Red Wing Business Systems, Inc.

Red Wing Cow-Calf Production System. *Version:* 6.0. Jan. 1992. *Compatible Hardware:* IBM PC & compatibles. *Operating System(s) Required:* PC-DOS, MS-DOS. *Language(s):* Compiled BASIC. *Memory Required:* 640k. *General Requirements:* 2 disk drives, or hard disk. *Customer Support:* 3 different technical support plans available.
disk $695.00.

TITLE INDEX

Assists Users with Herd Improvement by Heifer Selection, Increasing Weaning Weights, Selecting Best Bulls, Insuring Quality Records, Justifying Balance Sheet & Improved Forecasting. Allows Comparison of Management Practices & Works for Either Purebred or Commercial Systems. Reports Can Be User-Defined.
Red Wing Business Systems, Inc.

Red Wing General Ledger. *Version:* 6.1. Jan. 1991. *Compatible Hardware:* IBM PC & compatibles. *Operating System(s) Required:* MS-DOS, PC-DOS. *Language(s):* PDS 7.1. *Memory Required:* 640k. *General Requirements:* 2 disk drives or hard disk. *Customer Support:* 3 different technical support plans available. disk $495.00.
Available Management Information: Income Statements, Balance Sheets, Cash Flow Reports, 12-Month History, 12-Month Forecasts, Combined History/Forecast, Yearly Transaction List, End-of-Month Journal Entries, Trial Balance, Separate Family Living Expenses, Accounts Payable Transaction List. Integrates with the Following RED WING Programs: Accounts Payable, Accounts Receivable, Payroll, Asset Depreciation, Business Inventory, & Farm Inventory.
Red Wing Business Systems, Inc.

Red Wing Payroll. *Version:* 7.0. 1995. *Compatible Hardware:* IBM PC & compatibles. *Operating System(s) Required:* MS-DOS, PC-DOS. *Language(s):* PDS 7.1. *Memory Required:* 640k. *General Requirements:* 2 disk drives or hard disk. *Customer Support:* 3 different technical support plans available. disk $495.00.
Project & Piece Work Reporting & Management; Accommodates Taxes for 50 States; Handles 20 Earnings & Deductions Categories; Prints Checks; Prints W-2 Forms; Provides Information for Tax Forms 941 & 943; Prints Comparison & Accrued Taxes & Tax Limits after Each Payroll; Saves Yearly Detail; Includes Quick Check Feature.
Red Wing Business Systems, Inc.

Red Wing Project Cost. *Version:* 1.5. May 1985. *Compatible Hardware:* IBM PC & Compatible. *Operating System(s) Required:* MS-DOS, PC-DOS. *Language(s):* Interpretive BASIC. *Memory Required:* 640k. *General Requirements:* 2 disk drives or hard disk. *Customer Support:* 3 different technical support plans available. disk $395.00.
Available Management Information: Project ID, Description, Labor Hours (Bid, Actual Percent Complete), Labor Dollars (Bid, Actual, Percent Complete) Material Dollars (Bid, Actual Percent Complete) Last Activity Date, Comment Lines, Labor Detail Summarized by Category Code, Grand Total of All Labor Costs, Material Detail Summarized by Category Code, Grand Total of All Material & Project Totals. Integrates with Red Wing Payroll & Red Wing Accounts Payable.
Red Wing Business Systems, Inc.

REF. *Compatible Hardware:* TRS-80 Model I, Model III.
disk $24.95 (Order no.: D4REF).
Provides a Detailed Cross-Reference of All BASIC Variables.
The Alternate Source.

Reference. *Items Included:* Bound manual. *Customer Support:* Free hotline - no time limit; 30 day limited warranty; updates are $5/disk plus S&H.
MS-DOS. IBM & compatibles (256k). disk $39.95.
Combines Universal Data Search & Retrieval, Note Taking, & Reference Style Conversion in One Package. For Each Citation, All You Do Is Enter Author, Date, Title, Publisher, Volume, Page, Information, & As Many Notes As You Wish. Allows User to Search by First & Last Names of Senior & Junior Authors, Date of Publication, & up to 5 Keywords in the Title, Publisher's Name, Place of Publication, & Every Note or Quote in All References. The Results of Successful Searches Are Displayed, Printed, or Stored on Diskette for Minor Editing & Inclusion with Your Manuscripts. User Can Enter Data Sequentially As Prompted by REFERENCE or Use a Word Processor to Enter References Alphabetically & Keep Files up to Date.
Dynacomp, Inc.

Refinery I. *Version:* 2. Jan. 1988. *Compatible Hardware:* IBM PC. *Language(s):* BASIC. *Memory Required:* 128k.
disk $150.00 ea.
IBM. (Order no.: 05-201).
Covers Two Phase Flow Pressure Drop Analysis Based on Method of Lockhart & Martinelli & American Petroleum Institute's (API) - RP 530 Stress/Rupture Analsyis. If Zero Percent Vaporization Input - Calculates All Liquid Pressure Drop; If One Hundred Percent Vaporization Input - Calculates All Vapor Pressure Drop. For Two Phase Input Liquid Contribution & Vapor Contribution Are Calculated in Addition to Two Phase Results. API-RP 530 Stress/Rupture Analysis Calculates Elastic, Thermal & Rupture Stresses & Required Tube Thickness Including Thermal Stress Check at Arbitrary Thicker Wall.
Information Resource Consultants.

Reflection 8 Plus for DOS. *Version:* 5.0. Jun. 1994. *Items Included:* User guide, reference manual, technical reference (server versions only), online reference material, WRQ newsletter, Reflection mousepad. *Customer Support:* Free technical support & 90-day materials & workmanship warranty.
DOS. IBM PC, AT, XT, PS/2 or compatible. disk $229.00. *Addl. software required:* DOS 2.1 or higher. *Networks supported:* All popular LANs, including Banyan Vines, Novell, OfficeShare, & Ungermann-Bass.
Offers TN3270 Emulation Using Telnet Protocol over TCP/IP. Connects PCs to IBM Mainframes & Offers Special Features Including a CUA-Compliant GUI, Support for External Display & Field Attributes of 3270 Display Stations, HLLAPI Support, Keyboard Mapping, & Fast File Transfer Using IND$FILE or FTP. A TCP Option Is Also Available.
Walker, Richer & Quinn, Inc.

Reflection for the AS/400. *Version:* 4.1. Nov. 1994. *Items Included:* User guide, reference manual, technical reference (server versions only), online reference material, WRQ newsletter, Reflection mousepad. *Customer Support:* Free technical support & 90-day materials & workmanship warranty.
Windows. 386 or 486 PC (4Mb). disk $349.00. *Addl. software required:* Windows 3.1 or higher. *Optimal configuration:* 386 or 486 PC, color VGA, 4Mb memory or more. *Networks supported:* PC Support, NetWare for SAA, NS/Router, TCP/IP.
Provides 5250 Terminal Emulation over TCP/IP, PC Support, NetWare for SAA, or NS/Router. Includes Features for Easy Configuration & Management, & Offers Exceptional Programmability with Its Own Integrated Programming Language & Support for HLLAPI, Visual Basic, & C/C Plus Plus.
Walker, Richer & Quinn, Inc.

Reflection 4 for Windows. *Version:* 4.21. Jul. 1994. *Items Included:* User guide, reference manual, technical reference (server versions only), online reference material, WRQ newsletter, Reflection mousepad. *Customer Support:* Free technical support & 90-day materials & workmanship warranty.
Windows. 386 PC or higher (2Mb, or 4Mb min. running Microsoft Windows in standard mode). disk $399.00. *Addl. software required:* Microsoft Windows 3.1 or higher. *Networks supported:* All popular LANs including Banyan Vines, Novell, OfficeShare, & Ungermann-Bass.
Connects Windows PCs to Digital & UNIX Hosts & Offers Sixel & 16-Color ReGIS Graphics with VT340, VT320, Tektronix 4010/4014 Text Emulation. Includes Graphical Keyboard Mapping, Drag-&-Drop File Transfer, a Powerful Programming Language, & More Intuitive, Easy-to-Use Features.
Walker, Richer & Quinn, Inc.

Reflection 4 Plus for DOS. *Version:* 5.0. Jun. 1994. *Items Included:* User guide, reference manual, technical reference (server versions only), online reference material, WRQ newsletter, Reflection mousepad. *Customer Support:* Free technical support & 90-day materials & workmanship warranty.
DOS. IBM PC, AT, XT, PS/2 or compatible (256k). disk $329.00. *Addl. software required:* DOS 2.0 or higher, (3.0 or higher for the AT & PS/2). *Networks supported:* All popular LANs, including Banyan Vines, Novell, OfficeShare, & Ungermann-Bass.
Provides Complete Emulation of Digital's VT340, VT240, VT241, & Tektronix 4010/4014 Emulation. Offers a CUA-Compliant GUI, Fast, Accurate ReGIS & Sixel Graphics Support, Fast File Transfer, Keyboard Mapping, & Command Language.
Walker, Richer & Quinn, Inc.

Reflection 4 Plus for Macintosh. *Version:* 4.1. Oct. 1994. *Items Included:* User guide, reference manual, technical reference (server versions only), online reference material, WRQ newsletter, Reflection mousepad, keyboard template. *Customer Support:* Free technical support & 90-day materials & workmanship warranty.
System 6.0.5 or higher, System 7.x, Power Macintosh. Macintosh Plus or higher (2Mb). 3.5" disk $329.00. *Addl. software required:* Multifinder: required for multitasking. *Optimal configuration:* Macintosh Plus or higher, Color-capable Macintosh (68020 or higher processor) or a color-or gray-scale monitor, 2Mb memory minimum. *Networks supported:* Ethernet, token-ring, or gateway-equipped Localtalk networks.
Links Macintosh Computers to Digital & UNIX Machines Providing VT320 Text Emulation & VT340 ReGIS Graphics Allowing You to Run Programs Like RS/1, DECgraph, Vivid, & Others. Fast, Accurate File Transfer, a Powerful Programming Language, & Superb Graphics Are Provided with Macintosh Functionality.
Walker, Richer & Quinn, Inc.

Reflection Network Series. *Version:* 2.0. Feb. 1991. *Items Included:* Full set of manuals. *Customer Support:* 90 day materials & workmanship warranty along with free technical support.
DOS. IBM PC, XT, AT, PS/2 or compatible supported with Ethernet card. $99.00 to $299.00. *Addl. software required:* Reflection Series Products. *Networks supported:* Novell, 3COM, Microsoft LAN manager, Banyan Vines, HP LAN manager.
Macintosh. Macintosh Plus or higher. 3.5" disk $129.00. *Nonstandard peripherals required:* Hosts: TCP/IP. *Addl. software required:* MAC System 6.0.4 or higher, Apple's communicators Toolbox version 1.0, MAC TCP version 1.0.1 or higher, Reflection for MAC version 3.5 or higher. *Networks supported:* Ethernet, LocalTalk.

REFLECTION NETWORK SERIES FOR DOS

Family of Networking Products for the PC & Macintosh That Gives Access to a Variety of Hosts & Networks. The Series, for DOS, Is Composed of the LAT Connection, Telnet Connection, TCP Connection & 3000 Connection, & Works in Conjunction with Reflection Terminal Emulators. For the Macintosh, the Reflection Network Series Offers Telnet Connection for the Macintosh, for Network Connections to a Variety of Hosts over TCP/IP.
Walker, Richer & Quinn, Inc.

Reflection Network Series for DOS. Version: 2.11. Jul. 1994. *Items Included:* User guide, reference manual, technical reference (server versions only), online reference material, WRQ newsletter, Reflection mousepad. *Customer Support:* Free technical support & 90-day materials & workmanship warranty.
DOS. PC: 386 or higher running Windows 3.1x, host: HP 3000, UNIX, IBM, Digital VAX or Alpha hosts, & LAT based hosts. $99.00-$349.00. *Networks supported:* All popular LANs, including Banyan Vines, Novell, OfficeShare, Ungermann-Bass, & HP LAN Manager.
Options Are Available for Access to UNIX, Digital, HP, & IBM Hosts with Concurrent LAN Connections. Memory Requirements Are Low, Even with Multiple Sessions. NetBIOS, NetIPC, & TCP Sockets Support Is Provided, along with SLIP & an NFS Client Option.
Walker, Richer & Quinn, Inc.

Reflection Network Series for Windows. Version: 4.0. Jun. 1994. *Items Included:* User guide, reference manual, technical reference (server versions only), online reference material, WRQ newsletter, Reflection mousepad. *Customer Support:* Free technical support & 90-day materials & workmanship warranty.
Windows 3.1 or higher. PC: 386 or higher with supported network interface card. $99.00-$349.00. *Networks supported:* All popular LANs including Banyan Vines, Novell, OfficeShare, Ungermann-Bass, HP LAN Manager, Ethernet & Token-Ring networks.
Family of Networking Products That Provides Access to a Variety of Hosts & Networks. Provides Options for TCP/IP, Telnet, LAT, & NS/VT for Enterprise-Wide Connections. Powerful Applications & Management Features (FTP, & LPR/LPD) Are Included.
Walker, Richer & Quinn, Inc.

Reflection 1 for Windows. Version: 4.21. Jul. 1994. *Items Included:* User guide, reference manual, technical reference (server versions only), online programming language manual, WRQ newsletter, Reflection mousepad. *Customer Support:* Free technical support & 90-day materials & workmanship warranty.
Windows. 386 PC or higher (2Mb, or 4Mb min. running Microsoft Windows in standard mode). disk $399.00. *Addl. software required:* Microsoft Windows 3.1 or higher. *Networks supported:* All popular LANs including Banyan Vines, Novell, OfficeShare, & Ungermann-Bass.
Provides Accurate HP 700/92, 700/94, 2392A & ANSI Terminal Emulation, Linking Windows PCs to HP 3000s & 9000s. Includes Drag-&-Drop File Transfer, Graphical Keyboard Mapping, a Powerful Programming Language, & Many Intuitive, Easy-to-Use Features.
Walker, Richer & Quinn, Inc.

Reflection 1 Plus for DOS. Version: 5.0. Jun. 1994. *Items Included:* User guide, reference manual, technical reference (server versions only), online reference material, WRQ newsletter, Reflection mousepad. *Customer Support:* Free technical support & 90-day materials & workmanship warranty.
DOS. IBM PC, AT, XT, PS/2 or compatible (256k for text emulation, 384k for graphics emulation). disk $329.00. *Addl. software required:* DOS 2.0 or higher, (3.0 or higher for the AT & PS/2). *Networks supported:* All popular LANs, including Banyan Vines, Novell, OfficeShare, Ungermann-Bass, & HP LAN Manager.
Links PCs to HP Hosts with HP 2627A Color Graphics As Well As HP 700/92, 700/94, 2623A, Digital VT220, & Tektronix 4010 & 4014 Emulation, & Takes Minimal Memory. Includes a CUA-Compliant GUI, Support for Double-High, Double-Wide Characters, Feature Control, Keyboard Mapping, & Command Language.
Walker, Richer & Quinn, Inc.

Reflection 1 Plus for Macintosh. Version: 4.1. Oct. 1994. *Items Included:* User guide, reference manual, technical reference (server versions only), online reference material, WRQ newsletter, Reflection mousepad, keyboard template. *Customer Support:* Free technical support & 90-day materials & workmanship warranty.
System 6.0.5 or higher, System 7.x, Power Macintosh. Macintosh Plus or higher. 3.5" disk $329.00. *Addl. software required:* Multifinder: required for multitasking. *Networks supported:* Ethernet, token-ring, or gateway-equipped Localtalk networks.
Provides Precise HP 2392A, 700/92, 700/94, & 2623A Text & Graphics Emulation. Delivers High Speed, Reliable Terminal Emulation of HP Text, Graphics & ANSI Terminals. Fast, Accurate File Transfer, & a Powerful Programming Language Are Included. Communications Tools Support Apple, WRQ, & Third-Party Protocols. Includes Telnet, LAT, & NetWare for LAT.
Walker, Richer & Quinn, Inc.

Reflection 2 for Windows. Version: 4.21. Jul. 1994. *Items Included:* User guide, reference manual, technical reference (server versions only), online reference material, WRQ newsletter, Reflection mousepad. *Customer Support:* Free technical support & 90-day materials & workmanship warranty.
Windows. 386 PC or higher (2Mb, or 4Mb min. running Microsoft Windows in standard mode). disk $299.00. *Addl. software required:* Microsoft Windows 3.1 or higher. *Networks supported:* All popular LANs including Banyan Vines, Novell, OfficeShare, & Ungermann-Bass.
Provides Precise VT320, VT220 & VT102 Text Emulation for Windows PCs Connected to Digital & UNIX Hosts. Includes Graphical Keyboard Mapping, Drag-&-Drop File Transfer, a Powerful Programming Language, & Many Intuitive, Easy-to-Use Features.
Walker, Richer & Quinn, Inc.

Reflection 2 Plus for DOS. Version: 5.0. Jun. 1994. *Items Included:* User guide, reference manual, technical reference (server versions only), online reference material, WRQ newsletter, Reflection mousepad. *Customer Support:* Free technical support & 90-day materials & workmanship warranty.
DOS. IBM PC, AT, XT, PS/2 or compatible (256k). disk $229.00. *Addl. software required:* DOS 2.0 or higher, (3.0 or higher for the AT & PS/2). *Networks supported:* All popular LANs, including Banyan Vines, Novell, OfficeShare, & Ungermann-Bass.
Lets You Run Any Application Written for Digital's VT420, VT320, VT220, or VT102 Terminals on Your PC. Includes a CUA-Compliant GUI, Keyboard Mapping, Selective Feature Activation, Fast File Transfer, & Programming Language.
Walker, Richer & Quinn, Inc.

Reflection 2 Plus for Macintosh. Version: 4.1. Oct. 1994. *Items Included:* User guide, reference manual, technical reference (server versions only), online reference material, WRQ newsletter, Reflection mousepad, keyboard template. *Customer Support:* Free technical support & 90-day materials & workmanship warranty.
System 6.0.5 or higher, System 7.x, Power Macintosh. Macintosh Plus or higher (2Mb). 3.5" disk $229.00. *Addl. software required:* Multifinder: required for multitasking. *Optimal configuration:* Macintosh Plus or higher, a color- or gray-scale monitor, 2Mb Memory minimum. *Networks supported:* Ethernet, token-ring, or gateway-equipped Localtalk networks.
Precisely Emulates VT320, VT220, & VT102 Text Emulation, Linking Your Macintosh to Digital or UNIX Hosts. All Included Options Are Compatible with Popular VMS & UNIX Text Editors. Macintosh Functionality Is Offered with Communications Tools Support for Apple & Third-Party Protocols. Includes Telnet, LAT, & Fast File Transfer.
Walker, Richer & Quinn, Inc.

Reflection X. Version: 4.1. Oct. 1994. *Items Included:* User guide, reference manual, technical reference (server versions only), online reference material, WRQ newsletter, Reflection mousepad. *Customer Support:* Free technical support & 90-day materials & workmanship warranty.
Windows. 386, 486, or Pentium IBM PC-AT; PS/2 or compatible (4Mb). disk $469.00. *Addl. software required:* Windows 3.1 or higher. *Optimal configuration:* 386, 486, or Pentium IBM PC-AT; PS/2 or compatible, 4Mb memory or more recommended, high resolution VGA monitor with 256-color driver recommended. *Networks supported:* All popular LANs, including Banyan Vines, Novell, OfficeShare, Ungermann-Bass, & HP LAN Manager.
This 32-Bit PC X Server Is Available with VT320 Emulation & TCP Transport Options As the Reflection X Connectivity Suite. Offers Windows-Based FTP, a TCP/IP Stack with Management & Diagnostic Tools, & a Choice of Local (Microsoft Windows) or Remote Window Management.
Walker, Richer & Quinn, Inc.

Reflection 1 & Plus Version. Version: 4.12. Apr. 1992. *Items Included:* Full set of user manuals, including quick start guide. *Customer Support:* Registerd users of Walker Richer & Quinn products receive a 90-day materials & workmanship warranty along with free technical support.
MS-DOS (100k in minimum configuration). IBM PC, XT, AT, PS/2 & compatibles. $299.00-$369.00; quantity discounts available.
Offers Accurate HP 2392A Terminal Emulation from a PC. The Plus Version Allows PC Files to Be Backed up to the Host, & Provides Support for Network Connections As Well As Support for Direct & Dial-Up Connections. All Reflection Products Provide Error-Free File Transfer, Keyboard Remapping, Background Processing, & a Powerful Command Language.
Walker, Richer & Quinn, Inc.

Reflection 1 for Windows. Version: 3.71. Apr. 1992. *Items Included:* Full set of manuals. *Customer Support:* 90 day materials & workmanship warranty along with free technical support.
Windows; MS-DOS. IBM PC, XT, AT, PS/2 or compatibles (256k). disk $399.00. *Addl. software required:* Windows 3.X & MS-DOS 3.1 or higher. *Networks supported:* HP LAN Manager, OfficeShare, Ungermann-Bass, 3COM Novell, Star LAN, Reflection Network Series' Telnet Connection & 3000 Connection.
Provides Accurate HP 2392A & HP 700/92

TITLE INDEX

Terminal Emulation for the PC. Special Features Include 132-Column Support, Color Configuration of Host Attributes, Support for Dynamic Data Exchange (DDE), & Enhanced Printing Management. Additional Features Include Error-Free File Transfer, Keyboard Mapping, & a Powerful Command Language.
Walker, Richer & Quinn, Inc.

Reflection 1 Plus for the Macintosh. Version: 3.61. Dec. 1991. Compatible Hardware: Apple Macintosh. Memory Required: 512k. Customer Support: 90-Day materials & workmanship warranty along with free technical support.
3.5" disk $299.00.
Provides Accurate Hewlett Packard 2392A Alphanumeric Terminal Emulation to Access Data & Run HP 3000 Applications. Reflection 1 Plus Is Block- & Character-Mode Compatible. Supporting 132-Column Mode, Inverse Video, Underlining, Half Bright, & Security Options. Reflection 1 Plus Includes Apple's Communications Toolbox & Is System 7 Compatible. The Plus Feature Offers the Ability to Back up Important Macintosh Files to 1 File on the Host.
Walker, Richer & Quinn, Inc.

Reflection 2 (& Plus Version). Version: 4.13. Apr. 1992. Items Included: Full set of user manuals, including quick start guide. Customer Support: Registered users of Walker Richer & Quinn products receive a 90-day material & workmanship warranty along with free technical support.
MS-DOS 128k in minimum configuration. IBM PC, XT, AT, PS/2 & compatibles. $199.00-$269.00; quantity discounts available.
Offers PC Users Access to Data & Applications on Digital VAX or UNIX-Based Hosts. Allows Users to Run Any Application Written for Digital's VT320, VT220, or VT102 Terminals. The Plus Version Allows PC Files to Be Backed up to the Host, & Provides Support for Network Connections As Well As Support for Direct & Dial-Up Connections. All Reflection Products Provide Error-Free File Transfer, Background Processing, Powerful Command Language, & Keyboard Remapping.
Walker, Richer & Quinn, Inc.

Reflection 2 for the Macintosh. Version: 3.60. Compatible Hardware: Apple Macintosh. Memory Required: 420k.
3.5" disk $249.00.
Offers Macintosh Users Access to Data & Applications on Digital VAX or UNIX-Based Host Computers. Accurately Emulates VT320, VT220, VT102, or VT52 Terminals from Your Macintosh. Supports 132-Column Mode, Inversed Video, Underlining, Half Bright, & Security Options. Includes Apple's Communications Toolbox & Is System 7 Compatible. The Plus Feature Offers the Ability to Back up Your Macintosh Files to the Host.
Walker, Richer & Quinn, Inc.

Reflection 3 PLUS for the Macintosh. Version: 3.61. Compatible Hardware: Apple Macintosh. Memory Required: 420k. Customer Support: 90-day warranty & free tech support.
3.5" disk $399.99.
Offers Accurate HP 2392A & 2393A Terminal Emulation to Access Host Based HP 1000/3000/9000 Data, Graphics & Applications from the Macintosh. Is Block- & Character-Mode Compatible, Supporting 132-Column Mode Inverse Video, Underlining Half Bright & Security Options. Includes Apple's Communications Toolbox & Is System 7 Compatible. The Plus Feature Offers the Ability to Back up Important Macintosh Files to One File on the Host.
Walker, Richer & Quinn, Inc.

Reflection 4 (& Plus Version). Version: 4.13. Apr. 1992. Items Included: Full set of user manuals, including quick start guide. Customer Support: Registered Users of Walker Richer & Quinn products receive a 90-day material & workmanship warranty along with free technical support.
MS-DOS 204k in minimum configuration. IBM-PC, AT, XT, PS/2 & compatibles. $299.00-$369.00; quantity discounts available.
Emulates Digital VT320, VT220, VT102, VT330, VT340 & Tektronix 4014 Terminals with Full 16-Color ReGIS Graphics. The Plus Version Allows PC Files to Be Backed up to the Host, & Provides Support for Network Connections As Well As Support for Direct & Dial-Up Connections. All Reflection Products Provide Error-Free File Transfer, Background Processing, Powerful Command Language, & Keyboard Remapping.
Walker, Richer & Quinn, Inc.

Reflection 7 (& Plus Version). Version: 4.13. Apr. 1992. Items Included: Full set of user manuals, including quick start guide. Customer Support: Registered users of Walker Richer & Quinn products receive a 90-day material & workmanship warranty along with free technical support.
MS-DOS 225k mimium configuration. IBM PC & compatibles. $399.00-$469.00; quantity discounts available.
Provides the Graphics Capabilities of HP 2627A/2623A or Tektronics 4010/4014 As Well As Accurate HP 2392A Terminal Emulation from a PC. The Plus Version Allows PC Files to Be Backed up to the Host, & Provides Support for Network Connections As Well As Support for Direct & Dial-up Connections. All Reflection Products Provide Error-Free File Transfer, Keyboard Remapping, Background Processing, & a Powerful Command Language.
Walker, Richer & Quinn, Inc.

Reflection 3270. Version: 4.1. Oct. 1994. Items Included: User guide, reference manual, technical reference (server versions only), online reference material, WRQ newsletter, Reflection mousepad. Customer Support: Free technical support & 90-day materials & workmanship warranty.
Windows. 386 or 486 PC (4Mb). disk $299.00. Addl. software required: Windows 3.1 or higher. Optimal configuration: 386 or 486 PC, color VGA, 4Mb memory or more. Networks supported: TCP/IP networks, & support for Apertus, Fibronics, Interlink, McData 6100e, IBM 3172, IBM 8232, BusTech, NetLink, & Harris Adacom gateways.
Provides 3270 Terminal Emulation for TCP/IP Networks. Offers Support for Display & Field Attributes of 3270 Display Stations, Hotspots, Its Own Integrated Programming Language, & Support for HLLAPI, Visual Basic, & C/C Plus Plus.
Walker, Richer & Quinn, Inc.

Reflector & Lens Antennas: Analysis & Design. Version: 2.0. Jun. 1991. Items Included: 209 page user's manual.
IBM PC & compatibles. disk $200.00 (ISBN 0-89006-557-8).
Includes Descriptive Text & a Comprehensive Series of Programs for the Design of Metal-Plate Lens Antennas.
Artech Hse., Inc.

Reflex Plus: The Database Manager. Analytica, Inc. Compatible Hardware: Apple Macintosh. Memory Required: 512k.
3.5" disk $279.00.
Database Manager Which Combines Features of Flat-File & Relational Database Management Programs. Features Provided Include the Following: Accepts Any Number of Entry Forms for the Same Database; Permits Entry for More Than One Database in a Single Entry Form; Entry Form Can Display One Record at a Time or All Records at Once in a Table-Style View; Calculated Fields in Entry Forms; Display-Only Fields; Editable Default Fields; New Functions, Such As GROUPBY, Which Displays Records by Values in Common; Unlimited Font Selection; Selection of Templates, Including One to Generate Mailing Labels on ImageWriter or LaserWriter Printers; Choice of Record Sizes (1000, 2000, or 4000 Characters); WYSIWYG Design for Entry Forms & Reports; Text, Floating-Point, Number, Integer, Sequence Number, Date, Time, & Logical Data Types; Automatic Sorting by Key Fields; Sorting on As Many Fields As & in Any Way Desired; Size of Database Limited Only by Disk Capacity.
Borland International, Inc.

Reflex: The Analyst. Analytica Corp. Sep. 1985. Compatible Hardware: Apple Macintosh; IBM PC & compatibles, PC XT, PC AT. Operating System(s) Required: PC-DOS/MS-DOS 2.0, 2.1. Memory Required: 384k. General Requirements: CGA card, Hercules Monochrome Graphics Adapter, or equivalent with graphics display. Hard disk optional; mouse optional.
Contact publisher for price (ISBN 0-87524-145-X).
Data Base Management System Featuring Pop-Down Menus in a Macintosh-Like Format. The User Can: Choose Menu Commands with Cursor Keys, First Letter Keystroke, or Optional Mouse; Open up to Three Windows On-Screen at a Time; Expand a Window to Full-Screen View with One Keystroke. Data Can Be Entered & Changed in FORM or LIST Views. All Views Instantly Reflect Any Changes Made to the Database. Over 6000 Records Can Be Kept in the Working Database, with up to 65,000 Records on Disk, 128 Fields per Record, 254 Characters per Field. The Five Field Types Are Automatically Defined by Data. Query & Calculation Features Are Available.
Borland International, Inc.

Reflex: The Database Manager. Compatible Hardware: Apple Macintosh. General Requirements: External disk drive recommended.
3.5" disk $99.95.
Relational Database Manager. Incorporates a Spreadsheet Approach to Simplify Calculations. Allows Users to Draw Database Designs on Screen. Can Be Used in Managing Mailing Lists, Customer Files, Budgets, & Most Other Sets of Business Numbers Needs.
Borland International, Inc.

Reflex Workshop. Jun. 1986. Compatible Hardware: IBM PC & true compatibles, PC XT, PC AT, Portable PC, 3270 PC. Operating System(s) Required: PC-DOS/MS-DOS 2.0 or higher. Memory Required: 384k. General Requirements: CGA card, Hercules mono, or equivalent; 2 disk drives; Reflex 1.0 or higher. disk $69.95 (ISBN 0-87524-177-8).
Includes 22 On-Disk Models for a Broad Range of Business Applications Including Accounting, Financial Planning, Administration, Sales & Marketing, & Production & Operations. Each Chapter Supplies Step-by-Step Instructions for Customizing Databases, Graphs, Crosstabs, & Reports. Sample Analysis Problems Are Also Included.
Borland International, Inc.

Reformatter. Microtech Export. 1986. Compatible Hardware: TRS-80. Operating System(s) Required: TRSDOS. Memory Required: 32k. General Requirements: 2 disk drives.
disk $10.00.
Utility Which Gives the TRSDOS User Complete

Access to CP/M Formatted 8" Diskettes. Users Have the Ability to Copy Files Between TRSDOS Diskettes & Industry Standard CP/M 8" Diskettes.
TriSoft.

Reformatter Conversion Software: DEC R13 PCDOS2DEC-RT-11. *Version:* 2.12. Apr. 1981. *Operating System(s) Required:* MS-DOS. *Language(s):* Assembly.
8" disk $595.00.
Reads & Writes DEC RT-11 Single-Density Diskettes & Allows CP/M Users to Exchange Files on Floppy Diskette with DEC Equipment. Displays & Alters DEC RT-11 Directory; Exchanges Files to DEC Equipment Running RSTS/E, RSX-11M, & VAX/VMS Operating Systems As Internal Utilities on Those Systems Which Read & Write the RT-11 Format; Displays Records & Logical Blocks; Consolidates Fragmented DEC Diskettes.
MicroTech Conversion Systems.

Reformatter Conversion Software: R09 DOS2IBM. *Version:* 4.15. Jun. 1979. *Operating System(s) Required:* MS-DOS. *Language(s):* Assembly. *Memory Required:* 32k.
8" disk $695.00.
manual $25.00.
Reads & Writes IBM 3740 Formatted Diskettes (IBM Diskette 1, Basic Data Exchange Format) & Allows CP/M Users to Exchange Data on Floppy Diskette with IBM Mainframes & Any Equipment Accepting the IBM 3740 Diskette. All Conversion Functions Such As File Reorganization & ASCII to EBCDIC Character Translation, Are Automatically Handled. Gives CP/M Users Access to All IBM Diskette File Attributes & Provides Facilities for Examining & Altering All Data Areas, All Directory Entries, & All Fields Within Each IBM Data Set Table.
MicroTech Conversion Systems.

Reformatter Conversion Software: IBM PC/ IBM 3740. *Version:* 4.15. Apr. 1984. *Compatible Hardware:* IBM PC with 8" add-on soft-sectored disk drive. *Operating System(s) Required:* PC-DOS. *Language(s):* C, 8086 Assembly. *Memory Required:* 96k.
8" disk $695.00.
Allows IBM PC Users to Read & Write IBM 3740 Formatted Diskettes (IBM Diskette 1, Basic Data Exchange Format). Also Supports Five IBM Diskette 2 (Double-Sided), Diskette 2D (Double-Sided, Double Density) Format if the 8" Add-on Drive Has This Capacity. Blocked &/or Spanned Records on the IBM Diskette Can Be Read & Written. Users Can Exchange 8" Floppy Diskettes Containing Data Files & Source Code with IBM Mainframes or Other Mainframes Capable of Reading or Writing an IBM Formatted Diskette.
MicroTech Conversion Systems.

Reformatter Conversion Software: MS-DOS/ IBM 3740. *Version:* 3.04A. Jan. 1984. *Operating System(s) Required:* MS-DOS. *Language(s):* C, 8086 Assembly. *Memory Required:* 96k.
8" disk $350.00.
Enables Users of Microcomputers Running under the MS-DOS Operating System with at Least One 8" Floppy Drive, to Read & Write IBM 3740 Formatted Diskettes (IBM Diskette 1, Basic Data Exchange Format). Blocked &/or Spanned Records on the IBM Diskette Can Be Read & Written. Users May Exchange 8" Diskettes Containing Data Files &/or Source Code with IBM Mainframes or Any Other Mainframe Capable of Reading & Writing an IBM Formatted Diskette. User Interface Provides Control over IBM File Parameters.
MicroTech Conversion Systems.

Reformatter 9-Track Tape Software. *Version:* 4.20. *Items Included:* Pertec Tape controller. *Customer Support:* Yes.
MS-DOS, Unix, Xenix (512k). IBM PC XT, PC AT. 3.5" or 5.25" disk $1195.00 (Order no.: TAPE-PC). *Nonstandard peripherals required:* 9-track tape drive with Cipher/Pertec interface.
Nine-Track Tape Software & Controller Card to Read/Write ANSI & IBM-Labeled & Unlabeled Tapes.
MicroTech Conversion Systems.

REFRIG- Refrigeraton Box Loads. Jun. 1989. *Items Included:* Bound user manual. *Customer Support:* Unlimited telephone support.
MS-DOS (256k). IBM PC, PC XT, PC AT, AT 286, 386. disk $295.00 (Order no.: 800-648-9523). *Optimal configuration:* Hard disk (20Mb); color monitor; floppy drive.
Quickly Calculates Maximum Refrigeration Loads in BTU's per 24-Hour Period for All Types of Loads Including Roofs, Walls, Partitions, Floors, Products, Containers, Lights & More. Has Provision for Safety Factor Load. Designer Can Enter Product Name & Quantity to Get Automatic Product Cooling, Freezing, Sub-Cooling & Respiration Loads. Designer Can Also Specify Refrigerant & TD Desired So That Evaporator Coil & Compressor Can Be Quickly Selected from Built-In Library of Coils & Compressors.
Elite Software Development, Inc.

REFRIG: Refrigeration Box Loads Calculation. *Items Included:* Manual. *Customer Support:* Free toll free telephone support.
IBM PC & compatibles (256k). disk $395.00.
Calculates Maximum Refridgeration Loads in BTU's per 24 Hour Period for Any Size Walk-in Cooler, Freezer, Retail Display Case, Refrigerated Warehouse, etc. First Commercially Available Box Loads Program Ever Offered.
Elite Software Development, Inc.

Regard for the Planet LaserStack. *Items Included:* 1 floppy disk, instruction booklet. *Customer Support:* M-F 9 AM-5 PM Pacific Time (213) 451-1383.
Macintosh Plus, SE, II or Portable (1 Mb). 3.5" disk $59.95. *Nonstandard peripherals required:* Videodisc player, monitor & cables. *Addl. software required:* HyperCard 1.2.2 or higher.
Travel Through the 50,000 Images Contained on the Regard for the Planet Videodisc Using the Comprehensive Index That Lets User Search & Instantaneously Display Images from Any Geographical Area, or by Diverse Subjects Ranging from Transportation to Architecture to Ecology. An Interactive Game Tests User's Knowledge of Cultures & Locales, & a Slide-Show Feature Lets you Easily Select Specific Images for Illustrating Lectures or Making Presentations.
The Voyager Co.

Regions of the United States. 1984. *Customer Support:* Toll free customary service Hot Line 1-800-645-3739 (9a.m. - 5p.m. Eastern Time).
Apple II; IBM; Tandy (MS-DOS). $39.95, incl. 1 disk & documentaiton (Order no.: DB5000).
Geography Builds a Sense of Citizenship & Belonging. Part One Reviews All 50 States, Region by Region, by Means of a Beginner's or Super Quiz. Part Two Provides a More Complex Geography Game with the Computer Selecting a Region & Giving Clues about It. One or More Players.
Educational Activities Inc.

Register. Nov. 1989. *Items Included:* Instruction included on disk. *Customer Support:* 90 days unlimited warranty.
MS-DOS, Windows 3.1. IBM XT, AT or compatibles (512k). disk $24.95 plus $3.50 S&H (Order no.: 1075). *Addl. software required:* Lotus 1-2-3, Release 4.0 or higher. *Optimal configuration:* IBM AT, 640k RAM.
Check Register Which Allocates Expenditures to Proper Expense Categories & Produces an Analysis of Income & Expense for the Period.
Compiled Systems.

Register Sales. *Version:* 4.1. *Customer Support:* On site training unlimited support services for first 90 days & through subscription thereafter. Contact publisher for price.
Provides for Quick Check Out of Customer Through a Register. Prints a 40 Character Receipt with User-Defined Headings & Footings. Interfaces with a Cash Drawer If Desired. Support Cash, Credit Cards, Check & Charge Sale. Support a Bar Codes Reader with or Without Keyboard Entry.
Argos Software.

Registered Beef Herd & Herd Health Management System. *Compatible Hardware:* IBM PC, PC XT & compatibles.
$500.00.
Farm Management Systems of Mississippi, Inc.

Registered Dairy Herd & Herd Health Management Systems. *Compatible Hardware:* IBM PC, PC XT & compatibles.
$500.00.
Farm Management Systems of Mississippi, Inc.

Regress 2. *Items Included:* Bound manual. *Customer Support:* Free hotline - no time limit; 30 day limited warranty; updates are $5/disk plus S&H.
MS-DOS. IBM & compatibles (256k). disk $139.95.
Performs Regression Analysis. The Five Regression Solutions All Give User a Complete Anova Table Output, along with Regression Weights, T-Tests, & P-Values. The Stepwise Solution Gives a Summary of Steps Taken. All Solutions Produce Predicted & Residual Scores. Performs Correlation Analysis. User Can Easily Obtain Correlation & Covariance Matrices along with Descriptive Statistics, Multiple & Partial Correlations, & Serial Correlation of Residuals. Calculates Sum of Squares (SS), Mean Square (MS) Table, Multiple Correlation Coefficient, R2 with Error Estimate, Standard Error, Coefficients with Standard Error, Actual/Predicted/Residual Table, Serial Correlation & Serial Residuals, & Durbin-Watson Statistic. Produces Printer Reports of Results, Printer Copies of Data, & Plots & Bar Graphs on CRT or Disk.
Dynacomp, Inc.

Regression Analysis. *Compatible Hardware:* Commodore 64, IBM PC. *Memory Required:* Commodore 64k, IBM 128k.
disk $69.95, incl. manual.
Multilinear Regression Package.
Dynacomp, Inc.

Regression Analysis. *Compatible Hardware:* HP 85, 86/87 with Basic Statistics & Data Manipulation Software (HP 82805A for HP 85 & 82305A for HP 86/87).
HP 85. data cartridge, 3-1/2" or 5-1/4" disk $95.00 ea. (Order no.: 82806A).
HP 86/87. 3-1/2" or 5-1/4" disk $95.00 ea. (Order no.: 82836A).
Finds the Relationship Between a Dependent Variable & One or More Independent Variables. Polynomial & Multiple Linear Regression Routines (Including Four Variable-Selection Procedures) Are Provided. A Table of Residuals Is Printed.
Hewlett-Packard Co.

Regression Analysis 2. *Items Included:* Bound manual. *Customer Support:* Free hotline - no time limit; 30 day limited warranty; updates are $5/disk plus S&H.
MS-DOS. IBM & compatibles (256k). disk $39.95. *Nonstandard peripherals required:* Color graphics card; printer supported. *Addl. software required:* BASICA.
Commodore 64. disk $39.95.
Performs Bivariate or Multivariate, Linear or Nonlinear Regression Analysis. It Fits a User-Chosen Curve Type to a Given Set of Data Points Using the Least-Squares Method, Determines the Regression Coefficients, As Well As the Generalized Correlation Coefficient & the Standard Error of Estimate. User May Select the Names of the Variables to Be Used & Predefine Any Recurrent Constants, As Well As Review & Edit the Constants, Functionals, & Data.
Dynacomp, Inc.

Regression: Linear & non-linear. *Version:* 10.0. *Compatible Hardware:* Apple Macintosh, IBM PC & compatibles. *Items Included:* Disks, book, program instructions. *Customer Support:* Telephone.
disk $145.00 (ISBN 0-920387-90-X).
Include Simple Linear Regression, Four Multilinear Regression Programs, Ridge Regression, & Regression Using Orthogonal Polynomials. The Simple Linear Regression Program Provides the Analysis of Variance, Confidence Intervals on Regression Estimates & on Data Points, & So Forth. Multilinear Regression Programs Include a Fast & Accurate Algorithm (Max. 8 Independent Variables) Which Does Not Use Matrix Inversion Routine, Multilinear Regression for Weighted Data Points, a General Multilinear Regression Program Which Provides the Correlation Matrix, Beta Weights, T-Values, & So Forth, & a Multilinear Program which Uses the Cholesky Decomposition Techniques & Which Is Capable of Handling Interrelationships Between Independent Variables, etc.
Lionheart Pr., Inc.

Regression I. *Compatible Hardware:* Apple II with Applesoft; Macintosh; IBM PC. *Memory Required:* 48k, IBM 128k, Macintosh 512k. disk $19.95.
Complete & Coordinated Regression Curve-Fitting Package for the Analysis of Linear & Non-Linear, One-Dimensional Data. Analysis Is Interactive, Thereby Permitting the User Freedom in Experimenting with Fitting Functions & Orders of Approximation.
Dynacomp, Inc.

Regression 1: Polynomial Regression with Transformations. *Items Included:* Bound manual. *Customer Support:* Free hotline - no time limit; 30 day limited warranty; updates are $5/disk plus S&H.
MS-DOS Release 2.0; Others Release 1.0. Available for all computers (256k). $19.95-$29.95. *Nonstandard peripherals required:* For high resolution graphics, CGA (or equivalent) graphics capability is required.
Complete & Coordinated Polynomial Curve-Fitting Package for the Analysis of Linear & Nonlinear xy Data. Features: Easy Data Entry, Editing, Storage, & Retrieval; Automatic Data Sorting & Plotting (of Both the Data & Fitted Curve); Very Fast & Accurate Regression; A Choice of Many Data Transformations, Including Forms Supplied by the User; Standard Error of the Derived Coefficients & the Correlation Coefficient; Clear & Concise Manual with Step-by-Step Examples.
Dynacomp, Inc.

Regression 2 (Parafit). *Items Included:* Bound manual. *Customer Support:* Free hotline - no time limit; 30 day limited warranty; updates are $5/disk plus S&H.
Available for all computers. disk $29.95.
Parametric Least Squares Regression Program Designed Specifically for the Determination of the Nonlinear Coefficients in Complicated Mathematical Expressions. Features Included Are Automatic Plotting of the Data Fitted Function & Residuals; Cassette (or Diskette) Data Saving & Loading; & Data File Building/Editing.
Dynacomp, Inc.

Regression 3 (The Calibrator). *Items Included:* Bound manual. *Customer Support:* Free hotline - no time limit; 30 day limited warranty; updates are $5/disk plus S&H.
MS-DOS. IBM & compatibles (256k). disk $49.95.
Applications-Oriented Curve-Fitting Package Designed to Be Used for Generating Calibration Curves or Other Fits Based on the Mini-Max Principle. Features: Easy Data Entry & Editing; Full Data File Compatibility with REGRESSION I & REGRESSION II; A Choice of Many Data Transformations - the User May Even Program in His Own; Data Storage & Retrieval. The Outputs from REGRESSION III Are the Polynomial Co-Efficients & the Minimized Maximum Error. May Also Be Used to Generate Mini-Max Polynomial Approximations to Functions for Use in Applications Such As Replacing Tables or Providing Higher Speed Calculations.
Dynacomp, Inc.

Regular RV Park & Camp Reservation. Jul. 1992. *Items Included:* RunTime Cobol System; user manuals; tutorial manual. *Customer Support:* 90 day unlimited warranty; 90 days free telephone support. After 90 days training at $60.00 a hour.
MS-DOS. IBM PC or compatible (at least 386). disk $1995.00, multi-user version, ,595.00 single user version. *Nonstandard peripherals required:* 3.5" or 5.25" disk drive, printer, 90Mb hard disk. *Addl. software required:* WordPerfect. *Networks supported:* Novell.
Camp Ground Reservations, Collection of Monies, Check in/out Reporting, Mailing List, Confirmation Letters, Deposit Accounting, Trailer Supply Check List for Rent al Trailer/Cabins.
The James Gang.

Rehab. *Compatible Hardware:* Commodore 64, 128.
$199.95 (Order no.: REHC64-03-001).
Designed for Patients with Neuromotor Disorders. Displays Myoelectric Signals & Processes These Signals to Produce Audio & Visual Outputs Reflecting the Degree of Muscle Contraction & the Rate at Which It Changes.
Bodylog.

The Reincarnation of James: The Submarine Man. Rick Brown. Edited by Arlene Simmons. Mar. 1994. *Items Included:* Includes 212 page paperback book.
disk $11.95 (ISBN 1-57100-145-X).
Sublime Software.

Reinforced Concrete Beam Column Analysis. 1995. *Items Included:* Full manual. *Customer Support:* Free telephone support - 90 days, 30-day warranty.
MS-DOS 3.2 or higher. 286 (584k). disk $99.95. *Nonstandard peripherals required:* CGA/EGA/VGA.
RCB Provides a Unified Solution to Beam-Column Problems. It Is an All-Purpose Package Which Analyzes & Designs Rectangular Sections under Combined Axial Compressions & Any Axial or Biaxial Bending. It Accommodates Mixed Bar Sizes & Unsymmetrical Reinforcement Patterns. RCB Features a User Interface Equipped with a Full Screen Editor & Flexible Two-Way Screen Display Techniques.
Dynacomp, Inc.

Reinforced Concrete Beam Design. 1995. *Items Included:* Full manual. *Customer Support:* Free telephone support - 90 days, 30-day warranty.
MS-DOS 3.2 or higher. 286 (584k). disk $99.95. *Nonstandard peripherals required:* CGA/EGA/VGA.
RCBEAM Is a Comprehensive System Which Analyzes a Single or Doubly Reinforced Rectangular or T-Beam. Inputs Include Beam Dimensions, Reinforcements, & Loading. Outputs Include the Minimum/Maximum Reinforcement, Moments (Nominal, Cracked, & Ultimate Capacity), Curvature Gradient, & Modulus of Rupture.
Dynacomp, Inc.

Reinforced Concrete Laterally Loaded Piles. 1995. *Items Included:* Full manual. *Customer Support:* Free telephone support - 90 days, 30-day warranty.
MS-DOS 3.2 or higher. 286 (584k). disk $99.95. *Nonstandard peripherals required:* CGA/EGA/VGA.
LATPILE Will Analyze a Single Reinforced Concrete Pile for Lateral Loads. Inputs Include Pile Dimensions, Applied Lateral Load & Moment, & Lateral Resistance of Soil. Outputs at Various Locations along the Pile Include Horizontal Shear, Bending Moment, Actual Soil Pressure, & Allowable Soil Resistance.
Dynacomp, Inc.

Reinforced Concrete Pile Design. 1995. *Items Included:* Full manual. *Customer Support:* Free telephone support - 90 days, 30-day warranty.
MS-DOS 3.2 or higher. 286 (584k). disk $99.95. *Nonstandard peripherals required:* CGA/EGA/VGA.
Calculates the Penetration Depth Using STP (Standard Penetration Test) Readings, As Well As the Reinforcement of Reinforced Concrete Piles. Inputs Include Bore Log Data, Pile Shape (Circular, Rectangular, or Square), & Embedment Depth. Note That PILE Uses Metric Units.
Dynacomp, Inc.

Reinforced Concrete Two-Way Flat Plate Design. 1995. *Items Included:* Full manual. *Customer Support:* Free telephone support - 90 days, 30-day warranty.
MS-DOS 3.2 or higher. 286 (584k). disk $99.95. *Nonstandard peripherals required:* CGA/EGA/VGA.
FLATPL Designs Two-Way Flat Plates Using the Direct Design Method of Section 13.6 from ACI 318. Inputs Include Material Strengths, Column Size, Loading (Dead & Live), Number of Spans & Span Lengths. Outputs Include Slab Depth, Actual/Allowable Shear (Beam & Punching), & Required Reinforcement (Bar Size & Spacing, Column & Middle Strips, Positive & Negative).
Dynacomp, Inc.

Relate with Ease: Build & Keep Interpersonal Relationships. Feb. 1994. *Customer Support:* Toll-free telephone number for technical support. 90 days warranty for defects in materials & workmanship.
Macintosh System 7.0. Macintosh with 68040 processor (5Mb). CD-ROM disk $49.95 (ISBN 1-886806-06-3). *Nonstandard peripherals required:* Double speed CD-ROM drive. *Addl. software required:* QuickTime (included on CD-ROM disc).
Microsoft Windows 3.1. PC compatibles; 486/33 MHz (runs slow on 386/25MHz) (8Mb). CD-ROM disk $49.95. *Nonstandard peripherals*

required: 256 color display card (640x480); double speed CD-ROM drive. *Addl. software required:* QuickTime for Windows (included on CD-ROM disc).
Helps You Learn Key Interpersonal Skills You Can Use in Daily Interactions with Employees, Peers, Colleagues, & Family. You Will Learn How to Build Rapport, Listen Attentively, & Display Sensitivity to Others. This Highly Interactive CD-ROM Includes Full-Motion Video, Real-Life Simulations, a Self-Assessment, & Grand Mastery Simulation.
Wilson Learning Corp.

Relating Potential: M94. John Townley. 1984. *Compatible Hardware:* Apple II+; Commodore 64, PET; IBM PC. *General Requirements:* 2 disk drives, printer.
  disk $300.00 ea.
  Commodore 64. (ISBN 0-925182-23-0).
  IBM. (ISBN 0-925182-24-9).
  Apple. (ISBN 0-925182-25-7).
For the Professional Astrologer: Provides a Detailed Analysis of the Potential for Relationships of a Given Individual.
Matrix Software.

Relationship Report Writer. 1993. *Items Included:* 56 page manual. *Customer Support:* Full telephone support - free.
  PC-DOS/MS-DOS. IBM PC, XT, AT, PS/1, PS/2 & compatibles (320k). disk $295.00 (ISBN 0-933281-09-9). Optimal configuration: 2 disk drives or hard disk, printer.
Program Provides a Valuable Way to Explore Romantic Relationships Using the Science of Numerology. The Highly Insightful Reports Produced by This Program Are Full of Practical Suggestions That Can Help Couples to Have Stronger, More Meaningful Partnerships. The 14 to 18 Page Reports Include 11 Important Topics That Show the Dynamic Forces at Work in a Relationship.
Widening Horizons, Inc.

Relative Values for Dentists. *Version:* 92.0. Jan. 1992. *Items Included:* 3-ring print version of the data file.
  ASCII file. IBM compatible. disk $199.00. *Addl. software required:* Lotus 1-2-3, Excel, or other application.
  Macintosh. 3.5" disk $199.00.
Relative Values Are a Basis from Which to Derive Fair & Accurate Dental Fees, Perform Productivity Analysis, & Project Income/Cost Outlays. Data Was Developed by Survey of Practicing Dentists over 6 Year Period. Relative Value Studies, Inc. Also Produces Relative Values for Physicians Published by McGraw-Hill, Inc.
Relative Value Studies, Inc.

Relativistic Collision. 1995. *Items Included:* Full manual. *Customer Support:* Free telephone support - 90 days, 30-day warranty.
  MS-DOS 3.2 or higher. 286 (584k). disk $59.95. *Nonstandard peripherals required:* CGA/EGA/VGA.
Helps College Students Develop an Intuition for Relativistic Particle Interactions. It Allows Them to Analyze & Solve Exercises Regarding Such Phenomena As Particle Collisions, Pair Creation, Transformations, Decays, & Annihilations of Particles Moving in One or Two Spatial Dimensions.
Dynacomp, Inc.

Relax. *Compatible Hardware:* Apple II+, IIe, IIc; Atari 400, 800, XL series; Commodore 64; IBM PC, PC XT, PCjr. *Operating System(s) Required:* MS-DOS. *General Requirements:* IBM version requires graphics adapter & game control adapter.
  Apple. disk $139.95 (Order no.: UNI-6900).
  Atari/Commodore version on flip sides of same disk. $99.95 (Order no.: A/CDSK-6901).
  IBM. disk $139.95 (Order no.: UNI-6900).
  Body Sensors $39.95 (Order no.: SUP-6903).
Sensor Headband & Control Unit Graphically Monitors & Displays Changing Stress Levels, Which Can Be Charted with the Program Disk. Includes 200-Page Guide to Stress Reduction & a 30-Minute Audio Cassette. Optional Body Sensors Can Be Placed on Any Part of the Body to Measure Muscle Tension.
Broderbund Software, Inc.

Reliable Salon System. *Compatible Hardware:* Apple Macintosh Plus. *General Requirements:* Hard disk, printer.
  3.5" disk $1200.00.
Beauty Salon Management Program with Optional Cash Drawer.
Reliable Software & Consulting.

RELIEF. P. L. Mariam. Jun. 1985. *Compatible Hardware:* IBM PC & compatibles, PC XT, PC AT. *Operating System(s) Required:* PC-DOS/MS-DOS 2.X, 3.0. *Memory Required:* 256k. *General Requirements:* Printer.
  disk $149.95 (ISBN 0-935509-05-4, Order no.: 5375).
Computes the Required Size or Capacity of Relief Valves in Liquid, Gas, or Steam Service. Selects the Next Standard Size Orifice Automatically. If More Than One Valve Is Required, Program Will Automatically Determine the Number of Valves Required. Nozzle Coefficients May Be Changed for Most Manufacturers.
FlowSoft, Inc.

Religion Bookshelf. *Customer Support:* Free, unlimited.
  System 6 Mac. 030 Mac, 256 colors (4Mb). CD-ROM disk $24.95. *Nonstandard peripherals required:* Sound card, CD-ROM drive.
  Windows 3.1 PC. 486 PC (4Mb). *Nonstandard peripherals required:* Any Windows supported sound card, CD-ROM drive.
Contains the Complete English Language Versions of the King James Bible, the Book of Mormon, & the Koran. From Genesis to Revelation, Explore Christianity's Major Tenets Using the King James Version of the Bible. From Nephi to Moroni, Learn about the Book of Mormon, a Different Testament of Jesus Christ. From Al-Fatihah to Al-Nas, Explore the Islamic Holy Koran, the Most Important Text of the Muslims. Each of These Books Can Be Viewed Through an Easy-to-Use Browser Program Included on This Disc. You Can Even Search for Keywords & Phrases & the Browser Program Will Give You a List of All Matches As They Appear in Context. The Browser Program Also Allows You to Copy Text That You Select with Your Mouse & Copy It to the Clipboard So That You Can Later Paste It into Some Other Program.
BeachWare.

Religious Art Portfolio. *Version:* 2.0. Jun. 1986. *General Requirements:* External disk drive or hard disk drive. *Items Included:* Disk & manual. *Customer Support:* Complete telephone support; 90 days unlimited warranty; 1 year free maintenance.
  Macintosh (128K). 3.5" disk $24.95 (Order no.: 48842-590). *Addl. software required:* Macprint, Picturebase or Hypercard.
A Series of MacPAINT Documents & Hypercard Stacks Containing More Than 250 Images Including Handdrawn Symbols, Ornaments, Borders & Greeting Card Elements, As Well As Digitized Renditions of Religious Scenes, & Church Bulletin Symbols. Available in English or Spanish. Also Available in Picturebase Format.
Medina Software, Inc.

Relocatable Macro Cross Assembler: AA-555. 1989. *Operating System(s) Required:* PC-DOS, MS-DOS. *Memory Required:* 512k. *Items Included:* Reference manuals. *Customer Support:* Telephone support & customer/product service.
  disk $595.00.
American Automation.

Relocating Macro Assemblers: Assemblers & Virtual Assemblers. Stephen L. Russell. 1983-1985. *Operating System(s) Required:* CP/M. *Memory Required:* 40k.
  disk $49.95 ea.
  NSC800 Zilog Mnemonics. (Order no.: 101).
  NSC800 Intel Mnemonics. (Order no.: 102).
  HD64180 Zilog Mnemonics. (Order no.: 103).
  Intel Mnemonics 8085. (Order no.: 104).
  Virtual versions for each above system. disk $195.00 (Order no.: 151-154).
SLR Systems.

REMDISK-1. *Compatible Hardware:* TRS-80 Model I Level I. *Operating System(s) Required:* TRSDOS. *Language(s):* Assembly. *Memory Required:* 16k.
  disk $29.95.
Course in Inputting & Outputting with a Disk. Written in Assembly Language to Take Advantage of Its Diverse Applications. Includes 2 Lessons with Audio Cassettes & Voice-Keyed Images on the CRT, Turning the Screen into a Blackboard for the Lecturer. There Are 14 Examples on the Disk Which Can Be Integrated into the Programs.
REMsoft, Inc.

Remedy Practice Management System. 1980. *Language(s):* RM/COBOL 85/AccuCOBOL. *General Requirements:* 40Mb on hard disk. *Items Included:* User manual. *Customer Support:* 24 hrs/7 days a week.
  Texas Instruments Series 1000; IBM RS 6000 IBM PS/2 models 60, 80; Xenix/Unix (1Mb). contact publisher for price.
Comprehensive Medical Practice Management System Offering Patient Registration, Both Open-Item & Balance-Forward Accounting Methods, Accounts Receivable & Billing, Appointment Scheduling & Recalls, Medical Records, Both Electronic & Paper Insurance Claim Processing & Complete Practice Analysis Reporting.
LDS, Inc.

Remodeler's Dream. *Version:* 2.11r. Dan Heilman & Joe Applegate. *Items Included:* Quick reference card, educational manual. *Customer Support:* Unlimited, toll free number, 30 day unlimited warrantee.
  IBM PC & compatibles. 3.5" or 5.25" disk $99.00.
Estimating & Cutting List Software for Carpenter's, Homeowners, & Small Contractors. Estimates Materials & Generates Material Cutting Specifications for All Phases of Residential Construction & Remodelling.
Workhorses, Inc.

REMOTE. Jun. 1983. *Compatible Hardware:* IBM PC, PC AT, PC XT & compatibles. *Operating System(s) Required:* PC-DOS, MS-DOS. *Language(s):* BASIC. *Memory Required:* 512k.
  disk $100.00 (Order no.: REMOTE).
Gives Control of a Microcomputer to a Remote Terminal. The Target Computer Runs Remote. Password Protection Is Standard to Prevent Unauthorized Entry While the Program Is Running. Useful for Both Transmitting Data & Completing Computations from Afar.
Geostat Systems International, Inc. (GSII).

Remote 3270 AutoSync. 1988. *Compatible Hardware:* IBM PC, PS/2. *Operating System(s) Required:* PC-DOS/MS-DOS. *Memory Required:*

TITLE INDEX

256k. *General Requirements:* The host modem must have the same modem protocol but does not need AutoSync. At 1200 baud, any 212A modem that operates synchronously will work. At 2400 baud, any V.22 or V.22 bis modem that can connect to a Hayes will work. At 4800 & 9600 baud, a Hayes V9600 modem that uses V.32 half duplex must be used. *Items Included:* Software, manual. *Customer Support:* Free, 800-642-5888.
3.5" or 5.25" disk $595.00.
Supports the Hayes AutoSync Feature of High Speed Hayes Modems. Hayes AutoSync Support Allows the Use of a Standard Asynchronous Port on PC or PS/2 to Run Remote IBM 3270 Applications. This Support Is Available on All 3270 Remote Products. The Hayes AutoSync Feature Allows Mainframe Communications Without Communcations Hardware Adapters.
Micro-Integration Corporation.

Remote Bisync 3270. *Version:* 6.00. *Compatible Hardware:* IBM PC, PC XT. *Operating System(s) Required:* CP/M, CP/M-86, MS-DOS. *Language(s):* Assembler. *Memory Required:* 64k. *Customer Support:* Free, 800-642-5888.
disk $895.00.
Emulates a Bisync IBM 3270 Terminal for Screen Based Transaction Processing. Supported Devices Include 3271/3277, 3274/3278, & 3276. Features Full Screen & Keyboard Emulation of the 3270 Terminal & Includes Local Print Key Support, Logical 3284 or 3286 Printer Support. Supports Separately Addressable Printer & a Send File Capability Allows Off-Line Data Entry of 3270 Records & Subsequent Transmission on an Automatic or Semi-Automatic Basis. Standard Features Include a User-Initialization Module, Hardware Diagnostics, Line Trace, Error Checking, & EBCDIC/ASCII Translation.
Micro-Integration Corp.

Remote Draft-Wire Issuance System. 1989. MS-DOS 3.0 & higher, Windows. IBM PC, XT, PS/2, 386, 486 & compatibles. Contact vendor for price. *Networks supported:* Novell, Token Ring.
Enables a Bank's Customers (Corporates or Correspondents) to Issue Drafts or Originate Wires on the Bank's Accounts, Using Their Own Personal Computers. The System Operates in Conjunction with the Spot Systems' International Teller System, Acting As a Host Processor in the Bank's Offices.
Spot Systems, Inc.

Remote Entry/More Reports. *Version:* 3.6. *Compatible Hardware:* IBM PC, PC XT, PC AT & compatibles, PS/2. *Operating System(s) Required:* PC-DOS 2.1 or higher. *Language(s):* Pascal. *Memory Required:* PC-DOS 2.1 256k, PC-DOS 3.0 or higher 320k. *General Requirements:* Hard disk; Client Management System program. *Customer Support:* 60 days toll-free.
disk $495.00.
Includes & Performs the Following: Batch Style Billing Data Input (up to 250 Entries in 5 Batches at a Time); Data Input from Remote Computers; Transfer Function to Copy Billing Data from Remote Diskette to CMS Ledger Cards; Inserts Virtually Unlimited Memo into Billing Entries; Posted & Unposted Entry Reports & Audit Trails. Offers Ten New Management Reports Including: Attorney Time & Fees Analysis, Attorney Time per Case by Attorney, Income Distribution, Attorney Time per Service by Attorney, Missing Time, & Aged Costs Due.
CompuLaw, Ltd.

Remote 3270 Gateway. 1988. *Compatible Hardware:* IBM PC, PC XT, PC AT & compatibles, PS/2 Model 25, PS/2 Model 30, PS/2 Model 50, PS/2 Model 60, PS/2 Model 80. *Operating System(s) Required:* PC-DOS/MS-DOS 3.0 or higher. *Memory Required:* Gateway 200k, PC Node 175k. *General Requirements:* Synchronous I/O card or adapter. *Items Included:* Hardware, software, manual. *Customer Support:* Free, 800-642-5888.
3.5" or 5.25" disk $1995.00.
Allows PC to Function As a Remote Gateway into a NETBIOS Compatible Local Area Network (LAN). Eight Host Sessions Are Available Through One Gateway Server and up to Four Servers Can Operate on One Network. Can Connect PCs & PS/2s to One Host or up to Four Different Hosts at the Same Time.
Micro-Integration Corporation.

Remote 5250 Gateway. 1987. *Compatible Hardware:* IBM PC, PC XT, PC AT & compatibles, PS/2 Model 25, PS/2 Model 30, PS/2 Model 50, PS/2 Model 60, PS/2 Model 70, PS/2 Model 80. *Operating System(s) Required:* PC-DOS/MS-DOS 3.0 or higher. *Memory Required:* Gateway 70k, each PC Node 70k. *General Requirements:* SDLC communications card. *Items Included:* Software, hardware, manual. *Customer Support:* Free, 800-642-5888.
3.5" or 5.25" disk $1995.00 or $2995.00, depending on model (16-session or 64-session).
Allows PC to Function As a Remote Gateway into a NETBIOS Compatible Local Area Network. Handles All SNA/SDLC Layers & the NETBIOS Interface Between the Gateway & Workstation Nodes. LAN Workstations, As Gateway Nodes, Can Then Process the Same Information & Produce the Same Results As If they Were Real IBM 5250 Display or Printer Devices. IBM PC AT or PS/2 Recommended for Maximum Performance.
Micro-Integration Corporation.

Remote 3780 RJE. *Version:* 6.01. 1979. *Compatible Hardware:* IBM PC & compatibles with asynchronous serial port. *Operating System(s) Required:* CP/M, CP/M-86, MS-DOS. *Language(s):* Assembler. *Memory Required:* 64k. *Items Included:* Software, hardware, manual. *Customer Support:* Free, 800-642-5888.
$895.00, incl. hardware.
Full-Functioned IBM Bisync 2770/2780/3741/3780 Emulator Package Suitedfor RJE Applications.
Micro-Integration Corp.

Remote 3780 RJE: For Binary Synchronous Batch Communications. 1978. *Compatible Hardware:* IBM PC. *Operating System(s) Required:* PC-DOS/MS-DOS. *Memory Required:* 128k. *General Requirements:* Partial list of compatible remote systems: IBM S/370, 43 & 30 series computers; IBM Series 1, System/34, System/36 & System/38; DEC PDP-11 & VAX computers; Remote PCs equipped for bisync communications; cash registers & point of sale equipment. *Items Included:* Software, hardware, manual. *Customer Support:* Free, 800-642-5888.
disk $895.00.
Emulates IBM 3780, 3741, 2780 & 2770. Gives PC Full Remote Job Entry & Data Transfer Capability. Transmits & Receives Large Volumes of Batched Data. Easy Menu Configuration, Console Command Support, Printer Forms Control, & Unattended Operation Mode. Full Data Error Detection/Correction. National Language Support.
Micro-Integration Corporation.

Remote Squared. *Version:* 3.0. 1988. *Compatible Hardware:* AT&T 6300; Compaq; IBM PC, PC XT, PC AT; NEC; TeleVideo 1605. *Language(s):* Assembly. *Memory Required:* Caller 128k, Host 60k. *General Requirements:* Host software: 256k RAM, modem, DOS 2.1 or higher. Caller software: 128k RAM, modem, DOS 2.1 or higher. *Items Included:* Manual.
$195.00.
host $129.95.
caller $89.00.
Remote Console Communications Program That Allows Users to Make Calls to Their Microcomputer & Run Programs on It, from Any Location Where Terminal & Modem Are Available. Features Built-In Electronic Mail System & Secure Log-In Procedures; up to 50 Users Can Have Individual Passwords; Each User Can Send Private Mail to Other Users As Well As Public Messages; All Operations Are Automatic. Supports CROSSTALK & XMODEM File Transfer Protocols. Also Features an Activity Log, Support for CGA, EGA, & VGA & Hercules Monochrome Graphics, & Continuous Error Checking. Not Copy Protected.
Crosstalk Communications.

Remote Teller System. 1989.
MS-DOS 3.0 & higher, Windows. IBM PC, XT, PS/2, 386, 486 & compatibles. Contact vendor for price. *Networks supported:* Novell, Token Ring.
Allows Branches of International Banks to Buy & Sell Currency, Drafts, Checks, Wires, & Travelers' Checks. The System Operates in Conjunction with the Spot Systems' International Teller System, Acting As a Host Processor in the Bank's Offices.
Spot Systems, Inc.

Remote 3270. 1982. *Compatible Hardware:* IBM PC & compatibles. *Operating System(s) Required:* CP/M, CP/M-86, MS-DOS, PC-DOS. *Memory Required:* 128k. *General Requirements:* Modem, synchronous communications port. *Items Included:* Software, hardware, manual. *Customer Support:* Free, 800-642-5888.
disk $895.00 ea.
MS-DOS. (ISBN 0-924465-00-X).
PC-DOS. (ISBN 0-924465-01-8).
CP/M-86. (ISBN 0-924465-02-6).
CP/M. (ISBN 0-924465-03-4).
Full-Function IBM SNA/SDLC 3270 Terminal Emulator. Supports SNA/SDLC Communications of Batch Files Between Micros & an IBM or IBM Plug Compatible Host. Standard Features Include User-Friendly Configuration, Hardware Diagnostics, Line Trace, Error Checking & Correcting, Carriage Control Decoding, & Flexible EBCIC/ASCII Translation. Micro May Communicate over Point-to-Point or Multi-Point Telephone Communication Lines with a Mainframe. Includes Send File Capability.
Micro-Integration, Corp.

Remote 3270. 1984. *Compatible Hardware:* IBM PC, PC XT, PC AT & compatibles, PS/2 Model 25, PS/2 Model 30, PS/2 Model 50, PS/2 Model 60, PS/2 Model 80. *Operating System(s) Required:* PC-DOS/MS-DOS 2.0 or higher. *Memory Required:* 256k. *General Requirements:* SDLC communications card. *Items Included:* Software, hardware, manual. *Customer Support:* Free, 800-642-5888.
3.5" or 5.25" disk $895.00.
Full-Featured IBM 3270 Terminal Emulator That Allows PCs to Communicate, Using Bit Synchronous SNA/SDLC Protocol, with IBM or IBM Plug-Compatible Mainframes. A PC Equipped with Remote Appears to the Mainframe As a 3270 Control Unit with up to Eight 3270 Devices Attached. The Devices Can Be LU-2 Keyboard/Displays, LU-3 Printers (3270 DS) or LU-1 Printers (SCS).
Micro-Integration Corporation.

Remote 5250. 1985. *Compatible Hardware:* IBM PC, PC XT, PC AT & compatibles, PS/2 Model 25, PS/2 Model 30, PS/2 Model 50, PS/2

Model 60, PS/2 Model 80. *Operating System(s) Required:* PC-DOS/MS-DOS 2.0 or higher. *Memory Required:* 158k. *General Requirements:* SDLC communications card. Supports a variety of communications cards and/or modems. *Items Included:* Software, hardware, manual. *Customer Support:* Free, 800-642-5888.
3.5" or 5.25" disk $495.00.
Allows a PC to Emulate Devices Which Exchange Information with Remote System/3X Computer Systems. The PC Can Then Process the Same Information & Produce the Same Results As If It Were a Real IBM 5250 Cluster Controller with Attached Display Stations & Printers.
Micro-Integration Corporation.

Remote2. *Compatible Hardware:* IBM PC & compatibles. *Operating System(s) Required:* PC-DOS/MS-DOS 2.0 or higher. *Memory Required:* Monochrome 36k, color 48k.
disk Host $129.00.
Call $89.00.
both $195.00.
Enables Users to Remotely Operate Modem-Equipped IBM PCs. Consists of Two Modules: HOST & CALL. The HOST Is Installed on the Controlling Computer & Includes REMOTE2 MANAGER Used to Configure the HOST Software & Maintain the User Database. CALL Is a Communications Program That Calls REMOTE2 Hosts Providing Exact Screen & Keyboard Mapping of the Host Computer, File Transfers, Remote Printer Redirection, CGA Grahpics, & a Data-Compressed Link. Users May Call Files & Programs on LANs. Security Is Provided by Individual User Passwords.
Digital Communications Assocs.

RemoteVision. *Version:* 4.0.0. 1995. *Customer Support:* One year free maintenance, toll-free technical support, free upgrades.
DOS, Windows or OS/2. 16 user system $6995.00.
Provides Access to LAN Functions from Remote PCs or LANs. It Supports up to 64 Simultaneous Users Connecting to Either a Token-Ring or Ethernet LAN, & Can Support Multiple Protocol Stacks Concurrently over a Single Connection. Provides Remote Access for Any Network Application Based on NetBios, Named Pipes, APPC, 802.2, TCP/IP & IPX. Remote & Mobile Users Can Connect to LAN Applications via Asynchronous Direct-Dial & X.25 Packet Networks from DOS, Windows & OS/2 Workstations. Includes Data Compression Providing up to 70% Compression of All Data, a Powerful Menu-Driven Script Language, & Security Features, Including ID & Password Verification.
Telepartner International.

RemoteVision. *Version:* 4.0. 1995. *Customer Support:* One-year free maintenance, toll-free technical support, free upgrades.
Windows (4Mb). disk $295.00.
Provides Access to LAN Functions from Remote PCs or LANs. It Supports up to 64 Simultaneous Users Connecting to Either a Token-Ring or Ethernet LAN, & Can Support Multiple Protocol Stacks Concurrently over a Single Connection. Provides Remote Access for Any Network Application Based on NetBios, Named Pipes, APPC, 802.2, TCP/IP & IPX. Remote & Mobile Users Can Connect to LAN Applications via Asynchronous Direct-Dial & X.25 Packet Networks from DOS, Windows & OS/2 Workstations. Includes Data Compression Providing up to 70% Compression of All Data, a Powerful Menu-Driven Script Language, & Security Features, Including ID & Password Verification.
Telepartner International.

REMS Investor 3000: Investment Property Analysis. *Version:* 5.01. 1990. *Items Included:* 1 3-ring bound manual, 1 set diskettes, software license agreement. *Customer Support:* 1 hour free in the 1st 30 days on 214-713-6370; $50.00/hour in 15 minute increments on 214-713-6370; $150.00/year 5 hours over that year, toll-free number.
DOS 2.0 or higher. IBM or compatible (640k). disk $595.00.
Perform Fast, Easy and Accurate Financial Analyses and Reporting of Even the Most Complicated Project, Existing or Proposed. Forecast the Cash Flows from the Acquisition, Financing, Development, Operation, and Sale up to 25 Years in the Future. Includes All the Components for a Complete Analysis in One System. Provides for Participation in Income and/or Sale Proceeds by the Lenders. Provides for Fractional Ownership (Partnerships) for up to 10 Individuals or Groups, Allowing for Active and Passive Income, Losses Allowed, Ordinary and Capital Gains Tax Rates. Depreciation and Amortized Expense Handling Makes Reporting After-Tax Results Accurate and Easy. Provides Multiple Methods of Specifying the Property Sale Amount, Evaluate Lease vs. Buy, Exchanges, and Installment Sales. Reports Key Financial Ratios such as IRR, FMRR, ROI, ROE, NPV and Accumulation of Wealth. Reports May be Exported to a File and Imported into a Word Processor or Spreadsheet for Further Analysis or Customization.
Good Software Corp.

REMS Lessor 3000: Lease-By-Lease & Property Case Flow Analysis. *Version:* 1.2. 1988. *Items Included:* 1 3-ring bound manual, 1 set diskettes, product registration card, software, license agreement. *Customer Support:* 1 hour free in the 1st 30 days on 214-713-6370. $50.00/hour in 15 minute increments on the 214-713-6370 number. $150.00/year, 5 hours over that year, toll free number.
DOS 2.0 or higher. IBM or compatible (640k). $595.00.
Details Lease Income & Expenses Data for One to Five Hundred Leases for Office, Retail, Warehouse & Industrial Properties. Projects Cash Flows from Rents, Common Area Maintenance Charges, Pass-Throughs, Rent Escalations, Percentage Rents, etc. Rent Escalations May Be Based on Specified Dollar Amounts, Specified Percentage Increases, Increases in Market Rent, Increases Based on the Consumer Price Index (or Other Indexes) or Any Combination of These Types. Produces Complete Reports.
Good Software Corp.

REMS Property Manager: The Efficient System of Tenant & Property Management. *Version:* DOS: 3.5; Windows & Macintosh: 3.01. 1990. *Items Included:* 2 spiral bound manuals (Getting Started & Reference), 1 set diskettes, product registration card, software, license agreement. *Customer Support:* 1 hour free in the 1st 30 days on 214-713-6370; $50.00/hour in 15 minute increments on the 214-713-6370 number; $150.00/year, 5 hours over that year, toll free number; FAX Support 214-713-6308.
DOS 3.3 or higher. IBM or compatible (640k). $595.00-$2395.00.
Microsoft Windows; DOS 3.3 or higher. IBM or compatible (2Mb). $595.00. *Addl. software required:* Microsoft Windows 3.0 or higher.
Apple Macintosh System 6.0 or higher. Macintosh (2Mb). $595.00.
For the Owner/Manager of Any Number of Single-Family, Multi-Family, & Condominium Units. Adds the Ability to Manage an Unlimited Number of Rental Units & Provides for the Pass Through of Common Area Maintenance Expenses. Provides Accurate, Up-to-Date Information on Tenants, Vendors, Owners & Properties. Records Are Automatically Updated by Accounting Transactions. Tenant Information Includes: Recurring Tenant Charges, Late Fees, Number of NSF Checks & Late Charges, Deposit Balances; Past Tenants with Outstanding Balances & Forwarding Addresses. Automates Tasks Like Paying Recurring Expenses Such As Mortgage Payments, Creating Checks for Vendor Invoices, Calculating Management Fees & Owner Disbursements, Reconcilling Bank Statements, Billing Tenants, Creating Late Fees & Notices, & Increasing Rents. Network Version Available.
Good Software Corp.

Ren & Stimpy - Adventures in Space. Sep. 1995. *Items Included:* Installation instructions, registration card. *Customer Support:* Phone support by calling 302-234-1750, no charge. Fax support by faxing to 302-234-1760, no charge. E-Mail support at Compuserve ID 76004,3520 or MCI Mail/560-7116, no charge.
Windows 3.1 or higher. 386 or higher (4Mb). disk $4.99 (ISBN 1-887468-59-5).
Nonstandard peripherals required: Video for Windows, color VGA, mouse. *Optimal configuration:* SVGA, sound card.
Multimedia Collector's Disk Filled with Popular Cartoon Character Images & Sounds. Packaged in a Blister Pack & Features Nickelodean's Characters.
SWFTE International, Ltd.

Ren & Stimpy - Ren. Sep. 1995. *Items Included:* Installation instructions, registration card. *Customer Support:* Phone support by calling 302-234-1750, no charge. Fax support by faxing to 302-234-1760, no charge. E-Mail support at Compuserve ID 76004,3520 or MCI Mail/560-7116, no charge.
Windows 3.1 or higher. 386 or higher (4Mb). disk $4.99 (ISBN 1-887468-57-9).
Nonstandard peripherals required: Video for Windows, color VGA, mouse. *Optimal configuration:* SVGA, sound card.
Multimedia Collector's Disk Filled with Popular Cartoon Character Images & Sounds. Packaged in a Blister Pack & Features Nickelodean's Characters.
SWFTE International, Ltd.

Ren & Stimpy - Stimpy. Sep. 1995. *Items Included:* Installation instructions, registration card. *Customer Support:* Phone support by calling 302-234-1750, no charge. Fax support by faxing to 302-234-1760, no charge. E-Mail support at Compuserve ID 76004,3520 or MCI Mail/560-7116, no charge.
Windows 3.1 or higher. 386 or higher (4Mb). disk $4.99 (ISBN 1-887468-58-7).
Nonstandard peripherals required: Video for Windows, color VGA, mouse. *Optimal configuration:* SVGA, sound card.
Multimedia Collector's Disk Filled with Popular Cartoon Character Images & Sounds. Packaged in a Blister Pack & Features Nickelodean's Characters.
SWFTE International, Ltd.

Renaissance Masters, Vol. II. Feb. 1995. *Items Included:* CD-ROM booklet. *Customer Support:* Free technical support via phone as of release date.
MPC/Windows. 386.25 or higher IBM compatible (4Mb). CD-ROM disk $49.95 (ISBN 1-885784-02-3, Order no.: 1127). *Optimal configuration:* MPC CD-ROM player, S-VGA graphics card (640x480x256 colors) with compatible monitor, MPC compliant sound card, mouse, Windows 3.1.
Learn about the High Italian Renaissance, Mannerist & Baroque Periods. Study the Works of Michelangelo, Raphael, Titan & Their

Contemporaries. Explore Hundreds of Artistic Works Including Paintings, Mosaics, Sculpture & Architecture. Gain Insight into the Distinct Artistic Techniques of the Renaissance.
Technology Dynamics Corp.

Renaissance Masters, Vol. 1. Feb. 1995. *Items Included:* CD-ROM booklet. *Customer Support:* Free technical support via phone as of release date.
MPC/Windows. 386.25 or higher IBM compatible (4Mb). CD-ROM disk $49.95 (ISBN 1-885784-01-5, Order no.: 1110). *Optimal configuration:* MPC CD-ROM player, S-VGA graphics card (640x480x256 colors) with compatible monitor, MPC compliant sound card, mouse, Windows 3.1.
Discover the Art of the Late Gothic Through the Early Italian Renaissance. Interact with over a Thousand Artistic Works Including Paintings, Sculpture, Architecture & Mosaics. Study the Style of Botticelli, Piero della Francesca, Giotto & Their Contemporaries. Gain Insight into the Use of Paint, Stone, Wood & Bronze That Creates the Dramatic Look of Renaissance Art.
Technology Dynamics Corp.

RenderPrint. Mar. 1994. *Items Included:* 2 stapled manuals, 1 printer handbook, 2 3.5" disks. *Customer Support:* Free with registered service number.
DOS 3.3 or higher, Windows 3.1. IBM PC 386 or higher, VGA or better monitor (2Mb RAM, 4Mb recommended). disk $249.00. *Networks supported:* Novell Netware print queue.
Produces Fast, Photo-Realistic 3D Images on Any Printer at Full Resolution. DOS Version Works in ADI Protected Mode Within AutoCAD, 3D Studio, AutoVision & Other ADI Supported Applications, As a Standalone or TSR That Pops up Inside the Application. Select Images, Size, Placement, File Formats Supported, FIG, TIF, TGA, BMP), JPEG, PCX Dithering Method, Control Brightness, Contrast & Gamma for Professional Image Quality & Detail.
Insight Development Corp.

Renegade. Midnight Software Staff & SSI Special Project Group Staff. Feb. 1995. *Items Included:* Perfect bound manual & data card. *Customer Support:* 30 day limited warranty.
DOS 5.0 or higher. IBM PC & compatibles with CD-ROM drive, Hard drive & mouse (4Mb & 1Mb SVGA card). CD-ROM disk $69.95 (ISBN 0-917059-19-0, Order no.: 062181). *Nonstandard peripherals required:* Sound boards supported, Sound Canvas, Soundscape Wave blaster, SW 32/GW 32, Gravis Native mode, & Sound blaster family. *Optimal configuration:* 486/33 required, 486/66 recommended.
Tactical Space Combat Game Complete with SVGA Graphics, Number D Cinematics, & Realistic First-Person Flight Simulator Viewpoints.
Strategic Simulations, Inc.

Renegade: Battle for Jacob's Star. Midnight Software Staff. Sep. 1995. *Customer Support:* 30 Day Limited Warranty.
DOS 5.0 or higher. CD PC (4Mb). CD-ROM disk $9.95 (ISBN 0-917059-30-1, Order no.: 062531). *Optimal configuration:* 486/66.
Space Flight Command Game. Jewel Case Version.
Strategic Simulations Inc.

Renegade Legion: Interceptor. Scot Bayless & Mike Mancusso. *Items Included:* Rulebook. *Customer Support:* Technical support line: (408) 737-6850 (11am-5pm, PST); 14 day money back guarantee/30 day exchange policy.
DOS 2.11 or higher. IBM PC & compatible (512k). disk $59.95. *Nonstandard peripherals required:* Requires color monitor & graphic adaptor (i.e., CGA, EGA).
3.5" disk $59.95.
Engage in Exciting Ship-to-Ship Space Combat While You Wage A Campaign of Galactic Struggle Between the Terran Overlord Government & the Renegade Legion. Command Starfighters from 60 Existing Designs or Create Your Own Ships. Arm Them with High-Tech Weapons, Such As Mass-Driver Cannons, Lasers, Neutron Particle Guns, & Missiles. Mission Types Include: Fleet Intercepts, Space Station Strikes, Intelligence Gathering, & Wild Meles. You May Fly As a Single Player Against the Computer, ot Play Against Other Human Opponents & Fight Squadron!
Strategic Simulations, Inc.

Renegade: Return to Jacob's Star. Midnight Software. Mar. 1996. *Items Included:* 48 page manual. *Customer Support:* 30 day limited warranty.
PC-DOS CD-ROM. 486/66 (8Mb). CD-ROM disk $49.95 (ISBN 0-917059-08-5, Order no.: 062361). *Nonstandard peripherals required:* 1Mb SVGA, DOS 6.22 or higher, 2x drive, 20Mb hard drive space, supports soundscape, SW32/GW32, Gravis Native, sound blaster. *Optimal configuration:* 486 Pentium 90 or higher, 16Mb of RAM. *Networks supported:* Ten with Win 95, 14.4 ICBPS modem.
Sequel to Renegade: Battle for Jacob's Star Includes SVGA Graphics, Network Play, Digitized Jokes & Sound Effects. Fly New Missions with Head to Head Battles.
Strategic Simulations, Inc.

Rent-All Master. *Customer Support:* 800-929-8117 (customer service).
MS-DOS. IBM/PS2. disk $499.99 (ISBN 0-87007-446-6).
Point of Sale Management System for the All Round Rental Store. Has a Database of Usual Types of Implements Such as Lawn Care Equipment Already Built in. System will Save the Average Store over $4000 a Day. Has Extensive Error Checking Capabilities; It Sounds a Warning Horn to Alert User to Problems.
SourceView Software International.

Rent Control Compliance ("RCC"). Version: 2.1. May 1991. *Items Included:* User's Manual. *Customer Support:* Free initial on-site training; 90-day media defect warranty; 1-year maintenance is 15% of current purchase price which includes phone support & upgrades.
MS/PC DOS 3.0 or higher. Any IBM/AT (286) or compatible (640k). Base Price $1295.00, $295.00 per property, $2.75 per unit. *Optimal configuration:* IBM/AT-386DX/SX-20MHZ or higher, MS-DOS 5.0, 4MB RAM, Hewlett Packard LaserJet III/IIIP, QEMM 386.
Networks supported: Next Release Novell 3.1.
A Rent Control Expert System That Incorporates the D. C. Rent Control Law. Manages Multiple Properties & Units, Tracks Rent Histories for Each Unit, & Prints All Forms That Are Filable with the D. C. Government.
Software Engineering Technologies, Inc.

Rental Manager. Version: 2.1. David Coleman. Feb. 1984. *Compatible Hardware:* IBM PC & compatibles. *Operating System(s) Required:* MS-DOS. *Language(s):* Compiled BASIC. *Memory Required:* 256k. *Customer Support:* Telephone support.
disk $495.00.
General-Purpose Property Management System Which Handles All Tenant Activities, Automatically Posting a Built-In General Ledger. User Can Range from Simple Control of Receipts & Disbursements by Property, to More Complex Financial Reporting for Owners with Several Properties. Also Allows Tie-In to Electronic Spreadsheet & Word Processor Programs.
Coleman Business Systems.

Rental Record Keeper. *Compatible Hardware:* IBM PC & compatibles. *Memory Required:* 64k. *Customer Support:* Free telephone support, 1 month money back guarantee.
disk $179.00.
Tracks Data Needed to Manage Residential & Commercial Property. Provides P&L Statements for Each Property & for All Properties. Prints Rent Rolls, Federal Tax Figures & Many Other Reports.
MicroEase.

Rental Service Billing (Deliveries) System. *Compatible Hardware:* DECMate II, DECmate III, PDP 11-23. *Operating System(s) Required:* COS-310, MICRO-RSX. *Language(s):* DIBOL-83. $5000.00, incl. user guide (Order no.: 85-13).
Designed for Those Service Industries Who Need to Manage, Maintain, & Service Off-Site Equipment Rentals. Provides for Deliveries of Items to the Off-Site Businesses. Rental Industries Include Vehicle Equipment, Uniform Rental, Vending Machine Servicing, & Water & Gas Delivery Businesses. Provides Once a Month Billing for Off-Site Rentals As Well As Daily Deliveries. Includes Complete Accounting & Receivable Management, in Addition to Delivery Planning & Route Maintenance.
Corporate Consulting Co.

Renum-Compress. *Compatible Hardware:* TRS-80. *Language(s):* BASIC.
contact publisher for price.
Instant Software, Inc.

Renumber. Guerri F. Stevens. Aug. 1984. *Compatible Hardware:* Radio Shack Model 100, Tandy 200. *Language(s):* Machine. *Memory Required:* 3k.
cassette $24.95 (ISBN 0-932095-02-X).
Custom Software Engineering, Inc.

REOPN. 1982. *Compatible Hardware:* IBM PC. *Operating System(s) Required:* MS-DOS. *Language(s):* BASIC. *Memory Required:* 128k.
$350.00.
Calculates the Reinforcement Required Versus the Actual Reinforcement Existing for a Particular Configuration & Set of Design Conditions. Applies to Cylindrical, Elliptical & Spherical Shells. Provides a Weld Path Analysis. Designs for External Pressure. Provides a Formal Report with Formulas in Output.
Technical Research Services, Inc.

Repacking Your Bags: Lighten Your Load for the Rest of Your Life. Jan. 1995. *Items Included:* Repacking Journal. *Customer Support:* Toll-free telephone number for technical support, 90 days warranty for defects in materials & workmanship.
Macintosh System 7.0; Microsoft Windows 3.1. Macintosh with 68040 processor (5Mb); IBM compatibles (8Mb). CD-ROM disk $69.95 (ISBN 1-886806-01-2). *Nonstandard peripherals required:* Double-speed CD-ROM drive. *Addl. software required:* QuickTime (included on disc).
Helps You Understand How to Unpack & Repack Your "Life" Bags - What You Carry Around in Your Work, Relationships, Physical Space, & View of Life. This Highly Interactive CD-ROM Program Includes Information, Exercises, & Real-Life Examples to Help You Get Your Life under Control & Live It More Fully.
Wilson Learning Corp.

Repair. *Compatible Hardware:* IBM PC.
contact publisher for price.
Files on a Floppy Disk by Track or by Sector & Sets Files to Hidden System or Normal Status, Shows Hidden or Erased Files, & Adds or Changes a Directory.
Squire Buresh Assocs., Inc.

REPDATA System. *Compatible Hardware:* Apple II, TRS-80 Model II, Model 16.
contact publisher for price.
REPDATA.

Replay 4. Microdeal. Nov. 1988. *Compatible Hardware:* Atari ST. *Memory Required:* 512k.
3.5" disk $129.95.
Features Eight Different Sampling Speeds, up to 50 kHz, Realtime Oscilloscope Digital Filter, Two Midi Options, Cut, Paste, Move, Reverse, Fade in/Fade out Options. Includes Drum Beat Program for Creating Drum Kits.
MichTron, Inc.

Repo Smart. 1980. *Compatible Hardware:* IBM Micros & compatibles. *Language(s):* C. *Memory Required:* 640k. *Items Included:* Operator's manual. *Customer Support:* Onsite training, telephone support.
contact publisher for price. *Networks supported:* Novell, Banyan, etc.
Automated Repurchase Agreement System That Features: General Ledger Tickets; Client Confirmation Letters; Over 70 Standards of Reports; Client & Security Listings; Maturity; 1099 Tax Accounting; F.D.I.C. Breakouts; Regular, Pledge, & Broker Accounts; User Report Writer Sweep Accounting, Collateral Repricing & Reassigning with Client Notifications, Electronic GL Posting & Investing.
Wall Street Consulting Group.

REPORT. *Version:* 3.1. Jan. 1986. *Compatible Hardware:* IBM PC, PC XT, PC AT & compatibles. *Operating System(s) Required:* PC-DOS, MS-DOS. *Language(s):* FORTRAN. *Memory Required:* 512k. *General Requirements:* Printer.
disk $1250.00 (Order no.: REPORT).
Produces Grade/Tonnage Reports Using Either Standard Reserve Reporting Techniques or the Log Normal Short Cut Method. Using a Block File from KRIGE3 or SCREEN, the Program Prints a Summary of Estimated Reserves for Each Cut-Off Interval, Specified Level, Orebody Subportion & Orebody. Using a L3D Envelope from LIMIT3 or GENL3D, the User Can Target a Portion of the Model for Reporting.
Geostat Systems International, Inc. (GSII).

Report Card 2. *Version:* 2. Mark Ringuette. Jan. 1991. *Items Included:* Manual contained in 3-ring binder; program is shipped on both a 3.5" & 5.25" disk. *Customer Support:* No-charge customer support for registered users.
DOS 2.1 or higher. IBM & compatibles (256k).
disk $59.95 (ISBN 0-926776-25-8).
Nonstandard peripherals required: 80-column card. *Addl. software required:* BASIC.
Networks supported: Novell & other standard IBM networks.
Grading System for Teachers. Allows Teacher to Weight Activities According to Importance; Enter Student Names, I.D. Codes & Grades with Assignments Weighted Individually & in Groups (Such As Homework, Tests, etc.); up to 100 Activities Can Be Entered per Class; Each Student Is Given a Mark Out of Total Possible Points, & Report Card Calculates the Grades; No Grade Marks Accepted. Various Screen and/or Printer Reports Available. Hard Disk Compatible.
Sensible Software, Inc.

Report Writer (R/W). *Version:* 3.0. Intelligent Query, Inc. 1992. *Compatible Hardware:* IBM RS/6000, Sun SPARC, HP UX Data General Aviion; Altos; IBM PC AT, XT; Intel 286/386, NCR Tower. *Operating System(s) Required:* PC-DOS/MS-DOS, UNIX, XENIX, AIX, Sun OS SCO UNIX. *Items Included:* Documentation source code available. *Customer Support:* One year free maintenance included in initial license fees, annual maintenance available at app. $500-$675 per package per year, on-site customization, training & support available.
Unix, Xenix; MS-DOS (1.5Mb). IBM PC, PC XT, PC AT; Intel 286, 386; Altos 2000; NCR Tower & compatibles. contact publisher for price.
Produces Custom Reports & Screen Displays Using Data from Other MCBA Accounting, Distribution & Manufacturing Files. Features Prompts for Each Step. Report Data Can Be Bridged to Selected Word Processor, Graphic, Spreadsheet, Graphic & Database Packages.
MCBA, Inc.

Reporter. 1986.
PC-DOS 2.0, MicroSoft MS-DOS (256k). IBM PC, PC XT, PC AT & compatibles, PS/2. disk $62.00 (ISBN 0-89189-276-1).
3.5" disk $62.00 (ISBN 0-89189-278-8).
Microcomputer Laboratory Information System.
ASCP Pr.

The Requirements Analyst. *Version:* 2.2. Jun. 1992. *Compatible Hardware:* IBM PC & compatibles. *Memory Required:* 640k. *General Requirements:* Lotus 1-2-3 Releases 2 or 3. *Items Included:* Includes a 250 page guide to accounting software for microcomputers & a Lotus 1-2-3 template. *Customer Support:* Available as needed 1-800-433-8015.
$495.00.
Performs Needs Analysis & Decision Support for Selecting Micro Accounting Software Systems. Database Includes 20 Systems; Users May Add Others. Performs Analysis by Detailed System Elements, Lists Characteristics in Order of Priority, & Ranks Each System.
CTS.

ReRun Gamepak. 1985. *Compatible Hardware:* Commodore 64 with joystick. *Items Included:* Diskette & documentation booklet. *Customer Support:* Technical assistance at 800 number.
$5.49 special includes booklet.
Contains Action, Skill, Intrigue, & Suspense Game Programs. Includes Favorites Published in RUN Such As: Mystery of Lane Manor, Find-the-Word, & Tag; & Never-Before-Published Games Like: Ski, Hassle-Castle, & Trap Shoot.
IDG Communications/Peterborough.

Resale & Billback Series Feature Package B. Apr. 1984. *Compatible Hardware:* IBM PC, PC XT, PC AT. *Operating System(s) Required:* PC-DOS. *Language(s):* BASIC. *Memory Required:* 256k.
disk $2875.00 (ISBN 0-927905-11-6, Order no.: PT-70).
$5175.00 (ISBN 0-927905-12-4, Order no.: PT-150).
$6325.00 (ISBN 0-927905-13-2, Order no.: PT-500).
$7475.00 (Order no.: PT-1000).
Automatically Posts Telephone Charges to Clients' Accounts. Monitors All Extensions for Misuse & Abuse. Interfaces with Modern Business Telephone System to Automatically Analyze & Allocate Telephone Costs.
XIOX Corp.

Resale Store Management System. Nov. 1988. *Operating System(s) Required:* MS-DOS, UNIX, XENIX. *Memory Required:* 512k. *General Requirements:* 5Mb hard disk. *Customer Support:* Yes.
disk $2400.00.
Customer, Sales & Inventory Accounting. Ledger Accounts Updated Through Sales & Expense Transactions. Checks, Sales Tags, Mailing Labels Produced. Transaction Summaries, Financial Statement Printed. Customization Available.
Monterey Computer Consulting.

Rescue. *Version:* 1.1. *Compatible Hardware:* IBM PC & compatibles. *Customer Support:* Telephone hot-line.
disk $119.95.
Provides Solutions for Most 1-2-3/SYMPHONY File Loss Situations. Includes the Following Features: Automatic LOTUS Format Recovery - Recovers Files That Will Not Load Due to Damage; Recovery of Password Encrypted Files; LOTUS Data Search - Locates Lost 1-2-3 or SYMPHONY Files on Hard Disk or Floppy; LOTUS Data View/Audit - Decodes Disk & File Data into Cell References, Values, Formulas, etc., Helping Users to Pinpoint Damage or Find Pieces of a Lost Spreadsheet; Autosave/Backup Protection - Automatically Saves the 1-2-3 Worksheet at Timed Intervals & Backs Up Files Before Replacement.
Spectrum Computer Services, Inc.

Rescue Plus. *Version:* 1.3.
disk $129.95 Version 1.3 (Edition I) Lotus release 2 & Symphony; $149.95 Version 3.1 (Edition II) Lotus release 3. *Addl. software required:* Lotus 1-2-3 (all versions).
Recovery Utility for 1-2-3 & Symphony Files Includes Automatic Undelete Feature & Ability to Recover Data from One Drive to Another. Can Generally Retrieve More Than 95% of Damaged Data. Program Has Four Tools: ResQDisk Locates Lost File Data on Hard Disk or Floppy Drive; ResQView Pinpoints Damage & Can Find Missing Pieces of Lost Spreadsheets by Decoding Disk & File Data; ResQFile Unformats & Helps Recover Damaged Disks & Also Patches Damaged Directories or File Allocation Tables; & ResQPass Retrieves Forgotten Passwords.
Intex Solutions, Inc.

Rescue Squad. John F. Kutcher. Sep. 1983. *Compatible Hardware:* Commodore 64 with 1541 disk drive & joystick. *Operating System(s) Required:* CBM DOS. *Language(s):* Assembly. *Memory Required:* 64k.
disk $7.98, incl. reference card (ISBN 0-87190-023-8).
Action/Suspense Game in Which Player Maneuvers an Ambulance Through Traffic While Trying to Save People from a Burning Building.
Muse Software.

Research FORTRAN-77. *Compatible Hardware:* IBM PC. *Operating System(s) Required:* CP/M-86, MP/M-86, MS-DOS. *Memory Required:* 96k.
disk $500.00.
Implementation of the ANSI 77 Standard Programming Language. Can Be Used for Representing Algebraic Expressions, for Use in Vector & Matrix Arithmetic, & for Solving Problems Requiring Complex Arithmetic.
Digital Research, Inc.

Research Module: M65B. 1984. *Compatible Hardware:* Apple II, Commodore 64. *Memory Required:* 48k.
Apple. disk $250.00 (ISBN 0-925182-31-1, Order no.: M65B).
Commodore. disk $250.00 (ISBN 0-925182-32-X, Order no.: M65B).
Utilizes M65A Files As Database for Research.
Matrix Software.

Research: Series 900 to 2000. *Compatible Hardware:* IBM System/36, System/36 PC; AS/400.
contact publisher for price.
Classifies & Retrieves Client File Research, Opinions & Precedents.
Manac-Prentice Hall Software, Inc.

TITLE INDEX

Reservation & Billing System. *Version:* 1.1. *Customer Support:* 90 days of free telephone support.
IBM PC/XT, AT, PS/2 & compatibles (512k). disk $795.00.
Software Package for Managing Short Term Rentals. On Screen Calendar for Visual Tracking of Unit Status. Features Include Automated Guest Accounting for Payment in Advance, or Payment at Check out Making Program Appropriate for Vacation Rentals as Well as Hotels & Motels. Interfaces with DELUXE PROPERTY MANAGEMENT.
Yardi Systems.

RESICALC. Mar. 1986. *Operating System(s) Required:* MS-DOS, PC-DOS 2.XX. *Memory Required:* 256k.
disk $25.00 (ISBN 0-938087-01-0).
RAM Resident Programmable Scientific Calculator (Subset of MATRIX CALCULATOR). Can Handle Simple Matrix Operations & Scientific Functions, Including User Supplied Functions.
Soft Tech, Inc.

The RESIDENT. *Version:* 3.0. 1984. *Compatible Hardware:* Altos; AT&T; DEC; IBM PC AT & compatibles, NCR, Unisys, Texas Instruments. *Operating System(s) Required:* UNIX, XENIX, SCO XENIX. *Language(s):* C. *Memory Required:* 1000k.
contact publisher for price.
Practice Management Software Designed for Patient & Insurance Billing, Accounts Receivable, Practice Analysis, Patient Appointment Scheduling, Patient Charts & Telecommunications.
Wallaby Software Corp.

Resident Expert. *Customer Support:* 800-929-8117 (customer service).
MS-DOS. IBM/PS2. disk $99.99 (ISBN 0-87007-551-9).
A System That Records Over 100 Specific Characteristics About a Residenial Property, its Environs, the Type & Quality of the Neighborhood, & the Condition of the Property. Will Give the Probability of User Making Money Due to Appreciation or at Least "Breaking Even" & Warn User Away From Bad Buys.
SourceView Software International.

Resident Manager. Software Dynamics. *Operating System(s) Required:* MS-DOS 1.25. *Memory Required:* 128k. *General Requirements:* Printer, Winchester hard disk.
$995.00.
Texas Instruments, Personal Productivit.

Residential/Commercial Services. ADS Software, Inc. *Operating System(s) Required:* MS-DOS. *Memory Required:* 128k. *General Requirements:* 2 disk drives, printer.
$895.00.
Texas Instruments, Personal Productivit.

Residential Construction Symbols Library. *Version:* 2.0. *General Requirements:* PowerDraw or PowerCADD. *Items Included:* User manual, 3 diskettes. *Customer Support:* free with registration.
Macintosh Plus or higher. 3.5" disk $125.00 (ISBN 1-878250-03-5).
More Than 1,000 Architectural & Construction Symbols.
Engineered Software.

Residential Cooling & Heating. *Items Included:* Bound manual. *Customer Support:* Free hotline - no time limit; 30 day limited warranty; updates are $5/disk plus S&H.
MS-DOS. IBM & compatibles (448k). disk $395.00. *Nonstandard peripherals required:* Requires dot matrix (e.g., Epson, IBM, etc.) or laser printer.
demo diskette $5.00.
Calculates the Cooling & Heating Loads, Supply Air, Energy Requirements, & Heating/Cooling Costs for Houses, Apartments, Mobile Homes, & Light Industrial Applications.
Dynacomp, Inc.

Residential Cooling & Heating Loads Program: RHVAC. *Version:* 3.0. Saleem Chaudhary. May 1988. *Compatible Hardware:* IBM PC & compatibles. *Operating System(s) Required:* PC-DOS/MS-DOS. *Language(s):* CB-80. *Memory Required:* CP/M 64k, MS-DOS 256k. *General Requirements:* 2 disk drives, printer.
disk $395.00.
8" disk $395.00.
3.5" disk $395.00.
demo disk $38.00.
documentation $25.00.
Calculates Heating & Cooling Loads on Buildings Having As Many As 100 Zones & 100 Air Systems. Peak Loads & Air Quantities Calculated for Each Zone, System & the Residence As a Whole. Features Building Rotation, Exterior Shading, Psychrometrics, & Manual "J" Requirements, Table Values & Procedures from the 1981 ASHRAE Handbook of Fundamentals.
Elite Software Development, Inc.

Residential Cooling, Heating, Energy & Operating Cost - RL5M. *Version:* 03/1995. Mar. 1981. *Compatible Hardware:* IBM PC & compatibles. *Operating System(s) Required:* MS-DOS, PC-DOS. *Language(s):* Compiled & Assembly. *Memory Required:* 512k. *Customer Support:* Technical hotline, "Lifetime" support at no charge.
disk $349.00-$375.00.
Florida Version $75.00 (to automatically run the required Florida State Energy Efficiency Analysis.)
Uses latest ASHRAE Residential & ACCA Manual "J" Procedures to Calculate Residential/ Condominium/Light Commercial Cooling/Heating Loads, Annual Energy Requirements & Operating Cost. Allows Comparison of Different Equipment Selections & Fuels. Accepts User Inputs of Commercial Construction Materials as Well as Calling the Complete ACCA List of Materials Automatically. Handles Heat Pumps, Mobile Homes, Cathedral Ceilings, Building Rotation, Radiant or Hot Air Heating; R-Values to R-57. Gives Air CFM or Baseboard Heating Requirements. Bin Method for Energy. Automatic Weather & Bin Data for 900 Cities. State-of-the-Art Full-Function Interactive Prompted Input Screens with Windows, Pop-up Calculator, Defaults, Error Checking, Color or b/w, Almost 200 "Help" & Error Messages, etc. Prints Highly Personalized Presentation Offer for Client. English Units.
MC2 Engineering Software.

Residential Real Estate Tools. 1992.
Macintosh System 7 or higher. MAC Plus or higher (1Mb). 3.5" disk $195.00. *Addl. software required:* One of the following: 1.) ClarisWorks; 2.) MS-Works; 3.) Aldus Pagemaker & MS-Excel. *Optimal configuration:* Inkjet or Laser printer.
Postcards, Flyers, Newsletters, Sales Letters, CMA's, Value of Home, Seller's Estimate, Buyer's Estimate, etc.
RealData, Inc.

Resonance. *Items Included:* Bound manual. *Customer Support:* Free hotline - no time limit; 30 day limited warranty; updates are $5/disk plus S&H.
MS-DOS 2.0 or higher. IBM compatibles (256k). disk $99.95. *Nonstandard peripherals required:* Printer recommended, but optional.

RESOURCES FOR STRATEGIC ANALYSIS

Software Package for Determining the Resonant Frequencies of a Rotating Shaft or Beam, & What the Corresponding Mode Shapes Look Like. It Provides a Means for Designing Systems Which, for Example, Have Minimum Vibrations (Nodes) at Bearing Locations; Resonances Away from the Rotation or Loading Frequencies; Reinforcements at Maximum Stress Fatigue Points; Have Safeguards Against Whipping; etc.
Dynacomp, Inc.

Resort Manager. *Version:* 1.2. 1989. *Operating System(s) Required:* PC-DOS/MS-DOS. *Memory Required:* 512k. *General Requirements:* hard disk recommended. *Customer Support:* Telephone support.
disk $1750.00.
Management System for Resorts with Units Rented on The Behalf of Many Owners. Accommodates both Wholly-Owned & Time-Share Units, & Charges Guests Daily, Weekly or Monthly. Provides Statements & Checks to Unit Owners. Also Provides Guest Reservations, Automatic Charges (Taxes, Commissions & Fees) & Deposit Refund Checks.
Coleman Business Systems.

Resource Management System. Open Door Software Staff. 1995. *Items Included:* Manual. *Customer Support:* Call for info..
DOS. IBM & compatibles. disk $1299.00 (ISBN 1-56756-084-9, Order no.: OD1050I). *Optimal configuration:* 486 DX266, 5Mb free space on hard disk, 4Mb RAM-3Mb expanded usable, VGA monitor, 3.5" HD floppy, keyboard, mouse, tape back up & uninterruptible power supply.
Network Version. disk $2599.00 (ISBN 1-56756-086-5, Order no.: OD1052I). *Networks supported:* Novell Netware Lite.
A Rehabilitation Case Management Application Suited for Rehabilitative Services Personnel. RMS Uses Client & Claim Information to Print Invoices & Other Accounts Receivable Reports, Such As Age Analysis & Payment Histories. Handles Client, Adjustor, & Employee Provider Data to Provide a Comprehensive Case Management System for the Small Rehabilitative Services Firm. Many Company Defaults Help Speed the Billing Process by Providing Default Rates for Expert Witness, Worker's Compensations, & Mileage Expenses. Makes It Easy to File a New Claim, Work on an Existing Claim, & Close a Claim Efficiently, with Minimum Paperwork. Upon Completing the Claim Information, RMS Guides You Through Line Item Invoicing W/Pop Ups to Help Manage a Case From Start to Finish.
Advantage International.

Resource Manager. *Version:* 2.6. Jan. 1991. *Items Included:* Manuals. *Customer Support:* Free phone support.
MAC System 7.0 compatible. MAC Plus or higher (2Mb). 3.5" disk $395.00 (Order no.: RM-2.0). *Addl. software required:* Hypercard 2.0. *Optimal configuration:* MAC 68030 Processor, System 7.0, Hypercard 2.1 Hard disk, 2Mb RAM. *Networks supported:* AppleTalk.
A Collection of Maintenance & Inventory Databases for Hydrants, Hose, Appliances, Turnouts, SCBA'S, Communications Equipment, Tools, Personnel, Apparatus, All Linked to Provide Automated Schedules, Inventories & Budgeting.
Sound Advice, Inc.

Resources for Strategic Analysis. 1989. *General Requirements:* Lotus 1-2-3.
IBM. contact publisher for price (ISBN 0-538-80273-1, Order no.: GH80J8).
This Serves as a Companion Volume to Strategy: A Multi-Level Integrative Approach (GH80JA). It

RESPA+: REAL ESTATE SETTLEMENT

Links Computer Analysis to 12 Cases From the Main Text & Includes 4 Additional Cases. Package Consists of Text-Workbook & IBM Diskettes With Decision Tools & Lotus 1-2-3 Templates.
South-Western Publishing Co.

RESPA+: Real Estate Settlement Processing & Accounting System. Version: 6.0. 1983. *Compatible Hardware:* Barrister PC; IBM PC & compatibles, PC XT, PC AT. *Operating System(s) Required:* PC-DOS, MS-DOS. *Language(s):* RM-COBOL. *Memory Required:* 640k. *General Requirements:* Hard disk, printer.
$2500.00-$3500.00.
Consists of Software Systems for Real Estate Settlement Processing, Escrow Accounting, Management Reports, Generalized Forms Printing, &, in Some States, a State Forms Package. Prepares Disbursement Sheets, Checks HUD1 Closing System, FNMA, FHA, VA Notes, Mortgages, & Deeds. Includes Password Security Protection & Report Writer for User-Defined Reports & Inquiries. Forms Design Module Available. Network Version Available.
Barrister Information Systems Corp.

RESPIT. Version: 2.05. Oct. 1985. *Compatible Hardware:* IBM PC, PC XT, PC AT & compatibles. *Operating System(s) Required:* PC-DOS, MS-DOS. *Language(s):* FORTRAN. *Memory Required:* 512k. *General Requirements:* Printer.
disk $5000.00, incl. PITKOR, PSTPIT, & PREPIT (Order no.: RESPIT).
Reports the Minable Reserves within a Pit, Accounting for the Grade, Cost & Price Constraints Applied in PREPIT. RESPIT Forms a 3-D Envelope Which Constrains the Block Model from above (with the Original Topography), & from below (with the Final Pit Bottom) to Produce a Report of the Total Minable Reserves.
Geostat Systems International, Inc. (GSII).

Response Professional Mail Order. Version: 4.3. Jun. 1985. *Items Included:* Full user documentation (600 pages); DataFlex runtime license. *Customer Support:* 60 day limited warranty; voice, fax & modem support, maintenance plan- 14% of system value, annually.
DOS 3.X. IBM AT compatible 640k. $4495.00.
 Optimal configuration: 386 or 486. Networks supported: Novell.
Complete PC-Based Mail Order Processing Novell Netware Compatible. All Function for Mail Order Including NCOA Manifest & Merge Purge. On-Line Order Entry & Inventory Control.
Colinear Systems, Inc.

Response Time. B. Neiburger. 1983. *Compatible Hardware:* Apple II, IIc, IIe; Basis 6502; Franklin Ace. *Operating System(s) Required:* Apple DOS 3.3. *Language(s):* BASIC (source code included). *Memory Required:* 48k.
disk $20.00 (ISBN 0-914555-19-7).
Series of 10 Rapid Tests That Gives User a Response/Reaction Score Which Can Be Compared to an Easy, Verifiable Test for Levels of Disability, Fatigue, Intoxication & Dependability.
Andent, Inc.

Restaurant Accounts Payable. 1979. *Compatible Hardware:* IBM PC & compatibles, PC XT, PC AT. *Language(s):* BASIC, C, Compiled BASIC. *Memory Required:* 420k.
one-time fee $700.00.
lease $50.00, per mo.
maintenance $220.00, per yr.
Multi-Company, Divisional, & Departmental. Unlimited Transactions, Vendors, & Vendor History. Prints Checks, Aged AP Report, Cash Requirements, & Discounts Taken. Stands Alone or Integrates with Other Restaurant Programs.
Advanced Analytical/CharterHouse.

Restaurant & Bar Inventory. 1986. *Compatible Hardware:* IBM PC & compatibles, PC XT, PC AT. *Language(s):* GW-BASIC, BASICA, C, Compiled BASIC. *Memory Required:* 256k.
disk $99.00, incl. documentation.
Starter Kit for Restaurants. Reports Food, Liquor, Paper Usage & Cost, Items on Hand, Received. Prints Reorder & Checks Lists. Upgrades to Inventory, Menu, & Cost Control.
Advanced Analytical/CharterHouse.

Restaurant Comp. *Compatible Hardware:* Apple Macintosh, IBM PC & compatibles. *General Requirements:* Hard disk.
Food & Beverage Inventory. $1195.00.
Recipe Profit Analyzer. $495.00.
Sales & Food Cost Analyzer. $195.00.
Restaurant Management Program.
RestaurantComp.

Restaurant Express: Integrated Restaurant/Bar Management System. Version: 5.01. Bob Dombroski. Mar. 1985. *Compatible Hardware:* IBM PC XT & compatibles, PS/2. *Operating System(s) Required:* MS-DOS 3.3 or higher or UNIX. *Language(s):* MF/COBOL. *Memory Required:* 640k.
disk $1495.00-$4495.00.
Features Accounts Payable, Accounts Receivable, Inventory, Automatic Instant Food Costing by Menu/Recipe Item, Full Financial Statements. No Duplication of Entries. Generates Daily Cash Flow & All Essential Management Reports. Alphabetic Lookup Throughout Instantly Calls up Inventory, Menus, Suppliers, Customers. Optional Saladbar Module.
Systems Software Resource, Inc.

Restaurant Financial Management System: RFMS. Version: 3.0. Jan. 1991. *Items Included:* Operators manual. *Customer Support:* Telephone support (90 days free); 1 year support agreement $750.00 per call support at $100.00 per hour.
DOS. IBM PC or compatible (512k). disk $397.00. Nonstandard peripherals required: Requires color graphics & wide carriage printer.
 Optimal configuration: IBM PC, 640k memory, 40Mb hard disk, VGA monitor & printer.
A Complete Restaurant Accounting System, Including Payroll, Accounts Payable, General Ledger & Menu Costing. Includes Tip Allocation, Sales Entry by Category, Consolidation by Company- Restaurant & Bank Reconciliations. Modules Ca Be Bought Separately or All Together for Use by Restaurants from Alaska to Puerto Rico.
Rapp Industries, Inc.

Restaurant General Ledger. 1979. *Compatible Hardware:* IBM PC & compatibles, PC XT, PC AT. *Language(s):* GW-BASIC, BASICA, C, Compiled BASIC. *Memory Required:* 420k.
one-time fee $1000.00.
lease $50.00, per mo.
maintenance $220.00, per yr.
Multi-Company, Divisional, & Departmental. Features Unlimited Chart of Accounts, Unlimited Transactions, Two Years Detail On-Line, No Closing. Stands Alone or Integrates with Other Restaurant Programs.
Advanced Analytical/CharterHouse.

Restaurant Inventory & Food Cost, 6 programs. Harry Skolnik. Jun. 1984. *Compatible Hardware:* Apple Macintosh, IBM PC & compatibles. *Language(s):* Compiled dBASE III Plus. *Memory Required:* 512k. *General Requirements:* Hard disk, printer.
disk $395.00-$1195.00.
Series of 6 Inventory Programs for Food & Liquor Inventory & Food & Beverage Cost. Offers Versions for a Wide Range of Types & Sizes of Restaurant Operations.
RestaurantComp.

SOFTWARE ENCYCLOPEDIA 1996

Inventory I.
 disk $395.00.
 Does Inventory Extensions & Provides Inventory Checklists for Simplifying & Organizing Physical Inventories.
Inventory II.
 disk $495.00.
 Similar to INVENTORY I. Does Inventory Extensions & Provides Inventory Checklists for Simplifying & Organizing the Taking of Physical Inventories.
Inventory III.
 disk $795.00.
 Does Extensions & Calculates Quantities of Each Food & Beverage Item Used. Inventory Value & Usage Are Figured on Either an Average Cost or Last Cost Basis. Reports Price History & Multiple Vendors.
Inventory IV.
 disk $995.00.
 Does Extensions, Calculates Quantities of Each Food & Beverage Item Used, & Links to an Accounts Payable Program, So That Purchase Information Updates Both Inventory & Vendor Payables at the Same Time. Reports Price History & Multiple Vendors.
Inventory VI.
 disk $1095.00.
 Offers Multi-Outlet & Perpetual Inventory Capabilities; Keeps Track of Transfers of Food & Beverage Items from a Central Storage Area to As Many As 10 Sales Outlets or Departments. Reports Price History & Multiple Vendors.
Inventory VII.
 disk $1195.00.
 Offers Multi-Outlet & Perpetual Inventory Capabilities; Keeps Track of Transfers of Food & Beverage Items from a Central Storage Area to As Many As 10 Sales Outlets or Departments; Links to an Accounts Payable Program to Keep Track of Amounts Owed to Vendors & Write Payables Checks. Reports Price History & Multiple Vendors.

Restaurant Inventory, Menu & Cost Control. Version: 5.0. Jan. 1979. *Compatible Hardware:* IBM PC & compatibles, PC XT, PC AT. *Operating System(s) Required:* MS-DOS. *Language(s):* GW-BASIC, BASICA, C, Compiled BASIC (source code included). *Memory Required:* 420k. *General Requirements:* 132-column printer.
disk $1700.00.
lease $80.00, per mo.
maintenance $150.00, per yr.
Provides Management Information on Food Costs. Includes Perpetual Inventory, Food Cost Analysis, Sales Mix, & Menu Item Analysis for Standard Food Cost, Menu Explosion (Inventory Shortage Report), Current Menu Item Costing, Automatic Inventory Recorder, Theft Overportation Detection, Inflation Evaluation. Can Be Used with Any Point-of-Sales System. Restaurant Payroll, General Ledger, & Other Programs Are Also Available.
Advanced Analytical/CharterHouse.

Restaurant Management. Fisher Business Systems, Inc. *Operating System(s) Required:* MS-DOS. *Memory Required:* 128k. *General Requirements:* Printer.
$2500.00.
Texas Instruments, Personal Productivit.

Restaurant Management System. Jan. 1982. *Compatible Hardware:* IBM PC, PC AT & compatibles with 2 disk drives, 5-10Mb hard disk. *Operating System(s) Required:* PC-DOS, DOS 2.0. *Language(s):* BASIC. *Memory Required:* 256k.
 disk $5000.00 (Order no.: FBS-001).
 disk $2500.00 (Order no.: FBS-004).
 disk $4750.00 (Order no.: FBS-003).

TITLE INDEX

Performs the Functions of Food Costing/Inventory Control. Manages Daily Reporting, POS Interface, Payroll, Accounts Payable, General Ledger, Analysis, Labor Scheduling, Banquet & Catering.
Fisher Business Systems, Inc.

Restaurant Manager. *Compatible Hardware:* IBM PC, PC XT, PC AT. *Operating System(s) Required:* PC-DOS. *Memory Required:* 256k. *General Requirements:* Hard disk.
disk $3775.00.
Designed for Restaurant Business. Includes Accounts Payable, General Ledger, Payroll & Supplies Inventory. Accounts Payable Posts Directly to the Supplies Inventory for All Purchased Food, Beverage, & Paper Products. The Accounts Payable & Payroll Systems Post Directly to the General Ledger for Each Restaurant Location Maintained.
Business Computer Consultants/Merrill Street Software.

Restaurant Menu Management. *Compatible Hardware:* IBM PC; TRS-80 Model I Level II, Model III, Model 4, Tandy 1000. *Operating System(s) Required:* TRSDOS. *Language(s):* BASIC. *Memory Required:* 16k.
disk or cassette $79.95.
Tells User What to Charge According to Latest Input of Wholesale Food Prices. Capable of Handling Every Item on the Menu.
Viking, Inc.

Restaurant Payroll. *Version:* 8.0. Dec. 1985. *Operating System(s) Required:* MS-DOS. *Memory Required:* 128k. *Items Included:* Manual, training exercises, support. *Customer Support:* 3 months free.
disk $395.00 (Order no.: B28).
Payroll System Written for Small to Medium Size Businesses. Includes All of the Operations Required for Complete Payroll Accounting & Reporting. Handles Meals, Tips, Tip Allocation, & Minimum Wage Make-Up.
ADS Software, Inc.

Restaurant Payroll with Tip Allocation. *Version:* 6.0. Aug. 1983. *Compatible Hardware:* Casio FP 1000; Chameleon; Compaq; Corona; Eagle; Hyperion; IBM PC & compatibles, PC XT, PC AT; Litton Monroe; NCR PC; Stearns; Tava; Televideo 1605; TI Professional; TRS-80 Model I, Model II, Model III, Model 4, Model 12, Model 16, Tandy 2000; Victor 9000; Wang PC. *Language(s):* GW-BASIC, BASICA, C, Compiled BASIC. *Memory Required:* 420k.
disk one-time fee $1200.00 (ISBN 0-922121-07-9, Order no.: PR916).
lease $60.00, per mo.
maintenance $150.00, per yr.
Features Tip Allocation Computation in Accordance with IRS Regulations. Includes Employee Cash & Charge Sale Record Keeping, Pay Rates & Job Descriptions, User Definable Deductions & Tax Table.
Advanced Analytical/CharterHouse.

Resuba Disk Utilities. *Compatible Hardware:* IBM PC. *Language(s):* Assembly. *Memory Required:* 64k.
disk $24.95.
Designed for Use by Novice & System Programmers.
Resuba Digital Systems.

Resuba Print-Switch Utility. *Compatible Hardware:* IBM PC. *Operating System(s) Required:* MS-DOS. *Language(s):* Assembly. *Memory Required:* 64k.
disk $19.95.
Contains the Following Functions: LPT-Two Switches Printers One & Two on a System.

Allows the Second Printer to Act As Printer Number One (Printer Number One Changes to Printer Number Two LPT2). LPT-One Returns the Printers to Normal Assignments.
Resuba Digital Systems.

Resuba Print Utilities. *Compatible Hardware:* IBM PC. *Operating System(s) Required:* MS-DOS. *Language(s):* Assembly. *Memory Required:* 64k.
disk $24.95.
Designed to Allow the IBM PC to Control Most of the Various Print Modes Available on Printers.
Resuba Digital Systems.

Resuba Screen Utilities. *Compatible Hardware:* IBM PC with color monitor. *Operating System(s) Required:* MS-DOS. *Memory Required:* 64k.
disk $24.95.
Designed for Use by Novices & Systems Programmers on the IBM PC. Contains 2 Utilities: "Colors" Is a Series of Utilities That Is Used in Conjunction with DOS 2.00 to Produce Color Combinations When Working with DOS at the Command Level; "States" Are Utilities Supported by All IBM Compatible Monitors & Can Be Used with the Colors Utilities in Most Cases.
Resuba Digital Systems.

Resuba XT-Lock Utility. *Compatible Hardware:* IBM PC. *Language(s):* BASICA. *Memory Required:* 128k. *General Requirements:* Hard disk recommended.
disk $34.95.
Designed to Be Used by Novice & System Programmers. Locks the Keyboard Preventing Unauthorized Use of the Computer.
Resuba Digital Systems.

Results/Plus. *Version:* 5.0. Apr. 1990. *Items Included:* 2 manuals, word processing quick reference guide, keyCard index, training, tutorial, on-site installation. *Customer Support:* Annual support maintenance; includes toll free phone support, modem support, newsletter, free software upgrades, information bulletin board for $1200.00 annually.
DOS 3.x & higher. IBM & compatibles (380k). $3495.00, Stand alone; $4495.00, network version. *Networks supported:* Novell 286, 386.
Non-Profit Application Software Gears Towards Donor Receipting & Management. Personal Solicitations, Acknowledgements & Reminders Are Made Easy with an Internal Word Processing & Mail Management System. Unlimited Reporting Is Made Possible with the REPORT WRITER Which Allows User to Create Custom Reports. In Addition to Custom Reporting, More Than 100 Canned Fund-Raising Reports Are Provided That Provide the Necessary Feed Back on the Success of Users' Appeals & Campaigns.
Matafile Information Systems, Inc.

Resume Master.
Macintosh 512K or higher. 3.5" disk $39.95.
Resume Creation.
Brady Computer Bks.

Resume Profile System. *Compatible Hardware:* IBM PC & compatibles, PC XT, PC AT, PS/2. *Operating System(s) Required:* PC-DOS, MS-DOS 3.xx. *Language(s):* Foxbase PLUS (source code included). *Memory Required:* 640k. *General Requirements:* Hard disk.
disk $695.00.
demo & manual $49.50.
Maintains Applicant & Job Order Files. Matches in 3 Ways: 1) Applicant to All Job Orders, 2) Job Order to All Applicants & 3) Input Any Set of Requirements, Search & Match to All Applicants. Searches Large Applicant Files in Seconds. Matching Applicant Profiles Are Displayed or Printed. Search Criteria Is User-

RESUMES MADE EASY

Definable. Finds Applicants by Name, ID Number, Phone, Location, Salary Range, Skills, Whatever User Defines. Generates Labels. Interfaces with Word Processing Programs to Create Personalized Form Letters.
System Vision Corp.

Resume Profiles Plus. *Compatible Hardware:* IBM PC, PC XT, PC AT. *Operating System(s) Required:* PC-DOS, MS-DOS 3.XX. *Language(s):* Foxbase PLUS (source code included). *Memory Required:* 640k. *General Requirements:* Hard disk.
disk $695.00.
demo disk & manual $49.50.
Includes All the Features of RESUME PROFILE SYSTEM, Plus the Following New Features: Additional Screens for Keeping Confidential Information & Interview Tracking. Scratchpad Facility for Keeping Notes or Complete Resume Narratives. More Reports Including EEO Reports. Archive & Re-Activate Feature for Deleting Inactive Records from the Database & Storing on Floppy Disk for Later Reuse. User Definable Function Keys for Fast Data Entry. Built-In Word Processor. Autodial & a Tutorial System.
System Vision Corp.

Resumemaker Deluxe CD: PRO RWC. Aug. 1995. *Items Included:* User's guide, CD-ROM. *Customer Support:* Free 800-331-3313.
IBM & compatibles. Contact publisher for price (ISBN 0-918617-03-0).
The Ultimate in Complete Job Search Software on CD-ROM. Creates Professional Looking Resumes & Guided Letters, Tracks Target Companies, with Built-In Calendar to Manage Appointments & Contains a Virtual Interview with Job-Hunting Tactics & a Full Career Planning Exercise in Multimedia.
Individual Software.

Resumes Made Easy. Feb. 1996. *Items Included:* Program manual. *Customer Support:* Free technical support, 90 day warranty.
Single user. System 7.1 or higher. Mac, 16 MHz rating, 68030 or better processor (LC II or higher) (5Mb). 3.5" disk $99.95 (ISBN 1-57204-099-8, Order no.: APM155). *Nonstandard peripherals required:* 256 color monitor, 13" or larger.
Lab pack. System 7.1 or higher. Mac, 16 MHz rating, 68030 or better processor (LC II or higher) (5Mb). 3.5" disk $199.00 (ISBN 1-57204-122-6, Order no.: APM155LPK). *Nonstandard peripherals required:* 256 color monitor, 13" or larger.
Site license. System 7.1 or higher. Mac, 16 MHz rating, 68030 or better processor (LC II or higher) (5Mb). 3.5" disk $399.00 (ISBN 1-57204-128-5, Order no.: APM155SITE). *Nonstandard peripherals required:* 256 color monitor, 13" or larger.
Single user. Windows 3.1 or higher. IBM 386 (8Mb). disk $99.95 (ISBN 1-57204-100-5, Order no.: WIN155). *Nonstandard peripherals required:* 256 color monitor, mouse, sound card. *Addl. software required:* SVGA graphics.
Lab pack. Windows 3.1 or higher. IBM 386 (8Mb). disk $199.00 (ISBN 1-57204-123-4, Order no.: WIN155LPK). *Nonstandard peripherals required:* 256 color monitor, mouse, sound card. *Addl. software required:* SVGA graphics.
Site license. Windows 3.1 or higher. IBM 386 (8Mb). disk $399.00 (ISBN 1-57204-125-0, Order no.: WIN155SITE). *Nonstandard peripherals required:* 256 color monitor, mouse, sound card. *Addl. software required:* SVGA graphics.
Explains the different parts of the resume & why resumes are necessary.
Lawrence Productions, Inc.

ResumeWriter. Version: V1.0. Compatible Hardware: Apple Macintosh. Memory Required: 512k. General Requirements: External disk drive. Items Included: Start-up disk & manual. Customer Support: Lisa A. Kosloff 818-706-3887.
Professional version (multiple resumes) $100.00.
Student version (one name only) $30.00.
Desktop Publishing Tool for Personal Resumes.
Bootware Software Co., Inc.

Retail & Plus Management System. Version: 3.5. Aug. 1993. Items Included: User guide, reference manual. Customer Support: 1.) Over-the-shoulder support - 1 yr. subscription $595.00. 2.) Hot-line support - 1 yr. subscription $295.00. 3.) "Express" hardware exchange subscription: price varies with configuration.
MS-DOS. IBM PC XT, AT, PS/2 & compatibles (512k). disk $2995.00 1 location, 1 user licensed. Optimal configuration: Varies with each installation. Networks supported: Artisoft, Lantastic, Novell NetWare & most Net-BIOS LANs.
Fully Featured Retail Automation Package for Single or Multiple Store Locations. Integrates a Simple but Powerful Register & Point-of-Sale Management, Inventory, Order, Customer, End-of-Day & Data Transfer Management. New Enhancements Include a Custom Accounting Interface for General Ledger & Accounts Payable for BusinessWorks Software. Automated Credit Card/Check Processing Is a New Option in Version 3.5.
Paragon Retail Systems.

Retail Florist. ADS Software, Inc. Operating System(s) Required: MS-DOS. Memory Required: 128k. General Requirements: 2 disk drives, printer.
$895.00.
Texas Instruments, Personal Productivit.

Retail Florists Accounting Bundle. Version: 9.0. Jul. 1992. Compatible Hardware: IBM PC & compatibles. Operating System(s) Required: MS-DOS. Language(s): Microsoft BASIC. Memory Required: 640k. General Requirements: Hard disk 20Mb or higher. Items Included: Manual, training exercises. Customer Support: 6 months free.
disk $795.00. Nonstandard peripherals required: hard disk required.
Designed for the Small to Medium-Sized Retail Florist Who Requires Control over Accounts Receivable, Sales Analysis. Allows Posting of Daily Charges & Payments with Detail of All Charges & Sales Analysis up to 99 Sales Categories. Provides Wire Service Reconciliatitons of Daily Invoicing. Purchase History & Customer Files by Name Require Hard Disk, 640k Systems. Also Includes Accounts Payable, Payroll, & General Ledger. Also Available As an Add on Module - Point of Sale That Works with or Without a Cash Drawer.
ADS Software, Inc.

Retail Ice Cream Inventory & Cost Control. Compatible Hardware: IBM PC; TRS-80 Model II, Model III, Model 16. Operating System(s) Required: MS-DOS. (source code included).
contact publisher for price.
Advanced Analytical/CharterHouse.

Retail Inventory Program. Version: 96.1. (Inventory Management Ser.). 1979. Compatible Hardware: IBM PC & compatibles. Operating System(s) Required: PC-DOS/MS-DOS. Language(s): CB86. Memory Required: PD-DOS 128k.
$29.95 (ISBN 0-917081-31-5).
Performs Inventory Control, Purchasing, Labels & Keeps Track of Vendors & Customers. Includes Point-of-Sale. Very Fast & Easy.
CAP Automation.

The Retail Lease Management System. Version: 4.0. Oct. 1993. Items Included: User manual; 30 day warranty period; 30 day technical support. Customer Support: Annual maintenance agreement. Included: unlimited telephone and/or modem support. Free new version, updates, documentation, input on future enhancements, plus special offers on new products (15% of license fee).
MS-DOS. IBM & compatibles (386sx) (1Mb). $995.00-$9995.00 (based on number of properties/leases). Optimal configuration: 486 or higher, 2Mb of RAM or higher, 100Mb HD, Color VGA monitor, laser printer. Networks supported: Lantastic, Novell.
A Comprehensive, PC Based Database System Especially Designed to Assist Real Estate Managers in Managing Information Regarding Leased and/or Owned Property. The System Allows You to Catalog, Retrieve, & Process Information on Any or All Properties in the System. A Complete Reporting System Is Available.
Classic Real Estate Systems, L.L.C.

Retail Management System. Version: 6.1.4. Jun. 1992. Compatible Hardware: IBM PC & compatibles. Operating System(s) Required: MS-DOS. Memory Required: 640k. General Requirements: Hard drive & printer. Customer Support: 90 days free support; 2 optional support plans after that.
disk $649.00.
Point of Sale Inventory System Designed to Meet the Needs of Small Retail Businesses. Prints Out Customer Invoices As It Keeps Track of Inventory. Prints Out Suggested Orders, Inventory Value, & Period Sales Information. Part Numbers May Be up to 14 Characters Long. Report Generator Creates Custom Reports.
Westech Corp.

Retail Master. Nov. 1985. Memory Required: 256k.
disk $2795.00.
Point of Sale Package Including All Accounting Nodules. Alpha or Numeric Look up from All Modules. Serial Number Tracking, Promotional Prices & Product Bundling Are Included in Inventory. Also Includes Complete Order Entry with Pick Slips, Backorders & Invoicing. Point of Sale Provides A/R Interface for Real-Time Credit Checking. Bar Code Readers Are Supported.
Hurricane Systems, Inc.

The Retail Solution. Thomas J. Blaney. Jun. 1981. Compatible Hardware: RS/6000, RT/PC, 30286 & 30386. Operating System(s) Required: AIX, PC-DOS, Unix, Xenix. Language(s): COBOL & Microfocus COBOL. Memory Required: 2000k. General Requirements: Hard disk.
PC-DOS, MS-DOS. disk $2500.00.
Xenix & AIX. $5,000.00.
Provides Complete Inventory Control, Sales Management, Accounts Payable, Accounts Receivable, General Ledger, Mail List, Purchase Order & Inventory Entry Management. Utilizes Display Screen & Cash Drawers at the Point of Sale.
Small Business Management Systems, Inc.

Retail/Wholesale Inventory Control. Version: 1.0. 1988. Compatible Hardware: Altos; Compupro; Fujitsu; Heath-Zenith; HP; IBM PC, PC XT, PC AT; NEC; Tandy. Operating System(s) Required: MS-DOS, PC-DOS, Concurrent DOS, Unix, Xenix; Novell & Microsoft networks. Language(s): C. Memory Required: 512k. General Requirements: Hard disk & 132-column printer.
single-user $995.00.
multi-user $1295.00.
Unix, Xenix $1495.00.
demo disk & manual $20.00.
Produces Stock Report, Price List, Activity Report, Valuation Report, Recorder Report, Physical Inventory Worksheet, etc.
INMASS/MRP.

RetailFORCE. Version: 3.1. Jan. 1985. Compatible Hardware: IBM PC, PC XT, PC AT. Operating System(s) Required: PC-DOS, MS-DOS. Language(s): Compiled BASIC, Assembly. Memory Required: 256k. General Requirements: 132-column printer.
disk $2997.00.
Fully Integrated POS Retail Management System That Includes Inventory Control, Purchasing & Receiving, Accounts Payable & Receivable, Mailing List Management, Backorder Management, Rental/Loaner.
RetailFORCE, Inc.

Retailing. Version: 8B. (Vertical Software Ser.). Sep. 1993. Compatible Hardware: Altos, IBM PC & compatibles, UNISYS, NCR, IBM RT. Operating System(s) Required: PC-DOS/MS-DOS, Unix, Xenix; 3Com, Novell, AIX, Radio Shack networks. Language(s): COBOL 85. Memory Required: Multi-user 3Mb or higher, single-user 1000k. General Requirements: Integrated Accounting. Customer Support: Included with the support for the Integrated Accounting.
Single-User. disk $450.00.
Multi-User. disk $800.00.
Full Point-of-Sale Recording System Which Also Operates a Computer Terminal & Electronic Cash Drawer As a Cash Register. Retailing Handles Many Types of Payments (Cash, Checks, Charge, Gift Certificates, Coupon, Layaway) While Operating Cash Drawers at Many Locations Throughout the Store. It Uses Bar Code Readers. Performs Automatic Item Description & Price, Calculates Change, Inventory Control, Price & Quantity Look up, Sale of Non-Inventory Items, Drawer Maintenance & Reconciliation, Batch Discounts, Line Item Percent Mark-Down & Line Item Dollar Mark-Down, Inventory Availability Inquiry, Tracks Serialized Items, Corrects & Tracks over & under Rings.
Trac Line Software, Inc.

Retainwall. Jul. 1992. Items Included: Manual. Customer Support: 30 day money back guarantee; free telephone support.
Macintosh System 6. Macintosh Plus (1Mb). 3.5" disk $195.00.
Analysis & Design Cantilever Retaining Wall According to the 1991 UBC Building Code.
Daystar Software, Inc.

Retirement Planning. Version: 2.0. Floyd C. Henderson. Aug. 1982. Compatible Hardware: Atari 400, 800, 800XL, 1200; Commodore 64; IBM PC, PC AT & compatibles. Operating System(s) Required: Apple DOS 3.3. Language(s): BASIC (source code included). Memory Required: 48k.
disk $29.95 ea.
Commodore. (ISBN 0-917263-02-2).
Atari. (ISBN 0-917263-00-6).
Calculates Retirement Needs Fully Accounting for Inflation.
Advanced Financial Planning.

Retirement Solutions & Retirement Solutions PLUS. Version: 4.6. Nov. 1986. Compatible Hardware: IBM PC & compatibles, PC XT, PC AT. Operating System(s) Required: MS-DOS. (source code included). Memory Required: 2000k. General Requirements: Lotus 1-2-3 (Release 2.3 or higher for RS Plus). Customer Support: User manual, telephone support.
disk $250.00; $325.00 RS Plus.
Collection of 9 Separate Programs Covers

TITLE INDEX

Various Aspects of IRA & Retirement Planning. Designed for Use by the Professional Advisor (Financial Planner, Insurance Agent, Stock Broker, CPA). Reports Include: IRA PROPOSAL; IRA EXCHANGE; COST OF WAITING; BREAKEVEN; LUMP SUM DISTRIBUTION; & RETIREMENT CAPITAL.
Money Tree Software.

Retriever. *Compatible Hardware:* Apple Macintosh. *Memory Required:* 512k.
3.5" disk $89.95.
Database Desk Accessory.
Exodus Software.

Return of the Jedi AudioClips. *Version:* 1.7. Nov. 1994. *Items Included:* Manual, registration card, sound list. *Customer Support:* Phone technical support.
DOS 5.0, Windows 3.1. PC 286 or higher (2Mb). disk $14.95 (ISBN 1-57303-013-9). *Nonstandard peripherals required:* Sound card recommended. *Optimal configuration:* 286 or higher with 4Mb RAM, DOS 5.0 or later, Windows 3.1 or later, 4-7Mb HD space available, sound card.
AudioClips Are Exclusively Licensed High Quality Sound Files Consisting of Classic Sound Effects, Dialogue & Music from Original TV Shows & Movies. Also Included Is the "Whoop It Up" Audio Utility, Which Allows the User to Attach AudioClips to Various Windows Events.
Sound Source Interactive.

Return on Investment. *Version:* 1.00. *Compatible Hardware:* ALTOS Series 5-15D, Series 5-5D, 580-XX, ACS8000-XX; DEC Rainbow 100 with 2 disk drives, Rainbow 100+ with 10MB hard disk; IBM PC with 2 disk drives, PC XT, IBM compatibles; Kaypro 11/IV with 2 disk drives, Kaypro 10; Xerox 820 with 2 disk drives; ZILOG MCZ-250. *Operating System(s) Required:* CP/M, MP/M, CP/M-86/80, PC-DOS, MS-DOS.
License fee unit. $375.00 (Order no.: ROI).
License fee site. $590.00.
Maintenance unit. $75.00.
Maintenance site. $118.00.
Provides Four Methods for Computing the Internal Rate of Return for a Series of Cash Flows with a Specified Capital Gains Liability at Project Termination: Discounted Cash Flow Internal Rate of Return, Dual Terminal Rate of Return, Terminal Rate of Return, & the Sinking Fund Method. Also Handles Timed Investments & Timed Cash Flows. Once This Information Is Provided, Two Reports Are Printed: a Report Devoted to Internal & Terminal Rates of Return, Sinking Fund Report.
Coopers & Lybrand.

Return on Investment Analysis. 1982. *Compatible Hardware:* MS-DOS based machines. *Language(s):* Microsoft BASIC, BASICA.
disk $55.00 (Order no.: 260).
Analyzes the International Return on Investment Using the Discounted Cash Flow Technique to Determine a Compatible Criteria from Which to Analyze Different Investment Opportunities.
Resource Software International, Inc.

The Reunion Planner. Jun. 1992. *Items Included:* Staple bound manual. *Customer Support:* 30 day free technical support.
MS-DOS. IBM XT, AT, & compatible (640k).
disk $42.95 (ISBN 0-9630516-4-4).
Reunion Planning Software for Class, Family, or Other Large Group Reunions. Program Tracks Alumni/Guest Information, & Has Budgeting & Statistical Analysis Capabilities. Special Text Editor Is Included to Enable Design & Printing of Invitations & Notices.
Goodman Lauren Publishing.

Reveille Accounting: Advanced Revelation. *Version:* 5.4. Jul. 1992. *Items Included:* 4 user manuals & runtime version of Advanced Revelation DMGS. *Customer Support:* 30 days free support, $250.00 per 3 hour block thereafter.
MS-DOS, OS/2. IBM & compatibles, LAN's (512k). $495.00 for runtime; $1995.00 per 5 user LANPack; $4485.00 for source & runtime. *Addl. software required:* Advanced Revelation Development required for changing menus of screens. *Networks supported:* Novell, Banyan & LANtastic.
Complete Accounting System Consisting of General Ledger, Accounts Payable, Accounts Receivable & System Manager. User Definable GL Account Structure, Financial Reports, Subsidiary Ledgers. Variable Length Memos & Descriptions, Check Reconciliation, Cash or Accrual Checks & Vendor History. User Defined Invoices, Quotations. Customer Tracking & Sales Analysis. No Limit of Tax Authorities. Created in ADVANCED REVELATION.
Microx, Inc.

Reveille Distribution: Advanced Revelation. *Version:* 5.4. Jul. 1992. *Items Included:* 3 user manuals. *Customer Support:* 30 days free support, $250.00 for 3 hour block thereafter.
MS-DOS. IBM & compatibles, LAN's (512k). $495.00 single user, $1995.00 5 user, for runtime; $4485.00 for source & runtime. *Addl. software required:* Reveille Accounting. *Optimal configuration:* 386 DX33 for file server, 386 SX20 for workstations. *Networks supported:* Novell, Banyan & LANtastic.
Complete Distribution System Integrated with REVEILLE ACCOUNTING. Order Entry Screens May Be Customized. Inventory Has Short & Long Descriptions, Multiple Pricing Tables. Add Fields to Inventory Record Easily. Purchase Orders, Order Forms & Pick Tickets May Be Formatted to User's Requirements. 20 Character Part Numbers & Fractional Quantities Supported. Serial Number Tracking Supported. Created in Advanced Revelation.
Microx, Inc.

REVEILLE for Windows: Visual Basic. Sep. 1994. *Items Included:* User manual. *Customer Support:* Technical support - 30 days free, thereafter $250.00 for 3 hours or $750.00 for 10 hours.
Windows 3.1 or MS-DOS. 386/486 IBM compatible. $495.00 for Runtime, $1495.00 for LAN, $1995.00 for Source Code. *Addl. software required:* Windows 3.1. *Networks supported:* Novell.
Integrated Accounting & Payroll System Written in Visual BASIC Using the Access Data Base. Modules Include General Ledger, Accounts Payable, Accounts Receivable, Check Reconciliation & Payroll. GL Has 24 Months of On-Line Data, 12 Digit Account No's & Supports Departments. Payroll & Payables Support Conventional & Laser Checks. Source Code Available.
Microx, Inc.

Reveille Payroll: Advanced Revelation. *Version:* 5.4. Jul. 1992. *Items Included:* User manual. *Customer Support:* 30 days free support, $250.00 per 3 hour block thereafter.
MS-DOS, OS/2. IBM & compatibles, LAN's (512k). $495.00 single user, $1995.00 5 user, for runtime; $2495.00 for source & runtime. *Addl. software required:* Reveille Accounting GL. *Optimal configuration:* 386 DX33 for file server, 386 SX20 for workstations. *Networks supported:* Novell, Banyan & LANtastic.
Comprehensive Payroll with User Definable Paycodes, Check & Report Formats. Unlimited Deductions, Allowances, Tax, Department &

REVISED STANDARD VERSION TEXT

Workers Comp Codes. Extensive Employment History & Personnel Data. Users May Add Many Fields of Desired Length. Created in ADVANCED REVELATION 2.12.
Microx, Inc.

Revise. *Version:* 1.11. Mar. 1991.
PC-DOS, MS-DOS (64k). 3.5" or 5.25" disk $39.95 (ISBN 0-933737-03-3, Order no.: RMN).
Revises Files by Time & Date. Avoids Delays Caused by Unnecessary Copying of Files. Backs up to DOS Formatted Disks. Optionally Revises Only Matching Files & Copies Directory Trees. Can Also Flatten a Directory Tree to One Directory & Spread One Directory to Every Subdirectory at Once.
Hersey Micro Consulting, Inc.

Revised Standard Version. Mar. 1990. *Customer Support:* No fee is charged for our customer support: 30 day money back return guarantee; lifetime warranty on defective disk replacement; free telephone technical support.
PC or MS-DOS 2.0 or higher. IBM PC/XT/AT or compatible. 3.5" or 5.25" disk $49.95. *Addl. software required:* PC STUDY BIBLE. *Optimal configuration:* Hard disk with 1.5Mb hard disk space.
The Text of the Revised Standard Version of the Bible. Add-On Bible Version to Be Used with BIBLESOFT'S PC STUDY BIBLE.
Biblesoft.

Revised Standard Version. International Council of Religious Education & National Council of Churches. May 1993. *Customer Support:* No fee for customer support: (1) 30 day money back guarantee (2) Lifetime warranty replacement on defective disks (3) Free telephone technical support.
PC-DOS/MS-DOS 2.0 or higher. IBM PC, XT, AT/286/386/486 or 100% compatibles (640k). disk $49.95 (ISBN 1-56514-595-X). *Addl. software required:* PC Study Bible. *Optimal configuration:* Requires 5 1/4" 1.2Mb disk drive for installation & 3Mb of hard drive space. Mouse or pointer device recommended.
Text of the REVISED STANDARD VERSION of the Bible. Add-On Bible Version to Be Used with BIBLESOFT's PC Study Bible.

Revised Standard Version Text. *Items Included:* Disks, marketing literature, order form. *Customer Support:* No fee for customer support: 30 day money back guarantee, limited replacement warranty on diskettes defective at time of purchase, free telephone technical support.
PC-DOS/MS-DOS 3.0 or higher or Windows 3.1 or higher. IBM 386/486 or 100% compatible (Windows); Also AT/XT/286 (DOS) (640k DOS or 4Mb Windows). 3.5" disk $39.95 (ISBN 1-56514-213-6). *Addl. software required:* Biblesoft's PC Study Bible. *Optimal configuration:* 3.5" disk drive for installation & 1.5Mb of hard drive space, mouse or pointer device recommended.
The Text of the Revised Standard Version of the Bible - an Add-On Version to Be Used with Biblesoft's PC Study Bible.
Biblesoft.

Revised Standard Version Text. International Council of Religious Education Staff & National Council of Churches Staff. May 1993. *Items Included:* Disks, marketing literature, order form. *Customer Support:* No fee for customer support: 30 day money back guarantee, limited replacement warranty on diskettes defective at time of purchase, free telephone technical support.
PC-DOS/MS-DOS 3.1 or higher or MS Windows 3.0 or higher. 386/486 or 100%

873

IBM compatible (Windows); Also AT/XT/286 (DOS) (640k DOS or 4Mb Windows). disk $39.95 (ISBN 1-56514-595-X). *Addl. software required:* Biblesoft's PC Study Bible. *Optimal configuration:* Requires 5.25" 1.2Mb disk drive for installation & 1.5Mb of hard drive space, mouse or pointer device recommended.
The Text of the Revised Standard Bible - an Add-On Bible Version to Be Used with Biblesoft's PC Study Bible.
Biblesoft.

Revolution Brew. Annette Werle & Milton Honel. *Items Included:* Teacher's Guide.
Apple IIc, IIe, IIgs & MAC LC with a IIe card. 3.5" disk $49.99 (Order no.: RB02). *Addl. software required:* ProDOS.
(5) 5 1/2" floppy disks $49.99 (Order no.: RB01).
Covers All the Major Events in England & the Colonies Leading to the American Revolutionary War. Through Role-Playing, Makes the Events That Drove the American Colonists to Revolt Against England Personally Meaningful. Comprehension Questions Keep the Player on Course Throughout the Program. Scoring Is Used As an Incentive to High Performance. Record Keeping Is Done on a Data Disk.
Trillium Pr.

Revolution '76. Jun. 1989. *Compatible Hardware:* Apple IIgs & IBM (768k). *Items Included:* User manual, historical guide, catalog insert. *Customer Support:* 90-day money back guarantee, 30-day preview policy with purchase order number, backup disks $7.50, free replacement for damaged disks if under 90-day warranty.
disk $49.95. *Nonstandard peripherals required:* RGB monitor.
Engages Player in American Colonists' Struggle for Independence. Allows Player to Select Generals, Unite Colonies, Build Armies & Make or Break Alliances. Player's Aim Is to Force the British to Acknowledge Defeat.
Compton's NewMedia, Inc.

Rex Nebular: And the Cosmic Gender Bender. Sep. 1992. *Items Included:* 2 manuals. *Customer Support:* Free customer service, 1-410-771-1151, Ext. 350.
80286/80386/80486; hard disk required; 12MHz. IBM PC & compatibles (640k). disk $69.95. *Nonstandard peripherals required:* MCGA or VGA graphic cards. *Optimal configuration:* Joystick/mouse supported; supports Roland, Adlib, Sound Blaster & Corox sound cards. 80386/80486; 16MHz; 1-2Mb RAM; MS-DOS 5.0 Plus.
The Most Far-Out Animated Graphic Adventure Ever to Land on Store Shelves! Along with a Versatile New Interface System, the Game Combines Raucous Space Adventure & Comedy with the Most Dazzling Graphics Ever to Enhance a PC Screen.
MicroProse Software.

RGEN: Report Generator. *Version:* 3.0. Nov. 1985. *Compatible Hardware:* IBM PC. *Operating System(s) Required:* PC-DOS 2.0 or higher. *Language(s):* COBOL, Assembly. *Memory Required:* 256k.
disk $495.00 (Order no.: RGEN).
demo disk free (Order no.: PRI.RGX).
Developed Primarily to Be Used with the Library of CRS PC Accounting Packages to Produce Reports Using Data Items Contained in the Major Data Files. Also Gives Users the Ability to Create & Update Their Own Data Files & Reporting Requirements.
Computer Related Services, Inc.

Rhino Records Catalog, 1995. *Version:* 1.1. Mar. 1995. *Items Included:* Free software for accessing the catalog. *Customer Support:* One year free support via phone, mail, fax & BBS.
MS-DOS Version 3.3 or higher. Any IBM compatible (440k). disk $6.00.
Interactive Computer-Based Catalog for Rhino Records. Can Search for Individual Songs, Artists, Type of Music & More. Prints Reports & Automatically Handles Orders for CDs & Tapes.
PSG-HomeCraft Software.

Rhintek Pascal Compiler. 1977. *Compatible Hardware:* Data General. *Language(s):* Pascal. *Memory Required:* 32k. *Customer Support:* Telephone support.
Data General. $3000.00-$3500.00.
Compiler with Error Messages & 400 Lines/Minute Compile Speed Including Binding. Has 17-Digit Precision on Floating Variables & over 1400 Unique Identifiers.
Rhintek, Inc.

Rhintek Plot Package. 1977. *Compatible Hardware:* Data General; DEC. *Language(s):* FORTRAN (source code included). *Memory Required:* 4k.
computer tape $1050.00.
Set of Routines Supplied in Source Form Which Allows Any Printronix Printer Plotter or D6 LP2/TP2 Printer Plotter to Plot.
Rhintek, Inc.

RHUBARB: A Text Reconstruction Tool. *Version:* MS-DOS - Apple. Robert Leonard. 1987. *Items Included:* Disks - 5.25 or 3.50, documentation - registration agreement. *Customer Support:* Lifetime guarantee.
MS DOS, Apple IIe (64k). Single Copy, $69.95 - Site License, $139.95 (ISBN 0-940503-72-7). *Networks supported:* Network copy available.
Allows Teachers to Quickly & Easily Enter Reading Passages Tailored to Needs of Their Classes. Masks the Text & Students Solve the Passage, Has Help & Hint Features & Keep Scores That Can Be Printed Out. Can Also Be Used As a Learning Tool in the Home.
Research Design Assocs., Inc.

RHVAC: Residential HVAC Loads. *Items Included:* Manual. *Customer Support:* Free toll free telephone support.
IBM PC & compatibles (256k). disk $395.00.
Calculates Peak Heating & Cooling Loads for Residential & Small Commercial Buildings. Works in Full Accordance with the Methods Described in the Seventh Edition of the ACCA Manual J.
Elite Software Development, Inc.

Rhymer. Dec. 1990. *Items Included:* Workbook, bound manuals, templates. *Customer Support:* 800-541-5096 toll free phone number & support.
DOS 2.0 or higher. IBM PC & compatibles (34k). disk $89.00. *Optimal configuration:* Hard disk space: 500k.
Phonetic Word Finder. This Terminate-and-Stay-Resident Program Reviews Over 93,000 Words in Search of Specific Rhyme & Phonetic Word Patterns. Search Options Include Alliteration, First Syllable Sound Matching, Double & Triple Rhyme, & Beginning, Ending, & Internal Rhyme.
WordPerfect Corp.

RIA-III. 1983. *Compatible Hardware:* Apple II, IIe; IBM PC; TRS-80 Model I, Model II, Model III, Model 4, Model 12, Model 16. *Operating System(s) Required:* CP/M-80, PC-DOS. *Memory Required:* TRS-80 Model I, III 48k, others 64k. *General Requirements:* Printer.
TRS-80 Model II, 12, 16. disk $45.00.
CP/M. 8" disk $45.00.
disk $30.00 ea.
TRS-80 Model I, III, 4; IBM PC; Apple.

AMORT-I with any of the above $20.00.
Analysis of Commercial or Personal Home & Condominium Real Estate Investments. Makes Calculations for Projects & Prints Reports.
Documan Software.

Richard Scarry Series. Feb. 1995.
MS-DOS 3.1 or higher. 386 processor or higher (640k RAM). CD-ROM disk $99.90, Set (Order no.: R0999). *Nonstandard peripherals required:* CD-ROM drive. *Optimal configuration:* 386 processor or higher, MS-DOS 3.1 or higher, 20Mb hard drive, external speakers or headphones (with sound card) that are Sound Blaster compatible, VGA graphics & adapter, VGA color monitor.
Macintosh (4Mb). (Order no.: R0999A). *Nonstandard peripherals required:* 14" color monitor or larger, CD-ROM drive.
This Delightful Educational Adventure Challenges Creativity & Helps Children Develop Language & Social Skills, Exercise Creative Thinking, Build Memory, & Practice Problem Solving Through Games, Songs, Counting, Real Life Situations & More (Ages 3 & Up). 2 Volume Set.
Library Video Co.

Richard Scarry's How Things Work. (Richard Scarry Ser.). Feb. 1995.
MS-DOS 3.1 or higher. 386 processor or higher (640k RAM). CD-ROM disk $49.95 (Order no.: R1283). *Nonstandard peripherals required:* CD-ROM drive. *Optimal configuration:* 386 processor or higher, MS-DOS 3.1 or higher, 20Mb hard drive, external speakers or headphones (with sound card) that are Sound Blaster compatible, VGA graphics & adapter, VGA color monitor.
Macintosh (4Mb). (Order no.: R1283A). *Nonstandard peripherals required:* 14" color monitor or larger, CD-ROM drive.
This Delightful Educational Adventure Challenges Creativity & Helps Children Develop Language & Social Skills, Exercise Creative Thinking, Build Memory, & Practice Problem Solving Through Games, Songs, Counting, Real Life Situations & More (Ages 3 & Up).
Library Video Co.

Ricochet. EPYX, Inc. *Compatible Hardware:* HP 150 Touchscreen.
3.5" disk $39.95 (Order no.: 92243GB).
Strategic Game in Which You Test Your Wit Against the Computer or Another Opponent. The Screen Is Reminiscent of the Billiards Table, with Additional Barriers Which Increase the Difficulty of Judging the Ultimate Path of Each Projectile. You Shoot Your Launcher Against Your Opponent's Barriers. Each Projectile Causes the Barriers to Turn 90 Degrees Causing an Entirely New Board Layout for Each Shot. You Can Choose to Alter the Layout of Your Barriers in Exchange for a Launch at Any Point in the Game. Several Variances & Levels of Difficulty Are Available.
Hewlett-Packard Co.

RICS: Retail Inventory Control System. *Version:* 5.1. Jan. 1984. *Compatible Hardware:* IBM PC & compatibles. *Operating System(s) Required:* PC-DOS, MS-DOS. *Memory Required:* 640k. *General Requirements:* Wide carriage printer, DOS 5.0. *Customer Support:* 60 day free warranty, $500 per year for annual support & enhancements. Includes toll free number.
disk $2495.00 to $4495.00.
Designed Specifically for Shoe, Apparel & Athletic Retailers. Handles Tracking for Single or Multiple Stores & Multiple Sizes, Widths, or Colors Within the Same Item Number. Includes Analysis by Store, Department, Category, Vendor, Size, Width, Color & Salesperson. System Includes Purchase Order System, Stock

TITLE INDEX

Labels, Bar Coding, & Mail List. A Point-of-Sale Module & Networking Module Are Also Available.
C.S.I. Services Corp.

Ride for Your Life. *Compatible Hardware:* Commodore 64, 128. *General Requirements:* Pulse Rate sensor & Sensor Adapter Cable.
ROM cartridge $49.95 (Order no.: SOFC64-07-010/C).
After Inputing Personal Data, the Program Measures User's Heart Rate. It Then Determines & Provides the Most Ideal Aerobic Workout. A Continuous Progress Report of Heart Rate, Calories Burned, Session Time Remaining, & a Graph of Actual & Ideal Exercise Level Are Displayed. User Can Participate in a Video Game by Helping a Cyclist to Avoid Colliding with City Traffic.
Bodylog.

RIG Color Program: Computerized Color Pattern Selection. *Version:* 1.1. Gary Peek. Feb. 1993. *Items Included:* Fabric samples, manual. *Customer Support:* Unlimited warranty, free telephone support.
MS-DOS. IBM (640k). disk $14.95 (ISBN 0-915516-87-X, Order no.: RIGCOLOR). *Optimal configuration:* EGA or VGA color monitor.
Parachute Harness & Container Color Combinations May Be Viewed & Compared on the Screen. This Program Replaces Paper & Color Pencils.
Para Publishing.

RightWords: RightWriter Dictionary Utility.
Version: 2.1. Oct. 1985. *Compatible Hardware:* IBM PC & compatibles. *Operating System(s) Required:* PC-DOS/MS-DOS 2.0 or higher. *Language(s):* C. *Memory Required:* 256k.
General Requirements: Hard disk.
disk $29.95.
Allows Users to Customize Dictionaries by Adding up to 100,000 Words, Including Lists of Common, Uncommon, Buzz, & Slang Words. Features Expanded 45,000 Word Dictionary for Use with RIGHTWRITER & Seven Word Lists for Special Areas.
Que Software.

RightWriter. *Version:* 4.0. May 1989. *Compatible Hardware:* Chameleon; Columbia MPC & MPV-VP; Compaq, Compaq Plus, Compaq 286, Compaq Pro; Eagle PC; HP 150 Touchscreen, HP Vectra; IBM PC & compatibles, PC XT, PC AT; ITT XTRA, XTRA XP; NCR PC-4, PC-6, PC-8; Panasonic Sr. Partner; Seequa; Tandy 1000, 1200 HD, 2000; TI Professional. *Operating System(s) Required:* PC-DOS, MS-DOS, OS/2. *Language(s):* C. *Memory Required:* 384k. *Items Included:* 2 5.25" disks, 1 3.5" disk, 1 demo disk, manual. *Customer Support:* Free, via 800 number.
disk $95.00.
Automatic Document Proofreader Incorporating Artificial Intelligence Techniques to Analyze Documents for Errors in Grammar, Usage, Punctuation, & Style. Messages Are Inserted Directly into the Text to Point out Possible Errors & Problem Areas. Provides Indexes That Measure the Strength of Delivery, Readability, Use of Adverbs & Adjectives, & the Use of Jargon. Calculates the Reading Level of a Document Using the Fog, the Flesch, & the Flesch-Kinkaid Formulas. Works with Most Popular Word Processors.
Que Software.

RIMS-MPG.
contact publisher for price.
Micro Focus, Inc. (California).

The Rings of the Empire. *Compatible Hardware:* Atari 400, 800. *Language(s):* Atari BASIC (source code included). *Memory Required:* 32k. *General Requirements:* Joystick.
disk $18.95.
Space Arcade Game.
Dynacomp, Inc.

RIO. *Version:* 7.0. *Compatible Hardware:* IBM PC & compatibles. *Items Included:* RIO Software, 250 PostScript Type 1 fonts, including European characters, user guide, installation guide, devices & externals guide. *Customer Support:* Free customer support - only cost is phone charge. TARGA board. disk $995.00.
Targa, ATVista, Matrox, VGA.
A 2-D Design & Illustration Software Program Which Can Be Used to Generate Slides, Prints, Transparencies & Images for Video Production & Multimedia Presentations. It Provides Vector-Based Drawing Tools & Object-Oriented Technology to Enable Constant Revisions. Allows Users to Type & Edit On-Screen with a WYSIWYG Interface, & Offers Unlimited Layering of Graphics. Drivers Are Included for a Wide Range of Input & Output Devices As Well As Full Color Editable Previews.
AT&T Multimedia Software Solutions.

Rio.
MS-DOS 5.0 or higher. 386 or higher (8Mb). Contact publisher for price. *Nonstandard peripherals required:* 20Mb available on hard drive (additional space required for image storage), 3.5" high density (1.44Mb) disk drive, mouse and/or digitizing tablet, graphic display cards: VGA VESA 24-bit compliant or TARGA, TARGA Plus, ATVista, Matrox or compatible video display card.
Gives User the Smooth Movement That Only Frame-Accurate Animation Can Provide. User Can Animate Your Company's Logo, Actively Illustrate Sales Trends, Dramatically Demonstrate a New Product or Even Generate Sophisticated Broadcast-Quality Television Productions.
AT&T Multimedia Software Solutions.

Ripper! *Compatible Hardware:* Commodore 64/128.
disk $25.00 (Order no.: 47355).
Role Playing Adventure Game. Jack the Ripper Has Returned! It Is the Early 1900s & You Have Been Assigned to the Case. Some of the Greatest Minds of the Victorian Era Have Been Gathering at a Manor in Hyde Park to Assist You in Solving the Case... but You Suspect That Bloody Jack May Be One of Them. Capture Jack Before He Finds You!
Avalon Hill Game Co., The Microcomputer Games Div.

River Chase. *Compatible Hardware:* Commodore 64. *General Requirements:* Joystick.
disk $19.95.
Save Higgins from a Fleet of Deadly Gunboats.
Dynacomp, Inc.

RJE-PLUS. *Operating System(s) Required:* UNIX or UNIX-like environment. *Memory Required:* 1000k.
contact publisher for price.
Expands the Batch Processing Capabilities of the User's Computer. Emulates IBM's Remote Job Entry Hardware Devices Using Either SNA or BBC Protocols. The BSC Version Offers a Selectable Level of Emulation, 2780/3780/HASP. The SBA Version Emulates an IBM 3770 Workstation Fully Integratable with All Other Components in the Rabbit Family of Business Computing Software.
Rabbit Software Corp.

RLSM FLORIDA VERSION: A-C & HEATING

RJL Baseball Statbook. 1986. *Compatible Hardware:* IBM PC & compatibles. *Operating System(s) Required:* DOS 2.1 or higher. *Memory Required:* 256k.
disk $69.00 (Order no.: D9601).
Over 50 Standard & 6 User-Defined Player Statistics. Allows Multiple Teams. Automatically Calculates 12 Stats. Prints Player Lists in User-Specified Statistical Order, Custom Reports.
Briley Software.

RJL Basketball Stats. 1985. *Compatible Hardware:* IBM PC & compatibles. *Operating System(s) Required:* DOS 2.1 or higher. *Memory Required:* 256k.
disk $59.00 (Order no.: D9651).
Maintains Player & Team Records Year-to-Date. Allows Multiple Teams. Automatically Calculates 17 Statistics. Prints Player or Team Lists in User-Specified Statistical Order.
Briley Software.

RJL Football Stats. *Compatible Hardware:* IBM PC & compatibles. *Operating System(s) Required:* DOS 2.1 or higher. *Memory Required:* 256k. *General Requirements:* Printer.
disk $79.00 (Order no.: D9611).
Keeps Player & Team Records Year-to-Date. Allows Multiple Teams. Over 90 Standard & User-Defined Statistics. Prints Player Lists Ordered by Any Statistics, As Well As Team Lists.
Briley Software.

RJL Sports Statsbook. *Compatible Hardware:* IBM PC & compatibles. *Operating System(s) Required:* DOS 2.1 or higher. *Language(s):* BASIC. *Memory Required:* 256k.
disk $49.00 (Order no.: D9621).
Keeps Player & Team Records Year-to-Date. Allows for Multiple Teams. Auto-Calculation of 25 Statistics. Prints Player Lists Ordered by Any Statistic, As Well As Team Lists. This Product Is Intended for Those Sports Not Specifically Covered by Other Briley Software Packages, Such As Hockey, Soccer, etc.
Briley Software.

RLSM Florida Version: A-C & Heating Loads & Florida Special Energy Analysis. *Version:* 03/1995. Jul. 1993. *Items Included:* Detailed manuals, sample jobs, worksheets. *Customer Support:* Technical hotline, "Lifetime" support at no charge.
PC-DOS/MS-DOS. IBM & compatibles (512k).
disk $370.00. *Optimal configuration:* 386 or higher processor, color monitor, hard disk, dot matrix, laser or inkjet printer. *Networks supported:* Single user program.
Uses Latest ASRAE Residential & ACCA Manual "J" Procedures to Calculate Residential/Condominium/Light Commercial Cooling/Heating Loads, Annual Energy Requirements & Operating Costs. This New Florida Version Takes All Inputs Necessary for the New Florida Energy Efficiency Evaluation & Automatically Runs the Official Florida State Program "RES93". No Additional Inputs Are Necessary. Allows User Inputs of Commercial Construction Materials As Well As Calling the Complete ACCA List of Materials Automatically. Handles Heat Pumps, Mobile Homes, Cathedral Ceilings, Building Rotation, Radiant or Hot Air Heating; R-Values to R-57. Gives Air CFM or Baseboard Heating Requirements. Bin Method for Energy. Automatic Weather & Bin Data for 900 Cities. State-of-the-Art Full-Function Interactive Prompted Input Screens with Windows, Pop-Up Calculator, Defaults, Error Checking, Color or B/W, Almost 200 "Help" & Error Messages, etc. Prints Highly Personalized Presentation Offer for Client. English Units.
MC2 Engineering Software.

RM/CO* Nov. 1989. *Items Included:* Documentation, user's guide. *Customer Support:* Free 90-day introductory support, multitiered RM/CareWare support levels available.
MS-DOS, 2.1 or higher, UNIX. IBM PC, PC-compatible, IBM PS/2 micros (640K). disk call for price (Order no.: P10). *Addl. software required:* RM/COBOL-85 version 4.0 for MS-DOS, RM/COBOL-85 version 5.0 for UNIX or UNIX based. *Optimal configuration:* single diskette drive plus 10mb hard disk 80-column display.
Integrated COBOL Development Environment. Sets up a Fully Menu-Driven RM/COBOL-85 Environment with Hot Key Access to Compile, Execute, & Debug COBOL Programs. Also Provides Full Project Management Capabilities, Program Animation, & a Powerful Editor with Visible Diagnostics & Programmable Function Keys.
Liant Software Corp.

RM/COBOL. *Version:* 6.00.01. Aug. 1994. *Items Included:* User's guide, language reference manual, & syntax summary pamphlet. *Customer Support:* Free 90-day introductory support, multi-tiered RM/CareWare support levels.
PC-DOS/MS-DOS 3.0, UNIX, XENIX, SUN OS, HP UX. IBM PC & compatibles (256k). Call for price. *Optimal configuration:* 1Mb RAM, 40Mb fixed disk drive.
Modern COBOL Compiler/Runtime System Conforming to Both 1985 & 1974 ANSI Standards for the COBOL Language. An Error-Free, High Level Implementation of the ANSI X3.23-1985 Standard, RM/COBOL-85 Contains Language Extension Elements to Be X/Open Compliant. Allows the Compilation of Applications for Machine-Independent Portable Object That Can Be Rehosted without Access to th Original Source code. Has Object, Data, File, Human Factors, & Source Portability. Version 5 Includes New Features Such As Pop-up Windows, the READ PREVIOUS Statement, & the START LESS THAN Statement.
Liant Software Corp.

RM/Companion. *Version:* 2.5. Jul. 1994. *Items Included:* User's guide. *Customer Support:* 90 days of technical support at no charge; choice of multilevel support with RM/CareWare.
PC-DOS/MS-DOS. Will run under any operating system supported by RM/COBOL-85 and has substantially the same hardware & software requirements as RM/COBOL-85. contact publisher for price. *Addl. software required:* RM/COBOL-85 version 5 or later.
UNIX & UNIX-based systems. Will run under any operating system supported by RM/COBOL-85 and has substantially the same hardware & software requirements as RM/COBOR-85. contact publisher for price.
Report Writer That Is Fully Menu Driven with On-Screen Help. Supports Sorting, Selection, Calculations, Formating, Wildcards & Nesting of Conditional Decisions. Information Can Be Accessed From Multiple Files & Combined into a Single Report.
Liant Software Corp.

RM/Forte. May 1987. *Compatible Hardware:* IBM PC, 80286, 80386, 80486. *Operating System(s) Required:* PC-DOS. *Memory Required:* 64k. *General Requirements:* RM/Fortran 3.1. disk $595.00 (Order no.: F-DOS-DS).
Integrated Software Development Environment That Comes with RM/FORTRAN. Automatically Manages & Tracks All Program Files, Combining Several Development Tools into a Single Operating Environment & Simplifying the Software Testing Process. Integrates the Basic Programming Functions of Editing, Compiling, Linking & Debugging. Bundled with the Latest Release of RM/Fortran, Version 3.5.
Liant Software Corp.

RM-Fortran. *Version:* 3.10. May 1987. *Compatible Hardware:* IBM PC, 80286, 80386, 80486. *Operating System(s) Required:* PC-DOS, OS/2. *Memory Required:* 64k. disk $595.00 (Order no.: F-DOS-DS).
The Newest Release of RM/FORTRAN. Includes RM/Forte, an Integrated Software Development Environment. Also Includes a Syntax Checking-Only Capability, a Faster Math Coprocessor Emulation Library, Improved Inter-Language Communication & Enhanced Documentation. The 8087/80287 Emulator Has Been Enhanced to Make Programs Execute Almost Five Times Faster Than Earlier Versions of RM/FORTRAN.
Liant Software Corp.

RM/Panels. *Version:* 2.1.0. May 1994. *Items Included:* User's guide. *Customer Support:* Free 90-day introductory support, multi-tiered RM/CareWare support levels.
MS-DOS, UNIX & UNIX-based. IBM PC, PC-compatible, IBM PS/2, 68000-based system. Call for price. *Optimal configuration:* 1Mb RAM, 40-Mb fixed disk drive, version 5 of RM/COBOL-85.
Ryan McFarland's New Screen Management System That Gives the RM/COBOL-85 Programmer Capability in Developing a User Interface for Applications. Combines a Sohisticated Screen Painter with a Library of Functions & Adds Features Such As On-Screen Help & Screen Printing to an Application without Requiring Additional Coding.
Liant Software Corp.

RM/plus DB. *Version:* 2.00. Aug. 1993. *Items Included:* Spiral-bound user's guide. *Customer Support:* 90 days of technical support at no charge; choice of multilevel support with RM/CareWare.
UNIX (OG/UX, HP-UX, AIX, Interactive 386/ix, UNIX V SCO UNIX V/386, SCO XENIX 386, SUN OS). Data General, Hewlett-Packard, IBM RISC/6000, IBM PC & compatibles, NCR Tower 200/400/600, NCR Tower 300/500/700, NCR System, SUN Sparcstation. contact publisher for price. *Addl. software required:* Informix version 4, RM/COBOL-85 V5 or later. *Optimal configuration:* version specific.
Bi-Directional Gateway Between RM/COBOL-85 Applications & Industry-Standard Database Products. Allows the COBOL Program to Use Normal ANSI & X/Open COBOL Input-Output Statements to Access Either COBOL File System Data or Relational Databases.
Liant Software Corp.

RMS: Radiology Management System. *Version:* 5.0. Mar. 1992. *Items Included:* Video training tape, tutorial guide, 1 3-Ring manual. *Customer Support:* 1 year phone support, upgrades, maintenance, $1750.00 on-site training - $800.00/day plus expenses.
DOS (640k). IBM PC & compatibles (PS/2, XT, AT, 386, 486). $15,995.00. *Addl. software required:* Novell Netware for networks. *Optimal configuration:* Color monitor, 286 PC with 150Mb HD, Dot Matrix printer, tape backup, modem & UPS. *Networks supported:* Novell (all versions above & including 2.15).
Radiology Management Which Was Designed Specifically for Small Hospitals (300 Beds & Under). It Contains Modules for Scheduling, Transcription, Quality Control, Inventory, Standard Procedures, Billing, Film Tracking & Equipment Maintenance. Also Applicable to Clinics & Private Practices.
Swearingen Software.

RMS-II: A Resource Management System. *Version:* 9.0. 1980. *Compatible Hardware:* IBM PC & compatibles. *Operating System(s) Required:* MS-DOS, PC-DOS 2.1 or higher. *Language(s):* CB-86. *Memory Required:* 512k. *General Requirements:* Hard disk, 132-column printer.
$995.00.
Sub-System to PMS-II. Provides for the Definition of up to 192 Resource Centers, Each with Unique Capabilities, in Hours per Day, Wage Rate, & Burden Rate. Any Portion of Any Resource Can Be Allocated (up to 32,600 Allocations) to Any Activity in Any Project Defined under PMS-II, Reports Can Be Generated for One or Any Combination of Centers. Can Display Bar Graphs & Show Allocations As a Percent of Allocation Time.
North America MICA, Inc.

Road & Car Add-On Disk One: Test Drive III: The Passion. May 1990. *Items Included:* Catalog, copy protection device, manual, & a proof of purchase card. *Customer Support:* Technical support: 408-296-8400 & 90-day limited warranty.
IBM DOS 2.1 or higher, Tandy-DOS 8MHz or faster recommended (640k). IBM PC, XT, AT & compatibles, Tandy 1000 series, 3000, 4000. $24.95. *Addl. software required:* Test Drive III: The Passion. *Optimal configuration:* Hard drive installable, keyboard, joystick, graphics card, & sound board.
Driving Simulation. New England's Scenic Highways in Sports Cars That Can Be Mixed & Matched.
Accolade, Inc.

Road Engineering. *Items Included:* Bound manual. *Customer Support:* Free hotline - no time limit; 30 day limited warranty; updates are $5/disk plus S&H.
MS-DOS. IBM PC & compatibles (128k). disk $95.00. *Nonstandard peripherals required:* One drive & an 80-column printer.
Consists of Two Programs for Road Design & Construction. They Are Very User Friendly. Simply Answer the Prompts As They Appear on the Screen. CONSTRUCTION CURVES Computes Curve Details from the Deflection Angle & the Radius or Tangent. Results Are the Deflection, Radius, Arc, Chord, & External. You Can Print a Field Layout for Staking at Any Station Spacing & for Any Offset Desired. The Printout Lists the Deflections, the Long Arcs & Chords, & the Short Arcs & Chords at Each Station. ROAD GRADES Computes & Prints a Continuous List of Design Center & Gutter Elevations at Any Station Spacing, for Any Road Width & X-Fall % Specified. User Can Enter the Station & Elevation of Numerous Points, with or Without Vertical Curves. Automatically Saves Data to Disk for Later Revisions.
Dynacomp, Inc.

Road Racer. Oct. 1988.
Mac DOS (1Mb). Macintosh. 3.5" disk $69.95 (Order no.: 1019). *Nonstandard peripherals required:* Color monitor.
Macintosh Plus, SE, II.
High-Performance Corvette Simulation, Driving Through Five Environments Ranging from High-Speed Desert Flats to Twisting Mountain Roads. Numerous Detailed Sounds & Graphics, With Spectacular Scenery, Obstacles & Crashes, As You Fly over Hills & Around the Turns at up to 200 MPH. You Score Points for Fast Skillful Driving, by Steering & Accelerating with Your Mouse & Using Your Keyboard for Breaks & Shifting. Each Level Is Tougher Than the Last, with Unpredictable Road Hazards & Many Courses to Travel.
XOR Corp.

The Road to Compostela on Disk. (Historical Travel Guides Ser.). Edited by Ronald G. Musto & Eileen Gardiner. Jul. 1996.

TITLE INDEX

Windows. IBM. CD-ROM disk $25.00 (ISBN 0-934977-59-3).
Macintosh. CD-ROM disk $25.00 (ISBN 0-934977-58-5).
Texts, Maps, Photographs, Plans, & Travel Information Relating to the Medieval & Modern Pilgrimage Route to Santiago de Compostela.
Italica Pr.

Road Trips. *Version:* 1996. Nov. 1995. *Items Included:* CD-ROM with installation instructions, extensive on-line help. *Customer Support:* 90-day limited warranty, 90-day moneyback guarantee, update fee optional: to be determined, 800 number technical support.
Windows 3.1, Windows-95 or Windows-NT. IBM & compatibles (4Mb). CD-ROM disk $29.95 (ISBN 0-9649794-0-3). *Nonstandard peripherals required:* CD-ROM drive.
A Windows-Based Computer Software Program That Generates Point-to-Point Routes, Mileages, & Driving Instructions over the United States, Mexican, & Canadian Highway Systems.
TravRoute Software.

Road Trips: Door-to-Door. Jun. 1996. *Items Included:* 2 CD-ROMS w/installation instructions, extensive online help. *Customer Support:* 90-day limited warranty, 90-day moneyback guarantee, update fee optional (to be determined), 800-technical support.
Windows 95, 3.1, NT. OS/2. IBM-compatible. disk $99.95 (ISBN 0-9649794-1-1). *Nonstandard peripherals required:* 4x CD-ROM drive.
"Road Trips: Door-to-Door" is a windows-brand computer software program that generates detailed driving directions & maps for trips between exact addresses anywhere in the U. S. & parts of Mexico & Canada.
TraveRoute Software.

Roadsearch. *Version:* 3. 1989. *Compatible Hardware:* Apple II, II+, IIe, IIc; Commodore 64; IBM PC & compatibles. *Operating System(s) Required:* Apple DOS 3.3, MS-DOS. *Language(s):* Assembly. *Memory Required:* 64k. *Items Included:* Disk & manual. *Customer Support:* Yes.
disk $34.95.
Computerized Road Atlas That Helps Plan Trips. Produces Driving Routes, Mileage, Travel Times, & Fuel Usage in Different Formats. Contains a Database of 605 Cities & Road Junctions Located in the USA & Canada. Also Includes about 80,000 Miles of Road, Computes the Shortest Route Between Cities, Avoids Toll or Other Roads if Desired, & Lets Users Develop Routes Which May Be Longer, but More Suited to Their Needs.
Columbia Software (Maryland).

Roadsearch-Plus. *Version:* 3. 1989. *Compatible Hardware:* Apple II, II+, IIe, IIc; Commodore 64; IBM PC & compatibles. *Operating System(s) Required:* Apple DOS 3.3, MS-DOS. *Language(s):* Assembly. *Memory Required:* 64k. disk $74.95.
Computerized Road Atlas That Helps Plan Trips. Computes & Prints Detailed Driving Routes with Mileage, Travel Times & Fuel Usage. Determines the Shortest Route Between Cities, or Lets Users Develop Routes Which May Be Longer, but More Suited to Their Needs. Contains a Database of 605 Cities/Road Junctions Located in the USA & Canada, & About 80,000 Miles of Road. A ROADMAP DEVELOPMENT SYSTEM Lets Users Customize Their Roadmap with Their Own Towns/Road Junctions Anywhere in North America.
Columbia Software (Maryland).

Roadway Geometry. 1995. *Compatible Hardware:* IBM PC & compatibles. *Operating System(s) Required:* PC-DOS/MS-DOS. *Language(s):* QBASIC. *Customer Support:* Telephone assistance.
disk $47.00, incl. user guide.
disk $127.00, incl. source code.
Horizontal Alignment Disk Includes Design & Field Notes for Circular, Spiralized, & Compound Curves. Vertical Alignment Disk Includes Design & Elevations for Symmetrical & Unsymmetrical Parabolic Curves. No Data Storage Is Provided. Input Is Free-Format.
Systek, Inc. (Mississippi).

Roark & Young on Disk: Stress & Strain Calculations. 1995. *Items Included:* Full manual. *Customer Support:* Free telephone support - 90 days, 30-day warranty.
MS-DOS 3.2 or higher. 286 (584k). disk $599.95. *Nonstandard peripherals required:* CGA/EGA/VGA.
Since 1938, Roark's Formulas for stress & strain has been the most widely used Engineering Handbook in the World. Now the Entire 6th edition Published in 1989, Has Been Computerized. Includes over 5000 Formulas Grouped into Approximately 1500 Cases for Solving Problems Involving Beams, Columns, Plates, Pressure Vessels, etc.
Dynacomp, Inc.

Robert Mapplethorpe: An Overview. Robb Lazarus et al. Sep. 1995. *Items Included:* Instruction manual, upgrade card (if available). *Customer Support:* Call-in, 1-800, fax back & on-line support are available at no charge for the lifetime of the disk.
Macintosh with 68030 processor or higher. Macintosh, double speed CD-ROM drive (8Mb). CD-ROM disk $79.95 (ISBN 1-886664-00-5). *Nonstandard peripherals required:* 24-bit graphics card strongly recommended, Quick Time Movie.
Windows 3.1 or higher. Windows System 3.1 or higher (8Mb). CD-ROM disk $79.95 (ISBN 1-886664-01-3). *Nonstandard peripherals required:* 24-bit graphics card strongly recommended.
Discover the History & Context of Controversial Photographer Robert Mapplethorpe. Program Presents an Engrossing Introduction to This Important Artist. An Extensive Multimedia Presentation Includes a Narrated Artist's Biography Enhanced with Videotaped Interviews of Mapplethorpe & His Contemporaries. This Engaging, Well-Rounded Assessment of the Artist Constitutes One of the Most Complete Documents of His Life & Work Available to the General Public. You May Also Browse at Your Leisure in a Photo Gallery of over 400 Images on This Information-Rich CD.
Digital Collections, Inc.

Robert Mapplethorpe: An Overview: Jewel Case. Robb Lazarus et al. Jun. 1995. *Items Included:* Instructional manual, upgrade card (if available). *Customer Support:* Call-in, 1-800, fax back & on-line support are available at no charge for the lifetime of the disk.
Macintosh with 68030 processor or higher (8Mb). CD-ROM disk $49.95 (ISBN 1-886664-31-5). *Nonstandard peripherals required:* Double speed CD-ROM drive, 24-bit graphics card strongly recommended.
Windows 3.1 or higher (8Mb). CD-ROM disk $49.95 (ISBN 1-886664-32-3). *Nonstandard peripherals required:* 24-bit graphics card strongly recommended.
Digital Collections, Inc.

ROBERT MAPPLETHORPE: THE CONTROVERSY:

Robert Mapplethorpe: Catalogue Raisonne. Robb Lazarus et al. Sep. 1995. *Items Included:* Instruction manual, upgrade card (if available). *Customer Support:* Call-in, 1-800, fax back & on-line support are available at no charge for the lifetime of the disk.
Macintosh with 68030 processor or higher. Macintosh, double speed CD-ROM drive (8Mb). CD-ROM disk $495.95 (ISBN 1-886664-10-2). *Nonstandard peripherals required:* 24-bit graphics card strongly recommended, Quick Time Movie.
Windows 3.1 or higher. Windows System 3.1 or higher (8Mb). CD-ROM disk $495.95 (ISBN 1-886664-11-0). *Nonstandard peripherals required:* 24-bit graphics card strongly recommended.
View the Most Comprehensive Collection of Robert Mapplethorpe's Photographs Ever Made Available to the General Public. Over 2300 Artworks. An Entire Career on One Disk, This Expansive Collection of Editioned Prints & Unique Works Allows the Viewer to Gain Unparalleled Insight into the Evolution of This Prolific Artist. Developed in Conjunction with The Robert Mapplethorpe Foundation in New York, This Program Includes All of Mapplethorpe's Celebrated Prints - Including His Acclaimed Nudes, Flowers, Celebrities, Still-Lifes, & Self-Protraits - in Addition to His Equally Striking but Less Familiar Mixed-Media Pieces & Color Prints. The Controversial Photos Which Sparked Gallery Closings & National Debate Are Also Included.
Digital Collections, Inc.

Robert Mapplethorpe: The Controversy. Robb Lazarus et al. Aug. 1995. *Items Included:* Instruction manual, upgrade card (if available). *Customer Support:* Call-in, 1-800, fax back & on-line support are available at no charge for the lifetime of the disk.
Macintosh with 68030 processor or higher. Macintosh, double speed CD-ROM drive (8Mb). CD-ROM disk $129.95 (ISBN 1-886664-08-0). *Nonstandard peripherals required:* 24-bit graphics card strongly recommended, Quick Time Movie.
Windows 3.1 or higher. Windows System 3.1 or higher (8Mb). CD-ROM disk $129.95 (ISBN 1-886664-09-9). *Nonstandard peripherals required:* 24-bit graphics card strongly recommended.
View the Mapplethorpes That Shocked a Nation! Interactive CD-ROM is Available in a Second Version Suitable for an Adult Audience. Be among the First to Own This Unflinching Look at Robert Mapplethorpe, His Life & Work; See over 700 of His Photographs - Including the Most Provocative - in Your Own Private Photo Gallery. The CD Features an Electronic Reproduction of the Exhibit That Garnered International Headlines, "The Perfect Moment," As Well As a Multimedia Biography of the Artist.
Digital Collections, Inc.

Robert Mapplethorpe: The Controversy: Jewel Case. Robb Lazarus et al. Nov. 1995. *Items Included:* Instructional manual, upgrade card (if available). *Customer Support:* Call-in, 1-800, fax back & on-line support are available at no charge for the lifetime of the disk.
Macintosh with 68030 processor or higher (8Mb). CD-ROM disk $79.95 (ISBN 1-886664-39-0). *Nonstandard peripherals required:* Double speed CD-ROM drive, 24-bit graphics card strongly recommended.
Windows 3.1 or higher (8Mb). CD-ROM disk $79.95 (ISBN 1-886664-40-4). *Nonstandard peripherals required:* 24-bit graphics card strongly recommended.
Digital Collections, Inc.

Robert Winter's Crazy for Ragtime. Robert Winter. Mar. 1996.
MS Windows; Macintosh System 7.1 or higher. 486 or higher (8Mb); 040 Mac or Power Mac (16Mb). CD-ROM disk Contact publisher for price (ISBN 1-887701-03-6). *Nonstandard peripherals required:* CD-ROM drive & MPC-compatible Sound Card Video Card with 256 colors or higher; CD-ROM drive. *Optimal configuration:* 12Mb RAM.
The First in a Series of Titles Using Music As a New Way of Exploring the History of American Culture. In the First Two Decades of the 20th Century, Ragtime Took the Entire Country by Storm, Eventually Providing the Basis for Jazz & Virtually All American Popular Music up to Rap & Beyond.
Calliope Media.

Robo DESIGN. *Compatible Hardware:* IBM PC, PC XT, PC AT, PS/2; Compaq 286, 386. *Operating System(s) Required:* PC-DOS/MS-DOS. *Memory Required:* 640k. *General Requirements:* Hard disk, input device (mouse, digitizer), graphics display (EGA, VGA, Hercules). *Items Included:* Software, manual, quick-start tutorial. *Customer Support:* "800" number technical support.
disk $3000.00 (Order no.: 2612).
3.5" disk $3000.00 (Order no.: 5612).
Complete 2-D Drawing, Drafting, 3-D Solid Modeling Package. Shows Models from Any Angle, in Parallel or Perspective Projection. User Can Build Models from Drawings or Prepare Drawings from the Models. Automatic Parallel Lines, Advanced Editing, Mixed Drawing Units, Mathematical Expression Evaluation, Mass & Geometric Property Analysis, Time Management, Bill-of-Material Interface, etc.
Robo Systems International, Inc.

Robo IGES. *Version:* 1.0. Oct. 1988. *Compatible Hardware:* IBM PC, PC XT, PC AT, PS/2; Compaq 286, 386. *Operating System(s) Required:* PC-DOS/MS-DOS. *Memory Required:* 640k. *General Requirements:* Hard Disk, input device (mouse & digital), graphics display, (EGA, VGA, Hercules). *Customer Support:* "800" number technical support.
disk $1000.00 (Order no.: 2613).
3.5" disk $1000.00 (Order no.: 5613).
Bi-Directional Translation Between RoboCAD Drawings & the IGES Interface for Linking RoboCAD to Other CAD Software & Systems.
Robo Systems International, Inc.

Robo Utilities. *Compatible Hardware:* IBM PC, PC XT, PC AT, PS/2; Compaq 286, 386, or compatible. *Operating System(s) Required:* PC-DOS/MS-DOS. *Memory Required:* 640k. *General Requirements:* Hard disk, input device (mouse, digitizer), graphics display. *Items Included:* Software, manual. *Customer Support:* "800" number technical support.
3.5" or 5.25" disk $500.00 (Order no.: 2593).
Provides the Following Features: Time Logging & Reporting Function, Allowing Time Spent to Be Allocated to Projects, Cost Centers; Means of Analyzing the Content & Structure of Drawings; Neutral Format ASCII Drawing Data Interchange Function; & Means of Editing/Creating Drawing Text Fonts.
Robo Systems International, Inc.

RoboBuild. *Items Included:* Tutorial & reference manuals. *Customer Support:* Free "800" number.
PC-DOS/MS-DOS (640k). IBM PC/XT/AT, PS/2, Compaq 286/386 or compatible. disk $1995.00.
Takes a 2-D Plan from RoboCAD, & Automatically Converts it into a 3-D Solid. Surface Representation with Perspective, Hidden Line Removal, Shading, Etc. You Can Also Draw Directly in RoboBuild if You Wish. For Architects, a Solar Radiation & Shadow Package is Also Available.
Robo Systems International, Inc.

RoboCAD. *Version:* 20.0j. *Items Included:* Manual, & quick start tutorial. *Customer Support:* Free 800 # technical support.
PC-DOS/MS-DOS, DR-DOS 3.3+ & Macintosh that support DOS. IBM XT, AT, PS/2, 286, 386, 486 & compatibles (640k). disk $2000.00 (Order no.: 2669 (5 1/4"); 5669 (3.5")). *Optimal configuration:* 386; 3Mb RAM; VGA; math co-processor; mouse or other input device; DOS 3.3+ *Networks supported:* All popular networks; any network compatible with DOS file sharing.
Powerful, Full-Featured 2D CAD System with Pull-Down Menus, Palettes, & Icons. All Drawing Functions Are Instantly Available on Screen. Drawing & Editing Features are "Rubber-Banded" (See What You Are Doing Before Committing to It). Features Active Networking, Automatic Back-Up of Work in Process, Polygon Generation, Automatic Chamfer & Fillet, & a Comprehensive Built-In Multi-Page, Multi-Document Text Editor. DOS Support Includes Command Execution from Within RoboCAD & a DOS Shell. Supports All Popular File Formats Including RDF, RAF, HPGL, DXF, GEM, PCC & PCX. Interfaces with CAD, CAM, FEA, Desktop Pub S/W Through "Run Other" Menu or Through RoboUTILITY.
Robo Systems International, Inc.

RoboCAD 4. *Version:* 4.2. Jan. 1988. *Compatible Hardware:* IBM PC, PC XT, PC AT, PS/2; Compaq 286, 386 or compatible. *Operating System(s) Required:* PC-DOS/MS-DOS. *Memory Required:* 640k. *General Requirements:* Hard disk, input device (Mouse, Digitizer); graphics display. *Items Included:* Software, manual, quick-start tutorial. *Customer Support:* "800" number technical support.
disk $1500.00 (Order no.: 2556).
3.5" disk $1500.00 (Order no.: 5556).
Design & Drafting System with User Definable Auto Dimensioning, Rubberbanding; Cross Hatching; Angle & Grid Locus; Multiple Parallel Lines; Multiple Drawing Pages; Advanced User Interface; Auto Interface to Solid Modeling; Unique Microfiche Filing System, Multiple Units; Areas, Perimeters, etc.
Robo Systems International, Inc.

Robocop. Apr. 1995. *Customer Support:* Dedicated voice mail phone number; will respond back to consumer.
Windows 3.1 or higher; Macintosh. IBM or 100% compatible 486SX 25MHz (4Mb); 68030/68040 Color Mac System 7.1 or higher (4Mb). CD-ROM disk $19.99 (ISBN 1-57339-005-4, Order no.: ROM12983OR).
Nonstandard peripherals required: 2X CD-ROM drive.
Detroit...in the Not Too Distant Future. Officer Murphy, Brutally Murdered in the Line of Duty, Is Rebuilt As a Law Enforcement Cyborg. As His Memory Returns, He Seeks Revenge on Those Responsible for His Death.
Image Entertainment.

RoboFEM. *Items Included:* Manual. *Customer Support:* Free "800" number.
PC-DOS/MS-DOS (640k). IBM PC/XT/AT, PS/2, Compaq 286, 386, or compatibles. disk $300.00.
RoboFEM Makes a Finte Element Shell Mesh, of Triangular Elements, from a RoboSolid Model.
Robo Systems International, Inc.

RoboFEM/3D. *Items Included:* Manual. *Customer Support:* Free "800" number.
PC-DOS/MS-DOS (640k). IBM PC/XT/AT, PS/2, Compaq 286, 386, or compatibles. disk $500.00.
RoboFEM/3D Makes a Solid Finite Element 3D-Mesh of Tetrahedral Elements from a RoboSolid Model. The Output is a Neutral Format Mesh File Suitable for Processing by a Range of Finite Element Analysis Programs.
Robo Systems International, Inc.

RoboLink/CADL. *Items Included:* Manual. *Customer Support:* Free "800" number support.
PC-DOS/MS-DOS (640k). IBM PC, XT, AT, PS/2, Compaq 286, 386 or compatibles. disk $150.00.
Translates from RoboSolid to a 3-D Cadkey Wire-Frame.
Robo Systems International, Inc.

RoboLink/HPGL. *Items Included:* Reference manual. *Customer Support:* Free "800" support.
PC-DOS/MS-DOS. IBM PC, XT, AT, PS/2, Compaq 286, 386, & compatibles. disk $75.00.
Coverts Files in the Popular "HPGL" Graphics Format into RoboCAD Vector Files; Complements the HPGL Output Built-in to RoboCAD.
Robo Systems International, Inc.

RoboLink/SDRC. Jun. 1989. *Items Included:* Manual. *Customer Support:* Free "800" support.
PC-DOS/MS-DOS (640k). IBM PC, XT, AT, PS/2, Compaq 286, 386 & compatibles. disk $500.00.
Translates from RoboSolid to SDRC/Ideas Package & to a Neutral Format Compatible with Many Super-Mini & Mainframe Packages.
Robo Systems International, Inc.

RoboLink/3D. *Items Included:* Manual. *Customer Support:* Free "800" Support.
PC-DOS/MS-DOS (640k). IBM-PC, XT, AT, PS/2, Compaq 286, 386, or compatibles. disk $150.00.
Translates from RoboSolid to a 3-D DXF (ACAD Rel. 10) File Format.
Robo Systems International, Inc.

RoboMan. Brian Goble. Oct. 1990.
IBM PC & compatibles (256k). disk $39.95 (ISBN 0-945749-25-2, Order no.: 405).
IBM PS/2 & Laptops (256k). 3.5" disk $39.95 (ISBN 0-945749-24-4, Order no.: 403).
High Speed Action Arcade Game. User Acquires Points While Moving Through 50 Challenging Levels of Difficulty.
XOR Corp.

ROBOMATH. 1985-1991. *Items Included:* Disk(s), user's guide, poster, coloring book, warranty card, swap coupon. *Customer Support:* 90 day unlimited warranty; 800 toll free number, 800-221-7911, 8:00 a.m.-5:00 p.m. Arizona time; Updates $10.
Macintosh System 6 or higher. Macintosh (1Mb monochrome, 2Mb color). 3.5" disk $69.99 (ISBN 1-55772-021-5, Order no.: 0702). *Optimal configuration:* 2Mb color monitor, Macintosh LC. *Networks supported:* Digicard.
MS-DOS. IBM, Tandy, MS-DOS compatible (128k). disk $49.99 (ISBN 0-918017-13-0, Order no.: 0701). *Nonstandard peripherals required:* VGA or CGA card. *Optimal configuration:* 128k, color monitor, VGA card. *Networks supported:* Velan, Novell, Digicard.
DOS. Apple II, Apple IIe, Apple IIGS, Apple II Plus (48k). disk $49.99 (ISBN 0-918017-12-2, Order no.: 0700). *Optimal configuration:* Apple II, printer, color monitor, 48k. *Networks supported:* Digicard.
Award Winning ROBOMATH Combines Arcade Action to Inspire Robo-Mathematicians to Practice Multiplication & Division As They Close down Dr. Quark's Robomatic Machine. Choose Quick-Answer Method or Use the Screen to

Work Out More Difficult Problems Using Step-by-Step Prompts. Create Your Own Questions to Match Assignments. Ages 8 to 15.
Mindplay.

RoboSolid 2. Version: 2.0N. Mar. 1988. Compatible Hardware: IBM PC, PC XT, PC AT, PS/2; Compaq 286, 386, or compatible. Operating System(s) Required: PC-DOS/MS-DOS. Memory Required: 640k. General Requirements: Hard disk, input device, graphic display. Items Included: Software, manual, quick-start tutorial. Customer Support: "800" number technical support.
3.5" disk $2000.00 (Order no.: 5595).
disk $2000.00 (Order no.: 2595).
Solid Modeling System with Complete Hidden-Line Treatment, Shading (with Definable Light Source, Brightness, etc), Mass Property (Mass, C of Q, M of I, P of I) & Geometric (Volume, Surface Area) Analysis. Advanced Boolean Operations of Intersection, Union, Subtraction; Solids of Extrusion & Revolution; Automatic Interface to RoboCAD; Sectioning Supported, Advanced Extrusion Capabilities.
Robo Systems International, Inc.

RoboSolid 1.5. Version: 1.5. Mar. 1987. Compatible Hardware: IBM PC, PC XT, PC AT, PS/2; Compaq 286, 386 or compatible. Operating System(s) Required: PC-DOS/MS-DOS. Memory Required: 640k. General Requirements: Hard disk, input device (mouse, digitizer), graphics display. Items Included: Software, manual, quick-start tutorial.
disk $1500.00 (Order no.: 2500).
3.5" disk $1500.00 (Order no.: 5500).
Solid Modeling System with Complete Hidden Line Treatment, Solids of Extrusion & Revolution; Mass & Geometric Property Analysis; Advanced Boolgan Functions; Automatic Interface to RoboCAD.
Robo Systems International, Inc.

RoboSport. Ed Kilham. Mar. 1991. Items Included: Manual. Customer Support: 800-33-MAXIS for customer service technical support.
Macintosh system 6.02 or higher (1mb). $59.95.
Optimal configuration: Dual-packed with monochrome & color versions 1Mb required for monochrome version, & 2Mb required for color version; System 6.02 or higher.
Set in a Futuristic Time in Which Robots Do Battle for the Amusement of Humans. A Conflict Simulation Game That Combines the Tactical Challenge of Chess with the Intensity of Urban Guerilla Warfare. Players Program Maneuvers for Their Robot Teams & Set Them Loose Against Opposing Robots Controlled by the Computer or by Other Human Players. Simple, Point-and-Click Icon Construction Set Makes Programming Robots Easy to Learn & to Carry Out. Program Maneuvers for As Many As Four Teams, of up to Eight Robots Each.
Maxis.

Robot Control. Jan. 1985. Compatible Hardware: Commodore 64. Memory Required: 64k.
disk $29.95 (ISBN 0-931145-02-3).
Allows Owners of Commodore 64 with Morit 918 Robots & Microrenture C-64 Interface Cables to Program the Robot from Their C-64 Computer.
Sandlight Pubns.

Robot Odyssey. Compatible Hardware: Apple II, II+, IIe, IIc, IIgs; IBM PC, PCjr; Tandy 1000. Operating System(s) Required: MS-DOS. Memory Required: Apple 64k, IBM & Tandy 256k. General Requirements: CGA card for IBM.
disk $49.95, incl. backup.
backup disk $15.00.
Develops Advanced Logical Thinking Skills As Children Program Robots to Help Them Escape Robotropolis. Students Develop Strategies for Analyzing Problems, Forming Hypotheses & Refining Solutions in the Process. They Learn the Fundamentals of Digital Logic Circuit Design & Computer Programming.
The Learning Co.

Robot Readers: The Three Bears (Goldilocks). Jun. 1989. Customer Support: Free telephone, 90-day warranty.
Amiga DOS (512k). Commodore Amiga. 3.5" disk $29.95 (ISBN 0-925362-06-9, Order no.: CA006). Optimal configuration: Amiga 500.
Stories Help Children Learn to Read, Are Fun & Easy to Use. Features Include Reading Aloud with Each Word Changing Color As It Is Said. Adjustable Reading Speed. Children Hear Words Sounded Out As Letters Change Color, & Hear Animals' Names Spoken As They Glow. Includes "Find the Word" Game. Highly Interactive System Features Are Mouse Driven.
Hilton Android Corp.

Robotron. Compatible Hardware: Atari XL/XE. ROM cartridge $19.95 (Order no.: RX8033).
Atari Corp.

ROCKBASE. Version: 7.0. Items Included: Manual. Customer Support: Free phone & mail support, 30-day money back guarantee.
MS-DOS. IBM PC, PC XT, PC AT & compatibles. $199.00. Nonstandard peripherals required: EGA or VGA card. Optimal configuration: 386 with LaserJet II, dot matrix printers (Epson compatible).
Package Used to Generate Basemaps & Linearly & Non-Linearly Scaled Proportional Symbol Maps. Features Include Automatic Annotation, Slide Show Generation, Information Files, Ability to Read Either Free-Form or Fixed-Field Databases & User-Defined Scale Table.
RockWare, Inc.

Rockpecker: A Prospector's Mineral Identification Program. Items Included: "How to Use an Unknown Mineral's Physical Properties to Identify a Mineral". User is taken through the mineral pyrites from beginning to end. Copyright blank forms supplied for user photocopy use...as a guide. Customer Support: Fax & mail support - no charge. Voice not available. Program was extensively debugged for 12 months prior to release. In 6 months of user use, no bugs reported.
MS-DOS or IBM-DOS. IBM PC XT 486 with MS-DOS 3.3 or higher (640k). disk $59.00, v. 1 (without chemistry) (ISBN 1-886499-02-0, Order no.: ROCKPECKER). Addl. software required: MS-DOS 3.3 or higher.
disk $89.00, v. 2 (with chemical tests) (ISBN 1-886499-02-0).
Computerized 277 Mineral Description, Identification, Testing, DOS-XT/486 Program. User Can Identify Unknown Ore or Mineral; Then Pre-Assay Chemical Test for Elements to Confirm Identity-Finding. 277 Common Minerals Are Described in 17 Categories. (These Are the "Real World" Minerals Commonly Encountered in the Field).
Skill//Quest Co.

ROCKSOLID. Version: 3.0. Items Included: Manual. Customer Support: Free phone & mail support, 30-day money back guarantee.
IBM PC, PC XT, PC AT with at least 10Mb hard disk. disk $395.00. Nonstandard peripherals required: EGA or VGA card. Optimal configuration: 386 with LaserJet II, dot matrix printer (Epson compatible).
Solid Modeling Program That Generates a 3D Matrix. Includes User-Defined Scaling, Smoothing, Edge Enhancements, Extensive Collection of Solid Model Mathematical & Logical Utilities, 2 Algorithms, Trend Surface Analysis, Extensive Filtering Capabilities & Facit Smoothing.
RockWare, Inc.

ROCKSTAT. Customer Support: Free phone & mail support, 30-day money back guarantee.
IBM PC, PC XT, PC AT & compatibles. $299.00. Nonstandard peripherals required: EGA or VGA card. Optimal configuration: 386 with LaserJet II, dot matrix printers (Epson compatible).
Geostatistical Program That Performs Calculations & Diagram Plotting. Calculations Include: Population, Filtered Points, Min/Max/Mean, Skewness, Kurtosis, Median, Mode & Standard Deviation. Diagrams Available Include Linear/Linear, Log/Linear, Linear/Log, Log/Log Scattergrams, Ternary Plots, Piper & Stiff Diagrams. Data Can Be Plotted As Point to Point, Linear, 1st Through 10th Order Polynomial Curve Fitting, Histograms & Probability Diagrams.
Rockware, Inc.

RockWare Utilities. Version: 1.5. Aug. 1994. Items Included: Manual. Customer Support: First 30 mins. phone support is free, then a fee is charged. 30 day money-back guarantee.
MS-Windows. IBM PC & compatibles (4Mb). disk $249.00. Addl. software required: Windows. Optimal configuration: 486 PC with Windows 3.1 with 8Mb RAM.
A Collection of Windows-Based Geological Tools, Including 3 Point Problem Solver, Ternary Plots, Stereonets, Rose Diagrams, Hydrograph Diagrams, Bed Thickness Calculations, Survey Calculations, Coordinate Conversions, & More.
RockWare, Inc.

Rockworks. Jan. 1989. Items Included: Manuals. Customer Support: Free phone & mail support, 30-day money back guarantee.
MS-DOS (640k). IBM AT & compatibles, at least a 386 processor. disk $995.00. Nonstandard peripherals required: EGA or VGA card with at least 10Mb hard disk. Optimal configuration: 386 machine, LaserJet, dot matrix printers.
Integrated Collection of Geological Software Which Shares Standard Interface & Produces Cross-Compatible Graphics. Includes Following Programs: DIGITIZE, LOGGER, GEOPAL, GRIDZO, ROCKBASE, ROSE, ROCKSOLID, ROCKSTAT, STEREO.
RockWare, Inc.

Rocky Mountain Wildflowers: A Visual Plant Identification System. Version: 1.1. Walter Hartung et al. Jan. 1995. Customer Support: Free 30 day technical support, 90 day warranty.
Windows 3.1, Windows 95, Windows NT. 386 (4Mb). CD-ROM disk $29.00 (ISBN 1-885237-02-2, Order no.: 201-001). Nonstandard peripherals required: Mouse & CD-ROM, 8 bit color card, 8 bit sound card.
Macintosh 7.0. Mac II (4Mb). Nonstandard peripherals required: Mouse & CD-ROM, 8 bit color card.
Learn about the Beautiful Wildflowers of the Rocky Mountain States. Beautiful Full Screen Photos, Audio Descriptions, Glossaries & References Enhance Your Leanring Experience. A Flower Game Helps Test Your Knowledge.
Rocky Mountain Digital Peeks.

RODE-PC: Data Entry. Dec. 1984. Compatible Hardware: IBM PC & compatibles. Operating System(s) Required: PC-DOS 2.0 or higher. Memory Required: 256k.
disk $595.00 (ISBN 0-928582-03-5).
demo $40.00.
High-Speed, Full-Function Data Entry System for Networked & Stand-Alone PC's. Menu-Driven

Interface to Develop & Run Data Entry Applications. Stand-alone & LAN Versions Available.
DPX, Inc.

Rodin-Matisse Fonts. Parcway Corp. Aug. 1991. *Items Included:* Documentation in Japanese. *Customer Support:* Telephone technical support.
Macintosh KanjiTalk 6.0.7 or higher. Macintosh (2Mb). 3.5" disk $750.00 ea. *Nonstandard peripherals required:* Japanese-upgraded PostScript printer (e.g. NTX-J, RIP-J).
Japanese Type 1 PostScript Fonts; Come in 2 Typefaces & 5 Different Weights; Each Typeface & Weight Sold Separately.
Qualitas Trading Co.

Roland DPX Plotters.
Macintosh. disk DPX-2000 $2995.00. *Addl. software required:* Plotter driver such as MacPlot or MacPlot II.
disk DPX-3000 $4995.00.
DPX-200 Is an Eight-Pen Flatbed Plotter for ANSI-C/ISO-A2-Size Paper. Produces Fast, High-Quality Drawings at Maximum Plotting Speed of 450MM (16 Inches per Second) with Resolution of 0.0125 (0.0004 Inches per Step). Features Oversize Plotting Capability, XY Coordinate LED Displa, Built-In High-Capacity Data Buffer & More. DPX-300 Is an Eight-Pen Flatbed Plotter for ANSI-D/ISO-A1-Size Paper. Produces Fast, High-Quality Drawings at Maximum Speed of 450MM (18 Inches per Second) with Resolution of 0.125MM (0.004 Inches per Step). Features Secure Paper Setting, Automatic Pen Selection & More.
Roland Digital Group.

Roland DXY Plotters.
Macintosh. disk DXY-1100 $1295.00. *Addl. software required:* Plotter driver such as MacPlot or MacPlot II.
disk DXY-1200 $1895.00.
disk DXY-1300 $2495.00.
DXY-1100 Is an Inexpensive, Easy-to-Use Eight-Pen Plotter. Includes: Maximum Plotting Speed of More Than 16 Inches per Second, Mechanical Resolution of 0.0004 Inches per Step. Interfaces to Standard Centronics & RS-232 Hardware & Has HP-GL Emulation for Total Software Support. DXY-1200 Takes Basic Features of DXY-1100 & Adds Roland's Electrostatic Paper Hold System. This Eliminates Paper Slipping or Bubbling. DXY-1300 Takes all Features of the Other Two Machines & Adds 1Mb Plot Buffer. Entire Plot Can Be Captured & Replotted Independently of the Host Computer.
Roland Digital Group.

Rollerball. *Compatible Hardware:* Atari 400, 800. *Language(s):* Atari BASIC (source code included). *Memory Required:* disk 24k. *General Requirements:* Joysticks.
disk $21.95.
2-Player Combat Game.
Dynacomp, Inc.

Rolodex Live! *Version:* 2.0. Apr. 1991. *Items Included:* Manual, sample data, utilities disk. *Customer Support:* Advantage Club - 1 yr. maintenance & support - $25/yr.; Credit Card Support - $15 charge per call plus $1.50 per min. on all calls over 10 minutes; 900! Support - $1.50/minute phone charge with no minimum.
DOS 2.1 or higher. IBM or compatibles (256k). disk $49.95. *Nonstandard peripherals required:* Two 360k floppies or one 720k floppy or a hard disk; CGA, EGA monitor.
An Easy-to-Use Contact Management System That Makes Keeping Track of Your Regular Contacts Quick & Simple. It Includes a 22 Line Notepad for Each Record & It Prints Mailing Labels & Rolodex-Style Rotary Cards, Too. Also Includes an Autophone Dialer. (Requires Modem for Dialer).
DacEasy, Inc.

The Roman Empire: The Fall of Rome. Chris Butler & John Reinhardt. 1987. *Customer Support:* ECS offers technical support to registered users. Call (217) 359-7099. Other than the telephone call - technical support is no charge.
IBM. $49.95 single station/$250.00 network (Order no.: I-1227).
DOS 3.2 or higher.
This Social Studies Simulation Game Is Designed to Teach about the Factors in the Fall of the Ancient Roman Empire. The Student Is Placed in the Position of the Emperor of Rome. This Responsibility Includes Making Decisions about Itmes Such As Tax Rates, Number of Customs Officials & Tax Collectors, & Locations Where Legions Should Be Moved to Maintain Control of Conquered Territories. Factors Such As Plague, Climate & Trade Problems, Are Calculated by the Computer Based on the Frequency That These Actually Occurred in the Roman Empire. The Hall of Fame Lists the "Emperors" with the Highest Scores. Complete Teacher & Student Documentation Plus Worksheets Help Review Concepts of the Game.
Electronic Courseware Systems, Inc.

Romantic Encounters at the Dome. *Compatible Hardware:* Apple II, II+, IIe, IIc, IIgs; Atari ST; Commodore 64/128, Amiga; IBM PC.
$24.95.
A True-to-Life Adult Experience for Men & Women.
Microillusions, Inc.

Romeo & Juliet. *Version:* 1.5. Feb. 1995. *Items Included:* BookWorm Student Reader (diskette). *Customer Support:* 30 day MBG. Technical support (toll call) - no charge.
System 7.0 or higher. Macintosh (5Mb). CD-ROM disk $29.95 (ISBN 1-57316-022-9, Order no.: 16157). *Nonstandard peripherals required:* CD-ROM drive, 12" color monitor. *Optimal configuration:* 13" color monitor recommended.
Windows 3.1 or higher. IBM compatible (MPC) 386 DX (4Mb). CD-ROM disk $29.95. *Nonstandard peripherals required:* Standard multimedia compatible CD-ROM. *Optimal configuration:* 8Mb RAM recommended, 256 color monitor recommended.
The Ultimate Love Story & Still One of the Most Popular Tales Ever Told, Romeo & Juliet Touches All Who Read It. The BookWorm Version Features Complete Background Information, a Fully Annotated Text with All Difficult Words & Passages Explained, As Well As Plot Summaries, Theme Discussions, & Character Analyses.
Communication & Information Technologies, Inc. (CIT).

Romeo & Juliet & A Midsummer Night's Dream, Vol. 2. *Version:* 1.5. Feb. 1995. *Items Included:* BookWorm Student Reader (diskette). *Customer Support:* 30 day MBG. Technical support (toll call) - no charge.
System 7.0 or higher. Macintosh (5Mb). CD-ROM disk $59.95 (ISBN 1-57316-034-2, Order no.: 19002). *Nonstandard peripherals required:* CD-ROM drive, 12" color monitor. *Optimal configuration:* 13" color monitor recommended.
Windows 3.1 or higher. IBM compatible (MPC) 386 DX (4Mb). CD-ROM disk $59.95. *Nonstandard peripherals required:* Standard multimedia compatible CD-ROM. *Optimal configuration:* 8Mb RAM recommended, 256 color monitor recommended.
The Ultimate Love Story & Still One of the Most Popular Tales Ever Told, Romeo & Juliet Touches All Who Read It. Whether Seen As a Fantasy, a Romance, or a Nightmare, A Midsummer Night's Dream Has Long Been One of Shakespeare's Most Popular Works. Beautifully Illustrated with Pictures from Stage Performances & Art Masterpieces from Shakespeare's Day.
Communication & Information Technologies, Inc. (CIT).

Rookie Reporter. Mary B. Adams & Stephanie R. Briggs. Mar. 1995. *Items Included:* Teacher Resource Manual. *Customer Support:* Technical support phone number.
MS-DOS 5.0. 80486SX-20 (4Mb). CD-ROM disk $129.95 (ISBN 0-9639121-6-X). *Nonstandard peripherals required:* 16-Bit Sound Board, Double-speed CD-ROM drive, 17Mb free hard drive. *Addl. software required:* Microsoft Windows 3.1. *Optimal configuration:* 8Mb.
Students Enter the Fascinating World of Newspaper Publishing. Videos & Animations, Puzzles, & Hidden Surprises Challenge 11-to-14-Year Olds to Discover a Variety of New Information While Building Listening, Writing, Reading, & Critical Thinking Skills.
Meridian Creative Group.

Rookie Reporter. Marybeth Adams & Stephanie R. Briggs. Feb. 1996. *Items Included:* Teacher's resource manual, user guide. *Customer Support:* Technical support telephone number.
System 7.0. 68030 or PowerMac (8Mb). 3.5" disk $79.95. *Nonstandard peripherals required:* Double-speed CD-ROM drive, 10Mb free hard drive. *Optimal configuration:* 68040 or higher, or PowerMac.
Students Enter the Fascinating World of Newspaper Publishing. Videos & Animations, Puzzles, & Hidden Surprises Challenges 11-to-14-Year Olds to Discover a Variety of New Information While Building Listening, Writing, Reading, & Critical Thinking Skills.
Meridian Creative Group.

Roomer3. *Version:* 2.0. Nov. 1992. *Items Included:* 200 page manual, 90 minute VHS video. *Customer Support:* Free Telephone support.
DOS 3.0 or higher. DOS based machines (640k). $395.00. *Optimal configuration:* 12Mb or faster with a hard disk and a VGA monitor.
A 3D CAD Package Specifically Designed for People Who Need to Design Interior Spaces-Homes, Offices, Computer Rooms, Conferences, Parties, Crime Scene Reconstruction, Remodeling, etc.
Hufnagel Software.

Roots. *Compatible Hardware:* Apple II with Applesoft; IBM PC. *Memory Required:* 48k, IBM 128k.
$19.95.
Dynacomp, Inc.

Roots & Intersections of Curves. *Version:* 4. Sep. 1995. *Compatible Hardware:* IBM PC. disk $25.00 package.
Package of 2 Graphics Programs to Locate the Roots of Any Given Function & the Points of Intersection of Any Two Given Curves. Programs Allow for Both Graphical & Numerical Displays of Convergence.
MatheGraphics Software.

Rory Tycoon Portfolio Analyst. *Version:* 1.08. Dec. 1991. *Items Included:* Bound instruction manual. *Customer Support:* Telephone technical support, customizing available at an hourly fee.
MS-DOS (512k). IBM PC or compatible. $199.00. *Addl. software required:* Lotus 1-2-3 version 2.0 or later, or Symphony all releases. *Optimal configuration:* Graphic monitor (2 monitors preferred). *Networks supported:* Interfaces to Dow Jones News/Retrieval, CompuServe & Lotus signal.
Comprehensive Program Combining Portfolio

TITLE INDEX

Management, Historical & Real-Time Charting, & Electronic Quote Retrieval. Organizes, Tracks, & Reports on up to 2,500 Investments in 11 Investment Categories Including Stocks, Bonds, Mutual Funds, Options, & Futures. Also Available in Versions Offering Fewer Features.
Coherent Software Systems.

The Rosetta Stone Language Library: Deutsch Level I. *Version:* 2.0. Jul. 1993. *Items Included:* Spiral bound book with text, Glossary & Student Exercises; illustrated user's guide. *Customer Support:* 30 day moneyback guarantee of satisfaction, technical support.
Macintosh OS 6.07 or higher (system 7 compatible). Macintosh (8 bit color required) (2Mb). CD-ROM disk $395.00 (ISBN 1-883972-04-3). *Nonstandard peripherals required:* CD ROM drive; microphone will allow use of voice recording feature. *Optimal configuration:* 4Mb RAM, microphone.
Interactive Multimedia Immersion Program for Foreign Language Learning. Award-Winning Program Presents Thousands of Real Life Color Images, Native Speakers, & Text & Gives Immediate Feedback to Users. Takes Beginning Learners Age 8 Through Adult to Intermediate Levels. Also Available in English, Spanish, French, Russian & Dutch. Italian, Chinese & Japanese Are under Development.

The Rosetta Stone Language Library: Deutsch Level I. *Version:* 2.0. Jan. 1994. *Items Included:* Spiral bound book of text in German with Glossary & Student Exercises; illustrated user's guide. *Customer Support:* 30 day moneyback guarantee of satisfaction; technical support.
Windows. IBM 386 or higher (4Mb). CD-ROM disk $395.00 (ISBN 1-883972-16-7). *Nonstandard peripherals required:* CD-ROM drive, SVGA monitor, SVGA card, Sound Blaster compatible sound card, microphone will allow use of voice recording feature. *Addl. software required:* Windows 3.1 or higher. *Optimal configuration:* 486, 8Mb RAM, double speed CD-ROM drive. *Networks supported:* Novell Netware 3.12.
An Interactive Multimedia Immersion Program for Foreign Language Learning. Award-Winning Program Presents Thousands of Real Life Color Images, Native Speakers & Text & Gives Immediate Feedback to Users. Takes Beginning Learners Age 8 Through Adult to Intermediate Levels. Also Available in English, Spanish, French, Russian, & Dutch.
Fairfield Language Technologies.

The Rosetta Stone Language Library: Dutch Level I. *Version:* 2.0. Dec. 1995. *Items Included:* Spiral-bound book with text, glossary & student exercises; illustrated user's guide. *Customer Support:* 30 day money back guarantee of satisfaction, technical support.
Mac 6.07 or higher, System 7 & Power PC compatible. Macintosh (2Mb-Sys 6, 4Mb-Sys 7). CD-ROM disk $395.00 (ISBN 1-883972-25-6).
Windows 3.1 or higher. 386SX (4Mb). CD-ROM disk $395.00 (ISBN 1-883972-26-4). *Nonstandard peripherals required:* SVGA 256 colors 640 x 480, Soundblaster compatible sound card.
Interactive Multimedia Immersion Program for Foreign Language Learning. Award-Winning Program Presents Thousands of Real Life Color Images, Native Speakers, & Text, & Gives Immediate Feedback to Users. Takes Beginning Learners Age 8 Through Adult to Intermediate Levels. Also Available in English, Spanish, French, Russian, & German.
Fairfield Language Technologies.

The Rosetta Stone Language Library: English Level I. *Version:* 2.0. Jun. 1993. *Items Included:* Spiral bound book with English text, Glossary & Student Exercises; illustrated user's guide. *Customer Support:* 30 day moneyback guarantee of satisfaction, technical support.
Macintosh OS 6.07 or higher (system 7 compatible). Macintosh (8 bit color required) (2Mb). CD-ROM disk $395.00 (ISBN 1-883972-01-9). *Nonstandard peripherals required:* CD ROM drive; microphone will allow use of voice recording feature. *Optimal configuration:* 4Mb RAM, microphone.
An Interactive Multimedia Immersion Program for Foreign Language Learning. Award-Winning Program Presents Thousands of Real Life Color Images, Native Speakers & Text & Gives Immediate Feedback to Users. Takes Beginning Learners Age 8 Through Adult to Intermediate Levels. Also Available in English, Spanish, French, Russian, & Dutch.

The Rosetta Stone Language Library: English Level I. *Version:* 2.0. Jan. 1994. *Items Included:* Spiral bound book with English text, Glossary & Student Exercises; illustrated user's guide. *Customer Support:* 30 day moneyback guarantee of satisfaction; technical support.
Windows. IBM 386 or higher (4Mb). CD-ROM disk $395.00 (ISBN 1-883972-13-2). *Nonstandard peripherals required:* CD-ROM drive, SVGA monitor, SVGA card, Sound Blaster compatible sound card, microphone will allow use of voice recording feature. *Addl. software required:* Windows 3.1 or higher. *Optimal configuration:* 486, 8Mb RAM, double speed CD-ROM drive. *Networks supported:* Novell Netware 3.12.
An Interactive Multimedia Immersion Program for Foreign Language Learning. Award-Winning Program Presents Thousands of Real Life Color Images, Native Speakers & Text & Gives Immediate Feedback to Users. Takes Beginning Learners Age 8 Through Adult to Intermediate Levels. Also Available in Spanish, French, German, Russian, & Dutch.
Fairfield Language Technologies.

The Rosetta Stone Language Library: Espanol Level I. *Version:* 2.0. Jun. 1993. *Items Included:* Spiral bound book with text, Glossary & Student Exercises; illustrated user's guide. *Customer Support:* 30 day moneyback guarantee of satisfaction, technical support.
Macintosh OS 6.07 or higher (system 7 compatible). Macintosh (8 bit color required) (2Mb). CD-ROM disk $395.00 (ISBN 1-883972-02-7). *Nonstandard peripherals required:* CD ROM drive; microphone will allow use of voice recording feature. *Optimal configuration:* 4Mb RAM, microphone.
An Interactive Multimedia Immersion Program for Foreign Language Learning. Award-Winning Program Presents Thousands of Real Life Color Images, Native Speakers & Text & Gives Immediate Feedback to Users. Takes Beginning Learners Age 8 Through Adult to Intermediate Levels. Also Available in French, German, Russian, Dutch, & English (ESL).

The Rosetta Stone Language Library: Espanol Level I. *Version:* 2.0. Jan. 1994. *Items Included:* Spiral bound book with Spanish text, Glossary & Student Exercises; illustrated user's guide. *Customer Support:* 30 day moneyback guarantee of satisfaction; technical support.
MS-DOS. IBM 386 or higher (4Mb). CD-ROM disk $395.00 (ISBN 1-883972-14-0). *Nonstandard peripherals required:* CD-ROM drive, SVGA monitor, SVGA card, Sound Blaster compatible sound card, microphone will allow use of recording feature. *Addl. software required:* Windows 3.1 or higher. *Optimal configuration:* 486, 8Mb RAM, double speed CD-ROM drive. *Networks supported:* Novell Netware 3.12.
An Interactive Multimedia Immersion Program for Foreign Language Learning. Award-Winning Program Presents Thousands of Real Life Color Images, Native Speakers & Text & Gives Immediate Feedback to Users. Takes Beginning Learners Age 8 Through Adult to Intermediate Levels. Also Available in English, French, German, Russian, & Dutch.
Fairfield Language Technologies.

The Rosetta Stone Language Library: Francais Level I. *Version:* 2.0. Jun. 1993. *Items Included:* Spiral bound book with text, Glossary & Student Exercises; illustrated user's guide. *Customer Support:* 30 day moneyback guarantee of satisfaction, technical support.
Macintosh OS 6.07 or higher (system 7 compatible). Macintosh (8 bit color required) (2Mb). CD-ROM disk $395.00 (ISBN 1-883972-03-5). *Nonstandard peripherals required:* CD ROM drive; microphone will allow use of voice recording feature. *Optimal configuration:* 4Mb RAM, microphone.
An Interactive Multimedia Immersion Program for Foreign Language Learning. Award-Winning Program Presents Thousands of Real Life Color Images, Native Speakers & Text & Gives Immediate Feedback to Users. Takes Beginning Learners Age 8 Through Adult to Intermediate Levels. Also Available in English, Spanish, German, Russian, & Dutch.

The Rosetta Stone Language Library: Francais Level I. *Version:* 2.0. Jan. 1994. *Items Included:* Spiral bound book of text in French with Glossary & Student Exercises; illustrated user's guide. *Customer Support:* 30 day moneyback guarantee of satisfaction; technical support.
Windows. IBM 386 or higher (4Mb). CD-ROM disk $395.00 (ISBN 1-883972-15-9). *Nonstandard peripherals required:* CD-ROM drive, SVGA monitor, SVGA card, Sound Blaster compatible sound card, microphone will allow use of voice recording feature. *Addl. software required:* Windows 3.1 or higher. *Optimal configuration:* 486, 8Mb RAM, double speed CD-ROM drive. *Networks supported:* Novell Netware 3.12.
An Interactive Multimedia Immersion Program for Foreign Language Learning. Award-Winning Program Presents Thousands of Real Life Color Images, Native Speakers & Text & Gives Immediate Feedback to Users. Takes Beginning Learners Age 8 Through Adult to Intermediate Levels. Also Available in English, Spanish, German, Russian, & Dutch.
Fairfield Language Technologies.

The Rosetta Stone Language Library: Russian Level I. *Version:* 2.0. Feb. 1995. *Items Included:* Spiral-bound book with text, glossary & student exercises; illustrated user's guide. *Customer Support:* 30 day money back guarantee of satisfaction, technical support.
Mac 6.07 or higher, System 7 & Power PC compatible. Macintosh (2Mb-Sys 6, 4Mb-Sys 7). CD-ROM disk $395.00 (ISBN 1-883972-20-5). *Nonstandard peripherals required:* CD-ROM drive, microphone will allow use of voice recording feature.
Windows 3.1 or higher. 386SX (4Mb). CD-ROM disk $395.00 (ISBN 1-883972-21-3). *Nonstandard peripherals required:* CD-ROM drive, microphone will allow use of voice recording feature, SVGA 256 colors 640 x 480, Soundblaster compatible sound card.
Interactive Multimedia Immersion Program for Foreign Language Learning. Award-Winning Program Presents Thousands of Real Life Color Images, Native Speakers, & Text, & Gives

THE ROSETTA STONE POWER PAC

Immediate Feedback to Users. Takes Beginning Learners Age 8 Through Adult to Intermediate Levels. Also Available in English, Spanish, French, Dutch, & German.
Fairfield Language Technologies.

The Rosetta Stone Power Pac. Version: 2.0. Jun. 1994. Items Included: Spiral-bound book with text, glossary & student exercises; illustrated user's guide. Customer Support: 30 day money back guarantee of satisfaction, technical support. Mac 6.07 or higher. Macintosh (2Mb-Sys 6, 4Mb-Sys 7). CD-ROM disk $99.00 (ISBN 1-883972-17-5). Nonstandard peripherals required: CD-ROM drive, microphone.
Windows 3.1 or higher. 386SX (4Mb). Nonstandard peripherals required: CD-ROM drive, microphone will allow use of voice recording feature, SVGA 256 colors 640 x 480, Soundblaster compatible sound card.
Interactive Multimedia Immersion Program for Foreign Language Learning. Award-Winning Program Presents Real Life Color Images, Native Speakers, & Text, & Gives Immediate Feedback to Users. 22 Beginning-Level Chapters in Each of 6 Languages, Taken from the 92-Chapter Level 2 Programs: Spanish, French, German, Russian, Dutch, & English (ESL).
Fairfield Language Technologies.

Rosie's Lemonade Stand. Jan. 1994. Items Included: Program on CD-ROM, CD Booklet, & Registration Card. Customer Support: Free unlimited support via telephone.
Macintosh System 7.0 or higher. Macintosh LC or higher (4Mb). CD-ROM disk $49.00 (ISBN 1-57268-042-3, Order no.: 49003). Nonstandard peripherals required: 12 inch monitor or larger; CD-ROM drive. Optimal configuration: 5Mb RAM.
Managing a Lemonade Stand Requires a Variety of Skills, Such As Measuring Liquids, Counting Money, Making Comparisons, & Other Number-Related Skills. As Students Help Rosie Make Her Delicious Drink & Serve It to Her Friends in the Woods, They Have Fun Learning Important Math Fundamentals.
Conter Software.

Rosy.
Macintosh 512k or higher. 3.5" disk $175.00.
Two-Dimensional Orientation Analysis Program.
RockWare Data Corp.

ROTATE. Version: 2.0. May 1983. Compatible Hardware: IBM PC, PC XT, PC AT & compatibles. Operating System(s) Required: PC-DOS, MS-DOS. Language(s): FORTRAN. Memory Required: 512k. General Requirements: Printer.
disk $500.00 (Order no.: ROTATE).
In Three-Dimensional Space, This Program Will Rotate and/or Translate Coordinates. The Program Permits the Analyst to Look at Directions Oblique to a Plane of Coordinates. It Will Also Help the Analyst to Compare Different Coordinate Systems by Changing Them to a Common Coordinate System.
Geostat Systems International, Inc. (GSII).

Roulette. 1981. Compatible Hardware: Apple II, II+, IIe, IIc; Franklin Ace; Laser 128. Operating System(s) Required: Apple DOS 3.3. Language(s): Assembly. Memory Required: 48k.
disk $8.95.
instruction on disk avail.
Simulation of the Casino Game. Features High-Resolution Graphics & a Spinning Wheel. Bets Can Be Placed via the Keyboard or a Light Pen.
Artsci, Inc.

Route 488. Compatible Hardware: IBM PC, PC XT, PC AT & compatibles, PS/2. Operating System(s) Required: PC-DOS/MS-DOS 2.0 or higher. Memory Required: 96k. General Requirements: IEEE 488 board.
disk $125.00.
Memory-Resident BIOS-Level Device Driver Designed to Work with IEEE 488 Boards. Has the Capability of Transferring Data at Rates up to Four Times Faster Than the DOS Device Handler. Can Be Accessed from Any Language Running under MS-DOS.
Scientific Solutions.

Route Management: (Trash) Hauler's Billing System. Version: 4.5. 1987. Items Included: Step-by-Step instruction manual. Customer Support: Free support by phone, FAX, correspondence, or modems. On-site training and/or installation, $229.00 per day plus expenses.
MS/PC DOS 3.0 or higher. PC, 286, 386, 486; Tandy 3000 or higher (640k). disk $995.00 (Order no.: 1101). Nonstandard peripherals required: Interface to Touch-Tone requires our voice digitization board. Programs without Touch-Tone interface do not require non-standard peripherals, boards. Optimal configuration: 386SX computer with a fast hard disk & our telephone interface board. Networks supported: Novell.
Maintains a Route List, Prints Updates of Pages for Route Drivers, Prints Invoices & Shipping Lists. On-Board Module Tracks Items On/Off Truck & Returned. Excellent for Delivery Routes, Trash Haulers, etc. Customized to Fit Each Application.
Robert H. Geeslin (Educational Programming).

Route Stats. Version: 2.1. Jun. 1982. Items Included: Contact vendor. Customer Support: Contact vendor.
MS-Windows. 386 (4Mb). Contact publisher for price. Networks supported: Lantastic, Novell Netware, Microsoft LAN Manager, Microsoft Windows NT Advanced Server.
Collects Information about Riders & Drivers for Public Transportation. Maintains Date, Route, Vehicle, Rider Category, Number of Riders & Other Information Pertaining to Uses of Mass Transit. Driver Statistics for Vehicle, Route, Horus, Trips & Distance Are Recorded. Various Reports & Cross Tabulations Are Provided in Basic System.
Management Systems, Inc.

Rover Electronic DataBooks for Corrosion & Chemical Resistance. 1995.
Set. CD-ROM disk $995.00 (Order no.: 7395B).
CD-ROM disk $595.00 (Order no.: 7380B).
CD-ROM disk $395.00 (Order no.: 7442B).
CD-ROM disk $289.00 (Order no.: 7381B).
Corrosion Data Sets Include: PDLEM, Handbook or Corrosion DATA, Matcompat.
ASM International.

Roy's DOS Helper. David L. Campbell. Feb. 1986. Compatible Hardware: IBM PC & compatibles, PC XT, PC AT. Operating System(s) Required: MS-DOS 3.0 or higher. Memory Required: 256k.
disk $65.00 (Order no.: RDH-1).
Interfaces with DOS to Allow Non-Technical Computer Users to Perform Common DOS Functions Through Easy Menu Selections.
ROY G BIV Computer Consultants.

RPM for Windows: Rental Property Manager. Version: 1.1. Aug. 1994. Items Included: 1-bound users manual, RPM Product Facts Report. Customer Support: Free installation support. Enhanced support - $149 year/CPU 10am to 5pm Eastern Time - all questions from installation through usability. Premium support - $350 year/CPU 10am-10pm Eastern time - all questions from installation to consultative using remote compute software.
Microsoft Windows 3.1. 386 or higher processor (4Mb). disk $675.00. Nonstandard peripherals required: Scanner, mouse. Optimal configuration: 486 or higher, VGA monitor, 8Mb memory, scanner, Paradox 5.0 for Windows, Report Smith. Networks supported: Novell Netware, Windows NT, OS2.
UNIX, Windows 3.1. HP-UX, Sun OS, Solaris, IBM AIX, SCO. Contact publisher for price. Nonstandard peripherals required: Scanner, mouse. Addl. software required: Internet, Sybase, or Oracle.
Can Be Used for the Data Analysis/Reporting & Database Management of Commercial & Residential Rental Property. Makes It Easy to Manage Customer & Property Records, Expenses, Income, & Complex Reporting. Product Can Run in a Client Server Environment, LAN, or Stand Alone.
DBDS.

RPMAS: Residential Property Management Accounting System. Version: 3.11. Jun. 1987. Items Included: Manual. Customer Support: 90 days unlimited support; ongoing support $450/yr..
PC-DOS 3.30 (512k). PC AT & compatibles. $3000.00, Novell $4500.00 (ISBN 0-928246-06-X, Order no.: RPMAS). Nonstandard peripherals required: Modem for remote support. Addl. software required: "PC Anywhere" for remote support. Optimal configuration: Hard disk; EGA monitor; 690k RAM. Networks supported: Novell, PC NET.
Complete Property Management Accounting System Designed for the Professional Property Manager. Can Handle up to 46,000 Properties with Each Property Having up to 10,000 Units. Includes Unit Maintenance, Tenant Rent, Accounts Payable & General Ledger Modules.
HEL Custom Software, Inc.

R.SIMS: The Retail Sales & Inventory Management System. Steve White & Jeff Thomas. 1980. Compatible Hardware: IBM PC XT, PC AT. Operating System(s) Required: PC-DOS. Language(s): BASIC (source code included). Memory Required: 640k. General Requirements: Printer.
disk $1850.00.
Inventory Levels May Be Updated Daily with Sales & Sales Reports May Be Printed by Item, Department & Salesperson.
Advance Business Computer Corp.

RSNA: Selected Scientific Exhibits, 1992, 93, 94. Stephen Baker. Oct. 1994.
Mac/Windows PC (5Mb). disk $225.00, 1992 (ISBN 1-56815-036-9). Optimal configuration: PC Windows 3.1.
disk $225.00, 1993 (ISBN 1-56815-037-7).
disk $225.00, 1994 (ISBN 1-56815-049-0).
Mosby Multi-Media.

RSTRIP Exponential Decomposition & Parameter Estimation. Items Included: Bound manual. Customer Support: Free hotline - no time limit; 30 day limited warranty; updates are $5/disk plus S&H.
MS-DOS 2.0 or higher. IBM & compatibles (640k). disk $299.95. Nonstandard peripherals required: Two floppy drive (or one floppy & a hard disk), & CGA, EGA, or compatible graphics (for screen graphics). Supports an 80x87 math coprocessor (if present). Compatible with most printers (e.g., dot matrix, HP LaserJet), PostScript devices (e.g., Apple LaserWriter), & plotters (e.g., Epson HI-80, HP 7475, Houston Instruments DMP-029).
Applicable to the Analysis of Data Containing

Single or Multiple Exponential Dependencies Such As Found in Many Nuclear, Chemical, & Other Physical Processes Involving Reactions/ Interactions. Features Full-Screen Editing As Well As Interactive Graphics. Graphics Features Include Overlays, Zoom, Labeling, Scales, etc. Multiple Data Sets May Appear on the Same Plot, &, for Polyexponential Models, Two or More Model Curves May Be Plotted along with a Single Data Set. Grid Lines May Be Included, & the Multiple Plot Aspect Ratios Varied. Model Parameter Values May Be Stored/Retrieved, Residuals Plotted, Individual Points Weighted, & More. Data May Be Sent to or from Lotus, dBASE, DIFF, & ASCII Files.
Dynacomp, Inc.

RTCS-iSIM85: 8085 ISIS II Simulator. Version: 3.2. Nov. 1984. Compatible Hardware: IBM PC & compatibles, PC XT, PC AT. Operating System(s) Required: PC-DOS, MS-DOS 2.0 or higher. Memory Required: 256k. General Requirements: 2 disk drives, asynchronous communications adapter.
disk $500.00.
Allows Developers to Run Intel 8-Bit Software on IBM PC's & MS-DOS Systems. Includes Communications Software to Transfer Files. Supports All ISIS-II 8-Bit Software for 8085, 8080, 8048, & 8051 Processor Families.
Real-Time Computer Science Corp.

RTCS-UDI: Universal Development Interface. Version: 5.1. Aug. 1982. Compatible Hardware: IBM PC & compatibles, PC XT, PC AT. Operating System(s) Required: PC-DOS, MS-DOS. Memory Required: 256k. General Requirements: 2 disk drives.
disk $500.00.
Implementation of Intel's Universal Development Specification. Allows Software Developers to Run Intel Series III 16-Bit Software on PC-DOS & MS-DOS Systems.
Real-Time Computer Science Corp.

RTFile. Jan. 1985. Compatible Hardware: DEC Professional 300 Series, DEC Rainbow, DEC VAX, DEC PDP-11; IBM PC & compatibles; 3Com Networks. Operating System(s) Required: PC-DOS, MS-DOS, P-OS, VMS, RSX, RT-11, RSTS/E. Memory Required: 128k.
PC Version. $500.00, incl. RT Utility Library (Order no.: 1001).
Interactive Relational Database Management System Featuring a Menu-Driven Forms-Oriented End-User Interface. Enables Minimally Trained End-Users to Perform Many Commonly Needed Data Processing Tasks Without Applications Programming. Such Tasks Include Database Definition, CRT Forms Generation, Transaction Processing, & Report Generation, among Many Others. Also Includes an Object Library or Callable Subroutines Which Can Be Linked into User-Written Application Programs to Achieve Extended Functionality.
Contel Business Networks.

RTSORT. Operating System(s) Required: RT-11. TSX-Plus. Memory Required: 20k.
contact publisher for price.
S & H Computer Systems, Inc.

RTX 286: Real-Time Multitasking OS. Jan. 1986. Compatible Hardware: IBM PC AT. Memory Required: 512k. General Requirements: Hard disk.
disk $2395.00.
Implementation of Intel's IRMX 286 Real-Time Multitasking Operating System.Features 16MB Addressability & Runs in Protected Mode.
Real-Time Computer Science Corp.

Rubicon Alliance. Compatible Hardware: Commodore 64/128. Memory Required: 64k. disk $19.95 (ISBN 0-88717-213-X, Order no.: 16101-43499).
Galactic War Game. Player Assumes the Role of Space Fighter Who Has 8 Stages in His Mission, Each with a Specific Goal & Time Limit.
IntelliCreations, Inc.

Ruff's Bones. (Living Book Ser.). Eli Noyes.
MS-DOS 5.0 or higher, Windows 3.1 or higher. 386 processor or higher (4Mb). CD-ROM disk $49.95 (Order no.: R1185). Nonstandard peripherals required: CD-ROM drive. Optimal configuration: 386 processor operating at 16MHz or higher, MS-DOS 5.0 or higher, Windows 3.1 or higher, 30Mb hard drive, mouse, VGA graphic adapter & VGA color monitor (SVGA recommended), 4Mb RAM, external speakers or headphones (with sound card) that are Sound Blaster compatible.
Macintosh (4Mb). (Order no.: R1185).
Nonstandard peripherals required: 14" color monitor or larger, CD-ROM drive.
Highly Interactive Animated Stories for Children That Have Hundreds of Beautiful Animations & Have Received Countless Awards. In English & Spanish (Ages 3-8).
Library Video Co.

Rule of 78. Version: 6.0. Stroud. 1985. Compatible Hardware: Apple II, II+, IIc, IIe; IBM PC. Operating System(s) Required: Apple DOS 3.3, PC-DOS 2.1. Language(s): Applesoft BASIC, QuickBASIC 2.0 (source code included). Memory Required: 48k.
Apple. disk $39.95.
IBM. disk $59.95.
Performs the Calculation of Interest Due by the Rule of 78 When Loans Are Paid Out Prematurely.
Indian Head Data Systems.

RUN/C Professional. Age of Reason, Inc. Compatible Hardware: IBM PC or compatible or MS-DOS system with ansi.sys; Microsoft C or Lattice C for creation of loadable libraries. Memory Required: 320k.
contact publisher for price.
System for Creating Small to Medium-Sized Programs, Developing & Debugging Functions, Learning C, & for Writing & Testing Programs. Source Code Debugging Facilities Allow Users to Set Multiple Breakpoints, Single Step Through a Program, & View or Change Variables During Execution. Includes a Screen Editor & over 100 Sample Programs.
Lifeboat Assocs.

RUN/C-The Interpreter. Age of Reason, Inc. Compatible Hardware: IBM PC or compatible or MS-DOS computer with ansi.sys.
contact publisher for price.
C Interpreter with a User Interface Similar to That of a BASIC Interpreter. Includes a Full-Screen Editor. Over 100 Sample Programs Are Included on the Disk.
Lifeboat Assocs.

Run Master. Jul. 1993. Items Included: User manual. Customer Support: Free telephone support, customer satisfaction guarantee.
MS-DOS 3.21 or higher. IBM PC & compatibles (640k). disk $29.95. Optimal configuration: 2 disk drives; hard disk recommended. CGA, EGA, or VGA monitor.
Computerized Running Diary to Record, Analyze & Plot Distance, Pace, Time, Heart Rate & Weight. Also Includes Training Plans, Pace Charts, Marathon Time Prediction, Age Handicapping, Personal Fitness Evaluation, U.S.-Metric Conversions, a Tailored Weight-Reduction Running Program, an Extensive Glossary, Race Records, & Numerous Checklists. Easy to Use with Pull-Down Menus & On-Line Help. Print to Dot-Matrix or Laser Printers.
Bridget Software Co.

Running Score II. Version: 3.0. Jul. 1991. Compatible Hardware: IBM PC. Operating System(s) Required: PC-DOS. Language(s): C. Memory Required: 384k.
disk $200.00.
Allows the User to Hand Out Copies of Results to Runners After Crossing the Finish Line. Provides Results of All Finishers in the Order They Crossed the Line, Age, Sex, Team & Hometown, Time, Average Time per Mile, & Indicates Whether the Course Records Was Broken & Who Held the Old Record. Also Used for Scoring Triathlons.
RunTime Software.

Rural Water Billing. Compatible Hardware: Apple II+, IIe. Language(s): Applesoft BASIC. Memory Required: 48k.
disk $495.00.
Maintains Records for up to 850 Meters per Disk & Features Full Data Entry Editing. Includes Error Recovery & Allows Meters to Be Separated into Routes for 10 Different Rate Structures with 5 Steps per Rate.
REMsoft, Inc.

Russian Master Russian-English On-Line Dictionary. Items Included: Full manual. No other products required. Customer Support: Free telephone support - no time limit. 30 day warranty.
MS-DOS 3.2 or higher. IBM & compatibles (512k). disk $149.95. Optimal configuration: IBM, MS-DOS 3.0 or higher, hard disk (uses 1.8 Mb), CGA, EGA, or VGA (or compatible graphics capability, & 30k of free RAM.
Super-Fast Memory-Resident Language Utility for People Working with Russian to English Translations or Enlgish Students Studying Russian. Gives User Instant Access to over 48,000 Translations. All You Need to Do Is Press the "Hot Key", & up Pops the Dictionary. Press the Escape Key, & You Are Back to Your Application.
Dynacomp, Inc.

Russian Master: Russian-English On-Line Dictionary. 1992. Items Included: Detailed manuals included with all Dynacomp products. Customer Support: Free telephone support to original customer - no time limit; 30 day limited warranty.
MS-DOS 3.2 or higher. IBM PC & compatibles (512k). $149.95 (Add $5.00 for 3 1/2" format; 5 1/4" format standard). Optimal configuration: IBM, MS-DOS 2.0 or higher, a hard disk (uses 1.8Mb), CGA, EGA, or VGA or compatible graphics capability, & 30k of free RAM.
A Super-Fast Memory-Resident Language Utility for People Working with Russian to English Translations or English Students Studying Russian. It Gives You Instant Access to over 48,000 Translations. Not Only Are the Declinations of Many Nouns & Verbs Given, but the Declinations Are Also Listed Independently When They Differ Significantly from the Basic Form. Also, All Russian Words Are Shown with Proper Stress Marks.
Dynacomp, Inc.

Russian Tutor 1, Russian for Beginners, Vol. 1. (The/Language Tutor Collection). EDS USA staff & Elbe Space & Technology Staff. Mar. 1995. Language CD-ROM. disk $149.00 (ISBN 0-9650981-0-9).
Russian Tutor 1, Russian for Beginners is an interactive multi-media software product on CD-ROM.
ESA USA Incorporated.

Rusty & Rosy Read with Me, Vol. 1. Sep. 1995. *Customer Support:* Telephone support - free (except phone charge).
 Windows 3.1. IBM & compatibles (386 DX-20) (4Mb). CD-ROM disk $12.99 (ISBN 1-57594-008-6). *Nonstandard peripherals required:* 2x CD-ROM player, Sound Card, VGA monitor. *Optimal configuration:* 486 XS-33.
 Learning about Sounds, Words & Sentences.
 Kidsoft, Inc.

Rusty & Rosy Read with Me, Vol. 1. Sep. 1995. *Customer Support:* Telephone support - free (except phone charge).
 Windows 3.1. IBM & compatibles (386 DX-20) (4Mb). CD-ROM disk $12.99 (ISBN 1-57594-047-7). *Nonstandard peripherals required:* 2x CD-ROM player, Sound Card, VGA monitor. *Optimal configuration:* 486 SX-33.
 Learning about Sounds, Words & Sentences.
 Blister Pack Jewel Case.
 Kidsoft, Inc.

Rusty & Rosy Read with Me, Vol. 2. Sep. 1995. *Customer Support:* Telephone support - free (except phone charge).
 Windows 3.1. IBM & compatibles (386 DX-20) (4Mb). CD-ROM disk $12.99 (ISBN 1-57594-016-7). *Nonstandard peripherals required:* 2x CD-ROM player, Sound Card, VGA monitor. *Optimal configuration:* 486 XS-33.
 Learning about Sounds, Words & Sentences.
 Kidsoft, Inc.

Rusty & Rosy Read with Me, Vol. 2. Sep. 1995. *Customer Support:* Telephone support - free (except phone charge).
 Windows 3.1. IBM & compatibles (386 DX-20) (4Mb). CD-ROM disk $12.99 (ISBN 1-57594-055-8). *Nonstandard peripherals required:* 2x CD-ROM player, Sound Card, VGA monitor. *Optimal configuration:* 486 SX-33.
 Learning about Sounds, Words & Sentences.
 Blister Pack Jewel Case.
 Kidsoft, Inc.

Ruy Lopez Arkhangelsk Var. Van der Tak. 1993. *Items Included:* Book & disk with 500 or more games (over 200 annotated). *Customer Support:* Telephone support by appointment.
 MS-DOS 2.0 or higher (512k). 3.5" disk $25.00, incl. softcover text. *Nonstandard peripherals required:* Mouse, graphics, 3 1/2" drive.
 Atari ST (520k). Atari. disk $25.00.
 Nonstandard peripherals required: Monocrhome monitor DS/DD drive.
 Authoritative Introduction to & Analysis of an Important Chess Opening.
 Chess Combination, Inc.

RWB Answer. *Operating System(s) Required:* CP/M.
 contact publisher for price.
 RWB Assocs.

Rx-30 Pharmacy System. Jan. 1979. *Compatible Hardware:* DG Processors; IBM PC & compatibles. *Operating System(s) Required:* MS-DOS, DG-RDOS. *Language(s):* COBOL.
 disk $995.00.
 Handles Prescription Filling/Refilling, 3rd Party Claims, Generic Drugs Substitution, Allergy/ Interaction Checks, Patient Profiles, IRS Reports, DEA Reports, Inventory & More.
 Transaction Data Systems, Inc.

The Rx-80 Pharmacy System. *Version:* 4.12. 1978. *Operating System(s) Required:* MS-DOS, UNIX, Concurrent DOS. *Language(s):* COBOL.
 Memory Required: 1000k.
 disk $7500.00 ea., incl. user's guide.
 Pharmacy System That Automates Traditional & Unit Dose Dispensing in Hospitals, Nursing Homes & Retail Drug Store Pharmacies. Provides Third Party Claims Processing, Accounts Receivable & Perpetual Inventory. Produces All Required DEA Reports, Patient Profiles, & Gross Margin Reports. Features: On-Line Update of Patient, Drug, Doctor & SIG Files, Drug Interaction & Allergenic Reaction Checking, Interactive Maintenance Programs for Immediate Customizing of Menus, Screens & Labels, Optimized Data Storage, Self-Explaining Prompts & Pricing Formulas to Implement Strategy.
 Condor Corp.

RXWRITER. *Version:* L. 1990. *Compatible Hardware:* IBM PC & compatibles. *Operating System(s) Required:* MS-DOS, PC-DOS. *Memory Required:* 128k. *General Requirements:* Printer. *Items Included:* Manual, 75 pages, indexed. *Customer Support:* Telephone.
 disk $145.00.
 Prescription Writing Program Meant for Use in a Physician's Office. Will Produce Prescriptions Faster & More Accurately Than They Can Be Written by Hand, from the Physician's Own List of Drugs. A Disk File Is Created Which Can Later Be Searched to Find All the Prescriptions Written for a Patient, All the Patients with a Given Diagnosis, or All the Patients Who Have Been Given a Particular Drug.
 Hall Design.

Ryan Investment Planner. *Compatible Hardware:* IBM PC & compatibles. *Memory Required:* 512k. *General Requirements:* Lotus 1-2-3 Release 2.0 or higher.
 disk $249.00.
 Contains 18 Categories of Investments. After Users Name the Investments, They Choose How Much to Invest in Each Category (Percentage of Total Investment or Dollar Amount), & Select the Growth Rate, the Appreciation Rate, & the Tax Rate for Each Asset, or the Program Will Use Its Own Built-In Rates. The Program Computes a Five-Year Projection for the Portfolio. Users Can Also Input a Worst Case Percentage for Each Asset. Provides the Following Features: Tax Calculations, Special Input & Output Sections for Mutual Funds, Special Input Forms & Output Reports for Special Needs, & Built-In Inflation Factors. All Cash Generated by Investments (Except for IRA Contributions, Universal Life Insurance, & Mutual Funds) Is Invested in a Money Market Account Earning a Rate Specified by the User.
 Ryan Software, Inc.

The S-B Quotient. *Version:* 1.1. Dec. 1988. *Customer Support:* One-year money back guarantee, unlimited phone support.
 MS-DOS 2.0 or higher (360k). IBM PC & compatibles. disk $149.95. *Optimal configuration:* Monitor, printer.
 Predicts Likelihood of Any Business Going Bankrupt. Utilizes Altman's Z Score & Fulmer's H Score, Which Can Determine Bankruptcy with an Accuracy Rate Between 75% & 90%. Includes Other Ratios Measuring Financial Health in the Areas of Liquidity, Debt Solvency, Profitibility & Activity.
 Winning Strategies, Inc.

S-Plane Tutorial (SPT). (Plane Analysis Ser.: No. 4). *Operating System(s) Required:* Apple DOS 3.2, 3.3, MS-DOS. (source code included). *Memory Required:* Apple 48k, IBM 128k.
 disk $39.95.
 Discusses Development of Analog Filters Through the Use of Pole/Zero Representations.
 Dynacomp, Inc.

S20 Spec Forms II for Windows. Oct. 1994. *Items Included:* 2 manuals, S20 standard.
 DOS/Windows 3.X. PC compatible (4Mb). disk $240.00 (ISBN 1-55617-532-9, Order no.: 532-9). *Optimal configuration:* IBM 386, 4M RAM, 4Mb available on hard drive, VGA monitor. *Networks supported:* Multiple user option available.
 This Windows Application Automates the ISA S20 Standard for Instrument Specification Forms. The Product Uses the Popular Form Tool Gold Forms Generator. Users Are Supplied with 40 Forms on Disk. Form Filler, Designer, & a Database Are All Part of the Product.
 Instrument Society of America (ISA).

Sacred Ground. *Items Included:* Installation guide.
 Windows 95. CD-ROM disk Contact publisher for price (ISBN 0-87321-117-0, Order no.: CDD-3147).
 Macintosh. (ISBN 0-87321-118-9).
 Activision, Inc.

Sadako & the Thousand Paper Cranes.
 Intentional Education Staff & Eleanor Coerr. Apr. 1996. *Items Included:* Program manual. *Customer Support:* Free technical support, 90 day warranty.
 School ver.. System 7.1 or higher. Macintosh (4Mb). 3.5" disk contact publisher for price (ISBN 1-57204-189-7). *Nonstandard peripherals required:* 256 color monitor, hard drive, printer.
 Lab pack. System 7.1 or higher. Macintosh (4Mb). 3.5" disk contact publisher for price (ISBN 1-57204-190-0). *Nonstandard peripherals required:* 256 color monitor, hard drive, printer.
 Site License. System 7.1 or higher. Macintosh (4Mb). 3.5" disk contact publisher for price (ISBN 1-57204-191-9). *Nonstandard peripherals required:* 256 color monitor, hard drive, printer.
 School ver.. Windows 3.1 or higher. IBM/Tandy & 100% compatibles (4Mb). disk contact publisher for price (ISBN 1-57204-192-7). *Nonstandard peripherals required:* VGA or SVGA 640 x 480 resolution (256), mouse, sound device.
 Lab pack. Windows 3.1 or higher. IBM/Tandy & 100% compatibles (4Mb). disk contact publisher for price (ISBN 1-57204-193-5). *Nonstandard peripherals required:* VGA or SVGA 640 x 480 resolution (256), mouse, sound device.
 Site License. Windows 3.1 or higher. IBM/Tandy & 100% compatibles (4Mb). disk contact publisher for price (ISBN 1-57204-194-3). *Nonstandard peripherals required:* VGA or SVGA 640 x 480 resolution (256), mouse, sound device.
 This companion for young adult literature is ideal for students who don't know how to start that book report, or give that needed summary. Gentle prompts throughtout the guide section of the program include Warm-up Connections, Thinking about Plot, Quoting & Noting, Keeping a Journal, If I Were——'Responding to Questions, Using Quotations, Taking a Personal View, Write to Others, & Write a Sequel.
 Lawrence Productions, Inc.

Safari. Alpenglow & Jonathan Scott. Nov. 1994. *Items Included:* Run-time Video for Windows. *Customer Support:* Telephone support for installation/use problems.
 Windows 3.1 or higher. 386 or higher (4Mb). CD-ROM disk $49.95. *Nonstandard peripherals required:* CD-ROM drive (double speed preferred), VGA (SVGA preferred) with 256 colors, soundcard. *Optimal configuration:* Multimedia PC-486 or higher, 8Mb RAM, doublespeed CD-ROM drive, 16 bit soundcard, speakers or headphones.
 A Multimedia CD Exploring the Animals, Birds, & People of the Masai Mara/Serengeti National

TITLE INDEX

Parks of East Africa. There Is an Interactive 'Find the Animals' Section. There Are Narrated Slide Shows, Textual Stories & Guide Books for Animals & Birds. The Product Contains over 800 Photographs, 40 Video Clips, 60 Minutes of Music, Narration & Sounds.
Alpenglow.

Safari Collectables 1. Jul. 1992. *Customer Support:* 90 day unlimited.
Windows 3.1/MS-DOS or Windows 3.0 with ADOBE Type Manager. IBM PC or compatible (2Mb). disk $39.95 (Order no.: SAF-CO). *Addl. software required:* Windows 3.1 (for TRUETYPE) or ADOBE Type Manager (for Windows 3.0).
Apple Macintosh (2Mb). 3.5" disk $39.95 (Order no.: SAF-CM1). *Addl. software required:* ADOBE Type Manager (for Type 1's) or System 7 (for TRUETYPE).
Type 1 & TRUETYPE Faces, Includes Patriot, Surfside, Danelian Icequebe, Wedding Text, Motor City, & Plaques, Faces.
Computer Safari.

Safari Collectables 2. Jul. 1992. *Customer Support:* 90 day unlimited.
Windows 3.1/MS-DOS or Windows 3.0 with ADOBE Type Manager. IBM PC or compatible (2Mb). disk $39.95 (Order no.: SAF-C2). *Addl. software required:* Windows 3.1 (for TRUETYPE) or ADOBE Type Manager (for Windows 3.0).
Apple Macintosh (2Mb). 3.5" disk $39.95 (Order no.: SAF-CM2). *Addl. software required:* ADOBE Type Manager (for Type 1's) or System 7 (for TRUETYPE).
Type 1 & TRUETYPE Faces, Includes Crazydaze, Celebrate!, Milk Wagon, Sashimi, Rabbit Ears, Fireworks, & Motor City.
Computer Safari.

Safari Future Fonts. Jul. 1992. *Customer Support:* 90 day unlimited.
Windows 3.1/MS-DOS or Windows 3.0 with ADOBE Type Manager. IBM PC or compatible (2Mb). disk $39.95 (Order no.: SAF-FF1). *Addl. software required:* Windows 3.1 (for TRUETYPE) or ADOBE Type Manager (for Windows 3.0).
Apple Macintosh (2Mb). 3.5" disk $39.95 (Order no.: SAF-FFM). *Addl. software required:* ADOBE Type Manager (for Type 1's) or System 7 (for TRUETYPE).
Type 1 & TRUETYPE Typeface Collection. Includes Trek 6, Airlock, Telemetry, Sashimi, Atomic Age, & Shari Faces.
Computer Safari.

Safari Number 29 Font Collection. *Version:* 2.1. Dec. 1991. *Customer Support:* 90 day unlimited.
Windows 3.1/MS-DOS or Windows 3.0 with ADOBE Type Manager. IBM PC or compatible (2Mb). disk $39.95 (Order no.: SAF-29). *Addl. software required:* Windows 3.1 (for TRUETYPE) or ADOBE Type Manager (for Windows 3.0).
Apple Macintosh (2Mb). 3.5" disk $39.95 (Order no.: SAF-2M). *Addl. software required:* ADOBE Type Manager (for Type 1's) or System 7 (for TRUETYPE).
Type 1 & TRUETYPE Fonts, Includes NCC-17, NCC Inline, Romulus & Klinglish Faces.
Computer Safari.

Safari SFAN Special Edition Font Collection. *Version:* 2.6. Oct. 1991. *Items Included:* Instructions for creating name tags using the Egyptian Hieroglyphics font. *Customer Support:* 90 day unlimited.
Windows 3.1/MS-DOS or Windows 3.0 with ADOBE Type Manager. IBM PC or compatible (2Mb). disk $39.95 (Order no.: SAF-SE). *Addl. software required:* Windows 3.1 (for TRUETYPE) or ADOBE Type Manager (for Windows 3.0).
Apple Macintosh (2Mb). 3.5" disk $39.95 (Order no.: SAF-SM). *Addl. software required:* ADOBE Type Manager (for Type 1's) or System 7 (for TRUETYPE).
Type 1 & TRUETYPE Font Collection, Includes Classic Trek, Movie Star Trek Italic, Alien National, Klingan, Titles, Generations & Egyptian Hieroglyphics.
Computer Safari.

Safe Update. Open Door Software Staff. Apr. 1994. *Items Included:* Manual. *Customer Support:* Call for info..
DOS. IBM & compatibles. disk $24.99 (ISBN 1-56756-082-2, Order no.: OD10101). *Optimal configuration:* Any IBM or compatible w/a minimum of 640k of RAM.
Ideal for People Wanting to Ensure a Smooth Upgrade or Go Back to the Original Version Should the Upgrade Fail to Live up to Expectations. This Ingenius Utility Program Compresses the Files (of the Original Directory & Subdirectories) on Your Hard Drive Before the Update or Upgrade. Should the Upgrade Not Work, Safe Update Has a Companion Program Included That Restores the Program to Its Previous State. Can Eliminate Data Loss & Version Control Problems.
Advantage International.

SAFEGUARD. *Version:* 4.58. *Customer Support:* By phone Mon-Fri 8:30 AM-5:30 PM CST.
MS-DOS. IBM PC, PC XT, PC AT & compatibles, PS/2. disk $149.00 (Order no.: 455001).
Incorporates Uncopyable Magnetic Mark & Also Encrypts Program for Double Protection. Protects Software Developed by Others. Interrogation of Fingerprint, Decryption & Program Loading Is Performed by RUN Module. If System Fingerprint Is Not Available, RUN Will Not Allow Program to Execute. With HDCOPY, System Can Copy to a Hard Disk. Includes MASTER DISK Along with Appropriate Number of Disks. MASTER DISK Includes Necessary PROTECT & RUN Programs.
Glenco Engineering, Inc.

Safepark Advanced: Time-Resident Software. Eric Grasshoff & Norman Ivans. Aug. 1988. *Operating System(s) Required:* PC-DOS/MS-DOS. *Memory Required:* 64k.
disk $49.95 (Order no.: SP-1).
3.5" disk $49.95 (Order no.: SP-1/3).
Prevents Static Electricity, Turning Power on & off, Brownouts, Radio Frequency Interference, Electromagnetic Interference, Surges & Spikes from Destroying Data on the Hard Disk.
Disk Technician Corp.

Safety & Personnel Management. *Version:* 4.1. *Customer Support:* On site training unlimited support services for first 90 days & through subscription thereafter.
Contact publisher for price.
Maintains Data Specific to Your Personnel. This Includes a User-Definable Personnel Information & Action File Where Various Types of Records Can Be Defined & Analyzed. This Includes the Expiration of Certificates, Disciplinary Action, Awards, Vacation, Tardiness & More.
Argos Software.

The Safety Director. *Version:* 1.1. 1991. *Items Included:* One year of free telephone technical support, an operations manual in a 3-ring binder, the runtime version of Advanced Revelations. *Customer Support:* After the first year, additional technical support can be purchased if needed.
MS-DOS. IBM compatible PC's (512k). $4995.00 single user. *Networks supported:* Novell, IBM PC-Net, Banyan Vines, LAN Manager for MS-DOS, & most other DOS compatible networks.
Pathworks or Digital Equipment Corp.'s VMS. VAX (512k). $4995.00 single user. *Networks supported:* DECnet.
UNIX or SunOS. SPARC Station. Contact publisher for price.
An All-Inclusive Accident/Incident Record Keeping Software System That Offers Extensive Reports & Graphs to Provide the User with Powerful Tools for Analysis of Accident Trends. Also Generates the OSHA 200 Log & 101 Form. Even Enables the User to Record Those Accidents Where There Was No Injury.
Pro-Am Software.

The Safety Director. *Version:* 1.1. 1991. *Items Included:* One year of free telephone technical support, an operations manual in a 3-ring binder, the Runtime Version of Revelations. *Customer Support:* After the first year of free telephone technical support, additional tech support can be purchased if needed.
MS-DOS. IBM compatible PC's (512k). $4995.00 single user; $11,300.00 5 user network. *Networks supported:* Novell, IBM PC-Net, Banyan Vines, LAN Manager for MS-DOS, & most other DOS compatible networks.
Pathworks or Digital Equipment Corp.'s VMS. VAX (320k). $11,300.00 5 user; $16,725.00 10 user. *Networks supported:* DECnet.
UNIX or SunOS. SPARC Station. Contact publisher for price.
An All-Inclusive Accident/Incident Record Keeping Software System That Offers Extensive Reports & Graphs to Provide the User with Powerful Tools for Analysis of Accident Trends. Also Generates the OSHA 200 Log & 101 Form. Even Enables the User to Record Those Accidents Where There Was No Injury.
Pro-Am Software.

Safety Monkey: Help Make Swingland Safe. Mayo Clinic Staff. Oct. 1994. *Customer Support:* Free 800 Number Technical Support.
Windows. PC with 486SX 25MHz or higher (8Mb). disk $29.95 (ISBN 1-884899-09-9). *Optimal configuration:* 486SX 25MHz or higher PC, 8MB RAM, double-speed CD-ROM drive, VGA Plus 640x480 monitor displaying 256 colors, Windows 3.1, stereo headphones or speakers, hard disk space, Sound Blaster 16 or compatible sound card.
A Clever Character Named Safety Monkey Shows Young Children That Safety Isn't Something to Monkey Around With. Safety Monkey Helps Kids Identify & Correct Unsafe Conditions, & Learn How & When to Get a Grown-Up to Help. Animation & Sing-a-Long Songs Make Safety Tips Fun & Easy to Remember.
IVI Publishing, Inc.

SafeWord for Novell. *Items Included:* Manuals, optional PassWord generators. *Customer Support:* Hot line, on- & off-site training, BBS.
Contact publisher for price.
Protects a Novell File or Access Server. Access Is Granted Only after the User Supplies a Single-Use, Dynamic PassWord, Generated by an Electronic, Hand-Held PassWord Generator, or Token. Tokens Supported Include the SafeWord MultiSync Card, DES Gold Card, DES Silver Card, SafeWord AccessCard, WatchWord & SecureNet Key.
Enigma Logic, Inc.

SafeWord for VAX Systems. *Version:* 3.74. Mar. 1985. *Operating System(s) Required:* VAX VMS. *Memory Required:* 1000k. *General Requirements:* Users protected by dynamic PassWords will need a hand-held dynamic PassWord generator. *Items Included:* Supervisor,

user & installation guides, password generators (OPT). *Customer Support:* Hot-line, on & off-site training, BBS.
$500.00 to $30,000.00.
Computer Security System That Positively Verifies the Identify of Users Attempting to Logon to a VMS System. Accomplishes This Through Dynamic PassWord Technology, Permitting Logon Only After the User Provides a Single-Use, Dynamic PassWord, Available Only from a Registered PassWord Generator. Standard VMS Security Remains Unchanged. A Supervisor Can Further Restrict Access with Any Combination of Fixed Passwords, Password Aging, Time, Date, & Day-of-Week Locks, Logon Limits, & Attack Detection & Prevention.
Enigma Logic, Inc.

SafeWord PC-Safe II. *Version:* 1.20. Jul. 1989. *Compatible Hardware:* IBM PC XT, PC AT. *Memory Required:* 15k. *General Requirements:* Users protected by dynamic PassWords will need a hand-held dynamic PassWord generator. *Items Included:* Supervisor guide & user guide. *Customer Support:* Hot-line, on & off-site training, BBS.
3.5" or 5.25" disk $275.00.
Automatic Encryption & Access Control Program. Access Can Be Controlled by a Dynamic PassWord System Requiring a Single-Use, Dynamic PassWord Available Only from a Hardheld PassWord Generator. The Supervisor Can Further Restrict Access with Any Combination of Fixed Passwords, Access Limits, & Attack Detection & Protection. Maintains Audit Trails of All Access Attempts, Successful or Not. Both DES & Proprietary Encryption Is Available.
Enigma Logic, Inc.

SafeWord PC-Safe III. Jun. 1991. *Items Included:* Manuals. *Customer Support:* Manuals, telephone hot-line, BBS, on & off-site training.
PC-DOS or MS-DOS 3.0 or higher. IBM XT/AT or compatible (25K). 3.5" or 5.25" disk $275.00.
Provides Automatic File-by-File Encryption & Access Control for IBM PCs & Compatibles. Access to the PC's Hard Disk & Encrypted Diskettes Is Protected by Any Combination of Memorized, Fixed Passwords, Single-Use Dynamic Passwords, Password Use Count, Access Limits, & Attack Detection & Prevention.
Enigma Logic, Inc.

SafeWord Single Sign-On Server. Jul. 1992. *Items Included:* Supervisor & User manuals. *Customer Support:* Hot-line, on & off-site training, BBS.
MS/PC/DR DOS. IBM PC or compatible. disk $50.00. *Addl. software required:* Compatible with SafeWord PC-Safe II or III. *Networks supported:* Any accessible through an IBM PC or compatible.
A Utility That Securely Automates Logins from an IBM PC or Compatible. Users Provide Their ID & Password Once & Single Sign-On Automates All Subsequent Logins, Providing the User ID & Fixed & Dynamic PassWords for Other Logins.
Enigma Logic, Inc.

SafeWord SofToken. *Items Included:* User manuals. *Customer Support:* Hot line, BBS, on- & off-site training.
  MS-Windows. IBM & compatibles. Contact publisher for price. *Addl. software required:* Accesses SafeWord software on remote host computer.
  UNIX (SUN OS, Solaris, HP-UX, AIX & Others). Contact publisher for price.
A Software-Based Dynamic PassWord Generator That Emulates a Hand-Held Dynamic PassWord Generator, or Token. It Generates Single-Use, Non-Replayable Passwords, Without the Associated Cost of a Hardware Token, for Accessing Any System Protected by SafeWord Software. It Emulates the MultiSync Mode of the SafeWord MultiSync Token.
Enigma Logic, Inc.

SafeWord Stratus-Safe. *Version:* 3.74. Oct. 1988. *Operating System(s) Required:* Stratus VOS. *Memory Required:* 1000k. *General Requirements:* Users protected by dynamic PassWords will need a hand-held dynamic PassWord generator. *Items Included:* Supervisor guide, user guide, password generators (OPT). *Customer Support:* Hot-line, on & off-site training, manuals, BBS.
5000.00 to $30,000.00.
Computer Security System for Stratus Computer Systems. Access Is Controlled with Dynamic PassWord Technology, Which Requires the User to Supply a Different, Single-Use PassWord Each Time Access Is Requested. The User Can Obtain the Correct PassWord Only by Possession of a Registered Handheld PassWord Generator. A Supervisor Can Further Restrict Access with Any Combination of Fixed Passwords, Password Aging, Time, Date, & Day-of-Week Locks, Logon Limits, & Attack Detection & Prevention. Creates Complete Audit Logs, Available Only to the Supervisor.
Enigma Logic, Inc.

SafeWord Tandem-Safe. *Version:* 3.74. Nov. 1987. *Compatible Hardware:* Tandem Guardian 90. *Memory Required:* 260k. *General Requirements:* Users protected by dynamic PassWords will need a hand-held dynamic PassWord generator. *Items Included:* Supervisor guide, user guide, password generators (OPT). *Customer Support:* Hot-line, on & off-site training, manuals, BBS.
$5000.00 to $30,000.00.
Computer Security System Tailored for Tandem Computer Systems. Access to a Protected Area Is Controlled with Dynamic PassWord Technology, Which Requires the User to Supply a Different, Single-Use PassWord Each Time Access Is Requested. The User Can Obtain the Correct PassWord Only by Possession of a Registered Handheld PassWord Generator. A Supervisor Can Further Restrict Access with Any Combination of Fixed Passwords, Password Aging, Time, Date, & Day-of-Week Locks, Logon Limits, & Attack Detection & Prevention. Creates Complete Audit Logs, Available Only to the Supervisor.
Enigma Logic, Inc.

SafeWord UNIX-Safe. *Version:* 3.74. Feb. 1986. *Compatible Hardware:* Any CPU running UNIX Sys. III, V, ver. 7, BSD 4.2, 4.3, XENIX, ULTRIX, COSIX, POSIX, HPUX. *Operating System(s) Required:* UNIX Systems III, V, version 7, BSD 4.2, 4.3, Xenix, Ultrix, Cosix, Posix, HPUX. *General Requirements:* Users protected by dynamic PassWords will need a hand-held dynamic PassWord generator; some require a 'C' compiler. *Items Included:* Supervisor guide, user guide, password generators (OPT). *Customer Support:* Hot-line, on & off-site training, BBS.
$500.00-$30,000.00.
Computer Security System That Positively Verifies the Identity of Users Requesting Access to Any UNIX System. Accomplishes This Through Dynamic PassWord Technology, Granting Access Only After a User Provides a Single-Use, Dynamic PassWord, Available Only from a Handheld, Electronic PassWord Generator, Called a Token. A Supervisor Can Further Restrict Access with Any Combination of Fixed Passwords, Password Aging, Time, Date, & Day-of-Week Locks, Logon Limits, & Attack Detection & Prevention. Maintains Complete Audit Logs, Available Only to the Supervisor, of All Logons & Attempted Logons.
Enigma Logic, Inc.

SafeWord VTAM-Safe. *Version:* 3.74. *Items Included:* Supervisor guide, user guide, installation guide, PassWord Generators (optional). *Customer Support:* Hot-line, on & off-site training, 90-day warranty, BBS, extended warranty available.
MVS/VTAM (1Mb). $21,000.00-$50,000.00.
Computer Security System That Positively Verifies the Identity of Users Through Dynamic Password Technology, Requiring Users to Provide a Single-Use, Dynamic Password, Available Only from a Registered Hand-Held PassWord Generator.
Enigma Logic, Inc.

Safire Computer Program, Tape & Documentation. *Version:* 9.2. 1996. *Items Included:* 1 tape or disk & 7 manuals.
DOS. IBM PC's or compatible. disk $75.00 (ISBN 0-8169-0365-4).
A computer program for the Design of Emergency Pressure Relief Systems.
American Institute of Chemical Engineers.

S.A.I.L.B.O.A.T. *Compatible Hardware:* North Star Advantage. *Operating System(s) Required:* CP/M-86, CP/M, MS-DOS. *Language(s):* Assembly. *Memory Required:* 24k.
disk $70.00.
Supports Chaining to a COM File. Includes a Help Menu & Comprehensive Documentation. Lower Case May Be Used in Commands or Variable Names. Machine Language Disk File Sort Is Included. Programs Can Be Stored in Standard ASCII Text Files, Enabling User to Edit the Program with a Full Screen Editor.
S.A.I.L. Operating Systems Div.

Sailing Master. *Customer Support:* 800-929-8117 (customer service).
MS-DOS. Apple II. disk $69.99 (ISBN 0-87007-535-7).
An Advanced Version Where User Picks the Sailboat Characteristics from a Database Representing Almost Every Popular Brand. See "Learning to Sail".
SourceView Software International.

Sailplan-1. 1983. *Compatible Hardware:* IBM PC, PC XT, PC AT, PS/2. *Operating System(s) Required:* MS-DOS. *Language(s):* QuickBASIC. *Memory Required:* 640k. *General Requirements:* EGA, VGA, or Hercules card.
$95.00.
Interactive Design of Sailplan Layout Using Screen Graphics Display. Reports Sail Areas, Centers & Performance/Stability Ratios As User Alters Sail Corner Coordinates.
AeroHydro, Inc.

Salamandre Laserstack. *Items Included:* 1 Floppy Disk. *Customer Support:* M-F 9 AM-5 PM Pacific Time (213) 451-1383.
Macintosh Plus, SE, II or Portable (1 Mb). 3.5" disk $59.95. *Nonstandard peripherals required:* Videodisc player, monitor & cables; Salamandre videodisc. *Addl. software required:* HyperCard 1.2.2 or higher.
Compare Architectural Styles, Construction Methods, Collections of Art, & Chateaux Furnishings Using This Comprehensive Index to Salamandre: Chateaux of the Loire Which Chronicles the Evolution of Chateau Architecture During the Romanesque, Gothic, Renaissance & Baroque Periods.
The Voyager Co.

Salary Magic. *Version:* 2.0. *Compatible Hardware:* Apple Macintosh. *Memory Required:* 512k.
3.5" disk $495.00.
This Salary Management & Salary Negotiations Management Package Calculates, Records & Prints Virtually Any Information Needed at the

TITLE INDEX

Negotiating Table or for Salary Planning. Salaries, Fringe Benefit Packages, Changes (Increase or Decrease), or Completely New Salary Schedules or Guides Can Be Generated Using Dollars, Percentages, or a Combination of Both. Salary Information Can Be Generated in a Schedule of up to 30x40 Cells. Includes Rounding, Customizable Referencing, Off-Schedule Placement, & Calculating a Maximum Base from a Fixed Budget. Up to 20 Fringe Benefits Can Be Entered As a Percentage, a Dollar Amount, or Both. Calculation Options Recreate an Organization's Current Fringe Package Precisely. Selection Options Allow for Multiple Benefit Groups & for the Addition of New Fringes at Any Time. Employee Information May Be Entered in Two Ways. Specific Information for Each Employee May Be Entered, Including Additional Pay, Fringe & Insurance Information, & Cost Code.
Magic Software, Inc.

The Sale Manager. Gary Sande. 1985. *Compatible Hardware:* Apple II, II+, IIe, IIc. *Operating System(s) Required:* Apple DOS 3.3. *Memory Required:* 48k.
$79.50 (ISBN 1-55797-001-7, Order no.: AP2-AG30).
Helps Users Manage Sales Campaigns. Includes a Program Disk, Sales Data Disk, & a Customer Data Disk. Keeps Track of an Organization's Sales Data. Keeps Records of up to 500 Salespeople, Prints Customer Order Forms, Sales Summaries, Total Sales Orders, & a Final Summary.
Hobar Pubns.

Sales Achievement Predictor (SalesAp). *Version:* 1.010. Jotham Friedland et al. Nov. 1995. *Customer Support:* Free unlimited phone support.
Windows 3.X, Windows 95. 286 (4Mb). disk $275.00 (Order no.: W-1082). *Nonstandard peripherals required:* Printer.
Measures Traits That Are Critical to Success in Sales & in Related Fields Such As Customer Service, Sales Management, Marketing, & Public Relations. Meets All EEOC Guidelines. The Report Shows the Individual's Percentile Rank on the Folldwing Scales: Sales Disposition, Managerial Style, Initiative/Cold Calling, Assertiveness, Sales Closing, Personal Diplomacy, Achievement, Extroversion, Motivation, Patience, Competitiveness, Cooperativeness, Planning, Self Confidence, Related Style, Teamwork, & Goal Orientation.
Western Psychological Services.

Sales Analysis. *Compatible Hardware:* Radio Shack. *Operating System(s) Required:* CP/M. contact publisher for price.
Microtec Information Systems.

Sales Analysis: Optional Feature to A-R. *Version:* 4.5. 1978. *Compatible Hardware:* IBM PC & compatibles, PC XT, PC AT, 386, 486, Pentium, PS/2. *Operating System(s) Required:* PC-DOS/MS-DOS 3.X, 4X, 5X, 6X, Windows 3.1, Windows 95. *Language(s):* BASIC, C, Assembler. *Memory Required:* 640k. *General Requirements:* Stand-alone or 2Mb Network file server. *Customer Support:* 90 day warranty, onsite training, telephone support.
disk $200.00.
Sales & Summary Analysis Reports, Period Comparative, Product Type Profit Analysis Reports.
LIBRA Corp.

Sales Analysis Pro - Plus. *Version:* 5.11. Feb. 1992. *Items Included:* Disks & full documentation. *Customer Support:* 90 days free phone support, optional extended support plans available that include upgrades.
MS-DOS or compatible, Version 3.0 or higher. IBM PC or 100% compatible (640k). $195.00 Pro single user; $395.00 Plus single user. *Optimal configuration:* IBM PC or compatible, DOS 3.3 or higher 640k, printer laser or dot matrix. *Networks supported:* Novell, all NetBIOS compatible.
$295.00 Pro network version; $595.00 Plus network version.
Sales Figures Are Entered to Produce Ongoing Profitability & Menu Mix Reports for Any Period Specified. Powerful What-If Analysis Allows for Forecasting of Expected Revenues & Contributions by Menu Item or Category. Stand Alone or Integrates with Other Pro Software Modules. Interfaces to POS/Registers Available on Request. New Plus Module Allows Sales Mix to Deplete Inventory by Entering Sales Figures.
At Your Service Software, Inc.

Sales & Food Cost Analyzer. Harry Skolnik. Apr. 1986. *Compatible Hardware:* Apple Macintosh, IBM PC & compatibles. *Language(s):* Compiled dBASE III Plus. *Memory Required:* 512k. *General Requirements:* Hard disk.
disk $195.00 (Order no.: SPA).
Reports Menu Item Sales & Profits, Actual & Theoretical Food Costs, & Perpetual Inventory. Links to RestaurantComp's RECIPE PROFIT ANALYZER & INVENTORY PROGRAMS. Uses Sales Quantities for Each Menu Item, Typically Generated by an Electronic Point-of-Sale System.
RestaurantComp.

Sales & Market Forecasting. *Version:* 10.0. (Professional Ser.). 1989. *Compatible Hardware:* Apple Macintosh, IBM PC & compatibles. *Memory Required:* 512k. *Items Included:* Disks, book, program instructions. *Customer Support:* Telephone.
3.5" disk $145.00 (ISBN 0-920387-04-7).
3.5" disk $200.00, with Forecasting & Time Series.
Attacks the Very Practical Problem of How to Make a Forecast & What to Do with the Forecast Once It Is Made. The Starting Point Is the Preparation of a Demand Analysis & the Generation of a Company Time-Series. The Various Factors Which Might Appear in a Company Time-Series (Trends, Seasonality, & So Forth) Are Examined in Detail & Examples Are Given of the Appropriate Forecasting Techniques. The Problem of Relating the Company Time-Series to General Business & Economic Time-Series Is Covered, As Is the Development of the Forecast Itself, & Finally the Preparation of a Market Audit from the Various Materials Generated During the Forecasting Process. Sources of Information about Business Data Are Provided As Is an Extensive Data Base of about Fifty Yearly & Monthly Time-Series Obtained from U.S. Department of Commerce Publications. Numerous Examples Are Provided.
Lionheart Pr., Inc.

The Sales Assistant. *Items Included:* Bound manual. *Customer Support:* Free hotline - no time limit; 30 day limited warranty; updates are $5/ disk plus S&H.
MS-DOS 2.1 or higher. IBM & compatibles (128k). disk $59.95. *Nonstandard peripherals required:* 132-column printer, dual 360k drives, or one 360k drive & a hard disk.
Three Main Components Are: CLIENT INFORMATION: User Can Store Client Name, Address, Phone Number, Contact Person, Next Call/Visit Date, Last Sale/Sale Date, Running Total of Sales, Product Type, Credit Rating, & Account Number. This Database May Also Be Printed Several Convenient Ways; CAMPAIGN SCHEDULING: Use This to Plan a Sales Campaign Schedule. Includes a Graph; MAIL LABELS: User May Select Single or Double Wide Format. Using the CLIENT INFORMATION Database, You May Create Labels According to the Following Six Choices: 1. Entire Database; 2. By Selected Client; 3. By Selected City; 4. By Selected State; 5. By Selected ZIP Code; 6. By Selected Area Code.
Dynacomp, Inc.

SALES LEADS ANALYSIS

The Sales Associate System. *Version:* 2. Joseph M. Cerra. *Items Included:* The sales associate book, DBMS, instructions.
MS-DOS (384k). disk $79.95 (ISBN 0-927701-03-0, Order no.: SYSTEM). *Nonstandard peripherals required:* 1 hard disk, 1 floppy disk; printer.
Sales Software to Manage List, Sales Strategy, Call Records, Forecast, Orders, Commission Accounting, Time Management & Mass Marketing.
Evergreen Ventures, Inc.

Sales Express. *General Requirements:* External disk drive or hard disk drive.
Macintosh 512KE or higher. 3.5" disk $69.00.
Communication & Expense-Management Tool for Salespeople.
CP Software.

Sales History. *Version:* 5.2. 1992. *Compatible Hardware:* IBM RS/6000, Sun SPARC, HP UX Data General Aviion; Altos; IBM PC AT, XT; Intel 286/386, NCR Tower. *Operating System(s) Required:* PC-DOS/MS-DOS, UNIX, XENIX, AIX, Sun OS SCO UNIX. *Items Included:* Documentation, source code. *Customer Support:* One-year maintenance included in purchase price for resellers, annual maintenance available at app. $500-$675 per package per year, on-site customization, training & support available.
Unix, Xenix. Altos 2000; IBM PC, PC XT, PC AT; Intel 286, 386 & compatibles; NCR Tower. contact publisher for price. *Addl. software required:* MCBA Customer Order Processing & Accounts Receivable (Unix), contact publisher (Xenix).
Tracks & Produces Reports on Sales Information Provided by MCBA's Accounts Receivable, Customer Order Processing & Inventory Control Management Packages. Produces Analysis Reports to Locate Profit Sources, Comparison Reports to Monitor Cumulative Information Against Past Performance & Detailed Reports. Reports Can Be Selected by a Wide Range of Criteria.
MCBA, Inc.

Sales Invoice/Report Software. *Compatible Hardware:* IBM PC.
contact publisher for price.
Menu-Driven Program Can Be Used in Retail/ Wholesale Operations. Has the Capability to Print Invoices & Monthly/Annual Reports.
Antex Data Systems.

Sales Invoicing. (Service Management Ser.). 1996.
DOS, Unix. IBM PC. disk contact publisher for price.
Features include; Ability to edit previously entered line items, On-line credit limit checking as each line item is entered, Entry screen accommodates quotes, order, & invoices, etc.
Core Software, Inc.

Sales Leads Analysis. *Compatible Hardware:* DECmate, PDP 11-23. *Operating System(s) Required:* COS-310, MICRO-RSX. *General Requirements:* Hard disk.
disk $1200.00.
Provides Two Types of Analyses Designed to Answer the Question: "How Effective Was the Money Invested in Different Advertising Media,

in Generating Sales Leads & Sales Closings, & How Can It Be Made More Effective?" Media Source Analysis Targets the Most Profitable Investments by Showing Where & When Advertising Generates Leads & Sales. Closed Leads Analysis Interprets Sales by Source, Region, & Salesman, Providing Information on Where, When, & How the Company's Service or Product Groups Sell Best.
Corporate Consulting Co.

SALES LetterWorks. Sep. 1990. *Items Included:* Softcover book & computer disk. *Customer Support:* Free phone support no limitation. PC-DOS. IBM & compatible (256k). disk $79.98. *Addl. software required:* Word processor. Macintosh (128k). 3.5" disk $79.95. *Addl. software required:* Word processor.
300 Sales Letter, Proposals, Announcements & Other Documents to Help a Sales Person Sell More Effectively. User Finds the Document Requested in the Book & Calls It up from Within His Word Processor Using the System's Disks Which Contains Text (ASCII) Files of the Letters.
Round Lake Publishing Co.

Sales Management System. *Version:* 14.0. (Accounting Software Ser.). Aug. 1993. *Compatible Hardware:* IBM PC & compatibles. *Operating System(s) Required:* MS-DOS, PC-DOS. *Language(s):* MegaBASIC. *Memory Required:* 640k. *General Requirements:* Hard disk, wide carriage printer. *Customer Support:* (203) 790-9756.
disk $395.00, Network Option ,400.00 more. manual $50.00.
Territory Oriented, Providing Activity & Forecasting Features. Entry & Maintenance of Information on Salesmen, Customers, Prospects, & Manufacturers. Records Outstanding Quotes. Reports Include Projected Sales, Sales Activity, Active Jobs, Lead & Quote Analysis.
Applications Systems Group (CT), Inc.

Sales Management with dBASE III. Timothy Berry. *Operating System(s) Required:* MS-DOS. *General Requirements:* dBASE III.
$49.95, incl. manual (ISBN 0-934375-15-1).
Provides an Information System That Will Enable Users to Keep Track of Clients, Names, Addresses, Account Data, Pending Dates, etc. The System Organizes All the Day-to-Day Activities of Selling, & Includes Program Files, Format Files, Index Files, & Database Files. Documentation & Full Source Code Are Include for All the dBASE III Programs.
M & T Bks.

The Sales Manager's Tool Kit. *Compatible Hardware:* Apple Macintosh, IBM PC. *Memory Required:* 512k. *General Requirements:* Excel. 3.5" disk $59.95.
Designed to Help Sales & Marketing Professionals Be More Productive & Organized in Their Work. Kit Contains Five Templates: Sales Analyser, Sales Forecasting-Budgeting Form, Expense Report Calculator, Advertising Budget Form & Price Lister.
Wincom Data Systems, Inc.

Sales Order/Accounts Receivable: Accounts Receivable Service Billing.
$295.00.
Provides History Information for Customer Transactions. Information Can Be Displayed on a CRT or Printed.
Advanced Concepts, Inc.
   Auto-Assign Invoice Number at Time of Entry.
   $125.00.
   Auto-Assign Order Number Based upon Date.
   $125.00.
   Automatically Calculates Freight & Sales Tax.
   Compute Sales Tax on Freight.
   $75.00.
   Custom Invoices & Picking Slips.
   $150.00-$275.00.
   Display Multiple Invoice Payments.
   $125.00.
   During Entry of Cash Receipts, Payments for Multiple Invoices Will Be Displayed until Check Number Is Changed.
   Increase Ship-To Four Digits & Post to Sales History.
   $125.00.
   Line Item Discount Percentage.
   $200.00.
   During Order Entry the Unit of Measure Field Is Used to Input a Percentage Discount.
   Multiple Description Lines per Entry.
   $200.00.
   Description Field Allows up to 10 Lines of Description per Line Item Entry.
   Online History Inquiry.
   $295.00.
   Saleperson Commission.
   $295.00.
   Salesperson's Commission Can Be Calculated by Inventory Item.

Sales Order Entry. *Version:* 2.0. 1989. *Items Included:* Disks & manuals.
MS/PC DOS; Concurrent DOS, Xenix, Unix. IBM PC/XT/AT & compatibles, IBM PS/2 (512k). single-user $995.00. *Nonstandard peripherals required:* Hard disk, 132-column printer. *Networks supported:* Novell, Lantastic, Banyan VINES; all NETBIOS compatible.
multi-user $1295.00.
Sales Order Entry & Tracking System That Provides Management Information Essential for Keeping Response Time at Acceptable Levels & Identifying Bottlenecks. As Orders Are Prepared the Available Balance of Each Part Ordered Is Displayed. Order Quantity Can Be Adjusted to Match the Balance Available or the Remainder Can Be Backordered. Orders Can Be Released When Partially Held or Held until All Parts Are Available. Release Orders Can Be Billed & Shipped with Multiple Billings Possible. Billing Requires MC Software's Accounts Receivable System.
INMASS/MRP.

Sales Order Processing (a Part of ABECAS). *Version:* 3.3. Jan. 1989. *Customer Support:* On site training unlimited support services for first 90 days & through subscription thereafter.
PC/MS-DOS 3.1. IBM PC & compatibles. Contact publisher for price. *Nonstandard peripherals required:* Hard disk (30Mb or higher); 132 column printer.
Orders & Quotes May Be Entered & Managed. May Be Updated to Invoice, or Invoice May Be Entered Directly. New Customers May Be Added As Orders/Invoices Are Entered. Ship-To & Ship-By Information May Also Be Defined. Commissions May Be Based on Salesperson, Item, Product Group, or Order. Taxes May Be Tracked by Taxing Authority Based on Tax Code. Memo May Be Entered with Transaction. Numerous Reports Available to Analyze Current Orders & Invoices. Multi-User Version Available for Novell, NTNX, 10-Net, Unix/Xenix, Turbo DOS, & Others. Requires Accounts Receivable & Inventory Management Modules.
Argos Software.

Sales Plot. 1982. *Compatible Hardware:* MS-DOS, CP/M-80 based machines. *Language(s):* Microsoft BASIC.
3.5" or 5.25" disk $50.00 (Order no.: 265).
Plots Gross Sales for a Company by Month, Adjusts the Scale of the Graph to Be 100% for the Highest Month.
Resource Software International, Inc.

Sales Vision Field Sales: Information System for Sales Professionals. 1983. *Compatible Hardware:* IBM PC XT, PC AT, PS/2 & compatibles. *Operating System(s) Required:* MS-DOS, PC-DOS. *Language(s):* Foxbase PLUS or Foxpro (source code included). *Memory Required:* 640k. *General Requirements:* Hard disk, printer.
disk $295.00.
Designed for Individual Reps & Field Sales Organizations. Stores, Organizes & Retrieves Customer/Prospect Profiles, Contact History, Purchase History & Notes. Has Automatic Schedule/Calendar & Tickler Files. Produces Reports Including: Call Sheets, Forecasts, Expense Reports, Calendars & User-Definable Reports. Mailing Label Capability Interfaces to Word Processing for Follow-Up Letters & Mass Mailings. Handles 65,000 Customers with Quick Response. Other Features Include: Fast Data Entry Utilities, Global Update, User-Definable Fields.
System Vision Corp.

Sales Vision Telemarketing. *Compatible Hardware:* IBM PC XT, PC AT, PS/2 & compatibles. *Operating System(s) Required:* PC-DOS, MS-DOS. *Language(s):* Foxbase PLUS or Foxpro (source code included). *Memory Required:* 640k. *General Requirements:* Hard disk.
disk $495.00.
demo disk & manual $49.50.
Customer/Prospect Management System That Assists Telemarketing Representatives While on the Phone. Maintains Large Amounts of Data (Profiles, Contacts, Purchases, Notes, Qualifying Data) & Responds Quickly. Special Feature Operates with the Automatic Schedule/Calendar to Organize Daily Work & Presents All Records for Those Customers to Be Contacted. Fast Access to One Screen Showing Client's Most Current Activity. User-Definable Fields. Automatic Labels & Letters for Daily Follow-Up & Direct Mail. Over 20 Standard Reports Plus User-Definable Reports. Autodial & Scripting. Runs on a Local Area Network.
System Vision Corp.

Sales Yield Management (SYM). *Version:* 3.0. May 1991. *Items Included:* Spiral-bound manuals & on-line help; source code. *Customer Support:* 30 days unlimited warranty; maintenance 1 1/2% per month of license fee; training packages available; customization of software; hotline included.
MS-DOS, MS-Windows, Windows for PENS. IBM compatible (4Mb). $50,000.00-$100,000.00 (Order no.: SYM30). *Addl. software required:* SQL Database (SYBASE, GUPTA, INFORMIX, etc.). *Optimal configuration:* 4Mb of RAM, 110Mb disk storage, 486 microprocessor/33 MHz. *Networks supported:* Novell.
A Tactical Pricing Tool, Proactively Manages the Day-to-Day Pricing Process. Supplied with Updated Information about Customers & Competitors, Sales Organizations Can Objectively Evaluate Potential Deals. SYM Eliminates Pricing Guesswork. Companies Implementing This Powerful Profit Tool Typically Record a 2-5% Average Price Improvement in Booked Business.
MIT Group, Inc.

Sales Yield Management (SYM). *Version:* 3.0. May 1991. *Items Included:* Spiral-bound manuals & on-line help; source code. *Customer Support:* 30 days unlimited warranty; maintenance 1 1/2% per month of license fee; training packages available; customization of software; hotline included.
MS-DOS, MS-Windows; Windows for PENS.

TITLE INDEX

IBM compatible (2Mb). $50,000.00-$100,000.00 (Order no.: SYM30). *Addl. software required:* SYBASE. *Optimal configuration:* 4Mb of RAM; 110Mb disk storage; 386 microprocessor/33 MHz. *Networks supported:* Novell.
Tactical Pricing Tool Proactively Manages the Day-to-Day Pricing Process. Supplied with Updated Information about Customers & Competitors, Sales Organizations Can Objectively Evaluate Potential Deals. SYM Eliminates Pricing Guesswork. Companies Implementing This Powerful Profit Tool Typically Record a 2-5% Average Price Improvement in Booked Business.
MIT Group, Inc.

SalesMinder. *Version:* 4.0. Sep. 1985. *Compatible Hardware:* Columbia MPC; IBM PC, PC XT; Compaq; NCR PC; Epson QX-10; Leading Edge; Sperry PC; TI Professional. *Operating System(s) Required:* MS-DOS. *Language(s):* Microsoft BASIC.
$300.00.
Part of the STOREMINDER Series That Replaces the Cash Register with a Microcomputer. Sales Clerks Are Guided by Menus & Each Entry Is Defined on the Display. Automatically Keeps Track of Multiple Price Levels, Discount Structures, Commission Rates & Different Types of Sales. Price Item Description & Quantities On-Hand Are Automatically Looked-Up. Cash Drawer Access Is Monitored & Limited to Those Entering an Authorized Code.
Verifone, Inc.

SalesPower. *Version:* 3.01. *General Requirements:* Hard disk, 3Mb. *Customer Support:* 30 days free telephone support.
Macintosh Plus SE or II or compatibles (2Mb). Software price: $395.00 without word processing; $495.00 with word processing, Call for Multi-user pricing. *Nonstandard peripherals required:* 20 Mb Hard disk.
Sales Tracking & Lead Management, Extensive Sales & Marketing Reports. Manages Clients & Prospects, Sales Reps & Products. Generates Sales Quotes, 30-, 60-, 90-Day Sales Forecasts, Lead Source Reports. Includes a Report Writer & Label Generator. Multi-User Version Available.
Stanford Business Systems.

SalesTax Compliance System. *Compatible Hardware:* IBM PC & compatibles, PS/2. *Memory Required:* 2000k. *General Requirements:* Communications (download) software. *Items Included:* Monthly sales tax updates information for one year. One copy National SalesTax Rate Directory. Documentation. *Customer Support:* Customer support hotline - no charge.
Contact vendor for price.
Automates the Sales Tax Compliance Function: (1) Eliminates the Need to Research Sales Tax Rates & Return Information. Data File Contains Tax Rates for More Than 50,000 Locations in U.S. & Canada. (2) Automatically Calculates the Proper Tax to Be Applied to a Transaction. (3) Provides Management Reports for a Complete Audit Trail. (4) Automatically Generates State & Local Sales Tax Returns in Formats Accepted by Most States.
Vertex Inc.

SalesView. *Customer Support:* 800-929-8117 (customer service).
MS-DOS. IBM/PS2. disk $299.99 (ISBN 0-87007-789-9).
A Database Tool Intended for Salespersons Who Market Products That Are Not Sold on a One Call Basis. Letters May Be Mail Merged for Mass Mailings, & There Is Provision for Complete Account of All Activity on Each Account. Each Salesperson Can Use the Program on the Same Computer, with a Single Centralized Database. There Is Security on Names. Prospect Activity Can Be Scanned & Printed at Any Time. Files from Different Types of Databases Can Be Merged. A Complete Account of the Activity Per Prospect Is Kept Online for Immediate Recall. One of the Security Functions Prohibits Lower Level Access ID Holders from Making Copies of the Prospect Files on Floppy Disk.
SourceView Software International.

Salon Transcripts. *Version:* 5.1. *Compatible Hardware:* Apple Macintosh Plus or later. *Memory Required:* 1000k. *General Requirements:* 20Mb hard disk, ImageWriter II. *Items Included:* System customization; manuals in 3-ring binder, 415 (8.5 x 11") pages; free enhancements for 1 year. *Customer Support:* Toll-free hotline. $3865.00, 2 3.5" disks.
Salon Management System.
SST, Inc.

Sam. Jan. 1985. *Compatible Hardware:* IBM PC. *Operating System(s) Required:* PC-DOS. *Memory Required:* 512k. *General Requirements:* Hard disk.
Level 1. disk $3995.00.
Level 2. disk $9995.00.
Level 3. disk $14,995.00.
Controls & Handles Information Generated & Used in Chemical Laboratories. Facilitates Sample Scheduling, Tracking, & Control. Enables Users to Easily Implement & Maintain Quality Assurance & Quality Control Procedures. Performs Trend & Statistical Analysis of Data Results & Generates Reports Covering All Sample Analysis Results As Well As Financial Reports & Workload Status Reports.
Radian Corp.

S.A.M. Pacesetting Computers, Inc. *Operating System(s) Required:* CP/M. *Language(s):* CBASIC 86. *Memory Required:* 64k. *General Requirements:* Printer, Winchester hard disk. $2995.00.
Texas Instruments, Personal Productivit.

SAM-CD: Scientific American Medicine on CD-ROM. Oct. 1989. *Items Included:* An annual subscription to SAM-CD includes: four CD-ROM discs, a comprehensive user's guide & 8 new DISCOTEST II cases. *Customer Support:* Free unlimited phone support; unlimited free technical support 1-800-643-4351.
MS-DOS, Windows 3.1 or higher. 486 or higher (640k). CD-ROM disk institution $645.00; individual $395.00; contact publisher for network prices (ISBN 0-89454-009-2). *Nonstandard peripherals required:* CD-ROM drive. *Optimal configuration:* 486 or higher, 640k, Windows 3.1, CD-ROM drive. *Networks supported:* Contact publisher.
Macintosh (1Mb).
Contains the Full Text of Scientific American Medicine on a Single CD-ROM Disc. The Disc Provides the Same In-Depth Coverage of Internal Medicine As the Paper Version. All Tables & Illustrations from the Text Are Included (VGA Graphics Are Required to View Illustrations). The Disc Also Includes the Library of DISCOTEST II Patient Management Problems. The Disc Is Updated Quarterly.
Scientific American Medicine.

SAM: (Strategic A L Management Model). *Version:* 2.5. *Items Included:* Spiral bound manual. *Customer Support:* $700.00 to $1500.00. Training in our office.
MS-DOS 3.3 or higher (640k). IBM or compatibles. $1995.00 (Ver. LE); $3995.00 (Ver. SE); $7500.00 (SAM DE). *Optimal configuration:* 386-DX, MS-DOS 5.0 640k RAM, 2 Mb extended memory.
Dynamic Cash Flow Model with User-Definable Chart of Accounts. Simulates Effect of Changes in Interest Rates Has on Growth, Earnings, Gap, etc. Detailed Reports. Window-Like User-Interface. Add-ins Available for Graphics, Market Value, Decomposition Analysis.
Farin & Assocs.

Sambas; Threads. *Compatible Hardware:* Apple Macintosh. *Memory Required:* 512k.
Sambas $4500.00.
Threads $745.00.
Structural Analysis Package for Engineers.
Microneering.

Sammy's Science House.
Windows. 386 processor or higher (640k RAM). CD-ROM disk $49.95 (Order no.: R1359). *Nonstandard peripherals required:* CD-ROM drive. *Optimal configuration:* 386 processor or higher, MS-DOS 3.1 or higher, 20Mb hard drive, external speakers or headphones (with sound card) that are Sound Blaster compatible, VGA graphics & adapter, VGA color monitor.
Macintosh (4Mb). (Order no.: R1359). *Nonstandard peripherals required:* 14" color monitor or larger, CD-ROM drive.
Five Fascinating Activities Offer an Exciting Introduction to the Wonders of Science. Children Will Observe, Classify, Compare, Construct & Solve Problems As They Learn about Plants, Animals, Seasons & Weather.
Library Video Co.

Samna Plus IV. *Version:* 2.02. *Compatible Hardware:* Compaq Deskpro 386, AT&T 3B, NCR Tower 32, Convergent Technologies S/220, IBM RT PC. *Operating System(s) Required:* MS-DOS, Unix.
disk $745.00 to $11,900.00.
Word Processing & Office Automation Package. Allows Text, Graphics & Pictures Scanned into MS-DOS-Based PCs to Be Transferred into Unix-Based Small Computers.
Samna Corp.

Samna Word II. Samna Corp. *Operating System(s) Required:* MS-DOS. *Memory Required:* 192k. *General Requirements:* 2 disk drives, printer.
$450.00.
Texas Instruments, Personal Productivit.

Samna Word IV. *Version:* 3.0. *Compatible Hardware:* IBM PC, PC XT, PC AT, 3270 PC, PS/2 Models 30/50/60/80; TI Professional; other 80386-based computers.
contact publisher for price.
Samna Corp.

SAMPLE. *Version:* 1.01.
License fee unit. $300.00 (Order no.: SAMPLE).
License fee site. $450.00.
Maintenance unit. $60.00.
Maintenance site. $90.00.
Designed for Audit Sampling. Can Be Used in Compliance Testing to Determine the Required Sample Size for Testing the Deviation Rate of a Control, to Analyze the Results Achieved in a Sample or to Generate up to 3000 Random Items for Sample Selection. Used in Substantive Testing to Determine the Required Sample Size for Stratified Item Sampling. Also Provides Reports, Information Sheets, & Worksheets for Each Application.
Coopers & Lybrand.

SampleCell. Nov. 1990. *Items Included:* 1 spiral bound manual, 630Mb CD-ROM of samples, Sound Designer II SC sample editing software. *Customer Support:* Free technical phone support.
Macintosh II, IIx, IIcx, IIci, IIfx. $1995.00.
$2995.00 (8Mb).

16 Bit RAM-Based Stereo Sample Playback Card for the Mac II. Features 16 CD Quality Voices, 8 Polyphonic Outputs, & up to 8Mb of Standard Mac II RAM. Includes a 630Mb CD-ROM Sound Library Disk, Interface Software, & Sound Designer II SC Software for Sample Editing & Universal Sample Transfer. Additional Cards Add 16 More Voices Each, & the System Is Compatible with SOUND TOOLS or AUDIOMEDIA, Creating a Direct to Disk Digital & Recording & Sampling System on the Mac. RAM Upgrades Are Available.
Digidesign, Inc.

Sampler. *Items Included:* Instruction manual. *Customer Support:* Free Telephone support. DOS/Windows 95. IBM & compatibles (8Mb). Contact publisher for price. *Nonstandard peripherals required:* CD-ROM drive.
Digital Pictures, Inc.

Sampler. *Customer Support:* All of our products are unconditionally guaranteed.
DOS, Mac. CD-ROM disk Contact publisher for price (Order no.: SAMPLER). *Nonstandard peripherals required:* CD-ROM drive.
Samples of 44 Walnut Creek CDROMs Plus 5.00 Check to End User.
Walnut Creek CDRom.

Sampling Quality Control. *Customer Support:* 800-929-8117 (customer service).
MS-DOS. Apple II. disk $49.99 (ISBN 0-87007-654-X).
Sets up Simple Sampling Plans for Six Common Combinations of Alpha (Confidence Level) & Beta (Power of a Test) & Determines Minimum Sampling Size. This Package Will Determine Minimum Sampling Levels for Simple Sampling Plans That Meet Prescribed Protection Levels.
SourceView Software International.

The San Diego Zoo Presents: The Animals!
MS-DOS 5.0 or higher, Windows 3.1 or higher. 386 processor or higher (4Mb). CD-ROM disk $59.95 (Order no.: R1079). *Nonstandard peripherals required:* CD-ROM drive. *Optimal configuration:* 386 processor operating at 16Mhz or higher, MS-DOS 5.0 or higher, Windows 3.1 or higher, 30Mb hard drive, mouse, VGA graphic adapter & VGA color monitor (SVGA recommended) 4Mb RAM, external speakers or headphones (with sound card) that are Sound Blaster compatible.
Macintosh (4Mb). (Order no.: R1079A). *Nonstandard peripherals required:* 14" color monitor or larger, CD-ROM drive.
See & Hear over 200 Exotic Animals on Video, Plus 1300 Color Photos & Information on Other Animals, Facts & Habitat Descriptions.
Library Video Co.

The San Diego Zoo Presents The Animals!
IBM PC & compatibles (1Mb). CD-ROM disk $99.95. *Optimal configuration:* 16-MHz 286 IBM PC or compatible, 1Mb RAM (extended memory driver required), VGA with color monitor (256k video memory), CD-ROM drive (125k/second transfer rate), hard drive with 2Mb free space, MS-DOS 3.3 or higher, MSCDEX 2.1 or higher.
IBM PC or compatible with 80386sx processor or higher (2Mb). CD-ROM disk $99.95. *Optimal configuration:* IBM PC or compatible with 80386sx processor or higher, 2Mb RAM, MPC-compatible sound card, MPC-compatible CD-ROM drive, Super VGA graphics adapter & monitor, Microsoft-compatibe mouse recommended, DOS 3.1 or higher, Windows 3.1, MSCDEX 2.2 or higher.
Macintosh (4Mb). CD-ROM disk $99.95. *Optimal configuration:* Macintosh II series, LC series, Performa series or Macintosh Quadra,

12 inch RGB color monitor or 13 inch RGB color monitor (LC requires 512k or video RAM), Apple CD-ROM drive or compatibles (150k/sound transfer rate), 20Mb internal hard drive, System 6.07 or higher, QuickTime Extension, version 1.5 or higher, 32 bit color Quickdraw under System 6.07.
Discover the Liveliest Collection of Animal Sights, Sounds, & Statistics Ever to Appear on a Computer Screen. Visit the Zoo at Home Through Photos, Movies, Stories, and/or Text. Includes over an Hour of Motion Video with Synchronized Sound, More Than 1,300 Color Photographs, & Upwards of 2,500 Pages of Articles & Scientific Data. Activities of Special Interest for Younger Explorers Are Also Available in the Storybook Theater & Kid's Corner.
Software Toolworks.

Sands of Fire. Digital Illusions. Aug. 1989. *Items Included:* Thoroughly documented historical data in manual.
Apple Macintosh (512k). 3.5" disk $49.95 (Order no.: MCSF).
MS-DOS 2.0 or higher. IBM & compatibles. disk $49.95 (Order no.: PCSF). *Nonstandard peripherals required:* CGA, EGA or Hercules graphics board & matching monitor.
Welcome to the White-Hot Sands & Sweltering Intensity of WWII North Africa as Commander of the British & American Tank Units. Up to 48 Different Battle Engagements Can Be Played as Commander, Driver & Gunner. You Alone Can Influence the Outcome of WWII.
360, Inc.

Santa Fe Mysteries. *Items Included:* Installation Guide.
IBM PC. Contact publisher for price (ISBN 0-87321-064-6, Order no.: CDD-3106).
Activision, Inc.

Santa Fe Trail. David Allan Herzog. 1984. *Compatible Hardware:* Apple II+, IIe, MS-DOS. *Language(s):* BASIC. *Memory Required:* 256k. disk $65.00, incl. back-up disk & documentation (ISBN 0-89525-596-0, Order no.: DK-TRAIL).
Graphics, Animation, & Sound Effects Help Recreate Life on the Santa Fe Trail. A Trader Is in Search of Riches & High Adventure, Traveling Between Independence, Missouri & Santa Fe, New Mexico; the Years Are 1820-1829.
Educational Activities, Inc.

Santa's on His Way (to Your House): A Personalized Electronic Storybook. Peter Hannan & Jeremy Solomon. Jul. 1995. *Customer Support:* Limited, contact corporate office, no fee.
Windows 3.1 or higher. IBM 386 compatible or higher (4Mb). disk $14.95 (ISBN 0-9647659-0-X). *Nonstandard peripherals required:* 1 mouse & VGA monitor. *Optimal configuration:* IBM 486 compatible, 8Mb RAM.
Personalized Electronic Storybook about Santa Claus' Efforts to Reach the Reader's House on Christmas Eve. Reader's Must Help Santa Rescue Various Characters in Distress along the Way. Fun for Children Ages 2-10.
Granite Planet.

SAPANA: Cardfile. *Version:* 1.50. Kailash Chandra. 1984. *Compatible Hardware:* IBM PC & compatibles, PCjr, PC XT. *Operating System(s) Required:* PC-DOS 1.1, 2.0, 2.1. *Language(s):* Compiled BASIC. *Memory Required:* 128k. disk $195.00 (ISBN 0-918689-03-1).
Contains 11 Pre-Structured Fields. Stores Any Kind of Facts & Retrieves Them in Various Ways.
Sapana Micro Software.

SAP90. *Version:* 5.4. *Items Included:* Complete set of program documentation, including User & Verification manuals. *Customer Support:* 1 year maintenance, 15% of program price.
MS-DOS. IBM PC AT or compatible (1Mb). $2000.00-$7500.00. *Optimal configuration:* 4Mb RAM, 100Mb Hard disk.
Latest Program for the Three-Dimensional Static & Dynamic Finite Element Analysis of Structures Developed by Dr. Edward L. Wilson. The program Is Based on Modern Equation Solving Techniques & New Finite Element Formulations.
Computers & Structures, Inc.

Sarah, Plain & Tall. Intentional Education Staff & Patricia MacLachlan. Apr. 1996. *Items Included:* Program manual. *Customer Support:* Free technical support, 90 day warranty.
School ver.. System 7.1 or higher. Macintosh (4Mb). 3.5" disk contact publisher for price (ISBN 1-57204-326-1). *Nonstandard peripherals required:* 256 color monitor, hard drive, printer.
Lab pack. System 7.1 or higher. Macintosh (4Mb). 3.5" disk contact publisher for price (ISBN 1-57204-302-4). *Nonstandard peripherals required:* 256 color monitor, hard drive, printer.
Site license. System 7.1 or higher. macintosh (4Mb). 3.5" disk contact publisher for price (ISBN 1-57204-327-X). *Nonstandard peripherals required:* 256 color monitor, hard drive, printer.
School ver.. Windows 3.1 or higher. IBM/Tandy & 100% compatibles (4Mb). disk contact publisher for price (ISBN 1-57204-303-2). *Nonstandard peripherals required:* VGA or SVGA 640 x 480 resolution (256), mouse, hard drive, sound device.
Lab pack. Windows 3.1 or higher. IBM/Tandy & 100% compatibles (4Mb). disk contact publisher for price (ISBN 1-57204-328-8). *Nonstandard peripherals required:* VGA or SVGA 640 x 480 resolution (256), mouse, hard drive, sound device.
Site license. Windows 3.1 or higher. IBM/Tandy & 100 compatibles (4Mb). disk contact publisher for price (ISBN 1-57204-304-0). *Nonstandard peripherals required:* VGA or SVGA 640 x 480 resolution (256), mouse, hard drive, sound device.
This companion for young adult literature is ideal for students who don't know how to start that book report, or give that needed summary. Gentle prompts throughout the guide section of the program include Warm-up Connections, Think about Plot, Quoting & Noting, Keeping a Journal, If I Were ———' Responding to Questions, Using Quotations, Taking a Personal View, Write to Others, & Write a Sequel.
Lawrence Productions, Inc.

Sarah's Surprise. Nan Holcomb & Jane Steelman. Oct. 1993. *Items Included:* Directions on use of the program, registration card. *Customer Support:* 90 days limited warranty, replacement disks for fee of $10.00 & proof of purchase.
6.07. MAC LC (2Mb). 3.5" disk $29.95 (ISBN 0-944727-21-2). *Optimal configuration:* MAC LC, System 7.1, 4Mb RAM.
Sarah Is Unable to Talk but Wants to Sing "Happy Birthday". User Can Hear Sarah's Story Word by Word or Sentence by Sentence Using a Button on the Screen or a Switch. Text Is Highlighted in Color of Choice.
Jason & Nordic Pubs.

Sargon III. *Compatible Hardware:* HP 150 Touchscreen.
3.5" disk $49.95 (Order no.: 92243MA).
With the Touchscreen You Move the Chess Pieces by Simply Touching the Screen. Includes 45 Chess Problems & 107 Historical Chess Games. Its Algorithms Allow the Computer to Search Many Moves Ahead at Higher Levels of Play.
Hewlett-Packard Co.

TITLE INDEX

Sargon III. *Compatible Hardware:* Apple II+, IIe, IIc; Commodore 64; IBM PC. *Memory Required:* 128k. *Customer Support:* (617) 494-1220, (617) 494-1221.
$19.95 (Order no.: 300XX).
Computer Chess Game Which Features 9 Levels of Play & an Opening Library of Over 68,000 Moves. Offers Instructions to Beginners & Brain Teasing Problems to Masters. Players Can Receive Hints, Change Places with SARGON III & Have the Computer Finish the Game, Replay One of the 107 Greatest Games in History, & Have the Computer Play Against Itself.
Spinnaker Software Corp.

Sargon IV. May 1989. *Compatible Hardware:* Apple Macintosh; IBM PC, PC XT, PC AT, PS/2 & true compatibles. *Memory Required:* 640k. *Items Included:* Multiple chess sets crafted by professional artists, an on screen chess clock, a complete illustrated manual, "write a note," & many other capabilities. *Customer Support:* Unlimited free support: (617) 494-1220, (617) 494-1221.
disk $49.95. *Nonstandard peripherals required:* CGA, EGA, MCGA or VGA graphics, adaptor, two button mouse (optional).
16 Levels of Play, On-Line Help, 3d & 2d Graphics, Mouse or Keyboard Control, Piece Sculptor (Mac Only) to Handcraft User's Own Sets, Mood Files (IBM Only) to Customize Screen Colors & Text as Desired, & Many Other Features.
Spinnaker Software Corp.

Sargon V. *Items Included:* Installation Guide.
IBM. Contact publisher for price (ISBN 0-87321-065-4, Order no.: ID-231).
Activision, Inc.

Sargon V. *Items Included:* Installation Guide.
IBM PC. Contact publisher for price (ISBN 0-87321-066-2, Order no.: PD-231).
Activision, Inc.

SARVAL: Safety Relief Valve Sizing & Documentation. 1985. *Compatible Hardware:* IBM PC & compatibles. *Operating System(s) Required:* MS-DOS. *Language(s):* Compiled Advanced BASIC. *Memory Required:* 256k.
disk $595.00, incl. manual (ISBN 0-87664-905-3, Order no.: I905-3).
Performs Detailed Safety Relief Valve Sizing Calculations Using API & ASME Code Areas.
Instrument Society of America (ISA).

SAS/C Compiler. *Version:* 4.5. *Items Included:* Documentation included. *Customer Support:* Free software updates & enhancements; phone-in technical support; 24-hour on-line support; training courses available.
CMS, MVS. IBM 370/30XX/43XX/937X (512K). contact publisher for price.
C Compiler for the IBM 370 Architecture That Allows Users to Develop & Run C Programs in Mainframe Environments. The Compiler is Used by Other Software Developers, Systems Programmers & Applications Programmers.
SAS Institute, Inc.

SAS-CD: Scientific American Surgery on CD-ROM. Douglas W. Wilmore et al. Mar. 1996. *Items Included:* The annual subscription includes: four CD-ROM discs & a comprehensive user's guide. *Customer Support:* 800-291-5489.
Windows. 486 (33MHz) (8Mb). CD-ROM disk Institution $645.00; Individual $395.00; Contact publisher for network prices (ISBN 0-89454-022-X). *Nonstandard peripherals required:* CD-ROM drive.
Macintosh. 68020 (6Mb). *Nonstandard peripherals required:* CD-ROM drive.
Contains the Full Text & Graphics of the Loose-Leaf SCIENTIFIC AMERICAN SURGERY on a Single CD-ROM Disc. Sponsored by the American College of Surgeons for Use As a Practitioner's Guide to Comprehensive & Quality Surgical Care, Updated Quarterly.
Scientific American Medicine.

The SAS System. *Version:* 6. *Compatible Hardware:* IBM 370/30XX/43XX/937X; DEC VAX, PRIME 50, DG ECLIPSE MV; IBM PS/2 PC AT, UNIX Workstations from Silicon Graphics, HP, Sun, Solbourne, MIPS, DEC, IBM, DG, Apollo & Next. *Memory Required:* Mainframes & minicomputers, 512; microcomputers, 640k. *Items Included:* Documentation. *Customer Support:* Free software updates & enhancements; phone-in technical support; 24-hour online support; training courses available.
licensed on an annual basis; contact vendor; Renewals are available at lower rates. Discounts are available for degree-granting customers & other qualified sites.
The SAS System, an Integrated Suite of Information Delivery Software, Provides Enterprise-Wide Data Access, Management, Analysis, & Presentation. The System Includes More Than 125 Built-In Applications Grouped into Logical, Modular Components. These Applications Provide Capabilities for Client/Server Computing; Database Access, EIS, Applications Development, Graphics, Data Analysis, Report Writing, Quality Improvement, Project Management, Computer Performance Evaluation, Decision Support, & More.
SAS Institute, Inc.

Satellite Verdict. *Version:* 7.0. *Compatible Hardware:* IBM PC & compatibles. *Operating System(s) Required:* PC-DOS/MS-DOS.
disk $495.00.
Batch Posting System for Auxiliary Stations. Can Be Used in Conjunction with VERDICT.
Micro Craft, Inc.

Saturday Night Bingo. *Compatible Hardware:* TI-99/4A with speech synthesizer.
disk or cassette - contact publisher for price.
Computerized Multiplayer Bingo with Automatic or Manual Mode to Set the Pace of the Game.
Texas Instruments, Personal Productivit.

Saturday Night Live: Screen Saver. *Version:* 1.5. Dec. 1994. *Items Included:* Manual, registration card, promotional flyers. *Customer Support:* Phone technical support.
Windows 3.1. 386SX or higher (4Mb). disk $17.95 (ISBN 1-57303-014-7). *Nonstandard peripherals required:* Sound card recommended. *Optimal configuration:* 386 DX 25 w/4Mb RAM running Windows 3.1, 5Mb free hard disk space, sound card.
Slide Show Screen Saver Featuring Images & Audio from "Saturday Night Live" TV Series.
Sound Source Interactive.

SAUNA Modeling System: 3D Thermal Analysis. *Version:* 2.23. Michael Naughton. 1989. *Language(s):* Pascal. *Memory Required:* 512k. *Items Included:* 5.25" DS/DD, non-protected diskette (3.5" diskette available on special order). User's manual. *Customer Support:* 30 day unlimited warranty; 1-yr update service $898 & 1-day training at Ann Arbor including.
MS/PC-DOS. IBM PC/XT/AT & compatibles. disk $2995.00 (ISBN 0-927449-71-4, Order no.: T3PM). *Optimal configuration:* Hard disk, Coprocessor, EGA or VGA colorgraphing, mouse.
Apple/Finder. Macintosh II. disk $2995.00 (ISBN 0-927449-71-4, Order no.: T3MC).
A 3-D Thermal Analysis Program with Integrated Color Graphics Allowing the Plot of Thermal Gradients or Simple Clarifying the Various Thermal Components That Make up the Analysis. It Can Model Multilayer Circuit Boards, Plates, Heat Sinks, & Enclosures, Using All Heat Transfer Modes: Convection (Natural or Force Air), Radiation (Blackbody or Gray), & Conduction. It Also Provides Even Greater Modeling Power for Tough Thermal Analysis Problems. It Will Not Only Do Macro Thermal Analysis of the More Common Electronic Configurations But Also Has the Capability to Model Just about Any Type of Design: Potted Modules, Heat Sinks in "H" & "T" Configurations, & the Prediction of Junction-to-Case Thermal Resistance Are All Possible.
Tatum Labs, Inc.

SAUNA: 3D Thermal Analysis. *Version:* 2.23. Michael Naughton. 1989. *Language(s):* Pascal. *Memory Required:* 512k. *Items Included:* 5.25" DS/DD, non-protected diskette (3.5" diskette available on special order). User's manual. *Customer Support:* 30 day unlimited warranty; 1-yr update service $298.
MS/PC-DOS. IBM PC/XT/AT & compatibles. disk $995.00 (ISBN 0-927449-71-4, Order no.: T2PM).
Apple/Finder. Macintosh II. disk $995.00 (ISBN 0-927449-71-4, Order no.: T2MC). *Optimal configuration:* Hard disk, coprocessor, EGA or VGA color graphics, mouse.
3-D Thermal Analysis Program with Integrated Color Graphics Allowing the Plot of Thermal Gradients or Simply Clarifying the Various Thermal Components That Make up the Analysis. It Can Model Multilayer Circuit Boards, Plates, Heat Sinks, & Enclosures, Using All Heat TransferModes: Convection (Natural or Forced Air), Radiation (Blackbody or Gray), & Conduction. It is Interactive Menu Driven with Edit Features Which Makes it Easy to Learn & Use. It Has a Thermal Parameters Library That Includes Material Properties, Semiconductor Package Design Values, Mounting Method Parameters, etc. It Has Full Mouse Support. The Output Includes Full "Reports" of Materials, Node & Junction Temperatures, etc., As Well As Detailed Graphics.
Tatum Labs, Inc.

SAV KEY. *Compatible Hardware:* IBM PC XT & compatibles.
$89.00, incl. customized set of back-up labels, 3-ring binder & user's manual.
Hard Disk Backup System. Doesn't Require Making a Full Backup Each Time to Ensure Safety of All Data, So Backups Can Take Only Minutes Daily. Prompts the User to Backup Each Day & Specifies Which Diskettes to Use. Reports Keep Track of Backups by Type, Date, Time & Location. When Printed, These Reports Can Be Handed in for Backup Accountability Control. If Data Is Lost Because of Fire, Theft, Operator Error or Machine Failure, These Records Can Be Used with Step-by-Step On-Screen & Written Instructions to Restore Information.
Business-Pro.

Savage Island I & II. *Compatible Hardware:* TI-99/4A.
disk or cassette - contact publisher for price.
Texas Instruments, Personal Productivit.

Save the Planet, 1993: Database on Global Warming & Ozone Depletion. *Version:* 3.00. Roger Cox & Kathy Cox. Jan. 1992. *Items Included:* "IMAGES of a Changing Planet", a graphic display program featuring earth science images collected by NASA & other agencies; printed installation instructions. *Customer Support:* Free support by mail or phone to registered users; updates available to registered users for $17.95; program is updated annually.
MS-DOS 2.0 or higher. IBM PC & compatibles (640k). Single-user copy $24.95; Site licenses

start at $80.00 (Order no.: STP-PC5 (5.25"); STP-PC3 (3.5")). *Nonstandard peripherals required:* Graphics adapter: CGA, EGA, VGA or Hercules color or monochrome graphics monitor. *Optimal configuration:* 640k RAM, EGA or VGA graphics with color monitor, printer.
System 6 or 7. Macintosh (1Mb). Single-user copy $24.95; Site licenses start at $80.00 (Order no.: STP-MAC). *Addl. software required:* HyperCard 2.0 or higher.
Up-to-Date Information on Global Environmental Issues - Ozone Depletion, Climate Change, Deforestation, & Overpopulation - in an Engaging, Accessible Format, Using Computer Graphics, Maps, Charts, & Hypertext. Both Environmental Science & Public Policy Issues Are Covered. Software Includes a Global Warming Simulator & the Environmental Voting Records of Congress.
Save the Planet Software.

Saved. HiSoft. Dec. 1988.
TOS (512k). Atari ST. disk $39.95.
Desk Accessory Which Permits Deleting, Renaming & Copying of Files, Obtaining Information About a File or Disk, Formatting or Copying Disks & Printing of Text Files.
MichTron, Inc.

Savings. *Version:* 127A. *Compatible Hardware:* Sharp ZL-6100 System, ZL-6500 System. *Language(s):* Sharp Microcode.
$270.00.
Computes the Growth of a Certificate of Deposit & Finds Either Future Value or Required Deposit to Achieve a Certain Future Value. Computes Interest Earned, Federal Penalty for Early Withdrawal & Yield If Withdrawn. Computes Future Value of a Rollover I.R.A./Keogh, the Effective Annual Yield, etc.
P-ROM Software, Inc.

SayWhat?! *Version:* 4.0. *Compatible Hardware:* IBM PC & compatibles. *Operating System(s) Required:* PC-DOS/MS-DOS 3.0 or higher. *Memory Required:* 512k. *Items Included:* 1 program disk, 1 samples & utilities disk, 1 manual. *Customer Support:* Tech. Support: (510) 845-2110; BBS: (415) 697-1624; also CompuServe.
disk $79.00.
Enables Programmers to Draw Screens, Using the Included Editor, & Call Them from Inside Applications Written in Any Programming Language. Full Editor Mouse Support.
Software Science, Inc.

SB-86. *Operating System(s) Required:* SB-86. *Memory Required:* 64k.
disk $150.00.
Version of the Industry Standard MS-DOS Fully Compatible with PC-DOS. Provides a Proven Base of Support Applications. Recommended for the Software Development Community Only. Standard MS-DOS 1.25 Commands Apply.
Lifeboat Assocs.

SBACOUNT. *Version:* 5.0. *Compatible Hardware:* CP/M & MS-DOS based machines. *Operating System(s) Required:* CP/M, MS-DOS. *Language(s):* Quick Basic. *Items Included:* Manual disk & warranty card. *Customer Support:* 18 month via telephone.
disk $79.00.
demo disk & manual $20.00.
Accounting Program for Small Business/Self-Employed Individual.
Micro-Art Programmers.

SBM 86. *Version:* 1B. Mar. 1989. *Items Included:* Disk & Manual. *Customer Support:* Telephone Support - no charge.

MS-DOS (640k). IBM PC's XT/AT compatibles. $99.95 (Order no.: NI 1).
Inventory Control - Point of Sale System Designed to Operate in a Wholesale or Retail Environment. Will Produce Invoices, Purchase Orders, Statements, Mailing Labels, Price Labels, Quotes, Cash Register Receipts, Inventory Reports, Sales & Account Reports, etc. Tracks up to 30 Salespersons.
Newell Industries.

SBM ST. *Version:* 4B. Jun. 1989. *Compatible Hardware:* Atari ST. *Operating System(s) Required:* TOS ROM. *Language(s):* Machine. *Memory Required:* 512k. *General Requirements:* TOS in ROM, ST-compatible printer. *Items Included:* Manual. *Customer Support:* Yes.
3.5" disk $69.95.
Inventory Control - Point of Sale System Designed to Operate in a Wholesale or Retail Environment. Will Produce Invoices, Purchase Orders, Statements, Mailing Labels, Price Labels, Quotes, Cash Register Receipts, Inventory Reports, Sales & Account Reports, etc. Tracks up to 30 Salespersons. Capacity Varies with the Medium: 2,000 Records per Single-Sided Drive, 4,000 Records per Double-Sided Drive, 100,000 Records on 20Mb Hard Disk.
Newell Industries.

SBOS. *Version:* 6.1. *Compatible Hardware:* DEC PDP-11; IBM PC & compatibles. *Language(s):* BOS COBOL. *Memory Required:* 128k.
contact publisher for price.
Disk Operating System for Single User Operation.
BOS National, Inc.

SBT Professional Series. *Version:* 2.0. May 1992. *Language(s):* FoxPro/LAN 2.0. *Items Included:* Source code included. *Customer Support:* 90 day free start-up assistance (technical support) for new users. 5 yr. warranty. Executive Support Plan, 300 minutes for $395 with one hour callback. QuickTech, 60 minutes for $95 with one hour callback. 900 number for urgent problems, 900/454-9900.
DOS 5.0. IBM 386 & compatibles (4Mb). $1295.00 per application. *Networks supported:* NETBIOS or Novell.
Multi-User Accounting Software. Includes Seven Core Functions: Accounts Payable, Accounts Receivable, General Ledger, Inventory Control, Purchase Orders, Sales Orders, & System Manager. Links to SBT Series Six Plus to Expand Functionality & Include Applications Like Payroll. Information Available Instantly in Real Time from Any File in User-Definable Pop-Up Windows. Hotkey Accessible Help System Brings up Context-Sensitive Text about Any Data Field. (Over 100 User Configurable Default Settings Allow the Program to Be Personalized for Each User).
SBT Corp.

SBT Series Six Plus. *Version:* 6.35. Jan. 1992. *Items Included:* Includes source code for custom modifications, documentation, & sample data. *Customer Support:* 90 day free start-up assistance (technical support) for new users. 5 year warranty. Executive Support Plan, 300 minutes for $395 with one hour callback. QuickTech, 60 minutes for $95 with one hour callback. 900 number available for urgent problems, 900/454-9900.
DOS or UNIX. IBM AT, PS/2 or compatible (640k). $595.00 multi-user; $295.00 single-user. *Optimal configuration:* 640k. *Networks supported:* Novell or Novell-compatible network software, NetWare Version 2.15C or later.
Macintosh SE/30, LC or II (2Mb). $695.00 multi-user; $295.00 single-user. *Nonstandard peripherals required:* Multi-user FoxBASE Plus/

Mac Version 2.0 dated 8/4/89 or later required for source code product. *Networks supported:* EtherTalk is strongly recommended.
Modular & Modifiable Accounting Software. Includes 17 Functions: System Manager, General Ledger, Financial Reporter, Accounts Receivable, Accounts Payable, Sales Orders, Purchase Orders, Payroll, Laser Forms, Fixed Assets, Manufacturing, Job Cost, Time Billing, Property, Maintenance, Corporate Contact Manager, Communications Server. Business Status Report Gives Up-to-the-Minute Cash Position Statement in Real Time.
SBT Corp.

Scaleable Fonts. *Compatible Hardware:* IBM PC & compatibles.
per typeface $195.00.
Series Consists of 80 Typefaces Licensed from BITSTREAM. Series Include All Sizes from 3 to 240 Points, All Weights, & All Popular Character Sets.
SoftCraft, Inc. (Wisconsin).

ScaleTrac. Jun. 1992. *Items Included:* On-line help, documentation available. *Customer Support:* On-site training available. 60 day support included with purchase. Support for 1 year $600.00.
MS-DOS. IBM PC & compatibles (1Mb). disk $3000.00. *Addl. software required:* DOS 3.3 or higher. *Optimal configuration:* Modem. *Networks supported:* Novell, Token Ring, Lan Man.
Captures Weights from Electronic Weight Devices Directly into a Computer. Will Print a Scale Ticket (Weigh Ticket) & Calculate Dockage & Discounts Based on Quality Factors.
Vertical Software, Inc.

Scan-Connect. Greg M. Taylor. 1992. *Items Included:* Sample scan form, user's guide. *Customer Support:* 90 day warranty/support; $150.00 year renewable support.
MS-DOS & Windows. IBM PC & compatibles (512k). disk $1995.00 (Order no.: SCAN-CONNECT). *Addl. software required:* Ed-U-Keep II. *Optimal configuration:* VGA monitor & 486 computer, 80Mb hard disk. *Networks supported:* Novell.
Software Interface to Scantron Full Page Scanners. Allows Rapid Entry of Attendance, Testing, & Evaluations. Grades Tests & Gives Item Analysis of Tests & Evaluations.
The Edukeep Co.

ScanMan Color: Hand-Held Scanner. Sep. 1992. *Items Included:* Manuals; Windows 3.1 Help Engine; Foto-Touch Color Image Editing software; TWAIN-compliant scanning DLL. *Customer Support:* Tech support hotline (7-days-a-week); BBS; FaxBack; CompuServe; Limited lifetime warranty.
Microsoft Windows 3.0 or higher. IBM AT or compatible with 386SX processor or higher (4Mb). disk SRP $699.00. *Nonstandard peripherals required:* Scanner board included; graphics card (at least VGA); mouse. *Addl. software required:* All is included except Windows operating system. *Optimal configuration:* 5Mb free disk space; graphics card (256-color SVGA or higher recommended); mouse.
A 24-Bit Hand-Held Scanner That Captures 16.8 Million Colors. Features Graphical On-Line Interactive Help System, Customizable "Toolbox," a Variety of Image Editing Tools; Total System Calibration. FotoTouch Color Host Application Is TWAIN-Compliant & Functions As an OLE Server.
Logitech, Inc.

TITLE INDEX

ScanMan: Model 32 (for Macintosh). *Version:* 2.1. *Items Included:* Scanner head, cables, SCSI Box, Scanning software, Digital Darkroom Image Editing software.
Mac Plus or higher. disk $499.00.
Scanning Program That Works with Input from Hand-Held or Desktop Scanners. Offers True Gray-Scale Editing (32 Levels) & Advanced Half-Tone Capability, with Ability to Handle images at 100-, 200-, 300-, & 400-dpi Resolution. Error Diffusion Improves Better Image Resolution by Reducing Error among Adjacent Pixels. Includes Pop-Up Brightness & Contrast Controls & Zoom Possibilities for Greater Control During Image Editing. Note: 2 Bundle Options (Scanner Is Not Sold Alone) - 1. ScanMan & Digital Darkroom or 2. ScanMan & CatchWord Pro O.C.R. for Mac.
Logitech, Inc.

ScanMan Model 32 for PC with GrayTouch Image Editing Software. Jun. 1991. *Items Included:* 2 manuals. *Customer Support:* 7 day-a-week phone support; limited lifetime warranty.
Used with Logitech Hand-Held Scanner Requiring 1/2 Slot for Board (included with product).
IBM PC, XT, AT & compatibles; PS/2. disk $299.00.
Hand-Held Black & White Scanner Bundled with GrayTouch Image Editing Software That Achieves GrayScale (up to 32 Levels) Through Software & Can Edit Using a Palette of 256 Shades. Images Can Be Manipulated in a Variety of Ways & Stored in a Number of Popular File Formats. Users Can Scan Line Art or Photos. Features a Windowing Environment under DOS.
Logitech, Inc.

ScanMan Model 256 with FotoTouch Image Editing Software for Windows. *Version:* 1.2. Jun. 1991. *Items Included:* 2 manuals. *Customer Support:* 7 day-a-week phone support; limited lifetime warranty; BBS; CompuServe; FAXBack.
IBM AT or higher (for Windows to run effectively) Windows OS (1Mb). disk $499.00. *Nonstandard peripherals required:* Works with Logitech ScanMan Model 256 (1/2 slot for PC, full slot for microchannel).
Enables High-End Gray Scale Editing with Images Captured by ScanMan Model 256. User Can Resize, Rotate, Flip, Deskew, & Easily Achieve a Variety of Additional Image Manipulation. 256 Gray Scales Effectively Uses the Windows 3.0 or Higher Environment. Integrated Image Merging.
Logitech, Inc.

Scanning Software Package for the CBCL - 4-18, YSR, & TRF Machine Readable Forms. Thomas M. Achenbach. Jul. 1995. *Items Included:* Detailed manual. *Customer Support:* Free telephone support with no time limit.
MS-DOS. IBM & compatibles. disk $175.00 (ISBN 0-938565-40-0). *Nonstandard peripherals required:* NCS, Scantron, or SR scanner. *Addl. software required:* ScanTools, ScanBook, or TopScore.
Converts Data from CBCL/4-18, YSR, & TRF Machine-Readable Forms to Input for the CBCL/4-18, YSR, TRF, or Cross-Informant Scoring Programs.
University of Vermont, Dept. of Psychiatry.

ScanPro. *Version:* 4.2b. *Compatible Hardware:* IBM PC & compatibles & IBM PS/2. *Operating System(s) Required:* PC-DOS 2.0 or higher or OS/2. *Memory Required:* 512k. *General Requirements:* Hard disk. *Items Included:* Manual. *Customer Support:* Free, unlimited.
disk $495.00 (Order no.: 715-SCAN-3 (3.5"); 715-SCAN-5 (5.25")).
Reads Scanner-Produced Images Converting Them to Formats Readable by Computer-Aided Design (CAD) Systems Such as DesignCad, DesignCad 3D, AutoCad & Others. With a Scanner, Allows Engineers & Draftsmen to Read Existing Drawings from Paper into a Computer for Use with CAD Software.
American Small Business Computers, Inc.

ScanTerm. *Version:* 2.0. Feb. 1991. *Items Included:* Installation manual, 3.5" or 5.25" diskette. *Customer Support:* 30 day free phone support.
THEOS 386/486, THEOS 286 Plus. IBM PC & compatibles. disk $99.99. *Nonstandard peripherals required:* Serial line connection (RS-232).
DOS Software Terminal Emulator That Allows PCs & Compatibles to Act As ASCII or Scan-Code Compatible PC Term Terminals. Features Music & Sound Support. Transfers Multiple Files Between Systems Using Wildcard File Descriptions. Allows PCs to Upload/Download Any File to/from THEOS Host System. Uses YMODEM Protocol for File Transfer.
THEOS Software Corp.

The Scarlet Letter. *Version:* 1.5. Feb. 1995. *Items Included:* BookWorm Student Reader (diskette). *Customer Support:* 30 day MBG. Technical support (toll call) - no charge.
System 7.0 or higher. Macintosh (5Mb). CD-ROM disk $29.95 (ISBN 1-57316-026-1, Order no.: 16161). *Nonstandard peripherals required:* CD-ROM drive, 12" color monitor. *Optimal configuration:* 13" color monitor recommended.
Windows 3.1 or higher. IBM compatible (MPC) 386 DX (4Mb). CD-ROM disk $29.95. *Nonstandard peripherals required:* Standard multimedia compatible CD-ROM. *Optimal configuration:* 8Mb RAM recommended, 256 color monitor recommended.
Unlike Countless Volumes Before It, the BookWorm Edition of This Hawthorne Classic Offers a Timely Difference to the Reader Who Desires a Greater Range of Understanding. Includes the Novel's Colorful Text History, along with Many Full-Color Illustrations of Its Colonial America Setting. Features Complete Sound Allowing the User to Listen to All or Part of Each Work.
Communication & Information Technologies, Inc. (CIT).

Scattergrams. Frank D. Dennison et al. *Compatible Hardware:* IBM PC, PCjr, PC XT, PC AT, Portable PC with IBM Display & one double-sided disk drive. *Operating System(s) Required:* DOS 1.10, 2.00, 2.10, 3.00, 3.10. *Memory Required:* 128k.
disk $19.95 (Order no.: 6276653).
Word Game in Which Messages Typed or Already on File Are Split into Blocks of Characters & Scattered into a Screen Grid. To Solve the Scattergram the Player Must Rearrange the Blocks to Form the Original Message. The Program Diskette Contains 10 Files with Famous Quotations. The Game Can Be Played at Four Skill Levels.
Personally Developed Software, Inc.

ScatterPlot. *Customer Support:* 800-929-8117 (customer service).
MS-DOS. IBM/PS2. disk $49.99 (ISBN 0-87007-512-8).
Computes Simple Regression Between Two Arrays of Data & Plots up to 1000 Points. Reports Generated Include Scatter Plot, Smooth Plot, Plot of Residuals, Standard Deviation, R Square, b & Beta, Standard Error, Mean for Each Power of x, integration & Differentiation Results.
SourceView Software International.

SCENICWRITER

Scavenger Hunt Adventure Series: Africa. Oct. 1993. *Items Included:* CD-ROM; instruction/user manual; Quicktime 1.6 Extension. *Customer Support:* Total support available from distributor (Davidson), toll free telephone number/no charge involved.
Microsoft Windows 3.1. 80386 20Mhz (4Mb). CD-ROM disk $49.95 (ISBN 1-884282-00-8). *Nonstandard peripherals required:* CD-ROM drive, audio board. *Addl. software required:* QuickTime 1.1.
Macintosh System 7.0. MAC LC II (4Mb). CD-ROM disk $49.95. *Nonstandard peripherals required:* CD-ROM drive. *Addl. software required:* QuickTime 1.5. *Optimal configuration:* Macintosh LC 520 System 7.1, 8Mb RAM.
Interactive Multimedia Software Program That Utilizes the Scavenger Hunt Metaphor. Throughout the Adventure Explore & Discover the African Animals, Plants & Regions of Africa. Incorporates Three Basic Tools (Vica, the List & the Camera Icons), Interactive Puzzles & Guide Information Reinforce the Educational Content. Experience the Wonder of Virtual Landscape: 360 Degree, Eight Directional Point of View Navigation. Through Interactive Involvement, You Will Be Challenged, Encouraged to Explore & Discover, & Gain Knowledge & Information from the Full Character Animation, Audio Dialog, Sound Effects & Music That Makes the Learning Process Subtle, Fun & Entertaining. Africa Is Designed for Consumers & School Children Ages 6 Years & Older.
Swede Corp.

Scenic & Castles. Feb. 1995. *Items Included:* CD-ROM booklet. *Customer Support:* Free technical support via phone as of release date.
MPC Windows/DOS/UNIX; Macintosh; PhotoCD/CD-i. IBM 386 Processor or higher (4Mb); Mac System 6.07 or higher (4Mb). CD-ROM disk $24.95 (ISBN 1-885784-06-6, Order no.: 1014).
The Serenity of Nature Combined with the Timeless Architecture of Castles Is Stunningly Presented in This Photographic & Music Montage. This Collection Features 100 High-Resolution Scenic Images Orchestrated Music Selections That Can All Be Used Copyright Free for Desktop Publishing & Multimedia Presentations.
Technology Dynamics Corp.

ScenicWriter. *Version:* 7.9. 1985. *Compatible Hardware:* IBM PC XT, PC AT & compatibles. *Operating System(s) Required:* PC-DOS/MS-DOS 2.0 or higher. *Memory Required:* 384k. *General Requirements:* Hard disk, Hewlett-Packard LaserJet family laser printer & compatibles. *Items Included:* Disks & manual. *Customer Support:* 90 days support, 60 day money back warranty.
disk $1495.00.
Text Formatter That Lets Users Insert Codes to Format Text for Output to Hewlett-Packard LaserJet Family compatible Laser Printers. Uses the Embedded Dot & Backslash Commands to Control the Appearance of the Document, Including Margins, Text Alignment, & Bulletin Lists. Format Commands Can Be Saved As a Macro & Stored in a Library for Reuse. Supports Numerous Graphics Programs Including PC PAINTBRUSH, MICROTEK DEST, PANASONIC, & DATACOPY Scans from MACPAINT & ADOBE ILLUSTRATOR Can Be Included. The Program Also Draws Simple Graphic Elements Such As Ruled Lines, Boxes, & Gray Screens.
ScenicSoft, Inc.

ScenicWriter. Scenic Computer Systems Corp. *Operating System(s) Required:* UCSD p-System. *Memory Required:* 128k. *General Requirements:* Printer.
$575.00.
Texas Instruments, Personal Productivit

SCG22. *Version:* 2.2. Jan. 1982. *Operating System(s) Required:* CP/M 2.2. *Language(s):* CBASIC. *Memory Required:* 24k.
disk $45.00.
IBM 3740 format. 8" disk $45.00.
Aid to System Programmers, OEM's or Others Who Would Benefit from Detailed Knowledge of the Inner Workings of CP/M.
C.C. Software.

SCG3. *Version:* 3. Feb. 1984. *Operating System(s) Required:* CP/M Plus. *Language(s):* BASIC. *Memory Required:* 32k.
disk $75.00.
8" disk $75.00.
Generates Source Code for the CP/M (3.0) Operating System. Fully Labeled & Commented 8080 Assembly Code Compatible with RMAC. The CCP & BDOS Are Generated.
C.C. Software.

The Schedule Book. *Version:* 4.0. Jul. 1990. *Customer Support:* 24 hour/day, 7 day/week customer support; 90 day warranty; yearly maintenance fee approximately 15% of product cost.
MS-DOS/Novell/Windows. IBM & compatibles. $35,000.00-$45,000.00. *Nonstandard peripherals required:* 2400 baud Hayes compatible modem; 40 Mb hard disk. *Networks supported:* Novell.
Helps Coordinate the Central Scheduling Conflicts Between Patients, Doctors, Departments, Rooms, & Procedures When Making Appointments At a Central Location. Fully Configurable by the User & Features State-of-the-Art, Context Sensitive Help & Information Windows, Network Compatibility, Extensive Password Security, & Custom Reports.
LCI.

Schedule Graphics II: Software for Bar Chart Schedules. Oct. 1985. *Compatible Hardware:* IBM PC. *Operating System(s) Required:* PC-DOS, MS-DOS. *Memory Required:* 128k. *General Requirements:* Epson Compatible Dot Matrix Printer. *Items Included:* disks, user manual. *Customer Support:* (714) 472-2246.
disk $190.00.
Designed for Applications Which Require Quick Development & Custom Schedule Charts. Allows Users to Develop a Schedule from Dates Without Development of Activity Logic. The Program Features Many Graphic Bar & Milestone Symbols. Graphics & Text Are Combined for a Clear & Effective Schedule Presentation. Interfaces with LOTUS 1-2-3 & dBASE Are Provided. Works with Any Word Processor, or Spreadsheet Software That Can Create ASCII Files.
Project Dimensions, Inc.

Schedule Maker. *Version:* 3.0. *Compatible Hardware:* Apple Macintosh. *Memory Required:* 512k. *General Requirements:* Hard disk, Printer. *Customer Support:* Unlimited Phone.
3.5" disk $395.00.
Labor Management System.
Craig Management, Inc.

Schedule Planning System. Jan. 1979. *Compatible Hardware:* IBM PC & compatibles. *Operating System(s) Required:* MS-DOS. *Language(s):* BASIC. *Memory Required:* 256k. *Items Included:* Manual & demo.
disk $250.00.
Assigns Work Shifts & Days Off for Employees of Extended-Hours Services. Analyzes Staff Requirements Based on Daily Workload Levels/ Daily Minimum Staffing. Allocates On-Duty Employees. Calculates Deficit Staff Hours per Year Due to Absences of Scheduled Employees. Designs Various Types of Employee Schedules.
Prints Daily Rosters of On- & Off-Duty Employees in Calendar Form. Demo Disk Available.
Computing Power Applied.

Schedule Sculptor. *Version:* 3.0. 1990. *Items Included:* User's manual in 3-ring binder. *Customer Support:* 60 day no-risk trial period, telephone support during & after trial period.
MS-DOS 2.1 or higher. IBM PC, PS/2, or compatible (640k). disk $995.00.
Automatically Generates Work Schedules for Organizations That Assign Employees to Shifts. It Meets Departmental Staffing Requirements, While Accommodating Employee Workstretch/ Break/Rotation Preferences & Special Assignment Requests. An Interactive Capability Enables Users to Modify the Completed Schedules. Fifteen Reports Are Available, with Many Formatting Options.
Blue Ridge Creative Software.

The Scheduler. 1990. *Compatible Hardware:* IBM PC & compatibles, PC XT, PC AT, PS/2. *Operating System(s) Required:* MS-DOS. *Language(s):* Clipper. *Memory Required:* 512k.
disk $395.00.
Calendar Designed for the Professional Businessman, Accountant, or Lawyer, Schedules & Formats Data & Can Be Used As a Docket or an Appointment Book. Networking version available.
KIS Computer Corp.

SCHEDULER+. *Version:* 7.1. Jan. 1988. *Items Included:* Complete 3-ring binder manual with room for updates, help screens behind all input stages. *Customer Support:* Onsite training, unlimited telephone support & all new enhancements throughout the year.
MS-DOS 5.0 (2Mb). IBM AT/XT, PS/2 & compatibles, IBM System 36, 38 & AS400MS. single-user$3500.00; Local Area Network $5250.00. *Nonstandard peripherals required:* Dot matrix printer, 132-column-wide carriage. *Addl. software required:* LOANLEDGER+ *Networks supported:* Novell, 3-Com, IBM PC NET.
Allows User to Schedule a Stream of Negotiated Payments, Which Can Differ from the Original Contract Agreement. For Example: Have Interest Accrue at Original Note Rate, yet Collect at Different Pay Rate. Each Payment Can Vary from the Next. Schedule Fixed Principal Reduction, or No Payments for Any Given Period.
Dynamic Interface Systems Corp.

Scheduling & Control. Mel Tainiter. *Compatible Hardware:* IBM PC & compatibles, PC XT. *Operating System(s) Required:* PC-DOS 2.0 or higher. *Memory Required:* 128k.
disk $95.00 (ISBN 0-934577-07-2).
Designed for the PC Owner Who Wishes to Learn a Given Methodology & Immediately Utilize That Knowledge with a Software System. Covers All Aspects of Project Management.
Softext Publishing Corp.

Scholarships, Gra2ts & Loans. *Version:* 1.0. 1993. *Items Included:* Dual media (3.5" 1.44 Mb & 5.25" 1.2Mb) 360k available on request, 120 pg supporting manual. *Customer Support:* Unlimited customer support at no charge.
MS-DOS 3.2 or higher. IBM PC or PC compatible, XT, AT, 386SX, 386DX, 486SX, 486DX (640k & 7 Mb hard disk space). disk $79.95.
"How To" Audio Cassette series - $59.95.
Add-On Cassettes for Women, Graduates, Minorities, & Disabled Students - $19.95 each.
Up-TO-Date Comprehensive Reference Sources of Financial Aid. Enter Student Information into Easy Entry Screens. Program Searches Through Thousands of Awards. Identifies Those Specifically Applicable to User. Prints Request for Information Letters & Address Labels. Tracks Multiple Students. In Use by U.S. Dept. of Ed. Educational Opportunity Center Counselors. Fall Upgrade will Complete the Worksheet for the New Free Application for Federal Student Aid.
Pathfinders/College Affordability Productions, Inc.

Scholastic SuperPrint. 1987. *Compatible Hardware:* Apple II+, IIe, IIc, IIc Plus, IIgs; Tandy 1000 Plus; IBM & compatibles. *Memory Required:* Apple 128k, MS-DOS 256k. *Items Included:* 5.25"-one program disk, two graphics disks; 3.5"-one program/graphics disks (all disks not copy-protected); teaching guide. *Customer Support:* (800) 541-5513.
Net to educator. disk $79.95.
Retail/Home. disk $28.00.
Printing Program. Provides the Following Features: Almost 200 Graphics, from "Clip Art" Icons to 55" Displays; Each Graphic Prints in Four Sizes; Six Type Fonts, in Solid, Outline, & Bold Formats; Ten Pre-Designed Borders & an Unlimited Number of Custom Borders; Allows Users to Scroll Through Graphics & Stamp on an Unlimited Number of Different Graphic Elements; Displays Graphics on Screen Exactly As They Will Appear When Printed.
Scholastic Software.

School Attendance Manager. *Items Included:* Bound manual. *Customer Support:* Free hotline - no time limit; 30 day limited warranty; updates are $5/disk plus S&H.
Apple II Plus, IIe, IIc; TRS-80 Model I or III. $349.95-$359.95.
demo disk $25.00.
Program Will Automate the Attendance Needs of Any Size School. The Small-School Version Accommodates 800 Students. The Large-School Version Stores Data for 2400. Prints a Daily Absentee Report, an Individual Absentee Record for Any Student, State-Required Monthly Attendance Registers, Homeroom Lists, Class Rosters, Letters to Parents, Lists of Students Who Have Been Absent More Than a Specified Number of Days, & Mailing Labels. Keeps Track of Absences, Daily & Cumulative Tardies, Half Days, Religious Absences, Withdrawals, & Home Instruction.
Dynacomp, Inc.

School Discipline Manager. *Items Included:* Bound manual. *Customer Support:* Free hotline - no time limit; 30 day limited warranty; updates are $5/disk plus S&H.
MS-DOS. IBM & compatibles (128k). $249.95-$269.95. *Nonstandard peripherals required:* 80-column printer.
Apple; TRS-80 (48k). $249.95-$269.95.
demo disk $25.00.
Tracks 29 Different Infractions in up to 15 Different Locations by a Very Simple Coding System. It Includes: Dates of Infraction; Type of Infraction; Location of Infraction; Teacher Involved; Disposition; Administrator Involved. The Reports Available Include: A Single Student's Entire Discipline Record; All Infractions for a Particular Teacher; All Infractions for an Individual Administrator; The Number of Each Type of Infraction; Two Different Monthly Suspension Reports: A) Names of All Students; B) Number of Students, Broken down by Sex; Preaddressed Letters to Parents; Mailing Labels; Homeroom Lists; School or Class Rosters.
Dynacomp, Inc.

School Management Program. *Version:* 2. Aug. 1989. *Items Included:* 2 spiral-bound manuals. *Customer Support:* Free support.
DOS. IBM & compatibles (512k). disk $900.00. *Networks supported:* Novell, LANtastic.

Complete School Management Program. Includes Information on Students, Families & Teachers. Contains Scheduling, Medical & Grades Information, Extensive Reports Including Billing & Parent Teacher Conferencing.
Parish Data Systems, Inc.

School Spirit Disk. Sep. 1990. *Items Included:* 1 manual, 3.5" disk and warranty manual card.
Macintosh in Mac Paint format (1Mb). contact publisher for price.
Expand the Graphics Capabilites of Any Macintosh Publishing Program with the School Spirit Graphics Disk Featuring Over 200 New Graphics. A Full Pictorial Index Is Also Included. These Graphics Are in Mac Paint Format & Can Be Used with These Popular Titles: Mac Draw, Superpaint, Pagemaker, Microsoft Word, Hypercard, Macwrite & More.
Creative Pursuits.

School Transportation Manager. *Items Included:* Bound manual. *Customer Support:* Free hotline - no time limit; 30 day limited warranty; updates are $5/disk plus S&H.
MS-DOS. IBM & compatibles (128k). disk $549.95. *Nonstandard peripherals required:* One disk drive; 80-column (or wider) printer is supported.
Apple (64k). disk $549.95. *Nonstandard peripherals required:* Two disk drives.
Facilitates Bus-Route Planning. Helps Schedule Optimal Bus Runs by Allowing Manipulation of Bus Loads & Bus Stops. Keeps Bus Maintenance Records. In Addition, the Program Provides: The Bus-Driver Runs by Time of Pickup at Each Stop & a List of Students to Be Picked up at Each Stop; Transportation Reports That Contain All the Data Necessary to Obtain Reimbursement from the State; Student Bus Passes That List the Bus Stop, Time, & Bus Number; Addressed Bus Passes That Can Be Easily Mailed in Window Envelopes; Lists of All Walkers & Students Who Are Transported by Special Transportation, Such As Vans.
Dynacomp, Inc.

School Work Request & Preventive Maintenance. Version: 3.0. Feb. 1993. *Items Included:* Reference manual. *Customer Support:* 1 year free phone support; annual phone support - $250/yr..
Mac OS System 6 or 7. Macintosh (1Mb). Preventive Maintenance Module $995.00; Inventory Modules $1995.00. *Optimal configuration:* Mac Classic or better, 1Mb RAM, 20Mb HD. *Networks supported:* AppleTalk.
Preventive Maintenance Module $995.00.
A Cost Effective, Practical Solution for School Districts to Plan & Control Their Maintenance Activity. Provides for Work Request Tracking & Cost Analysis by School or Building. Requisitions Can Be Automatically Created from Work Order Information. Use the Preventive Maintenance Module to Implement a Scheduled Maintenance Program.
AD/C Solutions.

SchoolArt. *Compatible Hardware:* Apple Macintosh Plus. *Memory Required:* 1000k. *General Requirements:* HyperCard.
3.5" disk $39.00.
Electronic Clip-Board of School Topics.
P-Productions.

Sci-Fi. *Items Included:* Installation Guide.
IBM PC. Contact publisher for price (ISBN 0-87321-082-4, Order no.: MSD-3016).
Activision, Inc.

Sci-Fi Movie Machine. *Items Included:* CD-ROM booklet. *Customer Support:* Free technical support via phone as of release date.
MPC/Windows. 386 or higher (8Mb). CD-ROM disk $34.95 (ISBN 1-885784-49-X, Order no.: 1499). *Optimal configuration:* Double speed MPC CD-ROM player, S-VGA graphics card (640x480x256 colors) with compatible monitor, MPC compliant sound card, mouse, Windows 3.1 or higher, Windows 95 compatible.
System 7.0 or higher. Macintosh (8Mb). CD-ROM disk $34.95 (ISBN 1-885784-52-X, Order no.: 1529). *Optimal configuration:* CD-ROM drive, color monitor, mouse.
Blast off with the Sci-Fi Movie Machine & Make Your Own Science-Fiction Movie Creations! This Interactive CD-ROM Game Lets You Choose from Hundreds of Actual Hollywood Classic Sci-Fi Movie Clips. Click & Drag the Digitized Clips into Any Order, Any Length.
Technology Dynamics Corp.

Sci-Fi Movie Machine: Jewel. *Items Included:* CD-ROM booklet. *Customer Support:* Free technical support via phone as of release date.
MPC/Windows. 386 or higher (8Mb). CD-ROM disk $34.95 (ISBN 1-885784-70-8, Order no.: 1492). *Optimal configuration:* Double speed MPC CD-ROM player, S-VGA graphics card (640x480x256 colors) with compatible monitor, MPC compliant sound card, mouse, Windows 3.1 or higher, Windows 95 compatible.
System Version 7.0 or higher. Macintosh (8Mb). *Optimal configuration:* CD-ROM drive, color monitor, mouse.
Blast off with the Sci-Fi Movie Machine & Make Your Own Science-Fiction Movie Creations! This Interactive CD-ROM Game Lets User Choose from Hundreds of Actual Hollywood Classic Sci-Fi Movie Clips. Click & Drag the Digitized Clips into Any Order, Any Length.
Technology Dynamics Corp.

Sci-Fi Pack. *Items Included:* Installation Guide.
IBM PC. Contact publisher for price (ISBN 0-87321-083-2, Order no.: CDD-3016).
Activision, Inc.

Science. (Life Science Ser.). David Herzog. *Items Included:* CD-ROM, binder documentation & reproducible activity masters included with each unit. *Customer Support:* Toll free customer service Hot Line 1-800-645-3739 (9a.m. - 5p.m. Eastern Time) software guaranteed for two years.
System 6.07 or higher (2Mb); System 7.0 or higher (4Mb). Macintosh. CD-ROM disk $389.00 (Order no.: CDRLIFE2).
Detailed Tutorials with Logical Explanations Made in Small Enough Steps for Easy Comprehension. Simultaneous Colorful Graphics & Animated Sequences. Students Must Achieve Mastery of the Material Before Moving on to the Next Lesson. Included Are Classification of Living Things, Cells & Tissues, Green Plants, Genetics & Heredity, the Human Body.
Educational Activities Inc.

Science Adventure II.
MS-DOS 3.1 or higher, Windows. 386 processor or higher (640k). CD-ROM disk $69.95 (Order no.: R1182). *Nonstandard peripherals required:* CD-ROM drive. *Optimal configuration:* 386 processor or higher, MS-DOS 3.1 or higher, 20Mb hard drive, 640k RAM, external speakers or headphones (with sound card) that are Sound Blaster compatible, VGA graphics & adapter, VGA color monitor.
Learn All about the Earth, Space, Physics, Math, Science, Chemistry, Technology, Medicine & Biology Through This Interactive Program. 100 Video Clips, 1,000 Articles by Isaac Asimov & Computer Animation Make Learning about Science Fun. Features Adult & Children's Text (Ages 8 & Up).
Library Video Co.

Science & Engineering Programs for the IBM PC. Cass Lewart. Jan. 1984. *Compatible Hardware:* Compaq, IBM PC. *Operating System(s) Required:* PC-DOS 1.1, 2.0. *Language(s):* BASICA (source code included). *Memory Required:* 64k. *General Requirements:* CGA card for graphics displays (program will run without adapter but will only provide numeric output).
disk $39.95 (ISBN 0-13-794934-0).
26 Programs for Graphics, Probability & Statistics, Regression & Trend Analysis, Operations Research, Electrical Engineering & Math Applications.
Prentice Hall.

Science & Engineering Programs for the PCjr. Cass Lewart. Sep. 1984. *Compatible Hardware:* IBM PCjr. *Language(s):* Cartridge BASIC (source code included). *Memory Required:* 64k.
disk $29.95 (ISBN 0-13-794975-8).
bk. $14.95 (ISBN 0-13-794942-1).
26 Programs for Graphics, Probability & Statistics, Regression & Trend Analysis, Operations Research, Electrical Engineering & Math Applications.
Prentice Hall.

Science & Engineering Programs for the Macintosh. Cass Lewart. Sep. 1984. *Compatible Hardware:* Apple Macintosh. *Language(s):* BASIC (source code included). *Memory Required:* 400k.
3.5" disk $29.95, incl. bk. (ISBN 0-13-794801-8).
bk. $14.95 (ISBN 0-13-794793-3).
Collection of Programs Designed to Facilitate Problem-Solving in Science & Engineering. These Programs Fully Utilize the Macintosh's High Resolution Graphics Capabilities & Cover Graphics, Probability & Statistics, Regression & Trend Analysis, Operations Research, Electrical Engineering, & Math Applications.
Prentice Hall.

Science Library. *Customer Support:* All of our products are unconditionally guaranteed.
DOS. CD-ROM disk $39.95 (Order no.: SCIENCE). *Nonstandard peripherals required:* CD-ROM drive.
Large Collection of Technical & Scientific Shareware with Book.
Walnut Creek CDRom.

Science One: Human Body: an Overview. Dec. 1981. *Items Included:* Teacher's guide. *Customer Support:* 90-day limited warranty.
Apple-DOS 3.3. Apple II Family (48k). disk $89.00 (ISBN 0-917277-02-3).
Commodore 64/128 (64k). disk $89.00 (ISBN 0-917277-04-X).
The Systems of the Human Body - Respiratory, Circulatory, Digestive, Muscular, Skeletal & Nervous - Come Alive with Engaging & Animated Graphics to Illustrate the Text. Includes 7 Lessons & Review Test, & Concise Teacher's Guide Containing Additional Ideas for Reserach Topics & Student Projects. Ages 10 & Up.
BrainBank/Generation Ahead of Maryland.

Science Two: Skeletal System. Apr. 1983. *Items Included:* Teacher's guide. *Customer Support:* 90-day limited warranty.
Apple-DOS 3.3. Apple II Family (48k). disk $69.00 (ISBN 0-917277-05-8).
Commodore 64/128 (64k). disk $69.00 (ISBN 0-917277-07-4).
This Title Is a Follow-Up to the Program THE HUMAN BODY: AN OVERVIEW. The Lessons Include: A Bone to Pick, Major Skeletal Bones, Joints, & Ligaments & Cartilage, Plus a Review Test. For Ages 10 & Up.
BrainBank/Generation Ahead of Maryland.

The Scientific Desk. Version: 5. Apr. 1990. Compatible Hardware: Apple Macintosh Plus; DEC VAX; IBM PC, PC XT, PC AT, & compatibles, RT PC. Operating System(s) Required: MS-DOS 2.1 or higher, AIX. Language(s): FORTRAN (source code included). Memory Required: 256k. General Requirements: Fortran compiler.
$450.00 limited license.
$900.00 site license.
Includes a Library of over 600 FORTRAN Subroutines for Mathematics & Statistics.
C. Abaci, Inc.

Scientific Graphics Toolkit. General Requirements: True Basic Language. Macintosh, IBM PC. 3.5" disk $79.95. Produces Mathematical & Scientific Graphs from Data & Functions.
True BASIC, Inc.

Scientific Plotter. Compatible Hardware: Apple II+. Memory Required: 48k.
Plotter. disk $24.95.
Scientific Plotter Produces High-Resolution Graphs. Data Can Be Entered Through the Keyboard, from Disk Files, or Directly from BASIC Subroutines. The Scale & Endpoints of the Graph Are under the User's Control. Numeric Tables Are Automatically Added to the Axes. Text Labels Can Be Placed Anywhere On-Screen with Horizontal or Vertical Orientation. Scale Logarithmically, Scale Each Axis Independently, Plot Selectively in Quadrants of the Screen, Plot with Any 20 Symbols in 4 Different Sizes, & More.
Compuware.

SCIII Checkwriter. Compatible Hardware: Apple II+. Memory Required: 48k.
disk $29.95.
Prints Checks & Vouchers from Text Files Created by Super Checkbook III. Addresses Can Be Included on the Checks if the User Desires (for Mailing in Window Envelopes). Formatted for Use with the NEBS Brand All Purpose Check Forms Product #9022.
Powersoft, Inc.

SciTech Reference Plus. 1995. Customer Support: Information & Assistance Hotline; Electronic Bulletin Board.
DOS 3.1 or later. IBM & compatibles, 286 or higher (535k). CD-ROM disk $995.00 for 1 year. Nonstandard peripherals required: Hard disk (minimum 10 Mb free space); CD-ROM player running under MS-DOS extensions 2.0 or later.
CD-ROM disk $2836.00 for 3 years.
Portraits of 125,000 U.S. & Canadian Scientists & Engineers from AMERICAN MEN & WOMEN OF SCIENCE; Listings for 8,000 R & D Laboratories from the DIRECTORY OF AMERICAN RESEARCH & TECHNOLOGY; Profiles of Leading U.S. & International Technology Firms & Subsidiaries Found in the DIRECTORY OF CORPORATE AFFILIATIONS Series (Public, Private & International); Citations for 285,000 Sci-Tech & Medical Books from BOOKS IN PRINT; Records on 57,000 Sci-Tech & Medical Serials from ULRICH'S INTERNATIONAL PERIODICALS DIRECTORY.
R.R. Bowker.

SCO/ACCELL. Items Included: Manuals. Customer Support: 30-day warranty, hotline, newsletter, electronic bulletin board.
80386-based system under SCO Xenix 386 System V. $1295.00.
4GL (Fourth Generation Language) & Application Generator.
Santa Cruz Operation, Inc.

SCO FoxBASE: dBASE II Workalike. May 1986. Compatible Hardware: AT&T 6300+; IBM PC AT, PC XT. Operating System(s) Required: Xenix, Unix. Memory Required: 640k. Items Included: Manuals. Customer Support: 30-day warranty, hotline, newsletter, electronic bulletin board. disk $795.00.
UNIX-Based Multiuser Relational Database Management System That Offers User Interface & Functionally Identical to Ashton-Tate's dBASE II. Both Source Language & Data File Compatible with dBASE II, & Allows Full dBASE II Program Usage in Multiuser Operation, with Record & File Locking Data Security.
Santa Cruz Operation, Inc.

SCO FoxBASE+. Items Included: Manuals. Customer Support: 30-day warranty, hotline, newsletter, electronic bulletin board.
80386-based system under SCO Xenix 386 System V. $995.00.
Multi86 Version of Fox Software's Foxbase+.
Santa Cruz Operation, Inc.

SCO ImageBuilder. Items Included: Manuals. Customer Support: 30-day warranty, hotline, newsletter, electronic bulletin board.
80386-based system under SCO Xenix System V. $595.00.
Enable Users to Develop Presentation Graphics.
Santa Cruz Operation, Inc.

SCO Integra. Items Included: Manuals. Customer Support: 30-day warranty, hotline, newsletter, electronic bulletin board.
80386-based system under SCO Xenix 386 System V. $895.00.
SQL Relational Database.
Santa Cruz Operation, Inc.

SCO MasterPlan. Items Included: Manuals. Customer Support: 30-day warranty, hotline, newsletter, electronic bulletin board.
80386-based system under SCO Xenix 386 System V. $795.00.
Interactive Project Management Application. Employs the Critical Path Method.
Santa Cruz Operation, Inc.

SCO MultiView. Items Included: Manuals. Customer Support: 30-day warranty, hotline, newsletter, electronic bulletin board.
80386-based system under SCO Xenix 386 System V. $395.00.
Shell Providing a Multitasking Windowing Interface.
Santa Cruz Operation, Inc.

SCO Portfolio. Items Included: Manuals. Customer Support: 30-day warranty, hotline, newsletter, electronic bulletin board.
80386-based system under SCO Xenix 386 System V. $695.00.
Provides a Range of Desktop Tools. Integrates Applications.
Santa Cruz Operation, Inc.

SCO Portfolio Suite. Items Included: Manuals. Customer Support: 30-day warranty, hotline, newsletter, electronic bulletin board.
80386-based system under SCO Xenix 386 System V. $1995.00.
Integrates Word Processing, SQL Database, & Desktop Tools.
Santa Cruz Operation, Inc.

SCO Professional: Lotus 1-2-3 Workalike. May 1986. Compatible Hardware: AT&T 6300+ & compatibles; IBM PC AT, SUN. Operating System(s) Required: XENIX. Memory Required: 1024k. Items Included: Manuals. Customer Support: 30-day warranty, hotline, newsletter, electronic bulletin board. disk $995.00.
Offers Full LOTUS 1-2-3 Functionality under UNIX/XENIX. Existing Files & Floppies Can Be Read Directly by SCO Professional, & DOS-Readable Information Is Regenerated to Maintain Full Flexibility. Has Full Preview Character-Graphics Support for Any Standard Terminal, & Sparse Matrix Memory Management for Optimal Spreadsheet Storage.
Santa Cruz Operation, Inc.

SCO Statistician. Items Included: Manuals. Customer Support: 30-day warranty, hotline, newsletter, electronic bulletin board.
80386-based system under SCO Xenix 386 System V. $795.00.
Statistical Analysis System.
Santa Cruz Operation, Inc.

SCO UniPATH SNA 3270: Mainframe Communications Program. Pathway Design Inc. Apr. 1986. Compatible Hardware: AT&T 6300+ & compatibles; IBM PC AT, PC XT. Operating System(s) Required: XENIX, UNIX. Memory Required: 256k. Items Included: Manuals. Customer Support: 30-day warranty, hotline, newsletter, electronic bulletin board.
disk $695.00.
Allows UNIX Sytem Based Computers to Operate on IBM SNA Networks Through 3270 Emulation. The UNIX System Running UniPath Appears to the Host System As an IBM 3270 Communications Controller with Attached Display & Printer Devices or a 3270 Remote Job Entry Station. The Emulator Is Run As a Background Process Maintaining the Communications Line for Immediate, On-Demand Access to the Host System.
Santa Cruz Operation, Inc.

SCO Unix System V/386. Version: 3.2. Jun. 1989. Items Included: Manual. Customer Support: 90-day warranty, hotline, newsletter, electronic bulletin board.
80386-based systems with AT or Micro Channel bus. disk $895.00.
Multiuser, Multitasking System. Runs Applications Based on Xenix & Unix Systems, As Well As DOS (with SCO VP/ix or SCO's Open Desktop). Designed for C2 Security & Includes Menu-Based Administration, SCO Portfolio Compatibility, Conformance with FIPS 151.1 & X/Open's CAE, ANSI C 8-Bit Internationalization, MMDF II Mail, ACER Fast Filesystem (AFS) & Supports Many Standard Peripherals.
Santa Cruz Operation, Inc.

SCO VP/ix. Items Included: Manuals. Customer Support: 30-day warranty, hotline, newsletter, electronic bulletin board.
80386-based system. $495.00-$895.00.
Multitasking, Multiuser Operating System. Runs Both DOS & Unix Software Simultaneously.
Santa Cruz Operation, Inc.

SCO XENIX System V. Version: 2.3. Microsoft. Oct. 1985. Compatible Hardware: AT&T 6300+; IBM PC AT, PC XT & compatibles. Operating System(s) Required: UNIX, XENIX. Memory Required: 384k. Items Included: Manuals. Customer Support: 30-day warranty, hotline, newsletter, electronic bulletin board.
Operating System. disk $595.00-$795.00.
Development System. disk $795.00.
Text Processing System. disk $195.00.
Complete XENIX. $1395.00-$1695.00.
Enhanced Version of AT&T's UNIX Operating System. Multi-User, Multi-Tasking Operating System Which Allows File Sharing Between Independent Terminal Users or Between Any Application Programs under Control of One or More Users. Features Include Multi-Screens, Custom Installation Capability, Autoboot, Remote & Direct Networking, Multiple Printer Support & a DOS Cross-Development Environment.
Santa Cruz Operation, Inc.

TITLE INDEX

SCO XENIX Tutor. *Compatible Hardware:* IBM PC & compatibles. *Memory Required:* 128k. *General Requirements:* 2 disk drives or hard disk; IBM color, Hercules monochrome, or equivalent board. *Items Included:* Manuals. *Customer Support:* 30-day warranty.
disk $195.00.
DOS-Based XENIX. The Program Displays Instructions to the Student on One Half of the Screen, While the Other Half Emulates the XENIX System. There Are Five Modules: Introduction, XENIX File System, Manipulating Files & Directories, Mail, & Advanced XENIX Facilities. Concepts Are Illustrated with Color & Monochrome Graphics, As Well As with Animation. Can Track the Progress of up to 10 Students.
Santa Cruz Operation, Inc.

SCO Xenix 386, 16 disks (8 disks for the Operating System, 4 disks for the Development System, 2 disks for the Computer Graphics Interface, 2 disks for the Text Processing System) *Version:* 2.3. Santa Cruz Operations, Inc. & Microsoft, Inc. *Compatible Hardware:* Compaq Deskpro 386; 80386-compatible PC's; IBM PS/2 Model 80. *Memory Required:* 1024k, recommended 2048k. *General Requirements:* 1.2Mb floppy disk drive & 20Mb hard disk. *Items Included:* Manuals. *Customer Support:* 30-day warranty, hotline, newsletter, electronic bulletin board.
Complete system. $1495.00-$1695.00.
SCO Xenix Text Processing System (Xenix 286-compatible). $695.00-$795.00.
$195.00.
UNIX Implementation for 80386-Based Systems. Provides Multiuser & Multitasking Capabilities, & a UNIX Shell. The Development System Includes a C Compiler with lint, lex, & yacc & a DOS Cross-Development Environment for Creating DOS-Compatible .EXE Files. Also Included in the Development System Are Program Maintenance Tools & the SCO Computer Graphics Interface (CGI) Which Provides a Route for Developing Device-Independent Applications.
Santa Cruz Operation, Inc.

The Scoop. Jan. 1989. *Customer Support:* Unlimited free support: (617) 494-1220, (617) 494-1221.
PC-DOS/MS-DOS 3.0 or higher (512k). disk $39.95.
Apple IIe, IIe & Plus. disk $39.95.
Graphics & Text Game Where You're the New Reporter at the Daily Courier & There's Been a Murder. No One Knows Who Did It. Your Newspaper Rivals Beat You to the Story & Your Editor is Furious. Now to Save the Paper & Your Job You Must Solve the Murder & Scoop the Star. Features over 30 Animated Charaacters in over 80 Locations in & Around London.
Spinnaker Software Corp.

Score Board III. Richard Smith.
IBM PC (256k). $99.95.
Scoring Program for Duplicate Bridge Games.
Barclay Bridge Supplies, Inc.

SCORE Expert. *Items Included:* Bound manual. *Customer Support:* Free hotline - no time limit; 30 day limited warranty; updates are $5/disk plus S&H.
MS-DOS 2.1 or higher. IBM & compatibles (384k). disk $59.95. *Nonstandard peripherals required:* Printer is supported, but not required.
Uses Personal Computer to Score, Analyze, & Report the Results of Objective Tests. Provides Reporting Features to Help User Score Tests Quickly. Get All of the Statistical & Summary Reports Needed for the Most Exacting Analysis of Tests: Item Analysis; Summary Reports with Criterion-Referenced Sub-Tests; Individual Student Responses; Frequency Distributions; Automatic Conversion of Scores to Letter Grades; Test Statistics on Each Report.
Dynacomp, Inc.

Scorekeeper. *Compatible Hardware:* IBM PC. *Operating System(s) Required:* CP/M, MP/M, CP/M-86, Apple CP/M. *Language(s):* CBASIC. *Memory Required:* CP/M, MP/M, & Apple CP/M 64k, CP/M-86 & IBM 128k. *General Requirements:* 2 disk drives.
Multi-league version. disk $495.00.
Single league version. disk $49.00.
Multi-league version. demo disk $50.00.
Keeps Track of All Bowling Establishments Player/Team/League Statistics & Who Paid (or Who Owes) What Amount of Money.
Microsystems.

Scoreplan. *Memory Required:* 16k.
contact publisher for price.
Applications Generator for MSI's Portable Data Collection Terminals.
MSI Data Corp.

Scotch Opening. Jan Timman. 1994. *Items Included:* Book & disk with 500 or more games (over 200 annotated). *Customer Support:* Telephone support by appointment.
MS-DOS 2.0 or higher (512k). 3.5" disk $25.00, incl. softcover text. *Nonstandard peripherals required:* Mouse, graphics, 3 1/2" drive.
Atari ST (520k). Atari. disk $25.00. *Nonstandard peripherals required:* Monocrhome monitor DS/DD drive.
Authoritative Introduction to & Analysis of an Important Chess Opening.
Chess Combination, Inc.

Scout. *Version:* 4.1. Oct. 1989. *Items Included:* 250-page manual, complete tutorial, sample data. *Customer Support:* 60-day installation support, 30-day money back guarantee.
MS-DOS 2.0 or higher (512k). IBM PC, PC AT, PS/2 & compatibles. disk $74.95. *Nonstandard peripherals required:* Hard disk (10Mb); printer. *Optimal configuration:* Math coprocessor, UGA, color monitor.
Low-Cost Survey Management System for Organizing & Reporting on Small to Medium-Sized Surveys. Suitable for Non-Profit/ Educational/Service/Business Applications. Fully Featured, Priced for Limited Budgets. Creates Statistical Analyses, Count/Bar Graph Displays, Banner-Style Tabulation Tables. Low Learning Curve; Straightforward Operation.
Bruce Bell & Assocs., Inc.

Scram. Chris Crawford. *Compatible Hardware:* Atari 400, 600, 800, 800XL. *Memory Required:* Atari 400, 600, 800XL 16k; Atari 800 24k. *General Requirements:* Joystick, BASIC cartridge.
cassette $16.95 (Order no.: CX4123).
Try to Stop a Meltdown at a Nuclear Power Plant.
Atari Corp.

Scrapbook Plus for Windows. *Version:* 2.11. Jan. 1992. *Items Included:* Dual media. *Customer Support:* Free customer service.
Windows 3.0. IBM 286/386 (700k). disk $149.95.
Just Like What It Sounds Like - a "Scrapbook" for All of Your Images. It Allows User to Store & Find Clipart, Scanned Images, Computer Graphics, Text Charts, Spreadsheets, & Virtually Anything Else in Seconds. No More Searching Through Separate Files or Running Many Different Applications to Find the Image or Graphic You Want.
Eikon Systems.

SCREEN POWER SPEECH

ScratchPad with VoiceDrive. SuperSoft. Mar. 1984. *Operating System(s) Required:* MS-DOS. *Memory Required:* 128k. *General Requirements:* Speech Command System, printer, Winchester hard disk.
$495.00.
Texas Instruments, Personal Productivit.

SCREEN. *Version:* 2.2. Jul. 1985. *Compatible Hardware:* IBM PC, PC XT, PC AT & compatibles. *Operating System(s) Required:* PC-DOS, MS-DOS. *Language(s):* FORTRAN. *Memory Required:* 512k. *General Requirements:* Printer.
disk $1000.00 (Order no.: SCREEN).
Uses a Block Limit File to Select Either Sample Composites or Block Within Specific Geologic or Property Limits. The Program Can Be Used to Limit Data Before Variogram Computation or to Select Data Before or After Kriging.
Geostat Systems International, Inc. (GSII).

SCREEN. *Version:* 2.2. 1988. *Operating System(s) Required:* PC-DOS/MS-DOS 2.1 or higher. *Memory Required:* 256k. *Items Included:* User manual, 3.5" diskette. *Customer Support:* Free telephone support to registered users.
disk $295.00 (ISBN 0-932651-16-X).
Experimental Design Computer Program Using Plackett-Burman Saturated Fractional Factorial Screening Designs to Select the Most Significant Factors in an R&D or Manufacturing System. Generates the Specific Experimental Design & Analyzes the Results. Can Handle 35 Factors & 8 Responses.
Statistical Programs.

Screen Design. 1986. *Compatible Hardware:* Atari XL/XE. *Memory Required:* 48k. *General Requirements:* Advan BASIC.
disk $19.95.
Lets User Design Graphics Displays with Standard or Custom Modes. Custom Modes Allow Mixing Graphics Modes in One Display & Specifying Horizontal & Vertical Fine Scrolling. Draws Lines, Circles, Ellipses, Circular Arcs. Designs Alternate Character Sets. Fills in Figures. Reproduces Screen Figure at Another Location. Sets Color Registers. User Can Save Screen Display to a Disk, Load It, Plot to It & Fine-Scroll It.
Advan Language Designs.

Screen Dreams (Holy Lands). Parsons Technology.
3.5" disk Contact publisher for price (ISBN 1-57264-046-4).
Parsons Technology.

Screen Edit. *Compatible Hardware:* TRS-80.
disk $12.95 (Order no.: D8SED).
Assists with Duplicating Lines & Editing on Screen Data; Includes a Keyboard Driver.
The Alternate Source.

Screen Maker. *Compatible Hardware:* Atari XL/XE.
disk $6.95 (Order no.: AED80033).
Atari Corp.

Screen Master. *Compatible Hardware:* Atari 400, 800. *Language(s):* Atari BASIC. *Memory Required:* 32k.
disk $19.95.
Creates Text Displays & Writes BASIC Statement to Reproduce Them.
Dynacomp, Inc.

Screen Power Speech. *Compatible Hardware:* DOS-based computer & compatibles. *General Requirements:* Compatible speech synthesizer required.
$499.00 software-only.

Synthetic Speech Output System That Resides in the PC. Provides Audio Access to DOS Applications.
TeleSensory Corporation.

Screen Printer. *Compatible Hardware:* TRS-80 Model I with Level II BASIC. *Memory Required:* 16k.
disk $13.95.
Sends Contents of the Screen to the Printer.
Dynacomp, Inc.

Screen Scribe. *Compatible Hardware:* Apple.
contact publisher for price.
Instant Software, Inc.

Screening Test for Educational Prerequisite Skills (STEPS). *Version:* 1.011. Frances Smith. *Customer Support:* Free unlimited phone support.
Windows 3.X, Windows 95. 286 (4Mb). disk $89.50 (Order no.: W-1077).
The Kindergarten Screener That Prepares Schools to Meet the Needs of High-Risk Children. Based on Years of Research with Thousands of Children, "STEPS" Provides a Clear Picture of the Needs & Skills of Beginning Kindergarteners. Yet It Has None of the Problems Associated with Readiness Tests & Other Early Childhood Screeners.
Western Psychological Services.

Screenio, 2 disks. *Version:* 2.1. Jun. 1987. *Compatible Hardware:* IBM & compatibles, PC AT, 3270 PC, PS/2. *Operating System(s) Required:* PC-DOS/MS-DOS 2.0. *Language(s):* IBM COBOL/2, Micro Focus COBOL, Realia COBOL. *Memory Required:* Panel Editor 384k. *General Requirements:* Realia COBOL; hard disk recommended.
$400.00, incl. manual.
Panel Definition & Screen Management Facility for COBOL. Changes May Be Made to Existing Panels Without Requiring Changes to Existing Source Code. The PANEL EDITOR Will Allow Programmers to Design Screens with a "What-You-See-Is-What-You-Get" Approach, Showing Colors, Text, & Fields As They Will Look. Panel Images Are Stored in the User-Specified Libraries. A Library May Contain Any Number of Panel Images. Will Add about 40k to the Size of an Application, with 1-4k for Each Panel Used. There Are No Royalties or Runtime Fees for Including SCREENIO in Distributed Applications.
NORCOM (Northern Computing Consultants).

ScreenPower for Windows. *Version:* 1.47. Jan. 1996.
IBM compatible, Windows 3.1. 486-33 (8Mb). disk $995.00 (Order no.: SW1A). *Nonstandard peripherals required:* Requires compatible speech synthesizer and/or braille display.
Provides Tactile & Audio Access to Microsoft Windows for Blind Users. For Use with a Braille Display and/or Integrated Speech Output. The Numeric Pad & Braille Display Substitute for a Mouse. Information about Each Screen Element Is Readily Available So Users Can Identify Items & Their Relationship to Other Items.
TeleSensory Corp.

ScreenPower for Windows. *Version:* 2.0. Jun. 1996.
IBM compatible, Windows 3.1. 486-33 (8Mb). Contact publisher for price. *Nonstandard peripherals required:* Requires compatible speech synthesizer and/or braille display.
Provides Tactile & Audio Access to Microsoft Windows for Blind Users. For Use with a Braille Display and/or Integrated Speech Output. The Numeric Pad & Braille Display Substitute for a Mouse. Information about Each Screen Element Is Readily Available So Users Can Identify Items & Their Relationship to Other Items.
TeleSensory Corp.

Screenscapes. May 1993. *Items Included:* 3 diskettes, 82 page manual, & registration card. *Customer Support:* 60-day money-back guarantee, free technical support by phone, E-Mail or FAX.
Macintosh System 7 or higher. Macintosh (2Mb). 3.5" disk about $30.00 (ISBN 1-877777-04-8, Order no.: SSM1). *Optimal configuration:* Color monitor. *Networks supported:* Any.
Transforms Your Monitor with Spectacular Background Patterns over Which Your Work Windows "Float". Has 650 Professionally Designed Images, "Screenscape-A-Day," Convenient Cataloguing Features, & Innovative "Pattern Creation Modules" to Produce Extraordinary Patterns in Seconds. Requires No Extension or Control Panel.
Kiwi Software, Inc.

Script. *Compatible Hardware:* TRS-80.
contact publisher for price.
Instant Software, Inc.

Script Consultant. *Version:* 4.0. Feb. 1996. *Compatible Hardware:* IBM PC XT, PC AT, & compatibles. *Operating System(s) Required:* MS-DOS 3.0 or higher. *Language(s):* Compiled BASIC. *Memory Required:* 640k. *General Requirements:* Hard disk.
$295.00.
3 times a year $95.00.
Medication Management & Prescription Writing Program with Complete Drug Interaction Testing. Maintains Patient Medication & Allergy Files; Prints Complete Prescriptions, Patient Instructions & Information Consistent with the Standards of the National Council on Patient Information & Education; & Generates Custom Lists, Recall Notices, & Address Labels. Also Includes Drug-Drug, Drug-Food, & Drug-Alcohol Interaction Testing, with Automatic Testing As a Prescription Is Being Written. Provides All Utilities Needed for Maintaining the Data Base.
Rapha Group Software, Inc.

SCRIPT Professional: Multi-Language Word Processor. *Version:* 2.05. Locomotive Software. Apr. 1993. *Items Included:* Reference, user's guide, data base - Mail Merge, set-up & printer manual, sample data example files.
DOS 3.0 or higher. IBM & compatibles (512k). disk $225.00. *Optimal configuration:* One 720k floppy - hard drive recommended.
Multi-Language Word Processor That Can Use French, German, Spanish, Italian, Dutch, British & American English Dictionary & Thesaurus. Program Handles Foot & Endnotes, Newspaper Columns, Split Screen Editing, On-Line Help, Keyboards for Most European Languages, "Xtree" Style File Manager, Supports 9 Pin to Laser Printers (over 700), Drop down Menus, Automatic Date & Time Insertion, Scaleable Fonts, Page Preview & Handles Graphics.
Elliam Assocs.

Scriptor. *Compatible Hardware:* Apple Macintosh. *Memory Required:* 512k. *General Requirements:* Hard disk; supports daisywheel & LaserWriter printers.
3.5" disk $295.00.
Scriptwriting Utility. Automatically Reformats Documents As Changes Are Made. Works with MICROSOFT WORD.
Screenplay Systems, Inc.

Scriptr. *Compatible Hardware:* TRS-80 Model I, Model III. *Memory Required:* 32-48k. *General Requirements:* SCRIPSIT & compatible printer.
disk $34.95.
Printer Driver Adds Features to SCRIPSIT, Such As Single Letter Commands, Graphics, etc.
Instant Software, Inc.

Scripture Bits. *Version:* 1.4. *Compatible Hardware:* Apple Macintosh. *General Requirements:* Hard disk or external disk drive; MacWrite, Microsoft Word or compatible. *Items Included:* Disk & manual. *Customer Support:* Complete telephone support, 90-day warranty.
3.5" disk $12.95 (Order no.: 48842-600). demo disk $5.00.
Bible Reference & Calendar.
Medina Software, Inc.

Scriptures & the Heritage of the Sikhs. Prit M. Singh & Bhupinder Singh. Oct. 1995. *Items Included:* Inserted manuals. *Customer Support:* Free on-site training.
Windows 3.1 & higher. IBM & compatibles (4Mb). disk $99.00 (ISBN 0-9649439-0-5).
First Ever English Translation of Sikh Bible - Sri Guru Granth Sahib. Also Contains the Following Brief Date-Wise History - 200 Pictures of the Shrines, 31 Ragas of Indian Classical Nature As Included in the Holy Book, Punjabi Fonts, Lives of Gurus (the Teacher Founder of the Religion), More Than 2000 Quotations from the Holy Book on about 100 Topics: Life, Death, Caste, Ego, Women, Emancipation. Windows Screen Saver on Gurus.
Advanced Micro Supplies, Inc.

Scrolls of Talmouth. *Compatible Hardware:* Commodore Amiga, IBM PC, Apple Macintosh, Atari ST.
3.5" disk $24.95.
Quest Disk for Use with Paladin.
Omnitrend Software, Inc.

ScruTiny in the Great Round. Tennessee R. Dixon & Jim Gasperini. Nov. 1995. *Customer Support:* Free hot line for technical support.
MS Windows; Macintosh System 7.1 or higher. 486 or higher (8Mb); 040 Mac or Power Mac (8Mb). CD-ROM disk Contact publisher for price (ISBN 1-887701-02-8). *Nonstandard peripherals required:* CD-ROM drive & MPC-compatible Sound Card Video Card with 256 colors or higher; CD-ROM drive. *Optimal configuration:* 12Mb RAM.
A Captivating & Hypnotic Interactive Experience Based on a Limited Edition Book of Collage Art by New York Artist Tennessee Rice Dixon. Brought to Life in Collaboration with Multimedia Designer Jim Gasperini & Composer Charles Morrow, "ScruTiny" Offers a New Way to Think about & Interact with Art. Considered the First Full-Length Work in One of the Key Art Forms of the 21st Century, This Unique CD-ROM Title Incorporates Dixon's Images Depicting the Ebb & Flow of Life with an Eclectic Mix of Poetry & Music.
Calliope Media.

ScruTiny in the Great Round: Limited Edition. Tennessee R. Dixon & Jim Gasperini. *Customer Support:* Free hot line for technical support.
MS Windows; Macintosh System 7.1 or higher. 486 or higher (8Mb); 040 Mac or Power Mac (8Mb). CD-ROM disk Contact publisher for price (ISBN 1-887701-00-1). *Nonstandard peripherals required:* CD-ROM drive & MPC-compatible Sound Card Video Card with 256 colors or higher; CD-ROM drive. *Optimal configuration:* 12Mb RAM.
A Captivating & Hypnotic Interactive Experience Based on a Limited Edition Book of Collage Art by New York Artist Tennessee Rice Dixon. Brought to Life in Collaboration with Multimedia Designer Jim Gasperini & Composer Charles Morrow, "ScruTiny" Offers a New Way to Think about & Interact with Art. Considered the First Full-Length Work in One of the Key Art Forms of the 21st Century, This Unique CD-ROM Title Incorporates Dixon's Images Depicting the Ebb & Flow of Life with an Eclectic Mix of Poetry & Music.
Calliope Media.

SCS Netware. Sep. 1984. *Compatible Hardware:* IBM PC, PC XT, PC AT. *Memory Required:* 256k. *General Requirements:* Hard disk, PCnet Local Area Network Interface cards.
disk $1495.00.
Enhanced Network Operating System.
Santa Clara Systems, Inc.

SCSI Tool. *Version:* 1.3. *Compatible Hardware:* Apple Macintosh with SCSI. *Customer Support:* 800-346-6980.
3.5" disk $175.00.
Assists in the Development of SCSI Hardware & Software.
Arborworks, Inc.

Scuba Master. *Version:* 1.16. *Items Included:* Complete bound instruction guide. *Customer Support:* Free support for first 60 days; 1 year toll-free support, $295.00.
DOS. IBM & compatibles. $595.00-$1495.00.
   Optimal configuration: 486, 4Mb memory, fast hard disk. *Networks supported:* LANtastic, Novell.
This Software Handles the Entire Functions of a Typical Store from Renting Items & Invoicing down to Scheduling Classes & Trips. Allows for Rentals & Sales of Items As a Group or Individually. The Program Keeps Track of the History of Rental Items & Customers. Complete Retail Inventory Functions with Reorder Thresholds Alert When Stock Levels Are Low. Prints Receipts on Plain Paper or Custom Receipts.
Aphelion, Inc.

Sculpt-Animate 4D. *Compatible Hardware:* Commodore Amiga.
3.5" disk $499.95.
Professional 3D Animation, Scanline or Ray-Traced.
Byte by Byte.

Sculpt 3-D. *Compatible Hardware:* Commodore Amiga 500, 1000, 2000.
3.5" disk $99.95.
Graphics Development System Using the Standard AMIGA Environment & Mouse Control, Menus, & Windows. Includes the Following Features: Fully Multi-Tasking; Wire Frame Edit Mode; Library of Graphics Primitives; Tools Such As Spin, Grab, Extrude, Reflect, & Unslice. Gives User Control over the Color, Texture, Smoothing, & Shading of Every Surface of Every Object; Brightness, Color & Placement of Multiple Light Sources; Camera Position & Angle of View. Automatically Handles Shading, Smoothing, Anti-Aliasing, Shadows, & Texture. Includes a Painting Mode. Allows Users to Create Their Own Library of Primitives. All Images Are IFF Compatible. Script Mode Accepts ASCII Input. Supports All Resolution Modes, Videoframe Buffer Boards, & Genlocks. Not Copy Protected.
Byte by Byte.

Sculptor. *Compatible Hardware:* IBM PC & compatibles.
$149.00 to $15,000.00.
Free-Form, Command & Menu-Driven Database-Management System Featuring Help Screen, On-Disk Tutorial, Automatic Indexing & Split/Merge Files. Offers a Maximum of 32,767 Fields per Record, 32,767 Characters per Field, 16 Million Records per File, 32,767 Characters per Record, 160 Indexes per File, 16 Active Indexes & up to 160 Records Sorted. Allows User to Revise Field Descriptions at Will.
mpd U.S.A., Inc.

Sculptor.
   MS-DOS, Unix, Xenix (512k). IBM PC, PC XT, PC AT & compatibles. contact publisher for price.
   Database Designed for Business Applications. Query System Enables User to Extract Inquiries & Reports. Includes Fourth Generation Language for Manipulation of Data Files. System Can Run on Wide Range of Micros, Supermicros & Mini Computers.
Universal Data Research, Inc.

SD Accounting. Oct. 1985. *Compatible Hardware:* IBM PC & compatibles. *Operating System(s) Required:* MS-DOS. *Memory Required:* 256k. *Items Included:* Disk, manual, & demo data. *Customer Support:* Yes.
$50.00.
Provides Essentials of Effective Money Management for Home or Small Business Use from Balancing User's Checkbook to Providing Year End Figures for Taxes.
Software Design, Inc.

SDBOX: Box Rental, Data Base System, 2 disks. *Version:* 1.2. Harold L. Reed. Mar. 1987. *Compatible Hardware:* IBM PC. *Operating System(s) Required:* PC-DOS/MS-DOS 3.3 or higher. *Language(s):* Turbo Pascal. *Memory Required:* 256k. *General Requirements:* Hard disk, printer.
disk $400.00 (ISBN 0-924495-05-7).
Manages Safe Deposit Box Rental. Boxes Can Be Rented on Any Schedule the Renter Desires & Accounts Receivable Are Accumulated & Billing Is Automatic.
IDEA Computers, Inc.

Sea Strike. May 1988. *Compatible Hardware:* Apple IIgs. *Operating System(s) Required:* ProDOS. *Memory Required:* 512k.
3.5" disk $39.95.
Arcade Game Involving Oil Tankers under Attack.
PBI Software, Inc.

Sea War. *Compatible Hardware:* Atari 400, 800; IBM. *Language(s):* Atari BASIC, MS-DOS. *Memory Required:* Atari 48k, IBM 128k.
disk $16.95.
Battleship Game.
Dynacomp, Inc.

Seafox. *Compatible Hardware:* Apple II+, IIe. *General Requirements:* Joystick.
disk $34.95.
Submarine Game That Requires Maneuvering Abilities. Throughout the Game, the Player Has to Survive Exploding Depth Charges, Mines, & Torpedoes.
Broderbund Software, Inc.

The Seamless Lease-Loan Manag-r. *Version:* Fall, 1994. Sep. 1987. *Items Included:* Documentation, updates-two a year. *Customer Support:* 18-23% of Purchase Price per year; telephone hotline, documentation, bulletin board, training, annual conference, workshop.
MS-DOS 6.0, Windows 3.0 or higher. 486 PC (4-8Mb). disk $15,000.00 & up. *Optimal configuration:* 25Mb hard disk, 132-column printer. *Networks supported:* Novell, Plus most other standard LANs.
Comprehensive Lease & Loan Administration & Accounting System. Highlights of the System Include: Seamless Integration of Lease & Loan Contracts for Collection & Cash Application, Daily Interest Computations, Separate G/L Interfaces to Host Systems for Loans & Leases, Flexible Payment Schedules, Asset-Based Lending Concepts, Electronic Funds Transfer, Depreciation Schedules.
LeaseTek, Inc.

Search! *Compatible Hardware:* Apple IIe, IIc, IIgs. *Memory Required:* 64k.
disk $250.00.
Multiple-Level Program Designed for Retraining Visual/Spatial Perceptions, Assisting in the Following Areas: Eye-Hand Coordination, Form Constancy, Figure-Ground, Position in Space, Spatial Relationships, Organizational Skills, & Memory. Divided into 2 Tasks. In the First, the Client Is to Match the Right Column with the Left Column. In the Second Task the Client Is to Distinguish the Single Shape Which Comprises a Grouping of Shapes. 9 Different Maskings Are Available in Both Tasks.
Greentree Group, Inc.

Search Express/Legal. *Version:* 2.6. Apr. 1991. *Customer Support:* 30 day free phone support. Support Plan: 15% annual of the original purchase price of software. Includes unlimited phone support & free software upgrades.
MS-DOS, Windows. IBM & compatibles (640k). $2995.00. *Networks supported:* Novell, Banyon, 3COM, Lantastic, Starlan.
Full-Text & Fielded Data Index & Retrieval Software Package for Document Management & Litigation Support in Law Firms, Corporate Legal Departments, or Any Organization Needing Quick Retrieval of Documents Stored on (or off) the Network. Features Include Security, Concept Searching, Relevancy Ranking, Boolean Search Capabilities, Hypertext Linking, & Filters for Importing Documents from All the Major Word Processors. Uses Include Deposition Management, Work Product Retrieval, Resume Retrieval, On-Line Policy & Procedure Manuals, etc. Optional Document Imaging Module Available That Allows for High Speed Scanning & OCR of Hard Copy Documents.
Executive Technologies, Inc.

Search for Your Israeli Cousin. *Items Included:* Frommer's Israel (a tourist's guide to Israel). Macintosh Plus or higher. 3.5" disk $49.95 (Order no.: M809). *Addl. software required:* Hyper card 2.X. *Optimal configuration:* Macintosh Plus or higher, hard disk.
Combines Interesting & Useful Information about Famous Places in Israel with a Tantalizing Search for a Long-Lost Relative.
Davka Corp.

Search Master: Business Law Library. *Items Included:* The library is sold by annual subscription. Subscription includes Search Master System Software (& updates to the software at no additional charge), tutorial version of the software (allows learning the system without use of a CD-ROM drive), loose-leaf user's manual (including tutorial section, reference section, appendicies & installation), current Business Law Library CD-ROM disc & updated replacement CDs 5 times a year (old CDs must be returned). *Customer Support:* A users manual & context-sensitive on-screen help messages, subscription includes unlimited free assistance via toll-free telephone number.
PC-DOS or MS-DOS version 3.1 or higher, 3.3 or higher preferred (640k). IBM PC, AT, PS/2 or compatible; optional network support. CD-ROM disk Contact publisher for price. *Nonstandard peripherals required:* CD-ROM drive & compatible interface card appropriate for the drive & the user's computer. *Addl. software required:* Microsoft MS-DOS CD-ROM Extensions version 2.0 or higher, device drivers for the CD-ROM drive being used.
Allows a Subscriber to Use a PC to Search, Retrieve & Browse the Full Text of 'Current Legal Forms with Tax Analysis' (Rabkin & Johnson), 'Business Organizations with Tax Planning' (Cavitch), 'Debtor-Creditor Law', & three other Matthew Bender Business Law Publications Stored on CD-ROM (Compact Disc-Read Only Memory).
Matthew Bender & Co., Inc.

Search Master: California Library. *Items Included:* The library is sold by annual subscription. Subscription includes Search Master System Software (& updates to the software at no additional charge), tutorial version of the software (allows learning the system without use of a CD-ROM drive), loose-leaf user's manual (including tutorial section, reference section, & appendices), current California Library CD-ROM disc & updated replacement CDs 6 times a year (old CDs must be returned). *Customer Support:* A user's manual & context-sensitive on-screen help messages, subscription includes unlimited free assistance via toll-free telephone number. PC-DOS or MS-DOS version 3.1 or higher (640K). IBM PC/AT or compatible 80286-based or 80386-based personal computer or IBM PS/2 or compatible; Optional network support. CD-ROM disk publisher for price. *Nonstandard peripherals required:* CD-ROM drive & a compatible interface card appropriate for the drive & the user's personal computer. *Addl. software required:* Microsoft MS-DOS CD-ROM Extensions version 2.0 or higher, device drivers for the CD-ROM drive being used. *Allows a Subscriber to Use a PC to Search, Retrieve & Browse the Full Text of Bender's CALIFORNIA FORMS OF PLEADING & PRACTICE, CALIFORNIA LEGAL FORMS - TRANSACTION GUIDE, CALIFORNIA POINTS & AUTHORITIES, Bender's STANDARD CALIFORNIA CODES & the California Corporate & Penal Codes, CALIFORNIA INTELLECTUAL PROPERTY HANDBOOK, Bender's CALIFORNIA TAX CODE & REGULATIONS Stored on CD-ROM (Compact Disc-Read Only Memory).* Matthew Bender & Co., Inc.

Search Master: Collier's Bankruptcy Library. *Items Included:* The library is sold by annual subscription. Subscription includes Search Master System Software (& updates to the software at no additional charge), tutorial version of the software (allows learning the system without use of a CD-ROM drive), loose-leaf user's manual (including tutorial section, reference section, appendicies & installation), current Collier's Bankruptcy Library CD-ROM disc & updated replacement CDs 4 times a year (old CDs must be returned). *Customer Support:* A user's manual & context-senitive on-screen help messages, subscription includes unlimited free assistance via toll-free telephone number. PC-DOS or MS-DOS version 3.1 or higher (640K). IBM PC/AT or compatibles 80286-based or 80386-based personal computer or IBM PS/2 or compatible; Optional network support. CD-ROM disk publisher for price. *Nonstandard peripherals required:* CD-ROM drive & a compatible interface card appropriate for the drive & the user's personal computer. *Addl. software required:* Microsoft MS-DOS CD-ROM Extensions version 2.0 or higher, device drivers for the CD-ROM drive being used. *Allows a Subscriber to Use a PC to Search, Retrieve & Browse the Full Text of COLLIER on BANKRUPTCY, 15th EDITION (including the Bankruptcy Code & Rules), COLLIER BANKRUPTCY CASES, 2nd SERIES & Nine Other Matthew Bender Bankruptcy Publications Stored on CD-ROM (Compact Disc-Read Only Memory).* Matthew Bender & Co., Inc.

Search Master: Federal Practice Library. *Items Included:* The library is sold by annual subscription. Subscription includes Search Master system software (& updates to the software at no additional charge), tutorial version of the software (allows Learning the system without use of a CD-ROM drive), loose-leaf user's manual (including tutorial section, reference section, & appendicies), current Federal Practice Library CD-ROM disc & updated replacement CDs four times a year (old CDs must be returned). *Customer Support:* A User's manual & context-sensitive on-screen help messages, subscription includes unlimited free assistance via toll-free telephone number. PC-DOS or MS-DOS version 3.1 or higher (640K). IBM PC/AT or compatible 80286-based or 80386-based personal computer or IBM PS/2 or compatible; optional network support. CD-ROM disk contact publisher for price. *Nonstandard peripherals required:* CD-ROM drive & a compatible interface card appropriate for the drive & the user's personal computer. *Addl. software required:* Microsoft MS-DOS CD-ROM Extensions version 2.0 or higher, device drivers for the CD-ROM drive being used. *Allows a Subscriber to Use a PC to Search, Retrieve & Browse the Full Text of MOORE'S FEDERAL PRACTICE (Including the Federal Rules of Civil & Criminal Procedure), WEINSTEIN'S EVIDENCE, UNITED STATES RULES (Including the Federal Rules of Evidence), BENDER'S FORMS OF DISCOVERY & Eight Other Matthew Bender Federal Practice Publications Stored on CD-ROM (Compact Disc-Read Only Memory).* Matthew Bender & Co., Inc.

Search Master: Intellectual Property Library. *Items Included:* The Library is sold by annual subscription. Subscription includes Search Master system software (& updates to the software at no additional charge), tutorial version of the software (allows learning the system without use of a CD-ROM drive), loose-leaf user's manual (including tutorial section, reference section, & appendicies), current Intellectual Property Library CD-ROM disc & updated replacement CDs three times a year (old CDs must be returned). *Customer Support:* User's manual & context-sensitive on-screen help messages, subscription includes unlimited free assistance via toll-free telephone number. PC-DOS or MS-DOS version 3.1 or higher (640K). IBM PC/AT or compatible 80286-based or 80386-based personal computer or IBM PS/2 or compatible; optional network support. CD-ROM disk contact publisher for price. *Nonstandard peripherals required:* CD-ROM drive & a compatible interface card appropriate for the drive & the user's personal computer. *Addl. software required:* Microsoft MS-DOS CD-ROM Extensions version 2.0 or higher, device drivers for the CD-ROM drive being used. *Allows a Subscriber to Use a PC to Search, Retrieve & Browse the Full Text of NIMMER on COPYRIGHT, PATENTS (CHISM), TRADEMARK PROTECTION & PRACTICE (GILSON), MILGRIM on TRADE SECRETS, COMPUTER LAW & Eight Other Matthew Bender Intellectual Property Publications Stored on CD-ROM (Compact Disc-Read Only Memory).* Matthew Bender & Co., Inc.

Search Master: New York Library. *Items Included:* The library is sold by annual subscription. Subscription includes Search Master System Software (& updates to the software at no additional charge), tutorial version of the software (allows learning the system without use of a CD-ROM drive), loose-leaf user's manual (including tutorial section, reference section, appendicies & installation), current New York Library CD-ROM disc & updated replacement CDs 4 times a year (old CDs must be returned). *Customer Support:* A user's manual & context-sensitive on-screen help messages, subscription includes unlimited free assistance via toll-free telephone number. PC-DOS or MS-DOS version 3.1 or higher, 3.3 or higher preferred (640k). IBM PC AT, PS/2 or compatibles; optional network support. CD-ROM disk Contact publisher for price. *Nonstandard peripherals required:* CD-ROM drive & a compatible interface card appropriate for the drive & the user's computer. *Addl. software required:* MS-DOS CD-ROM extensions version 2.0 or higher, device drivers for the CD-ROM drive being used. *Allows a Subscriber to Use a PC to Search, Retrieve & Browse the Full Text of 'Bender's Forms for the Civil Practice', Bender's Section-by-Section Analysis of New York Civil Law (CPLR, EPTL, SCPA, Matrimonial Actions, & Equitable Actions, & Bender's Well-Known One-Volume "Colorbooks" of Primary Source Material on CD-ROM (Compact Disc-Read Only Memory).* Matthew Bender & Co., Inc.

Search Master: Personal Injury Library. *Items Included:* The library is sold by annual subscription. Subscription includes Search Master System Software (& updates to the software at no additional charge), tutorial version of the software (allows learning the system without use of a CD-ROM drive), loose-leaf user's manual (including tutorial section, reference section, appendicies & installation), current Personal Injury Library CD-ROM disc & updated replacement CDs 4 times a year (old CDs must be returned). *Customer Support:* A user's manual & context-sensitive on-screen help messages, subscription includes unlimited free assistance via toll-free telephone number. PC-DOS or MS-DOS version 3.1 or higher, 3.3 or higher preferred (640k). IBM PC AT, PS/2 or compatible; optional network support. CD-ROM disk Contact publisher for price. *Nonstandard peripherals required:* CD-ROM drive & a compatible interface card appropriate for the drive & the user's computer. *Addl. software required:* Microsoft MS-DOS CD-ROM Extensions version 2.0 or higher, device drives for the CD-ROM drive being used. *Allows a Subscriber to Use a PC to Search, Retrieve & Browse the Full Text of 'Attorneys' Textbook of Medicine' (Gray), 'Damages in Tort Actions', Proving Medical Diagnosis & Prognosis', Personal Injury-Actions, Defense, Damages, & 'Attorneys' Dictionary of Medicine' (Schmidt) Stored on CD-ROM (Compact Disc-Read Only Memory).* Matthew Bender & Co., Inc.

Search Master: Tax Library. *Items Included:* The library is sold by annual subscription. Subscription includes Search Master system software (& updates to the software at no additional charge), tutorial version of the software (allows learning the system without use of a CD-ROM drive), loose-leaf user's manual (including tutorial section, reference section, & appendicies), current Tax Library CD-ROM disc & updated replacement CDs monthly (old CDs must be returned). *Customer Support:* User's manual & context-sensitive on-screen help messages, subscription includes unlimited free assistance via toll-free telephone number. PC-DOS or MS-DOS version 3.1 or higher (640K). IBM PC/AT or compatible 80286-based or 80386-based personal computer or IBM PS/2 or compatible; optional network support. CD-ROM disk contact publisher for price. *Nonstandard peripherals required:* CD-ROM drive & a compatible interface card appropriate for the drive & the user's personal computer. *Addl. software required:* Microsoft MS-DOS CD-ROM Extensions version 2.0 or higher, device drivers for the CD-ROM drive being used. *Allows a Subscriber to Use a PC to Search, Retrieve & Browse the Full Text of BENDER'S*

FEDERAL TAX SERVICE (Including the Internal Revenue Code & Regulations), BENDER'S MASTER FEDERAL TAX HANDBOOK & Eight Matthew Bender State Tax Services (New York, California, New Jersey, Florida, Texas, Pennsylvania, Ohio & Illinois) Stored on CD-ROM (Compact Disc-Read Only Memory).
Matthew Bender & Co., Inc.

Search Master: Texas Library. *Items Included:* The library is sold by annual subscription. Subscription includes Search Master System Software (& updates to the software at no additional charge), tutorial version of the software (allows learning the system without use of a CD-ROM drive), loose-leaf user's manual (including tutorial section, reference section, appendicies & installation), current Texas Library CD-ROM disc & updated replacement CDs 3 times a year (old CDs must be returned). *Customer Support:* A user's manual & context-sensitive on-screen help messages, subscription includes unlimited free assistance via toll-free telephone number.
PC-DOS or MS-DOS version 3.1 or higher, 3.3 or higher preferred (640k). IBM PC AT, PS/2 or compatibles; optional network support. CD-ROM disk Contact publisher for price. *Nonstandard peripherals required:* CD-ROM drive & a compatible interface card appropriate for the drive & the user's computer. *Addl. software required:* Microsoft MS-DOS CD-ROM Extensions version 2.0 or higher, device drivers for the CD-ROM drive being used.
Allows a Subscriber to Use a PC to Search, Retrieve & Browse the Full Text of 'Texas Litigation Guide', 'Texas Transaction Guide - Legal Forms', & 'Dorsaneo's Texas Codes & Rules' stored on CD-ROM (Compact Disc-Read Only Memory).
Matthew Bender & Co., Inc.

Search Pro: Professional Approach to Lexis/Nexis. Richard Shoulberg. May 1986. *Operating System(s) Required:* PC-DOS, MS-DOS. *Memory Required:* 320k. *General Requirements:* Modem, RS-232C serial port.
disk $495.00 (Order no.: SP).
Accesses Lexis/Nexis Using Natural Language Interface. Supports English Query Building Program for Novices & Standard Query Building for Experts. Features Off-Line Query Building & Saving, Built-In Thesaurus, Ability to Save Retrieved Documents to Disk or Printer, Single Keystroke Access.
Direct-Aid, Inc.

SearchExpress - CD-ROM. *Version:* 3.4. *Compatible Hardware:* IBM PC AT, PS/2 & compatibles. *Operating System(s) Required:* MS Windows, DOS. *Memory Required:* 4000k. *Customer Support:* 1st month free phone support, then 15%/year of initial purchase price.
CD-ROM disk $6995.00.
A Royalty-Free CD-ROM Authoring & Retrieval Software Package. Allows Users to Prepare Databases Containing Both Text & Images for Subsequent Stamping on CD-ROM. There Are Two Aspects to SearchExpress: the Build & Retrieval Modules. Use the Build Module to Index & Organize Your Database of Text, Fielded Data, or Images. The Retrieval Module, Which May Be Distributed Royalty-Free, Is Sent on Every CD Disc & Provides the User with a Powerful yet Simple Interface for Quickly Retrieving Information. Lets One Quickly Search Any Combination of Fielded Databases, Full-Text and/or Images Using Boolean or Intelligent Search Techniques. Retrieval Module Features Include: Documents Ranking Order of Relevance, Full Boolean & Proximity Search Capabilities, Concept Search, & Fuzzy Search.
Executive Technologies, Inc.

SearchExpress Document Imaging System. *Version:* 3.4. *Compatible Hardware:* IBM PC & compatibles. *Operating System(s) Required:* MS Windows, DOS. *Memory Required:* 4000k. *General Requirements:* Hard disk, scanner. *Customer Support:* First 30 days free then 15% annual fee includes phone/modem support & free software updates.
disk $5995.00.
Allows for High-Speed Scanning of Documents & Optical Character Recognition (OCR) of the Scanned Images. The Images Are Compressed in TIFF Group IV Format. SearchExpress Uses a Sophisticated Parallel Processing System Allowing Thousands of Pages to Be Scanned & OCR'd Daily. Features Include an OCR Proofing Editor Which Displays Both the Image & OCR'd Test Simultaneously on the Screen. Full-Text As Well As Fielded Data Searches Will Retrieve Documents in Seconds. Also Supports All Major Optical Storage Devices. Features Concept Searching, Relevancy Ranked Searching, Fuzzy Searching, & Boolean Searching.
Executive Technologies, Inc.

SearchMAGIC Plus. *Customer Support:* Free for first 45 days. Microcomputers-$300.00 per year. MS-DOS 3.1 or higher. IBM PC & compatibles. first copy $395.00, each additional copy ,250.00.
$1350.00-$9200.00.
Searching Front End Designed for Use with Databases Created with Inmagic. Enables Novice or Occasional Users to Find Information Quickly & Easily Without Learning Search Commands or Knowing Anything about the Structure or Contents of Databases. Features Database Selection Menus, Fill-in-the-Blank Search Screens & Customized Help. Practical for Database Distribution. Image Version Also Available.
Inmagic, Inc.

Seasons & Holidays. *Compatible Hardware:* Apple IIgs. *Operating System(s) Required:* ProDOS 16. *Memory Required:* 768k. *General Requirements:* DeluxePaint II.
3.5" disk $29.95.
Provides Clip-Art for DELUXEPAINT II.
Electronic Arts.

Seastalker. Stu Galleg & Jim Lawrence. Jun. 1984. *Compatible Hardware:* Apple II; Atari XL/XE, ST; TRS-80; Commodore 64, Amiga. $14.95.
Interactive Story That Encourages Logical Thinking, Planning, & Organization. Also Stimulates the Players to Develop Creative Strategies for Problem-Solving While Encouraging Reading. You Have to Save the Aquadome, the World's First Undersea Research Station. But You Haven't Yet Tested the Sub in Deep Water, & the Crew of the Aquadome May Have a Traitor in Its Ranks. You'll Find Help in Your SEASTALKER Package, & You'll Need Every Last Scrap of It, Because If You Challenge the Deep Without Charting the Right Course, You Might Wind up As Shark Bait.
Activision, Inc.

SeaView!: Marine Instrument Display for PC. *Version:* 2.0. Sep. 1994. *Items Included:* Manual & interface cable. *Customer Support:* Free 90 day 800 number support.
Windows 3.1. IBM 386 or higher (2Mb). disk $495.00. *Addl. software required:* Windows 3.1. *Optimal configuration:* 386, Win 3.1, 4Mb RAM, serial port.
Display with Analog, Digital, Pie, Bar, & Other Forms of Display, Boat Speed, Wind Speed, Direction, Magnetic & True Direction. Apparent Angles, Depth, Navigation & Performance Information - Required NMMA0183 Input.
Fair Tide Technologies, Inc.

Second Front. Gary Grigsby. *Items Included:* Rulebook. *Customer Support:* Technical assistance line: (408) 737-6850 (11am-5pm, PST); 14 day money back guarantee/30 day exchange policy. DOS 2.11 or higher. IBM PC & compatible (512k, 640k). disk $59.95. *Nonstandard peripherals required:* Requires color monitor & graphic adaptor (i.e., CGA, EGA).
Workbench. Amiga (512k). disk $59.95.
A Division-Level Strategic Game on a Grand Scale. The Map Extends from Berlin in the West to Stalingrad in the East, & Covers the Entire Russian Front. Players Command Over 150 German Divisions & Over 200 Soviet Divisions, with Asset Information Available to the Individual Tank, Plane, & Infantry Squad Level. Direct a Variety of Air Operations Such As Interdiction Tank, Airlift, & Strategic Bombing. Use Pop-Up Menus to Exercise Complete Control Over Your Production Facilities or Sit Back & Let the Computer Handle Production. For One or Two Players.
Strategic Simulations, Inc.

Second Order Frame Analysis. *Items Included:* Full manual. No other products required. *Customer Support:* Free telephone support - no time limit, 30 day warranty.
MS-DOS 3.2 or higher. IBM & compatibles (512k). disk $89.95.
User-Interactive Program for Solving Multiple-Span Beams & Columns & Plane-Frame Structures in the Elastic Range, & Include the Secondary Effects of Deflected Shape under Load. Uses Non-Linear Elastic Analysis Theory, Including the P-Delta Effect, & Work for Tension As Well As Compression Axial Loads.
Dynacomp, Inc.

Second Sight BBS. *Version:* 3.0. *Compatible Hardware:* Macintosh Plus or higher. *General Requirements:* Hayes-compatible modem. *Items Included:* Manual. *Customer Support:* Available to registered users.
3.5" disk $199.00.
Multi-Line Bulletin Board Construction System Software.
The FreeSoft Co.

Secret. Vladislav Celik.
IBM & compatibles. disk $19.00 (ISBN 0-9624062-6-0).
3.5" disk $19.00 (ISBN 0-9624062-7-9).
Software That Can Code Text Entered in English into Understandable Code That Looks Just Like Some Other Language. It Can Be Printed on Paper or Just Displayed on Screen. Coded Text Can Be Converted into Standard English at Any Time.

The Secret Codes of C. Y. P. H. E. R: Operation U. S. Presidents. Oct. 1992. *Items Included:* PC Version - both 3.5" & 5.25" disks, documentation, code wheel (off-disk copy protection), quick start card, warranty/registration card. Mac Version - both 256-color & B&W versions, documentation, code wheel, warranty/registration card. *Customer Support:* Limited 90 day warranty; free technical support via telephone.
MS-DOS 3.0 or higher. IBM PC, XT & compatibles or higher (640k). disk $49.95 (ISBN 1-880006-10-3, Order no.: PC/OP/CNS). *Nonstandard peripherals required:* Hercules monochrome, EGA, VGA or MCGA graphics board. *Optimal configuration:* IBM PC AT or compatible running at 10MHz or faster, MS-DOS operating system, 640k RAM, VGA-256 color graphics, Roland sound card, mouse, hard disk drive.
Macintosh System 6.0.2 (B&W), 6.0.5 (color). Macintosh Plus or higher (1Mb B&W, 2Mb color). 3.5" disk $59.95 (ISBN 1-880006-15-4,

THE SECRET CODES OF C.Y.P.H.E.R:

Order no.: MAC/OP/CNS). *Optimal configuration:* Macintosh LC or higher, System 6.0.5, 2Mb RAM, hard disk drive.
Return to the World of C.Y.P.H.E.R. in This Exciting New Adventure. This Time Explore the Life & Times of the U.S. Presidents As You Race to Crack the Secret Codes. Your Colorful, Easy to Use FunCyclopedia Is the Latest in Secret Agent Resource Technology. Ages 8 Through Adult.
Tanager Software Productions.

The Secret Codes of C.Y.P.H.E.R: Operation Wildlife. Aug. 1991. *Items Included:* PC - both 3.5" & 5.25" diskette versions; Macintosh - both color & B&W versions. Documentation, code wheel (off-disk copy protection), quick start card, warranty/registration card. *Customer Support:* Limited 90 day warranty. Free technical support via telephone.
MS-DOS 3.0 or higher. IBM PC, XT or compatible or higher (IBM PC, XT, AT, PS/1, PS/2 compatibles, Tandy) (640k). $49.95 (ISBN 1-880006-00-6, Order no.: PC/OW/CNS). *Nonstandard peripherals required:* Hercules monochrome, EGA, VGA, or MCGA graphics board. *Optimal configuration:* IBM PC AT or compatible running at 10MHz or faster, MS-DOS operating system, 640k RAM, VGA-256 Color graphics, Roland Sound Card, mouse, hard disk drive.
Macintosh System 6.0.2 & higher - B&W; 6.0.5 & higher - color. Macintosh Plus & higher (1Mb - B&W) (2Mb - Color). $59.95 (ISBN 1-880006-05-7, Order no.: MAC/OW/CNS). *Optimal configuration:* Macintosh LC or higher, Macintosh System 6.0.5 operating system, 2Mb RAM, hard disk drive.
This Product Is an Educational Game. The Player Works for C.Y.P.H.E.R., an Undercover Organization Which Transmits Secret Coded Messages. The Product Teaches about Mammals, Communication Alphabets Such As Braille & Morse Code, & Promotes Language, Logic & Reasoning Skills, All in an Entertaining Secret Agent Theme. Ages 8 Through Adult.
Tanager Software Productions.

Secret*File. Daniel D. Stuhlman. Dec. 1985. *Compatible Hardware:* IBM PC & compatibles. *Operating System(s) Required:* MS-DOS 2.0 or higher. *Memory Required:* 256k.
disk $75.00, incl. documentation (ISBN 0-934402-18-3).
Encrypts Computer Files & Decodes Them. Includes Utilities to Run the Program.
BYLS Pr.

Secret Formula: Advanced. *Compatible Hardware:* Atari XL/XE.
disk $6.95 (Order no.: AED80022).
Atari Corp.

Secret Formula: Elementary. *Compatible Hardware:* Atari XL/XE.
disk $6.95 (Order no.: AED80020).
Atari Corp.

Secret Formula: Intermediate. *Compatible Hardware:* Atari XL/XE.
disk $6.95 (Order no.: AED80021).
Atari Corp.

The Secret Garden: Interactive Moviebook. *Version:* 1.5. Sep. 1994. *Items Included:* Manual, registration card, product flyer. *Customer Support:* Phone technical support.
Windows 3.1. 386 DX 25MHz or higher (4Mb). disk $19.95 (ISBN 1-57303-009-0). *Nonstandard peripherals required:* Sound card. *Optimal configuration:* 486 or higher with 8Mb RAM, Windows 3.1 or later, 15Mb free hard drive space available, sound card, 256 color monitor.
Interactive MovieBooks Are Exclusively Licensed Computer Storybooks for Children. Taken from the Movie Version, the Story Appears on the Computer Screen in Book Form Which the Child Can Read or, by Clicking the Mouse, Can Have Read to Them in a Boy's or Girl's Voice. Pictures Are Included Which, by Clicking the Mouse, Turn into Short Clips from the Actual Movie.
Sound Source Interactive.

The Secret Key. (Skillbuilders Ser.). Ellen Geist. Apr. 1986. *Compatible Hardware:* Apple II family. *Operating System(s) Required:* Apple DOS 3.3. *Language(s):* BASIC, Assembly. *Memory Required:* 48k.
disk $34.95, incl. tchr's. manual, wkshts., & bklt. (ISBN 0-88335-436-5, Order no.: SAP04). with back-up $49.95.
Lab pk.. 5 add'l. copies of same disk $75.00.
"Story Book" Adventure Game in Which 3 Gentle Wizards Help Students Work Their Way Through an Imaginary Land in Search of the Secret Key. When the Key Is Found, Students Can Alter the Imaginary Land by Adding Rooms, Riddles, or Ingredients to the Recipe of the Magic Potion.
Milliken Publishing Co.

The Secret Library Disk. *Compatible Hardware:* Atari. *Language(s):* BASIC.
disk $24.95 (ISBN 0-936200-34-0). $24.95.
Provides Utility Programs Including a Disk Editor, a Cassette Copier, a Routine to Create Binary Load Files from Any Code Which Can Be Loaded into Memory, & a BASIC Autorun Routine.
Blue Cat.

The Secret of Arendarvon Castle. Hal Renko et al. *Compatible Hardware:* Apple, Commodore, IBM.
contact publisher for price.
Apple. (ISBN 0-201-16484-1).
Commodore. (ISBN 0-201-16485-X).
IBM. (ISBN 0-201-16486-8).
Reader Becomes a Detective & Tries to Discover the Castle's Secret.
Addison-Wesley Publishing Co., Inc.

The Secret of Monkey Island.
IBM PC & compatibles (640k). CD-ROM disk $79.95 (ISBN 0-7911-0682-9, Order no.: 110682). *Optimal configuration:* IBM PC or compatible; DOS 3.1 or higher; Microsoft CD-ROM Extensions, 2.1 or higher; CD-ROM drive & software drivers; CD Audio; 640k RAM; keyboard, mouse or joystick; VGA/MCGA 256 colors.
This Adventure, Set in the Golden Age of Piracy in the Caribbean, Features Cinematic Storytelling in Brilliantly Colored Graphics & an Icon Inventory. Sling One-Liners with a Used Ship Salesman, a Sarcastic Sword Master, a Wisecracking Corpse, & a Prisoner Whose Breath Would Stop a Horse - All in the Effort to Become a Treasure-Seeking Pirate. Ahoy Mateys, You Get Stunning 3-D Graphics, Full CD Audio, Plus Engaging Tests, Trials, & Puzzles.
Software Toolworks.

Secret of the Lost City. (Math Blaster Ser.: Episode 2).
Windows. IBM & compatibles. CD-ROM disk $59.95 (Order no.: R1345). *Nonstandard peripherals required:* CD-ROM drive. *Optimal configuration:* 386 processor operating at 16Mhz or higher, MS-DOS 5.0 or higher, Windows 3.1 or higher, 30Mb hard drive, mouse, VGA graphic adapter & VGA color monitor (SVGA recommended), 4Mb RAM, external speakers or headphones (with sound card) that are Sound Blaster compatible.

SOFTWARE ENCYCLOPEDIA 1996

Teaches Children More Advanced Basic Math Concepts Such As Calculating Percentages, Logical Thinking, & Multiplication & Division with Two & Three Operands (Ages 8-13).
Library Video Co.

Secret of the Silver Blades. SSI Special Projects Team. *Customer Support:* Technical support line: (408) 737-6850 (11am-5pm, PST); 14 day money back guarantee/30 day exchange policy.
DOS 2.11 or higher. IBM PC or compatible (512k). disk $49.95. *Nonstandard peripherals required:* Requires a color monitor & graphic adaptor (CGA, EGA, Tandy 16-color).
Commodore 64/128 (64k). disk $39.95.
The Frigid Valleys of the Dragonspine Mountains Echo with the Desperate Plea of Terrified Miners: "Heroes of the Forgotten Realms, Save Us from Evil!" Explore the Largest 3-D Adventuring Expanse Ever in an AD&D Computer Game. Battle Monsters You've Never Before Encountered. Use Higher Character Levels, & Invoke New, Wondrous Spells!
Strategic Simulations, Inc.

Secret Weapons of the Luftwaffe.
IBM CD-ROM. IBM PC or compatible (640k). CD-ROM disk $79.95 (ISBN 0-7911-0681-0, Order no.: 110681). *Optimal configuration:* IBM PC or compatible; DOS 3.3 or higher; Microsoft CD-ROM Extensions, 2.1 or higher; CD-ROM drive & software drivers; supports AdLib & SoundBlaster; 640k RAM; keyboard, mouse or joystick recommended; VGA/MCGA 256-Color, EGA Tandy (AT) 80286 or faster graphics recommended.
This Is the Most Advanced World War II Air Combat Simulation Software Available for IBM PC Users. The Game Recreates the Campaign by the U.S. Eighth Air Force to Cripple the Industrial Might of Germany from 1943 to 1945. Fly American Planes & High-Tech German Aircraft, Some of Which Were Years Ahead of Their Time. Includes Four Tour-of-Duty Extensions. Technically, Historical, & Graphically Authentic.
Software Toolworks.

SecretAgent. *Version:* 3.1. Sep. 1994. *Items Included:* Approximately 120 pages of support documentation, license registration card. *Customer Support:* Free telephone support, the program is menu-driven with complete context-sensitive on-line help feature, approximately 120 pages of support documentation also included.
PC-DOS/MS-DOS, Windows, SCO UNIX, AT&T UNIX, AIX, Apple Macintosh System 7, A/UX, Sun, MIPS, DEC ULTRIX, HP-UX. IBM PC, XT, AT, PS/2 & compatible (256k), SCO UNIX V, Apple Macintosh, Sun, AT&T 3/B2 & s/B5, MIPS. $249.95 single unit commercial; $149.95 single unit government quantity discounts & site licenses also available (ISBN 0-923709-10-X). *Optimal configuration:* 512k RAM & microsoft mouse or compatible. *Networks supported:* all.
Apple A/UX, Apple MAC OS. Apple Macintosh 2Mb. $249.95 single unit commercial; $149.95 single unit government quantity discounts & site licenses also available (ISBN 0-923709-12-6). *Networks supported:* All.
SCO UNIX Systems V/3 86 or Open Desktop. 386 or higher (1Mb). $279.95 commercial single unit/$187.95 government single unit (ISBN 0-923709-14-2). *Networks supported:* All.
Public-Key Encryption Utility That Employs the Data Encryption Standard (DES) the ElGamal Public-Key Cryptosystem, & the NIST Digital Signature & Secure Hash Algorithms. It Provides Virtually Unbreakable Security for Sensitive Word Processing Documents, Spreadsheets, Databases, E-Mail, FAX Transmissions & Telex Transmissions. Also Offers Cross-Platform Compatibility Between MS-DOS, Windows, Macintosh & UNIX.

TITLE INDEX

Additional Features Include: Digital Signatures, Message Authentication, ASCII Conversion, Data Compression, File Erasure Utilities & a Complete Context-Sensitive On-Line Help System.
Information Security Corp.

SecretDisk II. *Version:* 1.06. *Compatible Hardware:* IBM PC & compatibles. *Operating System(s) Required:* PC-DOS/MS-DOS 2.0 or higher. *Memory Required:* 256k. *Customer Support:* Bulletin Board support; 30-day free technical support - subsequent support is available through a 900 number. FAX number available also.
disk $125.00 U.S. Version; $175.00 International Version.
Provides a "Software Only" Method to Protect Sensitive Data & Files. Creates New "Logical" Disk Drives Where All Data & Programs Are Always Encrypted. Protection Can Be Turned on & off at Any Time Without Rebooting. User Can Select Either the NBS or DES Algorithm or Lattice FAST Encryption Method Which Offers Virtually the Same Degree of Security but Is 40-50 Percent Faster. (International Version Does Not Provide DES Algorithm.) Password-Protected Access to "SECRETDISK" Files Is Provided Through a DOS Device Driver. Can Be Built Inside of Other "SECRETDISKS" for Multiple Levels of Security & the Encryption Algorithms Can Vary at Each Level. Provides Method to Shrink or Enlarge the Size of a Secret Disk. Files Can Be Copied in & Out of Protected Areas; All Application Programs Recognize These Drives; & Programs Will Also Run from Inside the Encrypted Areas.
Lattice, Inc.

SECT. *Version:* 3.12. Nov. 1985. *Compatible Hardware:* IBM PC, PC XT, PC AT & compatibles. *Operating System(s) Required:* PC-DOS, MS-DOS. *Language(s):* FORTRAN. *Memory Required:* 512k. *General Requirements:* Printer, plotter.
disk $2850.00 (Order no.: SECT).
Plots the Profile of Drill Holes As Projected on a Given Section Plane. There Are Five Ways to Select the Drill Holes to Be Plotted & Four Ways to Represent the Assay Intervals Along the Drill Holes. The Program Imposes No Limit on the Orientation & Location of the Section Plane.
Geostat Systems International, Inc. (GSII).

Section Properties. *Compatible Hardware:* IBM PC. *Memory Required:* 128k.
disk $39.95.
Provides Solutions for Cross Section Area, Location of Section Centroid, Moment of Inertia, Section Modulus Radius of Gyration, Product of Inertia, Polar Moment of Inertia, etc.
Dynacomp, Inc.

Section Properties 2 with Graphics. *Items Included:* Bound manual. *Customer Support:* Free hotline - no time limit; 30 day limited warranty; updates are $5/disk plus S&H.
MS-DOS 2.0 or higher. IBM & compatibles (128k). disk $99.95. *Nonstandard peripherals required:* CGA, EGA, VGA or Hercules graphics card (or equivalent).
Will Calculate Properties for Virtually Any Structural Member's Cross-Section. User May Determine Area, Centroids, Outer Fiber Distances, Torsion Constant, Moments of Inertia, Section Moduli, & Radii of Gyration about the Horizontal Axes, Vertical Axes, Polar Axes, Principal Axes, or about Any Given Angle Axes. Results May Be Sent to the Screen or to a Printer.
Dynacomp, Inc.

Sector Editor. *Compatible Hardware:* Apple II+. *Operating System(s) Required:* Apple DOS 3.2, 3.3. *Language(s):* Applesoft BASIC. *Memory Required:* 48k.
disk $39.95.
Utility That Helps Repair Damaged Disks & Modify Files, BASIC Programs, or System Programs Including Data. Also Allows User to Alter, Examine, Add, or Delete Information. Program Can Retrieve Data from the Disk by Supplying Track & Sector Information, & the User Can Search the Disk for a Specific Word up to 8 Characters Long.
Instant Software, Inc.

Securities Analysis. *Compatible Hardware:* TI Home Computer.
contact publisher for price (Order no.: PHM 3059).
Provides Stock Analysis, Call Options, Bond Analysis, Interest Calculations & More.
Texas Instruments, Personal Productivity Products.

The Securities Analyst. Oct. 1988. *Items Included:* Manual explaining technical analysis of stock market. *Customer Support:* Free technical support at 215-683-5699.
Amiga DOS (512k). 3.5" disk $79.95.
Stock Charting & Analysis Program with Nine Different Forms of Analysis.
Free Spirit Software, Inc.

Security. Sharon Lerch. 1990.
DOS. Any type of IBM (64k). $8.50 (ISBN 1-56178-003-0).
MAC. Any type of Macintosh (64k). $8.50 (ISBN 1-56178-020-0).
Novel: Contemporary Adult.
Connected Editions, Inc.

Security Safe-Keeping System. *Compatible Hardware:* IBM Micros & compatibles. *Operating System(s) Required:* PC-DOS/MS-DOS. *Language(s):* C. *Customer Support:* Onsite training, telephone support, first year maintenance free, annual maintenance after first year $900.00.
contact publisher for price.
Automated System Designed for Trust Departments & Bank Money Centers. Features Include: General Ledger Tickets, Various Reports, Accrued Interest/Brokers' Commission/Unlimited Fee Schedules, T-Bills, Bond or Stock Transactions, Maturity & Interest Look-Ahead, Separate Branch Accounting, Purchase/Sales/ Maturity Transactions, & Maturity Schedules.
Wall Street Consulting Group.

The Security Toolkit: System Security Assessment. *Version:* 2.0. 1985. *Compatible Hardware:* MicroVAX & VAX. *Operating System(s) Required:* VMS & MicroVMS 4.6 & higher. *Language(s):* Basic. *Memory Required:* 555k. *Items Included:* 1 year maintenance, quarterly newsletter. *Customer Support:* Available 6am-6pm, MST.
$582.00-$11,514.00.
Identifies Potential Security Risks. Used by System Security Managers, EDP, & Internal Auditors. System Reviews Several Different Areas Where VAX/VMS System Security May Be Compromised. By Using Summary Reports, User Can Quickly Diagnose Potential or Existing Security Problems & Provide Accurate Solution. Functions: Verifies Access Controls; Analyzes User Authorization Data Bases; Checks Directory, Device & Queue Protection; Assesses Network Security & Summarizes Overall Security Adequacy.
Raxco, Inc.

SELECT-A-FONT

See the U.S.A. Roger Shank. 1987. *Compatible Hardware:* Apple II, IBM PC. *Memory Required:* 256k. *Items Included:* Large full color wall map of US. *Customer Support:* 800-338-3224.
disk $49.95.
Educational Game to Help Children & Adults Learn More about the U.S.A. The Travelling Game Creates Cross-Country Trips. Over One Hundred Different Graphics Screens Depict Characteristics of Each State & Capital. The Quiz Section Is a Utility Enabling Creation of Questions to Test Player's Knowledge & Determine Computer's Response to Each Player's Input. The Player Answers the Question by Moving to the Correct Capital or State.
Compu-Teach, Inc.

SEED. SEED Software. *Operating System(s) Required:* MS-DOS. *Memory Required:* 320k. *General Requirements:* Printer, Winchester hard disk.
$1500.00.
Texas Instruments, Personal Productivit.

SeeMORE. *Version:* 2.0. *Compatible Hardware:* IBM PC, PC XT, PC AT, PS/2. *General Requirements:* CGA, EGA, VGA, Hercules, or compatible graphics card; Lotus 1-2-3 Release 2.
disk $99.95.
Screen Manager for 1-2-3 Capable of Displaying up to 180 Characters & 58 Lines with a Hercules Graphics Adapter. Allows Users to Zoom in & out As They Build & Manipulate a Worksheet. Compressed Screens Can Be Printed. Also Allows Users to Change Colors, Choose Normal or Reverse Video, & Select Mix Font Format (Normal Display for the Top Three Lines) Without Having to Exit the Application.
Personics Corp.

SEIHS. 1982. *Compatible Hardware:* IBM PC & compatibles. *Operating System(s) Required:* MS-DOS. *Language(s):* BASIC. *Memory Required:* 128k.
$260.00.
Used for Horizontal Vessels Mounted on Two Saddle Supports & Performs & Prepares a Complete Seismic Report on Forms Designed for This Program.
Technical Research Services, Inc.

SEILEGS. B. Fred Forman. 1985. *Compatible Hardware:* IBM PC & compatibles. *Operating System(s) Required:* MS-DOS. *Memory Required:* 128k.
disk $270.00.
Used in Design of Small Vertical Vessels with 4 Legs Welded Directly to the Vessel. The Required Angle or Wide Flange Shape Is Selected to Withstand Wind or Seismic Loading. Appropriate Bracing Is Selected When Needed for the Design.
Technical Research Services, Inc.

SEIVS. 1982. *Compatible Hardware:* IBM PC & compatibles. *Operating System(s) Required:* MS-DOS. *Language(s):* BASIC. *Memory Required:* 128k.
$230.00.
Used for Vertical Vessels Mounted on Four Lug-Type Supports Attached to the Shell Around Its Circumference. Performs & Prepares a Complete Report on Forms Designed for This Purpose.
Technical Research Services, Inc.

Select-A-Font. Robert G. Oesterlin. *Compatible Hardware:* IBM PC, PCjr, PC XT, PC AT, Portable PC, 3270 PC with IBM Display & IBM Graphics printer. *Operating System(s) Required:* DOS 1.10, 2.00, 2.10, 3.00, 3.10. *Memory Required:* 128k.
disk $19.95 (Order no.: 6276514).
Adds Nine Type Styles to the IBM Graphics Printer. User Can Choose from Three Type Sizes,

Nine Character Widths, & Two Print Densities for Each Type Style. Also Provides Basic Formatting Control, Such As Centering, Indenting, Justification of Text, Line Skipping, Tabbing, & Underlining.
Personally Developed Software, Inc.

Selected Works of Melville. *Version:* 1.5. Feb. 1995. *Items Included:* BookWorm Student Reader (diskette). *Customer Support:* 30 day MBG. Technical support (toll call) - no charge.
System 7.0 or higher. Macintosh (5Mb). CD-ROM disk $29.95 (ISBN 1-57316-032-6, Order no.: 16167). *Nonstandard peripherals required:* CD-ROM drive, 12" color monitor. *Optimal configuration:* 13" color monitor recommended.
Windows 3.1 or higher. IBM compatible (MPC) 386 DX (4Mb). CD-ROM disk $29.95. *Nonstandard peripherals required:* Standard multimedia compatible CD-ROM. *Optimal configuration:* 8Mb RAM recommended, 256 color monitor recommended.
Selections from Moby Dick, Billy Budd, & Bartleby the Scrivener Are among the Works by Melville Included in This Title. The BookWorm Edition Features a Fully Annotated Text with All Difficult Passages Explained, All the Topics You've Come to Expect in a BookWorm Edition Plus Complete Multimedia Coverage of Whaling in the Nineteenth Century. The BookWorm Edition Also Features Complete Sound Allowing the User to Listen to All or Part of Each Work.
Communication & Information Technologies, Inc. (CIT).

Selected Works of Poe. *Version:* 1.5. Feb. 1995. *Items Included:* BookWorm Student Reader (diskette). *Customer Support:* 30 day MBG. Technical support (toll call) - no charge.
System 7.0 or higher. Macintosh (5Mb). CD-ROM disk $29.95 (ISBN 1-57316-037-7, Order no.: 16037). *Nonstandard peripherals required:* CD-ROM drive, 12" color monitor. *Optimal configuration:* 13" color monitor recommended.
Windows 3.1 or higher. IBM compatible (MPC) 386 DX (4Mb). CD-ROM disk $29.95. *Nonstandard peripherals required:* Standard multimedia compatible CD-ROM. *Optimal configuration:* 8Mb RAM recommended, 256 color monitor recommended.
This Collection of Works by Poe, One of 19th Century America's Most Brilliant Writers of Prose & Poetry, Includes Some of His Most Popular Works: The Raven, Anabel Lee, The Fall of the House of Usher & More. Enhanced with Multimedia Annotations Covering Historical Context, Literary Devices, Biographies, Criticism, & More, This Volume Brings New Understanding to the Works of Poe. This Edition Features Complete Sound Allowing the User to Listen to All or Part of Each Work.
Communication & Information Technologies, Inc. (CIT).

Selective Copy. 1984. *Compatible Hardware:* IBM PC, PCjr, PC XT, PC AT & compatibles. *Operating System(s) Required:* DOS 1.0 or higher. *Memory Required:* 64k.
disk $19.00.
*Copy Selected Files with Two Keystrokes. Selective Copy Prompts User with Each File Name & Asks If the File Should Be Copied to Another Disk/Directory. Accepts the Global File Name Characters (? & *), Which Allows User to Pre-Screen the Types of Files to Be Copied.*
DataSource Publishing Co.

Selective Erase. *Version:* 4.1. PC Consulting. 1983. *Compatible Hardware:* IBM PC, PC XT, PC AT, PCjr & compatibles. *Operating System(s) Required:* PC-DOS 1.0 or higher. *Memory Required:* 32k.
disk $19.00.
File Erasing Utility Which Reads Directory Information from Diskette Then Displays the Name of Each File & Asks if File Should Be Erased.
DataSource Publishing Co.

SelectORE. Jul. 1984. *Compatible Hardware:* IBM PC, PC XT, PC AT & compatibles. *Operating System(s) Required:* PC-DOS, MS-DOS. *Language(s):* FORTRAN. *Memory Required:* 512k. *General Requirements:* Printer, plotter.
disk $17,000.00.
Streamlined Ore Grade Control Is Possible with the SelectORE Workstation. The System Is Data-Base Driven & Automatically Executes a Series of Programs for Fast Deposit Estimation. Grade Tonnage Reports for Any Time Period Can Be Produced by This Turnkey System. The System Accepts a Digitized Data Base & Will Post Values, Compute Variograms, Krige Estimates & Plot Contours & Block Maps for Any Portion of the Deposit. Customization of Program Is Available.
Geostat Systems International, Inc. (GSII).

SelectPAC: Action Arcade. Aug. 1995. *Customer Support:* Free technical support 810-477-1205.
MS-DOS 5.0 or higher. IBM 386 or higher, or compatible (4Mb). CD-ROM disk $12.95 (ISBN 1-57037-027-3). *Nonstandard peripherals required:* CD-ROM drive, 2Mb free hard disk space, SVGA card & monitor, mouse (recommended), sound card (optional), joystick (optional).
The Action Arcade Edition Brings Together Two of the Top Arcade Programs. Two Complete Games. LEMMINGS by Psygnosis Ltd. - The Wackiest Collection of Misdirected Rodents Ever Seen! DRAGON'S LAIR by ReadySoft Incorporated - Lead on Brave Adventurer - Your Quest Awaits!
SelectWare Technologies, Inc.

SelectPAC: Jet Set. Aug. 1995. *Customer Support:* Free technical support 810-477-1205.
MS-DOS 5.0 or higher. IBM 386 or higher, or compatible (2Mb). CD-ROM disk $12.95 (ISBN 1-57037-028-1). *Nonstandard peripherals required:* CD-ROM drive, 3Mb free hard disk space, SVGA card & monitor, mouse (recommended), sound card (optional), joystick (optional).
The Jet Set Edition Brings Together Two of the Top Flight Simulator Programs. Two Complete Games. SUPER-VGA HARRIER by Domark Software Inc. - The U.S. Marine Corps' Most Advanced Attack Fighter! & JETFIGHTER II by Velocity Incorporated - Fly over 100 Sweatdrenching Missions!
SelectWare Technologies, Inc.

SelectPAC: Sci-Fi Battles. Aug. 1995. *Customer Support:* Free technical support 810-477-1205.
MS-DOS 5.0 or higher. IBM 386 or higher, or compatible (4Mb). CD-ROM disk $12.95 (ISBN 1-57037-026-5). *Nonstandard peripherals required:* CD-ROM drive, 2Mb free hard disk space, SVGA card & monitor, mouse (recommended), sound card (optional), joystick (optional).
The Sci-Fi Battles Edition Brings Together Two fo the Top Science Fiction Programs. Two Complete Games. SPECTRE VR CLASSIC by Velocity Incorporated - This Is Not Just Another Game. It's Another Reality. NOVASTORM by Psygnosis Ltd. - The Fate of the Solar System Rests in Your Hands!
SelectWare Technologies, Inc.

SelectPAC: Super Sports. Aug. 1995. *Customer Support:* Free technical support 810-477-1205.
MS-DOS 5.0 or higher. IBM 386 or higher, or compatible (2Mb). CD-ROM disk $16.95 (ISBN 1-57037-025-7). *Nonstandard peripherals required:* CD-ROM drive, 2Mb free hard disk space, SVGA card & monitor, mouse (recommended), sound card (optional), joystick (optional).
The Super Sports Editions Brings Together Three of the Top Sports Programs. Three Complete Games. LINKS the Challenge of Golf by ACCESS Software, Inc. - Golf Simulation So Realistic, You'll Think You're There! TOM LANDRY STRATEGY FOOTBALL by Merit Studios, Inc. - Match Wits with One of the Best Minds in Pro Football! HARDBALL III by Accolade, Inc. - More of What Serious Baseball Fans Want in a Simulation!
SelectWare Technologies, Inc.

Selectra. *Version:* 91.02B. *Compatible Hardware:* IBM PC, HP Series 80. *Operating System(s) Required:* DOS 2.0 or higher. *Memory Required:* 128k.
contact publisher for price.
Collection of 3 Programs in the Field of Mechancial Power Transmission Given Working Condition. Roller Chain & Sprokets Program Determines a System of Standard ANSI Roller Chain Drive Components. V-Belt & Sheaves Program Selects Components for V-Belt Drives.
National Planning & Consulting Corp.

Self-Assessment in Biofeedback 1.5. *Version:* 1.5. *Compatible Hardware:* Apple II series, IBM PC. *General Requirements:* Monchrome or color monitor, 2 drives Apple II or 1 IBM.
disk per program $49.95.
These Two Programs Feature Multiple-Choice Test Questions over Theory, Physiology, Instrumentation, Research & Clinical Applications. Features Include Random Selection of Twenty-Five Question Multiple-Choice Tests with Immediate Feedback & Comprehensive Exams with Diagnostic Assessment.
Biosource Software.

Self-Assessment in Psychology. *Version:* 1.5. 1990. *Compatible Hardware:* Apple II, II+, IIe, IIc, IIgs. *Memory Required:* 64k. *General Requirements:* 2 disk drives Apple or 1 drive IBM PC.
$49.95 ea.
Student Mastery of Learning, Cognition, Sensation, Perception, Comparative, Personality, Abnormal, Clinical, Developmental, Social, History, Measurement, & Statistics Content Areas Is Comprehensive Tested.
Biosource Software.

Self-Exploration Series: IBM version. *Items Included:* Manual & 3 1/2" disk. *Customer Support:* 800-966-3382, Fax: 612-781-7753.
IBM & compatibles. disk $59.95.
32 reproducible pages $12.95 (ISBN 0-932796-58-3).
Students Interact with the Computer & Can Receive a Printout of Their Profiles on Each Inventory. Can Be Used Effectively in Middle, High School, & College Courses Concerned with Self-Awareness, Career Guidance, & Human Relationships. Includes: Career Planning Questionnaire; Occupational Orientation Matrix; What Are Your Occupational Values? Data, People, Things Occupational Survey; Internal vs. External Occupational Orientation Survey; Problem Solving Style; Parents Relationship Scale; How Do You Study? What Is Your Studying Attitude Quotient (A.Q.)? How Do You Learn? How Do You Think? Student Communication Orientation Scale; Self-Sufficiency Scale; Student Self-Esteem Scale.
Educational Media Corp.

TITLE INDEX

Sell to Needs: Sell the Way People Like to Buy. Mar. 1994. *Customer Support:* Toll-free telephone number for technical support. 90 days warranty for defects in materials & workmanship.
Macintosh System 7.0. Macintosh with 68040 processor (5Mb). CD-ROM disk $49.95 (ISBN 1-886806-04-7). *Nonstandard peripherals required:* Double speed CD-ROM drive. *Addl. software required:* QuickTime (included on CD-ROM disc).
Microsoft Windows 3.1. PC compatibles; 486/33 MHz (runs slow on 386/25MHz) (8Mb). CD-ROM disk $49.95. *Nonstandard peripherals required:* 256 color display card (640x480); double speed CD-ROM drive. *Addl. software required:* QuickTime for Windows (included on CD-ROM disc).
Helps You Increase Your Sales by Becoming a More Effective Problem-Solver. It Explores the Proven Skills, Techniques, & Knowledge of Successful Sales Professionals & Puts Them to Work for You. This Highly Interactive CD-ROM Includes Video Simulations & Exercises to Practce What You Learn.
Wilson Learning Corp.

SELLSTATION. *Version:* 3.0. May 1993. *Items Included:* Manuals. *Customer Support:* Training & maintenance available, hot line, electronic bulletin board & annual users' conference.
Microsoft Windows. 80386 SX processor minimum (6Mb). Enterprise license, Contact publisher for price. *Optimal configuration:* 80486, 8Mb RAM, 120Mb hard drive, color VGA moniotr, mouse, DOS 5.0 or higher, Windows for Workgroups 3.1.
Designed to Automate the Sales & Delivery of Retail Products. Takes Advantage of the Microsoft Windows Intuitive Graphical User Interface to Maximize Sales Effectiveness & Minimize the Time It Takes to Deliver a Bank's Products & Services.
Ampersand Corp.

SellWise. *Version:* 96.1. Jan. 1991. *Items Included:* Training disk & book. *Customer Support:* 30 days free support, additional support may be available from dealer, after free time $299.00 per year.
MS-DOS 3.3 or higher, OS/2, Windows. Any IBM compatible, 286 or higher (640k). $1495.00 single user, $2395.00 multi-user. *Optimal configuration:* DOS on a 386 with 640k RAM, color monitor, single user SellWise, Receipt printer with cash drawer, barcode CCD scanner, & 80 column printer. *Networks supported:* Novell, LANtastic.
Program That Is Simple to Track Serial Numbers, Suspend Service & Repair Invoices, Sell Kits, Analyze Sales & Do All the Required Reporting. There Are On-Line Help Files, a Note Pad for Every Customer or Inventory Item, Built-In Word Processor for Correspondence, One Key Method for Backup, Unique Tech Support Screen, Quantity Pricing, User Control of Look, Feel & Sound. Also Has Price Tags That Can Be Totally Designed by the User, from Printing Part Numbers & Prices, to Controlling the Height & Width of Barcodes. Captures Data at the Point-of-Sale & Reports Information with Microsoft ACCESS.
CAP Automation.

SEMA4 Financial Management System for A/E Industry. *Version:* 6.0. Ray King. Oct. 1991. *Compatible Hardware:* IBM PC XT, PC AT & 386 compatibles. *Operating System(s) Required:* MS-DOS, PC-DOS 2.0 or higher. *Memory Required:* 640k. *General Requirements:* Hard disk, printer, monitor. *Customer Support:* Manual, sample brochure of reports, disks (system), order form for checks & other forms. contact publisher for price. *Networks supported:* Lantastic, Novell.
Financial Management System Designed for Architects, Engineers & Designers. Suitable for Small & Large Firms. Features: Payroll, Automatic Invoicing, Time Analysis-Dollars & Hours Report, Budget Analysis, Project Cost Analysis, Reimbursable Expense Tracking, General Accounting, Local Area Network Capability in Software. Well-Organized Reports, Toll-Free Hotline Support & Periodic Updates.
Semaphore, Inc.

Seminar-on-a-Disc, Multimedia Edition: Windows 3.1 Fundamentals. *Version:* 3.1. *Items Included:* CD-ROM & installation guide. *Customer Support:* Toll-free, fee free technical support on the product & the subject software application.
Windows 3.1. IBM PC & compatibles (4Mb). CD-ROM disk $250.00. *Nonstandard peripherals required:* VGA or higher. *Optimal configuration:* IBM compatible PC, 386 or higher processor, 20MHz or higher speed clock, CD-ROM graphics adapter, MPC-compliant audio board or CD audio, 4Mb RAM.
Sound, Text, & Animation Guide Students Through a Number of Comprehensive Hands-On Lessons Presented in a Simulated Environment. Each Lesson Begins with an Overview. It Includes Practice Sessions & Quizzes.
Infosource, Inc.

Seminar-on-a-Disk: Approach Fundamentals. *Version:* 3.0. *Items Included:* Installation guide & diskettes. *Customer Support:* Toll-free, fee-free, technical support on the product title & the underlying application.
MS-DOS. IBM PC & compatibles. disk $160.00. *Nonstandard peripherals required:* VGA.
Part of an Integrated Curriculum of Computer-Based Training & Testing Products. Contact InfoSource for Course Contents.
InfoSource, Inc.

Seminar-On-A-Disk (Computer Based Training): Access Fundamentals. *Items Included:* Program diskette & installation guide. *Customer Support:* Toll-free fee free technical support on the product & the subject software application.
PC-DOS/MS-DOS 3.0 or higher. IBM PC & compatibles (450k). disk $160.00. *Nonstandard peripherals required:* VGA.
Learn the Basics of the Windows Environment, Queries, Form Wizard, Report Wizard.
Infosource, Inc.

Seminar-On-A-Disk (Computer Based Training): Access Fundamentals. *Version:* 2.0. *Items Included:* Program diskette & installation guide. *Customer Support:* Toll-free, fee free technical support on the product & the subject software application.
PC-DOS/MS-DOS 3.0 or higher. IBM PC & compatibles (450k). disk $160.00. *Nonstandard peripherals required:* VGA.
Learn the Basics of the Windows Environment, Queries, Form Wizard, Report Wizard.
Infosource, Inc.

Seminar-On-A-Disk (Computer Based Training): Approach Fundamentals. *Version:* 2.1. *Items Included:* Program diskette & installation guide. *Customer Support:* Toll-free, fee free technical support on the product & the subject software application.
PC-DOS/MS-DOS 3.0 or higher. IBM PC & compatibles (450k). disk $160.00. *Nonstandard peripherals required:* VGA.
Learn to Create - Modify - Save Databases, Specialize Searches, Link Multiple Databases, Design Forms, Mail Merge.
Infosource, Inc.

Seminar-On-A-Disk (Computer Based Training): Ami Pro Fundamentals. *Version:* 3.0. *Items Included:* Program diskette & installation guide. *Customer Support:* Toll-free, fee free technical support on the product & the subject software application.
PC-DOS/MS-DOS. IBM PC & compatibles (450k). disk $160.00. *Nonstandard peripherals required:* VGA.
Learn Formatting & Working with Multiple Documents, Creation & Use of Macros, SmartIcons, Search Tools & Layout Command.
Infosource, Inc.

Seminar-On-A-Disk (Computer Based Training): DOS Fundamentals. *Version:* 6.0. *Items Included:* Program diskette & installation guide. *Customer Support:* Toll-free, fee free technical support on the product & the subject software application.
PC-DOS/MS-DOS 3.0 or higher. IBM PC & compatibles (450k). disk $160.00. *Nonstandard peripherals required:* VGA.
Learn the Basics of DOS, DOS Utilities, DOS Shell, Error Messages & Their Causes.
Infosource, Inc.

Seminar-On-A-Disk (Computer Based Training): DOS Fundamentals - Intermediate. *Version:* 5.0. *Items Included:* Program diskette & installation guide. *Customer Support:* Toll-free, fee free technical support on the product & the subject software application.
DOS 5.0 or higher. Any PC, PC/XT, PC/AT, PS/2 (256k). disk $160.00. *Nonstandard peripherals required:* CGA.
Learn about Your Computer & DOS, Find Your Way Around Disks & Directories, Manage Your Disks, Protect Your Files & Data, DOSKEY, DOSSHELL, DOS Editing, Create & Edit Batch Files.
Infosource, Inc.

Seminar-On-A-Disk (Computer Based Training): dBASE IV Fundamentals. *Version:* 1.1. *Items Included:* Program diskette & installation guide. *Customer Support:* Toll-free, fee free technical support on the product & the subject software application.
DOS 2.0 or higher. Any PC, PC/XT, PC/AT, PS/2 (256k). disk $160.00. *Nonstandard peripherals required:* CGA.
Learn to Program up & running, Use the Control Center, Create a Database, Enter Data, Examine Structure & Contents, Set-Up/Generate Reports, Modify Report Format, Add-Edit-Delete Records, Sort Database, Change Structure, Create & Use Index.
Infosource, Inc.

Seminar-On-A-Disk (Computer Based Training): dBASE IV Intermediate. *Version:* 1.1. *Items Included:* Program diskette & installation guide. *Customer Support:* Toll-free, fee free technical support on the product & the subject software application.
DOS 2.0 or higher. Any PC, PC/XT, PC/AT, PS/2 (256k). disk $160.00. *Nonstandard peripherals required:* CGA.
Learn to Create Data-Entry Forms, Prepare Mailing Labels, Generate an Application, Link Databases, Use Advanced Reporting Features, Share Data with Other Programs, Use dBASE IV Command Mode, Update Databases, Develop & Enhance Your First dBASE Program.
Infosource, Inc.

Seminar-On-A-Disk (Computer Based Training): Excel for Windows. *Version:* 4.0. *Items Included:* Program diskette & installation guide. *Customer Support:* Toll-free, fee free technical support on the product & the subject software application.

PC-DOS/MS-DOS. Any PC that runs with Windows 3.0 or higher (450k). disk $160.00. *Nonstandard peripherals required:* EGA, VGA or higher monitor.
Learn to Start Excel, Move Around in Excel, Build Worksheets, Work with Ranges, Write Formulas & Functions, Work with Rows & Columns, Format Values & Worksheets, Print Worksheets, Create & Print Graphs.
Infosource, Inc.

Seminar-On-A-Disk (Computer Based Training): Excel for Windows Fundamentals. *Version:* 5.0. *Items Included:* Program diskette & installation guide. *Customer Support:* Toll-free, fee free technical support on the product & the subject software application.
PC-DOS/MS-DOS. Any PC that runs with Windows 3.0 or higher (450k). disk $160.00. *Nonstandard peripherals required:* EGA, VGA or higher monitor.
Learn to Start Excel, Move Around in Excel, Build Worksheets, Work with Ranges, Write Formulas & Functions, Work with Rows & Columns, Format Values & Worksheets, Print Worksheets, Create & Print Graphs.
Infosource, Inc.

Seminar-On-A-Disk (Computer Based Training): Freelance for Windows Fundamentals. *Version:* 2.0. *Items Included:* Program diskette & installation guide. *Customer Support:* Toll-free, fee free technical support on the product & the subject software application.
PC-DOS/MS-DOS 3.0 or higher. IBM PC & compatibles (450k). disk $160.00. *Nonstandard peripherals required:* VGA.
Learn the Basics of the Windows Environment, Create - Open - Close - View - Modify - Print - Show Presentations, Change Text & Objects, Create Charts, Create Shapes & Symbols, Design & Run Screen Shows.
Infosource, Inc.

Seminar-On-A-Disk (Computer Based Training): Harvard Graphics Fundamentals. *Version:* 3.0. *Items Included:* Program diskette & installation guide. *Customer Support:* Toll-free, fee free technical support on the product & the subject software application.
DOS 2.0 or higher. Any PC, PC/XT, PC/AT, PS/2 (256k). disk $160.00. *Nonstandard peripherals required:* EGA, VGA, or higher.
Learn to Get Harvard Graphics up & Running, Move Around in the Menus, Create Your First Title Chart, Set-Up a Bullet Chart, Create Column - Pie - Multiple Pie Charts, Design Bar, Line & Area Charts, Enhance Basic Charts, Develop Organization Chart.
Infosource, Inc.

Seminar-On-A-Disk (Computer Based Training): Lotus CC: Mail for Windows. *Items Included:* Program diskette & installation guide. *Customer Support:* Toll-free, fee free technical support on the product & the subject software application.
PC-DOS/MS-DOS 3.0 or higher. IBM PC & compatibles (450k). disk $160.00. *Nonstandard peripherals required:* VGA.
Learn How to Send Electronic Mail Through Your Network, Master the Basics for a Firm Working Foundation, Learn How to Edit - Send - Attach - Receive Archive Messages, Create Address Books, Folder, Bulletin Boards, Mailing Lists & Much More.
Infosource, Inc.

Seminar-On-A-Disk (Computer Based Training): Lotus Organizer Fundamentals. *Version:* 1.1. *Items Included:* Program diskette & installation guide. *Customer Support:* Toll-free, fee free technical support on the product & the subject software application.
PC-DOS/MS-DOS 3.0 or higher. IBM PC & compatibles (450k). disk $160.00. *Nonstandard peripherals required:* VGA.
Discover the Ease & Convenience of Recording Appointments in the Diary, Learn to Prioritize Tasks with the To Do List, Use the Address Book, Enter - Edit - Print Memos, Notes & Lists with the Note Pad, Create Timelines, Anniversary Calendar.
Infosource, Inc.

Seminar-On-A-Disk (Computer Based Training): Lotus 1-2-3 Database Management. *Version:* 2.0-2.2. *Items Included:* Program diskette & installation guide. *Customer Support:* Toll-free, fee free technical support on the product & the subject software application.
MS-DOS. IBM PC & compatibles (256k). disk $160.00. *Nonstandard peripherals required:* CGA.
Teaches You to Make a 1-2-3 Database, Sort a Database, Find & Extract Records, Use Formula Criteria, Use Compound Criteria, Importing Data from Other Programs, Create Statistics.
Infosource, Inc.

Seminar-On-A-Disk (Computer Based Training): Lotus 1-2-3 Graphics. *Version:* 2.0-2.2. *Items Included:* Program diskette & installation guide. *Customer Support:* Toll-free, fee free technical support on the product & the subject software application.
MS-DOS. IBM PC & compatibles (256k). disk $160.00. *Nonstandard peripherals required:* CGA.
Learn to Create a Lotus 1-2-3 Pie Chart, Print Graphs, Create Bar, Stacked-Bar & Line Charts, Use Important Graphics Options, Incorporate Graphs with WYSIWYG, Combine Text, Graphs, & Worksheets.
Infosource, Inc.

Seminar-On-A-Disk (Computer Based Training): Lotus 1-2-3 Macros. *Version:* 2.0-2.2. *Items Included:* Program diskette & installation guide. *Customer Support:* Toll-free, fee free technical support on the product & the subject software application.
MS-DOS. IBM PC & compatibles (256k). disk $160.00. *Nonstandard peripherals required:* CGA.
Learn to Use Range Names to Represent Cells, Set-Up & Use Macros.
Infosource, Inc.

Seminar-On-A-Disk (Computer Based Training): Lotus 1-2-3 Fundamentals. *Version:* 2.3. *Items Included:* Program diskette & installation guide. *Customer Support:* Toll-free, fee free technical support on the product & the subject software application.
MS-DOS. IBM PC & compatibles (256k). disk $160.00. *Nonstandard peripherals required:* EGA.
Basics for Setting-Up Applications: Getting 1-2-3 up & Running, Moving Around in a Spreadsheet, Commands, Setting-Up Headings, Entering Numbers, Printing, Function Key, Shortcuts, Formulas, & Much More.
Infosource, Inc.

Seminar-On-A-Disk (Computer Based Training): Lotus 1-2-3 Database Management. *Version:* 2.3. *Items Included:* Program diskette & installation guide. *Customer Support:* Toll-free, fee free technical support on the product & the subject software application.
MS-DOS. IBM PC & compatibles (256k). disk $160.00. *Nonstandard peripherals required:* EGA.
Teaches You to Make a 1-2-3 Database, Sort a Database, Find & Extract Records, Use Formula Criteria, Use Compound Criteria, Importing Data from Other Programs, Create Statistics.
Infosource, Inc.

Seminar-On-A-Disk (Computer Based Training): Lotus 1-2-3 Graphics. *Version:* 2.3. *Items Included:* Program diskette & installation guide. *Customer Support:* Toll-free, fee free technical support on the product & the subject software application.
MS-DOS. IBM PC & compatibles (256k). disk $160.00. *Nonstandard peripherals required:* EGA.
Learn to Create a Lotus 1-2-3 Pie Chart, Print Graphs, Create Bar, Stacked-Bar & Line Charts, Use Important Graphics Options, Incorporate Graphs with WYSIWYG, Combine Text, Graphs, & Worksheets.
Infosource, Inc.

Seminar-On-A-Disk (Computer Based Training): Lotus 1-2-3 Macros. *Version:* 2.3. *Items Included:* Program diskette & installation guide. *Customer Support:* Toll-free, fee free technical support on the product & the subject software application.
MS-DOS. IBM PC & compatibles (256k). disk $160.00. *Nonstandard peripherals required:* EGA.
Learn to Use Range Names to Represent Cells, Set-Up & Use Macros.
Infosource, Inc.

Seminar-On-A-Disk (Computer Based Training): Lotus 1-2-3 for Windows Fundamentals. *Version:* 1.1. *Items Included:* Program diskette & installation guide. *Customer Support:* Toll-free, fee free technical support on the product & the subject software application.
PC-DOS/MS-DOS. Any PC that runs Windows 3.0 or higher (640k). disk $160.00. *Nonstandard peripherals required:* EGA, VGA, or higher monitor.
Learn to Start-Up & Move Around in 1-2-3, Build a Worksheet, Work with Ranges, Formulas, Rows & Columns, Format Values, Print Worksheets, Create & Print Graphs.
Infosource, Inc.

Seminar-On-A-Disk (Computer Based Training): Lotus 1-2-3 for Windows Database. *Version:* 1.1. *Items Included:* Program diskette & installation guide. *Customer Support:* Toll-free, fee free technical support on the product & the subject software application.
PC-DOS/MS-DOS. Any PC that runs Windows 3.0 or higher (640k). disk $160.00. *Nonstandard peripherals required:* EGA, VGA, or higher monitor.
Learn to Construct a 1-2-3 Database, Sort, Find Records, Extract Database Records, Name Ranges, Import Data from Other Programs, Using Database Functions, Modify Records, Delete Records & Add Records.
Infosource, Inc.

Seminar-On-A-Disk (Computer Based Training): Lotus 1-2-3 for Windows Fundamentals. *Version:* 4.0. *Items Included:* Program diskette & installation guide. *Customer Support:* Toll-free, fee free technical support on the product & the subject software application.
PC-DOS/MS-DOS. Any PC that runs Windows 3.0 or higher (640k). disk $160.00. *Nonstandard peripherals required:* EGA, VGA, or higher monitor.
Learn to Construct a 1-2-3 Database, Sort, Find Records, Extract Database Records, Name Ranges, Import Data from Other Programs, Use Database Functions, Modify Records, Delete Records & Add Records.
Infosource, Inc.

Seminar-On-A-Disk (Computer Based Training): Lotus 1-2-3 Fundamentals. *Version:* 2.0-2.2. *Items Included:* Program diskette & installation guide. *Customer Support:* Toll-free,

TITLE INDEX

SEMINAR-ON-A-DISK (COMPUTER BASED

fee free technical support on the product & the subject software application.
MS-DOS. IBM PC & compatibles (256k). disk $160.00. Nonstandard peripherals required: CGA.
Basics for Setting-Up Applications: Getting 1-2-3 up & Running, Moving Around in a Spreadsheet, Commands, Setting-Up Headings, Entering Numbers, Printing, Function Key Shortcuts, Formulas, & Much More.
Infosource, Inc.

Seminar-On-A-Disk (Computer Based Training): Microsoft Mail Fundamentals. *Items Included:* Program diskette & installation guide. *Customer Support:* Toll-free, fee free technical support on the product & the subject software application.
PC-DOS/MS-DOS 3.0 or higher. IBM PC & compatibles (450k). disk $160.00. *Nonstandard peripherals required:* VGA.
Learn How to Open - Close - Move - Delete - Forward - Reply to Messages, Import Text, Make Folder & Sub-Folders, Enter Data into Appointment Book, Planner, Task List, Calendar.
Infosource, Inc.

Seminar-On-A-Disk (Computer Based Training): Paradox Fundamentals - Intermediate. *Version:* 3.5. *Items Included:* Program diskette & installation guide. *Customer Support:* Toll-free, fee free technical support on the product & the subject software application.
DOS 3.3 or higher. Any PC, PC/XT, PC/AT, PS/2 (256k). disk $160.00. *Nonstandard peripherals required:* CGA.
Learn to Start-Up Paradox, Move Around the Screen, Use Menus & Help, Create & Edit Tables, Sort & Key Tables, Employ Tools & Utilities, Ask Questions with Query Function, Write Scripts, Design & Print Reports, Set-Up Forms, Graph Data.
Infosource, Inc.

Seminar-On-A-Disk (Computer Based Training): PowerPoint for Windows Fundamentals. *Version:* 4.0. *Items Included:* Program diskette & installation guide. *Customer Support:* Toll-free, fee free technical support on the product & the subject software application.
PC-DOS/MS-DOS 3.0 or higher. IBM PC & compatibles (450k). disk $160.00. *Nonstandard peripherals required:* VGA.
Learn to Create Dynamic Presentations & High-Tech Slide Shows, Edit Text, Work with Fonts, Create & Import Photos, Graphs & Charts, Discover Powerful Drawing & Screen, Transition Capabilities.
Infosource, Inc.

Seminar-On-A-Disk (Computer Based Training): PC 386-486 Fundamentals. *Items Included:* Program diskette & installation guide. *Customer Support:* Toll-free, fee free technical support on the product & the subject software application.
PC-DOS/MS-DOS 3.0 or higher. IBM PC & compatibles (450k). disk $160.00. *Nonstandard peripherals required:* VGA.
Learn the Intricacies of the System, Keyboard, Mouse, Monitor, Solutions to Common Problems with Personal Computers.
Infosource, Inc.

Seminar-On-A-Disk (Computer Based Training): Quattro Pro Fundamentals. *Version:* 3.0. *Items Included:* Program diskette & installation guide. *Customer Support:* Toll-free, fee free technical support on the product & the subject software application.
MS-DOS. Any PC, PC/XT, PC/AT, PS/2 (256k). disk $160.00. *Nonstandard peripherals required:* EGA or VGA.
Learn to Get Quattro Pro up & Running, Moving Around in a Spreadsheet, Menu Mode, Setting-Up Headings, Entering Numbers in Your Spreadsheet, Printing, Using Function Keys, Writing Formulas & Functions, Copy Command.
Infosource, Inc.

Seminar-On-A-Disk (Computer Based Training): Quattro Pro Fundamentals. *Version:* 4.0. *Items Included:* Program diskette & installation guide. *Customer Support:* Toll-free, fee free technical support on the product & the subject software application.
MS-DOS. Any PC, PC/XT, PC/AT, PS/2 (256k). disk $160.00. *Nonstandard peripherals required:* EGA or VGA.
Learn to Get Quattro Pro up & Running, Moving Around in a Spreadsheet, Menu Mode, Setting-Up Headings, Entering Numbers in Your Spreadsheet, Printing, Using Function Keys, Writing Formulas & Functions, Copy Command.
Infosource, Inc.

Seminar-On-A-Disk (Computer Based Training): Quattro Pro for Windows Fundamentals. *Version:* 5.0. *Items Included:* Program diskette & installation guide. *Customer Support:* Toll-free, fee free technical support on the product & the subject software application.
MS-DOS 2.0 or higher. IBM PC & compatibles (450k). disk $160.00. *Nonstandard peripherals required:* VGA.
Learn to Get Quattro Pro up & Running, Moving Around in a Spreadsheet, Menu Mode, Setting-Up Headings, Entering Numbers in Your Spreadsheet, Printing, Using Function Keys, Writing Formulas & Functions, Copy Command.
Infosource, Inc.

Seminar-On-A-Disk (Computer Based Training): Quattro Pro Intermediate. *Version:* 3.0. *Items Included:* Program diskette & installation guide. *Customer Support:* Toll-free, fee free technical support on the product & the subject software application.
MS-DOS 2.0 or higher. Any PC, PC/XT, PC/AT, PS/2 (256k). disk $160.00. *Nonstandard peripherals required:* EGA or VGA.
Learn to Make a Quattro Pro Database, Sort, Locate Records with Specified Criteria, Create Graphs, Modify & Insert Graphs, Macros.
Infosource, Inc.

Seminar-On-A-Disk (Computer Based Training): Quattro Pro Intermediate. *Version:* 4.0. *Items Included:* Program diskette & installation guide. *Customer Support:* Toll-free, fee free technical support on the product & the subject software application.
MS-DOS 2.0 or higher. Any PC, PC/XT, PC/AT, PS/2 (256k). disk $160.00. *Nonstandard peripherals required:* EGA or VGA.
Learn to Make a Quattro Pro Database, Sort, Locate Records with Specified Criteria, Create Graphs, Modify & Insert Graphs, Macros.
Infosource, Inc.

Seminar-On-A-Disk (Computer Based Training): Windows Fundamentals. *Version:* 3.0. *Items Included:* Program diskette & installation guide. *Customer Support:* Toll-free, fee free technical support on the product & the subject software application.
PC-DOS/MS-DOS. Any PC that runs Windows 3.0 or higher (640k). disk $160.00. *Nonstandard peripherals required:* EGA, VGA, or higher.
Learn How to Get Started in Windows, Menus, Dialog Boxes - Lists - Messages, Organize Your Program, Program Manager, File Manager, Work with Files & Directories, Sharing Information, Help on Help.
Infosource, Inc.

Seminar-On-A-Disk (Computer Based Training): Windows Fundamentals. *Version:* 3.1. *Items Included:* Program diskette & installation guide. *Customer Support:* Toll-free, fee free technical support on the product & the subject software application.
PC-DOS/MS-DOS. Any PC that runs Windows 3.0 or higher (640k). disk $160.00. *Nonstandard peripherals required:* VGA or higher.
Learn How to Get Started in Windows, Menus, Dialog Boxes - Lists - Messages, Organize Your Program, Program Manager, File Manager, Work with Files & Directories, Sharing Information, Help on Help.
Infosource, Inc.

Seminar-On-A-Disk (Computer Based Training): WordPerfect for DOS Advanced. *Version:* 5.1. *Items Included:* Program diskette & installation guide. *Customer Support:* Toll-free, fee free technical support on the product & the subject software application.
DOS 2.0 or higher. Any PC, PC/XT, PC/AT, PS/2 (256k). disk $160.00. *Nonstandard peripherals required:* CGA.
Learn to Use Spell Checker & Thesaurus, Build & Use Columns, Use WordPerfect Math, Desktop Publishing Basics, Sort & Merge, Add Footnotes & Endnotes, Outlining in WordPerfect, Macros, File Management.
Infosource, Inc.

Seminar-On-A-Disk (Computer Based Training): WordPerfect for DOS Fundamentals. *Version:* 5.0-5.1. *Items Included:* Program diskette & installation guide. *Customer Support:* Toll-free, fee free technical support on the product & the subject software application.
DOS 2.0 or higher. Any PC, PC/XT, PC/AT, PS/2 (256k). disk $160.00. *Nonstandard peripherals required:* CGA.
Learn to Get WordPerfect up & Running, Move Around & Edit a Document, Create a Document, Save & Print a Document, Reformat Documents, Copy & Move Text, Use Search & Replace Commands, Macros.
Infosource, Inc.

Seminar-On-A-Disk (Computer Based Training): WordPerfect for DOS Fundamentals. *Version:* 6.0. *Items Included:* Program diskette & installation guide. *Customer Support:* Toll-free, fee free technical support on the product & the subject software application.
DOS 2.0 or higher. IBM PC & compatibles (450k). disk $160.00. *Nonstandard peripherals required:* VGA.
Learn to Get WordPerfect up & Running, Move Around & Edit a Document, Create a Document, Save & Print a Document, Reformat Documents, Copy & Move Text, Use Search & Replace Commands, Macros.
Infosource, Inc.

Seminar-On-A-Disk (Computer Based Training): WordPerfect for Windows. *Version:* 5.2. *Items Included:* Program diskette & installation guide. *Customer Support:* Toll-free, fee free technical support on the product & the subject software application.
PC-DOS/MS-DOS. IBM PC & compatibles (475k). disk $160.00. *Nonstandard peripherals required:* VGA.
Learn to Get WordPerfect up & Running, Move Around & Edit a Document, Create a Document, Save & Print a Document, Reformat Documents, Copy & Move Text, Use Search & Replace Commands, Macros.
Infosource, Inc.

Seminar-On-A-Disk (Computer Based Training): Word for Windows Fundamentals - Intermediate. Version: 2.0. Items Included: Program diskette & installation guide. Customer Support: Toll-free, fee free technical support on the product & the subject software application. PC-DOS/MS-DOS. Any PC that runs with Windows 3.0 or higher (640k). disk $160.00. Nonstandard peripherals required: EGA, VGA or higher monitor.
Learn to Start Program, Enter Data, Edit & Save Document, Formats, Print, Templates, Search & Replace Text, Check Spelling, Macros, Merging Documents & Files.
Infosource, Inc.

Seminar-On-A-Disk (Computer Based Training): Word for Windows Fundamentals. Version: 6.0. Items Included: Program diskette & installation guide. Customer Support: Toll-free, fee free technical support on the product & the subject software application. PC-DOS/MS-DOS. Any PC that runs Windows 3.0 or higher (450k). disk $160.00. Nonstandard peripherals required: EGA, VGA or higher.
Learn to Start Program, Enter Data, Edit & Save Document, Formats, Print, Templates, Search & Replace Text, Check Spelling, Macros, Merging Documents & Files.
Infosource, Inc.

Seminar-On-A-Disk (Computer Based Training): WordPerfect for Windows Fundamentals. Version: 6.0. Items Included: Program diskette & installation guide. Customer Support: Toll-free, fee free technical support on the product & the subject software application. PC-DOS/MS-DOS. IBM PC & compatibles (475k). disk $160.00. Nonstandard peripherals required: VGA.
Learn to Get WordPerfect up & Running, Move Around & Edit a Document, Create a Document, Save & Print a Document, Reformat Documents, Copy & Move Text, Use Search & Replace Commands, Macros.
Infosource, Inc.

Seminar on a Disk: Excel for Windows Intermediate. Version: 5.0. Items Included: 3.5" disk & installation guide. Customer Support: No charge, unlimited telephone support. MS-DOS. IBM PC & compatibles. disk $160.00. Addl. software required: Program that training is for.
CBTs (Training Tutorials).
InfoSource, Inc.

Seminar-on-a-Disk: Internet Fundamentals. Items Included: Installation guide & diskettes. Customer Support: Toll-free, fee-free, technical support on the product title & the underlying application. Windows 3.1 or higher. IBM PC & compatibles. disk $160.00. Nonstandard peripherals required: VGA.
Part of an Integrated Curriculum of Computer-Based Training & Testing Products. Contact InfoSource for Course Contents.
InfoSource, Inc.

Seminar-on-a-Disk: Lotus 1-2-3 for Windows Fundamentals. Version: 5.0. Items Included: Installation guide & diskettes. Customer Support: Toll-free, fee-free, technical support on the product title & the underlying application. Windows 3.1 or higher. IBM PC & compatibles. disk $160.00. Nonstandard peripherals required: VGA.
Part of an Integrated Curriculum of Computer-Based Training & Testing Products. Contact InfoSource for Course Contents.
InfoSource, Inc.

Seminar-on-a-Disk: Lotus 1-2-3 for Windows Intermediate. Version: 5.0. Items Included: Installation guide & diskettes. Customer Support: Toll-free, fee-free, technical support on the product title & the underlying application. Windows 3.1 or higher. IBM PC & compatibles. disk $160.00. Nonstandard peripherals required: VGA.
Part of an Integrated Curriculum of Training & Testing Products. Contact InfoSource for More Information.
InfoSource, Inc.

Seminar-on-a-Disk, Multimedia Edition: Databases Access for Windows Fundamentals. Version: 2.0. Items Included: CD-ROM. Customer Support: Toll-free, fee-free, technical support on the product title & the underlying application. Windows 3.1 or higher. PC 386-486 recommended (4Mb, 8Mb recommended). CD-ROM disk $250.00. Nonstandard peripherals required: Sound board must be installed, VGA or higher.
Part of an Integrated Curriculum of Computer-Based Training & Testing Products. Contact InfoSource for Course Content.
InfoSource, Inc.

Seminar-on-a-Disk, Multimedia Edition: Graphics & Presentations PowerPoint for Windows Fundamentals. Version: 4.0. Items Included: CD-ROM. Customer Support: Toll-free, fee-free, technical support on the product title & the underlying application. Windows 3.1 or higher. PC 386-486 recommended (4Mb, 8Mb recommended). CD-ROM disk $250.00. Nonstandard peripherals required: Sound board must be installed, VGA or higher.
Part of an Integrated Curriculum of Computer-Based Training & Testing Products. Contact InfoSource for Course Content.
InfoSource, Inc.

Seminar-on-a-Disk, Multimedia Edition: Operating Environments, Windows Fundamentals Upgrading to Windows 95. Version: 3.1. Items Included: CD-ROM. Customer Support: Toll-free, fee-free, technical support on the product title & the underlying application. Windows 3.1 or higher. PC 386-486 recommended (4Mb, 8Mb recommended). CD-ROM disk $250.00. Nonstandard peripherals required: Sound board must be installed, VGA or higher.
Part of an Integrated Curriculum of Computer-Based Training & Testing Products. Contact InfoSource for Course Content.
InfoSource, Inc.

Seminar-on-a-Disk, Multimedia Edition: Spreadsheets Excel for Windows Fundamentals. Version: 5.0. Items Included: CD-ROM. Customer Support: Toll-free, fee-free, technical support on the product title & the underlying application. Windows 3.1 or higher. PC 386-486 recommended (4Mb, 8Mb recommended). CD-ROM disk $250.00. Nonstandard peripherals required: Sound board must be installed, VGA or higher.
Part of an Integrated Curriculum of Computer-Based Training & Testing Products. Contact InfoSource for Course Content.
InfoSource, Inc.

Seminar-on-a-Disk, Multimedia Edition: Word Processing, Word for Windows Fundamentals. Version: 6.0. Items Included: CD-ROM. Customer Support: Toll-free, fee-free, technical support on the product title & the underlying application. Windows 3.1 or higher. PC 386-486 recommended (4Mb, 8Mb recommended). CD-ROM disk $250.00. Nonstandard peripherals required: Sound board must be installed, VGA or higher.
Part of an Integrated Curriculum of Computer-Based Training & Testing Products. Contact InfoSource for Course Content.
InfoSource, Inc.

Seminar-on-a-Disk: Paradox for DOS Fundamentals. Version: 4.5. Items Included: Installation guide & diskettes. Customer Support: Toll-free, fee-free, technical support on the product title & the underlying application. MS-DOS. IBM PC & compatibles. disk $160.00. Nonstandard peripherals required: VGA.
Part of an Integrated Curriculum of Computer-Based Training & Testing Products. Contact InfoSource for Course Contents.
InfoSource, Inc.

Seminar-on-a-Disk: Paradox for Windows Fundamentals. Version: 5.0. Items Included: Installation guide & diskettes. Customer Support: Toll-free, fee-free, technical support on the product title & the underlying application. MS-DOS. IBM PC & compatibles. disk $160.00. Nonstandard peripherals required: VGA.
Part of an Integrated Curriculum of Computer-Based Training & Testing Products. Contact InfoSource for Course Contents.
InfoSource, Inc.

Seminar-on-a-Disk: Upgrading to Windows 95. Items Included: Installation guide & diskettes. Customer Support: Toll-free, fee-free, technical support on the product title & the underlying application. MS-DOS. IBM PC & compatibles. disk $160.00. Nonstandard peripherals required: VGA.
Part of an Integrated Curriculum of Computer-Based Training & Testing Products. Contact InfoSource for Course Contents.
InfoSource, Inc.

Seminar-on-a-Disk: Word for Windows Intermediate. Version: 6.0. Items Included: Installation guide & diskettes. Customer Support: Toll-free, fee-free, technical support on the product title & the underlying application. MS-DOS. IBM PC & compatibles. 3.5" disk $160.00. Nonstandard peripherals required: VGA.
Part of an Integrated Curriculum of Computer-Based Training & Testing Products. Contact InfoSource for Course Contents.
InfoSource, Inc.

Seminar-on-a-Disk: WordPerfect for Windows Fundamentals. Version: 6.1. Items Included: Installation guide & diskettes. Customer Support: Toll-free, fee-free, technical support on the product title & the underlying application. MS-DOS. IBM PC & compatibles. disk $160.00. Nonstandard peripherals required: VGA.
Part of an Integrated Curriculum of Computer-Based Training & Testing Products. Contact InfoSource for Course Contents.
InfoSource, Inc.

Seminar-on-a-Disk: WordPerfect for Windows Intermediate. Version: 6.1. Items Included: Installation guide & diskettes. Customer Support: Toll-free, fee-free, technical support on the product title & the underlying application. MS-DOS. IBM PC & compatibles. disk $160.00. Nonstandard peripherals required: VGA.
Part of an Integrated Curriculum of Computer-Based Training & Testing Products. Contact InfoSource for Course Contents.
InfoSource, Inc.

TITLE INDEX

Semistructured Clinical Interview for Children & Adolescents Scoring Program for IBM PC Compatibles. Thomas M. Achenbach. 1994. *Items Included:* Detailed manual. *Customer Support:* Free telephone support with no time limit.
 MS-DOS. IBM PC & compatibles (512k). disk $135.00 (ISBN 0-938565-33-8). *Optimal configuration:* IBM PC compatible with 512k, & printer capable of 132-character lines if user wishes to print profiles.
 Provides for Entry & Verification of Data from the Semistructured Clinical Interview for Children & Adolescents. Scores Can Be Displayed on Printed Profile & Stored in Computer File.
 Univ. of Vermont, Dept. of Psychiatry.

Semitic Transliterator. *Version:* 3.1. Sep. 1994. *Items Included:* User manual, keyboard layout chart, keycap sticker sheet. *Customer Support:* Free telephone support, defective disks replaced.
 Macintosh. Macintosh (1Mb). 3.5" disk $99.95. *Addl. software required:* Any Word Processor. *Optimal configuration:* 4Mb RAM & a hard drive.
 ATM-Compatible, Type-1 & TrueType Plain, Bold, Italic & Bold-Italic Font. Includes All the Characters & Diacritics Necessary to Transliterate Semitic Languages & Greek, & to Type Turkish. The Characters in the Font Cover These Transliteration Methods: Hebrew - SBL, Blau, Greenberg, Harrison, LaSor, Prentice-Hall, TWOT, TDOT, Marks & Rogers, Weingreen, Eerdmans & Zondervan; Arabic - American Library of Congress (ALC), European, ALC with Persian, European with Persian, MESA, SBL, & Zondervan; Aramaic - SBL; Ugaritic - SBL & Zondervan; Greek - SBL & Prentice-Hall; Also, the Turkish Language. Other Methods of Transliteration Not Listed Here May Also Be Covered by TranslitLS.
 Linguist's Software, Inc.

Semitic Transliterator for Windows. *Version:* 2.2. Sep. 1994. *Items Included:* User manual, keyboard layout chart, keycap sticker sheet & ANSI chart. *Customer Support:* Free telephone support, defective disks replaced.
 Windows. IBM & compatibles (4Mb). disk $99.95. *Addl. software required:* Microsoft Windows or ATM. *Optimal configuration:* 4Mb RAM & 386.
 Includes All the Characters & Diacritics Necessary to Transliterate Semitic Languages & Greek, & to Type Turkish. The Characters in the Font Cover These Transliteration Methods: Hebrew - SBL, Blau, Greenberg, Harrison, Kautsch & Cowley, LaSor, TWOT, TDOT, Marks & Rogers, & Weingreen; Arabic - American Library of Congress (ALC), European, ALC with Persian, European with Persian, & SBL; Aramaic - SBL; Ugaritic - SBL; Greek - SBL & Prentice-Hall; Also the Turkish Language. Other Methods of Transliteration May Also Be Covered by TranslitLS.
 Linguist's Software, Inc.

Sendero A/L 1: Asset - Liability Management. Jun. 1995. *Items Included:* Documentation included. *Customer Support:* Toll-free telephone support (client use only), training, new releases, electronic bulletin board system, new client support, newsletter.
 Windows NT. 486 66 DX2 IBM compatible (16Mb); HD 500 Mb Free; 2X CD-ROM. $10,000.00. *Optimal configuration:* Depends on the number of transactions combined with the applications to be used. *Networks supported:* Netware, UNIX, LANManager, LANServer, Windows NT, AS/400, Dec-Net-Pathworks.
 Simulates Net Interest Income & Risk-Based Capital under Projected Interest Rate Movements. Provides Static Market Value Analysis, Static & Dynamic Gap, Rate Shocks, & Strategy/Scenario Combinations for "What If?" Analysis. Reports Are Generated in Both Detail & Summary Form for a 60-Month Forecast. Hedging, Consolidation, Dynamic Market Value & Dynamic Duration Are Optional.
 Sendero Corp.

Sendero A/L 3: Asset - Liability Management. Jun. 1995. *Items Included:* Documentation included. *Customer Support:* Toll-free telephone support (client use only), training, new releases, electronic bulletin board system, new client support, newsletter.
 Windows NT. 486 66 DX2 IBM compatible (16Mb); HD 500 Mb Free; 2X CD-ROM. $110,000.00. *Optimal configuration:* Depends on the number of transactions combined with the applications to be used. *Networks supported:* Netware, UNIX, LANManager, LANServer, Windows NT, AS/400, Dec-Net-Pathworks.
 A Sophisticated yet Flexible Simulation Model That Enables You to Model & Evaluate Your Institution Based on a True Reflection of the Balance Sheet. Use It for Measuring Interest Rate Risk, Evaluating Strategies, Budgeting & Planning, & Meeting Regulatory Compliance Requirements. It Contains Advanced Off-Balance Sheet Modeling Capabilities & Handles Embedded Options. Options Include Linear Path Space (Random-Path Generation) & CMO Analytics.
 Sendero Corp.

Sendero A/L 2: Asset - Liability Management. Jun. 1995. *Items Included:* Documentation included. *Customer Support:* Toll-free telephone support (client use only), training, new releases, electronic bulletin board system, new client support, newsletter.
 Windows NT. 486 66 DX2 IBM compatible (16Mb); HD 500 Mb Free; 2X CD-ROM. $50,000.00. *Optimal configuration:* Depends on the number of transactions combined with the applications to be used. *Networks supported:* Netware, UNIX, LANManager, LANServer, Windows NT, AS/400, Dec-Net-Pathworks.
 Supporting Unlimited Strategy/Scenario Combinations, A/L 2 Accesses Three Yield Curves & References 30 Key Rates. Pricing Spreads, Purchases & Sales, a Gap & Market Value Matrix, & Unlimited Prepayment Tables Are Featured in A/L2. Optional Modules Include Multicurrency, Linear Path Space (a Stochastic Modeling Technique), CMO Analytics, a 120-Month Forecast, Dynamic Market Value & Duration, Hedging, & the Ability to Build Rate Scenarios.
 Sendero Corp.

Sendero DMS: Data Management System. Jun. 1995. *Items Included:* Documentation included. *Customer Support:* Toll-free telephone support (client use only), training, new releases, electronic bulletin board system, new client support, newsletter.
 Windows NT. 486 66 DX2 IBM compatible (16Mb); HD 500 Mb Free; 2X CD-ROM. $50,000.00. *Optimal configuration:* Depends on the number of transactions combined with the applications to be used. *Networks supported:* Netware, UNIX, LANManager, LANServer, Windows NT, AS/400, Dec-Net-Pathworks.
 This Data Management System Channels Data from Various Sources into a Central Warehouse & Provides the Ability to Examine, Catalog & Manage Data at Transaction Detail or Summary Levels. The System Includes Extensive Data Editing, Correction & Auditing Features to Provide a Single Point of Reconciliation.
 Sendero Corp.

Sendero FTP: Funds Transfer Pricing. *Version:* 1.15. Aug. 1994. *Items Included:* Documentation included. *Customer Support:* Toll-free telephone support (client use only), training, new releases, electronic bulletin board system, new client support, newsletter.
 OS/2, UNIX, AS/400, PC-DOS/MS-DOS, Windows. 486 33 DX IBM compatible (16Mb). $72,500.00. *Optimal configuration:* Depends on the number of transactions combined with the applications to be used. *Networks supported:* Netware, UNIX, LANManager, LANServer, Windows NT, AS/400, Dec-Net-Pathworks.
 Supports a Match-Funded (Coterminous) Funds Transfer Pricing Methodology. It Allows Transfer Pricing of All Assets & Liabilities at the Appropriate Level of Detail to Support Products & Organization Profitability. The System Produces comprehensive Analytical & Management Reports to Support the Process & Offers a Sophisticated Tool for Interest Margin Management.
 Sendero Corp.

Senior High Mathematics I. 1992. *Items Included:* Detailed manuals included with all Dynacomp products. *Customer Support:* Free telephone support to original customer - no time limit; 30 day limited warranty.
 MS-DOS 3.2 or higher. IBM PC & compatibles (512k). $179.95 (Add $5.00 for 3 1/2" format; 5 1/4" format standard).
 Quadratic Equations; Trigonometry I; Trigonometry II; Simultan Equations (2x2); Simultan Equations (3x3); Geometrical Areas; Verbal Problems: Numbers; Verbal Problems: Coins; Verbal Problems: Ages; Verbal Problems: Interest; Verbal Problems: Mixtures; Verbal Problems: Geometry; Verbal Problems: Rates.
 Dynacomp, Inc.

Senior High Mathematics II. 1992. *Items Included:* Detailed manuals included with all Dynacomp products. *Customer Support:* Free telephone support to original customer - no time limit; 30 day limited warranty.
 MS-DOS 3.2 or higher. IBM PC & compatibles (512k). $179.95 (Add $5.00 for 3 1/2" format; 5 1/4" format standard).
 Verbal Problems: Digits; Verbal Problems: Work; Arithmetic Progressions I; Arithmetic Progressions II; Geometric Progressions I; Geometric Progressions II; Type of Variation; Linear Equations; Formula Evaluation; Coordinate Geometry; Exponents & Logarithms; Verbal Problems: General.
 Dynacomp, Inc.

SeniorPro: Senior Citizen Center Contact Manager. *Version:* 1.1. Aug. 1992. *Items Included:* Manual. *Customer Support:* 800 number support at $1/minute (1st 5 min/day free).
 MS-DOS 3.1. 386 or higher (1Mb). $1295.00 single user; $1595.00 multi-user. *Nonstandard peripherals required:* VGA color preferred. *Addl. software required:* FoxPro 2.0 runtime included. *Optimal configuration:* 386-25, VGA 4Mb RAM, mouse, 120Mb hard drive. *Networks supported:* All.
 Manages Lists & Provides Name/Talent Searching for Labels, Lists & Reports of All Persons, Businesses, etc. Associated with the Operation of a Senior Citizen Center. Links with SBT Database Accounting Library for Full Accounting Functions. Provides Instant Mail Merging of Letters & Forms.
 Terradise Computer Systems, Inc.

Sensible Soccer. *Version:* 3.0. Sensible Software & Renegade. Jan. 1994. *Items Included:* Instruction manual. *Customer Support:* 30 days limited warranty.

DOS. IBM PC & 100% compatibles (640k). disk $14.95 (ISBN 0-9641564-0-7). *Optimal configuration:* 386 processor & higher, DOS 5.0, 2Mb RAM.
PC Soccer Program Featuring Arcade & Strategy Action for 1 or 2 Players. Supports Both Keyboard & Joystick Controls & Major Sound Cards. Voted Game of the Year in Europe. Superb Graphics, Gameplay & Ball Control. Individual & World Cup Competition.
Everyware.

The Sensible Speller IV: School Pak. *Version:* 4.3. Charles Hartley. 1983. *Compatible Hardware:* Apple II, II+, IIc, IIe, IIgs; Franklin Ace. *Operating System(s) Required:* Apple DOS 3.2, 3.3. *Language(s):* Assembly. *Memory Required:* 48k.
disk $375.00 (ISBN 0-926776-20-7).
Proofreader & Dictionary to Remove Typos from Business & Personal Writing. Checks Against Dictionary & Shows Potentially Misspelled Words Not Found & Context of Usage. User Has Choice of Adding Word to Dictionary, Ignoring Errors, Marking As Misspelled or Making Correction. Random House Dictionary Contains 80,000 Words. Can Add 10,000 Words to Each Disk. Works with Most DOS 3.3, Apple-Pascal, & Apple CP/M Word Processors.
Sensible Software, Inc.

Sensible Speller ProDOS: School Pak. Charles Hartley. 1984. *Compatible Hardware:* Apple II+, IIe, IIc, IIgs, Laser 128. *Operating System(s) Required:* ProDOS. *Memory Required:* 64k.
disk $375.00 (ISBN 0-926776-05-3).
Any Time a Potential Misspelling Is Located User Is Given a Number of Options: Add the Word to the Dictionary, Ignore the Word, Look up the Correct Spelling in One of the Dictionary Diskettes, Ask the Computer to Suggest the Correct Spelling, Mark the Misspelled Word, Immediately Replace the Misspelled Word with the Correct Spelling. 10-Page Document Is Checked in 2-3 Minutes. Dictionary Contains 80,000 Words, Can Create Own Personal Dictionary. Gives Word Count & Word Usage.
Sensible Software, Inc.

Sensible Technical Dictionary, 2 disks. 1985. *Compatible Hardware:* Apple II, II+, IIe, IIc, IIgs. *Operating System(s) Required:* DOS, ProDOS. *Memory Required:* DOS 48k, ProDOS 64k. *General Requirements:* Sensible Speller program.
Set. disk $39.95 (ISBN 0-926776-04-5).
Contains Words from Life & Physical Sciences. Can Be Used Alone or with the Speller's Random House Dictionary. Contains over 47,000 Words.
Sensible Software, Inc.

Sensory Integration & Praxis Tests (SIPT). *Version:* 5.010. Jean Ayers. Jan. 1996. *Customer Support:* Free unlimited phone support.
Windows 3.X, Windows 95. 286 (4Mb). disk $225.00 (Order no.: W-1095). *Nonstandard peripherals required:* Printer.
Measure the Sensory Integration Processes That Underline Learning Behavior. By Showing You How Children Organize & Respond to Sensory Input, "SAPT" Helps Pinpoint Specific Organic Problems Associated with Learning Disabilities, Emotional Disorders, & Minimal Brain Dysfunction.
Western Psychological Services.

Sentimental Wings. *Customer Support:* All of our products are unconditionally guaranteed.
All Systems. CD-ROM disk $39.95 (Order no.: WINGS). *Nonstandard peripherals required:* CD-ROM drive.
Pictures in 4 Formats & Text Files of the History of Aircraft.
Walnut Creek CDRom.

Separations Calculations. 1995. *Items Included:* Full manual. *Customer Support:* Free telephone support - 90 days, 30-day warranty.
MS-DOS 3.2 or higher. 286 (584k). disk $289.95. *Nonstandard peripherals required:* CGA/EGA/VGA.
Determines the Conditions & Compositions at the Dew Point & at the Bubble Point for Multi-Component Mixtures. It Replaces Tedious Trial-&-Error Hand Calculations with Procedures to Interpolate Between Two Sets of Input Data. It Quickly Makes Binary & Multi-Component Flash Calculations to Determine the Compositions & quantities of Each Phase from Such Flashes.
Dynacomp, Inc.

Sequel. *Version:* 1.5. Richard Diemer. 1994. *Items Included:* 128-page manual; QuickStart sheet; Sample music & sound files. *Customer Support:* Phone (free).
Amiga DOS. Amiga, any model, minimum system (7MHz 68000) (0.5Mb). disk $139.95 (Order no.: SEQUEL). *Nonstandard peripherals required:* Hard drive not required, MIDI Interface required for recording. SMPTE-to-MTC converter required for SMPTE sync. *Optimal configuration:* Any Amiga.
32-Track MIDI Sequencer Lets You Record & Play Back Standard MIDI Files, Correct Mistakes, & Add Custom Music Production & Arrangement. Includes Multiple, Nested Playback Looping, Pattern Chaining, Quantizing, & More. Syncs to SMPTE Time Code, Allowing Film & Video Soundtrack Production, & Overdubbing of Acoustic Instruments on Tape. Supports the AMIGA's Built-In Digital Audio Channels As Well As External MIDI Instruments.
Diemer Development.

Sequence. Dec. 1988. *Compatible Hardware:* CI Music Computer.
contact publisher for price.
A MIDI Sequencing Program Developed to Take Full Advantage of the YAMAHA CI Music Computer's Hardware & Keyboard. Provides a Professional Sequencing Environment. Visually-Oriented. Uses Windows, Scroll Bars, Pull-Down Menus & Redundant Mouse & Keyboard Commands. Includes Full Range of Music-Editing Functions.
Yamaha Corp. of America.

The Serayachi Campaign. *Compatible Hardware:* Commodore Amiga, IBM PC, Apple Macintosh, Atari ST.
3.5" disk $24.95.
Combat Scenario Disk for Breach Game.
Omnitrend Software, Inc.

Serendipity. 1992. *Items Included:* Detailed manuals included with all Dynacomp products. *Customer Support:* Free telephone support to original customer - no time limit; 30 day limited warranty.
MS-DOS 3.2 or higher. Apple, Commodore 64 (48k). $19.95 (Add $5.00 for 3 1/2" format; 5 1/4" format standard).
Written by a Teacher & Field Tested in an Elementary School. It Consists of the Following Nine Subprograms: Alphabet Match Patch, Number Match Patch, Number Counting Patch, Waffle, Sour Apple, Math Invaders, Pinpoint, Estimation Baseball & Mineshaft. Written with Children in Mind. After Minimal Experience, the Child Usually Becomes Comfortable with the Format of the Package. The Programs Tackle Difficult Concepts in a Great Variety of Ways.
Dynacomp, Inc.

Serf City: Jewel Case CD. Blue Byte. Nov. 1995. *Customer Support:* 30 day limited warranty.
DOS 5.0 or higher. 386 CD-ROM with hard drive (2Mb). CD-ROM disk $9.95 (ISBN 0-917059-43-3, Order no.: 062641).
Command a Feudal Empire & Attempt to Dominate All Other Serfdoms, Place New Roads & Buidlings Effectively. Use Natural Resources & Maintain Food Supplies Which Will Sustain Your Settlement. Ultimate Goal Is Conquest!
Strategic Simulations, Inc.

Serial Control System. *Version:* 5.07. May 1995. *Compatible Hardware:* IBM PC & compatibles, PC XT, PC AT. *Operating System(s) Required:* MS-DOS or Windows. *Memory Required:* 640k.
Check-In/Claiming/Subscription Management, Holdings Lists. disk $1200.00.
Binder/Microfilm Management. disk $400.00.
Routing List Manager. disk $495.00.
Provides the Librarian with Control over the Ordering, Receiving, Preservation, & Renewal of Journals & Serialized Audio-Visuals. Tracks Subscriptions for Many Departments Other Than the Library.
Professional Software.

The Serials Directory: An International Reference Book, 5 Vols. Edited by Ann Talley. Set. MS-DOS 5.0 or higher (6.2 recommended), 286 CPU of better (386 recommended). CD-ROM disk quarterly $525.00. *Nonstandard peripherals required:* CD-ROM player(s), monitor & keyboard, printer, modem (optional). 640k of RAM, 5 mb available disk space. CD-ROM disk annually $339.00.
"The Serials Directory": An International Reference Book provides quality bibliographic coverage, current pricing information, & the most up-to-date, accurate information for more than 151,000 U. S. & international serials, including newspapers. The Serials Directory offers up to 60 elements of information composed of: Library of Congress Classification, Dewey Decimal Classification, Universal Decimal Code, National Library of Medicine Classification, CODEN. New to the ninth edition are entries which include wire service affiliations, publication size, photographs, advertising rates, & document delivery availability.
EBSCO Publishing.

Series CS1000, 6 modules. *Compatible Hardware:* IBM PC AT, PC XT. *Operating System(s) Required:* MS-DOS, PC-DOS. *Memory Required:* 256k. *General Requirements:* Printer.
Varies.
Accounts Receivable.
Accounts Payable.
Payroll.
General Ledger.
Decision support.
Fully Integrated Accounting Package Designed to Give Complete Control over Every Aspect of a Contractor's Business. Designed to Work for Both General & Specialty Contractors.
Concord Management Systems, Inc.

Series 5000. *Compatible Hardware:* Aegis, HP-UX, HP/Apollo, Unix OS Sun, & DEC work stations; VSM, Ultrix. *Items Included:* Documentation. *Customer Support:* Maintenance, training.
contact publisher for price.
General-Purpose CAD System. Includes 3-D Data Structures.
Auto-Trol Technology Corp.

Series Modular Banking. *Compatible Hardware:* Sharp ZL-6100 System. *Language(s):* Sharp Microcode.
Option A. $400.00.
additional option $90.00 ea.
Computes Installment Loans with Any Frequency of Payments, Odd Days, Origination Fee & Pack Fee, Credit-Life & Disability Insurance. Other Options Compute: Balloon Loans; Single Payment

TITLE INDEX

Loans; Installment Loan with Balloon; U.S. Rule Amortization Schedule; C/D Penalty & Yield-if-Withdrawn; Rule of 78's; I.R.A./Keogh Plan Growth & Withdrawal Projections; Effective Yield, Daily Factors & Amount of $1 Tables.
P-ROM Software, Inc.

Series 100-BASIC. Microsoft, Inc. *Compatible Hardware:* HP 150 Touchscreen, HP 110 Portable.
3.5" disk $300.00 (Order no.: 45445D).
BASIC Interpreter Including Features & Performance Found in Languages Operating on Large Minicomputers. Meets the Requirements for the ANSI Subset Standard for BASIC.
Hewlett-Packard Co.

Series Print. *Compatible Hardware:* TRS-80 Model II. *Operating System(s) Required:* TRSDOS. *Memory Required:* 64k. *General Requirements:* 2 disk drives.
disk $39.00.
Provides Continuous Printing of up to 100 Visicalc DIF Files, Selects the Files to Print (All or Just a Few) & Makes Single or Multiple Copies.
Computer/Business Services.

SERIES 2: Investment Management System. Dec. 1983. *Compatible Hardware:* IBM PC, PC XT, PC AT & compatibles; Prime. *Operating System(s) Required:* PC-DOS/MS-DOS, PRIMOS. *Language(s):* C, FORTRAN 77. *Memory Required:* 512k.
contact publisher for price.
Provides Securities Accounting, Portfolio Management, Operations & Trading Support for Mortgage-Backed Securities, Fixed & Variable Rate Investments, Equities, Futures, Options, & Money Market Securities. The System Also Addresses Dollar Rolls, Reverse Repurchase Agreements, CMOs, TBA, & Other Securitized Debt Instruments. SERIES 2 Further Provides Accrual-Based Accounting, Amortization Methods Including Level-Yield, Market Valuations, Missing Payments Tracking, Optimal Sale Allocation for MBS, Collateral Risk Monitoring, MBS Pool Prepayment Rate Statistics, Bond Swap Analysis, Report Writer, Lotus Downloads, System Generated Transactions Files, & a General Ledger Interface. Operates In-House or via Remote Processing.
Wismer Assocs., Inc.

Series 200-300 Utilities Package. *Compatible Hardware:* HP 9000 Series 200, 300. *Language(s):* BASIC (source code included).
10 utilities $195.00, incl. instr.
CALENDAR, Prints a Complete Calendar for Any Modern Year Which User Specifies. Holidays Are Marked. COMPARE, Compares Two Versions of the Same Program & Prints Out Their Differences. CRUNCH, Combines HP Programs FILE SIZER & REPACK with Automatic Operation to Reduce All Files on a Disk, Except Those User Specifies, to Their Minimum Length. Then Packs Each File Next to the Previous One at the Lowest Possible Address on the Disk. PROGRAM EXECUTION TIME HISTOGRAM, Prints Out the Percentage of the Total Program Execution Time Which Is Used by Each Line of the Program. Allows User to Find & Solve Execution Speed Bottlenecks Making the Program Run Faster. Printer Plot, Use HP Printers As an HPGL Plotter.
James Assocs.

Serpentine. *Compatible Hardware:* Apple; joystick optional. *Memory Required:* 48k.
disk $34.95.
Set Forth to Slay Their Slithering Cousins, the Snakes Lay Eggs & Fight to Protect Their Young. Takes the Serpent to Many Levels of Play.
Broderbund Software, Inc.

The Serpent's Star. Ultrasoft, Inc. *Compatible Hardware:* Atari 400, 800, XL, XE Series; Commodore 64.
Commodore. disk $39.95 (Order no.: COMDSK-257).
Atari. disk $39.95 (Order no.: ATDSK-139).
Mac Steele Travels to Tibet in Search of a Valuable Gem: The Serpent's Star. Features Animated Travel Sequences, Detailed Graphics, & Sound Effects.
Broderbund Software, Inc.

Service Billings. *Version:* 4.1. *Customer Support:* On site training unlimited support services for first 90 days & through subscription thereafter.
Contact publisher for price.
Allows Billings Units to Be Defined for Generating Service Orders As Well As for Repetitive Billing Purposes. The Billing Unit May Have a Location Separate from That of the Customer. Up to Six Repetitive Service Orders or Charges May Be Entered for Each Billing Unit. Numerous Reports Are Available for Analysis Purposes.
Argos Software.

Service Call Central. Jun. 1994. *Items Included:* User manuals. *Customer Support:* Free telephone support; training seminars - included in purchase price; rapid implementation services - fees vary with service provided.
DOS. 486 PC or compatible (8Mb). $9000.00 to $49,000.00. *Optimal configuration:* 486 PC with 8Mb RAM. *Networks supported:* Novell, NetBios, Banyan Vines.
Maintenance Management Program Designed for Retail Stores, Banks, Hotels & Other Chain-Type Organizations That Manage the Maintenance of Many Facilities from a Centralized Location. Customized for Each User, the Program Manages Corrective & Preventive Maintenance Activities, Offers a Wide Variety of Reports & Tracks Valuable Store Information.
OmniComp, Inc.

SERVICE CALL Maintenance Management. *Version:* 9. Jul. 1994. *Compatible Hardware:* CP/M computers; IBM PC or compatibles, 286 or higher. *Operating System(s) Required:* PC-DOS/MS-DOS 3.3 or higher. *Language(s):* Clipper. *Memory Required:* 640k. *General Requirements:* hard disk. *Customer Support:* Telephone support, training, rapid implementation services.
$2450.00-$10,000.00.
Corrective & Preventive Work Order Tracking Program. Aids in Work Scheduling, Tracks Cost Expenditures, Equipment Histories, Analyze Employee Performance, & Automatically Generates PM Work Orders.
OmniComp, Inc.

Service Dispatching. (Service Management Ser.). 1996.
DOS, Unix. IBM PC. disk contact publisher for price.
The Service Dispatch tracking module is one of three service modules that make-up Fastrak's Service Management Series. Work order & time information is entered after the service work is performed.
Core Software, Inc.

Service Inventory. *Version:* 5.0. Apr. 1984. *Compatible Hardware:* IBM PC, PC XT, PC AT, PS/2. *Operating System(s) Required:* PC-DOS. *Language(s):* Compiled BASIC (source code included). *Memory Required:* 512k. *General Requirements:* Hard disk, parallel printer. *Items Included:* Reference manual. *Customer Support:* Phone/modem support included first year, nominal fee thereafter.
disk $1200.00 (ISBN 0-924068-03-5, Order no.: SE1).

SERVICEWORKS

Inventory System Designed Specifically for Small Service Companies. Allows Addition of Labor & Overhead to Invoice, along with Materials from Inventory, & Features a Large Area on the Invoice to Describe Work Performed.
Fogle Computing Corp.

Service Management. (Service Management Ser.). 1996.
DOS, Unix. IBM PC. disk contact publisher for price.
Up to 99 Maintenance jobs at the same location on one work order.
Core Software, Inc.

Service Management Information System. *Version:* 4.00. Jan. 1990.
PC/MS-DOS 3.1 or higher. IBM PC, PSII, XT, AT or compatible (384k). disk $595.00 single-user $695.00 network version. *Nonstandard peripherals required:* 1 hard disk drive, 1 floppy disk.
Program That Allows Service Establishments to Store, Maintain & Retrieve Customer Names & Information. The Program Allows Several Report Formats As Well As Generating Service Orders & Invoices on a Variety of Forms. A Series of Menus Makes This Program Very Easy to Learn & Use. A Spanish/English Language Program Will Be Available in 1991. Registered Users Will Receive This Version Free of Charge When Completed.
Baud Room Computer Services.

Service Station Accountant. Stephen R. Krause. Apr. 1986. *Compatible Hardware:* IBM PC. *Operating System(s) Required:* PC-DOS, MS-DOS, XENIX. *Language(s):* Foxbase, dBASE IV, Foxpro. *Memory Required:* 640k. *General Requirements:* Hard disk, printer. *Customer Support:* 6 months free telephone support.
disk $2300.00 (Order no.: 4100-A).
Provides Accounts Receivable, Billing & Account Maintenance for Service Stations. Also Provides Servicing History, Meter & Stick Reading Analysis & Daily Cash Flow Accounting for Sales, Delivery, & Service.
Tele Vend, Inc.

Service Station Master. *Customer Support:* 800-929-8117 (customer service).
MS-DOS. IBM/PS2. disk $399.99 (ISBN 0-87007-449-0).
Keeps Track of Each Sale, Purchase, Charge & Collection of a Service Station. A Simplied Bookkeeping System, Provides Status on Station Stock & Gasoline Inventories. NOT for CPA's but Rather the Harried Station Owners Who Want a Minimal, Easy to Use System.
SourceView Software International.

Service Supply Pipe Sizing: SPIPE. *Version:* 1.1. William W. Smith. Aug. 1988. *Compatible Hardware:* IBM PC & compatibles. *Operating System(s) Required:* PC-DOS/MS-DOS. *Language(s):* CB-80. *Memory Required:* CP/M 64k, MS-DOS 256k. *General Requirements:* 2 disk drives, printer.
disk $495.00.
8" disk $495.00.
3.5" disk $495.00.
demo disk $38.00.
documentation $25.00.
Allows User to Optimally Size Hot & Cold Service Water Pipe Systems. Computes Optimum Minimum Pipe Sizes & Total System Pressure Drop. All ASHRAE Data for Pressure Drops Through Pipes & Fittings Is Used.
Elite Software Development, Inc.

ServiceWorks. *Compatible Hardware:* Apple Macintosh Plus.
3.5" disk $7995.00.
Field Service Management.
Xcel.

SES-Structural Expert Series:

SES-Structural Expert Series: Structural Engineering Software. *Items Included:* Manuals in 3 ring binder. *Customer Support:* Free 90 day warranty & support; Yearly Maintenance with toll free number for fee paid yearly; On-site training available.
UNIX/386. Intel 386/486 (8Mb). Call vendor for price. *Addl. software required:* CGI Graphics Drivers. *Optimal configuration:* Interactive UNIX/386, 8Mb RAM, VGA Monitor, 150Mb Tape Drive, 300Mb Hard disk. *Networks supported:* TCP/IP, NFS.
IBM AIX. IBM RS/6000 (16Mb). Call vendor for price. *Addl. software required:* Computer Graphics Interface Runtime. *Optimal configuration:* 16Mb RAM Min, 640Mb hard disk, 150Mb tape drive. *Networks supported:* TCP/IP, NFS.
MS-DOS. Intel 386/486 (640k). Call vendor for price. *Optimal configuration:* MS-DOS 3.3 or higher. 640k RAM, 80Mb hard disk, VGA monitor.
A Complete System of over Twenty Separate Structural Engineering Programs Which Encompass the Full Range of Analysis & Design of Structural Systems. Included Are Design Modules for Structural Steel & Reinforced Concrete Design of Beams, Columns & Foundations.
ECOM Assocs., Inc.

Sesame Street: Numbers.
MS-DOS 3.1 or higher. 386 processor or higher (640k). CD-ROM disk $54.95 (Order no.: R1360). *Nonstandard peripherals required:* CD-ROM drive. *Optimal configuration:* 386 processor or higher, MS-DOS 3.1 or higher, 20Mb hard drive, 640k RAM, external speakers or headphones (with sound card) that are Sound Blaster compatible, VGA graphics & adapter, VGA color monitor.
Children Can Learn about Numbers from Their Favorite "Sesame Street" Characters. Number Recognition, Counting, Classification, Sets & Various Math Concepts Are Reinforced Through Hours of Games, Activities & Amusing Animations (Ages 3-6).
Library Video Co.

SET-IT PLUS. Oct. 1985. *Compatible Hardware:* All MS-DOS/PC-DOS compatible printers. *Operating System(s) Required:* PC-DOS/MS-DOS. *Memory Required:* 128k. disk $49.95.
M.A.P. Systems, Inc.

Set Optometric System ("SOS"): For MS-Windows 3.1. *Version:* 2.1s. Sep. 1993. *Items Included:* User's manual. *Customer Support:* Free initial training; 90-day media defect warranty; 1-year maintenance is 20% of current purchase price which includes phone support & upgrades after the 1st 6 months.
PC-DOS/MS-DOS 5.0 or higher. Any IBM/AT (386) or compatible (4Mb). Base price: $895.00 Single User; $1295.00 Multi User. *Optimal configuration:* IBM/AT-386, DX/SX-20 MHZ or higher, MS-DOS 5.0, 8Mb RAM, Hewlett Packard LaserJet III/IIIP SVGA (800x600). *Networks supported:* Novell 3.1, Lantastic, Banyan.
An Optometric Management System Used to Manage All Aspects of the Optometric Practice. Patient Information-Billing, Scheduling, Recall Letters, Insurance Forms, Accounts Receivable-Payable, Prescriptions, Contact Lens Information & Service Agreements, Are Just Some of Its Capabilities. Highly Configurable to Your Practice's Needs.
Software Engineering Technologies, Inc.

Seven Cities of Gold. *Compatible Hardware:* Apple II+, IIe, IIc, IIgs, Macintosh; Atari XL/XE; Commodore 64, Amiga; IBM PC.
Apple, Atari, Commodore, IBM. disk $14.95.
Amiga, Macintosh. 3.5" disk $19.95 (Order no.: 85623).
Commodore 64. (Order no.: 85616).
Atari.
3.5" disk $39.95 ea., incl. back-up disk & tchr's. guide.
Macintosh.
Amiga.
Simulation of 16th Century Spanish Conquistadors. Players Journey to the New World, Deal with the Natives, Establish Missions, & Search for Gold.
Electronic Arts.

Sewer Man. *Customer Support:* 800-929-8117 (customer service).
MS-DOS, Commodore 64. disk $39.99 (ISBN 0-87007-454-7).
A Game that Requires Skill, Not Luck.
SourceView Software International.

SEWER: Sewer Design & Analysis Program.
Mar. 1984. *Compatible Hardware:* AT&T PC 6300; Compaq; IBM PC, PC XT. *Operating System(s) Required:* PC-DOS, MS-DOS. *Language(s):* Compiled BASIC, FORTRAN. *Memory Required:* 256k.
disk $495.00, incl. manual (ISBN 0-922920-14-1, Order no.: PR0037).
manual only $25.00.
May Be Used to Model an Existing or Proposed Sanitary or Sewage Collection System. Analyzes an Entire System or Only a Portion of a System. Includes Extensive Error Checking & Descriptive Error Messages. Uses Either Manning's or Hazen-Williams Coefficients. Allows for 800 Reaches, 500 Manholes, & 200 Labels.
Research Engineers.

Sewermania: Arcade Plus Series. *Compatible Hardware:* TI-99/4A with Milton Bradley's MBX System.
contact publisher for price (Order no.: PHM3150).
Defuse a Bomb, Flood the Sewer & Use a Shovel to Blow-Up, Drown & Bash Killer Rats & Alligators in a Sewer. Speech Synthesis & Voice Recognition.
Texas Instruments, Personal Productivit.

Sex-O-Scope Report. John Townley & Robert S. Hand. 1984. *Compatible Hardware:* Apple II with Applesoft, Apple II, IIe, IIc, III, Macintosh; Commodore 64 & 128, CP/M based machines; IBM PC. *Operating System(s) Required:* Apple DOS, CP/M-80, PC-DOS, MS-DOS, MacFinder. *Language(s):* BASIC. *Memory Required:* Apple & CP/M 48k, PC-DOS 256, MS-DOS 128k or 256k, Macintosh 512k, Commodore 64k. *General Requirements:* 2 disk drives, printer. *Items Included:* Manual. *Customer Support:* Free phone support.
disk $150.00 ea.
CP/M (Kaypro 2). (ISBN 0-913637-45-9).
IBM PC. (ISBN 0-913637-46-7).
MS-DOS. (ISBN 0-913637-62-9).
Macintosh. (ISBN 0-87199-042-3).
Apple. (ISBN 0-913637-44-0).
Commodore 64. (ISBN 0-87199-058-X).
Computes & Prints Natal Horoscope in an 1800-Word Interpretation Written from an R-Rated Point of View. Includes Batch Loader & License to Sell Printed Output.
Astrolabe, Inc.

Sex-O-Scope: Screen Version. (Ancient Arts Ser.). John Townley & Robert S. Hand. 1980. *Compatible Hardware:* Apple II with Applesoft, Apple II+, IIe, IIc, IIgs with 5-1/4" disk drive, III, Macintosh with 2 disk drives; Commodore 64; CP/M-based machines; IBM PC & MS-DOS compatibles. *Operating System(s) Required:* Apple DOS, Commodore DOS, CP/M, MacFinder, MS-DOS, PC-DOS. *Language(s):* BASIC. *Memory Required:* Apple & TRS-80 32k, Commodore & CP/M 64k, IBM PC & MS-DOS 128k, Macintosh 512k. *Items Included:* Manual. *Customer Support:* Free phone support.
disk $39.95 ea., incl. manual.
Apple. (ISBN 0-913637-40-8).
Commodore. (ISBN 0-87199-019-9).
CP/M (Kaypro 2). (ISBN 0-87199-017-2).
IBM PC & MS-DOS. (ISBN 0-87199-016-4).
Macintosh. (ISBN 0-87199-048-2).
Computes Natal Horoscope & Interprets It in 1500 Words or More from an R-Rated Viewpoint.
Astrolabe, Inc.

Sex Olympics. May 1991. *Customer Support:* 90 days defective warranty, free technical supports at 215- 683-5609.
Amiga DOS. Amiga (1Mb). $39.95. *Optimal configuration:* Amiga, 1Mb RAM, color monitor.
Combines Sexual, Tongue-in-Cheek Humor, Adult (R-Rated) Graphics, Unusual Sound Effects & an Icon-Drive Point-and-Click Interface to Create a Game That's a Little Different Than Your Usual Fare.
Free Spirit Software, inc.

Sex Vixens from Space. *Compatible Hardware:* Atari ST, Commodore Amiga, IBM PC. $39.95.
Free Spirit Software, Inc.

Sexpert. *Version:* 2.1. *Compatible Hardware:* IBM PC & compatibles. *Operating System(s) Required:* PC-DOS/MS-DOS. *Memory Required:* 256k. *General Requirements:* Hard disk recommended. *Items Included:* 32 pg. Thinking Software catalog.
3.5" or 5.25" disk $29.95.
Online Knowledgebase Prgram That Can Answer Queries on Most Sex-Related Topics. Includes a Random Browse Mode.
Thinking Software, Inc.

SF Library. *Version:* 2.0. May 1989.
IBM PC & compatibles (512k). disk $39.95.
Macintosh (512k). 3.5" disk $39.95.
Personal Library Software with Science Fiction, Fantasy & Horror Database.
Future Visions Software.

SF/X: Standard Form 254 & 255 Printing System. *Version:* 2. Scott Fischer. Sep. 1989. *Customer Support:* Free telephone support.
IBM & compatibles (512k). disk $795.00 (ISBN 0-922373-03-5).
Software Program for the Generation of Standard Forms 254 & 255. These Forms Are Used by Virtually All Architects & Engineers Seeking Professional Service Contracts from the Federal Government. Menu Driven Program Allows Producer to Simply Fill in the Necessary Blanks to Produce Each Form. Program Produces Each Form Quickly Using Plain Paper & a PostScript Compatible Laser Printer.
Parallel Resource, Inc.

SFIM: Sales Force Information Manager. *Version:* 1.1. Feb. 1989. *Items Included:* Documentation. *Customer Support:* Phone support, on-site training & consulting.
MS-DOS 3.0 or higher. IBM PC & compatibles (640k). $30,000.00 for home office; $795.00 per add'l CPU.
Automates Direct Selling Operations for Manufacturers & Financial Service Companies. Integrated Package Includes: Database, Report

Generator, Letter Writer, Personal Organizer, Home-Office Infolink. Facilitates Tracking of Extensive Information Regarding Contacts, Companies, & Applications. Provides Sales Professionals with an Administrative Assistant. Automated Selling Strategies.
XYZT Computer Dimensions, Inc.

sFINX. *Customer Support:* 800-929-8117 (customer service).
MS-DOS. IBM/PS2. disk $699.99 (ISBN 0-87007-256-0).
Integrated Financial & Statistical Modeling System. User Can Construct Complex Financial Models. Provides Users with Graphic & Numeric Reports. Supports the 8087 Math Coprocessor Chip.
SourceView Software International.

SFT NetWare. *Compatible Hardware:* IBM PC & compatibles, PC AT. *Operating System(s) Required:* PC-DOS/MS-DOS 2.0 or higher. *General Requirements:* 80286/80386-based server with at least 512k RAM, hard disk, 192k RAM in each workstation.
100-node system $4695.00.
Network OS Software Which Includes the Following Fault Tolerant Capabilities: Read after Write Verification, Hot Fix, Directory Repair Utilities, Redundant Directory Structures Valfix, etc.
Novell, Inc.

Shadow: Glass Shading Analysis. Richardo Cidale. *Compatible Hardware:* IBM PC, PC XT, & compatibles. *Operating System(s) Required:* MS-DOS. *Memory Required:* 256k. *General Requirements:* 2 disk drives. *Items Included:* Manual. *Customer Support:* Toll-free telephone support.
$149.00.
Calculates the Shaded Area for up to 1000 Glass Exposures, Each of Which May Have up to 11 Different Shading Devices. Intended As a Tool to Aid in the Initial Design of Overhangs, Fins, & Louvers That Shade Glass Exposures. In Addition It Can Calculate Shading from Nearby Buildings, Trees, Other Structures. Full Screen Input & Editing Features Are Provided for Fast & Easy Input. Printer Reports Contain Plots of the Isometric, Front, Right Side, & Top Views of the Glass Sections & Shading Devices. The Solar & Transmission Heat Gains for Each Glass Section Are Also Included in the Reports.
Elite Software Development, Inc.

Shakespeare. Dec. 1989. *Items Included:* Registration card. *Customer Support:* Creative Multimedia Corporation warrants the CD-ROM disc & diskettes to be free from defects in materials & workmanship under normal use & service for a period of 90 days from date of purchase. Creative Multimedia Corporation offers Technical Support to customers as needed.
MS-DOS 3.1 or higher. IBM PC & compatibles with VGA Monitor (640k). CD-ROM disk $29.99 (ISBN 1-880428-03-2, Order no.: 10149). *Optimal configuration:* SuperVGA with 512k video memory. *Networks supported:* All LAN.
System Software 6.0.5 or higher. Macintosh Plus or higher (2Mb). 3.5" disk $29.99 (Order no.: 10149). *Nonstandard peripherals required:* Images display on all systems. *Optimal configuration:* Color image display requires 8-bit color, 32-bit QuickDraw & Color monitor. *Networks supported:* All.
Complete Unabridged & Total Works of the World's Greatest Playwright of All Times. Includes Plays, Poems, & Sonnets in Both Queen's English & Modern Versions.
Creative Multimedia Corp.

SHANE Augmentative Communication Series. Howard Shane. Jul. 1987. *Compatible Hardware:* Apple II+, IIe, IIc, III; IBM PC. *Memory Required:* 64k. *General Requirements:* Epsom FX or selected laser printers.
contact publisher for price.
Provides a Means of Vital Communication Capabilities for the Non-Speaking. With Seven Microcomputer-Based Programs, the Series Opens the Door to Spoken Communication for Those People Unable to Speak. The Apple II Series Programs Are Designed to Be Used with the Most Popular Speech Synthesizers & Output Devices & Are Designed for Use by Severely Physically Handicapped Children, Adolescents, & Adults. The Seventh Program Is Designed for Use by Speech-Language Clinicians & Uses IBM & IBM-Compatible Microcomputers Only.
Harcourt Brace Jovanovich, Inc. (Psychological Corp.).

Shanghai. *Compatible Hardware:* Commodore Amiga.
3.5" disk $39.95.
Strategy Board Game.
TenPoint Zero.

Shanghai Great Moments. *Items Included:* CD Manual.
Win '95. IBM. Contact publisher for price (ISBN 0-87321-003-4, Order no.: CDD-3109).
Activision, Inc.

Shanghai Great Moments. *Items Included:* Installation Guide.
DOS. IBM PC. Contact publisher for price (ISBN 0-87321-067-0, Order no.: CDD-3056).
Activision, Inc.

Shanghai Great Moments. *Items Included:* Installation Guide.
IBM PC. Contact publisher for price (ISBN 0-87321-070-0, Order no.: CDD-3056-NFR).
Activision, Inc.

Shanghai Great Moments. *Items Included:* Installation Guide.
MAC. Contact publisher for price (ISBN 0-87321-068-9, Order no.: CDM-3056).
Activision, Inc.

Shanghai Great Moments Demo. *Items Included:* Installation Guide.
IBM PC. Contact publisher for price (ISBN 0-87321-069-7, Order no.: CDD-3056D).
Activision, Inc.

Shanghai Great Moments (Saturn). *Items Included:* Installation guide.
Contact publisher for price (ISBN 0-87321-143-X, Order no.: SAT-3109-000-U3).
Activision, Inc.

Shanghai II. *Items Included:* Installation Guide.
Windows. IBM PC. Contact publisher for price (ISBN 0-87321-073-5, Order no.: MS2-3044).
Activision, Inc.

Shanghai II. *Items Included:* Installation Guide.
IBM PC. Contact publisher for price (ISBN 0-87321-072-7, Order no.: ID-230).
Activision, Inc.

Shanghai II. *Items Included:* Installation Guide.
IBM PC. Contact publisher for price (ISBN 0-87321-071-9, Order no.: PD-230).
Activision, Inc.

Shanghai Triple Threat (Saturn). *Items Included:* Installation guide.
Contact publisher for price (ISBN 0-87321-144-8, Order no.: SAT-3052).
Activision, Inc.

Shape.
Macintosh 512K higher. 3.5" disk $150.00.
Draws Crystal Shapes.
RockWare Data Corp.

The Shape Magician. *Compatible Hardware:* Apple II with Applesoft. *Operating System(s) Required:* Apple DOS 3.2, 3.3. *Memory Required:* 48k.
disk $29.95.
Graphics Program That Simultaneously Displays Shapes & How They Will Look on High-Resolution Graphics Screen.
Dynacomp, Inc.

Shape Master. *Compatible Hardware:* Apple II+, IIe, IIc; Franklin Ace. *Memory Required:* 48k.
disk $24.95.
Utility That Allows the User to Create, Display, Combine, Save, Edit, & Print Out Hi-Res Shapes for Use in Apple Programs. 2 Separate Entry Methods on 5 User-Selected Grid Sizes Ranging from 13 x 23 to 39 x 69, Allow for Definition of Many Different Shapes. Built-In Character Set in 3 Different Sizes to Mix Text & Graphics in the Displays Is Included. Printout Routines Allow the User to Make a Hard Copy of the Shupes, Even with a Non-Graphic Printer. Reverse Command Allows a Mirror Image of Any One of the Shapes, & Edit Commands Allow User to Edit Shapes & Shape Tables, Thus Allowing User to Create, Merge, Delete, & Load Individual Shapes from the Shape Table.
Compuware.

Shape Mechanic. Bert Kersey & Mark Simonsen. Dec. 1985. *Compatible Hardware:* Apple II, II+, IIe, IIc, IIgs. *Operating System(s) Required:* Apple DOS 3.3, ProDOS. *Language(s):* Machine, BASIC. *Memory Required:* DOS 3.3 48k, ProDOS 64k.
disk $39.95.
Enhanced Version of the APPLE MECHANIC & TYPEFACES Programs. New Features Include: Shape Editor; a Shape Capture Feature That Lets Users Convert Part of Any Hi-Res Image That Can Be Drawn &/or Animated; a Hi-Res Learning Tool Featuring Three Demo Programs; & a Hi-Res Character Editor (30 Fonts Are Included on the Disk).
Beagle Brothers.

Shapes & Colors: Colorful Introduction to Shapes & Patterns. Oct. 1994. *Items Included:* Registration card, instruction sheet. *Customer Support:* 900 support number $2.00 per minute; limited 60 day warranty.
Windows. IBM PC & compatibles (1Mb). disk $9.95 (ISBN 1-57269-008-9, Order no.: 3202 42165). *Addl. software required:* Windows 3.1 or higher. *Optimal configuration:* 286 or higher CPU, VGA or higher monitor, single 3.5" disk drive, any mouse.
A Colorful World Comes Alive As Your Child Learns to Recognize Basic Shapes & Geometric Concepts.
Memorex Products, Inc., Memorex Software Division.

Shareware Breakthrough Desktop Publishing Collection. *Version:* 2.0. *Items Included:* Browser/installer front end software. *Customer Support:* 90 day warranty, free call back technical support.
Windows 3.1. IBM 386 (4Mb). CD-ROM disk $9.95. *Nonstandard peripherals required:* CD-ROM drive. *Optimal configuration:* IBM 486, 8Mb RAM.
BeachWare.

Shareware Breakthrough for Mac. *Version:* 2.0. *Items Included:* Browser/installer/player front-end program. *Customer Support:* 90 day warranty,

free call back technical support.
System 6. Mac (2Mb, 4Mb under System 7). CD-ROM disk $9.95. *Nonstandard peripherals required:* CD-ROM drive. *Optimal configuration:* 8Mb RAM. *Networks supported:* Apple File Sharing.
BeachWare.

Shareware Breakthrough Games & Education. *Version:* 2.0. *Items Included:* Browser/launcher/installer front end software. *Customer Support:* 90 day warranty, free call back technical support.
Windows 3.1. IBM 386 (4Mb). CD-ROM disk $9.95. *Nonstandard peripherals required:* CD-ROM drive. *Optimal configuration:* IBM 486, 8Mb RAM.
BeachWare.

Shareware Breakthrough Multimedia Collection. *Items Included:* Browser/installer/copier front end software. *Customer Support:* 90 day warranty, free call back technical support.
Windows 3.1. IBM 386 (4Mb). CD-ROM disk $9.95. *Nonstandard peripherals required:* CD-ROM drive, sound card. *Optimal configuration:* IBM 486, 8Mb RAM.
BeachWare.

Shareware Breakthrough Programmers Collection. *Customer Support:* 90 day warranty, free call back technical support.
System 6. Mac Plus or higher (2Mb, 4Mb under System 7). CD-ROM disk $9.95. *Nonstandard peripherals required:* CD-ROM drive. *Optimal configuration:* 8Mb RAM. *Networks supported:* Apple File Sharing.
BeachWare.

Shareware Breakthrough Programmers Collection. *Items Included:* Browser/launcher/installer front end software. *Customer Support:* 90 day warranty, free call back technical support.
Windows 3.1. IBM 386 (4Mb). CD-ROM disk $9.95. *Nonstandard peripherals required:* CD-ROM drive.
BeachWare.

Shareware Breakthrough Utilities & Productivity. *Version:* 2.0. *Items Included:* Browser/launcher/installer front end software. *Customer Support:* 90 day warranty, free call back technical support.
Windows 3.1. IBM 386 (4Mb). CD-ROM disk $9.95. *Nonstandard peripherals required:* CD-ROM drive.
BeachWare.

Shark Alert. Aug. 1994. *Items Included:* Run time version of video for Windows 1.1.
Windows 3.1, PC-DOS/MS-DOS 3.1 or higher. 386SX 25mhz (4Mb). CD-ROM disk $34.95 (ISBN 1-57272-950-3). *Nonstandard peripherals required:* Sound card, VGA display-256 colors, MS-DOS CD-ROM. *Addl. software required:* MSCDEX Version 2.2 or higher. *Optimal configuration:* 486/33 8Mb, double speed CD-ROM.
Offers Approximately 5 Hours of Audio & Video That Covers Sharks from Biology Through Folklore. The Role of Sharks in the Ocean Ecosystem & Threats to Their Continued Existence Are Also Explored. A Trivia Game Tests the Users Learning.
Capitol Multimedia, Inc.

SharpShooter. *Version:* 1.3.2. May 1992. *Items Included:* 3 spiral bound manuals, temporary license key, NFS response time monitor. *Customer Support:* 60 day free phone support; 1 yr. support/updates: 20%.

SunOS 4.0.3 & higher, Ultrix. Sun, DEC RISC, Auspex, Solbourne (16Mb). $4995.00 base price. *Networks supported:* TCP/IP.
AIM Technology's Client/Server Performance Monitor for UNIX TCP/IP Based Servers. Monitors via Agents on the Servers & Tracks: NFS Workload, Breaking down NFS Read/Write Activity by File Systems & Clients; Network Services, Categorizing According to Application (i.e., NFS, X-Windows, Telnet, etc.) by Network Interface & Client; Storage Device Utilization & File Aging by File System, User, & Group.
AIM Technology, Inc.

Shear Wall Design - ST14M. *Version:* 04/1990. Aug. 1983. *Compatible Hardware:* IBM PC & compatibles. *Operating System(s) Required:* MS-DOS, PC-DOS. *Language(s):* Compiled. *Memory Required:* 256k. *Customer Support:* Technical hotline, "Lifetime" support at no charge. $295.00.
Shear Wall Design - ST14M Uses ACI 318-77 Chapter 10 Methods to Design Reinforced Concrete Shear Walls. Computes Points for Interaction Curves, Reverses Wind, Quickly Recalculates for Other Steel Schedules at Other Building Levels. Allows Interactive Design. Fully Compiled. English Units Only.
MC2 Engineering Software.

Sheep Production: Decision Aid. Merle W. Wagner. 1982. *Compatible Hardware:* Apple II Plus, IIe, IIc; IBM. *Memory Required:* 48k, 640k. *General Requirements:* Monochrome monitor, printer.
disk $29.95 (ISBN 0-922900-19-1, Order no.: CFD-556).
Budget Analysis for a Ewe-Lamb Operation. 21 Data Entries & 10 Calculations.
Cherrygarth, Inc.

Sheep Production Records. Merle W. Wagner. 1981. *Compatible Hardware:* Apple II Plus, IIe, IIc; IBM. *Operating System(s) Required:* Apple DOS 3.3, MS-DOS 2.0. *Language(s):* BASIC. *Memory Required:* 48k, 640k. *General Requirements:* Printer.
disk $49.95 (ISBN 0-922900-05-1, Order no.: CFR-555).
Provides Income/Expense Information for a Complete Sheep Operation. 400 Ewes per Data Disk. Breeding & History Available for Each Ewe.
Cherrygarth, Inc.

Sheet Metal-Ductwork Estimating. Richard T. Scott. May 1981. *Compatible Hardware:* IBM PC XT, PC AT, PS/2 & compatibles. *Operating System(s) Required:* PC-DOS, MS-DOS. *Language(s):* BASIC. *Memory Required:* 128kk. *General Requirements:* 10Mb hard disk.
disk $1500.00 (ISBN 0-923933-12-3).
video tape demo avail.
source code avail.
Designed for Mechanical Contractors. Patented, Single-Key Parts Description Enables Users to Input Data Without Having to Key in Part Numbers, or Select Functions from a Series of Menus.
Esscomate.

Sheetmate. *Version:* 3.1. *Compatible Hardware:* HP 3000. *General Requirements:* Lotus 1-2-3 release 1A and 2.01.
$1250.00 to $3000.00.
Allows user to Take HP 3000 Printer Reports Out of the Queue & Put Them into Any WK1, WKS, or Delimited ASCII File So That They Don't Have to Be Re-Keyed Automatically Reformats the Spreadsheet to Duplicate the Report's Column Width, Negative Numbers, Headings, Integers, Decimals, & Currency. Pages Can Be Selected, Such As Those with Totals.
Computer Innovations Co.

Sherlock Holmes. *Items Included:* Registration card. *Customer Support:* Creative Multimedia Corporation warrants the CD-ROM disc & diskettes to be free from defects in materials & workmanship under normal use & service for a period of 90 days from date of purchase. Creative Multimedia Corporation offers Technical Support to customers as needed.
MS-DOS 3.1 or higher. IBM PC & compatibles with VGA Monitor (640k). CD-ROM disk $29.99 (ISBN 1-880428-04-0, Order no.: 10150). *Optimal configuration:* SuperVGA with 512k video memory. *Networks supported:* All LAN.
System Software 6.0.5 or higher. Macintosh Plus or higher (2Mb). 3.5" disk $29.99 (Order no.: 10150). *Nonstandard peripherals required:* Images display on all systems. *Optimal configuration:* Color image display requires 8-bit color, 32-bit QuickDraw & Color monitor. *Networks supported:* All.
World's Greatest Consulting Detective & Dr. Watson Solve Crimes in These Classic Stories of Detection. Linoleum Block Prints by Dr. George Wells Accent the Holmes Stories. Also Includes the Medical Casebook of Dr. Arthur Conan Doyle by Alvin E. Rodkin & Jack D. Key.
Creative Multimedia Corp.

Sherlock: Riddle of Crown Jewels. *Compatible Hardware:* Commodore Amiga.
3.5" disk $39.95.
Text Adventure with Sound & On-Line Hints.
Activision, Inc.

Sherwood Forest. 1983. *Compatible Hardware:* Apple II+, IIe, IIc, IIgs. *Language(s):* Assembly. *Memory Required:* 48k.
disk $34.95.
First in a Series of Softoon Adventures. Provides a Storyline with the Hi-Res Color Graphics. Features Full Color Animation.
American Eagle Software, Inc.

Shifty Sam. *Compatible Hardware:* Apple II+, IIe, IIc, with Applesoft. *Memory Required:* 48k.
disk $29.95 (ISBN 0-676-32195-X).
backup disk $2.95 ea.
In This Game The Big Winner Is the Player with the Best Vocabulary. Players Have 90 Seconds to Come up with New Words from the Seven-Letter Words Old Shifty Sam Deals Them.
Random House Schl. Div.

Shiloh. Intentional Education Staff & Phyllis R. Naylor. *Items Included:* Program manual. *Customer Support:* Free techncial support, 90 day warranty.
School ver.. Mac System 7.1 or higher. Macintosh (4Mb). 3.5" disk contact publisher for price (ISBN 1-57204-332-6). *Nonstandard peripherals required:* 256 color monitor, hard drive, printer.
Lab pack. Mac System 7.1 or higher. Macintosh (4Mb). 3.5" disk contact publisher for price (ISBN 1-57204-308-3). *Nonstandard peripherals required:* 256 color monitor, hard drive, printer.
Site license. Mac System 7.1 or higher. Macintosh (4Mb). 3.5" disk contact publisher for price (ISBN 1-57204-333-4). *Nonstandard peripherals required:* 256 color monitor, hard drive, printer.
School ver.. Windows 3.1 or higher. IBM/Tandy & 100% compatibles (4Mb). disk contact publisher for price (ISBN 1-57204-309-1). *Nonstandard peripherals required:* VGA or SVGA 640x480 resolution (256), mouse, hard drive, sound device.
Lab pack. Windows 3.1 or higher. IBM/Tandy & 100% compatibles (4Mb). disk contact publisher for price (ISBN 1-57204-334-2). *Nonstandard peripherals required:* VGA or

TITLE INDEX

SVGA 640x480 resolution (2156), mouse, hard drive, sound device.
Site license. Windows 3.1 or higher. IBM/Tandy & 100% compatibles (4Mb). disk contact publisher for price (ISBN 1-57204-310-5). *Nonstandard peripherals required:* VGA or SVGA 640x480 resolution (256), mouse, hard drive, sound device.
This companion for young adult literature is ideal for students who don't know how to start that book report, or give that needed summary. Gentle prompts throughout the guide section of the program include Warm-up Connections, Thinking about Plot, Quoting & Noting, Keeping a Journal, If I Were ———' Responding to Questions, Using Quotations, Taking a Personal View, Write to Others, & Write a Sequel.
Lawrence Productions, Inc.

Shiloh 1862. *Compatible Hardware:* Atari 400, 800. *Language(s):* Atari BASIC (source code included). *Memory Required:* 48k. *General Requirements:* Joystick.
disk $33.95.
Brigade Level 1-Player Simulation of 1st Day of Battle of Shiloh.
Dynacomp, Inc.

Shipley Institute of Living Scale. *Version:* 2.011. Walter C. Shipley. *Customer Support:* Free unlimited phone support.
IBM PC & 100% compatibles. 3.5" or 5.25" disk $210.00 (Order no.: W-1003 (5.25"); W-1028 (3.5")). *Optimal configuration:* DOS 3.0 or higher (512k), & hard disk with one Mb of free hard disk space, printer.
This Popular Measure of Intellectual Ability & Impairment Has Been Used with Millions of Individuals 14 Years of Age & Older. The SILS Measures the Discrepancy Between Vocabulary & Abstract Concept Formation Providing a Useful Measure of Cognitive Impairment.
Western Psychological Services.

"Shippers" System. *Version:* 10.0. *Operating System(s) Required:* PC-DOS, MS-DOS. *Language(s):* COBOL. *Memory Required:* 256k.
contact publisher for price.
Integrated Microcomputer/Mini Mainframe Data Base System That Automates: Tariff Rate Construction; Tariff Updating; Bill of Lading Rating; & the Audit/Payment of Freight Bills. Interfaces with Host Mainframe Computers for the Downloading & Uploading of Information. Outputs of the System Include: Transportation Reports; Accounting Reports; Rate Distribution (Electronic & Paper Rate Books); & Auditing & Reporting Controls.
Transportation Concepts & Services.

ShipSmartz. *Version:* 1.8. Aug. 1990. *Items Included:* Looseleaf bound manual, runtime Engine, PrintSmartz autoswitch INIT. *Customer Support:* Free phone support.
Macintosh system 6.0.5 or higher. Macintosh (4Mb). 3.5" disk $395.00-$999.00. *Nonstandard peripherals required:* Electronic scale & barcode wand option, auto printer switch option. *Optimal configuration:* 16mhz or higher MAC, 4Mb RAM, 14MS hard drive or higher, scale, barcode wand. *Networks supported:* Appletalk, Ethernet.
Full Function Shipping Program. UPS Approved Users. Comes with UPS Manifest, Summaries, COD Tags, Labels & Reports, Available with Fed Ex Airbill & Rates, US Mail Rates. Type in Unlimited Additional Carriers. Includes Rate Shopping Between Entered Carriers. SWOG (Ship with Other Goods), Extensive Reports, People Database, Mail Merge Lists, Labels, Letters & Envelopes, Notes & List Management, Powerful Query Capabilities & More. Comes with Printsmartz Printer Switch Control INIT for Automatic Multiple Form Printing.
Elefunt Software.

Shoe Retail Management System. *Version:* 1.0. L. Williams. 1982. *Compatible Hardware:* IBM PC, Cromemco, Kaypro, Eagle, Epson, Zenith. *Operating System(s) Required:* MS-DOS, MP/M, CROMIX, CP/M-86, CP/M 2.2, C-DOS. *Language(s):* BASIC. *Memory Required:* 48k.
disk $995.00.
Tracks Fast & Slow Selling Items in Time to Allow Ordering Adjustments & Price Changes. Zeros in on Size Structuring & Reduces Accounting & Clerical Expenses.
Microtec Information Systems.

The Shoebox Accountant. May 1984. *Compatible Hardware:* IBM PC & compatibles. *Operating System(s) Required:* PC-DOS/MS-DOS, TurboDOS, XENIX. *Language(s):* CYMA C-OPT. *Memory Required:* 128k.
disk $395.00.
Offers the Small Business a Fully-Integrated Accounting System Including: General Ledger, Accounts Receivable, Accounts Payable, & Payroll.
CYMA/McGraw-Hill.

Shoebox 3. *Operating System(s) Required:* PC-DOS/MS-DOS 3.1 or higher. *Memory Required:* 198k.
disk plus $350.00, 10.00 per workstation.
Time & Expense Management System. Lets the User Schedule a Meeting with Any or All Other Users. The Program Checks Everyone's Schedule & Avoids Conflicts. Can Also Give the User a Display of Their Appointments, Which Shows Only the Appointment Dates & Descriptions.
R Plus R Assocs., Inc.

Shogi Master: (Japanese Chess). Yoshikazu Kakinoki. Jun. 1991. *Items Included:* 5.25" & 3.5" diskettes, 28 page user guide with rules & strategies, game history. *Customer Support:* Telephone customer support at no charge available M-F 9:00-5:00 Pacific time.
MS-DOS. IBM compatible (512k). $49.95 retail (ISBN 0-923891-29-3, Order no.: GS21). *Optimal configuration:* Supports VGA, EGA, CGA & Hercules graphics. Mouse optional.
Easy Way to Learn Shogi. Play Against Your Computer. Program Features Outstanding Graphics, 6 Play Levels from Beginner to about 2Kyu. (Strong Enough to Challenge Most Amateur Players, It Allows User to Take or Give Handicaps.) Records & Replays Games, Including Commentary.
Ishi Press International.

Shoot Video Like a Pro. Oct. 1994. *Items Included:* For Windows/MPC - QuickTime for Windows 2.01 (on the CD-ROM); For Macintosh - QuickTime 2.0 (on the CD-ROM). *Customer Support:* Free online support on America online using key word Zelos; Toll free number 1-800-345-6777; 90 day money back guarantee.
Windows/MPC; Macintosh. 386, 33MHz, (486 recommended) double speed CD-ROM drive (8Mb); Macintosh 68030, 25MHz, double speed CD-ROM drive (8Mb). CD-ROM disk $29.95 (ISBN 1-883387-15-9). *Nonstandard peripherals required:* QuickTime-compatible, 640x480, 256 color SVGA display, Microsoft compatible mouse, SoundBlaster compatible sound card with 8-bit sound; 13" 256 color monitor. *Addl. software required:* DOS 5.0 or higher, Microsoft Windows 3.1, QuickTime for Windows 2.01; System 7.0, Quicktime 2.0.
Shoot Professional-Looking Videos with This Award-Winning & Easy-to-Use CD-ROM! Learn from a Team of Video Consultants, Directors, Camera People, & Lighting Experts. Through a "Virtual Camera," You'll Discover Composition, Lighting, & Sound Techniques. Receive Feedback, Tips, & Trade Secrets for Your Next Home or Business Video.
Zelos.

Shop-Aid. Jul. 1988. *Compatible Hardware:* IBM PC & compatibles. *Memory Required:* 256k.
disk $24.95.
For the Supermarket Shopping List, the User Selects a Basic Category, Such As Fruits & Vegetables or Dairy Products, & Then Picks Each Item from Detailed Lists That Appear on the Screen. After Making Selections, the List Is Printed out in an Organized Format.
Zephyr Services.

Shop Floor Control. *Operating System(s) Required:* MS/PC-DOS. *Language(s):* BASIC compiled. *Memory Required:* 128k.
disk $100.00.
Designed to Create & Edit Reports. Explodes Operation Records, Merges in the Shop Floor Control File, & Totals the Pending Workloads in Hours. Capable of Updating the Status of Operations & Printing Reports on the Status of Shop Orders.
Bernard Giffler Assocs.

Shop Floor Control. *Version:* 3.3. (Integrated Manufacturing & Financial System Ser.). *Compatible Hardware:* UNIBUS/VAX; IBM PC. *Operating System(s) Required:* MS-DOS, Novell, Micro/VMS, VAX/VMS, UNIX. *Language(s):* DIBOL.
MS-DOS. $750.00 single-user.
DEC PDP-11/VAX. multi-user $1500.00.
Designed to Coordinate & Control the Orderly Flow of Work after the Start of Production. Acts As a Control Center, Collecting & Compiling Daily Production Information. Records Hours Worked, Quantity Completed, Any Rework, Scrap, & down Time.
Primetrack.

Shop Projects Plans Index. *Items Included:* Bound manual. *Customer Support:* Free hotline - no time limit; 30 day limited warranty; updates are $5/disk plus S&H.
MS-DOS. IBM & compatibles (256k); TRS-80. disk $69.95.
Apple (48k). disk $69.95.
Allows the Class to Have a Computerized List of All the Shop Project Plans Available. Scan a List of As Many As Several Thousand Project Plans Available. The Computer Then Refers the Student to the Correct Book, Textbook, Notebook, or Magazine to Find the Complete Set of Plans.
Dynacomp, Inc.

Shop Projects Plans Index. 1992. *Items Included:* Detailed manuals included with all Dynacomp products. *Customer Support:* Free telephone support to original customer - no time limit; 30 day limited warranty.
MS-DOS 3.2 or higher. IBM PC & compatibles, Apple, TRS-80 (512k). $69.95 (Add $5.00 for 3 1/2" format; 5 1/4" format standard).
Allows the Class to Have a Computerized List of All the Shop Project Plans Available to Those Particular Shop Students. When Students Use the Excuse That They Don't Know What to Make, the Computer Is a Fun Way to Select a Project. They Can Scan a List of As Many As Several Thousand Project Plans Available in Their Own Shop. The Computer Then Refers the Student to the Correct Book, Textbook, Notebook, or Magazine to Find the Complete Set of Plans.
Dynacomp, Inc.

Shopkeeper Plus. *Version:* 5.5.6. *Items Included:* 3 spiral bound manuals. *Customer Support:* First 90 days free, $179.00 annually thereafter.
Macintosh (2Mb). single user $595.00 (ISBN 1-879815-00-1, Order no.: SK5S).
Macintosh (2.5Mb). multiuser $1150.00 (ISBN 1-879815-01-X, Order no.: SK5M). *Addl. software required:* Networking software. *Networks supported:* Tops, Ethernet,

Appleshare.
Billing, Point of Sale, Inventory, Accounts Receivable, Customer Data Base, Mailing Labels, & Price Labels in One Integrated Program. Credit Card Verifier.
Shopkeeper Software International, Inc.

Shopping Center DealMaker's Handbook: Practical Transaction Guide with Ready-to-Use Forms on Computer Diskettes. Bruce G. Zimmerman. Oct. 1993. *Items Included:* 630-page, indexed, hardbound manual. Custom "README" File on each separate format version of Forms Diskette (e.g., the WordPerfect version comes with a README file specific to WordPerfect. *Customer Support:* 90-day warranty diskette(s) free from defects in material & workmanship.
MS-DOS. IBM & compatibles (512k). 3.5" or 5.25" disk $140.00, incl. 630-page manual (ISBN 1-881250-90-3). *Addl. software required:* WordPerfect 5.0 or higher. *Optimal configuration:* 2.0Mb space available on hard drive.
MS-DOS. IBM & compatibles (512k). 3.5" or 5.25" disk $140.00, incl. 630-page manual (ISBN 1-881250-93-8). *Addl. software required:* Microsoft Word for DOS 5.5 or higher. *Optimal configuration:* 2.0Mb space available on hard drive.
MS-DOS. IBM & compatibles (2.0Mb). 3.5" or 5.25" disk $140.00, incl. 630-page manual (ISBN 1-881250-91-1). *Addl. software required:* Word for Windows (IBM). *Optimal configuration:* 2.0Mb space available on hard drive.
Apple Macintosh Sysytem 7.0 or higher. Apple Macintosh. 3.5" disk $140.00, incl. 630-page manual (ISBN 1-881250-94-6). *Addl. software required:* Macintosh Microsoft Word 5.0 or higher. *Optimal configuration:* 2.0Mb space available on hard drive.
manual avail. (ISBN 1-881250-88-1).
Word Processing Add-On for Shopping Center Professionals & Their Lawyers to Quickly Generate Sophisticated Proposals & Preliminary Agreements. Self-Installing Diskette Comes in a Variety of IBM-Compatible & Macintosh Formats & Includes 1 630-Page, Indexed Forms Manual. Eight-Page Product Brochure.
Business Source Publishing Co.

Shopping List. *Compatible Hardware:* IBM. *Operating System(s) Required:* MS-DOS.
contact publisher for price.
Dynacomp, Inc.

Short Circuit. (Series A).
All Apple IIs. disk $5.00. *Optimal configuration:* Apple II, joystick.
Here's Another Game That Combines a Scientific Environment with Problem Solving Challenges! Don't Worry about Finding the Doomsday Bomb; You're Inside It...As the Unstoppable Clock Ticks off Its Maddening Countdown! It's Another High-Voltage Creation by David Schroeder, Who Gave You Dino Eggs & Crisis Mountain. The Bomb Is Protected by Twelve Fuses, Each in an Increasingly Complex Microcircuit. You Have Been Transformed into a Random Electronic Particle So That You Can Make Your Hazardous Way Through the Circuits & Trip the Fuses. The Air Is Electric with Tension As You Try to Survive the Neutrons, Protons, Polarity Changes & Other Threats to Your Existence. It's a Race Against Time to See Which Will Blow First - the Fuses (You Hope)...or the Bomb.
Word Assocs., Inc.

Short Circuit Analysis Program: Short. *Version:* 4.0. William W. Smith. Jan. 1988. *Compatible Hardware:* IBM PC & compatibles. *Operating System(s) Required:* CP/M, CP/M-86, PC-DOS, MS-DOS. *Language(s):* CB-80. *Memory Required:* 256k. *General Requirements:* 2 disk drives, printer.
disk $595.00.
8" disk $595.00.
3.5" disk $595.00.
disk demo disk $38.00.
documentation $25.00.
Uses the "Per Unit" Method to Calculate Symmetrical & Asymmetrical Fault Currents at Each Bus in an Electrical Distribution System. Electrical Networks with As Many As 600 Buses & 25 Motors. Handles Networks with Many Voltage Transformations. Output Includes Not Only Fault Current, But All Supporting Information Such As per Unit "X" & "R" Values, Bus Voltage Levels, & "X" to "R" Ratios.
Elite Software Development, Inc.

Short Circuit Current & Voltage Drop Analysis. *Items Included:* Bound manual. *Customer Support:* Free hotline - no time limit; 30 day limited warranty; updates are $5/disk plus S&H.
MS-DOS 2.0 or higher. IBM & compatibles (384k). disk $699.95.
demo disk $5.00.
Allows User to Rapidly Calculate Symmetric, Asymmetric, & Instantaneous 3-Phase Bolted & Line-to-Ground Fault Currents & Voltage Drops Throughout Electrical Systems of Mixed Reactive & Resistive Loads. Tables of Resistance & Capacitance Characteristics Are Included on the Program Disk for over 30 Types of Devices.
Dynacomp, Inc.

Short Hand. Arnold Schaeffer. *Compatible Hardware:* IBM PC, PC XT, PC AT, Portable PC, 3270 PC with IBM Display. *Operating System(s) Required:* DOS 2.00, 2.10, 3.00, 3.10. *Memory Required:* 128k.
disk $14.95 (Order no.: 6276572).
Allows User to Redefine Keys &, Using the "Alt" Key, Call up Often-Used Long Sequences of Keystrokes. Up to 36 Keys Can Be Defined, & User Can Create Individual Online Help Messages for Each Keystroke.
Personally Developed Software, Inc.

SHORT: Short Circuit Calculations. *Items Included:* Manual. *Customer Support:* Toll free telephone support.
MS-DOS. IBM PC & compatibles (256k).
Contact publisher for price.
Allows the Designer to Quickly Obtain the Maximum Potential Short Curcuit Current at Each Node (bus) in a Radial Electric Power Distribution System with up to 500 Components. Computes Bolted Phase to Phase and Ground Faults & Uses the "Per Unit" Method of Calculation.
Elite Software Development, Inc.

Shotpoint. *Version:* 1.5. Apr. 1991. *Items Included:* Illustrated user manual. *Customer Support:* Free 30 day phone support.
MS/PC-DOS 2.0. IBM PC, PS/2 (105k). disk $89.00, for a license agreement (ISBN 0-945851-16-2). *Nonstandard peripherals required:* Digitizer. *Addl. software required:* Hotdij 3.0. *Optimal configuration:* IBM PC, PS/2, 640k, Serial Port, hard disk, printer.
A Geophysical Digitizing Program That Lets the Hotdij User Digitize Shot-Point Information from Maps into an ASCII Text File. Can Manage the Hotdij Coordinates & Other Data into Files for Use by Other Application Software. The User Can Import the Files into Quattro Pro, Lotus, or Wordperfect.
Geocomp, Ltd.

Show Off. Denis Friedman. Oct. 1987. *Compatible Hardware:* Apple IIgs. *Operating System(s) Required:* ProDOS. *Memory Required:* 512k. *General Requirements:* Printer recommended.
3.5" disk $59.95 (ISBN 1-55790-024-8, Order no.: 32852).
Allows User to Prepare Interactive Shows with Computer, Design & Print Overheads, etc.
Broderbund Software, Inc.

The Show That Never Aired. Eddie Cantor. 1993.
IBM. Contact publisher for price (ISBN 1-887958-02-9).
Gari Brian.

Showoff Graphics Collection: World Events. Aug. 1988. *Compatible Hardware:* Apple IIgs. *Memory Required:* 512k.
3.5" disk write for info.
Supplemental Disk of Icons, Graphics, & Backgrounds.
Broderbund Software, Inc.

ShuBox Medical Tracker II. *Version:* 3.0. Jan. 1991. *Customer Support:* Free by prepaid phone (904) 528-0371, 45 day unlimited warranty, updates $3.50 each w/disk.
Macintosh. Apple MacIntosh. 3.5" disk $30.00.
Optimal configuration: MAC compatible printer of any type, hard disk required.
Tracks Status of Medical Insurance Claims for Medical Services Rendered.
A. H. Nussel.

ShuBox Music Librarian II. *Version:* 3.0. *Compatible Hardware:* Macintosh. *General Requirements:* Hard disk, any MAC compatible printer. *Customer Support:* Free by prepaid phone (904) 528-0371, updates $3.50 with disks.
3.5" disk $25.00.
Music Classification, Cataloging, Inventory, Search & Retrieval.
A. H. Nussel.

ShuBox II. *Version:* 3.0. *Compatible Hardware:* Macintosh. *General Requirements:* Hard disk; any MAC compatible printer. *Customer Support:* Free by prepaid phone (904) 528-0371, updates $3.50 with disk, new manual $15.00.
3.5" disk $40.00.
Small Business Accounting.
A. H. Nussel.

Shuffle Mania! Paul M Murphy. Aug. 1989. *Memory Required:* For CGA 256k; for EGA 320k; for VGA 384k.
IBM PC & compatibles. disk $49.95 (ISBN 0-945749-22-8, Order no.: 205).
IBM PS/2 & Laptops. disk $49.95 (ISBN 0-945749-21-X, Order no.: 203).
Combines Nine Games Focusing on Strategy & Eye/Hand Coordination. Shufflegames, Bowling, Curling & More.
XOR Corp.

Shuttle Encyclopedia. *Customer Support:* All of our products are unconditionally guaranteed.
Windows, Mac. CD-ROM disk $39.95 (Order no.: SHUTTLE). *Nonstandard peripherals required:* CD-ROM drive.
3015 Gifs Plus 3779 Text Files All about the Space Shuttle.
Walnut Creek CDRom.

Shuttle II. *Compatible Hardware:* Atari ST. *General Requirements:* Color monitor.
3.5" disk $39.95.
It's the Late 1990's & This New Shuttle Can Take off & Fly with the Minimum of Controls. Decide the Launch & Landing Details Then Take the Seat of Flight Commander for Liftoff. Find a Faulty Satellite & Go Out with Your Jet Pack & Haul It In. Then Return to Earth.
MichTron, Inc.

TITLE INDEX

SI Plus. *Version:* 1.3. Feb. 1989. *Items Included:* Manual with conplete instructions & software. *Customer Support:* Free support, 60-day update on all documentation.
MS-DOS, OS/2 (161k). IBM PC & compatibles, PS/2. disk $99.00.
Conversion Utility Which Converts Units from One System to Another (e.g. Miles to Kilometers, Curies to Rutherfords, etc.). Over 90,000 Different Conversions Can Be Performed in 85 Classes of Units. Can Be Run in Conjunction with Any Other Program. Conversion Tables Can Be Customized So That User Only Sees the Necessary Table.
GEOCOMP Corp.

Sicilian: English Attack: Electronic Chessbook. K. Nikitin. *Items Included:* Softcover book. *Customer Support:* Free telephone support by appointment.
MS-DOS 2.0 or higher. 80086 (512k). disk $25.00. *Nonstandard peripherals required:* Mouse, any graphics.
Atari ST. 520. *Nonstandard peripherals required:* Monochrome monitor.
Study of Chess Opening.
Chess Combination, Inc.

Sicilian 2.f4. K. Langeweg. 1993. *Items Included:* Book & disk with 500 or more games (over 200 annotated). *Customer Support:* Telephone support by appointment.
MS-DOS 2.0 or higher (512k). 3.5" disk $25.00, incl. softcover text. *Nonstandard peripherals required:* Mouse, graphics, 3 1/2" drive.
Atari ST (520k). Atari. disk $25.00. *Nonstandard peripherals required:* Monocrhome monitor DS/DD drive.
Authoritative Introduction to & Analysis of an Important Chess Opening.
Chess Combination, Inc.

Sid Meier's Railroad Tycoon. Sid Meier & Bruce Shelley. *Items Included:* Technical insert, manual, player's aid car. *Customer Support:* Free customer service (301) 771-1151, ext. 350.
IBM PC & compatibles (512k). 3.5" or 5.25" disk $59.95. *Nonstandard peripherals required:* Color monitor is required, mouse is recommended, 640k is required for VGA/ MCGA.
Big Business, Tough Decisions. Excitement, Challenge & Compelling Attention to Detail. RAILROAD Tycoon Re-Creates the Golden Age of Railroads in Your Choice of Four Regions of the World, & Gives You Complete Control Over Every Aspect of Your Industrial Empire. Computer Gaming World's "Game of the Year.".
MicroProse Software.

Side-Swipe. Allan S. Meritt. *Compatible Hardware:* IBM PC, PCjr, PC XT, PC AT, Portable PC, 3270 PC. *Operating System(s) Required:* PC-DOS 2.00, 2.10, 3.00, 3.10. *Memory Required:* 128k. *General Requirements:* Color monitor.
disk $14.95 (Order no.: 6276563).
Guide Each Man Safely Through a Maze of Corridors - Each with a Fixed or Moving Escape Hatch & All Populated by Deadly Creatures. Win an Additional Man for Each Successful Escape & Each 5000 Points Scored.
Personally Developed Software, Inc.

Side-View Game Option Module. *Items Included:* Manual, catalog, update card. *Customer Support:* Always free over the phone, disks replaced free for first 30 days, disks replaced for $10.00 after 30 days.
MS-DOS. IBM PC & Compatibles (512k). $14.95.
Commodore 64, 128. $14.95.
Amiga 500, 1000, 2000 (512k). $14.95.
Down on the Hardwood You Lead Your Team As Its Center at All Times. There Is Cheerleader Entertainment As the Coach Sets Strategies, Lineups, & Makes Substitutions.
SportTime Computer Software.

SideKick. *Version:* 2.0. Feb. 1991. *Compatible Hardware:* IBM PC & compatibles, PC XT, PC AT, PS/2 & compatibles. *Operating System(s) Required:* PC-DOS 2.0 or higher. *Memory Required:* 512k.
disk $99.95 (ISBN 0-87524-224-3).
Resident Utilities Including Calculators, a Time Planner, an Address Book, a Notebook & More.
Borland International, Inc.

Sidekick: for the Macintosh. *Version:* 2.0. *Compatible Hardware:* Apple Macintosh. *Memory Required:* 512k.
3.5" disk $99.95.
upgrade to 2.0 $34.95.
Provides the Following Desk Accessories: "Outlook: The Outliner", "MacPlan: The Spreadsheet", Mini Word Processor, Calendar, Auto-Dialing & Phone Logging, Analog Clock, Alarm System, Calculator, Report Generator, & Telecommunications, Including XModem File Transfer Protocol. Enables Users to: Log-On to Services Like Dow Jones, MCI Mail, & CompuServe; Jot Notes While on the Phone; Balance Checkbook & Recalculate the Balance; Keep Reminders of Important Dates & Meetings; Edit Text Files; Do Word Processing; & Create Various Kinds of Charts for Spreadsheet Functions.
Borland International, Inc.

SideKick Plus. *Compatible Hardware:* IBM PC & compatibles.
disk $199.95.
Integrated Desktop Software Including 9 Memory-Resident Note-Pads/Editors, Calculator, ASCII Table, Disk Navigator/Manager, Clipboard/Cut-&-Paste Buffer, Outline Processor, Calendar/Alarm Clock & Appointment Scheduler, Telecommunications. Can Be Configured to Use LIM/EMS or to Write to Disk to Conserve RAM Usage. The Resident Portion Can Occupy As Little As 64k.
Borland International, Inc.

SideTalk II. *Version:* 2.0. May 1986. *Compatible Hardware:* IBM PC AT & compatibles. Supports Prometheus PRO MODEM 1200; Hayes Smartmodem 1200, 1400; USRobotics Password 1200, AutoDial 212A, Courier 2400, MicroLink 2400; Multitech Multimodem 1200. *Operating System(s) Required:* PC-DOS/MS-DOS 2.0 or higher. *Memory Required:* 512k. *General Requirements:* 2 disk drives, serial port & Hayes-compatible modem. *Customer Support:* BBS support; 30-day free technical support - subsequent support is available through a 900 number. FAX number available also.
disk $125.00.
Convenience of a Memory-Resident, Multi-Tasking Program & the Power of a Data Communications Language in a Single Package. Designed For All Levels of Users, & Can Operate as a Memory Resident or Stand Alone Program. Features Help Screens, Pre-Defined Function Keys, Pop-Up Communications Menu, Full Feature Dialing Directory, Complete File Transfer Capabilities, & Command Files for Pre-defined Uses. Product Gives User a Complete Basic-like Language with More Than 95 Functions Allowing User To Automate Simple & Complex Communication Processes. User Can Program Product To Retrieve Electronic Mail, Schedule Automatic Data Transfers, or Create Bulletin Board System. Also Adds Microcom Network Protocol (MNP) To User's Existing Modem.
Lattice, Inc.

SIGAR ACCOUNTING/INVOICING

SIDEVIEW III: Graphics PC-DOS Security Menu. *Version:* 3.10. Aug. 1992. *Compatible Hardware:* IBM PC XT, PC AT, PS/2. *Operating System(s) Required:* PC-DOS 2.0 or higher. *General Requirements:* Hard disk. *Items Included:* 70 pg. documentation, diskette. *Customer Support:* Unlimited toll-free telephone.
MS/PC/DR DOS 2.0 or higher. IBM PC/XT/AT, PS/2 or compatible. disk $79.00 (Order no.: SV). *Networks supported:* Novell, Banyan, LANtastic.
A Non-Memory Resident GUI Menu System to Launch 2000 Application Programs. Import Windows Icons to Create a Graphical User Interface for DOS. Windows Not Required. With a Mouse or Cursor Keys, Run Any DOS Command or DOS Application, Including Lotus, WordPerfect or Windows. Designed for the Corporate Information Center or Systems Consultant Who Wants to Create a Windows-Style, Icon-Based Front End for Any MS/PC/DR DOS System. Includes Passwords to Limit Access for up to 2000 Applications & Full Screen Editors for AUTOEXEC.BAT & CONFIG.SYS. Not Memory Resident, Thus Guaranteed to Run 100% of Your DOS Applications. Not Copy Protected.
Keller Software.

Sideways. *Version:* 3. *Compatible Hardware:* Apple II, IIe, IIc; Apple IIGS IBM PC, PCjr, PC XT, PC AT. *General Requirements:* Epson MX-80 or MX-100 printer with GraphTrax.
disk $69.95.
upgrade $20.00.
Allows a Spreadsheet Wider Than a Printer to Be Printed Sideways. Output Is Rotated by 90 Degrees While Printing. Can Print Any Printable File Including Pert Charts & Program Listings. Features Include: Choice of Two Character Fonts of Different Sizes, Double-Strike Option for Added Print Density, Control over Margins, & Character Spacing.
Funk Software.

SIG-ICS Inventory Control System. Nov. 1983. *Compatible Hardware:* IBM PC. *Operating System(s) Required:* MS-DOS. *Language(s):* Compiled BASIC. *Memory Required:* 1000k. *General Requirements:* Hard disk. *Customer Support:* $10/mo. or $100/yr..
disk $499.00.
Offers the Following Features: Retrieval of an Item by Stock Number or by All or Part of the Product's Description; Retrieval of a Vendor's Record by Vendor Alphanumeric Code or Record Number; Purchase Orders Based upon the Reorder Point & Quantity or a System Using Cumulative & Current Sales Figures; Lists Quantities On-Hand, on Order, on Backorder, & the Number of Weeks' Supply Desired On-Hand. Allows Costing of Each Item by LIFO, FIFO, Average, & Actual Cost with a Summary of the Last Four Different Actual Costs Retained for Each Line Item.
Signature Software Systems, Inc.

SIGAR Accounting/Invoicing. David R. Ottew. Jun. 1986. *Compatible Hardware:* IBM PC & compatibles, PC XT, PC AT. *Operating System(s) Required:* MS-DOS, PC-DOS. *Language(s):* Compiled BASIC. *Memory Required:* 1000k. *General Requirements:* Hard disk, printer. *Customer Support:* $10/mo. or $100/yr..
disk $499.00.
Tracks over 1,000,000 Accounts by Name & Number, As Charge Accounts, Payable Accounts & Inquiries or Customer List. Full Reports, Search & Sort.
Signature Software Systems, Inc.

"Sight" Survey for Windows. Stacy Hoggarth et al. Oct. 1995. *Items Included:* Full manual with tutorials & on-line help. *Customer Support:* 120 days free phone support; 90 day moneyback guarantee; unlimited phone support is available for $249/year.
Windows 3.1 or 3.11 or Win/95. 386 (8Mb). $699.00; $499.00 intro through June 30, 1996 (ISBN 0-932071-15-5). *Nonstandard peripherals required:* VGA. *Addl. software required:* Windows 3.1 or higher.
A Windows-Based Three-Dimensional Coordinate Geometry Program with Simplified Methods for Solving Any Commonly Encountered Coordinate Geometry or Construction Surveying Problem. On-Screen Graphics Provide Instant Feedback & Ease-of-Design. CADD Is Built-In So There Is No Need for Additional Programs. Drawings Are AutoCAD.DWG & DXF Compatible.
Simplicity Systems, Inc.

SigmaPlot: Scientific Graphing Software.
Version: DOS 5.0, MAC 4.1, Windows 1.0. 1985. *Items Included:* 2 perfect bound manuals, sample files. *Customer Support:* 90 day money back guarantee, free technical support.
DOS. 386 or higher (640k). disk $495.00 (Order no.: SSPDR508). *Nonstandard peripherals required:* Graphics card. *Networks supported:* Novell.
Macintosh. MacPlus or higher (2Mb). 3.5" disk $295.00 (Order no.: SSPMR413).
Windows. 386 or higher (4Mb). $495.00 (Order no.: SSPWR103). *Nonstandard peripherals required:* Graphics card. *Addl. software required:* Windows 3.1. *Networks supported:* Novell.
Includes Automatic Error Bars, Huge Dataset Handling, Mathematical Transforms, Axis Breaks, Regressions, Non-Linear Curve Fitting & More. With Extensive Scientific Features, Extraordinary Control & Advanced Data Analysis Capabilities, SigmaPlot Creates Outstanding Technical Graphs for Lectures, Poster Sessions & Journal Publication.
Jandel Scientific.

SigmaScan - Image: Scientific Measurement System. *Version:* 1.2. *Compatible Hardware:* IBM PC & compatibles. *Operating System(s) Required:* Windows 3.1 in enhanced mode. *Memory Required:* 4000k. *Items Included:* 1 perfect bound manual. *Customer Support:* Free telephone technical support; newsletter free, 90 day money-back guarantee.
$495.00.
Allows You to Make Accurate, Automatic On-Screen Measurements from Digitized Images, Charts, & Graphs with Simple Mouse Clicks. It Supports TIFF, TGA, BMP, PCX & GIF Image Files Obtained from Scanners, Diskettes, CD-ROMS & Other Sources. Splice Images Together, Enhance Contrast, or Apply Pseudocolor. Then Trace with Your Mouse or Automatically "Floodfill" Objects Based on Their Gray Levels to Obtain Area, Perimeter, Angle, Slope, Distance, Compactness, Shape Factor, Major/Minor Axes, Center of Mass, Line Intensity, Area Average Intensity, Pixel Intensity, & Many More.
Jandel Scientific.

SigmaStat: Statistical Software. Apr. 1993. *Items Included:* 2 perfect bound manuals, sample files. *Customer Support:* 90 day money back guarantee, free technical support.
DOS. 286 or higher (640k). disk $395.00 (Order no.: SSTDR103). *Networks supported:* Novell.
Windows. 386 or higher (4Mb). disk $495.00.
Efficiently Computes T-Tests, Analysis of Variance, Rates & Proportions, Nonparametric Methods, Regressions & More. Helps You Select the Most Appropriate Statistical Procedure for Your Data, Automatically Checks That Your Data Fit the Assumptions Underlying These Methods & Runs Tests on Missing or Unbalanced Data. Creates Detailed Reports & Interacts Directly with SigmaPlot to Create Graphs from Your Results.
Jandel Scientific.

The Sign of the Beaver. Intentional Education Staff & Elizabeth Spease. Apr. 1996. *Items Included:* Program manual. *Customer Support:* Free technical support, 90 day warranty.
School ver.. Mac System 7.1 or higher. Macintosh (4Mb). 3.5" disk contact publisher for price (ISBN 1-57204-378-4). *Nonstandard peripherals required:* 256 color monitor, hard drive, printer.
Lab pack. Mac System 7.1 or higher. Macintosh (4Mb). 3.5" disk contact publisher for price (ISBN 1-57204-354-7). *Nonstandard peripherals required:* 256 color monitor, hard drive, printer.
Site license. Mac System 7.1 or higher. Macintosh (4Mb). 3.5" disk contact publisher for price (ISBN 1-57204-379-2). *Nonstandard peripherals required:* 256 color monitor, hard drive, printer.
School ver.. Windows 3.1 or higher. IBM/Tandy & 100% compatibles (4Mb). disk contact publisher for price (ISBN 1-57204-355-5). *Nonstandard peripherals required:* VGA or SVGA 640 x 480 resolution, 256 monitor, mouse, sound device.
Lab pack. Windows 3.1 or higher. IBM/Tandy & 100% compatibles (4Mb). disk contact publisher for price (ISBN 1-57204-380-6). *Nonstandard peripherals required:* VGA or SVGA 640 x 480 resolution, 256 monitor, mouse, sound device.
Windows 3.1 or higher. IBM/Tandy & 100% compatibles (4Mb). disk contact publisher for price (ISBN 1-57204-356-3). *Nonstandard peripherals required:* or SVGA 640 x 480 resolution, mouse, sound device.
This companion for young adult literature is ideal for students who don't know how to start that book report, or give that needed summary. Gentle prompts throughout the guide section of the program include Warm-up Connections, Thinking about Plot, Quoting & Noting, Keeping a Journal, If I Were ———' Responding to Questions, Using Quotations, Taking a Personal View, Write to Others, & Write a Sequel.
Lawrence Productions, Inc.

Signal. *Compatible Hardware:* IBM PC, PC XT, PC AT, Portable PC. *Operating System(s) Required:* PC-DOS 2.0 or higher. *Memory Required:* 384k. *General Requirements:* Serial interface card (9600 baud).
$595.00.
Gives Access to Stock Market Data. Users Will Be Able to Track up to 600 Issues at One Time, Set Limit Alerts & Get News Alerts, Track the Market While the PC Is Turned Off. Users May Subscribe to NYSE, AMEX, NASDAQ, CBT, CME, CEC, KCBT, NYFE, Options from All Major Exchanges, Plus Major Indices & Market Statistics. 1-2-3 or Symphony Will Allow Plotting of Price Trend Lines, Real-Time Intra Day Interval Charting, Tracking of Moving Averages, Performing of Real-Time Portfolio Valuations, etc.
Lotus Development Corp.

Signal Integrity: Polaris. *Version:* 6.1. Jul. 1994. *Items Included:* Current Analysis Manual Set, Signal Integrity User's Guide. *Customer Support:* Free technical support with purchase. Maintenance may be purchased for a 1 year period of time from invoice. Updates available. Upgrades allow credit for exiting packages.
Windows 3.1 or higher. IBM-PC & compatibles. disk $4900.00 (Order no.: SI-PC3-350). *Addl. software required:* Design Center with Schematic Capture, Circuit Analysis & Simulation.
Analysis Tool for Extracting Transmission Line, Parasitic Capacitance, & Coupling Values from Printed Circuit Board (PCB) Layouts. Extracted Values Are Applied to Circuit Simulations in PSpice, Providing for Analysis of Crosstalk, Reflection, & Delay Effects in the Circuit Design. Gives the Designer the Ability to Verify That the Design Will Perform to Specification after the Layout Is Created & Before Boards Are Manufactured, Thus Reducing the Overall Cost of the Design.
MicroSim Corp.

Signature Generator. Dean Lance Smith. Dec. 1982. *Operating System(s) Required:* CP/M-80. *Language(s):* Assembly. *Memory Required:* 16k.
Single system license. 8" disk $150.00 (ISBN 0-918699-02-9).
Multi-system license. 8" disk $495.00 (ISBN 0-918699-03-7).
documentation $15.00 (ISBN 0-918699-01-0).
Calculates Most Free-Run & Some Second-Test Signatures. Calculates VCC, Address Line, ROM Output & Decoder Output Free-Run Signatures. Handles up to 16M Samples, 24 Address Lines, 64 Decoder Outputs & ROMs up to 32K Bytes. Results Can Be Displayed in Funny (0 to 9, A,C, F,H,P,U) or Standard Hexadecimal. Hewlett-Packard or a User Specified Feedback Tap Pattern Can Be Used.
Dean Lance Smith.

Signwriter Computer Program Package: the world's first sign processor. *Version:* 4.2. Valerie Sutton et al. Sep. 1993. *Items Included:* Four disks: Program Disk, Dictionary Disk (including Sutton's American Sign Language/English Dictionary on-line), Other Countries Disk (including 11 countries) and Lessons Disk (including Lesons in Sign Writing on-line). Also included: hard-backed, 3-ring notebook with 3 manuals teaching how to use the computer program, a second hard-backed, 3-ringed notebook with the second edition of Lessons in Sign Writing, & keyboard reference card. *Customer Support:* Free technical support by phone, TTY, FAX, or E-Mail for all registered users. A limited version of the program called Signwriter Shareware can also be downloaded on E—Mail without charge. User becomes automatically registered when complete package is purchased. There are no licensing fees.
MS-DOS (64K). IBM PC & compatibles. Non-members $130.00 (ISBN 0-914336-63-0). *Addl. software required:* CGA, EGA or VGA graphics.
Macintosh Plus or higher. Members & Bookstores $95.00. *Addl. software required:* SoftPC.
Annual Membership $10.00.
Word Processor for Eleven Signed Languages, Fingerspelling & Words. Symbols Can Be Rotated & Flopped with Simple Keystrokes. Typed Signs Automatically Wrap to the Next Line. Has Built-In Dictionary, Which Means Many Signs are Pretyped for User & Can Be Pasted into Document as it's Being Typed. Three Modes of Printing Included: Epson Compatible Dot Matrix Printing, Hewlett-Packard Compatible Ink-Jet or Laser, & Postscript Laser Printing.
Center for Sutton Movement Writing, Inc., The.

SIGSTAT. *Compatible Hardware:* Atari ST, Hewlett-Packard, IBM PC & compatibles. *Operating System(s) Required:* MS-DOS, TOS, Unix. *Language(s):* FORTRAN 77. *Memory Required:* 512k.
disk $595.00.
disk for education, non-profit $395.00.
Features Include the Following: Regressions on up to 80 Variables, Factor Analyses on 50 Variables, Analysis of Variance on Eight Way

TITLE INDEX

Designs, Missing Values, Residuals, Matrix Input/Output Options, Factor Scores & Cannonical Variables, Interactive Model Construction, Discriminant, Probit, & Time Series Analysis, Quality Control, Multi-Dimensional Scaling, Linear Programming, Cluster Analysis, Non-Parametrics, High Resolution on Graphics for Screen & Printer, 120 Programs in All.
Significant Statistics.

The Silence of the Lambs. Apr. 1995. *Customer Support:* Dedicated voice mail phone number; will respond back to consumer.
Windows 3.1 or higher; Macintosh. IBM or 100% compatible 486SX 25MHz (4Mb); 68030/68040 Color Mac System 7.1 or higher (4Mb). CD-ROM disk $19.99 (ISBN 1-57339-011-9, Order no.: ROMI2937OR). *Nonstandard peripherals required:* 2X CD-ROM drive.
Rookie FBI Agent Clarice Starling Strikes up an Uneasy Alliance with Hannibal Lector, a Jailed Psychotic Criminal, in the Hope That He May Help Catch a Serial Killer.
Image Entertainment.

Silent Butler. *Compatible Hardware:* Atari XL/XE. *Memory Required:* 64k. *General Requirements:* 1050 disk drive.
disk $24.95 (Order no.: DX5082).
Home Finances.
Atari Corp.

Silent Service. *Compatible Hardware:* Apple II, II+, IIe, IIc, IIgs; ST; Commodore 64/128, Amiga; IBM PC, PCjr; Tandy; Atari ST. *Customer Support:* Free customer service, (410) 771-1151, Ext. 350.
3.5" or 5.25" disk $19.95.
Simulation of an American World War II Submarine. The Player, As the Submarine Commander Must Sink the Enemy's Ships & Keep His Own Submarine from Being Destroyed.
MicroProse Software.

Silent Service II. *Items Included:* Manual, keyboard overlay, map. *Customer Support:* Free customer service, (410) 771-1151, Ext. 350.
3.5" or 5.25" disk $59.95. *Nonstandard peripherals required:* Supports CGA, EGA & Tandy 16-color; 640k is required for VGA/MCGA.
IBM PC & compatibles (512k).
World War II Submarine Simulation. Picks up Where Its Predecessor Left off -- with Enhanced, Digitized Graphics & Thrilling New Game Options -- Including Campaign Play -- That Give You Even More Decisions, Even More Intense Action.
MicroProse Software.

SilentPartner. *Version:* 7. Aug. 1990. *Customer Support:* 1 year free support & updates; After 1 year $150.
Mac Plus or higher (1Mb), IBM with Windows. 3.5" disk $1495.00. *Nonstandard peripherals required:* 20Mb hard disk.
demo $30.00.
Integrated Software That Combines Database & Word-Processing Capabilities with Accounting/Bookkeeping Capabilities. Designed for Commercial Photographers with Macintosh.
SilentPartner, Inc.

Silicon Salad. Bert Kersey & Mark Simonsen. *Compatible Hardware:* Apple II, II+, IIe, IIc, IIgs. *Operating System(s) Required:* Apple DOS 3.3.
disk $24.95, incl. Apple Command Chart.
Includes the Programs from Beagle's Tip Books #5, #6, & #7, & Tips & Tricks Chart #1 Also Includes Text Imprinter, Word Sorter, Beagle Blackjack, Disk Scanner, DOS-Killer, Two-Track Cat, Program Splitter, Undelete, etc.
Beagle Brothers.

SILVERRUN - Application Design Center & Distributed Application Generators. *Version:* 2.0. Aug. 1993. *Items Included:* One complete set of documentaiton.
Macintosh System 7; OS/2; Windows. Macintosh 386 or higher; IBM PS/2 & compatibles; IBM PC & compatibles. Contact publisher for price. *Networks supported:* Appletalk, TCIP, Ethernet.
Provides a Graphically Based Development & Maintenance Environment Across the Application Development Lifecycle. A Data/Object Model-Driven Approach Featuring an Object Repository, SILVERRUN ADC Builds Client/Server & Distributed Applications That Can Be Split among Host Machines & Workstations on a Network. A Single Application Definition Can Generate Source Code for Execution on Multiple Target Environments-Allowing SILVERRUN to Develop Applications That Are Uniform from Platform to Platform & Truly Portable for Broad Networking & Distribution.
Computer Systems Advisers, Inc.

SILVERRUN ERX, RDM, DFD, WRM. *Version:* 2.1. Apr. 1992. *Items Included:* Manuals. *Customer Support:* 90 days unlimited warranty & hot-line support; maintenance (1 yr), $375/module (ERX, DFD, WRM). RDM module $450.
Macintosh. Contact publisher for price.
Windows. IBM PC & compatibles.
OS/2. IBM PS/2 & compatibles.
Suite of Tools That Automate Key Steps in the Software Development Life-Cycle, Including Construction of the Underlying Models Necessary for Building Relational Database Applications. Available for the Macintosh, Windows & OS/2 PM. Modules Include the Following: Entity Relationship Expert (ERX), Relational Data Modeler (RDM), Data Flow Diagrammer (DFD), & Work Group Repository Manager (WRM).
Computer Systems Advisers, Inc.

Sim Farm Try & Buy. Maxis SimFarm & SimCity Staff. *Items Included:* The package includes a 3.5" diskette, a mini-manual & a Try & Buy Brochure.
Windows. IBM PC & compatibles, 386 or higher (4Mb). disk $29.99 (ISBN 1-57548-001-8).
SimFarm Is a Game.
IBM Software Manufacturing Solutions (ISMS).

SimAnt: The Electronic Ant Colony. Nov. 1991. *Items Included:* Comprehensive manual with science section on real ants. *Customer Support:* 90 days limited warranty, free technical support for registered customers.
System 6.0.2 or higher, System 7 compatible. Macintosh Plus, SE, SE/30, Classic, LC, II family, Portable. 3.5" disk $69.95 (ISBN 0-929750-52-7). *Optimal configuration:* Under 6.0.2: Color - Hard drive & 2Mb RAM required; B&W - 1Mb RAM required. Under System 7: Color - Hard drive & 2.5Mb RAM required; B&W - 2Mb RAM required.
MS-DOS 3.1 or higher. IBM PC AT, PS/1, PS/2; Tandy & 100% compatibles (640k). disk $59.95 (ISBN 0-929750-50-0).
Windows. IBM PC AT, 12mhz or higher - standard or enhanced mode (2Mb). disk $59.95 (ISBN 0-929750-51-9). *Optimal configuration:* Requires Windows 3.0 or 3.1, mouse required.
Puts You in Charge of an Ant Colony Out to Conquer a Suburban Back Yard. By Directly Controlling One Ant & Manipulating Ant Caste & Behavior, You Can Help Your Ant Colony Overcome Insect & Human Obstacles & Lead Your Fellow Ants to Victory-Invasion of the Human's House.
Maxis.

SIMEARTH: THE LIVING PLANET

SimCity Classic.
Macintosh Plus, Macintosh SE, Macintosh II (512k). Version 1.1 (02/1989) $49.95.
MS-DOS, Windows. IBM & compatibles, Tandy. (09/1989) $49.95. *Nonstandard peripherals required:* EGA, CGA, Hercules or Tandy card. *Optimal configuration:* Mouse optional.
Amiga (1Mb). Version 1.1 (04/1989) $44.95. *Nonstandard peripherals required:* Mouse.
Game Simulation Package.
Maxis.

SimCity Classic: The Original City Simulator.
Customer Support: 90 days limited warranty, free technical support for registered customers.
System 6.0.2 or higher, System 7 compatible. Macintosh Plus, (Classic, SE, LC, II, Quadra, Portable, PowerBook) series. 3.5" disk $59.95 (ISBN 0-929750-59-4). *Optimal configuration:* System 6.0.2: Color - Requires 2Mb RAM & hard drive; Monochrome - Requires 1Mb RAM. Under System 7: Color - Requires 2.5Mb RAM & hard drive; Monochrome - Requires 2Mb RAM.
MS-DOS. IBM PC, PC XT, PC AT, PS/2 & 100% compatibles (512k, EGA 640k). disk $49.95 (ISBN 0-929750-01-2). *Optimal configuration:* Mouse & printer optional.
Windows. IBM & 100% compatibles (2Mb). disk $59.95 (ISBN 0-929750-43-8). *Optimal configuration:* Requires Windows 3.1 standard or enhanced mode, hard disk. Supports keyboard & mouse.
Puts You in the Role of Mayor & Urban Planner As You Direct the Development of Your Own City. Fight Crime, Unemployment, & Pollution. Control Budgets, Taxes & Transit Systems. Deal with Disasters & Public Opinion.
Maxis.

SimCom 25. *Operating System(s) Required:* CP/M, MS-DOS. *Language(s):* BASIC. *Memory Required:* 64k.
disk $5000.00.
Complete Hotel Management System for the Small Hotel. Handles Reservations, Room Management, Guest Accounting, & Night Auditing, & Provides a Daily Revenue Report, a Management Report, & Accounts Receivable for up to 2,500 Reservations or Transactions.
New Systems, Inc.

SimCom 50. *Operating System(s) Required:* CP/M, MS-DOS. *Language(s):* BASIC. *Memory Required:* 64k.
disk $7500.00.
New Systems, Inc.

SimCom 75. *Compatible Hardware:* IBM PC XT with hard disk. *Operating System(s) Required:* CP/M, MS-DOS. *Language(s):* BASIC. *Memory Required:* 64k.
disk $10000.00.
Handles Unlimited Reservations, Room Management, Guest Accounting, & Night Audit, & Provides a Daily Revenue Report, Management Reports, Accounts Receivable, & a Special Guest History.
New Systems, Inc.

SimEarth: The Living Planet. Fred Haslam & Will Wright. Jan. 1991. *Items Included:* Manual. *Customer Support:* 800-33-MAXIS for customer support & tech assistant.
PC-DOS/MS-DOS 3.1 or higher, Windows. IBM PC & Tandy or compatibles dual-packed for 3.5" & 5.25" disks (640k). $69.95.
Macintosh system 6.0 or higher (1mb). $69.95. *Optimal configuration:* Dual-packed with monochrome & color versions.
Gives Players Control over the Evolution of a Planet, from the Origin of Life to the Development of Intelligence, Civilization, &

919

Interplanetary Travel. Players Can Create Their Own Planet from Scratch or Use One of Seven Pre-Built Planets: Aquarium; Stag Nation; Earth - Cambrian Era; Earth - Modern Day 1990; Mars; Venus; & DaisyWorld. Represents a Departure from Other Software Games in Its Design & Content. Players Can Explore the Game with no Set Goal, or Pursue Goals of Their Own - Developing a Civilization of Intelligent Dinosaurs, for Example, or Purposely Creating a Greenhouse World to See Which Species Survive.
Maxis.

SimLife: The Genetic Playground. Sep. 1992. *Items Included:* Comprehensive manual with suggested experiments, separate lab wkbk. *Customer Support:* 90 days limited warranty, free technical support for registered customers.
System 6.0.2 or higher, System 7 compatible. Macintosh SE, SE/30, Classic, LC, Portable, (PowerBook, II, Quadra) family. 3.5" disk $69.95 (ISBN 0-929750-58-6). *Optimal configuration:* Under 6.0.2: Color - 2.5Mb RAM required; B&W - 2Mb RAM required. Under 7: Color - 3Mb RAM required; B&W - 2.5Mb RAM required. Hard disk required.
An Advanced Biological Simulation That Allows You to Design Plants & Animals from the Genetic Level to Influence How They Look, Act & Eventually Evolve. Set Them Loose in Your Own Custom-Built Ecosystem & Test Your Species' Ability to Survive & Adapt.
Maxis.

Simon Hintbook. *Items Included:* Installation Guide.
IBM. Contact publisher for price (ISBN 0-87321-093-X, Order no.: HBK-3039).
Activision, Inc.

Simon the Sorcerer. *Items Included:* Installation Guide.
IBM PC. Contact publisher for price (ISBN 0-87321-076-X, Order no.: CDD-3039).
Activision, Inc.

Simon the Sorcerer. *Items Included:* Installation Guide.
IBM PC. Contact publisher for price (ISBN 0-87321-075-1, Order no.: MS2-3039).
Activision, Inc.

Simon the Sorcerer with Hintbook. *Items Included:* Installation Guide.
IBM PC. Contact publisher for price (ISBN 0-87321-074-3, Order no.: MS2-3039H).
Activision, Inc.

Simple Accounts. David Patch. 1985. *Compatible Hardware:* Apple II+, IIc, IIe, IIgs; IBM PC. *Operating System(s) Required:* Apple DOS 3.3, PC-DOS 2.0. *Language(s):* BASIC. *Memory Required:* Apple 48k, IBM 512k.
IBM. disk $39.95 (ISBN 0-942132-51-3, Order no.: I-1150).
Apple. disk $39.95 (ISBN 0-942132-50-5, Order no.: A-1150).
Administrative Computer Tool for Keeping Current Accounting Records for Various Money Accounts. As Many As Ten Accounts Allow Entry of Debits & Credits. Balances Are Kept Current at All Times. Statements of Accounts Can Be Printed.
Electronic Courseware Systems, Inc.

Simple Calc. David Patch. 1984. *Compatible Hardware:* Apple II+, IIc, IIe, IIgs; Commodore 64, 128; IBM PC. *Operating System(s) Required:* Apple DOS 3.3, PC-DOS 3.3. *Language(s):* BASIC. *Memory Required:* Apple 48k, Commodore 64k, IBM 640k. *General Requirements:* CGA card for IBM.
IBM. disk $39.95 (ISBN 0-942132-53-X, Order no.: I-1149).
Apple. disk $39.95 (ISBN 0-942132-52-1, Order no.: A-1149).
Commodore. disk $39.95 (ISBN 1-55603-003-7, Order no.: C-1149).
Calculator with Operations in Sequential Steps. Executes Addition, Subtraction, Multiplication, Division, Squares, & Square Roots. There Are Four Variables Available.
Electronic Courseware Systems, Inc.

Simple Log. Pete Charlton. 1980. *Compatible Hardware:* IBM PC & compatibles. *Operating System(s) Required:* MS-DOS. *Language(s):* BASIC. *Memory Required:* 512k.
disk $1295.00 to $995.00.
second station $125.00.
Traffic, Billing & Affidavits System for Radio.
The Management.

Simple Mailer. Dean Franks. 1985. *Compatible Hardware:* IBM PC. *Operating System(s) Required:* PC-DOS 2.0. *Language(s):* BASIC. *Memory Required:* 512k. *General Requirements:* CGA card for IBM.
disk $49.95 (ISBN 1-55603-015-0, Order no.: I-1160).
Administrative Computer Program Designed for Mailing Records. Allows the User to Store over 1000 Records & Specify up to 16 Different Parameters to Extract Information for Printing. The Records Sorting Feature Also Permits the User to Print Records in Zip Code or Alphabetical Order. In Addition to Printing Mailing Labels & Reports, It Can Be Used with MailMerge to Generate Form Letters.
Electronic Courseware Systems, Inc.

SimpleSpan Utilities I: Beam Analysis Disk Accessory Package.
Macintosh (512k or higher). disk $149.00.
Contains Two Structural Design Desk Accessories for Architects & Engineers. Enables User to Analyze & Select Sizes of Simply Supported or Cantilevered Wood Beams. Software Analyzes Shear, Deflection & Bending & Calculates Required Beam Size. Features Include Ability to Revise or Delete Individual Loads, Set User Options & Review Beam Calculations. Also Can Print Summary Report of Calculations & Allows Users to Enter Steel Stress Values. Adjusts Joist Spacing & Sizes Rough-Sawn Lumber & Draws Shear & Moment Diagrams.
Arch Software, Inc.

SIMPLEX-V: An Interactive Computer Program for Experimental Optimization. *Version:* 2.2. S. N. Deming. Jul. 1985. *Compatible Hardware:* IBM PC, PC XT, PC AT. *Operating System(s) Required:* PC-DOS/MS-DOS 2.1 or higher. *Language(s):* Turbo Pascal. *Memory Required:* 256k. *Items Included:* User manual, 5.25" disk. *Customer Support:* Free telephone support to registered users.
disk $295.00 (ISBN 0-932651-13-5).
Adjusts up to 12 Continuous Variables Simultaneously Using a Modified Sequential Simplex Algorithm.
Statistical Programs.

Simplicity Dental Software. *Version:* 7.406. *Compatible Hardware:* Apple Macintosh Plus. *General Requirements:* Hard disk, ImageWriter I or II.
$2450.00 includes Omnis 3 Plus Runtime single user & 60 days telephone support.
$2750.00 requires Omnis 3 Plus (not included).
demo & manual $65.00.
Schedules Appointments, Records Information.
Simplicity Dental Software Systems, Inc.

Simplicity Is Power: Make Using Your Macintosh Faster, Easier & More Fun!
Version: 1.1.8. Kirk A. Kerekes. Mar. 1993. *Customer Support:* 30 day M.B.G., 1st upgrade free, toll-free technical support.
Macintosh OS Version 6.0.7 or higher. All MACs (2048k). 3.5" disk $34.95, general volume discounts & site licenses available (ISBN 1-883757-00-2, Order no.: SIP393). *Optimal configuration:* System 7.X, color-capable MAC.
RoboType: Universal Auto-Glossary. MouseGears: Adjusts Mouse Speed Automatically. Pick-A-Letter: 60X Faster Than Key Caps! Monitors Minder: 80X Faster Than Monitors Control Panel. BullsEye: Finds "Lost" Cursor. GraVu!: Display Enhancer - Photos, Scans. DST Minder: Sets Clock for Daylight Savings Time & Back. Sleep Now: Instant Sleep/Backlight Control.

Simplicity Software: Accounting for Small Business. *Version:* 1.5. Dec. 1991. *Items Included:* 3.5" & 5.25" disks & manual. *Customer Support:* Free & unlimited by phone.
DOS 2.0 or higher. IBM & compatible (240k). $129.00. *Nonstandard peripherals required:* Hard disk with 3Mb avaialble.
Professional Accounting for Small Business. Includes: Accounts Payable, Payroll, Accounts Receivable, Billing, Inventory, Purchasing, General Ledger, Budgeting & Financial Reporting.
Simplicity Software, Inc.

Simplified Amiga Library. *Compatible Hardware:* Commodore Amiga.
3.5" disk $99.95.
Library Collection for Use With Benchmark Modula-2.
Avant-Garde Software.

SIMPLIFIER+. *Version:* 7.1. Jun. 1988. *Items Included:* Complete 3-ring binder manual with room for updates, HELP screens behind all input stages. *Customer Support:* On-site training available, unlimited telephone support & all new enhancements throughout year.
MS-DOS 5.0 (2Mb). IBM XT/AT, PS/2 & compatibles. single-user $2500.00; Local Area Network $3750.00; Wide Area Network $8750.00. *Nonstandard peripherals required:* Letter quality or Laser printer. *Addl. software required:* Qualifier+. *Networks supported:* Novell, 3-Com, IBM PC NET.
User Can Add Forms, Make Changes in Minutes & Generate Filled-Out Forms Directly from Electronic Customer Files. Also Create Forms Such As Payment Letter, Corporate Agreement, Tax Service Order, etc.
Dynamic Interface Systems Corp.

Simply Accounting for DOS. *Customer Support:* Support Agreement Available.
DOS. IBM PC & compatibles (512k). disk $89.00.
GL, AP, AR, Payroll, Inventory & Job Cost. AP/AR Uses Open Invoice Method. Handles Federal & State Deductions & Taxes. Allocates Revenue or Expenses up to 255 Projects or Departments per Entry. Handles Bank Reconciliation, Cash Sales & Purchases & On-Time Customers & Vendors. Includes Payroll Tax Tables for Income & Reporting on W-2s. Canadian, French-Canadian & U.S. Versions Available.
FourHome Productions.

Simply Accounting for the Macintosh.
Customer Support: Support Agreement Available.
Macintosh (1Mb). 3.5" disk $89.00.
GL, AP, AR, Payroll, Inventory & Job Cost. AP/AR Uses Open Invoice Method. Payroll Handles Federal & State Deductions. Manages 5,000 Accounts, Customers, Vendors, Employees, Items & Projects. Includes Password Security Option &

TITLE INDEX

Mailing Label Function. Supports Government Standards Required for Income & Deduction Reporting on W-2s & Incorporates Federal & State Government Payroll Tax Changes, Canadian, French-Canadian & U.S. Versions Available.
FourHome Productions.

Simply Accounting for Windows & OS/2. *Customer Support:* Support Agreement Available. Windows, OS/2. IBM PC & compatibles. disk $89.00.
GL/AP/AR/Payroll/Inventory/Job Cost Program. AP/AR Uses Open Invoice Method. Handles Federal & State Deductions. Allocates Revenue or Expenses up to 255 Projects or Departments from List of 999. Includes Payroll Tax Tables & Supports Standards Required for Income & Deduction Reporting on W-2s. Incorporates Federal & State Government Payroll Tax Changes. Canadian, French-Canadian & U.S. Versions Available.
FourHome Productions.

Simply Citizen. *Customer Support:* Available. Windows. disk $49.95.
Windows-Based Reference Tool to Help Users Learn about Current Political Issues. Contains Comprehensive, Non-Partisan Descriptions of Topical Issues, Lists Congressional Voting Records, & Profiles Key Leaders Promoting Sending Legislation. Provides Addresses, Phone & Fax Numbers, & Email Addresses to Send Elected Officials Your Political Comments. Helps Users Make Informed Decisions on Issues. A Monthly Update Plan Provides the Latest Information via CompuServe or Disk. The Hot Bills Feature Offers a Synopsis of the Most Controversial Topics for Debate on Capital Hill.
FourHome Productions.

Simply House: Features Advice from the Stanley Complete Step-by-Step Book of Home Repair & Improvement. 1994. *Customer Support:* Support Agreement Available. Windows. 486 CPU or higher (4Mb). disk $59.99.
Windows-Based, Multi-Media Graphical Presentation of Information Contained in the Stanley Complete Step-by-Step Book of Home Repair & Improvement. Allows Users to Navigate Through Actual House to Obtain Advice on Topics Such As Tools, Roofing, Insulation, Cabinets, Plumbing, Fireplaces, etc. Guides User Through Repairs & Includes Video, Sound Effects, & Audio to Aid in Explanation.
FourHome Productions.

Simply Tax: Featuring Tax Tips from the Ernst & Young Tax-Saving Strategies Guide, 1995, a John Wiley & Sons Publication. *Customer Support:* Support Agreement Available. Windows. IBM PC & compatibles (2Mb). disk $69.99.
Tax Preparation System. Assists Users in Preparing, Calculating, Storing & Printing Taxes. Includes Built-In Tax Preparation Checklist. Tax Form Locator, Context-Sensitive Help, Tax Savings Strategies, Alarm System for Deadlines, Automatic Print & File of Returns, Automatic Linking to Recalculate Entered Data on Correct Worksheets & Forms & Schedules. Provides Depreciation Monitor to Automatically Calculate & Record Depreciation of Assets.
FourHome Productions.

Simtek Business Games Library. *Version:* 2.0. Mar. 1989. *Customer Support:* On-site train-the-trainer $1,200.00, 1-year maintenance $100.00. MS-DOS, PC-DOS (384k). IBM-compatibles. disk $250.00 (Order no.: SBGL20). *Optimal configuration:* Printer & hard disk drive recommended.
Collection of Four (4) Management Simulations for Management Training. Two Simulations Illustrate the Retail Industry from the Point of View of Small & Large Supermarket Chains. The Third Dramatizes the Explosive Growth of the Pocket Calculator Industry. The Fourth Business Game Covers a Business Strategy Scenario.
Simtek.

Simtel MSDOS. *Customer Support:* All of our products are unconditionally guaranteed. DOS. CD-ROM disk $34.95 (Order no.: SIMTEL). *Nonstandard peripherals required:* CD-ROM drive.
1000 MB of the Best MSDOS Shareware. Now a 2-Disc Set.
Walnut Creek CDRom.

SIM3. *Version:* 1.2. Apr. 1983. *Compatible Hardware:* IBM PC, PC AT, PC XT & compatibles. *Operating System(s) Required:* MS-DOS, PC-DOS. *Language(s):* FORTRAN. *Memory Required:* 512k.
disk $2000.00 (Order no.: SIM3).
Using a Given Variogram, SIM3 Produces Simulated Values of Gaussian Deviates Either on a Fixed Grid or at Specific Points. The Variogram Used Can Be Any Combination of Nugget Effect, Spherical, Exponential, or Gaussian Models. Any Kind of Two- or Three- Dimensional Anisotropy, Geometric or Zonal, Can Be Accommodated. The Program Will Provide a Statistical Analysis of the Sample Point Distribution at Both Sample & Grid Points.
Geostat Systems International, Inc. (GSII).

SIM3C. *Version:* 1.1. Jun. 1983. *Compatible Hardware:* IBM PC, PC AT, PC XT & compatibles. *Operating System(s) Required:* MS-DOS, PC-DOS. *Language(s):* FORTRAN. *Memory Required:* 512k. *General Requirements:* Printer.
disk $1500.00 (Order no.: SIM3C).
Performs a Conditionalization of the Random Normal Deviates Produced by SIM3. This Conditionalization Process Transforms the Original Normalized Values to Grid Values That Closely Resemble the Original Sample Values. The New Values Are Interpolated from the Sample Points by Kriging.
Geostat Systems International, Inc. (GSII).

SimuDOS. *Version:* 2.0. James E. Potter. Sep. 1995. *Items Included:* Printed documentation & troubleshooting. *Customer Support:* Free through (800) 487-9868.
DOS. IBM & compatibles (453k). disk $19.95 (ISBN 1-885587-22-8). *Optimal configuration:* Color monitor. *Networks supported:* All.
A Set of Easy-to-Follow, Keystroke-by-Keystroke Lessons Teaching the Most Commonly Used DOS Commands & Functions. All Tutorial Functions Are Simulated. This Is a Self-Guided Way to Learn the Secrets of the DOS Operating System.
Bridge Learning Systems, Inc.

SimuDOS. *Version:* 2.0. James E. Potter. Sep. 1995. *Items Included:* Instructor's guide, spiral bound. *Customer Support:* Free through (800) 487-9868.
MS-DOS 3.0 or higher. IBM PC or compatibles (XT, 286, 386, 486, Pentium) (453k). disk $19.95 (ISBN 1-885587-22-8). *Nonstandard peripherals required:* Color monitor.
Set of Easy-to-Follow, Keystroke-by-Keystroke Tutorial Lessons Teaching the Most Commonly Used DOS Commands & Functions. All Tutorial Functions Are Simulated. This Is a Self-Guided Way to Learn the Secrets of the DOS Operating System.
Bridge Learning Systems, Inc.

Simulated Patient Encounters: Patients Who Need Help with Urinary Elimination, 5 disks. Gomez. Aug. 1985. *Compatible Hardware:* Apple II; IBM PC. *Memory Required:* Apple 64k, IBM 128k.
Apple set. disk $600.00, incl. user's guide (Order no.: 64-73508).
IBM set. $600.00, incl. user's guide (Order no.: 64-73516).
Designed to Teach Pertinent Content by Guiding the Learner Through an Encounter with a "Patient" Who Has Needs & Problems Consistent with a Medical Diagnosis Given on Admission to the Hospital.
J. B. Lippincott Co.

Simulated Solutions. *Version:* 2.30. Aug. 1987. *Compatible Hardware:* IBM PC & compatibles. *Memory Required:* 64k. *General Requirements:* Lotus 1-2-3 Releases 2 & 2.01, Symphony Releases 1, 1.01, 1.1, & 1.2.
$99.95.
Calculates the Average & Most-Likely Values of User's Defined Objective, As Well As the Standard Deviation, Based on the Specified Range & Distribution of Parameters. Provides & Displays a Profitability Distribution (with Accumulated Distribution) of the Objective Variable.
Enfin Software Corp.

Simulated Solutions-Plus. *Version:* 2.30. Aug. 1987. *Compatible Hardware:* IBM PC & compatibles. *Memory Required:* 320k. *General Requirements:* Lotus 1-2-3 Releases 2 & 2.01, Symphony Releases 1, 1.01, 1.1, & 1.2.
$295.00.
Finds the Probability & Accumulated-Probability Distributions of a Defined Objective. Performs Monte Carlo Simulations with As Many As 20 Variables. Analyzes & Calculates the Impact of Different Objective Scenarios. Calculates the Sensitivity of As Many As 25 Variables. Displays All Results Graphically.
Enfin Software Corp.

Simulating the Medical Office Software Getting Started & 7 Modules. Jerry Belch. 1993. *Items Included:* Handbook/workbook for Getting Started, Record Management, Correspondence, Appointments, Business Check Account, Office Purchase Orders, Patient Billing, Insurance Claims modules. Instructor's Guide for each or all modules. *Customer Support:* Technical support from editorial staff.
MS-DOS 3.21. IBM PC, Tandy & compatibles, (640k). $39.96 complete handbook (ISBN 0-89262-429-9). *Optimal configuration:* One-diskette, two-diskette, or hard disk systems & printer.
Instr's. guide $9.95 per module or $249.95 complete; Site license $129.95 per module or $695.00 complete.
$6.36 per module: Record Management, Correspondence, Appointments, Insurance Claims, Business Checking Account.
$7.16 Getting Started.
$5.95 Office Purchase Orders.
$7.96 Patient Billing.
Hands-On Material to Train Students for Employment in a Medical Front Office. Real World Examples. Open Entry/Open Exit. Modules Include Getting Started, Record Management, Correspondence, Appointments, Business Checking Account, Office Purchase Orders, Patient Billing, Insurance Claims.
Career Publishing, Inc.

Simultaneous PRINT & LPRINT. *Compatible Hardware:* TRS-80 Model I. *Language(s):* BASIC. contact publisher for price.
Allows All PRINT & LPRINT Statements to Go to Both the CRT & Printer at the Same Time.
Raymond L. Reynolds.

SimuNet. *Version:* 3.0. James E. Potter. Oct. 1994. *Items Included:* Documentation. *Customer Support:* Free phone support via (800)487-9868.
MS-DOS. IBM & compatibles (376k). $29.95 (Network/Workstation licenses avail.) (ISBN 1-885587-17-1). *Optimal configuration:* 286-486 CPU color monitor. *Networks supported:* All networks.
Windows. (ISBN 1-885587-19-8).
Macintosh. (ISBN 1-885587-15-5).
Teaches How to Use E-Mail; Conduct Internet Searches Using Telnet, Gopher, Carl, Archie, WWW, WAIS, Listserv, Usenet News & Veronica. Shows How to Upload, Download & Print Files.
Bridge Learning Systems, Inc.

SimuNET. *Version:* 3.0. James E. Potter. Oct. 1995. *Items Included:* Spiral bound user's guide or instructor's guide. *Customer Support:* Free through (800) 487-9868.
DOS. IBM or compatibles (XT, 286, 386, 486, Pentium) (451k). disk $29.95, incl. user's guide (ISBN 1-885587-17-1). *Nonstandard peripherals required:* Color monitor. *Optimal configuration:* 4Mb free disk space.
disk $29.95, incl. instr's. guide (ISBN 1-885587-11-2).
Macintosh 6.05 or higher. Macintosh Plus or higher (4Mb). 3.5" disk $29.95, incl. user's guide (ISBN 1-885587-18-X). *Optimal configuration:* 6Mb free disk space.
3.5" disk $29.95, incl. instr's. guide (ISBN 1-885587-15-5).
Windows 3.1. IBM PC or compatibles (386, 486, Pentium) (8Mb). disk $29.95, incl. user's guide (ISBN 1-885587-19-8). *Optimal configuration:* 6Mb free disk space.
disk $29.95, incl. instr's. guide (ISBN 1-885587-16-3).
Teaches How to Use the Text-Based Internet, Including E-Mail, & Conduct Information Searches Using Telnet, Gopher, Carl, Veronica, Archie, WWW, WAIS, WMOIS, Listserv & Usenet News. conduct File Retrieval Using FTP! Shows How to Upload, Download, Print Files. This Is an Off-Line Tutorial. No Modem Required.
Bridge Learning Systems, Inc.

SimuNet: (Demo Disk). James E. Potter & Alfred J. Garrotto. Aug. 1994. *Items Included:* Documentation. *Customer Support:* Free phone support via 800-487-9868.
MS-DOS. IBM-PC & compatibles (303k). $3.00 postpaid (ISBN 1-885587-03-1). *Optimal configuration:* 286-486 CPU, color monitor. *Networks supported:* Yes.
This Product Is a Partial Demonstration of the Features of the Full SimuNet Tutorial Program.
Bridge Learning Systems, Inc.

SimuWEB. James E. Potter. Nov. 1995. *Items Included:* Spiral bound user's or instructor's guide. *Customer Support:* Free (800) 487-9868.
Windows 3.1 or higher. IBM or compatibles (386, 486, Pentium) (8Mb). disk $39.95, incl. user's guide (ISBN 1-885587-23-6). *Optimal configuration:* 15Mb free disk space.
disk $39.95, incl. instr's. guide (ISBN 1-885587-10-4).
Macintosh 6.05 or higher. Macintosh II or higher (4Mb). 3.5" disk $39.95, incl. user's guide (ISBN 1-885587-12-0). *Optimal configuration:* 15Mb free disk space.
3.5" disk $39.95, incl. instr's. guide (ISBN 1-885587-24-4).
Teaches/Demonstrates How to Find Your Way Around the World Wide Web's Vast Internet Resources, Set up a "Home Page," Code Text Documents for Display Using HTML, Use FTP, Telnet, Gopher, & E-Mail on the Web. Point, Click, & Learn Your Way Around the Internet's Graphical WWW the Easy Way - Without Having to Be Online. No Modem Required.
Bridge Learning Systems, Inc.

Singly/Doubly Reinforced Beam Deflection. 1995. *Items Included:* Full manual. *Customer Support:* Free telephone support - 90 days, 30-day warranty.
MS-DOS 3.2 or higher. 286 (584k). disk $99.95. *Nonstandard peripherals required:* CGA/EGA/VGA.
S/D Solves the Tedious Problem of Determining Immediate & Long-Term Deflections of Rectangular/Non-Rectangular Sections. S/D Is Particularly Flexible & Analyzes Practically Any Singly or Doubly Reinforced Cross-Section, Even Cross-Sections That Vary along a Span.
Dynacomp, Inc.

Site Pro. Aug. 1992.
DOS. IBM PC & 100% compatibles. Contact vendor for price. *Nonstandard peripherals required:* Optimal modem.
Processes & Collects Resident Rents, Late Fees, & Deposits. Automatic Proration on Move in/Move Out. Reports on Traffic & Marketing Success. Tracks Amenities by Unit, Including Value of Amenity. Reconciles Gross Potential to Net Cash Received Automatically. Upload/Download Capabilities for Home Office Reporting & Control.
Timberline Software Corp.

Sitting on the Farm. Sanctuery Woods. Dec. 1995. *Customer Support:* Telephone support - free (except phone charge).
Windows 3.1. IBM & compatibles (386 DX-20) (4Mb). CD-ROM disk $12.99, Jewel (ISBN 1-57594-078-7). *Nonstandard peripherals required:* 2X CD ROM player, sound card, VGA monitor. *Optimal configuration:* 486 SX-33.
CD-ROM disk $12.99, Blister.
A Peaceful Picnic Quickly Turns into a Fun Fiasco for a Little Girl on a Farm. Sitting on the Farm Turns Reading into Entertainment. Your Children Can Read along, Have the Story Read to Them, or Sing Along. They Can Even Write Their Own Stories Using the Art Provided.
Kidsoft, Inc.

Sitting on the Farm. Sanctuery Woods. Dec. 1995. *Customer Support:* Telephone support - free (except phone charge).
Windows 3.1. IBM & compatibles (386 DX-20) (4Mb). CD-ROM disk $12.99 (ISBN 1-57594-078-7). *Nonstandard peripherals required:* 2X CD-ROM player, sound card, VGA monitor. *Optimal configuration:* 486 SX-33.
A Peaceful Picnic Quickly Turns into a Fun Fiasco for a Little Girl on a Farm. Sitting on the Farm Turns Reading into Entertainment. Your Children Can Read along, Have the Story Read to Them, or Sing Along. They Can Even Write Their Own Stories Using the Art Provided. Jewel Case.
Kidsoft, Inc.

6 Days of Creation Screen Saver.
Windows 3.1 or higher. 386 or higher IBM PC or compatibles (2Mb). disk $12.95 (Order no.: SW000-1B). *Optimal configuration:* 386 or higher IBM PC, Windows 3.1 or higher, 258 VGA or higher, 2Mb RAM & Mouse.
In the Beginning, God Created the Heavens & the Earth (Gen 1:1). Make Your Monitor a Captivating Statement of God's Truth & Power While Saving Your Screen. Seven Highly Graphical Sequential Images Depict Each Day of the Creation Complete with Bible Text! Created by Gospel Films Inc. & Knowlege Plus Publishing. God Saw Everything That He Had Made & It Was Very Good (Gen 1:31A).
Gospel Films Inc.

688 Attack Sub. John W. Ratcliff. Mar. 1989. *Items Included:* Manual or ref card. *Customer Support:* Customer hint hotline (415) 572-9560.
MS-DOS/PC-DOS (384k). disk $29.95 IBM; $49.95 Amiga. *Optimal configuration:* Graphics: Hercules, CGA, EGA, Tandy, VGA, MCGA.
Simulation That Puts User in Command of a Top Secret Billion Dollar Los Angeles Class U.S. Attack Sub. Pits You & Your Crew Against Deadly Fleets of Submerged, Surface & Airborne Targets Around the Globe. Unfolds the Dangers of Espionage, Evasion & Destruction.
Electronic Arts.

Six/25. *Version:* 2.01. Nov. 1987. *Compatible Hardware:* IBM PC & compatibles. *Operating System(s) Required:* PC-DOS. *Memory Required:* 400k. *General Requirements:* TDT Multiprotocol Adapter, IBM Co-Processor, UDS Sync-Up modem. *Items Included:* User manual. *Customer Support:* 1 year free.
disk $499.00 - $4999.00.
3174/3279/3770 SNA, SDLC, QLLC X.25 Terminal Emulation.
TDT Group, Inc.

68010 Super Sleuth. 1986. *Operating System(s) Required:* MS-DOS, UNIX, OS/9 68000. (source code included). *Memory Required:* 256k.
$200.00.
Generates Source Code with Labels from 68000/68010 Object Code.
Computer Systems Consultants.

68000 C Compiler. 1988. *Items Included:* Manuals. *Customer Support:* Included at no cost.
MS-DOS, UNIX, OS-9, SK-DOS (512k). $100.00.
K & R Standard C Compiler, Generates 68000 Assembler Language for Assembler Included. Source-Code Library Provided.
Computer Systems Consultants.

68000 Cross Assembler. Brian R. Anderson. *Operating System(s) Required:* MS-DOS. *Language(s):* Modula-2.
disk $25.00, incl. manual (ISBN 0-934375-71-2).
Two-Pass Cross Assembler for the Motorola MC68000 Microprocessor. Accepts Standard Motorola Syntax & Produces a Formatted Program Listing File & an Object File Consisting of Standard Motorola S-Records Which Is Fully Explained in the Manual. In Addition to the Assembler Program, the Software Supplied Also Includes OPCODE.DAT, a Data File Used to Initialize the Mnemonic Lookup Table for the Assembler.
M & T Bks.

64 Accounting. Mar. 1984. *Compatible Hardware:* Commodore 64 with printer. *Language(s):* Compiled BASIC. *Memory Required:* 180k. *Items Included:* Disk, manual, & demo data. *Customer Support:* Yes.
disk $50.00.
Provides Essentials of Effective Money Management for Home & Small Business Use from Balancing a Checkbook to Providing Year End Figures for Taxes.
Software Design, Inc.

64Forth. *Customer Support:* 800-929-8117 (customer service).
MS-DOS. Commodore 64. disk $49.99 (ISBN 0-87007-841-0).
A High Level Programming Language That Is Powerful, Flexible & Efficient. Used by Scientific Personnel, Including Most Astronomers in Universities & Sites Around the World. It Is a Threaded Language. An Interactive Language. Programs are Modular Premitting Structured Programming & Are Efficient in Memory Usage. Included Is a Full Virtual Disk Interface & a Full 6502 FORTH Assembler. This Is the Complete FIG (FORTH Interest Group) Version, it

TITLE INDEX

Maximizes Commodore 64 Graphics & Sound Capabilities, Has a Built-in Assembler & Debugger. An Instruction Manual Is Included.
SourceView Software International.

Size FE Flow Element Calculator. *Items Included:* Full manual. No other products required. *Customer Support:* Free telephone support - no time limit. 30 day warranty.
MS-DOS 3.2 or higher. IBM & compatibles (512k). disk $149.95.
Menu-Driven Flow Element Design Calculator. It Sizes Bore Diameter & Calculates the Flow or Pressure Differential for an Existing Device. User May Produce Flow vs. D/P Tables for Setting up Smart Transmitters or Data Acquisition System Software. Developed in a Real-Life Working Environment. Its Methodology Is Based on Sources Engineers Recognize As the Most Authoritative in the Field.
Dynacomp, Inc.

Size Planner. *Version:* 2.0. Jul. 1988. *Compatible Hardware:* IBM PC. *Operating System(s) Required:* PC-DOS 2.0 or higher.
$10,000.00 per year.
Projects Size of Software System on Front-End of Development. Uses Four Sizing Techniques: Fuzzy Logic, Standard Component, Function Points & New, Modified & Reused Source Code. By Combining These Methods, Program Produces Estimates That Vary by Only 7% with Actuals.
Quantitative Software Management, Inc.

SizeFE: Flow Element Calculator. 1995. *Items Included:* Full manual. *Customer Support:* Free telephone support - 90 days, 30-day warranty.
MS-DOS 3.2 or higher. 286 (584k). disk $149.95. *Nonstandard peripherals required:* CGA/EGA/VGA.
A Menu-Driven Flow Element Design Calculator. It Sizes Bore Diameter & Calculates the Flow or Pressure Differential for an Existing Device. You May Produce Flow vs. D/P Tables for Setting up Smart Transmitters or Data Acquisition System Software. Developed in a Real-Life Working Environment. Its Methodology Is Based on Sources Engineers Recognize As the Most Authoritative in the Field. Coefficients May Be Calculated via the ASME Fluid Meters Methodology, or from ASME MFC-3M-1989. Orifice Devices (Flange Tap, Corner Tap, Vena Contracta, 1- & 1/2-D Tap) As Well As Nozzles & Venturis Are Covered.
Dynacomp, Inc.

SK*DOS. *Operating System(s) Required:* SK-DOS. *Language(s):* Assembly. *Memory Required:* 32k.
contact publisher for price.
Disk Operating System Designed for Systems Based on the 6809 & 68000 Processors.
Star-K Software Systems Corp.

SK-Modules: Point of Sale. *Version:* 1.16. Mike Nudd. *Items Included:* 3 ring manual. *Customer Support:* First 90 days free - yearly prepaid contract or prepaid hourly contract.
Macintosh 7.0 or higher. Macintosh 68030 (8Mb). $595.00 single user; $1150.00 multiuser. *Nonstandard peripherals required:* Hard disk (80) printer.
A Series of Interconnected Applications for Business. In a Multi-User Network Server Situation the Employee Need Only Have the Modules on Their Computer That They Actually Use. The Receiving Department Only Needs "SK Receiving," a Cash Register Only Needs "SK Cash Register". No Need for an Employee to Learn Anything That Does Not Directly Effect Their Job & Nine Password Levels Insures That the Employee Only Has Access to the Modules That You Allow.
Shopkeeper Software.

SK: The System Kernel of the Tele Operating System Toolkit. Ken Berry. *Operating System(s) Required:* MS-DOS.
disk $49.95, incl. manual (ISBN 0-934375-30-5).
Provides Complete Documentation for Installing & Using the Tele Operating System Kernel on PCs with an 8086-Compatible Processor. Included Is the Preemptive Multitasking Algorithm, the Most Crucial Part of the Tele Operating System. Also Included Are: an Initialization Module, Utility Functions for String & Character Handling, Format Conversion, Terminal Support, & Machine Interface, along with a Real-Time Task Management System.
M & T Bks.

Skate or Die. *Compatible Hardware:* Commodore 64, 128; Apple IIgs; IBM PC.
Apple. disk $19.95.
Commodore. disk $14.95.
IBM. disk $14.95.
Competition Consisting of Five Skateboarding Events.
Electronic Arts.

Skeletal Muscle Anatomy & Physiology. 1985. *Compatible Hardware:* Apple II+, IIe, IIc, IIgs. *Operating System(s) Required:* Apple DOS 3.3. *Language(s):* BASIC. *Memory Required:* 48k. *General Requirements:* Monochrome or color monitor.
disk $49.95.
Contains Five Tutorials Which Allow Students to Progress at Their Own Pace. Topics Covered Include Three Muscle Categories, Sliding Filament Theory, Muscle Lever Systems, Skeletal Motor Units & Skeletal Muscle Microstructure. Students Choose a Ten Question Test Covering One Tutorial, or a 25 or 50 Question Comprehensive Exam Covering All Tutorials. When the 25 or 50 Question Comprehensive Exam Has Been Completed, They Will Receive a Breakdown of Performance on All Five Tutorials. Designed for High School & College Levels.
Biosource Software.

SketchPad. *Customer Support:* 800-929-8117 (customer service).
MS-DOS. Apple II. disk $49.99 (ISBN 0-87007-261-7).
A Simple Sketchpad Controlled by Cursor Keys.
SourceView Software International.

SKI-PACK: Ski Rental & Inventory. *Version:* 90.1. Jesse A. Tarshis & Kenneth Youngstrom. 1980. *Compatible Hardware:* IBM PC & compatibles. *Operating System(s) Required:* MS-DOS/PC-DOS/NETBIOS. *Language(s):* DBXL & Quicksilver. *Memory Required:* 640k. *General Requirements:* Hard disk. *Items Included:* Software, documentation. *Customer Support:* Toll free technical support.
$2195.00.
Creates Reservations Tied to Rental Inventory. Reports by Part Group, Number & Day. Lists Item Availibility for Any Day, Sets Warning Levels. Customer Data by Name, Family, Group & Date. Calculates Binding DIN Factor, Creates & Prints Reservation Confirmations, Rental Tickets, Labels & Envelopes.
Alpine Data, Inc.

Ski Rental Shops.
MS-DOS, Unix, Xenix (512k). IBM PC, PC XT, PC AT & compatible mini/micros. contact publisher for price.
Inventory Control for Reservation & Rental of Skis & Boots. Handles Customer Reservations, Overdue Returns, Tracks Frequency of Usage & Flags When Testing Is Due on Each Piece.
Universal Data Research, Inc.

SKILLS BANK 3: COMPLETE SET

Skills Bank 3: Complete Set. Mar. 1994. *Items Included:* Contents manual (Lesson & summaries), operations manual. *Customer Support:* Free 1-800 toll free line for technical support, 30 day full refund policy.
Mac. Mac Plus, SE, SE/30, Classic, Classic II, or any Mac II or LC (1Mb Sys 6, 2Mb Sys 7). 3.5" disk $1595.00 (ISBN 1-56985-073-9). *Optimal configuration:* At least 1 computer with 2 drives (a floppy & a hard drive or two floppies), color or monochrome monitor, hard drive space - 19Mb.
(Reading, Language, Mathematics, Writing, Study Skills) Provides Lessons, Quizzes & Tests for Mastering Basic Education Skills. It Contains a Management System for Recording Student Scores & Reporting Progress to Teachers, Parents & Administrators.
Skills Bank Corp.

Skills Bank 3: Complete Set. Mar. 1994. *Items Included:* Contents manual (Lesson & summaries), operations manual. *Customer Support:* Free 1-800 toll free line for technical support, 30 day full refund policy.
Mac/Network version. Mac Plus, SE, SE/30, Classic, Classic II, or any Mac II or LC (1Mb Sys 6, 2Mb Sys 7). 3.5" disk $4785.00 (ISBN 1-56985-103-4). *Optimal configuration:* At least 1 computer with 2 drives (a floppy & a hard drive or two floppies), color or monochrome monitor, hard drive space - 19Mb. *Networks supported:* Appleshare.
(Reading, Language, Mathematics, Writing, Study Skills) Provides Lessons, Quizzes & Tests for Mastering Basic Education Skills. It Contains a Management System for Recording Student Scores & Reporting Progress to Teachers, Parents & Administrators.
Skills Bank Corp.

Skills Bank 3: Complete Set. Mar. 1994. *Items Included:* Contents manual (Lesson & summaries), operations manual. *Customer Support:* Free 1-800 toll free line for technical support, 30 day full refund policy.
MS-DOS/Network. MS-DOS compatible (no PCjr), must have MS-DOS 3.1 or higher (512k). 3.5" disk $4785.00 (ISBN 1-56985-097-6). *Nonstandard peripherals required:* Color or monochrome monitor. Must be able to display graphics (CGA, Herc, EGA, MCGA, or VGA). *Addl. software required:* MS-DOS 3.1 or higher. *Optimal configuration:* At least 1 computer with 2 drives (a floppy & a hard drive or two floppies), color monitor that supports graphics, hard drive with appoximately 18Mb. *Networks supported:* Novell, Novell with ICLAS, LANtastic, Digicard & Velan. 5.25" disk $4785.00 (ISBN 1-56985-091-7).
(Reading, Language, Mathematics, Writing, Study Skills) Provides Lessons, Quizzes & Tests for Mastering Basic Education Skills. It Contains a Management System for Recording Student Scores & Reporting Progress to Teachers, Parents & Administrators.
Skills Bank Corp.

Skills Bank 3: Complete Set. Mar. 1994. *Items Included:* Contents manual (Lesson & summaries worksheets), operations manual. *Customer Support:* Free 1-800 toll free line for technical support, 30 day full refund policy.
MS-DOS. MS-DOS compatible (no PCjr), must have MS-DOS 3.1 or higher (512k). 3.5" disk $1595.00 (ISBN 1-56985-067-4). *Nonstandard peripherals required:* Color or monochrome monitor. Must be able to display graphics (CGA, Herc, EGA, MCGA, or VGA). *Addl. software required:* MS-DOS 3.1 or higher. *Optimal configuration:* At least 1 computer with 2 drives (a floppy & a hard drive or two floppies), color monitor that supports graphics,

923

SKILLS BANK 3: COMPLETE SET

hard drive with appoximately 18Mb. 5.25" disk $1595.00 (ISBN 1-56985-061-5). *(Reading, Language, Mathematics, Writing, Study Skills) Provides Lessons, Quizzes & Tests for Mastering Basic Education Skills. It Contains a Management System for Recording Student Scores & Reporting Progress to Teachers, Parents & Administrators.*
Skills Bank Corp.

Skills Bank 3: Complete Set. Mar. 1994. *Items Included:* Contents manual (Lesson & summaries), operations manual. *Customer Support:* Free 1-800 toll free line for technical support, 30 day full refund policy.
   Apple. Apple II2, IIc, IIgs, or MAC LC with Apple IIe card (128k). 3.5" disk $1595.00 (ISBN 1-56985-055-0). *Nonstandard peripherals required:* 80 column card. *Addl. software required:* Monitor must have 80 column card. *Optimal configuration:* One computer with 2 drives (floppy & hard drive with 13Mb or 2 floppies), color or monochrome monitor.
   5.25" disk $1595.00 (ISBN 1-56985-049-6). *(Reading, Language, Mathematics, Writing, Study Skills) Provides Lessons, Quizzes & Tests for Mastering Basic Skills. It Contains a Management System for Recording Student Scores & Reporting Progress to Teachers, Parents & Administrators.*
Skills Bank Corp.

Skills Bank 3: Complete Set. Mar. 1994. *Items Included:* Contents manual (Lesson & summaries), operations manual. *Customer Support:* Free 1-800 toll free line for technical support, 30 day full refund policy.
   Apple/Network. Apple II2, IIc, IIgs, or MAC LC with Apple IIe card (128k). 3.5" disk $4785.00 (ISBN 1-56985-085-2). *Nonstandard peripherals required:* 80 column card. *Addl. software required:* Monitor must have 80 column card. *Optimal configuration:* One computer with 2 drives (floppy & hard drive with 13Mb or 2 floppies), color or monochrome monitor. *Networks supported:* Appleshare, Corvus, Digicard, Velan.
   5.25" disk $4785.00 (ISBN 1-56985-079-8). *Provides Lessons, Quizzes & Tests for Mastering Basic Skills. It Contains a Management System for Recording Student Scores & Reporting Progress to Teachers, Parents & Administrators.*
Skills Bank Corp.

Skills Bank 3: Language. Mar. 1994. *Items Included:* Contents manual (Lesson & summaries), operations manual. *Customer Support:* Free 1-800 toll free line for technical support, 30 day full refund policy.
   Mac. Mac Plus, SE, SE/30, Classic, Classic II, or any Mac II or LC (1Mb Sys 6, 2Mb Sys 7). 3.5" disk $450.00 (ISBN 1-56985-069-0). *Optimal configuration:* At least 1 computer with 2 drives (a floppy & a hard drive or two floppies), color or monochrome monitor, hard drive space - 19Mb.
   Provides Lessons, Quizzes & Tests for Mastering Basic Education Skills in Language, Punctuation, Spelling & Capitalization. It Contains a Management System for Recording Student Scores & Reporting Progress to Teachers, Parents & Administrators.
Skills Bank Corp.

Skills Bank 3: Language. Mar. 1994. *Items Included:* Contents manual (Lesson & summaries), operations manual. *Customer Support:* Free 1-800 toll free line for technical support, 30 day full refund policy.
   Mac/Network version. Mac Plus, SE, SE/30, Classic, Classic II, or any Mac II or LC (1Mb Sys 7, 2Mb Sys 7). 3.5" disk $1350.00 (ISBN 1-56985-099-2). *Optimal configuration:* At least 1 computer with 2 drives (a floppy & a hard drive or two floppies), color or monochrome monitor, hard drive space - 19Mb. *Networks supported:* Appleshare.
   Provides Lessons, Quizzes & Tests for Mastering Basic Education Skills in Language, Punctuation, Spelling & Capitalization. It Contains a Management System for Recording Student Scores & Reporting Progress to Teachers, Parents & Administrators.
Skills Bank Corp.

Skills Bank 3: Language. Mar. 1994. *Items Included:* Contents manual (Lesson & summaries worksheets), operations manual. *Customer Support:* Free 1-800 toll free line for technical support, 30 day full refund policy.
   MS-DOS/Network. MS-DOS compatible (no PCjr), must have MS-DOS 3.1 or higher (512k). 3.5" disk $1350.00 (ISBN 1-56985-093-3). *Nonstandard peripherals required:* Color or monochrome monitor. Must be able to display graphics (CGA, Herc, EGA, MCGA, or VGA). *Addl. software required:* MS-DOS 3.1 or higher. *Optimal configuration:* At least 1 computer with 2 drives (a floppy & a hard drive or two floppies), color monitor that supports graphics, hard drive with appoximately 18Mb. *Networks supported:* Novell, Novell with ICLAS, LANtastic, Digicard & Velan.
   5.25" disk $1350.00 (ISBN 1-56985-087-9). *Provides Lessons, Quizzes & Tests for Mastering Basic Education Skills in Language, Punctuation, Spelling & Capitalization. It Contains a Management System for Recording Student Scores & Reporting Progress to Teachers, Parents & Administrators.*
Skills Bank Corp.

Skills Bank 3: Language. Mar. 1994. *Items Included:* Contents manual (Lesson & summaries), operations manual. *Customer Support:* Free 1-800 toll free line for technical support, 30 day full refund policy.
   MS-DOS. MS-DOS compatible (no PCjr), must have MS-DOS 3.1 or higher (512k). 3.5" disk $450.00 (ISBN 1-56985-063-1). *Nonstandard peripherals required:* Color or monochrome monitor. Must be able to display graphics (CGA, Herc, EGA, MCGA, or VGA). *Addl. software required:* MS-DOS 3.1 or higher. *Optimal configuration:* At least 1 computer with 2 drives (a floppy & a hard drive or two floppies), color monitor that supports graphics, hard drive with appoximately 18Mb.
   5.25" disk $450.00 (ISBN 1-56985-057-7). *Provides Lessons, Quizzes & Tests for Mastering Basic Education Skills in Language, Punctuation, Spelling & Capitalization. It Contains a Management System for Recording Student Scores & Reporting Progress to Teachers, Parents & Administrators.*
Skills Bank Corp.

Skills Bank 3: Language. Mar. 1994. *Items Included:* Contents manual (Lesson & summaries), operations manual. *Customer Support:* Free 1-800 toll free line for technical support, 30 day full refund policy.
   Apple. Apple II2, IIc, IIgs, or MAC LC with Apple IIe card (128k). 3.5" disk $450.00 (ISBN 1-56985-051-8). *Nonstandard peripherals required:* 80 column card. *Addl. software required:* Monitor must have 80 column card. *Optimal configuration:* One computer with 2 drives (floppy & hard drive with 13Mb or 2 floppies), color or monochrome monitor.
   5.25" disk $450.00 (ISBN 1-56985-045-3). *Provides Lessons, Quizzes & Tests for Mastering Basic Education Skills in Language, Punctuation, Spelling & Capitalization. It Contains a Management System for Recording Student Scores & Reporting Progress to Teachers, Parents & Administrators.*
Skills Bank Corp.

Skills Bank 3: Language. Mar. 1994. *Items Included:* Contents manual (Lesson & summaries), operations manual. *Customer Support:* Free 1-800 toll free line for technical support, 30 day full refund policy.
   Apple/Network. Apple II2, IIc, IIgs, or MAC LC with Apple IIe card (128k). 3.5" disk $1350.00 (ISBN 1-56985-081-X). *Nonstandard peripherals required:* 80 column card. *Addl. software required:* Monitor must have 80 column card. *Optimal configuration:* One computer with 2 drives (floppy & hard drive with 13Mb or 2 floppies), color or monochrome monitor. *Networks supported:* Appleshare, Corvus, Digicard, Velan.
   5.25" disk $1350.00 (ISBN 1-56985-075-5). *Provides Lessons, Quizzes & Tests for Mastering Basic Education Skills in Language, Punctuation, Spelling & Capitalization. It Contains a Management System for Recording Student Scores & Reporting Progress to Teachers, Parents & Administrators.*
Skills Bank Corp.

Skills Bank 3: Mathematics. Mar. 1994. *Items Included:* Contents manual (Lesson & summaries), operations manual. *Customer Support:* Free 1-800 toll free line for technical support, 30 day full refund policy.
   Mac. Mac Plus, SE, SE/30, Classic, Classic II, or any Mac II or LC (1Mb Sys 6, 2Mb Sys 7). 3.5" disk $450.00 (ISBN 1-56985-070-4). *Optimal configuration:* At least 1 computer with 2 drives (a floppy & a hard drive or two floppies), color or monochrome monitor, hard drive space - 19Mb.
   Provides Lessons, Quizzes & Tests for Mastering Basic Education Skills in Computation, Concepts, Word Problems, & Measurement & Introduction to Geometry & Algebra. It Contains a Management System for Recording Student Scores & Reporting Progress to Teachers, Parents & Administrators.
Skills Bank Corp.

Skills Bank 3: Mathematics. Mar. 1994. *Items Included:* Contents manual (Lesson & summaries), operations manual. *Customer Support:* Free 1-800 toll free line for technical support, 30 day full refund policy.
   Mac/Network version. Mac Plus, SE, SE/30, Classic, Classic II, or any Mac II or LC (1Mb Sys 6, 2Mb Sys 7). 3.5" disk $1350.00 (ISBN 1-56985-100-X). *Optimal configuration:* At least 1 computer with 2 drives (a floppy & a hard drive or two floppies), color or monochrome monitor, hard drive space - 19Mb. *Networks supported:* Appleshare.
   Provides Lessons, Quizzes & Tests for Mastering Basic Education Skills in Computation, Concepts, Word Problems, & Measurement & Introduction to Geometry & Algebra. It Contains a Management System for Recording Student Scores & Reporting Progress to Teachers, Parents & Administrators.
Skills Bank Corp.

Skills Bank 3: Mathematics. Mar. 1994. *Items Included:* Contents manual (Lesson & summaries worksheets), operations manual. *Customer Support:* Free 1-800 toll free line for technical support, 30 day full refund policy.
   MS-DOS/Network. MS-DOS compatible (no PCjr), must have MS-DOS 3.1 or higher (512k). 3.5" disk $1350.00 (ISBN 1-56985-094-1). *Nonstandard peripherals required:* Color or monochrome monitor. Must be able to display graphics (CGA, Herc, EGA, MCGA, or VGA). *Addl. software required:* MS-DOS 3.1 or higher. *Optimal configuration:* At least 1 computer with 2 drives (a floppy & a hard drive or two floppies), color monitor that supports graphics, hard drive with appoximately

TITLE INDEX

18Mb. *Networks supported:* Novell, Novell with ICLAS, LANtastic, Digicard & Velan. 5.25" disk $1350.00 (ISBN 1-56985-088-7). *Provides Lessons, Quizzes & Tests for Mastering Basic Education Skills in Computation, Concepts, Word Problems, & Measurement & Introduction to Geometry & Algebra. It Contains a Management System for Recording Student Scores & Reporting Progress to Teachers, Parents & Administrators.*
Skills Bank Corp.

Skills Bank 3: Mathematics. Mar. 1994. *Items Included:* Contents manual (Lesson & summaries), operations manual. *Customer Support:* Free 1-800 toll free line for technical support, 30 day full refund policy.
 MS-DOS. MS-DOS compatible (no PCjr), must have MS-DOS 3.1 or higher (512k). 3.5" disk $450.00 (ISBN 1-56985-064-X). *Nonstandard peripherals required:* Color or monochrome monitor. Must be able to display graphics (CGA, Herc, EGA, MCGA, or VGA). *Addl. software required:* MS-DOS 3.1 or higher. *Optimal configuration:* At least 1 computer with 2 drives (a floppy & a hard drive or two floppies), color monitor that supports graphics, hard drive with appoximately 18Mb.
5.25" disk $450.00 (ISBN 1-56985-058-5). *Provides Lessons, Quizzes & Tests for Mastering Basic Education Skills in Computation, Concepts, Word Problems, & Measurement & Introduction to Geometry & Algebra. It Contains a Management System for Recording Student Scores & Reporting Progress to Teachers, Parents & Administrators.*
Skills Bank Corp.

Skills Bank 3: Mathematics. Mar. 1994. *Items Included:* Contents manual (Lesson & summaries), operations manual. *Customer Support:* Free 1-800 toll free line for technical support, 30 day full refund policy.
 Apple. Apple II2, IIc, IIgs, or MAC LC with Apple IIe card (128k). 3.5" disk $450.00 (ISBN 1-56985-052-6). *Nonstandard peripherals required:* 80 column card. *Addl. software required:* Monitor must have 80 column card. *Optimal configuration:* One computer with 2 drives (floppy & hard drive with 13Mb or 2 floppies), color or monochrome monitor.
5.25" disk $450.00 (ISBN 1-56985-046-1). *Provides Lessons, Quizzes & Tests for Mastering Basic Education Skills in Computation, Concepts, Word Problems, & Measurement & Introduction to Geometry & Algebra. It Contains a Management System for Recording Student Scores & Reporting Progress to Teachers, Parents & Administrators.*
Skills Bank Corp.

Skills Bank 3: Mathematics. Mar. 1994. *Items Included:* Contents manual (Lesson & summaries), operations manual. *Customer Support:* Free 1-800 toll free line for technical support, 30 day full refund policy.
 Apple/Network. Apple II2, IIc, IIgs, or MAC LC with Apple IIe card (128k). 3.5" disk $1350.00 (ISBN 1-56985-082-8). *Nonstandard peripherals required:* 80 column card. *Addl. software required:* Monitor must have 80 column card. *Optimal configuration:* One computer with 2 drives (floppy & hard drive with 13Mb or 2 floppies), color or monochrome monitor. *Networks supported:* Appleshare, Corvus, Digicard, Velan.
5.25" disk $1350.00 (ISBN 1-56985-076-3). *Provides Lessons, Quizzes & Tests for Mastering Basic Education Skills in Computation, Concepts, Word Problems, & Measurement & Introduction to Geometry & Algebra. It Contains a Management System for Recording Student Scores & Reporting Progress to Teachers, Parents & Administrators.*
Skills Bank Corp.

Skills Bank 3: Reading. Mar. 1994. *Items Included:* Contents manual (Lesson & summaries), operations manual. *Customer Support:* Free 1-800 toll free line for technical support, 30 day full refund policy.
 Mac. Mac Plus, SE, SE/30, Classic, Classic II, or any Mac II or LC (1Mb Sys 6, 2Mb Sys 7). 3.5" disk $450.00 (ISBN 1-56985-068-2). *Optimal configuration:* At least 1 computer with 2 drives (a floppy & a hard drive or two floppies), color or monochrome monitor, hard drive space - 19Mb.
Provides Lessons, Quizzes & Tests for Mastering Basic Education Skills in Vocabulary, Word Knowledge, & Reading Comprehension. It Contains a Management System for Recording Student Scores & Reporting Progress to Teachers, Parents & Administrators.
Skills Bank Corp.

Skills Bank 3: Reading. Mar. 1994. *Items Included:* Contents manual (Lesson & summaries), operations manual. *Customer Support:* Free 1-800 toll free line for technical support, 30 day full refund policy.
 Mac/Network version. Mac Plus, SE, SE/30, Classic, Classic II, or any Mac II or LC (1Mb Sys 6, 2Mb Sys 7). 3.5" disk $1350.00 (ISBN 1-56985-098-4). *Optimal configuration:* At least 1 computer with 2 drives (a floppy & a hard drive or two floppies), color or monochrome monitor, hard drive space - 19Mb. *Networks supported:* Appleshare.
Provides Lessons, Quizzes & Tests for Mastering Basic Education Skills in Vocabulary, Word Knowledge, & Reading Comprehension. It Contains a Management System for Recording Student Scores & Reporting Progress to Teachers, Parents & Administrators.
Skills Bank Corp.

Skills Bank 3: Reading. Mar. 1994. *Items Included:* Contents manual (Lesson & summaries), operations manual. *Customer Support:* Free 1-800 toll free line for technical support, 30 day full refund policy.
 MS-DOS/Network. MS-DOS compatible (no PCjr), must have MS-DOS 3.1 or higher (512k). 3.5" disk $1350.00 (ISBN 1-56985-092-5). *Nonstandard peripherals required:* Color or monochrome monitor. Must be able to display graphics (CGA, Herc, EGA, MCGA, or VGA). *Addl. software required:* MS-DOS 3.1 or higher. *Optimal configuration:* At least 1 computer with 2 drives (a floppy & a hard drive or two floppies), color monitor that supports graphics, hard drive with appoximately 18Mb. *Networks supported:* Novell, Novell with ICLAS, LANtastic, Digicard & Velan.
5.25" disk $1350.00 (ISBN 1-56985-086-0). *Provides Lessons, Quizzes & Tests for Mastering Basic Education Skills in Vocabulary, Word Knowledge, & Reading Comprehension. It Contains a Management System for Recording Student Scores & Reporting Progress to Teachers, Parents & Administrators.*
Skills Bank Corp.

Skills Bank 3: Reading. Mar. 1994. *Items Included:* Contents manual (Lesson & summaries), operations manual. *Customer Support:* Free 1-800 toll free line for technical support, 30 day full refund policy.
 MS-DOS. MS-DOS compatible (no PCjr), must have MS-DOS 3.1 or higher (512k). 3.5" disk $450.00 (ISBN 1-56985-062-3). *Nonstandard peripherals required:* Color or monochrome monitor. Must be able to display graphics (CGA, Herc, EGA, MCGA, or VGA). *Addl. software required:* MS-DOS 3.1 or higher. *Optimal configuration:* At least 1 computer with 2 drives (a floppy & a hard drive or two floppies), color monitor that supports graphics,

SKILLS BANK 3: STUDY SKILLS

hard drive with appoximately 18Mb. 5.25" disk $450.00 (ISBN 1-56985-056-9). *Provides Lessons, Quizzes & Tests for Mastering Basic Education Skills in Vocabulary, Word Knowledge, & Reading Comprehension. It Contains a Management System for Recording Student Scores & Reporting Progress to Teachers, Parents & Administrators.*
Skills Bank Corp.

Skills Bank 3: Reading. Mar. 1994. *Items Included:* Contents manual (Lesson & summaries), operations manual. *Customer Support:* Free 1-800 toll free line for technical support, 30 day full refund policy.
 Apple. Apple II2, IIc, IIgs, or MAC LC with Apple IIe card (128k). 3.5" disk $450.00 (ISBN 1-56985-050-X). *Nonstandard peripherals required:* 80 column card. *Addl. software required:* Monitor must have 80 column card. *Optimal configuration:* One computer with 2 drives (floppy & hard drive with 13Mb or 2 floppies), color or monochrome monitor.
5.25" disk $450.00 (ISBN 1-56985-044-5). *Provides Lessons, Quizzes & Tests for Mastering Basic Education Skills in Vocabulary, Word Knowledge, & Reading Comprehension. It Contains a Management System for Recording Student Scores & Reporting Progress to Teachers, Parents & Administrators.*
Skills Bank Corp.

Skills Bank 3: Reading. Mar. 1994. *Items Included:* Contents manual (Lesson & summaries), operations manual. *Customer Support:* Free 1-800 toll free line for technical support, 30 day full refund policy.
 Apple/Network. Apple II2, IIc, IIgs, or MAC LC with Apple IIe card (128k). 3.5" disk $1350.00 (ISBN 1-56985-080-1). *Nonstandard peripherals required:* 80 column card. *Addl. software required:* Monitor must have 80 column card. *Optimal configuration:* One computer with 2 drives (floppy & hard drive with 13Mb or 2 floppies), color or monochrome monitor. *Networks supported:* Appleshare, Corvus, Digicard, Velan.
5.25" disk $1350.00 (ISBN 1-56985-074-7). *Provides Lessons, Quizzes & Tests for Mastering Basic Education Skills in Vocabulary, Word Knowledge, & Reading Comprehension. It Contains a Management System for Recording Student Scores & Reporting Progress to Teachers, Parents & Administrators.*
Skills Bank Corp.

Skills Bank 3: Study Skills. Mar. 1994. *Items Included:* Contents manual (Lesson & summaries), operations manual. *Customer Support:* Free 1-800 toll free line for technical support, 30 day full refund policy.
 Mac. Mac Plus, SE, SE/30, Classic, Classic II, or any Mac II or LC (1Mb Sys 6, 2Mb Sys 7). 3.5" disk $450.00 (ISBN 1-56985-072-0). *Optimal configuration:* At least 1 computer with 2 drives (a floppy & a hard drive or two floppies), color or monochrome monitor, hard drive space - 19Mb.
Provides Lessons, Quizzes & Tests for Mastering Basic Skills in High Order Thinking. It Contains a Management System for Recording Student Scores & Reporting Progress to Teachers, Parents & Administrators.
Skills Bank Corp.

Skills Bank 3: Study Skills. Mar. 1994. *Items Included:* Contents manual (Lesson & summaries), operations manual. *Customer Support:* Free 1-800 toll free line for technical support, 30 day full refund policy.
 Mac/Network version. Mac Plus, SE, SE/30, Classic, Classic II, or any Mac II or LC (1Mb Sys 6, 2Mb Sys 7). 3.5" disk $1350.00 (ISBN

1-56985-102-6). *Optimal configuration:* At least 1 computer with 2 drives (a floppy & a hard drive or two floppies), color or monochrome monitor, hard drive space - 19Mb. *Networks supported:* Appleshare.
Provides Lessons, Quizzes & Tests for Mastering Basic Skills in High Order Thinking. It Contains a Management System for Recording Student Scores & Reporting Progress to Teachers, Parents & Administrators.
Skills Bank Corp.

Skills Bank 3: Study Skills. Mar. 1994. *Items Included:* Contents manual (Lesson & summaries), operations manual. *Customer Support:* Free 1-800 toll free line for technical support, 30 day full refund policy.
MS-DOS/Network. MS-DOS compatible (no PCjr), must have MS-DOS 3.1 or higher (512k). 3.5" disk $1350.00 (ISBN 1-56985-096-8). *Nonstandard peripherals required:* Color or monochrome monitor. Must be able to display graphics (CGA, Herc, EGA, MCGA, or VGA). *Addl. software required:* MS-DOS 3.1 or higher. *Optimal configuration:* At least 1 computer with 2 drives (a floppy & a hard drive or two floppies), color monitor that supports graphics, hard drive with appoximately 18Mb. *Networks supported:* Novell, Novell with ICLAS, LANtastic, Digicard & Velan.
5.25" disk $1350.00 (ISBN 1-56985-090-9).
Provides Lessons, Quizzes & Tests for Mastering Basic Skills in High Order Thinking. It Contains a Management System for Recording Student Scores & Reporting Progress to Teachers, Parents & Administrators.
Skills Bank Corp.

Skills Bank 3: Study Skills. Mar. 1994. *Items Included:* Contents manual (Lesson & summaries), operations manual. *Customer Support:* Free 1-800 toll free line for technical support, 30 day full refund policy.
MS-DOS. MS-DOS compatible (no PCjr), must have MS-DOS 3.1 or higher (512k). 3.5" disk $450.00 (ISBN 1-56985-066-2). *Nonstandard peripherals required:* Color or monochrome monitor. Must be able to display graphics (CGA, Herc, EGA, MCGA, or VGA). *Addl. software required:* MS-DOS 3.1 or higher. *Optimal configuration:* At least 1 computer with 2 drives (a floppy & a hard drive or two floppies), color monitor that supports graphics, hard drive with appoximately 18Mb.
5.25" disk $450.00 (ISBN 1-56985-060-7).
Provides Lessons, Quizzes & Tests for Mastering Basic Skills in High Order Thinking. It Contains a Management System for Recording Student Scores & Reporting Progress to Teachers, Parents & Administrators.
Skills Bank Corp.

Skills Bank 3: Study Skills. Mar. 1994. *Items Included:* Contents manual (Lesson & summaries), operations manual. *Customer Support:* Free 1-800 toll free line for technical support, 30 day full refund policy.
Apple. Apple II2, IIc, IIgs, or MAC LC with Apple IIe card (128k). 3.5" disk $450.00 (ISBN 1-56985-054-2). *Nonstandard peripherals required:* 80 column card. *Addl. software required:* Monitor must have 80 column card. *Optimal configuration:* One computer with 2 drives (floppy & hard drive with 13Mb or 2 floppies), color or monochrome monitor.
5.25" disk $450.00 (ISBN 1-56985-048-8).
Provides Lessons, Quizzes & Tests for Mastering Basic Skills in High Order Thinking. It Contains a Management System for Recording Student Scores & Reporting Progress to Teachers, Parents & Administrators.
Skills Bank Corp.

Skills Bank 3: Study Skills. Mar. 1994. *Items Included:* Contents manual (Lesson & summaries), operations manual. *Customer Support:* Free 1-800 toll free line for technical support, 30 day full refund policy.
Apple/Network. Apple II2, IIc, IIgs, or MAC LC with Apple IIe card (128k). 3.5" disk $1350.00 (ISBN 1-56985-084-4). *Nonstandard peripherals required:* 80 column card. *Addl. software required:* Monitor must have 80 column card. *Optimal configuration:* One computer with 2 drives (floppy & hard drive with 13Mb or 2 floppies), color or monochrome monitor. *Networks supported:* Appleshare, Corvus, Digicard, Velan.
5.25" disk $1350.00 (ISBN 1-56985-078-X).
Provides Lessons, Quizzes & Tests for Mastering Basic Skills in High Order Thinking. It Contains a Management System for Recording Student Scores & Reporting Progress to Teachers, Parents & Administrators.
Skills Bank Corp.

Skills Bank 3: Writing. Mar. 1994. *Items Included:* Contents manual (Lesson & summaries), operations manual. *Customer Support:* Free 1-800 toll free line for technical support, 30 day full refund policy.
Mac. Mac Plus, SE, SE/30, Classic, Classic II, or any Mac II or LC (1Mb Sys 6, 2Mb Sys 7). 3.5" disk $450.00 (ISBN 1-56985-071-2). *Optimal configuration:* At least 1 computer with 2 drives (a floppy & a hard drive or two floppies), color or monochrome monitor, hard drive space - 19Mb.
Provides Lessons, Quizzes & Tests for Mastering Basic Education Skills in Language Usage, Language Mechanics, Sentence Structure, & Paragraphing. It Contains a Management System for Recording Student Scores & Reporting Progress to Teachers, Parents & Administrators.
Skills Bank Corp.

Skills Bank 3: Writing. Mar. 1994. *Items Included:* Contents manual (Lesson & summaries), operations manual. *Customer Support:* Free 1-800 toll free line for technical support, 30 day full refund policy.
Mac/Network version. Mac Plus, SE, SE/30, Classic, Classic II, or any Mac II or LC (1Mb Sys 6, 2Mb Sys 7). 3.5" disk $1350.00 (ISBN 1-56985-101-8). *Optimal configuration:* At least 1 computer with 2 drives (a floppy & a hard drive or two floppies), color or monochrome monitor, hard drive space - 19Mb. *Networks supported:* Appleshare.
Provides Lessons, Quizzes & Tests for Mastering Basic Education Skills in Language Usage, Language Mechanics, Sentence Structure, & Paragraphing. It Contains a Management System for Recording Student Scores & Reporting Progress to Teachers, Parents & Administrators.
Skills Bank Corp.

Skills Bank 3: Writing. Mar. 1994. *Items Included:* Contents manual (Lesson & summaries), operations manual. *Customer Support:* Free 1-800 toll free line for technical support, 30 day full refund policy.
MS-DOS/Network. MS-DOS compatible (no PCjr), must have MS-DOS 3.1 or higher (512k). 3.5" disk $1350.00 (ISBN 1-56985-095-X). *Nonstandard peripherals required:* Color or monochrome monitor. Must be able to display graphics (CGA, Herc, EGA, MCGA, or VGA). *Addl. software required:* MS-DOS 3.1 or higher. *Optimal configuration:* At least 1 computer with 2 drives (a floppy & a hard drive or two floppies), color monitor that supports graphics, hard drive with appoximately 18Mb. *Networks supported:* Novell, Novell with ICLAS, LANtastic, Digicard & Velan.
5.25" disk $1350.00 (ISBN 1-56985-089-5).
Provides Lessons, Quizzes & Tests for Mastering Basic Education Skills in Language Usage, Language Mechanics, Sentence Structure, & Paragraphing. It Contains a Management System for Recording Student Scores & Reporting Progress to Teachers, Parents & Administrators.
Skills Bank Corp.

Skills Bank 3: Writing. Mar. 1994. *Items Included:* Contents manual (Lesson & summaries), operations manual. *Customer Support:* Free 1-800 toll free line for technical support, 30 day full refund policy.
MS-DOS. MS-DOS compatible (no PCjr), must have MS-DOS 3.1 or higher (512k). 3.5" disk $450.00 (ISBN 1-56985-065-8). *Nonstandard peripherals required:* Color or monochrome monitor. Must be able to display graphics (CGA, Herc, EGA, MCGA, or VGA). *Addl. software required:* MS-DOS 3.1 or higher. *Optimal configuration:* At least 1 computer with 2 drives (a floppy & a hard drive or two floppies), color monitor that supports graphics, hard drive with appoximately 18Mb.
5.25" disk $450.00 (ISBN 1-56985-059-3).
Provides Lessons, Quizzes & Tests for Mastering Basic Education Skills in Language Usage, Language Mechanics, Sentence Structure, & Paragraphing. It Contains a Management System for Recording Student Scores & Reporting Progress to Teachers, Parents & Administrators.
Skills Bank Corp.

Skills Bank 3: Writing. Mar. 1994. *Items Included:* Contents manual (Lesson & summaries), operations manual. *Customer Support:* Free 1-800 toll free line for technical support, 30 day full refund policy.
Apple. Apple II2, IIc, IIgs, or MAC LC with Apple IIe card (128k). 3.5" disk $450.00 (ISBN 1-56985-053-4). *Nonstandard peripherals required:* 80 column card. *Addl. software required:* Monitor must have 80 column card. *Optimal configuration:* One computer with 2 drives (floppy & hard drive with 13Mb or 2 floppies), color or monochrome monitor.
5.25" disk $450.00 (ISBN 1-56985-047-X).
Provides Lessons, Quizzes & Tests for Mastering Basic Education Skills in Language Usage, Language Mechanics, Sentence Structure, & Paragraphing. It Contains a Management System for Recording Student Scores & Reporting Progress to Teachers, Parents & Administrators.
Skills Bank Corp.

Skills Bank 3: Writing. Mar. 1994. *Items Included:* Contents manual (Lesson & summaries), operations manual. *Customer Support:* Free 1-800 toll free line for technical support, 30 day full refund policy.
Apple/Network. Apple II2, IIc, IIgs, or MAC LC with Apple IIe card (128k). 3.5" disk $1350.00 (ISBN 1-56985-083-6). *Nonstandard peripherals required:* 80 column card. *Addl. software required:* Monitor must have 80 column card. *Optimal configuration:* One computer with 2 drives (floppy & hard drive with 13Mb or 2 floppies), color or monochrome monitor. *Networks supported:* Appleshare, Corvus, Digicard, Velan.
5.25" disk $1350.00 (ISBN 1-56985-077-1).
Provides Lessons, Quizzes & Tests for Mastering Basic Education Skills in Language Usage, Language Mechanics, Sentence Structure, & Paragraphing. It Contains a Management System for Recording Student Scores & Reporting Progress to Teachers, Parents & Administrators.
Skills Bank Corp.

Skills in Electromyography. *Compatible Hardware:* Apple II, II+, IIe, IIc, IIgs. *Memory Required:* 64k.
$49.95.

Skin Preparation, Reducing EMG Artifact, Testing a Myograph's Operation, Locating Surface Electrodes & Preventing Shock Hazards Are Reviewed.
Biosource Software.

Skills Inventory. *Items Included:* Bound manual. *Customer Support:* Free hotline - no time limit; 30 day limited warranty; updates are $5/disk plus S&H.
MS-DOS. IBM & compatibles (128k). disk $149.95. *Nonstandard peripherals required:* Hard disk or dual-floppy; printer recommended, but not required.
Database Program Written Specifically for Employment Agencies, Contract Programming Companies, & Personnel Departments of Companies Wishing to Maintain a File of Job Candidates & Their Associated Characteristics.
Dynacomp, Inc.

Skintite Bidding. Soft Software. May 1986. *Compatible Hardware:* Apple Macintosh. *Memory Required:* 512k. *General Requirements:* 2 disk drives, printer; Excell or Double Helix application software.
3.5" disk $395.00.
Estimates Costs for Milling or Lathe Parts, Calculates Feed, Speed, Elapsed Time, Integrated to Answer "What If" Questions to Allow Changes in Machining to Optimize Tool Wear, Maximize Accuracy in Quoting Job Costing.
Machinery Alternative.

Sky Shadow. *Version:* 1.1. 1987. *Items Included:* Instructions, reg. card. *Customer Support:* Free phone support.
6.02 & higher. Macintosh. 3.5" disk $31.95 (Order no.: M102).
Dreaded Blood-Thirsty Invaders Have All but Destroyed Your Home Planet. Only Your Audacious, White-Knuckled Bombing Raids over Enemy Territory Can Save It.
Casady & Greene, Inc.

Skyblaster. *Customer Support:* Back up disks available.
Amiga (512k). $14.95.
Fast Paced 3-D Air/Ground Combat Simulation. Battle Planes & Tanks from Your Helicopter.
DigiTek Software.

Skyclock Graphical Astronomical Clock. *Items Included:* Full manual. No other products required. *Customer Support:* Free telephone support - no time limit. 30 day limited warranty.
MS-DOS 3.2 or higher. IBM & compatibles (512k). disk $49.95. *Optimal configuration:* IBM, MS-DOS 3.3 or higher, CGA/EGA/VGA (or compatible) graphics capability, & 1.2Mb floppy or 720k (or higher) minidisk. Math coprocessor is supported, but not necessary.
Sophisticated Astronomy Package Which Integrates Time & Space. Accurately Displays the Major Celestial Bodies on the Face of a Clock in Accordance to Their Topocentric, Geocentric, or Heliocentric Coordinates. In Addition, Allows Quick Access to Numerical Astronomical Data & Planetary Positions in Ephemeris Format.
Dynacomp, Inc.

SkyClock: Graphical Astronomical Clock. 1992. *Items Included:* Detailed manuals included with all Dynacomp products. *Customer Support:* Free telephone support to original customer - no time limit; 30 day limited warranty.
MS-DOS 3.2 or higher. IBM PC & compatibles (512k). $59.95 (Add $5.00 for 3 1/2" format; 5 1/4" format standard). *Optimal configuration:* IBM, MS-DOS 3.3 or higher, CGA/EGA/VGA or compatible graphics capability, & a 1.2Mb floppy or 720k or higher minidisk. A math coprocessor is supported, but

not necessary.
A Sophisticated Astronomy Package Which Integrates Time & Space. It Accurately Displays the Major Celestial Bodies on the Face of a Clock in Accordance to Their Topocentric, Geocentric, or Heliocentric Coordinates. With SkyClock You May Determine the Phase of the Moon on a Particular Date; Find Eclipses; See Where to Look for Mars; View the Configuration of the Planets, etc. All Displays Can Be Printed.
Dynacomp, Inc.

Skydiving Formation Planner: Computerized RW Dive Creator. *Version:* 1.1. Gary Peek. 1995. *Items Included:* Instruction sheet. *Customer Support:* Free telephone support.
MS-DOS. 386 (640k). disk $19.95 (ISBN 1-56860-015-1). *Nonstandard peripherals required:* VGA.
Now You Can Plan Various Skydiving Formations & Save Them to Disk for Later Recall. There are up to 24 Skydivers, Eight Different Colors & 16 Different Rotational Positions. Slots Can Be Added or Deleted Either in the Middle of the Lineup or at the End. Grid Lines for Precise Alignment of the Slots Are Available.
Para Publishing.

SKYLINE: The Property Management System. *Version:* 3.4. The SOFTA Group, Inc. Oct. 1991. *Compatible Hardware:* IBM & compatibles 386 & higher. *Operating System(s) Required:* MS-DOS 3.1 & higher. *Language(s):* C. *Memory Required:* 20Mb hard disk, RAM 1000k. *General Requirements:* External hard disk. *Items Included:* Documentation included with package. *Customer Support:* Toll-free telephone support, local on-site or classroom training, consultation, & on-line help. Users can join one of many nationwide SKYLINE user groups. Annual updates & enhancement service available.
$2995.00 (ISBN 0-917391-00-4).
Designed for Professional Real Estate Property & Asset Managers. Handles Commercial, Retail, Residential, Industrial Properties. 4,000 Plus Systems Installed with over 12,000 Users. CCIM Recommended, IREM Certified. Integrates with Major Spreadsheet & Word Processing Programs. Additional Modules Available Include: BREAKPOINT, for Shopping Center Management; the SKYLINE Financial System; Site Manager & Site Controller, for On-Site Residential Property Management; Select, Query & Report Systems; SKYVIEW, for Financial Analysis & Reporting; Advance Commercial Escalations; SKYLINK, Multi-Site Management; MICR Laser Check Printing Module; LOCKBOX Interface; HUD Management Interface.
The SOFTA Group, Inc.

SKYvec. *Version:* 3.0. Jun. 1992. *Items Included:* Includes Linker, Assembler, Debugger/Simulator, Utilities, documentation, drivers, diagnostics, release notes 12-month warranty & updates.
UNIX. SKYbolt family. Contact publisher for price.
Helps Post Existing Application Solutions & Speeds Creation of New Ones for the SKY Computers, Inc. Family of Application Accelerators. Built upon Open Systems Principles, SKYvec Development Tools, Libraries & Multi-Tasking Operating Software Are Designed to Provide a Familiar & Congenial Environment for Users of UNIX-Based Workstations.
SKY Computers, Inc.

SL-MICRO. *Items Included:* Bound manual. *Customer Support:* Free hotline - no time limit; 30 day limited warranty; updates are $5/disk plus S&H.
MS-DOS. IBM & compatibles (256k). disk $149.95.
Easy-to-Use Statistical Language Which Should

Already Be Familiar to Many Users of Statistical Packages on Mainframes. Can Process Large Data Files Containing up to 32,600 Cases with 200 Variables. Professional Results Are Produced Very Rapidly. The Procedures Implemented Include Frequencies, Crosstabs, Condescriptive, Pearson Correlation & Multiple Regression, Breakdown, & ANOVA (up to 5-Way).
Dynacomp, Inc.

Slab-Column Unbalanced Moment Checker. 1995. *Items Included:* Full manual. *Customer Support:* Free telephone support - 90 days, 30-day warranty.
MS-DOS 3.2 or higher. 286 (584k). disk $99.95. *Nonstandard peripherals required:* CGA/EGA/VGA.
Calculates the Ultimate Shear Stresses Produced at the Slab-Column Interface for a Flat Plate Slab Which Is Subjected to a Downward Shear Combined with Moments in Two Directions. It Compares Those Stresses to the Nominal Shear Capacity of the Slab. May Be Used to Interactively Design or Analyze a Slab-Column Interface.
Dynacomp, Inc.

Slav Defence: Meran: Electronic Chessbook. *Version:* 2. Edited by Rini Kuijf. Sep. 1994. *Items Included:* Book & disk with 500 or more games (over 200 annotated).
3.5" disk $25.00, incl. softcover text (ISBN 0-917237-02-1).
Atari ST (520k). Atari. disk $25.00.
Nonstandard peripherals required: Monochrome monitor DS/DD drive.
Authoritative Introduction to & Analysis of an Important Chess Opening.
Chess Combination, Inc.

Slav Defense: Botvinnik: Electronic Chessbook. R. Kuijf. *Items Included:* Softcover book. *Customer Support:* Free telephone support by appointment.
MS-DOS 2.0 or higher. 80086 (512k). disk $25.00. *Nonstandard peripherals required:* Mouse, any graphics.
Atari ST. 520. *Nonstandard peripherals required:* Monochrome monitor.
Study of Chess Opening.
Chess Combination, Inc.

SLE - Business Series: Business Management Modules for dBASE III. Jan. 1986. *Compatible Hardware:* IBM PC & compatibles. *Operating System(s) Required:* PC-DOS. *Memory Required:* 256k. *General Requirements:* Hard disk.
contact publisher for price (Order no.: SLE 1000).
Enables Executives to Easily Convert Their dBASE III Software into a Ready-to-Use, Menu-Driven Business System. Modules Include: Accounts Payable, Accounts Receivable, Payroll, Personal Data Base, Client Data Base, Inventory Control, Price Lookup System, & Catalog Lookup System. New Modules Are Continually Being Added to the Series.
Software Lab East.

SLEd: Signature Logo Editor. *Version:* 2.2. Jul. 1992. *Compatible Hardware:* IBM PC, PC XT, PC AT. *Operating System(s) Required:* MS-DOS 2.X. *Memory Required:* 512k. *General Requirements:* Hard disk; HP, Cordata, Canon, NCR, or Ricoh laser printer. *Items Included:* VS laser word processor tool kit, clip art, manuals. *Customer Support:* Telephone/FAX/Mail/BBS (No charge).
disk $295.00.
Graphics Editor Which Provides a Way to Include Graphics with Any Word Processor That Can Select Laser Fonts. Has the Ability to Store a Graphic Image As a Series of Characters,

927

Creating a "Graphic Font." Prints Scanned Pictures, Drawings, Logos, & Signatures Inside Any Word Processor. Also Functions As a Graphics & Font Editor, & Can Save Images in GEM, TIF or PC PAINTBRUSH Format for Use with Desktop Publishers.
VS Software.

SleepLine CD-ROM Database for Sleep Disorders. Jun. 1993.
MS Windows 3.1 or higher. IBM & compatibles (4Mb). CD-ROM disk $325.00-$995.00; Networks $1895.00 & up. *Nonstandard peripherals required:* Magnetic or CD-ROM, using ISO 9660. *Optimal configuration:* IBM & compatibles, 80386 or higher, 4Mb RAM, 20Mb hard disk, mouse, MS Windows 3.1 or higher.
System 6.0.7 or higher. Apple Macintosh (3Mb). CD-ROM disk $325.00-$995.00; Networks $1895.00 & up. *Optimal configuration:* Apple Macintosh Plus or higher, 3Mb RAM, System 6.0.7 or higher.
SleepLine Is an Electronic Reference Database to the Sleep Disorders & Research Journal Literature. Sleep Disorders-Specific Excerpts (Including Abstracts) from the National Library of Medicine's MEDLINE Database Are Distributed on CD-ROM (Compact Disc, Read-Only Memory) Optical Disc. Knowledge Finder Search-&-Retrieval Software Makes Searching of the SleepLine Database Easy, Effective & Fast. After the User Types a Phrase or Sentence Describing the Information Needed, It selects the References in the Database That Appear to Best Match the Request, & Presents Them in Order of likely relevance. The SleepLine Archive CD-ROM Contains over 390,000 References to Articles Published in 115 Sleep Disorders & Research-Related Journals over the Most Recent 10 Full Years. Sleep Disorders Articles from More Than 2,500 Other Journals Are Also Included.
Aries Systems Corp.

Slender Concrete Wall Design. 1995. *Items Included:* Full manual. *Customer Support:* Free telephone support - 90 days, 30-day warranty.
MS-DOS 3.2 or higher. 286 (584k). disk $99.95. *Nonstandard peripherals required:* CGA/EGA/VGA.
Calculates the Reinforcement for a Slender Wall Using the P-Delta Method of Section 1914.8 of the UBC Coce. Inputs Include Wall Dimensions, Dead & Live Loads, Eccentricity, & Seismic & Wind Loads. Outputs Include Required Reinforcement, Stress Check at Mid-Height, Nominal Capacity, Service Deflection, & the P-Delta Moment.
Dynacomp, Inc.

SLIC-IV: Mesh Generation. *Version:* 4.50. Russell C. Greenlaw & Michael A. Gerhard. Mar. 1994. *Operating System(s) Required:* MS-DOS, PC-DOS, DEC VAX, Micro VAX, CDC NOS. *Customer Support:* Free.
MS-DOS or PC-DOS. $1995.00 & up.
DEC VAX, Micro VAX. $4265.00 & up tape.
CDC NOS (tape). $6398.00 & up.
Sun OS. Sun SPARC. $4265.00 & up.
Interactive/Graphic Parametric Layout of Finite Element Meshes for SAP-90, DYNA-3D & Similar 3D Stress Codes. Multitude of Features & Supported Objects.
Faast Software.

Slide Presentation Software. *Compatible Hardware:* IBM PC XT. *Memory Required:* 512k.
disk $150.00.
Presentation-Graphics Package for On-Screen Slide Shows. Features Dissolves, Wipes, & 32,768 User-Selectable Colors. Imports TGA File Formats. Allows TARGA Users to Create Slide Shows. Can Be Used for Video Production Using the Video Overlay Capabilities of TARGA.
Truevision, Inc.

Slide Write Presenter. *Items Included:* 76-page manual, SHOOT screen capture utility, routine version of Presenter (makes shows portable). *Customer Support:* Unlimited, free.
DOS 2.0 or higher. IBM PC & compatible (390k). contact publisher for price. *Nonstandard peripherals required:* EGA (25k memory) or VGA.
Displays PCX Files from Graphics Packages, Scanners & Paint Programs to Create Custom Slide Show Presentations with Special Effects on the Computer Screen. The Program Has a Graphical User Interface & Includes a Powerful Screen Capture Program.
Advanced Graphics Software, Inc.

SlideShow. *Customer Support:* 800-929-8117 (customer service).
MS-DOS. Apple II. disk $49.99 (ISBN 0-87007-260-9).
Enables User to Set up Colorful Slideshow Presentations on an Apple.
SourceView Software International.

SlideWrite Plus, 3 disks. *Version:* 3.1. *Compatible Hardware:* IBM PC & compatibles. *Operating System(s) Required:* MS-DOS 2.0 or higher. *Memory Required:* 390k. *General Requirements:* Mouse supported. *Items Included:* 400 page manual with tutorial & samples. *Customer Support:* Free, unlimited.
$445.00.
Slide Write Plus for the IBM PC Creates Graphs with X & Y Error Bars, Seven Curve Fits Including Spline & Polynomial, 16 Fonts, Greek/Math Characters, 4000 Points, 12 Data Series, Variable Marker Size & Line Thickness, Equation Plotting, Full Drawing Capability Including Scanned Images & Annotations.
Advanced Graphics Software, Inc.

SLIM: Software LifeCycle Management. *Version:* 3.0. Jul. 1988. *Compatible Hardware:* IBM PC, PC XT, PC AT, & true compatibles. *Operating System(s) Required:* PC-DOS, Windows 3.1. *Memory Required:* 640k. *General Requirements:* Hard disk, printer, color monitor.
$25,000.00 per yr.
Management Tool Used for Estimating, Planning & Controlling Large Software Development Projects. Designed to Help Companies Plan Before Project Begins & Avoid Cost Overruns & Schedule Slippages That Come As a Result of Poor Planning & Unreasonable Expectations. Features Extensive Reliability Prediction Function & Built-In Risk Assessment.
Quantitative Software Management, Inc.

Sling Psychrometer Psychometric Chart Evaluation. *Items Included:* Full manual. No other products required. *Customer Support:* Free telephone support - no time limit. 30 day warranty.
MS-DOS 3.2 or higher. IBM & compatibles (512k). disk $79.95.
Fully Menu-Driven, Easy-to-Use, & Exceptionally Accurate Software Replacement for Psychrometric Charts. No Longer Do You Need to Tediously Read & Interpolate Psychometric Charts. Just Enter Two Independent State Valuables, & the Rest Are Determined Automatically. Supports Both English & Metric Units.
Dynacomp, Inc.

Slip Stream. Ian Potts. Apr. 1989.
Amiga (512k). disk $39.95. *Addl. software required:* Joystick.
Fly Through the Stream Trying to Avoid Various Craft While Attempting to Destroy the Power Crystal at End of Stream.
MichTron, Inc.

Slope: Hansen Solubility Parameters & Interaction Energies. 1995. *Items Included:* Full manual. *Customer Support:* Free telephone support - 90 days, 30-day warranty.
MS-DOS 3.2 or higher. 286 (584k). disk $299.95. *Nonstandard peripherals required:* CGA/EGA/VGA.
Rapidly Estimates Hansen Solubility Parameters from Molecular Composition for Organic Molecules & Polymers. The Calculation Is Based on the Chemical Groups Present in the Molecule. Takes into Consideration That Hydrogen Bonding May Be Different in Mixed Association. Specific Hydrogen Bond Energies Are Used in Order to Predict More Appropriate Interaction Energies & Flory Chi Parameters. Interacts with the User in a Conversational Mode. It Provides Help Screens & Guidance When the User Needs to Make a Decision.
Dynacomp, Inc.

Slots & Cards. Nimbus. 1989.
IBM PC & Compatibles (512k). disk $39.95.
Amiga, Atari ST (512k). disk $39.95.
Collection of Slot Machines & Card Games.
MichTron, Inc.

SLRNK: SuperLinkers. Stephen L. Russell. 1983-1985. *Operating System(s) Required:* CP/M. *Memory Required:* 32k.
disk non-virtual $49.95 (Order no.: 131).
disk virtual version $195.00 (Order no.: 181).
SLR Systems.

Slurry Mass Transfer Analysis. *Items Included:* Bound manual. *Customer Support:* Free hotline - no time limit; 30 day limited warranty; updates are $5/disk plus S&H.
MS-DOS 2.1 or higher. IBM & compatibles (256k). disk $169.95. *Nonstandard peripherals required:* CGA, EGA, VGA, Hercules (or compatible) graphics card.
Tool for Solving Formulas Which Are Common in the Design of Slurry-Handling Systems. Define the Slurry in Terms of the Physical Properties & Mix Percentages of Each Component. Calculates the Specific Gravity, Dry Mass Flow Rate, Total Mass Flow Rate, Piping Head Loss, etc.
Dynacomp, Inc.

Small Assembler: An 80x86 Macro Assembler Written in Small C. James E. Hendrix. Jan. 1989. *Operating System(s) Required:* MS-DOS. *Language(s):* Small C.
disk $29.95, incl. manual (ISBN 1-55851-024-9).
Table-Driven Macro Assembler That Assembles Codes for All of the CPUs & Numeric Processors in the 80x86 Family & Is Compatible with Microsoft MASM, Providing an Example for Learning of How an Assembler Works. The Manual Provides an Overview of the Assembler & Its Capabilities, Surveys the Concepts & Facilities of the Assembler, Documents the Command Lines That Invoke the Programs in the Package, & Provides Appendixes of Reference Materials for the Programmer. Included Are the Small Assembler, Linkage Editor, CPU Configuration Utility, & a Program to Back up a File System. The Disk Contains a Fully Executable Assembler & Complete C Source Code.
M & T Bks.

Small Bookkeeping Services. *Version:* 9.0. Sep. 1990. *Operating System(s) Required:* MS-DOS. *Memory Required:* 640k. *General Requirements:* Hard disk. *Items Included:* Manuals, training exercises, support. *Customer Support:* 3 months free.
disk $695.00.
Designed for the Small to Medium-Sized Accountant. Small Bookkeeping Devices Contain Two Parts Which Are As Follows: Client Write-Up Features Valid Account Verification, Zero

TITLE INDEX

Proof of Each Transaction, Automatic Date Default with Override, Incrementing Reference Number, Integrated General Ledger Update, Latitude in Account Numbering, General Ledger Accounts Not Consumed for Report Formatting, Allows Departmental Profit Analysis & Consolidation, up to 13 Periods per Year, Operating Statement Features Percentage Calculations, This Year/Last Year Comparisons, &/or Budget Variances, Flexiblity in Setting up Any Journal (Cash Disbursements, Cash Receipts, Sales, etc.); Payroll Accounting Features After-the-Fact Payroll Recording, Multi-State Tax Reporting Capability, Quarterly Tax Return Worksheets, Year-End Turnaround W-2 Forms, Optional General Ledger Integration, Calculates Proper Tax Deductions but Allows Full Input.
ADS Software, Inc.

Small Bookkeeping Services & Public Accounts. ADS Software, Inc. *Operating System(s) Required:* MS-DOS. *Memory Required:* 128k. *General Requirements:* 2 disk drives, printer.
$895.00.
Texas Instruments, Personal Productivit.

Small Business. CYMA Corp. *Operating System(s) Required:* CP/M-86, MS-DOS. *Memory Required:* 64k. *General Requirements:* Printer.
$1095.00 (Order no.: SY P/N T039-065).
Texas Instruments, Personal Productivit.

The Small Business Accountant. Continental Software. *Compatible Hardware:* TI Professional. *Operating System(s) Required:* MS-DOS. *Language(s):* MSBASIC. *Memory Required:* 128k. *General Requirements:* Winchester hard disk, printer.
$195.00.
Texas Instruments, Personal Productivit.

Small Business Accounting System. *Compatible Hardware:* Apple Macintosh/PC compatible. *Memory Required:* 512k. *General Requirements:* Microsoft Excel.
3.5" disk $99.00.
Designed for Users Who Are Running Cash- or Accrual-Based Businesses Primarily Out of One or More Checking Accounts.
Heizer Software.

Small Business Accounts Payable. *Compatible Hardware:* TI 99/4A. *Operating System(s) Required:* DX-10. *Language(s):* Console BASIC. *Memory Required:* 16k.
cassette $31.95.
Creates & Maintains a List of Paid Bills & Open Accounts Payable. List Contains: Vendor Number & Name, Unpaid Balance, Date of Last Payment, etc. Various Reports Can Be Generated from This Information.
Eastbench Software Products.

Small Business Banking. 1984. *Compatible Hardware:* Apple II, II+, IIe, IIc; Franklin Ace. *Operating System(s) Required:* Apple DOS 3.3. *Language(s):* BASIC, Machine. *Memory Required:* 48k. *Customer Support:* Help at (305) 977-0686.
Disk set. $69.95, incl. manual (ISBN 0-87284-010-7).
Keeps Records of Bank Accounts & Provides Analysis of Receipts, Payments & Charges.
The Professor Corp.

Small Business Cash Flow Planner. 1984. *Compatible Hardware:* Apple II, II+, IIe, IIc; Franklin Ace. *Operating System(s) Required:* Apple DOS 3.3. *Language(s):* BASIC, Machine. *Memory Required:* 48k. *Customer Support:* Help at (305) 977-0686.
Disk set. $99.95, incl. manual (ISBN 0-87284-011-5).
Controls Cash Flow & Projects Future Available Cash.
The Professor Corp.

The Small Business Expert. Michael D. Jenkins. *Items Included:* Related resources available from PSI Research/The Oasis Press. *Customer Support:* 15 day unlimited warranty - telephone technical.
DOS 2.1 or higher. IBM PC, XT, AT, PS/2 & compatibles (256K). 3.5" or 5.25" disk $59.95. *Addl. software required:* Hard disk or 2-360K floppy drives or 1-720K floppy drive.
A Program to Help People Effectively Start or Operate a Business. It Instantly Provides Information on State & Federal Taxes & Laws. It Also Gives Expert Pointers on Hiring Staff, Marketing, & Purchasing a Business. In Addition, This Comprehensive Program Addresses Many Legal Questions, Including the Ramifications of Setting up a Partnership or Corporation. It Provides Checklists for: Purchasing an Existing Business; Leasing an Existing Business, Buying a Franchise, & More. Also Runs BallPark Calculations for Estimating Basic Personal, Estate, & Federal Taxes.
Oasis Pr.

Small Business Expert. *Customer Support:* Free technical support over phone; limited warranty.
DOS 2.0 or higher. IBM & compatibles (384k).
disk $34.95 (ISBN 1-55571-323-8, Order no.: SBXPSS/A31). *Nonstandard peripherals required:* Hard disk.
Provides State & Federal Laws, Regulations & Taxes on Your Specific Type & Location of Business. Great What-If Scenario Analyzer for Starting, Moving or Purchasing a Business. Covers over 125 Business Subject Areas.
Oasis Pr., The.

Small Business Invoicer. *Items Included:* Bound manual. *Customer Support:* Free hotline - no time limit; 30 day limited warranty; updates are $5/disk plus S&H.
MS-DOS 2.0 or higher. IBM & compatibles (128k). disk $89.95. *Nonstandard peripherals required:* Two disk drives (or one floppy & a hard disk), & an 80-column (or wider printer).
Designed for Businesses Which Charge for Both Time & Expenses, Work on a Project Basis, & Need to Show Considerable Itemized Detail on Their Invoices.
Dynacomp, Inc.

Small Business Legal Pro. *Version:* 2.0. Steingold. Oct. 1995.
Windows. IBM. disk $39.95 (ISBN 0-87337-313-8).
Mac. 3.5" disk $39.95 (ISBN 0-87337-317-0).
Formerly "Legal Guide to Starting & Running a Small Business on Disc".
Nolo Pr.

Small Business Management Using Lotus 1-2-3. 1987.
IBM/Tandy. contact publisher for price (ISBN 0-538-28402-1, Order no.: G268-1G).
Students Purchase Text-Workbook (G262) to Use With the Template Diskette. Shows How to Use Lotus For Many Small-Business Applications (e.g. Preparing a Business Plan, Financial Planning, Pricing, Inventory, Management, etc.).
South-Western Publishing Co.

Small Business Mini-Inventory. *Version:* 2. Jan. 1987. *Compatible Hardware:* IBM PC. *Operating System(s) Required:* MS-DOS. *Language(s):* Compiled BASIC. *Memory Required:* 256k.
disk $69.95.
Designed to Update Inventory with the

SMALL TIPS DESK ACESSORY

Occurrence of Each Sale or Item Restocked. Figures & Prints Inventory, Sales, & Reorder Data. There Are 2800 Items That Are Listed by Code, Name, Purchase, & Retail Price.
International Software.

Small Business System. *Compatible Hardware:* Atari 400, 800. *Memory Required:* 48k. *General Requirements:* 2 disk drives, printer.
disk $69.95.
Handles the Accounting, Examination & Scheduling of Chores in a Practice.
Dynacomp, Inc.

Small-C Compiler. Ron Cain. *Compatible Hardware:* IBM PC. *Operating System(s) Required:* CP/M. *Language(s):* C (source code included). *Memory Required:* 48k.
8" disk $19.95, incl. manual.
5-1/4" disk avail.
Supports a Limited Subset of C & Is 1/3 Faster As Q-C.
Jeffries Research.

A Small C Compiler: Language, Usage, Theory, & Design. James E. Hendrix. *Operating System(s) Required:* MS-DOS.
book & disk $39.95 (ISBN 0-934375-88-7).
book only $23.95 (ISBN 0-934375-97-6).
Contains a Presentation of the Design & Theory of the Small C Compiler & Programming Language. All Source Code for the Compiler Is Included. Provides a Full Compiler That Includes the Basics of How a Compiler Works, Making It a Tool for Learning Basic Compiler Theory.
M & T Bks.

Small Engine Part Numbers. Andrew Bear. 1987. *Compatible Hardware:* Apple II, II+, IIe, IIc. *Operating System(s) Required:* ProDOS. *Memory Required:* 64k. *General Requirements:* 2 disk drives, printer, 80-column card.
disk $34.50 (ISBN 1-55797-088-2, Order no.: AP2-AG298).
Designed to Supply the User with Information on Manufacturer's Part Numbers, Tune-Up Specifications, Torque Specifications, & Part Notes from the Six Major Manufacturers of Air-Cooled Small Gas Engines. The Manufacturers Are: Briggs & Stratton, Clinton, Tecumseh-Lauson (Two- & Four-Cycle), Koeler, & Power Bee. Each Engine Manufacturer Is Listed Individually, Allowing the User to Select Information Indexed by Model Number. The Printout Feature Includes Model Number, Part Name, & Notes.
Hobar Pubns.

Small Mac: An Assembler for Small-C. James E. Hendrix. Sep. 1985. *Operating System(s) Required:* CP/M.
manual & disk $29.95 (ISBN 0-934375-05-4).
Macro-Assembler Featuring a Simplified Macro Facility, C-Language Expression Operators, Descriptive Error Messages, Object File Visibility, & an Externally Defined Machine Instruction Table. Includes: Macro Assembler, Linkage Editor, Load-&-Go Loader, Library Manager, CPU Configuration Utility, & Dump Relocation Files.
M & T Bks.

Small Text. *Customer Support:* 800-929-8117 (customer service).
MS-DOS. IBM/PS2. disk $39.99 (ISBN 0-87007-386-9).
A Basic Subroutine for Programmers to Plug into Their Programs Which Calls the Subscript ROMS on Printers for Tiny Prints.
SourceView Software International.

Small Tips Desk Acessory. *Compatible Hardware:* Apple Macintosh. *Operating System(s) Required:* Finder 4.1, 5.3.

3.5" disk $19.50.
Stores & Displays "Tips" or Other Useful Information While Running an Application.
Kinko's.

Small Tools: Programs for Text Processing. James E. Hendrix. Sep. 1985. *Operating System(s) Required:* CP/M, MS-DOS, PC-DOS. manual & disk $29.95 (ISBN 0-934375-03-8).
Designed to Perform Specific Functions on Text Files, Including: Editing, Formatting, Sorting, Merging, Listing, Printing, Searching, Changing, Transliterating, Copying & Concatenating, Encrypting, Replacing Spaces with Tabs & Tabs with Spaces, Counting Characters, Words, or Lines, & Selecting Printer Fonts.
M & T Bks.

Small-Windows: A Library of Windowing Functions for the C Language. James E. Hendrix. *Operating System(s) Required:* MS-DOS. *General Requirements:* Microsoft C 4.0/5.0, Turbo C 1.5, Small C, or Lattice C compiler.
disk $29.95, incl. manual (ISBN 0-934375-35-6).
Library of C Language Functions for Creating & Manipulating Display Windows. Contained Are 41 Windowing Functions, Including Those That Allow to Clean, Frame, Move, Hide, & Scroll. A File Directory Illustrates the Use of Window Menu Functions, & Provides File Selection & Renaming & Deletion Capabilities. Two Test Programs Are Provided As Examples. Full Source Code Is Included.
M & T Bks.

Smalltalk-80. *Compatible Hardware:* Apple Macintosh, Macintosh Plus.
3.5" disk $995.00.
Programming Environment.
ParcPlace Systems.

Smalltalk/V. *Version:* 2.0. *Compatible Hardware:* IBM PC XT, PC AT, PS/2 & compatibles. *Operating System(s) Required:* PC-DOS, MS-DOS. *Memory Required:* 512k. *General Requirements:* CGA, EGA, VGA, AT&T 6300, Toshiba T3100 or IBM 3270 graphics board; Microsoft or compatible mouse (recommended). *Customer Support:* 60 day money-back guarantee, technical phone support, user newsletter, bulletin board support, reduced-price product upgrades.
disk $99.95, incl. manual.
EGA/VGA Extension Kit. $49.95. *Nonstandard peripherals required:* EGA board with 256k & IBM enhanced color monitor or compatible.
Communications Applications Pack. $49.95.
  Nonstandard peripherals required: Hayes compatible modem.
Goodies #1, Applications Pack. $49.95.
Goodies #2, Carleton Tools. $49.95.
Goodies #3, Carleton Projects. $49.95.
Programming Environment for Prototyping & Developing Applications. Features Include: Object-Oriented Programming; User-Extensible, Open-Ended Environment; Graphical User Interface; Support for Exploratory Programming & Prototyping; Class Hierarchy with Inheritance to Create Highly Re-Usable Code; Bit-Mapped Graphics with Bit & Form Editors; Source-Level Debugger; Optional Communications Interface to UNIX & Other Systems; Access to Other Languages & DOS Functions; DOS Command Shell; etc. Not Copy Protected.
Digitalk, Inc.

Smalltalk/V. *Compatible Hardware:* IBM PC & compatibles. *Operating System(s) Required:* PC-DOS/MS-DOS. *Memory Required:* 256k. *General Requirements:* Hard disk recommended. *Items Included:* 32 pg. Thinking Software catalog.
IBM PC version. 5.25" or 3.5" disk $99.95.
IBM PC AT version. $199.95.
Problem-Solving Tool Featuring Object-Oriented Programming. Users Program by Classifying Objects & Defining Interactions & Class Inheritance. Includes a Graphics Interface & Mouse Support.
Thinking Software, Inc.

Smalltalk/V Mac. *Version:* 1.1. *Compatible Hardware:* Apple Macintosh Plus, Macintosh SE, Macintosh II. *Memory Required:* 1500k. *Customer Support:* 60 day money back guarantee, technical phone support, user newsletter, bulletin board support, reduced-price product upgrades.
3.5" disk $199.95.
Delivers an Environment Suited to Problem Solving. Consists of a Development Language & an Interactive Development Environment. Users Can Create Smalltalk Code, Highlight It with a Mouse, & Immediately Test It Without Compilation & Linking Steps. Allows Users to Port Smalltalk/V or Smalltalk/V286 (for PCs) Applications Directly to Smalltalk/V Mac. The Resulting Application, Without Being Modified, Will Display Standard Macintosh Windows, as Well as Standard Zoom, Close, & Grow Boxes.
Digitalk, Inc.

Smalltalk/V PM. *Operating System(s) Required:* OS/2 1.1 or higher. *Items Included:* User manual, tutorial on object-oriented programming. *Customer Support:* 60 day money-back guarantee, technical phone support, user newsletter, bulletin board support, reduced price product upgrades.
$499.95.
Combines the Smalltalk/V Object-Oriented Programming Environment with Presentation Manager. Fully Integrated into the PM Environment. Provides Access to All PM Objects, Including Windows, Menus, Dialog Boxes & Scroll Bars. Applications Written in Other Smalltalk/V Environments Can Be Ported to Smalltalk/V PM. Provides Simplified Access to the Most Complex PM Features. Dynamic Data Exchange (DDE) Capabilities Allow Data to Be "Hot-Linked" to Applications Like Microsoft Excel with a Minimum of Programming. Any Dynamic Link Library (DLL) Call Can Be Made from Within Smalltalk/V PM. Compiler Generates Standalone Native Code Applications (.EXE) for Unrestricted Distribution, Requiring No Run-Time License Fees.
Digitalk, Inc.

Smalltalk V/286. *Version:* 1.1. *Compatible Hardware:* IBM PC AT, PS/2 & compatibles, 80386-based PCs. *Operating System(s) Required:* PC-DOS/MS-DOS, OS/2. *Memory Required:* 1500k. *General Requirements:* CGA, EGA, VGA, AT&T 6300, Toshiba T3100 or IBM 3270 graphics board; Microsoft or compatible mouse (recommended). *Customer Support:* 60 day money-back guarantee, technical phone support, user newsletter, bulletin board support, reduced-price product upgrades.
$199.95, incl. manual.
Communication Application Pack. $49.95.
  Nonstandard peripherals required: Hayes compatible modem.
Goodies #2, Carleton Tools. $49.95.
Goodies #3, Carleton Projects. $49.95.
Object-Oriented Programming System (OOPS) Tool for PCs. Features Debugging, Multi-Processing, Integrated Color Graphics, Class Library, & Access to 16Mb Protected Mode under DOS. Not Copy Protected.
Digitalk, Inc.

Smart Art.
System 6.02 or higher. Macintosh family of computers (1Mb). $99.00.
Four Libraries of Customized Headline Text & Graphic Effects.
Adobe Systems, Inc.

Smart Calendar. *Customer Support:* 800-929-8117 (customer service).
MS-DOS. Apple II. disk $49.99 (ISBN 0-87007-341-9).
Produces Several Kinds of Calendars, Including Graphics Depictions of User Provided Events, for Internal Distribution in a Friendly Format.
SourceView Software International.

The Smart Checkbook. *Version:* 2. 1990. *Compatible Hardware:* IBM PC, PC XT, PCjr; MS-DOS & CP/M based machines. *Operating System(s) Required:* PC-DOS/MS-DOS 1.1 or higher, CP/M, MP/M. *Language(s):* Compiled BASIC, Assembler. *Memory Required:* CP/M 56k; PC-DOS & MS-DOS 128k.
disk $75.00, incl. manual.
Financial Manager for Personal & Small Business Use That Keeps Financial Records, Writes Checks, Helps with Taxes, & Keeps Track of Budgets & Net Worth. Includes Search & Report Features & a Reconciliation Process That Locates Mistakes in an Account & Tells the User What They Are. Supports an Unlimited Number of Accounts, Including Checking, Cash, Money Market, Credit Card, Savings, Assets & Liabilities.
Softquest, Inc.

The Smart Data Manager. *Version:* 3.1. (The Smart Software System). Jan. 1987. *Compatible Hardware:* AT&T 6300 & compatibles, 3B; IBM PC, PC XT, PC AT, IBM 3270; Compaq, Compaq Plus; NCR Tower. *Operating System(s) Required:* DOS 2.0 or higher, UNIX V, SCO XENIX V. *Language(s):* C. *Memory Required:* 256k. *General Requirements:* 2 double-sided disk drives or hard disk; certain printers may require additional RAM.
disk DOS version $695.00, contact vendor for prices on other versions.
Part of the Smart Series of Integrated Software. Includes the Following Features: 1000 Characters per Field, 4000 Characters & 255 Fields per Record, 1,000,000 Records per File, up to 15 Key Fields Maintained for Sorting, up to 10 Files at Once, up to 50 Windows, up to 10 Screen Views, up to 15 Pages per Screen View, Security Password Entry at Screen & File Levels, 8 Field Types for Validation, "Read Only", & Must Enter" Fields, Temporary Keys for Output, Multiple Select Criteria Allowing Complex Queries of Files, Custom Defined Menus, & Many More.
Informix Software, Inc.

The Smart Data Manager. Innovative Software, Inc. Mar. 1984. *Compatible Hardware:* TI Professional. *Operating System(s) Required:* MS-DOS. *Memory Required:* 128k. *General Requirements:* 2 disk drives, printer.
$595.00.
Texas Instruments, Personal Productivit.

The Smart Database. *Operating System(s) Required:* MS-DOS/PC-DOS, OS/2, PC LAN, Xenix 386, Xenix 286.
$695.00.
Each Additional User License on PC LAN. $195.00.
Database Management System Provides On-Screen Help, Structured File Definition, Split & Merge Files, Built-in Editor, Debugging Facilities & Compiler. Features 255 Fields Per Record; 1000 Characters in Field; 1,000,000 Records Per File; 4,096 Characters in Record; Unlimited Indexes Per File; & up to 50 Active Indexes (1 Per Window). Offers 38 Commands, 150 Functions, Limited by Memory with Lines Per Command Field, & Memory is Depended with Variables. Data-Import/Export Capabilities Include Comma-Delimited ASCII, DIF, SYLK, & WKS.
Informix Software, Inc.

TITLE INDEX

Smart Expert Editor. Version: 3.1. John M. Smart. 1977. Compatible Hardware: IBM PS/2 or compatibles, DEC VAX, UNIX Workstations, IBM RS/6000, DEC 5000, SUN Sparcstation, HP900/700. Items Included: Training. Customer Support: Hot line, Internet.
MS-DOS, UNIX, SUN/OS, Solaris 2.1 Windows, DEC Alpha OSF/1, Motif, HP/UX. site license, $12,500.00.
Site & Network Licenses. contact publisher for price.
Critiques Technical Writing of Product Manuals for Controlled English, Grammar, Syntax, Vocabulary, Translatability, Good Style, etc. Produces a Report Showing Errors & Possible Corrections. Pre-Editor Smart Translations & Computer Translation of Technical Manuals into French, Spanish, German & Other Languages. Applications Include Writing of Technical Documentation for International Audiences in Controlled English.
Smart Communications, Inc.

Smart Keyboard. Compatible Hardware: Atari 400, 800. Language(s): Atari BASIC. Memory Required: 24k.
disk $19.95.
Execute Several Commands During System Startup or Program Keyboard to Expand a Single Keystroke into a Set of Characters.
Dynacomp, Inc.

The Smart LAN Performance Test. Jun. 1986. Compatible Hardware: IBM PC & compatibles. Operating System(s) Required: MS-DOS; Novell, 3Com. Memory Required: 256k, multiuser mode requires 384k. General Requirements: 2 disk drives or hard disk.
disk $49.95.
Standardized Test Program That Allows Users to Compare the Performance of Local Area Network Systems in a Simulated Working Environment. Included Is a Copy of the Smart Demo Pack, a Limited File Size Version of the Modularly Integrated Smart Software System. May Be Used on any IBM NETBIOS & DOS Call 3.1 or Higher LAN Operating System.
Informix Software, Inc.

Smart Menu. 1995. Items Included: Manual. Customer Support: One year of the CSAP is provided at n/c.
MS-DOS. IBM or compatibles (640k). 3.5" disk $29.95 if current w/CSAP; $99.95 if not current w/CSAP (ISBN 0-927875-70-5, Order no.: 1955). Addl. software required: Winnebago CIRC and/or CAT V 5.1 or higher. Optimal configuration: Same as Winnebago CIRC/CAT. Networks supported: IPX or Netbios compatible.
5.25" disk $29.95 if current w/CSAP; $99.95 if not current w/CSAP (ISBN 0-927875-71-3, Order no.: 1955).
With Smart Menu, User Can Select a Program from an Automatically Displayed Menu & Run It Without Typing a Single DOS Command. Files Are Named & Added to a Menu That Is Instantly Displayed When You Start Your Computer.
Winnebago Software Co.

Smart Notes. Compatible Hardware: IBM PC, PC XT, PC AT & compatibles. Operating System(s) Required: PC-DOS/MS-DOS 2.0 or higher. Memory Required: 80k.
disk $79.95.
Memory-Resident Program That Lets Users Attach Notes Anywhere on the Screen, in Almost Any Environment, Including Database Records, Spreadsheet Cells, or Word Processor Documents. The Note Pops up at the Touch of a Key & Can Be Removed at Any Time. Works with Lotus 1-2-3, dBASE, WordStar, Sidekick, & Other Popular Programs.
Personics Corp.

Smart Pulley Timer. David L. Vernier. 1987-88. Compatible Hardware: Apple II+, IIe, IIc, IIgs; IBM PC, PC XT, PC AT, PS/2. Operating System(s) Required: Apple ProDOS, MS-DOS. Memory Required: Apple 64k, IBM 256k. General Requirements: Smart Pulley Mechanics System avail. from PASCO Scientific; CGA card & game port (IBM only).
Apple. disk $39.95 (ISBN 0-918731-19-4).
IBM. disk $39.95 (ISBN 0-918731-26-7).
Collects, Analyzes & Graphs Data from the PASCO SMART PULLEY MECHANICS SYSTEM.
Vernier Software.

SMART: Sales Management Activity Reporting & Telemarketing. Items Included: On line help; customizable by non-programmer in minutes. Customer Support: 800 support & updates - 1% of cost of software per month, on site training - negotiable.
UNIX, XENIX, AIX. AT&T, DEC, HP, IBM RISC 6000, Sequent & other. contact publisher for price. Addl. software required: UNIFY ROBMS. Optimal configuration: 150Mb hard disk.
UNIX, ROBMS Based System for Increasing Sales, Sales Productivity & Customer Service for Prospects & Customers. Supports Quotation Tracking & Generation to Prospects; Activating Quotes into Orders, Prospects into Customers; Configuration Control (by Product or Customer Request), Schedule, Reschedule Dates, Reason for Reschedule. Integrates with Absolut Distribution & Accounting System.
Absolut Software, Inc.

The Smart Software System. Version: 3.1. Jan. 1987. Compatible Hardware: AT&T 3B, UNIX PC; IBM PC & compatibles, NCR Tower. Operating System(s) Required: MS-DOS, UNIX SCO, XENIX/286/386. Memory Required: 256k, multiuser mode requires 384k. General Requirements: 2 disk drives or hard disk.
IBM PC, AT&T. disk $895.00.
NCR Tower, 80286/80386 SCO XENIX. write for info.
Features THE SMART DATA BASE MANAGER, THE SMART WORD PROCESSOR with Optional SPELLCHECKER, & THE SMART SPREADSHEET with GRAPHICS. Also Included Is THE SMART PROGRAMMING LANGUAGE, Permitting Custom Applications Development, As Well As Built-In Time Manager & Full Asynchronous Communications. Can Be Used As Either Single or LAN Multiuser Product.
Informix Software, Inc.

The Smart Spreadsheet with Graphics. Version: 3.1. (The Smart Software System). Jan. 1987. Compatible Hardware: AT&T 3600 & compatibles, 3B; Compaq, Compaq Plus; IBM PC, PC XT, PC AT, IBM 3270; NCR Tower. Operating System(s) Required: DOS 2.0 or higher, UNIX V, SCO XENIX V. Language(s): C. Memory Required: 256k. General Requirements: 2 double-sided disk drives or hard disk; certain printers may require additional RAM.
DOS version $495.00, contact vendor for pricing of other versions.
Part of the Smart Series of Integrated Software Products. Spreadsheet Package Handles 999 Columns x 9,999 Rows in a Variety of Formats While Performing Many Different Commands. Also Has Project Processing So That an Entire Project Can Be Executed by the Touch of a Button. Three Confidence Levels Are Included in the Program So That a Beginner Can Work Through the Program Without Confronting the Complex Levels That Are Included for Advanced Use.
Informix Software, Inc.

THE SMART WORD PROCESSOR

The Smart Spreadsheet with Graphics. Innovative Software, Inc. Mar. 1984. Compatible Hardware: TI Professional. Operating System(s) Required: MS-DOS. Memory Required: 128k. General Requirements: 2 disk drives, color monitor, printer, 3-plane graphics.
$595.00.
Texas Instruments, Personal Productivit.

Smart Start. Ed Zaron. Dec. 1984. Compatible Hardware: Commodore 64 with 1541 disk drive. Language(s): Assembly. Memory Required: 64k.
disk $9.98 (ISBN 0-87190-034-3).
Includes Utilities for Customizing Computer's Border, Text, & Background Colors; Keep Track of Time with an On-Screen Digital Clock & Alarm; LOAD, RUN, SAVE & CATALOG Programs by Pressing the Cursor & RETURN; Design Sprite Graphics; Create Sound Effects; Automatically Generate BASIC Code for Sound & Sprite Program; Merge Multiple Programs into One; Print out Screens & Programs.
Muse Software.

The Smart Time Manager. Version: 3.1. (The Smart Software System). Jan. 1987. Compatible Hardware: AT&T 6300 & compatibles, 3B; Compaq, Compaq Plus; IBM PC, PC XT, PC AT, IBM 3270; NCR Tower. Operating System(s) Required: DOS 2.0 or higher, UNIX V, SCO XENIX V. Language(s): C. Memory Required: 256k. General Requirements: 2 double-sided disk drives or hard disk; certain printers may require additional RAM.
contact publisher for price.
Allows User to Schedule Appointments & Keep Track of Obligations. Can Be Accessed at Any Time from Any of the SMART Modules. Meetings & Tasks Can Be Displayed by Time & Priority. Meetings Can Be Changed, Appointments Rearranged, & Conflicts Checked on by the Touch of a Key.
Informix Software, Inc.

SMART TRANSLATORS: English-French-Spanish-German-Italian-Greek. Version: 3.1. Jan. 1990. Items Included: Includes Master Set of documentation training manual & other support items for translators & administrators. Customer Support: 12 month warranty hot-line & FAX support, updates by disk replacement.
UNIX, Sun Solaris 2.1 or Ultrix, MS-DOS, Windows 3.1, HP/UX. PC's 386, Sun Sparcstation, DEC Alpha, IBM RS/6000, UNIX workstations (32Mb). Base $25,000.00 Plus, 10-user Floating license, LAN or Network. Optimal configuration: UNIX workstations, 32Mb memory, Motif or Cose. Networks supported: Novell, LANastic, TC/ICP.
A Set of Sophisticated Computer Programs That Can Automatically Translate Technical English into French, Spanish, German, Greek & Other Languages. Reads Word Processing Files. Output with Embedded Codes for Publishing, Including INTERLEAF 5, MS-WORD, MS-WINDOWS, WORDPERFECT, PAGEMAKER, FRAMEMAKER & ASCII. Fast, Accurate Translation - 200,000+ Words per Hour.
Smart Communications, Inc.

The Smart Word Processor. Version: 3.1. (The Smart Software System). Jan. 1987. Compatible Hardware: AT&T 6300 & compatibles; Compaq, Compaq Plus; IBM PC, PC XT, PC AT, IBM 3270. Operating System(s) Required: DOS 2.0 or higher, UNIX V, SCO XENIX V. Language(s): C. Memory Required: 256k. General Requirements: 2 double-sided disk drives or hard disk; certain printers may require additional RAM.
DOS version $395.00, contact vendor for pricing on other versions.
Part of the Smart Series of Integrated Software Products. Word Processing Program Contains

THE SMART WORD PROCESSOR

Many Features Previously Found Only in Dedicated Word Processors, Such As: Screen Graphics, Multiple Windows, Flying Reform & On-Screen Math Capabilities. Also Has Project Processing So That an Entire Project Can Be Executed by the Touch of a Button. Three Levels Are Included So That a Beginner Can Work Through the Program Without Confronting Complex Levels That Are Included for Advanced Use.
Informix Software, Inc.

The Smart Word Processor. Innovative Software, Inc. Mar. 1984. *Compatible Hardware:* TI Professional. *Operating System(s) Required:* MS-DOS. *Memory Required:* 128k. *General Requirements:* 2 disk drives, printer.
$595.00.
Texas Instruments, Personal Productivit.

SMART.ALX, 2 disks. *Version:* 3.31. Jun. 1992. *Compatible Hardware:* IBM PC, PC XT, PC AT & PS 2. *Operating System(s) Required:* PC-DOS 2.1 or higher. *Memory Required:* 640k. *General Requirements:* 2 disk drives or hard disk, Hayes or compatible modem. *Customer Support:* Free of charge.
disk $395.00.
30 day free trial avail.
Enables Users to Obtain Credit Reports from All Major Credit Bureaus: EQUIFAX, TRANS UNION, & TRW. In the Interactive Mode Will Access TRW BUSINESS REPORT & DUN & BRADSTREET. Offers Instant Transmission As Well As Single-Screen Subject Entry. Operator Training Is Included on the Disk, Including an On-Screen Tutorial & Concurrent Help. Can Send Subjects in a Single Batch. Subjects Are Stored, So they Can Be Sent Again in Case There Is a Transmission Failure, or Rerouted to Another Bureau If Desired. Provides Password Security. Works with Most Database Management Programs (the DATABASE BRIDGE Program Is Required). Features Automatic Error Checking, Preventing Users from Sending in a Report until All the Correct Information Is Provided.
IQue, Inc.

Smartcom Two. *Version:* 3.0. *Compatible Hardware:* IBM PC & compatibles. *Operating System(s) Required:* MS-DOS 2.0-3.3. *Memory Required:* 512k. *General Requirements:* Hayes Smartmodem. *Items Included:* Connunications software, user's guide.
contact publisher for price.
This Version Suports the HAYES V-SERIES Products. Provides the Following Features: Menu Driven Operation; up to 26 Batch Commands Sets; Multiple Protocols, Including HAYES VERIFICATION, XMODEM, XMODEM CRC, XMODEM 1-K, YMODEM, YMODEM-G, & Stop/Start; VT100/102, VT52, TTY, or TeleVideo Terminal Emulation; Macro & Parameter Storage; Ability to Switch from Voice to Data & Back Within the Same Phone Connection; & Remote Access Operation.
Hayes Microcomputer Products, Inc.

Smartcom II for the Apple Macintosh.
Compatible Hardware: Apple Macintosh, Macintosh II. *Memory Required:* 128k, interactive graphics option requires 512k. *General Requirements:* Hayes modem.
3.5" disk $149.00.
Designed to Take Advantage of the Graphics Capabilities of the Macintosh. Provides the Following Features: Auto Dial/Auto Log-On; Easy File Transfer; Storage of Communication Documents for Accessing Different Computers; Prints, Stores, & Displays at the Same Time; Peruse Buffer Editing; Permits Transfer of Graphics to Remote Computer; Storage of Specific Instructions; Unattended Communications; HAYES Verification & XMODEM Protocols; VT100/102, VT52, & TTY Terminal Emulation; On-Line Help.
Hayes Microcomputer Products, Inc.

Smartcom III, 3 5-1/4" or 2 3-1/2" disks.
Compatible Hardware: IBM PC, PC XT, PC AT. *Operating System(s) Required:* MS-DOS 2.0-3.3. *Memory Required:* 512k. *General Requirements:* Hard disk, Hayes Smartmodem, including any V-series Smartmodem.
$249.00, incl. reference guide & quick reference card.
Stand-Alone Communications Program Which Features DOS-Level Commands, a Communications Programming Language, On-Line Editing, & Dual Communication-Session Capability. Beginners Can Use Menus, While the Experienced User Has Command Level Operations & Simple Communications Programming Environment (SCOPE) Options. SCOPE Lets Users Automate Repetitive & Unattended Tasks. Supports the Following File Transfer Protocols: XMODEM, XMODEM CRC, XMODEM-1K, YMODEM, YMODEM-G, & KERMIT.
Hayes Microcomputer Products, Inc.

Smartdecision. *Compatible Hardware:* DEC VAX. *Operating System(s) Required:* VMS. *General Requirements:* Smartstar Version 5.2 or higher.
$1050.00 to $8000.00, depending on configuration & CPU.
Optional Decision Support Component for the Company's Smartstar 4GL Application Development Software. Package Includes ANSI-Compliant SQL Capabilities & Lotus 1-2-3-Compatible Interfaces for Graphics & Spreadsheet Applications. EZ-Import Capability Lets Users Make General Queries Through a Query-by-Forms Interface Without Using Any Syntactical Language. The Results of the Query Are Then Imported into a Spreadsheet, & the Corresponding SQL Syntax Is Automatically Created.
Signal Technology, Inc.

Smartdisk Format Conversion. *Items Included:* Bound manual. *Customer Support:* Free hotline - no time limit; 30 day limited warranty; updates are $5/disk plus S&H.
MS-DOS 2.0 or higher. IBM & compatibles (256k). disk $39.95.
Read, Write, & Format over 200 CP/M & MS-DOS Disk Formats, Including All of Those Handled by MEDIA MASTER; Transfer Files from & to 96 TPI, 3 1/2" & 8" Drives; Read CP/M, CP/M-86, & CP/M-68 Disks, Including Individual (0-15) User Areas; Use Familiar Commands (e.g., DIR, TYPE, COPY, REN, & DEL); Read Wang 5503D Word Processor Files.
Dynacomp, Inc.

Smartdisk: Format Conversion. 1992. *Items Included:* Detailed manuals included with all Dynacomp products. *Customer Support:* Free telephone support to original customer - no time limit; 30 day limited warranty.
MS-DOS 3.2 or higher. IBM PC & compatibles (512k). $39.95 (Add $5.00 for 3 1/2" format; 5 1/4" format standard). *Optimal configuration:* IBM, MS-DOS 2.0 or higher.
With SMARTDISK You Can: Read, Wirte, & Format over 200 CP/M & MS DOS Disk Formats, Including All of Those Handled by MEDIA MASTER. Transfer Files from & to 96 TPI, 3 1/2-Inch & 8-Inch Drives. Read CP/M, CP/M-86, & CP/M-68 Disks, Including Individual (0-15) User Areas. Use Familiar Commands (E.G., DIR, TYPE, COPY, REN, & DEL). Read Wang 5503D Word Processor Files. Menu-Driven & Includes a Very Clear 96-Page Manual.
Dynacomp, Inc.

SOFTWARE ENCYCLOPEDIA 1996

SmartDisk with Safeboot. *Version:* 1.4. Jul. 1993. *Items Included:* 3.5" or 5.25" diskettes & manuals. *Customer Support:* Standard hotline support hours 8:00AM - 6:00PM EST, w/ emergency services provided 24 hours per day, 7 days a week.
PC-DOS/MS-DOS 3.1 or higher. IBM & compatibles (2Mb) w/3.5" or 5.25" disk drive & hard disk drive. disk $150.00. *Networks supported:* Network compatible.
Hardware Device That Requires No Additional Hardware Installation, Runs from the Existing 3.5" floppy drive. Secures the PC by Encrypting the data Stored on the PC's Hard Disk Using a Unique Encryption Key. The Encryption Key & Algorithm Are Stored on the SmartDisk & Can Only Be Read When the SmartDisk Password Has Been Entered Correctly. When a Computer Is Booted Using the SmartDisk, the Software Will Prompt for the Safeboot/SmartDisk Password & Then Read the Encryption Key & Algorithm into the PC's Memory. The SmartDisk Is Then Removed & the PC Can Be Used Normally. A Protected Computer Cannot Boot from Its Hard Disk Unless the Correct SmartDisk Is Inserted & the Correct Password Entered. If the Safeboot/Smart Disk Protected PC Is Booted from the Floppy Disk It Will Behave As Though It Had No Hard Disk.
Fischer International Systems Corp.

SmarTerm 320. *Version:* 2.0. Sep. 1989. *Items Included:* 1 binder, reference manual, installation folder with discs, reference card & technical support information. *Customer Support:* Unlimited phone support M-F 8:30 - 5:00 CST.
MS-DOS (320k). IBM PC, XT, AT, PS/2 or 100% compatible. single-user & multi-user versions $225.00 (Order no.: ST320).
Networks supported: DECnet CTERM & LAT, Excelan, Mobius, Bridge Communications EtherTerm, IBM LANACS, Network Products ACS2, Novell NACS, etc. All Ethernet networks.
A Full Featured Terminal Emulation Software Package Which Allows Your PC or Compatible to Function As a DEC VT320, VT220, VT102, VT100 or VT52 Text Terminal. It Includes Support for Advanced Terminal Features, Downloadable Character Sets, True Double-high/Double-wide Characters, 132-Column Text Screens & More. DEC International Character Set Support, 7-bit National Replacement Character Sets, 8-bit DEC Multinational & ISO LATIN-1 Sets Are Exactly Emulated. Split Baud Rates Are Available for European Users. Adds Many Convenience Features to Basic Terminal Emulation, Including Colorful Pop Up Menus, Color Choice in Text, Help Screens, & Much More. Softkeys & Smartfiles Can Automate Regular Log on or File Transfer Procedures. The Keyboard Can Be Easily Remapped to Suit the DEC User, Including the PF1-PF4 Keys. Special Keyboard Support Is Provided for Word Perfect Users.
Persoft, Inc.

SmarTerm 400. *Version:* 4.0. May 1983. *Compatible Hardware:* IBM PC & compatibles, PC XT, PC AT. *Operating System(s) Required:* PC-DOS, MS-DOS. *Language(s):* BASIC & Assembly. *Memory Required:* 320k. *Customer Support:* Phone support 8:30-5 M-F C.S.T.
disk $225.00.
Terminal Emulation & File Transfer Program That Allows IBM PC to Function As a Data General D100, D200, D210, D211, D214, D215, D400 or D410 Text Terminal. Features Multiple Set-up Configurations, Softkeys, Remappable Keyboard Layout, Online Screens, Compressed Display of 132 Column Video Board Support, Branch to DOS Key & European DOS Support. Full ASCII & Binary File Transfer Facilities Including "Error-Free" Protocol.
Persoft, Inc.

TITLE INDEX

SmarTerm 470. Version: 2.0. Jul. 1989. Customer Support: Unlimited phone support M-F 8;30 - 5:00 CST.
MS-DOS (512k). IBM PC, XT, AT, PS/2 or 100% compatible. $375.00 (Order no.: ST470). Nonstandard peripherals required: Hard disk or 360k floppy drive (if SETUP on separate disk) or 720k floppy drive; asynchronous I/O board with separate cabling; monochrome or 80 column color monitor; VGA or EGA for graphics; 132 column video display board for compressed display in text mode. Networks supported: Bridge Communications EtherTerm, IBM LANACS, Network Products ACS2, Novell NACS, Ungerman-Bass Net/One.
Provides Precise Terminal Emulation. It Emulates Data General Dasher D470 Color Graphics & D461, D460, D450 Monochrome Graphics Terminals & Most Text Terminals. File Transfer Protocols Supported Are Xmodem, Ymodem & Persoft's PDIP. Convenience Features Include: A Softkey Language for Automatic Log-ons & File Transfer, Back-ground Operations, Easy-to-use Menus, Automatic Installation, Multiple Configurations, Macro Language, Easy-to-understand Help Screens, Prompt, Courteous Technical Support, DG Style or Persoft Extended Color Mapping, Compressed Display Support, Host Control & Trace Mode.
Persoft, Inc.

SMARTEXT. Items Included: Manual. Customer Support: Unlimited toll free support, Compuserve forum.
MS-DOS. IBM PC compatible (640k). 495.00 for construction; 199.00 for readers only.
An Electronic Documentation Generator Which Reads Word Processing & Text Files & Generates an Electronic Outline, Index & Hypertext Lines. This Can Be Customized by the Author to Include Illustration Links & Customized Views. Lines Are Maintenance Updating.
Samna Corp.

SmartForecasts II Standard Edition. Version: 2.15. Sep. 1988. Compatible Hardware: IBM PC AT, PC XT & compatibles with color graphics adapter. Operating System(s) Required: PC-DOS 2.0 or higher. Memory Required: 256k.
disk $495.00.
Business Forecasting, Graphics & Data Analysis Program Makes Projections of Sales, Market Share, Revenues, Expenses, Inventory Levels & Other Time-Oriented Data. Combines a Stastical Expert System for Automatic Forecasting with Interactive Graphics for Judgemental Refinements.
Smart Software, Inc.

Smartkey/Smartprint Keyboard & Printer Utilities. Items Included: Bound manual. Customer Support: Free hotline - no time limit; 30 day limited warranty; updates are $5/disk plus S&H.
MS-DOS. IBM & compatibles (256k); CP/M. disk $69.95.
SMARTKEY Allows User to Re-Define the Keys on Keyboard to Be Commands, Phrases, etc. Its Features Include: Assign up to 60,000 Characters to a Single Key; Exclusive SuperShift Key Lets Each Key Have up to 7 Meanings; Lotus-Like Menu; User-Definable Windows; Keyboard Remapping; Definition Editor; DOS File Commands; Custom Menus. SMARTPRINT Gives User Access to All of a Printer's Features, Such As Wide, Bold, Condense, Underline, etc., from Within Any Program. Can Print Any Character (e.g., Greek) That Your Printer Is Capable Of. In Use, You Type One or Two Character Codes into Your Document, & at Print Time These Codes Are Translated into Print Commands.
Dynacomp, Inc.

Smartpath Hard-Disk Utility. Items Included: Bound manual. Customer Support: Free hotline - no time limit; 30 day limited warranty; updates are $5/disk plus S&H.
MS-DOS 2.0 or higher. IBM & compatibles (256k). disk $29.95.
Hard-Disk Utility Allows You & Your Software to Find Files, No Matter What Subdirectory They Are Located In. No Longer Will You Get "File Not Found" Errors When Running LOTUS, WordStar, & Other Programs. If the File Exists Somewhere, SMARTPATH Will Automatically Find It.
Dynacomp, Inc.

SmartStar. Compatible Hardware: DEC VAX/VMS.
$5,100.00-$55,000.00.
Family of Application Development Tools That Contains a Non-Technical Interface to the VIA Which Allows Users to Create Applications, Perform Data Management Operations Such As Adding & Retrieving Data, & Produce Formatted Reports Without Programming or Use of a Rigid Query Language Syntax. Contains Additional Database Administrator Tools & Programmer Productivity Tools to Provide a Relational Database Capability for Large, Demanding Applications. SmartStar/IBM Configuration Allows Access to IBM Mainframes.
Signal Technology, Inc.

Smartstuff Pop-Up Desk Tools. Items Included: Bound manual. Customer Support: Free hotline - no time limit; 30 day limited warranty; updates are $5/disk plus S&H.
MS-DOS 2.0 or higher. IBM & compatibles (256k). disk $39.95. Nonstandard peripherals required: Autodial feature requires a modem, & a general 80-column (or wider) printer is supported.
Set of "Pop-Up" Desk Tools Includes a Word Processor, Financial Calculator, Calendar, Alarm Clock, Autodialer, & Memory Partitioner.
Dynacomp, Inc.

SmartWare. Version: 3.1. Compatible Hardware: IBM PC XT. Memory Required: 384k. General Requirements: 10Mb hard disk.
$895.00 all modules.
$495.00 spreadsheet with graphics.
$695.00 database.
$395.00 word processor with spelling checker.
Integrated Software Program Featuring Word Processing, Spreadsheet, Database, Graphics, Communications & Programming Language Modules. Includes Mail/Merge Database Link, Built-In Language in All Modules, 999 by 9999 Spreadsheet Matrix Size & Context-Sensitive On-Screen Help. Pastes Spreadsheet Sections & Graphics into Word-Processing Files. Edits 50 Files Simultaneously & Links 50 Spreadsheets & 2 Database Tables in One Query. Imports & Exports ASCII, DCA, WKS & DIF File Formats.
Informix Software, Inc.

SmartWare for Xenix. Compatible Hardware: Xenix.
$1595.00.
Includes a Word Processor, Database & Spreadsheet with Graphics. Also Features Asynchronous Communications, a Time Manager & a Custom Applications Development Tool Called the SMART Programming Language.
Informix Software, Inc.

smARTWORK. Version: 1.4.7. Compatible Hardware: IBM PC, PC-XT, PC AT, PS/2 & 100% compatibles. Operating System(s) Required: PC-DOS 2.0 or higher. Memory Required: 640k. General Requirements: CGA, EGA or VGA card, IBM graphics printer or Epson FX/MX/RX series dot-matrix printer, Houston Instruments DMP-41, 42, 51, 52, or HP 7470, 7475, 7550, 7580, 7586 pen plotter; Microsoft mouse optional. Items Included: Autorouter. Customer Support: Free customer support on toll-free number & bulletin-board-system (BBS), 30-day money-back guarantee on package.
$895.00.
Printed-Circuit-Board Artwork Editor. Features Include: Complete Interactive Control over Placing & Routing, Quick Correction & Revision, Production-Quality 2X Artwork from a Pen-&-Ink Plotter, Prototype Quality 2X Artwork from a Dot-Matrix Printer. Single-Sided & Doubled-Sided Printed Circuit Boards up to 10x16 Inches, & Multicolor or Black-&-White Display. Features Include: Silkscreen Layer for Component Placement & Identification, Text Capabilities for All Three Layers, Selectable Trace Widths & Pad Shapes & Sizes, Ground Planes Created with a Single Command, Solder-Mask & Padmaster Plots Generated Automatically, Optional Drill-Tape & GERBER Photoplotter Utilities. AutoCAD DXF Files Output, Manual, & Free Technical Assistance.
Wintek Corp.

SMAS: Stock Market Advisor System. Compatible Hardware: TRS-80 Model I, Model III.
contact publisher for price.
Spiral Enterprises.

SMbasic. Operating System(s) Required: IRIS. Memory Required: 128k.
contact publisher for price.
Business BASIC Language Interpreter & Associated Utilities Which Runs under POINT 4's Multi-User IRIS Operating System.
Point 4 Data Corp.

SMDS: A Brief Overview. Version: 2. Oct. 1994. Items Included: User manual. Customer Support: Free technical support & a 30-day warranty (1-800-521-CORE).
MS-DOS. IBM & compatibles (512k). 3.5" disk $199.00 (ISBN 1-57305-001-6). Nonstandard peripherals required: High-density 3.5" disk drive; VGA color monitor. Addl. software required: MS-DOS version 3.3 or higher. Optimal configuration: IBM (512k), MS-DOS version 3.3 or higher, VGA color monitor, keyboard, Microsoft compatible mouse (optional).
Switched Multi Megabit Data Service (SMDS) Is a Computer-Based Training Package That Provides a Concise Overview of SMDS As a Service & How It Addresses High-Performance Interconnect Needs of Business Customers. This Training Package Explains What SMDS Is, the Characteristics & Features of This Service Offering, Applications of SMDS, the Overall Architecture of SMDS, SMDS Interface Protocol, & Reliability Issues of This Service.
Bellcore.

A Smile from Andy. Nan Holcomb & Jane Steelman. Oct. 1993. Items Included: Directions on use of the program, registration card. Customer Support: 90 days limited warranty, replacement disks for fee of $10.00 & proof of purchase.
6.07. MAC LC (2Mb). 3.5" disk $29.95 (ISBN 0-944727-22-0). Optimal configuration: MAC LC, System 7.1, 4Mb RAM.
Andy Is Shy, but Wants Attention & Friendship. User Can Read Andy's Story by Clicking a Button on the Screen or Use a Switch to Hear the Story Read Word by Word or Sentence by Sentence As the Text Is Highlighted in Color of Choice.
Jason & Nordic Pubs.

SMK GREEKKEYS

SMK GreekKeys. *Compatible Hardware:* Apple Macintosh. *Memory Required:* 512k.
ImageWriter. 3.5" disk $30.00.
LaserWriter. 3.5" disk $40.00.
Foreign Language Fonts for ImageWriter & LaserWriter. Allows a User to Type & Print the Characters & Diacritical Marks Used in Classical & Biblical Greek.
SMK.

SMU Electrical Engineering Library, 2 disks or 10 cassettes. *Compatible Hardware:* TI 99/4A.
contact publisher for price.
Teaching Aid for Students & Instructors Which Is Centered Around Basic Electrical Engineering Concepts. Can Be Used with Any College-Level Textbook on Introductory Circuit Analysis.
Texas Instruments, Personal Productivit.

SNA Gateway. *Operating System(s) Required:* UNIX or UNIX-like environments. *Memory Required:* 1000k.
contact publisher for price.
Forms the Basis for the Implementation of Multiple Applications Communicating over Distributed, Hybrid Networks. Ties Diverse Applications, Systems, & Environments Together by Providing a Common Networking Gateway Between Them. Provides a Set of SNA Physical Unit Type 2.1 Node Services, & Provides the End User with Facilities Designed to Simplify Access to Gateway Functions. Supports Several Applications Communicating with Multiple Hosts or Peer Nodes over Multiple Physical Links, Using SDLC,X.25, or Token Ring Procedures. System Is Portable & Can Be Integrated into Workstation Operating Systems & Application Support Environments.
Rabbit Software Corp.

Snap! *Version:* 3.1. Jun. 1989. *Items Included:* User reference manual with tutorial section. *Customer Support:* Free unlimited phone support, free bug-fixes, low-cost major version upgrades.
Macintosh (1Mb). 3.5" disk $695.00.
  Nonstandard peripherals required: Hard disk. *Networks supported:* Appletalk, TOPS.
demo disk $19.95.
General Purpose 2-D CAD Program. Features Include: Automatic Dimensioning, Built-In Plotter & LaserWriter Drivers, Symbol Libraries with Nested Symbols, a Mac-Like Text Editor, Fence & Group Manipulations, Reference File Overlays, User-Definable On-Screen or Digitizer Menus, & Virtual Windows.
Forthought, Inc.

SNAP. *Version:* 4.1. Mar. 1991. *Compatible Hardware:* IBM PC XT, PC AT, PS/2 & compatibles, Lap tops. *Operating System(s) Required:* PC-DOS/MS-DOS 3.1 or higher, OS/2 version 1.2 or higher in DOS mode. *Language(s):* Microsoft C with Btrieve database manager. *Memory Required:* 440k. *Items Included:* Software, documentation, implementation guide, sales kit. *Customer Support:* $300.00 per user (1200 minimum) for annual upgrade & support plan, optional 900 number.
$1200.00 per user (2,000.00 minimum) volume purchase plan available.
The Corporate Solution for Sales & Marketing Automation. From LANS to Laptops, It Links the Activities of a Distributed Sales Force to Management & to Marketing. Includes a Word Processor, a Report Generator, an Integrated Database Manager, Telemarketing, Direct Mail, Sales Cycle Analysis, Market Information & Analysis, Product Tracking & Forecasting, Lead Handling & Tracking & Field Sales Assistance.
SNAP, Inc.

SNAP/DXF Translator. Jun. 1990. *Items Included:* Reference manual, product registration forms. *Customer Support:* Free unlimited phone support.
Macintosh (1Mb). 3.5" disk $195.00. *Optimal configuration:* MAC II series, hard disk. *Networks supported:* Appletalk, Tops.
Provides 2-Way Translation of Files, from DXF Format to SNAP! to DXF. Drawings Can Be Scaled During the Translation Process. A Status Window Shows the Number & Type of Elements Being Translated. A Symbol Library Will Be Automatically Created if There is a Blocks Section in the DXF File.
Forthought, Inc.

SNAP Business System. Aug. 1986. *Compatible Hardware:* IBM PC & compatibles. *Operating System(s) Required:* PC-DOS, MS-DOS. *Memory Required:* 640k. *General Requirements:* Hard disk, printer. *Items Included:* General ledger, planner, payroll, AP/AR.
$595.00-$795.00.
Business Accounting Including: General Ledger, Profit Planner, & Payroll; Profit Centers, Budgets, & Check Writing; Accounts Receivable-Point of Sale, Inventory.
Countryside Data, Inc.

SNAP!/Intergraph Translator. *Version:* 3.1. Jun. 1989. *Items Included:* User reference manual. *Customer Support:* Free unlimited telephone support, free upgrades & bug fixes.
Macintosh (1Mb). 3.5" disk $195.00.
  Nonstandard peripherals required: Hard disk. *Networks supported:* Appletalk, TOPS.
Utility Which Provides Conversion of Drawings to & from Snap! Format & 2-D Intergraph IGDS Format. Public Domain Version of Kermit File Transfer Protocol Is Included. Features Include On-Screen Verification of Translated Elements, Font Substitution & Optional Scaling of Data.
Forthought, Inc.

Snap MAIL. Eric Braun & Adam King. 1992. *Items Included:* Manual, reg. card. *Customer Support:* Free phone support.
6.02 & higher - works in mixed System 6 & 7 environment. Macintosh (1Mb). 3.5" disk $200.00 5 packs; $320.00 10 packs; $1440.00 50 packs (Order no.: M700; M705, M710). *Networks supported:* Appletalk, Ethernet.
Hassle-Free Electronic Mail & Messaging System for the Macintosh. No Dedicated Server Required. Extremely Easy to Learn & Use.
Casady & Greene, Inc.

Snapshot Digital Storage Oscilloscope Demo Package. *Items Included:* Bound manual. *Customer Support:* Free hotline - no time limit; 30 day limited warranty; updates are $5/disk plus S&H.
MS-DOS 3.0 or higher. IBM & compatibles (640k). disk $14.95. *Nonstandard peripherals required:* CGA, EGA, VGA, AT&T, or Hercules graphics capability; math coprocessor is not needed, but is recommended to achieve maximum speed.
Package Consists of a Demonstration Disk & a 16-Page Quick-Reference Manual. Simulated Waveforms Are Used (You Do Not Need A/D Hardware for the Demo), & the Number of Points Is Limited to 500 (Instead of the 32k in the Full Package). The Demo Is Structured Like a Book: You Can Refer to Various Chapters to See How Particular Features Work.
Dynacomp, Inc.

Snapshots. Roy Buck. 1990.
DOS. Any type of IBM (64k). $4.95 (ISBN 1-56178-004-9).
MAC. Any type of Macintosh (64k). $4.95 (ISBN 1-56178-021-9).
Poetry: Anthology of Poems.
Connected Editions, Inc.

Sneggit. *Compatible Hardware:* TI-99/4A with PLATO interpreter solid state cartridge.
contact publisher for price (Order no.: PHM 3145).
Save the Eggs & Survive the Snake Attack.
Texas Instruments, Personal Productivit.

Snokie. *Compatible Hardware:* Atari.
disk $34.95.
cassette $34.95 (ISBN 0-915149-01-X).
Goal of Game Is to Help Reunite the Cute Little Sno-Bird with His Girlfriend While Avoiding Ice Lasers, Falling Stalagtites & Snow Boulders.
Blue Cat.

Snoopy Screen Saver. Jun. 1995. *Items Included:* Soft cover, stapled manual & registration card. *Customer Support:* Free customer service via our 800 number. Unlimited warranty on disk replacement.
System 7 or higher. Macintosh computers (Incompatible with MAC 128, 512, Plus, Classic, Powerbook & Portable) (4Mb). 3.5" disk $49.95 (ISBN 1-888046-19-8, Order no.: IS10024). *Nonstandard peripherals required:* Color monitor recommended, 7Mb hard disk space req.
Windows 3.1 or higher; 386 or higher. IBM, Tandy & 100% compatibles (4Mb). disk $49.95 (ISBN 1-888046-20-1, Order no.: IS10183). *Nonstandard peripherals required:* Super VGA; Sound Card: 100% Sound Blaster compatible; 5Mb hard disk space.
8 Screen Savers Featuring the Peanuts Characters; Start up Greetings & Magic Patterns; Icon Sticker & Peeler. Also Includes after Dark Control Panel.
Image Smith, Inc.

Snoopy Screen Saver: German Language Version. *Items Included:* Soft cover, stapled manual & registration card. *Customer Support:* Free customer service via our 800 number. Unlimited warranty on disk replacement.
System 7 or higher. Macintosh (incompatible with MAC 128, 512, Plus, Classic, Powerbook & Portable) 4Mb). 3.5" disk $49.95 (ISBN 1-888046-66-X, Order no.: IS10117). *Addl. software required:* Color monitor recommended, 7Mb hard disk space req.
Windows 3.1 or higher; 386 or higher. IBM, Tandy & 100% compatibles (4Mb). disk $49.95 (ISBN 1-888046-67-8, Order no.: IS10120). *Nonstandard peripherals required:* Super VGA, 100% Sound Blaster compatible sound card, 5Mb hard disk space.
8 Screen Savers Featuring the Peanuts Characters; Start up Greetings & Magic Patterns; Icon Sticker & Peeler. Also Includes after Dark Control Panel.
Image Smith, Inc.

Snoopy Screen Saver: Japanese Language Version. Sep. 1994. *Items Included:* Soft cover, stapled manual & registration card. *Customer Support:* Free customer service via our 800 number. Unlimited warranty on disk replacement.
System 7 or higher. Macintosh (incompatible with MAC 128, 512, Plus, Classic, Powerbook & Portable) 4Mb). 3.5" disk $49.95 (ISBN 1-888046-62-7, Order no.: IS10079). *Addl. software required:* Color monitor recommended, 7Mb hard disk space req.
8 Screen Savers Featuring the Peanuts Characters; Start up Greetings & Magic Patterns; Icon Sticker & Peeler. Also Includes after Dark Control Panel.
Image Smith, Inc.

Snow Report Writer. *Version:* 4.0. *Compatible Hardware:* Altos 1086/2086; AT&T 381, 382; DEC MicroVAX; IBM PC AT, RT PC 6150; NCR Tower, RS 6000, Daisys 5000, ICL DRS, DG,

TITLE INDEX

Sun, Siermers; Apple Macintosh, Microsoft Windows. *Operating System(s) Required:* Unix, SCO Xenix, Xenix, DOS, VMS, Mac System 7. *Memory Required:* 384k. *General Requirements:* Hard disk.
LAN. $995.00.
Unix. $1195.00.
Unix. $1295.00.
Can Create Custom Forms, Mailing Lists, Reports, & Business Graphics Using Data from Over 200 Programs & Languages. The Program Reads & Writes Data to & from Lotus 1-2-3, dBASE, WordStar, Several Versions of Basic & COBOL, & Various Accounting Programs. It Also Supports ASCII Files. Enables Users to Create A/R Aging, Transaction Summary, Expense, Sales Analysis, Debit & Credit, Billing History, Summary Total, & Cash/Bills Reports. Can Also Produce Invoices, Statements, Vouchers, Mailing Lists, Labels, & Form Letters. File-Protection & Record-Locking Capabilities Are Included.
Snow Software.

Snow Report Writer. *Version:* 4.0. *Compatible Hardware:* Altos, IBM, NCR, AT&T, DEC. *Items Included:* On-line tutorial, documentation. *Customer Support:* 30 days free, support subscription program available.
Xenix $1095.00.
Unix $1295.00.
NCR Tower $1495.00.
LAN $995.00.
Creates Customized Reports, Forms & Business Graphics, Reads and/or Writes to 200 Different Spreadsheet, Database, Accounting, & Word Processing Packages & Languages.
Snow Software.

Snow Report Writer: Network Version. *Version:* 4.0. *Compatible Hardware:* IBM PC & compatibles. Supports Novell, PC NET, Token Ring & 3-Com networks. *Memory Required:* 384k. *Items Included:* On-line tutorial, documentation. *Customer Support:* 30 days free, support subscription program available.
disk $995.00, for 8 workstations.
Merges Data from Multiple Sources. User Can Create Columnar Reports, Forms, Mailing Lists, Labels, Form Letters, & Business Graphics.
Snow Software.

Social Studies: States Game. Dec. 1981. *Items Included:* Teacher's guide. *Customer Support:* 90-day limited warranty.
Apple-DOS 3.3. Apple II Family (48k). disk $39.00 (ISBN 0-917277-08-2).
Commodore 64/128 (64k). disk $39.00 (ISBN 0-917277-56-2).
This Land Is Yours! Each of Our Fifty States Has Its Own Personality, History & Terrain. Learn Hard Facts While Guessing the States from Descriptive Clues. Includes 5 Games for 1 to 4 Players. Ages 8 & Up.
BrainBank/Generation Ahead of Maryland.

Socratix Diabetes. *Version:* 2.1. Nov. 1986. *Compatible Hardware:* IBM PC. *Language(s):* Quicksilver. *Memory Required:* 640k. *Customer Support:* Toll free telephone support.
$595.00.
Interviews & Re-Interviews Patients in an Extended Series of Teaching Activities to Assure Sound Knowledge about the Basics of Diabetes. Prints Homework Between Sessions.
SRC Systems, Inc.

SOD: Son of Donor Contribution Management System. Aug. 1986. *Items Included:* User manual. *Customer Support:* 90 days unlimited support after installation & training, ongoing support & maintenance $600/yr.
PC-DOS 3.30 (512k). PC AT & compatibles. disk $4000.00 (ISBN 0-928246-00-0, Order no.: SOD). *Nonstandard peripherals required:* Modem for remote support. *Addl. software required:* "PC Anywhere" for remote support. *Optimal configuration:* Hard disk, 640k RAM, WordPerfect or WordStar, EGA monitor. *Networks supported:* Novell.
Comprehensive Contribution Management System Designed for Not-for-Profits That Depend Upon Direct Solicitation of Funds. Consists of Three Modules: the First Is Development Office Which Handles Solicitation & Contribution Management; the Second Is Public Affairs Office Which Handles Tracking of Members, Friends, Volunteers, etc.; the Last Is the PAMS Module Designed to Track Legislative & Social Issues.
HEL Custom Software, Inc.

Soft Craft Graphical Custom Control. Nov. 1993. *Items Included:* Complete on-line help, file/manual with complete source code for sample. Demo sample showing product capabilities. *Customer Support:* Toll telephone - long distance charges only (608-257-3300); CompuServe forum - CompuServe charges only (WINAPB - SoftCraft Section); Internet - no charge (76702, 13.4 CompuServe.COM).
Windows 3.X. Windows (2Mb). disk $295.00 (Order no.: SGCC). *Addl. software required:* Visual BASIC.
Similar, but Much More Compable Than the VB Shape Control, This Control Provides Basic Shapes, Properties, Events, & Options Including Pure Colors & Graduated Fills. Shapes Include Rectangle, Circle, Ellipse, Polyline, Arbitrary Polygon, Regular N-Sided Polygon, Arc, Pie, & Bezier Curves. Events Include Click, DblClick, MouseUp, MouseDown, MouseMove, DragDrop, & DragOver. No Royalties.
Softcraft, Inc. (Wisconsin).

Soft Ledger. *Version:* 1.3. Marvin J. Andresen & Ronald W. Gatterdam. Dec. 1989. *Items Included:* Quick reference, tutorial, user manual. *Customer Support:* 30 days unlimited warranty. 1 yr. maintenance, $200.00.
MS-DOS 2.0 or higher (256k). $295.00.
Budget Balance Tracking for Department, Contract, Project Managers. Any Number of Accounts Can Be Added As Needed at Any Time. Budget Balances Are Reported for Each Account, Each Group of Accounts, & Total for All Accounts. Details of Any Purchase Order & Any Account is Available. Menu Driven. Written in Compiled Turbo Pascal.
AK-D Software.

SoftBackup II. *Version:* 4.16. Jun. 1991. *Items Included:* Includes manual. *Customer Support:* Free maintenance by phone, fax, & mail to registered users (technical support on the software).
Macintosh System Software 6.0.5 or higher. Macintosh Plus or higher (1Mb). 3.5" disk $149.95. *Nonstandard peripherals required:* Hard disk. *Optimal configuration:* System Software 6.0.7 or higher, the more RAM the better, SCSI Tape Drive, System 7 compatible. *Networks supported:* AppleShare, TOPS, System 7 FileSharing.
Backup Program for Backing up to DC2000 Tape, TEAC Tape, DC600 Tape, DAT, Exabyte 8mm Tape, Optical Disks, Mounted Volumes (Including Removable Hard Disks & Network Servers), & Floppies. It is Optimized for Backup Speed & Ease of Use. Can Do Unattended Backups. System 7 Compatible.
Diversified I/O, Inc.

The SOFTBOL Language System. *Version:* 2.1. Jun. 1985. *Operating System(s) Required:* MS-DOS, PC-DOS, CP/M-86, UNIX, XENIX, VMS, Reglus, Zeus, RSM-11M Plus, Netware. *Memory Required:* 128k.

contact publisher for price.
Language System Brings DEC DIBOL Software to Computers Using the CP/M-80, CP/M-86, MS-DOS, XENIX, UNIX, UNIX Look-Alike RSX-11M Plus, Netware & VAX/VMS Operating Systems. Consists of a Compiler, Runtime Systems, a Sort Package & Other DIBOL-Related Utilities Found in the DEC Environment. Programmers Have All the Necessary Tools to Migrate Their DIBOL Programs to SOFTBOL. A Portfolio of DIBOL Applications Is Also Available with No Changes to the Applications.
Omtool Corp.

Softcost. *Operating System(s) Required:* PC-DOS. *Language(s):* Microsoft BASIC (source code included). *Memory Required:* 64k.
disk $100.00 (Order no.: NPO-17936).
manual $38.00.
Cost Estimation Model Designed to Serve As a Financial Planner for Those in the Programming Industry. Estimates the Resource Requirements & Schedules of Software Development & Maintenance Efforts.
COSMIC.

SoftCraft Font Editor. Jun. 1987. *Compatible Hardware:* IBM PC & compatibles. *Memory Required:* 450k. *General Requirements:* 2 disk drives or hard disk; Hercules, CGA or EGA card or compatible.
contact publisher for price.
Mouse & Menu-Driven Graphics Font Editor. Edit & Create Custom Fonts in SoftCraft & HP Font Formats with up to 256 Characters. Design Logos & Print Them with a Word Processor. Allows Users to Open up to Five Windows to View a Single Character for Easy Editing, or Several Characters on Screen at Once. Allows Editing of Aldus/Microsoft TIFF Format Files & PC PAINTBRUSH Images.
SoftCraft, Inc. (Wisconsin).

SoftCraft Presenter. *Customer Support:* Free mail/fax/phone support.
Windows. disk $595.00. *Addl. software required:* Windows 3. *Optimal configuration:* Windows plus 2Mb plus mouse plus color display.
A Full-Featured Presentation Graphics Program with the Following Features: "Intelligent" Objects & Clip Art, Automatic Animation, Graphical Manipulation of Spreadsheet Data, Outliner, Slide Show, Slide Sorter, Business & Scientific Graphs, Slide Templates & Style Sheets, Dyanmic Data Exchange & Compound Document Support, & Extensive Drawing Tools.
SoftCraft, Inc. (Wisconsin).

SoftCraft Standard Series Fonts. *Compatible Hardware:* IBM PC & compatibles. *Memory Required:* 450k. *General Requirements:* Hercules, CGA, or EGA card or compatible.
disk $15.00 ea., (1-25 fonts per disk).
Font Libraries. Typefaces Available Include: Calligrapher, Classic (Roman), Elegant Script, Formal, Hershey Database Sample, Hershey Oriental Character Database, Indic Phonetic, Modern, Nouveau, Old English, Sans Serif, Script, & Tall Twist. Over 80 Disks Available.
SoftCraft, Inc. (Wisconsin).

Softerm PC. *Version:* 2.10. *Compatible Hardware:* IBM PC & compatibles; Data General AOS, AOS/VS; DEC VAX/VMS.
$195.00.
Communications & Terminal Emulation Package. Enhanced to Include Datapoint 8220, HP 2392A, IBM 3162, Prime PST100 & Televideo Exact Emulations.
Softronics, Inc.

Softerm 2. Version: 2.50. Oct. 1983. Compatible Hardware: Apple II, II+, IIc, IIe, IIgs. Operating System(s) Required: DOS. Language(s): Assembly. Memory Required: 64-128k. $195.00.
demo disk for dealers only $50.00.
Communications & Terminal Emulation Package for the Apple Series. Used to Access Information Services, Bulletin Boards, & Host Computers. Includes Exact Emulations of 24+ Terminals & Provides All Keyboard & Display Functions. Both Conversational & Block Modes Are Supported.
Softronics, Inc.

Softfile: A Memory Enhancer. Version: 2.3. Sep. 1989.
Xenix or Unix (Intel-based computers). 295.00 (demo disk & manual $25.00) (ISBN 0-918103-04-5).
SCO Xenix & SCO UNIX. AT compatibles (Intel 80386 or 80486). $295.00 (ISBN 0-918103-06-1).
Personal Database Which Stores Free-Form Text as Screen-Size Notes. Automatically Indexes the Words, Dates, & Numbers in Each Note. Notes Can Be Entered on a Form or on a Blank Screen. Each Note Can Be Linked To 9 Other Notes To Create Menus & Hypertext Documents.
RTG Data Systems.

Softforms. Compatible Hardware: Macintosh.
disk $39.95.
Twenty-Two Business Forms on Disk.
Artsci, Inc.

Softforms-Mac. Nov. 1984. Compatible Hardware: Apple Macintosh with MacPaint. Language(s): Mac Pascal. Memory Required: 128k.
disk $39.95 (ISBN 0-917963-03-2).
Provides Standard Business Forms.
Artsci, Inc.

Softgage. Version: 2.0. Compatible Hardware: Apple Macintosh (All); IBM PC, PC XT, PC AT. Memory Required: 512k. General Requirements: Hard disk or external disk drive; Microsoft Excel 3.0. Items Included: 65-page manual & diskette. Customer Support: Hotline.
$100.00 (ISBN 1-883467-04-7).
Engineering Program Designed to Replace Positional Functional (Metal) Gauges & Analyze Composite Positional Tolerances & N/C Machine Precision per ANSI Standards.
International Geometric Tolerancing Institute, Inc.

Softgage: Position Inspection. Version: 2.0. Sam Levy. Jan. 1991. Items Included: Manual in 6x9, 3 ring binder, membership card. Customer Support: 90 day unlimited warranty. Our site training $25.00/hr. Hot line (free) to caller; none returned.
PS/2, MS-DOS with Windows. IBM & compatibles. disk $100.00 (ISBN 1-883467-04-7, Order no.: IGTI 6-5 1/4 OR 3 1/2). Addl. software required: Microsoft Excel 3.0 or higher. Optimal configuration: Color monitor, printer, 2Mb RAM (extended on IBM).
Macintosh OS. Apple Macintosh (1Mb). 3.5" disk $100.00 (Order no.: IGTI 6-3 1/2 800K). Addl. software required: Microsoft Excel 3.0 or higher. Optimal configuration: Color monitor, 2Mb RAM, printer. Networks supported: Appletalk.
Productional Prograom That Can Be Used to Verify Feature Locations in Lieu of a (Hard) Positional Functional Gage When Used in Conjunction with an X, Y Coordinate Measuring Machine (CMM). Program Is Meant to Be a Workable Solution for the Composite Positional Verification of Holes or Studs/Pins. Measurements Taken from Any Origin May Be Translated to Determine Their Acceptability by the Computer. Although Designed for Ease of Use, Softgage Contains Many Sophisticated Transparent Routines, Such As Least Squares, Strategic Decision Making, Vector-Seeking Optimization, Slope/Distance Zone-Envelope Testing, Hand Tweaking & More. Includes an Interactive Graph of Actuals Verses Basics (Locations) & Color-Coded Cells. Program Is Not Copy Protected.

Softletters. Aug. 1985. Compatible Hardware: Apple II+, IIe, IIc, IIgs, Macintosh; Franklin Ace. Language(s): Assembly, Pascal (source code included). Memory Required: 48k.
$19.95.
Diskette Containing Business Letters, Personal Letters, & Forms. Contains over 50 Letters.
Artsci, Inc.

SOFTNET. Compatible Hardware: Apple; IBM PC. Memory Required: 48k, IBM 128k.
$149.95.
Dynacomp, Inc.

Softpoint PMS. Compatible Hardware: IBM PC. Operating System(s) Required: DOS. Memory Required: 192k.
$395.00, incl. demo disk & documentation.
Produces Time, Cost, Manpower & Progress Reports Based on CPM/PERT.
Softpoint Co.

SoftPolish. Version: 1.1. May 1992. Items Included: 1 manual. Customer Support: Free unlimited phone support.
Macintosh. Macintosh (2Mb). 3.5" disk $295.00.
Helps User Avoid Embarrassing Spelling Errors, Detect Incorrect or Incompatible Resources, & Improve the Appearance of Software. Examines Application Resources & Reports Potential Problems. Independent of Any Programming Language or Environment, SoftPolish Finds Errors & Improves the Quality of Any Macintosh Program.
Language Systems Corp.

Softspool. Version: 3.08. May 1985. Operating System(s) Required: MS-DOS, PC-DOS. Language(s): Assembly. Memory Required: 48k.
disk $59.95.
Spools Data to the Printer While Executing a Program. User Can Spool Multiple Copies of a Document (Up to 255).
Maverick Software, Inc.

SoftSwitch. Version: 9.2. Jun. 1987. Compatible Hardware: Apple IIgs. Language(s): Assembly. Memory Required: 256k. General Requirements: 512k RAM expansion card.
3.5" disk $49.95 (ISBN 0-927796-26-0).
Can Switch Between up to 9 ProDOS 8 & DOS 3.3 Programs on the Apple IIgs. Users Can Revert to a Previous State of a Program, or Interrupt a Program, Save It to Disk in Its Current State, & Return to That Exact Point Later. Can Also Copy & Paste Hi-Res & Double Hi-Res Screens into Programs Like PRINT SHOP & FANTAVISION. Installs Itself As an Apple IIgs Desk Accessory & If the Programs Allow Access to the Control Panel, They Are Compatible with SoftSwitch.
Roger Wagner Publishing, Inc.

Softsynth. Version: 2.1. Compatible Hardware: Apple Macintosh. Memory Required: 512k. General Requirements: MIDI interface.
3.5" disk $295.00.
Digital Additive FM Synthesis Software.
Digidesign, Inc.

Software Carousel. Version: 6.0. Apr. 1986. Compatible Hardware: IBM PC & compatibles with hard disk. Operating System(s) Required: PC-DOS/MS-DOS 2.0 or higher. Memory Required: 256k. Customer Support: 9:00 AM to 5:30 PM EST - (603) 644-5555.
disk $89.95.
Allows Background Printing While User Switches Instantly from Spreadsheet to Graphics to Database with a Touch of a Key. Have up to 12 Programs & Files Loaded & Hot Key Between Them Picking up Right Where User Left off. It Also Helps Solve Conflicts with Resident (TSR) Programs.
SoftLogic Solutions.

Software JukeBox: A Plus Grade Builder. Feb. 1993. Customer Support: Free technical support 810-477-1205.
MS-DOS 3.1 or higher. IBM AT or higher, or compatibles (640k). CD-ROM disk $9.95 (ISBN 1-57037-007-9). Optimal configuration: CD-ROM drive, 2Mb free hard disk space, VGA card & monitor, Supports Joystick; Mouse (recommended); Sound Blaster or compatible sound card (recommended).
The featured Software Packages Are: "Word Attack Plus" by Davidson & Associates - Children Will Learn Words & Sounds with Captivating Collection of Activities. "Memory Lane" by Stone & Associates - Fresh, Challenging & Positive Learning Experience! "2nd Math" by Stone & Associates - Make Learning Mathematics Easy & Fun! "Super Spellicopter" by Compton's NewMedia - Get Your Child's Spelling off the Ground.
SelectWare Technologies, Inc.

Software JukeBox: Fight, Flight & Might. May 1995. Customer Support: Free technical support 810-477-1205.
MS-DOS 5.0 or higher. IBM 386 or higher, or compatible (4Mb). CD-ROM disk $29.95 (ISBN 1-57037-020-6). Nonstandard peripherals required: CD-ROM drive, 2Mb free hard disk space, SVGA card & monitor, mouse (recommended), sound card (optional), joystick (optional).
The Fight, Flight & Might Edition Is Assembled from the Best Publishers of Flight Simulators Today. The Featured Software Packages Are: KNIGHTS OF THE SKY by MicroProse Software, Inc. - A Challenge to Dtermine World War I's Ace of Aces! F-14 TOMCAT by Activision, Inc. - Put Your Talents to the Test to Become the Top Gun! SUPER-VGA HARRIER by Domark Software Inc. - The U.S. Marine Corps' Most Advanced Attack Fighter! JETFIGHTER II by Velocity Incorporated - Fly over 100 Sweat-Drenching Missions!
SelectWare Technologies, Inc.

Software JukeBox: World Class Sports. Jun. 1995. Customer Support: Free technical support 810-477-1205.
MS-DOS 5.0 or higher. IBM 386 or higher, or compatible (4Mb). CD-ROM disk $29.95 (ISBN 1-57037-017-6). Nonstandard peripherals required: CD-ROM drive, 2Mb free hard disk space, SVGA card & monitor, mouse (recommended), sound card (optional), joystick (optional).
The World Class Sports Edition Is Assembled from the Best Publishers of Sports Games Today. Featured Software Packages Are: HARDBALL III by Accolade, Inc. - More of What Serious Baseball Fans Want in a Simulation! JACK NICKLAUS SIGNATURE EDITION by Accolade, Inc. - Finally, a Game with No Handicap! TOM LANDRY STRATEGY FOOTBALL by Merit Studios, Inc. - Match Wits with One of the Best Minds in Pro Football! INTERNATIONAL SOCCER by Merit Studios, Inc. - Outstandingly Realistic 11 Player Field Action! INTERNATIONAL TENNIS by Merit Studios, Inc. - Exciting Simulation of Top World Class Competition!
SelectWare Technologies, Inc.

TITLE INDEX

Software Maintenance Service. *Operating System(s) Required:* Data General.
contact publisher for price.
Information Fountain, Inc.

Software 1040. Jan. 1994. *Compatible Hardware:* IBM PC, PS/2 System 36, AS/400. *Operating System(s) Required:* PC-DOS/MS-DOS. *Memory Required:* 512k. *Items Included:* Software, operator's guide, tax preparer's guide. *Customer Support:* Unlimited telephone support via watts line.
contact publisher for price.
Tax Software for Use by Professional Tax Preparers in Computing & Producing Individual Tax Returns.
Prentice Hall Professional Software.

The Software Toolworks Presents Capitol Hill. Aug. 1993.
IBM CD-ROM. CD-ROM disk $49.95.
Macintosh. 3.5" disk $49.95.
You've Just Won Your Home State's Congressional Election by a Landslide & Now You're off to Washington! Experience What It's Like to Be a Member of Congress from Your Interactive Tour of the Capitol Building & Swearing-In, to Your Budget Reviews. Multiple Video Sequences & Photographs, along with Narration & Text Present a Full Spectrum of the Sights & Sounds of Government from the Inside. Capitol Hill Also Allows You to Test Your Knowledge of Congress in a Challenging Game Scenario.
Software Toolworks.

The Software Toolworks Presents Oceans Below. Aug. 1993.
IBM CD-ROM. CD-ROM disk $49.95 (Order no.: 111397).
MPC. CD-ROM disk $49.95.
MAC CD-ROM. CD-ROM disk $49.95 (Order no.: 111398).
Discover the World of Scuba Divers in This Exciting New Interactive Multimedia Experience! You'll Be Introduced to a Variety of Equipment Components & Underwater Environmental Factors, Then Provided with a Map of Exotic Locations from Which to Choose Your Ideal Dive Site. Learn about Local Sealife Through Video Clips & Photos, & Pursue a Number of Unique Diving Experiences. Explore Shipwrecks, Feed an Eel, Even Hitch a Ride on a Manta Ray! With over 45 Minutes of Video Clips - Plus Numerous Photos, Narration & Original Music - Oceans Below Is the Closest You'll Ever Come to Diving Without Getting Your Feet Wet.
Software Toolworks.

The Software Toolworks Presents Space Shuttle. Jun. 1993.
IBM CD-ROM. disk $49.95 (Order no.: 111358).
MPC. CD-ROM disk $49.95 (Order no.: 111360).
MAC CD-ROM. 3.5" disk $49.95.
Climb Aboard the Most Intriguing Spacecraft Ever Bulit, & Take Part in the Action As Though You Are a Member of the Crew! You'll Participate in a Fascinating Multimedia Tour of Every Aspect of the Most Advanced Space Program Ever Instituted: Examine the Design of the Module; Attend Crew Training; Observe the Launch Sequence; Monitor Conversations Between Astronauts & Mission Control. The Interactive Interface Lets You Choose Your Perspective. Full Motion Video, Stereo Soundtracks with Voice, Plus Thousands of Color Images & Volumes of Text Files Combine to Create an Unforgettable First-Hand Space Shuttle Experience.
Software Toolworks.

The Software Toolworks Travel Companion. Dec. 1992.
MS-DOS version 3.0 or higher. IBM PC-AT & compatibles (640k). 3.5" or 5.25" disk $79.95 (Order no.: 111161; 111159). *Optimal configuration:* IBM PC-AT or compatible (286 or higher); 640k RAM, hard disk required; VGA graphics adapter & monitor; mouse recommended.
The Ultimate Trip Planner & Electronic Travel Guide to the Most Popular Cities in the U.S.! Whether You're Traveling for Business or Pleasure, Travel Companion Puts an Astonishing Amount of Trip Information at Your Fingertips.
Software Toolworks.

The Software Toolworks U. S. Atlas. *Version:* 4. Nov. 1993.
MPC. disk $79.95 (Order no.: 111331).
IBM CD. disk $59.95.
Windows. 3.5" or 5.25" disk $59.95 (Order no.: 111323; 111322).
U.S. Atlas Puts the Country at Your Fingertips, with a Vast Array of Detailed Reference Maps & Reference Materials Containing Everything You Ever Wanted to Know about City, State, & U.S. Geography, Education, Health, Government, Economy, Crime, Agriculture, Travel & More! You Can Even Hear State Songs & View State Flags.
Software Toolworks.

The Software Toolworks U. S. Atlas. *Version:* 3. Jun. 1993.
MAC CD-ROM. CD-ROM disk $69.95 (Order no.: 111325).
Macintosh. CD-ROM disk $59.95 (Order no.: 111324).
Everything You Ever Wanted to Know about U.S. Geography, Government, Agriculture, Travel, & Transportation Is Just a Click Away! View the Whole Country As One Topographical Three-Dimensional Color Map, or Hop from State to State to Pick up County & City Information & Statistical Data. Includes over 1,000 State, County, & City Maps, Comprehensive City Data, Audio Pronunciation of Cities & States, & Aerial Movies of Major Geographic Wonders! Plus, You Can Hear State Songs & See Their Flags.
Software Toolworks.

The Software Toolworks World Atlas. *Version:* 4. Jun. 1993.
MPC CD-ROM. IBM PC or compatible with 80386 processor or higher (2Mb). CD-ROM disk $79.95 (Order no.: 111285). *Optimal configuration:* IBM PC or compatible with 80386 processor or higher; 2Mb, Hard disk; MPC compatible sound card & CD-ROM drive; Super VGA graphics adapter & color monitor; Fully Microsoft compatible mouse recommended; DOS 3.1 or higher; Microsoft Windows 3.1 or higher; MSCDEX 2.2 or higher.
IBM CD-ROM. CD-ROM disk $69.95 (Order no.: 111363). *Optimal configuration:* IBM PC or compatible with 80286, 80386, or 80486 processor; 640k RAM; hard disk; VGA graphics adapter & color monitor; CD-ROM drive; mouse highly recommended, AdLib, Sound Blaster, Pro Audio Spectrum sound cards supported; DOS 3.1 or higher; MSCDEX 2.1 or higher, EMS/XMS supported.
Windows. CD-ROM disk $79.95.
IBM. disk $59.95.
Gives You Instant Access to More Than 200 Fully Detailed Maps in Beautiful High-Resolution Graphics. Plus, a Huge Database of International Information Offers Valuable Facts on Hundreds of Topics Such As: Government, Demographics, Climate, Environment, Economic Indicators & More.
Software Toolworks.

The Software Toolworks World Atlas. *Version:* 3.
MAC CD-ROM. CD-ROM disk $89.95. *Optimal configuration:* Any Macintosh with 2Mb of memory or greater; CD-ROM drive; requires System 6.05 or higher; black & white or color monitor.
MAC. CD-ROM disk $79.95. *Optimal configuration:* Any Macintosh with 2Mb of memory or greater; Hard disk; requires System 6.05 or higher; black & white or color monitor.
Explore the World. It's Easy - & Its' Fun! Gives You Instant Access to More Than 200 Fully detailed Maps in Beautiful High-Resolution Graphics. Plus, a Huge Database of International Information Offers Valuable Facts on Hundreds of Topics Such As: Government, Demographics, Climate, Environment, Economic Indicators & More.
Software Toolworks.

Software Wedge Pro: For DOS or For Windows. *Version:* DOS 5.0, Windows 2.13. 1993. *Items Included:* Complete Manual (single book 100 pages). *Customer Support:* 90 day unlimited money back guarantee. Full, unlimited FREE phone support for all registered users.
DOS. Any - even 8088XT (8k). disk $295.00 (Order no.: SW50P). *Nonstandard peripherals required:* (Standard RS232 port required). *Addl. software required:* Any DOS application. *Optimal configuration:* Hard disk recommended, RS232 devices (Any). *Networks supported:* All.
Windows - OS/2. Min. 386 recommended for Windows (4Mb). disk $395.00 (Order no.: SW20WP). *Addl. software required:* Any Windows application. *Optimal configuration:* 8Mb RAM (or 16), Any RS232 devices. *Networks supported:* All.
Designed to Support Even the Most Complex Serial Input/Output Data Formats. It Has All the Powerful Features of the Standard Wedge Plus Additional Translation, Parsing, Filtering Functions, Faster Input/Output, & Built-In Diagnostic & Output Functions. It Is Recommended for Communication with More Sophisticated Medical, Scientific & Industrial Instruments & Controls.
T.A.L. Enterprises.

Software Wedge Standard Version: For DOS or For Windows. *Version:* DOS 4.0, Windows 1.1. 1992. *Items Included:* Complete Manual. *Customer Support:* 90 day unlimited money back guarantee. Full, unlimited FREE phone support for all registered users.
DOS. Any - even 8088XT (5k). disk $159.00 (Order no.: SW40A). *Nonstandard peripherals required:* (Standard RS232 port required). *Addl. software required:* Any DOS application. *Optimal configuration:* Hard disk recommended. *Networks supported:* All.
Windows - OS/2. Min. 386 recommended for Windows (286 o.k. but slow). disk $199.00 (Order no.: SW11W). *Addl. software required:* Any Windows or OS/2 application.
With the Software Wedge You Can Easily Input Real-Time Data from Any Serial Instrument (Bar Code Scanners, Measuring Tools, Electronic Scales, etc.). It Is Extremely Easy to Set-Up & Use, & Does Not Require Any Additional Hardware or Custom Programming.
T.A.L. Enterprises.

SoftwareVAULT: The Collection for Macintosh. Nov. 1994. *Customer Support:* Free phone technical support via 1-800 number.
MS-DOS; Windows. 386DX 40, MPC 1 (4Mb). CD-ROM disk $19.95 (ISBN 1-57600-012-5, Order no.: 50201). *Optimal configuration:* 386DX 40, 8Mb, 640 x 480 256-color Video Display, CD-ROM drive, 8bit sound card, MPC 2.

A Library of Shareware Collections on CD-ROM. Each Collection Includes Thousands of Programs & Resources from over 50 Categories of Interest. Includes Games, Business Applications, BBS Utilities, etc.
Digital Impact, Inc.

SoftwareVAULT: The Collection for Macintosh, Jewel Case. Nov. 1994. *Customer Support:* Free phone technical support via 1-800 number.
MS-DOS; Windows. 386DX 40, MPC 1 (4Mb). CD-ROM disk $19.95 (ISBN 1-57600-003-6, Order no.: 50201). *Optimal configuration:* 386DX 40, 8Mb, 640 x 480 256-color Video Display, CD-ROM drive, 8bit sound card, MPC 2.
A Library of Shareware Collections on CD-ROM. Each Collection Includes Thousands of Programs & Resources from over 50 Categories of Interest. Includes Games, Business Applications, BBS Utilities, etc.
Digital Impact, Inc.

SoftwareVAULT: The Diamond Collection. Jul. 1995. *Customer Support:* Free phone technical support via 1-800 number.
MS-DOS; Windows. 386DX 40, MPC 1 (4Mb). CD-ROM disk $19.95 (ISBN 1-57600-008-7, Order no.: 50112). *Optimal configuration:* 386DX 40, 8Mb, 640 x 480 256-color Video Display, CD-ROM drive, 8bit sound card, MPC 2.
A Library of Shareware Collections on CD-ROM. Each Collection Includes Thousands of Programs & Resources from over 50 Categories of Interest. Includes Games, Business Applications, BBS Utilities, etc.
Digital Impact, Inc.

SoftwareVAULT: The Diamond Collection, Jewel Case. Jul. 1995. *Customer Support:* Free phone technical support via 1-800 number.
MS-DOS; Windows. 386DX 40, MPC 1 (4Mb). CD-ROM disk $19.95 (ISBN 1-57600-007-9, Order no.: 50112). *Optimal configuration:* 386DX 40, 8Mb, 640 x 480 256-color Video Display, CD-ROM drive, 8bit sound card, MPC 2.
A Library of Shareware Collections on CD-ROM. Each Collection Includes Thousands of Programs & Resources from over 50 Categories of Interest. Includes Games, Business Applications, BBS Utilities, etc.
Digital Impact, Inc.

SoftwareVAULT: The Emerald Collection. May 1994. *Customer Support:* Free phone technical support via 1-800 number.
MS-DOS; Windows. 386DX 40, MPC 1 (4Mb). CD-ROM disk $19.95 (ISBN 1-57600-001-X, Order no.: 50107). *Optimal configuration:* 386DX 40, 640 x 480 256-color Video Display, CD-ROM drive, MPC 2, 8Mb, 8bit sound card.
A Library of Shareware Collections on CD-ROM. Each Collection Includes Thousands of Programs & Resources from over 50 Categories of Interest. Includes Games, Business Applications, BBS Utilities, etc.
Digital Impact, Inc.

SoftwareVAULT: The Games 2 Collection. Dec. 1994. *Customer Support:* Free phone technical support via 1-800 number.
MS-DOS; Windows. 386DX 40, MPC 1 (4Mb). CD-ROM disk $19.95 (ISBN 1-57600-010-9, Order no.: 50109). *Optimal configuration:* 386DX 40, 8Mb, 640 x 480 256-color Video Display, CD-ROM drive, 8bit sound card, MPC 2.
A Library of Shareware Collections on CD-ROM. Each Collection Includes Thousands of Programs & Resources from over 50 Categories of Interest. Includes Games, Business Applications, BBS Utilities, etc.
Digital Impact, Inc.

SoftwareVAULT: The Games 2 Collection, Jewel Case. Dec. 1994. *Customer Support:* Free phone technical support via 1-800 number.
MS-DOS; Windows. 386DX 40, MPC 1 (4Mb). CD-ROM disk $19.95 (ISBN 1-57600-005-2, Order no.: 50109). *Optimal configuration:* 386DX 40, 8Mb, 640 x 480 256-color Video Display, CD-ROM drive, 8bit sound card, MPC 2.
A Library of Shareware Collections on CD-ROM. Each Collection Includes Thousands of Programs & Resources from over 50 Categories of Interest. Includes Games, Business Applications, BBS Utilities, etc.
Digital Impact, Inc.

SoftwareVAULT: The Platinum Collection. Jan. 1994. *Customer Support:* Free phone technical support via 1-800 number.
MS-DOS; Windows. 386DX 40, MPC 1 (4Mb). CD-ROM disk $19.95 (ISBN 1-57600-000-1, Order no.: 50106). *Optimal configuration:* 386DX 40, 640 x 480 256-color Video Display, CD-ROM drive, MPC 2, 8Mb, 8bit sound card.
A Library of Shareware Collections on CD-ROM. Each Collection Includes Thousands of Programs & Resources from over 50 Categories of Interest. Includes Games, Business Applications, BBS Utilities, etc.
Digital Impact, Inc.

SoftwareVAULT: The Ruby Collection. Aug. 1994. *Customer Support:* Free phone technical support via 1-800 number.
MS-DOS; Windows. 386DX 40, MPC 1 (4Mb). CD-ROM disk $19.95 (ISBN 1-57600-002-8, Order no.: 50108). *Optimal configuration:* 386DX 40, 640 x 480 256-color Video Display, CD-ROM drive, MPC 2, 8Mb, 8bit sound card.
A Library of Shareware Collections on CD-ROM. Each Collection Includes Thousands of Programs & Resources from over 50 Categories of Interest. Includes Games, Business Applications, BBS Utilities, etc.
Digital Impact, Inc.

SoftwareVAULT: The Sapphire Collection. Jan. 1995. *Customer Support:* Free phone technical support via 1-800 number.
MS-DOS; Windows. 386DX 40, MPC 1 (4Mb). CD-ROM disk $19.95 (ISBN 1-57600-009-5, Order no.: 50111). *Optimal configuration:* 386DX 40, 8Mb, 640 x 480 256-color Video Display, CD-ROM drive, 8bit sound card, MPC 2.
A Library of Shareware Collections on CD-ROM. Each Collection Includes Thousands of Programs & Resources from over 50 Categories of Interest. Includes Games, Business Applications, BBS Utilities, etc.
Digital Impact, Inc.

SoftwareVAULT: The Sapphire Collection, Jewel Case. Jan. 1995. *Customer Support:* Free phone technical support via 1-800 number.
MS-DOS; Windows. 386DX 40, MPC 1 (4Mb). CD-ROM disk $19.95 (ISBN 1-57600-006-0, Order no.: 50111). *Optimal configuration:* 386DX 40, 8Mb, 640 x 480 256-color Video Display, CD-ROM drive, 8bit sound card, MPC 2.
A Library of Shareware Collections on CD-ROM. Each Collection Includes Thousands of Programs & Resources from over 50 Categories of Interest. Includes Games, Business Applications, BBS Utilities, etc.
Digital Impact, Inc.

SoftwareVAULT: The Windows 2 Collection. Dec. 1994. *Customer Support:* Free phone technical support via 1-800 number.
MS-DOS; Windows. 386DX 40, MPC 1 (4Mb). CD-ROM disk $19.95 (ISBN 1-57600-011-7, Order no.: 50111). *Optimal configuration:* 386DX 40, 8Mb, 640 x 480 256-color Video Display, CD-ROM drive, 8bit sound card, MPC 2.
A Library of Shareware Collections on CD-ROM. Each Collection Includes Thousands of Programs & Resources from over 50 Categories of Interest. Includes Games, Business Applications, BBS Utilities, etc.
Digital Impact, Inc.

SoftwareVAULT: The Windows 2 Collection, Jewel Case. Dec. 1994. *Customer Support:* Free phone technical support via 1-800 number.
MS-DOS; Windows. 386DX 40, MPC 1 (4Mb). CD-ROM disk $19.95 (ISBN 1-57600-004-4, Order no.: 50111). *Optimal configuration:* 386DX 40, 8Mb, 640 x 480 256-color Video Display, CD-ROM drive, 8bit sound card, MPC 2.
A Library of Shareware Collections on CD-ROM. Each Collection Includes Thousands of Programs & Resources from over 50 Categories of Interest. Includes Games, Business Applications, BBS Utilities, etc.
Digital Impact, Inc.

Solar & Lunar Returns: M-32. *Compatible Hardware:* Apple II+; Commodore 64, PET; TRS-80.
disk $50.00.
Commodore 64, PET; TRS-80. cassette $50.00.
Provides Solar & Lunar Returns in House System of Your Choice.
Matrix Software.

Solar Arc Directions: M-10. *Compatible Hardware:* Commodore 64, PET, VIC-20.
disk $30.00.
cassette $30.00.
Calculates Solar Arc Directions & Includes Directed Planet Positions.
Matrix Software.

Solar Arc Directions: M-35. *Compatible Hardware:* Apple II+; Commodore 64, PET; TRS-80.
Apple. disk $50.00.
Commodore 64, PET; TRS-80. cassette $50.00.
User Selects Chart Wheel or List of Planets' Positions & Angles for Radix.
Matrix Software.

Solar Astrological Font. Graham Dawson. 1995. *Items Included:* Brief manual. *Customer Support:* Free phone support.
Windows 3.1, Windows 95. disk $35.00 (ISBN 0-87199-132-2). *Addl. software required:* Word-Processing, Desktop Publishing, Graphics or other program that uses TrueType Fonts.
TrueType Font Has Same Bold Style As the Astrological Characters in the Solar Fire Program, but Places them on Ordinary Keys for Ease in Typing Them into Word-Processing, Desktop-Publishing & Graphics Documents.
Astrolabe, Inc.

Solar Collector F-Chart Calculation & Economic Analysis - SE1M. *Version:* 06/1988. 1979. *Compatible Hardware:* IBM PC & compatibles. *Operating System(s) Required:* PC-DOS/MS-DOS. *Language(s):* Compiled. *Memory Required:* 256k. *Customer Support:* Technical hotline, "Lifetime" support at no charge.
$265.00.
Solar F-Chart Calculation & Economic Analysis - SE1M Uses the U. Wisconsin F-Chart Method to Calculate the Monthly Heat Demanded/Supplied by the Solar Collector System, & Percent Solar. Does Life Cycle Economic Analysis of Payback on Investment. Menu Driven, Fully Prompted & Compiled. Detailed Printouts of All Inputs & Outputs. SI Metric or English Units.
MC2 Engineering Software.

TITLE INDEX

Solar Energy for the Home. *Compatible Hardware:* Apple II+. *Language(s):* Applesoft BASIC. *Memory Required:* 32k.
disk $34.95 (Order no.: 0235AD).
Computes Potential Cost/Benefits Comparison Between Solar & Conventional Heating Methods.
Instant Software, Inc.

Solar F-Chart & Economic Analysis. *Items Included:* Bound manual. *Customer Support:* Free hotline - no time limit; 30 day limited warranty; updates are $5/disk plus S&H.
MS-DOS. IBM & compatibles (256k). disk $249.95.
Calculates the Monthly Heat Demand, Heat Supplied by a Solar Collector System, & Percentage of Solar Using the University of Wisconsin F-Chart Method. It Treats Liquid or Air Systems, Combined Space-Heating & Water-Heating Systems, or Stand-Alone Water-Heating Systems. F-Chart Includes All the Factors Normally Applicable to the F-Chart Method Including the Off-South (Azimuthal) Correction.
Dynacomp, Inc.

Solar Fire: Astrological Calculations. *Version:* 2.1. Esoteric Technologies Pty. Ltd. Jul. 1993. *Items Included:* Manual. *Customer Support:* Free phone support.
Windows 3.0 or higher, running in 386 enhanced mode. IBM PC & MS-DOS & compatibles, 386 or higher (2Mb). disk $150.00 (ISBN 0-87199-128-4). *Nonstandard peripherals required:* Mouse; VGA or Super VGA monitor. *Optimal configuration:* 4Mb RAM, printer.
Astrological Calculation Program That Has Easy, Windows-Style Input Screens & Produces High-Resolution Graphic Horoscopes & Tables on the Screen or Printer. Features On-Screen Point-&-Click Interpretations of Each Part of the Birth Chart; These Can Also Be Sent to a Word Processor & Printed Out. Does Natal, Progressed, Directed, Return, Harmonic, Antisciion, Composite & Relationship Horoscopes; Dynamic Transit & Progression Listings; Aspect Tables & Analysis; & Traditional, Esoteric or Hierarchical Rulerships. Includes Tropical & Sidereal Zodiacs; 25 House Systems; Major Asteroids & the Mean or True Lunar Node; & up to 26 Aspect Types with User-Selectable Orbs. For Easier Data Input, Includes a User-Expandable Database of World Place Names & Time Zones.
Astrolabe, Inc.

Solar Fire Three. *Version:* 3.0. Graham Dawson & Stephanie Johnson. Jan. 1995. *Items Included:* 291-page manual, ACS Mini-Atlas on disk. *Customer Support:* Free phone support.
Windows 3.1, Windows 95. 386 (2Mb, 4Mb recommended). disk $250.00 (ISBN 0-87199-129-2). *Nonstandard peripherals required:* VGA.
Calculates a Wide Variety of Astrological Charts Using Many Zodiacs, House Systems & Techniques. Includes User-Definable Arabic Parts, Midpoints, 7 Asteroids & 11 Hypothetical or Experimental Points; Easily Customized Transit/Progression Lists & Graphs; User-Designable Wheels; Custom Ephemeris Generator; & Point-&-Click Interpretations of the Natal Chart, Transits & Stars.
Astrolabe, Inc.

Solar Maps. Graham Dawson & Stephanie Johnson. Mar. 1996. *Items Included:* Manual. *Customer Support:* Free phone support.
Windows 3.1, Windows 95. 386. disk $195.00 (ISBN 0-87199-134-9). *Nonstandard peripherals required:* VGA.
Produces Maps Showing How Astrological Influences Are Modified by One's Place on Earth. Imports Natal Charts or Casts Its Own; Draws the Chart's Astro-Mapping, Local Space, Paran & Geodetic Lines on Global or Country Maps in Several Projections. Includes Zoom Feature; Eclipse Paths; & Written Interpretations of the Astrogeographical Influences.
Astrolabe, Inc.

Solar Returns: M-7. *Compatible Hardware:* Commodore 64, PET, VIC-20.
disk $30.00.
cassette $30.00.
Calculates Exact Solar Return. Lists Planets & Houses.
Matrix Software.

Solar Spark. *Version:* 1.2. Graham Dawson & Stephanie Johnson. 1994. *Items Included:* Manual. *Customer Support:* Free phone support.
Windows 3.1, Windows 95. 386 (2Mb, 4Mb recommended). disk $95.00 (ISBN 0-87199-133-0). *Nonstandard peripherals required:* VGA.
Runs in Background; When Invoked, Displays Current Zodiacal Positions of Planets Updating in Real Time on an Astrological Wheel. Audible or Visual Alarms Can Be Set for Times of Aspects. Can Quickly Cast a Natal Chart, or Display & Print Charts from Nova, Solar Fire or Blue Star Files. "Sabian Oracle" Can Be Used Like the I Ching to Answer the Question of the Moment.
Astrolabe, Inc.

Solarsim. *Items Included:* Bound manual. *Customer Support:* Free hotline - no time limit; 30 day limited warranty; updates are $5/disk plus S&H.
MS-DOS. IBM & compatibles (256k); Z-100. disk $19.95.
3-D Graphic Simulation of Our Solar System & Nearby Star Systems. It Simulates the Motion of the Planets, 250 Asteroids & Comets (Including Halley's), & Includes over 800 Stars, Nebulae, & Galaxies (& You Can Add More!). View & Identify the Stars & Solar System from Any Point on Earth or Nearly Any Point in Space, & at Any Specified Time or Date.
Dynacomp, Inc.

Solicit Your Congress.
MS/DOS 2.0 or higher (512k). IBM PC & compatibles. disk $49.95. *Nonstandard peripherals required:* Hard disk drive. *Networks supported:* LAN (under NetBIOS 3.1).
Database with Names, Washington D.C. Addresses, Phone Numbers, & Committees of Every Member of the 102nd U.S. Congress. Program Can Print up to 100,000 Labels & Envelopes at One Time, & Therefore Is Suitable for Businesses or Lobbyists That Wish to Write Congress in Bulk. User Can Attach 105-Character Note to Each Address with a 1-7 Character Abbreviation for Special Committees or One-Time Hearings. Can Also Attach a Separate 630-Character Note to an Address for Recording Every Transaction with a Senator or Congressman.
T-Lan Systems.

Solicit Your Consumer Complaint. *Version:* 1.0. Sep. 1991. *Customer Support:* Unlimited free phone support.
PC/MS-DOS 2.1 or higher. IBM or compatible (512k). disk $39.95. *Nonstandard peripherals required:* Hard disk required. *Networks supported:* Net Bios 3.1.
Comes With the Names, Addresses & Phone Number for All of the Better Business Bureaus Throughout the U. S., State & Local Consumer Protection Agencies for Each State, & over 1,000 Companies That Provide Many of the Products Consumers Purchase. Users Can Print Labels, Envelopes, Index Cards, Post Cards, & Lists. Data Can Be Exported to Other Programs via Comma Delimited, Fixed Field or ASCII Text. Records Can Be Tagged for Quick Printing. One hundred Six Character Note Can Be Added to Each Record.
T-Lan Systems.

Solicit Your Editor. *Version:* 2.0. Nov. 1990. *Customer Support:* unlimited free support (phone).
MS/PC-DOS 2.1. IBM or compatibles (512k). $69.95 first year; $34.95 yearly update; 5 user Lan version $134.55. *Nonstandard peripherals required:* Hard disk required. *Networks supported:* NetBios 3.1.
Comes With the Names, Addresses, Phone & FAX Namers & Name of the Chief Editor of Every Daily Newspaper (1,603) & over 1,730 Magazines. The Program Allows You to Print Labels, Envelopes, Post Cards, Index Cards, Lists & Export the Data in Comma Delimited, ASCII Text & Fixed Field. A Small Word Processor is Included & Letters Can Be Started on the Fly. One Hundred Six Character Notes Can Be Added to Each Record. Names Can Be Searched for Using DOS'' Wildcard.*
T-Lan Systems.

Solid Dimensions II. *Compatible Hardware:* Apple Macintosh II.
$1395.00.
Graphics Processing Application. Takes Advantage of Mac II's Ability of Displaying Color.
Visual Information, Inc.

Solid State Physics: One-Dimensional Lattices. 1995. *Items Included:* Full manual. *Customer Support:* Free telephone support - 90 days, 30-day warranty.
MS-DOS 3.2 or higher. 286 (584k). disk $59.95. *Nonstandard peripherals required:* CGA/EGA/VGA.
Uses the Variational Method to Determine Energy States & Wave Functions of One-Dimensional Finite Square Crystal Lattices. These Lattices Are a Simple First Approximation to the Real Periodic Atomic Potentials Used in the Kronig-Penney Model. By Solving for Lattices of Any Finite Size, User Can Observe the Solutions for Individual Atoms, Small Groups of Atoms, & the Limiting Process in Approaching the Infinite Lattice of a Crystal.
Dynacomp, Inc.

Solitaire. John Weaver, Jr. 1985. *Compatible Hardware:* Sanyo MBC 555. *Memory Required:* 192k.
Sanyo. 5-1/4" disk $34.95 (ISBN 0-923213-24-4, Order no.: SA-SOI).
User Can Play Solitaire, Klondike, Poker Squares, Cribbage & Blackjack.
MichTron, Inc.

SOLITAIRE. Wayne Hammond. *Compatible Hardware:* IBM PC, PCjr, PC XT, PC AT, Portable PC, 3270 PC. *Operating System(s) Required:* PC-DOS 2.00, 2.10, 3.00, 3.10. *Memory Required:* IBM PCjr with DOS 3.00 or 3.10 256k, all others 128k.
disk $14.95 (Order no.: 6276565).
User Can Have the Computer Automatically Move the Card Chosen, If There Is Only One Position to Move to; Select the Multi-Pass Option to Repeatedly Go Through a Pair of Cards; Use the "Cheat" Options to See the Down Card on Each of the Card Columns, Move the Top Card of the Deck to the Bottom, Add Cards to the Top of the Column Instead of the Bottom, or Move Any Column to an Empty Column.
Personally Developed Software, Inc.

Solitaire Royale: Solitaire Card Games. *Version:* Amiga & Mac II 1.0, Mac 1.1 & IBM 1.5. Jul. 1987. *Compatible Hardware:* Apple

SOLOMON III

Macintosh 512K, Macintosh Plus, Macintosh SE, Macintosh II; Commodore Amiga 500, 1000, 2000, 2500; IBM PC, PC XT, PC AT, PS/2 & compatibles. *Operating System(s) Required:* Apple DOS 2.0, PC-DOS/MS-DOS 2.0 or higher, Amiga Kickstart 1.2 or above. *Memory Required:* IBM 256k; Apple Macintosh 512k, Mac II 1Mb, Amiga 512k. *General Requirements:* Color monitor.
Macintosh 1.1. 3.5" disk $39.95 (ISBN 0-928784-61-4).
Amiga. 3.5" disk $34.95 (ISBN 0-928784-63-0).
IBM. disk $34.95 (ISBN 0-928784-60-6).
MAC II. disk $34.95.
Collection of Solitaire Card Games. Provides Eight Kinds of Solitaire for Individual or Competitive Play. Users Can Choose from 10 Card Decks. Three Additional Games Are Included for Children.
Spectrum HoloByte.

Solomon III. *Version:* 2.0C. *Compatible Hardware:* IBM PC & compatibles, Novell Netware. *Memory Required:* 640k. *General Requirements:* Hard disk. *Customer Support:* support plans available. $495.00 to $1295.00 per module.
Financial/Accounting Software. Solomon III Is a Flexible Integrated Accounting Software Package. Modules Available Include General Ledger, Accounts Payable, Accounts Receivable, Payroll, Purchasing, Order Entry, Job Costing, Inventory, Report & Graph Designer, SolomoNotes, SolomonScript & External Systems Manager. Solomon III Has a Strong Audit Trail with Flexible Reporting Options. Four Levels of Fault Tolerance Help Insure Data Integrity.
Solomon Software.

Solomon IV. *Version:* 1.70. Oct. 1995. *Items Included:* Purchase of each module provides on line help, manuals & software. *Customer Support:* Support is based on list price 15% of list is maintenance only. 20%-maintenance & fax support; 25% telephone & maintenance & 30% of list price for guaranteed 1 hr. support & maintenance. No on site support provided from vendor. Resellers & Consultants provide on site support.
Windows or Windows for Workgroups. 486/Pentium (16Mb). CD-ROM disk $495.00. *Nonstandard peripherals required:* HP compatible printer, modem. *Networks supported:* Netware.
CD-ROM disk $1295.00-$13,995.00 server edition.
CD-ROM disk $1295.00-$13,995.00 NT server edition.
An Accounting Software Package That Offers Unrivaled Customization Capabilities & Provides a Unique Open Architecture. The Product Was Developed Using Industry-Standard Tools to Enable Extendibility & Compatibility Across the IS Enterprise. Users Can Quickly Create & Integrate Financial & Operational Solutions for All of Their Business Needs.
Solomon Software.

The Solution Machine So Simple It Works: The Creative Problem Solving Program That Harnesses the Power of Imagery. *Version:* 1.1. Jan. 1991. *Items Included:* Two disks 3.50 & 5.25 for IBM -PC version plus manual one disk 3.50 for MAC version plus manual. *Customer Support:* Custom training program for companies & groups, Site-licensing.
IBM PC-DOS 2.1 or more, MAC version 4.1 or better (DOS box in windows). IBM-PC or clone or Macintosh (256k). $149.00 (Order no.: 61245).
Creative Problem Solving Program That Harnesses the Power of Imagery. Assists Users in Getting New & Creative Insight into a Problem. It Uses the Power of Imagery & the Proven Techniques of Lateral Thinking. The Program Is Simple to Use & Complete, Step-by-Step Prompting Occurs Throughout. Time for an Average Problem Is About Twenty Minutes.
Gemini Group.

Solution 3000. *Compatible Hardware:* IBM PC & compatibles; Sun, SGI. *Items Included:* Documentation. *Customer Support:* Updates, hot-line, training.
disk $3500.00 & up.
Advanced Mechanical 3-D CAD-CAM for the Tooling Industry, PC & Workstation-Based.
Micro Engineering Solutions, Inc.

Solution 3000. *Version:* 5.3. Aug. 1992. *Items Included:* Documentation. *Customer Support:* Training, hot-line support, updates.
MS-DOS. 386/486. Contact publisher for price. *Optimal configuration:* 486 processor, 16Mb RAM, 200Mb hard disk. *Networks supported:* PC NFS.
UNIX. SUN Sparc, HP 9000/7xx, SGI Indigo, SGI IRIS, RS/6000. Contact publisher for price. *Optimal configuration:* 32Mb RAM, 600Mb hard disk. *Networks supported:* Ethernet.
Fully Integrated Design Through Manufacturing CAD/CAM System Designed Specifically for the Production of Molds, Dies, Patterns & Models. Surfacing Capabilities Include Section Cutting, Flow Cuts, Trimmed Surfaces, & Advanced Surface Editing Including NURBS Curves & Surfaces. NC Capabilities Include 2 Through 5 Axis Machining Including Surfaced Cavity Roughing & Gouge-Free Machining over Multiple Sculptured Surfaces. Also Includes CMM Verification & Programming.
Micro Engineering Solutions, Inc.

Solutions Waste Management Solutions Database. *Items Included:* Full manual. No other products required. *Customer Support:* Free telephone support - no time limit. 30 day warranty.
MS-DOS 3.2 or higher. IBM & compatibles (512k). $89.95-$539.95.
A "How-To" Database of Waste Management Solutions Which Have Been Developed from Real-World Industrial Situations. Provides a Comprehensive & Quick Means to Determine Approaches & to Develop Plans for Dealing with Environmental Problems. All Relevant Subjects Are Covered, Including Water, Wastewater, Air, Remediation, Waste Reduction, Recycling, & Cost Reduction.
Dynacomp, Inc.

!Solutions!Word! *Version:* 1.71. Jan. 1985. *Items Included:* Complete manual, tutorial & problem disk. *Customer Support:* Toll-free voice support "800" number.
MS-DOS (256k). IBM compatible. disk $395.00 (ISBN 0-929770-30-7). *Optimal configuration:* MS-DOS, 256k memory, 2 floppy disks or hard disk, printer.
Sorts, Calculates, Designs Languages, Has 90, 000 Word Spell Checker, Label Printing, Mail Merge, Word Counts, Storage.
!Solutions! Publishing Co.

Somos Asi One. Karen Grooms. *Items Included:* Software program guide. *Customer Support:* Customer support is available through our toll-free number 800-328-1452, ask for Technical Support. Free on-site training is also available through the same number.
MS-DOS. IBM & compatibles (256k). 3.5" disk $315.00 (ISBN 0-8219-1236-4, Order no.: 98110H). *Nonstandard peripherals required:* CGA or better graphics adaptor. *Optimal configuration:* Color monitor & printer. *Networks supported:* Not designed for networks, but can be installed to a network.
MS-DOS. IBM & compatibles (256k). 5.25" disk $315.00 (ISBN 0-8219-0988-6, Order no.: 98110G). *Nonstandard peripherals required:* CGA or better graphics adaptor. *Optimal configuration:* Color monitor & printer. *Networks supported:* Not designed for networks, but can be installed to a network.
Apple PRODOS. Apple IIe or higher (128k). disk $315.00 (ISBN 0-8219-0987-8, Order no.: 98110F). *Nonstandard peripherals required:* 80-column card for 64k Apple II's. *Optimal configuration:* Color monitor & printer. *Networks supported:* Not designed for networks, but can be installed to a network.
MAC OS 6.07 or higher. Macintosh (MAC SE 1Mb/MAC LC 2Mb). 3.5" disk $315.00 (ISBN 0-8219-1230-5, Order no.: 98110I). *Optimal configuration:* Color monitor & printer. *Networks supported:* Not designed for networks, but can be installed to a network.
Designed to Review, Drill, & Apply the Vocabulary, Structures, & Cultural Information Presented in the Textbook in an Easy-to-Use Interactive Environment.
EMC Publishing.

Somos Asi Two. Karen Grooms. *Items Included:* Software program guide. *Customer Support:* Customer support is available through our toll-free number 800-328-1452, ask for Technical Support. Free on-site training is also available through the same number.
MS-DOS. IBM & compatibles (256k). 3.5" disk $325.00 (ISBN 0-8219-1237-2, Order no.: 98120H). *Nonstandard peripherals required:* CGA or better graphics adaptor. *Optimal configuration:* Color monitor & printer. *Networks supported:* Not designed for networks, but can be installed to a network.
MS-DOS. IBM & compatibles (256k). 5.25" disk $325.00 (ISBN 0-8219-1005-1, Order no.: 98120G). *Nonstandard peripherals required:* CGA or better graphics adaptor. *Optimal configuration:* Color monitor & printer. *Networks supported:* Not designed for networks, but can be installed to a network.
Apple PRODOS. Apple IIe or higher (128k). disk $325.00 (ISBN 0-8219-1004-3, Order no.: 98120F). *Nonstandard peripherals required:* 80-column card for 64k Apple II's. *Optimal configuration:* Color monitor & printer. *Networks supported:* Not designed for networks, but can be installed to a network.
MAC OS 6.07 or higher. Macintosh (MAC SE 1Mb/MAC LC 2Mb). 3.5" disk $325.00 (ISBN 0-8219-1231-3, Order no.: 98120I). *Optimal configuration:* Color monitor & printer. *Networks supported:* Not designed for networks, but can be installed to a network.
Designed to Review, Drill, & Apply the Vocabulary, Structure, & Cultural Information Presented in the Textbook in an Easy-to-Use Interactive Environment.
EMC Publishing.

Sonar Bookends. *Version:* 3.5. Jul. 1992. *Customer Support:* (804) 739-3200.
Macintosh 6.0 & higher, Windows. Macintosh Plus & higher (1Mb), Power Mac, IBM. 3.5" disk $129.95. *Optimal configuration:* Macintosh, 4Mb RAM, hard disk.
Index & Table of Contents Generator for Popular File Formats Such As PAGEMAKER & QUARKXPRESS. Can Make an Index Based on Word Frequency, Proper Nouns, & a User Supplied List of Words & Phrases.
Virginia Systems, Inc.

Sonar Image. *Version:* 3.0. *Customer Support:* Free telephone support.
Macintosh System 7.0 or higher. All 68020 based or higher Macintosh (8Mb), Power Mac. 3.5" disk $1295.00 single user, $4216.00 5

pack (Order no.: IM001). *Optimal configuration:* System 7.1, Macintosh Power PC, scanner with document feeder, large hard disk or optical drive. *Networks supported:* All. Complete Document Imaging Product. Combines Scanner Control, Optical Character Recognition & High Speed Text Retrieval Functions in a Single, Comprehensive Package. Designed for Archiving, Researching & Annotating Large Bodies of Text, Allows User to Search Through Thousands of Documents in Seconds.
Virginia Systems, Inc.

SONAR Professional Text Retrieval System. *Version:* 9.0. *Compatible Hardware:* Apple Macintosh II, Plus, SE, Power Mac; IBM. *Customer Support:* (804) 739-3200.
3.5" disk $795.00.
Enables Users to Search the Contents of a Document - or Thousands of Documents - for a Particular Word or Phrase. Searches at 10,000 Pages per Second. Works with Text Files of Popular Word Processors Such As WORD, MACWRITE, WRITENOW, PAGEMAKER & WORDPERFECT. Excerpts & Notes Can Be Appended to the Clipboard. An Annotated Listing of All Paragraphs Selected by a Search Can Be Printed or Saved to Disk. Provides Indexing Capabilities. Supports Boolean, Proximity, Wildcard, Phonetic & Synonym Searching.
Virginia Systems, Inc.

Sonar Text Retrieval System. *Version:* 9.0. *General Requirements:* Hard disk. *Customer Support:* (804) 739-3200.
Apple, Windows. 3.5" disk $295.00.
Text Retrieval System Searches Thousands of Documents at 10,000 Pages per Second. Supports Popular Word Processors Such As WORD, PAGEMAKER, WRITENOW, WORDPERFECT, TEXT ONLY.
Virginia Systems, Inc.

SONET: An Overview. Sep. 1994. *Items Included:* User manual. *Customer Support:* Free technical support & a 30-day warranty (1-800-521-CORE).
MS-DOS. IBM & compatibles (512k). 3.5" disk $199.00 (ISBN 1-57305-006-7). *Nonstandard peripherals required:* High-density 3.5" disk drive; VGA color monitor. *Addl. software required:* MS-DOS version 3.3 or higher. *Optimal configuration:* IBM (512k), MS-DOS version 3.3 or higher, VGA color monitor, keyboard, Microsoft compatible mouse (optional).
This Computer-Based Training Course Describes the Impact SONET Will Have on Future Telecommunications Services. This Training Package Explains the Major Characteristics of the SONET Signal Format, SONET Network Elements, the Advantages & Applications of Synchronous Optical Transmission, & the Operations Benefits of SONET Overhead. It Is a Stand-Alone Course but Is Also a Helpful Prerequisite for a Variety of More Advanced Training.
Bellcore.

Sonic Digitizer Takeoff. Richard T. Scott. Aug. 1985. *Compatible Hardware:* IBM PC XT, AT, PS/2 & compatibles, SAC, SUMMAGRAPHICS. *Operating System(s) Required:* PC-DOS/MS-DOS. *Language(s):* BASIC. *Memory Required:* 128k. *General Requirements:* 10Mb hard disk, printer.
disk $500.00, ea., excluding hardware.
Sheet metal disk. (ISBN 0-923933-16-6).
Piping & Plumbing Disk. (ISBN 0-923933-08-5).
video tape demo avail.
Takeoff Entry Direct from Drawings Using Sonic Digitizer, As Opposed to Keyboard Entry.
Esccomate.

Sonic Spectrum Library. *Compatible Hardware:* Commodore Amiga.
contact publisher for price.
Over 700 Various Professionally-Sampled Sounds.
DataSound.

Sonshine Software for Amway Distributors. *Version:* 1.4. Sep. 1991. *Compatible Hardware:* IBM PC & compatibles. *Operating System(s) Required:* MS-DOS. *Language(s):* Machine. *Memory Required:* 640k. *Customer Support:* Product Price update subscriptions available.
disk $25.00.
Menu-Driven Program Aimed at Automating Amway Distribution & Ordering Processes. All Information Relevant to PV/BU Distribution Reports May Be Stored, Formatted & Printed.
Richcal Computing Services.

Sorcerer. Steve Meretzky. 1984. *Compatible Hardware:* Apple II, II+, IIe, IIc, Macintosh; Atari XL/XE, ST; Commodore 64, Amiga; IBM PC, PCjr; TRS-80 Model I, Model III; TI Professional, 99/4A. *Operating System(s) Required:* MS-DOS 2.0, CP/M.
$44.95.
Belboz the Necromancer, Your Friend & Mentor, Has Vanished, Leaving Behind Only a Cryptic Diary. There Are Signs That the Grand & Powerful Leader of the Guild of Enchanters Is in Thrall to Evil Sorcery. The Freedom of the Land & the Very Existence of the Guild of Enchanters, of Whom You Have Become a Full-Fledged Member, Could Be in Jeopardy. Can You Rescue the Kingdom & Locate Your Mentor Amid the Treacherous Mists of Time? Gaze Now into the Amulet of Aggathora & Let There Be Revealed the One Valorous Enough to Earn the Title of Sorcerer.
Activision, Inc.

Sorcerer. Infocom. *Compatible Hardware:* HP 150 Touchscreen, HP 110 Portable.
3.5" disk $44.95 (Order no.: 92243YA).
Belboz the Necromancer, Your Friend & Mentor, Has Vanished, Leaving Behind Only a Cryptic Diary. There Are Signs That the Grand & Powerful Leader of the Circle of Enchanters Is in Thrall to Evil Sorcery. The Freedom of the Land & the Very Existence of the Circle of Enchanters, of Which You Have Become a Full-Fledged Member, Could Be in Jeopardy. Can You Rescue the Kingdom & Locate Your Mentor Amid the Treacherous Mists of Time? Gaze Now into the Amulet of Aggthora & Let Be Revealed the One Valorous Enough to Earn the Title of Sorcerer.
Hewlett-Packard Co.

SORITEC. *Version:* 7.0. 1978. *Compatible Hardware:* Almost all platforms from a PC to a Cray. *Operating System(s) Required:* DOS 3.0. *Memory Required:* 512k.
$595.00-$30,000.00.
Sorites Group, Inc.

Sort Directory Utility. *Version:* 2.00. PC Consulting. 1983. *Compatible Hardware:* IBM PC, PCjr, PC XT, PC AT & compatibles. *Operating System(s) Required:* PC-DOS 1.0, 1.1, 2.0, 2.1. *Memory Required:* 32k.
disk $29.00.
disk with 5 add'l. utilities $59.95.
Sorting Utility Which Reads Directory Information from Diskette, Sorts Information by Filename, Extension, Date or Size, & Then Writes It Back to Diskette in Sorted Order. Also Available with 5 Additional Utilities As Time Savers.
DataSource Publishing Co.

Sort-Merge-Copy. *Compatible Hardware:* IBM PC, PCjr, PC XT, PC AT, PC compatibles.
disk $49.95.
Sort Utility. Can Be Used As a Stand-Alone, or Called from Any Language.
Software Matters.

Sort Routines. *Compatible Hardware:* TI 99/4A. *Operating System(s) Required:* DX-10. *Language(s):* Console BASIC. *Memory Required:* 16k.
contact publisher for price.
Any Alphanumeric or Alphabetic Data Input from a Disk, Cassette or Keyboard Can Be Sorted.
Eastbench Software Products.

Sorting & Searching Toolkit. *Compatible Hardware:* MAC, IBM PC.
3.5" disk $79.95.
True BASIC Library with Optimized Sorting & Searching Routines.
True BASIC, Inc.

S.O.S.! (Save Our Screen!). *Version:* 2. Feb. 1991. *Items Included:* Instructions, 3.5" & 5.25" disks. *Customer Support:* 90 days limited warranty.
MS-DOS/PC-DOS 2.0 or higher. IBM PC & compatible (128k). disk $29.95 (ISBN 1-881432-25-4).
Collection of 15 Programs Which Detect if a Key Has Not Been Pressed for a Specified Time Span & Then Replace the Current Screen with Another Colorful, Moving Screen. The Screen May Be Restored by Pressing a Key. There Is Also a "Passkey" Option.
BCS Publishing.

SOS (Super-Optimum Solutions) Decision-Aiding Software. *Version:* 8.7. Stuart S. Nagel et al. 1990. *Items Included:* A program disk. Over 100 Illustrative data files. A demonstration disk. A self-teaching tutorial. More specialized books for more specialized or advanced packages. *Customer Support:* A self-teaching tutorial. A detailed textbook. Workshops for associations, government agencies, law firms, business firms, etc. Hotline service. Journal articles. A support group.
DOS. Any IBM compatible computer (192k). disk $50.00, for the basic package & other prices for bigger packages. *Nonstandard peripherals required:* Non-standard peripherals or boards required. *Optimal configuration:* Optimum configuration is an IBM-compatible computer using DOS with at least 192k RAM & a graphics adapter.
Designed to Enable Disputants in Any Type of Controversy to Develop Super-Optimum Solutions Whereby All Sides Will Come Out Ahead of Their Best Initial Expectations Simultaneously. Such Solutions are Facilitated by Spreadsheet-Based Software Which Allows for a Multiplicity of Goals, Alternatives, Relations, & Other Inputs, As Well As Various Kinds of What-If Analysis.
SOS Group.

Sound Accelerator: Digital Signal Processing Card. *Version:* B. Sep. 1988. *Items Included:* Softsynth additive synthesis software, sound installer, manual(s).
MAC 6.0.2 (1Mb). Macintosh SE, SE/30, II, IIx, IIcx. $1295.00. *Addl. software required:* Softsynth (inc.), Turbosynth (opt.), Sound Designer II (opt.).
Gives User With MAC (SE/II) the Ability to Playback Co-Quality Audio. Its Motorola 56001 DSP Chip Facilitates Real-Time Audio Editing & Powerful DSP Functions Such as Time Compression/Exp, Digital Eq.
Digidesign, Inc.

Sound Clips. *Items Included:* Disks, manual & addendums. *Customer Support:* Free unlimited phone technical support, FAX & modem service. America Online, CompuServe, Applelink. Macintosh System 6.0.5 & higher. Mac Plus & higher (1Mb RAM). 3.5" disk $149.00.
Allows the User to Add Sound Effects to Any Presentation. Includes 10 Disks per Volume with

an Average of 100 Sounds per Volume. Sounds Range from Splashes, Lawn Mower, Phone Ring, Dial Tone, Saw, Drum Roll, Laugh, Police Car, Slot Machine, Football Noise, Planes, Trains, & More.
Olduvai Corp.

Sound Designer II. *Version:* 1.1. Jul. 1989. *Items Included:* Manual & reference card.
Mac 6.0.2 (1Mb). Mac Plus, SE, SE/30, II, IIx, IIcx. $595.00. *Optimal configuration:* Mac II, 2 meg RAM, 80 meg HD, sound accelerator.
Commodore 64, 128 (64k). contact publisher for price.
Stereo Waveform Editor for Use with the Apple Macintosh & Your Stereo or Mono Sampler. It Includes Advanced Sample Editing Tools & Powerful DSP Features, Such as Time Compression.
Digidesign, Inc.

Sound Designer Universal. *Version:* 1.5. *Compatible Hardware:* Apple Macintosh. *Memory Required:* 512k. *General Requirements:* 800k disk drive; MIDI interface; Digital sampling keyboard.
3.5" disk $395.00.
Visual Editing-Digital Signal Processing Software.
Digidesign, Inc.

Sound Sentences. Janet Payne. *Items Included:* CD-ROM binder & documentation. *Customer Support:* Toll free customer service Hot Line 1-800-645-3739 (9a.m. - 5p.m. Eastern Time) software guaranteed for two years.
System 6.07 or higher (2Mb); System 7.0 or higher (4Mb). Macintosh. CD-ROM disk $595.00 (Order no.: DK21041). *Nonstandard peripherals required:* CD-ROM drive.
Students Hear a Main Sentence, Related Vocabulary Words, & Questions Accompanied by an Appropriate Graphic. They Are Then Challenged by a Wide Variety of Activities (Correlated to CASAS) That Build upon the Basic Sentence: Including a Picture Glossary Related Questions & Answers & Sentence Reconstruction (Cloze).
Educational Activities Inc.

Sound Tools. *Version:* 2.0. Sep. 1990. *Customer Support:* Free technical phone support.
Macintosh SE/30, II, IIx, IIcx, IIci, IIfx. 3.5" disk $3285.00.
Stereo Direct-to-Disk CD-Quality Recording & Playback System with Extensive Editing Features & Digital Signal Processing Functions. Ideal for Music Editing & Mastering, Audio Post Production - Any Application That Requires High-Fidelity Audio & High-Speed, Flexible Editing. Consist of the Analog Interface Analog-to-Digital Converter, the Sound Accelerator Digital Signal Processing Card, & Sound Designer II Audio Editing Software.
Digidesign, Inc.

Sound Track Trolly. (Bright Beginning Ser.). *Compatible Hardware:* TI 99/4A with Milton Bradley MBX System.
contact publisher for price (Order no.: PHM3157).
Pick Up Musicians & Combine Their Tunes to Form a Band. Speech Synthesis & Voice Recognition.
Texas Instruments, Personal Productivit.

SoundEdit 16. May 1994. *Items Included:* Manuals. *Customer Support:* Registered users get first 90 days free phone support, fax & online support. Call Macromedia for information about Priority Access technical support.
Macintosh. Contact publisher for price.
Turns Your Macintosh into a Professional Sound Production Studio by Allowing You to Create, Edit, & Playback CD-Quality Soundtracks Without the Need for DSP Hardware. Lets You Record Directly to Your Hard Disk, Then Create Original Multitrack Soundtracks in 16-Bit, 44KHZ Quality. Diverse Feature Set Includes Special Effects, Multi-Track Mixing, Cross-Platform Capabilities, SMPTE Time Code Support, & QuickTime Soundtrack Creation & Editing.
Macromedia, Inc.

Sounder. Intentional Education Staff & William Armstrong. Apr. 1996. *Items Included:* Program manual. *Customer Support:* Free technical support, 90 day warranty.
School ver.. System 7.1 or higher. Macintosh (4Mb). 3.5" disk contact publisher for price (ISBN 1-57204-033-5). *Nonstandard peripherals required:* 256 color monitor, hard drive, printer.
Lab pack. System 7.1 or higher. Macintosh (4Mb). 3.5" disk contact publisher for price (ISBN 1-57204-034-3). *Nonstandard peripherals required:* 256 color monitor, hard drive, printer.
Site license. System 7.1 or higher. Macintosh (4Mb). 3.5" disk contact publisher for price (ISBN 1-57204-035-1). *Nonstandard peripherals required:* 256 color monitor, hard drive, printer.
School ver.. Windows 3.1 or higher. IBM/Tandy & 100% compatibles (4Mb). disk contact publisher for price (ISBN 1-57204-055-6). *Nonstandard peripherals required:* VGA or SVGA 640 x 480 resolution (256), hard drive, sound device, mouse.
Lab pack. Windows 3.1 or higher. IBM/Tandy & 100% compatibles (4Mb). disk contact publisher for price (ISBN 1-57204-056-4). *Nonstandard peripherals required:* VGA or SVGA 640 x 480 resolution (256), hard drive, sound device, mouse.
Site license. Windows 3.1 or higher. IBM/Tandy & 100% compatibles (4Mb). disk contact publisher for price (ISBN 1-57204-057-2). *Nonstandard peripherals required:* VGA or SVGA 640 x 480 resolution (256), hard drive, sound device, mouse.
This companion for young adult literature is ideal for students who don't know how to start that book report, or give that needed summary. Gentle prompts throughout the guide section of the program include Warm-up Connections, Thinking about Plot, Quoting & Noting, Keeping a Journal, If I Were ———' Responding to Questions, Using Quotations, Taking a Personal View, Write to Others, & Write a Sequel.
Lawrence Productions, Inc.

Soundhack. *Version:* 0.8. Tom Eibe. 1994. *Items Included:* Manual on disk.
MAC II or higher or Power PC. Macintosh (2Mb). 3.5" disk $50.00. *Nonstandard peripherals required:* None, but will work with Audiomedia card.
Software for Soundfile Manipulation. Includes Standard Features Plus Phase Vocoder, "Morphing," Binarial Location & Convolution, & Spectral Dynamics Processing. Recognizes All Soundfile Formats.
Frog Peak Music.

Sounds. Jun. 1982. *Compatible Hardware:* IBM PC, PCjr, PC XT, PC AT. *Operating System(s) Required:* DOS. *Language(s):* BASIC. *Memory Required:* 64k. *General Requirements:* CGA card, light pen.
disk $30.00.
Produces Sound Reproduction/Simulation.
Miracle Computing.

Sounds of Cyberspace: Rock, Pop, & Alternative Music on the Internet. Victoria Bell. Apr. 1996. *Items Included:* A 64-page companion booklet that reviews web sites & includes instructions on how to use the software. *Customer Support:* Access to the Go!Guides web site & FAQ, customer support by email at help goguides.com.
Macintosh System 7.0 or higher. Macintosh (4Mb). 3.5" disk $12.99 (ISBN 1-57712-013-2). *Nonstandard peripherals required:* Modem 14.4 or faster. *Addl. software required:* Internet account & connection. *Optimal configuration:* Macintosh System 7.0 or higher, at least 4Mb of RAM, at least 2Mb of free disk space, color monitor, 14.4 or 28.8 modem, Internet account.
Windows 3.1 or Windows 95. IBM or compatible (4Mb). disk $12.99. *Nonstandard peripherals required:* 14.4 or 28.8 modem. *Addl. software required:* Internet account. *Optimal configuration:* IBM-compatible running Windows 3.1 or Windows 95, at least 2Mb free space on hard drive, at least 4Mb RAM, color monitor, 14.4 or 28.8 modem, Internet account.
Sounds of Cyberspace Is Your Guide to Band Homepages, Music Zines, Discographies, Lyric Pages, Newsgroups, Sound Clips, Music, Videos & More on the Internet.
Motion Works Publishing.

Source Accounting. *Customer Support:* 800-929-8117 (customer service).
MS-DOS. Commodore 128; CP/M. disk $99.99 (ISBN 0-87007-038-X).
A Menu-Driven, Integrated Program. Includes Password Protection, Monthly, Quarterly & Annual Aging of Accounts & Personalization for Different Terminal Types.
SourceView Software International.

Source Code. *Customer Support:* All of our products are unconditionally guaranteed.
DOS, Unix. CD-ROM disk $39.95 (Order no.: SOURCE). *Nonstandard peripherals required:* CD-ROM drive.
600 MB of Unix & DOS Source Code.
Walnut Creek CDRom.

Source Level Debugger for Benchmark Modula-2. *Items Included:* 130 pages of documentation. *Customer Support:* Free telephone & mail technical support.
Amiga DOS (512k). $149.95. *Addl. software required:* Benchmark Modula-2.
Tool for Finding Bugs in User Created Programs. Provides Complete Program Control at the Source Level & Assembly Language Level.
Avant-Garde Software.

Source Maintenance System. Wayne R. Deniston. *Compatible Hardware:* IBM PC, PCjr, PC XT, PC AT, Portable PC. *Operating System(s) Required:* PC-DOS 2.00, 2.10, 3.00, 3.10. *Memory Required:* 128k.
disk $24.95 (Order no.: 6276568).
Provides a Structured Method of Making Individual or Multiple Changes to the Source Code in a Controlled Environment. Changes Can Be Made Without Duplicating or Damaging the Original Files. Changes Are Placed into Separate UPDATE CONTROL FILES & Combines the Changes with the Original Source File to Create a New Revised Version. Also Keeps a Summary Log of All Changes to Provide a Complete History of Program's Development.
Personally Developed Software, Inc.

SourceView Accountant's Time & Billing. *Version:* 2.1. *Operating System(s) Required:* CP/M, MS-DOS. *Language(s):* M Basic Compiler. *Memory Required:* 64k. *Customer Support:* 800-929-8117 (customer service).
MS-DOS. contact publisher for price (ISBN 0-87007-376-1).
Allows On-Line Editing & Updating of Master

TITLE INDEX

Files, Data Entry & Data Inquiry. Features: up to 999 User-Defined Service Codes, Interactive Time & Expense Transaction Entry, 3 Hourly Billing Rates. Accumulates Fixed Fee Job Activity for Final Billing & More.
SourceView Software International.

SourceView Accounting. Customer Support: 800-929-8117 (customer service).
MS-DOS. IBM/PS2. disk $299.99 (ISBN 0-87007-039-8).
An Accounting System Written in COBOL, & Migrated Down from Minicomputers to the Micro. Professional Double Entry System.
SourceView Software International.

SourceView Agenda Master. Version: 3. Michael Dean. Operating System(s) Required: CP/M, MS-DOS. Memory Required: CP/M 64k, MS-DOS 128k. Customer Support: 800-929-8117 (customer service).
MS-DOS. contact publisher for price (ISBN 0-87007-379-6).
Electronic Datebook. Able to Block Out Personal Time Such As Lunch Hours, Vacations & Holidays. Detects Concurrent Appointments. Utilizes Windowed Calendar Display. Allows Free-Form Notes of up to 250 Characters; Appointment Updating, Rescheduling or Canceling, etc.
SourceView Software International.

SourceView Attorney's Time & Billing. Version: 2.8. Customer Support: 800-929-8117 (customer service).
MS-DOS. IBM, Commodore 128 or compatible; CP/M. disk $599.99 (ISBN 0-87007-697-3).
Specially Designed for Law Firms Which Bill Their Time.
SourceView Software International.

SourceView Attorney's Time and Billing I. Customer Support: 800-929-8117 (customer service).
MS-DOS. IBM/PS2, Commodore 128 or compatible. disk $499.99 (ISBN 0-87007-375-3).
This System Has Been Reviewed for Appropriateness & Accuracy by the CPA Firm of Henning, Strouse, Jordan & Co., Designed for the Law Firm Which Bills Their Time.
SourceView Software International.

SourceView Attorneys's Time and Billing II. Customer Support: 800-929-8117 (customer service).
MS-DOS. IBM/PS2. disk $699.99.
Version 3.0 Is Written in C Programming Language. The Total Programs Take up Less Disk Space.
SourceView Software International.

SourceView Basic. Customer Support: 800-929-8117 (customer service).
MS-DOS. Apple II. disk $49.99 (ISBN 0-87007-455-5).
A Combination Interpreter & Compiler BASIC for the Apple Computer. With its Built-in Editor, Special Formats Are Made Online. The Editor Enables the Programmer to Build Large Subroutine Libraries & Load Them All Into Memory at Once. Code Is Compressed by Removing All Unnecessary Spaces. The System Then Formats User Code in a Strict Form the Compiler Recognizes & Matches up User's Structured Commands. Removes Every Possible Syntax Error with Few Exceptions & Translates User Program into a Form of Code Any Computer Can Use.
SourceView Software International.

SourceView Budget Trac. Compatible Hardware: IBM PC & compatible, Commodore 128, CP/M. Operating System(s) Required: CP/M, MS-DOS.
Memory Required: 64k. Customer Support: 800-929-8117 (customer service).
MS-DOS. contact publisher for price (ISBN 0-87007-561-6).
Fund Accounting System. Simplifies Record Keeping & Provides Immediate Access to Current Expense Information Relative to Budgeted Items.
SourceView Software International.

SourceView CommStar. Customer Support: 800-929-8117 (customer service).
MS-DOS. IBM/PS2. disk $799.99 (ISBN 0-87007-032-0).
Draws Together a Number of Useful Office Functions into One System. Send & Receive Facsimile Transmissions, Set up a Secure Voice Mailbox System for up to 9,999 Employees (Each with Their Own Password), Monitor Both Incoming & Outgoing Calls, Set up an Auto Attendant for Office in Users Own Voice, Provide Call Forwarding, Message Forwarding, Call Logging & Reporting, As Well As Many Other Specialized Telecommunications Tasks. Employ Product to Perform Automated Telephone Surveys or to Deliver Advertising Messages. Order Taking Either for Voice Orders or Through Menus Displayed on Customers' Monitors--Day or Night & Weekends.
SourceView Software International.

SourceView Conflict of Interest. Customer Support: 800-929-8117 (customer service).
MS-DOS. Commodore 128; CP/M. disk $299.99 (ISBN 0-87007-699-X).
IBM PC; PS/2. disk $299.00 (ISBN 0-87007-377-X).
Designed to Provide Law Firms with the Means to Avoid Conflicts Due to Present Litigation, Family Relationships, & Bankers Just to Name a Few. Based upon an Index of Client Names, the Process Is Designed to Interface with the SourceView Attorney's Time & Billing Program in Order to Avoid Double Entry of Information.
SourceView Software International.

SourceView Docket Control. Customer Support: 800-929-8117 (customer service).
MS-DOS. IBM PC; PS/2; Commodore 128; CP/M. disk $299.99 (ISBN 0-87007-698-1).
disk $299.99 (ISBN 0-87007-378-8).
Designed to Provide the Law Firm with an Easy & Comprehensive Means of Tracking Attorney Schedules & Office Functions As Well As Personal Activities. Complete Information Concerning Each Docket Record Is Stored for Quick Appointment Recall, Updating & Re-Scheduling. Designed to Interface with SourceView LawTab (Attorney Time & Billing).
SourceView Software International.

SourceView Flexi-Sort. Customer Support: 800-929-8117 (customer service).
MS-DOS. Commodore 128; CP/M. disk $99.99 (ISBN 0-87007-460-1).
Sorting Routine for Microsoft BASIC Database Programs.
SourceView Software International.

SourceView HotPack. Customer Support: 800-929-8117 (customer service).
MS-DOS. Commodore 128; CP/M. disk $299.99 (ISBN 0-87007-726-0).
IBM PC; PS/2. disk $199.00 (ISBN 0-87007-583-7).
A Package Developed to Help Users Better Operate Hotel or Motel. Designed to Help Managers, Owners, & Investors to Access Daily Operations, Prepare Budgets, & Make Operational Forecasts. Can Effectively Reduce Labor Costs, Increase Efficiency, & Guide a Hotel to Higher Profitablity.
SourceView Software International.

SOUTHERN CALIFORNIA BUSINESS

SourceView KnowConflicts. Customer Support: 800-929-8117 (customer service).
MS-DOS. IBM/PS2. disk $399.99 (ISBN 0-87007-746-5).
An Educational Scheduling Package Which Provides the School Administrator with a Master Schedule of the Lowest Possible Student & Course Conflicts. Provide Course & Teacher Master Files, Student Registration Reports with up to 8 Courses, Signals Errors in Registration, Reports by Department Code, by Number of Students in Course, Course by ID Code & Student/Course Conflict.
SourceView Software International.

SourceView Professional Time & Billing. Customer Support: 800-929-8117 (customer service).
MS-DOS. Commodore 128; CP/M. disk $599.99 (ISBN 0-87007-686-8).
IBM PC; PS/2. disk $499.99 (ISBN 0-87007-689-2).
Generalized for Nonlaw Professionals, But Provides All of the Same Benefits & Features of SourceView Attorney Time & Billing.
SourceView Software International.

SourceView Time & Billing System. Version: 2.1. Operating System(s) Required: CP/M, MS-DOS. Language(s): MBASIC. Memory Required: 64k. Customer Support: 800-929-8117 (customer service).
MS-DOS. contact publisher for price (ISBN 0-87007-375-3).
Allows Online Editing & Updating of Master Files, Data Entry & Data Inquiry. Features Interactive Time & Expense Transaction Entry Which Draws Information from the Master Files, up to 999 User-Defined Service Codes, 3 Hourly Billing Rates, & Accumulated Fixed Fee Job Activity for Final Billing.
SourceView Software International.

SOURCEWRITER. Compatible Hardware: 8-, 16-, & 32-bit machines. Operating System(s) Required: PC-DOS, MS-DOS, UNIX, CP/M-86. Memory Required: 256k. General Requirements: Minimum of 1Mb disk storage.
contact publisher for price.
Dictionary-Based Software Tool That Helps Programmers Design & Develop Internally Consistent & Error Free Systems at the Rate of 500-1000 Lines of COBOL Code per Day. Generated Applications Can Have: up to 20 Linked Files & Approximately 100 Modules (Each of Which Ranges from 200 to Several Thousand Lines of COBOL Source Code), File Sharing in a Multi-User Environment, Passwords, Multiple Menus.
Micro Focus, Inc. (California).

Southern California Business Directory, 1995: Database Prospect System. Jan. 1996. Items Included: 9 diskettes, User Manual. Customer Support: Free telephone hotline.
IBM PC & compatibles (640k). disk $795.00 (ISBN 0-929695-09-7).
This "Electronic Directory" Contains the Contents of the 1996 Southern California Business Directory & Buyers Guide, in Database Form, Together with Software That Enables the User to Select, Retrieve, Sort, & Output the Data. Forms of Output Include Complete Record, Short Record, Mailing Label & ASCII Files on Diskette. Data Is Provided on 27,600 Manufacturers, Wholesalers & Service Businesses Located in the 13 Southern Counties. Information Includes Company Name, Address, Parent, Telephone, FAX, WATS, Numbers; Year Established, Annual Revenues, Number of Employees, Plant Size, Business Description, Primary & Secondary SIC Codes, Import/Export Designators, Bank, Computers Used, Names & Titles of Key Executives, & Type of Ownership.
Database Publishing Co.

Sozobon Poker for Windows. Anthony Andrews & Johann Ruegg. May 1995. *Items Included:* 1 manual, 3.5" disk (free exchange for 5.25"). *Customer Support:* Limited phone support. Windows 3.1 or Windows 95. 386 (4Mb). Contact publisher for price (ISBN 1-886070-07-5, Order no.: 9507).
Allows Play of Casino Style Texas Hold'em Poker, & Seven Card Stud Including Single Table Tournaments. Accurate Simulation of Casino Poker. Configurable Computer Opponents.
ConJelCo.

SPACE: A Visual History of Manned Spaceflight. Jul. 1993.
Mac: System 7.X, 13-inch monitor (256 or better colors) (4Mb). CD-ROM disk $49.95 (ISBN 1-57047-007-3, Order no.: SPACE). *Nonstandard peripherals required:* CD-ROM drive with a sustained transfer rate of 150Kbps or higher.
CPU with 486/33 MHz or higher processor (6Mb). CD-ROM disk $49.95. *Nonstandard peripherals required:* CD-ROM drive with a sustained transfer rate of 150Kbps or higher.
The Multimedia Almanac of American Space Missions. Over one & a Half Hours of Narrated QuickTime Movies Feature the Best of NASA's Film Archive. Original Text by Author Anthony R. Curtis Includes Such Topics As Space-Based Science Experiments, Life in Zero Gravity, Mission Histories, Satellite Deployment, & Future Space Stations. Text-Search Capability, Time Lines, & a Movie Index Puts a Wealth of Information at Your Fingertips.
Sumeria, Inc.

Space Adventure II.
MS-DOS 3.1 or higher, Windows. 386 processor or higher (640k). CD-ROM disk $69.95 (Order no.: R1145). *Nonstandard peripherals required:* CD-ROM drive. *Optimal configuration:* 386 processor or higher, MS-DOS 3.1 or higher, 20Mb hard drive, 640k RAM, external speakers or headphones (with sound card) that are Sound Blaster compatible, VGA graphics & adapter, VGA color monitor.
A Fascinating Exploration of the Science & Mysteries of Space, Users Will Blast Through over 400 Articles, 20 Full-Screen Movies & Star Maps of Constellations, Planets & Galaxies. This Program Also Features the Latest NASA Footage, an Extensive Reference Section & Various Simulations.
Library Video Co.

Space & Astronomy. *Customer Support:* All of our products are unconditionally guaranteed.
All Systems. CD-ROM disk $39.95 (Order no.: SPACE). *Nonstandard peripherals required:* CD-ROM drive.
1000 Gif Images Plus 5000 Text Files Relating to Astronomy.
Walnut Creek CDRom.

Space Attackers. *Compatible Hardware:* TRS-80 Model I, Model III, Model 4 with Level II BASIC. *Memory Required:* 16k.
disk $16.95.
Space Action Game.
Dynacomp, Inc.

Space Bandit: Arcade Plus Series. *Compatible Hardware:* TI 99/4A with Milton Bradley's MBX System.
contact publisher for price (Order no.: PHM3149).
Snatch-Up Space Crystals in a 3-D Maze While Being Chased by Deadly Droid Guards. Speech Synthesis & Voice Recognition.
Texas Instruments, Personal Productivit.

Space Evacuation. *Compatible Hardware:* Apple II with Applesoft; IBM PC. *Memory Required:* Apple II 48, IBM 128k.
disk $19.95.
Find Worlds & Make Them Habitable Before Earth's Sun Explodes.
Dynacomp, Inc.

Space Frame Analysis with Graphics. *Items Included:* Bound manual. *Customer Support:* Free hotline - no time limit; 30 day limited warranty; updates are $5/disk plus S&H.
MS-DOS 2.0 or higher. IBM & compatibles (256k). disk $149.95. *Nonstandard peripherals required:* CGA, EGA, VGA, or Hercules Graphics (or equivalent). A printer is supported but not required.
Analyzes Three-Dimensional Frame Structures with up to 150 Nodes & 200 Members. It Will Calculate Node Displacements & Rotations, Member End Axial Forces & Stresses, Torsion Moments, Shear Forces, Bending Moments & Stresses about Two Perpendicular Axes, & Restraint Reactions. It Handles Unsymmetrical Beam Sections about Both Axes & Combined Stresses at Nine Locations on the Cross Section. Displays the Three-Dimensional Frame Model During the Development Process with Node, Member, Property, Material, Restraint Numbering, & Change-of-View Options.
Dynacomp, Inc.

Space Invaders. *Compatible Hardware:* Atari XL/XE.
ROM cartridge $6.95 (Order no.: CXL4008).
Atari Corp.

Space Lanes. *Compatible Hardware:* Apple II with Applesoft; IBM PC. *Memory Required:* Apple 48, IBM 128k.
$19.95.
Simulation of Economics of Space Transportation Industry.
Dynacomp, Inc.

Space M+A+X. *Version:* 2.1 Entertainment & 3.0 Educational. 1988. *Compatible Hardware:* IBM PC & compatibles. *Language(s):* Basic. *Memory Required:* 192k. *General Requirements:* CGA card & color monitor. Printer recommended; joystick optional. *Items Included:* 5.25" or 3.5" diskettes; 140-page illustrated manual. *Customer Support:* 805-943-5394.
$49.95, entertainment version (ISBN 0-9511267-0-9).
$74.95, educational version.
Project Management Simulation. Players' Task Is to Use Successful Resource Management to Build an Authentic Space Station Within Time & Budget Constraints.
Final Frontier Software.

Space Missions: An Insight into the Exciting World of Space Exploration. *Items Included:* Pamphlet of instructions. *Customer Support:* Tech support, 60-day money-back guarantee.
Windows 3.1 or higher. IBM PC compatible (2Mb). CD-ROM disk $49.95 (ISBN 0-924677-10-4). *Nonstandard peripherals required:* CD-ROM drive, Soundboard, SVGA display with 256 colors, mouse.
An Insight into the Exciting World of Space Exploration. Contains Nearly 500 Megabytes of Information. Learn about Space Missions Around the World. Images & Text Can Be Copied & Used in School Reports & Newsletters. Over 1600 Space Missions Recorded from Around the World.
IMSI (International Microcomputer Software, Inc.).

Space Pirates. *Compatible Hardware:* TRS-80 Model I, Model III, Model 4 with Level II BASIC. *Memory Required:* 16k.
disk $16.95.
cassette $12.95.
Space Action Game.
Dynacomp, Inc.

Space Quest (Chapter I: the Sarien Encounter). Mark Crowe & Scott Murphy. Sep. 1986. *Compatible Hardware:* Apple IIe, IIc, Macintosh; Atari ST; Commodore Amiga; IBM PC & compatibles, PCjr. *Memory Required:* Apple 128k, IBM 256k.
disk $49.95 ea.
Apple. (Order no.: 10290102).
Atari. (Order no.: 10290102).
Amiga. (Order no.: 27290102).
IBM. (Order no.: 31290102).
Macintosh. (Order no.: 10290102).
Features Roger Wilco, Sanitation Engineer Turned Space-Age Swashbuckler. Wilco Becomes the Sole Survivor Aboard the Research Ship ARCADA & Last Hope for His Planet, XENON. His Mission: Search Out & Destroy the Super-Secret Star Generator Which Has Been Violently Stolen from His Vessel, Then Carry Out ARCADA's First Objective: Initialize a New Star for His Paling Planet. As the Inexperienced Hero, the Player Will Assist Wilco As He Boards the Enemy Space Ships, Explores Alien Landscapes & Meets Creatures As Wierd As Anything Found in Star Wars. Features 3-D Graphics, Animation, & Arcade Sequences.
Sierra On-Line, Inc.

Space Robbers. *Compatible Hardware:* TRS-80 Model I, Model III.
disk $24.95.
Goal of the Game Is to Keep the Inter-Galactic Thieves Who Are After Your Fuel Supplies from Reaching the Cannisters.
Blue Cat.

Space Taxi. John F. Kutcher. Apr. 1984. *Compatible Hardware:* Commodore 64. *Operating System(s) Required:* Commodore. *Language(s):* Assembly. *Memory Required:* 64k. *General Requirements:* Commodore 1541 disk drive, joystick.
disk $7.98, incl. bklt. (ISBN 0-87190-030-0).
Game Set in the 23rd Century. 25 Multi-Action Screen Predicaments.
Muse Software.

Space Tilt. *Compatible Hardware:* Apple II with Applesoft; Atari 400, 800 with Atari BASIC. *Operating System(s) Required:* DOS 3.2, 3.3 for Apple. *Memory Required:* 48k.
disk $18.95.
Roll a Ball Through a Hole.
Dynacomp, Inc.

Space Trap. *Compatible Hardware:* Atari 400, 800. *Language(s):* Atari BASIC (source code included). *Memory Required:* 16k. *General Requirements:* Joystick.
disk $18.95.
cassette $14.95.
Space Arcade Game.
Dynacomp, Inc.

Space Truss Analysis with Graphics. *Items Included:* Bound manual. *Customer Support:* Free hotline - no time limit; 30 day limited warranty; updates are $5/disk plus S&H.
MS-DOS 2.0 or higher. IBM & compatibles (256k). disk $149.95. *Nonstandard peripherals required:* CGA, EGA, VGA, or Hercules Graphics (or equivalent). A printer is supported but not required.
Treats Three-Dimensional Truss Structures with up to 250 Nodes & 500 Members. It Will Calculate

TITLE INDEX

Node Displacements, Member Axial Forces & Stresses, & Restraint Reactions. Accepts Gravity Loading, Node Loads, & Applied Displacements in Three Directions. Calculated Results May Be Sent to the Screen or a Printer.
Dynacomp, Inc.

Space 1889. Paragon Software. Oct. 1990.
IBM PC & compatible (640k). 3.5" or 5.25" disk $49.95. *Nonstandard peripherals required:* Requires color monitor, supports VGA, EGA, CGA, Tandy 16-color.
Imagine Earth in the Victorian Era -- with One Small Difference. Outer Space Is Not A Vacuum, But Filled with a "ether" That Can Be Negotiated with Modified Sailing Ships. SPACE 1889 Lets You Control Five Characters as They Explore the Solar System with the Limited Technology of the 1800s.
MicroProse Software.

Spaceway 2000. 1993. *Items Included:* Instructions & reg. card. *Customer Support:* Free phone support.
6.05 & higher, Power Mac Native. Macintosh. 3.5" disk $49.95 (Order no.: M111).
Escape the High-Speed, Intergalactic, Alien-Infected Freeway.
Casady & Greene, Inc.

SPAM. *Compatible Hardware:* DEC Personal Computers.
contact publisher for price.
Zea Corp.

Spanish - English Math.
disk $99.95 (Order no.: MZ100).
Based on the Superior Design of the Long-Standing Math Sequences Program, This Package Takes It a Step Further by Presenting the Problems in English or Spanish. Addition, Subtraction, & Number Readiness Are Covered Extensively, with a Bonus Feature That Allows You to Print Exciting Worksheets with Graphics.
Milliken Publishing Co.

Spare Change. *Compatible Hardware:* Apple II, IIe; Atari 400, 800; Commodore 64.
disk $34.95.
Player Must Distract Zerks Who have Broken Loose & Are Trying to Save Enough Tokens in Their Piggy Bank to Retire. Player Has the Option of Several Distractions Including Playing a Juke Box, Ringing the Pay Phones & Popping Corn.
Broderbund Software, Inc.

Sparkle. Version: 4.0. Jul. 1990. *Compatible Hardware:* IBM PC, PC XT, PC AT, PC compatibles. *Operating System(s) Required:* PC-DOS/MS-DOS 3.0 or higher. *Language(s):* C. *Memory Required:* Workstation with modem needs 40k; with terminal emulator 220k; Sparkle Expert needs 512k. *General Requirements:* Serial card, asynchronous modem, NETBIOS-type network or Novell's Netware with IPX. *Customer Support:* 30 days free telephone support.
$895.00 for 5 concurrent connections (ISBN 1-877839-00-0).
$2195.00 for 20 concurrent connections (ISBN 1-877839-04-3).
Works As a Distributed Communications Server That Does Not Need a Dedicated PC. Any Workstation Can Be Used As a Terminal, Allows the Use of Any Modem on the LAN from Any Workstation, Any Computer Can Be Connected (Including Minicomputers), & Files Can Be Moved to & from Different Computers. Enables Computers to Emulate VT-100, VT-200, VT-102, VT-52, IBM 3101, DG D220, ADM 3A, or TeleVideo 912 Terminals. Supports ZMODEM, Kermit, SmartCom II, XON/XOFF, Delay-after-Line, & a Proprietary Protocol with Wild Cards & Automatic File Compression. Also Includes Remote Access Software so 5 PCs Can Run Programs on the Network from Afar.
CyberCorp, Inc.

Sparky's Spelling with Phonics.
IBM. CD-ROM disk $39.95 (ISBN 1-888419-01-6).
Spelling & Phonics Educational Game for Ages 6-9.
Firstlight Productions, Inc.

Sparky's Spelling with Phonics. May 1995.
IBM. CD-ROM disk $39.95 (ISBN 1-888419-00-8).
Spelling & Phonics Educational Game.
Firstlight Productions, Inc.

Sparrow Commander. *Compatible Hardware:* TRS-80.
contact publisher for price.
Instant Software, Inc.

SPARSEPACK. Apr. 1986. *Operating System(s) Required:* PC-DOS/MS-DOS 2.XX. *Memory Required:* 128k.
disk $49.95 (ISBN 0-938087-02-9).
Turbo Pascal Source Codes of Procedures & Functions for User Transparent Sparse Matrix Handling. Allows to Overcome 64k Size & Includes Matrix Editor, 8087/88 Translator, & Other Stand Alone Utiltiy Programs.
Soft Tech, Inc.

SPC Direct. Version: 3.0. Dec. 1995. *Compatible Hardware:* RS6000, Sun Sparc II, 386 Plus. *Operating System(s) Required:* AIX, MS-DOS, UNIX. *Language(s):* C. *Memory Required:* 4000k. *General Requirements:* Hard disk, printer. *Customer Support:* 800, BBS, FAX, Optional Training.
$1500.00-$5000.00.
On-Line Statistical Process Control Package. Collects 128 Channels of Data; Simultaneously Calculates & Monitors 32 Process Variables. Manual & Automatic Data Input. High Resolution Graphics for Histograms, Pareto Charts, & 13 Different Control Charts, & Process Capabilities.
Stochos, Inc.

SPC Orchestra. Version: 4.2. *Compatible Hardware:* IBM PC & compatibles, PS/2. *Memory Required:* 448k. *General Requirements:* Lotus 1-2-3 Release 2.X or Quattro Pro, Release 4 or higher.
$395.00.
Lets User Carry Out Statistical Process Control, the Technique That Analyzes Production, Manufacturing, & Administrative Processes Through Their Pattern Variations. User Can Generate Histograms & Shewhart X-Bar, Cumulative-Sum, Range-Control, Moving-Average, & Moving-Range Charts. The Program Automatically Enters Graph Titles & Suggests PIC-File Names Based on Column Headings.
D. A. Martin.

SPC-PC II. Version: 2.3. May 1991. *Compatible Hardware:* IBM PC & compatibles. *Operating System(s) Required:* MS-DOS 3.0 or higher. *Memory Required:* 640k. *General Requirements:* Graphics card. *Items Included:* Manual, binder, diskettes. *Customer Support:* 800-722-6154, 30 day money back guarantee, free technical support.
disk $795.00.
Statistical Process Control Package with Interactive Graphics. Contains All Popular Control Charts Including X Bar & Range, X & Moving Range, Moving Average & Moving Range. Other Calculations Include Descriptive Statistics, Histogram & Process Capability, & Non-Normal Data Analysis.
Quality America, Inc.

SPC-PC IV. Version: 3.0. Apr. 1993. *Items Included:* Manual, binder, diskettes. *Customer Support:* Free technical support, 30 day moneyback guarantee.
Microsoft Windows 3.0 & 3.1. IBM PC AT (286) (1Mb), 386 (4Mb) recommended. disk $995.00 Base RT or F&F Module $200.00 ea. *Addl. software required:* Microsoft Windows 3.0. *Networks supported:* IBM NetBios Compatible.
Statistical Process Control Package for Microsoft Windows 3.0 or higher. Contains All Popular Control Charts. Supports DDE & Multitasking. Data Can Be Imported from Other Software, Entered Directly from Gages or Through the Keyboard. The Program Supports Real-Time Capabilities. Fishbone (Cause & Effect) & Flow Charting Modules Also Available.
Quality America, Inc.

SPCS Chess. *Items Included:* Manual, customer specifies disk size. *Customer Support:* Unlimited telephone/FAX support.
IBM PC, PC XT, PC AT, PS/2, 386 (256k). 3.5" or 5.25" disk $34.95 (ISBN 1-878322-02-8, Order no.: SPCS CH.).
Program That Plays Chess with User. Very Quick, with International Chess Federation Rating of About 1800.
Scandinavian PC Systems, Inc.

SPCS Menu Program. *Items Included:* Manual, customer specifies disk size. *Customer Support:* Unlimited telephone/FAX support.
IBM PC, PC XT, PC AT, PS/2, 386 (256k). 3.5" or 5.25" disk $34.95 (ISBN 1-878322-03-6, Order no.: SPCS MENU).
Makes It Easier to Organize & Find Files While Using Hard Disk.
Scandinavian PC Systems, Inc.

SPCS PrimaBase: A 'Painless' Database for Windows. Version: 3.13. Pdata AB. May 1993. *Items Included:* Dual media (high density), single-user license, reference manual, exercise manual. Free with registration: Add-on, SPCS PrimaPAC, $49 value disk with pre-built forms & reports, & infobase of 103rd Congress. *Customer Support:* 90 day limited warranty on disks; unlimited telephone/fax technical support.
DOS 3.1 & higher; Windows 3.0 & higher. IBM AT, 286 or faster (1Mb). $199.00 single user; contact publisher for price of network version (ISBN 91-971839-3-8, Order no.: PB3). *Addl. software required:* Windows 3.0 or higher (or compatible). *Optimal configuration:* PC with Intel 386SX, 2Mb RAM, hard drive with minimum 2Mb free space, hi-res monitor (VGA), mouse or trackball. *Networks supported:* NetBIOS compatible.
demo disk avail.
Powerful Easy-to-Use Relational Database for Windows Operating Environment; Features Mail Merge, Automatic File Linking, Security Proprietary Encryption & Password Protection; 100 Plus Functions for Numeric, Date, Time & Text Operation; Maximum 16k Characters per Record, 200 Fields per Record, 15 Indexes (Five Levels) per File, Unlimited Records Possible. Reports Can Use All Fonts Available in User's Printer. Imports dBASE II/III/IV, Text, DIF EXPORTS: dBASE III/IV, Text, RTF, DIF. The Only Fully Relational Free Form Database for Windows to Offer Integrated Barcode Printing & Support - Including Postnet with DPBC, UPC-A, UPC-E, Code 39, Code 128, Interleaved 2 of 5, EAN-8 & EAN-13. Upgrade Adds Free Text (Memo Fields), Instant Searching in Indexed Fields, Word Wrapping.
Scandinavian PC Systems, Inc.

Speak. *Compatible Hardware:* TRS-80 Model III.
disk $39.95, incl. documentation & special utility programs.
Permits User to Add Speech to BASIC Programs.
The Alternate Source.

SpeakerSim. *Version:* 2.0. *Compatible Hardware:* Commodore Amiga. *Items Included:* Manual. *Customer Support:* 1 yr limited warranty, phone tech support.
3.5" disk $112.00.
CAD Package for Designing Loudspeaker Systems & Crossovers.
Dissidents.

Special Days, Footprints in History. *Version:* Special Days 2.8; Footprints 2.5.
MS-DOS 2.1 or higher (256k for Special Days, 320k for Footprints in History). IBM PC & compatibles. disk $44.95 ea. plus $3.00 ea. shipping.
Two programs for Viewing Anniversaries or an Entire Past. Special Days Allows User to Create One-Page Document for Birthdays, Anniversaries, etc. Document Can Be of Any Day from 1850 to Present. Includes Ability to Create Different Borders, ASCII File Creation & Portability to Desktop Publishing Programs. Footprints in History Lets User Highlight up to 200 Events in an Individual's, Family's or Company's Past. For Example, User Can Produce a Multi-Page Document Charting a Family's Growth. Also Supports Dates from 1850 to Present.
The Salinon Corp.

Special Effects with Slides. Larry Fischer. *Compatible Hardware:* IBM PC, PCjr, PC XT, PC AT, Portable PC, 3270 PC. *Operating System(s) Required:* PC-DOS 2.00, 2.10, 3.00, 3.10. *Memory Required:* 256k. *General Requirements:* Graphics editor that saves files in BSAVE format & text editor that creates standard ASCII files.
disk $24.95 (Order no.: 6276631).
Turns the Computer Display into a Presentation Tool by Combining Text & Graphics with Visual & Audio Effects. Features Numerous Display Commands, Including Color & Sound, & 16 Different Visual Effects. Slides Are Created with a Graphics Editor & a Text Editor. The Script Acts As a Show Director by Coordinating the Order of Presentation, Screen Color, & Sound.
Personally Developed Software, Inc.

Special Occasion Fax (aka Fax from Santa). *Version:* 1.0. Sep. 1995. *Items Included:* Manual, 2 3.5" diskettes. *Customer Support:* One year free technical support, 30 day unlimited warranty.
Windows 3.1. 20286(AT) (512k). 3.5" disk $29.95.
Your Kids Can Receive Unique Faxes on Holidays & Special Occasions. Set up Your Computer So Your Kids Receive a Fax from Santa on Christmas! or a Fax from Dracula on Halloween or Have Your Computer Surprise the Special Person in Your Life with a Love "Fax" on Valentine's Day--or on No Special Day at All (They'll Love It). No Phone or Fax Machine Is Required.
PSG-HomeCraft Software.

Specialized Fonts. *Version:* 1.1. Nov. 1988. *Compatible Hardware:* IBM PC & compatibles. *Operating System(s) Required:* PC-DOS/MS-DOS. *General Requirements:* HP LaserJet Plus or Series II printers or compatible. contact publisher for price.
Downloaded Soft Fonts: Calligraphy, Script, Custom Fonts, Business. Custom Font Service Available to Match Any Font.
Specialized Software.

SpecSelect: Spring Selection. 1995. *Items Included:* Full manual. *Customer Support:* Free telephone support - 90 days, 30-day warranty.
MS-DOS 3.2 or higher. 286 (584k). disk $10.00. Nonstandard peripherals required: CGA/EGA/VGA.
A Spring Selection Program for Compression & Extension Springs, As Well As Belleville, Curved, Finger, & Wave Washers Offered by Associated Spring Raymond Collection. You Select the Type of Spring & the Design Details, & SpecSelect Picks Out the Best Available Stock Item. This Is No Replacement for DYNACOMP's ULTIMATE SPRING DESIGNER, but Is a Handy Program.
Dynacomp, Inc.

SpectraCAM. *Version:* 3.21. Mar. 1995. *Items Included:* Three spiral bound manuals. *Customer Support:* 800/221-2763, No charge.
Windows platform 3.1. IBM & compatibles (4Mb). $1795.00 1st copy; $500.00 additional copies (ISBN 0-941791-10-6, Order no.: CAM-6701, CAM-6711). *Optimal configuration:* 486 DX/2 66MHz or higher, SVGA monitor, Microsoft compatible mouse, 8Mb. *Networks supported:* Novell compatible network.
MS-DOS platform - Version 5.0 or higher. IBM & compatibles (1Mb). $1495.00 1st copy; $500.00 additional copies (ISBN 0-941791-11-4, Order no.: CAM-6601, CAM-6611). *Optimal configuration:* 486 DX/2 66MHz or higher, SVGA monitor, Microsoft compatible mouse, 8Mb. *Networks supported:* Novell compatible.
Macintosh 6.0.8 or higher. Apple Macintosh (2Mb). $1495.00 1st copy; $500.00 additional copies (ISBN 0-941791-13-0, Order no.: CAM-6602, CAM-6612). *Optimal configuration:* 68030 processor, 4Mb RAM, System 7, color monitor.
A Complete Integrated CAD/CAM Package That Is Used As a Tool to Teach Computer-Aided Manufacturing with a Technology Education Class or a Vocational Trades Environment. Imports a CAD Geometry & Outputs an NC File That May, in Turn, Be Run on a CNC Mill or Lathe.
Light Machines Corporation.

Spectre VR; Project X. Velocity Development Corp. & Team 17 Software Ltd. Jan. 1996. *Items Included:* Set-up instruction sheet. *Customer Support:* 310-403-0043.
Spectre VR: DOS 2.1; Project X: DOS 3.0 or higher. IBM PC. disk $12.95 (ISBN 1-887783-17-2, Order no.: 5100-2005). *Optimal configuration:* Spectre VR: IBM PC 386 or higher, 640k RAM, DOS 2.1 or higher, VGA. Supports, but does not require, Soundblaster, Adlib, or mouse; Project X: IBM PC 386 or higher, DOS 3.0 or higher, VGA, 2Mb RAM, keyboard or joystick, Adlib, Soundblaster or Gravis compatible board, PC speakers.
Space Games. The Game Player Battles Against Aliens from Other Planets.
Entertainment Technology.

Spectre: 3-D Cyberspace Game Experience. Oct. 1994. *Items Included:* Registration card, instruction sheet. *Customer Support:* 900 support number $2.00 per minute; limited 60 day warranty.
DOS. IBM compatible 286/386/486 (16Mhz or higher) (640k). disk $9.95 (ISBN 1-57269-007-0, Order no.: 3202 42065). *Addl. software required:* MS-DOS 3.3 or higher. *Optimal configuration:* Supports (but does not require Sound Blaster, joystick & mouse.
Memorex Products, Inc., Memorex Software Division.

Speculation. *Compatible Hardware:* TRS-80 Model I, Model III, Model 4 with Level II; IBM. (source code included). *Memory Required:* 128k. $19.95.
Stock Market Simulation.
Dynacomp, Inc.

Speech Command Software Development Kit. Mar. 1984. *Operating System(s) Required:* MS-DOS. *Language(s):* MSBASIC, MSPascal, Lattice C. *Memory Required:* 256k. *General Requirements:* Speech command system, Winchester hard disk.
$8000.00 (Order no.: TI P/N 2237305-0001).
Texas Instruments, Personal Productivit.

Speech Command System. *Operating System(s) Required:* MS-DOS. *Memory Required:* 256k. *General Requirements:* Winchester hard disk.
$2600.00 (Order no.: TI P/N 2237363-0001).
Texas Instruments, Personal Productivit.

Speech Crafter. *Version:* 2.01. May 1989. *Customer Support:* 90 day warranty against defects in disk manufacture, immediate replacement of defective media.
PC-DOS/MS-DOS 3.1 or higher (256k). IBM PC/XT/AT/PS2 compatible. disk $59.95. Nonstandard peripherals required: Hard drive required. *Optimal configuration:* PC/AT or PS/2, hard disk, EGA or VGA graphics, 640k, one floppy drive. *Networks supported:* Novell.
Instant Recall of the Famous Sayings of Einstein, Freud, Plato, Socrtre, Christ, Comus, Shakespeare & a Hundred Other World Class Thinkers.
Thinking Software, Inc.

Speed & Stopping Distance Calculator. 1990. *Customer Support:* 1 year.
MS-DOS. IBM & compatibles (256k). disk $39.95 (Order no.: 5220-S). *Networks supported:* Novell.
Accurate, Rapid Determination of Stopping Distance (in Feet) At Any Selected Speed for Automobiles, Trucks, with Average, Poor Brakes. Allowance Made for Reaction Time.
Lawyers Software Publishing Co.

The Speed Handicapper. *Version:* 2. Oct. 1991. *Items Included:* Complete manual. *Customer Support:* 60 days limited warranty; telephone support, technical & handicapping.
MS-DOS. IBM compatible (512k). disk $249.00. *Optimal configuration:* IBM compatible with hard drive.
Contains All the Par Times for Every Track in North America. Automatically Adjusts Each Horse's Running Line for Track-to-Track, Distance-to-Distance, Daily Varient, etc. & Projects Its Running Time for Every Fraction of the Race. Removes all the "Grunt Work" from Speed/Pace Handicapping.
Cynthia Publishing Co.

The Speed Program. 1983. *Compatible Hardware:* IBM PC & compatibles. *Language(s):* BASIC. *Memory Required:* 10k.
disk or cassette $74.95.
Looks at Each Horse's Speed Ratings for up to the Last 4 Races. Designed for Any Speed Handicapper.
COM-CAP.

Speed Reader. *Compatible Hardware:* Atari XL/XE. *Memory Required:* 16k.
cassette $24.95 (Order no.: CX4126).
Atari Corp.

Speed Reading: The Computer Course. 1986. *Compatible Hardware:* Apple IIe, IBM PC, Apple Macintosh. *Memory Required:* Apple 64k, IBM 128k, Macintosh 512k.
disk $125.00 ea.
IBM PC. (Order no.: SRD9).
Apple. (Order no.: SAD7).
Macintosh. (Order no.: SMD4).
Teaches the User to Read Faster & More Efficiently & Explains the Theory & Basics of Speed Reading Through a Series of Interactive Exercises.
Bureau of Business Practice.

TITLE INDEX

Speed Reading Tutor IV. Kriya Systems, Inc. *Compatible Hardware:* Apple II, II+, IIe, IIc; Apple Macintosh, Macintosh Plus; IBM PC, PC XT, PC AT. *Operating System(s) Required:* ProDOS or Apple DOS 3.3 for Apple II; PC-DOS 1.1 or higher for IBM. *Memory Required:* Apple II 64k, IBM 128k Macintosh 512k.
Apple II, IBM. disk $39.95.
Macintosh. 3.5" disk $49.95.
Enables Users to Improve Their Reading Speed. The Program Determines Initial Level of Proficiency & Customizes Lessons Based on Current Abilities; Providing Feedback, Tracking Progress & Pacing As Abilities Improve.
Brady Computer Bks.

Spell. Scenic Computer Systems Corp. *Operating System(s) Required:* UCSD p-System. *Memory Required:* 128k. *General Requirements:* Printer.
$125.00.
Texas Instruments, Personal Productivit.

Spell-A-Rama. Selena Studios Staff. Oct. 1995. *Customer Support:* Tech support on-line at Selenay-AOL.COM.
486-66 Windows 3.1 or 95. Multimedia PC (8Mb). CD-ROM disk $14.95 (ISBN 1-55727-033-3, Order no.: SPCD01). *Nonstandard peripherals required:* 1Mb Video card.
Poor Buzz the Fly. In This Adventure Game, He's on the Way to a New Job & Has a Flying Accident. He Loses the Key to the Department Store That He Is Now Managing. It Seems It Has Fallen into the City's Underground 3-D Caves. Kids Will Have to Help Buzz Search for the Missing Key, While Encountering the Many Weird Cave-Dwellers. In Order to Search Their Domain, Children Will Have to Help Buzz Answer Spelling & Anagram Questions from a Built-In Data Base of 1st - 3rd Grade Words. Game-Play Varies Each Time. The Reward for Finding the Key Is a Visit into Mr. Bee's Insect Department Store.
Unicorn Educational Software.

Spell Master 2. *Items Included:* Bound manual. *Customer Support:* Free hotline - no time limit; 30 day limited warranty; updates are $5/disk plus S&H.
MS-DOS. IBM & compatibles (256k). disk $19.95.
Contains a Spelling Vocabulary of over 35,000 Words. Can Be Operated in Several Modes. Games: Standard Hangman; Unscramble; Guess the Missing Letter(s). Utilities: Scrabble Helper; Spelling Checker. Experimental: Create Your Own Use.
Dynacomp, Inc.

Spellbound. *Compatible Hardware:* TRS-80 Model I, Model III, Model 4. *Language(s):* Microsoft FORTRAN. *Memory Required:* 64k.
disk $10.00 (Order no.: D8SPS).
disk $19.95, incl. instructions (Order no.: D8SPB).
Word Game That May Be Played by the Entire Family.
The Alternate Source.

Spellbound. *Version:* 2.1. *Compatible Hardware:* Commodore Amiga.
3.5" disk $39.95.
Spelling Instruction, Drill & Practice.
Learners Image.

Spellbreaker. Dave Lebling. Oct. 1985. *Compatible Hardware:* Apple II, II+, IIe, IIc, Macintosh; Atari 400, 800, 1200, ST; Commodore 64, Amiga; IBM PC & compatibles; Kaypro. *Operating System(s) Required:* MS-DOS, CP/M.
disk $49.95.
Conclusion to the Enchanter Trilogy, in Which the Player Uses Magical Spells to Conquer Evil.
Activision, Inc.

Spellcasting Party Pak. Steve Meretzky. *Items Included:* CD-disk, game manual, package insert, warranty card, product catalog. *Customer Support:* Toll free technical assistance (1-800-658-8891). Computer operated pre-recorded hintline (1-900-PRO-KLUE). Hint books $9.95 each plus s/h.
MS-DOS 3.3 or higher. IBM & compatibles (640k). disk $59.95 (ISBN 1-880520-26-5, Order no.: SPPD). *Optimal configuration:* PC 80386 with 640k RAM & SVGA/VGA adapter & monitor, Microsoft compatible mouse, Sound Blaster compatible sound card.
A Series of Graphic Adventures in Which Ernie Eaglebeak Attends Sorcerer University & Has a Series of Delicious Romps Through the Magical Realm of Peloria. From the Bedrooms & Barrooms of Sorcerer University to Spring Break at Fort Naughtytail, Ernie Struggles to Win the Affection of His One True Love, Loloa Tigerbelly, & along the Way Experience the Opportunities of College Life.
Legend Entertainment.

Spellcasting Party Pak. Steve Meretzky. *Items Included:* CD-Disk, game manual, package insert, warranty card, product catalog. *Customer Support:* Toll free technical assistance (1-800-658-8891). Computer operated pre-recorded hintline (1-900-PRO-KLUE). Hint books $9.95 each plus s/h.
MS-DOS 3.3 or higher. IBM & compatibles. CD-ROM disk $59.95 (ISBN 1-880520-27-3, Order no.: SPPCD). *Nonstandard peripherals required:* CD-ROM. *Optimal configuration:* PC 80386 with 640k RAM & SVGA/VGA adapter & monitor, Microsoft compatible mouse, Sound Blaster compatible card.
A Series of Graphic Adventures in Which Ernie Eaglebeak Attends Sorcerer University & Has a Series of Delicious Romps Through the Magical Realm of Peloria. From the Bedrooms & Barrooms of Sorcerer Unviersity to Spring Break at Fort Naughtytail, Ernie Struggles to Win the Affection of His One True Love, Loloa Tigerbelly, & along the Way Experience the Opportunities of College Life.
Legend Entertainment.

Spellcasting 201 THE SORCERER'S APPLIANCE. Steve Meretzky. 1991. *Items Included:* Game manual, game map, copy protection codes, warranty card, additional scenario material. *Customer Support:* Toll-free technical assistance (1-800-658-8891). Computer operated pre-recorded Hint Line (1-900-776-5583). $.75 first minute, $.50 each additional minute. Hint Book - $9.95 plus s/h.
S201-5. MS-DOS 3.0 or higher. IBM PC & compatibles. 5.25" disk $69.95 (ISBN 1-880520-00-1). *Nonstandard peripherals required:* None, except for full sound support. Then an ADLIB, SOUNDBLASTER, or ROLAND MT-32 board is necessary.
S201-3. 1-880520-01-x. 3.5" disk $69.95.
Ernie Eaglebeak Returns to Sorcerer University for His Sophomore Year & Is Engrossed in a Battle of Wits with an Evil Pledgemaster & Professor as He Tries to Pledge the Hu Delta Phart Fraternity. As Ernie Is Forced to Master the Nuances of the Appliance, He Discovers the True Identity of the Villain & Once Again, Saves the University from Certain Destruction.
Legend Entertainment.

Spellcasting 301: Spring Break. Steve Meretzky. Sep. 1992. *Items Included:* Disks, game manual, package insert, warranty card & product catalog. *Customer Support:* Toll free technical assistance (1-800-658-8891). Computer operated pre-recorded hint line (1-900-776-5583); $.75 1st min., $.50 each additional minute. Hint book $9.95 plus s/h.
MS-DOS 3.3 or higher. IBM & compatible (640k). disk $59.95. *Optimal configuration:* IBM PC 80386 with 640k RAM & SVGA/VGA adapter & monitor, Microsoft compatible mouse & Soundblaster.
Third in a Series of Graphic Adventures Where Ernie Eaglebeak Takes a Spring Break Holiday with His Fraternity Pals.
Legend Entertainment Company.

The Speller. *Compatible Hardware:* HP 150 Touchscreen, HP 110 Portable.
3.5" disk $49.95 (Order no.: 35154D).
Helps Users Eliminate Spelling Errors in Their WRITER, MEMOWRITER, WORDSTAR, or Other ASCII Text Files. Includes over 20,000 of the Most Frequently Used English Words, Accounting for 97% of Total Word Usage. Examines a 15 Page Document in Less Than a Minute, Then Displays or Prints Either Suspect or Valid Words. User Can Accept or Change Suspect Words Individually or in Context Without Returning to the Word Processor, & Can Review Changes Before Saving Them to the Document. Allows User to Create Special Dictionaries. Can Be Merged with the WRITER & Executed Directly from the WRITER's Menu.
Hewlett-Packard Co.

Spelling Blizzard. (The/Talking Tutor Ser.). Windows. IBM & compatibles. CD-ROM disk $44.95 (Order no.: R1023). *Nonstandard peripherals required:* CD-ROM drive. *Optimal configuration:* 386 processor or higher, MS-DOS 3.1 or higher, 20Mb hard drive, 640k RAM, external speakers or headphones (with sound card) that are Sound Blaster compatible, VGA graphics & adapter, VGA color monitor.
Macintosh (4Mb). (Order no.: R1023A). *Nonstandard peripherals required:* 14" color monitor or larger, CD-ROM drive.
This Outstanding Series Uses Puzzles, Exciting Stories, Color-Animation & Music to Teach the Basics (Ages 9-12).
Library Video Co.

Spelling Coach Professional. *Version:* 4.0. 1992. *Compatible Hardware:* Apple Macintosh. *Language(s):* C. *Memory Required:* 2000k.
3.5" disk $195.00.
Interactive Spelling Checker Desktop Accessory. Provides Features Such As: Interactive Spelling & Grammar Checking; Batch Checking Mode That Scans Documents at over 150 Words per Second; Typo/Phonetic Correction System to Suggest the Correct Spelling; MERRIAM-WEBSTER's 91,000 Word Dictionary, 28,000 Word Legal & 35,000 Word Medical Libraries; + 25,000 Word Technical & Engineering; Built-In Interactive & Batch Hyphenation; the Ability to Add Words to the Dictionary, Including Words with Technical Symbols & Foreign Language Characters; Support for the Big Thesaurus 100, 000 Entry Point Thesaurus; 1,400,000 Words Synonyms, Antonyms Contrasted & Related Terms; Compatibility with Most Macintosh Software, Including PAGEMAKER 2.0, MORE, MICROSOFT WORKS, WORD 3.0, & EXCEL.
Deneba Software.

Spelling Jungle. (The/Talking Tutor Ser.). Windows. IBM & compatibles. CD-ROM disk $44.95 (Order no.: R1028). *Nonstandard peripherals required:* CD-ROM drive. *Optimal configuration:* 386 processor or higher, MS-DOS 3.1 or higher, 20Mb hard drive, 640k RAM, external speakers or headphones (with sound card) that are Sound Blaster compatible, VGA graphics & adapter, VGA color monitor.
Macintosh (4Mb). (Order no.: R1028A). *Nonstandard peripherals required:* 14" color monitor or larger, CD-ROM drive.
This Outstanding Series Uses Puzzles, Exciting Stories, Color-Animation & Music to Teach the Basics.
Library Video Co.

SpellStar. MicroPro International. *Compatible Hardware:* HP 86/87 with CP/M System (HP 82900A).
3-1/2" or 5-1/4" disk $125.00 ea. (Order no.: 45588A).
Spelling Checker That Works with WordStar. The 20,000-Word Dictionary Can Be Expanded, or Users Can Create Their Own Supplemental Dictionary.
Hewlett-Packard Co.

Spellswell Medical Dictionary. May 1987. *Compatible Hardware:* Apple Macintosh Plus. *Memory Required:* 1024k. *General Requirements:* Spellswell, Microsoft Works 2.0, Lookup, QuickLetter, Expert Writer, Expert Publisher.
3.5" disk $49.95 (ISBN 0-940331-01-2).
Includes over 40,000 Words for the Following Categories: Anatomical & Medical Terms, Major Drug Trade Names, Dental Terms, Psychiatric Terms, Pharmaceutical Drug Names, Major Pharmaceutical Co. Names, Nursing Terms, Veterinary Terms, Common Abbreviations.
Working Software, Inc.

Spellswell 7. *Version:* 1.0.7. Oct. 1986. *Compatible Hardware:* Apple Macintosh 512E, Mac Plus, Mac SE, Mac II. *Memory Required:* 512k.
3.5" disk $59.95 (ISBN 0-940331-00-4).
Spelling Checker & Proof Reader That Scans Documents Created by MACWRITE, WORD, & Other Programs. Provides the Following Features: Accepts Documents of Unlimited Size; Includes 93,000 Word User Modifiable Dictionary; Checks for Duplicate Words; Enforces Abbreviation Standards; Checks Homonyms; Maintains Capitalization; Provides Document Dictionaries; & Finds Capitalization Errors.
Working Software, Inc.

SPELLVUE: In-Context Spelling Checker. Chris Williams. 1982. *Operating System(s) Required:* THEOS286, THEOS386, OASIS. *Memory Required:* 128k. *General Requirements:* Hard disk.
THEOS286 or THEOS386. disk $195.00.
OASIS. disk or cartridge $195.00.
In-Context Spelling Checker & Corrector. While the Text Is Scrolling in the Screen, Program Checks Each Word Against 1, 2, or 3 Dictionaries. Words Not Found Are Highlighted, Prompting the User to Ignore, Correct, or Search for the Word. Corrected Words Are Updated at the End of the Scrolling Process. Program Updates the Text. OASIS/THEOS SCRIPT & SPELLBINDER Text Files Are Compatible.
Phase 1 Systems.

Spelunker. MicroGraphicImage, Inc. & Tim Martin. *Compatible Hardware:* Atari 400, 800, XL, XE Series; Commodore 64.
Commodore. disk $29.95 (Order no.: COMDSK-253).
Atari. disk $29.95 (Order no.: ATDSK-133).
Game about Cave Exploration Which Takes Place in Scrolling Subterranean Caverns Full of Treasures, Puzzles, & Surprises. Features 6 Levels & Sound Effects.
Broderbund Software, Inc.

SPF/PC: System Productivity Facility. *Version:* 2.1. May 1989. *Compatible Hardware:* IBM PC & true compatibles, 8088 & 80286. *Operating System(s) Required:* DOS 2.1. *Memory Required:* 256k. *Items Included:* Manual, disk, binder, quick reference card. *Customer Support:* Unlimited telephone support.
$295.00.
Provides Mainframe MVS Programmers with a Familiar ISPF/PDF Environment on Low-End DOS Machines. Features Instantaneous Response Time, Split Screen, Directory/Member Lists, Command Stacking, 4,000 Byte Lines & Large File Support, & More.
Command Technology Corp.

The Spice Hunter: Cookbook-on-Disk. Lucia Hunter. Jun. 1984. *Compatible Hardware:* Apple II, II+, IIe, IIc; Commodore 64, 128; IBM PC. *Operating System(s) Required:* Apple DOS 3.3, PC-DOS/MS-DOS 1.1. *Memory Required:* Apple DOS 48k, Commodore 64k, PC-DOS 128k.
General Requirements: Micro Kitchen Companion program.
disk $14.95 ea.
PC-DOS/MS-DOS. (ISBN 0-935745-83-1, Order no.: MK4).
Apple DOS. (ISBN 0-935745-84-X, Order no.: AK4).
Commodore 64. (ISBN 0-935745-86-6, Order no.: CK4).
Teaches User to Identify Flavorful Spices & Use Them to Enhance Meals.
Concept Development Assocs., Inc.

Spide Attack. Michael Head. Oct. 1983. *Compatible Hardware:* Apple II+, IIe; Commodore 64. *Operating System(s) Required:* Apple DOS 3.3. *Language(s):* BASIC, Assembly (source code included). *Memory Required:* Apple 48k.
Apple. disk $24.95.
Commodore. disk $24.95.
Game That Gives Children a Chance to Tangle in a Web of Fascinating Facts. Joins Gaming Theory with Drill & Practice. Children Learn As They Play Either Alone or in Their Competition with Another Player. The Problems Are Solved As Soon As a Player Speeds His Spide (or Beats His Opponent) to the Correct Answer - Avoiding Contact with the Fast Moving "Dit" along the Way. There Are Nine Fact Files Covering English & Mathematics on Varying Levels of Play. An Editorial Program Lets Users Design up to 26 of Their Own Quizzes for More Fact-&-Fun-Filled Competition on Any Subject of Their Choice.
Ahead Designs.

Spin-for-Money. Donald Sutherland. Jan. 1987. *Compatible Hardware:* IBM PC & compatibles, 8-bit CP/M machines. *Operating System(s) Required:* MS-DOS, PC-DOS. *Memory Required:* 128k. *General Requirements:* 2 disk drives or hard disk.
disk $24.95.
Word Game for 2-3 Players. Supplies Almost 2,000 Word Phrases on Disk, & Permits Players to Add Their Own Phrases & Categories. Allows for 1-5 Rounds of Play per Game, Plus a Bonus Round for the Player with the Most Dollars at the End of Regular Play. The High Score & Player's Name Are Saved to Disk. Provides Entertainment While Testing Players' Word Skills.
Generic Computer Products, Inc. (GCPI).

Spinfont. Dec. 1988. *Customer Support:* Free technical support (phone toll only).
PC- or MS-DOS 3.1 or higher (512k). IBM PC, AT or compatible. disk $95.00. *Addl. software required:* Fontware program (BFG, EXE) & at least one Fontware typeface outline file (with .BCO extension).
Creates Curved, Circular, Slanted, Rotated or Reversed Text Images from Bitstream Fontware Typeface Outlines for Logos, Insignias, & Special Text Effects for IBM-PC Compatibles with HP LaserJet Printers.
Softcraft, Inc. (Wisconsin).

Spinnaker Plus. *Version:* 2.0. 1991.
Macintosh System Software 6.0.2/Finder 6.1 or higher. Macintosh Plus, SE, SE/30, II, or higher (2Mb). Contact publisher for price. *Nonstandard peripherals required:* Two 800k floppy disk drives. *Addl. software required:* FDHD & Apple File Exchange software (or equivalent) required for disk based transfers to IBM computers. Color graphics card required for color display.
DOS 3.1 or higher (2Mb). Windows 3.0. PC with 80286 processor or higher. *Nonstandard peripherals required:* Hard disk & high density floppy disk. *Addl. software required:* FDHD & Apple File Exchange.
OS/2 Presentation Manager 1.1 or higher. PC with 80286 processor or higher (4Mb). *Nonstandard peripherals required:* Hard disk & HD floppy. *Addl. software required:* FDHD & Apple File Exchange.
Cross Platform Development System That Allows User To Create Graphically Intuitive Custom Applications That Look & Run Identically on Macintoshes & PCs Running Windows 3.0 or OS/2 Presentation Manager. Develop Application Just Once on a Mac or PC, & It's Instantly Available to Everyone via Disk or Network File Sharing.
Spinnaker Software Corp.

SpinRite II. *Version:* 2.0. *Compatible Hardware:* PC-DOS, MS-DOS. *Memory Required:* 192k. *Customer Support:* Technical support, BBS.
disk $89.00.
Identifies, Diagnoses & Repairs Every Form of Data & Low-Level Format Damage on Standard DOS Hard Disk. Detects Potential Errors. Determines Optimal Sector Interleave. Integrated Report Generator.
Gibson Research Corp.

SPIPE: Plumbing Service Supply Pipe Sizing. *Items Included:* Manual. *Customer Support:* Toll free telephone support.
IBM PC & compatibles (256k). disk $495.00.
Computes Optimal Pipe Sizes for Hot/Cold Domestic Water Supply Systems in Residential & Commercial Buildings. Will Handle Systems with up to 800 Pipes & Follows ASHRAE & ASPE Procedures. SPIPE Also Performs a Comprehensive Systems Analysis Complete with a Bill of Materials Showing Material & Labor Cost Estimates.
Elite Software Development, Inc.

Spirit of Excalibur. 1990. *Customer Support:* 90 day warranty.
MS-DOS 2.1 or higher. IBM, PC, XT, AT & Tandy & compatibles (640K). disk $49.99. *Nonstandard peripherals required:* VGA, EGA or Tandy Graphics Board required- 8Mhz or higher recommended.
Amiga (512K). 3.5" disk $49.99.
Atari (768K). 3.5" disk $49.99.
Years of Historical Research Ensure That This is the Definitive Game on Arthurian Legend. It Combines Elements of Traditional Fantasy Role Playing, Animated Adventure, & Strategy. With Five Major Quests & Dozens of Lesser Challenges, the Game is Played on Both Map & Scene Levels for Additional Variety.
Virgin Games.

SPITBOL 386. *Version:* 1.28. Mark B. Emmer et al. 1989. *Items Included:* Software & complete documentation. *Customer Support:* Free.
MS-DOS. 80386 or 80486 PC & compatibles (1Mb). disk $295.00 (ISBN 0-939793-09-1, Order no.: SPIT386).
OS/2 2.0. 80386 or 80486 PC & compatibles (1Mb). 3.5" disk $295.00 (ISBN 0-939793-10-5, Order no.: SPITOS2).
Complete Implementation of the SNOBOL4 Programming Language. Used for Complex Text Processing & Pattern Matching. Supports 32-Bit Protected Mode Programs, Binary & Direct Access Files, Built-In Sort, & Numerous Language Extensions. Includes Compiler, Tutorial & Reference Manual.
Catspaw, Inc.

TITLE INDEX

Spitfire 40. *Compatible Hardware:* Atari ST; Commodore 64/128.
disk $35.00.
You Control One of the World's Most Versatile Aircrafts. The Cockpit Has Working Dials, Gauges, & Compass. Users Can Choose Between Simulator & Game Scenarios.
Avalon Hill Game Co., The Microcomputer Games Div.

Splash! Jun. 1988. *Customer Support:* Unlimited support: (617) 494-1220, (617) 494- 1221. PC-DOS/MS-DOS 2.1 or higher (640k). disk $99.95. *Nonstandard peripherals required:* VGA or MGA graphics, VGA compatible monitor, IBM or Microsoft compatible mouse.
User Can Mix 256 Colors on Screen from a Palette of Over 256,000; Can Select from 60 Different Patterns & Brush Sizes. Text May Be Entered with up to 13 Different Fonts or Word Processor Text May Be Imported. Compatible with PageMaker, Ventura Publisher & Most Other Desktop Publishing Programs; Compatible with Computer Eyes Video Digitizer.
Spinnaker Software Corp.

Split Ink. *Compatible Hardware:* Atari XL/XE.
disk $24.95.
Printer Utility. Includes a Slide Show Capability & Can Load Pictures from ATARI ARTIST, FUN WITH ART, MICRO ILLUSTRATOR, MICRO PAINTER, or MICRO PACE. Gives the Ability to Flip, Move, or Invert the Loaded Images. Enables User to Create Fonts Beyond the 32 It Contains. Package Includes a Disk Sector Editor.
Digital Arts Software Assocs.

Spool-Master. *Version:* 5.0. *Compatible Hardware:* IBM PC, PCjr, PC XT, PC AT, PC compatibles.
disk $69.95.
RAM Printer Spooler. Produces Multiple Copies & Handles Single Sheets.
Software Matters.

SPORT!: Sports League Scheduler. *Version:* 5.3. Peter A. Bornstein. Feb. 1988. *Compatible Hardware:* IBM PC & compatibles, PC XT, PC AT. *Operating System(s) Required:* PC-DOS, MS-DOS. *Language(s):* Compiled BASIC. *Memory Required:* 128k. *Items Included:* Software, user manual. *Customer Support:* Telephone.
disk $99.00 (ISBN 0-918079-02-0).
Allows League Managers & Organizers of All Sports to Produce Season Schedules for up to 20 Leagues. Each League May Have from Four to Thirty-Six Teams & Ten Divisions. Sport! Maintains League & Team Names, Divisions, Length of Season, Days Played, Officials, Playing Facilities, Time & Date of Games, & Game Results. Team Standings & Several Other Reports Are Produced; Individual Player Statistics Module Is Also Included in the Package.
PRO Systems.

Sports. *Items Included:* Installation Guide.
IBM PC. Contact publisher for price (ISBN 0-87321-084-0, Order no.: MSD-3018).
Activision, Inc.

Sports & Games. (Studio Ser.). *Items Included:* Visual index, user's guide. *Customer Support:* Free & unlimited technical support to registered users; 60 day money-back guarantee.
Macintosh. Macintosh (Minimum required for program with which you want to use ClickArt). 3.5" disk $99.95. *Nonstandard peripherals required:* PostScript compatible printer. *Addl. software required:* Any desktop publishing, word processing or works application that accepts EPS files.
Windows V.3.0 or higher. IBM PC & compatibles (Minimum needed for application with which you will use ClickArt). 3.5" disk $99.95. *Addl. software required:* Any desktop publishing, word processing or works program that accepts CGM or WMF files.
MS-DOS V.3.3 or higher. IBM PC & compatibles (Minimum needed for application with which you will use ClickArt). 3.5" disk $99.95. *Addl. software required:* Any desktop publishing, word processing or works program that accepts WMF or CGM files.
Over 180 Images! Highest-Quality Full-Color Images Available; Ready-to-Use, or Changed in Appropriate Drawing Program; Designed in Full-Color (CMYK); Ready for Color Separations & Commercial Printing; Produced to Print in Detailed Greyscale on Black & White Printers.
T/Maker Co., Inc.

Sports Appeal: Trivia from Billiards to Baseball. Ralph Stoeber et al. *Compatible Hardware:* IBM PC, PCjr, PC XT, PC AT, Portable PC, 3270 PC with IBM Color Display & one double-sided disk drive. *Memory Required:* 128k.
disk $19.95 (Order no.: 6276608).
Trivia Game Including over 5000 Questions & 125 Topics to Choose From. One of Three Levels of Play Can Be Selected, & up to 14 Players Can Participate in Any Game. Score Can Be Displayed at Any Time.
Personally Developed Software, Inc.

Sports Bloopers. *Customer Support:* Free, unlimited.
System 6 Mac. 030 Mac, 256 colors (4Mb). CD-ROM disk $17.95. *Nonstandard peripherals required:* Sound card, CD-ROM drive.
Windows 3.1 PC. 486 PC (4Mb). *Nonstandard peripherals required:* Any Windows supported sound card, CD-ROM drive.
Contains over 220 Video Clips of the Funniest Mishaps in Your Favorite Sports. Check Out the Bad Turns in Auto Racing, the Errors in Baseball, & the Tricks a Racing Bike Can Do. Watch the Bungling Boxers, Tumbling Gymnasts, Hapless Hockey Players, & Hysterical Horse Racing. There Are Soccer Surprises & Antics in Water Sports.
BeachWare.

Sports Lover's Dream CD-ROM: 57 of the Best Shareware PC Computer Sports Programs.
Jan. 1996. *Items Included:* Directions booklet. DOS & Windows 3.1. PC (4k). CD-ROM disk $29.95 (ISBN 1-56087-114-8). Optimal configuration: 386, Windows 3.1 4k.
Over 50 Sports Programs Including Fantasy League. This Program Allows You to Create Your Own Players & Pit Them Against a Team of Your Choice. Programs for Baseball, Basketball & Football. Also Included Are Programs for Handicapping, Statistical Management, Little League Stats Manager, NFL Stats Tracker, & Several Sport Card Collection Programs & Databases.
Top of the Mountain Publishing.

Sports Memorabilia. Aug. 1985. *Compatible Hardware:* IBM. *Operating System(s) Required:* PC-DOS. *Memory Required:* 128k. *General Requirements:* 2 disk drives, printer.
disk $49.95 (ISBN 0-934453-00-4, Order no.: S-105).
Inventories Baseball, Football or Other Sports Cards, As Well As Sports Publications. Allows for Updating Prices So the User May Print a Profit & Loss Statement & Keep Track of Sports Shows.
River City Software, Inc.

Sports Pack. *Items Included:* Installation Guide.
IBM PC. Contact publisher for price (ISBN 0-87321-085-9, Order no.: CDD-3018).
Activision, Inc.

The Sports Statbook. *Operating System(s) Required:* MS-DOS, PC-DOS. *Memory Required:* 256k. *General Requirements:* Printer.
disk $49.00.
Maintains & Prints Game, Year-to-Date, & Lifetime Hockey, Soccer & Miscellaneous Sports Stats.
RJL Systems.

Sports Statistics I. *Compatible Hardware:* Apple II; IBM PC; TRS-80 Model I, Model II, Model III. contact publisher for price.
Educational Data Systems, Inc.

Spot the Computer Game. 1990. *Customer Support:* 90 day warranty.
MS-DOS 2.1 or higher. IBM (512K). disk $39.99. *Nonstandard peripherals required:* Requires EGA, Tandy or VGA Graphics.
Amiga (512K). 3.5" disk $39.99.
Commodore 64 (64K). disk $29.99. *Nonstandard peripherals required:* Joystick required.
Comes Alive in Full Animation & Boogies Across Your Computer Screen with Commercial-Quality Graphics & Sound. Play with up to 4 Human or Computer Players or a Combination of Both. There Are 9 Selectable Levels of Computer Skill. Select from the 512 Pre-Programmed Playfields or Design Your Own.
Virgin Games.

Spotlight. *Version:* 1.1. Jul. 1985. *Compatible Hardware:* IBM PC, PC XT, PC AT. *Operating System(s) Required:* DOS 2.0. *Memory Required:* 75k.
$75.00.
A Set of Desktop Accessories. Acessories Include an Appointment Book, a Phone Book with Appointment Audio Dialer, Notepad, Calculator, Index Card File, & DOS Filer.
Lotus Development Corp.

Spotlight. Jules Brenner. Aug. 1993. *Items Included:* Comb-bound manual. *Customer Support:* Free technical support - 90 days.
MS-DOS. IBM & compatibles (128k). disk $27.95 (ISBN 0-930437-32-2).
DOS Utility That Helps User Find Files on Drives in an Extraordinary Number of Ways Beyond DOS' DIR Command. Shows User Disk Space & Usage for up to 5 Drives on One Report; Shows Which Files Changed or Created Today or Within the Last X Number of Days; Will List Only New Files of a Certain Type; Will List Subdirectories & Show the Space Used in Each. Will Aid Housecleaning by Showing All Files on All Directories of Hard Drive That Have Been Changed on the Current Day. Identifies File Parameters Without the "" Wild Card, Eliminating All but One Shifted Character among All Its Parameters (Arguments); Will List As Many As Four Different File Parameters on One Command; Will Filter Out Specified File Parameters; Will List Files by Size & with Embedded Strings & Within an Alphabetical Range. Files Listed Are Color Coded for Easy Identification by Type. Files Are Listed in Two Columns to Put As Much Information on the Screen at One Time As Possible.*
NewTEK Industries.

SPP: Signal Processing Program. *Version:* 2. Apr. 1984. *Compatible Hardware:* Apple Macintosh; AT&T 6300; DEC Rainbow, DEC VT 180; HP-125; IBM PC, PC jr, PC XT, PC AT, & compatibles; Tandy 1000, 1200, 2000; TI Professional; Xerox 820, 820-II, 860. *Operating System(s) Required:* Apple DOS, PC-DOS/MS-DOS. *Language(s):* Compiled BASIC. *Memory Required:* IBM 256k, Macintosh 512k.
IBM PC. $195.00.
Macintosh. $350.00.
General Purpose Signal Processing Program

Containing an Integrated Set of Routines Which Analyze Linear & Non-Linear Systems & Circuits & Their Effects on User-Generated or User-Specified Time Domain Waveforms. The Basis for Much of SPP Is a 512-Point Fast Fourier Transform & Its Inverse. Linear Processing Is Conducted in the Frequency Domain & Non-Linear Processing Is Performed in the Time Domain. Has the Ability to Switch Rapidly Between the Time Domain & the Frequency Domain. Takes a System Described by a LaPlace Function & Computes the Time Domain Response of That System to Any User-Generated Input Waveform. Features Signal Input/Generation & Time/Frequency Domain Operations. Compatible with ACNAP, LOCIPRO, ACTFIL, & XFER.
BV Engineering.

SPF/PC. *Version:* 4.0. Jun. 1994. *Items Included:* 2 manuals, 2 disks, quick reference card. *Customer Support:* Unlimited telephone support. OS/2, DOS. Any computer running OS/2 version 2.1 or higher or 386 with 2Mb running DOS 3.1 or higher. $295.00. *Optimal configuration:* 386 4Mb.
Provides a Familiar Environment on the PC for Mainframe MVS Programmers. Features Full 3270 Compatibility, ISREDIT Macros via REXX, Modifiable Panels, Table Services, UNDO/REDO, Program Source Colorization, 132-Column Support, SUPERC File Comparison, COBOL Workbench Integration, & More.
Command Technology Corp.

SPREAD Financial Modeling Language: SPREAD. *Version:* 3.1. 1989. *Compatible Hardware:* IBM. *Operating System(s) Required:* MS-DOS. *Memory Required:* 384k.
disk $500.00.
Designed for Anyone Who Has a Need for Financial Reporting. Uses English-Like Commands & Parameters for Ease of Use Regardless of Computer Expertise. Is Flexible & Can Handle a Variety of Reports Whether It Be Forecasting & Tracking, Budgeting, or Hierarchical Consolidation. Key Features Include Direct Interface with Other Software Files, Readable Models, Auditable, On-Line Help Facility, & Built-In Functions for Complex Equations.
L & L Products, Inc.

Spread to DIF File Conversion Utility: DIF Converter. 1985. *Compatible Hardware:* IBM PC & compatibles; PC XT, PC AT; Wang PC. *Operating System(s) Required:* MS-DOS. *Language(s):* BASIC. *Memory Required:* 256k.
disk $250.00 ea.
Designed to Convert DIF Files Produced by Other Software into SPREAD Data Files or SPREAD Files to DIF Files.
L & L Products, Inc.

Spread Workstation. *Version:* 2.3a. 1989. *Compatible Hardware:* IBM PC & compatibles, PC XT, PC AT. *Operating System(s) Required:* MS-DOS. *Memory Required:* 512k. *General Requirements:* Hayes compatible modem. $900.00.
Allows File Transfers Between IBM PC or Compatibles to a Variety of Host Mini or Mainframe Computers Using a Modem. Features Include: Full Error Checking Protocol for Error Free File Transfers, Macros for Automating Log on & File Transfer Procedures, Status Display, & Command Processor for DOS, File Transformation, & PC Spread.
L & L Products, Inc.

SpreadSage. Mar. 1990. *Items Included:* Spiral-bound manual. *Customer Support:* Free telephone support.
HP 9000, series 200, 300, 520 (1-4Mb). disk $395.00. *Networks supported:* SRM.

MS-DOS. IBM PC & compatibles (640K). disk $395.00. *Addl. software required:* HT BASIC.
255 X 16383 Cell Spreadsheet with Graphics. Individual Cell Attributes of Color, Font, Borders, Alignment. Notes Attached to Individual Cells, Column Bar, Pie, Line, Point, or Contour Charts. Output to Print or Plotter, Natural Order Recalculation with Optional Alteration.
James Assocs.

Spreadsheet Connector. *Version:* 3.0. Dec. 1993. *Items Included:* Manual, demo, tutorials. *Customer Support:* free - phone, training available.
DOS & Netbios. Client IBM PC (512k); Table Server IBM PC (640k). $4995.00. *Addl. software required:* Netbios. *Networks supported:* Any running Netbios.
Module Allows Simultaneous Read/Write Access to Shared Data from 1-2-3 or Exiel on a Local Area Network. Suitable for On-Line Analytical Processing (OLAP).
Sinper Corp.

The Spreadsheet Forecaster. E. S. Gardner, Jr. Feb. 1990. *Items Included:* 84-page user's guide with examples. *Customer Support:* Free telephone support, 90 day unlimited warranty, consulting/training on-site available, customized programming.
MS-DOS 2.0 or higher (320k). IBM PC & compatible. $79.00.
The Program Is a Series of 23 Templates for 1-2-3 That Provide Models for Such Forecasting Tasks As Budgeting, Preparing Proforma Financial Statements, or Developing Marketing & Inventory Demand Forecasts. Each Model Is Accompanied by Sample Data, a Preset Graph, & Step-by-Step Instructions, Appropriate for the User Who Has No Background in Statistics or Forecasting.
Delphus, Inc.

Spreadsheet Junction. *Version:* 2.0. Apr. 1994. *Items Included:* One 3-ring binder & manual. *Customer Support:* Free phone support, FAX support, BBS.
MS-DOS/PC-DOS 2.0 or higher. IBM PC, XT, AT, 386, 486, PS/2 & compatibles (640k). $299.00 (ISBN 0-939283-06-9). *Networks supported:* All major networks.
PC 386/486, Sun Sparc OS, RS6000 (640k). $499.00 (ISBN 0-939283-06-9). *Networks supported:* All major networks.
Unix/Xenix.
Converts from/to Lotus, Supercalc, SylK, Enable, ASCII, & Uniplex Speadsheets. Converts Formats, Formulas, Data & Some Macros. Ideal for OEM Applications.
Tools & Techniques, Inc.

Spreadsheet Templates: Construction, Real Estate, Financial. Software Models. Jan. 1981. *Operating System(s) Required:* CP/M-80, MS-DOS. (source code included). *Memory Required:* 48k.
Construction. disk $59.95 (ISBN 0-923875-20-4).
Real Estate. disk $59.95 (ISBN 0-923875-22-0).
Financial. disk $59.95 (ISBN 0-923875-24-7).
Construction. 8" disk $59.95 (ISBN 0-923875-19-0).
Financial. 8" disk $59.95 (ISBN 0-923875-23-9).
Real Estate. 8" disk $59.95 (ISBN 0-923875-21-2).
Prebuilt Worksheets Using Figures from National Construction Estimator.
Elliam Assocs.

Spreadsheets & Linear Programs Disk to Accompany MANAGERIAL ECONOMICS. William F. Samuelson & Stephen G. Marks. Oct. 1992.
IBM. 3.5" disk $13.50 (ISBN 0-03-040597-1).
Dryden Pr.

Spring Design. Apr. 1985. *Compatible Hardware:* Apple II+, IBM PC. *Operating System(s) Required:* PC-DOS, Apple DOS 3.3. *Language(s):* BASIC (source code included). *Memory Required:* Apple 48k, IBM 128k. *Customer Support:* Telephone.
$125.00.
Design & Analysis of Helical & Belleville Springs. Includes Graphics.
PEAS (Practical Engineering Applications Software).

Spring Design with an IBM PC. Al Dietrich. Nov. 1985. *Compatible Hardware:* IBM PC. *Language(s):* BASIC. *Memory Required:* 64k. *Items Included:* 112 page manual with diskette.
disk $114.50, incl. manual (ISBN 0-8247-7349-7).
Helps User Design Compression, Extension & Torsion Springs. Takes Nearly All Variables & Operating Procedures into Consideration.
Marcel Dekker, Inc.

Springpac. *Version:* 5.1. Jan. 1983. *Compatible Hardware:* IBM PC, PC XT & compatibles. *Operating System(s) Required:* PC-DOS/MS-DOS. *Memory Required:* 512k. *General Requirements:* CGA card.
disk $495.00.
Solutions for Six Spring Types: Flat, Motor, Torsion, Extension, Compression & Belleville. Rectangular or Round Wire Calculates Number of Coils, Initial Tension, Coil Diameter, Spring Rate, Working Stress & 14 ASTM Material Specifications. Metric or British Units.
Engineering Software Co.

Sprinkler Selector. N. Aubuchon. Nov. 1986. *Operating System(s) Required:* MS-DOS 2.1. *Memory Required:* 256k. *General Requirements:* Printer.
disk $165.00 (ISBN 0-943065-01-1).
demo disk $20.00 (ISBN 0-943065-00-3).
Custom Database Containing Sprinkler Irrigation Products & List Prices, Allows Comparison of All Products by Listed Categories; or Selection of Products by User's Specified Requirements. Provides up to 15 Categories.
Larchsoft.

Sprint: The Professional Word Processor. *Compatible Hardware:* IBM PC & compatibles. *Operating System(s) Required:* DOS 2.0 or higher.
disk $195.95.
$595.00 network version.
Allows the User to Work Within the Command-Key Driven User Interface & Tailor It to Individual Needs. Offers Both a Function Key or Menu-Oriented Interface, with Logical Key Assignments That Can Also Be Reassigned. Includes an AutoSave Feature, Which Saves in Background Mode.
Borland International, Inc.

Sprite King. *Customer Support:* 800-929-8117 (customer service).
MS-DOS. Commodore 64. disk $49.99 (ISBN 0-87007-714-7).
Enables Developers to Produces Animated Sprites with up to 28 Frames in any Combination of Shape & Color. Features Pull-Down Menus, Scroll on-Screen Instructions & an Optional Grid.
SourceView Software International.

Sprite OS. *Customer Support:* All of our products are unconditionally guaranteed.
Unix. CD-ROM disk $29.95 (Order no.: SPRITE). *Nonstandard peripherals required:* CD-ROM drive.
UC Berkeley's Distributed OS for Sun Workstations.
Walnut Creek CDRom.

TITLE INDEX

SPROUT! *Version:* Windows 1.0, DOS 1.4, Macintosh 1.1.
Windows 3.1 or higher. disk $59.95 (Order no.: 744734 10560 9). *Optimal configuration:* Windows 3.1 or higher, 4Mb RAM, 5Mb hard drive space.
DOS 3.0 or higher. disk $59.95 (Order no.: 744734 10530 2). *Optimal configuration:* DOS, 640k, DOS 3.0 or higher, mouse & hard drive recommended.
Macintosh (1Mb). 3.5" disk $79.95 (Order no.: 744734 10550 0). *Optimal configuration:* Macintosh, 1Mb, hard drive recommended.
A Graphic Garden Design Program for Drafting Vegetable Garden Layouts with Pre-Drawn Vegetable & Garden Symbols, & a Planting Tool That Positions the Vegetables with Correct Row & Plant Spacings. Gives Comprehensive Growing Information, the Number of People the Garden Feeds, & a Calendar for Planting & Harvesting Times.
Abracadata, Ltd.

Sprout!: The Graphic Vegetable Garden Design Program. Jun. 1992. *Items Included:* Manual. *Customer Support:* No charge telephone tech support.
MS-DOS, Windows 3.1 or higher. IBM PC & all compatibles (640k). disk $59.95. *Optimal configuration:* Graphics card required, mouse recommended. Windows 3.1 or higher, 4Mb RAM & hard drive.
System 7. Macintosh (1Mb). 3.5" disk $79.95. *Optimal configuration:* Printer optional.
Complete Planning Tool for Vegetable Gardeners. Unique Planting Tool Produces a Graphic, Scalable Garden Plan with Correct Plant & Row Spacing. Contains a Fully Editable Database of Vegetables for 7 Climate Regions; & It Prints Out Garden Layouts, Calendars, Shopping Lists & Reports.
Abracadata, Ltd.

S.P.S. Statistical Pac. DBi Software Products. *Operating System(s) Required:* MS-DOS, CP/M-86. *Memory Required:* 64k. *General Requirements:* Printer, Winchester hard disk. $350.00.
Texas Instruments, Personal Productivit.

SPSS Data Entry II. Sep. 1993. *Compatible Hardware:* IBM PC. *Operating System(s) Required:* PC-DOS/MS-DOS 2.0 or higher. *Memory Required:* 512k. *General Requirements:* 10Mb hard disk; math co-processor recommended.
contact publisher for price (ISBN 0-918469-43-0).
Fully Integrated, Data Entry, Editing & File Translation Tool for Use with Most Microcomputer Software. Allows the User to Design Customized Screens Resembling the Paper Version, or Use the Spreadsheet Format to Enter Data. Cleaning Features Ensure the Integrity of the Data According to Rules Defined by the User. Also Features Skip Logic, Whereby Inapplicable Fields Are Skipped Over to the Next Appropriate Field.
SPSS, Inc.

SPSS Developer's Kit for Windows: Applications Development Software Tool.
386-based computer or higher (8Mb). Contact publisher for price. *Optimal configuration:* 386-based computer or higher, 8MB RAM recommended, 20Mb hard disk space, Microsoft Windows 3.1 or higher, VGA monitor or higher.
With the SPSS Developer's Kit for Windows, You Can Program Quickly & Easily Using Complete Components That Access, Manage & Analyze Your Data. Deliver Push-Button Statistical Reports & Interactive Data Analysis Using OLE 2.0 Automation. Get All the Statistical Functions & Graphs You Need.
SPSS, Inc.

SPSS for OS/2. Oct. 1989. *Items Included:* Complete system & statistical documentation. *Customer Support:* Value plus support plan & desktop freedom plan.
OS/2. IBM PS/2, IBM PC/AT & compatibles. contact publisher for price. *Optimal configuration:* Minimum 4 megabytes memory, 20Mb hard disk, & graphics supported by Presentation Manager, mouse & 8087 co-processor optional.
Statistical Program for Performing Both Simple & Complex Data Analysis Tasks. Runs under the Presentation Manager Interface. Includes Complete Data Management, Statistical & Reporting Functions. Statistical Functions Include: Descriptives, Cross Tabulation, Multiple Regression, Anova, Cluster & Factor Analyses, Nonlinear & Logistic Regression, Discriminant, Probit, & Survival Analyses, Optional Time Series Analysis & Forecasting Procedures.
SPSS, Inc.

SPSS for the Macintosh. *Version:* 6.1. *Items Included:* Software & documentation. *Customer Support:* Regular support, toll-free support & BBS available.
68030, 68040 (4Mb). contact publisher for price.
SPSS, Inc.

SPSS for the Macintosh: Statistical Data Analysis Software.
System 7.0 or higher. Macintosh, 68030 or 68040 based machines (8Mb). Contact publisher for price. *Optimal configuration:* 68030 or 68040 based machines, coprocessor, 8Mb RAM minimum, 16Mb RAM recommended, 13Mb hard disk space, System 7.0 or higher.
A Tightly Integrated Family of Products That Combines Ease of Learning, Ease of Use, In-Depth Statistical Features, Data Management & High-Resolution Graphics. Includes More Than 50 Chart Types & More Than 60 Statistical Procedures from Basic Exploratory Data Analysis to Advanced Procedures Such as MANOVA, Factor Analysis & Logistic Regression. Add-On Modules Provide Specialized Capabilities for Tabular Reporting, Correspondence Analysis & Perceptual Mapping, Forecasting & Much More.
SPSS, Inc.

SPSS for Windows: Statistical Data Analysis Software.
386-based computer or higher (8Mb). Contact publisher for price. *Optimal configuration:* 386-based computer or higher, 8Mb RAM recommended, 20Mb hard disk space, Microsoft Windows 3.1 or higher, VGA monitor or higher.
A Tightly Integrated Family of Products That Combines Ease of Learning, Ease of Use, In-Depth Statistical Features, Data Management & High-Resolution Graphics. Includes More Than 50 Chart Types & More Than 60 Statistical Procedures from Basic Counts & Crosstabulations to Advanced Procedures Such as MANOVA & Logistic Regression. Add-On Modules Provide Specialized Capabilities for Tabular Reporting, Correspondence Analysis & Perceptual Mapping, CHAID Analysis, Quality Improvement, LISREL & Much More.
SPSS, Inc.

SPSS/PC+. *Version:* 5.0. Sep. 1993. *Compatible Hardware:* IBM PC & compatibles, PC XT, PC AT. *Operating System(s) Required:* PC-DOS 2.0. *Memory Required:* 512k. *General Requirements:* Hard disk; 8087 co-processor optional; 512k, extended memory. *Items Included:* Software & documentation. *Customer Support:* Value Plus & Desktop Freedom plans.
Contact publisher for price (ISBN 0-918469-14-7).
Statistical Program for Performing Both Simple & Complex Data Analysis Tasks. Includes Fully Integrated Report Writing, Plotting, File Management, & Basic Statistics. Its Statistics Functions Include: Descriptives, Cross Tabulation, Exploratory Data Analysis, ANOVA. ADVANCED STATISTICS Performs Factor Cluster, Discriminant Analyses, MANOVA. TABLES Produces Presentation Quality Tabular Reporting, & Stub & Banner Tables; Handles Multiple Response Survey Data; Allows Complete Control over Content & Layout. Facilities Allow Transfer of Files to & from 1-2-3, dBASE III & IV, SAS, Symphony & Multiplan. Supports Token Ring & 3Com Networks.
SPSS, Inc.

Spycraft. *Items Included:* Installation guide.
IBM. CD-ROM disk Contact publisher for price (ISBN 0-87321-119-7, Order no.: CDM-3110-000-U3).
Activision, Inc.

SPYGRAF. 1984. *Compatible Hardware:* IBM PC, PCjr, PC XT, PC AT. *Operating System(s) Required:* PC-DOS 2.0 or higher. *Memory Required:* 128k. *Items Included:* Users manual. *Customer Support:* 90 day limited warranty.
disk $295.00 (ISBN 0-922928-58-4, Order no.: 1031).
Program Which, When Loaded Before Other Software Packages, Will Allow Text As Well Graphics to Be Enlarged at User's Command. Text & Graphics Enlarged up to 64 Times Their Normal Size May Be Displayed on Screen.
GemStar Partnership.

SpyProof. *Version:* 1.0. Jun. 1991. *Items Included:* Approximately 30 pages of support documentation, license registration card. *Customer Support:* Free telephone support, approximately 30 pages of support documentation also included.
MS-DOS, PC-DOS. IBM PC, XT, AT, PS/2 & compatible 256k. $99.95 single unit; quantity discounts & site licenses also available (ISBN 0-929609-06-9). *Optimal configuration:* 640k. *Networks supported:* All.
Data Encryption Utility for PC Users. It Uses the National Institute of Standards & Technology Endorsed Data Encryption Standard (DES) to Provide a High Level of Security for Sensitive Documents. The Encryption Engine Is Bundled with a WordPerfect Macro Which Makes the Program Easy to Use Even for WordPerfect Novices. SpyProof Can Be Used to Protect Sensitive Documents Stored on a Floppy or on a Local or Network Hard Disk. Encrypted Documents May Also Be Safely Transmitted via E-Mail. Original Documents May Be Optionally Erased to Department of Defense Security Guidelines.
Information Security Corp.

SQL & Relational Basics. Dec. 1989.
MS-DOS. IBM PC & compatibles. disk $23.95 (ISBN 1-55851-063-X).
Includes Explanation of the Relational Model, Clarification of the 12 Fidelity Rules Given by Dr. E.F. Codd (Inventor of the Model), Overview of Components & Features, Evaluation of System & Its Relational Fidelity & Practical Implications for the Selection & Use of PC Data Base Management Systems.
M & T Bks.

SQL for dBASE Programmers. Edward Dowgiallo. Sep. 1989. *Operating System(s) Required:* MS-DOS.
book & disk $39.95 (ISBN 1-55851-035-4).
book only $24.95 (ISBN 1-55851-034-6).
Provides a Detailed Introduction to the Structured

SQL NETWORK PRODUCT LINE: (SQL

Query Language (SQL). Among the Topics Discussed Are: Anatomy of the SQL Language, Facilities for Constructing Database Structures, How to Define Database Views, Set Manipulation Aspects, SQL Kernels, Application Generators, Multiple User Environments, Programming, etc.
M & T Bks.

SQL Network Product Line: (SQL Network for DB2); (SQL Network for Oracle). Version: (SQL Network for DB2); (SQL Network for Oracle); (SQL Network for SQL Server); (SQL Network for OS/2 EE Database Manager); (SQL Network for BHtreve). Items Included: Complete documentation in 3-ring binders. Customer Support: 90 days free support; Extended support depends on product from $75 to $375 annually. Technical training at Gupta, $995 per person, at customer site-$6000 + expenses.
  DOS, OS/2. IBM PC & compatibles & IBM mainframes, minicomputers. contact publisher for price. Addl. software required: Windows. Networks supported: All NetBOIS compatible networks, named pipes or TCP/IP LANS.
Gupta's Overarching Strategy for Providing Connectivity Across the Enterprise. The SQL Network Family Currently Consists of host, gateway & router software for DB2, Oracle, SQL Servers, OS/2 EE Database Manager & Btrieve. Products Make Minicomputer & Mainframe Databases Appear As Local Databases on the PC. Using SQL Database Gateways and/or the Appropriate SQLRouter, the Same Front-End Application on a PC; Stand-Alone or Hooked to a LAN, Can Now Simultaneously & Transparently Access Data in SQLBase Server, D82, SQL Server, Oracle. OS/2 EE Database Manager & Novell Btrieve. SQL Windows Is Now a Front-End for SQL Base Server Oracle, DB2, SQL Server, Oracle, OS/2 EE Database Manager & Novell Btrieve. SQLVision for Lotus 1-2-3, SQLVision for Excel & Library for Clipper. Other Available Front Ends Include C, COBOL, JAM/DBi, Quicksilver/SQL. VP-Expert, PC Nomad, SQL Commander, Access SQL, Forest & Trees & Q & A.
Gupta Technologies, Inc.

SQLBase Server. Version: 4.0.4. Compatible Hardware: IBM PC & compatibles. Items Included: complete documentation, SQL router software. Customer Support: 90 days free telephone support, extended support, on-site, off-site training & consulting.
  $2495.00 (DOS version).
  $3495.00 (OS/2 version).
An SQL Database Server Designed for Maximum Performance on PC LANs & Optimized to Run Mission Critical & Decision Support Applications. Can Run Within the Tight Memory Constraints of a PC. Supports DOS, OS/2, Unix, NetWare 386 & Can Operate on any NetBOIS compatible LAN. Shipping Fronts Ends for SQLBase Server Include Gupta's SQLWindows, SQLQuest, Vision for Lotus 1-2-3, SQLVision for Excel & Library for Clipper. Other Available Front Ends Include C, COBOL, JAM/DBi, Quicksilver/SQL, VP-Expert, PC Nomad, SQL Commander & Access SQL, Forest & Trees, & Q & A.
Gupta Technologies, Inc.

SQLWindows. Version: 3.0. Sep. 1991. Items Included: Complete documentation in 3-ring binders. Customer Support: 90 days free support; Extended support depends on product from $75 to $375 annually. Technical training at Gupta, $995 per person at customer site-$60000 + expenses.
  PC-DOS, MS-DOS 3.1 or higher; OS/2 1.2 or higher. IBM PC, AT, PS/2 model 30, 286 or higher & compatibles (2Mb). 3.5" or 5.25" disk $1295.00. Nonstandard peripherals required: Hard disk, IBM EGA monitor (or higher resolution). Addl. software required: Microsoft Windows 3.0, any mouse supported by MS Windows. Networks supported: All NetBOIS LANS, TCP/IP, APPC/LV6.2.
For Creating Powerful Microsoft Windows 3.0 & Presentation Manager Applications Quickly & Easily That Are Also Optimized for Client-Server Architecture. Can Access Multiple SQL Back-Ends Including Gupta's SQLBASE Server, IBM DB2, Oracle, SQL Server, OS/2 EE Database Manager & Novell Btrieve. Uses Point-and-Click Techniques & a Fourth Generation Language to Provide Developers with Complete Programming Functionality. It Does Not Require the Use of C or the Microsoft Windows Toolkit.
Gupta Technologies, Inc.

SquareNote. Version: 2.01. Compatible Hardware: IBM PC & compatibles. Operating System(s) Required: MS-DOS. Memory Required: 256k.
  disk $99.00.
Text Database-Management System with 2000 Characters per Field, 34,000 Characters per Record, 20 Designated Keyword Fields per Record & 64,000 Records per File. Supports Boolean Searches, & Searches Can Be Restricted to a Specific Field or Other Qualifier. Also Features Ability to Build Own Data Files; Run in Back ground under DesqView; Import & Append ASCII Tect Files; & Export ASCII, Wordperfect, WordStar & XYwrite Text Files.
Union Squareware.

Squeak: Learn How to Use the Mouse. Paul Rego. Nov. 1993. Customer Support: Free telephone support.
  6.0.7 or higher. Macintosh (2Mb). 3.5" disk $9.95 (ISBN 0-945876-07-6, Order no.: SQEK). Addl. software required: HyperCard 2.0 or higher. Optimal configuration: Macintosh 6.0.7 or higher 2Mb, HyperCard 2.0 or higher.
Teaches the Beginner How to Use the Mouse. Explains the Various Functions of the Mouse, Such As Clicking, Double-Clicking, Dragging & Moving. Allows the User to Practice These Functions While Overseeing the Results. Also Tests the User on These. Describes & Tests the User on Text Manipulation. Scores Are Maintained So the User Can Go Back Later & Improve Them.
Insight Data.

Squiggle. Version: 2.0. Oct. 1995. Items Included: 1 staple-stitched manual, 2 3.5" disks. Customer Support: Free with registered serial number.
  Windows 3.1. disk $99.00. Networks supported: No.
Transforms Hard-Line CAD Output for a Warmer Hand-Drawn Look. Preset & Custom Styles Put Your Personality into Your Presentation Graphics. Accepts HPGL & HPGL/2 Input. Print to HPGL or HPGL/2 Printer or Plotter Device or Using Windows Print Manager Drivers. Save As BMP or WMF Files.
Insight Development Corp.

SQZ! Plus: Spreadsheet File Utility System for Lotus.
  IBM PC/XT/AT, PS/2 or compatibles (50k). disk $99.95. Nonstandard peripherals required: Compatible with hardware supported by Lotus. Addl. software required: Lotus Release 1A, 2.0, 2.01 or Symphony for file compression & recovery. All other features require IBM PC versions of 1-2-3. (Release 2.0 or 2.01).
Spreadsheet File Utility System for Lotus. Reduces Size of Spreadsheet Files on Disk by up to 95%. Squeezes & Unsqueezes Files Automatically As They're Loaded by Lotus without Special Instructions. Other Features Include: File Back Up, History (Saves the Date & Time of File Changes), Recover, Password Option & More. Works with Programs Like SideKick, 4Views, The Cambridge Spreadsheet Analyst, Note-It Plus, & Lotus HAL.
Symantec Corp.

SS7: A Brief Look. May 1992. Items Included: User manual. Customer Support: Free technical support & a 30-day warranty (1-800-521-CORE).
  MS-DOS. IBM & compatibles (512k). 3.5" disk $125.00 (ISBN 1-57305-003-2). Nonstandard peripherals required: High-density 3.5" disk drive; VGA color monitor. Addl. software required: MS-DOS version 3.3 or higher. Optimal configuration: IBM (512k), MS-DOS version 3.3 or higher, VGA color monitor, keyboard, Microsoft compatible mouse (optional).
This One-Hour Computer-Based Training Package Provides an Overview of the Signaling system Seven (SS7) Network. The Course Provides a Concise, Yet Thorough Understanding of SS7 - Its Architecture & Applications. Special Attention Has Been Given to the Design of This Package, Including Colorful Graphics, to Make Learning Interesting for Students.
Bellcore.

SSP's PROMIS: Project Management Integrated System. Version: 4.1. May 1992. Compatible Hardware: IBM PC XT, PC AT, PS/2, 386 & 486 Based. Memory Required: 640k. Items Included: 90 day unlimited warranty, yearly maintenance plans, free technical support & updates for 1 year after purchase. Customer Support: 90 day unlimited warranty, yearly maintenance plans available.
  disk $3600.00.
Performs Resource Leveling, Complete Multi-Project Analysis Including Resource & Cost Roll-ups from Subnetwork Levels, Database Architecture, Data Interchange, Presentation Quality Reports & Graphics.
Cambridge Management Systems, Inc.

SST: The Seek Stopper. Version: 2.01. Compatible Hardware: IBM PC & compatibles. Operating System(s) Required: DOS 2.0 or higher. Memory Required: 256k; for 32Mb hard disk drives, 512k.
  $10.00 Shareware registration.
Shareware Disk Defragmenter & Packer. Not Copy Protected.
Alfred J. Heyman.

S2ASC: SuperSCRIPSIT to ASCII. 1989.
  PC/MS-DOS (384k). IBM PC & compatibles. $29.95.
Utility That Reads a SuperSCRIPSIT Document That Has Been Transferred to the PC & Creates an ASCII Version for Import by Any PC Word Processor. It Optionally Inserts Unique Place Markers While Removing Hidden Format Codes, Making Reformatting with PC Word Processor Much Easier Using Search Function.
Educational Micro Systems, Inc.

STAAD-III. Version: 21.0. Dec. 1995. Items Included: Manual, 120-day free maintenance. Customer Support: 1 yr. maintenance - 20% of the program price.
  MS-DOS, Windows 3.1, 95, NT (8Mb). $595.00 - $4000.00.
  UNIX (16Mb). Tape $5000.00.
An Integrated Software for Structural Analysis, Design & Drafting. Analysis Facilities Include Linear & Non-Linear 2D/3D Static/Dynamic/Seismic/P-Delta Analysis, Frame/Plate/Shell Elements & All Possible Loading & Support Conditions. Design Facilities Include Steel/Concrete/Timber/Aluminum Design per Current American & International Codes. May Be Utilized

TITLE INDEX

for Analyzing & Designing Practically All Kinds of Structures: Buildings, Bridges, Towers, Transportation, Industrial, & Various Utility Structures.
Research Engineers.

Stable Owners Option Module. *Items Included:* Manual, catalog, update card. *Customer Support:* Always free over the phone, disks replaced free for first 30 days, disks replaced for $10.00 after 30 days.
MS-DOS. IBM PC & Compatibles (512k). $14.95.
Commodore 64, 128. $14.95.
Amiga 500, 1000, 2000 (512k). $14.95.
Put Together Your Own Personal Stable of Claiming, Allowance & Stakes Horses. Hire Jockeys & Match Their Skills Against the Competition. Then Enter Your Steeds in the Races of Your Choice. Up to Four Human Players Can Participate at the Same Time Against Other Computer Opponents.
SportTime Computer Software.

StackSoft: Stacked Tolerance Analysis. 1995. *Items Included:* Full manual. *Customer Support:* Free telephone support - 90 days, 30-day warranty.
MS-DOS 3.2 or higher. 286 (584k). disk $599.95. *Nonstandard peripherals required:* CGA/EGA/VGA.
Handles the Tolerancing of One-, Two-, & Three-Dimensional Assemblies Involving Both Lineal & Angular Dimensioning. It Keeps the Dimensions & Tolerances Organized & Does All the Calculations, Reporting the Distributions of Tolerance. You Can Quickly See Which Parts or Manufacturing Processes Are Most (& Least) Influential.
Dynacomp, Inc.

Staff Scheduling. *Items Included:* Manuals, training exercises, quick reference guide.
IBM PC, XT, AT, & compatibles; PS/2. contact publisher for price.
Who Is to Be Working, When, & What Is Their Work Record.
Beechwood Software.

STAFFMASTER: Temporary Help. *Version:* 6.0. Aug. 1993. *Items Included:* Instruction manuals. *Customer Support:* First 90 days free, annually 15% of purchase price. Training customer site $800.00 per day plus expenses - training vendor office $500.00 per day.
MS-DOS, AIX, UNIX, VMS. Intel 486, IBM RS6000, DEC VAX (2Mb). disk $5800.00 (1-5 user) plus Progress. *Addl. software required:* Progress runtime. *Optimal configuration:* 486-50mhz 16Mb RAM, 1.44 Mb diskette, 525Mb QIC tape, 1.0 GB hard disk, 8 port MUX & printer. *Networks supported:* Lantastic, Novell, Powerfusion.
MS-DOS, AIX, UNIX, VMS. 486-50mhz (4Mb). disk $5800.00 (1-5 user) plus Progress. *Addl. software required:* Progress runtime. *Optimal configuration:* 486-50mhz 16Mb RAM, 1.44 Mb diskette, 5.25MB Qic tape, 1.0 GB hard disk, 8 port MUX & printer. *Networks supported:* Lantastic, Novell, Powerfusion.
Allows Managers to Record Customers & Employees, Record Contracts, Jobs, Work Orders, etc. Pay Can Be Dispatched Daily, Weekly, Biweekly, or Other Intervals. The System Automatically Bills Customers & Tracks Receivables, Includes Accounts Payable, General Ledger, & Staff Payroll. Provides for Skill Searching.
Automation Resources Corp.

Stage-Pro Module. May 1995. *Items Included:* Disks & manual. *Customer Support:* 90 day unlimited warranty.
Windows 3.1. 386 (8Mb). disk $1499.00. *Nonstandard peripherals required:* Microscope Auto Stage Controller. *Addl. software required:* Image-Pro Plus. *Networks supported:* No.
Media Cybernetics, L. P.

Stairs. *Version:* 2.0. *Compatible Hardware:* IBM PC. *Operating System(s) Required:* MS-DOS & AutoCAD. *Customer Support:* phone support. Contact publisher for price.
Automatically Creates Fabrication Drawings of Stair Stringers for PAN or Grating Tread Stairs.
Computer Detailing Corp.

Stamp Collector. D. Stein & E. Neiburger. 1981. *Compatible Hardware:* Apple II, IIc, IIe; Basis 6502; Franklin Ace; IBM PC, PC XT, PC AT. *Operating System(s) Required:* Apple DOS 3.3, MS-DOS 3.1. *Language(s):* BASIC (source code included). *Memory Required:* Apple 48k, IBM PC 256k.
disk $49.00 (ISBN 0-914555-18-9).
6 Programs in Which Collection Information Can Be Entered, Deleted, Changed, Searched, Sorted & Printed in Multiple Formats. Includes: Foreign Stamp List, Domestic Stamp List, Philatelist Meeting List, Sources List, Data Base & File Transfer.
Andent, Inc.

STAMPS. M. Mallon. Dec. 1985. *Operating System(s) Required:* MS-DOS, PC-DOS. *Memory Required:* 384k. *Items Included:* Complete database of U.S. stamps with prices, user's guide. *Customer Support:* Free tech support.
disk $95.00.
Enables Stamp Collectors to Catalog Their U.S. or United Nations Collection & Obtain Various Reports That Provide Personal Investment Information. A Data File with the Latest Prices for Nearly All Stamps Is Included with Annual Updates Available.
Compu-Quote.

Stamps. *Items Included:* Bound manual. *Customer Support:* Free hotline - no time limit; 30 day limited warranty; updates are $25/disk plus S&H.
MS-DOS. IBM & compatibles (256k). disk $49.95. *Nonstandard peripherals required:* Two drives; 80-column (or wider) printer is required for printing out reports.
Covers All U.S. Stamps Indexed by the Scott Catalogue Numbers. Virtually Every Issue Listed in Scott's National Album Is Included. Also Maintains a Want List, Complete with Prices.
Dynacomp, Inc.

Stamps World. *Compatible Hardware:* Apple Macintosh. *Memory Required:* 512k. *General Requirements:* ImageWriter or LaserWriter. *Items Included:* User's guide. *Customer Support:* Unlimited, free tech support.
3.5" disk $65.00.
Worldwide & Topical Stamp Inventory.
Compu-Quote.

Standard Coaxial Connection 3278-79. *Operating System(s) Required:* DOS 2.0. *Memory Required:* 96k.
disk $895.00.
Performs Full 3278/79 Emulation Enabling PCs to Access & Process 3270 Mainframe Computer Applications. Features Screen Print, Screen Save to Disk, & a Screen Control Application Program Interface. No Change to the Host or PC Software Is Required.
Novell, Inc.

Standard Pharmacy Software. *Version:* 110DA2. Mar. 1983. *Compatible Hardware:* Altos, IBM. *Operating System(s) Required:* CP/M-86, MP/M, MP/M-86, MS-DOS, Concurrent CP/M, Concurrent DOS. *Language(s):* CB-86. *Memory Required:* 512k. disk $995.00.
Designed to Satisfy the Needs of Small or Rural Pharmacies Serving up to 15 Third Party Plans & Dispensing an Average of under 75 Prescriptions per Day. Produces Labels, Receipts, Profiles, Daily & Narcotic Reports, Bilingual Label Instructions & Is Designed to Run in Menu-Format on Hard Disk Systems. Can Be Upgraded to the Expanded System or Universal System at a Later Time.
Dagar-Software Development Corp.

Standard Score Comparison: Learning Disabilities. *Version:* 2.0. Larry D. Evans. Sep. 1991. *Customer Support:* Technical assistance form (mail) is used for free support.
MS-DOS. IBM PC, XT, AT, 386, 486 & compatibles (512k). disk 5.25" disk $55.00 (ISBN 0-9633660-1-7).
3.5" disk $55.00 (ISBN 0-9633660-0-9).
Macintosh. Mac Plus, Classic, IIs, LC, SE & compatibles (1mb). 3.5" disk $55.00 (ISBN 0-9633660-3-3).
Apple II. Apple IIe/c/gs & compatibles (128k). 5.25" disk $55.00 (ISBN 0-9633660-2-5). *Optimal configuration:* 80 column video card.
Software & Manual for Analysis of IQ-Achievement Discrepancies That Are Characteristic of Students with Learning Disabilities.
W&L Publishing.

Standard Score Comparison: Mental Retardation. *Version:* 2.0. Larry D. Evans. Aug. 1992. *Customer Support:* Technical assistance form (mail) is used for free support.
MS-DOS. IBM PC, XT, AT, 386, 486 & compatibles (512k). 3.5" disk #contact publisher for price (ISBN 0-9633660-9-2).
MS-DOS. IBM PC, XT, AT, 386, 486 & compatibles (512k). 5.25" disk, contact publisher for price (ISBN 0-9633660-8-4).
Software & Manual for Analyses of IQ & Adaptive Behavior Scores to Determine Probabilities Student Scores Exceed Cut-Off for Mental Retardation.
W&L Publishing.

STANDING ORDERS. *Version:* 2.0. *Customer Support:* Toll free telephone support.
DOS 3.1 or higher. IBM PC & compatibles. disk $195.00.
This Solution Lets the Physician Write ONCE a Set of Orders for any Given Diagnosis, Then Use & Reuse That Document, as Written or Amended, Each Future Time a Set of Orders is Needed for the Same Diagnosis. With Each Encounter, the User Types the Name of the Patient for Whom the Orders are Being Written. User Scans a Vertical Window That Contains a Lightbar Menu of 1256 Diseases to Select Each Malady the Patient Suffers. As Each Illness Is Tagged, a Display Appears Showing all Orders Previously Used for that Disease. Line by Line, the User Keeps, Changes or Removes Each Order at Will. Thus the Content is Tailored Exactly to the Doctor's Specifications Just Before it is Printed as a Precise, Legible, Dated Document for the Patient's Chart. Additional Disease Names can be Added Easily if They are Needed. This Solution Gives Medicolegal Assurance That Nothing Has Been Overlooked & Acceptable Standards are Being Followed.
SRC Systems, Inc.

StandOut. *Compatible Hardware:* Apple Macintosh Plus. *Memory Required:* 1000k. 3.5" disk $295.00.
Presentation-Graphics Package for On-Screen Slide Shows with Transition Effects & Master Templates. Graphics & Chart-Making Features

Include Image Enlargement & Reduction & Undo Command; Bar, Line, Pie, Text & Scatter Charts; Pictograms; Multiple Charts on One Screen; & Free Positioning of Charts, Labels & Titles on Screen. Provides Unlimited Number of Typefaces & Font Sizes & 16.8 Million Colors of Which 256 Can Be Displayed Simultaneously. Outputs to PostScript Printer, Dot-Matrix Printer, Film Recorder, Plotter, Color Ink-Jet Printer & Thermal Printer. Imports TIFF, RIFF, EPSF, PICT I & II, MacPaint, MacWrite, Microsoft Word, WriteNow & ASCII File Formats. Also Features Style Sheets, Search & Replace, Glossaries, Template Library, Manual Kerning, Sorting by Title or Visually & Output of PICT Files.
Letraset USA.

STANFORM. *Version:* 2.0. *Compatible Hardware:* CP/M & MS-DOS based machines. *Operating System(s) Required:* CP/M, MS-DOS. *Language(s):* Quick Basic. *Items Included:* Manual, disk, warranty card. *Customer Support:* 18 month via telephone.
disk $79.00.
demo disk & manual $20.00.
Allows Variable Formatting for Printing on Standard & Non-Standard Forms.
Micro-Art Programmers.

STAP: Static Thermal Analysis Program. *Version:* 1.00. Jul. 1985. *Compatible Hardware:* AT&T 6300; DEC VT 180; HP-125; IBM PC, jr, PC XT, PC AT, & compatibles; Macintosh 512K or higher; Tandy 1000, 1200, 2000; TI Professional; Xerox 820, 820-II, 860; Apple Macintosh. *Operating System(s) Required:* PC-DOS/MS-DOS. *Memory Required:* 256k, Macintosh 512k.
$195.00.
General Purpose Two-Dimensional Steady State Heat Transfer Program with Particular Emphasis on the Analysis of Heatsinks in the Electronic Packaging Fields. After Entering the Heatsink Properties & Heat Input Characteristics, the Steady State Temperatures at All Nodes Are Calculated, Displayed & Saved to a Disk File. Designed for the Electrical Engineer Who Is Designing High Power Electronic Circuits; However, It Is a Fully Functional Two-Dimensional Thermal Analysis Program & Can Be Used to Solve Any 2-D Thermal Conduction Problem.
BV Engineering.

The Star Child. Feb. 1995. *Items Included:* CD-ROM booklet. *Customer Support:* Free technical support via phone as of release date.
MPC/Windows. 386.25 or higher IBM compatible (4Mb). CD-ROM disk $29.95 (ISBN 1-885784-11-2, Order no.: 1158). *Optimal configuration:* MPC CD-ROM player, S-VGA graphics card (640x480x256 colors) with compatible monitor, MPC compliant sound card, mouse, Windows 3.1.
Oscar Wilde's Story about a Baby Who Falls from the Sky & Is Discovered by a Woodcutter Is Even More Powerful As a Multimedia Storybook. Explore a Young Man's Search for Redemption As He Learns the Value of Being Human & Forgiving. Gain Important Insights into Human Nature. The Lessons Are Timeless & Moving.
Technology Dynamics Corp.

Star Con. *Compatible Hardware:* IBM; Macintosh. *Memory Required:* IBM 128k, Macintosh 512k.
disk $19.95.
Computer Board Game. Conquer All 20 Planets.
Dynacomp, Inc.

Star Control. Jul. 1990. *Items Included:* Catalog, copy protection device, manual, proof of purchase card. *Customer Support:* Technical support 408-296-8400, 90 day limited warranty.
IBM PC, XT, AT, & compatibles, Tandy 1000 series, 3000, 4000. $49.95. *Optimal configuration:* Hard drive, graphics card, & sound board.
Commodore C64/C128/1541/1541L/1571. $39.95. *Optimal configuration:* Hard drive, graphics card, & sound boards.
Amiga-Kickstart 1.2 or 1.3 (1Mb). Amiga 500, 1000, 2000, 2500, 3000. $49.95. *Optimal configuration:* Hard drive, graphics card, & sound boards.
Join Forces with the Alliance of Free Stars to Defend the Galaxy Against the Conquesting Armies of the Ur-Quan (Seven Alien Races Welded to Form the "Evil Empire"). Captains of Seven Fantastic Star-Fleets Await Your Orders for Battle.
Accolade, Inc.

Star Empire. *Compatible Hardware:* IBM PC, Commodore 64/128.
IBM PC. disk $29.95 (Order no.: 01004).
Commodore 64/128. disk $24.95 (Order no.: 05004).
An Imaginative, Action-Packed Graphic Interactive Fantasy Adventure Set in a Space Odyssey Where You Are the Space Pilot in an Exciting Trip Through Outer Space.
First Row Software Publishing.

Star Hawks: Earth Invasion, Spectre VR, Magnaflux Runner. ThreeDI Productions Staff & Velocity Development Group Staff. Aug. 1995. *Items Included:* Set up instruction sheet. *Customer Support:* (503) 639-6863.
DOS 2.1. IBM PC (640k). $14.95 Spectre VR (ISBN 1-887783-08-3, Order no.: 5300-4005). *Optimal configuration:* IBM PC 386 or higher, 640k RAM, DOS 2.1 or higher, VGA. Supports but does not require Soundblaster, AdLib, Joystick or mouse.
Windows 3.1 or higher, DOS 5.0. IBM PC. $14.95 Earth Invasion (Order no.: 5300-4005). *Optimal configuration:* IBM PC, Windows 3.1 or higher, DOS 5.0 or higher, 4Mb hard disk, joystick, mouse or keyboard, VGA or SVGA, Soundblaster, AdLib or Pro Audio Spectrum compatible.
Windows 3.1, DOS 5.0. IBM PC. $14.95 Magnaflux Runner (Order no.: 5300-4005). *Optimal configuration:* Windows 3.1 or higher, DOS 5.0, 3Mb hard disk, joystick, keyboard or mouse, VGA or higher, Soundblaster or Windows compatible sound card.
A Game Compilation of Space Games. The Game Player Battles Against Aliens from Other Planets.
Entertainment Technology.

Star Raiders. *Compatible Hardware:* Atari XL/XE, ST.
ST. 3.5" disk $29.95 (Order no.: DS5019).
XL/XE. ROM cartridge $6.95 (Order no.: CXL4011).
Atari Corp.

Star Raiders II. *Compatible Hardware:* Atari XL/XE.
disk $19.95 (Order no.: DX5084).
Atari Corp.

Star Saphire LISP. *Version:* 3.4. 1987. *Compatible Hardware:* IBM PC XT & BIOS compatibles, PC AT. *Language(s):* C (source code included). *General Requirements:* Hard disk, 1-8Mb RAM. *Items Included:* 100 pg. documentation, 0.5Mb online hypertext reference, emacs editor & LISP code examples, reference card. *Customer Support:* Free support via phone, fax or correspondence.
MS-DOS, Windows. disk $99.95. *Nonstandard peripherals required:* Extended memory option requires DOS 3.0 or higher & installed extended memory. Supports Microsoft compatible mouse.
An Implementation of the Common LISP Programming Language for the IBM PC & Compatibles. It Supports up to 8Mb Workspaces Using Either Extended or Virtual Memory. It Includes an Interpreter & a Compiler for a Large Subset of Common LISP.
Sapiens Software Corp.

Star Sentry. *Compatible Hardware:* Atari 400, 800. *Memory Required:* 24k.
contact publisher for price.
A.N.A.L.O.G., Inc.

Star Ship. 1996. *Customer Support:* Free telephone & BBS technical support; documentation.
MS-DOS. IBM/PC/XT/AT & compatibles. single-user basic $495.00, 695.00 multi-user or network basic, 995.00 single user enhanced, 1295.00 multi-user or network enhanced. *Networks supported:* Novell, Lantastic, Banyan VINES; all NETBIOS compatible.
This is a comprehensive shipping program for microcomputers. The system can be interfaced with the INMASS/MRP Sales Order Entry System. Calculates zones, rates & other charges automatically.
INMASS/MRP.

Star*Sprite. *Version:* 1.02. Apr. 1995. *Items Included:* Manual with boxed slipcover & free Glyphs desk accessory. *Customer Support:* Free unlimited phone support.
System 7 or higher. Macintosh (4Mb). 3.5" disk $129.50.
Dynamic Charting Tool with Extraordinary Full-Color Capabilities. Spin Charts Forward or Backward in Time at Actual or Accelerated Speeds. Halt Chart Motion at Any Instant in Time & Save for Future Use. Display & Print Charts in Full Color. Use Bi-Wheel Feature for Advanced Chart Analysis. Turn Any Chart into a Full Color Action Screen Saver.
Time Cycles Research.

Star Track. (Star Track Ser.). Robert S. Hand & Steve Hines. 1984. *Compatible Hardware:* Apple II with Applesoft, Apple II+, IIe, IIc, III. *Operating System(s) Required:* Apple DOS. *Language(s):* Applesoft BASIC (source code included). *Memory Required:* 48k. *General Requirements:* Printer. *Items Included:* Manual. *Customer Support:* Free phone support.
disk $150.00 (ISBN 0-913637-03-3).
Computes Natal, Progressed, Composite, Synastry & Solar/Lunar Return Horoscopes; Includes On-Screen Chart Module.
Astrolabe, Inc.

Star Track Extension Package (Midpoint Sort, Harmonics, Astro-Mapping, Solar Arc List). *Compatible Hardware:* Apple II with Applesoft, Apple II+, IIc, IIe, III. *Operating System(s) Required:* Apple DOS. *Language(s):* BASIC (source code included). *Memory Required:* 48k. *General Requirements:* Printer; Star Track or Natal Horoscope. *Customer Support:* Free phone support.
disk $50.00 (ISBN 0-87199-046-6).
Does a Variety of Supplemental Astrology Calculations.
Astrolabe, Inc.

Star Trek Classic AudioClips. *Version:* 1.7. Mar. 1995. *Items Included:* Registration card, certificate of authenticity, Quick installation reference card. *Customer Support:* Phone technical support.
DOS 5.0, Windows 3.1. PC 286 or higher (2Mb). disk $14.95 (ISBN 1-57303-018-X). *Nonstandard peripherals required:* Sound card recommended. *Optimal configuration:* 286 or

TITLE INDEX

higher with 4Mb RAM, DOS 5.0 or later, Windows 3.1 or later, 4-7Mb HD space available, sound card.
AudioClips Are Exclusively Licensed, High Quality Sound Files Consisting of Classic Sound Effects, Dialogue & Music from Original TV Shows & Movies. Also Included Is the Personal Desktop Audio Utility Which Allows the User to Attach AudioClips to Various Windows Events.
Sound Source Interactive.

Star Trek Motion Pictures AudioClips. *Version:* 1.7. Dec. 1994. *Items Included:* Manual, registration card, sound list. *Customer Support:* Phone technical support.
DOS 5.0, Windows 3.1. PC 286 or higher (2Mb). disk $14.95 (ISBN 1-57303-017-1). *Nonstandard peripherals required:* Sound card recommended. *Optimal configuration:* 286 or higher with 4Mb RAM, DOS 5.0 or later, Windows 3.1 or later, 4-7Mb HD space available, sound card.
AudioClips Are Exclusively Licensed, High Quality Sound Files Consisting of Classic Sound Effects, Dialogue & Music from Original TV Shows & Movies. Also Included Is the 'Whoop It Up' Audio Utility, Which Allows the User to Attach AudioClips to Various Windows Events.
Sound Source Interactive.

Star Trek: The Kobayashi Alternative.
MicroMosaics Productions, Inc. & Diane Duane. Oct. 1985. *Compatible Hardware:* Apple II+, IIe, IIc, Macintosh 512k, Macintosh Plus; Commodore; IBM PC, PCjr, PC XT, PC AT. *Operating System(s) Required:* Apple DOS 3.3 for Apple, PC-DOS 2.0 or higher for IBM. *Memory Required:* Apple II 64k, IBM 128k, Macintosh 512k.
disk $39.95 ea.
Interactive Text Adventure Based on the Characters & Situations True to the Star Trek Traditions. This New Cadet Performance Evaluation Exam Takes the Enterprise on a Mission to Recover an Inexplicably Missing Federation Ship under the Temporary Command of Lieutenant Sulu. Players Take on the Role of Captain James T. Kirk & Are Challenged to Solve a Mystery While the Fate of the Galaxy Hangs in the Balance.
Brady Computer Bks.

Star Trek: The Promethean Prophecy. TRANS Fiction Systems Corp. Oct. 1986. *Compatible Hardware:* Apple II+, IIe, IIc; Commodore 64, 128; IBM PC & compatibles, PCjr, PC XT, PC AT; AT&T; Compaq; Epson; Leading Edge; Tandy. *Operating System(s) Required:* PC-DOS 2.0 or higher for IBM; MS-DOS 2.11 or higher for PC compatibles. *Memory Required:* Apple 64k, IBM & compatibles 128k.
Apple, Commodore. disk $33.00, incl. manual.
IBM. disk $40.00.
Text Adventure Where You Play Captain Kirk. Your Enterprise Has Come under Attack & As a Result Your Entire Food Supply Is Contaminated. It Is up to You to Guide Your Crew Through the Strange Culture You Find As You Try to Find Food Before You All Starve.
Brady Computer Bks.

Star Trek: The Rebel Universe.
IBM PC (256k) under PC-DOS 2.0 with graphics display. $49.95.
Space Adventure. The Plot Uses the Original TV Series Characters.
Brady Computer Bks.

Star Wars. *Compatible Hardware:* Commodore Amiga.
3.5" disk $39.95.
Arcade Adventure Based on the Film.
Broderbund Software, Inc.

Star Wars Trilogy: Limited Edition CD-ROM. *Version:* 1.5. Jun. 1995. *Items Included:* Manual, registration card, certificate of authenticity. *Customer Support:* Technical support available on a phone-in (toll call).
Macintosh 6.0.7 or later; IBM PC compatible, Windows 3.1. Macintosh, LC or higher (4Mb); IBM, 386DX-25 or higher (4Mb). CD-ROM disk $29.95 (ISBN 1-57303-021-X). *Nonstandard peripherals required:* CD-ROM drive.
Features Digital Audio & Video Clips for Macintosh & IBM-Compatible Computers. The Clips Can Be Assigned to System Events, Allowing the User to Enjoy Sounds & Scenes from Star Wars, The Empire Strikes Back, & Return of the Jedi As They Perform Everyday Computer Tasks.
Sound Source Interactive.

Starbase 3.2. *Compatible Hardware:* Apple II with Applesoft; Macintosh; IBM PC. *Memory Required:* 48K, IBM 128k, Macintosh 512k.
disk $19.95.
Enhanced Classic Space Simulation.
Dynacomp, Inc.

Starcross. Dave Lebling. 1982. *Compatible Hardware:* Apple II, Macintosh; Atari XL/XE, ST; Commodore 64, Amiga; IBM PC, PCjr; Kaypro; TRS-80 Model I, Model III. *Operating System(s) Required:* MS-DOS, CP/M.
disk $14.95.
Launches You Headlong into the Year 2186 & the Depths of Space, Where You Are Destined to Rendezvous with a Gargantuan Starship from the Outer Fringes of the Galaxy. Upon Docking with the Strange Craft, You Must Succeed in Gaining Entry to the Mysterious Interior. Once Within, You Will Explore a Startling, Complex, & Engaging World Peopled with the Strangest Beings. But the Great Starship Serves a Far Larger Purpose Than Mere Cultural Exchange. It Conveys a Challenge That Was Issued Eons Ago, from Light Years Away - & Only You Can Meet It.
Activision, Inc.

Starcross. Infocom. *Compatible Hardware:* HP 150 Touchscreen, HP 110 Portable.
3.5" disk $49.95 (Order no.: 92243DA).
Launches You Headlong into the Year 2186 & the Depths of Space, Where You Are Destined to Rendezvous with a Gargantuan Starship from the Outer Fringes of the Galaxy. Upon Docking with the Strange Craft, You Must Succeed in Gaining Entry to Its Mysterious Interior. Once Within, You Will Explore a Startling, Complex, & Engaging World Peopled with the Strangest Beings. But the Great Starship Serves a Far Larger Purpose Than Mere Cultural Exchange. It Conveys a Challenge That Was Issued Eons Ago, from Light Years Away - & Only You Can Meet It.
Hewlett-Packard Co.

Stardyne. *Version:* 4.4. Sep. 1995. *Items Included:* Manual, 120-day free maintenance. *Customer Support:* 1 yr. maintenance - 20% of the program price.
Windows/NT (12Mb). $2995.00 - $3995.00.
UNIX (32Mb). $11,995.00 Tape.
A Powerful General Purpose Computer Aided Engineering Program That Performs Linear & Non-Linear, Static & Dynamic Analysis of Structures Using the Finite Element Analysis (FEA) Method. Facilities Are Included for Linear Static Analysis, Substructures, Non-Linear Foundation, P-Delta, Eigensolution & Buckling, Linear Dynamic Response with Missing Mass Correction, Non-Linear Statics, Non-Linear Time History Response, Fatigue for High-Cycle Loading, & Heat Transfer (Non-Linear) Time History.
Research Engineers.

THE STARPROOF BRIDGE

Starflight. Binary Systems. *Compatible Hardware:* IBM PC and compatibles.
disk $49.95.
Spaceship Simulation That Gives You the Opportunity to Explore New Worlds & New Civilizations. Features: a Galaxy of over 270 Unique Star Systems & 800 Planets to Discover; 7 Alien Civilizations, Languages, & Cultures; Role-Play 6 Starship Officers, All with Varying Degrees of Expertise; Animated Graphics Such As Rotating Planets & Landing Sequences; Full-Color Starmap & Security Coder.
Electronic Arts.

Starhawks II: Cadillacs & Dinosaurs; Buried in Time; Loadstar. General Motors Corp. et al. Feb. 1996. *Customer Support:* Area code telephone number (503) 639-6863 8AM-7PM PST M-F.
DOS 5.0 or higher (Cadillacs & Loadstar); Windows 95 or 3.1 (Buried in Time). 486 (4Mb) (Cadillacs & Loadstar); 486 (8mb, 10Mb HD) (Buried in Time). CD-ROM disk $14.95 (ISBN 1-887783-57-1, Order no.: 5300-4009). *Addl. software required:* Double-speed CD-ROM drive, IBM PC 486 or higher, sound blaster, Ad Lib, VGA, keyboard, joystick or mouse (Cadillacs); Speakers, SVGA, sound card (Buried in Time & Loadstar).
Networks supported: Yes.
A Game Compilation of Cadillacs & Dinosaurs, Buried in Time, & Loadstar Which Are Games of the Past & the Future.
Entertainment Technology.

Starhawks: Magnuflux Runner, Earth Invasion, Spectre VR. Three DI Productions & Velocity Development Group. Jan. 1996. *Items Included:* Set-up instruction sheet. *Customer Support:* 310-403-0043.
Spectre VR: DOS 2.1; Earth Invasion & Magnaflux: Win 3.1 or higher, DOS 5.0. IBM PC. disk $14.95 (ISBN 1-887783-23-7, Order no.: 5200-3005). *Optimal configuration:* IBM PC, Spectre VR: 386 or higher, 640k RAM, DOS 2.1 or higher, VGA. Supports but does not require Soundblaster, Adlib, joystick or mouse; Earth Invasion: Win 3.1 or higher, DOS 5.0 or higher, 4Mb HD, joystick, mouse, or keyboard, VGA/SVGA, Soundblaster, Adlib or Pro Audio Spectrum compatible; Magnaflux: Win 3.1 or higher, DOS 5.0, 3Mb HD, joystick, keyboard or mouse, VGA or higher, Soundblaster or Windows compatible soundcard.
A Game Compilation of Earth Invasion, Magnuflux Runner & Spectre VR Which Are "Space" Games. The Game Player Battles Against Aliens from Other Planets.
Entertainment Technology.

StarIndex. MicroPro International Corp. *Operating System(s) Required:* MS-DOS CP/M-86, Concurrent CP/M. *Memory Required:* 64k. *General Requirements:* Printer, Winchester hard disk.
$195.00 (Order no.: TI P/N 2311501-0001 SY P/N T134-045).
Texas Instruments, Personal Productivit.

The StarProof Bridge. Arnold Schaeffer. *Compatible Hardware:* IBM PC, PCjr, PC XT, PC AT, Portable PC, 3270 PC with IBM Display. *Operating System(s) Required:* DOS 2.00, 2.10, 3.00, 3.10. *Memory Required:* 128k.
disk $14.95 (Order no.: 6276536).
Takes a WordStar Document & Converts It to an ASCII Format So WORD PROOF Can Be Used to "Spell Check" the Document. After the Corrections Are Made, the Document Is Converted Back to the WordStar Format.
Personally Developed Software, Inc.

955

Starship Dogfight. *Compatible Hardware:* TRS-80 Model I, Model III, Model 4 with Level II BASIC. *Memory Required:* cassette 16k, disk 32k.
disk $23.95.
cassette $19.95.
Space Arcade Game.
Dynacomp, Inc.

Starship Landing Party Adventure. *Compatible Hardware:* Apple II with Applesoft; IBM. *Operating System(s) Required:* DOS 3.2, 3.3 for Apple. *Memory Required:* Apple 48, IBM 128k.
disk $19.95.
Find Energy Crystals on an Abandoned Mining Planet Before Ship's Power Gives Out.
Dynacomp, Inc.

Start a Business. *Version:* 1.1. Nov. 1993. *Customer Support:* Free technical support over phone; limited warranty.
DOS 3.1 or higher. IBM & compatibles (500k). Contact publisher for price (ISBN 1-55571-324-6, Order no.: SABZSS/A31). *Nonstandard peripherals required:* Hard disk with 3Mb free space. *Optimal configuration:* Printer beneficial.
Standalone Program for Calculating Profit/Loss & Cash Flow Projections for up to 10 Years. Maintains up to 5 Companies at One Time with 5 Budgets for Each Company. No Accounting Experience Is Necessary to Estimate the Potential of Your Business.
Oasis Pr., The.

Start to Sell: Find & Qualify Customers to Build Your Buisness. Sep. 1995. *Customer Support:* Toll-free telephone number for technical support, 90 days warranty for defects in materials & workmanship.
Macintosh System 7.0. Macintosh with 68040 processor (5Mb). CD-ROM disk $49.95 (ISBN 1-886806-09-8). *Nonstandard peripherals required:* Double speed CD-ROM drive. *Addl. software required:* QuickTime (included on CD-ROM disc).
Microsoft Windows 3.1. PC compatible; 486/33MHz (runs slow on 386/25MHz) (8Mb). *Nonstandard peripherals required:* 256 color display card (640x480); double speed CD-ROM drive. *Addl. software required:* QuickTime for Windows (included on CD-ROM disc).
Helps User Focus Your Time & Energy on Getting in Front of the People Who Will Best Help You Develop Your Business. You'll Learn to Identify & Qualify Prospects, Prioritize Your Selling Activities, Overcome Call Reluctance, & Establish & Track Sales Objectives.
Wilson Learning Corp.

Start to Sell Plus Sell to Needs: Two CD-ROMs to Improve Your Sales I. Q. Oct. 1995. *Items Included:* Two CD-ROMs in package: Start to Sell 1-886806-09-8; Sell to Needs 1-886806-04-7. *Customer Support:* Toll-free telephone number for technical support, 90 days warranty for defects in materials & workmanship.
Macintosh System 7.0. Macintosh with 68040 processor (5Mb). CD-ROM disk $49.95 (ISBN 1-886806-10-1). *Nonstandard peripherals required:* Double speed CD-ROM drive. *Addl. software required:* QuickTime (included on CD-ROM disc).
Microsoft Windows 3.1. PC compatible; 486/33MHz (runs slow on 386/25MHz) (8Mb). *Nonstandard peripherals required:* 256 color display card (640x480); double speed CD-ROM drive. *Addl. software required:* QuickTime for Windows (included on CD-ROM disc).
Start to Sell Helps You Focus Your Time & Energy on Getting in Front of the Right People. Sell to Needs Helps You Understand & Solve Customer Problems - to Make the Sale Once You Have a Qualified Prospect.
Wilson Learning Corp.

Starware Sky Mapper. *Items Included:* Bound manual. *Customer Support:* Free hotline - no time limit; 30 day limited warranty; updates are $5/disk plus S&H.
MS-DOS 2.1 or higher. IBM & compatibles (364k). disk $49.95. *Nonstandard peripherals required:* Requires an EGA (or compatible) graphics card. A mouse, math coprocessor, & printer are supported, but not necessary.
Terrestrial Sky Mapper Displays the Sky As Seen from Any Point on Earth & Calculates the Most Accurate Stellar Positions Possible for Any Time Within 5 Million Years of the Present. It Draws on a 2000-Star Database, Using the Newly Updated, Internationally Accepted Positions & Proper Motions. Every Star Visible to the Unaided Eye Is Shown (& More). The Positions of All the Planets (Including Pluto) Are Calculated. The Phases of the Moon Are Accurately Shown. The Position of Any Star, Any Planet, the Sun, or the Moon Can Be Displayed at Any Time. They May Also Be Found on the Sky Map by Just Typing in the Name. All 88 Constellations Are Shown, with Optional Line Drawings. Each May Be Stepped (by Pressing a Key) in 1000 Year Increments to See Changes over Time. Screen Displays May Be Saved to Disk for Later Printing or Display.
Dynacomp, Inc.

Starx. *Version:* 3.6. *Compatible Hardware:* All UNIX Platforms. *Operating System(s) Required:* All UNIX. *General Requirements:* Dot matrix printer. *Items Included:* Source.
3.5" disk $4995.00.
Pharmacy Package Designed to Serve Both Large Chains & Small Independent Pharmacies. User-Set Parameters Adjust the Size of the System to Any Size Store. It Is a Fully Functional Multiuser System with a High-Speed, Self-Correctable Database. Electronic Mail Is Written in the C Language & Runs Under UNIX/XENIX. Application Features Include: Third-Party Formulary Validation, Automatic Batch Refilling, Workman's Compensation Claims Processing, All State & Federal Regulation, Multiple Label Formats, Full-Screen Editing of RXs, Complete Detailed Patient Profiles, Drug Recall Reporting, a Full Set of Management Reports, Nursing Home Interface, Accounts Receivable Interface, Generic Pricing & Xref, HMO & Recap Interface, Universal Interface for Updates, Drug Interactions & Warnings, Multistore Configurations, Modern Controlled Updates, Multilingual Sig File, POS Interface, Alpha Key Access, Automatic Purge Control & Tape-to-Tape Claims Processing.
Sans Souci Consulting.

Stat 1 - A Statistical Tool Box. *Version:* 4. Jerry M. Brennan & Lawrence H. Nitz. Aug. 1989. *Items Included:* 200 page tutorial manual, statistical decision tree to help solve statistical tests appropriate for particular applications, glossary & reference trees. *Customer Support:* Free telephone support, training seminars at customer's site at cost.
PC-DOS (384k). PC, XT, AT, PS/2, & compatibles. $129.95 for Professional Version; $29.95 Student Version; $500.00 for laboratory site license. *Optimal configuration:* 640 RAM, hard disk or 2 floppies.
A Menu-Driven Statistical Package Designed for New Statistical/Analysts & Student Users. Comprehensive Menus Present Data Management Steps, Statistical Procedures & Variable Lists to Speed Work & Minimize Error. The Package Contains a Full Help System & Procedures for Transformations, Descriptive Statistics, Correlations, Cross Tabulations, Difference Costs, Regression, Factor Analysis & Smallest Space Analysis.
Sugar Mill Software Corp.

STAT-POWER. *Version:* 2.0. James L. Bavry. 1993. *Items Included:* Manual. *Customer Support:* Free technical support, 90 day limited warranty.
MS-DOS. IBM & compatibles. 3.5" disk $180.00, incl. manual (ISBN 1-56321-126-2). 214p. manual $30.00 (ISBN 1-56321-124-6).
Comprehensive, Menu-Driven Program for Statistical Power Analysis. Integrates the Procedures Necessary for Efficient Design of Data Analysis into One Simple System. Offers Scientific Analysts the Ease & Flexibility That Spreadsheet Programs Have Long Offered Financial Analysts.
Lawrence Erlbaum Assocs., Software & Alternate Media, Inc.

State Data on Demand. Aug. 1992. *Items Included:* Citations of all data sources of information to allow user to further pursue research of a particular topic. *Customer Support:* Includes free update of information in database in approximately six months.
Macintosh. 3.5" disk $149.95 (ISBN 1-880077-02-7). *Addl. software required:* Excel.
IBM PC & compatibles. disk $149.95 (ISBN 1-880077-03-5). *Addl. software required:* Lotus 1-2-3.
Contains over 700 Data Items Concerning the Fifty States. Demographics, Economics, Education, Health & Taxes Are a Few of the Topics Addressed. Each Section Contains Data for All Fifty States As Well As National Averages or Totals Where Applicable.
U.S. Data on Demand, Inc.

STATE 84. *Compatible Hardware:* IBM PC, TRS-80 Model II, Model 12, Model 16; Tandy 2000. *Operating System(s) Required:* PC-DOS, TRSDOS. *Language(s):* BASIC. *Memory Required:* 64k.
contact publisher for price.
Prepares Main State Income Tax Forms & Their Most Important Schedules. Forms Are Printed on Continuous Forms & Lined Paper & Are Based on a Model Approved by the IRS.
Computer Technical Services of New Jersey.

State Trends on Demand. Aug. 1992. *Items Included:* Includes all source citations for information contained on diskette for further research.
Macintosh. 3.5" disk $169.95 (ISBN 1-880077-04-3). *Addl. software required:* Excel.
IBM PC & compatible. disk $169.95 (ISBN 1-880077-05-1). *Addl. software required:* Lotus 1-2-3, Excel.
Contains over 150 Spreadsheets Containing over a Decade of Data for the Fifty States. Sections Cover Demographics, Economics, State Government, Taxes, Spending, Education, Health, Welfare & Transportation. This Allows User to See at a Glance, the State Trends in Any Given Area.
U.S. Data on Demand, Inc.

State Variables. *Compatible Hardware:* IBM. *Memory Required:* 128k.
disk $49.95.
Solves Systems of Ordinary Differential Equations (up to 10) Which Include a Forcing Function.
Dynacomp, Inc.

Statement Analysis. *Compatible Hardware:* TI 99/4A. *Operating System(s) Required:* DX-10. *Language(s):* Extended BASIC. *Memory Required:* 48k.
cassette $34.95.
Menu-Driven Financial Analysis Program Which Can Store up to 16 Financial Statements. Performs Several Types of Credit Analysis. 7 Trend Curves Can Be Found from up to 26 Financial Ratios & Statistics. Displays Any Financial Statement in "Common-Size" Format.
Eastbench Software Products.

TITLE INDEX

Statement Balancer.
disk $10.00 (Order no.: D8SB).
Helps Balance Checkbook & Does Not Save Data on Disk, but Requests Necessary Minimum Input As Needed.
The Alternate Source.

Statement Writer. *Compatible Hardware:* TRS-80 Color Computer. *Memory Required:* 32k.
cassette $34.95.
Supplements the Capabilities of the Disk Double Entry (DDE) Program. Allows the User to Select Certain DDE Accounts for Special Treatment, Add Supplemental Information for These Accounts, & Format the Ledgers for These Accounts to Satisfy Special Needs. Takes Receivable Accounts, Adds Full Customer Name & Address, & Produces Statements Suitable for Billing. Also Produces Summary Reports for Selected Accounts to Provide Overall Visibility of Account Status & Activity Designed & Documented to Allow Users Familiar with BASIC to Readily Change Formats to Accommodate Their Own Special Needs & to Provide Special Treatment for Accounts Other Than Receivables.
Custom Software Engineering, Inc.

Statgraphics Plus. *Version:* 7. *Customer Support:* 90 day free support.
DOS 3.3 or higher. IBM 386/486 & compatibles (4Mb). disk $1595.00.
Menu-Based Statistical Graphics System Optimized for 386/486 Computers. Fully Integrates Uniquely Interactive, Presentation Quality Graphics with a Wide Range of Statistical Procedures Including Descriptive Statistics, Regression, ANOVA, Multivariate Methods, Quality Control, Experimental Design, Time Series Analysis, & Nonparametric Methods. It Contains all of the Advanced Features Contained in STATGRAPHICS While Offering Substantially Increased Speed & Data Set Size.
Manugistics, Inc.

STATGRAPHICS Plus for Windows. Statistical Graphics Corp. Staff. Apr. 1994. *Items Included:* User manual. *Customer Support:* 90-day free support, telephone, fax, BBS, newsletter. Extended support plans available.
Windows 3.1 or higher. IBM 386, 486, or Pentium-based systems (4Mb). List price: $649.00 base system, $399.00 for each module. *Networks supported:* Banyan Vines, LANtastic, Novell, Netware, PCNet, Token-Ring.
A Powerful Statistical Analysis Tool That Combines a Broad Range of Procedures with Interactive Graphics. The Base System Gives Users All of the Day-to-Day Statistical Tools They Need: Regressions; ANOVA; Exploratory Data Analysis; Crosstabulation; & More. Additional Functionality Is Available in Optional Modules - Quality Control, Experimental Design, Time Series, & Multivariate Statistics.
Manugistics, Inc.

Statgraphics: Statistical Graphics System.
Version: 7. Nov. 1993. *Compatible Hardware:* IBM PC, PC AT, PC XT. *Operating System(s) Required:* MS-DOS, PC-DOS. *Memory Required:* 640k. *Customer Support:* 90 day free support, telephone, fax, BBS, newsletter.
disk $995.00 (ISBN 0-926683-06-3, Order no.: P121).
Statistical Graphics System Containing over 250 Procedures, Including Analysis of Variance, Regression Analysis, Estimation, Multivariate Techniques, Nonparametric Methods, Quality Control Procedures, & Forecasting & Time Series Analysis.
Manugistics, Inc.

Static Regain Duct Sizing: Duct. *Version:* 3.0. William H. Zaggle. Jan. 1988. *Compatible Hardware:* IBM PC & compatibles. *Operating System(s) Required:* PC-DOS/MS-DOS. *Language(s):* CB-80. *Memory Required:* CP/M 64k, MS-DOS 256k. *General Requirements:* 2 disk drives, printer.
Static Repair. disk $495.00.
Static repair. 8" disk $495.00.
Static repair. 3.5" disk $495.00.
demo disk $38.00.
Calculates Optimal Round & Rectangular Duct Sizes Using Either the Static Regain, Equal Friction, or Constant Velocity Method. Handles Duct System with As Many As 200 Trunks & Runouts. Trunks & Runouts Can Be Defined As Any Common Duct Material with Any Roughness Factor Desired. Height & Width Constraints on Trunk Sizes May Also Be Specified to Accommodate Special Space Considerations. Uses Standard Friction Loss Coefficients for All the Common Types of Fittings (Elbow, Tees, & Weyes) As Listed in ASHRAE Handbook of Fundamentals. Also Allows User Defined Friction Loss Coefficients So That Any Fitting, Standard or Not, Can Be Defined to the Program. Five Types of Reports Are Provided: Master Input Data, Trunk Output Data, Runout Output Data, Sheet Metal & Duct Fitting Bill of Materials with Cost & a Duct System Summary.
Elite Software Development, Inc.

Statics Problems Solved in BASIC. 1990. *Items Included:* Spiral manual contains theory, sample runs, program listings in BASIC. *Customer Support:* Free phone, on-site seminars.
MS-DOS. IBM (128k). disk $35.00. *Addl. software required:* BASIC.
Macintosh. Any Macintosh. 3.5" disk $35.00. *Addl. software required:* BASIC.
This Is a Book/Disk Package of 31 Programs That Solve Problems Encountered in a Course in Statics. Includes 2D & 3D Vectors, Force Resultants, Moment Resultants, Beams, Trusses, Ladders, Sliding Blocks, Centroids, Moments of Inertia.
Kern International, Inc.

Station 5. (Series A).
All Apple IIs. disk $5.00. *Optimal configuration:* Apple II, joystick optional; can be played on keyboard as well.
This Game Is Educational As Well As Fun! - Great for Problem Solving! The Energy Crisis on Earth Was Solved by Building Five Nuclear-Powered Generators in a Safe Spot - on the Moon. But Now There's Another Crisis: Four of the Reactors Have Been Destroyed, & the Fifth Station Has Been Crippled. It's up to You to Fix Station 5 & Feed Power to Earth. You've Got to Get the Reactor Going, Build Three New Transmitters, Beam Yourself to the Relay Station, & Repair the Dish Antennas.
Word Assocs., Inc.

Stationfall. Steve Meretzky. Jun. 1987. *Compatible Hardware:* Apple II, II+, IIe, IIc, Macintosh; Atari XL/XE, ST; Commodore 64, 128, Amiga; DEC Rainbow; IBM PC & compatibles; TI Professional. *Memory Required:* 48k.
disk $39.95.
This Adventure Begins Five Years after PLANETFALL. Since Then, Nothing of Interest Has Happened in the Stellar Patrol. Today's Assignment: Travel to a Nearby Space Station to Pick up a Supply of Trivial Forms. The Companion for Your Journey Is Your Old Buddy, Floyd. Arriving at the Space Station, You Find It Strangely Deserted. A Spooky Alien Ship Rests in a Docking Bay. A Commander's Log Describes the Mysterious Breakdown of Machinery. An Ostrich & an Arcturian Balloon Creature Are

STATISTICA - QC FOR WINDOWS:

Found, Abandoned but in Perfect Health. Luckily, Floyd Is on Hand to Help You Identify & Overcome the Dangerous Forces at Work. But Then Even He Begins Acting Oddly...
Activision, Inc.

STATISTICA/DOS. *Version:* 3.1. May 1992. *Customer Support:* Technical support.
DOS/VSE. PC's AT & higher (640k). disk $795.00. *Optimal configuration:* DOS Version 5.0 or higher. *Networks supported:* All.
Fully Integrated Statistics, Graphics, & Data Management System. Over 1,000 Graphs Integrated with All Analyses. 2D & 3D Graphs Feature Onscreen Drawing, Rotation, & Scalable Fonts. Interactive, Menu-Drive Operation Features Scrollable Output, Pop-Up Graphics, & Online Help. Supports Unlimited Size Data Files.
StatSoft, Inc.

STATISTICA/Mac. *Version:* 3. Aug. 1992. *Customer Support:* Technical support.
Macintosh System 6.X, 7.X. All Maintosh (1Mb). 3.5" disk $595.00. *Networks supported:* All.
Fully Integrated Statistics, Graphics, & Data Management System with Many Graphs Integrated with All Analyses. 2D & 3D Graphs Feature Onscreen Customization with MACDRAW-Like Tools. Data Management Features Include Fast Spreadsheet Editor, Merging/Splitting Files, Nested Sorting, Transformations. Supports Unlimited Size Data Files.
StatSoft, Inc.

STATISTICA/QC. *Version:* 4.1. Mar. 1993. *Customer Support:* Technical support for life of program.
Windows 3.X. Microcomputer, PC's 286 & higher (2Mb). disk $495.00. *Optimal configuration:* 4Mb RAM, Windows 3.1. *Networks supported:* Novell, Banyan-Vines, Lantastic.
Fully Integrated Statistics, Graphics, & Data Management System Which is Customized for Users of Industrial Statistics & Supports All Windows Conventions. Offers Hundreds of Types of 2D & 3D Graphs. On-Screen Customization Options Give the User Complete Control over Graph Specifications.
StatSoft, Inc.

STATISTICA - QC for DOS. *Version:* 3.1. 1993. *Items Included:* 1 loose-leaf & binder manual, Quick Start manual. *Customer Support:* Free technical support by phone, Fax, or mail; 14 day money back guarantee; service contract available.
MS-DOS (Version 3.1 or higher), DR DOS. PC/XT & compatibles with hard drive & 3 1/2" or 5 1/4" floppy drive (640k). Contact publisher for price (ISBN 1-884233-04-X). *Optimal configuration:* 386 SX/DX-25Mhz; MS-DOS 5.0 or higher; 640k RAM (expanded memory recommended); EGA or higher. *Networks supported:* Novell, Lantastic, Banyan Vines, & Others.
Specialized Statistics, Graphics, & Data Management System Which is Customized for Users of Industrial Statistics. Offers Many 2D & 3D Graphs. 2D & 3D Graphs Feature On-Screen Drawing, Rotation, & Scalable Fonts. Interactive Menu Driven Operation Features Scrollable Output, Pop-Up Graphics, & On-Line Help.
StatSoft, Inc.

STATISTICA - QC for Windows: Industrial Statistics Modules. *Version:* 4.5. 1993. *Items Included:* 1 bound manual. *Customer Support:* Free technical support by phone, Fax, or mail; 14 day money back guarantee; service contract available.
MS-Windows 3.0 or higher (version 3.1 recommended). 386DX with hard drive, 3 1/2" or 5 1/4" high density floppy drive (2Mb).

Contact publisher for price (ISBN 1-884233-07-4). *Optimal configuration:* 386DX-25Mhz; MS-Windows 3.1 (or higher); 4Mb RAM; VGA; mouse. *Networks supported:* Novell, Lantastic, Banyan Vines, Windows for Workgroups, & Others.
Fully Integrated Statistics, Graphics, & Data Management System Which Is Customized for Users of Industrial Statistics & Supports All MS Windows Conventions. Offers Hundreds of Types of 2D & 3D Graphs. On Screen Customization Options Give the User Complete Control over Graph Specifications.
StatSoft, Inc.

STATISTICA/w. *Version:* 4.1. Mar. 1993. *Customer Support:* Technical support for life of program.
Windows 3.X. Microcomputer, PC's 286 & higher (2Mb). disk $995.00. *Optimal configuration:* 4Mb RAM, Windows 3.1. *Networks supported:* Novell, Banyan-Vines, Lantastic.
Fully Integrated Statistics, Graphics, & Data Management System Which Completely Supports the Conventions of the Windows Environment (TT-Fonts, DDE, Clipboard Support, etc.). Offers Hundreds of 2D & 3D Graphics. On-Screen Customization Options Give the User Complete Control over Graphic Specifications.
StatSoft, Inc.

STATISTICA for DOS. *Version:* 3.1. 1991. *Items Included:* 3 loose-leaf & binder manuals, Quick Start manual, Addendum to the manual. *Customer Support:* Free technical support by phone, Fax, or mail; 14 day money back guarantee; service contract available.
MS-DOS (Version 3.1 or higher), DR DOS. PC/XT & compatibles with hard drive & 3 1/2" or 5 1/4" floppy drive (640k). Contact publisher for price (ISBN 1-884233-02-3). *Optimal configuration:* 386 SX/DX-25Mhz; MS-DOS 5.0 or higher; 640k RAM (expanded memory recommended); EGA or higher. *Networks supported:* Novell, Lantastic, Banyan Vines, & Others.
Fully Integrated Statistics, Graphics, & Data Management System. Over 1,000 Graphs Are Integrated with All Analyses. 2D & 3D Graphs Feature On-Screen Drawing, Rotation, & Scalable Fonts. Interactive, Menu Driven Operation Features Scrollable Output, Pop-Up Graphics, & On-Line Help. Supports Unlimited Size Data Files.
StatSoft, Inc.

STATISTICA for the Macintosh. *Version:* 4.0. 1993. *Items Included:* 2 bound manuals, Quick Start Manual. *Customer Support:* Free technical support by phone, Fax, or mail; 14 day money back guarantee; service contract available.
System 6.05. MAC Plus or higher (1Mb). Contact publisher for price (ISBN 1-884233-08-2). *Optimal configuration:* System 7, 4Mb RAM, color monitor, (co-processor not required). *Networks supported:* Yes.
System 6.05. Any Macintosh with a math coprocessor & hard drive (1Mb). Contact publisher for price. *Optimal configuration:* Macintosh with FPU; System 7; hard drive; 4Mb RAM; color monitor. *Networks supported:* Yes.
Fully Integrated Statistics, Graphics, & Data Management System with Many Graphs Integrated with All Analyses. 2D & 3D Graphs Feature On-Screen Customization via MACDRAW-Like Tools. Data Management Features Include Fast Spreadsheet Editor, Merging/Splitting Files, Nested Sorting, Transformations. Supplorts Unlimited Size Data Files.
StatSoft, Inc.

STATISTICA for the Macintosh. *Version:* 4.1. 1994. *Items Included:* 3 bound manuals, Quick Start Manual. *Customer Support:* Free technical support by phone, Fax, or mail; 14 day money back guarantee; service contract available.
System 6.0.5. Mac Plus or higher (1Mb). 3.5" disk $695.00 (ISBN 1-884233-32-5). *Optimal configuration:* Mac IIs; System 7; 4Mb RAM; color monitor; (co-processor not required). *Networks supported:* Yes.
A Fully Integrated Statistics, Graphics, & Data Management System with Many Graphs Integrated with All Analyses. 2D & 3D Graphs Feature On-Screen Customization via MacDraw-Like Tools. Data Management Features Include Fast Spreadsheet Editor, Merging/Splitting Files, Nested Sorting, Transformations. Supports Unlimited Size Data Files.
StatSoft, Inc.

STATISTICA for the Macintosh: Industrial Statistics Modules. *Version:* 5.0. 1993. *Items Included:* 1 bound manual. *Customer Support:* Free technical support by phone, Fax, or mail; 14 day money back guarantee; service contract available.
System 6.05. MAC Plus or higher (1Mb). Contact publisher for price (ISBN 1-884233-10-4). *Addl. software required:* STATISTICA for the Macintosh. *Optimal configuration:* System 7, 4Mb RAM, color monitor, (co-processor not required). *Networks supported:* Yes.
System 6.05. Any Macintosh with a math coprocessor & hard drive (1Mb). Contact publisher for price. *Optimal configuration:* Macintosh with FPU; System 7; hard drive; 4Mb RAM; color monitor. *Networks supported:* Yes.
Fully Integrated Statistics, Graphics & Data Management System Which Is Customized for Users of Industrial Statistics. 2D & 3D Graphs Feature On-Screen Customizaton via MACDRAW-Like Tools.
StatSoft, Inc.

STATISTICA for Windows. *Version:* 4.5. 1993. *Items Included:* 1 loose-leaf & binder manual, Quick Start manual. *Customer Support:* Free technical support by phone, Fax, or mail; 14 day money back guarantee; service contract available.
MS-Windows 3.0 or higher (version 3.1 recommended). 386DX with hard drive, 3 1/2" or 5 1/4" high density floppy drive (2Mb). Contact publisher for price (ISBN 1-884233-05-8). *Optimal configuration:* 386DX-25Mhz; MS-Windows 3.1 (or higher); 4Mb RAM; VGA; mouse. *Networks supported:* Novell, Lantastic, Banyan Vines, Windows for Workgroups, & Others.
Fully Integrated Statistics, Graphics, & Data Management System Which Completely Supports MS Windows Conventions (TT-Fonts, DDE, Clipboard Support, etc.). Offers a Full Selection of Statistical Analyses, Data Base Management, & Hundreds of 2D & 3D Graphs. On-Screen Customization Options Allow Complete Control over Graph Specifications.
StatSoft, Inc.

STATISTICA for Windows. *Version:* 5.0. 1994. *Items Included:* 4 bound manuals, Addendum, Quick Reference Manual. *Customer Support:* Free technical support by phone, Fax, or mail; 14 day money back guarantee; service contract available.
MS Windows 3.1. 386 DX with hard drive, 3 1/2" or 5 1/4" high density floppy drive (4Mb). disk $995.00 (ISBN 1-884233-33-3). *Optimal configuration:* 386 DX-25MHz; MSWindows 3.1 (or higher); 4Mb RAM; VGA; mouse. *Networks supported:* Novell, Lantastic, Banyan Vines, Windows for Workgroups; & others.
A Fully Integrated Statistics, Graphics, & Data Management System Which Completely Supports MS Windows Conventions (TT-Font, DDE, OLE, Clipboard Support, etc.). Offers a Full Selection of Statistical Analyses, Database Management & Hundreds of 2D & 3D Graphs. On-Screen Customization Options Allow Complete Control over Graph Specifications.
StatSoft, Inc.

STATISTICA/QC for Windows. *Version:* 5.0. 1994. *Items Included:* 4 bound manuals, Addendum, Quick Reference Manual. *Customer Support:* Free technical support by phone, Fax, or mail; 14 day money back guarantee; service contract available.
MS Windows 3.1. 386 DX with hard drive & 3 1/2" or 5 1/4" high density floppy drive (4Mb). disk $795.00 (ISBN 1-884233-35-X). *Optimal configuration:* 386 DX-25MHz; MSWindows 3.1 (or higher); 4Mb RAM; VGA; mouse. *Networks supported:* Novell, Lantastic, Banyan Vines, Windows for Workgroups; & others.
A Fully Integrated Statistics, Graphics, & Data Management System Which Is Customized for Users of Industrial Statistics & Supports All MS Windows Conventions. Offers Hundreds of Types of 2D & 3D Graphs. On-Screen Customization Options Give the User Complete Control over Graph Specifications.
StatSoft, Inc.

Statistical Consultant. *Items Included:* Full manual. No other products required. *Customer Support:* Free telephone support - no time limit. 30 day warranty.
MS-DOS 3.2 or higher. IBM & compatibles (512k). disk $9.95.
Advises You As to the Appropriate Statistical Procedure for Your Particular Application By Asking You a Series of Questions. It Not Only Suggests the Procedure, but Also Provides Some Explanation along with References. Includes a Printed Manual with Descriptions, Glossary, & Bibliography.
Dynacomp, Inc.

Statistical Consultant. 1992. *Items Included:* Detailed manuals included with all Dynacomp products. *Customer Support:* Free telephone support to original customer - no time limit; 30 day limited warranty.
MS-DOS 3.2 or higher. IBM PC & compatibles (512k). $9.95 (Add $5.00 for 3 1/2" format; 5 1/4" format standard).
Advises You As to the Appropriate Statistical Procedure for Your Particular Application by Asking You a Series of Questions. It Not Only Suggests the Procedure, but Also Provides Some Explanation along with References. Provided by DYNACOMP As a Service to Help Prospective Customers Choose the Right Software Package for Their Own Situations. Includes a Printed Manual with Descriptions, Glossary, & Bibliography.
Dynacomp, Inc.

Statistical Language for Microcomputers. *Compatible Hardware:* CP/M based machines with MBASIC, IBM. *Memory Required:* 48k, IBM PC version 128k.
disk $149.95.
Dynacomp, Inc.

Statistical Lottery Analysis. Ronald D. Jones. 1985. *Compatible Hardware:* Apple; Commodore; IBM; TRS-80 Model I, Model III, Color Computer. *Operating System(s) Required:* CP/M. *Memory Required:* 64k.
disk $79.95 ea.

TITLE INDEX

Apple. (ISBN 1-55604-150-0, Order no.: L001).
CP/M. (ISBN 1-55604-151-9, Order no.: L001).
Commodore. (ISBN 1-55604-152-7, Order no.: L001).
Color Computer. (ISBN 1-55604-153-5, Order no.: L001).
IBM. (ISBN 1-55604-154-3, Order no.: L001).
Model I & Model III. (ISBN 1-55604-155-1, Order no.: L001).
Helps Predict 3 & 4 Digit Numbers. Gives User the Ability to Track All Forms of Lottery & Compile the Most Probable Sets of Numbers Based on the Past. All "Mechanical" Systems Evoke Bias Which Can Be Statistically Evaluated & Isolated with Program.
Professor Jones Professional Handicapping Systems.

Statistical Lottery/Lotto Analysis. Ronald D. Jones. 1985. *Compatible Hardware:* Apple; Commodore; IBM; TRS-80 Model I, Model III, Color Computer. *Operating System(s) Required:* CP/M. *Memory Required:* 64k.
disk $99.95 ea.
Apple. (ISBN 1-55604-156-X, Order no.: L002).
CP/M. (ISBN 1-55604-157-8, Order no.: L002).
Commodore. (ISBN 1-55604-158-6, Order no.: L002).
Color Computer. (ISBN 1-55604-159-4, Order no.: L002).
IBM. (ISBN 1-55604-160-8, Order no.: L002).
Model I & Model III. (ISBN 1-55604-161-6, Order no.: L002).
Helps Predict 3 & 4 Digit Numbers for Lottery & Expands to 5 & 6 Digit Numbers for Lotto. Gives User the Ability to Track All Forms of Lottery & Lotto & Compile the Most Probable Sets of Numbers Based on the Past. All "Mechanical" Systems Evoke Bias Which Can Be Statistically Evaluated & Isolated with Program.
Professor Jones Professional Handicapping Systems.

Statistical Macro Package. *Compatible Hardware:* Apple Macintosh; IBM PC & compatibles. *General Requirements:* Microsoft Excel.
3.5" disk $79.00.
Collection of 12 Statistical Analysis Tools.
Heizer Software.

Statistical Masterfile. 1995. *Customer Support:* Quarterly Updated.
MS-DOS. IBM or compatibles. disk
Uncover statistics buried in millions of pages of information on a virtually limitless range of economic, demographic, social, & political subjects.
Congressional Information Service.

Statistical Methods for Improving Performance. *Version:* 3.1. 1992. *Operating System(s) Required:* PC-DOS/MS-DOS or Windows 3.1. *Memory Required:* Windows 4Mb, PC-DOS/MS-DOS 256k. *Items Included:* lesson disks, computer application program, testing kit, 1 student manual. *Customer Support:* 800-438-7647, 2 years free.
$1995.00 site license; $695.00 single.
Statistical Process Control Training for Production Employees, Supervisors, & All Employees Who Need to Know "How-To" Including Specific Material for General & Administrative Employees.
Concourse Corp.

A Statistical Package for Business, Economics, & the Social Sciences (Student). *Version:* 2.00. George H. Blackford. Aug. 1992.
MS-DOS 2.00 or higher. IBM XT & compatibles (512k). 5.25" disk $70.00 Registered Copy Version (ISBN 1-881564-52-5). *Networks supported:* All.
3.5" disk 3.5" disk $99.95 Registered Copy Version (ISBN 1-881564-53-3).
5.25" disk $34.95 Student Version, incl. ASP Tutorial & Student Guide (ISBN 1-881564-26-6).
3.5" disk 3.5" disk $39.95 Student Version, incl. ASP Tutorial & Student Guide (ISBN 1-881564-27-4).
A General Purpose Statistical Package That Is Menu Driven & Exceedingly Easy to Learn & Use. Included Are 13 Probability Distributions; 29 Summary Statistics; Numerous Hypothesis/ Nonparametric Tests; N-Way Analysis of Variance/Random Block & Covariance Designs with Unequal Samples; Frequency, Scatter, Box & Whisker, Stem & Leaf, Quantile, & Cumulative Plots; Ordinary, Generalized, Two Stage Least Squares, & Stepwise Regression; Control Charts; Factor Analysis; Time Series Analysis; & Much More.
DMC Software, Inc.

A Statistical Package for Business, Economics, & the Social Sciences. *Version:* 2.00. George H. Blackford. Jun. 1992.
MS-DOS 3.00 or higher. IBM 386 or 486 & compatibles (2000k). 5.25" disk $399.95 (ISBN 1-881564-54-1). *Networks supported:* All.
MS-DOS 3.30 or higher. 3.5" disk $249.95 (ISBN 1-881564-55-X).
A General Purpose Statistical Package That Is Menu Driven & Exceedingly Easy to Learn & Use. Included Are 13 Probability Distributions; 29 Summary Statistics; Numerous Hypothesis/ Nonparametric Tests; N-Way Analysis of Variance/Random Block & Covariance Designs with Unequal Samples; Frequency, Scatter, Box & Whisker, Stem & Leaf, Quantile, & Cumulative Plots; Ordinary, Generalized, Two Stage Least Squares, & Stepwise Regression; Control Charts; Factor Analysis; Time Series Analysis; & Much More.
DMC Software, Inc.

Statistical Power Analysis: A Computer Program. Michael Borenstein & Jacob Cohen. Nov. 1988. *Items Included:* User's manual. *Customer Support:* Free technical support.
MS-DOS. IBM & compatibles (512K). disk $125.00, incl. manual (ISBN 1-56321-011-8).
3.5" disk $125.00, incl. manual (ISBN 1-56321-009-6).
3.5" disk $115.00 (ISBN 1-56321-008-8).
5.25" demo disk $10.00 (ISBN 1-56321-010-X).
3.5" demo disk $10.00 (ISBN 1-56321-006-1).
This Program, Companion Software to the Text "Statistical Power Analysis, Second Edition", Includes the Following Features: Spreadsheet Input; Graphic Input; Active Help Screens; Simulations; Tables & Graphs; Procedures.
Lawrence Erlbaum Assocs. Software & Alternate Media, Inc.

Statistical Sample Planner. *Compatible Hardware:* Apple II with Applesoft, IBM PC. *Operating System(s) Required:* Apple DOS 3.2 or 3.3, MS-DOS. *Memory Required:* Apple 48k, IBM 128k.
disk $39.95.
Designed to Make It Easy to Find the Sample Size & Strategy That Best Meets Users Needs.
Dynacomp, Inc.

Statistical Software for Forecasting. *Version:* 2.0. Albert Bookbinder. Aug. 1993. *Compatible Hardware:* IBM PC. *Operating System(s) Required:* MS-DOS. *Language(s):* BASIC. *Memory Required:* 64kk. *Items Included:* Handbook. *Customer Support:* Telephone support.
disk $144.00 (ISBN 0-916106-11-X).
Includes 20 Interactive Statistical Programs Designed to Assist User in Making Forecasting Decisions. Programs Included Are: Arithmetic Mean, Median, Geometric Mean, Range, Standard Deviation, Mean Deviation, Coefficient of Variation, Range Coefficient, Moving Average, Exponential Moving Average, Exponential Smoothing of Forecasting, Secular Trend Projections, Growth Projections, Monthly Seasonal Index, Quarterly Seasonal Index, Monthly Link Relatives, Quarterly Link Relatives, Times Series Decomposition, Quarterly Time Series Decomposition, & Multiple Correlation & Regression.
Programmed Pr.

Statistical Toolbox. Namir C. Chammas. *Operating System(s) Required:* MS-DOS.
disk $39.95, incl. manual (ISBN 0-934375-22-4).
Provides Ways to Customize Statistical Programs. The Source Code on Disk & in the Manual Includes Functions & Procedures That Will Save Programming Time & Allow Users to Create Their Own Applications. Includes Statistical Distribution Functions, Random Number Generation, Parametric Statistical Testing, Non-Parametric Statistical Testing, Automatic Best Curve Selection, etc.
M & T Bks.

The Statistician PC. *Compatible Hardware:* IBM PC. *Operating System(s) Required:* PC-DOS. *Language(s):* FORTRAN. *Memory Required:* 128k.
disk $295.00.
Contains Approximately 100 FORTRAN Subroutines, Designed to Aid Mathematicians & Scientists in Performing Mathematical Functions. Subroutines Include Matrix Storage & Operations, Correlation & Regression, Design Analysis, Factor Analysis, Eigen Analysis, etc.
Alpha Computer Service.

Statistician's MACE. *Version:* 2.0. Carl F. Voelz. Oct. 1983. *Compatible Hardware:* IBM PC & compatibles. *Operating System(s) Required:* PC-DOS, MS-DOS. *Language(s):* Pascal. *Memory Required:* 128k. *General Requirements:* 2 disk drives.
disk $255.00.
Calculates Multiple Regression, Correlations, & Several ANOVA's, & Performs Nonparametric Tests, Descriptive Stats, Data Transformations, & Other Statistical Functions. Reads Data from Keyboard or Files Created by Spreadsheets, Data Base, Word Processors, etc.
The Matrix Calculating Engine, Inc.

Statistics. *Compatible Hardware:* TI 99/4A.
contact publisher for price (Order no.: PHM 3014).
Performs Statistical Calculations. Can Be Used to Analyze Data from Personal Record-Keeping Module. Includes Descriptive Statistics, Correlation & Linear Regression Functions.
Texas Instruments, Personal Productivit.

Statistics, Vol. 1. *Items Included:* Full manual. No other products required. *Customer Support:* Free telephone support - no time limit. 30 day warranty.
MS-DOS 3.2 or higher. IBM & compatibles (512k). disk $44.95.
Introduction to Descriptive & Inferential Statistics. Learn Random Sampling, Probability, Uses, & Interpretation of Statistics.
Dynacomp, Inc.

Statistics & Probability COM 3105A - COM 3109A, 6 programs on 9 disks. Bruce Trumbo. 1983. *Compatible Hardware:* Apple II+, IIe, IIc; Bell & Howell; Franklin Ace. *Operating System(s) Required:* Apple DOS 3.3. *Language(s):* BASIC. *Memory Required:* 48k.
Set. For both $270.00, Incl. documentation

(ISBN 0-933694-29-6).
Individual programs. $135.00 each.
Illustrates Concepts of Statistics & Probability with Color Graphics & Tutorial Problems & Simulations.
COMPress.

Statistics by Monte Carlo Analysis. *Items Included:* Bound manual. *Customer Support:* Free hotline - no time limit; 30 day limited warranty; updates are $5/disk plus S&H.
MS-DOS 2.0 or higher. IBM & compatibles (360k). disk $29.95.
Solve Both Simple & Complex Problems in Probability & Statistics. Applicable to Teaching & Demonstrating Statistical Procedures in Educational Settings Ranging from Junior High Through Graduate School. It Is Also Applicable to Business & Scientific Use.
Dynacomp, Inc.

Statistics for Business & Economics. John A. Ingram & Joseph G. Monks.
5 disks $15.00 (ISBN 0-15-583548-3).
Harcourt Brace Jovanovich, Inc. (College Div.).

Statistics Library, Pt. I, 5 disks. *Compatible Hardware:* HP Series 200 Models 216/220, 226/236, 217/237 Personal Technical Computers with BASIC 3.0. *Memory Required:* 260k.
HP 216/220, 217/237. 3-1/2" or 5-1/4 disk $925.00 ea. (Order no.: 98820B).
HP 226/236. 5-1/4" disk $925.00 ea.
Intended to Provide a Basic Library of General Statistics. Consists of Basic Statistics & Data Manipulation, General Statistics, Statistical Graphics, & Regression Analysis.
Hewlett-Packard Co.

Statistics Library, Pt. II, 5 disks. *Compatible Hardware:* HP 200 Series Models 216/220, 226/236, 217/237 Personal Technical Computers. *Language(s):* BASIC 3.0. *Memory Required:* 260k. *General Requirements:* Statistical Library, Pt. I program.
HP 216/220, 217/237. 3-1/2" or 5-1/4" disk $750.00 ea. (Order no.: 98820C).
HP 226/236. 5-1/4" disk $750.00 ea.
Advanced Statistical Analysis Library. Includes Monte Carlo Simulation, Analysis of Variance & Principal Components, & Factor Analysis.
Hewlett-Packard Co.

Statistics Module: M65S. *Compatible Hardware:* Commodore 64, PET; IBM PC.
disk $100.00.
Gives the Facts & Figures Needed to Back up Research Work. Includes File Handling & Printing of Tabular Results, Histograms & Scatter Plots. Covers All Major Univariate Techniques, Including: Analysis of Variance, Contingency Table Analysis (Chi-Square Tests), Multiple Regression, Tests of Hypotheses & Confidence Intervals for Means, Proportions & Variances & for Differences Between Means for Two Populations, Computation Probabilities & Quantities for the Most Common Statistical Distributions, Including Normal, Binomial, Chi-Square, T-Distributions & F-Distributions.
Matrix Software.

Statistics Series, 3 disks. *Compatible Hardware:* Apple II with Applesoft; IBM PC. *Language(s):* BASIC (source code included). *Memory Required:* 48k.
Disk set. $69.95.
Disk set.
Dynacomp, Inc.

Statistics Series. *Compatible Hardware:* Apple II, II+. *Language(s):* Applesoft II. *Memory Required:* 32k.

disk $34.95 (Order no.: 10030).
"Basic Statistics" Processes a Given Dataset of Univariate Numbers; "Statistics I" Computes Curve Fitting, Linear Regression Analysis, Logarithmic Curve Fitting & Exponential Curve Fitting.
Powersoft, Inc.

Statistics Software for Micros. Martha DiFazio. 1984. *Compatible Hardware:* Apple, IBM PC, Zenith. *Operating System(s) Required:* Apple DOS 3.3, PC-DOS 2.0. *Language(s):* BASIC (source code included).
disk & bk. $75.00.
IBM. (Order no.: 303-IK).
Z-100. (Order no.: 303-ZK).
Apple. (Order no.: 303-ZK).
19 Programs That Can Be Used to Perform a Variety of Statistical Procedures. Topics Include Summary Statistics, Binomial & Normal Probabilities, Chi-Square Test, One & Two Sample Hypothesis Testing & Confidence Intervals, Multi-Factor ANOVA, Comparison Procedures, Latin Squares, Crossover Designs, Repeated Measures Designs, Simple & Multi-Linear Regression Analysis, Regression Through the Origin & Logistic Response Analysis. Graphics Options Include Profiles of Means, Scatter-Plots, Residual Plots & Histograms.
Kern International, Inc.

Statistics with Stata. *Version:* 3. Lawrence Hamilton. *Items Included:* Two 3 1/2" disks, 172-page paperbound book. *Customer Support:* Unlimited technical support for registered users.
MAC. Macintosh. disk $43.25 (ISBN 0-534-18920-2). *Optimal configuration:* MAC System 6 or higher, 1Mb free.
DOS. 3.5" disk $43.25 (ISBN 0-534-18919-9).
Package Focus is on How to Do the Work of Data Analysis, Using Stata As a Tool. Student Stata Ha_ State-of-the-Art Graphics Capabilities & Is Easy to Learn. It Features a Consistent, Easily-Learned Command Structure; Extensive On-Line Help & The Ability to Shift to a Menu Mode at Any Time; a Full Range of Basic Procedures Such As Data Entry & Editing, Random Data Generation, Tables, Nonparametric Tests, ANOVA, & Regression; Flexible, Easy-to-Use, & the State-of-the-Art Analytical Graphics; Many Advanced Procedures, Including Logit, Probit, & Robust Regression; ANCOVA; Survival Analysis; Diagnostic Statistics, & Tests of User-Specified Hypothesis.
Brooks/Cole Publishing Co.

STATISTIX. *Version:* 4.0. *Compatible Hardware:* IBM PC & compatibles. *Items Included:* Software, manual, support. *Customer Support:* Free 612-628-0146.
IBM. disk $495.00 (ISBN 1-881789-00-4).
3.5" disk $495.00 (ISBN 1-881789-01-2).
Statistical System Featuring: Flexible Data Management & Transformations, Multiple Regression, ANOVA, SPC, Most Standard Parametric & Non-Parametric Tests; P-Values, Plots, Histograms, etc.
Analytical Software.

STATLAB: Mean & Standard Deviation. California State University et al. Aug. 1985. *Compatible Hardware:* Apple II, II+, IIe, IIc. *Memory Required:* 64k.
disk $49.95 (ISBN 0-07-831022-9).
The "Auto Calculator" Allows Students to Experiment with Statistical Concepts by Conducting Their Own "What If?" Experiments. Covers the Arithmetic Mean, the Root Mean, Deviation from the Mean, & the Standard Deviation.
McGraw-Hill, Inc.

STATLIB 1. Jack Prins. *Compatible Hardware:* IBM PC, PC XT, PC AT, Portable PC. *Operating System(s) Required:* DOS 1.10, 2.00, 2.10, 3.00, 3.10. *Memory Required:* 192k. *General Requirements:* Double-sided disk drive, 8087 math co-processor (80287 for PC AT), IBM Display (APL character chip required for monochrome display), IBM APL.
disk $149.95 (Order no.: 6276501).
Performs Statistical Analysis of Descriptive Statistics, Hypothesis Testing, Confidence Intervals, Analysis of Variance, Quality Control, Reliability, & Linear & Non-Linear Regression. Also Includes Some Financial Analysis Routines, & Incorporates Numerical Integration of Normal, t, f, & Chi-Square Distributions.
Personally Developed Software, Inc.

STATLIB 2. Jack Prins. *Compatible Hardware:* IBM PC, PC XT, PC AT, Portable PC with IBM Display (APL character chip required for monochrome display). *Operating System(s) Required:* DOS 1.10, 2.00, 2.10, 3.00, 3.10. *Memory Required:* 192k. *General Requirements:* Double-sided disk drive, 8087 math co-processor, IBM APL.
disk $149.95 (Order no.: 6276539).
Complements STATLIB 1 & Moves into More Advanced Analysis. Main Areas Covered Are Random Number Generators (Distributions), Multivariate Statistics, Time-Series Analysis, & Non-Parametric Statistics.
Personally Developed Software, Inc.

StatMaster. *Customer Support:* 800-929-8117 (customer service).
MS-DOS. IBM/PS2. disk $299.99 (ISBN 0-87007-368-0).
A Complete Statistical Analysis System, Including Data Collection & Design Analysis Components. Handles All Parametric & Non-Parametric Statistical Analysis Techniques, Including Factor Analysis, Regression, Linear Programming, Alpha & Beta Probability Tests, Item Analysis, F-Tests & Plotting of Results. A Comprehensive Package of Compatible Programs for Analyzing Data Sets Which Contain Extensive File Handling & Data Manipulation Features As Well As Data Analysis Programs. Three Types of Data Files Are Supported: ASCII, System Data & Matrix. Five Data Management Programs Are Provided: DATIN, ASCII, INPUT, RECODE, & REFILE. The Following Statistical Procedures Are Supported: DESCRIBE, FREQ, BREAK & BREAKOUT, CROSS, PLOT, COR, MDCOR, CORREG, FACTOR, DISCRIM, FORECAST.
SourceView Software International.

StatMaster U. S. Census Database. *Items Included:* Bound manual. *Customer Support:* Free hotline - no time limit; 30 day limited warranty; updates are $5/disk plus S&H.
MS-DOS 2.0 or higher. IBM & compatibles (640k). $99.95. Nonstandard peripherals required: Hard Disk.
Professional Version $399.95.
50-State Library of Statistics from the Bureau of the Census. It Includes Demographic, Economic, & Geographic Data for the Entire United States, Its Four Regions, 9 Divisions, 50 States, & Every County, City, & Place with a Population over 2500. It Is So User-Friendly That It May Be Left Running Unattended in Libraries So That the Casual User May Walk up & Retrieve Data in an Instant Without Any Fuss. 45 Major Categories; 900,000 Data Entries.
Dynacomp, Inc.

StatPac. *Version:* 6.0. David S. Walonick. 1981. *Compatible Hardware:* IBM PC, PC XT & compatibles; Kaypro; NCR; TI Professional Computer; TRS-80; Victor 9000. *Operating System(s) Required:* PC-DOS, MS-DOS, CP/M, DOS 1.1 or higher. *Language(s):* Compiled

BASIC. *Memory Required:* 192k. *General Requirements:* 2 disk drives.
disk $595.00 incl. user's manual.
manual $30.00.
demo disk & manual $50.00.
Math coprocessor-8087. $50.00.
Statistical Analysis Package for Professional Researchers. Features Batch Processing, Frequencies, Descriptive Statistics, Breakdown, Crosstabs & Banners, Correlation & Regression, Stepwise Multiple Regression, Probit Regression, Principal Components & Multicollinearity Analyses. Factor Analysis T-Tests, One & Two-Way Anova, & Multiple Variable Response. Printing Options, Including Graphics Are Available. Data Files May Contain 5000 Records & 255 Columns of Alpha or Numeric Information. Menu-Driven & Contains a Complete Data Base Manager Including Three Different Data Entry Techniques & a Built-In Word Processor for File Editing. Reads Fixed or Free Format ASCII Files Allowing Compatibility with Mainframe Files & Other Microcomputer Commands.
StatPac, Inc.

StatPac Gold IV. *Version:* 4.5. Mar. 1986. *Compatible Hardware:* IBM PC, PC XT, PC AT & compatibles. *Operating System(s) Required:* DOS 2.0 or higher. *Memory Required:* 640k. *General Requirements:* Hard disk. *Items Included:* Basic Statistics, Data Entry, Graphics.
$795.00.
Advance Statistics Module. $495.00.
Designed Exclusively for Survey Analysis & Marketing Research. Features Survey Design, Sample Selection, Data Entry & Management, CRT & Telephone Interviewing, Basic Analyses & Presentation Quality Graphics. Includes Frequencies, Tabs & Banners, Open-Ended Response Coding, Multiple Response, Descriptives, Breakdowns, Correlations & T-Tests. Advanced Analyses Available (Regression, Factor, Cluster, Conjoint, Perceptual Mapping, etc.). Complete tutorial.
StatPac, Inc.

Stats Plus. *Items Included:* Bound manual. *Customer Support:* Free hotline - no time limit; 30 day limited warranty; updates are $5/disk plus S&H.
MS-DOS. IBM & compatibles (256k). disk $179.95.
Accepts: 1 to 20 Variables per File, Keyboard or Disk-File Data, & Print-Format Files from VISICALC. Performs: Data Ranking, File Ranking, File Restructuring, 1-Way to 5-Way Crosstabulation, 1-Way to 4-Way Data-File Search, & File & Subfile Creation. Calculates: Descriptive Statistics, 14 Data Transformations, Frequncy Distribution, Cumulative Frequency & Percent, Percentiles, Correlation Matrix, Pearson r, Spearman Rho, Kendall Tau, Partial Correlation, 1 or 2 Predictor Regression, 1-Way or 2-Way Randomize Anova, t-Test for Independent Groups, t-Test for Correlated Groups, t-Test Against Population Mean, Chi-Square, Fisher Exact Test, Mann-Whitney/Rank-Sum Test, Signed-Ranks Test, Kruskall-Wallis, Wilcoxon Signed Ranks, & Friedman Anova by Ranks. Produces: Printed Reports of Results, Printed Copies of Data, & Plots & Bar Graphs on CRT or Disk.
Dynacomp, Inc.

Stats Tool Kit. *Version:* 6.0. *Compatible Hardware:* Apple Macintosh; Windows. *Memory Required:* 1000k. *Items Included:* Spiral bound manual. *Customer Support:* Free telephone support.
3.5" disk $99.00.
Statistical Analysis.
Sof-Ware Tools.

Statsort. *Compatible Hardware:* TRS-80. $39.95.
Dynacomp, Inc.

Stattest. *Compatible Hardware:* Apple II with Applesoft; Macintosh; IBM PC. *Memory Required:* 48k, IBM 128k, Macintosh 512k.
disk $49.95, incl. instr. bk.
Performs Statistical Tests of Hypotheses.
Dynacomp, Inc.

StatView. *Version:* 4.5. Jun. 1995. *Items Included:* Q2 soft bound manuals, program diskettes, product literature, shortcuts card. *Customer Support:* Free technical support by mail, FAX, phone & E-mail.
Macintosh System 7.0 or higher. Macintosh. 3.5" disk $595.00 (ISBN 0-944800-08-4). *Networks supported:* AppleTalk (Any Apple compatible network).
Win 95, Windows NT, Win 3.1, Win 32s. Windows PC. disk $595.00 (ISBN 0-944800-09-2).
Integrated Statistics, Data Management, Graphing & Presentation Software. Analysis Results Remain Dynamically Linked to Your Data - If You Change Your Date, Your Results Instantly Update. Any StatView Document May Be Saved As a Template & Reopened with the Original Dataset or Any Dataset of Interest. 100% Native for Power Macintosh.
Abacus Concepts, Inc.

Statview. *Version:* 2.05. Gordon Waite & Frederick Mensch. Jan. 1995. *Customer Support:* Unlimited telephone support.
MS-DOS. 286 (640k). disk $53.00 (ISBN 0-934777-18-7).
Allows Handicappers to Create Their Own Handicapping Systems Based on Data Files Downloaded from Racing Greyhounds BBS.
Pico Publishing.

StatXact: Statistical Software for Exact Nonparametric Inferency. Cyrus Mehta & Nitin Patel. Aug. 1991. *Items Included:* Manual, binder & 5.25" & 3.5" floppy diskettes. *Customer Support:* Phone support - technical & theoretical information - no fee.
MS-DOS. IBM XT, AT, 386 or compatibles (640K). disk $695.00 (ISBN 0-9624108-0-2). *Optimal configuration:* Arithmetic coprocessor desirable.
Computes Exact P-Values & Exact Confidence Intervals for Two-Sample Tests, R X C Contingency tables, Stratified 2 x 2 Contingency Tables & Stratified 2 x C Contingency Tables. A Supplement to Larger Statistical Packages When Data Sets Are Small, Imbalanced or Sparse & Conventional Large Sample Methods Are Unreliable.
Cytel Software Corp.

Stax! Helper. *Compatible Hardware:* Apple Macintosh. *Memory Required:* 1000k. *General Requirements:* 2 800k floppy disk drives; HyperCard, Hard disk recommended.
3.5" disk $59.95.
Aids in Developing or Modifying Stacks.
Stax!.

Stax! Sound Effects Studio. *Compatible Hardware:* Apple Macintosh. *Memory Required:* 1000k. *General Requirements:* 800k floppy disk; Hard disk; HyperCard.
3.5" disk $49.95.
Sound Effects Program.
Stax!.

Steady-State Continuous Distillation. *Items Included:* Full manual. No other products required. *Customer Support:* Free telephone support - no time limit. 30 day warranty.
MS-DOS 3.2 or higher. IBM & compatibles (512k). disk $2399.95.
Simulates Total & Partial Condensers, Including Two Liquid-Phase Condensers. Also Simulates Columns with Side Stream Products & Columns with Side Heaters or Coolers. You May Model Real Trays & Calculate Column Pressure Drop As an Option. You May Plot McCabe-Thiele Type Diagrams As Well As Plot Key Component Ratios. Has Equilibrium & Enthalpy Models for Both "Chemical" & Petroleum Systems. Included Is a Physical Property Databank of 240 Components, Which Can Be Modified & Expanded.
Dynacomp, Inc.

Stealth. Tracy LaGrone & Richard E. Sansom. *Compatible Hardware:* Atari 400, 800, XL, XE Series; Commodore 64.
Atari. disk $29.95 (Order no.: ATDSK-135).
Commodore. disk $29.95 (Order no.: COMDSK-256).
Pilot a Stealth Starfighter on a Mission to Destroy the Dark Tower & the Merciless Council of Nine. Battle Warp-Fighters While Avoiding Photon Tanks & Laser Artillery. Provides 3D Effects & 5 Difficulty Levels.
Broderbund Software, Inc.

STEAM. John Migliavacca. Dec. 1983. *Compatible Hardware:* IBM PC. *Operating System(s) Required:* PC-DOS 2.0. *Language(s):* BASIC. *Memory Required:* 256k.
disk $140.00 (ISBN 0-917405-00-5).
Calculates Pressure Loss in Piping, Steam Required for Desuperheating, Multiple Inlet Steam Drum Flashing, Steam Turbine Performance. Also Performs Steam Balance for Boiler/Deaerator/Flash Tank/Feed Pump System. Contains Internal Correlations for Thermodynamic Properties Such As Saturation Temperature & Specific Volumes for Both Saturated & Superheated Steam, So That the Designer Can Examine Conditions of Flow, Pressure, Temperature, etc.
Techdata.

Steam Boiler Efficiency Analyzer. *Items Included:* Full manual. No other products required. *Customer Support:* Free telephone support - no time limit. 30 day warranty.
MS-DOS 3.2 or higher. IBM & compatibles (512k). disk $389.95.
Calculates Both the Thermal & Overall Efficiency of Steam Boilers According to the ASME Power Test Code Heat Loss Method. Allows You to Analyze Your Boiler's Performance, Calculate Changes in Efficiency Using Parametric Studies, & Predict the Economic Changes Resulting from Operating Point Alterations or Capital Improvements. Results Are Presented in a Variety of Ways, Including Tables & Pie Charts.
Dynacomp, Inc.

Steam Boiler Efficiency Analyzer. 1992. *Items Included:* Detailed manuals included with all Dynacomp products. *Customer Support:* Free telephone support to original customer - no time limit; 30 day limited warranty.
MS-DOS 3.2 or higher. IBM PC & compatibles (512k). $379.95 (Add $5.00 for 3 1/2" format; 5 1/4" format standard). *Optimal configuration:* IBM, MS-DOS 2.0 or higher, 256k RAM, CGA or compatible graphics capability, & an Epson, IBM Prowriter, or compatible printer.
Calculates Both the Thermal & Overall Efficiency of Steam Boilers According to the ASME Power Test Code Heat Loss Method. It Allows You to Analyze Your Boiler's Performance, Calculate Changes in Efficiency Using Parametric Studies, & Predict the Economic Changes Resulting from Operating Point Alterations or Capital Improvements.
Dynacomp, Inc.

Steam Pipe Design & Calculations (Single Phase). *Items Included:* Full manual. No other products required. *Customer Support:* Free telephone support - no time limit. 30 day warranty.
MS-DOS 3.2 or higher. IBM & compatibles (512k). disk $895.00.
demo disk $5.00.
Quickly & Efficiently Sizes a Steam Line & Calculates the Pressure Drop Through an Already-Sized Line. You May Size Lines in a Steam System (Given a User-Defined Maximum Allowable Working Pressure, MAPD) When Only Steam Pressures & Temperatures Are Known. A Table May Be Printed Giving All Pipe Sizes Meeting the Stated Criteria. You May Also Size All Lines in a Liquid Piping System Using Maximum Velocity.
Dynacomp, Inc.

Steam Tables. *Items Included:* Bound manual. *Customer Support:* Free hotline - no time limit; 30 day limited warranty; updates are $5/disk plus S&H.
MS-DOS 2.11 or higher. IBM & compatibles (256k). disk $69.95. *Nonstandard peripherals required:* Monochrome or color monitor.
Calculate the Temperature, Pressure, Enthalpy, Entropy, & Specific Volume of Compressed Water, Saturated Water, Saturated Steam, & Super-Heated Steam over the Range of Pressures from 0 to 14,500 PSI & Temperatures from 32 Degrees to 1472 Degrees F (Excepting a Small Part of the Supercritical Region Between 662 Degrees & 850 Degrees F & above 4,000 PSIA). Various English & Metric Units Are Supported with Automatic Unit Conversion.
Dynacomp, Inc.

Stedman's Medical Dictionary, 3 disks. 1985. *Compatible Hardware:* Apple II, II+, IIe, IIc, IIgs. *Operating System(s) Required:* DOS, ProDOS. *Memory Required:* DOS 48k, ProDOS 64k. *General Requirements:* Sensible Speller program. disk $39.95 (ISBN 0-926776-03-7).
Three-Disk Dictionary Set That Contains over 65,000 Medical Terms. Can Be Used Alone or with the Random House Dictionary Which Is Included with Speller.
Sensible Software, Inc.

Stedman's-25 for WordPerfect. *Customer Support:* Free technical support for the life of product.
MS-DOS 2.1 or higher. IBM PC & compatibles. disk $99.00. *Addl. software required:* WordPerfect 5.0 & higher.
Macintosh. 3.5" disk $99.00. *Addl. software required:* WordPerfect 2.0.
Contains a Complete Medically-Enhanced Version of the WordPerfect Main Dictionary. There Are over 150,000 Medical Terms.
WordStar International, Inc.

Steel Assembly Weight Determination. Oct. 1983. *Compatible Hardware:* Apple II; HP Series 85; IBM PC. *Operating System(s) Required:* PC-DOS, Apple DOS 3.3. *Language(s):* BASIC (source code included). *Memory Required:* HP 32k, Apple 48k, IBM 128k. *Customer Support:* Telephone.
$125.00.
Determines Assembly Weights & Categorizes Piece Types from Itemized User Inputs of Piece Sizes & Structural Shape Lengths.
PEAS (Practical Engineering Applications Software).

Steel Beam Design - ST15M. *Version:* 01/1991. 1982. *Compatible Hardware:* IBM PC & compatibles. *Operating System(s) Required:* MS-DOS, PC-DOS. *Language(s):* Compiled. *Memory Required:* 256k. *Customer Support:* Technical hotline, "Lifetime" support at no charge. $195.00.
Steel Beam Design - ST15M AISC Manual of Steel Construction, Eighth Ed. Methods to Select Standard Prismatic Compact Steel Beams Using Standard AISC W, M, S, HP, C, & MC Shapes, & Any of the 33 Load Conditions Described in the Manual. Gives Optimum Beam Shape, Deflection, Lateral Support Spacing. Prompted & Interactive. Fully Compiled. SI Metric or English Units.
MC2 Engineering Software.

Steel Column Design - ST17M. *Version:* 11/1991. 1982. *Compatible Hardware:* IBM PC & compatibles. *Operating System(s) Required:* MS-DOS, PC-DOS. *Language(s):* Compiled. *Memory Required:* 256k. *Customer Support:* Technical hotline, "Lifetime" support at no charge. $195.00.
Steel Column Design - ST17M Uses ACI Methods to Select Optimum Sections for Steel Columns of W, M, S, HP, C, & MC Shapes. Allows Variable K-Factor Inputs & Axial Loads, with or Without End Bending Moments. Gives AISC Interaction Results. Prompted, Interactive. Fully Compiled. SI Metric or English.
MC2 Engineering Software.

Steel Panthers. Gary Grigsby. Sep. 1995. *Items Included:* Rulebook & Data card. *Customer Support:* 30 day limited warranty.
MS-DOS PC CD-ROM Ver 5.0 or higher. PC CD-ROM 2x CD drive 486/33 required (8Mb). CD-ROM disk $69.95 (ISBN 0-917059-06-9, Order no.: 062251). *Nonstandard peripherals required:* 512k-hi res VESA compatible SVGA card uncompressed hard drive required, requires 12Mb min hard drive space. *Optimal configuration:* 486/50 23Mb of hard drive space, soundblaster or soundscape boards 4 recommended.
A Tactical Tank-Based WWII War Game. Wargamers Will Fight Tank vs. Tank in This WW II Game, Leading a Single Platoon or up to an Entire Battalion Through Europe 1939-1945. You May Play As Either Germans or Allies.
Strategic Simulations, Inc.

Stellar Explorer. *Version:* V2.0b. Jan. 1994. *Items Included:* 8 page manual, 1 diskette, response card. *Customer Support:* 90 day limited warranty, support via phone, modem, fax.
DOS, Windows 3.1, Windows 95. IBM & compatibles (2Mb). disk $24.95 (ISBN 1-884791-01-8, Order no.: 01-2100-020B). *Optimal configuration:* Intel 386/486, 4Mb RAM, MPC-compatible sound card.
Single Player Entertainment Software for Microsoft Windows.
Technological Computer Innovations Corp.

Stellar 28. *Items Included:* Bound manual. *Customer Support:* Free hotline - no time limit; 30 day limited warranty; updates are $5/disk plus S&H.
MS-DOS. IBM & compatibles (128k). disk $29.95. *Nonstandard peripherals required:* Color graphics card.
Apple (48k). disk $29.95.
Learn to Identify Constellations & Prominent Stars Visible from the Northern Hemisphere. Uses High-Resolution Color-Graphics Star Maps to Teach User How to Find Constellations & How to Relate the Constellations to Each Other. Multiple Choice Questions & Questions That Require the Constellation or Star Names Are Used for Drill. User May Select Star Maps with or Without Lines Connecting the Constellation Stars. Options Include Learning the Zodiac Constellations, Learning Just the Prominent Constellations, or Learning All 50 Constellations.
Dynacomp, Inc.

Stenograph's BaronData Billing Address & Accounting System with The Scheduler.
contact publisher for price.
A Fully Integrated Scheduling, Billing & Accounting Systems Based on Open Systems Accounting Software. Highly Specialized for the Court Reporting Industry. This System Allows the User to Control the Financial Activities Within the Firm from the Point of Deposition Request to Producing Financial Statements Through the General Ledger. It Runs on a Variety of Operating Systems, Including: DOS, Xenix, Unix & Novell Networks.
Stenograph Corp.

Step-1 Data Base Manager/Application Generator. *Version:* 3.0. Sep. 1989. *Items Included:* Complete reference manual. *Customer Support:* 90 days limited warranty, subscription & telephone hotline support service available.
MS-DOS 2.0 & higher. $595.00 single-user, $995.00 network version. *Networks supported:* All Netbios LANS (Novell, 3Com, etc.) for MS-DOS, SuperDOS.
Comprehensive Data Base Management System Providing All Required Application Generator Features & Functions. Completely Integrated, with Modular Design That Ensures Flexibility. Employs Easy-to-Use Menus & Consistent Conventions to Ensure Quick Learning.
Webco Computers.

StepOne. Sep. 1991. *Items Included:* Software documentation/owners manual. *Customer Support:* Customer service is provided to all customers free of charge for 30 days after the purchase date. After that time, maintenance may be purchased at $125 per year.
IBM DOS. IBM compatible (640k). disk $249.00 Stand Alone Version (ISBN 0-943293-06-5). *Networks supported:* Novell, Lantastic & Banyon.
Estate Planning Software Designed for Professionals Just Starting in Estate Planning. It Creates a Visual, Flowchart Presentation Helping Ensure the Client Understands the Planner's Recommendations. Additionally, StepOne Can Display Four Different Estate Planning Scenarios; Includes Explanatory Text for Each Scenario.
ViewPlan, Inc.

Stepwise Multilinear Regression. *Items Included:* Bound manual. *Customer Support:* Free hotline - no time limit; 30 day limited warranty; updates are $5/disk plus S&H.
MS-DOS. IBM & compatibles (256k). disk $29.95. *Addl. software required:* Multilinear Regression (MLR).
disk $49.95, incl. Multilinear Regression module.
An Add-On Module to Be Used with MULTILINEAR REGRESSION (MLR). Performs an Analysis Somewhat Differently from MLR. It Fits Variables in the Order of Their Importance, Thereby Giving an Indication of What the Contribution Is of Each. If a Variable Does Not Significantly Reduce the Variance Between the Data & Fit, It Is Dropped. This Permits User to Determine the Main Variables Influencing Data. Can Handle Larger Data Sets Than MLR.
Dynacomp, Inc.

Stereo. *Customer Support:* Free phone & mail support 30-day money back guarantee.
MS-DOS. PC AT & compatibles. disk $299.00. *Nonstandard peripherals required:* EGA or VGA card. *Optimal configuration:* 386 with LaserJet II, dot matrix printers (Epson compatible).
3-D Orientation & Plotting Program with Choice of WULFF or Schmidt Projections. Features Include: Unlimited Number of Data Features on Same Stereonet Plot, Pattern-Coded Density-Contoured Plots, Eigenvector Analysis Routine,

TITLE INDEX

Multicolor Stereonets, Rotate & Plot Data About a Given Axis, Density-Contoured Plots of Rotated Data & Beta Intersection Plots. Optional Plotter Driver for H-P, Houston Instruments, Plotters.
Rockware, Inc.

STEREOCHEMICA. *Version:* 2.0. *Items Included:* Diskette & manual. *Customer Support:* Telephone Inquiries.
MAC-DOS (1Mb). Macintosh, all models. disk $49.95.
Graphics Template for Use with a Paint or Draw Type Program. Diskette Includes Pre-Drawn Templates for Newman Diagrams, Fischer Diagrams, Space-Filling Atoms, Porphyrins, Sawhorse Diagrams, Flying Wedge Diagrams, Rings & Heterocycles (Pict & Paint Files).
Atlantic Software.

Steve Leimberg's Financial Calculator. *Version:* 1.03. Stephan R. Leimberg. Mar. 1994. *Customer Support:* 30-day money-back guarantee, telephone support, facsimile service.
PC-DOS (256k). IBM PC, PC XT, PC AT & compatibles. disk $100.00.
Throw Away Your HP or Texas Instruments Calculator. This One Is Much Easier & Does Essential Financial Calculations Faster, Easier, & Prints What You See in Seconds. Over 50 Different Computations to Solve Your Clients' Mortgage, Investment, Finance, Loan, Depreciation Problems.
Leimberg Assocs.

STI Critical Date System (CDS). *Version:* 8. Dec. 1979. *Compatible Hardware:* IBM PC, PC XT, PC AT & compatibles. *Operating System(s) Required:* DOS Ver. 3.1 or higher. *Language(s):* Microsoft BASIC. *Memory Required:* 470k. *Items Included:* Binder with documentation. *Customer Support:* 1 yr. maintenance, $60.00, entitles users to phone support, quarterly newsletters & enhancements released during the year for their computer at no charge.
$300.00.
$35.00 demo disk, $60.00 maintenance fee, (optional).
Schedules Can Be Printed by Professional, Date, Time, Type of Activities and/or Client. Schedules May Be Printed for Individual or Entire Firm, Scheduling Feature Allows up to 99 Timekeepers to Be Scheduled for a Meeting at One Time. Searches for Conflicts, Displays the Conflicts & Will Make Note If They Were Entered As a Critical Function or Not. Includes Events Planner to Automatically Schedule Multiple Events from a Given Date. Integrates with TABS III.
Software Technology, Inc.

Sticky Bear Early Learning. Richard Hefter. 1992. *Items Included:* Home Version - manual, 1 set disks; Labpack - manual, 1 set disks, Lappack license for 6 computers; School version - manual, 2 set disks (2nd copy is back up set); Site licenese - manual, 1 set disks for unlimited number of computers in school. *Customer Support:* 90 day warranty from date of purchase.
Macintosh System 6.0.7 or higher. Color Mac with a hard drive. 3.5" disk $59.95 (Order no.: 46200). *Nonstandard peripherals required:* 2Mb RAM for Sys 6.0.7, 4Mb RAM Sys 7.0.
3.5" disk Lab Pack $149.95 (Order no.: 46212).
School Version $79.95 (Order no.: 46244).
$699.95 Site License (Order no.: 46242).
Bilingual (English & Spanish), 5 Preschool Activities to Include Alphabet, Shapes, Opposites, Colors & Graphing. Sound Effects & Speech.
Optimum Resource, Inc.

Sticky Bear Early Learning. Richard Hefter. 1995. *Items Included:* Home Version - manual, 1 set disks; Labpack - manual, 1 set disks, Lappack license for 6 computers; School version - manual, 2 set disks (2nd copy is back up set); Site licenese - manual, 1 set disks for unlimited number of computers in school. *Customer Support:* 90 day warranty from date of purchase.
Macintosh System 6.0.7 or higher. Color Mac with a hard drive. CD-ROM disk $59.95 (Order no.: 56200). *Nonstandard peripherals required:* 2Mb RAM for Sys 6.0.7, 4Mb RAM Sys 7.0.
CD-ROM disk $149.95, Lab Pack (Order no.: 56212).
CD-ROM disk 0.79.95, School Version (Order no.: 56244).
Bilingual (English & Spanish), 5 Preschool Activities to Include Alphabet, Shapes, Opposites, Colors & Graphing. Sound Effects & Speech.
Optimum Resource, Inc.

Sticky Bear Early Learning. Richard Hefter. 1995. *Items Included:* Home Version - manual, 1 set disks; Labpack - manual, 1 set disks, Lappack license for 6 computers; School version - manual, 2 set disks (2nd copy is back up set); Site licenese - manual, 1 set disks for unlimited number of computers in school. *Customer Support:* 90 day warranty from date of purchase.
Windows 3.1, Windows 95. 486SX 25MHz (4Mb). disk $59.95 (Order no.: 66200). *Nonstandard peripherals required:* Hrad drive, mouse, Super VGA display. *Addl. software required:* Windows compatible sound card.
Lab Pack $149.95 (Order no.: 66212).
School Version $79.95 (Order no.: 66244).
Site License $699.95 (Order no.: 66242).
Bilingual (English & Spanish), 5 Preschool Activities to Include Alphabet, Shapes, Opposites, Colors & Graphing. Sound Effects & Speech.
Optimum Resource, Inc.

Sticky Bear Early Learning. Richard Hefter. 1995. *Items Included:* Home Version - manual, 1 set disks; Labpack - manual, 1 set disks, Lappack license for 6 computers; School version - manual, 2 set disks (2nd copy is back up set); Site licenese - manual, 1 set disks for unlimited number of computers in school. *Customer Support:* 90 day warranty from date of purchase.
Windows 3.1, Windows 95. 486SX 25MHz (4Mb). CD-ROM disk $59.95 (Order no.: 56200). *Nonstandard peripherals required:* Hard drive, mouse, Super VGA display. *Addl. software required:* Windows compatible sound card.
CD-ROM disk $149.95, Lab Pack (Order no.: 56212).
CD-ROM disk $79.95, School Version (Order no.: 56244).
Bilingual (English & Spanish), 5 Preschool Activities to Include Alphabet, Shapes, Opposites, Colors & Graphing. Sound Effects & Speech.
Optimum Resource, Inc.

Sticky Bear Math Town. Richard Hefter. 1993. *Items Included:* Home Version - manual, 1 set disks; Labpack - manual, 1 set disks, Lappack license for 6 computers; School version - manual, 2 set disks (2nd copy is back up set); Site licnese - manual, 1 set disks for unlimited number of computers in school. *Customer Support:* 90 day warranty from date of purchase.
Macintosh System 7.0 or higher (4Mb). 3.5" disk $59.95 (Order no.: 46300). *Nonstandard peripherals required:* Color Mac (256 colors) with a hard drive.
Lab pack $149.95 (Order no.: 46312).
School Version $79.95 (Order no.: 46344).
Site License $699.95 (Order no.: 46342).
Bilingual (English & Spanish Program), 6 Levels of Add/Subtract/Multiply/Division. Sound Effects & Speech.
Optimum Resource, Inc.

STICKY BEAR READING ROOM

Sticky Bear Math Town. Richard Hefter. 1995. *Items Included:* Home Version - manual, 1 set disks; Labpack - manual, 1 set disks, Lappack license for 6 computers; School version - manual, 2 set disks (2nd copy is back up set); Site licnese - manual, 1 set disks for unlimited number of computers in school. *Customer Support:* 90 day warranty from date of purchase.
Windows 3.1 or Windows 95, hard drive, mouse, Super VGA display. Minimum 486SX 25MHz (4Mb). disk $59.95 (Order no.: 66300). *Addl. software required:* Windows compatible sound card.
Lab pack $149.95 (Order no.: 66312).
School Version $79.95 (Order no.: 66344).
Site License $699.95 (Order no.: 66342).
Bilingual (English & Spanish Program), 6 Levels of Add/Subtract/Multiply/Division. Sound Effects & Speech.
Optimum Resource, Inc.

Sticky Bear Math Town. Richard Hefter. 1995. *Items Included:* Home Version - manual, 1 set disks; Labpack - manual, 1 set disks, Lappack license for 6 computers; School version - manual, 2 set disks (2nd copy is back up set); Site licnese - manual, 1 set disks for unlimited number of computers in school. *Customer Support:* 90 day warranty from date of purchase.
Windows 3.1 or Windows 95, hard drive, mouse, Super VGA display. Minimum 486SX 25MHz (4Mb). CD-ROM disk $59.95 (Order no.: 56300). *Addl. software required:* Windows compatible sound card.
CD-ROM disk $149.95, Lab pack (Order no.: 56312).
CD-ROM disk $79.95, School Version (Order no.: 56344).
Bilingual (English & Spanish Program), 6 Levels of Add/Subtract/Multiply/Division. Sound Effects & Speech.
Optimum Resource, Inc.

Sticky Bear Reading Room. Richard Heffer. 1991. *Items Included:* Home Version - manual, 1 set disks; Labpack - manual, 1 set disks, Lappack license for 6 computers; School version - manual, 2 set disks (2nd copy is back up set); Site licnese - manual, 1 set disks for unlimited number of computers in school. *Customer Support:* 90 day warranty from date of purchase.
System 6.0.7 or higher. Macintosh. 3.5" disk $59.95 (Order no.: 46400). *Nonstandard peripherals required:* 2Mb RAM System 6.0.7 or 4Mb RAM System 7, black & white color monitor (256 colors).
Lab Pack $149.95 (Order no.: 46412).
School Version $79.95 (Order no.: 46444).
Site License $699.95 (Order no.: 46442).
Bilingual (English & Spanish), 4 Reading Exercises - WordBop, WordMatch, WordFind, Sentence Builder. Sound Effects & Speech.
Optimum Resource, Inc.

Sticky Bear Reading Room. Richard Heffer. 1991. *Items Included:* Home Version - manual, 1 set disks; Labpack - manual, 1 set disks, Lappack license for 6 computers; School version - manual, 2 set disks (2nd copy is back up set); Site licnese - manual, 1 set disks for unlimited number of computers in school. *Customer Support:* 90 day warranty from date of purchase.
MS-DOS. IBM PC or 100% compatibles (640k). disk $59.95 (Order no.: 96400). *Nonstandard peripherals required:* EGA, VGA, or equivalent grpahics with 256k. *Addl. software required:* DOS Version 3.1 or higher.
Lab Pack $149.95 (Order no.: 96412).
School Version $79.95 (Order no.: 96444).
Site License $699.95 (Order no.: 96442).
Bilingual (English & Spanish), 4 Reading Exercises - WordBop, WordMatch, WordFind, Sentence Builder. Sound Effects & Speech.
Optimum Resource, Inc.

Still Lifes. (Photopaedia Ser.: Vol. 3). Feb. 1995. *Items Included:* Warranty/registration card, game manual. *Customer Support:* Technical Support Number: 1-800-734-9466, 90 days limited warranty.
Windows 3.1; Macintosh System 7 or higher. IBM 33MHz i80486DX (8Mb); Macintosh 16MHz 68030 or higher, 25MHz 68LC040 or higher (5Mb). CD-ROM disk $59.99 (ISBN 1-888158-07-7). *Nonstandard peripherals required:* Double-speed CD-ROM drive. *Addl. software required:* MS-DOS 5.0 or higher.
World Renowned British Gallery Photographer Diane Wesson Debuts Her Work for the First Time in Any Published Medium. The Artistry of Wesson Evokes Feelings of Peace & Tranquility As She Narrates Her Work for the Active Audience. Over 100 Photographs Can Be Viewed by Artistic Theme or by Slideshow Option.
Synergy Interactive Corp.

Sting "All This Time". Oct. 1995. *Customer Support:* Toll-free technical support, on-line, fax back.
Windows 95. 486/66 or higher (8Mb). CD-ROM disk under $50.00 (ISBN 1-888104-01-5, Order no.: 7-14120-70901-8). *Nonstandard peripherals required:* 2x CD-ROM drive. *Optimal configuration:* 486/66 w/8Mb RAM, 2x CD-ROM drive, 16-bit color running Windows 95.
The Double CD-ROM "All This Time" Gives Music Fans a Personal Exploration Through the Mind, Soul & Music of One of Rock's Most Intriguing Performers, Sting. Including Exclusive Videos, New Songs, Candid Interviews & More.
Starwave Corp.

Stitch Crafts. *Version:* 2.31. Sep. 1992. *Items Included:* 70 page spiral bound manual. *Customer Support:* 30-day money back guarantee. Direct mail & telephone support, automatic update info.
Apple Macintosh (1Mb). $150.00. *Optimal configuration:* Mac II series (color) 4Mb Ram, hard drive.
Users Can Design Their Own Counted Cross Stitch & Other Needlecraft Charts. Allows Multiple Projects of Any Size with up to 50 User-Editable Symbols. Provides Tools for Drawing Symbols, Back Stitches, Area Fill, Moving, Copying & Flipping Motifs. Also Supports Several Grid Styles, Zoom Levels & Tools to Create Color Key Charts. Built-In 360 Color DMC Color Card. Automatically Converts Pictures to Finished Charts with DMC Color Matching.
Compucrafts.

Stitch Crafts Gold. *Version:* 4.0. Oct. 1995. *Items Included:* 173-page spiral bound manual. *Customer Support:* 30-day money back guarantee. Direct mail, email, & telephone support, automatic update info.
Windows 3.1 or higher (Windows 95). 386, 640x400x256 colors (4Mb). disk $190.00 (Order no.: SC-WIN-40).
Users Can Design Their Own Counted Cross Stitch & Other Needle Craft Charts. Allows Multiple Projects of Any Size with up to 120 User-Editable Symbols. Provides Tools for Drawing Symbols, Back Stitches, Satin Stitches, Area Free, Moving, Copying & Flipping/Rotating Motifs. Also Supports Several Grid Styles, Zoom Levels & Tools to Create Color Key Charts. Built-In 390 DMC Colors. 422 Anchor Colors, 290 JPCoats Colors. Automatically Converts Pictures to Finished Charts with DMC Color Matching.
Compucrafts.

The Stitch Grapher. *Version:* 3.2. *Compatible Hardware:* IBM PC & compatibles with VGA support, DOS. *Items Included:* Disk plus 75-pg. manual. *Customer Support:* Direct telephone & mail support-automatic update info.
IBM. disk $89.95.
Users Can Design Their Own Counted Cross Stitch & Other Needlecraft Charts. Allows Projects As Large As 640 x 640 Stitches with up to 30 Symbols with the Flexibility to Move, Copy, Mirror Image, Rotate, Erase, Save, & Reuse Designs. Automatically Converts Pictures to Charts with DMC Color Matching.
Compucrafts.

STNG Collection AudioClips. *Version:* 1.7. Mar. 1995. *Items Included:* Registration card, certificate of authenticity, Quick installation reference card. *Customer Support:* Phone technical support.
DOS 5.0, Windows 3.1. PC 286 or higher (2Mb). disk $14.95 (ISBN 1-57303-019-8). *Nonstandard peripherals required:* Sound card recommended. *Optimal configuration:* 286 or higher with 4Mb RAM, DOS 5.0 or later, Windows 3.1 or later, 4-7Mb HD space available, sound card.
AudioClips Are Exclusively Licensed, High Quality Sound Files Consisting of Classic Sound Effects, Dialogue & Music from Original TV Shows & Movies. Also Included Is the Personal Desktop Audio Utility Which Allows the User to Attach AudioClips to Various Windows Events.
Sound Source Interactive.

Stock Analysis. *Compatible Hardware:* Atari XL/XE. *Operating System(s) Required:* AOS. *Language(s):* Atari BASIC. *Memory Required:* 24k.
disk $9.95 (Order no.: CX8107).
Performs Portfolio Analysis Using Standard Methods of Arithmetic Mean & Standard Deviation of Log Returns. Computes the Annual Rates of Return for Specific Investments. Also Computes the Present Discounted Value of Estimated Dividends According to the Nicholas Molodovsky Method. Designed for the Long-Term Investor.
Atari Corp.

Stock & Options Analysis. *Compatible Hardware:* TRS-80 Model III, Model 4. *Operating System(s) Required:* TRSDOS. *Language(s):* BASIC. *Memory Required:* 32k.
disk or cassette $99.95.
Helps Plan & Test Future Strategies As Well As Organize & Evaluate Portfolios. OPTION Aids in Opening & Closing Call Options. OPGRAPH Shows Profit for Call, Put, & Stock Combinations with Graphs & Tables. Three Hedge Types Can Be Evaluated. Predicting Option Premiums Can Be Done with NEWPERM. PROTVAL Aids with Portfolio Services Such As Value Per Share. Commission, Margin Interest & Dividend Effects Are Also Included.
Compuware.

Stock Charting. *Compatible Hardware:* Atari XL/XE. *Operating System(s) Required:* AOS. *Language(s):* Atari BASIC. *Memory Required:* 24k.
disk $9.95 (Order no.: CX8108).
Full-Featured Stock Charting Program for the Market Investor. Displays the Calculated Price/Ratio, High, Low, Beginning, Close, Earnings & Dividends, & Volume up to 120 Trading Days May Be Viewed. A 10-Day Moving Average & a 6-Day Oscillator May Be Plotted on the Graph.
Atari Corp.

Stock Charting. *Version:* 6.20. Dec. 1984. *Compatible Hardware:* IBM PC XT, PC AT & 100% compatibles; Compaq; Leading Edge. *Operating System(s) Required:* PC-DOS. *Language(s):* BASICA (source code included). *Memory Required:* 128k.
disk $69.95.
demo disk $15.00.
Technical Analysis Package Which Provides the Investor a Price-Bar & Volume-Bar Chart. Will Access the Warner Computer System Data Base, & Automatically Retreive the Necessary Data to Construct the Charts. Other Manipulations of the Data Which Can Be Performed from the Main Menu Include: Deleting a Stock, Scaling the Data on File for Splits, Accessing the Warner Data Base for Information Other Than Simply Adding a Stock, & Printing All Data on File for a Stock.
Diamond Head Publishing.

The Stock Manager. *Version:* 7.2. *Compatible Hardware:* IBM PC & compatibles. *Operating System(s) Required:* MS-DOS 2.1. *Language(s):* C (source code included). *Memory Required:* 128k. *General Requirements:* 2 disk drives.
disk $200.00.
manual $25.00.
Portfolio Management Tool Designed for Private or Professional Investor Who Needs Accounting & Control System for Securities Portfolio, As Well As Small to Medium-Sized Institution Requiring Accounting & Reporting Capabilities. Accepts over 25 Items of Information on Each Stock. Prepares Necessary Information for Tax Returns at Year End, & Produces Several Other Reports.
Omni Software Systems, Inc. (Indiana).

Stock Market Bargains. *Items Included:* Bound manual. *Customer Support:* Free hotline - no time limit; 30 day limited warranty; updates are $5/disk plus S&H.
MS-DOS. IBM & compatibles (256k). disk $69.95.
Provides Two Tests for Categorizing, Evaluating, & Storing Statistics on Stocks Considered Under-Valued...& Ripe for Purchase by the Shrewd Investor. Test I - The Graham Approach: The First Test Is Based on Theories Benjamin Graham Set Forth in His Landmark Books Security Analysis & The Intelligent Investor. In This Test, a Stock's Investment Value Is "Graded" by Its Quick Liquidation Value. Test II - Pre-Set Values You Can Change As Needed. Test II Parameters: Price/Earnings Ratio; Number of Institutional Investors; Ratio of Current Assets to Current Liabilities; Change in Earnings per Share; Current Earnings per Share.
Dynacomp, Inc.

Stock Market Expert. *Version:* 5.1. *Compatible Hardware:* IBM PC & compatibles. *Operating System(s) Required:* PC-DOS, MS-DOS. *Memory Required:* 256k. *General Requirements:* Hard disk recommended. *Items Included:* 32 pg. Thinking Software catalog.
5.25" or 3.5" disk $59.95.
Provides a Specific Recommendation on the Investment Potential of Any Stock After a 20 Minute Consultation.
Thinking Software, Inc.

STOCK-MASTER. *Version:* II. David Powers. Jul. 1985. *Compatible Hardware:* IBM PC & compatibles. *Operating System(s) Required:* MS-DOS, PC-DOS. *Language(s):* Compiled Basic. *Memory Required:* 64k.
disk $49.95.
Stock Market Investment Aid Which Is Especially Useful for Mutual Fund Investment. Ideal for Casual Investor Who Needs Effective Buy-Sell Advice. Conservative Approach with Emphasis on Consistent Returns. Logs Transactions & Provides Investment Status.
Generic Computer Products, Inc. (GCPI).

Stock Master-Stock Plot. *Compatible Hardware:* Apple II with Applesoft. *Operating System(s) Required:* Apple DOS 3.2, 3.3. *Language(s):* BASIC (source code included). *Memory Required:* 48k. *General Requirements:* 2 disk drives.

disk $59.95, incl. manual.
Companion Programs Designed to Help the Investor Record Fiscal Data on Companies of Interest, Record Stock Transactions & Track Price Action.
Dynacomp, Inc.

Stock Options. *Customer Support:* 800-929-8117 (customer service).
MS-DOS. Apple II. disk $49.99 (ISBN 0-87007-810-0).
Analyzes Stock Options Using a Hedging Technique.
SourceView Software International.

Stock Portfolio. *Compatible Hardware:* TRS-80 Model III. *Memory Required:* 48k.
contact publisher for price.
Hancock Techtronics.

Stock Portfolio Reporter. *Compatible Hardware:* IBM PC, PC XT. *Operating System(s) Required:* MS-DOS. *Language(s):* Compiled BASIC. *Memory Required:* 128k. *General Requirements:* 2 disk drives, communications adapter card, modem, subscription to Dow Jones.
disk $279.00.
demo disk $15.00.
Designed to Give the Investor Portfolio Analysis of Stock Accounts. As Many As 200 Stocks Can Be Entered Using Menu-Type Choices & English Language Prompts. Market Price Updates Can Be Done Automatically from Log-On to Log-Off Using the Dow Jones News/Retrieval. This Includes Interface with with the Hayes Smartmodem to Auto-Dial the Call to Dow Jones.
Micro Investment Systems, Inc.

Stock Trader. *Compatible Hardware:* Apple II, II+, IIe, IIc. (source code included). *Memory Required:* 48k.
disk $9.95 (ISBN 0-918547-22-9).
illustration files on disk avail.
Simulation of the Stock Market with a Limited, but Diversified Portfolio. Based on a Trending Model of the Market, This Simulation Produces a Valid Experience for the Would-Be Trend Trader.
AV Systems, Inc.

Stock Watch II. *Compatible Hardware:* Apple Macintosh. *General Requirements:* ImageWriter or LaserWriter.
3.5" disk $59.00.
Investment-Management Program.
Encycloware.

Stock Watcher.
Macintosh Plus or higher. 3.5" disk $195.00.
Financial Market Technical Analysis Program.
Micro Trading Software, Inc.

Stockaid. *Compatible Hardware:* Atari, IBM PC. (source code included). *Memory Required:* Atari 48k, IBM 128k.
$69.95.
Dynacomp, Inc.

StockCharts Plus: For CD-ROM. Jun. 1995.
Items Included: 2 perfect bound manuals, 1 free month of data downloading. *Customer Support:* Free unlimited technical support for current shipping versions by phone, FAX, BBS, CompuServ, Prodigy, & American On-Line. FAX & BBS support for past versions for $19.95 per incident.
Windows. IBM 386-DX/33, hard drive, mouse, DOS 5, EGA (4Mb). CD-ROM disk $69.95 (ISBN 1-887286-01-2). *Nonstandard peripherals required:* CD-ROM drive & driver software. *Optimal configuration:* IBM 486-DX2/66, 8Mb RAM, DOS 6.2X or higher, Windows 3.11 for Workgroups, CD-ROM drive & driver software.
The First All-in-One Stock Charting Package Designed to Take Full Advantage of the Power & Ease of Microsoft Windows. It's Also the First to Include - Absolutely Free on CD - 5 Years of Price History on Every Stock & Mutual Fund on the NYSE, AMEX & NASDAQ - over 12,000 Symbols in All.
Omega Research, Inc.

StockExpert, MarketExpert. *Compatible Hardware:* IBM PC & compatibles. *General Requirements:* Hard disk, graphics card, modem. *Customer Support:* Free.
StockExpert, Version 4.1. $498.00.
MarketExpert, Version 4.1. $249.00.
Expert-System-Based End-of-Day Stock & Market Timing System That Signals What to Buy, When to Buy, & When to Sell. Programmed with a Knowledge Base of 25 Technical Indicators & Hundreds of Decision Rules Researched from Successful Market Experts. Automatically Connect by Modem to Financial Databases for Price & Volume Updating; MARKETEXPERT: Expert System That Signals When the Market Is Likely to Change Direction & Move up or Down. Tested Using 20 Years of Historical Data & Is Proven to Be 85% Reliable. Programmed with a Knowledge Base of 32 Technical Indicators & 400 Decision Rules That Represent the Knowledge of Many Experts of Market Timing.
AIQ, Inc.

StockMinder. *Version:* 4.0. Sep. 1985.
Compatible Hardware: IBM PC, PC XT; NCR PC; Compaq; Columbia MPC; Eagle Spirit; DEC Rainbow; Epson QX-10; Leading Edge; Sperry PC; TI Professional; Victor 9000; Zenith Z-100.
Operating System(s) Required: MS-DOS. *Language(s):* Microsoft BASIC. *Memory Required:* 256k.
contact publisher for price.
Inventory Management Package for Retail Businesses. Tracks up to 32,000 Inventory Items & Produces Status Reports for Items Such As Quantity On-Hand or On-Order. User Is Guided by a Menu, & Each Entry Is Defined on the Display. Reports Summarize the Inventory Status, Economic Order Points, Reconciliation Counts & Sales History (in Units & Dollars for Month-to-Date & Year-to-Date).
Verifone, Inc.

Stockroom Inventory. *Version:* 9.05. Jun. 1984.
Compatible Hardware: IBM PC, PC AT, PS/2. *Operating System(s) Required:* PC-DOS. (source code included). *Memory Required:* 512k.
Items Included: Reference manual. *Customer Support:* Phone/modem support included first year, nominal fee thereafter.
disk $1200.00 (ISBN 0-924068-01-9, Order no.: ST4).
Multi-User System Featuring a Universal Report Writer & Allocation of Inventory Usage to Departments Within the Corporation. Produces Detailed Reports on Usage of Inventory by Each Department at Month or Period End. Interfaces to Spreadsheets, & Other Applications Programs. Additional Reports Include: Back-Orders, Packing Lists, Year-to-Date & Life-to-Date Usage History, & Browse Recent Usage, & Utilizes LIFO, FIFO & Average Cost Methods.
Fogle Computing Corp.

Stockroom Manager. 1982. *Compatible Hardware:* Apple II, Commodore 64, IBM PC. *Memory Required:* 64k. *General Requirements:* Printer.
disk $39.00.
Intended for Businesses Which Maintain a Stockroom of Parts or Materials with Frequent in & out Transactions. There Are 5 Separate Files of 200 Items Each. Useful for Manufacturers, Wholesalers, Distributors or Retailers.
Navic Software.

Stomate Tutor. *Version:* 2.0. 1988. *Compatible Hardware:* Apple Macintosh. *Memory Required:* 512k. *General Requirements:* Hypercard.
3.5" disk $19.95 (ISBN 0-940119-04-8).
Interactive Video Animation of the Mechanism Used by Plants to Regulate Their Gaseous Environment.
Cooke Pubns.

Stone Fox. Intentional Education Staff & John Gardiner. Apr. 1996. *Items Included:* Program manual. *Customer Support:* Free technical support, 90 day warranty.
School ver.. System 7.1 or higher. Macintosh (4Mb). 3.5" disk contact publisher for price (ISBN 1-57204-234-6). *Nonstandard peripherals required:* 256 color monitor, hard drive, printer.
Lab pack. System 7.1 or higher. Macintosh (4Mb). 3.5" disk contact publisher for price (ISBN 1-57204-210-9). *Nonstandard peripherals required:* 256 color monitor, hard drive, printer.
Site license. System 7.1 or higher. Macintosh (4Mb). 3.5" disk contact publisher for price (ISBN 1-57204-235-4). *Nonstandard peripherals required:* 256 color monitor, hard drive, printer.
School ver.. Windows 3.1 or higher. IBM/Tandy & 100% compatibles (4Mb). disk contact publisher for price (ISBN 1-57204-211-7). *Nonstandard peripherals required:* VGA or SVGA 640 x 480 resolution (256), mouse, hard drive, sound device.
Lab pack. Windows 3.1 or higher. IBM/Tandy & 100% compatibles (4Mb). disk contact publisher for price (ISBN 1-57204-236-2). *Nonstandard peripherals required:* VGA or SVGA 640 x 480 resolution (256), mouse, hard drive, sound device.
Site license. Windows 3.1 or higher. disk contact publisher for price (ISBN 1-57204-212-5). *Nonstandard peripherals required:* VGA or SVGA 640 x 480 resolution (256), mouse, hard drive, sound device.
This companion for young adult literature is ideal for student's who don't know how to start that book report, or give that needed summary. Gentle prompts throughout the guide section of the program include Warm-up Connections, Thinking about Plot, Quoting & Noting, Keeping Journal, If I were ———' Responding to Questions, Using Quotations, Taking a Personal View, Write to Others, & Write a Sequel.
Lawrence Productions, Inc.

Stone's Reversible Games. *Compatible Hardware:* Apple II, II+. *Language(s):* Integer BASIC. *Memory Required:* 32k.
disk $24.95 (Order no.: 10039).
Action & Strategy Game.
Powersoft, Inc.

Store Front Retailing. *Version:* 8B. Sep. 1993.
Compatible Hardware: Altos, IBM PC & compatibles, NCR, UNISYS, Radio Shack.
Operating System(s) Required: PC-DOS/MS-DOS, UNIX, XENIX; 3Com, Novell. *Language(s):* COBOL 85. *Memory Required:* UNIX/XENIX 2Mb or higher, DOS 1000k. *General Requirements:* 40Mb hard disk for PC-DOS, 60Mb hard disk for Unix, Xenix; monochrome monitor, printer. *Customer Support:* $860.00 per year for 30 minutes per month.
NOVELL, 3COM. disk $500.00.
UNIX, XENIX. disk $700.00.
Complete Stand-Alone Point-of-Sale Accounting Package Designed for the Small Retailer. Functions As a Scaled-Down Version of Trac Line's Larger Point-of-Sale Integrated Accounting System. Integrates All Point-of-Sale Transactions into an Accounting System, Handling Accounts Receivable, Inventory Control, Sales Analysis, &

Purchasing. Also Operates Electronic Cash Drawers & Terminals As Cash Registers, & Can Operate Some Electronic Registers Tied into the Complete Computer System. Uses the Same Programs As Trac Line's Larger Software Products, Enabling the User to Upgrade Without Hardware Changes to a More Powerful System When Needed. Uses Bar Code Readers.
Trac Line Software, Inc.

The Store Manager. Version: 2.4. *Compatible Hardware:* IBM PC, PC XT, PC AT. *Memory Required:* 192k. *General Requirements:* 2 disk drives, printer.
disk $295.00.
Point-of-Sale Package That Is Also an Inventory Control System. Generates Invoices, Purchase Orders, Receiving Reports, Expense Vouchers, Packing Slips, Quotations.
High Technology Software Products, Inc.

StoreMinder. Version: 4.0. Sep. 1985. *Compatible Hardware:* IBM PC XT; Columbia MPC; Compaq; Sperry PC; Victor 9000; Zenith Z-100, or Z-150; TeleVideo; TI Professional; Eagle Spirit; Epson QX-10; Leading Edge; NCR PC; DEC Rainbow. *Operating System(s) Required:* MS-DOS, MmmOST. *Language(s):* Microsoft BASIC. *Memory Required:* 256k.
contact publisher for price.
Verifone, Inc.

Storm Across Europe. Dan Cermak. *Items Included:* Map card & rulebook. *Customer Support:* Technical support line: (408) 737-6850 (11am-5pm, PST); 14 day money back guarantee/30 day exchange policy.
Commodore 64/128 (64k). disk $59.95.
DOS 2.11 or higher. IBM PC & compatible (512k). disk $59.95. *Nonstandard peripherals required:* Requires a color monitor & a graphic adaptor (i.e., CGA, EGA).
Workbench. Amiga (512k). disk $59.95.
Atari ST (512k). 3.5" disk $59.95.
A Game That Allows You to Simulate World War II on a Grand Scale -- in As Short As One Evening! The Game Covers Every Part of That Raging Conflict -- from North Africa to Sweden, from Gibralter to the Ural Mountains in Russia. Each Game Turn Represents Three Months of Action. You Control Every Facet of the War: Move Armies Across the Map to Coquer Territory; Mount Amphibious Landings; Launch Huge U-Boat Campaigns in the Atlantic; Carry Out Strategic Bombing Strikes Against Enemy Production Centers; Send Fleets to Cripple Your Opponent's Shipping; & Drop Paratroop Forces on Enemy Positions. In As Little As One Night, You Can Determine the Fate of Europe!
Strategic Simulations, Inc.

Storm Plus: Storm Drain Analysis Program. Version: 1.21. Jan. 1992. *Compatible Hardware:* IBM PC, PC XT, PC AT & true compatibles. *Operating System(s) Required:* MS-DOS, PC-DOS. *Memory Required:* 640k. *General Requirements:* Hard disk, printer. *Items Included:* Manual, 120-day free maintenance. *Customer Support:* 1 year maintenance for $200. $495.00.
Hydraulic Analysis Program Which Computes Uniform & Nonuniform Steady Flow Water Surface Profiles & Pressure Gradients in Open Channels or Closed Conduits with Irregular or Regular Sections. Will Also Analyze Natural River Channels. Plotting Capabilities Included.
Research Engineers.

Story Time. *Compatible Hardware:* Apple II, II+, IIe. *Operating System(s) Required:* Apple DOS 3.3. *Language(s):* BASIC. *Memory Required:* 16k.
disk $24.95.
Uses Answers to Questions Like 'What's Your Name?', 'What Are You Afraid Of?', etc. to Make up Stories with Sound & Color Graphics. A Variety of Locales, Types of Weather, Time of Day, etc. Can Be Used for over 100,000 Story Variations.
Compuware.

Story Time & Don't Fall. *Compatible Hardware:* Apple II, II+, IIe; Franklin Ace. *Operating System(s) Required:* Apple DOS 3.3. *Language(s):* BASIC. *Memory Required:* 32k.
disk $24.95.
Uses Answers to Questions Such As 'What's Your Name?', 'What Are You Afraid Of?', etc. to Make up Stories with Graphics. Over 100,000 Variations. 'Don't Fall' Is a Version of Hangman. Words Are Chosen from Nine Categories. Each Letter Chosen Incorrectly Brings Player Closer to Falling in the Water. The Computer Has to Guess Words, Too. Three Skill Levels Are Included.
Compuware.

Storybook Capitals, 3 disks. Version: 2.1. *Compatible Hardware:* Commodore Amiga. *Customer Support:* By phone 206-733-8342.
3.5" disk $44.95.
Fonts.
CLASSIC CONCEPTS Futureware.

Storybook Maker. Jan. 1994. *Items Included:* Program on CD-ROM, CD Booklet, & Registration Card. *Customer Support:* Free unlimited customer support via telephone.
Macintosh System 7.0 or higher. Macintosh LC or higher (4Mb). CD-ROM disk $49.00 (ISBN 1-57268-082-2, Order no.: 20701). *Nonstandard peripherals required:* 12 inch monitor or larger; CD-ROM drive. *Optimal configuration:* 5Mb RAM.
Windows 3.1 or higher running under DOS 5.0 or higher. 386 SX (6Mb RAM; 500k low Dos Mem; 6Mb free disk space). CD-ROM disk $49.00 (Order no.: 20701). *Nonstandard peripherals required:* Sound card (either: Sound Blaster - 8, 16, PRO; Media Vision ProAudio Spectrum; or Microsoft Sound System; MPC compatible CD- ROM drive; VGA monitor; & microphone. *Optimal configuration:* 25 MHz 386 SX.
In This Engaging, Graphics-Based Product, Children Use a Variety of Elements, Such As Settings, Colorful Picture Cards, & of course, Words to Put Their Imaginations onto a Dynamic Canvas - the Computer. Storybook Maker Provides Eight Different Settings & Hundreds of Alphabetized Picture Cards, Featuring Animals & Objects.
Conter Software.

Storybook Maker. Jan. 1994. *Items Included:* Program on CD-ROM, CD Booklet, & Registration Card. *Customer Support:* Free unlimited customer support via telephone.
Windows 3.1 or higher running under DOS 5.0 or higher. 386 SX (6Mb RAM; 500k low Dos Mem; 6Mb free disk space). CD-ROM disk $49.00 (ISBN 1-57268-083-0, Order no.: 21701). *Nonstandard peripherals required:* Sound card (either: Sound Blaster - 8, 16, PRO; Media Vision ProAudio Spectrum; or Microsoft Sound System; MPC compatible CD-ROM drive; VGA monitor; & microphone. *Optimal configuration:* 25 MHz 386 SX.
In This Engaging, Graphics-Based Product, Children Use a Variety of Elements, Such As Settings, Colorful Picture Cards, & of course, Words to Put Their Imaginations onto a Dynamic Canvas - the Computer. Storybook Maker Provides Eight Different Settings & Hundreds of Alphabetized Picture Cards, Featuring Animals & Objects.
Conter Software.

Storybook Maker. Jan. 1994. *Items Included:* Program on CD-ROM, CD Booklet, & Registration Card. *Customer Support:* Free unlimited customer support via telephone.
Macintosh System 7.0 or higher. Macintosh LC or higher (4Mb). CD-ROM disk $49.00 (ISBN 1-57268-084-9, Order no.: 22701). *Nonstandard peripherals required:* 12 inch monitor or larger; CD-ROM drive. *Optimal configuration:* 5Mb RAM.
In This Engaging, Graphics-Based Product, Children Use a Variety of Elements, Such As Settings, Colorful Picture Cards, & of course, Words to Put Their Imaginations onto a Dynamic Canvas - the Computer. Storybook Maker Provides Eight Different Settings & Hundreds of Alphabetized Picture Cards, Featuring Animals & Objects.
Conter Software.

StoryBook Presents. Version: 1.0. Oct. 1986. *Compatible Hardware:* IBM PC & compatibles. *Operating System(s) Required:* PC-DOS/MS-DOS 2.X, 3.0. *Language(s):* C. *Memory Required:* DOS 2.X 384k, DOS 3.0 512k. *General Requirements:* CGA card, equivalent, or EGA card in the CGA mode.
disk $250.00.
Fonts Libraries. $60.00 ea.
Presentation Graphics Program Which Can Be Used to Create & Present Internal &/or Client Presentations, Product Demonstrations, & Other Applications That Require Good Communications Facilities. Can Be Menu or Command Driven. Users May Use the Keyboard or Mouse for Direct Input. To Aid in the Learning Process, It Makes Use of "OLE"" Documentation. Graphic On-Line Help Is Available for All Commands. Uses the "What You See Is What You Get" Concept for Ease of Use. Package Comes with One Keyboard Font with 7 Horizontal & Vertical Sizes. Text Color, Orientation, & Size Are All Selectable from the Keyboard. Additional Cut & Paste Fonts Are Available in the FONTS LIBRARY. Other Features Include Picture/Object Writing Modes - Overwrite, Superimpose, Reverse, Erase, & 5 Partial Negative or Positive Special Effects; Picture Materialization; Timing Controls - Automatic Play, Wait on Spacebar Response, etc.; Animation. Includes CAPTURE & MERGE Utilities. Runtime System Is Included.
Hypergraphics Corp.
  Computer Objects Library.
  US Maps Library.
  Borders/Fonts Library.
  People Library.
  World Maps Library.

Storymation. *Items Included:* CD-ROMs & manual or floppies & manual.
  Macintosh CD-ROM Deluxe. Macintosh (4Mb). CD-ROM disk $69.95 (Order no.: 08123). *Optimal configuration:* CD-ROM drive required, System 7.0 or higher, 256 color required. Optional: QuickTime & Microphone.
  Macintosh Floppy. Macintosh (4Mb). 3.5" disk $49.95 (Order no.: 08022). *Optimal configuration:* System 7.0 or higher, 256 colors required, 11Mb hard disk space. Optional: QuickTime & Microphone.
  Windows CD-ROM Deluxe (4Mb & extended memory). CD-ROM disk $69.95 (Order no.: 08113). *Optimal configuration:* Windows 3.1, 386/25 MHz or higher. SVGA card (Windows Accelerator recommended). Optional Windows compatible sound card. Video for Windows. CD-ROM drive required.
  Windows Floppy (4Mb & extended memory). disk $49.95 (Order no.: 08012). *Optimal configuration:* Windows 3.1, 386/25 MHz or higher. SVGA card (Windows Accelerator recommended). Optional: Windows compatible sound card. Video for Windows.

Windows CD-ROM (4Mb & extended memory). CD-ROM disk $49.95 (Order no.: 08013). *Optimal configuration:* Windows 3.1, 386/25 MHz or higher. SVGA card (Windows Accelerator recommended). *Optional:* Windows compatible sound card, Video for Windows. CD-ROM drive required.
Macintosh CD-ROM. Macintosh (4Mb). CD-ROM disk $49.95 (Order no.: 08023). *Optimal configuration:* CD-ROM drive required. System 7.0 or higher. 256 colors required. *Optional:* QuickTime & Microphone.
An Educational Program for the Kids with Ages Between 6 & 12 Years Old. Program Allows Children to Write Animated Stories with Sounds & Music.
ISM, Inc.

Storyspace. *Version:* 1.2. Jay David Bolter et al. Aug. 1991. *Items Included:* Manuals, research notes, StoryCard software. *Customer Support:* Toll-free tech support hotline, 30-day unlimited warranty.
Macintosh (System 6 or System 7). Macintosh Plus, Classic or higher (1Mb). 3.5" disk $215.00 (Order no.: STORYSPACE). *Optimal configuration:* Macintosh Plus or Classic or higher. Hard disk recommended. *Networks supported:* All Macintosh networks.
A Hypertext Writing Environment for the Process of Writing. Bringing Computer-Aided Design Tools to the Service of Writers & Analysts, Storyspace Provides Unique Linking, Mapping, & Path-Building Tools for Serious Writing. Supports All Media.
Eastgate Systems, Inc.

Stradiwackius. *Version:* CD-Mac. (Vroombooks Ser.). T-Maker Company.
Macintosh. Contact publisher for price (ISBN 0-918183-06-5).
Children's Software.
T/Maker Co., Inc.

Stradiwackius. *Version:* CD-Windows. (Vroombooks Ser.). T-Maker Company.
Windows. Contact publisher for price (ISBN 0-918183-07-3).
Children's Software.
T/Maker Co., Inc.

Stradiwalkius: The Counting Concert. (Vroombooks Ser.). T-Maker Co. Staff.
Contact publisher for price (ISBN 0-918183-03-0).
Children's Software.
T/Maker Co., Inc.

Strain-Graph. *General Requirements:* Microsoft Basic, MacPaint, ImageWriter.
Macintosh 512K higher. 3.5" disk $125.00.
Two-Dimensional Strain Analysis Program.
RockWare Data Corp.

Strange Odyssey. *Compatible Hardware:* TI-99/4A.
disk or cassette - contact publisher for price.
Texas Instruments, Personal Productivit.

A Stranger Came Ashore. Intentional Education Staff & Mollie Hunter. Apr. 1996. *Items Included:* Program manual. *Customer Support:* Free technical support, 90 day warranty.
School ver.. System 7.1 or higher. Macintosh (4Mb). 3.5" disk contact publisher for price (ISBN 1-57204-278-8). *Nonstandard peripherals required:* 256 color monitor, hard drive, printer.
Lab pack. System 7.1 or higher. Macintosh (4Mb). 3.5" disk contact publisher for price. *Nonstandard peripherals required:* 256 color monitor, hard drive, printer.
Site license. System 7.1 or higher. Macintosh (4Mb). 3.5" disk contact publisher for price (ISBN 1-57204-278-8). *Nonstandard peripherals required:* 256 color monitor, hard drive, printer.
School ver.. Windows 3.1 or higher. IBM/Tandy & 100% compatibles (4Mb). disk contact publisher for price (ISBN 1-57204-254-0). *Nonstandard peripherals required:* VGA or SVGA 640 x 480 resolution (256), mouse, hard drive, sound device.
Lab pack. Windows 3.1 or higher. IBM/Tandy & 100% compatibles (4Mb). disk contact publisher for price (ISBN 1-57204-279-6). *Nonstandard peripherals required:* VGA or SVGA 640 x 480 resolution (256), mouse, hard drive, sound device.
Site license. Windows 3.1 or higher. IBM/Tandy & 100% compatibles (4Mb). disk contact publisher for price (ISBN 1-57204-255-9). *Nonstandard peripherals required:* VGA or SVGA 640 x 480 resolution (256), mouse, hard drive, sound device.
This companion for young adult literature is ideal for students who don't know how to start that book report, or give that needed summary. Gentle prompts throughout the guide section of the program include Warm-up Connections, Thinking about Plot, Quoting & Noting, Keeping a Journal, If I Were ———' Responding to Questions, Using Quotations, Taking a Personal View, Write to others, & Write a Sequel.
Lawrence Productions, Inc.

STRATATREE. *Version:* ST (Stratatree). Dec. 1987. *Compatible Hardware:* IBM PC, PC XT, PC AT & compatibles; PS/2. *Memory Required:* 512k. *Customer Support:* Telephone.
3.5" or 5.25" disk $129.00.
Calculates Expected Value, Shows Optimal Paths to Solutions - Will Also Display Results Graphically.
Expert Choice, Inc.

STRATBASE Marketing Audit: Performance Support System. *Version:* 2.1. Prema Nakra & Robert E. Baker. Oct. 1992. *Operating System(s) Required:* MS-DOS, Windows 3.1 or higher, Windows 95, Windows NT. *Language(s):* Level 5. *Items Included:* Worksheets, user manual, text: Marketing Audit. *Customer Support:* 90 day unlimited warranty.
$995.00.
Windows 95. (ISBN 0-931755-06-9, Order no.: FS 110/2).
Windows NT. (ISBN 0-931755-07-7, Order no.: FS 110/3).
A Comprehensive, Systematic, Independent & Periodic, Examination of Company's - or Business Unit's - Marketing Capacity, & Performance with a View to Determining Problem Areas & Opportunities for Improvement. The Audit Is Central to Strategic Planning. An Effective Tool for Strategic Planners, Advertising Agencies, Marketing Consultants, Corporate Strategists, Educators.
Ellington Duval, Inc.

STRATBASE Marketing Controller: A Performance Support System. *Version:* 2.1. Perma Nakra & Robert E. Baker. Oct. 1992. *Compatible Hardware:* Digital Alpha, HP, IBM, 486 Pentium-based PCs & higher. *Operating System(s) Required:* MS-DOS, Windows, Windows 95, NT Server. *Memory Required:* 5000k. *General Requirements:* Hard disk, printer. *Items Included:* Text & worksheets, users manual. *Customer Support:* 90 day unlimited warranty, extended support-bulletin board $200.00 per year including updates.
Contact publisher for price.
Windows 3.1. (ISBN 0-931755-31-X, Order no.: FS 220/2).
Windows 95. (ISBN 0-931755-32-8, Order no.: FS 220/3).
Windows NT. (ISBN 0-931755-33-6, Order no.: FS 220/4).
Helps Marketers & Executives Collect, Review & Analyze Marketing Data; Provides Business Diagnostics, Marketing Essential to Analytics Central to Planning. Includes: Annual Plan Analysis; Financial Analysis; Budget Development Analysis Focusing on Long-Term Strategic Implications. The Controller Is a Marketing Communication Formidable Management, Evaluation, Control & Performance Support System.
Ellington Duval, Inc.

Strategic Conquest Plus. *Version:* 1.2. Jan. 1985. *Compatible Hardware:* Apple Macintosh. *Memory Required:* 512k.
3.5" disk $49.95.
Wargame of Global Domination. Includes an Instant Blackout Feature Enabling User to Escape Detection in the Office.
PBI Software, Inc.

Strategic Conquest II. *Compatible Hardware:* Apple Macintosh.
3.5" disk $59.95.
Multiplayer Version of STRATEGIC CONQUEST. Users Can Play Against the Computer or Against Each Other.
PBI Software, Inc.

Strategic Planning: Tax Minimization & Investment Strategy (Sixth Edition), 6 disks. Richard R. Sylvester. Apr. 1990. *Compatible Hardware:* IBM PC & compatibles, PC XT, PC AT. (source code included). *Memory Required:* 256k. *General Requirements:* 2 disk drives, Lotus 1-2-3.
Complete Set. $190.00, incl. bk., 6 diskettes.
$90.00, incl. bk., 3 disks.
bk. $59.00.
System for Long Range Investment Planning & Tax Minimization. Contents Include Tax Planning, Debt Planning, Cash Flow, Property Appraisal, Valuation of Firms, & Macroeconomic Forecasting. Includes New Provisions of 1986-89 Tax Act.
Ph.D. Publishing Co.

Strategic Retail Management: A Lotus 1-2-3 Based Simulation. 1989. *General Requirements:* Lotus 1-2-3.
IBM. contact publisher for price (ISBN 0-538-80290-1, Order no.: SF60A8).
This Simulation Consists of a Text-Workbook & 2 Lotus 1-2-3 Template Disks. Coverage Includes Major Areas of Retail Merchandising & Sales Management Principles Using Spreadsheet Applications. Students Make Decisions & Solve Problems Relating to Retail Sales Mgmt., Accounting/Finance, & Facilitating Functions.
South-Western Publishing Co.

Strategy! A Business Unit Simulation. 1987.
IBM/Tandy. contact publisher for price (ISBN 0-538-07723-9, Order no.: G72).
IBM PS/2. contact publisher for price (ISBN 0-538-07727-1, Order no.: G728).
This Team-Oriented Simulation Allows Students to Run 1 or More Companies (Each Team Can Run Up to 8 Different Companies) From 10 Different, Preprogrammed Industries. Decisions Are Made Based Upon Information From Preprogrammed Environmental Newsletters.
South-Western Publishing Co.

StratPlan Strategic Planning Model. Nov. 1985. *Compatible Hardware:* IBM PC & compatibles. *Memory Required:* 512k. *General Requirements:* Lotus 1-2-3 Releases 1A or higher, 132 column printer (or 80-column printer with compressed type). *Customer Support:* $100.00

STREAMLINED CNC: NUMERICAL CONTROL

per year.
$695.00, incl. first year of maintenance, support, & upgrades.
Evaluates Management Decisions That Affect Profitability Goals & Performance Objectives. Compares Forecast Assumptions with up to Five Years of Historical Data.
Farin & Assocs.

Streamlined CNC: Numerical Control Vertical Mill Trainer. *Items Included:* Bound manual. *Customer Support:* Free hotline - no time limit; 30 day limited warranty; updates are $5/disk plus S&H.
MS-DOS 2.1 or higher. IBM & compatibles (640k). disk $189.95. *Nonstandard peripherals required:* Two floppy drives (or one floppy & a hard disk); serial port (for communications); CGA, EGA, or equivalent graphics capability. Image Writer & laser printers are supported.
Macintosh Plus, SE, or II. 3.5" disk $189.95.
Trainer for Numerical Mill Control, Also a Working G-Code Generator. Includes a Syntax Checker (for Bridgeport Boss Level 3) & Graphical Simulator Which Allow You to Test Your G-Code Before Actually Sending It to the Machine. Bridgeport, Dyna, Cardinal, Tape Punch, & Text Communications Capabilities Are Built-In. Tool Paths May Be Plotted on the Screen or Sent to a Printer.
Dynacomp, Inc.

Streamliner. *Compatible Hardware:* IMS International Microcomputers. *Operating System(s) Required:* TurboDOS, CP/M. *Language(s):* Pascal.
contact publisher for price.
Integrated, Multi-User Subscription Fulfillment & Circulation Management System Specifically Designed for the Publishing Industry.
Computer Pubns. Group.

Streamlines: Fluid Flow in Networks. *Items Included:* Bound manual. *Customer Support:* Free hotline - no time limit; 30 day limited warranty; updates are $5/disk plus S&H.
MS-DOS 2.1 or higher. IBM & compatibles (360k). $59.95-$495.00. *Nonstandard peripherals required:* Two drives (one should be a hard disk or high-density floppy), & a math coprocessor.
Models the Steady-State Flow of Homogeneous Newtonian Fluids in Pipes, Ducts, Loops, Trees, & Networks. It Provides Accurate, Comprehensive, & Well-Documented Analyses of Duct & Pipe Sizing, Fan & Pumping Power, Pressure & Flow Control, & General System Performance.
Dynacomp, Inc.

Streets on a Disk. *Version:* 5.0. 1986. *Items Included:* 3 ring binder - manual, program disks (includes sample file), GPS Interface. *Customer Support:* Free Telephone Support.
DOS. IBM PC & compatibles (500k). disk $225.00. *Addl. software required:* Accessory maps ($40.00-$225.00 for each county) ($50.00-$100.00 for each USA layer) Available from Klynas Engineering. *Optimal configuration:* Disk Cache software & 1Mb RAM Disk.
Streets on a Disk Can Display Street Maps on a PC. It Can Read Mailing Lists, Automatically Locate Addresses, Generate Travel Directions, Calculate Distance, Mileage, Time Travel & Fuel Requirements. Accessory Map Files Are Available for Both U. S. Counties & USA. Also Available Is the New St-Batch Programmers Interface Language.
Klynas Engineering.

Streets on a Disk. *Version:* 6.0. *Items Included:* 200 plus page manual in a 3 ring binder. Sample map of New York (Manhattan) & the USA states. *Customer Support:* No charge for technical support (telephone).
$225.00 Base pkg.
$95.00 ea., County Maps.
$50.00 per layer, USA Series Maps.
Includes High Resolution Color Map Graphics, over 100 Windows Style Menus, Complete Search Capabilities, a Professional Map Editor, & the Ability to Overlay Database or Other Custom Information. Also Included Is a Router That Can Automatically Generate Travel Directions, a GPS Interface Able to Track a Fleet of Moving Vehicles, & Integrated Record/Playback of Keyboard MACROS. Allows User to Display Detailed Road Maps That Include Complete Map Graphics with Many Levels of Streets, Waterways, Boundaries, & Railroad Tracks. Most Maps Also Include Schools, Parks, Hospitals, Churches, & Other Landmarks. A Useful Companion for Salesmen, Delivery Services, Police & Fire Departments, Insurance Companies, Banks, & Motorists Everywhere.
Klynas Engineering.

Strength of Materials. Hari. 1985. *Items Included:* Spiral manual contains theory, sample runs. *Customer Support:* Free phone, on-site seminars.
MS-DOS. IBM (128k). disk $120.00. *Addl. software required:* BASIC.
6 Programs That Solve Problems in Strength of Materials Including 2 & 3D Combined Stress Using Mohr's Circle, Properties of Standard Beam Cross Sections, Beam Deflections with Shear & Bending Moments Displayed, Bending of a Curved Beam, Stress in a Thick Cylinder Caused by Shrink Fitting.
Kern International, Inc.

Stress. *Compatible Hardware:* Commodore 64, 128.
$199.95 (Order no.: STRC64-05-001).
EMG & Peripheral Skin Temperature (PST) Biofeedback Program for Treatment of Certain Vascular & Muscle Contraction Headaches, Hypertension, Anxiety & Many Other Disorders. Displays EMG and/or PST Signals & Processes These Signals to Produce Audio & Visual Outputs Reflecting the Degree of Muscle Contraction & Skin Temperature, & the Rate of Change in These 2 Parameters.
Bodylog.

Strike Fleet.
Apple II+, IIe, IIc. disk $14.95.
Commodore 64, 128. disk $14.95.
IBM. disk $14.95.
Simulation Which Lets You Control Battleships, Helicopters & Other Type of Transportation.
Electronic Arts.

Strings & Things. *Compatible Hardware:* IBM PC, PC XT, PC AT & compatibles.
disk $69.95.
Supports String Manipulations, Command Line Usage, DOS Call Capabilities, SHELL Generation & Data Transmission, BATCH File Control, Music Generation, PEEKs & POKEs, PORT Access, & General Register Manipulations. Versions Available for Microsoft, Supersoft, Ryan McFarland, IBM Professional, Lahev, & IBM FORTRAN.
Alpha Computer Service.

Strong's Greek-Hebrew Dictionary & Englishman's Concordance. Aug. 1989.
Customer Support: No fee is charged for our customer support: 30 day money back return guarantee; lifetime warranty on defective disk replacement; free telephone technical support.
PC or MS-DOS 2.0 or higher. IBM PC/XT/AT or compatible. 3.5" or 5.25" disk $69.95. *Addl. software required:* PC Study Bible & King James Version of Bible. *Optimal configuration:*

SOFTWARE ENCYCLOPEDIA 1996

Hard disk with 2.5Mb hard disk space for the Greek-Hebrew Dictionary.
Do Original Language Studies Without Prior Knowledge of Greek or Hebrew. View Strong's Definition of Any Greek or Hebrew Word; Find Every Occurrence of a Particular Greek or Hebrew Word in the Bible & Then View Each Verse in Context.
Biblesoft.

Strong's Greek-Hebrew Dictionary & Englishman's Concordance. May 1993. *Items Included:* Disks, marketing literature, order form. *Customer Support:* No fee for customer support: 30 day money back guarantee, limited replacement warranty on diskettes defective at time of purchase, free telephone technical support.
PC-DOS/MS-DOS 3.1 or higher or Windows 1.7 or higher. IBM 386/486 or 100% compatible (Windows); Also XT/AT/286 (DOS) (640k DOS or 4Mb Windows). disk $69.95 (ISBN 1-56514-545-3). *Addl. software required:* PC Study Bible & KJV text. *Optimal configuration:* Requires 5.25" 1.2Mb disk drive for installation & 3Mb of hard drive space, mouse or pointer device recommended.
Do Your Own Original Language Studies Without Prior Knowledge of Greek & Hebrew. View Strong's Definition of Any Greek or Hebrew Word, Find Every Occurrence of a Particular Greek or Hebrew Word in the Bible & Then View Each Verse in Content.
Biblesoft.

Strong's Greek-Hebrew Dictionary & Englishman's Concordance. James Strong. May 1995. *Items Included:* Disks, marketing literature, order form. *Customer Support:* No fee for customer support: 30 day money back guarantee, limited replacement warranty on diskettes defective at time of purchase, free telephone technical support.
DOS 3.0 or higher or PC Windows 3.1 or higher. IBM 386/486 or 100% compatible (640k DOS or 4Mb Windows). 3.5" disk $49.95 (ISBN 1-56514-303-5). *Optimal configuration:* Requires 3.5" 1.44Mb disk drive for installation & 3Mb of hard drive space, mouse or pointer device recommended.
Do Your Own Original Language Studies Without Prior Knowledge of Greek & Hebrew, View Strong's Definition of Any Greek or Hebrew Word, Find Every Occurrence or a Particular Greek or Hebrew Word in the Bible & Then View Each Verse in Content <end>
Biblesoft.

Strong's Greek-Hebrew Dictionary & Englishman's Concordance. James Strong. May 1993. *Items Included:* One addendum manual - perfect bound. *Customer Support:* No fee for customer support: (1) 30 day money back guarantee (2) Lifetime warranty replacement on defective disks (3) Free telephone technical support.
PC-DOS/MS-DOS 3.1 or higher. IBM PC, XT/AT/286/386/486 or 100% compatibles (640k). disk $69.95 (ISBN 1-56514-545-3). *Addl. software required:* PC Study Bible & KJV text. *Optimal configuration:* Requires 5 1/4" 1.2Mb disk drive for installation & 3Mb of hard drive space. Mouse or pointer device recommended.
Do Your Own Original Language Studies Without Prior Knowledge of Greek & Hebrew. View STRONG'S Definition of Any Greek or Hebrew Word; Find Every Occurrence of a Particular Greek or Hebrew Word in the Bible & Then View Each Verse in Context.

TITLE INDEX

STRSR. 1982. *Compatible Hardware:* IBM PC & compatibles. *Operating System(s) Required:* MS-DOS. *Language(s):* BASIC. *Memory Required:* 128k.
$190.00.
Solves All of the Problems Related to Shell Stress & Nozzle Wall Stress from External Loads on the Nozzle & Internal Pressure As It Applies to Square or Rectangular Attachments on Cylindrical Vessels. Relies on the Reference "Local Stresses in Pressure Vessels" for Input of Stress Coefficients, & Is Limited to the Range Contained in the Reference.
Technical Research Services, Inc.

STRSS. 1982. *Compatible Hardware:* IBM PC & compatibles. *Operating System(s) Required:* MS-DOS. *Language(s):* BASIC. *Memory Required:* 128k.
$395.00.
Solves All of the Problems Related to Shell Stress & Nozzle Wall Stress from External Loads on the Nozzle & Internal Pressure As It Applies to Round Nozzles on Spherical Vessels.
Technical Research Services, Inc.

STRUCT-I. 1983. *Compatible Hardware:* Apple II, IIe; IBM PC; TRS-80 Model I, Model II, Model III, Model 4, Model 12, Model 16. *Operating System(s) Required:* PC-DOS. *Memory Required:* TRS-80 Model I, III 48k, others 64k.
TRS-80 Model II, 12, 16. disk $45.00.
TRS-80 Model I, III, 4; IBM PC; Apple. disk $30.00 ea.
Designs Beams with Graphics. Considers Right Type of Loading, Material to Calculate Required Beam Size Deflection, Shear, Bending Moment of Inertia, Section Modulus, & Neutral Axis.
Documan Software.

Structural Analysis. *Version:* FASTRAN. 1989. *Compatible Hardware:* IBM PC & compatibles. *Operating System(s) Required:* PC-DOS/MS-DOS. *Language(s):* QBASIC. *Customer Support:* Telephone assistance.
disk $47.00, incl. user guide.
disk $127.00, incl. source code.
Accepts Input from a Previously Created Data File or Data May Be Input As the Program Requests It. Input Consists of Joint Coordinates, Member Incidences, Support Conditions (FIX, PIN, X-ROLLER, etc), Member Releases, Support Settlements (If Desired), Temperature Deformations (If Desired), & Joint & Member Loads. Output Consists of Joint Displacements & Rotations Plus the Member End Forces (Moments, Shears & Axial Forces) & Reactions. Uses a Virtual Memory Approach Allowing for "in Memory" Solutions for Smaller Problems While Automatically Switching to Disk Storage for Larger Problems.
Systek, Inc. (Mississippi).

Structural Analysis by Finite Elements: SAFE. *Version:* 7.0. Mar. 1990. *Compatible Hardware:* IBM PC, PC XT. *Operating System(s) Required:* MS-DOS. *Language(s):* FORTRAN. *Memory Required:* 256k. *General Requirements:* 2 disk drives.
disk $295.00, incl. instr's. manual.
General Purpose Finite Element Program for Static Stress Analysis in 2- & 3-Dimensional Structures. Will Calculate the Displacements at Each Node, the Reactions at All Designated Supports, & the State of Stress in Each Element According to Element Type. Maximums of 600 Nodes & 600 Elements Are Allowed, Plus 25 Sets of Different Characteristics. Element Types Available Include: Plane Truss, Plane Frame, Space Truss, Space Frame, Plane Stress Triangle & Rectangle, Plate Bending Triangle & Rectangle, Pipe/Shaft & Elastic Foundation Materials.
J. P. Axe.

Structural Analysis Software for Micros. 1987. *Compatible Hardware:* IBM PC, PC XT, PC AT, & compatibles. *Operating System(s) Required:* PC-DOS 2.0. *Language(s):* BASIC (source code included). *General Requirements:* CGA card.
disk $120.00.
(Order no.: 602-ID).
(Order no.: 602-B).
Analysis of 3D Frames with Concentrated Loads, Thermal Loads, Prescribed Displacements of Joints. 3D Graphics Show Structure with Deflections Overplotted.
Kern International, Inc.

Structural Concrete Beam Design. *Items Included:* Bound manual. *Customer Support:* Free hotline - no time limit; 30 day limited warranty; updates are $5/disk plus S&H.
MS-DOS. IBM & compatibles (384k). disk $349.95.
demo disk $5.00.
Designs Concrete Beams Using ACI 318-77 Ultimate Strength Method. Flexural & Shear Reinforcing Steel Requirements Are Computed for Rectangular & T-Sections. The Designer May Specify Beams Exposed to Weather, Cast in Place or Prefabricated, Cast Against Earth, or Cast in Formwork. The Beam Weight Is Computed Automatically & Applied As a Uniformly Distributed Load. Beams with Only Bottom, or Both Top & Bottom Steel Are Automatically Designed. An Extended Beam Can Be Simulated by Entering the End Moments.
Dynacomp, Inc.

Structural Concrete Column Design. *Items Included:* Bound manual. *Customer Support:* Free hotline - no time limit; 30 day limited warranty; updates are $5/disk plus S&H.
MS-DOS. IBM & compatibles (128k). disk $349.95.
demo disk $5.00.
Automatically Designs Near-Optimum Reinforced Concrete Columns of the Round-Spiral, Square-Tied, & Rectangular-Tied Types. SCCD Employs the Gaylord & Gaylord Method with a Generalization to Include Eccentric Axial Loads & Rectangular Column Designs. Meets ACI 1983 Concrete Design Code Requirements. Concrete Is Assumed to Be in Compression, with No Bending Other Than Eccentricity. Inputs Are Axial Dead Load & Live Load, Ultimate Strength & Weight of Concrete, Yield Strength of Longitudinal & Spiral Rebar, Eccentricity, Longest Laterally Unsupported Length, Total Column Length, & Column-End Fixity Factor. SCCD Tests Successive Sizes of Column & Determines the Smallest Column Meeting the Design Needs.
Dynacomp, Inc.

Structural Engineering Analysis on Personal Computers. *Version:* IBM. Fleming. *Compatible Hardware:* IBM PC. *Operating System(s) Required:* DOS. *Memory Required:* 64k. *Items Included:* Book & disk.
disk $32.52 (ISBN 0-07-079039-6).
Analyze Plane Trusses, Plane Frames, Space Trusses, & Space Frames. Accompanies Supplemental Text to Provide Programs Which the Students Can Use in a Variety of Structural Engineering Courses in Analysis & Design.
McGraw-Hill, inc.

Structural Engineering Library. *Compatible Hardware:* TI-99/4A.
contact publisher for price.
Helps Structural Engineers to Make Complex Calculations & Evaluations.
Texas Instruments, Personal Productivit.

Structural Engineering System. Sep. 1986. *Compatible Hardware:* Apple Macintosh; DEC; HP 80, HP 300, HP 200 series, IBM PC, PC XT, PC AT & compatibles; Wang PC, 2200. *Operating System(s) Required:* MS-DOS, CP/M, XENIX, UNIX. *Language(s):* C. *Memory Required:* 640k. *General Requirements:* Hard disk.
$300.00 to $2950.00.
Designed for Engineers Doing Analysis & Design of Commercial, Industrial, & Special Structures. Includes 2- or 3-Dimensional Analysis, Concrete Design, Steel Design, Shear Wall Analysis, Prestressed Beam Design, Concrete Footing Design, Bolted Beam Connections Design, & More.
ECOM Assocs., Inc.

Structural One-Way/Two-Way Concrete Slab Design. *Items Included:* Bound manual. *Customer Support:* Free hotline - no time limit; 30 day limited warranty; updates are $5/disk plus S&H.
MS-DOS. IBM & compatibles (256k). disk $369.95.
demo disk $5.00.
Designs One-Way & Two-Way Concrete Slabs under Applied Loads Using the Design Procedures of Winter & Nilson, the ACI 318-77 Direct Design Method, & ACI Moment Coefficients. Computes the Minimum Slab Thickness Required by Codes, Flexural Steel Bar Sizes, & Design Moments. Data Inputs for Two-Way Slabs Are the Short & Long Span Lengths, Minimum Desired Thickness, Live & Dead Loads, Reinforcing Steel Yield Strength, Concrete Density, & Compressive Strength. Two-Way Slab Design Also Requires the Column Dimensions & Interior & Exterior Beam Dimensions.
Dynacomp, Inc.

Structural Steel Beam Design. *Items Included:* Bound manual. *Customer Support:* Free hotline - no time limit; 30 day limited warranty; updates are $5/disk plus S&H.
MS-DOS. IBM & compatibles (256k). disk $179.95.
demo disk $5.00.
Selects Standard Prismatic Steel Beams According to the AISC Manual of Steel Construction (8th Edition) Using the Standard W, M, S, HP, C, & MC Shapes & Any of the 33 Load Conditions Described in the Manual. Inputs Are Span, Point, & Distributed Loads, Load Locations, & Material Yield Strength.
Dynacomp, Inc.

Structural Steel Column Design. *Items Included:* Bound manual. *Customer Support:* Free hotline - no time limit; 30 day limited warranty; updates are $5/disk plus S&H.
MS-DOS. IBM & compatibles (256k). disk $279.95.
demo disk $5.00.
Selects the Optimum Section for Steel Columns, Using the AISC Steel Construction Handbook Design Methods. A Family of Sections Is Offered, with the Optimum Section Indicated. Less Optimal Sections May Be Called up If Desired. The Column May Have Axial Loads, with or Without X- or Y-Axis Bending Moments at the Ends. A Data File Contains the Steel Beam Characteristics of W, M, S, HP, C, & MC Shapes. Axial Loads & Bending Moments about Both Ends Are Entered by the User. Other Inputs Are Beam Yield Strength, Laterally Unsupported Length along X- & Y-Axes, & Fixity Factor. Outputs Include AISC Designation of the Most Efficient Beam, Area, Depth, Flange Width, & Thickness, & a Family of Less Efficient Beams. SSCD Runs SI Metric or English Units.
Dynacomp, Inc.

StructurE: the Complete Toolkit for Structuring Assembly Language Programs. Kurt M. Schindler. Jun. 1989. *Items Included:* 256-page book: manual, user guide, technical information & source listings; disk containing working source

code for the required computer configuration. *Customer Support:* Free technical assistance available.
80x86, Z-80, 8051, 68xx. disk $39.95 (ISBN 0-9623669-2-7). *Addl. software required:* Macro-Assembler for target processor.
A Generic Software Tool That Raises Programming Productivity of Assembly Language Programmers by Aiding Them in Writing, Testing & Debugging. Helps Bridge the Gap Between Assembly & High-Level Languages.
Logical Solutions Research & Development, Inc.

Structured Assembler Translator. Wayne R. Deniston. *Compatible Hardware:* IBM PC, PCjr, PC XT, PC AT, Portable PC, 3270 PC with IBM Display, one double-sided disk drive, IBM Macro-Assembler (MASM). *Operating System(s) Required:* DOS 2.00, 2.10, 3.00, 3.10. *Memory Required:* 128k.
disk $34.95 (Order no.: 6246550).
Provides Many of the Structured Programming Facilities Provided by High-Level Languages While Retaining the Control of the Machine Language. Some of Its Features Include: Conditional Statements Such As IF, ELSE, ELSEIF, WHILE, & REPEAT to a Maximum Nesting Depth of 256; IMBED External Files That Are to Be Included & Need to Be Translated by the Preprocessor; Users Can Define Synonyms for Frequently Used Phrases, Define Customized Operators, & Choose or Switch Between SIGNED & UNSIGNED Comparisons.
Personally Developed Software, Inc.

Structured BASIC Facility. Scott T. Jones. *Compatible Hardware:* IBM PC, PCjr, PC XT, PC AT, Portable PC, 3270 PC with IBM Display & one double-sided disk drive. *Operating System(s) Required:* DOS 2.00, 2.10, 3.00, 3.10. *Memory Required:* 128k.
disk $54.95 (Order no.: 6276618).
Programming Development Tool Containing the Following Three Utilities: The EDITOR Helps Create & Edit Programs Using Both Line & Full-Screen Editing Capabilities; The PREPROCESSOR Converts Structured BASIC Source Files for Both the Interpreter & the BASIC Compiler; The GENERATOR Converts an Existing BASIC Source File into a Structured BASIC Source File.
Personally Developed Software, Inc.

STRUSAP Finite Element Structural Analysis. *Items Included:* Bound manual. *Customer Support:* Free hotline - no time limit; 30 day limited warranty; updates are $5/disk plus S&H.
MS-DOS 2.x, 3.x (640k); 4.x & higher (1Mb). IBM & compatibles. $169.95-$479.95.
Nonstandard peripherals required: Hard disk; CGA or EGA graphics capability; 80x87 math coprocessor. Compatible with HP7470, 7475, & other HPGL plotters, as well as IBM, HP, & Epson printers.
manual only $29.95.
Prepared by Engineers for Engineers. Even the Most Intricate Models Can Be Easily Designed & Analyzed. In Addition, the Color Graphics & Three-Dimensional Static, Dynamic, & Seismic Analyses Give Your PC Large-System Capabilities & Main-Frame Performance. Uses a Free-Format, Natural Engineering Language to Make Model Development Fast & Easy. Can Analyze Mechanical & Structural Systems Composed of (in Any Combination): Beams; Shells (Triangular, Rectangular); Springs; Equivalent Masses; Rotational Inertias; Forces, Moments, Gravity, Pressure, Thermal Stress. Features Include: Natural Modeling Language; Metric & English Units; 3-D Color Graphics with Virtual Device Interface; Bandwidth Minimization; Dynamic, Static, Response Spectra Analyses; Cartesian/Cylindrical Coordinates; Triangular & Quadrilateral Shell Elements; Automatic Joint/Member Generation.
Dynacomp, Inc.

Stuart Little. Intentional Education Staff & E. B. White. *Items Included:* Program manual. *Customer Support:* Free technical support, 90 day warranty.
School ver.. System 7.1 or higher. Macintosh (4Mb). 3.5" disk contact publisher for price (ISBN 1-57204-393-8). *Nonstandard peripherals required:* 256 color monitor, hard drive, printer.
Lab pack. System 7.1 or higher. Macintosh (4Mb). 3.5" disk contact publisher for price (ISBN 1-57204-369-5). *Nonstandard peripherals required:* 256 color monitor, hard drive, printer.
Site license. System 7.1 or higher. Macintosh (4Mb). 3.5" disk contact publisher for price (ISBN 1-57204-394-6). *Nonstandard peripherals required:* 256 color monitor, hard drive, printer.
School ver.. Windows 3.1 or higher. IBM/Tandy & 100% compatibles (4Mb). disk contact publisher for price (ISBN 1-57204-370-9). *Nonstandard peripherals required:* VGA or SVGA 640 x 780 resolution (256), mouse, hard drive, sound device.
Lab pack. Windows 3.1 or higher. IBM/Tandy & 100% compatibles (4Mb). disk contact publisher for price (ISBN 1-57204-395-4). *Nonstandard peripherals required:* VGA or SVGA 640 x 480 resolution (256), mouse, hard drive, sound device.
Site license. Windows 3.1 or higher. IBM/Tandy & 100% compatibles (4Mb). disk contact publisher for price (ISBN 1-57204-371-7). *Nonstandard peripherals required:* VGA or SVGA 640 x 480 resolution (256), mouse, hard drive, sound device.
This companion for young adult literature is ideal for students who don't know how to start that book report, or give that needed summary. Gentle prompts throughout the guide section of the program include Warm-up Connections, Thinking about Plot, Quoting & Noting, Keeping a Journal, If I Were ———' Responding to Questions, Using Quotations, Taking a Personal View, Write to Others, & Write a Sequel.
Lawrence Productions, Inc.

Stud Poker. *Compatible Hardware:* Atari 400, 800. *Language(s):* Atari BASIC. *Memory Required:* 16k.
disk $18.95.
2 Menu Selection of This Popular Game.
Dynacomp, Inc.

Student Adaptation to College Questionnaire. *Version:* 2.010. Robert W. Baker & Bohdan Siryk. *Customer Support:* Free unlimited phone support with a toll free number.
DOS 3.0 or higher. IBM or 100% compatible (512k). disk $150.00 (Order no.: W-1020 5.25"; W-1049 3.5"). *Optimal configuration:* Hard disk with 1Mb free disk space, printer.
Cost-Effective Way to Detect Problems Early in the Student's College Career. Indicates the Nature of Those Problems, & Provides Clear Guidelines for Subsequent Intervention. Particularly Useful in Identifying Potential Dropouts.
Western Psychological Services.

Student-Course Scheduling System. *Version:* V8.01. 1982. *Items Included:* 1 full manual. *Customer Support:* 90 days unlimited warranty; unlimited technical support via telephone for $225/system per year.
MS-DOS. IBM or compatible (640k). disk $995.00. *Optimal configuration:* MS-DOS 6.2 or higher, 15Mb including data, of space on a hard drive (to include all 5 systems). *Networks supported:* Novell, LANtastic, Windows NT.
Build a Master Schedule in Only Days! Enter Preliminary Section Data Once, Which May Be Used in Subsequent Years with Any Necessary Changes. Student Course Requests Are Entered with an Optical Scanner or Keyboard. Schedules May Be Printed 2 Different Ways. The Arena Method May Also Be Used.
Applied Educational Systems, Inc.

Student Guide to Weather Satellite Image Interpretation. Richard P. Behrens. 1993. *Items Included:* Spiral (3 ring) bound guide with five PCX images on two 3.5 disks. *Customer Support:* Telephone, no charge.
MS-DOS. IBM & compatibles (1Mb). disk $195.00 (ISBN 0-923854-08-8). *Nonstandard peripherals required:* Super VGA Graphics-capable of 800X600X256 colors. *Addl. software required:* SDSFAX PLUS Software $89.50. *Optimal configuration:* IBM compatible PC, hard drive, Super VGA graphics.
Interactive Guide Involves the Students in Computer Activities That Use Remote Sensing Images Captured by American Weather Satellites. These Activities Help Students Interpret Weather Phenomena & Geographic Features. A Detailed Explanation on How to Capture These Images Using the SDSFAX PLUS System Is Included.
Satellite Data Systems, Inc.

Student Organization Software: Complete Membership Management. Open Door Software Division. 1992.
IBM & compatible (512k). disk $69.00 (ISBN 1-56756-012-1, Order no.: OD250I).
Macintosh. 3.5" disk $69.00 (ISBN 1-56756-013-X, Order no.: ODS260M).
Management Software for Student Organization Leaders. Works Well with Multiple Organizational Management. For Student Organization That Needs to Report Current Officers, Phone, & Route Listings to a Central Office. Allows for Electronic Transfer of Information.
Advantage International.

Student's Marketing Edge.
IBM PC, PC XT, PC AT, PS/2 & compatibles (256k). disk $79.00. *Addl. software required:* Lotus 1-2-3 2, 2.01. 2.2 & 3.
Aimed at College & University Business School Students. Used for Industrial Marketing Courses Such As: Marketing Management, Strategic Market Planning, Entrepreneurial Classes & Computerized Marketing Decision Support Classes. Helps to Train Students in Real-World Market Planning Applications in Order to Make Better Decisions for: Selecting Target Markets, Pinpointing Customer Needs, Defeating Competitors, Developing Market Strategies, Pricing Products, Selecting Distribution Channels, etc.
Successware.

Studio of Greetings: Print Magic. *Version:* Greetings 3.5, Print Magic 2.0. *Items Included:* Design Idea Book illustrating over 700 greeting card designs, paper/envelopes, 3 3.5 diskettes (720k). Coupon for 5.25 diskettes (360k). *Customer Support:* 90-day warranty - customer support 8:30-5:30 PST (415) 368-3200.
DOS 2.1. PC/XT/AT, Hercules/CGA, EGA, VGA (512k). disk $64.95 (Order no.: 62705T). *Nonstandard peripherals required:* Printer required. *Optimal configuration:* DOS 5, 1Mb RAM, 386 VGA, mouse, laser printer.
All-in-One Toolkit Designs Greeting Cards, Flyers, Banners & More. Over 400 High Resolution Graphics Installable to New Print Shop .PCX Windows (.BMP) or Print Magic Format. 30 Plus Fonts. Includes New Print Magic 2.0 for Creating & Printing Cards. Design Ideas Book Illustrates 700 Plus Card Designs, Bonus 386 Accent Graphics & Sample Paper/Envelopes.
Epyx, Inc.

TITLE INDEX

Studio of Greetings!: Print Magic 2.0. Mar. 1992. *Items Included:* Design ideas book illustrating over 700 greeting card designs, paper/envelope samples. *Customer Support:* Telephone or mail warranty, no toll-free number.
DOS 2.1. PC/XT/AT, Hercules/CGA/EGA/VGA. disk $69.95 (Order no.: 62705D/T). *Nonstandard peripherals required:* Printer required. *Optimal configuration:* DOS 5, 1Mb RAM, 386 VGA mouse, laser printer.
All-in-One Toolkit for Design of Greeting Cards, Flyers, Banners, & More. Over 400 High Resolution Graphics Installable to New Print Shop, .PCX, Windows (.BMP) or Paint Magic Format. Includes New Paint Magic 2.0 for Creating & Printing Cards. Design Ideas Book Illustrates over 700 Card Designs Bonus 386 Accent Graphics & Sample Paper/Envelopes.
Epyx, Inc.

Studio of Greetings 3.5: Print Magic 2.0. *Items Included:* Design idea book illustrating over 700 greeting cards, signs, paper, envelopes, 3-3.5 diskettes (720k); coupon for 5.25 diskettes (360k). *Customer Support:* 90 day warranty, customer service available 8:30-5:30 PST (415) 368-3200.
DOS 2.1. PC/XT/AT, Hercules/CGA, EGA, VGA (512k). disk $64.95 (Order no.: 62705T). *Nonstandard peripherals required:* Printer required. *Optimal configuration:* DOS 5, 1Mb RAM, VGA, mouse, laser printer.
All-in-One Toolkit Designs Greeting Cards, Flyers, Banners & More. Over 400 High Resolution Graphics Installable to New Print Shop .PCX Windows (.BMP) or Print Magic Format. 30 Plus Fonts. Includes New Print Magic 2.0 for Creating & Printing Cards. Design Ideas Book Illustrates 700 Plus Card Designs, Bonus 386 Accent Graphics & Sample Paper/Envelopes.
Everbright Software.

Studio Series Design Group CD (CD-ROM). *Items Included:* User's guide, visual index. *Customer Support:* Free & unlimited technical support to registered users; 60 day money-back guarantee.
Macintosh. Macintosh (3Mb). CD-ROM disk $339.95 SRP. *Nonstandard peripherals required:* PostScript compatible printer. *Addl. software required:* Any word-processing, desktop publishing or works program that accepts EPS files.
Windows V.3.0 or higher. IBM PC & compatibles (4Mb). CD-ROM disk $339.95 SRP. *Addl. software required:* Any word processing, desktop publishing or works application that accepts CGM or WMF files.
Over 1100 Full-Color Images. Includes the following Studio Series Portfolios: Animals & Nature, Artistry & Borders, Business Art, Illustrations, Sports & Games. Also Includes SMART Gallery, The Intelligent Catalog - You Can Search by Name, Keyword, or Idea, & SMART Gallery Utilizes Artificial Intelligence Technology to Associate What You've Asked for with What You Really Want.
T/Maker Co., Inc.

Studio Sixteen - AD Five-Sixteen. Anthony I. Wood et al. *Items Included:* Documentation. *Customer Support:* 1 year warranty on parts & labor, free telephone support.
Amiga O.S. Commodore Amiga 2000, 2500, 3000 & 4000 (1Mb). $1495.00 (Order no.: STUDIO 16/AD516). *Optimal configuration:* Hard drive, 68020 or 68030 for best performance 2-3Mb of RAM.
Turns an Amiga into a Complete Digital Audio Workstation. The Built in SMPTE Time Code Reader Allows Easy Synchronization of Digital Audio to Video Tape. Can Record, Edit, & Play Back Direct to Hard Disk Allowing Almost Unlimited Sample Length. Supports Cut Copy, Paste As Well As More Advanced Functions Like Real-Time Echo. Can Be Used to Produce a CD Quality Master.
SunRize Industries.

Studio Sixteen-AD Ten-Twelve. Anthony J. Wood et al. Sep. 1991. *Items Included:* Documentation. *Customer Support:* 1 year warranty on parts & labor, free telephone support.
Amiga O.S. Commodore Amiga 2000, 2500, 3000 & 4000 (1Mb). $595.00 (Order no.: STUDIO 16/AD1012). *Optimal configuration:* Hard drive, 68020 or 68030 for best performance, 2-3Mb RAM.
Allows Amiga Owners to Record 12 Bit Audio Direct to Hard Disk. Built-In SMPTE Time Code Reader Allows Easy Synchronization of Digital Audio to Video Tape. Can Record, Edit, & Play Back Direct to Hard Disk Allowing Almost Unlimited Sample Length. The Supplied STUDIO 16 Editing Software Supports Cut, Copy, & Paste As Well As More Advanced Features, Like Multiband Graphic Equalizing. Provides a Perfect Low-Cost Audio for Video Post Production System.
SunRize Industries.

Studio/32.
Mac II (5Mb). 3.5" disk $695.00. *Nonstandard peripherals required:* 24-bit color card & color monitor for work with 16.8 million colors; 2Mb RAM, 8-bit color card & color monitor for 256-color display.
32-Bit Color Paint Program. Creates Photo-Quality Images with Thousands of Colors. Features Include: Scanner & Four-Color Separation Utilities, a Pantone Matching System, Special Effects Tools. Input-Output PICT, MacPaint, TIFF & Encapsulated PostScript Files.
Electronic Arts.

Studio/1.
Macintosh Plus or higher. 3.5" disk $149.95.
Black & White Paint & Graphics Program.
Electronic Arts.

Studio/8. *Compatible Hardware:* Apple Macintosh II. *General Requirements:* Hard disk, 4-bit color card & monochrome monitor for 2-color mode for 1Mb of RAM, 8-bit color card & color monitor for 2Mb of RAM.
3.5" disk $299.00.
256-Color Paint Program for Professionals in Graphics Design, Presentation, Desktop Publishing & Video Markets. Features Icon Toolbox, 9 Tool Modifiers, 8 Airbrushes, 4 Levels of Magnification, Dual-Mode Pencil, Variety of Polygons, French & Bezier Curves with Adjustable Anchor Points & Full Text Box-Style Editing Capabilities. Outputs to Tektronix 4693D Color Printer, Mirus 35mm Film Printer, Matrix 35mm Slide Imager & LaserWriter. Supports TIFF, PICT & PICT 2 File Formats.
Electronic Arts.

Study Quizfiles. 1994. *Customer Support:* Phone support - 90 day warranty.
Windows. IBM & compatibles (2Mb). disk $39.95. *Nonstandard peripherals required:* Mouse. *Optimal configuration:* 386 SX 2Mb RAM, Windows, Mouse. *Networks supported:* Yes.
Create Quizzes - No Programming Knowledge - Teacher, Parent, or Students Can Place Course on Disk, Which Can Be Retrieved, New or Revised, Lessons Are Scrambled. Hard Copy Printout. Word Match Format with Choices Displayed. Elementary-College.
Compu-Tations, Inc.

THE SUBLIMINAL SOFTWARE SERIES:

Stunt Driver. Version: 1.01. 1990. *Items Included:* manual. *Customer Support:* phone support.
IBM AT & compatibles (640k). disk $49.95.
With Amazingly Realistic 3-D Graphics & True-to-Life Sounds, Stunt Driver Delivers All the Action of Real Stunt Driving. Everything, That Is, But the Bruises. So Grab Your Helmet & Race to Your Favorite Retailer to Be First at the Starting Line for Stunt Driver.
Spectrum HoloByte.

STX: Shell & Tube Heat Exchanger Design & Rating Program. Heat Transfer Consultants. *Items Included:* Manual.
MS-DOS. IBM & compatibles. $3600.00.
Designs & Rates Shell & Tube Heat Exchangers.
Techdata.

Stylist. *Items Included:* User's manual, registration card. *Customer Support:* Unlimited support to registered users.
System 6.0 or higher. Macintosh Plus, SE/II. $99.95. *Addl. software required:* Microsoft Word 4.0 or higher.
Lets User Use the Full Power of Microsoft Word 4.0, by Taking the Mystery Out of Style Sheets. Displays & Prints Style Setting & Samples in Beautifully Organized Windows & Reports. Includes Auto-Formatting Templates & Dictionary of Computer Terms.
SNA, Inc.

Stylo-Type I. *General Requirements:* Second 800K drive.
Macintosh Plus or higher. 3.5" disk $295.00.
CRTronic/Linotronic Typesetting Program That Drives Typsetters in Their Native Command Language.
DeskTop Composition Systems.

STYLUS.
$2000.00.
user reference manual $18.00 (Order no.: A-0013).
installation document $5.00 (Order no.: X-0300).
Word Processing System.
Point 4 Data Corp.

Su 27: Flaulcer. Version: 1.1. Flying Legends. Jan. 1996. *Items Included:* Perfect bound manual, 4 color map. *Customer Support:* 30 day limited warranty.
Windows 95 or DOS 5.0 or higher. 486/66 (1Mb). disk $59.95 (ISBN 0-917059-37-9, Order no.: 052581). *Nonstandard peripherals required:* Uncompressed hard drive recommended. *Optimal configuration:* Pentium with 8Mb of hard drive space, SVGA card.
Military Russian Jet Flight Simulator.
Strategic Simulations, Inc.

Sub Battle Simulator. *Compatible Hardware:* Apple IIe, IIc, IIgs, Macintosh; Atari ST; Commodore 64/128, Amiga; IBM PC. *Memory Required:* Apple IIe/IIc 48k, Commodore 64k, IBM 128k, Apple IIgs, Macintosh, & Atari ST 512k.
disk $39.95.
Simulation of Submarine Warfare During War World II. Features Four Levels of Difficulty.
Epyx, Inc.

The Subliminal Software Series: Business Skills Series. Version: 1.0. Graeme Gibson. Jul. 1991. *Items Included:* Loading instructions; order form for other products; Manual is on the Disk. *Customer Support:* 7 day money back warranty; short phone questions answered free.
DOS 2.10 or higher. IBM or compatible, 1 disk drive 3.5 or 5.25 (256k). $14.99 (ISBN 0-916161-17-X, Order no.: S17). *Nonstandard peripherals required:* Does not work on Laptops with liquid crystal, needs CRT. *Addl. software*

THE SUBLIMINAL SOFTWARE SERIES:

required: DOS. *Optimal configuration:* AT or 386. *Networks supported:* All.
Interrupts Regular Applications People Are Using Then Flashing Affirmations for About 1/30th of a Second, Then It Returns the User to the Original Program with No Work Lost. Users Pick up Messages Subconsciously. Affirmations to Help with Promotions, Organization Reading, Public Speaking, etc. Well Behaved TSR.
Computer Training Corp.

The Subliminal Software Series: Personal Enrichment Series. *Version:* 1.0. Graeme Gibson. Jul. 1991. *Items Included:* Loading instructions, Order form for other products, manual is on the disk. *Customer Support:* 7 day money back warranty, short phone questions answered free.
DOS 2.10 or higher. IBM or compatible, 1 disk drive 3.5 or 5.25 (256k). disk $14.99 (ISBN 0-916161-03-X, Order no.: S03). *Nonstandard peripherals required:* Does not work on Liquid Crystal Displays; requires CRT. *Addl. software required:* DOS. *Optimal configuration:* AT or 386. *Networks supported:* All.
Interrupts Regular Applications People Are Using Flashing Affirmations for About 1/30th of a Second, Then It Returns the User to the Original Program with no Work Lost. Users Pick up Messages Subconsciously. Affirmations to Help with Weight, Diet, Smoking, Exercise, etc. Well Behaved TSR.
Computer Training Corp.

Submarine Blockade. *Compatible Hardware:* TRS-80 Model I, Model III, Model 4 with Level II BASIC. *Memory Required:* 16k.
disk $18.95.
Arcade Game.
Dynacomp, Inc.

Submarine Commander. *Compatible Hardware:* Commodore PET with Commodore BASIC. *Memory Required:* 16k.
disk $19.95.
Real-Time Submarine Simulation.
Dynacomp, Inc.

Subscription. *Operating System(s) Required:* All CP/M based machines.
contact publisher for price.
Business Computers, Inc. (Florida).

Subscription Manager. *Version:* 4.0. 1995. *General Requirements:* Hard disk, printer. *Items Included:* Disks, Complete illustrated instructions. *Customer Support:* Technical 8:30-4pm M-F telephone no Charge.
IBM PC, PC XT, PC AT, PS/2 (640k). disk $199.00 (ISBN 0-87132-953-0, Order no.: SUBCON).
IBM PC, PC XT, PC AT, PS/2 (640k). $399.00 Network version.
IBM. $219.00 Windows version (ISBN 0-87132-952-2).
$429.00 Windows Network version.
Keeps Track of Periodical Subscriptions: Subscription Title, Orders Placed, Number of Subscriptions Ordered. Will Maintain a File of Jobbers & Publishers. Prints Address Labels.
Right On Programs.

Subscription Manager. *Version:* 4.0.
DOS 5 or Win 3.1 (640K). DOS 199.00; DOS Network 399.00; Windows 219.00; Windows Network 429.00.
This program manages all periodicals whether they come once a week, once a month or once a season. It dosen't matter if you receive one copy of each or 4 copies. This program checks them in, tells you what's here & what's missing & then routes them any way you want.
Right on Programs.

Subscription Master. *Customer Support:* 800-929-8117 (customer service).
MS-DOS. IBM/PS2. disk $299.99 (ISBN 0-87007-817-8).
Start & Maintain an Accurate Alphabetic Order Membership List. Lists May Be Sorted by Zip Codes for Bulk Mailings or Divided into Convenient Geo Graphical Segments. Members Are Tracked So That Labels of Near-to-Expiration May Be Marked with a Set of Common Warning Signals for Any Number of Months Before & After Expiration. Letters May Also Be Generated to Follow up on These Lapses. Bills May Be Automatically Generated. New Subscriptions, & Old Subscriptions That Are Address Updates, Are Accessed at the Same Time & the Newest Address Is Automatically Updated to the File. Reports Related to New Subscribers, Revenues, etc. Are Generated. Menu-Driven.
SourceView Software International.

Subsidized Housing: Retirement Home Management. 1985. *Compatible Hardware:* DECmate, PDP 11-23. *Operating System(s) Required:* COS-310, MICRO-RSX. *General Requirements:* Hard disk.
disk $4000.00.
Combines Rental Accounting With Government Reporting to Serve the Needs of Rental Complexes Complying with HUD Subsidized Housing Contracts. ACCOUNTING SYSTEM Provides Automatic Monthly Rent Charging, & Processes Rental Receipts for Subsidized & Non-Subsidized Tenants. Monthly Income & Receipts Summary Separates Regular, Excess, & Subsidized Rental Income & Receipts. REPORTING SYSTEM Prints Two HUD Reports: Schedule of Assistance Payments Due (52670A - Part 1) & Excess Income Report (93104A).
Corporate Consulting Co.

Success Inc. *Customer Support:* 90 day warranty.
MS-DOS 2.1 or higher. IBM (256K). disk $129.99.
Leads User Through the Process of Preparing a Business Plan. Highly Detailed, The Plan Is Formatted in Standard Business Style. Program Is Totally Interactive.
Virgin Games.

Success on Stress: Computerized Stress Assessment. *Items Included:* Bound manual. *Customer Support:* Free hotline - no time limit; 30 day limited warranty; updates are $5/disk plus S&H.
MS-DOS 2.0 or higher. IBM & compatibles (128k). disk $69.95. *Nonstandard peripherals required:* 80-column printer; color graphics card.
Comprehensive Stress Assessment Designed to Enable Your Organization to: Measure Employee Stress Levels; Determine Which Type of Coping Response Is Being Used; Find Out How Well Stress Is Being Handled; Provide Individuals with Information on How to Make Stress Work for Themselves. May Be Used Alone or As Part of a Stress Management Program.
Dynacomp, Inc.

Successful Business Plan: (Standalone). *Version:* 2.01. Nov. 1993. *Items Included:* Combination package contains 3-ring binder edition of "Successful Business Plan: Secrets & Strategies" by Rhonda Abrams ISBN 1-55571-314-9. *Customer Support:* Free technical support over phone; limited warranty.
DOS 3.0 or higher. IBM & compatibles (640k). disk $99.95 (ISBN 1-55571-325-4, Order no.: SUBPSTXT31). *Nonstandard peripherals required:* Hard disk with 2Mb of free space. *Optimal configuration:* Mouse supported, printer beneficial.

SOFTWARE ENCYCLOPEDIA 1996

DOS 3.0 or higher. IBM & compatibles (640k). disk $125.95, incl. bk. (ISBN 1-55571-314-9, Order no.: SUBPBTXT31). *Nonstandard peripherals required:* Hard disk with 2Mb of free space. *Optimal configuration:* Mouse supported, printer beneficial.
This Easy to Use Program Includes an Outline Processor, Spreadsheet & Text Editor. Designed to Make the Process of Developing & Formatting a Business Plan Easy. No Previous Computer Experience Is Necessary. Combination Package Recommended for People Without Prior Experience Developing a Business Plan.
Oasis Pr., The.

Successful Job Interviewing. Feb. 1996. *Items Included:* Program manual. *Customer Support:* Free technical support, 90 day warranty.
Single user. Windows 3.1 or higher. IBM 386 (8Mb). disk $99.95 (ISBN 1-57204-102-1, Order no.: WIN153). *Nonstandard peripherals required:* 256 color monitor, mouse, sound card. *Addl. software required:* SVGA graphics.
Lab pack. Windows 3.1 or higher. IBM 386 (8Mb). disk $199.00 (ISBN 1-57204-127-7, Order no.: WIN153LPK). *Nonstandard peripherals required:* 256 color monitor, mouse, sound card. *Addl. software required:* SVGA graphics.
Site license. Windows 3.1 or higher. IBM 386 (8Mb). disk $399.00 (ISBN 1-57204-129-3, Order no.: WIN153SITE). *Nonstandard peripherals required:* 256 color monitor, mouse, sound card. *Addl. software required:* SVGA graphics.
Single user. System 7.1 or higher. Mac, 16MHz rating, 68030 or better processor (LC II or higher) (5Mb). 3.5" disk $99.95 (ISBN 1-57204-101-3, Order no.: APM153). *Nonstandard peripherals required:* 256 color monitor, 13" or larger.
Lab pack. System 7.1 or higher. Mac, 16 MHz rating, 68030 or better processor (LC II or higher) (5Mb). 3.5" disk $199.00 (ISBN 1-57204-126-9, Order no.: APM153LPK). *Nonstandard peripherals required:* 256 color monitor, 13" or larger.
Site license. System 7.1 or higher. Mac, 16 Mhz rating, 68030 or better processor (LC II or higher). 3.5" disk $399.00 (ISBN 1-57204-128-5, Order no.: APM153LPK). *Nonstandard peripherals required:* 256 color monitor, 13" or larger.
Shows students how to conduct themselves properly during an interview.
Lawrence Productions, Inc.

Suffixes One & Two. Jun. 1983. *Items Included:* Teacher's guide. *Customer Support:* 90-day limited warranty.
Apple-DOS 3.3. Apple II Family (48k). disk $59.00, Suffixes 1 (ISBN 0-917277-43-0).
disk $59.00, Suffixes 2 (ISBN 0-917277-45-7).
Five Computer Programs Teaching the Usage & Meaning of the Suffixes -Meter, -Gram, & Both in the Metric System. (Suffixes 1). Suffixes 2 Includes -Ess, -Fy, -Ize, -Ic, -Ical & -Ically. Both Complete with a Review Test. Ages 9 & Up.
BrainBank/Generation Ahead of Maryland.

Surgeon 3 - the Brain. *Items Included:* 2 manuals & 3 disks.
Macintosh Floppy Version. Macintosh (4Mb). 3.5" disk $59.95. *Optimal configuration:* Hard disk, color video/color monitor, System 6.07 or higher.
A Surgical Simulation Game Where a Player Attempts to Operate on a Patient's Brain. If the Player Succeeds He Gets Promoted. If the Player Fails He Will Face a Malpractice Suit.
ISM, Inc.

TITLE INDEX

Suicide Probability Scale (SPS). Version: 2.011. John G. Cull & Wayne S. Gill. Customer Support: Free unlimited phone support.
IBM PC & 100% compatibles. 3.5" or 5.25" disk $210.00 (Order no.: W-1012 (5.25"); W-1025 (3.5")). Optimal configuration: DOS 3.0 or higher (512k), & hard disk with one Mb of free hard disk space, printer.
Gives Clinicians a Rapid, Accurate, & Empirically Validated Measure of Suicide Risk in Adults & Adolescents over 13 Years of Age. Generates Three Summary Scores Which Give an Overall Indication of Suicide Risk.
Western Psychological Services.

Suit Yourself. Version: 3.0. Gail Florin. Jan. 1991. Items Included: Instruction manual.
DOS. IBM or compatibles. disk $189.00 (ISBN 1-56191-413-4, Order no.: 3226/3227). Optimal configuration: Software.
This Software Program, Designed for Men, Evaluates Body Measurements & Prints Out an Evaluation Form That Suggests Appropriate Styles of Clothing to Body Type.
Meridian Education Corp.

Suitcase II. Steve Brecker. Items Included: 1 Manual. Customer Support: Free, toll call.
Macintosh 512E. disk $79.00. Networks supported: Appletalk.
Provides Unlimited Access to Macintosh Fonts DA's F Keys & Sounds. It Allows the User to Break the Limit of 15 DA's, 500 Font Sizes While Providing Easy, "On-the-Fly" Opening of Resources.
Fifth Generation Systems, Inc.

Sum!Table. Compatible Hardware: IBM PC & compatibles, PS/2. General Requirements: Lotus 1-2-3 release 2, Symphony releases 1.1 or 1.2. $17.00 per Macro.
$45.00 for set.
Consists of Four Macros That Produce Various Tables of Results from Worksheets. The 1-Way Macro Allows to Tabulate Any Number of What-If Calculations Based on One Variable; 2-Way Calculates an Answer Based on Two Variables; 3-Way Is Similar to 1-Way, But User Can Put Data in More Than One File; & Transfer Place Data from Many Files into a Summary Table.
Rim Software.

SUM-UP. Compatible Hardware: TRS-80 Model I, Model III. Operating System(s) Required: TRSDOS, MULTI-DOS. Language(s): BASIC. $24.95.
Calculator That Stays in the Background Until Called Up. User Does Not Have to Leave the Application Program - Program Pauses Briefly & Then Returns.
Alpha Bit Communications, Inc.

Sumdij. Version: 1.1. Feb. 1995. Items Included: Illustrated user manual. Customer Support: Free 30 day telephone support.
PC-DOS 3.3 or higher. 386 (85k). Contact publisher for price (ISBN 0-945851-40-5). Nonstandard peripherals required: Any digitizing tablet.
An Estimating Program That Uses Hotdij, a TSR Digitizing Program. Captures the Hotdij Output from a Digitizer & Stores It in a File along with Other Sumdij Keyboard Data. You Can Then Use Sumdij to Identify & Sum Identical Items in the File & Print Reports.
Geocomp, Ltd.

Summary of Confirmation Coverage.
Compatible Hardware: Altos series 5-15D, series 5-5D, 580-XX, ACS8000-XX; DEC Rainbow 100 with 2 disk drives, Rainbow 100+ with 10MB hard disk; IBM PC with 2 disk drives, PC XT & compatibles; Kaypro 11/IV with 2 disk drives, Kaypro 10; Xerox 820 with 2 disk drives; ZILOG MCZ-250. Operating System(s) Required: CP/M, MP/M, CP/M-86/80, PC-DOS, MS-DOS. contact publisher for price (Order no.: CONFIRM).
Allows Auditor to List & Establishes Control over Confirmation Requests As They Are Mailed. When Replies Are Received, They Can Be Entered & Compared to Requests. Automatically Summarizes Differences Between Balances Carried by the Client & Amounts Confirmed by the Customers. Helps the Auditor to Obtain Confirmation Coverage Statistics Frequently & During the Engagement.
Coopers & Lybrand.

Summer Games II. Larry Clague et al. Compatible Hardware: Commodore 64, 128; IBM PC & compatibles. General Requirements: Joystick.
Call publisher for price.
Sports Game That Simulates the Summer Olympics. Contains 8 Additional Events Beyond Those Found in the SUMMER GAMES: Cycling, Equestrian Competitions, Fencing, High Jump, Javelin Throwing, Kayaking, Rowing, & Triple Jump. One to 8 Players Can Represent Any of 18 Countries.
Epyx, Inc.

Summit. Customer Support: 800-929-8117 (customer service).
MS-DOS. IBM/PS2. disk $1999.99 (ISBN 0-87007-690-6).
A General Accounting Package in Business Basic, Consisting of the Following Fully Integrated Systems: Order Processing & Sales Analysis, Accounts Receivable & Delinquent Accounts, Accounts Payable & Check Reconcilliation, General Ledger & Fixed Assets, Inventory Control & Open Order Reporting, & Payroll.
SourceView Software International.

SUMMUM: Sealed Except to the Open Mind.
Mar. 1994. Items Included: User's guide. Customer Support: 90 days limited warranty.
MS-DOS 3.3 or higher. PC compatible, high density floppy drive (512k). $15.00 plus shipping (ISBN 0-943217-05-9). Nonstandard peripherals required: Hercules monochrome or CGA/EGA/VGA graphics board. Optimal configuration: PC compatible, MS-DOS 3.3 or higher, 640k RAM, VGA graphics, hard disk.
This Is a Computerized Version of the Book, SUMMUM: Sealed Except to the Open Mind, Which Introduces the Summum Philosophy. The User Is Able to View the Book via a Computer.
Summum.

SunAccount. Version: 3.4. Compatible Hardware: IBM PC, IBM PC-based LANs, OS/2, IBM System/38; DEC VAX, All UNIX, AS400, IBM AIX (PS/2, RT6150, RS/6000). Memory Required: 512k. Items Included: Manuals, reference card, installation manual, demo database. Customer Support: Annual maintenance covering telephone, fax or modem support.
$6400.00.
site licenses are available.
Automatically Translates Different World Currencies in Various Accounts into a Selected Base Currency. Consolidates an Unlimited Number of Subsidiary Accounts, Each of Which May Be Based in Any Currency. Provides Journals & Account-Listings Audit Reports Showing Currency Values & Exchange Rates for Each Transaction & Generates a Trial Balance Sorted by Currency. Menu Selection Lets User Import & Export 1-2-3 PRN Files.
Systems Union, Inc.

Suncode-PC: Building Energy Load Simulation Program. Version: 5.7. Larry Palmiter & Terry Wheeling. Feb. 1985. Compatible Hardware: IBM PC & compatibles. Operating System(s) Required: MS-DOS 2.0. Language(s): MS FORTRAN (source code included). Memory Required: 384k. General Requirements: 2 disk drives, 8087 math coprocessor.
MS-DOS. object code disk $650.00 (ISBN 0-934478-30-9).
ringbinder $35.00, incl. documentation & manual (ISBN 0-934478-29-5).
Using Typical Weather Data, Program Simulates, on an Hourly Basis, Heating & Cooling Requirements of Residential & Small Commercial Buildings for Persons with or Without Technical Training.
Ecotope, Inc.

Sunday: Building Load Simulation. Version: 3.0. Nov. 1987. Compatible Hardware: IBM PC & compatibles. Operating System(s) Required: MS-DOS, PC-DOS. Language(s): Turbo Pascal. Memory Required: 128k.
disk object code $125.00 (ISBN 0-934478-28-7).
MS-DOS. (ISBN 0-934478-32-5).
object code $125.00.
Documentation & user's manual. ringbinder $35.00 (ISBN 0-934478-36-8).
Using Typical Weather Data, Program Simulates on a Daily Basis, Heating & Cooling Requirements of Residential & Small Commercial Buildings.
Ecotope, Inc.

SunDog: Frozen Legacy. Compatible Hardware: Apple II+, IIe, IIc; Atari ST.
disk $39.95.
You've Just Inherited SunDog, a One-Man Star Freighter from a Mysterious Uncle. Keeping It Is the Hard Part. Your Mission Is to Help Build a Space Colony - by Locating & Supplying the Cryogenically-Frozen Colonists & Delivering Them to Their New Home. But There Are Opponents Out There Bent on Stopping You Cold. The Game Features Zoom Action Windows, & Full Pop-Up Animation Allowing the Player to Explore over 50 Different Cities on 18 Inhabited Planets Clustered into 12 Star Systems.
FTL Games.

Sunpas. Version: 4.0. Oct. 1984. Compatible Hardware: Apple II+, IIe, Macintosh; IBM PC. Operating System(s) Required: MS-DOS, Apple OS. Language(s): Pascal. Memory Required: 64-512k. General Requirements: 2 disk drives.
disk $189.00.
Special California Version. disk $229.00.
Estimates a Building's Heating & Cooling Loads.
Solarsoft.

Sunpas/Sunop: Energy Analysis. Version: 4.0. Macintosh (512k or higher). disk $289.00.
Calculates Heating & Cooling Loads in Residential & Light Commercial Buildings. Calculation Method Involves Determination of Monthly Effective Day & Nighttime Indoor Temperatures. Program Uses Two analysis Methods: Variable Base Degree Day & Solar Load Ratio.
Solarsoft.

SunTracker Plus. Jul. 1988. Compatible Hardware: IBM PC & compatibles. Memory Required: IBM 256k. General Requirements: IBM: CGA.
disk $49.95.
Calculates Astronomical Conditions for Any Solar Eclipse & Displays a Map with Areas of Visibility. Provides Eclipse Elements, Accurate to 12 Miles on the Earth's Surface. Data for the Eclipse Includes Central Line Location, Width, Duration of Totality & Altitude of the Sun.
Zephyr Services.

Super Accounts Receivable. Customer Support: 800-929-8117 (customer service).
MS-DOS. Apple II. disk $49.99 (ISBN 0-87007-547-0).
A Menu-Driven Accounts Receivable System. Includes a Detailed Operations & User's Manual. Has the Flexiblity To Handle Different Payment & Credit Schemes. Emphasizes & Enhances Management Control & Integrates Sales Analysis with the Accounts Receivable. Salesperson-Oriented Reports Are Easily Generated As Well.
SourceView Software International.

Super Breakout. Compatible Hardware: Atari XL/XE.
ROM cartridge $6.95 (Order no.: CXL4006).
Atari Corp.

Super Carder. 1995. Compatible Hardware: Apple IIe, IIc, IIgs; IBM PC, PC XT, AT, PS/2, Macintosh. *Memory Required:* Apple 64k, IBM 520k. *Items Included:* Disks, Complete illustrated instructions. *Customer Support:* Technical 8:30-4pm M-F telephone no charge.
IBM. $159.00; Windows $199.00 (ISBN 0-87132-962-X).
Apple. $129.00 (ISBN 0-87132-963-8).
Creates Catalog Cards According to AACR II Rules for Books, AV Materials, etc. No Manual. All Done with On-Screen Prompts, On-Screen Editing, Previewing. Includes Starter Pack of Continuous Feed Catalog Cards.
Right On Programs.

Super Carder Expanded.
DOS or Win 3.1 (640K). IBM PC. DOS 179.00; Windows 199.00;.
This new program is the next generation of catalog card making software. It also fulfills another request librarians had regarding updating Catalog Carder. Choose Super Carder if your library does not require the second card or Super Carder Expanded if you need the extra lines & expanded fields for author, title, notes, & subjects.
Right on Programs.

Super Challenger. Steve Walker. 1984.
Compatible Hardware: Apple II+, IIc, IIe, IIgs; Commodore 64, 128; IBM PC; Macintosh. *Operating System(s) Required:* Apple DOS 3.3, MAC 6.03-7.1, PC-DOS 2.0. *Language(s):* QuickBasic. *Memory Required:* Apple 486k, Commodore 64k, IBM & MAC 512k.
disk $39.95 ea.
Apple. (ISBN 0-942132-18-1, Order no.: A-1114).
IBM. (ISBN 0-942132-19-X, Order no.: I-1114).
Commodore 64. (ISBN 1-55603-004-5, Order no.: C-1114).
MAC. disk $59.95.
Aural-Visual Game Designed to Increase the Player's Ability to Remember a Series of Pitches As They Are Played by the Computer. The Game Is Based on a 12-Note Chromatic Scale, an 8-Note Major Scale, & an 8-Note Minor Scale. Each Pitch Is Reinforced Visually on the Display with a Color Representation of a Keyboard.
Electronic Courseware Systems, Inc.

Super Challenger - MIDI. Steve Walker. 1985-86. Compatible Hardware: Atari ST; Apple, Commodore 64, IBM PC & compatibles. *Operating System(s) Required:* Apple DOS 3.3, PC-DOS 3.3. *Language(s):* QuickBasic. *Memory Required:* Apple 48k, Commodore 64k, IBM 640k, MAC 512k. *General Requirements:* MIDI Interface card, MIDI-compatible music keyboard. CGA card for IBM.
disk $39.95 ea.
Apple. disk $39.95 ea. (ISBN 0-942132-97-1, Order no.: MA-1156).
Commodore 64. disk $39.95 (ISBN 1-55603-011-8, Order no.: MC-1156).
IBM PC. disk $39.95 (ISBN 1-55603-030-4, Order no.: MI-1156).
Atari. disk $39.95 (ISBN 1-55603-079-7).
MAC. 3.5" disk $59.95.
Aural-Visual Game Designed to Increase the Total Memory of a Series of Pitches That Are Played by the Computer. The Game Is Based on a 12-Note Chromatic Scale, a Major Scale, & a Minor Scale. Each Pitch Is Reinforced Visually with a Color Representation of a Keyboard on the Display Screen.
Electronic Courseware Systems, Inc.

Super Checkbook. Compatible Hardware: Apple II, II+. *Language(s):* Applesoft II. *Memory Required:* 48k.
disk $24.95 (Order no.: 10041).
Maintains Checkbook with an Option to Produce Bar Graphs.
Powersoft, Inc.

Super Checkbook III. Compatible Hardware: Apple II, II+. *Language(s):* Applesoft II. *Memory Required:* 48k.
disk $49.95 (Order no.: 10001).
Revised Version of SUPER CHECKBOOK II.
Powersoft, Inc.

Super Checkbook III Checkwriter. Compatible Hardware: Apple II, II+ with printer. *Language(s):* Applesoft II. *Memory Required:* 48k.
disk $29.95 (Order no.: 10003).
Prints Checks & Vouchers from Text Files Created by SUPER CHECKBOOK III.
Powersoft, Inc.

Super Checkbook III Plus. Compatible Hardware: Apple II, II+. *Language(s):* Applesoft II. *Memory Required:* 48k. *General Requirements:* Printer.
disk $119.95 (Order no.: 10004).
Combination of SCIII, SCIII Checkwriter & Income Statement System.
Powersoft, Inc.

Super Circulation Control Expanded. 1995. *Items Included:* Disks, Complete illustrated instructions. *Customer Support:* Technical 8:30 am - 4:00 pm telephone-No Charge.
DOS & Windows. IBM & compatibles (512k). DOS $589.00; DOS Network $999.00; Windows $599.00; Windows Network $999.00. *Networks supported:* Novell, Banyan, etc.
See Complete Description for Circulation Control, Circulation Search & Circulation Reserve. Combines All Three & Gives User a Superb On-Line Circulation Program with Additional Search & Reserve Features. An Easy to Use, Friendly, Affordable On-Line Circulation Program for All Size & All Types of Libraries. This Version Expands Search to Three Authors, & Ten Subjects. Has Expanded & Annotation Fields. Prints to Laser Printer. 100% on Screen Prompts & Menu Driven.
Right On Programs.

Super Circulation Control Expanded. 1996.
DOS 5 or Win 3.1 (640K). DOS Version 589.00; DOS Network 999.00; Windows Version 599.00; Windows Network 999.00.
This software package is actually three programs in one: 1) Circulation, 2) Patrons' Online Books Catalog, 3) Overdue Books Manager. Compare ease of installation, ease & speed of learning, ease of use (100% on-screen prompts, 100% menudriven, availability & attitude of software support personnel, & cost of technical support.
Right on Programs.

Super Circulation Control with Carder. 1995.
Items Included: Disks, Complete illustrated instructions in 3 ring binder. *Customer Support:* Technical 8:30 am - 4:00 pm telephone-No Charge.
DOS & Windows. IBM & compatibles. DOS $589.00; DOS Network $999.00; Windows $599.00; Windows Network $999.00. *Networks supported:* Novell, Banyan, etc.
See Complete Description for Circulation Control, Circulation Search & Circulation Reserve. Combines All Three & Gives User a Superb On-Line Circulation Program with Additional Search & Reserve Features. An Easy to Use, Friendly, Affordable On-Line Circulation Program for All Size & All Types of Libraries. This Version Expands Search to Three Authors, & Ten Subjects. Has Expanded & Annotation Fields. Prints to Laser Printer. 100% on Screen Prompts & Menu Driven. Adds the Ability to Print Complete or Partial Sets of AACRII Catalog Cards.
Right On Programs.

Super Clerk. Version: 1.5. *Items Included:* Complete bound instruction guide. *Customer Support:* Free support for first 60 days; 1 year toll-free support, $295.00.
DOS. IBM & compatibles. $595.00-$1495.00. *Optimal configuration:* 486, 4Mb memory, fast hard disk. *Networks supported:* LANtastic, Novell.
General Purpose P.O.S. Package with Complete Inventory Functions Including Reorder & Stock Levels. The Software Tracks Inventory by Type Style or Category & Print Information with a Large Variety of Reports. Individual Client Accounts, Layaway, Credits, etc. Make Accounting Easy. Additional Features Include Commission Tracking, Coupon Tracking, Discounting by Client, or Category. Receipts Print on Plain Paper or Custom Forms.
Aphelion, Inc.

Super-Ed. Version: 3.0. Compatible Hardware: IBM PC, PCjr, PC XT, PC AT, PC compatibles.
disk $49.95.
Any DOS Command or Any Program Can Be RUN from Within SUPER-ED. Provides a Turbo Pascal-Like Environment for Any Language. Supports Multi-File Window Editing with the Ability to Move & Copy Between File Windows. Other Features Include On-Line Editing HELP, User-Definable Editing Commands & Colors, On-Line Language-Specific User-Definable HELP, WORDSTAR-Like Editor, Keyboard Macros Support.
Software Matters.

Super Fly: Arcade Plus Series. Compatible Hardware: TI 99/4A with Milton Bradley's MBX System.
contact publisher for price (Order no.: PHM3153).
Destroy the Alien Spiders Before the Next Batch Hatches & Gets You. Maneuver Your Fly Into Position & Zap the Spiders. Speech Synthesis & Voice Recognition.
Texas Instruments, Personal Productivit.

Super General Ledger. Customer Support: 800-929-8117 (customer service).
MS-DOS. Apple II. disk $49.99 (ISBN 0-87007-003-7).
An Easy Method for Keeping Multiple Sets of Double Entry Books of Account. Flexible & Totally Customizable General Ledgers. Menu-driven & Incorporates Alan G. Hill's AMPER-SORT Routine. A Detailed Manual is Included.
SourceView Software International.

Super Inventory. Customer Support: Telephone Support: 800-950-2059 (first 30 days), 900-776-6554 (after 30 days).
Apple II. disk $49.99 (ISBN 0-87007-811-9).
Easy to Use Inventory Control, Prints Labels.
SourceView Software International.

TITLE INDEX

Super MacroWorks. Randy Brandt. *Compatible Hardware:* Apple IIe, IIc, IIgs. *Operating System(s) Required:* ProDOS. *Memory Required:* 128k. *General Requirements:* AppleWorks 2.0 or higher.
disk $49.95.
Provides the Same AppleWorks Enhancements & Improvements as MacroWorks & Also the Following Features: Auto Startup, Directory Database, Integrated Compiler, Menu-Selected Pathnames, Linked Files, Global Cut-&-Paste, Local/Global Macros, & Time & Date Macros.
Beagle Brothers.

Super Mailer. *Version:* 2.0. 1983. *Compatible Hardware:* Atari. *Memory Required:* 48k.
disk $39.95.
Royal Software.

Super Mailing List. 1990. *Items Included:* Manual.
MS-DOS. IBM PC/XT/AT, PS/2 (256K). disk $14.95 (Order no.: 9500).
A Mailing List for PC or PC/XT. User Search by Any Field of the Address. This Makes Searching Very Easy. Since the Program is Written in the Language FORTH it is Very Fast Even with Large Amounts of Data. The Program Can Print Labels & Lists. Over 2000 Addresses per Floppy Disk.
Elcomp Publishing, Inc.

Super Payables. *Customer Support:* 800-929-8117 (customer service).
MS-DOS. Apple II. disk $49.99 (ISBN 0-87007-546-2).
Has the Capacity to Handle 100 Vendors & File as Many as 1500 Transactions at any Given Time on One Disk. It Is Menu-Driven & Includes an On Line Help File for Ready Access During Running.
SourceView Software International.

Super Payroll. *Customer Support:* 800-929-8117 (customer service).
MS-DOS. Apple II. disk $49.99 (ISBN 0-87007-787-2).
Easy to Use Payroll, May be Customized for any State or Province.
SourceView Software International.

Super PC-Kwik: Disk Accelerator. *Version:* 4.1. Jun. 1986. *Compatible Hardware:* IBM PC. *Operating System(s) Required:* PC-DOS. *Memory Required:* 64k. *Items Included:* Manual, diskette. *Customer Support:* Toll-free, unlimited support.
disk $79.95.
Gives Performance Improvement to Any PC, XT, 286, 386, 486, or PS/2 Running DOS. Super Uses Advanced Disk Cache Technology to Boost Disk Read & Write Throughout from Diskette, Hard, & Bernoulli Drives. Super Runs from the DOS prompt or from Batch Files in Conventional, Expanded, or Extended Memory.
PC-Kwik.

Super Plan. *Compatible Hardware:* Commodore Amiga.
3.5" disk $149.95.
Spreadsheet/Time Manager with ARexx Port.
Precision, Inc.

Super Quick DEX. *Version:* 2.056. Jun. 1992. *Customer Support:* Free phone support.
6.02 or greater. Macintosh. 3.5" disk $89.95.
Includes: Quick DEX II - Free Form Database; Print DEX II - Sorts, Merges, Duplicate Disks & Prints; Quick ELOPE - Single Envelope or Label Printer; Hot DA - Opens QDEX with Keystroke.
Casady & Greene, Inc.

Super-Ranker. *Compatible Hardware:* IBM & compatibles. *Operating System(s) Required:* MS-DOS, Windows. *Language(s):* BASIC, C & C Plus Plus. *Memory Required:* Windows 4Mb, DOS 640k. *General Requirements:* 386-VGA for Windows. *Items Included:* TV & radio ratings information. *Customer Support:* 800 number. varies.
Provides TV & Radio Station.
Strata Marketing, Inc.

Super Sleuth Disassembler Object-Only Version (B). *Operating System(s) Required:* OS-9. *Language(s):* Assembly (source code included). *Memory Required:* 64k.
disk $50.00.
Enables User to Examine &/or Modify Programs Interactively on Disk or in Memory on 6800/1/9 Systems. 6800/1/2/3/5/8/9 & 6502 Programs Can Be Disassembled into Source Code Format & Later Displayed, Printed or Saved on Disk. Labels Can Be Changed to Those of User's Own Preference. 6800/1/2/3/8/9 Object Codes May Be Converted to 680 Position-Independent Code.
Computer Systems Consultants.

Super Solvers Spellbound!
Windows. IBM & compatibles. CD-ROM disk $59.95 (Order no.: R1210). *Nonstandard peripherals required:* CD-ROM drive. *Optimal configuration:* 386 processor or higher, MS-DOS 3.1 or higher, 20Mb hard drive, 640k RAM, external speakers or headphones (with sound card) that are Sound Blaster compatible, VGA graphics & adapter, VGA color monitor.
This Program Includes Five Levels of Spelling-Bee Action That Becomes More Challenging As Word Power Improves. Through the Creation of Customized Weekly Spelling Lists, the Program Enhances Vocabulary & Language Development (Ages 7-12).
Library Video Co.

Super Sub Chase. *Compatible Hardware:* Apple II with Applesoft; Atari 400, 800. *Operating System(s) Required:* Apple DOS 3.2, 3.3. *Language(s):* Atari BASIC. *Memory Required:* 24k.
disk $23.95.
Lets You Take over the Controls of a Destroyer in Search of a Submarine.
Dynacomp, Inc.

Super Sunday. Jun. 1985. *Compatible Hardware:* Apple II, II+, IIe; Commodore 64/128; IBM PC & compatibles; Tandy 1000. *Memory Required:* 64-128k. *General Requirements:* CGA card for IBM.
disk $20.00 ea.
Apple. (Order no.: 48522).
IBM. (Order no.: 48534).
Commodore. (Order no.: 48855).
Features 20 Super Bowl Teams, Including All the Players' Names & Positions. Allows for More Than a Dozen Offensive & Defensive Plays. Individual Players' Performances & Statistics Are Updated Throughout the Game. Users Can View Them During & After the Game on the Screen, or Keep Permanent Records Using the Printer Option. There Are Three Modes of Play: Head-to-Head, Solitaire, & Autoplay. Expansion Disks Are Available Separately. For One or Two Players.
Avalon Hill Game Co., The Microcomputer Games Div.

Super Sunday Expansion Disk: Champions Disk. *Compatible Hardware:* Apple II+, IIe, IIc; Commodore 64/128; IBM PC & compatibles; Tandy 1000. *General Requirements:* Super Sunday software.
disk $20.00 ea.
Apple. (Order no.: 48522C).
IBM. (Order no.: 48834C).
Commodore. (Order no.: 48856C).
Provides 20 More Teams That Made It to the Top, Including the 17-0 Miami Dolphins, Lombardi's Packers from the '67 Season, & the '77 Denver Broncos. As a Bonus, Six Teams from the 1950s & 1960s Have Been Added.
Avalon Hill Game Co., The Microcomputer Games Div.

Super Sunday Expansion Disk: Season Disk 1984. *Compatible Hardware:* Apple II+, IIe, IIc; Commodore 64/128; IBM PC & compatibles; Tandy 1000. *General Requirements:* Super Sunday software.
disk $20.00 ea.
Apple. (Order no.: 48852A).
IBM. (Order no.: 48854A).
Commodore. (Order no.: 48855A).
Has 28 Teams That Played During the 1984 Season.
Avalon Hill Game Co., The Microcomputer Games Div.

Super Sunday Expansion Disk: Season Disk 1985. *Compatible Hardware:* Apple II+, IIe, IIc; Commodore 64/128; IBM PC & compatibles; Tandy 1000. *General Requirements:* Super Sunday software.
disk $20.00 ea.
Apple. (Order no.: 48522B).
IBM. (Order no.: 48834B).
Commodore. (Order no.: 48855B).
Has 28 Teams That Played During the 1985 Season.
Avalon Hill Game Co., The Microcomputer Games Div.

Super Tank Attack! *Compatible Hardware:* Atari 400, 800. *Language(s):* Atari BASIC. *Memory Required:* cassette 24k, disk 32k. *General Requirements:* Joysticks.
disk $21.95.
2 Player Action Game.
Dynacomp, Inc.

Super-Terminal. *Compatible Hardware:* TRS-80. *Memory Required:* 32k.
contact publisher for price.
Instant Software, Inc.

Super Tetris. Dec. 1991.
IBM/Windows. IBM & compatibles (640k). disk $49.95. *Networks supported:* Novell.
MAC. Color Classic or higher (2Mb). 3.5" disk $49.95.

Super-Text 40/80. *Compatible Hardware:* Apple II+, IIe; IBM PC. *Operating System(s) Required:* Apple DOS 3.3, PC-DOS. *Language(s):* Applesoft BASIC. *Memory Required:* Apple 48k, IBM 64k.
disk $19.98.
Full Featured Word Processor with a 40 or 80 Column Screen Display. Offers Letter Writing, Split Screen, & Expanded Math Modification. Character Designer, Lower Case on Screen, & Link Files for Search-&-Replace, & Printing Also Are Featured. Other Highlights Include a Preview Mode to Check Page Headings, Page Headers & Footers, Tutorial Documentation, & Quick Reference Card.
Muse Software.

Super-Text Home-Office. Ed Zaron. Mar. 1983. *Compatible Hardware:* Apple II+, IIe. *Operating System(s) Required:* Apple DOS 3.2, 3.3. *Language(s):* Assembly. *Memory Required:* 48k.
disk $19.98 (ISBN 0-87190-018-1).
Word Processing. Offers 40, 56, or 70 Column Display Without Additional Hardware.
Muse Software.

Super-Text Professional: Apple. Ed Zaron. Jun. 1984. *Compatible Hardware:* Apple II+, IIe, IIc with 80 column card. *Memory Required:* 48k.

disk $59.98, incl. Address Book mailing list & form letter (ISBN 0-87190-033-5).
disk w/o Address Book mailing list & form letter $19.98 (ISBN 0-87190-005-X).
Word Processor with Such Features As On-Screen Formatting, Help Reference Guides, Math Mode, & Split Screen.
Muse Software.

Super-Text Professional: Atari. Ed Zaron. Feb. 1984. *Compatible Hardware:* Atari 400, 800, 1200XL. *Operating System(s) Required:* Atari DOS 2.0. *Language(s):* Assembly. *Memory Required:* 48k.
disk $19.98, incl. reference card, back-up disk & wire bound manual (ISBN 0-87190-029-7).
Features 40-Column Screen Display; Disk Storage & Retrieval; Automatic Page Headings; Page & Chapter Numbering; Automatic Word Wrap; Single Key Commands; Unlimited Document Size; Multiple File Search & Replace; Copy, Save, Move or Delete Blocks of Text.
Muse Software.

Super-Text Professional: Commodore 64. Oct. 1983. *Compatible Hardware:* Commodore 64 with 1541 disk drive. *Language(s):* Assembly. *Memory Required:* 64k.
disk $19.98, incl. reference card, back-up disk & wire bound manual.
Features On-Screen Formatting; 40 or 80 Column Screen Display; Disk Storage & Retrieval; Automatic Page Headings; Page & Chapter Numbering; Automatic Word Wrap; Single Key Commands; Unlimited Document Size; Multiple File Search & Replace; Copy, Save, Move, Delete Blocks of Text; Split Screen.
Muse Software.

Super-Text Professional: IBM PC. Ed Zaron. Jun. 1983. *Compatible Hardware:* IBM PC, Columbia, Hyperion, Compaq & compatibles. *Operating System(s) Required:* DOS 1.1. *Language(s):* Assembly. *Memory Required:* 64k.
disk $19.98, incl. reference card, back-up disk & loose-leaf manual in binder (ISBN 0-87190-019-X).
Features Include: 80-Column Screen Display; Disk Storage & Retrieval; Automatic Page Headings; Page & Chapter Numbering; Automatic Word Wrap; Single Key Commands; Unlimited Document Size; Multiple File Search & Replace; Copy, Save, Move, Delete Blocks of Text; Split Screen.
Muse Software.

Super 3D Plotter II. R. Constan. 1985. *Compatible Hardware:* Atari XL/XE. *Memory Required:* 48k.
disk $29.95.
3D Image Design & Animation Package. Images May Be Enetered Via Numeric Data or Directly on the Screen with a Joystick. Features Include: True Hidden Surface Elimination & Solid Projection; Hi-Res Printout; Screen "Overlay" & "Save" Features; Compatibility with Most Drawing Programs. Package Includes 2 Editors.
Elfin Magic.

Super Utility Plus. *Compatible Hardware:* TRS-80 Model I, Model III. *Memory Required:* 48k.
disk $74.95 (Order no.: 5022RD).
Machine Language, Stand-Alone Program with Its Own I/O Routine.
Instant Software, Inc.

Super Zap. *Items Included:* Bound manual. *Customer Support:* Free hotline - no time limit; 30 day limited warranty; updates are $5/disk plus S&H.
MS-DOS; CP/M. IBM & compatibles (256k). disk $29.95.
Disk Dump & Patch Program. Provides Many Powerful Features, Yet It Combines Menu Control with Two-Dimensional Screen Interaction for Exceptional Ease of Use. It Features a Full Screen Display of Disk Records by Absolute Sector Number, or by File & Sector. It Displays Data in Hex, Octal, or ASCII. User Can Position the Cursor with Function Keys & Change Any Byte Using Any Data Format. Features Include: Searching for Sequence of Data Bytes in File or Entire Disk, Dump Sector Contents to Line Printer or Data File. CP/M Version Supports Display & Patch Program File by Memory Address. SAVE FILE Lets User Store Selected Sectors for Input by Other Programs.
Dynacomp, Inc.

SuperANOVA. *Version:* 1.11. *Items Included:* 1 soft bound manual, program diskettes, product literature. *Customer Support:* Free technical support by mail, fax, phone & e-mail.
System 6.0.2 or higher. Any Macintosh. 3.5" disk $495.00.
General Linear Modeling Program Designed to Solve Complex ANOVA, ANCOVA, MANOVA, MANCOVA, & Repeated Measures Models. Analysis Results Are Placed in a Complete Drawing Environment Where They May Be Customized & Annotated. All Results May Be Saved As Templates & Reopened with Any Data of Interest.
Abacus Concepts, Inc.

Superbase Personal. *Compatible Hardware:* Commodore Amiga.
3.5" disk $79.95.
File Manager.
Precision, Inc.

Superbase Personal II. *Compatible Hardware:* Commodore Amiga.
3.5" disk $149.95.
Includes Mail Merge, Telecommunications & Text Editing.
Precision, Inc.

Superbase Professional. *Version:* 4.01. *Compatible Hardware:* Commodore Amiga.
3.5" disk $349.95.
Relational Database.
Precision, Inc.

Superbase 4.
IBM PC XT (640k); under MS-DOS; with 20Mb hard disk; running Windows or GEM. Version 4.02 $695.00; 4-user LAN $895.00, add'l. nodes $225.00; without programming language & forms editor $249.00.
Integrated Software Package Featuring Word Processing, Database & Communications Modules. Other Applications Include Forms Editor, Report Writer & Program Editor. Features Context Switching, Mail/Merge Database Link, Built-In Language in All Modules & On-Screen Help. Pastes & Links Spreadsheet Sections & Graphics into Word-Processing Files. Imports & Exports dBASE II/III/III PLUS, Lotus 1-2-3, DIF, ASCII & Superplan Files.
Precision, Inc.

Superbase 64. *Compatible Hardware:* Commodore 64 with a 1541 disk drive or any large Commodore drive, including hard disk. *Language(s):* BASIC.
contact publisher for price.
Precision Software Products.

SuperBASIC. *Customer Support:* 800-929-8117 (customer service).
MS-DOS. Apple II. disk $49.99 (ISBN 0-87007-074-6).
Provides a Low-Cost Extension to User Resident Apple BASIC Interpreter. Allows Nested Macros with Substitutable Arguments, Symbolic Labels, Include Files, Deletion of Remarks Statements, No Line Numbers & Ability to Organize Output at a Specified Line Number. Includes These Commands: Case-of, If-Then-Else, While, Repeat-Until, Do, & Print Using. Specialized Error Messages are Included. Manual Included.
SourceView Software International.

SuperBatch. *Operating System(s) Required:* MS-DOS.
disk $79.95.
Automatically Provides Total Keyboard Input While Operating among Multiple Application Programs. Integrates Application Programs & MS-DOS Batch Filing Capabilities to Provide Turnkey Application System Capabilities for MS-DOS Microcomputers. Lets User Bypass All Commands When Calling up Programs. Stores an Infinite Number of Prompts That Can Be Generated by Tapping Several Keys.
Business Computer Consultants/Merrill Street Software.

Superbike Challenge. *Compatible Hardware:* IBM PC & compatibles. *Operating System(s) Required:* PC-DOS/MS-DOS. *Memory Required:* 256k.
3.5" disk $19.95 (Order no.: 80611).
Action Arcade Game for Two Players Racing on 12 of the Worlds Most Exciting Grad Prix Courses.
Broderbund Software, Inc.

SuperC. Donald M. Ludlow & Randy Black. *Compatible Hardware:* IBM PC, PCjr, PC XT, PC AT, Portable PC, 3270 PC with IBM Display & IBM Matrix printer (optional). *Operating System(s) Required:* DOS 2.00, 2.10, 3.00, 3.10. *Memory Required:* 128k.
disk $29.95 (Order no.: 6276575).
Enables User to Compare Files or Groups of Files & Determine Differences at the File, Line, Word, or Byte Level. Shows Text Differences in Document Files, Generates Output for Application Programs, Compares ASCII & Non-ASCII Data Files, Uses Unlimited File Sizes, Audits Files for Changes, & Creates/Changes Activity Reports.
Personally Developed Software, Inc.

SuperCAD: Schematic Diagram Entry. *Items Included:* Bound manual. *Customer Support:* Free hotline - no time limit; 30 day limited warranty; updates are $5/disk plus S&H.
MS-DOS 2.0 or higher. IBM & compatibles (256k). disk $89.95-$139.95. *Nonstandard peripherals required:* CGA, EGA, VGA, Hercules (or equivalent) graphics capability & a Microsoft (or compatible) mouse. Supports IBM, Okidata 192/193, Epson, or compatible dot matrix printers.
demo disk $5.00.
Schematic Entry Package. Includes the Following Features: Visually-Cued Command Entry; Library Support; Automatic Bus Generation; Auto-Incrementing Text; Snap Modes; Constraint Modes; Automatic Title Block Updating; Support Models; Style & Font Control.
Dynacomp, Inc.

SuperCalc 3. Sorcim Corp. *Compatible Hardware:* TI Professional. *Operating System(s) Required:* MS-DOS. *Memory Required:* 128k. *General Requirements:* Winchester hard disk, printer, plotter, color monitor.
$395.00 (Order no.: TI P/N).
Texas Instruments, Personal Productivit.

The Supercars: The Collection. *Customer Support:* 90 days limited warranties, customer support phone: (408) 296-8400, hrs: M-F 8-5 pm.
PC-DOS 2.1 or higher; Tandy-DOS (384k).

TITLE INDEX

$21.95.
Commodore (64k). $14.95.
Apple IIgs/ProDOS 16 (512k); Macintosh. $21.95.
Amiga-Kickstart 1.2 or 1.3 (512k); Atari. $21.95.
Macintosh 880 Drive, (1 Mb).
Add on Disk to the Duel; Test Drive II.
Accolade, Inc.

SuperCat Plus. *Compatible Hardware:* IBM PC, PC XT. *Memory Required:* 256k.
disk $89.95.
Cataloging System for Books, Cassettes, Records, etc. Catalogues by Author, Title, Subject, Call Number, Publisher, Publication Date, Acquisition Date & Price, with Customizable Fields for Other Methods of Organization. Data Can Be Sorted by Any Field & Displayed in 11 Card Catalogue Formats.
Zephyr Services.

SuperCharts. *Version:* 2.1. Jul. 1994. *Items Included:* 3 perfect bound manuals, 1 free month of data downloading. *Customer Support:* Free unlimited technical support for current shipping versions by phone, FAX, BBS, CompuServ, Prodigy, & American On-Line. FAX & BBS support for past versions for $19.95 per incident.
Windows. IBM 386-DX/33, hard drive, mouse, DOS 5, EGA (4Mb). disk $249.95 (ISBN 1-887286-02-0). *Optimal configuration:* IBM 486-DX2/66, 8Mb RAM, DOS 6.2X or higher, mouse, Windows 3.11 for Workgroups.
The World's Best-Selling Investment Charting Software for Windows Gives You the Power to Make More Profitable Decisions. By Combining State-of-the-Art Windows Charting & Automated Stock Scanning with State-of-the-Art System Testing & Optimization, It Makes Your Technical Analysis Easier, More Powerful & More Effective.
Omega Research, Inc.

SuperCharts Three: For CD-ROM. *Version:* 3.0. Jun. 1995. *Customer Support:* Free unlimited technical support for current shipping versions by phone, FAX, BBS, CompuServ, Prodigy, & American On-Line. FAX & BBS support for past versions for $19.95 per incident.
Windows. IBM 386-DX/33, hard drive, mouse, DOS 5, EGA (4Mb). CD-ROM disk $249.95 (ISBN 1-887286-03-9). *Nonstandard peripherals required:* CD-ROM drive & driver software. *Optimal configuration:* 486-DX2/66, 8Mb RAM, DOS 6.2X or higher, Windows 3.11 for Workgroups, 9600 baud modem.
Windows. IBM 386-DX/33, hard drive, mouse, DOS 5, EGA (4Mb). CD-ROM disk $249.95 (ISBN 1-887286-04-7). *Optimal configuration:* IBM 486-DX2/66, 8Mb RAM, DOS 6.2X or higher, Windows 3.11 for Workgroups.
The First Investment Charting Software to Provide Investors with Total Market Coverage. Combining 10 Years of Price History on Every Stock & Mutual Fund Traded on the NYSE, AMEX & NASDAQ with State-of-the-Art Windows Chartings & Powerful Stock Scanning & System Testing, It's the Best Way to Make More Profitable Investment Decisions.
Omega Reserach, Inc.

Supercode Barcode Reading & Printing. *Items Included:* Full manual. No other products required. *Customer Support:* Free telephone support - no time limit. 30 day warranty.
MS-DOS 3.2 or higher. IBM & compatibles (512k). disk $399.95.
High Quality Bar Code Pen Reader Lets User Scan Data into Computer with Perfect Accuracy, & at a Speed No Keyboard Operator Could Hope to Match. It Connects Between Your Keyboard & Computer & Requires No External Power Supply. The Bar Code Creator Part of Package Prints Popular Bar Code Labels: UPC-A, UPC-E, Standard 3 or 9, EAN-12, EAN-8, & ZIP Plus 4, All up to 2" High.
Dynacomp, Inc.

SuperConvert. *Version:* 3.0.1. Jason Harper & David Hecker. Mar. 1991. *Items Included:* Disk, manual. *Customer Support:* 11-5 Mon-Fri EST 904-576-9415 or on-line through AppleLink, America Online, GEnie, CompuServe, eWorld.
Apple IIGS (1Mb). disk $39.95 (ISBN 0-931277-16-7).
Convert Formats from Apple II, Macintosh, IBM, Atari ST, Amiga, Commodore 64/128. Transfer Graphics onto a IIGS Disk, via Modem or Other Means, Then Convert it with SuperConvert to Super Hi-Res. Product Also Has Powerful "Remap Image" Command to Convert a 320 Mode Image So it Appears Correctly in 640 Mode Programs. Or, Change a Color Image into a Grayscale or Black & White Picture.
Seven Hills Software Corp.

Superdraw. (Draw Utility, Graphics, Art Ser.). 1984. *Compatible Hardware:* IBM PC & compatibles, PCjr, PC XT, PC AT. *Operating System(s) Required:* PC-DOS 2.0 or higher, MS-DOS. *Language(s):* C. *Memory Required:* 128k. *General Requirements:* CGA card. *Items Included:* Users manual. *Customer Support:* 90 day limited warranty.
disk $195.00, incl. tchr's. guide (ISBN 0-922928-16-9, Order no.: 1006).
Draw Utility Program That Creates Detailed Diagrams, Rectangles, Circles, Mirror Images, Triangles, Color Swap, & More. Drawing Can Be Filled or Painted Using 8 Basic Colors. Colors Can Be Dithered to Create Combination of Shading. Zoom Function Will Blowup Sections. Images Can Be Temporarily Saved in a Buffer, Permanently Saved on Disk, or Incorporated into Any BASIC Program. Other Features Include: Custom Set of Character Fonts, Overlay Complex Shapes, Direct Transmission of Portions of Screen to Printer, On-Screen Display of Cursor Color, Draw Mode, X & Y Coordinates & Stack Coordinates.
GemStar Partnership.

SuperDup. Feb. 1993. *Items Included:* Product on 3.5" or 5.25" & manual. *Customer Support:* Product information available over phone, toll free; technical support provided, unlimited over telephone; 30 day money back guarantie.
DOS 3.1 or higher. IBM & compatibles (640k). disk $195.00. *Optimal configuration:* 386/486 640k Mem/RAM & 3Mb on hard drive free working on dBASE/ASCII Fixed Language files. *Networks supported:* Lantastic.
Will Allow Users to Find & Mark Duplicates for Deletion in up to Six Lists Against One Master List. Users Can Mark Records or Set the Program to Automatically Delete Duplicate Records. Program Checks at Exact, Near & Sound Alike Levels.
Mailer's Software.

SuperFile. *Version:* 3.0. FYI, Inc. May 1982. *Compatible Hardware:* Apricot; DEC Rainbow; HP 110, 150; IBM PC & compatibles; Victor. *Operating System(s) Required:* MS-DOS, CP/M-80. *Memory Required:* 64k. *General Requirements:* 2 disk drives.
disk $95.00.
Database Program Developed Specifically for Filing & Retrieving Free-Form Textual Information. Each SuperFile Database Can Manage up to 65,000 Entries, with up to 250 Key Words per Entry, & Can Span Many Disks. Searches Files for User-Assigned Key Words Which Can Be Combined with AND, OR & NOT to Retrieve Specific Information. Accepts Data from Word Processing Files or Downloaded from Online Sources.
Software Marketing Assocs.

SUPERHERO LEAGUE OF HOBOKEN

Superfile: Information. FYI Inc. Jan. 1981. *Operating System(s) Required:* CP/M-80, MS-DOS, PC-DOS. *Memory Required:* CP/M 64k, MS-DOS & PC-DOS 128k.
disk $49.95 (ISBN 0-923875-15-8).
$49.95 (ISBN 0-923875-14-X).
Information Retrieval System That Lets User Cross Index & Retrieve Anything That Can Be Typed with a Word Processing Program or Text Editor. Update Facility Automatically Re-Catalogs All New Entries.
Elliam Assocs.

SuperFont Sampler, 2 disks. *Version:* 2.1. *Compatible Hardware:* Commodore Amiga 500, 1000, 2000. *Items Included:* Reference charts, 40 page manual, Font Utilities, Icon Interface. *Customer Support:* Technical assistance provided by phone: (206)733-8342.
3.5" disk $44.95.
20 Professional Bitmap Fonts (60 Styles). Artist-Designed Monochrome & 2-Color Fonts From 7 to 32+ Lines, Many with European Characters. For Word Processing, Desktop Publishing, & Applications Requiring Small to Medium-Sized Fonts. Includes Icon Interface, Font Path & Moving Utilities.
CLASSIC CONCEPTS Futureware.

SuperGraphs. *Customer Support:* 800-929-8117 (customer service).
MS-DOS. IBM/PS2. disk $79.99 (ISBN 0-87007-168-8).
An Interactive, Flexible Plot Package with the Ability to Create, Save, Retrieve from Disk, Edit, Display & Print Graphs Whose Layout & Design Are Completely under the User's Control. Generates Bar Charts, Line Graphs, Pie Charts, Stick Plots & Symbol Plots. For Line, Symbol & Stick Plots any Combination of Linear & Logarithmic Horizontal & Vertical Scaling can be Obtained.
SourceView Software International.

Superhero League of Hoboken. Steve Meretzky. Aug. 1994. *Items Included:* Disks, game manual, warranty card, product catalog. *Customer Support:* Toll free technical assistance (1-800-658-8891). Computer operated pre-recorded hint line (1-900-933-CLUE). Hint book $9.95 plus s/h.
DOS 5.0 or higher. IBM PC 386/25 or higher (580k). disk $59.95 (ISBN 1-880520-25-7, Order no.: HOBO). *Nonstandard peripherals required:* Microsoft compatible mouse, Sound Blaster compatible audio card. *Optimal configuration:* 386/33 with 600k available conventional memory, Sound Blaster compatible audio card, microsoft compatible mouse.
A Comical Role-Playing & Adventure Game Combination That Follows a Band of Superheroes As They Wander the Wasteland of the Eastern United States Battling Villains & Solving Puzzles to Defeat the Evil Dr. Entropy.
Legend Entertainment.

Superhero League of Hoboken. Steve Meretzky. Dec. 1994. *Items Included:* CD-ROM disc, game manual, warranty card, product catalog. *Customer Support:* Toll free technical assistance (1-800-658-8891). Computer operated pre-recorded hint line (1-900-933-CLUE). Hint book $9.95 plus s/h.
DOS 5.0 or higher. IBM PC 386/25 or higher (580k available, conventional mem). CD-ROM disk $59.95 (ISBN 1-880520-18-4, Order no.: SLH-CD). *Nonstandard peripherals required:* CD-ROM, Microsoft compatible mouse, Sound Blaster compatible audio card. *Optimal configuration:* 386/33 w/600k available conventional memory, Sound Blaster compatible audio card, double-speed CD-ROM.
A Comical Role-Playing & Adventure Game Combination That Follows a Band of Superheroes

As They Wander the Wasteland of the Eastern United States Battling Villains & Solving Puzzles to Defeat the Evil Dr. Entropy.
Legend Entertainment.

SuperKey: Keyboard Enhancer - Security. Jun. 1985. *Compatible Hardware:* IBM PC & compatibles, PC XT, PC AT, PCjr. *Operating System(s) Required:* PC-DOS 1.0 or higher. *Memory Required:* 128k.
disk $69.95 (ISBN 0-87524-136-0). manual avail. (ISBN 0-87524-000-3).
Resident Utilities Include: Encryption for Confidential Files, Programmable Keys Allowing the User to Turn up to a Thousand Keystrokes into One, Keyboard Lock, Automatic Turn-Off of Screen after a Pre-Set Time, Password Protection, etc.
Borland International, Inc.

Superlabels. *Customer Support:* 800-929-8117 (customer service).
MS-DOS. Apple II. disk $59.99 (ISBN 0-87007-011-8).
Full Control of Label Production, Including 4-up Labels, Database Management, Combine Lines on Label, Choose any Cumulative Combination of Bold, Under-Lining, Proportional, Enhanced, Expanded, Compressed Type Styles.
SourceView Software International.

Superlog III. Pete Charlton. 1984. *Compatible Hardware:* IBM PC, PC AT & compatibles. *Operating System(s) Required:* MS-DOS 3.2 or higher. *Language(s):* BASIC. *Memory Required:* 512k.
IBM & Tandy. disk $2495.00 to $12995.00.
High Level Traffic, Billing, Affidavits, Accounts Receivable & Sales Aids System for Radio.
The Management.

Superman Cartoons, Vol. 1. Mar. 1995. *Customer Support:* Dedicated voice mail phone number; will respond back to consumer.
Windows 3.1 or higher; Macintosh. IBM or 100% compatible 486SX 25MHz (4Mb); 68030/68040 Color Mac System 7.1 or higher (4Mb). CD-ROM disk $14.99 (ISBN 1-57339-001-1, Order no.: ROMI2927BR). *Nonstandard peripherals required:* 2X CD-ROM drive.
The 17 Original Full-Color Superman Cartoons Released Theatrically Between 1941-1943. Includes "Superman," "Mechanical Monsters," "Billion Dollar Limited," "Arctic Giant," "Bulleteers," & "Magnetic Telescope".
Image Entertainment.

Superman Cartoons, Vol. 2. Apr. 1995. *Customer Support:* Dedicated voice mail phone number; will respond back to consumer.
Windows 3.1 or higher; Macintosh. IBM or 100% compatible 486SX 25MHz (4Mb); 68030/68040 Color Mac System 7.1 or higher (4Mb). CD-ROM disk $14.99 (ISBN 1-57339-002-X, Order no.: ROMI2928BR). *Nonstandard peripherals required:* 2X CD-ROM drive.
Six More of the Original Superman Theatrical Cartoons. Includes "Electric Earthquake," "Volcano," "Terror on the Midway," "Japoteurs," "Showdown," & "Eleventh Hour".
Image Entertainment.

Superman Cartoons, Vol. 3. Apr. 1995. *Customer Support:* Dedicated voice mail phone number; will respond back to consumer.
Windows 3.1 or higher; Macintosh. IBM or 100% compatible 486SX 25MHz (4Mb); 68030/68040 Color Mac System 7.1 or higher (4Mb). CD-ROM disk $14.99 (ISBN 1-57339-003-8, Order no.: ROMI2929BR). *Nonstandard peripherals required:* 2X CD-ROM drive.
The Final Five Theatrical Superman Cartoons Released Between 1941-1943. Includes "Destruction Inc.," "The Mummy Strikes," "Jungle Drums," "Underground World," & "Secret Agent." *Plus a Special Bonus, the Warner Bros. Wartime Parody "Snafuperman".*
Image Entertainment.

SUPERMIT. *Version:* 3.0. Apr. 1986. *Operating System(s) Required:* CP/M 2.2 or higher. *Language(s):* Assembly. *Memory Required:* 24k.
disk $40.00.
Utility That Brings BASIC to Batch (Submit) Jobs. The Result Is Batch Jobs That Employ GOTO's, IF...THEN...ELSE's, Arrays & Variables, & Other Constructs. Incorporates Diagnostics along with On-Line Instructions & Examples.
Logic Assocs.

SuperPrint. *Version:* 2.2. Apr. 1992. *Items Included:* Manual, 5 1/4" & 3 1/2" diskettes. *Customer Support:* On-line help files, on-line knowledge base, 24-hour automated FAX, 24-hour bulletin board, CompuServe forum, technical support operators 7:00 AM to 4:00 PM Monday-Friday (user pays toll charges, if any).
MS-DOS 3.0 or higher. PC AT or compatible or IBM PS/2. $149.00 & up. *Nonstandard peripherals required:* Some supported color devices require either SCSI or GPIB (IEEE-488) interface cards. *Addl. software required:* MS Windows 3.0 or higher. *Optimal configuration:* 80386-based (or better), 20 MHz (or better), 2Mb RAM (or more), Windows 3.1. *Networks supported:* All PC-based networks.
Provides Faster, Enhanced Printing from Any Windows-Based Application to Most Non-PostScript Devices, Including LaserJets, DeskJets, PaintJets, Other Laser, Dot Matrix, & Inkjet Printers. Separate Versions for Color Thermal & Dye-Sublimation Printers, Film Recorders, & Color Laser Copiers. Provides Efficient, Multi-Tasking Background Printing. Generates Scalable Screen & Printer Fonts from Any of These Typeface Outline Formats: Adobe Type 1, Bitstream Fontware & Facelift, Agfa Compugraphic Intellifont, & Digital Typeface Nimbus Q. Works Alongside TrueType & Adobe Type Manager Software.
Zenographics.

Superscope. *Items Included:* Manuals, documentation, free soft panels. *Customer Support:* Free tech support, upgrades.
Macintosh SE, II series. 3.5" disk $990.00 (Order no.: GWI-SS). *Nonstandard peripherals required:* MacADIOS hardware.
General Purpose Data Acquisition, Oscilloscope, XY Recorder, Stripchart, Spectrum Analyzer, Internal Word Processor, Transcendental, Statistical & DSE Operations, Post Processing Analysis. No Programming Required.
GW Instruments, Inc.

Superscreen. *Language(s):* Extended Color BASIC or Disk BASIC. *Memory Required:* 16k.
contact publisher for price.
Mark Data Products.

SuperScripsit Printer Driver.
disk $59.95 (Order no.: D4SPD).
The Alternate Source.

Supersked. Management Science Software Systems. Oct. 1982. *Compatible Hardware:* IBM PC, PC XT; NCR Decision Mate. *Operating System(s) Required:* MS-DOS. *Memory Required:* 320k. *General Requirements:* Printer.
$1395.00 ea.
IBM. (ISBN 0-931275-00-8, Order no.: 1001).
NCR. (ISBN 0-931275-01-6, Order no.: 1002).
Assigns Work Shifts to Employees for 1 Week Periods. Designed Especially for Supermarkets, Fast Food Restaurants, & Phone Reservation Offices Where Employee Availabilies May Be Restricted.
Management Robotics, Inc.

SuperSMITH. Robert Abernethy & Wes Fulton. Jul. 1994. *Items Included:* Copy of "The New Weibull Handbook". *Customer Support:* 30-day warranty.
MS-DOS. IBM (512k). disk $960.00 (Order no.: S107). *Optimal configuration:* 5Mb storage space on hard disk required.
Includes All Four Weibull Programs - WeibullSMITH, VisualSMITH, MonteCarloSMITH, & BiWeibullSMITH.
Gulf Publishing Co.

SuperSoft BASIC Compiler. *Items Included:* Bound manual. *Customer Support:* Free hotline - no time limit; 30 day limited warranty; updates are $5/disk plus S&H.
MS-DOS. IBM & compatibles (128k). disk $59.95.
Two-Pass Compiler Which Produces Relocatable Object Code. Linking This Code with the Necessary Runtime Support Routines from the Library Files Produces the Final Machine-Executable Program. No Assembler Is Needed in This Process, but with the Use of an Assembler, It Is Possible to Use Assembly-Language Subroutines. Includes These Features: Four Variable Types: Integer, String, & Single- & Double-Precision Floating Point (13-Digit BCD); Full PRINT USING for Formatted Output (Includes Asterisk Fill, Floating Dollar Sign, Scientific Notation, Trailing Sign, & Comma Insertion); Long Variable Names; Error Trapping; Matrices with up to 32 Dimensions; Boolean Operators OR, AND, NOT XOR, EQV, IMP; Supports Random & Sequential Disk Files with a Complete Set of File Manipulation Statements: OPEN, CLOSE, GET, PUT, KILL, NAME.
Dynacomp, Inc.

SuperSPREADing. *Compatible Hardware:* IBM PC XT, PC AT; Data General. *Operating System(s) Required:* AOS, RDOS, SuperDOS. *Language(s):* Business BASIC (source code included). *Memory Required:* 64k.
IBM. disk $450.00.
Data General. disk $450.00.
Interactive, Multi-User Spreadsheet, up to 250,000 Cells.
QAX International Systems Corp.

Supertax. 1985. *Compatible Hardware:* Apple II+, IBM PC & Sanyo MBC-550 Series, TRS-80 with 2 disk drives.
$149.00.
Personal Income Tax Programs to Calculate Tax Liability & Make Year-End Investment Decisions to Improve Financial Position.
Rockware Data Corp.

SuperVUE. *Version:* 3.0. Jun. 1986. *Compatible Hardware:* Alpha Micro, IBM PC. *Operating System(s) Required:* AMOS, MS-DOS. *Memory Required:* 70k.
IBM. contact publisher for price.
Alpha Micro. $1050.00-$3000.00 VCR tape.
Full-Featured Word Processor with Outline Editor. Journaling Restores Keystrokes after a System Failure. Includes Mail Merge, Programming Language, Sequential Forms Processing. Flexible Printing: Top & Bottom Titles, Special Highlights, Prints Double-Sided Documents, & Is Compatible with Postscript Laser Printers.
Provue Development Corp.

Supplies - Parts Inventory Tracking. *Version:* 4.1. *Customer Support:* On site training unlimited support services for first 90 days & through subscription thereafter.
Contact publisher for price.
Allows Supplies/Parts/Fuel to Be Entered into Inventory for Later Allocation to a Job Department Repair Order & So On. Items May Be Used in This Module or in Other Abecas

TITLE INDEX

Modules Such As Equipment Maintenance. A Special Screen Allows Fuel & Oil Usage to Be Entered by Vehicle for Transfer to EM & Trip Log Module As Appropriate.
Argos Software.

Supplies Inventory & Tracking. *Items Included:* Complete illustrated instructions. *Customer Support:* 90 days free replacement of damaged disks, free unlimited telephone customer assistance.
DOS 5 (640k). $349.00; Network $899.00.
Windows 3.1 (640k). $359.00; Network $899.00.
Handles All Details for All Supplies, Lists All Suppliers, Creates & Prints Orders, Checks in Supplies, Maintains Inventory, Checks Supplies in & Out for Users, Tells When to Reorder, & Prints Various Reports. User Can Enter & Personally Configure (Name) the Three Blank User Fields on the "Add an Item" Screen to Customize the Program to His/Her Needs. To Further Customize, the User Chooses the Fields to Print to Reports on Screen or Printer. Print New Orders, Outstanding Orders, Supply Details, Suppliers, & Their Products, Inventory Position (What's on Hand Right Now), Department Usage (Audit Trail) & More.
Right On Programs.

Support Tracking. Jan. 1992. *Items Included:* Manual on software, run-time version of Superbase 4. *Customer Support:* Training - $55.00/hour; phone support - $55.00/hour; 1 yr. maintenance - free of charge.
Microsoft (PC) MS-DOS. IBM & compatibles (640k). disk $200.00 (Order no.: SUPTRK). *Nonstandard peripherals required:* Mouse. *Addl. software required:* Windows 3.0 & higher. *Optimal configuration:* IBM compatible 386, 4Mb RAM, Windows 3.1, MS-DOS 5.0, at least 1Mb disk space for programs. *Networks supported:* Novell, LANtastic.
Support & Service Personnel Can Track Their Contacts with Customers. POS or Batch Billing Available for Time Billed & Items Sold. Allowed 400 Character Explanation on Each Contact. Easy Customer Problem History Search & Scan. Service/Support Manager Can Monitor Productivity of Employees.
Software Design, Inc.

Supra Accounting. *Customer Support:* 800-929-8117 (customer service).
MS-DOS. Commodore 128; CP/M. disk $169.99 (ISBN 0-87007-272-2).
A Complete Accounting System, Has Many Features Including: Accounts Payable, Accounts Receivable, Payroll, General Ledger, Bank Account Monitoring, Point of Sale for Sales Registers, Inventory Control & Special Buyers File.
SourceView Software International.

Supra Accounting System. *Customer Support:* 800-929-8117 (customer service).
MS-DOS. IBM/PS2. disk $349.99 (ISBN 0-87007-294-3).
Consists of Four Modules Integrated into a Cash Oriented & Single Entry System.
SourceView Software International.

Supra Accounts Payable. *Customer Support:* 800-929-8117 (customer service).
MS-DOS. Commodore 128; CP/M. disk $49.99 (ISBN 0-87007-194-7).
Has the Capacity to Handle 100 Vendors & File As Many As 1500 Transactions at Any Given Time on One Disk. It Is Menu-Driven & Includes an On-Line Help File for Ready Access During Running.
SourceView Software International.

Supra Billing. *Customer Support:* 800-929-8117 (customer service).
MS-DOS. Commodore 128, CP/M. disk $49.99 (ISBN 0-87007-189-0).
IBM PC, PS/2. disk $99.99 (ISBN 0-87007-196-3).
A Simple Billing Program Suited to Those Who Do Not Need to Keep Track of Time, & Do Not Need Detailed Aging of Their Accounts Receivable. Particularly Suited to Psychologists, Counselors, Doctors, Dentists & Anyone Who Bills with Date, Service Rendered, Charges, Payments, Balance. The Program Has an Automatic Billing Feature Which Allows Interest on Unpaid Balances to Be Calculated at the Beginning of Each Month. Allows Specified Scheduled Charges to Be Put into the Program Which Can Be Billed Automatically Each Month. User Can Set up to 99 Billing Codes, or Freehand a Description into the Entry. Also Has Several "Labels" Which Can Be Customized So Specific Messages Can Be Included on Bills.
SourceView Software International.

Supra General Ledger. *Customer Support:* 800-929-8117 (customer service).
MS-DOS. Commodore 128; CP/M. disk $49.99 (ISBN 0-87007-182-3).
Many Features Including: Categorizing Expenses & Income, Keeping a Running Monthly Total, Summarizing Expenses by Category, Printing Out Yearly Summaries, Producing Sorted, Itemized Printouts & Creating Profit & Loss Statements with Percentages.
SourceView Software International.

Supra Inventory. *Customer Support:* 800-929-8117 (customer service).
MS-DOS. Commodore 128; CP/M. disk $49.99 (ISBN 0-87007-178-5).
IBM PC, PS/2. disk $99.99 (ISBN 0-87007-184-X).
An Inventory Parts Status Report May Be Obtained Interactively, As Can All Inventory Functions. Management Reports That Can Be Generated on Demand Include: Inventory Part Status, Usage Value Rank, List of Inventory Transactions by Periods, Inventory Cost Reports, Aged Inventory Report & Stock Exception Reports.
SourceView Software International.

Supra Ledgers. *Customer Support:* 800-929-8117 (customer service).
MS-DOS. disk $99.99 (ISBN 0-87007-181-5).
Designed to Track Income & Expenses on a Continuing Basis & Helps Prepare Records for Submission to an Accountant. The Program Is Essentially an 8 Column Ledger in Checkbook Style (Allowing Check Numbers, Transaction Types, 99 Category Codes) Which Produces Monthly Cumulative Totals, Yearly Summaries, Profit & Loss Statements & a Checkbook Balance. Menu-Driven & Easy to Use.
SourceView Software International.

Supra Payables. *Customer Support:* 800-929-8117 (customer service).
MS-DOS. IBM/PS2. disk $99.99 (ISBN 0-87007-192-0).
Has the Capacity to Handle 100 Vendors & File As Many As 1500 Transactions at Any Given Time on One Disk. It Is Menu Driven & Includes an On-Line Help File for Ready Access During Running.
SourceView Software International.

Supreme Warrior. *Items Included:* Instruction manual. *Customer Support:* Free Telephone support.
Saturn. Sega Saturn. Contact publisher for price.
DOS/Windows 95. IBM & compatibles (8Mb). Contact publisher for price. *Optimal configuration:* CD-ROM drive.
MAC. Macintosh (4Mb). Contact publisher for price. *Optimal configuration:* CD-ROM drive.
Digital Pictures, Inc.

Surf-2-Cad. *Version:* 4.11. Mark D. Floan & Shirl A. Vonasek. Nov. 1988. *Items Included:* Manual. *Customer Support:* 120 days free phone support; 90 day moneyback guarantee.
MS-DOS 2.1 or higher (384k). IBM PC & compatibles. disk $75.00, incl. manual (ISBN 0-932071-06-6). *Nonstandard peripherals required:* 2 floppy drives or 1 floppy & 1 hard drive. *Addl. software required:* Surfer & Generic CADD Level 3, CADD 5.0 or CADD 6.0.
Transforms a Plot File As Produced by Surfer to a Batch File Readable by Generic CADD Level 3, CADD 5.0 or CADD 6.0. Transformation Process Ensures Correct Coordinate Translation & Drawing Scale.
Simplicity Systems, Inc.

Surface Modelling Software. Jun. 1992. *Items Included:* Spiral manual contains theory, sample runs. *Customer Support:* Free phone, on-site seminars.
MS-DOS. IBM (128k). disk $96.00.
Macintosh. Any Macintosh. 3.5" disk $96.00.
This Is a Book/Disk Package That Shows How to Write Software to Fit Surface Patches to 3 Dimensional Data Sets Using Parametric Surface Patchers. Includes Fitting Parametric Curves Through Boundary Data Points Using Splines, Fitting Parametric Surface Patches, Interpolating Between Patch Boundaries to Get Interior Surface Points.
Kern International, Inc.

Surface Plotter. Roy E. Myers. Nov. 1990. *Items Included:* Program disk & manual. *Customer Support:* Unlimited technical support for registered users.
Macintosh (512k). $50.00 for single user (ISBN 0-534-13716-4). *Optimal configuration:* Macintosh with 512k RAM & one disk drive.
IBM PC or 100% compatible (512k). $50.00 for single user (ISBN 0-534-13719-9). *Optimal configuration:* IBM PC or 100% compatible with one disk drive & CGA, EGA, or VGA graphics adapter.
Please call for site license information.
This Program Helps Users Understand Mathematical Concepts by Seeing Them. Helps Visualize Three-Dimensional Surfaces by Generating Images of Functions in Two Variables.
Brooks/Cole Publishing Co.

The Surfside Solution II. *Version:* 2. Apr. 1995. *Customer Support:* 30 day unlimited warranty, 90 days free tech support.
DOS. 386 or higher (640k). disk $695.00. *Nonstandard peripherals required:* VGA. *Networks supported:* Lantastic, Novell.
Complete Administration Package for Schools with Less Than 2000 Students.
Surfside Software, Inc.

SurgAnLine CD-ROM Database for Surgery & Anesthesia. Oct. 1991.
MS Windows 3.1 or higher. IBM & compatibles (4Mb). CD-ROM disk $235.00-$995.00; Networks $1895.00 & up. *Nonstandard peripherals required:* Magnetic or CD-ROM, using ISO 9660. *Optimal configuration:* IBM & compatibles, 80386 or higher, 4Mb RAM, 20Mb hard disk, mouse, MS Windows 3.1 or higher.
System 6.0.7 or higher. Apple Macintosh (3Mb). CD-ROM disk $235.00-$995.00; Networks $1895.00 & up. *Optimal configuration:* Apple Macintosh Plus or higher, 3Mb RAM, System 6.0.7 or higher.

SurgAnLine Is an Electronic Reference Database to the Surgery & Anesthesia Journal Literature. Surgery/Anesthesia-Specific Excerpts (Including Abstracts) from the National Library of Medicine's MEDLINE Database Are Distributed on CD-ROM (Compact Disc, Read-Only Memory) Optical Disc. Knowledge Finder Search-&-Retrieval Software Makes Searching of the SurgAnLine Database Easy, Effective & Fast. After the User Types a Phrase or Sentence Describing the Information Needed, It selects the References in the Database That Appear to Best Match the Request, & Presents Them in Order of Likely Relevance. The SurgAnLine Archive CD-ROM Contains More Than 645,000 References to Articles Published in 250 Surgery/Anesthesia-Related Journals over the Most Recent 10 Full Years. Surgery & Anesthesia Articles From More Than 2,500 Other Journals Are Also Included.
Aries Systems Corp.

SURGE: Pathology Laboratory Management System. *Customer Support:* 24 hour/day, 7 day/week.
  DOS or UNIX/MUMPS (language).
   Microcomputer (80386) server with networked PC workstations or multiplexed VT100-type terminals. $5000.00 & up. *Networks supported:* Novell Netware.
  A Comprehensive Pathology System That Provides Services for Accessioning, Word Processing, Histology, CAP's SNOMED Coding, Billing, Management Reporting, Statistics, Archiving, Clinician Services, Quality Control, & Ad Hoc Reporting. Multiple Laboratory Divisions Including Surgical Pathology, Cytology, & Autopsy May Be Supported on One System with Unique Numbering Systems & Separated Workflow & with Across Division Inquiry & Correlation Reporting. Allows Tailoring & Flexibility with a Full Range of User Defined Master Files, Parameters, Custom Screens, & Special Report Formatting. It Provides Efficiency with Expanded Phrases, Inquiry & Selection Windows, & Automated Archive Retrieval & Correlation Reporting. It Also Promotes Laboratory Marketability with Laser Perfect Reports, Follow-Up Letters, Quicker Turnaround Times, & Clinician Summary Reports.
LCI.

Surgeon 4.
  Windows CD-ROM. CD-ROM disk Contact publisher for price.
  A Surgical Simulation Game Where the Player Must Successfully Diagnose & Operate on a Diseased Heart.
ISM, Inc.

Surgeon 3: The Brain. *Version:* 1.1. *Compatible Hardware:* All Macintosh. *Customer Support:* Technical, (410) 560-0973.
  3.5" disk $49.95.
  Surgery Simulation Game.
ISM, Inc.

SURV-A-SOFT. *Version:* 4.0. A. Earl Smith. Aug. 1984. *Memory Required:* 512k. *General Requirements:* Hard disk. *Items Included:* Software & manual.
  disk $995.00.
  Land Surveying Program.
Surveyors Supply Co.

Surveillance for Windows Image Motion Detection. *Items Included:* Full manual. No other products required. *Customer Support:* Free telephone support - no time limit. 30 day warranty.
  MS-DOS 3.2 or higher. IBM & compatibles (512k). disk $495.00, One-Camera System ,995.00. *Optimal configuration:* 386/486 or Pentium (Intel-compatible), 4Mb RAM, 1Mb available disk space, Super VGA monitor (512k RAM/256 colors), Microsoft Windows 3.1 or higher.
  Ideal for Image Motion Sensing & Recording Applications Such As Low Cost Surveillance Systems; Remote Observation Posts; Monitoring Fire Alarm Panels in Buildings; Monitoring Patients in Nursing Homes & Hospitals; & More. You Can Display Live or Still Images. Images May Be Updated from 30 Times per Second to Once per Hour.
Dynacomp, Inc.

SURVEY. Charles F. Cicciarella. Sep. 1985. *Compatible Hardware:* IBM PC XT with 2 disk drives. *Operating System(s) Required:* PC-DOS. (source code included). *Memory Required:* 128k. *Items Included:* Disk, stable bound instructions.
  disk $99.00 (ISBN 0-926152-40-8, Order no.: 33).
  Designed for Collection & Analysis of Survey Data. Supports Branching Surveys, & Produces Breakdown, Cross-Tabulation, & Scale Interpretation of Survey Results.
Persimmon Software.

Survey Analyst.
  disk $99.00 (Order no.: D8SA).
  Designed for Profiling Survey Data That Can Be Important for Marketing a Product or Idea.
The Alternate Source.

Survey Calc I. *Compatible Hardware:* Commodore 64, IBM PC, TI 99/4A Home Computer. *Language(s):* Extended BASIC.
  TI. disk $74.95 (Order no.: 501XD).
  IBM, Commodore. write for info.
River City Software, Inc.

Survey Lite: Two-Dimensional Coordinate Geometry. *Version:* 4.02. Mark D. Floan. Dec. 1992. *Items Included:* Manual w/tutorial examples. *Customer Support:* 120 days free phone support; 1 yr unlimited (on all Simplicity Software), $249.00; 90 day moneyback guarantee.
  PC-DOS/MS-DOS 3.0 or higher. IBM PC, XT, AT, PS/2 & compatibles (640k). disk $199.00 (ISBN 0-932071-05-8). *Nonstandard peripherals required:* 1 hard drive & 1 floppy drive. *Optimal configuration:* VGA graphics card, mouse.
  Two-Dimensional (Northings & Eastings, No Elevations) Coordinate Geometry Programs for the Land Surveyor. Limited to 2000 Data Points per File. Easily Upgradable to Survey 4.0 When Extra Power and/or Point Capacity Is Needed.
Simplicity Systems, Inc.

A Survey of Western Art. Feb. 1995. *Items Included:* CD-ROM booklet. *Customer Support:* Free technical support via phone as of release date.
  MPC/Windows. 386.25 or higher IBM compatible (4Mb). CD-ROM disk $49.95 (ISBN 1-885784-00-7, Order no.: 1097). *Optimal configuration:* MPC CD-ROM player, S-VGA graphics card (640x480x256 colors) with compatible monitor, MPC compliant sound card, mouse, Windows 3.1.
  Macintosh. Macintosh (4Mb). CD-ROM disk $49.95 (ISBN 1-885784-26-0, Order no.: 1103). *Optimal configuration:* CD-ROM drive, color monitor with 256 plus colors, system version 6.07 or higher.
  Explore an Extensive Library of Art Featuring Hundreds of Paintings, Sculptures, Architecture & Other Works from Around the World. Gain Insight into More Than Eighty Schools of Art. Study Pieces from a Wide Variety of Periods, from Ancient Egypt to Modern America. A Powerful Resource for Scholars, Artists, Students & Art Enthusiasts.
Technology Dynamics Corp.

A Survey of Western Art: Jewel. *Items Included:* CD-ROM booklet. *Customer Support:* Free technical support via phone as of release date.
  MPC/Windows. 386MHz or higher (4Mb). CD-ROM disk $49.95 (ISBN 1-885784-62-7, Order no.: 1090). *Optimal configuration:* MPC CD-ROM player, S-VGA graphics card (640x480x256 colors) with compatible monitor, MPC compliant sound card, mouse, Windows 3.1 or higher, Windows 95 compatible.
  System 6.07 or higher. Macintosh (4Mb). *Optimal configuration:* Color monitor (256 plus colors), mouse, CD-ROM drive.
  Explore an Extensive Encyclopedia of Art Featuring Hundreds of Paintings, Sculptures, Architecture & Other Works from Around the World. Gain Insight into More Than Eighty Schools of Art. A Powerful Resource for Scholars, Artists, Students & Art Enthusiasts.
Technology Dynamics Corp.

Survey +. Feb. 1992. *Items Included:* 40 page documentation with diagrams. *Customer Support:* Free phone or mail support.
  PC-DOS/MS-DOS. IBM PC & compatibles (256k). disk $75.00. *Nonstandard peripherals required:* Color Graphics Card or Hercules Monochrome Graphics Card. *Addl. software required:* BASICA (provided).
  Provides 45 Functions to Locate Points, Perform Traverse Adjustments (Least Square or Compass Rule), Horizontal Alignments. Prints Traverse, Calculates Area & Displays Diagram of Surfaces with Linear or Curved Sides. 1400 Coordinate Points, Batch File or Interactive Command Entry, Input Error Detection, Variable Distances & Angles, & Arithmetic Mode Calculations.
Serge Loussarian.

Survey Pro. Nov. 1992. *Items Included:* User guide with tutorial & reference section, indexed. *Customer Support:* Free support hotline to registered owners, unlimited terms, 30 day unconditional guarantee.
  MS-DOS 2.0 or higher. IBM-PC or 100% compatibles (550k). Standard Edition $249.00; Advanced Edition $695.00. *Optimal configuration:* IBM PC or compatible, MS-DOS 5.0, 520-550k. *Networks supported:* Works on any network as a DOS standalone product, including on most servers.
  An All-in-One Product for Conducting Surveys. Features Automated Questionnaire Layout, Easy Data Entry, & Powerful Analysis Tools for Producing Reports. Available in Standard or Advanced Edition.
Apian Software.

Survey-Property I. Nov. 1983. *Compatible Hardware:* Sinclair ZX-80, TS-1000. *Language(s):* BASIC. *Memory Required:* 16k. *General Requirements:* Double-sided disk drive, CGA card.
  cassette $19.95 (Order no.: SN-1).
  8-Part Program Intended for Use by Professional or Amateur Surveyors. Computes Bearing to Azimuths, Adds Station Angles, Computes Traverse, Interior Angles, Error of Closure, Area by DMD Method, Area of a Triangle, & Azimuths to Bearings.
P. G. Billings.

Survey-Property II. Feb. 1986. *Compatible Hardware:* IBM PC & compatibles; Sanyo-55X; Tandy 100. *Operating System(s) Required:* MS-DOS. *Language(s):* BASIC (source code included). *Memory Required:* 24k.
  Sanyo. disk $29.95 (Order no.: SN-3).
  TI-99/4A. disk or cassette $29.95 (Order no.: TI-2, TI-3).
  Tandy 100. cassette $29.95 (Order no.: TRS-3).
  8-Part Program Intended for Use by Professional

or Amateur Surveyors. Computes Bearings to Azimuths, Adds Station Angles, Computes Traverse & Inverse, Coordinates, Interior Angles, Error of Closure with Adjustments to Azimuths & Distances, Area by DMD Method & Azimuths to Bearings Conversion.
P. G. Billings.

The Survey Sampler. Apr. 1988. *Operating System(s) Required:* PC-DOS/MS-DOS. *Memory Required:* 320k. *Items Included:* Indexed manual, tutorial. *Customer Support:* Unlimited phone support, warranty.
3.5" or 5.25" disk $149.00 (ISBN 0-918577-03-9).
System Creates Random Digit Telephone Samples for Marketing Research & Other Applications. The Samples Can Exclude Designated Numbers or Blocks of Numbers. Call List Formats Are Provided.
Creative Research Systems.

The Survey System. *Version:* 5.0. H. Zucker. 1994. *Compatible Hardware:* IBM PC & compatibles, PS/2. *Operating System(s) Required:* PC-DOS, MS-DOS. *Language(s):* Compiled BASIC, Assembly. *Memory Required:* 640k. *Items Included:* Indexed manual, tutorial. *Customer Support:* Unlimited phone support, warranty.
IBM PC, PS/2 & compatibles. $500.00-$1300.00 (ISBN 0-918577-00-4, Order no.: SS-PC).
Complete System Analyzes Market Research, Public Opinion, Customer Satisfaction, Employee Attitude Surveys. Easy to Learn & Use. Produces Presentation Quality Tables & Charts. Spell Checks Answers. Statistics Verbal, Computer Aided Interview & Phone Interview, Network Versions Available.
Creative Research Systems.

The Survey System. *Version:* 5.0. 1995. *Items Included:* Manual & tutorial. *Customer Support:* Unlimited telephone support.
PC-DOS/MS-DOS, OS/2. IBM & compatibles (640k). disk $500.00-$1300.00. *Optimal configuration:* PC-DOS/MS-DOS or OS/2, IBM or compatible (640k RAM). *Networks supported:* Novell, LANtastic, most others.
Designed to Enter, Process & Produce Results from All Types of Surveys. Accepts Mail, Phone, Personal & Computer Interviews. Produces Tables & Charts. Can Accept Open End Questions, Verbatim & Voice Responses. Spell Checks Answers. Can Export to Word Process & Spreadsheet. Modular Design to Suit All Needs. Evaluation Package $50 Applied to Purchase of System. Demo Disk & Sample Size Calculator Available.
Creative Research Systems.

Survey 3LX: COGO for the HP 95 LX. *Version:* 3.03. Mark D. Floan. Jun. 1991. *Items Included:* Manual w/tutorial examples. *Customer Support:* 120 days free phone support; 1 yr unlimited (on all Simplicity Software), $249.00; 90 day moneyback guarantee.
HP 95 LX DOS. HP 95 LX (512k). disk $199.00, incl. manual (ISBN 0-932071-05-8).
Nonstandard peripherals required: 512k RAM card. *Addl. software required:* HP Connectivity Pak. *Optimal configuration:* HP 95 LX w/ 1Mb RAM & 1Mb RAM card.
Advanced Three-Dimensional Coordinate Geometry Programs for the Land Surveyor for Use on the HP 95 LX Palmtop Computer. Compatible with Simplicity's Survey 4.0 on the PC.
Simplicity Systems, Inc.

Survey 4.0. *Version:* 4.01. Mark D. Floan. Dec. 1992. *Items Included:* Manual with examples & tutorial. *Customer Support:* 120 days free phone support; 90 day moneyback guarantee.
MS-DOS 3.0 or higher (640k). IBM PC & compatibles; including HP 100LX & 200LX. disk $299.00 incl. manual (ISBN 0-932071-05-8).
Nonstandard peripherals required: 1 floppy & 1 hard drive.
Advanced Three-Dimensional (Northings, Eastings & Elevations) Coordinate Geometry Programs for Land Surveyors. Menu-Driven Interactive Format.
Simplicity Systems, Inc.

Surveying. *Compatible Hardware:* HP 85, 86/87. HP 85. data cartridge, 3-1/2" or 5-1/4" disk $95.00 ea. (Order no.: 82813A).
HP 86/87. 3-1/2" or 5-1/4" disk $95.00 ea. (Order no.: 82843A).
Includes Programs to Aid Surveyors in Many Often-Encountered Computations.
Hewlett-Packard Co.

Surveying & Land Measurements. 1989. *Compatible Hardware:* IBM PC & compatibles. *Operating System(s) Required:* PC-DOS/MS-DOS. *Language(s):* QBASIC. *Customer Support:* Telephone assistance.
disk $47.00, incl. user guide.
disk $127.00, incl. source code.
Reduction of Differential Level Notes, Three-Wire Level Notes, Cross-Section Notes & Stadia Notes; Polaris Observation for Determination of Astronomical Azimuth and/or Bearing; Transverse Adjustment; & Taping Corrections. Data May Be Input in Free Form or May Be Drawn from a Previously Created Data File. Output May Be Sent to Both Monitor & Printer for User Verification.
Systek, inc. (Mississippi).

Surveying Calculations. Duane Bristow. *Compatible Hardware:* TRS-80 Model I, Model III. *Operating System(s) Required:* TRSDOS. *Language(s):* BASIC.
disk $249.95.
Surveyor Enters Land Boundaries & Computer Will Figure the Error of Closure of the Survey, Balance the Survey, Draw a Rough Sketch, & Calculate the Average.
Duane Bristow Computers, Inc.

Surveyor's Systems. *Version:* 3.0. Judson McClendon. Mar. 1976. *Compatible Hardware:* IBM PC. *Operating System(s) Required:* PC-DOS/MS-DOS. *Language(s):* BASIC, C (source code included). *Memory Required:* 256k. *Items Included:* Diskette, Manual. *Customer Support:* free phone support.
disk $295.00.
Menu-Driven Programs Assist in a Variety of Surveyor's Calculations & Operations.
Sun Valley Systems (Alabama).

Surveys & Questionnaires. *Version:* 10.0. 1989. *Compatible Hardware:* Apple Macintosh, IBM PC & compatibles. *Items Included:* Disks, book, program instructions (also includes "Marketing Statistics"). *Customer Support:* Unlimited telephone support.
Apple Macintosh, Commodore Amiga, IBM PC & compatibles (512k). $250.00.
This Package Contains Sophisticated, Yet Easy-to-Use Package for the Creation, Recording & Analysis of Surveys & Questionnaires, As Well As Formidable Statistical Techniques for Data Analysis.
Lionheart Pr., Inc.

Surview - Media Research Edition. *Version:* 4.2. Aug. 1989. *Items Included:* 250-page manual, complete tutorial, sample data. *Customer Support:* One-year technical support package including all free updates ($995 in subsequent years), 30-day money back guarantee.
MS-DOS 2.0 or higher (512k). IBM PC, PC AT PS/2 & compatibles. single-user license $6950.00, site license $9950.00 (Order no.: SURVIEW). *Nonstandard peripherals required:* Hard disk (10Mb); printer. *Optimal configuration:* UGA & color monitor; 640k; math coprocessor.
Complete Marketing Research System for Media Researchers & Marketeers Who Can Use Program to Create Exact Presentation Report Needed. Audience Reach/Frequency, Readership Profiles & Other Analyses Are Constructed Quickly. Most Cost-Effective Alternative to On-Line Data Services.
Bruce Bell & Assocs., Inc.

Survpac Boundary, Roadway, & Site Development. *Items Included:* Full manual. No other products required. *Customer Support:* Free telephone support - no time limit. 30 day warranty.
MS-DOS 3.2 or higher. IBM & compatibles (512k). disk $249.95. *Optimal configuration:* IBM, MS-DOS 3.2 or higher, 640k RAM & hard drive. Printer is optional. Can be interfaced to a digitizer.
demo disk $19.95 incl. manual.
Provides Complete Coordinate Geometry Routines for Boundary, Roadway & Site Development, & Generates Complete DXF Files for Use in AUTOcad. DXF Files Include All of the Text for Curves, Bearings & Distances. Curve Tables May Be Generated If the Arcs Are Too Short for Normal Notation.
Dynacomp, Inc.

Survtab. *Version:* 2.0. H. Foxwell. 1982. *Compatible Hardware:* IBM PC & compatibles, UNIX systems. *Operating System(s) Required:* MS-DOS 1.1, 2.0, 3.1; UNIX V. *Language(s):* C. *Memory Required:* 512k.
disk $249.00.
System for Tabulating Data from Survey Questionnaires.
Statistical Computing Consultants.

SUSAN: Simulator for Unsteady-State Analysis of Networks.
PC/MS-DOS (512k). IBM compatibles. disk $2295.00. *Nonstandard peripherals required:* Math coprocessor.
This Unsteady State Flow Analysis Program is Similar to PAULA, but Will Analyze Networked (Closed Loop & Branched) Systems in Addition to Straight Pipe. Pipes, Loops, Pumps, Valves, Variable Supply/Delivery Pressures or Flow Rates Can Be Modeled in Any Combination & Configuration. Changing Pressures & Flow Rates in Various Pipe Branches & at Every Time Step of the Simulation Are Calculated in Response to a Pressure or Flow Upset Somewhere in the Network. Pressure & Flow Upsets Are Normally Caused by Closing Valves or Pump Station Power Failures. Combinations of Pressure & Flow Variations May Also Be Used. Maximum Pressure, Cavitation, PRV & Surge Tank Summaries Are Reported. Has US/SI Units Options & a Full-Screen Input Editor, On-Line Help.
Techdata.

Suspect. David Lebling. Nov. 1984. *Compatible Hardware:* Apple Series, Macintosh; Atari XL/XE, ST; Commodore 64, Plus 4, Amiga; IBM; TI 99/4A; TRS-80 Model I, Model III, Color Computer, Tandy 2000. *Operating System(s) Required:* CP/M, MS-DOS 2.0.
$44.95.
Atari, Commodore 64 & Color Computer. $39.95.
You Are a Newspaper Reporter Invited to an Elegant Masquerade Ball & You Have but a Few Hours to Convince the Police That It Wasn't You Who Committed the Murder. You'll Need to Figure Out Who Committed the Crime & Why.
Activision, Inc.

Suspect. Infocom. *Compatible Hardware:* HP 150 Touchscreen, HP 110 Portable.
3.5" disk $44.95 (Order no.: 92244CA).
You Are a Reporter Who Gets the Scoop on the Society Event of the Year - the Murder of a Maryland Blue Blood Aristocrat at a Fancy Costume Ball. And You Couldn't Have a Closer Inside Source for Your Story. Because You're the Prime Suspect. You Know You're Not Guilty, but the Evidence Is Stacked Against You. Now You Must Prove Your Innocence & Find the Real Killer - or Risk Being Framed & Face the Consequences.
Hewlett-Packard Co.

Suspended. Michael Berlyn. 1983. *Compatible Hardware:* Apple II Seriesi; Atari XL/XE, ST; Commodore 64, Amiga; CP/M based machines; IBM PC; Kaypro; TRS-80 Model I, Model III.
disk $14.95.
You Are Buried Alive in a Cryogenic Capsule Deep Inside an Alien World. When an Earthquake Disrupts the Systems of the Underground Complex You Inhabit - Systems That Surface-Life Depends on - You Must Stabilize Conditions. However, You Can Only Do So by Commanding Your Six Robots, Each of Which Perceives the World Differently. If You Save Your World from Destruction, You Have Just Begun. Game Is Designed to Be Replayed Numerous Times, As You Optimize Your Strategies. You Can Also Go on to More Levels of Play, & There's an Option That Lets You Customize the Story.
Activision, Inc.

Suspended. Infocom. *Compatible Hardware:* HP 150 Touchscreen, HP 110 Portable.
3.5" disk $49.95 (Order no.: 92243FA).
Awaken after Being Buried in a Cryogenic Capsule to a Nightmare Landscape on a Mad Planet.
Hewlett-Packard Co.

Swamp War. *Compatible Hardware:* TRS-80.
contact publisher for price.
Instant Software, Inc.

Sweeps Keeper. *Version:* 4.00. *Items Included:* User manual, 2 sample leagues, 5 1/2 or 3 1/2 diskettes. *Customer Support:* Telephone support.
MS-DOS/PC-DOS (256k). IBM-PC/XT or 100% compatible. disk $650.00. *Nonstandard peripherals required:* Printer. *Optimal configuration:* Color monitor, hi speed dot matrix printer.
Designed Especially for Sweepstakes Bowling. It Computes, Adjusts, Records, & Files Scores, Maintains & Updates Handicaps, & Ranks Players & Teams for As Many As 60 Different Leagues, 6,000 Teams, & 18,000 Bowlers, at Once. Call up Individual or Team Scores & Rankings from Top to Bottom of Teams, Men's Singles, Women's Singles, Men's Doubles, Mixed Doubles, Women's Doubles & Special Doubles.
Data Research Processing, Inc.

SwiftCALC PC. *Version:* 3.0. *Items Included:* Manual. *Customer Support:* Unlimited technical support; 60 day moneyback guarantee.
DOS. IBM or compatibles (512k). disk $39.95. *Addl. software required:* DOS 2.1 or higher. *Optimal configuration:* One or more disk drives or a hard drive.
Easy-to-Learn, All-in-One Spreadsheet Program with an Easier-Than-Ever User Interface Designed for Personal & Small Business Use. User Interface Help Screens & Pull-Down Menus Keep You Going, Even If You've Never Used a Spreadsheet Before. Adds Life to Dull Statistical Information by Displaying & Printing Pie Charts, Multi-Level Bar or Line Charts or High-Low-Close Graphs.
Timeworks, Inc.

Swimsuit Review 94. *Items Included:* Browser/wallpaper installer/copier front end software. *Customer Support:* 90 day warranty, free call back technical support.
System 6. Color Mac (4Mb). CD-ROM disk $9.95. *Nonstandard peripherals required:* CD-ROM drive. *Optimal configuration:* 8Mb. *Networks supported:* Apple File Sharing.
Windows 3.1. IBM 386 (4Mb). CD-ROM disk $9.95. *Nonstandard peripherals required:* CD-ROM drive. *Optimal configuration:* IBM 486, 8Mb RAM.
BeachWare.

Swimsuit Review '94 & '95. *Customer Support:* Free, unlimited.
System 6 Mac. 030 Mac, 256 colors (4Mb). CD-ROM disk $24.95. *Nonstandard peripherals required:* Sound card, CD-ROM drive.
Windows 3.1 PC. 486 PC (4Mb). *Nonstandard peripherals required:* Any Windows supported sound card, CD-ROM drive.
Over One Hundred Photos of Stunning Models Await You in the Latest Swimwear, All Shot in Exotic, Tropical Settings. That's More Than Ninety Female & Ten Male Photos That You Can View. You Can Even Install Your Favorite Picture As a PC Wallpaper or a Macintosh Startup Screen.
BeachWare.

Swine Herd History. *Compatible Hardware:* Apple II Plus, IIe; IBM. *Language(s):* BASIC. *Memory Required:* Apple 48k; IBM 64k. *General Requirements:* Printer.
disk $49.95.
back-up disk $9.95.
manual $19.95.
Designed for Commercial or Purebred Operations. Each Data Disk Contains Records for 40 Sows for up to Ten Litters per Sow. Includes the Year & Sow Identification for Breeding Information, Breeding Date, Next Heat Date, Approximate Farrowing Date, & Actual Farrowing Date for the Sire Information. Litter History Information Includes the Following: Year, Sow & Litter Identification, Live & Dead Pigs Born, 21 & 60 Day Weight, Farrowing Ease, Sow & Litter Veterinarian Problems, Litter History, Pigs Sold & Price.
Cherrygarth, Inc.

Swine History Information. *Compatible Hardware:* Apple II+, IIe, III. *General Requirements:* Printer.
disk $49.50.
Assists in the Handling of Information about Each Sow & Litter. Accommodates up to 10 Litters for the Lifetime of the Sow. Along with Information about Each Litter, Data Includes Basic Breeding & Health Information about the Sow. The Report Generated by This Program Will Allow for Printing of Records of Any Sow or Sows, Litter or Litters, at Any Point in Time. Consists of a Program Disk & Data Disk. May Be Used on Either a Single or Dual Disk Drive System. Each Data Disk Contains Lifetime Records for 50 Sows.
Cherrygarth, Inc.

Swine Management. *Version:* 2.2. Farmhand Computer Systems. 1978. *Compatible Hardware:* IBM PC & compatibles, PC XT, PC AT, PS/2. *Operating System(s) Required:* MS-DOS, PC-DOS. *Language(s):* FORTRAN. *Memory Required:* 320k. *Items Included:* Manual. *Customer Support:* 1 hour per package purchased.
$395.00 5.25" or 8" disk, 3.5" disk.
Can Be Used for Any Hog Operation with 80 or More Sows Farrowed in Confinement. Provides Complete Sow & Litter Histories for Progeny Analysis.
MCC Software (Midwest Computer Ctr. Co.).

Swine Management. Agri-Management Services, Inc. *Compatible Hardware:* TI Professional. *Operating System(s) Required:* MS-DOS. *Memory Required:* 64k. *General Requirements:* Printer.
$995.00.
Texas Instruments, Personal Productivit.

Swine Ration Analysis. Merle W. Wagner. 1983. *Compatible Hardware:* Apple II Plus, IIe, IIc; IBM. *Operating System(s) Required:* Apple DOS 3.3, MS-DOS 2.0. *Language(s):* BASIC. *Memory Required:* 48k. *General Requirements:* Printer.
disk $49.95 (ISBN 0-922900-32-9, Order no.: CFR-190).
Designed for Use by Any Swine Operation. Provides 40 Nutrient Entries for Each Feed.
Cherrygarth, Inc.

SwineTRAK. *Version:* 5.0. *Operating System(s) Required:* MS-DOS. *Items Included:* Manual. *Customer Support:* 3 Different technical support plans are available.
disk $395.00.
Provides Hog Management Records for Large Herds. Furrowing & Finishing Capability. Tracks Bloodiness. Produces Crate Reports, Plus Additional Reports & Worksheets for Scheduling Herd Management Actions & Analyzing Herd Efficiencies & Profitability.
Red Wing Business Systems, Inc.

SwineTrak Plus. Red Wing Business Systems Inc. *Items Included:* Spiral bound manual. *Customer Support:* Available.
MS-DOS 2.0 or higher. IBM or PS/2 compatible (256k). contact publisher for price. *Optimal configuration:* 1 floppy drive with 80 column printer, hard drive requried.
Records Are Kept on Every Detail of Swine Breeding & Production. Individual Sow History & Statistics on Litters, Treatments, Disease & Breeding. Individual Boar Records & Whole Herd Stats on Breeding, Weanings, Inventory & Feed. Keeps Track of Herd Health & Feed Consumption Plus Gain. Tracks Sow & Boar Bloodlines, Also with a Variety of Reports.
Farmer's Software Assn.

Swiss Foreign Direct Investment in the United States 1974-1994. May 1995. *Items Included:* Spiral bound manual. *Customer Support:* Unlimited telephone support.
MS-DOS 6.0/Windows 3.1 or higher. PC Clone 486 or higher (4Mb). disk $125.00 (ISBN 1-878974-12-2). *Addl. software required:* Database Versions are available for MS Access 2.0, Excel, Lotus, Paradox, Foxpro, & dBASE. *Optimal configuration:* PC clone with MS-DOS 6.0/Windows 3.1 or higher. Must have MS Access 2.0, or Excel, or Lotus or Paradox or FoxPro or dBASE.
Database of All Swiss Foreign Investment Transactions in the United States 1974-1994.
Jeffries & Associates, Inc.

Swivel 3D Professional. *Version:* 1.5. Aug. 1990. *Items Included:* Manual. *Customer Support:* First 90 days free phone call, on line.
Apple Macintosh II line (4mb). 3.5" disk $695.00. *Nonstandard peripherals required:* Color monitor, 256 color board.
Enhanced Version of Swivel 3D, 24-Bit Color Output, 24-Bit Image Mapping, 8 Independent Light Sources, Environmental Mapping, MacRenderMan RIB & AutoCAD DXF Output. Hierchical Linking of Moving Parts, 3D Animation Capabilities.
Macromedia, Inc.

TITLE INDEX

The Sword of Altair. Version: 1.4.1. Sep. 1988. Compatible Hardware: Apple II series, IIgs. Memory Required: Apple II series 64k, Apple IIgs 256k.
  Apple II series. 3.5" disk $24.95 (ISBN 1-55616-014-3).
  Apple IIgs. 3.5" disk $24.95 (ISBN 1-55616-012-7).
  Adventure Game.
  DAR Systems International.

Sword of Aragon. Russell Shilling & Kurt Myers. Items Included: Rulebook & poster. Customer Support: Technical support line: (408) 737-6850 (11am-5pm PST); 14 day money back guarantee/30 day exchange policy.
  DOS 2.11 or higher. IBM PC & compatible (384k). disk $39.95. Nonstandard peripherals required: Requires a color monitor & a graphic adapter (i.e., CGA, EGA, Tandy 16-color).
  Workbench. Amiga (512k). 3.5" disk $39.95.
  As the Heir of the Late Duke of Aladda, It Is Your Duty to Fulfill Your Father's Lifelong Dream: Extend Aladda's Dominion & Unite the Entire Aragonian Empire Under Your Banner. This Fantasy Game Gives You More Than Flashing Swords & Arcane Sorcery. It Is Also a Strategy Game That Requires Plotting & Planning If You Are to Win. Raise & Equip an Army of Bowmen, Cavalry, Infantry, Mages, & Priests. Hire Mercenaries If You Must. Just Remember That, Even in a Magical World, You Still Have to Deal with the Harsh Realities of Limited Budgets & Resources. Assemble Your Army Wisely & Campaign with Vigor. Imagine How Glorious it Will Be to Sit on the Emperor's Throne & Call Aragon Yours!
  Strategic Simulations, Inc.

Sword of the Samurai. 1989. Items Included: Manual, keyboard template.
  MS-DOS. IBM PC, Tandy. $54.95. Optimal configuration: 384k, CGA, EGA, Hercules mono, VGA/MCGA, or Tandy 1000; joystick optional but recommended.
  Enter Japan In the Age of Warring States. At the Center of This Role-playing, Action-adventure Simulation of Combat, Statesmanship & Intrigue, Player Is a Samurai Warrior Struggling for Honor. More Than Life Itself, Honor is Critical to Acheiving Ultimate Goal: Unifying Feudal Japan Under Noble Rule.
  MicroProse Software.

SWPlan. Version: 2.0.
  Windows 3.1. IBM 386 (4 Mb). 3.5" disk $249.00. Nonstandard peripherals required: 4Mb hard disk space available; VGA or better; mouse (highly recommended).
  Design an integrated solid waste management system, evaluate an existing system, prepare or compare vendor proposals, compare your solid waste management system with others, or simulate a variety of management scenarios.
  Recycling Insights.

SW01W AudioClips: Star Wars. Version: 1.5. Aug. 1993. Items Included: Manual, registration card, sound list. Customer Support: Phone technical support.
  DOS 5.0, Windows 3.1. PC 286 or higher (2Mb). disk $14.95 (ISBN 1-57303-005-8). Nonstandard peripherals required: Sound card recommended. Optimal configuration: 286 or higher with 4Mb RAM, DOS 5.0 or later, Windows 3.1 or later, 4-7Mb HD space available, sound card.
  Exclusively Licensed High Quality Sound Files Consisting of Classic Sound Effects, Dialogue & Music from Original TV Shows & Movies. Also Included Is the 'Whoop It Up' Audio Utility, Which Allows the User to Attach AudioClips to Various Windows Events.
  Sound Source Interactive.

SW02W AudioClips: Empire Strikes Back. Version: 1.5. Jul. 1994. Items Included: Manual, registration card, sound list. Customer Support: Phone technical support.
  DOS 5.0, Windows 3.1. PC 286 or higher (2Mb). disk $14.95 (ISBN 1-57303-007-4). Nonstandard peripherals required: Sound card recommended. Optimal configuration: 286 or higher with 4Mb RAM, DOS 5.0 or later, Windows 3.1 or later, 4-7Mb HD space available, sound card.
  Exclusively Licensed High Quality Sound Files Consisting of Classic Sound Effects, Dialogue & Music from Original TV Shows & Movies. Also Included Is the 'Whoop It Up' Audio Utility, Which Allows the User to Attach AudioClips to Various Windows Events.
  Sound Source Interactive.

Symantec AntiVirus For Macintosh (SAM). Version: 3.0. Items Included: 1 disk & 1 manual. Customer Support: (408) 372-8100, 24 hr Virus Newsline.
  Macintosh Plus or higher. 3.5" disk $99.00.
  Offers Protection, Detection, & Elimination of Viruses. Works Against the Common Known Viruses: nVir, Scores, ANTI; Detects Irregularities That Occur on a System on the Chance That There Might Be Some Unknown Viral Infection at Work. Key Features: Detection Methods Spot Viruses Before They Have a Chance to Infect System; Scan Any File, Folder or Volume Capability to Determine If Virus Is Prsesent; If Virus is Detected, Program Makes It Easy for User to Delete File or Attempt to Repair It; Optionally Scans User-Specified Volumes & Folders at System Startup & Shutdown; Option to Automatically Scan Every Floppy Disk When Inserted into Macintosh; Works on Most Networks As on a Dedicated Machine; Wide Range of Options. Supports System 7.0.
  Symantec Corp.

Symantec Utilities for Macintosh. Version: 2.0. Compatible Hardware: Apple Macintosh. Operating System(s) Required: System 4.1 or higher, Finder 5.3 or higher. Items Included: 3 disks, 1 manual. Customer Support: (408) 372-8100.
  3.5" disk $75.00.
  Symantec Corp.

Symbol Library: Basic Home Design. Jun. 1987. Compatible Hardware: Apple Macintosh, IBM PC. Memory Required: 512k. General Requirements: 2 disk drives, graphics card, Generic CADD. Customer Support: Unlimited technical support to registered users.
  IBM. disk $49.95 (ISBN 1-55814-044-1, Order no.: F1250).
  IBM. 3.5" disk $49.95 (ISBN 1-55814-045-X, Order no.: T1250).
  Macintosh. 3.5" disk $49.95 (ISBN 1-55814-047-6, Order no.: M1250).
  Contains over 100 Pre-Drawn Symbols for Use in Drawing Plan & Elevation Views of Home Designs. A Variety of Symbols Are Included, Such As Kitchen Appliances, Bathroom Fixtures, Kitchen & Bathroom Cabinets, Doors, Windows, Electrical Outlets, Switches, etc.
  Autodesk, Inc.

Symbols Library: Bathroom Design. Dec. 1987. Compatible Hardware: Apple Macintosh, IBM PC. Memory Required: 512k. General Requirements: 2 disk drives, graphics card, Generic CADD. Customer Support: Unlimited technical support to registered users.
  IBM. disk $74.95 (ISBN 1-55814-135-9, Order no.: F2350).
  IBM. 3.5" disk $49.95 (ISBN 1-55814-136-7, Order no.: T2350).
  Macintosh. 3.5" disk $74.95 (ISBN 1-55814-

SYMBOLS LIBRARY: ELECTRICAL

038-7, Order no.: M2350).
  450 Symbols of Bathroom Cabinets, Fixtures, etc. Plan & Elevation Views.
  Autodesk, Inc.

Symbols Library: Clip Art. Jan. 1988. Compatible Hardware: IBM PC. Memory Required: 512k. General Requirements: 2 disk drives, graphics card, Generic CADD. Customer Support: Unlimited technical support to registered users.
  disk $24.95 (ISBN 1-55814-104-9, Order no.: F2000).
  3.5" disk $24.95 (ISBN 1-55814-105-7, Order no.: T2000).
  Apple.
  100 Art Type Symbols for Clip Art, Greeting Cards, Banners, etc.
  Autodesk, Inc.

Symbols Library: Commercial & Residential Electrical. Sep. 1987. Compatible Hardware: IBM PC. Memory Required: 512k. General Requirements: 2 disk drives, graphics card. Customer Support: Unlimited technical support to registered users.
  IBM. disk $49.95 (ISBN 1-55814-076-X, Order no.: F1650).
  IBM. 3.5" disk $49.95 (ISBN 1-55814-077-8, Order no.: T-1650).
  120 Symbols for Home & Commercial Electrical Wiring Diagrams: Architecture/Construction. Conforms to NECA Wiring Symbols Standards.
  Autodesk, Inc.

Symbols Library: Commercial & Residential Furnishings. Jun. 1987. Compatible Hardware: Apple Macintosh, IBM PC. Memory Required: 512k. General Requirements: 2 disk drives, graphics card, Generic CADD. Customer Support: Unlimited technical support to registered users.
  IBM. disk $49.95 (ISBN 1-55814-048-4, Order no.: F1300).
  IBM. 3.5" disk $49.95 (ISBN 1-55814-049-2, Order no.: T1300).
  Apple Macintosh. 3.5" disk $49.95 (ISBN 1-55814-051-4, Order no.: M1300).
  Contains Over 90 Predrawn Symbols, for Use in Interior Decorating & Professional Space Planning. A Variety of Symbols Are Included Such As Tables, Chairs, & Sofas, Beds & Chests, Home Electronics Equipment, Office Partitions, Desks & Conference Tables, Electrical Outlets, Switches etc. Users Rotate & Re-Size the Symbols As They Place Them Anywhere in Floor Plan Drawings.
  Autodesk, Inc.

Symbols Library: Commercial & Residential Plumbing. Dec. 1987. Compatible Hardware: Apple Macintosh, IBM PC. Memory Required: 512k. General Requirements: 2 disk drives, graphics card, Generic CADD. Customer Support: Unlimited technical support to registered users.
  IBM. disk $49.95 (ISBN 1-55814-080-8, Order no.: F1700).
  IBM. 3.5" disk $49.95 (ISBN 1-55814-081-6, Order no.: T1700).
  Macintosh. 3.5" disk $49.95 (ISBN 1-55814-083-2, Order no.: M1700).
  Over 100 Symbols for Home & Commercial Plumbing Drawings: Architecture/Construction.
  Autodesk, Inc.

Symbols Library: Electrical Engineering Power. Sep. 1987. Compatible Hardware: IBM PC. Memory Required: 512k. General Requirements: 2 disk drives, graphic card, Generic CADD. Customer Support: Unlimited technical support to registered users.
  disk $49.95 (ISBN 1-55814-040-9, Order no.:

F1200).
3.5" disk $49.95 (ISBN 1-55814-041-7, Order no.: T1200).
100 IEEE Symbols for Home & Commercial Plumbing Drawings; Architecture/Engineering.
Autodesk, Inc.

Symbols Library: Electronic II CMOS. Oct. 1987. *Compatible Hardware:* IBM PC. *Memory Required:* 512k. *General Requirements:* 2 disk drives, graphic card, Generic CADD or First CADD. *Customer Support:* Unlimited technical support to registered users.
disk $74.95 (ISBN 1-55814-024-7, Order no.: F1002).
3.5" disk $74.95 (ISBN 1-55814-025-5, Order no.: T1002).
100 Commonly Used Symbols from 4000 Series CMOS.
Autodesk, Inc.

Symbols Library: Electronic III: ECL. Oct. 1987. *Compatible Hardware:* IBM PC. *Memory Required:* 512k. *General Requirements:* 2 Disk drives, graphics card, Generic CADD. *Customer Support:* Unlimited technical support to registered users.
disk $74.95 (ISBN 1-55814-028-X, Order no.: F1003).
3.5" disk $74.95 (ISBN 1-55814-029-8, Order no.: T1003).
Over 100 Symbols from 10100 Through 1000170 of ECL Components.
Autodesk, Inc.

Symbols Library: Electronics I: IEEE. Sep. 1987. *Compatible Hardware:* Apple Macintosh, IBM PC. *Memory Required:* 512k. *General Requirements:* 2 disk drives, graphics card, Generic CADD. *Customer Support:* Unlimited technical support to registered users.
IBM. disk $24.95 (ISBN 1-55814-020-4, Order no.: F1001).
IBM. 3.5" disk $24.95 (ISBN 1-55814-021-2, Order no.: T1001).
Macintosh. 3.5" disk $24.95 (ISBN 1-55814-023-9, Order no.: M1001).
Offers Over 100 Logic Symbols, Diodes, ICs, Transistors, Resistors, etc. Most Symbols Conform to the IEEE STD 3315-1975 Standards.
Autodesk, Inc.

Symbols Library: Fasteners. Jan. 1988. *Compatible Hardware:* IBM PC. *Memory Required:* 512k. *General Requirements:* 2 disk drives, graphic card, Generic CADD. *Customer Support:* Unlimited technical support to registered users.
disk $74.95 (ISBN 1-55814-116-2, Order no.: F2100).
3.5" disk $74.95 (ISBN 1-55814-117-0, Order no.: T2100).
200 ASTM, NAS, & Miscellaneous Symbols. Includes Bolts, Nuts, Screws, Washers.
Autodesk, Inc.

Symbols Library: Flow Charts & Schedules. Jun. 1987. *Compatible Hardware:* Apple Macintosh, IBM PC. *Memory Required:* 512k. *General Requirements:* 2 disk drives, graphics card, Generic CADD. *Customer Support:* Unlimited technical support to registered users.
IBM. disk $24.95 (ISBN 1-55814-052-2, Order no.: F1350).
IBM. 3.5" disk $24.95 (ISBN 1-55814-053-0, Order no.: T1350).
Apple Macintosh. 3.5" disk $24.95 (ISBN 1-55814-055-7, Order no.: M1350).
Flow Charts & Schedules Symbol Library Containing Over 90 Pre-Drawn Symbols for Use in Professional Flow charts & Program Schedules. Symbols Are Included for Input & Output, Variable Assignments, Decisions & Iterations, Arrows & Pointers, Schedule Lines, Date Marks, etc.
Autodesk, Inc.

Symbols Library: Heating, Ventilation & Air Conditioning. Sep. 1987. *Compatible Hardware:* Apple Macintosh, IBM PC. *Memory Required:* 512k. *General Requirements:* 2 disk drives, graphics card, Generic CADD or First CADD. *Customer Support:* Unlimited technical support to registered users.
IBM. disk $49.95 (ISBN 1-55814-064-6, Order no.: F1500).
IBM. 3.5" disk $49.95 (ISBN 1-55814-065-4, Order no.: T1500).
Apple Macintosh. 3.5" disk $49.95 (ISBN 1-55814-067-0, Order no.: M1500).
130 HVAC Symbols for Residential & Commercial Buildings: Mechanical/Architecture/Construction.
Autodesk, Inc.

Symbols Library: Home Landscaping. Jan. 1988. *Compatible Hardware:* Apple Macintosh, IBM PC. *Memory Required:* 512k. *General Requirements:* 2 disk drives, graphics card, Generic CADD. *Customer Support:* Unlimited technical support to registered users.
IBM. disk $24.95 (ISBN 1-55814-092-1, Order no.: F1850).
IBM. 3.5" disk $24.95 (ISBN 1-55814-093-X, Order no.: T1850).
Apple Macintosh. 3.5" disk $24.95 (ISBN 1-55814-095-6, Order no.: W1850).
90 Symbols of Plan & Elevation Views of Common Landscaping Plants, Ground Covers, Pathways, Lawn Furniture & Hot Tubs.
Autodesk, Inc.

Symbols Library: Hydraulics. Jun. 1987. *Compatible Hardware:* IBM PC. *Memory Required:* 512k. *General Requirements:* 2 disk drives, graphics card, Generic CADD. *Customer Support:* Unlimited technical support to registered users.
disk $49.95 (ISBN 1-55814-056-5, Order no.: F1400).
3.5" disk $49.95 (ISBN 1-55814-057-3, Order no.: T1400).
Hydraulic Symbols Library Containing Over 90 Pre-Drawn Symbols, All Conforming to ANSI Standards. Includes: Line Components, Cylinders, Motors & Pumps, Valve Modes of Operation, Accumulators, Gages & Heaters.
Autodesk, Inc.

Symbols Library: Industrial Pipe Fittings. Jan. 1988. *Compatible Hardware:* Apple Macintosh, IBM PC. *Memory Required:* 512k. *General Requirements:* 2 disk drives, graphics card, Generic CADD. *Customer Support:* Unlimited technical support to registered users.
IBM. disk $69.95 (ISBN 1-55814-072-7, Order no.: F1600).
IBM. 3.5" disk $69.95 (ISBN 1-55814-073-5, Order no.: T1600).
Apple Macintosh. 3.5" disk $69.95 (ISBN 1-55814-075-1, Order no.: M1600).
160 ANSI Piping & Pipe Fittings Symbols: Mechanical/Civil/Architecture.
Autodesk, Inc.

Symbols Library: Kitchen Design. Jan. 1988. *Compatible Hardware:* Apple Macintosh, IBM PC. *Memory Required:* 512k. *General Requirements:* 2 disk drives, graphics card, Generic CADD. *Customer Support:* Unlimited technical support to registered users.
IBM. disk $49.95 (ISBN 1-55814-084-0, Order no.: F1750).
IBM. 3.5" disk $49.95 (ISBN 1-55814-085-9, Order no.: T1750).
Apple Macintosh. 3.5" disk $49.95 (ISBN 1-55814-087-5, Order no.: M1750).
Over 500 Symbols of Kitchen Cabinets, Appliances, Fixtures, etc. Plan & Elevation Views.
Autodesk, Inc.

Symbols Library: Landscape Architecture. Dec. 1987. *Compatible Hardware:* Apple Macintosh, IBM PC. *Memory Required:* 512k. *General Requirements:* 2 disk drives, graphics card, Generic CADD. *Customer Support:* Unlimited technical support to registered users.
IBM. disk $74.95 (ISBN 1-55814-100-6, Order no.: F1950).
IBM. 3.5" disk $74.95 (ISBN 1-55814-101-4, Order no.: T1950).
Apple Macintosh. 3.5" disk $74.95 (ISBN 1-55814-103-0, Order no.: M1950).
150 Symbols of Common Plants, Sprinkler System Components, Pathways, etc.
Autodesk, Inc.

Symbols Library: Microprocessors. Oct. 1987. *Compatible Hardware:* IBM PC. *Memory Required:* 512k. *General Requirements:* 2 disk drives, graphics card, Generic CADD. *Customer Support:* Unlimited technical support to registered users.
disk $74.95 (ISBN 1-55814-060-3, Order no.: F1450).
3.5" disk $74.95 (ISBN 1-55814-061-1, Order no.: T1450).
50 Symbols for Commonly Used Microprocessors & Peripheral Chips for 8, 16, 32 Bit.
Autodesk, Inc.

Symbols Library: Residential Framing Details. Jan. 1988. *Compatible Hardware:* IBM PC. *Memory Required:* 512k. *General Requirements:* 2 disk drives, graphics card, Generic CADD. *Customer Support:* Unlimited technical support to registered users.
disk $74.95 (ISBN 1-55814-088-3, Order no.: F1800).
3.5" disk $74.95 (ISBN 1-55814-089-1, Order no.: T1800).
100 Detail Views of Residential Framing, i.e. Windows, Door Frames, Floor Framing, Footings & Foundations, Stairs, Roof Framine & Trusses, etc. Architecture/Construction.
Autodesk, Inc.

Symbols Library: Steel Structural Shapes 1. Dec. 1987. *Compatible Hardware:* IBM PC. *Memory Required:* 384k. *General Requirements:* 2 disk drives, graphics card, Generic CADD. *Customer Support:* Unlimited technical support to registered users.
disk $69.95 (ISBN 1-55814-120-0, Order no.: F2151).
3.5" disk $69.95 (ISBN 1-55814-121-9, Order no.: T2151).
Over 500 AISC Standard Symbols of Steel Wide Flange Beams, Channels Pipes, etc. End & Top Views.
Autodesk, Inc.

Symbols Library: Steel Structural Shapes 2. Dec. 1988. *Compatible Hardware:* IBM PC. *Memory Required:* 384k. *General Requirements:* 2 disk drives, graphics card, Generic CADD. *Customer Support:* Unlimited technical support to registered users.
disk $69.95 (ISBN 1-55814-124-3, Order no.: F2152).
3.5" disk $69.95 (ISBN 1-55814-125-1, Order no.: T2152).
Over 500 Symbols of AISC Standard Channels & Angles.
Autodesk, Inc.

Symbols Library: Type Fonts 1. Dec. 1987. *Compatible Hardware:* IBM PC. *General Requirements:* 2 disk drives, graphics card, Generic CADD. *Customer Support:* Unlimited technical support to registered users.
disk $34.95 (ISBN 1-55814-108-1, Order no.: F2051).
3.5" disk $34.95 (ISBN 1-55814-109-X, Order

TITLE INDEX

no.: T2051).
10 Type Fonts for Presentation Graphics & Hand Lettering Styles.
Autodesk, Inc.

Symbols Library: Welding. Sep. 1987. *Compatible Hardware:* IBM PC. *Memory Required:* 512k. *General Requirements:* 2 disk drives, graphics card, Generic CADD. *Customer Support:* Unlimited technical support to registered users.
disk $49.95 (ISBN 1-55814-068-9, Order no.: F1550).
3.5" disk $49.95 (ISBN 1-55814-069-7, Order no.: T1550).
90 AWS Symbols of All Possible & Requalified Weld; Mechanical/Civil.
Autodesk, Inc.

SymEd. New Horizon Software Services. Feb. 1984. *Compatible Hardware:* TI Professional. *Operating System(s) Required:* MS-DOS. *Memory Required:* 128k. *General Requirements:* 2 disk drives, color monitor, printer, 3-plane graphics.
$79.95 (Order no.: TISY).
Texas Instruments, Personal Productivit.

The SYMIX Solution. *Version:* 4.0. Nov. 1994. *Compatible Hardware:* Over 400 platforms. *Operating System(s) Required:* DOS, Xenix, Unix, VMS, AIX, LANS. *Language(s):* PROGRESS, 4GL/RDBMS. *Memory Required:* 2Mb (DOS); other 4000k. *Items Included:* Manuals for each module. *Customer Support:* Telephone support, on-site & in-house training, implementation consulting, installation engineering (HW & SN), custom programming, systems integration.
Contact publisher for price.
Manufacturing Management System Designed for Manufacturers Who Compete by Focusing on the Specific Needs of Their Individual Customers. The Comprehensive Breadth & Depth of Functionality Allows Use of System to Efficiently Address Customer-Oriented Environments, Such As Engineer-to-Order, Make-to-Order, Assemble-to-Order, & Make-to-Stock, & Repetitive Requirements.
Symix Computer Systems, Inc.

The SYMIX System.
IBM PC & compatibles, UNIX, XENIX, HP-UX, AIX, VMS, DOS & LANS. Contact publisher for price.
Designed for Discrete Manufacturers in an Engineer-to-Order, Make-to-Order, Assemble-to-Order, Make-to-Stock, or Hybrid Environment. Integrates All Levels of the Manufacturer's Enterprise - from Business Planning & Operations Management to Manufacturing Control & Financial Analysis.
Symix Computer Systems, Inc.

Symphony. *Version:* 2.0. *Compatible Hardware:* IBM PC, PC XT, PC AT, PS/2 Models 30/50/60; Compaq Portable, Plus, Deskpro; AT&T 6300; other Lotus-certified compatibles. *Operating System(s) Required:* PC-DOS 2.0 or higher. *Memory Required:* 384k. *General Requirements:* Double-sided, double-density disk drive; 3-1/2" disk version requires PC-DOS 3.2 for IBM PC, PC XT, PC AT & PC-DOS 3.3 for PS/2.
3-1/2" or 5-1/4" disks $695.00.
Integrated Software System for Managers & Professionals. Combines Word Processing, Spreadsheet, Communications, Database, & Graphics. Release 1.2 Can Work with the New Expanded Memory Boards, Has a New Memory Allocation Scheme Which Provides Greater Flexibility & Eliminates the Need to Arrange Worksheets in Order to Conserve Memory. Supports 8087/80287 Math Processors, & Provides 1-2-3 Compatibility.
Lotus Development Corp.

Symphony Link. *Compatible Hardware:* IBM PC, PC XT, PC AT; Compaq Portable, Plus; other Lotus-certified compatibles. *Operating System(s) Required:* PC-DOS 2.0, 2.1, 3.0, 3.1.
contact publisher for price.
Enables the SYMPHONY User to Communicate with an IBM Mainframe.
Lotus Development Corp.

Symphony Spelling Checker. *Compatible Hardware:* IBM PC, PC XT, PC AT; Compaq Portable, Plus; other Lotus-certified compatibles. *Operating System(s) Required:* PC-DOS 2.0, 2.1, 3.0, 3.1. *Memory Required:* 150k, Symphony & Spelling Checker 576k. *General Requirements:* Symphony.
disk $139.00.
Companion Product for SYMPHONY That Screens Documents for Misspellings. Highlights Errors & Offers a List of Logical Alternatives to Misspelled Words.
Lotus Development Corp.

Symphony Text Outliner. *Compatible Hardware:* IBM PC, PC XT, PC AT; Compaq Portable, Plus; other Lotus-certified compatibles. *Operating System(s) Required:* PC-DOS 2.0, 2.1, 3.0, 3.1. *Memory Required:* 35k, Symphony & Text Outliner 448k.
disk $139.00.
Idea-Organizing Tool for Use with the SYMPHONY Word Processor.
Lotus Development Corp.

SYMPTOMASTER. *Version:* 2.0. *Customer Support:* Toll free telephone support.
DOS 3.1 or higher. IBM PC & compatibles. disk $595.00.
This Application Provides the Clinician a Flexible, Effortless Way to Design & Administer Patient Interviews to Assure a Fresh, Relevant Present Illness History During Each Medical Encounter. The Physician Complies a Portfolio of Patient Questionaires. A Set can be Constructed Quickly Because the Only Requirement is to Review & Tag Each Preferred Symptom from a Database of 382 (displayed on a Scrolling Lightbar Menu). The Number of Different sets is Unlimited.
SRC Systems, Inc.

SYN-CHECK. *Operating System(s) Required:* PC-DOS. Other versions can be developed. *Memory Required:* 256k. *General Requirements:* 2 360k disk drives or hard disk.
contact publisher for price.
Together with UPGRADE II, Allows Software Developers Who Have Developed Software Applications in RM/COBOL Syntax to Switch over to Micro Focus LEVEL II COBOL for Program Development. SYN-CHECK Evaluates RM/COBOL, Then Flags the Syntax Differences & Produces a Printed Report Describing What Modifications Are Needed to Compile the Source Code with a LEVEL II COBOL Compiler.
Micro Focus, Inc. (California).

SynCALC. Mike Silva & Joe Vierra. *Compatible Hardware:* Atari 400, 800, XL, XE Series; Commodore 64. *Language(s):* BASIC.
Atari & Commodore versions on flip sides of same disk. $49.95 (Order no.: A/CDSK-6112).
templates disk $19.95 (Order no.: A/CDSK-6113).
Menu-Driven Electronic Spreadsheet Which Features 128 Columns by 255 Rows, Individually Variable Column Widths, Fixed or Synchronous Windows, Logic Functions, & Alphabetic or Numeric Sorting. The On-Board Editor Allows the User to Edit Long, Complex Formulas Without Re-Typing. Multiple Spreadsheets Can Be Linked for Consolidation & Roll-Ups. Compatible with Other SYN-APPS (Synapse Applications) Programs.
Broderbund Software, Inc.

SYNDROMEASE: OCCULT SYNDROME

SynCHRON. Harry Guiremand. *Compatible Hardware:* Atari 400, 800, XL series.
disk $39.95 (Order no.: ATDSK-2114).
Keeps Track of User's Personal Calendar & Appointments. Stores up to 2 Years Worth of Entries, & Includes Personal Passwords for Privacy & Fine-Scrolling Text Window for Daily Journal.
Broderbund Software, Inc.

Synchrony. *Version:* 2.3. Oct. 1990. *Items Included:* Documentation, installation assistance. *Customer Support:* Toll free technical support; 1st year of maintenance free, thereafter 20% effective cost, training offered, contact vendor.
MS-DOS, OS/2, VTAM. IBM PC/XT/AT, PS/2, 3270 PC, IBM M/F (512k). $30,000.00 host component; $295.00 administrator (PC); $95.00 workstation (PC). *Nonstandard peripherals required:* IRMA, ICOT, Attachmate, IBM or any emulator supporting IBM 3270 API or Async comm PK+/3270 or FT/TERM.
An Electronic Software Distribution Management System That Automates the Delivery, Installation & Retrieval of Software & Data on Distributed Workstations & LANs. Provides a Timely, Reliable, Cost-Effective System for Managing Software Change in a Distributed Environment. Client/Server Architecture Delivers the High Performance, Reliability, & Management Controls Needed to Keep Distributed "Mission-Critical" Application in Sync. LAN Only Version Available Also.
Telepartner International.

SynCOMM. Pete Goodeve. *Compatible Hardware:* Atari 400, 800, XL series. *Language(s):* BASIC. *Memory Required:* 48k.
disk $99.95 (Order no.: ATDSK-2116).
Fine-Scrolling Communications Program Which Features Auto Dial Capabilities & Multiple Text Buffers. Hook up to Databases, Bulletin Boards, Other Computers (Including Mainframes).
Broderbund Software, Inc.

Syndesis 3D-ROM, Vol. I.
CD-ROM disk $99.95.
More Than 500 Models Stored on One CD-ROM. Each Model Is in 3D Studio, AutoCAD DXF, Lightwave, Imagine & Wavefront Formats, Unlocked & Ready to Use. Includes Demo Objects from Viewpoint Data Labs, Imagination Works, Noumenon Labs & VRS Media. It Also Includes More Than 400 Tileable, Seamless Texture Maps in TIFF, GIF & IFF-24.
Syndesis Corp.

Syndesis 3D-ROM, Vol. II. *Items Included:* 3 3.5" disks, manual.
CD-ROM disk $99.95.
Contains More Than 200 New Models. Each Model Is Pre-Translated to 3D Studio, AutoCAD DXF, Lightwave, Imagine & Wavefront Formats, All Unlocked & Ready to Use.
Syndesis Corp.

Syndromease: Occult Syndrome Identifier. *Version:* 1.5. G. B. Cook. Apr. 1987. *Compatible Hardware:* IBM PC. *Operating System(s) Required:* PC-DOS. *Language(s):* Quicksilver. *Memory Required:* 640k. *General Requirements:* Printer. *Customer Support:* Toll free telephone support.
disk $595.00.
Using Artificial Intelligence This System Allows the Physician to Sort Through a Group of Patient Symptoms to Learn If Any of 161 Syndromes May Be Present to Account for the Current Findings. Also Useful As a Teaching Aid for Physicians in Training.
SRC Systems, Inc.

Synergy DBL. *Version:* 5. 1993. *Language(s):* DIBOL, DBL. *Memory Required:* 256k. *General Requirements:* Hard disk. *Items Included:* Full set manuals; user guide; installation notes. *Customer Support:* 11 hour-daily telephone; user's manual; user's groups (local/national/international); bulletin board; 2 newsletters; co-op marketing fund; hardware vendor relationships co-op. contact publisher for price.
A Superset of the DIBOL Programming Language. Allows Applications Packages to Be Ported to Any of the Operating Systems, Including MS-DOS/PC-DOS, Novell's Netware, UNIX, TSX-Plus, VMS, RSX, & RSTS. Using Only One Version of Program Sources, Applications Written May Be Ported to a Number of Environments. Program Features Include: Software Virtual Memory Which Eliminates the Need for Program Overlaying, Multi-Key ISAM Support, a Fixed-Point Decimal Data Type, & Terminal Independent Screen Functions Which Increase Hardware Independence, Microsoft Windows compatible; GUI; Imaging. Data Dictionary & Report Generator.
DISC (California).

SynFILE Plus. Steve Ahlstrom & Dan Moore. *Compatible Hardware:* Atari 400, 800, XL, XE Series. *Language(s):* BASIC. *Memory Required:* 48k.
disk $49.95 (Order no.: ATDSK-2118).
Features up to 16 Disk Files, Free Screen Format, up to 66 Fields per Screen & Pop-Up Menus. Alpha, Numeric, Calculated, Date, Table Look-Up & Conditional Fields Are All Supported. Supports Single, Dual & Double-Density Formats & up to 4 Disk Files. Report Generator Prints/Lists Labels in Any Format, Provides Page/Level Breaks & Subtotals.
Broderbund Software, Inc.

SynSTOCK. Steven S. Weston. *Compatible Hardware:* Atari 400, 800, XL series; IBM PC, PCjr, PC XT. *Language(s):* BASIC. *Memory Required:* 48k.
Atari. disk $39.95 (Order no.: ATDSK-2124).
IBM. disk $99.95 (Order no.: IBMDSK-4124).
Stock Portfolio Management System. Analyzes & Displays Data & Trends in Color Charts in Three Formats: High/Low/Close, Moving Averages, & Oscillators. Built-In Data Entry System Allows Updates via Modem.
Broderbund Software, Inc.

The Syntel Math Toolbox. *Items Included:* Bound manual. *Customer Support:* Free hotline - no time limit; 30 day limited warranty; updates are $5/disk plus S&H.
MS-DOS. IBM & compatibles (128k). disk $19.95. *Nonstandard peripherals required:* Graphics card; one disk drive.
Programmable Calculator That Enables User to Do Sophisticated Mathematical Calculations Easily. User Enters Arithmetic Statements As Normally Written & Then, with a Keystroke, Asks the TOOLBOX for the Answer. The TOOLBOX Includes a Complete Set of Built-In Trigonometric, Logarithmic, & Exponential Functions. It Also Has a Powerful Programmable Feature. You Can Define Your Own Functions & Then Provide Parameter Values for These Functions for Solution. You Can Save All Your Computations on a Disk File & Load Them Back. The GRAPH Command Is a Flexible Tool for Creating Visual Representations of Mathematical Functions. You Can Create a Variety of Graphs. Features: Character/Bit-Map Graphs; Tables; Graph Labelling; Automatic Scaling; Graph Printing.
Dynacomp, Inc.

Synthesis III. *Customer Support:* 800-929-8117 (customer service).
MS-DOS. IBM/PS2. disk $99.99 (ISBN 0-87007-549-7).
A Menu-Driven, Interactive Database Manager. Create Files & Add, Review, Change, & Delete Records. Protects Against Entry Errors. Numeric Fields are Automatically Rightjustified. User can Generate Both Printed Reports & Screen Displays in Either Vertical or Horizontal Format. User can Choose Which Records & Information to Print. Rows, Columns, & Headings May be Custom-Designed to Suit the User's Needs. An Additional Feature Lets User Move Data from One File to Another. Records May Contain up to 1024 Bytes. Complete Manual is Included.
SourceView Software International.

Synthesis, Synthesis Runtime, Synthesis Enhancer. *Version:* 3.0T. Nov. 1988. *Items Included:* One manual, one digitizer tablet overlay. *Customer Support:* Free on-line support; one year maintenance agreement, 12% of programs price; training, $350.00.
MS-DOS (640k). IBM compatible PC. $5,500.00 for full program, $1,395.00 for Runtime, $345.00 for the Enhancer. *Addl. software required:* AutoCAD version 2.6, or release 9, or release 10. *Optimal configuration:* 386 IBM compatible PC, 2-3Mb RAM, 40Mb fast access hard disk, EGA or VGA video board, EGA or equivalent monitor.
Automated Design & Drafting System. Through Parametric Design, Synthesis will Automate the Process of Creating & Drafting New Designs That Are Basically Variations of Standard Parts. By Creating a "Model" or a Generic Design of a Product, It & Then Capturing the Engineering Rules Used to Design the Product Will Easily & Automatically Generate Designs for Whole Families of Products.
Synthesis, Inc.

SynTREND. Brian Lee et al. *Compatible Hardware:* Atari 400, 800, XL series. *Language(s):* BASIC. *Memory Required:* 48k.
disk $39.95 (Order no.: ATDSK-2132).
Graphing & Forecasting Package Takes Data & Generates Hi-Res, Full Color Line Graphs, Scatter Plots, Bar Graphs, & Pie Charts. Line & Scatter Graphs Can Display up to Three Factors of 100 Observations Each. Bar Graphs Display up to Three Factors & 32 Observations in Stacked or Clustered Format.
Broderbund Software, Inc.

SYS/MASTER. *Version:* 2.2. *Items Included:* Documentation included. *Customer Support:* Annual renewal fee 20% purchase price/yr..
MVS/ESA, MVS/XA, MVS/SP; VM/SP, VM/XA, VM/HPO;. DOS/VSE, DOS/VSE/SP; FUJITSU/MSP, FUJITSU/FSP. IBM system/370 & system/390 (and compatibles). SYS/MASTER .01,22,500.00-,45,000.00.
Simplifies & Improves Management of Complex MVS & VM Operations by Automating Many Manual & Tedious Tasks for Local & Remote Systems. Presents Single Console for Operating Systems, Network & Subsystems for Single or Multi-Site, Multi-CPU Operations. Expert Systems Foundation Provides Rule-Based Automation of Networks, Systems & Subsystems to Permit Capture of Expert Knowledge Without Systems Programming Expertise.
Sterling Software.

Sys V r4. *Customer Support:* All of our products are unconditionally guaranteed.
Unix. CD-ROM disk $59.95 (Order no.: SYS5). *Nonstandard peripherals required:* CD-ROM drive.
Tools (Compiler, Tex, Emacs) for Unix System V. r4.
Walnut Creek CDRom.

SYSKIT: Software Toolkit for Linear Systems, 3 disks for Apple, 2 disks for IBM. R. C. Rosenberg. *Compatible Hardware:* Apple II+; IBM PC, PC XT, PC AT. *Memory Required:* Apple 64K; IBM 256k. *General Requirements:* 2 disk drives. *Items Included:* 2 disks & documentation.
Apple. write for info. (ISBN 0-07-831093-8).
IBM. $49.24 (ISBN 0-07-831102-0).
Software Toolkit for System Dynamics, Controls & Vibration. Time Processor & Management Modules.
McGraw-Hill, Inc.

SYSLOG: System Log Utility. *Version:* 3.0. Sep. 1989. *Memory Required:* 384k.
SYSLOG. disk $129.95 (Order no.: ASW002). (Order no.: ASW003).
Monitors the Use of a Computer to Help Establish Effective Utilization. Monitors "Idle" Time for Sessions to Give True Productivity. Offers the Capability of Exporting Log Data to Spreadsheets or Database Programs.
Apex Software Corp.

SYSTAT. *Version:* 5.03 (DOS), 5.02 (Windows), 5.2 (Macintosh). *Compatible Hardware:* Apple Mac Plus or higher; IBM PC, 286 or higher & compatibles. *Operating System(s) Required:* MS-DOS, Macintosh, Microsoft Windows. *Items Included:* Documentation. *Customer Support:* Free technical support.
disk $895.00. *Optimal configuration:* Minimum 2Mb RAM required, Mac; 4Mb RAM, Windows; 640k RAM, DOS.
Statistics Package Which Includes: Full Screen Spreadsheet Data Editor; Missing Data, Arrays, Character Variables; Unlimited Cases; Rectangular & Triangular Files; Character, Numeric, & Nested Sorts; Merge & Append Large Files; Optional Programming Language; T-Tests; Pairwise/Listwise Missing Value Correlation, Covariance, Spearman, Gamma, Kendall Tau, Euclidean Distances; Extended Regression Diagnostics; Multi-Way ANOVA, ANOCOVA, MANOVA, Repeated Measures; Time Series; Nonlinear Estimation, etc.
Systat, Inc.

System Execution Manager: MS DOS Operation Scheduler. 1995. *Items Included:* Full manual. *Customer Support:* Free telephone support - 90 days, 30-day warranty.
MS-DOS 3.2 or higher. 286 (584k). disk $49.95. *Nonstandard peripherals required:* CGA/EGA/VGA.
Addresses the Need to Perform Computer Operations at Preset Times in the Future. Operations May Be Set up to Run & Repeat at Any Interval, Ranging from 1 to 64,000 Minutes. Execution May Also Be Scheduled to Begin at Any Specified Time & Date up to the Year 2095. Nested Batch Files May Also Be Executed.
Dynacomp, Inc.

SYSTEM FI. *Version:* 6.0. Jul. 1992. *Customer Support:* Telephone support.
PC-DOS. single-site license $4000.00 (Order no.: SYSTEM FI).
PC-DOS. disk $4000.00 (Order no.: FI MICRO).
Full-Featured Business Financial System. General Ledger, Accounts Receivable, Accounts Payable & Fixed Asset Management. Balanced Data Capture, Multiple Companies, Name & Address Label Printers, Operating Statements & Many More. Companion Custom Data Capture Generator FI MICRO Meets User-Specific Voucher Needs, International Currency & Language.
Data Index, Inc.

TITLE INDEX

System Installation Tracker. *General Requirements:* HyperCard 2.0 v2 or higher. Macintosh Plus or higher. 3.5" disk $25.00. *Creates a Schematic of a User's Network.*
Heizer Software.

System Manager (with Labels Plus): Module 1. *Version:* 7.11. Jeff Gold. Jul. 1991. *Items Included:* Perfect-bound manual. *Customer Support:* 90 days toll-free phone support; each additional year $150.
MS-DOS 3.1 or higher (384k). IBM PS/2, PC, PC XT, PC AT & compatibles. disk $95.00. *Networks supported:* PC-LAN, 3COM, Novell, Lantastic.
Handles Password Security, Company Information, & Various Utilities. Allows Use of Other Modules Separately or Combined into One Accounting Package. Includes LABELS PLUS, a Mailing Labels Program That Allows User to Produce Lists & Labels for Any Names Entered, as Well As for Employees, Customers or Vendors Entered in the Other Modules.
Manzanita Software Systems.

System MM. Jan. 1981. *Operating System(s) Required:* PC-DOS, Windows 3.11, Windows 95. *Memory Required:* 256k.
disk $4900.00.
Hansco Information Technologies, Inc.

System Monitor. *Compatible Hardware:* Commodore Amiga.
3.5" disk $49.95.
Monitors Memory Usage, Other Parameters.
Zen Software.

System Pump Sizing with Flash Protection. 1995. *Items Included:* Full manual. *Customer Support:* Free telephone support - 90 days, 30-day warranty.
MS-DOS 3.2 or higher. 286 (584k). disk $3299.95. *Nonstandard peripherals required:* CGA/EGA/VGA.
Now Your Design Engineers Can Make an Accurate Pump Selection & Specify All Required Control Valve Drops on a Twelve or Fifteen Branch Pumping System in Just One Hour, Using Only a P & I Diagram, a Piping Drawing, & the Liquid Characteristics.
Dynacomp, Inc.

System 34/36 Financial Software Packages. *Compatible Hardware:* IBM System 34/36. contact publisher for price.
Integrated Packages Include; Accounts Payable, Accounts Receivable, Fixed Assets, Payroll & General Ledger.
ACM Computer Services, Inc.

System 21 Blackjack. Ronald D. Jones. 1985. *Compatible Hardware:* Apple; Commodore; IBM; TRS-80 Model I, Model III, Color Computer. *Operating System(s) Required:* CP/M. *Memory Required:* 64k.
disk $49.95 ea.
Apple. (ISBN 1-55604-168-3, Order no.: S001).
CP/M. (ISBN 1-55604-169-1, Order no.: S001).
Commodore. (ISBN 1-55604-170-5, Order no.: S001).
Color Computer. (ISBN 1-55604-171-3, Order no.: S001).
IBM. (ISBN 1-55604-172-1, Order no.: S001).
Model I & Model III. (ISBN 1-55604-173-X, Order no.: S001).
Designed to Teach & Analyze Every Possible Card Combination. Hundreds of Simulated Games Can Be Run in Minutes to Test Strategy.
Professor Jones Professional Handicapping Systems.

System/2. *Version:* 6.1. Jul. 1991. *Compatible Hardware:* IBM compatible 386/486. *Operating System(s) Required:* OS/2 or WINDOWS NT. *Language(s):* MF/COBOL (source code included). *Memory Required:* 640k-2000k. *General Requirements:* Hard disk. *Customer Support:* Yes.
contact publisher for price.
Complete Turnkey Multi-User Based on Realworld 6.1 Business & Accounting Software.
ComputerPro of Miami.

System II Certified Payroll Management System. *Version:* 3.00 or higher. 1982. *Operating System(s) Required:* MS-DOS, PC-DOS. *Language(s):* MBASIC. *Memory Required:* DOS 512k. *General Requirements:* Hard disk, 132-column printer or compressed print capability, DOS.
disk $795.00.
Handles Weekly, Bi-Weekly, Semi-Monthly, & Monthly Pay Periods Simultaneously. Provides Full Labor Costing, Current & After the Fact Payroll. Certified Payroll Module Available. Prints Checks, W2, & 1099 Forms, 940, 941 & State Tax Reports for Any State. Integrates with The Boss Financial Accounting System.
Mesa Software.

System II Financial Accounting System. *Version:* DOS 3.0 or higher. 1979. *Operating System(s) Required:* MS-DOS, PC-DOS. *Memory Required:* 512k. *General Requirements:* Hard disk.
disk $1595.00.
Provides Fully Integrated General Ledger, Accounts Receivable, & Accounts Payable. Offers Logical, Single Screen Data Entry & Wide Variety of Management Reports. All Records & Reports Are As Current As the Last Transaction. LOTUS & MULTIPLAN Interfaces Are Available.
Mesa Software.

System II Inventory Accounting System. *Version:* DOS 3.0 or higher. 1983. *Operating System(s) Required:* MS-DOS, PC-DOS. *Memory Required:* 512k. *General Requirements:* Hard disk.
disk $1095.00.
Offers Point of Sale &/or Sales Order Entry. Tracks Sales Revenue & Calculates Cost of Goods Sold. Prints Purchase Orders, Sales Orders, Invoices, Packing Slips, Expected Receipts & Purchase Receipts All on One Form. Prints Management Reports, Reorder Reports, & Physical Inventory Worksheets. Integrates with THE BOSS Financial Accounting System.
Mesa Software.

System 2000 Data Management Software. *Version:* 11.6. *Items Included:* Documentation included. *Customer Support:* Free software updates & enhancements; phone-in technical support; 24-hour on-line support; training courses available.
CMS, MVS, CICS, OS-1100. IBM 370/30XX/ 43XX/937X; Unisys. contact publisher for price.
Offers Integrated Tools for Enhanced Data Management Including: Interactive Query/ Update, an Integrated Data Dictionary, Report Writing, Relational Data Base Access, High-Volume Batch & Interactive Production Processing, Accounting, Data recovery, Menu-Driven Data Manipulation, & Conversational Building of Data Bases.
SAS Institute, Inc.

System V/4 MP. Jan. 1995. *Customer Support:* 30 day money back guarantee; 90 day installation & warranty; $495.00 "Hotline" support; $1295.00 "Priority Hotline" support.
Unix System V Release 4.X. i80x86, Pentium (12Mb). $3095.00 - $12,390.00. *Optimal configuration:* Multi-processor Pentium. *Networks supported:* Ethernet; TCP/IP; IPX/ SPX; X.25.
A Complete Multi-Threaded Unix System V Release 4 Multi-Processor Operating System Designed for Symmetric Intel Hardware Platforms. Performance & Scalability Are Improved with Each Processor Addition. Includes Graphical User Interfaces, Enhanced Network Services, Application Compatibility & Standards Compliance. Ideally Suited for Enterprise Wide Network Servers.
Microport, Inc.

System V/386. 1987. *Compatible Hardware:* 80386-based systems. *Items Included:* Runtime - 2 user version to complete unlimited user package. *Customer Support:* 30 day installation warranty. 3.5" disk $329.00-$1198.00.
Unix System V Release 3 with Extensions Such As Shell Layering, Streams (RFS & NFS), Source Debugger, & Full Screen System Admin Menus & Korn Shell (ksh).
Microport, Inc.

SystemCommand: System Management Assistant. *Version:* 3.0. 1990. *Items Included:* Manual, quarterly newsletter. *Customer Support:* Customer support included in price.
VMS. VAX. $650.00-$10,950.00.
VAX/VMS System Management Assistant. Automatically Monitors Critical System Parameters in Real-Time to Help Maintain System & Application Availability. If Pre-Determined Performance Thresholds Are Exceeded, System Automatically Notifies Operators & Can Automatically Invoke User-Specified Commands to Take Corrective Action.
Raxco, Inc.

SystemPac. DBI Software Products. *Compatible Hardware:* TI Professional. *Operating System(s) Required:* MS-DOS, CP/M-86. *Memory Required:* 64k. *General Requirements:* Printer.
$395.00.
Texas Instruments, Personal Productivit.

SYSTRAK: Program Revision Traking System. *Version:* 1.03D. K. R. Plossl. Sep. 1988. *Compatible Hardware:* IBM PC, PC XT, PC AT, & compatibles. *Operating System(s) Required:* PC-DOS/MS-DOS 2.0 or higher. *Language(s):* C Basic. *Memory Required:* 64k. *General Requirements:* Printer.
360k dsdd disk $35.00.
Designed to Use the Operating System File Date Stamp to Keep Track of Program Revisions for One to Many Programs As a Series or Set. Automatically Updates Program Headers, Including Revision Numbering. Stores History of Who, When, & What Changed in a Separate History File.
K. R. Plossl & Co.

Sytos Autoloader: Support Module for OS-2. *Version:* 2.0. Sep. 1994. *Customer Support:* Tech support via BBS, & Fax.
OS/2 2.x (1Mb). disk $99.00. *Optimal configuration:* OS/2 2.x (1Mb), Mouse recommended. *Networks supported:* IBM LAN Server & Microsoft LAN Manager.
Device Support Utility for Multiple Tape Backup Devices Attached to OS/2 Workstations & Network Servers. As an Add-On Support Module for Sytos Premium, It Automates the Backup Process for Autoloaders, & Provides the Flexibility to Configure the Device As a Single Backup Device or As a Set of Backup Devices. Features Automated Operations, & the Ability to Access Tapes Sequentially or Partition Network Backups to Different Tapes for Each Server. Also, a Tape Cataloging Feature Identifies Volumes, Check Status & Reviews Volume Details.
Sytron Corp.

Sytos Plus for DOS: High-Performance DOS-Based Backup Also Offering Client-Based NetWare Backup. Version: 1.4x. Feb. 1990. *Customer Support:* Tech support via BBS, & Fax.
DOS 3.0 & higher, IBM 3.0 & higher (640k). disk $149.00. *Optimal configuration:* DOS 3.0 & higher, IBM 3.0 & higher (640k), 1.5Mb disk space, mouse is optional. *Networks supported:* NetWare 2.x, 3.x, 4.x, IBM PC LAN, NetBIOS.
High Performance Backup Software Offering DOS & DOS-Based Networking Environments a Fast, Reliable & Complete Backup Solution. Powerful, Feature-Rich Backup & Restore Application Supporting Storage Devices That Include: Diskette, Data Cassette, & 1/4" Tape, DAT, 8mm Helical & Optical Devices. Offers Full Support for IBM, Novell, LANtastic & Other NetBIOS Compatible Networks. Performs Complete Backup & Restore of Novell NetWare Binderies, Trustees, Access Rights, & File & Directory Attributes. Other Features Include: STAC Data Compression, Quick File Access (QFA), Error Correction Code, Compare & Password Protection. Available in English, French, German, & Japanese.
Sytron Corp.

Sytos Plus for OS/2: OS-2 2.x & OS-2 Server or Client-Based Network Backup Supporting IBM LAN Server & Microsoft LAN Manager. Version: 1.38. Aug. 1990. *Customer Support:* Tech support via BBS, & Fax.
MS OS/2 1.2, 1.3, IBM 1.2, 1.3, 2.x (1Mb). disk $175.00. *Optimal configuration:* MS OS/2 1.2, 1.3, IBM 1.2, 1.3, 2.x (1Mb), 1.5Mb disk space, Mouse is optional. *Networks supported:* Microsoft LAN Manager, IBM LAN Server.
Presentation Manager Backup Software Offering Full Support for the OS/2 Operation System Including IBM's OS/2 2.x & OS/2 Networking Environments. Offers Full Compatibility to IBM's LAN Server & Microsoft's LAN Manager. OS/2 Higher Performance File System (HPFS), Extended Attributes (EA), & Long Path Names Are Fully Supported. In a Networking Environment, It Performs Full Backup & Restore of Network File & Directory Access Control Lists (ACL's), File Permissions, & Network System Files. Other Features Include: STAC Data Compression, Quick File Access (QFA), Error Correction Code, Compare & Password Protection, Available in English, French, German, & Japanese.
Sytron Corp.

Sytos Plus for Windows: Windows Backup for Novell Networks. Version: 1.1. Jul. 1993. *Customer Support:* Tech support via BBS, & Fax.
DOS 5.0, Windows 3.1 (2Mb). disk $149.00. *Optimal configuration:* DOS 5.0, Windows 3.1 (2Mb), 1.5Mb disk space, mouse. *Networks supported:* Novell NetWare, NetBIOS.
Easy-to-Use Windows Backup Application Providing Novell NetWare 2.x & 3.x Server Backup. Standard Features Include: Point & Click Mouse Operations, Multi-Tasking Operations, Scheduler for Automated & Unattended Backups, Compare Option, Advanced Error Correction, STAC Data Compression, File Viewer, Password Protection & Multiple Backup Device Support. Network Backup Support Includes Complete Backup & Restore of All Trustee, Bindery, Extended Directory, & File Attribute Information & a Retry Busy File Option for Ensuring Complete Backup & Logging of Open Files. Available in English, French & German.
Sytron Corp.

Sytos Premium: OS-2 2.x & OS-2 Backup & Disaster Recovery Softare Offering Complete OS-2 Workstation & Network Server Data Protection. Version: 2.0. Sep. 1994. *Customer Support:* Tech support via BBS, & Fax.
OS/2 1.2 or higher, OS/2 2.x (1Mb). disk $295.00. *Optimal configuration:* OS/2 1.2 or higher, OS/2 2.x (1Mb), 2.5Mb disk space, OS/2 compatible mouse recommended. *Networks supported:* IBM LAN Server & Microsoft LAN Manager.
High Performance Backup & Disaster Recovery Software. OS/2 Workstations & Servers Are Protected from Total System Failure with Sytos Premiums's Recovery Featuring That Allows the User to Reboot with a Recovery Disk. All Operating System, Application & Data Files Are Recovered Within Minutes. Graphical Presentation Manager Interface Offers Simple Point & Click Functionality Using Icon & Tree Views. OS/2 High Performance File System (HPFS), Extended Attributes (EA), & Long Path Names Are Fully Supported. Backs up & Restores LAN Server & LAN Manager Network File & Directory Access Control Lists (ACL's), File Permissions, & Network System Files. Other Features Include: Multiple-Event Scheduler, File Groom, STAC Data Compression, Quick File Access (QFA), Error Correction Code, Compare & Password Protection. Available in English, French & German.
Sytron Corp.

Sytos Rebound: Disaster Recovery for OS-2. Version: 1.3. May 1993. *Customer Support:* Tech support via BBS, & Fax.
IBM OS/2 2.x, Microsoft OS/2 1.2 or higher (1Mb). disk $99.00. *Optimal configuration:* IBM OS/2 2.x, Microsoft OS/2 1.2 or higher (1Mb). *Networks supported:* LAN Manager, LAN Server.
Disaster Recovery Utility for OS/2 Workstations, & IBM LAN Server or Microsoft LAN Mangaer Servers. Together with the Backups Created by Sytos Plus, It Provides Rapid & Unattended Recovery of the OS/2 Operating System & Data Files in Case of a System Crash or Data Loss. Data Recovery Becomes an Automated Process That Circumvents the Normal Installation Prompts. In Less Than 10 Minutes Your Operating System Is Completely Restored. The Rest of Your Files Are Also Automatically Restored at a Rate of Speed Determined Solely by Your Storage Device. Can Be Used with IBM, Microsoft & Other Manufacturers' Versions of OS/2. Supports All the Industry-Standard Backup Devices Supported by Sytos Plus for OS/2, Including Quarter-Inch Tape, Data Cassette, 4mm Digital Audio Tape (DAT), 8mm Helical Scan & 3 1/2" Rewritable Optical. Available in English, French & German.
Sytron Corp.

Sytos Repro: System Duplication Utility for OS 2. Version: 1.1. Jan. 1994. *Customer Support:* Tech support via BBS, & Fax.
IBM OS/2 2.x, Microsoft OS/2 1.2 or higher, & CD-ROM OS/2 (1Mb). CD-ROM disk $99.00 (5 pack); $379.00 (10 pack); $995.00 (25 pack); $1995.00 (unlimited system built license). *Optimal configuration:* IBM OS/2 2.x, Microsoft OS/2 1.2 or higher, & CD-ROM OS/2 (1Mb). *Networks supported:* LAN Manager, LAN Server.
Duplication Utility for OS/2 Workstations, & IBM LAN Server & Microsoft LAN Manager Servers. Combined with Sytos Plus for OS/2 Backup Software, Sytos Repro Builds New OS/2 Systems from Backup Media Created by Sytos Plus. Developed for System Administrators & Integrators Who Build Multiple OS/2 Systems with the Same Configuration, It Is a Low Cost, Time Saving Duplication Solution. Offers Automated Duplication, Parallel Port Support, OS/2 Server Duplication, OS/2 Compatibility Including IBM OS/2 2.x, Sytos Plus Compatibility, & Multiple Device Support.
Sytron Corp.

Sytos Scheduler: Presentation Manager Scheduling Utility. Nov. 1993. *Customer Support:* Tech support via BBS, & Fax.
IBM OS/2 2.x, Microsoft OS/2 1.3 or higher (1.5Mb). disk $99.00. *Optimal configuration:* IBM OS/2 2.x, Microsoft OS/2 1.3 or higher (1.5Mb), mouse. *Networks supported:* LAN Manager, LAN Server.
Easy-to-Use Presentation Manager Scheduling Utility That Runs Automated or Background Events Including Command & Executable Files under OS/2, As Well As Sytos Plus for OS/2 Procedures. Can Be Used As Either a Standalone Scheduling Utility for OS/2, or As an Enhanced Scheduler for Sytos Plus for OS/2 Procedures. Features Point-&-Click Mouse Operations for Quick & Easy Selection of Events, Time, Frequency, Date & Year. Plan Single or Multiple Scheduled Events to Run Only Once, Daily, Weekly, During the Work Week, or Monthly.
Sytron Corp.

SYZYGY: Work Group Software for Managers. Aug. 1989. *Items Included:* 5 spiral-manuals, quick reference card, registration card. *Customer Support:* Toll-free 30-day telephone support, extended support $75 yr..
PC-DOS/MS-DOS 3.1 or higher (512k). IBM PC, XT, AT, PS/2 & compatibles. single user $395.00; 10 users $1295.00; 25 users $1995.00, unlimited users per server $2995.00. *Nonstandard peripherals required:* Hard disk. *Optimal configuration:* IBM AT or compatible (640k), color display, printer. *Networks supported:* All NetBIOS, including Novell, 3Com, Banyan & others.
MS-DOS Program to Manage Workgroup Information Activities, Budgets, Resources, Schedules & Due Dates. Holds Data in a Shared Workbase & Returns Relevant Responses to Workgroup Members Through Work Outlines & To-Do Lists, Group & Individual Calendars, Gant Charts & Over 50 Report Formats.
Information Research Corp.

T-BASE. Version: DOS 4.2, Windows 1.3. Apr. 1990. *Customer Support:* Free technical support via telephone, FAX.
DOS 3-5. 286, 386, 486 (640k). $495.00 DOS or Windows; $595.00 DOS/Windows Bundle. *Networks supported:* Any netbios compatible.
Programmer's Library That Adds Functions Needed to Work with Images. Three Basic Functions Provided Are Image Display, Image Printing, & Image Scanning. Includes: Automatic Scaling of Images to Fit the Screen or Window, Automatic Zooming of Images to Fit the Screen or Window, Multiple Images on a Screen, Automatic Optimized Palette Conversion for Multiple Images. Converts Between Image Formats, with Re-Sizing, Re-Scaling, & Color Reduction. Create Pictures with a Video Digitizer or a Color Scanner. Or Scan Documents with Any Black & White Scanner. Reads Most of the Popular Graphics Formats.
Videotex Systems, Inc.

T-Maker III. *Compatible Hardware:* TI Professional with 2 disk drives & printer. *Operating System(s) Required:* MS-DOS. *Memory Required:* 128k. $275.00.
Texas Instruments, Personal Productivit.

T, Script. Version: 3.4. Jan. 1994. *Items Included:* Spiral bound manual; 2 disks. *Customer Support:* 30 days unlimited warranty; free technical support over telephone.
Macintosh OS. Macintosh (2Mb). $85.00 for T Script Basic, $145.00 for T Script & $495.00 for T Script Delux (Order no.: FL2).
Software Raster Image Processor Capable of Interpreting PostScript & Driving a Variety of Non-PostScript Printers, Such As the HP LaserJet &

Apple LaserWriter SC. By Interpreting PostScript Directly, the Full Range of Macintosh Desktop Publishing & Graphics Programs Is Supported. Some Popular Macintosh Application Programs Supported Include Adobe Illustrator, Aldus Freehand, Quark XPress, PageMaker, ReadySetGo, Canvas, Microsoft Word, MacWrite, Microsoft Works, & MacDraw.
TeleTypesetting Co.

T Smooth Optimal Smoothing & Differentiation. *Items Included:* Full manual. No other products required. *Customer Support:* Free telephone support - no time limit. 30 day warranty.
 MS-DOS 3.2 or higher. IBM & compatibles (512k). disk $49.95. *Optimal configuration:* IBM, MS-DOS 3.2 or higher, 512k RAM, & 720k or higher disk drive.
Special Digital Filter Which Optimally Smoothes & Differentiates Equally-Spaced Data Sets of up to 5000 Points. Cubic Spline Model Is Used Which Also Provides Noise-Reduced estimates for the First & Second Derivatives. Although the Techniques Employed Is Very Sophisticated, No Knowledge of the Methodology Is Required. Emphasis Has Been Placed on Ease-of-Use. Manual Describes the Operation of TSMOOTH, As Well As the Algorithm (Severl References Are Included).
Dynacomp, Inc.

T201PC AudioClips: Terminator 2. *Version:* 1.5. Feb. 1993. *Items Included:* Manual, registration card, sound list. *Customer Support:* Phone technical support.
 DOS 5.0, Windows 3.1. PC 286 or higher (2Mb). disk $14.95 (ISBN 1-57303-003-1). *Nonstandard peripherals required:* Sound card recommended. *Optimal configuration:* 286 or higher with 4Mb RAM, DOS 5.0 or later, Windows 3.1 or later, 4-7Mb HD space available, sound card.
Exclusively Licensed High Quality Sound Files Consisting of Classic Sound Effects, Dialogue & Music from Original TV Shows & Movies. Also Included Is the 'Whoop It Up' Audio Utility, Which Allows the User to Attach AudioClips to Various Windows Events.
Sound Source Interactive.

Tab Talk: The Mnemonics Revolution. Jan. 1985. *Operating System(s) Required:* PC-DOS. *Memory Required:* 256k.
 disk $49.95.
Reduces the Use of a Computer to the Operation of 3 Keys. Eliminates the Need to Remember Computer Commands, Forces the Computer to Remember the Way User Works. Offers Word Processing, File Management, Character Graphics, Thought Processing & Practical Intelligence.
Software General Corp.

TableCurve 2D: Automated Curve Fitting Software. *Version:* DOS 3.1, Windows 1.0. Mar. 1992. *Items Included:* 1 3-ring manual, 5.25" & 3.5" disks. *Customer Support:* 90 day moneyback guarantee, free technical support.
 DOS 3.3 or higher. IBM PC & compatibles (4Mb). disk $495.00 (Order no.: STCDR313). *Nonstandard peripherals required:* Math coprocessor recommended. *Optimal configuration:* PC w/4Mb RAM & 2.5Mb free on hard disk & math coprocessor.
 Windows 3.1. IBM PC & compatibles, 386 or higher (4Mb). disk $495.00 (Order no.: STCWR103). *Nonstandard peripherals required:* Math coprocessor recommended & Microsoft compatible mouse required. *Addl. software required:* DOS 3.3 or higher. *Optimal configuration:* PC W/4Mb RAM & 2.5Mb free on hard disk & math coprocessor & MS compatible mouse.
Designed to Help Researchers Find the Best Equation to Fit to Their Experimental Data. Automatically Fits & Ranks All 3,400 Built-In & User-Defined Equations by Order of Best Fit in a Single, Rapid Processing Step. User Can Review Graphs & Complete Statistical Summaries, Including Full Parameter Values, of Any Selected Equation. The Built-In Equation Set Totals 3,456 Linear & Non-Linear Equations (15 User-Defined Equations Can Be Added). The Software Is Available on Both DOS & Windows.
Jandel Scientific.

TableCurve 3D. Jan. 1993. *Items Included:* 1 perfect bound manual. *Customer Support:* Free technical support, company newsletter, 90 day money back guarantee.
 Windows 3.1. 386-16 or higher (4Mb). disk $495.00 (Order no.: STC3R103). *Nonstandard peripherals required:* Microsoft compatible mouse, math coprocessor required. *Optimal configuration:* IBM-compatible 386-16 or higher, 4Mb RAM & 2.5Mb hard disk space. Windows 3.1.A Windows graphics coprocessor or video accelerator card & 256 Color VGA recommended.
Uses Automated Statistical Methods to Process X,Y,Z Data Tables for the Best Possible Surface Fits from More Than 450 Million Built-In Equations. Ranks Equations Automatically According to User-Selected Fit Criteria, Then Displays a List of Equations & a 3D Graph of the Best-Fit Surface for Your Review. Stepping Through the List of Ranked Equations Automatically Updates the Graph for Easy Visualization of Fit Quality. Produces Printed Graphs & Reports, Files for Use with SigmaPlot & Major Spreadsheets, & Ready-to-Compile Code (FORTRAN, Pascal, C & BASIC) of Best-Fit Equations.
Jandel Scientific.

TABS III - Report Writer. *Version:* 8. Sep. 1990. *Items Included:* Binder with documentation. *Customer Support:* Optional 1 year maintenance; $100 entitles users to free phone support & any enhancements released for their computer during the year at no charge.
 PC-DOS/MS-DOS Ver. 3.1 or higher. IBM PC & compatibles (530k). disk $500.00. *Addl. software required:* TAB III.
Allows Users to Define & Print Reports & Forms Based on Information in TABS III. Reports Can Be Saved in a Report Format, Fixed Field Format, Variable Field Format, dBASE III Format, or WordPerfect Format. The Forms Portion of the Software Is Ideal for Printing Mailing Labels, Rotary Index Cards, Client File Labels, & Much More. Most Fields in the Client File Are Accessible Including Work-in-Process Hours & Amounts Billed Hours & Amounts, & Accounts Receivable Figures.
Software Technology, Inc.

TABS III - Report Writer-M: M. *Version:* 8. Sep. 1989. *Items Included:* Binder with documentation. *Customer Support:* Optional 1 year maintenance; $100 for 9 timekeepers or $175 for 99 timekeeper version entitles users to free phone support for 1 year & any enhancement released for their machine during the 12 months period at no charge.
 DOS Ver. 3.1 or higher. IBM & compatibles (530k). disk $500.00 (9 timekeepers); $850.00 (99 timekeepers). *Addl. software required:* TABS III-M. *Networks supported:* Novell or IBM PC Network.
A True Multi-User Version of TABS III-RW Allowing up to 18 (9 Timekeepers) or 200 (99 Timekeepers) Terminals to Make, Define & Print Custom TABS III-M Forms & Reports.
Software Technology, Inc.

TABS III Jr. *Version:* 8. Aug. 1984. *Items Included:* Binder with documentation. *Customer Support:* 1 yr. $125 maintenance entitles user to phone support, newsletter & enhancements released during the year for their computer.
 DOS Ver. 3.1 or higher. IBM PC & compatibles (470k). disk $495.00. *Nonstandard peripherals required:* Hard drive. *Networks supported:* Novell, IBM PC Network & compatibles.
Time & Billing System for a 1 to 5 Timekeeper Firm. Allows up to 999 Transaction (Service) Codes, Categories That Are User Defined. Reports Include Detail & Summary Work-in-Progress, Accounts Receivable, Aged A/R, Productivity Reports by Client, Timekeeper, Category, Split Fee Billing, Spell Checker, Client Notes, Conflict of Interest, Bill Non-Refundable Retainers.
Software Technology, Inc.

TABS III-M Jr. *Version:* 8. Aug. 1984. *Items Included:* Binder with documentation. *Customer Support:* 1 yr. maintenance $250, entitles user to phone support, newsletter & enhancements released during the year for their computer.
 DOS Ver. 3.1 or higher. IBM PC & compatibles (470k). disk $995.00. *Nonstandard peripherals required:* Hard drive. *Networks supported:* Novell, IBM PC Network & compatibles.
Version of TABS III for the 1 to 5 Timekeeper Firm for Use on a Network Allowing up to 10 Workstations to Make Entries, Print Statements or Reports at the Same Time.
Software Technology, Inc.

TABS III-M (Time Accounting & Billing System III-M). *Version:* 8. 1985. *Compatible Hardware:* IBM PC XT, PC AT & compatibles. *Operating System(s) Required:* DOS Ver. 3.1 or higher; Novell NetWare or IBM PC Network software. *Memory Required:* 470k. *Items Included:* Binder with documentation. *Customer Support:* 1 yr. maintenance $450.00 entitles users to phone support, monthly user newsletter & any enhancements released during the year for their computer at no charge.
 disk $3995.00.
 $495.00 maintenance fee (optional).
 demo disk $45.00.
True Multi-User Version of TABS III Allowing 1 to 99 Timekeeper. Allows up to 200 Terminals to Make, Enter or Retrieve Client Billing Information at One Time. Provides Accounts Receivable, Client Employee & Area of Practice Productivity, etc. Reports Missing Time Entries in Timekeeper Hour Report, Split Fee Billing, Spell Checker, Conflict of Interest. First System Ever Approved by the ABA. Integrates with Case Master III-M (Case Management System), GLS-M, APS-M, CDS-M & TAS-M, TABS III Report Writer-M.
Software Technology, Inc.

TABS III-R (Time Accounting & Billing System III-R). *Version:* 8. Dec. 1979. *Compatible Hardware:* IBM PC, PC XT, PC AT & compatibles. *Operating System(s) Required:* DOS Ver. 3.1 or higher. *Memory Required:* 470k. *General Requirements:* 2 floppy drives (360k minimum) or hard disk; TABS III or TABS III-M. *Items Included:* Binder with documentation. *Customer Support:* 1 yr. maintenance $65.00 entitles users to phone support & enhancements released for their computer during the year at no charge.
 disk $350.00.
 maintenance fee (optional) $65.00.
Allows Remote Data Entry into TABS III Without the Use of a Network. Data Is Verified Both at the Time of Entry & During Batch Transfer into Main Data Files. Remote Site Has the Ability to Edit Data, Includes a Pop-Up Timer.
Software Technology, Inc.

TABS III (Time Accounting & Billing System III). Version: 8. Aug. 1984. Compatible Hardware: IBM PC XT, PC AT & compatibles. Operating System(s) Required: DOS Ver. 3.1 or higher. Memory Required: 470k. General Requirements: Hard disk. Items Included: Binder with documentation. Customer Support: 1 yr. maintenance, $295.00, entitles users to phone support, monthly user newsletters & any enhancements released for computer during the year at no charge.
disk $1995.00.
maintenance fee (optional) $295.00.
Allows 1 to 99 Timekeepers, 999 User-Defined Transaction Codes, Billing Categories & Professional Descriptions Allowing for Profession-Dependent Terminology. Reports Include Detail & Summary Work-in-Process, Accounts Receivable & Productivity Reports by Client, Timekeeper, Category, Trans Code, Timekeeper by Category & Timekeeper by Trans Code, Cash Receipts Allocation per Timekeeper. First System Ever Approved by the American Bar Association. Allows 25 Billing Cycles Including Billing on Demand, Split Fee Billing, Conflict of Interest, Notes, Spell Checker, Split Fee Billing. Integrates with STI's Case Master III (a Case Management System), GENERAL LEDGER, ACCOUNTS PAYMENT, TRUST ACCOUNTING & CRITICAL DATE SYSTEMS, TABS III Report Writer.
Software Technology, Inc.

T.A.C. (Tactical Armor Command). Compatible Hardware: Apple II+, IIe, IIc; Atari 800/XL/XE; Commodore 64/128. Operating System(s) Required: MS-DOS.
disk $40.00 ea.
Apple. (Order no.: 46052).
Commodore. (Order no.: 46055).
Armored Combat Game Designed for One or Two Players. Features Hi-Res Graphics & Sound with Five Different Scenarios from Meeting Engagement to Stalemate. Player Controls up to Eight Vehicles, Guns, & Squads Simultaneously, Utilizing Equipment of Either German, British, Russian, or American Forces.
Avalon Hill Game Co., The Microcomputer Games Div.

TACTIC: The Scheduler's Assistant. Version: 1.3. Nov. 1991. Items Included: Product manual. Customer Support: On or off site training, implementation assistance, telephone hot line support, remote operation support, computer bulletin board, product enhancements, consulting services.
DOS 5.0. PCs with 386 or 486 microprocessors (4Mb). Contact publisher for price. Addl. software required: Windows 3.1 or higher. Optimal configuration: Depends on application. Networks supported: All PC.
Finite Capacity Scheduling Software. Helps Manufacturing Companies Produce Detailed, Achievable Schedules Which Explicitly Consider Capacity Constraints. Through Its Sophisticated What-If Capability, Helps Manufacturers Choose the Best Scheduling Alternatives. Can Operate Stand Alone or Integrate with Other Computer Systems.
Waterloo Manufacturing Software.

Tactics for Lotus 1-2-3: Part One. Apr. 1986. Compatible Hardware: IBM PC & Compatibles. Memory Required: 20k.
$29.95.
parts 1 & 2 $49.95.
Training Guidebook with Worksheet-Application Disk. Includes LOTUS 1-2-3 Release 2 Features.
Computer Tutor.

Tactics for Lotus 1-2-3: Part Two. Apr. 1986. Memory Required: 20k.
$29.95.

Parts One & Two $49.95.
Training Guidebook with Worksheet-Application Disk. Includes LOTUS 1-2-3 Release 2 Features.
Computer Tutor.

TAG-IT. Version: 2.0. 1994. Compatible Hardware: IBM PC & compatibles. Operating System(s) Required: MS-DOS, PC-DOS. Language(s): Microsoft BASIC. Memory Required: 256k. General Requirements: 2 disk drives, printer. Items Included: Spiral bound Reference Manual. Customer Support: Free technical support.
disk $595.00.
This Program Complies with 1994 AAFCO Regulations & Produces the Text of Commercial Feed Labels, Mediated Labels, or Customer Formula Feed Labels. Calculates Guaranteed Analysis & Prints Common Names of Ingredients, Nutrients, Directions for Use, Precautionary & Claim Statements, etc. Text Files Can Be Edited, Printed, or Typeset. Warning Statements Triggered by Ingredient or Nutrient Levels. American & Metric Units.
Agricultural Software Consultants, Inc.

Take Control of Cholesterol. Items Included: Bound manual. Customer Support: Free hotline - no time limit; 30 day limited warranty; updates are $5/disk plus S&H.
MS-DOS. IBM & compatibles (128k). disk $19.95.
Macintosh (512k). 3.5" disk $19.95.
System Developed by Dr. Ron Goor, Former Coordinator of the National Cholesterol Education Program of the National Institutes of Health. On-Screen Directions Help You Determine Your Ideal Intake of Saturated Fats & Plan Menus Using 207 Special Recipes & Comprehensive Food Tables. Everything You Need Is Included.
Dynacomp, Inc.

Take-Stock. Compatible Hardware: Commodore Amiga.
3.5" disk $49.95.
Stock Monitoring & Analysis Program.
East/West Software.

Take Two Manager. Version: 2.1B. Compatible Hardware: IBM PC, PC XT, PC AT, PS/2. Items Included: Two 5.25" & one 3.5" disks, user documentation. Customer Support: Free telephone support.
$139.00.
avail. site & corporate Licensing.
Automatic File Backup & Recovery Progam Which Includes a Memory-Resident File Manager, File Annotation, File Recovery (Including Undelete) & Extensive Management Reporting Capabilities.
United Software Security, Inc.

Take Your Best Shot. Feb. 1995. Customer Support: Technical support is available free of charge through our technical support phone line by calling 214-437-5531 Monday through Saturday 8:00am-5:00pm, online via CompuServe by typing Go Seventh at any! prompt, or via Internet mail at Support-7thlevel.com.
Windows 3.1 or higher. IBM or compatible 486 25MHz or higher. CD-ROM disk $19.99 (ISBN 0-9641098-5-9, Order no.: 10018). Nonstandard peripherals required: 256-color display or higher, MPC-compatible sound card, amplified speakers, mouse, CD-ROM.
This Program Challenges You with Three Twisted Arcade Games Including a Tribute to Atari's Ground-Breaking Pong. Enjoy More Than 50 Levels of Game Play & Bonus Rounds. Play Best Shot to Relieve Your Stress. Customize Your Computer with Screen Savers, Wallpapers, Desktop Icons, & More Than 200 Audio Clips.
Seventh Level, Inc.

TAKEOVER. Version: 2.1. Mar. 1990. Items Included: A set of both 5.25" & 3.5" diskettes, four manuals. Customer Support: 60-day money back guarantee; free technical support at (904) 878-8564.
MS/PC-DOS. IBM (Guest PC: 480k; Host PC: 55-70k). disk $195.00. Nonstandard peripherals required: Modem.
Remote Control Software Package from the Developers of MIRROR III. Versatile Package That Lets User Control Another PC from a Remote Location. Supports Keyboard & Mouse.
SoftKlone Distributing Corp.

TAL (Timeslips Accounting Link). Version: 6.0. Compatible Hardware: 386 processor or higher. General Requirements: Hard disk; Timeslips 5 or higher. Items Included: Manual.
disk $79.95.
Links TIMESLIPS with Many Compatible Accounting Programs.
TIMESLIPS Corp.

The Tale of Peter Rabbit.
MS/PC-DOS 3.1 or higher. IBM, Tandy 1000RLX, Tandy 2500SX or compatible (640k). Contact publisher for price. Nonstandard peripherals required: 3 Mb Hard disk, Color VGA, Mouse. Optimal configuration: 386 PC & Sound Card.
Peter & His Companions Come Alive in This Interactive Storybook Featuring Original Watercolors by Award Winning Children's Illustrator Lonnie Sue Johnson, & the Complete Beatrix Potter Text. Each Word Is Highlighted as it Is Read Aloud. Individual Words & Phrases Can Be Repeated by Clicking the Mouse. Learning Proceeds at Whatever Pace Makes Young Readers Comfortable. Click on Objects on the Screen & Their Names Are Not Only Spoken, but also Spelled Out on the Screen (Some Even Have Sound Effects!). Spectacular 256-Color VGA Images & Stereo Sound.
Knowledge Adventure, Inc.

Tales of a Fourth Grade Nothing. Judy Blume. Items Included: Program manual. Customer Support: Free technical support, 90 day warranty.
School ver.. System 7.1 or higher. Macintosh (4Mb). 3.5" disk contact publisher for price (ISBN 1-57204-171-4). Nonstandard peripherals required: 256 color monitor, hard drive, printer.
Lab pack. System 7.1 or higher. Macintosh (4Mb). 3.5" disk contact publisher for price (ISBN 1-57204-172-2). Nonstandard peripherals required: 256 color monitor, hard drive, printer.
Site license. System 7.1 or higher. Macintosh (4Mb). 3.5" disk contact publisher for price (ISBN 1-57204-173-0). Nonstandard peripherals required: 256 color monitor, hard drive, printer.
School ver.. Windows 3.1 or higher. IBM/Tandy & 100% compatibles (4Mb). disk contact publisher for price (ISBN 1-57204-174-9). Nonstandard peripherals required: VGA or SVGA 640 x 480 resolution (256), mouse, hard drive, sound device.
Lab pack. Windows 3.1 or higher. IBM/Tandy & 100% compatibles (4Mb). disk contact publisher for price (ISBN 1-57204-175-7). Nonstandard peripherals required: VGA or SVGA 640 x 480 resolution (256), mouse, hard drive, sound device.
Site license. Windows 3.1 or higher. disk contact publisher for price (ISBN 1-57204-176-5).
This companion for young adult literature is ideal for students who don't know how to start that book report, or give that needed summary. Gentle prompts throughout the guide section of the program include Warm-up Connections,

TITLE INDEX

Thinking about Plot, Quoting & Noting, Keeping a Journal, If I Were ———,' Responding to Questions, Using Quotations, Taking a Personal View, Write to Others, & Write a Sequel.
Lawrence Productions, Inc.

Talespin. Timothy Purves & Mark Heator. May 1989.
TOS (512k). Atari ST. 3.5" disk $49.95.
Amiga (1Mb). 3.5" disk $49.95.
Combines Drawing, Texts & Sounds into a Series of Pages to Form an Interactive Adventure Game.
MichTron, Inc.

Talk to Me. *Compatible Hardware:* Atari. (source code included).
disk $19.95.
Dynacomp, Inc.

Talking Bartender. *Compatible Hardware:* TI 99/4A. *Operating System(s) Required:* DX-10. *Language(s):* Console BASIC. *Memory Required:* 16k.
disk $24.95.
Database of 100 Drinks Which Can Be Selected by Name or Type. Recipe Is Printed on the Screen. Recipe May Be Spoken by the Computer with Optional TEII Terminal Emulator Module & a Speech Synthesizer. Recipes Can Be Added to the Database Using AUTOMATIC FILER.
Eastbench Software Products.

Talking Home Inventory. *Compatible Hardware:* Atari. (source code included). *Memory Required:* 32k.
$19.95.
Dynacomp, Inc.

Talking PC Therapist. *Version:* 3.02. *Compatible Hardware:* IBM PC & compatibles. *Operating System(s) Required:* PC-DOS/MS-DOS. *Memory Required:* 256k. *Items Included:* 32 pg. Thinking Software catalog.
3.5" or 5.25" disk $59.95.
Features Natural Language Processing, Speech Synthesis & Machine Learning. Retains Everything Said, Conversational Ability Grows. Uses AI Sentence Parsing & Knowledgebase Technology, Plus 2000 Word Built-In Vocabulary. Talks Through PC Speaker Without Any Additional Hardware. Sample Turbo PROLOG Source Code Included.
Thinking Software, Inc.

Talking Phonebook. *Compatible Hardware:* Atari. (source code included). *Memory Required:* 32k.
$19.95.
Dynacomp, Inc.

The Talking Tutor Series.
Windows. IBM & compatibles. CD-ROM disk $269.70, Set (Order no.: R1022). *Nonstandard peripherals required:* CD-ROM drive. *Optimal configuration:* 386 processor or higher, MS-DOS 3.1 or higher, 20Mb hard drive, 640k RAM, external speakers or headphones (with sound card) that are Sound Blaster compatible, VGA graphics & adapter, VGA color monitor.
Macintosh (4Mb). (Order no.: R1022A). *Nonstandard peripherals required:* 14" color monitor or larger, CD-ROM drive.
This Outstanding Series Uses Puzzles, Exciting Stories, Color-Animation & Music to Teach the Basics. 6 Volume Set.
Library Video Co.

TALLTOWR. *Version:* 1.0. 1982. *Compatible Hardware:* IBM PC & compatibles. *Operating System(s) Required:* MS-DOS. *Language(s):* BASIC. *Memory Required:* 128k.
$435.00.
Provides Calculations for Wind Load, Seismic, Skirt & Base Design, & Deflection.
Technical Research Services, Inc.

Taming MS-DOS. *Version:* 2.0. Thom Hogan. *Operating System(s) Required:* MS-DOS.
book & disk $34.95 (ISBN 0-934375-92-5).
book only $19.95 (ISBN 0-934375-87-9).
MS-DOS Reference Guide. Covers Some of the More Complex Elements of MS-DOS, Including Time-Saving Tricks to Help Customize Any System. All Source Code Is Available on Disk.
M & T Bks.

T&M Optometric Plus. *Version:* 3.307. *Compatible Hardware:* Apple Macintosh Plus, SE, II. *Memory Required:* 1000k. *General Requirements:* Hard disk, ImageWriter. *Customer Support:* By optometrist.
Single user. 3.5" disk $3250.00.
Optometric Office Management Program.
T&M Systems, Inc.

Tanglewood. Microdeal. Nov. 1987. *Compatible Hardware:* Atari ST; Commodore Amiga. *Memory Required:* 512k.
Atari. 3.5" disk $39.95, (Demo Avail).
Commodore. 3.5" disk $39.95.
Player Has Ten Days to Win The Trust & Support of The Tanglians to Regain The Stolen Documents That Give You Exclusive Mining Rights to Their Planet. User Has Five Characters to Control in the Search. Each One with Differents Strengths & Weaknesses; over Twelve Thousand Locations.
MichTron, Inc.

Tangram. Elizabeth Wilkens. 1986. *Compatible Hardware:* IBM PC & compatibles. *Memory Required:* 256k.
disk $35.00 (ISBN 1-55763-016-X, Order no.: ML135D-PC).
Game in Which Seven Geometric Shapes Are Fitted Together in a Variety of Designs.
Micro Learningware.

Tangrams Puzzler. (Skillbuilders Ser.). Kenneth Coates. 1984. *Compatible Hardware:* Apple II family. *Operating System(s) Required:* Apple DOS 3.3. *Language(s):* BASIC, Assembly. *Memory Required:* 48k.
disk $34.95, incl. tchr's. manual, wkshts., & activities bklt. (ISBN 0-88335-280-X, Order no.: SMP05).
with backup $49.95.
Lab pk.. 5 add'l. copies of same disk $75.00.
Using 7 Geometric Shapes Out from a Single Square, Students Arrange the Pieces to Duplicate a Figure. Students May Create Their Own Figures. Stimulates Geometric Intuition & Artistic Ability.
Milliken Publishing Co.

Tankcalc. *Items Included:* Bound manual. *Customer Support:* Free hotline - no time limit; 30 day limited warranty; updates are $5/disk plus S&H.
MS-DOS 2.0 or higher. IBM & compatibles (128k). disk $89.95. *Nonstandard peripherals required:* 80-column printer; one 360k drive.
Tool to Assist in Liquids Inventory Control. It Creates Operating Tank Calibration (Gauging) Tables Quickly, Easily, & Accurately. TANKCALC Is Well Documented & Has a Variety of Applications Including: Determining Tank Contents Available for Use, Performing What-If Analysis for Tank Design, Checking Hand-Calculated Charts, & Calibrating Storage Tanks. Horizontal Cylindrical Tanks Can Be Level or Sloped with a Variety of Head Shapes. (Head & Sloped-Vessel Calculations Follow the American Petroleum Institute Standard 2551).
Dynacomp, Inc.

TANKQ. John Migliavacca. Dec. 1983. *Compatible Hardware:* IBM PC. *Operating System(s) Required:* DOS 2.0. *Language(s):* BASIC.
disk $180.00 (ISBN 0-917405-06-4).

Heat Transfer from Insulated Cone Roof Storage Tanks to Atmosphere. Finds Separate Heat Transfer from the Wetted Wall, Dry Wall, Bottom & Roof. Considers Wind & Surface Emissivity, Calculates Vapor Space Temperature. Output Includes Pertinent Heat Transfer Parameters in Addition to BTUs Lost.
Techdata.

Tap-It. G. David Peter. 1987. *Compatible Hardware:* Apple II, IBM PC & compatibles, Macintosh Plus or higher. *Operating System(s) Required:* Apple, DOS 3.3, Macintosh System 6.0.3 & 7.1, PC-DOS/MS-DOS 3.3. *Language(s):* QuickBasic. *Memory Required:* Apple 48k, IBM 640k, Macintosh 512k. *General Requirements:* CGA card for IBM.
disk $39.95 (ISBN 1-55603-055-X, Order no.: I-1245).
Apple. disk $39.95 (ISBN 1-55603-058-4, Order no.: A-1245).
Macintosh. 3.5" disk $59.95.
Rhythm Skills Program Which Teaches the Concepts of Beat & Tempo Through the Presentation of Rhythms & Tapping Drills Where Students Respond After Either Listening or Reading Rhythm Patterns. A Non-Stop Quiz at the End of Each Level Drills Rhythm Accuracy. The Lesson Has Three Skill Levels with an Option for a Final Quiz Using the Rhythms from Level Three. The Final Quiz Is Considered the All-Pro Level.
Electronic Courseware Systems, Inc.

TapDance: Skills Testing Software. *Version:* 1.8. Sep. 1994. *Items Included:* User's manual in 3-ring binder & cloth covered slipcase. *Customer Support:* Free telephone technical supprot for 90 days.
PC-DOS/MS-DOS 3.0 or higher. IBM PS/2, PC, AT & compatibles (256k). disk starts at $199.00.
Automatically Administers & Scores Tests for Typing, Statistical Typing, Data Entry, 10-Key, Math, Grammar, WORDPERFECT, WORD, LOTUS 1-2-3, & EXCEL. Comes with Sample Tests You Can Use, or You Can Create Your Own Custom Tests. Not a Simulation. Uses "Live" Versions of Software During Tests.
PRI Assocs., Inc.

TapeControl: Tape Management. *Version:* 2.2x. 1990. *Items Included:* Manual & quarterly newsletter. *Customer Support:* Customer support included in price.
VMS. VAX. $451.00-$1825.00.
Online Interactive Tape Management System Designed to Provide Protection for Magnetic Tape Storage in the VAX/VMS Environment. Manages the Tape Library by Monitoring Every Tape Mount, Dismount, & Initialization to Ensure the Integrity of All Tapes Within the Library. Data Retrieval & Management Functions Assist with File & Saveset (Dataset) Retrieval for Rapid Data Restoration.
Raxco, Inc.

TapeConvert: EBCDIC-ASCII Data Conversion. *Version:* 4.4. 1990. *Items Included:* Manual, quarterly newsletter. *Customer Support:* Customer support included in price.
VMS. VAX. $490.00-$880.00.
Enables Easy & Effective "Conversion" of Tapes Between VAX & IBM or Other Foreign Tapes. Will Read or Write an EBCDIC Standard Label or Non-Labeled Tape. A Useful Tool in Diverse User Environments with Various Combinations of Operating Systems & Processors.
Raxco, Inc.

Tapestry II. *Compatible Hardware:* IBM PC & compatibles, PC XT, PC AT, PS/2. *Memory Required:* 640k. *General Requirements:* 10Mb

hard disk, suitable networking hardware.
first workstation $695.00.
addl. workstations $250.00 ea.
Tapestry II LAN Manager Starter Pack $2995.00.
Tapestry/8 $795.00.
LAN Software with an Icon Interface. Electronic Mail, Networked Time Management System. Servers Are All Undedicated. Provides Central Storage for Applications, Automatic File Locking Enabling Users to Run Single-User Applications Not Originally Designed for Networks. Supports All Standards, Including IBM Token-Ring, PC Network, & 3Com Hardware So That Users Can Choose Themselves What LAN Hardware Will Suit Their Needs Best.
TORUS Systems, Inc.

Taranto General Ledger. *Version:* 6.5. 1995. *Operating System(s) Required:* MS-DOS, XENIX. *Language(s):* Compiled BASIC. *Memory Required:* 256k. *General Requirements:* Hard drive, printer. *Items Included:* Manual, disk, demo. *Customer Support:* Free phone support for 90-days; $25.00 per phone call after.
disk $200.00 ea. (ISBN 0-918185-02-5).
Transactions Entered Either Through Direct Posting, Cash Journal or External Sources Such As: Accounts Payable, Accounts Receivable, Payroll & Inventory Control. Retained Earnings Automatically Posted to User-Defined Account. Budgeting & Year-to-Year Comparisons. Report Generator. Prior Month Adjustment.
Taranto & Assocs., Inc.

Target Market Selector. Nov. 1988. *Items Included:* User manual & software tutorials. *Customer Support:* 30 day money back guarantee, free phone support, on line tutorials & help in software.
PC-DOS or OS/2 (256k). IBM PC, XT, AT, PS/2 or compatibles. $199.00 (US & Canada), $249.00 (International). *Nonstandard peripherals required:* CGA, EGA, VGA, or Hercules graphics board. *Addl. software required:* Lotus 1-2-3 release 2, 2.01, 2.2, or 3. *Optimal configuration:* IBM PC AT, DOS 2.1 or higher, 640k Ram, EGA board, 1-2-3 release 2 or higher. *Networks supported:* All that are supported by Lotus 1-2-3.
Assists Product Managers, Marketing Directors, Business Presidents, Entrepreneurs to Quickly Decide Whether or Not to Target/Enter a Market Segement. Prioritize/Rank up to 15 Market Segments for Targeting by Your Company, for Example: Industry/Vertical Segments, Product Segments, Company Size Segments, Income or Age Group Segments.
Successware.

TargetTeach. *Version:* VI. Oct. 1990. *Compatible Hardware:* IBM PS/2. *Operating System(s) Required:* PC-DOS/MS-DOS. *Language(s):* C (source code included). *Memory Required:* 640k. *Items Included:* Updates.
disk $5000.00.
Instructional Management Program Plus Curriculum Databases to Improve Test Scores.
Evans Newton, Inc.

Tarot Reader. 1985. *Compatible Hardware:* Apple II, Commodore 64, IBM PC.
disk report writer $300.00 ea.
Commodore. (ISBN 0-925182-26-5).
IBM. (ISBN 0-925182-27-3).
Designed to Throw a Ten or Sixteen Card Spread of Tarot Cards in the Traditional Coptic Cross Layout - Just As You Might Lay the Cards Out by Hand. The Computer Shuffles the Cards Using Its Random Number Generator, Then Lays Them Out & Provides an Interpretation.
Matrix Software.

TAS-M (Trust Accounting System-M). *Version:* 8. Dec. 1979. *Compatible Hardware:* IBM PC, PC XT, PC AT & compatibles. *Operating System(s) Required:* DOS Ver. 3.1 or higher; Novell Netware or IBM PC Network software. *Memory Required:* 384k. *General Requirements:* Hard disk. *Items Included:* Binder with documentation. *Customer Support:* 1 yr. maintenance, $144.00, entitles user to phone support, quarterly newsletters, & enhancements released for their computer during the year at no charge.
disk $700.00.
maintenance fee (optional) $144.00.
demo disk $35.00.
True Multi-User Version of TAS Allowing up to 200 Terminals to Enter or Retrieve Client Trust Account Information. User Can Print from Nine Separate Checking Accounts. Trust Details Remain in Clients Trust until Removed by User. Integrates with STI's TABS III-M.
Software Technology, Inc.

TAS Order Entry System. *Compatible Hardware:* TRS-80 Model 4. *Operating System(s) Required:* TRSDOS, MS-DOS.
disk $99.00 ea.
Model 4. (Order no.: D4TOES).
MS-DOS. (Order no.: DMTOES).
Model 4 source. (Order no.: D4STOE).
MS-DOS source. (Order no.: DMSTOE).
manual $5.00.
Supports up to a 300 Item Inventory, Invoicing & Automatic Address Conversion to MAILCALL.
The Alternate Source.

TAS Professional. *Version:* 4.03. Sep. 1993. *Items Included:* Tutorial, sample programs, full manual (3-ring binder). *Customer Support:* Free installation support (via phone) first 30 days; FAX & Bulletin Board: free, with response within 1-3 days; Phone support: 1 year, unlimited calls, 1-5pm M-F $150/year; Training is available from 3rd party.
DOS 3.3 or higher. PC compatibles/clones (2Mb). disk $599.00 (Order no.: TAS PRO 4.0). *Addl. software required:* Recommend an expanded memory manager. *Optimal configuration:* Intel 486 or clone, DOS 5.0, 4Mb RAM, 386 MAX memory manager, Novell 3.12 network (for multiuser). *Networks supported:* Any NetBIOS compatible network; recommend Novell or LANtastic.
Complete 4GL & Database Application Development System That Includes Screen Painter, Report Writer, Program Editor, Code Generator, & Utilities Like Import/Export. Produces Extremely Fast, Compact Compiled Code. Uses Btrieve Record Management System. Multiuser Ready Source Code for Integrated Accounting Package & Add-Ons Is Available.
Business Tools Software.

The TAS Public Domain Software Library, 19 disks. *Compatible Hardware:* TRS-80 Model I, Model III, Model 4.
disk $10.00 ea.
The Alternate Source.

TAS (Trust Accounting System). *Version:* 8. Dec. 1979. *Compatible Hardware:* IBM PC, PC XT, PC AT & compatibles. *Operating System(s) Required:* DOS Ver. 3.1 or higher. *Memory Required:* 384k. *Items Included:* Binder with documentation. *Customer Support:* 1 yr. maintenance, $108.00, entitles users to phone support, quarterly newsletters, & enhancements released for their computer during the year at no charge.
$500.00.
maintenance fee (optional) $108.00.
demo disk $35.00.
Provides Current Balance Information for Each Trust. Check Registers Can Be Printed for Individual Trusts or for Entire Trust Account. Records of Trust Activity Are Retained until Deleted by the User. Checks Can Be Manually or Computer Generated from 9 Separate Checking Accounts. Users Can Define Federal ID & a 1099 Field. Integrates with TABS III & TABS III-M.
Software Technology, Inc.

TAS Utility Package. *Compatible Hardware:* TRS-80 Model I Level II, Model III. *Operating System(s) Required:* LDOS. *Memory Required:* 48k.
disk $49.95.
Consists of Four Separate Utilities for TRS-80 Computers Using the LDOS Operating System. Also Included Are the Assembly Language Source Codes for Most of These Utilities.
The Alternate Source.

Task Force 1942. Sep. 1992. *Items Included:* Manual, keyboard overlay, map. *Customer Support:* Free customer service, 1-410-771-1151, Ext. 350.
80286, 16MHz, hard disk required, DOS 3.3 VGA, keyboard, sound card. IBM & 100% compatibles (640k). disk $69.95 (ISBN 1-55884-208-X). *Optimal configuration:* 386, 16MHz, hard disk, DOS 5.0, VGA, Joystick, Roland/Sound Blaster sound card.
Maneuver a Task Force Consisting of Destroyers, Cruisers & Battleships Against Enemy Forces in the South Pacific. Command Either American or Japanese Forces. Engage in an Entire Campaign or Quick Single Engagements & Ship-to-Ship Duels. 3-D Graphics & Special Effects Provide Unparalleled Realism.
MicroProse Software.

Task Monitor. *Version:* 4.207. *Compatible Hardware:* IBM PC XT, PC AT, PS/2. *Memory Required:* 640k.
disk $895.00.
Project-Management Package Featuring Automatic Resource Leveling, Context-Sensitive On-Screen Help, Task-by-Task Data-Entry Style, Plotter Support, 2500 Activities per Level & Disk Method of Data Storage. Produces Resource Distribution Histograms & Levels One Resource Simultaneously. Automatically Draws & Edits PERT Charts On-Screen. Three Simultaneous Criteria Can Be Used to Select Activities; Three Simultaneous Fields Can Be Used to Sort Activities. Interfaces with Artemis, Project/2 & Vision Software Without Additional Programming.
Monitor Software.

TaskCommand: Job Schedular. *Version:* 3.1. 1990. *Items Included:* Manual, quarterly newsletter. *Customer Support:* Customer support included in price.
VMS. VAX. $290.00-$1900.00.
Automated Job Scheduling Tool for VAX/VMS Systems. Automates the Scheduling of Routine & Repetitive Batch Jobs, Including Complex Schedules with Dependancies. Advanced Features Allow for Customized Calendars, Real-Time Monitoring, Cross Reference Reporting & Easy Schedule of Maintenance.
Raxco, Inc.

TaskMaker. Storm, Impact. Nov. 1989. Apple Macintosh (1Mb). 3.5" disk $49.95 (ISBN 0-945749-23-6, Order no.: 301).
Action Adventure Game.
XOR Corp.

TaskMaster. *Customer Support:* 800-929-8117 (customer service).
MS-DOS. IBM/PS2. disk $99.99 (ISBN 0-87007-088-6).
Allows Users to Organize Time & Projects. Two

TITLE INDEX

Files are Created: Today's Tasks - a Detailed Breakdown of Projects with Tasks; & Future Tasks - Users Sets Start & Completion Dates for Projects along with the Project's Relative Priority.
SourceView Software International.

TaskMaster-MAC. *Customer Support:* 800-929-8117 (customer service).
MS-DOS. Macintosh. disk $99.99 (ISBN 0-87007-566-7).
Designed to Provide the Manager, Employee, Entrepreneur & Professional with an Effective Way to Track & Manage the Various Tasks, & Contacts Required by Their Job. Structured to Meet the Needs of any Job or Profession by Allowing the User to Configure It to Reflect the Types of Tasks, Projects & Contracts that Are Relevant to Them in Their Profession. Automatically Generates Several Formats of "Things to Do" Lists, & Also Keeps Track of State Abbreviations, Area Codes, & Zip Codes as Permanent Reference Files. Has the Ability to Flexibly Categorize Tasks & Prioritize Them. Another Feature Is Its Use as a Prospecting Management & Telemarketing System. A 233-Page Manual Is Included.
SourceView Software International.

TASORT. *Compatible Hardware:* TRS-80 Model I, Model III. *Operating System(s) Required:* L-DOS, NEW-DOS-80 2.2, DOSPLUS, MULTI-DOS or TRSDOS. *Language(s):* BASIC. *Memory Required:* 1000k.
contact publisher for price.
Allows Sorting of up to 65 Arrays.
The Alternate Source.

Taste.
Macintosh Plus (1Mb). 3.5" disk $99.00.
Nonstandard peripherals required: Hard disk.
Word Processing Program for the Macintosh.
DeltaPoint, Inc.

Tate Fonts I. *Compatible Hardware:* Commodore Amiga.
3.5" disk $69.95.
Library with Tube, Slot & Prism Fonts.
Byte by Byte.

Tate Fonts II. *Compatible Hardware:* Commodore Amiga.
3.5" disk $69.95.
Library with Tronic, Chisel & Video Bold Fonts.
Byte by Byte.

Taurus. *Version:* 2.7. *Compatible Hardware:* IBM PC, PC XT. *Operating System(s) Required:* MS-DOS. *Language(s):* CBASIC. *Memory Required:* 64k. *General Requirements:* 5Mb hard disk, 132-column printer.
$600.00-$900.00.
free demo disk.
Includes the Following Features: Client Maintenance Allowing Adding, Updating & Deleting Information in up to 2000 Client Accounts. Security Maintenance of All Data up to Sixteen Different Types of Securities. Portfolio Maintenance of All Client Accounts. Portfolio Size Is Limited by the Capacity of the Computer Hardware. Realized Portfolio Maintenance Stores All Client Realized Transactions & Allows for Multiple Buys to One Sell or One Buy to Multiple Sells. Codes Maintenance Allows the User to Alter the Client Valuation Codes to Meet Individual Entries. Security Tickle Maintenance Flags the User of Securities Due, etc.
Taurus Computer Systems, Inc.

Tax Accrual Worksheet. *Compatible Hardware:* Altos Series 5-15D, Series 5-5D, 580-XX, ACS8000-XX; IBM PC, PC XT, PC AT (enhanced); Compaq with 2 disk drives, Compaq Plus with 10Mb hard disk; Hyperion with 2 disk drives; Chameleon Plus with 2 disk drives; Xerox 820 with 2 disk drives, Zilog MCZ-250. *Operating System(s) Required:* CP/M, MP/M, CP/M-86/80, PC-DOS, MS-DOS. *Memory Required:* 128k.
contact publisher for price.
Performs the Calculations & Prints the Necessary Workpapers for Deferred Tax Accounting. Helps Prepare the Income Tax Audit Workpapers to Support Total U. S. Income Tax Expense, Related Balance Sheet Liability & Deferred Tax Accounts, & Financial Statement Income Tax Disclosures.
Coopers & Lybrand.

Tax Authority. *Version:* 2.0. Apr. 1991. *Items Included:* Complete documentation; runtime version of Paradox. *Customer Support:* Free for first 90 days. Annual phone support optional for $150.00 per year.
MS-DOS 2.0 or higher. IBM compatible (640k). $695.00 single user; $1395.00 multi-user.
Networks supported: Novell, 3 Com, Vines, IBM PC LAN, others.
Tracks Corporate Tax Deadlines Including Filings, Estimated Payments & Extensions. Works for All Types of Taxes in All Jurisdictions. Offers Complete Due Date Monitoring & Office Automation & Organization.
Front Row Systems.

Tax Calendar. *Compatible Hardware:* Altos Series 15-5D, Series 5-5D, 580-XX, ACS8000-XX; DEC Rainbow 100 with 2 disk drives, Rainbow 100+ with 10MB hard disk; IBM PC with 2 disk drives, PC XT, IBM compatibles; Kaypro 11/IV with 2 disk drives, Kaypro 10, Xerox 820 with 2 disk drives, ZILOG MCZ-250. *Operating System(s) Required:* CP/M, MP/M, CP/M-86/80, PC-DOS, MS-DOS.
contact publisher for price.
Assists in Scheduling Tax Return Preparation & Review by Keeping Track of All Tax Return Due Dates. Establishes a Record for Each Return Due Date. Provides Reports Arranged by Tax Due Dates for a Particular Year, Client, Tax Form Number, Tax Partner, Tax Person, & Due Dates for a Particular Month. Operates under a Prepackaged Set of Commands Using the CONDOR Database Management System.
Coopers & Lybrand.

TAX CK-PRI, 2 disks. *Compatible Hardware:* TRS-80 Model I, Model II, Model III, Model 16, Tandy 6000. *Operating System(s) Required:* TRSDOS, DOSplus, XENIX 3.00. *Language(s):* BASIC (source code included). *Memory Required:* 48k.
Checking only. $500.00.
Checking & Printing. $1500.00.
Complete Checking & Printing of All Common Forms for Federal & N.C. State. Schedules Include: B, C, D, E, F, G, SE, W, 2106, 2210, 3903, 3468, 6251, 4922, 2119.
CK/PRI Co.

Taxbyte 1120 Software. Jan. 1995. *Items Included:* Operations manual, laser printing. *Customer Support:* Free telephone support; annual training meetings.
PC-DOS/MS-DOS 3.1 or higher. IBM & compatibles (640k). disk $400.00 (Order no.: 800-245-8299). *Optimal configuration:* 640k, DOS 3.1 or higher, laser printer, color monitor. *Networks supported:* Novell.
Computes & Prints Forms Used in Preparation of Corporation Returns. Includes Other Deductions Worksheet, On-Line Calculator with Note Pad Prints with Return.
Taxbyte, Inc.

Taxbyte 1120S Software. Jan. 1995. *Items Included:* Operations manual, laser printing. *Customer Support:* Free telephone support, annual training meetings.
PC-DOS/MS-DOS. IBM & compatibles (640k). disk $400.00 (Order no.: 800-245-8299). *Optimal configuration:* 640k, DOS 3.1 or higher, laser printer, color monitor. *Networks supported:* Novell.
Computes & Prints Sub S Corporation Returns; K1 Generator Includes On-Screen K-1 Summary; Other Deductions Worksheet, On-Line Calculator Includes Note Pad Feature, Prints Tape with Return.
Taxbyte, Inc.

Taxbyte 1040 Software. Jan. 1995. *Compatible Hardware:* IBM PC & compatibles. *Operating System(s) Required:* PC-DOS/MS-DOS 3.1 or higher. *Memory Required:* 640k. *General Requirements:* Hard disk & 640k RAM recommended. *Items Included:* Over 60 Federal Form, On-Line IRS Help. Built-In Calculator. *Customer Support:* Free telephone support.
PC-DOS/MS-DOS. $1000.00-$1500.00.
laser printing for federal forms $500.00.
$400.00 state software (specify state).
laser printing for state forms $100.00.
Computes & Prints up to 73 Federal Tax Schedules & Forms for 1040 Returns. Supports Individual or Batch Printing on Daisywheel or Dot Matrix Printers. Laser Printing Available at Additional Cost Includes 1040 PC Format. State Software Available for All States Having a State Income Tax & Florida Intangible Tax. State Laser Forms Available. Annual Training Meetings.
Taxbyte, Inc.

Taxbyte 1040X Software. *Compatible Hardware:* IBM. *Operating System(s) Required:* PC-DOS/MS-DOS 3.1 or higher. *Memory Required:* 256k. *General Requirements:* Hard or floppy disk system, printer. *Items Included:* Amended return software for previous 6 years, pop-up calculator, IRS help. *Customer Support:* Free telephone support.
disk $50.00.
Completes an Amended Return. Built-In IRS Help, Pop-Up Calculator, & the Ability to Enter Either "Correct" or "Net Change" Amounts Make It Very Easy to Use.
Taxbyte, Inc.

Taxbyte 1065-Partnerships. *Items Included:* On-line IRS help, pop-up calculator. *Customer Support:* Free telephone support, annual training meetings.
PC-DOS/MS-DOS 3.1 & higher. IBM & compatibles (640k). disk $400.00, incl. Laser Printing. *Optimal configuration:* 640k, DOS 3.1, Laser printer. *Networks supported:* Novell.
Complete Program to Produce a Partnership Return. Uses Same Design Criteria As 1040 to Maintain the Same Look & Feel. K-1 Generator Includes On Screen K-1 Summary. Other Deductions Worksheet, On Line Calculator Includes Note Pad Feature Prints Tape with Return.
Taxbyte, Inc.

Tax Database Manager. *Compatible Hardware:* Apple Macintosh. *Memory Required:* 512k. *General Requirements:* ImageWriter.
3.5" disk $8.00.
Tax Planning Program.
Gary Holmes.

Tax Deferred Exchange. 1978. *Compatible Hardware:* Apple II+, IIe, IIc, III; IBM PC & compatibles. *Operating System(s) Required:* MS-DOS, Apple DOS. *Language(s):* BASIC. *Memory Required:* 48k.
disk $75.00.
Module Showing the Total Financial Impact of a Tax Deferred, or Partially Deferred Property Exchange Enabling Investors to Make Informed Decisions When Trading Properties up or Down.
Realty Software.

Tax Department Financial Analysis. *Compatible Hardware:* Altos Series 15-5D, Series 5-5D, 580-XX, ACS8000-XX; DEC Rainbow 100 with 2 disk drives, Rainbow 100+ with 10Mb hard disk; IBM PC with 2 disk drives, PC XT, IBM compatibles; Kaypro 11/IV with 2 disk drives, Kaypro 10; Xerox 820 with 2 disk drives; ZILOG MCZ-250. *Operating System(s) Required:* CP/M, MP/M, CP/M-86/80, PC-DOS, MS-DOS. contact publisher for price (Order no.: TAX BUDGETS).
Designed for Projecting Tax Department Revenues. Performs Semimonthly Budget Projections for an Entire Year. Assists the Tax Department in Planning & Budgeting Their Staff Resources Most Effectively. Provides Quarterly Reports Detailing Charges in Personnel, Total Hours Worked, Client Chargeable Hours, Standard Revenue & Actual Revenue. Templates Produce: Semimonthly & Monthly Reports of Personnel Charges, Quarterly Reports, or Semimonthly & Monthly Totals, Annual Summary Showing Total Hours, Actual & Realized Revenue & Hourly Revenue.
Coopers & Lybrand.

TAX EASE. *Items Included:* On disk tutorial, instruction manual. *Customer Support:* 24 hour technical service line at no charge, 30 day limited warranty.
MS-DOS, OS/2 (256k-640k). IBM PC, PC XT, PS/2 or compatible. $79.00 individual program, $139.00 professional. *Addl. software required:* Spreadsheet: Lotus 1-2-3 or compatible.
Combines Both Federal & State Returns on a Single Disk. Computes & Prints Over 25 IRS Approved Forms As Well As the State Return for Any One of the Following States: AZ, CA, CT, CO,DC, GA, IL, IN, KS, KY, LA, MA, MD, MI, MN, MO, NC, NJ, NY, OH, OK, OR, PA, VA, WI.
Park Technologies.

Tax II: 1040 Tax Preparation & Planning System. Planery Systems, Inc. *Compatible Hardware:* TI Professional. *Operating System(s) Required:* MS-DOS, R/M COBOL Runtime. *Memory Required:* 128k. *General Requirements:* 2 disk drives printer.
$1295.00.
Texas Instruments, Personal Productivit.

Tax-Investment Record Keeping. *Compatible Hardware:* TI Home Computer, disk system. *Memory Required:* 32k.
contact publisher for price.
Organizes Tax & Investment Data.
Texas Instruments, Personal Productivity Products.

TAX/PACK: Professional 1040. *Version:* 95.1. Jesse A. Tarshis. Jan. 1980. *Compatible Hardware:* IBM PC, PC XT, PC AT, & compatibles. *Operating System(s) Required:* PC-DOS/MS-DOS. *Language(s):* Compiled Microsoft Professional BASIC. *Memory Required:* 640kk. *General Requirements:* Hard disk. *Items Included:* Software, documentation. *Customer Support:* Toll free technical support, updates via modem & disks.
$395.00.
Annual Update $245.00.
Corporations, S Corps, or Partnership $250.00 ea.
$150.00 to $200.00 41 State module.
avail. electronic filing.
laser software avail.
Prepares Federal 1040 Tax Returns Including 64 Forms & Schedules. Client Proforma, Pop-up Calculator, Attachments, Automatic Passive Loss & Batch Printing. Print Laser, Overlays, Continuous or Computer Generated. Electronic Filing, Laser Printing & States Optional.
Alpine Data, Inc.

Tax Partner. 1984. *Compatible Hardware:* IBM PC & compatibles. *Memory Required:* 512k. *General Requirements:* 2 disk drives, printer.
disk $995.00, incl. manual.
Designed to Be Used by Professional Tax Preparers. Calculates Taxes & Prints over 50 Forms & Schedules. Will Generate Client Worksheets, Transmittal Letters, & Invoices. Supports Hewlett Packard's LaserJet Printers. State Programs Are Available.
Best Programs.

Tax Planner. May 1986. *Compatible Hardware:* IBM PC & compatibles, PC AT, PC XT, PCjr. *Operating System(s) Required:* CP/M, CP/M-86, MS-DOS. *Language(s):* MBASIC. *Memory Required:* 128k.
disk $200.00.
add'l. state programs $50.00.
A 1-Year Tax Planner That Calculates Federal & State Taxes for 1986. Designed for the Professional Tax Advisor, This Menu-Driven Program Prints Out a Detailed & Summary Report. Input Sheets Are Included.
Pencil Pushers United, Inc.

Tax Planning 1990. Richard R. Sylvester. Mar. 1990.
IBM PC, PC XT, PC AT, PS/2 & compatibles.
disk $29.00 (ISBN 0-932010-60-1).
Nonstandard peripherals required: Color monitor, 2 floppy drives. *Addl. software required:* Lotus 1-2-3 version 1A or higher.
$59.00 book & diskette (ISBN 0-932010-59-8).
For 1989 Tax Return, Including Substantiation Schedules. Useful for Planning Minimum Tax Position for Future Years by Allocation of Investments.
Ph.D. Publishing Co.

Tax Planning, 1993: Calculation of Income Tax Due, Attachments, Gift Tax, Defense of Return. Richard R. Sylvester. Aug. 1993. *Customer Support:* Purchase money back if not satisfied.
MS-DOS. IBM PC & compatibles (640k). disk $49.50 (ISBN 0-932010-67-9). *Addl. software required:* Lotus 1-2-3 version 1A or higher, or Excel.
Spreadsheet Formats for LOTUS 1-2-3 or EXCEL Allows Accurate Calculation of Income Tax, with Attachments to the Return. Gift Tax Format Is Also Included. Word Processing Text Is Provided for Tax Court Petition, Stipulation, Appeals, & the U.S. Supreme Court Petition, for Defense of the Tax Return. On 3.5" Diskette with 1.2Mb of Program Material.
Ph.D. Publishing Co.

Tax Planning, 1996. Richard R. Sylvester. Jan. 1996. *Customer Support:* Telephone consultation 10 minutes no charge; $250 per hour thereafter. DOS. 286 (800k). disk $150.00. *Addl. software required:* Lotus 1-2-3.
Detailed Calculation Formats for the 1995 Tax Return, Including Attachments to the Return, Such As Depreciation, Auto Expense, R&D Tax Credit, & Capitalized Research Expenditures. Useful for Calculation of Alternative Tax Treatments, to Minimize Tax Due.
Ph.D. Publishing Co.

Tax Preparation Program. Jan. 1987. *Compatible Hardware:* IBM PC & compatibles, PC AT, PC XT. *Operating System(s) Required:* MS-DOS. *Language(s):* MBASIC. *Memory Required:* 128k.
Federal Program. disk $900.00.
Available States. write for info.
Tax Planner. write for info.
Designed for the Professional Tax Preparer to Do Individual Tax Returns. The Federal & State Is Completely Integrated. The Federal Prepares up to 33 Federal Forms with Multiple Schedule Capacity. Various Printing Options Include Laser Printing, Overlays, Originals, & Computer Generated Forms.
Pencil Pushers United, Inc.

Tax Preparer. 1994. *Compatible Hardware:* IBM PC & compatibles, Apple II series. *Operating System(s) Required:* MS-DOS for IBM version. *Memory Required:* Apple 128k, IBM 256k. *Items Included:* IRS accepted printouts, data organizers, batch processing, cover & billing letter. *Customer Support:* Available free.
IBM. disk $295.00, incl. manual.
Apple. $250.00.
$99.00 annual update.
Automates Preparation of Tax Returns by Not Only Looking up Numbers in the Tables & Performing the Arithmetic, but Automatically Completes & Computes Numerous IRS Worksheets to Handle the True Letter of the Law. Performs Math Not Only for Simple Return but for Complex Return That Is Typical of Investors, & Transfers Hundreds of Numbers Back & Forth among Forms, & Recalculates Entire Return As Often As Necessary to Get an Accurate Return. Handles Unlimited Record-Keeping & Unlimited Number of Stocks, Bonds, Rental, Accounts, & Depreciated Assets. Gives Accurate "What If" Capabilities with Tax Laws Built in Well Past Current Year. Gives Hundreds of Pages of Line-by-Line Detail So That You Aren't Left in the Dark about What the Software Is Doing, & Can Easily Handle Unusual Exceptions. All Depreciation Calculations Are Built-In As Well As Automated Handling of Passive Loss Rules. Available Options: Laser Graphics of All Forms & Electronic Filing.
HowardSoft.

Tax Preparer: California Supplement. 1994. *Compatible Hardware:* Apple II series; IBM PC & compatibles. *Operating System(s) Required:* MS-DOS for IBM version. *Memory Required:* Apple 128k, IBM 256k. *Customer Support:* Free phone support.
IBM. disk $129.00.
Apple. disk $129.00.
Provides the Same Automated Tax Preparation As TAX PREPARER for California State Income Taxes, Using the Federal Data As the Starting Point.
HowardSoft.

Tax Preparer: Partnership Edition. 1994. *Compatible Hardware:* IBM PC & compatibles. *Operating System(s) Required:* PC-DOS/MS-DOS. *Memory Required:* 256k. *Customer Support:* Free phone support.
disk $495.00.
$169.00 annual update.
Provides the Same Automation As TAX PREPARER for the Preparation of Form 1065 & Schedule K-1s & Supporting Forms for Business & Investment Partnerships. Not Only Prepares IRS-Accepted Partnership Returns but Also Helps Plan Tax Strategies & Keep Tax Records. Includes a Distribution Worksheet, Which Can Handle Complex Partnership Arrangements & Automatically Creates All the Partner's K-1s. All A.C.R.S. & Depreciation Calculations Are Built-In & Automatic. Generates IRS-Accepted Printouts on Dot-Matrix or Laser Printers.
HowardSoft.

Tax Pro. *Compatible Hardware:* Apple Macintosh, IBM & compatibles. *Memory Required:* 512k. *General Requirements:* Excel.
3.5" disk $49.95.
Tax Planning & Preparation Updated to Reflect the Tax Reform Act of 1986. Includes 13 Tax Forms & Numerous Worksheets. Also Prints IRS-Approved Forms, Including Form 1040.
Chesapeake Software.

TITLE INDEX

Tax Reference Library. Richard R. Hammar. IBM. CD-ROM disk $99.00 (ISBN 1-880562-22-7).
Christian Ministry Resources.

Tax Relief 1040 for Windows. Feb. 1994. *Items Included:* Bound manual. *Customer Support:* Product can be down loaded via bulletin board.
DOS 5.0 or higher; Windows 3.0 or higher. IBM PC, PS/2, 386, 486, 586 (4Mb). disk $995.00, incl. laser printer software & soft fonts, Network Pricing ,1245.00 (Order no.: 1040-WIN). *Nonstandard peripherals required:* Hard disk; HP-compatible laser printer. *Optimal configuration:* Hewlett Packard or compatible laser printer. *Networks supported:* Novell Netware; Lantastic, 3COM.
Comprehensive Professional Tax Preparation Program Which Simplifies All Aspects of the Tax Preparation Business. Supports 26 Forms & Schedules. State Programs Are Completely Integrated. Provides Automatic Billing. Choice of Four (4) User Editable Instruction Letter. Prepares Client, IRS, & State Mailing Labels. Options Include Electronic Filing, 1040 PC, Tax Practice Manager, Proforma/Client Organizer. Unique Input Engine Simplifies Data Entry & Provides Audit Trail. Other Features Include Speed Entry & Speed Print. On-Screen Display of Forms. Tax Planner Included. All Computations Including Passive Losses & AMT Are Done Automatically.
Micro Vision Software, Inc.

Tax Relief 1040 Plus. *Items Included:* Loose leaf manual with tutorial; one set of input sheets. *Customer Support:* Free on-site training; free telephone, fax & Bulletin Board support; updates to product can be downloaded via Bulletin Board.
MS-DOS 3.1 or higher (640k). IBM PC, XT, PS/2, 386, 486, 586. $595.00. Optional: laser software $350.00, state modules $99.00 to $249.00. Renewal prices: programs 50%; laser 70% of list price (Order no.: 1040+). *Nonstandard peripherals required:* Hard disk, Dot Matrix printer. *Optimal configuration:* Hewlett Packard or compatible laser printer. *Networks supported:* Novell Netware, IBM Token Ring, Lantastic, 3COM.
Supports 64 Forms & Schedules, Automatically Computes Alternative Minimum Tax, Self Employment Tax, Passive Activity Loss Limitations, Excess FICA, Earned Income Credit, Taxable Social Security, IRA & Keogh Worksheets, Kiddie Tax, Depreciation Supports MACRS (with Mid-Quarter), ACRS, ADS, DDB, SLD Year-to-Year Update of Client Personal Data, Business Information, Depreciation Items, Names of Interest & Dividend Payers, Rental Property & K-1 Information, Unused Passive Activity Loss, Prior Year Loss Carryovers, etc. Diagnostics, Tax Summary, Instruction Letter & Bill. Pop-Up Calculator & Note Pad. Integrated Tax Planner. Input Engine for Form Free Data Entry. Other Features Include Speed Entry & Speed Print. Optional: Laser Printing, Electronic Filing, Proforma/Client Organizer, State Modules.
Micro Vision Software, Inc.

Tax Relief 1065. *Items Included:* Looseleaf manual with tutorial; one set of input sheets. *Customer Support:* Free on-site training; free telephone, fax & Bulletin Board support; updates to product can be downloaded via Bulletin Board.
MS-DOS 3.1 or higher (512k). IBM PC, XT, PS/2, 286/386/486/586. $350.00. Optional: laser software $199.00, NY State module $195.00. Renewal prices: programs 50%; laser 70% of list price (Order no.: 1065). *Nonstandard peripherals required:* Hard disk, Dot Matrix printer. *Optimal configuration:* Hewlett Packard or compatible laser printer. *Networks supported:* Novell Netware, IBM Token Ring, Lantastic, 3COM.
Supports Forms 1065, 4562, 4797, 6252, 8825; Schedules A, D, F, K, K-1, L, M. Automatically Generates K-1's from Schedule K Data. Generates Supplemental Schedules for All Applicable Items. Depreciation Supports MACRS (with Mid-Quarter), ACRS, ADS, DDB, SLD. Year-to-Year Update of Partnership Information, Partners' Information, Partners' Capital Account, Depreciation & Balance Sheet. Transmittal Letter for Partnership & Letter of Instruction for All Partners. Pop-Up Calculator & Noted Pad. Handles Dollars in Billions. Other Unique Features Include: Part-Link, Direct Book Entry, Speed Entry & Speed Print. Optional: Laser Printing, NY State Module. Interfaces Directly with All Popular Client Write-Up Software Packages.
Micro Vision Software, Inc.

Tax Relief 1120 - 1120S. *Items Included:* Loose leaf manual with tutorial; one set of input sheets. *Customer Support:* Free on-site training; free telephone, fax and Bulletin Board support; updates to product can be downloaded via Bulletin Board.
MS-DOS 3.1 or higher. IBM PC, XT, AT, PS/2, 386, 486, 586. $495.00. Optional: laser software $199.00, 8 state modules $249.00 each. Renewal prices: program 50%; laser 70% of list price (Order no.: 1120). *Nonstandard peripherals required:* Hard disk, Dot Matrix printer. *Optimal configuration:* Hewlett Packard or compatible laser printer. *Networks supported:* Novell Netware, IBM Token Ring & 3COM.
Supports 27 Forms & Schedules, Calculates Alternative Minimum Tax, Professional Service Corporation Tax & Tax for Controlled Groups. Generates Supplemental Schedules for All Applicable Items. Depreciation Supports MACRS (with Mid-Quarter), ACRS, ADS, DDB, SLD. Year-to-Year Update of Corporation Information, Depreciation & Balance Sheet. Transmittal Letter. Pop-Up Calculator & Note Pad. Handles Dollars in Billions. Unique Direct Book Entry Allows Data Entry Directly from G/L Program or Trial Balance for Fast, Accurate Data Entry. Other Features Include Tax Planner, Proforma, Financial Statements & Speed Print. Optional: Laser Printing, NY & NJ State Modules. Interfaces Directly with All Popular Client Write-Up Software Packages.
Micro Vision Software, Inc.

Tax Shelter. 1982. *Compatible Hardware:* Apple II; Commodore 64; IBM PC. *Language(s):* BASIC. *Memory Required:* 64k. *General Requirements:* Printer.
disk $45.00.
Tax Planning & Estimating Tool Based on Current Federal Income Tax Rate Tables. Accepts Entries for Each of the IRS Specified Income Categories, Adjustments, Deductions, Credit & Payment Methods, & Projects Bottom-Line Tax Liability. Subsidiary Calculations Are Made on Income Averaging, Alternate Taxes, Capital Gains, & Exemptions Before Displaying a Summary of the Various Categories of Income & Expense.
Navic Software.

Tax Tool: Tax Productivity Tool, 8 disks. *Version:* 2.C. Andy Mau. Feb. 1981. *Compatible Hardware:* IBM PC. *Operating System(s) Required:* PC-DOS, MS-DOS. *Language(s):* QuickBASIC. *Memory Required:* 320k. *General Requirements:* 2 disk drives, hard disk, printer.
disk professional $495.00 (Order no.: TT001). disk personal $49.95 (Order no.: TT001).
Integrated Income Tax Package for the Federal, New York and New Jersey Returns. Includes the Non-Resident of Both States.
Mau Corp.

TAX TRACKING. *Compatible Hardware:* Altos Series 15-5D, Series 5-5D, 580-XX, ACS8000-XX; DEC Rainbow 100 with 2 disk drives, Rainbow 100+ with 10MB hard disk; IBM PC with 2 disk drives, PC XT, IBM compatibles; Kaypro 11/IV with 2 disk drives, Kaypro 10; Xerox 820 with 2 disk drives; ZILOG MCZ-250. *Operating System(s) Required:* CP/M, MP/M, CP/M-86/80, PC-DOS, MS-DOS.
contact publisher for price (Order no.: TAX TRACKING).
Schedule or Monitor the Preparation of Tax Returns. Functions As an On-Line Tax Calendar, Permitting User to Track Work in Progress As Returns Come In. Operates under a Prepackaged Series of Commands Using the CONDOR Database Management System.
Coopers & Lybrand.

TaxAide. *Items Included:* Form 1040 transparencies. *Customer Support:* Free tech support.
MS-DOS/PC-DOS 2.xx or higher. IBM XT, AT, PS/2 & compatibles, Zenith Z-100 (384k). disk $49.95.
Set of Integrated Income Tax Preparation Templates for Use with Lotus 1-2-3. Fully Integrated. Produces IRS Approved Forms.
Software Applications of Wichita.

Taxbyte - 1041 - Fiduciary Software. Jan. 1995. *Items Included:* Operation manual. *Customer Support:* Free telephone support, annual training meetings - $75, telephone training.
PC-DOS/MS-DOS. IBM & compatibles (640k). disk $400.00. *Optimal configuration:* 640k, DOS 3.1 or higher, laser printer. *Networks supported:* Novell.
Assists in Preparation of Federal Fiduciary Tax Returns. Comprehensive 500 Asset Depreciation; Laser Printing Included Free. Includes Most Often Used Forms & Schedules. On-Line Calculator Includes Note Pad Capability & Prints with Return. Unlimited Statements.
Taxbyte, Inc.

TaxLog & Pop-Up Calendar. *Version:* 3.0. *Compatible Hardware:* IBM PC, PC XT, PCjr. *Operating System(s) Required:* MS-DOS. *Memory Required:* 64k.
TaxLog & Pop-Up Calendar. disk $39.95 (ISBN 0-916435-09-1).
Pop-Up Calendar. disk $19.95 (ISBN 0-916435-13-X).
Popular Programs, Inc.

TAX$IMPLE. *Version:* 10.0. Jan. 1991. *Compatible Hardware:* IBM PC & compatibles, PC XT, PC AT, PS/2. *Operating System(s) Required:* MS-DOS, PC-DOS. *Language(s):* BASICA, etc.. *Memory Required:* 640k. *General Requirements:* Hard disk. *Items Included:* User's manual. *Customer Support:* 1-800-323-2662. disk $245.00-$495.00.
For Tax Professionals with a Minimum Knowledge of Computers. Offers Full Screen Input on IRS Forms (Adjusted for 80 Column Input) & Special Screens. Does Instantaneous Calculations, Transfers, Table Look Up & Redisplaying of Results. Offers On-Line Help, What If Capability, Overflow Schedules, Major ACRS, MACRS & Depreciation Methods, Year to Year Transfer, Transmittal Letter, Invoice, Labels, PAL, AMT, automatic calculations & All Printing Options. For 1040, 1065, 1120, 1120S & State Packages.
AJV Computerized Data Management, Inc.

TAXSTRAT. *Compatible Hardware:* IBM PC, Tandy 2000, Kaypro. *Operating System(s) Required:* PC-DOS, TRSDOS, CP/M, DOS. *Language(s):* BASIC. *Memory Required:* 64k. disk $150.00.

TAXTABLE TUTOR

Allows Flexible Income & Expense Forecasting for Tax Planning Purposes. Prints Reports with As Many As Three Options at a Time.
Computer Technical Services of New Jersey.

TaxTable Tutor. *Customer Support:* 800-929-8117 (customer service). MS-DOS. Apple II. disk $29.99 (ISBN 0-87007-806-2).
Tutorial Showing New Job Applicants Use of Sales Tax Table.
SourceView Software International.

TaxTime: California 540NR. *Version:* 92.01. Feb. 1992. *Items Included:* Manual, disk. *Customer Support:* 30-day money back guarantee less a $10.00 restocking fee. Technical support available on our regular phone lines.
PC-DOS/MS-DOS/DR-DOS. IBM PC & compatibles (512k). $65.00 first year, $45.00 annual renewal, $65.00 laser (Order no.: CA540NR). *Addl. software required:* Lotus 1-2-3, 2.01, 2.2 or 2.3, TaxTime 1040. *Optimal configuration:* 640k RAM & a hard disk. *Networks supported:* 3Com, Novell.
Features IRS (or State) Approved Template for Lotus 1-2-3 versions 2.01, 2.2 or 2.3 That Calculates & Updates Tax Forms. Form Include: 540 NR, 540 NR H. Sch CA (NR), Sch NRP, SI.
Austin Scientific, Inc.

TaxTime for 1-2-3: Alabama 40. *Version:* 92.01. Feb. 1992. *Compatible Hardware:* IBM PC & compatibles. *Operating System(s) Required:* PC-DOS/MS-DOS. *Memory Required:* 512k. *General Requirements:* Lotus 1-2-3 versions 2.01, 2.2 or 2.3, TaxTime 1040. *Items Included:* Manual, disk(s). *Customer Support:* 30 day money back guarantee less $10.00 restock fee. Tech support available on regular phone line.
PC-DOS/MS-DOS/DR-DOS. 3.5" or 5.25" disk $65.00.
renewal $45.00.
laser $65.00.
Features IRS Approved Template for Lotus 1-2-3 Versions 2.01, 2.2 or 2.3 That Calculates & Updates Tax Forms. Forms Include 40, Sch A, Sch BCR, Sch D, Sch E, 40ES.
Austin Scientific, Inc.

TaxTime for 1-2-3: California 100 Corp. *Version:* 92.01. Feb. 1992. *Compatible Hardware:* IBM PC & compatibles. *Operating System(s) Required:* PC-DOS/MS-DOS. *Memory Required:* 512k. *General Requirements:* Lotus 1-2-3 versions 2.01, 2.2 or 22.3, TaxTime 1120. *Items Included:* Manual, disk. *Customer Support:* 30 day money back guarantee less $10.00 restock fee, cost of phone call for tech support.
PC-DOS/MS-DOS/DR-DOS. 3.5" or 5.25" disk $195.00.
renewal $95.00.
laser $95.00.
Features IRS Approved Template for Lotus 1-2-3 Versions 2.01, 2.2 or 2.3 That Calculates & Updates Tax Forms. Forms Include 100, 100P, 100R, 5806, 3805Q.
Austin Scientific, Inc.

TaxTime for 1-2-3: California 540. *Version:* 92.01. Feb. 1992. *Compatible Hardware:* IBM PC & compatibles. *Operating System(s) Required:* PC-DOS, MS-DOS. *Memory Required:* 512k. *General Requirements:* Lotus 1-2-3 2.01, 2.2 or 2.3, TaxTime 1040 program. *Items Included:* Manual, disk. *Customer Support:* 30 day money back guarantee less $10.00 restock fee. Tech support available on regular phone line.
3.2" or 5.25" $95.00 (Order no.: 540).
annual updates $55.00.
laser $95.00.
IRS Approved Template for Lotus 1-2-3 Versions 2.01, 2.2 or 2.3 That Calculates & Updates Tax Forms. Includes 540, D1, H, P, RP, S, ES, X, Sch CA, Sch D, 3502, 3526, 3800, 3801, 3885A, 5805, Various Worksheets & Supporting Statements.
Austin Scientific, Inc.

TaxTime for 1-2-3: California 565. *Version:* 92.01. Feb. 1992. *Items Included:* Manual, disk. *Customer Support:* 30-day money back guarantee less a $10.00 restocking fee, technical support available on our regular phone lines.
PC-DOS/MS-DOS/DR-DOS. IBM PC & compatibles (512k). $195.00 first year, $95.00 annual renewal, $95.00 laser (Order no.: CA565). *Addl. software required:* Lotus 1-2-3, 2.01, 2.2 or 2.3, TaxTime 1065. *Optimal configuration:* 640k RAM & a hard disk. *Networks supported:* 3Com, Novell.
Features IRS (or State) Approved Template for Lotus 1-2-3 versions 2.0, 2.2 or 2.3 That Calculates & Updates Tax Forms. Forms Include: 565, Sch D, Sch K-1, 3885A.
Austin Scientific, Inc.

TaxTime for 1-2-3: Colorado 104. *Version:* 92.01. Feb. 1992. *Compatible Hardware:* IBM PC & compatibles. *Operating System(s) Required:* PC-DOS/MS-DOS. *Memory Required:* 512k. *General Requirements:* Lotus 1-2-3 versions 2.01, 2.2 or 2.3, TaxTime 1040. *Items Included:* Manual, disk. *Customer Support:* 30 day money back guarantee less $10.00 restock fee. Tech support available on regular phone line.
PC-DOS/MS-DOS/DR-DOS. 3.5" or 5.25" disk $65.00.
renewal $45.00.
laser $65.00.
Features IRS Approved Template for Lotus 1-2-3 Versions 2.01, 2.2 or 2.3 That Calculates & Updates Tax Forms. Forms Include 104, 104AMT, 104CR, 104EST, 204.
Austin Scientific, Inc.

TaxTime for 1-2-3: Connecticut 394. *Version:* 92.01. Feb. 1992. *Compatible Hardware:* IBM PC & compatibles. *Operating System(s) Required:* PC-DOS/MS-DOS. *Memory Required:* 512k. *General Requirements:* Lotus 1-2-3 versions 2.01, 2.2 or 2.3. *Items Included:* manual, disk. *Customer Support:* 30-day money back guarantee less $10.00 restock fee, technical support available on regular telephone line.
PC-DOS/MS-DOS/DR-DOS. 3.5" or 5.25" disk $50.00.
renewal $40.00.
laser $50.00.
Features IRS Approved Template for Lotus 1-2-3 Versions 2.01, 2.2 or 2.3 That Calculates & Updates Tax Forms. Forms Include 394, 394TA.
Austin Scientific, Inc.

TaxTime for 1-2-3: Georgia 500. *Version:* 92.01. Feb. 1992. *Compatible Hardware:* IBM PC & compatibles. *Operating System(s) Required:* PC-DOS/MS-DOS. *Memory Required:* 512k. *General Requirements:* Lotus 1-2-3 versions 2.01, 2.2 or 2.3, TaxTime 1040. *Items Included:* Manual, disk. *Customer Support:* 30 day money back guarantee less $10.00 restock fee. Tech support available on regular phone line.
PC-DOS/MS-DOS/DR-DOS. 3.5" or 5.25" disk $50.00.
renewal $40.00.
laser $50.00.
Features IRS Approved Template for Lotus 1-2-3 Versions 2.01, 2.2 or 2.3 That Calculates & Updates Tax Forms. Forms Include 500, 500ES, 500UET.
Austin Scientific, Inc.

TaxTime for 1-2-3: Illinois 1040. *Version:* 92.01. Feb. 1992. *Compatible Hardware:* IBM PC & compatibles. *Operating System(s) Required:* PC-DOS/MS-DOS. *Memory Required:* 512k. *General Requirements:* Lotus 1-2-3 versions 2.01, 2.2 or 2.3, TaxTime 1040. *Items Included:* Manual, disk. *Customer Support:* 30 day money back guarantee less $10.00 restock fee. Tech support available on regular phone line.
PC-DOS/MS-DOS/DR-DOS. 3.5" or 5.25" disk $80.00.
renewal $50.00.
laser $80.00.
Features IRS Approved Template for Lotus 1-2-3 Versions 2.01, 2.2 or 2.3 That Calculates & Updates Tax Forms. Forms Include 1040, 1040ES, Sch CR, 1299C, 2210, 4255, 4644.
Austin Scientific, Inc.

TaxTime for 1-2-3: Maryland 502. *Version:* 92.01. Feb. 1992. *Compatible Hardware:* IBM PC & compatibles. *Operating System(s) Required:* PC-DOS/MS-DOS. *Memory Required:* 512k. *General Requirements:* Lotus 1-2-3 versions 2.01, 2.2 or 2.3, TaxTime 1040. *Items Included:* Manual, disk. *Customer Support:* 30 day money back guarantee less $10.00 restock fee. Tech support available on regular phone line.
PC-DOS/MS-DOS/DR-DOS. 3.5" or 5.25" disk $65.00.
renewal $45.00.
laser $65.00.
Features IRS Approved Template for Lotus 1-2-3 Version 2.01, 2.2 or 2.3 That Calculates & Updates Fax Forms. Forms Include 502, 502CG, 502CR, 502 TP, 502UP, 502V.
Austin Scientific, Inc.

TaxTime for 1-2-3: Massachusetts 1. *Version:* 92.01. Feb. 1992. *Compatible Hardware:* IBM PC or compatibles. *Operating System(s) Required:* PC-DOS/MS-DOS. *Memory Required:* 512k. *General Requirements:* Lotus 1-2-3 versions 2.01, 2.2 or 2.3, TaxTime 1040. *Items Included:* Manual, disk. *Customer Support:* 30 day money back guarantee less $10.00 restock fee. Tech support available on regular phone line.
PC-DOS/MS-DOS/DR-DOS. 3.5" or 5.25" disk $65.00.
renewal $45.00.
laser $65.00.
Features IRS Approved Template for Lotus 1-2-3 Versions 2.01, 2.3 or 2.3 That Calculates & Updates Tax Forms. Forms Include 1, 1ES, M2210, Sch BD, Sch C, Sch EC, Sch EFNTS.
Austin Scientific, Inc.

TaxTime for 1-2-3: Michigan 1040. *Version:* 92.01. Feb. 1992. *Compatible Hardware:* IBM PC & compatibles. *Operating System(s) Required:* PC-DOS/MS-DOS. *Memory Required:* 512k. *General Requirements:* Lotus 1-2-3 versions 2.01, 2.2 or 2.3, TaxTime 1040. *Items Included:* manual, disk. *Customer Support:* 30-day money back guarantee, less $10.00 restock fee, Technical support available on regular telephone lines.
PC-DOS/MS-DOS/DR-DOS. 3.5" or 5.25" disk $80.00.
renewal $50.00.
laser $80.00.
Features IRS Approved Template for Lotus 1-2-3 Versions 2.01, 2.2 or 2.3 That Calculates & Updates Tax Forms. Forms Include MI1040, MI1040CR, 1040CR2, 1040CR5, 1040CR7, MI1040ES, MI2210, MI4797.
Austin Scientific, Inc.

TaxTime for 1-2-3: Missouri 1040. *Version:* 92.01. Feb. 1992. *Items Included:* Manual, disk. *Customer Support:* 30-day money back guarantee less a $10.00 restocking fee. Technical suppirt available on our regualr phone lines.
PC-DOS/MS-DOS/DR-DOS. IBM PC & compatibles (512k). $80.00 first year, $50.00 annual renewal, $80.00 laser (Order no.:

TITLE INDEX

M01040). *Addl. software required:* Lotus 1-2-3 2.01, 2.2 or 2.3, TaxTime 1040. *Optimal configuration:* 640k RAM & a hard disk. *Networks supported:* 3Com, Novell. *Features IRS (or State) Approved Template for Lotus 1-2-3 Versions 2.01, 2.2 or 2.3 That Calculates & Updates Tax Forms. Forms Include:* 1040, MO-Est, MO-2210, MO-A, MO-CRP, MO-CR, MO- NRI, MO-SC.
Austin Scientific, Inc.

TaxTime for 1-2-3: New Jersey 1040. *Version:* 92.01. Feb. 1992. *Compatible Hardware:* IBM PC & compatibles. *Operating System(s) Required:* PC-DOS/MS-DOS. *Memory Required:* 512k. *General Requirements:* Lotus 1-2-3 versions 2.01, 2.2 or 2.3, TaxTime 1040. *Items Included:* Manual, disk. *Customer Support:* 30 day money back guarantee less $10.00 restock fee. Tech support available on regular phone line.
PC-DOS/MS-DOS/DR-DOS. 3.5" or 5.25" disk $50.00.
renewal $40.00.
laser $50.00.
Features IRS Approved Template for Lotus 1-2-3 Version 2.01, 2.2 or 2.3 That Calculates & Updates Tax Forms. Forms Include NJ1040, NJ1040ES, NJ2450, Sch ABC.
Austin Scientific, Inc.

TaxTime for 1-2-3: New York IT-201. *Version:* 92.01. Feb. 1992. *Compatible Hardware:* IBM PC & compatibles. *Operating System(s) Required:* MS-DOS, PC-DOS. *Memory Required:* 512k. *General Requirements:* Lotus 1-2-3 versions 2.01, 2.2 or 2.3, TaxTime 1040. *Items Included:* Manual, disk. *Customer Support:* 30 day money back guarantee less $10.00 restock fee. Tech support available on regular phone line.
PC-DOS/MS-DOS/DR-DOS. 3.5" or 5.25" disk $95.00 (Order no.: IT-201).
annual updates $55.00.
laser $95.00.
IRS Approved Template for Lotus 1-2-3 Version 2.01, 2.2 or 2.3 That Calculates & Updates Tax Forms. Forms Include IT201, IT201-X 112R, ATT201, 214, 220, 360, 370, 399, 2105, 2105.9, NY C203.
Austin Scientific, Inc.

TaxTime for 1-2-3: New York IT-203. *Version:* 92.01. Feb. 1992. *Items Included:* Manual, disk. *Customer Support:* 30-day money back guarantee less a $10.00 restocking fee. Technical support available on our regular phone lines. PC-DOS/MS-DOS/DR-DOS. IBM PC & compatibles (512k). $65.00 first year, $45.00 annual renewal, $65.00 laser (Order no.: NY203). *Addl. software required:* Lotus 1-2-3 2.01, 2.2 or 2.3, TaxTime 1040. *Optimal configuration:* 640k RAM & hard disk. *Networks supported:* 3Com, Novell. *Features IRS (or State) Approved Template for Lotus 1-2-3 Versions 2.01, 2.2 or 2.3 That Calculates & Updates Tax Forms. Forms Include:* IT-203, IT-203-ATT, IT-203 A, NYC-203.
Austin Scientific, Inc.

TaxTime for 1-2-3: North Carolina D-400. *Version:* 92.01. Feb. 1992. *Compatible Hardware:* IBM PC & compatibles. *Operating System(s) Required:* PC-DOS/MS-DOS. *Memory Required:* 512k. *General Requirements:* Lotus 1-2-3 versions 2.01, 2.2 or 2.3, TaxTime 1040. *Items Included:* Manual, disk. *Customer Support:* 30 day money back guarantee less $10.00 restock fee. Tech support available on regular phone line.
PC-DOS/MS-DOS/DR-DOS. 3.5" or 5.25" disk $80.00.
renewal $50.00.
laser $80.00.
Features IRS Approved Template for Lotus 1-2-3 Versions 2.01, 2.2 or 2.3 That Calculates & Updates Tax Forms. Forms Include D400, D422, NC40, Sch A.
Austin Scientific, Inc.

TaxTime for 1-2-3: Ohio 1040. *Version:* 92.01. Feb. 1992. *Compatible Hardware:* IBM PC & compatibles. *Operating System(s) Required:* PC-DOS/MS-DOS. *Memory Required:* 512k. *General Requirements:* Lotus 1-2-3 versions 2.01, 2.2 or 2.3, TaxTime 1040. *Items Included:* Manual, disk(s). *Customer Support:* 30 day money back guarantee less $10.00 restock fee. Tech support available on regular phone line.
PC-DOS/MS-DOS/DR-DOS. 3.5" or 5.25" disk $50.00.
renewal $40.00.
laser $50.00.
Features IRS Approved Template for Lotus 1-2-3 Versions 2.01, 2.2 or 2.3 That Calculates & Updates Tax Forms. Forms Include IT 1040 IT 1040ES.
Austin Scientific, Inc.

TaxTime for 1-2-3: Oklahoma 511. *Version:* 92.01. Feb. 1992. *Compatible Hardware:* IBM PC & compatibles. *Operating System(s) Required:* PC-DOS/MS-DOS. *Memory Required:* 512k. *General Requirements:* Lotus 1-2-3 Versions 2.01. 2.2 or 2.3, TaxTime 1040. *Items Included:* Manual, disk. *Customer Support:* 30 day money back guarantee less $10.00 restock fee. Tech support available on regular phone line.
PC-DOS/MS-DOS/DR-DOS. 3.5" or 5.25" disk $65.00.
renewal $45.00.
laser $65.00.
Features IRS Approved Template for Lotus 1-2-3 Versions 2.01, 2.2 or 2.3 That Calculates & Updates Tax Forms. Forms Include 511, 538H, OW8ES, OW8PR, Sch D, Sch E, 508.
Austin Scientific, Inc.

TaxTime for 1-2-3: Pennsylvania 40. *Version:* 92.01. Feb. 1992. *Compatible Hardware:* IBM PC & compatibles. *Operating System(s) Required:* PC-DOS/MS-DOS. *Memory Required:* 512k. *General Requirements:* Lotus 1-2-3 versions 2.01, 2.2 or 2.3, TaxTime 1040. *Items Included:* Manual, disk(s). *Customer Support:* 30 day money back guarantee less $10.00 restock fee. Tech support available on regular phone line.
PC-DOS/MS-DOS/DR-DOS. 3.5" or 5.25" disk $80.00.
renewal $50.00.
laser $80.00.
Features IRS Approved Template for Lotus 1-2-3 Versions 2.01, 2.2 or 2.3 That Calculates & Updates Tax Forms. Forms Include 40, 40 ESR, Sch ABDG, Sch C, Sch D1, Sch EJ, Sch UE1, Sch UE2SP.
Austin Scientific, Inc.

TaxTime for 1-2-3: Utah 40. *Version:* 92.01. Feb. 1992. *Compatible Hardware:* IBM PC & compatibles. *Operating System(s) Required:* PC-DOS/MS-DOS. *Memory Required:* 512k. *General Requirements:* Lotus 1-2-3 versions 2.01, 2.2 or 2.3, TaxTime 1040. *Items Included:* Manual, disk. *Customer Support:* 30 day money back guarantee less $10.00 restock fee. Tech support available on regular phone line.
PC-DOS/MS-DOS/DR-DOS. 3.5" or 5.25" disk $50.00.
renewal $40.00.
laser $50.00.
Features IRS Approved Template for Lotus 1-2-3 Versions 2.01, 2.2 or 2.3 That Calculates & Updates Tax Forms. Forms Include TC40, TC636.
Austin Scientific, Inc.

TAXTIME FOR 1-2-3: 1041 FIDUCIARY

TaxTime for 1-2-3: Virginia 760. *Version:* 92.01. Feb. 1992. *Compatible Hardware:* IBM PC & compatibles. *Operating System(s) Required:* PC-DOS/MS-DOS. *Memory Required:* 512k. *General Requirements:* Lotus 1-2-3 versions 2.01. 2.2 or 2.3, TaxTime 1040. *Items Included:* Manual, disk. *Customer Support:* 30 day money back guarantee less $10.00 restock fee. Tech support available on regular phone line.
PC-DOS/MS-DOS/DR-DOS. 3.5" or 5.25" disk $65.00.
renewal $45.00.
laser $65.00.
Features IRS Approved Template for Lotus 1-2-3 Versions 2.01, 2.2 or 2.3 That Calculates & Updates Tax Forms. Forms Include 760, 760C, 760ES, 760F, 302, VAR.
Austin Scientific, Inc.

TaxTime for 1-2-3: 1040 Individual. *Version:* 92.01. Jan. 1992. *Compatible Hardware:* IBM PC & compatibles. *Operating System(s) Required:* MS-DOS, PC-DOS. *Memory Required:* 512k. *General Requirements:* Lotus 1-2-3 versions 2.01, 2.2 or 2.3. *Items Included:* Basic Guide, manual, disk. *Customer Support:* 30 day money back guarantee less $10.00 restock fee. Tech support available on regular phone lines.
PC-DOS/MS-DOS/DR-DOS. 3.5" or 5.25" disk $95.00 (ISBN 0-928399-14-1, Order no.: 1040).
$145.00 laser.
Annual updates $55.00.
IRS Approved Template for Lotus 1-2-3 Versions 2.01, 2.2 or 2.3 That Calculates & Updates Tax Forms. Forms Include 1040, 1040-ES, E1C, A, B, C, D, D-1, E, F, R, SE, 2106, 2210, 2441, 3800, 3903, 4562, 4797, 4952, 5884, 6251, 8582, 8615, 8801, 8829, Plus IRS Worksheets & Supporting Statements.
Austin Scientific, Inc.

Taxtime for 1-2-3: 1040 Master. *Version:* 92.01. Jan. 1992. *Compatible Hardware:* IBM PC & compatibles. *Operating System(s) Required:* PC-DOS/MS-DOS. *Memory Required:* 512k. *General Requirements:* Lotus 1-2-3 version 2.01, 2.2 or 2.3. *Items Included:* Basic Guide, manual, disk. *Customer Support:* 30 day money back guarantee less $10.00 restock fee. Tech support available on regular phone line.
PC-DOS/MS-DOS/DR-DOS. 3.5" or 5.25" disk $195.00.
renewal $95.00.
$295.00 laser.
Features IRS Approved Template for Lotus 1-2-3 Version 2.01, 2.2 or 2.3 That Calculates & Updates Tax Forms. Forms Include 1040X, 1116, 2119, 2120, 2688, 4136, 4137, 4255, 4684, 4835, 4868, 4972, 5329, 6198, 6252, 8271, 8283, 8332, 8606, 8814, 8829 & All Forms in the TaxTime 1040 Individual.
Austin Scientific, Inc.

TaxTime for 1-2-3: 1041 Fiduciary. *Version:* 92.01. Jan. 1992. *Compatible Hardware:* IBM PC & compatibles. *Operating System(s) Required:* MS-DOS, PC-DOS. *Memory Required:* 512k. *General Requirements:* Lotus 1-2-3 versions 2.01, 2.2 or 2.3. *Items Included:* Basic guide, manual, disk. *Customer Support:* 30 day money back guarantee, less $10.00 fee, technical support available on regular telephone lines.
PC-DOS/MS-DOS/DR-DOS. 3.5" or 5.25" disk $195.00 (Order no.: 1041).
annual updates $95.00.
$145.00 laser.
IRS Approved Template for Lotus 1-2-3 Version 2.01, 2.2 or 2.3 That Calculates & Updates Tax Forms. Forms Include 1041, C, F, D, K-1, E, J, 2210, 2758, 3800, 4255, 4562, 4797, 8271, 8582, 8656, 8736.
Austin Scientific, Inc.

TaxTime for 1-2-3: 1065 Partnership. *Version:* 92.01. Jan. 1991. *Compatible Hardware:* IBM PC & compatibles. *Operating System(s) Required:* PC-DOS, MS-DOS. *Memory Required:* 512k. *General Requirements:* Lotus 1-2-3 version 2.01 or higher. *Items Included:* Basic guide, manual, disk. *Customer Support:* 30 day money back guarantee less $10.00 restock fee. Tech support available on regular phone line.
PC-DOS/MS-DOS/DR-DOS. 3.5" or 5.25" $195.00 (Order no.: 1065).
annual updates $95.00.
$145.00 laser.
IRS Approved Template for Lotus 1-2-3 Version 2.01, 2.2 or 2.3 That Calculates & Updates Tax Forms. Forms Include 1065, F, D, K-1, 4255, 4562, 4797, 5884, 6252, 8271, 8736, 8825.
Austin Scientific, Inc.

TaxTime for 1-2-3: 1120 Corp. *Version:* 92.01. Jan. 1992. *Compatible Hardware:* IBM PC & compatibles. *Operating System(s) Required:* MS-DOS, PC-DOS. *Memory Required:* 512k. *General Requirements:* Lotus 1-2-3 versions 2.01, 2.2 or 2.3. *Items Included:* Basic guide, manual, disk. *Customer Support:* 30 day money back guarantee less $10.00 restock fee. Tech support available on regular phone line.
PC-DOS/MS-DOS/DR-DOS. 3.5" or 5.25" disk $195.00.
annual updates $95.00.
$145.00 laser.
IRS Approved Template for Lotus 1-2-3 Version 2.01, 2.2 or 2.3 That Calculates & Updates Tax Forms. Forms Include 1120, D, PH, W, X, 2220, 3800, 4255, 4562, 4626, 4684, 4797, 5884, 7004, 8801, 8827.
Austin Scientific, Inc.

TaxTime for 1-2-3: 1120 Sub-S Corp. *Version:* 92.01. Jan. 1992. *Compatible Hardware:* IBM PC & compatibles. *Operating System(s) Required:* MS-DOS, PC-DOS. *Memory Required:* 512k. *General Requirements:* Lotus 1-2-3 versions 2.01, 2.2 or 2.3. *Items Included:* Basic guide, manual, disk. *Customer Support:* 30 day money back guarantee less $10.00 restock fee. Tech support available on regular phone line.
PC-DOS/MS-DOS/DR-DOS. 3.5" or 5.25" disk $195.00 (Order no.: 1120S).
annual updates $95.00.
$145.00 laser.
IRS Approved Template for Lotus 1-2-3 Version 2.01, 2.2 or 2.3 That Calculates & Updates Tax Forms. Forms Include 1120S, D, K-1, 4255, 4562, 4797, 5884, 7004, 8271, 8825.
Austin Scientific, Inc.

TaxTime for 1-2-3: 706 Estate. *Version:* 91.01. Jul. 1992. *Compatible Hardware:* IBM PC & compatibles. *Operating System(s) Required:* MS-DOS, PC-DOS. *Memory Required:* 512k. *General Requirements:* Lotus 1-2-3 versions 2.01, 2.2 or 2.3. *Items Included:* Basic guide, manual, disk. *Customer Support:* 30 day money back guarantee less $10.00 restock fee. Tech support available on regular phone line.
PC-DOS/MS-DOS/DR-DOS. 3.5" or 5.25" disk $195.00 (Order no.: 706).
laser $195.00.
$95.00 renewal as needed.
IRS Approved Template for Lotus 1-2-3 Versions 2.01, 2.2 or 2.3 That Calculates & Updates Tax Forms. The Main Pages 1-28 Are Included.
Austin Scientific, Inc.

TB*Plus (Time & Billing). *Version:* 2.0. Mar. 1989. *Compatible Hardware:* IBM PC & compatibles. *Operating System(s) Required:* PC-DOS/MS-DOS 3.1 or higher. *Memory Required:* 640k. *Items Included:* Documentation manual; Quick Start Users Guide. *Customer Support:* 6 months toll free telephone support & updates; 90 day unlimited warranty; annual maintenance (support & updates) $200-$400.
$995.00-$1995.00.
Includes: Flexible Statement Formatting, WIP & A/R by Partner, up to 10 Billing Rates per Employee & Integrated Word Processor, Open Item & Balance Forward A/R.
UniLink.

TBLAYOUT. *Compatible Hardware:* IBM PC & compatibles. *Operating System(s) Required:* MS-DOS. *Language(s):* BASIC. *Memory Required:* 128k.
$165.00.
Determines Maximum Number of Tubes for a Given Shell Diameter. Handles Triangular, Square, or Rotated Square Pitch. Outputs Number of Tubes per Row, Total Tubes, & Outer Tube Perimeter.
Technical Research Services, Inc.

TBS Accounting Software, 6 modules. Jul. 1979. *Operating System(s) Required:* PC-DOS, MS-DOS. *Language(s):* Pascal. *Memory Required:* 128k.
disk $595.00.
Full Set of Accounting Software for Small to Medium Large Businesses. The Systems Stand-Alone or Can Work Together & Are Fully Integrated. Provides Almost All General Accounting Needs, Including Many Report Functions. They Are All Fully Menu Driven with Extensive Documentation.
Theta Business Systems.

TBS Five Integrated Accounting Systems, 5 modules. *Version:* 1.5. 1984. *Compatible Hardware:* IBM PC, PC XT, PC AT, & compatibles. *Operating System(s) Required:* MS-DOS, PC-DOS. *Language(s):* Pascal. *Memory Required:* 128k. *General Requirements:* 2 disk drives, printer.
disk $595.00.
Theta Business Systems.
  Accounts Payable.
    Features Vendor File Maintenance Including Alphabetical Vendor List, Accounts File Maintenance, On-Screen Entry of New Payables, Automatic Voucher Number Assignment & Batch Control Totals. Prints Accounts Payable Voucher Register, Cash Requirements Reports, Check Verification Report Prior to Check Printing, Check with Invoice Detail on Stubs, Check Register Showing All Checks, Accounts Payable Distribution Report in Detailed or Summarized Form, Accounts Payable Job Distribution Report & Cash Disbursements Report. Interfaces with the General Ledger Module.
  Accounts Receivable.
    Features On-Line Entry of Sales, Credit Memos & Manual Finance Charges with Batch Totals for Control of Transaction Flow. On-Line Entry of Cash Receipts Allows Partial Payments & Payments to More Than One Invoice. Accounts Receivable Open File Contains Transaction Details. Statements Can Be Selectively Printed with Aged Totals & Tear-Off Remittance. Prints Accounts Receivable History, & Sales & Cash Receipts. Automatically Interfaces to General Ledger Module.
  General Ledger.
    Prints Balance Sheets, Profit & Loss Statements, Supporting Schedules & Source & Application of Funds Reports, & Detailed or Summarized General Ledger Lists That Are Selected by Account Number or Date. Allows CRT Inquiry into accounts by Period. Automatically Interfaces to Accounts Receivable, Payroll & Accounts Payable Modules.
  Payroll.
    Maintains Employer Master File Containing Payroll & Personal Data. Automatically Calculates Gross & Net Pay for Hourly & Salaried Employees. Calculates FWT, SWT, FICA, FUI, City Tax & SUI. Reconciles Outstanding Checks. Prints the Following Forms & Reports: Paychecks with Payroll Register Detailing Payroll Calculations, Check Register, Labor Distribution Report, General Ledger Account Distribution Report, 941-A, State Tax Register, W-2 Forms, Payroll History Report & Hour History Report. Automatically Interfaces to General Ledger Module.

TBSHEET: TEMA. *Compatible Hardware:* IBM PC & compatibles. *Operating System(s) Required:* MS-DOS. *Language(s):* BASIC. *Memory Required:* 128k.
$350.00.
Calculates Required Thickness per TEMA. Handles Fixed, U-Tube & Floating Tube Sheets. Has Built-In Material Chart with Properties for Most Common Materials.
Technical Research Services, Inc.

TC-1 Time & Attendance. *Version:* 3.2. *Operating System(s) Required:* PC-DOS/MS-DOS. *Memory Required:* 580k. *General Requirements:* Hard disk.
IBM & compatibles. disk $800.00-$8000.00 depending on options (ISBN 0-87435-304-1).
Based on Management-by-Objective, This System Encourages Thorough Planning Which Establishes Objectives & Goals. Provides Management Reports & Documentation of the Activities of Sales Staff. Provides Salesman with Daily Planning Tools, Long Range Forecasting by Probability, Potential Problem Areas & Day-to-Day Administration Which Provides Updates, Communication, Documentation & Prioritizes Calls Efficiently.
Datamatics Management.

TC-1. *Version:* 3.2. Datamatics. Feb. 1986. *Compatible Hardware:* IBM PC & compatibles, PC XT. *Operating System(s) Required:* MS-DOS 3.1 or higher. *Memory Required:* 640k. *Items Included:* Various options. *Customer Support:* Available.
disk $495.00 plus options (Order no.: 370).
Proven to Save Payroll Costs & Administrative Time, Obsoleting Time Cards & Sign-In Sheets, & Offering More Efficiencies & Greater Flexibility Than Costly Electronic Time Systems. Correctly Applies User Definable Policies, Prepares Payroll Data, Simplifies Labor Cost Tracking & Makes Information about Attendance & Performance Available When Needed. It Records Entry & Exit from Work Using Keyboard, Bar-Code, Mag-Strip or & Other Devices. It Enforces Flex Time & Does Scheduling So the User Optimizes & Controls Labor Costs. Menu-Driven, Easy to Install, Learn & Use Regularly Regardless of Computer Experience. Expert System, Anticipating Common Errors Testing Parameter Ranges & Altering the Operator to Unusual Conditions.
Resource Software International, Inc.

TC-1 Time Clock. *Compatible Hardware:* IBM PC & compatibles. *Memory Required:* 512k. *General Requirements:* Hard disk, printer.
contact publisher for price.
Provides Payroll Preparation Forms, Time & Attendance Reports & a Database for Actual Applied Labor Time for Each Employee by Department, Task, Job or Machine. Electronic Time Sheets on Network.
Datamatics Management.

TITLE INDEX

Tcl/Tk. *Customer Support:* All of our products are unconditionally guaranteed.
Unix. CD-ROM disk $39.95 (Order no.: TCL). *Nonstandard peripherals required:* CD-ROM drive.
Tcl/Tk, X11 Programming Language Archive from Sprite.Berkeley.Edu.
Walnut Creek CDRom.

TCP - IP & the Internet: An Overview. Jul. 1995. *Items Included:* User manual. *Customer Support:* Free technical support & a 30-day money back guarantee.
MS-DOS. IBM & compatibles (640k). 3.5" disk $295.00 (ISBN 1-57305-021-0). *Nonstandard peripherals required:* High-density 3.5" disk drive; VGA color monitor. *Addl. software required:* MS-DOS version 3.3 or higher. *Optimal configuration:* IBM (640k), MS-DOS version 3.3 or higher, VGA color monitor, keyboard, Microsoft compatible mouse.
This Is a 2-Hour Computer-Based Training Program Introducing You to Accessing & Transferring Data on the Internet, Together with the Terminology & Technology Associated with the Internet.
Bellcore.

TCP/IP for DOS. *Items Included:* 3 spiral-bound manuals. *Customer Support:* Unlimited technical support.
DOS. IBM PC, XT, PS/2 & compatibles (256k). disk $295.00 (Order no.: DS-110). *Addl. software required:* PC-DOS/MS-DOS, Ver. 3.1 or higher. *Networks supported:* Ethernet.
Allows DOS-BASED PCs on the Network to Communicate with a Wide Range of Host Computers Through Standard IP Protocols. The Software Supports NDIS, ODI & Pocket Interface. TCP/IP Can Also Run Simultaneously with Network Operating Systems Such As NetWare & IBM LAN Support Program.
D-Link Systems, Inc.

TCS Integrated Accounting Package.
Compatible Hardware: IBM PC. *Operating System(s) Required:* CP/M 2.2, TRSDOS. *Language(s):* MBASIC. *Memory Required:* 48-128k.
8" disk $169.00 ea.
4 Modules: Accounts Receivable, Accounts Payable, General Ledger & Payroll.
Micro Architect, Inc.

TCS Q-Word. TCS Software, Inc. *Compatible Hardware:* TI Professional. *Operating System(s) Required:* MS-DOS. *Memory Required:* 64k. *General Requirements:* Printer.
contact publisher for price.
Texas Instruments, Personal Productivit.

Teach Your Kids Multimedia World History.
Windows. IBM & compatibles. CD-ROM disk $89.95 (Order no.: R1362). *Nonstandard peripherals required:* CD-ROM drive. *Optimal configuration:* 386 processor or higher, MS-DOS 3.1 or higher, 20Mb hard drive, 640k RAM, external speakers or headphones (with sound card) that are Sound Blaster compatible, VGA graphics & adapter, VGA color monitor.
Turn Your Computer into a Time Machine, Meet Heroes & Heroines from Every Age & Culture. Narrations, Audio-Enriched Animations, Maps, Photographs, Moving Pictures & over 120 Interactive Skits & Activities Allow Children to Learn World History.
Library Video Co.

Teach Yourself BASIC. *Compatible Hardware:* TI 99/4A with PLATO interpreter solid state cartridge.
contact publisher for price.
Teaches BASIC Programming with On-Screen Lessons.
Texas Instruments, Personal Productivit.

Teach Yourself BPI General Accounting.
(Training Power Ser.). *Compatible Hardware:* IBM & compatibles. *Operating System(s) Required:* CP/M, PC-DOS/MS-DOS 2.0 or higher. *Language(s):* CBASIC. *Memory Required:* 64k.
disk $75.00 (ISBN 0-922274-11-8, Order no.: I-30).
Split-Screen Interactive Simulation Tutorial Teaches How to Use BPI General Accounting Software.
American Training International, Inc.

Teach Yourself CP/M. (Skill Builder Ser.). *Compatible Hardware:* Apple II, IBM PC, PC-8000, DEC Rainbow 100. *Operating System(s) Required:* MS-DOS, CP/M-86, CP/M, PC-DOS, DOS 3.2. *Language(s):* CBASIC. *Memory Required:* 128k.
disk $49.95.
Teaches User the CP/M Operating System While Practicing Real CP/M Commands.
American Training International, Inc.

Teach Yourself dBASE III PLUS. *Version:* III. (Training Power Ser.). 1986. *Compatible Hardware:* IBM PC or compatibles. *Operating System(s) Required:* MS-DOS. *Memory Required:* 256k.
disk $75.00, incl. user's hdbk. (Order no.: TP03714).
Guide Users Step-by-Step in Creating & Modifying Reports Using Data from Multiple Databases. Edit Files & Create Customized Screens.
American Training International, Inc.

Teach Yourself dBASE IV, Vol. 1 & 2. *Version:* IV. (Training Power Ser.). *Compatible Hardware:* IBM PC & compatibles. *Operating System(s) Required:* MS-DOS, PC-DOS/MS-DOS 2.0 or higher, CP/M-86. *Memory Required:* 256k.
disk $75.00.
Teaches User Fundamental DBASE IV Commands. Contains Both Novice & Advanced Version.
American Training International, Inc.

Teach Yourself DisplayWrite 3. *Version:* 3.0. (Training Power Ser.). *Compatible Hardware:* IBM PC & compatibles. *Operating System(s) Required:* PC-DOS/MS-DOS 2.0 or higher. *Memory Required:* 256k.
disk $75.00, incl. user's hdbk. (ISBN 0-922274-47-9, Order no.: TP035).
Guides User Step-by-Step, So That with Each Command the Computer Responds Just As DISPLAYWRITE 3 Would. The Top Half of the Screen Simulates the Actual Program While the Bottom Half Contains the Explanation & Keying Instructions.
American Training International, Inc.

Teach Yourself DisplayWrite 4. *Version:* 4.0. (Training Power Ser.). *Compatible Hardware:* IBM PC & compatibles. *Operating System(s) Required:* PC-DOS/MS-DOS 2.0 or higher. *Memory Required:* 256k.
disk $75.00, incl. user's handbook.
Guides the User Step-by-Step, So That with Each Command, the Computer Responds Just As DISPLAYWRITE 4 Would. The Top Half of the Screen Simulates the Actual Program While the Bootom Half Displays the Explanations & Keying Instructions.
American Training International, Inc.

Teach Yourself DOS. *Version:* 3.2. *Compatible Hardware:* Convergent Technologies; DEC; IBM PC & compatibles; Texas Instruments. *Operating System(s) Required:* PC-DOS/MS-DOS 2.0 or higher. *Memory Required:* 256k.
disk $49.95.
disk "Quickref" program $59.95.
Introduces Users to the Operating System of the Computer.
American Training International, Inc.

TEACH YOURSELF LOTUS 1-2-3

Teach Yourself Enable. 1986. *Compatible Hardware:* IBM PC & compatibles. *Operating System(s) Required:* PC-DOS/MS-DOS 2.0 or higher. *Memory Required:* 256k.
3.5" or 5.25" disk $75.00 (Order no.: C-85).
Takes the User Step-by-Step Through the Program, On-Screen & Hands-On, Eliminating the Need to Study Manuals.
American Training International, Inc.

Teach Yourself Essentials of Accounting, 4 disks. Robert N. Anthony. Dec. 1983. *Compatible Hardware:* Apple II, II+, IIe; IBM PC, PC XT. *Memory Required:* 48k.
Apple Set. $129.95, incl. documentation (ISBN 0-201-15361-0).
IBM Set. $129.95, incl. documentation (ISBN 0-201-15328-9).
Interactive Self-Study Program. Course Requires 20 Hours to Complete. As User Works Through Plotted Exercises on the Screen the Program Demonstrates the Basic Concepts of Balance Sheets, Accounting Records & Systems, Revenues & Monetary Assets, Income Statements & Financial Statement Analysis.
Addison-Wesley Publishing Co., Inc.

Teach Yourself Excel. (Training Power Ser.). *Compatible Hardware:* Apple Macintosh Plus, 512. *Memory Required:* 128k.
disk $75.00 (ISBN 0-922274-49-5, Order no.: TPO06810).
Interactive Training Disk Which Instructs by Simulating the Actual Software. The User Is Guided Step-by-Step So That with Each Command, the Computer Responds Just As EXCEL Would. With the Split-Screen Approach, the Top Half Simulates the Actual Program While the Bottom Half Contains the Explanation & Keying Instructions.
American Training International, Inc.

Teach Yourself Extended BASIC. *Compatible Hardware:* TI 99/4A with extended BASIC cartridge.
contact publisher for price.
Tutorial Program Teaches Extended BASIC.
Texas Instruments, Personal Productivit.

Teach Yourself Framework, Vol. 1 & 2. (Training Power Ser.). *Compatible Hardware:* IBM PC & compatibles. *Operating System(s) Required:* PC-DOS/MS-DOS 2.0 or higher. *Memory Required:* 256k.
disk $75.00 (ISBN 0-922274-03-7, Order no.: C-50).
Split-Screen Interactive Simulation Tutorial. Contains Both Novice & Advanced Versions to Learn How to Use Framework Software.
American Training International, Inc.

Teach Yourself Jazz. (Training Power Ser.). *Compatible Hardware:* Apple Macintosh Plus, 512. *Operating System(s) Required:* Apple DOS. *Memory Required:* 64k.
disk $75.00, incl. user's hdbk. (ISBN 0-922274-46-0, Order no.: TP075).
Guides User Step-by-Step So That with Each Command the Computer Responds Just As JAZZ Would. The Top Half of the Screen Simulates the Actual Program While the Bottom Half Contains the Explanation & Keying Instructions.
American Training International, Inc.

Teach Yourself Lotus 1-2-3. *Version:* 2.0. (Training Power Ser.). *Compatible Hardware:* IBM PC & compatibles. *Operating System(s) Required:* PC-DOS/MS-DOS 2.0 or higher. *Memory Required:* 256k.
disk $75.00 (ISBN 0-922274-04-5, Order no.: C-10).
Guide Users Step-by-Step on How to Use the Spreadsheet Software.
American Training International, Inc.

TEACH YOURSELF MICROSOFT WORD

Teach Yourself Microsoft Word, Vol. 1.
Version: 5.0. (Training Power Ser.). *Compatible Hardware:* IBM PC & compatibles. *Operating System(s) Required:* PC-DOS/MS-DOS 2.0 or higher. *Memory Required:* 256k.
disk $75.00 (ISBN 0-922274-05-3, Order no.: E-50).
Split-Screen Interactive Simulation Tutorial, Teaches Individual How to Use Microsoft WORD Software. Contains Both Novice & Advanced Versions.
American Training International, Inc.

Teach Yourself MultiMate, Vol. 1 & 2.
(Training Power Ser.). *Compatible Hardware:* IBM PC & compatibles. *Operating System(s) Required:* PC-DOS/MS-DOS 2.0 or higher. *Memory Required:* 256k.
disk $75.00 (ISBN 0-922274-06-1, Order no.: E-20).
Split-Screen Interactive Simulation Tutorial, Teaches Individual How to Use MultiMate Word Processing Software. Contains Both Novice & Advanced Versions.
American Training International, Inc.

Teach Yourself Multiplan, Vol. 1 & 2. (Training Power Ser.). *Compatible Hardware:* IBM PC & compatibles. *Operating System(s) Required:* CP/M-80, CP/M-86, MS-DOS. *Memory Required:* 128k.
disk $75.00 (ISBN 0-922274-07-X, Order no.: F-10).
Simulates Multiplan & Guides User Through the Creation of a Customized Electronic Analysis Worksheets. User Can Correct Any Errors Made in the Entry. After User Designs a Spreadsheet Analysis, He or She Learns How to Link Worksheets, to Edit & Format the Information, & to Sort It According to Alphabetical or Numerical Order. Includes 5 Sample Worksheets, Simulates the Software It Teaches, Demonstrates Actual User Situations, Teaches Functions of Spreadsheet in Simplified Form in ATI's Advanced Educational Programs.
American Training International, Inc.

Teach Yourself 1-2-3 Macros. *Compatible Hardware:* IBM PC & compatibles. *Operating System(s) Required:* PC-DOS/MS-DOS 2.0 or higher.
disk $99.95.
Split-Screen, Interactive Tutorial Which Guides Users Step-by-Step Through 1-2-3 Commands. Shows Users How to: Set up a Menu (/XM), Go to a Subroutine (/XC), Return to a Subroutine (/XR), Enter Text (/XL), Enter Numbers (/XN), Go to Another Command (/XG), Loop Conditional Commands (/XI), Stop a Macro (/XQ), & Create Macro Applications. Average Training Time Is Two to Four Hours.
American Training International, Inc.

Teach Yourself Oracle for 1-2-3. 1988. *Compatible Hardware:* IBM PC & compatibles. *Operating System(s) Required:* PC-DOS/MS-DOS 2.0 or higher. *Memory Required:* 256k.
3.5" or 5.25" disk $75.00 (Order no.: C-35).
Takes First-Time ORACLE FOR 1-2-3 Users Step-by-Step Through This Database Program. Users Learn How to Create & Modify Reports Using Data from Oracle Tables, Edit Tables & Create Customized Applications.
American Training International, Inc.

Teach Yourself OS/2. *Compatible Hardware:* IBM PS/2. *Memory Required:* 256k.
3.5" or 5.25" disk $75.00.
Leads Users Step-by-Step Through the Features of This Operating System. Users Learn How to Examine the Contents of Directories, Copy Files, & Format Disks.
American Training International, Inc.

Teach Yourself Paradox, 2 disks. (Training Power Ser.). *Compatible Hardware:* IBM PC, PC XT, PC AT & compatibles. *Operating System(s) Required:* PC-DOS/MS-DOS 2.0 or higher. *Language(s):* C. *Memory Required:* 256k. $75.00.
Split-Screen Graphics Provide Users with a Simulation of PARADOX Screens As Well As Step-by-Step Instructions. Forward & Backward Paging, Place Marking, Menu Access, Branching, Activity Review, Content Summaries, & Skill-Building Exercises Facilitate Self-Directed Learning.
American Training International, Inc.

Teach Yourself PeachCalc. (Training Power Ser.). *Compatible Hardware:* IBM PC & compatibles. *Operating System(s) Required:* PC-DOS/MS-DOS 2.0 or higher. *Memory Required:* 256k.
disk $75.00 (ISBN 0-922274-16-9, Order no.: F-50).
Split-Screen Interactive Simulation Tutorial.
American Training International, Inc.

Teach Yourself Peachtext. (Training Power Ser.). *Compatible Hardware:* IBM PC & compatibles. *Operating System(s) Required:* PC-DOS/MS-DOS 2.0 or higher. *Memory Required:* 256k.
disk $75.00 (ISBN 0-922274-17-7, Order no.: E-60).
Split-Screen Interactive Simulation Tutorial.
American Training International, Inc.

Teach Yourself R:BASE for DOS. *Compatible Hardware:* IBM PC & compatibles. *Operating System(s) Required:* PC-DOS/MS-DOS 2.0 or higher. *Memory Required:* 256k.
3.5" or 5.25" disk $75.00 (Order no.: D-65).
Takes First-Time Users Step-by-Step Through This Database Program. Users Learn How to Create & Modify Reports Using Data from Multiple Tables, Edit Files & Create Customized Menus.
American Training International, Inc.

Teach Yourself R:BASE 5000. (Training Power Ser.). 1986. *Compatible Hardware:* IBM PC or compatibles. *Operating System(s) Required:* PC-DOS/MS-DOS 2.0 or higher. *Memory Required:* 256k.
disk $75.00, incl. user's handbook (ISBN 0-922274-51-7, Order no.: TP18614).
Interactive Training Disk Which Instructs Users by Simulating the Actual Software. The User Is Guided Step-by-Step So That with Each Command, the Computer Responds Just As R:BASE 5000 Would. With Its Split-Screen Approach, the Top Half Contains the Explanation & Keying Instructions.
American Training International, Inc.

Teach Yourself SuperCalc. *Compatible Hardware:* IBM PC & compatibles. *Operating System(s) Required:* CP/M, PC-DOS/MS-DOS 2.0 or higher. *Memory Required:* 256k.
disk $75.00.
Shows SUPERCALC Layout & Leads User Through the Creation of an Individualized Electronic Analysis Worksheet. Lets User Correct Any Errors Made in Entry Without Interrupting the Process. User Learns to Set up a Worksheet from Scratch, Enter Headings, Numbers & Formulas, Edit & Format Worksheet & Sort Information in Alphabetic or Numeric Order. Simulates the Software It Teaches, Demonstrates Actual User Situations, & Teaches Functions of Spreadsheets in Simplified Form.
American Training International, Inc.

Teach Yourself SuperCalc 3, Vol. 1 & 2.
(Training Power Ser.). *Compatible Hardware:* IBM PC & compatibles. *Operating System(s) Required:* PC-DOS/MS-DOS 2.0 or higher. *Memory Required:* 256k.
disk $75.00 (ISBN 0-922274-08-8, Order no.: C-20).
Split-Screen Interactive Simulation Tutorial, Teaches Individual How to Use SuperCalc 3 Software. Contains Both Novice & Advanced Versions.
American Training International, Inc.

Teach Yourself SuperCalc 4. *Compatible Hardware:* IBM PC & compatibles. *Operating System(s) Required:* PC-DOS/MS-DOS 2.0 or higher. *Memory Required:* 256k.
disk $75.00.
Leads Users Step-by-Step on the Use of Spreadsheet Software.
American Training International, Inc.

Teach Yourself Symphony, Vol. 1 & 2.
(Training Power Ser.). *Compatible Hardware:* IBM PC & compatibles. *Operating System(s) Required:* PC-DOS/MS-DOS 2.0 or higher. *Memory Required:* 256k.
disk $75.00 (ISBN 0-922274-09-6, Order no.: C-30).
Split-Screen Interactive Simulation Tutorial for SYMPHONY Software. Contains Both Novice & Advanced Versions.
American Training International, Inc.

Teach Yourself the Home Accountant. (Skill Builder Ser.). *Compatible Hardware:* IBM PC & compatibles. *Operating System(s) Required:* PC-DOS/MS-DOS 2.0 or higher. *Memory Required:* 256k.
disk $49.95 (ISBN 0-922274-40-1, Order no.: I-90).
Tutorial Simulation for the Home Accountant.
American Training International, Inc.

Teach Yourself TK! Solver. (Training Power Ser.). *Compatible Hardware:* IBM PC & compatibles. *Operating System(s) Required:* PC-DOS/MS-DOS 2.0 or higher. *Memory Required:* 256k.
disk $75.00 (ISBN 0-922274-25-8, Order no.: F-84).
Split-Screen Interactive Simulation Tutorial for TK! SOLVER.
American Training International, Inc.

Teach Yourself VisiCalc. *Compatible Hardware:* IBM PC & compatibles. *Operating System(s) Required:* PC-DOS/MS-DOS 2.0 or higher. *Memory Required:* 256k.
disk $49.95 (ISBN 0-922274-42-8, Order no.: F-20).
Split-Screen Simulation Tutorial.
American Training International, Inc.

Teach Yourself VolksWriter Deluxe. (Skill Builder Ser.). *Compatible Hardware:* IBM & compatibles. *Operating System(s) Required:* PC-DOS/MS-DOS 2.0 or higher. *Memory Required:* 256k.
disk $49.95 (ISBN 0-922274-43-6, Order no.: E-85).
Split-Screen Approach. Top Half Simulates Actual Software, Bottom Half Contains the Explanation & Keying Instructions.
American Training International, Inc.

Teach Yourself WordPerfect. Version: 5.0. (Training Power Ser.). 1988. *Compatible Hardware:* IBM PC & compatibles. *Operating System(s) Required:* PC-DOS/MS-DOS 2.0 or higher. *Memory Required:* 256k.
disk $75.00 (ISBN 0-922274-50-9, Order no.: TP03814).
Interactive Training Disk Which Instructs by Simulating the Actual Software. The User Is Guided Step-by-Step So That with Each

TITLE INDEX

TEAMEC

Command, the Computer Responds Just As WORDPERFECT Would. With the Split-Screen Approach, the Top Half Simulates the Actual Program, While the Bottom Half Contains the Explanation & Keying Instructions.
American Training International, Inc.

Teach Yourself WordStar, Vol. 1 & 2. *Version:* 2000. (Training Power Ser.). *Compatible Hardware:* IBM PC & compatibles. *Operating System(s) Required:* PC-DOS/MS-DOS 2.0 or higher. *Memory Required:* 256k.
disk $75.00 (ISBN 0-922274-10-X, Order no.: E-10).
Split-Screen Interactive Simulation Tutorial for WORDSTAR Word Processing Software. Contains Both Novice & Advanced Versions.
American Training International, Inc.

Teach Yourself WordStar 2000. *Compatible Hardware:* IBM PC & compatibles. *Operating System(s) Required:* PC-DOS/MS-DOS 2.0 or higher. *Memory Required:* 256k.
disk $75.00.
Split-Screen Simulation Tutorial.
American Training International, Inc.

Teacher/Trainer Turned Author. *Items Included:* Bound manual. *Customer Support:* Free hotline - no time limit; 30 day limited warranty; updates are $5/disk plus S&H.
MS-DOS 2.0 or higher. IBM & compatibles. $89.95-$374.95. Nonstandard peripherals required: 256k RAM & two drives for course creation; 128k & one drive for playback.
demo disk & literature $9.95.
Anyone with Elementary Typing Skills Can Now Create Courses with Color & Graphics in Minutes. User May Freely Mix Text, Color Graphics, & Questions on Any Page. Built-In Systems Are Provided for Fast Graphics Production. The Word-Processing Type Entry Has Instant Editing & Page Playback. User Has Full Control of All Page Sequencing, Branching, & Loops. True/False, Multiple Choice, & Fill-in-the-Blank Questions Are Supported with Embedded Student-Record Keeping. Course Playback Features Student Log-On, Log-Off, & Automatic Re-Entry at Page of Departure. User May Create Portable Courses That Play Back Without the Authoring System.
Dynacomp, Inc.

Teacher 2000. *Customer Support:* All of our products are unconditionally guaranteed.
DOS, Windows. CD-ROM disk $39.95 (Order no.: TEACHER). Nonstandard peripherals required: CD-ROM drive.
500 MB of Quality, Educational Programs for All Ages.
Walnut Creek CDRom.

Teacher's Aide. *Items Included:* Bound manual. *Customer Support:* Free hotline - no time limit; 30 day limited warranty; updates are $5/disk plus S&H.
All computers except C-64 (256k). disk $17.95.
Learning Tool Meant to Be Used for Grades 1-6 Mathematics. There Are Drills on Addition, Subtraction, Multiplication & Division. The Child Has the Choice of Five Levels of Difficulty for Each Procedure, & There Is the Option to Drill & Display Each Step in Long Division & Multiplication.
Dynacomp, Inc.

Teacher's Gradebook. *Items Included:* Bound manual. *Customer Support:* Free hotline - no time limit; 30 day limited warranty; updates are $5/disk plus S&H.
MS-DOS. IBM & compatibles (256k). disk $49.95.
Apple. disk $49.95.

For Each Class in Their Master File, Users Can Store, Retrieve, Summarize, Update or Otherwise Manipulate & Report Extensive Data Pertaining to Class Administration, Student Rosters, Grades, & Absences. To Evaluate the Performance of Students, up to Seven Distinct Grade Categories May Be Declared & Labelled for Each Class Individually, & As Many As 20 Marks May Be Entered for Each of Those Grade Categories. A Separate File of Absence Records May Also Be Maintained.
Dynacomp, Inc.

Teaching Assistance Package for Basic Lotus 1-2-3. Jul. 1986.
$990.00.
$75.00, set of 10 additional student handbooks.
Instructor-Led, Disk-Based Courseware Includes Instructor Outline & Narrative, Color Slides, Student Exercise Disk, Student Workbook, & Test Materials.
TAP Development Corp.

Teaching Assistant for AutoCAD Release 12. *Version:* 2.1. Jul. 1989. *Items Included:* 1 manual. *Customer Support:* Free telephone support; 90 day limited warranty.
DOS 3.3. IBM PC, 386, 486. disk $249.95 (ISBN 1-55603-179-3, Order no.: I-1313). Nonstandard peripherals required: EGA. Addl. software required: AudoCAD release 12.
An Embedded, On-Line Tutorial Introducing the full Range of Concepts User Must Use with AutoCad. The Menu, Commands, & On-Line Help Are Used from the Start. The Tutorial Takes Only 6-10 Hours to Complete & Practice Screens are Provided for Endless Review.
Electronic Courseware Systems, Inc.

Tealeafs: Just for Fun...with a Practical Twist. *Version:* 2.2. Jan. 1994. *Items Included:* Document included with package, manual on disk. *Customer Support:* Phone support, promotion item & site license(s), upgrade discounts.
MS-DOS 3.3 or higher, PC-DOS, DR-DOS, MS Windows. PC & compatibles (286 or higher) & DOS equipped MACs, Workstations (640k).
disk $21.95 (ISBN 1-884384-31-5, Order no.: 11165). Optimal configuration: PC 640k RAM, hard disk, MS-DOS 3.3 or higher, color monitor.
Finger Paint for the Young at Heart, Relaxation for Tired Eyes & Mind, Abstract Art for the Non-Technical, or Even Pattern Association While at Lunch or During Break. A Wonderful Little DOS "TSR" Program That Draws User Designated Patterns or Text on the Computer Screen after a User Specified Time of Keyboard Inactivity. User Can Specify Preferences for Pattern Displays, Write Text Displays, or Turn On/Off Audio. User Can Optionally Design Their Own Extended ASCII, or Graphics Display (Including Fractals), to Represent the Users Tastes & Artistic Insight.
Eugene L. Woods, PE.

Tealeafs: Just for Fun...with a Practical Twist. *Version:* 2.1. Jan. 1993. *Items Included:* Document included with package, manual on disk. *Customer Support:* Phone support, promotion item & site license(s), upgrade discounts.
MS-DOS 3.3 or higher, PC-DOS, DR-DOS, MS Windows. PC & compatibles (286 or higher) & DOS equipped MACs, Workstations (640k).
disk $21.95 (ISBN 1-884384-30-7). Optimal configuration: PC 640k RAM, hard disk, MS-DOS 3.3 or higher, color monitor.
Finger Paint for the Young at Heart, Relaxation for Tired Eyes & Mind, Abstract Art for the Non-Technical, or Even Pattern Association While at Lunch or During Break. A Wonderful Little DOS "TSR" Program That Draws User Designated Patterns or Text on the Computer Screen after a User Specified Time of Keyboard Inactivity. User Can Specify Preferences for Pattern Displays, Write Text Displays, or Turn On/Off Audio. User Can Optionally Design Their Own Extended ASCII, or Graphics Display (Including Fractals), to Represent the Users Tastes & Artistic Insight.
Eugene L. Woods, PE.

Team SAT. Peter Orton. Aug. 1995. *Items Included:* For Windows/MPC - QuickTime for Windows 2.01 (on the CD-ROM); For Macintosh - Sound Manager 3.0, QuickTime 2.0, Apple Multimedia Tuner 2 (also on the CD-ROM), Printed test booklet. *Customer Support:* Free online support on America online using key word Zelos; Toll free number 1-800-345-6777; 90 day money back guarantee.
Windows/MPC; Macintosh. 486, 25MHz, double speed CD-ROM drive (8Mb); Macintosh LCIII (68030 25MHz) or higher (8Mb). CD-ROM disk $29.95 (ISBN 1-883387-10-8). Nonstandard peripherals required: 640x480, 256 color SVGA display, Microsoft compatible mouse, 8 bit sound card; 13" 256 color monitor. Addl. software required: DOS 5.0 or higher, Microsoft Windows 3.1, QuickTime for Windows 2.01; System 7.0 or higher, QuickTime 2.0, Sound Manager.
Improve Your SAT Scores with This Dynamic, Comprehensive Test Preparation Title! Choose Your Own Study Partner to Give You Strategies & Critical Insights to Both Sections of the SAT Test. Contains Ten Tests Worth of Questions, & Give Immediate Feedback with Complete Explanations of Your Right & Wrong Answers.
Zelos.

TEAM-UP. *Version:* 2.2. Jan. 1989. *Items Included:* Full point of sale system with related applications, reports, menus, & documented procedural language which may be modified by the end-user; Team-Up's 4GL (procedural language), report generator, & importer are standard. *Customer Support:* 90 days free tech support from first call, following that it is $25.00/call or $250.00 for one year of unlimited calls; 24 hour service available at nominal charge.
DOS 3.1+ (150k). IBM compatibles, Texas Instruments. $795.00 (single-user), $1990.00 (multi-user licensed for 10 workstations on 1 file server), $895.00 (5 additional workstation license), $1395.00 (10 additional workstation license). Optimal configuration: Any network running DOS 3.1+ & NetBIOS, runs on unlimited number of workstations with no degradation in speed. Networks supported: All networks running DOS 3.1+ & NetBIOS, Novell, Banyan, 3Com, TokenRing, MS-NET, Lantastic, DNA, etc.
Multi-User, Transaction-Processing DBMS. It Includes an Extensive Report Generator, an Importer & an Inherent 4GL. Team-Up Also Features a Security System with 32 Groups & 10 Levels of Protection.
Unlimited Processing, Inc.

TeamEC. Jul. 1994. *Items Included:* Manual, 2 days of training & facilitation. Structuring, brainstorming & evaluation & choice. *Customer Support:* 2 years free support & software upgrades.
MS-DOS 5.0 or higher. IBM PC's & compatibles (640k). Contact publisher for price. Nonstandard peripherals required: Mouse & VGA monitor. Addl. software required: Can be used with hand-held keypads & a radio receiver.
Designed Especially for Group & Boardroom Decision Meetings, TeamEC Allows Every Member of the Group to Enter His or Her Input at Every Step of the Decision-Making Process.

1001

TEAMPLAN

From Identifying the Important Elements Affecting a Decision, to Designing the Structure of a Decision, to Making Judgments about the Relative Importance of the Elements of the Decision, TeamEC Is an Effective Tool That Leaves the Power of Decision-Making in the Hands of the Decision-Maker.
Expert Choice, Inc.

TEAMPLAN. *Version:* 9.0. 1985. *Compatible Hardware:* IBM PC & compatibles. *Operating System(s) Required:* MS-DOS, PC-DOS 2.1 & higher. *Language(s):* CB-86. *Memory Required:* 512k. *General Requirements:* Hard disk, 132-column printer.
contact publisher for price.
File Control Manager for PMS-II That Allows As Many As 2 to 26 Users to Run PMS-II Simultaneously in a LAN or Multi-User Environment. Separates Files for Each Unique User Are Maintained, Preventing File Contention.
North America MICA, Inc.

TeamTalk. *Version:* 2.0. Aug. 1994. *Customer Support:* 30 days money-back guarantee, 90 days free support, maintenance 15% of list price. Windows 3.1, Windows NT 3.1, OS/2 2.1. 286 IBM compatible (4Mb). $61.00-$79.00.
Optimal configuration: 386 running Windows 3.1 or NetWare Network. *Networks supported:* All Networks that support DOS Share.
A Group Discussion System That Facilitates Communication among Group Members. It Is a Forum for Group Collaboration & Decision Making. TeamTalk Organizes Information & Documents by Topic. Any Member Can Easily Create a New Public or Private Topic & Build the Member List.
Trax Softworks, Inc.

Tech. *Version:* 2.8. Jan. 1985. *Compatible Hardware:* Apple Macintosh. *General Requirements:* ImageWriter or LaserWriter. *Items Included:* User's manual, keyboard charts. *Customer Support:* Telephone support, defective disks replaced free.
3.5" disk $99.95.
Laser Tech. 3.5" disk $99.95.
8 Type-1 & TrueType Fonts. All Have Plain, Bold, Italic & Bold-Italic Styles Except City & CountryBlueprint, Which Have Plain Style Only. TechSymbol & TechSymbolSans Can Be Used with the Equation Editor in Microsoft Word to Produce Equations in Serif or Sans Serif with True Bold, Italic, & Bold-Italic Styles.
Linguist's Software, Inc.

Tech*Graph*Pad. *Version:* 4.0. *Compatible Hardware:* IBM PC & compatibles. *Operating System(s) Required:* PC-DOS/MS-DOS 2.1 or higher. *Memory Required:* 512k. *General Requirements:* CGA, EGA, VGA, Hercules, or compatible graphics card.
disk $395.00.
An Engineering & Scientific Graphing & Plotting Program. Reads Data Directly from Lotus 1-2-3, Symphony, ASCII Files, & Labtech Notebook. Creates Multiple X-Y Plots, Performs Curve Fitting & Data Smoothing, & Plots Linear, Log/Log, & Polar Plots. New 4.0 Features Includes Complete PostScript Support, Probability & Histogram Plot Types, Plotting from any Equation, & Automatic/Semi-Automatic Execution of Graphing. For Easily Integrated Text & Graphics, User Sends Graphs to WordPerfect V.5.X, & Other Word Processing & Desktop Publishing Packages. Supports Dozens of Laser Writers, Printers, & Plotters for Presentation Quality Output.
Binary Engineering Software, Inc.

Tech Help! *Version:* 6.0. Jan. 1994. *Items Included:* One page instruction sheet. *Customer Support:* Telephone support; 30 day money back guarantee.*
DOS 2.0 or higher. IBM PC/XT/AT & compatibles. disk $99.95. *Nonstandard peripherals required:* Hard disk recommended.
Hypertext Substitute for Printed Technical References for Programmers. 1.5 Mb of Technical Information Available with Point & Shoot Speed. Pop-Up Obscure but Essential Data from within the Editor/Debugger.
Flambeaux Software, Inc.

Tech/Word. *Items Included:* Bound manual. *Customer Support:* Free hotline - no time limit; 30 day limited warranty; updates are $5/disk plus S&H.
MS-DOS 2.0 or higher. IBM & compatibles (256k). disk $99.95. *Nonstandard peripherals required:* Two floppy disk drives (or one floppy & a hard disk), & a graphics card (CGA, EGA, Hercules, or equivalent).
Word Processor Designed Specifically for the Scientific Community. It Produces Professional Quality Mathematical Text, with Screen Displays That Show Exactly What Will Be Printed (Including Mathematical Symbols & Structures). Since TECH/WORD Includes This Within a Full-Featured Word Processor, User No Longer Needs to Laboriously Draw Symbols & Cut & Paste Equations into Printed Text. Allows Simultaneous Use of up to Nine Distinct Fonts (Seven Are Included: Three Math, One Script, One Greek, & Two IBM Graphics); a Font Creation Package; a Custom-Character Generator; Half Roll & In-Line Superscripts & Subscripts; Extensive Page Formatting; & All the Features You Would Expect of a High Quality Word Processor.
Dynacomp, Inc.

Tech/Word. 1992. *Items Included:* Detailed manuals included with all Dynacomp products. *Customer Support:* Free telephone support to original customer - no time limit; 30 day limited warranty.
MS-DOS 3.2 or higher. IBM PC & compatibles (512k). $199.95 incl. manual (Add $5.00 for 3 1/2" format; 5 1/4" format standard). *Optimal configuration:* IBM, MS-DOS 2.0 or higher, 256k RAM, two floppy disk drives (or one floppy & a hard disk), & a graphics card (CGA, EGA, Hercules, or equivalent).
An Intelligent Word Processor Designed Specifically for the Scientific Community. It Produces Professional Quality Mathematical Text, with Screen Displays That Show Exactly What Will Be Printed (Including Mathematical Symbols & Structures). For Creating Equations, Fractions, Roots, Subscripts, Superscripts, Integrals, & Summations Are Built Within One "Virtual" Line, with Automatic Adjustment of Their Positions During Editing. Standard Word Processor Features. Includes a Bound 342-Page Step-by-Step Manual.
Dynacomp, Inc.

TECHLIBplus. *Version:* 3.4. Feb. 1994. *Compatible Hardware:* CDC's Cyber Series; DEC ALPHA & VAX Series, IBM 370, 9370, 43xx, RS6000; HP 9000, Intel PCs, Sun SPARC, SGI Indigo, Unisys. *Operating System(s) Required:* AIX, MVS, IRIX, HP-UX, OSF/1, SunOS/Solaris 2, Ultrix, UnixWare, VMS/OpenVMS. *Language(s):* C, Assembler, FORTRAN. *Memory Required:* 140k. *Items Included:* Full documentation, training. *Customer Support:* Telephone support, training seminar, application development, installation. $20,000 & up.
Integrated Application Package for Automating Corporate, Special & Technical Library Functions, Including Cataloging Maintenance, Online Patron Access, Catalog COPAC Acquisitions, Circulation, Interlibrary Loan & Serials Control, MARC Interface, & Thesaurus. TECHUBplus Interfaces to Electronic Information & Collection Management Services, & to Internal Databases & services, Including ISI's Current Contents.
Information Dimensions, Inc.

Techman Volume One: Vol. 1.
Macintosh 512K or higher. 3.5" disk $59.95.
Clip Art of Computer Systems.
Alsek Productions, Inc.

Techmate. Szabo Software. Feb. 1987. *Compatible Hardware:* Atari ST. *Memory Required:* 520k.
3.5" disk $39.95 (ISBN 0-923213-59-7, Order no.: AT-TEL).
Chess Program with Graphics.
MichTron, Inc.

Technical Data Plotting. B. J. Korites. 1985. *Compatible Hardware:* Apple II; IBM PC, PC XT. *Operating System(s) Required:* Apple DOS 3.3, PC-DOS 2.0. *Language(s):* BASIC (source code included). *Memory Required:* 64k.
disk $120.00 incl. manual.
Collection of Data Management & Data Plotting Programs Specifically Written for Scientists & Engineers. Interfaces Are Available to Connect the IBM PC to Hewlett Packard & Houston Instruments Pen Plotters. Includes Regression, Function Fitting & Curve Fitting with Splines.
Kern International, Inc.

Technical Reference Programmers. Dave Williams. *Customer Support:* Free BBS support.
MS-DOS. IBM PC & compatibles. single user license $25.00 (Order no.: TECHREF). *Addl. software required:* Any word processor or text editor.
Complete Reference to Programming Under MS-DOS on the IBM PC. Cover Low & High Level Details. Disk-Based for Fast Access.
GRU Development.

TechniChart. *Version:* 2. *Compatible Hardware:* IBM PC & compatibles. *Operating System(s) Required:* MS-DOS 3.1 or higher. *Memory Required:* 640k. *General Requirements:* Hard disk. *Items Included:* Program disk & manual. *Customer Support:* 30 minutes free; Pay-per-call at $1.95/minute.
disk $2.95.
demo disk $10.00.
Commodity Charting & Analysis Program That Features: the Ability to Track Any Number of Commodities & Stocks, All the Popular Indexes & Some New Ones, Special Graphing Techniques Which Display More Days of Data on the Screen; Compatibility with SCI, Agri-Data Instant Update, & Farm Bureau ACRES; the TRADING STRATEGIST, Which Allows Users to Simulate Market Strategies & Determine Their Potential Profitability.
Harvest Computer Systems, Inc.

The Technician. *Version:* 5.2. Oct. 1990. *Compatible Hardware:* IBM PC, PC XT, PC AT, PS/2, & compatibles. *Operating System(s) Required:* PC-DOS 2.0 or higher. *Memory Required:* 640k. *General Requirements:* 2 disk drives or hard disk; CGA or EGA or VGA card. Dot matrix, laser, or color printer; Hayes Smartmodem 1200 or compatible recommended. *Items Included:* Extensive user manual. *Customer Support:* Full support at (801) 265-9998. $249.00.
Modem updating service from EQUIS $120.00/yr.
full functioning demo disk $5.00.
Market Timing Program Which Tracks, on a Daily Basis, the Sentiment, Momentum, Monetary, & Relative Strength of the Overall Market. Includes Fourteen Years of Daily Historical Data from 1979 On. Over 100 Pre-Programmed Technical

Indicators. The Indicators Provided Include the Advance/Decline Line, Odd Lot Ratios, Fed Funds, Stochastics, MACD, etc. The Indicators May Be Calculated on the DJIA, S&P 100 (OEX), S&P 500, NYSE, NY Futures Contracts, Value Line Composite. Includes a Profitability Tester to Test Trading Strategies. User-Defined Indicators May Be Used, or Custom Formulas May Be Calculated. Up to 1000 Days/Wks/Mos (in 36 Simultaneous Windows) May Be Displayed or Printed in a Desktop Publishing Format. Data May Also Be Exported in ASCII Format.
Equis International.

TechniFilter Plus. Version: 7.0. Mar. 1992. Compatible Hardware: IBM PC, PC XT, AT, PS/2. Operating System(s) Required: PC-DOS 3.1 or higher. Memory Required: 640k. Items Included: Documentation. Customer Support: For registered users only - one user per serial number.
$399.00.
Screening Program Designed for Use with the Dow Jones Market Analyzer, Savant's the Technical Investor, Computrac, EQUIS' Metastock or Inmark's Market Maker. Has the Capability of Automatically Screening the Data Base & Identifying Those Issues Which Satisfy the Technical Criteria. User Builds the Formulas Needed to Identify the Criteria & They Are Computed for All Issues in the Data Base. User Constructs Conditions Which Use These Computations & the Program Filters Out Those Issues Which Satisfy the Conditions. Computations Can Be Sorted, Weighted & Displayed in Various Formats. User Can Filter a Previously Filtered Set & Print Various Reports. The User Can Also Describe an Investment Strategy by Choosing a Buy & Sell Condition & Then Test the Strategy Historically Relative to an Individual Issue. This Same Test Can Be Performed over Varying Choices of Parameters to See Which Set of Parameters Would Have Given Optimal Results.
RTR Software, Inc.

Technology Plans on Disk. May 1994. Items Included: Full instructional manual with full text of program. Customer Support: Telephone help - free of charge.
Macintosh. Any Macintosh (2Mb). 3.5" disk $395.00 (ISBN 1-885717-00-8). Addl. software required: Any word processing package. Optimal configuration: MAC LC, LCII, LCIII, Performa or higher with any standard word processing package & hard drive.
MS-DOS. Any MS-DOS machine (2Mb). disk $395.00 (ISBN 1-885717-01-6). Addl. software required: Any standard word processing program. Optimal configuration: Any IBM PS-1, PS-2, Compaq, Dell, Tandy, etc. with 2Mb RAM, hard drive (2Mb free), any standard W-P program.
Windows. Any Windows capable machine (2Mb). disk $395.00 (ISBN 1-885717-02-4). Addl. software required: Any standard word processing package. Optimal configuration: Windows machine with 2Mb RAM, 5Mb free on hard drive, any standard W-P program.
Easy-to-Use, Multiple Choice, Fill-in-the-Blank Outline for Creating Technology Plans for Schools or Corporate Training Depts. Works on Any Word Processor. Covers All Aspects of Technology Planning from Overview to Funding, Software & Hardware Evaluation, Training, Budgets & Implementation.
Keith Philip A. & Assocs.

TechWords. Version: 2.0. Mar. 1990. Customer Support: 30 days free technical support via telephone, 60 day update on all documentation & software.
MS-DOS 2.1 or higher. IBM & compatibles. disk $99.00 (Order no.: 7102). Addl. software required: Word processor or editor. Optimal configuration: Mid-drive recommended.
Macintosh. 3.5" disk $99.00. Addl. software required: Word processor.
Network Version $495.00 1 site unlimited users
Listing of Technical Words Which Can Be Merged into the Spelling Checker of Most Word Processors Such As, WordPerfect & Microsoft Word. TechWords Contains Terms from Technical Areas Including: Aeronautical, Chemical, Civil, Electrical, Industrial, & Mechanical Engineering, As Well As the Computer Science, Scientific, Mathematical & Academic Disciplines.
GEOCOMP Corp.

Tecmath. 1987. Compatible Hardware: Apple II series. Memory Required: 48k. Items Included: 5 disks & 5 workbooks. Customer Support: Telephone support.
disk $250.00 (ISBN 0-939247-05-4, Order no.: T707).
Precalculus & Calculus: Graphing & Tutorial Programs.
Worldview Software.

Tecumseh Part Numbers, Craftsman 3 to 10 H.P. Andrew Bear. 1987. Compatible Hardware: Apple II, II+, IIe, IIc. Operating System(s) Required: Apple DOS 3.3, ProDOS. Memory Required: 64k. General Requirements: 2 disk drives, printer, 80-column card.
disk $34.50 (ISBN 1-55797-087-4, Order no.: AP2-AG297).
Designed to Supply the User with Information on Manufacturer's Part Numbers, Tune-Up Specifications, Torque Specifications, & Part Notes from the Six Major Manufacturers of Aircooled Small Gas Engines. Each Engine Is Listed Individually, Allowing the User to Select Information Indexed by Model Number. The Printout Feature Includes Model Number, Part Name, & Notes.
Hobar Pubns.

TEKCALC: Scientific Calculator Program. Version: 2. Rai C. Jaswa. Apr. 1986. Compatible Hardware: AT&T 6300; DEC VT 180; HP-125; IBM PC, PC jr, PC XT, PC AT, & compatibles; Tandy 1000, 1200, 2000; TI Professional; Xerox 820,820-II, 860. Operating System(s) Required: PC-DOS, MS-DOS. Memory Required: 256k.
$129.00.
Programmable Scientific Calculator for Solving Complex Mathematical Problems. Features Built-In Graphics, Statistics, User Extendable Functions, a Data Table Window, & Compatibility with Other BV Engineering Software. Formulas, Computations, & Data May Be Saved on Disk Permitting the Creation of a Customized Math Environment.
BV Engineering.

TeleAsync. Operating System(s) Required: CP/M-86, MS-DOS.
contact publisher for price.
Communications Software Package That Enables TeleVideo's Personal & Portable Computers to Transfer Disk Files to & from Other TeleVideo Systems. Also Provides Terminal Emulation for Communication with Any On-Line Timesharing System. Provides Direct Local File Management Commands to Eliminate the Need to Exit the Program.
TeleVideo Systems, Inc.

Teleform for Windows: Forms Design & Automatic Data Entry Software.
386-based computer or higher (8Mb). Contact publisher for price. Optimal configuration: 386-based computer or higher, 8Mb RAM recommended, 20Mb hard disk space plus 10Mb-20Mb for image files, compatible scanner, fax modem or fax server, MS-DOS 5.0 or higher, Microsoft Windows 3.1 or higher, VGA monitor or higher.
Complete Software Package for Forms Design, Distribution, Automatic Data Entry & Verification. With This Package, You Can Quickly & Easily Create Professional-Looking Forms On-Screen & Automatically Fax Them to Any Number of People. Completed Forms Can Be Faxed Directly to Your PC, Which Completely Eliminates Manual Data Entry. This Improves Response Time, Reduces Data Entry Errors, & Saves Money on Mailing & Outside Personnel. Your Resulting Data Can be Read into SPSS for Windows for Analysis.
SPSS, Inc.

Telelink I. Compatible Hardware: Atari XL/XE. Operating System(s) Required: AOS. Language(s): Machine. Memory Required: 16k. General Requirements: Atari Acoustic Modem.
ROM cartridge $4.95 (Order no.: CXL4015).
Allows Users to Communicate with Another Computer over Standard Telephone Lines. Data Received Can Be Printed on a Line Printer, but Program Cannot Download to a Disk Drive.
Atari Corp.

TeleMagic: Software for Success in Business. Version: 14. Jan. 1991. Items Included: User manual, release notes, installation guide. Customer Support: Annual hotline support contracts; 30 days free support.
UNIX/XENIX, DOS, Windows. 386, 486, Pentium. $2695.00.
DOS, UNIX. 286, 386, 486 (1Mb) Pentium. $495.00-$1995.00. Networks supported: Novell, 3COM, Lantastic, any Netbios compatible network.
IBM. IBM AS/400, IBM System 38 (2Mb). $6500.00-$33,000.00.
Contact Management & Tracking Group. Prospecting, Tracking Customer Sales, Service & Support, Telemarketing Campaigns, Order Entry, Maintaining Mailing Lists & More. Features Include: Appointment Scheduler, Tickler File, Multiple Pages of Notes for any Client, Built-In Wordprocessor, Alarm, Auto-Dialer, Quick List Generator, Telemarketing or Support "Scripting, Sales Quotes, & More.
Trajectory Software, Inc.

Telemetry Processing System. Nov. 1994. Items Included: Contact vendor. Customer Support: Contact vendor.
Windows 3.1 or higher. 386 (4Mb). Contact publisher for price. Nonstandard peripherals required: 640x480 VGA. Addl. software required: Paradox for Windows Ver. 5.0. Networks supported: Novell, Lantastic, Windows for Workgroups.
Program Reads & Processes Binary Files Created with Diamond Telemetry Traffic Counter Processing System, from High Leah Electronics in Oregon. Processed Data Is Saved to ASCII Files for Further Processing. An Optional Module Is Available That Leads the ASCII Files into Paradox for Windows Database Files.
Management Systems, Inc.

Telengard. Compatible Hardware: Atari 800/XL/XE, Commodore 64/128, IBM PC & compatibles, Tandy 1000. Language(s): BASIC. Memory Required: Commodore 64k, IBM 128k. General Requirements: CGA for IBM.
disk $12.99 ea.
IBM. (Order no.: 42654).
Commodore. (Order no.: 42655).
Fifty Levels of Dungeon Delving Fantasy. Your Explorer Has Strengths & Weaknesses, but Can Improve by Staying Alive & Knowing When to Run & Fight. Requires Quick Thinking & a Willingness to Search the Unknown Depths of the Underworld.
Avalon Hill Game Co., The Microcomputer Games Div.

TelePaint. *Version:* 2.2. Jan. 1986. *Compatible Hardware:* IBM PC & compatibles with 1 or 2 floppy disk drives & Microsoft compatible mouse. *Operating System(s) Required:* MS-DOS. *Language(s):* C. *Memory Required:* 256k.
disk $69.00 (ISBN 0-924862-01-7).
Full Color Enhancement Software Package That Allows User to Improve Charts & Graphs Created by His Personal Computer for the Making of Color Print-Outs, Slides & Overhead Transparencies for Peer Level Presentations. Key Features & Capabilities Include: A Full 8-1/2" x 11" Inch Page for the User to Work with; Over, Under & Replace Placement Modes; On-Line Screen Help, 16 Different Fonts; Variety of Print-Out Options (Full Page, 1/4 Page, Color & Black & White, Light & Dark Background); & the Ability to Clear The Icon Menu with the Press of a Function Key. Support for the Polaroid Palette. Freehand Drawing Capabilities for Creating Illustrations, Logos, Maps, & Charts.
LCS/Telegraphics.

Telescan Analyzer & Telescan Database: Stock Analysis Program. *Version:* 3.0. Richard Carlin. Jun. 1992. *Compatible Hardware:* IBM PC & compatibles with hard disk drives. *Operating System(s) Required:* MS-DOS 2.1 or higher. *Memory Required:* 640k. *Items Included:* Operations manual & reference manual. *Customer Support:* Free 800 number for support.
disk $99.00.
Stock Analysis Program Providing Both Individual or Professional Investors with Information for Performing Technical & Fundamental Analysis & Making Buy & Sell Decisions. Retrieves & Displays More Than 20 Years of Historical Stock Price & Volume Information. Accesses the Telescan Database Consisting of NYSE, AMEX & NASDAQ over the Counter Stocks & over 560 Market Indices, 1800 Mutual Funds, 35,000 Options & 197 Industry Groups. Special Features Include Multiple Graphs per Screen, Intra-Day Graphs, Reuters News Service Insider Trading Information, Composite Indicators, Save Feature for Analysis Off-Line, Industry Group Analyses, & Mutual Funds.
Telescan.

Telescan Investor's Platform: TIP. *Version:* 1.1. Dec. 1995. *Items Included:* Online tutorial, reference manual, Quick-Start manual. *Customer Support:* Toll-free customer support, seven days per week. Quarterly newsletter.
Windows 3.1. 486 (8Mb). CD-ROM disk $395.00. *Nonstandard peripherals required:* Modem (9600).
Provides Both Individual & Professional Investors with Information for Performing Technical & Fundamental Analysis, As Well As Making Buy/Sell Decisions. Retrieves & Displays over 20 Years of Historical Stock Price & Volume Information. Save Feature Allows User to Do Analysis Offline. Search for Stocks That Best Meet Investment Criteria.
Telescan.

Telescan ProSearch. *Version:* 4.0. Jul. 1993. *Items Included:* Operations manual & reference manual. *Customer Support:* Free customer support with 800 number: 7:00am-Midnight CST. DOS 2.1 or higher. IBM compatible (640k). disk $395.00, incl. Telescan Analyzer.
An Add-On to the Telescan Analyzer Stock Market Analysis Program, ProSearch Allows a User to Search the Telescan On-Line Database for Stocks Which Best Meet Their Investment Criteria. Users Can Search on up to 40 Variables Selected from a List of 207. The Program Scans over 11,000 Issues to Find the Ones Which Best Fit, Then Returns the List in Order of Best Fit. Users Can Search for Stocks, Industry Groups, Optionable Stocks or Stocks Within Certain Industries. Fundamental Data, Technical Data, Earnings Projections & Insider Trading Comprise the List of 50 Different Search Criteria.
Telescan.

Telescript. *Version:* 3.0a. Jul. 1991. *Items Included:* 2 bound manuals. *Customer Support:* On-site training - $750.00 per day; 1 year maintenance - $100.00; 30 days free technical support.
DOS version 3.1 or higher. PC XT, AT, PS/2 or compatible (640k). $850.00 single station. *Nonstandard peripherals required:* Low-end modem. *Networks supported:* All.
Sales & Marketing Software for Network Users. Fast Multi-User Preview Dialing Can Automatically Dial & Hang-Up up to 70 Calls Per Hour or More. Features Multiple Simultaneous Projects, In-Bound & Out-Bound, Scripts with Colors, Branching, Randomized Questions, Calculations, Multiple & Open-Ended Responses. Extensive Reporting, Both Realtime & Off-Line.
Digisoft Computers.

Teletype. *Customer Support:* 800-929-8117 (customer service).
MS-DOS. IBM/PS2. disk $99.99 (ISBN 0-87007-737-6).
Tutorial for Touch Typing the New 12 Function Key Standard Keyboard, With Exercises for the Function Keys, the ESC Key, & for all Other Keys. Can be Adjusted for the Dvorak Keyboards.
SourceView Software International.

TeleUSE. *Customer Support:* Customer support & training available.
D6/UX, ULTRIX. Sun 3, Sun 4, Dec 3100, Data General. contact publisher for price.
Complete Environment for the Development of Graphical User Interfaces for Applications Running under Unix & the X Windows System. Consists of a WYSIWYG Editor for Graphically Building Windows, Menus & Other Interaction Objects. OSF/Motif, Athens & User-Defined Widgets are Supported Within the Editor. Palettes of Colors & Fonts Allow Rapid Specification of Screen Layout.
Telesoft.

Telewand. *Items Included:* Telewand, headset, internal interface card, a 3-input switch box, users manual, software driver, easy key visual keyboard. *Customer Support:* One-year warranty. Customer support by telephone.
DOS/Windows 3.1. PC 286 (1Mb). disk $799.00. *Nonstandard peripherals required:* Switch with 1/8" plug compatibility, VGA.
An Assistive Input Device That Provides Complete Hands-Free Computer Operation. The Cursor Is Moved on the Computer Screen by Head Movements. Button Action Such As Clicking & Dragging Is Made Through External Switches. The EasyKey Visual Keyboard Allows Typing with No External Keyboard in Windows Applications.
Inkwell Systems.

TeleWriter. *Version:* 1.0, 2.0. Dec. 1981. *Compatible Hardware:* TRS-80 Color Computer. *Memory Required:* 16-32k.
contact publisher for price.
Cognitec.

Telewriter-64. *Version:* 1. Feb. 1983. *Compatible Hardware:* TRS-80 Color Computer. *Memory Required:* 16k-64k.
cassette $49.95, for disk 59.95.
Cognitec.

TeliSolar. Dennis R. Ellis. Apr. 1984. *Compatible Hardware:* Compaq; IBM PC. *Operating System(s) Required:* PC-DOS, MS-DOS. *Language(s):* Compiled BASICA. *Memory Required:* 128k. *General Requirements:* Graphics adapter, color monitor.
disk $50.00 (ISBN 0-923915-00-1, Order no.: PC-TS).
Management Tool to Aid Homeowners & Contractors in Making Decisions about Energy-Related Home Improvements & Investments. Used to Determine Hot Water Usage & Cost, Building Heat Loss, Solar Collector Sizing, Investment Payback, & Areas to Concentrate on to Reduce Energy Usage & Cost.
Tesseract Enterprises, Ltd.

TEMATH: Tools for Exploring Mathematics. *Version:* 1.5. Robert Kowalczyk & Adam Hausknecht. Apr. 1990. *Items Included:* One disk & paperback manual. *Customer Support:* Unlimited technical support for registered users.
Macintosh Plus, SE, II, or later model (1Mb). $50.00 single user package (ISBN 0-534-15533-2). *Optimal configuration:* Macintosh Plus, SE, II, or later model with one Mb of Memory (two Mb with Multifinder), System 6.0 or later, one 800k disk drive & a fixed disk or two 800k disk drive.
call for site license information (ISBN 0-534-15529-4).
Tool for Exploring Mathematical Concepts. TEMATH Makes Maximum Use of the Graphic Interface of the Macintosh, Representing Individual Numeric & Graphic Tools By Pictorial Icons. Aids the User in Relating Mathematical Concepts to Other Fields, Such As Physics, Engineering, & Business.
Brooks/Cole Publishing Co.

Temperature Cartridge. *Compatible Hardware:* Commodore 64, 128. *General Requirements:* Biofeedback Temperature sensor.
ROM cartridge $19.95 (Order no.: SOFC64-05-009).
Lets User Monitor External Body Temperature. Shows Variations to .05 Degrees Farenheit.
Bodylog.

Temperature Plotter III. David L. Vernier. Apr. 1988. *Compatible Hardware:* Apple II+, IIe, IIc, IIgs. *Operating System(s) Required:* ProDOS. *Language(s):* Applesoft BASIC, Machine (source code included). *Memory Required:* 64k. *General Requirements:* Temperature Probe System, avail. in parts or assembled from Vernier Software.
disk $39.95, incl. manual (ISBN 0-918731-12-7).
Allows the Apple Computer to Monitor up to Four Temperatures at Once. Temperature Data May Be Stored on Disk, Edited, & Graphed. Temperature Units, Delay Between Readings & Type of Clock Used Are under Program Control.
Vernier Software.

Template.
contact publisher for price.
3-D Subroutine Library for Engineering & Scientific Environments.
Template.

Template Software to Accompany FINANCIAL ACCOUNTING, 7th Edition. Ernest I. Hanson et al. Mar. 1993.
IBM. spreadsheet software 5.25" $20.00 (ISBN 0-03-097471-2).
spreadsheet software 3.5" $20.00 (ISBN 0-03-097470-4).
Dryden Pr.

Template Software to Accompany PRINCIPLES OF ACCOUNTING, 6th Edition. Ernest I. Hanson et al. Mar. 1993.
IBM. spreadsheet software 5.25" $13.50 (ISBN 0-03-097403-8).
spreadsheet software 3.5" $13.50 (ISBN 0-03-097402-X).
Dryden Pr.

TITLE INDEX

Templates of Doom. *Items Included:* Disk & documentation. *Customer Support:* Telephone (415)952-2375.
Lotus version. IBM PC (256k). (07/1985) $19.95.
PC Excel version. IBM PC (512k). (10/1987) $19.95.
Mac Excel version. Macintosh (1Mb). (02/1987) $19.95.
Adventure Game Teaches Spreadsheet Formulas & Command Structure While It Entertains. Worksheet Applications for Lotus 1-2-3, Quattro, & VP-Planner.
Solar Systems Software.

Temple of Apshai. EPYX, Inc. *Compatible Hardware:* HP 150 Touchscreen.
3.5" disk $39.95 (Order no.: 92243GA).
Adventure Taking You Back to the Days of Yore to Explore Unknown Depths Crawling with Monsters & Laced with Treasures. If You Are an Experienced Dungeon Adventurer, You Can Even Bring along Characters from Other Games. The Game Has Been Converted to Take Advantage of the Touchscreen's Features.
Hewlett-Packard Co.

Temple of Sun. *Compatible Hardware:* TRS-80.
contact publisher for price.
Instant Software, Inc.

TempleGraph. *Version:* 2.5. Apr. 1992. *Items Included:* Reference guide, user guides. *Customer Support:* 30 days free support for installation, etc.; 1 year maintenance available at 20% purchase price.
SunOS 4.x (8Mb), Solaris 1.0. Sun workstations. $1290.00.
Irix 4.x (8Mb). Silicon Graphics workstations. $1290.00.
Integrated Technical Graphing & Exploratory Data Analysis Tool for Scientists & Engineers. It Utilizes a Point & Click User Interface & Supports User-Defined Functions Written in C, Fortran, or Its Internal Language. It Is Live-Linked to FrameMaker & Mathematica & May Be Called from a User's Program. Its Curve-Fitting, Variable Transformation, Statistics & Calculus Operations are Performed Utilizing Novel Highly-Interactive Data Analysis & Visualization Tools.
Mihalisin Assocs.

TempleTracker. *Version:* 9.05. Feb. 1984. *Compatible Hardware:* IBM PC, PC AT, PC XT, PS/2. *Operating System(s) Required:* PC-DOS. *Language(s):* Compiled BASIC. *Memory Required:* 512k. *Items Included:* Reference manual, tutorial manual. *Customer Support:* Phone/modem support included first year, nominal fee thereafter.
disk $3500.00 (ISBN 0-924068-05-1, Order no.: TE5).
Multi-User System for Jewish Synagogues Which Includes Word Processing, Membership Management, General Ledger/Budget, Yahrzeit Control & Accounts Receivable.
Fogle Computing Corp.

The Templus Series. *Compatible Hardware:* IBM PC; Apple II+, IIe.
disk $74.95.
Includes Ready to Run Templates Which Allow Users to Solve Design & Financial Analysis Problems Without Setting up Models or Typing Lists. User Is Able to Perform the Following: Sales Forecasting, Cash Flow Analysis, Budget & Variance Analysis, Breakeven Analysis, Statistical Analysis & Annuity Calculations.
Prentice Hall.

Tempo EZ. *Items Included:* Manual.
Macintosh 6 & 7, 7.01X (512k). 3.5" disk $79.95.
Macro Utility. Allows Users to Record Any Series of Macintosh Commands or Keystrokes & Execute Any Macro Using a Single Key Code. Featurs "Intelligent" Capabilities Allowing Program to Perform Multiple Tasks Unattended. Macros Can Be Created & Edited with a Click of the Mouse. Features Step-by-Step Menu Commands & Dialog Boxes. Additional Features Include the Following; Users Can: Pause During a Macro Replay to Enter Text or Make a Selection; Record Macros up to the Limits of Disk Space on a Hard or Floppy Drive; Assign up to 450 Keyboard Commands in Each Application; Use Command Key Codes or Option Key Codes; Replay in Slow Motion, in Real Time, or at High Speed; Connect Macros Together, Sequentially; Repeat the Macro a Required Number of Times. Compatible with Most Macintosh Programs. Not Copy Protected.
Affinity Microsystems, Ltd.

Tempo 2 Plus. *Version:* 3.0. *Compatible Hardware:* Apple Macintosh 512k, Macintosh XL. *Memory Required:* 512k.
3.5" disk $179.95.
Macro Utility. Allows Users to Record Any Series of Macintosh Commands or Keystrokes & Execute Any Macro Using a Single Key Code. Features "Intelligent" Capabilities Allowing Program to Perform Multiple Tasks Unattended. Macros Can Be Created & Edited with a Click of the Mouse. Features Step-by-Step Menu Commands & Dialog Boxes. Additional Features Include the Following; Users Can: Pause During a Macro Replay to Enter Text or Make a Selection; Record Macros up to the Limits of Disk Space on a Hard or Floppy Drive; Assign up to 450 Keyboard Commands in Each Application; Use Command Key Codes or Option Key Codes; Replay in Slow Motion, in Real Time, or at High Speed; Connect Macros Together, Nested, Branched, or Sequentially; Repeat the Macro If or Until It Sees the Specified Text, or for a Required Number of Times. Compatible with Most Macintosh Programs. Not Copy Protected.
Affinity Microsystems, Ltd.

Temporary Nursing Personnel Agency System. *Compatible Hardware:* DECmate II, PDP 11-23. *Operating System(s) Required:* COS-310, MICRO-RSX. *Language(s):* DIBOL-83.
$6000.00, incl. user guide (Order no.: 85-11).
Self-Contained, Menu-Driven Invoicing, Payroll, & Planning System. Overwrite Entry Generates Accounting Information for Payroll & Billing Management. Planning System Maintains a Current Record of Nursing Availability at All Skill Levels. Designed for the Specialized Temporary Personnel Agent Which Provides Its Clients with Nursing Care at All Skill Levels & at All Shift & Pay Differentials. Prints Employee Pay Checks & Customer Invoices. Receivable Accounting Is Available. Customer Statements Can Be Printed at Any Time. Provides Separate Monthly Billing, Payroll & Cash Receipts Summaries.
Corporate Consulting Co.

Tempus II. *Version:* 2.0. Creative Computer Design. Jun. 1989.
TOS (512k). Atari ST. disk $79.95.
Text Editor with Many Options.
MichTron, Inc.

1041 Fiduciary. *Items Included:* Manual. *Customer Support:* Free 90 day maintenance.
PC-DOS, MS-DOS 2.0 or higher. IBM PC-XT, IBM PC-AT or compatible (512k). disk $189.00.
$89.00 2nd year renewal.
Spreadsheet Similar to IRS Layout for Tax Preparation.
Profitime, Inc.

1065 PARTNERSHIP TAX

The 1040 Solution. *Version:* 8.4. 1989. *Compatible Hardware:* IBM PC & compatibles, PC XT, PC AT, PS/2. *Operating System(s) Required:* PC-DOS/MS-DOS 3.0. *Language(s):* Pascal. *Memory Required:* 512k. *Customer Support:* Unlimited free.
contact publisher for price.
demo disk $49.00.
Facilitates In-House Tax Preparation of 1040's.
Creative Solutions, Inc. (Michigan).

The 1099 Package. *Version:* 1995. Aug. 1992. *Items Included:* Comprehensive manual in deluxe cloth binder & slipcase. Optional forms creation software available for those with laser printer & "T" cartridge. Optional magnetic media filing module $125.00. *Customer Support:* 2 hours no cost support to registered owners during 1st 6 months. Thereafter $60.00/hr with 1 hour minimum. annual maintenance $35.00, $100.00 with magnetic media filing.
PS-DOS/MS-DOS 2.1 or higher. IBM PC, XT, AT, PS/2 or 100% compatible micro-computer (384k). $125.00 (ISBN 1-877915-04-1, Order no.: 1055 (5.25"), 1053 (3.50")). *Nonstandard peripherals required:* Printer capable of printing 132 characters in condensed or normal mode, or Helwett-Packard Laserjet series II or 100% compatible laser. *Optimal configuration:* 604k, hard disk, DOS 3.3.
Magnetic Media Film $125.00 (Order no.: 1075 (5.25"), 1073 (3.50")).
Standalone Package Which Processes Form 1098, All Forms 1099, Form 5498 & Form 1096. Accumulates Forms 1098, 1099-Div, -INT, -MISC, -PATR, & -R over the Course of a Year. Allows up to 999 Multiple Clients & Can Process up to 5000 Forms per Client File. Will Import Comma-Delimited ASCII Files. Payee/Recipient Information Can Be Zeroed Out & Brought Forward from Year to Year. Has the Ability to Optionally Create an Audit Trail by Printing Each Transaction As It Is Posted. Audit Trail Can Be Stored for Printing Later. Also Validates & Formats Employer Identification Numbers & Social Security Numbers. Contains an 18 Character Account Number for the Purpose of Identifying Forms. Allows for Two Line Names for DBAs & Trusts. Provides Error-Checking During Input & Report Printing. Records Are Also Rechecked for Completeness & Non-Zero Money Prior to Printing Actual Forms. Allows Reprinting from Any Point in a Batch of Forms. Also Print a Single Form.
Phoenix Phive Software Corp.

1065 Partnership. *Items Included:* Manual. *Customer Support:* Free 90 day maintenance.
PC-DOS, MS-DOS 2.0 or higher. IBM PC-XT, IBM PC-AT or compatible (512k). disk $189.00.
$89.00 2nd year renewal.
Spreadsheet Similar to IRS Layout for Tax Preparation.
Profitime, Inc.

1065 Partnership Tax. *Compatible Hardware:* Altos Series 5-15D, 5-5D, 580-XX, ACS8000-XX; DEC Rainbow-100 with 2 disk drives, Rainbow 100+ with 10Mb hard disk; IBM PC, PC XT, PC AT (enhanced) with 2 disk drives; Compaq with 2 disk drives, Compaq Plus with 10Mb hard disk; Hyperion with 2 disk drives, Chameleon Plus with 2 disk drives; Kaypro 11/IV with 2 disk drives, Kaypro 10; Xerox 820; Zilog MXZ-250. *Operating System(s) Required:* CP/M, MP/M, CP/M-86/80, PC-DOS, MS-DOS. *Memory Required:* 128k.
contact publisher for price.
Prepares the U. S. Partnership Income Tax Form 1065 & Its Schedules. Includes On-Line Help Facilities. Can Be Used As a Stand-Alone or in Conjunction with the PRE-AUDIT Package.
Coopers & Lybrand.

Tenant File: For Residential & Commercial Property Management. Version: 3.0.0. Dec. 1992. Items Included: 2 manuals, registration card, check & forms information. Customer Support: No charge technical support. 30 day return policy guarantee.
MS-DOS. IBM & compatibles (512k). TF100 (for 100 units) $99.95; TF500 (for 500 units) $149.95 (Order no.: (512) 288-1305).
Ideal for Owners & Managers of Rental Property. Maintains Separate Tenant & Owner Ledger for Each Unit. Numerous Reports Include Date Sensitive Statements, Income/Expense, Property Features, Outstanding Balances, Vacancies, Even User Defined Report. Checks Easily Written to Screen, Printed, Posted to Ledgers. Vendor Listings with Automatic Payments. Powerful, Practical, & User Friendly.
W G Software.

Tenant Management. Version: 2.3. May 1986. Compatible Hardware: IBM PC AT, PC XT, PS/2 or IBM 100% compatibles. Operating System(s) Required: PC-DOS/MS-DOS. Language(s): C. Memory Required: 640k. Customer Support: 90 days free, additional support & maintenance available.
First station. Contact publisher for price.
Provides the Owner of One or Several Properties with the Tools to Quickly & Easily Track Tenants, Their Payment History, Properties & Individual Units. From Delinquency Reports to Property Profiles. Also Provides Information in Printed Reports or on the Screen Post Payments, Manages Move-Ins & Move-Outs, & Pinpoints Delinquencies.
Timberline Software Corp.

Tennessee Self-Concept Scale. Version: 3.011. William H. Fitts. Customer Support: Free unlimited phone support.
MS-DOS 3.0 or higher. IBM PC & 100% compatibles. disk $225.00 (Order no.: W-1046 (5.25"); W-1047 (3.5")). Optimal configuration: DOS 3.0 or higher (512k), & hard disk with one Mb of free hard disk space, printer.
One of the Most Popular Assessment Tools among Clinicians & Researchers. Designed for Individuals 12 Years of Age or Older, the TSCS Gives User a Multidimensional Description of Self-Concept. The Scale Can Be Used with Virtually Anyone - from Healthy Individuals to Psychotic Patients.
Western Psychological Services.

Tennis. Compatible Hardware: Atari XL/XE. ROM cartridge $16.95 (Order no.: RX8042).
Atari Corp.

Term-80. Compatible Hardware: HP 86/87 with serial interface (HP 82939A) & auxiliary preprocessor module.
3-1/2" or 5-1/4" disk $200.00 ea.
Converts the HP 86/87 into an Intelligent Terminal Able to Communicate with HP Mainframes in Multiple Operating Modes, Including Block & Format. Enables HP 86/87 to Emulate the HP 2622A Terminal.
Hewlett-Packard Co.

Terminal Emulation System. Dennis Allen. 1986. Compatible Hardware: TRS-80. Operating System(s) Required: TRSDOS 6.x. Memory Required: 64k.
disk $79.95 (Order no.: D4TES).
Enables the Model 4 to Emulate over 100 Different Terminals, & TSED, the Editor Which Allows User to Configure His Own Terminal Protocol.
The Alternate Source.

Terminal Emulator II. Compatible Hardware: TI Home Computer, telephone coupler, RS-232 interface, speech synthesizer.
contact publisher for price (Order no.: PHM 3035).
Links Home Computer to Telecommunications World.
Texas Instruments, Personal Productivit.

The Terminator. Mar. 1995. Customer Support: Dedicated voice mail phone number; will respond back to consumer.
Windows 3.1 or higher; Macintosh. IBM or 100% compatible 486SX 25MHz (4Mb); 68030/68040 Color Mac System 7.1 or higher (4Mb). CD-ROM disk $19.99 (ISBN 1-57339-014-3, Order no.: ROMI2941NSB). Nonstandard peripherals required: 2X CD-ROM drive.
Arnold Schwarzenegger Stars As a Cyborg from the Future Sent to Present Day Los Angeles to Kill the Mother of a Future Opposition Leader.
Image Entertainment.

Terminator. Compatible Hardware: IBM PC & compatibles. Operating System(s) Required: PC-DOS/MS-DOS 2.0 or higher. Memory Required: 38k. General Requirements: Hercules, CGA, or EGA card.
disk $39.95.
Enables Users to View, on a World Map, the Line That Separates the Day & Night at Any Time in the Future or Past. Features Variable Speed & the Ability to Display Selected Cities in a Zoom Mode.
TriDos Software Pubs.

Terminology for Allied Health Professionals. 1990.
IBM PC. write for info. (ISBN 0-538-70161-7, Order no.: RT 40BH81).
IBM PS/2. contact publisher for price (ISBN 0-538-70190-0, Order no.: RT40BH88).
Study Guide, to Accompany Terminology for Allied Health Professionals, Provides a Computerized Review of Chapter Material.
South-Western Publishing Co.

Termulator. Version: 3.10. Items Included: 1 manual. Customer Support: 1 free phone call.
MS-DOS to SCO UNIX Host. InTel Compatible (64k). $150.00. Optimal configuration: 8086 or higher, 256k, MS-DOS 64k available, Serial Port.
EmulaTec ANSI Console, WY60, PC-TERM & VT100 in MS-DOS Computers. Supports Color, Aux Serial Port, Background Printing & Two Way File Transfer.
Hansco Information Technologies, Inc.

Terpsichore. Richard E. Rae. Aug. 1986. Compatible Hardware: Apple Macintosh. Memory Required: 128k. General Requirements: Printer; ConcertWare+ or ConcertWare+MIDI software.
disk $49.95.
Collection of Renaissance/Baroque Music Transcribed & Arranged by Richard E. Rae. The Original Terpsichore, Named after the Greek Muse of Dance, Was Published in 1612 by Michael Praetorius, Who Collected Court Music from the French Dancemasters of the Court of King Henry IV. The 181 Music Files on These Disks Are Designed Exclusively for Use with ConcertWare+ & ConcertWare+MIDI, & Enable Much of This Music to Be Heard for the First Time. Many Baroque/Renaissance Instruments Designed for Concertware+ Are Included.
Great Wave Software.

TerraPro: Funeral Home Case Management. Version: 2.70. Jul. 1994. Compatible Hardware: IBM PC & compatibles. Operating System(s) Required: MS-DOS, Windows 3.1, Macintosh System 7. Language(s): FoxPro 2.6. Memory Required: 640k. General Requirements: 120Mb hard disk, printer. Items Included: Disks, manual. Customer Support: 800/373-5789, 1 year, renewable.
disk $1295.00 single user; $1595.00 multi-user.
Simplifies Bookkeeping of Accounts Receivable & Vital Statistics for the Funeral Director. It Also Prints All Forms, Allows Maintenance & Printing of Price Lists, & Produces a Sales Journal. Retrieves Information on Any Name Entered, Relationships Between Names; Also Includes Sales Analysis, Inventory Control, Word Processing (Editing of Obituary Information), Built-In Calculator, Calendar, & Appointment Scheduler. Information Is Stored on Floppy Disks, Allowing Unlimited Storage Capacity. Interfaces with SBT Accounting Library for Full Accounting Functions.
Terradise Computer Systems, Inc.

TerraView.
DOS, Windows, Unix. disk $3495.00.
Programmer's Toolkit for Developing Mapping Applications. Program Allows User to Write Applications Using Pascal, C, & Other Languages without Having Knowledge of Complex Cartographic Constructs. Optimized for Rapid Retrieval & Display of Spatial Data Accessed from Magnetic & CD-ROM Media. Toolkit Supports Data Types & Classification Systems Such As Mercator & Polyconic & Coordinate Systems Such As Longitude/Latitude & Most State Plane Coordinate Systems.
TerraLogics, Inc.

Tessel Mania. Sep. 1995. Customer Support: Telephone support - free (except phone charge).
Windows 3.1. IBM & compatibles (386 DX-20) (4Mb). CD-ROM disk $12.99 (ISBN 1-57594-032-9). Nonstandard peripherals required: 2x CD-ROM player, Sound Card, VGA monitor. Optimal configuration: 486 SX-33.
Art & Design Tool.
Kidsoft, Inc.

Tessel Mania. Sep. 1995. Customer Support: Telephone support - free (except phone charge).
Windows 3.1. IBM & compatibles (386 DX-20) (4Mb). CD-ROM disk $12.99 (ISBN 1-57594-071-X). Nonstandard peripherals required: 2x CD-ROM player, Sound Card, VGA monitor. Optimal configuration: 486 SX-33.
Art & Design Tool. Blister Pack Jewel Case.
Kidsoft, Inc.

TessSystem Three. Version: 3.8. M. Javed Aslam. Aug. 1985. Compatible Hardware: Macintosh. Memory Required: 512k. General Requirements: 10Mb hard disk. Customer Support: Yes.
3.5" disk $2995.00.
Comprehensive Medical Office Management System Designed to Automate Functions Such As Insurance Processing, Patient Billing, Accounts Receivable, Patient Transactions & Report Generation. Single-Doctor or Multidoctor/Single-User or Multiuser Practices.
Tess Data Systems.

Test Defier: The Business Letter. R. Leonard. Jun. 1987. Compatible Hardware: Apple II, IBM PC. Operating System(s) Required: Apple DOS 3.3, MS-DOS for IBM. Memory Required: Apple 64k, IBM 256k. General Requirements: 1.0. Customer Support: 800-654-8715, full lifetime guarantee.
Apple II. disk $69.95 (ISBN 0-940503-22-0).
IBM PC. disk $69.95 (ISBN 0-940503-23-9).
Apple II. site license disk $139.95.
IBM PC.
Research Design Assocs., Inc.

TITLE INDEX

Test Drive.
IBM PC & compatibles. disk $19.95.
Sports-Car Driving Simulation.
Accolade, Inc.

Test Drive III: The Passion. Oct. 1990. *Items Included:* Catalog, copy protection device, manual, proof of purchase card. *Customer Support:* Technical support 408-296-8400, 90 day limited warranty.
IBM DOS 2.1 or higher, Tandy-DOS (8Mhz or faster recommended). IBM PC, XT, AT, & compatibles, Tandy 1000 series, 3000, 4000 (640k). $59.95. *Optimal configuration:* Hard drive installable, keyboard, joystick, graphics card, & sound board.
Car Driving Simulation with New Features Including Snow, Rain, Night & Day Driving, Cross Traffic, Mountain Curves, Ocean Straightaways, Digitized Car Interiors, & More.
Accolade, Inc.

Test Master: A Series of Universal Game Templates for Training & Learning. Aug. 1995. *Items Included:* Runtime version for Windows or Mac. Index program to assist in content development. Document templates to assist in content development, on line tutorial. *Customer Support:* 30 day money-back guarantee, telephone support (no charge), on-line tutorial.
Windows 3.1 or higher, Windows 95. IBM & compatibles, 486 or higher (4Mb). $695.00 per template; $2000.00 all four templates, site licensing also avail. *Addl. software required:* Word processor. *Optimal configuration:* Pentium, 8Mb RAM, sound card. *Networks supported:* Allows multiple concurrent network access.
System 7.X or higher. Mac (4Mb). $695.00 per template; $2000.00 all four templates, site licensing also avail. *Addl. software required:* Word processor. *Optimal configuration:* PowerMac 8Mb RAM. *Networks supported:* Allows multiple concurrent network access.
A Series of Stimulating Game Templates/ Programs Whose Content Is Easily Adapted to Meet End-User Requirements Whether in a Corporate, Industrial, or Academic Environment. Designed to Reduce the Time Required to Successfully Trian & Educate Learners in Critical Subject Areas.
StillWater Media.

Test Quest. *Version:* 3.2. Chris Mayer. Apr. 1989. *Items Included:* Two 40 page manuals, site license. *Customer Support:* Context sensitive help menu, call collect if help is needed, no time-limit full money back if not satisfied.
PC or MS-DOS (384k). IBM or compatible, PC, XT, AT, PS/2. disk $99.00 (ISBN 1-56040-000-5, Order no.: TQ). *Nonstandard peripherals required:* 2 drives.
Test Generating Program for MS/PC-DOS Allows Educators to Gradually Develop Banks of Questions & Print Attractively Formatted Tests. Supports an Unlimited Number of Multiple Choice, Completion, True-False, Matching & Essay Questions. The Program Features an Efficient Text Editor, a Time-Saving On-Line HELP Function, Radomizing Answers to Prevent Cheating, & Automatic Answer Keys.
Snowflake Software.

Test Scoring System. *Version:* V8.01. *Items Included:* 1 full manual. *Customer Support:* 90 days unlimited warranty; unlimited technical support via telephone for $225/system per year.
MS-DOS. IBM or compatible (640k). disk $995.00. *Optimal configuration:* MS-DOS 6.2 or higher, 15Mb of space on a hard drive (to include all 5 systems). *Networks supported:* Novell, LANtastic, Windows NT.
This System Corrects Multiple Choice Tests of up to 100 Questions Using an Optical Scanner. It Correlates Responses with Objectives, Allowing Schools or School Districts to Monitor Student Progress in Competency Areas. This System Generates Reports by Student, Grade Level & School, or by Student, School, & District.
Applied Educational Systems, Inc.

Testat. *Compatible Hardware:* Apple Macintosh Plus or higher; IBM PC, 286 or higher & compatibles. *Items Included:* Documentation. *Customer Support:* Free technical support.
3.5" disk $110.00.
Test Summary Statistics, Reliability Coefficients, Standard Errors of Measurement, Item Analysis Statistics.
Systat, Inc.

TESTFACT. *Version:* 2.6. Douglas T. Wilson et al. 1993. *Items Included:* Manual. *Customer Support:* Free technical support, 90 day limited warranty.
MS-DOS. IBM & compatibles. 3.5" disk $465.00 386 DOS Extender (ISBN 1-56321-125-4). manual $30.00 (ISBN 1-56321-117-3).
Performs Item Analysis & Test Scoring According to the Principles of Classical Test Theory. Designed Originally for a National Testing Service, the Program Has All of the Features Needed for Processing Data from Binary Scored Tests, Subtests, or Scales.
Lawrence Erlbaum Assocs., Software & Alternate Media, Inc.

Testing Programs for Advanced Ear Training, 6 disks. Bruce Benward & Brian Moore. May 1986. *Compatible Hardware:* Apple II with Applesoft Firmware Card, II+, IIe. *Memory Required:* 64k. *General Requirements:* DAC board & headphones or speaker.
disk $150.00 (ISBN 0-697-00303-5).
Interactive Tests Which Require the Student to Identify Notes & Chords Played by the Computer. Keeps Track of a Running Score for the Individual Student.
Wm. C. Brown Pubs.

TestLab 2000. *Version:* 2.0. May 1990. *Items Included:* 3-Ring slipcase/binder. *Customer Support:* 60 day unlimited warranty; unlimited phone support; unlimited defective disk replacement.
MS-DOS. IBM PC & compatible (640k). $295.00 Single machine; $595.00 Network (Order no.: PS7234). *Addl. software required:* DOS. *Optimal configuration:* 640k RAM, Hard Disk. *Networks supported:* Yes.
Training Exam Creation, Delivery & Storage System. Creates Data Base of Exam Items, Allows Online or Hard Copy Administration. Stores Performance Data, Automatically Calculates Scores, Statistics. Stores Training Class Rosters, Allows Individual or Group Performance Review Online. Variety of Printouts Available.
A.U. Software.

Tetra Quest. Microdeal. Oct. 1988. *Compatible Hardware:* Atari ST; Commodore Amiga. *Memory Required:* 512k. *General Requirements:* Color monitor.
Atari. 3.5" disk $39.95, (Demo Avail.).
Commodore. 3.5" disk $39.95.
Arcade Game. Quest to Retrieve Six Phoenix Tablets Which Have Been Stolen by The Tetroids. They Have Split Each Tablet into Sixty-Four Pieces & Have Hidden Each of The Pieces in The Six Provinces of Their World. Various Obstacles Are Presented on The Quest.
MichTron, Inc.

TEXHELP: THE ON-LINE TEX HANDBOOK

Tetrad II: Tools of Casual Modeling. Richard Scheines et al. 1994. *Customer Support:* Free technical support, 90-day limited warranty.
DOS. disk $15.00, incl. manual (ISBN 1-56321-115-7).
A Powerful, Flexible Aid for Specifying Linear Structural Equation Models.
Lawrence Erlbaum Assocs. Software & Alternate Media, Inc.

TETRIS: The Soviet Challenge. *Version:* MAC 1.3, MAC II 1.0, Amiga 1.1, Apple II 1.1, Apple IIgs 1.1, AST 1.0, Commodore 64 1.0, IBM 1.1.
Amiga 500, 1000, 2000, 2500 (512k). 3.5" disk $34.95, backup ,10.00. *Addl. software required:* KickStart 1.2 or higher.
Apple II, II+, IIc, IIe, IIgs (requires 128k RAM for Side A or 48k RAM for Side B). disk $39.95, backup ,7.50.
Atari 520 ST, 1040ST, Mega 2, Mega 4 (512k). 3.5" disk $34.95, backup ,10.00. *Nonstandard peripherals required:* Color monitor.
Commodore 64, 128 (64k). disk $14.95, backup ,7.50. *Nonstandard peripherals required:* 1541/1571 disk drive; joystick.
IBM PC, PCjr, XT, AT or 99% compatible (256k). disk $34.95. *Nonstandard peripherals required:* One 5.25" disk drive or 3.5" disk drive; CGA, EGA or HGC graphics card, graphics monitor.
Mac 512k Enhanced, MacPlus, MacSE, SE/30, Mac II, IIx, IIcx, (512k; 1Mb for Mac II). 3.5" disk $39.95. *Nonstandard peripherals required:* 800k double-sided disk drive; RGB color monitor for Mac II.
First Game Ever to Come Out of the Soviet Union. User Rotates a Piece Shaped from Four Squares So That It Fits Precisely to Form a Solid Horizontal Row. User Can Move to a Higher Level after Successful Completion of Ten Rows. Offers Nine Levels of Play & Five Heights to Start From. Provides On-Screen Help. Displays Colorful Background Graphics. Allows User to Replay the Previous Game.
Spectrum HoloByte.

TeX. *Customer Support:* All of our products are unconditionally guaranteed.
DOS, Unix. CD-ROM disk $39.95 (Order no.: TEX). *Nonstandard peripherals required:* CD-ROM drive.
Professional Typesetting Program with 1000 MB of Code to Compile.
Walnut Creek CDRom.

Texas Corporation Formation Package & Minute Book. Wyman N. Bravard. May 1986. *Compatible Hardware:* IBM PC & compatibles. *Operating System(s) Required:* PC-DOS 2.0 or higher. *Memory Required:* 256k.
disk $39.95, incl. manual (ISBN 1-55571-010-7).
WORDSTAR-Compatible Word Processing Program Is Provided on the Disk, Together with the Text Files from the Book, Which Include All the Letters, Bylaws, Articles of Incorporation & Other Forms Incorporated in the Book.
Oasis Pr.

Texas Instruments General Ledger. *Compatible Hardware:* TI Professional. *Operating System(s) Required:* CP/M, MS-DOS. *Memory Required:* 64k. *General Requirements:* Printer.
$1095.00 (Order no.: SY P/N T039-015).
Stores Journal Transactions & Job Cost Entries with Complete Audit Trail. Provides 26 Different User-Defined Financial Statement Formats.
Texas Instruments, Personal Productivit.

TeXHelp: The On-Line TeX Handbook. Arvind Borde & Tomas Rokicki. Aug. 1993. *Items Included:* Brief manual & 1 disk. *Customer Support:* Support is available through the authors - no fee is charged.

DOS or Microsoft Windows 3.0, 286 or higher. IBM PC & compatibles (640k). disk $49.95 (ISBN 0-12-117640-1). *Addl. software required:* TeX Program. *Optimal configuration:* IBM PC or Clone 386 or 486 with Windows & color monitor, hard drive.
Provides TeX Users with a Set of Data Files & On-Line Access to Help Screens for Definitions & Explanations of all TeX Commands, & It Clearly Describes Which TeX Commands Are to Be Used for Which Typesetting Purposes. The Program Is Written in C & Runs on IBM PCs & Clones.
Academic Pr., Inc.

TEXIS. *Version:* 2.0. Sep. 1994. *Items Included:* Program, program manual (both hardcopy & on-line). *Customer Support:* Free unlimited phone tech support. Training/consulting $1200.00 per day, per person.
Unix. Any Unix (640k). Starting at $4395.00 with one client (quantity discount available). *Optimal configuration:* 4Mb hard disk, any Unix. *Networks supported:* Novell, Banyon, Ethernet.
MS-DOS/Windows. IBM PC & compatibles (640k). Starting at $4395.00 with one client (quantity discounts available). *Optimal configuration:* 4Mb hard disk, PC MS-DOS 2.1 or higher. *Networks supported:* Novell, Banyon, Ethernet.
OS/2 (640k). Starting at $4395.00 with one client (quantity discounts available). *Optimal configuration:* 4Mb hard disk. *Networks supported:* Novell, Banyon, Ethernet.
Allows User to Easily Bridge the Gully Between Traditional Databases & Document Driven Activities by Allowing the Import, Export, Management & Concept-Based Retrieval of Textual Information. ANSI SQL Driven; Binary Large Object Support; Unix, DOS & Windows & NT Servers; SGML Document Manipulation; Embedded SQL for C & C Plus Plus; UNIX Remote Procedure Call (RPC) Server; Microsoft ACCESS for Windows Compatible; Microsoft Open Database Connectivity (ODBC) Driver; Postscript File & Record Handling.
Thunderstone Software/Expansion Programs International, Inc.

Texis. *Version:* 2.01. *Items Included:* One binder manual. *Customer Support:* Unlimited phone support - free.
PC-DOS/MS-DOS, UNIX, Open VMS. IBM PC/XT/AT, PS/2 & compatibles, Midrange, Mainframe, Digital VAX Systems (300k). Starting at $4395.00. *Optimal configuration:* 500k hard disk. *Networks supported:* TCPIP, Banyan, Novell, Ethernet, Token Ring.
Merges the Power of Metamorph with a SQL Relational Database Server to Provide a Software Package That Tackles the Most Demanding Information Tasks. Allows Efficient Imaging of Gap Between Traditional Databases & Document Driven Activities by Allowing the Import, Export, Management & Concept-Based Retrieval of Textual Information.
Thunderstone Software/Expansions Programs International, Inc.

TexSys. *Compatible Hardware:* Apple Macintosh. 3.5" disk $69.00.
Text-Revision Control System.
ToolMasters, Ltd.

Text Adder & Shape Tables. 1984. *Compatible Hardware:* Apple II, II+, IIe. *Language(s):* Applesoft BASIC. *Memory Required:* 48k. disk $39.95 (Order no.: AU400).
Adds Text to Any Picture or Shape Table Figure. Also Includes Shape Tables with 141 Pre-Drawn Figures. Designed for Advanced Programmer Wanting to Expand His or Her Graphic Capabilities.
Amidon Pubns.

The Text Collector. *Version:* 2.0. *Compatible Hardware:* IBM PC & compatibles. *Operating System(s) Required:* PC-DOS/MS-DOS 2.0 or higher. *Memory Required:* 128k. *Items Included:* User's manual.
disk $69.00 (ISBN 0-931285-02-X).
Text-Retrieval System. Detects All Entries of Any String of Characters from Multiple Text Files & Saves them to a Separate Text File.
O'Neill Software.

Text Com. *Compatible Hardware:* IBM PC. *Customer Support:* Free product support. $989.00.
Textcom Transfers Documents Bisynchronously Between Wang VS, OIS, or Alliance Systems & the Following IBM PC Word Processing Formats: WordPerfect, OfficeWriter, Multimate, MicrosoftWord, DisplayWrite, PFS: Professional Write, Word Star & ASCII.
M/H Group.

Text Editing. *Compatible Hardware:* HP 85. data cartridge, 3-1/2" or 5-1/4" disk $115.00 ea. (Order no.: 82816A).
Write Memos, Outlines, & Reports on the Display Screen. Edit Copy, Save It on Tape, or Disc or Print It. Variable Input/Output of Text Files. Tab, Add, Delete, Replace, Renumber, & Move Lines. Matched String & Replace.
Hewlett-Packard Co.

Text Editor. May 1986. *Compatible Hardware:* IBM PC, PC XT, PC AT. *Operating System(s) Required:* PC-DOS 1.0 or higher, MS-DOS 1.1 or higher. *Language(s):* Compiled BASIC. *Memory Required:* 128k. *General Requirements:* Printer. CGA card & monitor recommended.
disk $20.00.
May Be Used to Create or Update Programs in BASIC, PL/1, Pascal, FORTRAN & Assembly or Any Other Language.
Robert L. Nicolai.

Text Editor-200. *Compatible Hardware:* HP Series 200 Models 216/220, 226/236, 217/237 Personal Technical Computers with BASIC 2.0 or 3.0. *Memory Required:* 512k.
HP 216/220, 217/237. 3-1/2" or 5-1/4" disk $275.00 ea. (Order no.: 45538B).
HP 226/236. 5-1/4" disk $275.00 ea.
Helps Users Create Reports, Memos, or Letters. Almost All Commands Are Executed Either from Menus or Softkeys. Features Include: Linking of Multiple Files for Printing, Alphabetic & Numeric Sorting, & Superscripts & Subscripts. Editing Functions Include Right & Left Justification, Word Wrap, Auto-Find of Words or Phrases, & Re-Forming Paragraphs to Declared Margins.
Hewlett-Packard Co.

Text Manager. *Operating System(s) Required:* Windows. *Memory Required:* 128k. $149.50.
Text Editor & Organizer That Runs under Microsoft Windows, Supports All Standard Windows Environment Features & Works Either with a Keyboard or Mouse. Program Functions Are Available in the Pull-Down Menus & Can Be Assigned to Accelerator Keys on the Fly. Also Available Are Text Templates for Legal, Accounting & Software Development Markets.
Solea Systems, Inc.

Text Master. *Compatible Hardware:* Apple II. *Memory Required:* 48k. $19.95.
Dynacomp, Inc.

Text Tanglers. V. Stevens & S. Millmore. Sep. 1987. *Compatible Hardware:* IBM PC. *Operating System(s) Required:* MS-DOS. *Memory Required:* 256k. *General Requirements:* 1 disk drive, color or mono monitor. *Customer Support:* 800-654-8715, full lifetime guarantee.
single site license disk $69.95 (ISBN 0-940503-21-2).
site license disk $139.95 (ISBN 0-940503-31-X).
Contains Five Text Reconstruction Programs.
Research Design Assocs., Inc.

Text-to-Speech. *Compatible Hardware:* TI 99/4A with speech synthesizer. *Language(s):* BASIC.
contact publisher for price (Order no.: PHD 5078).
Allows Computer to Speak Almost Any Word in the English Language. Operates with TI Extended BASIC Cartridge.
Texas Instruments, Personal Productivit.

Text Word Processing. 1978. *Compatible Hardware:* TRS-80. *Operating System(s) Required:* TRSDOS 1.3. *Language(s):* BASIC. *Memory Required:* 48k.
disk $24.95.
cassette $24.95.
Word Processor That Works with Lines & Pages.
Demi-Software.

Textbook Librarian. *Version:* 2.0. Oct. 1993. *Items Included:* Spiral bound 100 page manual, network sharing software for Multi User version. *Customer Support:* 24 Hour Support Hotline, Unlimited FAX/AppleLink Support, Software Updates, Version Upgrades, COMPanion Newsletters, User Group Sponsorship, & Area Training Seminars. The first year of support is included with purchase. Annual support renewal is $249.00.
Macintosh OS. Macintosh SE to Power Macintosh (1Mb). $995.00 Single user; $1745.00 site license. *Optimal configuration:* LC475 or Power Macintosh. *Networks supported:* AppleTalk, Ethernet, AppleShare, AllShare.
Offers a Complete Management Package for Your Textbook Bookroom, with Up-to-The Minute Information on Circulation, Inventory, & Management & Planning Details. Fines & Payments, Bar Code Labels, & Usage Reports Are Fully Integrated. Tabular Lists Such As Textbook Condition, Vendors, Teachers, & Courses Can Be Compiled Easily.
COMPanion Corp.

Texteditor. Duane Bristow. *Compatible Hardware:* TRS-80 Model I. *Operating System(s) Required:* TRSDOS. *Memory Required:* 32k.
disk $69.95.
Provides a Method for Storage & Manipulation of Text of All Kinds. Includes Line Edit, Screen Edit, Right Justify, Global Search & Replace.
Duane Bristow Computers, Inc.

TextScan. *Version:* 4.0. *General Requirements:* Apple Macintosh Plus, SE, II. *Items Included:* Complete comprehensive user's manual. *Customer Support:* Free Telephone technical support for 90 days.
3.5" disk $395.00.
Omni Font OCR Software Compatible with All Scanners Generating PICT & TIFF Images. Optional Saving of Font Tables to Increase Speed. Optional "Teach" Mode. Automatic Corrections Through 40,000 & Word Intelligent Dictionary. Reads Multiple Fonts & Sizes Within a Document. Dot-Matrix Capable.
Prism Enterprises, Inc.

Textures, 6 disks. *Compatible Hardware:* Apple Macintosh.
Set. $495.00, incl. user's guide & reference manual.
Allows the User to Compose & Typeset Documents up to Several Thousands of Pages in Length. Provides a Macro Programming Language for Complex Table Construction.
Addison-Wesley Publishing Co., Inc.

TITLE INDEX

TextWare: Instant Information Access. Version: 3.0. Compatible Hardware: IBM PC & LAN Environments (NetWare, Any NetBIOS compatible LAN); Macintosh Version 1.0. Operating System(s) Required: PC-DOS/MS-DOS. Memory Required: 640k. Items Included: Software & documentation. Customer Support: Software update service & phone support are available.
single user $495.00; with Images $745.00.
1-5 concurrent user LAN system $995.00; with Images $1495.00.
6-100 users $2995.00; with Imaging $4595.00.
Full Text Indexing & Retrieval Software for PC & LAN Environments. Each Word in a Text Database Can Be Indexed, & Users Can Then Retrieve, Display & Output Information Via Boolean, Phrase, Proximity or Field Searches. Images & Other Types of Data Can Be Tagged to Text to Create a Multimedia Environment. TextWare Is Ideal for the Creation & Maintenance of Online Manuals & Documentation, CD-ROM & Other Electronic Publishing Applications, & Image Storage & Retrieval Systems.
TextWare Corp.

TFLX. Version: 5.2. Nov. 1988. Compatible Hardware: Macintosh Plus & higher. Memory Required: 2500k. General Requirements: Hard disk with Apple Macintosh Plus, Macintosh SE, II Ser., Classic, SI, Quadra, Powerbook, etc. Items Included: H/W, cabling, disks, manual. Customer Support: Telephone/FAX.
disk $495.00, "starter set" to $1750.00, prof level.
Handles All Phone Tasks Such As Voice Mail, Surveys, Order Entry, Telemarketing, Technical Support, Fax on Demand, Without Supervision. Talks & Interacts with Incoming & Outgoing Calls. Uses Data Files to Merge & Speak Names, Prices, Greetings, Dates, Queries. Create Application with Magnum's PICTURE PROGRAMMING - Link Icons Together in Flowchart Format to Make Application. Includes Sample Templates, Voice Recordings, etc. Now Also Works with Pictures from Slowscan Video Phones.
Magnum Software Corp.

TGAUSS. Version: 3.2. Jun. 1983. Compatible Hardware: IBM PC, PC XT, PC AT & compatibles. Operating System(s) Required: MS-DOS, PC-DOS. Language(s): FORTRAN. Memory Required: 512k. General Requirements: Printer.
disk $1350.00 (Order no.: TGAUSS).
Completes the First Step in a Simulation Study: Analysis of the Sample Data Histogram & Normalization of the Model. The Model Relates the Histogram of the Data to the Histogram of Standard Gaussian Data. This Function Is an Expansion of Hermite Polynomials, Which Allows the Option of Disjunctive Kriging.
Geostat Systems International, Inc. (GSII).

TGRAF - TNET: TGRAF - TNET - 07, 4200, 05, 11, 15. Version: 2.4. Aug. 1994. Items Included: Media & user's guide. Customer Support: 1 year free technical support & updates.
DOS. IBM PC & compatibles (256k). Contact publisher for price. Networks supported: FTP's PC/TCP, PC NFS, DECNET LAT, Wollongong, Ethernet, Token Ring, Built-In TCP/IP, RS-232.
Enables a Personal Computer to Emulate a TEKTRONIX 4100 or 4200 Series Terminal (Depending on Which TGRAF You Choose), Performing Functions Include Drawing of Points, Vectors, Polygons, Segment Transformations, True Zoom & Pan, & Surfaces. Features Also Include, Graphics Input (GIN) Modes, Inking & Rubberbanding, Definable Cursor, Vector Fonts & Function Keys, & Pixel Operations for Such Tasks As Solid Modeling. Cutomers Using TGRAF Products Could Be Communicating with Mainframe Packages Like These: DISSPLA - Plotting Package; IDEAS - Mechanical Analysis; ARCINFO - Mapping GIS; MEDUSA - a CAD Package; & SASGRAPH Data Analysis.
Grafpoint.

TGRAF for Windows: TGRAF-05 Plus & TGRAF-07. Version: 1.2. Jul. 1991. Items Included: Media & user's guide. Customer Support: 1 year free technical support & updates.
MS-Windows 3.1. 286 (2Mb). disk $395.00-$795.00. Nonstandard peripherals required: VGA, mouse. Networks supported: Built-In TCP/IP, DEC LAT, DEC CTERM, LAN Workplace for DOS, INT 14, BAPI, RS-232.
Gives User the Power of a TEKTRONIX 4105, 4107, or 4207 Graphics Terminal at Your PC. User Has the Ability to Run Hundreds of Mainframe Applications Which Previously Required a Dedicated Graphics Terminal, Concurrently with All MS Windows Applications. A Valuable Engineering Tool for CAD/CAM, Data Analysis & Modeling, Molecular Design, Mapping & Application Development Software. Features Include; Arcs & Curves, Segments, Rubberbanding, Gridding, Pixel Operations. Communication Protocols Supported Are RS232, Grafpoint's Built-In TCP/IP, LAT, Interrupt 14, Telapi, & Other 3rd Party Networks Supported.
Grafpoint.

TGRAF-X: Tektronix Terminal Emulation Software. Version: 1.4. Jun. 1990. Items Included: Media & documentation. Customer Support: Free technical support & product updates for up to one year after date of purchase.
Virtually all UNIX platforms: Sun, VAX station, DEC station, HP, IBM RS/6000, Data General, Silicon Graphics, DEC Alpha. $995.00-$2995.00. Addl. software required: X-Window System (X11R4). Networks supported: Ethernet or RS-232.
Software Tool for Accessing Host-Based Applications (CAD/CAM, CAE, Mapping, & Business Graphics) on Your Workstation or X Terminal. Supports Both Graphic (Tektronix 4107/4207, 4211, or 4125/4225) & Alphanumeric (DEC VT52, VT100, VT220) Terminal Emulation. Runs in a Network, RS-232 or Standalone Environment.
Grafpoint.

TGS: The Graphic Solution. Version: 64.1. Sep. 1983. Compatible Hardware: Apple II series. Operating System(s) Required: Apple DOS 3.3. Memory Required: 64k. Items Included: Manual, Original & Backup of Software, Demo Disk & Sample Sequences.
disk $79.95.
Creates Animated Text & Graphics for Sales Product Demonstrations. Allows User to Develop Educational Materials & Training Aids That Mix Text, Programs, & Graphics on Screen. Images Can Be Displayed on Backgrounds Loaded from Other Programs. User Can Construct Custom Typesizes & Typefaces to Balance Visual Elements. Provides User with Colorful 3-D Perspectives for Charts. Can Create Interactive Materials & Can Be Used to Teach Computer Graphics & Animation at Art Schools & for Middle School Through University Age Levels.
Accent Software, Inc.

That's Interest-Ing. Compatible Hardware: TRS-80 Color Computer. Language(s): Extended Color BASIC. Memory Required: 32k.
cassette $30.95.
Computes Present Value of Stream of Payments or Receipts at Specified Interest Rate or Rate of Return Represented by Stream. Projects Future Values & Stream of Payments Equal to Stated Amount. Computes Current Bond Yield & Rate of Return to Maturity. Amortization Schedules May Specify Either Amount or Number of Payments, & Conditions May Be Changed Within Repayment Period.
Custom Software Engineering, Inc.

That's Life. Compatible Hardware: Atari. Memory Required: 48k.
disk $12.00.
Multiple Player Game for the Whole Family. Go to College, Choose a Career, Get Married, Raise a Family, Deal with the Crises of Every Day Living.
Athena Software.

Theatre Management System. Jul. 1989. Items Included: Training manual. Customer Support: 1 yr. maintenance $200.
MS-DOS (640k). IBM PC & compatibles, 386/486. disk $2995.00 assigned seats; $1995.00 unassigned seats. Addl. software required: WordStar Release 5 or WordPerfect. Networks supported: Novell.
MS-DOS. IBM PC host, 386 plus workstation keyboards & terminals. disk $2995.00 assigned seats; $1995.00 unassigned seats. Addl. software required: WordStar Release 5 or WordPerfect.
Manages Box Office Theatre Ticket Sales, Box Office Theatre Ticket Reservations, Group Sales Contracts, Ticket Reservations, Payment Collection, Theatre Mailing List for Leads & Communication, Subscriber Tickets & Gift Certificate Purchases.
The James Gang.

Thematic Applications: American History. Ron Dunaeisky. 1995. Items Included: CD-ROM in binder with documentation & activities. Customer Support: Toll free customer service Hot Line 1-800-645-3739 (9a.m. - 5p.m. Eastern Time) software guaranteed for two years.
Windows. IBM (8Mb). CD-ROM disk $99.00 (Order no.: CDR52004). Nonstandard peripherals required: CD-ROM drive. Addl. software required: MS Windows & MSworks for Windows.
Mac OS 7.0. Macintosh (8Mb). Nonstandard peripherals required: CD-ROM drive. Addl. software required: ClarisWorks 2.1 or higher or MS-Works 3.0 or higher.
Integrates Technology Directly into Content Area Curriculum. It Teaches Students to Locate, Manipulate, Organize & Analyze Data: to Draw Conclusions; & to Communicate Effectively Using Graphs, Mathematical Models Displays & Other Visual Media.
Educational Activities Inc.

Thematic Applications: American Pluralism. Ron Dunaeisky. 1995. Items Included: CD-ROM in binder with documentation & activities. Customer Support: Toll free customer service Hot Line 1-800-645-3739 (9a.m. - 5p.m. Eastern Time) software guaranteed for two years.
Windows. IBM (8Mb). CD-ROM disk $99.00 (Order no.: CDR52005). Nonstandard peripherals required: CD-ROM drive. Addl. software required: MS Windows & MSworks for Windows.
Mac OS 7.0. Macintosh (8Mb). Nonstandard peripherals required: CD-ROM drive. Addl. software required: ClarisWorks 2.1 or higher or MS-Works 3.0 or higher.
Integrates Technology Directly into Content Area Curriculum. It Teaches Students to Locate, Manipulate, Organize & Analyze Data: to Draw Conclusions; & to Communicate Effectively Using Graphs, Mathematical Models Displays & Other Visual Media.
Educational Activities Inc.

THEMATIC APPLICATIONS: ANCIENT

Thematic Applications: Ancient Civilizations.
Ron Dunaeisky. 1995. *Items Included:* CD-ROM in binder with documentation & activities. *Customer Support:* Toll free customer service Hot Line 1-800-645-3739 (9a.m. - 5p.m. Eastern Time) software guaranteed for two years.
Windows. IBM (8Mb). CD-ROM disk $99.00 (Order no.: CDR52002). *Nonstandard peripherals required:* CD-ROM drive. *Addl. software required:* MS Windows & MSworks for Windows.
Mac OS 7.0. Macintosh (8Mb). *Nonstandard peripherals required:* CD-ROM drive. *Addl. software required:* ClarisWorks 2.1 or higher or MS-Works 3.0 or higher.
Integrates Technology Directly into Content Area Curriculum. It Teaches Students to Locate, Manipulate, Organize & Analyze Data: to Draw Conclusions; & to Communicate Effectively Using Graphs, Mathematical Models Displays & Other Visual Media.
Educational Activities Inc.

Thematic Applications: General. Ron Dunaeisky. 1995. *Items Included:* CD-ROM in binder with documentation & activities. *Customer Support:* Toll free customer service Hot Line 1-800-645-3739 (9a.m. - 5p.m. Eastern Time) software guaranteed for two years.
Windows. IBM (8Mb). CD-ROM disk $99.00 (Order no.: CDR52001). *Nonstandard peripherals required:* CD-ROM drive. *Addl. software required:* MS Windows & MSworks for Windows.
Mac OS 7.0. Macintosh (8Mb). *Nonstandard peripherals required:* CD-ROM drive. *Addl. software required:* ClarisWorks 2.1 or higher or MS-Works 3.0 or higher.
Integrates Technology Directly into Content Area Curriculum. It Teaches Students to Locate, Manipulate, Organize & Analyze Data: to Draw Conclusions; & to Communicate Effectively Using Graphs, Mathematical Models Displays & Other Visual Media.
Educational Activities Inc.

Thematic Applications: Science I. Ron Dunaeisky. 1995. *Items Included:* CD-ROM in binder with documentation & activities. *Customer Support:* Toll free customer service Hot Line 1-800-645-3739 (9a.m. - 5p.m. Eastern Time) software guaranteed for two years.
Windows. IBM (8Mb). CD-ROM disk $99.00 (Order no.: CDR23001). *Nonstandard peripherals required:* CD-ROM drive. *Addl. software required:* MS Windows & MSworks for Windows.
Mac OS 7.0. Macintosh (8Mb). *Nonstandard peripherals required:* CD-ROM drive. *Addl. software required:* ClarisWorks 2.1 or higher or MS-Works 3.0 or higher.
Integrates Technology Directly into Content Area Curriculum. It Teaches Students to Locate, Manipulate, Organize & Analyze Data: to Draw Conclusions; & to Communicate Effectively Using Graphs, Mathematical Models Displays & Other Visual Media.
Educational Activities Inc.

Thematic Applications: Science II. Ron Dunaeisky. 1995. *Items Included:* CD-ROM in binder with documentation & activities. *Customer Support:* Toll free customer service Hot Line 1-800-645-3739 (9a.m. - 5p.m. Eastern Time) software guaranteed for two years.
Windows. IBM (8Mb). CD-ROM disk $99.00 (Order no.: CDR23002). *Nonstandard peripherals required:* CD-ROM drive. *Addl. software required:* MS Windows & MSworks for Windows.
Mac OS 7.0. Macintosh (8Mb). *Nonstandard peripherals required:* CD-ROM drive. *Addl. software required:* ClarisWorks 2.1 or higher or MS-Works 3.0 or higher.
Integrates Technology Directly into Content Area Curriculum. It Teaches Students to Locate, Manipulate, Organize & Analyze Data: to Draw Conclusions; & to Communicate Effectively Using Graphs, Mathematical Models Displays & Other Visual Media.
Educational Activities Inc.

Thematic Applications: World History. Ron Dunaeisky. 1995. *Items Included:* CD-ROM in binder with documentation & activities. *Customer Support:* Toll free customer service Hot Line 1-800-645-3739 (9a.m. - 5p.m. Eastern Time) software guaranteed for two years.
Windows. IBM (8Mb). CD-ROM disk $99.00 (Order no.: CDR52003). *Nonstandard peripherals required:* CD-ROM drive. *Addl. software required:* MS Windows & MSworks for Windows.
Mac OS 7.0. Macintosh (8Mb). *Nonstandard peripherals required:* CD-ROM drive. *Addl. software required:* ClarisWorks 2.1 or higher or MS-Works 3.0 or higher.
Integrates Technology Directly into Content Area Curriculum. It Teaches Students to Locate, Manipulate, Organize & Analyze Data: to Draw Conclusions; & to Communicate Effectively Using Graphs, Mathematical Models Displays & Other Visual Media.
Educational Activities Inc.

THEO Plus COM. 1994. *Customer Support:* 30 day free phone support.
THEOS. IBM & compatibles. disk $99.00.
Nonstandard peripherals required: Modem.
Plus Pak for THEOS 386/486 OS That Provides Easy-to-Use Menu-Driven Communications to Other THEOS Systems, Non-THEOS Systems, & Bulletin Boards. Includes Support for High Speed Modems, Unattended File Transfer, Terminal Emulation, & Popular Protocols to Connect with Non-THEOS Environments, Such As UNIX & Windows NT.
THEOS Software Corp.

THEO+DOS. *Version:* 2.0. Apr. 1989.
Compatible Hardware: 386/486/Pentium-based PC or compatible. *Operating System(s) Required:* THEOS 386/486. *Memory Required:* 1000k.
Items Included: Installation Manual, 3.5" or 5.25" diskette. *Customer Support:* 30 day free phone support.
disk $599.00.
Lets Users of the THEOS 386/486 Multiuser Operating System Run Programs That Were Previously Unavailable for Them. The THEOS 386/486 System Allows up to 240 Users to Share a Single Computer via Terminals. With THEO+DOS, Users Can Run 8088-Based DOS Applications & Programming Languages While Others Run THEOS Applications from Their Terminals. Also Lets Users Run Memory-Resident DOS Programs, Including Those That Require a Math Co-Processor or Address Expanded Memory, with Access to DOS Internal, External, & Batch Commands. Emulates DOS Networking Software. Users Can Share Printers, Queue Printing Tasks, & When Running Network Versions of DOS Applications, Share Files.
THEOS Software Corp.

THEO Plus DOS 32. *Version:* 3.2. 1994. *Customer Support:* 30 day free phone support.
DOS. IBM & compatibles (4Mb). $199.00 single user; $599.00 5 users; $999.00 9 users.
Multi-User OS That Turns Office Computers into Small Mainframes. Can Be Configured As Either a Stand-Alone Multiuser DOS Workgroup or a Network Companion. Up to 16 Users Can Run DOS Software & Access a Single 80386, 80486 or Pentium Host Computer. True DOS Compatibility, Built-In Multitasking Data Security & Simplified Maintenance.
THEOS Software Corp.

SOFTWARE ENCYCLOPEDIA 1996

THEO Plus GRAFX: TG - MAX. 1994. *Customer Support:* 30 day free phone support.
THEOS 386/486. IBM & compatibles. 2 port VGA Kit $1493.00; 2 port SuperVGA $1593.00; 4 port VGA Kit $2591.00. *Nonstandard peripherals required:* Maxpeed MaxStation.
TG/MAX Combines PC-Style Connectivity, Performance & VGA Multiuser Graphics Capability in a THEOS or THEO Plus DOS Workgroup Using Maxpeed Multiport Adapters & MaxStation Base Units. Sixteen Remote Consoles Can Be Located up to 300 Feet from the Host PC. Each Base Station Supports Serial & Parallel Peripherals with a Single Cable.
THEOS Software Corp.

Theorist. *Version:* 2. Dec. 1994. *Compatible Hardware:* Macintosh, Windows. *Memory Required:* 2000-4000k. *Items Included:* Learning manual, reference guide, program disks.
Customer Support: 519-747-2505.
disk $299.00.
Users Can Enter Equations Naturally & Manipulate Them with a Click of the Mouse. Theorist Files, Called Notebooks, Store the Equations, Their Graphs, & Supporting Text & Pictures. Supports Greek Letters by Using the Option Key on the Mac Keyboard. To Graph an Equation, Users Select the Equations Desired & Pick One of Six Menu Options for Graphs. There Are Five Different Types of Two-Dimensional Graphs Included, Along with One Three-Dimensional. Users Can Draw Graphs in Black & White or in Gray Scales or Color on the Mac II. Users Can Examine the Graphed Equations by Scrolling with a Hand Cursor, Which Moves the 2D Graph Sideways or Up & Down, & It Rotates the 3D Graph.
Waterloo Maple, Inc.

THEOS C. *Version:* 3.8. *Compatible Hardware:* IBM PC & compatibles. *Memory Required:* 512k.
General Requirements: Hard disk. *Customer Support:* 30 day free phone support.
disk $699.00.
A Powerful Programming Companion for THEOS 386/486 That Offers All the Functionality of ANSI C Plus over 250 Additional Functions for VDI Graphics, Multitasking, Windowing & File Access. Interfaces with MultiUser BASIC & EXEC Job Control Language. Supports Window Manager & ON KEY Features. Real-Time Extensions.
THEOS Software Corp.

THEOS MultiUser BASIC. 1993. *Customer Support:* 30 day free phone support.
THEOS 386/486. IBM & compatibles (1Mb). disk $799.00.
Structured Business BASIC for THEOS 386/486 OS That Includes 32-Bit Interpreter & Compiler. Allows Developers to Create Vertical Market or Mission Critical Applications. Provides Built-In Multilayered Text Windows Capability Which Implements Interface with Context-Sensitive Help. Features 32-Bit Word Addressing for Large Programs & for Accessing Large Amounts of Memory.
THEOS Software Corp.

THEOS 386/486. *Version:* 3.2. Feb. 1993.
Compatible Hardware: 386/486/Pentium based systems. *Items Included:* Quickstart, 3.5" or 5.25" diskettes, OS manual optional. *Customer Support:* 30 day free phone support.
$249.00 1 user.
$549.00 3 users.
$799.00 9 users.
Multiuser, Multitasking OS That Turns 386/486/Pentium PCs into Small Mainframes. Allows Workgroups of 2-200 Users to Share Resources, Compile Data & Run Different Programs. Features On-Line Help Screens, Security Features,

Shared Memory Between Users, Real-Time Processing, Built-In EXEC Job Control & Batch Processing Language & Built-In E-Mail & Message Utilities.
THEOS Software Corp.

There's A Worm in My Apple!! *Customer Support:* 800-929-8117 (customer service).
MS-DOS. Apple II. disk $69.99 (ISBN 0-87007-334-6).
Designed as a Detailed Tutorial to Help Beginning to Intermediate Programmers Develop Debugging Skills. Will Provide Exposure to Graphics, Music, File Handling, Animation & Game-Writing Techniques. Two Diskettes, Containing 15 Applesoft Basic Programs (Plus Necessary Binary & Text Files) Contain "Worms". The Programmer, with the Help of a 98 Page User's Guide, Must Correct the Worms in These Programs. Both Uncorrected & Corrected Versions are Supplied as Part of the Tutorials.
SourceView Software International.

Thermal Pipe & Plate Thermal Insulation. *Items Included:* Full manual. No other products required. *Customer Support:* Free telephone support - no time limit. 30 day warranty.
MS-DOS 3.2 or higher. IBM & compatibles (512k). disk $79.95.
Fully Menu-Driven & Exceptionally Easy-to-Use Steady-State Heat Flow Analysis Tool for Determining the Thermal Losses to the Environment from Bare & Insulated Flat Surfaces & Pipes. Handy Built-In Table of Schedule 40 & 80 Nominal Pipe Diameters Is Optionally Available, As Well As Optional Built-In Curve-Fits for the Thermal Conditivities of Several Common Insulating Materials. Both English & Metric Units Are Supported.
Dynacomp, Inc.

Thermal Stress Analysis Single Plane-Two Anchor. *Items Included:* Full manual. No other products required. *Customer Support:* Free telephone support - no time limit. 30 day warranty.
MS-DOS 3.2 or higher. IBM & compatibles (512k). disk $759.95.
Determine ASME/ANSI 831.1 Thermal Code Test Compliance for Two-Anchor, Single-Plane Unrestrained Systems. Program Allows User to Select Alloy & Type of Bend à Then Enter the Temperature. Stress Intensification & Thermal Factors Are Retrieved Automatically. On-Screen Instructions. Uses U.S. & SI Units. Includes Complete & Detailed Manual Which Describes All Procedures.
Dynacomp, Inc.

Thermodynamic & Physical Property Data. *Items Included:* Full manual. No other products required. *Customer Support:* Free telephone support - no time limit. 30 day warranty.
MS-DOS 3.2 or higher. IBM & compatibles (512k). disk $149.95.
Calculate 11 Thermodynamic & Physical Properties for Hydrocarbons & Other Organic Chemicals: Critical Properties & Acentric Factor, Heat Capacity of a Gas, Heat Capacity of a Liquid, Enthalpy of Vaporization, Vapor Pressure, Density of Liquid, Surface Tension, Enthalpy of Formation Gas, Gibb's Free Energy of Formation Gas, Solubility in Water, Henry's Law Constant for Compound in Water, Heat of Reaction & Reaction Feasibility (Gibb's Free Energy of Reaction Can Also Be Calculated). Included Are Data for Many Clean Air Act Compounds.
Dynacomp, Inc.

Thermodynamic Properties & Process Simulator. *Items Included:* Full manual. No other products required. *Customer Support:* Free telephone support - no time limit. 30 day warranty.
MS-DOS 3.2 or higher. IBM & compatibles (512k). disk $779.95.
Contains a Databank of Thermodynamic Properties for More Than 200 Hydrocarbons, 9 Non-Hydrocarbon Gases, Plus Carbon & Sulfur. For Each Component in the Databank There Are 25 Data Entries Relating to Property Constants. Accepts Mixtures Containing up to 30 Components. Uses U.S. & SI Units. Includes a Complete & Detailed Manual Which Describes Procedures.
Dynacomp, Inc.

Thermodynamics Lecture Demonstrations. 1995. *Items Included:* Full manual. *Customer Support:* Free telephone support - 90 days, 30-day warranty.
MS-DOS 3.2 or higher. 286 (584k). disk $49.95. *Nonstandard peripherals required:* CGA/EGA/VGA.
A Superb Lecture Aid for College-Level Physics & Engineering Students. This Set of Ten Computer Animations Displays the Relationships Between Volume, Pressure, Temperature, & Entropy for a Carnot or Heat Engine. Easy to Operate & Uncluttered, the Demonstrations Vary in Length, & Each Deals with a Single Concept. The Subjects Covered Include Isochoric & Adiabatic Processes, Isothermal Processes, Carnot Cycles, Otto Engines, & Diesel Engines.
Dynacomp, Inc.

Thermoelastic Crack Growth Analysis. A. Portela & M. H. Aliabadi. Sep. 1994. *Customer Support:* Fax.
MS-DOS 3.0 or higher. IBM PC & compatibles (4Mb). software pkg. $460.00 (ISBN 1-56252-269-8). *Addl. software required:* Crack Growth Analysis Using Boundary Elements Basic Package. *Optimal configuration:* Laser printer.
Unix. Sun, IBM (4Mb). software pkg. $460.00.
VMS. VAX (4Mb). software pkg. $460.00.
Thermoelasticity Module to Work with Basic Package Which Performs Crack Growth Analysis Using the Boundary Element Method.
Computational Mechanics, Inc.

Thermosim: Module 1: EQUIL: Thermodynamic Properties & Process Simulator. Wayne C. Edminister. Jan. 1990. *Compatible Hardware:* IBM PC, PC XT, PC AT & compatibles. *Operating System(s) Required:* PC-DOS/MS-DOS 3.1. *Language(s):* FORTRAN. *Memory Required:* 512k. *General Requirements:* 1Mb hard disk space. *Customer Support:* 30 day money-back guarantee.
3.5" or 5.25" disk $795.00, incl. 80-page manual (Order no.: 852).
Contains a Databank of Thermodynamic Properties for More Than 200 Hydrocarbons, 9 Non-Hydrocarbon Gases, Plus Carbon & Sulfur. For Each Component in the Databank, There Are 25 Data Entries of Property Constants. The First Module, EQUIL, Covers Single-Stage Vapor-Liquid Equilibrium Processes, Simulation of Gas Expansion, Gas Compression & Flow of Compressible Fluids, Thermodynamics of Chemical Reactions to Determine the Equilibrium Product Distributions & Heats of Reactions, & Absorption & Distillation Processes.
Gulf Publishing Co.

Thexder. *Compatible Hardware:* IBM. contact publisher for price.
Arcade Challenge in Which Players Are Given the Chance to Pilot an Armored Robot Through Multiple Attack Scenarios. Do Battle with over 20 Kinds of Aliens. Challenge & Music Escalates As the Game Progresses.
Sierra On-Line, Inc.

Think & Talk: French. Feb. 1992. *Items Included:* User manual. *Customer Support:* Registered users receive unlimited free technical support on toll line (615) 558-8270.
System 6.0.7 or higher; System 7 compatible. Macintosh Plus or higher (2Mb). 3.5" disk $199.00 (Order no.: 1220-000). *Nonstandard peripherals required:* Macintosh compatible CD-ROM drive. *Addl. software required:* HyperCard 2.0.2 or higher. *Networks supported:* AppleTalk.
MS-DOS 3.3 or higher. MPC or compatible with MPC upgrade kit (2Mb). disk $199.00 (Order no.: 1260-000). *Nonstandard peripherals required:* Sound board, CD-ROM drive. *Addl. software required:* Windows with Multimedia Extensions. *Networks supported:* Novell.
Features Lively Dialogue & Engrossing Scenes Filled with Sound Effects, Music & other Audio Cues. User Listens to Language & Repeats What He/She Hears. Sentences May Be Repeated as Many Times as Necessary. Fifty Lessons & an Online Bilingual Dictionary Are Included. Recording Feature Allows User to Record Voice into the Program.
HyperGlot Software Co., Inc.

Think & Talk: German. Feb. 1992. *Items Included:* User manual. *Customer Support:* Registered users receive unlimited free technical support on toll line (615) 558-8270.
System 6.0.7 or higher; System 7 compatible. Macintosh Plus or higher (2Mb). 3.5" disk $199.00 (Order no.: 1230-000). *Addl. software required:* Hypercard 2.0.2 or higher. *Networks supported:* AppleTalk.
MS-DOS 3.3 or higher. MPC or compatible with MPC upgrade kit. disk $199.00 (Order no.: 1270-000). *Nonstandard peripherals required:* Sound board, CD-ROM drive. *Addl. software required:* Windows with Multimedia extensions. *Networks supported:* Novell.
Features Lively Dialogue & Scenes Filled with Sound Effects, Music & Other Audio Cues. User Listens & Repeats What He/She Hears. Sentences May Be Repeated as Many Times as Necessary. Fifty Lessons & an Online Bilingual Dictionary Are Included. Recording Feature Allows User to Record Voice into the Program.
HyperGlot Software Co., Inc.

Think & Talk: Italian. Feb. 1992. *Items Included:* User manual. *Customer Support:* Registered users receive unlimited free technical support on toll line (615) 558-8270.
System 6.0.7 or higher; System 7 compatible. Macintosh Plus or higher (2Mb). 3.5" disk $199.00 (Order no.: 1240-000). *Nonstandard peripherals required:* Macintosh compatible CD-ROM drive. *Addl. software required:* HyperCard 2.0.2 or higher.
MS-DOS 3.3 or higher. MPC or compatible with MPC upgrade kit (2Mb). disk $199.00 (Order no.: 1280-000). *Nonstandard peripherals required:* Sound board, CD-ROM drive. *Addl. software required:* Windows with Multimedia Extensions.
Features Lively Dialogue & Engrossing Scenes Filled with Sound Effects, Music & Other Audio Cues. User Listens to Language & Repeats What He/She Hears. Sentences Can Be Repeated As Often As Necessary. Fifty Lessons & an Online Bilingual Dictionary. Recording Feature Allows User to Record Voice into Program.
HyperGlot Software Co., Inc.

Think & Talk: Spanish. Feb. 1992. *Customer Support:* Registered users receive unlimited free technical support on toll line (615) 558-8270.
System 6.0.7 or higher; System 7 compatible. Macintosh Plus or higher (2Mb). 3.5" disk $199.99 (Order no.: 1210-000). *Nonstandard peripherals required:* Macintosh compatible CD-

ROM drive. *Addl. software required:* HyperCard 2.0.2 or higher.
MS-DOS 3.3 or higher. MPC or compatible with MPC upgrade kit (2Mb). disk $199.00 (Order no.: 1250-000). *Nonstandard peripherals required:* Sound board, CD-ROM drive. *Addl. software required:* Windows with Multimedia Extensions. *Networks supported:* Novell.
Features Lively Dialogue & Engrossing Scenes Filled with Sound Effects, Music & Other Audio Cues. User Listens to Language & Repeats What He/She Hears. Sentences Can Be Repeated as Many Times as Necessary. Includes 50 Lessons & an Online Bilingual Dictionary. Recording Feature Allows User to Record Voice into the Program.
HyperGlot Software Co., Inc.

Think C. *Version:* 4.0. *Items Included:* 3 disks, 3 manuals. *Customer Support:* (408) 372-8100.
Macintosh (1Mb). disk $125.00. *Nonstandard peripherals required:* Source level debugger requires 2Mb.
Developed So That Programmers Can Derive Benefits of Object-Oriented Programming Without Learning a New Language. Syntax Is Upwardly Compatible with C++ but Independent of Changes in That Language. Programmer Can Write Cdevs (Control Panel Devices) & Multisegmented Code Resources. Includes Full Source-Level Debugger & Class Library.
Symantec Corp.

Think Like a Scientist!: Physical Science Skills. (Micro Learn Tutorial Ser.). *Items Included:* Teacher-learner materials. *Customer Support:* Free telephone support.
APP. Macintosh, Apple II series, (48K). 5.25" disk, $39.95 (Lab pack/5 $99.00). 3.5" disk, $44.95 (Lab pack/5 $115.00). Apple or Macintosh network, $249.00 (ISBN 0-939153-61-0).
MAC. (ISBN 1-57265-067-2).
Users Practice Thinking Like a Scientist As They Review Major Concepts in Electricity; Light; Force, Work & Energy; the Nature of Matter. The tutorial mode gives explanations for every answer choice, correct & incorrect (plus help/practice on important ideas). The test mode gives no help; after the score appears, it presents missed questions in the tutorial mode.
Word Assocs., Inc.

Think Pascal (formerly Lightspeed Pascal). *Version:* 3.0. *Items Included:* 3 disks & 3 manuals. *Customer Support:* (408) 372-8100.
Macintosh Plus or higher. 3.5" disk $125.00.
Professional Pascal Development Environment Including Source Level Debugger & Object Oriented Programming.
Symantec Corp.

Think Quick! Leslie Grimm. May 1987. *Compatible Hardware:* Apple II+, IIe, IIc, IIgs. *Memory Required:* 64k.
disk $49.95 (Order no.: 17050).
Adventure Game That Helps Children Develop Important Thinking Skills Needed for Future Learning. Players Overcome Increasingly Difficult Challenges As They Race Through over 100 Rooms in the Fascinating Castle of Mystikar. Helps Build Skills in Logical Thinking, Developing Strategies, Decision Making & Problem Solving. Six Increasingly Difficult Game Levels in the Regular Game, Plus an Expert Game.
The Learning Co.

Thinker. *Version:* 2.2. Alan Bombarger. Jul. 1995. *Items Included:* 100 page manual. *Customer Support:* 30 day return, free phone support.
Mac OS, Amiga. 68030 (750k). 3.5" disk $80.00. *Optimal configuration:* Apple Filesharing.
Combines Database Concepts with Outline Processing Using Hypertext. Modelled on the Work of Doug Englebart, Thinker Is the Most Flexible Hypertext Editor Available. Thinker Allows the Linking of Text, Pictures, Applications, & Sound into a Creative Process. Capable of Creating HTML Directly.
Poor Person Software.

The Thinker: Electronic Spreadsheet. *Version:* 3.0. May 1986. *Compatible Hardware:* IBM PC & compatibles. *Operating System(s) Required:* PC-DOS, MS-DOS. *Memory Required:* 128k. *Items Included:* Manual & disk. *Customer Support:* Yes.
disk $35.00.
A Lotus-Like Spreadsheet with 26 Columns & 125 Rows of Available Space. Lotus Command Structure Is Used & All Math, Financial & Statistical Functions of 1-2-3 Are Supported.
TexaSoft.

Thinkin' Things: Collection I.
Windows. IBM & compatibles. CD-ROM disk $59.95 (Order no.: R1363). *Nonstandard peripherals required:* CD-ROM drive. *Optimal configuration:* 386 processor or higher, MS-DOS 3.1 or higher, 20Mb hard drive, 640k RAM, external speakers or headphones (with sound card) that are Sound Blaster compatible, VGA graphics & adapter, VGA color monitor.
Macintosh (4Mb). (Order no.: R1363). *Nonstandard peripherals required:* 14" color monitor or larger, CD-ROM drive.
Six Thought-Provoking Activities Build Problem Solving, Creativity, Critical Thinking & Memory Skills. Activities Can Be Set to Various Levels of Difficulty to Challenge Children. Instruction Are Spoken for Pre-Readers (Ages 2-8).
Library Video Co.

The Thinking & Writing Process: A Process for All Ages, Level 2. *Version:* 2.0. Thea M. Holtan. Jul. 1994. *Items Included:* Instructions on how to operate the database & word processor; examples of each. *Customer Support:* Teacher's Guide; writer's guide, Level 2; inservices or university course.
Mac; DOS. Mac; IBM. disk $20.00 (ISBN 1-887071-10-5, Order no.: D-2). *Addl. software required:* MS Works 2.0 or higher. *Optimal configuration:* 4Mb RAM, Mac or IBM, Microsoft Works 2.0 or higher, a prepared database & word processor with instruction for use.
Database (in MS Works 2.0 Plus) Supports Steps of the Process. The Last Step Is Numbering the Notes & Sorting Them, Beginning with "1". Then, Database Is at the Top Half of the Screen, & the Word Processor Is Opened on the Bottom Half of the Screen. Writers Can Write Developed Thoughts from the Top of the Screen to the Bottom Half. Both Database & Word Processor Scroll until the Document Has Been Completed. Paper Is Needed Only for Forming a Topic Outline with Topic Paragraph & Topic Sentences.
Thea-Thot Pr.

The Thinking & Writing Process: A Process for All Ages, Level 3. *Version:* 2.0. Thea M. Holtan. Jul. 1994. *Items Included:* Instructions on how to operate the database & word processor; examples of each. *Customer Support:* Teacher's Guide; writer's guide, Level 2; inservices or university course.
Mac; DOS. Mac; IBM. disk $20.00 (ISBN 1-887071-11-3, Order no.: D-3). *Addl. software required:* MS Works 2.0 or higher. *Optimal configuration:* 4Mb RAM, Mac or IBM, Microsoft Works 2.0 or higher, a prepared database & word processor with instruction for use.
Database (in MS Works 2.0 Plus) Supports Steps of the Process. The Last Step Is Numbering the Notes & Sorting Them, Beginning with "1". Then, Database Is at the Top Half of the Screen, & the Word Processor Is Opened on the Bottom Half of the Screen. Writers Can Write Developed Thoughts from the Top of the Screen to the Bottom Half. Both Database & Word Processor Scroll until the Document Has Been Completed. Paper Is Needed Only for Forming a Topic Outline with Topic Paragraph & Topic Sentences.
Thea-Thot Pr.

Thinking Cap. *Compatible Hardware:* Commodore 64, 128. *General Requirements:* Bank Street Writer program, printer.
disk $49.95 (Order no.: COMDSK-268).
Outliner Able to Handle up to 7 Levels of Information with up to 16 Subtopics Within Each Level on an Outline up to 6 Pages Long. Users Have a Choice of Formats Including Roman Numerals, Prose, Technical, or Numeric. Templates for Five Outlines Are Included. Once the Levels Are Established, User May Enter Details Randomly Under the Appropriate Headings.
Broderbund Software, Inc.

3101 Emulator. Mar. 1984. *Compatible Hardware:* TI Professional. *Operating System(s) Required:* MS-DOS. *Memory Required:* 128k. contact publisher for price (Order no.: TI P/N 2234238-0001).
Allows Data to Be Sent 1 Character at a Time or in Blocks of Data & Remote Location Connection for Process Control, Inventorys Order Entry, Computer Based & Operator Training.
Texas Instruments, Personal Productivit.

3170 SNA. Mar. 1984. *Compatible Hardware:* TI Professional with modem. *Operating System(s) Required:* MS-DOS. *Memory Required:* 128k.
$675.00 (Order no.: TI P/N 2223182-0001).
Provides Access to an SNA Host Computer As a 3270-Type Terminal. Emulates IBM 3276/12 Cluster Control Unit with a Single 3279/2 Display. Supports Multiple Logical Units.
Texas Instruments, Personal Productivit.

3780 Communications. *Compatible Hardware:* TI Professional with modem. *Operating System(s) Required:* MS-DOS. *Memory Required:* 128k.
$150.00 (Order no.: TI P/N 2223124-0001).
Allows TI Professional Computer to Communicate with Other Computers.
Texas Instruments, Personal Productivit.

36 Developer Desktop. *Version:* 6.3. Jun. 1995. *Items Included:* Documentation. *Customer Support:* Technical support via fax, Bulletin Board System or CompuServe. 10 days free telephone support after 1st initial call.
Windows, Windows 95, DOS. PC 386 (4Mb). disk $750.00.
A Comprehensive Software Package That Allows RPG II Developers to Maintain & Run System/36 RPGII Applications on a Single Desktop or Home PC. The Product Supports the System/36 SSP Features (RPGC, SFGR, SEU, SDA, DSU, OCL, DFU, etc.) Replicated on the PC. Includes a Graphical Processor Which Automatically Creates Windows & Windows 95 Forms in Place of Previous Text Based RPG Screens Without Any Recoding. Converted Windows Can Be Further Enhanced Using a Point & Click Graphical Editor.
California Software Products, Inc.

3270/Elite. *Version:* 1.21. Oct. 1990. *Items Included:* Documentation.
DOS 2.0 or higher. IBM PC & compatibles, PC XT, PC AT, PS/2, Laptops (256k). disk $295.00. *Networks supported:* NetBIOS, 802.2, IPX/SPX.
Distributed Function Terminal (DFT) 3270 Single

Session Emulator That Uses 65k Workstation Memory. Supports One Logical Unit (LU) Terminal Session & a Second LU for a Printer Session. Features Include IND$FILE File Transfer, Supports EHLLAPI, EEHLLAP & PS/API.
Network Software Assocs. (NSA), Inc.

3270/Elite Plus. *Version:* 2.10. Jun. 1991. *Items Included:* Documentation.
DOS 2.0 or higher. IBM PC & compatibles, PC XT, PC AT, PS/2, Laptops. disk $395.00.
Networks supported: NetBIOS, 802.2, IPX/SPX.
Multisession Distributed Function Terminal (DFT) 3270 Emulator That Uses Only 77k Memory. Specifically Addresses the Problem of Limited Available Memory on DOS-Based PCs. Can Be Used with All Popular PC-to-Host Links, Including Coax, SDLC, AutoSync, Async, & X.25 Public Networks, As Well As LAN-to-Host Links Such As NetBIOS, NetWare IPX/SPX & 802.2 Token-Ring. The Software Can Be Used with NSA's AdaptSNA LAN Gateway, IBM's OS/EE 1.2 Communications Manager Gateway, or IBM's Personal Communications/3270 Gateway. Compatible with Most SDLC & Coax Adapter Boards, Including Those from Attachmate, DCA, IBM, AST, NSA & Others.
Network Software Assocs. (NSA), Inc,.

3270-PLUS. Mar. 1983. *Compatible Hardware:* UNIX & compatibles. *Operating System(s) Required:* UNIX.
disk $995.00.
Allows Users to Conduct Multiple SNA Sessions to Access Host Data Directly & Simultaneously onto Micros. Implements Functions Such As Application-to-Application Communications Between the Host & a Micro; Downloading, Uploading & Transferring of Host Files. Features Compatibility with IBM API & DISOSS.
Rabbit Software Corp.

Thoroughbred Gold Edition. Ronald D. Jones. 1983. *Compatible Hardware:* Apple; Commodore 64; IBM; TRS-80, Color Computer; CP/M machines. *Memory Required:* 64k.
Apple. disk $159.95 (ISBN 1-55604-000-8).
CP/M. disk $159.00 (ISBN 1-55604-001-6).
IBM. disk $159.00 (ISBN 1-55604-004-0).
Commodore. disk or cassette $159.00 (ISBN 1-55604-002-4).
Color Computer. disk or cassette $159.00 (ISBN 1-55604-003-2).
TRS-80. disk or cassette $159.00 (ISBN 1-55604-005-9).
Full-Featured Thoroughbred Analysis Program Designed for the Professional & the Serious Novice. Designed to Evaluate All Relevant Factors & Variables & Gives an Accurate Prediction of the Finish.
Professor Jones Professional Handicapping Systems.

Thoroughbred Professional Series Analysis Module. Ronald D. Jones. Jul. 1986. *Compatible Hardware:* Apple; Commodore; IBM; TRS-80 Model I, Model III, Color Computer. *Operating System(s) Required:* CP/M. *Memory Required:* 64k.
disk $249.95 ea.
Apple. (ISBN 1-55604-222-1, Order no.: PH01).
CP/M. (ISBN 1-55604-223-X, Order no.: PH01).
Commodore. (ISBN 1-55604-224-8, Order no.: PH01).
Color Computer. (ISBN 1-55604-225-6, Order no.: PH01).
IBM. (ISBN 1-55604-226-4, Order no.: PH01).
Model I & Model III. (ISBN 1-55604-227-2, Order no.: PH01).
Up to 11 Races on Each Horse Can Be Evaluated to Provide Results. Full Screen & Faster Input Makes for Quicker Entry. Artificial Intelligence Is Used to Learn More about Favored Factors. Contains Complete Betting Mode, Holding Tanks for Late Scratches & Entries, Track Record Adjuster & Multi Track Modules.
Professor Jones Professional Handicapping Systems.

Thoroughbred Professional Series Database Manager. Ronald D. Jones. Jul. 1986. *Compatible Hardware:* Apple; Commodore; IBM; TRS-80 Model I, Model III, Color Computer. *Operating System(s) Required:* CP/M. *Memory Required:* 64k.
disk $449.95 ea.
Apple. (ISBN 1-55604-234-5, Order no.: PH03).
CP/M. (ISBN 1-55604-235-3, Order no.: PH03).
Commodore. (ISBN 1-55604-236-1, Order no.: PH03).
Color Computer. (ISBN 1-55604-237-X, Order no.: PH03).
IBM. (ISBN 1-55604-238-8, Order no.: PH03).
Model I & Model III. (ISBN 1-55604-239-6, Order no.: PH03).
Essential Data on Every Horse Can Be Saved in a Data Base to Be Used in Conjunction with the Analysis Module. Includes Storage of the Last 10 Races of All Horses on Disk. Features Automatic Storage of Races & Complete Printouts of Previous Races.
Professor Jones Professional Handicapping Systems.

Thoroughbred Professional Series Factor Value Multiple Regression Module. Ronald D. Jones. Jul. 1986. *Compatible Hardware:* Apple; Commodore; IBM; TRS-80 Model I, Model III, Color Computer. *Operating System(s) Required:* CP/M. *Memory Required:* 64k.
disk $349.95 ea.
Apple. (ISBN 1-55604-228-0, Order no.: PH02).
CP/M. (ISBN 1-55604-229-9, Order no.: PH02).
Commodore. (ISBN 1-55604-230-2, Order no.: PH02).
Color Computer. (ISBN 1-55604-231-0, Order no.: PH02).
IBM. (ISBN 1-55604-232-9, Order no.: PH02).
Model I & Model III. (ISBN 1-55604-233-7, Order no.: PH02).
Provides Fast Multiple Regression Analysis, Deriving the Most Precise Weighting Formula Available. Includes Manual Factor Weighting Ability, Complete Multiple Regression of Target Races, a Holding Tank Link to Bet Module, As Well As True Low Level Artificial Intelligence.
Professor Jones Professional Handicapping Systems.

Thoughtline. *Version:* 3.32. Dan Burns. 1991. *Items Included:* User manual. *Customer Support:* Free telephone hotline.
PC-DOS & MS-DOS 2.1 or higher. IBM PC, PS/2 & compatible personal computers (640k). disk $79.95 (Order no.: 608). *Optimal configuration:* PC-DOS & MS-DOS 2.1 or higher & hard disk or laptop.
Cure Writer's Block Fast with This Easy-to-Use Program. Computer "Asks" Questions That Stimulate Creative, Organized, Thinking. Write Speeches, Articles, Presentation Documents. Links with WORDPERFECT & Other Word Processors.
Experience In Software, Inc.

Threads. Jan. 1988. *Compatible Hardware:* IBM PC, PC XT & compatibles. *Operating System(s) Required:* PC-DOS/MS-DOS. *Memory Required:* 512k. *General Requirements:* CGA card.
disk $295.00.
Calculates Dimensions for Most Thread Designs. Considers All the ANSI Thread Standards for Any Diameter or Pitch & Performs Calculations for Most Non-Standard Thread Designs. Internal or External Threads May Be Specified.
Engineering Software Co.

Threat Force. *Compatible Hardware:* Atari 400, 800. *Language(s):* Atari BASIC (source code included). *Memory Required:* cassette 32k, disk 48k. *General Requirements:* Joystick.
disk $33.95.
Simulation of Battle Between the U.S. Army in Europe & Invading Soviet/Warsaw Pact Forces.
Dynacomp, Inc.

3D/SIM: 3D Petroleum Reservoir Simulation for Vert. Horiz. & Dev. Wells. Wilson Chin. Jan. 1993. *Customer Support:* 30-day money-back guarantee.
DOS 3.0 (640k), 1Mb hard disk space required. disk $1495.00 (Order no.: S088).
New & Easier Way to Simulate Reservoir Drilling That Lets You Look at an Accurate Picture of Your Reservoir Without Typing an Endless Array of Numbers. Lets You Create Pictures of the Underlying Geology Using a Unique Graphical Interface, Drill with Your Keyboard or Mouse, & Immediately Simulate 4000 Gridblock Problems on Your PC in Minutes. Simulate the Darcy Flow of Liquids & Nonlinear Gases Through Complicated Reservoirs with General Anisotropic Heterogeneities. Can Easily Model Pressure Depletion in Confined Flows, Fluid Production under Aquifer Drives, & Problems with Mixed Boundary Conditions.
Gulf Publishing Co.

3D Color Graphics Program. *Compatible Hardware:* Apple; Commodore; IBM PC, PCjr.
disk $10.00.
Introduction to the Computer. Encourages Children to Play with the Keyboard by Producing Colorful Three Dimensional Shapes at the Stroke of a Key. Will Produce Pyramids, Cubes, Spheres, Circles, Points, Lines, & Other Shapes in Different Sizes & Colors. Will Teach Spatial Relations & Size, Color, & Shape Recognition. Includes a Color Key Overlay & Key Chart.
Disc (Washington, DC).

3-D Graphics Toolkit. *Compatible Hardware:* MAC, IBM PC.
3.5" disk $79.95.
3-D Contour Plots & Line Drawing.
True BASIC, Inc.

3D Studio: Release 2. *Version:* 2. Mar. 1992. *Items Included:* Reference manual, tutorials, CD-ROM with over 500 Mb of 3D objects, textures & animations. *Customer Support:* CompuServe, VAR support provided.
MS-DOS 3.3 or higher. IBM or Compaq 386/486 & compatibles (4Mb). 5.25" HD $2995.00 (ISBN 1-56444-007-9). *Nonstandard peripherals required:* Intel 80387 or WEITEK Math Co-processor; VGA device & pointing device.
3.5" HD $2995.00 (ISBN 1-56444-006-0).
Graphics Software Package for Creating High-Resolution 3D Models, Renderings, & Animations on 386/486 Based PC's. Provides Modeling, Materials Editing, Rendering, Animation, & Special Effects Power.
Autodesk, Inc.

3-D Tutor. 1993. *Items Included:* For Windows/MPC - QuickTime for Windows (on the CD-ROM); For Macintosh - QuickTime 1.6.1, Sound Manager (on the CD-ROM). *Customer Support:* Free online support on America online using key word Zelos; Toll free number 1-800-345-6777; 90 day money back guarantee.
Windows/MPC. 486, 25MHz, double speed CD-ROM drive (8Mb). CD-ROM disk $29.95 (ISBN 1-883387-07-8). *Nonstandard peripherals required:* 640x480, 256 color SVGA display, Microsoft compatible mouse, SoundBlaster compatible sound card with 8-bit sound. *Addl. software required:* DOS 5.0 or

higher, Microsoft Windows 3.1, QuickTime for Windows. *Optimal configuration:* MPC2.
Macintosh. Macintosh 68030, 25MHz (FPO required to run some demos) (8Mb). CD-ROM disk $29.95 (ISBN 1-883387-06-X).
Nonstandard peripherals required: 13" 256 color monitor - Macintosh compatible CD-ROM drive. *Addl. software required:* System 7.0, QuickTime 1.6.1, Sound Manager. *Optimal configuration:* Quadra or higher (Power Mac) - double speed CD-ROM drive, 12Mb RAM.
Let 3-D Tutor Be Your Guide & Look at Some of the Coolest 3-D Design & Animation Applications! Sample Numerous Programs & Develop Knowledge & Skills in the Basics of Modeling, Motion, Assembly, & Rendering. "Demo Library" Lets You Test-Drive Some of the Best Programs in the Field!
Zelos.

3 Dee-Q-Bee. *Compatible Hardware:* Commodore 64, 128. *General Requirements:* Standard EMG or Biofeedback EMG sensor.
ROM cartridge $29.95 (Order no.: SOFC64-03-003).
By Using Two Muscle Groups, the Player Is Required to Control a Ball in a Maze. There Are 30 Frames of Mazes Which Become Increasingly More Difficult. Requires Precise Muscle Coordination.
Bodylog.

Three-Dimensional Trapezoid Rule. *Version:* 2. Sep. 1995. *Compatible Hardware:* IBM PC. *Operating System(s) Required:* MS-DOS. *Language(s):* GWBASIC. *Memory Required:* 16k.
disk $20.00.
Offers a Method for the Evaluation of Double Integrals Using a 3-Dimensional Version of the Trapezoid Rule.
MatheGraphics Software.

387 FFT. *Version:* 1.0h. 1988. *Customer Support:* Free technical support for one year.
DOS. PC, XT, AT or 80386/486 system. $250.00. *Addl. software required:* Host Language: MicroSoft QuickBASIC, FORTRAN, C, or Pascal; Borland Turbo Pascal or Turbo C; Ryan McFarland FORTRAN; or Lattice C.
A Library of Optimized One & Two Dimensional FFT & Related Functions That Runs on PCs, & 80386-Based Systems Equipped with the Corresponding Intel Numeric Coprocessor. At Run Time, it Automatically Detects Whcih Coprocessor is Present & Makes the Best Use of the Available Coprocessor Instructions & Features. It is Callable from Most Popular 16-Bit Languages. Supports Both Single & Double Precision as Well as Real & Complex Data Types. Arrays of Real or Complex Numbers May Occupy up to 512K of Memory if the Host Language Supports Them. A Set of Standard in-Memory 2D FFT Functions, 2D Correlations, & 2D Convolutions, Includes DiskFFT, a Utility That Overcomes the Memory Limits Imposed by DOS. DiskFFT Performs Off-Disk 2D Transforms Directly on Disk Files.
Microway, Inc.

386 DOS Ada Compiler. *Version:* 4.2. Dec. 1988. *Compatible Hardware:* Compaq Deskpro 386; IBM PS/2 Model 80. *Operating System(s) Required:* PC-DOS/MS-DOS 3.0 or higher. *Language(s):* Ada. *Memory Required:* 512k.
disk $3095.00.
Includes All Required Software & Documentation. Permits an Application to Run in 80286 Protected Mode & Directly Access Extended Memory (up to 16 Mb). Also Offers Full 32-Bit Support. Includes Compiler, Multi-Library Environment, Binder & Run-Time Executive. Available Options Include Developer's Toolset, a Symbolic Source Level Debugger & Program Viewer; AdaXref, a Cross-Reference Generator; AdaMake, a Recompilation Unit; & AdaReformat, a Source Reformatter.
Alsys, Inc.

386 MAX. *Compatible Hardware:* 80386-based systems. *Operating System(s) Required:* PC-DOS/MS-DOS 3.0 or higher.
disk $74.95.
Allows Users to Utilize up to 1Mb of Memory, Accessed Either As Extended or Expanded Memory, or a Combination of the Two. Also Fills in DOS Memory above the Video Buffers & Makes It Available to DOS Through Standard Memory Allocations. Allows Software Modification of the Ratio Between Expanded & Extended Memory. Emulates the LOTUS/INTEL/MICROSOFT Expanded Memory Specifications (LIM/EMS) Using the 80386's Hardware Paging Tables & All Available Extended Memory.
Qualitas Trading Co.

386MAX Professional. Bob Smith. *Items Included:* Software & documentation. *Customer Support:* Technical support available to all registered users.
PC-DOS or MS-DOS 3.X or higher (256k extended memory starting at 1Mb). Any 80386 based computer. disk $129.95. *Networks supported:* Novell NetWare, 3COM 3+, Banyan, Vines, etc.
A Memory Manager & Program Loader for 386 Systems. Moves Memory-Resident Programs & Device Drivers, Including Many Network Shells, Above 640KB Freeing up Valuable Low DOS Memory for Direct Use by Your Applications. Automatically Determines the Resident & Initialization Sizes of the Programs to Relocate & Allows You Optimal Utilization of Small Fragmented Pieces of High DOS Memory. 386MAX Professional Also Includes All the Features of the Award Winning 386MAX; Backfills from the Top of Your System Board to the Start of Your Video Adapters on All Systems, Automatically Remaps Slow ROMs to Fast RAM, & Fully Emulates the Lotus-Intel-Microsoft (LIM) Expanded Memory Specification (EMS) Version 4.0 Using Fast Hardware Paging Tables & All Available Extended Memory. It Also Supports Both Extended Memory Specification (XMS) & Virtual Control Program Interface (VCPI).
Qualitas, Inc.

386 Unix Ada Compilation System & Toolset. *Version:* 4.2. Jan. 1989. *Items Included:* Media & documentation, including users guide, project development guide, installation guide, Ada reference manual, appendix F, Ada sampler, application developer's guide. *Customer Support:* Annual maintenance $560.00, mandatory for first year, includes phone support, basic upgrades, free customer newsletter.
Interactive Systems Unix, IBM PS/2 AIX, SCO Unix, or IBM Secure Xenix (4Mb). Compaq Deskpro 386, Multitech 1100, Prime EXC 320, IBM PS/2 Model 80. $3095.00 plus $800.00 for Developers's Toolset. *Optimal configuration:* 8Mb memory, 20Mb hard disk space above what is required for Unix. *Networks supported:* Novell.
A Production-Quality Ada Development System Capable of Handling Very Large Ada Applications. The Product Includes the Compiler, Multi-Library Environment, Binder, Run-Time Executive, & Full Documentation. Optionally Available Are the Developer's Toolset Including AdaProbe, a Symbolic Source Level Debugger & Program Viewer; AdaXref, a Cross-Reference Generator; AdaMake, a Recompilation Aid; & Ada Reformat, a Source Reformatter.
Alsys, Inc.

Three Mile Island. Richard Orban. Mar. 1981. *Compatible Hardware:* Apple II, II+, IIe, IIc. *Operating System(s) Required:* Apple DOS 3.2, 3.3. *Language(s):* Assembly. *Memory Required:* 48k.
disk $19.98 (ISBN 0-87190-006-8).
Take Charge of a Nuclear Reactor on Three Mile Island.
Muse Software.

3*16 Word Processor. *Compatible Hardware:* Data General; IBM PC, PC XT, PC AT & compatibles. *Operating System(s) Required:* RDOS, AOS, SuperDOS. *Language(s):* Business BASIC (source code included). *Memory Required:* 64k.
contact publisher for price.
Multi-User, Full Featured Word Processing System with Spelling Checker & Mail Merge.
QAX International Systems Corp.

Three Worlds. Cyberlore Studios Staff & Dreamforge Entertainment Staff. Apr. 1995. *Items Included:* 1 perfect bound manual, & 2 Data cards. *Customer Support:* 30 day limited warranty.
MS-DOS 5.0 or higher CD. IBM & compatibles (4Mb). CD-ROM disk $49.95 (ISBN 0-917059-00-X, Order no.: 062331). *Optimal configuration:* IBM 386/33 MHz with 4Mb of RAM, MS-DOS 5.0 or higher, VGA graphics & 20Mb of free hard drive space.
Product Contains Three Fantasy Role Playing Games in the Advanced Dungeons & Dragons (AD&D) World. The Player Controls from 1 to 4 Characters in a Battle Against Evil.
Strategic Simulations, Inc.

THREEDCOOR. Oct. 1985. *Compatible Hardware:* IBM PC, PC AT, PC XT & compatibles. *Operating System(s) Required:* MS-DOS, PC-DOS. *Language(s):* FORTRAN. *Memory Required:* 512k.
disk $500.00 (Order no.: 3DCOOR).
Used Interactively with a Drill Hole Database to Calculate the 3D Coordinates of Points along a Drill Hole. The Location Can Be Calculated for Any Point Down the Hole or at Regular Distances. The Original Drill Hole Database Can Be Modified or Appended at Any Time. Can Be Useful for Ongoing Drilling Projects in Which Drill Hole Data Is Continually Updated.
Geostat Systems International, Inc. (GSII).

3DTTT. *Customer Support:* 800-929-8117 (customer service).
MS-DOS. IBM/PS2. disk $39.99 (ISBN 0-87007-062-2).
A Three Dimensional Tic-Tac-Toe Game on a 4x4x4 Matrix, with Five Levels of Strategy.
SourceView Software International.

Threshold, Threshold-TM. *Version:* 2.0. Aug. 1982. *Compatible Hardware:* IBM PC. *Operating System(s) Required:* DOS 2.1. *Language(s):* COBOL. *Memory Required:* 320k.
Threshold. $3995.00.
Threshold-TM. $1995.00.
Consists of over 100 Programs Specifically Designed to Meet Office Management & Accounts Receivable Requirements of Private Medical Practice. Handles Paper & Electronic Claims, Including Blue Shield, Medicaid, & Medicare. Features Include Online Help & Audit Trails.
Physicians Practice Management, Inc.

Throw Five. *Customer Support:* 800-929-8117 (customer service).
MS-DOS. Apple II. disk $19.99 (ISBN 0-87007-486-5).
A Dice Game for up to Eight Players That Combines Skill & Luck.
SourceView Software International.

Thud Ridge. Acme Animation. *Items Included:* Manual - 32 pages. *Customer Support:* Free exchange for 5 1/4" for a 3.5" diskette, coupon enclosed in MS-DOS version.
MS-DOS 2.0 or higher (512k). IBM & compatibles. (11/1988) $39.95 (Order no.: PCTR). *Nonstandard peripherals required:* CGA/EGA or Hercules graphics board &

TITLE INDEX

matching monitor. *Addl. software required:* DOS 2.0 or higher.
Commodore. Commodore 64. (08/1989) $34.95 (Order no.: COTR).
You're Lead Wild Weasel in a Modified Thud, an F-105 Thunderchief. Only One Thing Stands Between You & Hanni--Thud Ridge--40 Miles of Rolling Terrain Leading Straight Downtown. Being a Thud Driver Demands Nerve, Skill & Raw Courage. Master 10 Missions. If You've Got the Guts, This is Your Game.
360, Inc.

Thumbelina.
MS-DOS 5.0 or higher, Windows 3.1 or higher. 386 processor or higher (4Mb). CD-ROM disk $59.95 (Order no.: R1364). *Nonstandard peripherals required:* CD-ROM drive. *Optimal configuration:* 386 processor operating at 16Mhz or higher, MS-DOS 5.0 or higher, Windows 3.1 or higher, 30Mb hard drive, mouse, VGA graphic adapter & VGA color monitor (SVGA recommended), 4Mb RAM, external speakers or headphones (with sound card) that are Sound Blaster compatible.
Macintosh (4Mb). (Order no.: R1364A). *Nonstandard peripherals required:* 14" color monitor or larger, CD-ROM drive.
Hans Christian Anderson's Story Comes Alive As Kids View the Spectacular Full-Motion Animated Story by Don Bluth, Read Through the Delightfully Interactive Pages, Paint Pictures from the Story & Play Games in Thumbelina's Play Land.
Library Video Co.

Thumbelina. Technopop. Aug. 1994. *Customer Support:* 800 Number.
Windows 3.1 386 Enhanced Mode. IBM & 100% compatibles, 386 or higher (4Mb). CD-ROM disk Contact publisher for price (ISBN 1-885932-01-4). *Nonstandard peripherals required:* 640x480 256 VGA, mouse, MPC CD-ROM. *Optimal configuration:* 8Mb RAM, sound card.
System 7.0 or higher. 68020 MAC (2.5Mb). CD-ROM disk Contact publisher for price (ISBN 1-885932-02-2). *Nonstandard peripherals required:* Color monitor, CD-ROM.
Thumbelina Is the Delightful Children's Fairy Tale by Hans Christian Anderson. In This Interactive Storybook, While Following Thumbelina on Her Adventure, Children Click on Numerous "Hot Spots," Each One with Its Own Humorous & Entertaining Animation.
Trimark Interactive.

Thunder Chief. 1985. *Compatible Hardware:* Sanyo MBC 555. *Memory Required:* 128k.
disk $34.95 (ISBN 0-923213-34-1, Order no.: SA-THU).
Three-D Action Game.
MichTron, Inc.

Thunder II. *Version:* 1.01. 1989. *Compatible Hardware:* Apple Macintosh with 2 400k disk drives or 1 800k disk drive. *Memory Required:* 512k.
Macintosh. 3.5" disk $79.95 (ISBN 0-922479-03-8, Order no.: BI1-2211).
Provides Three Programs in One: a Spelling Checker with 50,000-Word Dictionary, an Abbreviation Expander, Which Allows Users to Enter Pre-Set Abbreviations That Are Automatically Expanded into the Complete Word or Words, & Which Includes Built-In Abbreviations for Days, Months, U.S. States & Canadian Provinces; a Document Analyzer, Which Provides a Statistical Report, Including Number of Words, Average Sentence Length, FOG Score, & Other Data.
Electronic Arts.

Thunderboy. *Customer Support:* Back up disks available.
Amiga (512k). $14.95.
Battle the Dragon in the Dark Land Where Even the Butterflies are Deadly.
DigiTek Software.

Thunderscape. Jun. 1995. *Items Included:* 80 page perfect bound manual. *Customer Support:* 30 day limited warranty.
PC-DOS CD-ROM (DOS 5.0 or higher). 486/66 (8Mb). CD-ROM disk $39.95 (ISBN 0-917059-04-2, Order no.: 062301). *Nonstandard peripherals required:* 486/50 required, 486/66 recommended, hard drive, CD-ROM drive & mouse, with 20Mb of hard drive space. *Optimal configuration:* 486/66 with uncompressed hard drive & CD-ROM 4X.
A Fantasy Role Playing Game That Takes Place in the All New World of Aden. The Game Features 20 Different Play Levels, 24 Different Monsters, Blistering Combat & Brain Draining Puzzles. In Addition, The Game Includes Gorgeous Graphics Plus Amazing Sound Effects & Music.
Strategic Simulations, Inc.

Thwart! *Compatible Hardware:* Apple II+, IIe with Applesoft. *Operating System(s) Required:* Apple DOS 3.3. *Memory Required:* 48k.
disk $29.95 (ISBN 0-676-32207-7).
back-up disk $4.95.
Players Pick a Category. A Word Belonging to That Category Appears. Now They Must Think of As Many Words As They Can That Also Fit the Category. Added Words Automatically Intersect & Form a Crossword Puzzle.
Random House Schl. Div.

TI-Advanced Assembly Debugger. *Compatible Hardware:* TI 99/4A with editor/assembler cartridge. *Memory Required:* 32k.
contact publisher for price (Order no.: PHD 5099).
Texas Instruments, Personal Productivit.

TI-Count Business Packages. *Compatible Hardware:* TI Home Computer. *Language(s):* BASIC. *Memory Required:* 32k. *General Requirements:* 2 disk drives, printer, RS-232 interface.
contact publisher for price.
Integrated Accounting Package. Includes General Ledger, Accounts Receivable, Payroll, Mailing List, & Inventory Modules.
Texas Instruments, Personal Productivit.

TI-FORTH. *Compatible Hardware:* TI 99/4A with editor/assembler cartridge.
contact publisher for price (Order no.: PHD 5098).
Advanced Programming Language.
Texas Instruments, Personal Productivit.

TI Invaders. *Compatible Hardware:* TI-99/4A with PLATO interpreter solid state cartridge.
contact publisher for price (Order no.: PHM 3053).
Destroy an Armada of Nasty Creatures from Space with Your Missiles.
Texas Instruments, Personal Productivit.

TI-Mini-Writer. *Compatible Hardware:* TI Home Computer.
contact publisher for price (Order no.: PHT6103).
Word Processor with Full Screen Text Editing.
Texas Instruments, Personal Productivit.

TI-Othello. *Compatible Hardware:* TI-99/4A with PLATO interpreter solid state cartridge.
contact publisher for price (Order no.: PHM 3067).
Get As Many Disks of Your Color As Possible on the Board. Play Against Another or Against the Computer.
Texas Instruments, Personal Productivit.

TI-PILOT. *Compatible Hardware:* TI-99/4A with 32k memory expansion & P-Code card.
contact publisher for price (Order no.: PHD 5066).
Permits User to Run Programs in TI PILOT. Interpreter Supports Speech, Sound & Graphics Functions.
Texas Instruments, Personal Productivit.

TI Writer. *Compatible Hardware:* TI 99/4A with controller, TI impact printer & RS232 interface. *Memory Required:* 32k.
contact publisher for price (Order no.: PHM 3111).
Word Processor.
Texas Instruments, Personal Productivit.

Tic-Tac-Max. *Customer Support:* 800-929-8117 (customer service).
MS-DOS. Commodore 64. disk $39.99 (ISBN 0-87007-156-4).
A Challenging, New Variation of Tic-Tac-Toe with Each of the Original "Squares" Broken into Quadrants. Point Scoring Determines the Winner. Points are Earned by Filling the Similar Quadrant in the "Three-in-a-Row" Column. Players Can Take on Each Other or the Computer. Strategy Is Essential; Frustration Is Inevitable; Enjoyment Is Certain. Manual Is Included.
SourceView Software International.

TidBits. *Version:* 1990B. 1988. *Items Included:* manual. *Customer Support:* Free 90 days, annual updates.
PC-DOS, MS-DOS. IBM & compatibles, PC, XT, AT (128K). disk $79.95.
General Purpose Utility for Any Computer User. Two Sections, Calculation Section & Information Section. Calculation Section Performs Amortizations, Depreciation Schedules, Break Even Analysis, 36 Year I.R.A., Loan Comparison, Finance Charge Calculation, Percentage Calculation Plus 640 Conversions Including Metric & Others. Information Section Includes Area Codes, Consumer Price Index History, Postal & UPS Rates, Mileage Charts & Many Other Items.
Data Source One, Inc.

TideMaster. Jun. 1987. *Compatible Hardware:* IBM PC & compatibles, PC XT, PC AT. *Operating System(s) Required:* PC-DOS 2.1 or higher. *Memory Required:* 256k.
disk $39.95 (ISBN 0-918219-46-9).
Calculates Tide Times & Heights with Tables & Graphs for Any of 22 U.S. Coastal States.
Zephyr Services.

Tidy. *Compatible Hardware:* TRS-80 Model I Level II, Model III. *Operating System(s) Required:* TRSDOS. *Language(s):* Assembly. *Memory Required:* 16k.
cassette $14.95.
Renumbers BASIC Program over Any Legal Line Number Range Using Any Convenient Number Interval. Compacts Programs by Removing All Spaces &/or REMARK Statements. Result Is a Physically Smaller Program (Fewer Bytes of RAM Used) Which Executes Significantly Faster Than an Uncompacted Version.
Dynacomp, Inc.

Tiles & Tribulations. *Version:* V1.5. Jan. 1994. *Items Included:* 8 page manual, 1 diskette, response card. *Customer Support:* 90 day limited warranty, support via phone, modem, fax.
DOS, Windows 3.1, Windows 95, Windows 95 Japanese. IBM & compatibles (2Mb). disk $21.95 (ISBN 1-884791-02-6, Order no.: 01-

2101-010B). *Optimal configuration:* Intel 386/ 486, 4Mb RAM, MPC-compatible sound card. Macintosh.
Single Player Action/Arcade Entertainment Software for Microsoft Windows.
Technological Computer Innovations Corp.

T.I.M: Total Information Management.
Innovative Software, Inc. *Compatible Hardware:* TI Professional. *Operating System(s) Required:* MS-DOS. *Memory Required:* 128k. *General Requirements:* 2 disk drives, printer.
$495.00.
Texas Instruments, Personal Productivit.

TIMAS: Trucking Information Management, Accounting System. *Compatible Hardware:* IBM PC, PC XT. *Operating System(s) Required:* MS-DOS. *Language(s):* BASIC. *Memory Required:* 256k. *General Requirements:* 2 disk drives, printer. *Customer Support:* Mon-Fri EST 9:00AM-5:00PM, Modem support & on-site.
contact publisher for price.
Fully Automated, Menu-Driven Program Handles Local & Export Manifests & Produces Freight Bills for Runners by Location to Large Chains. Lists Probills by Number, Probills Still Open, Generates Over/Short Analysis, & Analysis of Shipping Dock Area. Once Products Are Shipped, the Program Provides a Claims System. Provides Tractor/Trailer Analysis Using a Fuel Inventory System, Fuel Usage by State, Tractor Analysis by Tractor, Preventive Maintenance, Inventory Control for Truck Parts, & Cost to Operate Each Truck. Automatic Rating Is Provided for Using Zip Codes & Rating Zones per ICC Guidelines. Management Report on Sales Analysis & Profitability Are Also Available. Full Set of Financials Are Provided.
M&C Systems, Inc.

Timberline Tax. Timberline Systems, Inc. *Compatible Hardware:* TI Professional. *Operating System(s) Required:* UCSD p-System. *Memory Required:* 512k. *General Requirements:* Winchester hard disk.
$1500.00.
Texas Instruments, Personal Productivit.

Timbuktu. *Version:* 4.0. *Compatible Hardware:* Apple Macintosh. *General Requirements:* Apple Talk. *Customer Support:* Free unlimited technical phone support, & 90 days warranty.
3.5" disk $195.00.
3.5" disk $995.00 10-pack; $1995.00 30-pack; $5500.00 100-pack.
Desk Accessory/Driver That Allows Remote Operation of Macintosh. Multiple Users Can Simultaneously Share Screens Across the Network for Workgroup Collaboration, User Support, Network Management etc. Includes File Transfer to Exchange Files & Password Protection Options. Now Supports Color & Color Features.
W O S Data Systems, Inc.

Timbuktu-Remote. *Version:* 3.0. 1988. *Customer Support:* Free unlimited phone support, 90-day warranty.
MAC-DOS or higher (1000). disk $195.00 (Order no.: SW401). *Optimal configuration:* 9600 bps. modems recommended. *Networks supported:* AppleTalk.
Allows User to Observe or Control Another Macintosh from User's Macintosh over Dial-Up Telephone Line, Serial Links, or ISDN Services. Includes Full Color Support, File Transfer to Exchange Files, "Chat" with Another User, Password Protection & Options. For Remote Access & Support, Training, Network Management, & Workgroup Collaboration.
W O S Data Systems, Inc.

Time Accounting & Billing. *Version:* 5.0. 1992. *Compatible Hardware:* IBM PC & compatibles. *Operating System(s) Required:* PC-DOS. *Language(s):* COBOL. *Memory Required:* 640k. *General Requirements:* Hard disk, 80-column printer. *Items Included:* Disks, manuals, 90 days of support. *Customer Support:* Direct from Morningstar.
$100.00 per timekeeper for single-user; $150.00 per timekeeper for multi-user.
Time & Expense Accounting & Billing Software in Which All Coding Is User-Definable Thereby Allowing User to 'Tailor' the System to Suit His Unique Method of Billing. Multiple Bill Formats, Account Aging, Past Due Statements & Vast Number of Firm Management Reports by Attorney, Area of Law, etc. Cash Receipts Integrate Back to the General Ledger System. Demo disk available.
Morningstar Technology Corp.

Time & Attendance. *Version:* 6.04. May 1987. *Compatible Hardware:* IBM PC XT & compatibles. *Operating System(s) Required:* MS-DOS. *Memory Required:* 512k.
disk $495.00.
disk $695.00, incl. Lotus 1-2-3 interface.
Gathers Time Information from a Variety of Time Clocks & Prints Daily, Weekly, Biweekly, & Semi-Monthly Reports on the Time & Attendance Data Including Regular Time, Overtime, 3 Pay Rates per Employee, Tips, Summary by Jobs & Depts., & Comparison to Schedule.
Kerkhoff Computers, Inc.

Time & Billing. *Operating System(s) Required:* MS-DOS. *Memory Required:* 128k. *General Requirements:* 2 disk drives, printer.
contact publisher for price.
Offers the Professional a Means to Effectively Manage Revenue & Expense. Monitors Time Spent (Both Billable & Non-Billable), Work-in-Process & Accounts Receivable. Reports Included in the System Assist User in Evaluating Client Profitability & Employee Productivity. Can Be Customized to Accommodate Any Professional's Practice.
Antech, Inc.

The Time & Billing Solution. *Version:* 4.14. 1987. *Compatible Hardware:* IBM PC & compatibles, PC XT, PC AT, PS/2. *Operating System(s) Required:* MS-DOS, OS/2. *Language(s):* Pascal. *Memory Required:* 256k. *Customer Support:* 3 hrs. in first year.
disk $995.00.
Helps Professional Accountants Manage Client Report & Billing Procedures. Handles up to 5,000 Clients, 100 Employees, 208 Billing & Work Codes & 15,000 Transactions per Period. Time May Be Billed in Minutes, Tenths of Hours, or Hundredths of Hours, & an Efficiency Factor of a Fixed Rate Can Be Incorporated.
Creative Solutions, Inc. (Michigan).

Time & Charges PASS, Vol. 2. Plenary Systems, Inc. *Compatible Hardware:* TI Professional. *Operating System(s) Required:* MS-DOS. *Language(s):* RM/COBOL runtime. *Memory Required:* 128k. *General Requirements:* 2 disk drives, printer.
$1995.00.
Texas Instruments, Personal Productivit.

Time & Materials. *Compatible Hardware:* Apple Macintosh Plus, SE, II. *General Requirements:* Hard disk; FileMaker II; ImageWriter I or II; LaserWriter optional (required for printing bar codes). *Items Included:* Software for bar code reader communications & user's manual, some customizing included.
3.5" disk $1495.00.
includes portable 16k bar-code reader, recharger-download station, connecting cable, download station power supply, bar-code keypad card, bar-code software & documentation.
Portable Battery-Operated Bar-Code Reader Used to Keep Track of Time for Client Billing. Employees Scan Their Bar Code, Scan a Client Bar Code, Scan a Project Bar Code & Then Scan a Bar Code for a Task or Product. The Bar-Code Reader Timestamps Each Bar-Code Scan with the Date & Time.
Computext.

Time & Materials Accounting: T.M.A. *Version:* 1.5. *Items Included:* Extensive documentation on-line, pop-up windows & printed manual. *Customer Support:* 800 line available to licensed users on software maintenance plan.
MS-DOS. PC, XT, AT & compatibles (256k). Contact publisher for price (Order no.: TMA). *Optimal configuration:* 80286 CPU, 450k RAM, 3Mb available hard disk space, Videx brand pocket portable bar code readers are optional & require one comm port. *Networks supported:* all.
Programmable, Service-Oriented System Which Accounts for Exact Time & Services & Materials Used by Employees. Sample Programs Are Included for Professionals (Lawyers, Doctors, etc.), Service (Catering, Retail, etc.), & Industry (Plant Maintenance, Hazardous Waste, etc.). A Maintenance Plan Program Is Included. Data Entry via Pocket Size Portable Bar Code Readers from Videx, Inc. Is Supported.
New Century Products.

Time & Task Management with dBASE III. Timothy Berry. *Operating System(s) Required:* MS-DOS. *General Requirements:* dBASE III.
$49.95, incl. manual (ISBN 0-934375-09-7).
Helps Users Organize Hours, Budgets, Activities, & Resources. Provides a Time-Management System & a Library of dBASE III Code & Macros. Includes Data Files to Keep Track of Hours, Projects, Budgets, Activities, & Resources; Program Files to Build a Menu; Report Files; & Index Files for Fast Access to Other Files. Source Code & Documentation Are Included.
M & T Bks.

Time Bandit. Bill Dunlevy & Harry Lafnear. May 1986. *Compatible Hardware:* Atari ST with color monitor & joystick; Commodore Amiga; IBM PC; Sanyo MBC. *Operating System(s) Required:* MS-DOS, TOS. *Memory Required:* 512k.
disk $39.95.
Atari. 3.5" disk $39.95 (ISBN 0-923213-04-X, Order no.: AT-TIM).
Sanyo. disk $39.95 (ISBN 0-923213-19-8, Order no.: SA-TIM).
You Are the Bandit: Rogue Traveller Through Time & Space. Battle the Evil Guardians, Collect the Treasures of Time, & Remove the Locks Blocking Your Escape. Features 16 Different Lands, Each with 16 Levels, Many with Multiple Floors & Secret Areas. There Are Also Three Built-In Text Aventures. Two Players Can Play at the Same Time, on Their Own Independent Screen Section.
MichTron, Inc.

Time Billing. *Version:* 1.5. *Compatible Hardware:* Apple Macintosh. *Memory Required:* 1000k. *Customer Support:* Free phone support.
3.5" disk $500.00.
With full intergrated accounting. 3.5" disk $2030.00.
Time Billing System.
Exceiver Corp.

Time Change Atlas: M25. *Compatible Hardware:* IBM PC.
disk $50.00.

TITLE INDEX

Provides the Longitude, Latitude, Time Zone & History of Time Changes for 1200 Cities in the U.S. & Around the World. When Entering Name & Birth Data, Just Choose the City & Specify the Date - the Atlas Automatically Enters the Geographic Coordinates & the Time Being Observed (Daylight Savings Time, Wartime, Double Summer Time, etc.).
Matrix Software.

Time Clock Computerized Punch-In - Out. *Items Included:* Full manual. No other products required. *Customer Support:* Free telephone support - no time limit. 30 day warranty.
MS-DOS 3.2 or higher. IBM & compatibles (512k). $199.95 single-user version; $299.95 network version. *Optimal configuration:* IBM, MS-DOS 3.3 or higher, 256k RAM.
Tracks Employee Hours & Computes Weekly Reports with Perfect Accuracy, Saving You the Hours Spent Doing the Job by Hand. Employees Key-In Unique I.D. Numbers Instead of "Punching" in & Out. Database Provides Daily, Weekly, & Hourly Reports. You Know Exactly When an Employee Starts & Leaves, & More. Built-In Security System Controls Access, So Only Authorized People Can See or Modify Your Confidential Data. Network-Compatible, 10,000 Employee Maximum.
Dynacomp, Inc.

Time Commando. *Items Included:* Installation guide.
Windows 95. IBM. CD-ROM disk Contact publisher for price (ISBN 0-87321-116-2, Order no.: CDD-3146).
Activision, Inc.

Time Frame: Your Contact Network Maximizer. *Version:* 2.1t. Jul. 1993.
DOS/Windows. IBM & compatibles (510k free). Contact publisher for price. *Optimal configuration:* 80386 or higher, 510 or more kilobytes of RAM free.
Personal Information Manager. Seven Screens per Contact. 22 Search Fields. Print Schedules, Activities, Contacts, Mailing Labels. Import/ Export Text/DBASE File Formats. Network Version Available. Password Security Available. 141 Page On-Line Manual. Context-Sensitive On-Line Help Windows.
Kruse Control Software.

Time is Money. *Compatible Hardware:* Apple II, II+, IIe. *Memory Required:* 48k.
write for info.
Turning Point Software.

Time Keeper. *Compatible Hardware:* IBM PC & compatibles. *Operating System(s) Required:* MS-DOS, PC-DOS, XENIX. *Language(s):* DBASE III Plus, DBASE IV, & FoxBase, Foxpro. *Memory Required:* 640k. *Customer Support:* 6 months free telephone support.
contact publisher for price.
Tele Vend, Inc.

Time: Legal Time Accounting & Billing System. *Version:* 1.3. Jan. 1988. *Compatible Hardware:* IBM PC & compatibles. *Operating System(s) Required:* PC-DOS. *Language(s):* Compiled BASIC. *Memory Required:* 128k.
disk $99.00.
Based upon Each Attorney Maintaining a Daily Time Sheet, Upon Which Time, File Number, Work & Expenses Are Recorded. At Any Time, an Inventory of Unbilled Time & Expenses Can Be Generated, Which Ages Time. Generates Draft & Final Bills (Where Fee Adjustments Can Be Made) & Alternate Bill Formats.
Simplified Legal Systems, Inc.

Time Line. *Version:* 4.0. Andrew Layman. *Compatible Hardware:* IBM PC, PC AT, PC XT, 3270 PC & compatibles. *Operating System(s) Required:* PC-DOS 2.X, 3.X. *Memory Required:* 640k. *General Requirements:* 2 disk drives. *Items Included:* 11 disks & 3 manuals. *Customer Support:* (408) 372-8100.
disk $249.00 (ISBN 0-928525-00-7).
Project Management System Which Can Be Used with Lotus 1-2-3, dBASE III & Others. Includes Features Such As Resource Leveling & Lead/Lag Scheduling That Are Necessary for Effective Planning & Control of Time, People & Costs. User Can Schedule over 1,000 Tasks per Project, Establish an Unlimited Number of Dependencies per Task, Schedule an Unlimited Number of Resources, & Partially Allocate Them to Tasks, Track Planned vs. Actual Performance, View the Schedule in Both Gantt & PERT Formats, Schedule Project "Backwards" from Deadline Dates, & Print Selective Reports. Include Graphics Module.
Symantec Corp.

Time Machine. *Compatible Hardware:* IBM PC AT, PC AT, PS/2. *Memory Required:* 256k.
disk $2500.00.
$2000.00 graphics module option.
Project Management Package Featuring Automatic Resource Leveling, On-Screen Help, Spreadsheet Data-Entry Style, Multi-User File Reading & Writing, 10,000 Activities per Level & Disk Method of Data Storage. The Number of Resources Leveled Simultaneously Is Only Limited by Memory. Produces Resource Distribution Histograms. Automatically Draws PERT Charts. Five Simultaneous Fields Can Be Used to Sort Activities. Interfaces with Artemis Mainframe & Mini-Based Software Without Additional Programming.
Diversified Information Services.

Time Recording & Management System: TRAMS. *Version:* 2.01. Oct. 1981. *Compatible Hardware:* IBM PC & compatibles, PC XT, PC AT, PS/2. *Operating System(s) Required:* MS-DOS, PC-DOS. *Language(s):* FORTRAN. *Memory Required:* 512k. *General Requirements:* Hard disk recommended. *Items Included:* Manual. *Customer Support:* 1 hour per package purchased.
$995.00 5.25" or 8" disk, 3.25" disk.
Comprehensive Billing & Time Management Package Providing Flexible Billing Formats, Personnel Productivity Reporting, Accounts Receivable, Project Management Accounting & Other Functions. May Be Interfaced to MCC's General Ledger Package.
MCC Software (Midwest Computer Ctr. Co.).

Time Runner. *Compatible Hardware:* Atari.
disk $29.95 (ISBN 0-915149-02-8).
cassette $29.95 (ISBN 0-915149-00-1).
Player Is Part of the 1st Intergalactic Space Rush, & Must Stake Out Territory As Fast As Possible Before Being Caught by the Defender Droids.
Blue Cat.

Time Saver Payroll. *Version:* 7.3. *Compatible Hardware:* Apple Macintosh Mac Plus or higher; IBM or compatible that will run Excel for Windows 3.0. *General Requirements:* ImageWriter or LaserWriter. *Items Included:* Disk & documentation. *Customer Support:* Yes.
Program. 3.5" disk $99.50.
Demo. 3.5" disk $15.00.
Full-featured Excel Payroll Template.
Western Software Assocs.

Time Series/Forecasting. *Items Included:* Bound manual. *Customer Support:* Free hotline - no time limit; 30 day limited warranty; updates are $5/ disk plus S&H.

Apple (48k). disk $49.95.
Menu-Driven Package Consisting of Several Programs for Data File Creation, Editing, & Analysis. The Analysis Routines Are Largely Based on the Methods Discussed in the Text by Freund & Williams. Files May Be Examined Using One of Three Trend Models: Linear, Quadratic, & Exponential. Detrended & Detrended/ Deseasonalized Data Files Can Be Set up While Running the Time Series Analysis, & They May Then Be Tested Using the Autocorrelation Routine (Included). This Allows You to Determine How Well the Model Works by Examining the Residual for Randomness.
Dynacomp, Inc.

Time Tracker. *Version:* 3.20. Jul. 1989. *Items Included:* Operating manual. *Customer Support:* Unlimited telephone support.
DOS 2.0 or higher (384k). IBM & compatibles. disk $99.00. *Optimal configuration:* IBM or compatible 286 hardware with 640k RAM & a hard disk drive, printer necessary for reports. *Networks supported:* Not multi-user but will run on all Netbios networks.
Time Billing Program with Complete Accounts Receivable Accounting. It Allows Unlimited Work Description Text & Handles Reimbursable Expenses & Pre-Payments (Retainers). It Has User-Friendly Pull-Down Menus, On-Line Help & Requires No Special Preprinted Forms. Perfect for CPAs, Lawyers & Consultants. Demo Disk $10.00.
Superior Micro-Techniques.

Time Traveler. *Items Included:* Bound manual. *Customer Support:* Free hotline - no time limit; 30 day limited warranty; updates are $5/disk plus S&H.
MS-DOS 2.0 or higher. IBM & compatibles (128k). disk $24.95.
Takes You on an Exciting Adventure Through American History. Along the Way You Will Meet Friendly & Unfriendly Travelers, Get Caught in Active Time Portals, & Navigate Secret Passages As You Attempt to Locate the Key of Time to Return to the Present. At Several Stops along Your Journey, You Must Answer Questions about American History Before You Can Continue. Correct Answers Allow You to Accumulate Gold Pieces. But Beware! There Are Many Pitfalls & Dangers Which May Cost You Some of That Precious Gold.
Dynacomp, Inc.

Time Traveler. *Compatible Hardware:* Apple II Plus, IIe, IIc.
$24.95 (ISBN 0-918349-38-9, Order no.: TT).
Adventure Game in Which You Are a Time Traveler Roving Across the Boundaries of the Ages, Searching for Magical Treasures Scattered Throughout History. Each Game Played Is Unique, Confronting You with the Need for Complex Decisions & Demands for Real Time Action.
Krell Software Corp.

The Time Traveller: M-77. *Compatible Hardware:* Apple II+; Commodore 64, PET; TRS-80.
disk $30.00.
Commodore 64, PET; TRS-80. cassette $30.00.
Calculates Planet Positions for Any Date from 4713 B.C. Forward.
Matrix Software.

Time Xtra, Time Xtra Plus. *Version:* 3.3. Nov. 1988. *Operating System(s) Required:* PC-DOS/MS-DOS. *Memory Required:* 380k. *General Requirements:* Hard disk. *Items Included:* Program disks & manual. *Customer Support:* Phone support.
Single user, network compatible. 3.5" or 5.25" disk $79.00.

TIMECARD

Network server package. 3.5" or 5.25" disk $295.00.
Calendar, Appointments, Memory Resident Alarms, To-Do-Lists, Tickler Files, Phones/ Addresses, AutoDialing, Mailing Labels, Text Notes of Any Length with Any Entry of Appointment, Thing-to-Do or Phone/Address. Note File Import/Export. Many Printing Options. Function Key Macros, Accesses Multiple Sets of Files, Networks/File Sharing. "Plus" Also Features Automatic Group Scheduling Meeting Functions, Graphic Display of Available Time, etc.
Park Software, Inc.

TimeCard. *Items Included:* Comes with program, desk accessory & manual. *Customer Support:* Initial 30 days free support from date of first call, annual plan: $80.00 per year, occasional support: $40.00/per hour, $5.00 minimum call.
Macintosh 6.0.2 or higher (390k). Mac Plus or above. Version 2.0.3 (12/1989) $199.00. *Optimal configuration:* SE, system 6.0.2 with hard disk.
MS-DOS 3.0 or higher (256k). IBM PC. Version 1.1 (06/1989) $199.00. *Optimal configuration:* IBM PC (384k), hard disk.
Aatrix TimeCard Is An Employee Time Tracking Software Program Which Allows Employees to Punch in & Punch Out on the Macintosh Computer. It Accumulates This Logged Time & Then Prints Payroll Reports at the End of Each Period Or Exports the Data to Aatrix Payroll for Payroll Calculations. TimeCard Also Works with a Magnetic Card Reader, Making "Punch-in to Paycheck" a Very Simple Process.
Aatrix Software.

Timecard. *Version:* 3.2. Mar. 1993. *Items Included:* 124 page user manual. *Customer Support:* 30 day free telephone support.
PC-DOS (320k). IBM PC. $335.00, (license fee) (ISBN 0-945851-29-4). *Nonstandard peripherals required:* Zon Credit Card Terminal.
Time & Attendance Program. Uses a Zon Credit Card Terminal to Monitor Each Card Pass & Approves Time-In, Time-Out by Card Holder. Program Stores Data & Can Access Later to Determine Total Hours Worked by Cardholder by Project.
Geocomp, Ltd.

Timecard: Job Cost Management System.
Version: 2.3. Gerald E. Johnson. Jun. 1982. *Compatible Hardware:* Altos; IBC; Onyx; Seiko. *Operating System(s) Required:* Oasis. *Language(s):* BASIC. *Memory Required:* 64k. *General Requirements:* 2 disk drives.
disk $2500.00 (ISBN 0-922660-02-6).
Tracks Time & Costs to Contract Limits with Comparative Analysis. Current Contract Status Is Available for Cost Control Management.
Business Design Software.

Timeclock II: Computerized Timeclock & Scheduler. 1995. *Items Included:* Full manual. *Customer Support:* Free telephone support - 90 days, 30-day warranty.
MS-DOS 3.2 or higher. 286 (584k). $199.95-$299.95. *Nonstandard peripherals required:* CGA/EGA/VGA.
Not Only a Complete Replacement for a Mechanical Time Clock, It Is Also a Powerful Time Management Tool. Turns Virtually Any PC into a Time Clock Which Can Maintain Detailed Records of Employee Comings & Goings. It Can Run As a TSR (Terminate & Stay Ready), Thereby Freeing up Your Computer for Other Activities, While Still Being Instantly Available to Log an Employee in or Out. The Employee May "Punch In/Out" by Entering a Code on the Keyboard (Standard Version), or by Using a Bar Code Reader (Optional). With the Network Version, Log-In/Out May Be Accomplished at Any Computer on the Network.
Dynacomp, Inc.

Timegraphs. *Version:* 2.0. *Items Included:* Manual. *Customer Support:* Free phone support.
MS-DOS 3.x (512k). disk $95.00 (ISBN 0-87199-087-3). *Nonstandard peripherals required:* Hard disk; 512k RAM Hercules, EGA or VGA graphics card; 8087 math processor recommended, dot-matrix or HP-compatible laser or inkjet printer. *Addl. software required:* Chartwheels I, Chartwheels II or other Nova-compatible program.
3.5" disk $100.00 (ISBN 0-87199-094-6).
Produces Ebertin-Style Graphic Ephemerides on Computer Screen or Printer; Does Transit, Progressed, Solar Arc & Declination Graphs Including Moving Midpoints; Geocentric, Heliocentric or Right Acensional Coordinates.
Astrolabe, Inc.

TIMEKEEP. *Compatible Hardware:* IBM PC, Tandy 2000, Kaypro. *Operating System(s) Required:* TRSDOS, CP/M, DOS. *Language(s):* BASIC. *Memory Required:* 64k.
disk $500.00.
Prepares Productivity Reports on Employees of Accounting & Law Firms at Various Levels of Supervision. Follows the Norms Recommended by the American Institute of Certified Public Accountants. Prepares Bills for Clients & Reports for Management.
Computer Technical Services of New Jersey.

TIMEKEEPER Central Software: TKC. Sep. 1985. *Compatible Hardware:* IBM PC with Serial Interface Card. *Operating System(s) Required:* PC-DOS 2.0 or higher. *Memory Required:* 512k.
contact publisher for price (Order no.: SD-00003-000).
Time Attendance Software Package. Software Automatically Communicates with Data Collection Terminals. The Menu-Driven Package Accesses Comprehensive Management Reports, Schedules, Employees & Applies to Payroll Policy Rules.
Kronos, Inc.

TimeLink: An Electronic Timesheet Import & Export Utility. *Version:* 2.0. Aug. 1994. *Items Included:* 6 months of free maintenance (updates & technical support) & manual. *Customer Support:* Annual maintenance (technical support & updates) fee of $100 (after first six months); 90 days unlimited warranty; telephone training available for $75/hr.; conferences available.
DOS 3.1 or higher. IBM & compatibles (640k). disk $295.00. *Networks supported:* Novell; Novell-Lite; Lantastic.
*An Electronic Timesheet, Export, & Import Utility That Integrates with UniLinks TB*Plus, Version 2. Contains Many Noteworthy Features. A Pop-Up (TSR) Utility Provides the Convenience of Tracking Time While in Other Programs. A Built in Stop-Watch Times Work Efficiently. Information Can Be Channelled in & Out of Popular Spreadsheet & Database Programs Through the Import & Export Utilities.*
UniLink.

TimeLink for Windows: Electronic Timesheet Import & Export Utility. *Version:* 2.0. Sep. 1994. *Items Included:* Manuals & 6 months of free maintenance (updates & technical support). *Customer Support:* Annual maintenance (technical support & updates) fee of $150 (after first six months); 90 days warranty; telephone training available for $75/hr.; conference training.
DOS 3.1 or higher & Windows. IBM & compatibles. $395.00 ($100.00 upgrade for existing TimeLink Users). *Networks supported:* Novell; Novell-Lite; Lantastic.
*An Electronic Timesheet, Export, & Import Utility That Integrates with UniLinks TB*Plus Version 2. TimeLink for Windows Is UniLink's Prototype for Windows Versions of Its Software & Takes Full Advantage of the Windows Environment. The Built-In Stopwatch Times Work Efficiently. Information Is Channelled into & Out of Popular Spreadsheet & Database Programs by the Import & Export Utilities.*
UniLink.

TimeMaker. *Version:* 2.2. May 1991. *Items Included:* Reports 2.0 runtime Hyper Card 2.0 runtime; Vinyl or leather zipper binder; index tab dividers for daily schedules (1-31), monthly calendars (Jan-Dec); & address lists (A-Z); Cassette audio tape; "How to Manage Time & Set Priorities" by Stephen Young; User's Guide & Tutorial. *Customer Support:* Thirty days free telephone support, 9am-5pm mountain standard time, Monday-Friday.
Macintosh OS 6.0.5 or higher. MAC Plus (2Mb). $149.00 software only; $199.00 with vinyl binder; $249.00 with leather binder (Order no.: 602-951-3812). *Nonstandard peripherals required:* Hard drive, laser printer. *Optimal configuration:* MAC II family computer with 2Mb RAM or higher, hard disk, laser printer.
Time & Contact Management System Which Replaces Manual Organizers. Prints Calendars, Prioritized Daily Schedules, & Address Lists on Plain Paper Ready to Place in a Zipper Binder. Prepares Letters, Envelopes, & Mailing Labels. Includes Software, Binder, Index Tabs, User's Guide with Tutorial, & Audio Cassette to Improve Time Management Skills.
First Wave.

Timemap. *Compatible Hardware:* IBM PC. (source code included). *Memory Required:* 128k.
disk $59.95.
Generalized Hard-Copy Schedule Generating Program Designed to Generate Printed Bar-Chart Schedules.
Dynacomp, Inc.

TimeMinder. *Version:* 2.1. *Compatible Hardware:* Apple Macintosh Plus or above. *Memory Required:* 512k.
3.5" disk $299.00.
Time-Tracking Utility Program Designed to Keep Track of Users' Time for Billing Purposes. Can Be Used for Professional Time Billing, Productivity Analysis, Job Costing, & Other Time Oriented Applications. Track Time While Working Using the DA, or Enter Time Manually Using Four Different Manual Entry Methods. Allows User to Fully Customize an Invoice With Multiple Fonts & a PICT Item for Logo. Program Offers a Powerful Reports Generator with Extensive Graphing Capabilities. Also Has Built in Text Processor for Attaching Notes to an Invoice Explaining the Charges.
Aatrix Software.

Timeout Desktools. *Compatible Hardware:* Apple II.
disk $49.95.
Provides Clock, Calendar, Appointment Scheduler, Task List, Calculator, Notepad, Dialer, Envelope, Addresser, Puzzle, & Other Tools.
Beagle Brothers.

Timeout Filemaster. *Compatible Hardware:* Apple II.
disk $49.95.
Allows Users to Manage All Their File & Disk Handling Needs from Within APPLEWORKS. Menus Allow Users to Copy, Compare, Rename, Lock, Unlock, & Delete Files. Users Can Read an Entire Disk at Once & Write out Multiple Copies Without Re-Reading the Original Disk.
Beagle Brothers.

Timeout Graph. *Compatible Hardware:* Apple II. *General Requirements:* Supports most dot-matrix printers.
disk $89.95.

Creates Graphs Direcly from Spreadsheets or Databases in Any of Nine Graph Types: Bar, Line, Pie, X-Y (Scatter), Stacked Bar, Area, Hi-Lo, Exploded Pie, & Point. Features Automatic or Manual Scaling of the X & Y Axes, Graph & Axes Titles, Legends, Grid Lines, & a Variety of Sizes.
Beagle Brothers.

Timeout QuickSpell. *Compatible Hardware:* Apple II.
disk $69.95.
Spell Checker. Allows Users to Correct Words in Context or in a Separate List. Includes an 80,000 Word Dictionary Which Also Accepts an Unlimited Number of Additional User-Supplied Words.
Beagle Brothers.

Timeout SideSpread. *Compatible Hardware:* Apple II. *General Requirements:* Supports most dot-matrix printers.
disk $49.95.
Rotates Spreadsheets 90 Degrees, Enabling Users to Print Sideways with No Limit on the Size of the File to Be Printed. Offers Users a Wide Choice of Font Sizes. Allows Printing of the Entire Spreadsheet or Any Portion.
Beagle Brothers.

Timeout SuperFonts. *Compatible Hardware:* Apple II. *General Requirements:* Supports most dot-matrix printers.
disk $79.95.
Prints APPLEWORKS Word Processor Files with Macintosh Fonts (6 to 27 Points in Size). Users Can Select from a Variety of Syles Including Bold, Italic, Underline, Shadow, Outline, Subscript, Superscript, & Negative. Allows Users to Incorporate Graphics into Their Documents & Includes a Page Preview Feature.
Beagle Brothers.

Timeout UltraMacros. *Compatible Hardware:* Apple II.
disk $59.95.
Macro Program Which Gives the User Complete Control over TIMEOUT & APPLEWORKS at a Single Keystroke. Also Allows Users to Define up to 500 Different Macros at a Time.
Beagle Brothers.

Timepoint Employee Scheduler. *Version:* 2.5a. Jan. 1994. *Items Included:* Reference manual, tutorial, set up/training workbook. *Customer Support:* 90 days free support (toll-free telephone); yearly toll-free is 15% of product price per year.
PC-DOS. IBM & compatibles (640k). disk $1195.00 up. *Optimal configuration:* IBM PC AT or higher, 640k RAM, printer, hard disk. *Networks supported:* Novell, Arcnet, Banyan.
Creates & Prints Optimized, Error-Free Shift Schedules for Professional, Retail or Service Employees (Nurses, Clerks, Bank Tellers, etc.). It Allows Unlimited Employees, Schedule Span, or Shift Lengths, & Tracks Skills, Availability, Vacations, Overtime, & Many Other Conflicts. Connects to Payroll or HRIS Systems.
Timepoint Corporation.

Timepoint Employee Scheduler for Windows. Jan. 1994. *Items Included:* 2 spiral bound, 1 loose leaf manuals; reference guide, tutorial & set up guide. *Customer Support:* 90 days free support (toll free telephone); yearly support is 15% of product price per year.
IBM PC with Windows 486-33 MHz or higher, 20Mb hard disk (8Mb). $1495.00 & up.
Timepoint Corp.

Timepoint "Equity" Scheduler. *Version:* 2.5a. Jan. 1994. *Items Included:* Supplemental reference manual. *Customer Support:* 90 days free support (toll-free telephone); yearly toll-free is 15% of product price per year.
PC-DOS. IBM & compatibles (640k). disk $2995.00. *Optimal configuration:* IBM PC AT or higher, 640k RAM, printer, hard disk. *Networks supported:* Novell, Arcnet, Banyan.
Automatically Creates "Equitable" Shift Schedules for Physicians & Other High-Skill Employees Working Undesirable Hours. Uses a "Difficulty Point" & "Last-Worked Rotation" Method. Allows Unlimited Employees, Schedule Span, & Shift Lengths; Checks 12 Different Conflicts Including Vacations, Skills, & Availability; Prints Charts, Graphs, & Management Reports.
Timepoint Corporation.

TimeSaver Client Billing System. *Version:* 4.5. Mar. 1985. *Compatible Hardware:* IBM PC or compatibles. *Operating System(s) Required:* PC-DOS/MS-DOS 2.0. *Language(s):* BASCOM 6.0. *Memory Required:* 384k. *Items Included:* Custom pre-configuration. *Customer Support:* Unlimited support first 90 days.
disk $980.00.
Offers Complete Client Billing for Secretarial Services & Executive Office Centers. Includes Timekeeping, Bill Preparation & Accounts Receivable.
Barnett & Assocs.

Timesavers: Quikey, On-Line, Help, RAM Driver, Sort Dir., Selective Erase. 1984. *Compatible Hardware:* IBM PC, PCjr, PC XT, PC AT & compatibles.
disk $59.95.
Package of Six Utilities Designed to Improve Operating Speed & Efficiency. Includes: QUIKEY to Redefine up to 485 Keys & Keystroke Combinations; Ram Driver to Use a Portion of Memory As an Electronic Disk; On-Line Help Offers Instructions on All PC-DOS 2.0/2.1 Commands; Sort Directory to Sort & Save Directions by Name, Date, Size or Extension; Selective Erase to Delete Files with Two Keystrokes; & Selective Copy to Copy Files with Two Keystrokes.
DataSource Publishing Co.

Timeshare Condominium System (TCS). *Version:* 8.00. 1981. *Compatible Hardware:* IBM PC, PC XT, PC AT or compatibles. *Operating System(s) Required:* MS-DOS 2.0. *Language(s):* Compiled Basic. *Memory Required:* 640k. *General Requirements:* Hard disk, printer.
$3000.00-$11,000.00 single-user.
$6000.00-$16,000.00 multi-user.
evaluation kit $95.00.
Specifically Designed for the Manager/Owner of a TIMESHARE Resort, Where 1 Condominium Is Sold to Multiple Individual Owners. Includes Owner Accounts Receivable, Commission Payable to Salespeople, Integrated General Ledger & Accounting System. Tracks Condominiums Available & Arrival & Departure Dates for All Owners.
Resort Data Processing, Inc.

Timeshare Resort Marketing System. Mary James. Jan. 1985. *Language(s):* COBOL. *Items Included:* User manual & tutorial manual. *Customer Support:* Yearly maintenance contract: $200.00.
MS-DOS. IBM PC (640k). disk $3250.00 (ISBN 0-928666-00-X, Order no.: TS MARK001). *Nonstandard peripherals required:* 3.5" or 5.25" disk drive, printer, 90Mb hard disk (640k). *Networks supported:* Networks supported: Novell.
386/486. disk $3250.00.
Timeshare Resort Industry Sales Tracking System.

Prints Sales Contracts & Sales Reports. Maintains Unit & Gift Inventories. Maintains Buyer, Non-Buyer, Salesperson & Source Information. Merges Data with WordStar or WordPerfect Word Processing Package.
The James Gang.

Timeshare Resort Receivables. Mary James. Jan. 1985. *Language(s):* COBOL. *Items Included:* User manual & tutorial manual. *Customer Support:* Yearly maintenance $200.00.
MS-DOS. IBM PC (640k). disk $3250.00 (ISBN 0-928666-06-9, Order no.: MAN01). *Nonstandard peripherals required:* 3.5" or 5.25" disk drive, printer, 90Mb hard disk. *Networks supported:* Networks supported: Novell.
386/486. disk $3250.00.
Maintains Monies Received for Outstanding Loans, & Maintenance Fees. Prints Investor Reports & Monthly Statements, Daily Accounting Reports & Aging of Accounts. Calculates Late Charges. Merges with WordStar or WordPerfect Word Processing for Late Notices, Year-End Notices & Other Correspondence.
The James Gang.

Timeshare Resort Reservations. Mary James. Oct. 1985. *Language(s):* COBOL. *Items Included:* User manual & tutorial. *Customer Support:* Yearly maintenance: $200.00.
MS-DOS. IBM PC (640k). disk $3250.00 (ISBN 0-928666-10-7, Order no.: RES01). *Nonstandard peripherals required:* 3.5" or 5.25" disk drive, printer, 90Mb hard disk. *Networks supported:* Networks supported: Novell.
386/486. disk $3250.00.
Maintains Reservations, Owner Rental, Exchanges, Float Time Usage & Billing/Receiving of Monies Charged by Resort Users. Prints Check In/Out List, Daily Charges, Unit Inventory & Description, & Reservation by Various Unit Types.
The James Gang.

TimeSheet Professional: Time & Expense Tracking for Projects & Clients. *Version:* 4.0. *Items Included:* Manual. *Customer Support:* 45 days free support starting with registration. 30 day money back guarantee (does not include shipping), $125 per year unlimited support & an 800 number.
DOS 3.3 or higher, hard disk recommended. 386 processor or higher. $199.95 single, $699.95 Network. *Networks supported:* Novell, TOPS, 3COM, Banyan, LANtastic & others.
Product to Track Time & Expenses for Projects & Clients. Links to Project Management, Payroll & Time & Billing.
TIMESLIPS Corp.

TimeSlicer. (ADVANTAGE Library Ser.). *Compatible Hardware:* IBM PC, PC XT, PC AT. *General Requirements:* Lattice C v.3.0G or later, assembly language or Microsoft C v.4.0 compiler.
disk $295.00.
Multitasking Library of C Functions That Gives Programmers the Ability to Develop Applications That Will Run an Unlimited Numer of Tasks Concurrently. Programmers Can Create Real-Time, Multi-Tasking Programs at the Application Level Rather Than Interfacing with the Operating System. Allows C Functions to Be Installed to Replace or Complement Any Interrupt Service Routine (ISR) & the Programmer Has Total Control over Whether & When the Original Service Routine Should Execute. Allows Tasks to Be Created, Suspended, Restarted, or Terminated at Run-Time. The Programmer Controls the Pre-Emption System. Critical Resource Management Functions Allow Non-Reentrant Code to Be Shared by Concurrent Tasks. Supports Small & Large Memory Models.
Lifeboat Assocs.

TIMESLIPS

Timeslips. *Version:* 6.0. May 1995. *Items Included:* Manual. *Customer Support:* 45 days free from date of registration; online support - AOL, CompuServe, Internet; 1 yr. toll-free single user $180.00.
Windows 3.1. 386 (4Mb). $180.00 single user.
Leading Time Tracking & Billing Product with Customizable Billing Formats. Stopwatch Timer & Customizable Reports.
TIMESLIPS Corp.

Timeslips Deluxe. *Version:* 6.0. *Compatible Hardware:* 386 processor or higher. *Memory Required:* 4000k. *Items Included:* Manual. *Customer Support:* 45 days free support starting with date of registration.
disk $299.95 single user; $699.95 network; $199.95 Network Expansion Kit.
Time & Expense Tracking, Professional Billing & Accounts Receivable System for Service Professionals & Small Businesses.
TIMESLIPS Corp.

Timeslips Remote. *Items Included:* 1 Perfect-bound manual.
DOS 3.3 or higher, Windows 3.1 or higher. $79.95 (Order no.: TSREM). *Addl. software required:* Timeslips version 5.1 or higher. *Optimal configuration:* 386 processor or higher. *Networks supported:* Any DOS 3.1 compatible network including Novell 3 COM, and others.
Time & Expense Tracking Module Featured in TIMESLIPS. For Laptops or Non Networked Offices That Have Multiple Users Tracking Time. Numerous Invoices & Managements Reports Can Be Created with Varying Levels of Detail Description.
TIMESLIPS Corp.

Timeslips: Time & Expense Tracking. 1995. *Items Included:* Full manual. *Customer Support:* Free telephone support - 90 days, 30-day warranty.
MS-DOS 3.2 or higher. 286 (584k). $299.95-$499.95. *Nonstandard peripherals required:* CGA/EGA/VGA.
The Most Widely Used Time & Billing System Available. It Includes Multiple Billing Rates, Work-in-Progress Reports, Client History Reports with YTD & Inception-to-Date Totals. The Accounts Receivable Module Has Four User-Definable Aging Periods, & Invoices May Be Customized. There Are 15 Custom Client Fields Which Can Be Sorted & Totalized. Up to 6 Billing Rates Are Available per User, per Client, & per Activity. Each Matter/Project May Have Separate or Consolidated Bills. Supports Canadian GST, & Is WordPerfect Library/Office Compatible.
Dynacomp, Inc.

Timeslips for the Mac. *Version:* 3.0. *Compatible Hardware:* Apple Macintosh. *General Requirements:* Hard disk. *Customer Support:* 45 days free tech support starting with registration. $299.95; $699.95 Network Edition (supports 5 stations); $139.95 Single Station Network Extension.
Upgrade of TIMESLIPS for Larger Businesses. Supports All Features of TIMESLIPS with Enhancements.
TIMESLIPS Corp.

Timespan Accounting. *Version:* 6.1. Apr. 1993. *Items Included:* 3 Wire O bound manuals, 3 5-1/4 & 3-1/2 disks, Checks/Forms Order Packet, Debit/Credit Reminder Stickers. *Customer Support:* Toll free telephone support included without charge.
MS-DOS 3.0 or higher. IBM-PC & compatibles & hard disk with 1Mb free (512k). $2000.00 Stand alone (Network licensing by quote) (Order no.: TIMESPAN ACCOUNTING 6.1).
Optimal configuration: IBM-PC compatible computer with 512Mb RAM; MS-DOS 3.0 Plus & hard disk with 3Mb free. *Networks supported:* Novell, MS-DOS Share.
A Comprehensive, General Business Accounting System Which Includes Fully-Integrated, Non-Batch, Real Time General Ledger, Accounts Receivable, Accounts Payable, Payroll & Job Costing for up to 10,000 Companies. It Is Well-Suited to Professional Bookkeepers, Accountants & Contractors & Allows for Multiple Users with Password Protection & Controlled Access Rights.
Timespan International, Inc.

Timestar. *Version:* 2.0. Oct. 1990. *Compatible Hardware:* Apple II+, IIc, IIe, IIgs, Atari (all but STS); IBM PC/XT/AT & compatibles; Commodore 64/128. *Memory Required:* 48k. *Items Included:* User's manual. *Customer Support:* Yes.
Apple; Atari; Commodore; IBM. disk $24.95 (ISBN 0-933596-10-3).
Turns the Computer into a Sequence Timer. Program up to 15 Separate Events, Each As Long As 99 Minutes. Define Warning Period Before Each Is Over. Counts down Events Giving On-Screen Data. Name of Event Being Timed, Position in Sequence, Minutes in Entire Sequence, & Minutes & Seconds Remaining in Timed Event. Manual or Automatic Operation Available. Many Applications in Photo Darkroom, Industry, Teaching, Testing, etc. Version 2.0 Stores an Unlimited Number of Sequences for Recall & Reuse.
F/22 Pr.

TimeTrac. *Version:* 91e. 1991. *Items Included:* Disk & manual. *Customer Support:* 90 days included in purchase price; support agreement available.
PC-MS/DOS 2.1 or higher. IBM PC & compatibles (200k). disk $50.00. *Nonstandard peripherals required:* 330k disk.
Site license available.
Allows Individuals in a Workgroup to Track Their Use of Time on Laptop Computers While in the Field & Then Export the Information to Accounting, Project Tracking, Spreadsheet & Database Programs. Uses Clock Time & Computes Time in Units That May Be Any Number of Whole Minutes up to One Hour. The User Chooses If It Will Round, Truncate, or Append Partial Units. Also Keeps Track of Multiple (nested) Interruptions.
Compass New England.

TimeTrax for Legal Professionals. *Version:* 2.0. Open Door Software Division. Oct. 1993. *Items Included:* Spiral manual, video (when available). *Customer Support:* 30 day free customer support; 900 line $2.00/min.; 1 yr. maintenance $400/mo. Includes: toll free line & fax back priority service.
DOS. IBM compatible 386, 25Mhz, 5Mb free space on hard disk, VGA monitor, 3.5" floppy, keyboard, mouse. disk $495.00 (ISBN 1-56756-047-4, Order no.: OD600I). *Addl. software required:* Operating system. *Optimal configuration:* IBM or compatible 486, 66Mhz, 5Mb free space on hard disk, 4Mb RAM-3Mb expanded usable, VGA monitor, 3.5" high density floppy, keyboard, mouse, tape backup, & uninterruptable power supply. *Networks supported:* Novell Netware Lite.
Windows. IBM compatible 386, 25Mhz, 5Mb free space on hard disk, VGA monitor, 3.5" floppy, keyboard, mouse. disk $495.00 (ISBN 1-56756-066-0, Order no.: OD605W). *Addl. software required:* Windows 3.1 or higher. *Optimal configuration:* IBM or compatible 486, 66Mhz, 5Mb free space on hard disk, 4Mb RAM-3Mb expanded usable, VGA monitor, 3.5" high density floppy, keyboard, mouse, tape backup, & uninterruptable power supply. *Networks supported:* Novell Netware Lite.
MAC. 3.5" disk $495.00 (ISBN 1-56756-048-2, Order no.: OD630M). *Addl. software required:* System 7.
Gives Lawyers & Paralegals the Ability to Manage Client Costs & Service Accounts by Differentiating Between What Is Billed As a Service & a Cost. Combines Case Management with Time Billing & Can Help the Legal Professional Manage Appointments & Billing with Efficiency & Accuracy. Stores Client Profiles, Client Case Notes & History, As Well As Expense & Billing Summaries. Has a Built in Automatic & Manual Timer Mechanism That Keeps Track of Billable Hours, Retainers & Has Reports for the Client, the Professional & the Accountant.
Advantage International.

TimeTrax for Time & Billing Professionals. *Version:* 2.0. Open Door Software Division. Oct. 1993. *Items Included:* Spiral manual, video (when available). *Customer Support:* 30 day free customer support; 900 line $2.00/min.; 1 yr. maintenance $400/mo. Includes: toll free line & fax back priority service.
DOS. IBM compatible 386, 25Mhz, 5Mb free space on hard disk. disk $495.00 (ISBN 1-56756-069-5, Order no.: OD620I). *Addl. software required:* Operating system. *Optimal configuration:* IBM or compatible 486, 66Mhz, 5Mb free space on hard disk, 4Mb RAM-3Mb expanded usable, VGA monitor, 3.5" high density floppy, keyboard, mouse, tape backup, & uninterruptable power supply. *Networks supported:* Novell Netware Lite.
Windows. IBM compatible 386, 25Mhz, 5Mb free space on hard disk. disk $495.00 (ISBN 1-56756-073-3, Order no.: OD625W). *Addl. software required:* Windows 3.1 or higher. *Optimal configuration:* IBM or compatible 486, 66Mhz, 5Mb free space on hard disk, 4Mb RAM-3Mb expanded usable, VGA monitor, 3.5" high density floppy, keyboard, mouse, tape backup, & uninterruptable power supply. *Networks supported:* Novell Netware Lite.
MAC. 3.5" disk $495.00 (ISBN 1-56756-070-9, Order no.: OD630M). *Addl. software required:* System 7.
Combines Job or Case Management with Time Billing & Can Help Any Billing Professional Manage Their Appointments & Billing with Efficiency & Accuracy. Stores Client Profiles, Client Notes & History, As Well As Expense & Billing Summaries. Has a Built in Automatic & Manual Timer Mechanism That Keeps Track of Billable Hours, Retainers & Has Reports for the Client, the Professional & the Accountant.
Advantage International.

Timewand I Communications Package. *Version:* 5.20. May 1992. *Compatible Hardware:* IBM PC & compatibles; Macintosh. *Operating System(s) Required:* MS-DOS 2.1 or higher, Macintosh. *Language(s):* C, Hyperscript. *Memory Required:* Macintosh 2Mb, PC 640k. *General Requirements:* TimeWand bar code reader. *Items Included:* MAC Hypercard. *Customer Support:* Free telephone support.
disk $100.00 (Order no.: TWS-000).
Designed to Download Information Gathered with the TimeWand Bar Code Reader & Deposit That Information onto a Disk in a Standard ASCII Text File. PC Version Also Controls the Use of Modems for Downloading from Remote Locations.
Videx, Inc.

TimeWand II Communications Software. *Version:* PC 1.4, Macintosh 3.0. Oct. 1991. *Items Included:* Instruction & operations manual included. *Customer Support:* Free customer phone support, 90 day warranty.

TITLE INDEX

MS-DOS (640k). disk $350.00. *Nonstandard peripherals required:* Requires TimeWand II portable bar code reader. *Optimal configuration:* MS-DOS 2.1 or greater.
Macintosh (2Mb). 3.5" disk $350.00. *Nonstandard peripherals required:* Requires TimeWand II portable bar code reader. *Addl. software required:* Hypercard. *Optimal configuration:* Macintosh (2Mb) & hard disk.
Programs the TimeWand II Portable Bar Code Reader. Allows User to Customize the LCD Display to Their Specification. Allows User to Preconfigure the Order of Data Entry. Also Receive Data from the TimeWand II & Stores It in an ASCII Text File.
Videx, Inc.

TimeWise. *Compatible Hardware:* Atari XL/XE. *Operating System(s) Required:* AOS. *Memory Required:* 32k.
disk $4.95 (Order no.: DX5047).
Offers 3 Ways of Tracking Appointments or Other Important Dates: by Use of a Calendar, by Calling up Appointments in Chronological Order, & by Calling up Specific Categories. Also Offers the Option of Flagging Appointments for Certain Individuals.
Atari Corp.

Tiny C. *Compatible Hardware:* Apple, DEC PC, TRS-80. *Operating System(s) Required:* CP/M.
contact publisher for price.
Tiny-c Assocs.

Tiny Pay. *Compatible Hardware:* TRS-80 Model I, Model III, Model 4. *Operating System(s) Required:* MS-DOS, TRSDOS.
disk $29.95 ea.
Model I & Model III. (Order no.: D8TP).
Model 4. (Order no.: D4TP).
MS-DOS. (Order no.: DMTP).
Source. (Order no.: D4TPSC).
upgrade fee $15.00.
Designed for Small Payrolls That Can Be Computed by Hand Normally Using the Pre-Computed Tables in IRS Schedule "E". Supports 20 Emplyees, Maintains Quarterly & Yearly Totals.
The Alternate Source.

Tip Disk #1. Bert Kersey. Aug. 1984. *Compatible Hardware:* Apple II, II+, IIe, IIc, IIgs. *Operating System(s) Required:* Apple DOS 3.3. *Language(s):* BASIC. *Memory Required:* 48k.
disk $20.00, incl. charts.
100 Programs That Illustrate & Demonstrate the Many Tricks & Tasks That the Apple Computer Can Perform. All of the Programs Are Listable & Copyable. A Peeks & Pokes Chart & Apple Command Chart Lists All Applesoft, Integer BASIC & DOS Commands & Their Functions.
Beagle Brothers.

TIPS. *Version:* X. Feb. 1992. *Items Included:* User's manual. *Customer Support:* On-site training at $65/hr.; on-site support at $150/mo. for annual contracts on S/W & H/W; on-site support at $120/hr. for non-contract work on S/W & H/W. 90 days warranty on TIPS products at no charge. UNIX V or MS-DOS. Any 386 or 486 platform.
disk $3500.00-$16,000.00. *Optimal configuration:* UNIX V, 4Mb RAM, 100 Mb hard disk, tape back-up. *Networks supported:* Yes.
Medical & Dental Office Management Program.
Programming & Systems Management, Inc.

TIPS-Dental S/W. Dec. 1983. *Compatible Hardware:* AT&T 3B2; IBM PC, PC AT & compatibles; Compaq; NEC. *Operating System(s) Required:* PC-DOS/MS-DOS, UNIX V. *Language(s):* FORTRAN. *Memory Required:* 4000k. *General Requirements:* 2 disk drives, hard disk, printer, modem.
IBM PC AT. single user $3500.00 (Order no.: 211D).
IBM PC AT. 4 users $5500.00 (Order no.: 212D).
IBM PC AT/MS-DOS. 8 disk set $6850.00 (Order no.: 213D).
AT&T/Unix V. 12 users $9000.00 (Order no.: 223D).
Multi-User, Multi-Tasking Office Management System for Solo or Multi-Dental Practices As Well As Large Clinics. Consist of Clinical History, Physical Exam, Treatment Plans, Process Billing, Insurance & Electronic Claims; As Well As Accounting & Management Reports. Features Data Compaction & No "End-of-the-Day" Updating Cycle.
Programming & Systems Management, Inc.

TIPS-Legal S/W, 5 disks. Sep. 1988. *Compatible Hardware:* AT&T 382; IBM PC, PC AT & compatibles. *Operating System(s) Required:* PC-DOS/MS-DOS, UNIX V. *Language(s):* FORTRAN. *Memory Required:* 512k. *General Requirements:* Hard disk, printer, modem.
IBM PC AT. $3500.00 (Order no.: 311L).
IBM PC AT. $5500.00 (Order no.: 312L).
AT&T. $6500.00 (Order no.: 322L).
Multi-User, Multi-Tasking Application Consisting of Detail Time-Keeping & Client-Matter Billing Information Such As Work-in-Process or Pre-Billing Reports, Complete Financial Reports by Attorneys, Docket Control & Keyword Search: All Fully Integrated. Programming Features Used Include Data Compaction Techniques, High-Speed & No "End-of-the-Day" Updating Cycle. Designed for Solo to Multi-Attorney Practices As Well As Medium-Sized Law Firms.
Programming & Systems Management, Inc.

TIPS-Medical S/W, 8 disks. Dec. 1981. *Compatible Hardware:* AT&T 3B2, IBM PC AT, NCR PC8. *Operating System(s) Required:* MS-DOS, UNIX. *Language(s):* FORTRAN. *Memory Required:* 512k. *General Requirements:* 2 disk drives, hard disk, printer, modem.
IBM PC AT/MS-DOS. $3500.00 (Order no.: 111M).
IBM PC AT/MS-DOS. $6850.00 (Order no.: 112M).
IBM PC AT/MS-DOS. $9850.00 (Order no.: 113M).
AT&T/Unix V. $12,000.00 (Order no.: 123M).
Multi-User, Multi-Tasking Office Management System Consisting of Medical History, Physical Exam, Lab Tests, Process Billing, Insurance & Electronic Claims, As Well As Accounting & Management Reports. Features Data Compaction Techniques, & No "End-of-Day" Updating Cycle.
Programming & Systems Management, Inc.

TIPS, RIO, TOPAS. *Compatible Hardware:* IBM PC, PC XT, PC AT & compatibles. *Operating System(s) Required:* MS-DOS.
contact publisher for price.
File Graphics for Slides, Print & Video Production.
Lyn Norstad & Assocs., Inc.

Titan. Apr. 1989.
MS-DOS (256k). disk $44.95. *Optimal configuration:* EGA or VGA video board.
Amiga 500, 1000, 2000 (512k). 3.5" disk $44.95. *Nonstandard peripherals required:* Joy stick.
Macintosh 512E, Plus, SE, II, IIx, IIcx (1Mb). 3.5" disk $69.95.
$39.95.
Strategic Puzzle with 80 Levels. Find the Tricks to Be Able to Win Each Level.
Titus Software Corp.

Title Company Automation Package: TCAP, 5 systems. *Version:* 2.5. 1988. *Compatible Hardware:* IBM PC & compatibles, PC AT, PC XT. *Operating System(s) Required:* MS-DOS. (source code included). *Memory Required:* 640k. *General Requirements:* Hard disk, printer. *Items Included:* Manual. *Customer Support:* Telephone & remote.
disk $1595.00-$15,000.00.
Package Consists of 5 Separate Systems: Automated Loan Closings, Commitment & Policy Preparation, Index of All Items Searched by Name, Automated Land Tract Index, Order Control & Tracking, & Mapping.
DTC Software.

TK! Solver. Software Arts. *Compatible Hardware:* HP Series 200 HP-UX Models 217, 220, 236, the Integral PC.
Single-user. 3.5" disk $499.00 (Order no.: 45515G).
Linus tape $624.00.
Multi-user. 3.5" disk $999.00 (Order no.: 45515H).
Linus tape $1124.00.
Equation Solving Software Package Allowing Users to Solve Complex Mathematical Models That Cannot Be Easily Done With Programming Languages, Spreadsheets, or Calculators. Users Define the Model with Equations Written in the Usual Form. All the Tools Needed for Problem-Solving Are Built into the Program, Including the Mathematical Functions, Facilities for Converting Units of Measurement, & the Ability to Produce Graphics & Tables. Four Additional Templates Are Available: Building Design & Construction, Financial Management, Introductory Science, & Mechanical Engineering.
Hewlett-Packard Co.

TK Solver for Motif. *Compatible Hardware:* IBM RISC System/6000, DECstation 3000 & 5000 Series, HP/Apollo 300 & 400 Series, & Sun SPARCstations & compatibles.
$995.00 & up.
Math Equation Solver & Graphing Program. Takes Advantage of the MOTIF Interface to Work in a Multiple Window Environment While Taking Advantage of Multitasking. User Can Run Two or More Models Simultaneously & Compare Their Results Side by Side. Product Also Allows User to Transfer Information Between Windows in a Single Application or Between Different Models.
Universal Technical Systems, Inc. (UTS).

TK Solver for Windows. Aug. 1994. *Compatible Hardware:* IBM PC & compatibles. *Operating System(s) Required:* Windows 3.1. *Items Included:* Disks & manuals. *Customer Support:* Free technical support - 815-963-2220, Fax support, CompuServe Forum.
contact publisher for price.
Interactive Program That Solves Equations Without Programming. Users Can Use Any of the Unknowns in an Equation Without Reformatting the Problem. Includes over 100 Built-In Functions & 200 Powerful Models. Features Conversions of Units of Measurement & Production of Tables & Graphs Using Values Produced by the List Solver. Includes Editing Commands to Assist in Entering & Modifying Data. Features Direct Data Exchange with WKS/WK1, ASCII & DIF Files.
Universal Technical Systems, Inc. (UTS).

TKR 5. *Version:* 2.20. *Operating System(s) Required:* PC-DOS, MS-DOS. *Language(s):* C. *Memory Required:* 640k. *Customer Support:* $375.00 single user - $625.00 network version annual support.
priced from $895.00 single user; $1645.00 network version.
Time & Billing System Designed for Small to

Large Sized Accounting, Engineering, Legal Practices. Keeps Track of Time & Expenses, Bills Clients & Tracks Receivables. Comprehensive Management Reporting Is Included. Add-On Modules Include Job Scheduling, CPE Tracking, Pop-Up Time & Expense Entry, SQL Report Writer & a Markeing System.
E. F. Haskell & Assocs.

TLC/96 for Windows: Total Life Care Planning. *Version:* 2.0. Robert L. Lessne. Jan. 1996. *Items Included:* Manual. *Customer Support:* Free customer support.
Windows (64k). disk $1495.00. *Networks supported:* Can be modified.
A Complete Life Care Planning Program Which Has an Extensive Data-Base & Is User Friendly. The Easy to Read Report Is Used in Litigation & Case Management & Supports Recommendations from Physicians for Products, Services & Medications.
ADA Compliance Specialists.

TLC Total Library Computerization. *Version:* 2.0. Dec. 1993. *Items Included:* Hardcopy spiral-bound manual & online manual. Customized minimenus. *Customer Support:* Free technical support via telephone, fax or E-Mail.
DOS. IBM PC & compatibles (640k). $2850.00 Basic System (6 modules); or per module $750.00 (first), $700.00 (each add'l.), $500.00 each for companion modules. *Optimal configuration:* PS/2 386 or higher, 1Mb RAM or more, modem. *Networks supported:* Any Net-Bios compatible network.
Integrated Software for Smaller Library Management & Smaller Library Budgets. Its Menu-Driven Modules for Cataloging, Circulation, Interlibrary Loan, Serials Control, Acquisitions, Work Product Identification, Full Text Documents Retrieval, Branch Office Holdings, & Work Timer (Client Billing for Library Research) May Also Be Purchased Separately.
On Point Pr.

TLDIS: Tape-Based Labelling Disassembler. *Compatible Hardware:* TRS-80.
contact publisher for price.
Instant Software, Inc.

TLG Engine. *Version:* 2.4. Jun. 1987. *Items Included:* User's manual, text editing program. *Customer Support:* Telephone support, defective disks replaced free.
Macintosh (512k). 3.5" disk $99.95. *Addl. software required:* MacGreek or LaserGreek or Macgreek, Hebrew & Phonetics.
Use Requires Thesaurus Linguae Graecae CD ROM or Tapes. Contains 42 Million Words of Greek Literature Before 600 A.D.: All the Major Classics, Church Fathers, Philo, Josephus... Will Convert Any Part of This Data Base into SuperGreek ASCII Code Conveniently Formatted for Reading. Also Converts Mainframe Tape Texts into SuperGreek ASCII Format, the Text Editing Software Edit. Includes SuperGreek 12 Point Font with Automatic Non-Deleting Backspacing Accents, Breathing Marks, Iota Subscripts, Plus TLG, Leiden, Nestle-Aland Plus UBS Text Critical Sigla. The Browser Portion of the TLG Engine Permits You to Browse Through the TLG Files Seeing the Texts in Fully Accented SuperGreek & Designate Which Portions of Which Works You Wish to Export in SuperGreek Format.
Linguist's Software, Inc.

TLN: The Total Logistics Network. Dec. 1992. *Items Included:* Quick reference guide, on-line documentation. *Customer Support:* 24 hrs/7 day week, training & maintenance available.
Xenix. RS 6000, IBM PS/2 model 80/95, HP 9000, 486 based PCs (2Mb). Contact publisher for price. *Optimal configuration:* Modem to access remotely.
UNIX. RS 6000, IBM PS/2, model 80/95, HP 9000, 486 based PCs (2Mb). Contact publisher for price. *Optimal configuration:* Model to access remotely.
AIX. RS 6000 (4Mb). Contact publisher for price. *Optimal configuration:* Modem to access remotely.
Comprehensive Tracking of Inventory from Manufacturer Through Freight Carriers, Warehouses, Distributors & End Destination. Accessible from Any Phone World-Wide via Modem. Designed to Read Use Inventory & Handling Costs While Increasing Customer Service.
LDS, Inc.

TLS Tutor for Lotus 1-2-3 Release 2. Oct. 1985. *Compatible Hardware:* IBM PC & compatibles. *Memory Required:* 128k.
$49.95.
Disk-Based Tutorial Available in Several Languages.
Damon International Corp.

TM/1 Perspectives. *Version:* 2.0. Nov. 1994. *Items Included:* Disks, manual, tutorial. *Customer Support:* Free phone, training available.
$795.00 & up.
Provides Shared Consistent Information & the Analytical Power of a Relational Spreadsheet to Workgroups Connected by LANs.
Sinper Corp.

TM/1. *Version:* 4.0. *Compatible Hardware:* IBM PC & compatibles. *Operating System(s) Required:* MS-DOS, PC-DOS. *Memory Required:* 370k. *Items Included:* Disks, user manual, tutorial, demo. *Customer Support:* Free.
disk $795.00.
Enables End User to Create Spreadsheet Based Systems for Multi-Dimensional Analysis Budgeting, Planning & Reporting Common to Financial Information Systems & Decision Support Systems.
Sinper Corp.

TMA-Workstation: Heat Exchanger Workstation. Robert P. Nealon. Jan. 1992. *Customer Support:* 30 day money-back guarantee.
DOS 3.0 (640k), 10Mb hard disk space required. disk $10,500.00 (Order no.: S049).
Get TMA-THERM, TMA-MECH, & TMA-AIRCOOLER for Less Than You Can Purchase the Programs Individually. Each Program Can Stand Alone or Be Used in Conjunction with Any or All of the Others. AIR-COOLER & THERM Can Both Access the Same Rigorous VLE Module & All Three Share the Databank Information As Well As Use the Databanks Unique to Proprietary. With All Three You Can Make Thermal Designs for Air-Cooled Heat Exchangers & Thermal & Mechanical Designs for Shell-and-Tube Heat Exchangers. All Programs Also Rate Existing Exchangers.
Gulf Publishing Co.

tMAP: Tutorial Map Analysis Package. *Version:* 4.0. Spatial Information System Inc. Staff. 1993. *Items Included:* Companion text Beyond Mapping (Berry 1993).
MS-DOS 3.1 or higher. IBM & compatibles (2Mb). disk $80.00. *Nonstandard peripherals required:* EGA/VGA Graphics, math coprocessor. *Optimal configuration:* 1 floppy, hard drive with 6Mb of free space.
Tutorial Version of PMAP Designed to Provide Introductory Concepts to GIS/Mapping & Spatial Analysis. Great Informational Tool. Fun & Easy to Learn.
Farmer's Software Assn.

TModel2: Transportation Modeling System. *Version:* 2.4. May 1992. *Compatible Hardware:* IBM PC, PC XT, PC AT, PS/2 & compatibles. *Operating System(s) Required:* PC-DOS/MS-DOS, or Windows. *Language(s):* Compiled BASIC. *Memory Required:* 512k. *General Requirements:* 2 disk drives, color graphics (CGA, EGA, VGA), mouse. Hard disk recommended. *Items Included:* NCAP (intersection capacity analysis package). *Customer Support:* Toll free support 1-800-T2MODLR EST or 1-800-T2MODEL PST.
Contact publisher for price.
Transportation Modeling Program Designed to Be Used by the Transportation Engineer & Planner. Program Is Menu-Driven & Contains On-Screen Directions. The Input Can Be Changed, Edited, or Corrected with Graphics. Planning Options Can Be Examined & Updated. Allows 1,000 Zones, 10,000 Link System with up to 2,500 Nodes to Be Run. Includes Matrix Manipulation & Plotting Routines. Other Features Include Calibration Scattergrams & Regression Analysis, Automatic External Zone Calibration, Integral Land Use & Trip Table Graphics, Fratering of Turn Movements, & More.
TModel Corp.

TMON Professional. *Version:* 3.0. *Compatible Hardware:* Apple Macintosh. *Memory Required:* 512k. *Customer Support:* Warranty for replacement of defective product, technical support & upgrade information for registered users.
3.5" disk $249.95.
A Multi-Window Object Level, Symbolic Debugger. The Monitor Is Invisible to the User Unless It Is Asked for by the Programmer. Its Sole Purpose Is to Reduce Development Time by Helping the User Track Down Implementation Flaws in a Program.
ICOM Simulations, Inc.

To Surf & Detect: Crime & Punishment on the Inte•net. Dennis Bolen. Apr. 1996. *Items Included:* A 64-page companion booklet that reviews web sites & includes instructions on how to use the software. *Customer Support:* Access to the Go!Guides web site & FAQ, customer support by email at help goguides.com.
Macintosh System 7.0 or higher. Macintosh (4Mb). 3.5" disk $12.99 (ISBN 1-57712-004-3). *Nonstandard peripherals required:* Modem 14.4 or faster. *Addl. software required:* Internet account & connection. *Optimal configuration:* Macintosh System 7.0 or higher, at least 4Mb of RAM, at least 2Mb of free disk space, color monitor, 14.4 or 28.8 modem, Internet account.
Windows 3.1 or Windows 95. IBM or compatible (4Mb). disk $12.99. *Nonstandard peripherals required:* 14.4 or 28.8 modem. *Addl. software required:* Internet account. *Optimal configuration:* IBM-compatible running Windows 3.1 or Windows 95, at least 2Mb free space on hard drive, at least 4Mb RAM, color monitor, 14.4 or 28.8 modem, Internet account.
Find the Crime Without Doing the Time. To Surf & Detect Takes the User to the Best Crime, Espionage, & Unsolved Mystery Sites on the Internet.
Motion Works Publishing.

Tolculator. *Version:* 4.0. *Compatible Hardware:* Apple Macintosh (All); IBM PC, PC XT, PC AT. *Memory Required:* 512k. *General Requirements:* Microsoft Excel 3.0. *Items Included:* 65 page manual. *Customer Support:* Hot line.
Macintosh or IBM (512k). $150.00 (ISBN 1-883467-06-3).
Macintosh Plus, SE, II, DOS/Windows. $150.00. $30.00 practice workbook; computer aided tolerance analysis (CATA) (ISBN 1-883467-

TITLE INDEX

02-0).
Geometric Tolerance & Mathematical & Inspection Analysis per ANSI for Engineering, Manufacturing & Inspection/Quality.
International Geometric Tolerancing Institute, Inc.

Tolculator: GD & T Design - Insp. Software.
Version: 4.0. Sam Levy. Jan. 1991. *Items Included:* Manual in 6x9, 3 ring binder, membership card. *Customer Support:* 90 day unlimited warranty. Our site training $25.00/hr. Hot line (free) to caller; none returned. Computer Aided Tolerance Analysis (CATA) Manual $34.00.
PS/2, MS-DOS with Windows. IBM & compatibles (640k). disk $150.00 (ISBN 1-883467-06-3, Order no.: IGTI 5-5 1/4 OR 3 1/2). *Addl. software required:* Microsoft Excel 3.0 or higher. *Optimal configuration:* Color monitor, printer, 2Mb RAM (extended on IBM).
Macintosh OS. Apple Macintosh (1Mb). 3.5" disk $150.00 (Order no.: IGTI 5-3 1/2 800K). *Addl. software required:* Microsoft Excel 3.0 or higher. *Optimal configuration:* Color monitor, 2Mb RAM, printer. *Networks supported:* Appletalk.
Designed to Automate Geometric Tolerance & Mathematical Analysis, (Such As Analytic Geometry, Trigonometry, etc.) per ANSI & ISO Standards for Design, Inspection & Quality Personnel. Used to Design Interchangeable Parts & Gages, Perform Probability & Tolerance Circuit Studies, Make Predictions on Hardware Tolerances & Do All Manner of Conversions, Including Metric. Also Automates Sampling, Histograms & Limits & Fits. Program Will Analyze Circularity (Roundness); Find the Least Squares Center; Analyze Flatness, Parallelism, Straightness of Elements or Axes; Find the Center of a Pattern; Do Shop Math, Sampling Studies, Figure Bonus Tolerances, & Much More. Program Is Not Copy Protected.

Tomahawk. *Compatible Hardware:* Apple II, IIgs; Atari; Commodore 64/128; IBM PC & compatibles. *Memory Required:* Apple II 64k, Apple IIgs 768k, Atari 64k, Commodore 64k, IBM 256k. *General Requirements:* Joystick Optional.
Apple II. disk $29.95 (ISBN 0-88717-199-0, Order no.: 15903-43499).
Apple IIgs. 3.5" disk $39.95 (ISBN 0-88717-228-8, Order no.: 15900-43499).
Atari. disk $29.95 (ISBN 0-88717-198-2, Order no.: 15900-43499).
Commodore. disk $29.95 (ISBN 0-88717-198-2, Order no.: 15906-43499).
IBM. $39.95 (ISBN 0-88717-206-7, Order no.: 15904-43499).
Game Tests User's Instincts, Reflexes, & Nerves While Challenging with Flight & Battle Stations. Features Include 3-D, Real-Time Graphics & Display; Offensive & Defensive Flight Maneuvers; Ground Attack & Air-to-Air Interception, Day & Night Vision Systems; Instrument-Only Flying; & Complete Weapons System.
IntelliCreations, Inc.

Tone Routine Generator. *Customer Support:* 800-929-8117 (customer service).
MS-DOS. Apple II. disk $29.99 (ISBN 0-87007-400-8).
AppleSoft Routine for Generating a Variety of Tones.
SourceView Software International.

Tony LaRussa's Baseball II: Jewel Case.
Stormfront Studios. Nov. 1995. *Customer Support:* 30 day limited warranty.
DOS 5.0 or higher. 386 CD-ROM with hard drive (2Mb). CD-ROM disk $9.95 (ISBN 0-917059-47-6, Order no.: 062681). *Optimal configuration:* 386, hard drive, CD-ROM, 256 color VGA.
Baseball Sports Strategy Game.
Strategic Simulations, Inc.

Tool Inventory. Version: 3.3. (Integrated Manufacturing & Financial System Ser.). *Compatible Hardware:* Micro/VAX, UNIBUS/VAX; IBM PC. *Operating System(s) Required:* MS-DOS, Novell, Micro/VAX, VAX/VMS, UNIX. *Language(s):* DIBOL.
MS-DOS. single-user $1000.00.
DEC PDP-11/VAX. multi-user $2500.00.
Manufacturing Tools Are Reserved & Then Tracked Through Requisitioning, Receiving, Issuing, Returning, & Disposition. The System Displays Supply, Usage, & Activity of Tools.
Primetrack.

Toolbelt. *Compatible Hardware:* TRS-80 Model 4. *Operating System(s) Required:* TRSDOS 6.X. contact publisher for price.
Powersoft, Inc.

Toolkit Linux 2.0. *Customer Support:* All of our products are unconditionally guaranteed.
Unix. CD-ROM disk $39.95 (Order no.: TOOLKIT). *Nonstandard peripherals required:* CD-ROM drive.
Slackware Distribution of Linux Plus Complete Archive. 2-CDs.
Walnut Creek CDRom.

Tools for Writers. *Compatible Hardware:* Apple Macintosh.
3.5" disk $17.00.
Allows Users to Perform Checks & Diagnostic Tests on Their Own Writing.
Kinko's.

Tools of the Trade. *Compatible Hardware:* IBM PC & compatibles. *Operating System(s) Required:* MS-DOS. *Memory Required:* 256k. contact publisher for price.
Set of Productivity Tools for Contractors. Applications Include Bid Time, Bid Notification, Submittal Control, Punch Lists, Bonding Reports, Tool Locator & Job Billings.
Concord Management Systems, Inc.

Toolworks Backup Pro. *Customer Support:* Technical support is available at 818-885-1078, 9AM-5PM PST.
IBM & compatibles. 3.5" or 5.25" disk $59.95. *Optimal configuration:* IBM PC/XT/AT; CGA, EGA, VGA; hard disk; keyboard or mouse.
Don't Get Caught Without a Back-Up! Takes Just Four Minutes for 10 Megabytes. Up to 90% Compression to Save Costly Floppies. Menus & Dialogs Are Clean, Crisp & Easy.
Software Toolworks.

Toolworks C Compiler. *Items Included:* Bound manual. *Customer Support:* Free hotline - no time limit; 30 day limited warranty; updates are $5/disk plus S&H.
MS-DOS. IBM & compatibles (256k). disk $49.95.
C MATHPAK $29.95.
Includes Virtually a Complete Subset of the C Programming Language. It Contains Structures, Pointers & Arrays, All Storage Classes, & Data Initialization. It Supports Char & 16-Bit Int & Unsigned Data Types; True Floats & Long Data Types Are Available with the Optional C MATHPAK. Compiles All C Operators & Control Statements. It Features a Complete Standard C Library, with the Sources for the Run-Time & Library Functions. The Library Functions Include Random/Sequential File I/O, Dynamic Storage Allocation, Character/String Manipulation, & Low-Level MS-DOS & Hardware Access. Generates LINK-Compatible .OBJ Files Directly & Command Line I/O Redirection.
Dynacomp, Inc.

TOOLWORKS REFERENCE LIBRARY

Toolworks C Compiler. 1992. *Items Included:* Detailed manuals included with all Dynacomp products. *Customer Support:* Free telephone support to original customer - no time limit; 30 day limited warranty.
MS-DOS 3.2 or higher. IBM PC & compatibles (512k). $49.95 (Add $5.00 for 3 1/2" format; 5 1/4" format standard).
Includes Virtually a Complete Subset of the C Programming Language. It Contains Structures, Pointers & Arrays, All Storage Classes, & Data Initialization. It Supports Char & 16-Bit Int & Unsigned Data Types; True Floats & Long Data Types Are Available with the Optional C MATHPAK. Compiles All C Operators & Control Statements. It Features a Complete Standard C Library, with the Sources for the Run-Time & Library Functions.
Dynacomp, Inc.

Toolworks Desk Reference.
DOS 3.1 or higher. IBM PC or 100% compatibles (640k). disk $69.95. *Optimal configuration:* IBM PC or 100% compatibles, 640k memory; EMS memory optional; DOS 3.1 or higher; hard drive; mouse (optional).
Windows. disk $79.95.
A Collection of the Most Frequently Sought Information at the New York Public Library. Twenty-Six Subjects; Everything from Who Won the Oscar for Best Actress in 1933 (Katharine Hepburn) to How Many Calories Are Burned in an Hour of Typing (110), It's the Ultimate, Instant Reference for Ideas, Advice, Details & Discoveries. Thousands of Entries Will Answer the Toughest Questions in the Least Amount of Time.
Software Toolworks.

Toolworks LengthWise.
IBM. disk $39.95.
Prints Your Spreadsheet or Other Data (No Matter How Wide or How Many Columns) Quickly & Easily, on One Continuous Piece of Paper. Guaranteed to Work with Any Dot Matrix & Most Laser Printers.
Software Toolworks.

Toolworks Lisp/80. *Items Included:* Bound manual. *Customer Support:* Free hotline - no time limit; 30 day limited warranty; updates are $5/disk plus S&H.
MS-DOS. IBM & compatibles (256k). disk $39.95.
Offers over 75 Built-In Functions Including Large Machine Features Like Trace, File I/O, & String Operations. It Comes with a Simple Editor, File Librarian, & Formatted Expression Print Routine, All Written in LISP, & a 36-Page Manual. Also Included Are Two Artificial Intelligence Demonstration Programs: A Guessing Game Which Learns As It Plays, & a Simple Version of the Famous ELIZA Psychiatrist Program.
Dynacomp, Inc.

Toolworks Office Manager.
IBM. disk $49.95.
Write a Business Letter, Spell-Check It, Merge It With Your Customer List. Even Add Your Financial Forecast...in about 10 Minutes! Office Manager Is a Word Processor, Spell Checker, Spreadsheet, & Database Filer in One Integrated Package. With No Messy DOS Commands.
Software Toolworks.

Toolworks Reference Library.
IBM CD-ROM. IBM PC or 100% compatibles (640k). CD-ROM disk $99.95. *Optimal configuration:* IBM PC or 100% compatibles, 640k memory; EMS memory optional; DOS 3.1 or higher; hard drive recommended; CD-ROM drive & driver; Microsoft CD-ROM Extensions (MSCDEX) Version 2.1 or higher; mouse (Optional).

Check Out Information from the New York Public Library - Without Leaving Your Home or Office! A Compilation of the Most Frequently Sought after Facts & Figures from That World Famous Library Can Be at Your Fingertips Today. One of the Fastest Multiple Reference Sources Available, You Can Quickly Refer to Webster's New World Dictionary & Thesaurus, The Dictionary of 20th Century History, Webster's New World Dictionary of Quotable Definitions, The National Directory of Addresses & Telephone Numbers, The Guinness Book of World Records, & J.K. Lasser's Legal & Corporation Forms for the Smaller Business. Uses Only 20K of Memory.
Software Toolworks.

ToothPics. *Version:* 2.5. *Compatible Hardware:* Apple Macintosh Plus, Quadra 950. *General Requirements:* Hard disk, ImageWriter II for color or LaserWriter. *Items Included:* Manual, software, 30-day money-back warranty. *Customer Support:* On-site training, $1295. As needed phone support available at $60 per hour (less than 5 minutes free) or by Annual Support Agreement, $695. Updates $395 or by Annual Update Agreement, $600. Combined Annual Update & Support Agreement, $995.
$3995.00 ToothPics Professional, single workstation; $1995.00 ToothPics Basic.
$750.00 each additional networked workstation.
Complete Dental Patient Management System with On-Screen Charting for Easy Entry of Existing Conditions, Treatment Plans, & Procedures Performed. Comprehensive Walkout Statement Includes a Graphic Odontogram, Printed in Color, to Reinforce Patient In-Office Education & Enhance Treatment Plan Retention & Acceptance. Custom Reports Available. Network Ready.
Class One, Inc.

Top 1000. *Compatible Hardware:* IBM PC & compatibles. *Operating System(s) Required:* PC-DOS 2.1 or higher. *Memory Required:* 512k.
standard edition $199.00.
elite edition $299.00.
Provides All the Data on 1,000 U.S. Corporations from the Annual Business Week Issue. A Program Included on the Disk Gives 25 Ways to Compare Some or All of the Companies' Data, Including Price/Earnings Ratios, Changes in Return-on-Equity, & Sales. Elite Edition Can Print a Mailing List to All 1,000 Companies' CEOs & CFOs. Menu Option Allows User to Export Data from Either Program to 1-2-3 or ASCII Files.
Business Week.

Top Two Hundred Drugs HyperCard Stack. *Version:* 8th Edition. Aug. 1992. *Items Included:* Manual. *Customer Support:* Telephone support free.
Apple Macintosh. Macintosh (1Mb). 3.5" disk $29.95 (ISBN 1-880579-05-7). *Addl. software required:* HyperCard Version 2.0 & higher.
Optimal configuration: Hard disk, 2Mb RAM.
The Top 200 HyperCard Stack Contains All the Information Included on Our Top 200 Study Cards in an Exciting New Format. At the Touch of a Button, Information on the Top 200 Prescription Drugs Appears & Disappears & Allows You to Quiz Yourself Efficiently. You Have the Option of Sorting the Cards by Different Fields. An Index Card Allows You to Quickly Go to the Card of Your Choice. There Is Also a Special "Custom Notes" Field That Gives You the Ability to Customize Each Card.
Sigler & Flanders, Inc.

TOPAZ. *Version:* 4.5. Apr. 1994. *Compatible Hardware:* IBM PC & compatibles. *Operating System(s) Required:* PC-DOS/MS-DOS. *Memory Required:* 256k. *General Requirements:* Borland Pascal 7.0 or Turbo Pascal Compiler 7.0 or 6.0. *Customer Support:* Tech. Support (510) 845-2110; BBS (415) 697-1624; CompuServe.
disk $199.00. *Networks supported:* Novell Netware, 3-COM, LANTASTIC, Invisible-Net, most (if not all) MS-Net compatible networks.
Allows Turbo Pascal Programmers to Write DOS or Windows Applications with dBASE-Like Syntax in Turbo Pascal. The Current Release Maintains Its Own Index Structure. Reads, Creates & Updates dBASE Data Files. Also Provides Additional Features That Have dBASE-Like Syntax but Go Beyond What dBASE III Itself Provides.
Software Science, Inc.

Topaz for C/C Plus Plus. *Version:* 4.5. May 1994. *Items Included:* Disks & manual. *Customer Support:* Free telephone tech support (510) 845-2110, BBS, CompuServe.
PC-DOS/MS-DOS or Windows. IBM PC & compatibles (640k). disk $299.00. *Addl. software required:* Borland (or Turbo) C/C Plus Plus compiler 3.0 or higher, Microsoft C/C Plus 7.0 or Visual C Plus Plus 1.0 or higher. *Networks supported:* Novell NetWare, 3-Com, LANTASTIC, Invisible-Net, other MS-Net compatible networks.
Comprehensive Toolkit for C & C Plus Plus to Create DOS & Windows Applications. Creates & Updates dBASE Data, Memo, & Index Files. Database, User-Interface, & Utility Features That Have dBASE-Like Syntax but Go Beyond What dBASE Provides.
Software Science, Inc.

TopDown. *Version:* 3.0. *Compatible Hardware:* Apple Macintosh. *General Requirements:* Hard disk recommended. *Items Included:* 800k disk, manual. *Customer Support:* Free technical support to registered owners.
3.5" disk $345.00.
A Drawing Tool for Creating Charts & Diagrams Quickly & Easily. Draw & Update Flowcharts, Organization Charts & Procedures. Connecting Lines Automatically Re-Route. Use the Many Symbols Included or Create Your Own. Multiple Drawing Levels, Text Importing & Notecards Make It Powerful, Yet Easy-to-Use.
Kaetron Software Corp.

TopHat. *Customer Support:* 800-929-8117 (customer service).
MS-DOS. IBM/PS2. disk $99.99 (ISBN 0-87007-396-6).
A Menuing System for MS-DOS Computers. Allows the Setup of 4 Pages of Single Keystroke Menus with up to 30 Menu Items per Page. Installing New Applications is Done Through a Simple to Use Menuing System. Includes an Easy to Use Batch File Maker, & A "Contacts" Database for Names & Addresses. Color is Supported Through Five Levels.
SourceView Software International.

TOPIC. *Version:* 3.1. *Compatible Hardware:* DEC, IBM, Macintosh, UNIX. *Operating System(s) Required:* DOS, UNIX, VMS, OS/2,. *Memory Required:* 3000k. *Customer Support:* Full support, training, consulting & maintenance.
$9290.00 per single user. *Networks supported:* Novell, 3COM, Banyan.
$795.00, network user.
$15,000.00 to 150,000.00 for VAX/VMS solution.
Text Database-Management System for Networked Computing Environments. Features Client/Server Architecture & Optional Real-Time System. Supports Concept Retrieval, Similarity Search, & Hypertex Links to Images, Annotation & Other Documentation. Also Features Ability to Index Existing DOS Files Without Importing or Converting; Import & Append ASCII, Frame, Interleaf & Other Text File Formats. Optional SQL-Gateway, SQL-Bridge Links to Popular RDBMS' Oracle, Ingres, Sybase, Informix.
Verity, Inc.

Topics. *Version:* 6.1. Kent Ochel & Bert Brown. Oct. 1989. *Items Included:* Tutorial disk; 3-ring binder with manual. *Customer Support:* Unlimited free technical support at (512) 251-75441.
Any DOS or Windows. IBM PC; XT; AT & compatibles (512k). disk $49.95.
Any Macintosh. 3.5" disk $49.95.
Topical Cross Reference of the Bible That Works with LIBRARIAN. Over 200 of the Most Frequently Discussed Subjects in Scripture Are Included. The Cross References Deal Not Only with the Word Content but Also with the Concept of the Subject.
Bible Research Systems.

Topics in Research Methods: Main Effects & Interactions. Russell H. Fazio & Martin H. Backler. 1984. *Compatible Hardware:* Apple II+, IIe, IIc; IBM PC, PCjr, PC XT. *Operating System(s) Required:* Apple DOS 3.3, PC-DOS 2.10-3.10. *Language(s):* Applesoft BASIC (source code included). *Memory Required:* Apple 48k, IBM 128k. *General Requirements:* Applesoft in ROM.
disk $60.00 ea., incl. instructor & student notes & backup.
Apple. (Order no.: PSY458A).
IBM. (Order no.: PSY458I).
add'l set of notes $3.00.
Gives Students Practice in Discerning Whether Two or More Independent Variables in a Given Experiment Are Exerting Main &/or Interactive Effects on the Dependent Variable. The Program Is Divided into Five Parts. PART 1 Introduces Students to Factorial Designs & Factorial Design Notation. PART 2 Concentrates on 2X2 Designs & Presents the Students with Two Strategies for Judging What Effects Are Apparent. PART 3 Describes a Specific Experiment's 2X2 Design & Then Presents a Series of Data Displays. After Each Display the Student Is Asked Whether There Exists a Main Effect of One Variable, a Main Effect of the Other, &/or Interaction of the Two. PARTS 4 & 5 Describe 2X2X2 Designs & the Two-Way & Three-Way Interactions That Are Tested in This Type of Design.
CONDUIT.

Topological Network Flow & Management Science Toolboxes: Business Process Re-Engineering. Jan. 1996. *Items Included:* Sample input & output files & users manuals on disk. *Customer Support:* Assistance in formulating inputs & understanding outputs, price free or variable.
MS-DOS. IBM PC (8Mb). disk $999.00 (Order no.: 203). *Nonstandard peripherals required:* Math coprocessor. *Addl. software required:* FORTRAN Compiler & Linker. *Optimal configuration:* Source code can be compiled & linked for execution on any machine with a FORTRAN compiler & linker.
A Business Process(BP) Re-Engineering Model - a Monte Carlo Simulation Model That Produces a Cumulative Total BP Timeline Distribution from the Component Tasks of the BP. In Particular, Each BP Task Is Described by a Statistical Model, in Which a Random Number Draw Is Made to Obtain a Specific Realization of the Time It Takes to Perform a BP Task. A Single Instance of the Total BP Timeline Is Obtained by Adding up the Time It Takes to Perform Each BP Task. A Statistical BP Timeline Distribution Is Obtained by Running the Model a Large Number of Times, e.g., 1000 Times, for Each BP.
Cane Systems.

TITLE INDEX

Topological Network Flow & Management Science Toolboxes: Minimum Cost Network Flow. Jan. 1996. *Items Included:* Sample input & output files & users manuals on disk. *Customer Support:* Assistance in formulating inputs & understanding outputs, price free or variable.
MS-DOS. IBM PC (8Mb). disk $1999.00 (Order no.: 202). *Nonstandard peripherals required:* Math coprocessor. *Addl. software required:* FORTRAN Compiler & Linker. *Optimal configuration:* Source code can be compiled & linked for execution on any machine with a FORTRAN compiler & linker.
Using Fast Polynomial Time Algorithms, This Tool Seeks a Least-Cost Flow in a Directed Network from a Supply Node to a Demand Node, Possibly Through Transhipment Nodes. The Following Outputs Are Generated for Each Feasible Flow: Total Network Flow Cost & for Each Network Link: Link Unit Flow Cost & Total Link Cost. If the Model Cannot Generate a Feasible Solution, e.g., Demand Exceeds Capacity, This Situation Is Noted in the Output File & on the Screen.
Cane Systems.

Topological Network Flow & Management Science Toolboxes: Maximum Network Flow. Jan. 1996. *Items Included:* Sample input & output files & users manuals on disk. *Customer Support:* Assistance in formulating inputs & understanding outputs, price free or variable.
MS-DOS. IBM PC (8Mb). disk $999.00 (Order no.: 201). *Nonstandard peripherals required:* Math coprocessor. *Addl. software required:* FORTRAN Compiler & Linker. *Optimal configuration:* Source code can be compiled & linked for execution on any machine with a FORTRAN compiler & linker.
Using Fast Polynomial Time Algorithms, This Tool Determines the Maximum Amount of Flow Possible from Each Transmission Node to Each Receiving Node Given the Capacity of the Network Links. Under User Control, Four Types of Maximum Flow Analysis Can Be Performed: All Sources to All Sinks, One Source to All Sinks, All Sources to One Sink, & One Source to One Sink. This Tool Generates Two Sets of Output: 1. The Maximum Flow on Each Link, the Number of Links That Are Saturated; 2. For Each Path the Links, That Have to Be Traversed on the Path, the Amount of Flow on the Link, & the Capacity of the Link.
Cane Systems.

TOPS. *Version:* 6.0. 1982. *Items Included:* Getting started manual, primer, system guide, security booklet & installation guide. *Customer Support:* Through Dealer.
MS-DOS. IBM & compatibles (640K). $3495.00 - $4995.00. *Nonstandard peripherals required:* Probe Box/Dallas Key.
Menu-Driven, Take-Off, Pricing & Bidding System Designed Specifically for Plumbing & Mechanical Contractors. Its Special Features Include Program Security, Probe or Digitizer, High Speed Price Extension & Advanced Assemblies Capability. The Program Also Handles Base Bid & Up to 74 Alternates Along with Subcontract & Quote Analysis.
Software Shop Systems, Inc.

TOPS FlashBox.
Macintosh. disk $189.00.
A Plug-In Device That Upgrades the Performance of AppleTalk Networks. Designed for Configurations in Which All Computers Communicate at FlashTalk Data Rates Using TOPS FlashBoxes (Macintosh) or TOPS FlashCard (PC).
Sitka Corp.

TOPS FlashCard.
IBM PC & compatibles; PS/2. disk $329.00. *Nonstandard peripherals required:* TOPS Teleconnector or compatible network connector.
A Network Interface Card That Allows PC's to Communicate with Other PC's & Macintosh Computers Using Twisted-Pair Cabling.
Sitka Corp.

TOPS for Sun Workstations. *Version:* 2.2.
Sun OS 4.x. Sun-4, SPARC, Sun 386i & Sun-3 workstations. $895.00 retail for 1-4 users; $1595.00 for 1-16 users. *Nonstandard peripherals required:* Ethernet Cabling or Kinetics FastPath.
File Server Software That Provides a Cost-Effective Way to Network PC's & Macintoshes to Sun Workstations.
Sitka Corp.

TOPS InBox Plus. *Version:* 3.0.
IBM PC & compatibles, Macintosh. disk $1995.00. *Nonstandard peripherals required:* LocalTalk or Ethernet connections.
Full-Featured Electronic Mail System Enabling Macintosh & DOS Users to Share Information & Communicate Across a Network & to Other Mail Systems When Used with Optional Third Party Gateways.
Sitka Corp.

TOPS NetPrint. *Compatible Hardware:* IBM PC & compatibles.
disk $189.00.
Spooler & Remote Printing Software That Enables DOS Users to Print Directly to an Apple LaserWriter.
Sitka Corp.

TOPS: Network Bundle for Macintosh. *Version:* 3.0. *Compatible Hardware:* Apple Macintosh Plus, SE, II. *Memory Required:* 370k.
3.5" disk $299.00.
Provides Software for One Macintosh Computer to Share Files, Print Spool Documents, & Send Electronic Mail on a TPOS Network.
Sitka Corp.

TOPS Repeater.
disk $189.00. *Nonstandard peripherals required:* Two TOPS TeleConnectors or compatible DB-9 network connectors. *Networks supported:* AppleTalk.
A Hardware Product That Amplifies the Electrical Signals in an AppleTalk or Compatible Network. Enables User to Extend the Maximum Length of Their Networks & to Change the Bus Configuration of These by Adding Branches or Daisy Chains.
Sitka Corp.

TopVest. *Version:* 1.32. Apr. 1992. *Items Included:* 600 page manual, tutorial. *Customer Support:* Price includes first year maintenance (updates & telephone support). After first year, $500/yr. individual & class training available.
DOS 3.3 or higher. IBM PC & compatibles with hard disk. disk $3500.00. *Optimal configuration:* 2Mb RAM, 80386, math co-processor, mouse, modem, printer.
Provides Technical & Fundamental Analysis of Stocks & Other Securities. Handles over 10,000 Securities per Data Directory with over 100 Built in Technical Indicators Including Moving Averages, RSI, Stochastics, MACD, Candlesticks, Point & Figure, Equivolume, Fourier & Adaptive Filtering. User Equations & User Studies Allow Creation of Indicators & Trading Systems Which Can Be Back Tested & Optimized. Screen on Technical & Fundamental Criteria. Powerful Macros Allow Complete Automation, Including Loops, Conditional Branching, Variables & Keyboard Entry.
Savant Software, Inc.

TOTAL BASEBALL

Tornado. Aug. 1993.
MS-DOS. IBM 16Mhz 80386SX & compatibles (1Mb). disk $79.95.

Tornado. *Version:* 1.8. *Compatible Hardware:* IBM PC, XT, AT, PS/2, Compaq, Laptops & compatibles; Tandy 1000, 2000, 3000. *Operating System(s) Required:* PC-DOS/MS-DOS 2.0 or higher. *Memory Required:* 60k. *Items Included:* Disk (5-1/4" or 3-1/2") & manual. *Customer Support:* (201) 342-6518.
$99.95.
RAM-Resident Windowing System Based on a System of Parallel Text Processing in Which Text Windows Are Simultaneously Viewed, Moved, & Accessed by Content. User Has Access to Notes Based on Any Word or Phrase Combination. The Built-In Editor Includes Cut & Paste, Time & Date Stamping, Sequence Numbering, Graphics Characters, & Embedded Printer Control Codes in Addition to Basic Editing Functions. A Windowing System Automatically Positions Several Note Windows on the Screen in a Way That Reduces Overlap.
Micro Logic Corp.

Tornado. *Version:* 1.0E. Digital Integration. Aug. 1994. *Items Included:* Manual, Maps. *Customer Support:* 800 Number.
MS-DOS 5.0 or higher. IBM & 100% compatibles, 386, 16MHz (1Mb). CD-ROM disk Contact publisher for price (ISBN 1-885932-00-6). *Nonstandard peripherals required:* 256 color, VGA, mouse, CD-ROM. *Optimal configuration:* 4Mb RAM, joystick, sound card.
Race at the Speed of Sound 200 Feet off the Desert Floor. Cripple Air Strips, Smash Bridges, & Plan Your Own Missions to Deal the Iraqi Forces a Crushing Blow.
Trimark Interactive.

Torricelli Editor. The, Answer in Computers. *Compatible Hardware:* TI Professional. *Operating System(s) Required:* MS-DOS. *Memory Required:* 64k. *General Requirements:* Printer.
$295.00.
Texas Instruments, Personal Productivit.

The Tortoise & the Hare. (Living Book Ser.).
MS-DOS 5.0 or higher, Windows 3.1 or higher. 386 processor or higher (4Mb). CD-ROM disk $49.95 (Order no.: R1046). *Nonstandard peripherals required:* CD-ROM drive. *Optimal configuration:* 386 processor operating at 16MHz or higher, MS-DOS 5.0 or higher, Windows 3.1 or higher, 30Mb hard drive, mouse, VGA graphic adapter & VGA color monitor (SVGA recommended), 4Mb RAM, external speakers or headphones (with sound card) that are Sound Blaster compatible.
Macintosh (4Mb). (Order no.: R1046). *Nonstandard peripherals required:* 14" color monitor or larger, CD-ROM drive.
Highly Interactive Animated Stories for Children That Have Hundreds of Beautiful Animations & Have Received Countless Awards. Aesop's Fables (Age 3-8) in English & Spanish.
Library Video Co.

Total Baseball, 1993 Edition: DOS-MAC Jewel Case. *Items Included:* Registration card. *Customer Support:* Creative Multimedia Corporation warrants the CD-ROM disc & diskettes to be free from defects in materials & workmanship under normal use & service for a period of 90 days from date of purchase. Creative Multimedia Corporation offers Technical Support to customers as needed.
MS-DOS 3.1 or higher, MS-CDEX or higher. IBM PC & compatibles with VGA monitor (500k). CD-ROM disk $69.99 (ISBN 1-880428-

11-3, Order no.: 10137). *Optimal configuration:* SuperVGA with 512k+ video memory capable of 640x480x256 color with VESA extensions recommended. *Networks supported:* All.
System Software 6.0.5 or higher. Macintosh Plus or higher (1Mb). 3.5" disk $69.99 (Order no.: 10137). *Nonstandard peripherals required:* Images display on all systems. *Optimal configuration:* Color requires 8-bit color display with 32-bit QuickDraw. *Networks supported:* All.
Comprehensive, Multimedia Baseball Encyclopedia on Disc Containing Text, Images, & Sound Clips of Some of Baseball's Most Exciting Moments. The Disc Compiles the Entire Text of Total Baseball, an Encyclopedia of over 2,600 Pages of Statistics & Articles - a Baseball Library Dating Back to 1871, Player, Pitch & Relief-Pitcher Registers, Top 100 All-Time Leaders, & Much More. Contains More Than 600 Photos & Images of Players, Teams & Ballparks.
Creative Multimedia Corp.

Total Baseball, 1993 Edition: DOS-MAC Retail Box. *Items Included:* Registration card. *Customer Support:* Creative Multimedia Corporation warrants the CD-ROM disc & diskettes to be free from defects in materials & workmanship under normal use & service for a period of 90 days from date of purchase. Creative Multimedia Corporation offers Technical Support to customers as needed.
MS-DOS 3.1 or higher, MS-CDEX or higher. IBM PC & compatibles with VGA Monitor (500k). CD-ROM disk $69.99 (ISBN 1-880428-24-5, Order no.: 10128). *Optimal configuration:* SuperVGA with 512k+ video memory capable of 640x480x256 color with VESA extensions recommended. *Networks supported:* All.
System Software 6.0.5 or higher. Macintosh Plus or higher (1Mb). 3.5" disk $69.99 (Order no.: 10128). *Nonstandard peripherals required:* Images display on all systems. *Optimal configuration:* Color requires 8-bit color display with 32-bit QuickDraw. *Networks supported:* All.
Comprehensive, Multimedia Baseball Encyclopedia on Disc Containing Text, Images & Sound Clips of Some of Baseball's Most Exciting Moments. The Disc Compiles the Entire Text of Total Baseball, an Encyclopedia of over 2,600 Pages of Statistics & Articles - a Baseball Library Dating Back to 1871, Player, Pitch, & Relief-Pitcher Registers, Top 100 All-Time Leaders, & Much More. Contains More Than 600 Photos & Images of Players, Teams & Ballparks.
Creative Multimedia Corp.

Total Control Diet. *Compatible Hardware:* Commodore Amiga.
3.5" disk $49.95.
A High Tech Approach to Weight Loss: Digitized Images, Recipes.
Lee Software.

Total Strength Systems Plus: The Complete Professional Strength Training System. *Version:* 2.0. Brian C. Elwood. Jan. 1994. *Items Included:* 3 master disks for up to 1998 people each, spiral bound manual.
MS-DOS version 2.0 or higher. IBM PC or 100% compatibles with a hard disk drive & printer (180k). disk $229.99 (ISBN 1-881432-38-6). *Nonstandard peripherals required:* CGA or higher video system. *Optimal configuration:* 8Mb free hard disk space, 200k available RAM, hard disk drive required, VGA monitor, printer.
An Easy to Use Powerful, Program Designed to Meet the Strength Training Needs of the Strength Coach or Fitness Director. You Will Be Able to Make Professional Strength Training Programs at an Extremely High Rate of Speed with Total Accuracy & Versatility.
BCS Publishing.

TotalNet. *Items Included:* Spiral manuals. *Customer Support:* Hotline, maintenance.
IBM PC; PS/2 & compatibles (640K). contact publisher for price.
Network Operating System Which Allows DOS, OS/2, & Xenix Clients to Access & Utilize the Powerful Resources of UNIX & VAX/VMS Machines Transparently.
OCS/Syntax.

TotalPhase CMA. *Operating System(s) Required:* PC-DOS/MS-DOS, OS/2. *Memory Required:* 256k. *General Requirements:* 132-column printer & 20Mb hard disk.
3.5" or 5.25" $2995.95.
Complete System for Management of the Dental Office. Package Includes Accounts Receivable, Paper & Electronic Claim Form Processing, General Ledger, Payroll Processing, Accounts Payable, Word Processing, Spreadsheet Analysis, Appointment Handling & Office Administration. Automatically Handles up to Ten Users.
CMA Micro Computer.

Totem Color Clip Art. *Items Included:* Color binder of art print-outs & index to diskettes. *Customer Support:* Telephone support for general assistance & advice.
Macintosh Plus or higher (1Mb), IBM PC, Next. (06/1988) $95.00/volume of 96 asst. images. $125.00 per selected category of 96 images. *Addl. software required:* Word processing, graphics or page lay-out. *Optimal configuration:* Laser printer, Mac II, color monitor, Adobe Illustrator 3.0, Freehand 3.0, or Pagemaker 4.0.
DOS, Windows (640k), NeXT. IBM compatible with 640k RAM, hard disk drive, 3 1/2 DS/DD floppy drive. (06/1989) $95.00/volume of 96 asst. images. $125.00 per selected category of 96 images. *Addl. software required:* Word processing graphics or page-layout. *Optimal configuration:* Laser printer with PostScript capabilities, Pagemaker, or Corel Draw, or Illustrator, windows version.
Color PostScript Clip-Art in 17 Categories: Birds, Business #1 & #2, Domestic Animals, Fish, Flowers, Food, Holidays, Insects, Nautical, Sports, Tools & Hardware, Wild Animals, & Women, Borders, Travel, Educucation. Available in Monthly Shipments of Assorted Images, or by Category. Macintosh Formats Available: Illustrator, Freehand, & EPSF. IBM Formats Available: Corel, EPS, Illustrator. Next Formats Available: Illustrator, EPS.
Totem Graphics, Inc.

Touch Games I. *Compatible Hardware:* HP 150 Touchscreen.
3.5" disk $39.00 (Order no.: 92248AA). *Includes:* 3D TIC-TAC-TOE, BLACKJACK, WUMPUS IV, Where You Must Defeat the Deadly Wumpus Dragon, or Die; & BIORHYTHMS, a Program That Charts the Ups & Downs of Your Physical, Emotional, & Cognitive Cycles.
Hewlett-Packard Co.

Touch 'n Go. *Version:* 1.06. Jun. 1990. *Items Included:* 3-ring binder with manual (tabbed & indexed); Automated installation program; Quick-reference card. *Customer Support:* Unlimited telephone support.
MS-DOS 2.1 or higher. IBM & compatibles (desktop or portable) (256K). disk $149.00 (Order no.: TG-100).
Business Travel Expense Management System. Generates Expense Reports During or After a Trip & Saves the Reports on Disk. Tracks Both Reimbursed & Unreimbursed Expenses for Tax Savings. Produces Summary Reports by Item, Credit Card, Car Mileage, 80/100% Deductibles, Account Numbers. Includes Full-Features Word Processor, Calendar, Clock, Calculator.
Quantic Corp.

TOUCHBASE PRO. *Version:* 3.0. Apr. 1993. *Items Included:* User manual. *Customer Support:* Free technical support.
Macintosh 6.0.5 or higher. Macintosh Plus or higher (2Mb). $79.95 (DATEBOOK/TOUCHBASE PRO Bundle $149.95). *Nonstandard peripherals required:* Hard drive. *Addl. software required:* System 7.0 required for integration with DATEBOOK PRO. *Optimal configuration:* System 7.0, Mac II family, 2Mb RAM, hard drive, color monitor. *Networks supported:* AppleTalk.
The Easiest Way to Manage Your Contacts. Can Print Envelopes, Labels, Address Books, Reports & Fax Cover Sheets. User Can Create Mail-Merge Letters with the Built-In FastLetter Feature. Can Even Directly Communicate with Your DATEBOOK PRO Calendar, Showing You All Your Contact's Meetings & To-Do Items in Your Calendar.
Aldus Corp. (Consumer Division).

Touchscreen Programmer's Tools. *Compatible Hardware:* HP 150 Touchscreen.
3.5" disk $295.00 (Order no.: 45435A).
Package Includes the HP 150 Programmer's Reference Manual; the Intel iAPX 8088 Reference Manual; the MS-DOS User's Guide, the MACRO-86 Macro Assembler Manual, & the MS-DOS Programmer's Reference Manual; a Diskette Including the MACRO-86 Assembler, the Linker, the Library, the Debugger, the Cross-Reference Utility, & a Line Editor, As Well As the File-Comparison, File-Conversion, SORT, & FIND Utilities.
Hewlett-Packard Co.

Tournament Bridge: Competition & Practice for the Serious Bridge Player. Paul A. Schwartz. 1985-86. *Compatible Hardware:* Apple II, II+, IIe, IIc; IBM PC. *Operating System(s) Required:* Apple DOS 3.3; PC-DOS 2.0, 2.1, 3.0. *Memory Required:* 64k.
disk $49.95 ea.
Apple. (ISBN 0-676-32440-1).
IBM. (ISBN 0-676-32441-X).
Improves Users' Bridge Game As They Play Challenging Hands, Receive Tutorial Advice, & Are Scored Master Points According to Professional Tournament Rules.
Random Hse., Inc.

Tournamentbowl. *Version:* B3. Ron Gunn. 1993. *Compatible Hardware:* Commodore 64, 128; IBM PC. *Operating System(s) Required:* CBM DOS, DOS 2.1 or higher. *Language(s):* BASIC, Compiled .EXE for IBM. *Memory Required:* Com 64k, IBM 512k.
Commodore 64, 128. disk $25.00 (Order no.: D022F).
IBM PC. disk $25.00 (Order no.: D0601).
Handles Data for a Tournament or Bowl-a-Thon of up to Hundreds of Mixed Teams. Keeps Scores by Individual Member, Team, etc. C64 Mode (400+ Teams), C128 Mode (700+ Teams), IBM (400+ Teams).
Briley Software.

Tower of Fear. *Compatible Hardware:* TRS-80. contact publisher for price.
Instant Software, Inc.

TITLE INDEX

The Tower of Myraglen. Compatible Hardware: Apple IIgs.
3.5" disk $44.95.
Battle the Forces of Evil to Save the Kingdom of Myraglen. Features Traps, Wizards, Monsters, Riddles, & Secret Passages. Integrates Graphics & Sound.
PBI Software, Inc.

TOXIPAC. Version: 2.0. Mar. 1985. Compatible Hardware: IBM PC, PC AT, PC XT & compatibles. Operating System(s) Required: PC-DOS, MS-DOS. Language(s): FORTRAN. Memory Required: 512k. General Requirements: Printer, plotter, digitizer.
disk $13,300.00 (Order no.: TOXIPAC).
Integrated Software System That Gives the Most Precise Estimate Possible of the Extent & Quantity of Hazardous Waste Contamination. Using Advanced Geostatistical Techniques, the System Maps Investigation Results, Assesses Contamination Fronts & Helps Determine Sampling Geometries.
Geostat Systems International, Inc. (GSII).

TPE Pipeline Estimator: Cost Estimating of Underground Gas Transmission Pipelines & Gas Gathering Systems. Harry Haines.
Customer Support: Maintenance, enhancement & support (first 6 months free); 30-day unlimited warranty.
  IBM PC, XT, XT, PS/2 & compatibles (640k), 10Mb hard disk space. $2500.00 (Order no.: 50081). Nonstandard peripherals required: Math coprocessor.
  (Order no.: 5008Z).
Estimate Construction Costs of Underground Pipeline & Gathering Systems, Sometimes within 15 Minutes. User Can Also Use the Program to Make Several Trial Estimates within a Short Time. The Program Allows Detailed Input of Costs for Particular Jobs. Thus Certain Unit Costs Can Be Used over & over for Many Different Jobs, Saving Much Input. The Program Also Comes with Libraries of Casing & Pipe Weights & Wall Thicknesses. This Program Will Cut Hundreds of Man-Hours from the Job of Cost Estimating & Makes Reestimates after Design Changes a Snap.
Gulf Publishing Co.

TPLAN: Transition Planning Tool. 1994. Items Included: User's manual, system disk, database disk of service providers (state). Customer Support: Free telephone support for 12 months after purchase.
  MS Windows. IBM PC or compatibles (2Mb). disk $130.00 (ISBN 1-888333-00-6). Nonstandard peripherals required: Mouse, color monitor. Optimal configuration: 3Mb of available space on hard disk drive.
  Macintosh System 7.1. Macintosh (5Mb). 3.5" disk $130.00 (ISBN 1-888333-02-2). Nonstandard peripherals required: Mouse, color monitor. Optimal configuration: 5Mb of available space on hard disk drive.
Interactive Computer-Based Transition Planning Environment Which Uses a Rule-Based Advisory & Information Management Approach to Assist in Making Decisions in Areas Including Education, Employment, etc., to Fulfill Almost All a Student's Transition Needs. Contains Service Provider Database for State by Subarea (County, Parish, Borough).
Analysis & Simulation, Inc.

TPLAN: Transition Planning Tool. 1994. Items Included: User's manual 3 copies; system disk 3 copies; database disk of service providers (state) 3 copies. Customer Support: Free telephone support for 12 months after purchase.
  MS Windows. IBM PC or compatibles (2Mb). disk $130.00, site license (ISBN 1-888333-01-4). Nonstandard peripherals required: Mouse, color monitor. Optimal configuration: 3Mb of available space on hard disk drive.
  Macintosh System 7.1. Macintosh (5Mb). 3.5" disk $130.00, site license (ISBN 1-888333-03-0). Nonstandard peripherals required: Mouse, color monitor. Optimal configuration: 5Mb of available space on hard disk drive.
Interactive Computer-Based Transition Planning Environment Which Uses a Rule-Based Advisory & Information Management Approach to Assist in Making Decisions in Areas Including Education, Employment, etc., to Fulfill Almost All a Student's Transition Needs. Contains Service Provider Database for State by Subarea (County, Parish, Borough).
Analysis & Simulation, Inc.

Track & Field. Compatible Hardware: Apple II with Applesoft. Operating System(s) Required: Apple DOS 3.2, 3.3. Language(s): Applesoft (source code included). Memory Required: 48k. General Requirements: Printer.
disk $39.95.
Maintains Athletic Event Records with up to 50 Names, 15 Different Meets, 8 Field Events & 12 Track Events.
Dynacomp, Inc.

Track & Field Records. Compatible Hardware: Apple II Plus, IIe, IIc; IBM. General Requirements: Printer.
disk $49.95.
Designed to Help the Coach Keep Up-to-Date Records & Placings on Individual & Relay Efforts. Data Entry Allows Distances, Meet Points, Times, & Placings of Each Individual for Each Meet. Total Points Are Calculated for the Individual Meet & Accumulated for the Season. No Comparison Is Made Concerning Distances & Times from One Meet to Another. All Individual & Relay Events Are Metric. The Individual Can Have Data Entered in Any Event in Any Meet. Reports Generated Include the Records of Any Player or Players & Meet or Meets. Designed So That It Can Be Used on a Single or Dual Disk Drive System. The Data Disk Can Be Copied So That the Program Can Be Used by Different Teams Within the Same School.
Cherrygarth, Inc.

Track Designer Option Module. Items Included: Manual, catalog, update card. Customer Support: Always free over the phone, disks replaced free for first 30 days, disks replaced for $10.00 after 30 days.
Commodore 64/128. $14.95.
Amiga 500, 1000, 2000 (512k). $14.95.
Create an Unlimited Quantity of Race Tracks That Differ from the Traditional Oval Variety in Shape, Distance & Difficulty. Special 3-D Graphics for Amiga Users Only.
SportTime Computer Software.

Track/Online. Items Included: Communications disk for ProComm Plus & user guide. Customer Support: Free by phone.
IBM & compatibles (256k). contact publisher for price. Optimal configuration: Modem-Hayes compatible. Networks supported: Telenet & Autonet, CompuServe.
Historical Quotes Dating Back to 1970 for Stocks & Futures Are Also Available. The News Database Provides Current & Historical News from Comtex Scientific Corp.'s ExecuGrid & Business Wire's Full Text Corporate News Releases. Other Financial Databases & Information Include: Mutual Fund Information & Performance Results from Investment Company Data; Insider Trading Data from INVEST/NET Group; Risk Arbitrage from Merrin Financial; Institutional Holdings & 144 Filings from Vickers Stock Research Corp.; Earnings Estimates from Zacks Investment Research; & Equity Analysis, Technical Indicators, Economic & Monetary Projections Bond Data & More from S&P MarketScope. Track/Online Provides Analysis on Put/Call Option Series, Volatility Analysis, Market Pulse & Market Monitoring.
Global Market Information, Inc.

Track Records. Compatible Hardware: Apple II+, IIe, IBM. Language(s): BASIC. Memory Required: Apple 48k; IBM 640k. General Requirements: Printer.
disk $49.95.
disk add'l. manual $19.95.
Can Be Used by Several Teams Within the Same School. Each Team Can Keep Its Statistics Separate on Different Data Disks. The Entry Information Includes the Following: Identification Code, Player, Opponent. Field Events Include: 100, 200, 400, & 800 Meter Dashes; 400, 800, 1600 & 3200 Meter Runs, 400 & 1600 Meter Relays; 100 High & 300 Low Hurdles.
Cherrygarth, Inc.

Track Simulator. Ronald D. Jones. 1985. Compatible Hardware: Apple; Commodore; IBM; TRS-80 Model I, Model III, Color Computer. Operating System(s) Required: CP/M. Memory Required: 64k.
disk $39.95 ea.
Apple. (ISBN 1-55604-174-8, Order no.: S002).
CP/M. (ISBN 1-55604-175-6, Order no.: S002).
Commodore. (ISBN 1-55604-176-4, Order no.: S002).
Color Computer. (ISBN 1-55604-177-2, Order no.: S002).
IBM. (ISBN 1-55604-178-0, Order no.: S002).
Model I & Model III. (ISBN 1-55604-179-9, Order no.: S002).
Using High Resolution Graphics Sound & Full Color, Program Provides a Full Day at the Races. Designed to Provide, & Improve, Fundamental Handicapping Skills along with the Excitement of "Being There." Spend an Exciting Race Day at Santa Anita Racetrack.
Professor Jones Professional Handicapping Systems.

Track Two Option Module. Items Included: Manual, catalog, update card. Customer Support: Always free over the phone, disks replaced free for first 30 days, disks replaced for $10.00 after 30 days.
MS-DOS. IBM & Compatibles (512k). $14.95.
Amiga 500, 1000, 2000 (512k). $14.95.
All New Racetrack & Stable with 128 Brand New Horses & Fresh Park Graphics. All Races Can Be Seen in EGA Graphics by IBM Users Only.
SportTime Computer Software.

Tracker. Operating System(s) Required: MS-DOS. Customer Support: On site training unlimited support services for first 90 days & through subscription thereafter.
contact publisher for price.
Records All Daily Activities Such As the Following: Crops, Livestock, Equipment, Employee Actions, Meetings. User-Defined Codes Are Used to Classify the When, Where, What, Who & How Information. These Codes with Their Descriptions, Are Displayed As Activities Are Entered.
Argos Software.

Tracker. Nov. 1989. Items Included: Instruction included on disk. Customer Support: 90 days unlimited warranty.
MS-DOS, Windows 3.1. IBM XT, AT or compatibles (512K). disk $24.95 plus $3.50 S&H (Order no.: 1076). Addl. software required: Lotus 1-2-3, Release 4.0 or higher. Optimal configuration: IBM AT, 640k RAM.
Produces Amortization Schedule for a Loan-Allows for Making Extra Payments.
Compiled Systems.

Tracker Cross-Reference System: M65J. 1984. *Compatible Hardware:* Commodore 64; IBM PC, PCjr. *Memory Required:* 64k. *General Requirements:* Printer.
disk $50.00 (ISBN 0-925182-39-7).
disk $50.00 (ISBN 0-925182-40-0).
Information Storage & Retrieval System with Cross-Reference Database.
Matrix Software.

TrackIt. *Customer Support:* Free, unlimited. Windows 3.1 or higher. 386 or higher (4Mb). disk $39.95.
The Ultimate Project Tracking Tool. Project Budgets, Track Materials Usage, & Keep Time Schedules for Home & Business. Ideal for Home Remodeling, Landscaping, Manufacturing, Product Development, Restoration Projects, New Construction, Business Projects, Plus Many Other Uses. The Easy to Use Timeline Will Keep Your Project Phases on Schedule, Not to Mention Keep Cost Overruns to a Minimum. Extremely Flexible File Formats Allow Importing from Chief Architect, 3D Home Architect, Floorplan Plus 3D, Estimator Plus, Land Designer, Quicken, Quickbooks, Microsoft Money, & Tab & Comma Delimited Files.
BeachWare.

Trackker. *Version:* 6.0. Stephen D. McGregor et al. Sep. 1992. *Items Included:* 1 loose-leaf user manual. *Customer Support:* Free customer support; 30 day money-back guarantee.
PC-DOS/MS-DOS Version 3.31 or higher. IBM PC, XT, AT, PS/2 or 100% compatible. disk $295.00 (ISBN 1-56433-072-9). *Optimal configuration:* IBM PC, XT, AT, PS/2 or 100% compatible; 640k RAM; hard disk with minimum 1Mb available; 1 floppy disk drive. *Networks supported:* Novell or compatible.
Monitors Due Dates for CPA Firms. Due Dates & Extension Dates Are Automatically Calculated Each Year. Flexible Reporting Allows Each Firm to Generate Needed Reports. Other Features Include Automatic Staff Assignments, Status Code Tracking, & One-Time Entry of Permanent Client & Firm Information.
Practitioners Publishing Co.

Trackmaster II. *Version:* 2.0. *Compatible Hardware:* MOTO680x0, AT&T, UNISYS, INTEL 80x86, IBM RS/6000. *Items Included:* Documentation in 3-ring manual. *Customer Support:* On-site training, 800 number, 90 day warranty, user's group, documentation, updates. Contact Publisher for price.
Enables Non-Profit Organizations to Maintain a Close Relationship with Major Donors & Prospects, Board Members, & Volunteers. By Classifying Donor Potential & by Assigning "Points" to Various Cultivation Activities, a Fund Raiser Is Able to Monitor Levels of Activity by Prospects, Board Members, Volunteers, & Staff. A Monthly Calendar System Is Also Provided to Assist the Fund Raiser in Knowing Which Activities Are Anticipated, of Immediate Interest, or Are Overdue. Complete Reporting & Recap Features Are Also Included Which Allow the Professional to Evaluate a Program's Progress to Date. Volunteer Activities Can Also Be Evaluated & Summarized for Volunteer Recognition Programs.
Master Systems.

TRACSTAR Integrated Software for Community Foundations. *Items Included:* Manual, Runtime Foxbase. *Customer Support:* With purchase of software, 30 days unlimited support. Yearly support plus $550.00 single user, $1100.00 multi-user.
MS-DOS (640k), 4mg RAM Optimal. DOS compatible 286 or 386 with hard disk. single user $3740.00. *Optimal configuration:* 486 with 120Mb hard disk, 4mg RAM. *Networks supported:* Novell/LANtastic.
multi-user $5390.00.
Integrated Fund Accounting, Donor & Grant Tracking Package Designed Specifically to Meet the Needs of a Growing Community Foundation. The Fund Accounting Module Includes Pooled Asset Allocation Capabilities & Management Fees Assessment. The Donor Tracking & Grant Tracking Keep Unlimited Histories of Gifts to the Foundation & Grants Made by the Foundation.
Technology Resource Assistance Ctr.

Trader's Money Manager: TMM. *Version:* 2.1. Robert C. Pelletier. Mar. 1993. *Items Included:* One program disk & ring-bound manual. *Customer Support:* Free telephone support.
PC-DOS/MS-DOS 2.0 or higher. IBM PC & compatibles (640k). disk $399.00. *Nonstandard peripherals required:* Math co-processor strongly recommended. *Optimal configuration:* Co-processor or 386.
Guides the Investor in Selecting a Profitable Trading System. It Tells the Probability of Reaching a Goal at Any Capital Level; Assigns a Numerical Rating Based on Return on Investment, Allowing Direct Comparison Between Trading Systems; & Tells When to Increase Market Exposure for Maximum Profit with Minimal Risk.
Commodity Systems, Inc. (CSI).

Traders Tool. James Diamond. Jan. 1996. *Items Included:* User guide. *Customer Support:* 60 days free support; free training video; yearly maintenance agreements with on-line service & 900 numbers.
DOS version 5.0 or higher, Microsoft Windows 3.1 or higher. IBM or 100% compatible PC (4Mb). disk $350.00 (ISBN 0-9650221-1-0). *Nonstandard peripherals required:* Mouse required; VGA card (640x480); 386 SX or higher; hard disk with 3Mb min free space.
A Comprehensive Program That Helps Businesses & Individuals Learn How to Barter. It Provides 7 Basic Operations: Trader Transaction Files; Trade Selection; Inventory Management; Fax Interface to Outside Databases; Windows Utilities Applications; Reminders for Expiration of Scrip or Services; & Currency Conversion.
The Word.

TRADES: Total Retail & Distribution System. *Version:* 0.2. Jan. 1994. *Items Included:* Manuals. *Customer Support:* 1 yr included. Renewal 48 hours $1000, ASAP $1200, FX-ASAP $1500, Modem (FX ASAP) $3600.
SCO UNIX, Novell, AIX. All RISC; 386, 486, Pentium (8Mb). $6000.00 - $60,000.00 dependant on number of users. *Optimal configuration:* RAM 20Mb; hard disk 250Mb; number terminals limited only by hardware. *Networks supported:* All.
Completely Integrated Back Office, Retailing, Point-of-Sale System for Single or Multi-Store Chains. Includes Delivery, Purchasing, Receiving, Inventory Control, Sales History & Reports. Module Options: High Speed Cash & Carry Point-of-Sale Transactions; Service & Warranty; Credit Authorization.
Trac Line Software, Inc.

TRADE$K. *Version:* 2.0. Feb. 1992. *Items Included:* Four program disks & ring-bound manual. *Customer Support:* Hotline support to customers; manual on magnetic media & hard bound manual.
MS-DOS. IBM Monochrome, CGA, EGA, VGA or compatible (640k). disk $149.00 with CSI Data Retrieval Service; $299.00 unrestricted use. *Optimal configuration:* 286 or 386 recommended.
Manages an Unlimited Number of Trading Accounts, Keeps Track of All Open Orders; Takes Daily Notes on Both Accounts & Individual Contracts & Allows for Review of All Interrelated Data in a Variety of Report Formats. Best Described As a Personal Information Manager Optimized for a Commodity Trader.
Commodity Systems, Inc. (CSI).

Trading Expert. *Version:* 3.2. Jan. 1992. *Items Included:* Program & Data disks, 3 spiral-bound manual with slip case.
DOS V3.0 or higher. IBM compatible. $996.00 unlimited, $88.00 Trial (fully functional) additional charge for Add-On Modules (Group/Sector, Options Analysis). *Optimal configuration:* Recommended 1Mb of memory & math coprocessor.
Expert System Combining Market Timing with Stock Selection. Overall Market Direction Is First Analyzed Then Individual Equities Are Screened for Buy or Sell Indication. Individual Stock Recommendations Are Then Filtered by Overall Market Direction & Trend Resulting in Dependable Buy & Sell Signals. Add-On Modules Are Available for Group/Sector Analysis & Option Analysis (Index & Equity).
AIQ, Inc.

Trading System Performance Evaluator (TSPE). *Version:* 1.0. 1991. *Items Included:* One program disk & manual. *Customer Support:* 91 page manual, hotline support to customers.
PC-DOS or MS-DOS. IBM PC, XT, AT, PS/2 or compatible (640k). disk $149.00. *Optimal configuration:* Math co-processor.
Draws upon Forecasting Theory & Random Simulation to Assess Trading System Performance. Will Take Any Profit & Loss (P&L) Input Record & Determine Whether a Similar Result Can Be Repeated by Chance with Randomly Drawn Samples from the Original P&L Set. Determines the Probability of Reaching a Goal at Varying Capital Levels.
Commodity Systems, Inc. (CSI).

Traffic Accident Analysis & Reconstruction. *Compatible Hardware:* North Star Horizon II. *Operating System(s) Required:* DOS 5.0. *Memory Required:* 48k.
disk $499.95 (Order no.: 0173ND).
Nine Programs for Solving Equations Involved in Accidents in Order to Reach Accurate Conclusions.
Instant Software, Inc.

Traffic Controller Personal. *Items Included:* Disks, manual & addendums. *Customer Support:* Free unlimited phone technical support, FAX & modem service. America Online, CompuServe, Applelink.
Macintosh System 7 & higher. Mac Plus & higher (2Mb RAM). 3.5" disk $195.00.
Will Provide the System 7 User with a Graphical Representation of All Publish & Subscribe Editions on a Single Macintosh. These Edition Files Can Be Accessed at Any Time for the User to Manipulate. Benefits Include the Saving of Each Iteration of Data Updated, Control of the Established Links, Quick Access to the Edition Data, Print Log of Editions, & More.
Olduvai Corp.

TrafficWatch 2. *Version:* 1.0. *Compatible Hardware:* Apple Macintosh. *Customer Support:* Free unlimited phone support, 90 days warranty. 3.5" disk $695.00.
For Network Managers Who Must Decide Where to Place Bridges or Peripherals on an AppleTalk Network. Measures Ethernet & Local Talk Network Traffic, Detects Bottlenecks, Low Traffic Areas, Network Errors, & with a Microsoft Excel Macro, View Traffic Flow in Real Time Bar Charts or Spreadsheet.
W O S Data Systems, Inc.

TITLE INDEX

The Tragedy of Hamlet. *Version:* 1.5. Feb. 1995. *Items Included:* BookWorm Student Reader (diskette). *Customer Support:* 30 day MBG. Technical support (toll call) - no charge.
System 7.0 or higher. Macintosh (5Mb). CD-ROM disk $29.95 (ISBN 1-57316-020-2, Order no.: 16155). *Nonstandard peripherals required:* CD-ROM drive, 12" color monitor. *Optimal configuration:* 13" color monitor recommended.
Windows 3.1 or higher. IBM compatible (MPC) 386 DX (4Mb). CD-ROM disk $29.95. *Nonstandard peripherals required:* Standard multimedia compatible CD-ROM. *Optimal configuration:* 8Mb RAM recommended, 256 color monitor recommended.
One of the Greatest of All Shakespearean Plays, Hamlet Has Engaged Audiences for 400 Years with Its Exciting Action, Profound Drama, & Intensely Conveyed Tragedy. Beautifully Illustrated with Pictures from Stage Performances & Art Masterpieces.
Communication & Information Technologies, Inc. (CIT).

The Tragedy of Macbeth. *Version:* 1.5. Feb. 1995. *Items Included:* BookWorm Student Reader (diskette). *Customer Support:* 30 day MBG. Technical support (toll call) - no charge.
System 7.0 or higher. Macintosh (5Mb). CD-ROM disk $29.95 (ISBN 1-57316-021-0, Order no.: 16156). *Nonstandard peripherals required:* CD-ROM drive, 12" color monitor. *Optimal configuration:* 13" color monitor recommended.
Windows 3.1 or higher. IBM compatible (MPC) 386 DX (4Mb). CD-ROM disk $29.95. *Nonstandard peripherals required:* Standard multimedia compatible CD-ROM. *Optimal configuration:* 8Mb RAM recommended, 256 color monitor recommended.
Shakespeare's Classic Tale of the Horrible Corruptions of Power. The BookWorm Edition Features Complete Background Information, a Fully Annotated Text with All Difficult Passages Explained, & Extensive Literary Discussions Drawn from the World's Best Scholars.
Communication & Information Technologies, Inc. (CIT).

TrAid-Names. Jan. 1988. *Items Included:* 1 bound users manual with example. *Customer Support:* Telephone support.
Macintosh (512k). 3.5" disk $159.00 (Order no.: 2001). *Optimal configuration:* Minimal configurations are suitable.
MS-DOS. IBM PC compatibles (512k). disk $159.00 (Order no.: 2003). *Optimal configuration:* Minimum configurations are suitable.
An Interactive Software Package That Develops New Product, Business or Service Names. Lists of Names Are Generated Based on Key Words & Descriptive Information about the Entity. Desired Prefixes, Suffixes or Word Parts May Also Be Utilized & May Be Locked into Various Positions Within the Created Names. Lists of Names Generated May Be Reviewed on Screen or Printed for Later Review.
Applied Systems & Technologies, Inc.

Trailblazer. *Items Included:* Manual. *Customer Support:* Unlimited technical support; 60 day moneyback guarantee.
Windows. IBM or compatibles (4Mb). disk $69.95. *Addl. software required:* MS Windows 3.0 or higer. *Optimal configuration:* 386/486 based DOS computer, hard disk with at least 3Mb disk space available, mouse.
Easy-to-Use File & Program Manager for Windows. Simple One-Stop File Management Window Improves Access to Directories for Easier File Manipulation. Find, Copy, Move & Erase Files Just by Dragging an Icon Across the Screen. Or Launch a File, & Its Associated Application by Double Clicking on the File Name. Electronic Notes Tell You the Contents of a File Before You Open It, & the Shredder Makes Erased Files Irretrievable. Makes Your PC Screen Come Alive with a Colorful Windows, Push Buttons & Scroll Bars, Time/Date Clock, Animated Icons & More.
Timeworks, Inc.

Train Engineer.
Windows, 3.1 or higher; DOS, 3.3 or higher. disk $49.95 (Order no.: 744734 50670 3). *Optimal configuration:* Windows, 3.1 or higher, 4Mb RAM, 4Mb hard drive space, 386 or higher; DOS, 3.3 or higher, 640k, 4Mb hard drive space.
System 6.0.7. Macintosh (1.7Mb). 3.5" disk $49.95 (Order no.: 744734 50650 5). *Optimal configuration:* Macintosh, System 6.0.7, 1.7Mb, hard drive. Sound Blaster-compatible sound board optional.
Allows Users to Design Track Layouts & Run Them from the Viewpoint of the Train's Engineer. After Choosing, Designing, or Importing a Layout, Players Can Schedule Various Cargos to Go to Different Destinations in Their Designs. Then, from the Engineer's Seat, They Race the Clock to Deliver Their Cargos to Their Destinations. Players Can Choose from Many User-Defined Options: e.g., Weather (Rain, Snow, Clear, Random), Time of Day, Number of Trains, Terrain, Pickup/Delivery Schedules, & More.
Abracadata, Ltd.

!Trak-IT AT. *Version:* 4. Feb. 1990. *Items Included:* Software & manual. *Customer Support:* Maintenance - annual fee depending on software purchased. 30-day warranty upon purchase.
Macintosh Plus or higher (2Mb). 3.5" disk $1295.00. *Networks supported:* AppleShare, Ethernet.
Multi-user $1990.00.
Applicant Tracking System Providing Skills, School & Past Employer Retrieval; Standard & Custom Letters; Routing Status; EEC; Recruiter Statistics; Applicant Profiles, & More. Provides over 80 Standard Reports & Includes a Custom Report Writer, a Custom Letter Generator & Multi-User Option.
Trak-It Solutions.

!Trak-IT HR. *Version:* 8. *Compatible Hardware:* Apple Macintosh Plus or larger.
3.5" disk $695.00 up.
Attendance Tracking Module. 3.5" disk $695.00.
Human Resource System.
Trak-It Solutions.

Trans Collect: Traffic Count System. Patrick Burcky. Aug. 1985. *Compatible Hardware:* IBM PC & compatibles PC XT. *Operating System(s) Required:* MS-DOS. *Language(s):* BASIC (source code included). *Memory Required:* 256k.
contact publisher for price (ISBN 0-925112-00-3).
System Which Collects Data from Remote Collection Stations via Phone Lines, Stores the Data on Disk & Recalls Stations As Required. Provides Reports During & after Data Collection, Data Deals with Traffic Counts at Various Locations Collected by Automatic Counting Equipment.
Management Systems, Inc.

TRANSACCT. *Version:* 4.0. *Items Included:* Reference manual & users manual. *Customer Support:* 1 year of support provided with purchase. Maintenance is 15% of purchase price per year or $50/hr. plus expenses.
UNIX & compatibles (6Mb). $27,000.00 & up, includes all. No separate modules. *Addl. software required:* Informix 4GL (4.0) or higher with run-time & SQL.
Fully Featured Management Accounting System That Utilizes Relational Data Base Management System (RDBMS). Fully Transactional, Real-Time System Allows Up-to-the-Minute Reports As Fresh As the Most Recent Transaction. No Posting To G/L Is Required. Enterprize-Wide Database & System Architecture Allows Complete Access to All Information in the Central Set of Tables. Includes G/L, A/P, A/R, O/E, Invoicing, Inventory Control, Payroll, Purchasing & Fixed Asset Management.
DataSpan International.

TransCyrillic. *Version:* 8.2. Apr. 1992. *Items Included:* User's manual, keyboard layout chart, key caps sticker sheet. *Customer Support:* Telephone support, defective disks replaced free.
Macintosh (1Mb). 3.5" disk $149.95 ($199.95 for TransCyrillic Professional which includes Sans Serif Fonts). *Nonstandard peripherals required:* Hard drive. *Addl. software required:* Any word processor.
Professional-Quality, Hinted Type 1 & TrueType TransCyrillic Plain, Bold, Italic, & Bold Italic Fonts & Polished Bitmaps in 8, 9, 10, 12, 14, 18, 24, 36, 48, & 96-Point Sizes Including All Major Current Cyrillic Languages. Includes Five Keyboard Layouts: Russian, Bulgarian, Ukran, Serbian & the AATSEEL-Recommended, Qwerty-Like Transliterated Keyboard layout. Specify If for System 6.
Linguist's Software, Inc.

TransCyrillic for Windows. *Version:* 6.3. Apr. 1992. *Items Included:* User's manual, keyboard layout chart, ANSI Chart, keycap sticker sheet. *Customer Support:* Free telephone support; defective disks replaced free.
Windows. IBM or compatibles (4Mb). disk $99.95 ($149.95 for TransCyrillic Professional for Windows which includes Sans Serif fonts). *Addl. software required:* MS Windows or ATM. *Optimal configuration:* 4Mb RAM & 386.
Professional-Quality, Hinted, Scalable Fonts in Both TrueType & Type 1 Formats: Times-Style TransCyrillic Plain, Bold, Italic & Bold-Italic. Type 1 Works with ATM & Windows 3.X & OS/2 & AutoCAD r.13. Includes Keyboard Switcher Windows Utility Providing Russian, AATSEEL Transliterated, Ukrainian, Serbian, & Bulgarian Keyboard Layouts in Windows Applications. Fonts Alone Work in Word 6 for DOS, WordPerfect 6.0b for DOS, or Newer, AutoCAD r.12 & 13; OS/2; NeXT. Must Upgrade to 6.0a or Newer to Type Overstrikes & Stress Marks. Includes All Major Current Cyrillic Languages: Avar, Azerbaijani, Bashkir, Belarus, Bulgarian, Buriat, Chechen, Chukchi, Chuvash, Dungan, Erzya, Evenki, Kabardian, Kalmyk, Kazakh, Kirghiz, Komi, Lak, Lezgin, Macedonian, Mari, Moksha, Moldavian, Mongolian, Mordvin, Nenets, Ossetian, Ostyak, Russian, Serbian, Tadzhik, Tatar, Turkmen, Tuvan, Udmurt, Ukrainian, Uzbek, Yakut, & Most Old Chruch Slavic Characters.
Linguist's Software, Inc.

TransCyrillic Sans Serif. *Version:* 8.2. Mar. 1992. *Items Included:* User's manual, keyboard layout chart, key caps sticker sheet. *Customer Support:* Telephone support, defective disks replaced free.
Macintosh (1Mb). 3.5" disk $99.95 ($199.95 for TransCyrillic Professional which includes Times-Style Fonts). *Nonstandard peripherals required:* Hard drive. *Addl. software required:* Any word processor.
Four Professional-Quality Fonts Including All Major Current Cyrillic Languages: Hinted Type 1 & TrueType TransCyrillic Plain, Bold, Italic, &

TRANSCYRILLIC SANS SERIF FOR WINDOWS

Bold-Italic Fonts with Polished Bitmaps in 8, 9, 10, 12, 14, 18, 24, 36, 48, & 96 Point Sizes. Includes Five Keyboard Layouts: Russian, Bulgarian, Ukran, Serbian & the AATSEEL-Recommended, Qwerty-Like, Transliterated Keyboard Layout. Specify If for System 6.
Linguist's Software, Inc.

TransCyrillic Sans Serif for Windows. *Version:* 6.3. Apr. 1992. *Items Included:* User's manual, keyboard layout chart, ANSI Chart, keycap sticker sheet. *Customer Support:* Free telephone support; defective disks replaced free.
Windows. IBM or compatibles (4Mb). disk $99.95 ($149.95 for TransCyrillic Professional for Windows which includes Times-Style fonts). *Addl. software required:* MS Windows or ATM. *Optimal configuration:* 4Mb RAM & 386.
Professional-Quality, Hinted, Scalable Fonts in Both TrueType & Type 1 Formats: Times-Style TransCyrillic Plain, Bold, Italic & Bold-Italic. Type 1 Works with ATM & Windows 3.X & OS/2 & AutoCAD r.13. Includes Keyboard Switcher Windows Utility Providing Russian, AATSEEL Transliterated, Ukrainian, Serbian & Bulgarian Keyboard Layouts in Windows Applications. Fonts Alone Work in Word 6 for DOS, WordPerfect 6.0b for DOS, or Newer, AutoCAD r.12 & 13; OS/2; NeXT. Must Upgrade to 6.0a or Newer to Type Overstrikes & Stress Marks. Includes All Major Current Cyrillic Languages: Avar, Azerbaijani, Bashkir, Belarus, Bulgarian, Buriat, Chechen, Chukchi, Chuvash, Dungan, Erzya, Evenki, Kabardian, Kalmyk, Kazakh, Kirghiz, Komi, Lak, Lezgin, Macedonian, Mari, Moksha, Moldavian, Mongolian, Mordvin, Nenets, Ossetian, Ostyak, Russian, Serbian, Tadzhik, Tatar, Turkmen, Tuvan, Udmurt, Ukrainian, Uzbek, Yakut, & Most Old Church Slavic Characters.
Linguist's Software, Inc.

Transend COMplete. Transend Corp. *Compatible Hardware:* HP 150 Touchscreen.
3.5" disk $230.00 (Order no.: 45414A).
Allows Exchange of Electronic Mail with Other Transend Users, or with Users of Mail Services Like THE SOURCE, Quick-Comm, & HPMail Using the XMODEM Protocol. Users Can Also Get Access to Information Services Like Dow Jones & Dialog. In Addition, It Features VT-100 Terminal Emulation.
Hewlett-Packard Co.

Transend 1. *Compatible Hardware:* Apple II, IIe, III. *Operating System(s) Required:* Apple DOS 3.3. *Language(s):* Assembly,. *Memory Required:* 48k.
disk $89.00.
Electronic Communications: Provides Instant Information Exchange with Other Apples, Mainframe Systems, & High Volume Public Networks.
Transend Corp.

Transend 2. *Compatible Hardware:* Apple II, IIe, III. *Operating System(s) Required:* Apple DOS 3.3. *Language(s):* Assembly, BASIC. *Memory Required:* 48k.
disk $149.00.
Transend 1 Options Plus the Ability to Send Large or Multiple Data Files in Complete Confidence over Any Distance. Automatically Checks for Errors & Retransmits Data to Insure Information Arrives Accurately.
Transend Corp.

Transfer. Tim Purves. *Compatible Hardware:* IBM; TRS-80 Model I, Model III, Model 4. *Operating System(s) Required:* MS-DOS 1.0. *Memory Required:* 64k. *General Requirements:* 2 disk drives.
disk $59.95 (ISBN 0-923213-23-6, Order no.: SA-TRA).
Transfers Files Between the TRS-80 & the IBM Using the TRS-80 As the Host Computer.
MichTron, Inc.

Transfer Function Analyzer. *Compatible Hardware:* Apple II with Applesoft; IBM PC. *Memory Required:* 48k, IBM 128k.
$29.95.
Dynacomp, Inc.

TransferTex. *Customer Support:* 800-929-8117 (customer service).
MS-DOS. IBM/PS2. disk $29.99 (ISBN 0-87007-719-8).
Helps Users Design T-Shirt Messages in Four Diffent Letter Sizes. Messages Are Printed Backwards on Regular Printer Paper with Heat Transfer Ink; When User Irons Design onto Cloth, the Letters Are in Readable Order! Users Supply a Color Printer Ribbon, & Color Monitor (& of Course the T-Shirt); TransferTex Does the Rest! Try Lettering Aprons, Team Shirts, Cloth Banners or Any Suitable Cloth Surface.
SourceView Software International.

TransFile-PC3780. *Version:* 6.0. *Compatible Hardware:* IBM PC, PC XT, PC AT, Portable PC, PC compatibles. *Operating System(s) Required:* PC-DOS/MS-DOS, Xenix 286/386. *Memory Required:* 128k. *General Requirements:* TDT Multiprotocol card or UDS Sync-Up modem. *Items Included:* User manual. *Customer Support:* 1 year free.
disk $499.00-$725.00.
File Transfer Program Allows Users to Send & Receive File Between the IBM PCs & Any Other Computer Supporting Any One of the Following Protocols: 2740, 3740, 3741, 2780, 3780. Operates at up to 9600 Baud. User May Define Record Size, Number of Records per Block, Record Separator As ITB or IRS, Trailing Character Supression Such As CR/LF at the End of Each Record, Suppression of Unwanted Characters in Receive, Space Compression, Automatic Error Correction. Remote Start up Is Possible. The PC Can Be Connected As a Slave or Master. Parameters Can Be Given Manually or Contained in a Command File. Programming Interface DOS, XENIX, UNIX V Supported.
TDT Group, Inc.

TransIndic Transliterator. *Version:* 3.0. Jun. 1993. *Items Included:* User's manual, keyboard layout chart. *Customer Support:* Free telephone support; defective disks replaced free.
Macintosh. Macintosh (1Mb). 3.5" disk $149.95. *Addl. software required:* Any word processor. *Optimal configuration:* 4Mb RAM, hard drive.
Professional-Quality, Hinted Times-Style Type-1 & TrueType Font. InduScript Input Method Allows Easy, Phonetic Input of All Characters, Including Conjuncts. Turn on an InduScript Transliteration Script & Type Transliterated Text Automatically. Contains Scripts for North or South Indian Languages. Simple Phonetic Input Method Follows Same InduScript Phonetic Keyboard Layout As Other InduScript-Controlled Languages. Includes Complete User's Manual & InduScript Phonetic Keyboard Chart.
Linguist's Software, Inc.

TransIndic Transliterator for Windows. *Version:* 1.2. Dec. 1994. *Items Included:* User's manual; keyboard layout chart; keycap sticker sheet. *Customer Support:* Free telephone support, defective disks replaced free.
Windows. IBM or compatibles (4Mb). disk $99.95. *Addl. software required:* MS Windows 3.1X or ATM.
Includes All the Characters & Diacritics Necessary to Transliterate Indian Languages & to Type French & German. The Font Includes Seventy-Four (74) Composite Characters Allowing Fast, Simple Placement of Characters with Diacritics for Most Characters Used in the Transliteration of Indian Languages, Using a Deadkey Input Method. The Twenty-Nine (29) Diacritical Marks Used to Create These Composite Characters Are Themselves Also Available Separately As Overstriking Characters Which May Be Combined with Any Character in Any Combination. Eight (8) Other Accents Necessary to Type French & German Are Also Included.
Linguist's Software, Inc.

Transit & Secondary Progressions: M-5. *Compatible Hardware:* Commodore 64, PET, VIC-20.
disk $30.00.
cassette $30.00.
Calculates Natal Chart & Secondary Chart (Transit or Secondary Progression).
Matrix Software.

Transit Search: Where & When: M-14. 1981. *Compatible Hardware:* Apple II; Commodore 64; IBM PC. *Memory Required:* 48k. *General Requirements:* Printer.
disk $100.00 ea.
Apple. (ISBN 0-925182-43-5, Order no.: M-14).
Commodore. (ISBN 0-925182-44-3, Order no.: M-14).
IBM. (ISBN 0-925182-45-1, Order no.: M-14).
Calculates a Natal Chart & Performs a Complete Transit Analysis.
Matrix Software.

Transits & Progressions: M-31. 1980. *Compatible Hardware:* Apple II, II+; Commodore 64, PET; TRS-80. *Memory Required:* 48k. *General Requirements:* Printer.
disk $50.00 ea.
Apple II. (ISBN 0-925182-46-X, Order no.: M-31).
Commodore 64. (ISBN 0-925182-47-8, Order no.: M-31).
TRS-80, Commodore. cassette $50.00.
User Can View Natal & Transit Simultaneously. Lists Angles (RAMC, MC, ASC, VTX) Plus Helio & Geo Longitude/Latitude.
Matrix Software.

Translate. Michael Wagner. *Compatible Hardware:* TRS-80. *Language(s):* BASIC.
disk $49.95.
Converts Any Character to Any Other Character or String. Allows Users to Create Their Own Shorthand & Print Special Characters.
Blue Cat.

Translate English to Spanish: The Ultimate English to Spanish Translation Tool. *Version:* 1.1. Jan. 1989. *Items Included:* 200 page bound manual. Bi-lingual, English & Spanish manual. *Customer Support:* 90 days free support, (305) 477-2750.
DOS 3.3 & 5.0 (640k). 8088 with hard disk (10Mb). 3.5" disk $139.00 (Order no.: TR3). *Optimal configuration:* 386, 80Mb hard disk, 1Mb RAM. *Networks supported:* Stand alone operation only.
5.25" disk $139.00 (Order no.: TR5).
Takes English Text from Your Favorite Word Processor or the Built in Full Featured Text Editor & Translates It into Spanish One Sentence at a Time. Correctly Translates Verbs Phrases & Idiomatic Expressions. Accurately Provides Number & Gender Agreement & Sentences in the Correct Word Order. 85000 Word English/Spanish Dictionary; Add Unlimited Words & Terminology to the Dictionary; Interactive & Batch Mode Translation; Integrated Full Featured Text Editor; Easily Handles Spanish Characters; Bilingual On-Line Help & Manual.
Finalsoft Corp.

TITLE INDEX

Translate It!: To-From (French, German, Spanish). Jun. 1993. *Items Included:* Manual. *Customer Support:* Unlimited technical support; 60 day moneyback guarantee.
DOS. IBM (550k). disk $99.95, German. *Addl. software required:* DOS 5.0 or higher. *Optimal configuration:* IBM 386 or higher compatible computer, 15Mb of avail. hard disk space recommended.
DOS. IBM (450k). disk $99.95, French. *Addl. software required:* DOS 5.0 or higher. *Optimal configuration:* IBM 386 or higher compatible computer, 15Mb of avail. hard disk space recommended.
DOS. IBM (450k). disk $99.95, Spanish. *Addl. software required:* DOS 5.0 or higher. *Optimal configuration:* IBM 386 or higher compatible computer, 15Mb of avail. hard disk spaced recommended.
Easy-to-Use, Whole Document Translation Program for the PC. Fast & Accurate, It Is Ideal for Personal or Business Use. Capable of Translating Whole Documents or Individual Words or Sentences at the Push of a Button. User Can Translate Documents As They Are Created with the Built-In Text Editor, or Import Them from Your Favorite Word Processor. Gives Full-Sentence, Idiomatic Accuracy, & Even Gives User Choices for Translating a World Based on Grammatical Usage. It's Like Having a Language Tutor Built into Your Computer.
Timeworks, Inc.

Translator. Sep. 1994. *Items Included:* Reference manual, example & tutorials. *Customer Support:* Update service - 18% annual covers all software & manual updates. Outside training - contact vendor.
Macintosh System 7 or AIUX3. Macintosh (6Mb). $495.00 copy - site licensing available. *Networks supported:* AppleTalk.
Sun or HP Unix with MAE (Macintosh Application Environment) (10Mb). $495.00 copy.
A Reengineering Utility for Use with the MacAnalyst & MacDesigner CASE Tools. Use It to Generate Structure Charts from C, Pascal, BASIC, or FORTRAN Source Code or Class Diagrams from C Plus Plus or Object-Pascal Code. It Also Populates the Data Dictionary & Allows Doubleclick Access from Diagrams to Code.
Excel Software.

Transport Analysis Using Boundary Elements. P. W. Partridge. Sep 1993. *Items Included:* Manual, including listings of each subroutine of the computer code, & four applications, along with relevant theory. Book: Dual Reciprocity Boundary Element Method.
MS-DOS 3.0 or higher. IBM PC & compatibles (640k). software pkg. $506.00 (ISBN 1-56252-122-5).
Solves the Transport Equation Using the Dual Reciprocity Method. Employs the Simple & Robust Fundamental Solution of the Laplace Equation As an Influence Function, Resulting in Two Boundary Integrals & a Series of Domain Integrals.
Computational Mechanics, Inc.

Transportation Accounting & Control System. 1983. *Compatible Hardware:* PC, PS/2 & compatibles, System 36, RS/6000. *Operating System(s) Required:* AIX, MS-DOS, SSP. *Language(s):* BASIC (source code included). *Memory Required:* IBM 512k, RS/6000 8Mb, S/36 256k. *General Requirements:* Printer, 320Mb - RS/6000, 120Mb - S/36. $5000.00-$18,000.00.
Comprehensive Accounting & Control System- Order Entry, Dispatch Aid, Automatic Freight Rating & Billing, Order Equipment Leasing Costing, Payroll, Owner/Operator Settlements, A/P, A/R & G/L.
Steppenwolff Corp.

Transportation System. *Version:* V8.01. 1994. *Items Included:* 1 full manual for district office & 1 full manual for each school. *Customer Support:* $225/per year per system. Unlimited telephone support, upgrades, new manuals.
MS-DOS 6.2 or higher. IBM-PC 486DX66 mhz (640k School, 8Mb District). Contact publisher for price. Nonstandard peripherals required: 9600 Baud Modem. *Addl. software required:* MS Windows (for the district office). *Networks supported:* Novell Netware, Artisoft Lantastic, Windows NT.
This System Is Used to Keep Track of Each Student's Method of Transportation, Who Should Be Picking Them up, Alternate Drop off Sights, etc. Once Each School Has Entered This Information, It Is Downloaded by Modem to the District Office for the Bus Department to Use. Both Pre-Set & User-Designed Reports Can Be Generated at the School or District Level.
Applied Educational Systems, Inc.

TransRoman. *Version:* 9.0. May 1993. *Items Included:* User's manual, keyboard layout chart. *Customer Support:* Free telephone support; defective disks replaced free.
Any system. Macintosh (1Mb). 3.5" disk $99.95; $50.00 for ea. additional typeface when purchased on the same invoice; $249.95 for TransRoman Professional which incls. all 5 typefaces. *Addl. software required:* Any word processor. *Optimal configuration:* 4Mb RAM, hard drive.
Over 130 Languages in 1 Font! TransRoman Keyboard Optimized for French, German & Spanish. ATM-Compatible, Type-1 & TrueType Plain, Bold, Italic & BoldItalic Fonts. Features 41 Overstrike Accents & Diacritical Mark Keys Each Having Automatic Non-Deleting Backspacing for Fast Typing over Any Letter or Symbol & in Any Combination. All European, Roman Language Characters & Many Others, Including Many American Indian & African Languages. Has 347 Kerning Pairs. EuroScript Allows You to Type the Accents & Special Characters fo 21 European Languages Using Only the Semicolon & Slash Keys to Produce the Special Characters. For Example, All of the Special Characters of Romanian Can Be Produced Just by Typing a Semicolon after the Special Character. Available in Times-Sylte, Helvetica-Style, Palatino-Style, Garamond-Style, & Zaph-Chancery-Style.
Linguist's Software, Inc.

TransRoman Dictionary Font. *Version:* 7.0. 1995. *Items Included:* User's manual; keyboard layout chart; keycap sticker sheet. *Customer Support:* Free telephone support, defective disks replaced free.
Macintosh. Macintosh (1Mb). 3.5" disk $99.95. *Addl. software required:* Any word processor.
ATM-Compatible, Type-1 & TrueType Plain, Bold, Italic & Bold-Italic Font. Features 41 Overstrike Accents & Diacritical Mark Keys Each Having Automatic Non-Deleting Backspacing for Fast Typing over Any Letter or Symbol & in Any Combination. All European, Roman Language Characters & Many Others, Including Many American Indian & African Languages. TransRoman Has 347 Kerning Pairs, TranSlavic 363. EuroScript Allows You to Type Quickly Using the Semicolon, Slash & Backslash Keys to Produce Accented Characters.
Linguist's Software, Inc.

TransRoman Dictionary Font for Windows. *Version:* 2.0. Jun. 1994. *Items Included:* User's manual; keyboard layout chart; keycap sticker sheet. *Customer Support:* Free telephone support, defective disks replaced free.
Windows. IBM or compatibles (4Mb). disk $99.95. *Addl. software required:* MS Windows 3.1X or ATM.

TRANSRUNIC FOR WINDOWS

Over 130 Languages in One Font! ATM-Compatible, Type-1 & TrueType Plain, Bold, Italic, & Bold-Italic Font. Features 41 Overstrike Accents & Diacritical Mark Keys Each Having Automatic, Non-Deleting Backspacing for Fast Typing over Any Letter or Symbol & in Any Combination. All European, Roman Language Characters & Many Others, Including Many American Indian & African Languages. Has 347 Kerning Pairs. TrueType Requires Microsoft Windows 3.1; Also Works with Word 6 for DOS, WordPerfect 6.0b for DOS & AutoCAD R. 13. Type 1 Works with ATM & Windows; Also Works with OS/2 & AutoCAD R.12 & 13. WordPerfect for Windows Users Must Upgrade to Version 6.0a or Newer. A NeXT Version Is Available.
Linguist's Software, Inc.

TransRoman for Windows. *Version:* 3.1. Jul. 1992. *Items Included:* User's manual, keyboard layout chart, ANSI Chart, keycap sticker sheet. *Customer Support:* Free telephone support; defective disks replaced free.
Windows. IBM or compatibles (2-4Mb). disk $99.95; ea. additional typeface family $50.00 when ordered at the same time as any full-priced TransRoman for Windows or TransSlavic for Windows typeface. Professional pack with all 5 typefaces, $249.95. *Addl. software required:* MS Windows or ATM. *Optimal configuration:* 4Mb RAM & 386.
Over 130 Languages in 1 Font! All European, Roman Language Characters & Many Others, Including American-Indian & African Languages. TransRoman Keyboard Optimized for French, German & Spanish. ATM-Compatible, Type-1 & TrueType Plain, Bold, Italic & BoldItalic Fonts. TransRoman & TransSlavic Contain Professional-Quality Hinted, Plain, Bold, Bold-Italic, & Italic Styles in Both TrueType & Type-1 Fonts. TrueType Requires Microsoft Windows 3.1; Also Works with Word 6 for DOS, WordPerfect 6.0b for DOS or Newer & AutoCAD r.13. Type 1 Works with ATM & Windows & OS/2 & AutoCAD r.12 & 13. Must Upgrade to Version 6.0a or Newer. A NeXT Version Is Available. Features 41 Overstrike Accents & Diacritical Mark Keys Each Having Automatic Non-Deleting Backspacing for Typing over Any Letter or Symbol & in Any Combination. TransRoman Has 347 Kerning Pairs. Available in Times-Style, Helvetica-Style, Garamond-Style, Palatino-Style, & Zaph-Chancery-Style.
Linguist's Software, Inc.

TransRunic. Apr. 1995. *Items Included:* User's manual; keyboard layout chart; keycap sticker sheet. *Customer Support:* Free telephone support, defective disks replaced free.
Macintosh. Macintosh (1Mb). 3.5" disk $99.95. *Addl. software required:* Any word processor.
Type-1 & TrueType RunicLS Font with Polished Bitmaps in 10, 12, 14, 18, & 24-Point Sizes. Includes Runes for Germanic, Anglo-Saxon, Kylver, Vadstena, Breza, Danish Runes & Swedo-Norwegian (Short-Twig) Runes.
Linguist's Software, Inc.

TransRunic for Windows. May 1995. *Items Included:* User's manual; keyboard layout chart; keycap sticker sheet. *Customer Support:* Free telephone support, defective disks replaced free.
Windows. IBM or compatibles (4Mb). disk $99.95. *Addl. software required:* MS Windows 3.1X or ATM.
Professional-Quality, Hinted, Scalable Font in Both TrueType & Type 1 Formats: RunicLS Plain. Includes Runes for Germanic, Anglo-Saxon, Kylver, Vadstena, Breza, Danish Runes & Swedo-Norwegian (Short-Twig) Runes. For All Windows 3.1X-Compatible Applications. Type 1 Works with ATM & Windows; Also Works with OS/2 &

TransSlavic. Version: 8.0. Apr. 1993. *Items Included:* User's manual, keyboard layout chart. *Customer Support:* Free telephone support; defective disks replaced free.
  Macintosh. Macintosh (1Mb). 3.5" disk $99.95; $50.00 for ea. additional typeface when purchased on the same invoice; $249.95 for TransSlavic Professional which incls. all 5 typefaces. *Addl. software required:* Any word processor. *Optimal configuration:* 4Mb RAM, hard drive.
Over 130 Languages in 1 Font! Keyboard Optimized for Slavic Languages. ATM-Compatible, Type-1 & TrueType Plain, Bold, Italic & BoldItalic Fonts. Features 41 Overstrike Accents & Diacritical Mark Keys Each Having Automatic Non-Deleting Backspacing for Fast Typing over Any Letter or Symbol & in Any Combination. All European, Roman Language Characters & Many Others, Including Many American Indian & African Languages. Has 363 Kerning Pairs. EuroScript Allows You to Type the Accents & Special Characters of 21 European Languages Using Only the Semicolon & Slash Keys to Produce the Special Characters. For Example, All of the Special Characters of Romanian Can Be Produced Just by Typing a Semicolon after the Special Character. Available in Times-Style, Helvetica-Style, Palatino-Style, Garamond-Style, & Zaph-Chancery-Style.
Linguist's Software, Inc.

TransSlavic for Windows. Version: 4.1. Jun. 1992. *Items Included:* User's manual, keyboard layout chart, ANSI Chart, keycap sticker sheet. *Customer Support:* Free telephone support; defective disks replaced free.
  Windows. IBM or compatibles (2-4Mb). disk $99.95; ea. additional typeface family $50.00 when ordered at the same time as any full-priced TransRoman for Windows or TransSlavic for Windows typeface. Professional pack with all 5 typefaces, $249.95. *Addl. software required:* MS Windows or ATM. *Optimal configuration:* 4Mb RAM & 386.
Over 130 Languages in 1 Font! All European, Roman Language Characters & Many Others, Including American-Indian & African Languages. TransRoman & TransSlavic Contain Professional-Quality, Hinted, Plain, Bold, Bold-Italic, & Italic Styles in Both TrueType & Type-1 Fonts. TrueType Requires Microsoft Windows 3.1; Also Works with Word 6 for DOS, WordPerfect 6.0b for DOS or Newer & AutoCAD r.13. Type 1 Works with ATM & Windows & OS/2 & AutoCAD r.12 & 13. Must Upgrade to Version 6.0a or Newer. A NeXT Version Is Available. Features 41 Overstrike Accents & Diacritical Mark Keys Each Having Automatic Non-Deleting Backspacing for Typing over Any Letter or Symbol & in Any Combination. Has 363 Kerning Paris. Available in Times-Style, Helvetica-Style, Garamond-Style, Palatino-Style, & Zaph-Chancery-Style.
Linguist's Software, Inc.

Transverter Pro. Version: 2.0. Nov. 1994. *Items Included:* Up to 3 3.5" floppy disks w/license, manual, misc. paper. *Customer Support:* Tech support available at no additional charge by phone: (216) 382-1787 9AM-4PM EST. via CompuServe: 72410,2053.
  Windows 3.1. 386 or higher (8Mb). disk $395.00 (ISBN 1-57459-200-9, Order no.: PT9). *Networks supported:* Works with all.
  Macintosh System 7.0. 68020 processor or higher (5Mb). 3.5" disk $395.00 (ISBN 1-57459-201-7, Order no.: PT10). *Networks supported:* Works with all.
Translate, Convert & View PostScript Files. This Complete Level 2, Software-Based, Interpreter & Softproofing Tool Transforms PostScript Print Files into Editable Graphics. RIPs Files to the Screen for Accurate Viewing & Document Portability. Built-In Error Log Identifies PostScript Errors That May Cause Imagesetter Failure.
TechPool Studios.

TrapWise: Domestic. Jan. 1993. *Customer Support:* For customer service, product registration, upgrades, technical support, & CustomerFirst service plans, customers may call Aldus Customer Services at (206) 628-2320.
  Macintosh. Contact publisher for price (ISBN 1-56026-158-7).
Aldus Corp.

Trash Man. *Compatible Hardware:* TRS-80. *Memory Required:* 16k.
  disk $23.95.
Arcade Game.
Dynacomp, Inc.

Traum Condex Brain & Behavior. May 1990. *Items Included:* Diskettes, instruction book.
  MS-DOS/PC-DOS 2.0 or higher. IBM & compatibles (540k). disk $49.95 (ISBN 0-945541-07-4, Order no.: 074).
Artificially Intelligent Program Designed To Diagnose & Prescribe Treatment For Common Neurological & Neuropsychological Deficits. User Communicates with the Program by Typing in Sentence Queries. Program Responds by Providing Precise Answers To the Questions Based on the Available Information.
CSY Publishing, Inc.

TRAUMATIX. Version: 2.0. *Customer Support:* Toll free telephone support.
  DOS 3.1 or higher. IBM PC & compatibles. disk $595.00.
This Solution is an Injury Registry That Gives a Private Physician all the Amenities Usually Restricted to Large Hospital-Based or Statewide Systems. To Register a New Case, the User Records Patient Demographies, then Labels Each Trauma Diagnosis from a Lightbar Menu to Quickly Select any of 440 Different ICD-9-CM Diagnosis Codes Stored in the System...Wounds, Fractures, Toxic Effects & all Forms of Injury. The Second Step Gives a Priority Grading to Record Acuteness. Next, all Stabilizing Modalities are Recorded, Sorted under Category Headings That Include Airway, Pulmonary, Vascular, etc. Finally, Patient Response is Registered. The Entire Process Takes Only a Minute or Two. Once Registered, any Record Can be Examined, Modified or Amended. Patterns of Information Across the Entire Registry are Found Using Simple Query Categories. Precise Parameters for Each Category are Typed & the System Displays Every Record That Fits the Chosen Criteria.
SRC Systems, Inc.

Travel Adventure. *Customer Support:* All of our products are unconditionally guaranteed.
  DOS, Mac. CD-ROM disk $39.95 (Order no.: TRAVEL). *Nonstandard peripherals required:* CD-ROM drive.
395 Quality Photos from Around the World. Plus 16-Page Book.
Walnut Creek CDRom.

Travel Expense Management System (TEMS). Version: 3.0. *Compatible Hardware:* Graphics card. *Operating System(s) Required:* PC-DOS/MS-DOS. *Memory Required:* 512k. *Customer Support:* 10% of purchase price.
  disk $7995.00.
Input & Approval of Employee Expense Information. Reconciles Credit Card Statements, Tracks Travel Advances, Payments by Checks or Wire Transfers. Maintains Budget & Interfaces with Mini or Mainframe Host Computer. Report Writer Allows for Graphing with Detail & History Reporting. Also Includes Security & Audit Trail.
Computer Related Services, Inc.

Traveler's Hotline Industry Database. Version: I. Dorthy DuBois. Mar. 1992. *Items Included:* 1 User Manual. *Customer Support:* 90-Day Unlimited warranty.
  MS-DOS 3.1 or higher. IBM Compatible (60k). disk $149.95 (ISBN 1-880581-00-0, Order no.: THIDB-001I). *Nonstandard peripherals required:* 1200 Baud Modem for Direct Telephone Dialing Access. *Addl. software required:* Word Processing with ASCII Format & Mail Merge Capabilities. *Optimal configuration:* DOS operating system Database.
  MS-DOS 3.1 or higher. Macintosh (60k). 3.5" disk $149.95 (ISBN 1-880581-01-9, Order no.: THIDB-002M). *Nonstandard peripherals required:* 1200 Baud Modem for Direct telephone dialing access. *Addl. software required:* Word Processing with ASCII Format & Mail Merge Capabilities.
Database of Over 12,000 Domestic & International Travel- Related Services. Toll-Free "800" Phone Numbers for Telephone Direct Dial Modem Access, for Reservations & Information. Operates on MS/DOS in ASCII Format for Use with Word Processing Mail Merge Operations. User-Friendly with Extensive Add-On Capabilities for Making Domestic & International Reservations & Maintenance Updated Mailing Lists.
Visions Resource Publishing, Inc.

Traveling SideKick. Dec. 1985. *Compatible Hardware:* IBM PC & true compatibles, PCjr, PC XT, PC AT, Portable PC. *Operating System(s) Required:* PC-DOS/MS-DOS 2.0 or higher. *Memory Required:* 256k. *General Requirements:* SideKick program, printer.
  $69.95 (ISBN 0-87524-149-2).
Combination of Binder & Software. The Software Prints Out Information Already in SideKick Files & Includes Report-Generating Software Able to Produce Up-to-Date Telephone Lists, Address Lists, Meeting Schedules, Travel Itineraries, Calendars, etc. Users Can Get Printed Daily/Weekly/Monthly/Yearly Calendar Forms, Alphabetized Address Book Forms, etc.
Borland International, Inc.

Travelrama U. S. A. Feb. 1996. *Customer Support:* Telephone support - free (except phone charge).
  System 6.0.7 or higher. 256 color Mac with 68030 processor (4Mb). CD-ROM disk $12.99 (ISBN 1-57594-120-1). *Nonstandard peripherals required:* 2x CD-ROM drive, mouse, 640/480 resolution monitor.
Using a Richly Detailed, Realistic Rand McNally Road Map As Their Guide, One to Four Players Scour the United States in Search of Monuments, National Parks, & Historical Locations. The Goal Is to Collect Postcards by Visiting Specified Locations & Playing Interactive Games.
Kidsoft, Inc.

Treasures of Russia. Intersoft, Inc. Jan. 1996. *Items Included:* Registration card. *Customer Support:* Tel 360-650-0534, 90 limited warranty.
  Windows. 386DX, 8-bit (4Mb). CD-ROM disk $69.95.
Tour of Russia's 5 Great National Museums. Art from 10-20th Centuries.
Cascade Marketing International, Inc.

TITLE INDEX

The Treasury of Scripture Knowledge. Thomas Scott et al. Mar. 1993. *Items Included:* Disks, marketing literature, order form, one Addendum Manual-perfect bound. *Customer Support:* No fee for customer support: 30 day money back guarantee, limited replacement warranty on diskettes defective at time of purchase, free telephone technical support.
PC-DOS/MS-DOS 3.1 or higher or Windows 3.1 or higher. 386/486 or 100% IBM PC compatible for Windows, Also AT/XT/286 for DOS (640k for DOS or 4Mb for Windows). disk $39.95 (ISBN 1-56514-775-8). *Addl. software required:* Biblesoft's PC Study Bible, DOS 3.0 or higher or Windows 1.7 or higher & KJV Text. *Optimal configuration:* 5.25" 1.2Mb disk drive for installation & 3.5Mb of hard drive space, mouse or pointer device recommended.
The Complete Set of Cross References from the Treasury of Scripture Knowledge. Nearly One Million Cross-References with the Ability to Add Your Own - an Add-On to Be Used with Biblesoft's PC Study Bible.
Biblesoft.

The Treasury of Scripture Knowledge. Canne et al. Apr. 1994. *Items Included:* Disks, marketing literature, order form. *Customer Support:* No fee for customer support: 30 day money back guarantee, limited replacement warranty on diskettes defective at time of purchase, free telephone technical support.
PC-DOS/MS-DOS 3.1 or higher or Windows 3.1 or higher. IBM 386/486 or 100% compatible for Windows, Also AT/XT/286 for DOS (640k for DOS or 4Mb for Windows). 3.5" disk $69.95 (ISBN 1-56514-773-1). *Optimal configuration:* 3.5" 1.44Mb disk drive for installation & 3.5Mb of hard drive space, mouse or pointer device recommended.
Nearly One Million Cross References attached to the Key Phrases in Every Bible Verse, Themes/ Thoughts Chained Together with Other Verses Using Similar Themes and/or Thoughts.
Biblesoft.

The Treasury of Scripture Knowledge. Thomas Scott et al. Mar. 1993. *Items Included:* One addendum manual - perfect bound. *Customer Support:* No fee for customer support: (1) 30 day money back guarantee (2) Lifetime warranty replacement on defective disks (3) Free telephone technical support.
PC-DOS/MS-DOS 3.1 or higher. IBM PC, XT/AT/286/386/486 or 100% compatibles (640k). disk $49.95 (ISBN 1-56514-775-8). *Addl. software required:* PC Study Bible 3.0 or higher & KJV text. *Optimal configuration:* Requires 5 1/4" 1.2Mb disk drive for installation & 3Mb of hard drive space. Mouse or pointer device recommended.
PC-DOS/MS-DOS 3.1 or higher. IBM PC, XT/AT/286/386/486 or 100% compatibles (640k). 3.5" disk $49.95 (ISBN 1-56514-773-1). *Addl. software required:* PC Study Bible 3.0 or higher & KJV text. *Optimal configuration:* Requires 3 1/2" disk drive for installation & 3.5Mb of hard drive space. Mouse or pointer device recommended.
Complete Set of Cross-References from The Treasury of Scripture Knowledge. Nearly One Million Cross-References with the Ability to Add Your Own.

Tree Charts. *Version:* 3.4. Alexander G. Smith. 1985. *Compatible Hardware:* Apple II+, IIe, IIc, IIgs; Commodore 64; IBM PC & compatibles. *Operating System(s) Required:* Apple DOS 3.3, ProDOS, PC-DOS/MS-DOS. *Language(s):* BASIC. *Memory Required:* Apple & Commodore-64k; IBM-128k. *General Requirements:* "Family Roots" or Lineages database; hard disk & printer optional. *Customer Support:* 60-day unlimited warranty, toll-free phone.
disk $39.00.
Apple DOS. (ISBN 0-917169-20-4).
Commodore. (ISBN 0-917169-12-3).
IBM. (ISBN 0-917169-36-0).
ProDOS. disk $39.00 (ISBN 0-917169-25-5).
Makes "English-Style" Box Charts (Like Organizational Charts) on Multiple Pages That Must Be Put Together to Form the Whole Chart. Works on Family Roots Data Base or on Data Imported via GEDCOM using FAMILY LINKS.
Quinsept, Inc.

Tree Easy. 1991.
MS-DOS 3.0 or higher. IBM PC compatibles (640k). $14.95. *Nonstandard peripherals required:* Hard drive or 2 diskette drives 5.25" or 3.5". *Optimal configuration:* 2 diskette drives or hard disk, color display (graphics OK but not required), any printer.
A Start-Up Genealogy System! Can Also Be Used As an Add-On to FAMILY REUNION or Vice Versa). Has a Graphical Based Data Entry Screen That Allows You to Easily Visualize Relationships As You Enter Them.
FAMware.

Tree86: The Hard Disk Management System. *Version:* 4.3. *Compatible Hardware:* IBM PC & compatibles. *Operating System(s) Required:* PC-DOS/MS-DOS 3.0 or higher. *Items Included:* Manual, diskette. *Customer Support:* Technical support, 9-5 Mon-Fri CST, 30 day moneyback guarantee.
disk $89.95.
A File Management Tool, Sophisticated, yet Easy to Use. Network Compatible. Options Accessed with Pull-Down Menus. Directories Displayed in a Graphic Format; Files Can Be Sorted in 10 Different Ways. Handles 16,000 Files in 2,000 Sub-Directories & Even Works Across Drives. Options Include Xcopy, Tag, Sort, Find Files, Text Search, Archive Files, Kill or Move Directories. Includes Alt/Edit, a Full-Featured, Pure ASCII Editor.
The Aldridge Co.

TreeSaver. *Version:* 3.1. Don Thomson. Aug. 1989. *Items Included:* License agreement, 3 1/2" diskette & 5 1/4" diskette, 112 page spiral bound manual, owners registration card. *Customer Support:* Telephone support to registered users (415) 769-2902 at no charge - weekdays 9 am-5 pm (PST).
PC-DOS/MS-DOS 2.1 or higher (25k), supports expanded memory. IBM PC, XT, AT, PS/2 & compatibles. $89.95 (ISBN 0-9623715-0-5). *Nonstandard peripherals required:* LaserJet Plus & LaserJet Series II, LaserJet IIp, LaserJet II-D, LaserJet III, IIID, IIIp, IIIsi, & compatible laser printers.
Memory-Resident Printing Utility for the HP LaserJet. It Allows Existing Software to Print Two, Three, Four or More Pages on One, Thereby Saving Paper, Copying, FAX & Storage Costs. Also "Photo-Reduces" Single Pages, Allowing Software Programs to Print "Shrink-to-Fit" Reports for Day-Timer & Other Organizers. Shrinks Graphic Images & Supports LaserJet Soft Fonts & Macros. Prints on Letter, Legal, Executive & A4 Paper. "Make Book" Feature Prints Pages in First-Last Sequence for Saddle Bound Books & Pamphlets.
Discoversoft, Inc.

Treetop. *Version:* 2.40. Oct. 1989. *Items Included:* Spiral bound manual.
MS-DOS (256k). IBM PC or compatible. disk $39.00.
General Purpose Software Utility That Helps User Organize Files & Directories on Hard Drive. Copy, Move, Sort, Print, Execute, Find, Delete, Rename, Display or Change the Date/Time of a File or Groups of Files, or Perform Similar Operations on Directories.
Kilgore Software.

TRG - Treatment Resource Guide: For NY, CA, PA, NJ. Michael G. Chan. Feb. 1989.
PC-DOS (512k). 3.5" or 5.25" disk $119.95 (Order no.: TRG89CD). *Nonstandard peripherals required:* 1 hard drive, 2 floppy drives.
Directory of All Licensed or Certified Facilities Treating Alcoholism, Drug Abuse or Other Addictions in New York, Pennsylvania, New Jersey & Connecticut. Proprietary Program Permits Searches by Type of Treatment Provided, Special Populations Served, Location (Zip Code, Town, County), Insurance Acceptances & Other Criteria. Windows & Help Menus Are Featured.
Morgan-Rand Publishing Co.

Trial Size Toolbox. *Version:* 1.0. *Compatible Hardware:* Apple II series. *Operating System(s) Required:* Apple DOS 3.3. *Memory Required:* 48k.
disk free (ISBN 0-927796-33-3, Order no.: 961).
Functional Demo Which Allows Users to Add Nearly 20 New Commands to Any Applesoft Program, Create Hi-Res Graphs & Charts, Musical Tones, & Format Text Sent to the Screen or Printer. Prints Its Own 50 Page Manual for Details on Using All Commands.
Roger Wagner Publishing, Inc.

Triflex: Pipe Stress Analysis. AAA Technologies & Specialties Co., Inc. Jan. 1988. *Compatible Hardware:* IBM PC, PC XT, PC AT & compatibles. *Operating System(s) Required:* PC-DOS/MS-DOS 3.1. *Language(s):* Assembler, C, FORTRAN. *Memory Required:* 640k. *General Requirements:* Hard disk, math coprocessor. *Customer Support:* 30 day money-back guarantee, MES available.
disk $7990.00, incl. 250-page manual (Order no.: 484).
Performs a Complete Static Analysis & Analysis of Mode Shapes & Natural Frequencies As Well As Response Spectra. Features Include Nonlinear Restraints, AUTOCAD Interface, Interactive Full-Screen Input or Key Word Line Input, Unlimited Problems Size & Code Compliance Reports. Output Includes System Deflections & Rotations, Forces & Moments, Stresses, Springer Hanger Design, & Analysis Summary.
Gulf Publishing Co.

Trig Expert. *Items Included:* Bound manual. *Customer Support:* Free hotline - no time limit; 30 day limited warranty; updates are $5/disk plus S&H.
MS-DOS. IBM & compatibles (128k). disk $69.95. *Nonstandard peripherals required:* IBM color graphics board (or equivalent).
Define the Geometry of the Problem, & TRIG EXPERT Accurately Figures Out Everything Else (the Lengths of the Unknown Sides, Unknown Angles, etc.). Architects, Draftsmen, Surveyors, Designers, & Many Others Can Save Huge Amounts of Time & Avoid Drudgery with TRIG EXPERT (& Be More Secure of Accurate Results!). Describe the Geometry of the Problem by Giving Coordinate Points, Line Lengths, and/ or Angles at Strategic Locations (e.g., Coordinates of the Intersections of Lines; Angles Between Lines; Tangent Points of Arcs; Tangent Points of Straight Lines & Arcs; Starting & Ending Points of Arcs; Foci of Ellipses; Centers of Circles & Arcs; Points on Lines, Circles, Chords, Curves, etc.). In Short, Describe the Problem, & TRIG EXPERT Will Supply the Missing Information.
Dynacomp, Inc.

Trig Expert. 1995. *Items Included:* Full manual. *Customer Support:* Free telephone support - 90 days, 30-day warranty.
MS-DOS 3.2 or higher. 286 (584k). disk $69.95. *Nonstandard peripherals required:* CGA/EGA/VGA.
You Describe the Geometry of the Problem, & TRIG EXPERT Accurately Figures Out Everything Else (the Lengths of the Unknown Sides, Unknown Angles, etc.) Architects, Draftsmen, Surveyors, Designers, & Many Others Can Save Huge Amounts of Time & Avoid Drudgery. You Describe the Geometry of the Problem by Giving Coordinate Points, Line Lengths, and/or Angles at Strategic Locations (e.g., Coordinates of the Intersections of Lines; Angles Between Lines; Tangent Points of Arcs; Tangent Points of Straight Lines & Arcs; Starting & Ending Points of Arcs; Foci of Ellipses; Centers of Circles & Arcs; Points on Lines, Circles, Chords, Curves, etc.).
Dynacomp, Inc.

Triggy! Donald L. Lloyd. Aug. 1988.
Sharp 1250A Pocket Computer. disk $165.00 (ISBN 0-9623900-0-3).
Performs Routine Shop Math Calculations.
Chips & Dips.

Trigonometry - Pre-Calculus. Jan. 1994. *Items Included:* Program on CD-ROM, CD Booklet, & Registration Card. *Customer Support:* Free unlimited support via telephone.
Windows 3.1 or higher running under DOS 5.0 or higher. 386 SX (4Mb RAM; 500k low Dos Mem; 6Mb free disk space). CD-ROM disk $49.00 (ISBN 1-57268-025-3, Order no.: 53105). *Nonstandard peripherals required:* Sound card (either: Sound Blaster - 8, 16, PRO; Media Vision ProAudio Spectrum; or Microsoft Sound System); MPC Compatible CD-ROM drive; VGA monitor; & microphone. *Optimal configuration:* 25MHz 386 SX.
High School Math for Windows. These Programs Offer Interactive Instruction for High-School-Aged Students. These CD-ROMs Contain Interactive Lessons Which Parallel the Pre-Algebra Concepts Taught in Eighth & Ninth Grades. Algebra 1 Reinforces Major Algebraic Concepts Your Child Must Master in School. Individual CD-ROMs for Geometry, Algebra 2, & Trigonometry Complement Programs for Grades Nine Through Twelve.
Conter Software.

Trillium Type Sender. Dale C. Jones. Jan. 1985. *Compatible Hardware:* Apple II, II+, IIc, IIe; IBM PC, PC XT, PC AT, PCjr; Wang PC. *Memory Required:* 48k.
disk $99.95 ea.
IBM. (ISBN 0-89824-135-9, Order no.: 135-9).
Wang. (ISBN 0-89824-136-7, Order no.: 136-7).
Apple. (ISBN 0-89824-134-0, Order no.: 134-0).
Transform Word Processed Material into Copy to Be Cast & Sent.
Trillium Pr.

Trilogy. Version: 1.3.0. Aug. 1988. *Compatible Hardware:* Apple II series, IIgs. *Memory Required:* Apple II series 64k, Apple IIgs 256k.
Apple II series. 3.5" disk $49.95 (ISBN 1-55616-052-6).
Apple IIgs. 3.5" disk $49.95 (ISBN 1-55616-053-4).
Adventure Games.
DAR Systems International.

TRIM. Sep. 1988. *Compatible Hardware:* IBM PC & 100% compatibles. *Operating System(s) Required:* PC-DOS/MS-DOS. *Memory Required:* 640k. *General Requirements:* 10Mb on hard disk, wide carriage printer with compressed print capabilities. *Customer Support:* Telephone support, regulatory compliance, product enhancements, newsletters.
$2995.00.
Processes Incoming Returned Items for Users. The System Processes Reclears & Charge Backs. The Tickler Feature Reminds Operators to Follow-Up on Large, "Called-In" Items. The System Generates Customer Notices Automatically & Prints Charges & Disbursements. Also Offers Consolidated Items & Multiple Customer Notices. Compliance with Regulation DD Included.
Learned-Mahn.

Trinity. Brian Moriarty. Jun. 1986. *Compatible Hardware:* Apple II, II+, IIe, IIc, Macintosh; Atari ST; Commodore 128, Amiga; IBM PC & compatibles.
Apple II, Macintosh, Atari ST, Amiga, IBM. disk $39.95.
Commodore 128. $34.95.
It's the Last Day of Your $599 London Vacation. Unfortunately, It's Also the First Day of World War III. Only Seconds Remain Before an H-Bomb Vaporizes the City... & You with It. Unless You Escape to a Secret Universe, a Plane Between Fantasy & Reality, Where Every Atomic Explosion Is Mysteriously Connected. You'll Crisscross Time & Space As You Explore This Fascinating Universe, Learning to Control Its Inexorable Power. TRINITY Takes You Back to the Dawn of the Atomic Age... & Puts the Course of History in Your Hands.
Activision, Inc.

Triple Blockade. *Compatible Hardware:* Atari 400, 800. *Language(s):* Atari BASIC (source code included). *Memory Required:* 48k.
disk $18.95.
Action Game for 2 or 3 Players.
Dynacomp, Inc.

Triple-Dump. Mark Simonsen & Rob Renstrom. Mar. 1986. *Compatible Hardware:* Apple II, II+, IIe, IIc, IIgs. *Operating System(s) Required:* Apple DOS 3.3, ProDOS. *Language(s):* Machine, BASIC. *Memory Required:* DOS 3.3 48k, ProDOS 64k.
disk $39.95.
"Print Anything" Utility That Lets Users Transfer Images from the Screen to Any Dot Matrix (Graphics Capable) Printer. Will Print Three Kinds of Images: Hi-Res & Double Hi-Res, Lo-Res & Double Lo-Res, 40 & 80-Column Text. Images May Be Cropped, Rotated, Reversed (Negative), Magnified & Printed in a Variety of Densities (Depending on the Printer). Includes a Banner Maker That Prints Signs with 8-Inch High Characters.
Beagle Brothers.

TripMaster/2000. Version: 2.01. May 1990. *Items Included:* Spiral-bound user's guide, self training tutorial & tutorial data. *Customer Support:* Telephone support: $2.00 per min (Master Card, Visa).
MS-DOS/PC-DOS 2.0 or higher. IBM XT, AT, PS/2 & compatibles (512k). disk $49.50 (Order no.: TM2000).
Manage Golfing Trips & Local Play Including Costs, Transportation, & Accommodations. Print/Display Computerized Scorecards Including Rating, Slope, & Hole by Hole Yardages, Par, & Handicap Information for Three Sets of Tees. Schedule Courses, Playing Groups & Tee Times. Prints Personalized Golfer Trip Sheets, Schedules. Prints Master Playing Schedule for Group Coordinator.
Focus/2000, Inc.

TriSpectives Professional: The New Standard for 3D. Sep. 1995. *Items Included:* 4 manuals: Getting Started Guide. User's Guide, Reference Manual, Advanced Tips & Tricks manual (Prof. version only). Computer-based tutorials. *Customer Support:* Telephone support at customer's cost after initial free call. Free electronic support (BBC, Fax, etc.).
Windows 95 or Windows NT 3.51 or higher. 486 or Pentium running at 33MHz or more; 15Mb hard disk (16Mb). disk $499.95 (ISBN 0-9648089-1-9). *Nonstandard peripherals required:* VGA, Super VGA, or other card supported by Windows 95 or Windows NT 3.51. *Optimal configuration:* Pentium computer with 16Mb RAM; CD-ROM drive. *Networks supported:* Windows 95/NT.
$499.95 25-user copy (ISBN 0-9648089-3-5).
$499.95 100-user copy (ISBN 0-9648089-5-1).
$499.95 1000-user copy (ISBN 0-9648089-7-8).
$499.95 Manual Set.
A Multi-Function 3D Drawing Program for Windows 95. It Combines Precise ACIS-Based 3D Modeling, Creative Page-Based 3D Illustration, Drag & Drop Real-Time 3D Animation, & Comprehensive Import/Export Features. It Is the Ideal Solution for All Product Designers, Graphics Illustrators, Artists & Multimedia Content Developers.
3D-Eye, Inc.

TriSpectives: The New Standard for 3D. Sep. 1995. *Items Included:* 3 manuals: Getting Started Guide. User's Guide, ReEference Manual, Computer-based tutorials. *Customer Support:* Telephone support at customer's cost after initial free call. Free electronic support (BBC, Fax, etc.).
Windows 95 or Windows NT 3.51 or higher. 486 or Pentium running at 33MHz or more; 15Mb hard disk (8Mb). disk $299.95 (ISBN 0-9648089-0-0). *Nonstandard peripherals required:* VGA, Super VGA, or other card supported by Windows 95 or Windows NT 3.51. *Optimal configuration:* Pentium computer with 8Mb RAM; CD-ROM drive. *Networks supported:* Windows 95/NT.
$299.95 25-user copy (ISBN 0-9648089-2-7).
$299.95 100-user copy; TriSpectives Professional $499.95 (ISBN 0-9648089-4-3).
$299.95 1000-user copy; TriSpectives Professional $499.95 (ISBN 0-9648089-6-X).
$299.95 Manual Set; TriSpectives Professional $499.95 (ISBN 0-9648089-8-6).
A Multi-Function 3D Drawing Program for Windows 95. With over 1,000 Professionally Designed 3D Clipart Models, You Can Use TriSpectives to Add Exciting 3D Animations to Your Presentations, Create Professional 3D Illustrations for Your Brochures, Flyers & Posters, & Produce High-Impact 3D Drawings for Your Diagrams & Reports.
3D-Eye, Inc.

Triton College Administrative Software: Student Records & Registration. Version: Current. 1980. *Items Included:* Completely documented, on-line help functions, source code included. *Customer Support:* Implementation & customization support.
MCP/AS. UNISYS - A-Series (12Mb). $36,750.00.
Performs Approximately 300 On-Line Real-Time Functions in the Following Major Areas: Student Records & Registration; Personnel; Payroll; Position Control; General Ledger, A/P, A/R; Career Planning & Placement; Electronic Mail; Voice Response Touch Tone Registration; Student Transfer Articulation.
MCS Management Corp.

TRITUS SPF. Version: 1.2.6. Jan. 1994. *Items Included:* 2 Tritus SPF manuals, 1 Tritus SPF Quick Reference Guide, & 1 License Agreement/Registration Card. *Customer Support:* Free technical support by phone.
AIX 3.2 or higher. any RISC processor running AIX. disk $425.00 (ISBN 1-882787-02-1).
A Text Editor That Provides True ISPF/PDF

Compatibility & an Excellent Programming Environment for OS/2, DOS & AIX Users. Supports Full-Featured REXX Macro Interface That Works in DOS, OS/2 & AIX. Macro & Built-In Commands May Be Assigned to Virtually Any Key Combination.
Tritus, Inc.

TRITUS SPF. Version: 1.2.5. Sep. 1993. *Items Included:* 2 Tritus SPF manuals, 1 Tritus SPF Quick Reference Guide, 1 REXX manual, & 1 License Agreement/Registration Card. *Customer Support:* Free technical support by phone.
DOS 2.1 or higher, Protected Mode DOS 3.3 or higher. IBM & true compatibles (512k). disk $124.00 (ISBN 1-882787-01-3). *Addl. software required:* TRITUS REXX. *Optimal configuration:* at least 2Mb of XMS. *Networks supported:* All.
OS/2 1.2 or higher. IBM & true compatible computers. disk $124.00. *Addl. software required:* TRITUS REXX. *Networks supported:* All.
A Text Editor That Provides True ISPF/PDF Compatibility & an Excellent Programming Environment for OS/2 & DOS Users. Supports Full-Featured REXX Macro Interface That Works in DOS & OS/2. Macro & Built-In Commands May Be Assigned to Virtually Any Key Combination.
Tritus, Inc.

TRITUS SPF. Version: 1.2.6. Jan. 1994. *Items Included:* 2 Tritus SPF manuals, 1 Tritus SPF Quick Reference Guide, 1 REXX manual, & 1 License Agreement/Registration Card. *Customer Support:* Free technical support by phone.
AIX 3.2 or higher. any RISC processor running AIX. disk $620.00 (ISBN 1-882787-03-X). *Addl. software required:* REXX/6000.
A Text Editor That Provides True ISPF/PDF Compatibility & an Excellent Programming Environment for OS/2, DOS & AIX Users. Supports Full-Featured REXX Macro Interface That Works in DOS, OS/2 & AIX. Macro & Built-In Commands May Be Assigned to Virtually Any Key Combination.
Tritus, Inc.

Trivia Challenge. *Items Included:* Bound manual. *Customer Support:* Free hotline - no time limit; 30 day limited warranty; updates are $5/disk plus S&H.
Apple (256k). disk $19.95.
From 1 to 4 Players or Teams Compete in Answering Questions in 5 Categories (Entertainment, Sports, History, Geography, & Miscellaneous). There Are over 1,600 Questions on the Data Disk. Included at No Extra Charge Is the Trivia Development System Which Allows You to Create Your Own Trivia Data Disk. You Can Generate Your Own Categories & Questions Even If You Have No Programming Knowledge.
Dynacomp, Inc.

Trivia Challenge. *Compatible Hardware:* Atari ST.
3.5" disk $39.95.
Nearly 4,000 Questions on International Sport, the Arts, Pop Music, Science & General Knowledge. Arcade Style Play Keeps the Game Quick. Users Can Add Their Own Questions.
MichTron, Inc.

Trivia Warehouse 2000. *Customer Support:* Free, unlimited.
System 6 Mac. 030 Mac, 256 colors (4Mb). CD-ROM disk $24.95. *Nonstandard peripherals required:* Sound card, CD-ROM drive.
Windows 3.1 PC. 486 PC (4Mb). *Nonstandard peripherals required:* Any Windows supported sound card, CD-ROM drive.
Contains Two Thousand Trivia Questions, from 45 Categories, in Several Game Formats. Test Your Memory with the Q&A, Concentration, & Multiple Choice Games! Categories Include: Animals, Bodies, Bond, Bugs, Cities, Comics, Computers, Firsts, Food, Games, Geography, Gilligan, Gross, Health, Holidays, Horrors, Kids, Knot's Landing, Math, Movies, Music, Novels, Pairs, People, Presidents, Puzzles, Royals, Scandals, Science, Sing, Space, Spare Parts, Sports, States, Talk Radio, TV, Twilight Zone, Wierd, & More.
BeachWare.

Trivia 102. Ralph Stoeber et al. *Compatible Hardware:* IBM PC, PCjr, PC XT, PC AT, Portable PC, 3270 PC with IBM Color Display & one double-sided disk drive. *Memory Required:* 128k. disk $19.95 (Order no.: 6276599).
Trivia Game Including over 2000 Questions & Almost 200 Categories to Choose From. Up to 14 People Can Play at One Time.
Personally Developed Software, Inc.

Trivia 103: Challenges for Young People. Ralph Stoeber et al. *Compatible Hardware:* IBM PC, PCjr, PC XT, PC AT, Portable PC, 3270 PC with IBM Color Display & one double-sided disk drive. *Memory Required:* 128k.
disk $19.95 (Order no.: 6276610).
Trivia Game Including 5000 Questions Which Cover More Than 150 Categories. Topics Range from Heroes to Hobbies, Cartoons to Colors, Ocean Life to Outer Space. Up to 14 People Can Play at One Time.
Personally Developed Software, Inc.

TRNSYS: A Transient System Simulation Program. Version: 13.1. 1991. *Compatible Hardware:* IBM & compatibles, Macintosh, & any computer with a Fortran-77 Compiler. *Memory Required:* 300k. *Items Included:* Manual. *Customer Support:* Phone line for questions & assistance.
$700.00.
Modular Simulation Program for Modeling Thermal Systems. User Creates a File Specifying the Components Used in the System & How They Are Connected & TRNSYS Simulates That Component System. TRNSYS Library Includes Many of the Components Commonly Found in Thermal Energy Systems, As Well As Component Routines to Handle Input of Weather Data or Other Time Dependent Forcing Functions & Output of Simulation Results. Users May Add Their Own Components to the Library. System Includes Utility Components, Solar Collectors, Thermal Storage Systems, Heating & Cooling Equipment, Hydronic Equipment, Building Loads & Structures, Controllers, Output, Heat Exchangers, & Combined Subsystems. Packet Includes: an Executable TRNSYS, Fifty Components, Debug - to Help Troubleshoot User Components, PTRNSYS - to Reduce the Size of TRNSYS, Prep- to Create Transfer Function Coefficients for Walls, Roofs, etc., & BID- to Create Multi-Zone Building Descriptions.
Univ. of Wisconsin-Madison Solar Energy Laboratory.

The Trojan War. John Kallas.
IBM. disk $29.99 (Order no.: 6075). disk $39.99, incl. backup disk (Order no.: 6075B).
Apple II. 3.5" disk $29.99 (Order no.: 6067). 3.5" disk $39.99, incl. backup disk (Order no.: 6067B).
Software Games on the History, Art, & Culture of Ancient Greece. Contains Four or Five Different Games. The Games Are Designed for One, Two, or Three Players. Players Are Given a Question & Challenged to Spell the Correct Answer Letter by Letter. Points Are Assigned by Letter & for Answering the Entire Word Correctly. The Answer Is Reinforced with Information. This Is Sophisticated Material in an Enjoyable Format.
Trillium Pr.

Trolls, Dragons & English Mechanics. Jun. 1994. *Items Included:* Program manual. *Customer Support:* Free technical support; 90 day warranty.
Consumer. MS-DOS 3.1 or higher. IBM or 100% compatible (1Mb). disk $59.95 (ISBN 1-882848-73-X, Order no.: 1B931). *Nonstandard peripherals required:* VGA or MCGA monitor & graphics card of 256 colors in 360 x 200 resolution, keyboard, Microsoft-compatible mouse, 3.5" disk drive (720k).
School ver.. MS-DOS 3.1 or higher. IBM or 100% compatible (1Mb). disk $69.95 (ISBN 1-882848-74-8, Order no.: 1B931T). *Nonstandard peripherals required:* VGA or MCGA monitor & graphics card of 256 colors in 360 x 200 resolution, keyboard, Microsoft-compatible mouse.
Lab pak. MS-DOS 3.1 or higher. IBM or 100% compatible (1Mb). disk $149.95 (ISBN 1-882848-75-6, Order no.: 1B931LPK). *Nonstandard peripherals required:* VGA or MCGA monitor & graphics card of 256 colors in 360 x 200 resolution, keyboard, Microsoft-compatible mouse.
Site license. MS-DOX 3.1 or higher. IBm or 100% compatible (1Mb). disk $699.00 (ISBN 1-882848-74-8, Order no.: 1B931SITE). *Nonstandard peripherals required:* VGA or MCGA monitor & graphics card of 256 colors in 360 x 200 resolution, keyboard, Microsoft-compatible mouse, 3.5" disk drive (720k).
Consumer. System 6.0.7 or higher. MAC LC or above (1Mb). 3.5" disk $59.95 (ISBN 1-882848-69-1, Order no.: APM931). *Nonstandard peripherals required:* 8-bit 256 color monitor.
Lab Pak. System 6.0.7 or higher. MAC LC or above (1Mb). 3.5" disk $149.95 (ISBN 1-882848-71-3, Order no.: APM931). *Nonstandard peripherals required:* 8-bit 256 color monitor.
Site license. System 6.0.7 or higher. MAC LC or above (1Mb). 3.5" disk $699.00 (ISBN 1-882848-72-1, Order no.: APM931SITE). *Nonstandard peripherals required:* 8-bit 256 color monitor.
School ed.. System 6.0.7 or higher. MC LC or above (1Mb). 3.5" disk $69.95 (ISBN 1-882848-70-5, Order no.: APM931T). *Nonstandard peripherals required:* 8-bit 256 color monitor.
Consumer. MS-DOS 3.1 or higher. IBM or 100% compatible (1Mb). disk $59.95 (ISBN 1-57204-066-1, Order no.: WIN931). *Nonstandard peripherals required:* VGA or MCGA monitor & graphics card of 256 colors in 360 x 200 resolution, keyboard, Microsoft compatible mouse, 3.5" disk drive (720k).
Welcome to the land of the enchanted, where the only way back to reality is by successfully crossing this mysterious, wonderous land. It won't be easy, however, because trolls control all the toll bridges you must cross, & you can suceed only by finding hidden gems to pay the tolls & solving the passwords that operate each of five bridges. So puzzles working with grammar, puncuation, parts of speech, spelling, sentence structure & analogies. Includes Lab Pak $149.95; Order # WIN931LPK; ISBN 1-57204-068-8; Site License $699.00; Order # WIN931SITE; ISBN 1-57204-069-6.
Lawrence Productions, Inc.

Trotter Professional Series Analysis Module. Ronald D. Jones. Jul. 1986. *Compatible Hardware:* Apple; Commodore; IBM; TRS-80 Model I, Model III, Color Computer. *Operating*

System(s) Required: CP/M. *Memory Required:* 64k.
disk $249.95 ea.
Apple. (ISBN 1-55604-258-2, Order no.: PT01).
CP/M. (ISBN 1-55604-259-0, Order no.: PT01).
Commodore. (ISBN 1-55604-260-4, Order no.: PT01).
Color Computer. (ISBN 1-55604-261-2, Order no.: PT01).
IBM. (ISBN 1-55604-262-0, Order no.: PT01).
Model I & Model III. (ISBN 1-55604-263-9, Order no.: PT01).
Up to 11 Races on Each Horse Can Be Evaluated to Provide Powerful Results. Full Screen & Faster Input Makes for Quicker Entry. Artificial Intelligence Is Used to Learn More about Favored Factors. Contains Complete Betting Mode, Holding Tanks for Late Scratches & Entries, Track Record Adjuster, & Multi-Track Modules.
Professor Jones Professional Handicapping Systems.

Trotter Professional Series Database Manager. Ronald D. Jones. Jul. 1986. *Compatible Hardware:* Apple; Commodore; IBM; TRS-80 Model I, Model III, Color Computer. *Operating System(s) Required:* CP/M. *Memory Required:* 64k.
disk $449.95 ea.
Apple. (ISBN 1-55604-270-1, Order no.: PT03).
CP/M. (ISBN 1-55604-271-X, Order no.: PT03).
Commodore. (ISBN 1-55604-272-8, Order no.: PT03).
Color Computer. (ISBN 1-55604-273-6, Order no.: PT03).
IBM. (ISBN 1-55604-274-4, Order no.: PT03).
Model I & Model III. (ISBN 1-55604-275-2, Order no.: PT03).
Essential Data on Every Horse Can Be Saved in a Data Base to Be Used in Conjunction with the Analysis Module. Includes Storage of Last 10 Races of All Horses, Attains Higher Win Percentage Due to More & Better Information, Automatic Storage of Races & Complete Printouts of Previous Races.
Professor Jones Professional Handicapping Systems.

Trotter Professional Series Factor Value Multiple Regression Module. Ronald D. Jones. Jul. 1986. *Compatible Hardware:* Apple; Commodore; IBM; TRS-80 Model I, Model III, Color Computer. *Operating System(s) Required:* CP/M. *Memory Required:* 64k.
disk $349.95 ea.
Apple. (ISBN 1-55604-264-7, Order no.: PT02).
CP/M. (ISBN 1-55604-265-5, Order no.: PT02).
Commodore. (ISBN 1-55604-266-3, Order no.: PT02).
Color Computer. (ISBN 1-55604-267-1, Order no.: PT02).
IBM. (ISBN 1-55604-268-X, Order no.: PT02).
Model I & Model III. (ISBN 1-55604-269-8, Order no.: PT02).
Provides Multiple Regression Analysis, Deriving the Most Precise Weighting Ability, Complete Multiple Regression of Target Races, a Holding Tank Link to Bet Module, As Well As True Low Level Artificial Intelligence.
Professor Jones Professional Handicapping Systems.

TRS-Test. *Compatible Hardware:* TRS-80 Model I. *Memory Required:* 16k.
cassette $14.95 (Order no.: 0184R).
TRS-80 Maintenance-Check ROM for Bad Bits, Keyboard for Defective Keys, & Data & Address Lines for Clean Signals.
Instant Software, Inc.

TRS-80 Model III Assembly Language. Hubert S. Howe, Jr. Sep. 1983. *Compatible Hardware:* TRS-80 Model III. *Operating System(s) Required:* TRSDOS. (source code included). *Memory Required:* 16k.
disk $29.95, incl. bk. (ISBN 0-13-931279-X).
disk only $22.95 (ISBN 0-13-931287-0).
Contains Completely Tested TRS-80 Programs & Subroutines. Details ROM, RAM & Disk Operating Systems, Flow Charts, Illustrations, Glossary & More.
Prentice Hall.

Trucker & Streets of the City. *Compatible Hardware:* Apple II, II+, IIe; Atari 800, 1200XL; Commodore; TRS-80 Model III, Model 4. *Operating System(s) Required:* Apple DOS 3.3, TRSDOS. *Language(s):* BASIC. *Memory Required:* 48k.
disk $24.95.
cassette $24.95.
Coast-to-Coast Hauls by a Trucker Are Simulated. Loads Can Be Oranges, Freight, or U.S. Mail. Each Haul Has Different Risks & Rewards. Bad Weather, Flat Tires, Construction, Tolls, Route Choices & Fuel Are Some of the Factors Involved. In 'Streets of the City', Grand Rapids, MI Is Site of a 10-Year Street & Transit Improvement Plan. User Has Task of Building & Repairing Streets, & Managing a Transit System. Labor Negotiations, Maintenance & On-Time Performance Are Some Factors.
Compuware.

Trucker's Road-Use Info Program: T.R.I.P. Pro Software, Inc. *Compatible Hardware:* TI Professional. *Operating System(s) Required:* MS-DOS. *Memory Required:* 64k.
$750.00.
Texas Instruments, Personal Productivit.

True BASIC: Advanced String Toolkit. (Library 1). 1987. *Compatible Hardware:* Apple Macintosh; IBM PC & compatibles. (source code included). *Memory Required:* Macintosh 1Mb, IBM 512k. *General Requirements:* True BASIC language system.
$79.95 ea.
Features Pattern Matching Routines, Expression Scanning, Associative Memories, Text Manipulation, Character Set Manipulation, English Text & Roman Numeral Conversion, & Other Routines. Includes a 38,000 Word English Dictionary.
True BASIC, Inc.

True BASIC: Communications Support Toolkit. 1988. *Compatible Hardware:* IBM PC & compatibles, PC XT, PC AT, Macintosh. (source code included). *Memory Required:* Macintosh 1Mb, IBM 512k. *General Requirements:* Asynchronous communications adapter or other add-in board with serial port for IBM PC.
$79.95.
Library Allows "True BASIC" Programs to Send & Receive Data via an Asynchronous Communication Port (RS-232C). Features Interrupt-Driven, Fully Buffered Input & Output; Speeds up to 92000 Baud; Simultaneous Use of Two COM Ports; Optional Use of Automatic XON/XOFF Protocol; Full Control of All Modem Signals (RTS, DTR, etc.); Fully Programmable Data Format, Including Parity & Stop Bits.
True BASIC, Inc.

True BASIC: Developer's Toolkit. 1988. *Compatible Hardware:* IBM PC & compatibles, PC XT, PC AT, Macintosh. *Operating System(s) Required:* PC-DOS/MS-DOS 3.1 or higher. (source code included). *Memory Required:* Macintosh 1Mb, PC 512k.
$79.95.
Collection of IBM-Specific Routines for Creating, Reading, & Removing Subdirectories, Hiding & Unhiding Files, & Switching Between Displays. Includes Functions for Dealing with Octal, Hexadecimal, & Binary Numbers; Support for MKDIR, CHDIR, RMDIR, & Other DOS Subdirectory Functions; Routines for Changing Cursor Shape, Switching Monitors, & Forcing Screen Dumps; Control of Caps Lock, Num Lock, & Scroll Lock Keys; "Chaining" to a .EXE or .COM File; Generalized Routines for Issuing DOS & BIOS Interrupts & Finding Memory Locations of Strings. MAC Version Provides Interface to Macintosh ROM Toolbox.
True BASIC, Inc.

True BASIC: Language System. John G. Kemeny & Thomas E. Kurtz. *Compatible Hardware:* Apple Macintosh, IBM PC & compatibles.
Language System. $99.95 Standard Edition.
$19.95 Student Edition.
$495.00 Professional Version.
Combines Features of BASIC with the Advantages of a Portable, Structured Programming Language. Supports Structures Such As SELECT CASE, Nested IF/THEN/ELSE, & DO/LOOP. Named Subroutines Accept Parameters Passed by Reference or by Value. Variables Can Be Local or Global, with Full Support for Recursion. Line Numbers & GOTO's Are Optional. Subroutines Can Be Separately Compiled & Saved in External Libraries. Supports Multiple Windows for Text or Graphics. Built-In 2-D Graphics Transformations Allow Users to Define an Image & Then Shift, Rotate, Scale, or Shear It. Follows the Proposed ANSI Standard for BASIC, Making Programs Portable Across a Wide Range of Machines. Includes Compiler Capable of Producing Intermediate b-Code & Enables Programs to Take Advantage of All the Memory Supported by the Operating System. Full-Screen Editor Includes Global Commands & Block Operations & Makes Use of Multiple Windows for Program Development.
True BASIC, Inc.
  IBM PC & compatibles version. *Memory Required:* 512k.
    The Full Screen Editor Includes Commands Like FIND & REPLACE, & Block Operations Such As MOVE & COPY. Multiple Windows Are Used for Program Development. Automatically Supports 8087 on the PC & 80287 on the AT. Supports up to 704k.
  Macintosh version. *Memory Required:* 1000k.
    Includes a Full-Featured Mouse-Based Text Editor. Commands May Be Entered Through Menus, a Special Control Panel, or the Keyboard in a Separate Command Window. Colors Are Mapped to Grey Scale. Program Output Goes to User-Sized Window or Uses Full Screen. Accesses Most Macintosh ROM Routines Including QUICKDRAW.

True BASIC: PC BASIC Converter. 1986. *Compatible Hardware:* IBM PC & compatibles, PC 6T, PC AT, Macintosh. *Operating System(s) Required:* PC-DOS/MS-DOS 2.X or 3.X. (source code included). *Memory Required:* MAC 1Mb, PC 512k. *General Requirements:* BASICA, GW-BASIC, QBASIC, & QuickBASIC, source code in ASCII format.
$39.95.
Translates Programs Written in BASICA, GW-BASIC, QBASIC, or QuickBASIC & Stored in ASCII Format. Every Statement, Format, & Function in the Original BASIC Is Either Converted to a True BASIC Equivalent or Flagged with Asterisks for Later Review. About 85-90% of the Original BASIC Is Automatically Translated. Features Include: Splits Multiple-Statement Lines into Multi-Line Structures; Inserts LET Statements; Directly Converts Features That Are Identical in Both Dialects; Substitutes Functions & Subroutines to Handle Unique BASICA Syntax; Handles Any Size BASIC Program (Within Hardware Memory Limitations).
True BASIC, Inc.

TITLE INDEX

True BASIC: Sorting & Searching Toolkit.
(Library 1). *Compatible Hardware:* Apple Macintosh, IBM PC & compatibles. (source code included). *Memory Required:* Macintosh 1Mb, IBM 512k. *General Requirements:* True BASIC language system.
$79.95.
Provides 14 Subroutines for Sorting Arrays. Routines Feature Fast, In-Place "Quicksort"; Users Can Define Their Own Customized Comparison Routines (Four Comparison Routines Included); Fast Pointer Sorts, with or Without Custom Comparison; Binary Search Routines; Heapsorts, Selection Sorts, & Bubble Sorts; Sample Programs with Cross Reference.
True BASIC, Inc.

True BASIC: 3-Dimensional Graphics Toolkit.
Compatible Hardware: Apple Macintosh, IBM PC & compatibles. (source code included). *Memory Required:* Macintosh 1Mb, IBM 512k. *General Requirements:* True BASIC language system.
$79.95.
Library Fully Supports Both Perspective & Parallel Projections. Other Features Include: Support for Circles, Rectangles, Grids, Polygons, Areas, Text Plotting, & Contour Plots; Special 3-D Animation Tools; Support for Cabinet & Cavalier Projections & Full Support for Arbitrary Oblique Projections.
True BASIC, Inc.

True-Image Software for Salons. *Items Included:* User manual, DBL-Runtime Utilities. *Customer Support:* 6-month warranty, training & hotline support, modifications & customizing available.
MS-DOS 2.1 or higher. AT Class, 80286 IBM PC Mono-Video & compatibles. contact publisher for price. *Nonstandard peripherals required:* Electronic cash drawer (serial), 80-column printer (parallel), 20Mb hard disk. *Addl. software required:* DBL-Runtime utilities. *Optimal configuration:* MS-DOS 3.3, 12 Mhz, monochrome monitor.
Credits Retail Sales & Services Performed to Client & Employee Files. Posts Inventory & Management Files at End-of-Day Process. Two Versions: (1) Single Salon: Includes Electronic Cash Drawer Management & Client, Employee, Inventory & Management Control Information, (2) Multi-Salon: Adds Automatic Polling & Corporate Office Consolidation of Remote Salon Sites.
MBA Computer Services, Inc.

Truerate% Nov. 1988. *Operating System(s) Required:* PC-DOS/MS-DOS. *Memory Required:* 256k. *General Requirements:* Lotus 1-2-3 release 2 or higher, or Symphony 1.1 or higher. Printer recommended. *Customer Support:* free by phone for 6 months; $100.00 annually thereafter.
3.5" or 5.25" disk $499.95.
Internal Rate of Return Calculator. Calculates the True Rate of Return by Using Math Corp.'s Own Proprietary Internal Rate of Return Calculation. Users Have the Choice of Calculating the TRUERATE%, the Original Cash Flow, or One of the Other Cash Flows by Entering the Other Data. Users May Enter As Many Cash Flows As Needed. Once a TRUERATE% Has Been Calculated Users May Verify the Figure by Using the Verification Facility. Has Its Own Help Screens & On-Disk Manual. Six Months of Technical Support Is Included in the Purchase Price.
Math Corp.

TrueSOUND. *Items Included:* User guide. *Customer Support:* 90 days limited warranty.
MS-DOS/PC-DOS 2.0 or higher (512k). IBM PC, PC XT, PC AT, PS/2 Model 30 & compatibles. disk $395.00. *Nonstandard peripherals required:* Webco Computers' TrueSOUND Card. *Networks supported:* All Netbios LANS (Novell, 3Com, etc.).
Makes Audio Files Interact with Author's Software Program to Enhance Application Effectiveness.
Webco Computers.

TruLynx/3270-PC. *Operating System(s) Required:* PC-DOS 2.0 or higher. *Memory Required:* 256k. *General Requirements:* Printer. *Items Included:* User guide. *Customer Support:* Phone support available 6 AM to 5 PM Pacific time; 90-day limited warranty.
3.5" or 5.25" disk $195.00.
Provides File Transfer & 3270 Terminal Emulation Functions.
Andrew Corp.

Trulynx/400. Nov. 1989. *Items Included:* User guide, 3.5" & 5.25" disk. *Customer Support:* Phone support 6AM to 5PM Pacific time; 90-day limited warranty.
PC-DOS 3.3. Host AS/400 with PC support; local/remote IBM PC or true compatible. contact publisher for price. *Nonstandard peripherals required:* Andrew Interlynx/5251 protocol converter.
Provides Complete Access for Local & Remote PC's in an Asynchronous Environment to AS/400 PC Support Programs, Functions & Features.
Andrew Corp.

TruLynx/5251. *Operating System(s) Required:* MS-DOS 2.0 or higher. *Memory Required:* 256k. *Items Included:* User guide. *Customer Support:* Phone support available 6 AM to 5 PM Pacific time; 90-day limited warranty.
3.5" or 5.25" disk $150.00.
File Transfer & Terminal Emulation of Providing Micro-to-System 34/36/38 Interface & Compatibility.
Andrew Corp.

Trust Account Management System. William D. Castagna. 1982. *Compatible Hardware:* Apple II+. *Operating System(s) Required:* Apple DOS 3.3. *Language(s):* Applesoft BASIC (source code included). *Memory Required:* 48k.
contact publisher for price.
Records All Transactions Made in Client Accounts, Including Deposits & Withdrawals & Continuously Maintains Both the Individual Client Account Balance & the Entire Trust Account Balance. Prints Check & Deposit Registers, Reconciles Bank Statements & Enables Attorney to Analyze an Entire Trust or Client Account.
Better Business Solutions.

Trust Accounting System Jr. *Version:* 8. Dec. 1979. *Items Included:* Binder with documentation. *Customer Support:* 1 yr. maintenance $65 entitles user to phone support, newsletter & enhancements released for their computer during the year at no charge.
DOS Ver. 3.1 or higher. IBM PC & compatibles (384k). disk $250.00. *Nonstandard peripherals required:* Hard drive.
Provides Current Balance Information for Each Trust & Grand Total for All of the Trusts Combined. Check Registers Can Be Printed for Individual Trusts or All of the Trusts Combined. Records for Each Trust Are Retained until Deleted by the User. Checks Can Be Manually or Computer Generated from 9 Separate Checking Accounts. Users Can Define Federal ID of Payee & 1099 Field. Users Can Also Elect to Combine Trust Account Activity with STI's Accounts Payable.
Software Technology, Inc.

Trust Accounting System Jr-M (TAS Jr-M).
Version: 8. Dec. 1979. *Items Included:* Binder with documentation. *Customer Support:* 1 yr. maintenance $85 entitles user to phone support,

THE TRUTH IS IN HERE: CONSPIRACIES

newsletters & enhancements made available for their computer at no charge.
DOS Ver. 3.1 or higher. IBM PC & compatibles (384k). disk $350.00. *Nonstandard peripherals required:* Hard drive. *Networks supported:* Novell, IBM PC Networks & compatibles.
Multi-User Version of TAS Jr Allowing up to 10 Workstations to Enter or Retrieve Client Trust Account Information. Users Can Either Manually or Computer Generate Checks from 9 Separate Checking Accounts. Trust Detail Remains until Deleted by the User. Print 1099 Information That Is Combined with STI's Accounts Payable System Jr-M. Integrates with STI's TABS III-MJr.
Software Technology, Inc.

Trust, Escrow & Fund Accounting System: TEFACS. *Version:* 2.00. 1984. *Compatible Hardware:* IBM PC & compatibles, PC XT, PC AT, PS/2. *Operating System(s) Required:* MS-DOS, PC-DOS. *Language(s):* FORTRAN. *Memory Required:* MS-DOS 320k. *Items Included:* Manual. *Customer Support:* 1 hour per package purchased.
5-1/4" or 8" disk, or 3-1/2" $395.00.
Manages over 500 Funds & Can Store 1700 Transactions per Single-Sided, Single Density Diskette. May Be Run Together with MCC's General Ledger Package.
MCC Software (Midwest Computer Ctr. Co.).

Trust Exec. 1984. *Compatible Hardware:* IBM PC & compatibles, PC XT, PC AT. *Operating System(s) Required:* MS-DOS 2.1 or higher. *Memory Required:* 256k. *General Requirements:* Hard disk, printer.
disk $495.00, incl. documentation.
Designed to Handle Fiduciary Trust Accounting in a Law Firm. Provides for Multi-Client Tracking from Single Bank Account Including the Printing of Checks.
Data Law.

Trust Exec. *Version:* 1.9. Aug. 1984. *Compatible Hardware:* IBM PC. *Operating System(s) Required:* PC-DOS, MS-DOS. *Language(s):* CB-86. *Memory Required:* 128k. *General Requirements:* Printer.
$399.95.
Provides Multi-Client Ledger Tracking Within a Single Checking or Bank Account.
Data Source One, Inc.

Trust Tracker. *Version:* 2.0. *Items Included:* Manual, disk, warranty card. *Customer Support:* 18 month via telephone.
3 1/2", 5 1/4" or 8" disk $89.00.
demo disk $20.00.
Tracks up to 400 Trust or Escrow Accounts. Up to 99 Types of Income & Expense Categories May Be Installed. Up to 9 Checking Accounts Can Be Installed. Prints Checks & Reconciles Checking Accounts. Prints Listing of Trusts, Statement of Each Trust Status, & Details of Any Trust. Generates a Detail Journal & Check Register for Audit Trail.
Micro-Art Programmers.

The Truth Is in Here: Conspiracies, Mysteries, Superstitions, Kooks & Cults on the Internet.
Karl Mamer. Apr. 1996. *Items Included:* A 64-page companion booklet that reviews web sites & includes instructions on how to use the software. *Customer Support:* Access to the Go!Guides web site & FAQ, customer support by email at help goguides.com.
Macintosh System 7.0 or higher. Macintosh (4Mb). 3.5" disk $12.99 (ISBN 1-57712-011-6). *Nonstandard peripherals required:* Modem 14.4 or faster. *Addl. software required:* Internet account & connection. *Optimal configuration:* Macintosh System 7.0 or higher, at least 4Mb of RAM, at least 2Mb of

1037

free disk space, color monitor, 14.4 or 28.8 modem, Internet account.
Windows 3.1 or Windows 95. IBM or compatible (4Mb). disk $12.99. *Nonstandard peripherals required:* 14.4 or 28.8 modem. *Addl. software required:* Internet account. *Optimal configuration:* IBM-compatible running Windows 3.1 or Windows 95, at least 2Mb free space on hard drive, at least 4Mb RAM, color monitor, 14.4 or 28.8 modem, Internet account.
Packed with Humourous & Out-of-the-Ordinary Sites, This Program Will Take You on the Stroll of Your Life Through the Back Alleys & Secret Passageways of the Internet Underworld.
Motion Works Publishing.

TR01PC AudioClips: Total Recall. *Version:* 1.5. Feb. 1993. *Items Included:* Manual, registration card, sound list. *Customer Support:* Phone technical support.
DOS 5.0, Windows 3.1. PC 286 or higher (2Mb). disk $14.95 (ISBN 1-57303-004-X). *Nonstandard peripherals required:* Sound card recommended. *Optimal configuration:* 286 or higher with 4Mb RAM, DOS 5.0 or later, Windows 3.1 or later, 4-7Mb HD space available, sound card.
Exclusively Licensed High Quality Sound Files Consisting of Classic Sound Effects, Dialogue & Music from Original TV Shows & Movies. Also Included Is the 'Whoop It Up' Audio Utility, Which Allows the User to Attach AudioClips to Various Windows Events.
Sound Source Interactive.

TS Graph. *Items Included:* manual.
Macintosh plus or higher (512K). 3.5" disk $49.95. *Nonstandard peripherals required:* ImageWriter or Apple LaserWriter.
Graphing Application. Written for Scientific Journal Style Graphs. Can Also Be Used in Many Other Graphing Applications. Allows a Graph Creator Flexibility in Customizing the Axes & Data Symbols. Has Data Entry, Editing, & Modification Capabilities.
Trimbur Software.

TS-Report-Gold. *Version:* 2.6. Oct. 1988. *Compatible Hardware:* IBM PC, 386, PS/2. *Operating System(s) Required:* OS/2. *General Requirements:* Hard disk, VGA monitor. *Customer Support:* 120 days free.
3.5" or 5.25" disk, contact vendor for price.
Provides Technology to Help Control Company Payables & Increase Cash Flow. Simplifies Cash Disbursements & Forecasts Cash Requirements. Checks Written Based on Designated Dates or a List Can Be Created of What & Who to Pay Based on Payment Methods. Also Features Intercompany Accounting, Tenant Pass-Throughs, & Property Charge-Backs.
Timberline Software Corp.

TSiGraphics. *Version:* 1.0.4. Jun. 1993. *Items Included:* TSi Manual. *Customer Support:* Unlimited free technical support.
Macintosh. Macintosh Plus or higher (2Mb). 3.5" disk $195.00 (Order no.: 800-252-6479).
Full-Featured Plotting Library. Line, Bar, Scatter, Pie, Contour, 3D Mesh, & Real Time Plots Are Supported. Up to 10 Graphics Windows Can Be Opened at once & Each May Contain Multiple Plots. Windows Are Fully Integrated with the Language Systems Application Shell.
Language Systems Corp.

TSP: Time Series Processor. B. Hall et al. Sep. 1986. *Compatible Hardware:* IBM PC & compatibles, 386 & Macintosh. *Operating System(s) Required:* PC-DOS. *Memory Required:* 640k. *General Requirements:* Hard disk, printer. *Customer Support:* Telephone, mail.
disk $325.00.

Estimation Methods Provided Are Ordinary Least Squares, 2- & 3-Stage Least Squares, Polynomial Distributed Lags, Regression with First Order Serial Correlation Correction, & Estimation of Nonlinear Simultaneous Models.
TSP International.

TSRman. *Version:* 1.8. *Compatible Hardware:* IBM PC, PCjr, PC XT, PC AT, 3270 PC & compatibles. disk $39.95.
Allows User to Remove Memory-Resident Programs to Provide More RAM for Large Applications.
Popular Programs, Inc.

TSRs & More. *Version:* 1.0. Nov. 1993. *Items Included:* 1 volume lay-flat perfect bound manual, pop-up help reference. *Customer Support:* 60 day money back guarantee, free technical support, CompuServe technical support, free electronic maintenance updates.
MS-DOS 3.3 or higher. Any PC compatible (1Mb). disk $189.00. *Addl. software required:* Borland C Plus Plus 3.1 or higher, Turbo C Plus Plus 3.0 or higher, Microsoft C/C Plus Plus 7.0 or higher.
A Programming Library for Writing Compact Memory Resident Programs in C or C Plus Plus. Supports Both Swapping & Conventional TSRs. TSRs Can Be Unloaded, Accessed from Other Programs, or Reconfigured Dynamically. Also Provides Keyboard Macros, Swapping Exec Manager, EMS & XMS Memory Manager, & Huge Virtual Arrays. Includes Complete Source Code & Numerous Example Programs.
TurboPower Software.

TsrTools: Pop-Up Desk Tools. *Items Included:* Bound manual. *Customer Support:* Free hotline - no time limit; 30 day limited warranty; updates are $5/disk plus S&H.
MS-DOS 2.0 or higher. IBM & compatibles (128k). disk $19.95. *Nonstandard peripherals required:* Both color & monochrome are supported.
A Collection of Terminate-&-Stay-Resident Utilities. CLIP & SAVE: Simply Use the Cursor to Define a Rectangular Area on the Screen, & Press a Key to Send That Area to the Printer or to a Disk File. Filter Out Graphics Characters, Control Codes, etc. Great for Picking Out Parts of a Screen Display for Inclusion in a Manual, Saving a Disk Directory to a Data File (So You Do Not Have to Enter the File Names by Hand), etc. SEEDIR: Look at a Directory or Subdirectory Whenever You Please Using "Point-&-Shoot." Limited to Non-Graphics Programs. RULERS: Includes a Horizontal Ruler, Vertical Alignment Gauge, Cursor Size Control, & a Pop-Up ASCII Chart. REMINDER: Programmed Alert Tool (Time to Save Data, Leave for Meeting, etc.).
Dynacomp, Inc.

TSSnet. *Items Included:* Spiral-bound documentation; 3.5 inch media (1/4" tape available). *Customer Support:* Standard support for TSS UNIX (AIX, SCO, SUN) products includes free telephone support & updates for one year from date of purchase. TSS Extended Maintenance Agreement ranges in price from $400/year to $1600/year.
System 7.0 or higher. Macintosh (2Mb). 3.5" disk $349.00 (Order no.: TNS1910000). *Nonstandard peripherals required:* Ethernet board. *Networks supported:* AppleTalk, DECnet, asychrenous.
IBM AIX. IBM RISC System/6000. $2400.00 to $9600.00. *Optimal configuration:* TSSnet operates on all IBM RISC System/6000 configurations.
SUN OS. All SUN models. $2400.00 to $9600.00. *Optimal configuration:* TSSnet operates on all SUN models. *Networks supported:* DECnet,

Ethernet.
SCO OpenDesktop/SCO UNIX. Any system running SCO OpenDesktop or SCO UNIX (2Mb). $2400.00 to $9600.00. *Nonstandard peripherals required:* Ethernet adapter. *Networks supported:* DECnet, Ethernet.
Provides a Cost Effective, Software Based Open Connectivity Solution Using Proven Protocols. TSSnet Not Only Provides DECnet & LAT Capabilities for UNIX, IBM AIX & Macintosh Systems, It Effectively Makes These Platforms Multi-Lingual. This Enables Them to Communicate Remotely with Their Native Protocols While Simultaneously Talking to UNIX, IBM AIX, Macintosh & VAX/VMS Systems Through the Use of TSSnet.
Thursby Software Systems, Inc.

TSSnet. *Items Included:* Spiral-bound documentation; 3.5" media (1/4" tape available). *Customer Support:* Standard support for TSS UNIX (AIX, SCO, SUN) products includes free telephone support & updates for one year from date of purchase. TSS Extended Maintenance Agreement ranges in price from $400/year to $1600/year.
System 7.0 or higher. Macintosh (2Mb). 3.5" disk $349.00 (Order no.: TNS1910000). *Nonstandard peripherals required:* Ethernet board. *Networks supported:* AppleTalk, DECnet, asychronous.
IBM AIX. IBM RISC System/6000. $2400.00 to $9600.00. *Optimal configuration:* Operates on all IBM RISC System/6000 configurations.
SUN OS, Solaris & Solaris for X86. All SUN models. $2400.00 to $9600.00. *Networks supported:* DECnet, Ethernet.
SCO OpenDesktop/SCO UNIX. Any system based running SCO OpenDesktop or SCO UNIX (2Mb). $2400.00 to $9600.00. *Nonstandard peripherals required:* Ethernet adapter. *Networks supported:* DECnet, Ethernet.
Provides a Cost Effective, Software Based Open Connectivity Solution Using Proven Protocols. TSSnet Not Only Provides DECnet & LAT Capabilities for UNIX, IBM AIX & Macintosh Systems, It Effectively Makes These Platforms Multi-Lingual. This Enables Them to Communicate Remotely with Their Native Protocols While Simultaneously Talking to UNIX, IBM AIX, Macintosh & VAX/VMS Systems Through the Use of TSSnet.
Thursby Software Systems, Inc.

TSSterm. *Version:* 2.0. 1993. *Items Included:* Media 3.5" or tape, documentation. *Customer Support:* 90 day warranty, with telephone support & updates, included at no cost. Annual maintenance available.
Solaris. Various. disk $495.00. *Networks supported:* TCP/IP, DECnet, LAT, Async.
AIX. IBM RISC System/6000. disk $495.00. *Networks supported:* TCP/IP, DECnet, LAT, Async.
HP/UX. HP 9000/700. disk $495.00. *Networks supported:* TCP/IP, DECnet, LAT, Async.
Provides Exact VT420 Terminal Emulation with Keyboard Mapping, Copy & Paste, Color & Blink Control, Double High & Wide Characters, Multiple Sessions, Macro & Scripting Language Support, True Representation of All Character Attributes, Print Capture, Session Logging & Comprehensive Customization Tools. TSSterm 420 Emulates Multiple DEC Terminal Types & Supports Virtual Terminal Protocols & Async Protocols.
Thursby Software Systems, Inc.

Tsushima. *Compatible Hardware:* Apple II+, IIe, IIc; Commodore 64/128.
disk $30.00 ea.
Commodore. (Order no.: 48252).

TITLE INDEX

Apple. (Order no.: 48255).
Recreates the Climax of the Russo-Japanese War of 1905 on Both Strategic & Tactical Levels. In the Strategic Game Sightings & Battles Are Resolved in Ship-to-Ship Maneuver & Combat. In the Tactical Game, Each Side Selects a Fleet Drawn from the 29 Ships Available. For One or Two Players.
Avalon Hill Game Co., The Microcomputer Games Div.

Tswing. Version: 2.2. Feb. 1984. Compatible Hardware: Apple II+, IIe. Operating System(s) Required: DOS 3.3P/M. Language(s): BASIC. Memory Required: 48k. General Requirements: 2 disk drives.
disk $425.00.
Thermal Simulation Element of Solarsoft Inc.'s Energy Design Series. By Inputting the Zone-by-Zone Characteristics & the Design Day Climate Data, User Can See the Projected Temperature Swings in Each Zone Defined in the Building.
Solarsoft.

TSX-NET LAN: License for up to 128 Nodes.
Version: 3.2. Sep. 1991. Items Included: 8 spiral bound manuals. Customer Support: $850/year for telephone consultation, updates $20.00, documentation $75.00.
PC/MS-DOS version 3.3 or higher (4Mb). IBM PC AT, PS/2 or compatible, 386 or 486 processor. $2500.00. Nonstandard peripherals required: Ethernet - Western Digital Etherarc Plus 16 "Elite". Optimal configuration: PC 386 AT, SCSI Disk Controller, 80Mb Disk. Networks supported: TCP/IP.
Peer-to-Peer Networking System. Offers Transparent Access to Remote Files, Peripherals, & Programs As Well As Remote Log-In, May Be Configured with Ethernet into a LAN and/or Over Async Serial Lines As a WAN. Incorporates the Standard TCP/IP Protocol & Is Interoperable with Other Systems with TCP/IP.
S & H Computer Systems, Inc.

TSX-Plus Version 5. Version: 6.5. Operating System(s) Required: RT-II, V5.0 or later. Memory Required: 128k. Items Included: Documentation, support for 1 year. Customer Support: 1 year, $500.00 year thereafter.
$2000.00.
RT-II Compatible Multi-User, Multi-Tasking OS W & U Real-Time Capabilities.
S & H Computer Systems, Inc.

TSX-32: Multi-User System. Version: 3.2. Sep. 1991. Items Included: 8 spiral bound manuals. Customer Support: 1 year $500.00 including telephone consultation, updates $20.00, new documentation $75.00.
MS/PC-DOS version 3.3. IBM PC AT, PS/2 or compatible with 386 or 486 processor (4Mb). $425.00-$1450.00. Optimal configuration: DOS 5.0, 8Mb RAM, 100Mb Disk, Intelligent serial multiplexers, SCSI disk controller. Networks supported: TCP/IP, Ethernet.
DOS Compatible, Multi-User, Multi-Tasking, Networking Operating System with Real-Time Capabilities for Computers Using the Intel 386, 486 & Compatible Microprocessors. Multi-Tasks Stabdard DOS Applications & 32-Bit Extended DOS & Native Applications At the Same Time.
S & H Computer Systems, Inc.

TSX-32: Single-User System. Version: 3.2. Sep. 1991. Items Included: 8 spiral bound manuals. Customer Support: $275/year - telephone consultation; updates - $20; new documentation $75.00.
PS/MS-DOS version 3.3 or higher. IBM PC AT, PS/2 or compatibles with 386 or 486 processor (4Mb). disk $450.00. Optimal configuration: 386 AT with 4Mb RAM, SCSI Disk Controller, 80Mb disk, DOS 5.0. Networks supported: TCP/IP Ethernet.
DOS Compatible Multi-Tasking, Networking Operating System with Real-Time Capabilities for Computers Using the Intel 386, 486 & Compatible Microprocessors. Multi-Tasks Standard DOS Applications & 32-Bit Extended DOS & Native Applications At the Same Time. Up to 10 Tasks May Be Controlled by a Single-User from the Consol or a Terminal.
S & H Computer Systems, Inc.

TTY Communications. Compatible Hardware: TI Professional. Operating System(s) Required: MS-DOS. Memory Required: 128k. General Requirements: Winchester hard disk, printer, modem, asynchronous communications interface.
$60.00 (Order no.: TI P/N 2223119-0001).
Texas Instruments, Personal Productivit.

Tube & Pipe Bending. Items Included: Bound manual. Customer Support: Free hotline - no time limit; 30 day limited warranty; updates are $5/disk plus S&H.
MS-DOS. IBM & compatibles (128k). disk $899.95. Nonstandard peripherals required: 80-column (or wider) printer.
demo disk $5.00.
Used to Properly Set Single-Plane Tube Bending Machines for Three-Dimensional Tube Bending. It Is Applicable to Tube Production for Industrial & Military Equipment; Steam Boiler Retubing; Tubular Lawn Furniture; & So On.
Dynacomp, Inc.

Tube & Pipe Bending - HP5M. Version: 05/1995. Feb. 1983. Compatible Hardware: IBM PC & compatibles. Operating System(s) Required: MS-DOS, PC-DOS. Language(s): Compiled & Assembly. Memory Required: 256k. Customer Support: Technical hotline, "Lifetime" support at no charge.
$995.00.
$1450.00, incl. graphics & CAD.
Tube-Pipe Bending Machine Setting Calculations - HP5M Takes Inputs of Bend Locations in X-Y-Z Coordinates or Angle & Length Format & Provides the Bending & Cutting Information Required to Fabricate 3-D Bent Tube Shapes in Single Plane Rotary Tube Bending Machines. Newly Equipped with a Graphics & CAD Module Displaying & Printing the Bent Tube in 3-Dimensions, Rotatable, Zoomable & Repositionable. Applies Elongation Factors, Fully Prompted, Compiled & Interactive. Also Does Miscellaneous Trigonometric Calculations, Arc Length & Others. Useful in Tube Bending. SI Metric or English Units.
MC2 Engineering Software.

Tune It II. Fred Willman. 1984. Compatible Hardware: Apple II Plus, IIc, IIe, IIgs; Commodore 64, 128; IBM PC; Macintosh. Operating System(s) Required: Apple DOS 3.3, Macintosh System 6.0.3-7.1, PC-DOS 3.3. Language(s): BASIC. Memory Required: Apple 48k, Commodore 64k, IBM 640k, MAC 512k. General Requirements: CGA card for IBM.
disk $39.95 ea.
Commodore 64. (ISBN 1-55603-005-3, Order no.: C-1118).
Apple. (ISBN 0-942132-22-X, Order no.: A-1118).
IBM. (ISBN 0-942132-23-8, Order no.: I-1118).
disk $59.95 (ISBN 1-55603-309-5, Order no.: MAC-1118).
Designed to Give Music Students Practice in Matching Pitches. Using a Graphic Representation of a Stringed Instrument Fingerboard, 2 Pitches Are Played, with the Second One Sounding Out of Tune with the First. The User Adjusts the Second Pitch until It Matches the First. The Level of Difficulty Can Be Chosen. Records Are Kept for Student Scores.
Electronic Courseware Systems, Inc.

TuneLand Starring Howie Mandel. Jan. 1994. Items Included: Free coloring book with lyrics to the songs. Customer Support: Technical support is available free of charge through our technical support phone line by calling 214-437-5531 Monday through Saturday 8:00am-5:00pm, online via CompuServe by typing Go Seventh at any! prompt, or via Internet mail at Support-7thlevel.com.
Windows 3.1 or higher. IBM or compatible 385 25MHz (4Mb). CD-ROM disk $39.99 (ISBN 0-9641098-0-8, Order no.: 10011). Nonstandard peripherals required: 256 color display or higher; mouse; CD-ROM drive; MPC-compatible sound card; amplified speakers.
The World's First Interactive Musical Cartoon CD-ROM. With Animation Clearly Superior to Any Other Comparable Product, TuneLand Is Close in Quality to Feature Films. Fantastic Fun & Learning for Kids of All Ages. A Perfect Product for Adults to Explore with Their Children.
Seventh Level, Inc.

Tunnels of Doom. Compatible Hardware: TI 99/4A.
contact publisher for price.
Be the Lone Hero or the Leader of a Party of Adventurers Fighting Monsters & Overcoming Danger in a Quest to Rescue the King & Gather Treasure.
Texas Instruments, Personal Productivit.

Turbo. (One-on-One Ser.). Compatible Hardware: Commodore Amiga.
$24.95.
Arcade Style Car Race Game Featuring Digitized Sounds & Music, Realistic Graphics, & Fast Action.
Microillusions, Inc.

Turbo Advantage Complex: Complex Number Routines for Turbo Pascal. Lauer & Wallwitz. Operating System(s) Required: MS-DOS.
disk $39.95, incl. manual (ISBN 0-934375-27-5).
Provides Procedures for Performing All the Arithmetic Operations & Necessary Real Functions with Complex Numbers. Each Procedure Is Based on Predefined Constants & Tupes, & Can Be Utilized to Build More Sophisticated Functions in a Program. Demonstrates the Use of These Procedures in Routines for Vector & Matrix Calculation with Complex Numbers & Variables, & Calculations of Convolution & Correlation Functions. Source Code & Documentation Is Included. Some of the Routines Are More Effectively Used with Routines Contained in Turbo Advantage.
M & T Bks.

Turbo Advantage Display: From Generator for Turbo Pascal. Lauer & Wallwitz. Operating System(s) Required: MS-DOS.
disk $39.95, incl. manual (ISBN 0-934375-28-3).
Makes It Easy to Design & Process Forms. The Package Includes a Form Processor, 30 Turbo Pascal Procedures & Functions to Facilitate Linking Created Forms to a Program, & Full Source Code & Documentation. Some of the Turbo Advantage Routines Are Necessary to Compile Turbo Advantage Display.
M & T Bks.

Turbo Advantage: Source Code Libraries for Turbo Pascal. Lauer & Wallwitz. Operating System(s) Required: MS-DOS.
disk $29.95, incl. manual (ISBN 0-934375-26-7).
Library with More Than 220 Routines Complete with Source Code, Sample Programs, & Documentation. Routines Are Organized & Documented in Categories Such As File Management, MS-DOS Support, String Operations, Data Compression, etc. The Manual Includes a Description of Each Routine, an Explanation of the Methods Used, & the Calling Sequence.
M & T Bks.

Turbo Almanac: Astronomical - Nautical - Calendar Almanac. *Items Included:* Full manual. No other products required. *Customer Support:* Free telephone support - no time limit. 30 day warranty.
 MS-DOS 3.2 or higher. IBM & compatibles (512k). disk $59.95. *Optimal configuration:* IBM, MS-DOS 2.0 or higher, 500k RAM, & EGA or VGA (or compatible) graphics capability. Math coprocessor, printer, & mouse are supported, but not necessary.
Astronomical, Nautical, & Calendar Almanac. Predicts the Locations, Rise Times, Set Times, & More for over 400 Celestial Objects, Including the Sun, Moon, & Planets. Accuracy Is Better Than One Minute of Arc. Also Predicts the Exact Times of Lunar Phases, Eclipses, & Much More, & Can Track the Path of Total Eclipses.
Dynacomp, Inc.

Turbo Almanac: Astronomical - Nautical - Calendar Almanac. 1992. *Items Included:* Detailed manuals included with all Dynacomp products. *Customer Support:* Free telephone support to original customer - no time limit; 30 day limited warranty.
 MS-DOS 3.2 or higher. IBM PC & compatibles (512k). $59.95 (Add $5.00 for 3 1/2" format; 5 1/4" format standard). *Optimal configuration:* IBM, MS-DOS 2.0 or higher, 500k RAM, & EGA or VGA or compatible graphics capability. A math coprocessor, printer, & mouse are supported, but not necessary.
An Astronomical, Nautical, & Calendar Almanac. It Predicts the Locations, Rise Times, Set Times, & More for over 400 Celestial Objects, Including the Sun, Moon, & Planets. The Accuracy Is Better Than One Minute of Arc. It Also Predicts the Exact Times of Lunar Phases, Eclipses, & Much More, & Can Track the Path of Total Eclipses. In Addition, It Provides Date & Time Calculations in the Gregorian, Jewish, & Islamic Calendars, & Identifies Holidays in All Three. Includes 75-Page Manual.
Dynacomp, Inc.

Turbo Analyst. *Version:* 7.0. Sep. 1995. *Compatible Hardware:* IBM PC, PC XT, PC AT & compatibles. *Memory Required:* 640k. *General Requirements:* Turbo Pascal 5.0, 5.5, 6.0, 7.0, or Turbo Pascal for Windows. *Items Included:* Perfect bound manual. *Customer Support:* Free technical support, 60 day money-back guarantee, free electronic maintenance updates, Compuserve technical support.
 disk $149.00.
Collection of Analytical Tools Which Automate Common Programming Tasks. They Help Programmers Write, Debug, & Fine Tune Code. Supports All of Turbo Pascal Features, Including Computed Constants & Implementation Uses. The Execution Timer Reports the Time Spent in Each Program Procedure. Fully Compatible with Borland's Turbo Pascal 7.0.
TurboPower Software.

Turbo ASM. *Compatible Hardware:* IBM PC & compatibles, 80386-based PCs.
 contact publisher for price.
Assembler Compatible with Several Versions of MICROSOFT MICRO ASSEMBLER. Provides Full '386 Support.
Borland International, Inc.

Turbo BASIC, 2 disks. *Compatible Hardware:* IBM PC & true compatibles, PC XT, PC AT. *Operating System(s) Required:* PC-DOS/MS-DOS 2.0 or higher. *Memory Required:* 320k.
 $99.95, incl. manual (ISBN 0-87524-180-8).
BASIC Compiler. Supports the Following Features: Full Recursion; Standard IEEE Floating-Point Format; Floating Point Support with Full 8087 Integration; Program Size Limited Only by Computer Memory; EGA & CGA Support; Access to Local, Static, & Global Variables; Full Integration of the Compiler, Editor, & Executable Program, with Separate Windows for Editing, Messages, Tracing, & Execution; Long Integer (32-Bit) Data Type; Full 80-Bit Precision; Pull-Down Menus; Full Window Management. BASICA Compatible. Package Includes MicroCalc, a Sample Spreadsheet That Can Be Compiled "As Is" or Be Modified.
Borland International, Inc.

Turbo BASIC Database Toolbox. *Compatible Hardware:* IBM PC & true compatibles, PC XT, PC AT. *Operating System(s) Required:* PC-DOS/MS-DOS 2.0 or higher. *General Requirements:* Turbo BASIC.
 disk $99.95.
The "Trainer" Module Will Show How B+ Trees Work. "Turbo Access" Will Locate, Insert, or Delete Records in a Database, Using B+ Trees. "Turbo Sort" Will Sort Data on Multiple Keys. Features Virtual Memory Management for Sorting Large Data Files. Source Code Is Included.
Borland International, Inc.

Turbo BASIC Editor Toolbox. *Compatible Hardware:* IBM PC & true compatibles, PC XT, PC AT. *Operating System(s) Required:* PC-DOS/MS-DOS 2.0 or higher. *General Requirements:* Turbo BASIC.
 disk $99.95.
Includes Source Code for Two Sample Editors. "First Editor" Is a Complete Editor That Can Be Included into Users' Own Programs, Featuring Windows, Block Commands, & Memory-Mapped Screen Routines. "MicroStar" Is a Text Editor with a Pull-Down Menu User Interface Featuring: Wordwrap; Undo Last Change; Auto-Indent; Find & Find/Replace with Options; Set Left/Right Margins; Block Mark, Move, & Copy; Tab, Insert, Overstrike Modes, Line Center, etc.
Borland International, Inc.

Turbo BASIC: Programming Techniques & Library Development. Namir C. Shammas. Sep. 1989. *Operating System(s) Required:* MS-DOS.
 book & disk $34.95 (ISBN 1-55851-015-X).
 book only $19.95 (ISBN 1-55851-016-8).
Guide for Advanced Programmers on the Syntax & Programming Features of Turbo BASIC. Introduces Programmers to the Turbo BASIC Environment, Programming Framework, & Data Types & the Use of Libraries, Functions & Subroutines to Permit More Structured Coding. The Techniques Discussed Are Then Put to Use Building a Selection of Libraries Including: General Utilities, String Handling, Numerical Analysis, Statistics, Data Structures, & File Manipulation.
M & T Bks.

Turbo BASIC Telecom Toolbox. *Compatible Hardware:* IBM PC & true compatibles, PC XT, PC AT. *Operating System(s) Required:* PC-DOS/MS-DOS 2.0 or higher. *General Requirements:* Turbo BASIC.
 disk $99.95.
Complete Communications Package Which Takes Advantage of the Built-In Communications Capabilities of BASIC. Features Include: Pull-Down Menus & Windows; XMODEM Support; VT100 Terminal Emulation; Captures Text to Disk or Printer; PhoneBook File; 200, 1200, 2400 Baud Support; Supports Script Files; Fast Screen I/O; Support Most of XTalk's Command Set; Manual Dial & Redial Operations. Can Be Used As Is or Modified by the Users to Embed Communications Capabilities into Their Own Programs and/or Build Their Own Communications Package. Source Code Included for All Toolbox Code & Sample Programs.
Borland International, Inc.

Turbo C. *Compatible Hardware:* IBM PC & true compatibles, PC XT, PC AT. *Operating System(s) Required:* PC-DOS/MS-DOS 2.0 or higher. *Memory Required:* 384k.
 disk $99.95 (ISBN 0-87524-184-0).
Includes One-Pass Compiler Generating Linkable Object Modules & Inline Assembler. The Object Module Is Compatible with the PC-DOS Linker. Supports Tiny, Small, Compact, Medium, Large, & Huge Memory Model Libraries. Can Mix Models with Near & Far Pointers. Includes Floating Point Emulator. The Interactive Editor Includes an Interactive Full-Screen Editor. A MAKE Routine Is Included. Links with Relocatable Object Modules. Supports Mixed-Model & Mixed Language Programming & Six Memory Models. ANSI C Compatible with Automatic 8087/80287 Support. Both Command Line & Integrated Environment Versions Included. Start-Up Routine Source Code Included.
Borland International, Inc.

Turbo C++. Mar. 1999.
 PC/MS-DOS 2.0 or higher. IBM PS/2 & compatibles (640k). disk $99.95 (ISBN 0-87524-228-6).
Turbo C++ Is Two Compilers in One: ANSI C & C++. Because C++ Is an Extension of C, User Can Program Now, & Move to C++ at His or Her Own Pace.
Borland International, Inc.

Turbo C: The Art of Advanced Program Design, Optimization, & Debugging. Stephen R. Davis. *Operating System(s) Required:* MS-DOS.
 book & disk $39.95 (ISBN 0-934375-45-3).
 book only $24.95 (ISBN 0-934375-38-0).
Provides Example Programs That Describe the Techniques Necessary to Program, Optimize, & Debug in Turbo C. Advanced Topics Such As Pointers, Direct Screen I/O, Inline Statements in Turbo C, & How to Intercept & Redirect BIOS Calls Are Covered. Outlined Are the Differences Between UNIX C & Turbo C; the Transition from Turbo Pascal to Turbo C; & the Superset of K&R C Features Implemented in Turbo C & Included in the Proposed ANSI C Standard.
M & T Bks.

Turbo CAD Symbols Library: Bathrooms. May 1991. *Items Included:* Manual. *Customer Support:* Unlimited free technical support, BBS 415-454-2893, 30 day unconditional guarantee.
 DOS 3.0 or higher. IBM PC, AT, PS/2 (512k).
 disk $49.95. *Nonstandard peripherals required:* Hard drive, graphics board.
Contains 290 Symbols of Plan & Elevation Views for Professional Bathroom Designing, Including Fixtures, Vanities, Sinks, Faucets, & Lighting. Standard Size Symbols Are Available for Wall Cabinets, Base Cabinets & Drawers with Four Different Door Styles.
IMSI (International Microcomputer Software, Inc.).

Turbo CAD Symbols Library: Home Furnishings II. May 1991. *Customer Support:* 30 day unconditional guarantee, unlimited free phone support, BBS 415-454-2893.
 MS-DOS 2.0 or higher. IBM PC, XT, AT, PS/2 (512k). disk $49.95. *Nonstandard peripherals required:* Hard drive, graphics board.
One Hundred Additional Symbols of Beds, Sofas, Tables, Chairs, Desks, Lamps, Small Appliances, Electronic Equipment, & More. For Use in Home Space Planning & Interior Designing.
IMSI (International Microcomputer Software, Inc.).

Turbo CAD Symbols Library: Kitchens. May 1991. *Items Included:* Manual. *Customer Support:* Unlimited free technical support, 30 day

TITLE INDEX

unconditional guarantee, BBS 415-454-2893.
MS-DOS 2.0 or higher. IBM PC, XT, AT, PS/2
(512k). disk $49.95. *Nonstandard peripherals
required:* Hard drive, graphics board.
*Includes Everything Required for Professional
Designing. Over 260 Plan & Elevation Views of
Kitchen Fixtures, Appliances, Sinks, Faucets. Wall
Cabinets, Base Cabinets & Drawers Are Included
in Many Standard Sizes & with Four Different
Door Styles.*
IMSI (International Microcomputer Software, Inc.).

**Turbo CAD Symbols Library: Office
Furnishings II.** May 1991. *Items Included:*
Manual. *Customer Support:* Unlimited free
technical support, BBS 415-454-2893, 30 day
unconditional guarantee.
MS-DOS 2.0 or higher. IBM PC, XT, AT, PS/2
(512k). disk $49.95. *Nonstandard peripherals
required:* Hard drive, graphics board.
*Two Hundred Fifty Additional Symbols of
Standard Size Panels, Work Surfaces, Desks,
Tables, Credenzas, Files, Shelves, Bookcases, etc.
Miscellaneous Symbols Are Also Included for
Drawing Lunch Rooms, Lobbies & Restrooms.*
IMSI (International Microcomputer Software, Inc.).

Turbo Champions. *Customer Support:* 90 day
warranty.
MS-DOS 2.1 or higher. IBM (256k). 3.5" disk
$12.99; 5.25" disk $9.99. *Nonstandard
peripherals required:* Requires CGA, EGA,
Tandy or VGA Graphics.
*Experience the Excitement of "Sports Car Road
Racing". Race on Eight Uniquely Different &
Challenging Courses, Round Chicanes, Through
Tunnels over Hills Overtaking Cars & Trucks at a
Very Fast Pace. Crashes, Overturning Vehicles,
360 Degree Slides Are All Depicted in Stunning
16 Color Graphics.*
Virgin Games.

Turbo Charge. Bruce Hansen. 1986. *Compatible
Hardware:* TRS-80 Model I, Model III, Model 4.
Operating System(s) Required: MS-DOS.
Memory Required: 64k.
disk $29.95 (Order no.: B8TURBO).
*Displays the Curving, Winding Roads of the Race
Track As Mathematically Perfect As Is Possible
with the Limited TRS-80 Graphics. Unprotected &
Operates As a /CMD File from Model I & III
Disk Operating Systems.*
The Alternate Source.

Turbo Database Toolbox. Jul. 1984. *Compatible
Hardware:* Apple; Apricot; DEC Rainbow, DEC
VT 180; Data General; Eagle; Generic; HP 125,
HP 150 Touchscreen; IBM PC, PC XT, PC AT,
PCjr; Kaypro, Morrow; NEC; North Star;
Osborne; Otrona; Radio Shack 4; Sanyo;
SuperBrain; TeleVideo; Victor 9000; Xerox.
Operating System(s) Required: PC-DOS, MS-
DOS, CP/M-80, CP/M-86. *Language(s):* Pascal.
Memory Required: 64-128k.
$54.95 ea.; MS-DOS (ISBN 0-87524-034-8);
CP/M-80 (ISBN 0-87524-057-7).
$69.95 ea.
Radio Shack 4. (ISBN 0-87524-058-5).
Sanyo. (ISBN 0-87524-059-3).
SuperBrain. (ISBN 0-87524-060-7).
TeleVideo. (ISBN 0-87524-061-5).
Xerox. (ISBN 0-87524-062-3).
manual avail. (ISBN 0-87524-005-4).
*Contains a Complete Library of Pascal
Procedures Allowing the User to Sort & Search
for Data, & Build Applications. Includes the
Source Code of a Working Database. Program Is
Not Copy-Protected.*
Borland International, Inc.

Turbo Debugger. Sep. 1988. *Compatible
Hardware:* IBM PC & compatibles, PS/2.
$149.95.
*Features 80386 Protected Mode Operation
Which Stores the Debugger above the 1Mb Limit
in Protected Memory. A Remote Debugging
Option Is Also Available, Where the Debugger
Runs on One Machine & Controls the Target
Program Via a Serial Port tto Another. Supports
Math Co-Processors & Integrates with TURBO
PASCAL & TURBO C, Allowing Users to Do Both
Source & Object Code-Level Debugging.*
Borland International, Inc.

Turbo Disk. Version: 4.0. Nov. 1988. *Items
Included:* User & technical manual. *Customer
Support:* Telephone; demo's.
$1250.00 to $25,000.00.
*Creates RAM Disk in Main Memory, Defined by
User. I/O Analyzer Is Part of Program &
Identifies "Hot Files". Package Is Easily Installed,
Completely Compatible & Transparent to VMS
Operating System. Data Is Protected by
"Shadowing" or Backup.*
EEC Systems, Inc.

Turbo Editor Toolbox. Dec. 1985. *Compatible
Hardware:* IBM PC & compatibles, PC XT, PC
AT, 3270, Portable. *Operating System(s)
Required:* PC-DOS, MS-DOS. *Language(s):*
Pascal (source code included). *Memory Required:*
128k.
$69.95, incl. manual (ISBN 0-87524-148-4).
*Includes MicroStar, a Full-Featured Word
Processor That Looks & Acts Like WordStar.
Features Windowing, & Gives User the Ability to
Customize Any Word Processor to Fit His
Particular Needs.*
Borland International, Inc.

Turbo Expert: Business Expert System Toolkit.
Version: 2.1. *Compatible Hardware:* IBM PC &
compatibles. *Memory Required:* 256k. *General
Requirements:* Hard disk recommended. *Items
Included:* 32 pg. Thinking Software catalog.
3.5" or 5.25" disk $49.95, incl. manual & quick
reference guide.
*Menu-Driven Approach to Generating Rule-Based
Backward Chaining Exppert Systems Based on
Confidence Factors. When Completed, the
System Will Ask the User to Ask a Series of
Questions to Be Answered on a Scale of 0 (No)
to 10 (Yes). At the Conclusion of the
Consultation, the Expert Will Draw a Graph of
the User's Responses, & Finally Display the
Correct Solution. Includes Demos (BABY,
COUNTRY, MICRO EXPERT).*
Thinking Software, Inc.

Turbo Expert Toolkit. *Compatible Hardware:* IBM
PC & compatibles. *Operating System(s)
Required:* PC-DOS/MS-DOS. *Memory Required:*
256k. *Items Included:* 32 pg. Thinking Software
catalog.
3.5" or 5.25" disk $59.95.
*Allows User to Create System Which Speaks.
Queries & Solutions Are Spoken in English by
Using the SPEECH THING from Covox ($69.95).
Presents Menu-Driven Approach to Generating
User's Rule-Based Backward Chaining Expert
System. Questions Asked, Yes & No Answers on
a Scale of 1 to 10 Provided. Graphs Used &
Solutions Displayed. Manual & Quick Reference
Guide Included.*
Thinking Software, Inc.

Turbo GameWorks. Oct. 1985. *Compatible
Hardware:* 8-bit & 16-bit micros. *Operating
System(s) Required:* PC-DOS, MS-DOS 2.0 or
higher. *Language(s):* Pascal (source code
included). *Memory Required:* 192k.
$69.95 (ISBN 0-87524-146-8).
Includes Three Games (Chess, Go-Moku, Bridge).

TURBO MATH FACTS

*Users Can Modify the Games Any Way They
Choose, While Learning Fundamental Concepts of
Programming & Game Design.*
Borland International, Inc.

Turbo Graphix Toolbox: Programming Aids.
Dec. 1984. *Compatible Hardware:* IBM PC, PC
XT, PC AT, PCjr; most other 8 & 16 bit micros.
Operating System(s) Required: PC-DOS, MS-
DOS 2.0 or higher. *Language(s):* Pascal (source
code included). *Memory Required:* 128k.
$69.95 (ISBN 0-87524-135-2).
manual avail. (ISBN 0-87524-001-1).
*Conatains a Complete Library of Pascal
Procedures & Functions Allowing the User to
Draw & Batch Pie Charts, Bar Charts, Circles,
Rectangles, & a Full Range of Geometric Shapes.
Also Includes Procedures That Save & Restore
Graphic Images to & from Disk.*
Borland International, Inc.

Turbo Lightning. Nov. 1985. *Compatible
Hardware:* IBM PC & true compatibles with 2
disk drives. *Operating System(s) Required:*
PC-DOS/MS-DOS 2.0 or higher. *Memory
Required:* 256k.
disk $99.95 (ISBN 0-87524-147-6).
*Instantly Checks Spelling As the User Types.
Program Is Resident in Memory, 100%
Concurrent, & Works with Any Other Program
(Word Processing, Communications, etc.). While
the Spell Checker Offers Sound-Alike
Alternatives, the Thesaurus Will Give Synonyms.
Includes the Engine, the 83,000 Word Random
House Speller & Word List, & the 50,000-Word
Random House Thesaurus.*
Borland International, Inc.

Turbo Lightning Word Wizard. Jun. 1986.
Compatible Hardware: IBM PC & compatibles.
Operating System(s) Required:
PC-DOS/MS-DOS 2.0 or higher. *Language(s):*
Pascal (source code included). *Memory Required:*
256k.
disk $69.95 (ISBN 0-87524-151-4).
*Source Code "Toolbox" for TURBO LIGHTNING.
Four Games & Solvers Are Documented with
Source Code. Games Feature Three or Four
Levels of Difficulty. Its Pascal Utilities Include a
Modular Help System with Data Compression &
High-Speed, Screen-Handling Routines. Over
Twenty TURBO PASCAL Procedures Unveil Many
of TURBO LIGHTNING's Engine Calls.*
Borland International, Inc.

**Turbo-Mac 2 Automotive Management
System.** Version: 1.3. *Compatible Hardware:* All
Apple Macintosh. *General Requirements:* Hard
disk, ImageWriter II, 2 MG ROM. *Items
Included:* On-site training included in purchase
price. Free 1st-year updates & software technical
support. After 1st year, $325/yr. technical
support & $325/yr. program updates. *Customer
Support:* 1 users manual, 800 service number.
3.5" disk $6200.00.
*Automotive Repair Shop Management System
Which Provides a Range of Management Tools
Designed to Improve Shop Effciency,
Productivity, & Profitability. Includes Tracking of
Customer & Vehicle Information; Generation of
Customer Invoices, Daily Performance Reports &
Extensive Management Reports & Service
Reminders.*
Micron Computer Co., Inc.

Turbo Math Facts. Version: 2.0. Feb. 1992. *Items
Included:* Manual & 1 diskette.
System 6.0.7 or higher. Macintosh Plus or higher
(1Mb). 3.5" disk $49.95 (ISBN 0-940081-
23-7).
Windows 3.1. 386SX or higher. 3.5" disk $49.95
(ISBN 0-940081-72-5). *Nonstandard
peripherals required:* Mouse, SVGA, sound

card.
Macintosh & Windows. CD-ROM disk $49.95 (ISBN 1-57374-012-8).
Develop Solid Math Skills in Addition, Subtraction, Multiplication, & Division. Correct Answers Earn Monetary Rewards. Buy the Fastest Race Car You Can Afford & Challenge Turbo Tom to a Race. Realistic Sound, Animation, & Color Combine to Create an Exciting Environment for Learning Math.
Nordic Software, Inc.

turbo Paragon. Version: 4.30. Compatible Hardware: IBM PC & compatibles. Memory Required: 384k. General Requirements: Hard disk. Items Included: GL, AR, AP, Invoicing, Financials, Payroll, Job Cost, Inventory. Customer Support: $90.00 per hour prepaid (telephone). $995.00 per package.
Automatic Posting from Other Modules, Report Format User Definable, Reports Comparative Statements, Ability to Jump Modules, Wild Card, Links with External Software Programs, Password Access, Encryption, Audit Trail, Error Recovery, Automatic Back-Up for Each Module, Log off Out-of-Balance, Reject Erroneous Account Numbers & On-Line Help.
P&L Assocs.

Turbo Pascal. Version: 3.0. Nov. 1983. Compatible Hardware: Commodore; IBM PC, PC jr, PC XT, PC AT. Operating System(s) Required: PC-DOS, MS-DOS, CP/M-80, CP/M-86. Language(s): Pascal. Memory Required: 128k. $69.95 ea.
CP/M-86 & MS-DOS (ISBN 0-87524-011-9); IBM PC, MS-DOS (ISBN 0-87524-131-x); Generic/SS, MS-DOS (ISBN 0-87524-132-8); IBM PC/SS, MS-DOS (ISBN 0-87524-133-6); DEC Rainbow, MS-DOS (ISBN 0-87524-134-4); Altos, CP/M-80 (ISBN 0-87524-138-7); Actrix, CP/M-80; Generic SS, MS-DOS (ISBN 0-87524-006-2); Data General, MS-DOS (ISBN 0-87524-007-0).
DEC Rainbow, CP/M-86 (ISBN 0-87524-012-7); CP/M-86, (ISBN 0-87524-013-5); Z-80, CP/M-80 (ISBN 0-87524-015-1); DEC VT 180, CP/M-80 (ISBN 0-87524-016-X); Eagle, CP/M-80 (ISBN 0-87524-017-8); Apple, CP/M-80 (ISBN 0-87524-014-3); Epson, CP/M-80 (ISBN 0-87524-018-6); HP 150, MS-DOS (ISBN 0-87524-008-9).
Heath Hard, CP/M-80 (ISBN 0-87524-019-4); Heath Soft, CP/M-80 (ISBN 0-87524-020-8); HP 125, CP/M-80 (ISBN 0-87524-021-6); Kaypro, CP/M-80 (ISBN 0-87524-022-4); Apricot, MS-DOS (ISBN 0-87524-009-7).
Morrow, CP/M-80 (ISBN 0-87524-023-2); NEC, CP/M-80 (ISBN 0-87524-024-0); North Star, CP/M-80 (ISBN 0-87524-025-9).
Osborne, CP/M-80 (ISBN 0-87524-026-7); Otrona, CP/M-80 (ISBN 0-87524-027-5).
with BCD & 8087 only $99.95.
manual avail. (ISBN 0-87524-003-8).
Borland International, Inc.

Turbo Pascal. Version: 4.0. Oct. 1987. Compatible Hardware: IBM PC & compatibles, PS/2. Operating System(s) Required: PC-DOS 2.0 or higher. Memory Required: 256k.
Turbo Pascal 4.0 Compiler. 5-1/4" or 3-1/2" disk $99.95 (upgrade $39.95) (ISBN 0-87524-170-0).
Turbo Pascal 4.0 Developer's Library. $395.00, (upgrade 150.00).
Turbo Pascal Tutor. $69.95, (upgrade 19.95).
Turbo Pascal Database Toolbox. $99.95, (upgrade 29.95).
Turbo Pascal Graphix Toolbox. $99.95, (upgrade 29.95).
Turbo Pascal Editor Toolbox. $99.95 (upgrade 29.95).
Turbo Pascal Numerical Methods Toolbox. $99.95, (upgrade 29.95).
Turbo Pascal Gameworks. $99.95, (upgrade 29.95).
Pascal Compiler - Able to Handle More Than 27,000 Lines of Code a Minute. Supports Program Larger Than 64k. Gives Programmers an Integrated Programming Environment with Pull-Down Menus, a Built-In Editor & an Interactive Debugger. Features Also Include a Command-Line Version of the Compiler & On-Line Help. Includes a Conversion Program to Help Users Convert Their 3.0 Programs to 4.0. Not Copy Protected.
Borland International, Inc.

Turbo Pascal Database Toolbox. Compatible Hardware: Apple Macintosh.
3.5" disk $99.95.
Provides Sort & Search Routines Needed for Pascal Database Applications. Also Provides TURBO PASCAL Routines for Reading & Writing Data to & from REFLEX for Macintosh Files. "Turbo Access" Locates, Inserts, or Deletes Records Using B+ Trees. "Turbo Sort" Uses the "Quicksort" Method to Sort Data on Single Items or Multiple Keys. Includes Source Code on Disk & a Free Sample Databse Using the Macintosh That Users Can Adapt to Their Individual Needs.
Borland International, Inc.

Turbo Pascal for the Macintosh. Compatible Hardware: Apple Macintosh.
3.5" disk $99.95.
Features Provided Include the Following: Compilation Speed of More Than 12,000 Lines per Minute; "Unit" Structure, Which Allows Users to Create Programs in Modular Form; Up to Eight Editing Windows at a Time; Compilation Options Which Include Compiling to Disk or Memory, or Compile & Run; No Need to Switch Between Programs to Compile or Run Program; Compatibility with LISA PASCAL & MACINTOSH PROGRAMMER'S WORKSHOP PASCAL (with Minor Changes); Compatibility with the Hierarchical File System of the Macintosh; Ability to Use All Macintosh Memory Without Limit; "Units" to Call All Routines Provided by MACINTOSH TOOLBOX.
Borland International, Inc.

Turbo Pascal for Windows. Mar. 1991.
Windows 3.0 or higher. IBM PC & compatibles. disk $249.95. Nonstandard peripherals required: EGA or VGA graphics & mouse (or other pointing device). 80286 or higher processor.
Program to Develop Microsoft Windows Applications.
Borland International, Inc.

Turbo Pascal Numerical Methods Toolbox for the Macintosh. Compatible Hardware: Apple Macintosh. Memory Required: 512k.
3.5" disk $99.95.
Collection of Routines & Programs for Solving Common Problems in Science & Engineering. Includes: Solutions to Equations; Interpolations; Matrix Operations - Inversions, Determinants, & Eigenvalues; Differential Equations; Least Squares Approximations; & Fourier Transforms. Source Code Can Be Included in User's Own Programs.
Borland International, Inc.

Turbo Pascal Numerical Methods Toolbox for IBM. Jan. 1987. Compatible Hardware: IBM PC & true compatibles; PC XT, PC AT. Operating System(s) Required: PC-DOS/MS-DOS 2.0 or higher. Memory Required: 256k. General Requirements: Turbo Pascal 2.0 or higher. Graphics Module requires graphics monitor with CGA, EGA, or Hercules compatible card; Turbo Graphix Toolbox. 8087 or 80287 recommended for optimal performance.
disk $99.95 (ISBN 0-87524-182-4).
Provides a Collection of TURBO PASCAL Routines for Mathematical & Engineering Problem Solving. The Collection Consists of Procedures, Sample Programs, & Source Code Covering: Zeros of a Function, Interpolation, Differentiation, Integration, Matrix Inversion, Matrix Eigenvalues, Differential Equations, Least Squares, Fourier Transforms, & Graphics. Source Code Is Provided for All Programs.
Borland International, Inc.

Turbo Pascal Tutor for the Macintosh. Compatible Hardware: Apple Macintosh. Memory Required: 512k.
3.5" disk $69.95.
Companion to TURBO PASCAL. Interactive Tutorial Which Teaches Users How to Program the Macintosh in Pascal, from the Basics to Advanced Programing on the Macintosh, in TURBO PASCAL, MPW Pascal, or Any Version of the Language Being Used. Includes the Following: a History of Pascal, & Step-by-Step Concepts for the Beginning Programmer; "Programmer's Guide" Explaining Aspects of the Language, from Program Structure to Data Types, Records, & Files; Advanced Programming Section Covering Linked Lists, Stacks, Sorting & Searching Algorithms, etc.; Guide to Using the Features of the Macintosh in Pascal Programming, from Use of the Visual Interface to Memory Management & Debugging; Source Code on Disk, Which Can Be Incorporated in Programs Created by the User, Without Having to Pay Royalties.
Borland International, Inc.

Turbo Pilot. Customer Support: 800-929-8117 (customer service).
MS-DOS. Apple II. disk $49.99 (ISBN 0-87007-807-0).
Pilot Programming Language, Based on Powerful Public Domain Version, Bur Significantly Enhanced, with Major Extensions.
SourceView Software International.

Turbo Plus. Version: 6.0. 1991. Items Included: Diskettes, Manual. Customer Support: 8-5 MST.
DOS. IBM compatible (350k). disk $199.00 or $349.00 with source code. Addl. software required: Turbo-Pascal version 5.5 or 6.0. Optimal configuration: 286 PC 640k.
A Turbo Pascal 5.5-6.0 Toolkit. Consists of Unit Libraries, Screen Painter, Source Code Generator, Prototyper, Sample Programs & Pop-Up Help System. Supports Both Standard & Object Oriented Programming. Complete Menu-Data Entry Form Objects Can Be Generated with the Turbo Plus Screen Painter. Source Code Is Available for the Turbo Pascal Units. Full 30 Day Guarantee.
Instant Replay Corp.

Turbo-Plus: Enhanced Support Package. Aug. 1983. Operating System(s) Required: Turbo DOS. Memory Required: 64k.
8" disk $350.00.
System Utility with Electronic Mail & Batch Processing.
Microserve, Inc.

Turbo Professional. Version: 5.2. Oct. 1993. Items Included: 2 lay-flat perfect bound manuals, pop-up online reference guide. Customer Support: Free technical support, 60 day money-back guarantee, free electronic maintenance updates, Compuserve technical support.
MS-DOS 2.0 or higher (360k). IBM PC, AT, PS/2, compatibles. disk $169.00. Addl. software required: Turbo Pascal 4.0, 5.0, 5.5, 6.0, 7.0. Optimal configuration: Hard disk, 640k RAM.
A Library of 600 Essential Procedures & Functions Optimized for Non-OOP Turbo Pascal.

Includes: Memory Resident Program Shell; Interrupt Service Routines; Keyboard Macro Processing; Sorting & Searching; String Manipulation; Arrays Larger Than 64K; Windows, Menus, & Virtual Screens; Help Systems, Pick Lists, Text Editing, & Validated Data Entry; Integrated Mouse Support; BCD Arithmetic; Advanced DOS Access; Runtime Error Recovery; & More. Also Supplied Are a Dozen Useful Demonstration Programs, Including a Menu System Source Code Generator. Includes Complete Source Code & a 750 Page Two Volume Manual.
TurboPower Software.

Turbo Prolog. Apr. 1986. *Compatible Hardware:* IBM PC & true compatibles, PC XT, PC AT, Portable PC, 3270 PC. *Operating System(s) Required:* PC-DOS/MS-DOS 2.0 or higher. *Memory Required:* 384k. *General Requirements:* 2 disk drives.
disk $99.95, incl. manual (ISBN 0-87524-150-6).
Includes an Incremental Compiler Generating Native In-Line Code & Linkable Object Module. Linking Format Is Compatible with PC-DOS Linker. System Also Includes an Interactive Editor. Supports an Object-Oriented Type System & Both Graphic & Text Windows. Has Complete Debug Trace Debugging Capabilities Allowing Single-Stepping of Programs. Package Includes the GeoBase Database Designed & Developed Around U.S. Geography.
Borland International, Inc.

Turbo Prolog Toolbox. *Compatible Hardware:* IBM PC & true compatibles, PC XT, PC AT. *Operating System(s) Required:* PC-DOS/MS-DOS 2.0 or higher. *Memory Required:* 512k. *General Requirements:* Turbo Prolog 1.10 or higher; dual floppy disk drive or hard disk.
disk $99.95 (ISBN 0-87524-183-2).
Enhances Turbo Prolog with More Than 80 Tools & Over 8,000 Lines of TURBO PROLOG Source Codes That Can Be Incorporated into User's Programs. Also Included Are about 40 Sample Programs. Includes the Following Features: Business Graphic Generation; Communications Package, File Transfers from REFLEX, dBASE III, 1-2-3, Symphony; Parser Generator, User-Interface Design Tools.
Borland International, Inc.

Turbo Prolog 2.0. *Compatible Hardware:* IBM PC, PC XT, PC AT & compatibles, PS/2. *Memory Required:* 384k. *General Requirements:* Hard disk recommended.
$149.95.
New Features Included in This Version Include: an External Database & a User Interface More Consistent with That of Other BORLAND Products. Included Is an Edinburgh-Style PROLOG Interpreter, the PROLOG INFERENCE ENGINE, Which Conforms to the Standard Edinburgh Dialect.
Borland International, Inc.

Turbo Screen Master. *Items Included:* User's manual.
MS-DOS 2.0 or higher (256k). IBM PC/XT/AT or 100% compatible. $69.95. *Addl. software required:* Turbo Pascal or Turbo C compiler from Borland International.
Screen Generation Utility for Turbo Pascal & Turbo C. Programmers Can Create Data Entry Screens & Help Windows Using a Simple Interactive Process. TSM Generates the Pascal or C Source Code to Implement Those Screens. Supports IBM PC Color & Graphics Character Capabilities.
Blue Bridge Software.

Turbo Shell: Generic Expert System. *Version:* 3. Apr. 1987. *Compatible Hardware:* IBM PC & compatibles. *Operating System(s) Required:* MS-DOS. *Language(s):* Turbo Prolog (source code included). *Memory Required:* 256k.
disk incl. manual $119.00.
Designed to Provide an Environment for the Development of Expert Systems. Provides Menu-Driven Facilities for Creating, Modifying, & Consulting Knowledge Bases. The System Is Based on EMYCIN Model Using Production Rules for the Classification of Knowledge & Calculation of Certainty Factors. Explanations of the System's Line of Reasoning Can Be Invoked Dynamically at Conclusion of Session. Will Provide a Knowledge Tree for Any Knowledge Base. Reports Can Be Directed to Disk File or Printer.
Berkshire Software Co.

Turbo Solitaire. *Items Included:* Bound manual. *Customer Support:* Free hotline - no time limit; 30 day limited warranty; updates are $5/disk plus S&H.
MS-DOS. IBM & compatibles (128k). disk $19.95. *Nonstandard peripherals required:* One disk drive; graphics not required.
Plays Five Fast-Paced & Strategy-Filled Versions of Solitaire. It Combines the Enjoyment of Card Games with the Challenge of Strategy Games in One Fun-Filled Program.
Dynacomp, Inc.

Turbo Spelling Tutor. *Items Included:* Bound manual. *Customer Support:* Free hotline - no time limit; 30 day limited warranty; updates are $5/disk plus S&H.
MS-DOS 2.0 or higher. IBM & compatibles (not available for PCjr) (128k). disk $39.95. *Nonstandard peripherals required:* One disk drive; CGA or equivalent; printer supported, but not required.
Spelling & Vocabulary Aid for Students of All Ages. It Is Suited to Any Subject That Involves Either Words Alone, or Words & Their Associated Meanings, Definitions, Dates, or Events. Features Include the Following: Word Randomizing & Test Scoring; Full Word & Definition List Editing; Search & Retrieve, or Page Through Definitions; A Variety of Practice & Test Methods; Directory & File Management Utilities.
Dynacomp, Inc.

Turbo Spring-Stat Multivariate Statistics. *Items Included:* Full manual. No other products required. *Customer Support:* Free telephone support - no time limit. 30 day warranty.
MS-DOS 3.2 or higher. IBM & compatibles (512k). $29.95-$195.00.
Designed to Meet the Data Analysis Needs of Business, Social Science, Market Research, Economics, Financial, Engineering, & Academic Professionals. While These Needs Have Been Met in the Past by Mainframe Packages (& More Recently by Downscaled or Expensive Versions of These Packages), SPRING-STAT Offers Some Unique Features. The 200 Plus Page Manual Covers All Aspects of the System. Sample Data & On-Screen Instructions Are Also Included.
Dynacomp, Inc.

Turbo Spring-Stat: Multivariate Statistics. 1992. *Items Included:* Detailed manuals included with all Dynacomp products. *Customer Support:* Free telephone support to original customer - no time limit; 30 day limited warranty.
MS-DOS 3.2 or higher. IBM PC & compatibles (512k). $29.95 each module; $29.95 manual plus demo disk; $399.95 Complete system incl. manual (Add $5.00 for 3 1/2" format; 5 1/4" format standard). *Optimal configuration:* IBM, MS-DOS 2.1 or higher, 256k RAM, two floppy disk drives (or one floppy & a hard disk), & an 80-column or wider printer.

Designed to Meet the Data Analysis Needs of Business, Social Science, Market Research, Economics, Financial, Engineering & Academic Professionals. While These Needs Have Been Met in the Past by Mainframe Packages (& More Recently by Downscaled or Expensive Versions of These Packages), SPRING-STAT Offers Some Unique Features: It's Comfortable to Learn & Use. The Entire System Is Prompt/Menu Driven & Interactive. The System Is Integrated & Modular. The 200 Plus Page Manual Covers All Aspects of the System. Sample Data & On-Screen Instructions Are Also Included. Data Is Stored in ASCII Format.
Dynacomp, Inc.

TURBO Spring-Stat: Statistical Analysis System. *Version:* 3.12. Feb. 1994. *Items Included:* Manual (hard copy), data base, spread sheet, text editor, expert system, math co-processor support, statistics modules, new HI-RES graphics module, trial disk available for $10.00. *Customer Support:* Free to get started; after that, $2.00 per minute, minimum of 10 minutes.
DOS 2.1 or higher (385k), Windows 3.X. PC/XT/AT/PS 2 or compatibles. $39.95 per module; $469.95 for whole system; $10.00 for trial disk; $39.95 evaluation package; $69.95 Windows evaluation package. *Optimal configuration:* 640k RAM, DOS 3.1 or up, hard disk, any printer, math co-processor, color monitor, (CGA, EGA, VGA, HGA, for HI-RES graphics module).
Modular, Integrated, Full Featured Statistical Package & Its 22 Modules Include Data Management, Graphics, a Text Editor, an Expert System, & Statistical Modules That Run the Gamut from Simple Descriptive Statistics to Sophisticated Multivariate Analysis. Uses Comfortable, Easy to Learn Point n' Pick Pop-up Menus & Dialog Boxes in User Interface. NEW: HI-RES graphics module.
Spring Systems, Inc.

Turbo Spring-Stat Text Editor II: ASCII Data File Editor. 1992. *Items Included:* Detailed manuals included with all Dynacomp products. *Customer Support:* Free telephone support to original customer - no time limit; 30 day limited warranty.
MS-DOS 3.2 or higher. IBM PC & compatibles (512k). $39.95 (Add $5.00 for 3 1/2" format; 5 1/4" format standard). *Optimal configuration:* IBM, MS-DOS 2.0 or higher, 512k RAM, CGA/EGA/VGA or compatible graphics capability. A mouse is optional. Does not require WINDOWS to operate.
A Powerful ASCII Data File Editor with a Very Extensive Complement of Features. It Supports a Mouse, a Clipboard, & As Many 64K Windows (Each Containing a Different File) As Free Memory Allows. Each of the Windows Is Accompanied by a Scroll Bar & Is Both Moveable & Resizable. You May Cut-&-Paste Both Within & Between Files.
Dynacomp, Inc.

Turbo Spring-Stat Text Editor 2 ASCII Data File Editor. *Items Included:* Full manual. No other products required. *Customer Support:* Free telephone support - no time limit. 30 day warranty.
MS-DOS 3.2 or higher. IBM & compatibles (512k). disk $39.95. *Optimal configuration:* IBM, MS-DOS 2.0 or higher, 512k RAM, CGA/EGA/VGA or compatible graphics capability.
Powerful ASCII Data File Editor with a Very Extensive Complement of Features. Supports a Mouse, Clipboard, & As Many 64K Windows (Each Containing a Different File) As Free Memory Allows. Each of the Windows Is Accompanied by a Scroll Bar & Is Both Moveable & Resizable.
Dynacomp, Inc.

TURBO TUTOR: PASCAL PROGRAMMING

Turbo Tutor: Pascal Programming Primer.
1984. *Compatible Hardware:* Apple; Apricot; Data General; DEC Rainbow; DEC VT 180; Eagle; Generic; HP 125, HP 150 Touchscreen; IBM PC, PC XT, PC AT, PCjr; Kaypro; Morrow; NEC; North Star; Osborne; Otrona; Radio Shack 4; Sanyo; SuperBrain; TeleVideo; Xerox. *Operating System(s) Required:* PC-DOS, MS-DOS, CP/M-80, CP/M-86. *Language(s):* Pascal. *Memory Required:* 64-128k.
 MS-DOS, CP/M-80, & CP/M-86 machines (ISBN 0-87524-063-1; 0-87524-091-7). $39.95.
 manual (ISBN 0-87524-004-6).
Borland International, Inc.

Turbo User Group (TUG). *Customer Support:* All of our products are unconditionally guaranteed.
DOS. CD-ROM disk $39.95 (Order no.: TUG).
 Nonstandard peripherals required: CD-ROM drive.
Entire Collection of TUG Source Code, News, & Utilities, C, Pascal, Ada, Etc.
Walnut Creek CDRom.

Turbo Windows. *Version:* 4.0. Jun. 1989. *Items Included:* User & technical manual. *Customer Support:* Yearly contract - pricing varies with CPO.
VMS V5.1 to V4.4 (4Mb). VAX. contact publisher for price. *Networks supported:* All.
Layered Software - Creates Multiple Windows on Std. Terminal. Concurrent Windows Can Be Viewed on One Window Full Screen. Allows Several Sessions Simultaneously on a Std. Terminal.
EEC Systems, Inc.

TurboCAD. *Version:* 3.1. Nov. 1990. *Compatible Hardware:* PC AT, PS/2, 286, 386, 486, & compatibles. *Operating System(s) Required:* MS-DOS 3.0 or higher. *Memory Required:* 640-1000k. *General Requirements:* Hard drive, graphics board. *Customer Support:* Unlimited free technical support, BBS 415-454-2893, 30 day unconditional guarantee.
3.5" or 5.25" disk $149.95.
Enables User to Create Simple or Complex Drawings Which Otherwise Would Be Created in Architectural Type Drawing Situations, Including Construction, Electrical, Plumbing, Landscape, Machine, Engineering, with Use of Layers, Different Line Types, Line Thicknesses, Auto Dimensioning, & DXF File Conversion. Includes 250 Free Drawing Symbols.
IMSI (International Microcomputer Software, Inc.).

TurboCad Designer for Windows: Fastest, Easiest Way to Draw. *Customer Support:* Tech support - free, 60-day money-back guarantee.
Windows 3.1 or higher. IBM compatible 386 or higher (2Mb). disk $49.95 (ISBN 0-924677-28-7). *Nonstandard peripherals required:* Mouse recommended. *Addl. software required:* Math Co-Processor recommended. *Optimal configuration:* IBM, VGA, EGA, SVGA.
The Ideal Drawing & Drafting Package for the Home Designer & Occasional User. Budget-Priced. Comes with 80 Professionally Drawn, True to Scale Home Design Symbols. You'll Quickly Discover a Full Complement of CAD Features Typically Reserved for High-End & High-Priced Packages Smart Cursors. Automatic Dimensioning, Snap Modes, 256 Layers & More.
IMSI (International Microcomputer Software, Inc.).

TurboGeometry. *Compatible Hardware:* Apple Macintosh Plus.
3.5" disk $149.95.
Library Featuring More Than 150 Two & Three-Dimensional Geometric Routines for CAD/CAM/ CAE Programmers. Features Equations of Lines, Circles & Planes, Intersection of Lines, Circles, Arcs & Planes, Decomposition of Polygon, Hidden Line Removal, Volume & Area Calculations, Perspectives, Line & Polygon Clipping, Composite Transformation Matrices & 2 & 3-Dimensional Transformations. Source Code Is Included.
Disk Software, Inc.

TurboGeometry Library. *Compatible Hardware:* Apple Macintosh Plus or higher; IBM PC, PC XT, PC AT, & compatibles. *Memory Required:* 256k. *General Requirements:* CGA or EGA card. Hard disk recommended.
$149.95, $199.95 with source code.
Includes More Than 150 Geometric Routines That Can Be Used in Creating Graphic Designs. Includes Routines to: Find the Intersection of Polygons, Circles, Arcs, & Planes; Determine the Coefficients of the Equations of Lines, Circles, Arcs, & Planes; Convert the Coefficients of One Equation to Another; Find the Distance Between Points, Lines, Circles, Arcs, & Planes; Create Perspective Drawings; Perform Two- & Three-Dimensional Transformations; etc.
Disk Software, Inc.

TurboSPC Software. *Version:* 3.3. Aug. 1990. *Customer Support:* Free life-time phone support; purchase training.
DOS 2.1 or higher. IBM PC or compatible (512k). $995.00 without data collector interface; $2995.00 with data collector interface. *Nonstandard peripherals required:* Hard disk required.
A Package to Help Professionals Manage Their Statistical Process Control Program. It Analyzes Variables or Attributes Data Collected Manually or by DataMyte Data Collectors. TurboSPC is a Database Program with Mouse-Supported Pull-Down Menus. It Includes Fifteen Different Statistical Control & Analysis Charts.
DataMyte Corp.

Turbosynth. *Version:* 2.0. *Compatible Hardware:* Apple Macintosh Plus, SE, SE/30, II, IIx, IIcx. *Memory Required:* 1000k.
3.5" disk $349.00.
Modular Synthesis-Signal Processing Software. Allows Users to Design & Edit Waveforms Using Object-Oriented Approach.
Digidesign, Inc.

Turnkey & Menu. *Compatible Hardware:* IBM. *Memory Required:* 128k.
disk $19.95.
Permits Selection of Any BASIC Program to Be Automatically Run at System Power-Up.
Dynacomp, Inc.

Turnstyle. *Version:* 2.0. *Customer Support:* Hot-line phone support.
MS-DOS/PC-DOS 3.0 or higher. IBM PC & compatibles. $395.00. *Networks supported:* Novell NetWare, Banyan Vines.
LAN Management Utility That Allows the Metering of Software Licenses on Novell Banyan LANs. After Completing a Few Simple Steps to Load the Program on the Network, Data Is Entered about Each Program, Then Program Automatically Controls the Number of Software Copies in Circulation. Software Is Metered by the Number of Copies Entered into the Data Base. Serial Numbers Can Be Entered to Keep a Complete Inventory of All Application Software in Use on the Network. Includes a Sophisticated Real Time Monitoring System That Lets the LAN Administrator See Which Programs Are Being Used by Network Users at Any Given Time. It Keeps Track of When Too Many Users Try to Access an Application & If They Cancel Their Request When All Licenses Are In Use.
Connect Computer Co., Inc.

SOFTWARE ENCYCLOPEDIA 1996

Turtle Toyland Jr. *Customer Support:* 800-929-8117 (customer service).
MS-DOS. Apple II. disk $29.99 (ISBN 0-87007-850-X).
A Pre-Logo Joystick-Operated Introduction to Programming for Ages 6 to 80. A Computerized Toybox Full of Fun! Learn Computer Concepts While Playing with Paints, Music Boxes, & Toys That Come to Life on the Screen. Guide a Real Turtle on the Screen to Create, Move & Store Pictures & Characters. A Gentle & Playful Introduction to Programming That Encourages Learning, Exploration & Creativity. Challenges Exploration & Thinking in Children Ages 6 & Beyond. It Allows the Older Child to Create Pictures, Train Sprites to Fly, & Compose Music. These Creations Can be Organized into a "Filmstrip" to be Played & Enjoyed Many Times.
SourceView Software International.

TUTCAD: Graphical User Interface. Sep. 1993. *Items Included:* Manual, examples. *Customer Support:* Technical support by phone at no cost.
DOS. IBM & compatibles (1.5Mb). disk Personal Multi Sheet $49.95, Professional Multi Sheet $149.95 (Order no.: TUTCAD). *Addl. software required:* TUTSIM. *Optimal configuration:* Same as TUTSIM.
Graphical User Interface (GUI) for the TUTSIM Block Diagram Simulation Program. Graphically Creates, Edits & Documents a TUTSIM Block Diagram Model. Hard Copy of the Model Can Be Printed on Any Epson Dot Matrix or HP Laser Jet or Compatible. Carries the Full Library of TUTSIM Functions & upon Conclusion Will Automatically Make a .SIM File into TUTSIM for Execution.
Tutsim Products.

Tutor-Tech Hypermedia Software. *Version:* 2.6. Daniel Lampert & David Lampert. Jan. 1985. *Items Included:* 3 disks (Teacher: for creating stacks, Student: for presenting stacks, & Samples, with sample stacks & art clippings); 1 spiral bound guide (200 pages), catalog of ready-made stacks. *Customer Support:* Free lifetime disk replacement, free telephone technical support at (407) 695-9000, 9am-5pm, EST, M-F; telephone technical support is also lifetime plan.
disk $195.00.
Apple II Hypermedia/Multimedia System Works Like the Macintosh HyperCard. Author (Stacks) Using Pull-Down Menus, Icons, Text, Graphics, & Buttons. Import Clip-Art from PrintShop, Newsroom, & Other Hi-res Pictures. Control Videodiscs, VCR, Video Overlay Card. Speech Synthesizers, Audio Tape Player, Touch Window, Alternative Keyboard, & More.
Techware Corp.

TUTORI/O. *Version:* 3.0. Jan. 1986. *Operating System(s) Required:* CP/M 2.2 or higher. *Language(s):* Assembly. *Memory Required:* 24k.
disk $35.00.
The Software "Breadboard" for CP/M File Functions. User Can Invoke Any I/O Function & See the Results with One Keystroke. I/O Interactions Can Be Analyzed & Debugged in Seconds, Instead of Hours. Also Doubles As a Disk Utility, Allowing Access to Any File by Name & Record Number.
Logic Assocs.

Tutorial Programs for Advanced Ear Training, 9 disks. Bruce Benward & Brian Moore. May 1986. *Compatible Hardware:* Apple II with Applesoft Firmware Card, II+, IIe. *Memory Required:* 64k. *General Requirements:* AppleSoft Firmware Card, DAC board & headphones or speaker.
disk $200.00 (ISBN 0-697-00400-7).
Provides Interactive Study Exercises Designed to Be Used As a Supplement to Classroom Instruction.
Wm. C. Brown Pubs.

TITLE INDEX

The Tutorial Set. *Compatible Hardware:* IBM & compatibles. *Operating System(s) Required:* Dos 2.0 or higher. *Memory Required:* 128k. *Items Included:* PC instructor, professor DOS, & smart guide for DOS. *Customer Support:* Call Individual Software (90 days).
disk $79.95.
Provides Training from Introduction to Computers Through DOS.
Individual Software.

Tutorials in Applied Physics: Self-Study Modules. Paul E. Tippens. Sep. 1987. *Compatible Hardware:* IBM PC, PC XT, PC AT. *Operating System(s) Required:* PC-DOS 2.0 or higher. *Memory Required:* 64k. *General Requirements:* Color graphics monitor with 340 x 200 resolution.
Set - Vols. 1-4. write for info., incl. user's guide (ISBN 0-07-838742-6).
$99.00 ea., vol.
Provides Self-Paced Tutorials & Problem-Solving Exercises in Physics. Each Topic Module Parallels Subject Matter Commonly Taught in Non-Calculus Technical & Applied Physics Courses in Post-Secondary Levels.
Gregg/McGraw-Hill.
   Vol. 1. Preparatory Physics.
   (ISBN 0-07-838733-7).
   Vol. 2. Vector Mechanics.
   (ISBN 0-07-838735-3).
   Vol. 3. Linear Kinematics.
   (ISBN 0-07-838737-X).
   Vol. 4. Rotational Motion.
   (ISBN 0-07-838739-6).

Tutsim Linear & Nonlinear System Simulator.
Items Included: Bound manual. *Customer Support:* Free hotline - no time limit; 30 day limited warranty; updates are $5/disk plus S&H.
MS-DOS 2.0 or higher. IBM & compatibles (256k, Evaluation & Collegiate versions; 384k, Professional version). $39.95-$649.95. *Nonstandard peripherals required:* CRT graphics require CGA, EGA, or Hercules graphics cards (or equivalent); math coprocessor supported, but not required.
Simulation Package Which Allows User to Logically Model a System (e.g., Electronic, Mechanical, Chemical, Production, Demographic, etc.) & Analyze the Response. Basically, You Describe Your System As a Collection of Functional Blocks Which Represent the Steps in the Process. Next, You Enter the Block Descriptions & Their Interconnections into TUTSIM & Perform the Simulation. You May Then Review the Results in Tabular Form or Examine Them Graphically.
Dynacomp, Inc.

TUTSIM, Professional Version: The Engineering Design Aid. *Version:* 7.11. Twente University of Technology, TUTSIM Products. Feb. 1992. *Language(s):* Assembly, C.
PC-DOS/MS-DOS. IBM PC & compatible (256k). Corporate $695.00 (Order no.: F1).
Personal $149.00.
$495.00 Academic.
disk Personal Version $149.00.
"C" User Blocks $435.00 (Order no.: USRC).
Fortran User Blocks $1600.00 (Order no.: USRF).
Simulation for Designing & Optimizing Continuous Systems. Permits Graphic, Numeric & Plotted Representation of Linear & Piecewise-Linear Systems. Lets User Solve Engineering Design Problems by Constructing a Block Diagram Simulation Model, Operating the Simulation & Evaluating Results. User Can Vary Model Design, Add or Delete Blocks, Change Parameters, Alter Interconnections, Change Timing, or Vary Method of Output Anytime During Simulation. User Defined Block Option Allows User to Write Custom Functions That Are Specific to Your Particular Application & Merge These Functions with the Full Power of TUTSIM Thus Enabling Virtually Unlimited Extensibility.
Tutsim Products.

TUTSIM Real Signal, Real Voltage, Realtime Option: RT-IO Option.
disk $385.00, incl. source code (Order no.: RT).
disk $870.00 incl. "plug & play" option ADC & DAC hardware (Order no.: RTPCL).
This Option Allows the User to Work with a System That is Partly Simulated & Partly Real Hardware. This May Be a Shaft Speed, a Liquid Level in a Vat or a Control Signal to a Furnace. Signals to & from the IN/OUT Blocks Are Conceptually Conducted by the Lines in a Block Diagram & Can Be Programmed to Convert These Values of Simulation to Real Voltages & Currents Which Can Operate Real Motors, Heaters, etc. Conversely, These Values May Be Converted by the IN Block to Values of the Simulation. This Option Includes User Modifiable Source Code, As Well As an Operating Module for the Data Translation 2800 Line of Analog Conversion Boards.
Tutsim Products.

Twain's World. Mark Twain. Jul. 1993. *Items Included:* CD ROM disc, Twain's World User's Guide, Registration Card, License Agreement. *Customer Support:* 1) 30 days to return product 2) Software will perform substantially in accordance w/accompanying written materials for 90 days from receipt date 3) Media containing software will be free from defects for 1 year from date of receipt 4) Technical support for all products.
DOS 3.30 or higher. 80386SX or higher processor (running at 16Mhz) 4-bit VGA graphics adapter w/color VGA monitor (2Mb). CD-ROM disk $39.95. *Nonstandard peripherals required:* MPC compatible CD-ROM drive, MPC-compatible audio board, headphones or speakers, Microsoft compatible mouse. *Addl. software required:* Microsoft Windows operating system 3.1 or higher (enhanced mode). *Networks supported:* Network version available through Bureau Development, Inc.
Twain's World Comes Alive Through This Complete Multimedia Collection of His Works. You Get All the Novels & Hard-to-Find Short Stories, Respected Literary Criticism, Voice Overs, Hundreds of Color Images & an Authoritative Biography. Works Include Huckleberry Finn, Tom Sawyer, Life on the Mississippi, Puddinhead Wilson, Mysterious Stranger, Prince & the Pauper, & Many Others.
Bureau Development, Inc.

'Twas the Night Before Christmas. *Compatible Hardware:* Apple II series; Commodore 64/128; IBM PC & compatibles. *Memory Required:* IBM 256k. *General Requirements:* CGA, EGA, or Hercules card for IBM.
disk $8.95.
Animated Musical Holiday Disk That Narrates the Classic Poem. It Also Allows Users to Send Personalized Disks As Gifts, Type & Print Letters to Santa, Print Christmas Cards, & Play a Chrismas Game in Jigsaw Format.
Brady Computer Bks.

Twelve-Bar Tunesmith. Fred Willman. 1985. *Compatible Hardware:* Apple II+, IIe, IIc, IIgs; Commodore 64, 128; IBM PC. *Operating System(s) Required:* Apple DOS 3.3, PC-DOS 3.3. *Language(s):* BASIC. *Memory Required:* Apple 48k, Commodore 64k, IBM 640k. *General Requirements:* CGA card for IBM.
disk $39.95 ea.
Apple. (ISBN 0-942132-98-X, Order no.: A-1174).
Commodore 64. (ISBN 0-942132-99-8, Order no.: C-1174).
IBM. (ISBN 1-55603-012-6, Order no.: I-1174).
Designed to Help the Young Compose & Play Simple Melodies Using Bar Graph Notation. The User Can Choose from Four Different Pitch Durations & Hear His/Her Tunes Played at Varying Tempos. The Eight Pitches Used Are Based on the C Major Scale. Iconic Notation Is Utilized on a Graphic System to Help the User Understand the Concepts of Pitch & Duration.
Electronic Courseware Systems, Inc.

Twelve Roads to Gettysburg. Feb. 1995. *Items Included:* CD-ROM booklet. *Customer Support:* Free technical support via phone as of release date.
MPC/Windows. 386.25 or higher IBM compatible (4Mb). CD-ROM disk $34.95 (ISBN 1-885784-05-8, Order no.: 1257). *Optimal configuration:* MPC CD-ROM player, S-VGA graphics card (640x480x256 colors) with compatible monitor, MPC compliant sound card, mouse, Windows 3.1.
Macintosh. Macintosh (4Mb). CD-ROM disk $34.95 (ISBN 1-885784-28-7, Order no.: 1271). *Optimal configuration:* CD-ROM drive, color monitor with 256 plus colors, system version 6.07 or higher.
Award-Winning Twelve Roads to Gettysburg Graphically Depicts the Details of the Battle of Gettysburg, the Monumental Turning Point of the Civil War. Using Animation, Narration, Photographs, Period Engraving, Military Terminology & Actual Period Music, This Interactive Reference Tool Provides more Gritty Detail Than Any Other Single Reference Study or Textbook.
Technology Dynamics Corp.

Twelve Roads to Gettysburg. *Version:* 2. *Items Included:* CD-ROM booklet. *Customer Support:* Free technical support via phone as of release date.
MPC/Windows. 386-25 or higher (4Mb). CD-ROM disk $29.95 (ISBN 1-885784-59-7, Order no.: 1597). *Optimal configuration:* MPC CD-ROM player, S-VGA graphics card (640x480x256 colors) with compatible monitor, MPC compliant sound card, mouse, Windows 3.1 or higher, Windows 95 compatible.
System 7.0 or higher. Macintosh (4Mb). CD-ROM disk $29.95 (ISBN 1-885784-60-0, Order no.: 1603). *Optimal configuration:* Macintosh with color monitor (256 plus colors) & a CD-ROM drive.
Graphically Depicts the Details of the Battle of Gettysburg, the Monumental Turning Point of the Civil War. Using Animation, Narration, Photographs, Period Engravings, Military Terminology & Actual Period Music, This Interactive Reference Tool Provides More Gritty Detail Than Any Other Single Reference Study or Textbook.
Technology Dynamics Corp.

Twelve Roads to Gettysburg: Jewel. *Version:* 2. *Items Included:* CD-ROM booklet. *Customer Support:* Free technical support via phone as of release date.
MPC/Windows. 386-25 or higher (4Mb). CD-ROM disk $29.95 (ISBN 1-885784-61-9, Order no.: 1590). *Optimal configuration:* MPC CD-ROM player, S-VGA graphics card (640x480x256 colors) with compatible monitor, MPC compliant sound card, mouse, Windows 3.1 or higher, Windows 95 compatible.
System Version 7.0 or higher. Macintosh (4Mb). *Optimal configuration:* Macintosh with a color monitor (256 plus colors) & a CD-ROM drive.
Graphically Depicts the Details of the Battle of Gettysburg, the Monumental Turning Point of the Civil War. Using Animation, Narration,

Photographs, Period Engravings, Military Terminology & Actual Period Music, This Interactive Reference Tool Provides More Gritty Detail Than Any Other Single Reference Study or Textbook.
Technology Dynamics Corp.

20th Century Faro. Dec. 1987. *Compatible Hardware:* IBM PC. *Memory Required:* 128k. *General Requirements:* Color Monitor & Adaptor. disk $20.00.
Written for One Player This Is the Video Version of the World's Oldest Gambling Game Played with Cards.
Robert L. Nicolai.

The Twentieth Century Video Almanac. Jun. 1993.
IBM CD-ROM. CD-ROM disk $99.95 (Order no.: 111314).
Travel Through the 20th Century in a Day! Land on the Moon, Attend Woodstock, Listen to President Kennedy's Inaugural Address, Witness the Wright Brothers in Flight, or Join the Crowd for the 1916 World Series. This Mutlimedia Reference Works Uses a Huge Archive of Motion Videos to Produce a Visual Encyclopedia of the Century, Including Audio, Photos & Text. Discover What Happened "On This Day" in History, or Explore Special Topics of Interest, Including Sports, War, Disasters, Science, Arts & Entertainment. Available As a Single Disc Overview, or 5-Disc Set Including the Overview & Four Special Topic Discs.
Software Toolworks.

2500AD C Compilers. *Items Included:* Assembler, Linker, Librarian, High Level Simulator/Debugger, Object Libraries, Macro Preprocessor, & Complete Documentation. *Customer Support:* Price of product includes a 90 day money back guarantee & full unlimited technical support.
MS-DOS, OS/2, 386 UNIX, XENIX, SUN 4, HP 700. IBM PC & compatibles. $650.00-$750.00 (most versions).
Supports In-Line Assembly Language. Produces Romable Code. Full Re-Entrant Libraries. All Data Types, Including Double & Single Precision Floating Point. Full Floating Point Library Functions.
2500AD Software, Inc.

2500AD Macro Cross Assemblers. *Items Included:* Linker, Librarian, & Complete Documentation. *Customer Support:* Price of product includes a 90 day money back guarantee & full unlimited technical support.
MS-DOS, OS/2, 386 UNIX, XENIX, SUN 4, HP 700. IBM PC & compatibles. $250.00-$350.00 (most versions).
Full Listing Control, Conditional Assembly & Built-In Cross Referencing. Predefined & User-Defined Sections. Listings Relocatable by Linker to Reflect Actual Run-Time Addresses. Creates Motorola S19, S28 & S37, Binary & Hex Code Files & Extended Microtek. Global, Rockwell, & Zax Symbol Tables.
2500AD Software, Inc.

2500AD Simulator/Debugger. *Customer Support:* Price of product includes a 90 day money back guarantee & full unlimited technical support.
MS-DOS, OS/2, 386 UNIX, XENIX, SUN 4, HP 700. IBM PC & compatibles. $150.00-$200.00 (most versions).
Full Color Menu Driven. Interrupts; I/O & Redirected I/O; Program, Register, Memory, Cycle-Count Breakpoints; Stack Control; Memory Traps; C & Assembly Language Source Code Display; Comprehensive C Variables Display; Full Control of Registers, Flags, Memory, Variables; Bank Switching.
2500AD Software, Inc.

Twenty-Five in One SoftCartridge: Software Equivalents of HP Fonts. Mar. 1991. *Items Included:* 1 manual, 1 set diskettes, software license agreement. *Customer Support:* Free telephone support on 214-713-6370 or FAX support on 214-713-6308.
DOS 3.1 or higher. IBM compatible 8088 or higher (384k). disk $129.95 (Order no.: 800-925-5700). *Nonstandard peripherals required:* Hewlett-Packard or compatible LaserJet printer. *Networks supported:* Novell.
Includes Soft Cartridges That Emulate Hewlett-Packard Font Cartridges A-Z. Designed Specifically for all Hewlett-Packard LaserJet Plus, Series II, IID, IIP, III, IIID or Compatible Laser Printers. Works with Virtually All Major Software Packages That Provide Support for Corresponding HP Cartridge. Includes Fonts for Business Forms, Tax Forms, Spreadsheets & Presentations.
Good Software Corp.

Twenty-Five In-1 SoftCartridge: Software Equivalents of the Hewlett-Packard Font Cartridges A-Z. *Version:* 1.0. Mar. 1991. *Items Included:* 1 wire bound manual.
MS-DOS 3.1 or higher. PC or AT Compatible with hard drive (384k). disk $129.95. *Addl. software required:* Any software package that includes support for ANSIP LaserJet with font cartridges. *Optimal configuration:* One of the following printers: NP LaserJet plus, II, IIO, 2000, IIP, III, IIID; IBM 4019 or 4019E Personae Laser printer (INISP mode); any HP LaserJet compatible.
Works with Any Hewlett-Packard or Compatible Printer & Can Be Used by Any Software Application That Supports HP Font Cartridges. The Convenient SoftCartridge Manager Utility Makes Downloading Fonts to Your Printer As Easy As Inserting a Cartridge.
The Font Factory.

2780 & 3780 RJE Terminal Emulator.
Compatible Hardware: B-20 series, B-22. *Operating System(s) Required:* BTOS. *Language(s):* PL/M. *Memory Required:* 256k. disk $750.00.
Enables B20 Workstation to Transmit Files to a Remote Host Suporting 2780/3780 Protocol for Processing. Sends Files to a B20 System or to a 2780/3780 Terminal. Permits Performance of Concurrent Tasks. Reads Transmitted Data from Disk Files Created by Editor, Word Processor or Application Program. Configuration Files Define Mode & Transmission Characteristics, Sign on to Host Computer & Specify Communications Facility.
Burroughs Corp.

Twenty Wargame Classics. SSI et al. Dec. 1995. *Items Included:* 4 CDs including playable demo of SSI's latest wargames. *Customer Support:* 30 day limited warranty.
PC DOS CD-ROM, DOS 5.0 or higher. 386/33 (4Mb). CD-ROM disk $59.95 (ISBN 0-917059-38-7, Order no.: 062591). *Nonstandard peripherals required:* Microsoft Mouse driver 5.0 or higher. *Optimal configuration:* 386/33 SVGA color monitor.
Includes 20 Top Hit Wargames from the Companies Strategic Simulations, Impressions & Strategic Studies Group. Tests Include SSI's Award Winning Panzer General, Pacific War & Wargame Construction Set II: TANICS. Impressions Conquest Japan & Enter Two World's War. SSG's Reach for the Stars & 2 Warlords, & Many More.
Strategic Simulations, Inc.

The Twilight Zone. Jan. 15/1989. *Compatible Hardware:* Apple II; Atari ST; Commodore 64/128, Amiga; IBM PC, PS/2.
IBM PC. disk $39.95 (Order no.: 01007).
IBM PS/2. 3.5" disk $39.95 (Order no.: 02007).
Amiga. 3.5" disk $39.95 (Order no.: 06007).
Commodore 64/128. disk $29.95 (Order no.: 05007).
Apple II. disk $39.95 (Order no.: 03007).
You're Traveling in Another Dimension. A Dimension Not Only of Sight & Sound, but of Mind. Participate in Several Stories That, at First, Seem Unrelated, But Eventually Weave Themselves into a Single Complex Plot, Complete with a Patented TWILIGHT ZONE Twist Ending. With Artwork & "World-Class Parse" Programmed by the Team Which Produced THE PAWN.
First Row Software Publishing.

The Twilight Zone: Screen Saver. *Version:* 1.5. Oct. 1994. *Items Included:* Manual, advertising brochure (2), registration card. *Customer Support:* Phone technical support.
Windows 3.1. 386 SX or higher (4Mb). CD-ROM disk $17.95 (ISBN 1-57303-011-2). *Nonstandard peripherals required:* Sound card recommended. *Optimal configuration:* 386 DX 25 w/4Mb RAM running Windows 3.1 or later, 5Mb free space on HD, CD-ROM, sound card.
Slide Show Screensaver Featuring Images & Audio from "The Twilight Zone" TV Series.
Sound Source Interactive.

TwinPak Plus. *Version:* 1.24. 1991. *Items Included:* 3 manuals. *Customer Support:* 30 days' free support, 1 yr. maintenance $250.
PC-DOS/MS-DOS. PC or PC-compatibles (640k). disk for TwinPak Plus $495.00.
Offers an Integrated Time & Billing Module & General Ledger Module for Small Law Firms (for 1-15 Attorneys/Timekeepers). The System Produces Client Bills & Financial Data; Includes Full Trust Accounting, Memory-Resident Alphabetized Client & General Ledger Account Lists.
Micro Craft, Inc.

Two-Dimensional Elastostatic Analysis Using Boundary Elements. J. C. Telles. 1987. *Compatible Hardware:* IBM PC & compatibles. *Operating System(s) Required:* MS-DOS 3.0 or higher. *Language(s):* FORTRAN 77. *Memory Required:* 256k. *Items Included:* Disk, manual, binder. *Customer Support:* Limited warranty. software pkg. $395.00 (ISBN 0-931215-14-5).
Uses a Free Format for Data Entry. All Numerical Data Are Introduced by the Respective Keyword in the Input-Data File. The Boundary Elements Implemented Are Linear with Linear Interpolation Functions for Surface Tractions & Displacements. The Loading Conditions Include Boundary Tractions & Displacements Prescribed (the Former Can Be Discontinuous), Self Weight, Centrifugal Load & Steady-State Thermal Load. In Addition, Symmetric Bodies (Finite & Infinite) under Symmetric Loads Can Be Analyzed by Taking Full Advantage of Symmetry Without Need to Discretize the Symmetry Axes. The Program Calculates Displacements & Stresses at Internal Points Requested by the User.
Computational Mechanics, Inc.

Two-Dimensional FFT. *Compatible Hardware:* TI 99/4A. *Operating System(s) Required:* DX-10. *Language(s):* Console BASIC. *Memory Required:* 16k.
disk or cassette $17.00.
Perform Fast Fourier Transform on 2-Dimensional Time Series Data Using a Length Which Must Be an Integer Power of 2. Forward or Reverse Transformation Can Be Done. Sample Data Which Can Be Transformed Is Included.
Eastbench Software Products.

TITLE INDEX

Two-Dimensional Potential Analysis Using Boundary Elements. L. C. Wrobel. 1987. *Compatible Hardware:* IBM PC & compatibles. *Operating System(s) Required:* MS-DOS 3.0 or higher. *Language(s):* Fortran 77. *Memory Required:* 256k. *Items Included:* Disk, manual, binder. *Customer Support:* Limited warranty. software pkg. $395.00 (ISBN 0-931215-13-7). Computer Code Employing Linear Continuous Boundary Elements, Described Routine by Routine. Provides a Free-Formatted Pre-Processor Which Facilitates Data Preperation. Results of Analyses Are Written to a File Created by the Program Which Can Be Printed or Displayed on the Screen.
Computational Mechanics, Inc.

286 DOS Ada Compilation System & Toolset. *Version:* 4.2. Dec. 1988. *Compatible Hardware:* IBM PC AT, PS/2 Model 60; Wang PC 280; Zenith Z-248; Hewlett-Packard Vectra. *Operating System(s) Required:* PC-DOS/MS-DOS 3.0 or higher. *Memory Required:* 512k.
$3595.00, incl. 4Mb RAM board.
Includes All Required Software, Documentation & 4Mb of Memory. Permits Application to Run in 80286 Protected Mode & Directly Access Extended Memory (up to 16Mb). Includes Compiler, Multi-Library Environment, Binder & Run-Time Executive. Available Options Are Developer's Toolset Including AdaProbe, a Symbolic Source Level Debugger & Program Viewer; AdaXref, a Cross-Reference Generator; AdaMake, a Recompilation Aid; & AdaReformat, a Source Reformatter.
Alsys, Inc.

220-ST. Tricom Software. Jul. 1987. *Compatible Hardware:* Atari ST. *Memory Required:* 512k. *General Requirements:* Modem.
3.5" disk $49.95.
Terminal Emulation Program That Combines the Power of the ST with the Flexibility of a VT220 Terminal. Four Terminal Modes Include VT52, VT100 & VT200.
MichTron, Inc.

Two-Phase Pressure Drop in Process Piping. *Items Included:* Bound manual. *Customer Support:* Free hotline - no time limit; 30 day limited warranty; updates are $5/disk plus S&H.
Apple (256k). disk $99.95.
Allows the Design Engineer to Quickly & Easily Calculate Pressure Drops in Process Piping for Either Single-Phase or Two-Phase Flow. Choose Either the Popular Ovid Baker or A. E. Dukler Methods for Horizontal Pipes, or the Widely Acclaimed Orkiszewski Method for Vertical Pipes. For Single-Phase Flow of Liquid or Non-Compressible Gas Flow, the Pressure Drop Is Calculated by the Familiar Darcy Equation. Covers Most Common Pipe Sizes from 2 to 20 Inches & Pipe Schedules of 10, 40, 80, & 160. Values Falling Outside This Range Can Be Readily Calculated by Entering the Actual Inside-Diameter of the Pipe.
Dynacomp, Inc.

Two-Port Analysis Tutorial. (Electrical Engineering Ser.: No. 7). *Compatible Hardware:* Apple II with Applesoft. *Operating System(s) Required:* Apple DOS 3.2, 3.3, MS-DOS. *Language(s):* BASIC (source code included). *Memory Required:* Apple 48k, IBM 128k.
disk $39.95.
Covers the Transfer Characteristics of "Black Boxes" Having 2 Ports.
Dynacomp, Inc.

2001 Quotes. *General Requirements:* HyperCard/Excel/Works.
Macintosh Plus or higher; IBM PC & compatibles. 3.5" disk $25.00.
Database of 2,001 Quotations for Writers & Speakers.
Heizer Software.

2000 True Type Fonts. *Customer Support:* All of our products are unconditionally guaranteed. DOS, Windows. CD-ROM disk $39.95 (Order no.: 2000TTF). *Nonstandard peripherals required:* CD-ROM drive.
2000 True Type Fonts Plus 5000 Clipart Images in PCX Format.
Walnut Creek CDRom.

II Write. 1987. *Compatible Hardware:* Apple IIe, IIc, IIgs. *Memory Required:* 128k.
disk $69.95, incl. back-up (ISBN 0-676-24958-2).
Word Processor with Macintosh-Like Features. Provides Pull-Down Menus, Rulers, Scroll Bars, & Dialog Boxes. Multiple Document Windows Permit up to Four Documents to Be Displayed at a Time, & Users Can Cut & Paste Between Documents. Offers a Variety of Fonts, Styles, & Sizes. Also Provides Online Help. Fully Usable with Keyboard or Mouse.
Random House Schl. Div.

TX802 & TX81Z Pro. *Compatible Hardware:* Apple Macintosh. *Memory Required:* 1000k. *General Requirements:* MIDI interface; Yamaha TX802 or TX81Z tone generator.
TX802 Pro. 3.5" disk $249.00.
TX81Z Pro. 3.5" disk $139.00.
Integrated Editor-Librarian Software Packages Designed for the Yamaha TX802 & TX81Z Synthesizers. Programs Allow Editing of All TX802 & TX81Z Parameters. Banks of Voices & Performances Can Be Transferred to the Synthesizer or to Disk for Storage.
Digital Music Services.

Tycoon: The Commodities Market Simulation. Blue Chip Software, Inc. *Compatible Hardware:* HP 150 Touchscreen, IBM PC.
3.5" disk $59.95 (Order no.: 92243HA).
Financial Simulation of the Commodities Market, Based on Actual Market Events & Price Trends. News Headlines, & a Wide Variety of Price-Trend Data Allow Both Novice & Expert Traders to Search for That Perfect Opportunity to Make a Fortune.
Hewlett-Packard Co.

Tyler's Dungeons. *Compatible Hardware:* Commodore 64.
contact publisher for price (Order no.: C-1508).
3-D Maze/Treasure Hunt Game.
Creative Equipment.

Tymekard: Timecard-Payroll Management. *Items Included:* Bound manual. *Customer Support:* Free hotline - no time limit; 30 day limited warranty; updates are $5/disk plus S&H. MS-DOS 2.0 or higher. IBM & compatibles (256k). disk $69.95. *Nonstandard peripherals required:* Two drives (or a hard disk), graphics card (CGA, EGA, or Hercules).
Timecard Management System for Small or Large Timecard Users. It Can Be Used Either with Payroll Programs or by Itself. Features: Easy Entry of Repeating Hour Values (Last Entry Is Default); Calculates Gross Hours & Gross Pay; Generates Reports & Summaries by Pay Period, Quarter to Date, & Year to Date for Regular & Overtime; Converts AM/PM to 24-Hour Format; Maintains Records for up to 999 Employees; Accepts up to 15 User-Defined Departments; Can Replace Mechanical Time Clocks.
Dynacomp, Inc.

TYP-PRT. *Compatible Hardware:* IBM PC; TRS-80 Model I, Model II, Model III, Model 4, Model 12, Model 16. *Operating System(s) Required:* TRSDOS, PC-DOS. *Memory Required:* 48-64k.
TRS-80 Model I, Model III, Model 4. disk $17.95.
IBM PC. disk $17.95.
Permits Use of Printer As a Typewriter & Allows Retention of Any Display Already on the Video. Make Notes from It or Copy It on the Printer Automatically. Runs Concurrently with Other Programs. Contains 6-Function Calculator.
Contract Services Assocs.

Type-a-Line. *Compatible Hardware:* HP 150 Touchscreen with HP 2601, 2602 or Diablo 620/630 or Qume 1140 printers.
3.5" disk $69.00 (Order no.: 45680A).
Makes Standard Forms & Envelopes Using the Touchscreen & a Character Mode Printer. Type Text from the Keyboard Directly to a Form in the Printer. Touch the Screen to Scroll the Paper up & down in the Printer. Use the Space Bar & Cursor Arrow Keys to Position the Print Head to the Correct Box or Space to Fill Out Forms, Invoices, & Other Blanks.
Hewlett-Packard Co.

Type Fonts 2. Jan. 1988. *Compatible Hardware:* Apple Macintosh. *Memory Required:* 384k. *General Requirements:* 2 disk drives, graphics card, Generics CADD. *Customer Support:* Unlimited technical support to registered users. disk $34.95 (ISBN 1-55814-112-X, Order no.: F2052).
3.5" disk $34.95 (ISBN 1-55814-113-8, Order no.: T2052).
Library of Type Fonts in Bold Outline Sytles for Adding to CADD Drawings.
Autodesk, Inc.

Typecase. Apr. 1992. *Customer Support:* Technical support free - phone/Fax/eMail. Windows 3.1 (2Mb). 3.5" disk $15.00. *Nonstandard peripherals required:* Printer. Collection of over 100 TrueType Fonts That Form the Foundation for Any Typeface Library. The Fonts Are Scalable from 1 to 999 Points, & Include a Bonus & PC Keys Font - Computer Symbols & Keycaps for Creating Manuals & Documents.
SWFTE International, Ltd.

Typecase III. Mar. 1993. *Customer Support:* Free technical support - Call/Fax/Mail, Phone: 305-567-9996, Fax: 305-569-1350.
Windows 3.1 (2Mb). disk $15.00. *Nonstandard peripherals required:* Printer.
Unique Collection of over 100 TrueType Fonts That Give a Typeface Library a Cutting Edge Element. These Fonts Have Been Seen Everywhere from Time Magazine to MTV! All Fonts Are Scalable from 1 to 999 Points. Includes Bonus 200 Holiday Symbol Fonts.
SWFTE International, Ltd.

Typecase II. Sep. 1992. *Customer Support:* Free technical support - Call/Fax/Mail, Phone: 305-567-9996, Fax: 305-569-1350.
Windows 3.1 (2Mb). disk $15.00. *Nonstandard peripherals required:* Printer.
Collection of over 100 TrueType Fonts That Complement Any Well-Rounded Typeface Library. Used As an Add-On to Typecase or As Stand Alone. Is Installed Through the Windows Control Panel. Fonts Are Scalable from 1 to 999 Points. Includes Bonus International Icons Font.
SWFTE International, Ltd.

Typecase 2001. Jul. 1995. *Items Included:* Installation instructions, registration card. *Customer Support:* Phone support by calling 302-234-1750, no charge. Fax support by faxing to 302-234-1760, no charge. E-Mail support at Compuserve ID 76004,3520 or MCI Mail/560-7116, no charge.
Windows. 386SX or higher & hard disk (2Mb). CD-ROM disk $19.95 (ISBN 1-887468-41-2).
Optimal configuration: PC-DOS/MS-DOS 3.1 or higher, Windows 3.1 or higher, CD-ROM

drive, 2Mb RAM, EGA, VGA or SVGA graphics adapter & monitor.
Macintosh. System 7. CD-ROM disk $19.95 (ISBN 1-887468-42-0). *Optimal configuration:* CD-ROM player, Adobe Type Manager (recommended).
A Complete Typeface Library with over 2000 Fundamental, Decorative, Script & Avant-Garde Typefaces to Suite Any Occasion. All Fonts Are Scalable from 1 to 999 Point.
SWFTE International, Ltd.

Typecase 2001. Jul. 1995. *Items Included:* Installation instructions, registration cards. *Customer Support:* Telephone 302-234-1750, Fax 302-234-1760, E-Mail, CompuServe 76004, 3520, E-mail, MCI mail 560-7116 - no charge.
Windows. 386SX or higher & hard disk (2Mb). CD-ROM disk $19.95 (ISBN 1-887468-41-2). *Optimal configuration:* PC-DOS/MS-DOS 3.1 or higher, Windows 3.1 or higher, CD-ROM drive, 2Mb RAM, EGA, VGA or SVGA Graphics Adapter & monitor.
Macintosh. System 7. CD-ROM disk $19.95 (ISBN 1-887468-42-0). *Optimal configuration:* CD-ROM player, Adobe Type Manager (recommended).
A Complete Typeface Library with over 2000 Fundamental, Decorative, Script & Avant-Garde Typefaces to Suit Any Occasion. All Fonts Are Scalable from 1 to 999 Point.
Swfte International, Ltd.

TypeNow. *General Requirements:* ImageWriter.
Macintosh. 3.5" disk $39.95.
Typewriter Desk Accessory.
Mainstay Software Corp.

TypeStyler. *Compatible Hardware:* Apple Macintosh. *Memory Required:* 512k.
3.5" disk $149.95.
Special Effects Program Enabling User to Bend, Squeeze, Stretch, Twist & Rotate Display Type. User Can Also Add Perspective, Such As Shadows, Shades, Patterns & Colors. Imports & Exports Paint, PICT & EPS Files.
Broderbund Software, Inc.

Typhoon Of Steel. Gary Grigsby. 1988. *Compatible Hardware:* Apple II series; Commodore 64/128. *Memory Required:* 64k. *Items Included:* rulebook, briefing manual. *Customer Support:* 14 day money back guarantee/30 day exchange policy; tech support line: (408) 737-6850 (11:00 - 5:00 PST); customer service: (408) 737-6800 (9:00 - 5:00 PST).
disk $49.95.
Sequel to PANZER STRIKE! Each Unit Symbol Represents Either One Tank/Gun or a Squad of Infantry; Each Square of the 60x60 Map, 50 Yards. Offers Play Flexibility Which Qualifies as a Construction Set. Tools Are Provided to Let You Easily Create Your Own Maps, Troops & Missions. Three Theaters Are Covered: The Pacific Theater; the Asian Theater; & European Theater Action Involving American Troops vs. German Troops. This Tactical Game Includes Practically Every Ground Weapon Used in Those Theaters - From Tanks, Tank Destroyers & Artillery to Trucks, Mortars & Machine Guns. Pillboxes, Minefields, Dragon's Teeth, Flamethrowers, & Naval Gun Support Are also Included.
Strategic Simulations, Inc.

Typhoon Thompson in Search for the Sea Child. Jul. 1988. *Compatible Hardware:* Atari ST. *Memory Required:* 512k. *General Requirements:* Color monitor.
3.5" disk $34.95 (ISBN 1-55790-146-5, Order no.: 13025).
Arcade Game Featuring State-of-the-Art 3-D Graphics. Features High-Resolution Graphics, Highly Detailed Animations, Mouse-Controlled Game, & a Feeling of Flying over the Water.
Broderbund Software, Inc.

Typing Keys to Computer Ease. Maetta Davis. 1984. *Items Included:* Instructions & binder.
Apple DOS 3.3. Apple II. $25.00 (ISBN 0-87879-450-6, Order no.: 450-6).
This Typing Method Takes Advantage of the Multisenasory Nature of Typewriting. It Develops Spelling & Reading Skills While Preparing Students for Computer Keyboards. Twenty Drill & Practice Lessons Lead Students Sequentially from the Home Keys Through Mastery of the Entire Keyboard.
Academic Therapy Pubns., Inc.,.

Typing Mastery. *Customer Support:* 800-929-8117 (customer service).
MS-DOS. Apple II. disk $29.99 (ISBN 0-87007-803-8).
Tutorial for Learning to Touch Type. Several Differnt Types of Exercises.
SourceView Software International.

TYPIST.
$2000.00.
user guide $45.00 (Order no.: A-0019).
manager manual $10.00 (Order no.: A-0021).
installation manual $12.00 (Order no.: A-0022).
Word Processing System.
Point 4 Data Corp.

TYPWTR: Computer Typewriter Program. Hall Associates. Sep. 1983. *Operating System(s) Required:* CP/M-80, MS-DOS, PC-DOS. *Memory Required:* CP/M 48k, MS-DOS & PC-DOS 128k.
disk 40 Track $29.95 (ISBN 0-923875-17-4).
disk 80 Track $29.95 (ISBN 0-923875-18-2).
8" disk $29.95 (ISBN 0-923875-16-6).
Has All the Features of a Word Processor on a Single Line Including Tabs, Margins, & Word Wrap. Print Head Follow Makes Filling Out Forms Easier.
Elliam Assocs.

T2S01W: Terminator 2: the Screen Saver. *Version:* 1.5. Oct. 1993. *Items Included:* Manual, registration card, sound list. *Customer Support:* Phone technical support.
DOS 5.0, Windows 3.1. PC 286 or higher (2Mb). disk $17.95 (ISBN 1-57303-008-2). *Nonstandard peripherals required:* Sound card recommended. *Optimal configuration:* 286 or higher with 4Mb RAM, DOS 5.0 or later, Windows 3.1 or later, 4-7Mb HD space available, sound card.
Exclusively Licensed High Quality Sound Files Consisting of Classic Sound Effects, Dialogue & Music from Original TV Shows & Movies. Also Included Is the 'Whoop It Up' Audio Utility, Which Allows the User to Attach AudioClips to Various Windows Events.
Sound Source Interactive.

U-Factor Calculation. *Version:* 2.0. William H. Zaggle. Dec. 1987. *Compatible Hardware:* Apple II; DEC Rainbow, DEC VT180; Hewlett-Packard; IBM PC; Kaypro; Morrow; North Star; Osborne; SuperBrain; TRS-80 Model I, Model III; Victor; Zenith. *Operating System(s) Required:* CP/M, CP/M-86, MS-DOS, PC-DOS. *Language(s):* CB-80. *Memory Required:* CP/M 64k, MS-DOS 256k. *General Requirements:* 2 disk drives, printer.
disk $99.00.
8" disk $99.00.
3.5" disk $99.00.
demo disk $38.00.
documentation $25.00.
References a File Containing the R-Values for over 200 Different Types of Building Materials As Listed in the ASRAE Handbook of Fundamentals. These R-Values Can Be Scrolled Through an On-Screen Window for Review & Selection. As Material Types Are Selected, the Program Instantaneously Displays the Resulting U-Factor. All Types of Air Firm & Air Space Resistances Are Allowed, & There Is Provision for the Non-Uniform Application of Materials Such As Furrings. All Input Data Is Stored on Disk & Can Be Reviewed & Revised at Any Time.
Elite Software Development, Inc.

UASM. *Version:* 3.5. *Compatible Hardware:* Apple Macintosh. *Memory Required:* 1000k. *Items Included:* Complete reference manual, Integrated Text editor, Cross Macro Assembler, & Communications Program. *Customer Support:* Telephone.
3.5" disk $149.95.
Microprocessor Software Development.
Micro Dialects, Inc.

UCSD Editor/Filer/Utilities. *Compatible Hardware:* TI 99/4A.
contact publisher for price (Order no.: PHD 5065).
Used for Screen Editing & File Management for the p-System.
Texas Instruments, Personal Productivit.

UCSD p-System Assembler-Linker. *Compatible Hardware:* TI 99/4A with p-Code card. *Memory Required:* 32k.
contact publisher for price (Order no.: PHD 5064).
Develops TMS9900 Assembly Language Programs Through the p-System.
Texas Instruments, Personal Productivit.

UCSD p-System Development with Pascal. Softech Microsystems. *Compatible Hardware:* TI Professional with Winchester second drive, color monitor, communications card. *Operating System(s) Required:* UCSD p-System Runtime. *Memory Required:* 64k.
$400.00 (Order no.: TI P/N 2232398-0001).
Texas Instruments, Personal Productivit.

UCSD p-System Runtime with Turtlegraphics. Softech Microsystems. *Compatible Hardware:* TI Professional with Winchester second drive, color monitor, communications card. *Memory Required:* 192k.
$350.00 (Order no.: TI P/N 2223135-0001).
Texas Instruments, Personal Productivit.

UCSD Pascal Compiler. *Compatible Hardware:* TI 99/4A with p-Code card. *Memory Required:* 32k.
contact publisher for price (Order no.: PHD 5063).
Permits User to Compile Pascal Programs into P-Code.
Texas Instruments, Personal Productivit.

UCSD Pascal for the IBM PC. Iain MacCallum. Jan. 1986.
disk $16.95 (ISBN 0-13-936048-4).
Prentice Hall.

UFACTOR: U-factor Calculations. *Items Included:* Manual. *Customer Support:* Free toll free telephone support.
IBM PC & compatibles (256k). disk $99.00.
Allows Designer to Quickly Calculate Roof & Wall "U-Factors" (Overall Heat Transfer Coefficients Required for Heating & Cooling Load Calculations). The Program Follows Exact ASHRAE Calculation Procedures.
Elite Software Development, Inc.

TITLE INDEX

The Ugly Duckling. Morgan Interactive Staff. Sep. 1995. *Customer Support:* Telephone support - free (except phone charge).
Windows 3.1. IBM & compatibles (386 DX-20) (4Mb). CD-ROM disk $12.99 (ISBN 1-57594-034-5). *Nonstandard peripherals required:* 2x CD-ROM player, Sound Card, VGA monitor. *Optimal configuration:* 486 SX-33.
Classic Children's Story.
Kidsoft, Inc.

The Ugly Duckling. Morgan Interactive Staff. Sep. 1995. *Customer Support:* Telephone support - free (except phone charge).
Windows 3.1. IBM & compatibles (386 DX-20) (4Mb). CD-ROM disk $12.99 (ISBN 1-57594-073-6). *Nonstandard peripherals required:* 2x CD-ROM player, Sound Card, VGA monitor. *Optimal configuration:* 486 SX-33.
Classic Children's Story. Blister Pack Jewel Case.
Kidsoft, Inc.

The Ugly Duckling. Jan. 1996. *Customer Support:* Telephone support - free (except phone charge).
System 7.0 or higher. 256 color capable Mac with a 68030 processor (4Mb). CD-ROM disk $12.99 (ISBN 1-57594-109-0). *Nonstandard peripherals required:* 2X CD ROM drive, 640/480 resolution monitor.
You Will Be Touched by the Ugly Duckling's Experiences As He Grows up in a World That Shuns Him Because He Doesn't Look Like All the Rest. This Exciting Story Includes Hundreds of Beautifully Animated Sequences, Original Musical Compositions & Lively Sound Effects. Entertaining for Hours While Developing Essential Reading Skills.
Kidsoft, Inc.

UGRAF. *Operating System(s) Required:* CP/M, CP/M-86, MS-DOS.
contact publisher for price.
Enables Users to Construct Graphs from Existing Data Files. Draws Pie, Bar, Scatter Line Graphs. Data from a Variety of Sources Can Be Used. Supports Several Terminals, Printers, & Plotters. User Does Not Need to Graph the Specifications or Obtain Additional Software in Order to Change Output Devices.
Transparent Data Systems, Inc.

Ulcers. (Patient Education Ser.).
MS-DOS 2.1 or higher. IBM PC & compatibles. disk $34.95 (Order no.: 6PE).
Provides Description & Animated Illustration of Acid Secretion Phases - Cephalic, Gastric & Intestinal. Discusses Primary Components of Gastric Mucosal Barrier & Elements That Disrupt It, & Action of Antacids, Histamine H2- Receptor Antagonists, & Sucralfate in Treatment of Peptic Ulcer Disease. Provides Percentage of Probability for Peptic Ulcer Disease in a Patient Whose Symptoms & Characteristics Are Entered by the User.
Cardinal Health Systems, Inc.

Ulrich's Plus. 1995. *Items Included:* Quarterly Updates. *Customer Support:* Information & Assistance Hotline; Electronic Bulletin Board.
DOS 3.1 or later. IBM & compatibles 286 or higher (535k). CD-ROM disk $595.00 for 1 year. *Nonstandard peripherals required:* Hard disk (minimum 10 Mb free space); CD-ROM player running under MS-DOS extensions 2.0 or later.
CD-ROM disk $1696.00 for 3 years.
The Bowker International Serials Database. This CD-ROM Includes Data on Some 190,000 Publications, Including 131,000 Periodicals & 62,000 Annuals & Irregulars - Both Active & Ceased. Includes Full Purchasing Information Plus Names, Addresses, & Phone Numbers for the 83,000 International Publishers Represented Throughout.
R.R. Bowker.

Ultima V; Warriors of Destiny. *Compatible Hardware:* Apple II Plus, IIe, IIc, IIgs; IBM PC compatibles XT/AT. *Items Included:* Full color cloth map; guide book, reference card, special extras.
disk $59.95.
Lord British, Britain's Benevolent Ruler, Has Been Lost on an Exploration of the Underworld. You Must Discover His Fate & Rescue Him to Save Your World.
Origin Systems, Inc.

Ultima III: Exodus. Richard Garriott. *Compatible Hardware:* Apple II Plus, IIe, Macintosh, Atari ST; Commodore 64, Amiga; IBM PC, PCjr, 286, XT/AT. *Language(s):* Assembly. *Memory Required:* 64k.
$59.95.
Takes User on Fantasy Role-Playing Journey Through Monster-Plagued Planet of Sosaria in Search of Elusive Exodus.
Origin Systems, Inc.

Ultima IV: The Quest of the Avatar. Richard Garriott. Oct. 1985. *Compatible Hardware:* Apple II, II Plus, IIe, IIc, Macintosh; Atari XL/XE, ST; Commodore 64, Amiga; IBM PC, PCjr, XT/AT. *Language(s):* Assembly. *Memory Required:* 64k. *Items Included:* Full color cloth map; guide book; reference card; special extras.
disk $59.95.
Enter Britannia, Kingdom of Lord British. Journey Through Terrain of Infinite Proportions, Conversing with Characters on Hundreds of Topics. Unravel the Mysteries of a Superior Magic System. At Each Turn Beware of Demons, Dragons, & Long-Dead Wizards Haunting the Most Tranquil of Places. Encounters with Parties of Mixed Enemy Types Test Strategic Abilities. Survive This Multi-Quest Fantasy, Then Begin the Final Conflict, Your Quest of the Avatar. The Ultimate Challenge - the Self - Awaits.
Origin Systems, Inc.

The Ultimate Human Body.
Windows. IBM & compatibles. CD-ROM disk $69.95 (Order no.: R1193). *Nonstandard peripherals required:* CD-ROM drive. *Optimal configuration:* 386 processor operating at 16Mhz or higher, MS-DOS 5.0 or higher, Windows 3.1 or higher, 30Mb hard drive, mouse, VGA graphic adapter & VGA color monitor (SVGA recommended), 4Mb RAM, external speakers or headphones (with sound card) that are Sound Blaster compatible.
This Blend of 3-D Images, Brilliantly Detailed Microphotography, Illustrations, Animations, Sounds & Text Helps Kids Learn What Every Part of the Body Is Called, See Where It Is Located, What It Looks Like & How It Functions.
Library Video Co.

Ultimate Payroll. Version: 7.0. *Compatible Hardware:* Macintosh Plus or above. *General Requirements:* Hard disk, System 6.0.5 or higher. *Items Included:* Tax tables for federal & all 50 states. *Customer Support:* Free for first 30 days, then $10.00 per month (includes tax tables).
3.5" disk $399.00.
All the Features of Payroll & in Addition Offers Unlimited Number of Deductions; Special Sections for Restaurant Tips Reporting, Unlimited Number of Pay Rates, Piecework, Commission & More. Provision for Printing Information on Federal Forms 940, 941, & 1099 or Any Federal or State Report Form. Also Has a Payroll Check Ledger for Tracking Net Check Amounts, & the Ability to Calculate & Accumulate Sick, Vacation, & Holiday Pay. Has the Ability to Print on Any Check Form As Well As Check Printing on Plain Paper. Both Payroll Programs Offer Automatic Payroll File Backup & Password Protection for Added Security.
Aatrix Software.

The Ultimate Spring Designer. *Items Included:* Bound manual. *Customer Support:* Free hotline - no time limit; 30 day limited warranty; updates are $5/disk plus S&H.
MS-DOS 2.0 or higher. IBM & compatibles (256k). $149.95-$199.95. *Nonstandard peripherals required:* 80-column (or wider) printer is recommended.
manual only $19.95.
Software Package for the Design of Springs. It Is Based on Field Experience & Includes a Built-In Database of 51 Materials & Heat Treatments (Based on the Latest Military, Federal, AMS, ASTM, & SAE Specifications). User Can Also Specify Your Own Material. Ten Helical Spring Types Are Handled: Compression Made of Round, Rectangular, Square, or Standard Round Wire; Compression Linear or Nonlinear Conical Made of Round Wire; Extension Made of Round Wire; Extension & Compression Garter; & Torsion Made of Round or Rectangular Wire.
Dynacomp, Inc.

The Ultimate Spring Designer 2. *Items Included:* Bound manual. *Customer Support:* Free hotline - no time limit; 30 day limited warranty; updates are $5/disk plus S&H.
MS-DOS. IBM & compatibles (256k). $395.00-$475.00.
manual only $19.95.
More Extensive Version OF THE ULTIMATE SPRING DESIGNER. Whereas the Smaller Version Handles 10 Spring Types, This Version Treats 30, Including Leaf, Belleville, Motor, Clock, Hair, Power, Spiral, & Washer Springs.
Dynacomp, Inc.

The Ultimate Worksheet Creator. *Items Included:* Program disk, clip art & curriculum disk & user's guide.
Apple II. disk $49.95 (Order no.: WC100).
MS-DOS. disk $49.95 (Order no.: WC100I).
Create Your Own Math Worksheets for Your Children. Now You Can Choose the Types of Problems Your Kids Need to Practice. Comes with a Huge Library of Clip Art That Borders Each Page. Problems Can Be Generated, with the Flexibility to Mix & Match Skills, Difficulty Levels, & Problem Types (Multiplication & Division, Addition & Subtraction, Computational Problems, & Word Problems, etc.). Answer Keys Can Be Printed Right along with the Worksheets for Your Convenience & since the Problems Are Randomly Generated, a Brand New Worksheet Is Only Minutes Away. A Perfect Complement to our Basic Math Diskettes.
Milliken Publishing Co.

Ultra Cat. Jul. 1991. *Customer Support:* Toll-free telephone support, 30 day unlimited warranty.
MS-DOS 2.10 or higher. IBM PC/XT, PS/2 & compatibles (640k). write for info.
Cataloging Software for Libraries Utilizing CD-ROM Discs Housing Appropriate Databases. Generation of MARC Cataloging Records, Card Sets & spine Labels.
Library Systems & Services, Inc.

Ultra F.A.R.M: (Farm Accounting & Records Management). Version: 3.0. May 1994. *Items Included:* 625 page perfect-bound manual. *Customer Support:* 90 days unlimited phone support.
MS-DOS 3.3. IBM & compatibles (640K). disk $550.00 (ISBN 0-918709-13-X). *Networks supported:* Novell, PC LAN.
A Cash Accounting System Providing Comprehensive Financial Reports Focusing on Taxes & Enterprise Profitability. Monthly Transactions Provide Concurrent On-Screen Balancing of Five Checkbooks with Vendors, Payroll, & Pull-Down Menus. Cashflow Plans, & Sales Analysis for Long Range Planning. Complete Inventory Control with Supporting Schedules for Book & Market Balance Sheet.
Specialized Data Systems, Inc.

Ultra Gold Dog Analysis. Ronald D. Jones. 1985. *Compatible Hardware:* Apple; Commodore; IBM; TRS-80 Model I, Model III, Color Computer. *Operating System(s) Required:* CP/M. *Memory Required:* 64k.
disk $399.90 ea.
Apple. (ISBN 1-55604-084-9, Order no.: D004).
CP/M. (ISBN 1-55604-085-7, Order no.: D004).
Commodore. (ISBN 1-55604-086-5, Order no.: D004).
Color Computer. (ISBN 1-55604-087-3, Order no.: D004).
IBM. (ISBN 1-55604-088-1, Order no.: D004).
Model I & Model III. (ISBN 1-55604-089-X, Order no.: D004).
Greyhound Analysis Uses Combination of Speed & Class Based upon the Grade of the Race. Master Bettor Evaluates Scores & Every Betting Combination of the Top 5 Dogs Are Given. Ultra Module Provides a True "Low Level" Intelligence Capable of Reweighting Variables Based on Results. Factors Relating to "Winning Dogs" Are Regressed Out of Actual Races to Be Used in Future Predictions.
Professor Jones Professional Handicapping Systems.

Ultra Gold Dog with Track Management. Ronald D. Jones. 1985. *Compatible Hardware:* Apple; Commodore; IBM; TRS-80 Model I, Model III, Color Computer. *Operating System(s) Required:* CP/M. *Memory Required:* 64k.
disk $479.85 ea.
Apple. (ISBN 1-55604-090-3, Order no.: D014).
CP/M. (ISBN 1-55604-091-1, Order no.: D014).
Commodore. (ISBN 1-55604-092-X, Order no.: D014).
Color Computer. (ISBN 1-55604-093-8, Order no.: D014).
IBM. (ISBN 1-55604-094-6, Order no.: D014).
Model I & Model III. (ISBN 1-55604-095-4, Order no.: D014).
Greyhound Analysis Uses Combination of Speed & Class Based upon the Grade of the Race. Master Bettor Evaluates Scores & Every Betting Combination of the Top 5 Dogs Are Given. Ultra Module Provides a True "Low Level" Intelligence Capable of Reweighting Vaiables Based upon Results. Factors Relating to "Winning Dogs" Are Regressed Out of Actual Races to Be Used in Future Predictions. Track Management Is Designed to Keep Records on All Dogs Running at a Track.
Professor Jones Professional Handicapping Systems.

Ultra Gold Thoroughbred. Ronald D. Jones. 1985. *Compatible Hardware:* Apple; Commodore; IBM; TRS-80 Model I, Model III, Color Computer. *Operating System(s) Required:* CP/M. *Memory Required:* 64k.
disk $399.95 ea.
Apple. (ISBN 1-55604-030-X, Order no.: H004).
CP/M. (ISBN 1-55604-031-8, Order no.: H004).
Commodore. (ISBN 1-55604-032-6, Order no.: H004).
Color Computer. (ISBN 1-55604-033-4, Order no.: H004).
IBM. (ISBN 1-55604-034-2, Order no.: H004).
Model I & Model III. (ISBN 1-55604-035-0, Order no.: H004).
A Full Featured Thoroughbred Analysis Designed to Evaluate All Relevant Variables & Give an Accurate Prediction of the Finish, Evaluating Scores & Giving Every Betting Combination of Top 5 Horses. Ultra Module Provides a True "Low Level" Artificial Intelligence Capable of Reweighting Variables Based on Results. Factors Relating to "Winning Horses" Are Regressed Out of Actual Races to Be Used in Future Predictions.
Professor Jones Professional Handicapping Systems.

Ultra Gold Thoroughbred with Track Management. Ronald D. Jones. *Compatible Hardware:* Apple; Commodore; IBM; TRS-80 Model I, Model III, Color Computer. *Operating System(s) Required:* CP/M. *Memory Required:* 64k.
disk $479.85 ea.
Apple. (ISBN 1-55604-036-9, Order no.: H014).
CP/M. (ISBN 1-55604-037-7, Order no.: H014).
Commodore. (ISBN 1-55604-038-5, Order no.: H014).
Color Computer. (ISBN 1-55604-039-3, Order no.: H014).
IBM. (ISBN 1-55604-040-7, Order no.: H014).
Model I & Model III. (ISBN 1-55604-041-5, Order no.: H014).
Full-Featured Thoroughbred Analysis Which Evaluates All Relevant Variables, Gives Prediction of the Finish, Evaluates Scores, & Gives Every Betting Combination of the Top Five Horses. Ultra Provides True "Low Level" Artificial Intelligence Capable of Reweighting Variables Based on Results. Factors Relating to "Winning Horses" Are Regressed Out of Actual Races to Be Used in Future Predictions. Track Management Is a Data Base Designed to Keep Records on All Horses Running at a Track.
Professor Jones Professional Handicapping Systems.

Ultra Harness Handicapper. Ronald D. Jones. 1985. *Compatible Hardware:* Apple; Commodore; IBM; TRS-80 Model I, Model III, Color Computer. *Operating System(s) Required:* CP/M. *Memory Required:* 64k.
disk $399.90 ea.
Apple. (ISBN 1-55604-210-8, Order no.: T004).
CP/M. (ISBN 1-55604-211-6, Order no.: T004).
Commodore. (ISBN 1-55604-212-4, Order no.: T004).
Color Computer. (ISBN 1-55604-213-2, Order no.: T004).
IBM. (ISBN 1-55604-214-0, Order no.: T004).
Model I & Model III. (ISBN 1-55604-215-9, Order no.: T004).
Full-Featured Harness Analysis Designed to Evaluate All Relevant Variables & Give a Prediction of the Finish. Evaluates Scores & Gives Every Betting Combination of the Top Five Horses. Ultra Module Provides a True "Low Level" Artificial Intelligence Capable of Reweighting Variables Based on Results. Factors Relating to Winning Horses Are Regressed Out of Actual Races to Be Used in Future Predictions.
Professor Jones Professional Handicapping Systems.

Ultra Harness Handicapper with Track Management. Ronald D. Jones. 1985. *Compatible Hardware:* Apple; Commodore; IBM; TRS-80 Model I, Model III, Color Computer. *Operating System(s) Required:* CP/M. *Memory Required:* 64k.
disk $479.85 ea.
Apple. (ISBN 1-55604-216-7, Order no.: T014).
CP/M. (ISBN 1-55604-217-5, Order no.: T014).
Commodore. (ISBN 1-55604-218-3, Order no.: T014).
Color Computer. (ISBN 1-55604-219-1, Order no.: T014).
IBM. (ISBN 1-55604-220-5, Order no.: T014).
Model I & Model III. (ISBN 1-55604-221-3, Order no.: T014).
Full-Featured Harness Racing Analysis Designed to Evaluate All Relevant Variables & Give a Prediction of the Finish. Evaluates Scores & Gives Every Betting Combination for the Top Five Horses. Ultra Module Provides a True "Low Level" Artificial Intelligence Capable of Reweighting Variables Based on Results. Factors Relating to "Winning Horses" Are Regressed Out of Actual Races to Be Used in Future Predictions. Track Management Is a Data Base Program Designed to Keep Records on All Horses Running at a Track.
Professor Jones Professional Handicapping Systems.

Ultra-Mac Games. *Customer Support:* All of our products are unconditionally guaranteed.
Mac. CD-ROM disk $39.95 (Order no.: U-GAMES). *Nonstandard peripherals required:* CD-ROM drive.
524 MB of Ready-to-Run Mac Games of All Types.
Walnut Creek CDRom.

Ultra-Mac Utilities. *Customer Support:* All of our products are unconditionally guaranteed.
Mac. CD-ROM disk $39.95 (Order no.: U-UTILS). *Nonstandard peripherals required:* CD-ROM drive.
630 MB of Ready-to-Run Mac Utilities Including Fonts, Desktop Apps, Much More.
Walnut Creek CDRom.

Ultra-Mon. *Compatible Hardware:* TRS-80.
contact publisher for price.
Instant Software, Inc.

UltraCAD. *Compatible Hardware:* Commodore Amiga.
3.5" disk $299.95.
Full-Scale CAD.
Progressive Peripherals & Software, Inc.

Ultracomp Probability & Scientific Calculator. *Items Included:* Bound manual. *Customer Support:* Free hotline - no time limit; 30 day limited warranty; updates are $5/disk plus S&H.
MS-DOS. IBM & compatibles (192k). disk $39.95.
Calculator Package with All the Capabilities of a Typical Hand-Held Scientific Calculator, Plus Several Extended Features. It Does Decimal Arithmetic with User-Selected Precision up to 800 Digits. It Can Handle Numbers with Magnitudes up to 10 to the 2 Billionth Power. It Computes Factorials up to 50,000 Factorial Quickly (Exact to Whatever Precision the User Selects). Exact Computations of Probabilities for Binomial, Hypergeometric, Poisson, Negative Binomial, Normal, F, & Student Are Performed by Built-In Functions. Calculations of Combinations & Permutations Are Also Built-In. Functions Include Trig Functions, Inverse Trig Functions, Exp, Log, Pi, Int, X to the Y Power, & Square Root. Other Features Include Ten Memories & Printing of the Results.
Dynacomp, Inc.

UltraFile. Continental Software. *Compatible Hardware:* TI Professional with printer. *Language(s):* MSBASIC. *Memory Required:* 128k.
$199.95.
Texas Instruments, Personal Productivit.

UltraPaint.
Mac Plus (black & white only), Mac II (color capabilities). disk $79.00.
Lets User Do Black & White & Color Painting, Grey-Scale Image Processing & Object Drawing in One Package. Program Supports 256 Colors, Blended Fills, Multi-Color Airbrush, Masking & Other Special Effects. Grey-Scale Capabilities Include Multiple Image Combination, Contrast & Brightness Control, Sharpen & Blur & Halftone Printing. Supports Bezier Curves, Scaling, 600-dpi Precision, Eight Layers & Auto-Tracing of Bitmap Images.
Deneba Software.

UltraScript PC+. Nov. 1988.
IBM PC & compatibles, PC AT, PS/2, Model 30-286. disk $495.00 (Order no.: 5250033-902).

TITLE INDEX

A Software Program Which Gives Dot Matrix & Ink Jet Printers PostScript Printing Capabilities. Works With Any Software Package That Supports PostScript Printers Without Affecting Printing from Applications Which Are Not Postscript Compatible. Uses Same Licensed Typefaces Found in Adobe Postscript-Based Printing & Typesetting Systems. Package Comes with Additional 22 Fully Scalable Typefaces.
Laser Connection.

Ultrex Quadro Maze. *Compatible Hardware:* Commodore 64.
contact publisher for price (Order no.: C-1512).
Eat All the Dots Before Being Squashed by the Hungry Squid.
Creative Equipment.

UMB Pro: High Memory Loader & Extended Memory Mgr. *Version:* 2.01. Scott Daniel et al. Sep. 1991. *Items Included:* 5.25" & 3.5" media; User Guide; Registration card; Network license registration card. *Customer Support:* Free customer support 9-6, M-F, 714-754-4017.
DOS. 286, 386, or 486 (1Mb). $89.95. *Optimal configuration:* Hard disk preferred.
Memory Manager for Windows 3.0 Users. A Full XMS (Extended Memory) Memory Manager Providing Upper Memory & Taking Only 8k of Total Memory. As a Straight Replacement for HIMEM.SYS. Gives Higher Performance. Recognizes 22 different "chipsets". Includes QUADTOOLS, RAMDisk, Disk Cache, Spooler. DOS 5.0 compatible.
Quadtel Corp.

UMI PA Library. 1994. *Items Included:* Manual. *Customer Support:* One year of CSAP is provided at N/C; 30 day no risk guarantee.
MS-DOS. IBM & compatibles (640k). 5.25" disk $1995.00 (ISBN 0-927875-56-X, Order no.: 1750). *Addl. software required:* Winn CIRC/CAT or Winn CAT V5.1 or greater, Winn Informational Database subscription Item No. 1760 for $299. *Optimal configuration:* Same as Winn CIRC/CAT or Winn CAT, an additional 500Mb of hard disk space per year. *Networks supported:* Netbios or IPX compatible.
3.5" disk $1995.00 (ISBN 0-927875-55-1, Order no.: 1750).
PA Library Database Is a Database of More Than 600 Information Sources Compiled for Public Libraries. Features Broad Subject Areas Including Social Sciences, Humanities, Business & Science. UMI Databases Are Distributed 3 Times Annually with an Annual Subscription Fee.
Winnebago Software Co.

UMI Resource/One. 1994. *Items Included:* Manual. *Customer Support:* One year of CSAP is provided at N/C; 30 day no risk guarantee.
MS-DOS. IBM & compatibles (640k). 5.25" disk $2495.00 (ISBN 0-927875-54-3, Order no.: 1740). *Addl. software required:* Winn CIRC/CAT or Winn CAT V5.1 or greater, Winn Informational Database subscription Item No. 1760 for $299. *Optimal configuration:* Same as Winn CIRC/CAT or Winn CAT, an additional 200Mb of hard disk space per year. *Networks supported:* Netbios or IPX compatible.
3.5" disk $2495.00 (ISBN 0-927875-53-5, Order no.: 1740).
A Database of More Than 140 Information Sources Compiled for High Schools & Public Libraries. UMI Databases Feature Broad Subject Areas Including Social Sciences, Humanities, Business & Science. Distributed 3 Times Annually with an Annual Subscription Fee.
Winnebago Software Co.

UMI-Resource/One Full Text. 1995. *Items Included:* Manual. *Customer Support:* One year of the CSAP is provided at n/c; 30 day no risk guarantee.
MS-DOS. IBM or compatibles (640k). disk $2495.00 (ISBN 0-927875-63-2, Order no.: 1745). *Addl. software required:* Winnebago CIRC and/or CAT V 5.1 or higher. *Optimal configuration:* Same as Winnebago CIRC/CAT or Winnebago CAT, an additional 2 GB hard disk space per year. *Networks supported:* IPX or Netbios compatible.
3.5" disk $2495.00 (ISBN 0-927875-62-4, Order no.: 1745).
Fully Searchable Full-Text Access to 100 Titles, & Abstracts & Indexing Available for 140 Titles. The Titles Were Selected Through a Survey of Public & High School Libraries.
Winnebago Software Co.

UMI-Resource/One Select Full Text. 1995. *Items Included:* Manual. *Customer Support:* One year of the CSAP is provided at n/c; 30 day no risk guarantee.
MS-DOS. IBM or compatibles (640k). disk $1495.00 (ISBN 0-927875-61-6, Order no.: 1735). *Addl. software required:* Winnebago CIRC and/or CAT V 5.1 or higher. *Optimal configuration:* Same as Winnebago CIRC/CAT or Winnebago CAT, an additional 1 GB hard disk space per year. *Networks supported:* IPX or Netbios compatible.
3.5" disk $1495.00 (ISBN 0-927875-60-8, Order no.: 1735).
Concentrated Coverage with Abstracts & Indexing of 60 Titles & Full ASCII Text of 50 Popular Periodicals. The Titles Were Selected Through a Survey of Public & High School Librarians.
Winnebago Software Co.

UMI-Resource/One Select. *Items Included:* Manual. *Customer Support:* One year of CSAP is provided at N/C; 30 day no risk guarantee.
MS-DOS. IBM & compatibles (640k). 5.25" disk $1495.00 (ISBN 0-927875-52-7, Order no.: 1730). *Addl. software required:* Winn CIRC/CAT or Winn CAT V5.1 or greater, Winn Informational Database subscription Item No. 1760 for $299. *Optimal configuration:* Same as Winnebago CIRC/CAT or Winnebago CAT, an additional 75Mb of hard disk space per year. *Networks supported:* Netbios or IPX compatible.
3.5" disk $1495.00 (ISBN 0-927875-51-9, Order no.: 1730).
Database of More Than 60 Information Sources Compiled for Middle Schools, High Schools, & Public Libraries. UMI Databases Feature Broad Subject Areas Including Social Sciences, Humanities, Business, & Science. UMI Databases are Distributed 3 Times Annually With an Annual Subscription Fee.
Winnebago Software Co.

Uncle Harry's Will. *Compatible Hardware:* IBM PC. *Memory Required:* 128k.
disk $24.95.
Poem Provides Clues to Treasures That Are Found by Travelling to over 300 Locations by Foot & Car.
Dynacomp, Inc.

Under a Killing Moon. Nov. 1994. *Items Included:* Manual. *Customer Support:* 90 day unlimited warranty, tech support 1-800-793-8324.
MS-DOS. 386/25 MHz CPU, SVGA Display (VESA compliant) (4Mb). SRP $99.95 (Order no.: 1204). *Nonstandard peripherals required:* CD Rom drive (150k/sec), hard drive with 2Mb available, mouse, sound board (supports all major boards). *Optimal configuration:* Pentium, 16Mb RAM, double spin CD Rom (300k/sec), hard drive with 10Mb available, 16 bit sound board.
Interactive Movie, Detective Adventure Using Brian Keith, Margot Kidder, Russell Means & James Earl Jones As the Main Stars. The User Plays the Role of Tex Murphy in This Hilarious Adventure with Complete Freedom to Move & Explore Each of over 40 Rooms While Personally Directing the Course of the Game by Choosing Different Attitudes of Response. Has a Full, Rich Score of Original Music, High Quality Digitized Voices & Sound Effects.
Access Software, Inc.

Under Fire!, 2 disks. *Compatible Hardware:* Apple II+, IIe, IIc; Commodore 64; IBM PC. *General Requirements:* Joystick for Apple II+ (optional for IIe & IIc).
disk $35.00, incl. rulebook (Order no.: 48532).
Simulates Tactical World War II Combat. Players Command an Army of Armor, Infantry, & Support Guns. Men & Weapons from the United States, Germany, & the Soviet Union Are Represented. The Map Is a Topographic Representation of the Ground Shown in Three Different Scales. Users May Choose the Traditional Map for the Strategic Flow of Battle, or the Tactical Screen. Extended Capabilities Disks Are Available. For One or Two Players.
Avalon Hill Game Co., The Microcomputer Games Div.

Under Fire!: Extended Capabilities Disk 1. *Compatible Hardware:* Apple II+, IIe, IIc. *General Requirements:* Under Fire!
contact publisher for price.
Adds British, Japanese, & Italian Armies & Gives More Vehicles for Each Nation.
Avalon Hill Game Co., The Microcomputer Games Div.

Under Fire!: Extended Capabilities Disk 2. *Compatible Hardware:* Apple II+, IIe, IIc. *General Requirements:* Under Fire!
contact publisher for price.
Allows UNDER FIRE Commanders to Build Companies & Battalions & Engage Them in Massive Battles. Each Country Has a Number of Infantry Companies, to Which Can Be Added Armored, Support Weapons, Special Leaders, & Supply Units. New Rules Cover Surrender, Retreats, & the Rebuilding of Broken Units. Pulling Units from the Line Is More Important with This Disk Because All Units Suffer Permanent Losses from Scenario to Scenario. Allows Faster Response Time for 128k Apple.
Avalon Hill Game Co., The Microcomputer Games Div.

The Underground CD-ROM Handbook for the SAT. Aug. 1995. *Items Included:* Installation instructions, registration cards. *Customer Support:* Phone support by calling 302-234-1750, no charge. Fax support by faxing to 302-234-1760, no charge. E-Mail support at Compuserve ID 76004,3520 or MCI Mail/560-7116, no charge.
CD-ROM disk $49.95 (ISBN 1-887468-02-1).
Windows 3.1. 386SX or higher (4Mb). *Nonstandard peripherals required:* Mouse-Microsoft compatible, SoundBlaster or compatible sound card. *Optimal configuration:* 486 processor, 8Mb RAM.
Macintosh. Macintosh running System 7 or higher (4Mb). *Nonstandard peripherals required:* 13" monitor or higher. *Optimal configuration:* 2.5Mb of free RAM.
A High-School Student's Guide to the SAT Written by 4 Real-Life High-School Students Who Aced the Test & Went on to Ivy League Schools. The 4 Authors Guide Students Through Fast-Paced Lessons on Verbal, Math, SAT Basics & the SAT II Writing Test, Giving Their Proven Strategies & Techniques.
SWFTE International, Ltd.

Underneath. Oct. 1988. *Operating System(s) Required:* PC-DOS/MS-DOS 2.0. *Memory Required:* 256k.
disk $495.00 (Order no.: UN1001).
PC Based Automation Tool. Provides a Script Language That Allows the User to Develop Solutions in a Practical, Cost-Effective Approach. "Super Macro" Development Tool for Automative & Software Applications. Supports Communication to IBM 3270, 5250, LU6.2, Unisys Poll/Select, DEC UT100 & Others. Includes: Quickstart Tutorial & Interactive Learn Mode.
Core Technology Corp.

Undersea Adventure.
MS-DOS 3.1 or higher, Windows. 386 processor or higher (4Mb). CD-ROM disk $69.95 (Order no.: R1148). *Nonstandard peripherals required:* CD-ROM drive. *Optimal configuration:* 386 processor or higher, MS-DOS 3.1 or higher, 20Mb hard drive, 640k RAM, external speakers or headphones (with sound card) that are Sound Blaster compatible, VGA graphics adapter, VGA color monitor.
Macintosh (4Mb). (Order no.: R1148A). *Nonstandard peripherals required:* 14" color monitor or larger, CD-ROM drive.
See How Sea Creatures Live, What They Eat, & How They Swim. Talking Books Improve Reading Skills & Promote Learning about Undersea Life. Includes Descriptioins of over 130 Organisms (Ages 3 & Up).
Library Video Co.

Understand Yourself. *Items Included:* Bound manual. *Customer Support*: Free hotline - no time limit; 30 day limited warranty; updates are $5/disk plus S&H.
All computers except Atari (256k). disk $29.95. disk $44.95, incl. bk.
Series of Tests Designed to Help You to Determine the Real You. Based on the Book "Test Yourself", by Dr. Harry Gunn, the Several Programs Which Compose This Package Designed to Disclose Your Character. The Computer Does All the Scoring. Each Test Is Simple to Take & Requires Nothing More Than a Press of a Key to Answer Any Question. A Full Set of Directions Is Built into Each Test & Messages Appear at the Bottom of the Screen Whenever You Are Required to Do Something.
Dynacomp, Inc.

Understanding Breast Cancer. *Customer Support:* CD-ROM & CD-ROM Operating System Pamphlet.
Windows CD-ROM (4Mb or more extended memory). CD-ROM disk $79.95. *Optimal configuration:* Windows 3.1 386/25 MHz or higher, SVGA card, (Windows Accelerator recommended) MPC compatible sound card, CD-ROM drive.
Macintosh CD-ROM (4Mb or higher). CD-ROM disk $79.95. *Optimal configuration:* System 7.0 or higher, 256 colors, CD-ROM drive.
First of Understanding Health Series. A Multimedia Program Which Informs the User of Causes, Diagnosis, Treatment & Prevention of Breast Cancer.
ISM, Inc.

Understanding Diabetes Mellitus. Jul. 1994. *Items Included:* CD-ROM & CD-ROM Operating System Pamphlet.
Windows CD-ROM (4Mb or more extended memory). CD-ROM disk $79.95. *Optimal configuration:* Windows 3.1, 386/25 MHz or higher, SVGA card, CD-ROM drive, (Windows Accelerator recommended) MPC compatible sound card.
Macintosh CD-ROM (4Mb or higher). CD-ROM disk $79.95. *Optimal configuration:* System 7.0 or higher, 256 colors, CD-ROM drive.
Part of the Understanding Health Series. This Multimedia Program Explains the Importance of Prevention & Treatment of Diabetes Mellitus.
ISM, Inc.

Understanding Exposure: How to Take Great Photographs. Bryan Peterson. *Items Included:* 144 page color book of same name, 16 page user manual. *Customer Support:* Telephone technical support, free.
Macintosh; Windows. Macintosh II or higher (4Mb); 80386SX or higher (5Mb). CD-ROM disk $79.95 (ISBN 1-886393-00-1). *Nonstandard peripherals required:* System 7.X or higher, CD-ROM drive; Windows 3.1 with MS-DOS 5.0 or higher, CD-ROM drive.
Includes More Than 400 Stunning Photogrpahs, Plus Videos & Narration. Award Winning Photographer & Author Bryan Peterson Shows You How Understanding the Interaction of Aperture Settings, Film Speed, Shutter Speed, & Lighting Enhances Your Own Photography.
DiAmar Interact.

Understanding Heart Attacks. May 1995. *Items Included:* CD-ROM & CD-ROM Operating System Pamphlet.
Windows CD-ROM (4Mb or more extended memory). CD-ROM disk $79.95. *Optimal configuration:* Windows 3.1 386/25 MHz or higher, SVGA card, CD-ROM drive, (Windows Accelerator recommended) MPC compatible sound card.
Macintosh CD-ROM (4Mb or higher). CD-ROM disk $79.95. *Optimal configuration:* System 7.0 or higher, 256 colors, CD-ROM drive.
Part of the Understanding Health Series. This Multimedia Program Explains Coronary Artery Diseases Such As Angina, Myocardial Infarction; Their Diagnoses, Treatment & Prevention.
ISM, Inc.

Understanding Prostate Disorders. May 1995. *Items Included:* CD-ROM & CD-ROM Operating System Pamphlet.
Windows CD-ROM (4Mb or more extended memory). CD-ROM disk $79.95. *Optimal configuration:* Windows 3.1 386/25 MHz or higher, SVGA card, (Windows Accelerator recommended) MPC compatible sound card, CD-ROM drive.
Macintosh CD-ROM (4Mb or higher). CD-ROM disk $79.95. *Optimal configuration:* System 7.0 or higher, 256 colors, CD-ROM drive.
Part of Understanding Health Series. This Multimedia Program Explains to the Users Prostate Disorders, Such As Prostate Cancer, Benign Prostatic Hypertrophy, & Other Diseases, Their Diagnosis, Treatment & Prevention.
ISM, Inc.

UNE-CON: File Recovery System. Aug. 1981. *Operating System(s) Required:* CP/M-80. *Memory Required:* 32k.
disk 40 TPI $49.95 (ISBN 0-923875-50-6).
disk 80 TPI $49.95 (ISBN 0-923875-51-4).
8" disk $49.95 (ISBN 0-923875-49-2).
Unerases Any File That Was Accidentally Erased. In Addition, It Indicates If User Will "Clobber" Another File When Unerasing.
Elliam Assocs.

Uni-Date System. 1983. *Memory Required:* 128k.
disk $95.00.
Appointment Scheduler & Datebook. Allows Operator to Define Descriptions for over 1000 Professional Staff Members & Resource-Units for Which Operator Can Schedule Time & Usage.
Univair, Inc.

Uni-File. 1983. *Operating System(s) Required:* CP/M. *Memory Required:* 128k.
disk $195.00.
maintenance fee $50.00.
Database Management System with Report Generator.
Univair, Inc.

Uni-Link. 1983. *Operating System(s) Required:* CP/M.
disk $75.00.
Provides a 'Master Control Menu' from Which All UNIVAIR Programs May Run Without Having to Remember Any Initial Start-Up Commands for a Specific Program. Program Can Also Automatically Interface into Various Other Popular Non-UNIVAIR Products.
Univair, Inc.

Uni-Sort Special Sorting Interface. 1983. *Operating System(s) Required:* CP/M, CP/M-86, MS-DOS. *Memory Required:* 128k.
disk $75.00.
Tool with Which to Extract Information Out of Databases That Already Exist & Create a 'Secondary' Database with Certain Pre-Selected Fields of Information Which Can Be Used to Perform Additional Functions.
Univair, Inc.

Unicenter for OpenView. *Customer Support:* Available.
Solaris, AIX, HP-UX, DYNIX/ptx, DG-UX. Contact publisher for price.
Integrates CA-Unicenter with HP OpenView Integrated Network & Systems Management Framework. Helps Enterprise Managers Monitor & Control All Networked Systems from Single Management Console. Provides Security, Backup, Scheduling, Report Distribution & SNMP Devices, & Performs Process-Oriented Problem Management. Provides Integration Through SNMP & Integration with HP Operations Center.
Computer Associates International, Inc.

Unicorn Collection Management System. Version: 5.0. Jun. 1991. *Items Included:* Full documentation is provided for all modules purchased. Application software is packaged with C-ISAM & BRS/Search. *Customer Support:* Software support is avilable on an annually renewable basis & includes software upgrades, remote diagnostic troubleshooting, & help desk access.
UNIX. Various computers supporting UNIX (16Mb). contact vendor for price. *Nonstandard peripherals required:* Dumb terminals or microcomputers act as workstations when connected to the host computer.
The Unicorn Collection Management System is an Integrated Library Management System with Bibliographic, Public Access, Circulation, Reserves, Acquisitions, Serials, Authority, Booking & E-Mail Modules. UNIX-Based Unicorn Runs on Anything from PCs to Mainframe, & is Available As a Turnkey System Combining Hardware & Software or As a Software-Only Package.
Sirsi Corp.

Uniforth. *Operating System(s) Required:* CP/M. contact publisher for price.
The FORTH-79 Standard Language Extended with over 500 New Words That Provide Full-Screen & Line-Oriented Editors, Enhanced Disk & Terminal I/O, Array & String Handling & an Assembler. Optional Features Include: a Floating Point Package with All Transcendental Functions (Logs, Tangents, etc.), the MetaFORTH Cross Compiler, Printer Plotting, CP/M File Transfer Utilities, Astronomical & Amateur Radio Application & Word Processing.
Unified Software Systems.

TITLE INDEX

UNIFY RDBMS. Version: 5.0. Compatible Hardware: All major UNIX systems V.3 & System V.4 Platforms; Motorola 680000. Operating System(s) Required: MS-DOS, UNIX, XENIX. Language(s): C. Memory Required: 4000k. Items Included: Software, Manuals, Release Notes. Contact publisher for price.
A High Performance Relational Database Management System Designed to Excel in Large, Multi-User Applications. UNIFY Optimizes Runtime Performance in Transaction Oriented Environments. Significant Features Include Full Internationalization, Enhanced Formatting & Performance, & Text-Binary Logging. Uses Four Different Access Methods to Ensure the Fastest Possible Performance in Database Queries Including Hashing, B-Trees, Links & Buffered Sequential.
Unify Corp.

UNIKEY. Compatible Hardware: TRS-80. disk $19.95 (Order no.: D4UKY).
Minimize User's Keystrokes When Entering Mode 4 BASIC Programming Listings. Supports Custom Keys.
The Alternate Source.

Union CAT. Version: 4.1. Items Included: Manual. Customer Support: One year is included in purchase price.
MS-DOS (640k). IBM AT, PS/2 or compatible. disk $2995.00 (ISBN 0-927875-10-1, Order no.: 450). Optimal configuration: 1 floppy disk drive, 1 hard disk drive, Epson or compatible printer. Networks supported: Netbios compatible.
District Level Union Catalog. Stores up to 300,000 Unique Titles Each with Unlimited Location Fields. Allows Search of Database by Subject, Title, Author, & Note Field. Uses Boolean Logic Search Capabilities. Is USMARC Compatible. Includes Interlibrary Loan Features.
Winnebago Software Co.

Union CAT with ILL (Interlibrary Loan). Version: 4.1. 1994. Items Included: Manual. Customer Support: One year of CSAP is included in purchase price; 30 day no risk guarantee.
MS-DOS. IBM & compatibles (640k). 5.25" disk $2995.00 (ISBN 0-927875-34-9, Order no.: 1920). Optimal configuration: 486 or greater processor 2/66 MHz clockspeed, MS-DOS 5.1 or greater 2-4Mb RAM, hard disk drive with access speed of less than 20 MS, 1 floppy disk drive, Epson or compatible printer. Networks supported: Netbios or IPX compatible.
3.5" disk $2995.00 (ISBN 0-927875-33-0, Order no.: 1920).
System-Wide Catalog Which Allows You to Share Resources Thus Reducing the Cost for New Acquisitions Because They Don't Have to Purchase Additional Copies. The ILL Feature Makes System-Wide Resources Available for All Libraries Quickly & Efficiently. The Program Also Maintains an ILL Log File.
Winnebago Software Co.

Union CAT with Interlibrary Loan. Version: 4.0. Apr. 1994. Items Included: 1 software manual 250 pg. in a 3 ring binder. Customer Support: Guaranteed 2 hr call-back; 1st year of support included with program purchase; toll-free 1-800 number; modem support; program updates & manual revisions; replacement program disks if necessary; subscription to the WUG Letter, 30 day money back guarantee.
MS-DOS. IBM or compatible PC-Based computer, DOS 3.0 or higher (640k). 3.5" disk $1995.00 (ISBN 0-927875-33-0, Order no.: 1920). Nonstandard peripherals required: Epson or compatible printer with tractor feed, barwand, & keyboard. 2Mb hard drive space. Optimal configuration: 486 or higher processor, MS-DOS 5.0 or higher, 1Mb RAM, 2Mb hard disk space for every 1,000 MARC records in database. Networks supported: Winnebago LAN, Novell, ICLAS, & LANtastic.
5.25" disk $1995.00 (ISBN 0-927875-34-9, Order no.: 1920).
A Multiple Library Site Library Automation Software System. The Libraries Share One Database So Both Patrons & Staff Can Immediately Know the Location of a Material for Any Library. Interlibrary Loan Allows You to Send & Receive Requests for Materials. A Variety of Reports Are Available.
Winnebago Software Company.

UniPlus Operating System. Jun. 1985. Compatible Hardware: AT&T. Operating System(s) Required: UNIX. Memory Required: 1024k.
contact publisher for price.
UniSoft Systems.

Unique 120. Customer Support: 800-929-8117 (customer service).
MS-DOS. IBM/PS2. disk $1999.99 (ISBN 0-87007-694-9).
Full Manufacturing Accounting Software. This Package is Composed of Various "Optima" Accounting Modules. Works in Multi-Company, Multi-Warehousing Environments.
SourceView Software International.

Unison Author Language. Version: 2.17. Jul. 1992. Compatible Hardware: IBM PC, PC XT, PC AT. Operating System(s) Required: PC-DOS 2.0. Memory Required: 384k. Items Included: Disk, tutorial manual, reference manual. Customer Support: 30 days phone support.
disk $345.00, incl. manual (ISBN 0-922394-02-4).
Command-Oriented Authoring Language Specifically Designed for the Production of Computer-Based Training Materials. Employs English-Like Commands Such As "At" & "Write". Can Be Used to Produce Lessons Such As Tutorials, Drills & Practice, Pre & Post Tests, Job Task Simulations, & Games. Includes a Complete Tutorial.
Courseware Applications, Inc.

Unison Draw. Version: 4.0. Nov. 1986. Compatible Hardware: IBM PC & compatibles. Operating System(s) Required: PC-DOS 2.0. Memory Required: 384k. General Requirements: Graphics card. Items Included: Disk, manual. Customer Support: 30 days phone support.
disk $195.00, incl. manuals (ISBN 0-922394-04-0).
Graphics Editor Which Allows Interactive Design of Computer Displays. The Program Is Designed to Be Used by People Producing Computer-Based Training Lessons. Once the Graphic Has Been Created, the Program Automatically Writes the UNISON AUTHOR LANGUAGE Program Needed to Recreate It in a Lesson.
Courseware Applications, Inc.

UNIT-CAD: A Unit Conversion Program. D. Edwards, Jr. Jan. 1992. Items Included: Manual, examples, a list of units in memory.
MS-DOS. IBM PC & compatibles (312k). disk $19.00.
Software Calculator for the PC That Handles Units. For Example, User Can Multiply 3cm x 2 ft. & Get the Answer in Square Meters or Any Other Area Unit. Has Stored Physical Constants & Allows the User to Add His Own.
Maple Leaf Software.

Unit Dose Calculation & Preparation. Ann M. Steves. 1996. Customer Support: Phone support by calling 1-800-748-7734 or 913-441-2881.
DOS 3.1 or higher. IBM or compatibles (512k). disk $150.00 (Order no.: MIS9026).
Educational Software Concepts, Inc.

U. S. Constitution Tutor. (Micro Learn Tutorial Ser.). Items Included: Manual includes worksheets, tests, help scens. Customer Support: Free telephone support.
MAC. IBM (128k), Macintosh, Apple series, (48k). 5.25" disk, $39.95 (Lab pack/5 $99.00). 3.5" disk, $44.95 (Lab pack/5 $115.00). Apple, IBM or Macintosh network, $249.00 (ISBN 0-939153-00-9).
DOS. Macintosh. Single copy, $44.95; Lab pack/5, $115.00; Network v., $249.00 (ISBN 0-939153-86-6).
APP. (ISBN 0-939153-41-6).
Instructs & Tests on Important Aspects of the U.S. Constitution & American Government. Select by Topic or by Difficulty Level. Topics Include Legislative, Executive & Judicial Branches, Amendments, Rights, Elections, Federalism, Separation of Powers, Checks & Balances. The tutorial mode gives explanations for every answer choice, correct & incorrect (plus help/ practice on important ideas). The test mode gives no help; after the score appears, it presents missed questions in the tutorial mode.
Word Assocs., Inc.

U. S. Government Periodicals Index. Items Included: Quarterly Updates.
MS-DOS. IBM or compatibles. disk
Detailed new index, first published in March 1994, reviews some 180 federal periodicals of major research, reference, & general-interest value - from air safety to cancer research to criminal justice.
Congressional Information Service.

U. S. Space Station Orbiter. Compatible Hardware: Commodore Amiga.
3.5" disk $69.95.
Object Library with Space Station/Orbiter Designs.
Byte by Byte.

Unitrust WKI. Jun. 1990.
MS-DOS. IBM & compatibles (512K). disk $84.50. Addl. software required: Lotus, 1-2-3 V. 2.01 or higher.
Calculates Remainder Interest for Unitrusts, Annuity Trusts, & Grantor Retained Income Trusts (Grits), per Internal Revenue Code Section 7520.
Serious Business Software.

Univair Payroll Management System. 1984. Operating System(s) Required: CP/M, CP/M-86, MS-DOS. Memory Required: 128k.
disk $500.00.
maintenance fee $100.00.
Provision for Storing Date of Hiring, Job Classification, Salary, Pay Frequency & up to 9 Standard Deductions.
Univair, Inc.

Univair Series 9000. Operating System(s) Required: CP/M, CP/M-86, MS-DOS, PC-DOS 2.0. Memory Required: 128k.
Univair, Inc.
Accounts Payable Management System.
    disk $500.00.
    demo disk $75.00.
    manual $30.00.
    Automatically Maintains a Company's Payables, Provides Cash Flow Projections & Generates Checks.
Dental Office Management System.
    disk $995.00.
    update serv. $200.00.
    demo disk $125.00.
    manual $30.00.
    Maintains Database on Each Dentist, Insurance Company & ADA Procedure Code That Is Being Used in the Practice, along with Standard Charges for Each Type of Service. All Charges & Activities Are Linked to Patient

Involved & Cross-Referenced by Dentist, Insurance Company, Diagnosis & Procedure Code. Automatically Prints Monthly Statements & Insurance Claims on the Standard ADA Form.
General Ledger Accounting System.
 disk $995.00.
 update serv. $200.00.
 demo disk $75.00.
 manual $30.00.
 Double-Entry Accounting That Verifies Valid Account Numbers, Displays the Descriptions, Calculates & Balances Each Journal Voucher Entry & Determines the Profit & Losses, As Well As the Company's Net Worth. Chart of Accounts Divided into Basic Categories: Current Liabilities, Long Term Liabilities, Equity, Income, Expenses & Cost of Sales.
Insurance Agency Management System.
 disk $1495.00.
 update serv. $200.00.
 demo disk $75.00.
 manual $30.00.
Legal-Professional Time & Billing System I.
 disk $995.00.
 update serv. $200.00.
 demo disk $125.00.
 manual $30.00.
 Contains a Full Accounts Receivable Package Which Allows Full Open-Item Accounting for Each File. User Can Define a Database of up to 999 Legal Categories, As Well As 999 Codes Specifying Type of Services Rendered.
Medical Office Management System.
 disk $995.00.
 update serv. $200.00.
 demo disk $75.00.
 manual $30.00.
 Maintains Database on Each Doctor, Insurance Companies, ICDA-9 Diagnosis Codes & CPT-4 Procedure Codes That Are Being Used in the Practice Along with Standard Charges for Each Type of Service. All Charges Linked to Patient & Cross-Referenced by Doctor, Insurance Companies, Diagnosis & Procedure Code. Prints Monthly Statements & Insurance Claims on Standard AMA Form OP-409.
On-Line Order-Entry with Inventory Control.
 disk $995.00.
 update serv. $200.00.
 demo disk $75.00.
 manual $30.00.
 Designed for User Who Sells Products from Inventory on a Cash or Credit Basis. Includes a Point-of-Sale Module As Well As a Fully Integrated Accounts Receivable Module for Regular Charge Customers. Vendor File Is Also Maintained for Input & Tracking of All Purchase Orders As Well As Current Inventory Status, YTD Sales Status, Items on Order & Amounts Owed to the Vendor.
Property Management System.
 disk $1150.00.
 update serv. $200.00.
 demo disk $125.00.
 manual $30.00.
 Allows User to Maintain an Exact Cost Accounting on Each Separate Building Within a Complex or Project As Well As Individual Lease or Rental Units within Each Building Itself. Maintains Fixed Asset Accounting on Buildings, Accounts Payable File for up to 99 Staff Members & 999 Local Suppliers & Accounts Receivable on Tenant. Report Categories Include: Inter-Office, Master Property, Master Tenant, Master Accounting, Monthly Statements & Forms.
Super Ledger Client Write-Up System.
 disk $650.00.
 update serv. $150.00.
 demo disk $75.00.
 manual $30.00.
 Combination of Univair's General Ledger Accounting System & Standard Accounts Payable Management System.

Universal & Sidereal Time Ephemeris. *Compatible Hardware:* TI 99/4A with Extended BASIC module. *Operating System(s) Required:* DX-10. *Language(s):* Extended BASIC. *Memory Required:* 48k.
 cassette $16.95.
 Calculates Sidereal Time for Any Geographic Location at Any Instant of Universal Time.
 Eastbench Software Products.

Universal Calculator. *Compatible Hardware:* Apple Macintosh Plus. *Customer Support:* Phone support.
 3.5" disk $98.00.
 Solves Common Design Calculations for Mechanical Designers & Engineers.
 Flight Engineering.

Universal Cartesian Plotting Program. *Compatible Hardware:* HP series 200, series 300. *Language(s):* BASIC 2.0, 3.0, 4.0 (source code included).
 $195.00, incl. 10 other utilities.
 Draws Graphs in Publication Style Format of Y Versus X &, If Desired, a Parameter. Data to Be Plotted Can Be Input from Keyboard, from a Data File, or from a Function Typed in from Keyboard. Also Includes: Execution Time Profiler, CRUNCH, COMPARE, RNDGRAPH, CALENDAR, & More.
 James Assocs.

Universal Cross Assembler. *Compatible Hardware:* Apple Macintosh Plus.
 3.5" disk $299.00.
 Flexible, Table-Based Cross-Assembler.
 Memocom Development Tools.

Universal Data Management. *Version:* 4.0. 1978. *Operating System(s) Required:* THEOS, UNIX. *Language(s):* THEOS BASIC, UX-BASIC.
 contact publisher for price.
 Data Base Management System Featuring Full Screen Entry.
 Comcepts Systems.

Universal Data Research General Ledger System. *Language(s):* Extended.
 contact publisher for price.
 Supports Broad Ranging Reporting & Control Requirements. Provides Ability to Integrate Other UDRI Data Base Packages.
 Universal Data Research, Inc.

Universal Data Research Payroll Package.
 write for info.
 Payroll System Generating All Information Necessary for Federal & State Financial Reports. Reports Include Check Printing, Employee List & Check History, W-2 Information, Quarterly Reports.
 Universal Data Research, Inc.

Universal Graphing. *Compatible Hardware:* TRS-80.
 contact publisher for price.
 Instant Software, Inc.

Universal Pharmacy Software Package. *Version:* 110DA2. 1979. *Compatible Hardware:* Altos; IBM. *Operating System(s) Required:* CP/M-86, MP/M-86, MS-DOS, Concurrent CP/M, Concurrent DOS. *Language(s):* CB-86. *Memory Required:* 512k.
 $7000.00.
 Provides Retail Pharmacies with a Single Entry, Menu-Driven System Which Produces Labels, Third Party Billing, Receipts, Patient Profiles, Bilingual Label Instructions, Daily & Narcotic Reports. Handles up to 62,000 Third Party Plans, over 1000 Price Plans, & Full Drug to Drug Interaction Checking. Available Options Include: Accounts Receivable, DME to Provide Inventory Control for Durable Medical Equipment, Nursing Home Service Options Such As Batch Refills, Programmable Med Sheets & Doctors Orders, & Membership Number Verification.
 Dagar-Software Development Corp.

UniVersions. Apr. 1991. *Items Included:* One spiral-bound manual. *Customer Support:* Free customer support, 800 number.
 Macintosh. disk List $50.00; Academic $50.00 (ISBN 0-8412-2060-3).
 Combines the Capabilities of a Physical Constant Database, Unit Conversion Facility, & Scientific Calculator. At the Heart of the Program Is a Database That Encompasses Many of the Important Physical Constants, Quantities, & Measurements of Interest to the Scientist, from Avogadro Number to Volumetric Flow & Weight. Automatic Features Include Tracking of Significant Digits of Physical Constants & Scaling of Quantities Using Magnitude Prefixes. Conversions Are Push-Button. Comes with Specialized Databases for NMR Spectroscopy, Photometrics, & Radiation Measurement. All Databases Are Extensible, Allowing User to Modify the Existing Properties. Features Include a Memory Register, Plus Log & Trig Functions.
 American Chemical Society.

UniWare Cross Assemblers. *Version:* 5.1. *Operating System(s) Required:* MS-DOS, UNIX, XENIX,. *Customer Support:* One full year support, updates & hot line telephone support.
 disk $800.00 & up.
 UniWare Cross Assemblers Generate ROMable, Relocatable Code for a Variety of Popular Microprocessors: Motorola - 68000-68040, CPU32, 68302, 68HC11, 6809, 6805, 6801, 6800; Intel - 8086/186/286, 8051, 8048, 8080/5, 8041; Hitachi - HD64180, 6305, 6301; Zilog - Z80/Z180, Z8; Others - 6502/c02, 1802, TMS7000/70C42, 3870/F8. Each Assembler Features Macros, File Inclusion, Versatile Listing Control, Cross Reference Listings, & Manufacturer Compatibility in Instruction Memonics & Operand Formats. A Linker, Librarian, & Downloader Are Provided with Each Assembler. The Downloader Converts Your Final Load into Industry Standard File Formats for Downloading to EPROM Programmers, Emulators, & Target Hardware. Custom Formats & Symbolics Are Supported.
 Software Development Systems, Inc.

UNIX MUMPS. *Version:* 2.1. Harlan Stenn. 1984. *Operating System(s) Required:* UNIX.
 contact publisher for price.
 A Character-String Oriented Data Manipulation Language That Adds Character String Operators & Key Indexed File Structures to UNIX. Features Include: Arbitrary Precision Character Arithmetic, Arbitrary Length Strings, Routines Prepared by Any Editor Available, Ability to Read & Write Standard UNIX Files.
 Plus Five Computer Services.

UNIX Programming on the 80286/80386. *Version:* 2.0. Alan Deikman. *Operating System(s) Required:* Unix, Xenix.
 book & disk $39.95 (ISBN 1-55851-062-1).
 book only $24.95 (ISBN 1-55851-060-5).
 Course on Running UNIX on an 80286/80386-Based Computer. Provides a Tutorial & Reference.
 M & T Bks.

UNIX SPITBOL. *Version:* 1.28. Mar. 1987. *Compatible Hardware:* SPARCstation, Sun 4, SGI. *Operating System(s) Required:* Sun O/S, Solaris, IRIX. *Memory Required:* 1000k. *Items Included:* Software & documentation. *Customer Support:* Free.
 UNIX, Single User. tape or disk $695.00 (ISBN 0-939793-06-7, Order no.: SPTSU).

TITLE INDEX

UNIX, Multi User. tape or disk $1995.00 (ISBN 0-939793-07-5, Order no.: SPTMU).
Implementation of the SNOBOL4 Programming Language. Used for Complex Text Processing & Pattern Matching. Supports Binary & Direct-Access Files, Pipes, Built-In Sort, & Numerous Language Extensions.
Catspaw, Inc.

Unlock. *Compatible Hardware:* Lifeboat. *Operating System(s) Required:* CP/M, SB-80. *Language(s):* BASIC-80 5.20. *Memory Required:* 64k.
disk $95.00.
Development Tool for the BASIC Programmer. Allows Listing & Editing of Files That Have Been Saved with the BASIC-80 "P". Eliminates the Need for Saving Source Codes.
Lifeboat Assocs.

Unprotect. *Compatible Hardware:* IBM PC, PCjr, PC XT, PC AT, PC compatibles.
disk $29.95.
Software Matters.

Unraveling Paths: Dreamers & Mystics. (The/Destiny Chronicles Ser.). William R. Stanek. Feb. 1995.
PC-DOS/MS-DOS, Novell DOS 3.1 or higher. IBM PC, XT, AT, PS/2 or 100% compatibles (640k). disk $11.95 (ISBN 1-57545-004-6). *Optimal configuration:* IBM PC, XT, AT, PS/2 or 100% compatibles, CGA/VGA or compatible graphics card & monitor, 640k minimum RAM, hard disk, PC-DOS/MS-DOS or Novell DOS 3.1 or higher. Will also run on Windows system.
PC-DOS/MS-DOS, Novell DOS 3.1 or higher. IBM PC, XT, AT, PS/2 or 100% compatibles (640k). disk $11.95 (ISBN 1-57545-005-4). *Optimal configuration:* IBM PC, XT, AT, PS/2 or 100% compatibles, VGA/SVGA or compatible graphics card & monitor, 640k minimum RAM, hard disk, PC-DOS/MS-DOS or Novell DOS 3.1 or higher. Will also run on Windows system.
Interactive Fiction on Floppy Disk.
Virtual Pr., The.

UNREL. *Version:* 1.0. John Calkins. Aug. 1983. *Operating System(s) Required:* CP/M, MP/M. *Language(s):* CBASIC. *Memory Required:* 48k.
disk $45.00.
8" disk $45.00.
Disassembles & Generates 8080 Assembly Code, from Relocatable Programs or Libraries.
C.C. Software.

UpFront. *Version:* 2.11. *Compatible Hardware:* IBM PC & compatibles. *Memory Required:* 512k.
disk $175.00.
Multifunction Program Integrates All Features Needed for Electronic Mail.
British Telecom.

Upgrade Amazonia Windows. 1994. *Items Included:* Teachers guide.
CD-ROM disk contact publisher for price.
Contains Level III software on CD-ROM, Level III teachers guide & software installation guide.
Computer Curriculum.

Upgrade the Virtual BioPack. 1994.
disk $299.00 (ISBN 1-57026-026-5).
Contains Level III software upgrade on CD-ROM, Level III Teacher's guide software installation guide.
Computer Curriculum Corp.

Upgrade II. *Compatible Hardware:* 8-, 16-, & 32-bit microcomputers. *Operating System(s) Required:* PC-DOS. *Memory Required:* 256k. *General Requirements:* 2 disk drives or hard disk. contact publisher for price.
Together with SYN-CHECK Allows Software Developers Who Have Developed COBOL Applications in RM/COBOL Syntax to Switch over to LEVEL II COBOL Compiler. Automatically Makes 60 to 80% or More of the Changes That SYN-CHECK Has Listed. Flags the Code Which Needs Programmer Attention, Converts COBOL Source Code to LEVEL II COBOL, Reformats RM Extensions to Make Them Compatible with Micro Focus Extensions, & Reconstructs the DISPLAY Instructions for Compatibility with MF DISPLAY Conventions.
Micro Focus, Inc. (California).

Upgrade III. *Compatible Hardware:* IBM RT PC. *Operating System(s) Required:* UNIX.
$400.00.
Preprocessor & Migration Aid for Applications Written in Ryan-McFarland COBOL Migrating to the Compact Level II COBOL/ET System.
Micro Focus, Inc. (California).

Uppers, Downers, All Arounders. Sep. 1995. *Customer Support:* 30 day money back guarantee, free technical help.
Windows (MPC 1) compatible sound board. 386SX33 CPU or higher, VGA (256 color) CD-ROM disk (4Mb). CD-ROM disk $170.00 (ISBN 0-926544-13-6). *Addl. software required:* 256 color screen driver, video for Windows. *Optimal configuration:* At least 1Mb hard drive.
7.1 or higher. Macintosh, 640x480 color monitor, audio, CD-ROM drive (4Mb). *Addl. software required:* Quicktime. *Optimal configuration:* At least 1Mb hard drive. *Networks supported:* Appletalk.
A Comprehensive Psychoactive Drug Education CD-ROM Based on the Textbook of the Same Name & Material from the Company's Various Awardwinning Drug Education Films & Videos. This Interactive Resource Can Be Used in Libraries, Media Centers, Counseling Sessions or at Home.
CNS Productions.

UR/FORTH. *Version:* 1.2. Oct. 1993. *Operating System(s) Required:* MS-DOS, Windows 3.1. *Memory Required:* 80386 2Mb, Windows 4Mb, MS-DOS 640k.
disk $495.00.
High Performance FORTH-83 Development System for MS-DOS, Windows 3.1 & 80386 32-Bit Protected Mode, Includes Graphics, Floating Point, Native Code Compiler.
Laboratory Microsystems, Inc.

Uranian Module: M65D. 1984. *Compatible Hardware:* Apple II+, IIe, IIc; Commodore 64, PET. *Memory Required:* 48k.
disk $50.00 ea.
Apple. (ISBN 0-925182-35-4, Order no.: M65D).
Commodore 64. (ISBN 0-925182-36-2, Order no.: M65D).
IBM. (ISBN 0-925182-37-0, Order no.: M65D).
Automatically Adds Uranian Planets.
Matrix Software.

USA Trivia. *Items Included:* Bound manual. *Customer Support:* Free hotline - no time limit; 30 day limited warranty; updates are $5/disk plus S&H.
MS-DOS. IBM & compatibles (128k). disk $19.95. *Nonstandard peripherals required:* Color graphics card.
Combines Game Format with the Presentation of Important Geographical & Historical Facts about the U.S.A.
Dynacomp, Inc.

USER MESSAGE

Uselog - Computer Use Log. *Version:* 3.00A. Keith R. Plossl. Sep. 1988. *Compatible Hardware:* IBM PC & compatibles. *Operating System(s) Required:* PC-DOS/MS-DOS. *Language(s):* C Basic. *Memory Required:* 64k. *General Requirements:* printer.
disk $35.00 ea.
IBM. (ISBN 0-934801-04-5).
CPM-86. (ISBN 0-934801-05-3).
CP/M-80. 8" disk $29.95 (ISBN 0-934801-06-1).
Designed to Track Computer Usage by Purpose. Keeps a Record by User, Purpose, Data & Time. Computes Elapsed Time by Purpose & Total Time Used.
K. R. Plossl & Co.

User Form. *Version:* 1.74. Apr. 1989. *Items Included:* Manual.
PC/MS-DOS 3.x (256k). IBM PC & compatibles. disk $25.00 (Order no.: UF). *Nonstandard peripherals required:* Hard disk. *Optimal configuration:* Printer.
Enables User to Create Own Forms. Use Variables to Insert Information Within Form. Store Information Within Data Base for Later Use. Variables Can Be Automatic, Required, Protected, Calculated or Come From Another Data Base. Forms Can Be Printed with Graphics & Shading, or Just Variable Data Can Be Printed on Existing Pre-Printed Forms.
Hansen Research & Development Corp.

User Help. *Version:* 1.81. Apr. 1989. *Items Included:* Manual.
PC/MS-DOS 3.x (256k). IBM PC & compatibles. disk $25.00 (Order no.: UH). *Nonstandard peripherals required:* Hard disk. *Optimal configuration:* 512k RAM, mouse.
Memory Resident Program for Storing Helpful Information. Can Be Used As a DOS Tutorial, Rolodex, Applications Note File, Data Reminder or Telephone List. Comes with "Cut" & "Paste" Functions for Passing Information Between Applications. If Computer Has EMS Memory, Program Will Only Need 10k of DOS Memory. "Hot" Key Is Redefinable. Program Can Access Multiple Files.
Hansen Research & Development Corp.

User Menu. *Version:* 2.55. Apr. 1989. *Items Included:* Printed material.
PC/MS-DOS 3.x (256k). IBM PC & compatibles. disk $25.00 (Order no.: UM). *Nonstandard peripherals required:* Hard disk. *Optimal configuration:* 512k RAM, mouse, printer.
Hard Disk Menu Program Allows Easy Access to Programs & Applications Stored in Computer. Also Has Passwords, DOS Shell, Easy-to-Use Installation Program, On-Line Help, User Tracking & Screen Saver. There Are Ten Categories with Ten Selections per Category. Menu Chaining Allows for User to Have Thousands of Selections Available.
Hansen Research & Development Corp.

User Message. *Version:* 1.74. Apr. 1989. *Items Included:* Manual.
PC/MS-DOS 3.x (256k). IBM PC & compatibles. disk $25.00 (Order no.: USERMSG). *Nonstandard peripherals required:* Hard disk. *Optimal configuration:* 512k RAM, mouse, printer.
Memory Resident Program to Store, Print & Archive Telephone Messages. Allows Receptionist to "Pop up" over Existing Application to Enter Telephone Message & Return to Application. Telephone Numbers Can Be Dialed Using a Telephone Modem Within the Computer. Messages Can Be Archived & Reviewed or Deleted with an Archive Viewing Utility. If Computer Has EMS Memory, Program Will Use Only 10k of DOS Memory.
Hansen Research & Development Corp.

USHARE

UShare. Compatible Hardware: Apple Macintosh Plus. Operating System(s) Required: Unix. 3.5" disk $1195.00.
Enables Macintosh Computers to Be Integrated with UNIX Workstations.
Information Presentation Technologies, Inc.

Using & Programming the Macintosh, Including 32 Ready-to-Run Programs. Frederick Holtz. 1984. Compatible Hardware: Apple Macintosh. Operating System(s) Required: Apple DOS. Language(s): MS BASIC. Memory Required: 128k.
disk $28.50, incl. bk. (ISBN 0-8306-5103-9, Order no.: 5103C).
Shows How to Manipulate the Mouse, Use Any of the Macintosh's 500 Built-In (ROM) Subroutines, Even Performs Complex Mathematical Questions in Seconds.
TAB Bks.

Using Applications Software: An Introduction Featuring FRAMEWORK. Donald Beil & Beil. Mar. 1986. Compatible Hardware: IBM PC, PC XT, PC AT. Memory Required: 256k. General Requirements: 2 disk drives.
disk $34.28 (ISBN 0-07-079651-3).
General Introductions Are Provided for Each Application, As Are Details of Working with FRAMEWORK. An Extended Case Study Is Featured, with Nine Related Assignments That Parallel the Presentation of the Text Material.
McGraw-Hill, Inc.

Using Microsoft Word 5: IBM Version. Version: 4 & 5. Bryan Pfaffenberger.
MS-DOS. IBM. disk $21.95 (ISBN 0-88022-409-6, Order no.: 943).
A Series of Examples & Applications Leads Readers from Word Processing Basics to the Advanced Features of Program.
Que.

Using Microsoft Word: 4. Bryan Pfaffenberger. Compatible Hardware: Macintosh. Memory Required: 320k.
$22.95 (ISBN 0-88022-451-7, Order no.: 987).
Step-by-Step Lessons, Power User Tips, & Keyboard Shortcuts Helps Users Optimize This Word Processor.
Que.

Using MS-DOS on a Hard Disk. Patricia A. Menges. 1987. Items Included: Quick Reference Guide, audio tapes. Customer Support: 30 day-right of return; Editorial support for course content/exercises.
DOS. IBM & compatibles. disk $125.00 (ISBN 0-917792-61-0, Order no.: 104). Addl. software required: MS-DOS.
Self-paced instruction for MS-DOS operating systems on computers with a hard drive.
OneOnOne Computer Training.

Using Multiplan for Marketing & Sales Problems. Michael V. Laric & Ronald Stiff. Jun. 1984. Compatible Hardware: IBM PC. Operating System(s) Required: PC-DOS. Memory Required: 64k. General Requirements: Printer recommended.
disk $34.95, incl. bk. (ISBN 0-13-605098-0).
Techniques for Spreadsheet Use in Solving Marketing & Sales Problems, Aimed at Primary Market of Professionals & Secondary Market of Business Schools.
Prentice Hall.

Using 1-2-3 Workbook & Disk, 2nd Edition. Items Included: Workbook & disk.
$175.00 (instructor's kit) (ISBN 0-88022-522-X, Order no.: 1017).
second edition $29.95 per workbook (disk included) (ISBN 0-88022-517-3, Order no.: 1064).
Courseware Designed to Accompany USING 1-2-3 Book. Instructor's Kit Includes Workbook, Disk, Reference Book, & Guide. Versions Available for LOTUS 1-2-3 Releases 1A & 2.
Que.

Using the Commodore 64 in the Home. Bill Behrendt & Hank Librach. Apr. 1984. Compatible Hardware: Commodore 64 or Portable 64. Language(s): BASIC (source code included). Memory Required: 64k.
disk $29.95 (ISBN 0-13-940099-0, Order no.: 04009-8).
20 Programs for the Home Including a Calorie Counter, Family Expense Monitor, Investment Analyzer, Checkbook Keeper & Games.
Prentice Hall.

Using the IBM Personal Computer: IBM EasyWriter. Ada W. Finifter. Edited by Paul Becker. Jul. 1984. Compatible Hardware: IBM PC. Operating System(s) Required: PC-DOS.
disk $39.95, incl. manual (ISBN 0-03-071782-5).
Tutorial/Reference Explains the Use & Applications of IBM's EASYWRITER Word Processing Program & Auxiliary Procedures Using the IBM DOS.
Dryden Pr.

Using the IBM Personal Computer: WordStar. C. J. Puotinen. Edited by Paul Becker. Oct. 1983. Compatible Hardware: IBM PC.
disk $39.95, incl. bk. (ISBN 0-03-063981-6).
Extensive Exercises & Examples to Guide the User Through Each of WordStar's Functions.
Dryden Pr.

Using the Lotus 1-2-3 Program. Oct. 1984. Memory Required: 192k. Items Included: Handbook & one training diskette.
$95.00 per package for 1 to 24 units. discounts for larger quantities.
Courseware Includes a Handbook & Disk for a Six-Hour to Eight-Hour Tutorial.
Science Research Assocs.

Using the Macintosh with System 7. Manthei & Associates Staff. 1991. Items Included: Quick Reference Guide, audio tapes, practice disk. Customer Support: 30 day-right of return; Editorial support for course content/exercises. Apple System. Macs. disk $175.00 (ISBN 0-917792-86-6, Order no.: 128). Addl. software required: System 7.0.
Self-paced training for Macintosh computer running System 7.0.X; covers desktop navigation, file management, initializing disks, networking, Hypercard, & much more - even Control panel, DAs & font.
OneOnOne Computer Training.

Using the PCjr in the Home. Hank Librach & Bill L. Behrendt. Sep. 1984. Compatible Hardware: IBM PCjr. Language(s): Cartridge BASIC (source code included). Memory Required: 64k.
bk. $10.95 (ISBN 0-13-937335-7).
disk contact publisher for price.
Collection of Home & Educational Programs Covering Educational, Financial & Recreational Topics.
Prentice Hall.

Using WordPerfect in Business. 1993. Compatible Hardware: IBM PC, PC XT, PC AT & compatibles. Operating System(s) Required: PC-DOS/MS-DOS. Memory Required: 640k. General Requirements: WordPerfect 5 or 5.1 WordProcessing Software.
disk $29.95 ea.
IBM. (ISBN 0-935987-22-3).
Apple. (ISBN 0-935987-23-1).
Self-Study Guide Which Consists of Student Guide & Diskette Containing Data Files. Student Guide Provides Step-by-Step Instructions in WORDPERFECT Word Processing. Topics Covered Include: Getting Started, Creating & Editing a Document, Save & Print, Copying & Moving Text, Spellchecker & Thesaurus, As Well As Customized Form Letters, Using Menus.
Edutrends, Inc.

Using Your PCjr: Beginning BASIC & Applications. Richard Swadley & Joseph Wikert. Jan. 1985. Compatible Hardware: IBM PCjr. Operating System(s) Required: PC-DOS 2.1. Language(s): Cartridge BASIC (source code included). Memory Required: 128k.
disk $24.95 (ISBN 0-13-939372-2).
bk. $13.95 (ISBN 0-13-937376-4).
Shows How to Set up & Run the PCjr, Introduces BASIC, Explains Computing Fundamentals, & Offers Additional Features. Provides a Variety of Home, Educational, Business, & Entertainment Applications Including Payroll Computations, Checkbook Balancing, a Math Tutorial, & a Game of Blackjack. Includes Directions for Modifying Applications & Extra Programming Tips.
Prentice Hall.

UT86. Lifeboat Associates. Compatible Hardware: TI Professional. Operating System(s) Required: MS-DOS. Memory Required: 64k.
$180.00.
Texas Instruments, Personal Productivit.

UTIL. Compatible Hardware: Apple.
contact publisher for price.
Dynacomp, Inc.

/Util: A UNIX-Like Utility Package for MS-DOS. Allen Holub. Operating System(s) Required: MS-DOS. General Requirements: The Shell from the On Command package (M&T Publishing, Inc.).
disk $29.95, incl. manual.
Collection of Utility Program Providing a Fully Functional Subset of the UNIX Environment. Many of the Utilities May Be Used Independently. Includes Complete Source Code on Disk. All Programs & Most of the Utility Subroutines Are Fully Documented in a UNIX-Style Manual.
M & T Bks.

UTILIBILL Customer History. 1986. Compatible Hardware: IBM. Operating System(s) Required: MS-DOS. Memory Required: 256k. General Requirements: 2 disk drives, UTILIBILL Utility IBM Billing System. Items Included: Diskettes, manual. Customer Support: 30 day toll-free telephone support.
disk $495.00.
Add-On Module for UTILIBILL, Provides a 13-Month History for Each Customer Showing the Billed Amounts, Bill Adjustments, Payments & Usages.
Tecnomics, Inc.

UTILIBILL FRS: Field Recorder System. 1983. Compatible Hardware: Psion Model L. General Requirements: UTILIBILL or UTILIBILL Plus System. Customer Support: 30 day toll-free telephone support.
disk $495.00.
Turns a Pocket Computer into an Electronic Meter Reading Device. MMeter Readings Are Recorded into the Computer in the Field. If the Reading Entered Is Out of Range for That Meter the Computer Will Alert the Reader So the Readding May Be Re-Entered. At the End of the Day, the Portable Computer Is Attached to the Office Computer for Automatic Transfer of the Readings.
Tecnomics, Inc.

TITLE INDEX

UTILIBILL IBM: Utility Billing System. 1982. *Compatible Hardware:* IBM. *Operating System(s) Required:* MS-DOS. *Memory Required:* 256k. *General Requirements:* Hard disk, tractor-feed dot matrix printer. *Items Included:* Diskettes, customization of titles, manual with tutorial session. *Customer Support:* 30 day toll-free telephone support; 3 support plans available. disk $995.00.
Prints Card Type Bills for 1 Metered & 2 Unmetered Services. Provides Financial & Water Use Management Reports. Up to 31 Different Flat or Stepped-Rate Structures May Be Used for the Metered Service, & up to 31 Flat Rates for the Unmetered Services. Billing May Be Performed Monthly, Bimonthly or Quarterly & Meter Readings May Be Estimated When Needed.
Tecnomics, Inc.

UTILIBILL Mailing Labels. 1984. *Compatible Hardware:* IBM. *Operating System(s) Required:* MS-DOS. *Memory Required:* 256k. *General Requirements:* 2 disk drives, printer, UTILIBILL IBM Utility Billing System. *Customer Support:* 30 day toll-free telephone support. disk $195.00.
Creates Mailing Lists of Customers for Small Utilities. Prints Labels for Individual Customers, All Customers or a Selected Group of Customers. For Use with UTILIBILL IBM.
Tecnomics, Inc.

UTILIBILL Plus: Utility Billing System. 1984. *Compatible Hardware:* IBM PC, PC XT, PC AT. *Operating System(s) Required:* MS-DOS. *Memory Required:* 256k. *General Requirements:* Hard disk, tractor-feed dot matrix printer. *Items Included:* Diskettes, customization of title, manual with demo session. *Customer Support:* 30 day toll-free telephone support; 3 support plans available.
disk $1595.00.
Prints Post Card Type Bills for up to Three Metered & Three Unmetered Services. Provides Financial & Water Use Management Reports. Includes a Mailing Label Generator, 13-Month Customer History, & Route Sheets. Field Recording System Option Available.
Tecnomics, Inc.

UTILIBILL Route Sheets. 1984. *Compatible Hardware:* IBM. *Operating System(s) Required:* MS-DOS. *Memory Required:* 256k. *General Requirements:* 2 disk drives, printer, UTILIBILL IBM Utility Billing System.
disk $195.00.
Add-On Module for UTILIBILL IBM. Meter Reading System for Utilities. Lists Account Number, Name, Address, Previous Reading, Average Use, Current Reading, & Reader's Comments.
Tecnomics, Inc.

UTILIFLEET: Fleet Monitoring System. 1985. *Compatible Hardware:* IBM PC, PC XT, PC AT. *Operating System(s) Required:* MS-DOS. *Memory Required:* 256k. *Items Included:* Diskettes, manual. *Customer Support:* 30 days toll-free support; 3 support plans available. disk $495.00.
Fleet Monitoring System for Utility & Other Companies with Vehicle Fleets. Monitors Operational Irregularities & Produces Cost per Mile, Per Hour Analysis for Each Vehicle & a Bar Graph Comparison for All Vehicles; Records Tag Number, Serial Number, Year, Make, Model, Odometer Reading at Purchase, Purchase Price, Date of Purchase, & Vehicle Weight; Details Costs for Fuel, Scheduled Maintenance, Insurance, License, Repairs, Taxes or Fees & Miscellaneous Vehicle-Specific Items; & Produces Reports Stating What Licenses & Insurance Are Correctly Due.
Tecnomics, Inc.

Utilities Management. *Compatible Hardware:* IBM PC, PC XT; with 10Mb hard disk. *Language(s):* BASIC. *Memory Required:* 256k. *Customer Support:* Mon-Fri EST 9:00AM-5:00PM, Modem support & on-site. contact publisher for price.
Allows for Postcard Invoice & Returns & Has No Provisions for Residential & Commercial Accounts. Enters/Updates Account Masters, Invoices, Accounts Receivable Cash Applications, Accounts Receivable Trial Balances, Statement Report by Type, & Budget Reporting. Handles Legal Searches by Attorneys & Prints Out the Search Letter Responses. All Financials Are Provided for in the Accounts Payable, Accounts Receivable, & General Ledger Modules.
M&C Systems, Inc.

Utilities Plus. Timothy Purves et al. Sep. 1988. *Compatible Hardware:* Atari ST. *Memory Required:* 512k.
3.5" disk $59.95.
Includes Desk Editor, Adjust File & Attributes. Formats Individual Tracks, Copies or Verifies Individual Sectors.
MichTron, Inc.

Utilities Watchdog. *Customer Support:* 800-929-8117 (customer service). MS-DOS. IBM/PS2. disk $79.99 (ISBN 0-87007-610-8).
Organizes Ten Years of User's Monthly Electric, Gas, Water & Sanitation Records. All Data Can Be Compared Month to Month, Year to Year Over Any Specified Period of Time. Information Can Be Displayed in Tables & Graphs. Full Documentation Is Provided.
SourceView Software International.

Utilities I. Gary Forghetti & Jack Gersbach. *Compatible Hardware:* IBM PC, PCjr, PC XT, PC AT, Portable PC, 3270 PC with IBM Display, fixed disk (optional). *Operating System(s) Required:* DOS 1.10, 2.00, 2.10, 3.00, 3.10. *Memory Required:* 128k.
disk $19.95 (Order no.: 6276517).
Includes Two Programs: FILE COMPRESS & EXPAND Compresses Files to Save Storage Space, Then Expands Them to Their Original Size When Needed; DOS COMMAND RETRIEVER Allows User to Display Commands, Edit Them, or Totally Revise Them. Frequently Used Commands Can Be Abbreviated to Save Keystrokes.
Personally Developed Software, Inc.

Utilities II. James Feeney et al. *Compatible Hardware:* IBM PC, PCjr, PC XT, PC AT, Portable PC, 3270 PC. *Operating System(s) Required:* DOS 2.00, 2.10, 3.00, 3.10. *Memory Required:* 128k. *General Requirements:* IBM Display; hard disk recommended.
disk $19.95 (Order no.: 6276520).
Includes Three Utilities: FILE LOCATER Locates & Displays a File by Dates of Entry Paths or Sizes; Data Can Also Be Prepared for "Piping" into Other Programs; BACKUP & UNMARK Simplifies File Maintenance by Automatically Finding & Copying Files That Have Not Been Backed Up; DOS TREE DISPLAY Simplifies the Search for Subdirectories by Showing Each of Them in a Graphic "Map" As They Occur Automatically Within a Directory Level.
Personally Developed Software, Inc.

Utilities III. Jack Gersbach & R. M. Ryan. *Compatible Hardware:* IBM PC, PCjr, PC XT, PC AT, Portable PC, 3270 PC. *Operating System(s) Required:* DOS 2.00, 2.10, 3.00, 3.10. *Memory Required:* 128k. *General Requirements:* 2 disk drives, IBM Display; hard disk recommended.
disk $19.95 (Order no.: 6276574).
Includes Five Utilities: SORT Reorders Files in Ascending or Descending Order with As Many As Ten Sort Keys; LOADRAM & SAVERAM Combines Multiple Files into a Single File for Transfer of Data Between Systems or for Archival Purposes; COMPARE Displays File Differences in Both HEX Notation & ASCII Symbols; ERRORLOG Can Alert User to the Need for Preventive Maintenance on the Disk Drives; PATCH Simplifies the Task of Correcting COM & EXE Files with Patch Files Provided by Program Developers.
Personally Developed Software, Inc.

Utility Billing (a Part of ABECAS). *Version:* 3.3. Jan. 1989. *Customer Support:* On site training unlimited support services for first 90 days & through subscription thereafter.
MS-DOS, PC-DOS. Contact publisher for price. *Nonstandard peripherals required:* Hard disk (30Mb); 132-column printer. *Networks supported:* Novell, NTNX, 10-Net, Unix, Xenix, Turbo DOS (Multi-User version for all).
Allows Billing Units to Be Defined to Include Information on Meters, Multiple Rate Pricing & Usage.
Argos Software.

Utility City. Bert Kersey. Aug. 1984. *Compatible Hardware:* Apple II, II+, IIe, IIc, IIgs. *Operating System(s) Required:* Apple DOS 3.3. *Language(s):* Machine, BASIC. *Memory Required:* 48k.
disk $29.50.
21 Programs to Assist Applesoft As Well As Printer Utilities, Program Changers & Copyright Protectors. Other Features Include Bigliner, Filename Zap, Invisible, Screenwriter, Multicat, Text Pump, Softfile, Run Counter, Date Counter & More.
Beagle Brothers.

Utility Programs. 1986. *Compatible Hardware:* Atari XL/XE. *General Requirements:* Advan BASIC.
disk $19.95.
Runtime System for Advan BASIC Programs, Crossref, Renumber, Matrix Commands & Special File Commands.
Advan Language Designs.

Utility II. *Compatible Hardware:* TRS-80. contact publisher for price.
Instant Software, Inc.

UVB-WARE: UV Calculator - Ozone Depletion Trend Database. Roger Cox & Kathy Cox. Mar. 1993. *Items Included:* Printed installation instructions, quick reference guide. *Customer Support:* Free support by mail or phone to registered users.
MS-DOS 2.0 or higher. IBM PC & compatibles (640k). disk $39.95 (Order no.: UVB-PC5 (5.25"); UVB-PC3 (3.5")). *Nonstandard peripherals required:* Hard disk drive (2.3Mb disk space). *Optimal configuration:* PC compatible with math co-processor, 640k, hard disk, printer.
Estimates the Strength of UV Rays & UVB Dosage, Based on User Location & Daily Schedule of Outdoor Activities. A Detailed Seasonal Ozone Trend Database Derived from 13 Years of NASA Satellite Data Is Used to Make Projections for over 350 Cities in the US & Canada.
Save the Planet Software.

V-COS. *Compatible Hardware:* Atari 1200XL. cassette $24.95 (ISBN 0-936200-53-7).
Transfers "Boot" Files & Binary DOS Files from Disk to Cassette. Will Not Work on Protected Copy but Will Work with ASSEMBLER EDITOR Cartridge.
Blue Cat.

V-for-Victory. *Version:* 4.01. Sep. 1995. *Items Included:* 2 manuals - reference & operation. *Customer Support:* Monday thru Friday 9AM to 6PM, limited warranty.
Macintosh System 6.05 or higher. Macintosh Plus or higher, B/W or color. CD-ROM disk Contact publisher for price (ISBN 1-57519-077-X).
Addl. software required: System 7 color version requires 32 bit QuickDraw.
V-for-Victory Series Has Set a New Standard for Computer War Games. Now Available As a Complete Series on a CD-ROM, It Is the Most Popular & Realistic Simulation of Large Scale WWII Ground Combat Ever Produced.
IntraCorp/Capstone.

V-UTILITY. *Compatible Hardware:* Apple II; IBM PC; TRS-80 Model I, Model III.
disk $129.95.
Consists of the Following Spreadsheet Data Processing Programs on One Disk Run by Index & Prompts. The Programs Include: V-Print (Select from 1 to 16 Columns & Print Them in Any Order, Specific Print Width of Each of the Columns, Select Spaces Between the Columns); V-Sort (User Selects Column for Numerical or Alpha Sort & Route to the Printer, to the Disk File, or to Both); V-Plot (Automatically Inputs Data from a VisiCalc Column, Performs Auto Scaling & Then Plots Either 1 or 2 Column on a Regular Line Printer); V-Stat (Collects Data Automatically from the VisiCalc Column & Calculates Numerical Distribution, Correlation, Coefficient, Regression Analysis, Chi Test & T-Test, Selects the Columns for Data Entry & Specifies the Row Number to Start & Row Number to End Data Collection); V-Overlay (Provides Selection of Overlays to Load on to the VisiCalc Sheet Such As Moving Averages, Exponential Smoothing, Equations, Time Series Trend Analysis & Data Columns).
Yucaipa Software.

Vacation Rental System (VRS). *Version:* 8.00. 1989. *Items Included:* Reference manual. *Customer Support:* $500.00 a day on-site training; year round support contract for 10% of purchase price; 24 hour, 365 day support contract available.
MS-DOS. IBM PC & compatibles (640K). $1500.00 - $9500.00; $3000.00 - $13,000.00 multi user. *Nonstandard peripherals required:* Printer. *Networks supported:* Novell.
Designed for Real Estate/Property Management Companies Whose Primary Business is the Short &/or Long Term Rental of Individually Owned Property Such as Condominiums, Yachts & RV's. Features Guest History, Statements, Receivables, & a Flexible Report Designing Ability.
Resort Data Processing, Inc.

Valdez. *Compatible Hardware:* Apple II with Applesoft; IBM PC. *Memory Required:* 48k, IBM 128k.
disk $19.95, incl. manual.
Simulation of Supertanker Navigation.
Dynacomp, Inc.

ValFORTH. *Compatible Hardware:* Atari 400, 800. *Memory Required:* 24k.
contact publisher for price.
Valpar International Corp.

Validated Telesoft Ada for MC68000-UNIX Systems. 1983. *Compatible Hardware:* Sun Microsystems. *Operating System(s) Required:* UNIX. *Language(s):* Ada. *Memory Required:* 512k.
contact publisher for price.
Allows Ada Compilation Integrated with UNIX File System; Can Be Used with UNIX Editor. Learning Materials Available.
Telesoft.

Validated Telesoft Ada for VAX-UNIX Systems & VAX-VMS. 1983. *Compatible Hardware:* Micro VAX II, VAX 11/780, 782, 785. *Operating System(s) Required:* UNIX, VMS. *Language(s):* Ada. *Memory Required:* 1000k.
contact publisher for price.
Ada-Compilation Integrated with UNIX & VMS File System; TeleSoft Ada Programs Make UNIX & VMS System Calls. Generates Fast VAX Machine Code & Uses UNIX & VMS Editor. Learning Materials for Ada Are Available under UNIX & VMS.
Telesoft.

Valley of the Kings. *Compatible Hardware:* Atari 400, 800. *Language(s):* Atari BASIC. *Memory Required:* 48k.
disk $29.95.
Adventurers Locate Objects & Passages.
Dynacomp, Inc.

Value Expert. *Version:* 6.0. Jun. 1993. *Compatible Hardware:* IBM PC. *Memory Required:* 512k. *Items Included:* Lotus 1-2-3 Version & Stand-Alone Version plus Documentation.
$195.00.
Menu-Driven Lotus Template Provides Desktop-Publishing Quality Reports for 30 Valuation Methods, Including Discounted Future Earnings Method. Incorporates Relevant Revenue Rulings. Automatic Data-Entry System Allows Input by Clerical Personnel. Prints Reports Using One Keystroke. Can Be Used in Conjunction with LOTUS 1-2-3 or As Stand-Alone DOS Program.
Innovative Professional Software, Inc.

Value Express. *Version:* 2.0. Feb. 1991. *Items Included:* 175 page manual, tutorial disk, data entry worksheet, automatic report writer, graphs. *Customer Support:* 60 days free.
MS-DOS. IBM PC compatible (640k). disk $245.00.
An Instant Business Valuation Program Which Offers Eight Different Valuation Approaches. Once the Value of Your Business Is Determined, Value Express Lets You Structure Financing & Purchasing Terms, & Also Calculates Monthly & Annual Post Sale Cash Flow Statements. The Software Then Automatically Produces a 3-10 Page Valuation Report.
Valusource.

Value/Screen II. Nov. 1988. *Compatible Hardware:* Apple II, Macintosh; IBM PC & compatibles, PC XT. *Operating System(s) Required:* MS-DOS. *Language(s):* C. *Memory Required:* Apple II 64k, IBM & Macintosh 512k. *General Requirements:* Modem for electronic delivery.
monthly update $396.00.
quarterly update $227.00.
weekly update $1500.00.
Screens 1600 Securities by Customer Specified Criteria from Statistical Information Supplied by Value Line Analysts on a Weekly, Monthly or Quarterly Basis. Includes Portfolio Analysis & the Ability to Load the Value Line Data into Popular Spreadsheet Programs.
Value Line, Inc.

ValuSource II: IRS Litigation Support Valuation System. Apr. 1991. *Items Included:* 250 page manual, tutorial, automatic report writer, data entry worksheet. *Customer Support:* One year free.
PC-DOS (640k). IBM PC, PS/2. $495.00 includes Automatic Report Writer.
Performs Formal Business Appraisals for IRS Compliance & Litigation Support. Offers 17 Different Valuation Methods & a Valuation Sensitivity Analysis. Provides Automatic Notations on Printed Schedules. Automatically Produces 20-50 Page Formal Appraisal Report.
ValuSource.

VALVE. *Version:* 15. P. L. Mariam. Jan. 1984. *Compatible Hardware:* IBM PC & compatibles, PC XT, PC AT. *Operating System(s) Required:* PC-DOS/MS-DOS 2.X, 3.0. *Memory Required:* 256k. *General Requirements:* Printer.
disk $149.95 (ISBN 0-935509-06-2, Order no.: 5310).
Sizes Liquid, Gas, Vapor, or Steam Control Valves. Predicts the Sound Pressure Level (SPL) Produced by Most Fisher Control Valves, Inline & Vent Diffusers on Gas, Steam, or Vapor Service. Automatically Computes the Pipe Wall Attentuation & Pipe Areas Using an Internal Pipe Table to Prevent Lookup Errors. Automatically Checks for Cavitation or Flashing of Liquids & Limits the Flow If Critical Drop Is Achieved.
FlowSoft, Inc.

Valve Sizing: Control Valve Sizing & Documentation. 1985. *Compatible Hardware:* IBM PC & compatibles. *Operating System(s) Required:* MS-DOS. *Language(s):* Compiled Advanced BASIC. *Memory Required:* 256k.
disk $595.00, incl. manual (ISBN 0-87664-904-5, Order no.: 1904-5).
Calculates Cv, Cg, or Cs; Back Calculates; Gas & Steam Calculations Based on ISA Control Valve Sizing Handbook; Fisher Formulas Used in Cg & Cs Calculation.
Instrument Society of America (ISA).

Vampire's Empire. *Customer Support:* Back up disk available.
Amiga (512k). $14.95.
Commodore 64/128 (64k). $14.95.
Atari (512k). $14.95.
Deep in the Transylvanian Forest, in the Depths of His Underground Lair, Count Dracula & His Minions Stir. Armed With Your Magic Light, Mirrors & Garlic You Must Fight Your Way Through the Vampire's Empire to Conquer the Evil Count.
DigiTek Software.

Van Greet Opening 1.Nf3. *Version:* 2. Van Geet. 1994. *Items Included:* Book & disk with 500 or more games (over 200 annotated). *Customer Support:* Telephone support by appointment.
MS-DOS 2.0 or higher (512k). disk $25.00. *Nonstandard peripherals required:* Mouse, graphics, 3 1/2" drive.
Atari ST (520k). Atari. 3.5" disk $25.00. *Nonstandard peripherals required:* Monochrome monitor DS/DD drive.
Authoritative Introduction to & Analysis of an Important Chess Opening.
Chess Combination, Inc.

Van Gogh Laserguide. *Items Included:* 1 floppy disk, instruction booklet. *Customer Support:* M-F 9 AM-5 PM Pacific Time (213) 451-1383.
Macintosh Plus, SE, II or Portable (1 Mb). 3.5" disk $59.95. *Nonstandard peripherals required:* HyperCard 1.2.2 or higher; videodisc. *Addl. software required:* Van Gogh Revisited or Van Gogh: A Portrait in two parts.
Explore the Many Facets of Van Gogh's Art--from His Use of Color to the Impact of Impressionism on His Work--Using This Comprehensive & Richly Detailed Index to Van Gogh Revisited. Works on the Videodisc Are Catalogued by Period, Theme, Medium, Title, Date & Key Words. An Illustrated Timeline of the Artist's Life is Also Available.
The Voyager Co.

VARCUT. Sep. 1985. *Compatible Hardware:* IBM PC, PC XT, PC AT & compatibles. *Operating System(s) Required:* MS-DOS, PC-DOS. *Language(s):* FORTRAN. *Memory Required:* 512k. *General Requirements:* Printer.
disk $1000.00 (Order no.: VARCUT).

Using the Affine Correction Method, VARCUT Will Calculate the Histograms of Grades of Mining Blocks from Sample Data. These Block Histograms Are Interpolated from the Composite Data by the Variance Correction Factor. The Blocks Considered in This Program Are the Selection Units Used to Compute Recoverable Reserves. The Output Can Be Displayed for a Given Rock Type, the Values above the Cut-Off & for the Entire Mining Block.
Geostat Systems International, Inc. (GSII).

Variable Feasts. Sof Talent. *Compatible Hardware:* Apple, IBM PC, Tandy. *Memory Required:* 128k. *General Requirements:* CGA, EGA, or Hercules monochrome card.
Apple. disk $49.95, incl. manual & cookbook (Order no.: APDSK-65).
IBM & Tandy. disk $59.95 (Order no.: IBMDSK-213).
Complete Guide to Party Planning & Entertaining with Food Based on Time-Life Books' Foods of the World Series. Rescales Requirements to Match the Number of Guests & Helps Plan for Special Needs Such As Vegetarian, Low-Calorie Meals, or No-Salt Diets. Includes Menus, Recipes & Shopping Lists.
Broderbund Software, Inc.

Variable Finder. *Compatible Hardware:* TRS-80 Model I, Model III.
disk $12.95 (Order no.: D8VF).
Provides a Detailed Cross-Reference of All BASIC Variables.
The Alternate Source.

Variable Interest Rate Loans. *Compatible Hardware:* TI 99/4A. *Operating System(s) Required:* DX-10. *Language(s):* Extended BASIC. *Memory Required:* 48k.
disk or cassette $31.95.
Database of the 200 Most Recent Changes in the Prime Rate. Interest Is Accrued for Loans at Prime or Any Other Rate. User Has the Option of 360 or 365 Day Based Rate. Increases & Decreases in Loan Balances Are Accommodated.
Eastbench Software Products.

Variable Rate Mortgage with PMI & Combined APR. *Compatible Hardware:* Sharp ZL-6100 system, ZL-6500 System. *Language(s):* Sharp Microcode.
$580.00.
Computes: Conventional Full-Term, Fixed-Payment & Variable Rate Mortgages; FHA 235 & 245 Types; Graduated Payment PMI; 4 Graduated-Equity Types. Prints Calendar-Year Interest & Principal Summaries. Includes Provisions for: Points, Application Fees, Prepaid Odd-Day Interest, Private Mortgage Insurance, Full Disclosure & Schedule of Payments & Year-End Balances. Computes Mortgages with up to 5 Years of Rate Changes for Variable Rates, Buy-Down Rates or Both.
P-ROM Software, Inc.

Variety Cookbook. *Compatible Hardware:* Commodore Amiga.
3.5" disk $14.95.
Recipes.
Meggido Enterprises.

Variety's Video Directory Plus. 1995. *Items Included:* Quarterly Updates. *Customer Support:* Information & Assistance Hotline; Electronic Bulletin Board.
DOS 3.1 or higher. IBM & compatibles 286 or higher. CD-ROM disk $495.00 for 1 year.
Nonstandard peripherals required: Hard disk (10 Mb free space); CD-ROM player running under MS-DOC extensions 2.0 or later.
CD-ROM disk $1411.00 for 3 years.
CD-ROM Contains Listings for over 93,000 Videos, Including some 55,000 Non-Entertainment Titles Such As Documentaries & Educational Videos. Features 578 Subject & Genre Classifications Covering All Non-Fiction Titles. Also Includes More Than 5000 Full-Text Film Reviews From VARIETY, & Complete Manufacturers/Distributors Information on Every Video Title.
R.R. Bowker.

VARIO3. *Version:* 2.5. Oct. 1985. *Compatible Hardware:* IBM PC, PC AT, PC XT & compatibles. *Memory Required:* 512k. *General Requirements:* Printer, plotter.
disk $1900.00 (Order no.: VARIO3).
Computes Variograms, Directional Graphs That Show How Samples Vary with Distance. In a Single Pass, It Computes the Absolute, General Relative, Local Relative, Logarithmic, & Indicator Variograms in Two or Three Dimensions. The Analyst Will Define the Computation Parameters & the Program Will Calculate the Variography of up to 25 Variables in Five Directions During a Single Run.
Geostat Systems International, Inc. (GSII).

Varipump. John Migliavacca. *Compatible Hardware:* IBM PC. *Operating System(s) Required:* PC-DOS. *Memory Required:* 128k. *General Requirements:* Printer, graphics card.
disk $100.00.
Analyzes the Performance of a Centrifugal Pump Operated at Variable Speed. Starting with a Given Pump Curve, VARIPUMP Will Use the Fan Laws to Predict the Speed Required in Order to Meet a Desired Condition of Flow & Head. A Pump Operated in This Way Can Be Controlled Using Speed Instead of an Energy-Consuming Control Valve. Also Calculates the Annual Energy Savings & the Time Required to Pay Back the Investment. Data to Form the Pump Curve at the New Speed Are Generated.
Techdata.

Vazhe Negar Farsi: Persian-Multilingual Document Processor. *Version:* 1.2. May 1993. *Items Included:* Persian/English manual; 25 Persian TrueType fonts, 1 English font; template; Persian keycap stickers. *Customer Support:* Free unlimited customer support to registered customers by telephone.
IBM DOS 3.1 or higher, Windows 3.1 or higher. IBM 386 compatible (1Mb). disk $495.00.
Nonstandard peripherals required: Windows compatible. *Optimal configuration:* 386, DOS 5.0, Windows 3.1, 16Mb RAM, mouse SVGA monitor. *Networks supported:* Novell.
Word Processing. Persian/Multilingual Document Processor.
Eastern Language Systems.

VB-Cert: Simulation of the Visual Basic Certified Professional Examination. Aug. 1994. *Items Included:* Guide & Owner's Manual. *Customer Support:* 30-day limited warranty.
Windows 3.1. IBM & compatibles (1Mb). disk $129.00 (ISBN 0-9635203-1-8). *Nonstandard peripherals required:* Printer & mouse optional. *Optimal configuration:* Windows 3.1, mouse.
Prepares Candidates to Take the Visual Basic Application Development Examination Given by Microsoft Corp. Gives Simulated Exams, Pinpoints Weak Areas, & Explains the Reasoning Behind the Answers. Includes Study Outline.
Transcender Corp.

Vbackup. *Version:* 2.0. *Items Included:* 1 Vbackup reference manual, install guide. *Customer Support:* Annual maintenance plans available; free customer service & updates for 60 days; 30-day money-back guarantee.
Unix, Ultrix. contact publisher for price.
Back-Up Utility for DEC Users. Allows User to Transfer VMS Save Sets onto a UNIX Platform.
Boston Business Computing, Ltd.

VCL. *Version:* 3.15. Jul. 1992. *Operating System(s) Required:* MS-DOS 2.0 or higher, UNIX, Xenix. *Memory Required:* 170k. *Customer Support:* 30 day money back guarantee, free customer support & updates for 60 days, annual maintenance plans available.
Contact publisher for price.
Implementation of DIGITAL's VAX/VMS Command Language for MS-DOS & UNIX Machines. Features over 100 DCL Commands & Switches, Complete DCL Syntax, an Extensible Command Set, Logicals, Symbol Names, Command History, Line Editing, etc. Includes Two New Features: TEACH & PASSTHRU to Assist in the Transition to an MS-DOS or UNIX Environment.
Boston Business Computing, Ltd.

VCN Concorde. *Version:* 3.0. 1988. *Compatible Hardware:* IBM PC, PC XT, PC AT & compatibles. *Operating System(s) Required:* PC-DOS/MS-DOS. *Memory Required:* 640k. *General Requirements:* Hard disk.
$695.00, incl. the icon library, Image Database.
Integrated Graphics Program Capable of Producing Medium & High Resolution Business Graphics, Freehand Screen Painting, Animation, & Self-Running Presentations. Offers a Variety of Applications Aimed at the Corporate Microcomputer User.
Visual Communications Network, Inc.

VCScreen. *Version:* 4.0. *Compatible Hardware:* IBM PC & true compatibles, PC XT, PC AT. *Operating System(s) Required:* PC-DOS/MS-DOS, OS/2. *Memory Required:* 380k. *General Requirements:* Vitamin C program. *Items Included:* Demo & Program Disks & Documentation. *Customer Support:* Included with proper registration of product.
disk $149.00.
Interactive Screen Editor That Lets User Draw Input, Output, & Constant Fields, Headings, Boxes, Lines, etc. Generates C Source Code Linkable to VITAMIN C-Developed Applications.
Creative Programming.

VDROP: Voltage Drop Calculations. *Items Included:* Manual. *Customer Support:* Toll-free telephone support.
MS-DOS. IBM-PC & compatibles (256k). disk $295.00.
Allows a Designer to Quickly & Accurately Obtain the Voltage Drop at Each Node (bus) in a Radial Electric Power Distribution System. The Voltage Drop Values are Calculated on a "Per Segment" & "Cumulative" Basis & Then Printed as a Percentage of the Source Voltage & as an Absolute Voltage Drop in Volts.
Elite Software Development, Inc.

Vector. Dec. 1989. *Compatible Hardware:* Apple Macintosh. *Memory Required:* 2000k.
3.5" disk $2595.00.
Appication Generator for Engineering Applications. The Programming Language Enables Users Access to Program's Open Architecture Database. Provides Entity Definition, Menu Creation, Icon Creation, User Definable Database Primitives, Associative Dimensioning, Layers & Level Control, Spline Curves, Bit Mapped & 3D Graphics Parametrics, DXF, & IGES I/O, HPGL & HI Plotting Output, etc.
Vector Systems, Inc.

Vectorpipe. *Compatible Hardware:* Aegis, HP/Apollo, Unix Sun, DEC work stations, Ultrix, VMS. *Customer Support:* Maintenance, training.
disk contact publisher for price.
3-D Process Plant Modelling System Integrated with a Relational Database System.
Auto-Trol Technology Corp.

Vectors. *Compatible Hardware:* Commodore 64, VIC-20. *Memory Required:* VIC-20 5k.
VIC-20. disk or cassette $9.95.
Commodore 64. disk or cassette $11.95.
Adds up to 25 Vectors. Magnitude & Angle for Each Vector Is Entered. Then the Program Computes the Resultant x, y & Total Magnitudes, & Resultant Angle.
Athena Software.

Vegas Casino. *Customer Support:* 90 day warranty.
MS-DOS 2.1 or higher. IBM (256K). 3.5" disk $12.99; 5.25" disk $9.99. *Nonstandard peripherals required:* CGA, EGA, VGA or Tandy Graphics card required.
Experience All the Excitement of Gambling Without Actually Losing Money. Try Your Hand with the Fruit Machine Vegas Jackpot or Pit Your Wits Against the Computer & Play Black Jack or Video Poker. Both Are Highly Skilled Card Games.
Virgin Games.

Vegas Casino 2. *Customer Support:* 90 day warranty.
MS-DOS 2.1 or higher. IBM (256K). 3.5" disk $12.99; 5.25" disk $9.99. *Nonstandard peripherals required:* CGA, EGA, Tandy, VGA or Hercules Graphics required.
Commodore 64 (64K). disk $9.99. *Nonstandard peripherals required:* Joystick required.
The Realism & Atmosphere of Vegas Gambling at Its Best Is So Accurately Simulated in This Program That You Almost Believe You Are Playing 'On the Strip'. Brings to your PC Two of the Best Loved & Exciting Casino Games - CRAPS & AMERICAN ROULETTE.
Virgin Games.

VEGAS CRAPS for Windows: Casino CRAPS Game. Peter A. Bornstein. Jul. 1993. *Compatible Hardware:* IBM PC & compatibles, PC XT, PC AT. *Operating System(s) Required:* PC-DOS/MS-DOS, Windows 3.1. *Language(s):* Visual BASIC. *Memory Required:* 256k. *Items Included:* 3 1/2" & 5 1/2" diskette, user manual. disk $25.00 (ISBN 0-918079-01-2).
Simulates All the Action of a Las Vegas Casino Craps Table. All Bets on a Craps Layout Are Supported, with Correct Odds Paid. Unique Money Manager Displays Odds & House Edge on Each Bet. User Manual Includes a Section on Betting Strategies.
PRO Systems.

The Vegetarian Game. Jon Shoemaker. Aug. 1993.
disk $19.95 (ISBN 0-931411-11-4).
Vegetarian Questions Including Categories of Health, Animals/Ethics, Environment, Food, & Famous Vegetarians.

Velocis Database Server. *Version:* 1.3.1. Aug. 1995. *Items Included:* Complete manuals. *Customer Support:* Support is provided by a team of engineers based at Raima, & cost 20 percent of software's list price. Support is provided via phone, fax, Internet e-mail, World Wide Web page (for upgrades, beta copies & patches) & BBS. Users also gain information on Raima products through an independent Listserv Internet mail group.
Windows 3.1. 386 (on Intel-based PC) (2Mb). $595.00 & up, depending on platform & number of users.
A High Performance SQL & ODBC Client-Server Database System That Naturally Manages Relational Data, Complex Object Data, & Sophisticated Multimedia Data with the Same Level of Scalability, Reliability, Accessibility, & Security. Velocis Provides Support for Industry-Standard Interfaces & Tools, Including C, C Plus Plus, ODBC, SAG CLI, ANSI SQL, & Object-Oriented Programming. Allows You to Create Databases Using the Relational Model, the Pointer-Based Network Model, or a Combination Model. Provides Server Extensions, in Which Application Code Is Hosted Directly on the Server, Reducing Network Traffic & Increasing Performance.
Raima Corp.

The Velveteen Rabbit or How Toys Become Real. Marshall Wheeler & Margery Williams. *Customer Support:* All necessary support is contained on the CD ROM itself.
386 SX or higher processor. IBM PC/MPC & compatibles (3Mb). disk $59.95 (ISBN 1-884117-00-7, Order no.: 07019301). *Nonstandard peripherals required:* Sound board recommended. *Addl. software required:* PC-DOS/MS-DOS 3.1 or higher, Microsoft Windows 3.1 or higher, MS Windows 3.0 with multimedia extensions. *Optimal configuration:* 486 SX, 4Mb RAM, 80Mb hard drive, CD ROM Drive, SuperVGA monitor & mouse & headphones or speakers connected to your system.
CD ROM Story Book That Runs Interactively or Passively, Original Music Scores in Digital Stereo, Digitized Real Life Voices of the Main Story Teller & Seven Characters, Colorful NTSC TV Quality Graphics with Animated Hot Characters, Word Defintions & Word Pronunciations Spoken by the Original Characters in the Story. A Built in Tutorial Produced for Use with Microsoft Windows on PC/MPC.

Vendor Histories: Purchasing-Accounts Payable. 1996. *Customer Support:* Free telephone & BBS technical support.
MS/PC DOS; Concurrent DOS, Xenix, Unix. IBM PC/XT/AT & compatibles; IBM PS/2 (512k). single or multi-user $795.00. *Networks supported:* Novell, Lantastic, Banyan VINES; all NETBIOS compatible.
"Vendor Histories" is an analytical business tool. It is designed to retain all Purchase Order & Payables invoice information for whatever period(s) desired. The "Vendor Histories" module captures & retains all historical dates from the period-end close in INMASS/MPR's Purchasing &/or "Accounts Payable" modules.
INMASS/MRP.

VENIX EDS. *Version:* UnixWare. Jun. 1994. *Items Included:* UnixWare operating system with NFS & TCP/IP. VenturCom's realtime & embedded extensions, & System Builder Exentsive Documentation. Free one year support & one week programming course. *Customer Support:* VenturCom has four levels of support. Prices start at $200.00 per year. In addition, there are seven courses which are held several times each year.
UnixWare (4Mb). $14,000.00. *Optimal configuration:* PC with 8Mb RAM, 200Mb hard disk, QIC 150 tape, VGA or higher. *Networks supported:* Netware, TCP/IP, NFS.
An Embedded Development System That Enables Developers to Embed the UnixWare Operating System - along with VenturCom's Embedded & Realtime Extensions - in Intel Microprocessor Based PCs & Single Board Configurations. Includes the General Purpose UnixWare Operating System Which Enables the Use of Widely Available Off-the-Shelf Software; the VENIX System Builder Which Allows Developers to Rapidly Build of Custom Tailored, Minimal-Sized Deployable UNIX Target Systems for ROM, Flash, Diskette, or Hard Disk Media; & X, TCP/IP, NFS & Motif Support. VenturCom's Feature Enhancements Include ROM Boot; Automated System Administration; Read Only File System; Automatic System Recovery; Remote Monitor & Debugging, & Console-Less & Unattended Operation.
VenturCom.

Ventilator Commitment. 1982. *Compatible Hardware:* Apple II+, IIe, IIc; IBM PC & compatibles. *Operating System(s) Required:* MS-DOS, Apple DOS 3.3. *Language(s):* BASIC. *Memory Required:* Apple 48k, IBM 512k. disk $200.00 (Order no.: CCS-8228).
Patient with Acute Restrictive Disease Is Presented. Respiratory Monitoring, ABG Interpretation, Oxygen Therapy & Assessment of Ventilator Commitment Are Stressed.
Educational Software Concepts, Inc.

Ventura Publisher. *Version:* 1.1. *Compatible Hardware:* IBM PC, PC XT, PC AT. *Memory Required:* 512k. *General Requirements:* Hard disk, mouse.
disk $895.00.
Handles Both Short & Long Documents with Text, Graphics, & Font Support & Broad Output Capability. Features Automatic Kerning, Support for Multicolumn Frames, Hyphenation, Cropping & Sizing of Art, On-Screen Rulers, Automatic Letter Spacing, etc. Pictures Are Anchored to Text During Batch Pagination. Can Handle Documents up to 128 Chapters in Length, Each Containing up to 300 Pages of Text. Supports Most Word Processing Packages, Including XYWRITE, DISPLAYWRITE III & IV, & DCA FILES. Provides Graphic Conversion for More Than 500 Graphics Packages Based on a Dozen File Formats, Including Macintosh "PICT" & Image Files. Also Provides Support for Downloaded POSTSCRIPT Fonts, Conversion of H-P Soft-Fonts, & Support for ADOBE Screen Fonts. Supports Both POSTSCRIPT & INTERPRESS Page Description Languages, Being Thus Compatible with All Popular Laser Printers.
Xerox Corp.

The Venture Search System. *Version:* 96.1. *Customer Support:* Free telephone support.
MS-DOS or Windows 3.0 or higher (384k). $250.00, for any one issue.
$700.00, for annual 6-issue subscription.
Consists of Windows or DOS Software Plus a Database of Names & Addresses of Approximately 1300 Venture Capital Firms. Users Can Print Cover Letters, Envelopes & Mailing Labels. Firms Can Be Selected by Investment Preferences with Respect to Industry, Geography, Dollar Investment. Database Updated 6 Times per Year.
Custom Databanks, Inc.

Venus Explorer. 1994. *Items Included:* 1 manual. *Customer Support:* 90 days unlimited warranty; free telephone support.
DOS CD-ROM. IBM 286 25MHz & higher (4Mb). CD-ROM disk $69.95 (ISBN 1-886082-15-4, Order no.: VECD-330). *Nonstandard peripherals required:* CD-ROM. *Optimal configuration:* 8Mb.
System 7. MAC (4Mb). CD-ROM disk $69.95 (ISBN 1-886082-16-2, Order no.: VEMACD-310). *Nonstandard peripherals required:* CD-ROM. *Optimal configuration:* 8Mb.
Exploration of Venus.
Virtual Reality Laboratories, Inc.

Verbal Reasoning. *Compatible Hardware:* Apple IIe, IIc; IBM PC, IIgs.
$250.00.
Multi-Level Package Designed to Retrain Verbal Skills of Brain Injured Individuals. Contains 6 Programs: "Synonyms", "Antonyms", "Homonyms", "Vocabulary", "Similarities", & "Analogies". Each Program Has 3 Formats, with Each Format Having 3 Levels of Difficulty.
Greentree Group, Inc.

Verdict & Multiuser Verdict. *Version:* 7.2. 1994. *Compatible Hardware:* IBM PC & compatibles. *Operating System(s) Required:*

TITLE INDEX

PC-DOS/MS-DOS; Networks such as Novell, Lantastic. *Customer Support:* 30 days' free support, 1 yr. maintenance $250.00 for Verdict, $400.00 for Multiuser Verdict.
disk $1695.00, Verdict.
disk $1995.00, Multiuser Verdict.
Verdict demo disk & manual $50.00.
Multiuser Verdict demo disk & manual $75.00.
Produces Itemized, Ready-to-Mail Bills for the 1-75 Person Law Firm Plus Pre-Bill Review Sheets, Aged Accounts Receivable, Monthly & Year-to-Date Financial & Timekeeping Summaries, Alphabetized Client Lists & Client Lists by Account Number. Choice of 7 Billing Categories & 16 Bill Formats for Bills. Memory-Resident Text Editor for Service Descriptions & Memory-Resident Account Lists. Integrated Trust, Audit Trail of Deletions & Changes, Archive System for Complete Detailed Account History & Ultra High Speed Sorts. User Can Create up to 500 Custom Paragraph Transaction Codes. Client Payments Can Be Allocated Between Reimbursement of Costs & Fees; Fees Can Be Allocated Between Responsible Attorney & Working Attorneys. Multiuser Verdict Is Available for Networked Systems.
Micro Craft, Inc.

Verdict Speller. *Version:* 1.5. 1994. *Customer Support:* 30 days' free support, 1 yr. maintenance $250.00.
Windows 3.1. 386, 486 (1Mb). disk $495.00.
Addl. software required: Verdict or Multiuser Verdict version 7.X. Optimal configuration: 4MB RAM. Networks supported: Novell, Lantastic.
A Windows Application That Spell Checks Services, Expenses & Payments Posted to Verdict & Automatically Writes the Corrections Back to the Verdict Data Files. Options Include the Ability to Spell Check All Postings, Just Postings for the Current Month, or Just Postings for a Particular Account. Includes a 50,000 Plus Word Legal Dictionary.
Micro Craft, Inc.

Vermont Views & Designer. *Version:* 2.0. Feb. 1990. *Compatible Hardware:* IBM PC & compatibles. *Operating System(s) Required:* PC-DOS/MS-DOS, OS/2, PC-XENIX, UNIX, VMS. *Language(s):* C (source code included). *Items Included:* No time limit money back guarantee. *Customer Support:* Free technical support.
PC-DOS. DOS with source 890.00 $495.00.
PC/XENIX. Binary Code $1795.00.
UNIX, VMS. contact publisher for price.
A C-Language User Interface Library for Data-Entry Forms, Menus, Windows, Help, & Keyboard Handling. An Attractive Editor Allows Easy Creation & Modification of Data-Entry Forms & Menus. Code Written with Vermont Views Is Fully Portable Between DOS, OS/2, UNIX, XENIX, & VMS.
Vermont Creative Software.

Versa Term. *Version:* 5.0. Abelbeck Software. *Compatible Hardware:* Macintosh 68k, Power Macintosh. *General Requirements:* Networks: TCP/IP, Appleshare. *Items Included:* Full documentation, disks. *Customer Support:* Free to registered en-users 610-779-0522, fax 610-370-0548, Internet tech syynergy.com.
3.5" disk $195.00 Retail; Educational pricing avail. (Order no.: SYNMAC555).
A Broad-Based Communications Application Combining High Quality Terminal Emulations, a Suite of TCP/IP Network Connections, & a Smoothly Integrated Graphical Interface for Mail, News, Directory, Telnet & FTP File Transfers to Exchange Data with the Internet Community. The Terminal Emulations Include: DEC VT100/VT220, Data General & Tektronix 4014 Emulations. File Transfer Protocols Include: Kermit, Xmodem, Ymodem, Zmodem & FTP (Client & Server). The VersaTerm SLIP Extension Transports TCP/IP Data over a Modem While Automating the Connection/Disconnection Process.
Synergy Software.

Versa Term-PRO. *Version:* 5.0. Abelbeck Software. *Compatible Hardware:* Macintosh 68k & Power Macintosh. *General Requirements:* Networks: TCP/IP, Appleshare. *Items Included:* Documentation & disks. *Customer Support:* Free to registered en-users 610-779-0522, fax 610-370-0548, Internet tech syynergy.com.
disk $295.00; Educational pricing avail. (Order no.: SYNMAC777).
Provides All the Features of VersaTerm & Adds the Following: Tektronix 4105 Graphics Terminal Emulation; Enhanced Tektronix 4014 Graphics Emulation; Zoom & Pan Graphics Interactively from Memory; View up to 32 Cleared Graphic Screens from Memory; & Print Graphics to Your Macintosh Printer. TCP/IP, ADSP, Modem & Serial Tools Are Also Included.
Synergy Software.

Versa-Till. *Version:* 2.01. Aug. 1988. *Operating System(s) Required:* PC-DOS/MS-DOS. *Memory Required:* 512k. *General Requirements:* 20Mb hard disk.
3.5" or 5.25" disk $750.00.
Point-of-Sale Application for Retailers. Set-Up Program Permits Adaptation to User's Business. Files for Prices, Bad Checks, Customer Charges. Operates with Two-Color Receipt Printer & Cash Drawer.
Advance Business Computer Corp.

Versaform XL. *Version:* 6.0. *Compatible Hardware:* IBM PC & compatibles.
single-user $495.00, multi-user $595.00.
Database Management System Provides On-Screen Help, Free-Form File Definition, Automatic Indexing, Split & Merge Files, Built-In Editor, & Compiler. Offers Comma-Delimited ASCII, DIF, DBF Import & Export Capabilities. VersaForm XL IS Fully Relational, Programmable & Can Be Customized for Any Application.
Applied Software Technology (California).

Versainventory. *Items Included:* Bound manual. *Customer Support:* Free hotline - no time limit; 30 day limited warranty; updates are $5/disk plus S&H.
MS-DOS. IBM & compatibles (256k). disk $99.95.
Apple (48k). disk $99.95.
Allows User to Instantly Add to, or Deduct from, Inventory Levels; Notifies User When an Item's Stock Level Falls to Reorder Point (Which You Have Previously Defined). Store Comprehensive Data for Every Item in Stock Using Item I.D. Number, Description, Vendor I.D., Vendor's Item Number, Stock Location, Department, Unit of Sale, Weight of Unit, Number of Items in Stock, Number on Back Order, Reorder Level & Quantity, Items Sold Period-to-Date & Year-to-Date, Latest Cost, Average Cost, Last P.O. Number & Date, Expected Delivery Date, Standard & Alternate Selling Prices, & Sales Period-to-Date & Year-to-Date; Print All Needed Inventory & Sales Reports, Including Master Inventory Listings, Items Below Reorder Point, Inventory Value Report, Period & Year-to-Date Sales Reports, Price Lists, & Physical Inventory Checklists.
Dynacomp, Inc.

Versainventory. 1995. *Items Included:* Full manual. *Customer Support:* Free telephone support - 90 days, 30-day warranty.
MS-DOS 3.2 or higher. 286 (584k). disk $99.95. Nonstandard peripherals required: CGA/EGA/VGA.

VERSAPRO BUSINESS SERIES

A Complete, Comprehensive, Inventory Control System That Keeps Track of Descriptions, Pricing, & Vendor Information for Every Item in Stock, What Is Being Sold (& Removed from Stock), What Stock Has Been Depleted to a User-Defined Reorder Point, & What Items Are Actually Out of Stock. Also Provides You with Essential Sales Reports That Tell You How Well Any Particular Product Has Been Selling.
Dynacomp, Inc.

Versaledger II. *Items Included:* Bound manual. *Customer Support:* Free hotline - no time limit; 30 day limited warranty; updates are $5/disk plus S&H.
MS-DOS. IBM & compatibles (256k). disk $99.95.
Apple II (48k). disk $99.95.
Maintain a Check Register Alone, Totally Independent from the System's General Ledger Features; Run a General Ledger Alone, Without Setting up a Check Register; Run One or More Checking Accounts & a General Ledger As a Complete, Integrated Accounting System; Get an Instant Balance at Any Time; Distribute a Single Check to More Than One Account (Unlimited Multiple Disbursements). Print Checks, Check Registers, Lists of Outstanding Checks, Journal Transaction Registers, Detailed & Summary Account Listings, Detailed & Summary Trial Balances, Check Register Posting Reports, Balance Sheets, & Income Statements. Store up to: 615 Accounts & 2400 Transactions per Month on the IBM PC; 615 Accounts & 500 Transactions per Month on the Apple II.
Dynacomp, Inc.

Versapayables. *Items Included:* Bound manual. *Customer Support:* Free hotline - no time limit; 30 day limited warranty; updates are $5/disk plus S&H.
MS-DOS. IBM & compatibles (256k). disk $99.95.
Apple (48k). disk $99.95.
Keep Complete Information on Each Vendor; Keep Track of Current & Aged Payables; Lets User Quickly Select Vouchers for Payment, or Automatically Suggest Which Vouchers Should Be Paid; Allow Partial Payments of Vouchers; Print Checks & a Check Register; Print All Needed Summary Reports, Including Vendor Data & Transaction Reports, Aged Payable Reports, Open Voucher Reports, & Automatic Voucher Selection Reports; Print Vendor Mailing Labels.
Dynacomp, Inc.

Versapayroll. *Items Included:* Bound manual. *Customer Support:* Free hotline - no time limit; 30 day limited warranty; updates are $5/disk plus S&H.
MS-DOS. IBM & compatibles (256k). disk $99.95.
Print Paychecks One at a Time, or Print an Entire Payroll at Once; Allows User to Intervene & Alter Any Figure on Any Paycheck; Gives User an Instant Summary of Any Employee's Year-to-Date Totals, or Totals for All Employees; Calculate All Federal, State, & Local Taxes; Allows for All Standard Deductions, Plus Three Miscellaneous Deductions; Take Amounts from Different Departments to Form One Paycheck; Print All Government-Required Reports; Permanently Store All Payroll Transactions; Integrate with VERSALEDGER II; Virtually Unlimited Capacity on Hard-Disk Systems.
Dynacomp, Inc.

VersaPro Business Series. *Items Included:* Manuals included. *Customer Support:* Free technical support for 60 days; after 60 days technical support is $75.00 for 6 months per module.
IBM & compatible (640k). contact publisher for

price.
Complete Accounting Series That Will Help the User Manage Personal Financial Assets, Control Critical Operations, & Integrate Company Accounting Information. Package Includes G/L, A/R, A/P, Payroll Inventory, Personnel, Points of Sale Property Management, Track/Barcoding. Network Versions Available.
Central Computer Products.

Versareceivables. *Items Included:* Bound manual. *Customer Support:* Free hotline - no time limit; 30 day limited warranty; updates are $5/disk plus S&H.
MS-DOS. IBM & compatibles (256k). disk $99.95.
Apple (48k). disk $99.95.
Accounts-Receivable System That Will Handle Your Invoicing & Billing Operations & Provide You With a Clear Picture of the Flow of Money Owed to Your Company. Will Store a Complete History for Each of Your Customers & Show You Who Owes Your Company, How Much, & Which Customers Are Delinquent in Their Payments.
Dynacomp, Inc.

VersaText Word Processing & Database System. TexaSoft, Inc. *Compatible Hardware:* TI Professional with 2 disk drives & printer. *Operating System(s) Required:* MS-DOS. *Memory Required:* 128k.
$199.95.
Texas Instruments, Personal Productivit.

VersaTilities. *Version:* 1.1. Abelbeck Software Staff. 1993. *Items Included:* 2 manuals (VersaTilities & VersaTerm-Link) & disks. *Customer Support:* Free to registered users.
Maintosh System 6.0.5 or higher including 7.5.
Macintosh 68k, Power Macintosh (1250k).
$145.00 Suggested Retail, Educational pricing available (Order no.: SYNMAC444). *Optimal configuration:* 1500k free RAM, 3Mb free hard drive. *Networks supported:* TCP/IP, Appleshare.
A Suite of Essential Network Connections with Special Emphasis on Solutions for TCP/IP Environments. VersaTerm-Link, the Cornerstone Application, Provides a Smoothly Integrated Graphical Interface for Accessing Mail, News, Directory, Telnet Terminal & File Transfer Functions. VersaTilities Focuses on Exchanging Data with the Exploding Internet Community over Ethernet, AppleTalk & Serial (SLIP) Connections. The VersaTerm SLIP Extension Transports TCP/IP Data over a Modem Connection While Automating the Connection/Disconnection Process.
Synergy Software.

VERSBASE. Jun. 1985. *Operating System(s) Required:* CP/M 2.2. *Memory Required:* 24k.
disk $38.00 (ISBN 0-924945-04-4, Order no.: 004).
Allows Inserting the Next Sequential Version Number Instead of ".BAK" into New Backup Files. Such File Versions Can Be Created or Erased by the User at Will, Without Impairing Operation.
Logic Assocs.

Verse Search. *Version:* 6.1. Kent Ochel & Bert Brown. Jan. 1991.
Any DOS or Windows. IBM PC; XT, AT & compatibles (512k), Macintosh. disk $99.95.
Any Macintosh. 3.5" disk $99.95.
Includes One Translation of the Bible (NIV; KJV; NKJ; RSV; NRS; TLB), a Bible Thesaurus. Searches Can Be Made for Any Word, Phrase, Sentence or String of Characters. Word Searches Are Found Instantly. A Bible Thesaurus Is Included for Concept Searches.
Bible Research Systems.

Verse Typist. *Version:* 6.1. Kent Ochel & Bert Brown. Aug. 1989. *Items Included:* Tutorial disk; 3-ring binder with manual. *Customer Support:* Unlimited free technical support at (512) 251-7541.
Any DOS. IBM PC; XT; AT & compatibles. disk $49.95.
Any Macintosh. 3.5" disk $49.95.
A 20k Memory Resident Program that Allows the User to Transfer Bible Text Directly into Their Word Processing Program. Browsing Through the Bible Text & Created Indexes Are Also Available. VERSE SEARCH is Required.
Bible Research Systems.

VersTrans Routing & Planning: VTRANS. *Version:* 6.2. Jan. 1996. *Compatible Hardware:* IBM 386DX, 486, Pentium & compatibles, PS/2. *Operating System(s) Required:* DOS 3.3 or higher. *Language(s):* Pascal. *Memory Required:* 640k. *General Requirements:* 120Mb hard disk storage, printer. *Items Included:* System installation, training & support. *Customer Support:* Annual fee.
contact publisher for price.
Loads, Routes, & Schedules School Buses. Prints Driver Direction. Mapping & Original Network Provided by CMI. Specialized Support Programs Include Grade Advancement, RFM Report Generator, Parent Letters/Bus Passes & Bus Stop Assignment.
Creighton Manning, Inc.

Vertical Shaft Furnace. *Version:* 2. Sep. 1988. *Compatible Hardware:* IBM PC. *Language(s):* BASIC. *Memory Required:* 256k.
disk $200.00 ea.
IBM PC. (ISBN 0-931821-26-6, Order no.: 06-251).
Performs a Material & Thermal Balance for Cooling Zones, Pre-Heat & Induration Zone, & Drying Zone Based on Desired Product Composition & Throughput, & Green Feed Composition & Input Stockline Dimensions. Determines Thermal Blow Ratio, Cooling Off Gas/Pellet Exit from Soak Zone Interface Temperature & Top Gas Temperature. Combustion Requirements Are a Function of Net Heat of Reaction & Upper Shaft Thermal Blow Requirements. Performs Combustion Analysis for 5 Fuels. Includes a Time (Distance)/Temperature Profile.
Information Resource Consultants.

Verticals. *Compatible Hardware:* IBM PC & compatibles. *Memory Required:* 512k. *General Requirements:* Hard disk recommended.
$686.00 to $1986.00 per module.
Posts Recurring Transactions, Automatic Posting from Other Modules, Report Format User Definable, Reports Comparative Statements, Ability to Jump Modules, Wild Card, Links with External Software Programs, Password Access, Audit Trail, Error Recovery, Automatic Back-Up for Each Module, Log off Out-of-Balance, Reject Erroneous Account Numbers & On-Line Help.
Bristol Information Systems.

Vessel Coster. *Items Included:* Manual - 3 ring box binder. *Customer Support:* $450/year updates & telephone support, 1st year free.
DOS. 386 or higher (2Mb). disk $3000.00.
Estimates the Cost of Pressure Vessels. It Operates from Libraries of Cost Data for Materials & Labor Data for Fabrication Operations. All of the Data Libraries & the Report Fromat Are User Modifyable.
Techdata.

Vessel Drafting Program. *Items Included:* Manual - 3 ring binder. *Customer Support:* $450/year updates & telephone support, 1st year free.

DOS. 486 (8Mb). disk $4000.00. *Addl. software required:* AutoCad.
Automatically Produces Fabrication Quality AutoCad Drawings for Pressure Vessels. The Drawings Include Nozzles, Flanges, Reinforcements, Weld Details, Vessel Support, Nozzle Schedule & Bill of Materials. Suitable for Both Proposals & Fabrication.
Techdata.

Vet Pac Practice Management. *Version:* 6.05. W. P. Ruemmler. Sep. 1983. *Compatible Hardware:* IBM PC & compatibles. *Operating System(s) Required:* PC-DOS/MS-DOS. *Language(s):* Pascal. *Memory Required:* 512k. *General Requirements:* 2 disk drives, printer. *Customer Support:* One year free.
disk $4995.00.
Integrated Business Package for the Small to Medium Sized Veterinary Practice. The Functions Provided Include: Invoice Billing, Inventory Management, Shot Reminders, Rabies Certificates, Daily Ledger, Bank Deposit, Pet Recall, Mailing List, Bad Accounts List, Medical History, Income Analysis. With a 10Mb Disk, Handles 10,000 Customers with 20,000 Pets. The Data Is Entered As Services Are Rendered, & All Information Is Available from the Computer. Various Reports Are Generated.
Vet Pac, Inc.

Veterinary Billing Accounts Receivable. *Version:* 2.0. 1979. *Compatible Hardware:* Apple II, IBM PC. *Operating System(s) Required:* Apple DOS 3.3, MS-DOS. *Language(s):* Applesoft BASIC, QuickBASIC (source code included). *Memory Required:* Apple 64k, IBM 256k. *General Requirements:* 10Mb hard disk for Apple, 20Mb hard disk for IBM.
$1295.00.
Veterinary Office Management System for Any Veterinarian Office. Includes Recalls, Receivables, Payroll, Inventory, Payables, & Mailing List.
Johnson Assocs. (Arizona).

Veterinary Office System. *Items Included:* Binder with complete user documentation is included. *Customer Support:* 6 mos. of maintenance/support is included. Subsequent annual maintenance cost is $250.00 per year which includes support & all program updates.
MS-DOS. IBM PC & compatibles. disk $995.00, single user. *Optimal configuration:* 512k RAM, hard drive, printer. *Networks supported:* Lantastic, Novelle, most PC Net compatible.
disk network version $2995.00.
Designed to Improve the Small to Medium Sized Veterinary Practice & Its Profits by Automating Customer/Patient Records, Invoicing, & Recall Functions. Special Attention Is Paid to Efficiency & Marketing Tools.
Computerware.

Veterinary Practice Management System. Professional Software Associates, Inc. *Compatible Hardware:* TI Professional. *Operating System(s) Required:* UCSD p-System. *Memory Required:* 128k. *General Requirements:* Winchester hard disk, printer.
$2495.00.
Texas Instruments, Personal Productivit.

VetLogic. *Version:* 4.0. 1983. *Compatible Hardware:* IBM PC XT or compatibles, 286, 386, 486. *Language(s):* Compiled BASIC. *Memory Required:* DOS 640k.
$1995.00.
Provides Management Reports, Accounts Receivable, Patient Data Storage, Recall Practice Analysis, Word Processing & Inventory.
Data Strategies, Inc.

TITLE INDEX

Vette! *Version:* 1.11. 1991. *Items Included:* manual. *Customer Support:* phone support.
IBM AT or compatible (512k). disk $49.95.
MAC Plus or higher (1Mb). disk $59.95.
Spectrum HoloByte.

VeZOT HaTorah. *Compatible Hardware:* Macintosh Plus or higher. *General Requirements:* HyperCard.
3.5" disk $39.95.
Jewish Knowledge.
Davka Corp.

Vi-Spy Professional Edition. *Version:* 12.0. Sep. 1989. *Items Included:* Manual includes "Computer Virus Primer & Troubleshooting Guide". *Customer Support:* Via 24 hour hot-line BBS, FAX, or telephone. Includes one free year of quarterly updates plus full support.
PC-DOS/MS-DOS 2.0-6.0, Windows. IBM PC, XT, AT, PS/2 & compatibles. disk $149.95.
site license pricing avail.
Finds, Erases and/or Cleans Computer Viruses on Networks, Hard Disk Drives, & Diskettes. Windows & Menu Interface. Unique Features Prevent File Infector Viruses & Boot Sector Viruses from Infecting the System. An On-Line Help File Provides On-the-Spot Details of Any Virus That Vi-Spy Detects. Automatic Virus Check on All File Movement, Including Modem Downloads, Uncompressing Files, File Transfers, etc.; Protection from "Unknown" Viruses.
RG Software Systems, Inc.

Vi-Spy Universal NIM: Network Installable Module. *Version:* V12. Mar. 1994. *Customer Support:* Value Added Support Program included in purchase price for one year. Renewable yearly. Includes updates/upgrades & full support via phone, Fax, BBS.
PC-DOS/MS-DOS, Novell 7. IBM PC's & compatibles. $995.00 per server (all workstations included w/o charge) multiple server discounts available. *Networks supported:* Novell, UNIX, Banyan, IBM Token Ring, IBM OS/2, 3-COM, Microsoft LANManager, DEC Pathworks.
Provides Virus Protection for All Network Platforms - Novell, UNIX, Banyan, IBM Token Ring, IBM OS/2, 3-COM, Microsoft LAN Manager, DEC Pathworks. All File Activity Between Workstations & Servers Is Monitored in Real-Time. Workstations Automatically Check for Boot Viruses on Diskettes. The Software Includes RG's Proprietary "Stealth-X Logic" for Instantaneous Detection & Recovery from Known & Unknown Partition Sector Infections, & "Integrity Checking" for Known Viruses & Any Virus-Like Activity. Incidents Are Reported to the Server via a Virus Incident Log. The NIM Is Network Software Independent, Adds No Processing Load, & Does Not Cause Network Crashes.
RG Software Systems, Inc.

ViaNet Networking Operating System. *Version:* 3.06. *Operating System(s) Required:* PC-DOS/MS-DOS 2.0 or higher. *Memory Required:* 128k.
$99.00.
Allows Any Workstation on the Network to Share Resources with the Network with Hard Disk Drives. Includes a Method of Displaying Available Resources. To Access These Resources the User Uses Standard DOS Commands. The System Also Has the Capability to Tie UNIX, Xenix & DOS Machines in a Resource Sharing Network.
Western Digital Corp.

VIANSOFT Church Contribution System. *Version:* 3.52. Jan. 1996. *Compatible Hardware:* IBM PC & compatibles. *Operating System(s) Required:* MS-DOS, PC-DOS. *Language(s):* Pascal. *Memory Required:* 256k. *General Requirements:* 80-column printer. *Items Included:* Tutorial on disk; user's manual. *Customer Support:* Telephone support. Tutorial.
3.5" or 5.25" disk $70.00 (Order no.: 06875).
Entry of Contributions Generates Member Summaries, Directories & Mailing Labels.
Vian Corp.

VIANSOFT Church Treasurer. *Version:* 1.72. Jan. 1996. *Compatible Hardware:* IBM PC & compatibles. *Operating System(s) Required:* PC-DOS/MS-DOS 2.0 or higher. *Memory Required:* 384k. *General Requirements:* Printer. *Items Included:* Tutorial; user's manual. *Customer Support:* Telephone support. Tutorial.
3.5" or 5.25" disk $85.00 (Order no.: 06876).
Designed to Meet the Accounting Needs of a Church. Allows User to Keep Track of Budget, Income & Expenses. Allows the Inexperienced Bookkeeper & Computer User to Keep Complex Records & Produce Reports.
Vian Corp.

Vibes II. *Version:* 2.0. Saul B. Dinman. Mar. 1986. *Compatible Hardware:* IBM PC XT & compatibles, PC AT. *Operating System(s) Required:* MS-DOS, PC-DOS. *Memory Required:* 320k. *General Requirements:* Hard disk.
disk $995.00 (ISBN 0-923440-01-1).
Provides Complete Video Inventory, Club Membership, & Rental Transaction Facilities, & Prints Invoices for Transactions. Tracks the Whereabouts of All Inventory Items & Produces Many Different Reports, Including Financial Management Statistics.
Custom Computer Services.

ViceVersa. *Version:* 2.21. Jan. 1993. *Items Included:* Approximately 100 pages of support document; license registration card. *Customer Support:* Free telephone support.
MS-DOS or PC-DOS. IBM PC, XT, AT, PS/2 & compatibles (256K). 3.5" or 5.25" disk $249.95.
PC Utility Which Allows User to Exchange Documents BiDirectionally Between Disk-Based Xerox Memorywriter Electronic Typewriter & Many of the Most Popular PC Word Processing Packages. Full Document Formatting Features Are Preserved. Conversions Are Performed By Simply Inserting the Typewriter Diskette Directly into the PC. Menu-Driven.
Information Conversion Services, Inc.

VictorDraft.
Macintosh Plus or higher (1Mb). disk $495.00. *Nonstandard peripherals required:* Hard disk drive recommended.
Full-Featured Two-Dimensional Production Drafting CAD Program. Vector-Based & Features Multiple Drawing "Sheets" That Can Be Open at One Time, Multiple Drawing Windows with Independent Scales on Each Sheet, User-Definable Reference Views, Internal Calculator for Inputting Equations & More.
Pictor Graphics, Inc.

Victory Pak CD-ROM Collection. Sep. 1995. *Items Included:* Manual, registration card. *Customer Support:* Tech support is available Monday thru Friday 9:00 AM to 6:00 PM EST.
DOS 5.0 or higher. IBM 486/SX or higher (4Mb). CD-ROM disk Contact publisher for price (ISBN 1-57519-051-6). *Nonstandard peripherals required:* CD-ROM player. *Addl. software required:* CD-ROM software. *Optimal configuration:* 486/66, 8Mb RAM.
The V-for-Victory Series Has Set a New Standard for Computer War Games. Now Available As a Complete Series on a Single CD-ROM, It Is the Most Complete, Accurate & Realistic Simulation of Large-Scale WWII Ground Combat Ever Produced. Beginners & Experts Alike Will Be Carried Away in the Rush of Events That Began on the Beaches of France in 1944.
IntraCorp/Capstone.

Video Chess. David Levy. *Compatible Hardware:* TI Home Computer.
contact publisher for price (Order no.: PHM 3008).
Learn Chess Playing Techniques by Choosing Your Own Level of Difficulty.
Texas Instruments, Personal Productivit.

Video Effects 3D. *Compatible Hardware:* Commodore Amiga.
3.5" disk $199.95.
Enables Users to Animate Eight-Color IFF Pictures from Paint, Image-Capture, or Text-Generation Programs. Can Animate As Many As 99 Objects Simultaneously, Controlling the 3-D Path, Rotation, Spin, Size, & Speed of Each. Two-Dimensional Objects Can Be Extruded into 3-D for Further Manipulation. Object Rotation Moves at 30 Frames per Second. Supports a Borderless Screen at a 704x480 Pixels Resolution. To Check the Animation Before Recording to Videotape, the Program Can Play Whatever Is in Memory at 60 Frames per Second.
InnoVision Technology.

Video Exec. *Version:* 4.30. *Items Included:* Complete bound instruction guide. *Customer Support:* Free support for first 60 days; 1 year toll-free support, $295.00.
DOS. IBM & compatibles. $595.00-$1495.00. *Optimal configuration:* 486, 4Mb memory, fast hard disk. *Networks supported:* LANtastic, Novell.
This Package Is a Complete Rental Tracking Package for Video Stores. Star Search Function Allows Finding a Film by Actor. Pay on Rent or Return Provides Flexibility. Complete Tape & Customer History Provided. Additional Features Include Coupons/Free Tape, Bonus Counter, Complete Retail Inventory Pricing by Day, Client, & Rental Category. Plenty of Reports Allow Information on Just about Any Information, with Password Protection.
Aphelion, Inc.

Video Fashion! News: Top One Hundred International Models. Jun. 1994. *Items Included:* License agreement & registration card. *Customer Support:* 1-900-420-5005, $3.00 per minute.
Windows 3.1 or System 7. IBM & compatibles & Macintosh (2.0Mb). CD-ROM disk $39.00 MSRP (ISBN 0-9634008-5-1). *Nonstandard peripherals required:* CD ROM drive. *Optimal configuration:* 386, 20MHz, 4Mb RAM, VGA monitor with 256 colors.
One Hundred Photo CD Images with Corel Utilities for Image Conversion & Screensavers for Windows & Macintosh.
Cascom International, Inc.

Video Games I. *Compatible Hardware:* TI 99/4A with PLATO interpreter solid state cartridge.
contact publisher for price (Order no.: PHM 3018).
Practice Your Aim at Post-Shot, Try Your Skill at Pinball or Trap Your Opponent with Doodle.
Texas Instruments, Personal Productivit.

Video Graphs. *Compatible Hardware:* TI 99/4A.
contact publisher for price (Order no.: PHM3005).
Helps Users Create Their Own Designs.
Texas Instruments, Personal Productivit.

Video Plotter. Compatible Hardware: TI 99/4A with Automatic Filer Program. Operating System(s) Required: DX-10. Language(s): Extended BASIC. Memory Required: 48k. cassette $19.95.
Creates Screen Plot of up to 28 Data Values; up to 10 Dependent Variables. User Has the Option of Linear or Logarithmic Axes & Automatic or User-Selected Scales. Categories & Number of Dependent Variables Are Prompted. Regression Equation Is Derived & the Coefficients Are Printed on the Screen.
Eastbench Software Products.

Video Rental Management System. Items Included: Bound manual. Customer Support: Free hotline - no time limit; 30 day limited warranty; updates are $5/disk plus S&H.
MS-DOS. IBM & compatibles (256k). disk $99.95.
Features Include: Invoice at Time of Rental - Just Enter the Account Number (If a Member) & the Video Number(s) & a Full Invoice Is Printed. Also, the Rental Is Recorded on Disk. There Is Also Room for Additional Charges & Credits. Tape Library Maintenance - Capable of Listing (& Printing) the Videos by Numerous Categories (i.e., VHS/Beta, Title, Actor, Director, Rating, etc.). Automatic Past-Due Calculation upon Return. Customer's Club Membership Information, Including Name, Address, Phone Number, Membership Date & More.
Dynacomp, Inc.

Video Rental Manager, MVP. Version: 5.1. Jan. 1994. Items Included: 1 - 9 x 11 inch 250 page manual. Customer Support: 1 year maintenance $395.00; $495.00 network version. 1st year support free with the purchase of software.
MS-DOS (512k). IBM PC or compatible. $495.00 limited single user; $995.00 full single user; $1495.00 Network version. Optimal configuration: IBM AT, 640k 40 meg hard drive, bar code reader, cash drawer, 80 col. printer. Networks supported: Novell Netware & Lantastic.
System Offers a Complete Solution for Video Store Operation. Features Include: Menu Driven Design, Context Sensitive Help, Complete Tracking & History on Members, Handles Inventory & Rental Items Independently, Allows Sell-through of Rental Inventory, Reports Depreciation, Bar Code Support, & GL & Payroll (optional).
MicroSpec.

Video Store Manage for the MAC. Version: 1.1. Rick Hallmark. Jan. 1993. Items Included: 1 hard bound manual. Customer Support: Free technical support. Customer pays for long distance call.
MAC 6.07 or higher. MAC Plus or higher (2Mb). Single User $695.00; Network Version $995.00. Optimal configuration: MAC 2 or higher, 7.1, 4Mb. Networks supported: AppleTalk.
A Complete Point of Sale/Rental Program Designed for Video Rental Industry. VSM/MAC Has Complete Business Management with Financial Analysis & Reporting Capabilities Which Provide User With the Information Needed for Good Business Management. Provides an Easy-to-Use Operating System That Macintosh Users Expect.
Ghost Software.

Video Store Management System, Oct. 1986. Operating System(s) Required: CP/M, MP/M, MS-DOS, PC-DOS, TurboDOS, XENIX, UNIX. Language(s): Dataflex. Memory Required: 8-bit systems 64k, 16-bit systems 256k.
MS-DOS, PC-DOS. disk $1200.00.
CP/M, MP/M, TurboDOS. 8" disk $1200.00.
Designed to Aid Video Retailers in Managing Their Operations. Keeps Track of Customer Information, Daily Transactions, & Will Alert the Operator When a Customer Owes Outstanding Fees. Maintains a Complete Inventory on All Movies, Blank Tapes, & Other Video Accessories. Also Generates a Report Listing All Movies from Most to Least Frequently Rented to Distinguish Those Which Are Most Popular.
Monterey Computer Consulting.

Video Store Manager. Version: 2.8. Feb. 1992. Items Included: 1 hard bound manual. Customer Support: Free Technical phone support.
DOS 3.1 or higher. IBM PC, XT, AT, 386 or compatible (512k). disk $395.00 single user; $545.00 network version. Optimal configuration: IBM or compatible with 640k, 20Mb hard disk, Dot Matrix printer. Networks supported: Net BIOS.
A Complete Rental/Point or Sale Program Designed for the Video Rental Industry. It Is a Business Management System with Financial Analysis & Reporting Capabilities Which Give You Control over Your Stores Operation. VSM Is Perfect for That up & Coming Video Store Looking for a Computer System to Automate Their Rental & Return Process.
Ghost Software.

Video Store Manager Plus. Version: 3.0. Feb. 1994. Items Included: 1 hard bound manual. Customer Support: Free phone technical support for 1st year. $125.00 per each additional year.
DOS 3.1 or higher. IBM AT, 386 or higher compatible (640k). disk $695.00 single user; $995.00 network version. Optimal configuration: IBM compatible with 640k, 40Mb hard disk & Dot Matrix printer. Networks supported: Net BIOS.
A Complete Rental/Point or Sale Program Designed for the Video Rental Industry. It Is a Business Management System with Financial Analysis & Reporting Capabilities Which Give You Control over Your Stores Operation. VSM Plus Contains All the Advanced Features a Larger Store Needs. Such As Employee Transaction Tracking, Multi Day Rentals, Bar Code Printing Capabilities & the Ability to Perform Most Functions at the Rental Screen. Unlimited Rental History, Unlimited Customers & Inventory.
Ghost Software.

Video Store Master. Customer Support: 800-929-8117 (customer service).
MS-DOS. IBM/PS2. disk $399.99 (ISBN 0-87007-618-3).
A Menu-Driven Program That Keeps Track of a Video Store's Inventory & Productivity. Up to 10,000 Titles & 2,000 Customers Can be Stored.
SourceView Software International.

Video Tape Rental. 1985. Compatible Hardware: IBM PC & compatibles. Operating System(s) Required: MS-DOS. Language(s): BASIC (source code included). Memory Required: 640k. General Requirements: 2 disk drives, 20Mb hard disk.
IBM. disk $399.00 (ISBN 0-924940-06-9, Order no.: LSC-2009).
Prints Sales Receipts & Keeps Records of Who Has Tapes. Handles Returns, Reservations, Late Charges, Free Tapes, Membership Fees & Checks Credit Card Expiration Date.
Lizcon Computer Systems.

Video Title Shop: A Computer + VCR Utility. Compatible Hardware: Atari ST, Commodore 64/128. General Requirements: Hard disk, printer.
disk $29.95.
Atari. (ISBN 0-88717-166-4).
Commodore. (ISBN 0-88717-167-2).
Designed to Enhance Video Productions. Combines VCR or Video Camera & Home Computer System to Create Specialized Video Productions for Home, School or Business. Screens Created Are Fully Usable for Video Applications Without the Clutter of Prompts or Cursors. Features Variety of Font Styles & Sizes, Creates Borders & Edits Work. Designs Fonts & Imports Picture Backdrops from Graphics Paint Programs.
IntelliCreations, Inc.

Video Titler. Compatible Hardware: Atari 400, 800. Language(s): Atari BASIC. Memory Required: 24k.
disk $29.95.
Creates Wide Variety of Screen Displays & Sounds.
Dynacomp, Inc.

Video Toolbox. Version: 8.9. 1985. Compatible Hardware: Apple II, II+, IIe, IIc, IIgs. Operating System(s) Required: Apple DOS 3.3, ProDOS 8. Language(s): Assembly, BASIC. Memory Required: 48k.
disk $39.95 (ISBN 0-927796-14-7).
Set of Screen Commands That Give User Control over the Appearance of the Text Screen. Formatting Screen Input & Text Display Commands Include: Input Using, Keyboard Scan, Lower Case Input, Number Format, Edit String, Key Click, Speed Control, Print Pause, Clear Format, Clear Screen, Four Way Scroller, & Print Repeat.
Roger Wagner Publishing, Inc.

Video Trak: Quick, Super, Senior, Master. Oct. 1983. Compatible Hardware: IBM PC & compatibles. Memory Required: 512k. General Requirements: Hard disk.
disk $995.00.
Used to Control/Manage Video Rental Applications. There Are 4 Systems: VIDEO TRAK QUICK for Convenience Stores & Small Stores, VIDEO TRAK SUPER for Supermarkets, VIDEO TRAK SENIOR for General Purpose Video Stores, & VIDEO TRAK MASTER for Larger Chains.
Cardinal Tracking Technics, Inc.-Video Trak.

Video Visions: Studio Set. Charles Voner. May 1990. Customer Support: Free phone tech support.
AmigaDOS 1.2 Or higher. Amiga 1Mb. 3.5" disk $199.00. Addl. software required: 3-D display for 3-D object disk. Optimal configuration: 1Mb & titler, or 3-D program.
This Set Encompasses All Vision Data to Date. Multi-Media Program "Multivisions" & Liberal Updates to Future Disks Included. Presently Includes 36 Full 3.5" Disks, Vol. 1-12 Coul ColorFont Collection, Animated Action Disks.
Charles E. Voner Designs.

Video Visions: The Animator Set. Jan. 1989. Customer Support: Free phone support, Customization of Package according to user needs.
Amiga DOS 1.2 or higher (512k). $49.95, (new) separate volumes $24.95 ea. Addl. software required: Sculpt 3-D, Imagine, or Lightwave 3D; Deluxe Paint 4 recommended.
Set Consists of 3-D Objects & Cel Images for Animating Presentation Programs. Includes Volume 2: 3D Animator, Volume 3: 2D Animator, Plus Animated Action Disks: Animated Intros & Animated Spots, Volume 10: The Illustrator (Entertainment - Game Sets).
Charles E. Voner Designs.

Video Visions: The Educator Set. Version: 1.0. Sep. 1991. Items Included: Short manual of video tips & techniques. Customer Support: Free phone support.
Amiga DOS 1.2 or higher. Amiga (1Mb).

TITLE INDEX

$39.95. *Addl. software required:* Display, paint program.
Four Disks of Data Suitable for DeskTop Video Themes of Education Pictorials. World Maps & School-Sports Scenes Useful for Video Yearbook Situations. Professors & Educators Can Use the Maps for Educational Purposes or a School TV Studio Can Use the Images in News & Sports Reports.
Charles E. Voner Designs.

Video Visions: The Mixed Set. *Customer Support:* Free phone support, customization of user needs.
Amiga DOS 1.2 or higher (512k). 3 volumes, $59.95; 4 volumes, $69.95; 5 volumes, $79.95. *Addl. software required:* Animation, Titler or Paint Program recommended. *Optimal configuration:* 2 disk drives (1Mb).
Package Consists of 3-D Objects & Backdrops Making up a Set of Choice, Any 3, 4, or 5 Volumes from the Video Vision Series.
Charles E. Voner Designs.

Video Visions: The Titler Set. *Customer Support:* Free phone support, customization of each package for user needs.
Amiga DOS 1.2 or higher (512k). $69.95; (new) separate volumes, $25.00 ea. *Addl. software required:* Display program Titler Type is recommended; especially suited for Pro Video Plus, Broadcast Titler. *Optimal configuration:* 2 disk drives (1.5Mb RAM).
Set Consists of Images for Use with Titler Programs. Included Are: Volume 1- the Titler (Backdrops-Fonts). Also Cool Colorfont Collection: Colofonts 1, Colorfonts 2, Colorfonts 3, Broadcaster (Business-Broadcast), Volume 7- the Advertiser, Volume 9- the Video-Musician (Jingle BG - Rock Scenes), 14 Disks Possible for Each Titler Set. Also Available As Videotape UHS Version.
Charles E. Voner Designs.

Video Visions: Wedding Set. Charles Voner. 1990. *Items Included:* Choice of optional Manual of multi-media tips. *Customer Support:* Free phone tech support.
AmigaDOS 1.2 or higher. Amiga (1Mb). 3.5" disk $39.95.
DOS 6.02 or higher. MAC II (1Mb). 3.5" disk $39.95. *Nonstandard peripherals required:* Color board. *Addl. software required:* Display program.
IBM VGA 3.0 or higher. 3.5" disk $39.95. *Nonstandard peripherals required:* VGA color board.
Wedding Pictures for Wedding Videos Feature Bar Mitzvah, Ceremonial & Wedding Occasion Data Screens. Full Overscan for Titler. Program Use or Display with the Included "Multivisions" Display Program. Note: (No Display Program or Script Disk with Mac Version).
Charles E. Voner Designs.

Video Voice Speech Training System. *Version:* Apple IIe, IIgs 4.0; IBM PC 2.0. 1991-92. *Compatible Hardware:* Apple II series, Apple IIgs; IBM PC, PC XT, PC AT, & compatibles, IBM PS/2. *Memory Required:* Apple II series 64k, Apple IIgs 256k, PC 640k. *Items Included:* Speech Analyzer Hardware, A-D card, microphone, software disks, training materials. *Customer Support:* 1-800-537-2182.
disk $2995.00 ea.
Combination of Specialized Hardware & Software Programs That Provide Visual Biofeedback on Speech That Helps Train Vowel Production, Word Articulation, Pitch & Inflection, Rate of Speech, etc. Demo Disk & Videotape Available on Request.
Micro Video Corp.

VideoBase. *Version:* 2.0. Paul Pearson. Oct. 1989. *Items Included:* Instructional manual, Hypercard software. *Customer Support:* Limited 90 day warranty on media, limited support with Professional package (technical support by telephone).
Macintosh (2Mb). $69.95; Professional $149.95. *Nonstandard peripherals required:* hard disk drive.
Database for Video Product Information. It's Main Purpose is to Aid in the Selection of a Program from a Large Library of Titles. Selection Criteria are Supplied by the End-User, Using a HyperCard Interface, & the List of Titles is Reduced to Those Meeting the Specifications.
Hyperworks Software Design & Development.

Videodisc Accessory Series. *Items Included:* 1 floppy disk, instruction booklet. *Customer Support:* M-F 9 AM-5 PM Pacific Time (213) 451-1383.
Macintosh Plus, SE, II or Portable (1 Mb). 3.5" disk $49.95. *Nonstandard peripherals required:* Videodisc player (Pioneer 2200, 4200, 8000, 6000, 6000A, 6010, 6010A, or Sony RS-232-equipped player), monitor & cables.
A Desk Accessory for Controlling All Standard Videodisc Functions from within Any Macintosh Application. Works with Most Pioneer & Sony RS-232 Players. (Please Specify Laserdisc Model Number).
The Voyager Co.

Videohound Multimedia 96 CD ROM. *Version:* 3.0. (Videohound Ser.). Oct. 1995.
IBM. CD-ROM disk $39.95 (ISBN 0-7876-0291-4, Order no.: 089533).
Movies on Video. Includes Biographies, Photos, Movie Stills, Sound Bites, & Other Movie Related Data.
Gale Research, Inc.

Videomatic. *Items Included:* Bound manual. *Customer Support:* Free hotline - no time limit; 30 day limited warranty; updates are $5/disk plus S&H.
MS-DOS 2.0 or higher. IBM & compatibles (256k). disk $39.95. *Nonstandard peripherals required:* Printer supported, but optional.
Organizes, Searches, Sorts, Edits, & Lists Your Video Collection. It Features Menu-Driven Operation, Full-Screen Entry & Editing, & Extensive Searching, Sorting, & List & Label Generation Capabilities. Any of the Pre-Defined Fields May Be Changed by the User. Can Generate Title Lists That Rival or Surpass Those Found in Rental Stores. Lists Can Be Organized by Any Field. List by Title, Category, Star, Studio, Rating, etc. You Can Also Select According to Key Words, Such as a Particular Star in a Particular Category of Film.
Dynacomp, Inc.

VideoPaint. *Version:* 1.1. *Items Included:* Disks, manual & addendums. *Customer Support:* Free unlimited phone technical support, FAX & modem service. America Online, CompuServe, Applelink.
Macintosh System 6.0.5 or higher (1Mb RAM). 8-bit color Mac LC & higher or SE/30 with 8-bit color. 3.5" disk $495.00. *Nonstandard peripherals required:* 2 versions: one for LC with 12" screen & no math co-processor & one for 13" screen with math co-processor. *Optimal configuration:* 030 with math co-processor.
Three-Dimensional Color Painting & Editing Program That Incorporates Sophisticated Special Effects & an Open Architecture. The Program's Features, on Top of the Regular Features Found in Most Color Paint Programs, Includes: More Than 40 Special Effects, Including Spherization, Blur, Smudge, Diffuse, Contour, Bezier Curves, Custom Shading, Dithering, Fractal, etc.; Stencil & Mask Tools Allow for Multilayer Creative Techniques; Built-In Color Separation Capabilities, Three-Dimensional Wire-Frame Creation & Rendering; Built-In Drivers for Apple, Microtek & Sharp Scanners; Advanced Built-In Import & Export Facilities, & a Fully-Documented Open Architecture That Allows Developers to Write New Special Effects & Input & Output Peripherals Easily.
Olduvai Corp.

VideoPrint: Photo-Realistic Printing. *Version:* 1.4. Jan. 1996. *Items Included:* Manual. *Customer Support:* Printer configuration, custom printer drivers.
Workbench 1.3 or higher. Any Amiga (512k). 3.5" 880k disk $25.00 (Order no.: AVP). *Addl. software required:* Paint or graphic text; or HoloCAD, MMBBS, MMTERM. *Optimal configuration:* Dot-addressable color graphics printer, 1Mb RAM.
MS-DOS 5.0 or higher. PC-286 or higher. 3.5" 720k or 5.25" 1.2M disk $30.00 (Order no.: PVP). *Optimal configuration:* Dot-addressable color graphics printer.
Photo-Realistic Printing of Images, Graphic Text. 256-Level Gray-Scale, 16M Colors. Smooth Edges, Blending. Brightness, Color Correction. Rotate, Enlarge, Reduce, Separations. Preferences Printer Drivers Compatible, or Use Ours for Best Results. NTSC, PAL, HDTV Conversion. Does Amiga IFF; PC TIFF 6.0, GIF; & MacPaint Conversions.
United ProCom Systems.

VideoShow HQ.
Macintosh Plus or higher. disk $4999.00.
Desktop Presentation Systems. Displays Images with up to 100,000 Simultaneous Colors with Patented Macrovision Resolution. Fully Portable - Connects to All Standard Monitors, Video Projectors & TVs. Simple Wireless Remote Control Operation.
General Parametrics Corp.

VideoShow Presenter.
Windows. IBM PC & compatibles. Contact publisher for price. *Addl. software required:* Microsoft PowerPoint, Harvard Graphics, or Lotus Freelance.
The World's First Remote Control with a Built-In Full Color Screen. Enjoy Total Confidence & Control of Your Presentation. Never Forget a Line Again. Because You'll Always Have Access to Your Notes. And You Can Privately Preview Your Next Image for Perfect Transitions. Get the Competitive Edge with the Most Powerful, Easy-to-Use Presentation Tool Ever.
General Parametrics Corp.

VIDEO4. *Compatible Hardware:* TRS-80.
disk $24.95 (Order no.: D8V4).
Utilizes the Features of TRS-80 Model 4 When in the Model III Mode.
The Alternate Source.

Vienna Game. R. Kuijf. 1994. *Items Included:* Book & disk with 500 or more games (over 200 annotated). *Customer Support:* Telephone support by appointment.
MS-DOS 2.0 or higher (512k). 3.5" disk $25.00, incl. softcover text. *Nonstandard peripherals required:* Mouse, graphics, 3 1/2" drive.
Atari ST (520k). Atari. disk $25.00. *Nonstandard peripherals required:* Monochrome monitor DS/DD drive.
Authoritative Introduction to & Analysis of an Important Chess Opening.
Chess Combination, Inc.

VIEWDAC. Jul. 1991. *Items Included:* Five manuals, three 5.25" high density floppy diskettes, three 3.5" high density floppy diskettes, one external DAS driver system & external DAS

driver manual. *Customer Support:* 90 day no-charge software support, free newsletter subscription.
DOS 3.0 or higher. IBM 386/386 SX/486 PC family of compatibles (6Mb). disk $2495.00 (ISBN 0-924729-17-1). *Nonstandard peripherals required:* Hard disk 15Mb available, hard disk 15Mb available, graphics display with EGA or greater resolution, 387 compatible math co-processor & Microsoft mouse or compatible device. *Optimal configuration:* 386/386SX/486 compatible with mouse, VGA color monitor.
An Integrated A/D, D/A Data Acquisition & GPIB & RS-232 Control, Analysis & Graphics on 386/386 SX/486. A Multitasking System with a Mouse-&-Menu Driven Windowing Interface.
Keithley Asyst.

ViewPoint with Windows Graphics. *Version:* 4.1. *Compatible Hardware:* IBM PC AT, PC XT, PS/2. *Memory Required:* 640k. *Customer Support:* Free product support; 2-day training, Hands-on available.
single user version $3500.00.
LAN version $8000.00.
3-user LAN pack $4500.00.
Features a New, Windows-Based Graphics System. ViewPoint Graphics Utilizes Windows' Intuitive Interface & Point-&-Click Features to Produce Presentation-Quality Output: Gantt & PERT Charts, Progress Plots, Resource Allocation Graphs & Much More. The New Software Allows the User to Open & Examine Several Windows, Load & Change Existing ViewPoint Files, Customize with Fonts & Colors, & Output to a Wide Variety of Printers, Plotters & Slide Systems. Used in Conjunction with ViewPoint's Powerful Project Planning & Management Capabilities, the New Software Turns ViewPoint into a Complete Management System.
Computer Aided Management.

Viking Data Entry System: VDE. *Version:* 3.5. 1981-93. *Compatible Hardware:* DEC VAX, Alpha, IBM PC & compatibles, DG, IBM RS 6000, Sun, 386 UNIX, HP. *Operating System(s) Required:* VMS, MS-DOS, UNIX, AIX, Solaris, HP/UX. *Language(s):* C. *Memory Required:* 512k. *Customer Support:* Hot line, newsletter, 90 day warranty.
contact publisher for price.
Full-Featured High-Speed Data Entry Package for Micros & Minis. Often Used for Replacing Keypunch & Key Disk Equipment in a "Heads-Down" Environment. Includes ReKey Verify, Balance & Cross-Foot & Flexible Field Edits.
Viking Software Services, Inc.

VIM: Vessel Inspection Manager. *Items Included:* Manual - 3 ring binder. *Customer Support:* $450/year updates & telephone support, 1st year free.
DOS. 386 or higher (2Mb). disk $1800.00.
Tracks & Manages OSHA-Required Data on Pressure Vessels. VIM Calculates Corrosion Rates for All Vessels in Your Plant & Forecasts Retirement Date & Next Required Inspection Date. Many Report Options Allow You to See Each Vessel's Current Status & Inspection History, Find the Nest Vessels to Inspect in a Plant Area, Show Results of Latest Inspections, etc. A Free Demo Illustrates the Program's Features.
Techdata.

Vine's Expository Dictionary of Biblical Words. W. E. Vine et al. Aug. 1991. *Customer Support:* No fee is charged for our customer support: 30 day money back return guarantee; lifetime warranty on defective disk replacement; free telephone technical support.
PC or MS-DOS 2.0 or higher. IBM PC/XT/AT or compatible. 3.5" or 5.25" disk $69.95. *Addl. software required:* PC STUDY BIBLE & GREEK-HEBREW DICTIONARY. *Optimal configuration:* 4.5Mb on the hard drive is required for the Greek-Hebrew Word Study Series.
Add-On Module for PC STUDY BIBLE'S GREEK-HEBREW DICTIONARY & ENGLISHMAN'S CONCORDANCE. It Provides a Powerful Combination of Vine's Expository Dictionary of NT Words & Nelson's Expository Dictionary of the Old Testament to the Module Containing Strong's Greek-Hebrew Dictionary & Englishman's Greek-Hebrew Concordance.
Biblesoft.

Vine's Expository Dictionary of Biblical Words. May 1993. *Items Included:* Disks, marketing literature, order form. *Customer Support:* No fee for customer support: 30 day money back guarantee, limited replacement warranty on diskettes defective at time of purchase, free telephone technical support.
PC-DOS/MS-DOS 3.1 or higher or Windows 3.1 or higher. IBM 386/486 or 100% compatible (Windows); Also AT/XT/286 (DOS) (640k DOS or 4Mb Windows). disk $39.95 (ISBN 1-56514-325-6). *Addl. software required:* Biblesoft's PC Study Bible, Strongs Greek/Hebrew Dictionary & King James Version text. *Optimal configuration:* 5.25 1.2Mb disk drive for installation & 4.5Mb of hard drive space, mouse or pointer device recommended.
Arranges Greek/Hebrew Words under English Translations. Provides Detailed Discussions of Major Bible Words; in Depth Articles on the Meanings & Usages of Key Bible Words.
Biblesoft.

Vine's Expository Dictionary of Biblical Words. May 1993. *Items Included:* Disks, marketing literature, order form. *Customer Support:* No fee for customer support: 30 day money back guarantee, limited replacement warranty on diskettes defective at time of purchase, free telephone technical support.
PC-DOS/MS-DOS 3.1 or higher or Windows 3.1 or higher. IBM 386/486 or 100% compatible (Windows); Also AT/XT/286 (DOS) (640k DOS or 4Mb Windows). 3.5" disk $39.95 (ISBN 1-56514-323-X). *Addl. software required:* Biblesoft's PC Study Bible, Strongs Greek/Hebrew Dictionary & King James Version text. *Optimal configuration:* 3.5" 1.44Mb disk drive for installation & 4.5Mb of hard drive space, mouse or pointer device recommended.
Arranges Greek/Hebrew Words under English Translations; in Depth Articles on the Meaning & Usage of Key Bible Words.
Biblesoft.

VINES UNLIMITED. *Version:* 4.10. Jan. 1990. *Compatible Hardware:* Compaq deskpro 386 486 capable of running DOS, IBM PCs, 80386-based & 80486-based OS/2 and/or Windows compatibles. *Items Included:* Assorted LAN drivers, file services, print services, StreetTalk naming service, security, NetBIOS interface, LAN bridging, global network administration. *Customer Support:* Various programs available. $7495.00.
Enterprise Wide Distributed Network Operating System for 80386-Based & 80486-Based Systems Running DOS, OS/2, and/or Windows. Communications with Asynchronous Hosts Is Provided via VT-100, VT-52, IBM3101, & TTY Terminal Emulation. Also Supports File Transfer Through the KERMIT Protocol.
Banyan Systems.

Vining Bond Swap System. *Compatible Hardware:* Apple III.
contact publisher for price.
Designed for Banks & Security Dealers to Evaluate the Consequence of Trading One Security for Another in a Portfolio, Estimating the Effect on Items Such As Account Income.
Vining Sparks Micro Software.

Vintage Production. *Compatible Hardware:* Apple Macintosh & IBM/clones. *General Requirements:* 10Mb hard disk, Flexware Run-Time.
$3500.00.
Monitors & Controls All Aspects of Wine Production from Crushing Through Bottling. Includes Ability to Cross-Reference by Vintage, Varietal & Vineyard. Calculates Varietal/Appellation Percentages. Maintains Bulk Inventory, Produces BATF 702 Reports, & Interfaces with Flexware Accounting Software. Features Code File, Workorders, Reports.
Pickering Winery Supply.

VinylCAD. *Version:* 2.0. *Items Included:* Sample drawings & manuals, Scanner Software for master to vector conversion. *Customer Support:* Free phone technical support.
DOS 3.0 or higher. IBM (2Mb). disk $799.95.
Combines the Power of CAD with Vinyl Sign Cutting. Allows User to Draw Any Object & Manipulate It, Then Turn It into a Vinyl Sign. 100 Fonts Are Included That Can Be Manipulated Any Number of Ways. Software That Utilizes a Scanner Is Included.
American Small Business Computers, Inc.

VinylCAD Extended Fonts Library. *Version:* 1.0. Robert Webster et al. Oct. 1992. *Items Included:* 1 perfect-bound manual. *Customer Support:* Unlimited free technical support via toll number; seminars (for fee).
MS-DOS. IBM & compatibles (2Mb). disk $795.00 (Order no.: 714-2000-3 (3.5"); 714-2000-5 (5.25")). *Nonstandard peripherals required:* VinylCAD 2.0 or higher. *Optimal configuration:* Faster the computer, the faster it runs.
Over 500 Outline Fonts to Complement VinylCAD's 110 Fonts. Every Font Reproduces at Any Size: No Need for Separate Fonts of Each Size. All Fonts Editable in VinylCAD. Never Again Turn down Jobs Because You Couldn't Match a Client's Font Wishes.
American Small Business Computers, Inc.

VIP-BASIC. *Version:* 2.0. Jan. 1996. *Items Included:* CD-ROM. *Customer Support:* Free technical support.
Mac System 7.5. Mac 030 (8Mb). CD-ROM disk $295.00.
Now You Can Create Full-Featured, Stand-Alone Macintosh & Power Macintosh Applications in Just Minutes-In Standard BASIC Code! Makes It Simple to Program Your Macintosh. Revolutionary Integrated Design, Gives You Everything You Need to Write Professional Applications-Right Out of the Box.
Mainstay.

VIP-C. *Version:* 2.0. Jan. 1996. *Items Included:* CD-ROM. *Customer Support:* Free technical support.
Mac System 7.5. Mac 030 (8Mb). CD-ROM disk $495.00.
Now You Can Create Full-Featured, Stand-Alone Macintosh & Power Macintosh Applications in Just Minutes. VIP-C Is the First Rapid Application Development System for Creating Complete Macintosh Programs in Standard ANSI C.
Mainstay.

VIP7200. *Compatible Hardware:* IBM PC & true compatibles, PC XT, PC AT, Portable PC. *Memory Required:* 128k. *General Requirements:* IBM asynchronous card or equivalent RS-232

TITLE INDEX

port, communications cable. *Items Included:* User manual. *Customer Support:* 1 year free.
disk $399.00.
Allows Terminal Emulation & File Transfer Capabilities for the Following HONEYWELL Bull Mainframes: Level 61, Level 62, Level 64, Mini 6, DPS 7, DPS 8. Operates at up to 9600 Baud. Can Be Configured for Different Terminal Types. Provides Transparent Printing, Is Installable onto the Hard Disk, Features Programmable Function Keys & Hayes Compatibility. Can Be Used with Either Primary or Secondary Port.
TDT Group, Inc.

Viraway. Jan. 1991. *Customer Support:* Free Phone Support.
IBM PC & compatible. 5.25" disk $50.00 (ISBN 1-879013-05-3).
3.5" disk $50.00 (ISBN 1-879013-06-1).
Computer Virus Detection, Prevention & Elimination.
T.C.P. Techmar Computer Products, Inc.

The Virtual BioPack. Jun. 1994. *Items Included:* NSTA Content Core, Teacher's Guide Level III, installation guide, laser disk, Pioneer MCI drivers (Windows).
Windows. IBM PC & compatibles (4Mb). CD-ROM disk Contact publisher for price (ISBN 1-57026-011-7). *Nonstandard peripherals required:* Pioneer laser disk player 2200, 2400, 4200. *Addl. software required:* Pioneer MCI driver (included).
Macintosh. Macintosh (4Mb). CD-ROM disk Contact publisher for price (ISBN 1-57026-008-7). *Nonstandard peripherals required:* Pioneer laser disk player.
An Interactive CD-ROM & Laserdisk Product That Explores the Relationship Between Animals & the Living Earth in Six Biomes.
Computer Curriculum Corp.

The Virtual BioPack, Level 1. Jun. 1994. *Items Included:* Teachers guide Level 1 with bar codes. laser disk Contact publisher for price (ISBN 1-57026-010-9). *Nonstandard peripherals required:* Pioneer laser disk player 2200, 2400, 4200.
Contains 30 Minutes of Visual Database for 6 Biomes. Interviews with Smithsonian Scientists & Screen Slots of the CD-ROM Product.
Computer Curriculum Corp.

The Virtual Body. Time Life Staff. Jan. 1995. *Customer Support:* Free 800 Number Technical Support.
Windows. PC with 486SX 33MHz or higher (8Mb). disk $29.95 (ISBN 1-884899-11-0). *Optimal configuration:* 486SX 33MHz or higher PC, 8Mb RAM, double-speed CD-ROM drive, VGA plus 640x480 monitor displaying 256 colors, Windows 3.1, stereo headphones or speakers, hard disk space, mouse or compatible positioning device, Sound Blaster 16 sound card or compatible.
This Comprehensive Science Exploration Title Answers 52 of the Most-Asked Questions about the Body. It Includes over 30 Actual Laboratory Experiments. Lifelike Illustrations & Detailed Animations Explain the Workings of the Human Body, from Circulation to Brain Development. For Ages 10-Adult.
IVI Publishing, Inc.

Virtual Guitar. Oct. 1994. *Items Included:* Bundled with game disk & cable. *Customer Support:* 90 day warranty.
MS Windows 3.1 Plus. IBM compatible Multimedia PC (MPC) (4Mb). CD-ROM disk $99.95 (ISBN 1-886022-00-3). *Nonstandard peripherals required:* Soundcard, CD-ROM (2x1, Speakers).
An Interactive CD-ROM Game That Lets You Be the Rock Star. Game Controller Lets You Jam - Even If You Never Have Played Guitar Before. Play Your Way from Obscurity to Center Stage with Aerosmith in This Rocking Game Which Has Been Described As "the Future of Interactive Multimedia".
Ahead, Inc.

Virtual Landscape: Winter Hiking in Rocky Mountain National Park. James N. Perdue. May 1994. *Items Included:* Documentation available on disc. *Customer Support:* 90-day warranty on defective disc. Telephone support to distributors & retailers - no charge.
7.0 or higher. Macintosh (4Mb). CD-ROM disk optical disk $29.00 (ISBN 1-885237-01-4, Order no.: RMDP 102-001). *Optimal configuration:* MAC II or higher, 6Mb or more RAM, 300k or faster CD-ROM, 8-bit color display card.
Interactively Explores the Winter Beauty of Rocky Mountain National Park Using a Navigation-Based Program Which Views Images in Natural Sequences, Such As Hiking along a Trail. At Each Position, the User Sees the Surrounding Views, Hears Sounds, Reads Explanatory Text & Graphics (Maps), & Views Video.
Rocky Mountain Digital Peeks.

Virtual Library at the Buzzard's Nest. Edited by C. W. Tazewell. Dec. 1995.
IBM. Contact publisher for price (ISBN 1-57000-044-1).
Comprehensive Library Collection on the Internet - Many Subjects (Somewhat Like a Worldwide Loose-Leaf Encyclopedia).
W. S. Dawson Co.

The Virtual Murder Series: MAC Retail Box. Shannon Gilligan. *Items Included:* Registration Card. *Customer Support:* Creative Multimedia Corporation warrants the CD-ROM disc & diskettes to be free from defects in materials & workmanship under normal use & service for a period of 90 days from date of purchase. Creative Multimedia Corporation offers Technical Support to customers as needed.
System Software 6.0.7 or higher. 8-bit color & color monitor, CD-ROM drive w/150k/sec transfer rate, 380ms or less access rate & extension. Macintosh Plus or higher (3.5Mb). CD-ROM disk $69.99 Suggested Retail Price (ISBN 1-880428-26-1, Order no.: 10518). *Optimal configuration:* Hard drive is recommended.
This Two-Disc Set of Challenging Interactive Mysteries Allows You to Investigate Crime Scenes, Interview Suspects & Solve the Murders Before Time Runs Out. In "The Magic Death", Elspeth Haskard, a Brilliant Anthropologist Has Been Killed in a Bizarre Ritualistic Fashion. In "Who Killed Sam Rupert?", You Are Asked to Solve the Murder of a Popular Restauranteur Who Is Found Dead in His Office.
Creative Multimedia Corp.

The Virtual Murder Series: MPC Retail Box. Shannon Gilligan. *Items Included:* Registration card. *Customer Support:* Creative Multimedia Corporation warrants the CD-ROM disc & diskettes to be free from defects in materials & workmanship under normal use & service for a period of 90 days from date of purchase. Creative Multimedia Corporation offers Technical Support to customers as needed.
MS-DOS 3.1 or higher, MS-CDEX 2.0 or higher. 386SX or higher (4Mb). CD-ROM disk $69.99 2 disk set (ISBN 1-880428-09-1, Order no.: 10400). *Nonstandard peripherals required:* Sound Blaster or Sound Blaster compatible board. CD-ROM drive with 150k/sec transfer rate, 380ms or less access rate. *Addl. software required:* Microsoft Windows 3.1. *Optimal configuration:* SuperVGA with 512k, video memory capable of 640x480x256 colors with Windows driver supported. *Networks supported:* All.
This Two-Disc Set of Challenging Interactive Mysteries Allows You to Investigate Crime Scenes, Interview Suspects & Solve the Murders Before Time Runs Out. In "The Magic Death", Elspeth Haskard, a Brilliant Anthropologist Has Been Killed in a Bizarre Ritualistic Fashion. In "Who Killed Sam Rupert?", You Are Asked to Solve the Murder of a Popular Restauranteur Who Is Found Dead in His Office.
Creative Multimedia Corp.

Virtual Tarot. Jeff A. Manning. Jun. 1994. *Customer Support:* 90 day unlimited - lifetime replacement for $10.00.
Mac System 7.0; Windows. Mac II; IBM 386DX 33MHz 640x480 256 monitor (5Mb). CD-ROM disk $69.95 (ISBN 1-886396-00-0, Order no.: UTRWLIL). *Nonstandard peripherals required:* CD-ROM & sound. *Optimal configuration:* 486DX 33 2x CD-ROM, sound, 8Mb 640x480, Quadra w/CD-ROM 13" color.
Explore Your Future Possibilities with Virtual Tarot, a CD-ROM Based Multimedia Experience That Blends the Ancient Mystic Art of the Tarot with Modern Computer Technologies. Entertaining, Provactive & Surprisingly Accurate.
Virtual Media Works, Inc.

Virtuoso Pianist. *Compatible Hardware:* Apple Macintosh.
Includes Classical Piano Library. 3.5" disk $549.00.
Music Instruction.
MacMIDI Distributing.

Viruscure PLUS. *Version:* 3.12. Sep. 1993. *Items Included:* Manual. *Customer Support:* Unlimited free technical support, 30 day unconditional support, BBS 415-454-2893.
MS-DOS, DOS 2.1 or higher. IBM PC, XT, AT (256k). disk $69.00, 10-PC LAN-Pack version for ,450.00 each, direct corporate site licenses are available.
Virus Scan Program. Scans Directories & DOS Partition Table. Memory Resident Module to Prevent Infection, Identifies & Removes Viruses, Repairs & Restores Damaged Files & Protects Against Viral Infections. Detects Over 700 Viruses & Strains. Reads Compressed Files.
IMSI (International Microcomputer Software, Inc.).

Visibility. *Compatible Hardware:* TI 99/4A with Extended BASIC module. *Operating System(s) Required:* DX-10. *Language(s):* Extended. *Memory Required:* 48k.
cassette $16.95.
Computes the Rising & Setting Times of Any Astronomical Body for Any Given Date & Location.
Eastbench Software Products.

The Visible Analyst Workbench, 3 disks. *Version:* 6.0 Windows. Jan. 1996. *Compatible Hardware:* Windows-compatible PC. *Operating System(s) Required:* MS-DOS; Novell NetWare, Windows 3.0. *Language(s):* C, C Plus Plus, COBOL. *Memory Required:* 4000k. *General Requirements:* 1 floppy & 1 hard disk drives, printer, Microsoft Mouse, Microsoft Windows; Pentium or 486-based system. *Items Included:* user manual, tutorial. *Customer Support:* technical support, maintenance & updates, education, consulting services available on a fee basis.
One Integrated Tool. $29.95 single-user license; under $2000.00 per seat for networked product.
Multi-User Case Tool for Developing Client/Server Applications & Databases. Supports Both

VISIBLE ANALYST WORKBENCH:

Traditional Structured & New Object-Oriented Design Techniques. Enables BPR Planning, Analysis, Design, Code Generation, Maintenance & Reverse Engineering.
Visible Systems Corp.

Visible Analyst Workbench: Educational Edition. *Version:* 5.3 Windows. Aug. 1994. *Items Included:* Textbook - Analysis & Design of Business Information Systems; Workbook - Introduction to Case.
MS-DOS & Windows. Windows compatible PC. disk $99.00 (Order no.: ED-1010). *Optimal configuration:* 1 floppy, 1 hard disk drive, printer, Pentium or 486-based system.
Step-by-Step Introduction to Building Real World Client/Server System with the Aid of a Case-Tool.
Visible Systems Corp.

VisiCalc. *Compatible Hardware:* Atari XL/XE.
disk $29.95 (Order no.: DX5049).
Spreadsheet.
Atari Corp.

VisiCalc. Paladin Software Corp. *Compatible Hardware:* HP Series 200 Models 216/220, 226/236.
HP 216/220. 3-1/2" or 5-1/4" disk $275.00 (Order no.: 98810A).
HP 226/236. 5-1/4" disk $275.00.
Hewlett-Packard Co.

VisiCalc Applications for Managerial & Cost Accounting. Sharon O'Reilly & Larry Armstrong. Apr. 1984. *Compatible Hardware:* Apple IIe, II+; IBM PC.
user's guide $12.95 (ISBN 0-03-071018-9).
disk $100.00, incl. manual (ISBN 0-03-071016-2).
Apple. disk $100.00, incl. manual (ISBN 0-03-071014-6).
Tutorial on VisiCalc & How to Apply the Spreadsheet in Solving Managerial & Cost Accounting Problems.
Dryden Pr.

VisiCalc PLUS. Paladin Software Corp. *Compatible Hardware:* HP 85 with ROM drawer (HP 82936A), plotter/printer ROM (HP 00085-15002), 16k memory module (HP 82903A), HP-IB interface (HP 82937A), plotter (HP 7225B with HP 17601A module, HP 9872C, or HP 7470A); HP 86/87 with 64k, ROM drawer, plotter/printer ROM, plotter.
HP 85. data cartridge, 3-1/2" or 5-1/4" disk $240.00 ea. (Order no.: 82800A).
HP 86/87. 3-1/2" or 5-1/4" disk $275.00 ea. (Order no.: 82830A).
The "PLUS" Is an Ability to Produce Line, Bar, & Pie Charts from Row & Column Information Without Entering New Data.
Hewlett-Packard Co.

Visionary Stampede: Dreams & Challenges of the '90s. Mar. 1995. *Items Included:* Includes tutorial of authoring program Apple Media Tool.
Macintosh 7.1 or higher. Macintosh (color) or Power PC (10Mb with Virtual Memory) (8Mb). CD-ROM disk $19.95 (ISBN 1-887107-01-0, Order no.: 01-0). *Optimal configuration:* 14" monitor, 256 color, double-speed CD-ROM drive.
Students from 9 High Schools Created & Produced Visionary Stampede, a Multimedia Magazine on CD-ROM That Explores Contemporary Issues of the '90s from the Viewpoint of Young Adults. It Demonstrates How Students Can Use Multimedia to Explore & Learn about a Variety of Subjects. Winner of a 1995 National Educational Media Award.
Opportune Pr.

Visionary Video. *Version:* 2.0. Jan. 1990. *Items Included:* spiral-bound manual. *Customer Support:* 30 day money back guarantee.
MS-DOS/PC-DOS. IBM & compatibles (512k). $350.00 (demo $15.00) (Order no.: VT-2).
Complete Software System for Managing a Video Rental Business. Includes Graphs, Password Security, Various Membership & Late Policies Plus Comprehensive Reports.
Visionary Technology.

Visions. *Customer Support:* All of our products are unconditionally guaranteed.
All Systems. CD-ROM disk $39.95 (Order no.: VISIONS). *Nonstandard peripherals required:* CD-ROM drive.
500 Royalty Free Photos in 640x480 & 600x800 GIF Formats.
Walnut Creek CDRom.

VisiSpell. VisiCorp. *Compatible Hardware:* TI Professional with Winchester second drive. *Operating System(s) Required:* MS-DOS. *Memory Required:* 128k.
$225.00 (Order no.: VC P/N 219495).
Texas Instruments, Personal Productivit.

Visitor Bureaus & Chambers of Commerce.
John Kremer. May 1995. *Customer Support:* Telephone support.
MS-DOS. IBM PC or compatible (256k). disk $29.95 (Order no.: 492). *Addl. software required:* Any database program.
Macintosh. 3.5" disk $29.95 (Order no.: 493). *Addl. software required:* Any database program.
This Computer Data File Lists the Addresses & Phone Numbers of More Than 4,450 Chambers of Commerce & Visitors Bureaus in the U.S., Canada & Foreign Countries. Use This List to Research Travel Books, to Target Potential Buyers for Your Books, & to Enhance the Value of Your Books by Providing a More Complete Resource Guide.
Open Horizons Publishing Co.

Vista. Oct. 1994. *Items Included:* Software Documentation/Owner Manual, Data Gathering Forms & Quick Reference Card. *Customer Support:* Customer Service is provided to all customers free of charge for 30 days after the purchase date. After that time, maintenance may be purchased at $150 per year.
Microsoft Windows. IBM & compatibles (4Mb). $695.00 Stand Alone Version (ISBN 0-943293-07-3). *Addl. software required:* Windows version 3.0 or higher. *Optimal configuration:* Mouse. *Networks supported:* Novell, Lantastic & Banyon.
Vista Is Designed to Allow Estate Planning Professionals to Demonstrate & Explain Estate Tax Planning Concepts & Approaches to Their Clients.
ViewPlan, Inc.

Vista Morph. 1991. *Items Included:* 1 manual. *Customer Support:* 90 days unlimited warranty; free telephone support.
DOS. IBM 386 25MHz & higher (4Mb). disk $69.95 (ISBN 1-886082-12-X, Order no.: VM-120). *Addl. software required:* Vista Pro. *Optimal configuration:* 8Mb.
Add on Program for Vista Pro Which Enables Animation of Any Object. Smoothly Transforms One Landscape Feature into Another Creating Stunning Results.
Virtual Reality Laboratories, Inc.

Vista Pro. *Version:* 3.0. 1990. *Items Included:* 1 manual. *Customer Support:* 90 days unlimited warranty; free telephone support.
DOS. IBM 386 & higher (4Mb). CD-ROM disk $129.95 (ISBN 1-886082-00-6, Order no.: VPD-102). *Optimal configuration:* 486 with 8Mb RAM. *Networks supported:* Not directly.
Windows. IBM 386 (4Mb). CD-ROM disk $129.95 (ISBN 1-886082-01-4, Order no.: VPW-150). *Optimal configuration:* 486, 8Mb RAM. *Networks supported:* Not directly.
DOS CD-ROM. IBM 386 (4Mb). CD-ROM disk $149.95 (ISBN 1-886082-02-2, Order no.: VPCD-402). *Optimal configuration:* 486, 8Mb. *Networks supported:* Not directly.
Windows CD-ROM. IBM 386 (4Mb). CD-ROM disk $149.95 (ISBN 1-886082-03-0, Order no.: VPWCD-155). *Optimal configuration:* 486, 8Mb RAM. *Networks supported:* Not directly.
System 7 & higher. MAC (4Mb). CD-ROM disk $149.95 (ISBN 1-886082-04-9, Order no.: VPMCD-180). *Optimal configuration:* 8Mb.
Power Mac. MAC Power PC (4Mb). CD-ROM disk $149.95 (ISBN 1-886082-05-7, Order no.: VPPMCD-185). *Optimal configuration:* 8Mb.
A Three Dimensional Landscape Simulation Program Which Enables the User to Accurately Recreate & Explore Landscapes on the Earth & Mars.
Virtual Reality Laboratories, Inc.

Visual Almanac Series.
Macintosh (4Mb). CD-ROM disk $69.90, Set (Order no.: R1106). *Nonstandard peripherals required:* 14" color monitor or larger, CD-ROM drive.
Two Volume Set.
Library Video Co.

Visual Aspects of the Moon. *Compatible Hardware:* TI 99/4A. *Operating System(s) Required:* DX-10. *Language(s):* Extended BASIC. *Memory Required:* 48k.
cassette $16.95.
Calculates the Moon's Age & Visibility, the Zodiac Constellation & the Fraction of the Moon Which Is Illuminated for Any Given Date. Also Computes Declination & Right Ascension.
Eastbench Software Products.

Visual Baler: Spreadsheet-Based Visual Development Tool. 1994. *Items Included:* All tools needed to create professional, stand-alone Windows programs. 500 pages of documentation. *Customer Support:* 90 days free support. Various paid support plans via CompuServe, fax & mail.
Microsoft Windows 3.1. 386 or higher (4Mb). disk $499.00 (Order no.: NEW). *Optimal configuration:* 486 with 4 Mb RAM & Windows 3.1. *Networks supported:* Novell.
First Spreadsheet-Based Development Tool for Building Stand-Alone, Professional Microsoft Windows Applications. No Programming Experience Is Required to Create Royalty-Free Windows Programs That May Be Distributed to Any Number of Users. Includes 3-D Spreadsheet Editor, Visual Interface Editor, Debugger, & On-Line Documentation.
Baler Software Inc.

Visual Basic Programming with Windows Applications. Douglas A. Hergert. *Items Included:* One 5.25" disk. *Customer Support:* Phone number available for technical support, 212-492-9832; free disk replacement within 90 days of purchase.
IBM PC & compatibles. disk $44.95 (ISBN 0-553-35317-9). *Addl. software required:* Visual Basic.
This Book/Disk Package Is a Hands-On Guide to Building Windows Applications with Microsoft's New Visual Basic, the First Object-Oriented Basic Programming Language for the Windows Environment. Provides Power-User Tips, Techniques to Increase Productivity. Includes over 100 Subroutines & Programming Tools for Visual Basic Programmers. Hergert Is a Bestselling Author & Basic Expert.
Bantam Bks., Inc.

Visual FX. *Version:* 2.0. Feb. 1994. *Customer Support:* First two hours of telephone technical support free, $75 per hour thereafter. 30 day money back guarantee.
Windows. 386. $199.00 application version. Commercial License available. *Optimal configuration:* MMPC. *Networks supported:* Yes.
Transitions Effect Library for Microsoft Windows Programmers. Over 100 Special Effects with Variations on Each to Choose from Like Explode, Slide, Puzzle, Grow, & Mosaic Can Add Value & Pizazz to Any Windows Application. Images Can Also Follow User Definable Paths. Transparency Is Supported for All Display Adapters & Display Modes. The Library Is Easy to Use with Visual C Plus Plus, Visual Basic, Borland Pascal or Any Language That Supports Windows DLLs. Available Through Royalty Free Dynamic Link Libraries (DLLs) & Supports Any Display Environment Available in Windows. You Can Replace Existing BitBlt Function Calls with BitBltFX. Extended Parameters Let You Select the Special Effect, Unlimited Grains, Speeds, & Paths. It Also Comes with Higher Level Functions to Load & Display DIBs, BMBs & WMF Files with the Special Effects.
Instant Replay Corp.

Visual MATRIX. *Version:* 2.0. Christopher A. Lane. 1995. *Items Included:* Complete end user & technical user system manual. *Customer Support:* Full service technological & hotline support available.
Windows 3.1x, Windows 95, Windows NT, OS/2, Unix. IBM PC & compatibles. contact publisher for price. *Networks supported:* Novell.
Features Include Lead Tracking, Forecasting, Sales Funneling, Sales Cycle Analysis, Data Distribution/Communications, & Contact, Opportunity, & Pipeline Management. Supports SPIN, Strategic Selling, & Other Sales Process Models & Virtually Any Database: xBASE, SQL Server, Oracle, DB2, Sybase, etc.
Market Power, Inc.

The Visual Plough. Roy Buck. 1990.
DOS. Any type of IBM (64k). $5.95 (ISBN 1-56178-005-7).
MAC. Any type of Macintosh (64k). $5.95 (ISBN 1-56178-022-7).
Anthology of "Visual" Poetry: Poems Whose Words Literally Form Visual Images.
Connected Editions, Inc.

Visual Statics. *Compatible Hardware:* IBM PC, Macintosh. *Language(s):* BASIC.
disk $120.00 ea. incl. bk.
IBM. (Order no.: 402-IK).
Z-100. (Order no.: 402-ZK).
Apple. (Order no.: 402-AK).
Graphically Illustrates Concepts in Mechanics. Intended to Be Used for Independent Study of Mechanics or As a Complement to a College Level Course in Statics. Emphasis Is on Concepts of Forces, Force Resultants, Particle Equilibrium, Moment of a Force about an Axis, Reduction of Forces to a Force & Moment, Rigid Body Equilibrium, Analysis of Trusses, Beams & Cables, & Friction.
Kern International, Inc.

Visual Stress & Strain. B. J. Korites & M. Novack. *Compatible Hardware:* Apple II, Macintosh; IBM PC. *Operating System(s) Required:* Apple DOS 3.3, Macintosh, PC-DOS 2.0 or higher. *Language(s):* BASIC (source code included).
disk $110.00 incl. bk.
IBM. (Order no.: 401-IK).
Z-100. (Order no.: 401-ZK).
Apple. (Order no.: 401-AK).
Solves Two- & Three-Dimensional Combined Stress Problems. Emphasis Is on Graphical Display of Elements & Stresses.
Kern International, Inc.

Visual Vibrations. 1985. *Compatible Hardware:* Apple, Macintosh; IBM PC. *Operating System(s) Required:* Apple DOS 3.3, Macintosh, PC-DOS 2.0. *Language(s):* BASIC (source code included).
disk $110.00, incl. bk. (Order no.: 405-IK).
Apple. (Order no.: 405-AK).
IBM.
Macintosh. (Order no.: 405-MK).
Collection of Programs That Solve Problems Associated with the Motion of a One- & Two-Degree-of-Freedom Damped Oscillator. Topics Covered Include Response to Applied Harmonic Force, Harmonic Foundation Motion, Impulse Loading & Step Loading, Damping Factor, Time Constant, Natural Frequency, Response Spectra, Log Plots & Other Quantities Associated with the Motion of Harmonic Oscillators.
Kern International, Inc.

Visualizer IIe. *Version:* 1.2. *Compatible Hardware:* Apple IIe, IIc. *Operating System(s) Required:* ProDOS. *Memory Required:* 128k.
Apple IIe, IIc. disk $89.95.
IIgs. disk $99.95.
Business Graphics Program Which Produces Line, Bar, Stacked-Bar, & Pie Charts from APPLEWORKS Files, or from Data Entered Directly by the User. Upgrade of GRAPHWORKS.
PBI Software, Inc.

VisualSMITH. Robert Abernethy & Wes Fulton. Jul. 1994. *Customer Support:* 30 days money-back guarantee.
MS-DOS. IBM (512k). disk $200.00 (Order no.: S104). *Optimal configuration:* 5Mb storage space required on hard disk.
This Program Provides Scientific Plotting Capability with Functions, Curve-Fitting, & Transforms. Also Includes Bar Graphs & Pie Charts. User Can Import Data from WeibullSMITH Files & Plot the PDF or Liklihood Contours, or Create/Display Histograms.
Gulf Publishing Co.

VisualSmith: Scientific Plotting. 1995. *Items Included:* Full manual. *Customer Support:* Free telephone support - 90 days, 30-day warranty.
MS-DOS 3.2 or higher. 286 (584k). disk $199.95. *Nonstandard peripherals required:* CGA/EGA/VGA.
Provides Scientific Plotting Capability with Functions, Curve Fitting (Including DUANE), & Transforms. It Includes Bar Graphs & Pie Charts. You Can Import Data from WeibullSMITH Files & Plot the PDF or Liklihood Contours or Create/Display Histograms.
Dynacomp, Inc.

Vital Signs. Michael P. Hansen. Jan. 1985. *Compatible Hardware:* Apple. *Memory Required:* 64k.
contact publisher for price (ISBN 0-931261-01-5).
Assists Students in Understanding the Concepts of Temperature, Pulse, Respiration, & Blood Pressure. Also Assists in Teaching Proper Methods of Taking These Readings.
Concord Regional Vocational Ctr.

Vitamin C. *Version:* IBM DOS 4.0; Unix, VMS, Xenix 1.61. *Compatible Hardware:* IBM PC, PC XT, PC AT & compatibles, OS/2. *Operating System(s) Required:* PC-DOS/MS-DOS, UNIX, VMS, XENIX. *Language(s):* C (source code included). *Items Included:* Libraries, tutorial, reference manual, demo, sample & example programs. *Customer Support:* Included with proper registration of product.
disk $395.00, DOS 4.0.
disk $495.00, OS/2 4.0.
disk $995.00, Unix/Xenix.
disk $1995.00, VMS 1.61.
Enables Users to Create Windows. Options Include: Titles, Borders, Colors, Pop-Up, Pull-Down, Zoom-In, Scroll Bars, Sizes up to 32k, etc; Windows May Be Moved & Resized at Run-Time. Data Entry Features Include: Protected, Invisible, Required, & Scrolling Fields; Picture Clause Formatting; Full Color/Attribute Control; Selection Sets; Single Field & Full-Screen Input; & Unlimited Animation Via Standard & User-Definable Routines. The Standard Help Handler Provides Context-Sensitive Pop-Up Help Messages. Other Features Include Multi-Level Macintosh- & Lotus-Like Menus & Text Editor Windows That Can Be Opened for Pop-Up Note Pads & General Purpose Editing.
Creative Programming.

Vitsie Visits Dinosaurs. (Vitsie Visits Ser.).
MS-DOS 5.0 or higher, Windows 3.1 or higher. 386 processor or higher (4Mb). CD-ROM disk $39.95 (Order no.: R1150). *Nonstandard peripherals required:* CD-ROM drive. *Optimal configuration:* 386 processor operating at 16Mhz or higher, MS-DOS 5.0 or higher, Windows 3.1 or higher, 30Mb hard drive, mouse, VGA graphic adapter & VGA color monitor (SVGA recommended), 4Mb RAM, external speakers or headphones (with sound card) that are Sound Blaster compatible.
Macintosh (4Mb). (Order no.: R1150). *Nonstandard peripherals required:* 14" color monitor or larger, CD-ROM drive.
Children Can Travel Back in Time to Visit Dinosaurs, Travel Through Outer Space or Go on an Underwater Adventure. Each Program Contains Video, Songs, Ideas, Games & Activities That Educate Children As Well As Encourage Creativity & Curiosity (Ages 3-8).
Library Video Co.

Vitsie Visits Series.
MS-DOS 5.0 or higher, Windows 3.1 or higher. 386 processor or higher (4Mb). CD-ROM disk $119.85, Set (Order no.: R1366). *Nonstandard peripherals required:* CD-ROM drive. *Optimal configuration:* 386 processor operating at 16Mhz or higher, MS-DOS 5.0 or higher, Windows 3.1 or higher, 30Mb hard drive, mouse, VGA graphic adapter & VGA color monitor (SVGA recommended), 4Mb RAM, external speakers or headphones (with sound card) that are Sound Blaster compatible.
Macintosh (4Mb). (Order no.: R1366). *Nonstandard peripherals required:* 14" color monitor or larger, CD-ROM drive.
Children Can Travel Back in Time to Visit Dinosaurs, Travel Through Outer Space or Go on an Underwater Adventure. Each Program Contains Video, Songs, Ideas, Games & Activities That Educate Children As Well As Encourage Creativity & Curiosity (Ages 3-8).
Library Video Co.

Vitsie Visits Space. (Vitsie Visits Ser.).
MS-DOS 5.0 or higher, Windows 3.1 or higher. 386 processor or higher (4Mb). CD-ROM disk $39.95 (Order no.: R1369). *Nonstandard peripherals required:* CD-ROM drive. *Optimal configuration:* 386 processor operating at 16Mhz or higher, MS-DOS 5.0 or higher, Windows 3.1 or higher, 30Mb hard drive, mouse, VGA graphic adapter & VGA color monitor (SVGA recommended), 4Mb RAM, external speakers or headphones (with sound card) that are Sound Blaster compatible.
Macintosh (4Mb). (Order no.: R1369). *Nonstandard peripherals required:* 14" color monitor or larger, CD-ROM drive.

Children Can Travel Back in Time to Visit Dinosaurs, Travel Through Outer Space or Go on an Underwater Adventure. Each Program Contains Video, Songs, Ideas, Games & Activities That Educate Children As Well As Encourage Creativity & Curiosity (Ages 3-8).
Library Video Co.

Vitsie Visits the Ocean. (Vitsie Visits Ser.). MS-DOS 5.0 or higher, Windows 3.1 or higher. 386 processor or higher (4Mb). CD-ROM disk $39.95 (Order no.: R1368). *Nonstandard peripherals required:* CD-ROM drive. *Optimal configuration:* 386 processor operating at 16Mhz or higher, MS-DOS 5.0 or higher, Windows 3.1 or higher, 30Mb hard drive, mouse, VGA graphic adapter & VGA color monitor (SVGA recommended), 4Mb RAM, external speakers or headphones (with sound card) that are Sound Blaster compatible. Macintosh (4Mb). (Order no.: R1368).
Nonstandard peripherals required: 14" color monitor or larger, CD-ROM drive.
Children Can Travel Back in Time to Visit Dinosaurs, Travel Through Outer Space or Go on an Underwater Adventure. Each Program Contains Video, Songs, Ideas, Games & Activities That Educate Children As Well As Encourage Creativity & Curiosity (Ages 3-8).
Library Video Co.

Vivaldi the Four Seasons. Feb. 1995. *Items Included:* CD-ROM booklet. *Customer Support:* Free technical support via phone as of release date.
MPC/Windows. 386.25 or higher IBM compatible (4Mb). CD-ROM disk $24.95 (ISBN 1-885784-18-X, Order no.: 1240). *Optimal configuration:* MPC CD-ROM player, S-VGA graphics card (640x480x256 colors) with compatible monitor, MPC compliant sound card, mouse, Windows 3.1.
Immerse Yourself in the Seasons of Nature Through Vivaldi's Musical Interpretation. With Full Color Scenes from Winter, Spring, Summer & Fall, The Four Seasons Concertos Are Presented in Illustrative, Interpretive, Informative & Thematic Styles. Explore the Music, the Instruments, the Works, & the Man Who Was Inspired to Create Them.
Technology Dynamics Corp.

Vivaldi: The Four Seasons (Jewel). *Items Included:* CD-ROM booklet. *Customer Support:* Free technical support via phone as of release date.
MPC/Windows. 386MHz or higher (4Mb). CD-ROM disk $24.95 (ISBN 1-885784-69-4, Order no.: 1243). *Optimal configuration:* MPC CD-ROM player, S-VGA graphics card (640x480x256 colors) with compatible monitor, MPC compliant sound card, mouse, Windows 3.1 higher, Windows 95 compatible.
Immerse Yourself in the Seasons of Nature Through Vivaldi's Musical Interpretation. With Full Color Scenes from Winter, Spring, Summer & Fall, "The Four Seasons" Concertos Are Presented in Illustrative, Interpretive, Informative & Thematic Styles. Explore the Music, the Instruments, the Works & the Man Who Was Inspired to Create Them.
Technology Dynamics Corp.

Vizawrite for the Amiga. Version: 1.09. 1987. *Compatible Hardware:* Commodore Amiga 500, 1000, 2000. *Memory Required:* 512k.
3.5" disk $79.95.
Word Processor Featuring WYSIWYG Display. IFF Pictures & Brushes Can Be Inserted & Resized Anywhere in the Document.
Progressive Peripherals & Software, Inc.

Vizawrite PC. 1987. *Compatible Hardware:* IBM PC. *Memory Required:* 256k.
disk $49.95.
Word Processor Which Allows Users to Edit Several Documents at a Time. Features Drop-Down Menus & Function Key Commands. Includes a Spelling Checker. Supports Mail-Merge Functions. Not Copy Protected.
Progressive Peripherals & Software, Inc.

Vmail. *Version:* 1.8. *Items Included:* 1 Vmail reference manual, Install Guide. *Customer Support:* 30-day money-back guarantee; free customer service & updates for 60 days; Annual maintenance plans available.
Unix, Xenix, Ultrix. contact publisher for price.
Electronic Mail for DEC VMS Users Moving to UNIX.
Boston Business Computing, Ltd.

VMD: Shear/Moment/Deflection. Micro Computations, Inc. Jan. 1986. *Compatible Hardware:* IBM PC & compatibles. *Operating System(s) Required:* MS-DOS. *Language(s):* BASIC. *Memory Required:* 256k.
disk $350.00, incl. demo & user's manual.
Analyzes Shears, Moments, & Deflections in Multiple Span Systems. Accounts for Loads over Supports, Downward Settlement of Supports, Fixed Ends of Spans, & User-Specified End-Shears & End-Moments. Allows User-Specified Moment of Inertia, Modulus of Elasticity, & Multiple Uniform, Concentrated, & Triangular Loads for Each Span, & Calculates Reaction on Each Span, Shear, & Moment at Each Support, As Well As Maximum Positive Moment & Maximum Deflection on Each Span. Plots Shear, Moment, & Deflections Across Spans.
Computing Power Applied.

VMMS. *Customer Support:* 800-929-8117 (customer service).
MS-DOS. IBM/PS2. disk $499.99 (ISBN 0-87007-620-5).
Vehicle Maintenance Management System (VMMS) Provides the Operator of a Vehicle Fleet with a Convenient Way to Enter, Record, Review, Edit & Print Information about Vehicle Maintenance Costs. With MS/DOS-Compatible (Hard Disk Preferred), User Can Keep Tabs on up to 9,999 Vehicles.
SourceView Software International.

VMRS Plus. Jun. 1986. *Compatible Hardware:* IBM PC XT, PC AT, PS/2. *Operating System(s) Required:* PC-DOS 3.3. (source code included). *Memory Required:* 320k. *General Requirements:* Hard disk, printer.
$1000.00.
Designed to Control Fleet Costs. This Is Accomplished by Providing On-Line Information on Efficiency of Vehicle Performance. Major Reporting Categories Include: Vehicle/Equipment, Parts Inventory, Preventive Maintenance Scheduling, Mechanic Statistics, Repair Order, System Performance Statistics, Fuel & Mileage Reporting.
Comsen Services, Inc.

VO-AG & FFA SOE Placement & Agribusiness Record. Gary Sande. 1985. *Compatible Hardware:* Apple II series, IBM PC & compatibles. *Operating System(s) Required:* Apple DOS 3.3, PC-DOS 2.0 or higher. *Memory Required:* Apple 48k, IBM 128k. *General Requirements:* 2 disk drives, printer.
Apple. disk $74.50 (ISBN 1-55797-186-2, Order no.: AP2-AG523).
IBM. disk $74.50 (ISBN 1-55797-187-0, Order no.: IBM-AG523).
Menu-Driven Program Which Allows FFA Members & VOAG Students to Maintain an Ongoing Record of Their Placement &
Agribusiness Ownership Enterprises. *The Program Is Designed to Be Used by Students on a Month-to-Month Basis. The Programs Save the Data for Four Years of Records on One Data Disk. One Disk (Copyable) Is Required for Each Area (Placement/Ownership). Students Create Disks As Needed.*
Hobar Pubns.

Vocabulary Booster: Middle School. Softwright.
IBM. disk $29.99 (Order no.: 1146).
disk $39.99, incl. backup disk (Order no.: 1146B).
Apple II. 3.5" disk $29.99 (Order no.: 1073).
3.5" disk $39.99, incl. backup disk (Order no.: 1073B).
Designed to Boost the Vocabulary & Word Usage Skills of Intermediate/Secondary Students. Useful for English & Foreign Languages. The Instructor Enters Sets of Nouns, Adverbs, Adjectives, & Verbs. The Students Are Challenged to Make Sentences from a Mixture of Words from Each Category. Level & Content Are Entirely Controlled by the Teacher. Can Be "Customized" for Slow, Average, or Bright Children. Fun for Learning the Specialized Vocabulary of Subjects Such As Biology, History, Earth Science, etc. Results of Student Built Sentences Are Frequently Hilarious. Much Loved by Students. An Eagerly Used Learning Tool That Can Be Constantly Renewed by Simply Changing Its Content.
Trillium Pr.

The Vocational Interest Inventory-Revised (VII-R). Patricia W. Lunneburg. *Customer Support:* Free unlimited phone support.
DOS 3.0 or higher. 286 or higher (512k). disk $150.00 (Order no.: W-1023). *Nonstandard peripherals required:* Printer.
Measures Students' Relative Interest in Roe's Eight Occupational Areas (Service, Buyness Contract, Organization, Technical, Outdoor, Science, General Culture, & Arts & Entertainment) Which Essentially Classify All Jobs.
Western Psychological Services.

Vocational Math Series: Prevocational Math Review. 1992. *Items Included:* Detailed manuals included with all Dynacomp products. *Customer Support:* Free telephone support to original customer - no time limit; 30 day limited warranty.
MS-DOS 3.2 or higher. IBM PC & compatibles, Apple (512k). $89.95 (Add $5.00 for 3 1/2" format; 5 1/4" format standard).
A Diagnostic & Teaching Program Consisting of 200 Arithmetic Problems Organized in Sets of 10 Problems in a Multiple-Choice Format. The Problems Cover Addition, Subtraction, Multiplication, & Division of Whole Numbers, Fractions, Decimals, & Percentages. Student Score for Each of the Sets Establishes a Profile of the Student's Skills & Weaknesses. Second Part of the Program Consists of Tutorials for Each of the Sets.
Dynacomp, Inc.

Vocational Math Series: Prevocational Math Review. 1995. *Items Included:* Full manual. *Customer Support:* Free telephone support - 90 days, 30-day warranty.
MS-DOS 3.2 or higher. 286 (584k). disk $119.95. *Nonstandard peripherals required:* CGA/EGA/VGA.
VMS:PMR Is a Diagnostic & Teaching Program Consisting of 200 Arithmetic Problems Organized in Sets of 10 Problems in a Multiple-Choice Format. The Problems Cover Addition, Subtraction, Multiplication, & Division of Whole Numbers, Fractions, Decimals, & Percentages. The Introduction Explains the Purpose of the Program & Gives Clear Instructions for Problems. Student Score for Each of the Sets Establishes a Profile of the Student's Skills & Weaknesses.
Dynacomp, Inc.

TITLE INDEX

Volcanoes: Life on the Edge. 1996. *Items Included:* Manual, registration card. *Customer Support:* Phone technical & customer support Mon-Fri 9:00-5:00 PST. Email & Web-site support.
Microsoft Windows 3.1, Windows 95. Multimedia PC with 486/33 or higher (8Mb). CD-ROM disk $45.00-$55.00 (ISBN 1-886802-04-1). *Nonstandard peripherals required:* 256-color Super VGA display, double-speed CD-ROM drive, 8-bit Windows-compatible sound card & speakers, mouse.
System 7.1. Macintosh 25MHz 68030 or higher (LCIII, IIVX, Centris, Quadra, performa, or higher) (8Mb, 12Mb for Power Mac). CD-ROM disk $45.00-$55.00 (ISBN 1-886802-05-X). *Nonstandard peripherals required:* Double-speed CD-ROM drive, 13" monitor or higher, 256 colors.
Fiery Explosions, Red-Hot Lava, Supernatural Power, Phenomenal Beauty - These Are the Seductive Lures That Draw Us to Volcanoes. Experience These Spectacular Wonders in an Engrossing CD-ROM That Explores Volcanoes Past & Present. Journey with Renowned Photojournalist Roger Ressmeyer As He Travels Worldwide During the Most Volcanically Active Period of the Century.
Continuum Productions.

Volcanoes Deluxe. *Version:* 1.2. 1988. *Items Included:* Manual, maps. *Customer Support:* After 90 days, new disk $10; rewrite $5.
Apple DOS 3.1. Apple IIgs (1.2Mb). disk $59.95 (ISBN 0-917979-12-5). *Optimal configuration:* Apple IIgs, mouse, color (RGB) monitor.
PC/MS-DOS. IBM PC & compatibles (640K). 3.5" or 5.25" disk $59.95 (ISBN 0-917979-09-5). *Optimal configuration:* 640K-monitor, VGA, CGA, etc, hard drive configurable.
This Program is a Simulation of Vulcanism in Game Format for 4 or 4 Teams of Players. Players Predict Eruptions of Volcanoes by Using Current Scientific Methods & Set Learning Levels. According to Accuracy of Predictions Players Win or Lose Game.
Earthware Computer Services.

Volleyball Statistics Program. *Version:* 95-1. Aug. 1995. *Items Included:* Users manual. *Customer Support:* 30 day money back guarantee, free phone support.
MS-DOS, Macintosh (512k). IBM & compatibles, Macintosh. $59.95 (ISBN 0-922526-38-9). *Nonstandard peripherals required:* 1 HD disk drive, dot matrix printer capable of compressed print.
Keeps Individual Player & Team Statistics for a Vollyball Team of 30 Players. Keeps Stats for Current Match, Season, & Conference. Prints Seventeen Reports Including Current Match Totals, Season Totals, per Match Averages, Serve Placement Diagrams, Attack Position Diagrams.
Big G Software.

Voltage Drop Calculations: VDROP. *Version:* 2.05. Jan. 1988. *Compatible Hardware:* IBM PC, PC XT, PC AT & compatibles. *Memory Required:* 256k.
3.5" or 5.25" disk $295.00.
Elite Software Development, Inc.

Voltage Plotter III. David L. Vernier. *Compatible Hardware:* Apple II+, IIe, IIc, IIgs. *Operating System(s) Required:* Apple ProDOS. *Language(s):* Applesoft BASIC, Machine (source code included). *Memory Required:* 64k. *General Requirements:* Voltage Input Unit or Advanced Interfacing Board avail. from Vernier Software.
disk $39.95 (ISBN 0-918731-15-1).
Allows the Apple to Be Used As a General Purpose Voltmeter, Chart Recorder, or Oscilloscope. The Accompanying Manual Describes Additional Circuits Which Allow Monitoring of pH, Force (with Strain Gauges) & Temperature (with Thermocouples). Works with Either Vernier's Voltage Input Unit ($40.00 Assembled or $30.00 Parts Kit) or Vernier's 12-Bit Advanced Interfacing Board ($225.00).
Vernier Software.

VOLUME. *Version:* 2.1. Mar. 1986. *Compatible Hardware:* IBM PC, PC XT, PC AT & compatibles. *Operating System(s) Required:* PC-DOS, MS-DOS. *Language(s):* FORTRAN. *Memory Required:* 512k. *General Requirements:* Printer.
contact publisher for price (Order no.: VOLUME).
Compares the Two Gridded Files & Calculates the Difference Between Them in Three Dimensions. The Output Can Be Reported in Bank Cubic Yards of Cut & or on a Block Map in Linear Feet. An Output File for a Dot Matrix Printer Is Also Generated, to Show Land Features, Cross Sections & Haul Distances.
Geostat Systems International, Inc. (GSII).

Volume Discount. *Version:* 8B. Sep. 1993. *Compatible Hardware:* PC-DOS, Xenix, Unix; 3COM & Novell. *Language(s):* COBOL 85. *Memory Required:* 512-3000k. *General Requirements:* Integrated Accounting & the Distributing module. *Customer Support:* Included with the support for the Integrated Accounting. 495.00-620.00.
Provides the Ability to Give Discounts Based on Quantity or Dollar Volume Purchased. Can Be Used As a Separate Method or in Conjunction with Distributing's Other Pricing Methods. eg: Gives Discounts to Customers Based on Quantity or Dollar Breakpoints for an Item or Group of Items; Can Assign Discounts for All Product Classes, Individual Product Classes, All Commodity Codes, Individual Commodity Codes etc. Can Assign up to 5 Discount Categories per Customer.
Trac Line Software, Inc.

VOLUMETRICS. *Version:* 2.1. Mar. 1986. *Compatible Hardware:* IBM PC, PC XT, PC AT & compatibles. *Language(s):* FORTRAN, BASIC. *Memory Required:* 512k. *General Requirements:* Printer, digitizer.
disk $3500.00 (Order no.: VOLUMETRICS).
Will Calculate the Volume of Cuts & Fills, Eliminating the Costly Guesswork of Manually Estimating Non-Rectangular Fills & Cuts. Using the Digitized Point Files of the Current & Proposed Topography, Volume Will Calculate the Difference Between the Two. Data Screening in Specific Areas & Three Dimensional Views of Both Topographies Are Available.
Geostat Systems International, Inc. (GSII).

Voodoo Castle. *Compatible Hardware:* TI 99/4A.
contact publisher for price.
Texas Instruments, Personal Productivit.

Voter Lists. *Compatible Hardware:* IBM PC, PC XT, PC AT or compatibles, Macintosh. *Language(s):* Machine. *Memory Required:* 640k. *General Requirements:* Printer; hard disk recommended. *Customer Support:* 24 hours/day toll free.
$500.00, incl. instr. manual.
Database Containing Name, Address & Phone Number of Every Registered Voter in the United States. Ideal for Mailings, Selecting Public Opinion Samples & Voters Registration.
Aristotle Industries.

THE VOYAGER CD AUDIOSTACK

Voter Lists on Compact Disc. Jan. 1996. *Items Included:* Documentation & media. *Customer Support:* Telephone 24 hours toll free.
MS-DOS, Windows. IBM PC (640k). disk $500.00. *Nonstandard peripherals required:* CD ROM Drive. *Networks supported:* Novell, 3-COMM.
A Current Listing of Every Registered Voter in the United States. Telephone Number, Parts Affiliations & Family Members Names Have Been Added. Includes Software to Search, Select Votes & Output Labels, Letters or Lists.
Aristotle Industries.

Voter IV. William R. Sipes. *Compatible Hardware:* IBM PC AT. *Operating System(s) Required:* PC-DOS 3.X. *Memory Required:* 512k. *General Requirements:* Wide-carriage printer.
disk $10,000.00.
Functions Provided Include: Geographical Location System, Redistricting, Absentee Ballot, Petition Check, Printing of Ballot Listings by Precinct, Registration Records, On-Line Review of Voter Records, Record Verification & Error Trapping, Multiple Sort Lists of Voter Records, Alphabetical Listings of up to 4 Items of Information from the Voter Record in Addition to Name & Address, Candidate Walk List, Polling Place Registers, Pre-Printed Mailing Labels, Automatic Printing of Cancellation Listings of Voters Who Have Not Voted or Registered Since Last General Election, etc.
Diversified Computing.

VOX: VAX Office Exchange. C. Harris et al. Jan. 1984. *Compatible Hardware:* VAX/II. *Operating System(s) Required:* VMS. *Language(s):* BASIC, Assembly. *Memory Required:* 62k.
magnetic tape $2,000.00-$13,000.00.
Complete Office Automation System That Includes Word Processing, Spreadsheet, Electronic Mail & Other Features.
Aquidneck Data Corp.

Voyager. *Version:* 3.51. *Customer Support:* 90 days free support, then $150.00 per year. 24 hour bulletin board system.
$199.00.
Complete Modem Communications Package. Includes Script Language, File Transfer, Terminal Emulation, & Dialing Directory. File Transfer Protocols Include X MODEM, Y MODEM, Z MODEM, Kermit, & Compuserve-B. Terminal Emulations Provided Include ADDS-A1, ADDS Viewpoint/60, ADM-3A, ANSI.SYS, IBM-3101, QUME QVT102, Televideo- 925, VIDTEXT (Compuserve), DEC VT-100, DECVT-52, Wyse 50, & Zenith Z-19. Detached (Background) Mode Available in Multiuser DOS & REAL/32 Version.
Logan Industries, Inc.

The Voyager CD AudioStack. *General Requirements:* Hard disk drive; CD-ROM drive; HyperCard. *Items Included:* 1 floppy disk, 1 CD audio disc, instruction booklet. *Customer Support:* M-F 9 AM- 5 PM Pacific Time (213) 451-1383.
Macintosh Plus, SE, II or Portable (1 Mb). 3.5" disk $99.95. *Nonstandard peripherals required:* Macintosh-compatible CD-ROM Drive, speakers or headphones with hard disk. *Addl. software required:* Hypercard 1.2.2 or higher, or SuperCard 1.0 or higher.
A Tool Kit for Using HyperCard with CD Audio Discs. Users Can Create Entertaining & Instructional HyperCard Stacks That Incorporate the Musical or Spoken Information Recorded on a CD. The Tool Kit's Main Element, the Audio Event Maker, Permits User to Define Audio Events, Create Buttons for the Events & Organize & Play Back Audio Events in Sequence; Also Includes Scripts, Sample Buttons, Online Manual of Audio Syntax & with the XCMDs & XFCNs necessary to Control the CD-ROM Drive.
The Voyager Co.

Voyager, the Interactive Desktop Planetarium. Version: 1.2. General Requirements: 800k disk drive.
Macintosh Plus or higher (1MB). 3.5" disk $124.50.
Astronomy Program.
Carina Software Systems.

The Voyager VideoStack. Version: 1.5. *Compatible Hardware:* Apple Macintosh Plus. *Memory Required:* 512k. *General Requirements:* HyperCard.
3.5" disk $99.95.
Designed for Developing Interactive Videodisc Applications with HYPERCARD. Features Include: Customization of More Than 35 Control Buttons; the Ability to Define Events & Then Make Buttons to Activate Those Events; Slide Tray to Load Still Frames & Play Them Back Manually or Automatically; & Automatic Installation of Video Drivers into Any HYPERCARD Stack.
The Voyager Co.

Vp ULTRA. Version: 1.0. *Compatible Hardware:* IBM PC & compatibles. *Memory Required:* 512k. *Items Included:* User's manual, registration card. *Customer Support:* Unlimited to registered users.
disk $169.00. *Addl. software required:* Ventura Publishing 2.0 Plus.
Stand-Alone Program. Add-On Utility for Ventura Publishing Document File Management & Style-Sheet Documentations.
SNA, Inc.

VP/WORKS for GEM PostScript. Version: 1.1. Jul. 1991. *Items Included:* 48 page manual; 3.5" & 5.25" disks; support for use under Windows 3.0 & 3.1. *Customer Support:* 30 day guarantee; 90 day media warranty; unlimited technical support.
MS-DOS/PC-DOS. IBM PC or compatible (128k). $99.00 volume discounts available (ISBN 1-879142-00-7). *Nonstandard peripherals required:* PostScript printer or interpreter. *Addl. software required:* GEM (GUI) based desktop publishing system. Ventura Publisher recommended. *Optimal configuration:* 286/386 PC with Ventura Publisher (GEM) 3.0 & PostScript printer.
Modifies PostScript Print Files Produced by GEM Desktop Publishing Programs to Provide Additional Print Options Including Two-Up, Facing-Pages, Page Scaling, Page Extraction, & Signature Construction for Saddle-Stitch or Case Binding. Also Eases Duplex Printing & Produces a Font Usage Summary.
Elirion, Inc.

VroomBooks Four Footed Friends. Dec. 1995. *Customer Support:* Telephone support - free (except phone charge).
Windows 3.1. IBM & compatibles (386 DX-20) (4Mb). CD-ROM disk $12.99, Jewel (ISBN 1-57594-081-7). *Nonstandard peripherals required:* 2X CD ROM player, sound card, VGA monitor. *Optimal configuration:* 486 SX-33.
CD-ROM disk $12.99, Blister.
Show Your Child the Wonder of Books, Words, Facts & Pictures Using the Activator. Take Your Child Beyond the Ordinary Book & Make Four Footed Friends Come Alive with Facts, 3D Animator, & Fun Learning Games in Four Different Languages.
Kidsoft, Inc.

VroomBooks: Four Footed Friends. Jan. 1996. *Customer Support:* Telephone support - free (except phone charge).
System 6.0.7 or higher. 256 color capable Macintosh (4Mb). CD-ROM disk $12.99 (ISBN 1-57594-105-8). *Nonstandard peripherals required:* 2X CD ROM drive, 640/480 resolution monitor.
Show Your Child the Wonder of Books, Words, Facts, & Pictures Using the Activator. Take Your Child Beyond the Ordinary Book & Make Four Footed Friends Come Alive with Facts, 3D Animations, & Fun Learning Games in Four Different Languages.
Kidsoft, Inc.

Vroombooks: Four Footed Friends. Feb. 1996. *Customer Support:* Telephone support - free (except phone charge).
Windows 3.1. IBM compatible 386 DX-20 (4Mb). CD-ROM disk $12.99 (ISBN 1-57594-094-9). *Nonstandard peripherals required:* 2x CD-ROM, sound card, VGA monitor. *Optimal configuration:* 486, SX-33.
Use the Activator to Learn the Wonder of Books, Words, Facts, & Pictures. Four Different Languages. Blister Pack.
Kidsoft, Inc.

VroomBooks Four Footed Friends. Dec. 1995. *Customer Support:* Telephone support - free (except phone charge).
Windows 3.1. IBM & compatibles (386 DX-20) (4Mb). CD-ROM disk $12.99 (ISBN 1-57594-081-7). *Nonstandard peripherals required:* 2X CD-ROM player, sound card, VGA monitor. *Optimal configuration:* 486 SX-33.
Show Your Child the Wonder of Books, Words, Facts & Pictures Using the Activator. Take Your Child Beyond the Ordinary Book & Make Four Footed Friends Come Alive with Facts, 3D Animation, & Fun Learning Games in Four Different Languages. Jewel Case.
Kidsoft, Inc.

VroomBooks' Four Footed Friends. *Items Included:* Parent's Guide, 4 Language User's Guide. *Customer Support:* Free & unlimited technical support to registered users; 60 day money-back guarantee.
Macintosh. Macintosh, System 6.0.7 or higher (4Mb). $49.95 CDROM. *Nonstandard peripherals required:* CDROM drive, color monitor.
Windows V.3.1 or higher. IBM PC & compatibles, 486, pentium or higher (4Mb, 8Mb rec). $49.95 CDROM. *Nonstandard peripherals required:* CDROM drive, Sound Blaster or compatible sound card, mouse, 256 VGA/SVGA color monitor.
An Interactive, Animated, Multimedia Storybook with Activities for Children Aged 3 & Up. Taken from an Enchanting Children's Book of Verse with Engaging Animal Illustrations, Four Footed Friends Can Be Run in Any of Four Languages - English, French, Spanish & Japanese. Lots of Point & Click Surprises, Too.
T/Maker Co., Inc.

VroomBooks Stradiwackius Counting Concert. Dec. 1995. *Customer Support:* Telephone support - free (except phone charge).
Windows 3.1. IBM & compatibles (386 DX-20) (4Mb). CD-ROM disk $12.99, Jewel (ISBN 1-57594-082-5). *Nonstandard peripherals required:* 2X CD ROM player, sound card, VGA monitor. *Optimal configuration:* 486 SX-33.
CD-ROM disk $12.99, Blister.
Spend Hours Showing Your Child the Wonder of Books, Words, Facts, & Pictures Using the Interactivator. Make Stradiwackius Come Alive with Interesting Facts, 3-D Animation, & Fun Learning Games in Four Different Languages.
Kidsoft, Inc.

VroomBooks Stradiwackius Counting Concert. Dec. 1995. *Customer Support:* Telephone support - free (except phone charge).
Windows 3.1. IBM & compatibles (386 DX-20) (4Mb). CD-ROM disk $12.99 (ISBN 1-57594-082-5). *Nonstandard peripherals required:* 2X CD-ROM player, sound card, VGA monitor. *Optimal configuration:* 486 SX-33.
Spend Hours Showing Your Child the Wonder of Books, Words, Facts, & Pictures Using the Interactivator. Make Stradiwackius Come Alive with the Interesting Facts, 3-D Animation, & Fun Learning Games in Four Different Languages. Jewel Case.
Kidsoft, Inc.

VroomBooks: Stradiwackius, the Counting Concert. Jan. 1996. *Customer Support:* Telephone support - free (except phone charge).
System 6.0.7 or higher. 256 color capable Mac with 68030 processor (4Mb). CD-ROM disk $12.99 (ISBN 1-57594-114-7). *Nonstandard peripherals required:* 2X CD ROM drive, mouse, 640/480 resolution monitor. *Optimal configuration:* 8Mb.
Spend Hours Showing Your Child the Wonder of Books, Words, Facts, & Pictures Using the Interactivator. Make Stradiwackius Come Alive with Interesting Facts, 3-D Animation & Fun Learning Games in Four Different Languages.
Kidsoft, Inc.

Vroombooks: Stradiwackius: The Counting Concert. Feb. 1996. *Customer Support:* Telephone support - free (except phone charge).
Windows 3.1. IBM compatible 386 DX-20 (4Mb). CD-ROM disk $12.99 (ISBN 1-57594-095-7). *Nonstandard peripherals required:* 2x CD-ROM, sound card, VGA monitor. *Optimal configuration:* 486, SX-33.
Show Your Child the Wonder of Books, Facts, & Pictures - Four Different Languages. Blister Pack.
Kidsoft, Inc.

VroomBooks' Stradiwackius The Counting Concert. *Items Included:* Parent's Guide, 4 Language User's Guide. *Customer Support:* Free & unlimited technical support to registered users; 60 day money-back guarantee.
Macintosh. Macintosh, System 6.0.7 or higher (4Mb, 8Mb recommended). CD-ROM disk $49.95 CD-ROM. *Nonstandard peripherals required:* CD-ROM drive, color monitor.
Windows V.3.1 or higher. IBM PC & compatibles, 486, Pentium or higher (4Mb, 8Mb rec). CD-ROM disk $49.95 CD-ROM. *Nonstandard peripherals required:* CD-ROM drive, SoundBlaster or compatible sound card, mouse, 256 VGA/SVGA color monitor.
An Interactive, Animated, Multimedia Storybook with Activities for Children Aged 3 & Up. Children Will Love Playing with the 10 Wacky Instrument Characters As They Are Exposed to Counting, Reading, Spelling & Music Through Delightful Animations & Informative & Fun Games. In English, French, Spanish & German.
T/Maker Co., Inc.

VS COBOL Workbench. *Compatible Hardware:* IBM PC, PC XT, PC AT, Portable PC, 3270 PC. *Operating System(s) Required:* PC-DOS 2.0, 2.1, 3.0. *Memory Required:* 256k.
disk $1200.00.
PC-Based Mainframe Application Environment Which Provides the Professional COBOL Programmer with Both IBM Mainframe & IBM PC Programming Facilities. The COBOL Compiler Generates 8086 Native Code. The Package Is a Synthesis of IBM's CSVS COBOL & VS COBOL II, Micro Focus' COBOL II & ANSI '85 COBOL. Supports the Full 12-Module ANSI '74 Standard, As Well As Micro Focus Extensions That Fully Supports the IBM PC Screen Attributes. Users Can Select from Any Combination of COBOL Dialects Supported During Syntax Checking.
Micro Focus, Inc. (California).

VS Com. *Version:* 7.6. *Compatible Hardware:* Apple Macintosh, IBM PC. *Customer Support:* Free product support.
terminal emulation & file transfer $395.00.
terminal emulation only $195.00.
Wang 2110 Terminal Emulation Program for an IBM PC, Wang PC or Macintosh Computer. In Addition, VS Com Also Provides File Transfer & Conversion Capability.
M/H Group.

VS Library of Laser Fonts. *Compatible Hardware:* IBM PC & compatibles. *Operating System(s) Required:* MS-DOS 2.X or higher. *General Requirements:* Laser printer. *Items Included:* VS laser word processor tool kit, manuals. *Customer Support:* Telephone/FAX/Mail/BBS (No charge).
$39.95, per point size.
$59.999 to $169.95, per family.
$549.95, per library.
The VS Library of Fonts Offers 1000 Carefully Crafted Downloadable Fonts from 6 to 30 Point. Included Are Well Known Type Styles from Compugraphic & ITC, Proportional & Fixed Pitch Fonts, Serif, Sans-Serif, Greek, Mathematical & Ornamental Styles. International Extended Characters Are Available. Fonts Are Packaged in Libraries, Families or by Point Size.
VS Software.

The VS Tool Kit. Sep. 1986. *Compatible Hardware:* IBM PC, PC XT, PC AT. *Operating System(s) Required:* MS-DOS 2.X. *Memory Required:* 256k. *General Requirements:* Hard disk; HP, Cordata, Canon, NCR or Ricoh laser printer. *Items Included:* Manuals. *Customer Support:* Telephone/FAX/Mail/BBS (No charge).
disk $150.00, (free with purchase of Fonts or FontGen V.1, or SLEd).
Creates Printer Driver Files for MICROSOFT WORD, XY-WRITE, & WORD PERFECT. Features "Fill-in-the-Blank" On-Screen Forms for Entering Font Names & Point Sizes, Batch File Downloading & Automatic PRD Creation. Also Provides Routines for the Creation of Landscape Fonts.
VS Software.

VS/VM. *Compatible Hardware:* Wang VS 6, VS 6E, VS 65, VS 75E, VS 85, VS 100, VS 300, VS 7000. *Operating System(s) Required:* VS, IN/ix.
$9,000.00 to $18,000.00 for license depending on VS processor.
Allows Multiple Operating Systems to Run Concurrently As Virtual Machines on One Wang 32-Bit VS Computer. On the VS 85, VS 100, VS 300 & VS 7000 Series computers, Supports a Combination of up to 15 VS Operating Systems & IN/ix, the Wang Version of Unix System V.2. Supports IN/ix & One VS OPerating System on the Low-End VS 6, VS 6E, VS 65 & VS 75E.
Wang Laboratories, Inc.

V64. *Version:* 2.0. 1989. *Items Included:* On-disk manual, tutorial & functional spec., reference card, complete source code. *Customer Support:* Free phone, fax or correspondence support.
MS-DOS. IBM PC, PS/2 or compatibles. disk $125.00. *Nonstandard peripherals required:* Extended memory option, requires DOS 3.0 or higher.& installed extended memory. *Addl. software required:* Microsoft C, or Turbo C.
Library of C Callable Functions Which Allows a Programmer to Manage an Arbitrarily Large Workspace & Still Run Their Program in MS-DOS Real Mode. The Workspace Can Be Stored Either in Extended Memory or in a Paged, Least Recently Used Virtual Memory Store.
Sapiens Software Corp.

VSORT: File Sort Utility. *Version:* 3.3. Apr. 1986. *Operating System(s) Required:* THEOS86, THEOS 286, THEOS386. *Memory Required:* 128k. *General Requirements:* Hard disk.
disk $225.00.
Merges & Sorts up to 17 Input Files; Can Output an Index Key, Record Number, Address, etc.; Skip the First 'N' Records; Display Records Which Are Formatted ; Output to Direct or Sequential Files; & Convert from ASCII to Binary or Vice Versa.
Phase 1 Systems.

VSTRESS3. *Version:* 1.2. Jun. 1990. *Compatible Hardware:* IBM PC & compatibles. *Operating System(s) Required:* MS-DOS. *Language(s):* FORTRAN77. *Memory Required:* 256k. *General Requirements:* Standard graphics board. *Items Included:* Complete users guide.
disk $965.00.
Foundations & Geotechnical Application Designed for the Computation of the Ultimate & Time-Rate of Consolidation Within a Stratified Soil System & to the Vertical Stresses Induced by Any Two- & Three-Dimensional Loading Conditions. Employs the Exact Theoretical Solutions Derived from the Boussinesq & Westergaard Theories for the Vertical Stresses Induced in an Elastic Continuum for Both Simple & Extremely Complex Load Cases.
Acumen Software Products.

VT 100 Terminal Emulator. *Compatible Hardware:* HP 150 Touchscreen.
3.5" disk $180.00 (Order no.: 45412A).
Allows the Touchscreen to Emulate a DEC VT 100 Terminal. Supports Most VT 100 & VT 52 Features with Comparable Speed & Performance (132-Column Mode Is Not Supported). User Can Keep a Host Terminal Session in the Background So That He/She Can Return, at the Touch of a Key, to Run Other Programs. Also Allows Incoming Text to Be Copied to a Local Disk File or Printer Attached to the Touchscreen, & Permits Error-Checked File Exchange with a Host Supporting the XMODEM Protocol.
Hewlett-Packard Co.

Vterm 4010. *Version:* 2.0. May 1985. *Compatible Hardware:* IBM PC, PC XT, PC AT & compatibles, PS/2. *Operating System(s) Required:* PC/MS-DOS 2.0 or higher. *Memory Required:* 256k. *General Requirements:* Monochrome or color graphics card.
disk $249.00.
Emulates Both the VT100 DEC Terminals & the 4010 Tektronix Graphics Terminals. Supports File Transfer with XMODEM, Kermit, or Proprietary VTRANS Protocol, for Which Free Host Software for Four Operating Systems Is Provided. Also Serves As a General Asynchronous Communications Program. Features: Scrollback Buffer to Save & Recall up to 80 Captured Screens, On-Line Help, Complete Support of EDT & Word-11, Compatibility with Several Different Printers & Plotters, Communications up to 19,200 Baud, 132 Column Display with Optional Video Card.
Coefficient Systems Corp.

Vterm/100. *Version:* 1.41. Dec. 1985. *Compatible Hardware:* IBM PC, PC XT, PC AT, & compatibles. *Operating System(s) Required:* PC-DOS/MS-DOS 2.0 or higher. (source code included). *Memory Required:* 192k.
non-copy protected $195.00 (Order no.: NCP).
Emulates a DEC VT100, VT101, VT102, or VT52 Terminal. Supports File Transfer with XMODEM, Kermit, or Proprietary VTRANS Protocol, for Which Free Host Software for Four Different Operating Systems Is Provided. Also Serves As a General Asynchronous Communications Program. Features Include: Scrollback Buffer to Save &
Recall up to 80 Captured Screens, Plug-Compatibility, On-Line Help, Complete Support of EDT & Word-11. User Programmable "Softkey" for Automated Dial up & Log on Procedures. 132 Column Display with Optional Video Board.
Coefficient Systems Corp.

VTLS. *Version:* 1994. 1985. *Items Included:* Documentation (paper and/or on-line). *Customer Support:* Toll-free number; 24-hour emergency support; turnkey installation in U.S. & Canada; annual site visits; on-site training; users groups; maintenance - contact VTLS Inc. for pricing; enhancements to software.
MPE/ix. HP3000. Contact publisher for price. *Networks supported:* Novell, TCP/IP, Token Ring, X.25, Ethernet, most any.
OSF/1. Digital's Alpha. Contact publisher for price. *Networks supported:* Novell, TCP/IP, Token Ring, Ethernet, X.25, most any.
UNIX (HP-UX) (IBM-AIX). HP9000, IBM RS6000. Contact publisher for price. *Networks supported:* Novell, TCP/IP, Token Ring, Ethernet, X.25, most any.
Integrated Library Automation Functions Are Based on National & International Standards. Ten Subsystems Are Included in the Base Software Package: Windows-Based GUI to Online Public Access Catalog EasyPAC, Keyword & Boolean Searching, Circulation, Reserve Room Control, Cataloging, Authority Control, Serials Control, Status Monitoring, Reporting & Parameters. Additional Fully Integrated Subsystems Available: Acquisitions & Fund Accounting, Document Delivery, Inventory Control, Journal Indexing & Materials Booking. User Interfaces Include: Locally Mounted Databases, Z39.50 Client, ADA Workstation, Cataloging Client, & Intelligent Workstation.
VTLS Inc.

VTLS InfoStation (VTLS-IS). *Version:* 3.3. *Items Included:* Documentation & floppy disk. *Customer Support:* On-site training, 30-day unlimited warranty.
NextStep 3.2-3.3. NeXT, 486 PCs (16Mb), HP-9000 700 series. disk $1200.00, first copy, ,10, 000.00 for installation & setup. *Nonstandard peripherals required:* HP 3000 or IBM 370 networked with NeXT. *Addl. software required:* VTLS or other library automation software. *Networks supported:* Ethernet, TCP/IP, NFS, FTP, Novell Netware.
Multimedia Information Access System with Hypermedia Links, Annotations & Authoring Capabilities for Library Automation. It Provides Seamless Integration Between Bibliographic & Multimedia Information. Lets User Connect to Multiple Distributed Databases via TCP/IP & Access Multimedia Objects on the Network via NFS, FTP & Novell Netware. Supports the Z39. 50 Standard.
VTLS, Inc.

VTX-On Line. Zaphodyne. Jul. 1989.
Amiga (512k). disk $79.95.
Full-Featured Graphics Oriented Telecommunications Package.
MichTron, Inc.

Vuman Ventura Link. *Version:* 0.9H. *Operating System(s) Required:* PC-DOS/MS-DOS, OS/2. *Memory Required:* 640k.
$295.00.
Provides a Multiple Character Set Text Editor, Plus Fonts Enabling the Addition of Scientific, Greek, Russian & European Language Characters to Ventura Publisher.
COSS.

W-4 Form Analyzer. Apr. 1987. *Compatible Hardware:* IBM PC & compatibles. *Memory Required:* 196k. *General Requirements:* Lotus 1-2-3 Release 1A or higher. *Items Included:* 5 1/4" diskette & user's guide.
$39.00.
Used for Calculating W-4, Tax to Be Withheld by Your Employer (Using Percentage Method) & Analyzing Tax Withholding to Help You Avoid Paying Too Much or Too Little Tax.
JPL Assocs.

The/W-4 Formula. *Version:* 1.2. Jul. 1987. *Items Included:* User guide. *Customer Support:* One-year money back guarantee, unlimited phone support, free 1991 update.
MS-DOS 2.0 or higher (360k). IBM PC & compatibles. disk $149.95. *Optimal configuration:* Monitor, printer.
Plans User's Federal Income Tax Refund. Accurately Estimates Federal Income Tax Liability & Automatically Finds Number of Employee Allowances to Claim to Achieve a Desired Tax Refund/Tax Due on April 15. Includes Mid-Year Analysis.
Winning Strategies, Inc.

W-Link. *Version:* 4.5. *Compatible Hardware:* IBM PC. *Customer Support:* Free product support.
$395.00.
Provides Disk to Disk Document Conversion Between Wang PC WP & the Following IBM PC Word Processing Formats: WordPerfect, Multimate, OfficeWriter, Microsoft Word, Display Write, PFS: Professional Write, Word Star & ASCII.
M/H Group.

W. P. Kingsfield. Christopher A. Williams.
PC-DOS (35k). 3.5" or 5.25" disk $19.95 (ISBN 0-926123-06-8, Order no.: WPK10). *Nonstandard peripherals required:* 1 hard disk or 1 floppy disk. *Addl. software required:* WordPerfect 4.1, 4.2 or 5.0.
Program Teaches WordPerfect Function Key Commands. Helps User Learn Correct Keystrokes to Manipulate Documents Faster.
Information Research Corp.

W-Poll: Wayne-Plus Interface. *Version:* 3.81. Jun. 1994. *Items Included:* User manuals & diskettes. *Customer Support:* 1st year support via modem.
MS-DOS 5.0 or higher. IBM PS/2 or compatible (640k). $1525.00. *Nonstandard peripherals required:* Serial Card 25 Pin. *Optimal configuration:* DOS 3.3, 640k RAM, hard disk, W-Poll. *Networks supported:* PC LAN.
Program Scheduler Activates Poller At Selected Times Throughout Day. Request Function Gets Sales Data. Program Function Allows User to Program the DOS Device from the PC. This Feature Permits PLU/SKU Prices to Be Changed As Well As Pump Prices. The Posting Function Places the Data into the Computerized Daily Book. Accepts Data from the CATS & SCANNERS.
Service Station Computer Systems, Inc.

W-2 & 1099 Generator. *Customer Support:* Free on-site training; free telephone, fax & Bulletin Board support; updates to product can be downloaded via Bulletin Board.
MS-DOS 3.1 or higher (512k). IBM PC, XT, AT, PS/2, 286/386/486/586. $95.00, with magnetic media $199.00. *Optional:* laser software $99.00. Renewal prices: program $65.00, with magnetic media $129.00, laser $70.00 (Order no.: W2). *Nonstandard peripherals required:* Hard disk & Dot Matrix printer. *Optimal configuration:* Hewlett Packard or compatible laser printer. *Networks supported:* Novell Netware, IBM Token Ring, 3COM.

With Our Generator, Payer/Employer Information Is Entered Only Once. The Screen Simulates Actual Forms for Easy Data Entry. Forms W-3 & 1096 Are Generated Automatically. Prints Letter Perfect W-2, 1099-DIV, 1099-INT, 1099-MISC, 1099-B, 1099-R, 1099-S & 1098. Optional: Laser Printing & Magnetic Media Filing.
Micro Vision Software, Inc.

W-2 Magnetic Filing. *Version:* 1.0. Jan. 1991. *Customer Support:* 90 days free support, $150/yr afterwards; on site training $200 per 1/2 day.
PC-DOS/MS-DOS. PC compatible (100k). $195.00. *Optimal configuration:* 640k, hard disk, floppy disks, mono. *Networks supported:* any.
Screen Entry of Company Data. Online Context Sensitive Help. Processes Variety of ASCISI W-2 Files, Including Printer Output & Produces PC Floppy.
Theta Business Systems.

WAIS-R Microcomputer Assisted Interpretive Report: D(WAIS-R Micro). *Version:* 1.2. 1986. *Compatible Hardware:* Apple II+, IIe, IIc; IBM PC. *Operating System(s) Required:* PC-DOS 2.0 or higher. *Memory Required:* Apple 64K, IBM 128k. *General Requirements:* Printer. *Items Included:* User's manual, IBM disk. *Customer Support:* 800-228-0752, 1 for Menu, 6 for Support.
$179.00.
Apple. (Order no.: 8992-505 (5.25")).
IBM. (Order no.: 8992-513 (5.25"); 8992-562 (3.5")).
Produces in-Depth Analysis of WAIS-R Results for Ages 16-74. The Program Generates a 3 to 4 Page Interpretive Report Based on Accepted WAIS-R Research. The Report Includes the Following: Descriptive Information, Individual Profile, Statistical Information (Confidence Intervals, Verbal/Performance Discrepancy, Idiographic Comparison), & Interpretive Information.
Harcourt Brace Jovanovich, Inc. (Psychological Corp.).

Wall Street Analyst. *Version:* 2. Aug. 1995. *Items Included:* 2 perfect bound manuals, 1 free month of data downloading. *Customer Support:* Free unlimited technical support for current shipping versions by phone, FAX, BBS, CompuServ, Prodigy, & American Online. FAX & BBS support for past versions for $19.95 per incident.
Windows. IBM 386-DX/33, hard drive, mouse, DOS 5, EGA (4Mb). disk $49.95 (ISBN 1-887286-05-5). *Optimal configuration:* IBM 486-DX2/66, 8Mb RAM, DOS 6.2X, Windows 95, mouse.
A Complete Stock Charting & Analysis Package Designed to Help the Individual Investor Make Better Investment Decisions. With Easy-to-Use Windows 95-Ready Interface, State-of-the-Art Charting Features, a Comprehensive Library of Classic Technical Indicators, & a Built-In Data Downloader, It Provides Everything Needed to Perform Market Analysis Like a Pro. The Program Also Includes Automatic Chart Scanning & a Built-In Expert System That Reveals & Explains the Bullish & Bearish Factors Affecting Any Chart Specified.
Omega Research, Inc.

Wall Street Analyst. Jul. 1994. *Items Included:* 3 perfect bound manuals, 1 free month of data downloading. *Customer Support:* Free unlimited technical support for current shipping versions by phone, FAX, BBS, CompuServ, Prodigy, & American On-Line. FAX & BBS support for past versions for $19.95 per incident.
Windows 3.1 or higher. IBM 386-DX/33, hard drive, mouse, DOS 5, EGA (4Mb). disk $99.00 (ISBN 1-887286-00-4). *Optimal configuration:* 486-DX2/66, 8Mb RAM, DOS 6.2X or higher, Windows 3.11 for Workgroups.
Allows Anyone to Perform Market Analysis Like the Pros on a Regular PC. The Secret Is a Revolutionary New Technology Called "Intelliguide" - an Intelligent & Interactive Encyclopedia of Market Analysis. The Program Also Includes an Easy-to-Use Windows Interface with Stunning Charting Abilities, a Built-In Data Downloader, Innovative Automation Features & One Free Month of Stock Data Downloading.
Omega Research, Inc.

Wall Street Commodities. *Compatible Hardware:* Apple Macintosh.
3.5" disk $195.00.
Commodities Management Program.
Pro Plus Software, Inc.

Wall Street Investor. *Version:* 3.0. *Compatible Hardware:* Apple Macintosh Plus; MS-DOS compatibles. *General Requirements:* Hayes-compatible modem. *Customer Support:* Free support.
disk $695.00.
Investment Management Program.
Pro Plus Software, Inc.

Wall Street Journal's Personal Finance Library. Dow Jones & Co. Jan. 1994. *Items Included:* On-line doc/help. *Customer Support:* No charge for support, toll free number - 800-942-2848, toll number 617-225-2136, calls received after working hours will be returned within 12 hrs. Support questions can be asked on Compuserve.
MS Windows 3.1 or higher. IBM compatible 386 or higher, 4Mb free hard disk, 256 color SVGA/VGA monitor or higher (4Mb). disk $49.95 (ISBN 1-57317-100-X, Order no.: V-WSJPFL-0001). *Optimal configuration:* 8Mb RAM, 486 machine, Windows 3.1 running enhanced mode, VESA local bus.
Advises Users on Personal Finance Subjects by Providing Detailed Articles from the "Your Money Matters" Column with Analytical Interactive Worksheets. The Combination of Content & Software Technology Enables Users to Apply Expertise & Guidance to Their Own Financial Situation. Topics Include Investing, Buying a Home, Choosing Life Insurance, & More.
Vertigo Development Group.

Wall Street Link: WSL. *Version:* 1990. *Operating System(s) Required:* OS/2. *General Requirements:* ChipChat & Microsoft Excel or Chipchat & Lotus 123/g.
disk $195.00.
Macros for Microsoft Excel & Lotus 123/g to Perform Dynamic Data Exchange with ChipChat: Communications Software for OS/2. A Typical Application is to Receive Stock Prices via Modem into Chipchat, then Dynamic Data Exchange (DDE) the Data to Excel or 123/g Allowing Immediate, Real Time Updating of Spreadsheet Data.
ChipChat-Cawthon Software.

Wall Street Pro's Secret Treasures CD-ROM: 147 of the World's Most Powerful Shareware Investment & Advisory Programs. Jan. 1996. *Items Included:* Instruction booklet.
DOS & Windows 3.1. PC (2k). CD-ROM disk $29.90 (ISBN 1-56087-124-5). *Optimal configuration:* 386, Windows 2k.
Easy-to-Use PC Computer Programs to Help You Turbo-Charge the Way You Handle Money. You Will Quickly Be Able to Download Quotes, Calculate Interest & Amortize Complicated Loans. Become a Master Market Strategist with: Spreadsheets, Bill Reminders, Investment

TITLE INDEX

Portfolios Manager, Dow Jones Forecaster, Credit Repair, & a Tracking System for Mutual Funds, Assets & Bonds. There's Even a Program on the National Debt!
Top of the Mountain Publishing.

Wall Street Raider. Michael D. Jenkins. May 1986. *Compatible Hardware:* IBM PC & compatibles. *Operating System(s) Required:* MS-DOS 2.0. *Memory Required:* 256k.
disk $39.95 (ISBN 1-55571-002-6).
Real-Time Simulation of Corporate Gamesmanship. Allows 1-4 Players to Invest in/ Manage Any One or More of 150 Companies in 26 Different Industry Groups in a Competitive "Smart" Financial Environment in Which There Are Almost No Limits Imposed on Financial Creativity. Program's Environment Consists of an Economic Model Within Which Everything Is Related to Almost Everything Else. Growth Rates, Oil Prices, Interest Rates, Bond Market Prices, Housing Starts & Other Economic Variables All Interact with Each Other & Affect Stock Prices & Consumer Growth Demand in 23 Industry Groups.
Oasis Pr.

Wall Street Trainer. *Items Included:* Bound manual. *Customer Support:* Free hotline - no time limit; 30 day limited warranty; updates are $5/disk plus S&H.
MS-DOS. IBM & compatibles (128k). disk $29.95. *Nonstandard peripherals required:* Printer supported, but optional.
Educational Financial Market Tutorial Which Simulates Fast Action, Long or Short "Ticker Tape" Trading in the Exciting Stock & Futures Markets. Eight Different Types of Put & Call Options May Be Traded on Low Margins. The Winning Strategy for This Game Is Based on Sound & Time-Tested Trading Practices of Successful Traders. Even After You Discover the Winning Strategy, It's Still a Challenge to Become Rich.
Dynacomp, Inc.

Wall Street Watcher. *Compatible Hardware:* Apple Macintosh. *Memory Required:* 2000k. *Items Included:* Free demo disk.
3.5" disk $495.00.
Stocks & Commodities Technical Analysis Program.
Micro Trading Software, Inc.

Wang Word Processing. *Compatible Hardware:* IBM PC, PC XT & compatibles. *Operating System(s) Required:* PC-DOS/MS-DOS 2.0, 2.1, 3.0 or 3.1. *Memory Required:* 256k.
$695.00.
Wang Laboratories, Inc.

Want Ads Composer. *General Requirements:* Second disk drive or hard disk drive; printer. Macintosh 512K or higher. 3.5" disk $995.00.
Generates Typeset-Quality Copy.
Microserve, Inc.

War in Russia: Jewel Case. Gary Grigsby. Nov. 1995. *Customer Support:* 30 day limited warranty.
DOS 5.0 or higher. 386 CD-ROM with hard drive (2Mb). CD-ROM disk $9.95 (ISBN 0-917059-41-7, Order no.: 062621).
Nonstandard peripherals required: VGA color monitor. *Optimal configuration:* 386/33, hard drive, mouse, CD-ROM, 256 color SVGA monitor.
World War II War Game Simulation/Strategy Game Covering Entire Eastern Front War. Includes Eight Historical Scenarios & One Hypothetical Scenario Offering 10-70 Hours of Intense War Gaming Excitement.
Strategic Simulations, Inc.

The War in Vietnam: A Multimedia Chronicle of the War That Divided America. Nov. 1995. *Customer Support:* 800 number (free), online support forums.
Windows 486SX, 25MHz; Macintosh. IBM & compatibles (8Mb); Performa 550 (33MHz 68030) (8Mb). CD-ROM disk $49.95 (ISBN 1-57595-005-7). *Nonstandard peripherals required:* Double-speed CD-ROM drive.
Experience the War Through the Archives of America's Premier News Organizations. Over an Hour of Original CBS News Video, Hundreds of Photos & Detailed Analysis from The New York Times. Searchable Database of the Wall.
Macmillan Digital U. S. A.

War of the Lance. David Landrey. *Customer Support:* Technical support line: (408) 737-6850 (11am-5pm, PST); 14 day money back guarantee/30 day exchange policy.
DOS 2.11 or higher. IBM PC & compatible (512k). disk $49.95. *Nonstandard peripherals required:* Requires color monitor & graphic adaptor.
Apple II (64k). disk $39.95.
Commodore 64/128 (64k). disk $39.95.
Prepare for Fierce Battles & All-Out War When the Forces of Whitestone Clash Against the Evil Highlord Dragonarmies. The Prize: Absolute Rule Over All Ansalon on the DRAGONLANCE Game World of Krynn. Choose Sides Against Another Human Opponent, or Command Whitestone Against the Computer. Send Forth Diplomats to Forge Treaties & Gain the Allies That Will Swell the Numbers of Your Troops. When Words Fail, Armies of Humans, Draconians, Elves, Dragons, & Other Creatures May Prove More Pursuasive. During the Course of the Game, Players Can Send Groups of Hero Characters on Quests to Discover Magic Items. Dragonlances, Dragonorbs, Gnomish Technology May Help to Defeat the Enemy.
Strategic Simulations, Inc.

Warehouse Distribution. *Version:* 8B. Sep. 1993. *Compatible Hardware:* PC-DOS, Xenix, Unix, 3COM, Novell. *Language(s):* COBOL 85. *Memory Required:* Single user 1Mb, multiuser 3000k. *General Requirements:* Integrated Accounting & The Distributing module. *Customer Support:* Included with the support for the Integrated Accounting.
Single user. Contact publisher for price
Multiuser. disk $1870.00.
Handles the Movement of Inventory Between a Company's Warehouses or Stores. Orders Can Be Taken from the Branches & Processed Similarly to the Way Customer Orders Are Processed. Many Reports & Inquiries Keep Track of All Shipments to & from the Branches. Inventory Distribution Also Expands the Warehouse Transfer Features for Companies with the Distributing Module. Includes: Shipping Analysis, Branch Orders & Billing Transfers.
Trac Line Software, Inc.

Warehouse for Distribution Companies (a Part of ABECAS). *Version:* 3.1. Jan. 1989.
MS-DOS, PC-DOS. Contact publisher for price. *Nonstandard peripherals required:* Hard disk (30Mb); 132-column printer. *Networks supported:* Novell, NTNX, 10-Net, Unix, Xenix, Turbo DOS (Multi-User version for all).
Allows Items Received by, Stored in & Shipped from a Distribution/Public Type Warehouse to Be Tracked in Detail. Options Include Warehouse Billing Sub Item/Sub-Lot/Serial Number Tracking & Warehouse Billing Customer Interface (Order Status Inquiry).
Argos Software.

WARRANTY (REPAIR) TRACKER

Warehouse for Storage Companies (a Part of ABECAS). *Version:* 3.3. Jan. 1989. *Customer Support:* On site training unlimited support services for first 90 days & through subscription thereafter.
MS-DOS, PC-DOS. Contact publisher for price. *Nonstandard peripherals required:* Hard disk (30Mb); 132-column printer. *Networks supported:* Novell, NTNX, 10-Net, Unix, Xenix, Turbo DOS (Multi-User version for all).
Allows Individual Lots & Containers to Be Tracked for Both Reporting & Billing Purposes. Options Include Warehouse Billing Sub-Item/Sub-Lot/Serial Number Tracking, Warehouse Billing Customer Interface (Allows Order Status Inquiry).
Argos Software.

Warehouse Locator System. 1992. *Compatible Hardware:* IBM PC, PS/2 & compatibles, System 36, RS/6000. *Operating System(s) Required:* AIX, MS-DOS, SSP. *Language(s):* BASIC (source code included). *Memory Required:* IBM 512k, RS/6000 8Mb, S/36 256k. *General Requirements:* 120Mb hard disk, printer, RS/6000 - 320Mb.
$5000.00-$10,000.00.
Tracks Location of All Items in Storage & the Availability of Empty Space. Assists in Applying Storage Rules for Putaway, Replenishment, Rewarehousing & Selection Operations.
Steppenwolff Corp.

Warehouse Manager, 2 disks. Organic Computing. May 1983. *Compatible Hardware:* TRS-80 Model II, Model 12, Model 16. *Operating System(s) Required:* PC-DOS, CP/M.
TRS-80. 8" disk $1200.00 (ISBN 0-925961-00-0).
PC-DOS based micros. disk $1200.00 (ISBN 0-925961-14-0).
CP/M. 8" disk $1200.00 (ISBN 0-925961-28-0).
Organic Computing.

Warehouse Scheduling & Control System. 1984. *Compatible Hardware:* PC, PS/2 & compatibles, System 36, RS/6000. *Operating System(s) Required:* AIX, MS-DOS, SSP. *Language(s):* BASIC (source code included). *Memory Required:* RS/6000 8Mb, 512k. *General Requirements:* 120Mb hard disk, printer, RS/6000 - 320Mb.
$10,000.00-$20,000.00.
Predicts Warehouse Labor Requirements on a Shift Basis & Monitors the Effectiveness of Warehousing Activities Relative to Predetermined Labor Standards.
Steppenwolff Corp.

Warlock. Infogrames. *Items Included:* Manual.
Macintosh (512k). (12/1988) $44.95 (Order no.: MCWL).
Apple IIgs (512K). (12/1988) $39.95 (Order no.: GSWL).
Commodore 64. (03/1989) $29.95 (Order no.: COWL).
Commodore Amiga. (12/1988) $34.95 (Order no.: AMWL).
Atari ST. (12/1988) $34.95 (Order no.: STWL).
You Alone Have Been Chosen to Rescue the Stolen Karna from the Depths of Darkness. Journey Through 20 Levels of Goulish Graveyards to Locate This Precious Jewel. Equipped with Only Your Wits & Sceptor, You'll Do Battle with as Motley an Assortment of Critters as You've Ever Imagined.
360, Inc.

Warranty (Repair) Tracker. *Version:* 4.5. 1989. *Items Included:* Step-by-Step instruction manual. *Customer Support:* Free support by phone, FAX, correspondence, or modem. On-site training and/or installation, $229.00 per day plus expenses.
MS/PC DOS 3.0 or higher. PC, 286, 386, 486;

1075

Tandy 3000 or higher (640k). disk $995.00 (Order no.: 8001). *Nonstandard peripherals required:* Interface to Touch-Tone requires our voice digitization board. Programs without Touch-Tone interface do not require non-standard peripherals, boards. *Optimal configuration:* 386SX computer with a fast hard disk & our telephone interface board. *Networks supported:* Novell.
HVAC Installers Can Track Units Installed & Mail Service Contract Renewals. Software Support Personnel Can Check for Registration Numbers. Customized for Each Installation.
Robert H. Geeslin (Educational Programming).

Warren Miller's Ski World: The Complete Multimedia Ski Experience. Sep. 1994. *Items Included:* Manual, registration card, flier describing all our titles, occasional promotional offers. *Customer Support:* Free telephone technical support.
DOS & Microsoft Windows 3.1. 12 MHz 80386SX. CD-ROM disk Contact publisher for price (ISBN 1-884014-12-7). *Nonstandard peripherals required:* MPC compatible. CD-ROM drive (680Mb) SVGA display, audio board, mouse, 486 DX processor. *Addl. software required:* Microsoft CD-ROM Extensions v.2.2.
Macintosh System 6.05. Color Macintosh (256 colors) (3.5Mb). CD-ROM disk Contact publisher for price (ISBN 1-884014-24-0). *Optimal configuration:* Single speed CD-ROM, 13" color monitor, 8 Mb RAM.
Resorts with Hundreds of Full-Color Photographs.
Multicom Publishing, Inc.

Wasteland. Interplay Productions. *Compatible Hardware:* Apple II, II+, IIe, IIc, IIgs; Commodore 64, 128; IBM PC.
Apple II. disk $14.95.
Commodore. disk $14.95.
IBM PC. disk $14.95.
Post World War III Fantasy Role-Playing Game. Your Band of Desert Rangers Must Outwit & Outgun the Seemingly Endless Variety of Mutants, Monsters, & Desert Outlaws of the Radiation Infested Southwest. With Luck, Your Party Will Be Well-Armed & Well-Skilled by the Time It Uncovers the Biggest Menace of All. The Game Combines State-of-the-Art Weaponry, Advanced Technology, & Your Most Advanced Survival Skills to Withstand This Nightmarish Civilization.
Electronic Arts.

Wastetrax. *Version:* 3.0. 1987. *Compatible Hardware:* IBM PC XT, PC AT; Sys 2; HP Vectra; Compaq. *Operating System(s) Required:* MS-DOS 3.0 & higher. *Language(s):* MBASIC, Machine, C. *Memory Required:* 512k. *General Requirements:* 5Mb hard disk, color display, CGA card; 10Mb hard disk recommended.
contact publisher for price.
Utilizes SRT Activated Sludge Control & Settling Flux Clarifier Control, Applicable to Diverse Wastewater Environments. The Settling Flux Control Strategy Allows Performance of a Clarifier to Be Predicted Based on Fundamental Principles & on Current Operating Data. Plant Personnel Can Generate Tabular Outputs for Any Time Period of Data Stored in the Main Data Manager Program. Generates Statistical Information for Each Parameter Tabularized & Prints a NPDES Report for Submittal to the Regulatory Agency. General X-Y Plotting, Trend Plotting & Probability Plotting Assist in Control of Laboratory Analyses While Additionally Providing a Tool for Short & Long-Term Monitoring of Treatment Processes. A Data Base for the Preventive & Breakdown Maintenance Programs Include Operational Facilities, Equipment Listings, & Inventories of Equipment Replacement Items.
Engineering Science, Inc.

Watchdog Armor. *Customer Support:* M-F 8AM - 6PM EST.
OS/2, PC-DOS/MS-DOS. IBM PC, PS/2, & compatibles. $150.00. *Addl. software required:* Watchdog PC Data Security Software.
Half-Card That Offers Additional Security Features That Work in Combination with the Watchdog PC Data Security Software. Product Provides a Hardware Implementation of DES (Data Encryption Standard) Algorithm, a Secure Clock That Prevents Tampering, & Hardware System Boot Protection.
Fischer International Systems Corp.

Watchdog Director LAN: Central Security Administration. *Version:* 7.02. Mar. 1992. *Items Included:* Software disks, installation, user & system administrator manual. *Customer Support:* M-F 8AM - 6PM EST.
PC-DOS/MS-DOS 3.0 or higher. IBM PC & compatibles, PS/2 (512k). Contact publisher for price. *Networks supported:* Novell, LAN Server, LAN Manager, Banyon Vines.
Provides Centralized Security Administration of All PCs on a Network Secured with Watchdog PC Data Security Software. This Allows a Single Master System Administrator to Initialize & Maintain the Watchdog Security Profiles for Local PCs Connected to the Network, from a Centralized Database, Without Leaving Their Office. Other Benefits Include Audit Activity on Each PC Reported to a Centralized Database & the Privacy & Authentication of the Security Permissions Downloaded to Each PC Is Ensured Using RSA-Public Key Encryption.
Fischer International Systems Corp.

Watchdog Keymaster. *Version:* 2.0. *Items Included:* Software & install/user manuals. *Customer Support:* M-F 8AM - 6PM EST.
PC-DOS/MS-DOS 2.0 or higher. IBM PC, PS/2, & compatibles. contact publisher for price. *Addl. software required:* Watchdog PC Data Security Software.
Working in Combination with Watchdog PC Data Security Software, Product Provides Secure System Administration, Password Management, & Retrieval of Lost or Forgotten Administration Passwords. Especially Useful Where Multiple Copies of Data Security Software Are Installed.
Fischer International Systems Corp.

WATCHDOG: PC Data Security. *Version:* 7.02. Jun. 1993. *Compatible Hardware:* AT&T; Compaq; IBM PC & compatibles. *Operating System(s) Required:* PC-DOS/MS-DOS 3.0, OS/2 1.3. *Language(s):* Assembly, C. *Memory Required:* 512k. *Items Included:* Software, install/user manuals. *Customer Support:* M-F 8AM - 6PM EST.
disk $295.00.
updates avail.
Security System That Prevents Unauthorized Use of the PC & It's Resources. Features Include ID & Password Access Control with a Single Sign-On Feature to LANs, Multiple Permission Levels, Automatic & Transparent Data Encryption of PC & Server Directories, Audit Trail Facility, System Boot & Format Protection, Logon Execs, Systems Administration, Object Reuse Protection, EMS Support & More. System Is Menu Driven, Is Completely Compatible with Windows 3.X & Third Party Menu Systems, & Provides Protection Against Virus Invasion.
Fischer International Systems Corp.

WATER. *Version:* 1.40. Mar. 1989. *Compatible Hardware:* AT&T PC 6300; Compaq; IBM PC, PC XT. *Operating System(s) Required:* PC-DOS, MS-DOS. *Language(s):* FORTRAN. *Memory Required:* 640k. *Items Included:* Manual, 120-day free maintenance. *Customer Support:* 1 year maintenance for $200.
disk $495.00.
Pipe Network Analysis Program Used for the Analysis of Water Systems. Can Be Used for Systems Containing up to 750 Pipes & Nodes. Flows May Be Defined in Either CFS, GPM, or LPS & Either Manning's N or Hazen William's Friction Factors May Be Used.
Research Engineers.

WATER. John Migliavacca. 1985. *Compatible Hardware:* IBM PC. *Operating System(s) Required:* DOS 1.1. *Memory Required:* 256k.
disk $100.00.
Calculates Langelier & Ryznar Indexes (Indicating a Tendency to Scale or Corrode), Hydroxide, Carbonate, & Bicarbonate Alkalinities, Electrical Conductivity, Total Dissolved Solids, Total Hardness, Ionic Balance, Ionic Strength, Internal Correlations Account for Effects of Temperature on PH & Ionization Constants. Solubility Products Are Computed & Compared with Maximum Allowable Values to Avoid Precipitation.
Techdata.

Water & Sewer Biller. *Compatible Hardware:* IBM PC.
contact publisher for price.
ASW Software.

Water Billing System. Pro Software, Inc. *Compatible Hardware:* TI Professional. *Operating System(s) Required:* MS-DOS. *Memory Required:* 64k. *General Requirements:* Printer.
$2000.00.
Texas Instruments, Personal Productivit.

Water Distribution: Loops. 1989. *Compatible Hardware:* IBM PC & compatibles. *Operating System(s) Required:* PC-DOS/MS-DOS. *Language(s):* QBASIC. *Customer Support:* Telephone assistance.
disk $47.00, incl. user guide.
disk $27.00, incl. source guide.
Standard Hardy-Cross Technique Handles Approximately 1000 Pipes. Loops Do Not Have to Be Identified. Runs Against a Data File Whioch May Be Modified for Changes in Demand, Line Size or Fire Flows. Output Includes Original Input Data, Head Losses, Velocities & Pressures. Input Is Free-Format.
Systek, Inc. (Mississippi).

Water Distribution: Nodes. 1989. *Compatible Hardware:* IBM PC & compatibles. *Operating System(s) Required:* PC-DOS/MS-DOS. *Language(s):* QBASIC. *Customer Support:* Telephone assistance.
disk $47.00, incl. user guide.
disk $127.00, incl. source code.
Hydraulic Analysis of Flows Based on a Simplified Newton-Raphson Method of Solution & Hazen-Williams Head Loss Formulations. Heads Are Adjusted to Meet Continuity Criteria. Input & Output Are Identical to the LOOPS Program. Additional Features Allowed Are Pressure Reducers, Opened & Closed Valves, Check Valves, Inline Booster Pumps, Pressure Sustaining Valves, Constant Flow Valves & Variable Outputs (i.e., Sprinklers). Limited to 600 Pipes.
Systek, Inc. (Mississippi).

Water Heater Selection. W. C. Dries. 1984. *Compatible Hardware:* IBM PC with printer. *Operating System(s) Required:* DOS. *Language(s):* BASIC (source code included). *Memory Required:* 64k.
disk $150.00 (ISBN 0-9606344-1-X).
Helps User Select Direct-Fired Water Heaters for Dormitories, Apartments, Motels, Nursing Homes, Restaurants, Schools & Offices.
Blitz Publishing Co.

TITLE INDEX

Water/Sewer/Trash Billing. *Compatible Hardware:* Apple Macintosh; IBM with Windows. *Memory Required:* 1000k. *General Requirements:* Hard disk, printer.
3.5" disk $695.00.
Water, Sewer & Trash Billing Management System.
S & J Enterprises.

Waterloo. Mirrorsoft Limited. *Customer Support:* Technical support line: (408) 737-6850; 14 day money back guarantee/30 day exchange policy.
DOS 2.11 or higher. IBM PC & compatibles (512k). disk $59.95. *Nonstandard peripherals required:* Requires color monitor & graphic adaptor (i.e., CGA, EGA).
Amiga (512k). 3.5" disk $69.95.
Atari ST (512K). 3.5" disk $59.95.
Napoleon, Wellington, & the Battle of Waterloo! The Most Famous Commanders in History Meet on the Most Famous battleground in the World. & You Are There, Living the Battle from the Commander's Perspective. Take the Place of Napoleon or Wellington & Lead the Forces That Changed History. Simple English Language Commands Give You Realistic Control Over Regiments of Infantry, Cavalry, & Artillary. The Historical Chains of Command, Battle Reports, & Commander's 3-D Perspective Keep You In the Thick of the Action. Can You Command the Victory That Eluded Napoleon's Grasp? The Fate of Nations Is in Your Hands!
Strategic Simulations, Inc.

Waterloo 1815. *Compatible Hardware:* Atari 400, 800. (source code included). *Memory Required:* cassette 32k, disk 48k. *General Requirements:* Joystick.
disk $33.95.
1-Player Simulation of the Battle of Waterloo.
Dynacomp, Inc.

WaveDisplay. *Version:* 1.10. Mar. 1986. *Compatible Hardware:* IBM PC with graphics card. *Operating System(s) Required:* MS-DOS, PC-DOS. *Language(s):* Assembly, BASIC. *Memory Required:* 128k.
disk $99.95.
Allows IBM PC to Be Used As an Intelligent Oscilloscope. Features Include: Displays Multiple Waveforms on the CRT, Selective Expansion of Captured Data, Direct Voltage & Time Readouts, Signal Averaging, Creating Waveshapes, Graphics Screen Dump to Dot Matrix Printers. Data Can Be Stored on Disk & Then Recalled for Future Analysis. Waveform to Be Displayed Can Be Positioned Anywhere on the Display Grid & Compressed to Any Size (Height) User Desires.
Epic Instruments, Inc.

Waveform Analysis. *Compatible Hardware:* HP 85, HP 86/87; HP Series 200 Models 216/220, 226/236 Personal Technical Computers with 320k, BASIC 2.0 & HP-IB printer.
HP 85. data cartridge, 3-1/2" or 5-1/4" disk $95.00 ea. (Order no.: 82809A).
HP 86/87. 3-1/2" or 5-1/4" disk $95.00 ea. (Order no.: 82839A).
HP 216/220. 3-1/2" or 5-1/4" disk $500.00 ea.
HP 226/236. 5-1/4" disk $500.00 ea.
Performs Fast Fourier Transforms on Either Frequency or Time Domain Data. Computes Correlation Function & Power Spectrum, Plus Fourier Series Coefficients. Supports Double Data Block Entry for Cross-Correlation, Power Spectrum & Convolution. Provides Plot or Print Output. The HP 85, 86/87 Versions Are a Subset of the Series 200 Package.
Hewlett-Packard Co.

WavePak. *Version:* 2.32. Oct. 1988. *Compatible Hardware:* IBM PC & compatibles. *Memory Required:* 640k. *General Requirements:* 2 expansion slots, math coprocessor. *Items Included:* Manuals. *Customer Support:* On-site training, in-house training center, 1 yr. free maintenance includes hardware/software updates, phone support & is extendable for a fee.
3.5" or 5.25" disk $6995.00 (Order no.: 1000).
Two Channel FFT Spectrum Analyzer Capable of Digital Oscilloscope Emulation, FFT Spectrum Analyzer Emulation, Data Recall & Analysis, Database Set-Up & Maintenance.
Computational Systems, Inc.

The Way Things Work.
Windows. IBM & compatibles. CD-ROM disk $69.95 (Order no.: R1197). *Nonstandard peripherals required:* CD-ROM drive. *Optimal configuration:* 386 processor operating at 16Mhz or higher, MS-DOS 5.0 or higher, Windows 3.1 or higher, 30Mb hard drive, mouse, VGA graphic adapter & VGA color monitor (SVGA recommended), 4Mb RAM, external speakers or headphones (with sound card) that are Sound Blaster compatible.
Macintosh (4Mb). (Order no.: R1197A). *Nonstandard peripherals required:* 14" color monitor or larger, CD-ROM drive.
Based on David Macaulay's Best-Selling Book "The Way Things Work," This Program, Through Sophisticated Animation & Audio, Brings Macaulay's Illustrations to Life with the Click of a Mouse. Get Ready to Embark on a Journey to the Greatest Scientific Discoveries from 700 B.C. to the Present (Ages 7 & Up).
Library Video Co.

WCL (Windows Communications Library). *Version:* 4.1.1. Nov. 1995. *Customer Support:* One month free support with each license, thereafter an optional annual maintenance/ support subscription & an optional upgrade pricing. Applies to both the Toolkit & runtime license.
Windows 3.1 or higher, Windows 95. 386. $995.00 per Toolkit, $70.00 per client. *Nonstandard peripherals required:* Hard disk. *Addl. software required:* 3270 or 5250 emulator.
Provides Windows Developers a High Level Toolkit & Function Set for Creating Client-Server Applications Against Existing Legacy Systems (3270 or 5250). Generation of Applications Is Provided for Both the Visual Basic & PowerBuilder Environments. Partial Generation & High Level Functions Are Provided for Most Other Development Environments.
Multi Soft, Inc.

WCL (Windows Communications Library). *Version:* 5.0. Feb. 1996. *Customer Support:* One month free support with each license, thereafter an optional annual maintenance/support subscription & an optional upgrade pricing. Applies to both the Toolkit & runtime license.
Sun Solaris (Unix). $70.00 per client. *Addl. software required:* I/O Concepts.
Provides Windows Developers a High Level Toolkit & Function Set for Creating Client-Server Applications Against Existing Legacy Systems (3270 or 5250). Generation of Applications Is Provided for Both the Visual Basic & PowerBuilder Environments. Partial Generation & High Level Functions Are Provided for Most Other Development Environments.
Multi Soft, Inc.

Wealth Insurance. Nov. 1988. *Items Included:* Paul Erdman's "Guide to Wealth Insurance", catalog insert sheet. *Customer Support:* 90-day money back guarantee, 30-day preview for schools with purchase order number, free replacement of damaged disks if under 90-day warranty.
MS-DOS 2.0 & higher (512k). IBM PC & compatibles. disk $39.95. *Nonstandard peripherals required:* CGA/EGA card; Epson printer recommended. *Optimal configuration:* 2 disk drives or one floppy & one hard disk.
Designed to Teach User Best Investments for the Years Ahead. Indicates When to Buy or Sell Stocks, Bonds, Precious Metals; How to Protect Earnings & Savings; How to Avoid Costly Investment Mistakes.
Compton's NewMedia, Inc.

WEATHER FORECASTER

The Weather Analyst. *Version:* 2.1. *Compatible Hardware:* Apple II, II+, IIe; IBM PC. *Operating System(s) Required:* AOS; Apple DOS 3.2, 3.3; MS-DOS; PC-DOS. *Language(s):* Machine. *Memory Required:* 48-64k. *Items Included:* disk, user's manual, & normal weather data. *Customer Support:* free telephone support.
disk $89.95.
Menu-Driven, Interactive Data Manager Which Allows User to Store & Analyze Local Weather Observation Such As Temperature & Precipitation Data. Includes Historical Weather & Average Conditions for the User's Locale Covering the Period from 1951 Through 1982. These Records Can Be Recalled to Compare with Current Weather Conditions & Are Also Used to Compute the Long-Term Normal Weather Conditions for the User's Location.
Climate Assessment Technology, Inc.

Weather Forecaster. *Items Included:* Bound manual. *Customer Support:* Free hotline - no time limit; 30 day limited warranty; updates are $5/ disk plus S&H.
MS-DOS. IBM & compatibles (128k). disk $39.95. *Nonstandard peripherals required:* Color graphics card.
Apple (48k). disk $39.95.
Statistically-Based Analysis Package That Will Predict Average Temperatures (30-Year Means) for Any Day of the Year As Well As Heating Degree Days, Cooling Degree Days, Number of Frost Free Days, Growing Seasons, & Corn Heat Units. It Will Give You a 3-Day Weather Forecast Based on Current Time Factors. In the Long Term It Will Simulate a 3-Day Weather Forecast Any Day of the Year for Your Location, Including 3-Day Weather Maps. Get an Average Forecast of Conditions at the Intermediate Upper Air Levels of 1,000, 850, 700, & 500 Millibars. Can Be Used for Regions Within the Following Geographic Coordinates: 0 Degrees to 90 Degrees North Latitude & 0 Degrees to 180 Degrees West Longitude. Predictions Displayed Include: Cloud Cover/Type/Height; Wind Direction & Speed; Weather Movement (Direction & Speed); Average Temperature & Deviation from Long Term Average; Air Mass Type; Storm Warnings.
Dynacomp, Inc.

Weather Forecaster. 1995. *Items Included:* Full manual. *Customer Support:* Free telephone support - 90 days, 30-day warranty.
MS-DOS 3.2 or higher. 286 (584k). disk $39.95. *Nonstandard peripherals required:* CGA/EGA/VGA.
A Statistically-Based Analysis Package That Will Predict Average Temperatures (30-Year Means) for any Day of the Years As Well As Heating Degree Days, Cooling Degree Days, Number of Frost Free Days, Growing Seasons, & Corn Heat Units. It Will Give You a 3-Day Weather Forecast Based on Current Time Factors. In the Long Term It Will Stimulate a 3-Day Weather Forecast Any Day of the Year for Your Location, Including 3-Day Weather Maps.
Dynacomp, Inc.

Weather Watch. *Compatible Hardware:* TRS-80 Model I, Model III. *Memory Required:* 32k. disk $24.95 (Order no.: 0316RD).
Two Programs - Weather Forecaster & Weather Plot (Charts, Graphs & Facts) on Local Weather for Every Major City in the U.S. & Its Possessions.
Instant Software, Inc.

Webster's Electronic Thesaurus. *Operating System(s) Required:* MS-DOS 2.0 or higher for IBM PC, XT & compatibles; MS-DOS 3.0 or higher for IBM PC AT & compatibles. *Memory Required:* 80k. *General Requirements:* 2 disk drives, 80-column monitor.
disk $59.00.
Provides 40,000 Entry Points, 470,000 Synonym Responses, Meanings, Inflection, & Spelling Correction. Enables Users to Place a Synonym Automatically in Their Text.
Proximity Technology, Inc.

Webster's New World On-Line Thesaurus. Korenthal & Assocs. Mar. 1986. *Compatible Hardware:* IBM PC, PC XT, PC AT. *Operating System(s) Required:* PC-DOS 2.0 or higher for IBM PC, PC XT; PC-DOS 3.0 or higher for IBM PC AT. *Memory Required:* 128k. *General Requirements:* Word processing software.
disk $69.95 (ISBN 0-671-60125-3).
Acts As an Extension of the Word Processor. At the Press of a Key, a Window Filled with Synonyms Is Displayed. Users Have the Option of Replacing the Original Word in the Text with One of the Available Synonyms.
Brady Computer Bks.

Webster's New World Spelling Checker. Korenthal & Assocs. Mar. 1986. *Compatible Hardware:* Apple II, II+, IIe, IIc; IBM PC, PCjr, PC AT, PC XT. *Operating System(s) Required:* PC-DOS 1.1 or higher for IBM PC, PC XT; PC-DOS 2.1 or higher for IBM PCjr; PC-DOS 3.0 or higher for IBM PC AT; Apple DOS 3.3; ProDOS for Apple IIe, IIc. *Memory Required:* 128k. *General Requirements:* Printer.
disk $59.95 ea.
IBM. (ISBN 0-671-54240-0).
Apple. (ISBN 0-671-61121-6).
Contains Database of 110,000 Words & Auxiliary Dictionary for Adding Words to Database. Offers 10 Possible Correct Word Choices. Allows User to View Document Being Corrected. Catches & Corrects Phonetic Misspellings.
Brady Computer Bks.

Webster's New World Writer. Korenthal & Assocs. Jun. 1986. *Compatible Hardware:* 2 disk drives; printer recommended. *Operating System(s) Required:* PC-DOS 2.0 or higher for IBM PC, PC XT; PC-DOS 3.0 or higher for IBM PC AT. *Memory Required:* 256k.
disk $150.00 (ISBN 0-671-54272-9).
Integrated Package Including Word Processor, Thesaurus, & Spelling Checker.
Brady Computer Bks.

Wedding Organizer. Sep. 1993. *Items Included:* Instruction manual, software disk.
DOS. IBM PC & compatibles (1Mb). disk $34.95. *Addl. software required:* No (unless other label desired then a mailing package such as Avery LabelPro). *Optimal configuration:* PC with 3 1/2" disk, hard drive & laser printer. (no inkjet printers) DBASE application.
Manage Wedding Plans: Guest List for Labels, Gifts, Guest Needs (Transportation & Lodging), Wedding Budget, Activities by Date - What Has to Be Done - When, Wedding Party, Bridal Registry & Gift List. Wedding Fact Sheet.
The James Gang.

Weekly Egg Production & Livability Tracking. *Version:* 4.3. Mar. 1980. *Compatible Hardware:* IBM PC & compatibles. *Operating System(s) Required:* MS-DOS 3.0 or higher. *Language(s):* BASIC (source code included). *Memory Required:* 256k. *Customer Support:* Telephone.
disk $30.00.
Allows Comparison of Weekly Egg Production & Livability to Other Egg Producers or Breeder Standards. Allows for up to 50 Flocks to Be Summarized on One Page.
Locus Systems.

Weekly Feed Consumed. *Version:* 1.4. Feb. 1980. *Compatible Hardware:* IBM PC & compatibles. *Operating System(s) Required:* MS-DOS 3.0 or higher. *Language(s):* BASIC (source code included). *Memory Required:* 128k.
disk $30.00.
Computes Actual & Expected Feed Consumption & Projects Amount & Date for Next Delivery. Provides Information on: Pounds of Feed on Hand Before First Delivery, Pounds of Feed Delivered, Pounds of Feed Available before Last Delivery, Pounds of Feed Expected to Last Flock for 1 Week, Date by Which Next Delivery Must Be Made, Number of Days Between Deliveries, Expected Pounds of Feed Consumed per Day for Flock, & Expected Consumption per 100 Birds.
Locus Systems.

Weibull Curve Fitter. *Items Included:* Bound manual. *Customer Support:* Free hotline - no time limit; 30 day limited warranty; updates are $5/disk plus S&H.
MS-DOS 2.0 or higher. IBM & compatibles (128k). disk $39.95.
Reliability Analysis Package Which Fits the Weibull Equation to the Failure History of a Sample of Test Specimens. The User Provides the Lifetimes at Failure, or at Removal from Test, of Each Specimen in the Test Sample. WCF Then Calculates the Mean Rank Estimates of the Cumulative Probability of Failure (or the User May Input an Alternative Set of Rank Estimates). Non-Failed Specimens May Also Be Included in the Data. The Calculated Results Are the Estimates of the Characteristic Lifetime, the Weibull Slope, & the Standard Deviation of the Fit.
Dynacomp, Inc.

WeibullSMITH. *Version:* 4.31. Jun. 1991. *Compatible Hardware:* IBM PC, PC XT, PC AT & compatibles. *Operating System(s) Required:* PC-DOS/MS-DOS 2.1 or higher. *Memory Required:* 512k. *General Requirements:* Printer, CGA, EGA, VGA or HERC card. *Items Included:* Program with file conversion utility & operator manual on disk. *Customer Support:* 213-548-6358 (answerphone).
version 4.31W, $200.00; version 4.31L, $300.00.
Probability Analysis Application That Handles Weibull & Log-Normal Distributions. Users Can Plot up to Three Sets of Data & Their Associated Confidence Limits on the Same Graph with up to 3000 Points Total. Imports/Exports Lotus 1-2-3 .PRN Data. The Program Automatically Scales Data Values in Increasing Order, Determines Their Median Rank Values, & Plots & Interprets Results. Compatible with Fulton Finding's VisualSMITH Program.
Fulton Findings.

WeibullSMITH. Robert Abernethy & Wes Fulton. Jul. 1994. *Customer Support:* 30-day limited warranty.
MS-DOS. IBM (512k). disk $440.00 (Order no.: S103). *Optimal configuration:* 5Mb storage space on hard disk required.
Program Implements Techniques Found in "The New Weibull Handbook." Can Quickly Evaluate Lifetime or Strength Data & Automatically Displays CDF Plots. Can Also Generate Median Rank Tables & Analysis Reports, Including Lognormal/Normal Analysis Capability. The Program Also Provides Built-In Probit Analysis for Sequential Inspections to Use on Probit Type Data.
Gulf Publishing Co.

WeibullSMITH: Reliability Engineering Analysis (RMS). 1995. *Items Included:* Full manual. *Customer Support:* Free telephone support - 90 days, 30-day warranty.
MS-DOS 3.2 or higher. 286 (584k). disk $439.95. *Nonstandard peripherals required:* CGA/EGA/VGA.
Based on the Methods, Techniques, & Applications found in the New Weibull Handbook, It Eliminates the Drudgery of Hand Calculations & Plotting, & Increases Both Accuracy & Productivity.
Dynacomp, Inc.

Weight Control & Nutrition. *Compatible Hardware:* TI Home Computer with cassette or disk data storage system.
contact publisher for price (Order no.: PHM 3021).
Assists Homeowners in Planning Balanced Meals to Help Improve Fitness Through Nutrition & Weight Control.
Texas Instruments, Personal Productivit.

Welcome Aboard: A Muppet Cruise to Computer Literacy. *Compatible Hardware:* Apple IIe, IIc; Commodore 64.
Apple. disk $39.95 (Order no.: APDSK-60).
Commodore. disk $24.95 (Order no.: COMDSK-260).
Kermit Teaches Programming As User Sets the Ship's Course to Pig or Frog Island, Gonzo Gives Miss Piggy a New "Look" with the Help of Computer-Aided Design, Scooter Explains the Basics of Word Processing & Electronic Mail So User Can Exchange Messages with a Muppet Crew Member, Fozzie Bear's Joke Library Introduces User to Data Management & Sam the Eagle's Game Room Contains a Selection of Arcade-Style Computer Games.
Broderbund Software, Inc.

Welcome to Africa. *Customer Support:* All of our products are unconditionally guaranteed.
Windows. CD-ROM disk $39.95 (Order no.: AFRICA). *Nonstandard peripherals required:* CD-ROM drive.
Educational & Entertaining Title about Life As African Villager.
Walnut Creek CDRom.

Welcome to Boydland: A Theme Park Where Every Ride Teaches Something New about the Human Body. Time-Life for Children Staff. Oct. 1994. *Customer Support:* Free 800 Number Technical Support.
Windows. PC with 486SX 33MHz or higher (8Mb). disk $29.95 (ISBN 1-884899-12-9). *Optimal configuration:* 486SX 33MHz or higher PC, 8Mb RAM, double-speed CD-ROM drive, VGA plus 640x480 monitor displaying 256 colors, Windows 3.1, stereo headphones or speakers, hard disk, mouse or compatible positioning device, Sound Blaster or compatible sound card.
Macintosh. Color capable Macintosh (5Mb). disk $29.95 (ISBN 1-884899-35-8). *Optimal configuration:* Color Macintosh computer, color monitor & video card supporting 256 colors at 640x480, 5Mb RAM, System 6.07 or higher, hard disk, double-speed CD-ROM drive, stereo headphones or speakers, mouse.
Kids Travel to Places Like Eyelands, Lung Loop & the Discovery Tower in This Entertaining Title.

Ricki & Her Parrot Companion, Hiccup, Guide the User Through a Tour of Bodyland, a Theme Park Based on the Human Body. Games & Activities Make It Fun to Learn How the Body Works.
IVI Publishing, Inc.

Wellness Check. *Compatible Hardware:* IBM PC, PC XT; Apple II+, IIe. *Language(s):* BASIC. contact publisher for price.
Health Risk Assessment Program Based on the Answers to 47 Questions Relating to a Person's Health Habits & Lifestyle.
Rhode Island Department of Health.

Welltris. 1989. *Items Included:* manual. *Customer Support:* phone support.
IBM PC or compatible (256k). $34.95. *Optimal configuration:* 5.25 or 3.5 disk drive.
MAC Plus or higher (1Mb). $39.95. *Optimal configuration:* one 800k 3.5" disk drive.
Amiga kickstart 1.2 or higher (512k). $34.95.
Step into Another Dimension! Is This Pit of Falling Welltris Pieces Really Drawing You Down into Its Very Depths or Is It Just Your Imagination? In This Latest Soviet Mind Teaser Alexey Pajitnov, the Designer of the Award-Winning Tetris Challenge, Transports Us into the Next Dimension. There's a New Angle At Every Turn. Welltris Pieces Can Be Rotated Within Each Wall, As Well As Around the Four Outer Walls While Falling Deeper into the Pit. With Three Difficulty Levels Containing Five Speeds Each, Few Will Be Able to Master the Challenge. There Is no Escape - If Tetris Didn't Get You, Welltris Will!
Spectrum HoloByte.

Wercs. HiSoft. Dec. 1988.
TOS (512k). Atari ST. disk $49.95.
Mouse-Driven GEM Resource File Editor for Creating Dialog Boxes, Menus, Icons & Alert Boxes.
MichTron, Inc.

WESTCheck / Automated Citation Checking Software. *Version:* 2.0. *Items Included:* Diskettes, user manual, quick reference guide, QuickScan mat. *Customer Support:* Free customer support; 1-800-WESTLAW; training provided.
MS-DOS version 3.0 or higher (PC's); MS-DOS version 3.1 or higher (LANs). IBM PS/2, IBM PC, or compatibles (384k). contact publisher for price. *Nonstandard peripherals required:* 1200, 2400 or 9600 baud modem. *Optimal configuration:* Hard drive, mouse (optional). *Networks supported:* Banyan VINES, EICON X.25 Gateway, IBM Asynchronous Communications Server, J&I NCS, Novell NACS, Network Products ACS2 & other servers using Interrupt 14 or LAT basic functions.
subscription charges per site for new version released after first year $25.00.
Automated Citation Checking Software Package. Allows Users to Verify Citations in a Brief or Other Document or a Manually Entered Citations List. Automatically Accesses WESTLAW, Verifies Citations & Retrieves Results from Insta-Cite, Shepards, Shepards' PreView, & QuickCite. Can Also Perform Content Verification to Ensure That Only Valid Citations Are Checked in WESTLAW. After the Citations Are Verified & Modified, the Citations List Can Be Checked in All Services by Performing a WESTCheck Run. Verifies the Citations & Creates an Easy-to-Read Concise Report That Can Be Printed Immediately or Downloaded for Later Use. Can Also Be Used to Retrieve the Full-Text of Documents from a List of Citations. This Software Is Also Available for Macintosh, Wang VS, & DEC VAX.
West Services, Inc.

Western European Tour. *Compatible Hardware:* Commodore Amiga, IBM & compatibles, Atari ST.
3.5" disk $29.95.
Scenery Disk for Use with Flight Simulator.
SubLOGIC.

Western Games. *Customer Support:* Back-up disks available.
Amiga DOS (512k). Commodore Amiga. $14.95.
Atari ST (512k). $14.95.
Commodore 64/128 (64k). $14.95.
Six Games of the Wild West with Optional Player Against Computer or Two Player Mode.
DigiTek Software.

Western Personality Inventory. *Version:* 1.000. Morse P. Manson. *Customer Support:* Free unlimited phone support.
IBM PC & 100% compatibles. 3.5" or 5.25" disk $125.00 (Order no.: W-1018 (5.25"); W-1044 (3.5")). *Optimal configuration:* DOS 3.0 or higher, DOS cannot be running in high memory, printer.
Combines Manson Evaluation & Alcadd Tests, Providing Single Instrument to Measure Both Susceptibility to & Extent of Alcohol Addiction.
Western Psychological Services.

Western Personnel Tests. *Version:* 1.500. Robert L. Gunn & Morse P. Manson. *Customer Support:* Free unlimited phone support.
IBM PC & 100% compatibles. 3.5" or 5.25" disk, contact publisher for price (Order no.: W-1004 (5.25"); W-1054 (3.5")). *Optimal configuration:* DOS 3.0 or higher, DOS cannot be running in high memory.
Widely Used Five-Minute Tests of General Intelligence. Ideal for Personnel Screening.
Western Psychological Services.

WESTLAW Custom Software for IBM's AS/400. *Version:* 2.0. *Items Included:* Media, installation instructions, user guide & templates. *Customer Support:* Free customer support 1-800-WESTLAW; training provided.
Operation System/400 version 1.2 or higher (some PTF's may be required). IBM's AS/400. contact publisher for price. *Nonstandard peripherals required:* Auto dial modem (1200, 2400, 9600 baud). *Networks supported:* SDLC dial or leased line to IBM's information network.
Product Can Access WESTLAW via SDLC Dial Through the IBM Information Network. Can be Accessed Through the IBM Information Network Using an Auto-Dial Modem. The WESTLAW IBM Information Network Interface Provides Many Useful Features Including: Highlighted Search Terms, Easy Editing of WESTLAW Queries, Function Keys for Frequently Used WESTLAW Commands, & Offline Printing to a System Printer or WESTLAW Custom Printer. Offline Printing Allows Users to Print Documents or Search Results After Signing off WESTLAW.
West Services, Inc.

WESTMATE. *Version:* 4.8. *Items Included:* Diskette, manual, user guide, templates. *Customer Support:* Free customer support 1-800-WESTLAW; training provided.
DOS 3.0 or higher. IBM PS/2 OR PC compatibles (350k). subscription charges of $25.00 per site for new versions released after the first year. *Nonstandard peripherals required:* 1200/2400/9600 baud modem. *Optimal configuration:* 350k of available memory required after DOS & other memory-resident programs are loaded; 500 bytes of free disk space. *Networks supported:* IBM ACS, Novell, Banyan Vines, Network Products' ACS2, 3COM, 3+ Share, AT&T Starlan, EICON X.25 Gateway, J&L NCS, & other servers using Interupt 14 & LAT basic Functioning.
Customizes Many Personal & Mini-Computers for Accessing West Publishing Company's Computer-Assisted Legal Research Service, WESTLAW. This Software Is Provided by West Services Inc., a Subsidiary of West Publishing. Advantages Include Store-to-Disk Capabilities, File Management Features, Expanded Print Capabilities, & Access to Other Online Services. Provides Pull-Down Menus & Function Key Support for Frequently-Used WESTLAW Commands. These Functions, Identified by a WESTLAW Template, Allow Users to Move Easily Within Search Results, Display a Query for Editing, Obtain a List of Retrieved Documents, & Access Such Services As Insta-Cite, Shepards, & Shepards' PreView. This Software Is Also Available for Wang VS, DEC VAX, Macintosh, Office Power, & UNIX Operating Systems.
West Services, Inc.

WetPaint.
Any Macintosh. 3.5" disk $89.95, per volume, 3 800k disks in FullPaint format.
Bit-Mapped Clip Art.
Dubl-Click Software.

What Color Is Your Mind? 1994. *Items Included:* Profile Worksheets. *Customer Support:* 30 day warranty.
IBM & compatibles (64k). disk $59.95 (ISBN 0-931847-00-1, Order no.: WCOLIB).
Apple II family (645k). disk $59.95 (ISBN 0-931847-00-1, Order no.: WCOLAP).
Analyze Yourself & Others. Learn How You Think. Are You A LeftBrain or Right-Brain Person? Thousands of Applications to Study or Research How We Think.
Chip Taylor Communications.

What Is a Bellybutton?
Windows. IBM & compatibles. CD-ROM disk $49.95 (Order no.: R1216). *Nonstandard peripherals required:* CD-ROM drive. *Optimal configuration:* 386 processor operating at 16Mhz or higher, MS-DOS 5.0 or higher, Windows 3.1 or higher, 30Mb hard drive, mouse, VGA graphic adapter & VGA color monitor (SVGA recommended), 4Mb RAM, external speakers or headphones (with sound card) that are Sound Blaster compatible.
Adapted from the Popular "Time-Life" Children's Book, This Program Helps to Answer Children's Earliest Questions about Their Bodies. The Storybook Format Is Entertaining & Easy to Understand (Ages 3-7).
Library Video Co.

What Is a Bellybutton?: Fun & Interactive Questions & Answers about the Human Body. Time-Life for Children Staff. Sep. 1995. *Customer Support:* Free 800 Number Technical Support.
Windows. PC with 386SX 33MHz or higher (4Mb). disk $29.95 (ISBN 1-884899-10-2). *Optimal configuration:* 386SX 33MHz or higher PC, 4Mb RAM, double-speed CD-ROM drive, VGA plus 640x480 monitor displaying 256 colors, Windows 3.1, stereo headphones or speakers, hard disk, mouse or compatible positioning device, sound card.
Macintosh. Color capable Macintosh (5Mb). disk $29.95 (ISBN 1-884899-34-X). *Optimal configuration:* Color Macintosh computer, color monitor & video card supporting 256 colors at 640x480, 5Mb RAM, System 6.07 or higher, hard disk, double-speed CD-ROM drive, stereo headphones or speakers, mouse.
"Why Do I Sneeze?" "What Happens to the Food I Eat?" Reach for This Engaging Title to Help Answer Children's Earliest Questions about Their Bodies. Sound Effects, Music & Humor Create a Whole New Learning Experience That Keeps Kids Involved As They Learn about Their Bodies, Visiting the Doctor & Staying Healthy.
IVI Publishing, Inc.

WHAT THEY DON'T TEACH YOU AT HARVARD

What They Don't Teach You At Harvard Business School. 1987. *Items Included:* Provided with each simulation is a manual describing the various simulation decisions & a facilitators guide that explains simulation set-up & terminology. *Customer Support:* Included in all entitles licensing Agreements is a service contract that Licensees to a Train-the-Trainer program & an 800 support phone number.
PC/MS-DOS 2.0 & higher. IBM PC/XT/AT & compatibles (256k). disk $59.95. *Nonstandard peripherals required:* 2 disk drives &/or a hard disk.
Management Simulation in the Art of Networking, Negotiating, & Management in a Competitive Industry.
Strategic Management Group, Inc.

What's Best!/Academic. General Optimization, Inc. Nov. 1987. *Compatible Hardware:* Compaq Portable, Plus, 286, DeskPro; IBM PC & compatibles, PC XT, PC AT. *Operating System(s) Required:* PC-DOS/MS-DOS 2.0 or higher. *Memory Required:* 256k. *General Requirements:* Hard disk, Lotus 1-2-3 Release 1A, VP-Planner, or Symphony Release 1.1 containing a valid COMMAND.COM file.
disk $29.95, incl. normal & pocket guide (ISBN 0-8162-3233-4).
Work-Along Utility for 1-2-3 Type Spreadsheets That Enhances the Microcomputer Spreadsheet with an Optimization System. It Is a General Purpose Linear Optimizer That Can Be Used for the Complete Range of Linear Programming Applications.
Holden-Day, Inc.

What's My Rule? *Compatible Hardware:* Apple II. *Memory Required:* 48k.
disk $34.95 (Order no.: INT 6013A).
Reasoning Game in Which Students Must Guess What Rules the Computer Is Using in a Given Logical Operation. For Example, the Computer Says, "I Like Red but I Don't Like Green. I Like Bananas but I Don't Like Apples." The Student Must Then Guess Which of the Following the Computer Likes: Butter, Penguins, or Geese. In This Case, the Computer's Rule Is That It Rejects Words with Double Letters. Students Get One Guess, More Examples, a Second Guess, & Then an Explanation. The Computer's Rules Become More & More Complex As the Student Progresses.
Intellectual Software.

What's My Story. *Items Included:* Instruction manual. *Customer Support:* Free Telephone support.
DOS/Windows 95. IBM & compatibles (8Mb). Contact publisher for price. *Nonstandard peripherals required:* CD-ROM drive.
MAC. Macintosh (4Mb). Contact publisher for price. *Nonstandard peripherals required:* CD-ROM drive.
Digital Pictures, Inc.

What's the Secret?, Vol. 2. Oct. 1995. *Customer Support:* Technical & customer support toll-free 1-800-219-9022, Direct dial (612) 737-8706, FAX (612) 736-5719.
MS-DOS 5.0 or higher, Microsoft Windows 3.1 or Windows 95. PC 486/25 SX or higher (4Mb). CD-ROM disk $59.95 (ISBN 1-886311-01-3, Order no.: 80-9550-2434-6).
Nonstandard peripherals required: Soundblaster (or compatible) Audio Card, speakers, double speed CD-ROM player or better. *Optimal configuration:* PC 486/33 SX, monitor: 256 color mode 640x480 resolution, MS-DOS 5.0 or higher, Microsoft Windows 3.1, 8Mb RAM, double speed CD-ROM player.
Apple System 7.1. Macintosh 030 CPU 25MHz or higher (8Mb). CD-ROM disk $59.95 (ISBN 1-886311-00-5, Order no.: 80-9550-2433-8). *Nonstandard peripherals required:* Double speed CD-ROM player or better. *Optimal configuration:* Macintosh 040 CPU 33MHz, monitor: 256 color mode 640x480 resolution, Apple System 7.1, 8Mb RAM, double speed CD-ROM player.
Follows the Successful Format of Volume 1 with All New Science Adventures to Explore & Is Based on "Newton's Apple," a PBS Science Show. A Sample of Topics Include: How Glue Sticks, How Airplanes Fly, How the Brain Thinks, & More.
ThreeM Software Media & CD-ROM Services.

Wheel Ease. *Compatible Hardware:* IBM PC & compatibles. *Operating System(s) Required:* PC-DOS 2.0 or higher. *General Requirements:* Lotus 1-2-3 Releases 1A, 2, & 2.01, dBASE III Plus 1.0, Microsoft Word 4.0,5.0; WordPerfect 4/4.2, 5.0, 5.1, WordStar Professional 4.0, MultiMate Advantage 3.6, DisplayWrite 4 1.0, CrossTalk XVI 3.6, MS-DOS 2.0.3.0, 40, MS-EXCEL 1.0/2.0, Ventura Publisher 1.0/2.0, MS-Windows 3.0.
$12.95.
Floppy-Disk Size Reference, Includes All Major Program Functions. Work-Related Items Are Grouped Together & Are Color-Coded for Easy Reference.
GP Technologies.

Whembly Castle Adventure. *Compatible Hardware:* IBM; Apple. *Memory Required:* Apple 48k, IBM 128k.
disk $19.95.
Treasure Hunt in a Large Castle.
Dynacomp, Inc.

Where in the USA Is Carmen Sandiego? K. Bull et al. *Compatible Hardware:* Apple II+, IIe, IIc, IIgs; Commodore 64, 128; IBM PC & compatibles, PCjr; Tandy. *Memory Required:* Apple & Commodore 64k; IBM & Tandy 128k; Commodore Amiga 512k. *General Requirements:* Joystick. IBM requires CGA, EGA, or Hercules monochrome card.
Apple. disk $44.95 (ISBN 0-922614-08-3, Order no.: 40150).
Commodore. disk $49.95 (ISBN 0-922614-09-1, Order no.: 40130).
IBM & Tandy. disk $44.95 (ISBN 0-922614-10-5, Order no.: 40110).
Apple. 3.5" disk $49.95 (ISBN 1-55790-231-3, Order no.: 40152).
Commodore. 3.5" disk $49.95 (ISBN 1-55790-236-4, Order no.: 40135).
IBM. 3.5" disk $44.95 (ISBN 1-55790-107-4, Order no.: 40111).
Carmen Sandiego's Gang of Eccentric Con Artists Has Grown Bigger & More Outrageous Than Ever. And They're Out to Steal Some of Our Most Precious National Treasures. You'll Start by Gathering All the Facts at the Scene of the Crime. Then You'll Be Off on a Wild Chase Across all the 50 States & the District of Columbia. As You Travel, You'll Learn about America's Cities, Coastlines, Mountain Ranges, Lakes, Deserts, History, etc. (the Program Includes the Fodor's USA Travel Guide). Features 16 Suspects, 50 States, & 1500 Clues.
Broderbund Software, Inc.

Where the Red Fern Grows. Intentional Education Staff & Wilson Rawls. Apr. 1996. *Items Included:* Program manual. *Customer Support:* Free technical support, 90 day warranty.
School ver.. Mac System 7.1 or higher. Macintosh (4Mb). 3.5" disk contact publisher for price (ISBN 1-57204-344-X). *Nonstandard peripherals required:* 256 color monitor, hard drive, printer.

SOFTWARE ENCYCLOPEDIA 1996

Lab pack. Mac System 7.1 or higher. Macintosh (4Mb). 3.5" disk contact publisher for price (ISBN 1-57204-320-2). *Nonstandard peripherals required:* 256 color monitor, hard drive, printer.
Site license. Mac System 7.1 or higher. Macintosh (4Mb). 3.5" disk contact publisher for price (ISBN 1-57204-345-8). *Nonstandard peripherals required:* 256 color monitor, hard drive, printer.
School ver.. Windows 3.1 or higher. IBM/Tandy & 100% compatibles (4Mb). 3.5" disk contact publisher for price (ISBN 1-57204-321-0). *Nonstandard peripherals required:* VGA or SVGA 640 x 480 resolution, 256 monitor, mouse, sound device.
Lab pack. Windows 3.1 or higher. IBM/Tandy & 100% compatibles (4Mb). 3.5" disk contact publisher for price (ISBN 1-57204-346-6). *Nonstandard peripherals required:* VGA or SVGA 640 x 480 resolution, 256 monitor, mouse, sound device.
Site license. Windows 3.1 or higher. IBM/Tandy & 100% compatibles (4Mb). 3.5" disk contact publisher for price (ISBN 1-57204-322-9). *Nonstandard peripherals required:* VGA or SVGA 640 x 480 resolution, 256 monitor, mouse, sound device.
This companion for young adult literature is ideal for students who don't know how to start that book report, or give that needed summary. Gentle prompts throughout the guide section of the program include Warm-up Connections, Thinking about Plot, Quoting & Noting, Keeping a Journal, If I Were ———' Responding to Questions, Using Quotations, Taking a Personal View, Write to Others, & Write a Sequel.
Lawrence Productions, Inc.

Whirlwind. Jan. 1994. *Items Included:* 8 page manual, 1 diskette, response card. *Customer Support:* 90 day limited warranty, support via phone, modem, fax.
DOS, Windows 3.1. IBM & compatibles (2Mb). disk $39.95 (ISBN 1-884791-03-4, Order no.: 01-2102-0100). *Optimal configuration:* Intel 386/486, 4Mb RAM, MPC-compatible sound card.
Single Player Arcade-Style Entertainment Software for Microsoft Windows.
Technological Computer Innovations Corp.

Whirly Bird Run. *Compatible Hardware:* Dragon Color Computer; MC-10; TRS-80 Color Computer, TDP-100. *Memory Required:* 16k. contact publisher for price.
Spectral Assocs.

Whistler's Brother. Louis Ewens. *Compatible Hardware:* Atari 400, 800, XL, XE series; Commodore 64. *General Requirements:* Joystick.
Commodore. disk $29.95 (Order no.: COMDSK-255).
Atari. disk $29.95 (Order no.: ATDSK-134).
You Must Keep Your Absent-Minded, Accident-Prone Brother, the Archaeologist Fenton Q. Fogbank, Out of Harm's Way. Features Simultaneous Control of 2 Characters, 13 Chapters, & 208 Levels.
Broderbund Software, Inc.

The White Horse Child. Feb. 1995. *Items Included:* CD-ROM booklet. *Customer Support:* Free technical support via phone as of release date.
MPC/Windows. 386.25 or higher IBM compatible (4Mb). CD-ROM disk $29.95 (ISBN 1-885784-10-4, Order no.: 1165). *Optimal configuration:* MPC CD-ROM player, S-VGA graphics card (640x480x256 colors) with compatible monitor, MPC compliant sound card, mouse, Windows 3.1.
Macintosh. Macintosh (4Mb). CD-ROM disk

TITLE INDEX

$29.95 (ISBN 1-885784-30-9, Order no.: 1295). *Optimal configuration:* CD-ROM drive, color monitor with 256 plus colors, system version 6.207 or higher.
Greg Bear, a Hugo & Nebula Award Winning Science Fiction & Fantasy Writer, Narrates His Story of The White Horse Child. Join a Boy As He Encounters the Excitement of His Own Imagination. Discover the Resulting Ignorance, Fear, Censorship He Faces from School, Home & Society. Learn the Power of Creative Thinking.
Technology Dynamics Corp.

White Knight. *Version:* 12. *Compatible Hardware:* Apple Macintosh Plus or higher; Power Macintosh for the Power. *General Requirements:* Modem. *Items Included:* Manual, Special offers from Delphi, CompuServe, Genie & ExMachina. *Customer Support:* Available for registered users.
3.5" disk $139.00.
Telecommunications Software.
The FreeSoft Co.

Whitesmiths Software Development Tools. *Compatible Hardware:* IBM PC, Sun Apollo, HP 9000, DEC VAX (VMS). *Operating System(s) Required:* MS-DOS, Unix, VMS. *Items Included:* C Cross Compiler, Cross Assembler, Utilities, libraries, & CXDB; a C source level cross debugger in a simulator & emulator version. *Customer Support:* Telephone hot-line, training, user documentation, 90 day unlimited warranty, yearly maintenance contracts available.
1 copy, IBM PC host: $2700.00.
Software Development Tools for Embedded Systems Designers Include Fully Integrated ANSI C Cross Compiler, Cross Assembler, Programming Utilities, Run-Time Libraries & CXDB, a C Source Level Cross Debugger (Simulator & Emulator Version). These Tools Allow the User to Produce Efficient, ROMable Reentrant Code for the 68HC11/16, 8051, 6809, Z80, & 64180. The Tools Are Available on the Following Host Computers: IBM PC, Sun, Apollo, HP 9000 Series 300 & the DEC VAX (VMS).
Intermetrics Microsystems Software, Inc.

Whitewater Resource Toolkit.
IBM PC AT (1Mb). disk $195.00. *Nonstandard peripherals required:* Hard disk drive. *Addl. software required:* Windows 2.1 or higher.
Includes Seven Editors for Creating, Editing & Managing a Microsoft Windows Application. User Can Create, Edit & Copy Standard Resources Such As Bitmaps, Icons, Cursors, Dialog Boxes, Menus, Accelerator Tables & String Tables from Within the Windows Environment. User Can Edit or Move Resources Directly from & into EXE & RES Files. String Table Editor Allows Translation of Applications into Foreign Languages Without Having Access to Application Source Code. Written in Actor (Whitewater's Object-Oriented Development Language) & Does Not Require SDK or RC. Supports Actor, C & Systems Integrating.
The Whitewater Group.

Who Framed Roger Rabbit. *Compatible Hardware:* Apple II series; Commodore 64/128 & Amiga; IBM PC & compatibles. *Memory Required:* Commodore 64/128 64k; Apple 128k; Commodore Amiga & IBM 512k. *Items Included:* Gag catalog, Quick Start card. *Customer Support:* (818)841-3326.
Apple. disk $39.95.
Amiga. 3.5" disk $44.95.
Commodore 64/128. disk $29.95.
IBM. 3.5" or 5.25" disk $39.95.
Go on a Madcap Race Through Tinseltown With Roger Rabbit As He Attempts to Save Toontown from the Evil Judge Doom. This Program Incorporates State-of-the-Art Graphics & Animation Plus Music & Sound Effects in Three Separate Games. Race Benny the Cab Through Tinseltown, Retrieve the missing Will at the Ink & Paint Club. Then High-Tail It to the Gag Factory for the Final Confrontation With Judge Doom. Succeed, & You Save Jessica & All of the Toontown; Fail, & Judge Doom Tuurns Toontown into a Freeway.
Walt Disney Computer Software, Inc.

Who Is Oscar Lake?: A French Interactive Language Learning Adventure. Sep. 1995.
Items Included: One (1) 160-page bound book. Runtime version of Windows or MAC. *Customer Support:* 30-day money-back guarantee plus free technical support.
Windows 3.1. 486 SX 25MHz or higher (40Mb). CD-ROM disk Contact publisher for price (ISBN 1-887684-02-6). *Nonstandard peripherals required:* 16 bit soundblaster compatible soundcard, double speed CD-ROM drive. *Optimal configuration:* 66MHz 486 DX, Quadspeed CD-ROM, 16 bit soundblaster compatible soundcard.
System 7.1 or higher. Macintosh 68030 or higher, 640x480x256 colors screen resolution. CD-ROM disk Contact publisher for price (ISBN 1-887684-03-4). *Nonstandard peripherals required:* Double speed CD-ROM drive. *Optimal configuration:* Macintosh 68040 or higher, quad speed CD-ROM drive.
CD-ROM Created & Produced for the Purpose of Teaching English or Foreign Languages by Using an Interactive Format.
Language Pubns.

Who Is Oscar Lake?: A Spanish Interactive Language Learning Adventure. Sep. 1995.
Items Included: One (1) 160-page bound book. Runtime version of Windows or MAC. *Customer Support:* 30-day money-back guarantee plus free technical support.
Windows 3.1. 486 SX 25MHz or higher (40Mb). CD-ROM disk Contact publisher for price (ISBN 1-887684-00-X). *Nonstandard peripherals required:* 16 bit soundblaster compatible soundcard, double speed CD-ROM drive. *Optimal configuration:* 66MHz 486 DX, Quadspeed CD-ROM, 16 bit soundblaster compatible soundcard.
System 7.1 or higher. Macintosh 68030 or higher, 640x480x256 colors screen resolution. CD-ROM disk Contact publisher for price (ISBN 1-887684-01-8). *Nonstandard peripherals required:* Double speed CD-ROM drive. *Optimal configuration:* Macintosh 68040 or higher, quad speed CD-ROM drive.
CD-ROM Created & Produced for the Purpose of Teaching English or Foreign Languages by Using an Interactive Format.
Language Pubns.

Who Is Oscar Lake?: An English Interactive Language Learning Adventure. Sep. 1995.
Items Included: One (1) 160-page bound book. Runtime version of Windows or MAC. *Customer Support:* 30-day money-back guarantee plus free technical support.
Windows 3.1. 486 SX 25MHz or higher (40Mb). CD-ROM disk Contact publisher for price (ISBN 1-887684-04-2). *Nonstandard peripherals required:* 16 bit soundblaster compatible soundcard, double speed CD-ROM drive. *Optimal configuration:* 66MHz 486 DX, Quadspeed CD-ROM, 16 bit soundblaster compatible soundcard.
System 7.1 or higher. Macintosh 68030 or higher, 640x480x256 colors screen resolution. CD-ROM disk Contact publisher for price (ISBN 1-887684-05-0). *Nonstandard peripherals required:* Double speed CD-ROM drive. *Optimal configuration:* Macintosh 68040 or higher, quad speed CD-ROM drive.
CD-ROM Created & Produced for the Purpose of Teaching English or Foreign Languages by Using an Interactive Format.
Language Pubns.

Who Killed Sam Rupert?: MPC Jewel Case. Shannon Gilligan. *Items Included:* Registration card. *Customer Support:* Creative Multimedia Corporation warrants the CD-ROM disc & diskettes to be free from defects in materials & workmanship under normal use & service for a period of 90 days from date of purchase. Creative Multimedia Corporation offers Technical Support to customers as needed.
MS-DOS 3.1 or higher, MS-CDEX 2.0 or higher. 386SX or higher (4Mb). CD-ROM disk $39.99 (ISBN 1-880428-10-5, Order no.: 10237). *Nonstandard peripherals required:* Sound Blaster or Sound Blaster compatible board. CD-ROM drive with 150k/sec transfer rate, 380ms or less access rate. *Addl. software required:* Microsoft Windows 3.1. *Optimal configuration:* SuperVGA with 512k, video memory capable of 640x480x256 colors with Windows driver supported. *Networks supported:* All.
In This First in a Series of Mysteries, You're Assigned the Case Just after Sam Rupert's Body Is Discovered in His Restaurant. You Have Access to the Crime Report, & Then You're on Your Own to Work the List of Suspects, & Match Your Crime-Solving Wits Against the Murderer. You'll Be Drawn into This Interactive Multimedia Mystery with Full-Motion Color Video, Sound & Animation. Your Challenge Is to Solve the Case Within Six Hours.
Creative Multimedia Corp.

Who Works When. *Version:* 1.1. *Compatible Hardware:* IBM PC AT, PC XT, PS/2, & compatibles. *Memory Required:* 640k. *Items Included:* Manual, diskettes, templates. *Customer Support:* 30-day free technical support.
disk $395.00.
Employee Scheduling Program That Quality-Matches Employees to Work Load Requirements.
Newport Systems.

The Whole Bit: Word Processing. *Version:* 2.1. 1983-1985. *Compatible Hardware:* Commodore 64. *Language(s):* Machine. *Memory Required:* 20k. *Items Included:* Vinyl case, documentation on disk.
disk $24.95.
Menu-Driven Word Processor Allows User to Print or Preview Any Portion of Text Held in the 20k Buffer. Package Includes 36 Pages of Documentation (Included on the Program Disk) Which Can Be Printed by the User If He/She Wishes.
Applied Technologies, Inc.

WHOLESALE DISTRIBUTION SYSTEM

Wholesale Distribution System. *Version:* 450.2. 1978. *Compatible Hardware:* IBM PC & compatibles. *Operating System(s) Required:* MS-DOS, PC-DOS. *Language(s):* QuickBASIC. *Memory Required:* 512k. *General Requirements:* Hard disk. *Items Included:* System diskettes, users guide, training tutorial. *Customer Support:* Telephone, annual contracts available.
$2995.00 to $3495.00.
Automates the Distribution Cycle from Purchasing of Inventory Through Collection of Receivables. Major Modules Include: Purchasing & Receivables, Inventory Control, Physical Inventory (Full & Cycle Counting), Serial & Lot Number Control, Customer Order Processing, Backorder Management, Rep Commissions, Accounts Receivable, & Both Territory & Corporate Budgeting. System Reports Company's Volume & Profitability by Product, Customer, & Sales Rep. Interfaces with IMS Manufacturing & General Ledger System. File Capacities Limited Only by Size of Hard Disk. The System May Be Run Single User or Multi-User on Many Networks.
International Micro Systems, Inc.

Wholesale Order Entry: Sales Counter Order Processing. Mike Flynn. Apr. 1987. *Operating System(s) Required:* MS-DOS, UNIX. *Memory Required:* 512k. *General Requirements:* Disk drive, hard disk, printer, modem.
MS-DOS. disk $5000.00.
UNIX. disk $10,000.
Designed for Distributors. Allows Clerks to Check on Customer Status, Item Inventory, & Pricing, Producing an Invoice on the Spot. Incomplete Invoices Can Be Held While Others Are Processed, Allowing Phone Order Taking, Will-Call Orders, Orders to Be Shipped, or Invoices for Customers Who Need More Time While Others Are Waiting.
Personal Systems Consulting.

The Wholesale Solution. Version: 5.0. 1980. *Operating System(s) Required:* Oasis or THEOS. *Language(s):* BASIC. *Items Included:* Software, documentation, 90 days support, on-site installation. *Customer Support:* Support contract available, call for pricing.
contact publisher for price.
Integrated Package of Accounting & Management Systems for Wholesalers, Distributors & Small Manufacturers.
Applied Solutions, Inc.

Whoops! 1986. *Compatible Hardware:* IBM PC & compatibles. *Operating System(s) Required:* PC-DOS. *Language(s):* Assembly. *Memory Required:* 256k.
disk $49.95.
site license avail.
Stand-Alone or Memory-Resident Program with On-Line Spelling Checking Capabilities. Features a 50,000 Word Dictionary. Not Copy Protected. Also Includes Thesaurus.
Cornucopia Software.

Who's Minding the Store? *Items Included:* Bound manual. *Customer Support:* Free hotline - no time limit; 30 day limited warranty; updates are $5/disk plus S&H.
MS-DOS. IBM & compatibles (256k). disk $19.95.
Game/Simulation Offers You the Chance of a Lifetime: to Own Your Own Business - a Neighborhood Grocery Store. Running the Store Is Not an Easy Business, However, As You Will Find Out the Very First Week. Brave the Perils of Spoiled Milk & Exciting Neighborhood Events (Such As the Neighborhood Reunion of a Very Large Italian Family, or the Local 4-H Club Conducting a Cooking Class). Dare to Bring High-Quality Merchandise & Low (?) Prices to Your Neighbors & Customers. "Beware" - Running the Store Is a Very Taxing Business, Especially since You Also Have Your Regular Job During the Week. You Have "Got" to Make the Store More Successful, So It Can Support You Full Time, Before You Have a Nervous Breakdown from Overwork! Ages 10 Through Adult.
Dynacomp, Inc.

Who.What.When. Version: 2.2. *Compatible Hardware:* IBM PC & compatibles. *Operating System(s) Required:* PC-DOS/MS-DOS 2.1 or higher. *Memory Required:* 512k. *General Requirements:* Hard disk. *Items Included:* Planner/organizer paper (optional). *Customer Support:* Yes, free.
disk $295.00.
Designed to Aid in People, Project & Time Management for Busy Executives. Enter the Who, What & When in a Familiar Daily Calendar Format...Information Instantly Updates All Personal Calendars, Project Schedules, Client & Account Histories, Time Lines (GANTT) & Project Task Lists. Complete with To-Do Lists, Task Delegation Tracking, Milestones & Deadlines, Appointment Move & Repeat, Meeting Maker, Conflict Checking, Alarms, Auto Dialer, Calendar Creator & 10 Calendar Reports to Fit Your Planner-Organizer Notebook.
Chronos Software, Inc.

The Wife of Bath's Prologue. Geoffrey Chaucer. Edited by Peter Robinson.
IBM. CD-ROM disk $240.00 (ISBN 0-521-46593-1).
Cambridge Univ. Pr.

WillMaker. Version: 4.0. Nolo Press Editors. Jun. 1990. *Operating System(s) Required:* System 4.1 or higher, DOS 2.1 or higher. *Language(s):* Assembly, QuickBASIC. *Customer Support:* Free technical support Monday-Friday, 9-5 PST; unlimited money back guarantee.
IBM PC or compatible (256k RAM). 3.5" & 5.25" disks $69.95 (ISBN 0-87337-147-X).
Macintosh 512k or higher (1Mb RAM). 3.5" disk $69.95 (ISBN 0-87337-146-1).
Users Can Draw Up Their Own Will. Prompts Through the Language of Wills in Easy Steps Designed for the Layman.
Nolo Pr.

WillPower. Apr. 1990. *Memory Required:* 512k. *Items Included:* User manual & Jacoby & Meyer's "Will & Estate Planning Guide" packaged together as one manual. *Customer Support:* Free phone support.
PC-DOS 2.0 or higher. disk $59.95 (ISBN 1-878834-00-2). *Nonstandard peripherals required:* Printer.
Designed for Home Users, This Program Will Allow Most Adult Americans to Safely & Privately Prepare a Legal Will.
Logicat, Inc.

WILSEARCH. *Compatible Hardware:* IBM PC & compatibles; Apple II series.
contact publisher for price.
Online Search Support Program Which Provides All of the Instructions & Suggestions Needed to Formulate & Carry Out a Search on the Wilson Online Databases. Instructions & Suggestions Appear On-Screen for Each Step of the Search Procedure. Includes Overview & Database Descriptions, Menu of Subject Areas, Database Menu, HELP Window, & HELP Command. Automatically Suggests Additional Related Terms (If Appropriate) When the Search Is Complete.
H. W. Wilson.

Win. Version: 2.0. Bob Nadler. Sep. 1985. *Compatible Hardware:* Apple II+, IIc, IIe, Atari 400, 800, 600XL, 800XL, 1200XL, 1400XL, 1450XLD, 65XE, 130XE; Commodore 64/128; IBM PC XT, AT & compatibles, PCjr. *Language(s):* Compiled Turbo BASIC. *Memory Required:* 48k; PC-DOS/MS-DOS 128k. *Items Included:* User's manual. *Customer Support:* Yes. disk $99.95 ea., incl. manual.
Apple. (ISBN 0-933596-27-8).
Atari. (ISBN 0-933596-28-6).
Commodore. (ISBN 0-933596-29-4).
IBM. (ISBN 0-933596-30-8).
reduced to $19.95 ea., if purchaser promises to pay F/22 Press 1% of his winnings over $100,000.00.
Generates LOTTO & Lottery Numbers, Offers 1- & 2-Digit LOTTO Numbers with Flexible Upper Limits, & Either 3, 4 or 5 Digit Lottery Numbers. Provides Data for As Many As 20 Games per Run. Handles 'Exotic' Games Such As New York's KENO.
F/22 Pr.

WIN/SYS Library. Dec. 1994. *Items Included:* Layflat manual, online help. *Customer Support:* 60 day money-back guarantee, free technical support, CompuServe technical support, free electronic maintenance upgrades.
Windows 3.1 or higher. 286 or higher (2Mb). disk $149.00. *Addl. software required:* Turbo Pascal for Windows 1.5, Borland Pascal 7.0, Borland C Plus Plus 3.1 or higher, Microsoft C/C Plus Plus 7.0 or higher, Borland Delphi 1.0.
WIN/SYS Library Is a Collection of System-Oriented Routines for Microsoft Windows Programming. Offers Comprehensive String Manipulation, International Date/Time Computation, Fast Arrays up to 64Mb, Sorting of up to 16Mb, General Purpose Data Structures (Lists, Collections, Dictionaries, Trees, Bitsets, etc.), DPMI Access, DOS Access, Exception Error Trapping & Recovery, & Heap Analysis Tools. Provides a DLL & Interfaces Callable from Delphi, Pascal, C, or C Plus Plus Programs; Also Provides Pascal Units for Direct Linking into Pascal & Delphi Programs. All Routines Optimized for Windows. Includes Full Source Code, Windows Help File, Comprehensive Documentation, & Plenty of Examples. No Royalties.
TurboPower Software.

Win Vegas. Centron Software Technologies Staff. Aug. 1995. *Items Included:* Set up instruction sheet. *Customer Support:* (503) 639-6863.
Windows 3.0 or higher. IBM PC. disk $14.95 (ISBN 1-887783-04-0, Order no.: 5300-4004). *Optimal configuration:* IBM PC, Windows 3.0 or higher, EGA, VGA, or SVGA, mouse, 640k RAM.
A Compilation of Various Casino Games That Allows the User to Learn How to Play the Games & Improve Their Skills.
Entertainment Technology.

Win Vegas. Centron Software Tech. Jan. 1996. *Items Included:* Set-up instruction sheet. *Customer Support:* 310-403-0043.
Win 3.0 or higher. IBM PC. disk $14.95 (ISBN 1-887783-22-9, Order no.: 5200-3004). *Optimal configuration:* IBM PC, Windows 3.0 or higher, EGA/SVGA, mouse, 640k RAM.
A Compilation of Various Casino Games That Allows the User to Learn How to Play the Games & Improve Their Skills.
Entertainment Technology.

Win Vegas, Vols. II & III. Centron Software Tech. Jan. 1996. *Items Included:* Set-up instruction sheet. *Customer Support:* 310-403-0043.
Windows 3.0 or higher. IBM PC. disk $12.95 (ISBN 1-887783-18-0, Order no.: 5100-2006). *Optimal configuration:* IBM PC, Win 3.0 or higher, EGA/VGA/SVGA, mouse, 640k RAM.
Casino Games That Allow the User to Learn How to Play the Games & Improve Their Skills.
Entertainment Technology.

WinCD Professional: The Ultimate CD Player. Brett McDonald. Oct. 1992. *Items Included:* Interactive help/on-line manual. *Customer Support:* Phone support.
MS-Windows 3.1 or higher. Intel '286, '386, '486 processor (2Mb). disk $49.95 (ISBN 1-882618-00-9, Order no.: WCDP). *Nonstandard peripherals required:* CD Rom drive. Multimedia sound card required for additional features. *Optimal configuration:* 386 PC, Windows 3.1, CD Rom drive, MPC compatible sound card.
A Complete, Professional CD Player for CD-ROM Drives. Unique Features Include CD Database, Track Sampling, Drag & Drop Programming, Multiple Saved Programs & More. Easy to Use Interface Mimics an Actual CD Player.
Apriori Software Corp.

WinConnect: for Microsoft Windows. Version: 1.0a. 1991. *Items Included:* 3.5" & 5.25" diskettes, 25 foot four-headed (9-pin & 25-pin)

serial cable, full documentation.
DOS 3.xxx or higher. IBM PC/XT/AT, PS/2 or compatible (60k). disk $99.95. *Addl. software required:* Microsoft Windows 3.0 (required on one machine).
Traveling Software, Inc.

Wind & Seismic Analysis. *Version:* 1.2. Jun. 1986. *Compatible Hardware:* IBM PC. *Operating System(s) Required:* PC-DOS. *Memory Required:* 96k.
disk $29.95.
Uses Wind & Seismic Building Code Data to Calculate the Forces & Moments Which Can Occur at Any Height on Any Size Structure. The Wind Data from the Building Codes, i.e. ANSI, UBC, etc., Is Entered in a Data File Which the User Can Modify.
Lbs Engineering, Inc.

Wind-2 Financial Management Software. *Version:* 4.4. *Memory Required:* 256k. *Items Included:* User manuals. *Customer Support:* After 60 days free. Hourly or yearly support contracts may be purchased.
MS-DOS. OS/2. IBM PC or compatible. write for info. *Optimal configuration:* Interfaces with Lotus & most word processors. *Networks supported:* Novell & 3-COM.
Specifically Designed for Engineers & Architects. Functions from the Input of Time & Expense to Provide Project Management, Profit Analysis, Overhead Cost Analysis, & Project Invoicing. Also Provides Accounts Receivable, General Ledger, Accounts Payable, Payroll, & a Custom Reporting Query Module.
Wind-2 Software, Inc.

WinDelete: The Safe & Simple Windows Uninstaller. *Items Included:* 1 Users Guide, 2 diskettes. *Customer Support:* Tech support.
Windows 3.1 or higher. IBM PC (4Mb, 2Mb hard disk). disk $49.95 (ISBN 0-924677-30-9). *Nonstandard peripherals required:* EGA, VGA or higher recommended. *Optimal configuration:* Mouse recommended.
Uninstalls Windows Applications Safely & Easily. By Using WinDelete to Uninstall Applications User Will Free up Hard Disk Space & Improve Windows Performance. The Easy Point & Click Interface & a Unique Color Coding System Make This Program Essential for Any Windows User.
IMSI (International Microcomputer Software, Inc.).

WinDings. Jul. 1992. *Items Included:* 3.5" & 5.25" diskettes, manual. *Customer Support:* Free lifetime technical support.
Windows & DOS. PC. disk $99.00.
Includes Automated ROLODEX That Holds 4000 Names, Auto Dialer, World Map Showing Time Zones & Direct Dial Country Codes, Personal Loan Calculator for Principle, Interest, Payments & More, Personal Info Filer for Account Numbers, Credit Cards & More - Password Protected.
Application Techniques, Inc.

Windmere Estate Adventure. *Compatible Hardware:* Apple II with Applesoft; IBM. *Memory Required:* Apple 48k, IBM 128k.
disk $29.95.
Exploration Simulation. Find Treasure & Deposit Safely at Treasure Drop.
Dynacomp, Inc.

Window Manager. *Version:* 2.1. 1994. *Customer Support:* 30 day free phone support.
THEOS 386/486. IBM & compatibles (4Mb). disk $399.00.
Plus Pak for THEOS 386/486 OS. Allows Developers To Design Applications That Feature Multiple Sessions, Windows & Color on Terminals. Features Include Multiuser BASIC Windows, EXEC Language Windows, 11 Windows per Session & up to 8 Sessions per Terminal.
THEOS Software Corp.

WINDOW: Multi Terminal Sessions. *Version:* 2.1. 1990. *Compatible Hardware:* MicroVAX & VAX. *Operating System(s) Required:* VMS, MICROVMS. *Language(s):* Basic, Macro. *Memory Required:* 25k. *Items Included:* 1 year maintenance, quarterly newsletter. *Customer Support:* 6:00 a.m.-6:00 p.m. MST. Included in ClydeSupport.
Enables the User to Create Multiple Interactive Sessions from a Single VT Terminal. Each Session is Active No Matter Which Session is Viewed on the Screen. Allows a User to Save Screen Contents to a File or Shared Print Queue.
Raxco, Inc.

WindowDOS. *Version:* 3.0. *Compatible Hardware:* IBM PC, PC XT, PC AT & compatibles; Tandy 1000, 1200. *Operating System(s) Required:* PC-DOS 3.3 or higher. *Memory Required:* 50k.
disk $69.95.
Resident Utility Gives Users Instant Access to DOS Functions & the Ability to Return to Where They Were. Up to 85 Files Can Be Displayed per Screen Page. Utilizes Pop up Windows & Single Keystroke Commands to Simplify Operation. The Printer Can Be Called Through Its Output Window & Given Commands from Inside Any Program. Text Editor for Editing Other Files Without Leaving Program You Are in.
Software of the Future, Inc.

WindowMagic. *Compatible Hardware:* Apple Macintosh. *Memory Required:* 512k.
3.5" disk $99.95.
Macintosh System Enhancement That Provides Users with Control over Windows.
Magnus Corp.

The Windows Disc. Feb. 1995. *Customer Support:* Telephone support, 30 day money back guarantee.
Windows 3.1. IBM & compatibles (2Mb). Contact publisher for price (ISBN 1-886770-04-2). *Optimal configuration:* VGA, Sound card, mouse recommended.
Collection of over 1500 Windows Programs - Games, Educational Programs, Business, Graphics, Icons, Fonts, & More.
Neon Publishing.

Windows DRAW. *Compatible Hardware:* IBM PC & compatibles. *Memory Required:* 320k.
disk $199.00.
Presentation Graphics Program That Runs under Microsoft's WINDOWS. Built into the Program Are Interfaces to LOTUS 1-2-3 & SYMPHONY. Graphs & Charts Produced by Either of These Programs Can Be Loaded Directly into WINDOWS DRAW, Enhanced, & Then Output to a Printer or Plotter. LOTUS 1-2-3 or SYMPHONY Files Are Loaded As a Group of Selectable Objects. Graph Elements Can Then Be Individually Manipulated & Enhanced. Other Drawings Can Be Incorporated from a Library of Pre-Defined Symbols.
Micrografx, Inc.

Windows Draw. *Version:* 3.0.
MS-DOS 3.1 or higher. IBM 386 or 486 & compatibles (2Mb). disk $149.00 (Order no.: DW3L30HD). *Addl. software required:* Windows 3.1. *Optimal configuration:* 4Mb.
Full-Featured Drawing Program for Anyone Who Uses Windows, Especially for Home or Office Use. Includes Freehand & Geometric Shape Tools with Bezier Curve Editing, Hundreds of Customizable Clip Art Images, an Editable Color Palette, OLE Support, More Than 12 TrueType Fonts, a Text along a Curve Feature, Context-Sensitive Help, & a Professional Technical Support Staff.
Micrografx, Inc.

Windows OrgChart. *Version:* 2.0.
MS-DOS 3.1 or higher. IBM 386 or 486 PC (2Mb). disk $149.00 (Order no.: OR2L20ENG). *Addl. software required:* Windows 3.1.
Create Sharp-Looking Organization Charts in Minutes. This Program Makes It a Snap to Create, Update, & Print Charts Using Windows. Just Click the Mouse & You're on Your Way to Creating Charts; Click & Drag the Mouse & You've Promoted or Reassigned Personnel to Another Location in the Chart. Can Even Cut, Paste, & Edit Multiple Charts While Viewing Them Simultaneously.
Micrografx, Inc.

Windows with Data Entry: Window Library Tools. *Version:* 2.21. Mar. 1986. *Operating System(s) Required:* PC-DOS, MS-DOS. *Memory Required:* 64k.
disk $99.00 (Order no.: 107001).
Productivity Enhancement Tool That Provides Commands to Handle the Keyboard More Efficiently. Debugging & Redesigning Screens, Altering Field Inputs, & Other Developmental Costs Are Greatly Reduced. Features Include a Window Editor to Create Several Windows & Menus Easily, & Window Librarian Which Allows Several Windows & Menus in One File, & a Snapshot Program That Allows Capture of Other Screens. This Product Includes Horizontal/Vertical Screens with Automatic Highlight & Supports the Following Data Types: Picture Strings, Date, Time, Integer, & Strings. Includes WINDOWS LIBRARY & a 220-Page Manual.
Glenco Engineering, Inc.

Windows 3.1 Power Tools for Windows 3.0 & 3.1: 2nd Edition. Geoffrey T. LeBlond & William B. LeBlond. *Items Included:* One 1.2Mb 3.5" high density disk. *Customer Support:* Phone number available for technical support, 212-492-9832; free disk replacement within 90 days of purchase.
IBM PC & compatibles. disk $49.95 (ISBN 0-553-35406-X). *Addl. software required:* Windows 3.1.
This Bestselling Book/Disk Package Has Been Updated to Cover the Latest Version of Windows. Details Tips/Techniques for Maximizing Windows Performance & Power. Covers: Memory Management, Control Panel, Using WIN.INI, Creating/Customizing PIF Files, DDE, Networking. Disk Features: Oriel 2.0 for Windows (a Graphics-Based Batch File Language), Command Post, Paint Shop. The LeBlonds' Bestselling Books Include "Using 1-2-3".
Bantam Bks., Inc.

WindowScript: The Interface Design Studio. *Version:* 1.5. *Items Included:* User manual. *Customer Support:* Phone, FAX, Apple Link, CompuServe, America On-Line.
Macintosh System 6.0.5 or higher. Macintosh Plus or higher (2Mb). 3.5" disk $149.00 (Order no.: 30-0500). *Addl. software required:* HyperCard 2.0v2 or higher.
Design Professional, Full-Color, Macintosh User Interfaces Within HyperCard. All Kinds of Dialog Boxes, Windows & Floating Palettes; Scrolling Lists of Text, Icons, Finder Icons & Pictures; QuickTime Movies; Standard, Tear-Off, Color Palette & Pop-Up Menus; Text Fields & Buttons, with Mixed Fonts, Styles, Sizes, Even Color; Icons, Including Color & Finder Icons; Color Pictures, Including Scrolling Pictures; Radio Buttons, Checkboxes & Round Rect Buttons; Lines & Boxes. WYSIWYG Interface Editor Lets You

Test As You Add or Change Objects. Advanced Programmers Can Add Custom MDEF, LDEF, CDEF & WDEF Resources to Expand WindowScript's Capabilities.
Heizer Software.

WindowsTeach. 1991.
Microsoft Windows 3.0. IBM PC & compatibles. disk $123.00.
Interactive System That Teaches MICROSOFT WINDOWS 3.0 Programming Techniques with Hypertext, Graphical Tutorials, & Source Code Annotations & Explanations.
IntelligenceWare, Inc.

Winery Production Management. *Compatible Hardware:* IBM PC. *Operating System(s) Required:* MS-DOS. *Language(s):* BASICA. *Memory Required:* 64k. *Customer Support:* Modem support.
disk $7800.00.
Manages Wine Production. Provides Crush & Invoice, Cellar Activity, Percent Composition & History, Tank System, Wine Chemistry, Barrel System, Cost Analysis & Government Forms.
Data Consulting Assocs.

Wines of the World. *Items Included:* Manual, registration card, flier describing all our titles, occasional promotional offers. *Customer Support:* Free telephone technical support.
DOS & Microsoft Windows 3.1. 12 MHz 80386SX. CD-ROM disk Contact publisher for price (ISBN 1-884014-23-2). *Nonstandard peripherals required:* MPC compatible. CD-ROM drive (680Mb) SVGA display, audio board, mouse, 486 DX processor. *Addl. software required:* Microsoft CD-ROM Extensions v.2.2.
Macintosh System 6.05. Color Macintosh (256 colors) (3.5Mb). CD-ROM disk Contact publisher for price (ISBN 1-884014-35-6). *Optimal configuration:* Single speed CD-ROM, 13" color monitor, 8 Mb RAM.
Enhance Your Enjoyment of Fine Wines. Search a 20,000 Wine Database Sorted by Vintage, Producer, Quality, Price at Release & Value. Video on Opening, Decanting, Production & Serving Wine.
Multicom Publishing, Inc.

Wines of the World Book Bundle. *Items Included:* Operating manual & book on wine. *Customer Support:* Free telephone technical support 1-800-850-7272.
DOS 3.1, Windows 3.1. 33Mhz 80486DX, VGA video/display at 256 colors (4Mb). CD-ROM disk $59.95 (ISBN 1-884014-59-3). *Nonstandard peripherals required:* CD-ROM drive, Sound Blaster compatible audio board. *Addl. software required:* Microsoft CD-ROM extensions 2.2. *Optimal configuration:* 8Mb, Dual speed CD-ROM.
DOS 3.1, Windows 3.1. 33MHz, 80486DX (4Mb). CD-ROM disk $49.95 (ISBN 1-884014-57-7). *Nonstandard peripherals required:* VGA video/display at 256 colors CD-ROM drive, Sound Blaster compatible audio board. *Addl. software required:* Microsoft CD-ROM extensions 2.2 or higher. *Optimal configuration:* 8Mb, Dual speed CD-ROM drive.
System 6.07 or higher. 68030 processor or higher Color Macintosh (256 plus colors, 13" monitor) (4Mb). CD-ROM disk $49.95 (ISBN 1-884014-58-5). *Nonstandard peripherals required:* CD-ROM drive. *Optimal configuration:* 8Mb, dual speed CD-ROM.
An Interactive Database of over 20,000 Wines. Full Motion Video & Photography Used to Illustrate Wine Serving. Coupled with the CD Is the Book on Wines of the World.
Multicom Publishing, Inc.

WINFIN - Financial Analysis for Windows: Investment Analysis. *Version:* 3.25. Russell C. Anderson. Nov. 1993. *Customer Support:* Free lifetime telephone support.
Windows 3.1 or higher. IBM compatible 386 (4Mb). $39.00 each plus $5.00 shipping & handling. *Optimal configuration:* Mouse & color monitor.
Analyze a Wide Range of Financial Instruments Involving Time & Money. The Unknown of Your Choice Is Computed along with Several Other Values Important to the Investment. Many Have "What-If" Analysis. Includes Mortgage & Rule-78 with Amortization. Bonds, Black-Scholes, IRR, MIRR, NPV, Portfolio Hedge, Auto Lease, Retirement Planning, Random Numbers, Days Between Dates, Calendar, T-Bills, CD's & BA's, Annuity & Compound Interest.
Gjetaas, Inc.

WinFlow. *Version:* 4.0. Oct. 1995. *Items Included:* Comprehensive manual, Runtime Viewer. *Customer Support:* Free technical support.
Windows 3.1 or Windows 95. 386 (4Mb). disk $295.00.
Use WinFlow to Produce Top-Quality Diagrams Fast, Without Tedious Drawing. Present Your Company's Organizational Structure or Design & Document the Flow of a Manufacturing Process. Develop Any Overall View of Work, Project, or Logic Flow in Just Minutes.
Mainstay.

WinForth. *Version:* 1.01. Oct. 1992. *Items Included:* 500-page reference manual. *Customer Support:* Electronic Mail, FAX, Bulletin Board, no charge.
Windows 3.1. Intel 386 or compatible, 486, Pentium. disk $495.00. *Optimal configuration:* 4Mb RAM, hard disk. *Networks supported:* All.
Forth-83 Program Development Environment for Windows 3.1. Includes Interpreter, Compiler, Assembler, Multiwindow Editor, Coprocessor, Support, Trace Utility, Many Example Programs, On-Line Hypertext Manual, & 500-Page Printed Manual.
Laboratory Microsystems, Inc.

Wings Out of Shadow. (Baen Software). Fred Saberhagen. May 1986. *Compatible Hardware:* Apple II, II+, IIe, IIc; Atari 800, 1200. *Memory Required:* 48k.
Apple. disk $34.95 (ISBN 0-671-30873-4).
Atari. disk $34.95 (ISBN 0-671-30876-9).
The Beserkers Come to Life in This Game Featuring Strategy, Tactics, Adventure & Arcade Action.
Brady Computer Bks.

Wingz. *General Requirements:* Two disk drives, hard disk recommended. *Items Included:* Documentation. *Customer Support:* Free technical support to registered users.
Macintosh Plus or higher (1Mb). 3.5" disk $499.00. *Nonstandard peripherals required:* Two disk drives, hard disk recommended.
OS/2 (packaged with windows). IBM 286 (1Mb). disk $499.00. *Nonstandard peripherals required:* Math coprocessor recommended. *Networks supported:* Novell.
Graphic Spreadsheet for the Business User. Features 32,768 Rows by 32,768 Columns; Quick Recalculations; a Search Function; Presentation Graphics; Access to up to 16 Million Colors; Charts, Art, Textures & Borders (in 2D & 3D); a Programming Language for Writing Applications; Import/Export Capabilities with Other Programs.
Informix Software, Inc.

WinJokes: The Greatest Joke Collection of All Time. *Version:* 1.1. Oct. 1993. *Items Included:* Installation guide. *Customer Support:* Free phone support.
DOS 3.0. IBM (512k). disk $29.95 (Order no.: DOSJOKES). *Optimal configuration:* Hard drive recommended.
Windows 3.0. IBM (1Mb). disk $29.95 (Order no.: WINJOKES). *Optimal configuration:* Hard drive recommended.
Mac System 6.05. Mac (512k). 3.5" disk $29.95 (Order no.: MACJOKES). *Optimal configuration:* Hard drive recommended.
Complete Collection of Some of the Funniest Jokes of All Time Is Now Shipping. Includes 1 MB of the Best One Liners, Stories, Compilations, & Outrageous Wit. Included Are Murphy's Complete Laws, Computing Funnies, Lawyer Jokes, & Hundreds of Hilarious Joke Lists. Great for Writers, Speakers, Comedians; Good for Reducing Stress; & Perfect for Kicking off Your Day in Just the Right Way.
Protronics Computer Systems.

Winnebago CAT. 1987. *Compatible Hardware:* IBM, PC AT, PS/2. *Memory Required:* 640k. *General Requirements:* hard disk. *Items Included:* Manual. *Customer Support:* One year included in purchase price.
3.5" or 5.25" disk $1495.00 (ISBN 0-927875-12-8, Order no.: 481).
On-Line Public Access Catalog. Allows Searches by Subject, Title, Notes, Call Number, & Author Using Key Word, Key Phrase & Boolean Logic Capabilities. Prints Bibliographic Reports. MARC-Record Compatible. Integrates with WINNEBAGO CIRC.
Winnebago Software Co.

Winnebago CAT for the Macintosh. *Version:* 3.0. Oct. 1992. *Items Included:* 3 ring bound manual included. *Customer Support:* Free on-site training, 1 year free customer support agreement, with purchase this includes 800 support 2 hour call-back guarantee.
Macintosh 6.05. Macintosh (4Mb). 3.5" disk $1495.00 (ISBN 0-927875-14-4, Order no.: 330). *Networks supported:* AppleTalk, EtherTalk.
This On-Line Catalog Is Fully Integrated with Circulation & Allows Users of the Library the Ability to Search Materials by Key Word, Key Phrase, with Boolean Options. It Gives the Ability to Look up Materials by Title, Author, Subject, Call Number, Series Titles, Joint Authors & Much More. It Is Designed to Be Very User Friendly Following the Apple Guidelines for User Interface.
Winnebago Software Co.

Winnebago CIRC. *Version:* 6.31. 1986. *Compatible Hardware:* IBM PC AT, PS/2. *Operating System(s) Required:* MS-DOS. *Language(s):* Turbo Pascal, C, Assembler. *Memory Required:* 640k. *General Requirements:* Hard disk, printer, bar wand. *Items Included:* Manual. *Customer Support:* One year included in purchase price.
disk $1495.00 (ISBN 0-927875-09-8, Order no.: 480).
Circulation Management Program Designed for the Smallest Library up to a Library with a Collection of 200,000 Items & 50,000 Patrons. Includes an Inventory Routine. Program Fully Integrates with Winnebago CAT.
Winnebago Software Co.

Winnebago CIRC/CAT. *Version:* Mac 3.0, IBM 6.31. Apr. 1994. *Items Included:* 2 manuals: Getting Started Manual (Mac - 100 pg, IBM - 100 pg); Software Manual (Mac - 260 pg, IBM - 428 pg) (3 ring binder). *Customer Support:* Guaranteed 2 hr call-back; 1st year of support included with program purchase; toll-free 1-800 number; modem support; program updates & manual revisions; replacement program disks if

necessary; subscription to the WUG Letter, 30 day money back guarantee.
MS-DOS. IBM or compatible PC-Based computer, DOS 3.0 or higher (640k). 3.5" disk $2990.00 (ISBN 0-927875-21-7, Order no.: 1000). *Nonstandard peripherals required:* Epson or compatible printer with tractor feed, barwand, & keyboard. 2Mb hard drive space. *Optimal configuration:* 486 or higher processor, MS-DOS 5.0 or higher, 1Mb RAM, 2Mb hard disk space for every 1,000 MARC records in database. *Networks supported:* Winnebago LAN, Novell, ICLAS, & LANtastic.
MS-DOS. IBM or compatible PC-Based computer, DOS 3.0 or higher (640k). 5.25" disk $2990.00 (ISBN 0-927875-22-5, Order no.: 1000). *Nonstandard peripherals required:* Epson or compatible printer with tractor feed, barwand, & keyboard. 2Mb hard drive space. *Optimal configuration:* 486 or higher processor, MS-DOS 5.0 or higher, 1Mb RAM, 2Mb hard disk space for every 1,000 MARC records in database. *Networks supported:* Winnebago LAN, Novell, ICLAS, & LANtastic.
System 6.0.5 or higher. Macintosh PC-Based (4Mb in addition to memory required by system software). 3.5" disk $2990.00 (ISBN 0-927875-23-3, Order no.: 2000). *Nonstandard peripherals required:* Laser printer or Apple Image Writer Printer, mouse, keyboard, barwand. *Optimal configuration:* Macintosh computer with a 68030 or higher processor, Macintosh System 7, 4Mb RAM, 1.4Mb floppy disk drive. *Networks supported:* Ethertalk, Local talk, & any other Apple Talk protocols.
An Integrated Library Automation System That Combines Both Circulation & Catalog. It Can Share One or Additional Databases So Both Patrons & Staff Can Immediately Know the Status of Materials. It Automates the Whole Library Process from Inventory & Checking in Materials to Numerous Reports & OPAC Searches.
Winnebago Software Company.

Winnebago Circ for the Macintosh. *Version:* 3.0. Jan. 1992. *Items Included:* 3 ring binder manual included. *Customer Support:* Free On-Site Training, 1 Year Free Customer Support Agreement with Program, This Includes 800 support 2 hour call-back guarantee.
Macintosh 6.05. Macintosh (4Mb). 3.5" disk $1495.00 (ISBN 0-927875-15-2, Order no.: 320). *Networks supported:* AppleTalk, Ethertalk.
This Product Controls the Circulation Functions of a Library Which Include Check-Out, Check-In, Fine Calculations, Reserves, All Revolving Around Specific Privilege & Loan Periods Set up by Librarians. It Comes with the Ability to Set up & Print Calendars for Library Hours. It Gathers Statistics As It Circulates. It Gives a Full Range of Report Options Including Lists of Notices for Over Dues Fines, Reserves & Materials Checked Out.
Winnebago Software Co.

Winnebago LAMP: Library Acquisition Management Program. 1991. *Customer Support:* One year included in purchase price.
DOS 3.1 or higher. IBM AT, PS/2, & compatible (640k). disk $695.00 (ISBN 0-927875-13-6, Order no.: 845).
Allows User to Organize & Manage the Ordering of Library Materials.
Winnebago Software Co.

Winnebago SLIP-IBM. *Version:* 2.1. 1993. *Items Included:* Manual. *Customer Support:* This program is listed with the CIRC/CAT which includes 1 year of customer support from purchase date. An inservice for CIRC/CAT is provided at no charge which includes the SLIP.

MS-DOS. IBM AT, PS/2 & compatibles (640k). disk $695.00 (ISBN 0-927875-31-4, Order no.: 8000). *Optimal configuration:* 386/486 processor, 2Mb RAM, hard disk drive access speed of less than 20 milliseconds, DOS 5.0 or higher. *Networks supported:* Any NetBIOS Network.
With Winnebago SLIP (Supply Library Information to the Patron) Users Can Automatically Produce a Variety of Slips from CIRC/CAT Programs Circulation Screen. Using a Small 40-Column Printer, Without One Extra Keystroke, User Can Print Circulation Receipts, Fine Notices, & Fine Receipts. May Also Print a Customized Message up to Five Lines in Length.
Winnebago Software Co.

Winnebago SLIP-MAC. 1993. *Items Included:* Manual. *Customer Support:* This program is listed with the CIRC/CAT which includes 1 year of customer support from purchase date. An inservice for CIRC/CAT is provided at no charge which includes the SLIP.
MAC. MAC w/68030 processor or higher (4Mb). 3.5" disk $695.00 (ISBN 0-927875-30-6, Order no.: 8000). *Optimal configuration:* 8Mb RAM, Version 7.0. *Networks supported:* Apple File Protocol Network.
With Winnebago SLIP (Supply Library Information to the Patron) Users Can Automatically Produce a Variety of Slips from CIRC/CAT Programs Circulation Screen. Using a Small 40-Column Printer, Without One Extra Keystroke, User Can Print Circulation Receipts, Fine Notices, & Fine Receipts. May Also Print a Customized Message up to Five Lines in Length.
Winnebago Software Co.

Winning Deal. *Compatible Hardware:* HP 150 Touchscreen.
3.5" disk $39.00 (Order no.: 92248CA).
Games Included Are Blackjack, Concentration, Accordion Solitaire, Streets & Alleys Solitaire, & Klondike Solitaire. Several Variations & Levels of Difficulty Are Available for Each Game.
Hewlett-Packard Co.

WinQL: Report Writer for Windows. *Version:* 4.0. Core Software. *Customer Support:* Sales support toll-free 1-800-451-3539 technical support.
MS-DOS Windows. IBM PC & compatibles (4Mb). disk $250.00 single user. *Networks supported:* Netware.
WinQL Is a Windows-Based Report Writer for Creating Custom Reports, Lists, & Forms Using Data from Your Existing Databases. WinQL Supports a Wide Variety of Formats Such As DataFlex, dBase, Btrieve, Paradox, Object Vision, ASCII FI6S & SQL-Based Systems.
Data Access Corp.

WinScope. *Version:* 1.20. Periscope Co. Staff. Jun. 1994. *Items Included:* 1 perfect-bound manual (100 plus pages) & disk. *Customer Support:* Free telephone support, BBS, CompuServe (Go Periscope).
DOS/Windows 3.1 or higher. 80386 or higher (enough to run Windows). disk $149.00.
Windows API Debugger & "Discovery" Tool for Developers. Non-Intrusively Captures & Stores API Calls, Messages, & Hooks - All with Parameter Names - As Well As Toolhelp Notifications & Debug Kernel Messages. This Gives the User a Meaningful, High-Level View of Any Windows Application.
Periscope Co.

WinSense. *Version:* 1.2. Jan. 1993. *Items Included:* One manual, diskettes, & registration card & box. *Customer Support:* Telephone support available from 9:00am to 5:30pm EST - 603-644-5555 No charge.

DOS 3.3 or higher. IBM PC, XT, AT, PS/2 & compatibles or clone (480k Windows RAM). disk $89.95. *Addl. software required:* Windows 3.1 or higher. *Networks supported:* Yes.
First Software to Offer the Windows User a Real Solution to the Confusion & Frustration of Fine-Tuning Windows Options. Has Automatic Optimizing of the Windows INI File Settings, a Sensible Appraoch to INI File Editing, Complete with Automatic Backup, a Comprehensive, Online, Windows Information System, & Much More. Everything You Need to Take Control of Windows.
SoftLogic Solutions.

Winter Games. *Compatible Hardware:* Macintosh; Atari ST. *General Requirements:* Joystick.
$39.95.
Includes Seven Winter Sport Events: Ski Jump, Hot Dog Aerials, Figure Skating, Free Skating, Speed Skating, Bobsled, & Biathlon. Includes Opening Ceremonies & Practice Training Sessions.
Epyx, Inc.

WINX. *Version:* 3.4.3. *Compatible Hardware:* Apple Macintosh, Macintosh Plus. *General Requirements:* Hard disk.
3.5" disk $3400.00.
Eyecare Management.
Medical Software, Inc.

WINX11. Nov. 1995. *Items Included:* 3-spiral-bound manual (175 pages). *Customer Support:* Free telephone support - 30 day money-back guarantee consulting/training available, custom programming.
Windows 3.1 or higher. IBM 486 or higher (1Mb). $1995.00 ($1295.00 with upgrade). *Nonstandard peripherals required:* VGA.
Provides Windows Interface to X11-ARIMA/88, a Sophisticated Seasonal Adjustment Package for the PC.
Delphus, Inc.

Wiremap. *Items Included:* Bound manual. *Customer Support:* Free hotline - no time limit; 30 day limited warranty; updates are $5/disk plus S&H.
MS-DOS. IBM & compatibles (256k). disk $59.95.
Apple (48k). disk $59.95.
Designed to Allow Electronic Circuits & Schematics to Be Computerized for the Purpose of Generating Parts Lists, Wire Lists, & Signal Lists. These Lists May Then Be Used for the Purposes of Production, Debugging, Trouble Shooting, & Documentation of the Circuit. Useful for Prototype, Wire-Map, & Point-to-Point Circuitry, since the Signal Listing May Be Used As a Guide to Correctly Wiring the Circuit.
Dynacomp, Inc.

Wiremaster. *Compatible Hardware:* IBM PC. *Operating System(s) Required:* CP/M-86, CP/M-80, MS-DOS.
contact publisher for price.
Afterthought Engineering.

WISC-III Compilation: What to Do Now That You Know the Score. Jeff Porter. Sep. 1993. *Items Included:* Instruction manual.
Macintosh. Macintosh (4Mb). 3.5" disk $70.00 (ISBN 0-87879-972-9, Order no.: 971-0). *Optimal configuration:* Apple System 5 or higher required. One double-sided disk drive required.
IBM PC AT or compatible (640k). disk $70.00 (ISBN 0-87879-970-2, Order no.: 970-2 (5 1/4")). *Optimal configuration:* One high-density disk drive (1.2Mb or 1.44Mb), DOS 3.3 or higher required.

(ISBN 0-87879-971-0, Order no.: 971-0 (3 1/2")).
Provides Long-Term Goals, Short-Term Objectives, Resources & Materials for Remediation of Deficit Areas Identified by WISC-III Test Scores. The Program Provides a Printout That Contains Test Scores with Goals & Objectives for Each Deficit Area, Significantly Reducing Report Preparation Time for Psychologists & Other Educational Diagnosticians.
Academic Therapy Pubns, Inc.

WISC-R Microcomputer-Assisted Interpretive Report: WISC-R Micro. Version: 1.2. The Psychological Corp. 1986. Compatible Hardware: Apple II+, IIe, IIc; IBM PC. Operating System(s) Required: PC-DOS 2.0 of higher. Memory Required: Apple 64K, IBM 128k. General Requirements: Printer. Items Included: User's manual, disk. Customer Support: 800-228-0752, 1 for Menu, 6 for Support.
$182.00.
Produces In-Depth Analysis of WISC-R Results for Ages 6-16. The Program Generates a 3 to 4 Page Interpretive Report Based on the Examinee's WISC-R Results, the Psychometric Characteristics of WISC-R Scores, & the Published Research Literature on the WISC-R. The Report Includes Descriptive Information, Individual Profile, Statistical Information (Confidence Intervals, Verbal/Performance Discrepancy, Idiographic Comparison), & Interpretive Information.
Harcourt Brace Jovanovich, Inc.

WISC-Three Compilation: What to Do Now That You Know the Score. Version: 2.0. Jeff Porter. Sep. 1994. Items Included: Instruction manual.
PC, IBM AT or compatibles (640k). disk $70.00 (ISBN 0-87879-970-2, Order no.: 970-2). Optimal configuration: One high-density disk drive (1.2Mb or 1.44Mb), DOS 3.3 or higher.
PC, IBM AT or compatibles (640k). 3.5" disk $70.00 (ISBN 0-87879-971-0, Order no.: 971-0). Optimal configuration: One high-density disk drive (1.2Mb or 1.44Mb), DOS 3.3 or higher.
Macintosh (4Mb). 3.5" disk $70.00 (ISBN 0-87879-972-9, Order no.: 971-0). Optimal configuration: Apple System 5 or higher, one double-sided disk drive.
Provides Long-Term Goals, Short-Term Objectives, Resources & Materials for Remediation of Deficit Areas Identified by WISC-III Test Scores. Provides a Printout That Contains Test Scores with Goals & Objectives for Each Deficit Area, Significantly Reducing Report Preparation Time for Psychologists & Other Educational Diagnosticians.
Academy Therapy Pubns, Inc.

WISEMAN. Compatible Hardware: Data General Micro-Products. Operating System(s) Required: RDOS. Language(s): Business BASIC.
disk $795.00.
Analyzes Existing Business BASIC Programs for 19 Possible Speed & Space Improvements.
QAX International Systems Corp.

Wishbringer. Brian Moriarty. Jun. 1985. Compatible Hardware: Apple II, II+, IIe, IIc, Macintosh; Atari XL/XE, ST; Commodore 64, 128, Amiga; DEC Rainbow; IBM PC & compatibles; Kaypro II; TI-99/4A, TI Professional; TRS-80 Model I, Model III, TRS-80 Color Computer. Operating System(s) Required: MS-DOS, CP/M.
disk $39.95.
You're an Ordinary Mail Clerk in an Ordinary Little Town. But There's Something Quite Extraordinary in Today's Mail. It's a Ransom Note for a Kidnapped Cat, & It Will Lead You Through Amazing Adventures to Wishbringer, a Stone Possessing Undreamed-Of Powers. For Although the Note Is Addressed to Someone in Your Town, It's Postmarked for Special Delivery to Parts Unknown. And Its True Destination Is Somewhere Beyond Your Wildest Dreams. You Can Solve the Story with the Help of Magic Wishes, or by the Use of Logic Alone.
Activision, Inc.

The Witness. Stu Galleg. 1983. Compatible Hardware: Apple Series; Atari XL/XE, ST; Commodore 64; IBM; Kaypro; TI-99/4A; TRS-80. Operating System(s) Required: MS-DOS, CP/M.
$39.95.
Why Should You, the Chief Police Detective, Give up Your Precious Spare Time to Work on This Case, Battling a 12-Hour Deadline? Could It Be the Self-Centered Soldier of Fortune Who Asked You So Urgently? Was His Wife's Death Really a Suicide? And What Makes His Daughter So Intriguing? And What about the Asian Butler, or the Lover Who Looks Like a Film Star? Armed with a Packet of Crucial Evidence, You Face a Tangled Web of Clues, Motives, & Alibis. The Only Testimony You Can Trust Is That of Your Own Eyes Because...You Are the Witness.
Activision, Inc.

The Witness. Infocom. Compatible Hardware: HP 150 Touchscreen, HP 110 Portable.
3.5" disk $39.95 (Order no.: 92243QA).
Reader Becomes a Detective in the 1930's.
Hewlett-Packard Co.

Wizard Medical Specialties. Version: 1.5. G. B. Cook. Jun. 1985. Compatible Hardware: IBM PC. Operating System(s) Required: PC-DOS. Language(s): Quicksilver. Memory Required: 640k. General Requirements: Printer.
disk $595.00 (Order no.: 285-06).
Provides 18 Different Interviews for the Medical Specialties. Saves Physician's Time in the Preliminary Interview & Avoids Costly Oversights. Questions May Be Modified or Amended.
SRC Systems, Inc.

Wizard of Wall Street. Multisoft Corp. & Synapse Software. Compatible Hardware: IBM PC & compatibles, PCjr, PC XT, PC AT. General Requirements: Graphics card.
disk $44.95 (Order no.: IBMDSK-4125).
Your Rich Uncle Has Left You $50,000 in His Will, with the Stipulation That You Must Play the Market. Buy & Sell Stock & Stock Options, Get Reports on Companies You Want to Invest in, Watch the Ticker Tape, & Chart Your Progress. You Can Buy & Sell from 12 to 24 Stocks & Options in 6 Different Industries. Three Levels Are Available.
Broderbund Software, Inc.

Wizardry - Bane of the Cosmic Forge. D W Bradley. Nov. 1990. Items Included: 125-Page manual, character reference sheet, system reference card, Magic Icon/Word list (copy protection). IBM PC package contains a disk exchange coupon. Customer Support: 30-day warranty free replacement if proof of purchase indicating purchase date is provided. If over 30-day warranty, please provide $12.50 replacement fee. Customer support hotline available Monday through Friday 4:00 PM to 8:00 PM, 12:00 noon to 4:00 PM weekends & holidays.
MS-DOS. IBM PC & 100% compatibles (640k). 3.5" or 5.25" disk $19.95. Optimal configuration: IBM PC & 100% compatibles, 2 disk drive, VGA, EGA, MCGA, CGA & Hercules, Full digitized sound, 640k RAM, hard drive optional.
System 7.0. MAC Plus & higher (1Mb-b/w; 2Mb-color). 3.5" disk $19.95. Optimal configuration: 1MB black & white, 2Mb color, One 3.5" 800k double-sided disk drive. Hard drive optional.
Amiga DOS. Amiga 500 & higher (1Mb). 3.5" disk $19.95. Optimal configuration: 1Mb RAM, one disk drive, hard drive optional.
The Truest Simulation Ever of FRP. From Its Novel-Like Plot to Its Calculated Die Rolls, Bane Offers Uncompromising Variety: 11 Races, 14 Professions, Weaponry, Physical & Academia Skills, a Researched Armament, 400 Items Strong, Six Spellbooks, & 462 Spell Combinations. Full-Screen, Animated Graphics & Digitized Sound Intensify the Gaming Experience.
Sir-Tech Software, Inc.

Wizardry Gold. Apr. 1995. Customer Support: Free hint line service available 4:00-8:00p.m. (EST) weekdays, 12:00-4:00p.m. (EST) weekends & holidays. Technical support on weekdays 9:00a.m.-5:00p.m. (EST), 30-day warranty with dated proof of purchase. After 30-day warranty expires, $12.50 replacement fee applied.
Windows 95. IBM PC 486/33 MHz (8Mb). CD-ROM disk Contact publisher for price (ISBN 0-926846-86-8). Nonstandard peripherals required: Double speed CD-ROM, SVGA display, Win-compatible. Addl. software required: MS Windows 3.1.
System 7.01. Macintosh LC-III (8Mb). CD-ROM disk Contact publisher for price (ISBN 0-926846-90-6). Nonstandard peripherals required: Double speed CD-ROM, 256 color monitor.
Multi-Faceted Wizardry Gold Includes a Complete Re-Engineered of Crusaders of the Dark Savant, the epic Story of a Planet on the Brink of War. The Fate of the World Lies in Your Hands, & Your Mission Is to Find the Astral Dominae, a Mystical Artifact That Holds the Secret of Life Itself. But Beware, You're Not the Only One After the Astral Dominae. The World into Which You Descend Is Populated with Creatures of Every Complexion. Some Will Beat You to the Prize. Others Will Beat You to a Pulp. From the Tension of a Perplexing Mindgame to the Intensity of Fullphased Combat, Wizardry Gold Serves up the Nastiest Foes & the Toughest Puzzles Ever Built into an Adventure Game. With High-End Graphics, Ear-Blasting Audio Effects, Full-Frame Animation Sequences, Multiple Endgames & Digitized Speech, Wizardry Gold Is a Total Experience That Will Sink Its Teeth into Your Ankles & Never Let go.
Sir-Tech Software, Inc.

Wizardry II: Knight of Diamonds (The Second Scenario). A. Greenberg & R. Woodhead. Nov. 1989. Customer Support: Hotline; disk repair or replacement.
Wizardry Runtime System (self booting). Tandy 1000 SX, EX, TX, HX, SL, TL. disk $19.95 (ISBN 0-926846-43-4, Order no.: 2022). Nonstandard peripherals required: CGA card.
Apple Pascal. Macintosh 512KE or higher (512k). 3.5" disk $19.95 (ISBN 0-926846-40-X, Order no.: 502).
The Second Scenario in the WIZARDRY Universe. It Requires the Use of Characters Originally Created in the First Scenario (Proving Grounds) or Those Transferred from Legacy of Llylgamyn, the Third Scenario. Characters Should Have Acquired At Least 13th Level of Experience Before Entering into the Knight of Diamonds. Only Those Surviving the Rigors of the Maze To Locate the Fabulous Missing Suit of Armor Will Be Worthy of the Title, the Knight of Diamonds.
Sir-Tech Software, Inc.

Wizardry III: Legacy of Llylgamyn (The Third Scenario). A. Greenberg & R. Woodhead. Nov. 1989. Items Included: Disk, manual, reference

TITLE INDEX

card, map plotting aid pad. *Customer Support:* Hotline; disk repair or replacement.
Wizardry Runtime System (self booting). Tandy 1000 SX, EX, TX, HX, SL, TL. disk $19.95 (ISBN 0-926846-44-2, Order no.: 2032). *Nonstandard peripherals required:* CGA card.
Apple Pascal. Macintosh (512k). (ISBN 0-926846-41-8, Order no.: 503).
The Third in the Wizardry Saga. In This Scenario, Wizardry Adventure Continues Through an Even More Daring Search for the Orb Taken by the Dragon L'kbtreth. Features Overlapping Window Graphics. Six Levels. Scenario Characters Are Descendents of Characters Developed in Wizardry I & II.
Sir-Tech Software, Inc.

Wizardry IV: The Return of Werdna (The Fourth Scenario). A. Greenberg & A. Woodhead. Nov. 1989. *Customer Support:* Hotline, disk repair or replacement.
Tandy 1000 SX, EX, TX, HX, SL, Tl. disk $19.95 (ISBN 0-926846-45-0, Order no.: 2052).
This Scenario Features a Role Reversal. Trebor & His Band of Do-Gooders Have Stolen Your Magic Amulet, Drained You into a Coma & Imprisoned Your Indestructible Body in a Convoluted Prison Maze, but Your Seething Lust for Revenge Has Re-Animated You. You Want Your Amulet Back!! Your Magical Powers Are As Week As a Babe's. Your Monster Allies Are Untrustworthy. Ultimately, to Escape & Wreak Revenge, You Must Depend on Your Wit & Skills As the Grandmaster of Wizardry.
Sir-Tech Software, Inc.

Wizardry: Proving Grounds of the Mad Overlord (The First Scenario). Andrew Greenberg & Robert Woodhead. Nov. 1989. *Customer Support:* Hotline; disk repair or replacement.
Wizardry Runtime System (self booting). Tandy 1000 SX, EX, TX, HX, SL, TL. disk $19.95 (ISBN 0-926846-42-6, Order no.: 2012). *Nonstandard peripherals required:* CGA card.
Proving Grounds is the First Scenario in the Wizardry Gaming System of Fantasy Role-Playing. Starting in the Castle, User Assembles a Party of Six Characters, Each with Their Own Characteristics to Explore the Magic & Mystery of the 10 Level, 3-D Maze. Characters May Be One of Five Races & One of Eight Professions. Under User's Command, Party Will Accumulate Experience & Treasures, Slay Dragons & Foes & Prepare Themselves For the Final Battle.
Sir-Tech Software, Inc.

Wizardry Trilogy: Proving Grounds, Knight of Diamonds, Legacy of Llylgamyn. Robert Woodhead & Andrew Greenberg. Nov. 1989. *Items Included:* Three software packages included in each Trilogy package, program disk, manual, reference card, map plotting aid, warranty/registration card. *Customer Support:* 30 day warranty, customer support hotline.
Apple Pascal. Apple II series (48k). disk $49.95 (ISBN 0-926846-50-7, Order no.: 100).
IBM PC & compatibles, 5.25" disk format (128k). disk $49.95 (ISBN 0-926846-51-5, Order no.: 200). *Nonstandard peripherals required:* CGA card.
IBM PC & compatibles, 3.5" disk format (128k). disk $49.95 (ISBN 0-926846-52-3, Order no.: 2003). *Nonstandard peripherals required:* CGA card.
Commodore 64/128 (64k). disk $39.95 (ISBN 0-926846-53-1, Order no.: 300).
Comprised of the First Three Scenarios in the Series of Fantasy Role-Playing Games.
Sir-Tech Software, Inc.

Wizardry: Trilogy Two. D. W. Bradley. Oct. 1993. *Items Included:* (4) 3.5" diskettes, manual, warranty registration card. *Customer Support:* Free hint line service available 4:00-8:00 p.m. (EST) weekdays, 12:00-4:00 p.m. (EST) weekends & holidays. Technical support - weekdays 9:00 a.m. to 5:00 p.m. (EST) 30-day warranty with dated proof of purchase. After 30-day warranty expires, $12.50 replacement fee applied.
MS-DOS. IBM PC/100% compatibles. disk $59.95 (ISBN 0-926846-72-8, Order no.: FD24103). *Optimal configuration:* Wizardry V - 2 floppy drives, 128k; Wizardry VI - 2 disk drives, VGA or EGA, PC Speaker, 640k RAM, hard drive; Wizardry VII - hard drive, PC/MS-DOS 3.X or 5.0, 10Mhz or faster.
Wizardry V-Heart of the Maelstrom, Wizardry VI-Bane of the Cosmic Forge & Wizardry VII-Crusaders of the Dark Savant combined in one package.
Sir-Tech Software, Inc.

Wizardry V: Heart of the Maelstrom. David W. Bradley. *Items Included:* 86 page manual, quick reference cards. *Customer Support:* Replacement disks after 30 days - $12.50, before 30 days - free, hotline.
Tandy 1000, SX, EX, TX, HX, SL, TL (128k). 3.5" disk $19.95 (ISBN 0-926846-46-9, Order no.: 2062).
Commodore 64/128 (64k). disk $19.95 (ISBN 0-926846-54-X, Order no.: 306).
Fifth Scenario in the Wizardry Gaming System, & is a Stand-Alone Scenario. Starting in the Castle, User Assembles a Party of Six Characters, Each with Their Own Characteristics to Explore the Magic & Mystery of the Monstrous Maze. Characters May Be One of Five Races & One of Eight Professions. Under Command, Characters Will Dive to the Depths of Pools, Talk & Barter with Interactive Creatures, Search for Hidden Items, Unlock (or Pick) Doors & Discover Treasure. Ultimately, User Must Rescue the Gatekeeper Who is Trapped at the Very Center of a Magical Vortex Deep Within the Caverns of the Maelstrom. His Keeper, the Evil Sorn, Waits with Gleaming Eyes & Hungry Heart.
Sir-Tech Software, Inc.

Wizardry 7: Crusaders of the Dark Savant. D. W. Bradley. Oct. 1992. *Items Included:* 111-page player's guide, four-color map, 8-page System Reference Card. 3.5" version contains 2 diskettes; 5.25" version contains 3 diskettes. *Customer Support:* Hint line available 4:00-8:00 p.m. EST Monday-Friday; 12:00-4:00 p.m. EST weekends & holidays. 30-day warranty - free replacement with dated proof of purchase. After 30 days, please provide $12.50 replacement fee.
PC-DOS/MS-DOS. IBM PC & 100% compatibles (640k). disk $39.95 (ISBN 0-926846-62-0). *Optimal configuration:* Hard disk drive, PC-DOS/MS-DOS 3.X or 5.0, 10Mhz or faster.
3.5" disk $39.95 (ISBN 0-926846-63-9).
Begin Your Adventure in Crusaders of the Dark Savant. Import Your Characters from Bane of the Cosmic Forge or Create a New Party Capable of Surviving the Rigors of a Strange Alien World. Both Friends & Foes You'll Discover As You Search for the Forgotten Secret of a once Madman - the Secret of the Very Universe Itself. And You Won't Be Alone in Your Search. Others As Enterprising As You Have Also Entered This Dimension. Only Your Actions - Both Past & Present - Will Determine Just How Well You Fare. From the Depths of a Dungeon to the Blue & Limitless Skies, You'll See It All - You'll Hear It All - in This Latest Wizardry Adventure.
Sir-Tech Software, Inc.

WLN CONSPECTUS DATABASE SOFTWARE

Wizard's Castle. *Compatible Hardware:* TRS-80 Model I, Model III, Model 4. *Memory Required:* 64k.
disk $14.95 (Order no.: D8WIZ).
Scenario for the Role Playing Warrior.
The Alternate Source.

Wizard's Cube. Cornerstone Computers Inc. *Compatible Hardware:* IBM PC. *Memory Required:* 64k.
disk $39.95.
Three Cubical-Lazer Games.
Brady Computer Bks.

Wizard's Toolbox. *Version:* 8.9. Peter Meyer et al. 1984. *Compatible Hardware:* Apple II, II+, IIe, IIc, IIgs. *Operating System(s) Required:* Apple DOS 3.3, ProDOS 8. *Language(s):* Assembly, BASIC. *Memory Required:* 48k.
disk $39.95 (ISBN 0-927796-13-9).
Assortment of Popular Commands That Can Be Used with Nearly Any Program User Develops.
Roger Wagner Publishing, Inc.

Wiziprint. A. Greenberg & R. Woodhead. May 1983. *Compatible Hardware:* Apple II, II+, IIe, IIc. *Language(s):* Pascal. *Memory Required:* 48k. *Customer Support:* Hotline; disk repair or replacement.
disk $24.95 (ISBN 0-926846-04-3, Order no.: 104).
Character Statistic Printout Utility That Prints the User's Wizardry Characters Possessions, Known Spells, & Attributes. Can Be Used with Almost Any Printer or Printer Interface Card & Is Compatible with All Wizardry Scenarios.
Sir-Tech Software, Inc.

WiziWord for Windows. *Version:* 3.1. Feb. 1993. *Items Included:* 2 spiral bound manuals. *Customer Support:* Telephone support, training (charge).
MS Windows 3.0. IBM PC & compatibles (2Mb). disk $595.00. *Addl. software required:* Windows 3.0. *Optimal configuration:* 386, VGA monitor, 4Mb RAM. *Networks supported:* Pathworks, Novell.
VMS, DECWindows/Motif. Digital VAXstation (16Mb). disk $695.00. *Addl. software required:* VMS, DECWindows/Motif. *Networks supported:* DECNet, Pathworks, TCP/IP.
Macintosh II (2mb). 3.5" disk $395.00.
WYSIWYG Word Processor That Runs on Multiple Platforms. Tables, Spell Checker, Graphics, Graphic Integration, Multi-Columns, Thesaurus, Advanced Macros, Plotting & More. File Format Is Identical on All Platforms to Ease Document Exchange & Charting & Plotting Capability, Technical Illustrator, Equation Editor Based on TEX Language.
Microsystems Engineering Co.

WLN - RLG Conspectus Software. Jan. 1993. *Items Included:* User's manual. *Customer Support:* 90 day warranty, on-going support, & periodic new releases.
MS-DOS 3.0 or higher. IBM compatible 3865X or higher (4Mb). disk $800.00 for single institution; $700.00 ea. for groups of three or more. *Optimal configuration:* IBM compatible IBM 3865X or higher, MS-DOS 3.0 or higher, 4Mb RAM & a 40-80Mb hard disk.
PC-Based Management Tool Designed to Support the RLG Conspectus. Manages Collection Assessment Data & Prints Text & Bar Graph Reports Which Demonstrate the Strengths & Weaknesses of a Single Library & Comparison Reports for Groups of Libraries.
WLN.

WLN Conspectus Database Software. *Version:* 5.0. Sep. 1993. *Items Included:* Users manual. *Customer Support:* 90 day warranty, on-going

support, & new releases annually.
MS-DOS 3.0 or higher. IBM AT compatible
(640k). $310.00 (small library); $625.00 (large
library); $800.00 (large library-multiple
branches); $1600.00 (consortium of libraries).
Provides a Library or Consortium with the
Capacity to Maintain & Update a Collections
Assessments Database In-House & to Print Ad-
Hoc Reports As the Need Arises. Local Collection
Assessment Records Can Also be Entered for
Comparative Reporting, Via Computer Diskette,
At No Charge.
WLN.

WLN Micro-Recon. Dec. 1984. *Compatible Hardware:* IBM PC. *Operating System(s) Required:* MS-DOS. *Memory Required:* 256k. *General Requirements:* 2 disk drives or hard disk. *Customer Support:* 800 number, no charge. disk $75.00.
Eliminates the User's Need to Be Concerned about Delimiters, Field Lengths, or Allowable Characters in Recon Records. User Types the Data & Micro-Recon Takes Care of the Format Details. User Can Concentrate on the Context of a Recon Record Rather Than the Form. Automatically Catches Certain Mistakes & Informs the User So Corrections Can Be Made.
WLN.

WMCS: WICAT Multi-User Control System. *Compatible Hardware:* WICAT Systems 1750, 1755, 1760, 7720. *Memory Required:* 1000k. contact publisher for price.
Operating System That Runs on All WICAT System Computers. Includes Networking (Ethernet), Editor, Sorter, KSAM Utility, & Other Utilities for Business As Well As Software Development.
Wicat Systems, Inc.

Wonderland. Jan. 1991. *Customer Support:* 90 day warranty.
MS-DOS 2.1 or higher. IBM (640K). disk $49.99. *Nonstandard peripherals required:* EGA, Tandy or VGA Graphics required. 8Mhz or higher recommended.
Amiga (1Mb). 3.5" disk $49.99.
Atari ST (1Mb). 3.5" disk $49.99.
Draws You into the Bizarre Logic of Lewis Carroll's. Game Creates a Radical New Text Adventure Environment with Stunning Graphics, Many of Them Animated. Features On-Screen Maps & Help, Multiple Windows, & Icons for Every Object & Room in the Adventure.
Virgin Games.

Wood-Ease. 1989. *Customer Support:* Free technical support (504) 649-0484.
Macintosh OS. MacPlus or higher (1Mb). 3.5" disk $2900.00. *Optimal configuration:* Mac IIcx, 2Mb RAM, 40Mb hard drive.
Produces a Cut List Either by the User Choosing Cabinets or from Output from Planit Kitchen Design Software. It Calculates Cabinet Component Sizes & Produces Cut Lists, Assembly Lists & Master Cut List.
CompServCo.

Wood Heat Calculator. *Customer Support:* 800-929-8117 (customer service).
MS-DOS. Apple II. disk $29.99 (ISBN 0-87007-401-6).
Calculates the Amount of Wood Required for Various Ambient Temperatures, Climates, & Insulation Levels.
SourceView Software International.

Word. 1981. *Compatible Hardware:* IBM PC. *Operating System(s) Required:* CP/M, PC-DOS. disk $48.00.
A Text Processor That Accepts Lines of Text Interspersed with Lines of Format Control

Information, & Formats the Text Into a Displayable Document. The User Can Prepare Manuals, Documents, Memos, & Books. Features Include: Vertical Spacing Control, Title & Page Numbering, Automatic Line Filling, Page Size, Line Width, Indent, Right Margin Justification & Centering Control. Supports All Printers That Use IPRINT. It Allows Upper/Lower Case Capabilities Without Modifying the Keyboard. Text File Merge Option Is Available. Data Records Can Be Selected, & Files Can Be Merged with the Text File.
Micro Architect, Inc.

Word City. Feb. 1996. *Customer Support:* Telephone support - free (except phone charge). System 6.0.7 or higher. 256 color Mac with 68030 processor (4Mb). CD-ROM disk $12.99 (ISBN 1-57594-121-X). *Nonstandard peripherals required:* 2x CD-ROM drive, mouse, 640/480 resolution monitor.
The First Multi-Level Arcade Game to Integrate Reading Comprehension, Vocabulary, & Spelling Skills & Even Keep Video Game Lovers Engaged. Kids Have a Great Time Learning & Playing at the Same Time. Jewel case.
Kidsoft, Inc.

Word Cruncher Index. *Compatible Hardware:* IBM PC & compatibles. *Operating System(s) Required:* MS-DOS. *Memory Required:* 512k. disk $395.00.
Text Database-Management System That Indexes Existing DOS Files Without Importing or Converting. Supports Boolean Searches, & Searches Can Be Restricted to a Specific Field or Other Qualifier. Also Features Ability to Import & Append ASCII & Other Text File Formats & to Export ASCII Files.
Johnston & Co.

Word Cruncher View. *Version:* 4.4. *Compatible Hardware:* IBM PC & compatibles. *Memory Required:* 512k, recommended: 640k. disk $395.00.
Text Retrieval Utility That Processes Unstructured Text. Boolean & Proximity Retrieval Capabilities Let the User Identify Occurrences of a Specific Word, Lists of Words, a Phrase, Part of a Word, or Two or More Words in a Defined Context. Features in Its Three Indexing Levels Include Command Truncation & the Ability to Generate Concordance Type Indexes.
Johnston & Co.

Word-C1. 1981. *Operating System(s) Required:* CP/M 2.2. *Language(s):* MBASIC compiled version. *Memory Required:* 56k.
8" disk $85.00 (Order no.: 801).
Text Processor with File/Merge Option.
Micro Architect, Inc.

Word-80. *Compatible Hardware:* HP 86/87. *Memory Required:* 128k.
3-1/2" or 5-1/4" disk $275.00 ea. (Order no.: 82823A).
Generates Memos, Letters, & Reports. Consists of an Editor to Create, Type, Print, & Store Documents & a Formatter to Format & Print Files Created with the Editor.
Hewlett-Packard Co.

Word Finder. 1992. *Items Included:* Detailed manuals included with all Dynacomp products. *Customer Support:* Free telephone support to original customer - no time limit; 30 day limited warranty.
MS-DOS 3.2 or higher. IBM PC & compatibles (512k). $39.95 (Add $5.00 for 3 1/2" format; 5 1/4" format standard). *Optimal configuration:* IBM, 128k RAM.
With WORD FINDER You Just Place Your Cursor on the Word You Want a Substitute for, & up

Pops a Window with a List of Alternate Words with Similar Meanings. Put the Cursor on the Word You Want, & Press the Return Key. The New Word Instantly Replaces the Old Word Right in the Document, Even Retaining the Exact Punctuation & Capitalization. You Can Even Use WORD FINDER for Confirming Both Word Meaning & Spelling.
Dynacomp, Inc.

Word for Word. *Version:* 5.2.
IBM PC & compatibles. disk $149.95.
Windows. disk $149.95.
Macintosh (256k). 3.5" disk $149.95. *Optimal configuration:* Macintosh Plus or higher; System Software 4.5 or higher; Finder 4.1 or higher, 256k RAM.
The Industry Standard. Automatically Converts Document Files from One Word Processor to Another. Like from MS Word to MultiMate or WordStar to WordPerfect. Keeps All Format Features Intact: the New Document Looks & Behaves As Though It Were Actually Created by the Target Word Processor.
Software Toolworks.

Word Functions. Apr. 1983. *Items Included:* Teacher's guide. *Customer Support:* 90-day limited warranty.
Apple-DOS 3.3. Apple II Family (48k). disk $69.00 (ISBN 0-917277-18-X).
Commodore 64/128 (64k). disk $69.00 (ISBN 0-917277-61-9).
Students Will Enhance Their Vocabularies by Learning to Distinguish Between Words That Sound Alike but Mean Different Things, Words with Almost the Same Meanings & Word with Opposite Meanings. This Title Also Includes Lessons on Correctly Using Commonly Troublesome Words Such As To/Too/Two & Its/It's. Age 8 Up.
BrainBank/Generation Ahead of Maryland.

Word Hunter. Ayumi Software. Aug. 1992. *Customer Support:* Telephone technical support. Macintosh KanjiTalk 6.0.7 or higher. Macintosh (2Mb). CD-ROM disk $599.00. *Nonstandard peripherals required:* CD-ROM drive.
12 Widely Used Japanese & Japanese/English Dictionaries on CD-ROM for Macintosh; Includes Full Application & Desk Accessory Version; Powerful Search Parameters.
Qualitas Trading Co.

WORD IV. 1980. *Compatible Hardware:* TRS-80 Model I, Model II, Model III, Model 4. *Operating System(s) Required:* TRSDOS. *Language(s):* BASIC. *Memory Required:* 32k. disk $49.00.
manual $10.00.
Word Processing for Preparing Letters, Memos, Reports, Manuals, etc.
Micro Architect, Inc.

Word-Link. *Version:* 2.5. *Compatible Hardware:* IBM PC & compatibles. *Memory Required:* 156k. *Customer Support:* Free product support. disk $149.00.
Converts Between All Major Word Processing Formats: MULTIMATE, WORDPERFECT, DISPLAYWRITE, ASCII, WORDSTAR, MICROSOFT, OFFICEWRITER, & PFS:PROFESSIONAL WRITE. WANG Conversions Are Available As Separate Options.
M/H Group.

Word List of the American Language I, II. 1984-1985. *Compatible Hardware:* IBM PC, PC XT, PC AT. *Operating System(s) Required:* PC-DOS/MS-DOS 1.1 or higher. *Memory Required:* 64k. *General Requirements:* Double-Sided disk drive.
American Language I. disk $20.00.
American Language II. disk $30.00.
ASCII List of Words from 3 to 15 Letters.
Robert L. Nicolai.

TITLE INDEX

Word Plus-PC. Professional Software, Inc. *Compatible Hardware:* TI Professional. *Operating System(s) Required:* MS-DOS. *Memory Required:* 128k. *General Requirements:* Winchester hard disk, printer.
$395.00.
Texas Instruments, Personal Productivit.

Word Processing. *Compatible Hardware:* IBM PC & compatibles, PC XT, PC AT. *Operating System(s) Required:* MOS. (source code included). *Memory Required:* 4 users 256k, 9 users 512k.
$995.00, incl. basic system.
Includes Automatic List Processing, Justification & Alignment of Text, Cut & Paste Options, Dictionary Facility, Find & Replace.
Hurricane Systems, Inc.

Word Processing Mailing List. *Compatible Hardware:* Onyx.
contact publisher for price.
Diamond Systems, Inc.

Word Processing Toolbox. *Items Included:* Bound manual. *Customer Support:* Free hotline - no time limit; 30 day limited warranty; updates are $5/disk plus S&H.
MS-DOS 2.0 or higher. IBM & compatibles (256k). disk $39.95. *Nonstandard peripherals required:* One drive & printer.
Package Contains 36 Word Processing Accessory Functions Designed to Augment Your Favorite Word Processor or Editor. Single-Sheet Feed Prompt; Encrypt & Decrypt Text Files; Create Forms & Form Letters; Format Text into Newspaper-Like Multiple (up to 20) Columns; Perform Character Substitutions for File Conversion (up to 200 Character Translations Can Be Defined per Run); Make Double-Sided Printouts (Print Odd Pages, Then Even); Remove Horizontal & Vertical Tabs; Perform Line Truncation, Wrapping, & Unwrapping (Lop Off Line Numbers, etc.); Cut & Paste Ranges of Lines or Pages in Text Files; Do Search-&-Replace Operations, up to 50 Patterns at a Time & More.
Dynacomp, Inc.

Word Processor File Translator. *Items Included:* Bound manual. *Customer Support:* Free hotline - no time limit; 30 day limited warranty; updates are $5/disk plus S&H.
MS-DOS. IBM & compatibles (256k). disk $9.95.
Collection of Utilities for Moving Files from One Word Processor to Another. Move Back & Forth Between ASCII, Multimate, WordPerfect, WordStar 3 (& 2000), & XyWrite. Additionally, User May Convert DCS, Display Write 2, & Volkswriter Files to ASCII.
Dynacomp, Inc.

Word Processor-Form Letters. Jun. 1985. *Compatible Hardware:* TRS-80 Model I Level II, Model III, Model 4; IBM PC & compatibles. *Operating System(s) Required:* TRSDOS, MS-DOS. *Language(s):* BASIC, Machine, Compiled BASIC (source code included). *Memory Required:* TRS-80 disk 32k, MS-DOS 128k. *Items Included:* Disk & 20-page manual. *Customer Support:* Free.
TRS-80. disk $12.00.
MS-DOS. disk $25.00.
Word Processor with a Variety of Features That Allow Editing, Deleting, Centering, etc. Also Included Are Scrolling & Graphic Capabilities. For Form Letters, First or Last Name & Address Can Be Inserted.
Hinrichs Software.

Word Quest. Nov. 1995.
IBM. CD-ROM disk $39.95 (ISBN 1-888419-02-4).
Fun with Words Game for Ages 7 to Adult.
Firstlight Productions, Inc.

Word Result. May 1985. *Compatible Hardware:* IBM PC & compatibles, PC XT, PC AT; Victor 9000. *Operating System(s) Required:* MS-DOS. *Memory Required:* 128k. *General Requirements:* 2 disk drives, printer.
disk $45.00.
Integrated package. $85.00, incl. Calc Result.
demo disk $5.00.
Word Processor with Full Editing Capabilities, Full Macro Commands, Search & Select Functions, & Unlimited Document Length. Built-In Register Allows User to Create a Mailing List with up to 13 Fields & 1,000 Records. Works in 9 Other Languages: Danish, Dutch, Finnish, French, German, Italian, Norwegian, Spanish, & Swedish.
ScanAm Enterprises, Inc.

Word Seeking. Jim Cyr & Ronald C. Thomas. *Compatible Hardware:* IBM PC, PCjr, PC XT, PC AT, Portable PC with IBM Display & IBM Matrix Printer. *Operating System(s) Required:* PC-DOS 1.10, 2.00, 2.10, 3.00, 3.10. *Memory Required:* 128k.
disk $19.95 (Order no.: 6276534).
After the Player Enters the Words, the Program Will Construct an Original Puzzle from Them. Puzzles May Be Organized Horizontally, Vertically, Diagonally, Even Backwards. Then the Player Must Detect the Words Within the New Arrangement.
Personally Developed Software, Inc.

Word Sleuth. Oct. 1985. *Compatible Hardware:* IBM PC, PC XT, PC AT. *Operating System(s) Required:* PC-DOS/MS-DOS 1.1 or higher. *Language(s):* Compiled BASIC. *Memory Required:* 64k. *General Requirements:* Double-sided disk drive.
disk $50.00.
Expanded Word List & Utility Program Designed Especially for Solving Crossword Puzzles.
Robert L. Nicolai.

Word Study Library. Aug. 1994. *Items Included:* Disks, marketing literature, order form. *Customer Support:* No fee for customer support: 30 day money back guarantee, limited replacement warranty on diskettes defective at time of purchase, free telephone technical support.
PC-DOS/MS-DOS 3.1 or higher & Windows 3.1 or higher. IBM XT/AT/286/386/486 or 100% compatibles (640k or 4Mb). 3.5" disk $79.95 (ISBN 1-56514-027-3). *Optimal configuration:* 3.5", 1.44Mb disk drive for installation, 13Mb hard drive space; mouse or pointer device recommended.
A Package Containing Strong's Greek Hebrew Dictionary, Englishman's Greek-Hebrew Concordance, Vine's Expository Dictionary of Biblical Words, & Interlinear Transliterated Bible with Lexicon Definitions from Thayer's & Brown-Driver-Briggs. Enables User to Conduct Word & Definition Searches of Greek & Hebrew Words Without User Having Prior Knowledge or Original Languages.
Biblesoft.

Word Study Series. Jun. 1994. *Items Included:* Disks, marketing literature, order form. *Customer Support:* No fee for customer support: 30 day money back guarantee, limited replacement warranty on diskettes defective at time of purchase, free telephone technical support.
DOS 3.0 or higher or Windows 3.1 or higher. IBM 386/486 or 100% compatible (Windows); Also XT/AT/286 (DOS) (640k DOS or 4Mb Windows). disk $99.95 (ISBN 1-56514-315-9).
Addl. software required: Biblesoft's PC Study Bible, & King James Version text. *Optimal configuration:* Requires 5.25" 1.2Mb disk drive for installation & 7Mb of hard drive space, mouse or pointer device recommended.
Package Containing Interlinear Bible (Displays Original Greek/Hebrew Texts). New Exhaustive Strong's (Word Definitions) & Vines Expository Dictionary (More Detailed Discussions of Major Bible Words).
Biblesoft.

Word Study Series. Jun. 1994. *Items Included:* Disks, marketing literature, order form. *Customer Support:* No fee for customer support: 30 day money back guarantee, limited replacement warranty on diskettes defective at time of purchase, free telephone technical support.
DOS 3.0 or higher or Windows 3.1 or higher. IBM 386/486 or 100% compatible (Windows); Also AT/XT/286 (DOS) (640k DOS or 4Mb Windows). 3.5" disk $99.95 (ISBN 1-56514-313-2). *Addl. software required:* Biblesoft's PC Study Bible, & King James Version text. *Optimal configuration:* Requires 3.5" 4Mb disk drive for installation & 7Mb of hard drive space, mouse or pointer device recommended.
Package Containing Interlinear Bible (Displays Original Greek/Hebrew Texts). New Exhaustive Strong's (Word Definitions) & Vines Expository Dictionary (More Detailed Discussions of Major Bible Words).
Biblesoft.

Word-to-Word. Lyle Anderson. Oct. 1983. *Compatible Hardware:* DEC VAX/II, Professional 350. *Operating System(s) Required:* VMS, CP/M. *Language(s):* FORTRAN. *Memory Required:* 62k.
magnetic tape $2000.00.
*Conversion Program for WORDSTAR, CT*OS & DECmate Word Processing Documents.*
Aquidnerk Data Corp.

Word Typer. *Compatible Hardware:* Apple Macintosh. *Memory Required:* 512k. *General Requirements:* ImageWriter or LaserWriter.
3.5" disk $79.00.
Word Processing Program.
Encycloware.

Word V. 1980. *Compatible Hardware:* TRS-80 Model I, Model II, Model III, Model 4. *Language(s):* BASIC. *Memory Required:* 48k.
disk $59.00.
manual $10.00.
Word Processing System Includes a File Merge Feature & Enhancement Possibilities.
Micro Architect, Inc.

WORD-X. *Compatible Hardware:* IBM PC, PCjr, PC XT. *Operating System(s) Required:* MS-DOS, PC-DOS. *Language(s):* Compiled BASIC. *Memory Required:* 128k. *General Requirements:* 2 disk drives, printer.
disk $48.00.
Includes a Screen Editor with Word Wrap & a Text Formatter. The User Can Merge Text Files with Data Files Created by IDM-X & EXEC1. A Color or Monochrome Display Can Be Used. Features Global Changes, Word Wrap, Multiple Text Files, File/Merge, Underline, Superscript & Italics, & Boldface.
Micro Architect, Inc.

Wordbench. *Compatible Hardware:* Apple IIe, IIc, IIgs; IBM PC & compatibles. *Operating System(s) Required:* MS-DOS 2.0 or higher, ProDOS 8. *Memory Required:* Apple 128k; IBM 256k.
Apple. disk $149.00.
IBM. disk $189.00.
Word Processing Package Consisting of an Outliner, Notetaker, Add-In Manager, Writer, Print Manager & Folder Manager. Desktop Tools Include a Spelling Checker, Thesaurus, Wordsearch, Format Tool & Viewer, & a Window That Allows the User to Work with 2 Documents at Once.
Addison-Wesley Publishing Co., Inc.

WordExec. Signature Software Corp. *Compatible Hardware:* TI Professional with printer. *Operating System(s) Required:* UCSD p-System. *Memory Required:* 64k.
$395.00 (Order no.: 5.03).
Texas Instruments, Personal Productivit.

Wordlister: The Online Glossary. Graeme Gibson. *Customer Support:* 7 day money back warranty. Short phone questions answered free. Contact publisher for price.
Online Glossary of Computer Terms. Provides Detailed Help for Hundreds of Computer Terms. Perfect for Support Staffers Having to Answer Definition Questions. Also Suited to Educational Uses.
Computer Training Corp.

WordMaker. Jun. 1989. *Items Included:* 1 spiral bound manual & disk. *Customer Support:* Free phone support.
Macintosh 512e, System 4.1 or higher (512k). Macintosh. $124.95. *Networks supported:* AppleShare & TOPS.
Includes Text Wrap Around Graphics, Graphics Movement with Text, Full Print Merge, Left & Right Headers & Footers, Color Capability, & a 100,000 Word Spelling Checker! Comprehensive Keyboard Cursor Control & Command Equivalents are Included. It Also Reads & Writes MacWrite Files.
New Horizons Software.

WordManager Advanced Word Processor. Nov. 1988. *Compatible Hardware:* IBM PC & compatibles. *Operating System(s) Required:* MS-DOS 2.1 or higher. *Memory Required:* 640k. *General Requirements:* Hard disk, printer. Modem optional.
disk write for info.
Word Processor Specifically Designed for Complex Document Production. Features Include: Spell Check with Coaching Option; Automatic Creation of Tables of Contents & Authorities; Background Functions Such As Printing, Paginating, Spell Check, Document Merge, & Document Assembly. Also Features Redlining, Keystroke Memory, & List File Merge Capabilities.
Barrister Information Systems Corp.

WordMARC Author. *Compatible Hardware:* AT&T 73000, IBM PC & many PC/MS-DOS based computers.
disk $295.00.
Word Processor That Incorporates the University of Chicago's Dissertation Office's Manual of Style Standards for Automatic Table of Contents, Indexing, Paragraph Numbering, Cross Referencing & Floating Footnotes.
MARC Software International, Inc.

WordMARC Composer+. *Version:* 6.2. *Items Included:* Learning WordMARC, Reference guide, technical reference manual, device manual, *Customer Support:* Annual maintenance fee 15% of current list price; 30 day warranty; Includes toll-free telephone support, software enhancements & updates, new printer & terminal drivers as available, newsletter, error corrections.
IBM PC or compatible (3.6 Mb). disk $495.00. *Networks supported:* Novell, Banyon, 3t, StarLan, Netware, IBM PC LAN.
UNIX, XENIX. Alliance, Apollo, AT&T, Decstation, HP 9000/800, IBM RS6000, NCR Tower, PRIME EXL, Pyramid, Sepuent, Sun, Unisys. $595.00-$19,000.00.
VAX VMS. DEC VAX VMS series. $595.00-$22,500.00. *Networks supported:* DECnet.
Full-Featured Word Processing Systems Designed to Provide Power & Ease of Use in Diverse Commercial, Educational, & Scientific Environments. Easily Integrate with Leading Business Software, Including Databases, Spreadsheets, Desktop Publishing, & Electronic Mail Packages.
MARC Software International, Inc.

WordPerfect. *Version:* 5.1. May 1988. *Compatible Hardware:* IBM PC, XT, AT, PS/2 & compatibles. *Operating System(s) Required:* PC-DOS 2.0 or higher. *Memory Required:* 384k required. Recommended 640k. *General Requirements:* Two 720k (or larger) floppy disk drives required. Hard disk recommended. Graphics adapter & matching monitor required for displaying graphics features. *Items Included:* Illustrated workbook, reference manual. *Customer Support:* Toll free customer support system. Contact publisher for price.
Can Print Images Anywhere on a Page, Rotate or Scale Graphics, & Wrap Text Around an Image. Can Directly Read PIC Files, As Well As the Formats of Most Other Popular Graphics & Paint Programs. For Those Formats It Cannot Read, It Comes with a Utility That Will Capture Images Directly from the Screen & Convert Them to Its Own Format. Includes Support for a Wide Range of Fonts & Print Attributes & a Kerning Feature for Adjusting Space Between Letters. Margins Can Be Set in Centimeters, Inches, or Points. User Can Electronically Compare Two Versions of a Document, & Automatically Update References to Pages, Footnotes, or Figures When the Length of Document Changes. Will Display Parallel Columns On-Screen, Even If They Extend Past a Page Break. Supports 700 Dot-Matrix, Daisy Wheel, & Laser Printers. Version 5.1 Also Includes PostScript Support.
WordPerfect Corp.

WordPerfect Advanced Features. 1993. *Operating System(s) Required:* PC-DOS/MS-DOS. *Memory Required:* 640k. *General Requirements:* WordPerfect 5 or 5.1 word processing software.
3.5" or 5.25" disk $29.95 (ISBN 0-935987-23-1).
Features Self-Study Guide Which Consists of Student Guide & Data Diskette Containing Data Files. Student Guide Provides Step-by-Step Instructions in the Advanced Word Processing Features of WordPerfect. Topics Include Advanced Mailmerge & Customized Form Letters, File Management, Outlines, Macros, Columns, & Desktop Publishing Features Including Making a Newsletter, Tables, Compose.
Edutrends, Inc.

WordPerfect Communications with ExpressFax 2.0 for DOS. *Version:* 2.0. Jul. 1993. *Items Included:* Registration card, manual, disks. *Customer Support:* (801) 228-9915 - free toll customer support.
DOS 3.0 or higher. IBM PC & compatibles (384k). $99.00 SRP; Upgrades $49.00 SRP. *Nonstandard peripherals required:* Class I & Class II, WorldPoint & SendFax modems required. *Optimal configuration:* 2Mb of hard disk space for full installation, low-density floppy drive required. *Networks supported:* Not networkable.
A Software Package That Provides Modular Telecommunications Capabilities for the PC or Laptop. The Software Has a 200 Entry Dialing Directory with an Auto-Logon Facility, & the Logical Area Code Feature Allows the Mobile User to Use the Same Directory. Several New Features Including ExpressFax Offer Additonal Functionality.
WordPerfect Corp.

WordPerfect for Desktop Publishing. Ralph Ruby, Jr. et al. 1994. *Items Included:* Package includes disk, reproducible teacher book (151pp) & 1 student activity text. Additional activity texts are $8.95, or $7.95 for 10 or more copies. *Customer Support:* Returnable if not satisfied. Call 1-800-341-6094 for technical support. 30-day preview available.
MS-DOS. IBM & compatibles (128k). disk $79.95 (ISBN 0-8251-2384-4, Order no.: 0-23844). *Addl. software required:* WordPerfect. *Students with a Basic Understanding of WordPerfect Can Use These Hands-On Lessons to Create Professional Resources. Students Modify Resource Files & Create Their Own. Clip Art Files Are Also Included.*
J. Weston Walch Pub.

WordPerfect for Desktop Publishing for Windows. *Version:* 6.0. Paula D. Ladd et al. 1996. *Items Included:* MS-DOS data disk; reproducible teacher book, 170 pp.; 1 student activity text, 145 pp. Additional copies of activity text available for $11.95; 10 or more copies, each $10.95. *Customer Support:* Call 1-800-341-6094 for free technical assistance, 30 day approval policy, money back guarantee.
MS-DOS. disk $84.95 (ISBN 0-8251-2776-9, Order no.: 0-27769). *Addl. software required:* WordPerfect 6.0.
Use These Self-Paced Lessons to Explore WordPerfect's More Advanced Desktop Publishing Features. Step-by-Step Instructions Show Students How to Modify Files on the Resource Disk & How to Create Their Own Professional-Looking Documents.
J. Weston Walch Pub.

WordPerfect for Macintosh. *Version:* 3.0. Jul. 1993. *Customer Support:* (800) 336-3614, weekdays between 7:00 a.m. & 6:00 p.m. MST. Macintosh (2Mb System 6.0.5, 4Mb System 7.X). Contact publisher for price. *Optimal configuration:* Any Macintosh with a hard drive, 2Mb RAM for System 6.0.5 or higher, 4Mb is required for System 7.x.
WordPerfect 3.0 for Macintosh Has a Powerful & Easy to Use Interface That Brings the Program's Power & Functionality Out to the User. The New Interface Simplifies the Menu Structure to Complex Features by Reducing the Number of Dialog's Needed to Edit Documents. New Interface Features Including the Button Bars, Ruler Bars & Status Bar Provide Quick Access to Both Basic & Advanced Features.
WordPerfect Corp.

WordPerfect for the Macintosh. *Version:* 2.1. 1991. *Compatible Hardware:* Apple Macintosh. Macintosh Plus, SE, & II. Contact publisher for price. *Nonstandard peripherals required:* Hard disk.
Word Processing Program. Includes the Following Features: Graphics & Drawing Package That Allows User to Create, Edit, Scale, & Crop Graphic Figures Without Leaving the Document, Macro Editor, Tables of Authorities, & Line Numbering. Program Allows User to Create Text Boxes, Inside of Which the User Can Change Font Size & Attributes. User Can Create Columns (Newspaper or Parallel) & Then Adjust the Column Settings, Align Text, Set Tabs, Change Line Spacing, Move Margins, & Other Formatting Changes. 36 Different Border Styles & New Enhancements to Merge, Search & Replace, & Macros. Printer Support for Apple ImageWriter, ImageWriter II, LaserWriter, & Other PostScript Printers.
WordPerfect Corp.

WordPerfect for Windows. *Version:* 5.1. Nov. 1991.
Windows 3.1. IBM PC & compatibles. Contact publisher for price.
Includes "Drop & Drag" to move text, Zoom Edit for Page Magnification, Macro Command Inserter, Macro Dialogs, On-Line Macro Help, & Remappable Alphanumeric Keys. Compatible with Windows 3.1.
WordPerfect Corp.

TITLE INDEX

WordPerfect for Windows. *Version:* 6.0. Aug. 1993.
Microsoft Windows 3.1. 386 or higher (4Mb) (preferably 6Mb). disk $495.00.
Offers Everything Needed to Create Professional-Looking Documents: Powerful Word Processing, Drawing, Charting, Spreadsheet Functionality Within Tables, & Direct Integration with Other Windows Applications. Designed to Give Users Complete Customization, the Easiest Transition to Windows, & a Product That Makes the Most of the Windows Environment.
WordPerfect Corp.

WordPerfect in Your Classroom for Windows: Starter Package. *Version:* 5.1. Ralph Ruby, Jr. et al. 1996. *Items Included:* Windows data disk; reproducible book, 170 pp., 1 student activity text, 115 pp. Additional copies of activity text available for $10.95; 10 or more copies, each $9.95. *Customer Support:* Call 1-800-341-6094 for free technical assistance, 30 day approval policy, money back guarantee.
IBM & compatibles. disk $79.95 (ISBN 0-8251-2725-4, Order no.: 0-27254). *Addl. software required:* WordPerfect 5.1.
Disk Files Allow Students to Explore Advanced Concepts Without Creating Their Own Documents. Students Learn to Use WordPerfect Functions at the Computer As They Manipulate Disk Files.
J. Weston Walch Pub.

WordPerfect InForms. Jul. 1993. *Items Included:* Manuals for both the Designer & the Filler, & a manual of the shared applications for all WordPerfect Corporation products for Windows. *Customer Support:* Toll support at (801) 228-9916 from within the United States, Puerto Rico, U.S. Virgin Islands, or Canada 7 a.m. to 6 p.m. Mountain Standard Time & After Hour Support at (801) 222-9010 Monday from 2 a.m. to 7 a.m., Monday-Thursday from 6 p.m. to 7 a.m., Friday from 6 p.m. to 10 p.m., & Saturday from 8 a.m. to 4 p.m..
MS Windows. 386 or higher (4Mb). disk $495.00 (Order no.: W3USWIN10).
Nonstandard peripherals required: VGA graphics adapter or higher. *Addl. software required:* MS-DOS 3.1 or higher, MS Windows version 3.1 or higher. *Optimal configuration:* Designer - 386-based PC or higher, 4Mb RAM, 15-19Mb hard disk space; VGA graphics adapter; mouse; MS DOS 3.1 or higher; & MS Windows 3.1. Filler - 386-based PC or higher; 4Mb RAM; 11.5-13Mb hard disk space; VGA graphics adapter; mouse; MS DOS 3.1 or higher; & MS Windows 3.1. *Networks supported:* Novell NetWare, Banyan Vines, TOPS, IBM LAN Network, NOKIA PC-NET, 3Com 3Plus Network, 10 NET, LANTASTIC, AT&T Star Group, Deck Pathwork, 3Com 3Plus OPEN, Street Talk.
An Intuitive Forms Package That Enables Users to Create & Fill in Even the Most Elaborate Electronic & Printed Forms. With WordPerfect InForms Data Handling Capabilities, Collected Information Can Be Written Directly to a Database. Will Be Sold As Two Separate Packages: a Designer Package to Create Forms & a Filler Package to Fill in Forms Created with the Designer.
WordPerfect Corp.

WordPerfect Office. *Version:* 4.0. *Compatible Hardware:* IBM PC & compatibles, Macintosh, UNIX.
$295.00 for the message server.
$495.00 5 users client.
Combines Electronic Mail, Personal Calendaring, Group Scheduling, & Electronic Forms into One Application. Version 4.0 Includes Rules-Based Message Management, Workflow Automation, Ordered Distribution, Task Management, Global Calendaring, Central & Distributed Administration, & Directory Synchronization.
WordPerfect Corp.

WordPerfect Presentations for DOS. *Version:* 2.0. Nov. 1992. *Customer Support:* (800) 541-5098, weekdays between 8 a.m. & 12 a.m. MST.
DOS 3.0 or higher. Intel 286 or higher processor (490k). Contact publisher for price. *Optimal configuration:* Intel 286 or higher processor, DOS 3.0 or higher, at least 490k free conventional memory (550k or higher recommended), extended or expanded memory recommended (up to 16Mb), hard disk with 6Mb minimum (14Mb for full installation), EGA, VGA or higher resolution graphics adapter & monitor.
A Significant Upgrade & Offers Capabilities That Are Completely New to the DOS Presentation Graphics Market. Developers Wanted to Give Users All the Functionality They Need to Produce Professional-Looking Presentations with One Software Package. Consequently, WP Presentations Includes Advanced Paint, Drawing, Charting, Text Handling & Presentation Tools & a Clip Art Library with More Than 1,000 Images.
WordPerfect Corp.

WordPerfect Presentations for Windows. *Version:* 2.0. *Customer Support:* (800) 541-5098, weekdays between 8 a.m. & 12 a.m. MST.
Windows 3.1 or higher, DOS 3.1 or higher (5.0 recommended). Intel 80386 or higher processor (4Mb). Contact publisher for price. *Optimal configuration:* Hard disk with at least 9Mb of free disk space (22 for full installation), EGA, VGA or higher resolution graphics adapter & monitor, mouse.
A Powerful, Easy-to-Use Presentation Graphics Program That Features Advanced Presentation, Drawing, Charting & Text Handling Tools & an Extensive Clip Art Gallery. Introduces Paint Tools & Direct Scanning Through TWAIN Support to Presentation Graphics. The Product Also Supports Object Linking & Embedding, Video & Sound. Developers Designed WordPerfect Presentations to Give Users All the Functionality They Need to Produce Professional-Looking Presentations in One Software Package.
WordPerfect Corp.

WordPerfect Presentations 2.0 for DOS & Windows. *Version:* 2.0. *Items Included:* Workbook, reference manual, color coded template.
Intel 286 or higher; DOS 3.0 or higher; at least 490k free conventional memory. disk $495.00.
WordPerfect Corp.

WordPerfect: Skills, Advanced Level 1, & Advanced Level 2. *Version:* 5.1. Jan. 1989. *Customer Support:* Hotline support.
IBM PC & compatibles (640k). starter pack $900.00 (Order no.: 40-353-PK). *Addl. software required:* WordPerfect 5.1.
Logical Operations.

Wordperfect: The McGraw-Hill College Version. Sep. 1989. *Items Included:* Spiral-bound manual & 5.25" disk.
IBM PC, AT, PCJr & true compatibles. disk $21.96 (ISBN 0-07-831502-6).
3.5" disk $19.95.
Simple Menu-Driven Program That Allows the Microcomputer to Be Used As a Typewriter. Allows for Inputting of Text, Changes or Deletion of Words, Movement of Sentences & Paragraphs & Other Operations Commonly Associated With Word Processing Programs.
McGraw-Hill, Inc.

WORDPICS CLINICAL PATIENT REPORT

The WordPerfect Video Training Course. *Version:* VHS. 1988. *Operating System(s) Required:* MS-DOS/PC-DOS. *Memory Required:* 640k. *General Requirements:* WordPerfect 5 software.
disk $99.00 (ISBN 0-935987-21-5).
Video & Disk Combination Which Teaches Both Basic & Advanced WordPerfect Word Processing Features. Topics Include Getting Started, Creating & Editing a Document, Columns, Math, Moving & Copying Text & Blocks, Spellchecker, Thesaurus, Style Sheets, Macros, Print & Saving, Keyboard Macros.
Edutrends, Inc.

WordPerfect Works. Jun. 1987. *Compatible Hardware:* IBM PC compatibles; PC XT, PC AT, PC Convertible PS/2; Toshiba T100+, T3100; NEC MultiSpeed; Compaq; Zenith; Data General One; DEC; Texas Instruments. *Operating System(s) Required:* MS-DOS 2.0 or higher. *Language(s):* Assembly. *Memory Required:* 512k. *General Requirements:* 720k mass storage on one or two floppies or hard disk. *Customer Support:* 800-321-3512 7 a.m. - 6 p.m.; 801-228-9902 after hours.
disk $159.00, incl. manual.
Integrates Word Processing with Spreadsheet, Appointment Calendar, Calculator, Note Cards, & Phone Directory. EXECUTIVE's Word Processor Is Similar to WORDPERFECT: Documents Created with the EXECUTIVE Can Be Used with WORDPERFECT & Vice-Versa.
WordPerfect Corp.

WordPerfect Works for Macintosh. *Version:* 1.2.1. Jun. 1993. *Items Included:* License, reference manual, tutorial workbook, quick reference card, & disks. *Customer Support:* Free customer support available at toll number - (801) 228-9901.
Macintosh. Mac Plus or higher (1Mb for Sys 6; 2Mb for System 7). $249.00 SRP.
Nonstandard peripherals required: Floppy disk & hard disk required. A modem is required for the communications module. *Networks supported:* Network ready.
An Integrated Program That Features the Following Six Modules: Word Processor, Database, Draw, Paint, Communications & Spreadsheet with Charting. Includes In-Context Editing, Which Lets You Make Changes to Linked Data from Any Module Without Leaving the Module You Are Working In.
WordPerfect Corp.

WordPerfect 5.1 Macros & Templates. Gordon McComb. *Items Included:* Two 5.25" disks. *Customer Support:* Phone number available for technical support, 212-492-9832; free disk replacement within 90 days of purchase.
IBM PC & compatibles. disk $44.95 (ISBN 0-553-34875-2). *Addl. software required:* WordPerfect.
The Expanded 5.1 Update of This Bestseller Covers: Shell Macros, Macro Programming Language, Keyboard Layouts, Mail Merge, Interactive Menus, Debugging. Disks Contain: 400 Ready-to-Use Macros, Letter Maker, with 88 Ready-to-Use Business Letters, Special Macros for Desktop Publishing & Law Practices.
Bantam Bks., Inc.

WordPICS Clinical Patient Report Generator & Database: Patient Data Manager. 1984. *Compatible Hardware:* IBM PC XT, PC AT, PS/2 Model 30. *Operating System(s) Required:* MS-DOS, PC-DOS. *Memory Required:* 640k.
contact publisher for price.
Enables Hospital Staff Members to Create Customized Reports on Most Types of Clinical Patient Procedures. Maintains an Accessed Database for Research Purposes, Patient Database.
Trinity Computing Systems, Inc.

WordPlay: Word Game. *Version:* 1.1. Aug. 1985. *Compatible Hardware:* Apple Macintosh. *Language(s):* Pascal. *Memory Required:* 128k. *Customer Support:* (512)854-8794.
3.5" disk $49.95.
Educational Vocabulary Program for Children & Adults. Provides More Than 50 Crossword Puzzles in Sizes from 4 x 4 up to 23 x 23, & Allows Users to Create Additional Ones. Diagramless Puzzles Are Also Included. Features On-Screen Help Menus.
Palsoft.

WordPort. *Version:* 4.1. Aug. 1990. *Items Included:* User Manual & registration. *Customer Support:* Free phone support.
MS-DOS, OS/2. IBM PC, XT, AT, PS/2 or compatible (256k). disk $149.00. *Optimal configuration:* 1 hard disk, 512k or higher RAM. *Networks supported:* Novell, 3Com.
Converts Document Files Between All Versions of WordPerfect, WordStar, Microsoft Word, Word for Windows, Word for Macintosh, Microsoft Works, DisplayWrite, WordStar-2000, Writing Assistant MultiMate, Samna Word, Ami Professional, pfs: Write, pfs: Professional Write, pfs: First Choice, Lotus Manuscript, Enable (Including OA) Programs, As Well As Brother Word Processors, IBM DCA/RFT, Microsoft RTF & ASCII File Formats (Except to Multimate, pfs, Writing Assistant or Samna). Converts the Document Text & Practically All Formatting As Well, Including Advanced Formatting Functions Like Multiple Columns, Font Size Changes, Automatic Paragraph Numbering, etc. The Converted Documents Rarely Require Any Touching up. The Program Has a Modern Easy-to-Use User Interface with On-Screen Help at All Times. Multiple Files May Be Converted in a Single Operation, Can Automatically Identify Document Files Created by the User's Word Processor. Users with Exacting Requirements May Customize WordPort.
Advanced Computer Innovations, Inc.

Words. *Compatible Hardware:* TRS-80 Model III. *Memory Required:* 32k.
$19.95.
Maintains a List of Several Hundred Words. Letters Are Scrambled & Player Is Given an Amount of Time Based on the Length of the Word to Unscramble & Correctly Spell the Word.
Duane Bristow Computers, Inc.

WordSearch Deluxe. Oct. 1991. *Items Included:* Manual & 1 diskette.
System 6.0.7 or higher. Macintosh Plus or higher (1Mb). 3.5" disk $39.95 (ISBN 0-940081-62-8).
Windows 3.1. 386SX or higher. 3.5" disk $39.95 (ISBN 0-940081-77-6). *Nonstandard peripherals required:* Mouse, SVGA, sound card.
Macintosh & Windows. CD-ROM disk $39.95 (ISBN 1-57374-015-2).
Create Hidden Word Puzzles form Lists Typed in or Imported from a Word Processing Program. Puzzles Can Be Solved on the Screen or Printed Out. Puzzles Can Be Exported to Page Layout Programs for Publishing. Puzzles to Be Solved on the Screen Can Include Color Graphics & Sound. Size & Shape of Puzzles Are Flexible.
Nordic Software, Inc.

Wordslinger. *Compatible Hardware:* TRS-80 Model I, Model III. *Memory Required:* 16k. *General Requirements:* Printer.
disk $29.95 (Order no.: 0129R).
Creates & Edits Texts & Saves Them on Tape.
Instant Software, Inc.

WordStar. MicroPro International. *Compatible Hardware:* HP 86/87 with CP/M System (HP 82900A), HP 150 Touchscreen, HP 110 Portable.
HP 86/87. 3-1/2" or 5-1/4" disk $350.00 ea. (Order no.: 45584A).
HP 150, HP 110. 3.5" disk $350.00 (Order no.: 45400D).
Text Is Displayed Directly on the Screen As It Is Entered, & Most Formatting Takes Place Immediately. Block & Column Move Commands Allow the Movement of Text Within the Document. Interfaces with SPELLSTAR & MAILMERGE.
Hewlett-Packard Co.

WordStar. *Version:* 7.0. Mar. 1992. *Compatible Hardware:* IBM PC & compatibles. *Operating System(s) Required:* PC-DOS/MS-DOS 2.11 or higher. *Language(s):* Assembly. *Memory Required:* For advanced page preview, 512k; graphics, 640k. *General Requirements:* 1 floppy drive & 1 hard disk. *Customer Support:* Life of product.
disk $495.00, incl. documentation.
Offers Comprehensive Support for Advanced Scalable-Font Printers, Such As the Hewlett-Packard LaserJet III & PostScript Printers. Features Typefaces Which Can Be Selected On-the-Fly, Special Effects Included Within Documents & Kerning to Produce Documents That Look As If They Were Typeset. Features of Earlier Versions Have Been Retained, Such As Text & Graphics Integration, Pull-Down Menus, Style Sheets for Automated Formatting, a Spelling Corrector with 100,000 Words, On-Line Thesaurus with 220,000 Words, Definitions, the Ability to Merge Data & Form Letters for Customized Mailings, Full Indexing & Table of Contents Generation, Word Processing File Conversion, Telecommunications Support, Powerful New Macro Capability & FAX Support.
WordStar International, Inc.

WordStar & MailMerge 3.3. MicroPro International Corp. *Compatible Hardware:* TI Professional. *Operating System(s) Required:* MS-DOS. *Memory Required:* 128k. *General Requirements:* 2 disk drives, printer.
$645.00.
Texas Instruments, Personal Productivit.

WordStar & SpellStar 3.3. MicroPro International Corp. *Compatible Hardware:* TI Professional with printer & 2 disk drives. *Operating System(s) Required:* MS-DOS. *Memory Required:* 128k.
$695.00.
Texas Instruments, Personal Productivit.

WordStar for Windows. *Version:* 1.5. Jul. 1992. *Customer Support:* Free technical support for the life of product; 30 day money back guarantee; free BBS service.
Windows 3.0 or higher, MS-DOS 3.1 or higher. IBM 286-based (or faster) PC or compatible (2Mb). disk $495.00. *Nonstandard peripherals required:* Windows compatible monitor & graphics card, mouse & printer. *Networks supported:* Novell NetWare, IBM PC LAN, 3COM 3 Plus Open, 3COM 3 Plus Share, Microsoft Network, LAN Manager & Banyan Vines.
Powerful WYSIWYG Text Editing. Superior Connectivity Including Client OLE Support & Full DDE Support, Network Support, File References & dBASE Support for Mailmerge. Highly Flexible Layout Tools Make It Easy to Create Columns, Place Graphics & Tables Anywhere You Like. WordStar & WordStar 2000 Keystroke Support. Support for over 50 Different Word Processors, Automatic Table Generation & Fully Integrated Graphic Tools.
WordStar International, Inc.

WordStar French Version. *Version:* 6.0. *Compatible Hardware:* IBM PC. *Operating System(s) Required:* PC-DOS/MS-DOS 2.0 or higher. *Language(s):* Assembly. *Memory Required:* 384k. For page preview 512k. *Customer Support:* Life of product.
disk $495.00.
Has All of the Features of the English Version. For the Convenience of the User a Series of Menus Can Be Displayed On-Screen Which List the Many Commands for Entering, Editing, & Printing Text, Including Page Breaks & Text Justification. They Appear on Screen Just As They Will Appear in Print.
WordStar International, Inc.

WordStar German Version. *Version:* 6.0. *Compatible Hardware:* IBM PC. *Operating System(s) Required:* MS-DOS, PC-DOS. *Language(s):* Assembly. *Memory Required:* 384k. For advanced page preview, graphics or outlining 512k. *Customer Support:* Life of product.
disk $495.00.
Has All the Features of the English Version. For the Convenience of the User a Series of Menus Can Be Displayed On-Screen Which List the Many Commands for Entering, Editing, & Printing Text, Including Page Breaks & Text Justification. They Appear on Screen Just As They Will Appear in Print.
WordStar International, Inc.

WordStar, MailMerge & SpellStar 3.3. MicroPro International Corp. *Compatible Hardware:* TI Professional with printer & 2 disk drives. *Operating System(s) Required:* MS-DOS. *Memory Required:* 128k.
$845.00 (Order no.: SY P/N T134-075).
Texas Instruments, Personal Productivit.

WordStar Professional 3.3. MicroPro International Corp. *Compatible Hardware:* TI Professional with 2 disk drives & printer. *Operating System(s) Required:* MS-DOS. *Memory Required:* 128k.
$695.00 (Order no.: TI P/N 2311504-0001 SY P/N T134-085).
Texas Instruments, Personal Productivit.

WordStar Professional 3.3 Option Kit. MicroPro International Corp. *Compatible Hardware:* TI Professional. *Operating System(s) Required:* MS-DOS. *Memory Required:* 128k. *General Requirements:* 2 disk drives, printer.
$295.00 (Order no.: TI P/N 2311502-0001).
Texas Instruments, Personal Productivit.

WordStar: Spanish Version. *Version:* 6.0. *Compatible Hardware:* IBM PC & compatibles. *Operating System(s) Required:* MS-DOS 2.0 or higher. *Memory Required:* 384k, for Advanced page preview, outlining & graphics 512k. *General Requirements:* 2 disk drives or hard disk or 1 disk drive & hard disk. *Customer Support:* Life of product.
$495.00.
Has Word Processing & Mail-Merge Capabilities, along with Complete Spanish Translations of Menu Screens, Tutors, & Documentation. Recognizes the Entire IBM Extended ASCII International Character Set. Advanced Page Preview Capabilities. On the Fly Scalable Font Capabilities.
WordStar International, Inc.

WordStar 2000. *Version:* 3.5. *Compatible Hardware:* IBM PC & compatibles. *Memory Required:* 512k, for Inset 640k. *Customer Support:* Free support.
disk $495.00.
Easy-to-Learn, Fast Word Processor Featuring a Built-In Graphics Program to Insert Charts, Graphs & Illustration, & Laser Printer Support.

TITLE INDEX

Advanced Page Preview Lets User View Single & Multiple Pages, Text Integrated with Graphics, & Exact Font Representations in Sizes up to 72 Points.
WordStar International, Inc.

WordStar 2000 Courseware. *Compatible Hardware:* IBM PC & compatibles.
disk $200.00.
wkbk. $25.00.
Three Courses Are Offered, Each Complete with a Leader's Guide, Workbook, & Exercise Disks. Available for Release 1.0 & 2.
WordStar International, Inc.

Wordwise. *Compatible Hardware:* HP 9000 Series 200, 300, 520, 9845.
3-1/2" single or double-sided disk, 5-1/4" disk $195.00.
Word Processing, Featuring Continuous Word Wrap & Continuous Screen Display of Text in Its Final Form. Includes Correspondence Features, Italics, Global or Single Search & Replace, Move, Copy & Sort, Mix Text & Graphics Output, Save or Retrieve on Any Disk Media Available, Table of Contents Generator, etc.
James Assocs.

Wordwise 300. *Version:* 8. *Compatible Hardware:* HP 9000 Series 200, 300, 520, MSDOS. *Language(s):* BASIC 2.0, 3.0, 4.0 (source code included).
disk $495.00, incl. manual.
upgrade kit (WORDWISE to WORDWISE 300) $345.00.
update to new version $50.00.
Features Word Processing Functions Such As Search & Replace, Exchange, Move, Copy, Left & Right Margin Indentation, Optional Right Margin Justification, Text File Chain Printing, Multiple Copy Printing, Automatic Page Numbering & Centering, Plus Graphics Printed with Text, User Definable Keys, Superscripts & Subscripts, Table of Contents Generator, Two Column Printing, Display & Printing of Roman Extension Character Set, Index Generator, Alpha & Numeric Sorting, Spell Check, Terminal Emulator, Mailing List Database.
James Assocs.

Wordworx. *Compatible Hardware:* Apple II+, IIe. *Memory Required:* 48k.
disk $30.00.
Consists of Two Word Games, Myspellery & Sentence Maker, Each on a Separate Disk. Each Game Can Be Played Competitively or Solo & Can Be Played at a Variety of Difficulty Levels. In Myspellery, the Player Must Decode a Mystery Word Using the Clues Provided by the Computer. In Sentence Maker, the Student Invents As Many Grammatically Correct Sentences As Possible When Presented with a String of Five Initial Letters. Each String of Initial Letters Is Based on a Secret Sentence, One of 150 Adages, Mottos, Famous Quotations, etc. Games Can Be Modified.
Prentice Hall.

Wordzzzearch. Jan. 1989. *Items Included:* Disk(s), user's guide, poster, coloring book, warranty card, swap coupon. *Customer Support:* 90 day unlimited warranty; 800 toll free number, 800-221-7911, 8:00 a.m.-5:00 p.m. Arizona time; Updates $10.
3.5" disk $49.95.
MS-DOS. IBM, Tandy, MS-DOS compatible (128k). disk $49.99 (ISBN 1-55772-073-8, Order no.: 6301). *Nonstandard peripherals required:* VGA or CGA card. *Optimal configuration:* 128k, color monitor, VGA card. *Networks supported:* Velan, Novell, Digicard.
DOS. Apple II, Apple IIe, Apple IIGS, Apple II Plus (48k). disk $49.99 (ISBN 0-918017-79-3, Order no.: 6300). *Optimal configuration:* Apple II, printer, color monitor, 48k. *Networks supported:* Digicard.
The Award Winning Puzzle Game for Playing & Creating Hidden Word Puzzles. Players Find Words Hidden in the 12 Different Puzzles (4 Puzzles on 3 Difficulty Levels). Also Features a Variable Grid Size with a Maximum of 10x18. With CHALLENGE UPGRADE, Wordzzzearch Can Fit the Needs of Individual Players. Ages 9 to Adult.
Mindplay.

W.O.R.K. at Home. *Compatible Hardware:* Apple, Commodore 64, IBM PC & compatibles.
disk $19.95.
Provides Users with the Necessary Tools for Simplifying Everyday Home Projects, Such As Preparing School Reports, Keeping Track of Expenses, & Maintaining Expenses.
Compton's NewMedia, Inc.

Work Force/Job Group Analyst for Windows. *Version:* 4.12. Jan. 1996. *Items Included:* Step-by-step manual in 3-ring binder with slipcase. *Customer Support:* 90 days telephone technical support included in purchase price. Extended telephone technical support including toll-free number is $150/year.
MS-DOS 2.1 or higher (8Mb). IBM PC, PS/2 & compatibles. $1000.00.
Performs Work Force & Job Group Analyses Required in Affirmative Action Plans. Individual Employee Information Can Be Imported from Mainframe or PC. Sorts Job Titles by Department for Work Force Analysis & by Job Group for the Job Group Analysis. Ranks Job Titles by Salary & Calculates Race & Gender Counts. Generates Printed Reports That Can Be Included in Final Copy of AAP, & Creates Export File So That Results Can Be Quickly Transferred to AAPlanner, a Companion Program. Prepares Lines of Progression & EEO Reports. Sorts & Searches Employee Information by Job Group, Job Title, Department, Employee ID Number, Name or EEO Code. Menu Driven. Requires No Programming Skills. Companion Program to AAPlanner & Adverse Impact Monitor.
PRI Assocs., Inc.

Work Order, 5 modules. May 1983. *Compatible Hardware:* IBM PC, PC XT, PC AT. *Operating System(s) Required:* PC-DOS. *Language(s):* COBOL. *Memory Required:* 192k. *General Requirements:* 2 disk drives.
$4675.00-$8600.00.
Five Modules Include: the Work Center & Router Modules Provide Labor Information for Each Work Center & the Operations Necessary to Produce an Item; Alternate Operations Are Supported & the Shop Calendar Supports 1000 Workdays; the Work Order Module Lists the Materials & Labor Requirements; Shop Floor Module Produces Reports by Work Center & Collects Labor Reporting Information; & the Capacity Planning Module Summarizes & Reports by Work Center, the Planned, Firmed & Released Work.
Twin Oaks, Inc.

Work Order System. *Operating System(s) Required:* CP/M.
$1500.00.
Masters Software Co.

Work Request & Asset Management. *Version:* 3.0. *Compatible Hardware:* Apple Macintosh Classic or higher. *General Requirements:* Hard disk.
$3795.00.
This Program Is a Cost Effective, Easy to Use Maintenance Program to Manage & Track Work Requests & Schedule Preventive Maintenance.

WORKFLOW ANALYZER: BUSINESS PROCESS

Work Requests Can Be Monitored by Status, In-House & Vendor Work Assignments/Costs, Start & Completion Dates, Projects & Cost Centers. Flexible Ad Hoc Reporting Capability for Complete Cost Analysis & Historical Reporting. Reduces Equipment Downtime Through Scheduled Preventive Maintenance with Work Orders Being Automatically Generated Based on Your Procedures & Cycles.
AD/C Solutions.

WorkBench Mac & WorkBench PC. *Compatible Hardware:* Apple Mac Plus, Classic, SE, SE/30, LC, IIsi, IIci, IIfx; IBM PC, PC XT, PC AT. *Operating System(s) Required:* PC-DOS 2.0, 3.0 or Apple DOS 3.3. *Language(s):* BASIC (source code included). *Memory Required:* Apple 48k, IBM 256k. *Customer Support:* Application engineers available.
contact publisher for price.
Data Acquisition & Control System with Hardware & Software. Measures & Controls Temperature, Pressure, Flow etc. for Laboratory & Industry.
Strawberry Tree, Inc.

Workbook. *Version:* 1.23. Kent Ochel & Jerry Spencer. Oct. 1989. *Items Included:* Tutorial Disk. *Customer Support:* Unlimited free technical support at (512) 251-7541.
MS/PC-DOS; 3.1 or higher. IBM PC, XT, AT or compatible (512K). disk $99.95. *Networks supported:* LAN.
Thought Organizer. Helps User Think As He/She Writes. Begin to Outline Thoughts in Any Order. In Simple Phrases, Then Re-Order the Priorities & Regroup the Ideas. Reshape Thinking While Writing. Workbook Includes Pull-Down Menus, Cut & Paste Features & 32 Levels of Hierarchy.
Business Resource Software.

Workers' Compensation Billing & Claims. *Version:* 2.1. 1984. *Items Included:* Contact vendor. *Customer Support:* Contact vendor.
MS-Windows 3.1. 386 (4Mb). Contact publisher for price. *Addl. software required:* Paradox for Windows Ver. 4.5 or 5.0. *Networks supported:* Artisoft Lantastic, Novell Netware.
Manages Companies, Corporations, Employees, & Dependents Charges for Workers' Compensation Insurance Coverage. Start up Billing & Monthly Re-Billing. Claims Tracking for All Employees Enrolled in Insurance Programs. Agent Commissions Are Calculated Based upon Paid Invoices. Various Reports Provided to Screen, File, or Printer. ICD-9 & CPT-4 Codes Recorded in Claim Service Records.
Management Systems, Inc.

WorkFlow Analyzer: Business Process Reengineering. 1993. *Items Included:* 2 manuals, 2 tutorials. *Customer Support:* 5 days consulting support included with purchase of product. Product phone support included with purchase.
Mac - System 7. Mac IIfx, Centeis, Quadra (32Mb). $34,995.00. *Addl. software required:* Excel.
HP-Unix 9.X. 9000/700 (32Mb). $34,995.00. *Addl. software required:* X11R4 or X11R5, XWindow System, Excel for MacOS or MS-Windows.
Sun OS 4.1.X or Solaris 2.X. Sparc (32Mb). $34,995.00. *Addl. software required:* X11R4 or X11R5, XWindows System, Excel for MacOS or MS-Windows.
Desktop Software Designed to Help Organizations Reengineer Their Business Processes to Achieve Dramatically Improved Performance in Costs, Quality, Service & Speed. The WorkFlow Analyzer Toolset Allows Business Users to Develop Graphical Models of Existing Workflows, for the Identificaiton of Bottlenecks, Resource Utilization, & Process Costs.
Meta Software.

WorkFlow.2020. 1994. *Items Included:* All User, Install, Administration Guides. *Customer Support:* Toll free phone support; 15% of current price for maintenance 1 year.
Windows 3.X, MS-DOS. IBM PC & compatibles (8Mb). disk $295.00. *Networks supported:* All.
Comprehensive GUI System Based on Object Oriented Programming That Electronically Automates Business Processes. Custom Electronic Forms Are Created Simply & Quickly with a Point, Click & Drag Toolbox of Objects, or You Can Use the Complete Set of Ready-to-Use Templates.
Fischer International Systems Corp.

WorkFlow.2000. 1993. *Items Included:* All User, Administrator, Install Guides. *Customer Support:* Toll free-24 hour phone support.
IBM S/370, VM/CMS, VM, MVS; MVS/TSO, MVS/XA, MVS/ESA, CICS, DOS/VSE, VTAM, IMS, OS/400, MS-Windows, OS/2, MS-DOS. IBM S/370, IBM PC & compatibles, Unix Workstations (8Mb). $18,000.00.
Networks supported: Novell, Banyan, Token-Ring, Ethernet.
Electronically Automates Paperwork. Intelligently Collects, Moves & Distributes Information & Data among a Number of Platforms & Allows Transactions Both Within & Across Organization. Provides Full Digital Signature Support for Security & Implements the Electronic Document Authorization Protocol Allowing for Immediate EDI Capability.
Fischer International Systems Corp.

Working Today & Tomorrow. Apr. 1991. *Items Included:* Teacher's manual/user guide.
DOS 2.10 or higher. IBM PC & compatible (256k). 5.25" disk $158.00 (ISBN 0-8219-0257-1, Order no.: 95428G). *Nonstandard peripherals required:* Color graphics adapter.
Apple DOS 3.3. Apple IIc or IIe (128k). disk $158.00 (ISBN 0-8219-0194-X, Order no.: 95428F).
Five Diskette Package That Includes Job Search Simulations, Interview Simulations, Personality Investigation to Match Compatibility with Jobs, Budget Spreadsheet.
EMC Publishing.

Working Watermarker. Sep. 1994. *Customer Support:* Free phone & E-Mail support.
Windows 3.1. PC (4Mb). disk $49.95.
Macintosh. All Macs (1Mb). 3.5" disk $49.95.
Lets User Print Any Graphic, Such As a Logo or "Draft" "Behind" Anything You Print from Any Application, to Any Printer. Sample Watermarks Include "Copy" "Draft" "Confidential".
Working Software, Inc.

WorkLog. *Version:* 2.0. 1985. *Compatible Hardware:* IBM PC, PC XT, PC AT & compatibles. *Operating System(s) Required:* PC-DOS/MS-DOS 2.0 or higher. *Language(s):* C, Assembly. *Memory Required:* 128k.
disk $95.00.
Automatically Maintains a Database of PC Usage by User, Activity & Project. Keeps Track of Keystrokes & Idle Time. Includes Report Generator.
WyssWare.

Workplace Vocabulary: Job Specific Literacy. *Version:* 2.0. Sep. 1991. *Items Included:* Operation manual; users manual; all hardware required to run courseware. *Customer Support:* 90 day unlimited warranty; toll free telephone 800-333-0054; 30 day free trial.
MS-DOS. IBM & compatible (640k). 250 word version - $9995.00 (Order no.: H245). *Nonstandard peripherals required:* CD-ROM drive & controller. *Addl. software required:* MS-DOS CD-ROM Extensions. *Optimal configuration:* Standard with CGA or VGA color monitor & CD-ROM drive. *Networks supported:* Yes if CD-ROM is supported on your system.
CD-ROM Based Computer Courseware Package Customized to Users Specific Needs. User Specifies 250 Job Specific Words, Definitions, Context Sentences, & Graphic Representation. Will Create User CD-ROM for His Exclusive Use. Will Increase Employee Productivity, Safety, Dependability, Understanding & Self-Esteem. Works Well with Reading HORIZONS.
HEC Software, Inc.

The Works of John Ruskin. John Ruskin. Edited by E. T. Cook & Alexander Wedderburn.
IBM. CD-ROM disk $750.00 (ISBN 0-521-56604-5).
Cambridge Univ. Pr.

The Worksheet Utilities. Jan. 1988. *Compatible Hardware:* IBM PC & compatibles, PS/2. *Memory Required:* 384k. *General Requirements:* Lotus 1-2-3 release 2/2.01.
3.5" & 5.25" disk $99.95.
Includes Six Utilities: Formula Editor, File Manager, Print Settings, Search & Replace, AutoSave, & Range Column Width. Formula Editor Lets User Edit & Debug Formulas, See the Whole Formula at Once, & Pick @Functions from a List. The File Manager Lets User Annotate a File Name with up to 240 Words, Perform DOS Functions, & Tag & Copy Files. One Utility Automatically Saves Work Periodically.
Funk Software.

WorksPlus Command. *Version:* 2.0. *Compatible Hardware:* Apple Macintosh.
3.5" disk $149.95.
Provides Pre-Programmed Commands Which Help Eliminate Repetitive Typing. Striking a Single Macintosh Command Key Enables Users to: Select a Style Rule, Set up Multi-Column Labels from a Data Base, Generate a Table of Contents or an Index, Log on to a Time-Sharing Service, etc. Also Allows Users to Create Custom Commands; Users Record the Keystrokes or Mouse Clicks & Program Creates the Command. Provides a Full Programming Language for Creating More Complex Macros. New Macros: Power Paste & Import Database. New Manual Complete with Examples & Illustrations.
Lundeen & Assocs.

WorksPlus Spell. *Version:* 2.0. *Compatible Hardware:* Apple Macintosh Plus, Mac SE, Mac II.
3.5" disk $99.95.
Spelling Checker. Main Directory Contains 73,000+ Words, & Users Can Add Words to Either the Main Dictionary or a Document's Personal Dictionary, As Well As Delete Words. Applies Rules for Spelling Exceptions, As Well As Verb Tenses, Plurals, Adjectives, & Adverbs. Users Can Find out the Correct Spelling of a Word by Typing in the First Few Letters; the Correct Word Can Then Be Selected & Inserted into the Document. Glossary Feature Permits Users to Abbreviate Frequently-Used Phrases; the Complete Phrase Will Be Inserted When the Abbreviation Is Typed In. Also Features Automatic Hyphenation, Word Count, & Checks for Double Words. New Feature: Smart Spelling.
Lundeen & Assocs.

Workstation Wizard. *Operating System(s) Required:* PC-DOS/MS-DOS 2.1 or higher. *Memory Required:* 256k.
disk $249.99.
Offers a Pop-Up Electronic Calculator, An Auto-Dialer, Security System, Audit Trails & Reporting Functions.
Leader Systems, Inc.

Workview. *Version:* 4.0. Jul. 1988. *Compatible Hardware:* IBM PC & compatibles, DEC VAX, SUN. *Operating System(s) Required:* PC-DOS/MS-DOS, VMS, UNIX. *Language(s):* C. *Items Included:* On-line help, tutorials (on-line), manual/documentation. *Customer Support:* Hot line support (toll free 12 hrs./day, electronic bulletin board 24 hrs./day), training courses, application/field engineers.
DOS or Unix. 80386, 80486 or compatibles, IBM RS 6000 (4Mb). contact publisher for price. *Networks supported:* Novell, NFS, TCP/IP, DECnet, Token Ring.
SUN-OS (Unix). Sun 3, Sparcstation, Sun 4 (8Mb). *Addl. software required:* X-windows. *Networks supported:* NFS, TCP/IP, DECnet.
DEC Ultric, DEC VMS. DECstation, VAXstation (16Mb). *Addl. software required:* DECwindows. *Networks supported:* DECnet, NFS, TCP/IP.
Electronic Design Entry (Schematic, Boolean, State, VHDL); Simulation (Mixed-Level, Mixed-Signal, Mixed Analog-Digital, VHDL; Synthesis (VHDL); Analysis (Analog & Digital Graphical Waveform Pre & Post Processing; CAE Framework for Integration, & Support for CAE Standards (VHDL, EDIF, CFI, UNIX, X-Windows, 386-DOS, Motif).
Viewlogic Systems, Inc.

World Biographical Dictionary of Artists on CD-ROM. *Items Included:* Annual Updates.
MS-DOS compatibility. IBM 386 or higher. CD-ROM disk $2100.00 for 1 year (Order no.: IAK110).
A research milestone in the world of art, this electronic database features nearly 180,000 artist documents, with biographies derived from the landmark Thieme-Becker/Volmer encyclopedia of artists. Covering painters, graphic artists, sculptors, architects, & applied arts practitioners from every epoch & culture sphere, the articles provide all the essential details of an artists life & development, along with characteristics of his or her work.
K G Saur.

World Biographical Index on CD-ROM. *Items Included:* Annual Updates.
MS-DOS. IBM 386 or higher. CD-ROM disk (Order no.: WBK110).
The indexes accompanying K. G. Saur's massive Biographical Archive series, which reproduces important biographical dictionaries from the 17 through 20th centuries on microfiche, have been transferred to CD-ROM. More than guides to the fiche archives, the indexes represent comprehensive biographical dictionaries in their own right, providing name; dates of birth & death; occupation; & references to the source work & microfiche entry. Although the reference sources date from 1601, the personalities appearing in the Archives date back to classical times, & represent men & women from every class & calling in Germany, the U. K., United States, Latin America, France, Italy, & Germany.
K G Saur.

The World Digitized World Outline Database. *Items Included:* Bound manual. *Customer Support:* Free hotline - no time limit; 30 day limited warranty; updates are $5/disk plus S&H.
MS-DOS 2.0 or higher. IBM & compatibles (256k). disk $19.95. *Nonstandard peripherals required:* CGA/EGA (or equivalent) graphics capability.
Composed of Six Disks Which Contain Geographical Data for the Entire World. The First Type of Display Starts with a World Globe. User May Choose to Zoom into Particular Regions According to State & National Capitals, Latitude/Longitude, or Area. Use the Cursor Keys to Move Around. Go in Close Enough & You Will See City Names. Calculate Distances &

TITLE INDEX

More! The Second Type of Display Contains Only Geographical Features (e.g., Rivers, Borders, Lakes, Islands, etc.), but at a Much Higher Resolution (the Data File Is over 1Mb). Choose to View Any Region on the Screen, & Move About at Will.
Dynacomp, Inc.

The World Digitized World Outline Database.
Items Included: Full manual. No other products required. *Customer Support:* Free telephone support - no time limit. 30 day warranty.
MS-DOS 3.2 or higher. IBM & compatibles (512k). disk $95.00.
Database Similar to COUNTY OUTLINE DATABASE, but on a Global Scale. Includes Continent, Island, & Lake Outline Data, As Well As Political Boundaries & the Locations of about 300 Cities.
Dynacomp, Inc.

The World Digitized: World Outline Database. 1992. *Items Included:* Detailed manuals included with all Dynacomp products. *Customer Support:* Free telephone support to original customer - no time limit; 30 day limited warranty.
MS-DOS 3.2 or higher. IBM PC & compatibles (512k). $95.00 (Add $5.00 for 3 1/2" format; 5 1/4" format standard).
A Database Similar to COUNTY OUTLINE DATABASE, but on a Global Scale. It Includes Continent, Island, & Lake Outline Data, As Well As Political Boundaries & the Locations of about 300 Cities. The Latest Version of MTRANS Also Allows the Conversion of Map Files from Degrees to the Mercator Projection.
Dynacomp, Inc.

World Games. 1986. *Compatible Hardware:* Apple II+, IIe, IIc, IIgs; Atari ST; Commodore 64, 128, Amiga; IBM PC & compatibles. contact publisher for price.
Features Eight Events: Cliff Diving, Bull Riding, Barrel Jumping, Weight Lifting, etc. Compete in Eight Different Countries. Provides Award Ranking & World Records Hall of Fame. Practice One Event or Compete in the World Circuit. One to Eight Players.
Epyx, Inc.

World Geography: Nigel's World Adventures.
MS-DOS 3.1 or higher. 386 processor or higher (4Mb). CD-ROM disk $49.95 (Order no.: R1231). *Nonstandard peripherals required:* CD-ROM drive. *Optimal configuration:* 386 processor or higher, MS-DOS 3.1 or higher, 20Mb hard drive, 640k RAM, external speakers or headphones (with sound card) that are Sound Blaster compatible, VGA graphics & adapter, VGA color monitor.
Macintosh (4Mb). (Order no.: R1231). *Nonstandard peripherals required:* 14" color monitor or larger, CD-ROM drive.
From Ecuador to Tanzania, Children Join Nigel As He Travels the World Snapping Pictures of Fascinating People, Places & Monuments. Helps Children Gain Geographic Literacy & Global Awareness. Includes More Than 40 Maps, 90 Photos, Native Folk Songs & More (Ages 7-12).
Library Video Co.

World of Odyssey. *Compatible Hardware:* Apple II, II+. *Language(s):* Applesoft II. *Memory Required:* 48k.
disk $24.95 (Order no.: 10040).
Adventure Game.
Powersoft, Inc.

The World of Totty Pig.
MS-DOS 5.0 or higher, Windows 3.1 or higher. 386 processor or higher (4Mb). CD-ROM disk $59.95 (Order no.: R1370). *Nonstandard peripherals required:* CD-ROM drive. *Optimal configuration:* 386 processor operating at 16Mhz or higher, MS-DOS 5.0 or higher, Windows 3.1 or higher, 30Mb hard drive, mouse, VGA graphic adapter & VGA color monitor (SVGA recommended), 4Mb RAM, external speakers or headphones (with sound card) that are Sound Blaster compatible.
Based on the Bank Street Ready-to-Read Series Book, "You Are Much Too Small," Children Can Interact with the Characters, Play Games, Solve Puzzles & Sing along with Songs. Highlighted Phrases Make Reading along Easy (Ages 3-8).
Library Video Co.

World Series of Poker Adventure. Wayne Russell. Aug. 1993. *Items Included:* Disk, manual, registration card. *Customer Support:* Free technical support, free sales support, guaranteed satisfaction or full refund.
MS-DOS 3.1 or higher. IBM & compatibles (640k) 1Mb hard disk. disk $39.99 (ISBN 1-882586-00-X). *Nonstandard peripherals required:* Mouse, supports all sound cards. *Optimal configuration:* Sound Card.
Simulation of the World Series of Poker Which Requires a $10,000 Buy-In. You Arrive with $5,000; the Balance You Must Win Playing Blackjack, Poker (Omaha, Texas Hold'Em or 7 Card Stud) Slots or Videopoker. Your Goal Is to Be the World Champion Poker Player & Receive $1,000,000 & a Gold Bracelet.

The World Shakespeare Bibliography, 1990-1993. Edited by James L. Harner.
IBM. CD-ROM disk $240.00 (ISBN 0-521-55627-9).
Cambridge Univ. Pr.

World View. *Compatible Hardware:* IBM PC & compatibles. *Operating System(s) Required:* PC-DOS/MS-DOS. *Memory Required:* 256k. *General Requirements:* Hard disks recommended. 3.5" or 5.25" disk $49.95.
Assists the User in Developing a Theory of Himself in the World. Topics Include Physical Health, Psychological Health, Creativity, Family & Friends, Philosophy of Life, Wealth & Success, Lifestyle & Goals.
Thinking Software, Inc.

World War II: A Compelling Exploration. *Items Included:* Pamphlet of instructions. *Customer Support:* Tech support, 60-day money-back guarantee.
Windows 3.1 or higher. IBM PC compatible (2Mb). CD-ROM disk $49.95 (ISBN 0-924677-09-0). *Nonstandard peripherals required:* CD-ROM drive, Soundboard, SVGA display with 256 colors, mouse.
A Compelling Exploration of the Last World War. Living Media Brings Life to History in This Dynamic Compilation of Images, Sound & Text Covering all Aspects of the War, from Europe to the Pacific Theater in the Effects of the War on Americans at Home. the Easy-to-Use Controls Allow You to Search on Specific Criteria or Use the Guided Tour for an Overview.
IMSI (International Microcomputer Software, Inc.).

The World Wide Web Encyclopedia. Ed Tittel et al. Mar. 1996. *Items Included:* Free Web Browser & Internet connect software. *Customer Support:* Free technical support, 30 day limited warranty, site licenses available.
Windows 3.1 or higher. IBM & compatibles (4Mb). CD-ROM disk $39.95 (ISBN 1-886801-44-4). *Nonstandard peripherals required:* CD drive. *Optimal configuration:* PC or compatible; 386 or higher; Windows 3.1 or higher; CD drive, 4Mb RAM (8 preferred).
Macintosh or compatibles. Performa, Power PCs (all models) Quadra, etc. (4Mb). *Nonstandard peripherals required:* CD drive. *Optimal configuration:* System 7.0 or higher; 4Mb RAM (8 preferred); CD drive.
MS-DOS or other DOS. IBM & compatibles (4Mb). *Nonstandard peripherals required:* CD drive. *Optimal configuration:* 386 or higher; CD drive; 4Mb RAM (8 preferred).
This Multiplatform CD (Windows/Mac/Unix) Provides Interactive Access to Thousands of Web Site, Information, Software, & Demonstrations. Useful for All Levels from Beginner to Advanced. Includes a Topical Search Function, a Large Gallery of Graphics, HTML Templates, & Thousands of Links to Internet Sites.
Charles River Media.

The World Wide Web Encyclopedia CD. Ed Tittel et al. Mar. 1996. *Items Included:* Free Web Browser & Internet Connect Software. *Customer Support:* Free technical support, 30 day limited warranty, site licenses available.
Windows 3.1 or higher; Macintosh; MS DOS or other DOS. IBM & compatibles, 386 (4Mb); Macintosh Performa, Power PC's, Quadra, System 7 or higher (4Mb). CD-ROM disk $39.95 (ISBN 1-886801-44-4). *Nonstandard peripherals required:* CD drive.
Provides Interactive Access to Thousands of Web Sites, Information, Software, & Demonstrations. Useful for All Levels from Beginner to Advanced. Includes a Topical Search Function, a Large Gallery of Graphics, HTML Templates, & Thousands of Links to Internet Sites.
Charles River Media.

World Writer PC. *Version:* 4.0. *Items Included:* Manual. *Customer Support:* Unlimited technical support; 60 day moneyback guarantee.
DOS. IBM or compatibles (512k). disk $39.95. *Addl. software required:* DOS 2.1 or higher. *Optimal configuration:* One or more disk drives or a hard drive.
Easy-to-Learn, High Performance Word Processing System That Includes Advanced Writing, Editing & Printing Tools. Includes a 100,000-Word Spell Checker with "Soundex" - You'll Never Waste Valuable Time Searching for the Correct Spelling of a Word. Also Includes a Convenient 240,000-Word Thesaurus & a Time-Saving Mail-Merge Feature That Helps Create Personalized Form Letters & Mass Mailings Quickly & Easily Using Data from Your Database or Word Writer.
Timeworks, Inc.

World's Best...Artistic Photography of Women. Feb. 1995. *Items Included:* CD-ROM booklet. *Customer Support:* Free technical support via phone as of release date.
MPC Windows/DOS/UNIX; Macintosh; PhotoCD/CD-i. IBM 386 Processor or higher (4Mb); Mac System 6.07 or higher (4Mb). CD-ROM disk $24.95 (ISBN 1-885784-07-4, Order no.: 1007).
The Intriguing Beauty of Woman Has Been the Subject of Countless Works of Art. This Photographic Art Collection Combines Stunning Photos of Women with Richly Orchestrated Music to Create an Exciting CD-ROM Entertainment Experience. Over 100 High-Resolution Images with Music Selections to Be Used for Multimedia Presentations & Desktop Publishing.
Technology Dynamics Corp.

The World's Easiest Database: Object Oriented Database. Feb. 1992. *Items Included:* 28 page manual.
MS-DOS. IBM PC, PC XT, PC AT, 386, 486 (256k). disk $9.95 (ISBN 0-911827-10-2, Order no.: 7602). *Optimal configuration:* MS-DOS computer, 1 disk drive, 1 hard drive.
If You've Ever Wanted to Just Enter Random Miscellaneous Information into Your Computer,

but Decided That It Was Too Much Trouble to Set up the Database, Then This Program Is Your Solution. Allows User to Type in Any Information on an Index Card on the Screen. Finding Something Is Easy. Just Type Any Character, Word or Partial Word & Every Card with That Combination Pops Up. Every Entry Is a Keyword! Unlimited Storage Capacity! Sort, Print, Search & Select for Any Entry. Very Fast. Very Easy to Use. Thousands of Database Applications.
Elcomp Publishing, Inc.

The World's Longest Melody. Version: 1.1. Larry Polansky. Nov. 1992. Items Included: Short documentation. Customer Support: Free phone, E-Mail & postal support.
Macintosh II or above (6.02 or higher). $10.00 for source code version; $25.00 for turnkey version. Nonstandard peripherals required: Needs at least a 12" monitor, requires MIDI interface & MIDI synthesizer. Addl. software required: HMSL for source code version. Optimal configuration: Mac II's or higher, MIDI interface, 16 channel MIDI synthesizer. Networks supported: Internet.
A "Portable" Experimental Music Graphic Screen. It Is Distributed As Source Code (Which Requires the Program HMSL, Available from Frog Peak Music) or As a Turnkey Application.
Frog Peak Music.

Worldwatch Database Disk 1996. Worldwatch Institute Staff. Jan. 1996.
IBM. Contact publisher for price (ISBN 1-85383-331-2).
Apple Mac. Contact publisher for price (ISBN 1-85383-336-3).
Excellent Teaching Resource Containing All the Data from Worldwatch Publications - "State of the World," "Vital Signs," Papers, Reports & Articles from "Worldwatch" Magazine, Plus the "Environmental Alert" Series - Set Out in Tables, Graphs & Figures in Easy-to-Use Formats. Data Are Readable in Almost Every Popular Spreadsheet Programme Including Lotus 1-2-3, Quattro & Quattro Pro, Supercalc & Microsoft Excel & Works. An Excellent Resource for Researchers, Libraries, University & College Departments Such As Geography, Politics & Environmental Sciences; Local Authorities & Research Institutes.
Island Pr.

WORLDWIDE BROCHURES: The Official Travel Brochure Directory. Mar. 1992.
IBM PC & compatible. disk $59.00. Nonstandard peripherals required: Hard drive.
Cross-Referenced Software Guide to Thousands of Leisure & Vacation Travel Brochures from Around the World. Entire Program Requires 7Mb of Hard Disk Space.
Travel Companions International, Inc.

WormStat. General Requirements: Macintosh. 3.5" disk $19.95.
Statistical Analysis.
Small Business Computers of New England, Inc.

WP-HELPER. Foleda Software. Feb. 1984. Operating System(s) Required: CP/M-80. Memory Required: 48k.
disk $29.95, 40 TPI (ISBN 0-923875-53-0).
disk 80 TPI $29.95 (ISBN 0-923875-54-9).
8" disk $29.95 (ISBN 0-923875-52-2).
One of the 10 Programs on the WP-HELPER Disk Will Catch Unmatched Print Control Codes in a Document. Match Program Allows User to Define Other Characteristics That Must Occur As Pairs. All Programs in This Package Use the Same User Interface. Programs May Be Executed with a Command Line or the Program Will Prompt for User Input.
Elliam Assocs.

WP Sift. Operating System(s) Required: PC-DOS/MS-DOS.
disk $180.00.
"Sifts" Out the WORDPERFECT Control Codes & Puts the Formatting Commands into PC Braille Format.
Arts Computer Products, Inc.

WPS Automated IEP System. Version: 1.200. Customer Support: Free unlimited phone support.
IBM PC & 100% compatibles. 3.5" or 5.25" disk (IBM); 5.25" disk (Apple); $99.50 (Order no.: W-1021 SPECIFY APPLE OR IBM PC 5.25" OR 3.5" DISK DRIVE)). Optimal configuration: DOS 3.0 or higher (512k), & hard disk with one Mb of free hard disk space.
Easy-to-Use Program Cuts IEP Writing Time in Half. Allows User to Customize IEPs to His District's Specifications, & to Revise or Update Them in Minutes. Also Gives User Access to Professionally Developed Goal Banks, Including Several Designed Specifically for Use with Well-Known Tests.
Western Psychological Services.

WRAP. Version: 2.00. Items Included: Manual. Customer Support: Technical support - first 60 days free, annual $495.00 via phone, Fax, E-Mail; 30 days limited warranty; training available.
Windows (2Mb). disk $129.00. Optimal configuration: IBM 486 66 DXZ Windows 16 RAM.
This Utility Gives Windows Developers On-the-Fly File Compression & Decompression from KPWin, Visual Basic, Visual C Plus Plus or Any Other Windows Development Tool Which Supports DLLs. Includes a Visual Front-End Written in Knowledge Garden's KPWin Plus Plus Development Tool. Useful for Creating Installation Routines, Help Systems & Comrpessed Hypertext Documents.
Knowledge Garden, Inc.

A Wrinkle in Time. Intentional Education Staff & Madeline L'Engle. Apr. 1996. Items Included: Program manual. Customer Support: Free technical support, 90 day warranty.
School ver.. System 7.1 or higher. Macintosh (4Mb). 3.5" disk contact publisher for price (ISBN 1-57204-293-1). Nonstandard peripherals required: 256 color monitor, hard drive, printer.
Lab pack. System 7.1 or higher. macintosh (4Mb). 3.5" disk contact publisher for price (ISBN 1-57204-268-0). Nonstandard peripherals required: 256 color monitor, hard drive, printer.
Site license. System 7.1 or higher. Macintosh (4Mb). 3.5" disk contact publisher for price. Nonstandard peripherals required: 256 color monitor, hard drive, printer.
School ver.. Windows 3.1 or higher. IBM/Tandy & 100% compatibles (4Mb). disk contact publisher for price (ISBN 1-57204-269-9). Nonstandard peripherals required: VGA or SVGA 640 x 480 resolution (256), mouse, hard drive, sound device.
Lab pack. Windows 3.1 or higher. IBM/Tandy & 100% compatibles (4Mb). disk contact publisher for price (ISBN 1-57204-294-X). Nonstandard peripherals required: VGA or SVGA 640 x 480 resolution (256), mouse, hard drive, sound device.
Site license. Windows 3.1 or higher. IBM/Tandy & 100% compatibles (4Mb). disk contact publisher for price (ISBN 1-57204-270-2). Nonstandard peripherals required: VGA or SVGA 640 x 480 resolution (256), mouse, hard drive, sound device.
This companion for young adult literature is ideal for students who don't know how to start that book report, or give that needed summary.

Gentle prompts throughout the guide section of the program include Warm-up Connection, Thinking about Plot, Quoting & Noting, Keeping a Journal, If I Were ———' Responding to Questions, Using Quotations, Taking a Personal View, Write to Others, & Write a Sequel.
Lawrence Productions, Inc.

Write & File. Compatible Hardware: Commodore Amiga.
3.5" disk $99.95.
Combines Word Processor & Database.
SoftWood Co.

Write Choice. Compatible Hardware: Apple II series. Operating System(s) Required: Apple DOS 3.3. Memory Required: 64k.
disk $64.95 (ISBN 0-927796-00-7).
Word Processing System Combines a Full-Featured Word Processor, a Hi-Res Typing Tutor, & a Documentation Package That Offers Guidelines for Style & Formatting of All Types of Letters, Outlines, Manuscripts & Reports. Includes TUT'S TYPER, a Combination Typing Tutorial & Arcade Game with Hi-Res Graphics, & THE ANALYST, a Program That Reads the Documents Created & Gives Users a Report Showing the Number of Characters & Minimum Grade Level Required to Read Document.
Roger Wagner Publishing, Inc.

Write In. Version: 1.3. Compatible Hardware: IBM PC & compatibles. Memory Required: 95k. General Requirements: Lotus 1-2-3, Rel 2.0, 2.1, 2.2, 2.3. Items Included: Diskette & manual. Customer Support: Unlimited phone support.
disk $129.95.
A Powerful Word Processing Add-In That Works in Conjunction with Lotus 1-2-3 to Produce Reports, Memos, Labels, & Form Letters That Incorporate Data & Graphs from Live Worksheets. Easy to Learn & Use Because It Operates with the Same Style Menus & Pointer Movement Keys As 1-2-3.
Blossom Software Corp.

Write 'n' Spell. Andres Escollor. 1985. Compatible Hardware: IBM & compatibles. Operating System(s) Required: PC-DOS/MS-DOS 2.0 or higher. Memory Required: 256k. General Requirements: Printer.
disk $129.00.
Full-Featured Word Processor & Integrated 90,000-Word Speller with Suggest & Auto-Correct Feature. Features Built-In Mail Merge, Cut & Paste, Word Wrap, On-Screen Bold & Underline, & Access to IBM Graphic Extended Character Set.
Professional Software, Inc.

The Write Stuff. (The Write Approach Ser. I & II). 1984. Compatible Hardware: Apple II Plus, IIe, IIc. Memory Required: 64k.
Apple. 14 disk $340.00 package price (ISBN 0-06-668001-8, Order no.: INT 2326A).
Word Processor Which Offers Two Formats in Which User Can Write & Edit. Features "Automatic Save" to Keep User from Losing Text & "Undo" to Reverse Changes in the Text.
Intellectual Software.

Write-Up Master. Version: 4.5. 1980. Compatible Hardware: IBM PC & compatibles, PC XT, PC AT, PS/2. Operating System(s) Required: MS-DOS. Language(s): CBASIC. Memory Required: 128k. Customer Support: Yearly support contract $300.00.
$995.00.
Designed for Accountants. Prepares & Unites Financial Statements. Includes Depreciation, Amortization, & Payroll Accumulation When Preparing the Financial Statements.
KIS Computer Corp.

TITLE INDEX

Write Up-Plus: Professional Client Write-Up.
Version: 6.35. Oct. 1990. *Items Included:* Documentation manual; Quick Start Users Guide. *Customer Support:* 6 months toll free support & updates; 90 day unlimited warranty; annual maintenance (support & updates) $300-$400. PC-DOS/MS-DOS 3.1 or higher. IBM PC & compatibles (512K). $1495.00 single-user.
Networks supported: Novell, Novell-Lite, Lantastic.
$1995.00 multi-user.
General Ledger with Quick Client Set-Up. Standard & Custom Financial Statement Formatting, After-the-Fact Payroll, Streamlined Data Entry, Cover Letter Generator, Data Export to Tax Programs.
UniLink.

The Write-Up Solution II. *Version:* 2.1.1. 1988. *Compatible Hardware:* IBM PC & compatibles, PC XT, PC AT, PS/2. *Operating System(s) Required:* PC-DOS/MS-DOS 4.X, Novell ELS I, ELS II, AFT, LANTASTIC 3.0 10 MBD cards. *Language(s):* C. *Memory Required:* 512k. *General Requirements:* Hard disk. *Items Included:* Extensive tutorial, manual with reference section management guide, 8 sample setup clients. *Customer Support:* 5 hrs. within first yr..
$1995.00.
demo disk $49.00.
Tool for Practicing Accountants to Automate Their Client Write-Up Work.
Creative Solutions, Inc. (Michigan).

WritePro. *Version:* IBM & compatibles 2.4, Macintosh 2.1.1. *Items Included:* Manuals. *Customer Support:* Help is available at no charge Monday-Friday, 9:00 am to 5:00 pm, 914-762-1255.
MS-DOS 2.0 & higher (256k); Macintosh MAC Plus or higher, System 6.0.5 or higher (512k), System 7 compatible; IBM PC & compatibles, Macintosh Plus or higher. $49.95 per disk (ea. disk contains two lessons).
Program for Profe6sional & Budding Fiction Writer. Shows How to Improve Character Development, Plot & Other Aspects of Novels & Stories. Developed by Sol Stein, Author of "The Magician." First Two Lessons Cover the Creation of Rounded Characters, Suspense, Plotting. Third Lesson Illustrates How to Start a Story with Character Conflict to Stimulate Reader Interest. Fourth Lesson Includes Dialogue Doctor, & Mastering Description, Narration, & Immediate Scenes. Lesson Five Covers Flab Editing, the Secrets of Cutting, How to Become Your Own Best Editor. Lesson Six Shows How to Make Dialogue Come Alive, Eliminate Echoes, Build Similes & Metaphors, Step up Pace. Lesson Seven Shows How to Write Marvelous Love Scenes, & Lesson Eight Shows How to Master Advanced Characterization. Has Its Own Word Processor & Shows Original & Revised Versions of What User Has Written on a Split Screen. Both Versions Can Also Be Printed &/or Exported to the User's Own Word Processor.
The WritePro Corp.

The Writer. *Compatible Hardware:* HP 150 Touchscreen, HP 110 Portable.
3.5" disk $49.95 (Order no.: 35153D).
Word Processor Providing the Occasional User with an Interactive Tutorial & "Help" Screens. Users Can Revise the Content & Organization of a Document While Viewing It on the Screen, As Well As Add, Move or Delete Words, Sentences or Entire Paragraphs. Additional Features Include Word Wrap, Centering, Boldface, Underline, Search & Replace, File Chaining, Headers & Footers, Right Justification, & a Mail Merge Capability.
Hewlett-Packard Co.

Writer's Helper. *Version:* 3.0. 1990. *General Requirements:* Word Processing Program.
Macintosh Plus (1Mb). 3.5" disk $135.00.
IBM PC (256k). disk $135.00.
Apple II (128k). disk $135.00.
Assists User in Writing a Paper or Document by Providing Pre-Writing, Drafting, & Revising Tools.
CONDUIT.

Writing K-2. Jan. 1994. *Items Included:* Program on CD-ROM, CD Booklet, & Registration Card. *Customer Support:* Free unlimited support via telephone.
Windows 3.1 or higher running under DOS 5.0 or higher. 386 SX (4Mb RAM; 500k low Dos Mem; 6Mb free disk space). CD-ROM disk $49.00 (ISBN 1-57268-017-2, Order no.: 57002). *Nonstandard peripherals required:* Sound card (either: Sound Blaster - 8, 16, PRO; Media Vision ProAudio Spectrum; or Microsoft Sound System); MPC Compatible CD-ROM drive; VGA monitor; & microphone.
Optimal configuration: 25 MHz 386 SX.
Writing & Keyboarding: These Programs Teach Students How to Manage Information & Effectively Communicate Their Ideas. The Creative Writing Skills Your Students Will Develop by Using These Grade-Level CD-ROM Programs Will Provide a Solid Foundation They'll Build upon Throughout Their Lives.
Conter Software.

Writing K-2. Jan. 1994. *Items Included:* Program on CD-ROM, CD Booklet, & Registration Card. *Customer Support:* Free unlimited customer support via telephone.
Windows 3.1 or higher running under DOS 5.0 or higher. 386 SX (4Mb RAM; 500k low Dos Mem; 6Mb free disk space). CD-ROM disk $249.00 (ISBN 1-57268-052-0, Order no.: 17020). *Nonstandard peripherals required:* Sound card (either: Sound Blaster - 8, 16, PRO; Media Vision ProAudio Spectrum; or Microsoft Sound System); MPC compatible CD-ROM drive; VGA monitor; & microphone.
Optimal configuration: 25 MHz 386 SX.
Writing & Keyboarding: These Programs Teach Students How to Manage Information & Effectively Communicate Their Ideas. The Creative Writing Skills Your Students Will Develop by Using These Grade-Level CD-ROM Programs Will Provide a Solid Foundation They'll Build upon Throughout Their Lives.
Conter Software.

Writing Process Workshop. Barbara Hombs & Priscilla Hamilton. 1994. *Items Included:* Diskettes, teachers guide & binders. *Customer Support:* Toll free customer service Hot Line 1-800-645-3739 (9a.m. - 5p.m. Eastern Time) software guaranteed for two years.
Mac 6.0 Plus. Macintosh (4Mb). 3.5" disk $249.00 (Order no.: DK40171).
This Sophisticated Prompted Writing Program Will Simultaneously Develop Your Students' Creativity, Writing, & Word Processing Skills. Brainstorming, Quickwriting & Drafting Help Them Master Fluency, the First Step in Becoming a Good Writer.
Educational Activities Inc.

Writing 3-4. Jan. 1994. *Items Included:* Program on CD-ROM, CD Booklet, & Registration Card. *Customer Support:* Free unlimited support via telephone.
Windows 3.1 or higher running under DOS 5.0 or higher. 386 SX (4Mb RAM; 500k low Dos Mem; 6Mb free disk space). CD-ROM disk $49.00 (ISBN 1-57268-018-0, Order no.: 57034). *Nonstandard peripherals required:* Sound card (either: Sound Blaster - 8, 16, PRO; Media Vision ProAudio Spectrum; or Microsoft Sound System); MPC Compatible CD-ROM drive; VGA monitor; & microphone.
Optimal configuration: 25MHz 386 SX.
Writing & Keyboarding: These Programs Teach Students How to Manage Information & Effectively Communicate Their Ideas. The Creative Writing Skills Your Students Will Develop by Using These Grade-Level CD-ROM Programs Will Provide a Solid Foundation They'll Build upon Throughout Their Lives.
Conter Software.

Writing 3-4. Jan. 1994. *Items Included:* Program on CD-ROM, CD Booklet, & Registration Card. *Customer Support:* Free unlimited customer support via telephone.
Windows 3.1 or higher running under DOS 5.0 or higher. 386 SX (4Mb RAM; 500k low Dos Mem; 6Mb free disk space). CD-ROM disk $249.00 (ISBN 1-57268-053-9, Order no.: 17340). *Nonstandard peripherals required:* Sound card (either: Sound Blaster - 8, 16, PRO; Media Vision ProAudio Spectrum; or Microsoft Sound System); MPC compatible CD-ROM drive; VGA monitor; & microphone.
Optimal configuration: 25 MHz 386 SX.
Writing & Keyboarding: These Programs Teach Students How to Manage Information & Effectively Communicate Their Ideas. The Creative Writing Skills Your Students Will Develop by Using These Grade-Level CD-ROM Programs Will Provide a Solid Foundation They'll Build upon Throughout Their Lives.
Conter Software.

Writing 5-6. Jan. 1994. *Items Included:* Program on CD-ROM, CD Booklet, & Registration Card. *Customer Support:* Free unlimited support via telephone.
Windows 3.1 or higher running under DOS 5.0 or higher. 386 SX (4Mb RAM; 500k low Dos Mem; 6Mb free disk space). CD-ROM disk $49.00 (ISBN 1-57268-019-9, Order no.: 57056). *Nonstandard peripherals required:* Sound card (either: Sound Blaster - 8, 16, PRO; Media Vision ProAudio Spectrum; or Microsoft Sound System); MPC Compatible CD-ROM drive; VGA monitor; & microphone.
Optimal configuration: 25MHz 386 SX.
Writing & Keyboarding: These Programs Teach Students How to Manage Information & Effectively Communicate Their Ideas. The Creative Writing Skills Your Students Will Develop by Using These Grade-Level CD-ROM Programs Will Provide a Solid Foundation They'll Build upon Throughout Their Lives.
Conter Software.

Writing 7-8. Jan. 1994. *Items Included:* Program on CD-ROM, CD Booklet, & Registration Card. *Customer Support:* Free unlimited support via telephone.
Windows 3.1 or higher running under DOS 5.0 or higher. 386 SX (4Mb RAM; 500k low Dos Mem; 6Mb free disk space). CD-ROM disk $49.00 (ISBN 1-57268-020-2, Order no.: 57078). *Nonstandard peripherals required:* Sound card (either: Sound Blaster - 8, 16, PRO; Media Vision ProAudio Spectrum; or Microsoft Sound System); MPC Compatible CD-ROM drive; VGA monitor; & microphone.
Optimal configuration: 25MHz 386 SX.
Writing & Keyboarding: These Programs Teach Students How to Manage Information & Effectively Communicate Their Ideas. The Creative Writing Skills Your Students Will Develop by Using These Grade-Level CD-ROM Programs Will Provide a Solid Foundation They'll Build upon Throughout Their Lives.
Conter Software.

Writing 7-8. Jan. 1994. *Items Included:* Program on CD-ROM, CD Booklet, & Registration Card. *Customer Support:* Free unlimited customer

support via telephone.
Windows 3.1 or higher running under DOS 5.0 or higher. 386 SX (4Mb RAM; 500k low Dos Mem; 6Mb free disk space). CD-ROM disk $249.00 (ISBN 1-57268-055-5, Order no.: 17780). *Nonstandard peripherals required:* Sound card (either: Sound Blaster - 8, 16, PRO; Media Vision ProAudio Spectrum; or Microsoft Sound System); MPC compatible CD-ROM drive; VGA monitor; & microphone. *Optimal configuration:* 25 MHz 386 SX.
Writing & Keyboarding: These Programs Teach Students How to Manage Information & Effectively Communicate Their Ideas. The Creative Writing Skills Your Students Will Develop by Using These Grade-Level CD-ROM Programs Will Provide a Solid Foundation They'll Build upon Throughout Their Lives.
Conter Software.

Writsit. Duane Bristow. *Compatible Hardware:* TRS-80 Model III. *Operating System(s) Required:* TRSDOS. *Language(s):* BASIC. *Memory Required:* 48k.
Wrisit disk. $59.95.
Mailit disk. $59.95.
Word Processor - Works with MAILIT Program to Merge Mailing Lists into Form Letters with Customized Inserts.
Duane Bristow Computers, Inc.

WSE-1. *Compatible Hardware:* IBM PC, PC XT, PC AT, PS/2. *Operating System(s) Required:* MS-DOS. *Language(s):* QuickBASIC. *Memory Required:* 256k.
$49.00.
Weight Schedule Editor Which Monitors Weight & Center of Gravity Position of Vessel During Design, Contruction, or Operation. Program Updates Weights & c.g. As Components Are Changed or Relocated.
AeroHydro, Inc.

WSVX80. *Customer Support:* 800-929-8117 (customer service).
MS-DOS. Commodore 128; CP/M. disk $39.99 (ISBN 0-87007-404-0).
Includes Creating & Printing on Empty Pages, Saving the Line Height, Chaining the Strikeover Character, Providing an Alternate Greek Character Set & Redefining Control Characters.
SourceView Software International.

W2 Program - 1099 Misc. Oct. 1987. *Operating System(s) Required:* PC-DOS/MS-DOS. *Memory Required:* 184k.
disk $49.95.
W2 Form & 1099 Misc Form Generator. Paint a W2 Form on Screen for Data Entry. Designed to Prepare 99 Company Accounts. Within Each Company, Prepares Unlimited W2 Records. Print User Report by Ctrol-Id (Employee No.), SSNN or Last Name, Support 1UP, 2UP W2 Forms, Formats A/B, Alternate, Standard, etc.
Mau Corp.

X11R5 & GNU. *Customer Support:* All of our products are unconditionally guaranteed.
Unix. CD-ROM disk $39.95 (Order no.: X11R5).
Nonstandard peripherals required: CD-ROM drive.
Complete X11R5 & GNU Distribution.
Walnut Creek CDRom.

X11R6. *Customer Support:* All of our products are unconditionally guaranteed.
Unix. CD-ROM disk $39.95 (Order no.: X11R6).
Nonstandard peripherals required: CD-ROM drive.
Official X11R6 Patch Level 3 X Window System. No GNU Distribution.
Walnut Creek CDRom.

X for Workgroups. *Version:* 4.0. May 1993. *Items Included:* Built-in TCP/IP, media & user's manual. *Customer Support:* 90 days free technical support & updates.
MS-Windows for Workgroups 3.1. 386 (4Mb). disk $249.00. *Nonstandard peripherals required:* Mouse. *Optimal configuration:* 486, 8Mb RAM, 3 Button Mouse, DOS 5.0, Hi-Res VGA board supporting 256 colors.
Server Software for Microsoft Windows for Workgroups. Lets PC Users Maximize Their Hardware Investment While Increasing Productivity. Turns 386-Or 486-Based PCs into X Terminals & Allows Users Access to the Work of X Windows Computing. Rather Than Buying a Dedicated X Terminal or Expense Workstation, Users Can Harness the Computing Power of Today's Popular PCs & Take Advantage of the X Applications Available on Their Network. Features Include, Built-In TCP/IP, Local and/or Remote Window Manger, XDM, Direct Access to Host System Through X Start Client Icon, Allows You to Simultaneously Run X Windows along with DOS & MS Windows Applications, Context-Sensitive Help, & Easy Installation.
Grafpoint.

X-One for DOS: X Server Software for PC's. *Version:* 2.4. 1991. *Items Included:* Built-in TCP/IP Networking software, Packet Drivers, complete user documentation, (Optional) THEdge - video graphics accelerator board. *Customer Support:* 90 days free technical support & updates.
MS-DOS 3.1 or higher. 386 or 486 based PC (2Mb). disk $249.00. *Networks supported:* Ethernet, Token Ring, Pathworks, PC NFC, FTP's PC/TCP, Beame & Whiteside, Wollongong Pathway.
Lets PC Users Maximize Their Hardware Investment While Increasing Productivity. Turns 386-Or 486-Based PCs into X Terminals & Allows Users Access to the World of X Windows Computing. Rather Than Buying a Dedicated X Terminal or Expensive Workstation, Users Can Harness the Computing Power of Today's Popular PCs & Take Advantage of the X Applications Available on Their Network. Features Include, Built-In TCP/IP along with Support for 3rd Party Network Software, Local Window Manager, DEC VT100 Terminal Capability, XDM, FTP, Context-Sensitive Help, & Easy Installation.
Grafpoint.

X-One for Windows. *Version:* 4.0. Aug. 1992. *Items Included:* Built-in TCP/IP, media, user guide. *Customer Support:* 90 days free technical support & updates.
MS-Windows 3.1. 386 (4Mb). disk $249.00. *Nonstandard peripherals required:* Mouse. *Optimal configuration:* 486, DOS 5, MS-Windows 3.1, 8Mb RAM, Hi-Res Graphics board w/ 256 colors. *Networks supported:* SUN PC-NFS, FTP PC/TCP, Novell LAN Workplace for DOS, Netmanage Chameleon, Winsocks.
Server Software for Microsoft Windows. Lets PC Users Maximize Their Hardware Investment While Increasing Productivity. Turns 386-Or 486-Based PCs into X Terminals & Allows Users Access to the World of X Windows Computing. Rather Than Buying a Dedicated X Terminal or Expensive Workstation, Users Can Harness the Computing Power of Today's Popular PCs & Take Advantage of the X Applications Available on Their Network. Features Include, Built-In TCP/IP along with Support for 3rd Party Network Software, Local and/or Remote Window Manager, XDM, Direct Access to Host System Through X Start Client Icon, Allows You to Simultaneously Run X Windows along with DOS & MS Windows Applications, Context-Sensitive Help, & Easy Installation.
Grafpoint.

X-Ray. *Version:* 1.3. Oct. 1988. *Compatible Hardware:* IBM PC, PC XT, PC AT, 80386-based PCs; DEC; HP; Sun; Apollo. *Operating System(s) Required:* MS-DOS, Unix, Ultrix, VMS. *Memory Required:* 640k.
$1750.00 to $6000.00.
Source-Code & Symbolic Debugger Integrated with C Compiler. Reads Microsoft .OBJ File Formats. Compatible Languages Are MS C; Intel & Microtec Research C, Pascal & FORTRAN. Supports 8086, 80186, 80286, 68000, 68010, 68020, 68030, Z80, 64180 & AMD 29000 Instruction Sets, Remote Debugging & 43-Line Mode. Features Full Screen & Command Line Interface; Code, Data, Stack Values & Register Values Windows Displays; & Simple, Complex, Access, Read/Write & Instruction Breakpoint Types. Also Includes Single-Step Execution, Single Step over Function, Limited Macro Capabilities, Multiple Viewports, up to 50 Programmable Windows & Multitasking Environment Support.
Microtec Research.

X-Stat: Statistical Experiment Design, Data Analysis & Non-Linear Optimization. *Version:* 2.0. John Murray. Aug. 1992.
disk $650.00 (ISBN 0-471-52444-1).
A Program That Runs under Microsoft Windows to Assist Design Engineers with Statistical Experiment Design, Data Anlaysis & Optimization Through Controlled Experimentation. Designed for Applications in Which Users Must Find the Combination of Independently & Continuously Adjustable Variables to Produce the Best Possible Product, Dramatically Reducing the Number of Experiments Needed to Achieve That Objective. Organized into a Reference Section & Tutorial Leading You Through Three Examples, It Catalogs All Available Options & Explains How to Use Them.
John Wiley & Sons, Inc.

X-STAT: Statistical Experiment Design, Data Analysis, Non-Linear Optimization. *Version:* 1.1. Softpower Inc. 1986. *Compatible Hardware:* IBM PC. *Operating System(s) Required:* PC-DOS 2.0 or higher. *Memory Required:* 256k. *General Requirements:* 2 disk drives.
disk $695.00 (ISBN 0-471-81119-X).
John Wiley & Sons, Inc.

XA. *Version:* 6.0. 1982. *Compatible Hardware:* Macintosh, PC, 80386, Sun, VAX. *Language(s):* C. *Memory Required:* 256k. *General Requirements:* Hard disk recommended. *Customer Support:* Telephone & FAX.
IBM PC. disk $2000.00.
$50.00 documentation.
evaluation disk $100.00.
Linear Programming System Which Includes Virtual Memory Techniques to Solve Large Problems, 32,000 x 100,000. Uses Double Precision Floating Point Numbers in All Calculations. Reads & Writes Formulations Directly from LOTUS 1-2-3 or SYMPHONY Worksheets.
Sunset Software.

XCELL+. Richard Conway. *Compatible Hardware:* IBM PC, PC XT, PC AT. *Memory Required:* 256k. *General Requirements:* Hard disk; EGA card.
disk $525.00 (ISBN 0-89426-093-6).
Enhanced Version of XCELL. Used to Evaluate the Design of a Factory.
Boyd & Fraser Publishing Co.

XDB. *Operating System(s) Required:* MS-DOS/PC-DOS, Unix, PC LAN.
MS-DOS Version. $495.00.
Database Management System Provides On-Screen Help, Free-Form & Structured File Definition, Automatic Indexing, Split & Merge

TITLE INDEX

Files, Built-In Editor, Debugging Facilities, Compiler, & Run-Time Version Available. Features 400 Fields per Record; 1,500 Characters in File; 2 Billion Records per File; 32,000 Characters in Record; 400 Indexes per File; & 200 Active Files. Offers 400 Variables. Data-Import/Export Capabilities Include Comma-Delimited ASCII, DIF, DBF, SYLK, Fixed ASCII, & User Defined Delimited ASCII. Languages Available Are Pascal, C, & COBOL.
XDB Systems, Inc.

XDT. *Operating System(s) Required:* CP/M. *Language(s):* Assembly. *Memory Required:* 16k.
disk $50.00, incl. source code.
Interactive Debugging Tool. Includes All the Features of DDT, Zilog Mnemonic Assemble/List Commands, Full Z80 Register Display, Support for Undocumented Instructions, I/O Port, Get/Put Commands, Multiple Breakpoints, Call Subroutine, & Address Arithmetic.
Aton International, Inc.

Xerion. Nov. 1988.
Macintosh (512E, Plus, SE, II, IIx, IIcx) (1Mb monochrome, 2Mb color). 3.5" disk $39.95.
36 Levels Color Breakout.
Titus Software Corp.

Xerox Ventura Publisher 2.0. *Compatible Hardware:* IBM PC & compatibles. *Operating System(s) Required:* PC-DOS/MS-DOS; 3Com, Novell, PC Lan.
$595.00.
upgrade from 1.0 or 1.1 $100.00.
network server $1295.00.
This Version Includes over 70 New Features, Including More Than 250 Context-Sensitive Help Screens in Dialog Boxes, a Combination of Pull-Down & Pop-Up Menus, & Increased Mouse Functionality. Also Features Enhanced Image Support & Color Controls, New Pagination & Page Makeup Tools, Typography Features Such As Discretionary Hyphenation, More Font Control, & Increased Printer Support. The PROFESSIONAL EXTENSION PACKAGE Is Designed for Users Creating More Sophisticated Documents Such As Contracts, Manuals, & Technical Documentation. Provides Expanded Memory Support for Long Documents. The PROFESSIONAL EXTENSION Provides WYSIWYG Generation of Equations & a Cross-Reference Feature That Lets Users Mark Locations for Later Insertion of Chapter & Page Numbers or Figures & Tables.
Xerox Corp.

Xess. *Compatible Hardware:* DEC VAX, Alpha AXP, HP 9000, SUN, IBM RS/6000, SGI, DG Aviion, Intel. *Operating System(s) Required:* X Windows/Motif, UNIX, VMS, OpenVMS, Windows NT.
$695.00 Single-User License.
Spreadsheet Designed Specifically for the X-WINDOWS/MOTIF Environment. Using a Point & Click Interface, Product Provides Full Range of Computational & Graphical Tools. Xess Connections API Allows Client/Server Applications to Be Fully Integrated with the Spreadsheet. Functions Include Matrix Operations, Fourier Transforms, Multiple Regressions, Linear Equation Solving, & Advanced Statistics. Graph Types Include Bar, Line, Scatter, X-Y, Polar, Pie, Histogram, High-Low, Contour, & 3D Surfaces. PostScript (EPS) Output. Date & Time Functions. Indirect Cell Reference Functions. Table Look-Ups. Dynamic Links with Other X Windows Programs, Even at Remote Locations. PostScript, ASCII or LaTeX Formats. Import/Export in LOTUS & EXCEL Formats. C & FORTRAN Programming Interfaces.
Applied Information Systems, Inc.

XFER: Transfer Function Analysis-Synthesis. *Version:* 2. K. J. Senn. Apr. 1986. *Compatible Hardware:* AT&T 6300; DEC Rainbow, DEC VT 180; HP-125; IBM PC & compatibles, PCjr, PC XT, PC AT; Apple Macintosh, Macintosh 512KE; Tandy 1000, 1200, 2000; TI Professional; Xerox 820, 820-II, 860. *Operating System(s) Required:* PC-DOS, MS-DOS. *Language(s):* Compiled BASIC. *Memory Required:* 256k, Macintosh 512k.
disk $150.00.
Uses Short Circuit Transfer Impedance Functions Around an Operational Amplifier Which Will Synthesize a Desired Transfer Function. Enables Users to Synthesize & Analyze Most Any Transfer Function Having Real Roots.
BV Engineering.

XF5700 Mantis Experimental Fighter. Aug. 1992. *Items Included:* Manual, technical supplement, free demo offer. *Customer Support:* Free customer service, 1-410-771-1151.
80286/80386/80486; hard disk required 16MHz. IBM PC & compatibles (640k). disk $69.95. *Nonstandard peripherals required:* VGA-256 Color. *Optimal configuration:* DOS 2.11 or higher; extended memory supported; Joystick recommended, mouse, keyboard; Roland, Adlib, Sound Blaster.
First State of the Art Space Simulation/Action Arcade Game to Feature a Unique & Innovative 3-D Graphic System, That Creates a Breathtaking Sensation of Space Flight. Players Will Pilot the Most Technologically Advanced Space Fighter Ever Created in a Quest to Save a Defenseless Earth.
MicroProse Software.

Xian, Chinese Chess for the IBM PC. *Version:* 3.0. Jan. 1989. *Items Included:* Manual. *Customer Support:* Free telephone support.
MS-DOS (384k). IBM PC, PC AT, PC XT, & compatibles. 5.25" disk $39.95 (ISBN 0-9623342-0-0). *Nonstandard peripherals required:* Graphics adapter. *Optimal configuration:* PC AT & compatibles.
MS-DOS (384k). IBM PC, PC AT, PC XT, PS/2 & compatibles. 3.5" disk $39.95 (ISBN 0-9623342-1-9). *Nonstandard peripherals required:* Graphics adapter. *Optimal configuration:* PS/2 & compatibles.
Plays the Classic Game of Chinese Chess. Can Also Teach the Game to Someone Unfamiliar with It. There Are 9 Skill Levels, Beginner to Expert.
Leong Jacobs, Inc.

Xian for Windows. Aug. 1992. *Items Included:* Manual. *Customer Support:* Free telephone support.
IBM PC, PC AT & compatibles (2Mb). disk $39.95 (ISBN 0-9623342-3-5). *Nonstandard peripherals required:* VGA graphics adapter, color VGA monitor. *Addl. software required:* Microsoft Windows Version 3.0 or higher. *Optimal configuration:* 80386 or 80486 PC, Microsoft Windows Version 3.1 or higher, 3Mb RAM, color VGA.
Plays the Classic Game of Chinese Chess, Can Also Teach the Game to Someone Unfamiliar with It. There Are 9 Skill Levels, Beginner to Expert.
Leong Jacobs, Inc.

Xilerator. 1987. *Compatible Hardware:* IBM PC & compatibles, PS/2. *Operating System(s) Required:* MS-DOS 3.X, OS/2 1.X. *Memory Required:* 192k.
disk $900.00.
Source-Code & Symbolic Debugger, Available As a Stand-Alone or Integrated with Compiler, Linker & Editor. Compatible with Micro Focus COBOL Language. Supports 8086, 8088, 80186, 80188, 80286, 80386, 8087, & 80287 *Instruction Sets. Features Full Screen Interface; Source, Object, Data & Register Windows Display; & Break & Break If Breakpoint Types. Also Includes Single Step in Source & ASM, Program Step in Source & ASM, Go to Next Breakpoint & Zooming.*
Micro Focus, Inc. (California).

XIOX Large Business Series. *Compatible Hardware:* IBM PC, PC XT, PC AT. *Operating System(s) Required:* PC-DOS. *Language(s):* BASIC. *Memory Required:* 256k.
disk $3900.00 (ISBN 0-927905-02-7, Order no.: TI 150).
$5400.00 (ISBN 0-927905-03-5, Order no.: TI 300).
$6400.00 (ISBN 0-927905-04-3, Order no.: TI 500).
$8000.00 (ISBN 0-927905-05-1, Order no.: TI 1000).
Monitors All Phone Extensions for Abuse. Print Reports on All Incoming & Outgoing, Date & Time Called, Length of Call. Prints Alarm When Unauthorized Calls Are Attempted. Has 20 Digit Account Code Capability to Allow Allocation of Telephone Charges to Departments or Clients.
XIOX Corp.

XIOX Resale & Billback Series BASIC Package. Nov. 1982. *Compatible Hardware:* IBM PC & compatibles, PC XT, TI-200. *Operating System(s) Required:* PC-DOS. *Memory Required:* 128k.
disk $2875.00 (ISBN 0-927905-19-1, Order no.: T1-200).
disk $5175.00 (ISBN 0-927905-20-5, Order no.: TI-750).
disk $7475.00 (ISBN 0-927905-21-3, Order no.: TI-2000).
Call Accounting for Hotels, Motels, Hospitals & Nursing Homes. Takes Advantage of Competitive Rates of Alternative Long Distance Services & "Resells" the Service. Prices Calls Immediately, Applies a Variable Markup Depending on the Call Type or Extension Class, Screens Calls for Excessive Cost, Length or Origin, & Produces Audit & Traffic Summary Reports.
XIOX Corp.

XIOX Resale & Billing Series Feature Package A. Nov. 1982. *Compatible Hardware:* IBM PC, PC XT, PC AT. *Operating System(s) Required:* PC-DOS. *Memory Required:* 256k. *General Requirements:* 2 disk drives.
disk $4025.00 (ISBN 0-927905-25-6, Order no.: MODEL 200).
Call Accounting for Hotels, Motels, Hospitals & Nursing Homes. Allows Property to Take Advantage of the Competitive Rates of Alternate Long Distance Services & "Resell" the Service. Prices Calls Immediately, Applies a Variable Markup Depending on the Call Type or Extension Class, Screens Calls for Excessive Cost, Length or Origin, & Produces Audit & Traffic Summary Reports.
XIOX Corp.

XPL Basic. *Customer Support:* 800-929-8117 (customer service).
MS-DOS. IBM/PS2. disk $99.99 (ISBN 0-87007-089-4).
XPL Means "Extendable Programming Language". Using the Same Kind of Block Structure as Highlevel Languages, Provides Ideal Programming of any Job Involving Data Structures, Byte Manipulation, or Lots of Logic. Support for the 8080, Z80, 6809 Chips are Provided for a Unique Cross-Assembler Solution.
SourceView Software International.

XPL Master. *Customer Support:* 800-929-8117 (customer service).
MS-DOS. IBM/PS2. disk $199.99 (ISBN 0-87007-299-4).
Basic XPL is Included, Along with Major Extensions. The Programmer is Given the Materials for Cross-Assembly Between 6809, 8080 & 8088 CPU's.
SourceView Software International.

XQL. *Version:* 2.01. Aug. 1988. *Compatible Hardware:* IBM PC & compatibles, PS/2. *Operating System(s) Required:* PC-DOS/MS-DOS 2.X or 3.X or 4.X, OS/2. *Language(s):* C, BASIC, PASCAL, COBOL, etc.. *Memory Required:* 196k. *General Requirements:* Btrieve 4.1X.
disk $795.00, incl. documentation.
Relational Data Management System Which Allows Access to Multiple Records at a Time & Provides True Relational Capabilities with Data Independence, Data Integrity & Security. There Are Two Interface Levels: XQL Primitives & SQL Statements -both Callable from Any Programming Language. An Interactive Editor Allows Users to Enter SQL Statements for DeBugging. DBMS Features Enable Users to Access Data by Name. Field Order Is Independent of Physical Location Within the Record - Fields Can Be Computed from Other Fields or Constants; Allows Manipulation of Composite Records Built from Multiple, Joined BTRIEVE Files. Includes LAN Support & Fault Tolerance. There Are No Royalties on XQL Applications.
Novell, Inc.

XRAY 68K. *Compatible Hardware:* DEC VAX, DG MV Series, Apollo, IBM PC & compatibles.
contact publisher for price.
Source Level Debugger.
Microtec Research.

Xref Plus. *Customer Support:* 800-929-8117 (customer service).
MS-DOS. IBM/PS2. disk $49.99 (ISBN 0-87007-321-4).
Produces a Formatted Listing of any Source Program. Also Produces a Cross Reference Listing of the Program & will Process any Number of Programs on a Single Diskette. Cross Reference any GW-BASIC Program.
SourceView Software International.

XS: The Index System. Ken Berry. *Operating System(s) Required:* MS-DOS. *General Requirements:* SK: The System Kernel & FS: The File System (M&T Publishing, Inc.).
disk $39.95, incl. manual (ISBN 0-934375-66-6).
Implements a Tree-Structured, Free-Form Database. Allows Names & Data of Variable Length with No Practical Limitations on Data Size. Names Can Be Inserted, Updated, & Deleted. Applications Can Also Adjust Memory Usage & Ensure That the Physical Device Has an Up-to-Date Copy of the Index. All C & Assembler Source Code, As Well As Precompiled Libraries, Are Included.
M & T Bks.

XT Net. *Version:* 2.0. May 1990.
PC-DOS/MS-DOS (256k). contact publisher for price (ISBN 0-937867-47-0). *Networks supported:* Novell.
Disk Management for Novell Network Supervisors & Users.
XTree Co.

XTAB Cross Tabulation. *Items Included:* Bound manual. *Customer Support:* Free hotline - no time limit; 30 day limited warranty; updates are $5/disk plus S&H.
MS-DOS 2.0 & higher. IBM & compatibles (320k). disk $59.95. *Nonstandard peripherals required:* One disk drive; will also use math coprocessor.
General-Purpose Cross-Tabulation Package for Analyzing & Tabulating Survey Data for Marketing Research, Demography, & Opinion Polls. If Data Is Organized According to Cities or States, User Can Get Separate Reports for Each & Add Them in Several Ways to Get Summary Totals. Analysis May Be Done on Multiple Variables by Both Rows & Columns. Weighted Means & Sample Standard Deviations May Be Computed Using Row Weights or Scores. The Difference Between Means of Pairs of Columns May Be Tested Using Student's t-Test with Different Confidence Levels.
Dynacomp, Inc.

XTERM. *Version:* 1.2. Jan. 1985. *Compatible Hardware:* IBM PC, PC XT, PC AT, PS/2 & compatibles; Data General One. *Operating System(s) Required:* PC-DOS/MS-DOS 2.X or 3.X. *Language(s):* Assembler. *Memory Required:* 48k. *General Requirements:* Modem optional.
disk $49.00.
Emulates the Following Terminals: DEC VT100, VT102, & VT52; IBM 3101; ADM3A; ADDS; HP 2624; WYSE50 & Televideo 95. Supports 300-9600 Baud Line Speed. Shows Time on Optional Status Bar (25th Line), with Uppercase/Lowercase & Num Lock. Program Is a "Pop up" (TSR).
Hawkeye Grafix.

xText: Hypertext Compiler & Toolkit. *Version:* 2.0. Aug. 1992. *Items Included:* 1 Comb-bound manual; unlimited distribution license. *Customer Support:* Telephone support; 30 day money back guarantee.
DOS 2.0 or higher. IBM PC XT, AT or compatible (256k). disk $199.95. *Nonstandard peripherals required:* Hard disk recommended. *Addl. software required:* Word processor or text editor.
Convert Text Created with any Word Processor into Hypertext, for Instant Online Access to Information Now Available Only in Printed Form.
Flambeaux Software, Inc.

XTPRO GOLD: Dutch. Jul. 1990.
MS-DOS/PC-DOS. IBM & compatibles. contact publisher for price (ISBN 0-937867-37-3).
Hard Disk File Manager.
XTree Co.

XTPRO GOLD: French. Jun. 1990.
MS-DOS/PC-DOS. IBM & compatibles. contact publisher for price (ISBN 0-937867-45-4).
Hard Disk File Manager.
XTree Co.

XTPRO GOLD: German. Jun. 1990.
MS-DOS/PC-DOS. IBM & compatibles. contact publisher for price (ISBN 0-937867-32-2).
Hard Disk File Management.
XTree Co.

XTPRO GOLD: Italian. Jul. 1990.
MS-DOS/PC-DOS. IBM & compatibles. contact publisher for price (ISBN 0-937867-14-4).
Hard Disk File Manager.
XTree Co.

XTPRO GOLD: Spanish. Jul. 1990.
MS-DOS/PC-DOS. IBM & compatibles. contact publisher for price (ISBN 0-937867-06-3).
Hard Disk File Management.
XTree Co.

XTPRO (International English). *Version:* 1.1. Jan. 1989. *Compatible Hardware:* IBM PC & compatibles. *Operating System(s) Required:* PC-DOS/MS-DOS. *Memory Required:* 100k. 3.5" or 5.25" disk $129.00 (ISBN 0-937867-04-7).
Hard Disk File Manager.
XTree Co.

Xtrapolator Time Series Forecasts. *Items Included:* Bound manual. *Customer Support:* Free hotline - no time limit; 30 day limited warranty; updates are $5/disk plus S&H.
MS-DOS. IBM & compatibles (128k). disk $99.95. *Nonstandard peripherals required:* One or two disk drives; printer supported but not required.
Apple (48k). disk $129.95.
Comprehensive & Multipurpose Forecasting System. The Analysis Framework Is Based upon Methodologies Encompassing Simple to Complex Extrapolative Techniques. Twelve Distinct Forecasting Methods Can Be Applied to a Data Series. In Addition, the Competing Methods Are Rated Based upon Their Best Fit & Likelihood of Accuracy.
Dynacomp, Inc.

XTree. *Version:* 2.0. Apr. 1985. *Compatible Hardware:* IBM PC & compatibles, PC XT, PC AT. *Operating System(s) Required:* MS-DOS 2.0, PC-DOS. *Memory Required:* 192k.
disk $49.95 (ISBN 0-937867-08-X, Order no.: XTREE).
Graphic File & Directory Management Program Designed to Simplify File & Directory Handling by Providing Single Keystroke Commands to Access, Delete, Rename, View, Move, List, or Print Any & All Files Within Any & All Directories on a Floppy & Hard Disk. Allows Users to View a Complete Disk Directory in a Single Display. Provides Menu at All Times Displaying All of Program Commands.
XTree Co.

XTree Gold. *Version:* 2.5. Dec. 1990.
PC-DOS/MS-DOS. IBM & compatibles. 3.5" or 5.25" disk $149.00.
Hard Disk File Management.
XTree Co.

XTree Mac. Jan. 1989. *Compatible Hardware:* Apple Macintosh 512KE, Macintosh Plus, Macintosh SE, Macintosh II. *Operating System(s) Required:* System 2.0, Finder 5.0.
3.5" disk $99.00 (ISBN 0-937867-39-X).
Integrated Disk Management. Provides File Management & File Undelete Functions.
XTree Co.

XTreePro. *Compatible Hardware:* IBM PC & compatibles.
disk $129.00.
Enhanced Version of XTree File Management Package Designed to Simplify File & Directory Handling Through Single Keystroke Commands That Execute Standard & Enhanced DOS Functions for Higher Power Users.
XTree Co.

Xtrieve. *Version:* 4.01. Aug. 1988. *Compatible Hardware:* IBM PC & compatibles, PS/2. *Operating System(s) Required:* PC-DOS/MS-DOS 2.X, 3.X, 4.X, OS/2. *Memory Required:* 384k. *General Requirements:* Btrieve 4.1X.
Single user. $245.00.
LAN, OS/2. $595.00.
Provides a Relational Database Interface to BTRIEVE Files, Allowing End Users to Access BTRIEVE Files & Generate Reports Without Writing a Program. Uses A Menu-Driven Query System to Allow Users to Catalogue, Retrieve, Analyze, & Update Information in BTRIEVE Files.
Novell, Inc.

XyWrite. *Version:* DOS 4.017. Apr. 1993. *Items Included:* Main reference manual, learning & installation guide, & customization guide, LAN Administration Guide, Making the Transition. *Customer Support:* One year free technical support, 30-day trial period available, money

TITLE INDEX

back guarantee.
DOS 4.0 or higher. IBM PC or compatible (386-class or higher recommended) (2Mb). $495.00 List, $99.00 upgrade, $129.00 competitive upgrade. *Nonstandard peripherals required:* Hercules, VGA EGA or better graphics adaptor. *Networks supported:* LAN, Novell.
MS Windows 3.1 or higher. IBM PC or compatible. $495.00 List, $99.00 upgrade, $129.00 competitive upgrade.
High-End Word Processor Targeted Towards Professional Writers. Features Pull-Down Menus & Dialog Boxes for Easy Learning. Features a Unique Command-Line Interface for Power Users & Ultimate Efficiency. Other Features Include ASCII File Format, Full Customization of All Program Elements, Editable WYSIWYG View, & a Very Fast Engine. Advanced Features Include a Command Stack, Multi-Level Undelete Buffer, Bookmarks, Redlining, & Optional Add-On Modules (Orbis, a Full-Text Search & Retrieval Engine, & Ibid, a Bibliography & Citation Manager).
Technology Group, Inc.

XYWrite for Windows. *Version:* 4.12. *Items Included:* Reference Manual, Installation & Learning Guide. *Customer Support:* Free technical support, 30 day trial, money back guarantee.
IBM PC & compatibles (640k). disk $495.00, Upgrade ,129.00, Competitive Upgrade ,149.00. *Nonstandard peripherals required:* Hard disk drive; EGA graphics adapter recommended.
Lets User View Document Page Layout & Edit in WYSIWYG Mode. New Font Definition & Type Size Commands Make It Easier to Specify Fonts Within a Document. Graphics Inclusion Feature of New Version Lets User Import Graphical Images & View them on Screen. User Controls Placement by Specifying Size, Location, Scale & Crop Areas of Image. Accepts Graphics in HPL, TIFF, PCX & ASCII Format. A la Carte Menus Have Been Added to Supplement Command-Line Interface. Now, They Are True Pull-Down Menus. User Can Still Toggle Between Command & Menu Interfaces.
Technology Group, Inc.

XyWrite III Plus. *Version:* 3.52. *Customer Support:* Pay per call basis, $15 per call.
PC/MS-DOS 3.0 or higher. IBM PC, XT, AT, & compatibles (384k). per license $180.00. (ISBN 0-927923-16-5).
New Features Added to This Release Include: 100,000-Word Spelling Checker & Dictionary to Which Another 10,000 Words Can Be Added; Thesaurus; & Text-Redlining & Word-Counting Capabilities. Users Can Check for Errors by Word, Phrase, Paragraph, File, or List of Files. Instant Spell-Checking Is Available. The Thesaurus Provides 220,000 Synonyms for 15,000 Key Words. Supports AT&T, 3Com, Novell, & Banyan Networks. Not Copy Protected.
Technology Group, Inc.

XYZ 3D. *Items Included:* Bound manual. *Customer Support:* Free hotline - no time limit; 30 day limited warranty; updates are $5/disk plus S&H.
MS-DOS. IBM & compatibles (512k). disk $269.95. *Nonstandard peripherals required:* Color graphics card, 8087 or 80287 math coprocessor.
Computer Program Which Draws Pictures at Any Level of Detail of Any Pictorial Data. Developed in the Early 1970s for Use on Mainframes. Provides Exact Visual Simulation, Producing Views of a Project from Any Viewpoint Selected, Including Those Within the Field of the Data. Successive Pictures Can Be Produced Which Show How a Project Would Look If You Were to Zoom in on It, Walk Around It, or Walk Through It. The Hidden-Line Removal Capability Is Completely General & Has No Restrictions. Cartographic Capability. User Can Easily Define a Surface Such As Terrain & Display It Using Any Line Pattern.
Dynacomp, Inc.

X.25 COMPAC, Level III. Oct. 1985. *Compatible Hardware:* CP/M-86 based micros; IBM PC, PC XT, PC AT. *Operating System(s) Required:* PC-DOS. *Language(s):* C. *Memory Required:* 64k.
disk $695.00.
Allows X.25 Communication Through the Frontier Technologies Advanced Communications Board. Implements All Three Levels of the CCITT X.25 Specification with 1980 Amendments.
Frontier Technologies Corp.

Yacht Race. *Compatible Hardware:* Atari 400, 800. *Language(s):* Atari BASIC (source code included). *Memory Required:* 48k. *General Requirements:* Joysticks or paddles.
disk $19.95.
Tactical Game of Navigation, Sailing Knowledge & Boat Handling Skills.
Dynacomp, Inc.

Yahtzee. *Compatible Hardware:* TI 99/4A.
contact publisher for price (Order no.: PHM3039).
Dice Game. Players Build Points by Rolling Certain Number Combinations.
Texas Instruments, Personal Productivit.

Yard Manager. *Compatible Hardware:* TRS-80 Model II, Model 12, Model 16. *Operating System(s) Required:* PC-DOS, CP/M 2.2. *Memory Required:* 64k. *General Requirements:* 2 disk drives.
TRS-80. 8" disk $1400.00 (ISBN 0-925961-01-9, Order no.: YMR).
PC-DOS. 8" disk $1400.00 (ISBN 0-925961-15-9, Order no.: YMP).
CP/M. disk $1400.00 (ISBN 0-925961-29-9, Order no.: YMC).
Integrated Menu Controlled System Featuring over 45 Programs Designed for the Wholesale Lumber Business. Maintains Inventory, Sales & Receivable Files.
Organic Computing.

YARDSTICK: ACM Lumber & Hardware Management Accounting System. *Compatible Hardware:* IBM System 36, 5265.
contact publisher for price.
Handles the Many Phases of Accounting Needs, Particular in Nature to Operating a Lumber & Hardware Retail Business.
ACM Computer Services, Inc.

Year Book Edition on CD-ROM, 1993: DOS-MAC. Feb. 1994. *Items Included:* Registration Card. *Customer Support:* Creative Multimedia Corporation warrants the CD-ROM disc & diskettes to be free from defects in materials & workmanship under normal use & service for a period of 90 days from date of purchase. Creative Multimedia Corporation offers Technical Support to customers as needed.
MS-DOS 3.1 or higher. IBM PC & compatibles with VGA monitor (350k). CD-ROM disk $295.00 Suggested Retail Price (ISBN 1-880428-36-9, Order no.: 10557). *Optimal configuration:* Super VGA with 512k video memory capable of 640x480x256 colors. *Networks supported:* All.
System Software 6.0.5 or higher. Macintosh Plus, SE, Classic, SE/30, LC & any Model II (2Mb). CD-ROM disk $295.00 Suggested Retail Price. *Optimal configuration:* Color display required 8-bit color, 32-bit QuickDraw & color monitor. *Networks supported:* All.
Contains the Complete Text of 33 Year Books from 1992-1993 from Mosby Year Book, Inc. Title for This CD-ROM Edition Are Year Books of: Dermatology, Diagnostic Radiology, Drug Therapy, Emergency Medicine, Family Practice Medicine, Neonatal/Perinatal Medicine, Obstetrics & Gynecology, Pediatrics, Psychiatry, & Sports Medicine. In Addition, Excerpts from The New England Journal of Medicine, the Journal of the AMA, Annals of Internal Medicine & Lancet Are Included All on a Single Disc.
Creative Multimedia Corp.

Year of International Organizations on CD-ROM. 1995. *Items Included:* Annual Updates.
MS-DOS compatibility. IBM 386 or higher. CD-ROM disk (Order no.: DIO110).
"Yearbook of International Organizations on CD-ROM" covers a total of 32,000 international Organizations within 225 countires, encompassing everything from intra-governmental & national bodies to more pheripheral conferences & religious orders.
K G Saur.

Yearn 2 Learn Flintstones Bedrock Art Gallery. Jun. 1995. *Items Included:* Soft cover, stapled manual & registration card. *Customer Support:* Free customer service via our 800 number. Unlimited warranty on disk replacement.
System 7 or higher. Any 256 color capable MAC (4Mb). 3.5" disk $14.95 (ISBN 1-888046-52-X, Order no.: ISFRG1001M). *Nonstandard peripherals required:* 13" monitor, 6Mb hard disk space, high density drive req.
Windows 3.1 or higher; 386 or higher. IBM, Tandy & 100% compatibles (4Mb). disk $14.95 (ISBN 1-888046-53-8, Order no.: ISFRG1001W). *Nonstandard peripherals required:* Super VGA, Sound Card: 100% Sound Blaster compatible, 4Mb hard disk space.
10 Coloring Book Pages Featuring the Flintstones Characters. Kids Can Color Existing Pages, or Draw & Save up to 120 of Their Own Pictures.
Image Smith, Inc.

Yearn 2 Learn Flintstones Coloring Book. May 1994. *Items Included:* Soft cover, stapled manual & registration card. *Customer Support:* Free customer service via our 800 number. Unlimited warranty on disk replacement.
System 6.0.7 or higher. Any 256 color capable MAC (4Mb). 3.5" disk $14.95 (ISBN 1-888046-41-4, Order no.: ISF1001). *Nonstandard peripherals required:* 4Mb hard disk space, high density drive required, 13" monitor or larger.
Windows 3.1 or higher; 386 or higher. IBM, Tandy & 100% compatibles (4Mb). disk $14.95 (ISBN 1-888046-42-2, Order no.: ISF1004). *Nonstandard peripherals required:* 256 colors req. 3.5 disk drive req., sound board. *Optimal configuration:* Latest drives, video cards: Trident, Diamond, AII, Orchid, Headlands. Sound boards: Audio Spectrum & SoundBlaster.
Interactive Coloring Book with 30 Coloring Pictures, Featuring the Flintstones Characters.
Image Smith, Inc.

Yearn 2 Learn Flintstones Family Fun Pack. May 1995. *Items Included:* Soft cover, stapled manual & registration card. *Customer Support:* Free customer service via our 800 number. Unlimited warranty on disk replacement.
System 7 or higher. Any 256 color capable MAC (4Mb). 3.5" disk $59.95 (ISBN 1-888046-43-0, Order no.: ISFFP1001M). *Nonstandard peripherals required:* 13" monitor, 6Mb hard disk space, high density drive req.
Windows 3.1 or higher; 386 or higher. IBM, Tandy & 100% compatibles (4Mb). disk $59.95 (ISBN 1-888046-44-9, Order no.:

ISFFP1001W). *Nonstandard peripherals required:* Super VGA, Sound Card: 100% Sound Blaster compatible, 4Mb hard disk space.
MAC: System 7.1 or higher; WIN 3.1 or higher; 386 or higher. MAC; any 256 color capable MAC or IBM, Tandy & 100% compatibles (4Mb). CD-ROM disk $59.95 (ISBN 1-888046-45-7, Order no.: ISFFP1001H). *Nonstandard peripherals required:* 13" monitor, mouse or Super VGA, 100% Sound Blaster compatible sound card, both formats require 1Mb hard disk space.
Six Learning Activities/Games, Including Spelling Games, Math Games, Art Games & Puzzles. All Activities Feature Hanna Barbera's Flintstones Characters.
Image Smith, Inc.

Yearn 2 Learn Flintstones Fashion Math Cave. Jun. 1995. *Items Included:* Soft cover, stapled manual & registration card. *Customer Support:* Free customer service via our 800 number. Unlimited warranty on disk replacement.
System 7 or higher. Any 256 color capable MAC (4Mb). 3.5" disk $14.95 (ISBN 1-888046-48-1, Order no.: ISFFM1001M). *Nonstandard peripherals required:* 13" monitor, 6Mb hard disk space, high density drive req.
Windows 3.1 or higher; 386 or higher. IBM, Tandy & 100% compatibles (4Mb). disk $14.95 (ISBN 1-888046-49-X, Order no.: ISFFM1001W). *Nonstandard peripherals required:* Super VGA, Sound Card: 100% Sound Blaster compatible, 4Mb hard disk space.
Math Games at Varying Levels of Difficulty, All Featuring the Flintstones Characters.
Image Smith, Inc.

Yearn 2 Learn Flintstones Fossil Foto Fixer. Jun. 1995. *Items Included:* Soft cover, stapled manual & registration card. *Customer Support:* Free customer service via our 800 number. Unlimited warranty on disk replacement.
System 7 or higher. Any 256 color capable MAC (4Mb). 3.5" disk $14.95 (ISBN 1-888046-50-3, Order no.: ISFFF1001M). *Nonstandard peripherals required:* 13" monitor, 6Mb hard disk space, high density drive req.
Windows 3.1 or higher; 386 or higher. IBM, Tandy & 100% compatibles (4Mb). disk $14.95 (ISBN 1-888046-51-1, Order no.: ISFFF1001W). *Nonstandard peripherals required:* Super VGA, Sound Card: 100% Sound Blaster compatible, 4Mb hard disk space.
Puzzles That Help Children Build Critical Thinking Skills, Logic & Perception. All Puzzles Feature the Flintstones Characters.
Image Smith, Inc.

Yearn 2 Learn Master Snoopy's Coloring Book. May 1995. *Items Included:* Soft cover, stapled manual & registration card. *Customer Support:* Free customer service via our 800 number. Unlimited warranty on disk replacement.
System 7 or higher. Any 256 color capable MAC (4Mb). 3.5" disk $24.95 (ISBN 1-888046-36-8, Order no.: ISMSCB1001M). *Nonstandard peripherals required:* 13" monitor or higher; 6Mb hard disk space; high density drive req.
Windows 3.1 or higher; 386 or higher. IBM, Tandy & 100% compatibles (4Mb). disk $24.95 (ISBN 1-888046-37-6, Order no.: ISMSCB1001W). *Nonstandard peripherals required:* Super VGA; 4.5Mb hard disk space; Sound Blaster compatible sound board. *Optimal configuration:* 486 & 5Mb RAM or higher.
MAC: System 7.0 or higher. Any 256 color capable MAC, 13" monitor, mouse (4Mb). CD-ROM disk $24.95 (ISBN 1-888046-38-4, Order no.: ISMSCB1001MCD).
Windows 3.1 or higher; 386 or higher. IBM, Tandy & 100% compatibles (4Mb). CD-ROM disk $24.95 (ISBN 1-888046-39-2, Order no.: ISMSCB1001WCD). *Nonstandard peripherals required:* 13" monitor, mouse, 100% Sound Blaster compatible sound card.
Macintosh or Windows. Macintosh or IBM, Tandy & 100% compatibles (4Mb). CD-ROM disk $24.95 (ISBN 1-888046-40-6, Order no.: ISMSCB1001H).
20 Coloring Book Pages & the Ability for Kids to Draw & Save up to 120 Pictures. The Coloring Book Pages Feature Snoopy & Other Peanuts Characters.
Image Smith, Inc.

Yearn 2 Learn Master Snoopy's Math. Nov. 1994. *Items Included:* Soft cover, stapled manual & registration card. *Customer Support:* Free customer service via our 800 number. Unlimited warranty on disk replacement.
System 7 or higher. Any 256 color capable MAC (4Mb). 3.5" disk $24.95 (ISBN 1-888046-26-0, Order no.: ISMS1001M). *Nonstandard peripherals required:* 13" monitor or higher; 6Mb hard disk space; high density drive req.
Windows 3.1 or higher; 386 or higher. IBM, Tandy & 100% compatibles (4Mb). disk $24.95 (ISBN 1-888046-27-9, Order no.: ISMS1001W). *Nonstandard peripherals required:* Super VGA; 4.5Mb hard disk space; Sound Blaster compatible sound board. *Optimal configuration:* 486 & 5Mb RAM or higher.
MAC: System 7.0 or higher. Any 256 color capable MAC, 13" monitor, mouse (4Mb). CD-ROM disk $24.95 (ISBN 1-888046-28-7, Order no.: ISMS1001MCD).
Windows 3.1 or higher; 386 or higher. IBM, Tandy & 100% compatibles (4Mb). CD-ROM disk $24.95 (ISBN 1-888046-29-5, Order no.: ISMS1001WCD). *Nonstandard peripherals required:* 13" monitor, mouse, 100% Sound Blaster compatible sound card.
Macintosh or Windows. Macintosh or IBM, Tandy & 100% compatibles (4Mb). CD-ROM disk $24.95 (ISBN 1-888046-30-9, Order no.: ISMS1001HCD).
3 Math Games for Kids Featuring Snoopy & Other Peanuts Characters.
Image Smith, Inc.

Yearn 2 Learn Master Snoopy's Spelling. Nov. 1994. *Items Included:* Soft cover, stapled manual & registration card. *Customer Support:* Free customer service via our 800 number. Unlimited warranty on disk replacement.
System 7 or higher. Any 256 color capable MAC (4Mb). 3.5" disk $24.95 (ISBN 1-888046-21-X, Order no.: ISMS1001M). *Nonstandard peripherals required:* 13" monitor or higher; 6Mb hard disk space; high density drive req.
Windows 3.1 or higher; 386 or higher. IBM, Tandy & 100% compatibles (4Mb). disk $24.95 (ISBN 1-888046-22-8, Order no.: ISMS1001W). *Nonstandard peripherals required:* Super VGA; 4.5Mb hard disk space; Sound Blaster compatible sound board. *Optimal configuration:* 486 & 5Mb RAM or higher.
MAC: System 7.0 or higher. Any 256 color capable MAC, 13" monitor, mouse (4Mb). CD-ROM disk $24.95 (ISBN 1-888046-23-6, Order no.: ISMS1001MCD).
Windows 3.1 or higher; 386 or higher. IBM, Tandy & 100% compatibles (4Mb). CD-ROM disk $24.95 (ISBN 1-888046-24-4, Order no.: ISMS1001WCD). *Nonstandard peripherals required:* 13" monitor, mouse, 100% Sound Blaster compatible sound card.
Macintosh or Windows. Macintosh or IBM, Tandy & 100% compatibles (4Mb). CD-ROM disk $24.95 (ISBN 1-888046-25-2, Order no.: ISMS1001HCD).
2 Spelling Games - Featuring Snoopy & Other Peanuts Characters.
Image Smith, Inc.

Yearn 2 Learn Master Snoopy's World Geography. May 1995. *Items Included:* Soft cover, stapled manual & registration card. *Customer Support:* Free customer service via our 800 number. Unlimited warranty on disk replacement.
System 7 or higher. Any 256 color capable MAC (4Mb). 3.5" disk $24.95 (ISBN 1-888046-31-7, Order no.: ISSWG1001M). *Nonstandard peripherals required:* 13" monitor or higher; 6Mb hard disk space; high density drive req.
Windows 3.1 or higher; 386 or higher. IBM, Tandy & 100% compatibles (4Mb). disk $24.95 (ISBN 1-888046-32-5, Order no.: ISSWG1001W). *Nonstandard peripherals required:* Super VGA; 4.5Mb hard disk space; Sound Blaster compatible sound board. *Optimal configuration:* 486 & 5Mb RAM or higher.
MAC: System 7.0 or higher. Any 256 color capable MAC, 13" monitor, mouse (4Mb). CD-ROM disk $24.95 (ISBN 1-888046-33-3, Order no.: ISSWG1001H).
Windows 3.1 or higher; 386 or higher. IBM, Tandy & 100% compatibles (4Mb). CD-ROM disk $24.95 (ISBN 1-888046-34-1, Order no.: ISSWG1001H). *Nonstandard peripherals required:* 13" monitor, mouse, 100% Sound Blaster compatible sound card.
Macintosh or Windows. Macintosh or IBM, Tandy & 100% compatibles (4Mb). CD-ROM disk $24.95 (ISBN 1-888046-35-X, Order no.: ISSWG1001H).
2 Games That Teach Kids Geography Featuring Snoopy & Other Peanuts Characters.
Image Smith, Inc.

Yearn 2 Learn Peanuts. *Version:* Mac 1.2.A, Win 1.2.1. Jun. 1992. *Items Included:* Soft cover, stapled manual & registration card. *Customer Support:* Free customer service via our 800 number. Unlimited warranty on disk replacement.
System 6.0.7 or higher. Macintosh (4Mb). 3.5" disk $59.95 (ISBN 1-888046-01-5, Order no.: IS10001). *Nonstandard peripherals required:* 14Mb hard disk space req. High density drive req. Low density disks available.
Windows 3.1 or higher; 386 or higher. IBM, Tandy & 100% compatibles (4Mb). disk $59.95 (Order no.: IS10009). *Nonstandard peripherals required:* 640 x 480 video display or higher, 256 colors min., 16Mb hard disk space; Sound Blaster compatible sound board.
MAC: System 7.1 or higher. Any 256 color capable MAC & color monitor (4Mb). CD-ROM disk $59.95 (ISBN 1-888046-02-3, Order no.: IS10035). *Nonstandard peripherals required:* Color monitor, 256 colors minimum, 2Mb hard disk space, CD-ROM drive, Sound Blaster compatbile sound board.
Windows 3.1 or higher; 386 or higher. IBM, Tandy & 100% compatibles (4Mb). CD-ROM disk $59.95 (ISBN 1-888046-03-1, Order no.: IS10040). *Nonstandard peripherals required:* 640x480 Video display or higher, 256 colors minimum, 2Mb hard disk space, CD-ROM drive, Sound Blaster compatible sound board.
Macintosh or Windows. Macintosh or IBM, Tandy & 100% compatibles (4Mb). CD-ROM disk $59.95 (ISBN 1-888046-04-X, Order no.: IS10064).
5 Different Activities Including Math, Reading, Coloring, & Geography Games. Also Teaches Kids Reading Comprehension Skills in a Fun Way. All Games & Activities Feature Charles Schulz's Peanuts Characters.
Image Smith, Inc.

Yearn 2 Learn Peanuts: Austrasian Version. May 1994. *Items Included:* Soft cover, stapled manual & registration card. *Customer Support:* Free customer service via our 800 number. Unlimited warranty on disk replacement.
System 6.0.7 or higher. Macintosh (4Mb). 3.5"

TITLE INDEX

disk $59.95 (ISBN 1-888046-68-6, Order no.: IS10036). *Nonstandard peripherals required:* 14Mb hard disk space, high density drive req., low denisty disks available.
Windows 3.1 or higher; 386 or higher. IBM, Tandy & 100% compatibles (4Mb). disk $59.95 (ISBN 1-888046-69-4, Order no.: IS10129). *Nonstandard peripherals required:* 640 x 480 video display or higher, 256 colors, 16Mb hard disk space, Sound Blaster compatible sound card.
5 Different Activities Including Math, Reading, Coloring & Geography Games. Also Teaches Kids Reading Comprehension Skills in a Fun Way. All Games & Activities Feature Charles Schulz's Peanuts Characters.
Image Smith, Inc.

Yearn 2 Learn Peanuts: Danish Language.
Items Included: Soft cover, stapled manual & registration card. *Customer Support:* Free customer service via our 800 number. Unlimited warranty on disk replacement.
System 6.0.7 or higher. Macintosh (4Mb). 3.5" disk $59.95 (ISBN 1-888046-81-3).
Nonstandard peripherals required: 14Mb hard disk space req.; high density drive req., low density disks available.
Windows 3.1 or higher, 386 or higher. IBM, Tandy & 100% compatibles (4Mb). disk $59.95 (ISBN 1-888046-82-1). *Nonstandard peripherals required:* 640 x 480 video display or higher, 256 colors, 16Mb hard disk space, 100% Sound Blaster compatible sound board.
Mac System 7.1 or higher; Windows 3.1 or higher, 386 or higher. 256 color capable Mac with color monitor; IBM, Tandy & 100% compatibles (4Mb). CD-ROM disk $59.95 (ISBN 1-888046-83-X). *Nonstandard peripherals required:* Mac: color monitor; Win: 640 x 480 video display or higher, 256 colors, 2Mb hard disk space, Sound Blaster compatible sound board.
5 Different Activities Including Math, Reading, Coloring, & Geography Games. Also Teaches Kids Reading Comprehension Skills in a Fun Way. All Games & Activities Feature Charles Schulz's Peanuts Characters.
Image Smith, Inc.

Yearn 2 Learn Peanuts: French Language. Jun. 1994. *Items Included:* Soft cover, stapled manual & registration card. *Customer Support:* Free customer service via our 800 number. Unlimited warranty on disk replacement.
System 6.0.7 or higher. Macintosh (4Mb). 3.5" disk $59.95 (ISBN 1-888046-75-9, Order no.: IS10166). *Nonstandard peripherals required:* 14Mb hard disk space, high density drive req., low denisty disks available.
Windows 3.1 or higher; 386 or higher. IBM, Tandy & 100% compatibles (4Mb). disk $59.95 (ISBN 1-888046-76-7, Order no.: IS10170). *Nonstandard peripherals required:* 640 x 480 video display or higher, 256 colors, 16Mb hard disk space, Sound Blaster compatible sound card.
5 Different Activities Including Math, Reading, Coloring & Geography Games. Also Teaches Kids Reading Comprehension Skills in a Fun Way. All Games & Activities Feature Charles Schulz's Peanuts Characters.
Image Smith, Inc.

Yearn 2 Learn Peanuts: German Language. Oct. 1993. *Items Included:* Soft cover, stapled manual & registration card. *Customer Support:* Free customer service via our 800 number. Unlimited warranty on disk replacement.
System 6.0.7 or higher. Macintosh (4Mb). 3.5" disk $59.95 (ISBN 1-888046-64-3, Order no.: IS10045). *Nonstandard peripherals required:* 14Mb hard disk space, high density drive req., low denisty disks available.
Windows 3.1 or higher; 386 or higher. IBM, Tandy & 100% compatibles (4Mb). disk $59.95 (ISBN 1-888046-65-1, Order no.: IS10106). *Nonstandard peripherals required:* 640 x 480 video display or higher, 256 colors, 16Mb hard disk space, Sound Blaster compatible sound card.
5 Different Activities Including Math, Reading, Coloring & Geography Games. Also Teaches Kids Reading Comprehension Skills in a Fun Way. All Games & Activities Feature Charles Schulz's Peanuts Characters.
Image Smith, Inc.

Yearn 2 Learn Peanuts: Japanese Language. May 1994. *Items Included:* Soft cover, stapled manual & registration card. *Customer Support:* Free customer service via our 800 number. Unlimited warranty on disk replacement.
System 6.0.7 or higher. Macintosh (4Mb). 3.5" disk $59.95 (ISBN 1-888046-60-0, Order no.: IS10012). *Nonstandard peripherals required:* 14Mb hard disk space, high density drive req., low denisty disks available.
Windows 3.1 or higher; 386 or higher. IBM, Tandy & 100% compatibles (4Mb). disk $59.95 (ISBN 1-888046-61-9, Order no.: IS10071). *Nonstandard peripherals required:* 640 x 480 video display or higher, 256 colors, 16Mb hard disk space, Sound Blaster compatible sound card.
5 Different Activities Including Math, Reading, Coloring & Geography Games. Also Teaches Kids Reading Comprehension Skills in a Fun Way. All Games & Activities Feature Charles Schulz's Peanuts Characters.
Image Smith, Inc.

Yearn 2 Learn Peanuts: Spanish Language.
Items Included: Soft cover, stapled manual & registration card. *Customer Support:* Free customer service via our 800 number. Unlimited warranty on disk replacement.
System 6.0.7 or higher. Macintosh (4Mb). 3.5" disk $59.95 (ISBN 1-888046-77-5, Order no.: IS10136). *Nonstandard peripherals required:* 14Mb hard disk space, high density drive req., low denisty disks available.
Windows 3.1 or higher; 386 or higher. IBM, Tandy & 100% compatibles (4Mb). disk $59.95 (ISBN 1-888046-78-3, Order no.: IS10139). *Nonstandard peripherals required:* 640 x 480 video display or higher, 256 colors, 16Mb hard disk space, Sound Blaster compatible sound card.
5 Different Activities Including Math, Reading, Coloring & Geography Games. Also Teaches Kids Reading Comprehension Skills in a Fun Way. All Games & Activities Feature Charles Schulz's Peanuts Characters.
Image Smith, Inc.

Yearn 2 Learn Peanuts: Swedish Language. Oct. 1994. *Items Included:* Soft cover, stapled manual & registration card. *Customer Support:* Free customer service via our 800 number. Unlimited warranty on disk replacement.
System 6.0.7 or higher. Macintosh (4Mb). 3.5" disk $59.95 (ISBN 1-888046-70-8, Order no.: IS10081). *Nonstandard peripherals required:* 14Mb hard disk space, high density drive req., low denisty disks available.
Windows 3.1 or higher; 386 or higher. IBM, Tandy & 100% compatibles (4Mb). disk $59.95 (ISBN 1-888046-71-6, Order no.: IS10103). *Nonstandard peripherals required:* 640 x 480 video display or higher, 256 colors, 16Mb hard disk space, Sound Blaster compatible sound card.
5 Different Activities Including Math, Reading, Coloring & Geography Games. Also Teaches Kids Reading Comprehension Skills in a Fun Way. All Games & Activities Feature Charles Schulz's Peanuts Characters.
Image Smith, Inc.

Yearn 2 Learn Peanuts: United Kingdom Version. Jun. 1994. *Items Included:* Soft cover, stapled manual & registration card. *Customer Support:* Free customer service via our 800 number. Unlimited warranty on disk replacement.
System 6.0.7 or higher. Macintosh (4Mb). 3.5" disk $59.95 (ISBN 1-888046-87-2, Order no.: IS10133). *Nonstandard peripherals required:* 14Mb hard disk space, high density drive req., low denisty disks available.
5 Different Activities Including Math, Reading, Coloring & Geography Games. Also Teaches Kids Reading Comprehension Skills in a Fun Way. All Games & Activities Feature Charles Schulz's Peanuts Characters.
Image Smith, Inc.

Yearn 2 Learn Snoopy. *Version:* Mac 1.1, Win 1.1. Dec. 1992. *Items Included:* Soft cover, stapled manual & registration card. *Customer Support:* Free customer service via our 800 number. Unlimited warranty on disk replacement.
System 6.0.7 or higher. Macintosh (4Mb). 3.5" disk $59.95 (ISBN 1-888046-07-4, Order no.: IS10032). *Nonstandard peripherals required:* 14Mb hard disk space req. High density drive req. Low density disks available.
Windows 3.1 or higher. 386 or higher. IBM, Tandy & 100% compatibles (4Mb). disk $59.95 (ISBN 1-888046-08-2, Order no.: IS10033). *Nonstandard peripherals required:* 640 x 480 video display or higher, 256 colors min., 16Mb hard disk space; Sound Blaster compatible sound board.
MAC: System 7.1 or higher. Any 256 color capable MAC & color monitor (4Mb). CD-ROM disk $59.95 (ISBN 1-888046-09-0, Order no.: IS10035). *Nonstandard peripherals required:* Color monitor, 256 colors minimum, 2Mb hard disk space, CD-ROM drive, Sound Blaster compatbile sound board.
Windows 3.1 or higher. 386 or higher. IBM, Tandy & 100% compatibles (4Mb). CD-ROM disk $59.95 (ISBN 1-888046-10-4, Order no.: IS10038). *Nonstandard peripherals required:* 640x480 Video display or higher, 256 colors minimum, 2Mb hard disk space, CD-ROM drive, Sound Blaster compatible sound board.
Macintosh or Windows. Macintosh or IBM, Tandy & 100% compatibles (4Mb). CD-ROM disk $59.95 (ISBN 1-888046-11-2, Order no.: IS10063).
Various Educational Games for Children: 3 Math Games; 5 Reading Games; Spelling Games; Drawing & Music Games. All Activities Feature Snoopy & Other Peanuts Characters.
Image Smith, Inc.

Yearn 2 Learn Snoopy: Danish Language.
Items Included: Soft cover, stapled manual & registration card. *Customer Support:* Free customer service via our 800 number. Unlimited warranty on disk replacement.
System 6.0.7 or higher. Macintosh (4Mb). 3.5" disk $59.95 (ISBN 1-888046-84-8).
Nonstandard peripherals required: 14Mb hard disk space req.; high density drive req., low density disks available.
Windows 3.1 or higher, 386 or higher. IBM, Tandy & 100% compatibles (4Mb). disk $59.95 (ISBN 1-888046-85-6). *Nonstandard peripherals required:* 640 x 480 video display or higher, 256 colors, 16Mb hard disk space, 100% Sound Blaster compatible sound board.
Mac System 7.1 or higher; Windows 3.1 or higher, 386 or higher. 256 color capable Mac with color monitor; IBM, Tandy & 100% compatibles (4Mb). CD-ROM disk $59.95 (ISBN 1-888046-86-4). *Nonstandard peripherals required:* Mac: color monitor; Win: 640 x 480 video display or higher, 256 colors, 2Mb hard disk space, Sound Blaster compatible sound board.

Various Education Games for Children: 3 Math Games; 5 Reading Games; Spelling Games; Drawing & Music Games. All Activities Feature Snoopy & Other Peanuts Characters.
Image Smith, Inc.

Yearn 2 Learn Snoopy: Japanese Language. Sep. 1995. *Items Included:* Soft cover, stapled manual & registration card. *Customer Support:* Free customer service via our 800 number. Unlimited warranty on disk replacement.
System 6.0.7 or higher. Macintosh (4Mb). 3.5" disk $59.95 (ISBN 1-888046-57-0, Order no.: IS10068). *Nonstandard peripherals required:* 14Mb hard disk space, high density drive req., low denisty disks available.
Windows 3.1 or higher; 386 or higher. IBM, Tandy & 100% compatibles (4Mb). disk $59.95 (ISBN 1-888046-58-9, Order no.: IS10069). *Nonstandard peripherals required:* 640 x 480 video display or higher, 256 colors, 16Mb hard disk space, Sound Blaster compatible sound card.
System 7.1 or higher. Any 256 color capable MAC & color monitor (4Mb). CD-ROM disk $59.95 (ISBN 1-888046-59-7, Order no.: IS10068). *Nonstandard peripherals required:* CD-ROM drive.
Various Educational Games for Children. 3 Math Games; 5 Reading Games; Spelling Games; Drawing & Music Games. All Activities Feature Snoopy & Other Peanuts Characters.
Image Smith, Inc.

Yearn 2 Learn Snoopy: Swedish Language. *Items Included:* Soft cover, stapled manual & registration card. *Customer Support:* Free customer service via our 800 number. Unlimited warranty on disk replacement.
System 6.0.7 or higher. Macintosh (4Mb). 3.5" disk $59.95 (ISBN 1-888046-72-4). *Nonstandard peripherals required:* 14Mb hard disk space req.; high density drive req., low density disks available.
Windows 3.1 or higher, 386 or higher. IBM, Tandy & 100% compatibles (4Mb). disk $59.95 (ISBN 1-888046-73-2). *Nonstandard peripherals required:* 640 x 480 video display or higher, 256 colors, 16Mb hard disk space, 100% Sound Blaster compatible sound board.
Hybrid-CD-ROM. Contact publisher for price (ISBN 1-888046-74-0).
Various Educational Games for Children: 3 Math Games; 5 Reading Games; Spelling Games; Drawing & Music Games. All Activities Feature Snoopy & Other Peanuts Characters.
Image Smith, Inc.

Yearn 2 Learn Snoopy's Geography. Version: 1.07. Nov. 1994. *Items Included:* Soft cover, stapled manual & registration card. *Customer Support:* Free customer service via our 800 number. Unlimited warranty on disk replacement.
System 6.0.7 or higher. Any 256 color compatible MAC (4Mb). 3.5" disk $59.95 (ISBN 1-888046-14-7, Order no.: ISSG1001M). *Nonstandard peripherals required:* 13" monitor or higher; 15Mb hard disk space; high density drive req.
Windows 3.1 or higher; 386 or higher. IBM, Tandy & 100% compatibles (4Mb). disk $59.95 (ISBN 1-888046-15-5, Order no.: ISSG1001W). *Nonstandard peripherals required:* Mouse, 15Mb hard disk space; Sound Blaster compatible sound board. *Optimal configuration:* 486; 5Mb or higher RAM.
MAC: System 7.0 or higher. Any 256 color capable MAC (4Mb). CD-ROM disk $59.95 (ISBN 1-888046-16-3, Order no.: ISSG1001MCD). *Nonstandard peripherals required:* Mouse, CD-ROM drive.
Windows 3.1 or higher; 386 or higher. IBM, Tandy & 100% compatibles (4Mb). CD-ROM disk $59.95 (ISBN 1-888046-17-1, Order no.: ISSG1001WCD). *Nonstandard peripherals required:* Mouse; CD-ROM drive, Super VGA; Sound card (100% Sound Blaster compatible).
Macintosh or Windows. Macintosh or IBM, Tandy & 100% compatibles (4Mb). CD-ROM disk $59.95 (ISBN 1-888046-18-X, Order no.: ISSG1001HCD).
5 Activities/Games That Teach Kids about Geography. All Games Feature Snoopy & Other Peanuts Characters.
Image Smith, Inc.

Yearn 2 Learn Snoopy's Geography: Japanese Language. Feb. 1995. *Items Included:* Soft cover, stapled manual & registration card. *Customer Support:* Free customer service via our 800 number. Unlimited warranty on disk replacement.
MAC: System 7.0 or higher; Windows 3.1 or higher, 386 or higher. Any 256 color capable MAC, or IBM, Tandy or 100% compatibles (4Mb). disk $59.95 (ISBN 1-888046-63-5, Order no.: ISSG1001HJL). *Nonstandard peripherals required:* Mac: mouse, CD-ROM drive; Win: Super VGA, 100% Sound Blaster compatible sound card.
5 Activities & Games That Teach Kids about Geography. All Activities & Games Feature Snoopy & Other Peanuts Characters.
Image Smith, Inc.

Yearn 2 Learn Spellasoarus Quarry. Jun. 1995. *Items Included:* Soft cover, stapled manual & registration card. *Customer Support:* Free customer service via our 800 number. Unlimited warranty on disk replacement.
System 7 or higher. Any 256 color capable MAC (4Mb). 3.5" disk $14.95 (ISBN 1-888046-54-6, Order no.: ISFSS1001M). *Nonstandard peripherals required:* 13" monitor, 6Mb hard disk space, high density drive req.
Windows 3.1 or higher; 386 or higher. IBM, Tandy & 100% compatibles (4Mb). disk $14.95 (ISBN 1-888046-55-4, Order no.: ISFSS1001W). *Nonstandard peripherals required:* Super VGA, Sound Card: 100% Sound Blaster compatible, 4Mb hard disk space.
Spelling Games with Varying Levels of Difficulty, All Featuring the Flintstones Characters.
Image Smith, Inc.

Yearn 2 Learn Tell-A-Tell Library. Jun. 1995. *Items Included:* Soft cover, stapled manual & registration card. *Customer Support:* Free customer service via our 800 number. Unlimited warranty on disk replacement.
System 7 or higher. Any 256 color capable MAC (4Mb). 3.5" disk $14.95 (ISBN 1-888046-46-5, Order no.: ISFTT1001M). *Nonstandard peripherals required:* 13" monitor, 6Mb hard disk space, high density drive req.
Windows 3.1 or higher; 386 or higher. IBM, Tandy & 100% compatibles (4Mb). disk $14.95 (ISBN 1-888046-47-3, Order no.: ISFTT1001W). *Nonstandard peripherals required:* Super VGA, Sound Card: 100% Sound Blaster compatible, 4Mb hard disk space.
Reading & Vocabulary Games Featuring the Flintstones Characters. Children Can Read Their Own Stories or Have a Story Read to Them.
Image Smith, Inc.

Yearn 2 Learn Peanuts Lab Pack. Version: MAC 1.2.A, WIN 1.2.1. Sep. 1994. *Items Included:* Soft cover, stapled manual & registration card. Also includes a teacher's guide for application in the classroom, & 5 sets of disks. *Customer Support:* Free customer service via our 800 number. Unlimited warranty on disk replacement.
System 6.0.7 or higher. Macintosh (4Mb). 3.5" disk $129.95 (ISBN 1-888046-05-8, Order no.: IS10126). *Nonstandard peripherals required:* 14Mb hard disk space req. High density drive req. Low density disks available.
Windows 3.1 or higher; 386 or higher. IBM, Tandy & 100% compatibles (4Mb). disk $129.95 (ISBN 1-888046-06-6, Order no.: IS10124). *Nonstandard peripherals required:* 640 x 480 Video display or higher, 256 colors min., 16Mb hard disk space; Sound Blaster compatible sound card.
5 Different Activities Including Math, Reading, Coloring, & Geography Games. Also Teaches Kids Reading Comprehension Skills in a Fun Way. All Games & Activities Feature Charles Schulz's Peanuts Characters.
Image Smith, Inc.

Yearn 2 Learn Snoopy Lab Pack. Version: MAC 1.1, WIN 1.1. Dec. 1994. *Items Included:* Soft cover, stapled manual & registration card. Also includes a teacher's guide for application in the classroom, & 5 copies of disks. *Customer Support:* Free customer service via our 800 number. Unlimited warranty on disk replacement.
System 6.0.7 or higher. Macintosh (4Mb). 3.5" disk $129.95 (ISBN 1-888046-12-0, Order no.: IS10125). *Nonstandard peripherals required:* 14Mb hard disk space req. High density drive req. Low density disks available.
Windows 3.1 or higher; 386 or higher. IBM, Tandy & 100% compatibles (4Mb). disk $129.95 (ISBN 1-888046-13-9, Order no.: IS10123). *Nonstandard peripherals required:* 640 x 480 Video display or higher, 256 colors min., 16Mb hard disk space; Sound Blaster compatible sound card.
Various Educational Games for Children: 3 Math Games; 5 Reading Games; Spelling Games; Drawing & Music Games. All Activities Feature Snoopy & Other Peanuts Characters.
Image Smith, Inc.

Yellow Brick Road. Oct. 1995. *Items Included:* Warranty/registration card, game manual. *Customer Support:* Technical Support Number: 1-800-734-9466, 90 days limited warranty.
Windows 3.1; Macintosh System 7 or higher. IBM 33MHz i80486DX recommended (8Mb); Macintosh 25MHz 68030 or higher, 33MHz LC040 or higher. CD-ROM disk $49.99 (ISBN 1-888158-09-3). *Nonstandard peripherals required:* Double-speed CD-ROM drive. *Addl. software required:* MS-DOS 5.0 or higher.
Team up with the Tin Man & the Cowardly Lion to Rescue the Scarecrow from the Palace in Emerald City. Pick up "Tools" with Special Powers to Help You on Your Journey. As You Venture on the Yellow Brick Road, You Meet Friends & Foes.
Synergy Interactive Corp.

Yellow Brick Road: Emerald Collection. *Items Included:* Warranty/registration card, game manual. *Customer Support:* Technical Support Number: 1-800-734-9466, 90 days limited warranty.
Windows 3.1, Windows 95. IBM i80486SX or higher, 33MHz i80486DX recommended (8Mb). CD-ROM disk Contact publisher for price (ISBN 1-888158-22-0). *Nonstandard peripherals required:* Double-speed CD-ROM drive. *Addl. software required:* MS-DOS 5.0 or higher. *Optimal configuration:* CD-ROM Extensions Ver 2.2 or higher; 3Mb plus open area in hard disk; display: 640 x 480/256 colors (SVGA); mouse.
Macintosh System 7 or higher. 25MHz 68030 or higher, 33MHz 68LC040 or higher (4Mb). CD-ROM disk Contact publisher for price. *Nonstandard peripherals required:* Double speed CD-ROM. *Addl. software required:*

Adaptability to QuickTime 1.6.1. *Optimal configuration:* 640 x 480 dots/256 colors; mouse.
Story Continues...The Tin Man, the Cowardly Lion, Scarecrow, & the Wizard Meet Again to Save Glinda. She Is Being Held by the Wicked Witch of the West Who Is Plotting to Take over the Land of Oz. The Emerald City Is in Grave Danger.
Synergy Interactive Corp.

Yellow Brick Road II. Oct. 1995. *Items Included:* Warranty/registration card, game manual. *Customer Support:* Technical Support Number: 1-800-734-9466, 90 days limited warranty.
Windows 3.1; Macintosh System 7 or higher. IBM i80486SX or higher, 33MHz i80486DX recommended (8Mb); Macintosh 25MHz 68030 or higher, 33MHz 68LC040 or higher (8Mb). CD-ROM disk $69.99 (ISBN 1-888158-12-3). *Nonstandard peripherals required:* Double-speed CD-ROM drive. *Addl. software required:* MS-DOS 5.0 or higher.
Story Continues: The Tin Man, the Cowardly Lion, Scarecrow, & the Wizard Meet Again to Save Glinda. She Is Being Held by the Wicked Witch of the West Who Is Plotting to Take over the Land of Oz. The Emerald City Is in Grave Danger.
Synergy Interactive Corp.

YidPix.
IBM PC or compatibles. disk $24.95 (Order no.: I211). *Addl. software required:* KidPix for DOS.
Macintosh. 3.5" disk $24.95 (Order no.: M211). *Addl. software required:* KidPix. *Optimal configuration:* Macintosh with color monitor.
Contains 27 Judaic Pictures User Can Color with Broderbund Software's KIDPIX. Each Picture Corresponds to a Different Letter of the Alef-Bet & Displays an Object Whose First Letter in Its Hebrew Form Is the Same As the Large Letter Displayed. Also Includes 56 Full-Color "Rubber Stamps" on a Variety of Judaic Themes.
Davka Corp.

Yields-1. *Compatible Hardware:* IBM PC, PCjr, PC XT. *Operating System(s) Required:* MS-DOS. *Language(s):* Compiled BASIC. *Memory Required:* 64k.
disk $45.00.
Incorporates the Complex Algorithms Required to Compute Yields to Maturity, Yields to Call, & Settlement Prices Based on Current Yields for Fixed Income Securities Such As Corporate Bonds, Municipal Bonds, etc.
R & M Assocs.

You & Your Checkbook. May 1983. *Compatible Hardware:* Coleco Adam. *Memory Required:* 18k. *General Requirements:* Printer.
cassette $24.95 (Order no.: 1001).
Multi-Colored, Graphically Enhanced Program for Balancing a Checkbook.
Micro 2.

You Be the Reporter. George Ridgeway. 1994. *Items Included:* CD-ROM, binder & documentation. *Customer Support:* Toll free customer service Hot Line 1-800-645-3739 (9a.m. - 5p.m. Eastern Time) software guaranteed for two years.
Mac 6.0 Plus. Macintosh (4Mb). CD-ROM disk $199.00 (Order no.: CDR002). *Nonstandard peripherals required:* CD-ROM drive.
Develops the Student's Ability to Organize Facts in Logical Order & to Write Active, Direct Sentences; Well Organized Paragraphs & News Articles.
Educational Activities Inc.

You Can Lead: Lead with Confidence. Sep. 1994. *Customer Support:* Toll-free telephone number for technical support. 90 days warranty for defects in materials & workmanship.
Macintosh System 7.0. Macintosh with 68040 processor (5Mb). CD-ROM disk $49.95 (ISBN 1-886806-08-X). *Nonstandard peripherals required:* Double speed CD-ROM drive. *Addl. software required:* QuickTime (included on CD-ROM disc).
Microsoft Windows 3.1. PC compatibles; 486/33 MHz (runs slow on 386/25MHz) (8Mb). CD-ROM disk $49.95. *Nonstandard peripherals required:* 256 color display card (640x480); double speed CD-ROM drive. *Addl. software required:* QuickTime for Windows (included on CD-ROM disc).
Designed to Help You Improve Your Ability to Take Charge of a Situation & Motivate Others to Participate. You Will Learn Proven Leadership Skills, Including Setting Objectives, Motivating Others, Delegating Tasks, & Providing Feedback. This Highly Interactive CD-ROM Includes Video Exercises & Simulations to Practice Your Skills.
Wilson Learning Corp.

You Could Already Be a Winner!: 101 Magazines on the Internet. Tracey Winters. Apr. 1996. *Items Included:* A 64-page companion booklet that reviews web sites & includes instructions on how to use the software. *Customer Support:* Access to the Go!Guides web site & FAQ, customer support by email at help goguides.com.
Macintosh System 7.0 or higher. Macintosh (4Mb). 3.5" disk $12.99 (ISBN 1-57712-008-6). *Nonstandard peripherals required:* Modem 14.4 or faster. *Addl. software required:* Internet account & connection. *Optimal configuration:* Macintosh System 7.0 or higher, at least 4Mb of RAM, at least 2Mb of free disk space, color monitor, 14.4 or 28.8 modem, Internet account.
Windows 3.1 or Windows 95. IBM or compatible (4Mb). disk $12.99. *Nonstandard peripherals required:* 14.4 or 28.8 modem. *Addl. software required:* Internet account. *Optimal configuration:* IBM-compatible running Windows 3.1 or Windows 95, at least 2Mb free space on hard drive, at least 4Mb RAM, color monitor, 14.4 or 28.8 modem, Internet account.
Stop Killing Trees, Start Saving Cash, & Get All Your Favorite Print Magazines, Plus a Few New Ones Online, Direct to Your Computer.
Motion Works Publishing.

You Know Fortran-Ada Is Simple. Mar. 1986. *Compatible Hardware:* IBM PC, PC XT, PC AT, PS/2 & compatibles. *Operating System(s) Required:* PC-DOS/MS-DOS 2.0 or higher. *Memory Required:* 150k.
disk $1200.00.
Features an Interactive, Computer-Aided Course, Specifically Designed for Programmers & Managers with Some Familiarity with FORTRAN. The Course Introduces the User to the Ada Language & Provides a Core of Concepts in Ada Programming. The Course Encompasses Approximately 20 Hours of Instruction Organized by Subject into 10 Lessons. The Lessons Are Designed to Maximize User Understanding & Interest.
Alsys, Inc.

Young Parent, Young Child, 8 disks. Control Data Corporation. Sep. 1986. *Operating System(s) Required:* Apple DOS 3.3. *Memory Required:* 48k.
Set. $295.00, incl. audio cassette, student's manual, tchr's. guide (ISBN 0-8219-0258-X, Order no.: 95450F).
Teaches Teenage Parents the Basic Knowledge of Infant & Toddler Development Stages. Encourages Physical, Intellectual, Verbal & Emotional Growth.
EMC Publishing.

Your Best Money Moves Now. Money Magazine. May 1994. *Items Included:* On-line doc/help. *Customer Support:* No charge for support, toll free number - 800-942-2848, toll number 617-225-2136, calls received after working hours will be returned within 12 hrs. Support questions can be asked on Compuserve.
MS Windows 3.1 or higher. IBM compatible 386 or higher, 4Mb free disk, 256 color SVGA/VGA monitor or higher (4Mb). disk $39.95 (ISBN 1-57317-003-8, Order no.: V-MONEY-0001). *Optimal configuration:* 8Mb RAM, 486 machine, Windows 3.1 running enhanced mode, VESA local bus.
Helps Users Maximize Personal Finances by Providing Detailed Text with Interactive Worksheets. The Combination of Content & Software Technology Enables Users to Apply MONEY's Expertise & Guidance to Their Own Personal Financial Situation. Subjects Include Picking Stocks, Finding the Best Values in Education, Saving for Retirement, & More.
Vertigo Development Group.

Your Biorhythms PC. Jan. 1996. *Items Included:* Instruction handbook.
DOS & Windows. PC (640k). disk $19.90 (ISBN 1-56087-129-6). *Optimal configuration:* Min. 286, DOS or Windows 3.1, 4k RAM.
Four Different Exciting PC Computer Shareware Programs That Disclose Your Secret Biorhythm Cycles. You Can Determine Your Compatibility with Others. Discover When You Can Get the Greatest Amount of Work Done. Understand When You Are at Your Point of Power, When Your Emotional, Physical & Intellectual Cycles Are at Their Peak. Plus an Interesting Program for Using Your Biorhythms to Win the Lottery <end>
Top of the Mountain Publishing.

Your Family Tree. *Version:* 1.1. *Compatible Hardware:* Commodore Amiga. *Memory Required:* 512k.
3.5" disk $49.95.
Designed for Genealogists.
MicroMaster, Inc.

Your Financial Advisor. *Version:* 3.00. Oct. 1992. *Operating System(s) Required:* PC-DOS/MS-DOS 2.11 or higher. *Memory Required:* 256k. *General Requirements:* 80-column printer. *Items Included:* Disk, manual, free support, free hard disk menu. *Customer Support:* 1 year telephone support.
3.5" or 5.25" disk $29.95.
Provides Loan Calculations & Displays a Table That Shows the Effects of Variations in Interest, Term & Loan Amount. Produces Amortization Tables That Include Prepayments. Provides Retirement Planning, College Cost Planning & Home Loan Calculations Based on the New Tax Law.
PSG-HomeCraft Software.

Your Ideal Silhouette. *Version:* 3.0. Gail Florin. Jan. 1991. *Items Included:* Instruction manual.
DOS. IBM or compatibles. disk $239.00 (ISBN 1-56191-414-2, Order no.: 3026/3025). *Optimal configuration:* Software.
This Software Program Evaluates Body Measurements & Prints Out an Evaluation That Suggests Appropriate Styles of Clothing to Wear According to Body Type. This Version Is for Women.
Meridian Education Corp.

Your Income Tax 1-2-3. Palmer Weyandt. Dec. 1984. *Operating System(s) Required:* MS-DOS. *Memory Required:* 256k.
disk $29.95 (ISBN 0-13-979584-7).
Features LOTUS 1-2-3 Spreadsheet Software That Leads User Through a Recommended Income/Expense Collection Procedure & Then Through the Calculation Process.
Prentice Hall.

Your Mutual Fund Selector. John Waggoner. Jul. 1994. *Items Included:* On-line doc/help. *Customer Support:* No charge for support, toll free number - 800-942-2848, toll number 617-225-2136, calls received after working hours will be returned within 12 hrs. Support questions can be asked on Compuserve.
MS Windows 3.1 or higher. IBM compatible 386 or higher, 4Mb free hard disk, 256 color SVGA/VGA monitor or higher (4Mb). CD-ROM disk $49.95 (ISBN 1-57317-004-6, Order no.: V-FUND-0001). *Nonstandard peripherals required:* MPC compatible CD-ROM drive, sound board & speakers. *Optimal configuration:* 8Mb RAM, 486 machine, Windows 3.1 running enhanced mode, VESA local bus.
Helps Individual Investors Assemble Fund Portfolios by Matching User's Specific Financial Objectives, Investment Preferences, & Tolerance for Risk with Detailed Ratings of 1,000 Top Mutual Funds from Morningstar, Inc. The Combination of Interactive Software, Video, Text, & Sound Allows Users to Apply Knowledge to Build a Solid Investment Plan. Topics Include Setting Investment Goals, Analyzing Risk, Understanding Fund Statistics, & More.
Vertigo Development Group.

Your Personal Computer Tutor. TexaSoft, Inc. *Compatible Hardware:* TI Professional. *Operating System(s) Required:* MS-DOS. *Memory Required:* 64k.
$59.95.
Texas Instruments, Personal Productivit.

Your Personal Cookbook. *Compatible Hardware:* Commodore Amiga.
3.5" disk $49.95.
Features Digital Images, Recipes.
MicroSearch.

Your Personal Habits. Feb. 1996. *Items Included:* Program manual. *Customer Support:* Free technical support, 90 day warranty.
Single user. Windows 3.1 or higher. IBM 386 (8Mb). disk $99.95 (ISBN 1-57204-108-0, Order no.: WIN451). *Nonstandard peripherals required:* 256 monitor, sound card, mouse. *Addl. software required:* SVGA graphics.
Lab pack. Windows 3.1 or higher. IBM 386 (8Mb). disk $199.00 (ISBN 1-57204-139-0, Order no.: WIN451LPK). *Nonstandard peripherals required:* 256 monitor, sound card, mouse. *Addl. software required:* SVGA graphics.
Site license. Windows 3.1 or higher. IBM 386 (8Mb). disk $399.00 (ISBN 1-57204-141-2, Order no.: WIN451SITE). *Nonstandard peripherals required:* 256 monitor, sound card, mouse. *Addl. software required:* SVGA graphics.
Single user. System 7.1 or higher. Mac, 16 MHz rating, 68030 or better processor (LC II or higher) (5Mb). 3.5" disk $99.95 (ISBN 1-57204-107-2). *Nonstandard peripherals required:* 256 color monitor, 13" or larger.
Lab pack. System 7.1 or higher. Mac, 16 MHz rating, 68030 or better processor (LC II or higher) (5Mb). 3.5" disk $199.00 (ISBN 1-57204-138-2, Order no.: APM451LPK). *Nonstandard peripherals required:* 256 color monitor, 13" or larger.
Site license. System 7.1 or higher. Mac, 16 MHz rating, 68030 or better processor (LC II or higher) (5Mb). 3.5" disk $399.00 (Order no.: APM451SITE). *Nonstandard peripherals required:* 256 color monitor, 13" or larger.
Guides the student through personal habits that make people effective on their jobs.
Lawrence Productions, Inc.

Your Personal Legal Guide. *Version:* 8.0. Jun. 1994. *Items Included:* GBC bound manual; legal document envelopes. *Customer Support:* One year free support via phone, mail, fax & BBS. MS-DOS 3.3 or higher. IBM compatible (512k). disk $39.95.
Advanced Artificial-Intelligence Based Legal Self-Help Software That Includes over 200 Legal Forms, Plus Tutorials & Annotated Text of Related Statutes.
PSG-HomeCraft Software.

Your Photo Here! *Version:* 1.1. Sep. 1995. *Items Included:* Routine version of Windows based application (1 disk), photo mailer, disk wallet. *Customer Support:* Free via phone.
Windows 3.1 or higher. IBM & compatibles (4Mb). disk $24.95 (ISBN 1-888120-00-2). *Optimal configuration:* PC, 4Mb RAM, 3Mb HD space.
Easy-to-Use Digital Imaging Screen Saver/Wallpaper Application That Lets the User Put Their Own Photos on Their Screens; "Create a Screen Saver & Wallpaper with Your Own Photographs".
Leisure Ware, Inc.

Your Work Habits. (Job Success Ser.). Feb. 1996. *Items Included:* Program manual. *Customer Support:* Free technical support, 90 day warranty.
Single user. System 7.1 or higher. Mac, MHz rating, 68030 or better processor (LC II or higher) (5Mb). 3.5" disk $99.95 (ISBN 1-57204-112-9, Order no.: APM452). *Nonstandard peripherals required:* 256 color monitor, 13" or larger.
Lab pack. System 7.1 or higher. Mac, 16 MHz rating, 68030 or better processor (LC II or higher) (5Mb). 3.5" disk $199.00 (ISBN 1-57204-142-0, Order no.: APM452LPK). *Nonstandard peripherals required:* 256 color monitor, 13" or larger.
Site license. System 7.1 or higher. Mac, MHz rating, 68030 or better processor (LC II or higher) (5Mb). 3.5" disk $399.00 (ISBN 1-57204-144-7, Order no.: APM452SITE). *Nonstandard peripherals required:* 256 color monitor, 13" or larger.
single. Windows 3.1 or higher. IBM 386 (8Mb). disk $99.95 (ISBN 1-57204-113-7, Order no.: WIN452). *Nonstandard peripherals required:* 256 color monitor, sound card, mouse. *Addl. software required:* SVGA graphics.
Lab pack. Windows 3.1 or higher. IBM 386 (8Mb). disk $199.00 (ISBN 1-57204-143-9, Order no.: WIN452LPK). *Nonstandard peripherals required:* 256 color monitor, mouse, sound card. *Addl. software required:* SVGA graphics.
Site license. Windows 3.1 or higher. IBM 386 (8Mb). disk $399.00 (ISBN 1-57204-145-5, Order no.: WIN452SITE). *Nonstandard peripherals required:* 256 color monitor, sound card, mouse. *Addl. software required:* SVGA graphics.
Emphasizes the importance of dependability & being a team player.
Lawrence Productions.

You're Hired!: The Ultimate Job Interview Simulator. *Version:* 1.32. Stu Tarquist. Feb. 1994. *Items Included:* Bound manual, free copy of CSHELL - a great disk file & directory management utility that is similar to many commercially available DOS Shell programs (XTree Gold, Norter Commander, PC Tools, etc.). *Customer Support:* 1 year of free support by telephone, fax, mail, CompuServe Mail or Internet E-Mail.
DOS 2.0 or higher. IBM & compatibles - any speed (450k). disk $26.95, Site license, volume discount & dealer pricing avail. (Order no.: 10876). *Optimal configuration:* IBM or compatible 286 or higher, hard drive, color monitor, 512k.
An Informative & Comprehensive Job Interview Simulator That Provides Realistic Training & Valuable Experience to Prepare You for Your Next Job Interview. The Program Asks You Common Challenging Interview Questions in a Lifelike Simulation & Records Elapsed Times As You Verbally Respond. Press a Key to Receive Professional Advice.
DataWell.

YOURsoft Conversion Process. *Version:* 2.0. Jun. 1995. *Items Included:* Complete indexed instruction manual, copyright forms, sample programs. *Customer Support:* Free phone support.
Windows. IBM PC or compatibles, 386 or higher. disk $89.00 (ISBN 0-923680-07-1). *Optimal configuration:* Any Windows system.
Spreadsheet Compiling Service That Provides a Complete Feature-Packed Stand-Alone Program, Instruction Manual & Royalty-Free Distribution. WKI Files from Lotus 1-2-3 & Compatible Programs Are Converted into Stand-Alone Programs That No Longer Require Lotus 1-2-3 to Run. Converted Programs Include Drop-Down Menus, Help Screens & More.
American ComVision, Inc.

Z-Com: CP/M BASIC Compiler. *Compatible Hardware:* Z80 based systems. *Memory Required:* 12k. *General Requirements:* Dual disk drive.
$2000.00.
Compiler System for CP/M BASIC.
Allen Ashley.

Z to I. *Operating System(s) Required:* CP/M. *Language(s):* Assembly (source code included). *Memory Required:* 16k.
disk $50.00.
Translates Zilog Z-80 to Intel 8080 Assembler Mnemonics. Only Those Source Code Lines for Which an Instruction Exists in 8080 Instruction Set Will Be Translated. Other Instructions & Macros Are Passed Through to Be Caught by Assembler Later On. Processes Z-80 & 8080 Pseudo-Ops for M80.
Aton International, Inc.

Z-Transform Tutorial. (Plane Analysis Ser.: No. 2). *Compatible Hardware:* Apple II with Applesoft, IBM. *Operating System(s) Required:* Apple DOS 3.2, 3.3, MS-DOS. (source code included).
disk $39.95.
Second Selection in Complex Plane Analysis Educational Series.
Dynacomp, Inc.

Zap...The Codefinder. Three Rivers Software Co. *Compatible Hardware:* IBM PC, PS/2.
IBM PC. disk $24.95 (Order no.: 01002).
IBM PS/2. 3.5" disk $24.95 (Order no.: 02002).
An Encyclopedia of ZIP Codes & Area Codes, Tucked Away Inconspicuously in Computer's Memory.
First Row Software Publishing.

Zapt. Jun. 1982. *Compatible Hardware:* Apple II, II+, IIe. *Operating System(s) Required:* ASM. *Memory Required:* 32k.
disk $12.95 (ISBN 0-926567-05-5, Order no.: ZAPT).
Allows Display in Hex-ASCII, ASCII or Disassembly. Edit by File or Track Sector. Allows Operation from Exec Files.
Rettke Resources.

TITLE INDEX

ZAS Software Development Package. *Version:* 2.5. Rick Hollinbeck. 1980. *Operating System(s) Required:* CP/M-80, ISIS II, MS-DOS. *Language(s):* C. *Memory Required:* 48k.
ISIS II. 8" disk $495.00.
CP/M. 8" disk $395.00.
Consists of a Macro Assembler (ZAS), a Linker (ZLK), Program Loading Utilities (ZLD) & a Run-Time Monitor (ZEX). Includes 36 Directives.
Western Wares.

Zaxxon. Peter Adams. *Compatible Hardware:* Commodore 64.
disk $39.95 (Order no.: COMDSK-3721).
3-D Graphics, a Diagonally-Scrolling Screen & Sound Effects Are Combined to Put You in the Cockpit of a Heavily-Armed Spacecraft.
Broderbund Software, Inc.

ZBASIC. *Version:* 5.0. Oct. 1985. *Compatible Hardware:* Apple IIe, IIc, Macintosh; IBM PC & compatibles; Kaypro, TRS-80 Model I, Model III, Model 4. *Operating System(s) Required:* CP/M 2.2, 3.0, MS-DOS 2.0 or higher, Apple DOS 3.3, TRSDOS 6.2 or higher, CP/M 2.2 or higher. *Language(s):* Compiled BASIC. *Memory Required:* TRS-80 Model I & Model III 48k; Kaypro & TRS-80 Model 4 64k; IBM & Apple 128k; Macintosh 512k.
Macintosh. disk $199.95.
Apple, IBM, Kaypro, TRS-80 Model I, Model III & Model 4. disk $89.95 ea.
Features Include: Structured BASIC, Device Independent Graphics, 6-54 Digits of Precision (Selectable by User), Built-In Interactive Editor & Compiler, Choice of Alphanumeric Labels or Line Numbers.
Zedcor, Inc.

ZDT. *Operating System(s) Required:* CP/M, SB-80. *Memory Required:* 64k.
disk $50.00.
Development/Testing Aid for Assembly Language Programs & Monitor Debugger That Sets Breakpoints & Examines Registers & Memory. Special Features Include Facility to Read & Write Blocks of Data from Specified Disk Locations; Input or Output of a Byte to a Specific Port; Moving Blocks of Data in Memory; a Full Memory with Specific Values & the Ability to Search for HEX or ASCII Strings. Supports up to 6 Breakpoints.
Lifeboat Assocs.

Zeddas: Servant of Sheol. Oct. 1995. *Items Included:* Warranty/registration card, game manual. *Customer Support:* Technical Support Number: 1-800-734-9466, 90 days limited warranty.
Windows 3.1; Macintosh System 7 or higher. IBM i80486SX or higher, 33MHz i80486DX recommended (8Mb); Macintosh 26MHz 68030 or higher, 33Mhz 68LC040 or higher. CD-ROM disk $69.99 (ISBN 1-888158-13-1). *Nonstandard peripherals required:* Double-speed CD-ROM drive. *Addl. software required:* MS-DOS 5.0 or higher.
Your Journey Begins at an Ancient Castle. Be Prepared to Put Your Courage & Wit to the Test. Evil Demons, Odious Spirits Await You. To Survive, You Must Believe in Yourself More Than Anything Else. Then, You May Discover the Secret Behind Those Clammy Walls.
Synergy Interactive Corp.

ZEE Compressibility. *Version:* .01. P. L. Mariam. Jun. 1980. *Compatible Hardware:* IBM PC & compatibles, PC XT, PC AT. *Operating System(s) Required:* PC-DOS/MS-DOS 2.X, 3.0. *Memory Required:* 256k. *General Requirements:* Printer.
disk $199.95 (ISBN 0-935509-07-0, Order no.: 5275).
Uses the Redlich Kwong Method to Predict the Base & Flowing Density & Compressibility of Fluids. Requires Input of Flowing Pressure & Temperature, Specific Gravity of Molecular Weight, & the Critical Pressure & Temperature. If the Fluid Is Similar to Natural Gas, the Program Can Compute the Critical Properties, Viscosity, & Specific Heat Ratio Based upon Generalized Equations.
FlowSoft, Inc.

Z80 UniWare C Compiler. *Version:* 5.1. *Items Included:* Software manual. *Customer Support:* One full year support, updates & hotline telephone support.
MS-DOS, UNIX, XENIX. IBM PC & compatible & all UNIX machines. $1600.00 & up.
Generates ROMable Code for the Zilog Z80 & Hitachi HD64180 Microprocessors. Compiler Output Code Is Split into Five Independent Memory Segments That Can Be Assigned into ROM or RAM As Needed. Sizes of Ints, Pointers, & Other Types Are User Selectable. ANSI Standard Language Features Are Provided. The Compiler Comes with a Fully Featured Zilog Style Assembler, a Linker That Can Handle Very Large Loads, & a Downloader That Can Convert Any Load into Intel Hex & Many Other File Formats. A Librarian, Symbol Lister, & Other Utilities Are Also Provided.
Software Development Systems, Inc.

ZEN. *Compatible Hardware:* TRS-80 Model I, Model III, Model 4. *Operating System(s) Required:* CP/M. *Memory Required:* 64k.
TRS-80. disk $39.95 (Order no.: D9Z).
CP/M. disk $39.95 (Order no.: DCZ).
Includes Text Editor, Monitor & Debugger & Fast Z-80 Assembler.
The Alternate Source.

Zenterprise Real Estate Investor. *Items Included:* Bound manual. *Customer Support:* Free hotline - no time limit; 30 day limited warranty; updates are $5/disk plus S&H.
MS-DOS. IBM & compatibles (256k). disk $69.95.
Analysis Package for Calculating the Profitability of Investment Real Estate. With It User May Compare the Potential Gains from Different Properties under Various Scenarios. User May Easily Change Assumptions Such As Appreciation Rate, Depreciation Term, Rental Income, Maintenance Expenses, etc. For Example, User Might Compare the Profits & Losses for an Investment Property Using Optimistic & Pessimistic Assumptions, or User Could Compare Several Properties under Uniform Assumptions. Computes the Monthly Before- & After-Tax Cash Flows & the After-Tax Rate of Return. Each Screen Shows the Financial Projections for Any Five-Year Period. Also, User May Calculate the Price in Order to Meet a Chosen Profitability Goal.
Dynacomp, Inc.

Zero Gravity. EAS Software. Nov. 1988. *Compatible Hardware:* Atari ST; Commodore Amiga. *Memory Required:* 512k.
3.5" disk $29.95.
Arcade Game Similar to Volleyball. One Player Is Placed on Each Side of the Cargo Bay in a Weightless Environment of Space. Side Panels Can Be Struck to Add or Detract Points from Your Score at Different Times. The Screen Is Divided to Present the View Point of Each Player.
MichTron, Inc.

Zero Zap. *Compatible Hardware:* TI 99/4A.
contact publisher for price (Order no.: PHM3036).
Computerized Pinball Game with Electric Lights & Sound Effects.
Texas Instruments, Personal Productivit.

ZFonts. *Compatible Hardware:* IBM PC & compatibles.
typeface $20.00-200.00 ea.
Font Libraries. Typefaces Available Include: Antique Olive, Artisan, Baskerville, Bodoni, Brush, Century, Century Textbook, CG Goudy Oldstyle, CG Omega, CG Palacio, CG Triumvirate, Courier, Dom Casual, Delegate (Trojan), Elite, Futura Book II, Garamond, Gill Sans Md, Hebrew, Helvetica, ITC Century Book, ITC Korinna, ITC Souvenir Medium, Letter Gothic, OCR-A, OCR-B, Old English, Omega, Optima, Orator, Palacio, Park Avenue, Pica, Prestige Elite, Script, Terminal, Tiffany, Times, & Titan. Also Includes 3 of 9 Bar Code, Postnet Bar Code, Ding Bats, Palatino, Presentation, Symbol, Math, Tax. Over 2000 Fonts in HP Soft Font Format.
StraightForward.

ZICK. *Version:* 1.0. 1982. *Compatible Hardware:* IBM PC & compatibles. *Operating System(s) Required:* MS-DOS. *Language(s):* BASIC. *Memory Required:* 128k.
$260.00.
Performs the Calculations to Determine Longitudinal Bending, Tangential Shear & Circumferential Compression Stresses for Horizontal Vessels with Two Saddles. Allows for Options of Varying Shell Thickness or Using Stiffening to Obtain Satisfactory Design.
Technical Research Services, Inc.

A Zillion Sounds. *Items Included:* Browser/sampler/installer front end software. *Customer Support:* 90 day warranty, free call back technical support.
System 6. Any Mac (1Mb). CD-ROM disk $20.00. *Nonstandard peripherals required:* CD-ROM drive. *Networks supported:* Apple File Sharing.
Windows 3.1. IBM 386 & compatibles (4Mb). CD-ROM disk $20.00. *Nonstandard peripherals required:* CD-ROM drive, sound card.
BeachWare.

ZIP-Data. Jul. 1990. *Items Included:* Disk & manual. *Customer Support:* By phone.
$495.00.
Same 8.5 Megabyte Database in ASCII Fixed Length Record Format. 78,000 Record File with ZIP, City, State, Area Code, County Number Number, Latitude & Longitude. A Second File Contains All U.S. Counties with FIPS Code & Time Zone. Third Is Set of Unique ZIP Codes & Assigned Organization.
Mailer's Software.

Zip-Phone *1. Jan. 1990. *Items Included:* Manual & disks, 3.5" & 5.25". *Customer Support:* By phone.
MS-DOS. IBM PC (256k). disk $69.00.
A Zip Code & Phone Number Location Finder. Type in a Zip Code & Get the City, State, Area Code & Time Zone. Or Type in the State & City Name to Get the Zip. If the User is Not Sure of the State, Type a "?" & System Finds All Matching Cities Nationwide. Enter an Area Code & Prefix & the System Displays the City, State, Zip & Time Zone.
Mailer's Software.

Zip*Select. Aug. 1993. *Items Included:* Product on 3.5" or 5.25" & manual. *Customer Support:* Product information available over phone, toll free; technical support provided, unlimited over telephone; 30 day money back guarantte.
DOS 3.1 or higher. IBM & compatibles (640k) 1 hard drive. $340.00; updates $95.00; auto updates $55.00 ea.; updates every 6 mos. *Optimal configuration:* 386/486 - 4Mb space free on hard drive, high density floppy disk drive. *Networks supported:* Lantastic.
Allows for the Lookup of All Zip Codes in a

Zippy Floppy. Jun. 1985. *Compatible Hardware:* Commodore 64. *Memory Required:* 64k.
disk $29.95 (ISBN 0-89824-137-5, Order no.: 1375).
Utilities Include Sprite-Builder, Headline-Builder, Character-Set Builder, Picture-Builder, More Than a Dozen Disk Data Files of Alphabet Letters, etc. Sample Subroutines, 4 Demonstrations, & a Tutorial.
Trillium Pr.

Radius, County or 3-Digit Zip Code Area. Will Also Look up All the Area Code & Prefix Combinations in an Area by Radius, County or 3-Digit Zip. Will Save Information Found to a File or Print a Hard Copy.
Mailer's Software.

ZIPPY Mail List Merger. *Version:* 1.06. Aug. 1986. *Compatible Hardware:* IBM PC, PC XT, PC AT, PS/2 & true compatibles. *Operating System(s) Required:* PC-DOS/MS-DOS 2.12 or higher. *Memory Required:* 128k. *Customer Support:* Yes.
IBM. disk $79.95 (ISBN 0-929800-20-6, Order no.: ZC5.25 OR ZC3.5).
Novell. disk $240.00 (Order no.: ZN5.25 OR ZN3.5).
Used to Create, Manage, Print, Update & Track a Mailing List Containing Names. Can Be Used by Any Company or Organization Wanting to Keep Track of Customers, Membership Lists, Zip Code Sorted Mailings, Single Labels, Partial User Specified Mailings or Whole File Mailings. Additional Features Include: Full Text Editing for Corrections & Updating, Comment Line for Information Regarding Name; Codes Allow the Selecting, Targeting & Tracking of Names; Zip Code &/or Alphabetic Search for Finding & Printing, Updating or Deleting Names; Print One Name, Print by Name Code, or Complete List. Label Set-Up for Different Size Labels & Margins; Print One-Up Shipping Labels or Address Labels from One-Up to Seven Across; Input of Control Codes to Activate Unique Printer Features; Archiving of Lists for Optimal Disk Storage. Can Store Mailing Lists on Hard Disk & under Subdirectories.
Electrosonics.

ZMAIL. *Compatible Hardware:* TRS-80 Model III, Model 4. *Operating System(s) Required:* TRSDOS. (source code included). *Memory Required:* Model III 48k, Model 4 64k.
Model III. disk $29.95 (Order no.: D3ZM).
Model 4. disk $29.95 (Order no.: D4ZM).
In-Memory Mailing System That Allows the Most Economical Use of Memory & Achieves the Greatest Speed in Time-Dependent Operations Such As Sorting, Searching & Disk I/O. Supports Various Line Sizes, Easy Merging of Files & Prints Labels & Lists.
The Alternate Source.

ZMATH. *Version:* 3.0. May 1985. *Compatible Hardware:* IBM & compatibles, PC XT, PC AT. *Operating System(s) Required:* DOS 1.10 or higher. *Memory Required:* 256k. *General Requirements:* Lotus 1-2-3 or Symphony, 2 double-sided disk drives or hard disk. *Items Included:* Manual, newsletters, & 6 months tech support. *Customer Support:* free for 6 months; $100.00 annually thereafter.
$499.95.
Collection of Application Templates that Calculate the Time Value of Money Sections Include Loan & Savings Calculations, Regulation Z Calculations, Amortization Schedule Production, Pre-Disclosures & Utilities.
Math Corp.

ZMDS: Z80 Development System. Zee Microwave. May 1984. *Operating System(s) Required:* CP/M-80. *Memory Required:* 48k.
disk 40 TPI $49.95 (ISBN 0-923875-26-3).
disk 80 TPI $49.95 (ISBN 0-923875-27-1).
8" disk $49.95 (ISBN 0-923875-25-5).
Advanced MARCO Asssembler That Produces Object Files in Either Intel HEX or Micro-Soft REL Formats for Zilog/Mostek Z-80 Mnemonics. Contains a Built-In Cross Reference Capability for Symbols, Op Codes & Marcos. Other Features Include Conditional Assembly, User-Defined Macros & Libraries, Source & Command Line Control of Assembly Functions, & Explicit Error Messages.
Elliam Assocs.

ZOA: Zone of Avoidance. John Calhoun & Jeffrey Robbin. 1993. *Items Included:* Instructions, reg. card. *Customer Support:* Free phone support.
6.02 & higher. Macintosh. 3.5" disk $49.95 (Order no.: M108).
3-Dimension Space-Flight Simulation. Use the State-of-the-Art Radar Console to Locate Incoming Raiders & Blow-Up the Mother Ship Before It's Too Late.
Casady & Greene, Inc.

Zodiac Castle Adventure. *Compatible Hardware:* Apple II with Applesoft. *Operating System(s) Required:* Apple DOS 3.2, 3.3. (source code included). *Memory Required:* 48k.
disk $29.95.
Treasure Hunt Game.
Dynacomp, Inc.

Zoo-Opolis. Sep. 1995. *Customer Support:* Telephone support - free (except phone charge). Windows 3.1. IBM & compatibles (386 DX-20) (4Mb). CD-ROM disk $12.99 (ISBN 1-57594-033-7). *Nonstandard peripherals required:* 2x CD-ROM player, Sound Card, VGA monitor. *Optimal configuration:* 486 XS-33.
Interactive Zoo Town with Movies, Games, Puzzles & Educational Fun.
Kidsoft, Inc.

Zoo-Opolis. Sep. 1995. *Customer Support:* Telephone support - free (except phone charge). Windows 3.1. IBM & compatibles (386 DX-20) (4Mb). CD-ROM disk $12.99 (ISBN 1-57594-072-8). *Nonstandard peripherals required:* 2x CD-ROM player, Sound Card, VGA monitor. *Optimal configuration:* 486 SX-33.
Interactive Zoo Town with Movies, Games, Puzzles & Educational Fun. Blister Pack Jewel Case.
Kidsoft, Inc.

Zoo-Opolis.
MS-DOS 5.0 or higher, Windows 3.1 or higher. 386 processor or higher (4Mb). CD-ROM disk $39.95 (Order no.: R1372). *Nonstandard peripherals required:* CD-ROM drive. *Optimal configuration:* 386 processor operating at 16Mhz or higher, MS-DOS 5.0 or higher, Windows 3.1 or higher, 30Mb hard drive, mouse, VGA graphic adapter & VGA color monitor (SVGA recommended), 4Mb RAM, external speakers or headphones (with sound card) that are Sound Blaster compatible.
Macintosh (4Mb). (Order no.: R1372).
Nonstandard peripherals required: 14" color monitor or larger, CD-ROM drive.
Tour a Real Zoo, Learn about Animals, Take Care of Zoo Animals with the Aid of Zoo Keepers, Play Games & Solve Puzzles with This Rewarding Program. Based on the Popular Children's Video (Ages 3 & Up).
Library Video Co.

Zoom Grafix. Dav Hole. 1982-88. *Compatible Hardware:* Apple with Applesoft, IIc, IIgs. *Operating System(s) Required:* Apple DOS 3.3. *Language(s):* Assembly. *Memory Required:* 48k. *General Requirements:* Printer.
disk $49.95.
Allows Selection from over 65,000 Possible Combinations & Allows User to Print Positive, Negative, Sideways, Size, Proportions-Almost Any Combination of Amplification of the Graphics.
American Eagle Software, Inc.

Zootopia. Dec. 1995. *Customer Support:* Telephone support - free (except phone charge). Windows 3.1. IBM & compatibles (386 DX-20) (4Mb). CD-ROM disk $12.99, Jewel (ISBN 1-57594-083-3). *Nonstandard peripherals required:* 2X CD ROM player, sound card, VGA monitor. *Optimal configuration:* 486 SX-33.
CD-ROM disk $12.99, Blister.
Kids Control This Learning Safari, Clicking along Routes Packed with Puns, Fun & Hip-Hop Animals Facts. Kids Can Create Their Own Animals in the Build-a-Beast Pavillion.
Kidsoft, Inc.

Zootopia. Jan. 1996. *Customer Support:* Telephone support - free (except phone charge). System 7.1 or higher. 256 color capable Mac with a 68030 processor (5.5Mb). CD-ROM disk $12.99 (ISBN 1-57594-107-4). *Nonstandard peripherals required:* 2X CD ROM drive, 640/480 resolution monitor.
Kids Control This Learning Safari, Clicking along Routes Packed with Puns, Fun & Hip-Hop Animals Facts. Kids Can Create Their Own Animals in the Build-a-Beast Pavillion.
Kidsoft, Inc.

Zootopia. Feb. 1996. *Customer Support:* Telephone support - free (except phone charge). Windows 3.1. IBM compatible 386 DX-20 (4Mb). CD-ROM disk $12.99 (ISBN 1-57594-096-5). *Nonstandard peripherals required:* 2x CD-ROM, sound card, VGA monitor. *Optimal configuration:* 486, SX-33.
Kids control This Learning Safari, Clicking along Routes Packed with Animal Facts. Kids Can Create Their Own Animals in the Build-a-Beast Pavillion. Blister Pack.
Kidsoft, Inc.

Zootopia. Dec. 1995. *Customer Support:* Telephone support - free (except phone charge). Windows 3.1. IBM & compatibles (386 DX-20) (4Mb). CD-ROM disk $12.99 (ISBN 1-57594-083-3). *Nonstandard peripherals required:* 2X CD-ROM player, sound card, VGA monitor. *Optimal configuration:* 486 SX-33.
Kids control This Learning Safari, Clicking along Routes Packed with Fun & Hip-Hop Animals Facts. Kids Can Create Their Own Animals in the Build-a-Beast Pavillion. Jewel Case.
Kidsoft, Inc.

Zootopia. 1995. *Items Included:* Program manual. *Customer Support:* Free technical support (800-421-4157), 90 day warranty.
Consumer. Windows 3.1; System 7.0 or higher. IBM 486 DX or faster (8Mb); Mac 040 processor or faster (8Mb). CD-ROM disk $59.95 (ISBN 1-57204-007-6, Order no.: CD941). *Nonstandard peripherals required:* CD-ROM drive, 13" or bigger 256 color monitor, SVGA video card.
School ver.. Windows 3.1; System 7.0 or higher. IBM 486 DX or faster (8Mb); Mac 040 processor or faster (8Mb). CD-ROM disk $69.95 (ISBN 1-57204-008-4, Order no.: CD941T). *Nonstandard peripherals required:* CD-ROM drive, 13" or bigger 256 color

TITLE INDEX

monitor, SVGA video card.
Lab Pack (5). Windows 3.1; System 7.0 or higher. IBM 486 DX or faster (8Mb); Mac 040 processor or faster (8Mb). CD-ROM disk $149.95 (ISBN 1-57204-009-2, Order no.: CD941LPK). *Nonstandard peripherals required:* CD-ROM drive, 13" or bigger 256 color monitor, SVGA video card.
Site license. Windows 3.1; System 7.0 or higher. IBM 486 DX or faster (8Mb); Mac 040 processor or faster (8Mb). CD-ROM disk $699.00 (ISBN 1-57204-011-4, Order no.: CD941SITE). *Nonstandard peripherals required:* CD-ROM drive, 13" or bigger 256 color monitor, SVGA video card.
The moment you enter the gates of "Zoopotia" you will know that this is no ordinary zoo. You'll listen to the lions talk radio show, sing the blues with Firebelly Toad, or even buy a used camel at "Camel Lot." In the temple of knowledge, watch informative videos & create your own exotic animal with "Build a Beast.".
Lawrence Productions, Inc.

Zork Hintbook. *Items Included:* Installation Guide. IBM. Contact publisher for price (ISBN 0-87321-094-8, Order no.: HBK-3034).
Activision, Inc.

Zork I. Infocom. *Compatible Hardware:* HP 150 Touchscreen, HP 110 Portable.
3.5" disk $39.95 (Order no.: 92243CA).
The Introduction to the Great Underground Empire, Challenging You to Find & Explore the Subterranean Ruins of an Ancient Civilization. The Object Is to Plunder Whatever Treasures Remain in the Catacombs & Live to Tell the Tale. But You Aren't the Only Explorer; a Hungry-Looking Thief Is after the Same Rich Bounty & He's a Formidable Enemy.
Hewlett-Packard Co.

Zork I: The Great Underground Adventure.
1979. *Compatible Hardware:* Apple II+, IIe, IIc, Macintosh; Atari XL/XE, ST; Commodore 64/128, Amiga; DEC Rainbow; IBM PC & compatibles; Kaypro; TI/99-4A; TI Professional; TRS-80 Model I, Model III, Color Computer. *Operating System(s) Required:* MS-DOS, CP/M. *Memory Required:* 32-48k.
Apple II, Macintosh, Atari ST, Amiga, DEC, IBM. disk $39.95.
Atari XL/XE, Commodore 64/128. $34.95.
TI 99/4A, TI Professional, TRS-80. disk $14.95.
This Interactive Adventure Takes You to the Ruins of an Ancient Empire Far Underground Where You Travel in Search of the Incomparable Treasures of Zork.
Activision, Inc.

Zork II. Infocom. *Compatible Hardware:* HP 150 Touchscreen, HP 110 Portable.
3.5" disk $44.95 (Order no.: 92243RA).
This Chapter Takes You Further into the Deepest Recesses of the Earth to Discover the Secrets of Sorcery. Confront the Wizard of Frobozz & His Evil Spells. He Will Attempt to Impede Your Quest with His Capricious Powers.
Hewlett-Packard Co.

Zork II. Infocom. *Compatible Hardware:* TI Professional. *Memory Required:* 64k. *General Requirements:* Printer.
$49.95 (Order no.: SS P/N 63T-002).
Texas Instruments, Personal Productivit.

Zork II: The Wizard of Frobozz. Marc Blank & Dave Lebling. 1981. *Compatible Hardware:* Apple II+, IIe, IIc, IIgs, Macintosh; Atari 400, 800, ST; Commodore 64, Amiga; IBM PC; Kaypro; TRS-80 Model I, Model III. *Operating System(s) Required:* CP/M, MS-DOS. *Memory Required:* 32-48k.
$44.95.
Second Adventure in the Zork Trilogy Puts You Back into the Subterranean Region with More Challenges.
Activision, Inc.

Zork III. Infocom. *Compatible Hardware:* HP 150 Touchscreen, HP 110 Portable.
3.5" disk $44.95 (Order no.: 92243TA).
The Final Chapter in the Trilogy, by Far the Most Difficult, Is the Test of Your Wisdom & Courage. Your Odyssey Culminates in an Encounter with the Dungeon Master Himself, & Your Destiny Hangs in the Balance.
Hewlett-Packard Co.

Zork III. Infocom. *Compatible Hardware:* TI Professional. *Memory Required:* 64k. *General Requirements:* Printer.
$49.95 (Order no.: SS P/N 63T-003).
Texas Instruments, Personal Productivit.

Zork III: The Dungeon Master. *Compatible Hardware:* Apple II+, IIe, IIc, IIgs, Macintosh; Atari XL/XE, ST; IBM PC; Commodore 64, Amiga; Kaypro; TRS-80 Model I, Model III. *Operating System(s) Required:* MS-DOS, CP/M. *Memory Required:* 32-48k.
$44.95.
Final Episode of the Zork Trilogy Pits the Reader Against the Dungeon Master.
Activision, Inc.

Zorlof Word Processing System. *Compatible Hardware:* IBM PC. *Operating System(s) Required:* MS-DOS.
disk $69.95.
Supports over 50 Printers & Most of Their Features & Lets User Compare Text & Format Commands with Actual Printed Results. Provides the Following Capabilities: Proportional Character Spacing, Underlining, Bolding, Superscripts & Subscripts, Condensed, Wide Lettering, Graftrax Italics, Margin Alignment, Center Any Line or Group of Lines, Set Tables, Indent Text on Left & Right Side Specify Different Margins for Even & Odd Papers.
Anitek Software Products.

Zorlof II. *Compatible Hardware:* TRS-80 Model I, Model III. *Memory Required:* Model III 24k, Model I 32k.
contact publisher for price.
Anitek Software Products.

Zorro. James Garon. Nov. 1985. *Compatible Hardware:* Apple; Atari; Commodore 64, 128. *Memory Required:* Atari 48k, Apple & Commodore 64k.
Atari & Commodore. disk $19.95 (ISBN 0-88717-127-3, Order no.: 1490WCF).
disk $19.95 (ISBN 0-88717-126-5, Order no.: 1490ADO).
Relive the Exploits & Adventures of the Legendary Zorro in Los Angeles of the 1800's As He Attempts to Rescue the Fair Maiden from the Clutches of the Evil Sergeant Garcia. His Quest Takes Him Through 20 Screens of Danger & Excitement As He Is Chased by Garcia's Soldiers.
IntelliCreations, Inc.

ZSAM: Z80 Assembler. Zee Microwave. Jun. 1984. *Operating System(s) Required:* CP/M-80. *Memory Required:* 48k. *General Requirements:* Printer.
disk 40 TPI $24.95 (ISBN 0-923875-32-8).
disk 80 TPI $24.95 (ISBN 0-923875-33-6).
8" disk $24.95 (ISBN 0-923875-31-X).
Assembler for Z-80 CP/M Microcomputers That Uses Zilog/Mostek Mnemonics. Designed for Assembling Small & Medium Sized Stand Alone Assembly Language Programs That Do Not Involve the Use of Macros, Libraries of Routines or Relocatable Code.
Elliam Assocs.

Z80 DEVELOPMENT PACKAGE

ZSIM. *Compatible Hardware:* TRS-80.
contact publisher for price.
Instant Software, Inc.

Z3PLUS/NZCOM Z-System for CP/M. *Operating System(s) Required:* CP/M Plus, 2.2. *Memory Required:* 64k.
3.5", 5.25" or 8" disk $69.95.
Command Processing That Provides Many Features Not Available in the Regular CP/M Operating System. Includes: Command Line Editing, Keyboard Reconfiguration, Batch (Submit) Files with IF, Shells, Name Directories, Redirection, Recall Previous Commands. No Assembling to Install.
Elliam Assocs.

Zurk's Rainforest Lab.
Windows. IBM & compatibles. CD-ROM disk $59.95 (Order no.: R1373). *Nonstandard peripherals required:* CD-ROM drive. *Optimal configuration:* 386 processor operating at 16Mhz or higher, MS-DOS 5.0 or higher, Windows 3.1 or higher, 30Mb hard drive, mouse, VGA graphic adapter & VGA color monitor (SVGA recommended), 4Mb RAM, external speakers or headphones (with sound card) that are Sound Blaster compatible.
Macintosh (4Mb). (Order no.: R1373A <END>). *Nonstandard peripherals required:* 14" color monitor or larger, CD-ROM drive.
Five Fun, Challenging Activities Motivate Children to Sharpen Reading Skills While Learning Life Science & Math. Children Can Explore, Discover & Learn at Their Own Pace As They Solve Puzzles, Categorize Various Animals & Much More.
Library Video Co.

Zy INDEX for DOS. *Version:* 4.0. *Compatible Hardware:* IBM PC & compatibles. *Operating System(s) Required:* MS-DOS 3.1 or higher. *Memory Required:* 512k. *Items Included:* Manual, newsletter. *Customer Support:* Free.
$395.00.
$995.00 Network 3 pack.
Full-Text Search & Retrieval System. Search Requests Include Boolean Operators, Proximity, & Wildcards. Search Terms Are Highlighted. Mark & Save Option Moves Text to a File or Printer. Also Features Option to Print.
ZyLAB.

ZyINDEX for Windows 5.0. *Version:* 5.0. Jul. 1992. *Items Included:* Manual. *Customer Support:* 60 day money back, free tech support, free BBS, free newsletter.
DOS 3.1 Plus, Windows 3.X. PC (2Mb). $395.00 single. *Optimal configuration:* 386, 4Mb RAM, HDD, VGA color monitor, mouse. *Networks supported:* Novell, Banyan, 3COM.
$995.00 Network 3 pack.
Full Text Search & Retrieval System. Search Requests Include Boolean Operators, Proximity, & Wildcards. Search Terms Are Highlighted. Mark & Save Option Moves Text to a File or Printer. Also Features Option to Print.
ZyLAB.

Z80 Development Package. *Operating System(s) Required:* CP/M, SB-80. *Memory Required:* 64k.
disk $130.00.
Helps User Create, Modify, & Implement Z80 Assembly Language Programs. Features a Z80 Relocating Assembler, Zilog/Mostek Mnemonics, Conditional Assembly, & Printed Symbol Table, a Disk File Line Editor with Global Inter & Intra Line Facilities, & Linker Loader That Produces Absolute Intel HEX Disk File Concentrates.
Lifeboat Assocs.

Z80 DIS: Z80 Disassembler. Stephen L. Russell. Feb. 1983. *Compatible Hardware:* TRS-80 Model I, Model II. *Operating System(s) Required:* CP/M 2.2. *Memory Required:* 32k. *General Requirements:* 2 disk drives.
$49.95 (Order no.: 190).
Disassembler with Labeling & Cross Referencing.
SLR Systems.

Z80ASM: Z80 Assembly Language Development.
$199.95.
manual only $30.00.
Absolute or Relocating Macro Assembler.
SLR Systems.

Z8000 FORTH Development System.
Compatible Hardware: TRS-80 Model II. *Operating System(s) Required:* CP/M, CDOS. *Language(s):* FORTH. *Memory Required:* 64k.
disk $450.00.
Includes a Cross-Compiler for CP/M or Cromemco CDOS.
Inner Access Corp.

Publisher/Title Index

A.A.H. Computer Graphics Productions, P.O. Box 610667, San Jose, CA 95161 Tel 408-980-7363.
Titles:
Bytes of Fright.
Classic Science Fiction.

AA Software Development, Div. of Automated Analysis, (0-922416), 429 S. Huntington Ave., Boston, MA 02130-4802 Tel 617-522-6531.
Titles:
Compare-A-Loan.

ABT Corp., 361 Broadway, New York, NY 10013-3998 Tel 212-219-8945; Toll free: 800-477-6532; FAX: 212-219-3925.
Titles:
ABT's Time Line Interface: Interface to Project Workbench System.
Function Point Manager.
Metrics Manager.
Project Bridge Modeler (for Windows).
Project Workbench PMW.

ACDA Corp., 220 Belle Meade Ave., Setauket, NY 11733 Tel 516-689-7722; FAX: 516-689-5211.
Titles:
Amiga FFT C Package.
Amiga View.
CS-Interface.
DigiScope.
Printer Drivers.

ACIUS, Inc., 20883 Stevens Creek Blvd., Cupertino, CA 95014 Tel 408-252-4444; FAX: 408-252-0831.
Titles:
File Force.
4D Write.
4th Dimension.

ACM Computer Services, Inc., 8303 SW Freeway, Suite 760, Houston, TX 77074-1601 Tel 713-644-9094.
Titles:
MARS/2000: ACM Manufacturing Software.
System 34/36 Financial Software Packages.
YARDSTICK: ACM Lumber & Hardware Management Accounting System.

ACS Pubns., (0-917086; 0-935127), P.O. Box 34487, San Diego, CA 92163-4487 Tel 619-297-9203; Toll free: 800-888-9983 (orders only); FAX: 619-297-9251. Do not confuse with ACS Publishing Co., also in San Diego or American Chemical Society in Washington, DC.
Titles:
The Electronic Astrologer: Reveals Your Horoscope.

ADA Compliance Specialists, 10765 SW 104th St., Miami, FL 33176 Tel 305-271-0012; FAX: 305-271-0011.
Titles:
ADAABC-ADA Compliance Program: The ABC's of the Americans with Disabilities Act.
TLC/96 for Windows: Total Life Care Planning.

AD/C Solutions, 1445 Grant Rd., Los Altos, CA 94024 Tel 415-969-3979.
Titles:
Office Services Inventory System.
School Work Request & Preventive Maintenance.
Work Request & Asset Management.

ADS Software, Inc., (0-922014), P.O. Box 13686, Roanoke, VA 24036 Tel 540-989-1273; Toll free: 800-672-4422; FAX: 540-989-4739.
Titles:
ADS Accounts Payable.
ADS Club Accounting.
ADS General Ledger.
ADS Light Accounting for Retail Florist.
ADS Payroll.
Restaurant Payroll.
Retail Florists Accounting Bundle.
Small Bookkeeping Services.

A E C Software, 22611 Markey Ct., Bldg. 113, Sterling, VA 20166 Tel 703-450-1980; Toll free: 800-346-9413; FAX: 703-450-9786.
Titles:
Fast Track Schedule: Simple Scheduling.
Impassive Power.
FastTrack Schedule.

AICorp., 404 Wyman, Suite 320, Waltham, MA 02254 Tel 617-891-6500.
Titles:
1st-Class.
KBMS: Knowledge Base Management System.

AIMS, Inc., (0-917677), 1810 Glenmar Ave., Monroe, LA 71201 Tel 318-323-2467; Toll free: 800-729-2467; FAX: 318-322-3472.
Titles:
Applied Information Payroll Package.
AUTOSEND.
AUTOSIR.
Complete Oil Marketers Perpetual Accounting System (COMPAS).

AIM Technology, Inc., (1-881351), 4699 Old Ironsides Dr., Suite 150, Santa Clara, CA 95054 Tel 408-748-8649; Toll free: 800-848-8649; FAX: 408-748-0161.
Titles:
AIM Resource Accounting.
AIM Suite III Multiuser Benchmark.
SharpShooter.

AIQ, Inc., P.O. Box 7530, Incline Village, NV 89452-7530; Toll free: 800-332-2999; FAX: 702-831-6784; 916 Southwood Blvd, Bldg. 3, Incline Village, NV 89450 Tel 702-831-2999.
Titles:
StockExpert, MarketExpert.
Trading Expert.

AIS Microsystems, Div. of Advanced Investment Strategies, Inc., (0-922031), 1007 Massachusetts Ave. NE, Washington, DC 20002 Tel 202-547-9113.
Titles:
Investment Tax Analyst.
Mortgage Switch Calculator.

AI Systems, Inc., 102 W. 500 S., No. 650, Salt Lake City, UT 84101 Tel 501-363-6119; Toll free: 800-733-8941.
Titles:
Autodraw.

AJV Computerized Data Management, Inc., 431 Rte. 10, Randolph, NJ 07869 Tel 201-989-8955; Toll free: 800-323-2662 (outside NJ); FAX: 201-366-5877.
Titles:
TAX$IMPLE.

AK Peters, Ltd., (1-56881), 289 Linden St., Wellesley, MA 02181 Tel 617-235-2210; FAX: 617-235-2404.
Titles:
Introductory Lectures on Data Parallel Computing.

ALOS Micrographics Corp., 118 Bracken Rd., Montgomery, NY 12549 Tel 914-457-4400; Toll free: 800-431-7105; FAX: 914-457-9083.
Titles:
ALOSWARE HD.

A.N.A.L.O.G., Inc., 565 Main St., Cherry Valley, MA 01611 Tel 508-892-9230; Toll free: 800-345-8112.
Titles:
Star Sentry.

ANTRIM Corp., 101 E. Park Blvd., 12th Flr., Plano, TX 75074 Tel 214-422-1022; Toll free: 800-767-3357; FAX: 214-516-3460.
Titles:
Blood Bank Systems.
Financial Systems.
Information Support Systems.
Laboratory Systems.

A.R.E. Pr., (0-87604), 68th St. & Atlantic Ave., Virginia Beach, VA 23451-0656 Tel 804-428-3588; Toll free: 800-723-1112; FAX: 804-422-6921; P.O. Box 656, Virginia Beach, VA 23451-0656.
Titles:
The Complete Edgar Cayce Readings.

ASAP Systems, (0-922054), 410 May Ave., No. 2, Santa Cruz, CA 95060-2968 Tel 408-476-3935; FAX: 408-476-9765.
Titles:
!Checkout.
Inventory System: !Assetrac - Bar Code Asset.

ASCP Pr., Div. of American Society of Clinical Pathologists, (0-89189), 2100 W. Harrison St., Chicago, IL 60612 Tel 312-738-1336; Toll free: 800-621-4142; FAX: 312-738-1619.
Titles:
Banko (Order).
Bleedo.
Casequiz.
ConverSIon: A Program for Medical SI Unit Conversion.
D.Tree.
Emergency Transfusion.
Intellipath.
Reporter.

ASM International, (0-87170), 9639 Kinsman Rd., Materials Park, OH 44073 Tel 216-338-5151; FAX: 216-338-4634. Do not confuse with ASM International, Inc. in Fort Lauderdale, FL.
Titles:
Comprehensive Index to ASM CD-ROM.
EnPlot.
Rover Electronic DataBooks for Corrosion & Chemical Resistance.

ASP, (1-878109), P.O. Box 1480, Hudson, OH 44236-0980 Tel 412-422-4134.
Titles:
ASP: The Integrity Shell.
MIT: Menu Integrity Tool.
Pat Mat: Pattern Matcher.

ASW Software, (0-922059), 117 Fairview Ave., Painted Post, NY 14870 Tel 607-936-8390.
Titles:
Water & Sewer Biller.

a/Soft Development, Inc., 1 Executive Pk. Dr., Bedford, NH 03110-6913 Tel 603-666-6699; FAX: 603-666-6460.
Titles:
nu/TPU.

A-Systems Corp., (0-922060), 339 E. 3900 S., Suite 101, Salt Lake City, UT 84107-1677 Tel 801-265-0600; Toll free: 800-365-6790; FAX: 801-265-0691.
Titles:
Contractor Three Lite.
Contractor III Plus.
Contractor III Standard.

AT&T Multimedia Software Solutions, Div. of AT&T, (1-886247), 2701 Maitland Ctr. Pkwy., Maitland, FL 32751 Tel 512-834-6935; Toll free: 800-448-6727; FAX: 800-826-5399.
Titles:
AT&T Multimedia Designer for Windows.
Multimedia Creation Collection Images CD.
Panorama.
RIO.

A.U. Software, (0-922068), 1735 S St., NW, Washington, DC 20009 Tel 202-265-6443; FAX: 202-265-6245.
Titles:
TestLab 2000.

AV Systems, Inc., (0-918547), Box 60533, Santa Barbara, CA 93160 Tel 805-569-1618.
Titles:
BASIC RAM Database.
The Big Apple.
The Car Disk.
Chess.
Concentration.
Convoy 1942.
Desert War 1991.
Dungeon of Danger.
Financial Analyst.
Football Simulation.
Gold Rush.
Golf Simulation.
The Graphic Programmer.
Halley's Comet.
Home Money Manager.
LifeGuard.
Nuclear Power Plant.
Stock Trader.

AWWA Research Foundation, (0-915295), 6666 W. Quincy Ave., Denver, CO 80235 Tel 303-794-7711.
Titles:
Electronic Watershed Management Reference Manual.

Aatrix Software, P.O. Box 5359, Grand Forks, ND 58206 Tel 701-746-7202; Toll free: 800-426-0854; FAX: 701-746-4249.
Titles:
Aatrix Payroll.
Checkwriter Pro.
TimeCard.
TimeMinder.
Ultimate Payroll.

Abacus, (0-916439; 1-55755), 5370 52nd St., SE, Grand Rapids, MI 49512 Tel 616-698-0330; Toll free: 800-451-4319 (orders only); FAX: 616-698-0325.
Titles:
CADPAK-64 Enhanced.
PowerLedger.

Abacus Concepts, Inc., (0-944800), 1918 Bonita Ave., Berkeley, CA 94704-1014 Tel 510-540-1949; Toll free: 800-666-7828; FAX: 510-540-0260.
Titles:
StatView.
SuperANOVA.

Abacus Data Systems, Inc., (1-877903), 6725 Mesa Ridge Rd., No. 204, San Diego, CA 92121 Tel 619-452-4245; Toll free: 800-726-3339; FAX: 619-452-2073. Do not confuse with Abacus Data Systems, Greensburg, PA.
Titles:
Abacus Law Plus.
FastPlan III.

Abacus, Inc., 1032 Irving St., No. 622, San Francisco, CA 94122-2200 Tel 415-759-9508.
Titles:
BeckerTools 4: Windows Disk & File Management Utilities.
MacPromo.
Marketing Management System.
No Mouse for Windows: Run Windows Without a Mouse!

Abiogenesis Software, P.O. Box 9, 1220 Central Ave., Bellingham, WA 98227-0009 Tel 360-650-9335.
Titles:
Lexicographer: Multimedia Dictionary Authoring.

Abracadata, Ltd., (0-939377), P.O. Box 2440, Eugene, OR 97402 Tel 503-342-3030; Toll free: 800-451-4871; FAX: 503-683-1925.
Titles:
Design Estimator.
Design Your Own Home, Architecture.
Design Your Own Home, Interiors.
Design Your Own Home: Landscape.
Design Your Own Home, Landscape: Landscape.
Design Your Own Railroad.
Design Your Own Train.
Everybody's Planner.
Graphics Supermarket with Source Code.
Mighty Draw.
SPROUT!
Sprout!: The Graphic Vegetable Garden Design Program.
Train Engineer.

Abraxas Software, Inc., 5530 SW Kelly, Portland, OR 97201 Tel 503-244-5253; Toll free: 800-347-5214; FAX: 503-244-8375.
Titles:
CODECHECK.
HyperTalk Language Toolkit.
MacYACC.
PCYACC: Professional Language Development Toolkit.

Absoft Corp., 2781 Bond St., Rochester Hills, MI 48309 Tel 810-853-0050; FAX: 810-853-0108.
Titles:
Absoft F77 SDK for Power Macintosh.
Absoft Fortran 90 for Power Macintosh.
Absoft FORTRAN 77 for 386/486.
Absoft FORTRAN 77.
FORTRAN 77.
MacFortran.
MacFortran II.
MacFortran/020.
Object-Oriented FORTRAN 77 for NeXT.

Absolut Software, (0-927965), 90 Rowe St., Auburndale, MA 02166-1531 Tel 617-964-3550; FAX: 617-964-2709.
Titles:
Absolut: Business & Inventory Management Software.
SMART: Sales Management Activity Reporting & Telemarketing.

Absolute Solutions, Inc., P.O. Box 232400, Encinitas, CA 92023-2400 Tel 619-966-8000; Toll free: 800-633-7666; 800-458-3399 (in California).
Titles:
Computerized Classic Accounting.
Computerized Classic Bookkeeping.

PUBLISHER/TITLE INDEX

AbTech Corp., 508 Dale Ave., Charlottesville, VA 22903 Tel 804-977-0686; FAX: 804-977-9615.
Titles:
AIM Problem Solver.

Academic Pr., Inc., Subs. of Harcourt Brace & Co., (0-12), 525 B St., Ste. 1900, San Diego, CA 92101 Tel 619-231-0926; FAX: 619-699-6715; Orders to: 6277 Sea Harbor Dr., Orlando, FL 32887; Toll free: 800-321-5068.
Titles:
Brain Browser.
The Desktop Fractal Design System.
The Desktop Fractal Design System: Macintosh Version.
Fractal Attraction: A Fractal Design System for the Macintosh.
HP 48SX Engineering Mathematics Library.
HYPERSTAT: Macintosh Hypermedia for Analyzing Data & Learning Statistics.
Microbe Base.
Molecular Graphics on the IBM PC Microcomputer.
TeXHelp: The On-Line TeX Handbook.

Academic Therapy Pubns., Inc., (0-87879; 1-57128), 20 Commercial Blvd., Novato, CA 94949-6191 Tel 415-883-3314; Toll free: 800-422-7249; FAX: 415-883-3720.
Titles:
Angling for Words in Bits & Bytes - Advance Level.
Angling for Words in Bits & Bytes - Intermediate Level.
Angling for Words in Bits & Bytes-Beginner's Program.
Typing Keys to Computer Ease.
WISC-III Compilation: What to Do Now That You Know the Score.
WISC-Three Compilation: What to Do Now That You Know the Score.

Accent Software, Inc., (0-922088), 4546 El Camino Real, Suite S, Los Altos, CA 94022 Tel 415-949-2711; FAX: 415-949-2716.
Titles:
TGS: The Graphic Solution.

Access Softek, (1-878687), 2550 9th St., Suite 206, Berkeley, CA 94710 Tel 510-848-0606; FAX: 510-654-4077.
Titles:
Dragnet.
Prompt! 1.2.

Access Software, Inc., 4910 W. Amelia Earhart Dr., Salt Lake City, UT 84116 Tel 801-359-2900; Toll free: 800-800-4880; FAX: 801-359-2968.
Titles:
Amazon: Guardians of Eden.
Links 386 Pro.
Mean Streets.
Under a Killing Moon.

ACCI Business Systems, Inc., (0-927962), 1415 Wagon Gap Trail, Houston, TX 77090-1801 Tel 713-872-4134; Toll free: 800-448-0601; FAX: 713-872-4908.
Titles:
ACCI Project Management Accounting System.

Accolade, Inc., (0-935345; 0-929579; 1-56042), 5300 Stevens Creek Blvd., San Jose, CA 95129 Tel 408-985-1700; FAX: 408-246-0885.
Titles:
California Challenge: The Collection.
The Duel: Test Drive II - The Collection.
Elvira II: The Jaws of Cerberus.
Elvira: Mistress of the Dark.
European Challenge: Test Drive II Scenery Disk - The Collection.
Grand Prix Circuit.
HardBall!
Hardball II.
Hoverforce.
Ishido: The Way of Stones.
Jack Nicklaus Course Designers Clip Art.
Jack Nicklaus' Greatest 18 Holes of Golf.
Jack Nicklaus Presents: The Great Courses of the U.S. Open.
Jack Nicklaus Presents the International Course Disk.
Jack Nicklaus Presents the Major Championship Courses of 1989.
Jack Nicklaus' Unlimited Golf & Course Design.
Les Manley: Lost in L.A.
Mean 18: Ultimate Golf.
Mike Dipka Ultimate Football.
The Muscle Cars: The Duel - Test Drive II Car Disk.
Road & Car Add-On Disk One: Test Drive III: The Passion.
Star Control.
The Supercars: The Collection.
Test Drive.
Test Drive III: The Passion.

Accounting Professionals Software, Inc., (0-927455), 4210 W. Vickery, Fort Worth, TX 76107 Tel 817-738-3122; FAX: 817-731-9704.
Titles:
Business Planning Model for Forecasts & Projections.
Business Valuation.
Cash Flow Planner.
Corporate Tax Planner.
Estate Tax Planner.
Financial Decisions.
Interest-NDL-Form 2210 Calculators.
Personal Financial Planner.
Real Estate Planner.

AccuTech Systems Corp., 125 E. Charles St., Suite 210, Muncie, IN 47305-2478 Tel 317-284-8213; Toll free: 800-686-0470; FAX: 317-284-3566.
Titles:
AccuFarm-MGR.
AccuTrust.

Activision, Inc., (0-922108; 0-87321), 11601 Wilshire Blvd., Suite 1000, Los Angeles, CA 90025 Tel 310-473-9200; FAX: 310-479-4005.
Titles:
Action Pack.
Activision Action Pack 2600: 7 Pack.
Atari Action Pack.
Atari 2600 Action Pack.
Atari 2600 Action Pack: 7 Pack.
Ballyhoo.
Battletech.
Beyond Zork.
Bureaucracy.
C-64 15 Pack.
Championship Baseball.
Championship Basketball.
Championship Golf.
Cornerstone.
Cutthroats.
Deadline.
Earthworm Jim.
Enchanter.
Enchanter Trilogy.
Floor Display.
Fooblitzky.
Game Pack II.
Gee Bee Air Rally.
GFL Championship Football.
The Great Game.
The Hitchhiker's Guide to the Galaxy.
Hockey Drome.
Hollywood Hijinx.
Infidel.
Infocom: Science Fiction Collection.
Inforcom: Adventure Collection.
Inforcom: Comedy Collection.
Inforcom: Fantasy Collection.
Inforcom: Mystery Collection.
Leather Goddesses of Phobos.
Lost Treasures.
Lost Treasures Hintbook.
Lost Treasures II.
The Lurking Horror.
Mac Best Sellers.
Mac Bestsellers.
MechWarrior 2.
MechWarrior 2: Australian Version.
MechWarrior 2 Ghost Bear Clan's Legacy.
MechWarrior 2: Singapore Version.
MechWarrior 2: U. S. Version.
Mighty Morphin Power Rangers Coloring Screens Box.
Mighty Morphin Power Rangers Coloring Screens Book.
Mighty Morphin Power Rangers Jigsaw Puzzle Book.
Mighty Morphin Power Rangers Print Kit Book.
Mighty Morphin Power Rangers Screen Scenes Box.
Mighty Morphy Power Rangers T. B. D. Book.
Mighty Morphy Power Rangers T. B. D. Box.
A Mind Forever Voyaging.
Moonmist.
Movies.
Movies Pack.
Muppet Treasure Island.
The Music Studio.
Net Mech Eight-Player Pack PCCD.
NetMech Eight-Player Pack.
Nord & Bert Couldn't Make Head or Tail of It: Eight Tales of Cliches, Spoonerisms, & Other Verbal Trickery.
Paparazzi.
Paparazzi Tales of Tinseltown.
Paparazzi Tales of Tinseltown: 7 Pack.
Pitfall.
Pitfall, Mayan Adventure with Hintbook.
Pitfall Strategy Guide.
Planetfall.
Plundered Hearts.
Powergames III.
R. Zork.
R. Zork Anthology.
R. Zork CD.
R. Zork CD Mac OEM.
R. Zork CD Mac with Anthology & Hintbook.
R. Zork CD OEM.
R. Zork MPEG CD OEM.
R. Zork Nemesis.
R. Zork with Anthology.
R. Zork with Anthology & Hintbook.
R. Zork with Hintbook.
Sacred Ground.
Santa Fe Mysteries.
Sargon V.
Sci-Fi.
Sci-Fi Pack.
Seastalker.
Shanghai Great Moments.
Shanghai Great Moments Demo.
Shanghai Great Moments (Saturn).
Shanghai II.
Shanghai Triple Threat (Saturn).
Sherlock: Riddle of Crown Jewels.
Simon Hintbook.
Simon the Sorcerer.
Simon the Sorcerer with Hintbook.
Sorcerer.
Spellbreaker.
Sports.
Sports Pack.
Spycraft.
Starcross.
Stationfall.
Suspect.
Suspended.
Time Commando.
Trinity.
Wishbringer.
The Witness.
Zork Hintbook.

Zork I: The Great Underground Adventure.
Zork II: The Wizard of Frobozz.
Zork III: The Dungeon Master.

Actuarial Micro Software, (0-922109), 353 Jonestown Rd., No. 512, Winston-Salem, NC 27104 Tel 910-759-3463.
Titles:
Monte Carlo Simulations (Advanced Version).

Acucobol, Inc., 7950 Silverton Ave., Suite 201, San Diego, CA 92126 Tel 619-689-7220; Toll free: 800-262-6585; FAX: 619-566-3071.
Titles:
Acuview.

Acumen Software Products, 8020 Barocco Dr., Harahan, LA 70123-4417.
Titles:
VSTRESS3.

Adapt, Inc., (0-918775), 616 N. Portia St., Nokomis, FL 34275 Tel 813-484-4686.
Titles:
MMED 3780.

Adaptive Software, 950 Skokie Blvd., Suite 310, Northbrook, IL 60062-4017 Tel 708-291-1413.
Titles:
Expense Account Manager.

Addison-Wesley Publishing Co., Inc., (0-201), 1 Jacob Way, Reading, MA 01867 Tel 617-944-3700; Toll free: 800-447-2226; FAX: 617-942-1117.
Titles:
The Antagonists.
Applesoft BASIC Toolbox.
BASIC Subroutines.
Energy Monitor: Energy Use Monitoring System.
The Fellowship of the Ring: A Software Adventure.
Gas Man.
HyperComposer.
Micro Decision Support System Analysis.
Micro-Decision Support System Finance.
Micro-Dynamo: System Dynamics Modeling Language.
Microcomputer Graphics.
MicroTEX.
MSX Software Sampler, Vol. 1: Entertainment & Home Applications.
MSX Software Sampler, Vol. 2: Business & Scientific Applications.
The Programmer's Online Companion.
Puppy Love.
The Secret of Arendarvon Castle.
Teach Yourself Essentials of Accounting.
Textures.
Wordbench.

Adisoft, Inc., P.O. Box 2094, 1298 E. 14th St., No. 322, San Leandro, CA 94577 Tel 510-483-5605; FAX: 510-483-7504.
Titles:
EasyShare.
Expense Report!

Adler Computer Technology, (0-922120), 14914 Mayall St., Mission Hills, CA 91345-2811 Tel 818-893-4196.
Titles:
Close.

Admark Systems, Inc., (0-922158), 2500 Mt. Moriah Rd., Suite F720, Memphis, TN 38115-1515 Tel 901-795-8200.
Titles:
"Agency" Advertising Management System.

Adobe Systems, Inc., 1585 Charleston Rd., Mountain View, CA 94039-7900 Tel 415-986-6530; Toll free: 800-344-8335; FAX: 415-961-3769.
Titles:
Adobe Illustrator Collector's Edition.
Adobe Illustrator: Windows Version.
Adobe Illustrator: with Adobe Type Manager.
Adobe Streamline.
Adobe Type Manager.
Adobe Type Reunion.
Adobe Type Set Packages.
Adobe TypeAlign.
Adobe Typeface Library.
Publishing Packs.
Smart Art.

Adra Systems, Inc., 2 Executive Dr., Chelmsford, MA 01854 Tel 508-937-3700; Toll free: 800-800-3702; FAX: 508-453-2462.
Titles:
CADRA Design Drafting Mechanical Design Software.
CADRA-NC: Numerical Control Graphics Programming Language.
CADRA-View: View Only Software for Engineer Drawing.

Advan Language Designs, P.O. Box 159, Baldwin, KS 66006 Tel 913-594-3551.
Titles:
Screen Design.
Utility Programs.

Advance Business Computer Corp., (0-917671), 1 Habbard Way., P.O. Box 654, Helena, MT 59624 Tel 406-443-2449.
Titles:
R.SIMS: The Retail Sales & Inventory Management System.
Versa-Till.

Advance Computer Concepts, Inc., 4832 Greencroft Rd., Sarasota, FL 34235-8234.
Titles:
Advanced Professional Services Monitor.

Advance Multimedia, 26600 Telegraph Rd., Suite 181, Southfield, MI 48034 Tel 810-350-2130.
Titles:
All-Time Favorite Dances: Macintosh CD-ROM.

Advanced A.I. Systems, P.O. Box 39-0360, Mountain View, CA 94039 Tel 415-948-8658; FAX: 415-948-2486.
Titles:
AAIS Full Control Prolog.

Advanced Analytical/CharterHouse, (0-922121), 22961 De Kalb Dr., Calabasas, CA 91302 Tel 818-591-0160; Toll free: 800-899-2227.
Titles:
AA Computer Systems Accounts Payable.
AA Computer Systems Club Accounts Receivable with Billing.
AA Computer Systems General Ledger.
CharterHouse Accounts Payable.
CharterHouse Accounts Receivable with Billing & Inventory.
CharterHouse Accounts Receivable with Billing.
CharterHouse Fixed Assets.
CharterHouse General Ledger.
CharterHouse Manufacturing Inventory/Bill of Materials.
CharterHouse Order Entry.
CharterHouse Payroll.
Employee Scheduling & Labor Costing.
QuikCost.
Restaurant Accounts Payable.
Restaurant & Bar Inventory.
Restaurant General Ledger.
Restaurant Inventory, Menu & Cost Control.
Restaurant Payroll with Tip Allocation.
Retail Ice Cream Inventory & Cost Control.

Advanced Computer Innovations, Inc., (0-923026), 30 Burncoat Way, Pittsford, NY 14534-2216 Tel 716-383-1939; FAX: 716-383-8428.
Titles:
R-Doc/X.
WordPort.

Advanced Concepts, Inc., (0-922131), 4129 N. Port Washington Ave., Milwaukee, WI 53212-1029 Tel 414-963-0999; FAX: 414-963-2090. Do not confuse with Advanced Concepts, West Palm Beach, FL.
Titles:
Advanced Concepts Accounts Payable.
Advanced Concepts Payroll.
General Ledger Multiple Company Reporting & Posting.
Inventory.
Multiple Bank Account Reconciliation.
Sales Order/Accounts Receivable: Accounts Receivable Service Billing.

Advanced Data Systems, Inc., (0-922134), 4010 Long Beach Blvd., Long Beach, CA 90807 Tel 310-426-8155.
Titles:
AVANTI.
General Accounting.
Job Cost I.
Job Cost II.
Manufacturing Job Cost II.
Order Distribution.
Payroll.

Advanced Financial Planning, (0-917263), 20922 Paseo Olma, El Toro, CA 92630 Tel 714-855-1578.
Titles:
College Funding.
Life Insurance Planning.
Retirement Planning.

Advanced Financial Planning Group, Inc., (0-929416), P.O. Box 817, New London, NH 03257; Rte. 114, New London, NH 03257 Tel 603-526-6885.
Titles:
College & Retirement Planning.
Federal Income Tax Planning for 1990 & 1991.
Personal Financial Planning Made Easy.

Advanced Graphics Software, Inc., 5825 Avenida Encinas, Suite 105, Carlsbad, CA 92008-4404 Tel 619-931-1919; FAX: 408-749-0511.
Titles:
Slide Write Presenter.
SlideWrite Plus.

Advanced Logical Software, 9903 Santa Monica Blvd., Suite 108, Beverly Hills, CA 90212 Tel 213-653-5786.
Titles:
Anatool.
Blue for System Flowcharts.
Blue/60: Data Modeling.

Advanced Micro Supplies, Inc., 780 Montague Expressway, No. 205, San Jose, CA 95131 Tel 408-383-0800.
Titles:
Scriptures & the Heritage of the Sikhs.

Advanced Systems Concepts, Inc., P.O. Box 6309, Altadena, CA 91001-2463 Tel 818-791-0983.
Titles:
ASCII Printer Sharing Switches.

PUBLISHER/TITLE INDEX

ALDUS CORP.

Advantage International, Inc., (1-56756), 14546 Bruce B. Downs Blvd., Tampa, FL 33613-2701 Tel 813-977-5739; Toll free: 800-837-8636; FAX: 813-972-7986.
Titles:
Big Brother.
C.A.R.-FREE.
Corporate Car Rental Sales Force Automator.
Fraternal Software: Complete Membership Management.
INFOQUEST Services Software: Student Services Software - Educational.
KEYMATE-RIDEMATE: Employee Services Software.
LaBrow.
LeadMan: Lead Management Software.
LISTMAN: Telemarketing & Direct Mail List Management.
Multiple Organizational Management.
Product Controller.
Quote Builder.
Resource Management System.
Safe Update.
Student Organization Software: Complete Membership Management.
TimeTrax for Legal Professionals.
TimeTrax for Time & Billing Professionals.

Advent Software, Inc., (0-931187), 301 Brannan St., Suite 600, San Francisco, CA 94107 Tel 415-543-7696; Toll free: 800-685-7688; FAX: 415-543-5070.
Titles:
Axys.

Aeolus Software, P.O. Box 11915, Saint Paul, MN 55111-0915 Tel 612-699-8672.
Titles:
Builder.

AeroHydro, Inc., (0-924909), P.O. Box 684, Main St., Southwest Harbor, ME 04679 Tel 207-244-7347; FAX: 207-244-7249.
Titles:
C3D.
FL/2B.
HYDRO-1.
HYDRO-2.
OFE3: Offset File Editor.
Sailplan-1.
WSE-1.

Affinity Microsystems, Ltd., 1900 Folsom St., Suite 205, Boulder, CO 80302-5723 Tel 303-442-4840; Toll free: 800-367-6771; FAX: 303-442-4999.
Titles:
AffiniFile.
Tempo EZ.
Tempo 2 Plus.

Afterthought Engineering, (0-922166), 7266 Courtney Dr., San Diego, CA 92111 Tel 619-279-2868.
Titles:
Wiremaster.

AG PLUS Consulting, (0-928480), 410 1/2 Second St., Ida Grove, IA 51445 Tel 712-364-2135.
Titles:
AG COUNT Extra.

AgData, (0-922020), 891 Hazel St., Gridley, CA 95948 Tel 916-846-6203.
Titles:
AgData Accounts Payable.
AgData Accounts Payable (Cash Basis).
AgData Accounts Receivable.
AgData Blue Skies Cost Accounting.
AgData Blue Skies General Ledger.
AgData Blue Skies Payroll.
AgData Check Reconciliation.
AgData Cost Accounting 1.
AgData Cost Accounting 2.
AgData Database Import-Export Utility.
AgData Enterprise Power Budgeting.
AgData Farm Labor Contractor's Payroll.
AgData General Ledger.
AgData Inventory.
AgData Land Leveling.
AgData Magnetic Media Reporting.
AgData Payroll Checkwriting.
AgData Payroll Reports.
AgData Small Farm Series.

Agents Processing Systems, Inc., Subs. of GAINSCO, 500 Commerce St., Fort Worth, TX 76102-5439 Tel 817-336-2500; Toll free: 800-438-4246; FAX: 817-335-1230.
Titles:
APS: Agents Processing Systems.
APS Premium Finance System.

Agile Manufacturing Enterprise Forum, (1-885166), 200 W. Packer Ave., 3rd Flr., Bethlehem, PA 18015 Tel 610-758-5510; FAX: 610-694-0542.
Titles:
Ramping Up: Becoming Agile by 2000: 1996 Agility Conference Proceedings.

Agricultural Software Consultants, Inc., (0-917265), P.O. Box 32, Kingsville, TX 78364 Tel 512-595-1937; FAX: 512-595-0446.
Titles:
Animal Data Disks.
BEEFPRO (Windows & DOS).
EGGPRO (Windows & DOS).
MILKPRO.
MINI-MAX.
MINI-MAX for Windows.
MIXIT Student Version.
MIXIT-2.
MIXIT-2+.
MIXIT-3.
MIXIT-3 plus.
MIXIT-4.
MULTIMIXIT.
PARAMETRICS.
PRICE-IT.
TAG-IT.

Ahead Designs, (0-922181), 1827 Hawk View Dr., Encinitas, CA 92024 Tel 619-942-5860; FAX: 619-436-4071.
Titles:
Spide Attack.

Ahead, Inc., (1-886022), 19A Crosby Dr., Suite 300, Bedford, MA 01730-1419 Tel 617-271-0900; FAX: 617-271-0711.
Titles:
Virtual Guitar.

Ajida Technologies, Inc., 613 Fourth St., Santa Rosa, CA 95404 Tel 707-545-7777; FAX: 707-575-3210.
Titles:
PlotView.

AK-D Software, (1-878509), P.O. Box 71912, Fairbanks, AK 99707 Tel 907-457-5303.
Titles:
Alaska Gunlog.
Soft Ledger.

Aker Corp., 1200 Main St., Irvine, CA 92714 Tel 714-250-1718; Toll free: 800-345-6244; FAX: 714-250-7404.
Titles:
Magic PC.

Alamo Publishing, (1-880075), 7083 Commerce Cir., Suite G, Pleasanton, CA 94588 Tel 415-463-3798.
Titles:
Quick Quant Plus.

Alcatel Servcom, P.O. Box 29039, Phoenix, AZ 85038 Tel 602-894-7000; Toll free: 800-448-8669 (Orders, outside Arizona).
Titles:
More About Lotus 1-2-3 Commands.

Alcor Systems, (0-922188), 1132 Commerce Dr., Richardson, TX 75081 Tel 214-238-8554; 800 W. Garland Ave., No. 204, Garland, TX 75040.
Titles:
Alcor Pascal.
Alcor Pascal & Advanced Development Package.
C Language.
Multi-Basic.

Alden Computer Systems Corp., (0-922190), P.O. Box 172, Kingfield, ME 04947-0172.
Titles:
APPS.

Aldridge Co., The, 2500 CityWest Blvd., Suite 575, Houston, TX 77042 Tel 713-953-1940; Toll free: 800-548-5019; FAX: 713-953-0806.
Titles:
Cache86 for DOS.
Cache86 for Windows & DOS.
CD-Cabin Pro: For Windows with Link'n Logging.
CD-Cabin: With Link'n'Logging for Windows.
PreCursor: Menu Program.
Tree86: The Hard Disk Management System.

Aldus Corp., (0-941719; 1-56026), 411 First Ave. S., Seattle, WA 98104-2871 Tel 206-622-5500.
Titles:
Aldus Dictionary for Macintosh.
Aldus Dictionary for Windows.
Aldus PageMaker for Macintosh.
Aldus PageMaker for Windows.
Aldus TechNotes for Aldus FreeHand for the Macintosh.
Commerical Printing Guide for Aldus FreeHand.
Kodak Precision Color Configure Users Guide: For Use with Aldus PhotoStyler.
Mac Aldus Home Publisher: Domestic.
Mac ChartMaker: Domestic.
Mac Classic Art, Vol. 2: Domestic.
Mac COSA After Effects: Domestic.
Mac DateBook Pro: Domestic.
Mac Fetch: Domestic.
Mac Fetch: International English.
Mac Fetch Trial Version: Domestic.
Mac FreeHand: Domestic.
Mac FreeHand: German.
Mac FreeHand: International English.
Mac FreeHand Japanese.
Mac FreeHand Korean.
Mac Gallery Effects User Manual.
Mac IntelliDraw: Domestic.
Mac PageMaker: Danish.
Mac PageMaker: Domestic.
Mac PageMaker: Dutch.
Mac PageMaker: Finnish.
Mac PageMaker: French.
Mac PageMaker: German.
Mac PageMaker: International English.
Mac PageMaker: Italian.
Mac PageMaker: Japanese.
Mac PageMaker: Norwegian.
Mac PageMaker: Spanish.
Mac PageMaker: Swedish.
Mac Persuasion: Domestic.
Mac PressWise: Domestic.
Mac PressWise: French.
Mac PressWise: German.
Mac Print to Video: Domestic.
Mac TouchBase Pro: Domestic.
Mac TrapWise: Domestic.

ALDUS CORP. (CONSUMER DIV.)

Mac TypeTwister: Domestic.
PageMaker: Korean.
PC Classic Art, Vol. 2: Domestic.
PC Gallery Effects User Manual.
PC InfoPublisher Database Edition.
PC IntelliDraw: Domestic.
PC PageMaker: Danish.
PC PageMaker: Domestic.
PC PageMaker: Dutch.
PC PageMaker: Finnish.
PC PageMaker: French.
PC PageMaker: German.
PC PageMaker: International English.
PC PageMaker: Italian.
PC PageMaker: Japanese.
PC PageMaker: Norwegian.
PC PageMaker: Spanish.
PC PageMaker: Swedish.
PC Photo Styler: Domestic.
PC PhotoStyler: French.
PC PhotoStyler: International English.
PC PhotoStyler Special Edition: Domestic.
PC PhotoStyler Special Edition: French.
PC PhotoStyler Special Edition: German.
PC PhotoStyler Special Edition: International English.
PC PhotoStyler Special Edition: Italian.
PC PhotoStyler Special Edition: Spanish.
PC PhotoStyler Trial Version: Domestic.
PC TouchBase: Domestic.
PC TrapWise Trial Version.
PC TypeTwister: Domestic.
PrePrint Japanese.
TrapWise: Domestic.

Aldus Corp. (Consumer Div.), Div. of Aldus Corp., P.O. Box 7900, Mountain View, CA 94039-7900.
Titles:
Aldus Digital Darkroom.
Aldus Gallery Effects: Classic Art, Volume 1.
Aldus IntelliDraw.
Aldus Personal Press.
Aldus Supercard.
Aldus SuperPaint.
DATEBOOK PRO.
TOUCHBASE PRO.

Alfred Publishing Co., Inc., (0-88284), 16380 Roscoe Blvd., Suite 200, Box 10003, Van Nuys, CA 91406-1215 Tel 818-891-5999; Toll free: 800-292-6122; FAX: 818-891-2182.
Titles:
Alfred's Adult Piano Theory: Level 1.
Alfred's Basic Band Computer Tutor.
Alfred's Basic Piano Theory: Levels 3-5.
Basic Piano Theory Level 1A, 1B & 2.
Music Achievement Series.
Music Made Easy.
Practical Theory.

Algo-Rhythm Software, 176 Mineola Blvd., Mineola, NY 11501 Tel 516-294-7590; Toll free: 800-645-4441.
Titles:
Cantus, the Music Improviser.

Algorithmic Assocs., 135 Everett St., Natick, MA 01760 Tel 617-237-7226.
Titles:
Animation.

Alisa Systems, Inc., 221 E. Walnut St., Suite 175, Pasadena, CA 91101 Tel 818-792-9474; Toll free: 800-628-3274 (Sales); FAX: 818-792-4068.
Titles:
AlisaMail.

All Easy Software Corp., P.O. Box 667, Dana Point, CA 92629-0667; Toll free: 714-364-2886; FAX: 714-240-7392.
Titles:
Datafax.
DATAFAX: Filing Software.
Hyperfile.
HYPERFILE: Windows Filing Software.

All-Tech Project Management Services, P.O. Box 25244, Rochester, NY 14625 Tel 716-385-3719.
Titles:
All-Tech Project Simulator.
Project Management Advantage.

Allan Computer Products, (0-9629699), P.O. Box 2177, Shawnee Mission, KS 66201; Toll free: 800-374-5725; FAX: 913-384-3451; 4805 W. 65th Terrace, Prairie Village, KS 66208 Tel 913-384-5725.
Titles:
Early Bird.

Alliance Manufacturing Software, (0-925850), P.O. Box 2009, Santa Barbara, CA 93120-2009 Tel 805-565-5126; Toll free: 800-490-2520; FAX: 619-454-3453.
Titles:
A2B: AutoCAD to BMP Interface System.
Bill of Materials Plus (BMP): Engineering Documentation Control System.
DAUDIT - Disk-Based Audit Trail System.
E-Z-CRP: Capacity Requirements Planning System.
E-Z-Lab.
E-Z MRP Junior: Material Requirements Planning System for Small Manufacturers.
E-Z-MRP: Material Requirements Planning System.
E-Z-PI: Physical Inventory System.
E-Z-PO: Purchase Order Module.

Allied Computer Group, (0-923566), P.O. Box 04039, Milwaukee, WI 53204-0039 Tel 414-223-0150.
Titles:
DOS Partner.

Alligator Technologies, 2900 Bristol St., Suite E101, Costa Mesa, CA 92626 Tel 714-850-9984; FAX: 714-850-9987.
Titles:
Prime Factor FFT for DOS.
Prime Factor FFT for Windows.

Allotype Typographics, 221 S. Washington St., Ypsilanti, MI 48197-8410.
Titles:
Allotype Typographics.

Alloy Computer Products, Inc., (0-922201), 25 Porter Rd., Littleton, MA 01460 Tel 508-486-0001; FAX: 508-486-4108.
Titles:
MultiNode.

Allyn & Bacon, Inc., Div. of Paramount Publishing, (0-205), 160 Gould St., Needham Heights, MA 02194-2310 Tel 617-455-1200; FAX: 617-455-1294; Orders to: Paramount Publishing (orders for College & Longwood Divs.), 200 Old Tappan Rd., Old Tappan, NJ 07675 Tel 201-767-5937; Toll free: 800-223-1360; Orders to: Allyn & Bacon (Individual purchases), 111 Tenth St., Des Moines, IA 50309 Tel 515-284-6751; Toll free: 800-666-9433.
Titles:
Personal STORM.

Alpenglow, (0-9643794), 14118 168th Ave., NE, Woodinville, WA 98072 Tel 206-485-3222; FAX: 206-485-3250.
Titles:
Safari.

Alpha Bit Communications, Inc., (0-922202), P.O. Box 20067, Ferndale, MI 48220 Tel 810-548-7643.
Titles:
LazyCalc.
LazyDoc.
LazyMerge.
LazyTab.
LazyType.
LazyWriter.
MULTIDOS.
Proportional Spacing.
Proportional Spacing for C. Itoh F10.
SUM-UP.

Alpha Computer Service, (0-922205), 4530 Eileen Ct., Colorado Springs, CO 80919-3176.
Titles:
ACS Time Series.
For-Winds.
Forlib-Plus.
FORTRAN Scientific Subroutine Package.
The Statistician PC.
Strings & Things.

Alpha Microsystems, (0-922211), 3501 Sunflower, Santa Ana, CA 92704 Tel 714-957-8500; Toll free: 800-253-3434.
Titles:
CaseLode (FKA PROMIS).

Alphametrics Corp., P.O. Box 2566, Bala Cynwyd, PA 19004; FAX: 610-667-8390; 111 Presidential Blvd., Suite 239, Bala Cynwyd, PA 19004 Tel 610-664-0386.
Titles:
Dataview: Data Management & Analysis Package.
Dataview Plus: Market Forecasting Package.
Foreign Exchange Dealer Support System: FXAT.
Modler Blue: Advanced Regression Package.
Modler MBA: Business Analysis Package Package.
Modler 100: Economic Finanical Analyses Package.
Modler: Statistical Information & Modelling System System.
Money Market Dealer Support System: FXAT.
Powerstation: Data Analysis Package.
Powerstation: Integrated Research Publishing System.

Alpine Data, Inc., Div. of Analytical Processes Corp., (0-922293), 737 S. Townsend Ave., Montrose, CO 81401 Tel 303-249-1400; Toll free: 800-525-1040; FAX: 303-249-8511.
Titles:
ASSET/PACK: Fixed Asset Manager.
FILMPATH: Audio Visual Scheduling.
OIL/PACK: Bulk Oil & Gas Billing & Inventory.
SKI-PACK: Ski Rental & Inventory.
TAX/PACK: Professional 1040.

Alpine Datasystems, Inc., Affil. of Teamco, (0-928390), 7320 SW Hunziker Rd., No. 310, Portland, OR 97223 Tel 503-624-0121; Toll free: 800-547-1837; FAX: 503-620-7817.
Titles:
Alpine Legal Management: Time Billing.
Alpine Project Time Management for Architects & Engineers: Time-Billing.

Alsek Productions, Inc., 5051 W. Boston Way, Chandler, AZ 85226 Tel 602-961-3686.
Titles:
Techman Volume One: Vol. 1.

PUBLISHER/TITLE INDEX

ALSoft, Inc., P.O. Box 927, Spring, TX 77383-0927 Tel 713-353-4090.
Titles:
Dietician.
DiskExpress II.
Font/DA Juggler Plus.
MacExpress.
MasterJuggler.
MultiDisk.
ProLink.

Alsys, Inc., 67 S. Bedford St., Burlington, MA 01803-5152 Tel 617-270-0030; FAX: 617-270-6882.
Titles:
Lessons on Ada.
Macintosh II A/UX Ada Compilation System & Toolset.
OS/2 Ada Compilation System & Toolset.
386 DOS Ada Compiler.
386 Unix Ada Compilation System & Toolset.
286 DOS Ada Compilation System & Toolset.
You Know Fortran-Ada Is Simple.

Alternate Source, The, (0-915363), 8500 S. Countyline Rd., Riga, MI 49276 Tel 517-486-2235; Toll free: 800-253-3200, Ext. 700.
Titles:
ABASIC Utility Pak.
Advanced BASIC Faster & Better.
The Adventure System.
ALE.
Alpha Window.
Alternate BASIC.
BAS34 Conversion Utility.
BAS43.
CHEKBOOK.
CLAN.
Cribbage.
Dennis Allen's ABASIC Combo.
DOStamer.
EDM Macro Editor.
EDM: The Programmable File Editor.
EDX.
GW-Convert.
HYPERCROSS.
HYPERZAP.
InfoScan.
INSIGHT.
ISAR.
LTERM4.
Mailcall.
The Memory Disk Driver: NEW-DOS/80.
Micro Memo.
Modem 80.
MODULA-2 for CP/M.
MultiDOS.
PLOT80.
Real Estate Investment Analysis.
REF.
Screen Edit.
Speak.
Spellbound.
Statement Balancer.
SuperScripsit Printer Driver.
Survey Analyst.
TAS Order Entry System.
The TAS Public Domain Software Library.
TAS Utility Package.
TASORT.
Terminal Emulation System.
Tiny Pay.
Turbo Charge.
UNIKEY.
Variable Finder.
VIDEO4.
Wizard's Castle.
ZEN.
ZMAIL.

Altos Computer Systems, (0-922231), 2641 Orchard Pkwy., San Jose, CA 95134 Tel 408-946-6700; Toll free: 800-258-6787.
Titles:
Altos Accountant Level III.
Altos Executive Financial Planner.
Altos Executive Word Processor.
AOM: Altos Office Manager Suite.
Informix SQL.

Altsys Corp., (1-881231), 269 W. Renner Rd., Richardson, TX 75080 Tel 214-680-2060; FAX: 214-680-0537.
Titles:
EPS Exchange.
Fontastic Plus.
Fontographer.
Metamorphosis Professional.

American Automation, (0-922239), 14281 Chambers Rd., Tustin, CA 92680-6909 Tel 714-731-1661.
Titles:
C-Language Cross Compilers: A-554.
Relocatible Macro Cross Assembler: AA-555.

American Avicultural Art & Science, (0-922238), 3268 Watson Rd., Saint Louis, MO 63139 Tel 314-645-4431.
Titles:
Bird Classification.
Chartics: Business-Science Graphic System.

American Chemical Society, Div. of ACS Bks. & Software, (0-8412), 1155 16th St., NW, Washington, DC 20036 Tel 202-872-4363; Toll free: 800-227-5558 (orders); FAX: 202-872-6067. Do not confuse with ACS Publishing Co., San Diego, CA.
Titles:
ChemStock: Database Management for Chemical Inventory.
NanoVision: Molecular Presentation Graphics.
Principles of Environmental Sampling.
UniVersions.

American ComVision, Inc., (0-923680), 9974 Scripps Ranch Blvd., Suite 21, San Diego, CA 92131-1899 Tel 619-566-8537.
Titles:
PLAN Strategist: Strategic Planning for Competitive Advantage.
PLAN Tactician: Business Planning for Healthcare Organizations.
PROplanner: Business Planning for Growing Companies.
YOURsoft Conversion Process.

American Eagle Software & Computer Hardware, Inc., (0-926199), P.O. Box 46080, Chicago, IL 60646 Tel 312-792-1227; FAX: 312-792-1228.
Titles:
Banner Magic.
The Elysian Fields.
Forms Foundry.
Kukulcan.
Masquerade.
Sherwood Forest.
Zoom Grafix.

American First Day Cover Society, (1-879390), P.O. Box 1335, Maplewood, NJ 07040-0456; 9 Cottage Ct., Maplewood, NJ 07040-2515 Tel 201-762-2012.
Titles:
First Days Cumulative Index, 1955-1991.

American Fundware, Inc., Div. of The Flagship Group, (0-928497), 1385 S. Colorado Blvd., Suite 400, Denver, CO 80222 Tel 303-756-3030; Toll free: 800-551-4458; FAX: 303-756-3514.
Titles:
Fundware.

American Geological Institute, (0-913312; 0-922152), 4220 King St., Alexandria, VA 22302-1507 Tel 703-379-2480; FAX: 301-379-7563; Orders to: AGI Publications Ctr., P.O. Box 205, Annapolis Junction, MD 20701 Tel 301-953-1744.
Titles:
Portrait U. S. A. CD-ROM.

American Heart Assn., Inc., (0-87493), 7272 Greenville Ave., Dallas, TX 75231-4596 Tel 214-706-1467.
Titles:
Cholesterol Education Group.

American Institute of Certified Public Accountants, (0-87051), Harborside Financial Ctr., 201 Plaza 3, Jersey City, NJ 07311; Toll free: 800-862-4272 (order dept.).
Titles:
Accountant's Trial Balance (ATB).
ATB Consolidations.
ATB Conversion.
ATB Financial Statements.
ATB Write-Up.
Audit Program Generator.
Depreciation.
Engagement Manager.
Interactive Data Extraction & Analysis.
PFP Partner.

American Institute of Chemical Engineers, (0-8169), 345 E. 47th St., New York, NY 10017 Tel 212-705-7107; FAX: 212-752-3294.
Titles:
Chempat: A Program to Assist Hazard Evaluation & Management.
Safire Computer Program, Tape & Documentation.

American Institute of Small Business, (0-939069), 7515 Wayzata Blvd., Suite 201, Minneapolis, MN 55426 Tel 612-545-7001; Toll free: 800-328-2906; FAX: 612-545-7020.
Titles:
How to Write a Business Plan.
Mergers & Acquisitions.

American Law Institute (ALI) & American Law Institute-American Bar Association (ALI-ABA), (0-8318), 4025 Chestnut St., Philadelphia, PA 19104-3099 Tel 215-243-1600; Toll free: 800-253-6397; FAX: 215-243-1664.
Titles:
Drafting the Federal Complaint, 1991.
Evidence for the Litigator, 1991.
The Hearsay Rule & Its Exceptions, 1991.

American Medical Assn., (0-89970), 515 N. State St., Chicago, IL 60610 Tel 312-464-5000; Toll free: 800-621-8335; FAX: 312-464-5600; Orders to: P.O. Box 109050, Chicago, IL 60610.
Titles:
CPT: Current Procedural Terminology.

American Small Business Computers, Inc., (0-922264), 1 American Way, Pryor, OK 74361-8801 Tel 918-825-7555; FAX: 918-825-6359.
Titles:
DesignCAD (DOS): DesignCAD 2D for DOS.
DesignCAD: The Expert Suite.
DesignCAD Windows: DesignCAD 2D for Windows.
DesignCAD 2D/3D Macintosh.
DesignCAD 3D.
DesignSYM: Professional Symbols Library.

AMERICAN SYSTEMS CORP.

ModelCAD.
ScanPro.
VinylCAD.
VinylCAD Extended Fonts Library.

American Systems Corp., (0-927986), 1632 Denniston Ave., Pittsburgh, PA 15217-1458 Tel 412-421-4446; FAX: 412-421-4446.
Titles:
F & I Billing System.

American Systems Development, (0-922271), P.O. Box 362, Germantown, MD 20874 Tel 301-972-2724.
Titles:
Medical Office Management.

American Training International, Inc., (0-922274), 12638 Beatrice St., Los Angeles, CA 90066 Tel 310-823-1129; Toll free: 800-955-5284; FAX: 310-827-1636.
Titles:
ATI Workshop Course: Lotus 1-2-3, Module 2 (Advanced).
ATI Workshop Course: Lotus 1-2-3, Module 1 (Introductory).
How to Use Apple IIe: Skill Builder Series.
How to Use Your PC/AT.
How to Use Your PC/XT.
How to Use Your PS/2.
LAN Administrators Kit.
MacCoach: How to Use Your Macintosh.
Managing with Lotus 1-2-3.
1-2-3 Support Library.
Teach Yourself BPI General Accounting.
Teach Yourself CP/M.
Teach Yourself dBASE III PLUS.
Teach Yourself dBASE IV.
Teach Yourself DisplayWrite 3.
Teach Yourself DisplayWrite 4.
Teach Yourself DOS.
Teach Yourself Enable.
Teach Yourself Excel.
Teach Yourself Framework.
Teach Yourself Jazz.
Teach Yourself Lotus 1-2-3.
Teach Yourself Microsoft Word.
Teach Yourself MultiMate.
Teach Yourself Multiplan.
Teach Yourself 1-2-3 Macros.
Teach Yourself Oracle for 1-2-3.
Teach Yourself OS/2.
Teach Yourself Paradox.
Teach Yourself PeachCalc.
Teach Yourself Peachtext.
Teach Yourself R:BASE for DOS.
Teach Yourself R:BASE 5000.
Teach Yourself SuperCalc.
Teach Yourself SuperCalc 3.
Teach Yourself SuperCalc 4.
Teach Yourself Symphony.
Teach Yourself the Home Accountant.
Teach Yourself TK! Solver.
Teach Yourself VisiCalc.
Teach Yourself VolksWriter Deluxe.
Teach Yourself WordPerfect.
Teach Yourself WordStar.
Teach Yourself WordStar 2000.

Amidon Pubns., Div. of Paul S. Amidon & Assocs., Inc., (0-89978), 1966 Benson Ave., Saint Paul, MN 55116-3299 Tel 612-690-2401; Toll free: 800-328-6502 (outside Minnesota); FAX: 612-690-4009.
Titles:
Text Adder & Shape Tables.

Ampersand, Div. of EDS, (0-918551), 128 S. George St., P.O. Box 15084, York, PA 17405-7084 Tel 717-845-5602; FAX: 717-854-1055.
Titles:
BRANCHBANKER.
BRANCHTELLER.
SELLSTATION.

Amphora Media, 110 Frederick Ave., Suite A, Rockville, MD 20850 Tel 301-251-0720.
Titles:
Congressional Portraits: Desktop Publishers' Collection.

Anaheim Technologies, Inc., 320 Fifth Ave., Troy, NY 12182 Tel 518-237-1474; FAX: 514-387-5290.
Titles:
Anaheim Bid.

Analysis & Simulation, Inc., (1-888333), 172 Holtz Rd., Buffalo, NY 14225 Tel 716-632-4932; Toll free: 800-632-0172; FAX: 716-632-4935.
Titles:
EPLAN/TPLAN: Individual Education - Transition Plan.
EPLAN: Individual Education Plan.
TPLAN: Transition Planning Tool.

Analytic Assocs., (0-917269), 4817 Browndeer Ln., Rolling Hills Estates, CA 90275 Tel 310-541-0418; Toll free: 800-959-3273.
Titles:
planEASe/Windows.
planEASe Financial Utilities.
planEASe Graphics Extension.
planEASe Monthly Extension.
PlanEASe Partnership Models.

Analytical Computer Service, Inc., 640 N. Lasalle Dr., Chicago, IL 60610 Tel 312-751-2815; FAX: 312-337-2551.
Titles:
A-Cross.
ACS-Query.
Juggler.
Knockout.

Analytical Service Assocs., (0-922294), 21 Hollis Rd., Lynn, MA 01904 Tel 617-593-2404.
Titles:
The Convertible Bond Analyst.

Analytical Software, (1-881789), P.O. Box 12185, Tallahassee, FL 32317-2185; FAX: 612-628-0148. Do not confuse with Analytical Software, Inc. of Dallas, TX.
Titles:
STATISTIX.

Analytical Software, Inc., (0-922295), 10939 McCree Rd., Dallas, TX 75238 Tel 214-340-2564. Do not confuse with Analytical Software of St. Paul, MN.
Titles:
Boardroom Graphics.
Executive Assistant.
The Financial Analyst.

Anawan Computer Services, (0-918553), 19K Winterberry Ln., Rehoboth, MA 02769 Tel 508-252-4537.
Titles:
PM-Status 111: Preventive Maintenance Scheduling.

Andent, Inc., (0-914555), 1000 North Ave., Waukegan, IL 60085 Tel 708-223-5077.
Titles:
Apple Alarm.
Appointments.
Coin Collector.
Coupon Collector.
Coupon Organizer.
Dental Insurance Form Writer.
Dental-Medical Office Data.
Encephalon.
Fit & Trim.
Histogram Plot.
Hypnosis.
Librarian List.
Medical Insurance Form Writer.

SOFTWARE ENCYCLOPEDIA 1996

Museum Collector.
Museum Collector Catalog.
Prescription Form Writer.
Reaction Time.
Recall List.
Response Time.
Stamp Collector.

Anderson Publishing Co., (0-87084), P.O. Box 1576, Cincinnati, OH 45201-1576 Tel 513-421-4142; Toll free: 800-582-7295; FAX: 513-562-8180; 2035 Reading Rd., Cincinnati, OH 45202-1416 Tel 513-421-4142. Do not confuse with companies with the same name in Novato, CA, Anacortes, WA, Burley, ID, Saginaw, MI, Branson, MO.
Titles:
Anderson's Bankruptcy Filing System.
Anderson's Ohio EPA on CD-ROM.
Anderson's Ohio Law on Disc.
ASH PLUS Automated Social History.
Automated Social History, Automated Social History II.
Economic & Hedonic Damages System.
Ohio Jury Instructions on CD-ROM.

Andrew Corp., (0-917343), 10500 W. 153rd St., Orland Pk., IL 60462.
Titles:
Bridge Manager Program.
TruLynx/3270-PC.
Trulynx/400.
TruLynx/5251.

Anitek Software Products, (0-922306), P.O. Box 361136, Melbourne, FL 32936 Tel 407-259-9397.
Titles:
LeScript.
Zorlof Word Processing System.
Zorlof II.

Annabooks, Div. of ANAV, Inc., (0-929392), 11838 Bernardo Plaza Ct., Suite 102, San Diego, CA 92128-2414 Tel 619-673-0870; Toll free: 800-462-1042; FAX: 619-673-1432.
Titles:
AnnaBios.
DOS Buttons.
PromKit.

Annual Reviews, Inc., (0-8243), 4139 El Camino Way, P.O. Box 10139, Palo Alto, CA 94303-0139 Tel 415-493-4400; Toll free: 800-523-8635 (including California, Alaska, Hawaii & Canada); FAX: 415-855-9815.
Titles:
Annual Reviews Index on Diskette for DOS.

Ansa Software, (0-941915), P.O. Box 660001, Scotts Valley, CA 95066-0001.
Titles:
Paradox.

Answer Software Corp., (0-928502), 20045 Stevens Creek Blvd., Cupertino, CA 95014 Tel 408-253-7515; FAX: 408-253-8430.
Titles:
HyBase (DBMS for Mac).
RBUG86: Symbolic Software Debugger.

Antech, Inc., (0-917957), 292 S. Atlanta St., Roswell, GA 30075-4961 Tel 404-993-7270.
Titles:
Computerized Operations Planning & Engineering (COPE).
Consultant.
FIPS: Financial Planning Simplified.
PROP: Project Planning & Reporting.
Time & Billing.

PUBLISHER/TITLE INDEX

Antex Data Systems, Div. of International Antex, Inc., (0-925340), 1346 Bordeaux Dr., Sunnyvale, CA 94089-1005.
Titles:
Sales Invoice/Report Software.

Anthony, S., Studios, 889 De Haro St., San Francisco, CA 94107 Tel 415-826-6193.
Titles:
LaserUp! Draw.
LaserUp! Fonts 1.
LaserUp! Plot.
LaserUp! Print.
LaserUp! Utilities 1.

Anthra Norell, Inc., (0-9642953), ; FAX: 202-775-0854; c/o Michaels & Wishner, 1140 Connecticut Ave., No. 900, Washington, DC 20036 Tel 202-223-5000.
Titles:
The Oberon System.

Apex Software Corp., 21 Old Main St., Suite 101, Fishkill, NY 12524 Tel 914-897-3025; FAX: 914-897-3729.
Titles:
SYSLOG: System Log Utility.

Aphelion, Inc., 1100 NASA Rd. 1, No. 606, Houston, TX 77058 Tel 713-333-9800; FAX: 713-333-9816.
Titles:
Fitness Manager.
R. A. M.
Scuba Master.
Super Clerk.
Video Exec.

Apian Software, P.O. Box 1224, Menlo Park, CA 94026 Tel 415-694-2900; Toll free: 800-237-4565; FAX: 415-694-2904.
Titles:
Decision Pad.
Decision Pad Lan Pack.
Survey Pro.

Apollon Engineering, Inc., P.O. Box 807, Columbia, MD 21044 Tel 410-747-0778; FAX: 410-747-8291; P.O. Box 807, Columbia, MD 21044.
Titles:
Grafeas.

Appaloosa Systems, 345 Flume Rd., Aptos, CA 95003 Tel 408-662-2473.
Titles:
MacTAE.

Application Techniques, Inc., (0-922333), 10 Lomar Park Dr., Pepperell, MA 01463 Tel 508-433-5201; Toll free: 800-433-5201 (Orders Only); FAX: 508-433-8466.
Titles:
PictureEze.
Pizazz Plus.
WinDings.

Applications Systems Corp., 323 W. Main St., No. 104, Tustin, CA 92680 Tel 714-838-8670.
Titles:
Pro-IV Accountant.

Applications Systems Group (CT), Inc., (0-927483), 97 Golden Hill Rd., Danbury, CT 06811-4632 Tel 203-790-9756; FAX: 203-790-5175.
Titles:
Accounts Payable.
Accounts Receivable Program.
Bill of Materials.
General Ledger.
Inventory.
Job Cost.
Name-Address Program.
Order Entry & Invoicing.
Payroll.
Point of Sale Register.
Purchasing.
Real Estate Management.
Sales Management System.

Applied Business Software, Inc., (0-917271), 2847 Gundry Ave., Long Beach, CA 90806 Tel 310-426-2188; Toll free: 800-833-3343; FAX: 310-426-5535.
Titles:
ABS Accounts Payable.
ABS Accounts Receivable.
ABS General Ledger.
ABS-IMS (Information Management System).
ABS/Inventory.
ABS Order Entry.
ABS Payroll.
Financier - Loan Escrow Servicing.
Financier/CAL - Financial Calculator.
Financier/CMO - Collateralized Mortgage Obligation.
Financier/DRE - Department of Real Estate Annual Report.
Financier/PSS - Partnership Servicing.
Financier-Trust Deed Servicing.
General Accounting Business Packages.
Magic - Property Management Software.

Applied Educational Systems, Inc., (0-917079), P.O. Box 2220, Concord, NH 03301 Tel 603-225-5511; Toll free: 800-237-5530; FAX: 603-225-2311.
Titles:
Daily Attendance Accounting System.
Discipline Tracking System.
District Attendance.
Electronic Grade Book.
Grade Reporting System.
Interim Reporting System.
Student-Course Scheduling System.
Test Scoring System.
Transportation System.

Applied Informatics, Inc., 15104 St. Thomas Church Rd., Upper Marlboro, MD 20772-8294 Tel 301-627-6650; Toll free: 800-272-0777.
Titles:
MicroSPEED.

Applied Informatics, Inc., (0-9639961), 295 Chipeta Way, Salt Lake City, UT 84108 Tel 801-584-3060; FAX: 801-584-3062. Do not confuse with Applied Informatics, Inc. in Upper Marlboro, MD.
Titles:
Medical HouseCall.

Applied Information Systems, Inc., (0-922350), 100 Europa Dr., Suite 555, Chapel Hill, NC 27514-2310 Tel 919-942-7801; Toll free: 800-334-5510; FAX: 919-493-7563.
Titles:
BURCOM: DEC - Unisys Communication System.
Xess.

Applied Logic Systems, Inc., P.O. Box 180, Newton Center, MA 02159-0902 Tel 617-965-9191; FAX: 617-965-1636.
Titles:
ALS Prolog.

Applied MicroSystems, Inc., (0-922357), P.O. Box 832, Roswell, GA 30077 Tel 404-552-9000; Toll free: 800-998-1979 (sales).
Titles:
Elements of Medical Terminology.
FasTracs.
PROTRACS PROFESSIONAL.

AQUARIUS INSTRUCTIONAL

Applied Publishing, Div. of Applied Software, Inc., (0-935679), 321 Waters Edge Dr., Chaska, MN 55318-1383 Tel 612-470-1837; Dist. by: The Distributors, 702 S. Michigan, South Bend, IN 46601 Tel 219-232-8500; Toll free: 800-348-5200 (except Indiana); Dist. by: Baker & Taylor Bks., Reno Service Ctr., 380 Edison Way, Reno, NV 89564 Tel 702-858-6700; Toll free: 800-775-1700 (customer service).
Titles:
Chameleon Remote.

Applied Research Consultants, (1-884796), 505 Clark St., Huntington, IN 46750 Tel 219-356-8205.
Titles:
Dance of the Planets.

Applied Software Technology, (0-914033), 591 W. Hamilton Ave., Suite 201, Campbell, CA 95008 Tel 408-370-2662; Toll free: 800-678-1111; FAX: 408-370-3393.
Titles:
Versaform XL.

Applied Solutions, Inc., (0-922363), 8485 Ramsey Rd., Gold Hill, OR 97525-9621 Tel 503-855-9891; FAX: 503-855-9892.
Titles:
The Wholesale Solution.

Applied Systems, (0-917147), 2500 Bond St., University Park, IL 60466 Tel 312-534-5575; Toll free: 800-999-5368; FAX: 312-534-1216.
Titles:
- The Agency Manager.

Applied Systems & Technologies, Inc., 227M Hallenbeck Rd., Cleveland, NY 13042 Tel 315-675-8584.
Titles:
MaxPage.
TrAid-Names.

Applied Technologies, Inc., Lyndon Way, Kittery, ME 03904 Tel 207-439-5074; FAX: 207-439-1061.
Titles:
BITS & PIECES.
Compu-U-Temp: Temperature Data Acquisition.
The File Converter.
MasterMenu.
MasterMenu Plus.
The Whole Bit: Word Processing.

Apriori Software Corp., (1-882618), 63 Washington Ave., Streamwood, IL 60107 Tel 708-830-6844.
Titles:
WinCD Professional: The Ultimate CD Player.

ApTech, Inc., 50 Front St., Binghamton, NY 13902 Tel 607-722-0350; Toll free: 800-443-3732; FAX: 607-722-0859.
Titles:
ABRAXAS.

Aquarius Instructional, (0-87354; 0-922368), P.O. Box 128, Indian Rocks Beach, FL 34635 Tel 813-595-7890; Toll free: 800-338-2644; FAX: 813-595-2685.
Titles:
Child Care.
Cooking & Baking.
Dermatology & Trichology.
Digestion Unit: Digestion.
Food Service Cluster.
Hair Shaping.
Home Management Unit.

Aquidneck Data Corp., (0-922369), 170 Enterprise Ctr., Middletown, RI 02840 Tel 401-847-7260.
Titles:
EAZY PC.
VOX: VAX Office Exchange.
Word-to-Word.

Arborworks, Inc., 431 Virginia Ave., Ann Arbor, MI 48103 Tel 313-747-7087; Toll free: 800-346-6980; FAX: 810-707-8775.
Titles:
SCSI Tool.

Arch Software, Inc., 1549 Teakwood Ave No. 24162, Cincinnati, OH 45224-2156 Tel 513-681-1642.
Titles:
SimpleSpan Utilities I: Beam Analysis Disk Accessory Package.

Archer, Stephen, Assocs., 31 Chestnut Hill Rd., Stamford, CT 06903 Tel 203-968-1156; FAX: 203-329-1358.
Titles:
Professional Corporate Financial Planning Models.

Archetype, Inc., 100 Fifth Ave., Waltham, MA 02154 Tel 617-890-7544; FAX: 617-890-3661.
Titles:
Archetype Designer.
Archetype InterSep.

Ares Software Corp., (1-879464), P.O. Box 4667, Foster City, CA 94404; 561 Pilgrim Dr., Suite D, Foster City, CA 94404 Tel 415-578-9090.
Titles:
FontFiddler: Kerning Editor.
FontMonger.
FontMonger Windows.

Argos Gameware, Div. of H&M Systems Software, Inc., (1-885936), 25 E. Spring Valley Ave., Maywood, NJ 07607-2150 Tel 201-845-3357; Toll free: 800-367-3366; FAX: 201-845-4638.
Titles:
Artapart Collectors Edition.
Entertainment Digest.

Argos Software, Div. of Argos, Inc., (0-927991), 4949 N. Crystal Ave., No. 140, Fresno, CA 93750-0208 Tel 209-227-1000; FAX: 209-227-9644.
Titles:
ABECAS Assets.
Accounts Payable (a part of ABECAS).
Accounts Receivable (a part of ABECAS).
Bill of Materials (a Part of ABECAS).
Contact Management (a Part of ABECAS).
Cost Manager Level I.
Cost Manager Level II.
Dispatch Management (a Part of ABECAS).
Equipment Maintenance (a Part of ABECAS).
Freight Bill Accounting (a Part of ABECAS).
General Ledger (a part of ABECAS).
General Ledger-Cost Accounting (a Part of ABECAS).
Grower Accounting (a Part of ABECAS).
Inventory Management (a Part of ABECAS).
Job Planner (a Part of ABECAS).
Material Requirements Planning (a Part of ABECAS).
Milkpay.
Payroll (a Part of ABECAS).
Process Server.
Production Management (a Part of ABECAS).
Purchase Orders Processing.
Register Sales.
Safety & Personnel Management.
Sales Order Processing (a Part of ABECAS).
Service Billings.
Supplies - Parts Inventory Tracking.
Tracker.
Utility Billing (a Part of ABECAS).
Warehouse for Distribution Companies (a Part of ABECAS).
Warehouse for Storage Companies (a Part of ABECAS).

Aries Systems Corp., 200 Sutton St., North Andover, MA 01845 Tel 508-975-7570; FAX: 508-975-3811.
Titles:
AIDSLINE CD-ROM Database.
CANCERLIT CD-ROM Database.
Cancerlit Knowledge Finder.
CardLine CD-ROM Database for Cardiology.
HEALTH Planning & Administration CD-ROM Database.
Knowledge Finder.
Knowledge Server.
MEDLINE Core Journals CD-ROM Database.
Medline Knowledge Finder.
Medline Knowledge Server.
MEDLINE Unabridged CD-ROM Database.
MIM-CD: Mendelian Inheritance in Man.
NeuroLine CD-ROM Database for Neurology.
OBGLine CD-ROM Database for Obstetrics-Gynecology.
OphthaLine CD-ROM Database for Ophthalmology.
OrthoLine CD-ROM Database for Orthopaedics.
PathLine CD-ROM Database for Pathology.
PediLine CD-ROM Database for Neurology.
RadLine CD-ROM Database for Radiology.
SleepLine CD-ROM Database for Sleep Disorders.
SurgAnLine CD-ROM Database for Surgery & Anesthesia.

Aristo Computers, Inc., 6700 SW 105th Ave., Suite 307, Beaverton, OR 97005 Tel 503-626-6333; Toll free: 800-327-4786; FAX: 503-626-6492.
Titles:
APSS Plus: Aristo Parcel Shipping System.
Aristo Parcel Shipping System.
Aristo Receiving Management System.

Aristotle Industries, (0-922379), 205 Pennsylvania Ave. SE, Washington, DC 20003 Tel 202-543-8345; Toll free: 800-243-4401; FAX: 202-543-6407.
Titles:
Campaign Manager III.
Constituent Service.
Voter Lists.
Voter Lists on Compact Disc.

Arity Corp., Damonmill Sq., Concord, MA 01742 Tel 508-371-1243; Toll free: 800-722-7489; FAX: 508-371-1487.
Titles:
Arity Combination Pack.
Arity/Expert System Development Package.
Arity OS/2 Integrated Prolog.
Arity/Prolog Compiler & Interpreter.
Arity/Prolog Interpreter.
Arity/Prolog32 Compiler & Interpreter.
Arity SQL Development Package.
Arity/Windows Toolkit.

Arlington Software & Systems Corp., (0-917681), 900 Mix Ave., Suite 14, Hamden, CT 06514 Tel 203-230-1733.
Titles:
PCAT Professional Contact & Tracking System.
PCAT System 6: Personal Computer Automated Telemarketing.

Armor Systems, Inc., (0-927995), 1626 W. Airport Blvd., Sanford, FL 32773-4814 Tel 407-323-9787; FAX: 407-330-0442.
Titles:
Armor Premier Accounting Software.

Armstrong Genealogical Systems, (0-927996), 5009 Utah, Greenville, TX 75401 Tel 214-454-8209.
Titles:
Compiling Roots & Branches.
Gensystems.

Ars Nova Software, (0-929444), P.O. Box 637, Kirkland, WA 98083-0637; Toll free: 800-445-4866; FAX: 206-889-0359; Dist. by: MacAmerica, 1360 Bordeaux Dr., Sunnyvale, CA 94089; Toll free: 800-535-0900.
Titles:
Practica Musica.

Artech Hse., Inc., Subs. of Horizon Hse. Microwave, Inc., (0-89006), 685 Canton St., Norwood, MA 02062 Tel 617-769-9750; Toll free: 800-225-9977; FAX: 617-769-6334.
Titles:
CAD for Linear & Planar Antenna Arrays of Various Radiating Elements.
DETPROB: Probability of Detection Calculation.
GasMap: Gallium Arsenide Model Analysis Program.
IONOPROP: Ionospheric Propagation Assessment.
MATCHNET: Microwave Matching Network Synthesis.
Reflector & Lens Antennas: Analysis & Design.

Artic Technologies, (0-928507), 55 Park St., Suite No.2, Troy, MI 48083-2753 Tel 810-588-7370; FAX: 810-588-2650.
Titles:
Artic Business Vision: Interactive Screen/Keyboard Processor.

Artificial Intelligence, Inc., (0-928508), 354 Upland Dr., Seattle, WA 98188 Tel 206-271-8633; Toll free: 800-533-8902; FAX: 206-575-2129.
Titles:
MicroVet: Veterinary Management.
PAS-3 PLUS Chiropractic.
PAS-3 PLUS System II Medical Practice Management.
PAS-3 System II: Anesthesiology Practice Management.
PAS-3 PLUS Dental Practice Management.

Artificial Intelligence Research Group, (0-917151), 921 N. La Jolla Ave., Los Angeles, CA 90046 Tel 213-656-7368.
Titles:
Eliza: The Computer Psychotherapist.

Artisoft, Inc., (0-927538), 2202 N. Forbes Blvd., Tucson, AZ 85745 Tel 602-670-7100; Toll free: 800-233-5564; FAX: 602-670-7101.
Titles:
LANtastic Network Operating System.

Arts Computer Products, Inc., (0-940285), P.O. Box 604, Cambridge, MA 02140-0005 Tel 617-547-5320; Toll free: 800-343-0095; FAX: 617-547-5597.
Titles:
Arts Info 1.0.
PC Braille.
PC Lens.
PC Sift.
WP Sift.

PUBLISHER/TITLE INDEX

Artsci, Inc., (0-917963), P.O. Box 1428, Burbank, CA 91507-1428 Tel 818-843-4080; FAX: 818-846-2298.
Titles:
Acecalc.
Acewriter II.
Apple '21'.
Calendar Magic.
Card Shop.
Card Shop: Greeting Cards for the Mac.
Craps.
Crosswords.
Hearts.
Magic Mailer.
Magic Memory.
Magic Office System.
Magic Window IIe.
Magic Words.
MagiCalc.
Microgammon II.
Roulette.
Softforms.
Softforms-Mac.
Softletters.

Artworx Software Co., Inc., (0-922395; 1-55662), 1844 Penfield Rd., Penfield, NY 14526 Tel 716-385-6120; Toll free: 800-828-6573.
Titles:
MailList.

Ashley, Allen, (0-922396), 395 Sierra Madre Villa, Pasadena, CA 91107 Tel 818-793-5748.
Titles:
Z-Com: CP/M BASIC Compiler.

Ashleywilde, Inc., (0-9627476), 23715 Malibu Road, Suite 132, Malibu, CA 90265 Tel 310-456-1277; Toll free: 800-833-7568; FAX: 310-456-8586.
Titles:
Plots Unlimited.

Ashwin Systems International, Inc., P.O. Box 1014, Dunedin, FL 34697; FAX: 813-787-1403; 1670 Curlew Rd., Palm Harbor, FL 34683 Tel 813-785-5844.
Titles:
PM-100 Professional Microsoftware for Physicians.

askSam Systems, P.O. Box 1428, Perry, FL 32347; Toll free: 800-800-1997; FAX: 904-584-7481; 119 S. Washington St., Perry, FL 32347 Tel 904-584-6590.
Titles:
askSam.
ASKSAM for Windows.
AskSam Network Version.
HyperSift.

Astrolabe, Inc., (0-87199; 0-913637), P.O. Box 1750, Brewster, MA 02631 Tel 508-896-5081; Toll free: 800-843-6682 (orders only); FAX: 508-896-5289; 350 Underpass Rd., Brewster, MA 02631 Tel 508-896-5081.
Titles:
Astro Edit I: Astrological Report Editor.
Astro Edit II: Astrological Report Editor.
Astro-Scope Report.
Astro-Scope: Screen Version.
Astro Star I.
The AstroAnalyst.
AstroDay: Personal Version.
AstroDay with Global Transits.
Astrolabe Font 1.
The Astrologer's Companion: An Astrological Clock Program.
Aztec Astro-Report.
Aztec Astrology.
The Blackwell Data Collection.
C-Star.
CCRS Horoscope Program 92: by Mark Pottenger.
Celeste I: Natal Horoscope Calculation Program.
Chartwheels II.
Composite Astro-Report.
Contact Astro-Report.
Daily Astro-Report.
Huang's I Ching.
Huang's I Ching 2000.
JigSaw.
Mackey-Saunders Data Collection: Contemporary American Horoscopes.
Monthly Astro-Report.
Natal Horoscope.
Nova.
Nova, Core Version.
Personal Numerology Report: Printing Version.
Personal Numerology Report 3.
Personal Numerology: Screen Version.
Printwheels.
Printwheels DTP.
Professional Natal Report.
Professional Relationship Report.
Professional Transit Report.
Progressed Astro-Report.
Sex-O-Scope Report.
Sex-O-Scope: Screen Version.
Solar Astrological Font.
Solar Fire: Astrological Calculations.
Solar Fire Three.
Solar Maps.
Solar Spark.
Star Track.
Star Track Extension Package (Midpoint Sort, Harmonics, Astro-Mapping, Solar Arc List).
Timegraphs.

At Your Service Software, Inc., 450 Bronxville Rd., Bronxville, NY 10708 Tel 914-337-9030; Toll free: 800-433-8368; FAX: 914-337-9031.
Titles:
Inventory Pro - Plus.
The Recipe Writer.
The Recipe Writer Pro - Plus.
Sales Analysis Pro - Plus.

Atari Corp., (0-915019), 1196 Borregas Ave., Sunnyvale, CA 94086 Tel 408-745-2000.
Titles:
Arcade Champ Kit.
Assembler Editor.
Asteroids.
AtariWriter Plus.
BASIC Tutor Kit.
Basketball.
Blackjack.
Bond Analysis.
Centipede.
CP/M Emulator.
DB Master One.
dBMann.
Defender.
Dig Dug.
Donkey Kong.
Donkey Kong, Jr.
Entertainer Kit.
Final Legacy.
1st Word.
Galaxian.
The Home Filing Manager.
Home Planetarium.
Joust.
Jungle Hunt.
LOGO Kit.
Macro Assembler.
Microsoft II.
Millipede.
Missile Command.
Ms. Pac Man.
Music II: Rhythm & Pitch.
NEOchrome.
Pac Man.
Pengo.
PILOT.
Player Maker.
Pole Position.
Proofreader for AtariWriter.
Qix.
R. S. Football.
Robotron.
Scram.
Screen Maker.
Secret Formula: Advanced.
Secret Formula: Elementary.
Secret Formula: Intermediate.
Silent Butler.
Space Invaders.
Speed Reader.
Star Raiders.
Star Raiders II.
Stock Analysis.
Stock Charting.
Super Breakout.
Telelink I.
Tennis.
TimeWise.
VisiCalc.

Athena Information Management, Inc., (1-57402), 7 Bridge St., Cameron, WV 26033 Tel 304-686-3344; Toll free: 800-895-8679; FAX: 304-686-3751.
Titles:
Any P. I. A. Software: Social Security Software.

Athena Software, (0-928511), 5 Brair Lane, Newark, DE 19711 Tel 302-738-6953.
Titles:
That's Life.
Vectors.

Atlantic Software, P.O. Box 299, Wenham, MA 01984-0699 Tel 508-922-4352; Toll free: 800-659-4584.
Titles:
CELLULA.
Cube & Tess.
DNA/RNA Builder.
Fractals.
MOLECULES.
N.N. Charge.
Protein Predictor.
STEREOCHEMICA.

Atlis Systems, Inc., 6011 Executive Blvd., Rockville, MD 20852 Tel 301-770-3000; Toll free: 800-638-6595.
Titles:
ATLIS/PC.

Aton International, Inc., (0-922410), 7654 Benassi Dr., Gilroy, CA 95020 Tel 408-847-3531.
Titles:
I to Z.
Micro-Remote 2780-3780 Emulator.
Micro-Remote 3270 Emulator.
XDT.
Z to I.

Atre Software, Inc., (0-937989), P.O. Box 727, Rye, NY 10580 Tel 914-967-2037; 16 Elm Pl., Rye, NY 10580.
Titles:
Information Center: Strategies & Case Studies.

Attachmate Corp., 3617 131st Ave., SE, Bellevue, WA 98006 Tel 206-644-4010; Toll free: 800-426-6283; FAX: 206-747-9924.
Titles:
Extra! Entry Level.
Extra! Extended for DOS.
EXTRA! for Macintosh.
EXTRA! for OS-2.
EXTRA! for Windows.
Extra! 3270 Gateway Option.
Host Graphics Option for DOS.
Host Graphics Option for Windows.
Now! PC/Host Autoware.

Auctoritas Software, 5012 Meadow Pass Way, Antelope, CA 95843 Tel 916-726-2025; Toll free: 800-355-9586; FAX: 916-726-4746.
Titles:
Lien Writer.

Augmentx, 9351 Grant St., Suite 430, Thornton, CO 80229 Tel 303-431-8991; Toll free: 800-232-4687; FAX: 303-431-9056.
Titles:
Document Administrator.

Aura CAD/CAM, Inc., Div. of Aura Systems, (0-9620874), 2335 Alaska Ave., El Segundo, CA 92045 Tel 310-536-9207; FAX: 310-643-8718.
Titles:
Aura CAD/CAM.

Austin Scientific, Inc., (0-928399), 695 Oak Grove, Suite 1B, Menlo Park, CA 94025 Tel 415-323-6338; Toll free: 800-433-1608; FAX: 415-323-6340.
Titles:
TaxTime: California 540NR.
TaxTime for 1-2-3: Alabama 40.
TaxTime for 1-2-3: California 100 Corp.
TaxTime for 1-2-3: California 540.
TaxTime for 1-2-3: California 565.
TaxTime for 1-2-3: Colorado 104.
TaxTime for 1-2-3: Connecticut 394.
TaxTime for 1-2-3: Georgia 500.
TaxTime for 1-2-3: Illinois 1040.
TaxTime for 1-2-3: Maryland 502.
TaxTime for 1-2-3: Massachusetts 1.
TaxTime for 1-2-3: Michigan 1040.
TaxTime for 1-2-3: Missouri 1040.
TaxTime for 1-2-3: New Jersey 1040.
TaxTime for 1-2-3: New York IT-201.
TaxTime for 1-2-3: North Carolina D-400.
TaxTime for 1-2-3: Ohio 1040.
TaxTime for 1-2-3: Oklahoma 511.
TaxTime for 1-2-3: Pennsylvania 40.
TaxTime for 1-2-3: Utah 40.
TaxTime for 1-2-3: Virginia 760.
TaxTime for 1-2-3: 1040 Individual.
Taxtime for 1-2-3: 1040 Master.
TaxTime for 1-2-3: 1041 Fiduciary.
TaxTime for 1-2-3: 1065 Partnership.
TaxTime for 1-2-3: 1120 Corp.
TaxTime for 1-2-3: 1120 Sub-S Corp.
TaxTime for 1-2-3: 706 Estate.

Auto-Graphics, Inc., 3201 Temple Ave., Pomona, CA 91768 Tel 909-595-7204; Toll free: 800-776-6939; FAX: 909-595-7004.
Titles:
IMPACT.

Auto Tell Services, Inc., 600 Clark Ave., King of Prussia, PA 19406 Tel 610-768-0200; Toll free: 800-523-5103; FAX: 610-337-1180.
Titles:
ATS Maintenance Management Systems.
ATS SPI System: Spare Parts Inventory Control.

Auto-Trol Technology Corp., 12500 N. Washington St., Denver, CO 80241-2400 Tel 303-452-4919; Toll free: 800-233-2882; FAX: 303-252-2249.
Titles:
Composite Image.
Electrical.
Facility Series: FL-I (Industrial); FL-O (Office-Commercial).
KONFIG.
Numerical Control.
Series 5000.
Vectorpipe.

Autodesk, Inc., (0-922414; 1-56444), 2320 Marinship Way, Sausalito, CA 94965 Tel 415-332-2344; Toll free: 800-445-5415; FAX: 415-491-8307.
Titles:
AutoCAD.
Autodesk Multimedia Explorer.
AutoShade.
Electronic IV.
Generic CADD.
Generic CADD for the Macintosh.
Generic 3D.
Geometric Positioning & Tolerancing: Geometric Positioning & Tolerance.
Hyperchem for Windows.
HyperChen for Windows: Upgrade Pack 1.2 MB Version.
HyperChen for Windows: Upgrade Pack 1.44 MB Version.
HyperChen for Windows: 1.2 MB Version.
HyperChen for Windows: 1.44 MB Version.
PenPlot.
Symbol Library: Basic Home Design.
Symbols Library: Bathroom Design.
Symbols Library: Clip Art.
Symbols Library: Commercial & Residential Electrical.
Symbols Library: Commercial & Residential Furnishings.
Symbols Library: Commercial & Residential Plumbing.
Symbols Library: Electrical Engineering Power.
Symbols Library: Electronic II CMOS.
Symbols Library: Electronic III: ECL.
Symbols Library: Electronics I: IEEE.
Symbols Library: Fasteners.
Symbols Library: Flow Charts & Schedules.
Symbols Library: Heating, Ventilation & Air Conditioning.
Symbols Library: Home Landscaping.
Symbols Library: Hydraulics.
Symbols Library: Industrial Pipe Fittings.
Symbols Library: Kitchen Design.
Symbols Library: Landscape Architecture.
Symbols Library: Microprocessors.
Symbols Library: Residential Framing Details.
Symbols Library: Steel Structural Shapes 1.
Symbols Library: Type Fonts 1.
Symbols Library: Welding.
3D Studio: Release 2.
Type Fonts 2.

Automate Computer Software, (0-928015), 11600 Huebner Rd., San Antonio, TX 78230 Tel 210-641-7863.
Titles:
Professional Manager.

Automated Financial Systems, (0-922418), 123 Summit Dr., Whiteland Bus Park, Exton, PA 19341 Tel 610-524-9300; FAX: 610-524-7977.
Titles:
AFS Asset-Based Lending.
AFS Combined Deposit System.
AFS Commercial Lending (Level III, II PLUS).
AFS Computer-Based Training.
AFS Consumer Lending (Level III, II PLUS).
AFS Customer Information File.
AFS Dealer Floor Plan.
AFS Executive Line of Credit.
AFS Interest Reporting System.
AFS Level III Mortgage Lending System.
AFS On-Line Collection System.
AFS Product Definition.
AFS Task Management System.
Check Services Model PLUS CSM PLUS.
CheckTrack PLUS.
PCDI Profit Source Computes Data Integration System.

Automated Ideas, Inc., 2375 W. 12th Ave., Hialeah, FL 33010 Tel 305-885-0338; Toll free: 800-451-5016.
Titles:
PC-Buddy.

Automated Reasoning Technologies, Inc., (0-936667), 2509 Willakenzie Rd., No. 4, Eugene, OR 97401-4846 Tel 503-345-0030; Toll free: 800-289-7638.
Titles:
Personal Finances with Lotus.

Automatic Forecasting Systems, Inc., (0-928400), P.O. Box 563, Hatboro, PA 19040 Tel 215-675-0652; FAX: 215-672-2534.
Titles:
Autobox.
Boxx.
MTS.

Automation Consultants, (0-928022), 39210 State St., No. 108, Fremont, CA 94538 Tel 510-794-7921. Do not confuse with Automation Consultants International, Mission Viejo, CA.
Titles:
House Keeper.
Job Cost System.

Automation Consultants, International, (0-917083), 23131 Tiagua St., Mission Viejo, CA 92692-1403 Tel 714-768-4544; FAX: 714-768-4548. Do not confuse with Automation Consultants, Fremont, CA.
Titles:
CataList.

Automation Counselors, Inc., P.O. Box 3917, Frederick, MD 21705-3917 Tel 301-663-3700; Toll free: 800-966-6725; FAX: 301-663-6692; 5728 Industry Ln., Frederick, MD 21701.
Titles:
Municipal.
Public Works Management.

Automation Resources Corp., (0-917683), 4830 W. Kennedy Blvd., Suite 665, Tampa, FL 33609-2571 Tel 813-287-2747; Toll free: 800-226-9336; FAX: 813-282-0601.
Titles:
AGENCYMASTER: Insurance Agency Accounting.
General Accounting.
Manufacturing Management: Manufacturing - Distribution.
MGA Paperless Office Policywriting: MGA Policywriting.
STAFFMASTER: Temporary Help.

Automatronics, 25-26 44th St., Long Island City, NY 11103 Tel 718-932-1086.
Titles:
Auto Journal System: Cash Flow Analyzer.
Auto Proofing System: Cash Flow Analyzer.
Autoform Print Utility.
Cash Reconcilement & Statement Proofing System: Cash Flow Analyzer.
Real Estate - Mortgage Analyzer: Loan Amortization.

Autoskill New York, Inc., (1-883919), Summit Rd., Carmel, NY 10512 Tel 914-225-5011; FAX: 912-225-8820.
Titles:
Academy of Reading.
Autoskill Component Reading Subskill Program.
Autoskill Mathematics Program.

Autospec, Inc., (0-922422), 504 King St., Santa Cruz, CA 95060 Tel 408-457-1430.
Titles:
AUTOCAST.
AUTOSPEC.

PUBLISHER/TITLE INDEX

Avalon Hill Game Co., The Microcomputer Games Div., (0-87276), 4517 Harford Rd., Baltimore, MD 21214 Tel 410-254-9200; Toll free: 800-999-3222.
Titles:
ABC Caterpillar.
B-1 Nuclear Bomber.
Beast War.
Circus Maximus.
Class Struggle.
Computer Acquire.
Computer Diplomacy.
Computer Stocks & Bonds.
Computer Third Reich.
Darkhorn.
Dr. Ruth's Game of Good Sex.
Guderian.
Gulf Strike.
Jupiter Mission 1999.
Legionnaire.
Macbeth.
Maxwell Manor.
Mission on Thunderhead.
NBA.
Office of the General Manager.
Panzer-Jagd.
Panzer's East!
Parthian Kings.
Quest of the Space Beagle.
Ripper!
Spitfire 40.
Super Sunday.
Super Sunday Expansion Disk: Champions Disk.
Super Sunday Expansion Disk: Season Disk 1984.
T.A.C. (Tactical Armor Command).
Telengard.
Tsushima.
Under Fire!
Under Fire!: Extended Capabilities Disk 1.

Avalon Software, (0-924641), 3716 E. Columbia, Suite 120, Tucson, AZ 85714 Tel 602-790-4214; Toll free: 800-282-5664; FAX: 602-750-0822.
Titles:
Avalon CIIM.
Interactive Financial Accounting.
Interactive Manufacturing Control.

Avant-Garde Software, 2213 Woodburn, Plano, TX 75075 Tel 214-964-0260.
Titles:
Benchmark Modula-2.
"C" Language Library for Benchmark Modula-2.
IFF Image Resource Library.
Simplified Amiga Library.
Source Level Debugger for Benchmark Modula-2.

Avant Software Enterprises, P.O. Box 1291, Addison, IL 60101.
Titles:
Avant Cards.

Aviation Analysis, Inc., (0-922234), P.O. Box 3570, Carson City, NV 89702-3570 Tel 702-882-1011; Toll free: 800-736-0392.
Titles:
Aviation Department Management System III ADMS III.

Aviation Data Service, Inc., (0-941024), Box 913, Wichita, KS 67201 Tel 316-262-1491; FAX: 316-262-5333; 312 E. Murdock, Wichita, KS 67214.
Titles:
AuData Business Turbine PC Package.

Avocet Systems, Inc., (0-928023), 120 Union St., P.O. Box 490, Rockport, ME 04856 Tel 207-236-9055; Toll free: 800-448-8500; FAX: 207-236-6713.
Titles:
AvCase 2 8051 Family Package.
AvCase 68000 Family C Package.
AVMACZ80: Z80, Z180, HD64180 Macro Assembler.
AVMAC05: 6805 Family Macro Assembler.
AVMAC09: 6809 Macro Assembler.
AVMAC11: 6811 Macro Assembler.
AVMAC18: 1802 Macro Assembler.
AVMAC48: 8048 Macro Assembler.
AVMAC65: 6500-6502 Macro Assembler.
AVMAC68: 6800-6301-6303-6801 Macro Assembler.
AVMAC85: 8085 Macro Assembler.
AVMAC04: 6804 Macro Assembler.
Avocet C Compiler Series.
AVSIM65.
AVSIMZ80: Z80 Simulator/Debugger.
AVSIM05: 6805 Simulator/Debugger.
AVSIM09: 6809 Simulator/Debugger.
AVSIM48: 8048 Simulator/Debugger.
AVSIM51: 8051 Simulator/Debugger.
AVSIM68: 6801 Simulator/Debugger.
AVSIM85: 8085 Simulator/Debugger.

Axcent Software, Inc., (0-938929), 4635 S. Lakeshore Dr., Tempe, AZ 85282-7167 Tel 602-838-3030; Toll free: 800-292-3687; FAX: 602-345-4109.
Titles:
AXCENT on Accounting: Accounts Payable.
AXCENT on Accounting: Client Write-Up.

Axe, J. P., 1429 Crownhill Dr., Arlington, TX 76012 Tel 817-277-2055; FAX: 817-277-2055.
Titles:
Machinery Kinematics & Dynamics: MKAD.
Network Analyzer for Piping Systems: NAPS.
Structural Analysis by Finite Elements: SAFE.

Azimuth Group, Ltd., 107 S. Front St., Hertford, NC 27944-1134.
Titles:
OPTIMA.

BBN Software Products Corp., (0-922436), 150 Cambridge Park Dr., Cambridge, MA 02140 Tel 617-873-5000.
Titles:
CDIBOL.
INFORMIX.
Level II COBOL.

BCS Publishing, Div. of B. C. Services, (1-881432), 1951 Sewell St., Lincoln, NE 68502-3845.
Titles:
MenuPro.
The PCAid Utilities.
S.O.S.! (Save Our Screen!).
Total Strength Systems Plus: The Complete Professional Strength Training System.

BIT Software, Inc., (0-922537), 47987 Fremont Blvd., Fremont, CA 94538-6508.
Titles:
BitCom.
The Forms Designer.

BMDP Statistical Software, (0-935386), 1440 Sepulveda Blvd., Los Angeles, CA 90025 Tel 310-479-7799; FAX: 213-312-0161.
Titles:
BMDP Statistical Software.

BOS National, Inc., Div. of I-Concepts, (0-922444), 2607 Walnut Hill Ln., Dallas, TX 75229 Tel 214-956-7722; FAX: 214-350-6688.
Titles:
AutoClerk.
BOS/Accounts Payable.
BOS/Accounts Receivable.
BOS COBOL.
BOS/COBOL Symbolic Debug: Delopment Pack.
BOS/Finder.
BOS/General Ledger.
BOS/Inventory Control.
BOS/Invoicing.
BOS/LAN.
BOS Office Products Package.
BOS/Planner.
BOS/WRITER.
MBOS.
SBOS.

BRB Software Systems, (0-922447), 7785 Baymeadows Way, Suite 101, Jacksonville, FL 32256 Tel 904-737-5554.
Titles:
MOM: Medical Office Manager.

BSO/Tasking, (0-922577), 333 Elm St., Dedham, MA 02026-4530 Tel 617-320-9400; Toll free: 800-458-8276; FAX: 617-320-9212.
Titles:
BSO/Assembler Microprocessor Relocating Assemblers.
BSO/C: BSO C Compiler.
BSO/Debug: Microprocessor Symbolic Debuggers.
BSO/Pascal Compiler.
BSO/PLM Compiler.
CrossView: CrossView Source Level Debugger.

BV Engineering, (0-87271), 2023 Chicago Ave., No. B13, Riverside, CA 92507 Tel 909-781-0252.
Titles:
ACNAP: AC Network Analysis Program.
ACNAP3.
ACTFIL: Active Filter Design/Realization.
COMCALC: Communications Design Spreadsheet.
DCNAP: DC Network Analysis Program.
DCNAP2.
LCFIL: L-C Filter Synthesis Program.
LOCIPRO: Root Locus Analysis.
LSP: Logic Simulation Program.
Matrix Magic: Matrix Manipulation Test Program.
PCPLOT: High Resolution Graphics Program.
PDP2: Scientific/Financial Graph Plotting Program.
SPP: Signal Processing Program.
STAP: Static Thermal Analysis Program.
TEKCALC: Scientific Calculator Program.
XFER: Transfer Function Analysis-Synthesis.

BYLS Pr., (0-934402), 6617 N. Mozart, Chicago, IL 60645 Tel 312-743-4241.
Titles:
Library Subject Headings Data Base System.
Print*File.
Secret*File.

BZ-Rights Stuff, Inc., Div. of BZ-Rights & Permissions, Inc., (1-884286), 125 W. 72nd St., New York, NY 10023 Tel 212-580-0615; FAX: 212-769-9224.
Titles:
The Mini-Encyclopedia of Public Domain Songs.

Bahr, James, Assocs., Ltd., (1-879115), 44450 Pinetree Dr., Suite 202, Plymouth, MI 48170 Tel 313-455-8260.
Titles:
ARIC: Allocation Resource Identification & Costing.

Baker CAC, 22001 N Park Dr., Kingwood, TX 77339 Tel 713-348-1000; FAX: 713-590-1028.
Titles:
Micro MAST-MT.
miniMast.

Baker Graphics, P.O. Box G826, Dept. C, New Bedford, MA 02742 Tel 508-996-6732; Toll free: 800-338-1753.
Titles:
BakerForms Accounting Applications.

Baker Street Software, (0-925087), P.O. Box 2712, Santa Clara, CA 95055-2712; 2871 Stevenson St., Santa Clara, CA 95051 Tel 408-296-3307.
Titles:
The Macintosh Holmes Companion: The Digital Sherlock Holmes.

Baler Software Corp., 1400 Hicks Rd., Rolling Meadows, IL 60008 Tel 708-506-9700; Toll free: 800-327-6108 (orders only); FAX: 708-506-1808.
Titles:
Baler Spreadsheet Compiler.
Baler XE.
Ice.
Visual Baler: Spreadsheet-Based Visual Development Tool.

Banner Blue Software, Inc., (1-886914), 39500 Stevenson Pl., Suite 204, Fremont, CA 94537 Tel 510-794-6850; FAX: 510-794-9152; Dist. by: Navarre Corp., 6750 W. Broadway, Brooklyn Park, MN 55428 Tel 612-535-8333.
Titles:
Family Tree Maker Deluxe: CD Edition.
Family Tree Maker for Windows.
Org Plus Advanced.

Bantam Bks., Inc., Div. of Bantam Doubleday Dell, (0-553), 1540 Broadway, New York, NY 10036-4094 Tel 212-354-6500; Toll free: 800-223-6834; FAX: 212-492-8941; Orders to: 414 E. Golf Rd., Des Plaines, IL 60016 Tel 312-827-1111.
Titles:
DOS Power Tools, 2nd Edition Revised for DOS 5.0: Techniques, Tricks & Utilities.
Dvorak's Guide to PC Connectivity.
Dvorak's Guide to PC Games.
FoxPro 2.0 Power Tools.
Novell Netware Power Tools.
The Official Arts & Letters Handbook: Covers Versions 3.0 & 3.1.
One-Two-Three Power Tools.
Visual Basic Programming with Windows Applications.
Windows 3.1 Power Tools for Windows 3.0 & 3.1: 2nd Edition.
WordPerfect 5.1 Macros & Templates.

Banyan Systems, 120 Flanders Rd., Westboro, MA 01581 Tel 508-898-1000; Toll free: 800-828-2404; FAX: 508-898-1755.
Titles:
VINES UNLIMITED.

Barclay Bridge Supplies, Inc., (0-87643), 3600 Chamberlain Ln., No. 230, Louisville, KY 40241-1989; Toll free: 800-274-2221.
Titles:
Bridge Champ I.
Bridge 5.0.
Score Board III.

Barnett & Assocs., 8870 Dunwoody Pl., Atlanta, GA 30350 Tel 404-552-7135; FAX: 404-518-0769.
Titles:
TimeSaver Client Billing System.

Barrington Systems, Inc., 150 E. Sample Rd., Pompano Beach, FL 33064 Tel 305-785-4555.
Titles:
Clarion.

Barrister Information Systems Corp., (0-922465), 45 Oak St., Buffalo, NY 14203 Tel 716-845-5010; Toll free: 800-345-3426; 800-458-8551 (in New York); FAX: 716-845-0077.
Titles:
ALFA: Automated Law Firm Accounting System.
B&TA: Billing & Time Accounting System.
The Barrister Financial Management System.
Barrister/Messager Electronic Mail.
Barrister/Publisher Document Finishing System.
The Barrister Relational Database Management System.
The Barrister Word Processing System.
DELTA: Docket Events & Legal Time Activities.
RESPA+: Real Estate Settlement Processing & Accounting System.
WordManager Advanced Word Processor.

Basics & Beyond, Inc., (0-922473), Box 4561, Lexington, KY 40544-4561 Tel 606-224-1060; FAX: 606-224-4385.
Titles:
Christa's Science Adventure, No. 1: The Manuscript.

Battelle, P.O. Box 999, MS K7-02, Richland, WA 99352 Tel 509-375-2360; FAX: 509-375-3778.
Titles:
FReditor.

Baud Room Computer Service, (0-9625825), 2200 Ocean Ave., No. 3L, Brooklyn, NY 11229 Tel 718-627-1292; Toll free: 800-223-6939.
Titles:
Service Management Information System.

Baudville, (0-930393; 1-56717), 5380 52nd St., SE, Grand Rapids, MI 49512-9765 Tel 616-698-0888; Toll free: 800-728-0888; FAX: 616-698-0554.
Titles:
Award Maker Plus (Apple Version).
Award Maker Plus (IBM).
Award Maker Plus (Macintosh Version).
BadgeMaker.
Laser Award Maker.
Laser Award Maker (IBM).

Baypointe Publishing, (1-886572), 13437 Crestwood Dr., Minnetonka, MN 55435 Tel 612-953-7810.
Titles:
Personal Financial Plan (PFP): A Guide.

Bayware, Inc., (1-883653), 1660 S. Amphlett Blvd., Suite 128, San Mateo, CA 94402 Tel 415-286-4492; Toll free: 800-538-8867; FAX: 415-578-1884.
Titles:
Kanji Moments.
Power Japanese.
Power Spanish.

BeachWare, 9419 Mount Israel Rd., Escondido, CA 92029 Tel 619-735-8945.
Titles:
Almanac of WWII.
Breakthrough Backgrounds.
Cheats, Hacks, & Hints.
Education Works.
Font Works for Macintosh.
Game Works for Macintosh.
Goldilocks Gamebook.
Multimedia Music Clips.
Multimedia Nursery Rhymes.
Multiware Multimedia Collection.
Nature Photo Collection.
Night Sky Interactive.
1000 Games for Macintosh.
1000 Games for Windows & DOS.
Photo Textures.
Religion Bookshelf.
Shareware Breakthrough Desktop Publishing Collection.
Shareware Breakthrough for Mac.
Shareware Breakthrough Games & Education.
Shareware Breakthrough Multimedia Collection.
Shareware Breakthrough Programmers Collection.
Shareware Breakthrough Utilities & Productivity.
Sports Bloopers.
Swimsuit Review 94.
Swimsuit Review '94 & '95.
TrackIt.
Trivia Warehouse 2000.
A Zillion Sounds.

Beacon Technology, Inc., P.O. Box 62669, Colorado Springs, CO 80962-2669 Tel 719-594-4884; Toll free: 800-777-1841; FAX: 719-594-4271.
Titles:
Begat.
Gems of the Word.
HyperBible: The Computerized Chain Reference Tool.

Beagle Brothers, (0-917085), P.O. Box 1941, Orem, UT 84059-1941; Toll free: 800-345-1750.
Titles:
Alpha Plot.
Apple Mechanic Type Face.
Beagle Bag.
Beagle BASIC.
Beagle Compiler.
Beagle Graphics.
Beagle Screens.
Big U.
D Code.
DiskQuick.
DOS BOSS.
Double-Take.
Extra K.
Fatcat.
FileMover.
Flex Type.
Font Mechanic.
Frame-Up.
G. P. L. E: Global Program Line Editor.
I. O. Silver.
MacroWorks.
Minipix.
Power Print.
Pro-Byter.
Pronto DOS.
Shape Mechanic.
Silicon Salad.
Super MacroWorks.
Timeout Desktools.
Timeout Filemaster.
Timeout Graph.
Timeout QuickSpell.
Timeout SideSpread.
Timeout SuperFonts.
Timeout UltraMacros.
Tip Disk #1.
Triple-Dump.
Utility City.

Beaman Porter, Inc., (0-917965), P.O. Box 201, Somers, NY 10589 Tel 914-276-0624.
Titles:
PowerText BookMaker.
PowerText Formatter.
PowerText Professional & BookMaker.

Beck-Tech, 1210 Marina Village Pkwy., No. 100, Alameda, CA 94501-1045.
Titles:
MacMovies.

PUBLISHER/TITLE INDEX

Beechwood Software, (0-922492), 975 Ebner Dr., Webster, NY 14580 Tel 716-872-6450.
Titles:
Accident/Incident Control.
Beechwood Accounts Payable Package.
Beechwood General Ledger Package.
Beechwood Payroll Package.
Care Plans.
Checking Account Package.
Infection Control.
Patient Assessment.
Patient Spending Account Package.
Patients Statistics & Accounts Receivable Package.
Physician Orders.
Quality Assurance Reports.
Staff Scheduling.

Behavioral Engineering, (0-922493), 343 Soquel Ave., No. 334, Santa Cruz, CA 95062-2305.
Titles:
Mind Master Introductory Software.
NLP "Anchoring" Software Package.
NLP Tools Volume 1.

Bell, Bruce, & Assocs., Inc., (0-917955), 425 Main St., Suite 10, P.O. Box 400, Canon City, CO 81212 Tel 719-275-1661; Toll free: 800-359-7738.
Titles:
ABtab.
Scout.
Surview - Media Research Edition.

Bellcore, (1-878108), 60 New England Ave., Piscataway, NJ 08854-4196 Tel 201-699-5802; Toll free: 800-521-2673.
Titles:
Advanced Intelligent Network: An Overview.
ATM: A Technical Overview.
ATM, F-R, SMDS: An Applications Overview.
ATM Local Area Networks: An Overview.
Broadband: An Overview.
Business Case for Implementing Broadband Networks.
CCS - SS7.
Fiber Optic Technology: An Overview.
Frame Relay: A Technical Overview.
Fundamentals of Protocols.
Introduction to Translations.
ISDN: A Closer Look.
ISDN Loop Qualification & Extension: An Overview.
ISDN Sales Planning: An Overview.
Local Area Networks: An Overview.
Open System Interconnection: An Overview.
Packet Switching Fundamentals.
SMDS: A Brief Overview.
SONET: An Overview.
SS7: A Brief Look.
TCP - IP & the Internet: An Overview.

Bellmore Software, (0-9621501), 2436 Kayron Ln., North Bellmore, NY 11710 Tel 516-221-0392.
Titles:
Hebrew - Signs, Banners, & Greeting Cards.
Introduction to Turbo Pascal: A Tutorial.
Math RCT Fun.

Bender, Matthew, & Co., Inc., Subs. of Times Mirror Co., (0-8205), Orders to: 11 Penn Plaza, New York, NY 10001 Tel 212-967-7707; Toll free: 800-833-9844; 800-422-2022 (in New York).
Titles:
California Wills & Trusts: CAPS Practice System Series.
Collier's Topform: Bankruptcy Filing Program.
Draft Master Software Series: California Business Incorporations.
Draft Master Software Series: California Deposition & Discovery on Disk.
Draft Master Software Series: California Marital Settlement Agreement.
Draft Master Software Series: California Personal Injury.
Search Master: Business Law Library.
Search Master: California Library.
Search Master: Collier's Bankruptcy Library.
Search Master: Federal Practice Library.
Search Master: Intellectual Property Library.
Search Master: New York Library.
Search Master: Personal Injury Library.
Search Master: Tax Library.
Search Master: Texas Library.

Benefit Analysis, Inc., (0-922509), 550 American Ave., Suite 100, King Prussia, PA 19401 Tel 610-992-1280; Toll free: 800-223-3601; FAX: 610-992-1204.
Titles:
Estate Resource.
Pension Resource.

Bennett, Loren, (0-922180), 1320 Notre Dame Dr., Davis, CA 95616 Tel 916-756-8946; FAX: 916-756-8946.
Titles:
Dairy Ration Evaluation.
Dairy Ration Formulation.
Professional Ration Package: For Beef, Swine, Dairy, Rabbits, Fish, Fertilizer, Poultry Load Sheet Calculator, Formula Pricing.

Berge Software, Subs. of Palmer Berge Co., (0-926065), P.O. Box 1343, Mercer Island, WA 98040-1343 Tel 206-236-1908; Toll free: 800-426-2135; FAX: 206-230-8664.
Titles:
Investment Analysis.
Real Estate Asset Management Software System.

Berkeley Softworks, Div. of Geoworks, 960 Atlantic Ave., Alameda, CA 94501-1018; Toll free: 800-443-0100, Ext. 234.
Titles:
DeskPack Plus.
FontPack Plus.
GeoCalc.
geoChart.
GeoFile.
geoProgrammer.
geoPublish.
GEOS: Graphic Environment Operating System.

Berkeley Systems, Inc., 2095 Rose St., Berkeley, CA 94709 Tel 415-540-5535.
Titles:
After Dark.
After Dark: For Windows.
inLARGE.
More After Dark: For Macintosh.
outSPOKEN: The Talking Macintosh Interface.

Berkshire Software Co., (0-938213), 44 Madison St., Lynbrook, NY 11563 Tel 516-593-8019.
Titles:
EQUIPD: The Equipment Management System.
Neuralog.
Perfect Merge.
Turbo Shell: Generic Expert System.

Berstis International, P.O. Box 181001, Austin, TX 78718 Tel 512-329-0639.
Titles:
Minnesota SNOBOL4.2.

Best, A. M., Co., (0-89408), Ambest Rd., Oldwick, NJ 08858 Tel 908-439-2200; FAX: 908-439-3296.
Titles:
Best ESP: Electronic Statement Preparation.

Best Case Solutions, Inc., 635 Chicago Ave., Suite 110, Evanston, IL 60202; Toll free: 800-492-8037; FAX: 708-492-8038.
Titles:
Best Case Bankruptcy Filing System.

Best Information Services, Div. of Best Programs, Inc., (0-922760), 11413 Isaac Newton Sq., Reston, VA 22090-5005; Toll free: 800-227-2437; FAX: 216-677-2541.
Titles:
CPAid Individual State Programs.
CPAid Individual Tax Planner.
CPAid Master Write-Up.
CPAid Master 1040.
CPAid Master 1065.
CPAid Master 1120.
CPAid Master 1120S.
CPaid Time & Billing Program.

Best Programs, (0-917685; 0-917791), 2700 S. Quincy St., Arlington, VA 22206 Tel 703-820-9300; Toll free: 800-842-4947; FAX: 703-379-7067.
Titles:
FAS: Fixed Asset System.
FAS 2000.
Fixed Asset System.
G & G GL: Client Write-Up.
G & G 1040.
G & G 1065: Partnership Return.
G & G 1120: Corporation Return.
G & G 1120S: Sub Chapter S Corporate.
Tax Partner.

BetaTool Systems, (0-926944), 1445 N. Amiron Way, No. B, Orem, UT 84057-8333.
Titles:
BASIC Development System: BDS.

Better Business Solutions, (0-917293), c/o Sharon Darling, 20505 U.S. Hwy. 19 N., No., Clearwater, FL 34624-6007.
Titles:
The Maintenance Authority-Facility Management.
Professional Timekeeping System.
Trust Account Management System.

Bible Research Systems, (0-917689), 2013 Wells Branch Pkwy., Suite 304, Austin, TX 78728 Tel 512-251-7541; Toll free: 800-423-1228; FAX: 512-251-4401.
Titles:
Chain Reference.
Chronological Bible.
The Greek Transliterator.
The Hebrew Transliterator.
Librarian.
People.
Personal Commentary.
Topics.
Verse Search.
Verse Typist.

Biblesoft, (1-56514), 22014 Seventh Ave., S., Seattle, WA 98198-6235 Tel 206-824-0682; Toll free: 800-877-0778; FAX: 206-824-1828.
Titles:
American Standard Version Add-On Module.
Biblesoft's Greek-Hebrew Word Study Series.
Greek-Hebrew Text for Windows.
Interlinear Transliterated Bible.
International Standard Bible Encyclopedia.
King James Version.
King James Version PC Study Bible King James Edition: PC Study Bible with Nave's - KJV.
King James Version Text.
The Living Bible.
The Living Bible Add-On Module.
Matthew Henry Commentary.
Naves Topical Bible & Cross Reference System.
Nelson's Bible Dictionary.
Nelson's Illustrated Bible Dictionary.
New International Version.

BIG BYTE SOFTWARE

New King James Version.
New King James Version Add-On Text.
New Unger's Bible Dictionary for Windows.
PC Study Bible for DOS: New American Standard Version.
PC Study Bible for Windows.
PC Study Bible for Windows: Discovery Plus Edition on CD-ROM.
PC Study Bible for Windows: King James Version Edition.
PC Study Bible for Windows: King James Version Edition CD-ROM.
PC Study Bible for Windows: King James Version on CD ROM.
PC Study Bible for Windows: KJV Discovery Edition on CD ROM.
PC Study Bible for WINDOWS KJV Edition.
PC Study Bible for WINDOWS MASTER Edition.
PC Study Bible for Windows: New American Standard Bible Discovery Edition on CD ROM.
PC Study Bible for Windows: New American Standard Bible Edition.
PC Study Bible for Windows: New American Standard Version.
PC Study Bible for Windows: New International Version Edition.
PC Study Bible for Windows: New Internatinoal Version Edition CD-ROM.
PC Study Bible for Windows: New King James Version.
PC Study Bible for Windows: New King James Version Edition.
PC Study Bible for Windows: New Master Edition CD-ROM.
PC Study Bible for Windows: New Master Edition.
PC Study Bible for Windows: New Reference Library.
PC Study Bible for Windows: New Reference Library CD-ROM.
PC Study Bible for Windows: New Reference Library Edition.
PC Study Bible for Windows: New Reference Library on CD-ROM.
PC Study Bible for Windows: NIV Discovery Edition on CD-ROM.
PC Study Bible for WINDOWS NIV Edition.
PC Study Bible for Windows: NKJ Discovery Edition on CD ROM.
PC Study Bible for Windows: Reference Library Plus.
PC Study Bible for WINDOWS Reference Library Edition.
PC Study Bible for Windows: Reference Library Plus with Matthew Henry CD-ROM.
PC Study Bible: King James Version.
PC Study Bible KJV Edition.
PC Study Bible: Master Edition.
PC Study Bible New International Edition: PC Study Bible with Nave's - NIV.
PC Study Bible: New International Version Edition.
PC Study Bible: New King James Version.
PC Study Bible NIV Edition.
PC Study Bible Reference Libary Edition.
PC Study Bible: Reference Library Edition.
Revised Standard Version.
Revised Standard Version Text.
Strong's Greek-Hebrew Dictionary & Englishman's Concordance.
The Treasury of Scripture Knowledge.
Vine's Expository Dictionary of Biblical Words.
Word Study Library.
Word Study Series.

Big Byte Software, (1-878081), 1814 Rosemount Ave., Claremont, CA 91711.
Titles:
The Nutrition Stack.
Recipe Master.

Big G Software, (0-922526), Rte. 2, P.O. Box 111, Alleyton, TX 78935 Tel 409-732-3904; Toll free: 800-222-3965; FAX: 409-732-3443.
Titles:
Football Statistics.
Volleyball Statistics Program.

Billings, P. G., 12134 Bonnie Terr., Seminole, FL 33542 Tel 813-398-1913.
Titles:
Survey-Property I.
Survey-Property II.

Binary Engineering Software, Inc., (0-932217), 100 Fifth Ave., Waltham, MA 02154 Tel 617-890-1812; FAX: 617-890-1340.
Titles:
Tech*Graph*Pad.

Bio-Rad Laboratories, (0-9618315), 2000 Alfred Nobel Dr., Hercules, CA 94547 Tel 510-741-1000; Toll free: 800-424-6723; FAX: 510-741-1060.
Titles:
Kinetic Collector/Macintosh.
Microplate Manager.

BioScan, Inc., 190 W. Dayton St., No. 103, Edmonds, WA 98020-4182 Tel 206-775-8000; Toll free: 800-635-7226; FAX: 206-775-3640.
Titles:
BioScan OPTIMAS.
BioScan SnapShot+.

Biosource Software, (0-944122), 4 Sunrise Ln., Kirksville, MO 63501 Tel 816-665-5751; FAX: 816-665-1657.
Titles:
Concepts in Electromyography.
Concepts in Thermography.
The Human Brain: Neurons.
Neuromuscular Concepts.
Principles of Pharmacology.
Self-Assessment in Biofeedback 1.5.
Self-Assessment in Psychology.
Skeletal Muscle Anatomy & Physiology.
Skills in Electromyography.

Biota Pubns., (0-9649044), 5353 Keller Springs, Suite 713, Dallas, TX 75248 Tel 214-407-8860.
Titles:
Bioinformation on the World Wide Web: An Annotated Directory of Molecular Biology Tools.
BioInformation on the World Wide Web: Annotated Directory of Molecular Biology Tools.

Bitmap, Inc., P.O. Box 237, Westwego, LA 70094 Tel 504-347-6317.
Titles:
Electronic Woodcuts & Holiday Clip Art.

Black Banana, Inc., 3930 S. Roosevelt Blvd., No. 310E, Key West, FL 33040-5201.
Titles:
Inventory Control & General Ledger.

BlackHawk Technology, P.O. Box 2013, Morgan Hill, CA 95038-2013 Tel 408-776-1106; Toll free: 800-528-9333; FAX: 408-776-1107.
Titles:
Parameter Manager Plus.

Blackman, Kallick, Bartelstein, Certified Public Accountants/Consulting, (0-916181), 300 S. Riverside Plaza, Suite 660, Chicago, IL 60606 Tel 312-207-1040; FAX: 312-207-1066.
Titles:
AuditCube.

Blanton Software Service, (0-922550), 410101 Grand Pk., San Antonio, TX 78239 Tel 210-657-3323.
Titles:
EZ-dBASE.
EZ Mail.
EZMENU.
EZSCRIP.
EZSCRIP PLUS.

Blitz Publishing Co., (0-9606344; 0-928404), 1600 N. High Point Rd., Middleton, WI 53562-3635 Tel 608-836-7550; FAX: 608-831-5598.
Titles:
Building Heat Gain & Heat Loss.
Building Heating Energy Use Estimator.
Office Building Load Estimator: Heating, Cooling, Electrical.
Water Heater Selection.

Bloom, E. J., Assocs., Inc., 115 Duran Dr., San Rafael, CA 94903 Tel 415-492-8443; FAX: 415-492-1239.
Titles:
Computer-Aided Design for Inductors & Transformers.

Bloom, Robert, (0-922554), Stoney Brook Professional Bldg., Lake Grove, NY 11755 Tel 516-588-3636.
Titles:
HAS (Health Assistance System).

Blossom Software Corp., 1 Kendall Sq., Bldg. 600, Cambridge, MA 02139 Tel 617-738-1516; FAX: 617-566-4936.
Titles:
Write In.

Blue Bridge Software, 7401 W. Canal Dr., Suite 343, Kennewick, WA 99336 Tel 509-627-6729.
Titles:
Turbo Screen Master.

Blue Byte Software, Inc., (1-888533), 33 S. Roselle Rd., Suite 201, Schaumburg, IL 60193 Tel 708-539-7950; FAX: 708-539-7951.
Titles:
Battle Isle 2220: Shadow of the Emperor.

Blue Cat, (0-936200; 0-932679), 469 Barbados, Walnut, CA 91789 Tel 909-594-3317; Dist. by: Ingram Bk. Co., 1 Ingram Blvd., La Vergne, TN 37086-1986 Tel 615-793-5000; Toll free: 800-937-8000 (orders only, all warehouses); Dist. by: Baker & Taylor Bks., Somerville Service Ctr., 50 Kirby Ave., Somerville, NJ 08876-0734 Tel 908-722-8000; Toll free: 800-775-1500 (customer service); Dist. by: Baker & Taylor Bks., Momence Service Ctr., 501 S. Gladiolus St., Momence, IL 60954-2444 Tel 815-472-2444; Toll free: 800-775-2300 (customer service); Dist. by: Baker & Taylor Bks., Commerce Service Ctr., 251 Mt. Olive Church Rd., Commerce, GA 30599-9988 Tel 706-335-5000; Toll free: 800-775-1200 (customer service).
Titles:
ABFAB Assembly Disk.
ABFAB Demo Applications Disk.
ABFAB Library Disks.
Aliens.
Apple Panic.
Atari Electric Pencil.
Auto-Exec: Accounts Receivable.
Auto-Exec: General Ledger.
Babble Terror.
BFBDEM.
BFBLIB.
The Black Hole.
Blue Pencil.
CASDIS.
CASDUP.
Cyberchess.
DEX-88 Spooler.

DFBLOAD.
DISASM.
DISDUP.
Diskmap.
DISKPAK.
DOSPLUS 2.0.
DOSPLUS 3.5.
DOSPLUS 4.0.
DOWNLD.
Electric Pencil.
Electric Pencil PC.
Electric Pencil PC Tutor.
Flag Race.
FULMAP.
IBM Superzap.
Interceptor.
Mad Mines.
Micro-Map.
Microterm.
PC Proofreader.
Pencil ACE.
Power Screen.
PROPAK.
RAMDISK PC.
Red Pencil.
The Secret Library Disk.
Snokie.
Space Robbers.
Time Runner.
Translate.
V-COS.

Blue Mountain Software, 958 Edwards Ave., Santa Rosa, CA 95401-4262. Do not confuse with Blue Mountain Software, Inc. in Port Angeles, WA.
Titles:
AutoTrace DOS.

Blue Ridge Creative Software, 12122 Holly Knoll Cir., Great Falls, VA 22066 Tel 703-444-5642.
Titles:
Schedule Sculptor.

BlueRithm Software, 21823 N. Glen Dr., Colbert, WA 99005-9415 Tel 509-468-1434; FAX: 509-467-2699.
Titles:
Aeris for Windows, Aeris for MS-DOS.

Blyth Software, Inc., Div. of Blyth Software, Ltd., (0-941299), 989 E. Hillsdale Blvd., Suite 400, Foster City, CA 94404 Tel 415-571-0222.
Titles:
Express.
Omnis II.
Omnis III.
Omnis III Plus.
Omnis Quartz.
Omnis Quartz: Windows Version.
Omnis V.

BNA Software, Div. of Bureau of National Affairs, Inc., (0-928513), 1231 25th St., NW, Washington, DC 20037 Tel 202-452-4453; Toll free: 800-424-2938; FAX: 202-452-7547.
Titles:
BNA Corporate Foreign Tax Credit Planner.
BNA Corporate Tax Spreadsheet.
BNA Estate Tax Spreadsheet.
BNA Fixed Asset Management System.
The BNA Income Tax Spreadsheet with Fifty State Planner.
BNA Real Estate Investment Spreadsheet.

Bodo Bodo & Co., Inc., (0-917789), 1205 Blackwood Mountain Rd., Chapel Hill, NC 27516-9201 Tel 919-929-5048.
Titles:
The Aerobics Master.

Bodylog, Inc., Div. of Medcomp Tech., Inc., 120 Kisco Ave., Mount Kisco, NY 10549 Tel 914-241-7121; Toll free: 800-233-2911; FAX: 914-241-7043.
Titles:
BASIC EMG #1.
Bodylink.
Bodyscope.
Crop Duster.
Data Retrieval for Rehab.
Data Retrieval for Stress.
Demo Program.
Dock-It.
Egg Roll.
Harry Helio.
Peace of Mind.
Rehab.
Ride for Your Life.
Stress.
Temperature Cartridge.
3 Dee-Q-Bee.

Books Nippan, Div. of Nippan Shuppan Hanbai, U.S.A., Inc., (0-945814; 1-56970), 1123 Dominguez St., Suite K, Carson, CA 90746 Tel 310-604-9701; Toll free: 800-562-1410; FAX: 310-604-1134.
Titles:
Nude Private Works.

Books on Business, (0-932355), P.O. Box 313G, Buena Park, CA 90621 Tel 714-523-0357.
Titles:
Commercial Credit Matrix: For Lotus 1-2-3 & Symphony.
Price Deflator Worksheet: For Lotus 1-2-3.

Bootware Software Co., Inc., 28024 Dorothy Dr., Agoura Hills, CA 91301 Tel 818-706-3887; FAX: 818-991-6485.
Titles:
ResumeWriter.

Boraventures Publishing, (1-883596), 18 Reef Rd., Fairfield, CT 06430 Tel 203-254-2953; FAX: 203-254-2368.
Titles:
America Remembered: Views You Can Use.
Rapunzel: A Retelling of the Brothers Grimm Fairy Tale.

Borland International, Inc., (0-87524), 1800 Green Hills Rd., P.O. Box 660001, Scotts Valley, CA 95066-0001 Tel 408-438-8400; Toll free: 800-543-7543.
Titles:
Borland C++.
dBASE III PLUS.
dBASE III PLUS LAN Pack.
dBASE IV.
Eureka: The Solver.
Framework IV.
MultiMate Local Area Network Versions.
MultiMate Professional Word Processor.
ObjectVision.
Paradox.
Paradox OS/2.
Paradox 386.
Quattro.
QUATTRO PRO.
RapidFile.
Reflex Plus: The Database Manager.
Reflex: The Analyst.
Reflex: The Database Manager.
Reflex Workshop.
SideKick.
Sidekick: for the Macintosh.
SideKick Plus.
Sprint: The Professional Word Processor.
SuperKey: Keyboard Enhancer - Security.
Traveling SideKick.
Turbo ASM.
Turbo BASIC.
Turbo BASIC Database Toolbox.
Turbo BASIC Editor Toolbox.
Turbo BASIC Telecom Toolbox.
Turbo C.
Turbo C++.
Turbo Database Toolbox.
Turbo Debugger.
Turbo Editor Toolbox.
Turbo GameWorks.
Turbo Graphix Toolbox: Programming Aids.
Turbo Lightning.
Turbo Lightning Word Wizard.
Turbo Pascal.
Turbo Pascal Database Toolbox.
Turbo Pascal for the Macintosh.
Turbo Pascal for Windows.
Turbo Pascal Numerical Methods Toolbox for the Macintosh.
Turbo Pascal Numerical Methods Toolbox for IBM.
Turbo Pascal Tutor for the Macintosh.
Turbo Prolog.
Turbo Prolog Toolbox.
Turbo Prolog 2.0.
Turbo Tutor: Pascal Programming Primer.

Boston Business Computing, Ltd., 13 Branch St., Methuen, MA 01844 Tel 508-725-3222; FAX: 508-725-3229.
Titles:
EDT+.
Vbackup.
VCL.
Vmail.

Boston Educational Computing, Inc., (0-917691), 78 Dartmouth St., Boston, MA 02116 Tel 617-536-5116.
Titles:
R.E. List: Real Estate Brokerage Program.

Bottom Line Software, (0-937973), P.O. Box 10545, Eugene, OR 97440 Tel 503-484-0520; FAX: 503-461-4634.
Titles:
Kitchen Help.
On-Hand Inventory.

Bourbaki, Inc., (0-922580), 615 W. Hays St., Boise, ID 83702 Tel 208-342-5849; Toll free: 800-289-1347 (orders only); FAX: 208-342-5823.
Titles:
1dir+ (Wonder Plus).

Bowker, R. R., A Reed Reference Publishing company, (0-8352; 0-911255), 121 Chanlon Rd., New Providence, NJ 07974 Tel 908-464-6800; Toll free: 800-521-8110; 800-431-1713 subscriptions to: Publishers Weekly, School Library Journal, Library Journal (in Ohio: 614-383-3141); 800-257-7894 subscriptions to: Library Hotline, Reviews-on-Cards (in New Jersey: 609-786-1160); FAX: 908-464-3553; Orders to: P.O. Box 1001, Summit, NJ 07902-1001.
Titles:
Advertiser & Agency Red Books Plus.
Books In Print Plus.
Books In Print Plus: With Book Reviews.
Books In Print with Book Reviews Plus.
Books Out Of Print Plus.
Books Out Of Print Plus: With Book Reviews.
Bowker/Whitaker Global Books In Print Plus.
Children's Reference Plus.
Christian Books In Print Plus.
Corporate Affiliations Plus.
Ingram Books In Print Plus.
Ingram Books In Print Plus: with Book Reviews.
Marquis Who's Who Plus.
Martindale-Hubbell Law Directory on CD-ROM.
Publishing Market Place Reference Plus.
SciTech Reference Plus.
Ulrich's Plus.
Variety's Video Directory Plus.

Bowker-Saur, A part of Reed Reference Publishing, (0-86291; 1-85739), 121 Chanlon Rd., New Providence, NJ 07974 Tel 908-464-6800; Toll free: 800-521-8110; FAX: 908-665-6707.
Titles:
ASSIA Plus: Applied Social Science Abstracts.
BHI Plus: British Humanities Index.
CTI Plus: Current Technology Index.
European R & D Plus.
Institute of Management International Databases Plus.
LISA Plus: Library & Information Science Abstracts.

Boyd & Fraser Publishing Co., Div. of International Thomson Publishing Education Group, (0-87835; 0-87709; 0-89426; 0-928763; 0-7895), One Corporate Pl., 55 Ferncroft Rd., Danvers, MA 01923 Tel 508-777-9069; Toll free: 800-225-3782; FAX: 508-777-9068; Orders to: Distribution Ctr., 7625 Empire Dr., Florence, KY 41042-2978 Tel 606-525-2230; Toll free: 800-354-9706.
Titles:
Asset Allocation Tools.
Decision Analysis for the Professional with Supertree.
GINO: General Interactive Optimizer.
LINDO: Linear Interactive & Discrete Optimizer.
MARKSTRAT: A Marketing Strategy Game.
XCELL+.

Bradford & Robbins, 606B Rio Grande, Austin, TX 78701; Toll free: 800-622-8727.
Titles:
MacAppraiser.

Brady Computer Bks., Div. of Prentice Hall Computer Publishing, (0-87618; 0-87619; 0-89303; 0-913486; 1-56686), 15 Columbus Cir., 14th Flr., New York, NY 10023 Tel 212-373-8500; FAX: 212-373-8192; Orders to: Prentice Hall Computer Publishing, 11711 N. College Ave., Suite 140, Carmel, IN 46032 Tel 317-573-2500; Toll free: 800-428-5331.
Titles:
Albert J. Lowry Real Estate Investment & Management.
Apple II Computer Graphics.
Games, Graphics & Sound for the IBM PC.
The Graphics Generator: Business & Technical Applications for the IBM PC.
The Great International Paper Airplane Construction Kit.
Hugh Johnson's Wine Cellar: A Wine & Food Companion.
Inside the IBM PC: Access to Advanced Features & Programming Techniques.
J. K. Lasser's Your Money Manager.
Jot It Down.
Laser Cycle.
The Mac Art Department.
The MacArt Department.
Nomination.
P&L.
Resume Master.
Speed Reading Tutor IV.
Star Trek: The Kobayashi Alternative.
Star Trek: The Promethean Prophecy.
Star Trek: The Rebel Universe.
'Twas the Night Before Christmas.
Webster's New World On-Line Thesaurus.
Webster's New World Spelling Checker.
Webster's New World Writer.
Wings Out of Shadow.
Wizard's Cube.

BrainBank/Generation Ahead of Maryland, (0-917277), 20649 Highland Hall Dr., Gaithersburg, MD 20879 Tel 301-869-0248; FAX: 301-869-6379.
Titles:
American History: Decades Game 1, 2 & 3.
Backaid Software.
Classes of Nouns.
Millionwaire.
Prefixes One & Two.
Reading One-Five: Four Skills, Practice A-D.
Science One: Human Body: an Overview.
Science Two: Skeletal System.
Social Studies: States Game.
Suffixes One & Two.
Word Functions.

Brainstorm Development, Inc., P.O. Box 26948, Austin, TX 78755 Tel 512-343-9482.
Titles:
Financial Utilities Pack.
Overture.

Breakthrough Productions, 210 Park Ave., Nevada City, CA 95959 Tel 916-265-0911; FAX: 916-265-8036.
Titles:
A Plus Electronic Flashcards.
Market Master for the Macintosh: Personal Version.
Market Master Manager.

Bridge Learning Systems, Inc., (0-9632069; 1-885587), 351 Los Altos, American Canyon, CA 94589 Tel 510-228-3177; Toll free: 800-487-9868; FAX: 510-372-6099; Orders to: 351 Los Altos, American Canyon, CA 94589; Toll free: 800-487-9868.
Titles:
Let's Do DOS Plus.
SimuDOS.
SimuNet.
SimuNet: (Demo Disk).
SimuWEB.

Bridgeport Machines, Inc., 219 Rittenhouse Circle, Bristol, PA 19007 Tel 215-788-0515; Toll free: 800-445-3479; FAX: 215-788-0734.
Titles:
EZ-CAM.

Bridget Software Co., (0-928043), 1309 Canyon Rd., Silver Spring, MD 20904 Tel 301-384-7875.
Titles:
Bicycle Master.
Fitness Master.
Graph Master (IBM).
Run Master.

Briggs Mountain Co., (0-934583), Box 363, R.D. 2, Red Hook, NY 12571 Tel 914-758-6735.
Titles:
Delivery Control & Accounting System: A Software Package for Fuel Distributors.

Briley Software, (0-922602), P.O. Box 2913, Livermore, CA 94551-2913 Tel 510-455-9139; FAX: 510-455-9139.
Titles:
Addresser.
Archivebowl.
BCS League Finance Manager.
Blackjack Tutor.
Leaguebowl.
MWS Baseball Stats.
MWS Basketball Stats.
MWS Bible Concordance: New Testament (KJV).
MWS Gymnastics.
MWS Volleyball Stats.
RECAPBOWL.
RJL Baseball Statbook.
RJL Basketball Stats.
RJL Football Stats.
RJL Sports Statsbook.
Tournamentbowl.

Bristol Information Systems, (0-922606), 11320 Lake Tree Ct., Boca Raton, FL 33498-6817.
Titles:
BIAS.
Bisiness Accounts Payable System.
Bisiness Accounts Receivable System (AR).
Bisiness Balance Forward Accounts Receivable (BFAR).
Bisiness Check Reconciliation System.
Bisiness Construction Accounting System.
Bisiness Equipment Management.
Bisiness Fixed Asset System.
Bisiness General Ledger System.
Bisiness Inventory Control System.
Bisiness Order Entry Billing System.
Bisiness Payroll System.
Bisiness Property Management System.
Bisiness Purchase Order System.
Verticals.

Bristow, Duane, Computers, Inc., (0-922609), Rte. 3, Albany, KY 42602 Tel 606-387-5884.
Titles:
Anti-Aircraft.
Auto Insurance.
Billboard.
Bristow Accounts Receivable.
Bristow Accounts Receivable II.
Calendar.
Cash Flow Plan.
Designs.
Equipment Inventory.
Farm Database Financial Analysis & Records.
Farm Enterprise Analysis.
Farm Simulator.
Forest Fire Dispatcher.
Forest Inventory Analysis.
Forest Sample Database.
General Ledger by Profit Center.
Grocery.
Keysort & Data Edit Package.
Maze.
Modules.
Nimrod.
Oil Accounting Package.
Oil Purchasing, Oil Accounting & Oil Well Reports to Interest Holders.
Oil Well Database.
100 Cards.
Population Simulation.
Rabbits.
Surveying Calculations.
Texteditor.
Words.
Writsit.

British Telecom, (1-878249), 2100 Reston Pkwy., Reston, VA 22091 Tel 703-715-7000.
Titles:
UpFront.

Brock Software Products, Inc., (0-922611), 8603 Pyott Rd., P.O. Box 799, Crystal Lake, IL 60014-0799 Tel 815-459-4210.
Titles:
Brock Disk Librarian for Macintosh.
Brock Keystroke Data Base.
Brock Keystroke Data Base Advanced-Encrypted.
Brock Keystroke Filer.
Brock Keystroke: Relational Data Base & Report Generator.

Broderbund Software, Inc., (0-922614; 1-55790; 1-57382), 500 Redwood Blvd., Novato, CA 94948-6121 Tel 415-492-3200; Toll free: 800-527-6263; Orders to: Software Direct, P.O. Box 6125, Novato, CA 94948-6125 Tel 415-492-3500.
Titles:
Airheart.
The Ancient Art of War.

PUBLISHER/TITLE INDEX

The Ancient Art of War at Sea.
Animate.
Arcade Game Construction Kit.
Bank Street Filer.
Bank Street Writer.
BannerMania.
Blue Max 2001.
Breakers.
Brimstone.
Broderbund Accounts Receivable.
Broderbund General Ledger with Payables.
Broderbund Payroll.
Captain Goodnight & the Islands of Fear.
The Castles of Doctor Creep.
Cauldron.
Championship Lode Runner.
Choplifter.
Cyborg.
David's Midnight Magic.
Dazzle Draw.
Directors Series.
DownHill Challenge.
Drawing Table.
Drol.
DTP Advisor.
Electronic Whole Earth Catalogue.
Essex.
Fantavision.
Fantavision - IIgs.
Financial Independence.
ForComment.
Jam Session.
Karateka.
Letterhead.
Lode Runner.
Lode Runner's Rescue.
The Mask of the Sun.
MemoryMate.
Mindwheel.
The Music Shop.
New York City - Air Support.
New York City - Electrician.
Omni-Med.
On Balance.
Operation Whirlwind.
Postermaker Plus.
PosterMaker Plus Graphic.
Postermaker Plus Graphics Library.
The Print Shop.
The Print Shop Companion.
The Print Shop Graphics Library.
The Print Shop Graphics Library: Holiday Edition.
Quasimodo - Air Support.
Quasimodo - Warriors of Zypar.
Raid on Bungeling Bay.
Rainbow Walker - Countdown.
Rainbow Walker - Doughboy.
Relax.
Seafox.
Serpentine.
The Serpent's Star.
Show Off.
Showoff Graphics Collection: World Events.
Spare Change.
Spelunker.
Star Wars.
Stealth.
Superbike Challenge.
SynCALC.
SynCHRON.
SynCOMM.
SynFILE Plus.
SynSTOCK.
SynTREND.
Thinking Cap.
TypeStyler.
Typhoon Thompson in Search for the Sea Child.
Variable Feasts.
Welcome Aboard: A Muppet Cruise to Computer Literacy.
Where in the USA Is Carmen Sandiego?
Whistler's Brother.
Wizard of Wall Street.
Zaxxon.

Brooks/Cole Publishing Co., Div. of International Thomson Publishing Co., (0-8185; 0-534), 511 Forest Lodge Rd., Pacific Grove, CA 93950 Tel 408-373-0728; FAX: 408-375-6414; Orders to: Int'l Thomson Publishing Distribution Ctr., 7625 Empire Dr., Florence, KY 41042-2978 Tel 606-525-2230; Toll free: 800-354-9706.
Titles:
Cabri: The Interactive Geometry Notebook.
GraphPlay.
Maple Five: Student Edition.
PhasePlane: The Dynamical System Too!
Statistics with Stata.
Surface Plotter.
TEMATH: Tools for Exploring Mathematics.

Brown, Wm. C., Pubs., Div. of Times Mirror Higher Education Group, Inc., (0-697), 2460 Kerper Blvd., Dubuque, IA 52001 Tel 319-588-1451; Toll free: 800-338-5578; FAX: 800-346-2377.
Titles:
Advanced Ear Training - Tutorial & Testing Programs.
Ear Training - A Technique for Listening.
Healthlines: Programs for Optimal Well-Being.
Music Fundamentals.
The Musician's Toolbox.
PSYCOM: Psychology on Computer: Simulations, Experiments & Projects.
Testing Programs for Advanced Ear Training.
Tutorial Programs for Advanced Ear Training.

Brown Bag Software, Div. of Software Resource Group, 2155 S. Bascom Ave., Campbell, CA 95008 Tel 408-559-4545; Toll free: 800-523-0764; 800-323-5335 (in California); FAX: 408-559-7090.
Titles:
Easy Presentation Graphics.
MindReader.
PC-Outline.
PowerMenu.

Bruzaud Assocs., (0-922627), 771 Rte. 15, S., Lake Hopatcong, NJ 07849 Tel 201-663-1522; FAX: 201-663-1713.
Titles:
The DEALMAKER: Automotive F&I.
The DEALMAKER: Automotive Leasing Systems.
The DEALMAKER: Data Conversion System.
The DEALMAKER: Management Reports.
The DEALMAKER: Vehicle Inventory System.

Bryley Systems, Inc., 12 Main St., Hudson, MA 01749 Tel 508-562-6077; FAX: 508-562-5680.
Titles:
Cash-Flow Forecaster Plus.

Buck Consultants, Inc., 2 Pennsylvania Plaza, New York, NY 10121 Tel 212-330-1000; FAX: 212-695-4184.
Titles:
Buck Actval.
Buck BENCAL/PC.
Buck IDP (Interactive Data Program).
Buck Recordkeeping Plus.
Buck Social Security.
Buck Tax Exclusion/PC.

BugByte, Inc., 3650 Silverside Rd., Wilmington, DE 19810 Tel 302-994-1502; Toll free: 800-284-9220.
Titles:
Balloon Stack.
Color Convert.
QuickPie 2.1.

Bullseye Systems, 2268 Westmoreland Dr., San Jose, CA 95124 Tel 408-266-9226.
Titles:
Helpdesk 1.

BUSINESS DESIGN SOFTWARE

Bureau Development, Inc., (1-878805), 141 New Rd., Parsippany, NJ 07054 Tel 201-808-2700; FAX: 201-808-2676.
Titles:
The Complete Dickens.
Twain's World.

Bureau of Business Practice, Div. of Simon & Schuster, Inc., A Viacom Co., (0-87622; 0-7896), 24 Rope Ferry Rd., Waterford, CT 06386 Tel 203-442-4365; Toll free: 800-243-0876; FAX: 203-437-0270.
Titles:
Building Productivity.
Communicating Safety Awareness.
Don Scott's Professional Selling the Computer Course, 72 Page Selling G.
George Plimpton's Great Speaker's File of Stories Jokes & Anecdotes.
Speed Reading: The Computer Course.

Burrelle's Information Services, (1-885601), 75 E. Northfield Rd., Livingston, NJ 07039 Tel 201-992-6600; Toll free: 800-876-3342; FAX: 201-992-7273.
Titles:
Burrelle's Media Directory 1994.
Burrelle's Media Directory 1995.
Burrelle's Media Directory 1996.

Burroughs Corp., (0-922640), 41100 Plymouth Rd., Bldg. No. 4, Plymouth, MI 48170 Tel 313-451-4680.
Titles:
B20 Asynchronous Terminal Emulator.
B20 BASIC Interpreter.
B20 COBOL Compiler.
B20 Customizer Package.
B20 Forms Facility.
B20 FORTRAN Compiler.
B20 Pascal Compiler.
B20 Poll-Select Data Communications Protocol.
B20 3270 Emulator.
B20 3270 SNA Emulator.
B22 Font Designer.
B20 X.25 Communications Manager.
Business Graphics.
Data Comm.
Data Manager.
Easy Accounts Payable.
Easy Accounts Receivable.
Easy General Ledger.
Easy Inventory Control.
Easy Order Entry-Invoicing.
Easy Public Institutions Payroll.
Executive Writeone System.
MT983 Emulator.
Multiplan.
2780 & 3780 RJE Terminal Emulator.

Business Computer Consultants/Merrill Street Software, (0-922647), 768 Oakland Ave., Birmingham, MI 48009-5755 Tel 810-649-9440.
Titles:
Contract Manager.
Job Manager.
Restaurant Manager.
SuperBatch.

Business Computers, Inc., (0-922654), 315 Inlet Ave., Merritt Island, FL 32952 Tel 407-452-2159.
Titles:
Membership.
Subscription.

Business Design Software, (0-922660), 1417 100th Ave., NE, Bellevue, WA 98004 Tel 206-455-0703.
Titles:
Account.
Estimate: Job Cost Estimating System.
Executive Interface.
Forecast.

**Business Forecast Systems, Inc., **68 Leonard St., Belmont, MA 02178 Tel 617-484-5050; FAX: 617-484-9219.
Titles:
ForeCalc.
Forecast Master Plus.
Forecast Pro.

**Business Planning Systems, Inc., **(0-922675), 10 Pennsylvania Ave., Rehoboth Beach, DE 19971 Tel 302-227-4322.
Titles:
Plan80.

**Business-Pro, **P.O. Box 44005, Phoenix, AZ 85064 Tel 602-256-7058; Orders to: 2131 Levanti St., Carlsbad, CA 92009 Tel 619-944-9073.
Titles:
SAV KEY.

**Business Resource Software, **2013 Wells Branch Pkwy., Suite 305, Austin, TX 78728 Tel 512-251-7541; Toll free: 800-423-1228; FAX: 512-251-4401.
Titles:
Business Insight.
Fetchit.
Plan Write for Marketing.
PlanWrite for Business.
Workbook.

**Business Source Publishing Co., **(1-881250), 412 N. Coast Hwy., Suite 136, Laguna Beach, CA 92651 Tel 714-376-1128; Toll free: 800-676-0230 (orders); FAX: 714-376-1129.
Titles:
Shopping Center DealMaker's Handbook: Practical Transaction Guide with Ready-to-Use Forms on Computer Diskettes.

**Business Systems Group/Merry Maid, Inc, **25 Messinger St., Bangor, PA 18013 Tel 610-588-0927.
Titles:
AgentBase.

**Business Tools Software, **1507 E. Franklin St., Suite 212, Chapel Hill, NC 27515; Toll free: 800-648-6258.
Titles:
Advanced Accounting.
Bill of Materials.
Job Cost Management System.
Point of Sale Management System.
TAS Professional.

**Business Week, **180 N. Stetson, Chicago, IL 60601 Tel 312-616-3304; Toll free: 800-553-3575.
Titles:
Top 1000.

**Byte by Byte, **8920 Business Park Dr., Suite 330, Austin, TX 78759-7405 Tel 512-343-4357.
Titles:
Animate 3-D.
Infominder.
Sculpt-Animate 4D.
Sculpt 3-D.
Tate Fonts I.
Tate Fonts II.
U. S. Space Station Orbiter.

**Bytel Corp., **(0-922698), 1029 Solano Ave., Albany, CA 94706 Tel 510-527-1157; Toll free: 800-777-0126; FAX: 510-527-6957.
Titles:
Genifer.

Timecard: Job Cost Management System.

**CADworks, Inc., **222 Third St., Suite 2300, Cambridge, MA 02142 Tel 617-868-6003; Toll free: 800-545-4223; FAX: 617-354-3057.
Titles:
Drawbase.

**CAMDE Corp., **449 E. Saratoga St., Gilbert, AZ 85296 Tel 602-926-2632; FAX: 602-926-2632.
Titles:
Nutri-Calc: Diet-Recipe Analysis Software.
Nutri-Calc HD.
NUTRI-CALC PLUS: Diet-Recipe Analysis Software.

**CAPS Software, **(0-922707), 4024 Alto St., Oceanside, CA 92056 Tel 619-724-0492.
Titles:
Artist Designer II.
Music Designer II.

**C. Abaci, Inc., **P.O. Box 2626, Raleigh, NC 27602-2626 Tel 919-832-4847.
Titles:
The Scientific Desk.

**C & G Software Systems, Inc., **7094 Peachtree Industrial Blvd., Suite 352, Norcross, GA 30071 Tel 404-446-0026; Toll free: 800-367-1157; FAX: 404-447-0530.
Titles:
CG-Survey for AutoCAD.
CG-Survey for DOS.
CG-Survey for MicroStation.

**CBE Services, Inc., **(1-888502), 245 Highland Ave., Arlington, MA 02174 Tel 617-646-1930; Toll free: 800-346-1930; FAX: 617-648-0491.
Titles:
Knowledge Quest.
Knowledge Quest Essentials.
Knowledge Quest Human Body & Health.
Knowledge Quest Literature.
Knowledge Quest Mathematics.
Knowledge Quest Science.
Knowledge Quest Science Fssentials.
Knowledge Quest United States.
Knowledge Quest World Geography.

**CBIS, Inc., **5875 Peachtree Industrial Blvd., Bldg. 100, Suite 170, Norcross, GA 30092 Tel 404-446-1332; Toll free: 800-344-8426; FAX: 404-446-9164.
Titles:
CD Connection.
NETWORK-OS.

**CCH ACCESS Software, **Div. of Commerce Clearing Hse., 4025 W. Peterson Ave., Chicago, IL 60646-6001; Toll free: 800-248-3248; FAX: 312-583-8312.
Titles:
IRS Interest.
Charitable Financial Planner.
Depreciation Calculator.
Estate Planning Tools.
Estimated Tax Penalties Calculator.
Financial Planning Tools.
IRS Factors Calculator.
Pension & Excise Tax Planner.

**C.C. Software, **(0-917279), 1907 Alvarado Ave., Walnut Creek, CA 94596 Tel 510-939-8153.
Titles:
Masterful Disassembler.
MD86, Masterful Disassembler 8086.
SCG22.
SCG3.
UNREL.

**CDE Software, **(0-928532), 4017 39th Ave., SW, Seattle, WA 98116 Tel 206-937-8927; Toll free: 800-767-8927 (orders only); FAX: 206-937-8562.
Titles:
Bowler's Diary.
Bowling League Secretary.
Checks & Balances.

**CEL Development, **P.O. Box 224, Penfield, NY 14526 Tel 716-377-3570.
Titles:
Race-Trac.

**CE Software, Inc., **Div. of CE Software Holdings, Inc., (0-922735; 0-918115), P.O. Box 65580, West Des Moines, IA 50265 Tel 515-221-1801; Toll free: 800-523-7638 (orders only); FAX: 515-221-1806.
Titles:
CalendarMaker.
CalendarMaker for Windows.
ProKey for DOS.
ProKey for Windows.
QuicKeys.
QuickMail.

**CISMAP/Industrial Information Resources, Inc., **11011 Richmond Ave., 4th Flr., Houston, TX 77042 Tel 713-783-5147.
Titles:
The Post-Soviet Industrial GeoLocator: SSS Industrial Atlas.

**CK/PRI Co., **(0-922744), 302 S. Center St., P.O. Box 107, Statesville, NC 28677 Tel 704-873-3356.
Titles:
TAX CK-PRI.

**CLASS (Cooperative Library Agency for Systems & Services), **(0-938098; 0-922745), 1415 Koll Cir., Suite 101, San Jose, CA 95112-4698 Tel 408-453-0444; FAX: 408-453-5379.
Titles:
Checkmate II.

**CLEO Communications, **Div. of Interface Systems, Inc., (0-917285), 3796 Plaza Dr., Ann Arbor, MI 48108 Tel 313-662-2002; Toll free: 800-233-2536; FAX: 313-662-1965.
Titles:
CLEO 3780Plus.

**CMA Micro Computer, **(0-88716), 55888 Yucca Trail, Box 2080, Yucca Valley, CA 92286-2080 Tel 619-365-9718; FAX: 619-228-1567.
Titles:
Client Dental Billing System.
The Client Medical Billing System.
CMA Dental for the Macintosh.
CMA Medical for the Macintosh.
Construction Accounting Systems.
Dental Account PAC.
Dental Office Management PC.
Dental Office Management PCE.
Dental Office Management PCH.
Dental Office Management PCHE.
Dental Office Management System PC-Oral Surgeon.
Dental Office Management I.
Dental Office Management II.
Dental WPC.
Dental WPCH.
Dental IIc.
Dental III.
Dental III H.
FutureWave.
Medical Office Management I.
Medical Office Management II.
Medical Office Management IIc.
Medical Office Management III H.
Medical Office Management PC.
Medical Office Management PCH.

PUBLISHER/TITLE INDEX

Medical Office Management PCHE.
Medicard.
Oral Surgery PC.
TotalPhase CMA.

CMV Software Specialists, Inc., (0-917701), P.O. Box 176, Hartford, SD 57033 Tel 605-338-6645; Toll free: 800-888-1649; FAX: 605-334-8521.
Titles:
Farm Credit Plan.
PROMAC.
Protrip.

CNS Productions, (0-926544), P.O. Box 96, Ashland, OR 97520-1962; Toll free: 800-888-0617; 130 Third St., Ashland, OR 97520 Tel 541-488-2805.
Titles:
Uppers, Downers, All Arounders.

COMAL Users Group, U.S.A., Ltd., (0-928411), 5501 Groveland Terrace, Madison, WI 53716-3251 Tel 608-222-4432.
Titles:
COMAL.
COMAL Starter Kit.
COMAL Super Chip.
COMAL 2.0.

COM-CAP, Div. of Midwest Mailorder, Inc., (0-928719), P.O. Box 6051, Omaha, NE 68106-6051 Tel 814-459-5995.
Titles:
COM-CAP Class.
COM-CAP Pace.
COM-CAP Racing Records.
Kaywood Method.
Mini-Pace.
Quirin.
The Speed Program.

COMPASS, (0-923006), 9509 U.S. Hwy. 42, Suite 108, Prospect, KY 40059 Tel 502-228-7805.
Titles:
Church Membership-Contribution.
Compass Accounts Payable.
Compass Accounts Receivable.
Compass Fixed Assets.
Compass General Ledger.
Compass Job Cost & Estimating.
Compass Job Queue.
Compass Material Requirements Planning (MRP).
Inventory Control.
Invoice Billing-Order Entry & Sales Analysis.
Purchase Orders.

COMPRO, Div. of Global Software, Inc., (0-928533), 6025 The Corners Pkwy., Suite 200, Norcross, GA 30092 Tel 404-662-8754; FAX: 404-441-0219.
Titles:
Foresight: Decision Support System.
Forestar Accounts Payable/Purchase Order Tracking System.
Forestar Accounts Receivable/Sales Analysis System.
Forestar Fixed Assets Systems.
Forestar General Ledger/Financial Reporting System.

CORGROUP Computer Operations Resource Group, Div. of Garde, P.O. Box 1265, Madison, CT 06443 Tel 203-458-9363.
Titles:
ESP - Accounting System.
ESP - Estimating & Proposal Creation System.
ESP (Executive Sensory Perception).
ESP Inventory & Purchase Order System.
ESP Office & Time Management.
ESP Payroll System.

COSS, Div. of The Doctors' Office, Inc., 1155 Central Ave., Mayo, MD 21106 Tel 301-261-7570.
Titles:
Vuman Ventura Link.

CPSA, 166 S. J St., Livermore, CA 94550 Tel 510-449-7744.
Titles:
DataFlash.

CP Software, 1501 Adams Ave., Milpitas, CA 95035 Tel 408-262-5182.
Titles:
Church Business Manager Plus.
Mac Church Assistant.
Mac Minister.
Match Maker Express.
Order Express.
Sales Express.

CPU Corp., The, (0-939119), 999 SW Pepperridge Terr., Boca Raton, FL 33486 Tel 407-338-0998.
Titles:
The Coordinated Financial Planning System: The CFP System.

CQ Computer Communications, Inc., 4695 N. Monroe St., Tallahassee, FL 32303-7009 Tel 904-562-4255; Toll free: 800-523-6807; FAX: 904-562-1221.
Titles:
CQ-3270-BSC.
CQ-3270-SNA.
CQ-3270-SNA LAN.
CQ-3770.
CQ-3770 LAN.
CQ-3780.
CQ-5250.
CQ-5250 LAN.

CR Software, Inc., (0-934599), 10621 Jones St., Suite 101A, Fairfax, VA 22030 Tel 703-934-9060; Toll free: 800-222-1722; FAX: 703-934-9430.
Titles:
Collection Resource System.

C.S.I. Services Corp., 4725 Merle Hay Rd., Suite 200, Des Moines, IA 50322 Tel 515-270-8182; Toll free: 800-654-3123; FAX: 515-270-1006.
Titles:
RICS: Retail Inventory Control System.

CSR Macmillan/McGraw-Hill, Div. of Macmillan/McGraw-Hill, (0-923252), Avon Park S., 40 Darling Dr., Avon, CT 06001 Tel 203-678-1212; Toll free: 800-922-1190; FAX: 203-677-5405.
Titles:
CSR TRAINER 4000.
Professional Data Center Curriculum.

CSY, Inc., (1-57585), 111 E. Capitol St., Suite 365, Jackson, MS 39201 Tel 601-352-0477; Toll free: 800-352-0477; FAX: 601-352-7644.
Titles:
Minorities in Science: Women & Minority Scientists Database CD-ROM Program.

CSY Publishing, Inc., (0-945541), P.O. Box 24463, Houston, TX 77229; 12670 Rip Van Winkle, Houston, TX 77024 Tel 713-468-4361.
Titles:
Condex United States Stamps (1902-1921).
Query Condex 10x1 - D Ramdrive.
Query Condex 10x1-C.
Query Condex 20x-D.
Query Condex 20x1 - D Ram Drive.
Traum Condex Brain & Behavior.

CTS, (0-917429), 11708 Ibsen Dr., Rockville, MD 20852 Tel 301-468-4800; Toll free: 800-433-8015; FAX: 301-468-2309.
Titles:
The Requirements Analyst.

C Ware, (0-922790), P.O. Box 428, Paso Robles, CA 93447 Tel 805-239-4620; FAX: 805-239-4620.
Titles:
DeSmet C 8086/8088 Development Package(DeSmet DC88).

CYMA/McGraw-Hill, Div. of McGraw-Hill, Inc., (0-923474), 1400 E. Southern, Tempe, AZ 85282 Tel 602-831-2607; Toll free: 800-292-2962.
Titles:
CYMA Chiropractic Practice Management.
CYMA Client Accounting.
CYMA Dental Practice Management.
CYMA General Business System.
CYMA Job Control.
CYMA Medical Practice Management.
CYMA Orthodontic Practice Management.
CYMA Patient Billing.
CYMA Professional Accounting Series.
Final Draft.
Professional Accounting Series.
The Shoebox Accountant.

CZ Software, (0-928048), 358 Forest Rd., South Yarmouth, MA 02664 Tel 508-362-8100; FAX: 508-362-5959.
Titles:
The Oddsmaker.

Cadkey, Inc., (0-925327), 4 Griffin Rd. N., Windsor, CT 06095 Tel 203-298-8888; FAX: 203-298-6401.
Titles:
CADKEY.
CADKEY Advanced Modeler.
DataCAD.

Caere Corp., 100 Cooper Ct., Los Gatos, CA 95030 Tel 408-395-7000.
Titles:
OmniPage.

CalComp, Inc., Subs. of Lockheed Group, 2411 W. La Palma Ave., Anaheim, CA 92801 Tel 714-821-2000; Toll free: 800-932-1212; FAX: 714-821-2832.
Titles:
CalComp ColorMaster Presenter.
DrawingMaster Plus (Model 52224).

Caldwell Software, (0-917703), General Delivery, Rio Rancho, NM 87124; FAX: 510-848-7642.
Titles:
Cost Estimating.
Performance Analysis of Passive Solar Heated Buildings.

Caldwell Software Solutions, 1564-A Fitzgerald Dr., Suite 408, Pinole, CA 94564 Tel 510-799-0101.
Titles:
PM-Turbo.

California Software Products, Inc., (0-922812), 525 N. Cabrillo Pk. Dr., No. 300, Santa Ana, CA 92701 Tel 714-973-0440; Toll free: 800-841-1532; FAX: 714-558-9341.
Titles:
Baby/4XX.
Baby/36 for Windows.
400 Developer Desktop.
400 Enterprise System.
400 Professional System.
36 Developer Desktop.

CALLIOPE MEDIA

Calliope Media, 1526 Cloverfield Blvd., Santa Monica, CA 90404-3502 Tel 310-829-1100; FAX: 310-829-7044.
Titles:
Robert Winter's Crazy for Ragtime.
ScruTiny in the Great Round.
ScruTiny in the Great Round: Limited Edition.

Caltexsoftwareinc, 3131 Turtle Creek Blvd., No 1101, Dallas, TX 75219 Tel 214-522-9840; FAX: 214-521-1836.
Titles:
D The Data Language.

Calyx Corp., Affil. of Flagship Group, (0-922932), 16745 W. Bluemound Rd., Suite 200, Brookfield, WI 53005 Tel 414-782-0300; Toll free: 800-866-1006; FAX: 414-782-3182.
Titles:
DDX.
MDX: Modular Medical Data-Management Software.

Cambridge Management Systems, Inc., P.O. Box 109, Onset, MA 02558-0109.
Titles:
Intelligent Report System (IRS).
Project Outlook.
SSP's PROMIS: Project Management Integrated System.

Cambridge Scientific Computing, Inc., 875 Massachusetts Ave., 6th Flr., Cambridge, MA 02139 Tel 617-491-6862; FAX: 617-491-8208.
Titles:
CSC ChemDraw.
CSC ChemDraw Plus.
CSC Chem3D.
CSC Chem3D Plus.

Cambridge Univ. Pr., (0-521), 40 W. 20th St., New York, NY 10011 Tel 212-924-3900; Toll free: 800-221-4512 (editorial & marketing); FAX: 212-691-3239; Orders to: 110 Midland Ave., Port Chester, NY 10573 Tel 914-937-9600; Toll free: 800-872-7423 (orders, returns, credit & accounting).
Titles:
A Dictionary of the English Language.
The Wife of Bath's Prologue.
The Works of John Ruskin.
The World Shakespeare Bibliography, 1990-1993.

Cambrix Publishing, (0-9634120; 1-885582), 6269 Variel Ave., Suite B, Woodland Hills, CA 91367 Tel 818-992-8484; Toll free: 800-992-8781; FAX: 818-992-8781.
Titles:
Learn To Play Guitar.

Cammock & Cammock, Inc., 5885 Landerbrook Dr., Suite 150, Cleveland, OH 44124 Tel 216-646-9494; FAX: 216-646-0046.
Titles:
Merrit Calc 2.

Campagne Assocs., Ltd., 491 Amherst St., Nashua, NH 03063 Tel 603-595-8774; Toll free: 800-582-3489; FAX: 603-595-8776.
Titles:
GiftMaker: (Entry Level System).
GiftMaker Pro.

Campbell Services, Inc., (0-943769), 21700 Northwestern Hwy., 10th Flr., Southfield, MI 48075 Tel 810-559-5955; Toll free: 800-345-6747; FAX: 810-559-1034.
Titles:
OnTime Enterprise.
OnTime for Windows.

Camtronics Software, P.O. Box 1, Camas Valley, OR 97416 Tel 503-445-2824.
Titles:
HyperShopper.

Cane Systems, 1600 Hagys Ford Rd., No. 6J, Narberth, PA 19072 Tel 610-660-9487.
Titles:
Broadcast Wan-Lan Simulation Toolbox: ADA Broadcast Wan-Lan Simulation.
Broadcast Wan-Lan Simulation Toolbox: BASIC Broadcast Wan-Lan Simulation.
Broadcast Wan-Lan Simulation Toolbox: "C" Broadcast Wan-Lan Simulation.
Broadcast Wan-Lan Simulation Toolbox: FORTRAN Broadcast Wan-Lan Simulation.
Broadcast Wan-Lan Simulation Toolbox: MODULA-2 Broadcast Wan-Lan Simulation.
Broadcast Wan-Lan Simulation Toolbox: PASCAL Broadcast Wan-Lan Simulation.
Enterprise Network Simulation Toolbox: Broadcast Wan-Lan Simulation.
Enterprise Network Simulation Toolbox: Network Link-by-Link Simulation.
Enterprise Network Simulation Toolbox: Network Link Simulation.
Enterprise Network Simulation Toolbox: Network Path Simulation.
Enterprise Network Simulation Toolbox: Network Response Time Simulation.
Initial Network Topology Toolbox: Array Shortest Path Initial Topology Generator.
Initial Network Topology Toolbox: Generator of Networks with Required Nodal Connectivity.
Initial Network Topology Toolbox: Input Network Topology Generator.
Initial Network Topology Toolbox: Minimum Distance Spanning Tree Initial Topology Generator.
Initial Network Topology Toolbox: Minimum Links Topology Generator.
Initial Network Topology Toolbox: Min-Max Spanning Tree Initial Topology Generator.
Initial Network Topology Toolbox: Minimum Weight Spanning Tree Initial Topology Generator.
Initial Network Topology Toolbox: Random File Shortest Path Initial Topology Generator.
Initial Network Topology Toolbox: Random Initial Network Topology Generator.
Lan Simulation Toolbox: IEE 802.5 Token Ring Simulation.
Least Cost Network Design Toolbox: Least Cost Access Network Design.
Least Cost Network Design Toolbox: Least Cost Multipoint Network Design.
Least Cost Network Design Toolbox: Least Cost Trunking Network Design.
Monte Carlo Analysis Toolbox: Monte Carlo BSC Throughput.
Monte Carlo Analysis Toolbox: Monte Carlo HDLC Throughput.
Monte Carlo Analysis Toolbox: Monte Carlo Intranodal Response Time.
Monte Carlo Analysis Toolbox: Monte Carlo One Way Link Delay.
Monte Carlo Analysis Toolbox: Monte Carlo One Way Path Delay.
Monte Carlo Analysis Toolbox: Monte Carlo Transmission Delay.
Network Analysis Toolbox: BSC Throughput.
Network Analysis Toolbox: HDLC Throughput.
Network Analysis Toolbox: Internodal Response Time Analysis.
Network Analysis Toolbox: Intranodal Response Time.
Network Analysis Toolbox: One Way Link Delay.
Network Analysis Toolbox: One Way Path Delay.
Network Analysis Toolbox: Transmission Delays.
Network Mathematics Toolbox: All Internodal Distances.
Network Mathematics Toolbox: Communications Traffic Profiles Generator.
Network Mathematics Toolbox: Erlang Analysis.
Network Mathematics Toolbox: Link Message Requirements.
Network Mathematics Toolbox: Message Arrival Time & Size Generator.
Network Mathematics Toolbox: Monte Carlo Cumulative Probability Analysis.
Network Mathematics Toolbox: Probability of Queueing.
Network Mathematics Toolbox: Specific Internodal Distances.
Network Topology Evaluation & Management Science Toolboxes: Acyclic Shortest Paths.
Network Topology Evaluation & Management Science Toolboxes: Cyclic Shortest Paths.
Network Topology Evaluation & Management Science Toolboxes: Euler Circuits in a Network.
Network Topology Evaluation & Management Science Toolboxes: Fundamental Circuits of a Network.
Network Topology Evaluation & Management Science Toolboxes: Hamilton Circuits of a Network.
Network Topology Evaluation & Management Science Toolboxes: Maximum Cardinality Matching.
Network Topology Evaluation & Management Science Toolboxes: Maximum Independent Sets of a Network.
Network Topology Evaluation & Management Science Toolboxes: Minimum Link Equivalent of a Network.
Network Topology Evaluation & Management Science Toolboxes: Min-Max Spanning Tree.
Network Topology Evaluation & Management Science Toolboxes: Minimum Weight Bipartite Matching.
Network Topology Evaluation & Management Science Toolboxes: Network Bridges.
Network Topology Evaluation & Management Science Toolboxes: Network Cliques.
Network Topology Evaluation & Management Science Toolboxes: Network Link Connectivity Analysis.
Network Topology Evaluation & Management Science Toolboxes: Optimal Acyclic Routing.
Network Topology Evaluation & Management Science Toolboxes: Optimal Cyclic Routing.
Network Topology Evaluation & Management Science Toolboxes: Strongly Connected Components of a Network.
Network Topology Evaluation & Management Science Toolboxes: Shortest Path Trees.
Topological Network Flow & Management Science Toolboxes: Business Process Re-Engineering.
Topological Network Flow & Management Science Toolboxes: Minimum Cost Network Flow.
Topological Network Flow & Management Science Toolboxes: Maximum Network Flow.

CAP Automation, (0-917081), 3737 Ramona Dr., Fort Worth, TX 76116-7001 Tel 817-560-7007; Toll free: 800-826-5009; FAX: 817-560-8249.
Titles:
CAP Accountant.
CAP BackOffice.
CAP Cash 'n Carry.
CAP Head Quarters.
CAP POS.
Quick Check with Accounts Payable & Receivable.
Retail Inventory Program.
SellWise.

Capital Enterprises, P.O. Box 716, West Springfield, MA 01090-0716 Tel 413-739-8231.
Titles:
Capital Cashflow Templates.
Capital Financial Templates.

PUBLISHER/TITLE INDEX

Capital Systems Group, Inc., (0-928406), 1355 Piccard Dr., Suite 350, Rockville, MD 20850 Tel 301-948-3033; FAX: 301-948-2242.
Titles:
Bookdex.
Mars.
MicroCTS: Corporate Treasurer's System.
Newsdex.

Capitol Multimedia, Inc., (1-57272), 7315 Wisconsin Ave., Suite 800E, Bethesda, MD 20814 Tel 301-907-7000; FAX: 301-907-7006.
Titles:
MegaMaze.
NFL Football Trivia Challenge.
Shark Alert.

Carberry Technology, Inc., 600 Suffolk St., Lowell, MA 01854 Tel 508-970-5358; FAX: 508-453-0336.
Titles:
CADleaf Plus.

Cardinal Health Systems, Inc., (0-933755), 4600 W. 77th St., Suite 150, Edina, MN 55435 Tel 612-835-6941; Toll free: 800-328-0180; FAX: 612-835-7141.
Titles:
Clinical Pharmacology.
Drug Actions in Hypertension.
Prescriptions for Type II Diabetes.
Preventive Methods in Coronary Artery Disease: Diet Analysis Tool.
Preventive Methods in Coronary Heart Disease: Exercise Prescription Tool.
Preventive Methods in Coronary Heart Disease: Life-Style Change Tool.
Preventive Methods in Coronary Heart Disease: Smoking Cessation Tool.
Ulcers.

Cardinal Point, Inc., (0-932065), 4999 W. Woodland Dr., Bloomington, IN 47404-8935; Toll free: 800-628-2828.
Titles:
Prints Charming.

Cardinal Software, (0-927765), 14800 Build America Dr., Woodbridge, VA 22191-3437 Tel 703-491-6502; FAX: 703-494-0744. Do not confuse with Cardinal Software of South Hamilton, MA.
Titles:
The Banner Machine.
Physical Exam for 1571, 1541, 8050, 4040 Disk Drives.

Cardinal Tracking Technics, Inc./Video Trak, (0-928537), 3207 Justin Rd., Lewisville, TX 75028 Tel 214-539-9650.
Titles:
Video Trak: Quick, Super, Senior, Master.

Care Information Systems, Inc., (0-922840), 155 W. Lake Dr., Springfield, IL 62703 Tel 217-529-0255; FAX: 217-529-8701.
Titles:
Care-DM.

Career Publishing, Inc., (0-89262), 910 N. Main St., Orange, CA 92667 Tel 714-771-5155; Toll free: 800-854-4014; FAX: 714-532-0180; P.O. Box 5486, Orange, CA 92613-5486.
Titles:
Desktop Publishing (PFS): First Publisher.
HyperCard Authoring Tool for Presentations, Tutorials & Information Exploration.
HyperCard (Mac) Creativity Tool: Student Version for Writing, Organizing & Multimedia.
IBM LinkWay Authoring Tool for Presentations, Tutorial, & Information Exploration.
IBM LinkWay Creativity Tool for Writing, Organizing, & Multimedia.
Powerful Presentations Using Your IBM-PC for the Classroom of the Future.
Powerful Presentations Using Your Macintosh for the Classroom of the Future: With Publish It! Easy.
Simulating the Medical Office Software Getting Started & 7 Modules.

CareerLab Bks., Div. of Career Lab, Ltd., (1-884087), 9085 E. Mineral Cir., Suite 330, Englewood, CO 80112 Tel 303-790-0505; Toll free: 800-723-9675; FAX: 303-790-0606.
Titles:
Instant Job Winning Letters.

Carina Software Systems, 322 Natchez Ct., Jupiter, FL 33477 Tel 407-747-9195.
Titles:
Carina BBS.
Voyager, the Interactive Desktop Planetarium.

Carleton Corp., (0-922844), 8 New England Executive Pk., Burlington, MA 01803 Tel 617-272-4310; Toll free: 800-832-8348; FAX: 617-272-2910.
Titles:
CQS-Linkware.

Carrera, Don, 50 Suhan Dr., R.D. 11, Irwin, PA 15642 Tel 412-744-4347.
Titles:
Astronomy: Planet Orbits 1500-2400 AD.

Cartesia Software, (0-929401), P.O. Box 757, Lambertville, NJ 08530 Tel 609-397-1611; Toll free: 800-334-4291; FAX: 609-397-5724.
Titles:
HyperAtlas.
MapArt: EPS Format.
MapArt: Paint (MAC) or.PCX (PC).
MapArt: PICT (MacDraw II Format).
MapArt: Volumes 1 - 4.
QuickMap.

Casady & Greene, Inc., (0-943573; 1-56482), 22734 Portola Dr., Salinas, CA 93908-1119 Tel 408-484-9228; Toll free: 800-359-4920; FAX: 408-484-9218.
Titles:
AME: Access Managed Environment.
Conflict Catcher II.
Crash Barrier.
Crystal Crazy.
Crystal Quest with Critter Editor.
Eastern European Library.
Fluent Laser Fonts: True Type Starter Set.
Glasnost Cyrillic Library Two.
Glider.
Glider Pro.
Mission Starlight.
Pararena 2.0.
Sky Shadow.
Snap MAIL.
Spaceway 2000.
Super Quick DEX.
ZOA: Zone of Avoidance.

Cascade Graphics Systems, Subs. of KTI, (0-922851), 5000 Birch St., Suite 500, Newport Beach, CA 92660-2132.
Titles:
CADlab.
Cascade I.

Cascade Marketing International, Inc., (1-57307), 115 E. School Rd., Wenatchee, WA 98801 Tel 509-663-9523; Toll free: 800-892-3338; FAX: 509-664-7398.
Titles:
The Hermitage Art Treasures Tour.
The Hermitage, Vol. 2: The Winter Palace.
Treasures of Russia.

Cascom International, Inc., (0-9634008; 1-885759), 806 Fourth Ave., S., Nashville, TN 37210 Tel 615-242-8900; FAX: 615-256-7890.
Titles:
Bikini Open.
5000 Plus Image Library.
Lingerie International 100.
Video Fashion! News: Top One Hundred International Models.

Cashmaster Business Systems, Inc., (0-917797), 15009 Eighth Pl., W., Lynnwood, WA 98037 Tel 206-742-7120; Toll free: 800-999-4593; FAX: 206-742-2897.
Titles:
Microsoft Excel Business Sourcebook.

Casio, Inc., Subs. of Casio Computer Co., Ltd., Tokyo, (1-878532), 570 Mt. Pleasant Ave., Dover, NJ 07801 Tel 201-361-5400; FAX: 201-361-3819.
Titles:
OAG Travel Planner.

Catspaw, Inc., (0-939793), P.O. Box 1123, Salida, CO 81201 Tel 719-539-3884; FAX: 719-539-4830; 9395 County Rd. 160, Salida, CO 81201 Tel 719-539-3884.
Titles:
Algorithms in SNOBOL4.
MaxSPITBOL: The SNOBOL4 Language for the Mac User.
SPITBOL 386.
UNIX SPITBOL.

cc-Mail, Div. of Lotus, 2141 Landings Dr., Mountain View, CA 94043-0845 Tel 415-961-8800; Toll free: 800-448-2500; FAX: 415-961-8400.
Titles:
cc:Mail LAN Package.

CD Solutions, Inc., 111 Speen St., Suite 202, Framingham, MA 01701 Tel 508-879-0006.
Titles:
The Internet for Everybody.

Celestial Software, Div. of Robert L. Cloud Assocs., Inc., (0-928055), 2150 Shattuck Ave., Suite 1200, Berkeley, CA 94704 Tel 510-843-0977; FAX: 510-848-9849.
Titles:
Images - Thermal.
Images-AISC.
Images-2D.
Images-3D.

Celestin Co., (1-886545), 1152 Hastings Ave., Port Townsend, WA 98368 Tel 206-385-3767; Toll free: 800-835-5514; FAX: 206-385-3586.
Titles:
Apprentice: Definitive Collection of Source Code & Utilities for Mac Programmers.

Cen-Tex Data Systems, Inc., (0-922864), 128 E. Main St., Fredericksburg, TX 78624 Tel 210-997-3320.
Titles:
Inventory & Gold Adjustment.

Centaurus Systems, Inc., (0-922866), 4425 Cass St., Suite A, San Diego, CA 92109 Tel 619-270-4552; FAX: 619-273-7769.
Titles:
ARGUS.
PEGASUS.

Ctr. for Sutton Movement Writing, Inc., The, (0-914336), P.O. Box 517, La Jolla, CA 92038-0517 Tel 619-456-0098.
Titles:
Signwriter Computer Program Package: the world's first sign processor.

Central Coast Software, P.O. Box 164287, Austin, TX 78716-4287.
Titles:
DOS-2-DOS.
MAC-2-DOS Package.
QuarterBack.
Quarterback Tools.

Central Computer Products, 387 Zachary Ave., Bldg. 103, Moorpark, CA 93021 Tel 805-532-9171; Toll free: 800-456-4123; FAX: 805-524-4026; Toll free: 800-431-2818.
Titles:
VersaPro Business Series.

Central Point Software, Inc., (0-929282), 15220 Greenbrier Pkwy., Suite 150, Beaverton, OR 97006 Tel 503-690-8090; Toll free: 800-964-6896; FAX: 503-690-8083.
Titles:
Central Point Anti-Virus.
Central Point Anti-Virus for Macintosh.
Central Point Anti-Virus for NetWare.
Central Point Anti-Virus for Windows.
Central Point Backup for DOS.
Central Point Backup for Windows.
Mactools.
PC Tools.
PC Tools for Windows.

Century Analysis, Inc., (0-917699), 114 Center Ave., Pacheco, CA 94553 Tel 510-680-7800; FAX: 510-676-6857.
Titles:
CAI Integration Toolset.

Century Software Systems, (0-922872), 11664 Gateway Blvd., West Los Angeles, CA 90064 Tel 310-477-4505.
Titles:
Business Management, Pt. V: Econometrics.

Cer-Comp, (0-922874), 5566 Ricochet Ave., Las Vegas, NV 89110 Tel 702-452-0632.
Titles:
Data Pack & Disk Pack.

Champion Business Systems, Inc., (0-922880), 6726 S. Revere Pkwy., Englewood, CO 80112-3907 Tel 303-792-3606; Toll free: 800-243-2626; FAX: 303-792-0255.
Titles:
Champion Accounting Software.
Champion Accounts Payable.
Champion Accounts Receivable.
Champion Business Accounting System Bookkeeper.
Champion Controller - Integrated Accounting Software: Business Accounting.
Champion General Ledger: Business Accounting.
Champion Inventory.
Champion Payroll.
Champion Report Writer.
The Password Security System.

Chang Laboratories, Inc., (0-922582), 10228 N. Stelling, Cupertino, CA 95014 Tel 408-727-8096; FAX: 408-252-3081.
Titles:
C.A.T. III.

Channelmark Corp., 2929 Campus Dr., Suite 400, San Mateo, CA 94403 Tel 415-345-5900; Toll free: 800-851-2917.
Titles:
Calendar Creator.

Charles River Media, (1-886801), P.O. Box 417, Rockland, MA 02370; FAX: 617-871-4376; 403 VFW Dr., Rockland, MA 02370 Tel 617-871-4184.
Titles:
CD Helpdesk Series: Novell Products.
HTML Template Master CD.
Internet Simulator CD Package.
The Internet Watch Dog.
The World Wide Web Encyclopedia.
The World Wide Web Encyclopedia CD.

CharterHouse Software Corp., (0-925894), 4195 Thousand Oaks Blvd., No. 235, Westlake Village, CA 91362 Tel 805-494-5191; Toll free: 800-767-7638; FAX: 805-494-8191.
Titles:
CharterHouse Accounting Systems.
CharterHouse Accounts Payable System: A-P.
CharterHouse Accounts Receivable, Billing & Inventory Control System: A-R.
CharterHouse Fixed Assets System.
CharterHouse General Ledger System: G-L.
CharterHouse Manufacturing Inventory Control System.
CharterHouse Order Entry System: Order Entry.
CharterHouse Payroll System.
CharterHouse Purchase Order System.
Fixed Assets & Depreciation.
Job Costing.
Levinson Lyon Business Accounting Systems: A-R, A-P, G-L, Inventory.
Levinson Lyon Data Link & Report Writer: D-L & R-W.
Levinson Lyon Fixed Assets: F-A.
Levinson Lyon Manufacturing Inventory.
Levinson Lyon MICR Check Writer: MICR.
Levinson Lyon Order Entry: O-E.
Levinson Lyon Payroll: P-R.
Levinson Lyon Purchase Order: P-O.
Levinson Lyon UPS Computerized Manifest: UPS.
Manufacturing Inventory Control.
OCC-Accounts Receivable, Billing & Inventory Control.
OCC-General Ledger: Client Write-Up.
Occupational Computing Accounts Payable.
Occupational Computing General Ledger.
Order Entry.
Payroll.

Chaudhry, Amanat U., (1-881433), 9235 Westheimer Ave., Plantation W., No. 260, Houston, TX 77063 Tel 713-952-6604; FAX: 918-831-9555; Dist. by: Pennwell Bks., 1421 S. Sheridan, Tulsa, OK 74112 Tel 918-831-9421; Toll free: 800-752-9764 (orders only).
Titles:
GWBasic Total Well Production Systems Optimization Manual: GWBasic TWPSOM Software.

CheckMark Software, Inc., 724 Whalers Way, Bldg. H, Fort Collins, CO 80525 Tel 303-225-0522; Toll free: 800-444-9922; FAX: 303-225-0611.
Titles:
Cash Ledger.
CheckMark MultiLedger.
Payroll.

Cherrygarth, Inc., (0-922900), 101 S. Dewey St., Auburn, IN 46706 Tel 219-925-1093.
Titles:
Baseball Records.
Beef Herd History.
Beef Herd Management: Decision Aid.
Beef History Information.
Beef Production Records.
Broiler Production: Decision Aid.
Cattle Ration Analysis.
Crop Production: Decision Aid.
Crop Production Records.
Crops Records.
Dairy Herd Management: Decision Aid.
Dairy Production Records.
Farm Accounting System.
Farm Budget Planning System.
Farrow-Finish Hog Production: Decision Aid.
Finishing Feeder Cattle: Decision Aid.
Finishing Feeder Lambs: Decision Aid.
Finishing Feeder Pigs Decision Aids.
Football Records.
Growing Dairy Calves Decision Aids.
Hay-Pasture Production: Decision Aid.
Hog Production Records.
Laying Flock Production: Decision Aid.
Sheep Production: Decision Aid.
Sheep Production Records.
Swine Herd History.
Swine History Information.
Swine Ration Analysis.
Track & Field Records.
Track Records.

Cherrystone Productions, Inc., 733 Lakefield Rd., Suite AA, Westlake Village, CA 91361 Tel 805-497-8865.
Titles:
Janet & Judy's Mission from Planet N.

Chesapeake Software, 303 Seventh St., NE, Washington, DC 20002 Tel 202-546-9479.
Titles:
Tax Pro.

Chess Combination, Inc., (0-917237), 2423 Noble Sta., Bridgeport, CT 06608 Tel 203-367-1555; Toll free: 800-354-4083; FAX: 203-380-1703.
Titles:
Budapest Gambit: Electronic Chessbook.
French Advance Variation: Electronic Chessbook.
King's Indian Classical System: Electronic Chessbook.
NicBase3.
Nicpublish.
Ruy Lopez Arkhangelsk Var.
Scotch Opening.
Sicilian: English Attack: Electronic Chessbook.
Sicilian 2.f4.
Slav Defence: Meran: Electronic Chessbook.
Slav Defense: Botvinnik: Electronic Chessbook.
Van Greet Opening 1.Nf3.
Vienna Game.

Chilton Bk. Co., Subs. of Capital Cities/ABC, Inc., (0-8019; 0-87069), 201 King of Prussia Rd., Radnor, PA 19089-0230 Tel 610-964-4000; Toll free: 800-695-1214; FAX: 610-964-4745; Orders to: 1 Chilton Way, Radnor, PA 19089-0230.
Titles:
CasCode Component Application Guide, 1966-1993.

Chip Taylor Communications, (0-931847; 1-57192), 15 Spollett Dr., Derry, NH 03038 Tel 603-434-9262; Toll free: 800-876-2447; FAX: 603-432-2723.
Titles:
Learning Guitar Overnight.
What Color Is Your Mind?

ChipChat-Cawthon Software, (0-922857), 24224 Michigan Ave., Dearborn, MI 48124-1897 Tel 313-565-4000; FAX: 313-565-4653.
Titles:
ChipChat: Communications Software for OS/2.
Wall Street Link: WSL.

Chips & Dips, (0-9623900), 14905 Willis St., Houston, TX 77039 Tel 713-590-8023; FAX: 713-590-8024.
Titles:
Triggy!

Christensen Computer Co., Inc., (0-922908), 12005 N. Panorama Dr., Suite 204, Fountain Hills, AZ 85268 Tel 602-837-7173; Toll free: 800-222-6102.
Titles:
AlphaLEDGER: Complete Business Accounting System.
Realtime Information Management System (RIMS): Point of Sale Tire Software.

PUBLISHER/TITLE INDEX

Christian Ministry Resources, (1-880562), 617 Greenbrook Pkwy., Matthews, NC 28105 Tel 704-846-8704; FAX: 704-846-5923.
Titles:
Legal Reference Library.
Tax Reference Library.

Christian Science Publishing Society, The, (0-87510; 0-87952), One Norway St., P411, Boston, MA 02115 Tel 617-450-2773; Toll free: 800-288-7090; Orders to: P.O. Box 1875, Boston, MA 02117; Toll free: 800-877-8400.
Titles:
Concord: A Study Package.

Chronologic Corp., 4925 N. Camino Antonio, Tucson, AZ 85718-6005 Tel 602-293-3100; FAX: 602-293-0709.
Titles:
Instant Recall.
Instant Recall OFFICE.

Chronos Software, Inc., 19 Homestead, San Francisco, CA 94114 Tel 415-920-6900; FAX: 415-661-6857.
Titles:
Enterprise.
Who.What.When.

Church Software, (0-922911), 1636 Sierra St., Seaside, CA 93955 Tel 408-394-0759.
Titles:
Church Administration/Accounting.

Citation Systems, (0-922918), 683 Cumberland Rd., NE, Atlanta, GA 30306 Tel 404-874-3282.
Titles:
Expense Management.

Clarion Software, 150 E. Sample Rd., Pompano Beach, FL 33064 Tel 305-785-4555; Toll free: 800-354-5444; FAX: 305-946-1650.
Titles:
Clarion Personal Developer.
Clarion Professional Developer.
Clarion Report Writer.

Claris Corp., Subs. of Apple Computer, (0-929774), 5201 Patrick Henry Drive, Santa Clara, CA 95052-8168 Tel 408-987-7000; FAX: 408-987-3932.
Titles:
Claris Emailer.
Claris Organizer for Macintosh.
ClarisDraw for Macintosh.
ClarisDraw for Windows.
ClarisImpact for Windows, Macintosh & Power Macintosh.
ClarisWorks.
Easy Business Cards for Windows.
FileMaker Pro.
FileMaker Pro Server.
MacDraw Pro.
MacPaint.
MacWrite Pro.

Class One, Inc., 431 E. Ellis Dr., Tempe, AZ 85282 Tel 602-820-3696.
Titles:
ToothPics.

CLASSIC CONCEPTS Futureware, P.O. Box 786, Bellingham, WA 98227-0786 Tel 206-733-8342.
Titles:
A*Video: Professional Font System.
Cyrillic Alphabets.
EuroFonts Video.
Professional Font Library.
Quick-Art Borders & Vignettes.
Storybook Capitals.
SuperFont Sampler.

Classic Real Estate Systems, L.L.C., 3305 Breckinridge Blvd., Suite 115, Atlanta, GA 30136 Tel 404-921-5200; FAX: 404-921-2616.
Titles:
The Corporate Real Estate Management System.
The Farmers Home Property Management System.
The OREO Manager.
The Retail Lease Management System.

Claybrook Co., The, P.O. Box 744182, 7306 Claybrook Dr., Dallas, TX 75374 Tel 214-341-9438.
Titles:
MacOrg.

Cleaning Management Institute, Div. of National Trade Pubns., Inc., (0-9609052), 13 Century Hill Dr., Latham, NY 12110-2197 Tel 518-783-1281; FAX: 518-783-1386.
Titles:
Maclean.

Clear Lake Research, 5615 Morningside, 127, Houston, TX 77005 Tel 713-523-7842.
Titles:
CLR Anova.
CLR HyperArrays.
CLR StatCalc.

Client-Server Campaigns, Inc., (0-9644117), P.O. Box 1489, Coppell, TX 75019-1489; 625 E. Parkway Blvd., No. 1112, Coppell, TX 75019 Tel 214-393-3586.
Titles:
PowerBuilder 3 Application Development for Windows.

Climate Assessment Technology, Inc., P.O. Box 25262, Houston, TX 77265 Tel 713-528-7707; FAX: 713-529-2695.
Titles:
Crop Weather Analyst.
Crop Weather Analyst - Irrigator.
The Weather Analyst.

Coefficient Systems Corp., (0-922948), 2039 Palmer Ave., Larchmont, NY 10538 Tel 212-777-6707; FAX: 212-228-3137.
Titles:
Vterm 4010.
Vterm/100.

Cognitec, Div. of 3rd Force Software, Inc., (0-922950), 341 14th St., No. A, Del Mar, CA 92014-2557 Tel 619-755-1258.
Titles:
TeleWriter.
Telewriter-64.

Cognition Corp., 209 Burlington Rd., Bedford, MA 01730-1406 Tel 617-271-9300; FAX: 617-271-0813.
Titles:
Cost Advantage.
Design Advantage.
Mechanical Advantage 2.

Coherent Software Systems, 1012 Elkgrove Ave., Venice, CA 90291 Tel 310-452-1175.
Titles:
Rory Tycoon Portfolio Analyst.

Colbert's Medico, 2808 Castle Bar Dr., Las Vegas, NV 89134; FAX: 702-255-8005.
Titles:
Colbert's Medico.

Coleman Business Systems, 3654 Arcadian Dr., Castro Valley, CA 94546 Tel 510-581-7125.
Titles:
Condo Manager.
Rental Manager.
Resort Manager.

COMMERCIAL INVESTMENT ASSOCS.

Colinear Systems, Inc., 1000 Johnson Ferry Rd., Suite F130, Marietta, GA 30068 Tel 404-578-0000; FAX: 404-565-7881.
Titles:
Response Professional Mail Order.

Collector Software, 1535 W. Holt, Pomona, CA 91768 Tel 714-620-9014.
Titles:
BearWare.

College Board, The, (0-87447), 45 Columbus Ave., New York, NY 10023-6992 Tel 212-713-8000; Toll free: 800-323-7155 (for Visa, Discover & Mastercard only); FAX: 212-713-8143.
Titles:
College Cost Explorer Fund Finder, 1993.
College Explorer Plus, 1993.
College Explorer: 1994.
College Planner.

Columbia Software, (0-917287), 5461 Marsh Hawk Way, Columbia, MD 21045 Tel 410-997-3100.
Titles:
Roadsearch.
Roadsearch-Plus.

Comcepts Systems, (0-922973), P.O. Box 468, Indio, CA 92201 Tel 619-345-7008; FAX: 619-347-5790.
Titles:
AdvanTax: 1040 Tax Preparation System.
Gear Calculations.
Green Recipe.
Library Assistant.
Office Manager.
Pack Master.
Universal Data Management.

Comedy Software, Ltd./Disktop Publishing, Inc., P.O. Box 3605, Beverly Hills, CA 90212-0605 Tel 310-275-7826; Toll free: 800-645-8432.
Titles:
Milton Berle's Private Joke File.

ComGrafix, Inc., 620 E St., Clearwater, FL 34616-3342 Tel 813-443-6807; Toll free: 800-448-6277; FAX: 813-443-7585.
Titles:
MapGrafix Mapping System.
MapStar: Communications-Vehicle Training System.

Comlink, 485 Brown Briar Cir., Horsham, PA 19044 Tel 215-672-9396.
Titles:
Benoit.
Creator XCMD: (Developer's Version).

Command Technology Corp., (0-925583), 1040 Marina Village Pkwy., Alameda, CA 94501-1041 Tel 510-521-5900; Toll free: 800-336-3320 (orders only); 800-648-6700 (demo disks only); FAX: 510-521-0369.
Titles:
COBOL Source Analyst.
COBOL Source Analyst for SPF-PC.
SPF/PC: System Productivity Facility.
SPF/PC.

Commercial Investment Assocs., (0-931815), 3440 Gulf of Mexico Dr., Longboat Key, FL 34228 Tel 813-383-7173; FAX: 813-383-7583.
Titles:
Carol's Big Helper: Interest on Deposits.
RateChart.

1135

Commercial Legal Software, Inc., 170 Changebridge Rd., Suite D4, Montville, NJ 07045 Tel 201-575-5450; Toll free: 800-435-7257; FAX: 201-575-7442.
Titles:
Collection-Master: Legal Collection-Master.

Commercial Software Systems, Inc., (0-917717), 7689 W. Frost Dr., Littleton, CO 80123 Tel 303-973-1325.
Titles:
Real Estate Models for the Eighties.

Commodity Systems, Inc. (CSI), (0-922989), 200 W. Palmetto Pk. Rd., Boca Raton, FL 33432 Tel 407-392-8663; Toll free: 800-274-4727; FAX: 407-392-1379.
Titles:
Quickplot/Quickstudy.
QuickTrieve/QuickManager.
Trader's Money Manager: TMM.
TRADE$K.
Trading System Performance Evaluator (TSPE).

Commonwealth Veterinary Consultants, 23 St. James Blvd., Springfield, MA 01104 Tel 413-543-2772.
Titles:
OmniVet.

Communication & Information Technologies, Inc. (CIT), (1-57316), 777 N. Fifth Ave., Knoxville, TN 37917-6722 Tel 615-927-4601; Toll free: 800-845-1755; FAX: 615-673-0024; Dist. by: Ingram Bk. Co., 1 Ingram Blvd., La Vergne, TX 37086-1986 Tel 615-793-5000; Toll free: 800-937-8000 (orders only, all warehouses).
Titles:
The Adventures of Huckleberry Finn.
The Adventures of Tom Sawyer.
After the Fire: American Literature in the Age of Expansion, 1865-1914.
The Artistry of Henry James.
The Awakening.
Canterbury Tales.
Frankenstein.
Frankenstein & Selected Works of Poe.
Hamlet & MacBeth.
Huckleberry Finn & Tom Sawyer.
Little Women.
Making the Modern: 19th Century Poetry in English.
A Midsummer Night's Dream.
Romeo & Juliet.
Romeo & Juliet & A Midsummer Night's Dream.
The Scarlet Letter.
Selected Works of Melville.
Selected Works of Poe.
The Tragedy of Hamlet.
The Tragedy of Macbeth.

CompuSports, Inc., (0-928065), P.O. Box 1340, Frederick, MD 21702 Tel 301-663-3257; Toll free: 800-691-4555.
Titles:
Easy-D-Scout: Defensive Football Scouting System.
Easy Scout.

COMPanion Corp., 1831 Fort Union Blvd., No. 200, Salt Lake City, UT 84121-3041 Tel 801-943-7277; Toll free: 800-347-6439; FAX: 801-943-7752.
Titles:
Alexandria.
Lancaster: The Teaching Partner for the Computerized Classroom.
Textbook Librarian.

Compass New England, P.O. Box 117, Portsmouth, NH 03802 Tel 603-431-8030.
Titles:
PC Canary.
RealShar.
TimeTrac.

Compiled Systems, 4528 S. Parkhill Ave., Springfield, MO 65810-1674.
Titles:
Comparison.
Database Preparer.
Federal Income Taxes.
Flow.
Labels.
Macro Library.
MailMerge.
Mortgage.
Mutual.
Receivables.
Register.
Tracker.

COMPLETE Machine, The, Div. of TCM Integrated Systems, (0-928407), 365 S. Bayview Ave., Suite 202, Freeport, NY 11520-5316 Tel 516-868-7820.
Titles:
Cash Management for Holding Companies (CMS).
The Dictator.
The Not-So-Fancy Menu System.

COMPress, Div. of Queue, Inc., (0-933694; 0-88720), 338 Commerce Dr., Fairfield, CT 06430 Tel 203-335-0908; Toll free: 800-232-2224; FAX: 203-336-2481.
Titles:
Cardiac Muscle Mechanics.
Chemistry Laboratory Simulations Parts I & II COM 4030B.
Completely Randomized Designs: One-Way Analysis of Variance.
Continuous Probability Distributions.
Discrete Probability I: Shape of Well-Known Distributions.
Discrete Probability II: Simulations, Limit Theorems & Distribution Functions.
Graphical Approaches to Multivariate Data Analysis.
Microcomputer Assisted Heat Transfer Analysis - Professional COM 4403B.
Prostat.
Statistics & Probability COM 3105A - COM 3109A.

CompServCo, 1921 Corporate Sq., Suite 1, Slidell, LA 70458 Tel 504-649-0484; FAX: 504-649-3849.
Titles:
HyperGene.
MacCad.
Planit.
Wood-Ease.

Compton's NewMedia, Inc., (0-916281; 1-55730; 0-923843; 1-55731; 0-922555), 2320 Camino Vida Roble, Carlsbad, CA 92009-1504 Tel 619-929-2500; FAX: 619-929-2511.
Titles:
The American Investor: The Official Simulation of the American Stock Exchange.
Complete Multimedia Bible.
Design to Print.
The Doctor's Book of Home Remedies.
The Interactive Encyclopedia.
Jigsaw! The Ultimate Electronic Puzzle.
Let's Go: The Budget Guide to Europe.
Millionaire II.
Revolution '76.
Wealth Insurance.
W.O.R.K. at Home.

Compu-Arch, 1954 Cotner, Los Angeles, CA 90025 Tel 310-312-6632; FAX: 310-444-9577.
Titles:
ADS-MGMStation-Architecture.
ADS-MGMStation-Electronics.
ADS-MGMStation-Interiors.
ADS-MGMStation-Mechanical.

Compu-Literate, 265 Oakland Ct. No. 9, Ramsey, NJ 07446-1176.
Titles:
Insertion Order.
Media Flow Charts.

Compu-Nette, Inc., 1409 Almont Dr., SW, Atlanta, GA 30310 Tel 404-753-4796.
Titles:
Churchware.

Compu-Quote, (0-923027), 6914 Berquist Ave., Canoga Pk., CA 91307 Tel 818-348-3662; Toll free: 800-782-6775.
Titles:
Card/Fax.
Coins/Plus.
STAMPS.
Stamps World.

Compu-Share, Inc., (0-917967), Sentry Plaza III, 5214 68th St., Lubbock, TX 79424 Tel 806-794-1400; Toll free: 800-356-6568; FAX: 806-794-1110.
Titles:
Accounts Payable.
Bill of Materials Processor.
Compu-Share General Ledger.
Compu-Share Receivables Management RE/CS.
Fixed Assets: FA.
GL - Rdb Financial Management System: GL - Rdb.
Human Resources Management & Imaging System: HR.
Inventory Control: IC.
Job Cost: JC.
Order Entry: OE.
Payroll.
Purchase Order: PO.

Compu-Soft, (1-886102), 2022 Avenue A, Suite 31, Kearney, NE 68847 Tel 308-234-9243; FAX: 308-234-2566.
Titles:
Compu-Soft's Pro-Performance Management Series: Service Performance.

Compu-Tations, (0-917729), P.O. Box 487, Southfield, MI 48037-0487 Tel 810-855-0224.
Titles:
Card-Cat.
Computer Literacy.
Get Your Affairs In Order.
The Loan Arranger.
Mail-Phone List.
Study Quizfiles.

Compu-Teach, Inc., (0-915813), 16541 Redmond Way, Suite 137C, Redmond, WA 98052 Tel 206-885-0517; Toll free: 800-448-3224; FAX: 203-624-0900.
Titles:
See the U.S.A.

CompuCepts, Inc., P.O. Box 137, Plymouth, VT 05056 Tel 802-672-5194; FAX: 802-672-3222.
Titles:
Follow-Up.

Compuco, Inc., (0-9627047), 93 Grove St., Ramsey, NJ 07446-1343 Tel 201-236-0025.
Titles:
LogoWriter Activities for Readers.

PUBLISHER/TITLE INDEX

CompuConsultants, (1-879185), P.O. Box 194546, San Juan, PR 00919-4546; FAX: 809-731-1616; HCR-1, Box 29030, Suite 464, Caguas, PR 00725-8900 Tel 809-731-1616.
Titles:
Correspondence Control System.
Correspondence Control System: Control of In-House Referrals.

Compucrafts, P.O. Box 6326, Lincoln Center, MA 01773-6326 Tel 508-263-8007; Toll free: 800-263-0045; FAX: 508-264-0619.
Titles:
Stitch Crafts.
Stitch Crafts Gold.
The Stitch Grapher.

CompuData, Inc., (0-923045), 10501 Drummond Rd., Philadelphia, PA 19154 Tel 215-824-3000; Toll free: 800-223-3282; FAX: 215-824-4423.
Titles:
Brother John.

CompuDent, Inc., 4954 Lincoln Dr., Edina, MN 55436 Tel 612-926-0238.
Titles:
Joey Software for Dental Office Management.

CompuLaw, Ltd., P.O. Box 67720, Los Angeles, CA 90067-0720; Toll free: 800-444-0020; FAX: 310-558-4486.
Titles:
Ca$hFlow.
The Client Management System.
CoCounsel III.
CompuCite.
Docket Calendar/Critical Dates.
DocuLiner.
Legal Ledger.
Network Docket.
Remote Entry/More Reports.

Compumax, Inc., (0-923055), P.O. Box 7239, Menlo Park, CA 94026 Tel 415-854-6700.
Titles:
Bill of Materials.
Maxiledger.
Microbiz 6-Pak.
MicroBOMP Bill of Materials Processor.
Microinv.
Microledger.
Micropay.
Micropers.
Microrec.
MRP-II Manufacturing Resource Planning.
Order Entry.

Compusense, 2711 Village Dr., Avenel, NJ 07001 Tel 908-396-9291.
Titles:
Client Database.
Powersheet.

CompuServe, inc., (0-941269), 5000 Arlington Centre Blvd., Columbus, OH 43220 Tel 614-457-0802; Toll free: 800-848-8199; FAX: 614-457-0348.
Titles:
CompuServe Navigator.

CompuSystems, Inc., (0-923067), 1 Science Ct., Columbia, SC 29203-9344 Tel 803-735-7700; Toll free: 800-922-5528.
Titles:
CompuSystems Payroll System.

Computational Engineering Assocs., 3525 Del Mar Heights Rd., Suite 183, San Diego, CA 92130 Tel 619-259-8863.
Titles:
MATFOR: A System for Numerical Computations.

Computational Mechanics, Inc., (0-931215; 0-945824; 1-56252; 1-85312), 25 Bridge St., Billerica, MA 01821 Tel 508-667-5841; FAX: 508-667-7582.
Titles:
Applied Environmetrics: Hydrological Tables.
Applied Environmetrics: Meteorological Tables.
Applied Environmetrics: Oceanographic Tables.
Applied Environmetrics: Set of 3 Tables & Dust Emissions Software.
Beasy: Acoustic Design.
Beasy: Corrosion & CP.
Beasy: Fatigue & Crack Growth.
BEASY-Mechanical Design: Boundary Element Analysis System.
BEM Starter Pack for Acoustics.
BEM Starter Pack for Fracture Mechanics & Crack Growth.
BEM Starter Pack for Stress Analysis.
Boundary Element Starter Packs.
Complex Variable Boundary Elements.
Crack Growth Analysis in Anisotropic Materials.
Crack Growth Analysis in Stiffened Sheets.
Crack Growth Analysis Using Boundary Elements: Basic Package.
Crack Growth Analysis Using Boundary Elements: Three-Module Package.
Database of Stress Intensity Factors.
Dust Emissions: Dustcon & Stockpile Software.
PRISE: Plume Rise & Dispersion Model.
Thermoelastic Crack Growth Analysis.
Transport Analysis Using Boundary Elements.
Two-Dimensional Elastostatic Analysis Using Boundary Elements.
Two-Dimensional Potential Analysis Using Boundary Elements.

Computational Methods, Inc., (0-9626943), 2693 Fairfax Dr., Columbus, OH 43220 Tel 614-451-6204.
Titles:
Numerical Methods Software: Computational Software Library (CSL).

Computational Systems, Inc., 835 Innovation Dr., Knoxville, TN 37932 Tel 615-675-2110; FAX: 615-675-3100.
Titles:
MasterTrend.
WavePak.

Computech, Subs. of BK System, Ltd., (0-923076), 975 Forest Ave., Lakewood, NJ 08701 Tel 201-364-3005.
Titles:
Pony Express.

Computer Age, Inc., (0-923089), 1811 W. Altorfer, Peoria, IL 61615 Tel 309-693-6200; FAX: 309-693-8644.
Titles:
EOS Accounting: Record-Keeping & Accounting System.
EOS Construction Job Costing.
EOS Manufacturing: Manufacturer Accounting.

Computer Aid Corp., P.O. Box 1074, Vienna, VA 22183 Tel 703-281-7486; Toll free: 800-327-4243; FAX: 703-281-3461.
Titles:
Computer Aid Payroll: PayMaster for Hotels, Restaurants & Multi Location Businesses.
Inventory Control & Cost Analysis for Restaurants.
Inventory Control & Menu Analysis.
Paymaster Payroll.
PayMaster Plus: Automated Time & Attendance.
PayMaster Plus Time Clock.
PayMaster's Direct Deposit.

Computer Aided Management, Inc., 1318 Redwood Way, Suite 115, Petaluma, CA 94954 Tel 707-795-4100; Toll free: 800-635-5621; FAX: 707-795-0441.
Titles:
ViewPoint with Windows Graphics.

Computer Aided Technology, Inc., 10132 Monroe Dr., Dallas, TX 75229 Tel 214-350-0888.
Titles:
Cat Reader OCR Software for Hand-Held Scanners.

Computer Assistance, Inc., (0-918567), 82277 Weiss Rd., Creswell, OR 97426 Tel 503-895-3347; FAX: 503-895-3999.
Titles:
Garage Keeper Inventory Control & Invoicing System: Garage Keeper I.
Garage Keeper System III.
Garage Keeper 500.
Motive Power for Mitchell.

Computer Assisted Library Information Co., Inc., (0-916625), P.O. Box 6190, Chesterfield, MO 63006-6190 Tel 314-863-8028; Toll free: 800-367-0416; FAX: 800-367-0416.
Titles:
LION (Library Information Online).
LION OPAC Inventory Module.
LION-Union Catalog.

Computer Assocs. International, Inc., (0-923108; 0-918317; 0-928104; 0-922344; 0-926530; 0-922091), One Computer Associates Plaza (Headquarters), Islandia, NY 11788 Tel 516-342-5224; Toll free: 800-225-5224; FAX: 516-342-5734; 909 E. Las Colinas Blvd., Irving, TX 75039.
Titles:
ACCPAC Plus Accounting.
ACCPAC Plus Accounting Accounts Payable.
ACCPAC Plus Accounting Accounts Receivable.
ACCPAC Plus Accounting DynaView.
ACCPAC Plus Accounting General Ledger & Financial Reporter.
ACCPAC Plus Accounting Inventory Control & Analysis.
ACCPAC Plus Accounting Job Costing.
ACCPAC Plus Accounting LanPak.
ACCPAC Plus Accounting Order Entry.
ACCPAC Plus Accounting Purchase Orders.
ACCPAC Plus Accounting Retail Invoicing.
ACCPAC Plus Accounting Sales Analysis.
ACCPAC Plus Accounting ScanPAC.
ACCPAC Plus Accounting U. S. Payroll.
ACCPAC Plus Accounting Windowing System Manager.
CA ACCESS Library.
CA-Accpac/2000 Accounts Payable.
CA-Accpac/2000 Accounts Receivable.
CA-Accpac/2000 General Ledger.
CA-Accpac/2000 Lanpak.
CA-Accpac/2000 System Manager.
CA-Accpac/2000 U. S. Payroll.
CA-ACCPAC/2000.
CA-ACF2/PC PC Only Option.
CA-ACF2.
CA-ACF2/DB2.
CA-ACF2/PC.
CA-ACF2/Secman for VAX.
CA-ACF2/Viewpoint.
CA-ADS.
CA-ADS/PC.
CA-APCDDS.
CA-APCDOC.
CA-Archiver.
CA-ASM/Archive.
CA-ASM/Workstation.
CA-ASM2.
CA-Blockmaster.
CA-BPI Accounting II.
CA-CAS/AD Manufacturing & Logistics Management System for Aerospace & Defense.

COMPUTER ASSOCS. INTERNATIONAL, INC.

CA-CAS:AP.
CA-CAS:AR.
CA-CAS:BOM.
CA-CAS:COE.
CA-CAS:COST.
CA-CAS:Data Collection.
CA-CAS:FA.
CA-CAS:GL.
CA-CAS:INV.
CA-CAS Logistics & Financial Management System.
CA-CAS Manufacturing & Logistics Management System.
CA-CAS:MPS.
CA-CAS:MRP.
CA-CAS:PUR.
CA-CAS:SFC.
CA-CICSORT.
CA-Classic/Open: FlexComp.
CA-Classic/Open: Payroll.
CA-Classic/Open.
CA-Classic/Open: Personnel/Benefits.
CA-Clipper.
CA-Clipper/Compiler Kit for dBASE IV.
CA-Clipper/ExoSpace.
CA-Clipper Tools.
CA-Consol.
CA-Consol/PC.
CA-Consol/WS.
CA-Convertor.
CA-Corporate Tie.
CA-Cricket Draw III.
CA-Cricket Graph III.
CA-Culprit.
CA-DADS/Plus.
CA-DASDCheck.
CA-Datacom/PC Runtime.
CA-Datacom/PC Runtime Server.
CA-Datacom/STAR.
CA-Datacom/STAR PC.
CA-Datacom/UNIX.
CA-Datacom/CICS Services.
CA-Datacom/DB.
CA-Datacom/DL1 Transparency.
CA-Datacom Fast Restore.
CA-Datacom/IMSDC Services.
CA-Datacom/PC.
CA-Datacom/PC Lanpack.
CA-Datacom Presspack.
CA-Datacom Resource Analyzer.
CA-Datacom Server.
CA-Datacom/SQL Option.
CA-Datacom/Total Transparency.
CA-Datacom/Transparency for DB2.
CA-Datacom/VSAM Transparency.
CA-Datacom VSE/ESA Option.
CA-Datamacs/II.
CA-Dataquery.
CA-Dataquery for VAX.
CA-Dataquery/PC.
CA-DataVantage.
CA-Director.
CA-Dispatch.
CA-Dispatch/Notepad.
CA-Dispatch/PC.
CA-Dispatch/Viewpoint.
CA-Disspla.
CA-Disspla COBOL.
CA-Driver.
CA-DUO.
CA-Dynam/B.
CA-Dynam/D.
CA-Dynam/FastVTOC.
CA-Dynam/FI.
CA-Dynam/T VM.
CA-Dynam/T VSE.
CA-Dynam/TLMS.
CA-Dynam/TLMS/Copycat.
CA-Dynam/TLMS/Viewpoint.
CA-Earl.
CA-EasyProclib.
CA-Easytrieve/IQ.
CA-Easytrieve/Online.
CA-Easytrieve Plus.
CA-Easytrieve/Toolkit.
CA-Easytrieve/Workstation.
CA-EDP Auditor.
CA-11.
CA-11/Disaster Recovery Planning.
CA-11/Notepad.
CA-11/Reports+.
CA-11/Viewpoint.
CA-eMail+.
CA-eMail+ Companion.
CA-eMail+ X.400 Option.
CA-ESP/Upgrade.
CA-Estimacs.
CA-ETC.
CA-Examine.
CA-Examine/PC.
CA-Eztest/CICS.
CA-FastDASD.
CA-Filesave/RCS.
CA-FPXpert.
CA-Gener/OL.
CA-Graphics Connection.
CA-HRISMA.
CA-Ideal.
CA-Ideal DB2 Option.
CA-Ideal/PC.
CA-IDMS/PC Runtime.
CA-IDMS/PC Runtime Server.
CA-IDMS/UNIX.
CA-IDMS/ADS Alive.
CA-IDMS/ADS Trace.
CA-IDMS/APPC.
CA-IDMS/CMS Option.
CA-IDMS/Database Extractor.
CA-IDMS/DB.
CA-IDMS/DB Analyzer.
CA-IDMS/DB Audit.
CA-IDMS/DB Reorg.
CA-IDMS/DBOMP Transparency.
CA-IDMS/DC.
CA-IDMS/DC Sort.
CA-IDMS/DDS.
CA-IDMS/Dictionary Migrator.
CA-IDMS/Dictionary Module Editor.
CA-IDMS/DLI Transparency.
CA-IDMS/DML Online.
CA-IDMS/Enforcer.
CA-IDMS/Journal Analyzer.
CA-IDMS/Log Analyzer.
CA-IDMS/Masterkey.
CA-IDMS/PC.
CA-IDMS/PC Lanpack.
CA-IDMS Performance Monitor.
CA-IDMS Presspack.
CA-IDMS/SASO.
CA-IDMS/Schema Mapper.
CA-IDMS Server.
CA-IDMS SQL Option.
CA-IDMS/Task Analyzer.
CA-IDMS/Total Transparency.
CA-IDMS/UCF.
CA-IDMS/VSAM Transparency.
CA-IDMS VSE/ESA Option.
CA-Infopoint.
CA-Infopoint Account Analysis.
CA-Infopoint Accounts Payable System.
CA-Infopoint Automated Clearing House.
CA-Infopoint Cashtran.
CA-Infopoint Collection Management.
CA-Infopoint Combined Interest Reporting.
CA-Infopoint Combined Statement.
CA-Infopoint De-Dupe.
CA-Infopoint Deposits.
CA-Infopoint Desktop Budgeting.
CA-Infopoint Exception Administrator.
CA-Infopoint Financial Control System.
CA-Infopoint Household Marketing.
CA-Infopoint Integrated Commercial Loans.
CA-Infopoint Integrated Installment Loans.
CA-Infopoint Multisort.
CA-Infopoint Profitability.
CA-Infopoint Recovery Management.
CA-Infopoint Relationship CIF.
CA-Infopoint Relationship Pricing.
CA-Infopoint Scrub.
CA-Infopoint Super MICR.
CA-Infopoint Teller/Transaction Gateway.
CA-Infopoint Time Investment.
CA-InterTest.
CA-InterTest/Batch.
CA-ISS/Three.
CA-JARS.
CA-JARS/CICS.
CA-JARS/DSA.
CA-JARS IDMS.
CA-JARS/IMS.
CA-JARS/Interface for VAX.
CA-JARS/Reports+.
CA-JARS/SMF.
CA-JCLCheck.
CA-JobWatch.
CA-KBM.
CA-KBM Accounts Payable.
CA-KBM Accounts Receivable.
CA-KBM Bar Code.
CA-KBM Business Planning.
CA-KBM Cash Management.
CA-KBM Detail Capacity Planning.
CA-KBM EDI.
CA-KBM Financial Statements.
CA-KBM Financials.
CA-KBM General Ledger.
CA-KBM Inventory Management.
CA-KBM Manufacturing.
CA-KBM Master Production Schedule.
CA-KBM Material Requirements Planning.
CA-KBM Multi-Manufacturing Planning.
CA-KBM Process.
CA-KBM Product Structure.
CA-KBM Purchase Order Management.
CA-KBM Rough Cut Capacity Planning.
CA-KBM Sales Order Management.
CA-KBM Shop Floor Control.
CA-KBM Standard Product Cost.
CA-KBM Windows.
CA-KBM Work Order Management.
CA-Librarian.
CA-Librarian/JCL Validation.
CA-Link.
CA-Look.
CA-MANMAN/X:Distribution & Inventory Location Management.
CA-MANMAN/X:Sales & Purchasing Management.
CA-MANMAN/X.
CA-MANMAN/X Accounts Payable.
CA-MANMAN/X Accounts Receivable.
CA-MANMAN/X Capacity Requirements Planning.
CA-MANMAN/X Cost Center Administration.
CA-MANMAN/X Distribution Requirements Planning.
CA-MANMAN/X Drawing Control.
CA-MANMAN/X Electronic Data Interchange.
CA-MANMAN/X Financial Management System.
CA-MANMAN/X Financial Statements.
CA-MANMAN/X Fixed Asset Registration.
CA-MANMAN/X General Ledger.
CA-MANMAN/X Hours Accounting.
CA-MANMAN/X Inventory Location Control.
CA-MANMAN/X Lot Control.
CA-MANMAN/X Manufacturing Planning & Execution.
CA-MANMAN/X Master Production Scheduling.
CA-MANMAN/X Material Requirements Planning.
CA-MANMAN/X Product Classification.
CA-MANMAN/X Product Configurator.
CA-MANMAN/X Production Control.
CA-MANMAN/X Production Master Data.
CA-MANMAN/X Production Planning.
CA-MANMAN/X Project Budgeting.
CA-MANMAN/X Project Control.
CA-MANMAN/X Project Management.
CA-MANMAN/X Project Network Planning.
CA-MANMAN/X Purchase Quotations.
CA-MANMAN/X Purchasing Statistics.
CA-MANMAN/X Return Material Administration.

PUBLISHER/TITLE INDEX

CA-MANMAN/X Sales & Marketing Information.
CA-MANMAN/X Sales & Purchase Control.
CA-MANMAN/X Sales Contracts.
CA-MANMAN/X Sales Quotations.
CA-MANMAN/X Sales Statistics.
CA-MANMAN/X Service Management.
CA-MANMAN/X Service Order Processing.
CA-Manufacturing Workbench.
CA-Masterpiece/2000 Accounts Payable.
CA-Masterpiece/2000 Accounts Receivable.
CA-Masterpiece/2000 Fixed Assets.
CA-Masterpiece/2000 Fund Accounting.
CA-Masterpiece/2000 General Ledger.
CA-Masterpiece/2000 Inventory Control.
CA-Masterpiece/2000 Job Cost.
CA-Masterpiece/2000 Labor Distribution.
CA-Masterpiece/2000 Order Processing.
CA-Masterpiece/2000 Purchasing.
CA-Masterpiece/2000 Workbench.
CA-Masterpiece/2000.
CA-Mazdamon.
CA-MetaCOBOL+.
CA-MetaCOBOL+/PC.
CA-Metrics.
CA-Migrate/COBOL.
CA-Mindover.
CA-Netman.
CA-Netman/Workbench.
CA-Netman/Bar Code.
CA-Netman/DB.
CA-Netman for VAX.
CA-Netman/OLCF.
CA-Netman/PC.
CA-Netman/Reports+.
CA-9/R+.
CA-OLQ.
CA-1.
CA-1/Copycat.
CA-1/Viewpoint.
CA-OpenIngres.
CA-OpenIngres/Desktop.
CA-OpenIngres/DTP.
CA-OpenIngres/Enhanced Security.
CA-OpenIngres/Enterprise Access.
CA-OpenIngres/Net.
CA-OpenIngres/Object Management Extension & Spatial Object Library.
CA-OpenIngres/Server.
CA-OpenIngres/Star.
CA-OpenIngres Replicator.
CA-OpenRoad.
CA-Opera.
CA-Opera/PC.
CA-Optimizer.
CA-Optimizer/II.
CA-Pan/LCM.
CA-Pan/LCM Configuration Manager.
CA-Pan/Merge.
CA-PanAPT.
CA-PanAPT DB2 Option.
CA-PanAPT JCLCheck Option.
CA-PanAudit Plus.
CA-PanAudit Plus CPS.
CA-PanAudit Plus PC.
CA-Panexec.
CA-Panvalet.
CA-PFF.
CA-Planmacs.
CA-Plot Optimizer.
CA-PMA/ChargeBack.
CA-PMA/ChargeBack for VAX.
CA-PMA/Look.
CA-Power/Bench.
CA-PRMS:Accounts Payable.
CA-PRMS:Accounts Receivable.
CA-PRMS:Capacity Requirements Planning.
CA-PRMS:CIM Series.
CA-PRMS:Distribution Requirements Planning.
CA-PRMS Distribution Solution.
CA-PRMS Enterprise Solution.
CA-PRMS Financial Solution.
CA-PRMS:Fixed Assets.
CA-PRMS:Forecasting Workbench.
CA-PRMS:General Ledger.
CA-PRMS:Human Resources.
CA-PRMS:Inventory Control.
CA-PRMS Manufacturing Solution.
CA-PRMS:Master Production Scheduling.
CA-PRMS:Material Requirements Planning.
CA-PRMS:Order Desk.
CA-PRMS:Order Entry & Billing.
CA-PRMS:Order Entry Configurator.
CA-PRMS:Payroll.
CA-PRMS:Product Costing.
CA-PRMS:Product Structure.
CA-PRMS:Purchasing & Receiving.
CA-PRMS:Quality Control.
CA-PRMS:Replenishment Orders.
CA-PRMS Sales Analysis Workbench.
CA-PRMS: SCAN for Windows.
CA-PRMS: Shop Floor Control.
CA-PRMSVision.
CA-ProAudit.
CA-ProBuild.
CA-ProEdit.
CA-ProOptimize.
CA-ProSecure.
CA-Quickserv.
CA-Ramis.
CA-Raps.
CA-Realia CICS.
CA-Realia COBOL.
CA-Realia DL/I.
CA-Realia/MS.
CA-Realia JCL.
CA-Realia ScreenIO.
CA-Realia II Workbench for MVS Batch.
CA-Realia II Workbench for MVS CICS.
CA-Realia II Workbench for VSE CICS.
CA-Realia II Workbench.
CA-Realia 370.
CA-Realizer.
CA-Roscoe.
CA-RSVP.
CA-Scheduler.
CA-Scheduler/Notepad.
CA-Scheduler/Report Balancing.
CA-Scheduler/Reports+.
CA-Scheduler/Smart Console.
CA-Scheduler/Viewpoint.
CA-7.
CA-7 for AS/400.
CA-7/Notepad.
CA-7/Report Balancing.
CA-7/Reports+.
CA-7/Smart Console.
CA-7/Viewpoint.
CA-ShareOption/5.
CA-Sort.
CA-Spoolman.
CA-SRAM.
CA-Stabilize/CICS.
CA-SuperProject.
CA-SuperProject for DOS.
CA-SuperProject for VAX.
CA-SymDump.
CA-System/Manager.
CA-Teleview.
CA-Tellagraf.
CA-Telon.
CA-Telon AS/400 Target Option.
CA-Telon PWS.
CA-Telon UNIX Target Option.
CA-Telon VSE Target Option.
CA-Top Secret.
CA-Top Secret/PC-PC Only Option.
CA-Top Secret/DB2.
CA-Top Secret/PC.
CA-Top Secret/Secman for VAX.
CA-Top Secret/Viewpoint.
CA-Transit.
CA-Traps.
CA-Ucandu.
CA-UFO.
CA-Unicenter.
CA-Unicenter/Agent Factory.
CA-Unicenter/AHD Advanced Help Desk.

COMPUTER CONTROL SYSTEMS, INC.

CA-Unicenter/DB Alert.
CA-Unicenter/OSM Open Storage Manager.
CA-Unicenter/Software Delivery.
CA-Unicenter/Systems Alert.
CA-Unicenter/TNG.
CA-Unicenter for VMS.
CA-Unicenter/II.
CA-Unicenter SSO Single Sign-On.
CA-Unicenter/STAR.
CA-Verify.
CA-Verify/EEO.
CA-VISA: VAX Integrated System Administration.
CA-Visual Express.
CA-Visual Express/Easytrieve Server.
CA-Visual Express/Host Server.
CA-Visual Objects.
CA-Visual Objects Lite.
CA-Visual Objects SDK.
CA-Visual Realia.
CA-Visual Telon.
CA-Vivid.
CA-Vman.
CA-VMLib.
CA-Vollie.
CA-Vterm.
CA-Warehouse Boss.
CA-1 for VAX.
CA-7 for VAX.
CA-Ramis/PC.
Unicenter for OpenView.

Computer Broadcasting International, (0-923112), 1106 Pippin Cir., Santa Rosa, CA 95407-6772 Tel 707-542-6957.
Titles:
Music Index.

Computer/Business Services, (0-923115), 28333 Suburban Dr., Warren, MI 48093 Tel 810-751-6291.
Titles:
Case Load.
InvoiceM.
InvoiceR.
Ninvoice.
Series Print.

Computer Ctr., Div. of Process, Inc., (0-923123), 370 U.S. Rte. 1, Falmouth, ME 04105 Tel 207-781-2260; FAX: 207-781-3585.
Titles:
Fund Accountant.
MUNIS.

Computer Co., The, (0-923125), 1905 Westmoreland St., Richmond, VA 23230 Tel 804-254-2200; Toll free: 800-446-2612.
Titles:
ARS-A Reporting System.

Computer Consultants, 98 Main St., No. 526, Tiburon, CA 94920 Tel 415-435-9585; Toll free: 800-435-9585; FAX: 415-435-9224.
Titles:
The Marina Program.

Computer Consulting Ctr., Inc., 309 E. 87th St., Apt. 7N, New York, NY 10128-4813 Tel 212-564-9088.
Titles:
LOTS: Loan Origination Tracking System.

Computer Continuum, (0-931169), 75 Southgate Ave., Daly City, CA 94015 Tel 415-755-1978.
Titles:
PC Scope.

Computer Control Systems, Inc., (0-918569), Rte. 3, Box 168, Lake City, FL 32055 Tel 904-752-0912; FAX: 904-752-6873.
Titles:
Autosort-86M.
DB-FABS-DABL.
FABS PLUS.

Computer Curriculum Corp., Div. of Paramount Publishing, (1-57026), 1287 Lawrence Station Rd., Sunnyvale, CA 94089 Tel 408-745-6270; FAX: 408-980-0609.
Titles:
Amazonia.
Amazonia Macintosh Installation Guide.
Amazonia Teacher's Guide.
Amazonia Teachers Guide: Level III.
Amazonia Windows Installation Guide.
The Little Turtle.
Ocean Escape.
Upgrade Amazonia Windows.
Upgrade the Virtual BioPack.
The Virtual BioPack.

Computer Decisions Corp., (0-923143), 5004 Petaluma Blvd., N., Petaluma, CA 94952 Tel 707-762-9630; FAX: 707-763-1142.
Titles:
Docket.
EASY: Estate & Trust Fiduciary Accounting System.

Computer Detailing Corp., (0-923148), 80 Second St. Pike, Southampton, PA 18966 Tel 215-355-6003; FAX: 215-355-6210.
Titles:
Beams & Columns.
Plans & Elevations.
Stairs.

Computer Friends, 14250 NW Science Pk. Dr., Portland, OR 97229-5417 Tel 503-626-2291; Toll free: 800-547-3303; FAX: 503-643-5379.
Titles:
Modern Artist.

Computer Guidance & Support, (0-922739), P.O. Box 620127, Littleton, CO 80162 Tel 303-973-4035.
Titles:
Church Directory & Financial Records System.
Coin Collection & Inventory Valuation System.
Law Office Accounting & Timekeeping.
Manufacturing Job Cost Accounting.

Computer Innovations Co., 9405 Braemar Terr., Charlotte, NC 28210 Tel 704-543-1402.
Titles:
Sheetmate.

Computer Innovations, Inc., (0-923167; 0-923793), 1129 Broad St., Shrewsbury, NJ 07702-4314; Toll free: 800-922-0169; FAX: 908-542-6121.
Titles:
C86 C Compiler for QNX.
Computer Innovations C++.
Debug 2000.
EDIT 2000.
FlexeLint.
FlexeLint for the QNX Operating System.
Introducing C.

Computer Insights, (0-942199), 2090 Main St., Concord, MA 01742 Tel 508-369-9306.
Titles:
Directory of Free Computer Publications.

Computer Investment Advice, Inc., (0-923170), 505 Mill St., Coraopolis, PA 15108 Tel 412-262-5661; Toll free: 800-536-2367; FAX: 412-262-2693.
Titles:
CIA EMS Management Software.
CIA Interstate Fuel & Mileage Software.
CIA Relational Data Base System.
CIA Vehicle Maintenance Software.

Computer Law Systems, Inc., 11000 W. 78th St., Eden Prairie, MN 55344 Tel 612-941-3801; Toll free: 800-328-1913; FAX: 612-942-3450.
Titles:
CLS Law Office Management System.

Computer Logics, Ltd., (0-924561), 31200 Carter St., Solon, OH 44139 Tel 216-349-8600; Toll free: 800-828-0311; FAX: 216-349-8620.
Titles:
LinkUp 3270 Unisession for Windows.

Computer Management Technologies, 9 Nat's Farm Cane, Box 897, West Tisbury, MA 02575-0897 Tel 508-693-7921.
Titles:
PhotoAlbum the ScreenSaver: For Windows.

Computer Power Group, 630 Third Ave., New York, NY 10017 Tel 212-986-7600.
Titles:
LAWTRAC.

Computer Pubns. Group, (0-928081), 6011 Broadmeadow, San Antonio, TX 78240-5305.
Titles:
Streamliner.

Computer Related Services, Inc., (0-923201), Pembroke V., Suite 108, Virginia Beach, VA 23462 Tel 804-499-8911; FAX: 804-490-5932.
Titles:
Facts & Figures.
JCM: Job Cost Management.
PCAP: Accounts Payable.
PCAR: Accounts Receivable.
PCGL: General Ledger.
PCINV: Inventory Control.
PCOE: Order Entry-Invoicing.
PCPR: Payroll.
RGEN: Report Generator.
Travel Expense Management System (TEMS).

Computer Safari, 353 W. Main St., Suite K, Woodland, CA 95695-5013 Tel 916-666-1813; Toll free: 800-824-2547 (orders only).
Titles:
Safari Collectables 1.
Safari Collectables 2.
Safari Future Fonts.
Safari Number 29 Font Collection.
Safari SFAN Special Edition Font Collection.

Computer Security Corp., P.O. Box 2215, Huntington Beach, CA 92647 Tel 714-840-4656.
Titles:
Dr. Solomon's Audit.
Dr. Solomon's RingFence.

Computer Services, (0-923209), 1050 E. 800 S., Provo, UT 84601 Tel 801-377-2100. Do not confuse with Computer Services, Orrum, NC.
Titles:
Family Ties.

Computer Software Consultants, Inc., (0-918571), 1567 Congdon Ln., Cortland, NY 13045-9512.
Titles:
Account Sales Receivables.

Computer Software for Professionals, Inc., (0-917737), 1615 Broadway, 14th Flr., Oakland, CA 94612 Tel 510-444-5316; FAX: 510-444-5344.
Titles:
Legalex.
Legalmaster.
Legalmaster Conflicts Standalone: Conflicts of Interest.
Legalmaster: Standard Version.
Legalmaster S4 Timekeepers.
Legalmaster S8 Timekeepers.

Computer Support Corp., (1-883515), 15926 Midway Rd., Dallas, TX 75244 Tel 214-661-8960; FAX: 214-661-5429.
Titles:
Arts & Letters Apprentice.
Arts & Letters Editor.
Arts & Letters Jurassic ART.
Arts & Letters Picture Wizard.
Arts & Letters Scenerio.
Picture Perfect.

Computer Systemics, 806 Hill Wood Dr., Austin, TX 78745 Tel 512-441-4583; FAX: 512-443-6211.
Titles:
GeoView: Contour Mapping & Analysis.

Computer Systems Advisers, Inc., 50 Tice Blvd., Woodcliff Lake, NJ 07675 Tel 201-391-6500; Toll free: 800-537-4262; FAX: 201-391-2210.
Titles:
SILVERRUN - Application Design Center & Distributed Application Generators.
SILVERRUN ERX, RDM, DFD, WRM.

Computer Systems Consultants, (0-917741), 1454 Latta Ln., Conyers, GA 30207 Tel 404-483-4570.
Titles:
Cmodem Telecommunications Program.
Cross-Assemblers.
Full Screen Forms Display (A).
Full Screen Inventory-MRP (A).
Full Screen Mailing List (A).
68010 Super Sleuth.
68000 C Compiler.
Super Sleuth Disassembler Object-Only Version (B).

Computer Technical Services of New Jersey, (0-923253), 825 N. Broad St., Elizabeth, NJ 07208 Tel 201-353-5283.
Titles:
CORP 84.
Insurance.
Matching.
STATE 84.
TAXSTRAT.
TIMEKEEP.

Computer Training Corp., (0-916161), 610 W. Maple Ave., Independence, MO 64050 Tel 816-252-4080; Toll free: 800-329-0911; FAX: 816-252-5545.
Titles:
Batchwork Quilt: The Menu Control Program.
The Subliminal Software Series: Business Skills Series.
The Subliminal Software Series: Personal Enrichment Series.
Wordlister: The Online Glossary.

Computer Tutor, 1 Newton Executive Pk., Newton, MA 02162 Tel 617-954-5858. Do not confuse with companies with the same name in Fort Collins, CO, Santa Barbara, CA, Dallas, TX.
Titles:
Tactics for Lotus 1-2-3: Part One.
Tactics for Lotus 1-2-3: Part Two.

Computerized Micro Solutions, (0-923353), 7966 Arjons Dr., Suite 220, San Diego, CA 92126 Tel 619-578-2664; Toll free: 800-255-7407; FAX: 619-578-2688.
Titles:
ProEST.
ProScale.

ComputerPro of Miami, (0-917745), 4961 S.W. 75th Ave., Miami, FL 33155 Tel 305-667-3556; FAX: 305-667-0545.
Titles:
System/2.

PUBLISHER/TITLE INDEX

Computers A Z, Inc., Div. of KinnicKinnic Agri-Sultants, Inc., (1-880762), P.O. Box 37763, Raleigh, NC 27627-7763; FAX: 919-460-8707; 120 Abbotts Glen Ct., Cary, NC 27511 Tel 919-467-3963.
Titles:
ANOVA PACKAGE.

Computers & Structures, Inc., 1995 University Ave., Suite 210, Berkeley, CA 94704 Tel 510-845-2177.
Titles:
ETABS.
SAP90.

Computersmith, Inc., The, 141 Kimball Hill Rd., Hudson, NH 03051 Tel 603-889-2670; Toll free: 800-370-2670; FAX: 603-889-0476.
Titles:
Benchmark Survey System.

Computervision Corp., 100 Crosby Dr., Bedford, MA 01730 Tel 617-275-1800.
Titles:
Personal Architect.
Personal Designer.

Computerware, (0-923283), 4403 Manchester Ave., Suite 101, Encinitas, CA 92024 Tel 619-436-3512.
Titles:
Check Ledger.
Computerware Accounts Payable.
Computerware Accounts Receivable.
Computerware General Ledger.
Computeware Payroll.
Manufacturer's Inventory Control System.
Point of Sale Inventory System.
Veterinary Office System.

Computext, 911 NE Lawndale Pl., Corvallis, OR 97330 Tel 503-754-1100.
Titles:
Bar Code Factory.
Inventory.
Library.
Point of Sale.
Time & Materials.

Computing!, (0-913733), 20 Prescott Ct., San Francisco, CA 94133 Tel 415-398-8093; FAX: 415-986-4429.
Titles:
Docupower!
Laser Design!
Menu.
Power!

Computing Power Applied, 206 Straightoak, Ballwin, MO 63021 Tel 314-227-5488.
Titles:
Beat Design & Analysis System.
Employee Scheduling System.
Patrol Deployment Planning System.
PCM: Project Cost Monitor.
Pedigree.
PHYSCHED: Physician Scheduling System.
PORTAL.
Schedule Planning System.
VMD: Shear/Moment/Deflection.

Computools, Inc., 803 W. Big Beaver Rd., Suite 202, Troy, MI 48084-4734 Tel 313-643-9220.
Titles:
Checkwriter+: The Electronic Pegboard.

CompuTrac, A Telerate Co., Div. of Telerate Systems, Inc., (0-944173), P.O. Box 15951, New Orleans, LA 70175; 1017 Pleasant St., New Orleans, LA 70115 Tel 504-897-1934.
Titles:
COMPUTRAC-PC.
Intra Day Analyst/PC.
Quote Capture.

Computx, (0-918575), 14 Pierce Ave., Oak Ridge, NJ 07438 Tel 201-697-3141.
Titles:
AMORT-ZIT.
Bank*Count*Calc.
C-D-Calc.
CLUB-PLAN-CALC.
MAI-L-ET LIST.
PA-ROLL.

Compuware, 15 Center Rd., Randolph, NJ 07869 Tel 201-366-8540.
Titles:
Action & Bumping Games.
Action Games.
Advanced Air Traffic Controller.
Business Address & Information System.
Curve Fitter.
Diet.
Disk Doctor.
Hail to the Chief.
Market.
Microgolf.
Milestone.
Original Adventure.
Rats.
Scientific Plotter.
Shape Master.
Stock & Options Analysis.
Story Time.
Story Time & Don't Fall.
Trucker & Streets of the City.

Comsen Services, Inc., (0-923302), P.O. Box 457, Camp Hill, PA 17001-0457 Tel 717-691-8123.
Titles:
Comsen Energy Distribution System.
Comsen Trucking System.
VMRS Plus.

Comshare, Inc., (0-923303), 3001 S. State St., Ann Arbor, MI 48108 Tel 313-994-4800; Toll free: 800-922-7979; 800-541-1780 (in Canada); FAX: 313-769-6943.
Titles:
Commander FDC.
Commander Software for Managerial Applications.
One-Up.

ComTrain, 103 Providence Mine Rd., Suite 202, Nevada City, CA 95959 Tel 916-265-0300; Toll free: 800-758-7246; FAX: 916-265-6550.
Titles:
FastHelp.
FastStart Legal: For WordPerfect (Versions 5.0 & 5.1).
FastStart Plus: For dBASE IV.
FastStart Plus: For DOS (2.01 to 3.3 or Release 5.0).
FastStart Plus: For Lotus 1-2-3 (rel. 2.01, 2.2 & 2.3).
FastStart Plus: For WordPerfect (ver. 4.2, 5.0, 5.1).

Comtronic Systems, Inc., (0-917751), 205 N. Harris Ave., Cle Elum, WA 98922 Tel 509-674-7000; FAX: 509-674-2383.
Titles:
Comtronic Contract Collector.
Comtronic Debtmaster: Debt Collection System.
Comtronic Property Manager for Windows.

Concentric Data Systems, Inc., Sub. of Wall Data, Inc., (0-923310), 110 Turnpike Rd., Westborough, MA 01581 Tel 508-366-1122; Toll free: 800-325-9035; FAX: 508-366-2954.
Titles:
R & R Code Generator.
R&R Report Writer.
R & R Report Writer for Paradox.
R&R Report Writer: SQL Edition.
R&R Report Writer: XBase Edition.
R&R Report Writer for 1-2-3, Symphony, & Quattro Pro.
R&R Report Writer Xbase.

Concept Development Assocs., Inc., (0-935745; 1-55610), 63 Orange St., Saint Augustine, FL 32084-3628 Tel 904-825-0220; FAX: 904-825-0223; Dist. by: Lifestyle Software Group, 63 Orange St., Saint Augustine, FL 32084 Tel 904-825-0220; Toll free: 800-289-1157.
Titles:
America Cooks American: Cookbook-on-Disk.
America Cooks Chinese: Cookbook-on-Disk.
America Cooks French: Cookbook-on-Disk.
America Cooks Italian: Cookbook-on-Disk.
America Cooks Mexican: Cookbook-on-Disk.
Great Chefs-Master Collection.
Micro Kitchen Companion.
Micro Wine Companion.
Official Mr. Boston - New Edition.
The Spice Hunter: Cookbook-on-Disk.

Conceptual Software, Inc., (0-923315), P.O. Box 56627, Houston, TX 77256 Tel 713-667-4222; Toll free: 800-782-8969; FAX: 713-667-3329.
Titles:
DBMS/Copy.
DBMS/Copy Lite.
DBMS/Copy plus.
PRODAS DATABASE.
PRODAS Evaluation System.

Concord Management Systems, Inc., (0-923316), 5301 W. Cypress St., Tampa, FL 33607 Tel 813-875-4492; Toll free: 800-851-1115; FAX: 813-287-0730.
Titles:
Concord Management System: CS1000, CS2000.
Series CS1000.
Tools of the Trade.

Concord Regional Vocational Ctr., (0-931261), Warren St., Concord, NH 03301 Tel 603-225-0808.
Titles:
Blood Review.
Vital Signs.

Concourse Corp., (0-928567), 1313 Fifth St., SE, Minneapolis, MN 55414-4504 Tel 612-379-3955; Toll free: 800-438-7647; FAX: 612-379-3935.
Titles:
Statistical Methods for Improving Performance.

Condor Computer Corp., (0-923319), 555 E. William, Ann Arbor, MI 48104 Tel 313-971-8880; Toll free: 800-451-3267; FAX: 313-663-8514.
Titles:
Condor Jr.
Condor 3.

Condor Computing, Inc., (0-925374), P.O. Box 17276, Huntsville, AL 35810-7276 Tel 205-852-4490; FAX: 205-837-8714.
Titles:
Nursery Inventory Control System (N*I*C*S).

Condor Corp., (0-923320), 2060 Oak Mountain Dr., P.O. Box 189, Pelham, AL 35124 Tel 205-664-0454; Toll free: 800-347-7980; FAX: 205-664-2878.
Titles:
The Rx-80 Pharmacy System.

CONDUIT, Div. of Univ. of Iowa, (0-937332; 1-57136), Univ. of Iowa, 100 Oakdale Campus, M306-OH, Iowa City, IA 52242-5000 Tel 319-335-4100; Toll free: 800-365-9774; FAX: 319-335-4077.
Titles:
Baffles II.
Laboratory in Cognition & Perception.
Matrix Calculator.
Topics in Research Methods: Main Effects & Interactions.
Writer's Helper.

Confluence Creations, (0-9643689), 2130 S. Emerson St., Denver, CO 80210-4505 Tel 303-722-9461; FAX: 303-722-0385.
Titles:
Chaco: Canyon of Mystery.

Congressional Information Service, Inc., A Reed Reference Publishing company, (0-912380; 0-88692), 4520 East-West Hwy., Suite 800, Bethesda, MD 20814 Tel 301-654-1550; Toll free: 800-638-8380; FAX: 301-654-4033.
Titles:
Congressional Masterfile 1.
Congressional Masterfile 2.
Environmental Abstracts.
Statistical Masterfile.
U. S. Government Periodicals Index.

ConJelCo, (1-886070), 132 Radcliff Dr., Pittsburgh, PA 15237 Tel 412-492-9210; Toll free: 800-492-9210; FAX: 412-492-9031.
Titles:
Blackjack Trainer.
Ken Elliott's Crapism Professional.
Ken Elliott's Crapsim Interactive.
Percentage Hold'em.
Sozobon Poker for Windows.

Connect Computer Co., Inc., 9855 W. 78th St., Eden Prairie, MN 55344 Tel 612-944-0181; FAX: 612-944-9298.
Titles:
Lanscope.
Turnstyle.

Connect, Inc., (0-9643690), 7 Riversville Rd., Greenwich, CT 06831 Tel 203-531-8082; FAX: 203-531-8298.
Titles:
Grow.

Connected Editions, Inc., (1-56178), 65 Shirley Ln., White Plains, NY 10607 Tel 914-428-8766.
Titles:
The Age of Choice: Commentaries on Public & International Affairs.
The Birdhouse Cathedral.
Decisions: Computers & the Democratic Process.
Deuce of a Time.
Essays on Cyberspace & Electronic Education.
The Evolution of Technology.
Fellow Travellers.
The Loom & the Keyboard: Working Environment & Life on the Job.
OnLines: Chronicles of Electronic Days.
Security.
Snapshots.
The Visual Plough.

Connecticut Information Systems, Inc., (0-923323), 218 Huntington Rd., Bridgeport, CT 06608 Tel 203-579-0472.
Titles:
Mail List of Computer Dealers & Retailers.
Mail List of Congressmen & Senators.

Consolidated Micro Technology, 9400 Hall Rd., Downey, CA 90241 Tel 310-803-4685; FAX: 310-803-6164.
Titles:
CMT Personal Movie Database.

Construction Concepts, P.O. Box 232, Placentia, CA 92670 Tel 714-528-0711.
Titles:
EZ-EST.
The Force: Construction Estimating Program.

Construction Data Control, Inc. (CDCI), (0-923328), 4000 DeKalb Technology Pkwy., Suite 220, Atlanta, GA 30340 Tel 404-457-7725; Toll free: 800-285-3929.
Titles:
Basic Builder II.
The Bid Team.
Profit Builder.
ProfitCAD.

Construction Estimating Co. (ConEstCo), (0-917753), 443 Springs Rd., Vallejo, CA 94590 Tel 707-552-5476.
Titles:
The ConEstCo Contractor: AI/I.

Constructive Computing Co., Inc., (0-923331), 5600 Inland Dr., Kansas City, KS 66106 Tel 913-596-2113; Toll free: 800-456-2113; FAX: 913-287-7652.
Titles:
Quick DIRT.
QuickAccount.
QuickEST.
QuickEST/CAD.
QuickREPORT.

Consulair Corp., Box 2192, Ketchum, ID 83340 Tel 208-726-5846; FAX: 208-726-1401.
Titles:
Consulair MacC Jr.
Consulair MacC/MacC Toolkit.
Consulair MacC 68020/68881.
Consulair 68000 Development System.
Consulair 68020/68881 C Compiler.
Consulair 68020/030 Assembler.
MacC-MacC Toolkit.

Contact Software International, Inc., 10201 Torre Ave., Cupertino, CA 95014-2132; Toll free: 800-365-0606.
Titles:
Act!
ACT! for Windows.
ACT! Network.
First ACT!

Contel Business Networks, Subs. of Continental Telecom Inc., (0-923340), 14012 Parkeast Cir., Chantilly, VA 22021-2225.
Titles:
RTFile.

Conter Software, Jostens Learning Co., (1-57268), 9920 Pacific Heights Blvd., Suite 100, San Diego, CA 92121-4430 Tel 619-587-0087; Toll free: 800-521-8538; FAX: 619-622-7873.
Titles:
Algebra 1.
Algebra 2.
Community Exploration.
Early Learning English.
Early Learning Math.
Early Learning Spanish.
Forgetful Freddy.
GED Assessment.
GED Literature.
GED Math.
GED Science.
GED Social Studies.
GED Studies.
GED Writing.
Geometry.
Home, Sweet Home.
Learning English: Home & Family.
Learning English: Neighborhood Life.
Learning English: Primary.
Learning English: Primary Rhymes.
Math - Reading - Writing K-8.
Math - Reading K-8.
Math - Reading Kindergarten.
Math 1.
Math 1-2.
Math 2.
Math 3.
Math 3-4.
Math 4.
Math 5.
Math 5-6.
Math 6.
Math 7.
Math 7-8.
Math 8.
Me, Myself & I.
Mischievous Marvin.
Pre-Algebra.
Reading 1.
Reading 1-2.
Reading 2.
Reading 3.
Reading 3-4.
Reading 4.
Reading 5.
Reading 5-6.
Reading 6.
Reading 7.
Reading 7-8.
Reading 8.
Rosie's Lemonade Stand.
Storybook Maker.
Trigonometry - Pre-Calculus.
Writing K-2.
Writing 3-4.
Writing 5-6.
Writing 7-8.

Continental Business Computers, Inc., (0-923347), 165 DuBois St., Suite A, Santa Cruz, CA 95060 Tel 408-426-8161.
Titles:
IRIS.

Continuum Productions, (1-886802), 15395 SE 30th Pl., Suite 300, Bellevue, WA 98007 Tel 206-641-4505; FAX: 206-643-9740.
Titles:
Critical Mass: America's Race to Build the Atomic Bomb.
A Passion for Art: Renoir, Cezanne, Matisse, & Dr. Barnes.
Paul Cezanne: Portrait of My World.
Volcanoes: Life on the Edge.

Contour Software, Inc., (0-928089), 700 W. Hamilton Ave., Campbell, CA 95008-6611 Tel 408-370-1700; Toll free: 800-777-1718; FAX: 408-370-0366.
Titles:
The Credit Reporter.
The Loan Closer.
The Loan Finder.
Loan Handler.
The Loan Tracker.

Contract Services Assocs., (0-917755; 0-928569), 507 Lead, Kingman, AZ 86401 Tel 602-753-1133.
Titles:
CBook.
Formlet.
LoanComp.
PC-TAX.
TYP-PRT.

PUBLISHER/TITLE INDEX

Control Automation, Inc., 2350 Commerce Park Dr. N.E., Suite 4, Palm Bay, FL 32905-7722 Tel 407-676-3222; FAX: 407-676-4388.
Titles:
ModelMate Plus +.

Control Data Business Management Services, Div. of Control Data Corp., 8100 34th Ave., S., Minneapolis, MN 55440 Tel 612-853-4224.
Titles:
Human Resources Management System: HRMS.
Orchestrator.
Orchestrator Premier.

Conway Data, Inc., (0-910436), 40 Technology Pk./Atlanta, No. 200, Norcross, GA 30092 Tel 404-446-6996; Toll free: 800-554-5686; FAX: 404-263-8825.
Titles:
IDRC/rpm Software.

Cooke Pubns., (0-940119), P.O. Box 4448, Ithaca, NY 14852-4448 Tel 607-257-8148; FAX: 607-257-2820.
Titles:
MacElastic.
MacPoisson.
PC-Elastic.
PC-Poisson.
Stomate Tutor.

Coopers & Lybrand, (0-923363), 1251 Ave. of the Americas, New York, NY 10020 Tel 212-536-2000; Toll free: 800-223-0535.
Titles:
Adjustments Scoresheets.
Book & Tax Depreciation.
COMBO.
Coopers & Lybrand Effective Analytical Review System: CLEAR.
Corporate Quarterly Estimated Tax Payments.
DEBT.
Deferred Charges.
Depreciation-Amortization Estimator.
1120 TAX ASSEMBLY.
Engagement Management Templates.
FASB13.
HCFA2522 Simulator.
Home Health Agency Cost Report System.
Individual Retirement Account.
Inputed Interest.
Installment Sales.
Interest Expense Estimator.
Investment Tax Credit Options.
Leasepur.
Lower Cost of Market.
Lumpsum Distribution.
Mediplan Input Screens.
MERGER.
Monetary Unit Sampling.
Multi-Level Financing Calculations.
Net Present Value.
Optimum Tax Shelter Determination.
Ordinary Income Acceleration.
Original Issue Discount.
Pre-Audit.
R&D Partnership Analysis.
REALPLAN.
Return on Investment.
SAMPLE.
Summary of Confirmation Coverage.
Tax Accrual Worksheet.
Tax Calendar.
Tax Department Financial Analysis.
TAX TRACKING.
1065 Partnership Tax.

Copia International, Ltd., 1342 Avalon Ct., Wheaton, IL 60187 Tel 708-682-8898; Toll free: 800-689-8898; FAX: 708-665-9841.
Titles:
AccSys for Paradox.
AccSys for xBASE.
FaxFacts.

Corbel & Co., 1660 Prudential Dr., Jacksonville, FL 32207 Tel 904-399-5888; Toll free: 800-326-7235; FAX: 904-399-5551.
Titles:
The Corbel Connection: Online.
PentaxPlus.
Quantech.

Core Software, Inc., (0-923368), 26303 Oak Ridge Dr., Spring, TX 77380-1918 Tel 713-292-2177; FAX: 713-298-1492.
Titles:
Accounts Payable.
Accounts Receivable.
Alternate Pricing.
Contract Processing.
Extended Payments.
Fastrak.
FasTrak Accounting.
FasTrak: Accounting with Inventory & Order Entry.
FasTrak: Accounting with Serialized Inventory.
FasTrak: General Ledger with Report Writer.
FasTrak: Service Management Series.
FasTrak 2.32: Service Management Software.
General Ledger.
Inventory.
Prospect - Contact Manager.
Purchase Order Processing.
Sales Invoicing.
Service Dispatching.
Service Management.

Core Technology Corp., 7335 Westshire Dr., Lansing, MI 48917 Tel 517-627-1521; Toll free: 800-338-2117; FAX: 517-627-8944.
Titles:
CTC Bridge: CTC Burroughs Micro to Mainframe Communication (Mac, Burroughs & Sperry connection).
QUICKEY: CTC Data Entry-Micro.
Underneath.

Cornsoft Group, (0-923370), 6008 N. Keystone Ave., Indianapolis, IN 46220 Tel 317-257-3227.
Titles:
Frogger.

Cornucopia Software, (0-917969), 626 San Carlos Ave., Albany, CA 94706 Tel 510-528-7000.
Titles:
Electric Webster.
Whoops!

Corporate Consulting Co., (0-923373), 43 White St., Belmont, MA 02178 Tel 617-484-1709; FAX: 617-489-3665.
Titles:
Client Write-Up General Ledger Accounting Module.
Contractor Cost Accounting System.
Cost Center Reporting System.
Health Care (Nursing Home) Patient Billing.
Lawn Service Routing & Accounting System.
Manufacturers Bill of Material Invoicing & Inventory Control Module.
Manufacturers Job Cost-Inventory Control Module.
Medical Laboratory-Third Party Billing & Accounts Receivable Package.
Musical Instrument Rental.
Project Cost Accounting System.
Rental Service Billing (Deliveries) System.
Sales Leads Analysis.
Subsidized Housing: Retirement Home Management.
Temporary Nursing Personnel Agency System.

COURSEWARE APPLICATIONS, INC.

Corporate Safety & Health Systems, (0-923374), 175 Green St., Brooklyn, NY 11222 Tel 718-383-8730.
Titles:
Hearing Management System, Industrial Safety System.

Corvus Systems, Inc., (0-923383), 160 Great Oaks Blvd., San Jose, CA 94119-1347 Tel 408-281-4100; FAX: 408-578-4102.
Titles:
Constellation III For Macintosh.
Corvus Omninet.
PC/NOS.
Readynet.

COSMIC, Univ. of Georgia, 382 E. Broad St., Athens, GA 30602 Tel 706-542-3265; FAX: 706-542-4807.
Titles:
ACTOMP - AutoCAD to Mass Properties.
AKSATINT - Satellite Interference Analysis & Simulation Using Personal Computers.
ARAM - Automated Reliability-Availability-Maintainability.
CLIPS.
EIVAN - An Interactive Orbital Trajectory Planning Tool.
General Thermal Analyzer.
Softcost.

Cosmos International, Inc., P.O. Box 775, Jenison, MI 49429-0775 Tel 616-457-7538; FAX: 616-667-2474.
Titles:
Club Receivables/Membership.
Golf Handicapping.
Golf Time Reservation System.
Golf Tournament Management System.
Proshop Retail.

Cotton Software, Inc., 2325 Anderson Rd., Suite 364, Covington, KY 41017 Tel 606-727-1600.
Titles:
BOXCALC 1000.
NFL Forecaster.

Cougar Mountain Software, Inc., (0-923390), P.O. Box 6886, Boise, ID 83707 Tel 208-344-2540; Toll free: 800-388-3038; FAX: 208-343-0267.
Titles:
Act 1 Plus.
Act 4 Plus.
ACT1 Plus Series.
ACT2 Plus Series.
Fund Accounting 4+.
Fund Accounting One Plus.
Fund Accounting 2+.
Lynx.

Countryside Data, Inc., (0-923393), 1500 Pancheri Dr., Suite 5, Idaho Falls, ID 83402 Tel 208-523-2641.
Titles:
AG Finance.
AG Payroll.
AG Planner.
Farm Management Series.
Field Manager.
SNAP Business System.

Courseware Applications, Inc., (0-923394), One Appletree Square, Suite 1541, Bloomington, MN 55425 Tel 612-854-8909; FAX: 217-359-1880.
Titles:
Drawbridge.
Unison Author Language.
Unison Draw.

Cra Z Software, P.O. Box 6379, Haverhill, MA 01831.
Titles:
MacAuto.

Cragsmoor Interactive, Inc., (0-9637769), 605 W. 112th St., Suite 6B, New York, NY 10025 Tel 212-864-7547; FAX: 212-866-8744.
Titles:
The Line & the Shape Eater: An Interactive Adventure in New York City.

Craig Systems, Inc., 16717 Monitor Ave., Baton Rouge, LA 70817 Tel 504-756-2322.
Titles:
Schedule Maker.

Crawford, Chris, Games, (0-9625733), P.O. Box 360872, Milpitas, CA 95036 Tel 408-946-4626.
Titles:
Balance of the Planet.

Creative Equipment, (0-923411), 5555 W. Flagler St., Miami, FL 33134-1065 Tel 305-261-7866.
Titles:
Commander Ultra Terminal-64.
Falconian Invaders.
Lazer Cycles.
Maze Man.
Tyler's Dungeons.
Ultrex Quadro Maze.

Creative Multimedia Corp., (1-880428), 514 NW 11th St., Suite 203, Portland, OR 97209 Tel 503-241-4351; Toll free: 800-262-7668; FAX: 503-241-4370.
Titles:
American Family Physician on CD-ROM: DOS-MAC.
Annal of Internal Medicine, 1992-1994.
Beyond the Wall of Stars: MPC Jewel Case.
Beyond the Wall of Stars: MPC-MAC Jewel Case.
Beyond the Wall of Stars: MPC-MAC Retail Box.
The C. H. A. O. S. Continuum: MAC Jewel Case.
The C. H. A. O. S. Continuum: MPC Jewel Case.
The C. H. A. O. S. Continuum: MPC Retail Box.
The Chaos Continuum: MAC Retail Box.
The Classic Collection Plus: 4 Disc Set Jewel Case.
The Complete Audubon: DOS-MAC Retail Box.
The Complete Works: Shakespeare & Sherlock Holmes.
Dinosaur Safari: MAC Jewel Case.
Dinosaur Safari: MAC Retail Box.
Dinosaur Safari: MPC Jewel Case.
Dinosaur Safari: MPC Retail Box.
Family Doctor: MAC Jewel Case.
The Family Doctor: MAC Retail Box.
Family Doctor: MPC Jewel Case.
Family Doctor: MPC Retail Box.
The Magic Death: MAC Jewel Case.
The Magic Death: MPC Jewel Case.
Multimedia Audubon's Birds: DOS-MAC Jewel Case.
Multimedia Audubon's Mammals: DOS-MAC Jewel Case.
The New England Journal of Medicine on CD-ROM: DOS-MAC.
Parenting: Prenatal to Preschool: DOS-MAC Jewel Case.
Parenting: Prenatal to Preschool: DOS-MAC Retail Box.
The Pediatric Infectious Disease Journal on CD-ROM: DOS-MAC.
Pediatrics on CD-ROM: DOS-MAC.
Pediatrics Review & Education Program (PREP) on CD-ROM: DOS-MPC.
Shakespeare.
Sherlock Holmes.
Total Baseball, 1993 Edition: DOS-MAC Jewel Case.
Total Baseball, 1993 Edition: DOS-MAC Retail Box.
The Virtual Murder Series: MAC Retail Box.
The Virtual Murder Series: MPC Retail Box.
Who Killed Sam Rupert?: MPC Jewel Case.
Year Book Edition on CD-ROM, 1993: DOS-MAC.

Creative Programming, P.O. Box 112097, Carrollton, TX 75011-2097 Tel 214-245-9139; Toll free: 800-726-6447; FAX: 214-245-9717.
Titles:
VCScreen.
Vitamin C.

Creative Pursuits, (1-878928), 12151 La Casa Ln., Los Angeles, CA 90049 Tel 708-884-7040; Toll free: 800-624-2926; FAX: 708-884-9227.
Titles:
School Spirit Disk.

Creative Research Systems, (0-918577), 140 Vista View, Suite 100, Petaluma, CA 94952-4728 Tel 707-765-1001; FAX: 707-765-1068.
Titles:
The Survey Sampler.
The Survey System.

Creative Software, (0-928574), 526 Maple Ave., Madison, WI 53704-5843.
Titles:
CSI Business System.

Creative Solutions, (0-923419), 4701 Randolph Rd., Suite 12, Rockville, MD 20852 Tel 301-984-0262; Toll free: 800-367-8465; FAX: 301-770-1675. Do not confuse with companies with the same name in Dexter, MI, Bellevue, WA.
Titles:
Mac II Tools.
MacFORTH Plus.
MacForth 3-D Library.

Creative Solutions, Inc., (0-917973), 7322 Newman Blvd., Dexter, MI 48130 Tel 313-426-5860; FAX: 313-426-5946. Do not confuse with companies with the same name in Rockville, MD, Bellevue, WA.
Titles:
The Checkbook Solution.
The Depreciation Solution II.
The 1120 Solution.
The 940/941 Solution.
1065 Solutions.
The 1040 Solution.
The Time & Billing Solution.
The Write-Up Solution II.

Creighton Manning, Inc., (0-928575), 500 Kenwood Ave., Delmar, NY 12054-1822 Tel 518-439-4991; Toll free: 800-383-4369; FAX: 518-439-7094.
Titles:
Fleetmax.
Fleetmax for Windows.
VersTrans Routing & Planning: VTRANS.

Crescent Software, Inc., 11 Bailey Ave., Ridgefield, CT 06877-4505 Tel 203-438-5300; Toll free: 800-352-2742; FAX: 203-431-4626.
Titles:
GraphPak Professional.
LaserPak.
P.D.Q.
PDQComm.
QB Plus.
QuickHelp.
QuickMenu.
QuickPak Professional.
QuickPak Scientific.
QuickScreen.

Cromemco, Inc., 39899 Balentine Dr., Apt. 117, Newark, CA 94560-5361; FAX: 408-737-7488.
Titles:
BAS.
CCC.
COB-XS.
CROMIX Plus.
FOR.
PAS.

Crosstalk Communications, Div. of Digital Communications Assocs., (0-925424), 1000 Alderman Dr., Alpharetta, GA 30202-4199 Tel 404-442-4000.
Titles:
Crosstalk for Windows.
Crosstalk Mark 4.
Crosstalk XVI.
Crosstalk XVI: Network Version.
Remote Squared.

Crosstech Systems, Inc., 95 Old Country Rd., Hicksville, NY 11801 Tel 516-932-8020; FAX: 516-932-8063.
Titles:
Financial Accounting Package.
Manufacturers Software.
Profit Series Accounts Payable.
Profit Series Accounts Receivable.
Profit Series for Accountants.
Profit Series for General Business Accounting.
Profit Series for Wholesalers/Distributors.
Profit Series Inventory-Bill of Materials.
Profit Series Job Estimating & Tracking.
Profit Series Payroll.
Profit Series Purchase Order.
Profit Series SalesTrak: Order Entry/Billing/Sales Analysis.
Profit Series Time Management & Billing With AR.

Crowe Chizek, (0-923427), 330 E. Jefferson Blvd., P.O. Box 7, South Bend, IN 46624 Tel 219-232-3992; Toll free: 800-523-2799; FAX: 219-236-8612.
Titles:
FAMAS (Financial Analysts Management & Authoring System).

Crownsoft Applications, Inc., (0-918581), 350 S. Main St., Suite 211, Doylestown, PA 18901 Tel 215-340-2626.
Titles:
Club-Pak.
Loan-Pak.

Crunch Software Corp., (0-923431), 7677 Oakport St., Suite 470, Oakland, CA 94621-1917 Tel 510-562-9900; Toll free: 800-999-7828; FAX: 510-562-9919.
Titles:
Crunch Interactive Statistical Package: Crunch.
eHOP: Electronic Handbook of Probability.

CSC; Artemis Products & Services, Subs. of Computer Sciences Corp., 3702 Pender Dr., Suite 300, Fairfax, VA 22030 Tel 703-277-1050; Toll free: 800-477-6648; FAX: 703-277-1053.
Titles:
Artemis ProjectView.
Artemis Schedule Publisher.
Artemis 7000.

Cultural Resources, Inc., (0-9624372), 30 Iroquois Rd., Cranford, NJ 07016 Tel 908-709-1574; FAX: 908-709-1590.
Titles:
Culture: The Multi-Media Guide to Western Civilization.

PUBLISHER/TITLE INDEX

Current Clinical Strategies Publishing, (0-9626030; 1-881528), 9550 Warner Ave., Suite 213, Fountain Valley, CA 92708-2822 Tel 714-965-9400; Toll free: 800-331-8227; FAX: 714-965-9401.
Titles:
Prescription Writer: Current Clinical Strategies.

Custom Computer Services, (0-923440), 15 Moonakis Rd., East Falmouth, MA 02536-7725.
Titles:
Vibes II.

Custom Data, (0-923442), 2505 Aspen Dr., Alamogordo, NM 88310-4201 Tel 505-434-1096.
Titles:
Attendance.
Church Denominations.
Church Donations.
Church Ledger.
Custom Ledger.
Directory.
Formlet.
Profile.

Custom Databanks, 13925 Esworthy Rd., Germantown, MD 20874-3313 Tel 301-990-4010; Toll free: 800-445-3557; FAX: 301-990-4011.
Titles:
The College Majors Search System.
Executive Search System.
The Growth Search System.
The Venture Search System.

Custom Software Consulting Services, Inc., 2 Split Rock Ct., Melville, NY 11747 Tel 516-692-4500.
Titles:
Business Manager.

Custom Software Engineering, Inc., (0-928095), 807 Minutemen Causeway, Dept. B, Cocoa Beach, FL 32931 Tel 407-783-1083.
Titles:
Alpha-Draw.
Assembler.
Command Stream Processor.
Data-O-Base Calendar.
Disk Data Handler 64k.
Disk Double Entry.
Graphic Screen Print Program: GSPR.
Let's Play Monopoly.
Melody Maker.
Renumber.
Statement Writer.
That's Interest-Ing.

CyberCorp, Inc., (1-877839), P.O. Drawer 1988, Kennesaw, GA 30144 Tel 404-424-6240; FAX: 404-424-8995.
Titles:
Cyberdesk.
Sparkle.

Cybernetics Technology Corp., (0-923458), 1370 Port Washington Blvd., Port Washington, NY 11050-2628 Tel 516-883-7676.
Titles:
PC CYACCT.
PC CYLAW.
PC CYPRO.
PINS: Personal Injury Negligence System.
The Real Estate Closing System.

Cynthia Publishing Co., (0-9614168), 11390 Ventura Blvd., No. 5, Studio City, CA 91604 Tel 818-509-0165; FAX: 818-509-1602.
Titles:
All-in-One V2.
Betting Analyst.
PEH (Positive Expection Handicapper).
The Speed Handicapper.

Cytel Software Corp., (0-9624108), 137 Erie St., Cambridge, MA 02139 Tel 617-661-2011; FAX: 617-661-4405.
Titles:
StatXact: Statistical Software for Exact Nonparametric Inferency.

DATALEX, (0-917299), 100 Pine St., Suite No. 1600, San Francisco, CA 94111 Tel 415-362-4466; Toll free: 800-962-8888; FAX: 415-362-5733.
Titles:
Entrypoint for Windows.
Entrypoint 90.
Entrypoint 90/Plus.

D & L Software, R.R. 1, Box 26, Gunter, TX 75058-9801 Tel 214-991-1801.
Titles:
PCAS: Personal Computer Accounting System.

D & M Software Pubs., (0-917765), 1510 S. 97th St., Tacoma, WA 98444 Tel 206-537-8155.
Titles:
Easy Computing Greatest Hits.

DCD Co., Div. of Borg Enterprises, (0-928097), 1000 Shelard Pkwy., Suite 400, Minneapolis, MN 55426 Tel 612-544-7077; Toll free: 800-457-3015; FAX: 612-544-8253.
Titles:
DCD Job Shop Control System.

DCM Data Products, 1710 Two Tandy Ctr., Fort Worth, TX 76102 Tel 817-870-2202.
Titles:
Mactran Plus.

DDA Software, (0-923491), P.O. Box 477, Long Valley, NJ 07853 Tel 908-876-5580; FAX: 908-876-5579.
Titles:
The Apple Pie Series.
The Know It All Series.
NAS2: Nutrient Analysis System 2.

DDI, Inc., 6201 W. Howard St., No. 202, Niles, IL 60714 Tel 708-647-2222.
Titles:
DDI*Amor: Loan Amortization.
DDI*Assets: Fixed Asset Accounting.
DDI*LAW: Legal Time & Billing.
DDI-Mailbag: Mailing List/Labels.
DDI*TIMETRAK: Professional Time & Billing Scheduling.

D.D.S., Inc., (0-923492), P.O. Box 850, Severna Park, MD 21146 Tel 410-544-1800.
Titles:
Dental Office Solution.

DHA Systems & Software, 333 I St., Fremont, CA 94536 Tel 510-795-9522.
Titles:
FastPak Mail.

DINE Systems, Inc., (0-923713), 586 N. French Rd., Suite 2, Amherst, NY 14228 Tel 716-688-2400; FAX: 716-688-2505; Dist. by: Publishers Distribution Service, 6893 Sullivan Rd., Grawn, MI 49637 Tel 616-276-5196; Toll free: 800-345-0096 (orders only).
Titles:
DINE Right for Windows.
MacDINE Perfect.
Medicine Monitor.

DWC COMPUTER SOLUTIONS, INC.

DISC, 11070 White Rock Rd., Suite 210, Rancho Cordova, CA 95670 Tel 916-635-7300; Toll free: 800-366-3472; FAX: 916-635-6549. Do not confuse with D I S C Washington, DC.
Titles:
Down to Earth Business Software.
Synergy DBL.

DISC, 1725 K St., NW, Washington, DC 20006 Tel 202-785-8585. Do not confuse with D I S C Rancho Cordova, CA.
Titles:
3D Color Graphics Program.

D-Link Systems, Inc., 5 Musick, Irvine, CA 92718 Tel 714-455-1688; Toll free: 800-326-1688; FAX: 714-455-2521.
Titles:
D-Manager.
D-View, SNMP Network Management Program.
LANsmart Network OS.
TCP/IP for DOS.

DMA, Inc., (0-923755), 1776 E. Jericho Tpke., Huntington, NY 11743 Tel 516-462-0440; FAX: 516-462-6652.
Titles:
ASCOM IV.
PC Anywhere III.

DMC Software, Inc., (1-881564), 6169 Pebbleshire Dr., Grand Blanc, MI 48439 Tel 810-695-6131.
Titles:
A Statistical Package for Business, Economics, & the Social Sciences (Student).

DNS Assocs., Inc., (1-877748), 6 New England Executive Pk., Burlington, MA 01803-5080 Tel 617-272-4252; Toll free: 800-624-6354; FAX: 617-272-5820.
Titles:
DNS Crew Requirements Model.
EDI - EDGE - LAN.
EDI - ENTRY.
EDI/EDGE.
Fast EDI.
microBOCS.
microTOCS.
microURCS.

DPX, Inc., (0-928582), 490 S. California Ave., Palo Alto, CA 94306-1605 Tel 415-323-8195.
Titles:
RODE-PC: Data Entry.

DSP Development Corp., 1 Kendall Sq., Cambridge, MA 02139 Tel 617-577-1133; FAX: 617-577-8211.
Titles:
DADiSP: Data Analysis & Display.

DTC Software, (0-923511), P.O. Box 1503, Janesville, WI 53545 Tel 608-752-0017; Toll free: 800-637-3382; FAX: 608-752-1918.
Titles:
Title Company Automation Package: TCAP.

DWB Assocs., (0-917157), 9360 SW Gemini Dr., Beaverton, OR 97005 Tel 503-626-3081; Toll free: 800-275-6284; FAX: 503-641-6012.
Titles:
The Profiler.

DWC Computer Solutions, Inc., 2355 Harrodsburg Rd., Lexington, KY 40504-3363 Tel 606-233-2316; FAX: 606-223-1846.
Titles:
Membership Management System: MEMSYS.

DWN, (0-918741), 2840 Lancaster Dr., Boise, ID 83702 Tel 208-345-2387.
Titles:
Basic Accounting Course.
BET-A-BIT.
Depreciation Schedule.
File Plus.
Postall.

DacEasy, Inc., Div. of Sage Group, (0-942113; 1-56366), 17950 Preston Rd., Suite 800, Dallas, TX 75252 Tel 214-248-0305; Toll free: 800-992-7779; FAX: 214-250-3752.
Titles:
DacEasy Accounting.
DacEasy Bonus Pack.
DacEasy Instant Accounting.
DacEasy Light.
DacEasy Payroll.
DacEasy Payroll Self Paced.
DacEasy Point of Sale.
DacEasy Self Paced.
Rolodex Live!

Dagar/Software Development Corp., (0-923512), 649 Amity Rd., Bethany, CT 06525 Tel 203-393-2000; Toll free: 800-233-3711.
Titles:
Dagar Home Health Care.
DME by Dagar.
Expanded Pharmacy Software.
MD-REBS.
Standard Pharmacy Software.
Universal Pharmacy Software Package.

Dalex Pubns., (0-9610300), Rte. 1, Box 970, King George, VA 22485 Tel 703-663-2694.
Titles:
Computerized Stock Market Analysis.

DALTONWARE, 2800 Greenridge Ct., Mexico, MO 65265 Tel 314-581-4334.
Titles:
Football Guide, 1994.

Damon International Corp., P.O. Box 11854, Fort Lauderdale, FL 33339 Tel 305-563-5590; Toll free: 800-433-4530.
Titles:
TLS Tutor for Lotus 1-2-3 Release 2.

Danscores, (1-878084), 1215 Krise Cir., Lynchburg, VA 24503 Tel 804-384-8212.
Titles:
The Adventures of Notationman: A Computerized Introduction to Labanotation.

Dapple-Tech Computers, P.O. Box 1098, Laurel, MD 20725-1098 Tel 410-792-2735.
Titles:
MacHorse.

DAR Systems International, (0-916163; 1-55616), P.O. Box 521598, Miami, FL 33152-1598 Tel 305-529-3572; Toll free: 800-633-3506; FAX: 305-262-3195; Dist. by: Baker & Taylor Bks., Momence Service Ctr., 501 S. Gladiolus St., Momence, IL 60954-2444 Tel 815-472-2444; Toll free: 800-775-2300 (customer service).
Titles:
Casino Games.
DARAD IIe.
DARAD IIe Report Generator.
The Gem of Zephyrr.
Mines of Moria II.
The Mines of Moria.
The Pits of Doom!
The Quest for Varsar.
The Sword of Altair.
Trilogy.

DARcorporation, 120 E. Ninth, Suite 2, Lawrence, KS 66044 Tel 913-832-0434.
Titles:
Advanced Aircraft Analysis (AAA).

Darvish Systems, 2000 Dwight Way, Suite D, Berkeley, CA 94704 Tel 510-843-4341.
Titles:
Harmony.

Data Access Corp., (0-923531), 14000 SW 119th Ave., Miami, FL 33186 Tel 305-238-0012; Toll free: 800-451-3539; FAX: 305-238-0017.
Titles:
DataFlex.
FlexQL.
WinQL: Report Writer for Windows.

Data Analysis Group, (0-936677), P.O. Box 128, Cloverdale, CA 95425-0128; FAX: 916-333-1247.
Titles:
Computer Industry Forecasts: The Source for Business Information on Computers, Peripherals, & Software.

Data Base System, 295 Mohawk Rd., Owens Cross Roads, AL 35763 Tel 205-518-9957.
Titles:
Genealogical Data Base System: GDBS.

Data-Basics, Inc., (0-923543), 11000 Cedar Rd., Suite 110, Cleveland, OH 44106 Tel 216-721-3400; Toll free: 800-837-7574; FAX: 216-721-2398.
Titles:
Architectural/Engineering Master Accounting System Plus (AEMAS Plus).
Construction Master Accounting System Plus (CMAS Plus).

Data Consulting, (0-923549), 18 Hector Ln., Novato, CA 94949 Tel 415-883-2300.
Titles:
Data*Easy PC Accounts Payable.
Data*Easy PC Cash Register.
Data*Easy PC Data Entry & Edit.
Data*Easy PC Elementary A/R.
Data*Easy PC Inventory Control A, B & C.
Data*Easy PC Names & Labels A.
Data*Easy PC Mail Order System.
Data*Easy PC Menu/Item Costing.
Data*Easy PC Names & Labels B.
Data*Easy PC Open Item A/R.
Data*Easy PC Product Invoicing.
Data*Easy PC Purchase Orders.
Data*Easy PC Tax Organizer.
Data*Easy PC Time Accounting.

Data Consulting Assocs., (0-923548), 18000 Coleman Valley Rd., Occidental, CA 95465 Tel 707-874-3067.
Titles:
Winery Production Management.

Data Description, Inc., (0-935321), P.O. Box 4555, Ithaca, NY 14852 Tel 607-257-1000; FAX: 607-257-4146.
Titles:
Data Desk.

Data East U.S.A., Inc., 1850 Little Orchard St., San Jose, CA 95125-1041 Tel 408-286-7074; FAX: 408-286-2071.
Titles:
ABC's Monday Night Football.
Bo Jackson Baseball.
Drakkhen.

Data Image, (0-9649980), 6262 Blossom Park Dr., Dayton, OH 45449 Tel 513-435-1103.
Titles:
Lighthouse Bibliography: Database.

Data Index, Inc., (0-923560), 7131 Chipperton, Dallas, TX 75225-1708 Tel 214-739-1703.
Titles:
Catch Weight 2001: CW2001.
Custom Auto-Pricing System: CAPS.
SYSTEM FI.

Data Law, Div. of Sulcus Law Management Corp., (0-923563), 41 N. Main St., Greensburg, PA 15601 Tel 412-836-5737; Toll free: 800-433-3438; FAX: 412-836-1440.
Titles:
Calendar/Docket System.
Collection Ledger Accounting System.
DATALAW-PC.
Litigation Support.
Trust Exec.

Data Management Assocs. of New York, Inc., 275 N. Plank Rd., Newburgh, NY 12550 Tel 914-565-6262.
Titles:
Draw-Forms.
Framework Fonts.
Mac-Tally.
MacQC.
PC MacTerm.

Data Pro Accounting Software, Inc., 5439 Beaumont Ctr. Blvd., Suite 1050, Tampa, FL 33634; Toll free: 800-237-6377.
Titles:
Data Pro Accounting Series.

Data Research Processing, Inc., 5121 Audrey Dr., Huntington Beach, CA 92649 Tel 714-840-7186.
Titles:
Sweeps Keeper.

Data Source One, Inc., 310 E. Harrison St., Tampa, FL 33602 Tel 813-221-1100.
Titles:
Check Exec.
Escrow Exec.
TidBits.
Trust Exec.

Data Strategies, Inc., (0-917767), 9645 Granite Ridge Dr., Suite 230, San Diego, CA 92123 Tel 619-514-0300; Toll free: 800-875-0480; FAX: 619-514-0322.
Titles:
Compumedic.
DentalWare.
VetLogic.

Data Team Corp., (0-923592), 4121 W. 83rd, No. 243, Prairie Village, KS 66208 Tel 913-642-8812; Toll free: 800-359-6840.
Titles:
Data Team DDS: Dental Office Management.

Data Transforms, Inc., Div. of Solarstatics, Inc., (0-917297), 790 Washington St., Denver, CO 80203 Tel 303-832-1501.
Titles:
Apple Utility Pak.
Fontpak.
Fontrix (Apple).
Fontrix (IBM).
Graphtrix.
Laser Fontpak.
Printrix.

Data Translation, 100 Locke Dr., Marlboro, MA 01752 Tel 508-481-3700; Toll free: 800-525-8528; FAX: 508-481-8620.
Titles:
Global LAB Color: HSI Color Image Processing.
Global Lab Data Acquisition.
Global LAB Image: Image Processing for Microsoft Windows.

Data Transport Systems, Div. of DTS, Manila, (0-923597), 347 E. 62nd St., New York, NY 10021 Tel 212-888-6931.
Titles:
Branch - HQ Integrated System.

Data Trek, Inc., Subs. of Dawson Holdings PLC Group, (0-929795), 5838 Edison Pl., Carlsbad, CA 92008-6596 Tel 619-431-8400; Toll free: 800-876-5484; FAX: 619-431-8448.
Titles:
Manager Series Audio/Visual Handler Module: Manager Series Library Automation System.
GLAS Acquisitions Module: Graphical Library Automation Systems.
GLAS Cataloging Module: Graphical Library Automation Systems.
GLAS Circulation Module: Graphical Library Automation Systems.
GLAS Databridge Module: Graphical Library Automation Systems.
GLAS EasySearch Utility: Graphical Library Automation Systems.
GLAS Serials Module: Graphical Library Automation Systems.
GoPAC Module (Graphical Online Public Access Catalog): Library Automation System.
ImageLink Module: Library Automation System.
Manager Series Acquisitions Module: Manager Series Library Automation System.
Manager Series Cataloging Module: Manager Series Library Automation System.
Manager Series Circulation Module: Manager Series Library Automation System.
Manager Series Databridge Module: Manager Series Library Automation System.
Manager Series OPAC Module (Online Public Access Catalog): Manager Series Library Automation System.
Manager Series Report Generator Module: Manager Series Library Automation System.
Manager Series Serials Module: Manager Series Library Automation System.
NetPAC.
Professional Series Acquisitions Module: Professional Series Library Automation System.
Professional Series Cataloging Module: Professional Series Library Automation System.
Professional Series Circulation Module: Professional Series Library Automation System.
Professional Series Databridge Module: Professional Series Library Automation System.
Professional Series OPAC Module (Online Public Access Catalog): Professional Series Library Automation System.
Professional Series Serials Module: Professional Series Library Automation System.

Data Workshop, 935 Main St., Suite H9, Manchester, CT 06040-6050 Tel 203-647-8625.
Titles:
Real Prospects.

Database International, Inc., P.O. Box 2432, Framingham, MA 01701 Tel 508-820-0018.
Titles:
Aware.
Dual Currency Aware.
MultiCurrency Aware.

Database Publishing Co., (0-911510; 0-929695; 0-937628), 1590 S. Lewis St., Anaheim, CA 92805-6423 Tel 714-778-6400; FAX: 714-778-6811.
Titles:
1996 California Manufacturers Register: Database Prospect System.
1996 California Wholesalers, Distributors & Services Companies: Database Prospect System.
Southern California Business Directory, 1995: Database Prospect System.

DataCompatible, (0-938793), 2423 Willowbend Dr., Richmond, TX 77469 Tel 713-232-4372.
Titles:
The Professional Bailbondman.
Quick Docket.

Datacount, Inc., (0-923609), 508 S. Seventh St., P.O. Box 3078, Opelika, AL 36801 Tel 334-749-5641; FAX: 334-749-5666.
Titles:
DARTS: Traffic & Billing System for Radio Broadcasters.
Datacount Music Box: Music Management & Scheduling System.
General Ledger Rev. 3.05.

Datacut, Inc., (1-887777), 466 Saw Mill River Rd., Ardsley, NY 10502 Tel 914-693-6000; Toll free: 800-882-2288; FAX: 914-693-6738.
Titles:
The CAD - CAM Starter Kit.
GRAF-X Plus.
GRAFX II.
GRAFX II: Limited Edition.
NCTALK.

DataEase International, Inc., (0-918111), 7 Cambridge Dr., Trumbull, CT 06611 Tel 203-374-8000; Toll free: 800-243-5123; FAX: 203-365-2317.
Titles:
Data Ease.
DataEase.
DataEase Developer.

Dataflight Software, 10573 W. Pico Blvd., Suite 68, Los Angeles, CA 90064 Tel 310-471-3414; Toll free: 800-421-8398.
Titles:
Concordance.

Dataflow Technologies, Inc., 1300 York Rd, Suite 30, Lutherville, MD 21093 Tel 410-296-2630; FAX: 410-321-6524.
Titles:
Bar Code Generator & Reader Software.
DFWEDGE.
LASerDEV.

DataFund Systems, Inc., (0-9623482), 11150 Santa Monica Blvd., Suite 1400, Los Angeles, CA 90025 Tel 310-273-9689; FAX: 310-273-0422.
Titles:
DataFund Systems.

DataHouse, Inc., 1 Perimiter Pk. S., Suite 100, Birmingham, AL 35243 Tel 205-972-9292.
Titles:
DME-XPRESS.

Datalight, 307 N. Olympic Ave., No. 201, Arlington, WA 98223-1338 Tel 205-435-8086; Toll free: 800-221-6630; FAX: 206-435-0253.
Titles:
C Thru ROM.

Datamatics Management Services, Inc., Affil. of Resource Software International, (0-87435), 330 New Brunswick Ave., Fords, NJ 08863 Tel 908-738-9600; Toll free: 800-673-0366; FAX: 201-738-9603.
Titles:
Performance Measurement: PMS.
TC-1 Time & Attendance.
TC-1 Time Clock.

Datamed Research, Inc., (0-923620), 1433 Rosecomore Rd., Los Angeles, CA 90077 Tel 310-472-8825.
Titles:
Asset.
MedAccount.

DataMyte Corp., Subs. of Allen-Bradley Co., Inc., (0-930345), 14960 Industrial Rd., Minnetonka, MN 55345 Tel 612-935-7704; FAX: 612-935-0018.
Titles:
FANII Software Program.
TurboSPC Software.

DataPak Software, Inc., 11815 NE 99th St., Suite 1200, Vancouver, WA 98682 Tel 360-891-0542; Toll free: 800-327-6703; FAX: 360-891-0743.
Titles:
PAIGE.

Datasmith, Inc., Affil. of LPI Information Systems, (0-917769), 10020 Fontana, Overland Park, KS 66207 Tel 913-381-9118.
Titles:
Custom Payroll.
Datasmith Payroll.

DataSound, 28 Westbrook Ln., Roosevelt, NY 11575-1016.
Titles:
Sonic Spectrum Library.

DataSource Publishing Co., Div. of DataSource System Marketing Corp., (0-926001), 5230 W. 73rd St., No. A, Edina, MN 55439-2204; Toll free: 800-328-2260.
Titles:
Auto Mac.
On-Line Help Utility.
Quikey.
RAM Driver 2.0.
Selective Copy.
Selective Erase.
Sort Directory Utility.
Timesavers: Quikey, On-Line, Help, RAM Driver, Sort Dir., Selective Erase.

DataSpan International, 3143 W. 7300 S., Spanish Fork, UT 84660-4517; Toll free: 801-226-2200; FAX: 801-226-0225.
Titles:
TRANSACCT.

Datastorm Technologies, Inc., P.O. Box 1471, Columbia, MO 65205 Tel 314-443-3282; FAX: 314-875-0595.
Titles:
ProComm.
ProComm Plus.
ProComm Plus Network Version.

Dataverse Corp., P.O. Box 937, New Paltz, NY 12561 Tel 914-657-2645; FAX: 914-255-9077.
Titles:
Accountant's Practice Management.
The Club Controller: Health & Country Club Management System.
The Importer: Import Distribution System.

DataViz, Inc., (0-918583), 55 Corporate Dr., Trumbull, CT 06611 Tel 203-268-0030; Toll free: 800-733-0030 (sales info. only); FAX: 203-268-4345.
Titles:
Conversion Plus.
MacLinkPlus/Easy Open Translators.
MacLinkPlus/HP Palmtop.
MacLinkPlus/PC Connect.
MacLinkPlus/Translators Pro.
MacOpener: For Windows.

DataWell, 13852 Echo Park Ct., Burnsville, MN 55337-4776 Tel 612-432-5109.
Titles:
You're Hired!: The Ultimate Job Interview Simulator.

Davidson Software Systems, Inc., (0-918587), 834 W. Grand River Ave., Williamston, MI 48895 Tel 517-655-5985; Toll free: 800-678-3367; FAX: 517-655-5191.
Titles:
Funeral Directors Management & Accounting System.

Davka Corp., (0-923644), 7074 N. Western Ave., Chicago, IL 60645 Tel 312-465-4070; Toll free: 800-621-8227.
Titles:
Afikoman Adventure.
AllPage.
AllScript.
Catch a Hamantash.
Catskills.
Crumb Eater.
Davka Bats.
DavkaGraphics: Bitmaps.
DavkaGraphics EPS: Jewish Holidays.
DavkaGraphics EPS: Judaica.
Dreidel Drama.
Eshkolit.
Hebrew CalendarMaker.
Hebrew DAvka.
Hebrew LaserWriter Fonts.
HyperHebrew.
HyperSeder.
Jericho.
Jerusalem Stores.
The Lion's Share.
MacShammes.
Milon Plus.
Otzar Plus.
PC Hebrew Writer.
The Philistine Ploy.
Purimaze.
Search for Your Israeli Cousin.
VeZOT HaTorah.
YidPix.

Dawson, J. B., (0-9615084), 4328 E. Lapuente Ave., Phoenix, AZ 85044 Tel 602-893-0108.
Titles:
Application Tool Kit Diskette to Accompany "Understanding the TI PC: A Programming Digest".
Key Matic.
Programmer's Line Editor.

Dawson, W.S., Co., (1-878515; 1-57000), P.O. Box 62823, Virginia Beach, VA 23466; FAX: 804-490-0922; 4709 Jeanne St., No. 103, Virginia Beach, VA 23462 Tel 804-499-6271.
Titles:
Virtual Library at the Buzzard's Nest.

Dayflo Software Corp., (0-923649), P.O. Box 19243, Irvine, CA 92713-9243 Tel 714-474-2901; Toll free: 800-367-5369; FAX: 714-474-0217.
Titles:
DayFlo TRACKER.

Daystar Software, Inc., 8120 NW Hillside Dr., Kansas City, MO 64152 Tel 816-741-4310; FAX: 816-421-1956.
Titles:
DS-Concrete.
DS-Steel2D.
DS-Wood.
Retainwall.

DBDS, P.O. Box 3312, Cincinnati, OH 45201 Tel 513-333-0482.
Titles:
RPM for Windows: Rental Property Manager.

De-Lux'O Consumer Productions, 3700 Ingelwood Blvd., No. 8, Los Angeles, CA 90066 Tel 310-391-5897.
Titles:
Bar-Min-Ski: Consumer Product.

De Novo Systems, Inc., 3910 NE 42nd St., Suite 100, Vancouver, WA 98661 Tel 206-695-9372.
Titles:
Legal Case Manager.

Dealership Systems, 11225 Midlothian Pike, Richmond, VA 23235 Tel 804-379-2466.
Titles:
Dealerwerks.

DecComp, Inc., (0-928108), 14752 Sinclair Cir., Tustin, CA 92680 Tel 714-730-5116.
Titles:
Pro-Accountant: Integrated Business System.

Decision Aids, Inc., 1720 Parkhaven Dr., Champaign, IL 61820 Tel 217-359-8541; FAX: 217-244-5712.
Titles:
Policy/Goal Percentaging: A Decision-Aiding Program.

Decision Graphics, Inc., 210 Exchange Pl., Suite C, Huntsville, AL 35806 Tel 205-837-7710; Toll free: 800-352-7859; FAX: 205-837-7712. Do not confuse with Decision Graphics, Inc., Littleton, CO.
Titles:
ACI.
ACS.

Decision Graphics, Inc., (0-932779), P.O. Box 2776, Littleton, CO 80161 Tel 303-796-0341. Do not confuse with Decision Graphics, Inc. of Huntsville, AL.
Titles:
The DGI Cryptogram.
DGI LOTTO MGR.
DGI Organization Chart Manager.
PRO DGI Word Search.

Deep River Publishing, Inc., (1-885638), P.O. Box 9715-975, Portland, ME 04104 Tel 207-871-1684; FAX: 207-871-1683; 565 Congress St., Suite 200, Portland, ME 04104 Tel 207-871-1684. Do not confuse with Deep River Pr. in Omaha, NE.
Titles:
Adventures.
Complete House.
Everywhere U. S. A. Travel Guide.
Explore America!
Fractal Ecstasy.
Great Restaurants, Wineries & Breweries.

Dekker, Marcel, Inc., (0-8247), 270 Madison Ave., New York, NY 10016 Tel 212-696-9000; Toll free: 800-228-1160; FAX: 212-685-4540.
Titles:
Mechanical Design Failure Analysis.
QCPAC Statistical Quality Control on the IBM PC.
Spring Design with an IBM PC.

Delphi Noetic Systems, Inc., P.O. Box 7722, Rapid City, SD 57709 Tel 605-348-0791; FAX: 605-342-2247.
Titles:
F-BASIC.
F-BASIC System SLDB.

Delphi Redshaw, Div. of Delphi Information Systems, Inc., (0-926547), 680 Andersen Dr., Foster Plaza 10, Pittsburgh, PA 15220-2770 Tel 412-937-3661; Toll free: 800-999-1115; FAX: 412-937-3688.
Titles:
PC-ELITE.

Delphus, Inc., 103 Washington St., Suite 348, Morristown, NJ 07960 Tel 201-267-9269; Toll free: 800-335-7487; FAX: 201-285-9248.
Titles:
AUTOCAST II- Expert Forecasting.
AUTOCAST II/BATCH: Volume Forecasting.
Peer Planner for Windows.
The Spreadsheet Forecaster.
WINX11.

Delta Research, P.O. Box 151051, San Rafael, CA 94915 Tel 415-461-1442.
Titles:
J-Forth Professional.
JForth.

DeltaPoint, Inc., 2 Harris Ct., Suite B1, Monterey, CA 93940 Tel 408-648-4000; FAX: 408-648-4020.
Titles:
Taste.

Deltek Systems, Inc., 8280 Greensboro Dr., McLean, VA 22102 Tel 703-734-8606; Toll free: 800-456-2009; FAX: 703-734-0346.
Titles:
Deltek Government Contractor Accounting & Job Cost System.
Deltek Pro Pricing & Estimating System.

Demi-Software, (0-923684), 62 Nursery Rd., Ridgefield, CT 06877 Tel 203-431-0864.
Titles:
Mail.
Plan Project Management.
Text Word Processing.

DeMichele Systems, Inc., (0-923685), 6432 E. McDowell Rd., Mesa, AZ 85205 Tel 602-985-4926.
Titles:
Data Entry Optimize, Store Front & Estimating.

Deneb, Inc., 201 Riverside Dr., Suite 2C, Dayton, OH 45405 Tel 513-223-4849; FAX: 513-223-1548.
Titles:
DENEB Construction Accounting & Estimating: Accounts Payable.
DENEB Construction Accounting & Estimating: Accounts Receivable.
DENEB Construction Accounting & Estimating: Bank Reconciliation.
DENEB Construction Accounting & Estimating: Contact Organizer & Mailing List.
DENEB Construction Accounting & Estimating: Estimating.
DENEB Construction Accounting & Estimating: Equipment Control.
DENEB Construction Accounting & Estimating: General Ledger.
DENEB Construction Accounting & Estimating: Item Billing.
DENEB Construction Accounting & Estimating: Inventory Control.
DENEB Construction Accounting & Estimating: Job Cost.
DENEB Construction Accounting & Estimating: Order Entry.
DENEB Construction Accounting & Estimating: Office Tools.
DENEB Construction Accounting & Estimating: Payroll.
DENEB Construction Accounting & Estimating: Purchase Order.
DENEB Service Management.

PUBLISHER/TITLE INDEX

Deneba Software, 7400 SW 87th Ave., Miami, FL 33173 Tel 305-596-5644; Toll free: 800-622-6287; FAX: 305-273-9069.
Titles:
BigThesaurus.
Canvas.
Canvas: Windows Version.
Deneba ArtWORKS.
Spelling Coach Professional.
UltraPaint.

Dennis Publishing, (1-886009), 25 W. 39th St., No. 1103, New york, NY 10018 Tel 212-302-2626; FAX: 212-302-2635.
Titles:
Blender Magazine.

Denpac Systems, Inc., (0-928113), 809 Wall St., Valparaiso, IN 46383 Tel 219-462-2564.
Titles:
DENPAC 80.

Denslow, V. A., & Assocs., 4151 Woodland Ave., Western Springs, IL 60558 Tel 708-246-3365.
Titles:
Common Stock Decision Aide.
Financial Needs for Retirement.
Mutual Fund Decision Aide.

Dentcom, Inc., Benjamin Fox Pavillion, Suite A101, Jenkintown, PA 19046; Toll free: 800-523-2494.
Titles:
DentaLab.

DeScribe, Inc., 4047 N. Freeway Blvd., Sacramento, CA 95834 Tel 916-646-1111; FAX: 916-923-3447.
Titles:
DeScribe Word Processor.

Design Science, Inc., (1-884799), 4028 Broadway, Long Beach, CA 90803 Tel 310-433-0685; Toll free: 800-827-0685; FAX: 310-433-6969; Dist. by: SciTech International, Inc., 2525 N. Elston Ave., Chicago, IL 60647-2003 Tel 312-472-0444; Toll free: 800-622-3345; Dist. by: PC Micro Distributors, 3042 Remington Ave., Baltimore, MD 21211; Toll free: 800-448-8892.
Titles:
MathType - the Equation Editor Upgrade: For Macintosh.
MathType - the Equation Editor Upgrade: For Windows.
MathType: For Macintosh.
MathType: For Windows.

Design Software, 4227 E. 83rd St., Tulsa, OK 74137 Tel 918-481-5855.
Titles:
D-Screen.
DS Backup Plus.
DS Optimize.

Desktop Architect, 27 E. Russell St., Suite 201, Columbus, OH 43215 Tel 614-469-9906.
Titles:
Desktop Architect.

DeskTop ComPosition Systems, 336 Greenbrae Dr., Sparks, NV 89431-3242 Tel 702-355-7503.
Titles:
Stylo-Type I.

Desktop Video Productions, 1316 63rd St., Emeryville, CA 94608 Tel 510-428-1035.
Titles:
Clip Animation Sampler.
Desktop Video Productions Clip Art.

Desops, Ltd., (1-887215), P.O. Box 1200, Purcellville, VA 22132-9109 Tel 540-338-9147.
Titles:
Horticopia: Perennials & Annuals.
Horticopia Trees, Shrubs & Groundcovers.

Devonian International Software Co., Div. of Devonian Industries, P.O. Box 2351, Montclair, CA 91763 Tel 909-621-0973; FAX: 909-621-2117.
Titles:
Artagenix: Planes of Fame.
Fontagenix.
Foreign Fonts Edition.
Lasergenix: Sverdlovsk, Riverside, IPA, Newport News, Fontana, Fractional, Cracow, Chef Dijon, Bryansk.

Dexter & Chaney, Inc., 3200 NE 125th St., Seattle, WA 98125 Tel 206-364-1400; Toll free: 800-875-1400; FAX: 206-367-9613.
Titles:
FOREFRONT Construction Management System: Accounts Payable.
FOREFRONT Construction Management System: Accounts Receivable.
FOREFRONT Construction Management System: Equipment Control.
FOREFRONT Construction Management System: Esti-Link.
FOREFRONT Construction Management System: Fixed Assets.
FOREFRONT Construction Management System: General Ledger.
FOREFRONT Construction Management System: Inventory Control.
FOREFRONT Construction Management System: Info-Link.
FOREFRONT Construction Management System: Order Processing.
FOREFRONT Construction Management System: Preventive Maintenance.
FOREFRONT Construction Management System: Purchase Order.
FOREFRONT Construction Management System: Sales Analysis.
FOREFRONT Construction Management System: Service Contracts.
FOREFRONT Construction Management System: Small Tools.
FOREFRONT Construction Management System: Time & Materials-Billing.
FOREFRONT Construction Management System: Work Order.

Diacad Assocs., (0-927513), Stinson Lake Rd., Rumney, NH 03266 Tel 603-786-2700.
Titles:
QCal.
QCRYPT: CP/M File Decipher & Encipher Program.

Diamante Software, 3027 Brookshire Dr., Plano, TX 75075 Tel 214-964-5444.
Titles:
CaseFlow Management System.
MacPlantManager.

Diamond Chip Technologies, Inc., (0-929490), 711 S. Bayview Ave., Freeport, NY 11520 Tel 516-379-4432; FAX: 516-868-2187.
Titles:
Personnel Management Software.

Diamond Group, (0-9644900), 9648 Olive Blvd., Suite 212, Saint Louis, MO 63132 Tel 314-928-0393.
Titles:
Forms2000 for Windows Reference Manual: General Manager's Handbook.

DIGITAL COLLECTIONS, INC.

Diamond Head Publishing, Div. of Diamond Head Software, (0-917771), 1101 E. El Caminito Dr., Phoenix, AZ 85020-3725; FAX: 808-732-9418.
Titles:
Stock Charting.

Diamond Systems, Inc., (0-923702), P.O. Box 48301, Niles, IL 60648 Tel 312-763-1722.
Titles:
Word Processing Mailing List.

DiAmpar Interactive, (1-886393), 1107 First Ave., Suite 1802, Seattle, WA 98101 Tel 206-340-5975; FAX: 206-340-1432.
Titles:
Understanding Exposure: How to Take Great Photographs.

Diehl Graphsoft, Inc., 10270 Old Columbia Rd., Suite 100, Columbia, MD 21046 Tel 410-290-5114; FAX: 410-290-8050.
Titles:
Azimuth.
Blueprint.
MiniCad.

Diemer Development, 12814 Landale St., Studio City, CA 91604-1351 Tel 818-762-0804.
Titles:
C-Zar.
Sequel.

Digidesign, Inc., 1360 Willow Rd., Suite 101, Menlo Park, CA 94025 Tel 415-688-0600; FAX: 415-327-0777.
Titles:
Audiomedia 2.
DECK.
Pro Tools.
Q-Sheet A-V.
SampleCell.
Softsynth.
Sound Accelerator: Digital Signal Processing Card.
Sound Designer II.
Sound Designer Universal.
Sound Tools.
Turbosynth.

Digisoft Computers, (0-928139), 245 E. 92nd St., New York, NY 10128 Tel 212-289-0991.
Titles:
Telescript.

Digital Arts Software Assocs., 3878 Bradwater St., Fairfax, VA 22031 Tel 703-978-3867.
Titles:
Split Ink.

Digital Collections, Inc., (1-886664), 1301 Marina Village Pkwy., 2nd Flr., Alameda, CA 94501 Tel 510-814-7200; Toll free: 800-449-6220; FAX: 510-814-6100.
Titles:
Ancient Egyptian Art: The Brooklyn Museum: Jewel Case.
Ancient Egyptian Art: The Brooklyn Museum.
Great Paintings Renaissance to Impressionism: The Frick Collection.
Great Paintings Renaissance to Impressionism: The Frick Collection: Jewel Case.
Masterworks of Japanese Painting: The Etsuko & Joe Price Collection.
1000 Years of Russian Art: The State Russian Museum, St. Petersburg.
Robert Mapplethorpe: An Overview.
Robert Mapplethorpe: An Overview: Jewel Case.
Robert Mapplethorpe: Catalogue Raisonne.
Robert Mapplethorpe: The Controversy.
Robert Mapplethorpe: The Controversy: Jewel Case.

Digital Communications Assocs., (0-927467), 1000 Alderman Dr., Alpharetta, GA 30201 Tel 404-442-4000; Toll free: 800-241-4762.
Titles:
IRMAcom-RJE.
IRMAcom-3270.
IRMAcom-3270B.
IRMAcom-3770.
IRMAlink DBX-CICS.
IRMAlink FT-TSO.
IRMA2.
MacIRMA API.
MacIRMA Graphics.
Remote2.

Digital Destinations, 2719 Quail St., Davis, CA 95616 Tel 916-757-2323.
Titles:
Destination Japan: Multimedia Business & Education Reference.

Digital Impact, Inc., 6506 S. Lewis, Suite 250, Tulsa, OK 74136 Tel 918-742-2022.
Titles:
ImageVAULT.
ImageVAULT Pro.
ImageVAULT, Vol. 1: General Interest.
The Maximum Six.
Ozzie's Travels Destination Japan.
Ozzie's Travels Destination: Japan Lab Pack.
Ozzie's Travels Destination Mexico.
Ozzie's Travels Destination: Mexico Lab Pack.
Ozzie's Travels: First Grand Tour.
Ozzie's Travels: Mexico.
Ozzie's World.
Power Bytes Action & Arcade.
Power Bytes Board & Strategy.
Power Bytes Business & Office Utilities.
Power Bytes Card & Casino Games.
Power Bytes Crossword Challenge.
Power Bytes Desktop Tools & Personal Organizers.
Power Bytes Drawing & Publishing.
Power Bytes Education for All Ages.
Power Bytes Money & Finance.
Power Bytes Multimedia Tools.
Power Bytes Pro Football Guru.
Power Bytes Utilities for Windows.
Professor C. D. Smart.
SoftwareVAULT: The Collection for Macintosh.
SoftwareVAULT: The Collection for Macintosh, Jewel Case.
SoftwareVAULT: The Diamond Collection.
SoftwareVAULT: The Diamond Collection, Jewel Case.
SoftwareVAULT: The Emerald Collection.
SoftwareVAULT: The Games 2 Collection.
SoftwareVAULT: The Games 2 Collection, Jewel Case.
SoftwareVAULT: The Platinum Collection.
SoftwareVAULT: The Ruby Collection.
SoftwareVAULT: The Sapphire Collection.
SoftwareVAULT: The Sapphire Collection, Jewel Case.
SoftwareVAULT: The Windows 2 Collection.

Digital Learning Systems, Inc., (0-923708), 401 State Rte. 24, 3rd Flr., Chester, NJ 07930-2904.
Titles:
KeyNotes Associated Press Stylebook.
KeyNotes Financial Mathematics Handbook.
KeyNotes Writer's Handbook.

Digital Matrix Services, Inc., 3191 Coral Way, Suite 900, Miami, FL 33145 Tel 305-445-6100; FAX: 305-442-1823.
Titles:
DiGiCAD.
InFoCAD.
InFoCASE.
InFoIMAGE.
InFoTERM.
InFoTRACE.
InFoTRAN.

InFoVIEW.

Digital Music Services, 2310 Lake Forest Dr., Suite D334, Laguna Hills, CA 92653 Tel 714-951-1159.
Titles:
DMP7 & DMP11 Pro.
DX11 & TX81Z Pro.
DX7 II & TX802 Pro.
FB Pro.
TX802 & TX81Z Pro.

Digital Pictures, 1825 S. Grant St., Suite 900, San Mateo, CA 94402 Tel 415-345-5300.
Titles:
Corpse Killer.
Double Switch.
Kids on Site.
Kids on Site Demo.
Maximum Surge.
Night Trap.
Prize Fighter.
Quarterback Attack.
Sampler.
Supreme Warrior.
What's My Story.

Digital Research, Inc., (0-917581), 2180 Fortune Dr., San Jose, CA 95131-1815 Tel 408-649-3896; Toll free: 800-443-4200.
Titles:
Assembler Plus Tools.
CBASIC.
CBASIC Compiler.
Concurrent DOS 386.
CP/M Plus.
CP/M 2.2.
FlexNet.
FlexOS 386.
FORTRAN 77.
GEM Artline.
The GEM Collection.
GEM Desktop Publisher.
GEM Draw.
Gem Draw Plus.
GEM 1st Word Plus.
GEM Graph.
GEM Presentation Team.
GEM WordChart.
GEM/3: Graphics Environment Manager.
Pascal-MT Plus.
PL/1.
Research FORTRAN-77.

Digital Wisdom, Inc., (1-883481), P.O. Box 2070, Tappahannock, VA 22560; Toll free: 800-800-8560; FAX: 804-758-4512; 419 Water Ln., Tappahannock, VA 22560 Tel 804-758-0670.
Titles:
Body Shots - Business.

Digitalk, Inc., 5 Hutton Centre Dr., 11th Flr., Santa Ana, CA 92707-5754 Tel 310-645-1082; Toll free: 800-922-8255; FAX: 310-645-1306. Do not confuse with Digitalk, Inc. in Huntsville, AL.
Titles:
Smalltalk/V.
Smalltalk/V Mac.
Smalltalk/V PM.
Smalltalk V/286.

DigiTech Systems, 34684 Richard O. Dr., Sterling Heights, MI 48310 Tel 810-264-3039.
Titles:
Imagebank EPS Maps.
Imagebank Professional ClipArt Images.

DigiTek Software, 1916 Twisting Ln., Wesley Chapel, FL 33543 Tel 813-973-7733; Toll free: 800-783-8023; FAX: 813-973-7888.
Titles:
Amegas.
Clever & Smart.

Dino Wars.
Drum Studio.
Final Mission.
Gunshoot.
Hole-In-One Miniature Golf.
Hole-In-One Miniature Golf, Extra Course Disk 3.
Joe Blade.
Powerstyx.
Skyblaster.
Thunderboy.
Vampire's Empire.
Western Games.

Dilloware, Inc., 1395 Bear Creek Rd., New Braunfels, TX 78132 Tel 210-899-2100; Toll free: 800-880-0887; FAX: 210-899-2124.
Titles:
Billing Clerk with Accounts Receivable.

Dimension Software Systems, Inc., (0-917307), 1717 Walnut Hill Ln., Suite 104, Irving, TX 75038 Tel 214-580-1045; FAX: 214-580-0794.
Titles:
FREEFORM(R).

Dimensional Insight, Inc., 99 S. Bedford St., Burlington, MA 01803 Tel 617-229-9111.
Titles:
CrossTarget.

Direct-Aid, Inc., (0-928153), 31332 Via Colinas, Suite 102, Westlake Village, CA 91362 Tel 818-889-1013; Toll free: 800-443-8080.
Titles:
Direct Connect.
The Impersonator.
Law Search.
Lawsearch Plus: Natural Link Access to WESTLAW.
Search Pro: Professional Approach to Lexis/Nexis.

Direct Imagination, 745 Earlham St., Pasadena, CA 91101 Tel 818-793-8387.
Titles:
The Grammar of Ornament, Compact Edition.
The Grammar of Ornament, Professional Artist's Edition.

Direct Systems, Inc., 7846 Forest Hill Ave., P.O. Box 13753, Richmond, VA 23225 Tel 804-320-2040; FAX: 804-330-4748.
Titles:
Direct Plus.

Discoversoft, Inc., (0-9623715), 1516 Oak St., Suite 307, Alameda, CA 94501 Tel 510-769-2902; FAX: 510-769-0149.
Titles:
TreeSaver.

Discovery Systems, (0-925452), 7001 Discovery Blvd., Dublin, OH 43017 Tel 614-761-2000; FAX: 614-761-4258.
Titles:
HyperSearch.

Disk-Count Software, Inc., 1751 W. County Rd. B, Suite 107, Saint Paul, MN 55113 Tel 612-633-2300.
Titles:
Multiple Checkbook System.
Portfolio Manager.

Disk Software, Inc., 109 S. Murphy Rd., Murphy, TX 75094 Tel 214-423-7288.
Titles:
TurboGeometry.
TurboGeometry Library.

PUBLISHER/TITLE INDEX

Disk Technician Corp., (0-929594), 1940 Garnet Ave., San Diego, CA 92109 Tel 619-274-5000.
Titles:
Disk Technician.
Disk Technician Advanced.
Disk Technician Advanced: Automated A1 Software System.
Disk Technician: Automated A1 Software System.
Disk Technician Gold.
Disk Technician +.
Disk Technician Pro.
Safepark Advanced: Time-Resident Software.

Disney, Walt, Computer Software, Inc., Div. of Walt Disney Co., (0-927806; 1-57350), 500 S. Buena Vista St., Burbank, CA 91521 Tel 818-543-4300; FAX: 818-547-6737.
Titles:
Who Framed Roger Rabbit.

Dissidents, 730 Dawes Ave., Utica, NY 13502 Tel 315-797-0343.
Titles:
disED.
MIDI Sample Wrench.
SpeakerSim.

Distributed Planning System Corp., (0-923725), 23501 Park Sorrento, No. 106, Calabasas, CA 91302 Tel 818-222-3881; FAX: 818-992-4289.
Titles:
Bankreporter I.
Call Reporter I.
GARMANAGER I.
ProfitManager I.

Diversified Computer Applications, P.O. Box 1142, Du Quoin, IL 62832 Tel 618-357-3619.
Titles:
Document Storage System (DSS).
MiniWareHouse Manager: Rentals Management for the MAC & DOS Platforms.

Diversified Computers Systems, 3775 Iris Ave., Suite 1B, Boulder, CO 80301 Tel 303-447-9251; FAX: 303-447-1406.
Titles:
EM4105-Plus.
EM4105.
EM320-DOS.
EM320 for Windows.
EM340 for Windows.
EM4010.

Diversified Computing, (0-928737), 509 First Ave., W., Kalispell, MT 59901-4837 Tel 406-752-7166; Toll free: 800-227-3775; FAX: 406-752-7165.
Titles:
Budgetary Accounting-General Ledger.
Budgetary Planning-Financial Modeling.
Diversified Computing Payroll.
Fixed Asset Inventory.
Local Governmental Administration: BA-GL, PAY, WILL, TAXES, VOTER.
Voter IV.

Diversified I/O, Inc., P.O. Box 230948, Encinitas, CA 92023-0948; FAX: 415-961-6405.
Titles:
Hard Disk Utilities-Optical Disk Utilities.
SoftBackup II.

Diversified Information Services, (0-944381), P.O. Box 6057, Sitka, AK 99835; 107C Cathedral Way, Sitka, AK 99835 Tel 907-747-5578.
Titles:
Time Machine.

Doane Agricultural Services Co., 4900 SW Griffith Dr., Suite 125, Beaverton, OR 97005 Tel 503-646-5581; Toll free: 800-367-7082; FAX: 503-646-0622.
Titles:
Doane/Equipment.
Doane System for Nurseries & Landscape.

Dr. T's Music Software, Inc., (1-885769), 124 Cresent Rd., Needham, MA 02194 Tel 617-455-1454; Toll free: 800-989-6434; FAX: 617-455-1460.
Titles:
Around the World.
The Copyist D.T.P.
The Copyist Professional DPT with QuickScore Deluxe.
Dr. T's Sing-A-Long Around the World.
Dr. T's Sing-A-Long Kids' Classics.
KCS Level II.
Kids Classics.

Documan Software, Div. of Documan Pr., (0-928170), Box 387-M, Kalamazoo, MI 49005 Tel 616-344-0805.
Titles:
Amort-I.
Depreciate-II.
FINDISK-III.
RIA-III.
STRUCT-I.

Dogwood Software, (0-928171), 3905 Dogwood Dr., Greensboro, NC 27410 Tel 910-299-3369.
Titles:
Portfolio Management.

Domain, Inc., Information Managers Div., (1-877805), 800 S. Field St., Lakewood, CO 80226 Tel 303-987-8511.
Titles:
Contacts & Facts.

DOMICO, (0-925231), 2608 Ninth St., Berkeley, CA 94710 Tel 510-841-4155; Toll free: 800-688-6181; FAX: 510-644-3156.
Titles:
Property Management.

Douglas Electronics, 2777 Alvarado St., San Leandro, CA 94577 Tel 510-483-8770; FAX: 415-483-6453.
Titles:
Douglas CAD/CAM Layout Systems: Printed Circuit Board Design & Manufacturing.
Douglas CAD/CAM Professional System: Integrated CAD-CAM for Electronic Design & Manufacturing.

Dow Jones Information Services, Div. of Dow Jones & Co., Inc., (0-928175), P.O. Box 300, Princeton, NJ 08543-0300 Tel 609-452-1511; Toll free: 800-815-5100; FAX: 609-520-4660.
Titles:
Dow Jones Market Analyzer PLUS.
Dow Jones Spreadsheet Link.

Dragon Group, Inc., The, 148 Poca Fork Rd., Elkview, WV 25071 Tel 304-965-5517.
Titles:
The Amiga Coloring Book: Borders.
The Amiga Coloring Book: Sampler.
The Amiga Coloring Book: The World.
4xFORTH.

Draves & Barke Systems, Inc., (0-928600), 6866 Washington Ave. S., Eden Prairie, MN 55344 Tel 612-835-2728; Toll free: 800-846-0110; FAX: 612-941-1557.
Titles:
FoodTrack/InnaTrack.
InnaTrack/FoodTrack.

Drew, Dennis, (0-924122), P.O. Box 101, Joplin, MO 64802 Tel 417-781-4248.
Titles:
Employee Management System: Reduce Employee Turnover.

Dryden Pr., Div. of Harcourt Brace College Pubs., (0-03; 0-8498; 0-15), 6277 Sea Harbor Dr., Orlando, FL 32887; Toll free: 800-782-4479 (orders, inquiries); 800-544-6678 (claims); 301 Commerce St., Fort Worth, TX 76102 Tel 817-334-7500.
Titles:
Computerized Test Bank to Accompanby INTERNATIONAL MARKETING, 3rd Edition.
Computerized Test Bank to Accompany CONTEMPORARY BUSINESS, 7th Edition.
Computerized Test Bank to Accompany CONCEPTS OF TAXATION, 1993 Edition.
Computerized Test Bank to Accompany FINANCIAL ACCOUNTING, 2nd Edition.
Computerized Test Bank to Accompany FINANCIAL INSTITUTIONS, MARKETS, & MONEY, 5th Edition.
Computerized Test Bank to Accompany MONEY, BANKING, & FINANCIAL MARKETS, 2nd Edition.
Computerized Test Bank to Accompany PROMOTION MANAGEMENT & MARKETING COMMUNICATIONS, 3rd Edition.
Computerized Test Bank to Accompany PROFESSIONAL SELLING.
Computerized Test Bank to Accompany STRATEGIC MANAGEMENT: TEXT & CASES, 5th Edition.
Data Disk to Accompany STEPPING THROUGH WORD 2.0 FOR WINDOWS.
The DEC Rainbow 100: Use Applications & BASIC.
Econograph II.
Executive Computing in BASIC: The IBM Personal Computer.
General Ledger Software to Accompany FINANCIAL ACCOUNTING, 7th Edition.
General Ledger Software to Accompany PRINCIPLES OF ACCOUNTING, 6th Edition.
Instructor's Manual on WordPerfect 5.1 to Accompany FINANCIAL ACCOUNTING, 7th Edition.
Instructor's Manual on WordPerfect 5.1 to Accompany PRINCIPLES OF ACCOUNTING, 6th Edition.
Instructor's Manual to Accompany FINANCIAL ACCOUNTING, 7th Edition.
Instructor's Manual to Accompany PRINCIPLES OF ACCOUNTING, 6th Edition.
Interactive Computer Library to Accompany Production & Operations Management.
Joe Spreadsheet Statistical.
Programming the IBM Personal Computer: BASIC.
Programming the IBM Personal Computer: COBOL.
Programming the IBM Personal Computer: FORTRAN 77.
Programming the IBM Personal Computer: Pascal.
Spreadsheets & Linear Programs Disk to Accompany MANAGERIAL ECONOMICS.
Template Software to Accompany FINANCIAL ACCOUNTING, 7th Edition.
Template Software to Accompany PRINCIPLES OF ACCOUNTING, 6th Edition.
Using the IBM Personal Computer: IBM EasyWriter.
Using the IBM Personal Computer: WordStar.
VisiCalc Applications for Managerial & Cost Accounting.

DST Belvedere, Subs. of DST Systems, Inc., 470 Atlantic Ave., No. 900, Boston, MA 02210-2208 Tel 617-482-8800; FAX: 617-482-8878.
Titles:
Global Portfolio System (GPS).
OpenPerformance.

Dubl-Click Software, Inc., (1-884447), 20310 Empire Ave., Suite A102, Bend, OR 97701 Tel 541-317-0355; FAX: 541-317-0430.
Titles:
Calculator Construction Set.
Calx.
ClickChange.
Icon Manial.
MacTut/ProGlyph: Wet Paint Volume 19.20.
MenuFonts.
WetPaint.

Dun & Bradstreet Computing Services, Div. of Dun & Bradstreet Corp., (0-923746), 2 Trap Falls Rd., Suite 4, Shelton, CT 06484-4656; Toll free: 800-362-7587.
Titles:
DunsPlus.

Dun & Bradstreet Credit Services, Div. of Dun & Bradstreet Corp., 1 Diamond Hill Rd., Murray Hill, NJ 07974-0027 Tel 908-665-5000.
Titles:
Duns Market Manager.
Duns Print/PC.
Industry Norms & Key Business Ratios on Diskette.

Durham Technical Images, P.O. Box 72, Durham, NH 03824-0072 Tel 603-868-5774.
Titles:
PC Data Master.

Dusek Pharmacy, P.O. Box 431, Cameron, TX 76520 Tel 817-697-2112.
Titles:
Amalgamated Pharmomatic Mark II.

Duval, Ellington, Inc., (0-931755; 1-55505), 250 Beechwood Ave., M/S A16, Poughkeepsie, NY 12601-5216 Tel 914-485-2017; Toll free: 800-834-2064 (in New York); FAX: 914-485-1540.
Titles:
Adult Parole Management.
Alternative Sentencing: Criminal Justice Application System.
Central Offender Processing System: Criminal Justice Application System.
Correction Administration - Health Services Administration: Criminal Justice Application System.
Correction Administration - Management Analysis: Criminal Justice Application System.
Correction Administration - Offender Classification: Criminal Justice Application System.
Correction Administration - Offender Finance: Criminal Justice Application System.
Correction Administration - Offender Profile: Criminal Justice Application System.
Correction Administration - Offender Productivity Management: Criminal Justice Application System.
Correction Administration - Offender Scheduling: Criminal Justice Application System.
Correction Administration - Operations Management: Criminal Justice Applications System.
Correction Administration System Offender Administration: Criminal Justice Application System.
Detention Center Management: Correction Administration System.
Info Trust: Client Information Trust.
Info Trust: Personal Information Trust.
Internal Funds Tracking & Commissary: Correction Administration System.
Juvenile & Adult Probation Parole System.
STRATBASE Marketing Audit: Performance Support System.
STRATBASE Marketing Controller: A Performance Support System.

Duxbury Systems, Inc., (0-923747), 435 King St., P.O. Box 1504, Littleton, MA 01460 Tel 508-486-9766; FAX: 508-486-9712.
Titles:
The Braille Editor (Edgar).
Duxbury Braille Translator.

Dykes Consulting, Inc., (0-922652), 500 N. Meridian, Suite 108, Oklahoma City, OK 73107 Tel 405-946-0260.
Titles:
Lease Oil & Gas Accounting Systems.

Dynacomp, Inc., (1-55697), 4560 E. Lake Rd., Livonia, NY 14487 Tel 716-346-9788.
Titles:
ABC's of Americans with Disabilities Act.
ACAP-Active Circuit Analysis Spice Circuit Simulation.
Accudraw Computer-Aided Design System.
Active Circuit Analysis Program (ACAP).
ADA Compliance Kit.
The Adam Osborne Software Collection.
Adaptive Filters: Filter Design & Analysis.
Advanced Disk Editor (ADE).
Advanced Math Graphics.
Advanced Scientific Analysis & Graphics.
AGA Orifice Flow Element Calculations.
AI Logo.
Air Defense.
AIRCON Pneumatic Conveying System Analysis.
Airflow.
Algebra I, Vol. 1: Sets & Notation.
Algebra I, Vol. 2: Number Systems.
Algebra III, Vol. 1: Polynomials.
Algebra II, Vol. 1: Equations & Formulas.
Algebra II, Vol. 2: Linear Relations.
All Track Applicant Tracking System.
Alley Stats.
Alphacat.
Alvin.
Ambulance.
Amine Process Simulator Absorption & Stripping.
Analog.
Analysis of Continuous Beams.
Analysis of Continuous Beams II with Graphics.
Analysis of Continuous Beams 2 with Graphics.
Analysis of Large Deflection Frames with Graphics.
Analysis of Plane Frames.
Analysis of Plane Frames II with Graphics.
Analysis of Plane Frames 2 with Graphics.
Analysis of Plane Grids.
Analysis of Plane Grids II with Graphics.
Analysis of Plane Grids 2 with Graphics.
Analysis of Plane Trusses.
Analysis of Plane Trusses II with Graphics.
Analysis of Plane Trusses 2 with Graphics.
Analysis of Three-Dimensional Frames.
Analysis of Three-Dimensional Trusses.
Analysis of Variance (ANOVA).
The Animator.
Anova 2.
ANSI-66 Fortran Compiler.
Argus Perceptual Mapper.
The Art of Negotiating 2.
Astroquest.
Atari Utilities.
Baccarat.
Backflow Records.
Backgammon.
Bar Code Printer.
Barney O'Blarney's Magic Spells.
Basic Dispersion Models.
Basic Gas & Liquid Flow Calculator.
Basic Photography.
Basic Primer.
BASIC Scientific Subroutines.
Basic Scientific Subroutines, Vol. 3, Chapter 1: Basic Probability Distributions.
Basic Statistical Subroutines.
Basketball Coach's Assistant.
Batch Distillation.
Battlefield!!!
Beam-Column Analysis & Second Order Frame Analysis.
Beam-Column Analysis: Second Order Frame Analysis.
Beam Deflection.
Beam Deflection 2.
Beams One-Two-Three.
The Bean Machine.
Beginner's Adventures.
Best Choice 3 Decision Making.
Best of Wok Talk.
BestChoice3: Decision Making.
Betty Crocker's Fortieth Anniversary Cookbook.
Betty Crocker's Microwave Cookbook.
Betty Crocker's Old-Fashioned Cookbook.
The Bible on Disk.
Bilinear Transform Tutorial.
Binary Phase Equilibria Curve Fitting.
Biology, Vol. 1: Respiration.
Biology, Vol. 2: Digestion & Nutrition.
Biology, Vol. 3: Reproduction & Development.
Biology, Vol. 4: Circulation & the Heart.
Biquad Filter Design Tutorial.
BiWeibullSMITH: Dual Weibull Analysis.
Black Hole.
Blackjack Analyzer: Rules & Strategy Simulation.
Blackjack Coach.
Boa.
Bookkeep.
Bowler's Database.
Bowling League Record System 2.
Breakup.
Bridge Baron.
Bridge Master.
Bridge Master 2.
Bridge Parlor.
Bridge Partner Alice.
Bridge Scorer.
Budget Model Analyzer.
Business Pack: Business Program Collection.
Buy Low-Sell High.
Buysel.
Cactus League Baseball.
CADPAK.
The Calcugram Stock Options System.
Calfex & Calfex G-T.
Cam Master: Kinematic Cam Design.
Canis Dog Owner's Database.
Canostat Statistical Process Control.
Casino Craps.
CAT (Computer-Aided-Teaching).
Catalog Card & Label Writer.
Celestial BASIC.
Centrifugal Compressor Design & Rating.
Centrifugal Pump Selection & Rating.
Certificate Master-Award Certificate Creation.
Chaos Data Analyzer.
Chaos Demonstrations.
Chaos Simulations.
Chaotic Mapper: Linear - 2D Iterative Maps.
Check Writer.
Checkers 3.0.
Chef's Accountant.
Chemcalc Multiphase & General Fluid Flow.
Chemical Compounds Databank.
Chemical Engineering 1: Chemical & Process Engineering.
Chemistry, Vol. 1: The Atom.
Chemistry, Vol. 2: The Periodic Table.
Chess Master.
Children's Carrousel.
Child's Play One.
Chinese Checkers.
Chirp Invaders.
Chompelo.
Class Record.
Class Scheduling System.
Client-Sales Master.

PUBLISHER/TITLE INDEX

DYNACOMP, INC.

Coach's Corner.
Codegen: DSP Filter Code Generator.
Coindata & Stampdata.
COINS.
Collection One: Collections for Dental & Medical Offices.
Collector's Paradise.
Color Presentation Magic Simplified Graphics Generation.
Commercial Building Energy Consumption.
Commercial Cooling & Heating.
Commodore 64 Tutorial.
Complex Matrix Master.
Compu-Chart EGA: Technical-Graphic Market Analyzer.
Compu-Opoly.
Compuledger: Single-Entry General Ledger.
Compusec Portfolio Manager.
Computer Aided Design System.
Computer Aided Drafting.
Computer Chef.
Computer Generated Chemistry Exams & Homework Assignments.
Computhello.
Conceptual Process Cost Estimator Labor, Materials, & Subcontracts.
Concrete Retaining Wall Analysis.
Concrete Shear Wall & Column Design.
Concrete Spread Footing Design.
CONPLOT Contour Plotter.
Continuous Concrete Beam Design.
Contractor Management Program.
Control Valve Sizing Fluid Control Analysis.
Convective Heat Transfer.
Corporate Telephone Directory.
Correlation.
Cosmos.
County Outline Database.
Covered Options.
CP/M Emulator for MS-DOS.
CP/M-MS DOS Teaching Testing & Training Program.
CP/M-80 Emulator for the IBM PC.
Cranston Manor Adventure.
Crazy Chase.
The Credit Rating Booster.
Cribbage.
Criterion CAE/CAD Schematic & PC-Board Design System.
Critical Path Project Management.
Crosswords Scrabble & Crossword Helper.
Crystals.
Curve Fit Utility.
Curve Fitting & Data Manipulation.
Customer Profile.
Customer Profile II: Customer-Client Tracking.
Customer Profile 2: Customer - Client Tracking.
The Data Acquisition Hardware Expert.
Data Aid.
Data Plotter.
Data Retrieval System (DRS).
Data Smoother.
Data Smoother: Semi-Spline - Polynomial Data Smoothing.
DataCAD 128: 3-D Architectural Design & Drafting.
Datamax.
Datasurf.
Datebook.
dBarcode: dBase Bar Code Printing.
Decision Analysis.
Deep Space.
Dental One: Dental Office Management System.
Descriptions Write Now!: ADA-Ready Job Descriptions.
Design-Ease Design of Experiments.
Design Expert Response Surface Methods & Design of Experiments for Mixtures.
Design Your Own Home: Architecture.
Design Your Own Home: Interiors.
Design Your Own Home: Landscape.
Design Your Own Train: Train-Transit System Construction Set.
Desktop Bibliography.

Dfile.
Di-Graph Scientific Plotting.
Di-Man: Mandelbrot Fractal Graphics.
Diamond Hunter.
Dictionary.
Diet Analyzer.
Differential Equations.
Differential Equations with Parameter Estimation.
Diffusion Model Library for LaPlace Transform Tools.
Diggerbonk.
Digital Filter.
Digital Filter Design Tutorial.
Digital Image Processing (DIP).
Digitze Digitizer Software Interface.
Diskette Inventory System.
Diversi-DOS.
Do-It-Yourself Adventure Kit & Dormac's Castle.
Domino.
Doodle Drawer.
Dot Matrix & Laser Printer Utilities.
Double-Deck Pinochle.
Dragonblast.
Duct System Design.
Dynabase Database Program.
The Dynacomp Battle Trilogy: Leipzig 1813, Waterloo 1815, Shiloh 1862.
DynaFORTH.
Dynamic & Continuous Distillation.
Dynamic System Analyzer: Linear & Nonlinear Systems.
Dynamics & Vibration Analysis.
Dynamind Neural Network Processor.
Dynaword Document Creator.
Easy Access.
EBASIC with Starbase 3.2.
ECM Turing Machine.
Economic Insulation Sizing.
EGA Paint 2005: Graphics Generation-Editing.
Eigen Analyzer.
Electrical Contractor Calculator.
Eliza II.
EMF: Electromagnetic Fields.
EMIS: Editor & Machine Interface for CNC.
Employee Policy Manual On-a-Disk.
Engineering Collection.
Engineering Collection VIII: The Energy Analyst.
Engineering Collection VI: Fluid, Mechanical, Energy & Cost Calculations.
Engineering Collection 4: Fluid, Mechanical Energy & Cost Calculations.
Engineering Collection 4: Practical Engineering Calculations.
Engineering Collection 7: Metal Fabrication - Machining.
Engineering Sketchpad.
The Engineer's Companion Mechanical Engineering Analysis.
Enhanced Structural & Finite Element Analysis.
EPA Emissions Analysis Above-Ground Storage Tanks.
The Equator II: Equation Evaluation & Plotting.
The Equator 2: Equation Evaluation & Plotting.
Equil: Chemical Equilibrium Calculations for Solutions.
Equilibrium Flash Calculations.
Escape from Volantium.
Estamore: Cost Estimating for Single Family Housing.
Euchre.
Everybody's Planner: Scheduling & Flowcharting.
Executive Phone-Mailer.
Expert Ease.
Expert System Tutorial.
EZ Barcode III: Bar Code Printer.
EZ Barcode II: Bar Code Printer.
EZRes: Memory Resident Bar Code Printing.
f(Z) Complex Variable Graphics.
Faculty-Staff Attendance Manager.
The Family Budget.
Family Tree.
FANSIM: Frequency Domain Analysis & Simulation.
Fast Fourier Transform Master.

Fast Fourier Transform Tutorial.
Feedback Linear Systems Simulator.
Files.
Filter Analysis.
Filter Analysis: Passive Filter Evaluation.
Final Assembly.
FinanceMaster Personal Finance & Budgeting.
Financial Management System.
Findit.
Fire Hose Records.
Fire Sprinkler Grid Design.
Fire Sprinkler System Design.
Five Weeks to Winning Bridge.
Fixed Geometry Calculations.
Flare Network Analysis.
Fleet Control.
Flexitext.
Flight Plan.
Flight Simulator.
Flipsketch.
Flowmaster: Pipes, Ditches & Open Channels.
Fluid/Gas Flow Collection I: Steam, Gas, Liquid, & Paper Stock.
The Forecasting Edge Box-Jenkins Automated Time Series Forecasting.
Forest Fire.
Fortune Telling with Dice & Numerology.
Four Toes.
Fourier Analysis Forecaster.
Fourier Analyzer.
Fourier Toolkit Transform, Correlation, Filtering, & Time Series Analysis.
Fourier Transform Series.
Fractalscope.
Fractionation Tray Design & Rating.
Frequency Domain Filtering Tutorial.
Frog Master.
Fun & Games.
Functions.
Fundamentals of Heat Transfer.
Fundwatch.
Fuse-Circuit Breaker-Wire Coordination Analysis.
F(Z) Complex Variable Graphics.
Galactic Battles.
Games Pack I & II.
GB-Stat Statistics As Graphs.
Geardesign.
Generis Data Retrieval System.
Genesis: The Adventure Creator.
Geometry, Vol. 1: Basic Geometrical Notions.
Geometry, Vol. 2: Introduction to Plane & Space Geometry.
German & Russian Practice.
Ghostprinter Printer-to-Disk Spooler.
Gin Rummy.
Go Fish.
Go4000 Advanced Computer Go.
Goldspread Statistical.
Golf Handicapper: Slope Index System.
Golf Pro.
Golfer's Database.
Gomoku II.
Grafix.
Graph-in-the-Box Executive: Professional Graphics & Charting.
Graph Scientific Plotting & Data Transformation.
Graphics Conversion & Printing Utilities.
Great Chefs of PBS Master Collection.
Gridzo Contour & Perspective Mapper.
Gumball Rally Adventure.
Handicapper II.
Handwriting & Numerology.
Hansen-Predict.
Hardy Cross Network Analysis.
Harmonic Analyzer.
Harness Handicapper.
Hearts 2.0.
Heat & Mass Transfer Equilibrium Calculations.
Heat Exchanger Design Shell-&-Tube.
Heat Exchanger Network Analysis Single-Phase, Shell-&-Tube.
Heat Exchanger Network Optimizer.
Heat Loss.
Hercules Graphics Utilities.

DYNACOMP, INC.

HiScore Database.
Hodge Podge.
Home Appraiser.
Home Doctor.
The Home Insurance Inventory.
Home Insurance Protector.
Home Management 2.
The Homeowner.
Hometown Demographics.
Hopper.
HP Plotter Emulator.
Hydrant Flow Records.
Hydraulic Pipe Design.
Hydro-Pack Hydraulics Analysis.
Hydropac 2 Storm Drainage Design.
Hydroworks: Hydraulic & Pneumatic Schematics.
Hyperdom.
I Ching: Canon of Change.
The Idea Generator Plus: Structured Brainstorming.
INPAC Customer-Client Tracking.
The Ins & Outs of Diets Multimedia Diet Education.
Instrucalc.
Instrument Specification Data Sheets.
Interactive Cluster Analysis: Multidimensional Statistics.
The Interactive Diabetic Cookbook.
Interactive Multiple Prediction: Multiple Linear Regression.
Interactive Questionnaire Analysis: Questionnaire Response Statistics.
Interactive Source Debugger.
Interactive Waveform Analysis: Fourier Series Decomposition, Filtering & Reconstruction.
International Classification of Diseases: ICD - Latest Revision.
Introductory Calculus.
Introductory Chemistry I.
Introductory Chemistry II.
Introductory Physics I.
Introductory Physics II.
Intruder Alert.
Inventory Control.
Inventory Management System.
Inverse Fast Fourier Transform Tutorial.
The Investing Advisor.
Invomax: Inventory Profit Optimizer.
IRMA: Investment Records Management Aid.
Ironclads.
The Job Coster Automatic Job Estimating.
Jobmaster.
Junior High Mathematics.
King's Indian Defense.
The Labyrinth of Zyr.
Ladder Network.
Land Survey Calculator.
Landscape Plant Manager.
Language Drill.
Laplace Transform Tools Numerical Inversion Utilities.
Las Vegas Keno.
Laser Manager: Laser Printer Enhancements.
Laserjet Printing Utilities.
Leipzig 1813.
LEM Lander.
Let's Make a Wheel.
The Librarian.
Life Cycle Analysis & Depreciation.
Life Cycle Cost Analysis.
Life Cycle Cost Optimization for Piping Insulation.
Life Style Analyzer.
Lighting Design.
Li'l Men from Mars.
Linear Algebra.
Linear Circuit Analysis: LINCAP.
Linear Ordinary Differential Equations.
Linear Programmer.
Linear Programmer Minimax.
Linear Transient & AC Circuit Analysis.
Liquid-Liquid Extraction.
Liquid Pipeline Network Surge Analysis.
Liquid Pipeline Surge Analysis.
Liquid Pumping System Interactive Analysis & Balance.
Loan Analysis.
The Loan Arranger.
Locomotion.
Logic Designer.
Logic Simulator.
Lotto Master.
Lqiuid Pipeline Surge Analysis.
Lunar Voyager.
M-Master.
MCSS-Automated Search Software Containing Annually Updated CPT, ICD-9 & HCDC Codes.
Mail Master.
Major League Handicapper.
Make Your Day's Multiuser Calendar & Appointment Scheduler.
Management Simulator.
MAPIT.
The Market Forecaster.
Market Model.
Market Timer.
Master Drill.
Master Genealogist.
Mastermatch.
MATCHNET.
Math Pack.
Mathematics Collection.
Mathomatic 2: Algebraic Equation Processor.
Mathplot Numerical Data Analysis.
Matrix Laboratory.
Matrix Master.
Matrix Processor.
Matrix Tutorial.
Matrix 100.
Maxwell Electromagnetic Fields.
Mechanical Engineering.
Media Master.
Medical One: Medical Office Management System.
The Member Tender.
Member Tender II: Membership Management System.
Member Tender 2 Membership Management System.
Metric Unit Conversions Engineering Unit Conversions.
Metrix: U. S. - Metric Conversion System.
Metrix U.S. - Metric Conversion System.
Micro Bridge Companion.
Micro Cap Microcomputer Analysis Program.
Micro CAP: Microcomputer Circuit Analysis Program Advanced Version.
MICRO CAP 2: Microcomputer Circuit Analysis Program, Advanced Version.
Micro-Cap 3.
Micro Kitchen Companion.
Micro Logic II.
Micro Logic 2.
Micro-Mech: Planar Mechanism Analysis.
MICROBJ: Box Jenkins Forecasting, Arima Modeling.
Microcomputer Bond Program (MBP).
Microcomputer Chart Program.
Microcomputer Circuit Analysis Program II.
Microcomputer Logic Design Program II.
Microcomputer Stock Program (MSP).
Microphys Computer-Generated Physics Exams & Homework Assignments.
Microphys Geometrical Optics: Optics Simulations.
Microphys Inorganic Equation Balancer: Computer-Aided Chemistry.
Microphys Physic-Al: Computer-Aided Physics Experiments.
Microphys Physics Laboratory Experiments.
Microphys Waves & Superposition: Physics Simulations.
Midway.
Minicomputer Chart Program.
MINSQ Chemical Kinetic Library.
MINSQ Nonlinear Curve Fitting & Model Development.
MINSQ Pharmokinetic Library.
Mission: Intergalactic Diplomacy.
Mr. Boston Official Bartenders' Guide.
Molecular Modeling.
Molecular Modeling 2: Molecular Graphics.
Monarch.
Monarch Digital Signal.
Monarch: Digital Signal Processing.
Money.
Money Decisions.
Monkey Business Typing Tutor.
MonteCarloSMITH: Monte Carlo Probability Analysis.
Moonprobe.
MS DOS Graphics Screen Printing Utilities.
MTBASIC.
Multicomponent Separations Process.
Multilayer Interference.
Multilinear Regression.
Multilingual Word Processor.
Multiphase Flow in Pipeline Networks & Wells.
Multiphase Flow in Pipelines & Oil Wells.
Multiple Factor Analysis: Multidimensional Statistics.
Multiple Integration.
Multiple Precision Math Subroutines for BASIC & FORTRAN.
Multiple Regression & Multiple-Partial Correlation.
Multivariate Non-Linear Regression & Optimization.
Multivariate Regression Analysis.
MYDIET Nutrition & Diet Helper.
NBA Wager Analyzer.
Nebs.
Network Multiphase Flow with Total Energy Balance.
NFL Forecaster.
NFL Handicapper.
Non-Linear Parameter Regression (Parafit II).
Non-Prismatic Concrete Beams Analysis.
Nonlinear Parametric Regression (Parafit II).
Nonlinear Systems.
North Star Utilities Package.
Nuametrics Econometric Analysis.
Number Kruncher I.
Number Kruncher II.
Numerical Data Analysis.
Numerology.
NYINDEX.
Objects in Motion: Physics Simulation.
Off-the-Wall.
The Olde Gin Parlour (Gin Rummy).
Omni-Fit.
On the Dotted Line: Legal Forms.
On Time! Business Calendar.
One-Minute Convection: Convective Heat Transfer.
Open Channel Flow: Network Irrigation & Water Drainage.
Operations Research Tutorial.
Optics One.
Optimac.
The Optimizer Linear Programmer.
Options Analysis.
Orbits: Orbital Motion Simulation.
The Original Adventure.
Paper Boy.
Paratest: Non-Parametric Statistics.
Paratest Two Non-Parametric Statistics.
Parimutuel Betting Bet Management for Golf & Other Events.
Paul Whitehead Teaches Chess.
Payfive.
PC ANOVA: Analysis of Variance.
PC Assembly Screens.
PC Calculator Plus.
PC Chart Plus: Technical Analysis Software.
PC Chord Primer.
PC Estimator Construction Cost Estimation.
PC File 'N' Report Integrated Database.
PC Graphics.
PC-Mathematics: Mathematical Software Library.
PC Planetarium.
PC Regression: Multiple Regression & Correlation.
PC Secretary.
PC Statistician (by HSD).

PUBLISHER/TITLE INDEX

Performance Now!: Computer Aided Performance Review.
Personal Balance Sheet.
Personal Computer Automatic Investment Management.
Personal Finance Manager.
Personal Finance Planner.
Personal Finance System.
Personal Real Estate Manager.
Personal Task Manager.
Petroleum Transportation Marketing Emissions Analysis.
Phase Locked Loop Tutorial.
Phone Directory.
Physical Properties of Hydrocarbon Liquids.
Physician Fee Analyzer Plus.
Physics Simulation.
Physics, Vol. 1: Motion.
Physics, Vol. 2: Heat & Light.
Picaresque: The Graphic Novel Publisher.
Picnic.
Pipe Stress II: Piping Through Stress Analysis Single Plane, Two Anchor.
Pipecalc.
Pipeflow.
Pipeline Multiphase Flow with Total Energy Balance.
Pipeline Pressure Loss.
Pipemate Piping Project Cost Estimation.
Pipestress 1: Pipe Wall Thickness Specification.
Play Bridge with Sheinwold.
Player-Missile Graphics Tool Kit.
Player-Missile Player Editor.
Player Piano.
Plot!
PlotSmith.
The Plumber's Helper: Job Cost Estimation.
Point & Shoot.
Poker Machine.
Poker Party.
Polyps from Pluto.
Pool & Billiards.
Portfolio Data Manager.
Portfolio Decisions.
Portfolio Manager.
Portfolio Status.
Portview 2020.
Power Amplifier Design Tutorial.
Powerpak Electrical Distribution.
Practical Pipeline Hydraulics Gas & Liquid Networks.
Principal Component & Factor Analysis.
Print File.
Private Pilot Written Test Simulator.
Pro Predictions.
Probability & Statistics.
Probaloto.
Process Engineer's Conversion Kit.
Product Idea Evaluator - Questionnaires.
Professional-Class Golf.
Profile Grade, Street, Sewer & Water Line Profiler.
Program Animator for BASIC.
Programming Tools for Quickbasic.
Project Control One.
Project Task Control & Scheduling.
Project Time Reporting System.
Prolook QuickBASIC Subroutine Library.
Property Manager.
Protracs Project Tracking - Reporting.
Protracs Project Tracking/Reporting.
Pyramids of Gar.
QC Plot Statistical Process Control.
Query: Opinion Surveys & Questionnaires.
Quintominoes.
Ratios.
The Reading Professor: Faster Reading with Comprehension.
Real Estate Resident Expert.
Real Net Cost Ownership - Depreciation.
Rectangular Combined Footings.
Reference.
Regress 2.
Regression Analysis.

Regression Analysis 2.
Regression I.
Regression 1: Polynomial Regression with Transformations.
Regression 2 (Parafit).
Regression 3 (The Calibrator).
Reinforced Concrete Beam Column Analysis.
Reinforced Concrete Beam Design.
Reinforced Concrete Laterally Loaded Piles.
Reinforced Concrete Pile Design.
Reinforced Concrete Two-Way Flat Plate Design.
Relativistic Collision.
Residential Cooling & Heating.
Resonance.
The Rings of the Empire.
River Chase.
Road Engineering.
Roark & Young on Disk: Stress & Strain Calculations.
Rollerball.
Roots.
RSTRIP Exponential Decomposition & Parameter Estimation.
Russian Master Russian-English On-Line Dictionary.
S-Plane Tutorial (SPT).
The Sales Assistant.
School Attendance Manager.
School Discipline Manager.
School Transportation Manager.
SCORE Expert.
Screen Master.
Screen Printer.
Sea War.
Second Order Frame Analysis.
Section Properties.
Section Properties 2 with Graphics.
Senior High Mathematics I.
Senior High Mathematics II.
Separations Calculations.
Serendipity.
The Shape Magician.
Shiloh 1862.
Shop Projects Plans Index.
Shopping List.
Short Circuit Current & Voltage Drop Analysis.
Singly/Doubly Reinforced Beam Deflection.
Size FE Flow Element Calculator.
SizeFE: Flow Element Calculator.
Skills Inventory.
Skyclock Graphical Astronomical Clock.
SL-MICRO.
Slab-Column Unbalanced Moment Checker.
Slender Concrete Wall Design.
Sling Psychrometer Psychometric Chart Evaluation.
Slope: Hansen Solubility Parameters & Interaction Energies.
Slurry Mass Transfer Analysis.
Small Business Invoicer.
Small Business System.
Smart Keyboard.
Smartdisk Format Conversion.
Smartkey/Smartprint Keyboard & Printer Utilities.
Smartpath Hard-Disk Utility.
Smartstuff Pop-Up Desk Tools.
Snapshot Digital Storage Oscilloscope Demo Package.
SOFTNET.
Solar F-Chart & Economic Analysis.
Solarsim.
Solid State Physics: One-Dimensional Lattices.
Solutions Waste Management Solutions Database.
Space Attackers.
Space Evacuation.
Space Frame Analysis with Graphics.
Space Lanes.
Space Pirates.
Space Tilt.
Space Trap.
Space Truss Analysis with Graphics.
SpecSelect: Spring Selection.
Speculation.

Spell Master 2.
StackSoft: Stacked Tolerance Analysis.
Stamps.
Star Con.
Starbase 3.2.
Starship Dogfight.
Starship Landing Party Adventure.
Starware Sky Mapper.
State Variables.
Statistical Consultant.
Statistical Language for Microcomputers.
Statistical Sample Planner.
Statistics.
Statistics by Monte Carlo Analysis.
Statistics Series.
StatMaster U. S. Census Database.
Stats Plus.
Statsort.
Stattest.
Steady-State Continuous Distillation.
Steam Boiler Efficiency Analyzer.
Steam Pipe Design & Calculations (Single Phase).
Steam Tables.
Stellar 28.
Stepwise Multilinear Regression.
Stock Market Bargains.
Stock Master-Stock Plot.
Stockaid.
Streamlined CNC: Numerical Control Vertical Mill Trainer.
Streamlines: Fluid Flow in Networks.
Structural Concrete Beam Design.
Structural Concrete Column Design.
Structural One-Way/Two-Way Concrete Slab Design.
Structural Steel Beam Design.
Structural Steel Column Design.
STRUSAP Finite Element Structural Analysis.
Stud Poker.
Submarine Blockade.
Submarine Commander.
Success on Stress: Computerized Stress Assessment.
Super Sub Chase.
Super Tank Attack!
Super Zap.
SuperCAD: Schematic Diagram Entry.
Supercode Barcode Reading & Printing.
SuperSoft BASIC Compiler.
Surveillance for Windows Image Motion Detection.
Survpac Boundary, Roadway, & Site Development.
The Syntel Math Toolbox.
System Execution Manager: MS DOS Operation Scheduler.
System Pump Sizing with Flash Protection.
T Smooth Optimal Smoothing & Differentiation.
Take Control of Cholesterol.
Talk to Me.
Talking Home Inventory.
Talking Phonebook.
Tankcalc.
Teacher/Trainer Turned Author.
Teacher's Aide.
Teacher's Gradebook.
Tech/Word.
Text Master.
Thermal Pipe & Plate Thermal Insulation.
Thermal Stress Analysis Single Plane-Two Anchor.
Thermodynamic & Physical Property Data.
Thermodynamic Properties & Process Simulator.
Thermodynamics Lecture Demonstrations.
Threat Force.
Tidy.
Time Clock Computerized Punch-In - Out.
Time Series/Forecasting.
Time Traveler.
Timeclock II: Computerized Timeclock & Scheduler.
Timemap.
Timeslips: Time & Expense Tracking.
Toolworks C Compiler.
Toolworks Lisp/80.

Track & Field.
Transfer Function Analyzer.
Trash Man.
Trig Expert.
Triple Blockade.
Trivia Challenge.
TsrTools: Pop-Up Desk Tools.
Tube & Pipe Bending.
Turbo Almanac: Astronomical - Nautical - Calendar Almanac.
Turbo Solitaire.
Turbo Spelling Tutor.
Turbo Spring-Stat Multivariate Statistics.
Turbo Spring-Stat Text Editor II: ASCII Data File Editor.
Turbo Spring-Stat Text Editor 2 ASCII Data File Editor.
Turnkey & Menu.
Tutsim Linear & Nonlinear System Simulator.
Two-Phase Pressure Drop in Process Piping.
Two-Port Analysis Tutorial.
Tymekard: Timecard-Payroll Management.
The Ultimate Spring Designer.
The Ultimate Spring Designer 2.
Ultracomp Probability & Scientific Calculator.
Uncle Harry's Will.
Understand Yourself.
USA Trivia.
UTIL.
Valdez.
Valley of the Kings.
Versainventory.
Versaledger II.
Versapayables.
Versapayroll.
Versareceivables.
Video Rental Management System.
Video Titler.
Videomatic.
VisualSmith: Scientific Plotting.
Vocational Math Series: Prevocational Math Review.
Wall Street Trainer.
Waterloo 1815.
Weather Forecaster.
Weibull Curve Fitter.
WeibullSMITH: Reliability Engineering Analysis (RMS).
Whembly Castle Adventure.
Who's Minding the Store?
Windmere Estate Adventure.
Wiremap.
Word Finder.
Word Processing Toolbox.
Word Processor File Translator.
The World Digitized World Outline Database.
XTAB Cross Tabulation.
Xtrapolator Time Series Forecasts.
XYZ 3D.
Yacht Race.
Z-Transform Tutorial.
Zenterprise Real Estate Investor.
Zodiac Castle Adventure.

Dynamic Financial Logic Corp., 401 City Line Ave., Bala Cynwyd, PA 19004; Toll free: 800-396-2642; FAX: 215-688-8220.
Titles:
Estate Maximizer.
Personal Financial Planner.

Dynamic Graphics, Inc., (0-939437; 1-56157), 6000 N. Forest Park Dr., Peoria, IL 61614 Tel 309-688-8800; Toll free: 800-255-8800; FAX: 309-688-3075.
Titles:
Designer's Club.
Electronic Clipper.
Electronic Print Media Service.

Dynamic Information Systems Corp. (DISC), 5733 Central Ave., Boulder, CO 80301 Tel 303-444-4000; Toll free: 800-444-4953; FAX: 303-444-6960.
Titles:
Omniview.

Dynamic Interface Systems Corp., (0-931813), 5959 W. Century Blvd., Suite 1200, Los Angeles, CA 90045-6513 Tel 310-568-4567; FAX: 310-578-0740.
Titles:
ANALYZER+.
BOTTOM$LINE+.
BUILDER PLUS.
COLLECTOR PLUS.
FLEX-RATE+.
FLOATING-RATE+.
INTERE$Tplus.
Loanledger+.
M/BANKER+.
MARGIN+.
More $ales.
OPEN$LINE.
SCHEDULER+.
SIMPLIFIER+.

Dynaware USA, Inc., Affil. of Dynaware Corp., (1-888372), 111 Anza Blvd., Suite 115, Burlingame, CA 94410 Tel 415-696-8333; Toll free: 800-280-6108; FAX: 415-696-8339.
Titles:
DynaPerspective.

DynoTech Software, Div. of Carlson Home Industries, (1-885708), 1105 Home Ave., Waynesville, MO 65583-2231 Tel 314-774-5001; FAX: 314-774-3052.
Titles:
Boxes: Champion Edition.
Dino Match: A Mind-Building Game for Windows.
Dino Numbers: A Math Game for Windows.
Dino Spell: A Spelling Game for Windows.
Dino Trilogy: Three Educational Windows Games.

E&IS SignWare, P.O. Box 521, Cedar Falls, IA 50613; FAX: 319-266-7800.
Titles:
CAV-ASL: Computerized Animated Vocabulary of ASL.
Elementary Signer: Elementary Signer.
FingerSpeller.
FingerZoids.

E & M Software Co., 1347 E. Desert Trumpet Rd., Phoenix, AZ 85048 Tel 602-460-0283.
Titles:
Astronomy.
Equilibrium.
MathLab.
PolyMath.
Reactions.

EBSCO Publishing, Div. of EBSCO Industries, Inc., (1-882248), P.O. Box 2250, Peabody, MA 01960; FAX: 508-535-8545; 83 Pine St., Peabody, MA 01960 Tel 508-535-8500.
Titles:
The Serials Directory: An International Reference Book.

ECOM Assocs., Inc., (0-923762), 8324 N. Steven Rd., Milwaukee, WI 53223 Tel 414-365-2100; Toll free: 800-558-5137; FAX: 414-365-2110.
Titles:
SES-Structural Expert Series: Structural Engineering Software.
Structural Engineering System.

EDCO Services, Inc., 12410 N. Dale Mabry Hwy., Tampa, FL 33618 Tel 813-962-7800.
Titles:
LetrTuck.

EEC Systems, Inc., (0-928198), 327-E Boston Post Rd., Millbrook Pk., Sudbury, MA 01776 Tel 508-443-5106; FAX: 508-443-9997.
Titles:
Turbo Disk.
Turbo Windows.

EKD Computer Sales & Supplies Corp., P.O. Box Y, 770 Middle Country Rd., Selden, NY 11784 Tel 516-736-0500; FAX: 516-736-2209.
Titles:
Business in a Box.
EZ Backup.
EZ-BLUMNOTE.
KeyWords: A Return to Readability.
ODBS - The O'Hanlon Database Solution.
pcCOMMANDER.
pcSECRETARY: The Ultimate Information Utility.

EMC Publishing, Div. of EMC Corp., (0-88436; 0-912022; 0-8219), 300 York Ave., Saint Paul, MN 55101 Tel 612-771-1555; Toll free: 800-328-1452; FAX: 800-328-4564.
Titles:
Deutsch Aktuell One.
Deutsch Aktuell Two.
Economics: Principles & Applications.
Le Francais Vivant One.
Le Francais Vivant Two.
Introduction to Economics.
Parenting Three to Six.
Somos Asi One.
Somos Asi Two.
Working Today & Tomorrow.
Young Parent, Young Child.

EME Corp., (0-923820; 0-923646; 1-56348), P.O. Box 2805, Danbury, CT 06813-2805; Toll free: 800-848-2050; FAX: 203-798-9930; 41 Kenosia Ave., Danbury, CT 06810 Tel 203-798-2050.
Titles:
Geodynamics Multimedia Database.
Home Energy Conservation.
Nutrition-A Balanced Diet.

ERM Assocs., P.O. Box 1032, Agoura Hills, CA 91301-1032 Tel 818-707-3818; Toll free: 800-288-3762; FAX: 818-707-1510.
Titles:
ERMASOFT Easy Fonts.
Laser Envelopes.

ESD USA, Inc., Div. of Elbe Space & Technology Dresden GmbH & Co., (0-9650981), 3000 N. Atlantic Ave., Suite 207, Cocoa Beach, FL 32931 Tel 407-783-6332; Toll free: 800-313-6334; FAX: 407-783-6397.
Titles:
Russian Tutor 1, Russian for Beginners.

ESHA Research, (0-940071), P.O. Box 13028, Salem, OR 97309; FAX: 503-585-5543; 4263 Commercial St. SE, Suite 200, Salem, OR 97302 Tel 503-585-6242.
Titles:
Fitness Analyst.
The Food Processor, Basic: Nutrient Analysis.
The Food Processor Plus.
Genesis: Nutrition Analysis-Labeling Software: Nutrient Analysis Labeling Aid.
Nutrition Pro!: Exercise, Nutrient Analysis Software.

PUBLISHER/TITLE INDEX

EWDP Software, Inc., (0-923775), P.O. Box 40283, Indianapolis, IN 46240 Tel 317-872-8799.
Titles:
Filebase.

E-Z Data, Inc., 918 E. Green St., Pasadena, CA 91106-2935; Toll free: 800-777-9188; FAX: 818-458-9097.
Titles:
Client Data System (CDS).

EZ Soft, 21125 Chatsworth St., Chatsworth, CA 91311 Tel 818-341-8681.
Titles:
EZ-Backup.

EZ Systems, Inc., 1001 18th Ave., S., Nashville, TN 37212 Tel 615-329-2815; FAX: 615-321-3601.
Titles:
Re: Members.

Eagle Point Software, 4131 Westmark Dr., Dubuque, IA 52002-2627; Toll free: 800-678-6565.
Titles:
Eagle Point Advantage Series for AutoCAD & MicroStation.

Earthware Computer Services, (0-917979), P.O. Box 30039, 2386 Spring Blvd., Eugene, OR 97403 Tel 503-683-1940; FAX: 503-344-3383.
Titles:
Volcanos Deluxe.

Easel Corp., 25 Corporate Dr., Burlington, MA 01803-5150 Tel 617-221-2100; FAX: 617-221-2199.
Titles:
Layout/CUA for DOS.

East Coast Sheet Metal Fabricating Corp., (0-923783), 740 Broadway, New York, NY 10003 Tel 212-477-9110; Orders to: 4000 Arlo Ln., Peekskill, NY 10566 Tel 914-739-0100.
Titles:
CADvent Integrated System: Computer-Aided Drafting-Design System.
CADvent Piping System: Computer-Aided Drafting-Design System.
CADvent Sheet Metal System: Computer-Aided Drafting-Design System.
MAKER: Sheet Metal Shop Fabricating System.

East Hampton Industries, Inc., (0-934556), 81 Newtown Ln., P.O. Box 5069, East Hampton, NY 11937 Tel 516-324-2224; Toll free: 800-645-1188; FAX: 516-324-2248.
Titles:
A >Recipes.
PSP - The Parcel Shipping Program for UPS Shipments.

East/West Software, 73 Lorna Ln., Suffern, NY 10901 Tel 914-627-2831.
Titles:
Take-Stock.

Eastbench Software Products, (0-923784), 1290 Cliffside Dr., Logan, UT 84321 Tel 801-750-2981.
Titles:
Automatic Filer.
The Calendar Program.
Celestial Body Angular Distance.
Checkbook Manager.
Complex Mathematics.
Computerized Telephone Directory.
Curve Fitter.
Data Converter.
Daylight.
The Daylight Ephemeris Program.
Disassembler.
Disk Manager.
Diurnal Arc.
Doctor.
Equation Solver.
Equinox-Solstice.
Fast Fourier Transform.
Home Budget-II.
Home Budget-III.
Home Budget-IV.
Income & Expense Report: Non-Profit Organizations.
Introduction to the Daylight Ephemeris.
Local & Greenwich Sidereal Time.
Local Horizontal Coordinates.
Local Sidereal Time.
Lunar Phases.
Master Disk Catalog.
Minor Planet Ephemeris.
Multiple Statement Program Generator.
Music Analyzer-Synthesis.
Navigational Star Identification.
The Navigational Star Program.
Numerical Integration.
Personal Income & Expense Report.
Planetary Ephemerides.
Planetary Orbital Elements.
Position of the Comet Halley.
Pretty Printer.
Printer Plotter.
Small Business Accounts Payable.
Sort Routines.
Statement Analysis.
Talking Bartender.
Two-Dimensional FFT.
Universal & Sidereal Time Ephemeris.
Variable Interest Rate Loans.
Video Plotter.
Visibility.
Visual Aspects of the Moon.

Eastern Computers, Inc., 596 Lynnhaven Pkwy., Virginia Beach, VA 23452-7303 Tel 804-671-8000.
Titles:
Forword Word Processor.

Eastern Language Systems, P.O. Box 502, Provo, UT 84603-0502 Tel 801-377-4558; Toll free: 800-729-1254; FAX: 801-377-2200.
Titles:
Alkaatib International.
Vazhe Negar Farsi: Persian-Multilingual Document Processor.

Eastgate Systems, Inc., (1-884511), 134 Main St., Watertown, MA 02172 Tel 617-924-9044; Toll free: 800-562-1638; FAX: 617-924-9051.
Titles:
Fontina.
Hypergate Writer.
Hypertext '87 Digest.
Labels & Envelopes Deluxe.
Storyspace.

Easy-As, Inc., (0-923789), 201 N. Charles St., No. 1501, Baltimore, MD 21201 Tel 410-539-5540; FAX: 410-539-6228.
Titles:
FEDTAX92: Federal Income Tax Calculator.
PAS: Personal Accounting System.
PMS: Personal Mailing System.

Ecological Linguistics, (1-879910), P.O. Box 15156, Washington, DC 20003-0156; 316 A St. SE, Washington, DC 20003 Tel 202-546-5862.
Titles:
Ecological Linguistics Fonts.

Economics Research, Inc., (1-879995), 1361 Valencia Ave., Tustin, CA 92680-6459 Tel 714-641-3955; FAX: 714-434-0595.
Titles:
MACRO.
ParGRADE.
ParSCORE.
ParSURVEY-GST: General Survey Tool.
ParSURVEY-SEI: Student Evaluation of Instruction.
ParSURVEY SITE License.
ParSURVEY-TABulator.
ParSYSTEM SITE License.
ParTEST.
ParTEST On-Line.

Ecosoft, Inc., 8295 Indy Ct., Indianapolis, IN 46214 Tel 317-271-5551; Toll free: 800-952-0472; FAX: 317-271-5561.
Titles:
Microstat-II.

Ecotope, Inc., (0-934478), 2812 E. Madison, Seattle, WA 98112 Tel 206-322-3753; FAX: 206-325-7270.
Titles:
Suncode-PC: Building Energy Load Simulation Program.
Sunday: Building Load Simulation.

Eden Pr., P.O. Box 8410, Fountain Valley, CA 92728 Tel 714-556-2023.
Titles:
Privacode.

Edison Design Group, 4 Norman Rd., Upper Montclair, NJ 07043 Tel 201-744-2620.
Titles:
EDG C Front End.
EDG C++ Front End.
EDG FORTRAN Front End.

Edmark Corp., (0-916031; 1-56926), P.O. Box 3218, Redmond, WA 98073-3218; Toll free: 800-426-0856; FAX: 206-556-8998; 6727 185th Ave., NE, Redmond, WA 98073 Tel 206-556-8400.
Titles:
KidDesk.
Millie's Math House.

Edrington Data, 2801 Westminster, Dallas, TX 75205 Tel 214-691-1594.
Titles:
Medical Accounts Receivable.

Educational Activities, Inc., (0-914296; 0-89525; 1-55737; 0-7925), 1937 Grand Ave., Baldwin, NY 11510 Tel 516-223-4666; Toll free: 800-645-3739; FAX: 516-623-9282; Orders to: P.O. Box 392, Freeport, NY 11520.
Titles:
Arithmetic Skills Assessment Test.
Basic Math Competency Skill Building.
Core-Reading & Vocabulary Development.
Diascriptive Cloze Set Program: Diascriptive Cloze I-IV.
Diascriptive 2010 Reading Programs: Diascriptive II.
Diascriptive 2010 Reading Programs: Diascriptive I.
Informal Reading.
Learning Styles Inventory.
Math Baseball.
Math for Beginners.
Math for Everyday Living.
Math Map Trip.
Mystery Games.
Mystery Mazes: High Tech Detective Adventures Through Reading.
Reading for Beginners.
Reading in the Workplace.
Reading Programs: Diascriptive Reading in the Content Area Social Studies.
Regions of the United States.
Santa Fe Trail.
Science.
Sound Sentences.
Thematic Applications: American History.
Thematic Applications: American Pluralism.

EDUCATIONAL DATA SYSTEMS, INC.

Thematic Applications: Ancient Civilizations.
Thematic Applications: General.
Thematic Applications: Science I.
Thematic Applications: Science II.
Thematic Applications: World History.
Writing Process Workshop.
You Be the Reporter.

Educational Data Systems, Inc., (0-923819),
4661 Pinewood Dr. E., Mobile, AL 36618
Tel 334-342-6021.
Titles:
Baseball Book Statistics.
Occupational Skills Analysis System: Job Match-Job Placement.
Sports Statistics I.

Educational Media Corp., (0-932796), 4256
Central Ave., NE, Minneapolis, MN 55421-2920
Tel 612-781-0088; FAX: 612-781-7753; Orders
to: P.O. Box 21311, Minneapolis, MN 55421
Tel 612-781-0088.
Titles:
Activity Log System: Instructional Enterprises.
Counseling Data Base System: Instructional Enterprises.
Self-Exploration Series: IBM version.

Educational Micro Systems, Inc., (0-923821),
P.O. Box 471, Chester, NJ 07930 Tel 201-879-5982.
Titles:
AUTOFLOW.
Conv III to PC: Convert Model I-III BASIC to PC.
Conv 4 to PC: Convert Model 4 BASIC to PC.
EDITBAS.
S2ASC: SuperSCRIPSIT to ASCII.

Educational Programming, Inc., (0-923822),
P.O. Box 81264, Mobile, AL 36689 Tel 205-342-5591.
Titles:
Education Management II.
POS Record Package I.

Educational Software Concepts, Inc.,
(0-925016), P.O. Box 13267, 660 S. Fourth St.,
Edwardsville, KS 66113 Tel 913-441-2881; Toll
free: 800-748-7734; FAX: 913-441-2119.
Titles:
Basic Lung Volume Calculation.
Cardio-Pulmonary Exercise Testing.
Critical Care Nursing Simulations: Endocrine System.
Cystic Fibrosis.
Dietary Intervention - Hypertension.
Evaluation of Obstructive Lung Disease by Pulmonary Function Testing.
Head Trauma.
Introduction to Radiopharmacy.
Medical Imaging Sciences: Additional Radiographic Procedures.
Medical Imaging Sciences: Advanced Concepts Exposure - Image Quality.
Medical Imaging Sciences: Alimentary Cancer: Pathology & Treatment.
Medical Imaging Sciences: Basic Radiographic Physics.
Medical Imaging Sciences: Case Studies in Ethics.
Medical Imaging Sciences: CT Registry Preparation.
Medical Imaging Sciences: Ethical Decision Making.
Medical Imaging Sciences: Integration of Radiographic Physics.
Medical Imaging Sciences: Introduction to Patient Care for Radiological Procedures.
Medical Imaging Sciences: Introduction to Radiation Biology: Theoretical Considerations.
Medical Imaging Sciences: Introduction to Radiologic Technology.
Medical Imaging Sciences: MR Registry Preparation.
Medical Imaging Sciences: Patient Care During Procedures Using Contrast Media.
Medical Imaging Sciences: Patient Protection During Diagnostic Radiography Procedures.
Medical Imaging Sciences: Personnel Protection During Diagnostic Radiography Procedures.
Medical Imaging Sciences: Radiation Biology: Theoretical Considerations & Clinical Applications.
Medical Imaging Sciences: Radiation Exposure - Image Quality.
Medical Imaging Sciences: Radiologic Technology Registry Preparation.
Medical Imaging Sciences: Radiologic Technology Test Bank & Test Generator.
Medical Laboratory Sciences: Erythrocyte Morphology & Inclusions.
Medical Laboratory Sciences: Essential Concepts in Immunology.
Medical Laboratory Sciences: Ethical Dilemmas: Approaches to Resolution.
Medical Laboratory Sciences: Ethical Dilemmas: Case Studies.
Medical Laboratory Sciences: Guidelines for Laboratory Safety.
Medical Laboratory Sciences: Laboratory Math: Solution Concentrations.
Medical Laboratory Sciences: Leukemia: A Primer for Laboratory Scientists.
Medical Laboratory Sciences: Principles of Therapeutic Drug Monitoring.
Medical Laboratory Sciences: Renal Function & Routine Urinalysis.
Medical Laboratory Sciences: The Plasma Coagulation System.
Medicolegal & Psychological Aspects of Patient Care.
Near Drowning.
Neonatal Distress.
Preparation of Technetium-99m Labeled Radiopharmaceuticals.
Quality Control of Molybdenum-99 Technetium-99m Generator Eluate.
Quality Control of Technetium-99m Labeled Radiopharmaceuticals.
Radionuclide Generators.
Unit Dose Calculation & Preparation.
Ventilator Commitment.

Educational Testing Service, (0-88685), P.O.
Box 6108, Princeton, NJ 08541-6108 Tel 609-771-7243; FAX: 609-734-5410.
Titles:
The Official Software for GMAT Review.

Educulture, Inc., (0-89000), 689 W. Schapville
Rd., Scales Mound, IL 61075 Tel 815-777-9697;
Toll free: 800-553-4858; FAX: 815-777-9699.
Titles:
Medical Terminology: General Terms.

Edukeep Co., The, (0-925200), R.R. 16, Box
652, Bedford, IN 47421-9438 Tel 812-275-8111; Toll free: 800-338-5337; FAX: 812-275-8118.
Titles:
Badge-Scan System.
Ed-U-Keep II: Professional Record Keeping System for Educators.
ED-U-KEEP 2000 for Windows.
Scan-Connect.

Edutrends, Inc., (0-935987; 1-57068), 25 Clifton
Rd., Milton, NJ 07438 Tel 201-697-7007; Toll
free: 800-252-8736; FAX: 201-697-7638.
Titles:
Computers in Business.
Data Communications: Basics.
Data Communications: Equipment.
Data Communications: Networks.
dBASE III Plus in Business.
dBASE IV for Everyone.
Local Area Networks I: Fundamentals, Technologies & PCs.
Local Area Networks II: Resource Sharing, Interconnections & Products.
Lotus 1-2-3 Advanced Features.
Lotus 1-2-3 for Everyone.
Lotus 1-2-3 Trainer's Kit: Parts I & II.
Microsoft Word for Everyone: Basics.
PC Networks Fundamentals, Communications & LANS.
PC to Host Networks & Applications.
Using WordPerfect in Business.
WordPerfect Advanced Features.
The WordPerfect Video Training Course.

Eigenware Technologies, 513 S. Neponsit Dr.,
Venice, FL 34293-1120.
Titles:
C Scientific Libraries: CSL.
CSL: C Scientific Programming Library.

800 Software, Inc., (0-923476), 918 Parker St.,
Berkeley, CA 94710 Tel 510-644-3611; Toll
free: 800-888-4880; FAX: 510-644-8226.
Titles:
R-Maker.

Eikon Systems, 989 E. Hillsdale Blvd., Suite 260,
Foster City, CA 94404 Tel 415-349-4664.
Titles:
Scrapbook Plus for Windows.

Elan Computer Group, Inc., 888 Villa St., 3rd
floor, Mountain View, CA 94041 Tel 415-964-2200; Toll free: 800-536-3526; FAX: 415-964-8588.
Titles:
Avalon Publisher.

ELAN Software Corp., 17383 Sunset Blvd., Suite
101, Pacific Palisades, CA 90272; Toll free: 800-654-3526; FAX: 310-454-4848.
Titles:
GoldMine.

Elastic Reality, Inc., 92 Stewart St., Madison, WI
53713 Tel 608-273-6585; FAX: 608-271-1988.
Titles:
The Art Department.
Art Department Professional.
FACC II.
Professional ScanLab.

Elcomp Publishing, Inc., (0-911827), 4650
Arrow Hwy., No. E6, Montclair, CA 91763
Tel 909-626-4070; FAX: 909-624-9574.
Titles:
Busipack.
HelpDir: File Manager.
Index Cards for IBM PC/XT/AT.
Invoices & Sales Slips.
Mail-Merge with Formletters.
Mailing List with Notepad.
PC-Letter.
Property Manager: Instant Relief from Landlord's Headaches.
Super Mailing List.
The World's Easiest Database: Object Oriented Database.

Electret Scientific Co., (0-917406), P.O. Box
4132, Star City, WV 26504 Tel 304-594-1639.
Titles:
Musician Royal.

Electronic Arts, (0-914535; 1-55543; 0-7845),
1450 Fashion Island Blvd., San Mateo, CA
94404 Tel 415-571-7171; Toll free: 800-245-4525 (orders); FAX: 415-571-7995.
Titles:
Abrams Battle Tank.
Art Parts.
The Bard's Tale.
The Bard's Tale II: The Destiny Knight.
Cartooners.
Caveman Ugh-Lympics.
Chuck Yeager's Advanced Flight Trainer.
Dark Lord.

PUBLISHER/TITLE INDEX

Deluxe Music Construction Set.
Deluxe Recorder.
DeluxePaint II.
DeluxePrint II (with Art Disk, Vol. 2).
DeluxeVideo 1.2.
Earl Weaver Baseball.
Earl Weaver Baseball Data Disk.
F/A-18 Intercepter.
Ferrari Formula One.
Grand Slam Bridge.
Hot & Cool Jazz.
Instant Pages.
It's Only Rock 'N Roll.
John Madden Football.
Julius Erving & Larry Bird Go One-on-One.
Marble Madness.
PaperClip Publisher (Commodore Version).
Patton Versus Rommel.
Pinball Construction Set.
Seasons & Holidays.
Seven Cities of Gold.
688 Attack Sub.
Skate or Die.
Starflight.
Strike Fleet.
Studio/32.
Studio/1.
Studio/8.
Thunder II.
Wasteland.

Electronic Courseware Systems, Inc., (0-942132; 1-55603), 1210 Lancaster Dr., Champaign, IL 61821 Tel 217-359-7099; Toll free: 800-832-4965; FAX: 217-359-6578.
Titles:
Adventures in Musicland.
Appleworks Management Templates.
Audio Mirror for SoundBlaster.
Aural Skills Trainer.
Barnstorming Microstation 3-D.
Block It.
Brass Instrument Tutor.
CD TimeSketch.
Chemistry Facts.
Clef Notes.
Comparative Market Analysis.
Digital Music Mentor.
Double Reed Fingerings.
Ear Challenger Windows.
Early Music Skills - MIDI.
Echos - MIDI.
Echos II.
Elements of Mathematics.
Elements of Music.
English Series.
Functional Harmony - MIDI: Basic Chords.
Functional Harmony: Basic Chords.
The Gourmet Computer Cookbook.
Graphics Are Easy.
Harmonic Progressions.
Hear Today...Play Tomorrow: Find That Tune, Ear Training Skills, Descending-Ascending Intervals, Melodic Dictation (Beginner), Melodic Dictation (Intermediate).
Image Maker.
Instant Keyboard Fun I - MIDI.
Keyboard Arpeggios-MIDI.
Keyboard Blues - MIDI.
Keyboard Chords - MIDI.
Keyboard Extended Jazz Harmonies - MIDI.
Keyboard Fingerings.
Keyboard Intervals - MIDI.
Keyboard Jazz Harmonies - MIDI.
Keyboard Kapers.
Keyboard Kapers - MIDI.
Keyboard NAMEGAME.
Keyboard Note Drill - MIDI.
Keyboard Tutor.
Keyboard Tutor - MIDI.
KIDS - MIDI: Getting Ready to Play.
Lime.
Listen!: A Music Skills Program.
Magic Mountain Memory.
Maple: Music Applications Programming Language Extension.
Math Facts Lottery.
Math Grapher.
MIDI Bass Works.
MIDI Jazz Improvisaton Series.
MIDI Screen Saver.
Music Appreciation - A Study Guide: The Musical Language/Music History.
Music Composer Quiz.
Music Flash Cards.
Music History Review: Composers.
Music Room.
Music Terminology.
Music Terminology for Bands, Orchestras & Choirs.
Musicus.
Note Detective.
Patterns in Pitch: Level 1, Level II, Level III.
Perspectives in Music History.
Pinball Math.
The Roman Empire: The Fall of Rome.
Simple Accounts.
Simple Calc.
Simple Mailer.
Super Challenger.
Super Challenger - MIDI.
Tap-It.
Teaching Assistant for AutoCAD Release 12.
Tune It II.
Twelve-Bar Tunesmith.

Electronic Learning Systems, Inc., (0-9621393), 2622 NW 43rd St., Suite B4, Gainesville, FL 32606 Tel 904-375-0558; Toll free: 800-443-7971; FAX: 904-375-5679.
Titles:
Menu Master.

Electrosonics, (0-929800), 36380 Garfield, Suite 1, Clinton Township, MI 48035 Tel 810-791-0770; Toll free: 800-858-8448; FAX: 810-791-3010.
Titles:
Exec-Amort - Loan Amortizer Plus.
Labelets.
Link Com.
ZIPPY Mail List Merger.

Elefunt Software, 724 Allston Way, Berkeley, CA 94710 Tel 510-843-7725; FAX: 510-486-1818.
Titles:
Order House.
RateFinder.
ShipSmartz.

Elfin Magic, 23 Brook Pl., East Islip, NY 11730 Tel 516-581-7657.
Titles:
Checking Account Manager.
Circuit Database II.
Super 3D Plotter II.

Eliot Software Co., P.O. Box 337, Eliot, ME 03903 Tel 207-439-9361; Toll free: 800-755-9887; FAX: 207-439-4517.
Titles:
MacInn.

Elirion, Inc., (1-879142), P.O. Box 771, Naugatuck, CT 06770-0771 Tel 203-720-0070.
Titles:
VP/WORKS for GEM PostScript.

Elite Data Processing, 3415 S. Sepulveda Blvd., Suite 500, Los Angeles, CA 90034-6061 Tel 213-398-4000 Tel 213-398-4966.
Titles:
The Elite System.

Elite Software, (0-928606), P.O. Box 11224, Pittsburgh, PA 15238 Tel 412-795-8492; Toll free: 800-745-8491; FAX: 412-337-8611.
Titles:
BlackJack Master.
Elite Mail for Windows or DOS: Direct Mail Planning Tool.
Elite-Menu: Fast Program Access with File Security.
Elite-Xfer: Color Computer File Transfer Utility.

Elite Software Development, Inc., (0-923873), P.O. Box 1194, Bryan, TX 77806 Tel 409-846-2340; Toll free: 800-648-9523; FAX: 409-846-4367.
Titles:
AUDIT.
AUDIT: Residential Energy Analysis.
Best Friend.
CB80 Language Utilities.
CHVAC: Commercial HVAC Loads Calculation.
Commercial Cooling & Heating Load Program: CHVAC.
Critical Path Method & Job Scheduling Program: CPMPERT.
DPIPE: Waste Drainage Pipe Sizing.
Drainage Pipe Sizing: DPIPE.
DUCTSIZE: Static Regain & Equal Friction.
Earth Coupled Pipe Loop Sizing: ECA.
ECOORD: Fuse & Breaker Coordinator.
ENERGY: Commercial Energy Analysis.
ETOOLS: Electric Tools.
Faser-Energy Accounting: FASER.
FIRE: Fire Sprinkler Hydraulic Calculations.
Fire Sprinkler Design.
Fludware: Lighting 2 Axis Point by Point.
HPIPE: Hydronic Pipe Sizing.
HVAC Tools: A Collection of HVAC Utilities.
Job Cost Accounting: JOBCOST.
Life Cycle Economics Program.
Lighting Fixture Program: LIGHT.
PANEL- Panel Design & Component Sizing.
PANEL: Panel Design & Component Sizing.
PARTS: Electronic Catalog.
PC-Sweep.
PSYCHART: Psychometric Analysis.
Psychrometric Analysis: PSYCHART.
QHVAC: Quick Commercial HVAC Loads.
QUICK QUOTE: HVAC Sales Tool.
REFRIG- Refrigeraton Box Loads.
REFRIG: Refrigeration Box Loads Calculation.
Residential Cooling & Heating Loads Program: RHVAC.
RHVAC: Residential HVAC Loads.
Service Supply Pipe Sizing: SPIPE.
Shadow: Glass Shading Analysis.
Short Circuit Analysis Program: Short.
SHORT: Short Circuit Calculations.
SPIPE: Plumbing Service Supply Pipe Sizing.
Static Regain Duct Sizing: Duct.
U-Factor Calculation.
UFACTOR: U-factor Calculations.
VDROP: Voltage Drop Calculations.
Voltage Drop Calculations: VDROP.

Elite Systems, Inc., R.1, Box 3215 Hayward Rd., Bangor, ME 04401 Tel 207-848-5771.
Titles:
Elite Accounting System: ELITEAR, ELITEAP, ELITEGL, ELITEPA, ELITEWP.

Elliam Assocs., (0-923875), 4067 Arizona Ave., Atascadero, CA 93422 Tel 805-466-8440; FAX: 805-461-1666.
Titles:
BackGrounder II Task Switching System for CP/M.
EZ Text.
EZDSX: Z80 Disassembler.
EZDT: Z80 Dynamic Debugger.
File-Buster.
Forms 4: Form Fill in Program.
HDIS: CP/M 8080 Disassembler.
MM-ENTR: Mail Merge Entry Program.

OKARA: CP/M Shell Programs.
PDIR.
SCRIPT Professional: Multi-Language Word Processor.
Spreadsheet Templates: Construction, Real Estate, Financial.
Superfile: Information.
TYPWTR: Computer Typewriter Program.
UNE-CON: File Recovery System.
WP-HELPER.
ZMDS: Z80 Development System.
ZSAM: Z80 Assembler.
Z3PLUS/NZCOM Z-System for CP/M.

Elwyn, Inc., (0-923879), 111 Elwyn Rd., Elwyn, PA 19063 Tel 610-891-2084; FAX: 610-891-2088.
Titles:
Reaching Out with Sign: A Basic Sign Language Phrase Manual.

Emerald Intelligence, P.O. Box 4540, Ann Arbor, MI 48106-4540 Tel 313-663-8757; FAX: 313-663-5284.
Titles:
Magellan.
Magellan Interface Toolkit.
Mahogany External Development Guide.
Mahogany Introductory.
Mahogany Professional.

Emerging Market Technologies, Inc., 1230 Johnson Ferry Rd., Suite F1, Marietta, GA 30068 Tel 404-973-2300; FAX: 404-973-3003.
Titles:
Invest Now!

Emerging Technology Consultants, (0-918599), 2888 Bluff St., No. 263, Boulder, CO 80301-1200 Tel 303-447-9495; FAX: 303-447-9241.
Do not confuse with Emerging Technology Consultants, Saint Paul, MN.
Titles:
EDIX.

Enable Software, Inc., (0-927009), 313 Ushers Rd., Ballston Lake, NY 12019-1591 Tel 518-877-8600; Toll free: 800-888-0684; FAX: 518-877-5225.
Titles:
Enable OA.
Enable Office.
Enable 4.5.
Higgins Mail.
Higgins Productivity.

Encycloware, 712 Washington St., Ayden, NC 28513 Tel 919-746-4961.
Titles:
MacBible NIV or King James.
MacChurch Data II.
Stock Watch II.
Word Typer.

Enertech Information Systems, (0-928218), 310 W. Wall, Suite 700, Midland, TX 79701 Tel 915-685-1753.
Titles:
Oil & Gas Accounting System Depletions Reporting.

Enfin Software Corp., 6920 Miramar Rd., Suite 106A, San Diego, CA 92121 Tel 619-549-6606; Toll free: 800-922-4372; FAX: 619-695-1806.
Titles:
Budget Solutions.
Business Planner.
Decision Support I.
Goal Solutions.
Goal Solutions-Plus.
Optimal Solutions.
Optimal Solutions-Plus.
Simulated Solutions.
Simulated Solutions-Plus.

Engineered Software, (1-878250), 615 Guilford-Jamestown Rd., Greensboro, NC 27409 Tel 910-299-4843; FAX: 910-852-2067; 615 Guilford Jamestown Rd., Greensboro, NC 27409 Tel 910-299-4843.
Titles:
Advanced Drafting Tools 1.
Advanced Drafting Tools 2.
Landscape Library.
Machinery Designers Library 1.
Machinery Designers Library 2.
PowerCADD: Power Macintosh Version of PowerDraw.
PowerDraw: Advanced CAD Drafting Design System.
Powerdraw Translator.
Residential Construction Symbols Library.

Engineered Software, Inc., (0-918601), 4531 Intelco Loop SE, Lucey, WA 98503 Tel 360-412-0702; Toll free: 800-786-8545 (pre-sales only); FAX: 360-412-0672.
Titles:
The Flo Series.

Engineering/Analysis Corp., (0-923903), 3450 E. Spring St., Suite 112, Long Beach, CA 90806 Tel 310-373-1234; FAX: 310-427-7431.
Titles:
EASE 2.

Engineering & Management Pr., (0-89806), 25 Technology Pk./Atlanta, Norcross, GA 30092 Tel 404-449-0461; FAX: 404-263-8532.
Titles:
Decision Inventory Package.

Engineering Design Analysis Consultants, Inc., 3414 Deerwood Ln., Missouri City, TX 77459 Tel 713-437-1155.
Titles:
IRIS*FLANGE: Design of bolted flange connections.
IRIS*NOZZLE: Local stress analysis due to external loading per WRC-107.
IRIS*VESSEL: Pressure Design & Analysis per ASME Sec VIII, Div. 1.

Engineering Science, Inc., Subs. of Parson Co., (0-918665), Bldg. 57, Executive Park South NE, Suite 590, Atlanta, GA 30329 Tel 404-325-0770; FAX: 404-325-8369.
Titles:
Plantrax 3.
Plotrax.
Wastetrax.

Engineering Software Co., Div. of Infotech, (0-923905), 2418 Cales Dr., Arlington, TX 76013 Tel 817-861-2296; FAX: 817-861-0405.
Titles:
Concrete.
Integrated Structural Design.
Mechanisms.
QuickBeam: Finite Analysis of Beams.
QuickColumn.
QuickFrame Design Package.
Springpac.
Threads.

Engineering Software, Inc., (0-923906), 2000 Washington St., Wilmington, DE 19802-4026 Tel 302-571-9575; FAX: 302-656-3701.
Titles:
Process Engineering Software Package.

Enigma Logic, Inc., 2151 Salvio St., Suite 301, Concord, CA 94520 Tel 510-827-5707; FAX: 510-827-2593.
Titles:
SafeWord for Novell.
SafeWord for VAX Systems.
SafeWord PC-Safe II.
SafeWord PC-Safe III.
SafeWord Single Sign-On Server.
SafeWord SofToken.
SafeWord Stratus-Safe.
SafeWord Tandem-Safe.
SafeWord UNIX-Safe.
SafeWord VTAM-Safe.

Ensign Systems, Inc., 26 N. Main, Suite B, Layton, UT 84041 Tel 801-546-1616; FAX: 801-546-6490.
Titles:
POS-IM.

Enterprise Computer Systems, Inc., (0-923914), P.O. Box 2383, Greenville, SC 29602-2383 Tel 803-234-7676; Toll free: 800-992-6309; FAX: 803-281-3249.
Titles:
Business Management System.

Enterprising Solutions, Inc., P.O. Box 31, Cottleville, MO 63338; Toll free: 800-831-6610; 3930 Old Hwy. 94 S., Suite 107, Saint Charles, MO 63304 Tel 314-939-0374.
Titles:
Business Architect: For the Business You Imagine.

Entertainment Technology, 18000 Studebaker Rd., Suite 200, Cerritos, CA 90703 Tel 310-403-0039; FAX: 310-403-0049.
Titles:
Aces, Eagles & Birdies: Picture Perfect Golf; Tom Kite-Shotmaking; Best Places to Play.
As Times Go: Concise Encyclopedia, Our Century in Depth (Sci-Tech).
Battlefield Warriors: Jetfighter II, Operation Combat, Project X.
Block & Tackle: Fantasy Football, Tom Landry Football, Pro Football Scorecard.
Crosswords.
Dark Passages I: The Psychotron; Wrath of the Demon; Dark Seed.
Dark Passages II: Crusaders of the Dark Savant; The C. H. A. O. S. Continuum; Demoniak.
Fantasy Football.
Jet Fighter II; Earth Invasion.
Jetfighter II.
Kid Smarts: Learning Library, Alien Arcade, My Coloring Book.
KidSmarts: My Coloring Book Learning Library, Alien Arcade.
Klotski; Gemstorm.
Mud Pies: Mario's Early Years, Card Shop, It's a Bird's Life.
Operation Combat; Magnuflux Runner.
Phantom Stormers: Alien Logic, Arc of Doom, Command Adventures Starship.
Portraits in History: The Best of Our Century, Encyclopedia of the JFK Assassination, Encyclopedia of West, Lawmen & Outlaws.
Puzzle Antics.
Puzzle Antics: Gemstorm, Puzzle Master, Klotski.
Puzzle Master; Crosswords.
Spectre VR; Project X.
Star Hawks: Earth Invasion, Spectre VR, Magraflux Runner.
Starhawks II: Cadillacs & Dinosaurs; Buried in Time; Loadstar.
Starhawks: Magnuflux Runner, Earth Invasion, Spectre VR.
Win Vegas.

Entex Information Services, 1000 Boone Ave., N., Golden Valley, MN 55427 Tel 612-797-0068; FAX: 612-557-7545.
Titles:
Microworx Courseware for Lotus.

Entropy Assocs., Inc., 1747 S. Field Ct., Lakewood, CO 80232-6537; FAX: 303-237-1103.
Titles:
Monte Carlo Simulation.

PUBLISHER/TITLE INDEX

Environmental Telesis & Controls, Inc., P.O. Box 180206, 2801 Denton Dr., Austin, TX 78718 Tel 512-835-0330; FAX: 512-832-1775.
Titles:
The Environmental Manager: TEM.

Epcon International, 110 North St., Woodsfield, OH 43793 Tel 614-472-5300; Toll free: 800-367-3585; FAX: 614-472-1553.
Titles:
Engineers Aide II: Mechanical.
Engineer's Aide I: Process.

Epic Instruments, Inc., 279 Lawrence Ave., South San Francisco, CA 94080 Tel 415-588-2260.
Titles:
WaveDisplay.

Epyx, Inc., (0-923920), 1979 Palomar Oaks Way, Carlsbad, CA 92009-1307; FAX: 415-369-2999.
Titles:
Bible Builder.
California Games.
California Games II.
Chips Challenge.
Create a Calendar.
Fast Load.
Getaway: Laptop Entertainment Six Pack.
Getaway Windows: Windows Entertainment 6-Pack.
Graphics Scrapbook.
Impossible Mission.
Studio of Greetings: Print Magic.
Studio of Greetings!: Print Magic 2.0.
Sub Battle Simulator.
Summer Games II.
Winter Games.
World Games.

Equine Computer Software, P.O. Box 9103, Evansville, IN 47724-7103 Tel 812-464-2931.
Titles:
EquiMac.

Equis International, (1-885439), 3950 S. 700 E., Suite 100, Salt Lake City, UT 84107 Tel 801-265-9996; Toll free: 800-882-3040; FAX: 801-265-3999.
Titles:
The Downloader.
The/DownLoader-Dial/Data.
MetaStock.
MetaStock RT: Real-Time Technical Analysis Charting Software.
Pulse Portfolio Management System.
The Technician.

Erlbaum, Lawrence, Assocs. Software & Alternative Media, Inc., Div. of Lawrence Erlbaum Assocs., Inc., (1-56321), 10 Industrial Ave., Mahwah, NJ 07430 Tel 201-236-9500; Toll free: 800-926-6579; FAX: 201-276-0072. Do not confuse with Lawrence Erlbaum Associates, Inc at same address.
Titles:
The Active Eye.
Advanced Basic Meta-Analysis.
Advanced Logo: A Language for Learning.
Applied Multivariate Statistics for the Social Sciences.
Author's Guide to Journals in the Behavioral Sciences.
Auxal 2: A PC Program for Auxological Analysis of Longitudinal Measuremenets of Human Stature.
BILOG.
BIMAIN.
Contour.
Creating a Memory of Casual Relationships: An Integration of Empirical & Explanation-Based Learning Methods.
DSTAT: Software for the Meta-Analytic Review of Research Literatures.
Engines for Education.
Experimental Methods in Psychology.
A First Course in Factor Analysis.
A First Course in Grammar & Usage for Psychology & Related Fields: Electronic Edition.
Handbook of Research in Language Development Using Children.
Intermediate Statistics: A Modern Approach.
International Problem Solving Using Logo.
LISCOMP.
LISREL 8 & PRELIS 2: Comprehensive Analysis of Linear Relationships in Multivariate Data.
MULTILOG.
Multivariance.
PARSCALE.
Pepper: Examine Phonetic & Program to Phonologic Evaluation Records.
Photojournalism: An Ethical Approach.
STAT-POWER.
Statistical Power Analysis: A Computer Program.
TESTFACT.
Tetrad II: Tools of Casual Modeling.

Ernst & Young, (1-879161), 2001 Ross Ave., Suite 2800, Dallas, TX 75201 Tel 214-979-1674; Toll free: 800-421-0004; FAX: 214-979-2333.
Titles:
EY/FastPlan.

esccomate, (0-923933), P.O. Box 461, Fort Collins, CO 80522-0461 Tel 303-484-8200.
Titles:
Accounting-Job Costing.
Payroll-Labor Costing.
Piping-Plumbing Estimating.
Sheet Metal-Ductwork Estimating.
Sonic Digitizer Takeoff.

Essex Systems, P.O. Box 1818, Bloomfield, NJ 07003 Tel 201-743-1818.
Titles:
Omnitrax.

Estima, P.O. Box 1818, Evanston, IL 60204 Tel 708-864-8772; Toll free: 800-822-8038; FAX: 708-864-6221.
Titles:
EZX-11.

Etlon Software, 1936 Quail Cir., Louisville, CO 80027 Tel 303-665-3444; FAX: 303-665-2282.
Titles:
MacStronomy.

Etreby Computer Co., Inc., (0-923937), 17870 Castleton St., Suite 235, Industry, CA 91748 Tel 818-917-7244; Toll free: 800-843-7988; 800-292-5590 (in California); FAX: 818-918-1076.
Titles:
Entreby System 2000.

Eugenides, Jan, R.R. 1, Box 9463, Waterbury Center, VT 05677 Tel 802-244-5946.
Titles:
Oasis.

Evans Economics, Inc., 901 N. Washington St., No. 708, Alexandria, VA 22314-1535.
Titles:
ENS Electronic News Service.

Evans Newton, Inc., (0-928612), 14255 N. 76th Pl., Scottsdale, AZ 85260 Tel 602-998-2777; Toll free: 800-443-0544; FAX: 602-951-2895.
Titles:
TargetTeach.

Everbright Software, P.O. Box 8020, Redwood City, CA 94063-1524 Tel 415-368-3200.
Titles:
Bible Builder Software.
Getaway Windows: Windows Entertainment 6-Pack.
Studio of Greetings 3.5: Print Magic 2.0.

Evergreen Ventures, Inc., (0-927701), P.O. Box 445, Voorhees, NJ 08043; 1 Addington Ct., Voorhees, NJ 08043 Tel 609-753-0758.
Titles:
The Sales Associate System.

Everyware, (0-9641564), 1119 Colorado Ave., Santa Monica, CA 90401 Tel 310-319-3736; FAX: 310-391-3755. Do not confuse with EveryWare Bks. in Salt Lake City, UT.
Titles:
Sensible Soccer.

Evolution Computing, 437 S. 48th St., Suite 106, Tempe, AZ 85281 Tel 602-967-8633; Toll free: 800-874-4028; FAX: 602-968-4325.
Titles:
EasyCAD 2.
FastCAD.
FastCAD 3D.

Evolution, Inc., (0-918623), 13632 W. 95th St., Lenexa, KS 66215 Tel 913-599-4646.
Titles:
Health Specialist.
Masterfile.
Premium Finance.

Evolutionary Commercial Systems, P.O. Box 639, Friendswood, TX 77546 Tel 713-996-0061.
Titles:
ExpressForm.

Excalibur Sources, Inc., (0-925924), P.O. Box 467220, Atlanta, GA 31146 Tel 404-518-8898.
Titles:
EXSELL.
EXSELL (LAN).

Excalibur Systems, Inc., (0-923945), 27281 Las Ramblas, Suite 155, Mission Viejo, CA 92691; Toll free: 800-932-9320; FAX: 619-723-9076.
Titles:
The Compu-Counter Accounts Payable: Business Accounting Software.
The Compu-Counter Accounts Receivable: Business Accounting Software.
The Compu-Counter General Ledger: Business Accounting Software.
The Compu-Counter Payroll: Business Accounting Software, Payroll.
Compu-Cutter: Paper Cutting Calculator.
The Compu-Printer Customer History Module.
The Compu-Printer: Paper Inventory.
The Compu-Printer: Print Shop Estimating-Quoting.
The Compu-Printer: Print Shop Management System.

Excalibur Technologies Corp., (0-923946), 9255 Towne Centre Dr., 9th Flr., San Diego, CA 92121 Tel 619-625-7900; Toll free: 800-788-7758; FAX: 619-625-7901.
Titles:
PixTex/EFS: Electronic Filing Software.

Exceiver Corp., 14688 County Rd. 79, Elk River, MN 55330 Tel 612-441-8166; FAX: 612-441-6457.
Titles:
Builder's Apprentice.
Construction Contractor Management.
Mailbase.
Time Billing.

Excel Software, P.O. Box 1414, Marshalltown, IA 50158 Tel 515-752-5359; FAX: 515-752-2435.
Titles:
Mac A & D.
MacAnalyst.
MacDesigner.
Translator.

Excelsior Software, Inc., (1-878401), P.O. Box 3416, Greeley, CO 80633 Tel 303-353-8311; Toll free: 800-473-4572; FAX: 303-353-8340; 960 37th Ave. Ct., Greeley, CO 80634 Tel 303-353-8311; Dist. by: Forsythe Computers, 8514 Eager Rd., Saint Louis, MO 63144 Tel 317-638-8888. Do not confuse with companies with the same name in New York, NY, New Milford, NJ.
Titles:
Excelsior Quiz 2.

Execplan, Inc., (0-926721), 777 Alexander Rd., No. 204, Princeton, NJ 08540-6301 Tel 609-987-5000; Toll free: 800-850-8444 (sales only); FAX: 609-987-0707.
Titles:
EXECPLAN.

Execudata, Inc., 6850 Canby Ave., Suite 108, Reseda, CA 91335 Tel 818-343-1300; Toll free: 800-343-0011 (outside state); FAX: 818-343-8456.
Titles:
HORIZON - TWO SERIES: General Ledger, Accounts Payable, Property Management.
HORIZON - TWO SERIES: Job Cost, General Ledger, Accounts Payable.
Horizon Two Series: General Ledger, Accounts Payable, Job Cost.
Horizon Two Series: General Ledger, Accounts Payable, Property Management.
Horizon-2 Series: Job Cost General Ledger, Accounts Payable.
Horizon-2 Series: Property Management, General Ledger, Accounts Payable.
Quality Plus: Customer Service Management & Warranty Control.

Executive Data Systems, Inc., (0-923955), 1640 Powers Ferry Rd., Bldg. 27, Marietta, GA 30067 Tel 770-955-3374; Toll free: 800-272-3374; FAX: 770-955-1975. Do not confuse with Executive Data Systems, Inc. of Avon, CT.
Titles:
Donor Records.
Fund Accounting Software Series.
Ledgermaster: Client Write Up.

Executive Micro Systems, Inc., (0-926580), 27 Parsonage Lot Rd., Lebanon, NJ 08833 Tel 908-832-6300; FAX: 201-335-7365.
Titles:
MCBA Classic Software.

Executive Productivity Systems, (0-9625299), 2305 Miller Ct., Lakewood, CO 80215 Tel 303-232-0225.
Titles:
EPS Linker.
EPS Personal Manager System.
EPS Records Management System: The Central Filing Solution.

Executive Software, (0-9640049), 701 N. Brand Blvd., 6th Flr., Glendale, CA 91203 Tel 818-547-2050; Toll free: 800-829-4357; FAX: 818-545-9241.
Titles:
Diskeeper.
Diskeeper Performance Edition.
File Alert for Windows NT.
Filemaster.
I/O EXPRESS.

Executive Technologies, Inc., 2120 16th Ave. S., Birmingham, AL 35205 Tel 205-933-5494; FAX: 205-930-5509.
Titles:
Search Express/Legal.
SearchExpress - CD-ROM.
SearchExpress Document Imaging System.

Exeter Software, (0-925031), 100 N. Country Rd., Bldg. B, Setauket, NY 11733 Tel 516-689-7838; Toll free: 800-842-5892; FAX: 516-689-0103.
Titles:
C2D: Spatial Autocorrelation in 2 Dimensions.
NTSYS-pc: Numerical Taxonomy system.
RAMAS/age: Modeling Fluctuations in Age-structured Populations.

Exodus Software, 800 Compton Rd., No. 11, Cincinnati, OH 45231-3848 Tel 513-522-0011.
Titles:
Retriever.

Experience In Software, Inc., (0-928615), 2000 Hearst Ave., Suite 202, Berkeley, CA 94709-2176 Tel 510-644-0694; Toll free: 800-678-7008; FAX: 510-644-3823.
Titles:
The Art of Negotiating.
The Idea Generator Plus.
Project KickStart.
Project KickStart for Windows.
Thoughtline.

Expert Choice, Inc., (0-917305), 5001 Baum Blvd., Suite 650, Pittsburgh, PA 15213 Tel 412-682-3844; FAX: 412-682-7008.
Titles:
Expert Choice.
Newtech Expert Choice.
STRATATREE.
TeamEC.

Expert Systems, Inc., (0-9636716), 2616 Quebec Ave., Melbourne, FL 32935-8744 Tel 407-242-0140.
Titles:
Metrics.

Expertelligence, (0-923117), 203 Chapala St., Santa Barbara, CA 93101 Tel 805-962-2558; FAX: 805-962-5188.
Titles:
ExperLink.
ExperLogo.

Expressware Corp., (1-878012), P.O. Box 1800, Duvall, WA 98019 Tel 206-788-3774; Toll free: 800-753-3453 (orders only); FAX: 206-788-4493.
Titles:
Express Check.
ExpressCalc.
ExpressGraph.
File Express.
On-Side.

Exsys, Inc., 1720 Louisiana Blvd. NE, Suite 312, Albuquerque, NM 87110 Tel 505-256-8356; Toll free: 800-676-8356; FAX: 505-256-8359.
Titles:
EXSYS EL: Expert System Development Package.
Exsys Professional-Expert Systems Development Tool.

Eyring Corp., (0-923972), 6912 South 185 West, Midvale, UT 84047-0816 Tel 801-561-1111; Toll free: 800-937-7367; FAX: 801-565-4692.
Titles:
Absoft FORTRAN 77.
BASIC.
BSDnet.
C.
PASCAL.
PDOS Full Spectrum Development Kit.
PDOS InSpector.
PDOS-MRI ANSI C & Cplus plus Compiler.
PxRay & XRAY/MTD: Source Level Debugger.

FAS, Inc., 2400 Lake Park Dr., Smyrna, GA 30080-7644.
Titles:
FAST.
FASTC.
FASTG.

FGM, Inc., 131 Elden St., Suite 308, Herndon, VA 22070 Tel 703-478-9881; FAX: 703-478-9883.
Titles:
PICTure This.

FORTH, Inc., (0-924076), 111 N. Sepulveda Blvd., Manhattan Beach, CA 90266 Tel 310-372-8493; Toll free: 800-553-6784; FAX: 310-318-8493.
Titles:
PolyFORTH.

F1 Software, (0-942439), 208 Ridgefield Dr., Asheville, NC 28806 Tel 704-665-1818; Toll free: 800-486-1800; FAX: 704-665-1999.
Titles:
PowerChurch Plus.

FTG Data Systems, (0-923986), 8381 Katella Ave., P.O. Box 615, Stanton, CA 90680 Tel 714-995-3900; Toll free: 800-962-3900; FAX: 714-995-3989.
Titles:
EMU-TEK.

FTL Games, Div. of Software Heaven, 6160 Lusk Blvd., Suite C-206, San Diego, CA 92121 Tel 619-453-5711.
Titles:
Dungeon Master.
Oids.
SunDog: Frozen Legacy.

F/22 Pr., (0-933596), P.O. Box 141, Leonia, NJ 07605 Tel 201-568-6250.
Titles:
BestBet.
ClearingHouse.
Darkstar.
Darkstar Plus (Combines Both Darkstar & Timestar).
Lotto-Five-Wheeler.
Lotto Wheeler.
Timestar.
Win.

FWB Software, Inc., 2040 Polk St., Suite 215, San Francisco, CA 94109 Tel 415-474-8055; FAX: 415-775-2125.
Titles:
Hard Disk Toolkit.

Faast Software, 3062 East Ave., Livermore, CA 94550 Tel 510-455-8086.
Titles:
Faast-3.
SLIC-IV: Mesh Generation.

FaceWare, 1310 N. Broadway, Urbana, IL 61801 Tel 217-328-5842.
Titles:
FaceIt.

Facts on File, Inc., Subs. of Infobase Holdings, Inc., (0-87196; 0-8160), 460 Park Ave. South, New York, NY 10016 Tel 212-683-2244; Toll free: 800-322-8755; FAX: 212-213-4578.
Titles:
Public Domain Software on File Collection.

Fair Tide Technologies, Inc., 18 Ray Ave., Burlington, MA 01803 Tel 617-229-6409; Toll free: 800-732-3284; FAX: 617-229-2387.
Titles:
Navigate!
SeaView!: Marine Instrument Display for PC.

PUBLISHER/TITLE INDEX

FairCom Corp., (0-923990), 4006 W. Broadway, Columbia, MO 65203-0100 Tel 573-445-6833; Toll free: 800-234-8180.
Titles:
c-tree Plus File Handler.
d-tree.
FairCom ODBC Driver.
FairCom Server.
R-Tree Report Generator.

Fairfield Language Technologies, (1-883972), 122 S. Main St., Suite 400, Harrisonburg, VA 22801 Tel 540-432-6166; Toll free: 800-788-0822; FAX: 540-432-0953.
Titles:
The Rosetta Stone Language Library: Deutsch Level I.
The Rosetta Stone Language Library: Dutch Level I.
The Rosetta Stone Language Library: English Level I.
The Rosetta Stone Language Library: Espanol Level I.
The Rosetta Stone Language Library: Francais Level I.
The Rosetta Stone Language Library: Russian Level I.
The Rosetta Stone Power Pac.

Family Care Software, Subs. of Lundin Laboratories, Inc., 7071 Orchard Lake Rd., Suite 235, West Bloomfield, MI 48322 Tel 810-851-8282; Toll free: 800-426-8426; FAX: 810-851-8294.
Titles:
Personal Pediatrician.
Personal Physician.

FAMware, (0-918065), 1580 E. Dawn Dr., Salt Lake City, UT 84121 Tel 801-943-6908; FAX: 801-943-6908.
Titles:
Family Fortune.
Family Reunion.
Tree Easy.

Far West Systems, Inc., 5445 Balboa, No. 112, Encino, CA 91316 Tel 818-905-1410; FAX: 818-905-1429.
Titles:
PBAR-PC: Patient Billing & Accounts Receivable.

Farin & Assocs., 6506 Schroeder Rd., Madison, WI 53711 Tel 608-273-1004; Toll free: 800-236-3724; FAX: 608-273-2374.
Titles:
Interest Rate Risk Analyzer-Regulatory Performance Monitor: IRRA-RPM.
Managers Toolbox.
SAM: (Strategic A L Management Model).
StratPlan Strategic Planning Model.

Farm Management, Inc., (0-924000), 1200 E. Haven Ave., New Lenox, IL 60451-2021 Tel 815-485-4955; Toll free: 800-992-2814; FAX: 815-485-4011.
Titles:
The Financial Manager.

Farm Management Systems of Mississippi, Inc., (0-923999), P.O. Box 646, McComb, MS 39648 Tel 601-684-6402.
Titles:
Beef Herd & Herd Health Management.
Broiler Management.
Crop Management System.
Embryo Transfer Management.
Least Cost Nutrition.
Registered Beef Herd & Herd Health Management System.
Registered Dairy Herd & Herd Health Management Systems.

Farmer's Software Assn., (0-928111), P.O. Box 660, Fort Collins, CO 80522 Tel 970-493-1722; Toll free: 800-237-4182; FAX: 970-493-3938.
Titles:
AgChek IV: Crop & Livestock Modules & Pesticide.
AgChek IV: General Ledger.
Horizon Accounting.
Horizon Preceptions: Crop, Inventory, Orders, Modules.
Mapinfo for Windows: Desktop Mapping - GIS.
Pmap: Professional Map Analysis Package.
Red River Crop & Livestock Accounting.
SwineTrak Plus.
tMAP: Tutorial Map Analysis Package.

FastTrax International, 880 Ensenada Ave., Berkeley, CA 94707-1850 Tel 510-525-3510.
Titles:
FastTrax.

Faxon Co., The, (0-87305), 15 Park Cir., Westwood, MA 02090-1725; Toll free: 800-826-8200.
Titles:
MicroLinx Check-In.
MicroLinx Route.

Faxon Institute, Div. of The Faxon Co., (0-9631061), 15 SW Park, Westwood, MA 02090 Tel 617-329-3350; Toll free: 800-766-0039; FAX: 617-329-9875.
Titles:
Creating User Pathways to Electronic Information: Synopsis of the 1991 Faxon Institute Annual Conference.
Listening to Users: Case Studies in Building Electronic Communities: 1992 Faxon Institute Annual Conference Proceedings.

Feith Systems & Software, Inc., (0-924011), 425 Maryland Dr., Fort Washington, PA 19034 Tel 215-646-8000.
Titles:
Feith Document Database: Document Storage & Retrieval System.

Felsina Software, Incorporated, (1-884992), 4440 Finley Ave., No. 108, Los Angeles, CA 90027 Tel 213-669-1497; Toll free: 800-300-1803; FAX: 213-669-1893.
Titles:
A-Talk for Windows.
A-Talk for Windows NT.

Ferox Microsystems, Inc., (0-918541), 901 N. Washington St., Suite 204, Alexandria, VA 22314 Tel 703-984-1660; FAX: 703-684-1666.
Titles:
EIS Toolkit.
Encore! Plus.

Field Multimedia, 222 Spring Rd., Malvern, PA 19355-3416 Tel 610-296-2577.
Titles:
For Mice Only!: Three Beatrix Potter Mouse Tales.
For Rabbits Only!: Three Beatrix Potter Rabbit Tales.
For Squirrels Only!: Two Beatrix Potter Squirrel Tales.

Fifth Generation Systems, Inc., 10049 N. Reiger Rd., Baton Rouge, LA 70809 Tel 504-291-7221; Toll free: 800-873-4384; FAX: 504-295-3268.
Titles:
Brooklyn Bridge.
Disklock.
Fastback Plus.
File Director.
Pyro!
Suitcase II.

Final Frontier Software, 541 Sugar Loaf Dr., Palmdale, CA 93551-7953; FAX: 805-723-6637.
Titles:
Space M+A+X.

Finalsoft Corp., (1-878133), P.O. Box 114629, Miami, FL 33111-4629 Tel 305-477-2703; Toll free: 800-232-8228; FAX: 305-477-0680.
Titles:
Finalsoft Executive: Groupware for Windows.
Translate English to Spanish: The Ultimate English to Spanish Translation Tool.

Financial Aid Finders, Div. of IAB, Inc., (1-884002), 77 Gristmill Rd., Randolph, NJ 07869 Tel 201-361-2567; FAX: 201-361-9815.
Titles:
College Money Finder Program: Financial Aid Software.

Financial Computer Support, Inc., (0-923313), 145 Commerce Dr., Oakland, MD 21550 Tel 301-334-1800; FAX: 301-334-1896.
Titles:
Client Asset Management System (dbCAMS+).

Financial Feasibilities, 9454 Wilshire Blvd., Beverly Hills, CA 90212 Tel 310-278-8000; FAX: 310-679-2263.
Titles:
CFO Advisor.

Financial Microware, P.O. Box 40, Cupertino, CA 95015 Tel 408-446-5639.
Titles:
Loan Qualifier.

Financial Navigator International, 254 Polaris Ave., Mountain View, CA 94043 Tel 415-962-0333; Toll free: 800-824-9827; FAX: 415-962-0730.
Titles:
Financial Navigator.

Finot Group, The, P.O. Box 11497, Piedmont, CA 94611-0497; Toll free: 800-748-6480.
Titles:
KeepTrack Plus.

FinPlan Co., 100 E. Cuttriss, Park Ridge, IL 60068 Tel 708-823-4169; Toll free: 800-777-2108.
Titles:
Divorce Planner.

1st Aid Software, 42 Radnor Rd., Boston, MA 02135 Tel 617-783-7118; Toll free: 800-943-3497.
Titles:
The Anti-Virus Kit.
1st Aid Kit.

First Byte, Div. of Davidson & Assocs., (0-931819), 19840 Pioneer Ave., Torrance, CA 90503-1660 Tel 310-793-0610; FAX: 310-793-0611.
Titles:
Monologue for Windows 32.

1st Class Expert Systems, Inc., P.O. Box 9156, Waltham, MA 02254-9156.
Titles:
1st Class Fusion.
1st Class HT (Hypertext).

First DataBank, Div. of The Hearst Corp., 1111 Bayhill Dr., San Bruno, CA 94066-3035 Tel 415-588-5454; Toll free: 800-633-3453.
Titles:
Auto-Nutritionist IV.
Nutritionist IV: Diet Analysis.
Nutritionist IV: Food Labeling.

1st Desk Systems, Inc., Div. of Micro Group Co., 7 Industrial Park Rd., Medway, MA 02053 Tel 508-533-2203; Toll free: 800-522-2286; FAX: 508-634-0269.
Titles:
DataModeler.
1st BBS-II.
1stBase-II.
1stPort-II.
1stVue-II.

First Food Cost Expert, (0-9623044), SW 818 Crestview, Pullman, WA 99163 Tel 509-334-2638.
Titles:
First Food Cost Expert.

First Reference, Inc., 1 Bridge St, Irvington, NY 10533-1513.
Titles:
CBT Development Stacks.

First Row Software Publishing, 257 St. James Pl., Philadelphia, PA 19106 Tel 215-662-1400.
Titles:
Dr. Dumont's Wild P.A.R.T.I.
The Honeymooners.
Moses #1.
Prime Time.
Star Empire.
The Twilight Zone.
Zap...The Codefinder.

First Wave, (0-9624533), 9449 N. 90th St., Suite 213, Scottsdale, AZ 85258-1400 Tel 602-860-4300; FAX: 602-860-2501.
Titles:
Information Rainbow.
MacTunes.
TimeMaker.

Firstlight Productions, Inc., (1-888419), 15353 NE 90th St., Redmond, WA 98052 Tel 206-869-6600; Toll free: 800-368-1488; FAX: 206-869-6605.
Titles:
Sparky's Spelling with Phonics.
Word Quest.

Fiscal Systems, Inc., (0-928227), 102 Commerce Cir., Madison, AL 35758 Tel 205-772-8920; FAX: 205-772-8590.
Titles:
The FIS-CAL Accounts Payable System.
The FIS-CAL Accounts Receivable System.
Fis-Cal Business System: FIS-CAL Point-of-Sale Manager's Workstation Software.
The FIS-CAL General Ledger System.
The FIS-CAL Inventory Control System.
The FIS-CAL Payroll System.
The FIS-CAL Purchase Order Processing System.
The FIS-CAL Sales Order Processing System.

Fischer International Systems Corp., 4073 Mercantile Ave., Naples, FL 33942 Tel 813-643-1500; Toll free: 800-237-4510; 800-331-2866 (in Florida); FAX: 813-643-6357.
Titles:
EMC2/TAO.
MailSafe: Public Key Encryption Software.
SmartDisk with Safeboot.
Watchdog Armor.
Watchdog Director LAN: Central Security Administration.
Watchdog Keymaster.
WATCHDOG: PC Data Security.
WorkFlow.2020.
WorkFlow.2000.

Fisher Business Systems, Inc., (0-924051), 900 Cir. 75 Pkwy. NW, Suite 1700, Atlanta, GA 30339-3095 Tel 404-578-1771.
Titles:
Medical Practice Management System.
The Practitioner.
Restaurant Management System.

Flambeaux Software, Inc., 1147 E. Broadway, Suite 56, Glendale, CA 91205 Tel 818-500-0044; Toll free: 800-833-7355; FAX: 818-957-0194.
Titles:
DOS Help!
Tech Help!
xText: Hypertext Compiler & Toolkit.

Flight Engineering, 615 Forrest Dr., No. 206, Miami, FL 33166 Tel 305-884-1475.
Titles:
Elements Plus.
PACK-ER II.
Universal Calculator.

Flight Training Devices, P.O. Box 91723, Anchorage, AK 99509-1723 Tel 907-276-6719; Toll free: 800-321-9139.
Titles:
Pilot.

Florida Funding Pubns., Inc., Div. of John L. Adams & Co., Inc., (1-879543), 9350 S. Dixie Hwy., Suite 1560, Miami, FL 33156 Tel 305-670-2203; FAX: 305-670-2208.
Titles:
Grantseeker's F.I.N.D: Florida Information Network Database.

FlowSoft, Inc., (0-935509), 5 Oak Forest Ct., Saint Charles, MO 63303 Tel 314-441-1022; FAX: 314-441-7752.
Titles:
BulkMail.
FloCurve.
GAS.
ORIFICE: Flow Element Sizing.
PLATE, Orifice PLATE.
RELIEF.
VALVE.
ZEE Compressibility.

Fluent, Inc., Div. of Aavid Thermal Technologies, Inc., Centerra Resource Pk., 10 Cavendish Ct., Lebanon, NH 03766 Tel 603-643-2600; Toll free: 800-445-4454; FAX: 603-643-3967.
Titles:
FLUENT.
Fluent/UNS.
NEKTON.
RAMPANT.

Focus/2000, Inc., P.O. Box 3479, Shawnee, KS 66203 Tel 913-631-1171.
Titles:
Golf Resort Diskettes.
GolfMaster/2000.
TripMaster/2000.

Fogle Computing Corp., (0-924068), 101 W. Saint John St., No. 202, Spartanburg, SC 29306 Tel 803-582-3718; Toll free: 800-845-7594; FAX: 803-582-4147.
Titles:
ChurchMaster.
Fogle Accounts Payable.
Fogle Accounts Receivable.
Fogle General Ledger.
Fogle Payroll.
HarbourMaster.
Purchase Order.
Records Retention.
Service Inventory.
Stockroom Inventory.
TempleTracker.

Follett Software Co., Div. of Follett Corp., (0-88153; 0-924917), 1391 Corporate Dr., McHenry, IL 60050-7041 Tel 815-344-8700; Toll free: 800-323-3397; FAX: 815-344-8774.
Titles:
Alliance Plus.
Catalog Plus.
Circulation-Catalog Plus Multiuser.
Circulation Plus (Apple).
Circulation Plus (MS-DOS).
PHD+: Portable Handheld Device.
Quick Card (Apple).
Quick Card MS-DOS.

Font Factory, The, Subs. of Good Software Corp., 4125 Keller Springs Rd., Suite 156, Dallas, TX 75244-2035 Tel 214-239-6085; Toll free: 800-272-4663; FAX: 213-239-4643.
Titles:
Twenty-Five In-1 SoftCartridge: Software Equivalents of the Hewlett-Packard Font Cartridges A-Z.

Foresight Resources Corp., (0-945535), 10725 Ambassador Dr., Kansas City, MO 64153 Tel 816-891-1040; Toll free: 800-231-8574; FAX: 816-891-8018. Do not confuse with Forsight Bks., Unionville, CT.
Titles:
Drafix CAD Professional.
Drafix CAD Ultra.
Drafix Network Symbols Library.
Planix Home Architect.
Planix Office.
Professional Symbol Libraries.

Forte Communications, Inc., 2010 Fortune Dr., No. 101, San Jose, CA 95131-1823 Tel 408-945-9111; Toll free: 800-233-3278.
Titles:
Forte Twinax.

Forthought, Inc., P.O. Box 32, Sunset, SC 29685 Tel 803-878-7484.
Titles:
HPGL Spooler.
Snap!
SNAP/DXF Translator.
SNAP!/Intergraph Translator.

Fortnum Software, 16742 Gothard St., Huntington Beach, CA 92647 Tel 714-841-1562.
Titles:
MacChemistry.
MacNest.

Foundation Pubns., Inc., (0-910618; 1-885217), P.O. Box 6439, Anaheim, CA 92816 Tel 714-630-6450; Dist. by: Riverside/World, P.O. Box 370, 1500 Riverside Dr., Iowa Falls, IA 50126 Tel 515-648-4271; Toll free: 800-247-5111; Dist. by: Spring Arbor Distributors, 10885 Textile Rd., Belleville, MI 48111 Tel 313-481-0900; Toll free: 800-395-5599 (orders); 800-395-7234 (customer service).
Titles:
Bible/Master: Cross References & Marginal Notes.
Bible/Master: King James Version Computer Bible.
Bible/Master: La Biblia de las Americas.
Bible/Master: NAS Computer Bible.
Bible/Master: NAS Hebrew-Greek Transliterated Dictionary.
Bible/Master: New International Version.
Bible/Master: New Revised Standard Version.
Bible/Master: Topical Studies.
Bible/Master: Treasury of Scripture Knowledge.
BibleMaster for Macintosh: Bible Bundle.
BibleMaster for Windows: Bible Bundle.
BibleMaster on CD-ROM.

PUBLISHER/TITLE INDEX

4Home Productions, Div. of Computer Associates International, Inc., (0-923108; 0-918317; 0-928104; 0-922344; 0-926530; 0-922091), One Computer Associates Plaza, Islandia, NY 11788 Tel 516-342-2000; Toll free: 800-773-5445.
Titles:
Kiplinger's Simply Money.
Parents Magazine's Simply Kids.
Simply Accounting for DOS.
Simply Accounting for the Macintosh.
Simply Accounting for Windows & OS/2.
Simply Citizen.
Simply House: Features Advice from the Stanley Complete Step-by-Step Book of Home Repair & Improvement.
Simply Tax: Featuring Tax Tips from the Ernst & Young Tax-Saving Strategies Guide, 1995, a John Wiley & Sons Publication.

Franklin Electronic Pubs., Inc., (0-945731; 1-56712), 1 Franklin Plaza, Burlington, NJ 08016-4907 Tel 609-261-4800; Toll free: 800-762-5382; FAX: 609-261-2984.
Titles:
Franklin Big League Baseball Encyclopedia: HRS-100.

Franks, D. V., 3721 Sue Ellen Dr., Raleigh, NC 27604 Tel 919-872-5379.
Titles:
ArtDisk 7 "Christian Images".
ArtDisks 1, 2, 3, & 4.

Franz, Inc., 1995 University Ave., Berkeley, CA 94704 Tel 510-548-3600; Toll free: 800-333-7260; FAX: 510-548-8253.
Titles:
Allegro CL.
Allegro CL for Windows: Object Oriented Development Systems.
Allegro Composer.
CLIM: Common Lisp Interface Manager.

Fraternal Software, (0-939321), 106 Busch Hill Dr., Wetumpka, AL 36092 Tel 334-567-2763.
Titles:
Blue Lodge Program Package.

Free Spirit Software, Inc., 244 N. College Ave., Indianapolis, IN 46202-3702.
Titles:
Ami...Alignment System.
Doctor Ami.
1541/1571 Drive Alignment.
Planet of Lust.
The Securities Analyst.
Sex Olympics.
Sex Vixens from Space.

Freeman, W. H., & Co., Subs. of Scientific American, Inc., (0-7167), 41 Madison Ave., E. 26th, 35th Flr., New York, NY 10010 Tel 212-576-9400; FAX: 212-689-2383; Orders to: 4419 W. 1980, S., Salt Lake City, UT 84104 Tel 801-973-4660.
Titles:
Apple Assembly Language.
Apple Pascal: A Self-Study Guide for the Apple II Plus, IIe, & IIc.
Commodore 64 Assembly Language Diskette.
Computing Without Mathematics: BASIC, Pascal, Applications.
Learning Apple FORTRAN.
Macintosh Pascal: Student's Diskette.
Macintosh Pascal: Teacher's Diskette.
Program Solving in Apple Pascal.

Freemyers Design, 575 Nelson Ave., Oroville, CA 95965 Tel 916-533-9365.
Titles:
A-Z Form Templates for Excel.
Ad/Art/Plus: Architectural Graphics.
Ad/Art/Plus: Borders.
Ad/Art/Plus: Cartoon Designer.
Ad/Art/Plus: Forms.
Ad/Art/Plus: LaserArt-Borders.
ART EPS: Borders 1.
Art EPS: Cartoon Characters.
ART EPS: Cartoon Critters.
ART EPS: Designs 1.
ART EPS: Designs 2.
ART EPS: Holiday (Christmas).
Art EPS: Industry 1.
ART EPS: Patterns 1.
Art EPS: Restaurant & Foods.
ART EPS: Symbols 1.
ART EPS: Symbols 2.
Art EPS: Trees.
Clip*Video*Art "Animation Effects".
Clip*Video*Art "Presentation Animation".
Invoice & List It for Excel: Time & Billing System.

FreeSoft Co., The, 105 McKinley Rd., Beaver Falls, PA 15010 Tel 412-846-2700; FAX: 412-847-4436.
Titles:
OKyto.
Second Sight BBS.
White Knight.

Frey, Donald R., & Co., Inc., (0-924098), 40 N. Grand Ave., Suite 303, Fort Thomas, KY 41075-1765 Tel 606-441-6566; Toll free: 800-659-3739; FAX: 606-441-7152.
Titles:
Budgetary Control System: BUCS.
Comprehensive Integrated Payroll System: CHIPS.
Comprehensive Utility Billing & Control System: CUBIC.

Friedman Computing & Publishing, 2347 Pine Terr., Sarasota, FL 34231 Tel 813-924-3238; FAX: 813-924-4652.
Titles:
HyperLibrary.

Friendlysoft, Inc., (0-918605), 3638 W. Pioneer Pkwy., Arlington, TX 76013 Tel 817-277-9378; Toll free: 800-527-6530; FAX: 817-277-7126.
Titles:
Friendly Writer with Friendly Speller.
FriendlyRider Speller.
FriendlyWare.
Friendlyware Checkbook.
FriendlyWare PC Arcade.

Frog Peak Music, (0-945996), P.O. Box 1052, Lebanon, NH 03766 Tel 603-448-8837.
Titles:
HMSL.
Soundhack.
The World's Longest Melody.

Front Desk Systems, Div. of Comprehensive Engineering Corp., (0-944896), P.O. Box 178504, San Diego, CA 92177 Tel 619-273-9498; Toll free: 800-877-2917; FAX: 619-483-9428.
Titles:
Front Desk: 104 Rooms.
Front Desk: 600 Rooms.

Front Row Systems, P.O. Box 550346, Atlanta, GA 30355 Tel 404-231-1120; Toll free: 800-864-1120; FAX: 404-261-1350; 3033 Maple Dr., Atlanta, GA 30305.
Titles:
CPA Tickler Database.
Tax Authority.

Frontier Technologies Corp., (0-924107), 10201 N. Port Washington Rd., Mequon, WI 53092-5752 Tel 414-241-4555.
Titles:
Async COMPAC.
C Subroutines.
COMPAC Z.
HDLC/SDLC COMPAC.
Micro Graphic Kernal System: MGKS.
X.25 COMPAC.

Full Phase Software, P.O. Box 17045, Seattle, WA 98107 Tel 206-325-2112.
Titles:
MacAstrologer.

Fuller, M. E., P.O. Box 655, Alamo, CA 94507 Tel 707-746-8087.
Titles:
The Landscaper.

Fuller Computer Systems, Inc., P.O. Box 9222, Mesa, AZ 85214 Tel 602-497-6070; FAX: 602-497-6071.
Titles:
Project D.

Fulton Findings, 1251 W. Sepulveda Blvd., Suite 800, Torrance, CA 90502 Tel 310-548-6358.
Titles:
WeibullSMITH.

Funk Software, (0-924113), 222 Third St., Cambridge, MA 02142 Tel 617-497-6339; Toll free: 800-822-3865; FAX: 617-547-1031.
Titles:
Allways.
InWord.
Noteworthy.
P.D. Queue.
Sideways.
The Worksheet Utilities.

Funsoft, Inc., (0-915149), 591 Constitution Ave., Camarillo, CA 93012-9106; Dist. by: Softsel Computer Products, Inc., 546 N. Oak St., Inglewood, CA 90302 Tel 310-412-1700; Toll free: 800-645-7777; 800-645-7778 (orders only).
Titles:
Flak.
Mad Mines.

Funsten, James W., Pub., 140 Second St., 5th Flr., San Francisco, CA 94105 Tel 415-974-6201.
Titles:
BARE BONES Accounting.
CRISP-R Real Estate Accounting.
CRISP Real Estate Accounting.

Future Visions Software, (0-9623956), 10630 NW Freeway, Houston, TX 77092 Tel 713-682-4212; Dist. by: Dreamhaven Bks. & Art, 1309 Fourth St., SE, Minneapolis, MN 55414 Tel 612-379-8924.
Titles:
Collector's Bookcase.
SF Library.

G&Z Systems, Inc., 22 Saw Mill River Rd., Hawthorne, NY 10532-1533 Tel 914-741-0011; Toll free: 800-333-5373.
Titles:
Dataquick.

GHQ, Ltd., (0-924132), 1082 Grand Oaks Glen, Marietta, GA 30064-5423 Tel 404-423-0700.
Titles:
Dairy Cattle Recordkeeping.

GIS World, Inc., (0-9625063; 1-882610), 155 E. Boardwalk Dr., Suite 250, Fort Collins, CO 80525 Tel 303-223-4848; FAX: 303-223-5700.
Titles:
GIS World Source CD 1996.

G-N-G Software, 919 W. Canadian, Vinita, OK 74301 Tel 918-256-8598.
Titles:
Catalog Card/Labels Program.

GO Graphics, Inc., 18 Ray Ave., Burlington, MA 01803 Tel 617-229-8900; Toll free: 800-237-5588 (outside Massachusetts); FAX: 617-229-2387.
Titles:
Desket Design Edition.
DeskSet PS Edition.

GO Technologies, P.O. Box 4535, Incline Village, NV 89450; 770 Northwood, Suite 10, Incline Village, NV 89450 Tel 702-831-3100.
Titles:
MacTree Plus.

GP Publishing, Inc., (0-87683), 7410 E. 64th St., Tulsa, OK 74133-7505 Tel 918-496-2773; FAX: 918-749-8274. Do not confuse with G P Publishing, Inc. Pontiac, MI.
Titles:
Applications of Logs & Exponentials for the Nuclear Industry.

GP Technologies, 160 Meister Ave., Somerville, NJ 08876 Tel 908-722-7165; Toll free: 800-523-1809; FAX: 908-722-9401.
Titles:
Wheel Ease.

GRC International, Inc., 5383 Hollister Ave., Santa Barbara, CA 93111 Tel 805-964-7724; Toll free: 800-933-5383; FAX: 805-967-7094.
Titles:
GRCCOM/Quest.
LaserGuide: Patron Access Catalog.
LaserQuest.

GRU Development, (1-878830), P.O. Box 181, Jacksonville, AR 72076-0181; 111 Pulaski Dr., Jacksonville, AR 72076 Tel 501-982-0753.
Titles:
Technical Reference Programmers.

GTCO Corp., (0-924144), 7125 Riverwood Dr., Columbia, MD 21046 Tel 410-381-6688; FAX: 410-290-9065.
Titles:
Graphic Analysis Package.

GTEK Development Hardware/Software, P.O. Box 2310, 399 Hwy. 90, Bay Saint Louis, MS 39521-2320 Tel 601-467-8048; Toll free: 800-282-4835; FAX: 601-467-0935.
Titles:
CP/Emulator.
Programmer's Tool Kit.

GW Instruments, Inc., 35 Medford St., Somerville, MA 02143 Tel 617-625-4096; FAX: 617-625-1322.
Titles:
MacAdios Manager II.
MacInstruments.
MacSpeech Lab I.
MacSpeech Lab II.
Superscope.

Gabriel Publishing Co., (0-945659), 1469 Rosena Ave., Madison, OH 44507-1099 Tel 216-428-4409. Do not confuse with Gabriel Publishing in Comfort, TX.
Titles:
Directory of the State Legislature.
Directory of the U.S. Congress.
Directory of U.S. Government Buying Offices.

Gale Research, Inc., Subs. of The Thomson Corp., (0-8103; 0-7876), 835 Penobscot Bldg., Detroit, MI 48226-4094 Tel 313-961-2242; Toll free: 800-877-4253; FAX: 313-961-6083.
Titles:
Companies International IBM CD ROM Plus PK.
Companies International IBM Manual Plus.
Companies International IBM Plus Help.
Companies International IBM 96.
Contemporary Authors CD-ROM DOS-MAC 96 Manual.
Contemporary Authors 96 Mac Help Card.
Discovering Authors, 1995.
Discovering Jobs.
Encyclopedia of Associations CD-ROM 95-1.
Encyclopedia of Associations: National 95 IBM CD ROM.
Gale Business Resource, 1995.
Gale Business Resource, 1995 Box.
Gale Career Guidance System.
Videohound Multimedia 96 CD ROM.

Gamma Productions, Inc., (0-924162), 2130 Sawtelle Blvd., No. 305, Los Angeles, CA 90025 Tel 310-478-6774; FAX: 310-478-7765.
Titles:
Multi-Lingual Scholar.

Gantt Systems, Inc., (0-918607), 16 Pearl St., Metuchen, NJ 08840-1816 Tel 908-494-9550; FAX: 908-321-5203.
Titles:
GANTT LAB MANAGER.
GANTT-PACK: Work Processor.
GANTT SAMPLE LOG.

Gari, Brian, (1-887958), 650 West End Ave., New York, NY 10025 Tel 212-799-2592.
Titles:
The Eddie Cantor Radio Show, 1942-1943.
The Original Complete Carnegie Hall Concert.
The Show That Never Aired.

Garland Publishing, Inc., (0-8240; 0-8153), 717 Fifth Ave., Suite 2500, New York, NY 10022-8102 Tel 212-751-7447; FAX: 212-308-9399; Orders to: 1000A Sherman Ave., Hamden, CT 06514 Tel 203-281-4487; Toll free: 800-627-6273 (orders).
Titles:
HyperCELL, 1995: A Hypermedia Presentation of Cell Biology.

Gaskins, Stern & Assocs., Ltd., 176 Thomas Jefferson Dr., Suite 205, Frederick, MD 21702 Tel 301-698-9777; FAX: 301-698-9779.
Titles:
Paylode.

Gateway Communications, Inc., 2941 Alton Ave., Irvine, CA 92714 Tel 714-553-1555; Toll free: 800-367-6555; FAX: 714-553-1616.
Titles:
G/Async Gateway.
G/Remote Bridge 64.
G/SNA Gateway.
G/X25 Gateway.

Geeslin, Robert H., (Educational Programming), (0-934649), P.O. Box 1717, Sapulpa, OK 74067 Tel 918-224-0065; FAX: 918-224-0005.
Titles:
Cataloger.
Collection Management System: ColMan System.
Donations Tracking.
Facilities Scheduling: Room Reservations.
Library Information Management System: On-Line Catalog-Circulation.
Med-Sheets: With Doctor's Orders.
Route Management: (Trash) Hauler's Billing System.
Warranty (Repair) Tracker.

Gem Island Software, P.O. Box 804, Carlisle, MA 01741 Tel 508-369-6162.
Titles:
The Professional Recipe Manager.
The Recipe Manager.

Gemini Group, (0-9628982), Little Old Farm, 333 Pinebrook Rd., Bedford, NY 10506 Tel 914-764-4938.
Titles:
The Solution Machine So Simple It Works: The Creative Problem Solving Program That Harnesses the Power of Imagery.

GemStar Partnership, (0-922928; 0-929857), P.O. Box 050228, Staten Island, NY 10305-0004 Tel 201-579-5484; FAX: 201-579-5377NY 10305.
Titles:
Action Art.
AIDS: CHOICES.
SPYGRAF.
Superdraw.

General Micro Systems, P.O. Box 44247, Eden Prairie, MN 55344-1247.
Titles:
PC220: VT220 Terminal Emulator.
PC102: Terminal Emulator.
PC4010: Graphics Terminal Emulator.

General Parametrics Corp., (0-932233), 1250 Ninth St., Berkeley, CA 94710 Tel 510-524-3950; Toll free: 800-223-0999; FAX: 510-524-9954.
Titles:
EasyShow 2 for Windows.
PhotoMetric SlideMaker - PrintMaker.
PictureIt.
VideoShow HQ.
VideoShow Presenter.

General Programming, Inc., 2000 W. Hedding St., San Jose, CA 95128 Tel 408-248-5320; FAX: 408-244-9336.
Titles:
PayBreeze.

Generic Computer Products, Inc., (0-918611), P.O. Box 790, Dept. MD-105, Marquette, MI 49855 Tel 906-226-7600; FAX: 906-226-8309.
Titles:
Archive.
CATALOG-MASTER.
Cursor & Keypad Editor: C.A.K.E.
Depreciation-Master II.
F-Trans.
FCEU: File Compress & Encryption Utility.
File Edit.
Financial Pak.
Football.
Football-Picks.
Forms-Kit.
Inte-Print.
INVESTMENT-MASTER.
Loan-Master.
MAIL-PLUS.
Night Rider: Pinball Simulation Game.
PRNSPOOL.
Spin-for-Money.
STOCK-MASTER.

Genium Publishing Corp., (0-931690), 1 Genium Plaza, Schenectady, NY 12304 Tel 518-377-8857; Toll free: 800-243-6486; FAX: 518-377-1891.
Titles:
Chemical Laser Labels.
Chemical Week Buyers' Guide, 1996.
Genium MSDS Collection on CD-ROM.
International Metallic Materials Cross-Reference.
Modern Drafting Practices & Standards Manual on CD-ROM.
MSDS Form.
1-Minute Convection.

Genline CAD/CAM Systems, Div. of Southeastern Die Co., Inc., 343 Salen Gate Dr., Suite 201, Conyers, GA 30208 Tel 404-918-0640; Toll free: 800-358-2388; FAX: 404-593-1180.
Titles:
Genline PC.

GenMicronics, 5900 Shore Blvd., No. 401, Saint Petersburg, FL 33707 Tel 813-345-5020.
Titles:
Financial Decisions.

GEOCOMP Corp., (0-924202), 10 Craig Rd., Acton, MA 01720-5405 Tel 508-635-0012; Toll free: 800-822-2669; FAX: 508-635-0266.
Titles:
GEOCONTOUR.
GEOFLOW.
GEOGRAF Level One.
GEOSIN.
GEOSLOPE.
SI Plus.
TechWords.

Geocomp, Ltd., (0-945851), 749 Van Gordon Ct., Golden, CO 80401-4715 Tel 303-233-1250; FAX: 303-233-4837.
Titles:
EASYDIJ.
HOTDIJ.
Shotpoint.
Sumdij.
Timecard.

Geodesic Pubns., P.O. Box 956068, Duluth, GA 30136 Tel 404-822-0566; FAX: 404-339-9995.
Titles:
Illumilink.

George Lithograph, (0-924204), 650 Second St., San Francisco, CA 94107 Tel 415-397-2400; FAX: 415-267-4626.
Titles:
atp: Code Free Typesetting.

Geostat Systems International, Inc., (0-928236), P.O. Box 1193, Golden, CO 80402 Tel 303-277-0070; FAX: 303-278-4749.
Titles:
BLKPLOT, BLKMAP: BLOCKPLOT, BLOCKMAP.
CMINER.
COMPOS.
CORREL.
CPRS: Coal Preparation Response Surfaces.
DCLUST.
DIGIT.
ECONRISK.
GENL3D.
GRIDDER.
HGRAM.
HISTO.
IN2CAD.
ISOPOLY.
ITGAUSS.
KRIGE3.
KRIJAC.
KRIREC.
KRIVAR.
LIMIT3.
LIMNEW.
MAP3D.
MineORE.
MRCS.
OREntry.
PENPLOT.
PITKOR.
PLOT2D.
POLYGON.
POLYSIM.
PREPIT.
PREPLOT.
PSTPIT.
QuickEST.
REMOTE.
REPORT.
RESPIT.
ROTATE.
SCREEN.
SECT.
SelectORE.
SIM3.
SIM3C.
TGAUSS.
THREEDCOOR.
TOXIPAC.
VARCUT.
VARIO3.
VOLUME.
VOLUMETRICS.

Gestetner Corp., 599 W. Putnam Ave., Greenwich, CT 06836 Tel 203-625-7600; Toll free: 800-431-2455.
Titles:
Gestetner Integration Manager.

Ghost Software, Inc., 12600 S. Belcher Rd., Suite 103D, Largo, FL 34643 Tel 813-530-7400; Toll free: 800-443-5806; FAX: 813-530-9061.
Titles:
Payroll Manager.
Video Store Manage for the MAC.
Video Store Manager.
Video Store Manager Plus.

Gibbs & Assocs., 5400 Tech Cir., Moorpark, CA 93021 Tel 805-523-0004; FAX: 805-523-0006.
Titles:
The Gibbs System.

Gibson Research Corp., (1-880814), 35 Journey, Aliso Viejo, CA 92656-3333 Tel 714-830-2200; FAX: 714-830-0300.
Titles:
SpinRite II.

Giffler, Bernard, Assocs., 34 Linda Ln., Warrington, PA 18976 Tel 215-343-0194.
Titles:
Material & Resource Requirements Planning System (MR2PS-II).
Product Costing (Quotation) System.
Shop Floor Control.

Gimpel Software, 3207 Hogarth Ln., Collegeville, PA 19426 Tel 610-584-4261; FAX: 610-584-4266.
Titles:
The C Shroud.
C-Vision for C/C Plus Plus.
FlexeLint for C/C Plus Plus.
PC-lint for C/C Plus Plus.

Gjetaas, Inc., 7251 Mount Baker Hwy., Deming, WA 98244 Tel 206-599-2418.
Titles:
WINFIN - Financial Analysis for Windows: Investment Analysis.

Gleiter Computer Services, Inc., (0-9622124), 1324 New Garden Rd., Greensboro, NC 27410 Tel 910-294-3338.
Titles:
Household Inventory System.

Glenco Engineering, Inc., (0-924216), 270 Lexington Dr., Buffalo Grove, IL 60089; Toll free: 800-562-2543; FAX: 708-808-0313.
Titles:
Communications Library.
Coupon Padlock.
CRYPT LIBRARY.
HDCopy.
HDPRTCT.
Key Tag.
Padlock II.
PC Padlock.
SAFEGUARD.
Windows with Data Entry: Window Library Tools.

Global Market Information, Inc., (0-917319), 56 Pine St., New York, NY 10005 Tel 212-422-1600; FAX: 212-248-9162.
Titles:
Dial-Data.
Track/Online.

Global MediaNet Corp., 12121 Wilshire Blvd., No. 1001, Los Angeles, CA 90025 Tel 310-442-7144; FAX: 310-442-7128.
Titles:
Jack's Adventures Beyond the Beanstalk.
Leonard Nimoy Science Fiction.

Gold Hill, Inc., (0-917589), 26 Landsdowne St., Cambridge, MA 02139 Tel 617-621-3300; FAX: 617-621-0656.
Titles:
GCLISP: Golden Common LISP.
GCLISP 286 Developer.
GCLrun.
GoldWorks II.

Golightly Cos., (0-925010), 22 Central St., Hingham, MA 02043 Tel 617-749-7622; FAX: 617-749-9221.
Titles:
Labsearch.

Good News Marketing, Inc., 18 Peacock Farm Rd., Lexington, MA 02173-6330.
Titles:
Market Nicher.

Good Software Corp., (0-924233), 4125 Keller Springs, Suite 156, Dallas, TX 75244 Tel 214-713-6370; Toll free: 800-925-5700; FAX: 214-713-6308.
Titles:
Amortizer Plus: Professionals Count on It.
Easy Loans.
Easy Time & Billing.
REMS Investor 3000: Investment Property Analysis.
REMS Lessor 3000: Lease-By-Lease & Property Case Flow Analysis.
REMS Property Manager: The Efficient System of Tenant & Property Management.
Twenty-Five in One SoftCartridge: Software Equivalents of HP Fonts.

Goodman Lauren Publishing, (0-9630516), 11661 San Vicente Blvd., Suite 505, Los Angeles, CA 90049 Tel 310-820-5554; FAX: 310-820-8341.
Titles:
The Reunion Planner.

Gospel Films, Inc., (1-55568), Box 455, Muskegon, MI 49443-0455 Tel 616-773-3361; Toll free: 800-253-0413; FAX: 616-777-1847.
Titles:
Conflict in Jerusalem: Jesus' Last Days.
Dead Sea Scrolls Revealed.
Logos Bible Atlas.
Logos Bible Clips.
Logos Bible Crosswords.
Logos Bible Software Add-On Modules: ASV - American Standard Version (1901).
Logos Bible Software Add-On Modules: BYZ Greek - The New Testament in the Original Greek According to the Byzantine-Majority Textform.
Logos Bible Software Add-On Modules: BHS (Hebrew) - Biblia Hebraica Stuttgartensia.
Logos Bible Software Add-On Modules: Greek 4-Pack - NA-UBS, BYZ, TR Scrivener's, TR Stephen's.
Logos Bible Software Add-On Modules: NASB - New American Bible.
Logos Bible Software Add-On Modules: NA-UBS Greek - The Greek New Testament.

Logos Bible Software Add-On Modules: TR Scrivener's - Textus Receptus Scrivener's 1891 (Greek).
Logos Bible Software Collection.
Logos Bible Software: KJV-ASV American Standard Verison.
Logos Bible Software: KJV-NASB The New American Standard Bible.
Logos Bible Software: KJV-NCV The New Century Version.
Logos Bible Software: KJV-NIV The New International Version.
Logos Bible Software: KJV-NKJV New King James Version.
Logos Bible Software: KJV-NRSV The New Revised Standard Version.
Logos Bible Software: KJV-RSV The Revised Standard Version.
Logos Bible Software: KJV-The King James Version.
The One-Minute Bible for Windows.
6 Days of Creation Screen Saver.

Gotoless Conversion, P.O. Box 835910, Richardson, TX 75083 Tel 214-625-2323; Toll free: 800-617-2323; FAX: 214-370-2612.
Titles:
BAS-C: BASIC to C Converter.
BAS-C 286: BASIC to C Translator.
BAS-C386 XENIX: Basic to C Translator.
BAS-PAS: BASIC to Pascal Converter.

Grafica Multimedia, Inc., 1777 Borel Pl., Suite 500, San Mateo, CA 94402 Tel 415-358-5555.
Titles:
A House Divided: The Lincoln-Douglas Debates.

Grafpoint, 1485 Saratoga Ave., San Jose, CA 95129 Tel 408-446-1919; Toll free: 800-426-2230; FAX: 408-446-0666.
Titles:
TGRAF - TNET: TGRAF - TNET - 07, 4200, 05, 11, 15.
TGRAF for Windows: TGRAF-05 Plus & TGRAF-07.
TGRAF-X: Tektronix Terminal Emulation Software.
X for Workgroups.
X-One for DOS: X Server Software for PC's.
X-One for Windows.

Graftech, 99 Jacklin Ct., Milpitas, CA 95035-3565.
Titles:
Premiere Video Rental Management System.

Graham Software Co., 8609 Ingalls Cir., Arvada, CO 80003 Tel 303-422-0757.
Titles:
Disk Ranger - Ranger Reader.

Granite Planet, 2040 N. Milwaukee Ave., Chicago, IL 60647 Tel 312-278-8868.
Titles:
Santa's on His Way (to Your House): A Personalized Electronic Storybook.

Graphic Applications, Inc., 7031 Halpert Pike Rd., Suite 101, Greensboro, NC 27409 Tel 910-852-1608; Toll free: 800-365-7883; FAX: 910-855-6931.
Titles:
Embroidery Expert.
Embroidery Plus.
Laser Positive.

Graphic Software Systems, Inc., Div. of Spectragraphics Corp., (0-924250), 9590 SW Gemini Dr., Beaverton, OR 97005 Tel 503-641-2200; Toll free: 800-800-9599; FAX: 503-643-8642.
Titles:
Graphics Development Toolkit for DOS.
GSS*CGM.
GSS-Toolkit Kernel System.
PC-Xview.

Graphware, Inc., (0-924253), P.O. Box 373, Middletown, OH 45042 Tel 513-424-6733.
Titles:
Charts Unlimited.

Gray, Herbi, (0-9608406), P.O. Box 2343, Olympia, WA 98507 Tel 206-491-4138.
Titles:
Handweavers' Input Program for the Commodore 64.

Great Game Products, (0-935307), 8804 Chalon Dr., Bethesda, MD 20817 Tel 301-365-3297; Toll free: 800-426-3748.
Titles:
Bridge Baron II.
5 Weeks to Winning Bridge.
Micro Bridge Companion.
Play Bridge with Dorothy Truscott.
Play Bridge with Sheinwold.

Great Plains Software, (0-924261), 1701 SW 38th St., Fargo, ND 58103 Tel 701-281-0550; Toll free: 800-456-0025; FAX: 701-282-4826.
Titles:
Great Plains Accounting Series: Accounts Payable.
Great Plains Accounting Series: Accounts Receivable.
Great Plains Accounting Series: General Ledger.
Great Plains Accounting Series: Inventory.
Great Plains Accounting Series: Network Manager.
Great Plains Accounting Series: Order Entry with Point of Sale.
Great Plains Accounting Series: Payroll.
Great Plains Accounting Series: Purchase Order.
Great Plains Executive Advisor.
Great Plains Import Manager.
Great Plains Report Maker Plus.
Job Cost.
Plains & Simple One-Write Accounting.
Printers Inc.

Great Wave Software, 5353 Scotts Valley Dr., Scotts Valley, CA 95066-3523 Tel 408-438-1990; FAX: 408-438-7171.
Titles:
ConcertWare+.
ConcertWare+ MIDI.
ConcertWare+ Music, Vol. 1: Instrumental Favorites.
ConcertWare+ Music, Vol. 2: Die Kunst der Fuge.
ConcertWare+ Music, Vol. 3: Christmas Favorites.
ConcertWare+ Music, Vol. 4: Early Music.
ConcertWare+ Music, Vol. 5: Classical Selections.
ConcertWare+ Music, Vol. 6: Popular Music 1900-1930.
ConcertWare+ Music, Vol. 7: Jazz with a French Twist.
Crystal Paint.
Terpsichore.

Greenleaf Software, Inc., 16479 Dallas Pkwy., Suite 570, Dallas, TX 75248 Tel 214-248-2561; Toll free: 800-523-9830; FAX: 214-248-7830.
Titles:
Greenleaf ArchiveLib.
Greenleaf Comm Plus Plus.
Greenleaf CommLib Level 2.
Greenleaf DataWindows.
Greenleaf Financial Mathlib.
Greenleaf MakeForm.
Greenleaf SuperFunctions.
Greenleaf Viewcomm.

Greentree Group, Inc., (0-928245), RD No.1, Box 1044, Leesport, PA 19533.
Titles:
Find It.
Parables Plus.
Purposeful Patterns.
Purposeful Symbols.
Search!
Verbal Reasoning.

Gregg/McGraw-Hill, (0-07), 1221 Sixth Ave., New York, NY 10020 Tel 212-512-2000; Toll free: 800-722-4726.
Titles:
Accounting Applications for the Microcomputer.
Computer Applications for Introduction to Business.
McGraw-Hill Database.
McGraw-Hill Integrated Software: Spreadsheet, Database, Graphing, Word Processing.
McGraw-Hill Spreadsheet.
McGraw-Hill Word Processing.
Tutorials in Applied Physics: Self-Study Modules.

GRiD Systems Corp., (0-924270), P.O. Box 57005, Irvine, CA 92619-7005; Toll free: 800-222-4743.
Titles:
GRiD Debug.
GRiDPrint/GRiDPlot/GRiDFile/GRiDWrite/ GRiDMaster/GRiDPaint/GRiDTask.
GRiDReformat.

GRIST On-Line, P.O. Box 20805, Columbus Cir. Sta., New York, NY 10023-1496 Tel 212-787-2861.
Titles:
Gleanings: Uncollected Poems of the Fifties.
Poems of the Place.

Grossman & Assocs., Inc., 5 Dunlap Court, Savoy, IL 61874; Toll free: 800-779-1978; FAX: 217-398-1983.
Titles:
Commodity Merchandising.
Grossman Accounting Software: for the Agribusiness Industry.
Inventory Control.
LAND TRUST.
Order Entry - Invoicing.

Groundwater Services, Inc., (1-882713), 5252 Westchester, Suite 270, Houston, TX 77005 Tel 713-663-6600; FAX: 713-663-6546.
Titles:
RBCA Tool Kit: RBCA Spreadsheet System.

Gryphon Microproducts, (0-924278), 12808 Ruxton Rd., Silver Spring, MD 20904 Tel 301-946-2585.
Titles:
DBRx.

GTM Software, 293 E. 950 S., Orem, UT 84058 Tel 801-235-7000; FAX: 801-235-7099.
Titles:
Back-It for Windows.
Back-It 4.
Collect-a-Debt.
Collections Plus.
OPTune.
Q-DOS 3.
RAPID: File Manager for Windows.

Guenzi Surveys, P.O. Box 127, No. 38CDR, Glendive, MT 59330 Tel 406-365-3527.
Titles:
CogoMaster II.

PUBLISHER/TITLE INDEX

Gulf Publishing Co., (0-87201; 0-932012; 0-87719; 0-88415), P.O. Box 2608, Houston, TX 77252-2608 Tel 713-520-4444; Toll free: 800-231-6275 (except Alaska & Hawaii); 800-392-4390 (in Texas); FAX: 713-525-4647.
Titles:
BiWeibullSMITH.
CHAMPIPE: Piping Materials Inventory & Control.
Chemcalc 2: Gas & Liquid Flow Calculation.
Chemcalc 3: Heat Transfer Calculations.
Chemcalc 4: Multiphase Flow & General Fluid Calculations.
Chemcalc 5: Heat Exchanger Network Optimization.
Chemcalc 6: Heat Exchanger Design (Shell-&-Tube).
Chemcalc 7: Chemical Compound Databank.
Chemcalc 8: Centrifugal Pump Selection & Rating.
Chemcalc 10: Heat & Mass Transfer Equilibrium Calculations.
Chemcalc 11: Amine Process Simulator.
Chemcalc 12: Flare Network Analysis.
Chemcalc 14: Boiler Efficiency Analysis.
Chemcalc 15: Centrifugal Compressor Design & Rating.
Chemcalc 16: Liquid-Liquid Extraction.
Chemcalc 17: EPA Storage Tank Emissions Analysis.
Column: Multicomponent Separation Processes.
Instrucalc.
Instruwire: Electrical & Instrument Wiring Design & Documentation.
MicroOHMTADS (Oil & Hazardous Materials Technical Assistance Database).
MonteCarloSMITH.
Page's CONCEPTUAL COST ESTIMATOR.
Petrocalc 14: Horizontal & Vertical Borehole Modeling.
Petrocalc 2: Drilling Engineering.
Petrocalc 3: Reservoir Economics & Evaluation.
Petrocalc 6: Wellbore Stimulation.
Petrocalc 7: Applied Well Log Analysis.
Petrocalc 12: Joint Interest Billing with dBASE III+.
Petrocalc 13: Quik-Flo Gas Volume & Flow Calculation.
Pipecalc 1: Practical Pipeline Hydraulics.
Pipemate.
PROJCON: Project Management & Control System.
SuperSMITH.
Thermosim: Module 1: EQUIL: Thermodynamic Properties & Process Simulator.
3D/SIM: 3D Petroleum Reservoir Simulation for Vert. Horiz. & Dev. Wells.
TMA-Workstation: Heat Exchanger Workstation.
TPE Pipeline Estimator: Cost Estimating of Underground Gas Transmission Pipelines & Gas Gathering Systems.
Triflex: Pipe Stress Analysis.
VisualSMITH.
WeibullSMITH.

Gupta Technologies, Inc., (1-881253), 1040 Marsh Rd., Menlo Park, CA 94025 Tel 415-321-9500; FAX: 415-321-5471.
Titles:
Quest.
SQL Network Product Line: (SQL Network for DB2); (SQL Network for Oracle).
SQLBase Server.
SQLWindows.

H&D Leasing, 5500 Mabry Dr., Clovis, NM 88101 Tel 505-762-3324.
Titles:
Church Stewardship Program.
Direct Mail.
Fuel Tax Specialist.
Keep on Trucking.
MacNurse.

HBO & Co., Inc., (0-928499), 301 Perimeter Ctr. N., Atlanta, GA 30346 Tel 404-393-6000.
Titles:
Case Mix Library.
Clinical Cost Accounting.
COSTREP+.

hDC Computer Corp., 6742 185th Ave. N.E., Redmond, WA 98052 Tel 206-885-5550; FAX: 206-881-9770.
Titles:
HDC FirstApps.
HDC Windows Express.

HEC Software, Inc., (0-928424), 3471 S. 550 W., Bountiful, UT 84010 Tel 801-295-7054; Toll free: 800-333-0054; FAX: 801-295-7088.
Titles:
Workplace Vocabulary: Job Specific Literacy.

HEL Custom Software, Inc., (0-928246), 485 Devon Park Dr., No. 103, Wayne, PA 19087-1815 Tel 610-293-1855.
Titles:
Clinic Management System (CMS).
HUPBEN: Hospital & University Personal Benefits System.
PAMS: Political Activist Monitoring System.
PILAW: Personal Injury Legal Care Management System.
RPMAS: Residential Property Management Accounting System.
SOD: Son of Donor Contribution Management System.

HFK Software, (0-918813), 68 Wells Rd., Lincoln, MA 01773 Tel 617-259-0059; FAX: 617-259-0626.
Titles:
The QWERTY Text Merge.
QWERTY Word Processor.

HMS Computer Co., 3422 Lakeshore Cove, Chaska, MN 55318-1021 Tel 612-368-7512.
Titles:
Mortgage Loan Calculator.
ProClass.
Professional Warranty System.
Prospect Tracking System.

Ha, Khanh, (0-9624854), 14912 Village Gate Dr., Silver Spring, MD 20906 Tel 301-598-0557.
Titles:
EASY TABLE: An Operation Manual.

Hakotev Systems, P.O. Box 612, Provo, UT 84603-0612 Tel 801-377-2045; Toll free: 800-347-1588; FAX: 801-375-9063.
Titles:
Hakotev.

Hall Design, (0-924312), 250 Maple Ave., Wilmette, IL 60091 Tel 312-337-1612; FAX: 312-337-2721.
Titles:
RXWRITER.

Hamilton Software, Inc., 6432 E. Mineral Pl., Englewood, CO 80112 Tel 303-770-9607; Toll free: 800-733-9607.
Titles:
Easy ROR.
FUNDWATCH PLUS.
The Investor's Accountant.
Market Strategist.
MARKETWATCH.
Portfolio Analyzer.

Hancock Techtronics, Subs. of Radio Shack, (0-924323), 101 E. Main St., Hancock, MD 21750 Tel 301-678-6000.
Titles:
Stock Portfolio.

Hanley-Wood, Inc., One Thomas Cir., Suite 600, Washington, DC 20005 Tel 202-452-0800.
Titles:
Guide to Building Products from Builder Magazine, 1996.

Hansco Information Technologies, Inc., (0-924328), P.O. Box 477, 185 West Ave., Suite 304, Ludlow, MA 01056 Tel 413-547-8991; Toll free: 800-548-9754.
Titles:
AdPack Classified Management System.
Compu-Crete.
Construction Management.
System MM.
Termulator.

Hansen Research & Development Corp., (0-924330), 6042 W. Bellfort, Houston, TX 77035 Tel 713-723-8129.
Titles:
User Form.
User Help.
User Menu.
User Message.

Harcourt Brace & Co., Subs. of Harcourt General Corp., (0-15), 1250 Sixth Ave., San Diego, CA 92101 Tel 619-231-6616; Toll free: 800-346-8648; 800-543-1918; 800-237-2665; FAX: 619-699-6320; 555 Academic Ct., San Antonio, TX 78204 Tel 210-299-1061; 1627 Woodland Ave., Austin, TX 78741 Tel 512-440-5700; Trade Dept. Customer Service, 6277 Sea Harbor Dr., Orlando, FL 32887; P.O. Box 819077, Dallas, TX 75381-9077 Tel 214-245-1118; 7555 Caldwell Ave., Chicago, IL 60648 Tel 312-647-8822; 3551 Esters Blvd., Irving, TX 75063.
Titles:
California Verbal Learning Test (CVLT) Research Edition.
Computer Resource Guide, Third Edition: Principles of Accounting.
Microcomputer Use.
The Psychology Experimenter.
SHANE Augmentative Communication Series.
Statistics for Business & Economics.
WAIS-R Microcomputer Assisted Interpretive Report: D(WAIS-R Micro).
WISC-R Microcomputer-Assisted Interpretive Report: WISC-R Micro.

Hartley Courseware, Inc., Div. of Jostens Learning Corp., (1-55582; 1-56498), 9920 Pacific Heights Blvd., No. 500, San Diego, CA 92121-4334.
Titles:
The Cognitive Rehabilitation Series: Categorization, Sequencing, Association, Memory, Authoring Program.
E-Z Pilot II: Training Package.

Hartley Data Systems, Ltd., (0-924344), 1807 Glenview Rd., Glenview, IL 60025 Tel 708-724-9280.
Titles:
MP System.

Harvard Assocs., Inc., (0-924346), 10 Holworthy St., Cambridge, MA 02138 Tel 617-492-0660; Toll free: 800-776-4610; FAX: 617-492-4610.
Titles:
Desk Toppers.
Mac Manager.
MacManager.

HARVEST COMPUTER SYSTEMS, INC.

Harvest Computer Systems, Inc., Subs. of FMS Marketing, Inc., (0-924349), 118 N. Harrison St., Alexandria, IN 46001 Tel 317-724-4429; Toll free: 800-284-8483; FAX: 317-724-5073.
Titles:
Beef Manager.
Business Horizon: Small Business Accounting.
Depreciation Log.
Field Manager.
Hog Manager.
Home Inventory Manager.
Horizon Accounting.
Horizon Inventory.
Horizon Invoicing.
Horizon Order/Inventory.
Horizon Payroll: For IBM.
Machinery Manager.
TechniChart.

Hasbro, Inc., 1027 Newport Ave., Pawtucket, RI 02862 Tel 401-727-5612.
Titles:
Mr. Potato Head Saves Veggie Valley.
Playskool Puzzles.

Haskell, E.F., Software, Div. of E. F. Haskell & Assocs., Inc., (0-928247), 9700 N. 91st St., Suite C130, Scottsdale, AZ 85258-5036 Tel 602-391-0740; Toll free: 800-732-3688; FAX: 602-391-2122.
Titles:
Client Write-Up.
Fixed Asset Management Accounting System.
TKR 5.

Hauppauge Computer Works, (0-928637), 91 Cabot Ct., Hauppauge, NY 11788-3706.
Titles:
87 Software Pak.

HavenTree Software, Ltd., P.O. Box 470, Fineview, NY 13640 Tel 613-544-6035; Toll free: 800-267-0668; FAX: 613-544-9632.
Titles:
EasyFlow.

Hawk Scientific Systems, Inc., 170 Kinnelon Rd., Suite 8, Kinnelon, NJ 07405 Tel 201-838-6292.
Titles:
Molecular Presentation Graphics (MPG).

Hawkeye Grafix, (0-924354), P.O. Box 1400, Oldsmar, FL 34677 Tel 813-855-8687; FAX: 813-854-1948.
Titles:
BASIC Windows.
Business Board System.
COMMX.
COMMX-M.
CONSOLX.
DES-PAC.
Inside Trac.
Programmers' PAC 1 Z80 Assembler.
Quick Base.
XTERM.

Hayes Microcomputer Products, Inc., (0-924356), P.O. Box 105203, Atlanta, GA 30348 Tel 404-449-8791; FAX: 404-441-1238.
Titles:
InterBridge.
Smartcom Two.
Smartcom II for the Apple Macintosh.
Smartcom III.

Headbone Interactive, (1-886503), 1520 Bellevue Ave., Seattle, WA 98122 Tel 206-323-0073; FAX: 206-323-0188.
Titles:
AlphaBonk Farm.

Headway Solutions, P.O. Box 1027, Simsbury, CT 06070 Tel 203-658-7789.
Titles:
The Micro Integrated Planner.

Health & Habitation, Inc., (0-924358), 1938 E. Santa Rita Dr., Sierra Vista, AZ 85635-3336.
Titles:
Chubby Checker.

Health Professions Div./McGraw-Hill, Inc., Div. of McGraw-Hill, Inc., (0-07), 1221 Avenue of the Americas, 28th Flr., New York, NY 10020 Tel 212-512-4484; Toll free: 800-262-4729 (Individuals); 800-722-4726 (Bookstores, Libraries & Distributors).
Titles:
Harrison's CD-ROM - Harrison's Plus.

HealthCare Communications, 210 Gateway, Suite 200, Lincoln, NE 68505 Tel 402-466-8100; Toll free: 800-627-4344; FAX: 402-466-9044.
Titles:
ChiroMac.
DentalMac.
FilePad.
MediMac.
PowerForms.

Heizer Software, P.O. Box 232019, Pleasant Hill, CA 94523 Tel 510-943-7667; Toll free: 800-888-7667; FAX: 510-943-6882.
Titles:
Chinese Clip Art.
CompileIt!
MasterScript: Dedicated to the Flawless Scripting.
Payroll Partner.
Small Business Accounting System.
Statistical Macro Package.
System Installation Tracker.
2001 Quotes.
WindowScript: The Interface Design Studio.

Helmsman Corp., 666 Plainsboro Rd., Suite 505, Plainsboro, NJ 08536 Tel 609-275-9416; FAX: 609-275-6512.
Titles:
HELMSMAN for Windows.

Helu Software Corp., (0-924296), 18232 N. 66th Ln., Glendale, AZ 85308-1013.
Titles:
HELU Accounts Payable.
HELU General Ledger.
HELU Payroll.
Inventory Control.
Perfect Balance.
Property Management.

Hersey Micro Consulting, Inc., (0-933737), P.O. Box 811686, Boca Raton, FL 33481-1686 Tel 407-994-3829.
Titles:
FANSI-Console: The Integrated Console Utility.
Revise.

Hershey Consultants, Inc., 570 W. DeKalb Pike, No. 108, King of Prussia, PA 19406-3070 Tel 610-962-0130; FAX: 610-962-0162.
Titles:
H.C.I. Phone Biller.

Hertzler Systems, Inc., 17482 Eisenhower Dr. N., Goshen, IN 46526 Tel 219-533-0571; FAX: 219-533-3885.
Titles:
CMS/Advantage.
GageTrol: Gage Calibration & GR&R Software System.
GageTrol NET: GR & R Software System Network Version.
Q-Track Corrective Action & Inspection Software.
QA/S Net Statistical Process Control Software: Full System: Network Version.
QA/S Statistical Process Control Software: Defect Management System.
QA/S Statistical Process Control Software: Full System.
QA-S Variable Process Capability System: Short Run & Variable SPC.

Hessel Group, The, (0-9636296), 44 Old Ridgefield Rd., Wilton, CT 06897 Tel 203-762-0365; FAX: 203-834-9625.
Titles:
Domestic Relocation Gross-Up Procedure.
Domestic Relocation Tracking System (DRTS).
Lump-Sum.

Hewlett-Packard Co., (0-9612030), 3000 Hanover St., Palo Alto, CA 94304 Tel 408-746-5000; Toll free: 800-367-4772.
Titles:
AC Circuit Analysis.
Action Games.
Advanced Programming ROM.
AdvanceLink.
Adventure.
Assembler ROM.
BARON: The Real Estate Simulation.
BASIC Programmer's Library.
Basic Statistics & Data Manipulation.
BPI Accounts Payable.
BPI Accounts Receivable.
BPI General Accounting.
BPI Inventory Control.
BPI Job Cost.
BPI Payroll.
BPI Personal Accounting System.
Calculator HP-UX.
The Calendar.
Charting Gallery.
COBOL.
Compiled BASIC.
Condor 1.
Condor 3.
Context MBA.
Cross Reference Utility.
Cutthroats.
Data Communications.
Data Grapher 200.
DataComm Software.
DataFax.
Datebook II.
dBASE II.
Deadline.
Deluxe VisiCalc.
Digital Filter Design.
Dow Jones Spreadsheet Link.
Drawing Gallery.
Electronic Disk ROM.
Enchanter.
Executive MemoMaker.
File-80.
File Manager.
Financial Calculator.
Financial Decisions.
Forecasting.
Forms Master.
FORTRAN.
Galaxy Patrol.
The Gallery Collection.
Gallery Picture Library.
Games.
Games II.
Games-200.
General Statistics.
Graphics Editor 200.
The Graphics Gallery.
Graphics Presentations.
GraphPlan.
Graphwriter Basic Set.
GW-BASIC.
Hewlett-Packard ColorPro Graphics Plotter.
The Hitchhiker's Guide to the Galaxy.
Home Budget Manager.
HP AdvanceWrite Plus.
HP Softfonts.

HP TechWriter.
HP-UX BASIC.
HP-UX C Compiler.
HP-UX Development System.
I/O ROM.
Icon Design System.
Infidel.
Information Management (IMPac).
Lattice C Compiler.
Linear Programming.
Linear Systems Analysis.
The List Manager.
MailMerge.
Mass Storage ROM.
Math.
Matrix ROM.
MemoMaker.
MicroPlan.
MicroPlan Consolidation Module.
Microsoft Word.
MicroTrak.
MIKSAM ROM.
Milestone.
Milky Way Merchant.
Millionaire: The Stock Market Simulation.
MONITOR-IBM PC.
MultiMate.
Multiplan.
Numerical Analysis Library.
PASCAL.
Personal Card File.
Personal Datebook.
PFS:FILE & PFS:REPORT.
PFS:GRAPH.
PFS:WRITE.
Planetfall.
The Planner.
Plotter-Printer ROM.
Plotter ROM.
Portfolio Management.
Professional Communications.
Programmer's Tools.
Project Management.
Rags to Riches Ledger.
Rags to Riches Payables.
Rags to Riches Receivables.
Rags to Riches Sales.
Regression Analysis.
Ricochet.
Sargon III.
Series 100-BASIC.
Sorcerer.
The Speller.
SpellStar.
Starcross.
Statistics Library.
Surveying.
Suspect.
Suspended.
Temple of Apshai.
Term-80.
Text Editing.
Text Editor-200.
TK! Solver.
Touch Games I.
Touchscreen Programmer's Tools.
Transend COMplete.
Tycoon: The Commodities Market Simulation.
Type-a-Line.
VisiCalc.
VisiCalc PLUS.
VT 100 Terminal Emulator.
Waveform Analysis.
Winning Deal.
The Witness.
Word-80.
WordStar.
The Writer.
Zork I.
Zork II.
Zork III.

Hexcraft, Inc., 48 Brattle St., Cambridge, MA 02238 Tel 617-876-5570.
Titles:
Fact-Stractor.
MacBraille.

Heyman, Alfred J., P.O. Box 50087, Nashville, TN 37205 Tel 615-352-0490; FAX: 615-352-0491.
Titles:
SST: The Seek Stopper.

Hi Tech Expressions, Inc., 584 Broadway, Suite 509, New York, NY 10012 Tel 212-941-1224; Toll free: 800-447-6543; FAX: 212-941-1521.
Titles:
Astro-Grover.
AwardWare.
Big Bird's Special Delivery.
Ernie's Big Splash.
Ernie's Magic Shapes.
Grover's Animal Adventure.

High Caliber Systems, Inc., (0-934899), 171 Madison Ave., Suite 806, New York, NY 10016 Tel 212-684-5553; FAX: 212-532-2362.
Titles:
peopleBASE.

High Mountain Pr., Inc., (0-934605; 1-56690), 2530 Camino Entrada, Santa Fe, NM 87505-4835 Tel 505-471-8822; FAX: 505-438-9633. Do not confuse with High Mountain Publishing, Inc. in Irasburg, VT.
Titles:
Inside MapInfo.
101 ArcView/Avenue Scripts: The Disk.
101 MDL Commands Disks.

High Performance Systems, Inc., 45 Lyme Rd., Suite 300, Hanover, NH 03755 Tel 603-643-9636; Toll free: 800-332-1202; FAX: 603-643-9502.
Titles:
Eightthink: The Visual Thinking Tool for the 90s.

High Technology Software Products, Inc., (0-924391), P.O. Box 60406, Oklahoma City, OK 73146 Tel 405-848-0480; FAX: 405-848-0489.
Titles:
Doctor's Office Companion.
Gusher.
Harmonic Motion Workshop.
The Store Manager.

Highland Software, Inc., P.O. Box 555, Atlantic Highlands, NJ 07716 Tel 908-291-2991.
Titles:
LABELS + FORMS.
Printer Genius.
Printer Genius: Printer Driver.

Hilgraeve, Inc., (0-924396), 111 Conant Ave., Suite A, Monroe, MI 48161 Tel 313-243-0576; Toll free: 800-826-2760; FAX: 313-243-0645.
Titles:
HyperACCESS/5.

Hilton Android Corp., (0-925362), 35 Esplanade, Irvine, CA 92715 Tel 714-651-8024; Dist. by: American Software, 502 E. Anthony Dr., Urbana, IL 61801 Tel 217-384-2050; Toll free: 800-225-7941; Dist. by: Comprehend Software Distributors, 23151 Verdugo, No. 115, Laguna Hills, CA 92653 Tel 714-581-7677.
Titles:
Robot Readers: The Three Bears (Goldilocks).

HindSight, P.O. Box 4242, Highland Ranch, CO 80126 Tel 303-791-3770.
Titles:
InView.
InVue.

Hinrichs Software, 2116 SE 377th Ave., Washougal, WA 98671-9732 Tel 360-835-2983.
Titles:
FontPrint.
Fourier Analysis & Synthesis.
Mandelbrot/Julia Set.
Multi-Variable Regression Analysis.
Word Processor-Form Letters.

Hinsch, H. M., & Co., Inc., 347 Clinton St., Brooklyn, NY 11231 Tel 718-237-1977; FAX: 718-237-1990.
Titles:
Hinsch Time Planner.

Historical Enterprises, (0-9639502), 12003 Ridge Knoll Dr., No. 12, Fairfax, VA 22033 Tel 703-591-2522.
Titles:
Ambrose's Chronology of History.

Hobar Pubns., Div. of Hobar Enterprises, Inc., (0-913163; 1-55797), 1234 Tiller Ln., Saint Paul, MN 55112 Tel 612-633-3170; FAX: 612-633-2020.
Titles:
Bill of Material Record.
Certificates & Awards Designer.
Chains & Belts.
Contest Tabulator & Scorecard Program I.
Copyfitting.
E-Z Plot.
Farm Business Analysis.
FFA Leadership Record.
Halftone Computer.
Home Inventory.
Ink Trapping Computer.
Management Calendar Creator.
The Sale Manager.
Small Engine Part Numbers.
Tecumseh Part Numbers, Craftsman 3 to 10 H.P.
VO-AG & FFA SOE Placement & Agribusiness Record.

Holden-Day, Inc., (0-8162), 1259 SW 14th St., Boca Raton, FL 33486-5311 Tel 407-750-9229.
Titles:
Microsolve - Network Flow Programming.
Microsolve Operations Research.
What's Best!/Academic.

Hollow Earth Publishing, (1-879196), P.O. Box 1355, Boston, MA 02205; Toll free: 800-473-8735; 708 White Cedar Blvd., Portsmouth, NH 03801 Tel 603-433-8735.
Titles:
Bed & Breakfasts & Country Inns.

Holm-Dietz Computer Systems, Inc., 545 E. Alluvial Ave., No. 112, Fresno, CA 93720-2800 Tel 209-431-8100; Toll free: 800-444-8301; FAX: 209-431-0731.
Titles:
FAMOUS: Farm Management Accounting System.
FAMOUS: Produce System.

Holmes, Gary, 1003A Cherry Ave., Suite 4, Charlottesville, VA 22903 Tel 804-293-4688.
Titles:
Tax Database Manager.

HomeStyles Publishing & Marketing, Inc.,
(0-9616155; 0-945471; 1-56547), 275 Market St., No. 521, Minneapolis, MN 55405-1626 Tel 612-338-8155; Toll free: 800-547-5570; FAX: 612-338-1626; Dist. by: Kable Bks., 11 W. 42nd St., New York, NY 10036 Tel 212-768-1000; Dist. by: Publishers Group West, 4065 Hollis St., Emeryville, CA 94608 Tel 510-658-3453; Toll free: 800-788-3123.
Titles:
HomeStyles' HomeDesigns Multimedia Encyclopedia: 1,001 Best-Selling Home Plans on CD-ROM.
HomeStyles' HomeDesigns Multimedia Encyclopedia: 3,003 Best-Selling Home Plans on CD-ROM.

Hoops, P.O. Box 310, Bloomington, IN 47402 Tel 812-332-0664.
Titles:
Hoops.

Hopkins Technology, (1-886649), 421 Hazel Ln., Hopkins, MN 55343 Tel 612-931-9376; FAX: 612-931-9377.
Titles:
The Herbalist CD-ROM.

Horizon Nine Keys Publishing, (1-885802), 21062 Brookhurst St., Huntington Beach, CA 92646 Tel 714-964-6334; Toll free: 800-862-5648; FAX: 714-964-6814.
Titles:
Horizon Nine Keys Personality Profile.

Hosts Corp., (1-886010), 8000 NE Parkway Dr., Suite 201, Vancouver, WA 98662-6459 Tel 206-260-1995; Toll free: 800-833-4678; FAX: 206-260-1783.
Titles:
Help One Student to Succeed (HOSTS) Language Arts: A Diagnostic-Prescriptive-Structured Mentoring Instructional Delivery System.

Houston Computer Services, (0-924431), 3207 Ashfield Dr., Houston, TX 77082-2205 Tel 713-558-9900; Toll free: 800-445-9980; FAX: 713-558-1880.
Titles:
OCTACOMM - LINK.
OCTACOMM-PC.

Houston Directional Software, 7127 Mobud Dr., Houston, TX 77074 Tel 713-776-8835; Toll free: 800-835-0213.
Titles:
Oil Well Blowout.
Oil Well Directional Package.
Oil Well Screen Plot.

HowardSoft, (0-924434), 1224 Prospect St., Suite 150, La Jolla, CA 92037 Tel 619-454-0121; Toll free: 800-248-2937; FAX: 619-454-7559.
Titles:
Real Estate Analyzer.
Tax Preparer.
Tax Preparer: California Supplement.
Tax Preparer: Partnership Edition.

Howell, Gene, 270 Evergreen Dr., Springboro, OH 45066-9714 Tel 513-748-1109.
Titles:
PhotoOffice II.

Howell Pr., (0-9616878; 0-943231; 1-57427), 1147 River Rd., Suite 2, Charlottesville, VA 22901-4172 Tel 804-977-4006; Toll free: 800-868-4512; FAX: 804-971-7204. Do not confuse with Howell Pr., Louisville, KY, nor with Howell Bk. Hse., New York, NY.
Titles:
Airline 500.
Commercial Aircraft: History & Specifications.

Hubbard Scientific, Div. of American Educational Products, (0-8331), P.O. Box 760, Chippewa Falls, WI 54729-1468; Toll free: 800-323-8368; FAX: 715-723-8021.
Titles:
Astronomy Data Bytes.
Computer Starfinder.

Hufnagel Software, P.O. Box 747, 501H Main St., Clarion, PA 16214 Tel 814-226-5600; FAX: 814-226-5551.
Titles:
Roomer3.

Hunt, Earl R., & Assocs., Inc., 3810 Medical Pkwy., Suite 235, Austin, TX 78751 Tel 512-452-2822; Toll free: 800-251-7270.
Titles:
Information Manager/6000 for Justice.
Information Manager/6000 for Law Firms.

Hurricane Systems, Inc., (0-925457), P.O. Box 1171, Orlando, FL 32802.
Titles:
Electronic Mail.
Inventory Accounting.
Microbol Accounts Payable.
Microbol Accounts Receivable.
Microbol General Ledger.
Payroll Accounting.
Point of Sale.
Retail Master.
Word Processing.

Hutch Computer Industries, Inc., 555 Third Ave., NW, Hutchinson, MN 55350 Tel 612-587-2940; Toll free: 800-424-5566; FAX: 612-587-2302.
Titles:
Compulize: Accounts Payable.
Compulize: Accounts Receivable.
Compulize: Cash Crop Breakeven.
Compulize: Data Base Reports.
Compulize: Formulation.
Compulize: Invoicing & Inventory Central.
Compulize: Lab Telecommunications.
Compulize: Prepay.
Compulize: Soil-Field History.
Compulize: Soil Test Recommendation.

Hydrosphere Data Products, Inc., (1-884632), 1002 Walnut St., Suite 200, Boulder, CO 80302 Tel 303-443-7839; Toll free: 800-949-4937; FAX: 303-442-0616.
Titles:
Climatedata Hourly-Precipitation.
Climatedata Monthly Summary GIS.
Climatedata Quarter-Hourly Precipitation.
Climatedata Summary of the Day.
Hydrodata Monthly Summary GIS.
Hydrodata STORET GIS.
Hydrodata USGS Daily Values.
Hydrodata USGS Peak Values.

Hyperbole Studios, (1-885835), 1756 114th Ave. SE, Suite 204, Bellevue, WA 98004 Tel 206-441-8334; FAX: 206-441-9134.
Titles:
The Madness of Roland.

HyperGlot Software Co., Inc., (1-881192; 1-57373), 314 Erin Dr., Knoxville, TN 37919 Tel 615-558-8270; Toll free: 800-800-8270; FAX: 615-588-6569.
Titles:
Learn to Speak Series (French or Spanish).
Think & Talk: French.
Think & Talk: German.
Think & Talk: Italian.
Think & Talk: Spanish.

HyperGraphics Corp., (1-881483), 308 N. Carroll Blvd., Denton, TX 76201 Tel 817-565-0004; Toll free: 800-369-0002; FAX: 817-565-0959.
Titles:
Ole' BASIC: On-Line Encyclopedia.
Ole' DOS: On-Line Encyclopedia.
StoryBook Presents.

Hyperworks Software Design & Development, Div. of PM Enterprises, (1-878364), 15448 Mayall St., Mission Hills, CA 91395 Tel 818-891-0066.
Titles:
Hyperworks.
VideoBase.

ICMS, Div. of Wills-van den Bergh, Inc., (0-931167), 1150 Bayhill Dr., San Bruno, CA 94066 Tel 415-583-3714; FAX: 415-583-7013.
Titles:
ICMS: Integrated Cash Management System.

ICOM Simulations, Inc., (0-929528), 648 S. Wheeling Rd., Wheeling, IL 60090 Tel 708-520-4440; Toll free: 800-877-4266; FAX: 708-459-7456.
Titles:
On Cue II.
TMON Professional.

ICOT Corp., (0-926100), 3801 Zanker Rd., San Jose, CA 95150 Tel 408-433-3300; Toll free: 800-762-3270; FAX: 408-433-0260.
Titles:
OmniPATH Gateway.
OmniPATH PC.

IDAC, Inc., P.O. Box 397, Rte. 101, Amherst, NH 03031 Tel 603-673-0765; FAX: 603-673-0767.
Titles:
IDAC-A-Stac.
IDAC-Chrome.
Macontrol.

IDEA Computers, Inc., (0-924495), 300 Jackson St., Richmond, TX 77469 Tel 713-342-5846; FAX: 713-232-3810.
Titles:
IACCT: Base Accounting & Database.
IHOME: Home Accounting/Data Base.
IMAN: I Manufacture.
IRETAIL: With Product Inventory.
SDBOX: Box Rental, Data Base System.

IDG Communications/Peterborough, Subs. of CW Communications, Inc., (0-928579), 80 Elm St., Peterborough, NH 03458 Tel 603-924-9471; Toll free: 800-343-0728; FAX: 603-924-9384.
Titles:
ReRun Gamepak.

IEP Pubs., (0-941457; 0-917089), Rte. 671, P.O. Box 546, Fork Union, VA 23055 Tel 804-842-2000; Toll free: 800-294-2759; FAX: 804-842-2000.
Titles:
Goal Rush.
IEPSystem/Bonanza.

PUBLISHER/TITLE INDEX

IFDS, Inc., (0-918615), P.O. Box 888165, Atlanta, GA 30356-0165 Tel 404-256-6447; Toll free: 800-554-8004.
Titles:
IFDS Graphics Presentation System.
IFDS Professional Series/2.
IFDS Professional Series/3.
IFDS Word Processing Interface.
Penny Pincher II.

IGS International, 130 Redwood Pl., Scotts Valley, CA 95066 Tel 408-438-2276; FAX: 408-438-2276.
Titles:
Flight Plan.
Frequent Flyer Calculator.

ILAR Systems, Inc., (0-927251), 334 Baywood Dr., Newport Beach, CA 92660 Tel 714-759-8987.
Titles:
The Bookkeeper.
Bottomline Capitalist.
Bottomline GRAF.
Business Valuation Template.
d-Marketcom.

IMPACC Assocs., Inc, (0-917987), P.O. Box 93, Gwynedd Valley, PA 19437 Tel 215-699-7235. Do not confuse with IMPACC, Inc. in Greenville, ME.
Titles:
Communications Central.
Interactive-C.

IMRS, Inc., (0-924469), 777 Long Ridge Rd., Stamford, CT 06902 Tel 203-321-3500; FAX: 203-321-3893.
Titles:
FASTAR.
Hyperion.
IMRS Forms.
IMRS OnTrack.
Micro Control.

IMSI (International Microcomputer Software, Inc.), (0-924677), 1938 Fourth St., San Rafael, CA 94901 Tel 415-454-7101; Toll free: 800-833-4674; FAX: 415-454-8901.
Titles:
Barry the Bear: Explore the Polar World with Your New Friend Barry.
EZ Language French: The Simple Vocabulary & Pronunciation Tutor.
EZ Language German: The Simple Vocabulary & Pronunciation Tutor.
EZ Language Italian: The Simple Vocabulary & Pronunciation Tutor.
EZ Language Japanese: The Simple Vocabulary & Pronunciation Tutor.
EZ Language Russian: The Simple Vocabulary & Pronunciation Tutor.
EZ Language Spanish: The Simple Vocabulary & Pronunciation Tutor.
EZ Language: The Simple Vocabulary & Pronunciation Tutor.
FormTool Small Business Edition: Create Forms, Easily.
Graphics Converter Gold for Windows.
Graphics Transformer.
IMSI Mouse - Combo: PS-2 & Serial.
IMSI Publisher.
Kevin the Kangaroo: Explore the Land down under with Your New Friend Kevin.
Louis the Lion: Explore the African Savanna with Your New Friend Louis.
MasterClips 6000: The Art of Business.
MasterClips 3000: The Art of Business.
Peter & Santa: Enchanting Fun in Santa's Interactive Wonderland of Toys, Games & Crafts.
Peter's Alphabet Adventure: Learn the ABCs in over 60 Interactive Games, Rhymes & Activities.
Peter's Colors Adventure: Explore & Discover the Wonder of Colors in an Interactive Journey to Faraway Lands.
Peter's Magic Adventure: Explore the Wonders of the World in an Interactive Journey of Learning & Fun.
Peter's Numbers Adventure: Explore 10 Enchanted Islands on an Interactive Voyage of Learning & Fun.
Pok the Little "Artiste": Explore the World of Art & Colors with Your New Friend Pok.
Premium Mouse Black: Three-Button.
Premium Mouse White: Three-Button.
Ready Set Grow!: A Fun, Interactive & Informative Guide for Expecting & New Parents.
Space Missions: An Insight into the Exciting World of Space Exploration.
Turbo CAD Symbols Library: Bathrooms.
Turbo CAD Symbols Library: Home Furnishings II.
Turbo CAD Symbols Library: Kitchens.
Turbo CAD Symbols Library: Office Furnishings II.
TurboCAD.
TurboCad Designer for Windows: Fastest, Easiest Way to Draw.
Viruscure PLUS.
WinDelete: The Safe & Simple Windows Uninstaller.
World War II: A Compelling Exploration.

INTUSOFT, (0-923345), P.O. Box 710, San Pedro, CA 90733-0710 Tel 310-833-0710; FAX: 310-833-9658.
Titles:
IS-SPICE/386.

ISICAD, Inc., P.O. Box 61022, 1920 W. Corporate Way, Anaheim, CA 92803-6122 Tel 714-533-8910; FAX: 714-533-8642.
Titles:
CADVANCE.

ISM, Inc., 2103 Harmony Woods Rd., Owings Mills, MD 21117 Tel 410-560-0973; FAX: 410-560-1306.
Titles:
G-NETIX.
Oncolib.
Storymation.
Surgeon 3 - the Brain.
Surgeon 4.
Surgeon 3: The Brain.
Understanding Breast Cancer.
Understanding Diabetes Mellitus.
Understanding Heart Attacks.
Understanding Prostate Disorders.

IVI Publishing, Inc., (1-884899), 7500 Flying Cloud Dr., 4th Flr., Minneapolis, MN 55344 Tel 612-996-6000; Toll free: 800-952-4773; FAX: 612-996-6001.
Titles:
AnnaTommy: An Adventure into the Human Body.
Blown Away: Twisted Villain, Twisted Logic, Twisted Games.
Eco East Africa: A Virtual Simulation Game.
Hometime Weekend Home Projects: Your Interactive Guide to Home Improvement.
May Clinic Family Pharmacist, 1996 Edition: Your Ultimate Guide to Medications, Early Detection & First Aid.
Mayo Clinic - the Total Heart: The Ultimate Interactive Guide to Heart Health.
Mayo Clinic Family Health, 1996 Edition: The Ultimate Interactive Guide to Health.
Mayo Clinic Health Encyclopedia 1996 Edition: Your 4 CD-ROM Health Library.
Mayo Clinic Sports Health & Fitness: Your Personal Guide to Physical Fitness.
Next Step: Mars?: An Exciting Learning Adventure about Space.
Safety Monkey: Help Make Swingland Safe.
The Virtual Body.
Welcome to Boydland: A Theme Park Where Every Ride Teaches Something New about the Human Body.
What Is a Bellybutton?: Fun & Interactive Questions & Answers about the Human Body.

IatroCom, 7159 Navajo Rd., Suite E, San Diego, CA 92119 Tel 619-698-6927.
Titles:
Mac On-Call.

Ibidinc, P.O. Box 2574, Springfield, MA 01101.
Titles:
The Alpine Encounter.

Ibis Communications, Inc., (0-9637731), 9350F Snowden River Pkwy., Suite 251, Columbia, MD 21045 Tel 410-290-9082; FAX: 410-290-6589.
Titles:
American Journey 1896-1945.

IBM Software Manufacturing Solutions, 6300 Dragonel Hwy., Boulder, CO 80301 Tel 303-939-3307.
Titles:
Ace File Try & Buy.
At Home Household Organizer Try & Buy.
At Home Personal Post Office Try & Buy.
Calendar Creater Plus Try & Buy.
Daz-Zle Plus Try & Buy.
First Aid Try & Buy.
Lode Runner Try & Buy.
MapLinx Try & Buy.
Print Artist Try & Buy.
Sim Farm Try & Buy.

Icas Systems, Inc., (0-924489), 44 N. Morris St., Dover, NJ 07801 Tel 201-366-1900; FAX: 201-366-7450.
Titles:
Pacesetter.

ICONIX Software Engineering, Inc., 2800 28th St., Suite 320, Santa Monica, CA 90405 Tel 310-458-0092; FAX: 310-396-3454.
Titles:
AdaFlow.
CoCoPro.
Iconix PowerTools.
An Overview of Object-Oriented Analysis & Design Methods.

Ideaform, Inc., (0-934077), P.O. Box 1540, Fairfield, IA 52556 Tel 515-472-7256; FAX: 515-472-9795.
Titles:
Bird Brain: The Birding Database for Macintosh.

Ideascapes, 323 Curacao Cove, Niceville, FL 32578 Tel 904-897-6407.
Titles:
ComedyWriter.

Iliad Software, Inc., 495 W. 920 N., Orem, UT 84057-3043 Tel 801-226-3270.
Titles:
Athena II.

Illini Data Systems, Subs. of Illinois Drilling Corp., (0-924502), 3640 Union Ave., Steger, IL 60475 Tel 312-755-1300.
Titles:
Credit Union Management System.

Image Entertainment, (1-57339), 9333 Oso Ave., Chatsworth, CA 91311 Tel 818-407-9100; Toll free: 800-473-3475; FAX: 818-407-9111. Do not confuse with Image Entertainment, Tampa, FL.
Titles:
Body Chemistry 3: Point of Seduction.
Carnasaur.
Dominion-Tank Police.
Robocop.
The Silence of the Lambs.
Superman Cartoons.
The Terminator.

Image Group International, (1-887494), 14550 28th Ave., N., Minneapolis, MN 55447 Tel 612-559-5557; Toll free: 800-509-5556; FAX: 612-559-5696.
Titles:
Library!: Personal Edition for Windows.

Image Mapping Systems, 516 S. 51 St., Omaha, NE 68106 Tel 402-553-2246.
Titles:
MacChoro II with Map Animation.

Image Processing Software, Inc., (0-924507), 6409 Appalachian Way, Madison, WI 53705 Tel 608-233-5033; 4414 Regent St., P.O. Box 5016, Madison, WI 53705.
Titles:
ProofWriter Color Graphics.
ProofWriter Enhanced Color Version.
ProofWriter Hercules Graphics.
ProofWriter International-Scientific.
ProofWriter Standard.

Image Smith, Inc., 1313 W. Sepulveda Blvd., Torrance, CA 90501 Tel 310-325-5999; Toll free: 800-876-6679; FAX: 310-539-9784.
Titles:
Darby My Dalmatian.
Flintstones Coloring Book: Spanish Version.
M. C. Escher Screen Saver.
The Native Americans.
Snoopy Screen Saver.
Snoopy Screen Saver: German Language Version.
Snoopy Screen Saver: Japanese Language Version.
Yearn 2 Learn Flintstones Bedrock Art Gallery.
Yearn 2 Learn Flintstones Coloring Book.
Yearn 2 Learn Flintstones Family Fun Pack.
Yearn 2 Learn Flintstones Fashion Math Cave.
Yearn 2 Learn Flintstones Fossil Foto Fixer.
Yearn 2 Learn Master Snoopy's Coloring Book.
Yearn 2 Learn Master Snoopy's Math.
Yearn 2 Learn Master Snoopy's Spelling.
Yearn 2 Learn Master Snoopy's World Geography.
Yearn 2 Learn Peanuts.
Yearn 2 Learn Peanuts: Austrasian Version.
Yearn 2 Learn Peanuts: Danish Language.
Yearn 2 Learn Peanuts: French Language.
Yearn 2 Learn Peanuts: German Language.
Yearn 2 Learn Peanuts: Japanese Language.
Yearn 2 Learn Peanuts: Spanish Language.
Yearn 2 Learn Peanuts: Swedish Language.
Yearn 2 Learn Peanuts: United Kingdom Version.
Yearn 2 Learn Snoopy.
Yearn 2 Learn Snoopy: Danish Language.
Yearn 2 Learn Snoopy: Japanese Language.
Yearn 2 Learn Snoopy: Swedish Language.
Yearn 2 Learn Snoopy's Geography.
Yearn 2 Learn Snoopy's Geography: Japanese Language.
Yearn 2 Learn Spellasoarus Quarry.
Yearn 2 Learn Tell-A-Tell Library.
Yearn 2 Learn Peanuts Lab Pack.
Yearn 2 Learn Snoopy Lab Pack.

ImageBuilder Software, Inc., 7300 SW Hunziker Rd., Tigard, OR 97223 Tel 503-684-5151.
Titles:
ImageBuilder.

Imager, Inc., (1-883221), 767 Knollwood Terr., Westfield, NJ 07090 Tel 908-233-9155; FAX: 908-654-5925; Dist. by: Broderbund Software, Inc., 500 Redwood Blvd., Novato, CA 94948-6121 Tel 415-492-3200; Toll free: 800-527-6263.
Titles:
KIDART: School Pac 1.

Imagine That, Inc., 6830 Via Del Oro, Suite 230, San Jose, CA 95119 Tel 408-365-0305; FAX: 408-629-1251.
Titles:
Extend.
Extend Plus BPR: Business Process Reengineering.
Extend + Manufacturing.

Imaging Technology, Inc., 55 Middlesex Tpke., Bedford, MA 01730 Tel 617-275-2700; Toll free: 800-356-4216 (west of the Mississippi); 800-532-3500 (east of the Mississippi); FAX: 617-275-9590.
Titles:
ITEX-ALIGN.

Impulse, Inc., 8416 Xerxes Ave., N., Brooklyn Park, MN 55444 Tel 612-425-0557; Toll free: 800-328-0184; FAX: 612-425-0701.
Titles:
Digimax: Hardware.
Imagine.

IMS-Scandura, Div. of Intelligent Micro Systems, Inc., 1249 Greentree, Narberth, PA 19072 Tel 610-664-1207; FAX: 610-664-7276.
Titles:
Code Visualizer re/Nu Sys Workbench.

IN-TEC Equipment Co., P.O. Box 123, D. V. Sta., Dayton, OH 45406 Tel 513-276-4077.
Titles:
The Ewe-Ram Productivity System.
General Homesteader.
The Rabbitry System.

Indian Head Data Systems, (0-924513), 1002 Indian Head Dr., Snow Hill, NC 28580 Tel 919-747-2839.
Titles:
Rule of 78.

Indiana Digital Corp., P.O. Box 1878, Bloomington, IN 47402 Tel 812-332-1110.
Titles:
Perform II.

Individual Software, (0-918617), 5870 Stoneridge Dr., No. 1, Pleasanton, CA 94588 Tel 510-734-6767; Toll free: 800-822-3522; FAX: 510-734-8337.
Titles:
Anytime Windows: PRO AT3.
Individual Training for Lotus 1-2-3.
Individual Training for PageMaker.
Individual Training for Project Management.
Learn to Use Windows 95.
Multimedia Typing Instructor.
PC Instructor.
Power Macros for the Lotus 1-2-3 User.
PowerMacros for the Excel User.
Professor DOS with SmartGuide for DOS.
Professor Multimedia.
Professor Office (Excel 5.0, Word 6.0, Learn Mac): PRF OM2.
Professor Windows Multimedia.
Professor Windows Multimedia with Windows for Dummies: PRF 31C.
Professor Windows 95 Deluxe CD: PRF 95C.
Professor Windows 95 Deluxe CD.
Professors for Microsoft Office.
Resumemaker Deluxe CD: PRO RWC.
The Tutorial Set.

Individualized Operand (IO), Div. of Cassidy Research Corp., (0-918619), 2280 Airport Blvd., Santa Rosa, CA 95403 Tel 707-546-6781.
Titles:
AccuRec Time Recording-Wage Totalling System.

Industrial Programming, Inc., (0-924521), 100 Jericho Quadrangle, Jericho, NY 11753 Tel 516-938-6600; Toll free: 800-365-6867; FAX: 516-938-6609.
Titles:
MTOS-UX/68k, MTOS-UX/386, MTOS-UX/88k, MTOS-UX/AT 386, MTOS-UX/860, MTOS-UX/R3k.

Infeld Software, (0-924523), 1117 Lexington Dr., Sunnyvale, CA 94087-1708.
Titles:
Infemed: Medical Management - Macintosh.

Infinite Graphics, Inc., 4611 E. Lake St., Minneapolis, MN 55406 Tel 612-721-6283; FAX: 612-721-3802.
Titles:
Flex/Hybrid System.
In-CAD.
InfiNit.
Pro-Vision.

Info-Tec, Inc., (0-940017), P.O. Box 40092, Cleveland, OH 44140 Tel 216-333-3155; FAX: 216-331-3171; 20545 Center Ridge Rd., SW 39, Cleveland, OH 44140.
Titles:
Magic Gradebook.

InfoAccess, Inc., 2800 156th Ave., SE, Bellevue, WA 98007 Tel 206-747-3203; FAX: 206-641-9367.
Titles:
Guide Professional Publisher.

Infodex, Inc., 7000 Blvd. E., Guttenberg, NJ 07093-4808 Tel 201-662-7020.
Titles:
Automax.
Filemax.
Macrolock.

Infoquest, (0-924535), 5503 Lemonwood Dr., Austin, TX 78731-2649 Tel 512-346-8040.
Titles:
The Quest.

Information Analysis Corp., (0-924538), 865 Tahoe Blvd., No. 112, Incline Village, NV 89451 Tel 702-832-4442; FAX: 415-948-9388.
Titles:
MEDLOG.

Information Analysis, Inc., 2222 Gallows Rd., Suite 300, Dunn Loring, VA 22027 Tel 703-641-0955; FAX: 703-641-0201.
Titles:
Fast File.

Information Analysis Systems Corp., (0-917823), 2 Brookside, Mansfield Center, CT 06250 Tel 203-429-1691; FAX: 203-429-2684.
Titles:
Genterm/ADM3.
Genterm/3101.
GenTerm/TV9.

Information Builders, Inc., (0-924541), 1250 Broadway, New York, NY 10001 Tel 212-736-4433.
Titles:
DBMS Interface.
EQL (English Query Language).
FOCTALK.
Focus.
Focus for Unix 4GL/DBMS.
Focus 4GL/DBMS.
Focus Interface.
Level5.
Level5 Macintosh.
PC/FOCCALC.
PC/Focus.
PC/Focus Multi-User.

PUBLISHER/TITLE INDEX

PC/Focus Multiuser.

Information Conversion Services, Inc., (0-929609), 1141 Lake Cook Rd., Suite D, Deerfield, IL 60015 Tel 847-405-0501; FAX: 847-405-0506.
Titles:
KeyCap.
ViceVersa.

Information Dimensions, Subs. of Online Computer Library Ctr., 5080 Tuttle Crossing Blvd., Dublin, OH 43016-3569 Tel 614-761-8083; Toll free: 800-328-2648; FAX: 614-761-7290.
Titles:
BASIS Desktop.
BASIS SGMLserver.
BASIS WEBserver.
BASISplus.
TECHLIBplus.

Information Fountain, Inc., (0-917403; 0-927362), 46 Oakwood Dr., Chapel Hill, NC 27514-5652.
Titles:
Software Maintenance Service.

Information Intelligence, Inc., (0-924544), P.O. Box 31098, Phoenix, AZ 85046 Tel 602-996-2283; Toll free: 800-228-9982.
Titles:
A-C-C-E-S-S: Microcomputer Network System.
Invoice Writer.

Information Legal Systems, Inc., Div. of BaronData Co., 2111 E. Highland Ave., Phoenix, AZ 85016 Tel 602-224-0855.
Titles:
Legal-Pro Billing & Accounts Receivable: Level 1.
Legal-Pro Billing & Accounts Receivable: Level 2.
Legal-Pro Billing & Accounts Receivable: Level 3.
Legal-Pro Billing & Accounts Receivable: Level 4.
Legal-Pro Checkwriting/Disbursements System.
Legal-Pro Conflict of Interest System.
Legal-Pro Docket Control System.
Legal-Pro General Ledger System.
Legal-Pro Remote Time Entry.
Legal-Pro Report Writer.

Information Management Corp., P.O. Box 391, Grafton, MA 01519; FAX: 508-839-2354; 1 Grafton Common, Grafton, MA 01519 Tel 508-839-6445.
Titles:
IMC Quest.
MPS Station Management.
Professional Service Manager I.

Information Management Pr., Inc., (0-9606408), P.O. Box 19166, Washington, DC 20036 Tel 202-293-5519; FAX: 202-223-5534.
Titles:
InfoMapper: Information Resources Management Online Support System.

Information Management Solutions, Inc., (0-917825), P.O. Box 13263, Research Triangle Pk., NC 27709 Tel 919-382-0166; FAX: 919-382-0166.
Titles:
PD2 POWERPak.
R/C RaceTrak.

Information Marketing Businesses, Inc., (0-918381), 18 Hurley St., Cambridge, MA 02141 Tel 617-864-1115; FAX: 617-868-3221.
Titles:
PEOPLE-PLANNER Labor Forecaster.
People-Planner Schedule Manager.
PEOPLE-PLANNER Scheduler & Time & Attendance System.

Information Presentation Technologies, Inc., 23801 Calabasas Rd., Suite 2008, Calabasas, CA 91302.
Titles:
UShare.

Information Research Corp., Div. of Sprigg Lane Investment Corp., (0-926123), 2421 Ivy Rd., Charlottesville, VA 22901 Tel 804-979-8191; Toll free: 800-368-3542; FAX: 804-977-1949.
Titles:
ActionTracker.
SYZYGY: Work Group Software for Managers.
W. P. Kingsfield.

Information Resource Consultants, (0-931821; 1-55804), 1556 Walpole Dr., Chesterfield, MO 63017 Tel 314-530-7966; Toll free: 800-858-7966.
Titles:
Air Pre-Heat.
Cement Pyro Processing.
Fired Heater.
Heat Exchanger.
Hydro-Metallurgical Fundamentals: Metropro.
Hydro-Metallurgical Leaching Process Equipment: Hydropro.
Iron Blast Furnace.
RATS: Rapid Assessment & Treatment Strategies.
Refinery I.
Vertical Shaft Furnace.

Information Resources, Inc., Div. of Software Products Group, (0-925106), 200 Fifth Ave., Waltham, MA 02154 Tel 617-890-1100; FAX: 617-890-4660. Do not confuse with Information Resources, Inc. in Craryville, NY.
Titles:
PcEXPRESS.

Information Resources, Inc., (0-917323), 319 Decker Rd., M/S R. R. 1, Craryville, NY 12521 Tel 518-851-2815; Toll free: 800-333-7678; FAX: 518-851-9822. Do not confuse with Information Resources, Inc. in Waltham, MA.
Titles:
COSORT.

Information Security Corp., Subs. of ICS, 1141 Lake Cook Rd., Suite D, Deerfield, IL 60015 Tel 847-405-0500; FAX: 847-405-0506.
Titles:
DSA Signature Software.
SecretAgent.
SpyProof.

Information Systems Design of Stuart, Inc. (ISD), 370 NW Alice St., Stuart, FL 34994 Tel 407-692-0400; FAX: 407-220-9605.
Titles:
Managing a Private Practice: Software for the Professional Therapists.
Multi-Pro: Accounts Payable.
Multi-Pro: Club Management & Accounts Receivable.
Multi-Pro: General Ledger.
Multi-Pro: Payroll.
Multi-Pro: Point-of-Sale.
Multi-Pro: Resort Management.
Multi-Pro: Tee Time Reservations.

Information Transform, Inc., (1-879701), 502 Leonard St., Madison, WI 53711 Tel 608-255-4800; Toll free: 800-824-6272; FAX: 608-255-2082.
Titles:
MITINET/Marc.

Informix Software, Inc., (0-924587), 16011 College Blvd., Lenexa, KS 66219 Tel 913-599-7100; Toll free: 800-438-7627; FAX: 913-599-7350; 4100 Bohannon Dr., Menlo Park, CA 94025 Tel 415-926-6300.
Titles:
Informix-ESQL/Ada.
Informix-ESQL/C.
Informix-4GL.
Informix-4GL.
Informix-4GL Rapid Development System & Interactive Debugger.
Informix-SQL.
The Smart Data Manager.
The Smart Database.
The Smart LAN Performance Test.
The Smart Software System.
The Smart Spreadsheet with Graphics.
The Smart Time Manager.
The Smart Word Processor.
SmartWare.
SmartWare for Xenix.
Wingz.

InfoSource, Inc., 6947 University Blvd., Winter Park, FL 32792 Tel 407-677-0300; Toll free: 800-393-4636; 800-253-2995 (in Canada only); FAX: 407-677-9226.
Titles:
InfoCheck: Custom Test Maker, Designer.
InfoCheck: Databases Access 2.0 for Windows Fundamentals & Intermediate.
InfoCheck: Designer.
InfoCheck: Graphics & Presentations, PowerPoint 4.0 for Windows Fundamentals.
InfoCheck: Operating Environments Windows 3.1 Fundamentals, Windows 95 Fundamentals.
InfoCheck: Spreadsheets, Excel 5.0 for Windows Fundamentals & Intermediate, Lotus 1-2-3 Rel. 5 for Windows Fundamentals & Intermediate.
InfoCheck: Word Processing Word 2.0 for Windows, Word 6.0 for Windows Fundamentals & Intermediate, WordPerfect 6.1 for Windows Fundamentals & Intermediate.
Presenter Series: Access Fundamentals.
Seminar-on-a-Disc, Multimedia Edition: Windows 3.1 Fundamentals.
Seminar-on-a-Disk: Approach Fundamentals.
Seminar-On-A-Disk (Computer Based Training): Access Fundamentals.
Seminar-On-A-Disk (Computer Based Training): Ami Pro Fundamentals.
Seminar-On-A-Disk (Computer Based Training): DOS Fundamentals.
Seminar-On-A-Disk (Computer Based Training): DOS Fundamentals - Intermediate.
Seminar-On-A-Disk (Computer Based Training): dBASE IV Fundamentals.
Seminar-On-A-Disk (Computer Based Training): dBASE IV Intermediate.
Seminar-On-A-Disk (Computer Based Training): Excel for Windows.
Seminar-On-A-Disk (Computer Based Training): Excel for Windows Fundamentals.
Seminar-On-A-Disk (Computer Based Training): Freelance for Windows Fundamentals.
Seminar-On-A-Disk (Computer Based Training): Harvard Graphics Fundamentals.
Seminar-On-A-Disk (Computer Based Training): Lotus CC: Mail for Windows.
Seminar-On-A-Disk (Computer Based Training): Lotus Organizer Fundamentals.
Seminar-On-A-Disk (Computer Based Training): Lotus 1-2-3 Database Management.
Seminar-On-A-Disk (Computer Based Training): Microsoft Mail Fundamentals.
Seminar-On-A-Disk (Computer Based Training): Paradox Fundamentals - Intermediate.
Seminar-On-A-Disk (Computer Based Training): PowerPoint for Windows Fundamentals.
Seminar-On-A-Disk (Computer Based Training): PC 386-486 Fundamentals.
Seminar-On-A-Disk (Computer Based Training): Quattro Pro Fundamentals.

INFOSOURCE MANAGEMENT, INC.

Seminar-On-A-Disk (Computer Based Training): Quattro Pro for Windows Fundamentals.
Seminar-On-A-Disk (Computer Based Training): Quattro Pro Intermediate.
Seminar-On-A-Disk (Computer Based Training): Windows Fundamentals.
Seminar-On-A-Disk (Computer Based Training): WordPerfect for DOS Advanced.
Seminar-On-A-Disk (Computer Based Training): WordPerfect for DOS Fundamentals.
Seminar-On-A-Disk (Computer Based Training): WordPerfect for Windows.
Seminar-On-A-Disk (Computer Based Training): Word for Windows Fundamentals - Intermediate.
Seminar on a Disk: Excel for Windows Intermediate.
Seminar-on-a-Disk: Internet Fundamentals.
Seminar-on-a-Disk: Lotus 1-2-3 for Windows Fundamentals.
Seminar-on-a-Disk: Lotus 1-2-3 for Windows Intermediate.
Seminar-on-a-Disk, Multimedia Edition: Databases Access for Windows Fundamentals.
Seminar-on-a-Disk, Multimedia Edition: Graphics & Presentations PowerPoint for Windows Fundamentals.
Seminar-on-a-Disk, Multimedia Edition: Operating Environments, Windows Fundamentals Upgrading to Windows 95.
Seminar-on-a-Disk, Multimedia Edition: Spreadsheets Excel for Windows Fundamentals.
Seminar-on-a-Disk, Multimedia Edition: Word Processing, Word for Windows Fundamentals.
Seminar-on-a-Disk: Paradox for DOS Fundamentals.
Seminar-on-a-Disk: Paradox for Windows Fundamentals.
Seminar-on-a-Disk: Upgrading to Windows 95.
Seminar-on-a-Disk: Word for Windows Intermediate.
Seminar-on-a-Disk: WordPerfect for Windows Fundamentals.
Seminar-on-a-Disk: WordPerfect for Windows Intermediate.

Infosource Management, Inc., (0-942915), P.O. Box 33458, Raleigh, NC 27636; 5312 Sendero Dr., Raleigh, NC 27612 Tel 919-782-0229.
Titles:
JMACS: Job Manufacturing & Accounting Control System.

Infosphere, 12134 SW Tryon Hill Rd., Portland, OR 97219-9303 Tel 503-226-3515; Toll free: 800-445-7085.
Titles:
ComServe.
LaserServe.
Liaison.
MacServe.

Inkwell Systems, (0-928649), P.O. Box 1318, Taient, OR 97540-1318 Tel 541-535-1210; FAX: 541-535-2061.
Titles:
Amiga 184-A Light Pen & Driver.
EasyKey Visual Keyboard.
Flexidraw.
Flexifont.
Graphics Gallerias 1/11.
Graphics Integrator.
170-C & 184-C.
PCPro Light Pen System.
Telewand.

INLEX, Inc., 80 Garden Ct., Suite 200, Monterey, CA 93940 Tel 408-646-8600; Toll free: 800-553-1202 (outside California); FAX: 408-646-0651.
Titles:
The Assistant: Integrated Library Automation Software.

Inmagic, Inc., (0-918621), 800 W. Cummings Pk., Woburn, MA 01801-6372 Tel 617-938-4442; Toll free: 800-229-8398; FAX: 617-938-6393.
Titles:
Inmagic DB/SearchWorks.
Inmagic DB/TextWorks.
INMAGIC Image.
INMAGIC Plus.
SearchMAGIC Plus.

Inmark Development Corp., 2065 Landings Dr., Mountain View, CA 94043 Tel 415-691-9000.
Titles:
The Market Maker.

INMASS/MRP, (0-928703), 2127 E. Speedway Blvd., No. 205, Tucson, AZ 85719-4744 Tel 602-795-6800; FAX: 602-323-2505.
Titles:
Accounts Payable.
Accounts Receivable.
Assemble to Order: Through Sales Order Entry.
Bar Coding.
Bill of Materials.
Contract Management.
Customer Histories: Order Entry-Accounts Receivable.
EDI: Electronic Data Interchange.
Fixed Assets Management.
Forecasting.
General Ledger.
INCOME II: Integrated Company Management.
INMASS II: Integrated Manufacturing Software Series.
INMASS-MRP.
Inquire - Report Writer.
Inventory.
Inventory Control.
Job Cost-Work-in-Process.
Material Requirements Planning.
Materials Requirements Planning.
MC Software General Ledger.
Order Entry.
Payroll.
Point of Sale.
Purchasing.
Retail/Wholesale Inventory Control.
Sales Order Entry.
Star Ship.
Vendor Histories: Purchasing-Accounts Payable.

Inner Access Corp., (0-924575), P.O. Box 888, Belmont, CA 94002 Tel 415-591-8295; FAX: 415-593-0542.
Titles:
8080/Z80 MetaFORTH Cross Compiler.
Power-Sort.
Z8000 FORTH Development System.

Inner Media, Inc., 60 Plain Rd., Hollis, NH 03049 Tel 603-465-3216; Toll free: 800-962-2949; FAX: 603-465-7195.
Titles:
Collage Complete.
Collage PM.

Innovative Data Design, Inc., (0-929610), 1820 Arnold Industrial Way, Suite L, Concord, CA 94520-5325 Tel 510-680-6818; FAX: 510-680-1165.
Titles:
MacDraft.
MacDraft for Windows.

Innovative Electronics, Inc., Subs. of Dynatech Corp., 10110 USA Today Way, Miramar, FL 33025 Tel 305-432-0300; FAX: 305-432-0705.
Titles:
The NETMASTER System.

SOFTWARE ENCYCLOPEDIA 1996

Innovative Professional Software, Inc., 7140 East Heritage Pl., N., Englewood, CO 80111 Tel 303-220-5730.
Titles:
Value Expert.

Innovative Programming Assocs., Inc., (0-924584), 303 Wall St., Princeton, NJ 08540 Tel 609-924-7272; Toll free: 800-472-7638; FAX: 609-924-0875.
Titles:
Labcat.

InnoVision Technology, 1933 Davis St., Suite 238, San Leandro, CA 94577 Tel 510-638-0800; FAX: 510-638-6453.
Titles:
Alpha Paint.
Broadcast Titler 2.
Broadcast Titler 2: Font Enhancer.
Broadcast Titler 2: Font Pack 1.
MONTAGE for the Video Toaster.
MONTAGE 24 for the Amiga.
PrimeTime.
PrimeTime with Animation.
Video Effects 3D.

InnServ Co., Rte. 1, Box 68, Redkey, IN 47373 Tel 317-369-2245.
Titles:
InnServ B&B HyperGuide.

Inset Systems, Inc., (0-927984), 71 Commerce Dr., Brookfield, CT 06804-3405 Tel 203-740-2400; Toll free: 800-374-6738; FAX: 203-775-5634.
Titles:
HiJaak for DOS.
HiJaak Graphics Suite.

Insight Advantage, (0-9627172), 4509 Yellowleaf Dr., Fort Worth, TX 76133 Tel 817-346-9116.
Titles:
Math Lab.

Insight Data, (0-945876), P.O. Box 2297, Candler, NC 28715 Tel 704-665-0638.
Titles:
Lottery Leprechaun: A Software Guide for Selecting Numbers.
Squeak: Learn How to Use the Mouse.

Insight Development Corp., 2420 Camino Ramon, Suite 205, San Ramon, CA 94583 Tel 510-244-2000; Toll free: 800-825-4115; FAX: 510-244-2020.
Titles:
PrintAPlot Pro.
RenderPrint.
Squiggle.

Insight Software Solutions, P.O. Box 354, Bountiful, UT 84011-0354 Tel 801-295-1890; FAX: 801-299-1781.
Titles:
The Debt Analyzer.
The Interest Analyzer.
The Mortgage Analyzer.

Inspiration Software, Inc., (0-928539), 2920 SW Dolph Ct., Suite 3, Portland, OR 97219 Tel 503-245-9011; Toll free: 800-877-4292; FAX: 503-246-4292.
Titles:
Inspiration.

Instant Replay Corp., P.O. Box 1750, Saint George, UT 84771 Tel 801-634-7648; Toll free: 800-388-8086; FAX: 801-634-7640.
Titles:
Carets & Cursors.
Instant Replay Professional (IRPRO).
No Blink-Accelerator.

PUBLISHER/TITLE INDEX

Turbo Plus.
Visual FX.

Instant Software, Inc., Subs. of Wayne Green Enterprises, (0-924592), 70 Rte. 202, N. Bldg., Peterborough, NH 03458-1130 Tel 603-924-9646.
Titles:
ABE.
Adventure Game.
Air Flight Simulation.
Airmail Pilot.
Alien Attack Force.
All Stars.
Apple Clinic.
Archimedes Apprentice.
Assem-Zsim.
Astrology.
Ball Turret Gunner.
BASIC Programming Assistant.
Battleground.
Bowling League Secretary.
Bowling League Statistics System.
Business Analysis.
Business Cycle Analysis.
Cassette Scope.
Client Record-Bill Preparation.
The Communicator.
Compression Utility Pack.
Cosmic Patrol.
Danger in Orbit.
Disk Editor.
Disk Library.
Disk Scope.
Disk-Tape Exchange.
DLDIS: Disk-Based Labeling Disassembler.
Dr. Chips.
Domes of Kilgari.
DOS Customizer.
DOSPLUS 3.4.
Dynamics Device Drivers.
Easy Calc.
The Electronic Breadboard.
Electronics Design Calculator.
Electronics Engineer Assistant.
Energy Audit.
Enhanced BASIC.
Find It Quick.
Flight Path.
Football Forecaster.
HAM Package.
Hi-Res Plus.
Key Commander.
Kitchen Sink.
Label.
Mailing List.
Master Directory.
Master Plot.
Master Revival.
Mission: Mud.
Model Rocket Analyzer & Preflight Check.
Mountain Pilot.
Mountain Pilot-Precision Approach Radar.
NFL Prognosticator.
Oil Tycoon.
Personal Bill Paying.
Phasor Belt.
Programmers Converter.
QSL Manager.
Renum-Compress.
Screen Scribe.
Script.
Scriptr.
Sector Editor.
Solar Energy for the Home.
Sparrow Commander.
Super-Terminal.
Super Utility Plus.
Swamp War.
Temple of Sun.
TLDIS: Tape-Based Labelling Disassembler.
Tower of Fear.
Traffic Accident Analysis & Reconstruction.
TRS-Test.
Ultra-Mon.
Universal Graphing.
Utility II.
Weather Watch.
Wordslinger.
ZSIM.

Institute for Scientific Information, (0-941708), 3501 Market St., Philadelphia, PA 19104 Tel 215-386-0100; Toll free: 800-523-1850; FAX: 215-386-6362.
Titles:
Current Contents on Diskette (available in 7 editions).

Instrument Society of America, (0-87664; 1-55617), P.O. Box 12277, 67 Alexander Dr., Research Triangle Pk., NC 27709 Tel 919-549-8411; FAX: 919-549-8288.
Titles:
AutoSim: A Process Control Software Lab.
FLOWEL: Flow Element Sizing & Documentation.
INDEX+: Instrument Index.
ISA Dictionary on Disk: Electronic Dictionary of Measurement & Control.
ISA Standards Library CD-ROM: Guidelines for Quality & Safety.
P & ID Clip Symbols.
S20 Spec Forms II for Windows.
SARVAL: Safety Relief Valve Sizing & Documentation.
Valve Sizing: Control Valve Sizing & Documentation.

Insurance Rating Systems, Inc., (0-924596), 433 Kitty Hawk, No. 211, Universal City, TX 78148 Tel 512-658-4691; Toll free: 800-876-1466; FAX: 512-658-2220.
Titles:
Agency Information Management System.

Insurance Technology Consultants, 2101 E. Fourth St., Suite 285B, Santa Ana, CA 92705 Tel 714-836-0671; FAX: 714-836-0737.
Titles:
Agency Accounting.
Automobile Rating & Policy Issuance.

Integral Quality, Inc., (0-924599), 6265 20th Ave., NE, Seattle, WA 98115-6907 Tel 206-527-2918.
Titles:
IQLISP.

Intel Corp., (0-917017; 1-55512), 2200 Mission College Blvd., Santa Clara, CA 95052-8119 Tel 408-765-1711; Toll free: 800-548-4725; Orders to: P.O. Box 7620, Mount Prospect, IL 60056-9960.
Titles:
DB86.

Intellectual Software, Div. of Queue, Inc., (0-87200; 0-87492; 0-7827), 338 Commerce Dr., Fairfield, CT 06430 Tel 203-335-0908; Toll free: 800-232-2224; FAX: 203-336-2481.
Titles:
Chain 4.
Gymnastics.
Music Appreciation.
What's My Rule?
The Write Stuff.

IntelliCreations, Inc., (0-923625), 60 Leveroni Ct., Novato, CA 94949-5746 Tel 415-346-4114; FAX: 818-772-6809.
Titles:
Alternate Reality: The City.
Alternate Reality: The Dungeon.
Battledroidz.
Bismarck-The North Sea Chase.
Bruce Lee.
Conan.
Cosmic Relief.
Dark Lord.
Force VII.
Global Commander.
The Hunt for Red October.
Mercenary: Escape from Targ.
Mind Pursuit.
Napoleon in Russia-Borodeno 1812.
The Never-Ending Story.
Rubicon Alliance.
Tomahawk.
Video Title Shop: A Computer + VCR Utility.
Zorro.

IntelligenceWare, Inc., (0-945877), 5933 W. Century Blvd., Los Angeles, CA 90045 Tel 310-216-6177; Toll free: 800-888-2996; FAX: 310-417-8897.
Titles:
Auto-Intelligence.
Corporate Vision: The Super Spreadsheet.
Database/Supervisor.
DVT: Database Visualization Tool.
Experteach-III.
Iconic Query.
IDIS: The Information Discovery System.
IXL: The Discovery Machine.
NEURAL/QUERY.
WindowsTeach.

Intelligent Business Systems, Div. of Computerland Corp., 403 W. Main St., Clarksburg, WV 26301 Tel 304-624-7488.
Titles:
Point of Sale.

Intelligent Environments, 2 Highwood Dr., Tewksbury, MA 01876 Tel 508-640-1080; Toll free: 800-669-2797; FAX: 508-640-1090.
Titles:
AM Professional.

Intelligent Machines, (0-924626), 1440 W. Broadway, Missoula, MT 59802 Tel 406-728-0332.
Titles:
Clone.
Control-Net.
DataEze: For the Pharmacist.
DosNet.
DOS386.

Intelligent Manufacturing Solutions, Inc., 4065A N. Calhoun Rd., No. 201, Brookfield, WI 53005-1316 Tel 414-781-3334; FAX: 414-781-5335.
Titles:
Intellimaint.

Intelligent Technology Group, (0-923376), 115 Evergreen Heights Dr., Pittsburgh, PA 15229 Tel 412-931-7600; Toll free: 800-333-4844; FAX: 412-931-4429.
Titles:
ClienTrak.

Intellimedia Sports, (1-882284), 2 Piedmont Ctr., Suite 300, Atlanta, GA 30305 Tel 404-261-8330; Toll free: 800-842-6848; FAX: 404-872-8343.
Titles:
Cowboy Casino.
ESPN & Pop Warner Interactive Football.
ESPN Baseball: Hitting.
ESPN Golf Lower Your Score with Tom Kite: Shotmaking.
ESPN Interactive Baseball Playing the Field.
ESPN Interactive Golf: Tom Kite Shotmaking.
ESPN Interactive Soccer: Skills & Strategies by Intelliplay.
ESPN Let's Go Skiing.
ESPN Let's Play Baseball.
ESPN Let's Play Beach Volleyball.
ESPN Let's Play Soccer.
ESPN Let's Play Tennis.

INTERACTIVE ARTS

Interactive Arts
ESPN Lower Your Score with Tom Kite: The Full Swing & Putting.
ESPN Winning Hoops with Coach K.
Intelliplay Cowboy Casino.
Interactive Fly Fishing School.

Interactive Arts, 7140 SW Fifth St., Plantation, FL 33317-3811.
Titles:
The P.A.C.K (Programmer's Assembly-Language Construction Kit).

Interactive Business Systems, Ltd., (0-924638), 380 Madison Ave., 7th Flr., New York, NY 10017 Tel 212-856-4499.
Titles:
POS.
RECOS.

Interactive Network Technologies, Inc., 11 Longmeadow Rd., Lincoln, MA 01773 Tel 617-259-1320.
Titles:
Donor Room.
Legal Aide.

Intercomputer Communications Corp., (0-924655), 8230 Montgomery Rd., Cincinnati, OH 45236 Tel 513-745-0500; FAX: 513-745-0327.
Titles:
ICC-Intercom 102-FileXpress: Burroughs Term Emulation & File Transfers.
ICC-Intercom 500/600: Sperry Terminal Emulation Mapper File Transfers, SDF File Tranfers.

Intergraph Corp., 1 Madison Industrial Pk., Huntsville, AL 35807-4201 Tel 205-772-2000; Toll free: 800-8276-3515.
Titles:
MicroStation PC.

Intergraphics, Inc., 106-A S. Columbus St., Alexandria, VA 22314 Tel 703-683-9414.
Titles:
Personal Publishing.

Interkom, (0-928658), 3900 Lakeshore Dr., Suite 19E, Chicago, IL 60613 Tel 312-472-0713.
Titles:
Address Pro.
Foreign Language Library: Teacher Authored Games in French, German, Russian, Spanish, Italian.
Foreign Language Word Processing.

Interleaf, Inc., Prospect Pl., 9 Hillside Ave., Waltham, MA 02154 Tel 617-290-0710; FAX: 617-290-4955.
Titles:
Interleaf Publisher.

Intermetrics Microsystems Software, Inc., Subs. of Intermetrics, Inc., 733 Concord Ave., Cambridge, MA 02138 Tel 617-661-0072; Toll free: 800-356-3594; FAX: 617-868-2843.
Titles:
Intertools.
PassKey Source Level Cross Debugger.
Whitesmiths Software Development Tools.

International Assn. of Fire Chiefs, 4025 Fair Ridge Dr., Fairfax, VA 22033-2868 Tel 703-273-0911; FAX: 703-273-9363.
Titles:
ICHIEFS Communication Network.

International Business Software, Inc., 100 Pleasant St., Worcester, MA 01609 Tel 508-757-6555.
Titles:
Destiny: Business Info & Planning.

International Computer Consultants, 1311 Clegg St., Petaluma, CA 94952 Tel 707-765-9200.
Titles:
Mac-3000.

International Computer Shop, The, 188-29 Keeseville Ave., Jamaica, NY 11412 Tel 718-454-6463.
Titles:
Medicaid Patient Billing System (MPBS).
Merchants Automated Business System (MABS).

International Geometric Tolerancing Institute, (1-883467), 2943 Cortina Dr., San Jose, CA 95132 Tel 408-251-7058; FAX: 408-272-2329.
Titles:
GD&T-E-BOD: Electronic Book on Disk.
Metri-Pak.
Softgage.
Softgage: Position Inspection.
Tolculator.
Tolculator: GD & T Design - Insp. Software.

International Logic Corp., (0-924673), 100 Pine St., No. 2760, San Francisco, CA 94111-5213 Tel 415-989-7223; FAX: 415-989-0252.
Titles:
IAS-H: Insurance Agent System-Health.

International Loss Control Institute, Inc., (0-88061), P.O. Box 1898, Loganville, GA 30249 Tel 404-466-2208; Toll free: 800-486-4524; FAX: 404-466-4318.
Titles:
Computer Assisted Loss Management System (CALMS): Intelligent Query.
Computer Assisted Loss Management System (CALMS): Task Analysis Module.

International Micro Systems, Inc., (0-924675), 1520 Erie St., Kansas City, KS 64116-3805; Toll free: 800-255-6223.
Titles:
Accounts Payable.
Church Management System.
Dental Office Management System.
Fund Accounting.
General Ledger.
Inventory Control with Purchasing.
Manufacturing Inventory Control System.
Medical Office Management System.
Accounts Receivable.
Order Processing.
Payroll.
Wholesale Distribution System.

International Software, (0-918625), 1954 Nob Hill, P.O. Box 747, Running Springs, CA 92382 Tel 909-867-2436.
Titles:
Daily Reminder.
Small Business Mini-Inventory.

International Technology Group, Inc., 5 Greentree Ctr., No. 111, Marlton, NJ 08053-3422.
Titles:
Factmatcher: Search & Find.

Internet, 11 Longmeadow Rd., Lincoln, MA 01773 Tel 617-965-5239. Do not confuse with Internet in Chapel Hill, NC.
Titles:
intermail.

Interpretive Software, Inc., (1-885837), 1932 Arlington Blvd., Suite 107, Charlottesville, VA 22903 Tel 804-979-0245; Toll free: 800-746-8587; FAX: 804-979-2454.
Titles:
AutoSim: The Marketing Laboratory.
The Feeling's Mutual.
PharmaSim: A Brand Management Simulation.

Intersecting Concepts, 30851 Agoura Rd., Suite 200, Agoura Hills, CA 91301 Tel 818-879-0086; Toll free: 800-959-2657; FAX: 818-879-0623.
Titles:
Diskmizer.

Intersolv, 5540 Centerview Dr., Suite 324, Raleigh, NC 27606 Tel 919-859-2220; Toll free: 800-876-3101; FAX: 919-859-9334.
Titles:
DataDirect Developer's Toolkit.
DataDirect ODBC Pack.
Intersolv Q&E.
DataDirect MultiLink/VB.

Interval Software, 278 E. 650 S., Kaysville, UT 84037 Tel 801-544-2314.
Titles:
Fast-Flex Pro.
Fast-Flex Pro Network: The Flexible Spending Plan Administration Kit.

Intex Software Systems International, Ltd., P.O. Box 3068, Stamford, CT 06905-0068 Tel 203-975-7412; FAX: 203-975-7317.
Titles:
Intext.

Intex Solutions, Inc., 35 Highland Cir., Needham, MA 02194 Tel 617-449-6222; FAX: 617-444-2318.
Titles:
Intex Bond Calculations.
Intex CMO Analyst.
Intex Mortgage-Backed Calculations.
Portable Troll.
Rescue Plus.

Intra Day Analyst, (0-924697), 1021 Ninth St., New Orleans, LA 70175 Tel 504-895-1474; Toll free: 800-895-1474.
Titles:
Intra Day Analyst.

IntraCorp/Capstone, 501 Brickell Key Dr., 6th Flr., Miami, FL 33131 Tel 305-373-7700; Toll free: 800-468-7226; FAX: 305-577-9875.
Titles:
Anyone for Cards?
BridgeMaster Championship Edition.
Business Card Maker: Small Office Home Office.
Grandmaster Championship Chess.
Harpoon II.
Harpoon II Battleset, No. 2: WestPac.
Harpoon II Battleset, No. 3: Cold War.
V-for-Victory.
Victory Pak CD-ROM Collection.

Intro-Logic, Inc., (0-924698), 24293 Telegraph, Suite 250, Southfield, MI 48034 Tel 810-948-8100.
Titles:
Manufacturing II & Inventory Control.

Intuit, Inc., (0-929804; 1-57338), P.O. Box 2143, Menlo Park, CA 94026; FAX: 415-329-2786; 155 Linfield Ave., Menlo Park, CA 94025 Tel 415-329-3698.
Titles:
Quicken.
Quicken CheckArt.
Quicken for the Macintosh.
Quicken Tax Reform Analyzer.
Quicken Transfer Utility.

Inverted-A, Inc., (0-938245), 6500 Main St., No. 226, Houston, TX 77030-1402 Tel 214-264-0066.
Titles:
AB-RK (Soft Alphabet).
ADDITOR (Arithmetic Editor).
FED: Font Editor.
LANDSCAPER (Font Conversion Utility).
MINISIMULATOR IIc.

PUBLISHER/TITLE INDEX

OBRIEF (Hebrew Brief).
OBRIT: Hebrew Printing.

Investek, Inc., (0-928260), P.O. Box 1006, Jackson, MS 39205 Tel 601-355-1335; FAX: 601-949-3177.
Titles:
BondScholar.

ION, 3301 Kerner Blvd., Suite 260, San Rafael, CA 94901 Tel 415-455-1466.
Titles:
The Individualist: Computer Box.
The Individualist: Jewel Case.

IQue, Inc., 65F Gate Five Rd., Sausalito, CA 94965 Tel 415-289-4036; Toll free: 800-257-6963; FAX: 415-332-2416.
Titles:
SMART.ALX.

Iron Mountain Software, 5320 Hwy. 49N, No. 5, Mariposa, CA 95338 Tel 209-742-5000; FAX: 209-966-3117.
Titles:
Dawn.

Ishi Pr. International, (0-923891), 76 Bonaventura Dr., San Jose, CA 95134 Tel 408-944-9900; Toll free: 800-859-2086 (orders); FAX: 408-944-9110.
Titles:
East Meets West Nutrition Planner.
Endgame Software: Mathematical Go Endgames.
Goliath: Computer GO for the Macintosh.
GoScribe.
The Many Faces of GO, 1992.
Shogi Master: (Japanese Chess).

Island Graphics, (0-924710), 4000 Civic Ctr. Dr., 4th Flr., San Rafael, CA 94903 Tel 415-491-1000.
Titles:
Productivity Series.

Island Pr., Div. of Center for Resource Economics, (0-933280; 1-55963), 1718 Connecticut Ave., NW, Suite 300, Washington, DC 20009 Tel 202-232-7933; FAX: 202-234-1328; Star Rte. 1, Box 38, Covelo, CA 95428 Tel 707-983-6432; Orders to: P.O. Box 7, Covelo, CA 95428; Toll free: 800-828-1302.
Titles:
Worldwatch Database Disk 1996.

Italica Pr., (0-934977), 595 Main St., Suite 605, New York, NY 10044 Tel 212-935-4230; FAX: 212-838-7812.
Titles:
Guide to the Holy Land for Mac & Windows.
Hell on Disk: An Interactive Tour of the Infernal Otherworld.
Marvels of Rome for Windows.
Norman London for Mac & Windows.
The Road to Compostela on Disk.

Ithaca Software, 1301 Marina Village Pkwy., Alameda, CA 94501-1042 Tel 510-523-5900; FAX: 510-523-2880.
Titles:
HOOPS.

J&KH Software, (0-924723), 242 Beechwood Rd., Fort Mitchell, KY 41017 Tel 606-344-0780.
Titles:
PStext-plus: PostScript Print Utility for Unix Systems.

JIAN Tools for Sales, Inc., (1-56811), 1975 W. El Camino Real, Suite 301, Mountain View, CA 94040 Tel 415-254-5600; Toll free: 800-346-5426; FAX: 415-941-9272.
Titles:
AgreeMentor.
BizPlanBuilder.
Business GuardDog.
Ca$hCollector.
Forecast Express: Forecast Management System.
Investimator: Investment Analysis Worksheets.
JobSketch.
Living TrustBuilder.
Manufacturer's 9-Pack.
Operations - Integrator.
PartnersLTD.
P.P. Memo.

JMI Software Systems, Inc., (0-924733), 904 Sheble Ln., Spring House, PA 19477 Tel 215-628-0840; FAX: 215-628-0353; P.O. Box 481, Spring House, PA 19477.
Titles:
BASTOC.
C EXECUTIVE.
JMI Portable C Library.
National Semiconductor Series 32000 C Cross Compiler.

JOMURPA Publishing, Inc., (0-932599), P.O. Box 1708, Spring Valley, NY 10977; FAX: 914-426-0802; 7 South Myrtle Ave., Spring Valley, NY 10977 Tel 914-426-0040.
Titles:
Directory on Computer.

JPL Assocs., 18 Sequoia Way, San Francisco, CA 94127 Tel 415-469-8862.
Titles:
GetMemo.
W-4 Form Analyzer.

J.P. Programs, 852 Kallas Ct., Valley Stream, NY 11580 Tel 516-825-2132.
Titles:
Knitting Instruction.

JTW Computer Systems, Inc., (0-917171), 12015 NE Marx St., Portland, OR 97220-1061 Tel 503-223-5691; FAX: 503-294-4433.
Titles:
Flexibilty-Plus.

Jacobsen Software Designs, 1590 E. 43rd Ave., Eugene, OR 97405 Tel 503-343-8030.
Titles:
The Baseball Database.

Jam Technologies, 685 Market St., Suite 860, San Francisco, CA 94105 Tel 415-442-0795.
Titles:
AutoDialog.
Convert.
MacList.
Medical Electronic Desktop (MacM.E.D.).

James Assocs., (0-924740), 7329 Meadow Ct., Boulder, CO 80301 Tel 303-530-9014.
Titles:
Adventure: The Original by Crowther & Woods.
Calendar.
Classic BASIC Games.
Concentrator Solar Cell Modelling.
Execution Time Profiler.
FORTRAN to BASIC Syntax Translator.
Multi-Layer Dielectric Optical Filter Design.
Optical Concentrator of Solar Energy.
Series 200-300 Utilities Package.
SpreadSage.
Universal Cartesian Plotting Program.
Wordwise.
Wordwise 300.

James Gang, The, (0-928666), P.O. Box 3298, Tega Cay, SC 29715 Tel 803-547-7630; Toll free: 800-297-0212; FAX: 803-547-7630.
Titles:
Membership RV Park & Camp Reservations.
Membership RV Park & Camp-Resort Marketing.
Membership RV Park & Camp-Resort Receivables.
Regular RV Park & Camp Reservation.
Theatre Management System.
Timeshare Resort Marketing System.
Timeshare Resort Receivables.
Timeshare Resort Reservations.
Wedding Organizer.

Janac Enterprises, 1725 Fleetwood Dr., Elgin, IL 60123-7130.
Titles:
OmniBooks.
OmniMailer.
OmniPay.

Jance Assocs., 1632 Par Causeway, Wescosville, PA 18106-9633.
Titles:
Powerload.
The Real Estate Investor.

Jandel Scientific, Div. of Jandel Corp., 2591 Kerner Blvd., San Rafael, CA 94901 Tel 415-453-6700; Toll free: 800-874-1888; FAX: 415-453-7769.
Titles:
Mocha Image Analysis Software.
PeakFit: Chromatography-Spectroscopy Analysis.
SigmaPlot: Scientific Graphing Software.
SigmaScan - Image: Scientific Measurement System.
SigmaStat: Statistical Software.
TableCurve 2D: Automated Curve Fitting Software.
TableCurve 3D.

Jasik Designs, 343 Trenton Way, Menlo Park, CA 94025 Tel 415-322-1386.
Titles:
The Debugger VZ & MacNosy.

Jasmine Multimedia Publishing, (1-885415), 6746 Valjean Ave., No. 100, Van Nuys, CA 91406 Tel 818-780-3344; Toll free: 800-798-7535; FAX: 818-780-8705.
Titles:
How To Create Multimedia.

Jason & Nordic Pubs., Affil. of Blue Bunny Productions, (0-944727), P.O. Box 441, Hollidaysburg, PA 16648 Tel 814-696-2920; FAX: 814-696-4250.
Titles:
Andy Finds a Turtle.
Andy Opens Wide.
Fair & Square.
Patrick & Emma Lou.
Sarah's Surprise.
A Smile from Andy.

Javelin Products Group, Div. of Information Resources, Inc. (IRI), 200 Fifth Ave., Waltham, MA 02154 Tel 617-890-1100; Toll free: 800-528-3546; FAX: 617-890-1020.
Titles:
Javelin PLUS.

Jeffries & Assocs., Inc., (1-878974), 17200 Hughes Rd., Poolesville, MD 20837 Tel 301-972-8034.
Titles:
British Foreign Direct Investment in the United States 1974-1994.
Canadian Foreign Direct Investment in the United States 1974-1994.
Dutch Foreign Direct Investment in the United States 1974-1994.

Export by Mail.
Foreign Direct Investment in the United States.
French Foreign Direct Investment in the United States 1974-1994.
German Foreign Direct Investment in the United States 1974-1994.
Global Information Access & Management.
International Language Quick Look.
Japanese Foreign Direct Investment in the United States 1974-1994.
Swiss Foreign Direct Investment in the United States 1974-1994.

Jeffries Research, (0-922946), P.O. Box 5519, Santa Maria, CA 93456-5519 Tel 805-934-1056; FAX: 805-934-2320.
Titles:
O C Compiler.
Q-C Compiler.
Small-C Compiler.

Jerome Headlands Pr., (0-9618438), P.O. Box N, Jerome, AZ 86331; Old High Schl., Hwy. 89A, Jerome, AZ 86331 Tel 602-634-8894; Dist. by: Putnam Publishing Group, 200 Madison Ave., New York, NY 10016 Tel 212-576-8900; Toll free: 800-631-8571; Dist. by: Music Sales Corp., 257 Park Ave., S., New York, NY 10010 Tel 212-254-2100.
Titles:
PC-Talk III.

Jessup, E., & Assocs., (0-918627), 4977 Canoga Ave., Woodland Hills, CA 91364 Tel 818-884-3997; FAX: 818-884-5471.
Titles:
F-Chart 1-2-3.
HPAC Details.
Load 1-2-3.

Jewell ComputerEase, 3712 Seasons Dr., Antioch, TN 37013-4937 Tel 615-399-1533.
Titles:
The Institutional Real Estate Investor, Junior: For Individual Ownerships.

JobTime Systems, Inc., (0-927901), 181 Second Ave., Suite 321, San Mateo, CA 94401 Tel 415-343-3900; FAX: 415-343-3935.
Titles:
JobTime Plus: Production Scheduling System.

Johnson Assocs., (0-917331), P.O. Box 42073, Phoenix, AZ 85080-2073 Tel 602-993-7440.
Titles:
Dental Billing Accounts Receivables.
Medical Billing Accounts Receivable.
Veterinary Billing Accounts Receivable.

Johnston & Co., P.O. Box 6627, Bloomington, IN 47407-6627 Tel 812-339-9996; FAX: 812-339-9997.
Titles:
Word Cruncher Index.
Word Cruncher View.

Jones Interactive Systems, Inc., Div. of Jones International, Ltd., (1-885400), P.O. Box 3309, Englewood, CO 80155-3309; Toll free: 800-525-7002; FAX: 303-784-8510; 9697 E. Mineral Ave., Englewood, CO 80112 Tel 303-792-3111.
Titles:
Charlton Heston Voyage Through the Bible: A Voyage of Discovery on CD-ROM.
Jones Multimedia Encyclopedia: Your Guide to the Information Superhighway.

Jonson, Ernest A., & Co., (0-928668), 216 Queen Anne Ave., N., Seattle, WA 98109 Tel 206-285-2100; Toll free: 800-541-3539; FAX: 206-281-4165.
Titles:
Flex-Screen.
General Ledger.

Payroll Program.

Jurisoft, Div. of LEXIS-NEXIS, 955 Massachusetts Ave., Cambridge, MA 02139 Tel 617-864-6151; Toll free: 800-262-5656; FAX: 617-661-0630.
Titles:
CiteRite II.
CompareRite: The Instant Redliner.
FullAuthority: The Intelligent Table of Authorities Generator.
The Legal Toolbox.

K&H Professional Management Services, Inc., 435 Devon Park Dr., Suite 300, Wayne, PA 19087 Tel 610-293-3504; FAX: 610-293-3523.
Titles:
Prestige PC.

K.C. Data Program Services, Inc., (0-924776), P.O. Box 1054, Mattoon, IL 61938 Tel 217-235-1919.
Titles:
KC-TRUST: Trust Accounting System.

KCI Computing, Inc., 2221 Rosecrans Ave., No. 136, El Segundo, CA 90245-4911 Tel 310-643-0222; Toll free: 800-824-3920.
Titles:
CONTROL/EXCEL or CONTROL for Lotus 1-2-3.

KDA Systems, (0-925812), 13115 Washington Blvd., Suite 100, Mar Vista, CA 90066 Tel 310-396-5632.
Titles:
BarGen.
GenGen.
LogGen: Logmars Label Generating Software.

KDS Corp., 934 Cornell St., Wilmette, IL 60091 Tel 847-251-2621; FAX: 847-251-6489.
Titles:
KDS Development System.
KDS-VOX-PM.

KFS Software, Inc., P.O. Box 897, Corning, CA 96021-0897; FAX: 813-530-0481.
Titles:
The Accountant.
DAY-2-DAY Pro.

KIDASA Software, Inc., (0-9623182), 1114 Lost Creek Blvd., Suite 300, Austin, TX 78746 Tel 512-328-0167; Toll free: 800-765-0167; FAX: 512-328-0247.
Titles:
MILESTONES, ETC.

KMS Systems, Inc., P.O. Box 7264, Woodlands, TX 77387 Tel 713-363-9154; FAX: 713-298-1911.
Titles:
AC: Access Control.
Direct Information.
FC: Fire Control.

K-Talk Communications, (0-927609), 1260 Windham Rd., Columbus, OH 43220 Tel 605-451-1306.
Titles:
K-TALK FileDISPATCHER: Data Aquisition & Gateway.
K-TALK FullFeatured.
MathEdit.

K-12 MicroMedia Publishing, Inc., (0-943646; 1-56419), 6 Arrow Rd., Ramsey, NJ 07446 Tel 201-825-8888; Toll free: 800-292-1997; FAX: 201-825-0582.
Titles:
Catalog Card & Label Maker.
Catalog Card & Label Writer: V6Pro.
Microstats: Sports Statistics Programs.
OfficeWorks.

Kaetron Software Corp., 12777 Jones Rd., Suite 445, Houston, TX 77070 Tel 713-890-3434; FAX: 713-890-6767.
Titles:
TopDown.

Kalish, Mark, 3131 Camino del Rio N., Suite 270, San Diego, CA 92108 Tel 619-282-7172; FAX: 619-282-7626.
Titles:
Forensic Provider.
The Provider.

Kampong Pubns., (0-9628087), 1870 Sunrise Dr., Vista, CA 92084 Tel 619-726-0990.
Titles:
Cornucopia: A Source Book of Edible Plants.

Kandu Software Corp., 2305 N. Kentucky St., Arlington, VA 22205 Tel 703-532-0213; FAX: 703-533-0291.
Titles:
CADMover.

Karatz-Nogle Accountancy Corp., 100 Spear St., Suite 1630, San Francisco, CA 94105 Tel 415-882-7373.
Titles:
LC Tracker.

KASE Systems, Inc., Div. of Intelligent Systems Corp., 1 Meca Way, Suite 150, Norcross, GA 30093 Tel 404-564-5696; FAX: 404-564-5679.
Titles:
KASE:C Plus Plus for OS/2.
KASE:VIP for OS/2.
KASE:VIP for Windows.

Kaz Business Systems, 10 Columbus Cir., Suite 1620, New York, NY 10019 Tel 212-757-9566.
Titles:
FrontEnd.

Keiland Corp., (1-885797), 7500 E. Butherus Dr., Suite J, Scottsdale, AZ 85260 Tel 602-948-3198; FAX: 602-948-5689.
Titles:
Arizona High Tech Directory, 1996: ACT for Windows Electronic Database Edition.
Arizona High Tech Directory, 1996: Electronic Database Edition.

Keith, Philip A., & Assocs., (1-885717), 15 Stephen Halsey's Path, Water Mill, NY 11976 Tel 516-726-2541; FAX: 516-726-5049.
Titles:
Technology Plans on Disk.

Keithley Asyst, Div. of Keithley Instruments, Inc., (0-924729), 440 Myles Standish Blvd., Taunton, MA 02780-7324; Toll free: 800-348-0033.
Titles:
ASYST.
ASYSTANT.
ASYSTANT - Student Version.
ASYSTANT GPIB.
EASYEST LX.
VIEWDAC.

Keller Software, (0-924801), 3857 Birch St., No. 108, Newport Beach, CA 92660 Tel 714-854-8211; Toll free: 800-544-5939; FAX: 714-756-8648.
Titles:
SIDEVIEW III: Graphics PC-DOS Security Menu.

Kent Engineering & Design, P.O. Box 178, 4215 Jordan Rd., Mottville, NY 13119-0178 Tel 315-685-8237.
Titles:
MacroModem.

PUBLISHER/TITLE INDEX

Kent Homeopathic Assocs., P.O. Box 39, Fairfax, CA 94978 Tel 415-457-0678; FAX: 415-457-0688.
Titles:
MacRepertory.

Kentary, Inc., 9034 Arrow Grass Way, Highlands Ranch, CO 80126 Tel 303-791-2077.
Titles:
Mac Art Library.

Kerchner, C. F., & Assocs., Inc., (0-917335), 5507 Louise Ln., E. Allen Township, Northampton, PA 18067-9076 Tel 610-837-0700; FAX: 610-837-7978.
Titles:
Manufacturing Inventory Control with MRP & BOMP.

Kerkhoff Computers, Inc., (0-924808), 775 S. Kirkman Rd., Suite 109, Orlando, FL 32811 Tel 407-291-4145; FAX: 407-291-4342.
Titles:
Time & Attendance.

Kern International, Inc., (0-940254; 1-55948), 190 Duck Hill Rd., Duxbury, MA 02332 Tel 617-934-2452.
Titles:
Advanced Machine Design.
Basic Aircraft Performance.
Beam Analyzer.
Beam Sections.
C-Graphics.
C Math Functions.
CAM Design Software.
Computer Models of Epidemiology.
Computer Models of Pattern Formation in Biology.
Computer Models of Population Dynamics.
Computer Models of the Chemostat.
Computer Models of the Environment.
Curve Fitting Software.
Data Plotting Software for Micros.
Dynamics.
Fiber Optic Design.
Finite Element Analysis.
Geometric Principles of CAD Graphics.
GFlow: Fluid Mechanics Software.
Graphics for the Apple.
Graphics for the IBM PC.
Helical Spring Design.
Math Lib: Math Library.
Matman: Robot Manipulator Design.
Measurement & Display of Ecological Diversity.
Mechanism Design.
Optical RayTracing Software: Ray Trace.
Promal: Mechanics of Composites.
Quality Control Charts: QC Charts.
Statics Problems Solved in BASIC.
Statistics Software for Micros.
Strength of Materials.
Structural Analysis Software for Micros.
Surface Modelling Software.
Technical Data Plotting.
Visual Statics.
Visual Stress & Strain.
Visual Vibrations.

Keyboard Publishing, Inc., (1-57349), 482 Norristown Rd., Suite 111, Blue Bell, PA 19422 Tel 610-832-0945; Toll free: 800-945-4551; FAX: 610-832-0948.
Titles:
The Acid-Base Diagnostician.
Hematology VideoReview.
Histology QuizBank.
Histology TextStack.
Histology Video Review.
Histology VideoIndex.
Immunology QuizBank.
Immunology TextStack.
Keyboard Histology Series: Student Edition.
Keyboard Immunology Series: Student Edition.
Keyboard Microbiology Series: Student Edition.
Keyboard Pathology Series: Student Edition.
The Merck Manual TextStack: Professional Edition.
The Merck Manual TextStack: Student Edition.
Microbiology QuizBank.
Microbiology TextStack.
Microbiology VideoIndex.
Molecular Cloning.
Pathology QuizBank.
Pathology TextStack.
Pathology VideoIndex.
Pharmacology TextStack: Professional Edition.
Pharmacology TextStack: Student Edition.

Kidsoft, Inc., (1-57594), 10275 N. DeAnza Blvd., Cupertino, CA 95014 Tel 408-342-3522; FAX: 408-342-3500.
Titles:
Alien Arcade.
America Adventure.
A Bear Family Adventure.
Bug Adventure.
Compton's Concise Encyclopedia.
Dr. T's Sing-a-Long Around the World.
Dr. T's Sing-a-Long Kid's Classics.
Elementary Science: The Human Body.
Even More Incredible Machine.
Foo Castle.
Games in English.
Games in French.
Games in German.
Games in Japanese.
Games in Spanish.
Gus & the Cyberbuds Go to the Kooky Carnival.
Gus & the Cyberbuds Sing, Play & Paint A-Long.
Gus Goes to Cyber Town.
Gus Goes to Cyberopolis.
Gus Goes to CyberStone Park.
Imaginator.
The Incredible Toon Machine.
Isaac Asimov's Library of the Universe.
Isaac Asimov's Library of the Universe: The Solar System.
Isaac Asimov's: The Solar System.
It's a Bird's Life.
Jigsaw-It, Jr.
Kaboom, Jr.
Kid's Zoo.
Lenny's Multimedia Circus.
Lenny's Music Toons.
Lenny's Time Machine.
The Lost Tribe.
Mental Math Games.
Monster Lab.
Morgan's Trivia Machine, Jr.
Nigel's World Adventure in World Geography.
Nighlight.
Night Light.
Nightlight.
Nightlite.
Ozzie's Fun Time Garden.
Ozzie's Funtime Garden.
Professor Wise & His X-Ray Eyes.
Professor Wise X-Ray Eyes.
Real World Math Adventures in Flight.
Rusty & Rosy Read with Me.
Sitting on the Farm.
Tessel Mania.
Travelrama U. S. A.
The Ugly Duckling.
VroomBooks Four Footed Friends.
VroomBooks Stradiwackius Counting Concert.
VroomBooks: Stradiwackius, the Counting Concert.
Word City.
Zoo-Opolis.
Zootopia.

Kilgore Software, (0-9624863), P.O. Box 2291, West Sacramento, CA 95691; 2964 Ironwood Way, West Sacramento, CA 95691 Tel 916-371-3715.
Titles:
Treetop.

Kinetic Corp., 250 Distillery Commons, Louisville, KY 40206-1990 Tel 502-583-1679; FAX: 502-583-1104.
Titles:
Kinetic Access II.
Kinetic CADConvert.
Kinetic Menu.
Kinetic Microlok.
Kinetic U.S. Maps-3D.
Kinetic Words, Graphs & Art.

Kinko's, (1-55577), P.O. Box 8000, Ventura, CA 93002; Toll free: 800-235-6919; 800-292-6640 (in California); 255 W. Stanley Ave., Suite A, Ventura, CA 93002 Tel 805-652-4000.
Titles:
ALPAL & Big ALPAL.
Create.
DAFRAC-The Diffraction Calculation Tool.
Drexel Plot.
FEMG: A Finite Element Mesh Generator.
FunPlot.
FunPlot-3D.
KSIMS.
Laser Terminal.
MacDiet-Student Version.
MacSimplex.
MacStereo (R-S).
MacVoice.
MindLab.
Model Neuron.
Molecular Editor.
Molecular Weight Calculator.
Neuranotomy Foundations.
Pascal Pointers.
Small Tips Desk Acessory.
Tools for Writers.

KIS Computer Corp., (0-925363), P.O. Box 62334, King of Prussia, PA 19406-0376 Tel 610-354-0244; FAX: 610-354-9144.
Titles:
Accountant's 1040.
ESQ-1.
PROMOT.
The Scheduler.
Write-Up Master.

Kiwi Software, Inc., (1-877777), 6546 Pardall Rd., Santa Barbara, CA 93117-4842 Tel 805-968-7432; FAX: 805-565-1086.
Titles:
Kiwi POWER MENUS.
Kiwi POWER WINDOWS.
KiwiEnvelopes!
Screenscapes.

Klex Software, Inc., 25633 Branchester, Farmington, MI 48336 Tel 810-473-0347.
Titles:
MacConcept.

Klynas Engineering, P.O. Box 499, Simi Valley, CA 93062 Tel 805-583-1029.
Titles:
Streets on a Disk.

Knick Drafting, Inc., 914 Saint Clair St., No. M17, Melbourne, FL 32935 Tel 407-253-3500.
Titles:
MacPerspective.

Knoware Learning Systems, Inc., (0-924836), 219 Vassar St., Cambridge, MA 02139 Tel 617-576-3821; Toll free: 800-843-5669.
Titles:
Knoware.

Knowledge Adventure, Inc., (1-56997), 4502 Dyer St., La Crescenta, CA 91214 Tel 818-542-4200; FAX: 818-542-4475.
Titles:
Dinosaur Adventure.
The Tale of Peter Rabbit.

Knowledge Dynamics Corp., (1-56747), P.O. Box 1558, Canyon Lake, TX 78130; Toll free: 800-331-2783; FAX: 210-964-3958; HC4, Box 185H, Canyon Lake, TX 78133 Tel 210-964-3994.
Titles:
INSTALL OWNER'S MANUAL.

Knowledge Garden, Inc., 127 Wildernedd Rd., Saint James, NY 11780 Tel 516-862-0600; FAX: 516-862-0644.
Titles:
KnowledgePro Database Toolkit.
KnowledgePro for DOS/DOS Gold.
KnowledgePro for Windows KPWin/KPWin Gold.
KPWin Plus Plus.
KPWin SQLKIT.
WRAP.

KnowLedgePoint, 1129 Industrial Ave., Petaluma, CA 94952 Tel 707-762-0333.
Titles:
Descriptions Now!
Performance Now!
Policies Now!

KnowWare, (0-9642108), 40559 Encyclopedia Cir., Fremont, CA 94538 Tel 510-770-4900; FAX: 510-656-9979.
Titles:
Chadwick & the Sneaky Egg Thief.

Koala Acquisitions, Inc., (0-928431), P.O. Box 1924, Morgan Hill, CA 95038-1924 Tel 408-776-8181; FAX: 408-776-8187.
Titles:
MacVision Color Video Digitizer with MacVision Image Processing Software 4.1.
MacVision Image Processing Software.
MacVision Video Digitizer with MacVision Image Processing Software 4.1.

Komputerwerk, 851 Parkview Blvd., Pittsburgh, PA 15215 Tel 412-782-0384; Toll free: 800-423-3400.
Titles:
Finally! Modules.
Finally! Subroutines.
Finally! Xgraf.

Komstock Co., P.O. Box 485, Washburn, ND 58577-0485.
Titles:
AgAccounts.
Komstock's MapCalc.
MapBase.

Kraft Systems Co., (0-928672), 450 W. California Ave., Vista, CA 92083 Tel 619-724-7146; Toll free: 800-854-1923.
Titles:
Executive Cursor Control: Joystick Support Software.

Krell Software Corp., (0-918349), P.O. Box 1252, Lake Grove, NY 11755 Tel 516-689-3500; Toll free: 800-245-7355; FAX: 516-689-3549.
Titles:
GMAT: Exam Preparation Series.
Krell's GED Prep.
Odyssey in Time.
Plague Fighters.
Time Traveler.

Krohm International, Ltd., (1-878190), 4216 S. Hocker Dr., Suite 200, Independence, MO 64055-4766 Tel 816-373-7828; FAX: 816-373-8990.
Titles:
KI/Composer.

Kronos, Inc., (0-924847), 62 Fourth Ave., Waltham, MA 02154 Tel 617-890-3232; Toll free: 800-225-1561.
Titles:
CRT Emulator.
File Transfer.
Host 35-70.
Kronos Controller.
TIMEKEEPER Central Software: TKC.

Kroy, Inc., 14555 N. Hayden Rd., Scottsdale, AZ 85260 Tel 602-951-1593; Toll free: 800-521-4997.
Titles:
Kroy Sign Studio.

Kruse Control Software, 30 Ridge Rd., Suite 21, Ridgewood, NJ 07450 Tel 201-670-0677.
Titles:
Time Frame: Your Contact Network Maximizer.

LA Business Systems, Inc., 1866 Sheridan Rd., Suite 216, Highland Park, IL 60035 Tel 708-433-6477; FAX: 708-433-7676.
Titles:
CAN-FAX.

LAS Systems, Inc., (0-917993), 21703 Timber Ridge Ct., Kildeer, IL 60047 Tel 312-438-3811.
Titles:
LAS AIMS: Agency Information & Management System for Independent Insurance Agents.
LAS-FIMS: LAS Food Industry Management System for the Processed Food Industry.

L & L Products, Inc., (0-924975), Wheeler Professional Pk., P.O. Box A-57, Hanover, NH 03755 Tel 603-643-4503.
Titles:
SPREAD Financial Modeling Language: SPREAD.
Spread to DIF File Conversion Utility: DIF Converter.
Spread Workstation.

Lbs Engineering, Inc., 1320 Lincoln St., Hollywood, FL 33019 Tel 305-920-1584.
Titles:
Wind & Seismic Analysis.

LCI, (0-924863), 2702 International Ln., Madison, WI 53704 Tel 608-241-4151; FAX: 608-241-0361.
Titles:
Blood Bank Archives.
Chameleon Laboratory Information Management System.
Chameleon Laboratory Information System.
HIV Tracking System.
Hummingbird Laboratory System.
Micro for OMCARE Microbiology System.
O. R. Suite Management & Scheduling System.
The Schedule Book.
SURGE: Pathology Laboratory Management System.

LCS/Telegraphics, (0-924862), 150 Rogers St., Cambridge, MA 02142 Tel 617-225-7970; FAX: 617-225-7969.
Titles:
TelePaint.

LDS, Inc., (0-925014), 10323 W. 84th Terr., Lenexa, KS 66214-1639 Tel 913-492-5700; Toll free: 800-255-1912; FAX: 913-492-3506.
Titles:
Accuplus Integrated Distribution Logistics System.
EMPATH.
Remedy Practice Management System.
TLN: The Total Logistics Network.

LHR Assocs., (1-880967), P.O. Box 851, Marietta, GA 30060; 409 Church St., Marietta, GA 30060 Tel 404-424-1451.
Titles:
Express.

LIBRA Corp., (0-924915), 4001 S. 700 E., Suite 301, Salt Lake City, UT 84107-2177 Tel 801-281-0700; Toll free: 800-453-3827; FAX: 801-284-9182.
Titles:
Accounts Receivable.
Billing.
Cost Accounting.
Inventory Control.
LIBRA Accounts Payable.
LIBRA General Ledger.
LIBRA Payroll.
Order Entry.
Perspectives by Libra: P2.
Property Management.
Sales Analysis: Optional Feature to A-R.

LTD Software, P.O. Box 3176, Chatsworth, CA 91313 Tel 818-998-6840.
Titles:
Personal Financial Forecaster.

Laboratory Microsystems, Inc., (0-924864), 12555 W. Jefferson Blvd., Suite 313, Los Angeles, CA 90066 Tel 310-306-7412; FAX: 310-301-0761.
Titles:
LMI FORTH-83 Metacompiler.
UR/FORTH.
WinForth.

Laboratory Technologies Corp., 400 Research Dr., Wilmington, MA 01887 Tel 508-657-5400; Toll free: 800-879-5228; FAX: 508-658-9972.
Titles:
LABTECH CONTROL.
LABTECH NOTEBOOK.
Realtime Vision: Operator Interface.

Lahey Computer Systems, Inc., P.O. Box 6091, Incline Village, NV 89450 Tel 702-831-2500; Toll free: 800-548-4778; FAX: 702-831-8123.
Titles:
F77L-EM/32.
F77L-Lahey-FORTRAN.
Lahey Fortran 90 (LF90).
Lahey Personal FORTRAN '77 (LP77).
LP77 Toolkit Library.

Lake Avenue Software, (0-924869), 2406 N. Lake Ave., Altadena, CA 91001 Tel 818-445-6526; FAX: 818-799-3406.
Titles:
Advanced Job Shop System.
Advanced Manufacturing System.
The Assistant Controller: Order Entry/Invoicing.
The Assistant Controller Series.
Bank Reconciliation.
Golf Handicapping System.
Golf Tournament Scoring.
Lake Avenue Accounting Collection.
Multi-Company.
Point of Sale System.

PUBLISHER/TITLE INDEX

Purchase Order System.

Land of Canaan Communications, (0-9622875), 8916 Reading Rd., No. 4, Cincinnati, OH 45215-3256 Tel 513-731-0707.
Titles:
Horror in Hocking County.

LANDCADD International, Inc., 7388 S. Revere Pkwy., Bldg. 900, Suite 901-902, Englewood, CO 80112-3942 Tel 303-799-3600; FAX: 303-799-3696.
Titles:
Landcadd Complete.

Landtech Data Corp., (0-922497), 120 S. Olive Ave., Suite 303, West Palm Beach, FL 33401 Tel 407-833-0454; FAX: 407-835-0326.
Titles:
Landtech 86 Real Estate Closing System.

Langenscheidt Pubs., Inc., Subs. of Langenscheidt KG, (0-88729; 3-468), 46-35 54th Rd., Maspeth, NY 11378 Tel 718-784-0055; Toll free: 800-432-6277; FAX: 718-784-0640.
Titles:
Correct Behavior: The Japanese Way.
Duden: Das Herkunftsworterbuch.
Duden: Das Stilworterbuch.
Duden: Das Worterbuch Medizinischer Fachausdruke.
Duden: Die Deutsch Rechtschreibung.
Duden: Dt. Universal WB, Duden Oxford GWB, Englisch.
Duden Multimedia: Mein Ertes Lexikon (for Pre-Readers).
Duden PC Bibliothek: Das Bedeutungsworterbuch.
Duden PC Bibliothek: Das Fremdworterbuch.
Duden PC Bibliothek: Die Sinn und Sachverwandten Worter.
Duden: Redewendungen und Sprichwortliche Redensarten.
Duden: Richtiges und Gutes Deutsch.
Duden: Zitate und Ausspruche.
Earthwords for Alien Dinosaurs Super Media.
Earthwords for Alien Dinosaurs Superplanetary.
Langenschedit PC Worterbuch Englisch.
Langenschedits CD-ROM Bibliothek: PC Worterbuch Englisch, Duden Bedeutungsworterbuch, Meyers Grosses Hand Lexikon.
Langenscheidt: Euroworterbuch Englisch.
Langenscheidt: Euroworterbuch Franzosisch.
Langenscheidt: Euroworterbuch Italienisch.
Langenscheidt: Euroworterbuch Spanisch.
Langenscheidt PC Bibliothek: 100 Musterbriefe Englisch.
Langenscheidt PC Bibliothek: 100 Musterbriefe Franzosisch.
Langenscheidt: Taschenworterbuch Englisch.
Langenscheidt: Taschenworterbuch Franzosisch.
Langenscheidt's: (Basic Vocabulary) Grundwortschatz Englisch.
Langenscheidt's: (Basic Vocabulary) Grundwortschatz Franzosisch.
Langenscheidt's: (Basic Vocabulary) Grundwortschatz Italienisch.
Langenscheidt's: (Basic Vocabulary) Grundwortschatz Spanisch.
Langenscheidt's: Englisch Worterbuch Fur DOS - An Wender.
Langenscheidt's: Euro-Set Englisch 1 Franzosisch - Italienisch - Spanisch.
Langenscheidt's: Handworterbuch Englisch for PC Windows & Mac.
Langenscheidt's: Handworterbuch Franzosish for PC Windows & Mac.
Langenscheidt's: Taschenworterbuch Englisch Mit Sprachausgabe.
Langenscheidt's: Taschenworterbuch Russisch.
LexiROM Meyers, Duden & Langenscheidt's.
Meyer Multimedia: Das Flaggschiff des Konigs.
Meyers Lexikon: Das Wissen A-Z.
Meyers Lexikon: Die Okologie.
Meyers Lexikon: Informatik.
Meyers Lexikon: Politik und Gesellschaft.
Meyers Multimedia: Das Wunder un Seres Korpers.
Meyers Multimedia: Wie Funktioniert Das?
Polyglott Stadtefuhrer Berlin.
Polyglott Stadtefuhrer London.
Polyglott Stadtefuhrer New York.
Polyglott Stadtefuhrer Paris.

Language Engineering Corp., (1-882465), 385 Concord Ave., Belmont, MA 02178 Tel 617-489-4000; FAX: 617-489-3850.
Titles:
Ambassador English-Japanese for the Macintosh.
Ambassador French-Japanese for the Macintosh.

Language Pubns. Interactive, Inc., 121 W. 27th St., Suite 801, New York, NY 10001 Tel 212-620-3193.
Titles:
Who Is Oscar Lake?: A French Interactive Language Learning Adventure.
Who Is Oscar Lake?: A Spanish Interactive Language Learning Adventure.
Who Is Oscar Lake?: An English Interactive Language Learning Adventure.

Language Systems Corp., (1-885644), 100 Carpenter Dr., Sterling, VA 20164 Tel 703-478-0181; Toll free: 800-252-6479; FAX: 703-689-9593.
Titles:
FORTRAN Tools for AppMaker.
LS FORTRAN Professional.
LS FORTRAN Standard.
Math77: Matehmatical Subprograms for FORTRAN 77.
SoftPolish.
TSiGraphics.

Lansing Computer Assocs., Inc., Div. of Professional Technical Development, (0-924878), 501 N. Marshall St., Suite 101, Lansing, MI 48912; FAX: 517-482-8896.
Titles:
Homeowners.

LapCAD Engineering, 1568 Diablo Point Ct., Chula Vista, CA 92011 Tel 619-421-1236.
Titles:
LapCAD: Finite Element Modeler.

Larchsoft, (0-943065), 2025 E. Downing, Mesa, AZ 85203 Tel 602-834-3999.
Titles:
Sprinkler Selector.

Lascaux Graphics, (0-943189), 3771 E. Guthrie Mountain Pl., Tucson, AZ 85718 Tel 520-299-0661; Toll free: 800-338-0993; FAX: 520-299-9588.
Titles:
Fields & Operators.
Lascaux 1000: The Intelligent Calculator.

Laser Connection, Subs. of QMS, Inc., P.O. Box 850296, Mobile, AL 36685 Tel 334-633-7223; Toll free: 800-523-2696; FAX: 334-633-4866.
Titles:
MacKiss.
UltraScript PC+.

LaserGo, Inc., (1-878388), 9715 Carroll Center Rd., Suite 107, San Diego, CA 92126 Tel 619-450-4600; FAX: 619-450-9334.
Titles:
GoFonts.
GoScript.
GoScript Plus.
GoScript Select.
LaserGo Type Commander TrueType Fonts for Windows 3.1: Blue Ribbon Collection.
LaserGo Type Commander TrueType Fonts for Windows 3.1: Harvest Collection.

LAWRENCE PRODUCTIONS, INC.

LaserGo Type Commander TrueType Fonts for Windows 3.1: Springtime Collection.

LaserWare, Inc., P.O. Box 668, San Rafael, CA 94915 Tel 415-453-9500; Toll free: 800-367-6898 (outside California).
Titles:
LaserPaint.
LaserPaint Color II: The Integrated Graphics Workshop.

Lassen Software, Inc., (0-924883), 5923 Clark Rd., Suite F, Paradise, CA 95969 Tel 916-877-0408; Toll free: 800-338-2126; FAX: 916-877-1164.
Titles:
Diskette Manager II.
Diskette Manager Plus.
Financial Ratios.
Loan Manager.
Personal Lawyer-Power of Attorney & Statement of Guardianship.
Personal Lawyer-Promissory Notes.
Personal Lawyer-Residential Real Estate Lease.
Personal Lawyer-Wills.
Personal Lawyer-Wills Professional Version.
Program Manager Plus.

Lattice, Inc., (0-917382; 1-55544), 3020 Woodcreek Dr., Suite D, Downers Grove, IL 60515 Tel 708-769-4060; Toll free: 800-444-4309 (Sales only); FAX: 708-769-4083.
Titles:
CodeProbe Debugger for RPG.
Communications Library.
dBC III Library.
DFE-DFU: Data File Editor-Data File Utility.
400D-RPG Development Tools for DOS.
HighStyle.
Lattice C Compiler for DOS & OS/2.
Lattice ES68K C Development System.
Lattice ES78 C Development System: MS-DOS to NEC uPD78310, uPD78312, or uPD78312-A Cross Development System.
Lattice ES80 C Development System: MS-DOS to Zilog Z80 C Cross Development System.
Lattice RPG II Development System.
Lattice 80286 C Development System for DOS & OS-2.
SecretDisk II.
SideTalk II.

Law Firm Management, Inc., 406 SW 96th Ct., Miami, FL 33174 Tel 305-920-5605; Toll free: 800-578-6345; FAX: 602-991-7087.
Titles:
MiniNEIL Time/Cost Billing System.
The Neil Legal System for Microcomputers.
Neil Legal Time/Cost Billing System.
Neil Legal Time/Cost Billing with General Ledger, Accounts Payable with Check Writing.

Law Management Systems, 975 N. Michilinda, Pasadena, CA 91107 Tel 818-351-8921.
Titles:
Law & Order: Litigation Support.
LAWMAN Calendar: Calendar-Docket Control.
LAWMAN Case Management.
LAWMAN Conflict of Interest.
LAWMAN Document Manager.
LAWMAN Litigation Support.
LAWMAN SST.
Lawman 7: Law Office Management System.
Layman Probate Accounting.

Lawrence Productions, Inc., (0-917999; 1-882848; 1-57204), 1800 S. 35th St., Galesburg, MI 49053 Tel 616-665-7075; Toll free: 800-421-4157; FAX: 616-665-7060.
Titles:
Abel's Island.
Across Five Aprils.
Amos Fortune Free Man.
... and now Miguel.

Bridge to Terabithia.
The Cat Ate My Gymsuit.
The Cay.
Charlotte's Web.
Child of the Owl.
The Chocolate War.
The Cricket in Times Square.
Dear Mr. Henshaw.
Dicey's Song.
Filling Out Job Applications.
First Days on the Job.
Freaky Friday.
From the Mixed-up Files of Mrs Basil E. Frankweiler.
The House of Dies Drear.
The House of 60 Fathers.
The Incredible Journey.
Island of the Blue Dolphins.
James & the Giant Peach.
Job Attitudes: Assessment & Improvement.
Job Readiness Series.
Job Success Series.
Julie of the Wolves.
Katie's Farm.
Kid McGee.
Kid McGee II.
Lawrence Productions' Discovering America.
The Lion, the Witch & the Wardrobe.
Looking Good.
The Lost Tribe.
Luck Everlasting.
McGee.
McGee at the Fun Fair.
McGee School Days.
The McGee Series.
Mathology.
Mathology II: Fractions.
Mind Castle: The Spell of the Word Wizard.
Mrs. Frisby & the Rats of NIHM.
Mystery Math Island.
Nigel's World: Adventures in World Geography.
Number the Stars.
Old Yeller.
The Phantom Tollbooth.
Philip Hal Likes E, I Reckon Maybe.
The Pushcart War.
Rabbit Hill.
Resumes Made Easy.
Sadako & the Thousand Paper Cranes.
Sarah, Plain & Tall.
Shiloh.
The Sign of the Beaver.
Sounder.
Stone Fox.
A Stranger Came Ashore.
Stuart Little.
Successful Job Interviewing.
Tales of a Fourth Grade Nothing.
Trolls, Dragons & English Mechanics.
Where the Red Fern Grows.
A Wrinkle in Time.
Your Personal Habits.
Your Work Habits.
Zootopia.

Lawyers Software Publishing Co., Div. of Compilex Corp., (0-926030), 1095 Klish Way, Del Mar, CA 92014 Tel 619-481-5944; Toll free: 800-247-5327; FAX: 619-755-8517; P.O. Box 2765, Del Mar, CA 92014-5744.
Titles:
Economic Loss Program.
Future Damage & Present Value Calculator.
Personal Injury Case Evaluation Program.
PLEAS - Personal Injury Litigation Evaluation & Accounting System.
Speed & Stopping Distance Calculator.

Leader Systems, Inc., 4200 Northside Parkway, Atlanta, GA 30067 Tel 404-816-3325.
Titles:
Workstation Wizard.

Leadership Software, Inc., (0-944222), 4611 Evergreen, Bellaire, TX 77401 Tel 713-668-4130.
Titles:
MPO: Managing Participation in Organizations.

Learned-Mahn, Subs. of National Data Corp., (0-922092), 1109 Main St., Boise, ID 83702 Tel 208-336-2281; Toll free: 800-727-5009; FAX: 208-342-0964.
Titles:
ACHWorks.
Bank-On-It.
Collections Manager.
Contract Collection Manager.
Contract Express.
ECMLink.
EMCI: Electronic Media Claims Interface.
ERA/Link.
HealthPay.
TRIM.

LearnerFirst, 1075 13th St., S., Birmingham, AL 35205 Tel 205-934-9182.
Titles:
Benchmarking with Dr. H. James Harrington.
Getting Started with Quality Management.
How to Implement ISO 9000.
Process Breakthrough.
Process Management.

Learners Image, P.O. Box 3669, Logan, UT 84321; Toll free: 800-255-8791; FAX: 801-753-8417; 560 W. 600 N., Logan, UT 84321 Tel 801-752-5608.
Titles:
Miniature Math.
Spellbound.

Learning Co., The, (0-917995; 1-879093), 6493 Kaiser Dr., Fremont, CA 94555 Tel 510-792-2101; Toll free: 800-852-2255; FAX: 510-792-9628.
Titles:
Math Rabbit.
Robot Odyssey.
Think Quick!

Lease Star, Ltd., 1650 Old Country Rd., Plainview, NY 11803-5088 Tel 516-694-3700; Toll free: 800-782-7234; FAX: 516-694-0239.
Titles:
LeaseStar 2000.

LeaseTek, Inc., 300 Penn Center Blvd., Suite 500, Pittsburgh, PA 15235-5505 Tel 412-829-3080; FAX: 412-829-0840.
Titles:
The Analyz-r.
The LeaseManag-r.
The Quote-r.
The Seamless Lease-Loan Manag-r.

LeBaugh Software Corp., (0-929977), P.O. Box 371074, Omaha, NE 68137-5074; FAX: 402-593-0381.
Titles:
LePrint.

Lee Software, P.O. Box 742644, Dallas, TX 75374-2644 Tel 214-530-2864.
Titles:
Health Med.
Total Control Diet.

Legal Data Systems, Inc., 960 C. Harvest Dr., Blue Bell, PA 19422; Toll free: 800-341-4012; FAX: 617-426-9286.
Titles:
RainMaker: Legal Data's Client Accounting Software.

Legal Technologies, Inc., 59 Hidden Turn, Newtown, PA 18940-1126.
Titles:
Paperchaser Computer System.

Legend Entertainment, (1-880520), P.O. Box 10810, Chantilly, VA 22021-0810 Tel 703-222-8500; Toll free: 800-658-8891; FAX: 703-968-5151; Dist. by: Accolade, Inc., 550 S. Winchester Blvd., Suite 200, San Jose, CA 95128 Tel 408-985-1700.
Titles:
Companions of Xanth.
Death Gate.
Eric The Unready.
Frederik Pohl's GATEWAY.
Mission Critical.
Spellcasting Party Pak.
Spellcasting 201 THE SORCERER'S APPLIANCE.
Spellcasting 301: Spring Break.
Superhero League of Hoboken.

Legisoft, Inc., (1-879530), 3430 Noriega, San Francisco, CA 94122 Tel 415-566-9136; FAX: 415-566-1168.
Titles:
Lawyer's WillWriter II.

Lego Dacta, Div. of Lego Systems, Inc., (0-914831; 1-57056), 555 Taylor Rd., Enfield, CT 06083-1600 Tel 203-749-2291; Toll free: 800-527-8339; FAX: 203-763-2466.
Titles:
LEGO TC Logo Starter Pack.

Financial Data Ctr., P.O. Box 1332, Bryn Mawr, PA 19010 Tel 610-527-5216; FAX: 610-527-5226.
Titles:
Financial Planning TOOLKIT.
NumberCruncher.

Leimberg Assocs., (0-9644565), P.O. Box 601, Bryn Mawr, PA 19010 Tel 610-527-5216; FAX: 610-527-5226; 207 Rawles Run Ln., Bryn Mawr, PA 19010.
Titles:
Steve Leimberg's Financial Calculator.

Leisure Ware, Inc., 1530 Locust St., Philadelphia, PA 19102 Tel 215-735-6815.
Titles:
Your Photo Here!

Lemain, Inc., 7420 Shellborn Dr., Loomis, CA 95650 Tel 916-791-7884; Toll free: 800-227-7881; FAX: 916-989-9466.
Titles:
Corporate MBA.

Lender Support Systems, Div. of LSSI, 2565 Camino del Rio South, Suite 102, San Diego, CA 92108-3771 Tel 619-291-7172; FAX: 619-291-5654.
Titles:
LOANbase DocPrep II.
LOANbase III PLUS.

Leong Jacobs, Inc., (0-9623342), 2729 Lury Ln., Annapolis, MD 21401 Tel 410-224-2346.
Titles:
Xian, Chinese Chess for the IBM PC.
Xian for Windows.

Lerman Assocs., 12 Endmoor Rd., Westford, MA 01886 Tel 508-692-7600; Toll free: 800-233-4671.
Titles:
Extra K.

PUBLISHER/TITLE INDEX

Letraset U.S.A., Div. of Esselte Pendaflex Corp., (0-944289), 40 Eisenhower Dr., Paramus, NJ 07653 Tel 201-845-6100; FAX: 201-845-5351.
Titles:
ImageStudio.
LetraFont Type Library & LetraStudio.
Letraset Design Solutions.
Letraset Design Templates.
Letraset Type Library.
LetraStudio.
Ready, Set, Go! 3.0.
Ready, Set, Go! 4.0.
StandOut.

Lewis Pubs., Subs. of CRC Pr., Inc., (0-87371; 1-56670), Tel 313-475-8619; FAX: 313-475-8650; Orders to: CRC Pr., Inc., 2000 Corporate Blvd., NW, Boca Raton, FL 33431 Tel 407-994-0555; Toll free: 800-272-7737. Lewis Pubs. Out of Print titles are available through Franklin Book Co., Inc.
Titles:
EPA's Sampling & Analysis Methods Database.

Lexikon Services, (0-944601), P.O. Box 1328, Elverth, CA 95626 Tel 916-331-3046.
Titles:
Accounting & Finance Abbreviations & Acronyms.
Computer Glossary of Abbreviations: SuperGlossary.
History of Computing: An Encyclopedia of the People & Machines That Made Computer History.

Liant Software Corp., (0-926638), 959 Concord St., Framingham, MA 01701 Tel 508-872-8700; Toll free: 800-237-1873; FAX: 508-626-2221.
Titles:
C Plus Plus/Views.
C-scape.
CodeWatch.
LPI-C.
LPI - C++.
LPI-COBOL.
LPI-FORTRAN.
Open PL/I.
RM/CO*
RM/COBOL.
RM/Companion.
RM/Forte.
RM-Fortran.
RM/Panels.
RM/plus DB.

Libraries Unlimited, Inc., (0-87287; 1-56308), P.O. Box 6633, Englewood, CO 80155-6633 Tel 303-770-1220; Toll free: 800-237-6124; FAX: 303-220-8843.
Titles:
C. A. Cutter's Three-Figure Author Table.
C. A. Cutter's Two-Figure Author Table.
Cutter-Sanborn Tree-Figure Author Table.

Library Educational Institute, Inc., (1-879359), R.R. 1, Box 219, New Albany, PA 18833 Tel 717-746-1842; FAX: 717-746-1114.
Titles:
Library Border Book.
Library of ClipArt: Disk Version.
Library Symbol Clip Art.

Library Systems & Services, Inc., 200 Orchard Ridge Dr., Gaithersburg, MD 20878 Tel 301-975-9800; Toll free: 800-638-8725; FAX: 301-975-9844.
Titles:
LOANet.
Ultra Cat.

Library Video Co., P.O. Box 1110, Bala Cynwyd, PA 19004; Toll free: 800-843-3620; FAX: 610-667-3425; 521 Righters Ferry Rd., Bala Cynwyd, PA 19004 Tel 610-667-0200.
Titles:
Alge-Blaster 3.
Allie's Activity Kit.
Allie's Activity Series.
Allie's Playhouse.
Alphabet Blocks.
Amanda Stories.
America Adventure.
Annatommy.
Anno's Learning Games.
Arthur's Birthday.
Arthur's Teacher Trouble.
Bailey's Book House.
Beginning Reading.
Big Anthony's Mixed-Up Magic.
The Big Bug Alphabet Book.
Bug Adventure (3-D).
Busytown.
Countdown.
Counting on Frank.
Creepy Crawlies.
Cyberboogie with Sharon, Lois & Bram.
Dangerous Creatures.
Dinosaur Adventure (3-D).
Dinosaur Discovery.
Dinosaur Safari.
Dinosaurs (Microsoft).
Dinosaurs: The Multimedia Encyclopedia.
The Discoverers.
Early Math.
The Everything You Wanted to Know about Sports Encyclopedia.
Eyewitness Encyclopedia of Science.
Firefighter.
George Shrinks.
Harry & the Haunted House.
If You Give a Mouse a Cookie.
In Search of Spot.
Jump Start Kindergarten.
Junior Encyclopedias: The Farm.
Just Grandma & Me.
Kid's Typing.
Kid's Zoo: A Baby Animal Adventure.
Little Monster at School.
Living Book Series.
Lost & Found.
Lost & Found Series.
Lyric Language French.
Lyric Language German.
Lyric Language Series.
Lyric Language Spanish.
Macmillan Multimedia Dictionary for Children.
The Magic School Bus Explores the Human Body.
The Magic School Bus Explores the Solar System.
Magic School Bus Series.
Mammals: A Multimedia Encyclopedia.
Math Blaster Mystery: The Great Brain Robbery.
Math Blaster Series.
Math Rabbit.
Merriam Webster's Dictionary for Kids.
Millie's Math House.
Multimedia Animals Encyclopedia.
My First Incredible Amazing Dictionary.
The New Kid on the Block.
Oregon Trail.
Ozzie's World.
Peter & the Wolf.
Peter Pan: Kids Creative Reader.
Picture Atlas of the World.
Planetary Taxi.
The Presidents: A Picture History.
Professor Iris Fun Field Trip: Animal Safari.
Putt-Putt Goes to the Moon.
Random House Kid's Encyclopedia.
Reader Rabbit.
Reading Blaster.
Recess in Greece.
Richard Scarry Series.
Richard Scarry's How Things Work.
Ruff's Bones.
Sammy's Science House.
The San Diego Zoo Presents: The Animals!
Science Adventure II.
Secret of the Lost City.
Sesame Street: Numbers.
Space Adventure II.
Spelling Blizzard.
Spelling Jungle.
Super Solvers Spellbound!
The Talking Tutor Series.
Teach Your Kids Multimedia World History.
Thinkin' Things: Collection I.
Thumbelina.
The Tortoise & the Hare.
The Ultimate Human Body.
Undersea Adventure.
Visual Almanac Series.
Vitsie Visits Dinosaurs.
Vitsie Visits Series.
Vitsie Visits Space.
Vitsie Visits the Ocean.
The Way Things Work.
What Is a Bellybutton?
World Geography: Nigel's World Adventures.
The World of Totty Pig.
Zoo-Opolis.
Zurk's Rainforest Lab.

Lichtman Industries, 4 Taylor St., Millburn, NJ 07041 Tel 201-467-0010; Toll free: 800-545-5564; FAX: 201-467-0440.
Titles:
EZ-PrintSet.

Lieberman, Philip, & Assocs., Inc., (0-923941), 1010 S. Weinbach Ave., Evansville, IN 47714 Tel 812-479-5064; FAX: 812-479-8295.
Titles:
AIM for Utility Companies: Utility Company Processing for Digital Equipment Corporation Systems.
Labels.

Life Science Assocs., (0-9610148), 1 Fenimore Rd., Bayport, NY 11705-2115 Tel 516-472-2111; FAX: 516-472-8146.
Titles:
Computer Programs for Cognitive Rehabilitation.
Discovering Psychology.
ESP: Precognition, Clairvoyance & Telepathy.
Perception: A Computerized Approach.
Pharmacological Calculations-Research.
Psychological Experiments & Research.
Randt Memory Test.

Lifeboat Assocs., Affil. of Lifeboat Assocs., Italy, France, Japan, (0-924918), 1163 Shrewsbury Ave., Shrewsbury, NJ 07702 Tel 201-389-8950; Toll free: 800-847-7078.
Titles:
ADVANTAGE C++.
ADVANTAGE Disassembler.
ADVANTAGE Graphics.
ADVANTAGE Link.
ADVANTAGE Make.
ADVANTAGE 386 C.
ADVANTAGE 386 Pascal.
ADVANTAGE Version Control Management System (VCMS).
The C-Food Smorgasboard.
Disilog.
Distel.
Emulator 86.
Executive Alert System.
MagicPrint.
MathStar.
MathStar PC.
PANEL Plus.
PLINK.
PLINK II.
PLINK-86.
PMATE.
PMATE PC.
PMATE 86.

Precision BASIC.
Programmer's Apprentice MailMerge Option.
QuickScreen.
Reclaim.
RUN/C Professional.
RUN/C-The Interpreter.
SB-86.
TimeSlicer.
Unlock.
ZDT.
Z80 Development Package.

Light Machines Corp., (0-941791), 444 E. Industrial Pk. Dr., Manchester, NH 03109-5317 Tel 603-625-8600; Toll free: 800-221-2763; FAX: 603-625-2137.
Titles:
EnLIGHT Multimedia Milling Curriculum.
EnLIGHT Multimedia Turning Curriculum.
SpectraCAM.

Linguistic Products, P.O. Box 8263, Woodlands, TX 77387 Tel 713-298-2565; FAX: 713-298-1911.
Titles:
PC-Translator.

Linguist's Software, Inc., P.O. Box 580, Edmonds, WA 98020-0580 Tel 206-775-1130; FAX: 206-771-5911.
Titles:
AfroRoman.
AfroRoman for Windows.
AnyText II: Full Proximity Boolean Search Engine & Index Generator.
Bible - RSV, NRSV, KJV, RVR (Spanish Bible), RLB (German), NVSR (French), or Vulgate for Windows.
Bible: RSV, NIV, KJV, Vulgate, NRSV, RLB, or RVR (Spanish Bible), (German), NVSR (French).
Biblical Hebrew Grammar.
Cyrillic II.
Cyrillic II for Windows.
EuroScript.
EuroScript Text Converter.
EuroSlavic.
EuroSlavic for Windows.
Foreign-Language Fonts.
Greek New Testament for Windows.
Greek New Testament with Grammatical Tags for Windows.
Greek Old Testament for Windows.
Greek Old Testament with Grammatical Tags for Windows.
Hebrew Scriptures (BHS) for Windows.
InduScript Text Converter.
IT.
Laser Cambodian.
Laser Georgian.
Laser IPA.
Laser Laotian.
Laser Persian.
Laser THAI.
Laser Tibetan.
LaserAmharic.
LaserArabic & Farsi.
LaserArmenian.
LaserArmenian for Windows.
LaserBengali.
LaserBurmese.
LaserBurmese for Windows.
LaserCambodian for Windows.
LaserCherokee.
LaserCherokee for Windows.
LaserCoptic.
LaserCoptic for Windows.
LaserCree.
LaserFrench German Spanish.
LaserGaelic.
LaserGaelic for Windows.
LaserGeorgian.
LaserGeorgian for Windows.
LaserGeorgian Professional.
LaserGeorgian Professional for Windows.
LaserGlagolitic.
LaserGlagolitic for Windows.
LaserGreek.
LaserGreek & Hebrew.
LaserGreek & Hebrew for Windows.
LaserGreek for Windows.
LaserGreek, Hebrew & Phonetics.
LaserGujarati.
LaserGujarati for Windows.
LaserGwich'in.
LaserHebrew.
LaserHebrew for Windows.
LaserHebrewII.
LaserHindi Sanskrit.
LaserHindi Sanskrit for Windows.
LaserHulquminum.
LaserHulquminum for Windows.
LaserInukititut.
LaserInuktitut for Windows.
LaserIPA for Windows.
LaserKannada.
LaserKorean.
LaserKorean for Windows.
LaserKwakwala.
LaserKwakwala for Windows.
LaserLaotian.
LaserLaotian for Windows.
LaserLaotian Sukanya.
LaserLittera.
LaserLittera for Windows.
LaserMalayalam.
LaserPunjabi.
LaserPunjabi for Windows.
LaserSinhalese.
LaserSyriac.
LaserSyriac for Windows.
LaserSyriacII.
LaserTamil.
LaserTelugu.
LaserTewa.
LaserTewa for Windows.
LaserThai for Windows.
LaserTibetan.
LaserTibetan for Windows.
LaserTransliterator.
LaserTransliterator for Windows.
LaserTurkish.
LaserVietnamese.
LaserVietnamese for Windows.
LaserYukon.
LaserYukon for Windows.
MacAkkadian.
MacBurmese.
MacCherokee.
MacChinese Cantonese.
MacChinese Mandarin.
MacGaelic.
MacGreek New & Old Testaments; MacHebrew Scriptures.
MacGreek New Testament Dictionary.
MacHebrew Scriptures Converter.
MacHebrew Scriptures Dictionary.
MacHieroglyphics.
MacKana & BASIC Japanese Kanji.
MacPhonetics.
MacSemitic Coptic.
MacTamil.
Modern Greek for System 7.
ModernGreek for Windows.
OldSlavonic.
OldSlavonic for Windows.
Optina Slavonic for Windows.
OptinaSlavonic.
Semitic Transliterator.
Semitic Transliterator for Windows.
Tech.
TLG Engine.
TransCyrillic.
TransCyrillic for Windows.
TransCyrillic Sans Serif.
TransCyrillic Sans Serif for Windows.
TransIndic Transliterator.
TransIndic Transliterator for Windows.
TransRoman.
TransRoman Dictionary Font.
TransRoman Dictionary Font for Windows.
TransRoman for Windows.
TransRunic.
TransRunic for Windows.
TransSlavic.
TransSlavic for Windows.

Linksware Corp., 641 Lily St., Monterey, CA 93940 Tel 408-372-4155; Toll free: 800-879-5465; FAX: 408-646-9104.
Titles:
Linksware.

Lionheart Pr., Inc., P.O. Box 20756, Mesa, AZ 85277 Tel 602-396-0899; FAX: 602-396-0932.
Titles:
Biometrics.
Business Statistics.
Cluster Analysis.
Decision Analysis Techniques.
Econometrics.
Experimental Statistics.
Exploratory Data Analysis.
Forecasting & Time-Series.
Inventory.
Linear & Non-Linear Programming.
Matrix Operations.
Multivariate Analysis.
Optimization, Risk, Simulations.
Parameter Design & Tolerance Design.
Project Planner (PERT & CPM).
Quality Control & Industrial Experiments.
Regression: Linear & non-linear.
Sales & Market Forecasting.
Surveys & Questionnaires.

Lipa Software, 125 La Sandra Way, Portola Valley, CA 94025 Tel 415-324-7728.
Titles:
GraphPack.

Litek, Inc., 4326 Fish Hatchery Rd., Grants Pass, OR 97527 Tel 503-479-6633; FAX: 503-479-1442.
Titles:
Personal Estimator: Computer Aided Estimating.

Liticom, Ltd., Affil. of ICON, 3475 Edison Way, No. J, Menlo Park, CA 94025-1813 Tel 415-366-4999; Toll free: 800-548-4266; FAX: 415-366-8333.
Titles:
Best Access.

Liturgical Pubns., Inc., (0-940169; 0-941850), 2875 S. James Dr., New Berlin, WI 53151 Tel 414-785-1188; Toll free: 800-876-4574; FAX: 414-785-9567.
Titles:
ConCensus.

LIVE Studios, Inc., (1-878590), 30151 Branding Iron Rd., San Juan Capistrano, CA 92675 Tel 714-661-8337; FAX: 714-661-4076.
Titles:
Future Classics Collection.

Livingsoft, Inc., P.O. Box 970, Janesville, CA 96114 Tel 916-253-2700; Toll free: 800-626-1262; FAX: 916-253-2703.
Titles:
Dress Shop.

Lizcon Computer Systems, (0-924940), 1434 S. 2100 E., Salt Lake City, UT 84108 Tel 801-583-2049.
Titles:
Car Sales & Rental Software.
Equipment Rental Software.
Equipment Sales & Rental Software.
LSC-2020 Fully Integrated Accounting Software.
Medical Appointment & Billing Software.

Medical Laboratory Management Software.
Video Tape Rental.

Llewellyn Pubns., Div. of Llewellyn Worldwide, Ltd., (0-87542; 1-56718), P.O. Box 64383, Saint Paul, MN 55164-0383; Toll free: 800-843-6666; FAX: 612-291-1908; 84 S. Wabasha, Saint Paul, MN 55107 Tel 612-291-1970.
Titles:
The Electric Tarot.
Magical Diary.

Locus Computing Corp., 9800 La Cienega Blvd., Inglewood, CA 90301 Tel 310-670-6500; Toll free: 800-955-6281; FAX: 310-670-2980.
Titles:
Merge 386.
PC-Interface for DOS - Windows.
PC-Interface for Macintosh.
PC-Interface Plus.

Locus Systems, Div. of Chick Haven Feed Service, Inc., (0-928678), 2265 Flint Hill Rd., North Wilkesboro, NC 28659 Tel 910-838-4166.
Titles:
Egg Production Pricing.
Flock Service Report.
Grade Out Analysis.
Monthly Feed Consumed.
Weekly Egg Production & Livability Tracking.
Weekly Feed Consumed.

Logan Industries, Inc., 2115 Palm Bay Rd. NE, No. 7, Palm Bay, FL 32905 Tel 407-984-1627; FAX: 407-951-7292.
Titles:
Callme.
Mimic.
PTERM.
Real/32: Multiuser DOS-Windows Operating System.
Voyager.

Logic Assocs., (0-924945), 1433 W. Thome, Chicago, IL 60660 Tel 312-262-5927.
Titles:
BENCHMARK.
COLUMNS.
DISKGUISE.
SUPERMIT.
TUTORI/O.
VERSBASE.

Logical Operations, Div. of Ziff Technology Group, A Ziff Communications Co., 595 Blossom Rd., Rochester, NY 14610 Tel 716-482-7700; Toll free: 800-456-4677; FAX: 716-288-7411.
Titles:
Advanced HyperCard Skills.
dBASE IV: Introduction Level 1, Introduction Level 2 & Advanced.
Microsoft 4.0 (Macintosh).
1-2-3: Database Graphics.
1-2-3: Macro Programming.
1-2-3 Release 2.2; Advanced; 1-2-3 Release 3.1; Advanced.
1-2-3: Spreadsheets.
Pagemaker: Introduction Level 1 & Level 2.
WordPerfect: Skills, Advanced Level 1, & Advanced Level 2.

Logical Solutions Research & Development, Inc., (0-9623669), 615 Anderson Ct., Satelite Beach, FL 32937 Tel 407-773-8356.
Titles:
StructurE: the Complete Toolkit for Structuring Assembly Language Programs.

Logicat, Inc., (1-878834), 201 E. 16th St., 5th Flr., New York, NY 10003 Tel 212-529-1840; FAX: 212-353-3392.
Titles:
PassMaster: CPA Review.
WillPower.

Logicraft Information Systems, Inc., (0-927767), 22 Cotton Rd., Nashua, NH 03060 Tel 603-880-0500; Toll free: 800-722-8299; FAX: 603-880-7229.
Titles:
CDexecutive.
LanCD.

Logitech, Inc., (0-932799), 6505 Kaiser Dr., Fremont, CA 94555 Tel 510-795-8500; Toll free: 800-231-7717; FAX: 510-792-8901.
Titles:
CatchWord.
CatchWord Pro: OCR Software for Windows.
FotoMan Camera for the Computer with FotoTouch Gray Image Editing Software.
ScanMan Color: Hand-Held Scanner.
ScanMan: Model 32 (for Macintosh).
ScanMan Model 32 for PC with GrayTouch Image Editing Software.
ScanMan Model 256 with FotoTouch Image Editing Software for Windows.

Loglan Institute, Inc., The, (1-877665), 3009 Peters Way, San Diego, CA 92117-4313 Tel 619-270-1691.
Titles:
LIP, the Loglan Interactive Parser, 2nd ed.

Looking Glass Learning Products, Inc., (1-877666), 276 E. Howard Ave., Des Plaines, IL 60018-1906 Tel 708-296-0292; Toll free: 800-545-5457; FAX: 708-296-0294.
Titles:
Readability Formulas, 2nd ed.

Lotus Development Corp., (0-924968; 0-926966), 55 Cambridge Pkwy., Cambridge, MA 02142 Tel 617-577-8500; Toll free: 800-343-5414; 800-635-6887 (orders); P.O. Box 9172, Cambridge, MA 02139; Orders to: 61 Medford St., Somerville, MA 02143 Tel 617-623-6672.
Titles:
BlueFish.
Freelance Graphics for Windows.
Freelance Maps Facts.
Freelance Plus.
Jazz.
Lotus Agenda.
Lotus Express: PC Communications Software for MCI Mail.
Lotus Graphwriter: Combination Set.
Lotus Graphwriter II.
Lotus HAL.
Lotus Manuscript.
Lotus Measure.
Lotus 1-2-3.
Lotus 1-2-3 for Windows: Add-in Development Kit.
Lotus 1-2-3/G.
Lotus 1-2-3 Networker.
Lotus Report Writer.
Lotus 1-2-3 for Macintosh.
Magellan.
Metro.
Modern Jazz.
Signal.
Spotlight.
Symphony.
Symphony Link.
Symphony Spelling Checker.
Symphony Text Outliner.

Louisiana State Univ. Pr., (0-8071), P.O. Box 25053, Baton Rouge, LA 70894-5053 Tel 504-388-6294.
Titles:
Historical Collections of Louisiana.

Loussarian, Serge, 2050 Starlight Dr., Marietta, GA 30062 Tel 404-971-0917.
Titles:
Survey +.

Lucid Corp., (1-56678), 101 W. Renner Rd., Suite 450, Dallas, TX 75082-2017 Tel 214-994-8100; FAX: 214-994-8103.
Titles:
Lightning.

Lucid, Inc., P.O. Box 1838, San Leandro, CA 94577-0718; Toll free: 800-843-4204; 800-225-1386 (in California); FAX: 415-329-8480.
Titles:
Lucid Common LISP/DEC system.
Lucid Common LISP/386.

Lugaru Software, Ltd., 5843 Forbes Ave., Pittsburgh, PA 15217 Tel 412-421-5911; FAX: 412-421-6371.
Titles:
Epsilon Programmer's Editor.

Lundeen & Assocs., P.O. Box 2900, Alameda, CA 94501-0029; Toll free: 800-255-0996; FAX: 510-769-2078; 1000 Atlantic Ave., Suite 107, Alameda, CA 94501 Tel 510-769-7701.
Titles:
Command.
WorksPlus Command.
WorksPlus Spell.

Lundin Laboratories, Inc., 7071 Orchard Lake Rd., Suite 235, West Bloomfield, MI 48322 Tel 810-851-8282; Toll free: 800-559-4560; FAX: 810-443-5191.
Titles:
FamilyCare Software.

Lyriq International Corp., (1-882486), 1701 Highland Ave., No. 4, Cheshire, CT 06410 Tel 203-250-2070; Toll free: 800-433-4464; FAX: 203-250-2072.
Titles:
Lyriq Crosswords: Crossword Magazine Edition.
Lyriq Crosswords: Washington Post Edition.

M.A.P. Systems, Inc., (0-924986), 18100 Upper Bay Rd., Suite 100, Houston, TX 77058 Tel 713-333-9640; Toll free: 800-527-2851; FAX: 713-333-9579.
Titles:
BigPrint.
Lines, Boxes, etc.
MAP's Printer Tool Kit.
Paperscreen Plus.
Print-It.
SET-IT PLUS.

MARC Software International, Inc., (0-925134), 260 Sheridan Ave., Palo Alto, CA 94306 Tel 415-326-1971; Toll free: 800-835-2400; 800-854-9900 (in California); FAX: 415-323-5892.
Titles:
WordMARC Author.
WordMARC Composer+.

M&C Systems, Inc., (0-924992), 1 Bethany Rd., Suite 80, Hazlet, NJ 07730 Tel 908-739-9080; FAX: 908-739-6993.
Titles:
Auto-Laws-Automatic Legal, Administrative Word Processing System.
Automated Document Tracking System.
Non-Profit & Membership.
RAMFAS: Route Accounting & Manufacturing Financial Accounting System.
TIMAS: Trucking Information Management, Accounting System.
Utilities Management.

M & D Systems, Inc., (0-925011), 3885 N. Buffalo Rd., Orchard Park, NY 14127 Tel 716-662-6611.
Titles:
Myte Myke Business & Manufacturing Software.
Myte Myke Business Sys.
Myte Myke Comparative Sales Report Writer.
Myte Myke Manpower Planning.
Myte Myke Material Requirements Planning.
Myte Myke Production Costing.
Myte Myke Production Forecasting-Sched.
Myte Myke Production Order Processing.
Myte Myke Shop Floor Control.
Myte Myke Standard Cost Module.
Myte Myke Wholesale Distribution System: Accounts Payable.
Myte Myke Wholesale Distribution System: Accounts Receivable.
Myte Myke Wholesale Distribution System: General Ledger.
Myte Myke Wholesale Distribution System: Inventory Control.
Myte Myke Wholesale Distribution System: Order Entry-Billing.
Myte Myke Wholesale Distribution System: Purchase Order Processing.
Myte Myke Wholesale Distribution System: Sales Analysis.

M & T Bks., Div. of M&T Publishing, Inc., (0-934375; 1-55851), 411 Borel, San Mateo, CA 94022 Tel 415-358-9500; Toll free: 800-688-3987; FAX: 415-366-1685; Dist. by: Ingram Bk. Co., 1 Ingram Blvd., La Vergne, TN 37086-1986 Tel 615-793-5000; Toll free: 800-937-8000 (orders only, all warehouses); Dist. by: Baker & Taylor Bks., Reno Service Ctr., 380 Edison Way, Reno, NV 89564 Tel 702-858-6700; Toll free: 800-775-1700 (customer service).
Titles:
Blueprint of a LAN.
Building Local Area Networks.
C Chest & Other C Treasures from Dr. Dobb's Journal.
C Programming for MIDI.
DESQview: A Guide to Programming the DESQview Multitasking Environment.
Dr. Dobb's Essential HyperTalk Handbook.
Dr. Dobb's Toolbook of Forth.
Dr. Dobb's Toolbook of 80286/80386 Programming.
Dr. Dobb's Z80 Toolbook.
DS: Display Window.
Fractal Programming in C.
FS: The File System.
Graphics Programming in C.
LAN Troubleshooting Handbook.
MIDI & Sound Book for the Atari ST.
MIDI Programming for the Macintosh.
MIDI Sequencing in C.
Netware User's Guide.
NR: An Implementation of the UNIX NROFF Word Processor.
On Command: Writing a UNIX-Like Shell for MS-DOS.
PageMaker 3 by Example.
PC Accounting Solutions.
The PC User's Survival Guide.
Program Interfacing for MS-DOS.
The Programmer's Essential OS/2 Handbook.
QuickBASIC: Programming Techniques & Library Development.
Sales Management with dBASE III.
68000 Cross Assembler.
SK: The System Kernel of the Tele Operating System Toolkit.
Small Assembler: An 80x86 Macro Assembler Written in Small C.
A Small C Compiler: Language, Usage, Theory, & Design.
Small Mac: An Assembler for Small-C.
Small Tools: Programs for Text Processing.
Small-Windows: A Library of Windowing Functions for the C Language.
SQL & Relational Basics.
SQL for dBASE Programmers.
Statistical Toolbox.
Taming MS-DOS.
Time & Task Management with dBASE III.
Turbo Advantage Complex: Complex Number Routines for Turbo Pascal.
Turbo Advantage Display: From Generator for Turbo Pascal.
Turbo Advantage: Source Code Libraries for Turbo Pascal.
Turbo BASIC: Programming Techniques & Library Development.
Turbo C: The Art of Advanced Program Design, Optimization, & Debugging.
UNIX Programming on the 80286/80386.
/Util: A UNIX-Like Utility Package for MS-DOS.
XS: The Index System.

MBA Business Accounting Software, (0-925296; 0-922776), 2025 Centre Pointe Blvd., Suite 210, Mendota Heights, MN 55120-1259 Tel 612-686-5141; Toll free: 800-431-1416; FAX: 612-686-5020.
Titles:
Accounting Database-Word Processor-Programmer Interface.
The MBA Accountant.
MBA Accounts Payable.
MBA Accounts Payable with Check Writing.
MBA Accounts Receivable with Invoicing.
MBA Fixed Asset Accounting.
MBA General Ledger with Financial Report Writer.
MBA Inventory Control with Invoicing.
MBA Job Cost.
MBA Multi-Company Option.
MBA Payroll Multi-state, Local with Check Writing.
MBA PhD Data Utility.
MBA Professional Time Accounting.
MBA Professional Time Accounting with Billing.
MBA Purchase Orders & Requisitions for Inventory.
MBA Sales Order Entry.
Micro Business Applications Accounting Software.
Multi-State-Local Payroll.

MBA Computer Services, Inc., (0-924996), 3819 100 St., SW, No. 6, Tacoma, WA 98499-4425 Tel 206-581-3262; FAX: 206-582-2287.
Titles:
Lumberman III.
True-Image Software for Salons.

MBP Software & Systems Technology, Inc., (0-924999), 1131 Harbor Bay Pkwy., Suite 260, Alameda, CA 94501 Tel 510-769-5333; Toll free: 800-231-6342; FAX: 510-769-5735.
Titles:
MBP Visual COBOL 85.

MBS Software, (0-917345), 2410 S.E. 121st Ave., No. 2B, Portland, OR 97216 Tel 503-760-2620; Toll free: 800-962-9310; FAX: 503-761-8311.
Titles:
The DataFiler.

MCBA, Inc., (0-925002), 330 N. Brand Blvd., Glendale, CA 91204-1269 Tel 818-242-9600; FAX: 818-500-4805.
Titles:
Lot & Serial Tracking.
MCBA Accounts Payable (A-P).
MCBA Accounts Receivable (A-R).
MCBA Bill of Materials Processor (BOMP).
MCBA Business Software.
MCBA Capacity Requirements Planning (CRP).
MCBA Customer Order Processing (COP).
MCBA Fixed Assets & Depreciation (A-D).
MCBA General Ledger (G-L).
MCBA Inventory Management (I-M).
MCBA Job Costing (J-C).
MCBA Labor Performance (L-P).
MCBA Manufacturing Resource Planning: MRP II.
MCBA Master Scheduling.
MCBA Material Requirements Planning (MRP).
MCBA Payroll (PR).
MCBA Purchase Order & Receiving (P-O).
MCBA Shop Floor Control (SFC).
MCBA Standard Product Costing (SPC).
MCBA Standard Product Routing (SPR).
Multi-Currency.
Report Writer (R/W).
Sales History.

MCC Software (Midwest Computer Ctr. Co.), (0-925594), 5785 Merle Hay Rd., P.O. Box 188, Johnston, IA 50131 Tel 515-276-3387.
Titles:
Accounts Receivable.
Automotive Information Management System: AIMS.
Bill of Material Processor: BOMP.
Customer Profile System.
Farm Accounting System: FAS.
General Ledger.
Inventory Accounting.
Inventory Management.
MCC Accounts Payable.
MCC Financial Analysis.
MCC Job Costing/Job Budgeting.
Payroll.
Purchase Order Management System.
Swine Management.
Time Recording & Management System: TRAMS.
Trust, Escrow & Fund Accounting System: TEFACS.

MCI International, International Dr., Rye, NY 10573; Toll free: 800-826-7902; 800-826-6300.
Titles:
Comm Desk.

MCS Management Corp., 5 Keuka Ct., Hawthorn Woods, IL 60047-1905 Tel 708-680-3707; FAX: 708-680-3742.
Titles:
Triton College Administrative Software: Student Records & Registration.

MEAA, Inc., 1432 W. 11th St., Pomona, CA 91766 Tel 909-949-6854; FAX: 909-949-1328.
Titles:
MacInventory.

MECA Software, Inc., (0-925349), 55 Walls Dr., P.O. Box 912, Fairfield, CT 06430-0912 Tel 203-255-1441; FAX: 203-256-5159.
Titles:
Andrew Tobias' Managing Your Money.
Andrew Tobias' TaxCut.
Hyatt Legal Services: Home Lawyer.

MEGAS Corp., (0-925019), P.O. Box 12292, Tallahassee, FL 32317 Tel 904-878-6568.
Titles:
Medical Billing Package.

MFE Assocs., P.O. Box 851, Amherst, MA 01004 Tel 413-549-7626.
Titles:
Exchange Calculator.
Mac EarthWorks.

M/H Group, 300 W. Adams St., Chicago, IL 60606 Tel 312-443-1222; FAX: 312-443-1377.
Titles:
Archive-Link.
Text Com.
VS Com.
W-Link.
Word-Link.

PUBLISHER/TITLE INDEX

MIDITALK, P.O. Box 211, Averill Park, NY 12018-0211.
Titles:
Editor/Librarian for Yamaha TX81Z.

MIPS, Inc., 1309 Evergreen Rd., Wausau, WI 54401-2029.
Titles:
Automated Infection Control II.
Automated Nurse Staffing.
Medical Record Release of Information Manager.
Medical Record Tracker.

MIT Group, Inc., P.O. Box 615, Laurel, MD 20725-0615 Tel 301-854-3258; FAX: 301-854-2965.
Titles:
Empower.
MYM (Media Yield Management for Spot TV).
Sales Yield Management (SYM).

MIX Software, (1-879810), 1132 Commerce Dr., Richardson, TX 75081 Tel 214-783-6001; Toll free: 800-333-0330; FAX: 214-783-1404.
Titles:
ASM Utility.
Ctrace Debugger.
MIX C Compiler.
MIX Split Screen Editor.
Power C.
Power Ctrace.

MLSI, 16365 Park 10 Pl., Suite 200, Houston, TX 77084 Tel 713-578-8800.
Titles:
LITIDEX: Litigation Support/Document Management System.

mpd U.S.A., Inc., 2440 Minton Rd., Hamilton, OH 45013-4334 Tel 513-868-2233.
Titles:
Sculptor.

MPM Computing, 6135 York Blvd., Los Angeles, CA 90042 Tel 213-254-2806.
Titles:
The Property Manager.

M.P.S. Co., (0-925041; 0-925007), 8 N. Grant Dr., Addison, IL 60101 Tel 312-543-1748.
Titles:
Ditch Hydraulics.
Earthwork.
MCOGO.

MSC Technologies, Inc., (0-928712), 47575 Seabridge Dr., Fremont, CA 94538 Tel 510-656-1117.
Titles:
Designer Pop-up-Menu Software.
FieldMouse.
PC Paint Plus.

MSI Data Corp., (0-925051), 340 Fischer Ave., Costa Mesa, CA 92626 Tel 714-549-6000; Toll free: 800-854-7835.
Titles:
Appgen.
Autogen.
MSI BASIC.
MSI TMS-PC.
MSI TMS-1, TME.
MSI UBASIC.
Scoreplan.

MST Software, Div. of Mortgage Service Tools, Inc., 25541 Indian Hill Ln., No. Q, Laguna Hills, CA 92653-6059 Tel 714-837-3664; FAX: 714-768-0736.
Titles:
Personnel Master III.
Personnel Master Lite.
Personnel Supervisor.

M2, Ltd., (1-877996), 9210 Wightman Rd., Suite 300, Gaithersburg, MD 20879 Tel 301-977-4281; Toll free: 800-927-4281; FAX: 301-926-5046.
Titles:
MainPlan/EQ.

MTS, Inc., (0-918001), 917 Hospital Dr. P.O., Box 596, Niceville, FL 32578 Tel 904-678-3328; Toll free: 800-826-7072.
Titles:
Compuchurch Plus Combo Pak.

Maasta Software, 444 Nevada St., Auburn, CA 95603 Tel 916-885-4686.
Titles:
Movie Match.

MacAcademy, Div. of Florida Marketing International, Inc., 477 S. Nova Rd., Ormond Beach, FL 32174 Tel 904-677-1918; Toll free: 800-527-1914; FAX: 904-677-6717.
Titles:
INNCharge.

MacDaddy Entertainment, 10128 Emptyrean Way, No. 202, Los Angeles, CA 90067 Tel 510-552-4854.
Titles:
Beverly Hills Models.
Crystal Fantasy.

Mace, Paul, Software, (0-929462), 400 Williamson Way, Ashland, OR 97520 Tel 503-488-2322; Toll free: 800-944-0191; FAX: 503-488-1549.
Titles:
Grasp.

MacGAMUT Music Software International, (1-886997), 98 Brevoort Rd., Columbus, OH 43214-3824 Tel 614-263-9359; Toll free: 800-305-8731; FAX: 614-263-9359.
Titles:
MacGAMUT Instructor Disk.
MacGAMUT: Intervals, Scales, & Chords & Melodic Dictation Instructor Disk.
MacGAMUT: Intervals, Scales, & Chords & Melodic Dictation User Disk.
MacGAMUT User Disk.

McGraw-Hill, Inc., (0-07; 0-390), 1221 Ave. of the Americas, New York, NY 10020 Tel 212-512-2000; Toll free: 800-262-5755 (retail); 800-338-3987 (college); 800-722-4726 (consumer); Orders to: Princeton Rd., Hightstown, NJ 08520; Toll free: 800-338-3987 (college only); Orders to: 13311 Monterrey Ave., Blue Ridge Summit, PA 17294-0850; Toll free: 800-822-8138; 800-722-4726.
Titles:
Electric Machinery Examples.
Engincomp.
Fluid Mechanics Programs for the IBM PC.
Handheld Calculator Programs for Rotating Machinery Equipment Design.
Heat Transfer Software.
I.V. Meds for Kids: Basic Nursing Procedures.
Micro, Inc: Computerized Audit Practice Case.
MicroExpert.
Nursing Diagnosis: Basic Concepts.
A Pascal Tutorial with PMS.
STATLAB: Mean & Standard Deviation.
Structural Engineering Analysis on Personal Computers.
SYSKIT: Software Toolkit for Linear Systems.
Using Applications Software: An Introduction Featuring FRAMEWORK.
Wordperfect: The McGraw-Hill College Version.

MACOLA SOFTWARE

Mach One Software, L.L.C., (0-9643722), 6104 Calm Meadow Rd., Dallas, TX 75248 Tel 214-233-0890; Toll free: 800-845-2762; FAX: 214-233-0128.
Titles:
The Generator: The Universal Test Data Generator.

Machinery Alternative, (0-928438), 638 N. Poinsettia, Santa Anna, CA 92701-3939 Tel 714-542-4100.
Titles:
MGM-Station: Micro Graphic Manufacturing Station.
Professional CAD for Mac.
Skintite Bidding.

MacHunter, Div. of Micro J. Systems, Inc., 2020 Broadway, Santa Monica, CA 90404 Tel 310-453-5059.
Titles:
MacHunter RMS.
PCHunter RMS.

MacMedic Pubns., Inc., 5177 Richmond Ave., Suite 1040, Houston, TX 77056 Tel 713-621-6900; FAX: 713-621-2408.
Titles:
MacAnatomy.
MacAnatomy Volumes 1-A.
MacSurgery.
MacSurgery: Laparoscopic Cholecystectomy.

MacMIDI Distributing, 18 Haviland St., Boston, MA 02115 Tel 617-598-8929.
Titles:
BigEars.
Virtuoso Pianist.

Macmillan Digital U. S. A., 1633 Broadway, 6th Flr., New York, NY 10019 Tel 212-654-8500.
Titles:
Best of Breed: The American Kennel Club's Multimedia Guide to Dogs.
The Fighting Irish: The History of Notre Dame Football.
Macmillan Digital World Atlas.
Macmillan Visual Dictionary: Multimedia Edition.
Planet Earth: Explore the Worlds Within.
Politically Correct Bedtime Stories: Cyber Sensitivity for Our Life.
The War in Vietnam: A Multimedia Chronicle of the War That Divided America.

Macmillan New Media, Div. of Macmillan, Inc., (1-56574), 124 Mt. Auburn St., Cambridge, MA 02138 Tel 617-661-2955; Toll free: 800-342-1338; FAX: 617-661-2403; Dist. by: Compton's NewMedia, Inc., 722 Genevieve, Suite M, Solana Beach, CA 92075 Tel 619-259-0444.
Titles:
BEACON: The Multimedia Guidance Resource.

MacNeal-Schwendler Corp., (0-931313), 815 Colorado Blvd., Los Angeles, CA 90041 Tel 213-258-9111; Toll free: 800-336-4858; FAX: 213-259-3838.
Titles:
MSC - NASTRAN.

Macola Software, 333 E. Center St., Marion, OH 43302 Tel 614-382-5999; Toll free: 800-468-0834; FAX: 614-382-0239.
Titles:
Macola Accounting Software.
Macola Accounting Software: Accounts Payable (A-P).
Macola Accounting Software: Accounts Receivable (A-R).
Macola Accounting Software: Assets & Depreciation (A-D).
Macola Accounting Software: Bill of Material Processor (BOMP).
Macola Accounting Software: Customer Order Processing (COP).

Macon Systems, Inc.

Macola Accounting Software: General Ledger (G-L).
Macola Accounting Software: Inventory Management (I-M).
Macola Accounting Software: Payroll (PR).
Macola Accounting Software: Purchase Order & Receiving (P-O).
Macola Accounting Software: Report Writer (R-W).

Macon Systems, Inc., 724 S. Tejon St., Colorado Springs, CO 80903 Tel 719-520-1555; FAX: 719-520-0715.
Titles:
Advanced DB Master Level IV.

MacPDS, P.O. Box 85097, Seattle, WA 98105 Tel 206-524-8888; FAX: 206-524-1616.
Titles:
Medical Application ClipArt, Vol. 1.

MacPoint Pubns., 1374 E. 57th St., Chicago, IL 60637 Tel 312-955-1954.
Titles:
MacBits.
MacBits Supplement.
Macindex.
MacPoint Shareware Collection.

Macro World Research Corp., 4265 Brownsboro Rd., Suite 170, Winston-Salem, NC 27106 Tel 910-759-0600; Toll free: 800-841-5398; FAX: 910-759-0636.
Titles:
Macro*World Forecaster.
Macro*World Investor.

Macromedia, Inc., 600 Townsend St., Suite 310W, San Francisco, CA 94103 Tel 415-252-2000; Toll free: 800-288-4797; FAX: 415-626-0554.
Titles:
Action!
Authorware.
MacroMedia Director.
MacroModel.
ModelShop II: 3D Spatial Design & Presentation.
SoundEdit 16.
Swivel 3D Professional.

Macsyma, Inc., 20 Academy St., Arlington, MA 02174 Tel 617-646-4550; Toll free: 800-622-7962; FAX: 617-646-3161.
Titles:
Macsyma.

Mader Consulting Co., (1-878936), 1049 Kamehame Dr., Honolulu, HI 96825-2860 Tel 808-396-9855; FAX: 808-396-9855.
Titles:
MCC Explosive Modeling Package.
MCGRAPH: A Library of OS-2 & DOS Graphics & Print Screen Routines for FORTRAN & C Programs.

Magic Software, Inc., 12138 Del Verde, Yuma, AZ 85367 Tel 602-342-7496; FAX: 602-342-7496.
Titles:
AutoSave II.
Salary Magic.

Magnum Software Corp., (0-944310), 21115 Devonshire St., Suite 337, Chatsworth, CA 91311 Tel 818-701-5051; FAX: 818-701-5459.
Titles:
McPic!; McPic!
McPic!: Push Button Art.
Natural Sound "Sound Effects".
TFLX.

Magnus Corp., 9025 61st Pl., W., Mukilteo, WA 98275-3337 Tel 206-467-5738.
Titles:
FileMagic.
FlashCrypt.
MultiMagic.
WindowMagic.

Magreeable Software, Inc., (0-925088), 5925 Magnolia Ln., Plymouth, MN 55442 Tel 612-559-1108.
Titles:
B-Tree HELPER.

Mailer's Software, (0-937467), 970 Calle Negocio, San Clemente, CA 92673 Tel 714-492-7000; Toll free: 800-800-6245; FAX: 714-492-7086.
Titles:
Fone*Data.
Mailer's GeoCode.
Mailer's +4.
Mailer's Look-Up.
Quick*Locate.
SuperDup.
ZIP-Data.
Zip-Phone *1.
Zip*Select.

Mainstay, 591A Constitution Ave., Camarillo, CA 93012 Tel 805-484-9400; FAX: 805-484-9428.
Titles:
Captivate.
MacFlow.
MarcoPolo.
MarkUp.
Phyla.
Plan & Track.
VIP-BASIC.
VIP-C.
WinFlow.

Mainstay Software Corp., (0-928413), 7853 E. Arapahoe Ct., Suite 2500, Englewood, CO 80112 Tel 303-220-8780.
Titles:
MAINSTAY.
MarkUp.
TypeNow.

Maintenance Automation Corp., (0-925095), 3107 W. Hallandale Blvd., Hallandale, FL 33009 Tel 305-962-8800; FAX: 305-962-9046.
Titles:
The Chief Software.

Malvino, Inc., (1-56048), 809 Cuesta Dr., No. 208B, Mountain View, CA 94040-3605 Tel 415-961-2019.
Titles:
Quik-Lab Three for Digital Electronics.

Manac-Prentice Hall Software, Inc,, Div. of Simon & Schuster Professional Information Group, 29100 Northwestern Hwy., Southfield, MI 48034-1046; FAX: 516-861-7109.
Titles:
Accounts Payable: Series 900 to 2000.
Accounts Receivable Collections: Series 900 to 2000.
Case & File Management (Mailings & Records Management): Series 900 to 2000.
Client & Lawyer Financial: Series 500 & 600.
Client Files, Conflict & Dates: Series 500 & 600.
Client Financial Management: Series 900 to 2000.
Client Statements: Series 900 to 2000.
Conflict of Interest: Series 900 to 2000.
Dates: Series 900 to 2000.
Information Systems for Attorneys: Series 500, 600.
Law Firm Financial-G/L: Series 500 & 600.
Law Firm Financial Management: Series 900 to 2000.
Lawyer Financial Management: Series 900 to 2000.
Library Management: Series 900 to 2000.
Litigation & Resource Library: Series 500 & 600.
Litigation Support: Series 900 to 2000.
Omnilaw: Series 500 to 2000.
Research: Series 900 to 2000.

Management Graphics, Inc., 1401 E. 79th St., Minneapolis, MN 55425 Tel 612-854-1220; FAX: 612-854-6913.
Titles:
Easy Slider.

Management Robotics, Inc., (0-931275), 485 Baseline Rd., Boulder, CO 80302 Tel 303-440-4191.
Titles:
Supersked.

Management Systems, Inc., (0-925112), P.O. Box 272323, Fort Collins, CO 80527 Tel 970-223-1530.
Titles:
AVLIB.
Branch Marketing.
CPA Client Master.
DB*CONVERT.
Due Process.
Job Tracker.
Project Reporter.
Route Stats.
Telemetry Processing System.
Trans Collect: Traffic Count System.
Workers' Compensation Billing & Claims.

Management, The, Div. of Electric Works Corp., (0-918005), P.O. Box 1-36457, Fort Worth, TX 76136 Tel 817-625-9761; Toll free: 800-334-7823.
Titles:
CTV-Plus.
EZ-Log.
Simple Log.
Superlog III.

Mansfield Software Group, Inc., (0-925126), P.O. Box 532, Storrs, CT 06268 Tel 203-429-8402; FAX: 203-487-1185.
Titles:
KEDIT.

Manufacturing & Consulting Services, Inc., 7560 E. Redfield Rd., Scottsdale, AZ 85260 Tel 602-991-8700; FAX: 602-991-8732.
Titles:
ANVIL-5000.

Manugistics, Inc., (0-926683), 2115 E. Jefferson St., Rockville, MD 20852 Tel 301-984-5123; Toll free: 800-592-0050; FAX: 301-984-5094.
Titles:
APL*Plus III for Windows.
APL*Plus-PC.
APL*Plus-PC Financial & Statistical Library.
APL*Plus-PC TOOLS.
APL*Plus for UNIX.
APL*Plus II for DOS.
Pocket APL System.
Statgraphics Plus.
STATGRAPHICS Plus for Windows.
Statgraphics: Statistical Graphics System.

Manx Software Systems, (0-925129), P.O. Box 980, Freehold, NJ 07728-0980; Toll free: 800-221-0440; FAX: 201-542-8386.
Titles:
Aztec C.
Aztec C86.
Aztec C65.
Aztec C68k/Am-p Professional System 3.6.
Aztec ROM Systems: 6502/65C02, 8080/Z80, 8086/80x86, 680x0.
Manx Aztec CII.

PUBLISHER/TITLE INDEX

Manx Aztec SDB for Amiga.

Manylink, P.O. Box 350, Redmond, WA 98073 Tel 206-881-5060.
Titles:
Manylink.

Manzanita Software Systems, 2130 Professional Dr., No. 150, Roseville, CA 95661-3751 Tel 916-781-3880; FAX: 916-781-3814.
Titles:
Accounts Payable: Module 3.
Accounts Receivable: Module 4.
BusinessWorks Bundle (Apple).
BusinessWorks Inventory Control: Module 6.
BusinessWorks PC Bundle.
General Ledger: Module 2.
Order Entry: Module 7.
Payroll: Module 5.
System Manager (with Labels Plus): Module 1.

Maple Leaf Software, 90 Brook Haven Dr., Apt. 3B, Attleboro, MA 02703-5127.
Titles:
UNIT-CAD: A Unit Conversion Program.

Marcam Corp., 95 Wells Ave., Newton, MA 02159 Tel 617-965-0220; Toll free: 800-343-2088; FAX: 617-965-7273.
Titles:
PRISM Business Planning & Control Systems.

Marietta Systems, Inc., P.O. Box 71506, Marietta, GA 30007 Tel 404-565-1560.
Titles:
The Marietta Libraries.

Marigold Computer Consultants, (1-878608), 40 Douglas Rd., Delmar, NY 12054-3122 Tel 518-439-4845.
Titles:
Deduct!: Payroll Processing.

Mark Data Products, (0-925141), 24001 Alicia Pkwy., No. 207, Mission Viejo, CA 92691 Tel 714-768-1551.
Titles:
Astro Blast.
Calixto Island.
Cosmic Clones.
Glaxxons.
Superscreen.

Mark of the Unicorn, (0-925142), 222 Third St., Cambridge, MA 02142 Tel 617-576-2760.
Titles:
The Final Word.
Hex.
Mince.
PC-Intercomm.
Performer.
Professional Composer.

Market Power, Inc., (0-925148), 101 Providence Mine Rd., Suite 104, Nevada City, CA 95959 Tel 916-265-5000; Toll free: 800-468-1117; FAX: 916-265-5171.
Titles:
Visual MATRIX.

Marketing Resources Plus, A VNU Business Information Services Co., Div. of VNU Business Information Services, (0-925454), 151 N Delaware St., Suite 1750, Indianapolis, IN 46204-2526 Tel 317-321-2600; Toll free: 800-488-7544; FAX: 317-321-2636.
Titles:
Adman.
The Adman System.

MarketWare Corp., 3100 Medlock Bridge Rd., Bldg. 500, Norcross, GA 30071-1441 Tel 404-246-1700; Toll free: 800-752-6647; FAX: 404-246-1750.
Titles:
Pegman Space Management Software.

Marsh, Kent, Ltd., 3260 Sul Ross, Houston, TX 77098 Tel 713-522-5625; Toll free: 800-325-3587; FAX: 713-522-8965.
Titles:
CryptoMactic with EasyTrash & Incinerate: Integrated Desktop Encryption Shredding & Trash Management.
FolderBolt for Windows: Integrated Security for Windows Directories.
FolderBolt: Integrated Security for the Macintosh Desktop.
NightWatch 2.
QuickLock.

Marsh Media, (0-925159; 1-55942), P.O. Box 8082, Shawnee Mission, KS 66208 Tel 816-523-1059; Toll free: 800-821-3303 (for orders/customer service only); FAX: 816-333-7421; Orders to: 5901 Main St., Kansas City, MO 64113 Tel 816-523-1059.
Titles:
Me & My Body.
Me & My Family.

Martin, D. A., P.O. Box 52848, Knoxville, TN 37950-2848 Tel 615-693-1476; FAX: 615-588-6922.
Titles:
SPC Orchestra.

Martin, Roger, Co., P.O. Box 9099, Portland, OR 97207 Tel 503-245-7441.
Titles:
REA/L Estate Analysis.

Masque Publishing, (0-9624419; 1-882586), P.O. Box 5223, Englewood, CO 80155; Toll free: 800-765-4223; FAX: 303-290-6303; 7200 E. Dry Creek Rd., Suite F103, Englewood, CO 80155 Tel 303-290-9853.
Titles:
Casino Lite Omaha Hold'Em.
Casino Lite Seven Card Stud.
Casino Lite Texas Hold'Em.
CHESSNET for Windows.
Masque Blackjack.
Masque Video Poker.
World Series of Poker Adventure.

Master Data Ctr., Inc., Div. of Viacom, (0-925171), 29100 Northwestern Hwy., Suite 300, Southfield, MI 48034-1095 Tel 810-352-5810; FAX: 810-352-0754.
Titles:
PC Master for Windows.
PC MASTER Lite.

Master Software, 20618 Cypress Way, Lynnwood, WA 98036 Tel 203-672-8708.
Titles:
Bear Essentials.
Bibliography Builder.

Master Systems, (0-925173), 1249 Pinole Valley Rd., Pinole, CA 94564-1348 Tel 510-724-1300; Toll free: 800-827-7214; FAX: 510-724-5382.
Titles:
Donormaster II.
Grantmaster.
Membermaster II.
PremiumMaster.
Trackmaster II.

Masters Software Co., (0-918009), 9930 Albury Rd., Sandy, UT 84092-3733 Tel 801-571-7590.
Titles:
Accounting Package.
Cost Accounting.
Planned Maintenance System.
Plant Management Package.
Work Order System.

Math Corp., (0-922643), P.O. Box 644, Green Lake, WI 54941-0644 Tel 414-294-0180; FAX: 414-294-0174.
Titles:
Best Bid.
The MathCorp Engine.
Truerate%
ZMATH.

MatheGraphics Software, 61 Cedar Rd., East Northport, NY 11731 Tel 516-368-3781.
Titles:
Differential Equations Graphics Package.
Graphical Regression Analysis.
Graphics for Engineering Math.
Interpolation.
Roots & Intersections of Curves.
Three-Dimensional Trapezoid Rule.

Mathematical Software Co., (0-917163), 3529 Cannon Rd., No. 2B-613, Oceanside, CA 92056-4980 Tel 619-940-0343.
Titles:
Interactive Multiple Prediction.
Interactive Questionnaire Analysis.
Multiple Factor Analysis.

MathSoft, Inc., (0-942075; 1-57682), 101 Main St., Cambridge, MA 02142 Tel 617-577-1017; Toll free: 800-628-4223; FAX: 617-577-8829.
Titles:
MathCAD.

Matrix Calculating Engine, Inc., (0-925070), 2313 Center Ave., Madison, WI 53704 Tel 608-244-3331.
Titles:
Statistician's MACE.

Matrix Software, (0-925182), 315 Marion Ave., Big Rapids, MI 49307 Tel 616-796-2483.
Titles:
Astro Logical Chart Package: M-30.
Astro Talk: M-11.
Astrological Chart Service: M65A.
Astrological Horoscope Interpreter.
Astrological Transit Reporter: M91.
Beginners Charts: M-309 Printing Package 1.
Bi-Wheel Printer: M-311 Printing Package 3.
Biorhythm Graph & Interpreter.
Blue Star.
Blue Star 64.
Blue Star Time Change Atlas.
Chart Printer: Printing Package 3.
Composite & Relationship Charts: M-17.
Composite & Relationship Charts: M-34.
Designer Series.
Horary Astro Clock: M-65H.
Horoscope Program: M-1.
Local Space (Advanced Package): M-33.
Local Space & Coordinates: M-4.
Lucky Day-Lottery Number Report: M-197.
Lunar Returns: M-8.
Matrix Layout.
M65 Astrological Chart Service.
M65 Home Chart Service.
The M65 Screen Module: M65C.
Natal Horoscope Interpreter: M90J.
Natal Starter Package: M-0.
Numerology Report Writer: M93.
One Page Printer: M-310 Printing Package 2.
Relating Potential: M94.
Research Module: M65B.
Solar & Lunar Returns: M-32.
Solar Arc Directions: M-10.

Solar Arc Directions: M-35.
Solar Returns: M-7.
Statistics Module: M65S.
Tarot Reader.
Time Change Atlas: M25.
The Time Traveller: M-77.
Tracker Cross-Reference System: M65J.
Transit & Secondary Progressions: M-5.
Transit Search: Where & When: M-14.
Transits & Progressions: M-31.
Uranian Module: M65D.

Matrix Systems, (0-925183), 916 Via Nogales, Palos Verdes, CA 90274 Tel 310-375-7784.
Titles:
Property Management System III (PMS III).

Matthews, G. E., Assocs., Inc., 2900 Fourth St. N., Suite 202B, Saint Petersburg, FL 33704 Tel 813-823-1080.
Titles:
Pension Profile.

Mau Corp., (0-928682), 27 Harrier Ct., Wayne, NJ 07470; FAX: 718-359-3075.
Titles:
Mailing List System.
Tax Tool: Tax Productivity Tool.
W2 Program - 1099 Misc.

Maverick Software, Inc., (0-926595), P.O. Box 998, Melrose, MA 02176 Tel 617-662-0856; Toll free: 800-248-3838.
Titles:
Keyswap.
ProCrypt.
Softspool.

Mavis Computer Systems, Div. of Mavis Industries, Inc., (0-925185), 2976 Alhambra Dr., Cameron Park, CA 95682-8819 Tel 916-985-0373.
Titles:
Mavis Accounting System.
Mavis Pharmacy Computer System.

Max 3, Inc., P.O. Box 11935, San Rafael, CA 94912-1935.
Titles:
CineWrite.
Computer Bidding.
Edit Lister.
MacToolkit.
PostCard/Tape Vault.

Maxis, (0-929750; 1-56754), Two Theatre Sq., Suite 230, Orinda, CA 94563-3041 Tel 510-254-9700; Toll free: 800-336-2947; FAX: 510-253-3736.
Titles:
RoboSport.
SimAnt: The Electronic Ant Colony.
SimCity Classic.
SimCity Classic: The Original City Simulator.
SimEarth: The Living Planet.
SimLife: The Genetic Playground.

MaxThink, Inc., 2425 Channing Way No. 592B, Berkeley, CA 94704-2209 Tel 510-428-0104.
Titles:
Houdini.
MaxThink.
MaxThink 89.
PC-Hypertext.

MC2 Engineering Software, (0-918637), 8107 SW 72nd Ave., Suite 425E, Miami, FL 33143 Tel 305-665-0100; FAX: 305-665-8035; P.O. Box 430980, Miami, FL 33143.
Titles:
Commercial Cooling & Heating Load - CL4M.
Concrete Beam Design - ST16M.
Concrete Column Design - ST18M.
Critical Path Project Management - M2M.

Duct Design - DD4M.
Energy Consumption for Heating & Cooling in Commercial Buildings & Economic Analysis of Alternatives - EN4M.
Enhanced Finite Element Analysis - ST10MB.
E3M: Short Circuit Current & Voltage Drop Calculation.
Finite Element Analysis - ST10M.
Fire Sprinkler Grid System Design - HP4M.
Fire Sprinkler Tree System Design - HP6M.
Fuse & Breaker Coordination - E4M.
Hardy Cross Water Distribution System Analysis - HP3M.
Hydraulic Pipe Design - HP2M.
Life Cycle Cost - LC2M.
Lighting Design - E5M.
One-Way Two-Way Concrete Slab Design - ST19M.
Residential Cooling, Heating, Energy & Operating Cost - RL5M.
RL5M Florida Version: A-C & Heating Loads & Florida Special Energy Analysis.
Shear Wall Design - ST14M.
Solar Collector F-Chart Calculation & Economic Analysis - SE1M.
Steel Beam Design - ST15M.
Steel Column Design - ST17M.
Tube & Pipe Bending - HP5M.

Means, R. S., Co., Inc., A Southam Co., (0-911950; 0-87629), 100 Construction Plaza, Kingston, MA 02364 Tel 617-585-7880; Toll free: 800-448-8182; FAX: 617-585-7466.
Titles:
Means Data for Spreadsheets: Construction Costs for Spreadsheet Estimating.

Med Man Simulations, (0-9628045), P.O. Box 67-160, Chestnut Hill, MA 02167 Tel 617-277-2117; FAX: 617-732-6798.
Titles:
GASMAN: Understanding Anesthesia Uptake & Distribution.

MEDformatics, Inc., 1306 Fort Bragg Rd., Fayetteville, NC 28305 Tel 910-323-1748; Toll free: 800-745-1767; FAX: 910-323-1534.
Titles:
MEDformation.

Media Computing Corp., (0-917775), P.O. Box 185, Lombard, IL 60148-0185; 1920 S. Highland Ave., Suite 300, Lombard, IL 60148-0185 Tel 708-916-3126.
Titles:
Powerful Business Software.

Media Cybernetics, L.P., (0-87525), 8484 Georgia Ave., Silver Spring, MD 20910 Tel 301-495-3305; Toll free: 800-992-4256; FAX: 301-495-5964.
Titles:
Dr. HALO IV Imaging Pak.
Gel-Pro Analyzer.
Halo Imaging Library.
Image-Pro Plus.
Materials-Pro Analyzer.
Prints-Pro.
Stage-Pro Module.

Medical College of Pennsylvania, Div. of Allegheny Health, Education & Research Foundation, (1-884901), P.O. Box 5692, Philadelphia, PA 19129; Toll free: 800-666-7737; FAX: 215-843-5589; 3200 Henry Ave., Philadelphia, PA 19129 Tel 215-842-4091.
Titles:
NSNA NCLEX EXCEL! Computerized Nursing Q & A.
NSNA NCLEX EXCEL! Computerized Nursing Q & A: Nursing & Pharmacology Combined.
NSNA NCLEX-RN EXCEL! Computerized Pharmacology Q & A.

Medical Economics Data, Inc., (1-56363), 5 Paragon Dr., Montvale, NJ 07645-1742 Tel 201-358-7500; Toll free: 800-442-6657; FAX: 201-573-4956.
Titles:
Physicians' Desk Reference on CD-ROM.

Medical Office Management Systems, 631 Pennsylvania Ave., Washington, DC 20003 Tel 202-546-0887; Toll free: 800-466-0887; FAX: 202-546-0890.
Titles:
MedBill.
MEDSYS.

Medical Software, Inc., 215 Second Ave., NE, Waseca, MN 56093 Tel 507-835-7677; FAX: 507-835-8892.
Titles:
WINX.

Medicus Systems Corp., (0-925218), 1 American Plaza, Evanston, IL 60201 Tel 708-570-7500; FAX: 708-570-7518.
Titles:
Emerge: Emergency Department Classification & Information Systems.
LADPAQ: Labor & Delivery Productivity & Quality.
NPAQ: Nursing Productivity & Quality.

Medina Software, Inc., P.O. Box 521917, Longwood, FL 32752-1917 Tel 407-260-1676; FAX: 407-260-1636.
Titles:
Correctamente.
Electro Bits.
MacConcord I (KJV).
MacGospel (KJV)/HyperGospel.
MacScripture (KJV).
Medina Spelling Dictionary.
Religious Art Portfolio.
Scripture Bits.

Medispec Management Services, Inc., (0-925220), P.O. Box 20406, Columbus, OH 43220 Tel 614-538-2400.
Titles:
Anespec.

Medsoft, Inc., Div. of Deluxe Corp., (0-925222), P.O. Box 7049, 925 N. Lake Blvd., Suite B301, Tahoe City, CA 96145-7049 Tel 916-583-2994; Toll free: 800-343-5653; FAX: 916-583-1532.
Titles:
ChartEx.
Optimizer.

Mega CADD, Div. of Design Futures, Inc., 65 Marion St., Seattle, WA 98104 Tel 206-623-6245; FAX: 206-623-5721.
Titles:
MegaAEC.
MegaDraft.
MegaModel.

Megacom, (0-924264), Fifth Ave., Frankfort, NY 13340-1402 Tel 315-894-9261.
Titles:
PC-Softsource: Directory of Software Information.

Megamata, Inc., (0-925228), P.O. Box 1753, Beverly Hills, CA 90213 Tel 213-278-5249; Toll free: 800-747-6342.
Titles:
Law Time Management.

MegaWest Systems, Inc., (0-925233), 345 Bearcat Dr., Salt Lake City, UT 84115 Tel 801-487-0788; Toll free: 800-999-0788.
Titles:
MegaMed Medical Management System.

Meggido Enterprises, 7900 Limonite Ave., Suite G-191, Riverside, CA 92509 Tel 909-683-5666.
Titles:
Desserts Cookbook.
Recipe-Fax.
Recipe-FAX Plus.
Variety Cookbook.

Memocom Development Tools, 1301 Denton Dr., Suite 204, Carrollton, TX 75006 Tel 214-446-9906.
Titles:
Universal Cross Assembler.

Memorex Products, Inc., Memorex Software Div., Div. of Hanny Magnetics Holdings, H.K., Ltd., (1-57269), 1200 Memorex Dr., Santa Clara, CA 95050 Tel 408-957-1000; Toll free: 800-225-5679; FAX: 408-957-1145.
Titles:
At the Movies: The Complete Resource on over 10,000 Movies.
Computer Casino: The Most Realistic Gaming Experience Ever.
Computer Slots: Realistic Casino Slots Action.
Cosmos II: Your Guide to the Celestial Sphere.
Counting & Adding: Colorful Introduction to Numbers.
Doc in the Box: The Medical Self-Diagnosis Program.
Floor Plan Designer: The Do-It Yourself Architectural & Landscape Design Tool.
Household Cash Planner: A Planning Guide to Household Finances.
International Recipes: World of Exciting Cuisines at Your Fingertips.
JetFighter: The Ultimate Combat Flight Simulator.
PC Home Bartender: Ultimate Guide to Expertly Prepared Cocktails.
Shapes & Colors: Colorful Introduction to Shapes & Patterns.
Spectre: 3-D Cyberspace Game Experience.

Menlo Business Systems, Inc., 201 Main St., Los Altos, CA 94022 Tel 415-948-7920; FAX: 415-949-6655.
Titles:
CT Spool.
CTAccess.
CTXfer.
Foundation Graphics Toolbox.
Foundation Vista.
Foundation Vista Translator.
Mac Menlo T65xx.
MAX.

Mentor Technologies, Inc., (1-56494), 500 W. Wilson Bridge Rd., No. 130, Worthington, OH 43085-2238 Tel 614-265-3170; Toll free: 800-227-5502; FAX: 614-262-0738.
Titles:
Mentor Notes, Advanced Wordperfect.
Mentor Notes, Intermediate dBASE IV (Working Title).
Mentor Notes, Intermediate DOS (Working Title).
Mentor Notes, Intermediate Lotus.
Mentor Notes, Introduction to dBASE IV (Working Title).
Mentor Notes, Introduction to DOS (Working Title).
Mentor Notes: Introduction to Lotus.
Mentor Notes: Introduction to OS 2 2.0.
Mentor Notes, Introduction to Windows.
Mentor Notes, Introduction to Wordperfect.
Mentor Notes, Wordperfect Equations.
Mentor Notes, Wordperfect Macros & Merge (Working Title).
Mentor Notes, Wordperfect Manuscript & Report Writing.
Mentor Notes, Wordperfect Tables (Working Title).
Mentor Notes, Wordperfect Word Publishing (Working Title).

Meredith Bks., (0-696), 1716 Locust St., Des Moines, IA 50309-3023; Toll free: 800-678-8091; FAX: 515-284-3371. Do not confuse with Meredith Pr. in Skaneateles, NY.
Titles:
Better Homes & Gardens Cool Crafts.

Meridian Creative Group, Div. of Larson Texts, Inc., (0-9639121), 5178 Station Rd., Erie, PA 16510 Tel 814-898-2612; FAX: 814-898-0683.
Titles:
Rookie Reporter.

Meridian Education Corp., (0-936007; 1-877844; 1-56191), 236 E. Front St., Bloomington, IL 61701 Tel 309-827-5455; Toll free: 800-727-5507; FAX: 309-829-8621.
Titles:
Career Compass.
Suit Yourself.
Your Ideal Silhouette.

Merriam-Webster, Inc., Subs. of Encyclopaedia Britannica, Inc., (0-87779), P.O. Box 281, Springfield, MA 01102; Toll free: 800-828-1880; FAX: 413-731-5979; 47 Federal St., Springfield, MA 01102 Tel 413-734-3134. Do not confuse with Webster's International, Inc., Parent Education, Brentwood, TN.
Titles:
The Language Pack.
Merriam-Webster's Word Crazy: Electronic Edition, Windows.

Mesa Graphics, Inc., P.O. Box 600, Los Alamos, NM 87544 Tel 505-672-1998.
Titles:
Mesa Graphics Plotter Utility.
Mesa Graphics Terminal Utility: Text Term + Graphics.

Mesa Software, (0-922457), 3435 Greystone Dr., Suite 106, Austin, TX 78731 Tel 512-346-1771; Toll free: 800-531-5483; FAX: 512-345-2450.
Titles:
Boss 1-2-3.
System II Certified Payroll Management System.
System II Financial Accounting System.
System II Inventory Accounting System.

Mescon Multimedia, (1-885929), 303 Peachtree St., Suite 1620, Atlanta, GA 30328 Tel 404-656-1929; Toll free: 800-656-1932; FAX: 404-393-9853.
Titles:
Clark Howard's Consumer Survival Kit.

Meta Software, Corp., 125 CambridgePark Dr., Cambridge, MA 02140 Tel 617-576-6920; Toll free: 800-227-4106; FAX: 617-661-2008.
Titles:
Design/CPN: CPN Analysis Methods.
Design/IDEF.
Design/OA.
MetaDesign.
WorkFlow Analyzer: Business Process Reengineering.

Meta Venture Technology, 247 E. Colorado Blvd., Suite 253, Pasadena, CA 91101 Tel 818-796-5479.
Titles:
Real Estate Partners.

Metafile Information Systems, Inc., (0-926778), 421 First Ave. S.W., Rochester, MN 55902 Tel 507-286-9232; Toll free: 800-638-2445; FAX: 507-286-9065.
Titles:
METAFILE.
Metaview.
Results/Plus.

Metagroup Consultants, 12103 S. Brookhurst, Suite E-410, Garden Grove, CA 92642-3065 Tel 714-638-8663.
Titles:
Mail Business Manager (MBM).

MetaWare, Inc., 2161 Delaware Ave., Santa Cruz, CA 95060-5706 Tel 408-429-6382; FAX: 408-429-9273.
Titles:
High C/C Plus Plus 386 Compiler.
High C-286.

Metro ImageBase, Inc., 18623 Ventura Blvd., No. 210, Tarzana, CA 91356 Tel 818-881-1997; Toll free: 800-525-1552; FAX: 818-881-4557.
Titles:
Metro ImageBase Electronic Art.

Metropolis Software, Inc., 505 Hamilton Ave., No. 305, Palo Alto, CA 94301 Tel 415-322-2001; FAX: 415-327-5579.
Titles:
DB/write.
The Mortgage Office.
MSI Access.

Metrowerks, Inc., 8920 Business Park Dr., Suite 315, Austin, TX 78759-7405 Tel 514-458-2018; FAX: 514-458-2010.
Titles:
Metrowerks CodeWarrior.
Metrowerks Modula-Two Startpak.
Metrowerks Modula-2 MPW Edition.
Metrowerks Modula-2 Professional Standalone Edition.

MGlobal International, Inc., P.O. Box 459, Orange, TX 77631 Tel 409-883-3721; FAX: 713-960-1522.
Titles:
Comp Computing Standard MUMPS (CCSM).
MGM - MacMUMPS 2.
MGM PC MUMPS: 386-486 Window 3.1 Required.

Mica Accounting Software, (0-918641), 2349 Memorial Blvd., Port Arthur, TX 77640 Tel 409-983-2051; Toll free: 800-448-6422; FAX: 409-983-5106.
Titles:
MICA Accounting Series.
MICA-Accounts Payable.
MICA-Accounts Receivable.
MICA-Applications Manager.
MICA-General Ledger.
MICA-Inventory Control.
MICA-Job Cost.
MICA/Network Manager.
MICA-Order Entry.
MICA-Payroll.
MICA-Productivity Interface.
MICA/PS-Point of Sale.
MICA-Sales Invoicing.
Mica 4 Accounting Series.
Mica 4 Accounts Payable.
Mica 4 Accounts Receivable.
Mica 4 Bank Reconciliation.
Mica 4 General Ledger.
Mica 4 Inventory Control.
Mica 4 Job Cost.
Mica 4 Payroll.
Mica 4 Purchase Order Processing.
Mica 4 Sales Order Processing.

MiccaSoft, Inc., 1395 Fm 2722, New Braunfels, TX 78132 Tel 210-629-4341; Toll free: 800-950-7943.
Titles:
Accounts Payable.
The Invoicer with Accounts Receivable.
The Invoicer with Sales Tracking/Inventory.

MichTron, Inc., (0-923213; 0-944500), 12685 Overseas Hwy., Marathon, FL 33050 Tel 305-743-8372.
Titles:
Airball.
Airball Construction Set.
alt.
Amas.
Business Agreements.
Business Tools.
C. Breeze.
Calendar.
Cards.
Cashman.
Cornerman.
Demon Seed.
DFT: Direct File Transfer.
DOS Shell.
DS-DOS Plus 2.11.
Easy Record.
Echo: Environment Controller.
Eight Ball.
Fleet Street Publisher.
Flip Side.
Freeze Frame.
Fright Night.
GFA Artist.
Goldrunner II.
Hard Drive Turbo Kit.
HiSoft BASIC.
HiSoft BASIC Professional.
HiSoft C Interpreter.
HiSoft Dev Pac.
Hit Disks.
Hyperfont.
International Soccer.
Invasion.
Journey to the Lair.
The Juggler.
K-Graph3.
Karate Kid Part II.
Leatherneck.
M-Disk.
Major Motion.
Master CAD 3-D.
Master Graph III.
Match Point.
MI-KEY.
MI-Print.
MI-Term.
Michtron BBS.
Mighty Mail.
Perfect Match.
Personal Money Manager.
Pinball Factory.
Protext.
R.A.I.D.
Replay 4.
Saved.
Shuttle II.
Slip Stream.
Slots & Cards.
Solitaire.
Talespin.
Tanglewood.
Techmate.
Tempus II.
Tetra Quest.
Thunder Chief.
Time Bandit.
Transfer.
Trivia Challenge.
220-ST.
Utilities Plus.
VTX-On Line.
Wercs.
Zero Gravity.

Micro Analysis & Design, Inc., (0-937197), 4900 Pearl East Cir., No. 201E, Boulder, CO 80301-6108 Tel 303-442-6947; FAX: 303-442-8274.
Titles:
Animation.
Micro SAINT 3.1.

Micro Architect, Inc., (0-925287), 3 Sleeper Dr., Burlington, MA 01803-3029 Tel 617-273-5658.
Titles:
ACCT-M2.
ACCT-III.
IDM-C1.
IDM-IV.
IDM-V.
IDM-X.
Integrated Accounting Package for TRSDOS 2.0.
INV-V.
INV-X.
L216.
Mail-V.
Mail-X.
Purchase Order Processor: Add-On Option.
TCS Integrated Accounting Package.
Word.
Word-C1.
WORD IV.
Word V.
WORD-X.

Micro-Art Programmers, (0-925289), 1500 Miramar Beach, No. D, Santa Barbara, CA 93108-2913 Tel 805-962-0922.
Titles:
Electronic Typewriter.
$Finance.
MAILLIST.
MBACOUNT.
MBADATA.
PROFBILL/PC.
SBACOUNT.
STANFORM.
Trust Tracker.

Micro Business Systems, (0-925301), 2907 Timberline Dr., Eugene, OR 97405-1233.
Titles:
MBS Temp Package One.

Micro Craft, Inc., (0-918019), 6703 Odyssey Dr., Suite 102, Huntsville, AL 35806-3301 Tel 205-922-9746; Toll free: 800-225-3147; FAX: 205-922-9749.
Titles:
Accounts Payable & Accounts Payable-M.
Check Write & Check Write-M.
Docket & Multiuser Docket.
The General Ledger for Professionals & General Ledger-M.
LegalPad.
Litigator & Litigator-M.
Satellite Verdict.
TwinPak Plus.
Verdict & Multiuser Verdict.
Verdict Speller.

Micro Data Base Systems, Inc. (m d b s), (0-925335; 0-917425; 0-924482), 1305 Cumberland Ave., P.O. Box 2438, West Lafayette, IN 47906 Tel 317-463-7200; Toll free: 800-445-6327; FAX: 317-463-1234.
Titles:
GURU.
MDBS IV.
Object/1.

Micro Decision Systems, (0-917349), P.O. Box 1392, Pittsburgh, PA 15230 Tel 412-854-4070.
Titles:
ConvertaCalc.
DocuCalc.
LoadCalc.

Micro Decisionware, Inc., (0-925342), 3035 Center Green Dr., Boulder, CO 80301-5405 Tel 303-443-2706; Toll free: 800-221-3634; FAX: 303-443-2797.
Titles:
Database Gateway.
PC/SQL-link for Windows.

Micro Dialects, Inc., P.O. Box 190, Loveland, OH 45140 Tel 513-271-9100; FAX: 513-271-4922.
Titles:
UASM.

Micro Dynamics, Ltd., 8555 16th St., 7th Flr., Silver Spring, MD 20910 Tel 301-589-6300; Toll free: 800-634-7638.
Titles:
Micro Dynamics MARS.
PostHaste.

Micro-Ed, (0-925348), 31 Marshall Dr., Edison, NJ 08817 Tel 201-572-3415 Tel 201-572-2149.
Titles:
AIDS Information Game.
In the Promised Land.

Micro-80, Inc., (0-925350), P.O. Box 372, Oak Harbor, WA 98277-0372.
Titles:
Generations, the Genealogy Program.

Micro Engineering Solutions, Inc., 26200 Town Center Dr., Novi, MI 48375 Tel 810-347-9650; Toll free: 800-832-9592; FAX: 810-347-6220.
Titles:
Solution 3000.
Solution 3000.

Micro Entertainment, 914 Highland Ave., South Portland, ME 04106 Tel 207-767-2664; Toll free: 800-255-5217.
Titles:
The Golden Pyramid.

Micro Focus Publishing, Div. of Micro Focus Group, PLC, (1-56928), 2465 E. Bayshore Rd., Suite 400, Palo Alto, CA 94303 Tel 415-856-4161; Toll free: 800-551-5269; FAX: 415-856-3724.
Titles:
Animator.
CIS COBOL.
CIS COBOL with FORMS-2 for Apple.
CO-Graphics.
CO-Math.
COBOL Developer's Toolkit.
Compact Level II COBOL/ET.
Forms 2.
High Performance Level II COBOL.
High Performance Level II COBOL with animator.
Level II COBOL.
Mac COBOL.
Micro Focus COBOL/2.
Micro Focus COBOL/2 Workbench.
Micro Focus COBOL/2 for UNIX.
Micro Focus COBOL/2 Toolset.
Professional COBOL.
RIMS-MPG.
SOURCEWRITER.
SYN-CHECK.
Upgrade II.
Upgrade III.
VS COBOL Workbench.
Xilerator.

Micro-Integration Corp., (0-913831; 0-924465; 0-918719), 1 Science Prk., Frostburg, MD 21532 Tel 301-689-0800; Toll free: 800-832-4526; FAX: 301-689-0808.
Titles:
Local 3270.
Local 3270 DFT: 3270 Distributed Function Terminal.
Local 5250.

Local 5250 for DOS, Windows, or OS-2.
Local 5250 Gateway.
Remote 3270.
Remote 5250.
Remote 3270 AutoSync.
Remote Bisync 3270.
Remote 3270 Gateway.
Remote 3780 RJE.
Remote 3780 RJE: For Binary Synchronous Batch Communications.
Remote 5250 AutoSync.
Remote 5250 Gateway.

Micro Investment Systems, Inc., (0-925367), P.O. Box 8599, Atlanta, GA 30306 Tel 404-892-3194.
Titles:
Stock Portfolio Reporter.

Micro Learningware, (1-55763), Rte. 1, Box 162, Amboy, MN 56010-9762 Tel 507-674-3705; FAX: 507-674-3705.
Titles:
Ag. Marketing & Commodity Futures.
Charts for Agricultural Commodities (Price Charting).
Computerized Farm Records "Farmware".
Field File Program.
Market Trend Charting.
Picture It with Words.
Rat Maze.
Tangram.

Micro Logic Corp., P.O. Box 70, Hackensack, NJ 07602 Tel 201-342-6518; Toll free: 800-342-5930 (orders only); FAX: 201-342-0370.
Titles:
InfoSelect.
Tornado.

Micro-MRP, Inc., Div. of Kewill Systems, (0-925373), 1065 E. Hillsdale Blvd., Foster City, CA 94404 Tel 415-345-6000; Toll free: 800-338-6921; FAX: 415-345-3079.
Titles:
Micro-MAX MRP.

Micro Magic, 1461 Gretel Ln., Mountain View, CA 94040-3702.
Titles:
Forms in Flight 2.
Forms in Flight: 3D Drawing & Animation.

Micro Mode, Inc., (0-925392), 4006 Mt. Laurel, San Antonio, TX 78240 Tel 210-341-2205; FAX: 210-697-0489.
Titles:
Integrated Financial Management-General Accounting.

Micro Planning International, 3801 E. Florida Ave., Suite 507, Denver, CO 80210 Tel 303-757-2216; Toll free: 800-852-7526; FAX: 303-757-2047.
Titles:
InstaPlan.
MICRO PLANNER Manager.
Micro Planner Professional.
MICRO PLANNER X-Pert.

Micro Trading Software, Inc., Box 175, Wilton, CT 06897 Tel 203-762-7820.
Titles:
Portfolio Watcher.
Stock Watcher.
Wall Street Watcher.

Micro 2, (0-922553), 888 E. Clinton St., Apt. 1067, Phoenix, AZ 85020-5807.
Titles:
You & Your Checkbook.

Micro Video Corp., (0-917359), 210 Collingwood, Suite 100, P.O. Box 7357, Ann Arbor, MI 48107 Tel 313-996-0626; Toll free: 800-537-2182; FAX: 313-996-3838.
Titles:
Video Voice Speech Training System.

Micro Vision Software, Inc., (0-925433), 368 Veterans Memorial Hwy., Commack, NY 11725 Tel 516-543-1040; Toll free: 800-829-7354; FAX: 516-543-1175.
Titles:
Fixed Assets Relief.
Tax Relief 1040 for Windows.
Tax Relief 1040 Plus.
Tax Relief 1065.
Tax Relief 1120 - 1120S.
W-2 & 1099 Generator.

Micro-W Corp., (0-925445), 614 Trenton Ave., Point Pleasant Beach, NJ 08742 Tel 908-899-4256; Toll free: 800-767-6108; FAX: 908-899-7459.
Titles:
The Clone Machine.
Font Downloader & Editor.
Mr. Tester.
QRS Music Rolls.

MicroArt Corp., (0-925453), 111 SW Columbia St., No. 960, Portland, OR 97201-5841 Tel 503-228-1148; Toll free: 800-642-7627.
Titles:
Image Word-Graphics Processor.

Microbridge Computers, Sky Way Bldg., 655 Sky Way, Suite 123, San Carlos, CA 94070 Tel 415-593-8777; FAX: 415-593-7675.
Titles:
Bridge-It 3.5.
CPYAT2PC.
Rear Guard.

MicroCase Corp., (0-922914), 1301 120th Ave., NE, Bellevue, WA 98005 Tel 206-635-0293; Toll free: 800-682-7367; FAX: 206-635-0953.
Titles:
MicroCase Analysis System.

MicroCompatibles, Inc., (0-925310), 301 Prelude Dr., Silver Spring, MD 20901 Tel 301-593-0683; FAX: 301-593-5151.
Titles:
N-See: NC Verification Software.

Microcomputer Consulting Services, (0-925478), 1750 Alma Rd., Suite 112, Richardson, TX 75081-1863 Tel 214-699-7783; Toll free: 800-697-7783 (sales only); FAX: 214-699-7795.
Titles:
MCS Appraisal System.

MicroEase, 7110 44th Ave., SW, Seattle, WA 98136 Tel 206-932-6448.
Titles:
Rental Record Keeper.

Microfinancial Corp./FLEXWARE, (0-925502), 23622 Shadow Dr., Auburn, CA 93602-8358; Toll free: 800-527-6587.
Titles:
FlexShare Database Server.
FLEXWARE Accounts Payable.
FLEXWARE Accounts Receivable.
FLEXWARE Application Development System.
FLEXWARE Database Development System.
FLEXWARE General Ledger.
FLEXWARE Integrated Accounting System.
FLEXWARE Inventory.
FLEXWARE Job Costing.
FLEXWARE Order Processing.
FLEXWARE Payroll.
FLEXWARE Point of Sale.
FLEXWARE Purchasing.
FLEXWARE Sales Analysis System.
FLEXWARE Spreadsheet.

Micrografx, Inc., (0-918653), 303 Arapaho, Richardson, TX 75081 Tel 214-234-1769; Toll free: 800-272-3729.
Titles:
ABC Flowcharter.
Amazing Art Adventure.
Art Studio.
Designer.
Eating the Chocolate Elephant: Take Charge of Change Through Total Process Management.
Graphics Works.
PhotoMagic.
Picture Publisher.
Windows DRAW.
Windows OrgChart.

MicroHealth-NursePerfect Software & Publishing, (1-883441), P.O. Box 98471, Raleigh, NC 27624-8471; 2101 Osprey Cir., Raleigh, NC 27615 Tel 919-954-0807.
Titles:
NurseWorks.

Microillusions, Inc., P.O. Box 9148, Marina Del Rey, CA 90295-1548; FAX: 818-787-7345.
Titles:
Blackjack Academy.
Craps Academy.
Discovery.
Ebonstar.
The Faery Tale Adventure.
Fire Power.
Galactic Invasion.
GENESIS The Third Day.
Mainframe.
Music-X.
Photon Paint.
Photon Paint Expansion Disks.
Photon Video: CellAnimator.
Photon Video: Transport Controller.
Romantic Encounters at the Dome.
Turbo.

Microlite Corp., 1021 Sutherland St., Pittsburgh, PA 15204 Tel 412-771-4901.
Titles:
CTAR.

MicroMaster, Inc., 1289 Brodhead Rd., Monaca, PA 15061 Tel 412-775-3000.
Titles:
Digital Building System.
Your Family Tree.

Micron Computer Co., Inc., 401 Mobil Ave., Suite 8, Camarillo, CA 93010 Tel 805-482-0702; FAX: 805-388-1542.
Titles:
Turbo-Mac 2 Automotive Management System.

Microneering, 211 E. Culver Blvd., Suite Q, Playa Del Rey, CA 90293 Tel 310-306-0878; Toll free: 800-423-0814.
Titles:
Sambas; Threads.

Micronetics, Inc., (0-925531), 621 NW 53rd St., No. 240, Boca Raton, FL 33487 Tel 407-995-1477; FAX: 407-995-0856.
Titles:
The Accounting XPert.

Microport, Inc., 108 Whispering Pines Dr., Scotts Valley, CA 95066-4784 Tel 408-438-8649; Toll free: 800-367-8649; FAX: 408-438-7560.
Titles:
DOS Merge 286.
DOS Merge 386.
Microport System V/4.
System V/4 MP.

MICROPROSE SOFTWARE

System V/386.

MicroProse Software, (0-928289; 1-55884), 180 Lakefront Dr., Hunt Valley, MD 21030 Tel 410-771-1151; Toll free: 800-876-1151 (orders only); FAX: 410-771-1174.
Titles:
Airborne Ranger.
Ancient Art of War in the Skies.
ATAC: Advanced Tactical Air Command.
Challenge of the Five Realms: Spellbound in the World of Nhagardia.
Covert Action.
Darklands: Heroic Role-Playing Adventures in Medieval Europe.
David Leadbetter's Greens: The Instructional 3D Golf Game.
F-15 Strike Eagle.
F-19 Stealth Fighter.
F-15 Strike Eagle II.
F-15 Strike Eagle II: Operation Desert Storm Scenario Disk.
F-15 Strike Eagle III.
F-117A Nighthawk Stealth Fighter 2.0.
Flying Fortress B-17.
Gunship.
Gunship 2000.
Gunship 2000: Islands & Ice Scenario Disk.
Jump Jet.
Knights of the Sky.
Lightspeed.
Mega Traveller 3: The Unknown Worlds.
Megatraveller: The Zhodani Conspiracy.
M1 Tank Platoon.
Pirates.
Red Storm Rising.
Rex Nebular: And the Cosmic Gender Bender.
Sid Meier's Railroad Tycoon.
Silent Service.
Silent Service II.
Space 1889.
Sword of the Samurai.
Task Force 1942.
XF5700 Mantis Experimental Fighter.

Microrim, Inc., Subs. of Abacus Software Group, (0-916937), 15395 SE 30th Pl., Bellevue, WA 98007-6537 Tel 206-649-9500; Toll free: 800-628-6990 (sales only); 800-248-2001 (customer service only); FAX: 206-746-9350.
Titles:
R:BASE: For DOS.
R:BASE: For OS-2 PM.
R:BASE: For Windows.
R:WEB.

MicroSearch, 9000 Southwest Freeway, Suite 330, Houston, TX 77074-1521 Tel 713-988-2818.
Titles:
Art Companion.
Citi Desk.
City Desk.
Database 4.
Head Coach: Football Simulation.
Perfect Sound: Digital Sound Sampler.
Your Personal Cookbook.

Microserve, Inc., (0-925549), 276 Fifth Ave., New York, NY 10001 Tel 212-683-2811.
Titles:
Estimator Plus.
MacProspect.
Turbo-Plus: Enhanced Support Package.
Want Ads Composer.

MicroServices, Inc., (0-925408), P.O. Box 40, Brooksville, ME 04617 Tel 207-326-4847.
Titles:
Fleet Management System.
Police Records System.
Real Estate System.

MicroSim Corp., 20 Fairbanks, Irvine, CA 92718 Tel 714-770-3022; Toll free: 800-245-3022; FAX: 714-455-0554.
Titles:
Design Center - with Circuit File Entry: Direct Program Management.
Design Center - with Extended DOS Control Shell.
The Design Center with Paragon: Analog Performance Optimization.
Design Center with Schematic Capture: Schematic Capture Front-End.
PLSyn: Programmable Logic Synthesis.
Signal Integrity: Polaris.

Microsmith Computer Technology, (0-932289), P.O. Box 1473, Elkhart, IN 46515 Tel 219-522-6807; FAX: 219-522-8602.
Titles:
I'm No Accountant: Business Journal Template for LOTUS 1-2-3.

Microsoft Pr., Div. of Microsoft Corp., (0-914845; 1-55615; 1-57231; 0-925550; 1-879021), One Microsoft Way, Redmond, WA 98052-6399 Tel 206-936-0055; FAX: 206-823-8101; Dist. by: Publisher Resources, Inc., 1224 Heil Quaker Blvd., P.O. Box 7001, La Vergne, TN 37086-7001 Tel 615-793-5090; Toll free: 800-937-5557.
Titles:
Business BASIC Compiler.
C Optimizing Compiler.
COBOL.
CodeView.
FORTRAN Optimizing Compiler.
FoxBASE+.
FoxBASE+/LAN.
FoxBASE+/Mac.
FoxBASE+/386.
FoxGraph.
FoxPro.
Learning DOS.
MASM.
Microsoft BASIC Interpreter.
Microsoft Bookshelf.
Microsoft C Optimizing Compiler.
Microsoft Chart (IBM).
Microsoft Chart (Mac).
Microsoft COBOL Compiler.
Microsoft Excel.
Microsoft File.
Microsoft Flight Simulator (Mac).
Microsoft Flight Simulator 3.0.
Microsoft FORTRAN Compiler.
Microsoft Macro Assembler 5.1.
Microsoft Mail.
Microsoft Multiplan.
Microsoft Pascal Compiler.
Microsoft PowerPoint.
Microsoft Project.
Microsoft QuickBASIC for the Macintosh.
Microsoft QuickBASIC 4.5.
Microsoft QuickC.
Microsoft Windows.
Microsoft Windows Excel.
Microsoft Windows 386.
Microsoft Word.
Microsoft Word for the Macintosh.
Microsoft Word for Xenix.
Microsoft Works.
Microsoft WRITE.
MS-FORTRAN.
OS/2.
Quick C Compiler.

MicroSpec, (0-925558), 1809 Avenue K, Plano, TX 75074 Tel 214-881-0030; Toll free: 800-451-3363; FAX: 214-881-1809.
Titles:
PC-POS.
Video Rental Manager, MVP.

SOFTWARE ENCYCLOPEDIA 1996

Microsystems, (0-925565), 7201-87 SE, Mercer Island, WA 98040 Tel 206-236-1513.
Titles:
Discounted Cash Flow.
House Manager, Scorekeeper.
Scorekeeper.

Microsystems Engineering Co., Div. of Freedom Solutions Group, (0-925567), 2500 S. Highland Ave., Suite 350, Lombard, IL 60148-5390 Tel 708-261-0111; Toll free: 800-359-3695; FAX: 708-261-9520.
Titles:
Mass-11 CLASSIC Document Processor.
Mass-11 Draw.
Mass-11 Manager.
MASS-11 SuperCom.
Mass-11 CLASSIC Document Processor: Microsystems Administrative Support System for Personal Computers.
The Network Illustrator.
WiziWord for Windows.

Microtec Information Systems, (0-918033), 2802 Martinbrook Ln., Jonesboro, AR 72401 Tel 501-972-1793.
Titles:
Clothing Retail Management System.
Sales Analysis.
Shoe Retail Management System.

Microtec Research, (0-925573), 2350 Mission College Blvd., Suite 500, Santa Clara, CA 95054 Tel 408-733-2919; Toll free: 800-551-5554; P.O. Box 60337, Sunnyvale, CA 94088.
Titles:
Microtec ASM68K.
Microtec MCC68K C Cross Compiler.
Microtec 68020 Cross Assembler.
Paragon ASM186 Cross Assembler System.
Paragon HC86 Cross Compiler System.
X-Ray.
XRAY 68K.

MicroTech Conversion Systems, (0-925575), 940 Industrial Ave., Palo Alto, CA 94303 Tel 415-424-1174; Toll free: 800-223-3693; FAX: 415-424-1176.
Titles:
MasterMaker.
PolyTape.
Reformatter Conversion Software: DEC R13 PCDOS2DEC-RT-11.
Reformatter Conversion Software: R09 DOS2IBM.
Reformatter Conversion Software: IBM PC/IBM 3740.
Reformatter Conversion Software: MS-DOS/IBM 3740.
Reformatter 9-Track Tape Software.

Microtemp, 318 Mendocino Ave., Suite 22, Santa Rosa, CA 95404 Tel 707-575-1459.
Titles:
Microtemp Financial Calculators.

Microware Systems Corp., (0-918035), 1900 NW 114th St., Des Moines, IA 50325-7077 Tel 515-224-1929; FAX: 515-224-1352; 2041 Mission College Blvd., Santa Clara, CA 95054 Tel 408-980-0201.
Titles:
OS-9000.
RAVE.

Microway, Inc., (0-925446), P.O. Box 79, Kingston, MA 02364 Tel 508-746-7341; FAX: 508-746-4678.
Titles:
NDP C-C Plus Plus 386.
NDP C/C++ 486.
NDPFFT.
NDP FORTRAN-486.
NDP Fortran-386.

PUBLISHER/TITLE INDEX

NDP Fortran 90.
NDP Pascal-386.
NDP Pascal 486.
NDP Plot.
387 FFT.

Microx, Inc., 9821 Katy Freeway, Suite 260, Houston, TX 77024-1205 Tel 713-467-7000; Toll free: 800-622-4990; FAX: 713-461-7095.
Titles:
Reveille Accounting: Advanced Revelation.
Reveille Distribution: Advanced Revelation.
REVEILLE for Windows: Visual Basic.
Reveille Payroll: Advanced Revelation.

Middle Coast Publishing, (0-934523), P.O. Box 2522, Iowa City, IA 52244 Tel 319-354-8944; Dist. by: Baker & Taylor Bks., Somerville Service Ctr., 50 Kirby Ave., Somerville, NJ 08876-0734 Tel 908-722-8000; Toll free: 800-775-1500 (customer service); Dist. by: Quality Bks., Inc., 1003 W. Pines Rd., Oregon, IL 61061 Tel 708-295-2010; Toll free: 800-323-4241 (libraries only).
Titles:
Double Agent: For Making & Breaking Secret Codes.

Midisoft Corp., P.O. Box 1000, Bellevue, WA 98009 Tel 206-881-7176; Toll free: 800-776-6434; FAX: 206-883-1368.
Titles:
Attitude for Success.
Communicate!
Manage Stress.
Manage Time.
Midisoft Studio: Advanced Edition.
Midisoft Studio: Standard Edition.
Midisoft Windows DLL.
Organize for Success.

Midwest Agribusiness Services, Inc., (0-940135; 1-56719), 4565 Hwy. 33 W., West Bend, WI 53095-9108 Tel 414-629-5577; Toll free: 800-523-3475; FAX: 414-629-9628.
Titles:
Agri-Quiz: Conduct of Meetings.
Agri-Quiz: FFA Instruction.
Agri-Quiz: Floriculture.
Agri-Quiz: Greenhouse I.
Agri-Quiz: Greenhouse II.
Agri-Quiz: Horticulture I.
Agri-Quiz: Horticulture II.
Agri-Quiz: Nursery - Landscape.
Agri-Quiz: Parliamentary Procedure II.
Agri-Quiz: Small Engine.

Mighty Byte Computer, Inc., (0-925601; 0-925603), 6040-A 6 Forks Rd., Twin Forks Office Pk., Suite 223, Raleigh, NC 27609 Tel 919-846-0345; Toll free: 800-237-7072; FAX: 919-676-0500.
Titles:
Baseball League Statistics.
Basketball League Statistics.
Bowling League Secretary.
Golf League Secretary.

Mihalisin Assocs., 600 Honey Run Rd., Ambler, PA 19002 Tel 215-646-3814; FAX: 215-643-4896.
Titles:
TempleGraph.

Millennium Media Group, Inc., (0-9645142), 234 N. Columbus Blvd., Philadelphia, PA 19106 Tel 215-625-8888; Toll free: 800-892-6848; FAX: 215-625-2567.
Titles:
Dell Magazines Diabolical Digits.

Millennium Software, 1970 S. Coast Hwy., Laguna Beach, CA 92651 Tel 714-497-7439.
Titles:
HyperX.

Miller, R. H., Assocs., 483 N. 4154 E., Rigby, ID 83442 Tel 208-745-9249; FAX: 208-745-9249.
Titles:
Financial Analysis Template.

Miller Assocs., (0-941847; 1-56188), 11 Burtis Ave., Suite 200, New Canaan, CT 06840 Tel 203-972-0777; Toll free: 800-654-5472; FAX: 203-966-7547.
Titles:
APBA Baseball/Baseball Wizard.
APBA Baseball Classic Deluxe.
APBA Baseball Classic: Master Edition.
APBA Baseball for Windows Ballparks Disks.
APBA Baseball General Manager.
APBA Baseball/Old Timers.
APBA Baseball/Original Franchise All-Stars.
APBA Baseball StatMaster.
APBA Presents Baseball for Windows.
Bill James All Time All-Stars.
Bill James Electronic Baseball Encyclopedia.
Classic Season Disks.
MicroManager Editor.

Miller Microcomputer Services, (0-918039), 61 Lake Shore Rd., Natick, MA 01760-2099 Tel 508-653-6136.
Titles:
DATAHANDLER.
DATAHANDLER-PLUS.
FORTHCOM: Communications Module.
FORTHWRITE.
MMSFORTH.
MMSFORTH GAMES.
MMSFORTH General Ledger.
MMSFORTH Utilities.

Millett Software, 146 W. 255, S., Orem, UT 84058 Tel 801-224-6841.
Titles:
Learn about the Solar System & Halley's Comet.

Milliken Publishing Co., (0-88335; 1-55863; 0-7877), 1100 Research Blvd., Saint Louis, MO 63132-0579 Tel 314-991-4220; Toll free: 800-325-4136; FAX: 800-538-1319.
Titles:
The Animal Tales Electronic Books.
The Big Bug Alphabet Book.
Golf Classic-Battling Bugs.
Marvin the Moose.
Math Gulper.
The Milliken Storyteller Children's Classics.
The Secret Key.
Spanish - English Math.
Tangrams Puzzler.
The Ultimate Worksheet Creator.

Milum Corp., P.O. Box 163985, Austin, TX 78716-3985 Tel 512-327-2255; Toll free: 800-257-2120.
Titles:
Business Letter Base.
Business Letters Go!
Copyrights, Trademarks & Patents.
Exporting Guide for Business.
50 Classic Business Contracts.
In-Out.

Min Microcomputer Software, Inc., (0-939015), P.O. Box 3561, Frederick, MD 21701; 1319 Johnson Ferry Rd., Suite 209, Marietta, GA 30068 Tel 404-971-0643.
Titles:
The Landlord.
The Landlord Plus.
The Landmaster: Property Management Software.

MindPlay, Div. of Methods & Solutions, Inc., (0-918017; 1-55772), 160 W. Fort Lowell Rd., Tucson, AZ 85705-3812 Tel 602-888-7904; Toll free: 800-221-7911.
Titles:
Bake 'n Taste.
Cotton Tales.
Crozzzwords.
Dyno-Quest.
Easy Street.
Jumblezzz.
Math Magic.
Puzzle Series: Jumblezzz; Crozzzwords; Wordzzzearch.
ROBOMATH.
Wordzzzearch.

MiniLab Bks., (0-9621208), P.O. Box 21086, Daytona Beach, FL 32121-1086; 1035 Green Acres Cir., N., Daytona Beach, FL 32119 Tel 904-761-2436.
Titles:
D-PLOT: For Amiga or IBM.
MININEC for Radio amateurs.
Practical Antenna Design & Analysis: Volume 1.

Minitab, Inc., (0-925636), 3081 Enterprise Dr., State College, PA 16801 Tel 814-238-3280; Toll free: 800-448-3555; FAX: 814-238-4383.
Titles:
Minitab Statistical Software.

Miniware, Inc., (0-925637), 205 Winchester Rd., Annapolis, MD 21401 Tel 410-757-5626.
Titles:
Bounded Linear Program: RAMLP.

Minuteman Software, (0-925641), P.O. Box 171, Stow, MA 01775 Tel 508-897-5662; Toll free: 800-223-1430; FAX: 508-897-7562.
Titles:
GPSS/PC.
GPSS/PC Animator.

Miracle Computing, (0-918657), P.O. Box 336, Perry, KS 66073-0336.
Titles:
Sounds.

Miramar, Ltd., (0-925472), 2441 Peppertree Ct., Lisle, IL 60532-3335 Tel 708-369-5177.
Titles:
CARS: Computer Assisted Repair System.
LOF: Lube, Oil & Filter.
QCARS: Quick Computer Assisted Repair System.

MIS Technology, (0-928078), 10335 W. Oklahoma Ave., Milwaukee, WI 53227 Tel 414-327-7560; FAX: 414-327-5618.
Titles:
PROFIT.

Mission Accomplished Software Services, Inc., 10615 Bradbury Rd., Los Angeles, CA 90064 Tel 213-870-2441.
Titles:
Mail-Dex.
Pro-Desk.
Psych-Log.

Mitchell & Gauthier Assocs., Inc., (0-925649), 200 Baker Ave., Concord, MA 01742-2112 Tel 508-369-5115; FAX: 508-369-0013.
Titles:
ACSL-PC: Advanced Continuous Simulation Language-PC.

Mitchell Management Systems, (0-927259), 2298 16th Ave., San Francisco, CA 94116; Toll free: 800-336-3661.
Titles:
Mapps: The Management & Project Planning System.

Quick-Plan: Executive Project Planning System.

MMCAD Systems, P.O. Box 360845, Milpitas, CA 95036 Tel 510-770-0858; FAX: 510-770-0116.
Titles:
C Programmer's Toolbox.
McCLint: C Programmer's McTool Series Tool 2.
McCPrint: C Programmer's McTool Series Tool No. 1.

Mnemotech Financial Systems, Inc., (0-925653), 269 W. 40th St., New York, NY 10018 Tel 212-398-1155.
Titles:
Commercial Finance Lending System.

Mobius Corp., (1-878842), 405 N. Henry St., Alexandria, VA 22314 Tel 703-684-2911; Toll free: 800-426-2710; FAX: 703-684-2919.
Titles:
Electronic Builder.
Electronic Easel.
Farm.
KIDWARE 2 Plus Learning Center: (For Two Computer in One Classroom).
KIDWARE 2 Plus Single Station.
Mural Maker.
Music Maker.

Mobius Pr., (0-9637970), P.O. Box 3339, Boulder, CO 80307; Toll free: 800-529-5627; FAX: 303-499-5289. Do not confuse with Mobius Pr. in Madison, SD.
Titles:
FirmMerge.

ModaCAD, Inc., 1954 Cotner Ave., Los Angeles, CA 90025 Tel 310-312-6632; FAX: 310-444-9577.
Titles:
ENVISION.
ModaCAD.
ModaCAD Design System.

Modern Computer Aided Engineering, Inc., 8425 Woodfield Crossing Blvd., Suite 221, Indianapolis, IN 46240 Tel 317-469-4140; Toll free: 800-444-6223; FAX: 317-469-4130.
Titles:
Inertia.

Modern Microcomputers, (0-925663), 7302 Kim Shelly Court, Mechanicsville, VA 23111-4261 Tel 804-746-4352.
Titles:
MODBIL.
MODFIN.
MODMAIL 3.
MODSTAT.

Modtec, Software Div., (0-925666; 0-925665), 45 Williamsburg Dr., Fairport, NY 14450 Tel 716-425-1651.
Titles:
AUTO-GRAPH.
Automatic Graphing of Functions.
Biorhythm.
Copy-Tape.

Molarbyte Data Systems, Div. of Molarbyte, 92 Old Brook Rd., Dix Hills, NY 11746 Tel 516-586-0962.
Titles:
Molarbyte Manager.

Monagle, George, Graphic Partners, 120 Walton St., Syracuse, NY 13202 Tel 315-426-0513; FAX: 315-426-1890.
Titles:
LaserLogo Credit Card Symbol Font.

Money Tree Software, (0-925679), 1753 Wooded Knolls Dr., No. 200, Philomath, OR 97370 Tel 503-929-2140; FAX: 503-924-2787.
Titles:
Easy Money - Easy Money PLUS.
Money Tools.
MoneyCalc IV.
Retirement Solutions & Retirement Solutions PLUS.

Monitor Software, 960 N. San Antonio Rd., Suite 210, Los Altos, CA 94022 Tel 415-949-1688.
Titles:
Task Monitor.

Monterey Computer Consulting, (0-925689), 501 Webster, Monterey, CA 93940-3232 Tel 408-646-1147.
Titles:
Resale Store Management System.
Video Store Management System.

Morgan Interactive, 160 Pine St., Suite 509, San Francisco, CA 94111 Tel 415-693-9596.
Titles:
Morgan's Trivia Machine.
Recess in Greece.

Morgan-Rand, Inc., (0-913061; 0-925133), 1800 Byberry Rd., Mason's Mill II Business Pk., Huntingdon Valley, PA 19006 Tel 215-938-5500; FAX: 215-557-8414.
Titles:
TRG - Treatment Resource Guide: For NY, CA, PA, NJ.

Morningstar Technology Corp., P.O. Box 5370, Greenville, SC 29606 Tel 803-232-2170.
Titles:
Attorney's Trust Accounting: ATAS.
Conflict of Interest.
Docket Control-Calendaring.
Legal Accounts Payable.
Morningstar General Ledger: MGLS.
Morningstar Payroll.
Time Accounting & Billing.

Mosby/Multi-Media, Div. of Times Mirror Co., (0-8016; 0-940122), 11830 Westline Industrial Dr., Saint Louis, MO 63141 Tel 314-872-8370; Toll free: 800-325-4177.
Titles:
Color Spectral Doppler Ultrasound of the Carotid Arteries & Peripheral Vessels: An Interactive Compendium.
General Radiology: An Interactive Compendium.
RSNA: Selected Scientific Exhibits, 1992, 93, 94.

Motion Works Publishing, 330 Townsend St., Suite 123, San Francisco, CA 94107 Tel 415-541-9333.
Titles:
Get It Free on the Internet: The Penny-Pincher's Guide to Online Bargains.
Get the News on Usenet: Using Newsgroups to Join the Conversation, Which Is Always in Progress.
How to Get on the Internet: Finding, Installing, & Using Internet Connection Software to Get Online.
How to Publish on the Internet: Build Your Own Home Page on the World Wide Web.
How to Use Internet Email: Installing & Using Eudora to Get the Most Out of Electronic Mail.
The Internet Business Guide: Essential Online Resources.
Internet Family Guide: Resources for Learning & Playing Online.
The Internet Media Guide: News & Entertainment in Cybersapce.
Internet Travel Guide: Practical Business & Adventure Resources.
A Night Out on the Internet: Entertainment, Fun, & Excitement on the World Wide Web.
Sounds of Cyberspace: Rock, Pop, & Alternative Music on the Internet.
To Surf & Detect: Crime & Punishment on the Internet.
The Truth Is in Here: Conspiracies, Mysteries, Superstitions, Kooks & Cults on the Internet.
You Could Already Be a Winner!: 101 Magazines on the Internet.

Motivational Developers, (0-9623859), 108-24 Fern Pl., Jamaica, NY 11433 Tel 718-706-4034.
Titles:
On Family Life.

Mt. Xinu, 2560 Ninth St., Suite 312, Berkeley, CA 94710 Tel 510-644-0146; FAX: 510-644-2680.
Titles:
Mach386.

Mountain View Pr., Div. of Epsilon Lyra, Inc., (0-914699), Box 429, Rte. 2, LaHonda, CA 94020 Tel 415-747-0760; Toll free: 800-321-4103 (orders only). Do not confuse with Mountain View Pr. in South Hadley, MA.
Titles:
MVP-FORTH Cross Compiler.
MVP-FORTH Expert-2 System.
MVP-FORTH Meta Compiler.
MVP-FORTH PADS.
MVP-FORTH Programmer's Kit.
MVP-FORTH Programmer's Kit (HP).
MVP-FORTH Programming Aids.

Multi-Ad Services, Inc., 1720 W. Detweiller Dr., Peoria, IL 61615-1695 Tel 309-692-1530; Toll free: 800-447-1950; FAX: 309-692-5444.
Titles:
Multi-Ad Creator.
Multi-Ad Search.
ProArt Professional Art Library.

Multi Soft, Inc., Subs. of Multi Solutions, Inc., (0-925716), P.O. Box 3359, Princeton, NJ 08543-3359; FAX: 609-895-0072.
Titles:
EasySAA.
Hyper-Action.
Infront.
WCL (Windows Communications Library).

Multi-Tech Systems, Inc., (0-918047), 2205 Woodale Dr., Mounds View, MN 55112 Tel 612-785-3500; Toll free: 800-328-9717; FAX: 612-785-9874.
Titles:
MultiExpress for DOS: Data Communications Software.
MultiExpress for Windows: Communications Software.
MultiExpressFAX for DOS: Facsimile Software.
MultiExpressFAX for Windows: Facsimile Software.

Multicom Publishing, Inc., (1-884014), 1100 Olive Way, Suite 1250, Seattle, WA 98101 Tel 206-622-5530; Toll free: 800-850-7272 (orders only); FAX: 206-622-4380; Dist. by: Electronic Arts, 1450 Fashion Island Blvd., San Mateo, CA 94404 Tel 415-571-7171; Toll free: 800-245-4525 (orders).
Titles:
Americans in Space.
Astrology Gift Pack.
Astrology Source.
The Best Food & Wine, Vol. 1: MPC - Stand-Alone.
The Best of Food & Wine.
The Best of Food & Wine, Vol. 1: Mac-MPC Book Bundle.
The Best of Multimedia.
The Best of Multimedia: CD-ROM Sampler.
Better Homes & Gardens Complete Guide to American Cooking.

Better Homes & Gardens Complete Guide to Gardening.
Better Homes & Gardens Cool Crafts: Incredible Activities for Kids.
Better Homes & Gardens Health Cooking CD Cookbook.
Better Homes & Gardens Planning Your Home.
Cooking for Today: Chicken.
Cooking for Today: Chicken (Hybrid Book Bundle).
Cooking for Today: Pasta.
Cooking for Today: Pasta (Hybrid Book Bundle).
Cooking for Today: Stir Fry.
Cooking for Today: Stir Fry (Hybrid Book Bundle).
Cooking for Today: Vegetarian.
Cooking for Today: Vegetarian (Hybrid Book Bundle).
Dandy Dinosaurs: A Max the Dragon CD-Storybook.
Dandy Dinosaurs: A Max the Dragon Interactive Storybook.
Exploring America's National Parks.
Exploring America's National Parks: Mac-MPC Book Bundle.
Exploring America's National Parks: Stand-Alone (Hybrid).
Gardening Gift Pack.
Gourmet Gift Pack.
Home Improvement 1-2-3.
Home Improvement 1-2-3: Hybrid Kit.
Home Improvement 1-2-3: Mac-MPC Kit.
Journey to the Planets.
Legends of Oz.
National Parks of America.
Warren Miller's Ski World: The Complete Multimedia Ski Experience.
Wines of the World.
Wines of the World Book Bundle.

Multisoft Resources, (0-9624552), P.O. Box 235, Washington Grove, MD 20880-0235; 7405 Cliffbourne Ct., Derwood, MD 20855 Tel 301-977-6972.
Titles:
Federal JobLink: The Complete SF 171 & Supportive Forms Package.

Mumford Micro Systems, (0-925723), 3933 Antone Rd., Santa Barbara, CA 93110 Tel 805-687-5116.
Titles:
Macintize.
Micro-Set.
PostCode.

Murray, Nick, 608 W. Colorado St., Hammond, LA 70401 Tel 504-345-2332.
Titles:
Classified! II.

Muse Software, (0-87190), P.O. Box 283, Monrovia, MD 21770 Tel 301-831-7090.
Titles:
ABM.
Address Book.
Advanced Blackjack.
The Best of Muse.
Beyond Castle Wolfenstein.
Castle Wolfenstein.
The Caverns of Freitag.
Data Plot.
The Eating Machine.
Form Letter Module.
International Gran Prix.
Rescue Squad.
Smart Start.
Space Taxi.
Super-Text 40/80.
Super-Text Home-Office.
Super-Text Professional: Apple.
Super-Text Professional: Atari.
Super-Text Professional: Commodore 64.
Super-Text Professional: IBM PC.
Three Mile Island.

Music Institute of California, (0-9624062; 1-883993), P.O. Box 3535, Vista, CA 92085-3535; 1930 W. San Marcos Blvd., Suite 308, San Marcos, CA 92069 Tel 619-727-3424; Dist. by: Brodart Co., 500 Arch St., Williamsport, PA 17705 Tel 717-326-2461; Toll free: 800-233-8467; Dist. by: Baker & Taylor Bks., Somerville Service Ctr., 50 Kirby Ave., Somerville, NJ 08876-0734 Tel 908-722-8000; Toll free: 800-775-1500 (customer service); Dist. by: Baker & Taylor Bks., Momence Service Ctr., 501 S. Gladiolus St., Momence, IL 60954-2444 Tel 815-472-2444; Toll free: 800-775-2300 (customer service); Dist. by: Baker & Taylor Bks., Commerce Service Ctr., 251 Mt. Olive Church Rd., Commerce, GA 30599-9988 Tel 706-335-5000; Toll free: 800-775-1200 (customer service); Dist. by: Baker & Taylor Bks., Reno Service Ctr., 380 Edison Way, Reno, NV 89564 Tel 702-858-6700; Toll free: 800-775-1700 (customer service).
Titles:
Secret.

Music Systems for Learning, (0-941849), P.O. Box 1387, Boca Grande, FL 33921 Tel 813-964-1030; FAX: 813-964-1030.
Titles:
MusicShapes.

MusiKrafters Music Services, P.O. Box 14124, Louisville, KY 40214 Tel 502-361-4597.
Titles:
ExampleKrafter.

Mutrax, 2227 Cameron Ave., North Merrick, NY 11566 Tel 516-868-0042.
Titles:
Mutrax Monitor.

Myers, Howard W., & Assocs., 361 Virginia St., Crystal Lake, IL 60014 Tel 815-459-0100.
Titles:
AMAS: Agency Management Automation System.
ELCAD: Intelligent Computer Aided Design Software Package.
Micro Manufacturer.
PAL-DOC.

NBI, Inc., (0-925736), 65 Bellevue Dr., Boulder, CO 80302 Tel 303-444-5710; Toll free: 800-624-1111; FAX: 303-938-2591.
Titles:
Legacy.

N.B. Informatics, Inc., (0-928178), 285 W. Broadway, No. 600, New York, NY 10013; Toll free: 800-969-6922; FAX: 212-334-0845.
Titles:
Nota Bene.

NCR Corp., Personal Computer Div., 1601 S. Main, PCD-1, Dayton, OH 45479 Tel 513-445-7478.
Titles:
NCR PC2PC.

NCS/MEMTRAC, 400 Northridge Rd., Atlanta, GA 30350 Tel 404-642-5041; Toll free: 800-847-3563, Ext. 504.
Titles:
Membership Management, Program Management, Auction Management, General Ledger, Accounts Receivable, Accounts Payable, Fixed Assets, Project Cost, Data Writer.

NCSS-PC, (0-917373), 329 N. 1000 E., Kaysville, UT 84037-1731 Tel 801-546-0445; FAX: 801-546-3907.
Titles:
NCSS-PC.

NDX Corp., (0-928713), P.O. Box 337, Oakton, VA 22124 Tel 703-502-9800; Toll free: 800-232-8345; FAX: 703-502-9805.
Titles:
CREATEABASE.
DocuSystem.

NEC Technologies, Subs. of NEC America, Inc., (0-925739), 1255 Michael Dr., Wood Dale, IL 60191-1094 Tel 708-860-9500; Toll free: 800-632-7638; FAX: 312-860-5523. Same company as N E C Technologies in Boxborough, MA.
Titles:
Crowley Manor.
DEMO.

NORCOM (Northern Computing Consultants), P.O. Box 020897, Juneau, AK 99802-0897 Tel 907-780-6464; FAX: 907-790-2779.
Titles:
Screenio.

NSP, Inc., (0-925749), 3509 E. Atherton Ln., Baneberry, TN 37890-4915.
Titles:
C. S. M. S.

Namestormers, The, 4347 W. Northwest Hwy., Suite 1040, Dallas, TX 75220-3864 Tel 214-350-6214; FAX: 214-350-7617.
Titles:
Headliner.
NamePro.
Namer.

Nanosecond Systems, Inc., (0-918645), P.O. Box 81, Woodland, CA 95776 Tel 916-662-4334; FAX: 916-662-4334.
Titles:
NANOS.

Nappo Computer Service, (0-925756), 696 Amity Rd., No. A3, Bethany, CT 06524-3006 Tel 203-878-8770.
Titles:
Certified Dental Assistant.

National Business Institute, (0-925761), P.O. Box 3067, Eau Claire, WI 54702 Tel 715-835-8525.
Titles:
Elementary Computer Literacy System.

National Computer Systems, Inc., (0-89878; 0-932402; 0-924186), 4401 W. 76th St., Edina, MN 55435 Tel 612-893-8143; Toll free: 800-431-1421.
Titles:
Employ-EASE.
Local Government-Education & Other Not for Profit Organizations.

National Guest Systems Corp., (0-925766), 2096 Gaither Rd., Suite 100, Rockville, MD 20850 Tel 301-926-2500; Toll free: 800-456-6472; FAX: 301-926-3500.
Titles:
Gaither: Restaurant POS System.
Innstar Hotel-Restaurant Management System.
IS4: Hotel Property Management System.
Meetings Catering System.
Millennia Hotel Management System.
Miracle Regional Sales Lead System.
Miracle Sales & Catering System.

National Information Systems, Inc., (0-925768; 0-927470), 4040 Moorpark Ave., Suite 200, San Jose, CA 95117-1852 Tel 408-985-7100; Toll free: 800-441-5758; FAX: 408-246-3127.
Titles:
ACCENT GraphicVUE: Visual Project Management.
Accent R.
ACCENT RDM: User Application Developer.
ACCENTR Fourth Generation Language: SQL-Based 462.

National Instruments, (0-925769), 6504 Bridge Point Pkwy., Austin, TX 78730-5039 Tel 512-794-0100; Toll free: 800-433-3488; FAX: 512-794-8411.
Titles:
Lab Windows CVI.
HiQ.
LabVIEW: Laboratory Virtual Instrument Engineering Workbench.
LabWindows.
NI-DAQ.
NI-488.2 Software.
NI-VXI.

National Intelligence Bk. Ctr., (1-878292), Lock Box Mail Unit 18757, Washington, DC 20036-8757; FAX: 202-331-7456; 2020 Pennsylvania Ave., NW, Suite 165, Washington, DC 20006 Tel 202-797-1234.
Titles:
Bowen Digital Bibliography of Works on Intelligence, Security, & Covert Activities.

National Planning & Consulting Corp., (0-928717), P.O. Box 140489, Coral Gables, FL 33114-0489 Tel 305-442-1133; FAX: 305-558-2374.
Titles:
Selectra.

Natural Language, Inc., 2910 Seventh St., Berkeley, CA 94710 Tel 510-841-3500; Toll free: 800-654-5858; FAX: 510-841-3628.
Titles:
Natural Language.

Natural Software Ltd., 129 Pearsall Pl., Ithaca, NY 14850 Tel 607-272-0157; Toll free: 800-626-2511.
Titles:
CouponOmizer.
NSL Diet Analyzer.

Nautasoft, Inc., P.O. Box 282, Rockland, DE 19732; Toll free: 800-441-0360, Ext. 1009.
Titles:
MacTides.

Navic Software, (0-925781), P.O. Box 441161, Aurora, CO 80044-1161.
Titles:
Business Analyst.
Cash Controller.
Christmas Mail.
Client List.
Client List II.
Compute Pursuit.
Family Medical Advisor.
Jury Trial II.
List-N-Label.
Mortgage Maker.
Portfolio II.
Stockroom Manager.
Tax Shelter.

Nelson, Michael E., & Assocs., Inc., (1-886917), 1315 College Ave., Conway, AR 72032 Tel 501-329-9204; FAX: 501-329-1960.
Titles:
Designer Bath Plans.
Designer Kitchen & Breakfast Plans.
Designer Kitchen & Breakfast Room Plans.
Kitchen & Breakfast Room Plans.

Nelson Data Resources, Inc., (0-925786), 4901 F St., Omaha, NE 68117 Tel 402-733-2700; Toll free: 800-745-4712; FAX: 402-733-2288.
Titles:
General Accounting System.
Hospital Management System.
Local Government Accounting System.

NeMMaR, (1-887450), P.O. Box 151, Rye, NY 10580-0151; 15 E. Putnam Ave., Suite 151, Greenwich, CT 06830-5424 Tel 914-967-2226.
Titles:
The Home Inspection Business from A to Z On-Site Checklist: The Narrative Checklist the Other's Don't Have!
The Home Inspection Business from A to Z Report Writing Document.

Neon Publishing, (1-886770), 14220 Carlson Cir., Tampa, FL 33626 Tel 813-854-5515; FAX: 813-854-5516.
Titles:
Amusement Trivia!
The Education Disc.
Edutainment Trivia!
The/Games Disc '95.
Jokes & Quotes.
The Windows Disc.

Network Management, Inc., 6101 Stevenson Ave., Alexandria, VA 22304 Tel 703-461-2400; FAX: 212-797-3817.
Titles:
LANshadow.
LANtrack.
LANtrail.

Network Research Corp., 4000 Via Pescador, Camarillo, CA 93012-5014; Toll free: 800-541-9508 (outside California); FAX: 805-485-8204.
Titles:
Fusion Network Software.

Network Software Assocs., Inc. (NSA), 31 Technology Dr., 2nd Flr., Irvine, CA 92718-2322; Toll free: 800-352-3270.
Titles:
AdaptSNA.
AdaptSNA APPCplus 3270.
AdaptSNA LU6.2/APPC.
AdaptSNA 3270.
3270/Elite.
3270/Elite Plus.

Neuron Data, Inc., 156 University Ave., Palo Alto, CA 94301 Tel 415-321-4488; Toll free: 800-876-4900; FAX: 415-321-3728.
Titles:
Neuron Data Open Interface.
Nexpert Object.
Nextra.

New Century Products, P.O. Box 27011, MS RB, San Diego, CA 92198 Tel 619-486-2505.
Titles:
Computer Assisted Charting: Nurse Charting.
Time & Materials Accounting: T.M.A.

New England Software, Inc., (0-945830), 411 W. Putnam Ave., No. 280, Greenwich, CT 06830-6233 Tel 203-625-0062; FAX: 203-625-0718.
Titles:
GB-Analytic.
GB-STAT.
Graph-in-the-Box Executive.
Graph-in-the-Box Release 2.

New Horizons Software, P.O. Box 164260, Austin, TX 78716-4260 Tel 512-328-6650; FAX: 512-328-1925.
Titles:
Flow: Idea Processor.
ProFonts: Decorative.
ProFonts: Professional.
ProScript.
ProWrite.
WordMaker.

New Riders Publishing, Div. of Macmillan Computer Publishing, (0-934035; 1-56205), 201 W. 103rd St., Indianapolis, IN 46290; Toll free: 800-428-5331.
Titles:
AutoCAD Reference Guide Disk: 2nd Edition.
Inside AutoCAD Disk: 6th Edition.

New Systems, Inc., (0-925808), 6486 S. Quebec St., Englewood, CO 80111.
Titles:
SimCom 25.
SimCom 50.
SimCom 75.

Newell Industries, 1213 Devonshire Ln., Wylie, TX 75098-5284 Tel 214-442-6612.
Titles:
SBM 86.
SBM ST.

NewHouse Medical Systems, 50 S. 18th St., Easton, PA 18042 Tel 610-252-0548; Toll free: 800-323-3002; FAX: 610-559-7677.
Titles:
MacMed.

Newport Systems, Div. of Care Computer Systems, Inc., P.O. Box 3705, Bellevue, WA 98009-3705 Tel 206-451-0537; Toll free: 800-782-1233; FAX: 206-455-4895.
Titles:
Who Works When.

Newstar Software, (0-928450), 904 Carl Rd., Lafayette, CA 94549-4807.
Titles:
New Word 3.
NewWord.

NewTEK Industries, Subs. of Coastar Publishing Co., (0-930437), P.O. Box 46116, Hollywood, CA 90046-0116 Tel 213-874-6669.
Titles:
Commission Comparisons.
Commission Comparisons for Windows.
Compu/Chart.
Spotlight.

Nicolai, Robert L., (0-925825), 4038 N. Ninth St., Saint Louis, MO 63147-3441 Tel 314-621-7618; Toll free: 800-642-6524.
Titles:
Arcade Poker.
BASIC Cross Reference Facility.
Basic Gramarcy: The Word Game.
Basic Program Mender.
BASIC Program Printer.
Casino Poker.
The Cheapware Tax Record.
Five Year Personal Diary.
Form Letter Writer.
Label Maker Version II.
Note Pad.
Odds Calculator for Draw Poker.
Personal Mailing List.
Text Editor.
20th Century Faro.
Word List of the American Language I, II.
Word Sleuth.

NightOwl Software, Inc., Rte. 1, Box 7, Hwy. 12, Fort Atkinson, WI 53538 Tel 414-563-4013; Toll free: 800-648-3695; FAX: 414-563-5060.
Titles:
MEX-PC.

Nikrom Technical Products, Inc., (0-925826), 330 Fort Pond Rd., Lancaster, MA 01523 Tel 508-537-9970; Toll free: 800-835-2246.
Titles:
Electronic Rolodex.
LaserCraft Images.
Master Diagnostics.
Quick-Copy.

Niles & Assocs., Inc., 800 Jones St., Berkeley, CA 94710 Tel 510-559-8592; FAX: 510-559-8683.
Titles:
Endlink.
Endnote Plus: Enhanced Bibliographic Software.

Nisus Software, Inc., 107 S. Cedros, Solana Beach, CA 92075 Tel 619-481-1477; Toll free: 800-922-2993; FAX: 619-481-6154.
Titles:
Easy Alarms.
Laser TechFonts.
Mac TAG Teacher's Assistant Grader.
MacQwerty.
Nisus.
Nisus Compact.
Qued-M.

Nite Owl Productions, 5734 Lamar Ave., Shawnee Mission, KS 66202 Tel 913-362-9898.
Titles:
DAS Editor.
Developer Disk 1.
Developer Disk 2.
The Nite Owl Journal #1.

Nolan, Robert E., Co., Inc., (0-925834), 17746 Preston Rd., Dallas, TX 75252 Tel 214-248-3727; FAX: 214-733-1427.
Titles:
AQM: Automated Quality Measurement.
ASET: Advanced Staff Evaluation Techniques.
ATC: Advanced Teller Controls.
Auto-AOC: Automated Advanced Office Controls.

Nolo Pr., (0-917316; 0-87337), 950 Parker St., Berkeley, CA 94710 Tel 510-549-1976; Toll free: 800-992-6656; FAX: 510-548-5902.
Titles:
California Incorporator.
The California Nonprofit Corporation Handbook.
How to Form Your Own New York Corporation, Computer Edition.
How to Form Your Own Texas Corporation, Computer Edition.
Nolo's Living Trust.
Nolo's Personal Recordkeeper.
Small Business Legal Pro.
WillMaker.

Nordic Software, (0-940081; 1-57374), P.O. Box 6007, Lincoln, NE 68506-0007 Tel 402-488-5086; FAX: 402-488-2914; 6911 Van Dorn, Lincoln, NE 68506 Tel 402-488-5086.
Titles:
Clock Shop.
Coin Critters.
Language Explorer.
MacKids Christmas Pack.
MacKids Jungle Quest.
MacKids Preschool Pack.
MacKids Word Quest.
Preschool Parade.
RadioView.
Turbo Math Facts.
WordSearch Deluxe.

Norris Software, Ltd., 3208 W. Lake St., Suite 65, Minneapolis, MN 55416 Tel 612-827-2766; FAX: 612-922-4426.
Titles:
norgen.

Norstad, Lyn, & Assocs., Inc., (0-925847), 2470 E. Oakton St., Arlington Heights, IL 60005 Tel 312-640-6400; FAX: 312-640-1677.
Titles:
TIPS, RIO, TOPAS.

North America MICA, Inc., (0-928721), 11772 Sorrento Valley Rd., Suite 152, San Diego, CA 92121 Tel 619-792-1012; FAX: 619-792-1014.
Titles:
BPS-II (Batch Processing).
GPS-II (Graphics Printer Support).
MMS-II (Materials Management System).
PMS-II (Project Management System).
RMS-II: A Resource Management System.
TEAMPLAN.

North River Pr., Inc., (0-88427), P.O. Box 567, Great Barrington, MA 01230; Toll free: 800-486-2665.
Titles:
Executive Challenge: OPT Thoughtware.

North Shore Systems, Inc., (0-9625126), P.O. Box 8687, Incline Village, NV 89452 Tel 702-831-1108; FAX: 702-831-8553.
Titles:
CursorPower.

North Winds, P.O. Box 671, Greensburg, PA 15601 Tel 412-832-9799; FAX: 412-832-9759.
Titles:
Formall.
FormZ.

Northwest Analytical, Inc., (0-917369), 519 SW Park Ave., Portland, OR 97205 Tel 503-224-7727; FAX: 503-224-5236.
Titles:
NWA Quality Analyst.
NWA Quality Monitor: Real-Time SPC Workstation Software.

Northwest Geophysical Assocs., Inc., P.O. Box 1063, Corvallis, OR 97339-1063 Tel 503-757-7231.
Titles:
GM-SYS: Gravity-Magnetics Modeling Software.

Norton, Peter, Computing, Inc., (0-917371), 2500 Broadway, Suite 200, Santa Monica, CA 90404 Tel 310-453-4600; Toll free: 800-451-0303, Ext. 40.
Titles:
Dan Bricklin's Demo II.
The Norton Commander.
The Norton Commander 2.0.
The Norton Editor.
The Norton Guides: BASIC.
The Norton Guides: BIOS/DOS/Assembly.
The Norton Guides: C.
The Norton Guides: OS/2.
The Norton Guides: Pascal.
Norton Utilities.
Norton Utilities Advanced Edition 4.5.
Norton Utilities Standard Edition 4.5.

Norton-Lambert Corp., (0-934083), P.O. Box 4085, Santa Barbara, CA 93140 Tel 805-964-6767; FAX: 805-683-5679.
Titles:
Close-Up/LAN Pro.
Close-Up: Remote.
Close-Up Remote Communications: Host & Remote.
LYNC: Telecommunications Software.

Nova Media, Inc., (0-9618567; 1-884239), 1724 N. State St., Big Rapids, MI 49307-0414 Tel 616-796-7539; 1724 N. State, Big Rapids, MI 49307 Tel 616-796-7539.
Titles:
AIDS "Trivia" Update for Nineties: The AIDS Prevention & Education Game.
AIDS Trivia Update for Nineties Updated: PC IBM Windows Version.
Drug Culture Monopoly.
Employee Application Resume Rating & Categorizing Scale: EARRCS.
Racial Attitude Survey.

Nova Publishing Co., (0-935755), 1103 W. College St., Carbondale, IL 62901 Tel 618-457-3521; Toll free: 800-748-1175; FAX: 618-457-2541; Dist. by: National Bk. Network, 4720A Boston Way, Lanham, MD 20706-4310 Tel 301-459-8696; Toll free: 800-462-6420. Do not confuse with Nova Publishing in Madison, TN.
Titles:
Divorce Yourself: The National No-Fault Divorce Kit.
Incorporate Your Business: The National Corporation Kit.
Prepare Your Own Will: The National Will Kit.

Nova R&D, Inc., 1525 Third St., Suite A201, Riverside, CA 92507 Tel 909-781-7332.
Titles:
Mac LawnMan.

Novell, Inc., Affil. of Safeguard Scientific's, (0-918663; 0-926928), P.O. Box 5900, Provo, UT 84601-5900 Tel 801-379-5900; Toll free: 800-453-1267.
Titles:
Advanced Netware: Network Operating System.
Advanced Netware-286 Network Operating System.
Btrieve.
Developer's Kit.
NetWare-ACS: Gateway Software.
NetWare-ARCNET: Starter Kit.
NetWare-BI-286.
NetWare for the Macintosh.
NetWare-G-Net: Starter Kit.
NetWare-ProNET: Starter Kit.
NetWare-RM: Runtime.
NetWare-S-Net: Basic System.
NetWare-SNA: Gateway Software.
NetWare VMS.
SFT NetWare.
Standard Coaxial Connection 3278-79.
XQL.
Xtrieve.

Numerical Algorithms Group, Inc., Subs. of Numerical Algorithms Group, Ltd., (1-85206), 1400 Opus Pl., Suite 200, Downers Grove, IL 60515-5702 Tel 708-971-2337; FAX: 708-971-2706.
Titles:
AXIOM: Scientific Computation System.
Genstat.
GLIM.
IRIS Explorer: Visualization.
NAG FORTRAN Workstation Library.
NAGWare f90 Compiler.

Nussel, A. H., 260 NE Sixth Blvd., Williston, FL 32696 Tel 904-528-0371.
Titles:
Muscial Words Game.
ShuBox Medical Tracker II.
ShuBox Music Librarian II.
ShuBox II.

NutriPlan, (0-925523), 187 Gardiners Ave., Levittown, NY 11756 Tel 516-579-6392; Toll free: 800-872-7522.
Titles:
MacNutriplan.
Nutriplan.

OCS/Syntax, Div. of OCS Technolgies, (0-927328), 840 S. 333rd St., Federal Way, WA 98003-6343; FAX: 206-833-1368.
Titles:
The Criminal Justice System.
Law Enforcement Management: LEMS.
LMserver.
TotalNet.

OHM Software, 98 Long Pasture Way, Tiverton, RI 02878 Tel 401-253-9354; Toll free: 800-346-9034.
Titles:
FormsProgrammer.

OITC, Inc., P.O. Box 73, Melbourne Beach, FL 32951 Tel 407-984-3714.
Titles:
Checkup Rx.
DeClass.
Doc Monitor.
File Zero.
File Zero INIT.
Macomo.

OMD, (0-928729), P.O. Box 6760, Jefferson City, MO 65102-6760; FAX: 314-893-3487; 3705 Missouri Blvd., Jefferson City, MO 65109 Tel 314-893-8930.
Titles:
OMD Management Information System.

OMM Corp., (0-918659), 733 Bishop St., Suite 170-406, Honolulu, HI 96813-4093 Tel 808-528-4751; Toll free: 800-428-2783; FAX: 808-528-4751.
Titles:
CONEXUS: MIST Plus Communications NEXUS.
MIST (Microcomputer Information Support Tools) Plus.

OMNI Systems Co., (0-925885), 5431 Logan Ave. North, Minneapolis, MN 55430 Tel 612-566-8437.
Titles:
Basics of Servomechanisms & Operational Amplifiers.

OR-D Systems, 1414 Brace Rd., Cherry Hill, NJ 08034 Tel 609-795-8300; Toll free: 800-722-6731; FAX: 609-795-8302.
Titles:
OR-D Dental System.
OR-D Medical System.
OR-D Tutorial System.

OTC Corp., (1-883260), 17300 17th St., Suite J-117, Tustin, CA 92680 Tel 714-832-4833; Toll free: 800-769-6344; FAX: 714-832-4563.
Titles:
KingCOM.

Oak Manor Pr., Div. of Jan MacDougal Creates, (0-9628535), P.O. Box 31611, Charleston, SC 29417-1611; 1 New Town Ln., Charleston, SC 29407 Tel 803-556-0154.
Titles:
CA51 Cross Assembler for 8051 Microcontrollers.

Oak Software, Inc., (0-925889), P.O. Box 400, Indian Rocks Beach, FL 34635-0400 Tel 813-596-0262; FAX: 813-593-0204.
Titles:
OakWord.

Oakland Group, Inc., (0-925522), 959 Concord St., Framingham, MA 01701-4682; Toll free: 800-233-3733.
Titles:
C-scape.

Oasis Pr., The, Subs. of Publishing Services, Inc., (0-916378; 1-55571), 300 N. Valley Dr., Grants Pass, OR 97526 Tel 503-479-9464; Toll free: 800-228-2275; FAX: 503-476-1479; Dist. by: Publishers Group West, 4065 Hollis St., Emeryville, CA 94608 Tel 510-658-3453; Toll free: 800-788-3123.
Titles:
Business Plan Package.
California Corporation Formation Package & Minute Book.
California Corporation Software: (Text Files).
CashPlan.
Colorado Corporation Formation Package & Minute Book.
A Company Policy & Personnel Workbook.
Company Policy Manual Package.
Company Policy Manual (Standalone).
Company Policy: (Standalone).
CPR Professional: Customer Profile & Retrieval.
Delaware Corporation Formation Package & Minute Book.
Develop Your Business Plan.
Financial Management for Small Businesses.
Financial Management Techniques.
Financial Management Tools for Small Business.
Financial Templates for Small Business.
Florida Corporation Formation Package & Minute Book.
The Small Business Expert.
Start a Business.
Successful Business Plan: (Standalone).
Texas Corporation Formation Package & Minute Book.
Wall Street Raider.

Oasys, Inc., (0-925891), 1 Cranberry Hill, Lexington, MA 02173-7397 Tel 617-862-2002; FAX: 617-863-2633.
Titles:
Glockenspiel C++.
Grenn Hills C++.
Microsoft C Cross Compiler, Assembler, Linker Package.
MULTI.
OASYS 88000 C, C++ Pascal & FORTRAN Cross Compilers.
OASYS 88000 Cross Assembler/Linker.
OASYS 680x0 C, C++, Pascal & FORTRAN Cross Compilers.
OASYS 680x0 Cross Assembler/Linker.

Octree Software, Inc., 1955 Landings Dr., Mountain View, CA 94043-0801.
Titles:
Caligari.

Odesta Corp., (0-910787; 1-56084), 4084 Commercial Ave., Northbrook, IL 60062 Tel 312-498-5615; Toll free: 800-323-5423; FAX: 312-498-9917.
Titles:
Odesta ODMS.

Odyssey Interactive, 1326 Hanley Industry Ct., Saint Louis, MO 63144 Tel 314-997-8515.
Titles:
Apollo 13: A Week to Remember.

Oedware, P.O. Box 595, Columbia, MD 21045 Tel 410-997-9333; FAX: 410-997-2143.
Titles:
PC-Key-Draw.

O'Hanlon Computer Systems, Subs. of Technology Capital Partners, Inc., (0-925897), 14400 Bel Red Rd., No. 204, Bellevue, WA 98007-3952 Tel 206-747-2345; FAX: 206-747-0172.
Titles:
O'Hanlon Development Solution: Professional Programming Language.

Oklahoma State Univ., College of Osteopathic Medicine, 1111 W. 17th St., Tulsa, OK 74107 Tel 918-582-2681.
Titles:
Automated Cognitive Rehabilitation Laboratory: ACRe Lab.

Olduvai Corp., 9200 S. Dadeland Blvd., Suite 725, Miami, FL 33156 Tel 305-670-1112; Toll free: 800-822-0772; FAX: 305-670-1992.
Titles:
ArtClips.
ArtFonts.
Icon-It! Pro.
Magic Typist.
MasterFinder.
MultiClip.
Read-It! Personal OCR.
Read-It! Personal OCR for Windows 3.X (IBM).
Read-It! Pro: Macintosh Version.
Read-It! Pro OCR for Windows 3.X (IBM).
Read-It!: Windows Version.
Sound Clips.
Traffic Controller Personal.
VideoPaint.

Olympic Media Information, (0-88367), P.O. Box 190, West Park, NY 12493 Tel 914-384-6563.
Titles:
Educational Media Locator.
Healthcare Media Locator.
Nature Meditations from the Essays of John Burroughs.

Omega Research, Inc, 9200 Sunset Dr., Miami, FL 33173; Toll free: 800-292-3454.
Titles:
StockCharts Plus: For CD-ROM.
SuperCharts.
SuperCharts Three: For CD-ROM.
Wall Street Analyst.

Omega Star Software, 6044 Chisolm Rd., Johns Island, SC 29455.
Titles:
Amiga BASIC Companion.
The Amiga Companion Series.

Omen Technology, 17505V NW Suavie Island Rd., Portland, OR 97231 Tel 503-621-3406; FAX: 503-621-3735.
Titles:
Professional-YAM.

Omni Computer Systems, Inc., (0-925920), P.O. Box 162 Hearthstone Plaza, Chestnut Hill, MA 02167 Tel 617-277-2962; Toll free: 800-525-1055.
Titles:
Flash Com.

Omni Software Systems, Inc., (0-925923), 702 N. Ernest, Griffith, IN 46319 Tel 219-924-3522; Toll free: 800-473-3524.
Titles:
Accountant's Pac I.
Accountant's Pac II.
Accountant's Stock System.
After-the-Fact Payroll.
Amortization-Plus.
The Checkwriter.
Church Contribution Record System.
Form 1099 Generator.
The Form 1099 Printer.

PUBLISHER/TITLE INDEX

Inventory-Plus.
The Invoicer-Plus.
Loan Amortization-Plus.
Omni Accounts Receivable-Plus.
PC Client Accounting.
PC Payroll.
The Portfolio Management System.
Professional Billing System.
The Stock Manager.

OmniComp, Inc., (0-931195), 220 Regent Ct., State College, PA 16801 Tel 814-238-4181; Toll free: 800-726-4181; FAX: 814-238-4673.
Titles:
Comfort Call.
FASER Energy Accounting: Fast Accounting System for Energy Reporting.
Service Call Central.
SERVICE CALL Maintenance Management.

Omnitrend Software, Inc., (0-932549), 15 Winchester Ct., Farmington, CT 06032-3423 Tel 203-678-7679.
Titles:
Breach.
OmniTrend's Universe.
OmniTrend's Universe II.
OmniTrend's Universe III.
Paladin.
Scrolls of Talmouth.
The Serayachi Campaign.

OmniVerse Software Corp., P.O. Box 370, Hadlock, WA 98339-0370; Toll free: 800-365-7627; FAX: 206-385-5960.
Titles:
Galaxy.

Omtool Corp., 2 Manor Pkwy., Salem, NH 03079-2841.
Titles:
The SOFTBOL Language System.

On-Going Ideas, (0-918667), R.D. 1, Box 810, Starksboro, VT 05487 Tel 802-453-4442.
Titles:
OGI Development System Linker.
OGI Fig-FORTH.
OGI FORTH-79.
OGI Pascal Development System VI: Pascal Level 1.
OGI Pascal Development System V2: OGI Pascal2.
OGI ProFORTH.

On Point Pr., (0-9619323), P.O. Box 1969, Jackson, MS 39215; 810 Gillespie St., Jackson, MS 39202 Tel 601-944-1950.
Titles:
TLC Total Library Computerization.

On the Mark Computer Software Co., (1-877766), 1762 Westwood Blvd., No. 460, Los Angeles, CA 90024-5608.
Titles:
Dentist's Appointment Scheduler & Projects Organizer.
Dentist's Checklist & Tray Setup System.
Dentist's Employee Record.
Dentist's Fee Schedule Analyzer.
Dentist's Humorous Side.
Dentist's Insurance Organizer.
Dentist's Management System.
Dentist's Management System for the IBM.
Dentist's Patient Literature & Handouts.
Dentist's Recall System.
Dentist's Songs, Poetry, & Nursery Rhymes.
Dentist's Technique Manual.
Dentist's Tray Setup Checklist System.
Doctor's Collections Manager & Bookkeeper.
Doctor's Computer Organizer.
Doctor's Contacts & Filebox Address & Phone Manager.
Doctor's Demo Disk.
Doctor's Inventory Organizer.
Doctor's Legal Aid.
Doctor's Master Menu.
Doctor's Modem & Bulletin Boards.
Doctor's Ordering Supplies System.
Doctor's Prescription Organizer.
Doctor's Psychology Manual.
Doctor's Real Estate Analyzer.

One Step Records, (1-888057), P.O. Box 6087, Auburn, CA 95604 Tel 408-622-9441; Toll free: 800-770-9292; FAX: 408-622-9439.
Titles:
An Earth with One Spirit: Stories from Around the World for the Child Within Us All CD.
A People with One Heart: Stories from Around the World for the Child Within Us All CD.
A Planet with One Mind; A People with One Heart; An Earth with One Spirit: Stories from Around the World for the Child Within Us All CD.
A Planet with One Mind: Stories from Around the World for the Child Within Us All CD.

O'Neill Software, (0-931285), P.O. Box 26111, San Francisco, CA 94126 Tel 415-398-2255.
Titles:
Electra-Find.
The Text Collector.

OneOnOne Computer Training, Div. of Mosaic Media, Inc., (0-917792; 1-56562), 2055 Army Trail Rd., Suite 100, Addison, IL 60101 Tel 708-628-0500; Toll free: 800-424-8668; FAX: 708-628-0550.
Titles:
Advanced Training for dBase 4.
Advanced Training for Lotus 1-2-3 for Windows: Graphs & Charts.
Advanced Training for Lotus 1-2-3 for Windows: Macros.
Advanced Training for Lotus 1-2-3 Rel. 1 for Windows: Functions & Analysis.
Advanced Training for Lotus 1-2-3 Rel. 5 for Windows.
Advanced Training for Microsoft Excel for Windows 95.
Advanced Training for Microsoft Excel for Windows.
Advanced Training for Microsoft Word for Windows.
Advanced Training for Paradox: Managing Data.
Advanced Training for Paradox: Personal Programmer.
Advanced Training for Quattro Pro: Graphs & Charts.
Advanced Training for Quattro Pro: Macros.
Advanced Training for Quattro Pro (Versions 2 & 3): Formulas & Functions.
Advanced Training for WordPerfect.
Advanced Trianing for WordPerfect for Windows.
Desktop Publishing with WordPerfect.
How to Use dBase III Plus.
How to Use dBase 4.
How to Use Excel for Windows.
How to Use Freelance Windows.
How to Use Harvard Graphics for Windows.
How to Use Harvard Graphics 3.0.
How to Use Lotus Freelance Plus.
How to Use Lotus One-Two-Three.
How to Use Lotus One-Two-Three for Windows.
How to Use Lotus 1-2-3 for DOS.
How to Use Lotus 1-2-3 for Windows.
How to Use Microsoft Access for Windows 95.
How to Use Microsoft Excel for Windows 95.
How to Use Microsoft Windows 3.0.
How to Use Microsoft Windows 3.1.
How to Use Microsoft Word.
How to Use Microsoft Word for Windows.
How to Use Microsoft Word for Windows 95.
How to Use Microsoft Word Mac.
How to Use Microsoft Word PC.
How to Use MS-DOS.
How to Use MS-DOS 5.
How to Use Novell Netware.
How to Use Novell NetWare 286 & SFT.
How to Use PageMaekr 5 for Mac.
How to Use PageMaekr 5 for Windows.
How to Use PageMaker Mac.
How to Use PageMaker PC: With Story Editor.
How to Use Paradox.
How to Use Paradox for Windows.
How to Use PowerPoint for Windows.
How to Use PowerPoint for Windows 95.
How to Use QuarkXPress.
How to Use Quattro Pro.
How to Use Quattro Pro for Windows.
How to Use UNIX & XENIX.
How to Use Windows 95.
How to Use WordPerfect.
How to Use WordPerfect for Windows.
Using MS-DOS on a Hard Disk.
Using the Macintosh with System 7.

Online Computer Systems, Inc., Div. of Reed Elsevier Group, (1-56953), 20251 Century Blvd., Germantown, MD 20874 Tel 301-428-3700; Toll free: 800-922-9204; FAX: 301-428-2903.
Titles:
OPTI-NET Lite.

Ontario Systems Corp., (0-923062), 201 E. Jackson, Muncie, IN 47305 Tel 317-284-7131.
Titles:
Accufarm Plan.
Breaktrust Accounting System.

Ontrack Computer Systems, Inc., 6321 Bury Dr., Suites 13-21, Eden Prairie, MN 55346 Tel 612-937-1107; Toll free: 800-752-1333; FAX: 612-937-5815.
Titles:
Disk Manager.
Disk Manager Mac & Kits.
Disk Manager-N.
Dr. Solomon's Anti-Virus Toolkit.
DosUtils.
Drive Rocket.
NetUtils 2.
NetUtils 3.
Ontrack Data Recovery for NetWare.
Ontrack Netshield: VLM Protection for Novell Netware File Savers.
RecoverEase: Data Recovery & Protection Utilities for UNIX Systems.

Open Horizons Publishing Co., (0-912411), P.O. Box 205, Fairfield, IA 52556-0205 Tel 515-472-6130; Toll free: 800-796-6130; FAX: 515-472-1560.
Titles:
Mail Order Spreadsheet Kit.
Publicity & Promotional Events Data File.
Visitor Bureaus & Chambers of Commerce.

Open Systems Holdings Corp., Inc., Subs. of UCCEL Corp., (0-925944), 7626 Golden Triangle Dr., Eden Prairie, MN 55344 Tel 612-829-0011; Toll free: 800-328-2276.
Titles:
Material & Production Management.
Merge 386.

Opportune Pr., (1-887107), 232 E. Blithedale, Suite 210, Mill Valley, CA 94941 Tel 415-381-7566; FAX: 415-381-7571.
Titles:
Legends & Myths.
MultiMedia Cookbook for Hyper Studio.
Visionary Stampede: Dreams & Challenges of the '90s.

Opt-Tech Data Processing, (0-925946), P.O. Box 678, Zephyr Cove, NV 89448 Tel 702-588-3737; FAX: 702-588-7576.
Titles:
Opt-Tech Sort.

Optilearn, Inc., (1-886471), P.O. Box 997, Stevens Point, WI 54481; Toll free: 800-850-9480; FAX: 715-344-1066; 15 Park Ridge Dr., Suite 200, Stevens Point, WI 54481 Tel 715-344-6060.
Titles:
Environmental Views Series CD-ROM.

Optimization Software, Inc., (0-911575), 1100 Glendon Ave., Suite 1447, Los Angeles, CA 90024 Tel 310-208-5674.
Titles:
Kalman Filtering Software.

Optimum Resource, Inc., (0-911787; 1-55913), 5 Hiltech Ln., Hilton Head, SC 29926 Tel 803-689-8000; Toll free: 800-327-1473; FAX: 803-689-8008.
Titles:
First Steps Counting & Thinking Games.
Sticky Bear Early Learning.
Sticky Bear Math Town.
Sticky Bear Reading Room.

Options-80, (0-917375), P.O. Box 471, Concord, MA 01742 Tel 508-369-1589.
Titles:
Options-80A: Advanced Stock Option Analyzer.

OptionVue Systems International, Inc., (0-918711), 175 E. Hawthorne Pkwy., Suite 180, Vernon Hills, IL 60061 Tel 708-816-6610; Toll free: 800-733-6610; FAX: 708-816-6647.
Titles:
OptionVue IV.

Oracle Corp., 500 Oracle Pkwy., Redwood Shores, CA 94065 Tel 415-506-7000.
Titles:
Oracle for Macintosh.
Oracle Quicksilver.
Oracle SQL*Tutor.
ORACLE Tools & Database.
Professional Oracle.

Orange Fortune, (1-877928), 10221 Slater Ave. Suite 103, Fountain Valley, CA 92708 Tel 714-842-8721; Toll free: 800-766-6772; FAX: 714-841-1200.
Titles:
Manufacturing Resource Planning - Decision Support System: MRP-DSS.
Quik BOM: Bill of Materials Processor in dBASE.
Quik MAN: Manufacturing Management System in dBASE.

OrCAD, 9300 SW Nimbus Ave., Beaverton, OR 97008-7137 Tel 503-671-9500; Toll free: 800-671-9505; FAX: 503-671-9401.
Titles:
OrCAD Capture for Windows.
OrCAD Layout for Windows.
OrCAD Layout Ltd. for Windows.
OrCAD Layout Plus for Windows.
OrCAD PCB: OrCAD Printed Circuit Board Layout Tools 386.
OrCAD PCB 386Plus: Printed Circuit Board Tools 386Plus.
OrCAD PCR 386Plus: Placement & Critical Route 386Plus.
OrCAD/PLD.
OrCAD PLD 386: OrCAD Programmable Logic Design Tools 386.
OrCAD PLD386Plus: Programmable Logic Design 386Plus.
OrCAD/SDT.
OrCAD SDT386Plus: Schematic Design Tools 386Plus.
OrCAD Simulate for Windows.
OrCAD STD 386: OrCAD Schematic Design Tools 386.
OrCAD Verification & Simualtion Tools 386.
OrCAD/VST.
OrCAD VST386Plus: Verification & Simulation Tools 386Plus.

Organic Computing, (0-925961), 96 Caddo Peak, Joshua, TX 76058.
Titles:
Budget System.
Mail Manager: Craft-Antique Mail Point of Sale & Accounts Payable.
Warehouse Manager.
Yard Manager.

Origin Systems, Inc., (0-929373), 12940 Research Blvd., Austin, TX 78750 Tel 512-335-5200; FAX: 512-328-3825.
Titles:
Moebius.
Ultima V; Warriors of Destiny.
Ultima III: Exodus.
Ultima IV: The Quest of the Avatar.

Orion Computer Systems, Inc., 980 Jolly Rd., Blue Bell, PA 19422-1962 Tel 717-741-4536; Toll free: 800-451-5059; FAX: 717-741-9176.
Titles:
Orion Chiropractic.
Orion Dental.
Orion Family Practice.
Orion Optometric.
Orion Psychiatric.
Orion Radiology Information Management.
Orion Surgical.

Orion Microsystems, Inc., Fifth & Chestnut Sts., Lafayette Bldg., Suite 910, Philadelphia, PA 19106 Tel 215-928-1119; FAX: 215-925-3700.
Titles:
GLOWS Client Accounting System.
GLOWS Practice Management System: GLOWSPM.
Glowsap.
Glowsar.
Glowspr.

Orion Publishing, LLC, (0-9647699), P.O. Box 174, Dover, NH 03820 Tel 603-749-1164; FAX: 603-742-9884; 324 Tolend Rd., Dover, NH 03820.
Titles:
Annual Horse Chronicles, 1996.

Orion Software, 17303 Glenhew Rd., Humble, TX 77396 Tel 713-454-5285. Do not confuse with companies with the same name in Ossining, NY, Auburn, AL.
Titles:
Black Hawk.

Orthodontic Processing, 386 E. H St., Suite 209-404, Chula Vista, CA 92010 Tel 619-691-1280.
Titles:
Quick Ceph.

Outlook Software, Inc., (0-922692), 4125 Keller Springs Rd., Suite 15G, Dallas, TX 75244 Tel 214-713-6370; Toll free: 800-925-5700; FAX: 214-713-6308.
Titles:
buttonFile.
Easy Landlord.
PC-File.

OverDrive Systems, Inc., 23980 Chagrin Blvd., Suite 200, Cleveland, OH 44122 Tel 216-292-3425; FAX: 216-292-4888.
Titles:
Overdrive 2 for WordPerfect.

Ovid Technologies, (0-922624), 333 Seventh Ave., New York, NY 10001 Tel 212-563-3006; Toll free: 800-950-2035; FAX: 212-563-3784.
Titles:
BRS/Search.

Oxxi, Inc., (0-938385), P.O. Box 90309, Long Beach, CA 90809-0309 Tel 310-427-1227; FAX: 310-427-0971; 1339 E. 28th St., Long Beach, CA 90806 Tel 310-427-1227.
Titles:
A-Talk.
A-Talk III.
Aegis Animagic.
Aegis Audiomaster III.
Aegis Express Paint.
Aegis Oran 2000.
Aegis Showcase FX.
Aegis Sonix.
Aegis Videoscape 3D.
Aegis Videotitler 3D.
Amiga Graphics Starter Kit.
Nimbus.

PADS Software, Inc., 165 Forest St., Marlborough, MA 01752-3048 Tel 508-485-4300; FAX: 508-485-7171.
Titles:
PADS-Logic.
PADS-Perform.
PADS-WORK.

PAR Publishing, Co., 6054 Sadring Ave., Woodland Hills, CA 91367 Tel 818-340-8165; FAX: 818-340-8165.
Titles:
Page Designs Quick!
Page Designs Quick! 5.

P&L Assocs., 4642 E. Chapman Ave., No. 349, Orange, CA 92669 Tel 714-974-6560; Toll free: 800-843-3997; FAX: 714-532-8204.
Titles:
Paragon.
turbo Paragon.

PBC ENterprises, P.O. Box 925, Wallingford, CT 06492 Tel 203-269-6903.
Titles:
DentalStack.

PBI Software, Inc., (0-944045), 1592 Union St., No. 295, San Francisco, CA 94123.
Titles:
Alien Mind.
Cavern Cobra.
CommWorks.
HD Back-Up.
HD 20 & 30 Back-Up.
HFS Locator Plus.
Monte Carlo.
Sea Strike.
Strategic Conquest Plus.
Strategic Conquest II.
The Tower of Myraglen.
Visualizer IIe.

PC Flight Guide, 5 Argent Circle, Irvine, CA 92714 Tel 714-651-9405.
Titles:
PC Flight Guide.

PCM Cambridge Imaging Technology, 1430 Spring Hill Rd., McLean, VA 22102 Tel 703-356-4600; Toll free: 800-654-5845; FAX: 703-356-1260.
Titles:
DataEdge.
PC Album.
PC Album Network.

PUBLISHER/TITLE INDEX

PC Software, (0-926012), 11627 Calamar Ct., San Diego, CA 92124 Tel 619-576-8223.
Titles:
Championship Blackjack.

PC Software Solutions, Sub. of Ready Computer Solutions, P.O. Box 163, Clarksville, MD 21029 Tel 410-531-3314.
Titles:
Bidsheet.

PDC Pension Templates, 1400 Fashion Island Blvd., Suite 307, San Mateo, CA 94404-1584 Tel 415-341-3322; FAX: 415-341-7409.
Titles:
PC-Trust.

PDS, (0-926078), 359 Enterprise Ct., Bloomfield Hills, MI 48302 Tel 810-335-7475; Toll free: 800-886-6736; FAX: 810-335-7346.
Titles:
PDS-ADEPT.
PDS-C Source Generator.
Preferred Series Accounts Payable.
Preferred Series Accounts Receivable.
Preferred Series General Ledger.
Preferred Series Inventory Control.
Preferred Series Order Entry.
Preferred Series Payroll.
Preferred Series Purhcase Order.

PEAS (Practical Engineering Applications Software), (0-926020), 7208 Grand Ave., Pittsburgh, PA 15225 Tel 412-264-3553.
Titles:
Area Moment of Inertia.
Beam Analysis.
Beam Analysis with Selection.
Column Buckling.
Continuous Span.
Cylinder & Shock Absorber Analysis.
Heat Transfer Analysis.
Power Transmission I.
Spring Design.
Steel Assembly Weight Determination.

PLE, Inc., 6931 W. Palmer Lake Dr., Brooklyn Center, MN 55429 Tel 612-566-4252.
Titles:
CICS/pc.
PC-HIBOL.

P-Productions, 2514 Illinois St., Racine, WI 53405 Tel 414-554-9688.
Titles:
SchoolArt.

PRI Assocs., Inc., (0-922012), 1905 Chapel Hill Rd., Durham, NC 27707 Tel 919-493-7534.
Titles:
AAPlanner for Windows.
Adverse Impact Monitor.
TapDance: Skills Testing Software.
Work Force/Job Group Analyst for Windows.

P.R.N. Medical Software, Div. of Computeam, Inc., (0-87132; 1-55812), 755 New York Ave.., Huntington, NY 11743 Tel 516-424-7777; FAX: 516-424-7207.
Titles:
Acquisitions Manager.
Basic Diet Analysis.
Hospital Staff Scheduler.
Medical Office Scheduler.

P-ROM Software, Inc., (0-926034), 1820 Shelburne Rd.,Box 4027, Burlington, VT 05401 Tel 802-862-7500; Toll free: 800-843-7766; FAX: 802-862-8357.
Titles:
APR Check & Dealer Reserve.
Autofinance.
Constant-Payment-to-Principal Loan.
Finance Charge & Insurance Premium Rebates.
Interest-Only-Balloon-Payment Loan.
Interest Only Installment Loan.
Irregular Skip Loan.
Leasing Program.
Loan Pricing & Profitability-Yield on Funds Used.
Mortgage Banking.
Savings.
Series Modular Banking.
Variable Rate Mortgage with PMI & Combined APR.

PRS-Software, (0-918669), 25425 Knoll Ln., Carmel, CA 93923 Tel 408-625-6168.
Titles:
PRS Legal Billing System.

PSDI (Project Software & Development, Inc.), 20 University Rd., Cambridge, MA 02138 Tel 617-661-1444; Toll free: 800-366-7734; FAX: 617-661-1642.
Titles:
MAXIMO Series Five.

P/Soft Consulting, 1155 Camino Del Mar, No. 405, Del Mar, CA 92014 Tel 619-259-8643.
Titles:
PC-PAROT: Production Analysis Reports on Time.

P3, Inc., 1202 Foothill Dr., Champaign, IL 61821-5618.
Titles:
The Investor.

Pac Corp., Subs. of Alta Summa Corp., (0-926043), 1617 St. Mark's Plaza, Suite B, Stockton, CA 95207 Tel 209-951-8697; FAX: 209-951-0740.
Titles:
Construction Software.
Midas Software.
Property Management System.

Pacer Software, Inc., 7911 Herschel Ave., Suite 402, La Jolla, CA 92037 Tel 619-454-0565; FAX: 619-454-4267.
Titles:
DAL Server for UNIX.
PacerConnect.
PacerForum.
PacerLink.
PacerPrint.
PacerShare.
PacerTerm.

Pacific Basin Graphics, 1577 Ninth Ave., San Francisco, CA 94122 Tel 415-564-5416.
Titles:
PBG 100.
PBG 300: Business Graphics Package.

Pacific Data Systems, Inc., (0-926051), 48021 Warm Springs Blvd., Fremont, CA 94539-7497; Toll free: 800-343-9194.
Titles:
MoneyMaster.

Pacific Research Pubns., (0-926606), 23441 Golden Springs Dr., Suite 216, Diamond Bar, CA 91765 Tel 714-993-7446.
Titles:
Database of Accounting Research-Search Software.

Packaged Solutions, Inc., (0-918671), 2 Twelvepence Ct., Melville, NY 11747-3410 Tel 516-253-2500.
Titles:
BiComM-3270.
BiComM-3700.

PAPERCLIP PRODUCTS

Packard Bell Interactive, Div. of Packard Bell Electronics, (1-888646), 1201 Third Ave., No. 2380, Seattle, WA 98101 Tel 206-654-4180; FAX: 206-654-4188.
Titles:
PBI Goldilocks & the Three Bears.
PBI Little Red Riding Hood.
PBI Milly Fitzwilly's Mousecatcher.
PBI Storybook Library: Bundle Trio of The Pirate Who Wouldn't Wash, Wrong Way-Around the World & The Friends of Emily Culpepper.
PBI The Little Engine.
PBI There's a Dinosaur in the Garden.

Page Studio Graphics, 3175 N. Price Rd., Suite 1050, Chandler, AZ 85224 Tel 602-839-2763.
Titles:
PIXymbols Special Purpose Pictorial Symbol Fonts & EPS Packages: 60 Specific Titles.

Palisade Corp., 31 Decker Rd., Newfield, NY 14867 Tel 607-277-8000; Toll free: 800-432-7475; FAX: 607-277-8001.
Titles:
@RISK.
@RISK for Project.
BestFit.

Palmer & Palmer, (0-926064), 510 Tenth St., SE, Hampton, IA 50441 Tel 515-456-3608.
Titles:
Concrete Mix Designs.
Games, Games, & More Games.

Palo Alto Software, 144 E. 14th, Suite 8, Eugene, OR 97401 Tel 541-683-6162; Toll free: 800-229-7526; FAX: 541-683-6250.
Titles:
Business Plan Pro.
Business Plan Toolkit.
DecisionMaker.
Marketing Plan Pro.

Palomar Software, Inc., 2964 Oceanside Blvd., Suite D, Oceanside, CA 92054; FAX: 619-721-7000.
Titles:
Colorizer.
On the Road.
PICT Detective.
PLOTTERgeist.

Palsoft, (0-926063), P.O. Box 60053, Corpus Christi, TX 78466-0053 Tel 512-883-3636; Dist. by: Ingram Software, 900 W. Walnut Ave., Compton, CA 90220; Toll free: 800-847-6383.
Titles:
Mactype.
Palantir Filer for Windows.
Palantir Spell for Windows.
Palantir Word Processor.
WordPlay: Word Game.

PaperClip Products, (1-883757), 4308 S. Peoria, Suite 763, Tulsa, OK 74105 Tel 918-749-7417; Toll free: 800-495-5508.
Titles:
Simplicity Is Power: Make Using Your Macintosh Faster, Easier & More Fun!

Para Publishing, (0-915516; 1-56860), P.O. Box 8206-P, Santa Barbara, CA 93118-8206 Tel 805-968-7277; Toll free: 800-727-2782 (orders); FAX: 805-968-1379; 530 Ellwood Ridge, Santa Barbara, CA 93117-1047 Tel 805-968-7277; Dist. by: Publishers Group West, 4065 Hollis St., Emeryville, CA 94608 Tel 510-658-3453; Toll free: 800-788-3123; Dist. by: Baker & Taylor Bks., Reno Service Ctr., 380 Edison Way, Reno, NV 89564 Tel 702-858-6700; Toll free: 800-775-1700 (customer service); Dist. by: Baker & Taylor Bks., Commerce Service Ctr., 251 Mt. Olive Church Rd., Commerce, GA 30599-9988 Tel 706-335-5000; Toll free: 800-775-1200 (customer service); Dist. by: Baker & Taylor Bks., Somerville Service Ctr., 50 Kirby Ave., Somerville, NJ 08876-0734 Tel 908-722-8000; Toll free: 800-775-1500 (customer service); Dist. by: Baker & Taylor Bks., Momence Service Ctr., 501 S. Gladiolus St., Momence, IL 60954-2444 Tel 815-472-2444; Toll free: 800-775-2300 (customer service); Dist. by: Pacific Pipeline, Inc., 8030 S. 228th St., Kent, WA 98032-2900 Tel 206-872-5523; Toll free: 800-444-7323 (Customer Service); 800-677-2222 (orders); Dist. by: Quality Bks., Inc., 1003 W. Pines Rd., Oregon, IL 61061 Tel 708-295-2010; Toll free: 800-323-4241 (libraries Only); Dist. by: Bookpeople, 7900 Edgewater Dr., Oakland, CA 94621 Tel 510-632-4700; Toll free: 800-999-4650; Dist. by: Ingram Bk. Co., 1 Ingram Blvd., La Vergne, TN 37086-1986 Tel 615-793-5000; Toll free: 800-788-3123.
Titles:
Business Letters for Publishers.
Canopy Color Program: Computerized Color Pattern Selection.
Canopy Formation Planner: Computerized CRW Formation Planner.
Jumpsuit Color Program: Computerized Color Pattern Selection.
Publishing Contracts, Sample Agreements for Book Publishers on Disk.
RIG Color Program: Computerized Color Pattern Selection.
Skydiving Formation Planner: Computerized RW Dive Creator.

Paracomp, Inc., (0-926074), 27 Walnut St., Upton, MA 01568 Tel 508-529-3175; Toll free: 800-633-0610.
Titles:
Camping One.
Camping II.
PC-Aid.
PC-Trend.

Paradise Software Corp., P.O. Box 50996, Phoenix, AZ 85076 Tel 602-759-0335.
Titles:
MacScuba.

Paragon Media, Div. of the Paragon Group, Inc., (1-882949; 1-57634), 2115 Sixth Ave., Seattle, WA 98121 Tel 206-441-4500; Toll free: 800-874-9044; FAX: 206-441-0556.
Titles:
America's Cup.
Color Digital Photos.
Color Digital Photos, Vol. 1: Premier.
Color Digital Photos, Vol. 2: Space.
Color Digital Photos, Vol. 3: Floral.
Color Digital Photos, Vol. 4: Planes.
Color Digital Photos, Vol. 5: Paramount.
Color Digital Photos, Vol. 6: Glamour.
Color Digital Photos, Vol. 7: Underwater.
English As a Second Language (ESL): After the Auction.
The Interactive Guide to Soccer.
The Interactive Guide to Volleyball.
Kittens to Cats.
Puppy to Dogs.

Paragon Retail Systems, (0-926077), 6421 Congress Ave., No. 110, Boca Raton, FL 33487-2858 Tel 407-994-8361; Toll free: 800-544-8364; FAX: 407-994-8363.
Titles:
Retail & Plus Management System.

Paragon Software Corp., (0-944937; 1-56528), 1004 Ligonier St., 3rd Flr., Latrobe, PA 15650-1837; FAX: 412-834-4279. Do not confuse with Paragon Software, Inc. Boca Raton, FL.
Titles:
Alien Fires 2199 A.D.

Parallel Resource, Inc., (0-922373), P.O. Box 2488, Auburn, AL 36831 Tel 334-821-9000.
Titles:
SF/X: Standard Form 254 & 255 Printing System.

ParcPlace Systems, 999 E. Arques Ave., Sunnyvale, CA 94086 Tel 408-481-9090; Toll free: 800-822-7880.
Titles:
Objectworks For Smalltalk-80.
Smalltalk-80.

Parish Data System, Inc., (0-926085), 14425 N. 19th Ave., Phoenix, AZ 85023 Tel 602-789-0595; Toll free: 800-999-7148 (orders only); FAX: 602-789-0597.
Titles:
Facility Scheduler.
Parish Data System Census-Contribution Program.
Payroll Management Program.
PDS Ledger/Payable Program.
PDS Religious Education Management Program.
School Management Program.

Park Row Software, Div. of Park Row, (0-935749), 1418 Park Row, La Jolla, CA 92037-3710; Toll free: 800-747-5589.
Titles:
CBT Analyst.
Cost/Benefits.
Easy Expert.
MacCarols: The Christmas Disk.
Problem Analysis.
Publish or Perish: Macintosh Version.

Park Software, Inc., P.O. Box 710, Milwaukee, WI 53201-0710 Tel 414-797-7911.
Titles:
Time Xtra, Time Xtra Plus.

Park Technologies, P.O. Box 1317, Clifton Park, NY 12065 Tel 518-877-5881; Toll free: 800-423-3189.
Titles:
TAX EASE.

Parrot Software, (0-942763), 6505 Pleasant Lake Ct., West Bloomfield, MI 48322 Tel 810-788-3223; Toll free: 800-727-7681; FAX: 810-788-3224.
Titles:
Aphasia I: Noun Associations.
Aphasia II: Opposites & Similarities.
Aphasia III: Categories.
Aphasia IV: Reading Comprehension.
Cognitive Disorders I: Category Naming & Completion.
Cognitive Retraining with Print Shop Pictures.
Minimal Contrast Therapy.

Parsons Technology, (1-57264), P.O. Box 100, Hiawatha, IA 52233-0100; Toll free: 800-833-3241; FAX: 319-395-0386; One Parsons Dr., Hiawatha, IA 52233 Tel 319-395-9626; Dist. by: Spring Arbor Distributors, 10885 Textile Rd., Belleville, MI 48111 Tel 313-481-0900; Toll free: 800-395-5599 (orders); 800-395-7234 (customer service).
Titles:
American History Atlas for Windows.
Appointment Calendar: Word for the Day.
Bible Illustrator for DOS.
Bible Illustrator for Windows.
Christian Images.
Christian Images Bundle.
Christian Products Video.
Daily Journal for Windows.
Family Origins.
Family Origins for Windows.
Holman Bible Dictionary for Windows.
It's Legal.
Membership Plus Deluxe.
Membership Plus Demo.
Money Plans.
MoneyCounts.
Nave's Topical Bible.
New Scofield Study Bible.
PC Bible Atlas.
PC Bible Atlas for Windows.
QuickVerse Bible Concordance.
QuickVerse Bible Reference Collection.
QuickVerse Bible Text: King James Translation.
QuickVerse Bible Text: New American Standard Bible Translation.
QuickVerse Bible Text: New Century Version Translation.
QuickVerse Bible Text: New International Version Translation.
QuickVerse Bible Text: New King James Translation.
QuickVerse Bible Text: New Revised Stanard Version Translation.
QuickVerse Bible Text: Revised Standard Version Translation.
QuickVerse Bible Text: The Living Bible Translation.
QuickVerse for DOS: King James Translation with Naves.
QuickVerse for DOS: Living Bible Translation with Naves.
QuickVerse for DOS: New American Standard Translation with Naves.
QuickVerse for DOS: New Century Translation with Naves.
QuickVerse for DOS: New International Translation with Naves.
QuickVerse for DOS: New King James Translation with Naves.
QuickVerse for DOS: New Revised Standard Translation with Naves.
QuickVerse for DOS: Revised Standard Translation with Naves.
QuickVerse for Windows Demo.
QuickVerse for Windows: King James Translation with Naves.
QuickVerse for Windows: Living Bible Translation with Naves.
QuickVerse for Windows: New American Standard Translation with Naves.
QuickVerse for Windows: New Century Translation with Naves.
QuickVerse for Windows: New International Translation with Naves.
QuickVerse for Windows: New King James Translation with Naves.
QuickVerse for Windows: New Revised Standard Translation with Naves.
QuickVerse for Windows: Revised Standard Translation with Naves.
QuickVerse Home Bible Study Collection.
QuickVerse Strong's Concordance: With Transliterated Hebrew-Greek Dictionary.
QuiteWrite.
Screen Dreams (Holy Lands).

PUBLISHER/TITLE INDEX

Passport Designs, Inc., (0-926096), 100 Stone Pine Rd., Half Moon Bay, CA 94019 Tel 415-726-0280; FAX: 415-726-2254.
Titles:
Clicktracks.
Master Tracks Jr!
Master Tracks Pro.

Pathfinders/College Affordability Productions, Inc., (0-9629535), 6047 N. Ninth Ave., Phoenix, AZ 85013-1407 Tel 602-246-8761.
Titles:
Scholarships, Gra2ts & Loans.

Pattern Systems International, Inc., (0-926103), 200 Valley Rd., Suite 302, Mt. Arlington, NJ 07856 Tel 201-770-3800; Toll free: 800-225-7804; FAX: 201-770-0053.
Titles:
Cut Planner 10, 20, 30.
DrawPower 3D (AutoCAD).
Drill-Mate.
Label Planner.
Product Planner 10.
Product Planner 20.
Pulsar Cuisitech.

Paynter, E. F., & Assocs., Inc., (0-918675), 6140 N. College Ave., Indianapolis, IN 46220 Tel 317-257-7561.
Titles:
Computer-Aided Construction Take-Off & Estimating System: CACTES.

PC-Kwik, (0-925722), 3800 SW Cedar Hills Blvd., Suite 260, Beaverton, OR 97005 Tel 503-644-5644; Toll free: 800-274-5945; FAX: 503-646-8267.
Titles:
PC-Kwik Power Disk.
PC-Kwik Power Pak.
Super PC-Kwik: Disk Accelerator.

PC World New Media, 501 Second St., San Francisco, CA 94107 Tel 415-975-2668.
Titles:
PC World Interactive.

PCollier Systems, 7925-A N. Oracle Rd., Suite 390, Tucson, AZ 85704; Toll free: 800-522-2060.
Titles:
Modula-2PC.

Peachpit Pr., (0-938151; 1-56609), 2414 6th St., Berkeley, CA 94710 Tel 510-548-4393; Toll free: 800-283-9444; FAX: 510-548-5991; Dist. by: Publishers Group West, 4065 Hollis St., Emeryville, CA 94608 Tel 510-658-3453; Toll free: 800-788-3123; Dist. by: Golden-Lee Bk. Distributors, Inc., 1000 Dean St., Brooklyn, NY 11238 Tel 718-857-6333; Toll free: 800-473-7475; Dist. by: Ingram Bk. Co., 1 Ingram Blvd., La Vergne, TN 37086-1986 Tel 615-793-5000; Toll free: 800-937-8000 (orders only, all warehouses); Dist. by: Baker & Taylor Bks., Somerville Service Ctr., 50 Kirby Ave., Somerville, NJ 08876-0734 Tel 908-722-8000; Toll free: 800-775-1500 (customer service); Dist. by: Baker & Taylor Bks., Momence Service Ctr., 501 S. Gladiolus St., Momence, IL 60954-2444 Tel 815-472-2444; Toll free: 800-775-2300 (customer service); Dist. by: Baker & Taylor Bks., Commerce Service Ctr., 251 Mt. Olive Church Rd., Commerce, GA 30599-9988 Tel 706-335-5000; Toll free: 800-775-1200 (customer service); Dist. by: Baker & Taylor Bks., Reno Service Ctr., 380 Edison Way, Reno, NV 89564 Tel 702-858-6700; Toll free: 800-775-1700 (customer service).
Titles:
ColorCourse/Imagesetting.
FileMaker Pro 3: Training on CD.
PageMill: Training on CD.

Peachtree Software, Subs. of ADP, Inc., (0-926111), 1505 Pavilion Pl., Norcross, GA 30093 Tel 404-564-5800; Toll free: 800-247-3224; FAX: 404-564-5888.
Titles:
Peachtree Accounting for Macintosh.
Peachtree Accounting for Windows.
Peachtree Complete Accounting: Easy to Use Accounting for Small Businesses.
Peachtree Insight Accounting for Macintosh.

Peacock Systems, Inc., 1730 N. Lynn St., No. A11, Arlington, VA 22209-2004.
Titles:
CB Tree.
CBTree.

Peak Media, Inc., (0-9639134), 418 N. River St., P.O. Box 925, Hailey, ID 83333 Tel 208-788-4500; Toll free: 800-769-1055; FAX: 208-788-5098.
Titles:
Mount Everest: Quest for the Summit of Dreams.

Pencil Pushers United, Inc., (0-926126), 10 New England Executive Pk., Burlington, MA 01803-5214 Tel 617-861-6962; Toll free: 800-348-5563.
Titles:
Tax Planner.
Tax Preparation Program.

Peoplesmith Software, P.O. Box 384, North Scituate, MA 02060 Tel 617-545-7300; Toll free: 800-777-2460; 18 Damon Rd., North Scituate, MA 02060 Tel 617-545-7300.
Titles:
DynaKey.LIB.

Performance Technologies, Inc., Subs. of The Charles Schwab Corp., 4814 Old Wake Forest Rd., Raleigh, NC 27609 Tel 919-876-3555; Toll free: 800-528-9595; FAX: 919-876-2187.
Titles:
Centerpiece.
Performance Monitor.

Periscope Co., (0-923537), 1475 Peachtree St., Suite 100, Atlanta, GA 30309 Tel 404-888-5335; Toll free: 800-722-7006; FAX: 404-888-5520.
Titles:
Periscope-EM.
Periscope I.
Periscope IV.
WinScope.

Permutations Software, Inc., (0-9630781), 323 W. Fourth St., Apt. 5C, New York, NY 10014 Tel 212-727-0457.
Titles:
LoveTies.

Perrysburg Software Corp., 109 1/2 W. Indiana Ave., Perrysburg, OH 43551-1578 Tel 419-874-8502; FAX: 419-874-9313.
Titles:
LabelSoft.

Persimmon Software, (0-926152), 8611 Wilshire Dr., Amarillo, TX 79110 Tel 806-351-1149.
Titles:
Attitude Scales.
Diving Scorer.
Event Log.
Mailer PC.
SURVEY.

Persoft, Inc., (0-918063), 465 Science Dr., Madison, WI 53711 Tel 608-273-6000; Toll free: 800-368-5283; FAX: 608-273-8227.
Titles:
SmarTerm 320.
SmarTerm 400.

PERSONAL TRAINING SYSTEMS

SmarTerm 470.

Personal Bibliographic Software, Inc., (0-928453), 525 Avis Dr., Suite 10, Ann Arbor, MI 48108 Tel 313-996-1580; FAX: 313-996-4672.
Titles:
Biblio-Link II Packages.
Biblio-Link II.
Pro-Cite.
Pro-Cite (IBM).
ProCite: For Windows.

Personal Systems Consulting, (0-926172), 8507 Melrose Ln., El Cajon, CA 92021 Tel 619-443-5353.
Titles:
Mexinur Policy Writing Station.
Wholesale Order Entry: Sales Counter Order Processing.

Personal Tex, Inc., (0-9631044), 12 Madrona Ave., Mill Valley, CA 94941 Tel 415-388-8853; Toll free: 800-808-7906; FAX: 415-388-8865.
Titles:
PC TEX.
PC Tex: Personal Computer Typesetting Software.
PCTex for Windows.

Personal Training Systems, (0-944124; 1-57217), 173 Jefferson Dr., Menlo Park, CA 94105 Tel 415-462-2100; Toll free: 800-832-2499; FAX: 415-462-2105.
Titles:
Beginning Word.
Intermediate Word.
Personal Training for Adobe Illustrator 5.0.
Personal Training for Adobe Photoshop.
Personal Training for Excel.
Personal Training for FileMake Pro.
Personal Training for Fonts.
Personal Training for FreeHand.
Personal Training for HyperCard.
Personal Training for Intuit Quicken.
Personal Training for Lotus 1-2-3.
Personal Training for Macintosh Performa.
Personal Training for Microsoft Office.
Personal Training for Microsoft PowerPoint.
Personal Training for Microsoft Works.
Personal Training for PageMaker.
Personal Training for Persuasion.
Personal Training for QuarkXPress.
Personal Training for the Macintosh System 7.
Personal Training for Word.
Personal Training for WordPerfect.
Personal Training Systems Claris Works.
Personal Training Systems Software Made Easy: Advanced Adobe Illustrator.
Personal Training Systems Software Made Easy: Advanced Adobe Photoshop.
Personal Training Systems Software Made Easy: Advanced Claris Filemaker Pro.
Personal Training Systems Software Made Easy: Advanced Excel Spreadsheets.
Personal Training Systems Software Made Easy: Advanced Excel 5.0.
Personal Training Systems Software Made Easy: Additional Features Word.
Personal Training Systems Software Made Easy: Advanced Lotus Spreadsheets.
Personal Training Systems Software Made Easy: Adobe Photoshop.
Personal Training Systems Software Made Easy: Aldus PageMaker 5.0 Mac.
Personal Training Systems Software Made Easy: Advanced Quattro Pro Features.
Personal Training Systems Software Made Easy: Advanced System Features.
Personal Training Systems Software Made Easy: Advanced Word.
Personal Training Systems Software Made Easy: Advanced Word 6.0.
Personal Training Systems Software Made Easy: Beginning Access.

Personal Training Systems Software Made Easy: Beginning Aldus Freehand.
Personal Training Systems Software Made Easy: Beginning Adobe Illustrator.
Personal Training Systems Software Made Easy: Beginning Adobe Photoshop.
Personal Training Systems Software Made Easy: Beginning Claris Filemaker Pro.
Personal Training Systems Software Made Easy: Beginning Excel Spreadsheets.
Personal Training Systems Software Made Easy: Beginning Excel 5.0.
Personal Training Systems Software Made Easy: BEGINNING Lotus AMIPRO.
Personal Training Systems Software Made Easy: Beginning Lotus Notes.
Personal Training Systems Software Made Easy: Beginning Lotus Spreadsheets.
Personal Training Systems Software Made Easy: BeginningQuattro Pro.
Personal Training Systems Software Made Easy: Beginning Power Point.
Personal Training Systems Software Made Easy: Beyond the Basics.
Personal Training Systems Software Made Easy: Beginning Word.
Personal Training Systems Software Made Easy: Beginning Word Perfect.
Personal Training Systems Software Made Easy: Beginning Word 6.0.
Personal Training Systems Software Made Easy: Beginning XPress Quark.
Personal Training Systems Software Made Easy: Charts & Databases Excel 5.0.
Personal Training Systems Software Made Easy: Cards & Stacks.
Personal Training Systems Software Made Easy: Color & Type Quark.
Personal Training Systems Software Made Easy: Creating Excel Business Graphs.
Personal Training Systems Software Made Easy: Creating Special Affects.
Personal Training Systems Software Made Easy: Creating Special Effects.
Personal Training Systems Software Made Easy: Converting to System 7-P1.
Personal Training Systems Software Made Easy: Excel Graphs & Business.
Personal Training Systems Software Made Easy: Excel Macros.
Personal Training Systems Software Made Easy: Excel Powerful Spreadsheets.
Personal Training Systems Software Made Easy: Excel 5.0 Mac CD-ROM.
Personal Training Systems Software Made Easy: Excel 5.0 Windows CD-ROM.
Personal Training Systems Software Made Easy: Getting Started.
Personal Training Systems Software Made Easy: Getting Started with Windows.
Personal Training Systems Software Made Easy: GETTING STARTED 3.1.
Personal Training Systems Software Made Easy: Intermediate Access.
Personal Training Systems Software Made Easy: Intermediate Aldus Freehand.
Personal Training Systems Software Made Easy: Intermediate Adobe Illustrator.
Personal Training Systems Software Made Easy: Intermediate Adobe Photoshop.
Personal Training Systems Software Made Easy: Intermediate Claris Filemaker.
Personal Training Systems Software Made Easy: Intermediate Excel.
Personal Training Systems Software Made Easy: Intermediate Excel 5.0.
Personal Training Systems Software Made Easy: Intermediate Lotus.
Personal Training Systems Software Made Easy: Intermediate Lotus Notes.
Personal Training Systems Software Made Easy: Integrating MS Office 4.20.
Personal Training Systems Software Made Easy: Integrating Office PRO 4.0 MAC.
Personal Training Systems Software Made Easy: Introduction to Claris Works.
Personal Training Systems Software Made Easy: Introduction to DOS 6.2.
Personal Training Systems Software Made Easy: Integrating the Microsoft Office.
Personal Training Systems Software Made Easy: Introduction to Persuasion.
Personal Training Systems Software Made Easy: Introduction to Quicken.
Personal Training Systems Software Made Easy: Introduction to Works.
Personal Training Systems Software Made Easy: Intermediate Windows.
Personal Training Systems Software Made Easy: Intermediate Word Perfect.
Personal Training Systems Software Made Easy: Intermediate Word 6.0.
Personal Training Systems Software Made Easy: Microsoft Office Pro (Windows).
Personal Training Systems Software Made Easy: Microsoft Office Standard.
Personal Training Systems Software Made Easy: MS Office 4.2Mac CD-ROM.
Personal Training Systems Software Made Easy: Master Pages Quark.
Personal Training Systems Software Made Easy: Office 4.0 Mac.
Personal Training Systems Software Made Easy: Precision Drawing Tech.
Personal Training Systems Software Made Easy: PTS MacPAK.
Personal Training Systems Software Made Easy: PTS Productivity Pack.
Personal Training Systems Software Made Easy: Quattro Pro Presentation.
Personal Training Systems Software Made Easy: System 7.5 - Macintosh Basics.
Personal Training Systems Software Made Easy: System 7 Mac CD-ROM.
Personal Training Systems Software Made Easy: Tips & Techniques Quark.
Personal Training Systems Software Made Easy: "The Basics-Classic, SE, Plus".
Personal Training Systems Software Made Easy: The Basics-Mac II.
Personal Training Systems Software Made Easy: The Basics-2 Floppy Drives.
Personal Training Systems Software Made Easy: Text Formats Quark.
Personal Training Systems Software Made Easy: Using HyperCard.
Personal Training Systems Software Made Easy: Using Macintosh ATM Fonts.
Personal Training Systems Software Made Easy: Using Macintosh Fonts.
Personal Training Systems Software Made Easy: Using Macintosh TrueType.
Personal Training Systems Software Made Easy: Using Quattro Pro For Windows.
Personal Training Systems Software Made Easy: Using Quicken 3.0 Windows.
Personal Training Systems Software Made Easy: Using the Mac Interface.
Personal Training Systems Software Made Easy: Using Windows ATM Fonts.
Personal Training Systems Software Made Easy: Using Windows Fonts.
Personal Training Systems Software Made Easy: Using Windows TrueType.
Personal Training Systems Software Made Easy: Word 6.0 Mac CD-ROM.
Personal Training Systems Software Made Easy: Word 6.0 Windows CD-ROM.

Personalized Business Resources, 10247 SE 224, Kent, WA 98031 Tel 206-852-2308.
Titles:
QwikBid Residential Estimating System.

Personally Developed Software, Inc., P.O. Box 3280, Wallingford, CT 06494; Toll free: 800-426-7279.
Titles:
Alley Cat.
Backgammon.
Beyond Basic BASIC.
Blackjack.
Browstext.
Crypto-Mania.
Crypto-Mania Puzzle Pac.
Daily Organizer.
DOS Enhanced Debug.
DOS File Tracker.
DOS File View.
DOS Memories.
Executive Phone Directory.
Executive Phone Directory Build Your Own.
Executive Phone Directory with Message Feature.
Extended BASIC Programming.
File Conversion Utility.
FileCommand II.
FORTRAN Tutor.
Freddy's Rescue Roundup.
Introductory Editor.
JoyMouse.
JustEdit.
Kaleidoscope.
Language Extension System-Assembler.
Lines Plus.
Liptocoe.
Lite Editor.
Matrix Madness.
Member Services.
Morse Code Drills.
Multimedia Presentation Aid.
Object Library Maintenance.
PC Checkbook.
PC Morse Code.
PC Palette.
PC Palette Utility.
PC Print.
Personal Computer Picture Graphics.
Personal Correspondence Manager.
Personal Editor III.
Personal Scientific Calculator.
Phone Directory On-Line.
Picture Draw.
Plan-a-Year.
Portfolio Management System.
PrintDW.
Project Planning & Scheduling.
Scattergrams.
Select-A-Font.
Short Hand.
Side-Swipe.
SOLITAIRE.
Source Maintenance System.
Special Effects with Slides.
Sports Appeal: Trivia from Billiards to Baseball.
The StarProof Bridge.
STATLIB 1.
STATLIB 2.
Structured Assembler Translator.
Structured BASIC Facility.
SuperC.
Trivia 102.
Trivia 103: Challenges for Young People.
Utilities I.
Utilities II.
Utilities III.
Word Seeking.

Personics Corp., 234 Ballardvale St., Wilmington, MA 01887-1032; Toll free: 800-445-3311; FAX: 508-897-1519.
Titles:
@Base.
Laptop UltraVision.
Monarch.
SeeMORE.
Smart Notes.

Peterson Enterprises, 7 Grove St., Haydenville, MA 01039 Tel 413-268-9232.
Titles:
C-Light.

Peterson's Guides, Inc., (0-87866; 1-56079), P.O. Box 2123, Princeton, NJ 08543-2123; Toll free: 800-338-3282; FAX: 609-243-9150; 202 Carnegie Ctr., Princeton, NJ 08540 Tel 609-243-9111.
Titles:
Peterson's Career Options.
Peterson's College Selection Service, Peterson's College Selection Service 2 (with Financial Aid File).
Peterson's College Selection Service: 1995 Four-Year Colleges.
Peterson's College Selection Service: 1995 Two-Year Colleges.
Peterson's Financial Aid Service 1995.

Pharmacy Management Systems, Inc., 6297 Westover Rd., West Palm Beach, FL 33417 Tel 407-697-3911.
Titles:
Pharmacy.

Phase 1 Systems, (0-926187), 2950 Merced St., Suite 101, San Leandro, CA 94577 Tel 510-895-0832; FAX: 510-895-0828.
Titles:
Control Plus.
SPELLVUE: In-Context Spelling Checker.
VSORT: File Sort Utility.

Ph.D. Publishing Co., (0-932010), 11606 Charnock Rd., Los Angeles, CA 90066 Tel 310-391-2080.
Titles:
Financial Planning: Long Range Economic Forecast, International GNP, Valuation.
Financial Planning, 1996.
Strategic Planning: Tax Minimization & Investment Strategy (Sixth Edition).
Tax Planning 1990.
Tax Planning, 1993: Calculation of Income Tax Due, Attachments, Gift Tax, Defense of Return.
Tax Planning, 1996.

Phelps, C. M., & Co., 3525 Piedmont Rd. NE, No. 500-8, Atlanta, GA 30305-1561 Tel 404-325-7346.
Titles:
Credit Committee.

Phoenix Phive Software Corp., (1-877915), 7830 E. Gelding Dr., Suite 400, Scottsdale, AZ 85260-3488 Tel 602-483-0991; Toll free: 800-331-1811; FAX: 602-948-1379.
Titles:
Industrial Strength Payroll.
Inventory Control.
Mail.
Payroll.
The 1099 Package.

Physician Micro Systems, Inc., (0-926202), 2033 Sixth Ave., Suite 707, Seattle, WA 98121 Tel 206-441-8490; FAX: 206-441-8915.
Titles:
Practice Partner Appointment Scheduler.
Practice Partner Medical Billing III.
Practice Partner Medical Writer.
Practice Partner: Patient Records.

Physicians Office Computer, (0-926339), 1240 Kona Dr., Rancho Dominguez, CA 90220 Tel 310-603-0555; Toll free: 800-782-5214; FAX: 310-603-0581.
Titles:
Physician's Office Computer.

Physicians Practice Management, Inc., (0-918071), 350 E. New York St., No. 300, Indianapolis, IN 46204-2134 Tel 317-634-8080; Toll free: 800-428-3515.
Titles:
PC*Claim Link.
PC-Claim, PC-Claim Plus.
Threshold, Threshold-TM.

Piano Partners, Inc., (1-878391), 531 E. 72nd St., Suite 3A, New York, NY 10021 Tel 212-628-3912; Toll free: 800-742-6677.
Titles:
Piano Partners Music Learning System.

Pick Systems, 1691 Browning, Irvine, CA 92714 Tel 714-261-7425; Toll free: 800-367-7425; FAX: 714-250-8187.
Titles:
Pick PC System.

Pickering Winery Supply, 1300 22nd St., San Francisco, CA 94107 Tel 415-821-2400; FAX: 415-821-0811.
Titles:
Vintage Production.

Pico Publishing, (0-934777), 5906 Tenth Ave., Kenosha, WI 53140 Tel 414-652-3278; FAX: 414-652-2906.
Titles:
Browse.
Counters.
DogPak.
G-Spell.
G-Whiz.
RacePro for Windows.
Racing Greyhounds Combo.
Statview.

Pictor Graphics, Inc., 800 E. Campbell Rd., Suite 199, Richardson, TX 75081 Tel 214-437-9043.
Titles:
VictorDraft.

PictureWare, Inc., 5400 NW Grand Blvd., No. 450, Oklahoma City, OK 73112-5654.
Titles:
PicturePower.
PicturePower HC.

Pilot Research Assocs., 1953 Gallows Rd., Vienna, VA 22182 Tel 703-883-2522.
Titles:
Check*Mate.

Pinnacle Publishing, Inc., (1-880935), 18030 72nd Ave., S., Kent, WA 98032 Tel 206-251-1900; Toll free: 800-231-1293; FAX: 206-251-5057. Do not confuse with companies with the same name in Santa Barbara, CA, Branson, MO.
Titles:
Graphics Server for Actor 4.0.

Pinnell/Busch, Inc., (0-926210), 6420 SW Macadam Ave., Suite 330, Portland, OR 97201 Tel 503-293-6280; FAX: 503-243-2289.
Titles:
PMS80 Project Management Application Software.

Pinpoint Publishing, (0-917413), P.O. Box 7329, Santa Rosa, CA 95407-0329 Tel 707-523-0400; FAX: 707-523-0469.
Titles:
Micro CookBook.

Plenary Systems, Inc., (0-926218), P.O. Box 181629, Dallas, TX 75218-8629 Tel 214-840-1140; Toll free: 800-841-1070; FAX: 800-841-1070.
Titles:
Plenary Express: Checkwriting Payroll.
Plenary Express: Client Write-Up.

Plossl, George, Educational Services, Inc., (0-926219), P.O. Box 671316, Marietta, GA 30066 Tel 404-973-6361.
Titles:
MFGCON: Manufacturing Control Training System.

Plossl, K. R., & Co., (0-934801), P.O. Box 669681, Marietta, GA 30066 Tel 404-973-6361.
Titles:
SYSTRAK: Program Revision Traking System.
Uselog - Computer Use Log.

Plus Five Computer Services, (0-928741), P.O. Box 1634, Manchester, MO 63011 Tel 314-991-3330.
Titles:
UNIX MUMPS.

POC-IT Management Services, Inc., (0-928742), 429 Wilshire Blvd., No. 460, Santa Monica, CA 90401 Tel 310-393-4552; FAX: 310-451-2888.
Titles:
MicroMan Esti-Mate.
MicroMan II Project & Staff Management System.

Point 4 Data Corp., (0-926227), 130 McCormick Ave., Suite 106, Costa Mesa, CA 92626 Tel 714-755-6550.
Titles:
Electronic Office System (EOS).
FORCE.
IRIS (Interactive Real-Time Information System).
PC Connection.
SMbasic.
STYLUS.
TYPIST.

Point of Sale Systems Corp., (0-918153), 706 Chippewa Sq., Marquette, MI 49855 Tel 906-228-7623; Toll free: 800-487-7620; FAX: 906-228-7622.
Titles:
Manager's Assistant: Retail Point of Sale Inventory Control System.

Polestar, Inc., 1716 Tipton Dr., Crofton, MD 21114 Tel 301-261-3529.
Titles:
MapVision.

Polyglot Software, 884 W. Melrose Ln., Boise, ID 83706 Tel 208-336-4583.
Titles:
Crossword Creator.
4-In-One: Easy But Fun.

Polygon, Inc., (0-918075), 1015 Corporate Sq., Suite 100, Saint Louis, MO 63132 Tel 314-432-4142; FAX: 314-997-9696.
Titles:
Poly-COM/320.
Poly-LINK.
Poly-Net.
Poly-STAR/G: PC-to-VAX Communication Software.
Poly-XFR Plus.

Polygon Software Corp., 330 Seventh Ave., New York, NY 10001 Tel 212-376-3200.
Titles:
Crossword Creator.
Dominoes.

Poor Mans Software, 3620 Little Chief Ct., North Highlands, CA 95660 Tel 916-332-9224.
Titles:
HyperAlarms.

POOR PERSON SOFTWARE

Poor Person Software, 3721 Starr King Cir., Palo Alto, CA 94306 Tel 415-493-7234.
Titles:
Thinker.

Popular Programs, Inc., (0-916435), 6915 LaGranada, Houston, TX 77083 Tel 713-530-1195; Toll free: 800-447-6787 (orders only); FAX: 713-530-1358.
Titles:
Pop-Up Alarm Clock.
Pop-Up Calculator & Financial Calculator.
Pop-Up DeskSet & DeskSet PLUS.
Pop-Up DeskSet Plus.
Pop-Up PopDOS & Pop-Up Anything.
Pop-Up TeleComm.
TaxLog & Pop-Up Calendar.
TSRman.

Popular Technology, Div. of Branden Publishing Co., (0-927210), 17 Station St., Box 843, Brookline, MA 02147 Tel 617-734-2045; FAX: 617-734-2046.
Titles:
Macro Manager: For WordPerfect 5.0, 5.1.
Pages & Windows.

Portfolio Software, Inc., P.O. Box 1010, 1 Millet St., Richmond, VT 05477-1010 Tel 802-434-6400.
Titles:
Day-to-Day Calendar.
Day-to-Day Complete Organizer.
Day-to-Day Contacts.
Day-to-Day Notepad.

Power System Engineering, Inc., (0-934795), 2000 Engel St., Suite 100, Madison, WI 53713 Tel 608-222-8400; FAX: 608-222-9378.
Titles:
DISTANL: Distribution Circuit Analysis.
Guying: Guying & Anchoring.
Linecost: Construction Material & Cost Estimating.
Outage Plus.

PowerBase Systems, Inc., Subs. of Compuware, (0-924138), 31440 Northwestern Hwy., Farmington Hills, MI 48018 Tel 810-540-2398.
Titles:
PowerBase.
PowerBase Application Templates.

Powersoft, Inc., (0-926257), 12 Tiros Ave., Sewell, NJ 08080-1924.
Titles:
Address File Generator.
Automotive Diagnosis.
BASIC-S.
Black Jack Tutorial.
Business Utility I.
Business Utility II.
Check Writer.
Cubik.
Disk Access Supervisor.
Electrical Engineering Series.
FeatureFormat.
Function Graphs & Transformations-Vector Analysis.
Hi-Res Graphics Utilities.
Income Statement System.
Perquackey.
PowerDot II.
PowerDraw.
PowerMail.
PowerMail Plus.
Real Estate Analysis.
Real Estate Analysis Program.
SCIII Checkwriter.
Statistics Series.
Stone's Reversible Games.
Super Checkbook.
Super Checkbook III.
Super Checkbook III Checkwriter.
Super Checkbook III Plus.

Toolbelt.
World of Odyssey.

Practical Computer Applications, Inc., 18056 Valley View Rd., Eden Prairie, MN 55346-4125.
Titles:
MacCourses.
MacGolf.
MacRacquetball.

Practical Solutions, Inc., (0-926262), 70 Merrick Rd., Lynbrook, NY 11563 Tel 516-599-6600.
Titles:
BillMaster.
Listmaster.

Practice Management Information Corp., (1-878487; 1-57066), 4727 Wilshire Blvd., Suite 300, Los Angeles, CA 90010 Tel 213-954-0224; Toll free: 800-633-4215; FAX: 213-954-0253.
Titles:
CPT 1996 Codes on Disk.
ICD-9-CM 1996 Codes on Disk.

Practitioners Publishing Co., Div. of Warren, Gorham & Lamont, (1-56433; 0-7646), P.O. Box 966, Fort Worth, TX 76101 Tel 817-332-3709; Toll free: 800-323-8724; FAX: 817-336-2433; 3221 Collinsworth, Fort Worth, TX 76107.
Titles:
GuideView.
GuideWare.
Trackker.

Practorcare, Inc., (0-926263), 4115 Sorrento Valley Blvd., San Diego, CA 92121-1406 Tel 619-450-0553; Toll free: 800-421-9073; FAX: 619-458-0920.
Titles:
Dietcare.
Foodserve.
Free & Reduced Planner.
Menumodifier.
Nutrilabel.
Nutriplanner.
Nutripractor.
Nutristatus.

Preceptor Systems, Inc., P.O. Box 3941, Frederick, MD 21701 Tel 301-662-6883.
Titles:
Cassandra: Medical Office Manager.

Precision Computer Systems, 123 W. Birch Ave., No. 100, Flagstaff, AZ 86001-4515 Tel 602-779-5341.
Titles:
Precision Inventory Control & Order Entry.
Precision Time & Cost Billing System.

Precision, Inc., P.O. Box 54983, Santa Clara, CA 95056-0983.
Titles:
Logistix.
Super Plan.
Superbase Personal.
Superbase Personal II.
Superbase Professional.
Superbase 4.

Precision Software Products, (0-922380), 432 Holyoke St., San Francisco, CA 94134-1735.
Titles:
Instant Install with Keys Please!
Superbase 64.

Premium Review Assocs., 35 Green Heron Ln., Nashua, NH 03062 Tel 603-888-9361; FAX: 603-891-0646.
Titles:
PRA's Experience Modification System.

SOFTWARE ENCYCLOPEDIA 1996

Prentice Hall, Div. of Simon & Schuster, Inc., (0-13), 113 Sylvan Ave., Rte. 9W, Englewood Cliffs, NJ 07632 Tel 201-592-2000; Toll free: 800-922-0579; Orders to: Paramount Publishing, 200 Old Tappan Rd., Old Tappan, NJ 07675 Tel 201-767-5937.
Titles:
Analyst/Designer Toolkit.
Animation Games & Sound for the Apple IIe.
Apple II/6502 Assembly Language Tutor.
Applestat: Regression-Correlation Programs on the Apple II, IIe.
BASIC Fun for the Commodore 64 Beginner.
Beanstalk.
Bounce.
Business Problem Solving Using the IBM PC & PC XT.
Cash Flow Management with Lotus 1-2-3.
Cash Flow Management with Symphony.
Computer Applications in Retail Management & Entrepreneurship for the Apple II Series.
Conquering the Commodore 64 Kingdom: 25 Original Games in Dazzling Sight & Sound.
Conquering the PCjr Kingdom: 25 Original Games in Dazzling Sight & Sound.
Construction Estimator.
Cross Reference Utility (CRF): A Programming Aid for the IBM PC.
Darius IV.
dBASE II Programming: Making dBASE Work for Your Small Business.
Dolphin's Pearl.
The Electric Address Book.
The Executive's Guide to the IBM PC: BASIC Programming & VisiCalc.
Fancy Programming in Applesoft.
Fun & Games on the PCjr.
Graphics Programming on the IBM Personal Computer.
Histcon.
IBM PC: An Introduction to the Operating System, BASIC Programming & Applications.
IBM PC-Apprentice: Dollars & Sense, Tutorial Workbook.
IBM PC-Apprentice: Easybusiness System General Ledger, Tutorial Workbook.
IBM PC-Apprentice: FORTRAN-77-Beginning, Tutorial Workbook.
IBM PC-Apprentice: Open Access, Tutorial Workbook.
IBM PC-Apprentice: SuperCalc III, Tutorial Workbook.
IBM PC-Apprentice: UCSD Pascal-Beginning, Tutorial Workbook.
IBM PC Assembly Language Tutor.
IBM PC 8080 Assembly Language Tutor.
IBM PC XT Assembly Language: A Guide for Programmers.
IBM PC XT Graphics Book.
Infomanager.
Key Business Measures.
Learning LISP.
Lotus 1-2-3 for Marketing & Sales.
LSF: Least Square Curve Fitter.
Mastering Your Atari Through 8 Basic Projects.
Mastering Your Commodore 64 Through 8 Basic Projects.
MINIX Operating System.
Mouthpiece.
Movie Maker.
The Multiplan Teach Program.
Music & Sound for the Commodore 64.
Music & Sound for the PCjr.
Pascal for the Apple.
Pascal Programming for IBM PC.
The Personal Financial Manager.
The Personal Financial Planner.
The Personal Financial Planner: Professional Edition.
The Power of: Construction Management Using Multiplan.
The Power of: Construction Management Using 1-2-3.
The Power of: Financial Calculations for Lotus 1-2-3.

PUBLISHER/TITLE INDEX

The Power of: Financial Calculations for Multiplan.
The Power of: Multiplan.
The Power of: 1-2-3.
The Power of: Professional Tax Planning Using Multiplan.
The Power of: Professional Tax Planning Using 1-2-3.
The Power of: Word by Microsoft.
Preparing Your Business Budget with Framework.
Preparing Your Business Budget with Symphony.
Preparing Your Business Plan with Lotus 1-2-3.
Preparing Your Business Plan with Multiplan.
The Profit Center Accounts Payable.
The Profit Center Accounts Receivable.
The Profit Center Business Word Processor.
The Profit Center General Accounting.
The Profit Center Information Query for General Accounting.
The Profit Center Job Costs.
The Profit Center Job Estimator.
The Profit Center Master Menu.
The Profit Center NEAT: The Time & Information Managers.
The Profit Center Spellproof.
Science & Engineering Programs for the IBM PC.
Science & Engineering Programs for the Macintosh.
The Templus Series.
TRS-80 Model III Assembly Language.
UCSD Pascal for the IBM PC.
Using Multiplan for Marketing & Sales Problems.
Using the Commodore 64 in the Home.
Using the PCjr in the Home.
Using Your PCjr: Beginning BASIC & Applications.
Wordworx.
Your Income Tax 1-2-3.

Prentice Hall Professional Software, Subs. of Simon & Schuster, Inc., P.O. Box 723597, Atlanta, GA 31139 Tel 404-432-1996; Toll free: 800-241-3306; FAX: 404-435-5036; 2400 Lake Park Dr., P.O. Box 723597, Atlanta, GA 30339.
Titles:
Business Ties.
Fast! Advantage.
Financial Reporting.
Plan 1040.
Practice Advantage.
The Prentice Hall Tax Advantage System - 1120, 11205, 1065.
Software 1040.

Primavera Systems, Inc., (0-926282; 1-57408), 2 Bala Plaza, Bala Cynwyd, PA 19004 Tel 610-667-8600; Toll free: 800-423-0245; FAX: 610-667-7894.
Titles:
Expedition.
Finest Hour.
Parade.
Primavera Project Planner: Project Management & Control Software.

Prime Computer, Inc., 201 Burlington Ave., Bedford, MS 01730 Tel 617-275-1800.
Titles:
Merge '386.

Primetrack, (0-923136), 136 Old Farms Rd., Box 368, West Simsbury, CT 06092 Tel 203-651-9756.
Titles:
Accounts Payable.
Accounts Receivable.
Bill of Materials-Routing.
General Ledger.
Integrated Manufacturing System.
Job Costing.
Material Requirements Planning.
Materials Inventory-Purchasing.
Order Entry-Invoicing.
Payroll.
Production Planning.
Quotation.
Shop Floor Control.
Tool Inventory.

Printers Software, Inc., (0-926288), 3665 Bee Ridge Rd., Suite 112, Sarasota, FL 34233 Tel 813-923-9010.
Titles:
Estimate.
Job Control.

Prism Enterprises, Inc., 14703-E Baltimore Ave., Suite 248, Laurel, MD 20707 Tel 301-604-6611; FAX: 301-604-6613.
Titles:
MacScan.
NetCounter.
ReadingEdge: O. C. R. Software.
TextScan.

Pro-Am Software, 551 Keystone Dr., Warrendale, PA 15086 Tel 412-776-1818; Toll free: 800-852-7316; FAX: 412-776-2263.
Titles:
Confined Space Entry Tracking.
The Director Plus Modules.
Rainbow Bar Code Data Collection Kits: Inspection-Scan, SCBA-Scan.
Rainbow Bar Code Data Collection Kits: SCBA-Scan, Inspection-Scan.
Rainbow MSDS Module.
Rainbow Safety.
Rainbow SARA Module.
The Safety Director.

Pro Data Systems, Inc., (0-926290), 13944 Cabana N., Corpus Christi, TX 78418 Tel 512-949-0333.
Titles:
Mega-Farming.
Personal Property Inventory.

Pro-Mation, Inc., Affil. of The Flagship Group, (0-926292), 5242 S. College Dr., Suite 200, Salt Lake City, UT 84123 Tel 801-261-8595; Toll free: 800-521-4562; FAX: 801-261-8599.
Titles:
Critical Path Scheduling.
The Pro-Mation Advantage: Accounts Payable.
The Pro-Mation Advantage: Accounts Receivable.
The Pro-Mation Advantage: Equipment Control.
The Pro-Mation Advantage: General Ledger.
The Pro-Mation Advantage: Inventory Control-Purchase Orders.
The Pro-Mation Advantage: Job Costing.
The Pro-Mation Advantage: Payroll.

Pro Plus Software, Inc., P.O. Box 4640, Scottsdale, AZ 85261-4640; FAX: 602-834-0461.
Titles:
Pro Plus Accounting.
Wall Street Commodities.
Wall Street Investor.

PRO Systems, Subs. of Procor, Inc., (0-918079), 6561 Gillis Dr., Suite 333, San Jose, CA 95120-4626 Tel 408-997-1776.
Titles:
SPORT!: Sports League Scheduler.
VEGAS CRAPS for Windows: Casino CRAPS Game.

Pro/Tem Software, (0-926295), 3790 El Camino Real, Suite 389, Palo Alto, CA 94306 Tel 415-323-4083; Toll free: 800-533-6922; FAX: 415-323-0611.
Titles:
NoteBuilder: The Cornerstone of Your Data.

Prodata, Inc., (0-926300), 3350 Americana Terr., Boise, ID 83706 Tel 208-342-6878. Do not confuse with Prodata Inc., Albuquerque, NM.
Titles:
Easyscreen-PC.
Insure.
KSAM-PC.

Prodata, Inc., (0-926299), 12101 Menaul Blvd., NE, Albuquerque, NM 87112 Tel 505-294-1530. Do not confuse with Prodata, Inc., Boise, ID.
Titles:
MJA Accounting.

Production Systems Technologies, Inc., 5001 Baum Blvd., Pittsburgh, PA 15213 Tel 412-683-4000.
Titles:
OPS/83.
OPS/83 for OS/2.

Productivity Computing Services, 1625 Waverly Rd., San Marino, CA 91108 Tel 818-281-7079.
Titles:
RATE: Risk Analysis Template Evaluation System.

Productivity Performance, Inc., 214 Colton St., Newport Beach, CA 92663 Tel 714-631-0515.
Titles:
Connex Professional Correspondence Manager.

Productivity Software International, Inc., 211 E. 43rd St. No 2202, New York, NY 10017-4707 Tel 212-818-1144; FAX: 212-818-1197.
Titles:
PRD+: (Productivity Plus).

Professional Computerware, (0-918681), Rte. 3, Box 20, Bloomfield, IN 47424.
Titles:
Apple II Security.
Chiropractic Data System.
The Librarian.

Professional Data Corp., (0-918083), 6449 Goldbranch Rd., Columbia, SC 29206 Tel 803-782-5376.
Titles:
ESTAX.
MFM/Medical Financial Management.

Professional Software, (0-926331), 21 Forest Ave., Glen Ridge, NJ 07028 Tel 201-748-7658; FAX: 201-680-9536.
Titles:
Acquisition Manager.
Circulation Manager.
Online Catalog.
Serial Control System.

Professional Software, Inc., (0-926334), 599 North Ave., No. 7, Wakefield, MA 01880-1616 Tel 617-246-2425; FAX: 617-246-1443.
Titles:
Fleet Check.
Fleet Filer.
Fleet System 2+.
Fleet System 3.
Fleet System 4.
Pro Tutor Accounting.
Write 'n' Spell.

Professor Corp., The, Affil. of Computerre, Inc. Canada, (0-87284), 3411 NW 21st St., Coconut Creek, FL 33066 Tel 305-977-0686; FAX: 305-977-5264.
Titles:
The Apple's Core: An Introduction to Applesoft Computer Programming.
The Apple's Core, Pt. II: The Seed.
The Apple's Core, Pt. III: Advanced BASIC.
DOS Helper.
Family Banking.

Family Cash Planning.
Multi-Lingual Word Processor: The Math & Science Disk.
Small Business Banking.
Small Business Cash Flow Planner.

Professor Jones Professional Handicapping Systems, (1-55604), 1940 W. State St., Boise, ID 83702 Tel 208-342-6939.
Titles:
Bookie Buster I Football Analysis.
Bookie Buster II Football Analysis.
Eleven Rule Greyhound.
Enhanced Gold Dog Analysis.
Enhanced Gold Dog with Track Management.
Enhanced Gold Horse - Thoroughbred.
Enhanced Gold Quarterhorse.
Enhanced Gold Thoroughbred with Track Management.
Enhanced Lottery/Lotto Analysis.
Enhanced Master Harness Handicapper with Track Management.
Football Addition.
Football Predictor with Data Base.
Football Predictor Without Data Base.
Gold Dog Analysis.
Gold Harness Handicapper.
Greyhound Professional Series Analysis Module.
Greyhound Professional Series Database Manager.
Greyhound Professional Series Factor Value Multiple Regression Module.
Greyhound Track Record Adjustor.
Limited Gold Dog Analysis.
Limited Gold Dog with Track Management.
Limited Gold Thoroughbred.
Limited Gold Thoroughbred with Track Management.
Limited Harness Handicapper.
Limited Harness Handicapper with Track Management.
LOT: Lottery Analysis.
Master Harness Handicapper Enhanced.
Master Harness Handicapper Limited.
Milano Quinella Analysis.
Mini-Pro Analysis Professional Series Thoroughbred Version.
NBA Basketball Addition.
NBA Basketball Analysis.
NBA Basketball Analysis with College Version.
Pro-Bookie Combo.
Professional Lottery/Lotto.
Professional Lottery-Lotto with ACS.
Professional Series Football.
Professor Pix Football.
Quarterhorse Gold Edition.
Statistical Lottery Analysis.
Statistical Lottery/Lotto Analysis.
System 21 Blackjack.
Thoroughbred Gold Edition.
Thoroughbred Professional Series Analysis Module.
Thoroughbred Professional Series Database Manager.
Thoroughbred Professional Series Factor Value Multiple Regression Module.
Track Simulator.
Trotter Professional Series Analysis Module.
Trotter Professional Series Database Manager.
Trotter Professional Series Factor Value Multiple Regression Module.
Ultra Gold Dog Analysis.
Ultra Gold Dog with Track Management.
Ultra Gold Thoroughbred.
Ultra Gold Thoroughbred with Track Management.
Ultra Harness Handicapper.
Ultra Harness Handicapper with Track Management.

Profile Technologies, Inc., 2350 Airport Freeway, Suite 200, Bedford, TX 76022 Tel 817-354-1704.
Titles:
The Profile.

Profitime, Inc., 22 Beaver St., Ambridge, PA 15003 Tel 412-266-4330; FAX: 412-266-4278.
Titles:
1120 Corporation.
1120S Subchapter S Corporation.
PACorp: PA Corp. Tax Returns.
Profitime/Plus: Professional Time & Billing.
ProfitTime Plus: Time & Billing.
1041 Fiduciary.
1065 Partnership.

Profitkey International, Inc., 382 Main St., Salem, NH 03079 Tel 603-898-9800; Toll free: 800-331-2754; FAX: 603-898-7554.
Titles:
Rapid Response Manufacturing System.

Program Systems, Inc., (0-926356), 2806 Ruffner Rd., No. 202, Birmingham, AL 35210-3927 Tel 205-956-9436; Toll free: 800-873-7744.
Titles:
The Fixed Asset Package.

Program Workshop, Inc., The, 301 Health Park Blvd., No. 328, St. Augustine, FL 32086 Tel 904-829-6500; FAX: 904-824-3989.
Titles:
MedQuest.

Programmed Pr., (0-916106), 599 Arnold Rd., West Hempstead, NY 11552 Tel 516-599-6527.
Titles:
Bonds & Interest Rates Software.
Commodities & Futures Package.
Computer-Assisted Investment: Handbook.
Foreign Exchange Software.
Investment Software.
Option Arbitrage Software.
Statistical Software for Forecasting.

Programmers & Analysts, Ltd., (0-928751), P.O. Box 3355, Oak Park, IL 60303 Tel 312-848-8623.
Titles:
Arena.
DCI: Dry Cleaner Inventory.

Progamming & Systems Management, Inc., (0-926361), 5257 Ackerman Blvd., Dayton, OH 45429 Tel 513-439-0228; FAX: 513-293-0230.
Titles:
TIPS.
TIPS-Dental S/W.
TIPS-Legal S/W.
TIPS-Medical S/W.

Progress Software Corp., (0-923562), 5 Oak Park, Bedford, MA 01730 Tel 617-275-4500; Toll free: 800-327-8445; FAX: 617-275-4595.
Titles:
LAN Progress.
Progress.
Progress D.
Progress: Database & 4GL Application Development System.
Progress Fast Track.

Progressive Peripherals & Software, Inc., (0-941689), 4026 Youngfield St., Wheat Ridge, CO 80033-3862.
Titles:
Access-64.
CLImate.
DiskMaster.
Dr. Term Professional.
IntroCAD.
Math-Amation.
Microlawyer.
Pixmate.
UltraCAD.
Vizawrite for the Amiga.
Vizawrite PC.

ProGroup, (0-922906), P.O. Box 349, Sedro-Woolley, WA 98284 Tel 206-855-1031; Toll free: 800-772-4545.
Titles:
Bionutritional Blood Analysis.
P S Graph.
Practice Star.

Project Control Systems, 13000 SW Foothill Dr., Portland, OR 97225-4850 Tel 503-644-3572.
Titles:
PlanFlow.

Project Dimensions, Inc., 5 Park Plaza, Suite 1170, Irvine, CA 92714 Tel 714-476-2246.
Titles:
Schedule Graphics II: Software for Bar Chart Schedules.

Prolific, Inc., 1808 W. Southgate Ave., Fullerton, CA 92633 Tel 714-447-8792; FAX: 714-522-5655.
Titles:
Pro-Board.
Pro-Net.

Promark, Ltd., 6207 Pan American Freeway, NE, Albuquerque, NM 87109 Tel 505-345-7701; FAX: 505-344-0189.
Titles:
Control Panel.
MAI Integrated Accounting Software.

Prose Software, Subs. of Noland & Assocs., (0-926377), 2921 Brown Trail, Suite 230, Bedford, TX 76021 Tel 817-656-5927; FAX: 817-656-5928.
Titles:
Dental-Rx: Dental Office Management System.
Medi-Rx: Medical Office Management for Anesthesiology.
Medi-Rx: Medical Office Management System.
Medi-RX: Office Management System for Podiatry.
Medi-Rx: Oral & Maxillo Facial Office Management System.

Protosoft, P.O. Box 16756, Seattle, WA 98116 Tel 206-628-0791.
Titles:
Idea-Tree.
PC-Date.

Protronics Computer Systems, 499 Northside Cir. NW, Suite 420, Atlanta, GA 30309-2112 Tel 404-351-1055; FAX: 404-605-0865.
Titles:
Personal Best: The Mental Breakfast of Champions.
WinJokes: The Greatest Joke Collection of All Time.

Provue Development Corp., (0-928280), 18411 Gothard St. Unita, Huntington Beach, CA 92648 Tel 714-841-7779; FAX: 714-841-1479.
Titles:
DataVUE.
OverVUE.
OverVue Mail Manager Template.
Panorama.
SuperVUE.

PUBLISHER/TITLE INDEX

Proximity Technology, Inc., Subs. of Franklin Computer Corp., (0-926390), 3511 NE 22nd Ave., Fort Lauderdale, FL 33308 Tel 305-566-3511; Toll free: 800-323-0023; FAX: 305-566-2088.
Titles:
Friendly Finder.
Language Master.
Webster's Electronic Thesaurus.

PSG-HomeCraft Software, Div. of HCP Services, Inc., P.O. Box 974, Tualatin, OR 97062 Tel 503-692-3732; FAX: 503-692-0382.
Titles:
Complete Catalog of Forty-Fives.
I'm Out - Screen Saver - Business Version.
I'm Out - Screen Saver - Personal Version.
A Little Painter.
Mega Guide to LPs.
Megaguide to CDs.
Megaguide to LPs.
Megaguide to Singles.
Organize! Your Art Collection.
Organize! Your Books & Magazines.
Organize! Your Books & Magazines in Windows.
Organize! Your Business.
ORGANIZE! Your Business - Industrial Version.
Organize! Your CDs & Albums in Windows.
Organize! Your Classical Music.
Organize! Your Coin Collection.
Organize! Your Coin Collection in Windows.
Organize! Your Comic Books.
Organize! Your Fabrics (for Sewing).
Organize! Your Guns.
Organize! Your Home (Home Inventory).
Organize! Your Home in Windows.
Organize! Your Jazz Collection.
Organize! Your Memorabilia.
Organize! Your Model Railroad.
Organize! Your Music.
Organize! Your Phone Cards in Windows.
Organize! Your Photographs & Slides.
Organize! Your Plants & Garden.
Organize! Your Professional Books.
Organize! Your Sports Cards - Windows Version.
Organize! Your Stamp Collection.
Organize! Your Stamps in Windows.
Organize! Your Token Collection.
Organize! Your Video Games in Windows.
Organize! Your Video Tapes.
Organize! Your Video Tapes in Windows.
Organize! Your Wines.
PC-Bartender for Windows.
PhotoRobot.
Play 'n' Learn in Windows.
Rhino Records Catalog, 1995.
Special Occasion Fax (aka Fax from Santa).
Your Financial Advisor.
Your Personal Legal Guide.

Psion, Inc., Subs. of Psion PLC, 555 Virginia Rd., No. 5CONC, Concord, MA 01742-2727; Toll free: 800-548-4535; FAX: 203-274-7976.
Titles:
Psion Chess.

PsychStat, (0-9631763), 1003 Justin Ln., No. 2118, Austin, TX 78757 Tel 512-451-8152.
Titles:
PsychStat MAX 2.11: Psychometric - Statistical Programs.

PsyLogic Systems, (0-945317), P.O. Box 315, Tolland, CT 06084.
Titles:
An Electronic Holmes Companion.

Publishing International, P.O. Box 70790, Sunnyvale, CA 94086-0790 Tel 408-738-4311; FAX: 408-773-1791. Do not confuse with Publishing International, Williamsville, NY.
Titles:
Hometown U. S. A.

Publishing Solutions/MacTography, 15927 Indian Hills Terr., Derwood, MD 20855-2626.
Titles:
PostScript Type: Volumes 1-17.

Pugh-Roberts Assocs., Inc., (0-926398), 41 Linskey Way, Cambridge, MA 02142-1104 Tel 617-864-8880; FAX: 617-661-7418.
Titles:
Professional DYNAMO Plus.

Puma Software, Inc., P.O. Box 35373, Albuquerque, NM 87176 Tel 505-296-0950.
Titles:
Matrix Workshop.

Pyramid Media Group, (0-944188), 168 Prospect Ave., Sea Cliff, NY 11579 Tel 516-674-0769.
Titles:
Airline 500: A Buyer's Guide.
Commercial Aircraft: History & Specifications.

QAX International Systems Corp., (0-923001), 4273 Cavehill Rd., Spring Hill, FL 34606 Tel 904-596-2090.
Titles:
Inquiry Action Express: Salesman's Marketing & Management.
PC-Advantage.
SuperSPREADing.
3*16 Word Processor.
WISEMAN.

Q-M Consulting Group, Inc., 141 Fifth Ave., New York, NY 10010 Tel 212-995-5287; FAX: 212-995-5415.
Titles:
Q-M Secure/Net.
QM Filer for FoxPro: FoxPro File Manager.
The QM Library for FoxPro.

Quadmation, Inc., 1120 Stewart Court, Suite L, Sunnyvale, CA 94086 Tel 408-733-5557; Toll free: 800-733-5557; FAX: 408-733-1938.
Titles:
Mac Personal Class.

Quadratron Systems, Inc., (0-926417), 31368 Via Colinas, No. 108, Westlake Village, CA 91362-3917 Tel 818-865-6655; FAX: 818-865-6644.
Titles:
CliqAccessories.
CliqCalc.
CliqDCA.
CliqPage.
CliqWord.

Quadtel Corp., 2575 McCabe Way, Irvine, CA 92714-6243.
Titles:
QMAPS: Premium Memory Management for 386-486.
UMB Pro: High Memory Loader & Extended Memory Mgr.

Qualitas, Inc., 8314 Thoreau Dr., Bethesda, MD 20817 Tel 301-469-8848.
Titles:
386 MAX.
386MAX Professional.

Qualitas Trading Co., 2029 Durant Ave., Berkeley, CA 94704-1512 Tel 510-848-8080; FAX: 510-848-8009.
Titles:
EGWord.
Excel-Japanese.
JapanEase, Vol. 1: Katakana.
JapanEase, Vol. 2: Hiragana Grammar.
MacKojien.
Pagemaker-Japanese.
Rodin-Matisse Fonts.
Word Hunter.

Quality America, Inc., (0-930011), 7650 E. Broadway, Tucson, AZ 85710 Tel 602-722-6701; Toll free: 800-729-0867; FAX: 602-722-6705.
Titles:
DOE - PC IV.
SPC-PC II.
SPC-PC IV.

QUANT IX Software, 5900 N. Port Washington Rd., No. 142A, Milwaukee, WI 53217 Tel 414-961-1991; Toll free: 800-247-6354.
Titles:
QUANT IX Portfolio Evaluator.

Quantic Corp., 21 Mount Airy Rd., Pipersville, PA 18947-1631.
Titles:
Touch 'n Go.

Quantitative Micro Software, (1-880411), 4521 Campus Dr., No. 336, Irvine, CA 92715 Tel 714-856-3368; FAX: 714-856-2044.
Titles:
MicroTSP: For Macintosh.
MicroTSP: For PC Compatibles.

Quantitative Software Management, Inc., (0-926426), 1057 Waverly Way, McLean, VA 22101 Tel 703-790-0055; FAX: 703-749-3795.
Titles:
PADS: Productivity Analysis Database System.
Size Planner.
SLIM: Software LifeCycle Management.

Quark, Inc., (0-926432), 1800 Grant St., Denver, CO 80203 Tel 303-894-8888; Toll free: 800-788-7835; FAX: 303-894-3399.
Titles:
QuarkXPress.

Quarterdeck Office Systems, (0-926433), 150 Pico Blvd., Santa Monica, CA 90405 Tel 310-392-9851; Toll free: 800-354-3222 (orders only); FAX: 310-314-4219.
Titles:
API C Library.
API Reference.
DESQview Companions 1: Calculator, Datebook, Link, Notepad.
DESQview: The Multi-Window Software Integrator.
QEMM 7.

Que, Div. of Prentice Hall Computer Publishing, (0-88022; 1-56529; 0-7897), 201 W. 103rd St., Indianapolis, IN 46290-1094 Tel 317-581-3500; Toll free: 800-428-5331; FAX: 317-573-2583. Do not confuse with Que Software, also a division of Prentice Hall Computer Publishing, same address.
Titles:
1-2-3 Macro Library, 3rd Edition.
1-2-3 Release 3 Business Applications.
Using Microsoft Word 5: IBM Version.
Using Microsoft Word: 4.
Using 1-2-3 Workbook & Disk, 2nd Edition.

Que Software, Div. of Prentice Hall Computer Publishing, (0-929964), 201 W. 103rd St., Indianapolis, IN 46290-1094 Tel 317-573-2500; FAX: 317-573-2656. Do not confuse with Que, also a division of Prentice Hall Computer Publishing, same address.
Titles:
RightWords: RightWriter Dictionary Utility.
RightWriter.

QuesTech, Inc., (0-926440), 7600 Leesburg Pike No. A, Falls Church, VA 22043-2004; Toll free: 800-336-0354.
Titles:
FORTH-32.
It's My Business (with Simplex).

Queue, Inc., (0-87200; 0-87492; 0-7827), 338 Commerce Dr., Fairfield, CT 06430 Tel 203-335-0908; Toll free: 800-232-2224; FAX: 203-336-2481.
Titles:
Q-Art.

Quilt Computing, 7048 Stratford Rd., Woodbury, MN 55125 Tel 612-739-4650.
Titles:
MacSRMS.

QuinnEssentials, Inc., 141 Fifth Ave., New York, NY 10010 Tel 212-995-5287; FAX: 212-995-5415.
Titles:
The Five A's.

Quinsept, Inc., (0-917169), P.O. Box 216, Lexington, MA 02173 Tel 617-862-0404; Toll free: 800-637-7668; FAX: 617-860-0550.
Titles:
Family Connections.
Family Links.
Family Roots.
Lineages.
Lineages/Advanced.
Lineages/Standard.
Tree Charts.

Quintus Computer Systems, Inc., 47212 Mission Falls Ct., Fremont, CA 94539-7820.
Titles:
FLEX (Forward-Chaining Logical EXpert) System Toolkit.
MacProlog.
Quintus Prolog for IBM PS/2.
Quintus Prolog For 80386.

Quistory, Ltd., (0-9642091), P.O. Box 1064, Beverly Hills, CA 90213-1064; FAX: 310-659-2774; 8316 Melrose Ave., Los Angeles, CA 90069 Tel 213-782-1390; Dist. by: Inland Bk. Co., 140 Commerce St., East Haven, CT 06512 Tel 203-467-4257; Toll free: 800-243-0138.
Titles:
Queers in History Classic.
Queers in History Deluxe.

R & M Assocs., (0-926458), P.O. Box 377, Sea Girt, NJ 08750 Tel 201-449-2210.
Titles:
Capgain.
Portfol1.
Yields-1.

REMsoft, Inc., (0-926471), 571 E. 185th St., Euclid, OH 44119 Tel 216-531-1338; FAX: 216-481-6483.
Titles:
REMDISK-1.
Rural Water Billing.

REPDATA, (0-926472), 59 Middlesex Tpke. SR 300, Bedford, MA 01730 Tel 617-275-0355.
Titles:
REPDATA System.

RG Software Systems, Inc., 6900 E. Camelback Rd., No. 630, Scottsdale, AZ 85251 Tel 602-423-8000; FAX: 602-423-8389.
Titles:
No More #*!$ Viruses.
Vi-Spy Professional Edition.
Vi-Spy Universal NIM: Network Installable Module.

RIX SoftWorks, Inc., 17811 Sky Park Cir., No. B, Irvine, CA 92714-6109; Toll free: 800-345-9059; 800-235-3754; FAX: 714-476-8486; 3053 Church St., Burlington, NC 27215 Tel 910-584-4886.
Titles:
ColoRIX-VGA Paint.

RJG Software & Training, 126 Fox Run Cir., Clarks Summit, PA 18411 Tel 717-586-2316.
Titles:
Lotus Demo & Exercise Set: Release 4.

RJL Systems, 106 New Haven Ave., Milford, CT 06460 Tel 203-878-0376.
Titles:
The Baseball Statbook.
The Basketball Statbook.
The Football Statbook.
Mr. QuarterMaster.
Mr. QuarterMaster Jr.
The PriceBook.
The Sports Statbook.

RPH Assocs., (0-918101), P.O. Box 1155, Weston, CT 06883 Tel 203-227-7970.
Titles:
Converticalc.

R Plus R Assocs., Inc., 154 E. Boston Post Rd., Mamaroneck, NY 10543 Tel 914-698-1232.
Titles:
Shoebox 3.

RR Software, Inc., (0-926479), P.O. Box 1512, Madison, WI 53701 Tel 608-251-3133; Toll free: 800-722-3248; FAX: 608-276-6009.
Titles:
JANUS-Ada AdaVid.
The JANUS-Ada B-Pak Tools Kit: Development Package.
JANUS-Ada Compiler.
JANUS-Ada Cross Compilers.
The JANUS-Ada Pascal to Ada Translator (PASTRAN).

RTG Data Systems, (0-918103), 2665 30th St., Suite 105, Santa Monica, CA 90405 Tel 310-399-6452.
Titles:
LTB: Legal Time & Billing.
Softfile: A Memory Enhancer.

RTR Software, Inc., (0-926484), 19 W. Hargett St., No. 204, Raleigh, NC 27601 Tel 919-829-0786; FAX: 919-829-0891.
Titles:
TechniFilter Plus.

RWB Assocs., (0-926486), 5112 River Ave., Newport Beach, CA 92663 Tel 714-631-2683.
Titles:
RWB Answer.

Rabbit Software Corp., 7 Great Valley Pkwy., E., Malvern, PA 19355 Tel 610-647-0440; Toll free: 800-722-2482; FAX: 610-640-1379.
Titles:
APPC-PLUS.
DIA-PLUS.
RJE-PLUS.
SNA Gateway.
3270-PLUS.

Radian Corp., Subs. of Hartford Steam Boiler Inspection & Insurance Co., P.O. Box 201088, Austin, TX 78720-1088 Tel 512-454-4797; FAX: 512-450-0583.
Titles:
CHARM.
CPS/PC.
Sam.

Radio Shack, Div. of Tandy Corp., (1-55508), 1800 One Tandy Ctr., Fort Worth, TX 76102 Tel 817-390-3011; FAX: 817-390-2774.
Titles:
DeskMate.

Raima Corp., (0-928469), 1605 NW Sammamish Rd., No. 200, Issaquah, WA 98027-5378 Tel 206-557-0200; Toll free: 800-327-2462; FAX: 206-557-5200.
Titles:
db—QUERY.
Raima Database Manager.
Raima Database Manager Plus Plus.
Raima Database Manager System.
Raima Database Server: Client-Server Database Engine.
Raima Object Manager.
Velocis Database Server.

Raised Dot Computing, Inc., 408 S. Baldwin St., Madison, WI 53703 Tel 608-257-9595; Toll free: 800-347-9594; FAX: 608-257-4143.
Titles:
BEX.
Flipper.
MegaDots.

Ram/Tek, 2580 Azurite Cir., Newbury Park, CA 91320-1201; Toll free: 800-338-5952.
Titles:
RamCam.

Rambow Enterprises, (0-926496), 200 W. 34th Ave., Suite 410, Anchorage, AK 99503 Tel 907-272-9484.
Titles:
Boring Logs.
Construction Estimating.
Health Care: Patient Management.
Job Costing.
Maintenance Management.
Parts Inventory.
Parts Inventory (Warehouse Version).

Ranac Computer Corp., (0-926499), 4181 E. 96th St., Suite 280, Indianapolis, IN 46240 Tel 317-844-0141; Toll free: 800-844-0141; FAX: 317-848-2269.
Titles:
CompreMED.

Random Access, 62 Birdsall St., Greene, NY 13778 Tel 607-656-7584.
Titles:
Front Desk.
Letterip.
Lettertip.
Newsflow.

Random Hse., Inc., (0-394; 0-676; 0-375; 0-679; 0-87665), Random Hse. Publicity, (11-6), 201 E. 50th St., 22nd Flr., New York, NY 10022 Tel 212-751-2600; Toll free: 800-733-3000 (orders); 800-726-0600 (credit, inquiries, customer service); Orders to: 400 Hahn Rd., Westminster, MD 21157 Tel 410-848-1900.
Titles:
APBA Major League Players Baseball.
Peanuts Picture Puzzlers.
Tournament Bridge: Competition & Practice for the Serious Bridge Player.

Random Hse. Schl. Div., Div. of Random Hse., Inc., (0-394; 0-676), 201 E. 50th St., New York, NY 10022 Tel 212-751-2600; FAX: 212-872-8026; Orders to: 400 Hahn Rd., Westminster, MD 21157 Tel 410-848-1900; Toll free: 800-733-3000 (orders).
Titles:
Peanuts Math Matcher.
Peanuts Maze Marathon.
Shifty Sam.
Thwart!

PUBLISHER/TITLE INDEX

II Write.

Rapha Group Software, Inc., (0-925214), 433 Carson Rd.,, Saint Louis, MO 63135 Tel 314-521-0808.
Titles:
Blood Gas Consultant 2.0.
Byte 'N Bass.
Drug Master Plus.
Script Consultant.

Rapp Industries, Inc., (0-924790), 885 Lincoln Ave., Glen Rock, NJ 07452 Tel 201-670-9084; Toll free: 800-999-1159; FAX: 201-444-4595.
Titles:
Menu Costing System.
Restaurant Financial Management System: RFMS.

Rational Software Corp., 2800 San Tomas Expressway, Santa Clara, CA 95051 Tel 408-496-3600; FAX: 408-496-3636.
Titles:
Rational Apex.
The Rational Environment.

Rational Systems, Inc., 220 N. Main St., Natick, MA 01760 Tel 508-653-6006; Toll free: 800-666-2585; FAX: 508-655-2753.
Titles:
Instant-C.

Raxco, Inc., 2440 Research Blvd., Suite 200, Rockville, MD 20850 Tel 301-258-2620; Toll free: 800-284-7832; FAX: 301-330-5756; 371 E. 800 S., Orem, UT 84058 Tel 801-227-3768; 420 Bedford St., Lexington, MA 02173 Tel 617-861-6262; 12007 Sunrise Valley Dr., Reston, VA 22091 Tel 703-715-9251.
Titles:
ArchiveCommand.
AUDIT: Background User Session Monitoring.
CALOUT PLUS: Computer-to-Computer Communications.
CARBONCopy.
ClydeSENTRY.
ClydeSupport.
CONTRL: Security Monitoring.
DataLock.
DIALBACK: Secures Dial-in Lines.
FRAMER: Display Document Files.
INSTRUCTOR.
KBLock.
PerfectCache: File Caching & Virtual Disk.
PerfectDisk: Disk Defragmentation & Optimization.
PerfectTune: Dynamic Online System Tuning.
Rabbit-8 Report Architect: (R-8).
Rabbit-9 VAX Acceleration Software Technology.
RABBIT-1: Resource Accounting, Auditory & Billing System.
RABBIT-2: System Performance-Capacity Planning.
Rabbit-2 VMS Know-It-All.
RABBIT-5: High Speed VMS Archiving Backup.
RABBIT-7: Disk Optimizer.
RaxManager: Resource Management System.
RaxMaster: Comprehensive Performance Enhancement Solution.
The Security Toolkit: System Security Assessment.
SystemCommand: System Management Assistant.
TapeControl: Tape Management.
TapeConvert: EBCDIC-ASCII Data Conversion.
TaskCommand: Job Scheduler.
WINDOW: Multi Terminal Sessions.

Raxsoft, Inc., (1-884379), 1781 Barcelona St., Livermore, CA 94550 Tel 510-449-9079; Toll free: 800-377-4686; FAX: 510-449-3519.
Titles:
Picture Factory Set 1.

Rays Computers & Energy, (0-936561), 169 NW 44th St., No. L-9, Fort Lauderdale, FL 33309-3923 Tel 305-946-4160; FAX: 305-946-5113.
Titles:
Degree Day Handler.
Energy Owl.
Professional Energy Analyst Deluxe.

ReadiWare Systems, Inc., (0-926516), P.O. Box 413, Rapid City, MI 49676-0413.
Titles:
ReadiWriter.

Real-Comp, Inc., (0-926518), P.O. Box 1210, Cupertino, CA 95015 Tel 408-996-1160.
Titles:
Real Analyzer.
Real Property Management II.

Real-E-Data, Inc., (0-918107), 2634 S. Carrier Pkwy., Suite 107, Grand Prairie, TX 75052 Tel 214-660-1373; Toll free: 800-543-8992.
Titles:
Real-t-PRO.

Real Soft Systems, Inc., (0-926523; 0-918109), 1722 14th St., No. 200, Boulder, CO 80302 Tel 303-442-2855; Toll free: 800-999-9595; FAX: 303-442-3608.
Titles:
RealSoft Integrated Appraisal System.

Real-Time Computer Science Corp., (0-926483), 1273 S. Rice Rd. No. 49, Ojai, CA 93023-3468.
Titles:
AT-RTX.
C86.
Pascal 86.
PC-RTX.
RTCS-iSIM85: 8085 ISIS II Simulator.
RTCS-UDI: Universal Development Interface.
RTX 286: Real-Time Multitasking OS.

RealData, Inc., (0-926529), 78 N. Main St., South Norwalk, CT 06854 Tel 203-838-2670; Toll free: 800-899-6060; FAX: 203-852-9083.
Titles:
Commercial-Industrial Real Estate Applications.
Comparative Lease Analysis.
Real Estate Connections.
On Schedule.
Property Management III.
Real Estate Investment Analysis.
Residential Real Estate Tools.

Realsoft, Inc., (0-926531), 1305 Rio Vista, Fort Myers, FL 33901 Tel 813-936-5145.
Titles:
Amortizer.
Cash Flow Pro.
Land Investor.

Realty Software, (0-926534), P.O. Box 4285, Park City, UT 84060 Tel 801-649-6149.
Titles:
APR Loan Analysis.
Construction Cost-Profit.
Home Purchase.
Income Property Analysis.
Loan Amortization.
Loan Sales/Purchase.
Maintenance Manager.
Property Listings Comparables.
Property Management.
Property Management Plus.
Property Managers Option.
Property Sale.
REAP Plus: Real Estate Analysis Program.
Tax Deferred Exchange.

REGISTER DATA SYSTEMS

RealWorld Corp., (0-926537), P.O. Box 9516, Manchester, NH 03108-9516 Tel 603-641-0200; Toll free: 800-678-6336; FAX: 603-641-0232.
Titles:
CashTrax Point of Sale.
FAS - Fixed Assets.
FAS2000.
IQ Report Writer.
Job Cost Accounting Software.
Real World Sales Analysis.
RealWorld Accounting & Business System.
RealWorld Accounts Payable.
RealWorld Accounts Receivable.
RealWorld Check Reconciliation.
RealWorld General Ledger.
RealWorld Inventory Control.
RealWorld Order Entry-Billing.
RealWorld Payroll.
RealWorld Professional Invoicing.
RealWorld Professional Time & Billing.
RealWorld Purchase Order.
RealWorld Sales Management Solutions.

Reco, Inc., 8649 W. 45th St., Lyons, IL 60534 Tel 708-447-6177; Toll free: 708-447-9303; FAX: 708-447-9307.
Titles:
General Ledger File.
Payroll Ease: Reco, Inc. Payroll System.

Recycling Insights, c/o CPM, Inc., 8317 Scott Ave., N., Brooklyn Park, MN 55443-2226.
Titles:
SWPlan.

Red Wing Business Systems, Inc., (0-87265; 0-932250; 0-924340), P.O. Box 19, Hwy. 19, Red Wing, MN 55066 Tel 612-388-1106; Toll free: 800-732-9464; FAX: 612-388-7950.
Titles:
AgCHEK Accounting.
Asset Depreciation.
Red Wing Accounts Payable.
Red Wing Accounts Receivable.
Red Wing Business Inventory System.
Red Wing Cow-Calf Production System.
Red Wing General Ledger.
Red Wing Payroll.
Red Wing Project Cost.
SwineTRAK.

Reference Software International, (0-9626212), 1555 N. Technology Way, No. CA343-09, Orem, UT 84057-2395 Tel 801-225-5000; Toll free: 800-872-9933; FAX: 801-228-5077.
Titles:
Grammatik Mac.
Grammatik UNIX.
Grammatik V.
Grammatik Windows 2.0.

Regents/ALA Co., Subs. of American Language Academy, (0-934270), 1401 Rockville Pike, Suite 550, Rockville, MD 20852 Tel 301-309-1400; Toll free: 800-346-3469; FAX: 301-309-0202.
Titles:
ALA Lab System.

Register Data Systems, P.O. Box 980, 404 General C. Hodges Blvd., Perry, GA 31069 Tel 912-987-2501; Toll free: 800-521-5222; FAX: 912-987-7595.
Titles:
RDS System Seven.
RDS System Six.
RDS Traffic Master I.
RDS Traffic Master II.
RDS Traffic Master III.

Rehi Bks., (0-938273), 734 McGill Dr., Rochester, MI 48309 Tel 810-375-0629; Orders to: 54 N. Adams, Suite 130-R, Rochester Hills, MI 48309.
Titles:
8088 Tutor Monitor: IBM PC-8088 Assembly Language Programming.

Reichert Digital Systems, (0-926554), P.O. Box 2046, Brevard, NC 28712-2046.
Titles:
Complete Personal Accounting (CPA).

Relational Database Systems, Inc., (0-926556), 4100 Bohannon Dr., Menlo Park, CA 94025 Tel 415-926-6300.
Titles:
C-ISAM.
File-It!
Informix.
INFORMIX-ESQL/C.
INFORMIX-SQL.

Relational Technology, (0-926559), 1 Computer Associate Plaza, Islandia, NY 11788-7000 Tel 516-342-5224; Toll free: 800-446-4737.
Titles:
INGRES.

Relationship Software, (1-887867), 1393 W. 9000 S., Suite 348, West Jordan, UT 84088 Tel 801-253-2252; FAX: 801-235-7099.
Titles:
Exciting Experiences of Love.
More Loveplay.

Relative Value Studies, Inc., (1-879298), P.O. Box 6431, Denver, CO 80206; 180 Cook St., Suite 110, Denver, CO 80206 Tel 303-329-9787.
Titles:
Relative Values for Dentists.

Reliable Software & Consulting, P.O. Box 335, Fort Calhoun, NE 68023 Tel 402-468-5700.
Titles:
Reliable Salon System.

Remote Measurement Systems, Inc., 2633 Eastlake Ave., Suite 200, Seattle, WA 98102 Tel 206-328-2255; FAX: 206-328-1787.
Titles:
ADControl.

Research Design Assocs., Inc., (0-940503), 35 Crooked Hill Rd., Suite 200, Commack, NY 11725 Tel 516-499-0053; Toll free: 800-654-8715; FAX: 516-499-0389.
Titles:
Bati-Texte: French Storyboard.
Crossword Challenge.
Crossword Master.
Double Up.
DROPIN.
Rapid Recall II.
RHUBARB: A Text Reconstruction Tool.
Test Defier: The Business Letter.
Text Tanglers.

Research Engineers, Inc., (0-922920), 22700 Savi Ranch Pkwy., Yorba Linda, CA 92687-4613 Tel 714-974-2500; Toll free: 800-367-7373; FAX: 714-974-4771.
Titles:
AutoCIVIL.
AutoProject.
CadPLUS 3D.
COGO PC Plus: Coordinate Geometry Program.
CONTOUR Plus: Contour Plotting Program.
HDP: Highway Design Program.
HEC-1.
HEC-2.
SEWER: Sewer Design & Analysis Program.
STAAD-III.
Stardyne.
Storm Plus: Storm Drain Analysis Program.
WATER.

Resolutions Now, P.O. Box 443, Blue Island, IL 60406-0443 Tel 312-994-6450; FAX: 312-994-6450.
Titles:
GeeWiz: Wizard Maker.
Raffle Do.

Resort Data Processing, Inc., (0-926571), 1650 E. Vail Valley Dr., Suite C-1, Vail, CO 81657 Tel 303-476-9244.
Titles:
Condominium Control System: Reservations Only, Front Desk, General Ledger, Accounts Payable & Owner Billing & Receivables, Group-Company Billing, Guest History, Enhanced Report Writer.
Hotel Control System (HCS).
Inn Control System (ICS).
Timeshare Condominium System (TCS).
Vacation Rental System (VRS).

Resource Analysis International Corp., 1125 Cardiff Ave., Apt. 4, Los Angeles, CA 90035-1336 Tel 310-390-7661; Toll free: 800-877-6788.
Titles:
Compile 1-to-C.

Resource Control Systems Corp., (0-926573), 99 Park Ave., 9th Flr., New York, NY 10016 Tel 212-697-0735.
Titles:
Placement Power.

Resource Optimization, Inc., 1685 Chevron Way, Atlanta, GA 30350-4431 Tel 404-394-8125; FAX: 404-394-3526.
Titles:
The Least Cost Formulator.

Resource Software International, Inc., Affil. of Datamatics Management, (0-87539), 330 New Brunswick Ave., Fords, NJ 08863 Tel 908-738-8500; Toll free: 800-673-0366; FAX: 908-738-9603.
Titles:
Bond Value.
Breakeven Analysis.
Building Cost Analysis.
Depreciation Comparison.
Executive's Time Value.
Financial Ratio Calculations.
Installment Loan Payment.
Interest Rate Calculation.
Internal Rate of Return.
Lease-Buy Analysis.
Professional Marketing System: Prospect Ranking.
Return on Investment Analysis.
Sales Plot.
TC-1.

RestaurantComp, 5 Echo Pl., Larkspur, CA 94939 Tel 415-924-6300; FAX: 415-924-6399.
Titles:
Recipe Profit Analyzer.
Restaurant Comp.
Restaurant Inventory & Food Cost.
Sales & Food Cost Analyzer.

Resuba Digital Systems, (0-926577), P.O. Box 440, Dept. 9, Blackwood, NJ 08012 Tel 609-228-5666.
Titles:
Flip-Ello.
Resuba Disk Utilities.
Resuba Print-Switch Utility.
Resuba Print Utilities.
Resuba Screen Utilities.
Resuba XT-Lock Utility.

RetailFORCE, Inc., (0-922959), P.O. Box 399, Bloomfield Hills, MI 48303 Tel 810-332-4536.
Titles:
ColorBIZ Biorhythm.
ColorBIZ Gambler.
ColorBIZ Inventory.
ColorBIZ Loan.
RetailFORCE.

Rettke Resources, (0-926567), 630 Riverview Ln., Appleton, WI 54915-1272 Tel 414-749-9447.
Titles:
APT-ZAP.
DUMP: Hex-ASCII Memory Dump.
DUSC: Disk Utility Sort Catalog.
NFC: Non-Flashing Cursor.
Padlock.
Zapt.

Revelation Technologies, Inc., (0-923387), 181 Harbor Dr., Stamford, CT 06902 Tel 203-973-1000; Toll free: 800-262-4747; FAX: 206-975-8744.
Titles:
Advanced Revelation.
Advanced Revelation: Runtime.

Reynolds, Raymond L., (0-926587), 384 Hyacinth St., Fall River, MA 02720 Tel 508-673-4968.
Titles:
Banner Printer.
Bartender's Friend.
Bowler.
Home Inventory Management.
Mailer.
Municipal Accounting Package: General Ledger, Accounts Payable, Budget.
Pilot Interpreter.
PRINT to LPRINT & LPRINT to PRINT Utilities.
Simultaneous PRINT & LPRINT.

Rhintek, Inc., (0-918113), P.O. Box 220, Columbia, MD 21045-0220 Tel 410-730-2575; FAX: 410-730-5960.
Titles:
EMU/470 Data General Terminal Emulator for IBM Micros & Personal Computers.
EMU 220.
Rhintek Pascal Compiler.
Rhintek Plot Package.

Rhode Island Dept. of Health, (0-926589), 75 Davis St., Providence, RI 02908 Tel 401-277-6957.
Titles:
Wellness Check.

Richcal Computing Services, (0-926593), 607 Holmes Ave., Placentia, CA 92670 Tel 714-996-6506.
Titles:
Sonshine Software for Amway Distributors.

Richmond Software Corp., (0-929963), 3960 Fallbrook Dr., Duluth, GA 30136 Tel 404-623-4898; Toll free: 800-222-6063.
Titles:
Mac the Librarian.

Right Answers Group, The, Box 3699, Torrance, CA 90510 Tel 310-325-1311.
Titles:
The Director.

RIGHT ON PROGRAMS, Div. of Computeam, Inc., (0-87132; 1-55812), 755 New York Ave., Huntington, NY 11743 Tel 516-424-7777; FAX: 516-424-7207.
Titles:
Collectibles Manager.
Equipment Scheduler.
EZ Ledger.

PUBLISHER/TITLE INDEX

Home Library Catalog.
Interlibrary Loan Control.
Interlibrary Loan Manager.
Item Inventory & Tracking.
Magazine Article Filer.
MARC Record Reader.
On-Line Catalog Expanded.
On-Line Catalog with Carder.
Outward Bound: Book Delivery Manager for the Housebound.
Outward Bound for Shut Ins.
Overdue Books Manager.
Periodical Indexing Manager.
Periodical Manager.
Personnel Scheduler.
Records Management Control.
Subscription Manager.
Super Carder.
Super Carder Expanded.
Super Circulation Control Expanded.
Super Circulation Control with Carder.
Supplies Inventory & Tracking.

Rim Software, 58 Strong Rd., West Granby, CT 06090-1211 Tel 203-653-5656.
Titles:
Sum!Table.

Ringling Multimedia Corp., (1-888489), 1753 Northgate Blvd., Sarasota, FL 34234 Tel 941-355-2201; FAX: 941-358-8802.
Titles:
Let's Pretend: Our World Is a Playground.

Ritam International, Ltd., (0-926598), P.O. Box 1180, Fairfield, IA 52556 Tel 515-472-8262; FAX: 515-472-5524.
Titles:
MONTY Plays Monopoly.
MONTY Plays Scrabble.

River City Software, Inc., (0-926601; 0-934453), 2836 Melhollin Dr., Jacksonville, FL 32216 Tel 904-737-0687.
Titles:
Annuity Table.
Appointment Calendar.
Bond Computation.
Call Option Writing.
Investment Club I.
Investment Club II.
Mailing List.
Mailing List & Appointment Calendar.
Personal Investment Package.
Sports Memorabilia.
Survey Calc I.

Riverdale Software, Inc., 10501 Riverdale, SE, Middleville, MI 49333 Tel 616-891-1859.
Titles:
MacLocus.

Riverdale Systems Design, Inc., (0-939545), P.O. Box 25, New Milford, NJ 07646-0025 Tel 201-836-5170; FAX: 201-836-6707.
Titles:
The Entrepreneur's Financial Workplate.
The Entrepreneur's Inventory Workplate.
The Entrepreneur's Marketing Workplate.
The Entrepreneur's Personnel Workplate.
The Entrepreneur's Sales Workplate.
The Hospital Financial Workplate.
The Hospital Market Workplate.
The Hospital Medical Staff Workplate.
The Hospital Space Planning Workplate.
The Hospital Utilization Workplate.
MEDCAPS Plus: Credential & Planning System.

Roberts-Slade, Inc., 619 N. 500 West, Provo, UT 84601 Tel 801-375-6847; Toll free: 800-433-4276.
Titles:
Enhanced Chartist.
Master Chartist.

Robo Systems International, Inc., (0-922901), 408 S. State St., No. 4, Newtown, PA 18940-1947 Tel 215-579-1344; Toll free: 800-221-7626; FAX: 215-860-6993.
Titles:
CAD-1+.
Robo DESIGN.
Robo IGES.
Robo Utilities.
RoboBuild.
RoboCAD.
RoboCAD 4.
RoboFEM.
RoboFEM/3D.
RoboLink/CADL.
RoboLink/HPGL.
RoboLink/SDRC.
RoboLink/3D.
RoboSolid 2.
RoboSolid 1.5.

Rochelle Communications, Inc., (0-9629249), P.O. Box 141189, Austin, TX 78714 Tel 512-794-0088; Toll free: 800-542-8808; FAX: 512-794-0908.
Titles:
Caller ID Developer Toolkits: Single Line & Multi-Line.
Caller ID+ Plus, Single Line & Multi-Line.

Rockware Data Corp., (0-926609), P.O. Box 866307, Plano, TX 75023 Tel 214-596-0588.
Titles:
Grav2D.
Rosy.
Shape.
Strain-Graph.
Supertax.

RockWare, Inc., 2221 East St., Suite 100, Golden, CO 80401 Tel 303-278-3534; Toll free: 800-775-6745; FAX: 303-278-4099.
Titles:
DIGITIZE.
GEOPAL+.
GRIDZO.
LOGGER.
MacGridzo.
MacInstrain.
MacMohr.
MacSection.
Mineral Data Bases for the Macintosh.
Piper-Stiff.
ROCKBASE.
ROCKSOLID.
ROCKSTAT.
RockWare Utilities.
Rockworks.
Stereo.

Rocky Mountain Digital Peeks, (1-885237), P.O. Box 1576, Nederland, CO 80466-1576 Tel 303-258-3779; Toll free: 800-266-7637; FAX: 303-258-7170.
Titles:
Calculated Beauty: A Journey Through Mandelbrot Space.
Earth Observatorium: Mission to Planet Earth.
Rocky Mountain Wildflowers: A Visual Plant Identification System.
Virtual Landscape: Winter Hiking in Rocky Mountain National Park.

Roeing Corp., (0-923028), 2433 S. Ninth St., Lafayette, IN 47905 Tel 317-474-5402; FAX: 317-474-4485.
Titles:
LT-Family of Software: Long Term Family of Software.

ROY G BIV COMPUTER CONSULTANTS

Roland Digital Group, 7200 Dominion Cir., Los Angeles, CA 90040-3647 Tel 213-685-5141.
Titles:
GRX 300-400.
Micro Modeler.
Roland DPX Plotters.
Roland DXY Plotters.

Rosehips Ink, Affil. of The Tarot Gypsy, (1-878490), HC 1, Box 406, Spirit Lake, ID 83869-9704 Tel 208-263-2093; Hoo Doo Valley, Spirit Lake, ID 83869.
Titles:
PC Gypsy.

Rosen, Larry, Co., 7008 Springdale Rd., Louisville, KY 40241 Tel 502-228-4343; FAX: 502-228-4782.
Titles:
Bond Portfolio Manager.
Complete Bond Analyzer.
Financial & Interest Calculator.
Investment IRR Analysis (after Taxes) for Stocks, Bonds, & Real Estate.
Mortgage Loans -- to Refinance or Not.
Options Valuation.

Ross Systems, Inc., (0-926626; 0-928379), 555 Twin Dolphin Dr., Redwood City, CA 94065 Tel 404-851-1872; FAX: 415-592-9364.
Titles:
Accounts Payable.
Accounts Receivable.
Encumbrance Accounting.
Fixed Assets.
General Ledger.
MODEL: Financial Modeling.
Purchase Order.

Round Lake Publishing Co., (0-929543), 31 Bailey Ave., Ridgefield, CT 06877 Tel 203-431-9696.
Titles:
LetterWorks.
SALES LetterWorks.

Routledge, Chapman & Hall, Inc., Subs. of International Thomson Organization, Inc., (0-416; 0-7100; 0-87830; 0-04; 0-86861), 29 W. 35th St., New York, NY 10001-2291 Tel 212-244-3336; FAX: 212-563-2269.
Titles:
CODA.

Rovak, Inc., (0-925420), 3549 Lake Elmo Ave. N., Lake Elmo, MN 55042 Tel 612-779-9444; Toll free: 800-672-2999; FAX: 800-428-5819.
Titles:
O. M. S. Optical Mark System.

Rowlette Enterprises, Inc., (0-926631), P.O. Box 363, Eldon, MO 65026 Tel 314-392-5876.
Titles:
Client Accounting System.
MSS Payroll System.

Roxbury Research, Inc., (0-933631), R.D. 1, Box 171A, Roxbury, NY 12474 Tel 607-326-4822.
Titles:
Greetingware Christmas Medley: Electronic Xmas Gift-Card.
Greetingware Do-It-Yourself Kit: GW Promotional Kit.

ROY G BIV Computer Consultants, 1531 S. Eufaula Ave., Eufaula, AL 36027 Tel 334-687-2810.
Titles:
Roy's DOS Helper.

Royal Recovery Systems, Inc., P.O. Box 1468, Plainfield, NJ 07061 Tel 201-753-2835.
Titles:
Instant ImageTalk.

Royal Software, (0-926633), 1474 W. Sixth St., Eugene, OR 97402 Tel 541-683-5361.
Titles:
EZ CALC.
Inventory Master.
Paroll Master.
Super Mailer.

Rubel Software, Subs. of Andrew Rubel & Assocs., Inc., (0-918117), P.O. Box 1035, Cambridge, MA 02140-0009 Tel 617-876-7993.
Titles:
BLOX Graphics Builder.

Rubicon Publishing, 4030 Braker Ln., W.. Suite 350, Austin, TX 78759 Tel 512-794-8533; Toll free: 800-688-7466; FAX: 512-794-8520.
Titles:
Dinner at Eight.

RunTime Software, (0-926636), 3717 Wildwood Dr., Endwell, NY 13760 Tel 607-754-2339; FAX: 607-777-2288.
Titles:
Running Score II.

Rupp Brothers, P.O. Drawer J, Lenox Hill Sta., New York, NY 10021 Tel 212-517-7775.
Titles:
FastWire II.

Ryan Software, Inc., 271 North Ave., No.1216, New Rochelle, NY 10801-5120 Tel 914-633-0130.
Titles:
Ryan Investment Planner.

S.A.I.L. Operating Systems Div., (0-926640), 1136 S. Grand St., Mesa, AZ 85201-3629.
Titles:
S.A.I.L.B.O.A.T.

S.A.M. Designs, (0-9623179), P.O. Box 7969, Tyler, TX 75711 Tel 903-592-5465; FAX: 903-592-5465. Do not confuse with S.A.M. in Dallas, TX.
Titles:
DRP Addresses.
DRP Stocks.

SASI Software Corp., P.O. Box 457, Sherwood, OR 97140 Tel 503-625-5384.
Titles:
Market Edge.

SAS Institute, Inc., (0-917382; 1-55544), SAS Campus Dr., Cary, NC 27513-2414 Tel 919-677-8000; FAX: 919-677-8123.
Titles:
JMP Statistical Discovery Software.
SAS/C Compiler.
The SAS System.
System 2000 Data Management Software.

S & H Computer Systems, Inc., (0-926641), 1027 17th Ave., S., Nashville, TN 37212 Tel 615-327-3670; FAX: 615-321-5929.
Titles:
COBOL-Plus.
EDIT-32.
MessageNet: Advanced E-Mail System.
RTSORT.
TSX-NET LAN: License for up to 128 Nodes.
TSX-Plus Version 5.
TSX-32: Multi-User System.
TSX-32: Single-User System.

S&H Software, (0-926642), 58 Van Orden Rd., Harrington Park, NJ 07640 Tel 201-768-3144.
Titles:
The DOS Enhancer.

S & J Enterprises, Incorporated, (0-926643), P.O. Box 1134, Bettendorf, IA 52722 Tel 319-332-1188; Toll free: 800-508-4410; FAX: 319-332-4252.
Titles:
Inventory Control Program.
Maintenance Management.
Water/Sewer/Trash Billing.

S&J Software, 62 Plaza Dr., New Albany, IN 47150 Tel 812-948-8521.
Titles:
CMOS.COM: CMOS Save - Restore - Compare.

SBT Corp., (0-926869), 1 Harbor Dr., Sausalito, CA 94965 Tel 415-331-9900; Toll free: 800-944-1000; FAX: 415-331-1951.
Titles:
SBT Professional Series.
SBT Series Six Plus.

SK Data, Inc., P.O. Box 413, Burlington, MA 01803 Tel 617-229-8909.
Titles:
FindFile.
Golden Retriever 2.0.

SLR Systems, (0-926667), 1622 N. Main St., Butler, PA 16001-1599 Tel 412-282-0864; FAX: 412-282-7965.
Titles:
DSD80: Debugger.
Relocating Macro Assemblers: Assemblers & Virtual Assemblers.
SLRNK: SuperLinkers.
Z80 DIS: Z80 Disassembler.
Z80ASM: Z80 Assembly Language Development.

SMK, P.O. Box 15399, Atlanta, GA 30333-0399 Tel 404-727-2320.
Titles:
SMK GreekKeys.

SMS (Southern Micro Systems), (0-916461), 3545 S. Church St., Burlington, NC 27215-9100 Tel 910-584-5552; Toll free: 800-888-8555.
Titles:
LH 'O': Library Helper 'Overdues'.

SNA, Inc., 2200 NW Corporate Blvd., Suite 404, Boca Raton, FL 33431 Tel 407-241-0308; Toll free: 800-628-6442; FAX: 407-241-3195.
Titles:
Offline.
Stylist.
Vp ULTRA.

SNAP, Inc., 175 Canal St., Manchester, NH 03101-2320 Tel 603-623-5877; FAX: 603-623-5562.
Titles:
SNAP.

SOFTA Group, Inc., The, (0-917391), 707 Skokie Blvd., Northbrook, IL 60062 Tel 708-291-4000; Toll free: 800-445-7638; FAX: 708-291-4022.
Titles:
BREAKPOINT: For Shopping Center Management.
LOCKBOX Interface.
SKYLINE: The Property Management System.

SOS Group, Univ. of Illinois, 361 Lincoln Hall, Urbana, IL 61801 Tel 217-359-8541; FAX: 217-244-5712.
Titles:
SOS (Super-Optimum Solutions) Decision-Aiding Software.

SPS, Inc., (0-926672; 0-926698), 75 Worthington Rd., White Plains, NY 10607 Tel 914-682-0333; FAX: 914-592-1167.
Titles:
The Personnel System - TPS.

SPSS, Inc., (0-918469; 0-923967; 1-56827), 444 N. Michigan Ave., Chicago, IL 60611 Tel 312-329-2400; Toll free: 800-543-6609; FAX: 312-329-3668.
Titles:
QI Analyst: Statistical Process Control Software.
SPSS Data Entry II.
SPSS Developer's Kit for Windows: Applications Development Software Tool.
SPSS for OS/2.
SPSS for the Macintosh.
SPSS for the Macintosh: Statistical Data Analysis Software.
SPSS for Windows: Statistical Data Analysis Software.
SPSS/PC+.
Teleform for Windows: Forms Design & Automatic Data Entry Software.

SRC Systems, Inc., (0-925210), 14785 Omicron Dr., San Antonio, TX 78245-3201 Tel 210-677-6010; FAX: 210-677-6090. Do not confuse with SRC International in Bala Cynwyd, PA.
Titles:
AIDSaide.
ANESafe.
CAche.
Calorix Savant.
Care Plan.
CLINICALL.
Conflix-A.
First Opinion.
GALENUS: Disease Processor.
HISTORYMAKER IV.
Microbes Savant: Antimicrobial Treatment Advisor.
Obesity Savant: Obesity Diagnostic Screening.
Omnicoder: ICD-9-CM code finder.
PEARLMASTER.
Socratix Diabetes.
STANDING ORDERS.
SYMPTOMASTER.
Syndromease: Occult Syndrome Identifier.
TRAUMATIX.
Wizard Medical Specialties.

SSD (Small System Design), Inc., (0-934621), 7464 Arapahoe Ave., No. A-7, Boulder, CO 80303 Tel 303-442-9454; Toll free: 800-272-0053; FAX: 303-442-7881.
Titles:
Bid Lite.
Construction Management Software Plus.
Equipment Boss: Equipment Tracking.
Job Boss.

SST, Inc., 9460 Owensmouth Ave., Chatsworth, CA 91311 Tel 818-718-0062; Toll free: 800-766-4778; FAX: 818-718-2421.
Titles:
Salon Transcripts.

SWFTE International, Ltd., Sub. of Expert Software, Inc., (1-887468; 1-57714), 722 Yorklyn Road, Hockessin, DE 19707-8701 Tel 302-234-1740; Toll free: 800-237-9383; FAX: 302-234-9104.
Titles:
Archibald's Guide to the Mysteries of Ancient Egypt.
Bicycle Baccarat.
Bicycle Casino.
Bicycle Classics.
Bicycle Gin.
Bicycle Limited Edition - CD-ROM.
Brain Quest CD - Grades 1-2.
Brain Quest CD - Grades 2-3.
Brain Quest CD - Grades 3-4.

PUBLISHER/TITLE INDEX

Brain Quest CD - Grades 4-5.
Brain Quest CD - Grades 5-6.
Brain Quest CD - Grades 6-7.
Brain Quest CD - Preschool & Kindergarten.
Brain Quest CD: Grades 1-2.
Brain Quest CD: Grades 2-3.
Brain Quest CD: Grades 3-4.
Brain Quest CD: Grades 4-5.
Brain Quest CD: Grades 5-6.
Brain Quest CD: Grades 6-7.
Brain Quest: Grade 1.
Brain Quest: Grade 2.
Brain Quest: Grade 3.
Brain Quest: Grade 4.
Brain Quest: Grade 5.
Brain Quest: Grade 6.
Brain Quest: Grade 7.
Brain Quest: Grades 1-2.
Brain Quest: Grades 3-4.
Brain Quest: Grades 4-5.
Brain Quest: Grades 6-7.
Brain Quest Interactive Software.
Gettysburg.
Gettysburg Multimedia Battle Simulation.
The Multimedia Bird Book.
The Multimedia Bug Book.
New York Times Crosswords.
Real Monsters - Ickis.
Real Monsters - Krumm.
Real Monsters - Oblina.
Ren & Stimpy - Adventures in Space.
Ren & Stimpy - Ren.
Ren & Stimpy - Stimpy.
Typecase.
Typecase III.
Typecase II.
Typecase 2001.
The Underground CD-ROM Handbook for the SAT.

SZ Software Systems, (0-926687), 1269 Rubio Vista Rd., Altadena, CA 91001 Tel 818-791-3202.
Titles:
North Star BASIC, Utlity Set, North Star Sort Statement.

Safety Software, Inc., (1-880147), 2030 Spottswood Rd., Suite 200, Charlottesville, VA 22903-1245 Tel 804-296-8789; Toll free: 800-932-9457; FAX: 804-296-1660.
Titles:
OSHALOG Four PC Pro.
OSHALOG.200.
OSHALOG.200 Manager.
OSHALOG.200 Manager Plus.
OSHALOG.200 Plus.
OSHALOG.4PC.

Sah Research, Inc., (0-9626417), 5801 S. Dorchester Ave., Apt. 10A, Chicago, IL 60637-1768; Dist. by: Spreadsheet Solutions Co., P.O. Box 231296, Great Neck, NY 11023-0296 Tel 516-222-1429; Toll free: 800-634-8509.
Titles:
Option Valuation & Implied Volatility.

St. Benedict's Farm, (0-926695), P.O. Box 366, Waelder, TX 78959 Tel 210-540-4814.
Titles:
BeefUp.
Pedigree.

Salinon Corp., The, 7424 Greenville Ave., Suite 115, Dallas, TX 75231 Tel 214-692-9091; FAX: 214-692-9095.
Titles:
Special Days, Footprints in History.

Sammamish Data Systems, Inc., P.O. Box 70382, Bellevue, WA 98007 Tel 206-867-1485; FAX: 206-861-0184.
Titles:
Census Data System '90.
GeoSight Professional.

Samna Corp., (0-918687), 1000 Abernathy Rd., Bldg. 400, Suite 1700, Atlanta, GA 30328 Tel 404-851-0007; Toll free: 800-831-9679; FAX: 404-255-9460.
Titles:
Ami.
Ami Professional.
Samna Plus IV.
Samna Word IV.
SMARTEXT.

Samsara, Ltd., P.O. Box 1705, Sandpoint, ID 83864 Tel 208-263-3543.
Titles:
Clerk of the Works: Accounting Software for Architects & Engineers.

San Francisco Legal Systems, 240 Stockton St., Suite 410, San Francisco, CA 94108 Tel 415-397-8666; FAX: 415-397-9801.
Titles:
Litigation Express.

Sandlight Pubns., (0-931145), 6832 Toluca Dr., El Paso, TX 79912-1716 Tel 915-581-1483.
Titles:
Kids' Assembler.
Robot Control.

Sans Souci Consulting, (0-927212), 330 Chestnut Ave., Bakersfield, CA 93305 Tel 805-327-1172; FAX: 805-327-9299.
Titles:
Com/ment.
Starx.

Santa Clara Systems, Inc., (0-926705), 1610 Berryessa Rd., San Jose, CA 95133 Tel 408-729-6700.
Titles:
SCS Netware.

Santa Cruz Operation, Inc. (SCO), (0-928332), 400 Encinal St., Box 1900, Santa Cruz, CA 95061 Tel 408-425-7222; Toll free: 800-726-8649; FAX: 408-458-4227.
Titles:
Lyrix Word Processing System.
Micro Focus COBOL/2.
Microsoft BASIC Interpreter.
Microsoft FORTRAN Compiler.
Microsoft Pascal Compiler.
Microsoft Word.
Multiplan: Electric Spreadsheet.
SCO/ACCELL.
SCO FoxBASE: dBASE II Workalike.
SCO FoxBASE+.
SCO ImageBuilder.
SCO Integra.
SCO MasterPlan.
SCO MultiView.
SCO Portfolio.
SCO Portfolio Suite.
SCO Professional: Lotus 1-2-3 Workalike.
SCO Statistician.
SCO UniPATH SNA 3270: Mainframe Communications Program.
SCO Unix System V/386.
SCO VP/ix.
SCO XENIX System V.
SCO XENIX Tutor.
SCO Xenix 386.

SAVE THE PLANET SOFTWARE

Sapana Micro Software, (0-918689), 1305 S. Rouse, Pittsburg, KS 66762 Tel 316-231-5023.
Titles:
Expense-Track-II.
Household-Inventory-Track-I.
Mail-Bulk-Rate II.
Mail-Bulk-Rate-III.
Mail-Second-Class-II.
Mail-Second-Class-III.
Mail-Star-One.
Mail-Track-I with LetterMerge.
Mail-Track-II with LetterMerge II.
Mail-Track-III.
SAPANA: Cardfile.

Sapiens Software Corp., P.O Box 3365, Santa Cruz, CA 95063-3365 Tel 408-458-1990; FAX: 408-425-0905.
Titles:
Star Saphire LISP.
V64.

Satellite Data Systems, Inc., (0-923854), P.O. Box 219, Cleveland, MN 56017 Tel 507-931-4849; FAX: 507-931-4849.
Titles:
Electro-Services Weather Fax.
Student Guide to Weather Satellite Image Interpretation.

Satellite Technology & Research (S.T.A.R.), (0-927939), 530 S. Commerce Rd., Orem, UT 84058 Tel 801-225-7000.
Titles:
Lettronics 731.

Satori Software, (0-926713), 2815 Second Ave., Suite 295, Seattle, WA 98121 Tel 206-443-0765; FAX: 206-728-7068.
Titles:
Bulk Mailer.
Components Accounts Payable.
Components Accounts Receivable with Invoicing.
Components General Ledger.
Legal Billing II.
Legal Billing II+.
Project Billing.

Saunders, W. B., Co., Subs. of Harcourt Brace & Co., (0-7216), Curtis Ctr., Independence Sq., W., Philadelphia, PA 19106-3399 Tel 215-238-7800; FAX: 215-238-7883; Orders to: 6277 Sea Harbor Dr., Orlando, FL 32821; Toll free: 800-545-2522.
Titles:
Cecil Textbook of Medicine CD-ROM.

Saur, K. G., A part of Reed Reference Publishing, (3-598; 3-7940), 121 Chanlon Rd., New Providence, NJ 07974 Tel 908-464-6800; Toll free: 800-521-8110; FAX: 908-665-6707.
Titles:
World Biographical Dictionary of Artists on CD-ROM.
World Biographical Index on CD-ROM.
Year of International Organizations on CD-ROM.

Savant Software, Inc., (0-917387), 120 Bedford Center Rd., Bedford, NH 03110 Tel 603-471-0400; Toll free: 800-231-9900.
Titles:
The Investor's Portfolio.
TopVest.

Save the Planet Software, (1-885023), P.O. Box 45, Pitkin, CO 81241 Tel 970-641-5035; 513 River St., Pitkin, CO 81241 Tel 970-641-5035.
Titles:
CD-ROM Selector: A Directory of CD-ROMs for DOS & Windows.
ECOMAP: A Global View of Major Terrestrial Ecosystems.
Save the Planet, 1993: Database on Global Warming & Ozone Depletion.

UVB-WARE: UV Calculator - Ozone Depletion Trend Database.

ScanAm Enterprises, Inc., Subs. of Langtry Assocs., Inc., (0-924324), P.O. Box 661, Westwood, NJ 07675; FAX: 201-358-6509; 11 Madison Ave., Westwood, NJ 07675 Tel 201-358-6620.
Titles:
Calc Result.
Calc Result Advanced.
Calc Result Easy.
Real Estate 64.
Word Result.

Scandinavian PC Systems, Inc., (1-878322), P.O. Box 3156, Baton Rouge, LA 70821-3156 Tel 504-338-9580; Toll free: 800-487-7727; FAX: 504-338-9670.
Titles:
Corporate Voice.
John C Dvorak's PC Crash Course & Survival Guide.
SPCS Chess.
SPCS Menu Program.
SPCS PrimaBase: A 'Painless' Database for Windows.

Scarecrow Pr., Inc., Subs. of Grolier, Inc., (0-8108), 52 Liberty St., Box 4167, Metuchen, NJ 08840 Tel 908-548-8600; Toll free: 800-537-7107; FAX: 908-548-5767.
Titles:
LH Online.
LH Online: On-Line Public Access Catalog.
The Librarian's Helper.

ScenicSoft, Inc., P.O. Box 909, Edmonds, WA 98020 Tel 206-776-7760; Toll free: 800-422-2994.
Titles:
ScenicWriter.

Schemers, Inc., (0-9628745; 1-888579), 2136 NE 68th St., Suite 401, Fort Lauderdale, FL 33308 Tel 954-776-7376; FAX: 954-776-6174.
Titles:
EdScheme: A Modern Lisp.

Schmidt Enterprises, 7448 Newcastle Ave., Reseda, CA 91335 Tel 818-342-5930; Toll free: 800-232-6777 (orders only).
Titles:
The Accountant.
Apollo.
Fastword.

Scholastic Software, Div. of Scholastic, Inc., (0-590), 740 Broadway, 11th Flr., New York, NY 10003 Tel 212-505-6006; FAX: 212-353-8219.
Titles:
Operation: Frog.
Scholastic SuperPrint.

School Management Arts, Inc. (SMARTS), (0-932743), P.O. Box 1, Boston, MA 02195 Tel 617-969-0966.
Titles:
FundMaster: Activity Fund Accounting.

Schroeppel, Tom, (0-9603718), 4705 Bay View Ave., Tampa, FL 33611 Tel 813-831-0947.
Titles:
AVScripter.

Science Academy Software, (0-9623926), 65 Loring Ave., Yonkers, NY 10704-2732 Tel 914-422-1100.
Titles:
BasketMath.
BasketMath: For IBM Computers.
MathVolley: For Apple II Computers.

Science Research Assocs., Div. of Macmillan/McGraw-Hill School Publishing Co., (0-574; 0-88120), 250 Old Wilson Bridge Rd., Suite 310, Worthington, OH 43085 Tel 614-438-6600; Toll free: 800-468-5850; FAX: 312-984-7988.
Titles:
Using the Lotus 1-2-3 Program.

Scientific American Medicine, Div. of Scientific American, Inc., (0-89454), 415 Madison Ave., New York, NY 10017 Tel 212-754-0550; Toll free: 800-545-0554; FAX: 212-980-3062.
Titles:
DISCOTEST II.
SAM-CD: Scientific American Medicine on CD-ROM.
SAS-CD: Scientific American Surgery on CD-ROM.

Scientific Solutions, Subs. of Tecmar, Inc., 6225 Cochran Rd., Solon, OH 44139 Tel 216-349-4030; FAX: 216-349-0851.
Titles:
Route 488.

Scitor Corp., (0-926752), 393 Vintage Park Dr., Suite 140, Foster City, CA 94404 Tel 415-570-7700; FAX: 415-570-7807.
Titles:
Project Scheduler Five.

Score Bk. Software, P.O. Box 3677, Estes Park, CO 80517 Tel 303-586-0781.
Titles:
Complete League Series.
Complete Team Series.

Scorpion Systems, Inc., (0-926755), 103 S. Carroll St., No. 400, Frederick, MD 21701-5608 Tel 301-663-0539.
Titles:
Cruiser: Records Management for Law Enforcement.

Scott, Foresman & Co., Subs. of HarperCollins Pubs., Inc., (0-673), 1900 E. Lake Ave., Glenview, IL 60025 Tel 708-729-3000; FAX: 708-729-8910.
Titles:
Complete Church Management Applications.
The Deacon System.

ScreenMagic, Inc., 820 Florida St., San Francisco, CA 94110 Tel 415-648-8056.
Titles:
Etch-A-Sketch Magic Screen Machine.

Screenplay Systems, Inc., (0-918973), 150 E. Olive Ave., Suite 305, Burbank, CA 91502 Tel 818-843-6557.
Titles:
Movie Magic.
Movie Magic Scheduling/Breakdown.
Scriptor.

Scripture Pr. Pubs., Inc., (0-88207; 0-89693; 1-56476), 1825 College Ave., Wheaton, IL 60187 Tel 708-668-6000; Toll free: 800-323-9409; FAX: 708-668-3806.
Titles:
Play...Childrens Bible.

SelectWare Technologies, Inc., (1-57037), 29200 Vassar, Suite 200, Livonia, MI 48152 Tel 810-477-7340; Toll free: 800-342-3366; FAX: 810-477-6488.
Titles:
Classic Collection: Adventure - Fantasy.
Classic Collection: Greatest Air Battles.
MusicROM Perspectives: Blues.
MusicROM Perspectives: Jazz.
MusicROM Perspectives: R & B.
MusicROM Perspectives: Reggae.
MusicROM Perspectives: Special Edition.
SelectPAC: Action Arcade.
SelectPAC: Jet Set.
SelectPAC: Sci-Fi Battles.
SelectPAC: Super Sports.
Software JukeBox: A Plus Grade Builder.
Software JukeBox: Fight, Flight & Might.
Software JukeBox: World Class Sports.

Semaphore, Inc., 3 E. 28th St., 11th flr., New York, NY 10016 Tel 212-545-7300; Toll free: 800-545-7484; FAX: 212-545-7443.
Titles:
SEMA4 Financial Management System for A/E Industry.

Sendero Corp., Subs. of Flserv, Inc., 7272 E. Indian School Rd., No. 300, Scottsdale, AZ 85251 Tel 602-941-8112; Toll free: 800-321-6899; FAX: 602-946-8224.
Titles:
Sendero A/L 1: Asset - Liability Management.
Sendero A/L 3: Asset - Liability Management.
Sendero A/L 2: Asset - Liability Management.
Sendero DMS: Data Management System.
Sendero FTP: Funds Transfer Pricing.

Senecio Software, Inc., (1-884386), 720 Wallace Ave., Bowling Green, OH 43402 Tel 419-352-4371; FAX: 419-352-4281.
Titles:
Flo-Stat.
Flo-Stat: An Elementary Statistics, Mapping Graphics System.
IPSS: Interactive Population Statistical System.
MaCATI: Macintosh Assisted Telephone Interviewing.

Sensible Designs, (0-926775), 4508 Calle De Vida, San Diego, CA 92124 Tel 619-268-0123.
Titles:
AutoBASE.
dProgrammer.

Sensible Software, Inc., (0-926776), 20200 E. Nine Mile Rd., Suite 150, Saint Clair Shores, MI 48080 Tel 810-774-7215; Toll free: 800-394-4669.
Titles:
Black's Law Dictionary.
Bookends Extended.
Bookends Extended-SP: School Pak.
Bookends II.
Bookends PC.
Report Card 2.
The Sensible Speller IV: School Pak.
Sensible Speller ProDOS: School Pak.
Sensible Technical Dictionary.
Stedman's Medical Dictionary.

Serious Business Software, 2113 E. Huntington Dr., Tempe, AZ 85282 Tel 602-838-5063.
Titles:
Unitrust WKI.

Service Station Computer Systems, Inc., (0-934537), 1212 S. Main St., Suite 101, Salinas, CA 93901 Tel 408-755-1800; Toll free: 800-972-7727; FAX: 408-422-0314.
Titles:
Computerized Daily Book.
D.S.D. - Direct Store Delivery Physical Inventory: Telxon PTC-710.
G-Poll: Gilbarco Interface.
W-Poll: Wayne-Plus Interface.

Seven Hills Software Corp., (0-931277), 2310 Oxford Rd., Tallahassee, FL 32304 Tel 904-575-0566; Toll free: 800-200-4555; FAX: 904-575-2015.
Titles:
The Character Factory.
Drive Cleaner.
Font Factory GS.

PUBLISHER/TITLE INDEX

Funny Fruit Faces.
GATE.
GraphicWriter III.
SuperConvert.

7th Level, Inc., (0-9641098), 1771 International Pkwy., No. 101, Richardson, TX 75081 Tel 214-437-4858; FAX: 214-437-2717.
Titles:
Monty Python's Complete Waste of Time.
Monty Python's Flying Circus Desktop Pythonizer.
Take Your Best Shot.
TuneLand Starring Howie Mandel.

Shadduck & Sullivan, (0-935975), 3508 45th Ave. S., Minneapolis, MN 55406-2927 Tel 612-729-1292.
Titles:
Filer Finder: Index to Information Management Software for Microcomputers.

Shaherazam, P.O. Box 26731, Milwaukee, WI 53226 Tel 414-442-7503.
Titles:
Brass.
Mac-A-Mug.
Mac-A-Mug Pro.
MusicType.

Shannon, J. H., Assocs., Inc., P.O. Box 597, Chapel Hill, NC 27514 Tel 919-929-6863.
Titles:
Metamorphosis.

ShareData, 250 Sobrante Way, Sunnyvale, CA 94086 Tel 408-746-3666; Toll free: 800-783-3388.
Titles:
ESP: (Employee Stock Purchase).
ITC: (Investor Tracking Capability).
The OTC Software Products: (Option Tracking Capability).

SharpImage Software, P.O. Box 373, Prince St. Sta., New York, NY 10012 Tel 212-998-7857.
Titles:
HIPS.

Sheldon, Tom, Publishing, (0-927907), P.O. Box 947, Cambria, CA 93428-0947.
Titles:
DOSShell.

Shenandoah Software, (0-918693), 1427 S. Main St., P.O. Box 776, Harrisonburg, VA 22801 Tel 703-433-9485; Toll free: 800-527-6856.
Titles:
Puzzle Master.

Shepard's/McGraw-Hill, Inc., Div. of McGraw-Hill, Inc., (0-07), 555 Middle Creek Pkwy., P.O. Box 35300, Colorado Springs, CO 80935-3530 Tel 719-488-3000; Toll free: 800-525-2474; FAX: 800-525-0053.
Titles:
The Blackacre Conveyancer.
Blackacre's Foreclosure System.
Blackacre's RESPA.
Determining Damages: Economic Loss in Personal Injury & Wrongful Death Cases.
Drafting Wills & Trust Agreements on CAPS.
Estate Practice Assistant.
Federal Estate Tax Returns: Calculation & Preparation.
Federal Gift Tax Returns: Calculation & Preparation.
Fiduciary Accounting for Trusts & Estates.
Fiduciary Income Tax Returns: Calculation & Preparation.
Fiduciary Income Tax Returns: Calculation & Preparation: Core Program, Laser Versions (HP, HP Center Piece, Canon LBP-8II & Xerox 4045).
New York Net Worth.

Sher-Mark Products, Inc., 11 Ramleh Rd., R.F.D. 4, Mount Kisco, NY 10549 Tel 914-241-6262.
Titles:
Eye Chart Generator.

Shirley Software Systems, (0-926808), P.O. Box 3758, Idyllwild, CA 92549-3758.
Titles:
MISTER.
MRBARS.
MRPLOTA.
MRPLOTP.

Shopkeeper Software, (1-879815), 1005 Lakewood Ln., Round Rock, TX 78681 Tel 512-388-3290; FAX: 512-310-9855.
Titles:
Bill-It.
Quick Ship.
QuickLookups.
Shopkeeper Plus.
SK-Modules: Point of Sale.

Showker Graphic Arts & Design, 15 Southgate Ct., Harrisonburg, VA 22801 Tel 703-433-8402.
Titles:
The Graphics Warehouse.
Monster Fonts.

Sidereal Technolgies, Inc., (0-926255), 263 Center Ave., P.O. Box 30, Westwood, NJ 07675 Tel 201-666-6262; Toll free: 800-544-2483; FAX: 201-666-8119.
Titles:
dms4Cite: Document Management System for Citations.

Sierra On-Line, Inc., (0-87177), P.O. Box 485, Coarsegold, CA 93614; FAX: 209-683-7830; 40033 Sierra Way, Oakhurst, CA 93644 Tel 209-683-4468.
Titles:
King's Quest I.
Oil's Well.
Space Quest (Chapter I: the Sarien Encounter).
Thexder.

Sigler & Flanders, Inc., (1-880579), P.O. Box 3578, Lawrence, KS 66046; 1420C Kasold Dr., Lawrence, KS 66049 Tel 913-749-5259.
Titles:
Top Two Hundred Drugs HyperCard Stack.

Signal Technology, Inc., (0-926819), 104 W Anapamu St., No. J, Santa Barbara, CA 93101-3126.
Titles:
ILS-Interactive Laboratory System.
ILS-PC 1.
ILS-SKY.
PACS PLUS.
Smartdecision.
SmartStar.

Signature Software Systems, Inc., 6125 Yarbrough Ln., Lakeland, FL 33813-4173 Tel 941-646-0759.
Titles:
EZ-Rx System.
SIG-ICS Inventory Control System.
SIGAR Accounting/Invoicing.

Significant Statistics, 625 East, 3180 North, Provo, UT 84604 Tel 801-377-4860.
Titles:
SIGSTAT.

Signum Microsystems, Inc., 11 Mountain Ave., Bloomfield, CT 06002-2343 Tel 203-726-1911; FAX: 203-242-4520.
Titles:
IpsoFacto Litigation Support System.

SIMPLICITY SOFTWARE, INC.

SilentPartner, Inc., 180 Black Rock Rd., Oaks, PA 19456 Tel 215-625-4986.
Titles:
SilentPartner.

Silver Software, 1922 Purchase Brook Rd., Southbury, CT 06488 Tel 203-264-2583.
Titles:
DNA Music.
Eye Play 2.
Fractal Music.
Golden Music.
Mouse Bowling.
Protein Music.

SilverPlatter Education, Div. of SilverPlatter Information, (1-57276), 100 River Ridge Dr., Norwood, MA 02062 Tel 617-769-2599; Toll free: 800-343-0064; FAX: 617-769-8763.
Titles:
Adult Airway Management: Principles & Techniques.
Allergy Case Studies.
American College of Allergy & Immunology.
Anatomy & Anesthesia of the Mandibular Nerve.
Atlas of Clinical Rheumatology.
Biological Age.
Case Studies in Gastroenterology: GastroMaster.
Core Curriculum in Primary Care: Asthma & Allergy Section.
Core Curriculum in Primary Care: Gastroenterology Section.
Core Curriculum in Primary Care: Metabolic Diseases Section.
Core Curriculum in Primary Care: Nephrology Section.
Core Curriculum in Primary Care: Office Surgery & Urology Section.
Core Curriculum in Primary Care: Ophthalmology & Neurology Section.
Core Curriculum in Primary Care: Preventive Medicine Section.
Core Curriculum in Primary Care: Psychiatry & Pain Management Section.
Core Curriculum in Primary Care: Pulmonary Medicine & ENT Section.
Dental Development.
The Diagnosis of Pulmonary Embolus: A Clinician's Approach.
The Etiology of Cancer.
Masticatory Muscles.
The Nature of Genes.
Oral & Cutaneous Manifestations of HIV.
Pediatric Airway Obstruction.
Pigmented Lesions of the Skin.
Primary Cancers of the Skin.

Simmons Computing Service, Inc., 800 N. Pearl St., Albany, NY 12204 Tel 518-436-0129.
Titles:
Product Management System for Architects/Engineers.
Productivity Analysis: Piecework/Payroll Reporting.

Simplicity Dental Software Systems, Inc., 9 S. Ridge Ave., Ambler, PA 19002 Tel 215-646-3382.
Titles:
Simplicity Dental Software.

Simplicity Software, Inc., (0-9633170), 4699 N. Federal Hwy., Pompano Beach, FL 33064 Tel 305-946-5891; Toll free: 800-346-3215; FAX: 305-946-5691.
Titles:
Simplicity Software: Accounting for Small Business.

SIMPLICITY SYSTEMS, INC.

Simplicity Systems, Inc., (0-932071), 1621 Second Ave. NE, P.O. Box 556, East Grand Forks, MN 56721-0556 Tel 218-773-8917; Toll free: 800-777-7978; FAX: 218-773-3849.
Titles:
CogoMate.
Collector Connector: Data Collector Communications for Your PC.
DigiMate: A Coordinate Point Digitizer Interface.
Draftsman DXF.
DrainCalc.
LegalEase: Legal Description Writer.
METES & Bounds.
"Sight" Survey for Windows.
Surf-2-Cad.
Survey Lite: Two-Dimensional Coordinate Geometry.
Survey 3LX: COGO for the HP 95 LX.
Survey 4.0.

Simplified Legal Systems, Inc., 3200 Southwest Freeway, Suite 1170, Houston, TX 77027-7523 Tel 713-629-0670; FAX: 713-621-4060.
Titles:
Time: Legal Time Accounting & Billing System.

Simpson, Orval D., Scientific Consultant, 965 Syringa Dr., Idaho Falls, ID 83401 Tel 208-529-0963.
Titles:
Radiological Safety Analysis.

Simtek, (0-933836), P.O. Box 105, Carlisle, MA 01741-0105 Tel 508-369-5538.
Titles:
Simtek Business Games Library.

Sinauer Assocs., Inc., (0-87893), 23 Plumtree Rd., P.O. Box 407, Sunderland, MA 01375-0407 Tel 413-549-4300; FAX: 413-549-1118.
Titles:
MacClade.

Sinper Corp., 513 Warrenville Rd., Warren, NJ 07059 Tel 201-755-9880; Toll free: 800-822-1596; FAX: 201-755-9230.
Titles:
Spreadsheet Connector.
TM/1 Perspectives.
TM/1.

Sir-Tech Software, Inc., (0-926846), P.O. Box 245, Ogdensburg, NY 13669; Toll free: 800-447-1230 (sales only); FAX: 315-393-1525; Ogdensburg Business Ctr., Suite 2E, Ogdensburg, NY 13669 Tel 315-393-6633.
Titles:
CPA: The Clan Practical Accountant.
Crypt of Medea.
Deep Space - Operation Copernicus.
Druid.
Freakin' Funky Fuzzballs.
Jagged Alliance.
Nemesis: A Wizardry Adventure.
Realms of Arkania: Blade of Destiny.
Realms of Arkania: Shadows over Riva.
Realms of Arkania: Star Trail.
Wizardry - Bane of the Cosmic Forge.
Wizardry Gold.
Wizardry II: Knight of Diamonds (The Second Scenario).
Wizardry III: Legacy of Llylgamyn (The Third Scenario).
Wizardry IV: The Return of Werdna (The Fourth Scenario).
Wizardry: Proving Grounds of the Mad Overlord (The First Scenario).
Wizardry Trilogy: Proving Grounds, Knight of Diamonds, Legacy of Llylgamyn.
Wizardry: Trilogy Two.
Wizardry V: Heart of the Maelstrom.
Wizardry 7: Crusaders of the Dark Savant.
Wiziprint.

Sirius Publishing, Inc., (1-57418), 7320 E. Butherus, Suite 100, Scottsdale, AZ 85260 Tel 602-951-3288; Toll free: 800-247-0307; FAX: 602-951-3884. Do not confuse with companies with the same name in Shutesbury, MA, Eagle River, AK.
Titles:
5 Ft. 10 Pak Special Edition.

Sirsi Corp., 689 Discovery Dr., Huntsville, AL 35806 Tel 205-536-5884; FAX: 205-536-8345.
Titles:
Unicorn Collection Management System.

Sitka Corp., Subs. of Sun Microsystems, 2 Elizabeth Dr., Chelmsford, MA 01824-4112.
Titles:
InBox.
Network Bundle for DOS.
TOPS FlashBox.
TOPS FlashCard.
TOPS for Sun Workstations.
TOPS InBox Plus.
TOPS NetPrint.
TOPS: Network Bundle for Macintosh.
TOPS Repeater.

6502 Program Exchange, (0-918137), 2920 W. Moana Ln., Reno, NV 89509 Tel 702-825-8413.
Titles:
MC-Matrix Calculator.

Skill//Quest Co., (1-886499), 675 Fairview Dr., Suite 246, Carson City, NV 89701 Tel 619-233-7211; FAX: 619-233-1964.
Titles:
Rockpecker: A Prospector's Mineral Identification Program.

Skills Bank Corp., (0-9616781; 0-939673; 1-56985), 15 Governor's Ct., Baltimore, MD 21244 Tel 410-265-8855; Toll free: 800-451-5726; FAX: 410-265-8874.
Titles:
Skills Bank 3: Complete Set.
Skills Bank 3: Language.
Skills Bank 3: Mathematics.
Skills Bank 3: Reading.
Skills Bank 3: Study Skills.
Skills Bank 3: Writing.

SKY Computers, Inc., (0-926853), 27 Industrial Ave., Chelmsford, MA 01824 Tel 508-250-1920; FAX: 508-250-0036.
Titles:
SKYvec.

SLACK, Inc., (0-913590; 0-943432; 1-55642), 6900 Grove Rd., Thorofare, NJ 08086-9447 Tel 609-848-1000; Toll free: 800-257-8290; FAX: 609-853-5991.
Titles:
COTA Examination Review Check.

Small Business Computers of New England, Inc., P.O. Box 397, Amherst, NH 03031 Tel 603-673-0228; FAX: 603-673-0767.
Titles:
WormStat.

Small Business Management Systems, Inc., (0-924545), 92 Walling Rd., Warwick, NY 10990 Tel 914-258-4844; FAX: 914-258-6097.
Titles:
The Retail Solution.

Small Computer Co., Inc., (0-918697), 41 Saw Mill River Rd., Hawthorne, NY 10532 Tel 914-769-3160; Toll free: 800-847-4740; FAX: 914-769-3653; 40 W. Ridgewood Ave., Ridgewood, NJ 07450.
Titles:
FilePro Plus.
FilePro 16.
FilePro 16 Plus Network.
Medical Office System: MOS.

Smart Communications, Inc., (0-918139), 885 Third Ave., 29th Flr., New York, NY 10022 Tel 212-486-1894; FAX: 212-826-9775.
Titles:
Smart Expert Editor.
SMART TRANSLATORS: English-French-Spanish-German-Italian-Greek.

Smart Software, Inc., (0-928773), 4 Hill Rd., Belmont, MA 02178 Tel 617-489-2743; Toll free: 800-762-7899; FAX: 617-489-2748.
Titles:
SmartForecasts II Standard Edition.

Smith, Dean Lance, (0-918699), 10907 Cedarhurst, Houston, TX 77096.
Titles:
Signature Generator.

Smith Micro Software, Inc., (0-926884; 0-923426), 51 Columbia, Aliso Viejo, CA 92656-1456 Tel 714-362-2345; Toll free: 800-964-7671; FAX: 714-362-2300.
Titles:
Cross Connect.
Cross Connect Inbound.
Cross Connect Outbound.
CrossConnect.
HotFax.
HotLine.
QuickLink Gold.

Snow Software, Div. of Snow International Corp., 2360 Congress Ave., Clearwater, FL 34623 Tel 813-784-8899; FAX: 813-786-1904.
Titles:
Snow Report Writer.
Snow Report Writer: Network Version.

Snowflake Software, (1-56040), 8 Cedar Heights Rd., Rhinebeck, NY 12572 Tel 914-876-3328.
Titles:
Test Quest.

Snyder, Tom, Productions, Inc., (0-926891; 1-55998), 80 Coolidge Hill Rd., Watertown, MA 02172 Tel 617-926-6000; Toll free: 800-342-0236; FAX: 617-926-6222.
Titles:
The Other Side: A Global Conflict Resolution Kit.
Reading Magic Library: Fizz & Martina in "Tough Krudd".
Reading Magic Library: Flodd, the Bad Guy.
Reading Magic Library: Hansel & Gretel.
Reading Magic Library: Hilary & the Beast.
Reading Magic Library: Jack & the Beanstalk.

Sof-Ware Tools, P.O. Box 8751, Boise, ID 83707 Tel 208-343-1437; FAX: 208-336-2536.
Titles:
Engineering Tool Kit.
Lab Partner.
Process Control Chart Tool Kit.
Stats Tool Kit.

SofSolutions, 5078 S. 108th St., No. 163, Omaha, NE 68137-6310 Tel 210-735-0746.
Titles:
dBASE On-Line.

Soft & Friendly, (0-926897), P.O. Box 65, Rte. 2, Solsberry, IN 47459 Tel 812-825-7384.
Titles:
Print-Characters.
Print Screen.
ProWriter Utilities.

PUBLISHER/TITLE INDEX

Soft Estate, (0-928463), 1400 Nottingham Ct., No. 1A, Wheeling, IL 60090-6960.
Titles:
Real Estate Investment Analysis Customizing Kit.

Soft GAMs Software, P.O. Box 1311, Mendocino, CA 95460 Tel 707-961-1632.
Titles:
DOG: Disk OrGanizer.

Soft Images, Div. of Decision Systems, Inc., (0-926904), 200 Rte. 17, Mahwah, NJ 07430 Tel 201-529-1440; FAX: 201-529-3163.
Titles:
Pandemonium.

Soft Path Systems, (0-933009), Cheshire Hse., 105 N. Adams, Eugene, OR 97402 Tel 503-342-3439.
Titles:
BrainStormer.

Soft Tech, Inc., (0-938087), 30003 Hickory Ln., Franklin, MI 48025-1566.
Titles:
Matrix Calculator.
RESICALC.
SPARSEPACK.

Soft Warehouse, Inc., (0-926919), 3660 Waialae Ave., Suite 304, Honolulu, HI 96816-3236 Tel 808-734-5801; FAX: 808-735-1105. Do not confuse with Soft Warehouse, Fort Wayne, IN.
Titles:
Derive, A Mathematical Assistant.
muLISP-90.

SoftCraft, Inc., (0-926927), 16 N. Carroll St., Madison, WI 53703 Tel 608-257-3300; Toll free: 800-351-0500; FAX: 608-257-6733. Do not confuse with SoftCraft, Inc., Austin, TX.
Titles:
Fancy Font.
Fancy Word.
Font Effects.
Font Solution Pack.
Font Special Effects Pack.
Laser Fonts.
Scaleable Fonts.
Soft Craft Graphical Custom Control.
SoftCraft Font Editor.
SoftCraft Presenter.
SoftCraft Standard Series Fonts.
Spinfont.

Softdisk, Inc., (1-55801), P.O. Box 30008, Shreveport, LA 71130-0008; Toll free: 800-831-2694; 606 Common St., Shreveport, LA 71130-0008 Tel 318-221-8718.
Titles:
The Compleat Alfredo: Animated Adventures.
Diskworld.
First Encounter: The Ultimate Earthling Challenge.
Mail-Outs.

Softek Design, Inc., P.O. Box 2100, Telluride, CO 81435 Tel 303-728-5252; FAX: 303-728-6767.
Titles:
A4.

SofterWare, Inc., (0-926937), 540 Pennsylvania Ave., No. 200, Fort Washington, PA 19034 Tel 215-628-0400; Toll free: 800-220-4111; FAX: 215-628-0585.
Titles:
DonorPerfect.
EZ-Camp.
EZ-Care.
Mac CARE.

Softext Publishing Corp., (0-934577), 50 Sagamore Dr., Syosset, NY 11791 Tel 212-682-2773.
Titles:
Art & Science of Decision Making.
Basic Business Finance.
Basic Business Forecasting.
Basic Business Graphics.
File Xfer.
Forecasting Software System.
MTplus Tools for Pascal MTplus-86.
Scheduling & Control.

Softflair, Inc., 7389 Lilac Ln., Victoria, MN 55386-9768.
Titles:
AmPack.
FinPlan-10.
LoanLease Library.

SoftKlone Distributing Corp., 327 Office Plaza Dr., Suite 100, Tallahassee, FL 32301 Tel 904-878-8564; Toll free: 800-634-8670; FAX: 904-877-9763.
Titles:
Mirror-Fax with Voice.
MIRROR for Windows.
MIRROR III.
MIRROR III LAN.
MIRROR 3-FAX.
MIRROR-VFMS (Voice - Fax - Messaging System).
TAKEOVER.

SoftLogic Solutions, P.O. Box 4840, Manchester, NH 03108-4840 Tel 603-627-9900; Toll free: 800-272-9900.
Titles:
@Liberty.
CUBIT.
Disk Optimizer.
Disk Optimizer for Windows.
DoubleDOS.
Open Link Extender: (OLE').
Software Carousel.
WinSense.

Softool Corp., (0-926942), 340 S. Kellogg Ave., Goleta, CA 93117 Tel 805-683-5777; FAX: 805-683-4105.
Titles:
Change & Configuration Control (CCC) Enterprise Wide Life-Cycle Management.

Softouch Software, Inc., 5200 S.W. Macadam, Suite 255, Portland, OR 97201 Tel 503-241-1841; Toll free: 800-829-1841.
Titles:
Cost Management System.
Customer Profile System.

Softpoint Co., (0-926909), 1003 Crest Ln., Carnegie, PA 15106 Tel 412-279-4130.
Titles:
Project Management Systems I.
Softpoint PMS.

Softquest, Inc., (0-918701), P.O. Box 3456, McLean, VA 22103 Tel 703-281-1621.
Titles:
The Smart Checkbook.

SofTrak Systems, 1574 W. 1700 S., Salt Lake City, UT 84104-3469 Tel 801-973-9610; FAX: 801-973-9725.
Titles:
CustomGantt Plus.
MicroTrak.
MultiGantt.
PlotTrak.

SOFTWARE DESIGN, INC.

Softronics, Inc., (0-926952), 5085 List Dr., Colorado Springs, CO 80919 Tel 719-593-9540; Toll free: 800-225-8590.
Titles:
Instant Terminal.
Softerm PC.
Softerm 2.

SoftServe Pr., Div. of Rohrbough-Houser, (1-877855), 7000 Bianca Ave., Van Nuys, CA 91406-3512 Tel 818-996-7000; Toll free: 800-777-8710; FAX: 818-996-0008.
Titles:
FastTrack.

SoftShell International, Ltd., 715 Horizon Dr., No. 390, Grand Junction, CO 81506-8727 Tel 303-242-7502; FAX: 303-242-6469. Do not confuse with SoftShell, Bel Air, MD.
Titles:
ChemIntosh.
ChemWindow.
ChemWindow Classic.

Softsync, Inc., Subs. of Expert Software, (0-918145), 56 Technology Dr., Irvine, CA 92718-2301; Toll free: 800-933-2537; FAX: 305-443-3255.
Titles:
Accountant, Inc.

Software AG, (0-926961), 11190 Sunrise Valley Dr., Reston, VA 22091 Tel 703-860-5050; Toll free: 800-336-3761.
Titles:
Adabas.
Natural.
Natural-Connection.
Natural Construct.

Software Applications of Wichita, 2204 Winstead Cir., Wichita, KS 67226 Tel 316-684-0304.
Titles:
TaxAide.

Software Complement, 8 Pennsylvania Ave., Matamoras, PA 18336 Tel 717-491-2492; FAX: 717-491-2443.
Titles:
Logos On-Line.

Software Constructors, Inc., P.O. Box 1305, Franklin, TN 37065 Tel 615-791-7778.
Titles:
Accounting 4 Construction.
Estimating 4 Construction.

Software Creations, (0-926987), 550 Carson Plaza Ct., Suite 222, Carson, CA 90746 Tel 310-324-7032; FAX: 310-324-9577. Do not confuse with Software Creations, Aiea, HI.
Titles:
Bill-85.

Software Design, Inc., (0-918149), 1945 Mitchell Ave., Waterloo, IA 50702 Tel 319-235-1314; Toll free: 800-553-0002; FAX: 319-232-8903.
Titles:
ACCESS Accounts Payable.
ACCESS Accounts Receivable.
ACCESS General Ledger.
ACCESS Order Entry-Inventory.
ACCESS Payroll.
Prospect Tracking: Sales Control.
SD Accounting.
64 Accounting.
Support Tracking.

Software Designs 2000, (0-928464), P.O. Box 13238, Albuquerque, NM 87192 Tel 505-294-2165.
Titles:
Large-Integer Programming Subprograms (LIPS).
Linear Least Squares FORTRAN Subprogram.
Linear Programming Subprograms in ANSI FORTRAN (LPSUBS).
LP-2000.

Software Development Group, P.O. Box 18027, Boulder, CO 80308 Tel 303-444-8789.
Titles:
ProcessTerm.

Software Development Systems, Inc., 815 Commerce Dr., Oak Brook, IL 60521-8838 Tel 708-368-0400; Toll free: 800-448-7733; FAX: 708-990-4641. Do not confuse with Software Development Corp., Milwaukee, WI.
Titles:
CrossCode C for the 68000 Microprocessor Family.
FreeForm Debugger.
UniWare Cross Assemblers.
UniWare Z80 C Compiler.

Software Discoveries, Inc., 137 Krawski Dr., South Windsor, CT 06074 Tel 203-872-1024.
Titles:
MergeWrite.
RecordHolderPlus.

Software Engineering Technologies, Inc., 1725 K St. NW, Suite 611, Washington, DC 20006 Tel 202-785-8585; FAX: 202-659-8544.
Titles:
Menu Control System ("MCS").
Rent Control Compliance ("RCC").
Set Optometric System ("SOS"): For MS-Windows 3.1.

Software Enterprise, Ltd., (0-9638498), P.O. Box 91370, Portland, OR 97291-1370; FAX: 503-629-4984; 15455 NW Greenbrier Pkwy., Suite 210, Beaverton, OR 97006 Tel 503-645-6760.
Titles:
Daniel the Dinosaur Teaches Concepts: Same & Different.

Software Factory, Inc., The, 7042 S. Blue Creek Rd., Evergreen, CO 80439-6306 Tel 303-674-9430; FAX: 303-674-9428.
Titles:
EZ-INSTALL Installation Aid.

Software General Corp., Subs. of J. Vilkaitis Consultants, (0-927761), P.O. Box 26, Thomaston, CT 06787 Tel 203-283-4232.
Titles:
Tab Talk: The Mnemonics Revolution.

Software Lab East, 121 Gordon St., Ridgefield Park, NJ 07660 Tel 201-440-9593.
Titles:
Fire Reporter.
SLE - Business Series: Business Management Modules for dBASE III.

Software Link, Inc., The, (0-927031), 5575 Chamblee Dunwoody Rd., No. 205B, Atlanta, GA 30338-4142; FAX: 404-263-6474.
Titles:
LANLink 5X.
LANLink Laptop.
PC EmuLink.
PC-MOS 3.0.
PC-MOS 4.0.

Software Machine, Inc., (0-9626705), P.O. Box 270269, Tampa, FL 33688-0269; Toll free: 800-658-8484; FAX: 801-483-1199.
Titles:
AutoPLOT 1.
AutoPLOT 2.
AutoPLOT 3.

Software Marketing Assocs., (0-932701), 1100 Snowy Owl Ct., Austin, TX 78746-5253 Tel 512-327-3091.
Titles:
FYI 3000 Plus.
SuperFile.

Software Matters, Inc., (0-927035), 7803 Meadowbrook Dr., Indianapolis, IN 46240 Tel 317-253-8088; Toll free: 800-253-5274.
Titles:
Buffer-Master.
Calc-Pad.
Flash, the Disk Accelerator.
Sort-Merge-Copy.
Spool-Master.
Super-Ed.
Unprotect.

Software Models, (0-927037), P.O. Box 3610, Crestline, CA 92325 Tel 909-338-5075.
Titles:
Construction Job Cost Estimating.
Finance Models.
Finance Projections.
Home Finance Management.
Real Estate Investment Comparisons.

Software of the Future, Inc., (0-927517), P.O. Box 531650, Grand Prairie, TX 75053 Tel 214-264-2626; Toll free: 800-766-7355; FAX: 214-262-7338.
Titles:
MarketForce Corporate: Telemarketing, Direct Marketing & Client Management Software.
MarketForce Plus: Telemarketing, Direct Marketing & Client Management Software.
WindowDOS.

Software Options, Inc., (0-927042), 473 Sylvan Ave., Englewood Cliffs, NJ 07632-2915 Tel 201-568-6664; FAX: 201-568-6992.
Titles:
C.O.T.S/BOSS.
COTS/DEALER Options System.

Software Power Co., P.O. Box 14133, Fremont, CA 94539 Tel 510-490-6086.
Titles:
Power Disk.

Software Products International, (0-927048), 6620 Flanders Dr., San Diego, CA 92121 Tel 619-450-1526.
Titles:
Open Access.
Open Access II.
Open Access II Plus.

Software Resources, (0-927057), 750 Washington St., No. 345, Boston, MA 02111-1533.
Titles:
Cue.
ESP.

Software Science, Inc., 168 S. Park St., No. 500, San Francisco, CA 94107-1809 Tel 415-697-0411; Toll free: 800-468-9273; FAX: 415-697-1916. Do not confuse with Software Science Pr., Inc., Oak Brook, IL.
Titles:
EZTOUCH.
SayWhat?!
TOPAZ.
Topaz for C/C Plus Plus.

Software Shop Systems, Inc., (0-927068; 0-927067), P.O. Box 1973, 1340 Campus Pkwy., Wall, NJ 07719-1973 Tel 908-938-3200; Toll free: 800-554-9865; FAX: 908-938-5631.
Titles:
ACE.
The Construction Manager.
ESTMAT 2000.
TOPS.

Software Solutions, Inc., 3425B Corporate Way, Duluth, GA 30136 Tel 770-418-2000; Toll free: 800-232-2999; FAX: 770-418-2022. Do not confuse with Software Solutions, Inc., Lebanon, OH.
Titles:
FACTS.
PRO$PER.

Software Solutions, Inc., (0-927073), 420 E. Main St., Lebanon, OH 45036-2234 Tel 513-932-6667; FAX: 513-932-4058. Do not confuse with Software Solutions, Inc., Duluth, GA.
Titles:
Municipal Management System.

Software Sorcery, (1-883189), 5405 Morehouse Dr., Suite 200, San Diego, CA 92121-4724 Tel 619-452-9901; Toll free: 800-541-4489; FAX: 619-452-5079.
Titles:
AEGIS: Guardian of the Fleet.
Jutland.

Software Teacher, Inc., The, (0-928781), P.O. Box 650, Montrose, AL 36559 Tel 334-928-3711.
Titles:
Film Writing.

Software Technology, Inc., (0-926681), 1621 Cushman Dr., Lincoln, NE 68512 Tel 402-423-1440; FAX: 402-423-2561. Do not confuse with Software Technology, Portland, OR.
Titles:
Accounts Payable System.
Accounts Payable System Jr.
Accounts Payable System-M.
APS (Accounts Payable System).
Case Master III.
Case Master III-M.
Case Master III.
CDS-M (Critical Date Systems-M).
Critical Date System Jr.
Critical Date System JR-M.
General Ledger System Jr.
General Ledger System-M Jr.
GLS (General Ledger System).
GLS-M (General Ledger System-M).
Profit$ource.
STI Critical Date System (CDS).
TABS III - Report Writer.
TABS III - Report Writer-M: M.
TABS III Jr.
TABS III-M Jr.
TABS III-M (Time Accounting & Billing System III-M).
TABS III-R (Time Accounting & Billing System III-R).
TABS III (Time Accounting & Billing System III).
TAS-M (Trust Accounting System-M).
TAS (Trust Accounting System).
Trust Accounting System Jr.
Trust Accounting System Jr-M (TAS Jr-M).

Software Toolworks, (0-88718; 0-935029; 0-87085; 0-7911), 60 Leveroni Ct., Novato, CA 94949 Tel 415-883-3000; Toll free: 800-234-3088; FAX: 415-883-3033.
Titles:
AccuWeather.
Captain Blood.
Casino Pack One.
CD Game Pack.

PUBLISHER/TITLE INDEX

CD Game Pack Two.
The Chessmaster 3000.
Contraption Zack.
Crossword Magic.
D/Generation.
Four Crystals of Trazere.
Game Pack Three.
Game Pak One.
The Guinness Disc of Records, 1993.
The Hunt for Red October.
Life & Death.
Life & Death II: The Brain.
Loom.
Mario Is Missing.
Mario Is Missing! CD Deluxe.
Mario Is Missing!: City Disk.
Mario's Time Machine.
Mavis Beacon Teaches Typing!
The New Grolier Multimedia Encyclopedia.
Newsweek Interactive.
Paperboy Two.
The San Diego Zoo Presents The Animals!
The Secret of Monkey Island.
Secret Weapons of the Luftwaffe.
The Software Toolworks Presents Capitol Hill.
The Software Toolworks Presents Oceans Below.
The Software Toolworks Presents Space Shuttle.
The Software Toolworks Travel Companion.
The Software Toolworks U. S. Atlas.
The Software Toolworks World Atlas.
Toolworks Backup Pro.
Toolworks Desk Reference.
Toolworks LengthWise.
Toolworks Office Manager.
Toolworks Reference Library.
The Twentieth Century Video Almanac.
Word for Word.

Software Ventures Corp., (0-924169), 2907 Claremont Ave., Berkeley, CA 94705 Tel 510-644-3232; Toll free: 800-336-6477; FAX: 510-848-0885.
Titles:
MicroPhone II.
MicroPhone LT for Macintosh.
MicroPhone Pro for Macintosh.
MicroPhone Pro for Windows.

Software Visions, Inc., 12625 La Tortola, San Diego, CA 92129 Tel 619-538-6263; Toll free: 800-527-7014. Do not confuse with Software Visions in Cypress, CA.
Titles:
Microfiche Filer Plus.
Microfiche Filer: The Graphic Database.

Softwood Co., (0-943533), 3850 Royal Ave., Simi Valley, CA 93063 Tel 805-522-9800; Toll free: 800-775-4100; FAX: 805-522-7300.
Titles:
Write & File.

Solana Software International, 3751 Sixth Ave., San Diego, CA 92103 Tel 619-291-1533; Toll free: 800-748-5596; FAX: 619-291-9748.
Titles:
Imaging for DataEase (IFD).

Solar Systems Software, 8105 Shelter Creek Ln., San Bruno, CA 94066-3829 Tel 415-952-2375; FAX: 415-952-7507.
Titles:
Ed-U-Games Cultural Literacy Edition.
Templates of Doom.

Solarsoft, Div. of Kinetic Software, Inc., (0-927108), 12672 Skyline Blvd., Woodside, CA 94062 Tel 415-851-4484.
Titles:
Daylite.
Sunpas.
Sunpas/Sunop: Energy Analysis.
Tswing.

Solea Systems, Inc., 61 Bennington, Irvine, CA 92720-2708 Tel 714-551-1852.
Titles:
Text Manager.

Solid State Software, Inc., (0-925069), 1401 N. Jesse James Rd., Excelsior Springs, MO 64024 Tel 816-637-8638; FAX: 816-637-4101. Do not confuse with Solid State Software of Foster City, CA.
Titles:
Capacity Planning.
MPAC: Manufacturing Planning & Control.

Solomon Software, Div. of TLB, Inc., (0-927413), 200 E. Hardin St., P.O. Box 414, Findlay, OH 45839 Tel 419-424-0422; Toll free: 800-476-5666; FAX: 419-424-3400.
Titles:
Solomon III.
Solomon IV.

Solutions, Inc., 4526 Fountain Dr., Wilmington, NC 28403 Tel 910-395-0233.
Titles:
Professional Layout Templates Collection I for Pagemaker 2.0.

Solutions! Publishing Co., (0-929770), 8016 Plainfield Rd., Cincinnati, OH 45236 Tel 513-891-6145; Toll free: 800-255-6643.
Titles:
Complete Property Manager-II.
Complete Real Estate Investor.
Professional Property Manager.
!Solutions!Word!

Somerville Assocs., 1093 S. Governors Ave., Dover, DE 19901-6907 Tel 302-678-2131.
Titles:
Classical Compact Disc Guide.
Mac 'n Med II Medical Office Management System.
Mac 'n Med Spelling Checker.

Sorites Group, Inc., (0-927134), 8136 Old Keene Mill Rd., Suite A-309, P.O. Box 2939, Springfield, VA 22152 Tel 703-569-1400.
Titles:
SORITEC.

Sound Advice, Inc., P.O. Box 278, Cazadero, CA 95421 Tel 707-632-5911; FAX: 707-632-5751.
Titles:
Drill Report.
FirePlan.
MACCFIRS.
Resource Manager.

Sound Decisions, (0-926911), 6646 Clearhaven Cir., Dallas, TX 75248-4020 Tel 214-404-9445.
Titles:
Appraisal Management System.
Multilayer Thin Film Interference Program: (MIP).

Sound Source Interactive, 2985 E. Hillcrest Dr., No. A, Westlake Village, CA 91362 Tel 805-494-9996.
Titles:
The Adventures of Batman & Robin: Interactive MovieBook.
Babe: Interactive MovieBook.
Babylon 5: Limited Edition CD-ROM Entertainment Utility.
Black Beauty: Interactive Moviebook.
ExoSquad: Interactive MovieBook.
Free Willy 2: The Adventure Home.
Lassie: Interactive MovieBook.
Little Rascals.
Return of the Jedi AudioClips.
Saturday Night Live: Screen Saver.
The Secret Garden: Interactive Moviebook.
Star Trek Classic AudioClips.
Star Trek Motion Pictures AudioClips.
Star Wars Trilogy: Limited Edition CD-ROM.
STNG Collection AudioClips.
SW01W AudioClips: Star Wars.
SW02W AudioClips: Empire Strikes Back.
T201PC AudioClips: Terminator 2.
TR01PC AudioClips: Total Recall.
The Twilight Zone: Screen Saver.
T2S01W: Terminator 2: the Screen Saver.

SourceMate Information Systems, Inc., 20 Sunnyside Ave., Mill Valley, CA 94941 Tel 415-381-1011; Toll free: 800-877-8896; FAX: 415-381-6902.
Titles:
AccountMate Professional.

SourceView Software International, Subs. of The SourceView Corp., (0-87007; 0-87017), P.O. Box 578, 1663B Willow Pass Rd., Concord, CA 94522-0578 Tel 510-689-5668; FAX: 510-689-5669.
Titles:
Active Investor.
Agenda Master.
Apartment Mortgage Analysis.
AppleWriter Enhancer.
Armageddon.
Author's Aid.
Baseball Power.
Biorhythm Master.
BisPlan Master.
Blackjack Tutor.
Bowling Secretary.
Brain Damage.
Breeze.
Bulk Mailing Master.
Bulletin Board Construction Set.
BusBASIC.
Business Planning Master.
Business Pro-Pak.
Business Utility Master.
Cal LottoMaster.
Capital Investment Analysis.
Cardio Pulmonary Master.
Cash Flow Analysis.
Catacombs.
Cinema Master.
Construction Cash Flow Master.
Construction Master.
Conversion Master.
CP/M Emulator Master.
CPNIX.
Critical Path Analysis.
Db.Bas.
dbSecure II.
Dental Master.
Depreciation Master.
DesignMaster.
Desktop Accountant.
Desktop Time and Billing.
Diet Analysis.
DirLabel.
Disk Master.
Dispatch Route Sales.
DriveAlyne.
Edifice.
Electronic BillBoard.
EPRINT.
EpsWord.
The Estimator.
Executive Chess.
Executive Mastery Accounting.
Executive Plus.
F77Lib.
Facilities Scheduler.
Facility Master.
Family Budget Analysis.
Farm Accounting.
Finance I.
Finance Manager.
Flex-i-Term.
Flight Master.
Flight Plan.
Flow Master.

SOUTH-WESTERN PUBLISHING CO.

FLX-I-SORT.
The Football Book.
Football Master.
Forecaster.
Fun City.
Gambler's Game Pak.
Garden Master.
GemStar.
GhostWriter 128.
Graphics BASIC.
Graphics Master.
Halley's Comet Locator.
HealthMaster.
Hello Master.
HES MON 64.
Home Budgetor.
Household Expenses Profile.
HVAC Design.
Icarus.
Icarus87.
Infodex.
Interactive Appointments.
Interactive Bibliography.
Interactive Catalog.
Interactive Cobol Generator.
Interactive Cobol Generator (IBM).
Interactive Options.
Interactive StatPak.
Interactive Stock.
Interactive Warranty.
Investment Analyzer.
I.R.A. Selector.
Language Collection.
LawStar.
Learning to Sail.
LibMan.
Library!: Personal Edition for Windows.
Linear Programming Master.
Linear Regression Master.
List Handler.
Lister.
Lock & Key.
Love Games.
Lynngyde.
Machine Engineering I.
MacroCircuits.
Market Master.
Master the Market.
Membership Master.
MicroMain.DB.
MicroMind Knowledge Engineering Tool.
Micronics Accounts Payable.
Micronics Balance Forward.
Micronics General Ledger.
Micronics Integrated.
Micronics Inventory.
Micronics Open Account.
Micronics Payroll.
Milky Way Merchant.
Mines of Morell.
Model Railroaders.
MSI Print.
MUNI Water Billing.
Music Master.
NetPoint.
Normal-Aid.
Omnibase.
OmniCalc.
OmniFiler.
OmniWriter & OmniSpeller.
Optima Accounting.
Optima Accounts Payable.
Optima Accounts Receivable.
Optima General Ledger.
Optima Inventory.
Optima Load Scheduling.
Optima Order Processing & Sales Analysis.
Optima Payroll.
Optima Production & Cost Control System.
Optima Project Cost Control System.
Optima Requirements Generation System.
Organization Master.
Oubliette.
P-Lisp.
Patch Com.
PC Accountant.
PC Forms.
PC Home Checkbook.
PC Line Monitor.
PC Mailer.
PC Screen.
PC Secure.
PC Word.
PCBanner.
Perpetual Calendar.
Personal Budget System.
Pilot Master.
Portfolio Master.
Professional Patient Scheduling.
Profit Projection Analysis.
ProfitShare.
Project Master.
ProMaster.
ProTex.
Publishing Production Design.
Quicksearch.
Real Estate Aids.
Real Estate Collection.
Rent-All Master.
Resident Expert.
Sailing Master.
SalesView.
Sampling Quality Control.
ScatterPlot.
Service Station Master.
Sewer Man.
sFINX.
64Forth.
SketchPad.
SlideShow.
Small Text.
Smart Calendar.
Source Accounting.
SourceView Accountant's Time & Billing.
SourceView Accounting.
SourceView Agenda Master.
SourceView Attorney's Time & Billing.
SourceView Attorney's Time and Billing I.
SourceView Attorneys's Time and Billing II.
SourceView Basic.
SourceView Budget Trac.
SourceView CommStar.
SourceView Conflict of Interest.
SourceView Docket Control.
SourceView Flexi-Sort.
SourceView HotPack.
SourceView KnowConflicts.
SourceView Professional Time & Billing.
SourceView Time & Billing System.
Sprite King.
StatMaster.
Stock Options.
Subscription Master.
Summit.
Super Accounts Receivable.
Super General Ledger.
Super Inventory.
Super Payables.
Super Payroll.
SuperBASIC.
SuperGraphs.
Superlabels.
Supra Accounting.
Supra Accounting System.
Supra Accounts Payable.
Supra Billing.
Supra General Ledger.
Supra Inventory.
Supra Ledgers.
Supra Payables.
Synthesis III.
TaskMaster.
TaskMaster-MAC.
TaxTable Tutor.
Teletype.
There's A Worm in My Apple!!
3DTTT.
Throw Five.
Tic-Tac-Max.
Tone Routine Generator.
TopHat.
TransferTex.
Turbo Pilot.
Turtle Toyland Jr.
Typing Mastery.
Unique 120.
Utilities Watchdog.
Video Store Master.
VMMS.
Wood Heat Calculator.
WSVX80.
XPL Basic.
XPL Master.
Xref Plus.

South-Western Publishing Co., Subs. of International Thomson Organization, Inc., (0-538), 5101 Madison Rd., Cincinnati, OH 45227 Tel 513-271-8811; Toll free: 800-543-0487; FAX: 513-527-6194; Dist. by: Van Nostrand Reinhold, 115 Fifth Ave., New York, NY 10003 Tel 212-254-3232.
Titles:
Accounting Tutorial.
The Adventures of Ricky Racoon: Lost in the Woods.
Alphabetic Keyboarding.
BriefCASE: The Collegiate Systems Development Tool.
Business Communication for the Microcomputer.
Business Law, Comprehensive Volume.
Business Mathematics for Colleges.
Business Simulator Collegiate Edition w Business Week Articles.
College Accounting - Practice Sets.
Computerized Inventory Procedures.
COST ACCOUNTING: Planning & Control - Practice Case.
DisplayWrite 3 Tutorial.
Electronic Spreadsheet Applications for Cost Accounting.
Electronic Spreadsheet Applications for Intermediate Acctg.
Financial Calculator.
Financial Cookbook: A Consumer's Guide.
Human Resources Simulation for Lotus 1-2-3.
Integrated Accounting on Microcomputers.
Investor.
Keyboarding Skill Development.
Keymates: A Color Keyboarding System.
Let's Color: Coloring Book Software.
Lotus 1-2-3: Principles & Applications.
The Magic Applehouse.
Marketing Decision Making Using Lotus 1-2-3.
MicroType Pro.
The MultiMate Advantage.
Multimedia Reference for Writers.
Music Boosters: An Entrepreneurial Adventure.
Numeric Keyboarding.
Numeric Keypad Operation.
Paws in Typing Town.
Payroll Accounting for Microcomputers.
Personal Finance.
Principles of Cost Accounting - Computerized Practice Set.
Productivity Tools for the Microcomputer.
Resources for Strategic Analysis.
Small Business Management Using Lotus 1-2-3.
Strategic Retail Management: A Lotus 1-2-3 Based Simulation.
Strategy! A Business Unit Simulation.
Terminology for Allied Health Professionals.

Southeastern Software, (0-927146), 667 Missimer Ln., Vinton, VA 24179.
Titles:
Data Capture.
Data Capture IIe.
Data Capture III.
Data Capture PC.
Mac Transfer.
The Movie Stack.

Southern Computer Systems, Inc., (0-918157), 2732 Seventh Ave., S., Birmingham, AL 35233 Tel 205-251-2985; Toll free: 800-533-6879; FAX: 205-322-4851.
Titles:
ImageKey.
KeyEntry III: PC-Based Software Data Entry System.

Southern Software Systems, Inc., (0-927152), 2411 Edenborn, Metairie, LA 70001 Tel 504-552-9204. Do not confuse with Southern Software of Ocean Springs, MS.
Titles:
COMIS.
PHARMIS: Pharmacy Information System.

Southland Assocs., (0-928353), 655 Sky Way, Suite 207, San Carlos, CA 94070 Tel 415-595-4992.
Titles:
EASY!ROUTE II: Amusement Route Management System.

Southwest Data Systems, (0-932721), 3017 San Fernando Blvd., Burbank, CA 91504 Tel 818-841-1610; Toll free: 800-325-3488.
Titles:
Pluto: Business BASIC & Interpreter.

Southwest Music Systems, Inc., 91 Ann Lee Rd., Harvard, MA 01451 Tel 508-772-9471.
Titles:
MIDI Stack.
MidiPaint.
MidiShare.
One-Step.

Space Remote Sensing Ctr., Div. of Institute for Technology Development, Bldg. 1103, Suite 118, Stennis Space Center, MS 39529 Tel 601-688-2509; FAX: 601-688-2861.
Titles:
Mac Grass.

Spartan Software Systems, P.O. Box 7405, Endicott, NY 13760 Tel 607-748-9491.
Titles:
Guitar Master.
Keyboard Master.
MidiFile Reader.

Speak Softly, Inc., (0-918161), 303 Calvert Ave., Clinton, SC 29325 Tel 803-833-5407.
Titles:
Card & Label Manager (CALM).

Specialized Computer Systems, 4016 Quartz Dr., Santa Rosa, CA 95405 Tel 707-539-9003.
Titles:
Edit Worx: Video Editing & Production Management.

Specialized Data Systems, Inc., (0-918709), P.O. Box 8278, Madison, WI 53708 Tel 608-241-5050; FAX: 608-241-3353.
Titles:
Farm Biz.
Farm Sense.
GEMIDEX: PC Data Entry.
Ultra F.A.R.M: (Farm Accounting & Records Management).

Specialized Software, 24050 Timberlane Dr., Beachwood, OH 44122 Tel 216-292-5260.
Titles:
Altar Boy Scheduler.
Borlog.
Camp Planning System.
Hebrew Enhancement of First Word Plus.
Hyperwedding Planner.
Specialized Fonts.

Specialized Systems Consultants, Inc., (0-916151), P.O. Box 55549, Seattle, WA 98155 Tel 206-527-3385; FAX: 206-527-2806.
Titles:
PubliCalc.

Spectra Publishing, Div. of PC Software Interest Group, (0-915835), 1030 E. Duane, Suite D, Sunnyvale, CA 94086 Tel 408-730-9291; Toll free: 800-245-6717; FAX: 408-730-2107.
Titles:
Power BASIC.

Spectral Assocs., (0-918163), 3418 S. 90th St., Tacoma, WA 98409 Tel 206-581-6938.
Titles:
Android Attack.
Galax Attax.
Ghost Gobbler.
Keys of the Wizard.
Lancer.
Lunar Rover Patrol.
Planet Invasion.
Whirly Bird Run.

Spectrum Computer Services, Inc., 32 David St., Holliston, MA 01746-1556 Tel 617-891-1450; Toll free: 800-541-4370.
Titles:
Rescue.

Spectrum Computing, Inc., P.O. Box 141097, Coral Gables, FL 33114 Tel 305-665-0404.
Titles:
Chameleon.

Spectrum HoloByte, Inc., (0-928784; 0-928299; 1-57190), 2490 Mariner Sq. Loop., Alameda, CA 94501 Tel 510-614-1288; FAX: 510-614-8431.
Titles:
Faces.
Falcon.
Falcon: F-16 Fighter Simulation.
Falcon MC.
Flight of the Intruder.
GATO: World War II Submarine Simulation.
Iron Helix.
Mi6-29: Deadly Adversary of Falcon.
National Lampoon's Chess Maniac 5 Billion & 1.
Orbiter: Space Shuttle Simulation.
PT-109: WWII Patrol Torpedo Simulation.
Solitaire Royale: Solitaire Card Games.
Stunt Driver.
Super Tetris.
TETRIS: The Soviet Challenge.
Tornado.
Vette!
Welltris.

SPECTRUM Human Resource Systems Corp., 1625 Broadway, Suite 2600, Denver, CO 80202 Tel 303-534-8813; Toll free: 800-334-5660; FAX: 303-592-3227.
Titles:
HRVantage.
HRVantage for Client/Server.

Spectrum Software, (0-927178), 1021 S. Wolfe Rd., Suite 130, Sunnyvale, CA 94086 Tel 408-738-4387; FAX: 408-738-4702. Do not confuse with Spectrum Software, Silver Spring, MD.
Titles:
Micro-Cap IV.
Micro-Logic II.

Spinnaker Software Corp., (0-917649; 1-55541; 0-923391; 0-929575), 201 Broadway, Cambridge, MA 02139-1901 Tel 617-494-1200; Toll free: 800-826-0706; FAX: 617-494-1219.
Titles:
Better Working Desktop.
BetterWorking Eight-in-One.
The BetterWorking One Person Office.
BetterWorking: The Resume Kit.
BetterWorking Word Processor.
BetterWorking Word Publisher.
Easy Working: The Filer.
Easy Working: The Planner.
Easy Working: The Writer.
Pinstripe Presenter.
Quadralien & Stargoose.
Sargon III.
Sargon IV.
The Scoop.
Spinnaker Plus.
Splash!

Spiral Enterprises, (0-927185), 308 Crown Rd., Willow Pk., Wetherford, TX 76087 Tel 817-441-8901.
Titles:
SMAS: Stock Market Advisor System.

Spirit of St. Louis Software Co., 18067 Edison Ave., Chesterfield, MO 63005 Tel 314-530-0757.
Titles:
Baseball the Series: Pitching Clinic.
Golf the Series: The Full Swing.

Splash Studios, 8573 154th Ave., NE, Redmond, WA 98052 Tel 206-882-0300.
Titles:
Piper: A VideoActive Adventure for Children of All Ages.

SportTime Computer Software, Div. of Jamner Enterprise, (1-877658), 324 S. P.C.H., No. 201, Redondo Beach, CA 90277 Tel 310-543-0501; Toll free: 800-752-9426 (orders only); FAX: 310-543-0503.
Titles:
College League Option Module.
College Season Disk 1990.
Jockey Competition Option Module.
OMNI-PLAY Basketball.
OMNI-PLAY Horse Racing.
Pro League Option Module.
Side-View Game Option Module.
Stable Owners Option Module.
Track Designer Option Module.
Track Two Option Module.

Spot Systems, Inc., (0-927186), 180 Montgomery St., Suite 1550, San Francisco, CA 94104-4230 Tel 415-982-8150; FAX: 415-982-2502.
Titles:
Foreign Exchange Trading System.
Global Limits Reporting System.
International Loan/Deposit Accounting System.
International Teller System.
Multi-Currency General Ledger.
Remote Draft-Wire Issuance System.
Remote Teller System.

Spreadsheet Solutions Corp., P.O. Box 231296, Great Neck, NY 11023-0296; Toll free: 800-634-8509; FAX: 516-222-1517.
Titles:
At Ease.
At Fixed Income.
FinCalc.

Spring Branch Software, Inc., (0-9625582), P.O. Box 342, Manchester, IA 52057 Tel 319-927-6532; FAX: 319-927-2979.
Titles:
GS Numerics.
MacNumerics.
MacNumerics Two.

Spring Systems, Inc., P.O. Box 10073, Chicago, IL 60610 Tel 312-275-5273.
Titles:
ARGUS: Perceptual Mapper.
MktSim: Marketing Simulation Model.

Squire Buresh Assocs., Inc., (0-927192), 27 Endmoor Rd., Westford, MA 01886-1450.
Titles:
Freecopy, Freeformat, Freemode, etc.
Repair.

Stafford Financial Services Corp., (0-925044), 9707 E. Colorado Ave., No. 107, Denver, CO 80231-3000.
Titles:
Professional Business Barometers.
Professional College Planner.
Professional Retirement Planner.
Professional Retirement Toolbox.
Professional Social Security Planner.

Stanford Business Systems, Inc., 400 Corporate Pointe, Suite 415, Culver City, CA 90230-7615 Tel 310-215-8444.
Titles:
SalesPower.

Stanograph Corp., 1500 Bishop Ct., Mount Prospect, IL 60056 Tel 510-352-8101; Toll free: 800-323-4247.
Titles:
BaronData Personal CAT: Computer Aided Transcription System.

Stansfield & Assocs., (0-927207), 101 Rainbow Dr., No. 3992, Livingston, TX 77351-9300.
Titles:
P&RC: Performance & Resource Chart.

Stanton Consulting, Inc., P.O. Box 28762, Saint Louis, MO 63146 Tel 314-542-0075; FAX: 314-638-2687.
Titles:
DentalChip.

Star-K Software Systems Corp., (0-927213), P.O. Box 209, Mount Kisco, NY 10549 Tel 914-241-0287; FAX: 914-241-0287.
Titles:
HUMBUG.
SK*DOS.

Star Micronics America, Inc., 420 Lexington Ave., Suite 2702, New York, NY 10170 Tel 212-986-6770.
Titles:
MacStar II.

Star Software, Inc., 220 Orange Ave., E., Longwood, FL 32750-4292; Toll free: 800-331-8125.
Titles:
The Perfect Word.

Starcom Microsystems, 25 W. 1480 N., Orem, UT 84057 Tel 801-225-1480.
Titles:
Family Heritage File.
Life History Disk.

Starlite Software Corp., (0-926447), P.O. Box 370, Hadlock, WA 98339 Tel 206-437-2650; Toll free: 800-888-8088; FAX: 206-437-0362.
Titles:
PC-Browse.
PC-Write Advanced Level.
PC-Write Standard Level.

Starwave Corp., 13810 SE Eastgate Way, Bellevue, WA 98005 Tel 206-957-2000.
Titles:
Eastwood.
The Muppet CD-ROM: Muppets Inside.
The Muppets CD-ROM: Muppets Inside.
Sting "All This Time".

State Business Systems, Inc., 78 Alwat St., Woodbridge, NJ 07095 Tel 201-634-7137.
Titles:
LISTER: Alternative to Spread Sheets.

State Of The Art, Inc., (0-918167), 56 Technology Dr., Irvine, CA 92718-2301 Tel 714-753-1222.
Titles:
M-A-S 90 Accounting Software.
M.A.S. 90 EVOLUTION/2: Import Master.
M.A.S. 90 EVOLUTION/2: Post Master.
M.A.S. 90 EVOLUTION/2.
M.A.S. 90 EVOLUTION/2: Accounts Payable.
M.A.S. 90 EVOLUTION/2: Accounts Receivable.
M.A.S. 90 EVOLUTION/2: Bank Reconciliation.
M.A.S. 90 EVOLUTION/2: General Ledger.
M.A.S. 90 EVOLUTION/2: Inventory Management.
M.A.S.90 EVOLUTION/2: Job Cost.
M.A.S. 90 EVOLUTION/2: Library Master & Report Master.
M.A.S. 90 EVOLUTION/2: Payroll.
M.A.S. 90 EVOLUTION/2: Purchase Order Processing.
M.A.S. 90 EVOLUTION/2: Sales Order Processing.
M.A.S. 90 EVOLUTION/2: Time & Billing.

Statistical Computing Consultants, (0-918169), 9804 Ward Ct., Fairfax, VA 22032-3933 Tel 703-250-9513.
Titles:
Survtab.

Statistical Programs, (0-932651), 9941 Rowlett, Suite 6, Houston, TX 77075 Tel 713-947-1551; FAX: 713-947-0604.
Titles:
BOX-B.
C-COMP.
EXPERIMENTAL DESIGN.
FACTORIAL-DESIGN.
LSQR.
MIXTURE-DESIGN.
SCREEN.
SIMPLEX-V: An Interactive Computer Program for Experimental Optimization.

StatPac, Inc., (0-918733), 4532 France Ave., S., Minneapolis, MN 55410 Tel 612-925-0159; FAX: 612-925-0851.
Titles:
Forecast Plus.
Goodness-of-Fit.
StatPac.
StatPac Gold IV.

StatSoft, Inc., (1-884233), 2325 E. 13th St., Tulsa, OK 74104-4405 Tel 918-583-4149; FAX: 918-583-4376.
Titles:
CSS/3.
CSS/3.
CSS:GRAPHICS.
Megafile Manager.
Quick CSS.
Quick STATISTICA/Mac.
Quick STATISTICA/w.
Quick STATISTICA for DOS.
Quick STATISTICA for the Macintosh.
Quick STATISTICA for Windows.
STATISTICA/DOS.
STATISTICA/Mac.
STATISTICA/QC.
STATISTICA - QC for DOS.
STATISTICA - QC for Windows: Industrial Statistics Modules.
STATISTICA/w.
STATISTICA for DOS.
STATISTICA for the Macintosh.
STATISTICA for the Macintosh: Industrial Statistics Modules.
STATISTICA for Windows.
STATISTICA/QC for Windows.

Stax!, 8008 Shoal Creek Blvd., Austin, TX 78758 Tel 512-467-4563; Toll free: 800-622-7829.
Titles:
The Macintosh Bible: Stax! Edition.
Stax! Helper.
Stax! Sound Effects Studio.

Stenograph Corp., Subs. of Quixote Co., (0-937112), 1500 Bishop Ct., Mount Prospect, IL 60056 Tel 708-803-1400; Toll free: 800-323-4247; FAX: 708-803-1089.
Titles:
Cimarron.
OmniCat.
Stenograph's BaronData Billing Address & Accounting System with The Scheduler.

Steppenwolff Corp., (0-924166), 82 Horatio St., 1B, New York, NY 10014 Tel 212-645-9618; FAX: 212-463-0050.
Titles:
Job Cost Accounting System.
Manufacturing Accounting & Control System.
Transportation Accounting & Control System.
Warehouse Locator System.
Warehouse Scheduling & Control System.

Stepstone Corp., The, 75 Glen Rd., Suite 115, Sandy Hook, CT 06482 Tel 203-426-1875; Toll free: 800-289-6253; FAX: 203-270-0106.
Titles:
Objective-C Compiler.

Sterling Castle, 56089 29 Palms Hwy., Suite 254, Yucca Valley, CA 92284 Tel 619-228-9653; Toll free: 800-776-3818; FAX: 619-369-1185.
Titles:
BestChoice 3.

Sterling Software, 1800 Alexander Bell Dr., Reston, VA 22091 Tel 703-264-8000; Toll free: 800-533-5128; FAX: 703-476-0328.
Titles:
INFO/MASTER.
NET/MASTER.
NET-MASTER: Advanced System Management (ASM).
SYS/MASTER.

Sterling Software Co., 202 E. Airport Dr., No. 280, San Bernardino, CA 92408 Tel 909-889-0226.
Titles:
Intelligent Backup.

Stevens Creek Software, 21346 Rumford Dr., Cupertino, CA 95014 Tel 408-725-0424; Toll free: 800-823-4279.
Titles:
The Athlete's Dairy.
PlotView.

Stiller Research, 2625 Ridgeway St., Tallahassee, FL 32310-5169; Toll free: 800-788-0787; FAX: 314-966-1833.
Titles:
Integrity Master: Anti-Virus - Data Integrity System.

StillWater Media, P.O. Box 789, Northport, NY 11768 Tel 516-261-4599.
Titles:
Test Master: A Series of Universal Game Templates for Training & Learning.

Stochos, Inc., (0-927236), 14 N. College St., Schenectady, NY 12305 Tel 518-372-5426; Toll free: 800-426-4014; FAX: 518-372-4789.
Titles:
Custom/QC.
Factor Extractor.

PUBLISHER/TITLE INDEX

SPC Direct.

Stokes Imaging Services, 7000 Cameron Rd., Austin, TX 78752 Tel 512-458-2201; FAX: 512-458-2309.
Titles:
Professional Image II.

Stolzberg Research, Inc., (0-918171), 3 Seabrook Ct., Stony Brook, NY 11790 Tel 516-751-4277; Toll free: 800-568-4634; FAX: 516-689-6671.
Titles:
Chemical Manufacturing Control System.
Cosmetics Manufacturing Control System.
Manufacturing Control System.
Pharmaceutical Manufacturing Control System.
Public Opinion Survey.

Stone & Assocs., (0-918173), 7910 Ivanhoe Ave., Suite 319, La Jolla, CA 92037 Tel 619-693-6333; Toll free: 800-733-1263; FAX: 619-693-6337.
Titles:
Catalist: File Manager Support for Your Word Processor.

STORM Software, Inc., 24100 Chagrin Blvd., Cleveland, OH 44122 Tel 216-464-1209; Toll free: 800-847-8249; FAX: 216-464-4222.
Titles:
Professional STORM.

Storm-Tech, (1-882873), Box 58331, Louisville, KY 40268-0331; FAX: 502-933-2361; 1731 Cloverbrook Dr., Louisville, KY 40268 Tel 502-366-7824.
Titles:
Prime Numbers: Generating Prime Numbers, Testing & Factoring Numbers.

Straightforward, 11918 Millpond Ct., Manassas, VA 22111-3283; FAX: 310-834-2377.
Titles:
ZFonts.

Strata Marketing, Inc., (0-927246), 540 N. Lake Shore Dr., Chicago, IL 60611-3414 Tel 312-222-1555; Toll free: 800-222-8482; FAX: 312-222-2510.
Titles:
Super-Ranker.

Strategic Management Group, Inc., (0-939465), 3624 Market St., University City Science Ctr., Philadelphia, PA 19104 Tel 215-387-4000; Toll free: 800-445-7089; FAX: 215-387-3653.
Titles:
Business Learning System.
Business Simulator.
Business Week's Business Advantage.
Export To Win!
Financial Learning System.
What They Don't Teach You At Harvard Business School.

Strategic Mapping, Inc., (1-879124), 3135 Kifer Rd., Santa Clara, CA 95051 Tel 408-970-9600; FAX: 408-970-9999.
Titles:
ATLAS*GIS.
Atlas MapMaker: For Windows.
Atlas Pro: For DOS.
Atlas Pro: For Macintosh.
Local Expert: Where to Go, What to Do, How to Get There.

Strategic Planning Systems, P.O. Box 4019, Simi Valley, CA 93093-4019 Tel 805-254-5897; Toll free: 800-488-5898.
Titles:
Quote Master.

Strategic Simulations, Inc., (0-917059), 675 Almanor Ave., Suite 201, Sunnyvale, CA 94086-2901 Tel 408-737-6800; FAX: 408-737-6814.
Titles:
AL-Qadin: The Genie's Curse (Jewel Case CD).
Alien Logic.
Allied General Power Mac.
Allied General Win 95.
Battles of Napoleon.
Carrier Strike: Jewel Case CD.
Champions of Krynn.
Clash of Steel: Jewel Case.
Critics Choice.
Curse of the Azure Bonds.
Cyclones.
Dark Legions.
Dark Sun II: Wake of the Ravage (Jewel Case CD).
Dark Sun: Shattered Lands (Jewel Case CD).
Deathkeep 3DO.
Definitive Wargame Collection.
Dragons of Flame.
Dragonstrike.
Dungeon Masters Assistant, Vol. I: Encounters.
Dungeon Masters Assistant, Vol. II: Characters & Treasures.
Entomorph MAC: Plague of the Darkfall.
Fantasy Fest.
Fantasy General.
First Over Germany.
Gettysburg: The Turning Point.
Great Naval Battles II: Guadal Canal 1942-43.
Great Naval Battles, Vol. III: Fury in the Pacific.
Heroes of the Lance.
Hillsfar.
Kampfgruppe.
Menzoberranzan.
Overrun!
Pacific War: Jewel Case CD.
Panzer General.
Panzer General for Sony Playstation.
Panzer General 3DO.
Pool Of Radiance.
Ravenloft: Stone Prophet.
Ravenloft Stone Prophet Cluebook.
Red Lighting.
Renegade.
Renegade: Battle for Jacob's Star.
Renegade Legion: Interceptor.
Renegade: Return to Jacob's Star.
Second Front.
Secret of the Silver Blades.
Serf City: Jewel Case CD.
Steel Panthers.
Storm Across Europe.
Su 27: Flaulcer.
Sword of Aragon.
Three Worlds.
Thunderscape.
Tony LaRussa's Baseball II: Jewel Case.
Twenty Wargame Classics.
Typhoon Of Steel.
War in Russia: Jewel Case.
War of the Lance.
Waterloo.

Strategy Plus, Inc., Five Independence Way, Princeton, NJ 08540 Tel 609-452-1345; Toll free: 800-452-1832; FAX: 609-452-7792.
Titles:
EXECUSTAT.

Strawberry Tree, Inc., 160 S. Wolfe Rd., Sunnyvale, CA 94086 Tel 408-736-8800; Toll free: 800-736-8810; FAX: 408-736-1041.
Titles:
WorkBench Mac & WorkBench PC.

Structural Research & Analysis Corp., (0-927260), 12121 Wilshire Blvd., Suite 700, Los Angeles, CA 90025 Tel 310-207-2800; FAX: 310-207-2774.
Titles:
COSMOS/M Designer II.
COSMOS/Works: Phase 1.
COSMOS/Works: Phase 2.
COSMOS-M CAD Interface.
COSMOS-M Designer.
COSMOS/M: Finite Element System.

Studio Magic Corp., 1690 Dell Ave., Campbell, CA 95008-6901 Tel 408-378-3838; FAX: 408-378-3577.
Titles:
Personal Video Studio.

Sublime Software, (1-57100), P.O. Box 1358, Glendora, CA 91740; 345 W. Foothill Blvd., Suite 12, Glendora, CA 91740 Tel 818-963-3108.
Titles:
The Reincarnation of James: The Submarine Man.

SubLOGIC, (0-927267; 1-55602), 501 Kenyon Rd., Champaign, IL 61820 Tel 217-359-8482; Toll free: 800-637-4983; FAX: 217-352-1472.
Titles:
Flight Simulator: Scenery Disk #7.
Flight Simulator: Scenery Disk #11.
Western European Tour.

Suburban Machinery, Software Div., 37127 Ben Hur Ave., Willoughby, OH 44094 Tel 216-951-8974.
Titles:
PCNC.

Successful Money Management Software, Inc., 10180 SW Nimbus, J6, Portland, OR 97223 Tel 503-620-8284; Toll free: 800-326-7667; FAX: 503-639-0199.
Titles:
LIFE Goals.

Successware, 203 Annandale Dr., Cary, NC 27511 Tel 919-469-0119.
Titles:
Advertising Edge.
The Executive's Market Decision Kit.
Marketing Edge Issue 4.0: The Market Planning Expert.
1,2,3 Lead Prioritizer.
Pricing Edge.
Student's Marketing Edge.
Target Market Selector.

Sugar Mill Software Corp., 1180 Kika Pl., Kailua, HI 96734 Tel 808-261-7536; Toll free: 800-729-7536.
Titles:
Stat 1 - A Statistical Tool Box.

Sulcus Law Management Services, Inc., Sub. of Sulcus Computer Corp., 41 N. Main St., Courthouse Sq., Greensburg, PA 15601 Tel 412-836-2000; Toll free: 800-245-7900; FAX: 412-836-8441.
Titles:
Financial.
Legal.
Real Estate.

Sumeria, Inc., (1-57047), 329 Bryant St., Suite 3D, San Francisco, CA 94107 Tel 415-904-0800; Toll free: 800-478-6374; FAX: 415-904-0888.
Titles:
Exploring Ancient Cities.
OceanLife, Vol. 2: Micronesia.
OceanLife, Vol. 3: Hawaii.
OceanLife, Vol. 4: The Great Barrier Reef.
QuickTime: The CD 1992.

SUMMIT SYSTEMS, INC.

QuickTime: The CD 1992-1993.
QuickTime: The CD 1993.
QuickTime: The CD 1994.
SPACE: A Visual History of Manned Spaceflight.

Summit Systems, Inc., 22 Eisenhower Dr., South Easton, MA 02375-1048.
Titles:
DbsPay.

Summum, (0-943217), 707 Genesee Ave., Salt Lake City, UT 84104 Tel 801-355-0137; FAX: 801-355-2320.
Titles:
SUMMUM: Sealed Except to the Open Mind.

Sun Microsystems, Inc., 2 Federal St., Billerica, MA 01821 Tel 508-667-0010.
Titles:
DOS Windows.

Sun Valley Systems, (0-927276), 329 37th Ct., NE, Birmingham, AL 35215 Tel 205-853-8440.
Titles:
Surveyor's Systems.

Suncom Technologies, Div. of Wico Distribution Corp., 6400 W. Gross Point Rd., Niles, IL 60648 Tel 708-647-4040; FAX: 312-647-7828.
Titles:
Animation Station: Computer Design Pad & Graphics Program.

SunRize Industries, 2959 S. Winchester Blvd., Suite 204, Campbell, CA 95008 Tel 408-374-4962; FAX: 408-374-4963.
Titles:
Studio Sixteen - AD Five-Sixteen.
Studio Sixteen-AD Ten-Twelve.

Sunset Software Technology, (0-918181), 1613 Chelsea Rd., Suite 153, San Marino, CA 91108 Tel 818-441-1565; FAX: 818-441-1567.
Titles:
XA.

Sunstar Systems, (0-934075), Rte. 4, Box 368, Ogdensburg, NY 13669 Tel 315-393-7117.
Titles:
Dairy Cooperative Accounting.

Suntex National Corp., P.O. Box 772868, Houston, TX 77215 Tel 512-389-8060.
Titles:
Monte Carlo Plus.
Profit Planner.

Superior Micro-Techniques, 5510 Orchard St. W., Suite B1473, Tacoma, WA 98467 Tel 206-564-0807.
Titles:
Time Tracker.

Suran Systems, Inc., 627 Deerfield Dr., Versailles, KY 40383 Tel 606-873-1504.
Titles:
Church Data Master Plus.

Suresoft!, (0-925455), 160 Washington SE, Suite 69, Albuquerque, NM 87108 Tel 505-293-4776.
Titles:
Proneat.

Surfside Software, Inc., (0-925705), P.O. Box 1112, East Orleans, MA 02643; Toll free: 800-942-9016; 79 Finlay Rd., Orleans, MA 02653 Tel 508-255-1120.
Titles:
The Surfside Solution II.

Surveyors Supply Co., (0-927305), P.O. Box 809, Apex, NC 27502 Tel 919-362-7000; Toll free: 800-334-0095; FAX: 919-362-7077.
Titles:
SURV-A-SOFT.

Survivor Software, Ltd., 11222 LaCienega Blvd., Suite 450, Inglewood, CA 90304 Tel 310-410-9527; FAX: 310-338-1406.
Titles:
InvoicIt.
MacMoney.

Swanson Analysis Systems, Inc., P.O. Box 65, Johnson Rd., Houston, PA 15342-0065 Tel 412-746-3304; Toll free: 800-937-3321; FAX: 412-746-9494.
Titles:
ANSYS.
ANSYS-PC/Linear: Finite Element Analysis.

Swearingen Software, Inc., (0-927309), 10235 W. Little York, Suite 418, Houston, TX 77040 Tel 713-849-2026; Toll free: 800-992-1767; FAX: 713-849-4201.
Titles:
RMS: Radiology Management System.

Swede Corp., (1-884282), 19600 Fairchild, Suite 270, Irvine, CA 92715-2510; FAX: 714-640-7719; Dist. by: Davidson & Assocs., 19840 Pioneer Ave., Torrance, CA 90503-1660 Tel 310-793-0600; Toll free: 800-545-7677.
Titles:
Scavenger Hunt Adventure Series: Africa.

Swiftware Corp., (0-927311), 318 Country Club Rd., Newton Centre, MA 02159 Tel 617-332-2776.
Titles:
Computer Crossword.
Fast-Finance.

Sygenex, Inc., 15446 Bel-Red Rd., Suite 450, Redmond, WA 98052-5507 Tel 206-881-5500; FAX: 206-869-2837.
Titles:
Criterium.

Sylvia Products, (0-928357), P.O. Box 3515, Lantana, FL 33465 Tel 407-367-9856.
Titles:
The Advertizer.

Symantec Corp., (0-928525), P.O. Box 51755, Pacific Grove, CA 93950 Tel 408-372-8100; FAX: 408-372-2041.
Titles:
The Budget Express.
GrandView.
Just Enough Pascal.
MacSQZ!
More II.
Q&A.
Q&A Write.
Q&A 386.
SQZ! Plus: Spreadsheet File Utility System for Lotus.
Symantec AntiVirus For Macintosh (SAM).
Symantec Utilities for Macintosh.
Think C.
Think Pascal (formerly Lightspeed Pascal).
Time Line.

Symix, Inc., (0-925380), 2800 Corporate Exchange Dr., Columbus, OH 43231 Tel 614-523-7000; FAX: 614-895-2504.
Titles:
The SYMIX Solution.
The SYMIX System.

SOFTWARE ENCYCLOPEDIA 1996

Symmetry Corp., 8603 E. Royal Palm Rd., Suite 110, Scotsdale, AZ 85258 Tel 602-844-2190; Toll free: 800-624-2485.
Titles:
HyperEngine.

Synaptec Software, Inc., 425 S. Cherry St., Suite 230, Denver, CO 80222 Tel 303-320-4420; Toll free: 800-569-3377; FAX: 303-320-4860.
Titles:
FileBase.
LawBase.
The Legal System - Series 1.

Syndesis Corp., P.O. Box 65, 235 S. Main St., Jefferson, WI 53549 Tel 414-674-5200; FAX: 414-674-6363.
Titles:
InterChange.
InterChange for Windows.
InterFont.
InterFont Upgrade.
Syndesis 3D-ROM.

Synergy Interactive Corp., Sub. of Synergy, Inc., (1-888158), 444 De Haro St., Suite 123, San Francisco, CA 94107 Tel 415-437-2000; Toll free: 800-734-9466; FAX: 415-431-3684.
Titles:
Alice.
Faces of Summer.
Gadget.
Iron Angel of the Apocalypse.
Iron Angel of the Apocalypse: The Return.
L-Zone.
100 Japanese Photographers.
Still Lifes.
Yellow Brick Road.
Yellow Brick Road: Emerald Collection.
Yellow Brick Road II.
Zeddas: Servant of Sheol.

Synergy Software, Div. of Maxwell Resources, Inc., 2457 Perkiomen Ave., Reading, PA 19606 Tel 610-779-0522; Toll free: 800-876-8376; FAX: 610-370-0548. Do not confuse with Synergy Software in Chicago, IL.
Titles:
KaleidaGraph.
Versa Term.
Versa Term-PRO.
VersaTilities.

Synex, (1-880773), 692 Tenth St., Brooklyn, NY 11215-4502 Tel 718-499-6293; Toll free: 800-447-9639; FAX: 718-768-3997.
Titles:
Bar Code Pro.
Bar Code Pro Filemaster.
Bar Code Pro Reader: User's Guide.
Label Press: Label Printing Software Tamed.
MacEnvelope.
MacPhonebook.

Syntactics, (0-918177), P.O. Box 50036, Palo Alto, CA 94303-0036; Toll free: 800-626-6400; FAX: 408-727-0309.
Titles:
CrystalLaser Laser Typesetting.
CrystalWriter Plus.

Synthesis, Inc., 2120 Ellis St., Bellingham, WA 98225 Tel 206-671-0417; FAX: 206-671-0458.
Titles:
Synthesis, Synthesis Runtime, Synthesis Enhancer.

Syscom, Inc., 230 Hilton Ave., Suite 217, Hempstead, NY 11550 Tel 516-481-8201; FAX: 516-565-9042. Do not confuse with Syscom, Inc., Fort Lauderdale, FL.
Titles:
The Legal Eagle.

PUBLISHER/TITLE INDEX

Systat, Inc., (0-928789), 444 N. Michigan Ave., Chicago, IL 60611-3903.
Titles:
Design.
FASTAT.
Logit.
Probit.
SYSTAT.
Testat.

Systec Computer Services, P.O. Box 7533, San Jose, CA 95150-7533 Tel 408-723-2264; Toll free: 800-237-8209; FAX: 408-978-6096.
Titles:
Front Office.

Systek, (0-932507), 13641 Smoke Creek Ave., Bakersfield, CA 93312 Tel 805-588-1417.
Titles:
CurveFit: Curve Fitting Program.
FLPROP.
GASMOD: Gas Pipeline Simulation.
LIQPIPE: Pipeline Hydraulic Simulation.
LIQTHERM.
ORIFLO: Orifice Meter Calculation.
PIPECON: Liquid Pipeline Economics.
PUMPCURV.
PUMPERF.

Systek, Inc., (0-927343), P.O. Box 6234, Mississippi State, MS 39762-6234 Tel 601-325-7192; FAX: 601-325-7189.
Titles:
Continuous Beam Analysis.
Coordinate Geometry.
Earthwork.
Pressure Sewer.
Quantity Estimation.
Roadway Geometry.
Structural Analysis.
Surveying & Land Measurements.
Water Distribution: Loops.
Water Distribution: Nodes.

System Vision Co., (0-927355), 180 Stanley Ave., Pacifica, CA 94044-3942; FAX: 415-355-9214.
Titles:
Resume Profile System.
Resume Profiles Plus.
Sales Vision Field Sales: Information System for Sales Professionals.
Sales Vision Telemarketing.

Systems Plus, Inc., (0-917555), 500 Clyde Ave., Mountain View, CA 94043 Tel 415-969-7047; Toll free: 800-222-7701; FAX: 415-969-0118.
Titles:
Accounting Plus.
The Medical Manager.

Systems Software Resource, Inc., 11 A-S Meridian, Kalispell, MT 59901 Tel 406-752-9696; FAX: 406-756-1110.
Titles:
Restaurant Express: Integrated Restaurant/Bar Management System.

Systems Union, Inc., Div. of Systems Union Group, 10 Bank St., White Plains, NY 10606-1933 Tel 914-948-7770; FAX: 914-948-7399.
Titles:
SunAccount.

Sytron Corp., Subs. of Renon, Inc., 134 Flanders Rd., P.O. Box 5025, Westboro, MA 01581-5025 Tel 508-898-0100; Toll free: 800-877-0016 (sales); FAX: 508-898-2677.
Titles:
ProServe CX: Automated, Server-Based NLM Backup for Novell NetWare.
ProServe CX Lite: Automated, Server-Based NLM Backup for Novell NetWare.
Sytos Autoloader: Support Module for OS-2.
Sytos Plus for DOS: High-Performance DOS-Based Backup Also Offering Client-Based NetWare Backup.
Sytos Plus for OS/2: OS-2 2.x & OS-2 Server or Client-Based Network Backup Supporting IBM LAN Server & Microsoft LAN Manager.
Sytos Plus for Windows: Windows Backup for Novell Networks.
Sytos Premium: OS-2 2.x & OS-2 Backup & Disaster Recovery Softare Offering Complete OS-2 Workstation & Network Server Data Protection.
Sytos Rebound: Disaster Recovery for OS-2.
Sytos Repro: System Duplication Utility for OS 2.
Sytos Scheduler: Presentation Manager Scheduling Utility.

TAB Bks., Div. of McGraw-Hill, Inc., (0-8306; 0-07), P.O. Box 40, Blue Ridge Summit, PA 17294-0850 Tel 717-794-2191; Toll free: 800-233-1128; FAX: 717-794-2080.
Titles:
Advanced Programming Techniques for Your ATARI Including Graphics & Voice Programs.
Atari ST Graphics & Sound Programming.
Commodore 64/128 Graphics & Sound Programming.
Database Manager in MICROSOFT BASIC.
Fundamentals of IBM PC Assembly Language.
Graphics Programs for the IBM PC.
How to Create Your Own Computer Bulletin Board.
IBM PC Graphics.
Investment Analysis with Your Microcomputer.
Music & Speech Programs for the IBM PC.
101 Programming Surprises & Tricks for Your Apple II or IIe Computer.
101 Ready-to-Run Programs & Subroutines for the IBM PCjr.
1001 Things to Do with Your Commodore 128.
1001 Things to Do with Your Amiga.
1001 Things to Do with Your TRS-80, Apple II, IIe, IBM PC, Commodore 64 & Macintosh.
PayCalc: How to Create Customized Payroll Spreadsheets.
Programming with dBASE III Plus.
Putting Pascal to Work.
Using & Programming the Macintosh, Including 32 Ready-to-Run Programs.

T.A.L. Enterprises, 2027 Wallace St., Philadelphia, PA 19130 Tel 215-763-5096; Toll free: 800-722-6004.
Titles:
B-Coder: For DOS or For Windows.
Software Wedge Pro: For DOS or For Windows.
Software Wedge Standard Version: For DOS or For Windows.

TAP Development Corp., 1055 E. Tropicana, Suite 450, Las Vegas, NV 89119 Tel 702-798-4888; Toll free: 800-231-5455; FAX: 702-798-0037.
Titles:
Teaching Assistance Package for Basic Lotus 1-2-3.

T & M Computing, (0-927393), 4914 Rainford Ct., Saint Louis, MO 63128 Tel 314-892-3248.
Titles:
MAT One Interpreter.

T&M Systems, Rte. 1, Box 116, Birch Tree, MO 65438 Tel 314-292-3822.
Titles:
MacLunchroom.
T&M Optometric Plus.

TCI Software, (0-917099), 6107 W. Mill Rd., Flourtown, PA 19031 Tel 215-836-1406; FAX: 215-233-5009.
Titles:
Mailtrak: List Management System.

TSP INTERNATIONAL

T.C.P. Techmar Computer Products, Inc., (1-879013), 8502 79th St., Woodhaven, NY 11421-1102 Tel 718-997-6666; Toll free: 800-922-0015; FAX: 718-520-0170.
Titles:
AntivirusPlus.
Viraway.

TDT Group, Inc., 940 Park Ave., No. 106, Lake Park, FL 33403-2418 Tel 407-842-0079; FAX: 407-863-6020.
Titles:
Honey Bunch.
Six/25.
TransFile-PC3780.
VIP7200.

T-Lan Systems, 11 Meadow Rd., No. 1, Augusta, ME 04330 Tel 207-397-5511.
Titles:
Solicit Your Congress.
Solicit Your Consumer Complaint.
Solicit Your Editor.

T/Maker Co., Inc., Subs. of Deluxe Corp., (0-918183), 1390 Villa St., Mountain View, CA 94041 Tel 415-962-0195; Toll free: 800-395-0195; FAX: 415-962-0201.
Titles:
Animals & Nature.
Artistry & Borders.
Beastly Funnies: ClickArt Cartoons.
Bulletins & Newsletters: ClickArt Cartoons.
Business Art.
Business Illustrations: ClickArt.
Christian Illustrations: Bookstore Edition.
Christian Illustrations: ClickArt.
ClickArt EPS Symbols & Industry.
Company & Business: ClickArt Cartoons.
Four Footed Friends.
Illustrations.
Incredible Image Pak 2000: ClickArt.
Marvin the Ape: European, Dual.
My Very First CD, Hybrid.
Newsletter Art: ClickArt.
Occasions & Celebrations: ClickArt.
On the Job: ClickArt Cartoons.
Parties & Events: ClickArt Cartoons.
Sports & Games.
Stradiwackius.
Stradiwalkius: The Counting Concert.
Studio Series Design Group CD (CD-ROM).
VroomBooks' Four Footed Friends.
VroomBooks' Stradiwackius The Counting Concert.

TNT Software, 34069 Hainesville Rd., Round Lake, IL 60073 Tel 708-223-8595.
Titles:
The Creator.
My Word!

TORUS Systems, Inc., 9706 Sagamore Rd., Leawood, KS 66206-2314.
Titles:
Tapestry II.

TPS Electronics, 2495 Old Middlefield Way, Mountain View, CA 94043 Tel 415-988-0141; Toll free: 800-526-5920; FAX: 415-856-3843.
Titles:
Macintosh Bar Code Printing Program.
PostScript UPC Version A Bar Code Font.

TSP International, (0-925435), P.O Box 61015, Sta. A, Palo Alto, CA 94306 Tel 415-326-1927.
Titles:
TSP: Time Series Processor.

Tallysheet Corp., 2816 Rowena, No. 3, Los Angeles, CA 90039 Tel 213-665-5891; FAX: 213-660-6080.
Titles:
Greggway HVAC-PC.
Greggway PIPE-PC.
GW HVAC-PC.
GW Pipe-PC.

Talon Software, Inc., P.O. Box 3165, Auburn, AL 36831-3165 Tel 334-821-4892.
Titles:
IMPACT.

TalonSoft, Inc., 1107 Kenilworth Dr., Suite 307, Towson, MD 21204 Tel 410-821-7282.
Titles:
Battleground: Ardennes: Battle of the Bulge.

Tanager Software Productions, Affil. of Baker & Taylor Distribution, (1-880006), 1933 Davis St., Suite 208, San Leandro, CA 94577-1200 Tel 510-430-0900; Toll free: 800-841-2020; FAX: 510-430-0917.
Titles:
The Secret Codes of C. Y. P. H. E. R: Operation U. S. Presidents.
The Secret Codes of C.Y.P.H.E.R: Operation Wildlife.

TanData Corp., (0-928470), 5200 S. Harvard Ave., Tulsa, OK 74135-3500 Tel 918-748-9000; Toll free: 800-365-3316; FAX: 918-748-9099.
Titles:
Parcel Manifest System.
Partnership.
Progistics.

Tangible Vision, Inc., 1933 Loomis Ave., Downers Grove, IL 60516 Tel 708-969-7517.
Titles:
Imprimis.

Taranto & Assocs., Inc., (0-918185), P.O. Box 6216, San Rafael, CA 94903 Tel 415-472-2670; Toll free: 800-522-8649; FAX: 415-473-2673.
Titles:
Accounts Payable-Purchase Order.
Accounts Receivable Balance Forward.
Accounts Receivable-Invoicing-Sales Analysis.
The AUCTIONEER.
Inventory Control.
Membership Accounts Receivable.
Order Entry.
Payroll.
Point-of-Sale.
ProAUCTIONEER.
Taranto General Ledger.

Tardis Software, 2817 Sloat Rd., Pebble Beach, CA 93953 Tel 408-372-1722.
Titles:
Amiga Programmer's Library.

Tatum Labs, Inc., (0-927449), 1287 N. Silo Ridge Dr., Ann Arbor, MI 48108-9562 Tel 313-663-8810; FAX: 313-663-3640.
Titles:
ACTIVE: Active Filter Design.
Curve-F: Polynomial Curve Fitting.
ECA-2: Electronic Circuit Analysis.
ECA-2.
LCA-1: Logic Circuit Analysis.
Logic Tutor: Self-Instruction in Digital Switching Logic.
PLOT-D: Plotter Interface.
SAUNA Modeling System: 3D Thermal Analysis.
SAUNA: 3D Thermal Analysis.

Taurus Computer Systems, Inc., (0-927982), 2120 Corporate Sq. Blvd., No. 6, Jacksonville, FL 32216 Tel 904-725-2929.
Titles:
Taurus.

Taxbyte, Inc., 1801 Sixth Ave., Moline, IL 61265 Tel 309-764-7245; Toll free: 800-245-8299; FAX: 309-764-0976.
Titles:
Taxbyte 1120 Software.
Taxbyte 1120S Software.
Taxbyte 1040 Software.
Taxbyte 1040X Software.
Taxbyte 1065-Partnerships.
Taxbyte - 1041 - Fiduciary Software.

Taylor-Gray, (1-883671), 15 E. 26th St., Suite 1807, New York, NY 10010-1505.
Titles:
Digital System Design Using VHDL.
One Hundred One Financial Spreadsheet Templates: Excel for Macintoosh.

Teach Yourself by Computer Software, Inc., (0-918187), 3400 Monroe Ave., Rochester, NY 14618 Tel 716-381-5450; Toll free: 800-724-4691; FAX: 716-427-7628.
Titles:
EduClip Images Five: Educational Borders.
EduClip Images Four - Technology, Math, Science.
EduClip Images 1 - Sports, Holidays, School Items.
EduClip Images 2 - Initials & Numbers with Graphics.
EduClip Images 3 - Curriculum Logos, Social Studies, Sports, Holidays.

Teacher Support Software, Inc., (0-927461; 1-55676), 1035 NW 57th St., Gainesville, FL 32605 Tel 904-332-6404; Toll free: 800-228-2871; FAX: 904-332-6779.
Titles:
Read-a-Logo: Concentration.
Read-a-Logo: Group-a-Logo.
Read-a-Logo: Rebus Stories.
Read-a-Logo: Write-about-Logos.

Team Visionics Corp., 667 Madrone Ave., Sunnyvale, CA 94086-3040; Toll free: 800-553-1177; FAX: 408-492-1380.
Titles:
The Designer.
EE Designer III.
Fabmaster.
MaxRoute.

Tech Hackers, Inc., 50 Broad St., New York, NY 10004 Tel 212-344-9500.
Titles:
@nalyst.

Techdata, (0-917405), 11221 Richmond, C103, Houston, TX 77082 Tel 713-497-5704; FAX: 713-497-5839.
Titles:
ACT: Activated Sludge.
ACX: Air Cooled Heat Exchanger Design & Rating Program.
COMPRESS.
DEMIN.
Flare.
Micro Hardy Cross.
ORIFICE.
PAULA: Pipeline Algorithm for Unsteady Liquid Analysis.
PIG.
PIPEDP.
PIPEQ.
PUMP.
STEAM.
STX: Shell & Tube Heat Exchanger Design & Rating Program.
SUSAN: Simulator for Unsteady-State Analysis of Networks.
TANKQ.
Varipump.
Vessel Coster.
Vessel Drafting Program.
VIM: Vessel Inspection Manager.
WATER.

Technical Research Services, Inc., (0-927471), 9122 S. Florence Ave., Tulsa, OK 74137 Tel 918-299-0928; FAX: 918-299-3007.
Titles:
AISCBEAM.
ALODS.
APITANK.
CGCAL.
CONTRN.
DBLTS.
EXPRFR.
FLGH.
FLGL.
INPRFR.
LAYOUT.
MICA.
NOZZLE.
REOPN.
SEIHS.
SEILEGS.
SEIVS.
STRSR.
STRSS.
TALLTOWR.
TBLAYOUT.
TBSHEET: TEMA.
ZICK.

Technological Computer Innovations Corp., (1-884791), 255 N. Cherrywood Dr., Lafayette, CO 80026-2726 Tel 303-673-9046; FAX: 303-673-9085.
Titles:
At Play for Windows.
Stellar Explorer.
Tiles & Tribulations.
Whirlwind.

Technology Concepts, Inc., Subs. of Bell Atlantic Co., 40 Tall Pine Dr., Sudbury, MA 01776 Tel 508-443-7311; Toll free: 800-777-2323; FAX: 508-443-7310.
Titles:
CommUnity: DECnet for Non-DEC Systems.

Technology Dynamics Corp., (1-885784), 2716 Ocean Park Blvd., Suite 3085, Santa Monica, CA 90405 Tel 310-452-6720; FAX: 310-452-6722.
Titles:
Aesop's Fables.
California Travel.
California Travel: Jewel.
A Christmas Carol.
Don Quixote.
Goferwinkel's Adventure.
ImageKit Cities Disk.
ImageKit Earth Disk.
ImageKit Foliage Disk.
ImageKit Illustrations Disk.
ImageKit Miscellaneous Disk.
ImageKit Objects Disk.
ImageKit People Disk.
ImageKit ScreenRez.
ImageKit Skies Disk.
ImageKit Ten CD Set.
ImageKit Water Disk.
Impressionism & Its Source.
Jazz Greats.
Jazz Greats: From Louis Armstrong to Duke Ellington (Jewel).
Kaa's Hunting.
Motion Commotion.
Motion Commotion: Jewel.
Mowgli's Brother.

Mozart.
Mozart: Jewel.
The Nutcracker: An Interactive Holiday Fantasy (Jewel).
Peter & the Wolf.
Pyotr Ilyich Tchaikovsky: A Multimedia Music Production.
Pyotr Ilyich Tchaikovsky: A Multimedia Music Production (Jewel).
Renaissance Masters.
Scenic & Castles.
Sci-Fi Movie Machine.
Sci-Fi Movie Machine: Jewel.
The Star Child.
A Survey of Western Art.
A Survey of Western Art: Jewel.
Twelve Roads to Gettysburg.
Twelve Roads to Gettysburg: Jewel.
Vivaldi the Four Seasons.
Vivaldi: The Four Seasons (Jewel).
The White Horse Child.
World's Best...Artistic Photography of Women.

Technology Group, Inc., (0-927923), 36 S. Charles St., Suite 2200, Baltimore, MD 21201 Tel 410-576-2040; FAX: 410-576-1968.
Titles:
XyWrite.
XYWrite for Windows.
XyWrite III Plus.

Technology Resource Assistance Ctr., Inc., 530 Oak Grove Ave., Suite 101, Menlo Park, CA 94025 Tel 415-853-1100; Toll free: 800-676-5831; FAX: 415-853-1677.
Titles:
MacTrac Fund Raising Software.
TRACSTAR Integrated Software for Community Foundations.

Technology with Ease, Inc., P.O. Box 840355, Pembroke Pines, FL 33084 Tel 405-431-0364.
Titles:
Easy-Checking.
Easy-Checking +.
Easy Pieces SA.
Easy Sales - ASI.
Plain-Payroll.

Technovation Corp., (0-927715), 1201 Tenth St. NW, No. 308, Saint Paul, MN 55112-6786 Tel 612-636-2980.
Titles:
CashWise Retail Systems.

TechPool Studios, (1-57459), 1463 Warrensville Ctr. Rd., Cleveland, OH 44121 Tel 216-382-1234; Toll free: 800-543-3278; FAX: 216-382-1915.
Titles:
LifeART Collections.
Transverter Pro.

Techware Corp., (1-55781), P.O. Box 151085, Altamonte Springs, FL 32715-1085 Tel 407-695-9000; Toll free: 800-347-3224.
Titles:
Tutor-Tech Hypermedia Software.

Tecnomics, Inc., 100 Ardmore St., Blacksburg, VA 24060 Tel 703-552-5609; Toll free: 800-456-9808.
Titles:
UTILIBILL Customer History.
UTILIBILL FRS: Field Recorder System.
UTILIBILL IBM: Utility Billing System.
UTILIBILL Mailing Labels.
UTILIBILL Plus: Utility Billing System.
UTILIBILL Route Sheets.
UTILIFLEET: Fleet Monitoring System.

Tektronix, Inc., (0-927489), P.O. Box 1000, 63-830, Wilsonville, OR 97077 Tel 503-627-7111; Toll free: 800-547-1512.
Titles:
CAT200.

Tele Vend, Inc., (0-918189), 111 Croydon Rd., Baltimore, MD 21212 Tel 410-532-7517; FAX: 410-532-7818.
Titles:
Association Accounter: Accounting for Associations.
Cash & Credit.
Med-Lab.
Service Station Accountant.
Time Keeper.

Telepartner International, 135 South Rd., Farmington, CT 06032 Tel 203-674-2640; Toll free: 800-935-3270; FAX: 203-674-8234.
Titles:
Flash!
Packet/PC for Windows.
Packet/Main.
Packet/PC for Windows.
PACKET/3270.
RemoteVision.
Synchrony.

TeleRobotics International, Inc., 7325 Oak Ridge Hwy., Knoxville, TN 37931 Tel 615-690-5600; FAX: 615-690-2913.
Titles:
Course Builder.

Telescan, (0-928473), 5459 Corporate Dr., Suite 2000, Houston, TX 77036 Tel 713-588-9700; Toll free: 800-324-8246; FAX: 713-588-9797.
Titles:
Telescan Analyzer & Telescan Database: Stock Analysis Program.
Telescan Investor's Platform: TIP.
Telescan ProSearch.

TeleSensory, (0-936409), 455 N. Bernardo Ave., Mountain View, CA 94043 Tel 415-960-0920; Toll free: 800-286-8484; FAX: 415-969-9064.
Titles:
Oscar: Reading Software for the Blind.
Screen Power Speech.
ScreenPower for Windows.

TeleSoft, (0-927500), 10251 Vista Sorrento Pkwy., Suite 300, San Diego, CA 92121-2718 Tel 619-457-2700; FAX: 619-452-1334.
Titles:
TeleUSE.
Validated Telesoft Ada for MC68000-UNIX Systems.
Validated Telesoft Ada for VAX-UNIX Systems & VAX-VMS.

TeleTypesetting Co., Inc., (1-881387), 311 Harvard St., Brookline, MA 02146 Tel 617-734-9700; FAX: 617-734-3974.
Titles:
Digital Gourmet Classic.
Digital Gourmet Deluxe.
T, Script.

TeleVideo Systems, Inc., 550 E. Brokaw Rd., P.O. Box 49048, San Jose, CA 95161-9048 Tel 408-954-8333; FAX: 408-954-0622.
Titles:
TeleAsync.

Tellan Software, Inc., 2670 S. White Rd., No. 281, San Jose, CA 95148 Tel 408-274-1110; Toll free: 800-483-5526; FAX: 408-274-8392.
Titles:
MacAuthorize.
MacAuthorize - Hub.

Template Graphics Software, 9920 Pacific Heights Blvd., Suite 200, San Diego, CA 92121 Tel 619-457-5359.
Titles:
Template.

10-K Pr./Janal Communications, (1-879572), 1063 Morse Ave., Suite 7-301, Sunnyvale, CA 94089 Tel 408-734-2092.
Titles:
How to Publicize High Tech Products & Services.

10.0, Div. of Mediagenic, (1-877746), 11440 San Vicente Blvd., No. 300, Los Angeles, CA 90049-6242.
Titles:
Focal Point II.
Open It.
Shanghai.

Tensor Laboratories, P.O. Box 9723, Stanford, CA 94309 Tel 707-763-7873.
Titles:
McFace Package.

Terradise Computer Systems, Inc., (0-928794), 2063 Beechmont Ave., Cincinnati, OH 45230 Tel 513-231-4468; Toll free: 800-373-5789; FAX: 513-231-4051.
Titles:
SeniorPro: Senior Citizen Center Contact Manager.
TerraPro: Funeral Home Case Management.

TerraLogics, Inc., 131 Daniel Webster Hwy. S., Suite 348, Nashua, NH 03060 Tel 603-889-1800; FAX: 603-880-2022.
Titles:
TerraView.

Terrapin Software, Inc., (0-927510), 10 Holworthy St., Cambridge, MA 02138 Tel 617-547-5646; Toll free: 800-972-8200; FAX: 617-492-4610.
Titles:
Commodore Logo.
LOGO Data Toolkit.
Logo Plus.

TerraVision, Inc., 2351 College Station Rd., Suite 563, Athens, GA 30605 Tel 706-769-5641; Toll free: 800-523-1796; FAX: 706-769-8013.
Titles:
The Graphics Link Plus.
PHIPS-Professional Hi-Resolution Image Processing System.

Tess Data Systems, (0-928364), 14340 Torrey Chase Blvd., Suite 340, Houston, TX 77014-1021 Tel 713-440-6943; Toll free: 800-440-6943; FAX: 713-440-6526.
Titles:
TessSystem Three.

Tesseract Enterprises, Ltd., (0-923915), P.O. Box 8144, The Woodlands, TX 77387-8144.
Titles:
Contour PLOT.
TeliSolar.

Texas A&M Univ., Real Estate Ctr., (1-56248), Texas A&M Univ., Real Estate Ctr., No. 628, College Station, TX 77843-2115 Tel 409-845-2031.
Titles:
CS-4: Residential Buy-Rent Software Package.

Texas Instruments, Personal Productivity Products, (0-927518), P.O. Box 6102, Temple, TX 76503-6102 Tel 817-774-6001; Toll free: 800-848-3927.
Titles:
A-Maze-Ing.
AC Circuit Analysis Library.

TEXAS INSTRUMENTS, PERSONAL

ADS Accounts Payable.
ADS Accounts Receivable.
ADS General Ledger.
ADS Payroll.
Advanced SystemPac.
Adventure International Series.
Adventureland.
Alpiner.
Anesthesia Practice Management System.
Arborist.
ASCOM 86.
ATI Training Modules.
The Attack.
AutoCAD-86.
Basketball Statistician.
Beef Cattle Management.
Big Foot: Arcade Plus Series.
Blackjack & Poker.
Blasto.
BPI Accounts Payable.
BPI Accounts Receivable.
BPI Payroll.
Bridge Bidding I.
Bridge Bidding II.
Bridge Bidding III.
Btrieve.
Business Aids Library - Cash Management.
Business Aids Library - Financial Management.
Business Aids Library - Inventory Management.
Business Aids Library - Invoice Management.
Business Aids Library - Lease-Purchase Divisions.
Business Management System.
Calc Merge.
Cars Wars.
CertiFLEX.
CertiFLEX Accounts Payable with Check Writing.
CertiFLEX Accounts Receivable with Billing.
CertiFLEX Fixed Assets-Depreciation.
CertiFLEX General Ledger.
CertiFLEX Payroll with Check Writing.
Championship Baseball: Arcade Plus Series.
Checkbook Manager.
Chiropractic.
Chiropractic Practice Management System.
Chisholm Trail.
Church Financial Accounting.
Churchstar.
CIS COBOL.
Client Accounting.
Client Write-Up System.
Client Write-Up System: PASS.
CodeWriter.
Computerized Practice Management System: CPMS.
Connect Four.
Construction.
Contractor Microcomputer Software.
CP/M-86 & CBASIC 86.
CPplus.
Crops Management.
Crossdata.
CYMA Accounts Payable.
CYMA Accounts Receivable.
CYMA Payroll.
Dairy Management.
Data Merge.
Datatree.
Dax Plus with Voicedrive.
The dBASE Door.
The dBASE Window.
Dental.
Dental Practice Management System.
Distribution Management System.
dMERGE.
Dr. LOGO.
DR Graph.
Draw Poker.
DREP.
Easy Dealer.
EasyPost Insurance Agency Management System.
EasySales Pro.
EasyWriter I System Legal.
EasyWriter I System Medical.
EasyWriter II System.

EasyWriter II System Legal.
Editor-Assembler.
Electrical Engineering Library.
EM-8086.
Embryo Transfer.
Emulator-86.
Entrapment.
Entrypoint.
Equipment & Supply Dealer Package.
Ethermail Server Kit.
Etherprint Server Kit.
Etherseries User Kit.
Ethershare Server Kit.
Extended BASIC.
FABS.
Faster-Raster.
Feed Plant Management.
Feedlot & Swine Finish Floor Management.
Fertilizer Plant Management.
FilePac.
Financial Planning System.
Fixed Assets-Depreciation.
Football.
The Formula Plus G.A.S.
GarageKeeper.
General Ledger-Client Write-Up.
Ghost Town.
The Golden Voyage.
Graphing Package.
Great Plains Accounts Receivable.
Great Plains Software Accounts Payable.
Great Plains Software General Ledger.
Great Plains Software Payroll.
Hangman.
Herdsman.
Home Financial Decisions.
Honey Hunt: Bright Beginning Series.
Horse Farm Management.
Horse Show Management.
Household Budget Management.
Housing Assistance Pac.
Hunt the Wumpus.
Hustle.
IFPS-Personal.
I'm Hiding.
Indoor Soccer.
Informa.
International Software Sales General Ledger.
Inventory.
Inventory Control.
Inventory with Point of Sale.
Investment Evaluator.
Invoicing with Accounts Receivable & Inventory.
Jewel Accounting System.
Job Cost Estimator.
KnowledgeMan.
LAN-DataCore.
LAN-DataStore.
Law Office Management System.
Livestock Auction.
LogiQuest III.
MAG-Base1.
MAG/Base2.
MAG/Base3.
MAGIS Plus.
Mailing List.
The Main Street Filer.
Maintenance Package.
The Management Tool Kit.
Manufacturing Management System.
Market Simulation.
MASH.
Math Routines Library.
MedAccount.
Medical.
Medical Billing System.
Medical Practice Management.
Medical Practice Management System.
Meteor Belt: Arcade Plus Series.
MICA-Accounts Payable.
MICA-Accounts Receivable.
MICA-General Ledger.
MICA-Inventory Control.
MICA-Payroll.

MICA-Sales Invoicing.
Micro-Host Payroll Program.
Micro-SPF.
MicroGANTT.
Micropix.
MicroSpell.
Mind Challengers.
Mini-Memory.
Mission Impossible.
MoonMine.
MS-BASIC.
MS-BASIC Compiler.
MS-COBOL.
MS-DOS 2.1.
MS-DOS 1.25.
MS-FORTRAN Compiler.
MS-Pascal.
MS-Pascal Compiler.
Multiplan for TI.
Munch Mobile.
MunchMan.
Music Maker.
Mystery Fun House.
Mystery Melody.
NaturaLink Access to Dow Jones News-Retrieval.
931 Emulator.
Oldies but Goodies Games I.
Oldies but Goodies Games II.
Open Systems General Ledger.
Open Systems Payroll.
Optimum Data Management System.
ORACLE.
Orchard & Grove Management.
Order Entry.
Orthodontic.
Orthodontic Practice Management System.
Pages Plus with VoiceDrive.
Panel-86.
Parsec: Speech Synthesizer.
Pascal Development System.
PC Focus.
PC Scheme.
Peachtree Accounts Payable.
Peachtree Accounts Receivable.
Perfect Writer/Speller.
Perfect Writer/Speller/Calc.
Personal BASIC.
Personal Consultant Easy (PC Easy).
Personal Consultant Plus (PC Plus).
Personal Finance Aids.
Personal Real Estate.
Personal Record Keeping.
Personal Report Generator.
Personal Tax Plan.
Personnel Agency Management System.
Physical Fitness.
PL/1.
Planfin.
Plant Nursery Management.
PLINK-86.
PMATE 86.
Poultry Layer Management System.
Print Man Spooler System.
Printers Bid System.
PRISM.
Private Membership Club.
Pro Bookkeeper.
ProCalc.
Productivity Pack.
PROFIN.
Programming Aids I.
Programming Aids II.
Programming Aids III.
ProKey.
Property Management for Commercial Real Estate.
Pyramid of Doom.
Quick Register.
QuickCalc Loan Analyzer.
Rapid Transfer.
Resident Manager.
Residential/Commercial Services.
Restaurant Management.
Retail Florist.

SOFTWARE ENCYCLOPEDIA 1996

PUBLISHER/TITLE INDEX

S.A.M.
Samna Word II.
Saturday Night Bingo.
Savage Island I & II.
ScenicWriter.
ScratchPad with VoiceDrive.
Securities Analysis.
SEED.
Sewermania: Arcade Plus Series.
Small Bookkeeping Services & Public Accounts.
Small Business.
The Small Business Accountant.
The Smart Data Manager.
The Smart Spreadsheet with Graphics.
The Smart Word Processor.
SMU Electrical Engineering Library.
Sneggit.
Sound Track Trolly.
Space Bandit: Arcade Plus Series.
Speech Command Software Development Kit.
Speech Command System.
Spell.
S.P.S. Statistical Pac.
StarIndex.
Statistics.
Strange Odyssey.
Structural Engineering Library.
Super Fly: Arcade Plus Series.
SuperCalc 3.
Swine Management.
SymEd.
SystemPac.
T-Maker III.
Tax II: 1040 Tax Preparation & Planning System.
Tax-Investment Record Keeping.
TCS Q-Word.
Teach Yourself BASIC.
Teach Yourself Extended BASIC.
Terminal Emulator II.
Texas Instruments General Ledger.
Text-to-Speech.
3101 Emulator.
3170 SNA.
3780 Communications.
TI-Advanced Assembly Debugger.
TI-Count Business Packages.
TI-FORTH.
TI Invaders.
TI-Mini-Writer.
TI-Othello.
TI-PILOT.
TI Writer.
T.I.M: Total Information Management.
Timberline Tax.
Time & Charges PASS.
Torricelli Editor.
Trucker's Road-Use Info Program: T.R.I.P.
TTY Communications.
Tunnels of Doom.
UCSD Editor/Filer/Utilities.
UCSD p-System Assembler-Linker.
UCSD p-System Development with Pascal.
UCSD p-System Runtime with Turtlegraphics.
UCSD Pascal Compiler.
UltraFile.
UT86.
VersaText Word Processing & Database System.
Veterinary Practice Management System.
Video Chess.
Video Games I.
Video Graphs.
VisiSpell.
Voodoo Castle.
Water Billing System.
Weight Control & Nutrition.
Word Plus-PC.
WordExec.
WordStar & MailMerge 3.3.
WordStar & SpellStar 3.3.
WordStar, MailMerge & SpellStar 3.3.
WordStar Professional 3.3.
WordStar Professional 3.3 Option Kit.
Yahtzee.
Your Personal Computer Tutor.

Zero Zap.
Zork II.
Zork III.

Texas Software, (0-941433), 10165 Phelan Blvd., Beaumont, TX 77713 Tel 409-866-9765; Toll free: 800-727-9765; FAX: 409-866-9765.
Titles:
Client Information Management System: CIMS.

TexaSoft, (0-927523), P.O. Box 1169, Cedar Hill, TX 75106-1169 Tel 214-291-2115; Toll free: 955-8392; FAX: 214-291-3400.
Titles:
KWIKSTAT BASIC.
The Thinker: Electronic Spreadsheet.

Textco, Inc., 27 Gilson Rd., West Lebanon, NH 03784 Tel 603-643-1471.
Titles:
The DNA Inspector IIe.
Gene Construction Kit.

TextWare Corp., P.O. Box 3267, 1910 Prospector Ave., Park City, UT 84060 Tel 801-645-9600; FAX: 801-645-9610.
Titles:
TextWare: Instant Information Access.

The Examiner Corp., (0-928275), 1327 Delaware Ave., Saint Paul, MN 55118-1911 Tel 612-451-7360; FAX: 612-451-6563.
Titles:
The Examiner: Item Banking & Examination Administration.

The Word, P.O. Box 12666, Scottsdale, AZ 85267 Tel 602-951-6828.
Titles:
Traders Tool.

Thea-Thot Pr., (1-887071), 206 Saratoga Ln., N., Minneapolis, MN 55441-6221 Tel 612-545-6789.
Titles:
The Thinking & Writing Process: A Process for All Ages, Level 2.

THEOS Software Corp., 1777 Botelho Dr., Suite 110, Walnut Creek, CA 94596 Tel 510-935-1118; Toll free: 800-600-5660; FAX: 510-938-4367.
Titles:
ScanTerm.
THEO Plus COM.
THEO+DOS.
THEO Plus DOS 32.
THEO Plus GRAFX: TG - MAX.
THEOS C.
THEOS MultiUser BASIC.
THEOS 386/486.
Window Manager.

Theta Business Systems, (0-927526), 9636 Via Torino, Burbank, CA 91504-1405 Tel 818-547-3480; FAX: 818-547-3479.
Titles:
Order Entry & Inventory Control.
Purchase Order System.
TBS Accounting Software.
TBS Five Integrated Accounting Systems.
W-2 Magnetic Filing.

Think Educational Software, Inc., (0-942845), 1030 E. El Camino Real, No. 401, Sunnyvale, CA 94087-3759.
Titles:
MacEdge 2.
Mind over Mac.

THOUGHTWARE, INC.

Think Technologies, Div. of Symantec Corp., (0-927529), 135 South Rd., Bedford, MA 01730 Tel 617-275-4800; Toll free: 800-648-4465.
Titles:
InBox.
LaserSpeed.
Lightspeed C 3.0.
Lightspeed Pascal.

Thinking Software, Inc., Div. of Business Computer Systems, Inc., 46-16 65th Pl., Woodside, NY 11377 Tel 718-424-7711; FAX: 718-898-3126.
Titles:
AI Learning Lab.
Alvin.
The Art of Negotiating.
AutoWriter.
Eliza.
Encrypt.
Executive Health Expert.
Expert 87.
Expert System Six Pack.
The Hunter.
Hypertext.
Idea Generator.
If/Then.
Investment Expert.
LawPlan: Artificial Intel Database.
Lifeplan.
LISP Database.
Management Expert.
Neural Networks.
Neuron Expert.
Neuron Expert Professional II.
NeuroShell.
PC Expert.
PC-LISP.
PC-PROLOG.
PC Purchase Advisor.
Personality Prober.
PL/D.
PROLISP.
The Protector.
The Psychiatry Expert.
The Psychology Expert.
Sexpert.
Smalltalk/V.
Speech Crafter.
Stock Market Expert.
Talking PC Therapist.
Turbo Expert: Business Expert System Toolkit.
Turbo Expert Toolkit.
World View.

Investext Pubns., (0-927469), 11 Farnsworth St., 4th Flr., Boston, MA 02210 Tel 617-345-2000; FAX: 617-330-1986.
Titles:
PORTIA.

Thomson Semi Conductors-Mostek Corp., Subs. of Thomson CSF, (0-925702), 1310 Electronics Dr., Carrollton, TX 75006 Tel 214-466-6000.
Titles:
ANSI BASIC Software Interpreter.
ASM-68000.
M/OS-80.
Process BASIC Software Interpreter.

Thoroughbred, Div. of Concept Omega Corp., (0-9620847), P.O. Box 6712, 19 Schoolhouse Rd., Somerset, NJ 08875-6712 Tel 201-560-1377; Toll free: 800-524-0430; FAX: 201-722-7958.
Titles:
Eight-User Thoroughbred/OS.

Thoughtware, Inc., 200 S. Biscayne Blvd., Suite 2750, Miami, FL 33131-2321 Tel 305-854-2318; FAX: 305-374-2718.
Titles:
Lightyear.
Management Diagnostic Series.

3G GRAPHICS, INC.

Management Training Library.
Management Training Series.

3G Graphics, Inc., 114 Second Ave. S., Suite 104, Edmonds, WA 98020 Tel 206-774-3518; Toll free: 800-456-0234.
Titles:
Images With Impact! Accents & Borders 1.
Images with Impact! Business 1.
Images with Impact! Graphics Symbols 1.

3M, (1-886311), 3M SM&CDS, Bldg. 223-SN-01, Saint Paul, MN 55144-1000 Tel 612-733-5773; Toll free: 800-219-9022; FAX: 612-736-5719.
Titles:
What's the Secret?

360, Inc., 2105 S. Bascom Ave., Suite 290, Campbell, CA 95008 Tel 408-879-9144; FAX: 408-879-9739.
Titles:
Dark Castle.
Harpoon.
Sands of Fire.
Thud Ridge.
Warlock.

3D-Eye, Inc., (0-9648089; 1-888159), 1050 Craft Rd., Ithaca, NY 14850 Tel 607-257-1381; FAX: 607-257-7335.
Titles:
TriSpectives Professional: The New Standard for 3D.
TriSpectives: The New Standard for 3D.

Thunderstone Software/Expansion Programs International, Inc., 11115 Edgewater Drive, Cleveland, OH 44102 Tel 216-631-8544; FAX: 216-281-0828.
Titles:
FileFinder.
Its-Writer.
METAMORPH.
TEXIS.

Thursby Software Systems, Inc., 5840 W. Interstate 20, Suite 100, Arlington, TX 76017 Tel 817-478-5070; FAX: 817-561-2313.
Titles:
MacNFS: NFS Client for Macintosh.
TSSnet.
TSSterm.

Tiara Computer Sysems, (0-924091), 1091 Shoreline Blvd., Mountain View, CA 94043 Tel 415-965-1700; Toll free: 800-638-4272; FAX: 415-965-2677.
Titles:
IONET Plus LAN Operating System.

Timberline Software Corp., (0-927550), 9600 SW Nimbus, Beaverton, OR 97005 Tel 503-626-6775; Toll free: 800-628-6583; FAX: 503-526-8050.
Titles:
Accounts Payable Gold.
AEasy.
AEasy Plus.
Budget Analysis.
Medallion Accounts Payable.
Medallion Accounts Receivable.
Medallion Equipment Management.
Medallion General Ledger.
Medallion General Ledger Plus.
Medallion Gold Accounts Payable.
Medallion Gold General Ledger.
Medallion Gold, Job Cost.
Medallion Gold Payroll.
Medallion Gold TS Report.
Medallion Inventory.
Medallion Job Cost.
Medallion Payroll Plus.
Medallion Property Management Gold.
Medallion Starter Set.
Medallion TenanTrac.
Medallion TS-Bridge.
Medallion/TS-Report I.
Medallion/TS-Report II.
On-Site Management.
On-Site Residential.
Precision Bid Analysis.
Precision Buyout.
Precision CAD Integrator.
Precision Digitizer.
Precision Estimating.
Precision Estimating Extended: Student Workbook.
Precision Estimating Plus.
Precision Estimating Plus: Student Workbook.
Precision Estimating: Student Workbook.
Precision Extended.
Precision Unit Price.
Progress Billing.
Property Management Gold.
Purchasing Management.
Site Pro.
Tenant Management.
TS-Report-Gold.

Time Arts, Inc., 1152 State Farm Dr., Santa Rosa, CA 95403-2717 Tel 707-576-7722; Toll free: 800-959-0509; FAX: 707-576-7731.
Titles:
Lumena.

Time Cycles Research, 375 Willetts Ave., Waterford, CT 06385 Tel 860-444-6641; Toll free: 800-827-2240; FAX: 860-442-0625.
Titles:
Famous Charts: Graphic Astrology.
Io Atlases: Graphic Astrology.
Io Edition: Graphic Astrology.
Io Forecast: Graphic Astrology.
Io Horoscope: Graphic Astrology.
Io Relationship: Graphic Astrology.
Penn Dragon Fonts: Graphic Astrology.
Star*Sprite.

Timephaser Corp., 9171 Towne Center Dr., No. 330, San Diego, CA 92122 Tel 619-554-1020; Toll free: 800-959-7095; FAX: 619-554-1028.
Titles:
Integrated Project Management System (IPMS).

Timepoint Corp., 304 Grand Ave., Suite 208, South San Francisco, CA 94080 Tel 415-952-6617; Toll free: 800-875-6617; FAX: 415-952-6618.
Titles:
Timepoint Employee Scheduler.
Timepoint Employee Scheduler for Windows.
Timepoint "Equity" Scheduler.

Times Mirror Multimedia, (1-885551), 1 Maynard Dr., Park Ridge, NJ 07656 Tel 201-307-8866; FAX: 201-307-8884.
Titles:
CyberBoogie with Sharon, Lois & Bram.
Food & Wine's Wine Tasting.
Food & Wine's Wine Tasting: An Interactive Experience.

TIMESLIPS Corp., (1-881182), 239 Western Ave., Essex, MA 01929 Tel 508-768-6100; Toll free: 800-285-0999; FAX: 508-768-7660.
Titles:
TAL (Timeslips Accounting Link).
TimeSheet Professional: Time & Expense Tracking for Projects & Clients.
Timeslips.
Timeslips Deluxe.
Timeslips Remote.
Timeslips for the Mac.

Timespan International, Inc., 4200 Scotts Valley Dr., Suite G, Scotts Valley, CA 95066 Tel 408-438-4005; FAX: 408-438-4806.
Titles:
Timespan Accounting.

Timeworks International, (0-927555), 70 W. Madison St., Suite 2300, Chicaog, IL 60602-4206; Toll free: 800-535-9497.
Titles:
Color It!
Data Manager PC.
Data Manger for Windows.
Paint It!
Publish It!
Publish It! Easy.
Publish It! for Windows.
Publish It! Lite.
SwiftCALC PC.
Trailblazer.
Translate It!: To-From (French, German, Spanish).
World Writer PC.

Timon, Inc., (0-927558), P.O. Box 383, Kennett Square, PA 19348 Tel 610-444-4332.
Titles:
Construction Cost Control System CCS/PMS.
Daily Manager: Accounts Payable.
Daily Manager: Funds Development System.
Daily Manager: General Accounting System.
Daily Manager: Horse Management.
Daily Manager: Accounts Receivable with Optional Inventory/Billing.
Daily Manager: Manufacturing Management Systems.
Daily Manager: Name & Address System.
Daily Manager: Payroll System.
The Deacon System: Church Management System.

Tin Man Software, (0-933735), P.O. Box 48823, Wichita, KS 67201-8823 Tel 316-264-3830.
Titles:
Air Systems.
Automan.
DAS-Security.
DASTOOLS.
The Firm.

Tiny-c Assocs., (0-927560), 10 Powderhorn Ct., Holmdel, NJ 07733 Tel 201-671-2296.
Titles:
Tiny C.

Tischrede Software, P.O. Box 79594, North Dartmouth, MA 02747 Tel 508-994-7907.
Titles:
Lexegete A/B/C.
Lexeqete: Matthew, Luke, & Mark.

Titus Software Corp., 20432 Corisco St., Chatsworth, CA 91311 Tel 818-709-3692; FAX: 818-709-6537.
Titles:
Crazy Cars.
F40 Pursuit Simulator.
Fire & Forget.
Galactic Conqueror.
Knight Force.
Off Shore Warrior.
Titan.
Xerion.

TModel Corp., P.O. Box 1850, Vashon, WA 98070-1850 Tel 206-463-3768; Toll free: 800-826-6335; 800-826-6357; FAX: 206-463-5055; P.O. Box 3327, Annapolis, MD 21403.
Titles:
NCAP: Intersection Capacity Analysis.
TModel2: Transportation Modeling System.

PUBLISHER/TITLE INDEX

Tobias, Daniel, (0-943871), 447 Merrick St., Shreveport, LA 71104-2305 Tel 318-222-3474.
Titles:
Planet of the Robots: Adventure Game for Fido-Opus Systems.

ToolMasters, Ltd., 600 Herndon Pkwy., Herndon, VA 22070 Tel 703-478-9808; FAX: 703-787-6720.
Titles:
TexSys.

Tools & Techniques, Inc., (0-939283), 2201 Northland Dr., Austin, TX 78756 Tel 512-459-1308; Toll free: 800-580-4411; FAX: 512-459-1309.
Titles:
Data Junction.
Spreadsheet Junction.

Top Banana, Inc., 1501 E. Chapman Ave., Suite 261, Fullerton, CA 92631 Tel 714-449-7777.
Titles:
The Forms: WordPerfect Version.
Grants: Financial Grant Management Forms.

Top of the Mountain Publishing, (0-914295; 1-56087), P.O. Box 2244, Pinellas Park, FL 34665-2244 Tel 813-530-0110; FAX: 813-536-3681; Dist. by: Quality Bks., Inc., 1003 W. Pines Rd., Oregon, IL 61061 Tel 708-295-2010; Toll free: 800-323-4241 (libraries only); Dist. by: New Leaf Distributing Co., 5425 Tulane Dr., SW, Atlanta, GA 30336-2323 Tel 404-691-6996; Toll free: 800-326-2665; Dist. by: Baker & Taylor Bks., Commerce Service Ctr., 251 Mt. Olive Church Rd., Commerce, GA 30599-9988 Tel 706-335-5000; Toll free: 800-775-1200 (customer service); Dist. by: The Distributors, 702 S. Michigan, South Bend, IN 46601 Tel 219-232-8500; Toll free: 800-348-5200 (except Indiana); Dist. by: Unique Bks., Inc., 4230 Grove Ave., Gurnee, IL 60031 Tel 708-623-9171; Dist. by: Ingram Bk. Co., 1 Ingram Blvd., La Vergne, TN 37086-1986 Tel 615-793-5000; Toll free: 800-937-8000 (orders only, all warehouses); Dist. by: Brodart Co., 500 Arch St., Williamsport, PA 17705 Tel 717-326-2461; Toll free: 800-233-8467; Dist. by: Pacific Pipeline, Inc., 8030 S. 228th St., Kent, WA 98032-2900 Tel 206-872-5523; Toll free: 800-444-7323 (Customer Service); 800-677-2222 (orders); Dist. by: Upper Access, Inc., P.O. Box 457, 1 Upper Access Rd., Hinesburg, VT 05461 Tel 802-482-2988; Dist. by: Emery-Pratt Co., 1966 W. Main St., Owosso, MI 48867-1372 Tel 517-723-5291; Toll free: 800-762-5683 (Library orders only); 800-248-3887 (Customer service only).
Titles:
Astrological Professional PC Computer Shareware Pack: Software for Personalized Astrological Charts & Accessories Programs.
Beginning Tarot PC.
ESP Test Researcher & Ancient Oracles PC.
57 Cookbooks CD-ROM: Thousands of the World's Greatest Recipes.
Home School CD-ROM: Two Hundred Ninety-Nine of the Best Educational Shareware Computer Programs.
Internet Marketing, Print & Electronic Publishing Software CD-ROM.
Internet Navigation Simulator: An Interactive Tutor-on-Disk.
Learn Ten Foreign Languages CD-ROM.
Lottery Winners' Secrets CD-ROM.
Mystical Tarot PC.
97 Golf Courses CD-ROM.
Numerology Pro PC.
100 Best Computer Games CD-ROM.
101 More of the World's Golf Courses to Play on Your Computer.
Sports Lover's Dream CD-ROM: 57 of the Best Shareware PC Computer Sports Programs.
Wall Street Pro's Secret Treasures CD-ROM: 147 of the World's Most Powerful Shareware Investment & Advisory Programs.
Your Biorhythms PC.

Total Quality Innovators, (0-9642801), 7301 Forest Ave., Richmond, VA 23226 Tel 804-673-2253; Toll free: 800-603-8326; FAX: 804-282-3066.
Titles:
FasTeam Diskette (Templates): TQM Templates for Work Teams.

Totem Graphics, Inc., 6200F Capitol Blvd., Tumwater, WA 98501 Tel 206-352-1851; FAX: 206-352-2554.
Titles:
Totem Color Clip Art.

Toucan Valley Pubns., Inc., (0-9634017; 1-884925), 142 N. Milpitas Blvd., Suite 260, Milpitas, CA 95035 Tel 408-956-9492.
Titles:
Profiles of America: An Informational, Statistical, & Relocation Encyclopedia of All U. S. Cities, Towns, Counties.

Touch Technologies, Inc., (0-943013), 9988 Hibert St., Suite 310, San Diego, CA 92131-2480 Tel 619-566-3603; Toll free: 800-525-2527; FAX: 619-566-3663. Do not confuse with Touch Technology, Annapolis, MD.
Titles:
DLB/Plus.
Dynamic Tape Accelerator.
InTouch NSA - Network Security Agent.
PC Menu.

Tower Publishing, (1-881758; 0-89442), 588 Saco Rd., Standish, ME 04084-6239 Tel 207-642-5400; FAX: 207-642-5463. Do not confuse with Tower Publishing Co. in Chula, GA.
Titles:
EasyData: NH Business & Professional Directory on Disk.

Trac Line Software, Inc., (0-927585), 1767-38 Veterans Memorial Hwy., Islandia, NY 11722 Tel 516-348-4300; Toll free: 800-872-2546; FAX: 516-348-4312.
Titles:
Alternate Inventory.
Branch Store Retailing.
Distributing.
Floor Planning.
IAP Supplement.
Integrated Accounting.
Mailing List.
PC Register.
PC Register Interface.
P.O.S. Supplement.
Purchase Order Module.
Retailing.
Store Front Retailing.
TRADES: Total Retail & Distribution System.
Volume Discount.
Warehouse Distribution.

Trajectory Software, Inc., 45 Whitney Rd., Suite B-8, Mahwah, NJ 07430 Tel 201-847-8880; FAX: 201-847-8899.
Titles:
Lex Elite Word Processing/Database System.
TeleMagic: Software for Success in Business.

Trak-It Solutions, 485 Pala Ave., Sunnyvale, CA 94086 Tel 408-737-9454; FAX: 408-737-9456.
Titles:
!Trak-IT AT.
!Trak-IT HR.

Transaction Data Systems, Inc., (0-927595), 6355 Metrowest Blvd., No. 100, Orlando, FL 32811-6206.
Titles:
Rx-30 Pharmacy System.

TRAVROUTE SOFTWARE

Transcender Corp., (0-9635203; 1-888750), 242 Louise Ave., Nashville, TN 37203-1812 Tel 615-726-8779; FAX: 615-320-6594.
Titles:
Examinator: Simulation of the MS Windows Certified Professional Examinations.
VB-Cert: Simulation of the Visual Basic Certified Professional Examination.

Transend Corp., (0-926678), 444 Kipling St., Palo Alto, CA 94301-1529.
Titles:
Easy Com Easy Go.
PC Complete.
Transend 1.
Transend 2.

Transkrit Corp., P.O. Box 500, Brewster, NY 10509 Tel 914-278-7000.
Titles:
MAILERMATE II.

Transparent Data Systems, Inc., P.O. Box 18276, San Jose, CA 95158.
Titles:
UGRAF.

Transportation Concepts & Services, (0-927600), 20 Highland Ave., Metuchen, NJ 08840 Tel 201-548-1200.
Titles:
"Shippers" System.

Transpower Corp., (1-880845), 3444 Rose Ave., Trevose, PA 19053 Tel 215-355-7011; Toll free: 800-678-8632; FAX: 215-355-7804.
Titles:
Optimal Engineer.
Optimal Manager.
Optimal Scientist: Designs & Analyzes Optimal Experiments.

TransWorld Intertainment, (1-884117), 133 Woodhill Dr., Redding, CA 96003-2917 Tel 916-246-0738; Toll free: 800-578-1545; FAX: 916-246-0738.
Titles:
The Velveteen Rabbit or How Toys Become Real.

Travel Companions International, Inc., (1-880624), 1227 Kenneth St., Detroit Lakes, MN 56501 Tel 218-847-1694; Toll free: 800-852-6752; FAX: 218-847-7090; Dist. by: EBSCO Industries, Inc., P.O. Box 830409, Birmingham, AL 35283-0409 Tel 205-991-1479.
Titles:
WORLDWIDE BROCHURES: The Official Travel Brochure Directory.

Traveling Software, Inc., (0-927603), 18702 N. Creek Pkwy., No. 102, Bothell, WA 98011 Tel 206-483-8088; Toll free: 800-343-8080; FAX: 206-487-1284.
Titles:
Battery Watch Pro for DOS & Windows: Release IV.
DeskLink: Release II.
LapLink Mac III.
LapLink 4.
WinConnect: for Microsoft Windows.

TravRoute Software, Div. of ALK Assocs., Inc., (0-9649794), 1000 Herrontown Rd., Princeton, NJ 08540 Tel 609-252-8117; FAX: 609-683-0290.
Titles:
Road Trips.
Road Trips: Door-to-Door.

Trax Softworks, Inc., (0-927604), 5840 Uplander Way, Culver City, CA 90230-6620 Tel 310-649-5800; Toll free: 800-367-8729; FAX: 310-649-6200.
Titles:
Cypress for Dow Jones News-Retrieval.
EdWord.
EdWordVision.
Electronic Spreadsheet System (ESS).
TeamTalk.

TreeAge Software, Inc., 1 Post Office Sq., 23rd flr., Boston, MA 02109 Tel 617-426-5819; FAX: 617-338-2880.
Titles:
Decision Analysis by TreeAge.

Trend Computer Systems, (0-928800), 828A Dodsworth Ave., Covina, CA 91724 Tel 818-331-4114.
Titles:
CNC.
General Ledger.
MOMS: Medical Office Management System.

Tri-L Data Systems, Inc., (0-927607), 94-871 Farrington Hwy., 2nd Flr., Waipahu, HI 96797-3146 Tel 808-671-5133.
Titles:
Legal Billing System.

Triad Computers, P.O. Box 436, Cambridge, MD 21613 Tel 410-228-3118.
Titles:
Accounting Trial Balance Worksheets.

Tridata Corp., (0-927614), 121 N. Cedar Crest Blvd., Allentown, PA 18104 Tel 610-820-9577.
Titles:
Programmer Aptitude.

TriDos Software Pubs., 4875 S.W. 19th Dr., Portland, OR 97201.
Titles:
ImageBuilder.
Terminator.

Trigram Systems, (0-927617), 5840 Northumberland St., Pittsburgh, PA 15217 Tel 412-422-8976; FAX: 412-422-3793.
Titles:
Datasafe.
Microspell.

Trillium Pr., (0-89824), First Ave., Unionville, NY 10988 Tel 914-726-4444; FAX: 914-726-3824. Do not confuse with Trillium Pr. in Saint Albans, WV.
Titles:
Brain Booster: Reasoning by Visual Analogy.
Concept Booster.
Drawing Discovery.
Greek History & Culture.
Greek Mythology.
Hangman.
The Odyssey.
Revolution Brew.
Trillium Type Sender.
The Trojan War.
Vocabulary Booster: Middle School.
Zippy Floppy.

Trilog, Subs. of CIGNA, (0-923305), 1 Logan Sq., Suite 1700, Philadelphia, PA 19103 Tel 215-564-3404; FAX: 215-564-5135.
Titles:
Micro Share Thrift-401(k): MST.

Trimark Interactive, (1-885932), 2644 30th St., Santa Monica, CA 90405 Tel 310-314-2000; Toll free: 800-424-7070; FAX: 310-392-8170.
Titles:
Emperor's New Clothes.
National Lampoon's Blind Date.

Thumbelina.
Tornado.

Trimbur Software, 200 Pleasant Grove Rd., Ithaca, NY 14850 Tel 607-257-2070; Toll free: 800-328-2252; FAX: 607-257-2657.
Titles:
TS Graph.

Trinity Computing Systems, Inc., (0-918201), 3346 E T C Jester Blvd., No. G3, Houston, TX 77018-7135 Tel 713-621-6911; Toll free: 800-231-2445.
Titles:
Cardionet.
The Cath Lab Support System.
The Critical Care Support System.
The Electrophysiology System.
IntensiveNet.
Micro Radiology Manager.
The Pacemaker Followup System.
WordPICS Clinical Patient Report Generator & Database: Patient Data Manager.

Trionics, (0-927621), 111 Croydon Rd., Baltimore, MD 21212 Tel 410-532-9079; FAX: 410-532-7818.
Titles:
General Business.

TriSoft, (0-927623), 1825 E. 38 1/2, Austin, TX 78722 Tel 512-472-0744; Toll free: 800-531-5170; FAX: 512-473-2122.
Titles:
BASIC-68k.
CP/M-2.2mH.
CP/M-68k.
FORTRAN-77.
MacSLIP.
Pascal-68k.
RAMD: Memory Disk.
Reformatter.

Tritus, Inc., (1-882787), 3300 Bee Caves Rd., Suite 650, Austin, TX 78746-6663 Tel 512-794-5800; Toll free: 800-321-2100; FAX: 512-794-3833.
Titles:
TRITUS SPF.

True BASIC, Inc., (0-939553), 12 Commerce Ave., West Lebanon, NH 03784-1669; Toll free: 800-436-2111; FAX: 603-298-7015.
Titles:
Advanced String Library.
Business Graphics Toolkit.
Communications Support Toolkit.
Forms Management Toolkit.
MacFunction.
Mathematician's Toolkit.
Scientific Graphics Toolkit.
Sorting & Searching Toolkit.
3-D Graphics Toolkit.
True BASIC: Advanced String Toolkit.
True BASIC: Communications Support Toolkit.
True BASIC: Developer's Toolkit.
True BASIC: Language System.
True BASIC: PC BASIC Converter.
True BASIC: Sorting & Searching Toolkit.
True BASIC: 3-Dimensional Graphics Toolkit.

Truevision, Inc., 7351 Shadeland Sta., Suite 100, Indianapolis, IN 46256 Tel 317-841-0332.
Titles:
Slide Presentation Software.

TurboPower Software, Sub. of Casino Data Systems, P.O. Box 49009, Colorado Springs, CO 80949 Tel 719-260-9136; Toll free: 800-333-4160; FAX: 719-260-7151.
Titles:
ASYNC Professional.
Async Professional for Delphi.
Async Professional for Windows.

B-Tree Filer.
Data Entry Workshop.
Object Professional.
Object Professional for C Plus Plus.
Orpheus.
TSRs & More.
Turbo Analyst.
Turbo Professional.
WIN/SYS Library.

Turner Hall Publishing, Div. of Symantec Corp., 10201 Torre Ave., Cupertino, CA 95014 Tel 408-253-9600.
Titles:
Note-It Plus: One Two Three Documentation Utility.

Turning Point Software, (0-926228), 1 Gateway Ctr., Newton, MA 02158-2802.
Titles:
Time is Money.

Turtle Creek Software, 118 Prospect St., Babcock Hall, Suite 201, Ithaca, NY 14850 Tel 607-272-1008; FAX: 607-272-5446.
Titles:
Bid Magic.
Hyper Estimator.
Hyper Remodeler.
MacNail.

Tutsim Products, (0-922348), 200 California Ave., No. 212, Palo Alto, CA 94306 Tel 415-325-4800; FAX: 415-325-4801.
Titles:
FANSIM: Frequency ANalysis & SYnthesys.
Personal Fansim.
Personal Tutsim.
TUTCAD: Graphical User Interface.
TUTSIM, Professional Version: The Engineering Design Aid.
TUTSIM Real Signal, Real Voltage, Realtime Option: RT-IO Option.

2500AD Software, Inc., 109 Brookdale Ave., Buena Vista, CO 81211 Tel 719-395-8683; Toll free: 800-843-8144; FAX: 719-395-8206.
Titles:
2500AD C Compilers.
2500AD Macro Cross Assemblers.
2500AD Simulator/Debugger.

Twin Oaks, Inc., (0-927639), 1079 Regency Dr., St. Paul, MN 55125. Do not confuse with Twin Oaks Bks. in Greenfield, WI or Twin Oaks, Inc. in Louisa, VA.
Titles:
Bill of Materials.
Cost Development.
Inventory.
Item Master & Control File.
Material Planning.
Purchasing.
Work Order.

UNICOM, Div. of United Camera, (0-917409), 297 Elmwood Ave., Providence, RI 02907 Tel 401-467-5600; FAX: 401-467-5607.
Titles:
dbMed/Mac.

USD, Inc., (0-9633595), 2075A W. Park Pl., Stone Mountain, GA 30087 Tel 404-469-4098; FAX: 404-469-0681.
Titles:
EPI Info.

Unified Software Systems, (0-927662), 6336 E. Willow Loop, Flagstaff, AZ 86004 Tel 602-526-4285.
Titles:
Uniforth.

PUBLISHER/TITLE INDEX

Unify Corp., (0-927664), 3901 Lennane Dr., Sacramento, CA 95834 Tel 916-928-6400; Toll free: 800-248-6439; FAX: 916-928-6401.
Titles:
ACCELL-IDS.
ACCELL/SQL.
UNIFY RDBMS.

Unik Assocs., 4065A N. Calhoun Rd., No. 201, Brookfield, WI 53005-1316 Tel 414-781-3334; FAX: 414-781-5335.
Titles:
51 Ready to use Engineering Programs.
General Engineering Software.
Hydro-Pack.
Machine Shop.
Maintenance Crib Simulator: MCS.
Maintenance Management System (MMS II).
Manufacturing Inventory Control.

UniLink, P.O. Box 1630, Jackson Hole, WY 83001 Tel 307-733-1666; Toll free: 800-456-8321; FAX: 307-733-5934.
Titles:
AP*Plus (Accounts Payable).
AR*Plus (Accounts Receivable).
Due Date*Plus: Duedate Monitoring.
GL*Plus (General Ledger).
PR*Plus (Payroll).
TB*Plus (Time & Billing).
TimeLink: An Electronic Timesheet Import & Export Utility.
TimeLink for Windows: Electronic Timesheet Import & Export Utility.
Write Up-Plus: Professional Client Write-Up.

Union Squareware, 60 E. Chestnut, No. 342, Chicago, IL 60611 Tel 617-623-3023; Toll free: 800-428-2032.
Titles:
SquareNote.

UniPress Software, Inc., 2025 Lincoln Hwy., Edison, NJ 08817 Tel 908-287-2100; Toll free: 800-222-0550 (orders Only); FAX: 908-287-4929.
Titles:
eXclaim! RealTime Spreadsheet.
eXclaim! Spreadsheet.
Q-CALC RealTime Spreadsheet.
Q-Calc Standard.

UniSoft Systems, (0-927671), 1250 Bayhill Dr., No. 200, San Bruno, CA 94066-3049.
Titles:
UniPlus Operating System.

Unison World Software, Div. of Kyocera Electronics, Inc., (0-928475), 1321 Harbor Bay Pkwy., Alameda, CA 94501 Tel 415-748-6670; Toll free: 800-444-7553; FAX: 510-748-6964.
Titles:
Art Gallery I & II.
AVAGIO Publishing System.
FaxBuilder.
Fonts & Borders.
NewsMaster II.
PrintMaster Plus.

United ProCom Systems, (0-927681), 3237 Dupont Ave. S., No. 3, Minneapolis, MN 55408-3513 Tel 612-825-5628.
Titles:
HoloCAD: Holographic Computer Aided Design.
Multi Media Bulletin Board System: MMBBS.
Multi Media Terminal: MMTERM.
VideoPrint: Photo-Realistic Printing.

United Software Industries, (0-944233), 1888 Century Park. E., No. 1500, Los Angeles, CA 90067-1719.
Titles:
ASCII Express: Mouse Talk.
ASCII PRO.

United Software Security, Inc., 3547 Padaro Ln., Carpinteria, CA 93013-1119.
Titles:
MasterKey.
OnGuard.
PC Librarian.
Privacy Plus.
Take Two Manager.

U. S. Data on Demand, Inc., (1-880077), R.D. 1, Box 445D, McConnellsburg, PA 17233 Tel 717-485-5348; FAX: 717-485-3813.
Titles:
State Data on Demand.
State Trends on Demand.

U. S. Robotics, Inc., (0-918727; 0-917721), 8100 N. McCormick Blvd., Skokie, IL 60076 Tel 312-982-5001; Toll free: 800-342-5877; FAX: 312-982-5235.
Titles:
BLAST: Blocked ASynchronous Transmission.
BLAST Professional.
BLAST II: Blocked ASynchronous Transmission.
MacBlast.

United Systems Software Corp., (0-927691), 955 E. Javelina Ave., No. 106, Mesa, AZ 85204 Tel 602-892-7974; Toll free: 800-544-1004; FAX: 602-892-9877.
Titles:
High Per Form.
HighPerForm Appraisal Processor.

Univair, Inc., (0-918205), 9024 St. Charles Rock Rd., Saint Louis, MO 63114 Tel 314-426-1099.
Titles:
Office-Star Secretarial-Office Management System.
Uni-Date System.
Uni-File.
Uni-Link.
Uni-Sort Special Sorting Interface.
Univair Payroll Management System.
Univair Series 9000.

Universal Data Research, Inc., (0-927692), 8517 Sugar Palm Ct., Orlando, FL 32835-8039; FAX: 716-759-2013.
Titles:
Accounts Payable-Purchase Order-Vendor Programs.
Accounts Receivable Package.
Dental Laboratory System.
FTK-File Management System.
Inventory.
Job Shop/Manufacturing.
Maintenance System.
Manufacturer's Inventory.
P.O.S.-Auto & Truck Parts Dealers/Retailers.
Sculptor.
Ski Rental Shops.
Universal Data Research General Ledger System.
Universal Data Research Payroll Package.

Universal Technical Systems, Inc. (UTS), 1220 Rock St., Rockford, IL 61101 Tel 815-963-2220; Toll free: 800-435-7887; FAX: 815-963-8884.
Titles:
TK Solver for Motif.
TK Solver for Windows.

Univ. of Texas Pr., (0-292), P.O. Box 7819, Austin, TX 78713-7819 Tel 512-471-7233; Toll free: 800-252-3206.
Titles:
Handbook of Latin American Studies, CD-ROM: 1936-1994.

UTILITY BILLING SPECIALISTS

Univ. of Vermont, Dept. of Psychiatry, (0-9611898; 0-938565), 1 S. Prospect St., Burlington, VT 05401 Tel 802-656-8313; FAX: 802-656-2602.
Titles:
Bibliography of Published Studies Using the Child Behavior Checklist & Related Materials, 1995.
Client-Entry Program for the CBCL - 4-18, YSR, & TRF.
Cross-Informant Program for the CBCL/4-18, YSR, & TRF.
Direct Observation Form Scoring Program - Apple II Version.
Direct Observation Form Scoring Program - IBM PC Version.
Program for the CBCL/4-18 Profile, 1991 - Apple II Version.
Program for the 1992 CBCL/2-3 Profile - IBM PC Version.
Program for the 1993 CBCL/4-18 Profile - IBM Version.
Program for the 1993 Teacher's Report Form Profile - IBM Version.
Program for the 1993 YSR Profile - IBM Version.
Program for the Teacher's Report Form, 1991 - Apple II Version.
Program for the Youth Self-Report, 1991 - Apple II Version.
Scanning Software Package for the CBCL - 4-18, YSR, & TRF Machine Readable Forms.
Semistructured Clinical Interview for Children & Adolescents Scoring Program for IBM PC Compatibles.

Univ. of Wisconsin-Madison, Solar Energy Laboratory, 1500 Johnson Dr., 1339 Engineering Research Bldg., Madison, WI 53706 Tel 608-263-1589; FAX: 608-262-8464.
Titles:
TRNSYS: A Transient System Simulation Program.

University Quality Software Co., (0-9628332), 8518 Chevy Chase Dr., La Mesa, CA 91941 Tel 619-464-4350.
Titles:
Logical Reasoning: A Guide to Clear Thinking.

University Software Assocs., Inc., (0-927704), R.F.D. 1, Box 6, Fitchville, CT 06334 Tel 203-889-5641.
Titles:
Master Select Copy.
Master String Editor.
Master Word Processor.

Unlimited Processing, Inc., (0-922076), 112 W. Adams St., Suite 1802, Jacksonville, FL 32202-3837 Tel 904-292-9113; Toll free: 800-874-8555; FAX: 904-292-4468.
Titles:
Perfect-Assistant.
TEAM-UP.

Upper Access, Inc., (0-942679), P.O. Box 457, Hinesburg, VT 05461 Tel 802-482-2988; Toll free: 800-356-9315; FAX: 802-482-3125.
Titles:
PIIGS: Publishers' Invoice & Information Generating System.

Utilico, 3377 Solano Ave., Suite 352, Napa, CA 94558 Tel 707-965-2290.
Titles:
Essential Data Duplicator 4 (EDD 4).
Essential Data Duplicator 4 Plus (EDD 4 Plus).

Utility Billing Specialists, 1101 SSW loop 323, Tyler, TX 75701 Tel 903-535-8222.
Titles:
DMS - III.

VIDI, 136 W. Olive Ave., Monrovia, CA 91016 Tel 818-358-3936.
Titles:
Presenter Professional.

VS Software, Div. of VideoSoft, Inc., 3323 Center St., Suite 810, Little Rock, AR 72201 Tel 501-376-2083; FAX: 501-376-1377.
Titles:
FontGen V.1.
SLEd: Signature Logo Editor.
VS Library of Laser Fonts.
The VS Tool Kit.

VTLS, Inc., (0-9627016), 1800 Kraft Dr., Blacksburg, VA 24060 Tel 703-231-3605; Toll free: 800-468-8857; FAX: 703-231-3648.
Titles:
Micro-VTLS.
VTLS.
VTLS InfoStation (VTLS-IS).

VT Productions, Inc., (1-884076), P.O. Box 339, Soquel, CA 95073; FAX: 408-464-1554; 511 Calle Serra Rd., Aptos, CA 95003 Tel 408-464-1552.
Titles:
The Exotic Garden: The Ultimate Guide to Growing Plants.

Valpar International Corp., (0-927722), 2450 W. Ruthrauff Rd., No. 180, Tucson, AZ 85705-1935 Tel 602-293-1510.
Titles:
ValFORTH.

Value Line, Inc., (0-928809), 711 Third Ave., New York, NY 10017 Tel 212-687-3965.
Titles:
Value/Screen II.

ValuSoft, Inc., (0-926536), P.O. Box 10519, 1 Salem Tower, Winstom-Salem, NC 27108 Tel 910-721-0233; Toll free: 800-367-7970.
Titles:
ATV2: Real Estate Valuation Software.

ValuSource, 7222 Commerce Ctr. Dr., Suite 210, Colorado Springs, CO 80919-2632; Toll free: 800-825-8763.
Titles:
Competitive Review.
DealMaker III, Senior Analyst.
Loan Express.
Value Express.
ValuSource II: IRS Litigation Support Valuation System.

Vamp, Inc., 6753 Selma Ave., Los Angeles, CA 90028 Tel 213-466-5533.
Titles:
McCAD EDS Electronic Design Systems.
McCAD Software: Electronic & Printed Circuit-Board Design.

Vanilla Software, 3345 Lakeshore Ave., Dept. L., Oakland, CA 94610 Tel 510-482-4756.
Titles:
Diskette Cookbook Series.

Vano Assocs., Inc., P.O. Box 12730, New Brighton, MN 55418 Tel 612-788-9547.
Titles:
MacChuck.

Varcon Systems, 10509 San Diego Mission Rd., Suite K, San Diego, CA 92108 Tel 619-563-6700; FAX: 619-563-1986.
Titles:
Great Gantt!
Manage THAT!

Vector Automation, Inc., 5100 Falls Rd., Suite 250, Baltimore, MD 21210 Tel 410-433-4200; FAX: 410-433-0305.
Titles:
CADMAX 3D.
CADMAX TrueSurf.

Vector Systems, Inc., 3700 Vanguard, Fort Wayne, IN 46809 Tel 219-478-8088; FAX: 219-747-5894.
Titles:
Absolute Coordinate Dimensioning Plus.
Customizable Screen Symbol Library.
The Master Menu.
MicroConcepts Digitizer Overlay.
Vector.

Vegetarians Resource Group, The, (0-931411), P.O. Box 1463, Baltimore, MD 21203 Tel 410-366-8343; Dist. by: New Leaf Distributing Co., 5425 Tulane Dr., SW, Atlanta, GA 30336-2323 Tel 404-691-6996; Toll free: 800-326-2665; Dist. by: Inland Bk. Co., 140 Commerce St., East Haven, CT 06512 Tel 203-467-4257; Toll free: 800-243-0138; Dist. by: Golden-Lee Bk. Distributors, Inc., 1000 Dean St., Brooklyn, NY 11238 Tel 718-857-6333; Toll free: 800-473-7475.
Titles:
The Vegetarian Game.

Ventura Educational Systems, (0-917623; 1-57116), 910 Ramona Ave., Suite E, Grover Beach, CA 93433 Tel 805-473-7383; Toll free: 800-336-1022; FAX: 805-473-7382.
Titles:
Balancing Act.
Computer Concepts.
Dr. Know.
Geometry Toolkit.
GraphPower.
Hands-On Math.
Music Concepts.
Probability Toolkit.

VenturCom, Inc., (0-927733), 215 First St., Cambridge, MA 02142 Tel 617-661-1230; Toll free: 800-334-8649; FAX: 617-577-1607.
Titles:
E-VENIX/386.
Embedded TCP IP & NFS.
VENIX EDS.

Verifone, Inc., (0-927919), 3080 Airway Ave., Costa Mesa, CA 92626 Tel 714-979-1870; Toll free: 800-654-1674; FAX: 714-434-2498.
Titles:
MailMinder.
SalesMinder.
StockMinder.
StoreMinder.

Verite Corp., 22 Park Terr., West Caldwell, NJ 07006 Tel 201-226-7072; Toll free: 800-800-7622; FAX: 201-226-4609.
Titles:
PMACS - Physicians Management & Control System.

Verity, Inc., 1550 Plymouth St., Mountain View, CA 94043-1230 Tel 415-960-7600; FAX: 415-960-7698.
Titles:
TOPIC.

Vermont Creative Software, Pinnacle Meadows, Richford, VT 05476 Tel 802-848-7731; Toll free: 800-848-1248; FAX: 802-848-3502.
Titles:
Vermont Views & Designer.

Vernier Software, (0-918731), 2920 SW 89th St., Portland, OR 97225 Tel 503-297-5317; FAX: 503-297-1760.
Titles:
DHMA Plotter.
Graphical Analysis.
Graphical Analysis III.
Multipurpose Lab Interface.
Precision Timer III.
Smart Pulley Timer.
Temperature Plotter III.
Voltage Plotter III.

VersaSoft, 4340 Almaden Expressway, Suite 110, San Jose, CA 95118-2034 Tel 408-723-9044; FAX: 408-723-9046.
Titles:
dBMAN.
dBMAN: Amiga Version.
dBMAN: IBM Version.
DBMAN 5.

Versatile Group, Inc., The, (0-928079), 4410 Spring Valley Rd., Dallas, TX 75244 Tel 214-991-1370; FAX: 214-980-8136.
Titles:
Certiflex Dimension Accounting Software.

Versys Corp., 1 Post St., Suite 400, San Francisco, CA 94104 Tel 415-274-4300; FAX: 415-274-4301.
Titles:
Legal Insight.

Vertex, Inc., 1041 Old Cassatt Rd., Berwyn, PA 19312 Tel 610-640-4200; Toll free: 800-355-3500; FAX: 610-640-1207.
Titles:
CommTax Telecommunication Tax Compliance System.
PayrollTax Calculation System.
SalesTax Compliance System.

Vertical Software, Inc., 3100 W. Harmon Hwy., No. 200, Peoria, IL 61604-5917 Tel 309-682-7070; FAX: 309-685-2081.
Titles:
FlourTrac.
Grain Clerk.
GrainTrac.
ScaleTrac.

Vertical Solutions, P.O. Box 7535, Olympia, WA 98507 Tel 206-352-2097; Toll free: 800-942-4008.
Titles:
FastLabel.

Vertigo Development Group, (1-57317), 58 Charles St., Cambridge, MA 02141 Tel 617-225-2065; Toll free: 800-942-2848; FAX: 617-225-0637.
Titles:
Jonathan Pond's Personal Financial Planner.
Wall Street Journal's Personal Finance Library.
Your Best Money Moves Now.
Your Mutual Fund Selector.

Vet Pac, Inc., 42 Goethals Dr., Richland, WA 99352 Tel 509-946-4138.
Titles:
Vet Pac Practice Management.

Vian Corp., (0-927747), 452 W. Hill Rd., Glen Gardner, NJ 08826-3253 Tel 908-537-4642.
Titles:
VIANSOFT Church Contribution System.
VIANSOFT Church Treasurer.

Vicarious Entertainment, Inc., (1-884906), 2221 Broadway, Suite 205, Redwood City, CA 94063 Tel 415-610-8300; FAX: 415-610-8302.
Titles:
Our Times Multimedia Encyclopedia of the 20th Century.

Videotex Systems, Inc., (0-928381), 11880 Greenville Ave., Suite 100, Dallas, TX 75243-3568 Tel 214-231-4200; Toll free: 800-888-4336; FAX: 214-231-2420.
Titles:
ChromaTools.
T-BASE.

Videx, Inc., (0-928814), 1105 NE Circle Blvd., Corvallis, OR 97330 Tel 503-758-0521; FAX: 503-752-5285.
Titles:
Bar Code Labeler.
Bar Code Labeler 2.
Timewand I Communications Package.
TimeWand II Communications Software.

Viehmann Corp., (0-927758), 35 Lucerne Dr., Andover, MA 01810 Tel 508-475-5591; FAX: 508-475-6785.
Titles:
Make-to-Order Net Requirements Planning: On-Target Job Shop Software.
ON-TARGET Job Shop Management.

Viewlogic Systems, Inc., 293 Boston Post Rd., W., Marlborough, MA 01752 Tel 508-480-0881; Toll free: 800-422-4660; FAX: 508-480-0882.
Titles:
Workview.

ViewPlan, Inc., Div. of MEM Systems, Inc., (0-943293), P.O. Box 80788, San Diego, CA 92138-0788 Tel 619-239-3141; Toll free: 800-826-2127; FAX: 619-497-0192.
Titles:
BeneQuick.
DATA+.
DATA Plus: For Windows.
Estate Forecast Model.
Factuary.
Progeny.
StepOne.
Vista.

Viking, Inc., 910 Soo Blvd., Suite 25, Rice Lake, WI 54868 Tel 715-234-2680; Toll free: 800-622-4070.
Titles:
El Cheapo Mail Program.
Fortune Telling.
Meat Cutting.
Menu Management.
Nifty Note Handler.
Party Program.
Restaurant Menu Management.

Viking Software Services, Inc., (0-927759), 6804 S. Canton, Suite 900, Tulsa, OK 74136-3419 Tel 918-491-6144; Toll free: 800-324-0595; FAX: 918-749-2701.
Titles:
ImagEntry.
Portal.
Viking Data Entry System: VDE.

Vining Sparks Micro Software, 6077 Primacy Pkwy., Suite 427, Memphis, TN 38119; Toll free: 800-829-0321; FAX: 901-762-5368.
Titles:
Vining Bond Swap System.

Virgin Games, 18061 Fitch Ave., Irvine, CA 92714 Tel 714-833-8710; Toll free: 800-874-4607 (orders only).
Titles:
Barbarian.
Conflict.
Double Dragon.
Greg Norman's Shark Attack: The Ultimate Golf Simulator.
House of Cards.
Magic Johnson's Basketball.
Mega Pack.
NY Warriors.
Opel Hershiser's Strike Zone.
Overload.
Spirit of Excalibur.
Spot the Computer Game.
Success Inc.
Turbo Champions.
Vegas Casino.
Vegas Casino 2.
Wonderland.

Virginia Systems, Inc., 5509 W. Bay Ct., Midlothian, VA 23112 Tel 804-739-3200; FAX: 804-739-8376.
Titles:
Sonar Bookends.
Sonar Image.
SONAR Professional Text Retrieval System.
Sonar Text Retrieval System.

Virtual Entertainment, Inc., (1-886031), 200 Highland Ave., Suite 401, Needham, MA 02194 Tel 617-449-7567; FAX: 617-449-4887.
Titles:
Body Park.
IQ Test for Windows.

Virtual Media Works, Inc., (1-886396), P.O. Box 70030, Sunnyvale, CA 94086; FAX: 408-739-5551; 665 Town & Country Village, Sunnyvale, CA 94086 Tel 408-739-0301.
Titles:
Virtual Tarot.

Virtual Pr., The, (1-57545), 534 Wright Ave., Wahiawa, HI 96786 Tel 808-624-7228; Orders to: 408 Division St., Shawano, WI 54166.
Titles:
At Dream's End: A Kingdom in the Balance.
Best Fantasy 1996.
Best Mystery 1996.
Best Sci-Fi 1996.
Chaos Path: The Hands of over Earth.
Unraveling Paths: Dreamers & Mystics.

Virtual Reality Laboratories, Inc., (1-886082), 2341 Ganador Ct., San Luis Obispo, CA 93401 Tel 805-545-8515; FAX: 805-473-3053.
Titles:
Distant Suns.
Formbuster.
Make Path Flight Director.
Mars Explorer.
Venus Explorer.
Vista Morph.
Vista Pro.

Visatex Corp., 1745 Dell Ave., Campbell, CA 95008 Tel 408-866-6596.
Titles:
Compusketch.
Facts & Faces of U.S. Presidents.

Visible Software, (0-941897), P.O. Box 949, Drawer Q, Newark, DE 19715-0949 Tel 302-455-9400.
Titles:
Dr. Pascal.

Visible Systems Corp., (0-924146), 300 Bear Hill Rd., Waltham, MA 02154-1019 Tel 617-890-2273; Toll free: 800-847-4253; FAX: 617-890-8909.
Titles:
Application Browser.
The Visible Analyst Workbench.
Visible Analyst Workbench: Educational Edition.

Vision Technologies, 6133 Sixth Ave., S., Seattle, WA 98108 Tel 206-762-0761.
Titles:
The Body System: Complete Personal Fitness Program.

Vision X Software, Inc., (1-888331), 761 Sproul Rd., No. 211, Springfield, PA 19064 Tel 610-892-9766; FAX: 610-566-3342.
Titles:
Digiday Electronic Daily Calendar: 365 Days of Classic Quotes.
Digiday Electronic Daily Calendar: 365 Days of Great Words to Know.
Digiday Electronic Daily Calendar: 365 Days of Off-the-Wallpaper.

Visionary Technology, (0-9625936), 185 E. 206th St., Apt. 3C, Bronx, NY 10458-1126.
Titles:
Comic-Pro.
Visionary Video.

Visions Resource Publishing, Inc., (1-880581), 606 Third Ave., Suite 418, San Diego, CA 92101.
Titles:
Traveler's Hotline Industry Database.

Visual Communications Network, Inc., (0-927719), 238 Main St., Cambridge, MA 02142 Tel 617-497-4000; FAX: 617-491-4260.
Titles:
VCN Concorde.

Visual Information, Inc., 136 W. Olive Ave., Monrovia, CA 91016-3410.
Titles:
Design Dimensions.
Dimensions.
Dimensions Presenter.
Solid Dimensions II.

Vitalograph, (0-927772), 8347 Quivira Rd., Lenexa, KS 66215 Tel 913-888-4221; Toll free: 800-255-6626.
Titles:
Office Spirometry Program.

VITREX Corp., (0-9627731), P.O. Box 260, Huntsville, UT 84317; 7150 E. 1000 North, Huntsville, UT 84317 Tel 801-745-2517.
Titles:
I.Q. Quest.

Voner, Charles E., Designs, 11 Spring St., Reading, MA 01867-2640 Tel 617-942-0209.
Titles:
Video Visions: Studio Set.
Video Visions: The Animator Set.
Video Visions: The Educator Set.
Video Visions: The Mixed Set.
Video Visions: The Titler Set.
Video Visions: Wedding Set.

Voyager Co., The, (0-931393; 1-55940), 578 Broadway, Suite 406, New York, NY 10012 Tel 212-431-5199; Toll free: 800-446-2001.
Titles:
Amanda Stories.
CD Companion Series: Igor Stravinsky, The Rite of Spring.
CD Companion Series: Ludwig Van Beethoven, Symphony No. 9.
Dream Machine Laserstack.

Eadweard Muybridge Laserstack.
The Great Quake of '89 Hypercard Stack.
The National Gallery of Art Laserguide.
Regard for the Planet LaserStack.
Salamandre Laserstack.
Van Gogh Laserguide.
Videodisc Accessory Series.
The Voyager CD AudioStack.
The Voyager VideoStack.

Voyetra Technologies, (1-888743), 5 Odell Plaza, Yonkers, NY 10701-1406 Tel 914-966-0600; Toll free: 800-233-9377; FAX: 914-966-1102.
Titles:
Digital Orchestrator Plus.
Digital Sound Gallery.
Discovering Music.
Midi Music Gallery.

W&L Publishing, (0-9633660), 6929 JFK Blvd., Suite 20-120, North Little Rock, AR 72116.
Titles:
Standard Score Comparison: Learning Disabilities.
Standard Score Comparison: Mental Retardation.

WD Templates, 13701 Riverside Dr., No. 400, Sherman Oaks, CA 91423 Tel 818-981-4315; FAX: 818-981-4304.
Titles:
QUID: The QUIck Depreciation Template.

W G Software, P.O. Box 3829, Austin, TX 78764 Tel 512-288-1305.
Titles:
Tenant File: For Residential & Commercial Property Management.

WLN, (0-9633700), P.O. Box 3888, Lacey, WA 98503-0888; Toll free: 800-342-5956; FAX: 206-923-4009; 4224 Sixth Ave., SE, Bldg. No. 3, Lacey, WA 98503 Tel 206-923-4000.
Titles:
Bridge-It.
Laser Bridge.
WLN - RLG Conspectus Software.
WLN Conspectus Database Software.
WLN Micro-Recon.

Wagner, Roger, Publishing, Inc., (0-927796), 1050 Pioneer Way, Suite P, El Cajon, CA 92020 Tel 619-442-0522; Toll free: 800-421-6526; FAX: 619-442-0525.
Titles:
Assembly Lines.
Chart 'N Graph Toolbox.
The Graphic Exchange.
Hyperstudio.
HyperStudio (IIgs).
Invisible Tricks Toolbox.
Macromate.
Merlin.
Merlin 8/16.
Merlin Pro.
Merlin 64.
Merlin 128.
MouseWrite.
P8CDA.
Printographer.
SoftSwitch.
Trial Size Toolbox.
Video Toolbox.
Wizard's Toolbox.
Write Choice.

Walch, J. Weston, Pub., (0-8251), P.O. Box 658, Portland, ME 04104-0658 Tel 207-772-2846; Toll free: 800-341-6094 (US & Canada only); FAX: 207-772-3105. Canadian address: P.O. Box 158, St. Stephen NB E3L 2X1.
Titles:
Apple Graphics Made Easy.
AppleWorks in Your Classroom: A Student Introduction.
ClarisWorks in Your Classroom: A Student Introduction.
The Computer Geoboard: Visualized Geometry.
Espionage at International Electronics: Exploring WordPerfect.
Microsoft Windows in Your Classroom: A Student Introduction.
Mystery at Laser-Age Hardware: Exploring Microsoft Works for MS-DOS.
Pagemaker in Your Classroom for Macintosh & Windows: Starter Package.
QuattroPro in Your Classroom: A Student Introduction.
Reading for Facts, Information, & Details: The Cloze Reading Tutor Starter Package.
WordPerfect for Desktop Publishing.
WordPerfect for Desktop Publishing for Windows.
WordPerfect in Your Classroom for Windows: Starter Package.

Walker, Richer & Quinn, Inc., 1500 Dexter Ave. N., Seattle, WA 98109-3051.
Titles:
NS Connection.
Reflection 8 Plus for DOS.
Reflection for the AS/400.
Reflection 4 for Windows.
Reflection 4 Plus for DOS.
Reflection 4 Plus for Macintosh.
Reflection Network Series.
Reflection Network Series for DOS.
Reflection Network Series for Windows.
Reflection 1 for Windows.
Reflection 1 Plus for DOS.
Reflection 1 Plus for Macintosh.
Reflection 2 for Windows.
Reflection 2 Plus for DOS.
Reflection 2 Plus for Macintosh.
Reflection X.
Reflection 1 & Plus Version.
Reflection 1 for Windows.
Reflection 1 Plus for the Macintosh.
Reflection 2 (& Plus Version).
Reflection 2 for the Macintosh.
Reflection 3 PLUS for the Macintosh.
Reflection 4 (& Plus Version).
Reflection 7 (& Plus Version).
Reflection 3270.

Wall Street Consulting Group, 89 Millburn Ave., Millburn, NJ 07041 Tel 201-762-4300.
Titles:
Bond Smart.
Funds Smart.
InvestNet.
Money Smart.
Repo Smart.
Security Safe-Keeping System.

Wall Street Graphics, Inc., (0-927800), 1575 E. 12th St., Brooklyn, NY 11230-7101 Tel 718-645-7717.
Titles:
Chart Eas-Alyzer.
Market EAS-Alyzer.

Wallaby Software Corp., (0-927802), 10 Industrial Ave., Mahwah, NJ 07430 Tel 201-934-9333; FAX: 202-934-5538.
Titles:
The RESIDENT.

Walnut Creek CDRom, (1-57176), 1547 Palos Verdes Mall, Suite 260, Walnut Creek, CA 94596 Tel 510-674-0783; Toll free: 800-786-9907; FAX: 510-674-0821.
Titles:
Ada Programming.
Amazing Animations.
Aminet.
Beer.
Best Aps.
C-User Group.
CICA.
Clipart Cornucopia.
Clips for QuickTime.
La Coleccion.
CP-M.
Doom - Shareware.
Doom - Toolkit.
East Asian Text Processing.
4.4 BSD Lite.
4.4 BSD Lite (Export).
Fractal Frenzy.
FreeBSD.
Garbo.
GEMini Atari.
Gif Galore.
Giga Games II.
GigaGames.
GNU.
Hobbes OS/2 Archived.
Hobbes Ready-to-Run.
Info-Mac V.
Internet Info.
Kirk's - Comm.
Linux.
Linux Bible.
Mastering OS/2 Warp Book.
Music Workshop.
Nebula NeXTSTEP.
Nova.
Perl.
POV-Ray.
Project Gutenberg.
QRZ! Ham Radio.
Sampler.
Science Library.
Sentimental Wings.
Shuttle Encyclopedia.
Simtel MSDOS.
Source Code.
Space & Astronomy.
Sprite OS.
Sys V r4.
Tcl/Tk.
Teacher 2000.
TeX.
Toolkit Linux 2.0.
Travel Adventure.
Turbo User Group (TUG).
2000 True Type Fonts.
Ultra-Mac Games.
Ultra-Mac Utilities.
Visions.
Welcome to Africa.
X11R5 & GNU.
X11R6.

Waltech, (1-886019), P.O. Box 2991, Carroll Station, MD 21229 Tel 410-644-0819.
Titles:
Page-A-Ranger: Book Making Software.
Page-A-Ranger: Book Making Software.

Walton Group, The, (0-927807), 10 W. Hill Pl., Boston, MA 02114-3265.
Titles:
Portfolio Manager.

Wang Laboratories, Inc., (0-927809), 836 North St., Tewksbury, MA 01876 Tel 508-459-5000; Toll free: 800-225-0654.
Titles:
ClearView.
Find-It.
Random House Electronic Thesaurus.
VS/VM.
Wang Word Processing.

Warner, S. E., Software, Inc., (1-57094), 2225 E. Murray-Holladay Rd., Suite 103, Salt Lake City, UT 84117-5382 Tel 801-277-9444; Toll free: 800-722-5185; FAX: 801-277-2795.
Titles:
Micro-Formatting Software.
Micro-Typewriter Software.

PUBLISHER/TITLE INDEX

Warner Bks., Inc., A Time Warner Co., (0-446; 0-445), 1271 Avenue of the Americas, New York, NY 10020 Tel 212-522-7200; FAX: 212-522-8700; Orders to: Little, Brown & Co., 200 West St., Waltham, MA 02154; Toll free: 800-759-0190.
Titles:
The Desk Organizer.

WarnerVision Entertainment, Inc., (1-56832), 75 Rockefeller Plaza, New York, NY 10019 Tel 212-275-2902; FAX: 212-765-0899.
Titles:
Penthouse: CD-ROM Virtual Photo Shoot 2.

Warriner, R. F., Assocs., (0-927814), 1621 Carver St., Redondo Beach, CA 90278 Tel 310-376-5004.
Titles:
I-EMP: Interactive Engineering Math Pack.
I-TAS: Interactive Thermal Analysis System.

Waterloo Manufacturing Software, 10574 Ravenna Rd., Twinsburg, OH 44087 Tel 216-425-2466; FAX: 216-425-8086.
Titles:
TACTIC: The Scheduler's Assistant.

Waterloo Maple, Inc., 939 Howard St., San Francisco, CA 94103 Tel 415-543-2252; Toll free: 800-827-6284; FAX: 415-882-0530.
Titles:
Expressionist.
Theorist.

Wave Communications, Inc., (1-885364), Box 296, Alexandria, VA 22313; Toll free: 800-836-5397; FAX: 703-836-1489; 509 Colecroft Ct., Alexandria, VA 22314 Tel 703-836-1488.
Titles:
Financial Healthcheck for Windows.

Webco Computers, (1-878414), 16011 Webco Place, Grass Valley, CA 95945-4314 Tel 916-274-9390; FAX: 916-274-9392.
Titles:
ProAssist.
Step-1 Data Base Manager/Application Generator.
TrueSOUND.

Weber & Sons, Inc., P.O. Box 104PR, Adelphia, NJ 07710 Tel 908-431-1128; Toll free: 800-225-0044; FAX: 908-431-9578.
Titles:
MacDisk Manager.

WEKA Publishing, Inc., (0-929321), P.O. Box 886, Shelton, CT 06484-0886; Toll free: 800-222-9352; FAX: 203-622-4187.
Titles:
Computer Upgrades & Repair.
DOS/Windows Secrets.
Fax Modems & Online Services.
FotoROM: The Superior Photo Collection on CD-ROM.
Graphics Charts & Graphs.
Keys to the Internet.
The Modern IC-Databook: A Key Aid for Every Electronics Amateur & Professional.
PhotoPaq.
Quality Clip Art Collection.

Welcom Software Technology, 15995 N. Barkers Landing, Suite 275, Houston, TX 77079 Tel 713-558-0514; FAX: 713-584-7828.
Titles:
COBRA.
Open Plan.
Opera.

West Coast Consultants, (0-927829), 11272 Pabellon Circle, San Diego, CA 92124 Tel 619-565-1266; FAX: 619-565-8610.
Titles:
CURVE.
CURVE Appleplotter.
Curve Copy.
Curve Digitizer.
Curve-Fit.
Curve Perspective.
Curve 3-D.
Curve 3-D CRT.
Curve II.
Curve II CRT.

West End Film, Inc., 5125 MacArthur Blvd. NW, No. 31, Washington, DC 20016-3300 Tel 202-232-7733.
Titles:
Artwork.
Brushwork.
CHARTWORK.
PAGEWORK.

West Services, Inc., Subs. of West Publishing Co., 620 Opperman Dr., Eagan, MN 55123 Tel 612-687-5605; Toll free: 800-328-9963.
Titles:
WESTCheck / Automated Citation Checking Software.
WESTLAW Custom Software for IBM's AS/400.
WESTMATE.

Westcon, Inc., 150 Main St., Eastchester, NY 10707 Tel 914-779-4773.
Titles:
ARC-Monitor Plus.

Westech Corp., (0-927833), 57 Sparta Ave., Sparta, NJ 07871 Tel 201-729-4378; Toll free: 800-829-4767; FAX: 201-729-0431.
Titles:
Retail Management System.

Western Digital Corp., 8105 Irvine Center Dr., Irvine, CA 92718 Tel 714-932-5000; FAX: 714-932-6294.
Titles:
ViaNet Networking Operating System.

Western Psychological Services, Div. of Manson Western Corp., (0-87424), 12031 Wilshire Blvd., Los Angeles, CA 90025 Tel 310-478-2061; Toll free: 800-648-8857; FAX: 310-478-7838.
Titles:
Achievement Motivation Profile (AMP).
Bell Object Relations & Reality Testing Inventory.
Developmental Profile II.
Education Applications of the Wise-III.
Endler Multidimensional Anxiety Scales (EMAS).
Halstead Russell Neuropsychological Evaluation System.
Interpersonal Styles Inventory.
Learning Styles Inventory.
Learning Styles Inventory (LST).
Logical Patient Billing.
Louisville Behavior Checklist.
Luria-Nebraska Neuropsychological Battery (Adult & Child Forms).
Manson Evaluation-Revised (ME).
Marital Satisfaction Inventory (MSI).
The Marks Adolescent Feedback & Treatment Report for the MMPI-A & MMPI.
The Marks Adolescent Interpretive Report for the MMPI-A & MMPI.
The Marks Adult Clinical Report for the MMPI-2 & MMPI.
The Marks Adult Feedback & Treatment Report for the MMPI-2 & MMPI.
Menstrual Distress Questionnaire-Form C.
Multiscore Depression Inventory for Adolescents & Adults.
Offer Self-Image Questionnaire for Adolescents-Revised (OSIQ-R).
Parent-Child Relationship Inventory (PCRI).
Personal Experience Inventory for Adults (PEI-A).
Personal Experience Inventory (PEI).
Personality Inventory for Children (PIC).
Piers-Harris Children's Self-Concept Scale.
Psychiatric Diagnostic Interview-Revised.
Sales Achievement Predictor (SalesAp).
Screening Test for Educational Prerequisite Skills (STEPS).
Sensory Integration & Praxis Tests (SIPT).
Shipley Institute of Living Scale.
Student Adaptation to College Questionnaire.
Suicide Probability Scale (SPS).
Tennessee Self-Concept Scale.
The Vocational Interest Inventory-Revised (VII-R).
Western Personality Inventory.
Western Personnel Tests.
WPS Automated IEP System.

Western Software Assocs., 110 El Dorado Rd., Walnut Creek, CA 94595 Tel 510-932-3999.
Titles:
Time Saver Payroll.

Western Wares, (0-918735), P.O. Box C, Norwood, CO 81423 Tel 303-327-4898.
Titles:
AFTOFF.
CC-RIDER Professional: The C-CH Programmer's Companion.
CC-RIDER: The C & C Plus Plus Programmers Companion.
ICX-File Transporter.
ISE-ISIS II Emulator.
ZAS Software Development Package.

Westgard Quality Corp., (1-886958), P.O. Box 2026, Ogunquit, ME 03907; 112 Shore Rd., Ogunquit, ME 03907 Tel 207-646-1553.
Titles:
QC Validator.

Weston & Muir, P.O. Box 868, Del Mar, CA 92014 Tel 619-752-7812; Toll free: 800-487-5655.
Titles:
Bank Accounts Payable.
Financial Statement Analyzer.
IConSys: Interim Construction Lending System.
Personnel Management II.

White Pine Software, Inc., 40 Simon St., Suite 201, Nashua, NH 03060-3043 Tel 603-886-9050; Toll free: 800-241-7463; FAX: 603-886-9051.
Titles:
Exodus for the Macintosh.
Mac320.
Mac330.
Mac340.

Whitewater Group, The, 7516 Lyons St., Morton Grove, IL 60053-1159.
Titles:
ACTOR.
ObjectGraphics.
Whitewater Resource Toolkit.

Wicat Systems, Inc., (0-87357), 1875 S. State St., Orem, UT 84058 Tel 801-224-6400; P.O. Box 539, Orem, UT 84058.
Titles:
WMCS: WICAT Multi-User Control System.

Widening Horizons, Inc., (0-933281), 21713 NE 141st St., Woodinville, WA 98072-5849 Tel 206-869-9810; FAX: 206-869-1821.
Titles:
Intimacy.
The Numerologist.
Numerologist Report Writer.
Personal Numerologist.
Relationship Report Writer.

Wild Hare Computer Systems, Inc., (0-927857), P.O. Box 3581, Boulder, CO 80307 Tel 303-442-0324; FAX: 303-440-7916.
Titles:
Choice!

Wiley, John, & Sons, Inc., (0-471; 0-8260), 605 Third Ave., New York, NY 10158-0012; FAX: 908-302-2300; Orders to: John Wiley & Sons, Inc., United States Distribution Ctr., 1 Wiley Dr., Somerset, NJ 08875-1272 Tel 908-469-4400; Toll free: 800-225-5945 (orders).
Titles:
C Language Scientific Subroutine Library Version 2.0.
FORTRAN Scientific Subroutine Library.
X-Stat: Statistical Experiment Design, Data Analysis & Non-Linear Optimization.
X-STAT: Statistical Experiment Design, Data Analysis, Non-Linear Optimization.

William Andrew, Inc., (1-884207), P.O. Box 443, Morris, NY 13808-0443; FAX: 607-263-2446; Pegg Rd., R.R. 1, Morris, NY 13808 Tel 607-263-2318; Dist. by: ASM International, 9639 Kinsman Rd., Materials Park, OH 44073 Tel 216-338-5151.
Titles:
A Database for Chemical & Environmental Compatibility of Plastics: POLCOM.

Williams AG Products, 9749 Paseo Montril, San Diego, CA 92129 Tel 619-494-9653; Toll free: 800-321-9193.
Titles:
Professional Series Drafting Symbols.

Williams & Wilkins, Div. of Electronic Media, (0-683; 0-8121), 428 E. Preston St., Baltimore, MD 21202 Tel 410-528-4000; Toll free: 800-527-5597; 800-638-0672; FAX: 410-528-4422; 200 Chester Field Pkwy., Malvern, PA 19355-9725 Tel 610-251-2230; Orders to: P.O. Box 1496, Baltimore, MD 21203; Dist. by: Majors Scientific Bks., Inc., 4004 Tradeport Blvd., Atlanta, GA 30354 Tel 404-608-2660; Toll free: 800-241-6551; Dist. by: Majors Scientific Bks., Inc., 1851 Diplomat Dr., P.O. Box 819074, Dallas, TX 75381 Tel 214-247-2929; Toll free: 800-633-1851; Dist. by: Login Brothers Bk. Co., 1436 W. Randolph St., Chicago, IL 60607 Tel 312-738-0016; Toll free: 800-621-4249; Dist. by: Login Brothers Bk. Co., P.O. Box 2700A, 4 Sperry Rd., Fairfield, NJ 07004 Tel 201-882-0440; Dist. by: Login Brothers Bk. Co., 1550 Enterprise Pkwy., Twinsburg, OH 44087 Tel 216-425-9600; Toll free: 800-321-8778; 800-621-0800 (in Ohio); Dist. by: Login Brothers Bk. Co., 2 Keith Way, Hingham, MA 02043 Tel 617-749-8570; Toll free: 800-225-8233; 800-232-1902 (in Massachusetts); Dist. by: Rittenhouse Bk. Distributors, Inc., 511 Feheley Dr., King of Prussia, PA 19406 Tel 215-277-1414; Toll free: 800-345-6425; Dist. by: Matthews Medical Bk. Co., 11559 Rock Island Ct., Maryland Heights, MO 63043 Tel 314-432-1400; Toll free: 800-633-2665 (Med-Book); Dist. by: Majors Scientific Bks., Inc., 9464 Kirby Dr., Houston, TX 77054 Tel 713-662-3984; Toll free: 800-458-9077.
Titles:
Arrhythmias: Case Studies in Management.
Arterial Blood Gases.
DIGITALIS.
Drug Interactions Advisor.
Hypertension Management.
Hypertensive Emergencies.

Wilson, H. W., (0-8242), 950 University Ave., Bronx, NY 10452 Tel 718-588-8400; Toll free: 800-367-6770; FAX: 718-590-1617.
Titles:
WILSEARCH.

Wilson Learning Corp., (1-886806), 7500 Flying Cloud Dr., Eden Prairie, MN 55344 Tel 612-944-2880; Toll free: 800-328-7937; FAX: 612-828-8835; Dist. by: Navarre Corporation, 6750 W. Broadway, Brooklyn Park, MN 55428 Tel 612-535-8333.
Titles:
Connect for Success: Connect with Others & Influence Them.
Connect for Success Plus Repacking Your Bags: Two CD-ROMs to Improve Your Family Life.
Create Your Dream Job: Four Key Questions to Design Your Life's Work.
Decide for Sure: Add Certainty to Your Decision Making.
Keep Your Cool: Manage Your Emotions.
No Trust? No Sale!: Build Lasting Customer Relationships.
Prosper in the '90s on the Job & at Home: Wilson Learning CD-ROM Sampler.
Relate with Ease: Build & Keep Interpersonal Relationships.
Repacking Your Bags: Lighten Your Load for the Rest of Your Life.
Sell to Needs: Sell the Way People Like to Buy.
Start to Sell: Find & Qualify Customers to Build Your Buisness.
Start to Sell Plus Sell to Needs: Two CD-ROMs to Improve Your Sales I. Q.
You Can Lead: Lead with Confidence.

Wilson WindowWare, Inc., 2701 California Ave. SW, No. 212, Seattle, WA 98116 Tel 206-937-9335; Toll free: 800-762-8383; FAX: 206-935-7129.
Titles:
Command Post.

Wincom Data Systems, Inc., P.O. Box 1037, Manhasset, NY 11030 Tel 516-365-6547.
Titles:
The Sales Manager's Tool Kit.

Wind-2 Software, Inc., (0-928817), 1901 Sharp Point Dr., Suite A, Fort Collins, CO 80525 Tel 303-482-7145; Toll free: 800-779-4632; FAX: 303-493-4578.
Titles:
Wind-2 Financial Management Software.

Winnebago Software Co., (0-927875), 457 E. South St., Caledonia, MN 55921 Tel 507-724-5411; Toll free: 800-533-5430; FAX: 507-724-5711.
Titles:
Advance Booking.
Bookmobile Software.
Catalog Card Maker IV.
Cross-Reference Words Database.
Directory of National Helplines.
Facts on File - Public Library Database.
Facts on File-College Library Database.
Facts on File-School Library Database.
Guide to Wide Area Networks: A Step-by-Step Introduction.
Informational Databases.
Internet Video Starter Kit.
Local ACE - Authority Control Edit.
A Matter of Fact Database.
Multilingual CAT.
Multilingual On-Line Catalog - French.
Multilingual On-Line Catalog - Spanish.
Multilingual Online Catalog.
PC Cardmaker.
Quick Reference Guide: Marc Coding & Tagging Booklet.
Smart Menu.
UMI PA Library.
UMI Resource/One.
UMI-Resource/One Full Text.
UMI-Resource/One Select Full Text.
UMI-Resource/One Select.
Union CAT.
Union CAT with ILL (Interlibrary Loan).
Union CAT with Interlibrary Loan.
Winnebago CAT.
Winnebago CAT for the Macintosh.
Winnebago CIRC.
Winnebago CIRC/CAT.
Winnebago Circ for the Macintosh.
Winnebago LAMP: Library Acquisition Management Program.
Winnebago SLIP-IBM.
Winnebago SLIP-MAC.

Winning Strategies, Inc., 105 Rye Ct., Mc Kees Rocks, PA 15136-1574; FAX: 412-921-0489.
Titles:
The IRA Investment Analyzer.
IRS-InterestCalc.
The S-B Quotient.
The/W-4 Formula.

Wintek Corp., (0-927877), 1801 South St., Lafayette, IN 47904-2993 Tel 317-448-1903; Toll free: 800-742-6809; FAX: 317-448-4823.
Titles:
HiWire II.
smARTWORK.

Wintergreen Software, P.O. Box 15899, New Orleans, LA 70175 Tel 504-899-0378; Toll free: 800-321-9479; FAX: 504-899-9974.
Titles:
The Computerized D.O.T.
The Computerized D.O.T. Plus.
Handwriting Analyst.

Winterhalter, Inc., (0-927878), P.O. Box 2180, Ann Arbor, MI 48106; Toll free: 800-321-7785; 3796 Plaza Dr., Ann Arbor, MI 48108 Tel 313-662-2002.
Titles:
DataTalker 3270.

Wismer Assocs., Inc., Subs. of SunGard Data Systems, Inc., (0-928819), 22134 Sherman Way, Canoga Park, CA 91303 Tel 818-884-5515; FAX: 818-346-5044.
Titles:
CASHMAX: Investment Management System.
MONEYMAX: Investment Management System.
PENSIONMAX: Investment Management System.
SERIES 2: Investment Management System.

Wolfram Research, Inc., (1-880083), 100 Trade Center Dr., Champaign, IL 61820-7237 Tel 217-398-0700; Toll free: 800-441-6284; FAX: 217-398-0747.
Titles:
Mathematica.
Mathematica for Students.

Wolmut, Peter, (0-918737), P.O. Box 11426, Portland, OR 97211 Tel 503-284-7248.
Titles:
Precious Metals Evaluator.

Woodchuck Industries, Inc., (0-942455), 340 W. 17th St., New York, NY 10011 Tel 212-206-6490.
Titles:
P-tral: BASIC to Pascal Translation Software.

Woods, Eugene L., , PE (1-884384), 8817 Hillery Dr., P.O. Box 6, San Diego, CA 92126-2808; Toll free: 800-242-4775 (credit card orders only); FAX: 619-558-7850.
Titles:
FONE800: Your Toll-Free Telecommunications Resource.
FONE: Manage Communication Costs.
FONE900: Your Audiotex Cost Management Resource.
FONE: Your Call Pricing Program of Choice.
FONE800: Your Personal Toll-Free Data Base.
FONE900: Your Personal AUDIOTEX Data Base.
Tealeafs: Just for Fun...with a Practical Twist.

PUBLISHER/TITLE INDEX

Woolf Software Systems, Inc., (0-927888), 23842 Archwood St., West Hills, CA 91307 Tel 818-703-8112.
Titles:
Medi/Claims.
Move-It.
ProFont: Editing for Laser Printers.

Word Assocs., Inc., (0-939153; 1-57265), 3226 Robincrest Dr., Northbrook, IL 60062 Tel 708-291-1101; FAX: 708-291-0931.
Titles:
Algebra: Equation-Solving Skills.
American History: Becoming a World Power, 1865-1912.
Assistant Coach: Basketball.
Boulder Dash.
C. A. S. Classroom Administration System.
Crisis Mountain.
Death in the Caribbean.
Dino Eggs.
Economics: Who's Got the Goods?
English SAT I.
English SAT II.
Geometry: Concepts & Proofs.
Geometry: Planely Simple.
Geometry: Right Triangles.
The Heist.
Highrise.
Highrise Math.
HomeFiler.
The Learning System.
Life Skills Math.
Math SAT I.
Miner 2049er.
Miner 2049er II.
More Myths, Magic & Monsters.
More Powers to You!: Exponents & Scientific Notation.
Myths, Magic & Monsters: Comprehensive Reading Skills.
Phraze Maze: Grammar Through Phrases.
Short Circuit.
Station 5.
Think Like a Scientist!: Physical Science Skills.
U. S. Constitution Tutor.

Wordcraft, (0-917419), 3827 Penniman Ave., Oakland, CA 94619 Tel 510-534-2212. Do not confuse with Wordcraft, Union, OR.
Titles:
The C Workshop.

WordPerfect Corp., (1-55692), 1555 N. Technology Way, Orem, UT 84057-2399 Tel 801-225-5000; Toll free: 800-451-5151; FAX: 801-222-5077.
Titles:
Black's Law Dictionary Legal Word Speller.
Collins Electronic English Dictionary & Thesaurus.
DataPerfect.
Dorland's Electronic Medical Speller.
Grammatik.
LetterPerfect.
LetterPerfect for Macintosh.
PlanPerfect: Spreadsheet.
Random House Webster's Electronic Dictionary & Thesaurus: College Edition.
Rhymer.
WordPerfect.
WordPerfect Communications with ExpressFax 2.0 for DOS.
WordPerfect for Macintosh.
WordPerfect for the Macintosh.
WordPerfect for Windows.
WordPerfect InForms.
WordPerfect Office.
WordPerfect Presentations for DOS.
WordPerfect Presentations for Windows.
WordPerfect Presentations 2.0 for DOS & Windows.
WordPerfect Works.
WordPerfect Works for Macintosh.

WordStar International, Inc., (0-925537), 201 Broadway, Cambridge, MA 02139-1955 Tel 415-382-8000; Toll free: 800-227-5609; FAX: 415-883-1617.
Titles:
The American Heritage Dictionary.
Correct Grammar.
Correct Letters.
Correct Quotes.
Correct Writing.
Easy Extra.
Stedman's-25 for WordPerfect.
WordStar.
WordStar for Windows.
WordStar French Version.
WordStar German Version.
WordStar: Spanish Version.
WordStar 2000.
WordStar 2000 Courseware.

WordTech Systems, Inc., Box 1747, Orinda, CA 94563 Tel 510-254-0900.
Titles:
dBXL.
Quicksilver.
Quicksilver Diamond Release.

Work Management Solutions, Inc., 119 Beach St., Boston, MA 02111-2520 Tel 617-482-6677; FAX: 617-482-6233.
Titles:
The MULTITRAK Enterprise-Wide Work Management System.
MULTITRAK Work Request System.
PlanView.

Workhorses, Inc., 805-B 14th St., Golden, CO 80401 Tel 303-279-8551; Toll free: 800-777-2477; FAX: 303-278-4029.
Titles:
Contractor's Dream.
Mathpack for Lotus 1-2-3.
Remodeler's Dream.

Working Computer, 4755 Oceanside Blvd., No. 200, Oceanside, CA 92056 Tel 619-945-4334; FAX: 619-945-2365.
Titles:
Clients & Profits for Advertising Agencies.

Working Software, Inc., (0-940331), P.O. Box 1844, Santa Cruz, CA 95061-1844 Tel 408-423-5696; Toll free: 800-229-9675; FAX: 408-423-5699.
Titles:
Findswell.
Geographical Dictionary.
Last Resort.
Last Resort: Typing Retrieval System.
Legal Dictionary.
Lookup.
QuickLetter.
Spellswell Medical Dictionary.
Spellswell 7.
Working Watermarker.

World Software Corp., 124 Prospect St., Ridgewood, NJ 07450 Tel 201-444-3228; Toll free: 800-962-6360; FAX: 201-444-9065.
Titles:
Extend-a-Name Plus.

Worldview Software, (0-939247; 1-57055), 76 N. Broadway, Suite 4009, Hicksville, NY 11801 Tel 516-681-1773; Toll free: 800-347-8839; FAX: 516-822-0950.
Titles:
Tecmath.

WritePro Corp., The, (1-879584), 43 S. Highland Ave., Ossining, NY 10562 Tel 914-762-1255; Toll free: 800-755-1124; FAX: 914-762-5871.
Titles:
FictionMaster: For Novelists & Short Story Writers.
FirstAid for Writers.
WritePro.

WyssWare, 19504 47th Ave., NE, Seattle, WA 98155 Tel 206-362-4447.
Titles:
WorkLog.

XDB Systems, Inc., 14700 Sweitzer Ln., Laurel, MD 20707 Tel 301-317-6800.
Titles:
XDB.

XIOX Corp., (0-927905), 577 Airport Blvd., Suite 700, Burlingame, CA 94010 Tel 415-375-8188; FAX: 415-342-1139.
Titles:
Resale & Billback Series Feature Package B.
XIOX Large Business Series.
XIOX Resale & Billback Series BASIC Package.
XIOX Resale & Billing Series Feature Package A.

XOR Corp., (0-945749), 7241 Ohms Ln., Edina, MN 55439-2148; FAX: 612-888-0640; Dist. by: ABCO Distributing, 300 Tall Pines, Industrial Pkwy., Monsey, NY 10942 Tel 914-368-1930.
Titles:
Basketball Challenge.
Lunar Rescue.
MacCourses.
MacGolf.
MacGolf Classic.
MacRacquetball.
MacSki.
NFL Challenge.
PRO Challenge.
Road Racer.
RoboMan.
Shuffle Mania!
TaskMaker.

XYZT Computer Dimensions, Inc., (0-927908), 150 Broadway, Suite 1001, New York, NY 10038 Tel 212-608-6655; FAX: 212-385-4831.
Titles:
IWS: Integrated Work Station.
SFIM: Sales Force Information Manager.

Xcel, 1600 W. Sixth St., Mishawaka, IN 46544 Tel 219-259-7804.
Titles:
ServiceWorks.

Xerox Corp., 101 Continental Blvd., Suite 500, El Segundo, CA 90245 Tel 310-333-3436; FAX: 310-333-6919.
Titles:
Analyst.
ASP.
Humble Expert System Shell.
Ventura Publisher.
Xerox Ventura Publisher 2.0.

Xiphias, (0-927915), Helms Hall, 8758 Venice Blvd., Los Angeles, CA 90034 Tel 310-841-2790; FAX: 310-841-2559; Dist. by: Compton's NewMedia, Inc., 722 Genevieve, Suite M, Solana Beach, CA 92075 Tel 619-259-0444.
Titles:
The National Directory of Addresses & Telephone Numbers.

XPrime Corp., (0-937185), 15202 Otsego St., Sherman Oaks, CA 91403-1511; FAX: 310-470-8672.
Titles:
KeyLISP: The Language (Apple II Edition).

Xram Xpert Systems, 9 Vail Pl., Suite 100, Methuchen, NJ 08840; Toll free: 800-358-8559.
Titles:
Lexa System.

XTree Co., (0-937867), 15220 NW Greenbrier Pkwy., Suite 200, Beaverton, OR 97006-5762; Toll free: 800-964-2490.
Titles:
HOT.
Hot Runtime Module.
XT Net.
XTPRO GOLD: Dutch.
XTPRO GOLD: French.
XTPRO GOLD: German.
XTPRO GOLD: Italian.
XTPRO GOLD: Spanish.
XTPRO (International English).
XTree.
XTree Gold.
XTree Mac.
XTreePro.

Xysys, Inc., 32500 Telegraph Rd., No. 201, Bingham Farms, MI 48025-2463 Tel 810-433-1730.
Titles:
CAD-Access.

Yale Graphics, 228 Mill St., Milford, OH 45150-1072; FAX: 513-791-0574.
Titles:
ImageStation.

Yale Univ., Schl. of Medicine, Ctr. for Advanced Instructional Media, (1-884012), Biomedical Communications, 333 Cedar St., New Haven, CT 06510 Tel 203-785-4088; FAX: 203-785-3291.
Titles:
Atlas of Myocardial Perfusion Imaging.
Introduction to Cardiothoracic Imaging.

Yamaha Corp. of America, P.O. Box 6600, Buena Park, CA 90622 Tel 714-522-9011.
Titles:
DX7 Voicing Program.
FM Music Composer.
FM Music Macro.
FM Voicing Program.
Sequence.

Yardi Systems, 819 Reddick St., Santa Barbara, CA 93103 Tel 805-966-3666; Toll free: 800-866-1144; FAX: 805-963-3155.
Titles:
Basic Property Management.
Construction Accounting.
Deluxe Property Management.
The Estimator.
General Accounting.
Payroll Accounting.
Real Estate Office Management.
Real Estate Tool Kit: Financial Analysis Software.
Reservation & Billing System.

Yucaipa Software, (0-927932), 12343 12th St., Yucaipa, CA 92399 Tel 908-797-6331.
Titles:
V-UTILITY.

Z-Law Software, Inc., P.O. Box 40602, Providence, RI 02940 Tel 401-421-5334; Toll free: 800-526-5588.
Titles:
Real Estate Lawyer.

Zaki Corp., Forestside Ofc. Pk., 30 Turnpike Rd., Southboro, MA 01772 Tel 508-480-0201; Toll free: 800-874-2731; FAX: 508-481-0595.
Titles:
PC SHARE/VM.
PC SHARE/VM-2.
PC SHAREplus.

Zangsoft, Inc., (0-9643229), P.O. Box 3337, Urbana, IL 61801; 1504 Trails Dr., Urbana, IL 61801 Tel 217-384-0066.
Titles:
CookSoft.

Zea Corp., (0-927937), 100 Hanover Ave., 3rd Flr., Cedar Knolls, NJ 07927.
Titles:
SPAM.

Zedcor, Inc., 4500 E. Speedway, Suite 22, Tucson, AZ 85712-5305 Tel 602-881-8101; Toll free: 800-482-4567; FAX: 602-881-1841.
Titles:
Desk.
DeskPaint & DeskDraw.
ZBASIC.

Zelos, Div. of Zelos Ventures, Inc., (1-883387), 535 Pacific Ave., San Francisco, CA 94133 Tel 415-788-0566; FAX: 415-788-0562.
Titles:
Escape from Management Hell.
Inc. Magazine's How to Really Start Your Own Business.
Shoot Video Like a Pro.
Team SAT.
3-D Tutor.

Zeltner Assocs., Inc., (0-927941), 4600 S. Michigan St., South Bend, IN 46614 Tel 219-299-0322; FAX: 219-291-7834.
Titles:
Cemetery Accounting.
Factory Manager.
Foundry & Die Cast Management System.

Zen Software, 1205 Bethel St. N.E., Olympia, WA 98506-4320.
Titles:
System Monitor.

Zenographics, Four Executive Cir., Suite 200, Irvine, CA 92714 Tel 714-851-6352.
Titles:
Pixie.
SuperPrint.

Zephyr Services, (0-918219), 1900 Murray Ave., Pittsburgh, PA 15217 Tel 412-422-6600; FAX: 412-422-9930.
Titles:
ArtPack.
Astro-Aid Plus.
Astrobase Plus.
Astrocalc Plus.
AstroTutor.
Bearings.
Bio-Data.
Financer Super.
GraphMaster.
Gravitator Plus.
Headliner.
HomeVentory.
Horoscopics Plus.
LifeLines.
LodeStar Plus.
Numberscope Plus.
Prophet-East.
Shop-Aid.
SunTracker Plus.
SuperCat Plus.
TideMaster.

Zoom Telephonics, Inc., (0-928823), 207 South St., Boston, MA 02111 Tel 617-423-1072; Toll free: 800-631-3116.
Titles:
NetMaster.
PFS:ACCESS with Zoom Disk.

ZSoft Corp., (1-877728), 450 Franklin Rd., Suite 100, Marietta, GA 30067 Tel 404-428-0008; FAX: 404-427-1150.
Titles:
PC Paintbrush IV.
PC Paintbrush IV+.
Publisher's Paintbrush.
Publisher's Type Foundry.

ZyLAB, (0-927958), 19650 Club House Rd., Gaithersburg, MD 20879 Tel 301-590-0900; Toll free: 800-544-6339; FAX: 301-590-0903.
Titles:
Zy INDEX for DOS.
ZyINDEX for Windows 5.0.